JAPAN
An Illustrated Encyclopedia

2

M······▸Z

JAPAN
An Illustrated Encyclopedia

2

M······Z

KODANSHA

Distributed in the United States and Canada by Kodansha America, Inc., 114
Fifth Avenue, New York, N.Y., 10011, and in the United Kingdom and continental
Europe by Kodansha Europe Ltd., Gillingham House, 38-44 Gillingham Street,
London, SW1V 1HU, and in Asia, Australia, and New Zealand by Kodansha
International Ltd., 17-14, Otowa 1-chome, Bunkyo-ku, Tokyo 112.

Published by Kodansha Ltd., 12-21, Otowa 2-chome, Bunkyo-ku, Tokyo 112.

Library of Congress Cataloging-in-Publication Data

Japan: an illustrated encyclopedia / Kodansha—1st ed.
    p.   cm.
  Includes bibliographical references and indexes.
  ISBN 4-06-931098-3
  1. Japan—Encyclopedias. I. Kōdansha.
 DS805.J263 1993
 952'.003—dc20   93-20512
                                                        CIP

ISBN 4-06-206490-1 (Volume 2)
ISBN 4-06-931098-3 (Set)

JAPAN
An Illustrated Encyclopedia

M

ma 間

Term widely used in traditional Japanese arts—especially music, dance, and the theater—to designate an artistically placed interval in time or space. By its very absence of sound or color, *ma* helps accentuate the overall rhythm or design. Originally a musical term, it later assumed metaphorical meanings and came to be used in many other arts as well.

Japanese music uses various types of *ma* to create effects in roughly the same way that Western music does. Traditionally, however, Japanese musicians have had a greater liberty in lengthening or shortening a rest according to their interpretation of a given composition. In dance and drama also, performers have considerable freedom to insert or extend a pause in their singing, speech, and bodily movement, even when doing a time-honored classical piece. In NŌ drama, an actor is expected to attain highly dramatic expression when he stops all motion momentarily during an act. In KABUKI, too, intervals between words or gestures are acted out in such a way that the effect of stillness may be maximized. One such interval has been codified as *mie*, a moment of emotional intensity when the actor stops all motion and, without speaking, turns toward the audience. In more popular forms of entertainment like RAKUGO and MANZAI, *ma* plays an important role in achieving the intended comic effect.

The concept of *ma* is also utilized outside the performing arts. Traditional Japanese painters try to create a "meaningful void" by the deliberate use of blank space. In landscape gardening open space is used strategically to enhance the effect of the whole design. In poetry, ideas like YOJŌ ("overtones") and YŪGEN ("mystery and depth") can be seen as variations of the same concept.

Mabechigawa 馬淵川

River in Iwate and Aomori prefectures, northern Honshū. It originates in northeastern Iwate Prefecture, flows north between the Kitakami and Ōu mountains, and enters the Pacific Ocean at the city of Hachinohe, Aomori Prefecture. The water is used by Hachinohe for industry. Length: 142 km (88 mi); area of drainage basin: 2,050 sq km (792 sq mi).

Mabe Manabu 間部学

(1924–). Painter. Born in Kumamoto Prefecture, Mabe emigrated with his parents to Brazil in 1934. While working as a farmer in the state of São Paulo, he devoted himself to painting. Internationally known for works characterized by a lyrical romanticism, he held individual exhibitions in Europe and America and won a number of prizes.

Mabuchi Motor Co, Ltd マブチモーター[株]

(Mabuchi Mōtā). Manufacturer of small electric motors. Incorporated in 1926. Supplying more than half the world market, the company produces 2.8 million motors daily and over 700 million annually, most manufactured overseas. Its products are forwarded directly to its end users. The firm has overseas production bases in Hong Kong, Taiwan, and China and overseas sales offices in New York, Frankfurt, Singapore, Hong Kong, and Taipei. Sales for the fiscal year 1990 totaled ¥60.4 billion (US $452.3 million), and capitalization stood at ¥13.6 billion (US $101.8 million). Headquarters are in the city of Matsudo, Chiba Prefecture.

MacArthur, Douglas マッカーサー, D.

(1880–1964). Commander of the US Army forces in the Far East and supreme commander for the Allied powers (SCAP) during the Allied OCCUPATION of Japan until 1951. MacArthur was born near Little Rock, Arkansas, the son of a prominent army general. He graduated first in his class from West Point in 1903 and served extensively in the Philippines and East Asia. He was wounded twice in World War I and participated in the occupation of the German Rhineland. He was superintendent of West Point between 1919 and 1922 and army chief of staff from 1930 to 1935. MacArthur then returned to the Philippines as chief military adviser to the new commonwealth. He resigned his US Army commission in 1937 in order to complete the reorganization of the Philippine Army.

On 28 July 1941, he was recalled to active duty by President Franklin D. Roosevelt and appointed commander of the US forces in the Far East. After being driven from the Philippines by Japanese forces in 1942, he dramatically proclaimed, "I shall return." Directing a counteroffensive of "island-hopping" campaigns, he fulfilled his promise and returned to Leyte in October 1944. On 2 September 1945 he accepted the surrender of Japan on the USS *Missouri*. Appointed supreme commander of the Allied forces, MacArthur headed the Allied Occupation of Japan, commanding some 500,000 troops and supervising over 5,500 military and civilian bureaucrats engaged in remodeling Japanese society.

After the outbreak of the KOREAN WAR on 25 June 1950, MacArthur staged a massive amphibious landing at Inch'ŏn, behind North Korean lines, on 15 September 1950. When China entered the war MacArthur insisted on retaliatory action, in open disagreement with US policy. On 11 April 1951 MacArthur was relieved of his command by President Harry S. Truman. In Japan, where he was generally respected, MacArthur's dismissal was received with shock. Upon his return to the United States he was greeted as a hero. In speeches before Congress, at West Point, and at the Republican National Convention, MacArthur appealed to patriots, and it was thought that he might become a candidate for president; however, he ended his life in retirement, keeping his rank as a five-star general.

MacDonald, Ranald マクドナルド, R.

(1824–94). Adventurer who traveled to Japan in the 1840s. Born in Astoria, Oregon, of an American father and a Chinook Indian mother, he first became interested in Japan as a child. In 1847 he left the Hawaiian Islands in the whaler *Plymouth*. On 27 June 1848 he jumped ship off the western coast of Hokkaidō and made his way alone by boat to the islands of Yagishiri and Rishiri, where he was arrested under Japan's NATIONAL SECLUSION policy and sent to Nagasaki. From mid-October until the following April, MacDonald was held captive in a small room in a Nagasaki temple. During that time he taught English to MORIYAMA TAKICHIRŌ and others and is now regarded as the first instructor of English in Japan. He left Japan in April 1849 and wandered from place to place. In 1885 he finally settled in Fort Colville, Washington, where he worked on his memoir, *Japan: Story of Adventure*. He died before it reached print. His manuscript, edited by William S. Lewis and Murakami

Naojirō (1868–1966), was published in 1923 as *Ranald MacDonald, 1824–1894*.

McDonald's Co (Japan), Ltd
日本マクドナルド[株]

(Nihon Makudonarudo). Fast-food restaurant chain. Established in 1971 as a joint venture between McDonald's Corporation of the United States and Fujita and Co. The first McDonald's restaurant in Japan was opened in Tōkyō's Ginza district in 1971. As of 1991, the company operated 792 outlets throughout Japan and ranked first in sales among Japanese restaurant chains. For fiscal year 1990, sales totaled ¥175.4 billion (US $1.3 billion) and capitalization stood at ¥1.0 billion (US $7.4 million). Headquarters are in Tōkyō.

machi bugyō
町奉行

(city commissioners). Officials of the Tokugawa shogunate (1603–1867) responsible for urban commoners' (CHŌNIN) affairs; they had administrative, judicial, and police duties. The term *machi bugyō* is commonly used to mean the EDO MACHI BUGYŌ, the commissioners of Edo (now Tōkyō), the shogunal capital. Several other *machi bugyō*, collectively known as *ongoku bugyō* (commissioners of distant places), were stationed in Kyōto, Ōsaka, and other cities and major towns under direct shogunate control. All were drawn from families of HATAMOTO rank and had staffs, office procedures, and functions roughly analogous and proportional to those of the Edo city commissioners. The *machi bugyō*, the KANJŌ BUGYŌ (commissioners of finance), and the JISHA BUGYŌ (commissioners of temples and shrines) were known collectively as the *sambugyō* (three commissioners). See also SADO BUGYŌ; URAGA BUGYŌ; BUGYŌ.

machibure
町触

Official notices issued by the shogunate or by *daimyō* to townsmen (CHŌNIN) during the Edo period (1600–1868). The shogunate issued them in Edo (now Tōkyō) and other towns under direct shogunate control; daimyō issued them in their own castle towns. In Edo *machibure* were issued by the MACHI BUGYŌ (city commissioners). See also OFUREGAKI; MACHI YAKUNIN.

Machida
町田[市]

City in southern Tōkyō Prefecture. Machida developed in the 12th century as a post-station town. It is now principally a residential suburb, with many housing complexes, and a commercial center. Pop: 349,050.

Machida City Museum of Graphic Arts
町田市立国際版画美術館

(Machida Shiritsu Kokusai Hanga Bijutsukan). Municipal museum established in 1987 in the city of Machida, Tōkyō Prefecture. The collection houses a broad range of both Japanese and Western prints from the 15th century to the present, including works by KOBAYASHI KIYOCHIKA, MUNAKATA SHIKŌ, IKEDA MASUO, Dürer, Rembrandt, and Munch. The museum also has a collection of research materials related to printmaking.

machine tool industry
工作機械産業

(*kōsaku kikai sangyō*). Japan's machine tool industry has recorded remarkable growth since the 1970s. In the decade between 1976 and 1985, annual production grew from ¥326.2 billion (US $1.1 billion) to ¥1.3 trillion (US $5.3 billion), an increase of about four times in yen figures. In 1982 Japan became the world's leading producer of machine tools, and as of 1990 Japan held that position for nine years, accounting for 24.2 percent of total worldwide production of US $45.3 billion.

Technological developments in the machine tool industry are today diverging in two main directions. One is toward fully automated factories and unmanned production. This trend is apparent in such technologies as flexible manufacturing cells, flexible manufacturing systems, and advanced factory-automation technology utilizing computer-aided design and computer-aided manufacturing (CAD/CAM) as well as factorywide local area networks (LAN). The other trend is toward extremely high precision and high speed processing technologies. Developments in these areas have helped Japan maintain its world leadership position in both the technology and production of machine tools.

machine translation
機械翻訳

(*kikai hon'yaku*). Translation from one language into another by computer. In Japan machine translation has followed one of two basic approaches. The "direct" method uses analysis of syntax and grammar to translate one language into another, while the "transfer" approach employs an internal, intermediate language as a bridge between the source language and the target language.

Several Japanese high-technology firms launched English-to-Japanese translation systems based on the direct method in 1984. The same year a small Tōkyō firm began marketing the country's first commercial Japanese-to-English translation system, based on a transfer method pioneered by an American computer software company. Since that time the computer dictionaries and syntax-analysis programs used have become increasingly sophisticated; by 1990 machine translation software for the personal computer had come on the market. Increasing interest has developed in Japanese-to-English machine translation in other countries, particularly the United States, because of the need to disseminate a large volume of information from Japan. Despite continuing progress, the widespread commercial application of machine-translation technology has not yet been realized. The assistance of human translators is still required because major problems remain with the quality of the output. Current systems work best when the input is edited into a form likely to be correctly understood by the machine translation system.

machishū
町衆

Townspeople of the Muromachi (1333–1568) and Azuchi-Momoyama (1568–1600) periods, primarily those of Kyōto. Also denotes the inhabitants of SAKAI, ISHIYAMA HONGANJI, and other urban areas. A *machi* consists of rows of houses facing each other across a street. In the 15th and 16th centuries *machi* assumed a social role, integrating several sectors of society into a communal aggregate, the *machishū*. As the authority of the Muromachi shogunate declined after the Kakitsu Disturbance of 1441, these communities took on responsibility for internal security and defense against incursions of armed peasants (TSUCHI IKKI) into Kyōto; between 1532 and 1536 a confederation of townsmen and temples of the Nichiren sect, the Hokke Ikki, was the effective power in the city (see TEMMON HOKKE REBELLION), ruling through "assemblymen" (*shūe no shū*); by

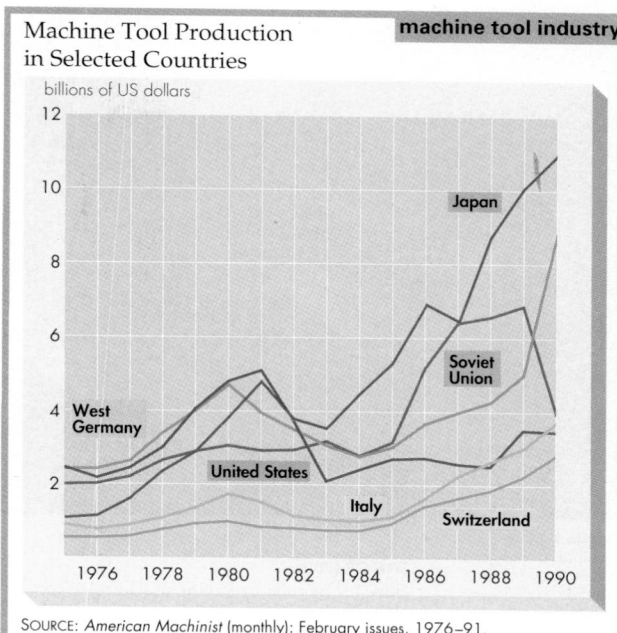

Machine Tool Production in Selected Countries

machine tool industry

billions of US dollars

Japan
Soviet Union
West Germany
United States
Italy
Switzerland

1976 1978 1980 1982 1984 1986 1988 1990

SOURCE: *American Machinist* (monthly): February issues, 1976–91.

the mid-16th century several extended associations (*machigumi*), each comprising some dozen *machi*, had appeared.

machiya → minka

machi yakko
町奴

Also known as *otokodate*. A type of town rowdy or hoodlum of the Edo period (1600–1868). In contrast to HATAMOTO YAKKO, who claimed association with particular *hatamoto* houses, *machi yakko* had no formal affiliation with feudal authorities. They often assumed the responsibility for, and profits from, providing *daimyō* and *hatamoto* houses with day laborers from the ranks of the urban unemployed. *Machi yakko* were bound by a code of honor and usually recognized by their dandified attire. They were given to fighting, especially with *hatamoto yakko;* the shogunate sometimes used stern measures to check them, although it also used their services in hunting down criminals. See also KYŌKAKU.

machi yakunin
町役人

City and town officials of commoner (CHŌNIN) status during the Edo period (1600–1868). The shōgun's city commissioners (MACHI BUGYŌ) had a small staff to administer the commoners' section of town (*machi yashiki*), but because it was so small, the *machi bugyō* relied heavily on the cooperation of *machi yakunin*. The titles and remuneration of these officials and their specific functions varied from town to town, but their basic character as minor functionaries and intermediaries between the rulers and urban populace was everywhere the same.

In Edo (now Tōkyō), *machi yashiki* affairs were administered by officials titled *machi nanushi, tsuki gyōji,* and *yanushi. Machi nanushi* acted as the senior spokesmen representing city wards, dealing directly with the *machi bugyō.* Through this hierarchy they helped the Edo *machi bugyō* supervise a multiplicity of urban affairs, including maintaining censuses (NIMBETSU ARATAME), guard patrols (JISHIMBAN AND TSUJIBAN), and fire-fighting organizations (HIKESHI).

Douglas MacArthur
The supreme commander for the Allied powers during the Occupation of Japan, MacArthur presided over the dismantling of the Japanese military and the promotion of American-style democratic principles.

Maeda Seison
A painter of historical scenes, Maeda here depicted the 12th-century warrior Minamoto no Yoritomo with his men. The two-panel folding screen is titled *Yoritomo in the Cave.* 1929. Colors on silk. 191 × 270 cm. Ōkura Shūkokan Museum, Tōkyō.

mackerel   鯖

(*saba*). The *saba* or Pacific mackerel (*Scomber japonicus*) is a littoral migratory fish of the family Scombridae, order Perciformes, class Osteichthyes. It grows to over 40 centimeters (16 in). It is thought to be distributed roughly in the temperate to subarctic zones of the northern Pacific Ocean and adjoining waters, moving north and south along the continental shelf in large schools. A closely related form, *S. tapeinocephalus*, caught commercially in Japan, is called either *saba* or *gomasaba.* The two are used for food, either raw or cooked, canned or dried, and are among the cheapest fish in Japan. They are caught by angling, purse seine, and scoop net.

macrobiotics   マクロバイオテックス

(*makurobaiotekkusu*). Diet-centered regimen purported to promote health and longevity. Macrobiotics was developed in Japan in the 1950s by Sakurazawa Nyoichi (1893–1966), later known as George (or Georges) Ohsawa, and introduced to the West, where it became popular in the late 1960s and early 1970s among young people associated with what was known as the counterculture. It continues to be well known in the West among those concerned with maintaining a healthy lifestyle, but has received relatively little attention in Japan itself.

The diet consists chiefly of unpolished cereals, especially brown rice (*gemmai*), which are eaten with seasonal vegetables, beans, and seaweed. Practitioners of macrobiotics range from pure vegetarians to those who eat fish and shellfish and those who eat some meat. All foods must be raised organically and are not to be processed, preserved, or prepared using additives that are deemed injurious to health. Foods, methods of preparation, and the practitioner's body type are evaluated on the basis of *yin* and *yang,* concepts borrowed from traditional Chinese philosophy, and appropriate diets are prescribed for each stage of the individual's development toward an ideal state of health.

Madre de Deus Incident
マードレ・デ・デウス号事件

(*Mādore de Deusu gō* Jiken). Also called *Nossa Senhora de Graça* Incident. International incident of the early 17th century that resulted from rivalry in the Southeast Asian sea trade and helped to harden the attitude of the Tokugawa shogunate (1603–1867) against European traders and their religion. In 1608 the crews of two ships belonging to the Christian *daimyō* ARIMA HARUNOBU became involved in a fracas with the Portuguese at Macao. The disturbance was forcibly suppressed by the governor, André Pessoa, who had one of the Japanese ringleaders executed. When Pessoa came to Nagasaki in July 1609 as captain-major of the carrack *Madre de Deus* (also called *Nossa Senhora de Graça*), his explanation of the imbroglio was at first accepted by the local authorities and by TOKUGAWA IEYASU, then semiretired at Sumpu (now the city of Shizuoka, Shizuoka Prefecture). After Arima protested on behalf of his men, Ieyasu ordered Pessoa seized, dead or alive. When the *Madre de Deus* was finally boarded on the night of 6 January 1610, Pessoa decided to blow it up rather than surrender. The Portuguese from Macao were allowed to renew their trade in 1611. See also VERMILION SEAL SHIP TRADE.

Maebara Issei   前原一誠

(1834–76). *Samurai* activist of the Chōshū domain (now Yamaguchi Prefecture). An official in the early Meiji government and later leader of the HAGI REBELLION of 1876. Like ITŌ HIROBUMI, KIDO TAKAYOSHI, and other leaders of the MEIJI RESTORATION (1868), Maebara attended the private school of YOSHIDA SHŌIN, the antishogunate intellectual and activist. He held several offices in the new government, but resigned in 1870 due to illness. Maebara became increasingly dissatisfied with the government's dismantling of samurai privileges (see SHIZOKU). In October 1876 Maebara organized a group of former Chōshū samurai and led them in an armed revolt known as the Hagi Rebellion. It was quashed by government forces, and Maebara was caught and executed.

Maebaru   前原[町]

Town in northwestern Fukuoka Prefecture, Kyūshū. In existence since prehistoric times, Maebaru is thought to correspond to the place called Itokoku in the Chinese history WEI ZHI (*Wei chih*). Today it is a growing commuter suburb for the city of Fukuoka. Pop: 50,250.

Maebashi   前橋[市]

Capital of Gumma Prefecture, central Honshū; on the river TONEGAWA. A provincial center since the 8th century, in the Edo period (1600–1868) it developed as a castle town and as a distribution center for silk cocoons and raw silk. From the Meiji period (1868–1912) until after World War II, the silk-spinning industry flourished in Maebashi. Today, its main industries are transport machinery, electrical appliances, and lumber. Pop: 286,261.

Maeda Corporation   前田建設工業[株]

(Maeda Kensetsu Kōgyō). Firm engaged in general construction and public works projects. Since it was founded in 1919, Maeda has participated in large-scale energy projects, as well as urban and littoral developments. Sales for the fiscal year ending March 1991 were ¥475.0 billion (US $3.5 billion), and capitalization stood at ¥17.1 billion (US $124.6 million) in the same year. Headquarters are in Tōkyō.

Maeda family   前田氏

(Maedashi). DAIMYŌ family of the Edo period (1600–1868). MAEDA TOSHIIE was awarded Noto Province (now part of Ishikawa Prefecture) by ODA NOBUNAGA in 1581, and the family rapidly increased its power and wealth through later alliances with TOYOTOMI HIDEYOSHI and TOKUGAWA IEYASU. Based at Oyama Castle in what is now the city of Kanazawa, the Maeda controlled the provinces of Kaga (now part of Ishikawa Prefecture), Noto, and Etchū (now Toyama Prefecture). Income from these lands, more than 1.2 million *koku* (see KOKUDAKA), was the greatest of any daimyō domain, and the Maeda were renowned throughout Japan as the masters of the "million *koku* of Kaga" (Kaga *hyakuman-goku*). The Maeda daimyō, especially MAEDA TSUNANORI, encouraged Confucian scholarship, gardening, and pottery.

Maeda Kanji   前田寛治

(1896–1930). Western-style painter. Born in Tottori Prefecture. Graduate of Tōkyō Bijutsu Gakkō (now Tōkyō University of Fine Arts and Music), where he studied under FUJISHIMA TAKEJI. Between 1922 and 1925 he studied in Paris and was particularly inspired by the realist paintings of Gustave Courbet (1819–77) and others. In 1926, after returning to Japan, he organized the 1930-nen Kyōkai (1930 Association) and began to exhibit works that revealed his own individual mixture of realism and fauvism.

Maedakō Hiroichirō   前田河広一郎

(1888–1957). Author. Active member of Japan's PROLETARIAN LITERATURE MOVEMENT. Born in Sendai, Miyagi Prefecture. He dropped out of school to go to Tōkyō, where he became a disciple of the eccentric Tolstoyan writer TOKUTOMI ROKA. Maedakō left for the United States in 1907. In Chicago and later in New York he supported himself with odd jobs and occasionally published prose pieces in English in literary journals. Meeting little success, he abandoned writing in English and returned to Japan in 1920. In 1923 Maedakō joined the coterie that published the magazine TANE MAKU HITO, and the following year he joined the magazine BUNGEI SENSEN. After the mid-1930s, he concentrated on writing biographical accounts of Tokutomi Roka, autobiographical novels, and autobiographies. His major works include *Daibōfūu jidai* (1924, The Age of Storm), a novel, and *Jūnenkan* (1930, Ten Years), a collection of critical essays.

Maeda Magoemon 前田孫右衛門

(1818–64). *Samurai* from the Chōshū domain (now Yamaguchi Prefecture) active in the movement to overthrow the Tokugawa shogunate (see MEIJI RESTORATION). An inspector in the domainal government, he supported the proimperial, antishogunate movement in Chōshū. With the ascendancy of conservative forces within the domain following the first shogunate expedition against Chōshū (see CHŌSHŪ EXPEDITIONS) in 1864, Maeda was imprisoned and executed.

Maeda Road Construction Co, Ltd 前田道路[株]

(Maeda Dōro). Firm specializing in road construction, concrete and asphalt paving, and production of asphalt mixtures. Incorporated in 1930. The company is affiliated with MAEDA CORPORATION. Sales for the fiscal year ending March 1991 totaled ¥162.2 billion (US $1.2 billion); capitalization stood at ¥17.7 billion (US $129.0 million). Headquarters are in Tōkyō.

Maeda Seison 前田青邨

(1885–1977). Japanese-style painter. Real name Maeda Renzō. Born in Gifu Prefecture, he went to Tōkyō in 1901. He was a member of the artist group Kōjikai and of the reorganized JAPAN FINE ARTS ACADEMY (Nihon Bijutsuin). In 1935 he was appointed to the Imperial Fine Arts Academy (Teikoku Bijutsuin). Influenced by the native YAMATO-E and RIMPA styles, he is noted for his paintings on historical themes. In 1944 he was appointed as a court artist (*teishitsu gigeiin*) and in 1946 as a judge of the Nitten exhibitions. He was a professor of art at the Tōkyō Bijutsu Gakkō (now Tōkyō University of Fine Arts and Music), where he taught until 1959. He received the Order of Culture in 1955.

Maeda Tamon 前田多門

(1884–1962). Bureaucrat and politician. Viewed as one of Japan's leading "internationalists," Maeda served in many public and private offices, both national and international. Born in Ōsaka, he graduated from Tōkyō University in 1909. He worked for the Home Ministry from 1909 until 1920, when he was appointed deputy mayor of Tōkyō under GOTŌ SHIMPEI. From 1928 to 1938 he was an editorial writer for the newspaper *Tōkyō asahi shimbun*. During the war years he served as governor of Niigata Prefecture.

Maeda is best remembered for his activities as minister of education just after the war (August 1945–January 1946). Working closely with Prime Minister SHIDEHARA KIJŪRŌ, he worked on the draft of the rescript in which the emperor renounced his divinity (see EMPEROR, RENUNCIATION OF DIVINITY BY). Soon after the rescript was issued, Maeda was "purged" by Allied OCCUPATION authorities for having served as a governor during the war. He was rehabilitated in 1950, and, until his death in 1962, he engaged in various civic and international causes, most notably UNESCO and the movement for "clean elections."

Maeda Toshiie 前田利家

(1538?–99). *Daimyō* of the Azuchi-Momoyama period (1568–1600). The son of a petty baron of Owari Province (now part of Aichi Prefecture), Toshiie became a page of the presence (KOSHŌ) of ODA NOBUNAGA in 1551 and eventually became one of Nobunaga's major captains, taking part in most of his important military operations. Toshiie became a daimyō in 1581 when Nobunaga allotted him Noto Province (now part of Ishikawa Prefecture). In the succession struggle after Nobunaga's assassination in 1582 (see HONNŌJI INCIDENT), Toshiie tried to mediate between SHIBATA KATSUIE and TOYOTOMI HIDEYOSHI. When the two rivals confronted each other in 1583 at the Battle of SHIZUGATAKE, Toshiie deserted Katsuie, thereby ensuring Hideyoshi's victory. Rewarded by Hideyoshi with two districts in Kaga Province (now part of Ishikawa Prefecture), Toshiie moved his residence to Kanazawa; in 1585, after he helped Hideyoshi defeat Sassa Narimasa (d 1588), the daimyō of Etchū (now Toyama Prefecture), most of that province was transferred to Toshiie. Toshiie became a member of Hideyoshi's council of "Five Great Elders" (Gotairō) in 1595. Upon Hideyoshi's death in 1598 Toshiie assumed responsibility for protecting his young heir, TOYOTOMI HIDEYORI. Toshiie's own death the next year removed one of the chief pillars of the Toyotomi house and helped to set in motion the struggle for succession to the hegemony over Japan won by TOKUGAWA IEYASU in 1600.

Maeda Tsunanori 前田綱紀

(1643–1724). *Daimyō* of the Kanazawa domain (now Ishikawa Prefecture). He became daimyō at the age of two following the death of his father and ruled until his retirement in 1723. Guided first by his grandfather Maeda Toshitsune (1593–1658) and later by his father-in-law, HOSHINA MASAYUKI, he initiated reforms to increase domainal control over the peasantry. This he accomplished by converting all *samurai* fief holders into salaried (see KIRIMAI) samurai-bureaucrats and placing all land under direct domainal administration; carrying out rigorous surveys and holding each village responsible for a fixed amount (JŌMEN) of taxes; and giving more responsibility to peasant officials (see also KAISAKUHŌ). Tsunanori was associated with outstanding Confucian scholars. He invited one of them, KINOSHITA JUN'AN, to collect, preserve, and edit old books and documents; these materials formed the core of what is now the SONKEIKAKU LIBRARY, a collection of more than 100,000 Japanese and Chinese works.

Maeda Yūgure 前田夕暮

(1883–1951). TANKA poet. Real name Maeda Yōzō. Born in Kanagawa Prefecture. Associating with writers such as TAYAMA KATAI and SHIMAZAKI TŌSON, he established his name around 1910 as a *tanka* poet of the naturalist school (see NATURALISM). His poems, some written in free verse, are fluid and impressionistic. His principal collections are *Shūkaku* (1910) and *Suigen chitai* (1932).

Maehata Hideko 前畑秀子

(1914–). Swimmer. Married name Hyōdō Hideko. Born in Wakayama Prefecture. Maehata won a silver medal in the women's 200-meter breaststroke at the 1932 Los Angeles Olympic Games and became the first Japanese woman to receive a gold medal when she won the same event in the 1936 Berlin Olympic Games.

Maejima Hisoka 前島密

(1835–1919). Founder of the Japanese postal service. Real name Ueno Fusagorō. Born in the village of Shimo Ikebe in Echigo Province (now part of Niigata Prefecture). In 1870 he was appointed to the Mimbushō (Ministry of Popular Affairs), where his ability brought him to the attention of ŌKUMA SHIGENOBU and ITŌ HIROBUMI. Maejima proposed creation of a national postal service, which began operations in April 1871 with daily mail linking 65 post offices between Tōkyō and Ōsaka. There were 5,099 post offices by 1881, when Maejima resigned. Maejima hired an American, Samuel M. Bryan, to negotiate a postal exchange treaty with the United States (ratified 18 April 1874) and effected the admission, in 1877, of Japan to the Universal Postal Union.

Maejima took the lead in organizing postal savings (1874) and money order (1875) systems, revising weights and measures (1871) and the land tax (1878), and holding the first National Industrial Exhibition (1877). In 1872 he founded a daily newspaper, the YŪBIN HŌCHI SHIMBUN (renamed *Hōchi shimbun* in 1894; combined with *Yomiuri shimbun* in 1942). He also advocated simplifying the Japanese writing system by replacing Chinese characters with KANA syllabic script. See JAPANESE LANGUAGE REFORMS.

Maejima aided his friend Ōkuma in founding the Tōkyō Semmon Gakkō (renamed Waseda University in 1901) and served as its second president (1886–90). He and Ōkuma also helped found the RIKKEN KAISHINTŌ (Constitutional Reform Party). He was vice-minister of communications (1888–91) and a member of the House of Peers (1904–10).

Maejima Hisoka The father of Japan's postal service, Maejima coined the Japanese equivalents for such English terms as "mail" (*yūbin*) and "stamp" (*kitte*).

Maekawa Haruo 前川春雄

(1911–89). Businessman and governor of the BANK OF JAPAN (1979–84). Born in Tōkyō. After graduating from Tōkyō University in 1935, he entered the Bank of Japan and distinguished himself in the international finance department. He promoted the liberalization and internationalization of the money market. As a specialist in international finance, he acted as chairman of the "Task Force on Economic Structural Adjustment for International Cooperation" that released the MAEKAWA REPORT in 1986. He served as chairman of Kokusai Denshin Denwa Co, Ltd (1986–89), and was a member of the Economic Council of the Economic Planning Agency (1975–79; 1985–89).

Maekawa Kunio 前川国男

(1905–86). Architect. Born in the city of Niigata. Upon graduation from Tōkyō University in 1928, he studied in Paris under the French architect Le Corbusier. He worked in the office of Antonin RAYMOND before starting his own firm in 1935. Maekawa was internationally recognized as one of the foremost advocates of modern architecture in Japan. His noted works include the Harumi Apartment House (1958), the Tōkyō Metropolitan Festival Hall (1961), the Saitama Prefectural Museum (1971), the Tōkyō Kaijō Building (1974), the Tōkyō Metropolitan Art Museum (1975), and the Miyagi Museum of Art (1981).

Maekawa Report 前川レポート

(Maekawa Repōto). Report submitted in April 1986 by the Advisory Group on Economic Structural Adjustment for International Harmony, a private advisory group to Prime Minister NAKASONE YASUHIRO. The report is named after the group's chairman,

Maekawa Haruo (1911–89), former governor of the Bank of Japan.

The Maekawa Report stated that Japan's huge trade surplus had its roots in the nation's export-dependent economic structure and recommended that Japan aim at changing to an economic structure more in keeping with harmonious development of the world economy. It recommended the following policies: (1) stimulation of demand in the domestic market; (2) change to an industrial structure that would contribute to international harmony; (3) further improvement of access to the Japanese market for foreign nations, coupled with stimulation of imports; (4) stabilization of international exchange rates and liberalization and internationalization of financial markets; and (5) promotion of international cooperation and contributions to the world economy commensurate with Japan's international status. The government accepted these proposals and formulated its basic economic policies in the following years largely in line with the recommendations of the report.

Maeno Ryōtaku   前野良沢

(1723–1803). Physician and scholar of WESTERN LEARNING. Born in Edo (now Tōkyō). He began his medical career as a doctor of Chinese medicine (*kampō*) but in his late forties developed an interest in Western medicine and studied Dutch. In 1771, with SUGITA GEMPAKU and other scholars, Maeno observed a human dissection (at the time only those of the lowest classes handled corpses), using a Dutch anatomy text, *Ontleedkundige Tafelen* (1734, Anatomical Tables), as a reference. Impressed by the accuracy of the Dutch book, which was a translation of the German work *Anatomische Tabellen* (1722) by Johann Adam Kulmus (1639–1745), the group decided to translate it. The translation was completed three years later under the title KAITAI SHINSHO (New Book of Anatomy).

Mafune Yutaka   真船豊

(1902–77). Playwright. Born in Fukushima Prefecture; studied at Waseda University. He was influenced by Irish theater and wrote one-act plays. He joined the leftist agrarian movement in the late 1920s. A number of his plays, such as *Itachi* (1934, Weasel), depict the distortions of human nature among the peasant class. The play *Hadaka no machi* (1936, Naked City) focuses on city life and was made into a movie by director UCHIDA TOMU. After World War II, Mafune turned to comedy and farce as a means of exploring what it means to be Japanese. He also wrote scripts for radio broadcasts.

magatama → beads, ancient

magazines   雑誌

(*zasshi*). Since the first Japanese magazines were published in the years following the Meiji Restoration in 1868, periodicals have had a major, independent role in shaping ideas and behavior. The history of Japanese magazines can be divided into three stages: the emergence of the first magazines of opinion and general readership in the Meiji period (1868–1912); the growth of commercial publishing during the Taishō (1912–26) and early Shōwa (1926–89) periods; and the post–World War II period of mass communications.

Meiji-Period Magazines——The first periodical in Japan to use the word *zasshi* (literally, "miscellaneous writings") in the modern sense of magazine was *Seiyō zasshi* (The Western Magazine), which appeared in 1867 under the editorship of YANAGAWA SHUNSAN. It consisted primarily of translations from Dutch magazines. Several other periodicals were begun but soon ceased publication as a result of government controls on freedom of the press.

In the following decades opinion magazines in the true sense of the word began to appear. In 1887 TOKUTOMI SOHŌ, leader of the Min'yūsha group, founded KOKUMIN NO TOMO (The Nation's Friend), the first of a genre known as *sōgō zasshi*, or general interest magazines. *Taiyō* (The Sun), a magazine begun by the HAKUBUNKAN publishing company in 1895, established the standard format for the *sōgō zasshi*. The journal *Hanseikai zasshi* (1887, Magazine of the Self-Examination Society), established by the temperance movement, changed its name to CHŪŌ KŌRON (Central Review) in 1899 and set a new standard for editorial practices. In the world of belles lettres, the KEN'YŪSHA literary group led by OZAKI KŌYŌ began *Garakuta bunko* (Library of Odds and Ends), the first of Japan's literary magazines.

Taishō and Early Shōwa Periods——The Taishō years marked the beginning of intense competition among magazines in the areas of entertainment, arts, women's topics, and children's interests. The 1920s saw the commercialization of magazine publishing. KŌDANSHA, LTD, began *Kōdan kurabu* (Story Club) in 1911. In the midst of the TAISHŌ DEMOCRACY movement, YAMAMOTO SANEHIKO founded KAIZŌ (Reconstruction) in 1919. KIKUCHI KAN'S BUNGEI SHUNJŪ (Literary Annals), begun in 1923, cultivated literary talent. Kōdansha's KINGU (King) offered a varied content of serialized fiction, moralistic stories, and practical information. It reached a record circulation of over one million.

As Japan embarked on an imperialist course and militarists gained influence on politics, restrictions were imposed on free speech. Magazines were called on to promote patriotism, and those that took a critical stance toward the authorities, such as *Chūō kōron* and *Kaizō*, were forced to discontinue publication.

Post–World War II——With the end of World War II, *Chūō kōron*, *Bungei shunjū*, and *Kaizō* reappeared, and several other *sōgō zasshi* were inaugurated. The appearance of *Ōru yomimono* (All Reading Matter) in 1945 and *Shōsetsu shinchō* (New Currents in Novels) in 1947 marked the start of a class of magazines concentrating on light fiction with an emphasis on entertainment. A new term, CHŪKAN SHŌSETSU (middlebrow fiction), was coined to describe such reading matter. The biggest development in the publishing world, however, was the sudden growth in WEEKLY MAGAZINES.

Current Trends——WOMEN'S MAGAZINES have flourished in recent years. In 1990 there were 61 monthlies for female readers, from *An-an* and *Non-no*, which have been major fashion trendsetters since the 1970s, to *Kurowassan* (Croissant), *More*, and *With*, targeted at women in their 20s and 30s, and *Katei gahō* (Family Illustrated) and *Shufu no tomo* (The Housewife's Friend), aimed at a slightly more mature audience. Popular men's magazines include the fashion journals *Men's Non-no* and *Checkmate*, as well as *Popeye* and *Hot Dog Press*, whose editorial policy is directed toward the tastes and interests of a youthful market. One new development is the video magazine: inexpensive videocassettes released on a periodic basis and covering a variety of topics from cars to music and business information. Another comparatively recent genre is the urban entertainment guide, pioneered by the magazine *Pia* in the 1970s, offering comprehensive listings of films, plays, concerts, and other events. In 1989, 112 new magazines began publication, while 56 suspended or ceased their operations.

magemono 曲物
Round or oval containers made from slips of cypress or Japanese cedar. The slips are made by shaving with the grain along the circumference of a log. They are then held over flames or softened in boiling water and bent into shape. Joints are bound with strips of cherry bark, and slats of thicker wood are used to make the bottom. Lacquer is applied to some *magemono;* others are fashioned to serve as ladles, food steamers, or containers for meals.

mago 馬子
(packhorsemen). Men who led packhorses carrying freight or passengers. After the establishment of POST-STATION TOWNS under the RITSURYŌ SYSTEM in the 8th century, peasants were required to furnish horses and labor. From the late Kamakura period (1185–1333) they were called BASHAKU (teamsters) and became the principal transporters of rural products to the towns. By the Muromachi period (1333–1568) they virtually monopolized haulage on the highways through well-organized associations. These groups became known for uprisings (BASHAKU IKKI) against the erection of toll barriers, involvement in peasant revolts (TSUCHI IKKI), and terrorism toward travelers. In the Edo period (1600–1868) the term *mago* referred to those packhorsemen permanently assigned to post stations (*shukuba*). *Mago* songs (*mago uta*) are an important type of Japanese FOLK SONG.

Magome Pass 馬籠峠
(Magome Tōge). Located in southwestern Nagano Prefecture, central Honshū. The nearby post-station town of Magome prospered during the Edo period (1600–1868) because of its location on the highway Nakasendō but declined with the opening of a national highway and a railway line. Vestiges of the post-station town still remain. Altitude: 801 m (2,628 ft).

Magoshi Kyōhei 馬越恭平
(1844–1933). Businessman. Born in Bitchū Province (now part of Okayama Prefecture). In 1873 he entered a Tōkyō trading company established by MASUDA TAKASHI; the firm was reorganized as the MITSUI Trading Company (Mitsui Bussan Kaisha) in 1876, with Magoshi as Yokohama branch manager and a company director. In 1896 he left Mitsui to become managing director of the Nippon Brewery Company, which in 1906 became Dai Nippon Brewery Company; it soon became the largest brewery in Japan. Popularly referred to as the "King of Beer," Magoshi was associated with over 100 companies, including Tōkyō Electric and the SOUTH MANCHURIA RAILWAY. He was named to the House of Peers in 1924.

magusaba 秣場
Term used in the Edo period (1600–1868) for areas, usually fields and mountains, designated for collecting vegetation to be used as fertilizer and fodder. Most of these areas were collectively owned, with their use restricted to a certain village or group of villages. For the right to collect, supplementary taxes (*komononari*) were usually paid to the shogunal or domainal government. See also IRIAI.

Mahiru no ankoku 真昼の暗黒
(1956, Darkness at Noon). Film directed by IMAI TADASHI. (It bears no relation to the Arthur Koestler novel of the same title.) The screenplay by HASHIMOTO SHINOBU is based on *Saibankan* (1955, The Judge), an account of the YAKAI INCIDENT written by Masaki Hiroshi (1896–1975), a defense lawyer involved in the actual incident. In the film a group of young working-class men are framed by the police and pressured into confessing to a murder they did not commit. The film achieved notoriety because it was released while the courts were trying the murder case resulting from the Yakai Incident. The film clearly advocated acquittal by attempting to demonstrate that the defendants could not possibly have committed the crime. Imai is concerned here, as in his other films, with exposing the injustice that persists in Japanese society. The film's finest sequence is the surreal, satiric enactment of the murder in a flashback that employs a variety of cinematographic techniques to make a mockery of the case against the boys.

Mah-Jongg 麻雀
(J: *mājan*). Game of Chinese origin usually played by four persons with 136 pieces called tiles. The two Chinese characters for Mah-Jongg literally mean "house sparrow," and the name is said to derive from the way the shuffling of the tiles sounds like the twittering of sparrows. It is thought that the game itself derives from tarot cards introduced to China from Europe. Mah-Jongg is similar to the Western card game of rummy in that the object is to collect combinations of sequences and sets of identical tiles.

Mah-Jongg was introduced to Japan early in the 20th century. By the 1920s it had become especially popular in urban areas, and it achieved an unprecedented level of popularity after World War II. Today there are more than 25,000 Mah-Jongg parlors in the country and more than 14 million players. In Japan Mah-Jongg has traditionally been a man's game, frequently played for money.

Maihara 米原[町]
Also known as Maibara. Town in eastern Shiga Prefecture, central Honshū, on the eastern bank of Lake Biwa. A port town since the 17th century, it is served by several highways and lines of JR (Japan Railways). Agriculture is the main industry. The Samegai district is known for its trout fisheries. Pop: 12,536.

Maiko 舞子
Also known as Maikonohama. Coastal district in Tarumi Ward, Kōbe, Hyōgo Prefecture, western Honshū, along the Akashi Strait. Maiko was famous for its pine trees, but they have largely been destroyed by automobile exhaust fumes and land development.

maiko 舞妓
Apprentice GEISHA in the area around Kyōto and Ōsaka; those in the Tōkyō area are called *hangyoku.* During their apprenticeship as traditional entertainers, *maiko* are schooled in such arts as classical dance and the playing of traditional drums. Until they attain full geisha status, *maiko* maintain a distinctive hairstyle and dress for entertaining and wear high round clogs (*pokkuri*) when outdoors. Young women entering the profes-

maiko Apprentice *geisha* walk along a Kyōto street in full costume. Holding the hems of their long *kimono* and wearing high round clogs, the *maiko* make popular photo subjects.

Maki Fumihiko An aerial view of the architect's Tōkyō Metropolitan Gymnasium (1990), showing the large, circular Main Arena.

sion of geisha were traditionally apprenticed as *maiko* between the ages of about 13 and 18; however, the few women who enter the profession today typically do so at a slightly later age and without undergoing the *maiko* apprenticeship.

Mainichi Broadcasting System, Inc (MBS)　　　[株]毎日放送

(Mainichi Hōsō). An Ōsaka-based commercial radio and television broadcasting company serving the Kinki (west-central Honshū) region. Established in 1950 with backing from the MAINICHI SHIMBUN, one of Japan's largest national daily newspapers, as the New Japan Broadcasting Company (Shin Nippon Hōsō), it was one of the first commercial radio stations to operate in Japan. In 1956 it joined with ASAHI BROADCASTING CORPORATION (ABC) to form the Ōsaka Broadcasting Corporation (Ōsaka Terebi). Later it withdrew its capital funds from Ōsaka Broadcasting and founded the present Mainichi Broadcasting System in 1958. Although under the aegis of the *Mainichi shimbun*, for many years it shared a network affiliation with Nippon Educational Television (now known as ASAHI NATIONAL BROADCASTING CO, LTD), a Tōkyō-based television company affiliated with the ASAHI SHIMBUN, another leading newspaper. In 1975 it switched affiliation to the Japan News Network (JNN) belonging to the *Mainichi shimbun*–affiliated TŌKYŌ BROADCASTING SYSTEM, INC (TBS), group. It has operated since then as a secondary affiliate.

Mainichi shimbun　　　毎日新聞

One of Japan's leading national daily newspapers. The history of the *Mainichi* dates back to the *Nihon rikken seitō shimbun*, an early political news organ of the Rikken Seitō (Constitutional Government Party), a spin-off of the JIYŪTŌ (Liberal Party), which began publishing in 1882. In 1888 the name was changed to the *Ōsaka mainichi shimbun*, and the paper emerged as a general news publication aimed at the Ōsaka merchant community. MOTOYAMA HIKOICHI, who took over as company president in 1903, transformed the *Mainichi* into a first-class na-

tional news publication. In 1943 the *Tōkyō nichinichi shimbun* and the *Ōsaka mainichi shimbun* were consolidated under the present *Mainichi shimbun* banner. Along with the ASAHI SHIMBUN and YOMIURI SHIMBUN, it ranked as one of Japan's three largest national newspaper companies. Its circulation was 4.1 million in 1991. In addition to its regular daily edition, the *Mainichi* publishes special newspapers for primary- and middle-school students, the English-language *Mainichi Daily News*, and numerous periodicals and books.

Maisaka　　　舞阪[町]

Town in western Shizuoka Prefecture, central Honshū, on Lake HAMANA. Maisaka developed as a post-station town on the highway TŌKAIDŌ. Its main industry is fishing; eels, *nori* (a kind of seaweed), and snapping turtles (*suppon*) are raised. The town is also noted for its musical-instrument industry. Attractions include the Bentenjima Hot Spring and the Hamanako boat races. Pop: 11,492.

Maitreya → Miroku

Maizuru　　　舞鶴[市]

City in northern Kyōto Prefecture, central Honshū, on the Sea of Japan. A castle town and port in the Edo period (1600–1868), it has been the site of a naval base since 1901. After World War II, it handled Japanese repatriates from overseas. It is an important port for trade with Russia, South Korea, China, and Southeast Asia. Principal industries are spinning, lumbering, shipbuilding, plate glass, and chemicals. Pop: 96,333.

Majima Rikō　　　真島利行

(1874–1962). Organic chemist known for his extensive research on urushiol, the chief component of Japanese lacquer (*urushi*), safflower (*benibana*) and other vegetable pigments, and alkaloids. Born in Kyōto, he graduated from Tōkyō University. He studied in Europe from 1907 to 1911, when he returned to Japan and became professor at Tōhoku University. He moved to Ōsaka University in 1932 and served as its president from 1943 to 1946. He was influential in founding the Tōkyō Institute of Tech-

nology (Tōkyō Kōgyō Daigaku) and in establishing the faculties of science at Tōhoku and Ōsaka universities. He received the Order of Culture in 1949.

Maki　　　巻[町]

Town in central Niigata Prefecture, central Honshū. A commuter suburb of the city of Niigata, it is surrounded by rice-producing farmland and has several food-processing plants. Pop: 29,020.

maki　　　牧

(pasture land). Little is known about the regulation of pasturage for horses and cattle until the TAIKA REFORM of 645, when they were put under the control of the Ministry of Military Affairs (Hyōbushō). Provincial governors (*kokushi*) were made responsible for the raising of these animals, which were used for transportation, farming, and military purposes. As the power of the central government declined from the 9th century onward, such official pasture lands were increasingly absorbed by private estates (*shōen*) and sometimes converted to farmland; horses raised on these estates were sent to the proprietors rather than to the government. Pasture land was again strictly regulated under the Tokugawa shogunate (1603–1867). The eighth shōgun, TOKUGAWA YOSHIMUNE, established major government-controlled pasture areas at Kogane and Sakura in Shimōsa Province (now part of Chiba Prefecture), and many *daimyō* followed suit in their own domains.

Maki Aritsune　　　槙有恒

(1894–1989). Pioneer of modern Japanese mountain climbing. Born in Miyagi Prefecture. In 1921, after graduating from Keiō University, Maki made the first ascent of the east ridge of the Eiger in the Bernese Alps. Four years later he made the first ascent of Mt. Alberta in the Canadian Rockies. In 1956 he led the Japanese party that made the first ascent of Mt. Manaslu (Nepal).

maki-e　　　蒔絵

(literally, "sprinkled picture"). Term for a class of decorative techniques used in LACQUER WARE, all employing sprinkled powders or filings, usually of gold or silver. The powder is applied to lacquered designs while the lacquer is still damp. The first record of their use in Japan dates from the 8th century AD. During the Heian period (794–1185), *maki-e* became the dominant method of Japanese lacquer decoration. By the Kamakura period (1185–1333) three major *maki-e* techniques had evolved: *togidashi maki-e* ("polished-out sprinkled picture"), *hiramaki-e* ("level sprinkled picture"), and *takamaki-e* ("relief sprinkled picture"), each of which varied the texture of the finished product. In the Muromachi period (1333–1568) hereditary lines of *maki-e* craftsmen, such as the Kōami and Igarashi families, emerged, and *maki-e* techniques reached a high level of development. In the Azuchi-Momoyama period (1568–1600) a new form called KŌDAIJI MAKI-E became popular, and in the Edo period (1600–1868) *namban maki-e*, which mixes *maki-e* with *raden* (MOTHER-OF-PEARL INLAY) was exported in large quantities to Europe. The RIMPA artists contributed to *maki-e*'s popularity with their unusual designs.

Maki Fumihiko　　　槙文彦

(1928–). Architect and urban designer. Born in Tōkyō. After graduating from the architecture department of Tōkyō University in 1952, he pursued advanced studies at Cranbrook Academy and Harvard University. He is known for his study of urban morphology entitled *Investigations in Collective Form* (1960). Maki began his career with the Toyota Memorial Auditorium at Nagoya University (1960). His designs include the Risshō University Kumagaya campus (1968), the Daikan'yama Hillside Terrace Apartments (1969–76), the Ōsaka Prefectural Sports Center (1972), the Okinawa Aquarium (1975), the Spiral Building (1985), the Nippon Convention Center (Makuhari Messe; 1989), and the Tōkyō Metropolitan Gymnasium (1990).

Makiguchi Tsunesaburō 牧口常三郎

(1871–1944). Religious leader and educator. Founder and first president of the SŌKA GAKKAI, a lay organization of the Nichiren Shōshū sect of Buddhism (see NEW RELIGIONS). Born in Niigata Prefecture, he graduated from the Sapporo Normal School in 1893. He worked as an elementary-school teacher and later became a principal. He wrote several books, including *Sōka kyōikugaku taikei* (1930, The System of Value-Creating Pedagogy). In his many writings Makiguchi strongly emphasized his concept of value creation (*kachiron*), an assertion that true happiness can be attained through the "creation of values." He became convinced that Buddhist ideas were exactly what he had been striving to achieve in the classroom. In 1930 he formed what became the Sōka Gakkai to promote his educational reforms. He and others of his organization were jailed during World War II for opposing the government's war policies and the enforced belief in STATE SHINTŌ. Makiguchi died in prison in 1944, but Sōka Gakkai became the largest of Japan's new religions.

Makihatayama 巻機山

Mountain on the border of Niigata and Gumma prefectures, central Honshū. Popular for skiing and mountain climbing, it is also the focus for worship of the guardian deity of weaving. Height: 1,962 m (6,437 ft).

Maki Izumi 真木和泉

(1813–64). Activist in the antishogunate movement of the late Edo period (1600–1868). Also known as Maki Yasuomi. He wrote pamphlets for the antishogunate cause. In 1864 he joined an army of proimperial loyalists in the Chōshū domain (now Yamaguchi Prefecture) in an unsuccessful attempt to retake Kyōto (see HAMAGURI GOMON INCIDENT). The insurgents retreated and Maki committed suicide.

Makino Eiichi 牧野英一

(1878–1970). Scholar of criminal law and legal theory; prominent advocate of reform in the theory and practice of the administration of Japan's Penal Code (see CRIMINAL LAW and CRIMINAL PROCEDURE. Born in Takayama, Gifu Prefecture, Makino graduated from the law department of Tōkyō University in 1903 and subsequently secured appointments there as lecturer and assistant professor. From 1910 to 1913 he studied abroad in Germany, England, and Italy. In 1913 he was appointed professor at Tōkyō University, a position he held for 25 years. He actively sought the adoption of modernist criminal law and theory, stressing the importance of rehabilitation rather than retribution as the focus of punishment. He served on a number of legal reform advisory committees.

Makino served as longtime editor in chief of *Kikan keisei* (Quarterly Journal of Criminal Law and Criminology) and was himself a prolific writer. Among his more than 100 published works are *Nihon keihō* (1916, The Penal Code of Japan) and *Keihō kenkyū* (20 vols, 1919–67, Studies in Criminal Law).

Makinohara 牧ノ原

Upland on the west bank of the river Ōigawa, southern Shizuoka Prefecture, central Honshū. An elevated fan formed by deposits from the Ōigawa. It has been a tea-growing area since the late 19th century. Average elevation: 90 m (35 ft); area: 50 sq km (20 sq mi).

Makino Masahiro マキノ雅裕

(1908–). Film director. One of the primary creators of period films during the 1920s and 1930s and a leading director of action films until the 1970s. His father, MAKINO SHŌZŌ, was a pioneer of early Japanese cinema. Young Makino grew up in Kyōto movie studios. He directed his first film at age 18 and made his first masterpiece when he was only 20: *Rōningai* (1928, Street of Masterless Samurai), a devastating look at the decadent society of the Edo period (1600–1868). Makino's period films have always been vehicles for comment on contemporary society, expressing a certain degree of nihilism that has carried over into his later films about gamblers and gangsters. His films have usually featured heroes who are loners, often masterless *samurai* or outlaws, who find themselves compelled to right an injustice simply out of a sense of personal obligation. These heroes are usually opponents of conventional society. Makino directed 261 films from 1926 to 1972, including nine films in the series *Nihon kyōkaku den* (1964–71, Tales of Japanese Chivalry).

Makino Nobuaki 牧野伸顕

(1861–1949). Politician and diplomat. Also known as Makino Shinken. Born in the Satsuma domain (now Kagoshima Prefecture), the second son of ŌKUBO TOSHIMICHI; adopted by the Makino family. In 1871 Makino went abroad on the IWAKURA MISSION. He entered the Ministry of Foreign Affairs in 1880 and served in such posts as ambassador to Italy, minister of education in the first SAIONJI KIM-

MOCHI cabinet (1906–08), and minister of foreign affairs in the first YAMAMOTO GONNOHYŌE cabinet (1913–14) before attending the Paris Peace Conference (see VERSAILLES, TREATY OF) in 1919. Beginning in 1921, first as imperial household minister and then as lord keeper of the privy seal, Makino assisted Prince Saionji in mediating among the political parties, the military, the bureaucracy, and big business. In the early 1930s, Makino came under criticism for his support of a cooperative, nonexpansionist foreign policy and was forced to leave office in 1935. He narrowly escaped assassination in the FEBRUARY 26TH INCIDENT of 1936. Prime Minister YOSHIDA SHIGERU was his son-in-law.

Makino Shin'ichi 牧野信一

(1896–1936). Author. Born in Kanagawa Prefecture. Graduate of Waseda University. While working as a magazine editor in Tōkyō, he wrote in the autobiographical style (see I-NOVEL), as in his short-story collection *Chichi o uru ko* (1924). Progressive alcoholism and emotional exhaustion forced him to return to his rural hometown in 1927. There he developed the style peculiar to him—a combination of dream and reality, of Greek mythological figures and fantasized landscapes. Such short stories as "Mura no sutoa ha" (1928) and "Zēron" (1931) revealed his antipathy toward his family. He committed suicide in 1936.

Makino Shōzō 牧野省三

(1878–1929). Director and producer. Born in Kyōto. Considered the father of Japanese film. Makino was manager of a small theater when he met Yokota Einosuke (1872–1943), head of the company that later became NIKKATSU CORPORATION. Yokota hired him to direct films, the first of which was *Honnōji-gassen* (1908). Makino later went on to direct 60 to 80 films a year for the next 10 years with ONOE MATSUNOSUKE as his leading man. These films—thrilling tales of masterful swordsmen and nonsensical, absurd monster stories—had immediate popular appeal. He left Nikkatsu in 1921 to work independently and in 1925 established Makino Productions. He popularized realis-

Makino Eiichi This scholar of criminal law stressed the importance of rehabilitation over retribution.

Makuhari A baseball stadium and the Makuhari Messe, a huge convention and exhibition hall (behind the stadium), are key elements of the international trade complex being developed here.

Makino Tomitarō The pioneer of Japanese plant taxonomy.

tic period dramas, starring actors such as BANDŌ TSUMASABURŌ. His son MAKINO MASAHIRO also became a director.

Makino Tomitarō 牧野富太郎

(1862–1957). Plant taxonomist. Born in Kōchi Prefecture. After dropping out of elementary school, he studied botany on his own. In 1893 he became an assistant instructor at Tōkyō University and later an instructor. He helped publish *Shokubutsugaku zasshi* (The Botanical Magazine) and wrote *Nihon shokubutsu zukan* (1940, Illustrated Flora of Japan). He contributed greatly to the development of plant taxonomy in Japan and identified as many as 1,000 new species of plants. He was posthumously awarded the Order of Culture.

Maki Ryōko 巻菱湖

(1777–1843). Calligrapher of the late Edo period (1600–1868). He was born in Echigo (now Niigata Prefecture) in a post-station town called Maki, from which he took his surname. He took his art name, Ryōko, from a nearby lake full of water chestnuts (*ryōko*). He became the pupil of KAMEDA BŌSAI. Ryōko's calligraphy follows that of Bōsai but is less dynamic, showing instead the fluid style and grace of various Chinese masters. With ICHIKAWA BEIAN, he was considered one of the two master calligraphers in Edo (now Tōkyō), but while Beian attracted followers from the governing elite, Ryōko appealed to Edo townsmen. Their influence on succeeding generations, however, was equal.

Makita Corporation [株]マキタ

(Makita). Manufacturer of electric power tools and pneumatic tools. Established in 1915. In 1958 Makita developed Japan's first portable power plane. The company has 15 overseas subsidiaries and operations in more than 100 countries. Sales for the fiscal year ending March 1991 totaled ¥122.4 billion (US $892.1 million), and the company was capitalized at ¥23.9 billion (US $174.2 million). Headquarters are in Anjō, Aichi Prefecture.

makoto 誠

(sincerity; Ch: *cheng* or *ch'eng*). In Chinese philosophy, *cheng* is the cardinal virtue and metaphysical principle underlying the Five Virtues of Confucian teaching. Expounded as a central concept in the Confucian classic *Doctrine of the Mean* (Ch: *Zhongyong* or *Chung yung*; J: *Chūyō*), it came to mean both the essence of humanity and the Way of Heaven. The school of the Chinese Neo-Confucian philosopher Zhu Xi (Chu Hsi; J: Shushi) emphasized *cheng*, interpreting it as truthfulness.

In Japan, ITŌ JINSAI and other nonorthodox

Confucian thinkers interpreted *cheng* or *makoto* as sincerity of mind or heart that should rule relationships between individuals. At the same time in the native SHINTŌ tradition, *makoto* (*ma*, true or genuine; *koto*, words or conduct) was considered an essential virtue that underscored purity and honesty of mind or heart, and the term was often used by Shintoists and KOKUGAKU (National Learning) scholars of the Edo period (1600–1868).

Maksimovich, Karl Ivanovich マキシモビッチ, K. I.

(1827–91). Russian botanist. Born near Moscow, the son of a doctor. Studied medicine and botany at the university in Dorpat (now Tartu). In 1853 he studied the flora of the Amur River region, and in 1860 he came to Japan, where he studied the distribution of plants in various areas of the country. Maksimovich is said to have been consulted by many Japanese botanists of the time, and his findings influenced subsequent Japanese plant taxonomy.

Makuhari 幕張

Name given to the northwestern section of the city of Chiba, Chiba Prefecture, central Honshū. Formerly a fishing village on Tōkyō Bay, Makuhari is now being developed into a center for international trade. The Makuhari Messe, an international convention and exhibition complex, was completed here in 1989.

makura kotoba 枕詞

("pillow words"). Conventional epithets used in WAKA poetry to modify certain fixed words. *Makura kotoba* were used for images or tonal elevation and usually occupied one 5-syllable line, modifying the first word in the following line. For example, in the following poem (GOSEN WAKASHŪ no. 659) by Taira no Sadabumi (also called Taira no Sadafun; d 923), *chihayaburu* ("mighty") is a *makura kotoba* modifying *kami* ("gods"):

Nanigoto o
Ima wa tanoman
Chihayaburu
Kami mo tasukenu
Waga mi narikeri

What remains
On which I might rely?
Abandoned, I
Find even mighty gods refuse
To lend a helping hand.

Makura kotoba appear in the poetry of the 8th-century chronicles KOJIKI and NIHON SHOKI and were popular in the MAN'YŌSHŪ (compiled ca 759). Afterward, the technique of KAKEKOTOBA, or "pivot words," gained predominance, and the original meanings of many *makura kotoba* were lost. The device continued to be used by later poets, however, to elevate the language of a poem by recalling the glories of bygone days.

Makura no sōshi 枕草子

(996–1012; tr *The Pillow Book of Sei Shōnagon*, 1967). The first example of the ZUIHITSU (random jottings) genre, written by a court lady of the Heian period (794–1185), SEI SHŌNAGON (fl late 10th century). A slender volume of short eyewitness narratives, casual essays, impressions, reflections, lists, and imagined scenes, the *Makura no sōshi* gives a detailed account of events and customs at the Heian court; at the same time, it hints at the inner reality of court life as ex-

perienced by its author. Matters of love and the beauty of nature are predominant themes, but issues of taste and the foibles of the uncouth are delineated with sharp and often ruthless wit. A motif characteristic of the author, text, and genre is the list (of likes and dislikes, interesting names, natural phenomena, or items of passing interest), while the unfinished sentence consisting of a noun clause is a typical mode of expression. In discussing love, Sei Shōnagon avoids the tragic tone of the classical tradition, offering a vision that is realistic, satirical, and, above all, amusing. The deft vignettes she paints in her section on the four seasons, capturing the moods and hours of the day that best exemplify each, have been much admired and imitated by Japanese authors over the years. All in all, the *Makura no sōshi* is a vehicle for its author's vivacious personality and style, rendering her impressions of the passing scene with unsparing wit and sharp economy.

Makurazaki 枕崎[市]

City in southern Kagoshima Prefecture, Kyūshū. A base for bonito fishing, it also produces tea. A tea experimental station is here. The ancient port of BŌ NO TSU is nearby. Pop: 28,794.

Malayan Campaign マレー作戦

(Marē Sakusen). Japanese invasion and conquest of the Malay Peninsula and Singapore at the beginning of World War II. The commanding officers were Lieutenant General YAMASHITA TOMOYUKI and Vice Admiral Ozawa Jisaburō (1886–1966). A surprise landing made on 8 December 1941 at the base of the Malay Peninsula and landings in southern Thailand caught British forces off guard. Japanese troops swiftly moved down the peninsula through territory considered impassable and captured Singapore on 15 February 1942. In the Battle of the SOUTH CHINA SEA on 10 December, the major defending forces of the British Royal Navy were destroyed. See also WORLD WAR II.

Malaysia and Japan マレーシアと日本

(Marēshia *to* Nihon). Japan's earliest contact with the Malay Peninsula dates back to the 15th century, when the Ryukyuan kingdom traded with Portuguese at Malacca. After the Tokugawa shogunate (1603–1867) established its NATIONAL SECLUSION policy in 1636, there was little intercourse between Japan and Malaya except for the continued exchange of goods through Ryukyuan traders at the port of Malacca.

Contacts increased after the Meiji Restoration of 1868, and by the end of the Meiji period (1868–1912) there were more than 2,300 Japanese in Malaya, the majority of whom were KARAYUKI SAN (women sold into prostitution and sent abroad). An increasing number of Japanese were attracted by economic opportunities, and a boom in the market for rubber marked the beginning of Japanese economic interests in Malaya. Fluctuations in the rubber industry led to Japanese involvement in the iron-mining industry, and before long iron mining became a Japanese monopoly. The last of the three major industries in which Japan asserted control was the fishing industry.

In the 1920s and 1930s Chinese in peninsular Malaya became actively engaged in an anti-Japanese boycott movement, and, when the Japanese army invaded Malaya in 1941–42, the *kempeitai* (military police) executed many Malayan Chinese suspected of anti-

Japanese activity. Japanese atrocities committed during the military occupation period (1942–45) eventually led to the "BLOOD DEBT" INCIDENT in 1962. The Japanese occupation also spurred the rise of the postwar communist movement. Communist leaders of the anti-Japanese nationalist movement went into the jungle after the fall of Singapore to the Japanese in February 1942 and organized the Malayan People's Anti-Japanese Army (MPAJA). The MPAJA, composed primarily of ethnic Chinese, harassed the Japanese and murdered their Malay collaborators, contributing to the outbreak of bitter and bloody racial strife between the two ethnic groups in the postwar years. Another legacy of the Japanese occupation was the indoctrination and training of Malay youths at schools in Malaya and Japan, fostering a spirit of self-discipline and anticolonialism integral to the process of nation building following World War II.

In 1957 the Federation of Malaya gained its independence within the British Commonwealth and established diplomatic relations with Japan. When Indonesian-Malaysian conflicts occurred following the formation of Malaysia in 1963, Japanese prime ministers served as mediators and were instrumental in preventing the conflicts from expanding further. Japan's mediation role and mutual economic needs in the 1960s further paved the way for closer economic relations. In 1966 Japan extended its first yen credit to Malaysia, equivalent to US $50 million worth of goods and services, for project aid. Between 1966 and 1989 the Japanese government granted Malaysia total yen credits equivalent to US $3.4 billion (in 1989 dollars). The Japanese have been involved in a wide range of activities including investment in manufacturing for natural resource development, construction of dams and irrigation projects, Youth Volunteer Corps assistance, and educational support for Japanese studies, as well as agricultural and vocational training.

In 1990 Malaysia's trade balance with Japan, its largest trade partner, shifted from surplus to deficit. That year Japan purchased US $5.4 billion worth of goods from Malaysia, mostly in the form of raw materials and primary products as well as crude oil and natural gas, while Malaysia imported US $5.5 billion worth of manufactured goods from Japan, mostly heavy industrial and chemical goods and machinery. As of 1989 Japanese investment in Malaysia totaled US $2.5 billion, with the majority of Japanese firms operating in Malaysia as joint ventures.

Several hundred Malaysians have studied at Japanese universities under scholarship programs sponsored by the Japanese Ministry of Education and other organizations, while the JAPAN FOUNDATION actively promotes Japanese studies in Malaysia. The Japan-Malaysia Association in Tōkyō is active in promoting friendship and mutual understanding between the two nations.

Mamiya Rinzō   間宮林蔵

(1775–1844). Explorer. Born in Hitachi Province (now Ibaraki Prefecture), Rinzō studied cartography under the geographer INŌ TADATAKA, and from 1800 worked as a surveyor for the shogunal administration in EZO (now Hokkaidō) and the southern Kuril Islands. In 1807 he was wounded in a Russian raid on Etorofu (Iturup). Ordered to reconnoiter Karafuto (Sakhalin), he explored its eastern periphery in 1808. The following

year he traveled alone up the west coast and discovered that, contrary to prevailing theories, Sakhalin was separated from the continent by a strait. He then crossed over to the mainland and ascended the Amur River to within 128 kilometers (80 mi) of the present Soviet city of Komsomolsk. Rinzō's reports, *Kita Ezo zusetsu* (An Illustrated Account of Sakhalin) and *Tōdatsu kikō* (Travels in Tartary), made important contributions to ethnographic and geographic knowledge. Rinzō later became a shogunal spy and is thought to have been instrumental in bringing about the arrest of the cartographer TAKAHASHI KAGEYASU in 1828, after the latter had secretly exchanged some maps with the Bavarian naturalist Philipp Franz von SIEBOLD. Rinzō died alone, impoverished, and ostracized by many former colleagues. After returning to Europe Siebold publicized Rinzō's discoveries, which were duly recorded on Western maps.

mammals   哺乳類

(*honyūrui*). In Japan there are about 110 kinds of land mammals. The only surviving large carnivores are two species of BEARS: the brown bear in Hokkaidō and the Himalayan black bear in the mainland. (The wolf of Hokkaidō and the Japanese wolf of the mainland were extinct by about 1905.) Ungulates are limited to three forms of *shika* (sika deer) in the mainland, Tsushima, and Hokkaidō; the KAMOSHIKA (Japanese serow) and *inoshishi* (Japanese wild boar) in the mainland; and the small, primitive Ryūkyū *inoshishi* (Liukiu wild boar) of the Ryūkyū Islands (see WILD BOAR).

Among Japan's medium- or small-sized mammals are the TANUKI (raccoon dog), distributed throughout the mainland, Hokkaidō, Korea, and China; the yellow-furred *ten* (yellow marten; *Martes melampus*), of the mainland and Tsushima; the mainland's *musasabi* (the larger of Japan's FLYING SQUIRRELS); and the *saru* (Japanese macaque), found in the mainland and Yakushima. Japanese MONKEYS are the northernmost monkeys in the world. Among fruit bats, the world's northernmost are two species of *ōkōmori* (flying foxes; see BATS) in the Ryūkyū and Ogasawara islands.

Rare Ryūkyū Species—The Ryūkyūs are inhabited by such rare endemic species as the arboreal *kenaganezumi* (bristled rat; *Rattus legatus*) and the terrestrial *togenezumi* (Amami spiny mouse; *Tokudaia osimensis*). The rarest are the Amami *no kurousagi* (Amami rabbit) and the Iriomote *yamaneko* (Iriomote cat). The Amami rabbit is a remnant of the subfamily Palaeolaginae that flourished in the Tertiary period; the Iriomote cat, found on the islands of Amami Ōshima and Tokunoshima, is a remnant of the tribe Metailurini that flourished in the Miocene period in China and is quite dif-

ferent from the leopard cat of the tribe Felini found in Tsushima, Taiwan, China, and elsewhere.

Mainland Small Mammals—The smallest mammals of the mainland include the *kawanezumi* (Himalayan water shrew; *Chimarrogale platycephala*); the *kayanezumi* (harvest mouse; *Micromys minutus*), which makes a spherical nest in tall grass; the *okojo* (stoat; *Mustela erminea*); and numerous kinds of bats, house mice, and rats. Of the MOLES, the *himehimizu* (furry-snouted shrew mole) and *himizu* (Japanese shrew mole) are closely allied to the American shrew mole (genus *Neurotrichus*) of the western United States. The *yamane* (see DORMOUSE, JAPANESE) hibernates rolled into a ball and remains undisturbed even when rolled around; its genus (*Glirulus*) appears to have been distributed widely on the Eurasian continent, and fossils of the same genus have been unearthed from the Pliocene and Lower Pleistocene in Europe. Endemic species commonly found in cultivated fields and on plains in the mainland include the *akanezumi* (Japanese field mouse; *Apodemus speciosus*), the *hatanezumi* (Japanese vole; *Microtus montebelli*), the Azuma *mogura* (Japanese mole), and the *jinezumi* (dzinezumi shrew; *Crocidura dsinezumi*); in Hokkaidō are found species that also inhabit the continent, including the *yukiusagi* (snow hare), the *shimarisu* (chipmunk; *Tamias sibiricus*), the Ezo *yachinezumi* (red-backed vole; *Clethrionomys rufocanus*), and the *ōashi togarinezumi* (big-clawed shrew; *Sorex unguiculatus*).

Marine Mammals—The rarest of Japan's MARINE MAMMALS is the dugong of the Ryūkyū Islands. Dugongs were once plentiful in the sea around the Yaeyama Islands but in recent years are seldom found. The *sunameri* (black finless porpoise; *Neomeris phocaenoides*), only 1.0 to 1.8 meters (3.3 to 5.9 ft) long, is found in large numbers along the coast of Honshū in south-central Japan and sometimes swims up large rivers. The *ashika* (Japanese sea lion; *Zalophus japonicus*) is endemic to the coast of the mainland, but it is feared to be on the verge of extinction.

See also CATS; CATTLE; DEER, JAPANESE; DOG, JAPANESE; FLYING SQUIRRELS; FOXES; HORSES; JAPANESE SPANIEL; JAPANESE TERRIER; KAWAUSO; RABBITS; RATS AND MICE; TOSA DOG; WEASELS; WHALES; WILDCATS; WOLF, JAPANESE.

Mampukuji   万福寺

Head temple of the ŌBAKU SECT of ZEN Buddhism, located in Uji, Kyōto Prefecture. Founded in 1661 by the Chinese monk INGEN, the temple complex is especially noted for the stylistic influence of Ming-dynasty (1368–1644) China in its BUDDHIST ARCHITEC-

Mampukuji
1 This wooden fish gong is struck to call the temple's monks to meals.
2 The Daiō Hōden, the main hall, was built in 1668 in the style of Buddhist architecture characteristic of Ming-dynasty China.

Mamiya Rinzō
Geographic and ethnographic knowledge about Sakhalin and the Amur River region was significantly expanded by this cartographer's early-19th-century explorations.

TURE, carvings, calligraphy, paintings, and statuary. Among the temple's large collection are many statues by the Chinese craftsman Han Dōsei (Ch: Fan Daosheng or Fan Tao-sheng; 1637–70), including those of the eccentric monk Hotei (see SEVEN DEITIES OF GOOD FORTUNE); Idaten (Skt: Skanda), a guardian deity of monks; and the 16 RAKAN, or worthy ones. Its noted paintings include a portrait of Ingen done by the NAGASAKI SCHOOL master Kita Genki and paintings by KANŌ TAN'YŪ, IKE NO TAIGA, and ITSUNEN. Most of the present temple buildings date from the 1660s.

Since 1786 only Japanese monks have succeeded to the abbacy at Mampukuji, but until 1740 the abbacy was held exclusively by Chinese. In the 46-year interim, Japanese and Chinese monks alternated as monastery superiors.

Manabe Akifusa　　　　　間部詮房

(1667–1720). Adviser to the sixth and seventh Tokugawa shōguns, TOKUGAWA IENOBU and Ietsugu (1709–16; r 1713–16). Born in Oshi, Musashi Province (now Saitama Prefecture). Manabe was appointed Ienobu's page in 1684. When Ienobu was made shogunal heir, Manabe accompanied him to Edo Castle. Appointed SOBAYŌNIN (grand chamberlain) in 1709, he had direct access to the shōgun at all times. After Ienobu died in 1712, Manabe conducted governmental affairs during the short reign of the child shōgun Ietsugu, but in 1716 TOKUGAWA YO-SHIMUNE became shōgun, and Manabe lost his position. In 1717 he was transferred to Murakami (in what is now Niigata Prefecture) where he died.

Manabe Akikatsu　　　　　間部詮勝

(1802–84). Senior councillor (rōjū) of the Tokugawa shogunate (1603–1867). He was a supporter of the great elder (tairō) II NAOSUKE and a leader in the suppression of critics of the shogunate (see ANSEI PURGE). Manabe, who was daimyō of the small Sabae domain (now part of Fukui Prefecture), obtained imperial approval for the ANSEI COMMERCIAL TREATIES, but eventually lost Ii's favor and was forced into retirement.

management　　　　　経営管理

(keiei kanri). In Japan, the origins of the professional manager go back to the pre–World War II period. As the ZAIBATSU (the large prewar financial combines) expanded and diversified, the families owning them began to turn over the operation of these vast enterprises to professional managers, and by the 1930s professional managers had come to assume the major management responsibilities. This trend became firmly established in the postwar era, as the zaibatsu were dissolved and stock ownership became widely disbursed. With few exceptions, large Japanese enterprises are now managed by professional managers. Entry into a managerial career is based almost entirely on education. A college education has become all but essential, and graduates of prestigious universities are preferred. There are few women in senior managerial positions.

Personnel Practices—One of the most prominent features of the Japanese managerial system is the practice of lifetime employment. Management trainees are recruited directly from colleges yearly to begin work in April and are expected to stay with the company for their entire working careers. There is little intercompany managerial mobility. One is not dismissed for any reason short of serious moral misconduct. Incompetence or poor performance does not usually constitute grounds for dismissal (see also EMPLOYMENT SYSTEM, MODERN).

Another distinct characteristic of Japanese employment practices is the reward system. The most critical criterion is seniority. At least up through the middle management ranks, advancement is almost automatic. By the time one reaches the middle management ranks, advancement is accelerated for those with proven capacity and performance, and in the upper middle management ranks, differences in advancement patterns become quite notable. Promotion to top management ranks is highly selective and competitive.

The lifetime commitment and seniority-reward system requires mechanisms to ensure a regular turnover. For this reason, compulsory RETIREMENT for all but top management comes fairly early, usually between 55 and 60. Another mechanism frequently employed is transfer to the company's subsidiaries, related firms, and suppliers. Some workers will look for postretirement work elsewhere. For high-ranking financial, corporate, and government officials, it is possible to find well-paying jobs with other institutions after retirement (see AMAKUDARI).

Just as career advancement is carefully paced within the overriding framework of seniority, so is compensation. Compensation consists of cash payment and fringe benefits, the latter being an important element. Major fringe benefits may include housing, recreational facilities, and liberal expense accounts. The cash compensation consists of base salaries and semiannual bonuses. The bonuses have become a regular part of the compensation system and are sometimes as high as 50 percent of the total annual salary.

Organizational Structure and Decision Making—In Japan the individual, at least historically, existed only as a member of a group and not as a strong, clearly identifiable, and distinct entity. The basic unit of Japanese organizations remains the group. A task is assigned to and performed by a group rather than by individuals. The task is defined on the basis of the group, the assignment is carried out by the group, and the responsibility is shared by all. Under such an organizational arrangement, a leader must first create and then maintain a climate in which every member of the organization can work together harmoniously.

The decision-making process commonly followed in large bureaucratic organizations is known as the RINGI SYSTEM, which has often been described as an approval-seeking process. In it a proposal, known as a ringisho, is prepared by a lower functionary. The ringisho works its way up through the organizational hierarchy in a highly circuitous manner, often at a snail's pace, and at each step is examined by the proper officials, whose approval is indicated by affixing a seal. Out of this process a decision emerges. The dynamic but informal interaction that characterizes every stage of decision making is the essence of the ringi system. From the very stage during which a decision is first being shaped, various ideas and alternatives are explored, albeit very informally. Different interests are accommodated, and compromises are sought. At the same time, a process of education, persuasion, and coordination among various groups takes place.

An elusive element in the ringi system is the role of the formal leader. In this system the formal leader is not a decision maker in the classical sense. In the Japanese organization, while the status of a leader is meticulously defined, his role in the decision-making process is little differentiated from that of other members of the organization. In other words, the leader participates with his subordinates in the decision-making process. Thus, the degree to which the leader's view is incorporated into a decision depends largely on how well he is accepted and respected by his subordinates and on the kind of relationships he enjoys with them.

Another basic condition for making the ringi system effective is the need for a high degree of shared understanding and values among the participants. In large Japanese companies, the development of such shared understanding and organizational commitment begins with the recruiting system and is reinforced through subsequent personnel practices. Young men are carefully selected from among the graduates of the best universities and have thus already survived a series of rigorous screening processes and are highly homogeneous in ability, training, background, and values. Once they have been recruited by a company, they go through an intensive socialization process during which they are indoctrinated with the values of a particular firm and through which, after a number of years, they develop a high degree of shared understanding and commitment. Japanese practices are undergoing gradual change, but the patterns outlined here are found today in almost every large Japanese corporation.

Management and Coordination Agency　　　　　総務庁

(Sōmuchō). Cabinet-level agency of the national government formed in July 1984 on the basis of a 1983 report of the SECOND PROVISIONAL COMMISSION FOR ADMINISTRATIVE REFORM. The new agency combines the organization and functions of the Administrative Management Agency (which no longer exists) with certain functions of the PRIME MINISTER'S OFFICE. The chief purpose of this reorganization was to provide more effective overall administrative coordination of government departments. The Management and Coordination Agency is made up of five bureaus, two taken over from the Administrative Management Agency (the Administrative Management Bureau and the Administrative Inspection Bureau) and the other three from the Prime Minister's Office (the Personnel Bureau, the Pension Bureau, and the Statistics Bureau).

managerial ideology　　　　　経営理念

(keiei rinen). Ideas and values that attempt to legitimize the power of industrial managers, elicit the cooperation of the work force, and provide a defense against outside intervention into labor relations.

In Japan prior to World War II, managerial ideology was based upon service to the nation, the samurai spirit, PATERNALISM (onjō shugi) or familism (kazoku shugi) within an enterprise, and a sense of the uniqueness of Japanese culture. The emphasis on service to the nation and the samurai spirit emerged early in the Meiji period (1868–1912). It was claimed the modern businessman (jitsugyō-ka; "man of enterprise") deserved government support and public trust precisely because he, like the public-spirited samurai heroes of the past, was willing to put the national interest before self-interest. Western doctrines of economic individualism and the centrality of the profit motive were implicitly or explicitly rejected.

Paternalism and Japan's cultural uniqueness became central themes only at the turn of the 20th century, when industrial managers faced the threat of government intervention into labor relations. Most business spokesmen claimed that foreign models of labor legislation would be harmful to national progress, that survival in the international arena depended upon keeping labor costs low, and that Japanese managers—unlike Western capitalists—were motivated by a deep concern for the well-being of their workers, with whom they enjoyed a family-like relationship within the company enterprise.

Postwar managerial ideology has retained many of the tenets of prewar ideology at the same time that private enterprise has accepted a place within a pluralistic institutional framework that includes a widespread, powerful labor movement, comprehensive regulatory legislation, and cooperative business-government planning of industrial structure and investment. See also CORPORATE CULTURE; EMPLOYMENT SYSTEM, MODERN.

Manase Dōsan 曲直瀬道三

(1507–95). Also known as Ikkei Dōsan. Physician of the Sengoku (1467–1568) and Azuchi-Momoyama (1568–1600) periods. Orphaned at the age of nine, he became an acolyte (*kasshiki*) at the Zen monastery Shōkokuji in Kyōto in 1519. In 1528 he was sent to study Confucianism at the Ashikaga Gakkō, medieval Japan's only secular institution of higher learning. Three years later he became a disciple of TASHIRO SANKI, a physician trained in China in the medical tradition of the Yuan (Yüan) period (1279–1368) scholars Li Dongyuan (Li Tung-yüan) and Zhu Danxi (Chu Tan-hsi). In 1545 Dōsan returned to Kyōto. Though he had a prominent clientele that included members of the imperial family, it was his pioneering role as medical educator that earned Dōsan a place in Japanese medical history. In his private academy, the Keitekiin, Dōsan trained several hundred students in Li-Zhu medicine; his writings, including *Keitekishū* (1574, Enlightening Teachings) and 17 other extant medical treatises, confirmed the Li-Zhu school's preeminence in Japan. Dōsan also practiced the arts: he was an accomplished amateur of the tea ceremony, scholar of Chinese classics, and rhetorician. In 1584 he became a Christian, baptized as Belchior.

Manatsuru 真鶴[町]

Also known as Manazuru. Town in southwestern Kanagawa Prefecture, central Honshū. Situated on the Manazuru Peninsula, it is a fishing port. The entire peninsula forms a natural park with recreational facilities and camping grounds. Pop: 9,588.

Manchukuo 満州国

(J: Manshūkoku). Puppet state established by the Japanese GUANDONG (KWANTUNG) ARMY after its conquest of Manchuria in 1931 (see MANCHURIAN INCIDENT). For 13 years, from its founding in 1932 until Japan's surrender in World War II in August 1945, Manchukuo remained a dependency of Japan.

The Land and People—Geographically, Manchukuo comprised all of Manchuria and a portion of Inner Mongolia. At the time of its founding it consisted of China's "three northeastern provinces," Liaoning, Jilin

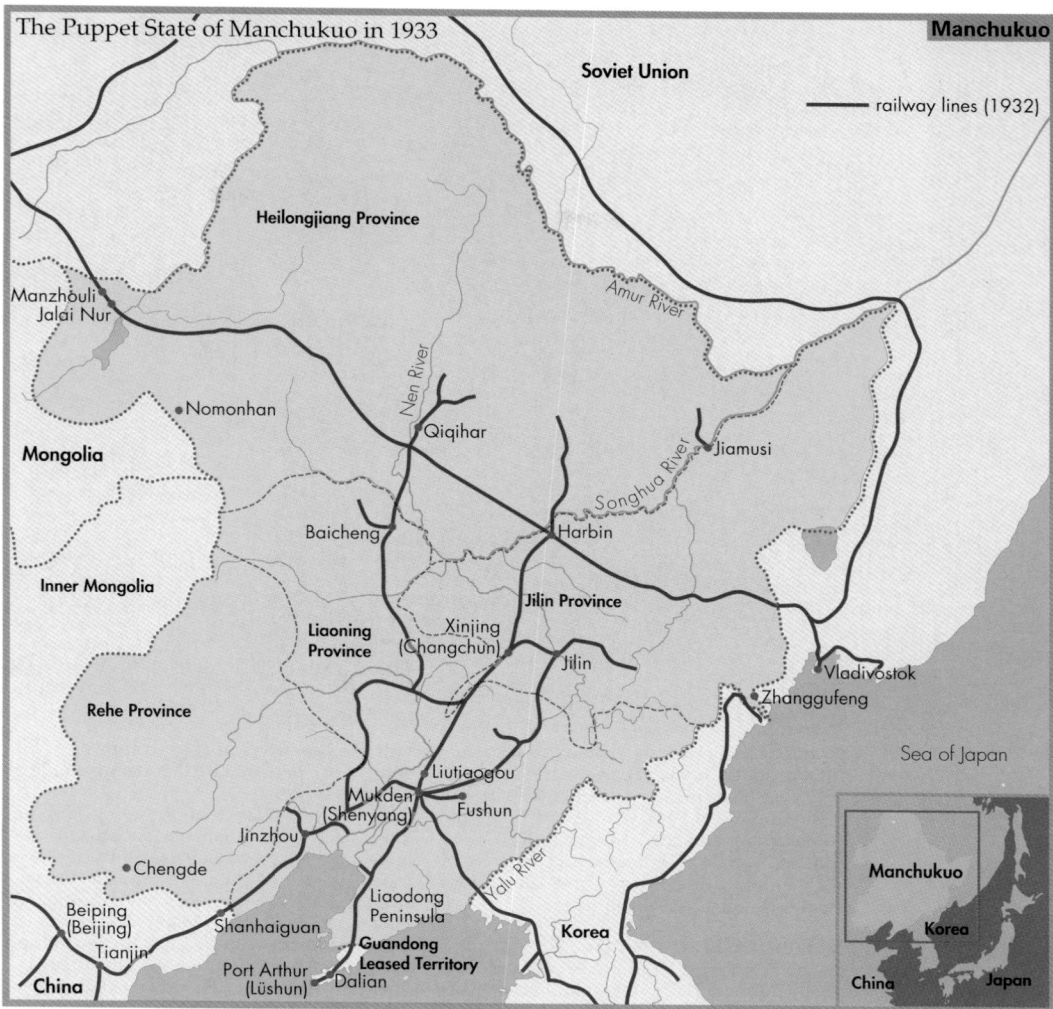

The Puppet State of Manchukuo in 1933

railway lines (1932)

(Kirin), and Heilongjiang (Heilungkiang). The province of Rehe (Jehol) was annexed in 1933.

The land was populated mainly by Manchus, Chinese, and Mongolians. There were also many Koreans; some White Russians; and a few Japanese, Tibetans, and people of Central Asian stock. Its population was estimated at about 43.2 million in the early 1940s.

Formation of the Puppet State—PUYI (P'u-i), who had been the last emperor of the Qing (Ch'ing) dynasty of China (1644–1912), was brought out of seclusion by DOIHARA KENJI of the Guandong Army and installed as regent of Manchukuo in March 1932. Changchun was selected as the new capital and renamed Xinjing (Hsinking; J: Shinkyō).

US Secretary of State Henry L. STIMSON applied a NONRECOGNITION POLICY to Manchukuo. The LYTTON COMMISSION report to the League of Nations of October 1932, which condemned Japan's action as aggressive, caused Japan to withdraw from the League the following year.

Even in Japan itself, Premier INUKAI TSUYOSHI resented the arbitrary acts of the Guandong Army, perpetrated in defiance of the Japanese government, and hoped to delay recognition. In May 1932, however, the premier was killed by extremist officers. His successor, SAITŌ MAKOTO, had no alternative but to recognize Manchukuo for fear of further terrorist acts.

The Protocol between Japan and Manchukuo (Nipponkoku Manshūkoku Kan Giteisho; usually called Nichiman Giteisho) was concluded on 15 September 1932. It was agreed that the Japanese government would

be solely responsible for the internal security and defense of Manchukuo. However, it was the Guandong Army that actually directed the affairs of Manchukuo. In March 1934 Puyi was made emperor. Manchukuo received recognition from about a dozen countries.

Immigration—Between 1932 and 1935 five contingents recruited from among Japanese army reservists settled in Manchukuo. The Guandong Army also initiated immigration from Japan, but as of 1940, fewer than 20,000 Japanese households had settled in Manchukuo. Korean immigration was promoted, and the Korean population grew to over 2 million by 1945.

Industries—The South Manchuria Railway Company, which had spearheaded the penetration and expansion of Japan's interests in Manchuria, had reached the proportions of an empire by the 1930s. After 1937, however, over 80 of its affiliated companies were combined with AIKAWA YOSHISUKE's Nissan combine to form the Guandong Army–backed Manchuria Heavy Industry Company (Manshū Jūkōgyō Kaihatsu Kaisha).

The War Years—Following Japan's invasion of China in 1937, border clashes with the forces of Outer Mongolia and the Soviet Union became more frequent. These included the artillery duel at Zhanggufeng (Chang-ku-feng) in July 1938 and the air and tank battle at Nomonhan in May 1939 (see ZHANGGUFENG [CHANG-KU-FENG] INCIDENT; NOMONHAN INCIDENT).

With the commencement of World War II in the Pacific in December 1941, Manchukuo reduced imports from Japan and increased

915
Manchukuo

Manchurian Incident
1 Soldiers of the Japanese Guandong Army man a light machine gun at Mukden on 23 September 1931.
2 Members of the League of Nations' Lytton Commission investigate the bombing of the South Manchuria Railway that initiated the Manchurian Incident. The bombing was staged by Japanese and imputed to Chinese troops.
3 After the incident, the Japanese satellite state of Manchukuo was established in 1932. This photograph was taken on 11 April 1934 to commemorate Japanese ambassador Hishikari Takashi's presentation of his credentials to Emperor Puyi.

production of minerals, metals, and agricultural products to aid Japan's war effort. Assaults on Manchuria by US bombers began in the summer of 1944. On 9 August 1945 the Soviet Union invaded Manchukuo. On 18 August 1945 Puyi abdicated and the state of Manchukuo passed into history along with Japan's domination of the region.

Manchurian Incident   満州事変

(Manshū Jihen). The conquest and pacification of Manchuria by the GUANDONG (KWANTUNG) ARMY, Japan's field army in Manchuria, from September 1931 to January 1933 or, more narrowly, the initial attack on the Chinese garrison in Mukden (now Shenyang) on the night of 18–19 September 1931 by elements of the Guandong Army (see LIU-TIAOGOU [LIU-T'IAO-KOU] INCIDENT).

Background—The Manchurian affair arose from the intensifying struggle in the late 1920s between Japan and China to gain a predominant position in Manchuria. At the end of the 19th century tsarist Russian penetration into southern Manchuria included the development of numerous commercial enterprises, the acquisition of mining concessions, the construction of major rail systems, and eventually the granting by China to Russia of a leasehold on the Liaodong (Liaotung) Peninsula, known as the Guandong Leased Territory. In the Treaty of PORTSMOUTH, which concluded the RUSSO-JAPANESE WAR of 1904–05, these interests, concessions, and territories in southern Manchuria were ceded to Japan (see GUANDONG [KWANTUNG] TERRITORY), though Manchuria outside the Guandong Leased Territory was still considered to be under the nominal control of China.

Japanese colonists in southern Manchuria were growing in number and were urging their government to be more active in the region. The SOUTH MANCHURIA RAILWAY Company, a Japanese concern, not only came to control "attached lands"—ill-defined rights-of-way alongside the railway—but also began to exercise jurisdiction over adjacent towns and villages. After 1919 Japanese railway guard units and military garrisons came under the control of the Guandong Army,

with headquarters at PORT ARTHUR (Ch: Lüshun; now part of Lüda) in the Guandong Leased Territory.

After the collapse of the Qing (Ch'ing) dynasty in 1912, Manchurian warlord elements had begun to exercise political power independent of China. For most of the decade of the 1920s this power was consolidated under a single warlord, Marshal ZHANG ZUOLIN (Chang Tso-lin). But by 1928 the Guandong Army staff had grown so jealous of his influence in southern Manchuria that it contrived to assassinate Zhang by blowing up his train outside Mukden. Zhang was succeeded by his son, "the Young Marshal," ZHANG XUELIANG (Chang Hsüeh-liang).

By this time the great tide of Chinese nationalism, the reunification drive by Chiang Kai-shek and the Guomindang (Kuomintang; KMT; Nationalist Party), had begun to approach the borders of Manchuria. By 1930, under pressure from the Chinese government in Nanjing (Nanking), Zhang Xueliang formally acknowledged the authority of Nationalist China. By 1931, therefore, the stage was set for a confrontation in Manchuria between China and Japan—the Chinese in an effort to reclaim actual as well as nominal control of Manchuria as an integral part of China, and the Japanese in an attempt to preserve their rights and properties in southern Manchuria by separating Manchuria from China once and for all.

The Takeover—Led by Colonels ISHIWARA KANJI and ITAGAKI SEISHIRŌ, the Guandong Army staff over a two-year period laid careful plans for the conquest of Manchuria. These plans, conceived without authorization of central headquarters or the civilian government in Japan, culminated in a sudden attack by elements of the Guandong Army on the main Chinese garrison at Mukden on the night of 18–19 September 1931. The Guandong Army justified the assault as retribution for a supposed Chinese attempt to destroy the tracks of the South Manchuria Railway just north of the city, an act secretly perpetrated by Guandong Army staff officers.

This initial attack set in motion a runaway campaign for the conquest of southern Manchuria and the annihilation or intimidation of regional Chinese armies, despite the ef-

forts of the Japanese civilian government and military high command in Tōkyō to limit the field initiatives of the Guandong Army staff. By the beginning of December 1931 the Guandong Army held most of southern Manchuria and controlled the capitals of all three Manchurian provinces. Denied authorization to annex Manchuria formally as a Japanese territory, the Guandong Army staff negotiated with pliable Chinese leaders in Manchuria to establish an "autonomous" satellite state, eventually dubbed MANCHUKUO. These political maneuvers had also been undertaken over the express opposition of the political and military establishment in the home islands.

Two developments in December 1931 affected the Guandong Army. First, a resolution by the League of Nations urged restraint pending the establishment of a neutral commission of inquiry (the LYTTON COMMISSION), but sanctioned Japanese operations against "bandits" and other "lawless elements." Second, the political climate in Japan became more favorable to expansion with the downfall of the more liberal cabinet of WAKATSUKI REIJIRŌ, the succession of Premier INUKAI TSUYOSHI, who was less adamant in his opposition to the use of force to maintain Japanese interests in Manchuria, and changes in the military high command. By January 1933 the Guandong Army had completed the conquest of Manchuria. The occupation of neighboring Rehe (Jehol) occurred early in 1933.

The Manchurian Incident may be linked not only to increasingly strident extremist elements in Japan who called for radical and violent solutions to Japan's foreign problems but also to the emergence of a widely shared conviction that the survival of the nation in a divided and unstable world depended on the forceful and unilateral creation of hegemony in East Asia to the exclusion of all other national and international interests there. However, the Guandong Army's adventure in Manchuria in 1931–32 brought Japan neither the military security nor the economic self-sufficiency its advocates had hoped for, but instead propelled the nation along a perilous new path of foreign confrontation. See also SINO-JAPANESE WAR OF 1937–1945.

Manchurian-Mongolian Independence Movement 満蒙独立運動

(Mammō Dokuritsu Undō). Name given to a series of Japanese plans during the first two decades of the 20th century to detach Manchuria and Mongolia from China by promoting separatist movements. After the overthrow of the Manchu Qing (Ch'ing) dynasty in 1911, Kawashima Naniwa (1865–1949), a Japanese adventurer (see TAIRIKU RŌNIN) in China, and elements in the Japanese General Staff decided to form a Manchu state in Manchuria. They brought their candidate for ruler, Prince SU, to the Japanese GUANDONG (KWANTUNG) ARMY headquarters in PORT ARTHUR. They also persuaded some Mongol princes from Inner Mongolia to agree to Japanese dominance of their country in exchange for military and financial aid. Word of their plans, however, reached the foreign ministry in Tōkyō. Kawashima was recalled to Japan, and the plans came to nothing. In 1916, taking advantage of the political turmoil in China caused by an announcement by President Yuan Shikai (Yüan Shih-k'ai) of his intention to declare himself emperor, General TANAKA GIICHI, then deputy chief of staff, decided to resurrect Kawashima's plans, but they were abandoned when Yuan died in June 1916.

mandala 曼荼羅

(J: mandara; from Skt: maṇḍala). A symmetrically arranged symbolic diagram used in Hinduism and ESOTERIC BUDDHISM to express fundamental religious doctrine for the purposes of ritual and meditation. Buddhist mandalas range from simple geometric diagrams or arrangements of sacred words to complex configurations in which many Buddhas and bodhisattvas are depicted.

The word mandala has many meanings; no translation can do it justice. The original Sanskrit word maṇḍala meant "circle," "group," "collection," or "company." It was interpreted in the esoteric Buddhist scripture Mahāvairocana-sūtra (J: Dainichikyō) and in commentaries on the scripture as consisting of maṇḍa (essence) and la (possession or attainment), essence being taken to mean supreme enlightenment, the state of inner enlightenment (J: SATORI) achieved by the Buddha. The mandala was a symbolic representation of satori meant to be used as an object of contemplation. It came to be expressed two- and three-dimensionally; that is, as painting and sculpture.

In Tibetan Buddhism the word maṇḍala was translated into Tibetan by a word meaning "circle," but in Chinese Buddhism it was transliterated by use of Chinese characters whose sound approximated the sound of the Sanskrit word. The Japanese word mandara is also a transliteration based on the Japanese pronunciation of the Chinese characters. In India a mandala was originally an earthen platform, built for the ordination rite, which was destroyed after the ceremony was completed. In China the mandala was a graphic representation on silk, often depicting Buddhas and bodhisattvas, which was hung on the wall or spread on the floor. In Japan, too, this interpretation generally prevailed.

Mandalas can be divided into four types: (1) dai mandara (Skt: mahā-maṇḍala), in which Buddhas and bodhisattvas are diagrammatically represented with iconographically prescribed hand gestures (mudrā) and attributes; (2) sammaya mandara (Skt: samaya-mandala), in which objects (e.g.,

sword, wheel, or lotus) symbolic of the nature and vows of different Buddhas and bodhisattvas are depicted; (3) hō mandara (Skt: dharma-maṇḍala), in which Buddhas and bodhisattvas are symbolically represented by the Sanskrit script; and (4) kuyō or katsuma mandara (Skt: karma-mandala), a three-dimensional mandala employing statuaries arranged on a platform in which various actions of divinities are depicted. Mandalas of these four types can be further classified under three Japanese terms as besson, bue, and toe. In besson mandara one central divinity and his retinue are depicted. In bue mandara divinities belonging to the same family are depicted. In toe mandara all families of divinities are depicted. Among the various families of divinities are Buddhas, bodhisattvas, MYŌŌ (Skt: vidyārāja; mostly fierce-natured deities), and ten (Skt: deva; heavenly beings; see TEMBU).

Among all the different mandalas, the most fundamental are the Taizō mandara and Kongōkai mandara, both of which are of the toe type (see also RYŌBU MANDARA). These two fundamental mandalas, based on the two most important sutras of esoteric Buddhism, were transmitted to Japan by the monk KŪKAI (774–835) and became the basis of the SHINGON SECT.

mandarin duck 鴛鴦

(oshidori). Aix galericulata. A waterfowl of the family Anatidae that is a relative of the North American wood duck (A. sponsa). It is about 45 centimeters (18 in) in length. The breeding plumage of the drake is exceptionally colorful, with a pair of orange-yellow, fan-shaped wings ("sails") rising at the lower back. The hen is a dull gray-brown with white rings around its eyes and a black bill. Living in streams, ponds, and marshes, they nest in the hollows of old tree trunks. They are distributed throughout China, Japan, and the Ussuri region of southwestern Siberia.

Although the Japanese, influenced by Chinese literary works, have traditionally viewed pairs of mandarin ducks as a symbol of faithfulness and marital harmony, mandarin ducks actually change their partners each year. In a story from the 13th-century anthology KOKON CHOMONJŪ, a hunter takes holy orders after discovering that the mate of a drake he killed has died of grief.

M&As → mergers and acquisitions

Mandokoro 政所

Originally, private administrative offices established by great noble houses of the Heian period (794–1185) to deal with family business, especially the administration of their private estates (SHŌEN). Temples, shrines, and individual shōen also established such offices. The Mandokoro of the FUJIWARA FAMILY included a KUMONJO, which handled documents, and a KURŌDO-DOKORO, or secretariat. Early in the Kamakura period (1185–1333) MINAMOTO NO YORITOMO established a Mandokoro that absorbed the functions of the existing Kumonjo in Kamakura, appointing ŌE NO HIROMOTO as its first administrator (bettō). As the HŌJŌ FAMILY took control of the shogunate the duties of the Mandokoro were restricted to financial matters. The MUROMACHI SHOGUNATE (1338–1573) established a Mandokoro as well.

manekineko 招き猫

(literally, "beckoning cat"). Figurine in the shape of a sitting cat with one paw upraised,

mandarin duck The Chinese made this bird, found throughout northeast Asia, a symbol of conjugal fidelity. In fact, however, it takes a new mate every year. Drake, left; hen, right.

as though making the customary Japanese gesture used in beckoning to people. Often displayed prominently at the front of shops and businesses that rely on heavy customer traffic, such as eateries and drinking establishments. It is believed to "beckon" good fortune and business success. Usually constructed of papier-mâché or pottery, some manekineko have the right front paw raised and some the left front paw. Some temples and shrines give out miniature copies of manekineko as protective amulets (GOFU) to those making their first shrine or temple visit of the new year. Manekineko are also sold commercially as coin banks.

Man'en gannen no futtobōru 万延元年のフットボール

(tr The Silent Cry, 1974). Novel by ŌE KENZABURŌ; published 1967. One of Ōe's major novels, Man'en gannen no futtobōru tells the story of two very different brothers who, in the wake of the failed protests against the revision of the United States–Japan Security Treaty in 1960, search for new directions in their lives. They return to the remote village where they were born, a setting of mythic proportions that has been an enduring element in Ōe's fiction. There the younger and more impetuous Takashi organizes a group of local men into a militaristic football team. Obsessed with power, Takashi rapes and kills a woman and then commits suicide. Mitsusaburō, the older and more introspective of the pair, decides to mend his marriage and leave Japan for Africa. The work, which deals with such topics as the emperor, individuality, and authority, expresses the sense of disillusionment with regard to politics experienced by many left-wing intellectuals during the 1960s.

Man'en Kembei Shisetsu → United States, mission of 1860 to

manga 漫画

(comic pictures). The word manga, which originally meant "random sketches," has become a general term for comic or satiric pictures, cartoons, or comic strips.

Ancient Period——The oldest examples of Japanese comic art are found in the SHŌSŌIN repository in Nara. It contains drawings of funny faces on cloth with the eyes cut out (fusakumen) and a caricature called the Daidairon (see GRAFFITI), which is drawn on the corner of a document dated 745. Comic drawings have also been found in temples and shrines, indicating religious elements in the comic-picture tradition. During the Heian period (794–1185) the oko-e, a type of comic drawing, was popular. Toward the end of the period, the caricatures of the

manekineko The "beckoning cat" is thought to invite prosperity and good fortune and is often displayed at traditional bars and restaurants.

manga

▶ This early-Edo-period painting depicting demons at a party is from the *Kibune no honji*, a Nara-ehon picture book illustrating the origins of the Shintō deity Kibune Daimyōjin. 17 × 25 cm. Daitōkyū Memorial Library.

▶ A satirical cartoon by the Meiji-period painter and woodblock-print designer Kobayashi Kiyochika. 1881.

▼ A political cartoon from the magazine *Tōkyō Puck* satirizes the leaders of the 1912–13 Movement to Protect Constitutional Government by portraying them as characters in the *kabuki* play *Kanjinchō*.

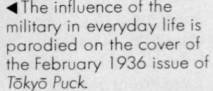

◀ The influence of the military in everyday life is parodied on the cover of the February 1936 issue of *Tōkyō Puck*.

▲ A playful depiction by the artist Hokusai of overweight people in various poses. From the 8th volume, published in 1818, of *Hokusai manga*. 22 × 16 cm. Tōkyō National Museum.

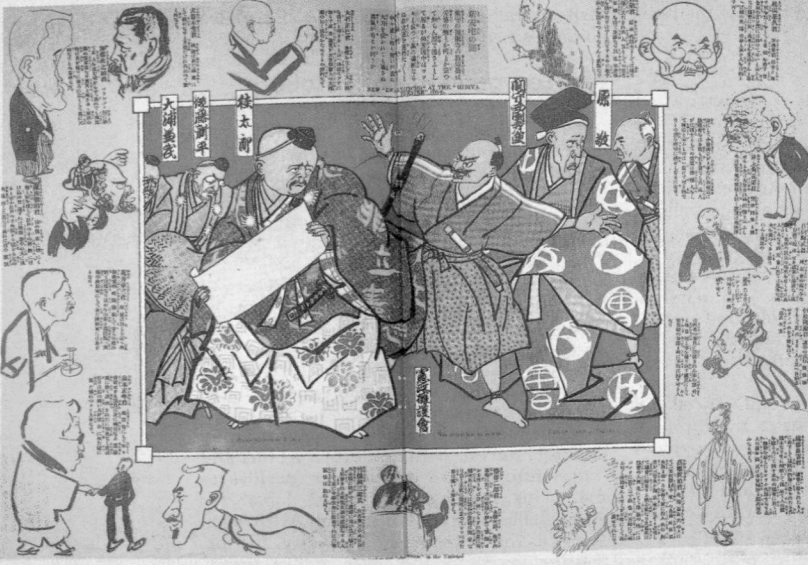

◀ This 1919 political cartoon by Kitazawa Rakuten satirizes the inability of world leaders to reach agreement on the creation of the League of Nations.

CHŌJŪ GIGA picture scroll were drawn, probably by the monk TOBA SŌJŌ. The SHIGISAN ENGI EMAKI and the BAN DAINAGON EMAKI, both outstanding picture scrolls from the period, contain comic elements. See also EMAKIMONO.

Medieval Period——From the Kamakura period (1185–1333), illustrated scrolls depicting Buddhist teachings and scenes of suffering, such as the JIGOKU-ZŌSHI scenes of hell, showed a bold imagination. The exaggerated depictions of figures bring a sense of humor even to the ugly and grotesque. Other examples of comic art include the pictures found in the collections of popular short stories called OTOGI-ZŌSHI from the Muromachi period (1333–1568).

Edo Period——The growth of a popular culture in the Edo period (1600–1868) brought about a surge in comic pictures and FŪZOKUGA genre painting. ŌTSU-E paintings, *toba-e* drawings with their exaggerated human features, and the genre paintings of Kuwagata Keisai (also known as Kitao Masayoshi; 1764–1824) and Yamaguchi Soken (1759–1818) are examples of comic

works from this period. UKIYO-E artists such as SHARAKU also produced many comic works. Those of HOKUSAI are well known under the general title of *Hokusai manga*. Literati painters such as BUSON and WATANABE KAZAN and the Zen monks SENGAI GIBON and HAKUIN also produced humorous works.

Modern Times——Western artists who came to Japan after the opening of the country to the West in 1854, such as Charles WIRGMAN of England (the founder of *Japan Punch* in 1862) and Georges BIGOT of France, exerted a large influence on Japanese comic artists, including the *ukiyo-e* master KOBAYASHI KIYOCHIKA. In 1905 Kitazawa Rakuten (1876–1955) founded the magazine *Tōkyō pakku* (Tōkyō Puck), leading to the emergence of many *manga* artists and *manga*-related periodicals in the years thereafter.

Newspaper comics and cartoons gained importance during the Taishō period (1912–26), and artists like OKAMOTO IPPEI attained fame in this field. In the Shōwa period (1926–89) there was a trend toward so-called *ero-guro-nansensu* (erotic, grotesque, nonsense) *manga*. Just before World War II, the militaristic slant in comic material increased, as

can be observed in *Norakuro* by TAGAWA SUIHŌ. Following World War II and the wide introduction of American culture, comic content changed to respond to the new society. Representative artists of this period include HASEGAWA MACHIKO, YOKOYAMA RYŪICHI, and TEZUKA OSAMU. In the 1960s a new genre of *manga* called *gekiga* ("narrative comics") emerged, and readership expanded to include college students and other adults. With numerous weekly and monthly comic magazines now being published, *manga* have established a position as a significant medium of mass communication halfway between print and television. See also COMIC MAGAZINES.

Manjirō, John→Nakahama Manjirō

manjū　　　　　　　　　　饅頭
Confection made by wrapping a core of sweetened red bean paste (*an*) in a skin of wheat- or buckwheat-flour dough and steaming. Yam or *amazake* (sweet nonalcoholic *sake*) may be added to the dough to soften its consistency, or baking powder for leavening. *Manjū*, the preparation of which

was transmitted from China, were first made in the Muromachi period (1333–1568). *Chūka manjū,* or Chinese *manjū,* are made with a thicker wrapping of well-leavened dough about a core of meat or Chinese-style bean paste.

Mannō Pond　満濃池

(Mannō Ike). Reservoir in Kagawa Prefecture, Shikoku, located on the northern slopes of the Sanuki Mountains. Its water is used to irrigate the Marugame Plain. First constructed in the beginning of the 8th century, it underwent extended repairs in 1959. Area: 1.4 sq km (0.5 sq mi); circumference: 20 km (12.4 mi); depth: 31 m (102 ft); storage capacity: 15.4 million cu m (543.8 million cu ft).

manryō　万両

(spearflower). *Ardisia crenata.* An evergreen shrub of the family Myrsinaceae that grows wild in the shady woods and warm regions of central Honshū, Shikoku, and Kyūshū. Its average height is 50–60 centimeters (19.7–23.6 in), but some grow to 2 meters (6.6 ft). The leaves are alternate, thick, and glossy with serrated edges. In summer small, star-shaped white flowers appear in clusters at the tips of the branches. Small, round, pendulous red fruit appear in autumn. Because of its beauty and auspiciousness (*manryō* literally means "10,000 gold pieces"), the cut or potted plant is used as a New Year's decoration.

Mansai　満済

(1378–1435). Also pronounced Manzei. Buddhist priest of the Shingon sect; statesman. Son of Imakōji (Fujiwara) Morofuyu, he entered the temple DAIGOJI near Kyōto and became its abbot in 1395. Mansai was a confidant of the shōgun ASHIKAGA YOSHIMITSU (r 1369–95), who made him his *yūshi* (adopted son without right of inheritance). He also served shōguns Ashikaga Yoshimochi (1386–1428; r 1395–1423) and ASHIKAGA YOSHINORI (r 1429–41). In 1428 he was granted the honorary title *jugō,* normally reserved for empresses and imperial princes. Mansai's diary, *Mansai jugō nikki,* covers 1411–35 and is an important source for the period's political and religious history.

mansaku→witch hazel

Mansfield, Michael Joseph
マンスフィールド, M. J.

(1903–). US politician and diplomat. Born in New York City, he graduated from the University of Montana in 1933. He was elected as a Democrat from Montana to the House of Representatives in 1942 and then to the Senate in 1952. He served as Senate majority leader from 1961 to 1977, a position he held longer than any other senator. Mansfield was appointed by President Jimmy Carter as US ambassador to Japan in 1977. During his tenure there, which ended in 1988, he dealt successfully with numerous economic and political frictions between the United States and Japan. His description of the US-Japanese relationship as "the most important bilateral relationship in the world, bar none" has been widely quoted.

manshon　マンション

Rented or privately owned apartments or condominiums. Until the early 1950s, collective housing in Japan was built almost exclusively by the publicly run Japan Housing Corporation (now the HOUSING AND URBAN DEVELOPMENT CORPORATION). However, during the construction boom of the 1960s, which

was set in motion partly by the 1964 Tōkyō Olympics, private developers began to build apartment buildings. In an attempt to distinguish their apartments from public housing projects, or *kōdan apāto,* the private developers borrowed the English word "mansion," hoping to convey a sense of spaciousness and comfort. As land prices soared in the late 1970s, *manshon* construction grew more vigorous. Multiple-room *manshon* units aimed at families were introduced, and one-room units for single people also became popular. In 1989 the price of a typical *manshon* in the Tōkyō Metropolitan Area averaged ¥55 million (US $401,459), while some luxury *manshon* units were selling for more than ¥100 million (US $725,847).

Manshū Jihen→Manchurian Incident

Manshūkoku→Manchukuo

Mantetsu→South Manchuria Railway

mantra　真言

(J: *shingon;* literally, "truthful utterance"). Also known in Japanese as *ju, mitsuju, mitsugon.* Mantras are verses and words that are considered to have sacred, mystical, or magical power and are transmitted in secret from master to disciple. In Buddhism, mantra refers to sacred utterances considered to contain the substance of the enlightenment of the Buddhas and bodhisattvas and their vows. The mantra has a special importance in Japanese esoteric Buddhism, as indicated by the name of the SHINGON SECT, Mantrayāna. Mantras, especially longer verses, are also called *darani* (Skt: *dhāraṇī*) and have been kept untranslated. These are written in Chinese transliteration of the Sanskrit and recited in a Japanese pronunciation.

Manufactured Imports Promotion Organization　製品輸入促進協会

(MIPRO; J: Seihin Yunyū Sokushin Kyōkai). Nonprofit organization established in 1978 by the joint efforts of the Japanese government and the private sector to promote the import of foreign products. MIPRO's activities include holding trade exhibitions for buyers and the general public at which foreign products are sold and disseminating information regarding imported products and the Japanese market.

Man'yōshū　万葉集

The earliest extant collection of Japanese poetry. Divided into 20 books, it contains 4,516 numbered WAKA poems, the last and most recent of which is dated New Year's Day of the Japanese year corresponding to AD 759. The earliest ascriptions are a set of four to Empress Iwanohime, who lived in the early 5th century—though all attributions earlier than the early 7th century are best regarded with skepticism. There are also extended headnotes, footnotes, prose settings, letters, and other compositions—all in Chinese—and a few Chinese poems, to which no numbers have been assigned. Of the three Japanese poetic forms represented in the anthology, there are approximately 4,200 TANKA ("short poems"), 265 CHŌKA ("long poems"), and 60 *sedōka* ("head-repeated poems"). The figure for *tanka* includes the *hanka* or envoys that occur at the end of many *chōka.* The *Man'yōshū* contains the overwhelming majority of poems preserved from before the end of the 8th century, which is to say almost all of what the Japanese of those days regarded as literature in their own language, and it

stands alone as the monument of Japan's first literary flourishing, whose span can be defined as more or less the century preceding this anthology's terminus of 759.

During this century Japan was in a ferment of growth and change, importing Chinese culture and institutions in a deliberate attempt to catch up with the most advanced country in the world. Although 8th-century Japan was rapidly acquiring a modernism of which the *Man'yōshū* was one product, it was still close to its primeval preliterate roots. Partially because the poetry that interested the compilers was not as totally aristocratic in outlook as tended to be true of the later commissioned IMPERIAL ANTHOLOGIES, and because the poetic voice of the aristocrats was not uniformly imbued with the Chinese ideal of elegant indirection that later became so influential, the total effect of Man'yō, or Man'yōshū, poetry is one of wholeheartedness, sincerity, and robust passion—precisely the qualities that admirers of the anthology have pointed to over the centuries and that still draw readers to it as one of the most revered treasures of the national literature. The Japanese people feel that they can hear their own voices in the collection and not merely those of a high-toned literary clique. A more careful and critical reading of the anthology, however, will quickly reveal highly complex artistry and more than a little of the elegant outlook supposedly characteristic of later ages.

Title and Compilation—The name *Man'yōshū* is written with Chinese characters meaning "Collection of Ten Thousand Leaves." This title has an obvious poetic appeal, whether "leaves" is taken as a metaphor for "poems" (not for "pages," since the original manuscripts were in scroll form) or a sinicization of the Japanese word *kotonoha,* meaning "word," but literally "leaf of word." It has been plausibly argued, however, that the character for "leaf" is used here in its well-attested sense of "age" or "generation" and that the title therefore should be understood as "Collection for Ten Thousand Generations."

Unlike some of the imperial anthologies, the *Man'yōshū* has no preface, nor is it mentioned in contemporary documents. Internal evidence indicates that the anthology is the culmination of a process dating back at least several decades and that the person most extensively involved in its compilation was the poet ŌTOMO NO YAKAMOCHI. There are recurrent references in the *Man'yōshū* to older anthologies and to collections of the work of individual poets; however, none of these works has survived outside the *Man'yōshū.*

Ōtomo no Yakamochi, with over 400 extant poems, is the best preserved of Man'yō poets. The last 4 of the 20 books of the *Man'yōshū* are definitely his compilation, chronologically arranged by him, and with personal notes on the circumstances of composition of each poem. The large number of poets of the Ōtomo family included in the anthology supports the hypothesis that at least one member was instrumental in assembling the collection. Yakamochi is the most obvious candidate for the culminating role in what must have been a long process.

Native Tradition and Chinese Influence—The earliest examples of Japanese verse are found not in the *Man'yōshū,* but in the KOJIKI (Records of Ancient Matters; tr *Kojiki,* 1969) and the NIHON SHOKI (Chronicle of Japan; tr *Nihongi,* repr 1972), the old-

manjū
1 A selection of *manjū* filled with sweetened red bean paste.
2 The savory Chinese-style *chūka manjū* contains a meat and vegetable filling.

manryō Considered auspicious, this evergreen shrub is used as a New Year's decoration.

Michael Joseph Mansfield During his tenure as the US ambassador to Japan (1977–88), Mansfield was a popular figure in his host country.

est Japanese books, histories of Japan dating respectively to 712 and 720. What apparently are the oldest songs are lacking in a set prosodic structure, that is, a sense of set line-lengths and poetic forms. They are usually exclamatory, declarative, or narrative in mode, or sometimes dramatic, as if they were acted out while they were being recited. The *jo*, or JOKOTOBA (imagistic preface), is already a dominant technique. There seems to have been from earliest times a predilection for working into the song's subject by the roundabout path of wordplay, and elaborate structures leading up to a key word are found frequently in early verse.

This penchant for preposited imagery continued to be developed in Man'yō poetry. There is also an observable tendency to alternate shorter and longer lines, and the range of verse in the chronicles includes examples of perfectly regular *tanka* in the syllabic pattern of 5–7–5–7–7. There are also several old-style *chōka* in more or less loose alternation of long and short lines, but lacking the final 7–7 couplet of the form as it eventually came to be defined. At this point the content of the *Man'yōshū* begins to overlap that of the chronicles. There is no completely irregular verse, but a number of old *chōka* are included. Most of the *chōka* follow the classical form and are followed by one or more *tanka* as envoys (*hanka*). Another form found in the *Man'yōshū* is the *sedōka*. The 62 examples in the *Man'yōshū* are the largest surviving corpus of this form. Its syllabic pattern of 5–7–7–5–7–7 seems to be based on a repetition of the ancient "half-poem" (*katauta*) in 5–7–7. The over 4,000 *tanka*, however, are clearly the numerically dominant form of Man'yō poetry. When the *chōka* and *sedōka* fell into desuetude after the 8th century, it was the *tanka* that continued as the classic poetic form for centuries to come.

Chinese books began to come into Japan in the 5th century, and Buddhist scriptures followed in the 6th. Knowledge of their contents was at first limited to a tiny elite, instructed by Korean and then by Chinese masters. The Japanese quickly became aware of the high value placed in China on the composition of poetry, some skill at which was a virtual requirement for a position in the bureaucracy. As part of their own training in reading and writing Chinese, the Japanese began in the late 7th century to experiment with writing *shih* (J: *shi*), the most common form of Chinese poetry. By the mid-8th century the Nara court had developed enough literati for a collection to be made of their poems in Chinese, the KAIFŪSŌ, whose date of 751 is eight years earlier than the last poem in the *Man'yōshū*. See POETRY AND PROSE IN CHINESE.

Efforts to write in Chinese, however, did not satisfy the literary urges of the Japanese. They wished to record a literature of their own, and the *Man'yōshū* was their first product. The ancient songs of the oral tradition already existed and could now be put down on paper. Moreover, at the same time that the Japanese gained literacy, their reading of Chinese poetry made them aware of poetry as an art, of literary form, mode, and point of view. It is probably from this time that the basic alternation of short and long lines in the native prosody began to regularize itself into five- and seven-syllable units, and that the set forms of the *tanka*, *chōka*, and so

forth started to evolve. The basic preference for preposited forms of modification and figurative expansion remained and was further developed. Long imagistic *jokotoba* and one-line "pillow words" (MAKURA KOTOBA) continued to be standard techniques, but their possibilities were fully realized only around the end of the 7th century. Increased use of parallelism—particularly of the pattern a-b-a' -b', where the structure of a couplet is echoed and its sense altered in a contiguous couplet (for example, "In spring the mountains / Deck themselves with blossoms // In autumn the river / spreads itself with fallen leaves")—undoubtedly owes much to the influence of balanced contrastive structures in Chinese, both prose and poetry. This mannered style of writing had been particularly popular in China during the Six Dynasties (222–589), a period whose literary ideals are reflected in the *Wenxuan* (*Wen-hsüan*; J: *Monzen*; early 6th century), an anthology very influential in Japan.

Japanese poetry thus became conscious of itself as an art, developed its native techniques, and adapted foreign ones, under what can only be called a beneficent Chinese influence. Other aspects of this influence have sometimes been looked at askance as corrupting the purity of the native Japanese spirit. The *kotodama*, or "word-soul," of the Japanese language speaks most truly, it is held, in the accents of true love, loyalty, and honesty. Anything more devious or roundabout would be a regrettable foreign intrusion. However, the great size and variety of the *Man'yōshū* represent a world of diversity and growth. Simple emotions straightforwardly expressed are certainly part of that world, but only part. The effect of a poem in which a country girl speaks of her hands being chapped by hulling rice, or a fisher boy likens his girl to a sea lentil (*nanoriso*), is all the greater in a total context that includes the experiments of courtiers in writing Chinese-style plum-blossom poems. The sea lentil is humble and native, the plum blossoms elegant and foreign, but in both cases the poems exploit the technique of analogy. The sea lentil poem, which also employs irony, is actually very artistic—that is, as much based on fully poetic stratagems as the plum-blossom poems, if not as self-consciously "literary."

Pretended or "elegant" confusion (in such phrases as "Are they plum blossoms, or is it snow?") makes its first appearance in Japanese poetry of the *Man'yōshū*, in the poems of ŌTOMO NO TABITO and his circle, in 730. This kind of elegant artfulness was to be deeply influential on the poetry of the Heian period (794–1185), but it is important to realize that the poets of the 8th century were already indulging in it. A poet like Ōtomo no Tabito leaves a very different impression than does his great predecessor KAKINOMOTO NO HITOMARO. Hitomaro, who did most of his work in the last two decades of the 7th century, speaks with the voice of the ancient bard, perfecting the traditions of his native verse. He seems very "Japanese," very close to the rootstock of his country's archaic essence. Tabito, by contrast, resembles more a Chinese literatus. The two were contemporaries at the end of the 7th century, but Tabito lived on, and his surviving work is from his old age. A great hinge of time seems to turn on the decades before and after the foundation of Heijōkyō (now Nara) in 710.

Content and Structure—The first 2 of the 20 books of the *Man'yōshū* form a

pair. Each is arranged chronologically, as are many of the books, starting with poems attributed to figures of remote antiquity and coming down with poems attributed to the early 8th century. Together these two books present three of the anthology's main typological categories—*zoka*, *sōmon*, and *banka*. *Zōka* ("miscellaneous poems"), a term adopted from the *Wenxuan*, refers to verses that cannot be categorized as either love poems or elegies. The term *sōmon*, also borrowed from the *Wenxuan*, refers to love poems. The word implies an exchange of endearments; in practice, however, the poetry is predominantly one of longing. *Banka* are poems occasioned by death. The term originally referred to dirges accompanying the pulling of a funeral hearse and also derives from a category found in the *Wenxuan*. It is thought that, at least until Kakinomoto no Hitomaro's time at the end of the 7th century, dirges were actually sung at court funerals in Japan, and some of the Man'yō funeral songs are public elegies on the deaths of court nobles. Other *banka* in these books are private laments over the loss of a loved one, usually the poet's wife. As Buddhist ceremonies and music came to replace old native rites, *banka* declined.

Hiyuka are poems containing analogies, varying from metaphor to allegory, and dealing chiefly with the subject of love. *Kibutsu* ("referring to things"), a subcategory of *hiyuka*, is a love analogy in which the "thing" referred to functions as metaphor or extended allegory (the sea standing for love, the boat for the lover, and the oars for his driving passion). *Eibutsuka* ("poems on things"), a subcategory of *zōka*, deal descriptively or allegorically with natural phenomena.

The various volumes of the *Man'yōshū* are hardly of a piece. Book 5, for example, is half prose, all of it in Chinese, and is basically a collection of the writings of the circle of Ōtomo no Tabito and his friend YAMANOUE NO OKURA, whose interest in a Chinese style in life and letters emerges strongly in the *Man'yōshū*. Book 16 is of special literary interest because it contains the forerunners of fictional forms combining prose and poetry and features highly informal, even comic material that relates to the later poetic genres of *haikai* (see HAIKU) and KYŌKA. The final four volumes, books 17 through 20, are definitely the compilation of Ōtomo no Yakamochi and form a kind of personal poetic diary.

Major Poets—The *Man'yōshū* is famed for its social range. There are poems by members of the imperial family and by members of the peasantry. Most of the named poets, however, are middle- or lower-ranking courtiers, and it is to them one must turn for a list of major poets.

Kakinomoto no Hitomaro is the poet whose creativity dominates the late 7th century and, in large measure, the entire tradition of Man'yō poetry. He was a courtier-official, probably of low to middling rank, whose time was likely divided between service in provincial and central bureaucracies. He is known as an author of *banka*, or elegies, and he perfected the techniques of the earlier poetry, the formulaic style developed from the oral tradition, the use of metaphorical, preposited, imagistic structures, the parallelism, and the long prosodic units. He created and maintained a lofty and majestic style, flexible and varied, laced through with compassionate irony, that brought to the *chōka* its best moments. His themes were the

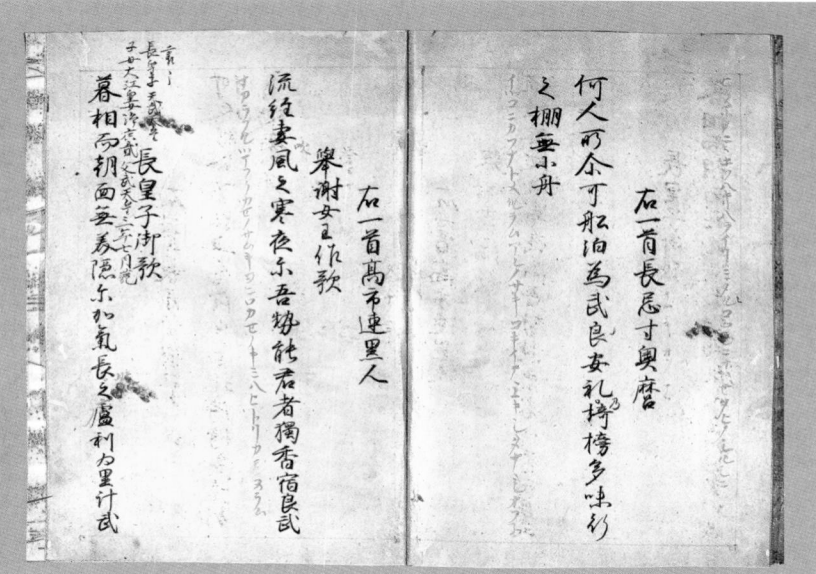

sadness of parting, whether in life or death, the awesomeness of the imperial institution, and the mystery of man's fate. His surviving poems total 18 *chōka* and 67 *tanka*.

KASA NO KANAMURA is known to have been active from 715 to 733 and left a small body of poems largely dealing with his travels in the imperial train. YAMABE NO AKAHITO brought to poetry an aesthetic appreciation of nature and a descriptive lyricism in the *tanka*, new and recognizably his own, which were in the long run more influential than Hitomaro's grandeur. TAKAHASHI NO MUSHIMARO was of all the Man'yō poets the most interested in local legends and in mountains. His notable poems include celebrations of Mt. Fuji, described as a living god, and the narrative account of the legend of the fisherman Urashima (URASHIMA TARŌ). Ōtomo no Tabito was more of a personage on the political scene than most other major Man'yō poets. While serving as governor-general at DAZAIFU in northern Kyūshū he presided over a poetically active circle of subordinates and acquaintances from 727 or 728 to 730. His work, primarily *tanka*, shows a mind attuned to the elegance of Six Dynasties prose and poetry; he was one of the earliest Japanese poets to display a consistent and dominant interest in Chinese themes and attitudes.

Yamanoue no Okura can usefully be viewed in comparison with his friend Tabito. He too left mostly the poetry of his old age. It shows him to be a crotchety, moralistic, but also humorous and loving character, with a strong sense of social outrage. Okura is the only major Man'yō poet known to have visited China. He was a member of the official embassy of 702 and returned in 707. His poetic manner is angular, personal, sometimes angry, as in his "Dialogue on Poverty." At the same time he experimented with the hugely popular imported theme of the lover stars Altair and Vega, who can meet only once a year (see TANABATA FESTIVAL).

Ōtomo no Yakamochi was the eldest son of Tabito. One in every 10 Man'yō poems is by him and he is the leading candidate for compiler of the anthology. Yakamochi is a poet of great variety and amplitude. As a young man he acquitted himself well in the mode of amorous *tanka* and he also wrote *chōka* in the grand manner. A note of delicate sadness is apparent in his late nature poetry and he was, like his father, an early practitioner of "elegant confusion." He also struck some of the first self-conscious notes

in Japanese poetry of specifically Buddhist awareness of life's illusory character.

It is surprising to find a large number of poems in the *Man'yōshū* by people outside the circle of the court, in some cases people one would hardly suspect were literate. There are, for instance, the rustic poems from Azuma (northeast Japan) in book 14 and the poems (SAKIMORI UTA) in book 20 by conscripts from the northeast stationed in Kyūshū. At the lowest estimate, 1,851 poems in the anthology are, in fact, anonymous. This great mass of verse must have come from a variety of sources, written and—directly or indirectly—oral. Internal evidence, such as it is, suggests that some of this material is by courtiers and some by commoners or by courtiers writing in a commoner mode, with a very large proportion representing a kind of universal viewpoint that could be shared by both.

The Man'yō Writing System——Japan did not invent a writing system, but adapted the script of China, the first one it encountered. The Chinese writing system was not a phonetic script, such as an alphabet or syllabary, but was composed of complex graphic units representing entire words. Each graph, however, by virtue of representing a monosyllabic Chinese word, was associated with the pronunciation of that word. If meaning was discarded the character could be used to represent its sound alone. This phonetic application is known as *man'yōgana*. Furthermore, as Chinese graphs represented common objects and qualities, they could also be used semantically. Thus the graph for "hand" could be read as if it were the Japanese word for the same thing. A further complication was that once the semantic application of a graph was established, for example the Japanese reading *te* of the graph for "hand," it could be used to write the syllable *te* in any other word. The consequence of this experience with graphomania was that by the 10th century when the syllabaries, or KANA, had become established, poets were no longer able to read the *Man'yōshū* with assurance.

Decipherment and Exegesis——Although the first work on decipherment of the *Man'yōshū* was undertaken at imperial command in 951, the earliest complete extant manuscript of the anthology is the Nishi Honganji text in book form, which dates from the latter part of the Kamakura period (1185–1333). It was not until the Edo period (1600–1868), however, that *Man'yōshū* studies came into their own as one of the chief

scholarly endeavors of the National Learning (KOKUGAKU) movement. The first important figure in Edo Man'yō studies was SHIMOKŌBE CHŌRYŪ, whose work was carried on after his death in 1686 and completed by the priest KEICHŪ. *Man'yō daishō ki* (ca 1683–90), the work he produced, is a complete commentary on the *Man'yōshū*, and displays great erudition and original research. The most voluminous premodern commentary on the anthology, *Man'yōshū kōgi* (141 vols, 1856), was written by KAMOCHI MASAZUMI. In the 20th century Man'yō studies have flourished as never before, and numerous multivolume commentaries have made the anthology ever more accessible to the reading public.

Manza Hot Spring 万座温泉

(Manza Onsen). Located on the western slope of Shiranesan at an altitude of 1,760 m (5,774 ft), northwestern Gumma Prefecture, central Honshū. A sulfur spring; water temperature 60°–95°C (140°–203°F). It attracts numerous skiers in winter.

manzai 漫才

Performing art in which a comic dialogue is carried on by two comedians. Said to have had its beginnings in the Nara period (710–

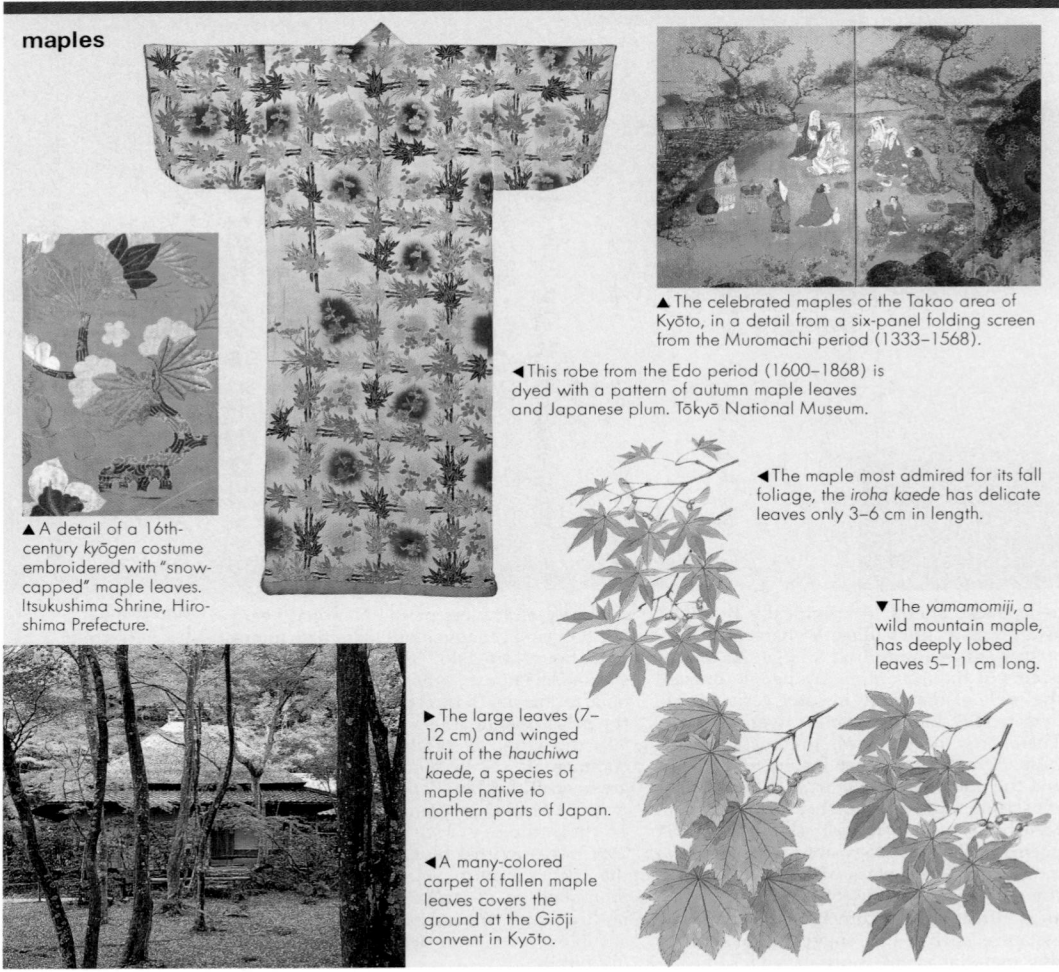

▲ A detail of a 16th-century *kyōgen* costume embroidered with "snow-capped" maple leaves. Itsukushima Shrine, Hiroshima Prefecture.

▲ The celebrated maples of the Takao area of Kyōto, in a detail from a six-panel folding screen from the Muromachi period (1333–1568).

◄ This robe from the Edo period (1600–1868) is dyed with a pattern of autumn maple leaves and Japanese plum. Tōkyō National Museum.

◄ The maple most admired for its fall foliage, the *iroha kaede* has delicate leaves only 3–6 cm in length.

▼ The *yamamomiji*, a wild mountain maple, has deeply lobed leaves 5–11 cm long.

► The large leaves (7–12 cm) and winged fruit of the *hauchiwa kaede*, a species of maple native to northern parts of Japan.

◄ A many-colored carpet of fallen maple leaves covers the ground at the Giōji convent in Kyōto.

794), *manzai* spread throughout Japan in the Edo period (1600–1868). The custom arose for a wit (*tayū*) and a straight man (*saizō*) to go from house to house at New Year's engaging in congratulatory repartee accompanied by comical hand and body gestures and a rhythm tapped out on a small drum (see KADOZUKE).

Toward the close of the Edo period, *manzai* was performed in makeshift theaters, and by the first decade of the 20th century its popularity, especially in Ōsaka, increased rapidly. In 1930 the *manzai* pair Yokoyama Entatsu (1896–1971) and Hanabishi Achako (1897–1974) began to perform in Ōsaka. Their dialogues, without musical accompaniment and based on scripts that dealt with contemporary events and social customs, were broadcast nationwide and established the standard for today's *manzai*. After World War II, passing from the age of radio to that of television, *manzai* has continued to flourish. Today the repartee of *manzai* performers—the wit is now called *tsukkomi* and the straight man *boke*—is distinguished by its fast pace, its use of current events, and its swift shifts, often by bizarre association, from topic to topic.

Manzanar Relocation Center
マンザナー収容所

(Manzanā Shūyōjo). Wartime relocation facility for Japanese Americans from California and Washington State; located near Lone Pine, Inyo County, California. In operation from 21 March 1942 until 21 November 1945, it held a maximum of 10,046 inmates at any one time; 11,062 persons were confined there in all. The first of the relocation centers to open, it also functioned as an assembly center. The first major disturbance of the relocation program, the so-called Manzanar Riot, occurred here on 7 December 1942. See also JAPANESE AMERICANS, WARTIME RELOCATION OF; WAR RELOCATION AUTHORITY.

Mao Zedong (Mao Tse-tung)
毛沢東

(1893–1976; J: Mō Takutō). Chinese communist leader and founder of the People's Republic of China. Born in Hunan Province. As a student Mao read widely on contemporary affairs. In 1918 he went to Beijing (Peking), where he met Li Dazhao (Li Ta-chao), later a founder of the Chinese Communist Party (CCP). Mao participated in the MAY FOURTH MOVEMENT of 1919 and by 1920 he had committed himself to Marxism. In July 1921 he helped found the CCP.

By 1931 Mao headed the government of a communist base area in Jiangxi (Kiangsi) Province. In late 1934 the Guomindang (Kuomintang; KMT) siege of Jiangxi forced the communists to abandon their base. During the retreat of the Red Army northwest to Yan'an (Yenan), known as the Long March, Mao emerged as party leader. The CCP led by Mao sought cooperation with the KMT in resistance to Japanese aggression in North China. In 1937 the rival parties agreed on a united front against Japan (see SECOND UNITED FRONT). The alliance was never very firm, and after Japan's defeat in World War II civil war broke out again in 1946. By 1949 the CCP had defeated the KMT, and the People's Republic of China was established with Mao as chairman.

maples
楓・紅葉

(*kaede; momiji*). *Acer* spp. Deciduous trees of the genus *Acer*, family Aceraceae, include more than 100 species, more than 20 of which are indigenous to Japan. The beauty of their autumn foliage has been a frequent subject in literature and art. Many trees in the genus *Acer* have palmate leaves, but some varieties have leaves that are not lobed, including various oval, elliptic, and three-part compound types. All have opposite leaves and two-seeded, long-winged fruits.

The *iroha kaede* (Japanese maple; *A. palmatum*), also called Takao *momiji*, is widely distributed in Japan's mountain areas and extensively planted around houses. The doubly-serrated leaves are small, have 5–7 palmate lobes, and turn a beautiful red in autumn. The *yamamomiji* (mountain maple; *A. palmatum* var. *matsumurae*) grows wild in mountain areas; the large leaves have 7–9 deeply indented lobes. The *hauchiwa kaede* (*A. japonicum*; also called *meigetsu kaede*) is indigenous to Hokkaidō, northern Honshū, and the central Honshū mountain area; it has large, doubly-serrated leaves with 9–11 relatively shallow lobes. There are several other wild species and numerous horticultural varieties.

mappō→eschatology

maps
地図

(*chizu*). The oldest existing maps in Japan—india ink drawings of reclaimed land that are preserved in the SHŌSŌIN repository in Nara—date from the late Nara period (710–794). However, mapmaking began to flourish only in the early 17th century, following the introduction of European maps and improvements in woodblock printing techniques. At various times during the Edo period (1600–1868), the shogunate ordered the domains (*han*) to make maps of their territories, which became the basis for comprehensive maps of the country.

In 1775 the first known Japanese latitudinal map—the *Nihon yochi rotei zenzu*—was completed by geologist NAGAKUBO SEKISUI. Far superior to all previous maps was the *Dai Nihon enkai yochi zenzu* completed in 1821. Using European techniques, it was the result of 16 years of surveying under the direction of INŌ TADATAKA.

From the late 1800s until the end of World War II, the sole government body responsible for the making of standard maps was the Land Survey Department of the Army General Staff Office. After the war, however, the GEOGRAPHICAL SURVEY INSTITUTE of the Ministry of Construction was made responsible for surveying and mapmaking. By 1978 it had completed a set of 1:25,000-scale maps based on aerial surveys and covering the entire country.

marathons
マラソン

(*marason*). The marathon race is one of the most popular sports events in Japan, with the number of participants ranking among the highest in the world. Japan's first real marathon was held in 1911 as a trial meet for the Stockholm Olympic Games the following year. At these trials, Kanaguri Shizō (1891–1983) set a new world record with a time of 2 hours 32 minutes 45 seconds. Since then a number of new records have been established by Japanese runners. In the post–World War II period, Japanese athletes have competed with good results in the Boston Marathon and other foreign marathons, as well as in the Olympic Games. As of 1990, three men's and three women's marathons in Japan have been recognized by the International Amateur Athletic Federation.

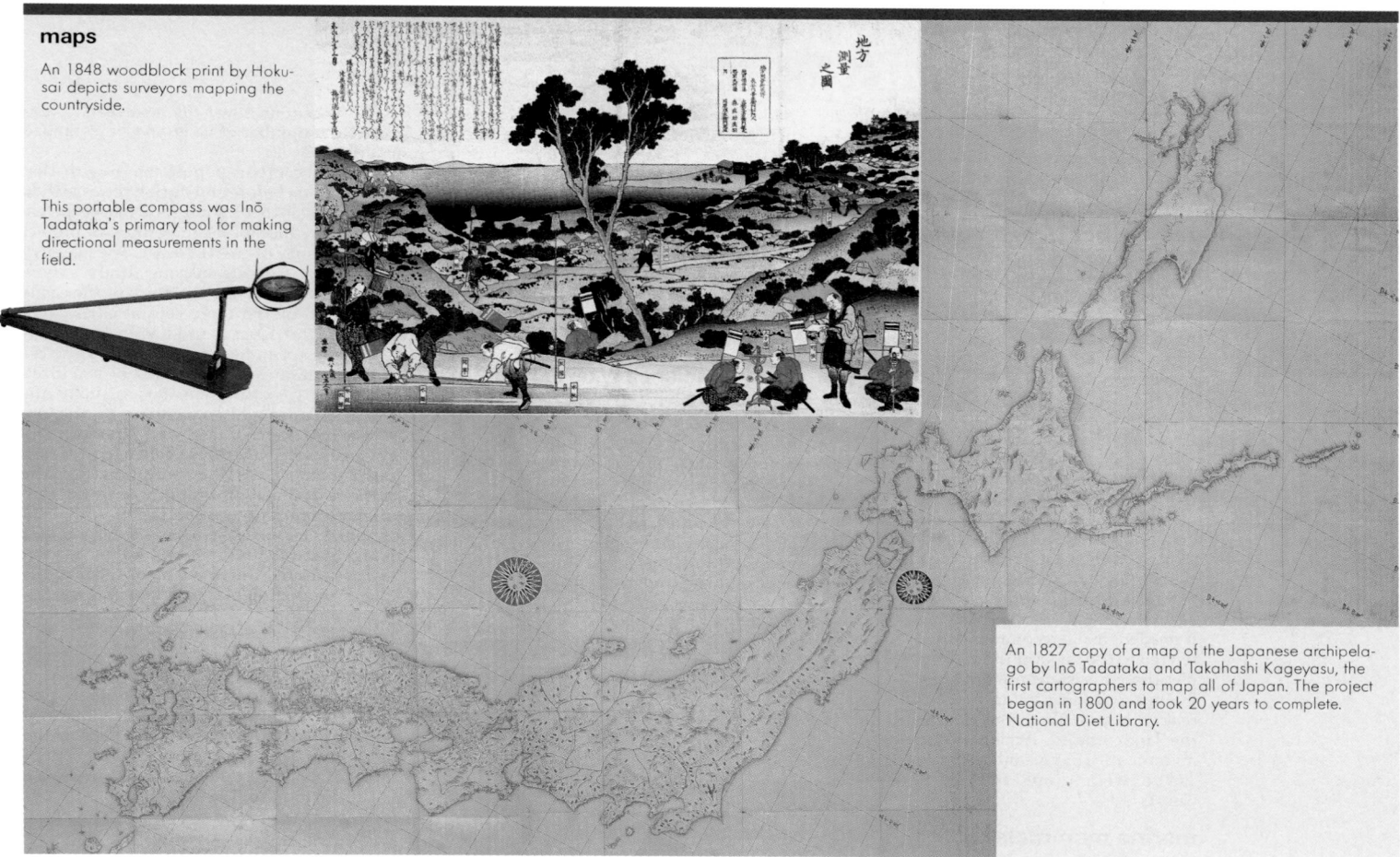

maps

An 1848 woodblock print by Hokusai depicts surveyors mapping the countryside.

This portable compass was Inō Tadataka's primary tool for making directional measurements in the field.

地方測量之圖

An 1827 copy of a map of the Japanese archipelago by Inō Tadataka and Takahashi Kageyasu, the first cartographers to map all of Japan. The project began in 1800 and took 20 years to complete. National Diet Library.

March 15th Incident　三・一五事件

(San'ichigo Jiken). Mass arrests throughout Japan on 15 March 1928, in which about 1,600 people suspected of being communists were apprehended. The incident was the government's response to the renewed activities of the outlawed JAPAN COMMUNIST PARTY, which had become highly visible in support of legal leftist parties during the first national election under the new Universal Manhood Suffrage Law (see UNIVERSAL MANHOOD SUFFRAGE MOVEMENT) in February 1928. These arrests constituted the government's third invocation of the PEACE PRESERVATION LAW OF 1925.

About 500 of those arrested were ultimately prosecuted. The conservative cabinet of TANAKA GIICHI used the exposed inner workings of the Communist Party as an excuse to ban the Labor-Farmer Party (RŌDŌ NŌMINTŌ), the All Japan Proletarian Youth League (Zen Nihon Musan Seinen Dōmei), and the Council of Japanese Labor Unions (Nihon Rōdō Kumiai Hyōgikai) and to revise the Peace Preservation Law of 1925, adding a death penalty. The March 15th Incident, the first of a number of mass arrests aimed at destroying communism, is deeply etched in the Japanese consciousness. See also APRIL 16TH INCIDENT.

March Incident　三月事件

(Sangatsu Jiken). Attempted coup d'état by rightist army officers and civilians in March 1931. Participants included HASHIMOTO KINGORŌ and other field-grade officers belonging to his SAKURAKAI (Cherry Blossom Society); members of the General Staff, such as KOISO KUNIAKI and TATEKAWA YOSHITSUGU; and the rightist civilians ŌKAWA SHŪMEI and Kamei Kan'ichirō (b 1892). Convinced of the need for national reform along totalitarian lines, they hoped to overthrow the cabinet and establish a military government headed by General UGAKI KAZUSHIGE. Their plans were aborted because of logistic difficulties, opposition from military men concerned with the Manchuria-Mongolia problem, and Ugaki's own reluctance to accept the post. This incident, the first of many military interventions in politics (see also OCTOBER INCIDENT; FEBRUARY 26TH INCIDENT; MAY 15TH INCIDENT), was kept secret by the army until the end of World War II.

Marco Polo Bridge Incident　蘆溝橋事件

(Rokōkyō Jiken). Clash between Japanese and Chinese troops that led directly to the SINO-JAPANESE WAR OF 1937–1945. On the night of 7 July 1937, Japanese troops conducting maneuvers near the Marco Polo Bridge (J: Rokōkyō), 19 kilometers (12 mi) southwest of Beiping (Peiping; now Beijing or Peking), engaged in a skirmish with Chinese forces under General SONG ZHEYUAN (Sung Cheyüan). On 11 July a local cease-fire agreement was concluded. However, the KONOE FUMIMARO cabinet announced a plan to mobilize five divisions for possible service in North China, and Army Minister SUGIYAMA HAJIME dispatched one division from Korea and two brigades from the Japanese GUANDONG (KWANTUNG) ARMY to the area. On 23 July the Chinese government at Nanjing (Nanking) had Song's troops reenter Beiping. On 29 July the Japanese commander, General Katsuki Kiyoshi, attacked and occupied Beiping and Tianjin (Tientsin). Thus began the second Sino-Japanese War.

marebito　客人

(literally, "guests"). Also known as marōdo. Divine visitors believed to bring blessings of luck and wealth from the other world (TOKOYO). The folklorist ORIKUCHI SHINOBU (1887–1953) described marebito as deified ancestral spirits who appear in human guise, equipped for a journey. He held that itinerant monks, ascetics, artists, or faith healers were welcomed by people as possible divine visitors in disguise. He noted that the belief in supernatural beings who bring favors was closely linked to the idea that hospitality should be extended to a visitor from afar who might bear new technical knowledge. Such a notion would be especially strong in remote communities.

Maria Luz Incident　マリア・ルーズ号事件

(Maria Rūzu gō Jiken). A diplomatic crisis that occurred early in the Meiji period (1868–1912). On 9 July 1872 the Peruvian ship Maria Luz, bound for Peru carrying 229 Chinese coolies, sailed into Yokohama for repairs. Two coolies escaped to a British warship, complaining of inhuman conditions on the Maria Luz. The acting British minister, R. G. Watson, asked Foreign Minister SOEJIMA TANEOMI to look into the matter. It was decided to set up a special court representing the Ministry of Foreign Affairs and to appoint ŌE TAKU as judge. Two American legal experts, E. P. Smith and G. W. Hill, served as advisers and largely determined Japan's position in the case. The court declared the captain of the Maria Luz guilty of illegally confining the coolies. It commuted his sentence but ruled that he must file with the court for permission to execute his contract for carrying the coolies. On 25 August, Ōe ruled that the contract was invalid.

The case became a dispute under international law, and in February 1873 the Peruvian government demanded compensation for damages and a formal apology. On 25 June 1873 Japan and Peru agreed to submit to arbitration by Tsar Alexander II of Russia.

On 29 May 1875 the tsar upheld the decisions of the Japanese court. The *Maria Luz* case compelled the Western powers to recognize Japan as an equal before international law.

marine accidents inquiry 海難審判

(*kainan shimpan*). Investigation conducted by the Marine Accidents Inquiry Commission (Kainan Shimpan Chō) into the causes of accidents at sea. Marine accidents are defined by law as the infliction of damage to a vessel or related facilities; death or injury in connection with a vessel's construction, facilities, or operations; and the impairment of the safety or operation of a vessel (Marine Accidents Adjustment Law, 1947).

The commission is part of the MINISTRY OF TRANSPORT. The system attempts to prevent the recurrence of accidents. The inquiry commission establishes the cause of the accident and announces its conclusion by issuing a ruling. When the accident is caused intentionally or by the negligence of a pilot or a technician in the course of his duties, the agency will take disciplinary measures and, if needed, make recommendations to parties related to the cause of the accident. In principle, these decisions are not supposed to influence civil and criminal proceedings, but in reality they do. Decisions can be appealed to the High Marine Accidents Inquiry Commission in Tōkyō, and from there to the Tōkyō High Court and to the Supreme Court.

marine mammals 海獣類

(*kaijūrui*). Japan's marine mammals, with the exception of WHALES, are found in two principal habitats: the shores of Hokkaidō and northern sections of the Tōhoku area of Honshū, where seals and sea lions are found; and the waters off Okinawa, where dugongs (sea cows) are seen. In other parts of the country, marine mammals are extremely rare.

Mammals of the suborder Pinnipedia, the *todo* (Steller's sea lion), the *wamon azarashi* (ringed seal), the *kurakake azarashi* (ribbon seal), and the *gomafu azarashi* (harbor seal), are seen in relatively large numbers. Colonies of *ottosei* (fur seal), which breed on the Komandorski Islands off the Kamchatka Peninsula, appear from fall to winter in the waters of Hokkaidō and the Tōhoku area; by April and May they return northward. The dugong of Okinawa is sometimes seen; many are believed to exist, but their habits are unknown.

marine parks 海中公園

(*kaichū kōen*). Government-designated ocean areas featuring distinctive seabed topography and an abundance of marine life, along with recreational and educational facilities located on adjoining coastal areas. The first 10 Japanese marine parks, designated in 1970, were mostly in subtropical areas such as Sabiura in the town of Kushimoto, Wakayama Prefecture. Additional areas were designated later, including sites in the Ogasawara Islands and Hokkaidō, bringing the total to 58 at the end of 1990.

Japan's marine parks may be loosely divided into three groups on the basis of the dominant ocean current. There are 27 marine parks located on the fringe of the warm KUROSHIO current in the Okinawa Islands, the Ogasawara Islands, Kyūshū, Shikoku, and the Kii Peninsula of central Honshū. These parks contain subtropical coral reefs and many varieties of soft coral. Along the coast of the Sea of Japan 30 marine parks are washed by the warm TSUSHIMA CURRENT. They are noted for their vast beds of sargassum and other seaweeds. The Kesennuma Marine Park is the only one bordering the cold OYASHIO current, which flows along the east coasts of northern Honshū and Hokkaidō. It is noted for huge laminaria kelp and for marine mammals such as seals. See also KUSHIMOTO MARINE PARK.

Marine Science Museum of Tōkai University 東海大学海洋科学博物館

(Tōkai Daigaku Kaiyō Kagaku Hakubutsukan). A privately run aquarium in the city of Shimizu, Shizuoka Prefecture. The museum was established in 1970 as part of the Social Education Center of Tōkai University. Its extensive facilities include one of the world's largest completely glass-walled oceanariums, and the "mechquarium," in which robots simulate undersea creatures.

markets 市

(*ichi*; also called *ichiba*). Markets of ancient Japan are thought to have developed at the sites of festivals or song and dance gatherings (UTAGAKI); in fact, the word *ichi* may have evolved from *itsuki*, meaning ceremony.

Following the TAIKA REFORM of 645, markets were established in the east and west districts of the successive capital cities. Government-sponsored markets were also held near administrative offices in provincial capitals (KOKUFU). Toward the end of the Heian period (794–1185) shops opened in settlements, forming MARKET TOWNS. With the rise of landed estates (SHŌEN), rent collection centers and entrepôts developed, especially in port towns. Other markets grew up in front of major temples and shrines (see MONZEN MACHI).

With the growing use of money from the mid-Kamakura period (1185–1333), periodic one-day markets (*higiri ichi*) became an important means of converting the estates' grain tax (NENGU) into cash. Following the Ōnin War of 1467–77, it became common to hold markets called *rokusaiichi* in villages six times a month. The Muromachi shogunate (1338–1573) encouraged trade, and many markets were opened by local *daimyō* to enrich their CASTLE TOWNS. The national unifiers ODA NOBUNAGA and TOYOTOMI HIDEYOSHI established "free markets" (*rakuichi*) and abolished the monopolistic privileges of merchants in the ZA (guilds; see RAKUICHI AND RAKUZA). In large cities permanent small shops and wholesalers (TOIYA) began to compete for business with the periodic markets. Special rice markets and wholesale markets also appeared. Traditional markets with many small booths still operate in a number of towns, especially during festivals.

market towns 市場町

(*ichiba machi*). Settlements authorized to sell goods to the public on specified days every month. Often providing some services as well as commercial opportunities, each marketing center established a link with urban life for residents of nearby villages and served as the basic, small-scale trading arena for itinerant merchants. Urban markets existed as early as the Nara period (710–794), but only in the Kamakura period (1185–1333) did they proliferate outside of administrative centers. Over the next several centuries the number of *ichiba machi* expanded enormously.

With the urban population growth that occurred just before and during the early Edo period (1600–1868), some local markets were closed to reduce local competition or protect the prosperity of CASTLE TOWNS. The majority of periodic markets became firmly subordinated as commercial outposts of the castle towns and of the three central cities—Edo (now Tōkyō), Ōsaka, and Kyōto (see RAKUICHI AND RAKUZA). In the 18th century the estimated number of market towns stabilized at close to 1,500 and remained virtually unchanged for roughly a century. By the late Edo period merchants in well-situated market areas posed a serious challenge to castle-town interests. At the same time periodic markets declined or disappeared in the face of more efficient transportation and daily shopping in village stores. Representing a bridge between urban and rural, market towns reflected the dramatic changes in the role of marketing places in Japan.

Marquat, William Frederic マーカット, W. F.

(1894–1960). Army major general who from 1945 to 1952 was chief of the Economic and Scientific Section of SCAP (the headquarters of the Allied OCCUPATION of Japan), one of the most successful Occupation activities. Born in St. Louis, Missouri, he served in France during World War I and with General Douglas MACARTHUR in the Pacific throughout World War II.

marriage 婚姻

(*kon'in*). Marriage in Japan has been characterized as centering on arranged marriage (*miai kekkon*), in which a man, a woman, and their families are formally introduced to each other by a go-between, or NAKŌDO, and a marriage is celebrated while the bride and groom are still comparative strangers. Allied to this is the traditional Japanese concept of marriage as the creation of links between two households, or IE, rather than the joining of two individuals. Put simply, marriage has traditionally been more of a family affair in Japan than it has in most Western cultures.

Through the years, however, and especially since the end of World War II, the legal requirements and personal expectations for marriage in Japan have changed in response to a host of new social situations, some of which are the result of influence from the West. While traditional ideas concerning the mechanics of making a match in Japan have not been completely abandoned, they exist chiefly as a framework for changing attitudes and preferences. Marriage in contemporary Japan is much more of a private decision between two people than it was before World War II; households, in particular the parents of a couple contemplating marriage, do not have as final a say in the matter as they did 50 years ago; and the function of the *nakōdo*, while still important, has in many cases shrunk to a largely ceremonial role.

Marriage in the Premodern Period— During much of the Heian period (794–1185) endogamous marriage (marriage within a group of households) and marriage to cousins were features of all levels of society. Among the court aristocracy marriage was essentially matrilocal, with a man moving into his wife's house at some point after they were married (see ᴍUKOIRIKON). Men of rank and importance could divide their time between two or three different houses, and marriage practices among the ruling elite are thought to have been largely polygynous; that is, a powerful man was not bound at any time to a single wife in monogamous marriage. He could, however, build a separate residence in which he lived and to which he brought one wife, giving a degree of permanence to their relationship.

An aristocratic woman usually conducted herself with discretion, since her pregnancies needed recognition by a man (not necessarily the father of the child) for her children to have any importance in society. Children might be confirmed to the rank of their father, or they could rely on their mother's father or brother to make public gestures indicating the child was of the mother's rank. ADOPTION into other households to achieve rank was also very common.

It was much more difficult for social classes of meager means to follow the marriage practices of the Heian elite. Farmers, artisans, and low-ranking warriors had a better chance of maintaining their status through permanent marriage with one wife. Still, almost any man, regardless of social status, could change wives without difficulty if his wife's family was not in a position to challenge his right to do so.

Change to Permanent Marriage—By the late 12th century the SAMURAI class had become the ruling elite in both central and provincial affairs throughout Japan. The political imbalances, warring factions, and military reprisals that had brought the samurai to power and that continued until about the late 1500s frequently involved households related through marriage. It was during this politically unsettled time that marriage began to assume importance as a means of ceremonially establishing or cementing military alliances between families, reaching the height of its importance in the period of intense interfamily political struggle known as the Sengoku period (1467–1568).

The marriage practices of the samurai, like much of their military ethic, were supported by Confucianism. Among samurai families the practice of maintaining multiple wives became less common (concubines, however, were considered separate from wives and were permitted). Samurai marriage customs also stressed the immediate transfer of the wife from her parents' home to her husband's residence (see YOMEIRIKON). Family concerns became important in the selection of a spouse, and in high-status marriages wives began to be taken from households at some distance, breaking with the older pattern of marriage within a close group and intensifying the need for professional nakōdo to ensure an appropriate match.

The marriage practices of rural commoners were less affected by the rise of the military elite. Practices that lent a more casual air to marriage customs, such as night visiting (YOBAI) and multiple liaisons, continued in the provinces.

The establishment of the Tokugawa shogunate in 1603 signaled the end of widespread warfare and the return of political stability. The samurai emphasis on arranged marriage continued throughout the Edo period (1600–1868) and urban commoners increasingly emulated samurai custom. The MIAI, a formal meeting of prospective marriage partners and their families, became popular at this time. The YUINŌ, a ceremonial exchange of engagement gifts between families, also became an important part of marriage practice among urban commoners, who

began to celebrate marriages with lavish WEDDINGS in the samurai style.

Legally, marriage in the Edo period was subject to a number of rules and regulations designed to preserve the status quo of the ruling military elite. Central among the many laws created was the mandatory reporting of proposed marriages before any ceremonies took place. Marriages had to be cleared through officials and the appropriateness of the match confirmed. Since all households were registered (see HOUSEHOLD REGISTERS), it was possible to monitor the population's adherence to the strict regulations.

Marriage and Industrialization—After the Meiji Restoration of 1868, Japan began an all-out effort to industrialize and catch up with the West. Cities, the centers of industry, also became centers of migration from all parts of Japan, further increasing the need for a nakōdo to ensure the appropriateness of a marriage.

The increased mobility of the population during the Meiji period (1868–1912) was a key factor in changing attitudes toward marriage in many (though not all) rural areas. As in urban centers, the miai, yuinō, the use of nakōdo, and other practices that had originated with the samurai became more common in rural areas. Parental arrangement of and authority over marriages increased, and, with the help of nakōdo, marriage negotiations began to be conducted over long distances.

An important legal codification of marriage was effected during the Meiji period. Under the CIVIL CODE of 1898 marriage was legally conducted under the so-called ie system (ie seido), which had necessitated the agreement of the heads of the two households involved in a marriage, rather than the man and woman to be married. Under Meiji civil law husband and wife were far from equal: through marriage, the wife lost her legal capacity to engage in property transactions; management of her own property came under her husband's control; and only the wife had the duty of chastity. The Meiji Civil Code remained the law of the land

until after World War II, when the new Civil Code of 1947 abolished the ie system and eliminated the legal inequality of husband and wife. See also MARRIAGE LAW; CONSTITUTION OF JAPAN.

Post–World War II Japan—Though the legal requirements of marriage in Japan changed radically after the war, largely as a result of OCCUPATION directives, marriage practices in the immediate postwar period were slower to respond to outside influence. While many Japanese were exposed to Western ideas about dating and marriage, mainly through movies and books, the traditional marriage pattern beginning with formal introduction through a nakōdo continued relatively unchanged, especially in high-status families. Very few Japanese of the mid-20th century expected to find a spouse through casual meeting or dating.

Even in contemporary Japan, where Western marriage practices seem to have affected the way a sizable number of Japanese think about marriage, the traditional system has not completely disappeared. Rather, Western influence has worked its way into a traditional system that has modified itself to meet contemporary preferences. Many people still seek, or perhaps are urged to seek, the advice of a nakōdo on a potential spouse; dating then confirms or disallows previous judgments concerning the individual's suitability. The nakōdo is especially useful when a person is near or past what is considered the "appropriate" age for marriage, which, as in the West, has changed over the years (statistically, the average age at marriage has been on the rise since 1970; in 1990 it was 25.9 for females and 28.4 for males). Additional examples of the ways in which the traditional system has opened itself to modern-day preferences are the matchmaking networks that operate among large companies and their affiliates, as well as many college alumni associations. These networks often make use of sophisticated computers to aid in the search for a marriage partner.

Still, marriage in contemporary Japan has

markets An early-17th-century screen painting of a bustling Kyōto market. Among the many merchants depicted are fan and kimono dealers.

adjusted in certain key areas to the influence of Western ideas, especially the importance of conjugal love as a fundamental aspect of marriage. More Japanese now say they prefer a *ren'ai kekkon*, or "love marriage," over the traditional arranged marriage. Individual choice has in many cases become the deciding factor in settling on a marriage partner, and the level of familial involvement in the marriage process has come to resemble that found in Western countries; that is, not completely absent, but not nearly as deep as it was in prewar Japanese society.

marriage law 婚姻法

(*kon'inhō*). The legal term for marriage in Japan, *kon'in*, refers to the socially sanctioned relationship for sexual union between a man and a woman and the contract that legalizes such a union. Modern Japanese marriage law is based on monogamy and legally protects as marriages only those unions between a man and a woman that meet certain legally established requirements.

Under the CIVIL CODE of 1898, marriage in Japan was conducted largely within the *ie* (family system), which was controlled by the *koshu* (head of the family). Thus, marriage involved one of the parties leaving his or her *ie* (family) as a *yome* (bride, daughter-in-law) or *muko* (groom, son-in-law) to become part of the other party's family. In order to do this, agreement between the heads of both households was necessary. In this system, husband and wife were far from equal: through marriage, the wife lost her legal capacity to engage in property transactions; management of her own property came under her husband's control; and only the wife had the duty of chastity. Following the provisions set down in the 1947 constitution, which protected individual dignity and the essential equality of the sexes, the Civil Code of 1947 abolished the *ie* system and eliminated the inequality of husband and wife.

Requirements for Marriage—Japanese civil law recognizes only marriages based on the fulfillment of the legal requirements. For the establishment of a marriage, the following requirements (the first formal, the rest substantial) must be fulfilled: (1) In accordance with the Family Registration Law (Koseki Hō; see HOUSEHOLD REGISTERS), notification in writing, properly witnessed, or in person by the two parties or their proxies, and two adult witnesses or guarantors is required (the guarantors need not actually accompany the two parties or their proxies). Even when the husband-wife relation has already been established by a formal ceremony or by living together, it is not recognized as a marriage without this notification. (2) The parties must have agreed upon marriage. A marriage is invalid if the intent to marry is lacking, as in cases of mistaken or false identity. Marriages involving fraud or intimidation may be annulled. (3) Men must be at least 18 years old, women at least 16. (4) When a woman remarries, at least six months must have passed since the day of dissolution or cancellation of her previous marriage. This is to determine paternity in case of pregnancy. (5) A marriage must not be bigamous. (6) Marriage cannot be consanguineous. Marriages between lineal relatives by blood, between collateral natural relatives within the third degree of relationship by blood, and between lineal relatives by mar-

riage (even after the relationship has ended through divorce or dissolution) are forbidden. (7) Minors (those under 20 years of age) must obtain the consent of their parents. If one parent objects or is incapable of expressing intent, the agreement of only one parent is sufficient. Marriages that violate any of conditions 3 through 6 may be canceled (*torikeshi*).

Results of Marriage—Establishment of the marriage relationship results in the following. Both husband and wife are called by one of their surnames. Each becomes a relative by marriage of the other's blood relatives. Each assumes the duties of cohabitation, cooperation, and support. Each assumes the duty of fidelity. Minors who marry are considered to have attained their majority. Contracts between husband and wife may be annulled while they are married. Mutual rights of inheritance are recognized. Children born are rebuttably presumed legitimate. Husband and wife may each hold property separately, but property whose ownership is unclear is rebuttably presumed to be held in common ownership.

Legal marriage is dissolved by the death or a declaration of disappearance of one of the parties or by divorce. See also DIVORCE; INHERITANCE LAW; MARRIAGE.

marshal 執行官

(*shikkōkan*). Court officer in charge of the service of judicial documents and execution in civil cases dealing with movables. The Marshal Law (Shikkōkan Hō) of 1966 sets forth the details of the office. Marshals belong to the district courts and are subject to supervision by the court.

martial arts 武術

(*bujutsu*). Also called *bugei;* now usually called *budō* or "the martial Way." The Japanese terms encompass such martial arts as KENDŌ (fencing), JŪDŌ, and KYŪDŌ (archery). The old expression BUGEI JŪHAPPAN (the 18 martial arts) refers to the arts of archery, horsemanship, spearmanship (SŌJUTSU), fencing, swimming, IAI (sword drawing), the short sword, the truncheon (*jitte*), dagger throwing (SHURIKEN), needle spitting, the halberd (NAGINATA), gunnery, roping, *yawara* (present-day *jūdō*), NINJUTSU (spying), the staff, *mojiri* (a staff with numerous barbs on one end), and the chained sickle (KUSARIGAMA). KARATE is not considered one of the traditional Japanese martial arts, although it is sometimes referred to as such outside of Japan. In the Edo period (1600–1868), in addition to academic subjects, warriors were required to learn six martial arts: fencing, spearmanship, archery, horseback riding, *jūjutsu* (now known as *jūdō*), and firearms. These six, together with military strategy, were called the seven martial arts. These were taught under the name BUSHIDŌ (the Way of the warrior).

After the Meiji Restoration (1868) the content of martial arts changed greatly, reflecting the fact that they were no longer meant to be used in combat and were no longer exclusive attainments of the warrior class. Reflecting this new circumstance, *bujutsu* was replaced by the term *budō*, implying that one would be trained in spiritual principles rather than for combat.

Modern *budō* seeks the development of skills through physical exercise and, by establishing objective standards of skills, provides opportunities for competition. In this sense it can be considered a form of sport. Yet behind the martial arts lie the philoso-

phies of Confucianism, Buddhism, and Taoism. Japanese martial arts started with *waza* (skills) for killing and fighting and, through searches for *kokoro* (or *shin*, heart), the heart that transcends victory and defeat, were led to the Buddhist view of life and death and the Confucian way of natural harmony, *yawara* (pliancy).

The basis of the martial arts resides in posture and body movement. The fundamental postures of the martial arts are standing upright and sitting upright. These are expressed as "natural body" in *jūjutsu* and "no stance" in swordplay and are related to an etiquette that forms a correct attitude toward life. YOSHIDA SHŌIN stated that "ceremony is defense," and MIYAMOTO MUSASHI added that it is important to "make your daily self your martial self, your martial self your daily self." These principles illustrate the essence of the martial arts.

The martial arts entail danger. As soon as one has dodged the enemy's attack through proper posture and body movement, one counters by attacking when the enemy is off guard. The means and methods for this are the basis for classification of the various martial arts. They can be roughly divided into those that use weapons and those that use the hands. Skills employing weapons aim to "strike and kill." Even when attacking the enemy empty-handed, the purpose of blows, thrusts, and kicks is to "strike and kill." On the other hand, unarmed skills such as throwing, restraining, squeezing, and immobilizing do not necessarily aim to kill and injure, but to "control violence yet not hurt life." However, these too, depending upon how they are employed, can be dangerous.

During the Sengoku period (1467–1568) the battlefield served as a place for application of skills, whether of swordsmanship or of *jūjutsu.* However, the peaceful Edo period (1600–1868) provided neither wars nor battles. Having lost the arena of actual combat, practitioners concentrated on the forms. In time, however, they became preoccupied with detail and began losing real effectiveness. This was held in contempt by purists who described such methods as *kahō kempō* ("flower-school swordplay"). In order to remedy this trend, new training methods were developed.

However, even after these new methods were initiated, it was difficult to dislodge the idea that training on the actual battlefield was superior. Furthermore, the conversion of combat into a game still involved physical danger, and the feeling persisted that martial training was something to engage in at the risk of one's life. The martial arts required a trained attitude toward death before actual battle and came to be considered religious achievements through which one could become absolutely invincible regardless of the result of combat. Moreover, they became secret methods guarded from outsiders.

In the development of the martial arts, the religious, secretive, and sectarian aspects made significant contributions, but they were accompanied · by exclusiveness, self-importance, and blind faith, qualities that do not suit modern society. After World War II, there was a need to modify certain views of the martial arts, and the emphasis shifted from practical arts intended for national defense to sports that stress harmony and universality.

martial law 戒厳令

(*kaigenrei*). The present CONSTITUTION OF JAPAN has no provision for martial law, al-

though article 78 of the Self Defense Forces Law (Jieitai Hō) of 1954 empowers the prime minister to mobilize the SELF DEFENSE FORCES for the preservation of public peace. Regulations were issued in 1882 by the Grand Council of State (DAJŌKAN) providing for martial law during times of war or internal dissension. Subsequently, the Meiji Constitution of 1889 (art. 14) reserved for the emperor the right to invoke martial law. Full martial law was declared in Ujina in Hiroshima Prefecture following the onset of the SINO-JAPANESE WAR OF 1894–1895; it was invoked again in Nagasaki, Sasebo, Tsushima, and Hakodate, as well as in Taiwan (then a Japanese colony), during the RUSSO-JAPANESE WAR of 1904–05. Martial law regulations were partially applied in Tōkyō in 1905 at the time of the HIBIYA INCENDIARY INCIDENT, after the TŌKYŌ EARTHQUAKE OF 1923, and in 1936 following the FEBRUARY 26TH INCIDENT.

Marubashi Chūya 丸橋忠弥

(?–1651). One of the principals in the RŌNIN (masterless *samurai*) cabal behind the KEIAN INCIDENT of 1651. An expert lancer who ran a school of this martial art, Chūya joined YUI SHŌSETSU in plotting a public disorder, if not the overthrow of the TOKUGAWA SHOGUNATE (1603–1867). Their plan allegedly included blowing up the shogunate's arsenal, burning the city of Edo (now Tōkyō), killing the shogunate's chief ministers, and even seizing Edo Castle. But the plot was exposed, apparently through Chūya's own boastfulness, and he was arrested and executed together with 33 other plotters and their relatives.

Marubeni Corporation 丸紅[株]

(Marubeni). One of Japan's leading GENERAL TRADING COMPANIES. Although the company is primarily engaged in international and domestic trade, its operations also include contracting and financing of construction work, underwriting of property insurance, and leasing of real and movable properties. The company is a key member of the Fuyō group, one of the major industrial-financial groups in Japan. The company originated in 1858 and was reorganized in its present form in 1949. It has 40 domestic and 128 overseas branches and subsidiaries, with 166 affiliates in Japan and 125 abroad. The company's plans emphasize the improvement of material and product distribution systems; promotion of plant exports; and development of sources of energy, food, and other basic materials. Sales for the fiscal year ending March 1991 totaled ¥19.0 trillion (US $138.5 billion), of which imports and exports accounted for 29.0 percent; offshore trade, 30.4 percent; and domestic trade, 40.6 percent. Capitalization in the same year was ¥193.1 billion (US $1.4 billion). Headquarters are in Tōkyō.

Marudai Food Co, Ltd 丸大食品[株]

(Marudai Shokuhin). Meat processor producing ham and sausages. Incorporated in 1958. Initially the firm produced fish sausages, but in the 1960s it turned to meat processing. In the 1970s the firm entered the field of prepared foods, enabling it to become a comprehensive food processor. The firm has set up a direct-sales system of retail outlets, avoiding the use of wholesalers. Sales for the fiscal year ending March 1991 totaled ¥197.1 billion (US $1.4 billion), and capitalization was ¥6.7 billion (US $48.8 million). Headquarters are in Ōsaka.

Maruetsu, Inc [株]マルエツ

(Maruetsu). Supermarket chain. Incorporated in 1943. Maruetsu operates 176 stores in the Tōkyō Metropolitan Area. For the fiscal year ending March 1991, sales totaled ¥296.5 billion (US $2.2 billion) and capitalization stood at ¥23.5 billion (US $171.3 million). Headquarters are in Tōkyō.

Marugame 丸亀[市]

City in western Kagawa Prefecture, Shikoku; includes part of the Shiwaku Islands. Marugame developed as a castle town with the construction of Marugame Castle, of which ruins remain, in 1597. In the Edo period (1600–1868) it prospered as the landing point for pilgrims visiting KOTOHIRA SHRINE. Industries include textiles and chemicals; *uchiwa* (fans) are also made here. Pop: 75,606.

Maruichi Steel Tube, Ltd 丸一鋼管[株]

(Maruichi Kōkan). Manufacturer of welded steel pipe and tubing. Founded in 1913. The company is well known overseas by its trade name, MKK. The firm owns 12 plants in Japan and has established 5 overseas plants. Sales for the fiscal year ending March 1991 totaled ¥131.6 billion (US $959.2 million), and capitalization was ¥8.1 billion (US $59.0 million). Headquarters are in Ōsaka.

Marui Co, Ltd [株]丸井

(Marui). Firm operating a chain of department stores known for its system of installment payment. Incorporated in 1937. It was the first domestic firm to issue credit cards. In 1989 the firm owned 33 stores, centered in the Tōkyō metropolitan area. Marui credit card holders number over 10.4 million, and the company maintains a vast data base concerning them. All stores are connected by an on-line computer system to give them access to the latest sales and marketing information. Sales for the fiscal year ending January 1991 totaled ¥565.8 billion (US $4.2 billion). In the same year capitalization stood at ¥35.3 billion (US $263.7 million). Headquarters are in Tōkyō.

Maruki Iri 丸木位里

(1901–). Japanese-style (NIHONGA) painter. Born in the city of Hiroshima. Maruki was almost completely self-taught. He and his wife, the Western-style painter Maruki Toshi (b 1912), received the 1953 International Peace Cultural Award for their collaborative *Gembaku no zu* (Hiroshima Murals), a series of folding screens dealing with the atomic bombing. In 1966 the Maruki Gallery for the Hiroshima Murals opened in the city of Higashi Matsuyama, Saitama

Prefecture, to house the series. In recent years Maruki has turned to ink painting, producing a number of bold, improvisational landscapes in this medium.

Marunouchi 丸ノ内

Business district in the eastern part of Chiyoda Ward, Tōkyō, between Tōkyō Station and the Imperial Palace. During the Edo period (1600–1868) mansions of the largest DAIMYŌ dominated the area. At the beginning of the Meiji period (1868–1912) it was an army parade ground, but in 1890 the land was transferred to the Mitsubishi industrial conglomerate, and it became a financial and business center. It remains so today, and the headquarters of many major Japanese corporations are located here.

Maruoka Hideko 丸岡秀子

(1903–90). Researcher on social problems, particularly the lives of rural women. Original name Ishii Hide. Born in Nagano Prefecture and raised in the countryside, she graduated from the Nara Women's Higher Normal School (now Nara Women's University), where she later taught. She worked with the survey division of the Sangyō Kumiai Chūōkai (Central Organization of Production Unions; see AGRICULTURAL COOPERATIVE ASSOCIATIONS) so she could study rural women. Her pioneering book was *Nihon nōson fujin mondai* (1937, The Problems of Women in Japanese Farming Villages). After World War II, Maruoka became concerned with educational problems. She worked for the establishment of parent-teacher associations (PTAS), campaigned in the antinuclear movement, and in 1955 helped start the JAPANESE MOTHERS' CONGRESS (Nihon Hahaoya Taikai).

Maruyama Kaoru 丸山薫

(1899–1974). Poet; often called the poet of the sea. Born in Ōita Prefecture. In 1917 he was admitted to the Tōkyō Shōsen Gakkō (now Tōkyō University of Mercantile Marine) but had to withdraw because of poor health. His unrealized dream of becoming a sailor affected him for much of his life. His first book, *Ho, rampu, kamome* (1932, Sails, Lamps, Seagulls), which conveyed a deep sense of yearning and loss, established his later reputation. *Tenshō naru tokoro* (1943, Where the Bell Rings) describes his experiences aboard a four-masted bark in 1941. Poems about his two-month cruise on board a freighter in 1955 are collected in his anthology of sea poems, *Tsuresarareta umi* (1962, The Sea That Was Taken Away). In 1934 Maruyama joined HORI TATSUO and

Maruki Iri *Bamboo Grove* by Maruki Iri and Maruki Toshi. Detail from a pair of folding screens, one of 15 pairs of screens known as the *Gembaku no zu* (Hiroshima Murals). 1954. Colors on paper. 180 × 360 cm. Maruki Gallery for the Hiroshima Murals, Saitama Prefecture.

Maruyama Kaoru This lyric poet is well known for his poems about the seafaring life.

Maruyama Ōkyo *View of the Banks of the River Yodogawa.* Detail. 1765. Handscroll. Colors on silk. 40 × 1,690 cm. Hara Museum, Tōkyō.

Maruya Saiichi This writer-critic's accomplishments include several finely crafted novels as well as translations of works by Graham Greene and James Joyce.

MIYOSHI TATSUJI in publishing the poetry magazine *Shiki* (Four Seasons). "Watashi to shiyū" (1970, My Poet Friends and I) is an account of his associations with other poets in connection with this influential magazine.

Maruyama Kenji   丸山健二

(1943–). Author. Born in Nagano Prefecture. Graduated from a technical high school. Maruyama began to write while supporting himself as a telegraph operator. He received the Akutagawa Prize for his novella *Natsu no nagare* (1966), a dry, impersonal account of a convict's execution as seen through the eyes of a veteran executioner. Influenced by Hemingway, Maruyama depicts young working-class people trying to escape from their humdrum and sometimes violent lives. A recent work is *No ni furu hoshi* (1990, Field of Fallen Stars).

Maruyama Masao   丸山真男

(1914–). Political scientist; known for his study of the history of political thought in Japan. Born in Ōsaka Prefecture. After graduation from the law department of Tōkyō University in 1937, he joined its faculty, becoming a full professor in 1950 and retiring in 1971. Maruyama contributed greatly to the development of political science in Japan from the end of World War II and undertook a penetrating analysis of Japan's social and ideological situation from the viewpoint of a democratic humanism. Particularly noteworthy is his *Chōkokka shugi no ronri to shinri* (1946, The Logic and Psychology of Ultranationalism), an analysis of the spiritual structure underlying the premodern and antidemocratic nature of the Japanese emperor system. He also wrote *Nihon seiji shisōshi kenkyū* (1952; tr *Studies in the Intellectual History of Tokugawa Japan*, 1974), *Gendai seiji no shisō to kōdō* (1956–57; tr *Thought and Behavior in Modern Japanese Politics*, 1963), and *Senchū to sengo no aida* (1976, Between the War and Postwar Eras).

Maruyama Ōkyo   円山応挙

(1733–95). Painter and founder of the Maruyama school. Real name Maruyama Mondo. Born into a poor farming family in Tamba Province (now part of Kyōto Prefecture). In his youth he was sent to Kyōto, where he studied painting with the KANŌ SCHOOL master Ishida Yūtei (1721–86). Ōkyo was influenced by the artist WATANABE SHIKŌ, as well as by Western-derived techniques,

RIMPA and TOSA SCHOOL elements, the NAGASAKI SCHOOL, and Chinese BIRD-AND-FLOWER PAINTING.

His combination of realistic perspective and chiaroscuro together with traditional Kanō-school compositional techniques and decorative elements, such as gold leaf backgrounds, was received enthusiastically. Though he was skilled in all categories of painting, he was perhaps most adept at painting flowers and trees. Ōkyo did many large-scale screen-and-wall paintings.

He attracted many followers, the most notable of whom were Nagasawa ROSETSU, WATANABE NANGAKU, and MATSUMURA GOSHUN (the founder of the Shijō school). Ōkyo's influence on later generations of painters was great, and practically all the developments of the MARUYAMA-SHIJŌ SCHOOL can be traced to sources in Ōkyo's vast oeuvre.

Maruyama Park   円山公園

(Maruyama Kōen). Municipal park located at the western foot of Higashiyama in Higashiyama Ward, Kyōto. The park was created in the early Meiji period (1868–1912) and has been expanded several times since then. The temples An'yōji and Chōrakuji are located in the park; the temple Chion'in borders it to the north and Yasaka Shrine is to the east. The park is famous as a spot for nighttime cherry-blossom viewing in the spring. Area: 8.6 hectares (21 acres).

Maruyama-Shijō school   円山四条派

(Maruyama-Shijō Ha). Major movement in Japanese painting in the Kyōto area in the late 18th and 19th centuries. Derived in large part from the Maruyama school, which was founded in Kyōto by MARUYAMA ŌKYO (1733–95). Ōkyo's student MATSUMURA GOSHUN (1752–1811) founded the Shijō school, named after his studio on Shijō Street in Kyōto. The artists, such as MATSUMURA KEIBUN (1779–1843) and OKAMOTO TOYOHIKO (1773–1845), who followed in the tradition of Ōkyo and Goshun have become known collectively as the Maruyama-Shijō school, a designation that probably dates from the end of the Edo period (1600–1868). The painters of the movement incorporated realistic aspects based on Western-influenced perspective and shading and on direct sketching from life, but they never broke completely with traditional techniques and themes.

Of the traditional schools of painting in 19th-century Kyōto, many were heavily influenced by the Maruyama-Shijō style, including the Kishi, Mori, and later Rimpa

schools, as well as the FUKKO YAMATO-E SCHOOL. By the beginning of the Meiji period (1868–1912), the similarities among these schools far outweighed their differences. Even today, artists working in the tradition of Japanese-style painting (NIHONGA) recognize a debt to the Maruyama-Shijō legacy.

Maruya Saiichi   丸谷才一

(1925–). Novelist and critic. Real name Nemura Saiichi. Born in Yamagata Prefecture. Maruya graduated from Tōkyō University, where he majored in English. In 1952 he and the critic Shinoda Hajime (1927–89) founded the coterie magazine *Chitsujo* (1952–63). This magazine serialized Maruya's first novel, *Ehoba no kao o sakete* (1952–60). In 1968 he won the Akutagawa Prize for his short story "Toshi no nokori." In his fiction Maruya uses the depiction of the outward surface of daily life as a vehicle for exploring the deeper levels of human psychology. His most important works of fiction include *Tatta hitori no hanran* (1972; tr *Singular Rebellion*, 1986) and *Yoko shigure* (1974; tr *Rain in the Wind*, 1990). His critical works include *Go-Toba In* (1973; winner of the Yomiuri Literary Prize in the same year), *Bunshō tokuhon* (1977), *Chūshingura to wa nani ka* (1984), and "Jueitan" (1987). Maruya has also been an outspoken commentator on issues relating to the Japanese language.

Maruzen Co, Ltd   丸善[株]

(Maruzen). One of Japan's leading companies engaged in the import, publishing, and sale of Western books and a well-known purveyor of stationery and office supplies. Founded in Yokohama as the Maruya Shōsha in 1869 by Hayashi Yūteki (1837–1901), a student of FUKUZAWA YUKICHI, the company began as an importer of Western books, magazines, stationery, and medical supplies. In 1893 it was moved to Tōkyō and its name was changed to Maruzen Co, Ltd. Today Maruzen continues to import and sell Western literature and maintains a high reputation in the publishing world.

Masakadoki → Shōmonki

Masamune Hakuchō   正宗白鳥

(1879–1962). Prominent writer of the naturalist school (see NATURALISM), whose work extends over the late Meiji (1868–1912), Taishō (1912–26), and Shōwa (1926–89) periods. Real name Masamune Tadao. Eldest son in a prosperous family of 10 children in Okayama Prefecture, he studied English at a school in the city of Okayama run by American Protestant missionaries. Because of anxiety and a fear of death engendered by his frail health, his religious interest deepened, and he derived much solace from the works of the Japanese Christian UCHIMURA KANZŌ.

In February 1896 Hakuchō went to Tōkyō, enrolling in the English department of the Tōkyō Semmon Gakkō (now Waseda University). During this same period he heard the sermons of the noted Protestant preacher UEMURA MASAHISA, and in 1897 he was baptized and became a church member. Through his encounter with the prominent naturalist critic SHIMAMURA HŌGETSU, he became a writer of a literary column for the YOMIURI SHIMBUN, one of Japan's leading national daily newspapers, and served in this capacity from 1903 until 1910.

The first story truly proclaiming Hakuchō's emergence as a naturalist writer of note was "Jin'ai" (1907; tr "Dust," 1970). In this short story he skillfully captures the bleakness of the life of a proofreader in a newspaper office. This and the stories that followed, such as "Doko e" (1908, Whither?), were deeply pessimistic, apparently negating his Christian faith. *Shisha seisha* (1916, The Dead and the Living) treats the breakdown of the family system in the face of the self-ishness and insensitivity of contemporary urban life. From 1924 he produced a succession of plays on much the same nihilistic theme as his narrative fiction, including his best-known play, *Jinsei no kōfuku* (1924, The Joys of Life). He also traveled extensively within Japan, Asia, and Europe. His major postwar output was in the area of criticism and drama. In 1948 he published *Shizen shugi seisuishi* (A History of the Rise and Fall of Naturalism). His death in 1962 caused a stir in the Japanese literary world because the minister who attended him on his death-bed, UEMURA TAMAKI, daughter of the man who had baptized him, wrote an essay contending that Hakuchō had regained his faith in the face of death. He received the Order of Culture in 1950.

Masanobu →Kanō Masanobu

Masaoka Shiki 正岡子規

(1867–1902). Poet and critic. Through his successful advocacy of a new realism for HAIKU and TANKA, the traditional verse forms, he made them viable genres in the postfeudal culture of Meiji-period (1868–1912) Japan. Shiki, whose given name was Tsunenori, was born in Matsuyama in what is now Ehime Prefecture to a modest *samurai* family. In 1883 Shiki went to Tōkyō to prepare himself for a career in philosophy or politics, but his exposure to literature changed his goals. Forfeiting a scholarship, he withdrew from Tōkyō University in 1892 to devote the 10 remaining years of his life to literature.

Shiki spent much effort on the reform of haiku verse. Contemporary haiku, which Shiki attacked vigorously from 1892 in a series of articles in the newspaper *Nihon*, was sterile and imitative, employing limited diction and subject matter. The master poet BASHŌ, who by this time was honored by monuments and in quasi-religious shrines, was the supreme model. Shiki, who denigrated the bulk of Bashō's haiku, advocated freedom of diction and subject matter, the scholarly study of haiku history, the treatment of haiku as serious literature, and the importance of realism or immediacy, which he termed *shasei* ("sketch from life"). Among his disciples was TAKAHAMA KYOSHI, who became the most influential haiku figure of his day. The haiku magazine HOTOTOGISU, founded under Shiki's auspices, was still being published in 1990.

By 1898, when the preeminence of Shiki's Nihon school of haiku was established, he turned to discussion of the *tanka* in a series of newspaper articles. The enervating effects of tradition were even more marked for this courtly form than for the haiku. Shiki attacked the style of the KOKINSHŪ (ca 905), the first imperial anthology, and found little to his taste in the SHIN KOKINSHŪ. He urged a return to the standards of the MAN'YŌSHŪ, the 8th-century anthology, which he admired for its manly vigor, artlessness of tone, and directness of mode. Shiki attracted a devoted group of followers, known as the Negishi Tanka Society, which included ITŌ SACHIO, whose transmission of Shiki's thought to SAITŌ MOKICHI, a leading modern *tanka* poet, established Shiki as the founder of the modern *tanka* tradition.

In 1889, when Shiki spat blood for the second time, he adopted the pen name Shiki, the Chinese pronunciation of the characters used to write the word *hototogisu*, the cuckoo, which in legend sang until it coughed blood. His illness was gravely aggravated by his trip to China as a war correspondent in 1895, and he soon realized he was terminally ill with tuberculosis. He continued to write vigorously. By 1898 he was bedridden. In three journals dated 1901–02 (*Bokujū itteki*, *Byōshō rokushaku*, and *Gyōga manroku*), the agonizing progress of his physical deterioration is given in realistic, clinical detail. Interspersed among the prose entries are series of haiku and *tanka*, including some of his most appreciated verse.

However innovative Shiki's theory seemed to his contemporaries, he himself generally kept to the formal elements of both the haiku and *tanka* forms, unlike his more revolutionary followers. The best of his mature work is marked by an austerity that has a unique freshness, which has established him as one of the four masters of haiku along with Bashō, BUSON, and ISSA. While his position as a *tanka* poet is not so clearly established, the same bareness of statement lends his *tanka* force and poignance.

masculine language 男性語

(*danseigo*). A variety of Japanese that is typically used by males as a reflection of their masculinity. Linguistic studies of the JAPANESE LANGUAGE have made more references to FEMININE LANGUAGE than to the masculine variety. The implication is that masculine Japanese is included as part of the language proper and that feminine Japanese is a deviant variety.

At an early age, Japanese children become aware of gender differentiation overtly reflected in language. For example, while there are a number of neutral terms and patterns that can be used by all children in referring to themselves, only a boy is expected to refer to himself as *boku* (I).

Lower pitch, distinctive voice quality and articulation, and particular sentence-final intonations are common in masculine speech. Other typically masculine features include several terms of self-reference and address; sentence particles; interjections; and plain, nondeferential forms of the verb and copula.

Masculine language communicates assertiveness, strength, toughness, and vigor. In its most marked form, it occurs among males in situations where these qualities are appropriate and important. In many all-male communication situations, however, gender-neutral language would be considered more fitting. When communication involves both sexes, the language of males varies even more markedly: it may be an obviously masculine style (when the user is signaling authority, toughness, and strength); or a gender-neutral style (signaling the linguistic neutrality typical of conferences or lectures); or even what has traditionally been identified as feminine style (when the male wishes to convey gentleness and empathy toward the addressee). Recently, many so-called male speech patterns are increasingly being used among women to signal strength, assertiveness, and self-assurance, paralleling the use of gentle patterns by men. These are examples of setting replacing gender as a style determinant.

Mashiko 益子[町]

Town in southeastern Tochigi Prefecture, central Honshū. It is known primarily for its

Mashiko ware
A modern teapot, decorated with a *sansui* (mountain and water) scene.

local pottery, MASHIKO WARE, produced here since 1853 and made famous by HAMADA SHŌJI. The Mashiko Sankōkan has a permanent display of Hamada's collection of folk arts. The town is also known for its tobacco leaves. Food, machinery, and watch factories have been established recently. Of note are the temples Saimyōji and Entsūji and the Tsuna Shrine. Pop: 24,317.

Mashiko ware 益子焼

(*mashiko-yaki*). Folk-style pottery made in the town of Mashiko, Tochigi Prefecture. Mashiko became famous as the home of potter HAMADA SHŌJI (1894–1978). In the late Edo period (1600–1868) Mashiko produced teapots, *suribachi* (mortars), cooking pots, and other kitchenware for the Kantō area. In 1853 local potters began producing a Shimotsuke ware, similar to the SŌMA WARE of what is now Fukushima Prefecture. During the early 20th century Mashiko fell into a decline but recovered after Hamada settled there in 1924. Hamada's son carries on his father's tradition, and several of Hamada's former students still live and work there. As a result of Hamada's fame many foreign potters have studied in Mashiko. It is now a prosperous town and a tourist attraction, and the home of a number of serious potters. Both the handmade and mass-produced wares of Mashiko are utilitarian tablewares.

Mashū, Lake 摩周湖

(Mashūko). Caldera lake in eastern Hokkaidō. Located on the eastern fringe of Akan National Park, this lake is said to be one of the most transparent in the world. It is surrounded by cliffs averaging 300 m (984 ft) in height. Kamuishu Island, a lava dome, lies in the center of the lake. Rainbow trout have been released into the lake. Fog occurs frequently in summer. Area: 19.6 sq km (7.6 sq mi); circumference: 21 km (13 mi); depth: 212 m (695 ft); transparency: 35.8 m (117.4 ft); altitude: 351 m (1,152 ft).

masks 面

(*men*). Masks made of clay, dry lacquer, cloth, paper, or wood have long been an integral part of Japanese dance, ritual, FESTIVALS (*matsuri*), and religious ceremony. They reflect traditions from the Asian continent as well as indigenous ones. Masks from as early as the 7th century are preserved in temples, shrines, and museums, and new ones are still being modeled on them for performances today. Although clay masks dating from the late Jōmon period (ca 10,000 BC–ca 300 BC) have been unearthed, the majority of Japanese masks are carved from wood and sometimes painted with a layer of lacquer. They are primed with kaolin or powdered chalk and finally coated with polychrome pigments. The modern mask

Masamune Hakuchō
The fiction of this prominent naturalist writer is marked by its nihilistic themes and the ennui of its characters.

Masaoka Shiki An advocate of *shasei*, or "sketches from life," as a literary technique, this poet played a central role in the modern revival of traditional poetic forms.

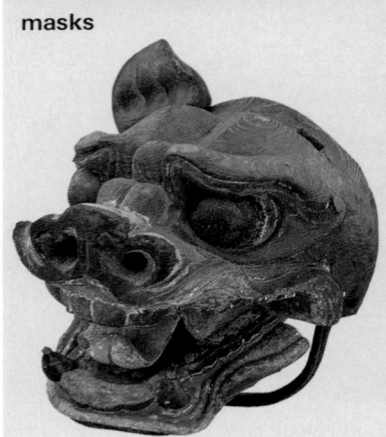

A *gigaku* lion mask said to have been used in the 752 dedication ceremonies for the Great Buddha at Tōdaiji, Nara. Painted wood. Shōsōin, Nara Prefecture.

A *gigaku* mask of an elderly man, said to have been used for the Great Buddha dedication ceremonies. Painted wood. Shōsōin, Nara Prefecture.

A 12th-century *bugaku* mask representing Batō, a character from Indian mythology. Painted wood. Itsukushima Shrine, Hiroshima Prefecture.

In a procession held each May at the temple Taima-dera in Nara, *gyōdō* masks are used to represent the 25 bodhisattvas who are said to have escorted the soul of the lady Chūjō (753–781) to heaven.

A 12th-century *gyōdō* mask representing Ken-dabba (Skt: Gandharva), one of a group of eight Buddhist guardian deities. Painted cypress wood. Hōryūji, Nara Prefecture.

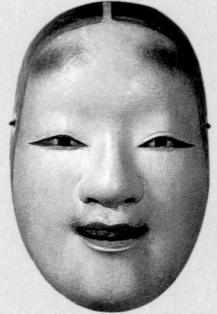

A Muromachi-period (1333–1568) *koomote* (young woman) Nō mask. Known as the *hana* (flower) *koomote*, it was owned by Toyotomi Hideyoshi. Painted wood. Mitsui Bunko, Tōkyō.

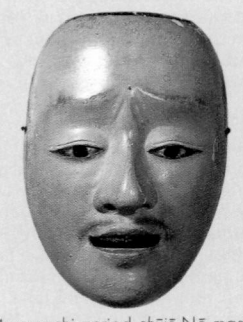

A Muromachi-period *chūjō* Nō mask used to represent a nobleman. Painted wood. Mitsui Bunko, Tōkyō.

A Muromachi-period *gyōdō* mask of a bodhisattva. Painted paulownia wood. The gilt-bronze crown was added later. Hōryūji, Nara Prefecture.

Two masks used in comical *kagura*, a type of Shintō dance performance. Painted wood.

An early-16th-century *kobuaku*-type *kyōgen* mask with typically distorted features and silly expression. Painted wood. Tōkyō National Museum.

A mid-Edo-period (1600–1868) *kyōgen* mask of the deity Bishamonten. Painted wood. Itsukushima Shrine, Hiroshima Prefecture.

carver uses essentially the same techniques developed 500 years ago.

Gigaku Masks—The oldest types of wooden masks still preserved are those used in GIGAKU, a procession followed by skits performed on temple grounds. The masks and bits of costume that have been preserved serve as valuable clues to the nature of the now-lost practice of *gigaku*.

Massive and sculptural, *gigaku* masks measure 20 to 30 centimeters (7.9 to 11.8 in) wide, 30 to 40 centimeters (11.8 to 15.7 in) tall, and 18 to 35 centimeters (7.1 to 13.8 in) deep and are constructed so as to cover the top of the head as well as the face. The outer rim of the mask extends back to include ears, a feature unusual on other Japanese masks. A *gigaku* program required 14 different types of masks, which together made up one set.

Some *gigaku* masks are made of dry lacquer, but most are carved from paulownia wood (*kiri*), painted with lacquer, and then polychromed on a base of kaolin; many have an oil finish. They have shaded areas, black outlines around the features, and hair pasted on and held down with bronze disks.

Bugaku Masks—These masks were used in court dance (*bugaku*) from the 9th century. Each face captures an attitude or emotion. *Bugaku* masks vary greatly in size, measuring 19 to 33 centimeters (7.5 to 13.0 in) tall, 16 to 24 centimeters (6.3 to 9.4 in) wide, and 10 to 18 centimeters (3.9 to 7.1 in) deep. They are typically made of cypress (*hinoki*) and are placed in front of the face. Many do not have ears. The oldest *bugaku* mask, the only dry-lacquer example extant, probably dates from the 8th century.

Very few of the *bugaku* masks bear the names of their carvers. Many of these carvers—Jōkei, Inshō, Inken—were also sculptors of Buddhist statues. Indeed, the techniques and styles used in *bugaku* mask carving parallel those of Buddhist sculpture.

Gyōdō Masks—*Gyōdō* masks represent Buddhist figures. Worn in outdoor temple processions, these masks of superhuman size and engulfing form serve primarily as a visual reminder of the figure they represent.

Nō and Kyōgen Masks—The uniquely Japanese masks used in NŌ and KYŌGEN plays emerged in the 14th and 15th centuries and drew on existing folk types. About 80 different masks constitute the necessary stock of a theater, but well over 200 are commonly used. Shallow in construction, most Nō masks are smaller than the average adult Japanese face. Central to their dramatic quality is a mutable expression that centers in the eyes, so carved that they seem to move, to sadden, to brighten with the play of shadows caused by slight shifts of the head. Early Nō masks were carved freely with simple, open expressiveness, but the masks were standardized in form and use during the 17th century. Masks for the *kyōgen* comedies, performed between Nō plays, have a joyous extroversion marked by distorted features.

Mason, Luther Whiting
メイソン, L. W.

(1818–96). US music educator who introduced Western music to Japanese schools as an adviser to the Ministry of Education from 1880 to 1882. Born in Turner, Maine, Mason had for many years been a teacher of music when in 1879 he accepted an invitation from the Japanese government to visit Japan, extended through his former pupil IZAWA SHŪJI. Mason advanced the popularity and technical understanding of Western music through the music education system that he and Izawa developed for Japan's new normal and elementary schools. Mason also laid the foundation for a national music school, later called the Tōkyō Ongaku Gakkō (now Tōkyō University of Fine Arts and Music). His published texts include *National Music Course* (4 vols, 1887–97).

mass communications   マスコミ

(*masukomi*). Japan has been a world leader in the development of mass communications, which is typically defined as the rapid and inexpensive transmission of large quantities of news, opinion, educational and cultural information, and entertainment to all groups of the population by large-scale, complex organizations using advanced technology.

Historical Development—The Edo period (1600–1868) left Japan with a superb social base for modern mass communications in its geographically compact, culturally homogeneous, politically centralized, education-oriented, and increasingly urbanized population. The spread of democratic institutions, university education, and urban lifestyle in the 20th century created enormous markets for newspapers, magazines, and books and for the electronic media introduced directly following their development in the West: radio broadcasting in 1925, television in 1953, FM radio in 1959, and regular color television service in 1960.

Structures and Functions—In organization, scale, and allocation of functions, the Japanese mass media have developed uniquely out of the indigenous economic and social structure and philosophical bent. Both newspapers and book publishing display the same intensive oligopolistic competition among gigantic, tightly knit enterprise groups that is characteristic of modern Japanese business as a whole. Television broadcasting illustrates the Japanese preference for government initiative in nurturing a new industry and setting general standards before throwing it open to private enterprise, eventually maximizing social benefits through a dual public and commercial system.

Competitive pressures in a basically unitary national newspaper market have led to a striking uniformity of format, content, editorial viewpoint, and reportorial style. The limited local competition consisting of single prefectural and three regional "bloc" papers, takes its cue from the five national dailies (the YOMIURI SHIMBUN, ASAHI SHIMBUN, MAINICHI SHIMBUN, SANKEI SHIMBUN, and NIHON KEIZAI SHIMBUN) in a top-heavy configuration dictated by geographical intimacy and the predominance of Tōkyō and Ōsaka. With a total daily publication of 52 million, Japan ranked first in the world in per capita circulation of newspapers in 1991.

Radio broadcasting was begun in 1925 by the private Tōkyō Broadcasting Station, with strong government backing. In 1926 the Japan Broadcasting Corporation (NHK) was granted a broadcasting monopoly under the firm control of the Ministry of Communications. In 1950 the new BROADCASTING LAW made provision for a commercial sector and reorganized NHK as a strictly public service organization. Since television broadcasting started in 1953, there has been much competition between the public and private sectors of Japan's dual system. NHK is the most popular news source and provides lavish cultural and informational programming on both its general and educational channels.

The five commercial chains are NIPPON TELEVISION NETWORK CORPORATION (NTV); TŌKYŌ BROADCASTING SYSTEM, INC (TBS); TELEVISION TŌKYŌ CHANNEL 12, LTD; FUJI TELECASTING CO, LTD; and ASAHI NATIONAL BROADCASTING CO, LTD. These five have been strengthened by tie-ups with the five national newspapers.

The functions of wire services, weekly magazines, and monthly journals in Japan have all been affected by the character of the newspapers. With the national dailies relying mainly on their own domestic and foreign news bureaus, Japan's two news agencies, KYŌDŌ NEWS SERVICE and JIJI PRESS, play a supplementary role except for the local press.

Journalists and Their Audience—The journalists in Japan's major media firms enjoy high professional status, and they are joined by a broad public forum (*rondan*) of intellectual critics (*hyōronka*) who fuel debate through daily columns, television symposia, and monthly commentaries. Japan's highly literate public, deferential toward intellectual authority and eager for information and guidance in the pursuit of personal and corporate uplift, sustains an extensive high-grade sector of "mass quality" newspapers and television programs. The surprising homogeneity, especially in news coverage, derives not only from market rivalries but also from the unique organization of news gathering in Japan. The typical reporter writes not so much independent stories as raw material for reprocessing at the departmental desk, and the correspondents themselves are organized into exclusive PRESS CLUBS (*kisha kurabu*) attached to all major government institutions and public figures.

News, Opinion, and Politics—The Japanese press was under constant regulation and periodic suppression from the time of the PRESS ORDINANCE OF 1875 through the militaristic regime of the 1930s, the war years, and then the censorship of the Allied OCCUPATION authorities. Democratization during the Occupation nevertheless left the press in 1952 in a far more liberated state than it had ever before experienced, and for some years it adopted an almost reflex policy of unofficial opposition to the Japanese government and the United States. Today, Japanese journalism continues to enjoy great freedom from statutory restraint in the areas of libel, slander, parliamentary privilege, and official secrets. However, the press has often failed to attack government and business promptly and head-on over major evils such as graft or pollution. The collaborative ties between the press and its sources in the press clubs, among club members, and between media management and big business have all joined with general group psychology to produce a more comfortable relation between journalism and established power than would be deduced from their formal adversarial relationship.

Education, Culture, and Society—Newspaper companies have sponsored and provided vast funds for art exhibits, symphony orchestras, academic symposia, and research projects, as well as more lucrative public-relations investments such as amusement parks and baseball teams. In television, the Broadcasting Law requires all stations to carry balanced cultural and educational as well as news and entertainment programming.

Mass communications has contributed to political and social stability in postwar Japan. Television has virtually eliminated

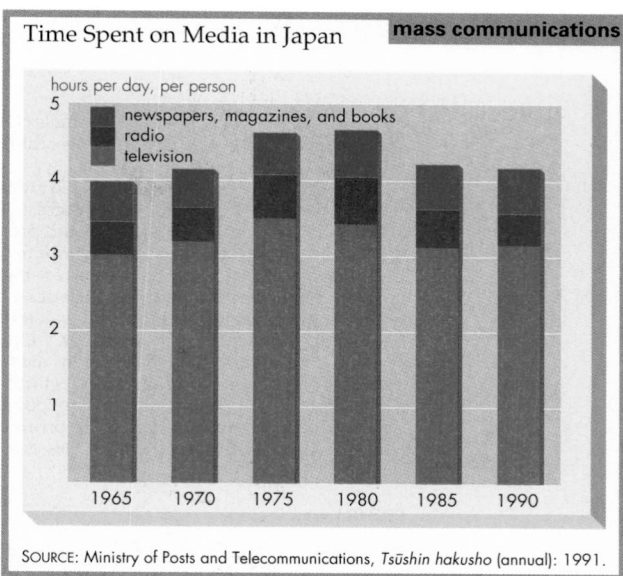

Time Spent on Media in Japan

hours per day, per person

newspapers, magazines, and books
radio
television

1965 1970 1975 1980 1985 1990

SOURCE: Ministry of Posts and Telecommunications, *Tsūshin hakusho* (annual): 1991.

the urban-rural cultural gap, a divisive factor in the prewar period. The mass media and educational system together have greatly reduced the potential for class cleavage by spreading a uniform, middlebrow, middle-class culture throughout Japan. Recent social concerns have included information glut and "data pollution," technological threats to privacy and individual freedom, and the gradual loss of psychological space in a post-industrial society dominated by computers, telecommunications, and hyperproductive mass media. The Japanese, who already inhabit one, have done a great deal to develop the concept of the "information society" (*jōhōka shakai*) both as a popular notion and as a new academic discipline.

In a continuing effort to reduce the depiction of sex and violence, standards of ethics, decency, and taste are monitored by the Newspaper Content Evaluation Center, the JAPAN ADVERTISING REVIEW ORGANIZATION, several broadcasting program consultative committees for television, the MOTION PICTURE CODE COMMITTEE, and the National Mass Communications Ethics Council.

Recent Trends—The 1980s saw Japan enter the so-called New Media Age, a term that refers to the development of new information technology through the use of computer and telecommunications hardware. A major stimulus for this was the deregulation of the telecommunications industry in April 1985.

In the late 1980s major dailies computerized page production by inputting articles into computers and editing them on video display terminals. TELECOMMUNICATIONS SYSTEMS could then be used to forward these articles in the form of digital signals for print publication anywhere in the world. Japanese newspapers were thus able to bring out same-day editions by satellite in Europe and the United States. Newspaper companies developed new enterprises utilizing this information as videotex and data bases.

Broadcasting industry developments included satellite broadcasting, multiplex broadcasting, HIGH-DEFINITION TELEVISION, and digital broadcasting. As of April 1991, three satellite broadcast channels were being operated, two by NHK, and one by Japan Satellite Broadcasting, Inc (JSB). CABLE TELEVISION (CATV) has also been made available via satellite relay, and 77 stations were operating in 1990 with a further 26 planned. In the public sector, as of 1991 there were 109 television channels, 1 satellite channel, 47 AM channels, 35 FM channels, 1 commercial shortwave channel, and numerous cable television channels.

The publishing industry has shifted from metal type to computerized word processing and typesetting, and most editorial and production functions are also fully computerized. The use of new electronic hardware has enabled publishers to produce varieties of nonprint publications such as audiocassette books and videocassette "magazines." Up-to-date dictionaries have also been made available on compact disc. The new technology has brought publishing to the point where it is no longer limited to the printed page. See also BROADCASTING; NEWSPAPERS; PUBLISHING.

masu → salmons

Masuchi Yōjirō   増地庸治郎

(1896–1945). Scholar of management economics. Born in Kyōto, he was a graduate of Tōkyō Higher Commercial School (now Hitotsubashi University). After working with Sumitomo Ltd, Masuchi became a professor at his alma mater in 1921. He helped establish the Japan Management Studies Association in 1926 and in 1928 started publishing *Keiei keizaigaku kenkyū* (Management Economics Studies). He also went to Germany and studied under H. Nicklisch. Masuchi focused on management's internal structure and its external relations. His main works include *Keiei keizaigaku* (1929, Management Economics), *Kabushiki kaisha* (1937, Joint-Stock Company), and *Chingin ron* (1939, On Wages).

Masuda   益田[市]

City in western Shimane Prefecture, western Honshū, on the Sea of Japan. Principal industries are textiles and lumber processing. Kakinomoto Shrine, dedicated to the poet KAKINOMOTO NO HITOMARO, is located here. Pop: 52,412.

Masuda Mizuko   増田みず子

(1948–). Novelist. Born in Tōkyō; graduate of Tōkyō University of Agriculture and Technology. Masuda's writing explores the relationship of the individual to society from a cool and unsentimental perspective. Her works include *Mugibue* (1981, Straw Whistle), *Jiyū jikan* (1984, Free Time), winner of the Noma Prize for New Talent, and *Shinguru seru* (1986, Single Cell).

Masuda Takashi   益田孝

(1848–1938). Businessman; leader of the MITSUI financial combine. Born in Sado Province (now part of Niigata Prefecture), the son of a minor official. Masuda and his father accompanied the 1864 Tokugawa shogunate mission to France (see SHOGUNATE MISSIONS TO THE WEST). In 1872 he entered the Ministry of Finance at the invitation of Vice-Minister of Finance INOUE KAORU but resigned with Inoue the following year. Under Inoue's direction, Masuda headed the Senshū Kaisha trading company, which in 1876 was taken over by Inoue's business allies, the Mitsui merchant house. The business was reorganized as the Mitsui Trading Company (Mitsui Bussan Kaisha), and Masuda helped to build the Mitsui financial empire. His ventures included the purchase of the MIIKE COAL MINES and the acquisition of resources in China. He was a noted art collector and connoisseur of the tea ceremony.

Masukagami   増鏡

Historical tale attributed to NIJŌ YOSHIMOTO; probably written between 1338 and 1376. Beginning with the birth of Emperor Go-Toba in 1180, it traces 154 years of court history through the reigns of 15 emperors up to the return of Emperor Go-Daigo from exile in 1333, including the relationship of the imperial court with the ruling shogunate government in Kamakura. The narrator, an old woman reminiscing about the past (a device used in the earlier ŌKAGAMI and IMAKAGAMI), paints the world of the Kyōto court nobility in nostalgic tones. The elegant classical prose style is apparently modeled on that of the TALE OF GENJI (*Genji monogatari*).

Masumoto Hakaru   増本量

(1895–1987). Physical metallurgist. Developed the stainless alloy Invar (1929), New KS Magnetic Steel (together with HONDA KŌTARŌ in 1933), and numerous other metal alloys. Born in Hiroshima Prefecture. After graduating from Tōhoku University in 1922, Masumoto carried out research at the Research Institute for Iron, Steel, and Other Metals at the same university, under the direction of Honda Kōtarō. He became a professor there in 1933 and director of the research institute in 1950. In 1955 he was awarded the Order of Culture.

Masumura Yasuzō   増村保造

(1924–86). Film director. Born in Yamanashi Prefecture, he graduated from Tōkyō University. After working for Daiei Co, Ltd, as an assistant director, he went to Rome to study at the Centro Experimentale de Cinema. After returning to Japan, he made his directorial debut in 1957. He became a pioneering leader of the Japanese *nouvelle vague* with his fast-paced, penetrating studies of human relationships and society and its ills. Among his major works are *Hyōheki* (1958, Wall of Ice), *Kyojin to gangu* (1958, The Buildup), and *Kuro no shishōsha* (1962, The Black Test Car).

Masutomi Hot Spring   増富温泉

(Masutomi Onsen). Located in the town of Sudama, northwestern Yamanashi Prefecture, central Honshū. A radioactive mineral spring noted worldwide for the volume of its radium emanation; water temperature 30°C (86°F). The waters are said to be effective for gastrointestinal disorders and neuralgia. This hot spring has been designated as a National Health Resort Hot Spring.

Matabei → Iwasa Matabei

Matagi   またぎ

A people inhabiting the highlands of the Tōhoku (northern Honshū) region who live mainly in mountain huts and subsist almost totally by collective hunting; formerly called Yamadachi. Some Matagi still maintain their traditional lifestyle, strictly observing customs and taboos and speaking a unique "mountain dialect" (*yama kotoba*).

matchlocks → hinawajū

maternity passbook   母子健康手帳

(*boshi kenkō techō*). A pregnancy and child care logbook and manual issued to pregnant women who have registered with a local ward office. The issuance of the passbook is provided for by the 1965 Maternal and Child Health Law (Boshi Hoken Hō). The maternity passbook serves as a register for data on the course of pregnancy, childbirth, newborn and infant medical examinations, vaccinations, and other medical treatment. It also contains practical information on pregnancy and child care. The maternity passbook system had its origins in the *ninsampu techō* ("pregnancy logbook"), first issued in 1942.

mathematics, modern   現代数学

(*gendai sūgaku*). From the 17th century to the first half of the 19th century, Japanese mathematics was dominated by WASAN, a traditional system of calculation unique to Japan. Modern mathematics in Japan came entirely from Europe, having been introduced soon after the Meiji Restoration (1868) by KIKUCHI DAIROKU and FUJISAWA RIKITARŌ, who had both studied abroad. *Wasan* was eliminated from the Japanese school curriculum in 1873.

The Tōkyō Mathematical Society (Tōkyō Sūgakusha), originally founded in 1877 to promote modern mathematics in Japan, was reorganized as the Tōkyō Mathematical and Physical Society in 1884 to include physicists. Membership spread nationwide and resulted in a second reorganization in 1918, this time as the Mathematical and Physical Society of Japan (Nihon Sūgaku Butsuri Gakkai).

Mathematical research had been carried out at Japanese universities since the 1870s, but the first modern Japanese mathematician to win international recognition was TAKAGI TEIJI for his work on class field theory, presented in 1920 and 1922. Ōsaka University established a reputation as a center for abstract mathematics in the 1930s.

Shortly after World War II, the Mathematical and Physical Society of Japan split into the Mathematical Society of Japan (Nihon Sūgakkai) and the Physical Society of Japan (Nihon Butsuri Gakkai). The 11th International Mathematics Conference, held at Harvard University in 1950, marked the return of Japanese mathematicians to the international scene after the war. In 1954 KODAIRA KUNIHIKO received the prestigious Fields Medal, as did HIRONAKA HEISUKE in 1970.

Mathematical research in Japan is of the highest standards, and Japanese mathematicians have published extensively abroad. The *Sūgaku jiten* (1985), edited by the Mathematical Society of Japan, has been translated into English as the *Encyclopedic Dictionary of Mathematics* (1990). The two major mathematical research institutes in Japan are the Institute of Statistical Mathematics (Tōkei Sūri Kenkyūjo), founded in 1944 under the Ministry of Education, and the Research Institute for Mathematical Science (Sūri Kaiseki Kenkyūjo), which was established in 1963 and is affiliated with Kyōto University. Recent developments in research include the stochastic calculus applied to probability theory developed by Itō Kiyoshi (b 1915) and the algebraic analysis originated by Satō Mikio (b 1928). In 1990 the International Congress of Mathematicians was held in Kyōto. In 1990 MORI SHIGEFUMI was awarded the Fields Medal for his research in algebraic geometry, a field in which Japan has become a world leader.

Despite its many achievements, Japanese mathematics is not without its problems. A rapid increase in the number of mathematicians in recent years has not been matched by a corresponding expansion of job opportunities, and the flood of papers written by these researchers cannot be accommodated by the existing magazines and journals. On the other hand, in some areas such as combinatorics and classical analysis, there is a shortage of specialists.

mathematics, traditional → wasan

matsu → pines

Matsubara　松原［市］
City in Ōsaka Prefecture, central Honshū. It developed early on as a junction of the roads connecting the ancient capitals of NANIWAKYŌ and ASUKA. In recent years much of its farming has been replaced by light industries. There are several ancient mounded tombs (KOFUN) in the area. Pop: 135,919.

Matsubayashi Keigetsu　松林桂月
(1876–1963). Japanese-style (NIHONGA) painter. Born Matsubayashi Atsushi in Yamaguchi Prefecture, he studied under the *nihonga* painter Noguchi Yūkoku (1827–89). His work was first shown at the BUNTEN (Ministry of Education Fine Arts Exhibition) in 1908. In 1960 he formed the Nihon Nangain (Japan Academy of Southern School Painting), and as its chairman played a crucial role in the promotion of contemporary works done in the traditional style of literati painting known as NANGA or BUNJINGA. He also served as director of the Japan Art Association (Nihon Bijutsu Kyōkai). He received the Order of Culture in 1958.

Matsuda Gonroku　松田権六
(1896–1986). Lacquerer. Born in Kanazawa, Ishikawa Prefecture. Matsuda graduated from Tōkyō Bijutsu Gakkō (now Tōkyō University of Fine Arts and Music) and studied under the lacquerer Rokkaku Shisui (1867–1950). He developed a new technique for making MAKI-E—pictures, often on lacquered box covers, using gold, silver, or powdered lacquers of various colors. Matsuda won the highest award at the Teiten (Exhibition of the Imperial Fine Arts Academy) in 1929. In 1955 he was designated a Living National Treasure and in 1976 he received the Order of Culture.

Matsudaira family → Tokugawa family

Matsudaira Ietada　松平家忠
(1555–1600). Also known as Matsudaira Tonomo no Suke Ietada. Warrior vassal of TOKUGAWA IEYASU (1543–1616). A collateral kinsman of Ieyasu, he distinguished himself in Ieyasu's campaigns against TAKEDA KATSUYORI (1546–82) and in the KOMAKI NAGAKUTE CAMPAIGN against TOYOTOMI HIDEYOSHI (1537–98) in 1584. Ietada died defending Fushimi Castle, Ieyasu's residence in the Kyōto area, when it fell to forces mobilized by ISHIDA MITSUNARI (1560–1600) in a prelude to the Battle of SEKIGAHARA. Ietada's diary, *Ietada nikki*, is a valuable historical source for the years 1577–94.

Matsudaira Katamori　松平容保
(1835–93). *Daimyō* of the Aizu domain (now part of Fukushima Prefecture) and military governor of Kyōto (KYŌTO SHUGOSHOKU); one of the leaders of the MOVEMENT FOR UNION OF COURT AND SHOGUNATE. In order to quell antishogunate extremist *samurai* controlling Kyōto and to bolster the shogunate, Katamori advocated closer cooperation between the court and the shogunate. He also made use of special police units, such as the

maternity passbook
This English-language version of the maternity passbook is available to foreign women who give birth in Japan. **1** Cover. **2** Table of contents.

SHINSENGUMI, to patrol the streets of Kyōto. In 1863 the combined forces of the Satsuma (now Kagoshima Prefecture) and Aizu domains succeeded in driving the extremists from Kyōto (see COUP D'ETAT OF 30 SEPTEMBER 1863). When the extremists attempted to retake Kyōto the following year, Katamori again led Aizu and Satsuma troops and repelled them (see HAMAGURI GOMON INCIDENT). After the restoration of imperial rule in 1868 (see MEIJI RESTORATION), Katamori returned to Aizu and resisted the imperial takeover. Supported by an alliance of northeastern domains (the ŌUETSU REPPAN DŌMEI) and reorganizing his army along Western lines, he made a last-ditch effort to defend Tokugawa interests. He surrendered when Wakamatsu Castle was taken by imperial troops (see BOSHIN CIVIL WAR).

Matsudaira Nobutsuna　松平信綱
(1596–1662). A leading administrator of the early TOKUGAWA SHOGUNATE (1603–1867). Known as Chie Izu (Clever Izu) from his title Izu no Kami. Nobutsuna was assigned to serve TOKUGAWA IEMITSU at the latter's birth and remained his intimate throughout Iemitsu's term as shōgun (1623–51). Nobutsuna became a senior councillor (RŌJŪ) in 1633 and continued under the next shōgun, TOKUGAWA IETSUNA. In 1637–38 he served as special commissioner in charge of suppressing the SHIMABARA UPRISING; subsequently he inspected parts of Kyūshū associated with Christianity and with foreign contacts, and his observations contributed to the formulation of the shogunate's NATIONAL SECLUSION policy in 1638–39. Nobutsuna played an important part in the suppression of abortive plots to overthrow the government in the KEIAN INCIDENT of 1651 and the Jōō Incident of the following year. Nobutsuna is also remembered for the innovative agricultural techniques he introduced to his domain at Kawagoe in Musashi Province (now Saitama Prefecture).

Matsudaira Sadanobu　松平定信
(1759–1829). *Daimyō* of the Shirakawa domain (now part of Fukushima Prefecture) and a senior councillor (*rōjū*) of the TOKUGAWA SHOGUNATE (1603–1867); best known as the initiator of the KANSEI REFORMS (1787–93). Born in Edo (now Tōkyō), he was the seventh son of TAYASU MUNETAKE and grandson of TOKUGAWA YOSHIMUNE, the eighth shōgun. As a member of one of the three junior collateral houses of the Tokugawa family (GOSANKYŌ), he was in line for the position of shōgun in the event of a succession problem, but in 1774 Sadanobu fell victim to a political scheme of the *rōjū* TANUMA OKITSUGU and was ordered to be adopted by Matsudaira Sadakuni, daimyō of Shirakawa. Sadanobu later returned to the center of power as chief senior councillor

(*rōjū shuseki;* 1787–93) and shogunal regent (*hosa;* 1788–93).

In the 1780s, in the wake of Tanuma's centralizing policies and ruthless extravagance, the shogunate faced a financial crisis. After Tanuma's resignation, Sadanobu was appointed *rōjū* in 1787 and immediately began a purge of Tanuma's clique. Sadanobu reversed Tanuma's mercantilist policies, enforced sumptuary laws, canceled the debts of shogunal retainers, and built up Edo's cash and rice supplies.

Sadanobu's most controversial measure was the "Ban on Heterodoxy" (Kansei Igaku no Kin) of 1790, which limited the curriculum of the shogunal academy, the SHŌHEIKŌ, to a narrow version of the Zhu Xi (Chu Hsi) school of Neo-Confucianism (see SHUSHIGAKU). In the Laxman Affair (see ADAM LAXMAN), Sadanobu was able to maintain the Tokugawa policy of NATIONAL SECLUSION and avoid a clash with Russia by promising token trade in Nagasaki. In the Title Incident of 1789 (Songō Jiken), Sadanobu refused a request from Emperor Kōkaku (1771–1840; r 1780–1817) to grant the title of *daijō tennō* (reserved for retired emperors) to the emperor's father, Prince Sukehito (1733–94). Sadanobu's unpopular decision contributed to his dismissal from his shogunate posts in 1793. He retired to Shirakawa to direct domainal affairs.

Matsudaira Tadanao　松平忠直
(1595–1650). *Daimyō* of the early Edo period (1600–1868); grandson of TOKUGAWA IEYASU. In 1607 Tadanao succeeded his father Yūki Hideyasu (1574–1607) as daimyō of Echizen (now Fukui Prefecture). He fought in the Ōsaka campaigns of 1614–15 (see ŌSAKA CASTLE, SIEGES OF) but felt that he was not adequately rewarded and became increasingly unruly after Ieyasu's death in 1616. He tyrannized his retainers and defied the shogunate's rules on many occasions. In 1623 he was deprived of his domain and exiled.

Matsudaira Tadayoshi　松平忠吉
(1580–1607). Fourth son of TOKUGAWA IEYASU, the founder of the Tokugawa shogunate (1603–1867). While still an infant, Tadayoshi was made head of the Tōjō Matsudaira, a branch of Ieyasu's collateral kinsmen. Tadayoshi distinguished himself in the Battle of SEKIGAHARA (1600). He received the 520,000-*koku* (see KOKUDAKA) fief of Kiyosu in Owari Province (now Kiyosu Chō, Aichi Prefecture).

Matsudaira Yoshinaga　松平慶永
(1828–90). Known also as Matsudaira Keiei and by his pen name Shungaku. *Daimyō* of the Fukui or Echizen domain (now part of

Matsui Sumako The pioneering Western-style stage actress in costume for the title role in Hermann Sudermann's *Magda.*

Fukui Prefecture) and adviser to the Tokugawa shogunate during its final years; leader of the MOVEMENT FOR UNION OF COURT AND SHOGUNATE. Born into the Tayasu family, he was adopted by Matsudaira Nariyoshi, the daimyō of Echizen. In the 1840s he carried out progressive reforms in his domain, and in the 1850s he repeatedly urged the shogunate to open Japan to foreign trade but at the same time to improve coastal defenses and modernize its military forces. In 1862 he was appointed to the new office of shogunal prime minister (*seiji sōsaishoku*). With TOKUGAWA YOSHINOBU, who had become shogunal regent (*kōkenshoku*) in 1862, he attempted to reform the shogunate; he abolished the costly SANKIN KŌTAI system and hoped to shore up the prestige of the shogunate by bringing the imperial court closer to the workings of government. He was dismissed from office, however, for urging the resignation of the shōgun TOKUGAWA IEMOCHI. Yoshinaga then withdrew from political affairs, although he later served as the head of several ministries in the new Meiji government.

Matsuda Mitsuhiro 松田光弘

(1934–   ). Fashion designer. Born in Tōkyō. Graduate of Waseda University and Bunka Fashion College. In 1971 he founded the company Nicole. With his Madame Nicole line, he introduced a simple, sophisticated look for mature women. Since 1982 he has marketed his clothes abroad under the Matsuda label.

Matsudo 松戸[市]

City in northwestern Chiba Prefecture, central Honshū, on the river EDOGAWA. During the Edo period (1600–1868) it was a prosperous river port and a post-station town on the highway Mito Kaidō. Since World War II, metal and machinery industries have flourished here. It has also become a residential suburb of Tōkyō. Pop: 456,210.

Matsue 松江[市]

Capital of Shimane Prefecture, western Honshū, on Lake Shinji. A castle town during the Edo period (1600–1868), Matsue is now a part of the so-called Nakaumi New Industrial City and has machinery and textile industries. Of interest are Fudoki no Oka Park; the temple KOKUBUNJI; Matsue Castle; the temple Gesshōji; Kanden'an, an 18th-century tea house; and the Koizumi Yakumo Kinenkan, a museum in honor of Lafcadio HEARN, who lived in Matsue. Pop: 142,956.

Matsue Plain 松江平野

(Matsue Heiya). Located in northeastern Shimane Prefecture, western Honshū. Situated between Lake Shinji in the west and the lake called Nakaumi in the east, this low-lying plain is formed by sediment from the river Ōhashigawa. The major city Matsue covers much of the plain; numerous industrial development projects are under way. Area: approximately 40 sq km (15 sq mi).

Matsue Shigeyori 松江重頼

(1602–80). HAIKU poet and disciple of MATSUNAGA TEITOKU. A major figure in the establishment of haiku as a poetic genre independent of the older RENGA, he published the pioneering haiku anthology *Enokoshū* (1633) and he wrote *Kefukigusa* (1638), an extensive guide to the vocabulary, rules, and techniques of haiku.

Matsugi Nobuhiko 真継伸彦

(1932–   ). Novelist. Born in Kyōto; graduate of Kyōto University. Using his extensive knowledge of Buddhism, in *Same* (1963, Shark) Matsugi depicts the conversion to that faith of a man born into the outcaste *hinin* class during the Ōnin War (1467–77). The sequel to that work, *Mumyō* (1970, Spiritual Darkness) is the story of the agony that ensues when man questions his faith. Matsugi's other works include *Hikaru koe* (1966, Shining Voice).

Matsui Sumako 松井須磨子

(1886–1919). Japan's first Western-style actress; original name Kobayashi Masako. Born in Nagano Prefecture. After a brief first marriage she moved to Tōkyō and married a teacher, Maezawa Seisuke (d 1923). In 1909 she joined the drama group Bungei Kyōkai, led by TSUBOUCHI SHŌYŌ, which was introducing Western theater into Japan. She is probably best remembered for her 1911 portrayal of Nora in Ibsen's *A Doll's House.* Her acting was directed and inspired by Shōyō's protégé SHIMAMURA HŌGETSU, who eventually left his wife and children for her. In 1913 they left the Bungei Kyōkai and started a new drama company, the Geijutsuza. A recording of Matsui singing "Katusha's Song," from a play based on Tolstoy's *Resurrection,* became extremely popular. Just two months after Hōgetsu's death, Sumako committed suicide.

Matsukata fiscal policy 松方財政

(Matsukata *zaisei*). Policy of retrenchment, deflation, and currency and banking reform adopted by the Meiji government in 1880–81. In the years immediately preceding the appointment of MATSUKATA MASAYOSHI as finance minister in October 1881, the Japanese economy was in the throes of a serious inflation triggered by the huge issue of inconvertible paper currency in 1877 and 1878. Matsukata policies, implemented from 1881 to 1885, attacked both inflation and paper currency depreciation. Their immediate objective was to restore the value of paper money and their long-range goal was to establish a unified convertible currency system. These goals were to be achieved by creating a budget surplus with which to redeem inconvertible paper notes and to build up specie reserves and by founding a central bank, the BANK OF JAPAN.

The Matsukata Reform—In May 1880 ŌKUMA SHIGENOBU, who had been finance minister until February of that year, came forward with a radical plan for redeeming the outstanding paper notes by raising a loan of ¥50 million in London. His proposal was defeated, and in September 1880 the government decided instead to embark on a program of currency reform through financial retrenchment and increased taxation. Ōkuma and Councillor ITŌ HIROBUMI then jointly hammered out the details of this program. With Ōkuma's ouster from the government in the POLITICAL CRISIS OF 1881, Matsukata replaced SANO TSUNETAMI, Ōkuma's hand-picked successor, as finance minister. Matsukata advocated the gradual withdrawal of inconvertible notes, together with the accumulation of specie, until paper currency was restored to face value, followed by the gradual replacement of the outstanding notes with convertible notes issued by a central bank.

Matsukata cut administrative expenditures, increased indirect taxes, and began

selling off government enterprises (see KAN'EI JIGYŌ HARAISAGE). He thereby generated a budget surplus between 1882 and 1884 of ¥40.1 million and succeeded in reversing the inflationary trends of the 1878–81 period.

The Bank of Japan, established in 1882 as the central bank and given a monopoly of note issue in 1883, began issuing convertible Bank of Japan notes in May 1885. In the meantime, the government had set up a program for the conversion of NATIONAL BANKS into ordinary commercial banks and for the gradual liquidation of their inconvertible bank notes. Matsukata's policies, which sacrificed short-run growth for long-term stability, severely depressed the economy, causing a wave of bankruptcies and forced mergers among small, speculative ventures and led to a serious depression in agriculture. Between 1883 and 1890 nearly 368,000 peasant proprietors, or something on the order of 10 percent of all independent holders, were dispossessed for failure to pay taxes. An even larger number of farmers lost their holdings through mortgage foreclosure, an estimated one-seventh of total arable land being foreclosed in the years 1884 and 1885 alone. However, Matsukata's policies placed the government on a sound financial basis and provided the stability necessary for sustained industrial growth.

Matsukata Masayoshi 松方正義

(1835–1924). Finance minister, prime minister, and GENRŌ (elder statesman) of the Meiji period (1868–1912). Born in the Satsuma domain (now Kagoshima Prefecture). At age 13 Matsukata entered the Zōshikan, the domainal Confucian academy. There he was introduced to ideas based on the Wang Yangming interpretation of Confucianism (see YŌMEIGAKU), which helped determine the course of his life. These ideas were banned by the Tokugawa shogunate for their emphasis on loyalty to the emperor.

After 1862 he rose rapidly in the Satsuma bureaucracy. In 1866 he went to Nagasaki to study Western science, mathematics, and surveying. ŌKUBO TOSHIMICHI and SAIGŌ TAKAMORI, who were in Kyōto plotting the overthrow of the shogunate, used him as their liaison with the domainal government. At the time of the Meiji Restoration (1868), Matsukata helped maintain order in Nagasaki, which was left in turmoil after shogunate authorities fled.

In 1868, Ōkubo, on behalf of the new central government, appointed Matsukata governor of Hita Prefecture (now part of Ōita Prefecture). Matsukata moved to Tōkyō in 1871 and worked for the next few years drafting the laws for the LAND TAX REFORM OF 1873–1881 and supervising their implementation.

Matsukata became minister of finance in 1881, at a time when the Japanese economy was in critical inflationary trouble. The deflationary measures he undertook were a daring and successful experiment. They established confidence in the currency and financial institutions, thus creating the conditions under which modern economic growth could begin (see MATSUKATA FISCAL POLICY). When the cabinet system was created in 1885, Matsukata continued as finance minister and served in 7 out of the first 10 cabinets, occupying this critically important position for 18 out of 20 years between 1881 and 1901. In the Meiji Constitution of 1889, his chief contributions were in the articles on finance (arts. 62–72).

Matsukata followed YAMAGATA ARITOMO as

Matsukata Masayoshi This Meiji-period finance minister is remembered as the architect of the modern Japanese fiscal system.

prime minister from 6 May 1891 to 8 August 1892 and succeeded ITŌ HIROBUMI from 18 September 1896 until 12 January 1898. In 1898 he was named an elder statesman (*genrō*), and in 1905 he was promoted from count to marquis. Finally in 1922 he was given the highest noble rank, prince. He served from 1903 to 1912 as president of the International Red Cross of Japan.

Matsukawa Incident   松川事件

(Matsukawa Jiken). A controversial criminal incident of the OCCUPATION period. On 17 August 1949 a train of the Japanese National Railways was sabotaged and overturned near the village of Matsukawa in Fukushima Prefecture. Three crew members were killed. The Japanese government subsequently arrested and charged 20 Japanese citizens, 19 men and 1 woman, all of them leaders or members of either the National Railway Workers' Union (NRWU) or the Tōshiba Electric Co's Matsukawa factory union, and all but one of them members of the Japan Communist Party. The trial and appeals turned into a muddle of challenged evidence, revolving above all around the use of confessions in Japanese criminal law. In 1961 the Sendai High Court found all of them not guilty, and in 1963 the Supreme Court upheld this verdict. In 1970 the Tōkyō High Court awarded damages to the Matsukawa defendants and their families and ordered the government to pay them ¥76,259,833 (US $211,832). The Matsukawa Incident was one of three violent encounters in 1949 (see also MITAKA INCIDENT; SHIMOYAMA INCIDENT).

During the 1960s various writers, including the novelist MATSUMOTO SEICHŌ, sensationalized the case, suggesting that the sabotage was actually caused by the American Occupation authorities to discredit the communist trade-union movement. Although the statute of limitations covering the Matsukawa case has precluded further prosecution, there are no untried suspects, and the case remains formally unsolved.

Matsukaze   松風

(Wind in the Pines). NŌ play by KAN'AMI; adapted by ZEAMI. It is classified as a *sambamme-mono* ("part-three play"). On a fall evening an itinerant Buddhist priest (the *waki* or subordinate character) arrives at the beach of Suma, where he seeks overnight lodging at a salt maker's cottage. While he waits for the proprietor to return, two sisters who dip salt water appear before him, and a conversation begins in the moonlight. Gradually the sisters reveal that they are the ghosts of Matsukaze and Murasame, once loved and then forsaken by the poet Ariwara no Yukihira (818–893). Overcome with longing for her former lover, Matsukaze dons the court robes he once gave her and dances a mad dance. As dawn breaks, the priest sees that the sisters have gone, leaving behind them only the wind in the pines.

Matsukura Shigemasa   松倉重政

(?–1630). *Daimyō* of the early Edo period (1600–1868). A hereditary vassal of the Tsutsui family (see TSUTSUI JUNKEI) of Yamato and Iga provinces (now Nara Prefecture and part of Mie Prefecture, respectively), Shigemasa distinguished himself on the Tokugawa side at the Battle of SEKIGAHARA, and in 1608 was made lord of a domain at Futami Gojō (now the city of Gojō) in Yamato. In 1616 he was promoted to a much larger domain at Shimabara in Hizen Prov-

ince (now Nagasaki Prefecture), a region Christianized under its previous lords, the Arima (see ARIMA HARUNOBU). Shigemasa was instructed by the Tokugawa shogunate to apply stringent measures against Christians, and by 1628 "all the domain's peasants had reformed." The persecution of Christianity and extortionate taxation by the Matsukura sowed the seeds of the SHIMABARA UPRISING of 1637–38. Shigemasa's son Katsuie succeeded him as daimyō, but Katsuie was held responsible for the Shimabara Uprising and sentenced to death by the shogunate in 1638.

Matsumae   松前[町]

Formerly Fukuyama. Town in southwestern Hokkaidō. From 1606 it became the castle town of the MATSUMAE FAMILY and served as a base for colonizing EZO, as Hokkaidō was then called. The principal occupation is fishing. Pop: 13,546.

Matsumae family   松前氏

(Matsumaeshi). Warrior family who, during most of the Edo period (1600–1868), were given nominal authority over the region known as EZO (now Hokkaidō, southern Sakhalin, and the southern Kuril Islands). The Matsumae family were descended from the Kakizaki family, warriors who established control over the Oshima Peninsula in the 15th century and took the surname Matsumae in 1599, when they pledged fealty to the future shōgun TOKUGAWA IEYASU. Until 1869 the name Matsumae also referred to the region of southwestern Hokkaidō, centering on the Oshima Peninsula, that the Japanese had first occupied and that was the core of the Matsumae family domain; settlement was restricted in the rest of the island, which was inhabited by the AINU people.

With the appearance of Russian ships along the Kuril Islands in the second half of the 18th century, Matsumae and Ezo became sensitive frontier regions and were twice placed under direct shogunal rule (1799–1821 and 1855–67). As a result, the Matsumae family were relocated in scattered domains in northern and eastern Honshū. After the Meiji Restoration (1868) they briefly resumed authority over their ancestral lands until the domains were abolished and the new prefectural system established in 1871.

Matsumoto   松本[市]

City in central Nagano Prefecture, central Honshū. A provincial capital from the 8th century, it was the base of the Ogasawara family during the 14th and 15th centuries and a prosperous castle town in the Edo period (1600–1868). Industries include traditional woodwork and silk reeling, electrical machinery, and dairy products. Shinshū University is located here. Attractions include Matsumoto Castle, the Matsumoto Folk Arts Museum, and Kaichi Gakkō, one of Japan's first modern elementary schools, built in 1876. With numerous hot-spring resorts, Matsumoto is the base for trips to the Northern Alps and the highlands called UTSUKUSHIGAHARA. Pop: 200,715.

Matsumoto Basin   松本盆地

(Matsumoto Bonchi). Also called Azumidaira. In central Nagano Prefecture, central Honshū. Flanked by the Hida and Chikuma mountains, it consists of piedmont alluvial fans below the fault scarp and river terraces. The area is known for horseradish (*wasabi*) and rice. Light industries are also being developed here. The major city is Matsumoto. Length: 60 km (37 mi); width: 10 km (6 mi).

Matsumoto Castle   松本城

(Matsumotojō). Formerly known as Fukashi Castle. Castle located in the city of Matsumoto, Nagano Prefecture. Construction of the original castle was begun in 1504 by the Shimadate, a small Sengoku-period (1467–1568) *daimyō* family who were vassals of the powerful OGASAWARA FAMILY. The castle was under the control of the TAKEDA FAMILY from 1555 to 1582, when the Ogasawara regained possession. Later it was occupied by the Ishikawa family, who completed the presently surviving five-story main keep about 1595. The donjon, composed of the main keep, a smaller keep, and a turret tower, has been designated a National Treasure.

Matsumoto Jōji   松本烝治

(1877–1954). Legal scholar and statesman. Born in Tōkyō, Matsumoto graduated from Tōkyō University in 1900. In 1903 he became an associate professor at Tōkyō University.

Matsumoto Castle
One of the best preserved of Japan's feudal castles, Matsumoto Castle in Nagano Prefecture is also known as Karasujō (Raven Castle) because of its black wainscoting.

Matsumoto Shunsuke *Self-Portrait.* 1942. Oil on canvas. 142 × 130 cm. Kamakura Museum of Modern Art, Kanagawa Prefecture.

From 1913 he served concurrently as an adviser (*sanjikan*) to the government's Legislative Bureau (Hōseikyoku). He left the university in 1919 to serve as vice president of the SOUTH MANCHURIA RAILWAY. In 1923 he became director general of the Legislative Bureau and in 1934 minister of commerce and industry in the SAITŌ MAKOTO cabinet. As minister of state in the SHIDEHARA KIJŪRŌ cabinet in 1945, he was charged with the task of constitutional revision, though his draft for a new constitution was essentially a rewording of the Meiji Constitution and was rejected by the Occupation authorities. After 1950, he was chairman of the Public Utilities Commission (Kōeki Jigyō Iinkai). His works include commercial law texts such as *Kaishōhō* (1914, Maritime Commercial Law) and collections of monographs such as *Shihō rombunshū* (1926, Essays in Private Law).

Matsumoto Kōshirō   松本幸四郎

One of the most distinguished names among the traditional acting families in the KABUKI theater. Matsumoto Kōshirō I (1674–1730), who specialized in *aragoto* ("rough business," or active, masculine roles) and *jitsugoto* (the realistic style), was ranked with the great Ichikawa Danjūrō II (see ICHIKAWA DANJŪRŌ). Kōshirō IV (1737–1802), a pupil of Ichikawa Danjurō IV, specialized in *wagoto*

(love stories) and *jitsugoto*, and in his later years he also performed in *jitsuaku* (tales of evil deeds). Kōshirō VII (1870–1949), with his splendid appearance and sonorous voice, gave a definitive realization of Benkei in the play KANJINCHŌ, performing the role some 1,600 times. Kōshirō VIII (1910–82) studied under Nakamura Kichiemon I (see NAKAMURA KICHIEMON), later becoming his son-in-law. He specialized in *jidaimono* (historical plays). In 1975 Kōshirō VIII was designated a Living National Treasure, and he received the Order of Culture in 1981. Kōshirō IX (b 1942) starred in musicals in the popular theater under his first professional name, Somegorō. He took the name Kōshirō IX in 1981. In kabuki he specializes in heroic roles.

Matsumoto Seichō   松本清張

(1909–92). Novelist. Real name Matsumoto Kiyoharu. Born in Fukuoka Prefecture. He worked as a commercial artist for the newspaper *Asahi shimbun* from 1937 to 1957, after which he devoted himself full time to the writing that he had begun in his early forties. He won the Akutagawa Prize in 1952 for "Aru *Kokura nikki* den," a short story about a man who searches all his life without success for the *Kokura nikki*, the diary of a famous Meiji-period (1868–1912) novelist. He soon shifted his energies to mystery writing and produced "Kao" (1956; tr "The Face," 1980), *Ten to sen* (1957–58; tr *Points and Lines*, 1970), *Me no kabe* (1957), and *Suna no utsuwa* (1960–61; tr *Inspector Imanishi Investigates*, 1989)—becoming the most successful mystery writer in Japan. Other works include *Nihon no kuroi kiri* (1960, Black Mist over Japan), a mystery; *Kodaishi gi* (1966–67), a work on ancient history; and *Shōwashi hakkutsu* (1956–71), a 13-volume series on the history of the Shōwa period (1926–89).

Matsumoto Shigeharu   松本重治

(1899–1989). Journalist and contributor to international cultural exchange. Born in Ōsaka. After graduating from Tōkyō University, he studied in Europe and North America. In 1933 he became a bureau chief for Japan Associated Press in China, and in 1936 broke the story of the XI'AN (SIAN) INCIDENT. After World War II, he assisted in the establishment of INTERNATIONAL HOUSE OF JAPAN, an institution dedicated to facilitating cultural exchange, and became its director. He was acting chairman of International House from 1965 to 1989 and received the Japan Foundation Award in 1979. Memoirs of his experiences as a journalist in China are contained in *Shanhai jidai* (3 vols, 1974–75, Shanghai Days).

Matsumoto Shunsuke   松本竣介

(1912–48). Western-style painter. Born in Tōkyō. Matsumoto studied under the artists associated with the Taiheiyō Gakai (Pacific Painters' Society). His work was first shown at the Nikaten (Exhibition of the Nika Society) in 1935. His paintings depict the complex interweaving of human activity and the urban environment. After World War II he was active in the avant-garde Jiyū Bijutsu Kyōkai (Free Artists' Association).

Matsumura Goshun   松村呉春

(1752–1811). Painter in the BUNJINGA (literati painting) tradition who founded the Shijō school; also a HAIKU poet and a calligrapher. Goshun was born to an established Kyōto family, but he left his inherited position at the

government mint to pursue in earnest the study of painting with the literati painter and haiku poet Yosa BUSON. In 1781 family tragedy and financial troubles seem to have led Goshun to move to Ikeda in Settsu Province (now part of Ōsaka Prefecture). Although Buson had died several years earlier, Goshun returned to Kyōto in 1789. He eventually joined the workshop of MARUYAMA ŌKYO, apparently as an equal. After Ōkyo's death, Goshun established his atelier at Shijō in Kyōto. Goshun's students and later followers included his younger brother, MATSUMURA KEIBUN, and OKAMOTO TOYOHIKO. See also MARUYAMA-SHIJŌ SCHOOL.

Matsumura Jinzō   松村任三

(1856–1928). Botanist. Born in Hitachi Province (now part of Ibaraki Prefecture), the son of the *karō* (family elder) of the Matsuoka domain in Hitachi. After leaving the Daigaku Nankō (now part of Tōkyō University) without completing his studies, he worked from 1877 at the Tōkyō University botanical gardens (now KOISHIKAWA BOTANIC GARDEN). He later taught at Tōkyō University, where he contributed to the introduction into Japan of methodologies in academic fields such as plant taxonomy and plant anatomy. He wrote numerous books and articles, including *Nihon shokubutsu meii* (1884, Glossary of the Plants of Japan).

Matsumura Keibun   松村景文

(1779–1843). Painter of the Shijō school; a follower of his elder brother, MATSUMURA GOSHUN, the school's founder. Keibun lived and worked in Kyōto. Along with Goshun and OKAMOTO TOYOHIKO, Keibun is generally considered one of the three most important artists of the Shijō school. He also studied with MARUYAMA ŌKYO, whose stylistic influence is strong. His finest and best-known work is in BIRD-AND-FLOWER PAINTING (*kachōga*). In his best paintings he employs bright, distinctive colors in his birds, which are seen against a background of equally brilliant foliage. See also MARUYAMA-SHIJŌ SCHOOL.

Matsumura Kenzō   松村謙三

(1883–1971). Politician. Born in Toyama Prefecture; graduate of Waseda University. Matsumura entered politics after working for the newspaper *Hōchi shimbun* and served 13 consecutive terms (1928–69) in the House of Representatives, apart from a brief period (1946–51) when he was barred from public office during the OCCUPATION PURGE. He served as minister of welfare and minister of education in the cabinet of Prince HIGASHIKUNI NARUHIKO (1945), as minister of agriculture and forestry in the SHIDEHARA KIJŪRŌ cabinet (1945–46), and as minister of education in the second HATOYAMA ICHIRŌ cabinet (1955). He promoted normalization of relations with the People's Republic of China.

matsumushisō   松虫草

(Japanese scabiosa). *Scabiosa japonica.* Biennial herb of the family Dipsacaceae (teasel) that grows wild in sunny mountain areas throughout Japan. The plant is 90 centimeters (35 in) high, has opposite, palmate leaves, and produces purple flowers (4–5 cm [1.5–2.0 in] across) in summer and fall. In high mountain areas the *takane matsumushisō* (*Scabiosa japonica* var. *alpina*), a shorter variety with large flowers, is found. Western varieties of scabiosa are imported and cultivated.

Matsushima Sunrise over the pine-covered islands of Matsushima Bay, traditionally considered one of the three most scenic spots in Japan.

Matsunaga Goichi　松永伍一

(1930–). Poet and critic. Born in Fukuoka Prefecture. Matsunaga is known for his poems dealing with the subject of farm life. His first collection of poetry was *Aotenjō* (1954, The Sky's Blue Vault), which was soon followed by *Kusa no jōheki* (1955, Ramparts of Grass). Matsunaga has also published a number of critical essays, including *Nihon nōminshi shi* (1967–70, The History of Japanese Rural Poetry) and *Dozoku no kōzu* (1977, The Composition of Folkways).

Matsunaga Sekigo　松永尺五

(1592–1657). Neo-Confucian scholar of the early Edo period (1600–1868); also known as Matsunaga Shōsan. Born in Kyōto, son of the literary figure MATSUNAGA TEITOKU. Sekigo was a leading disciple of the Neo-Confucian scholar FUJIWARA SEIKA. He opened his own school in 1648 and is said to have trained more than 5,000 students, including KINOSHITA JUN'AN.

Matsunaga Teitoku　松永貞徳

(1571–1653). Classical scholar and poet. Founder of the Teimon school of *haikai* (the prototype of HAIKU). Born in Kyōto. He studied with HOSOKAWA YŪSAI, SATOMURA JŌHA, and scholars close to TOYOTOMI HIDEYOSHI, whom he served as secretary. The principal encyclopedist of his time, Teitoku compiled lexicons and commentaries on classics such as the *Tsurezuregusa* of YOSHIDA KENKŌ. He strove to liberate classical learning from the tradition of secret oral transmission. His most important *haikai* work is *Gosan* (1651), in which he elaborated the rules of *haikai* composition, thus establishing *haikai* as a genre of poetry. Among Teitoku's disciples were KITAMURA KIGIN and YASUHARA TEISHITSU.

Matsunaga Yasuzaemon　松永安左衛門

(1875–1971). Businessman and a leader of the ELECTRIC POWER industry. Born in Nagasaki Prefecture, he studied at Keiō Gijuku (now Keiō University). He established Fukuhaku Electric Railways Co (later Kyūshū Electric Railways Co) in 1909 and Kyūshū Hydroelectric Co in 1910. He took control of a majority of the public utility corporations in northern Kyūshū in about 1915. In 1924 he was elected president of the Japan Electric Association. The same year he established the Tōkyō Electric Power Co, merging it in 1928 with the Tōkyō Electric Lighting Co. In 1936 he strongly opposed the nationalization of electric power companies. When nationalization took place in 1938, Matsunaga retired. After World War II, he staged a comeback, championing private ownership of power companies and bringing about the present network of nine regional power companies.

Matsuo Bashō → Bashō

Matsuoka Eikyū　松岡映丘

(1881–1938). Japanese-style painter in the classical Japanese YAMATO-E style. Given name Teruo. Born in Hyōgo Prefecture. A pupil of the KANŌ SCHOOL artist HASHIMOTO GAHŌ and the *yamato-e* artist Yamana Tsurayoshi (1836–1902), he graduated from and taught at the Tōkyō Bijutsu Gakkō (now Tōkyō University of Fine Arts and Music). He participated in the establishment of three *yamato-e* artists' groups: the Kinrei-

sha in 1916, the Shinkō Yamato-e Kai in 1921, and the Kokugain in 1935. He was a member of the Imperial Fine Arts Academy (Teikoku Bijutsuin).

Matsuoka Joan　松岡恕庵

(1669–1747). Specialist in *honzōgaku* (traditional pharmacognosy) who continued studies begun by INŌ JAKUSUI. Born in Kyōto, he first studied Confucianism, guided by YAMAZAKI ANSAI and ITŌ JINSAI. Later he studied pharmacognosy under Inō Jakusui. Matsuoka taught ONO RANZAN and Toda Kyokuzan (1696–1769).

Matsuoka Komakichi　松岡駒吉

(1888–1958). Prewar labor leader. Born in Tottori Prefecture. A mechanic, he became involved in the labor movement around 1912 and joined YŪAIKAI, Japan's earliest labor group, founded by SUZUKI BUNJI. In 1929 Matsuoka represented Japanese labor at a meeting of the International Labor Organization (ILO). He helped organize the union SŌDŌMEI and in 1932 became its chairman. After World War II, he reorganized Sōdōmei and again served as chairman. In 1946 he was elected to the House of Representatives and in 1947 and 1948 served as speaker of the house. After 1950 he represented Japan at many international labor conferences.

Matsuoka Yōsuke　松岡洋右

(1880–1946). Diplomat and foreign minister. Born in the village of Murozumi, Yamaguchi Prefecture. In 1893 he went to the United States. After graduating from the University of Oregon School of Law in 1900, he returned to Japan, where he entered the Foreign Ministry in 1904. For the next 17 years he served in a variety of diplomatic posts in China, Russia, and the United States and acted as the information officer for the Japanese delegation to the Paris Peace Conference ending World War I.

Dissatisfied with the diplomatic service, Matsuoka joined the Japanese-owned SOUTH MANCHURIA RAILWAY (SMR) as a director from 1921 to 1926 and as vice-chairman from 1927 to 1929. In 1930 he was elected to the House of Representatives as a RIKKEN SEIYŪKAI candidate. Calling Manchuria and Inner Mongolia "Japan's lifeline," Matsuoka became a strong advocate of the creation of a satellite state in Manchuria (see MANCHUKUO). In 1932 he was sent to Shanghai to negotiate a truce to end the SHANGHAI INCIDENT. The same year he became Japan's chief delegate to the League of Nations. In the face of international censure of Japanese aggression in Manchuria (see MANCHURIAN INCIDENT), Matsuoka initially favored Japan's remaining in the league, but

when the proceedings went against Japan (see LYTTON COMMISSION), Matsuoka led his delegation out of the league in 1933.

Matsuoka resigned from the Diet in December 1933 and embarked on a movement to dissolve the political parties and rid Japan of what he saw as the baneful influence of partisan politics. He abandoned these efforts upon being named president of the SMR in 1935, a post he held until 1939. From July 1940 to July 1941 Matsuoka was foreign minister in KONOE FUMIMARO's second cabinet. In this capacity he concluded the TRIPARTITE PACT with Germany and Italy on 27 September 1940 and the SOVIET-JAPANESE NEUTRALITY PACT on 13 April 1941. His resistance to negotiations between Japan and the United States eventually led to his forced resignation from the Konoe cabinet and the end of his active political career. After Japan's defeat in World War II, Matsuoka was indicted as a class-A war criminal, but he died of illness in June 1946, before the trial was concluded.

Matsuratō　松浦党

A league (*tō*) of warriors (see BUSHIDAN) who controlled the Matsura region (in what is now Nagasaki and Saga prefectures) from the 12th through the 15th centuries. These several dozen warrior families, bound by both real and fictitious kinship ties, apparently stemmed from pirate groups. They fought on the losing side at the Battle of DANNOURA in 1185 but soon submitted to the victorious MINAMOTO NO YORITOMO and received appointments as officials in local private estates (SHŌEN).

matsuri → festivals

Matsusaka　松阪〔市〕

Also known as Matsuzaka. City in central Mie Prefecture, central Honshū. It developed as a castle town and was also an important post-station town. It is known for its hardworking merchants (the MITSUI originally came from here). It has cotton textile, lumber, and glass industries, and the surrounding area is known for its beef. Of interest are Suzunoya, the home of the scholar MOTOORI NORINAGA; the remains of Matsusaka Castle; and the complex of mounded tombs (KOFUN) at Takarazuka. Pop: 118,725.

Matsushima　松島

A group of more than 260 tiny but scenic islands in Matsushima Bay, Miyagi Prefecture, northern Honshū. Known as one of the so-called Nihon Sankei (Japan's three most

Matsumoto Seichō The most successful mystery writer in Japan, also known for his historical writing.

matsumushisō The blooms of this wild herb, a member of the teasel family.

Matsuoka Yōsuke As foreign minister, Matsuoka concluded the Tripartite Pact with Germany and Italy in 1940 and the Soviet-Japanese Neutrality Pact in 1941.

Matsushita Kōnosuke
The founder of the Matsushita group of electrical appliance companies was known as a "businessman-philosopher."

beautiful sights), Matsushima was celebrated by the 17th-century *haiku* poet Matsuo Bashō. The temple Zuiganji, said to have been built in 838, has been designated a National Treasure. Activities include tourism and the cultivation of oysters and seaweed (*nori*).

Matsushima Bay   松島湾

(Matsushima Wan). Part of northwestern Sendai Bay, Miyagi Prefecture, northern Honshū. Dotted with more than 260 small islands, Matsushima Bay has been a noted scenic spot since ancient times. Marine products are *nori* (a kind of seaweed) and oysters.

Matsushiro   松代

District in the southern part of the city of Nagano, Nagano Prefecture, central Honshū. During the Edo period (1600–1868), it was a castle town. During World War II, the Imperial Headquarters of the armed forces was constructed underground here; it is now being used as a seismological observatory.

Matsushita Communication Industrial Co, Ltd   松下通信工業[株]

(Matsushita Tsūshin Kōgyō). Manufacturer of data processing, audiovisual, and telecommunication equipment; measuring and control devices; and car stereos and other automotive instruments. Incorporated in 1958. Its products are sold by MATSUSHITA ELECTRIC INDUSTRIAL CO, LTD, under the Panasonic brand name. Sales for the fiscal year ending March 1991 totaled ¥441.8 billion (US $3.2 billion), and capitalization was ¥22.1 billion (US $161.1 million). Headquarters are in Yokohama.

Matsushita Daisaburō   松下大三郎

(1878–1935). Japanese-language scholar. Born in Shizuoka Prefecture, Matsushita graduated from and later taught at Kokugakuin University. He established a theory of Japanese grammar that bears his name. It is based on the three units *genji*, *shi*, and *danku*, which closely approximate morphemes, words, and sentences, respectively. He also wrote grammatical studies of spoken Japanese. His principal works are *Nihon zokugo bunten* (1901, A Grammar of Japanese Colloquialisms); *Kaisen hyōjun Nihon bumpō* (1928, Revised Standard Japanese Grammar); and *Hyōjun Nihon kōgohō* (1930, A Standard Grammar of Spoken Japanese).

Matsushita Electric Industrial Co, Ltd   松下電器産業[株]

(Matsushita Denki Sangyō). One of the world's largest manufacturers of consumer electric and electronic products. Established in 1918. Most of the company's products are marketed under the Panasonic and Quasar brand names in the United States and Canada; under the Panasonic name in Europe, Latin America, and Oceania; and under the National trademark in the rest of the world. High fidelity audio equipment is marketed worldwide under the Technics trademark.

Matsushita Electric features the integrated production of components and finished products. It has an active research and development program with basic and applied research conducted in 44 laboratories. The company operates 71 manufacturing and 28 sales organizations in 36 countries. It exports a wide range of products to more than 160 countries around the world. Sales for the fiscal year ending March 1991 totaled

¥4.7 trillion (US $34.3 billion), of which video equipment accounted for 20 percent; communication and industrial equipment, 25 percent; home appliances, 15 percent; electronic components, 17 percent; audio equipment, 7 percent; and other products, 16 percent. The company was capitalized at ¥195.5 billion (US $1.4 billion) in the same year. Headquarters are in Kadoma, Ōsaka Prefecture.

Matsushita Electric Works, Ltd   松下電工[株]

(Matsushita Denkō). Manufacturer of a wide variety of electrical and building products. A member of the Matsushita group, the company was founded in 1918 by MATSUSHITA KŌNOSUKE. Products include precision controls, switches, relays, and various construction and building materials. The company has 20 subsidiaries in Japan and overseas. Sales for the fiscal year ending November 1990 totaled ¥971.5 billion (US $7.5 billion). In 1990 it was capitalized at ¥77.9 billion (US $603.5 million). Headquarters are in Kadoma, Ōsaka Prefecture.

Matsushita Electronic Components Co, Ltd   松下電子部品[株]

(Matsushita Denshi Buhin). Manufacturer of electronic components. Incorporated in 1950 as a member of the Matsushita group. It has subsidiaries in Malaysia, Singapore, the United States, Brazil, Germany, and the United Kingdom. The firm also has equity in 17 companies in 15 countries, all subsidiaries of MATSUSHITA ELECTRIC INDUSTRIAL CO, LTD. Sales for the fiscal year ending March 1990 totaled ¥346.1 billion (US $2.3 billion), and capitalization stood at ¥13.0 billion (US $84.9 million). Headquarters are in the city of Kadoma, Ōsaka Prefecture.

Matsushita Electronics Co   松下電子工業[株]

(Matsushita Denshi Kōgyō). Manufacturer of electron tubes, semiconductors, and electric lamps. Incorporated in 1952 as a joint venture of MATSUSHITA ELECTRIC INDUSTRIAL CO, LTD, and N. V. Philips. It has overseas manufacturing subsidiaries in Singapore for semiconductors and fluorescent lamps and in the United States and China for cathode-ray tubes. Sales for the fiscal year ending March 1990 totaled ¥444.4 billion (US $2.9 billion); capitalization stood at ¥41.0 billion (US $267.8 million). Headquarters are in the city of Takatsuki, Ōsaka Prefecture.

Matsushita Kōnosuke   松下幸之助

(1894–1989). Founder of the Matsushita electric companies. Born in Wakayama Prefecture. In 1918 he opened a small electric fixture shop in Ōsaka, where he had huge success in developing small bicycle lamp batteries. He enlarged this into a home electrical appliance plant in 1933 and reorganized it as MATSUSHITA ELECTRIC INDUSTRIAL CO, LTD, in 1935. He established contractual ties with N. V. Philips's Gloeilampenfabriken in 1952 and had the highest personal income in Japan for that year. Always seeking innovations, Matsushita developed a series of home electrical appliances and pushed his company to the forefront of the industry through introduction of mass-production systems and clever sales tactics. By taking full advantage of the boom in home electronics from the late 1950s, Matsushita led his company to spectacular growth by aggressively producing and marketing televisions, washing ma-

chines, and refrigerators. He also placed strong emphasis on exports and made "National" an internationally known brand name.

Even when American-style management swept through Japan in the postwar years, Matsushita stuck to traditional Japanese management practices. Matsushita launched the Peace and Happiness through Prosperity (PHP) Movement in 1946 and advocated a management philosophy aimed at attaining peace and prosperity for society through business and cultural activities. He presided over establishment of the Asuka Conservation Association, promoted Shintō studies, and created the Matsushita Institute of Government and Management for cultivating new political leaders for the 1980s.

Matsushita-Kotobuki Electronics Industries, Ltd   松下寿電子工業[株]

(Matsushita-Kotobuki Denshi Kōgyō). Manufacturer of electronic, heating, and acoustic equipment. A member of the Matsushita group of companies, it was incorporated in 1948. Its three chief products are color television sets, tape recorders, and electrical versions of the traditional *kotatsu* (a small, quilt-covered table with a heating device underneath that is used to warm the feet and legs). MATSUSHITA ELECTRIC INDUSTRIAL CO, LTD, controls 57.4 percent of the firm's stock. Sales for the fiscal year ending March 1991 totaled ¥273.7 billion (US $2.0 billion), and capitalization was ¥7.9 billion (US $57.6 million). Headquarters are in the city of Takamatsu, Kagawa Prefecture.

Matsushita Refrigeration Co   松下冷機[株]

(Matsushita Reiki). Manufacturer of refrigerators, freezers, air conditioners, and related parts; member of the Matsushita group. Incorporated in 1939 as Nakagawa Machinery, Inc. In 1952 it was absorbed by MATSUSHITA ELECTRIC INDUSTRIAL CO, LTD, and began producing household refrigerators sold under the domestic brand name "National." In 1962 it expanded into the fields of commercial refrigeration, freezing cabinets, and household freezers. The firm took its present name in 1972. It has a compressor plant in Singapore. Matsushita Electric Industrial Co, Ltd, holds 50.7 percent of Matsushita Refrigeration stock. Sales for the fiscal year ending March 1991 totaled ¥97.7 billion (US $1.4 billion), and capitalization stood at ¥11.9 billion (US $86.7 million). Headquarters are in Ōsaka.

Matsushita Seikō Co, Ltd   松下精工[株]

(Matsushita Seikō). Manufacturer of electrical appliances and equipment. A member of the Matsushita group. Incorporated in 1956, the company assumed its current name in 1962. The firm exports its products through Matsushita Electric Industrial Co. Sales for the fiscal year ending March 1991 totaled ¥93.7 billion (US $683.0 million), of which consumer electronics accounted for 25 percent; residential air-conditioning equipment, 51 percent; industrial air-conditioning equipment, 22 percent; and other products, 2 percent. The company was capitalized at ¥12.1 billion (US $88.2 million) the same year. Headquarters are in Ōsaka.

matsutake   松茸

Tricholoma matsutake. A mushroom of the family Tricholomataceae that grows chiefly in the wild in the sandy, granitic soil of red

pine (*Pinus densiflora*) forests (the literal meaning of *matsutake* is "pine mushroom"). As the *matsutake* grows, its pileus (cap) gradually changes shape from convex to flat, eventually reaching a diameter of 8–20 centimeters (3.2–7.9 in). The upper surface of the pileus is light yellowish brown to dark brown and the stem is 10–20 centimeters (3.9–7.9 in) long. The characteristic flavor and aroma of the *matsutake* have made it the most highly prized mushroom in Japanese cooking. Some people still go on autumn outings, known as *matsutake-gari*, to gather *matsutake*.

Matsutani Miyoko　　　松谷みよ子

(1926–). Author of children's books. Born in Tōkyō. Matsutani won the Hans Christian Andersen Award for her book *Tatsu no ko Tarō* (1960; tr *Tarō, the Dragon-Boy*, 1967), which was based on a folktale from Nagano Prefecture. She gathered folktales from all over Japan for her *Nihon no mukashi-banashi* (1967–68, Old Tales of Japan). Her Momo chan series—including *Chiisai Momo chan* (1964; tr *Little Momo-chan*, 1985), *Momo chan to Akane chan* (1969; tr *Momo-chan and Akane-chan*, 1987), and *Momo chan to Pū* (1970; tr *Momo-chan and Poo*, 1986)—has gained popularity both at home and abroad.

Matsuura　　　松浦[市]

City in northern Nagasaki Prefecture, Kyūshū, on the Genkai Sea. What was once a flourishing coal-mining town has become, under government sponsorship, a farming and industrial area. Pop: 24,184.

Matsuura Takeshirō　　　松浦武四郎

(1818–88). Explorer of EZO (now Hokkaidō). Born in Ise Province (now Mie Prefecture), he explored Ezo three times from 1845 and made several maps. It was at his suggestion that Ezo was renamed Hokkaidō. He served as an official in the Hokkaidō Colonization Office (1869).

Matsuyama　　　松山[市]

Capital of Ehime Prefecture, Shikoku. It developed as a castle town after the construction of a castle in 1603. Petrochemical and soda factories are here, and citrus fruits are grown on nearby mountain slopes. Visitors are drawn to the DŌGO HOT SPRING and Matsuyama Castle. Matsuyama is the birthplace of the poets MASAOKA SHIKI and TAKAHAMA KYOSHI and provides the setting for NATSUME SŌSEKI's popular novel *Botchan*. A traditional product is *iyogasuri*, a cotton cloth. Pop: 443,322.

Matsuyama Plain　　　松山平野

(Matsuyama Heiya). Located in central Ehime Prefecture, Shikoku. Bordering the Inland Sea and located along the Median Tectonic Line, it consists of alluvial fans of the river Shigenobugawa. Mandarin oranges are cultivated in the hills surrounding the rice-producing lowlands. Along the coast are oil refineries and petrochemical plants. The major city is Matsuyama, and a well-known resort is Dōgo Hot Spring. Area: approximately 100 sq km (40 sq mi).

Matsuyama Zenzō　　　松山善三

(1925–). Screenwriter and film director. He has written frequently for directors KINOSHITA KEISUKE and KOBAYASHI MASAKI, among others. He joined SHŌCHIKU CO, LTD, in 1948, starting as an assistant director and working in the script department. He assisted Kinoshita Keisuke for several years. One of his

fellow assistants was Kobayashi Masaki, with whom he later collaborated on several important projects, writing the screenplays for *Anata kaimasu* (1956, I'll Buy You); *Kuroi kawa* (1957, Black River); and Kobayashi's acclaimed masterpiece, *Ningen no jōken* (1959–61, The Human Condition). Matsuyama's favorite themes deal with important social issues, often involving individuals who suffer injustice. His film debut as a director, *Na mo naku mazushiku utsukushiku* (1961, Nameless, Poor, Beautiful), about the struggles of a deaf couple to lead normal, productive lives, was highly praised. *Haha* (1988, Mother) is a representative recent work.

Matsuzakaya Co, Ltd　　　[株]松坂屋

(Matsuzakaya). One of the leading department stores in Japan. Started business in Nagoya as a *kimono* shop in 1611; it was incorporated in 1910. In 1989 Matsuzakaya had 12 domestic stores in principal cities including Tōkyō, Nagoya, and Ōsaka, with 4 overseas stores in Hong Kong, Paris, and Los Angeles. The company has 54 affiliated companies in various businesses, including supermarkets, restaurants, and furniture manufacturers. The annual sales turnover for the fiscal year ending February 1991, not including the affiliated companies, was ¥466.4 billion (US $3.6 billion). Capitalization was ¥9.8 billion (US $75.1 million) in the same year. Headquarters are in Nagoya.

Mattō　　　松任[市]

City in central Ishikawa Prefecture, central Honshū, on the river Tedorigawa. Mattō developed as a distribution center for rice and is now the site of a JR (Japan Railways) factory. The temple Shōkōji maintains the reputed grave of the poet KAGA NO CHIYO. Pop: 58,142.

mawari-dōro　　　回り灯籠

(revolving shadow lantern). A lantern designed to create shadow pictures. Introduced from China, the *mawari-dōro* was popular during the Edo period (1600–1868) for viewing on summer nights. Heated air from a lighted candle inside a cylinder covered with silhouettes causes the cylinder to rotate inside a circular frame, producing moving images on a translucent outer cover.

Max Factor KK　　　マックスファクター[株]

(Makkusu Fakutā). Cosmetics manufacturer. Originally established in 1953, the company was replaced by a new Max Factor KK in 1987. The company markets cosmetics, toiletries, perfume, wigs, and pharmaceuticals. For the fiscal year ending December 1990, sales totaled ¥69.3 billion (US $518.9 million) and capitalization stood at ¥8.6 billion (US $64.4 million). Headquarters are in Tōkyō.

mayaku → drug abuse

Mayama Seika　　　真山青果

(1878–1948). Playwright, essayist, and novelist. Born in Sendai, Miyagi Prefecture. After an unsettled youth, he went to Tōkyō to pursue a literary career and served his literary apprenticeship with OGURI FŪYŌ. He attracted attention as a promising naturalist writer with *Minami Koizumi Mura* (1907), a novel about peasant life. He subsequently spent a number of years in obscurity as a SHIMPA playwright before reemerging onto the literary scene in 1924 with a short his-

Matsuyama The Dōgo Hot Spring in Matsuyama is one of the oldest in Japan. The main building, the wooden Shinrokaku bathhouse, dates from 1894.

torical play, *Gemboku to Chōei*, which was highly acclaimed. Over the next 18 years there followed a continuous stream of historical plays that were distinguished for their combination of historical accuracy and interplay of personalities. His most famous play cycle, *Genroku chūshingura* (1934–41), is a realistic retelling of the celebrated FORTY-SEVEN RŌNIN INCIDENT of 1703. Mayama was also noted for his scholarly studies of the writers SAIKAKU and Takizawa BAKIN.

May Day Incident　　　メーデー事件

(Mēdē Jiken). Confrontation between demonstrators and police in Tōkyō on 1 May 1952. In Japan May Day is traditionally observed by radical labor groups and students to honor labor. There had been growing antigovernment and anti-American senti-

mawari-dōro Watching the moving pictures of the revolving shadow lantern was a popular pastime on warm summer nights during the Edo period.

May Fourth Movement Student-led anti-Japan rallies, such as the one pictured here at Beijing's Tiananmen Square in December 1919, were representative of the increasing nationalism associated with this early-20th-century Chinese intellectual movement.

mayoke Small cloth amulets such as this one, sold at shrines and temples, are one of the many varieties of charms and talismans employed to ward off misfortune.

ment following the signing of the SAN FRANCISCO PEACE TREATY and the United States–Japan Security Treaty in September 1951. The treaties had become effective three days earlier, on 28 April, and frustration and dissatisfaction turned to anger when permission to hold a May Day rally in front of the Imperial Palace grounds was denied. After officials dispersed a rally held in Hibiya Park, several thousand participants clashed with police. Two civilians died and over 2,000 were injured. Under the Riot Law, 1,232 people were arrested and 261 were indicted. On 28 January 1970 the Tōkyō District Court found 93 people guilty of breaking the Riot Law. On appeal the Tōkyō High Court, on 21 November 1972, found all defendants not guilty of violation of the Riot Law. However, 16 were convicted on other charges. See also UNITED STATES–JAPAN SECURITY TREATIES.

Mayet, Paul マイエット, P.

(1846–1920). German economist and one of many FOREIGN EMPLOYEES OF THE MEIJI PERIOD (1868–1912) who advised the government. Invited to Japan in 1875, Mayet assisted various government departments in formulating financial and economic policies, including plans for a postal savings system, fire and farm insurance, public bond issues, and an independent Board of Audit. He also made an important study of contemporary Japanese agriculture, pointing out the hardships faced by small farmers and the possibility of relief through land-tax reform. He returned to Germany in 1893.

May 15th Incident 五・一五事件

(Goichigo Jiken). Attempted coup d'état by young naval officers on 15 May 1932; their assassination of Prime Minister INUKAI TSUYOSHI led to the demise of the party cabinet system. As a result of the ratification of the 1930 London Naval Treaty (see LONDON NAVAL CONFERENCES), a movement grew among young military officers to reorganize the state. In the OCTOBER INCIDENT of 1931 army staff officers failed in their attempt to form a military government. Within the navy, officers established contacts with the ultranationalist INOUE NISSHŌ with the aim of effecting a "SHŌWA RESTORATION" by assassinating leading political and business figures. Inoue and his terrorist group carried out a series of murders (see LEAGUE OF BLOOD INCIDENT). Naval officers reinforced by TACHIBANA KŌZABURŌ and his students from the AIKYŌJUKU, plus army cadets and remnants of the League of Blood, on 15 May attacked and killed Prime Minister Inukai and attacked the residence of Lord Keeper of the Privy Seal MAKINO NOBUAKI, the headquarters of the RIKKEN SEIYŪKAI party, the Mitsubishi Bank, and several transformer substations. Apart from the assassination of the prime minister,

nothing was accomplished, and all the participants surrendered to military police. See also MILITARISM.

May Fourth Movement 五・四運動

(Goshi Undō). The 4 May 1919 student demonstrations in Beijing (Peking) against the decision of the Paris Peace Conference to transfer German rights in Shandong (Shantung) Province to Japan (see VERSAILLES, TREATY OF) and against China's own officials for collaborating with the Japanese. Also, the intellectual movement of the 1910s and 1920s of which the 4 May demonstrations became a symbol. The movement was associated with the growth of nationalism, the development of a new literature written in the vernacular language, and an accelerated political radicalism.

Some 5,000 students participated in the 4 May demonstrations, marching from the Gate of Heavenly Peace to the Legation Quarter and then burning the residence of CAO RULIN (Ts'ao Ju-lin), the official regarded as the mastermind of government collaboration with Japan. Student organizers, among them MAO ZEDONG (Mao Tse-tung) and ZHOU ENLAI (Chou En-lai), staged subsequent demonstrations in Beijing and in other cities, resulting in the dismissal of three high government officials and the refusal of Chinese delegates in Paris to sign the peace treaty.

The outcome of the demonstrations fueled a nationalistic intellectual movement that had been underway since the middle of the decade. Foreign-educated men such as Chen Duxiu (Ch'en Tu-hsiu; 1879–1942), who established the magazine *Xin qingnian* (*Hsin-ch'ing-nien;* New Youth), and LU XUN (Lu Hsün) condemned traditional Chinese values, including Confucianism, and promoted Western ideas of romantic love, the nuclear family, democratic government, technological development, and Marxism. Two important political consequences of the May Fourth Movement were increased antagonism toward Japan as the embodiment of foreign aggression and growing discontent with China's warlord governments. More significantly, the intellectual and political ferment of the time gave birth to the Chinese Communist Party.

mayoke 魔除け

Talismans or rituals believed to dispel evil spirits and demons and the personal misfortunes and natural disasters presumably caused by these agents. Hanging charms from gates and eaves to prevent evil spirits from entering one's home or placing a sword at the pillow of a corpse are examples of *mayoke.* There are special forms of *mayoke* for the protection of children. These include embroidering brightly colored protective insignia on the back of a child's *kimono* or tracing an *X* or the Chinese character for "dog" (the natural enemy of malevolent spirits) on a child's forehead with ash. The charms and amulets (GOFU) issued at temples and shrines are also believed to ward off evil spirits, as are other special appurtenances, such as the HAMAYA AND HAMAYUMI (lucky bow and arrow) sold at shrines at the NEW YEAR.

May 30th Incident 五・三〇事件

(Gosanjū Jiken). On 30 May 1925 British police at the SHANGHAI INTERNATIONAL SETTLEMENT fired on Chinese workers and students who were demonstrating against the killing of a Chinese worker in a Japanese textile mill by a Japanese foreman. The death of 13 protest-

ers prompted nationwide strikes, demonstrations, and boycotts that collectively became known as the May 30th Movement. The movement marked a new height in agitation against foreign privileges and exploitation in China. It saw the growth of a vigorous labor movement in Shanghai and other treaty ports. It also prompted modification of the privileges of foreign powers in China that had been made possible by unequal treaties. In 1925–26 the foreign powers finally held the tariff conference originally called for at the WASHINGTON CONFERENCE of 1921–22. The Japanese government sent a delegation guided by the conciliatory policies of Foreign Minister SHIDEHARA KIJŪRŌ. These negotiations were disrupted by the Nationalist Party's Northern Expedition (1926–28), however, and Chinese tariff autonomy was not regained until 1933.

Mayuzumi Toshirō 黛敏郎

(1929–). Composer. Born in Yokohama. Mayuzumi completed postgraduate studies at the Tōkyō School of Music (now Tōkyō University of Fine Arts and Music) and studied at the Paris Conservatory. He is responsible for introducing electronic music to Japan, and his *XYZ* (1953) was the first Japanese work composed in the manner of *musique concrète.* Influenced by Buddhism and Asian cultures, in 1958 he composed the symphony *Nehan* (Nirvana) and in 1963 the cantata *Keka* (Repentance). In 1976 he composed an opera based on MISHIMA YUKIO's novel KINKAKUJI that was first performed by the Berlin Opera.

Mazaki Jinzaburō 真崎甚三郎

(1876–1956). Army officer. Born in Saga Prefecture. He graduated from the Army Academy in 1897. He was made a general in 1933 and appointed inspector general of military education a year later. Together with General ARAKI SADAO, Mazaki was considered a leader of the KŌDŌHA army faction. Suspected of complicity in a Kōdōha plot to assassinate political figures, he was dismissed in 1935. The following year, when Kōdōha officers attempted a coup d'état (see FEBRUARY 26TH INCIDENT), he was indicted on suspicion that he had assisted them but was exonerated for lack of evidence.

Mazda Motor Corporation
マツダ[株]

(Matsuda). Manufacturer of Mazda automobiles. Founded in 1920 as Tōyō Cork Kōgyō Co, Ltd, the firm assumed its present name in 1984. In 1967 Mazda introduced the world's first twin-rotor rotary engine automobile (the Cosmo Sports/110S), becoming the only automotive manufacturer in the world to mass-produce vehicles powered by three different types of engine: the conventional piston engine, the rotary engine, and the diesel engine. Mazdas are exported to more than 120 countries. Mazda cars are also produced in the United States at Mazda's wholly owned subsidiary, Mazda Motor Manufacturing (USA) Corporation (MMUC). In addition, Mazda vehicles are assembled at 18 other plants overseas. Mazda Motor Corporation has established research and development bases in Japan, North America, and Europe. Factory production in calendar year 1990 totaled 1,422,626 cars and trucks. Sales for the fiscal year ending March 1991 totaled ¥2.2 trillion (US $16.0 billion), and the company was capitalized at ¥92.9 billion (US $677.1 million). Headquarters are in Aki, Hiroshima Prefecture, and in Tōkyō.

Meakandake
雌阿寒岳

An active volcanic group in the Chishima Volcanic Zone, eastern Hokkaidō. It consists of stratovolcanoes with complex features. The foothills are covered with primeval forests of Yeddo spruce (*ezomatsu*) and Sakhalin fir (*todomatsu*). Meakandake is part of Akan National Park. Height: 1,503 m (4,931 ft).

meakashi
目明し

(private investigators). Agents hired by city commissioners (MACHI BUGYŌ) during the Edo period (1600–1868) to help the basic police force (*dōshin*) in tracking down criminals. Because many of them were former offenders, they were knowledgeable about the underworld; they were notorious for their skill in extracting confessions, for accepting bribes, and for otherwise abusing their position. Although the Tokugawa shogunate repeatedly prohibited the use of *meakashi*, they were considered indispensable, with as many as 381 *meakashi* in the regular employ of the city commissioners of Edo (now Tōkyō) in 1867.

Meckel, Klemens Wilhelm Jakob
メッケル, K. W. J.

(1842–1906). German military officer and adviser to the Japanese army. Born in Cologne, Meckel graduated from the Prussian Army Staff College in 1869. After the Japanese army decided to adopt the German model of military organization, Meckel was invited by the Japanese government in 1885 to teach at the Army War College and to advise the General Staff. He assisted KATSURA TARŌ and KAWAKAMI SŌROKU in modernizing military structure and strategy. Meckel's contributions (which included revising the universal conscription system, establishing a divisional system and a supreme command, and strengthening logistic systems) helped lay the groundwork for Japan's victory in the SINO-JAPANESE WAR OF 1894–1895. His emphasis on the infantry in offensive campaigns, however, is said to have led to enormous casualties in the RUSSO-JAPANESE WAR (1904–05). He returned to Germany in 1888.

medals of honor
褒章

(*hōshō*). One of two categories of official medals awarded by the emperor, on the nomination of the cabinet, to living people who have made distinguished contributions to society in various fields. The other category is DECORATIONS (*kunshō*).

When the awarding of official medals was first established in 1881 by proclamation of the Grand Council of State (DAJŌKAN), there were three kinds—the Medal with Red Ribbon, the Medal with Green Ribbon, and the Medal with Blue Ribbon. Today there are six Medals: the Red Ribbon awarded for lifesaving; the Green Ribbon for extraordinarily virtuous conduct; the Yellow Ribbon for excellence in the field of business and industry; the Purple Ribbon in academics and the arts; the Blue Ribbon in the field of social welfare; and the Dark Navy Blue Ribbon in the field of philanthropy. Although these six are equally ranked, the Yellow Ribbon, Purple Ribbon, and Blue Ribbon are awarded twice a year, in spring and fall, while the Red Ribbon, Green Ribbon, and Dark Navy Blue Ribbon are given only when appropriate.

medical and health insurance
医療保険

(*iryō hoken*). Central component of Japan's medical care security system, designed to provide nationwide health care coverage. The cornerstone of the present system of public health insurance is the 1922 Health Insurance Law, providing coverage primarily for factory workers and miners. Over the years, various other basic health and social welfare statutes have followed. These measures have been supplemented by hundreds of amendments and auxiliary rules and regulations, and since 1961 all Japanese citizens and aliens resident in Japan have been entitled to coverage under one of six alternative health insurance plans. Chief among them are EMPLOYEES' HEALTH INSURANCE, which covers most private-sector employees, and NATIONAL HEALTH INSURANCE, for people ineligible for employee health insurance. Other plans provide coverage for seamen, national public-service employees, local public-service employees, and private-school teachers and employees. The 1982 LAW CONCERNING HEALTH AND MEDICAL SERVICES FOR THE AGED provides for medical care for citizens aged 70 and over. By 1980, 99.3 percent of the total population was covered under one of the six plans; the remaining 0.7 percent was covered by the medical assistance program provided under the 1950 LIVELIHOOD PROTECTION LAW or by other special public programs. Under most Japanese medical insurance plans, members are required to pay 10 to 30 percent of their medical expenses, depending on the type of treatment provided; the insurance carrier then remunerates the doctor, hospital, clinic, or other medical care provider directly for the remainder on a fee-for-service basis determined by the MINISTRY OF HEALTH AND WELFARE.

The nationwide cost of health care has been rising faster than NATIONAL INCOME, with medical costs accounting for 3.1 percent of national income in 1960 and 6.3 percent in 1985. Increased costs incurred by the aged, hospital inpatients, and hospital outpatients accounted for the majority of this growth. The rapid expansion of Japan's aged population since the 1970s and its effects on medical care and costs is one of the major issues that the medical and health insurance system must face in coming decades.

medical care expenses
医療費

(*iryōhi*). Japan spent nearly ¥21 trillion (US $142.3 billion) on medical care in 1990, amounting to about 5 percent of the gross national product (GNP), and ¥166,700 (US $1,151) per capita. By comparison, Western European countries spent 7–8 percent of their GNPs on medical care, and the United States spent about 10 percent.

The aging of the population is one problem confronting the Japanese medical system that is expected to pose an expanding cost burden in the future. In 1990, medical costs for those 65 years of age and older reached ¥7.5 trillion (US $51.5 billion), an increase of 6.7 percent over the previous year. With costs rising at such a pace, there is concern that the nation will be facing a serious social problem by the late 1990s, when medical insurance is predicted to be inadequate to cover the cost.

Another problem cited is the high proportion of pharmaceuticals among medical costs, amounting to some 30 percent. This is attributed to the relative lack of separation between dispensary facilities and medical practice in Japan in comparison to Europe and the United States. Income from dispensing medicines is used to cover a hospital's operating costs. Medicines may therefore be overprescribed for the purpose of maintaining the hospital's income, a tendency that is a major factor in boosting medical costs. The MINISTRY OF HEALTH AND WELFARE is pursuing policies designed to ensure that increases in medical costs are held below increases in national income levels. It is also proceeding with improvements in the pharmaceutical distribution system and the separation of medical functions and is conducting a review of health care for the elderly. See also MEDICAL AND HEALTH INSURANCE.

medicine
医学

(*igaku*). Systematized medical care in Japan dates from the introduction of Chinese medicine in the 6th century. Chinese medicine was at first exclusively reserved for the imperial family, but treatment spread gradually among the people. This medical tradition produced many noted Japanese physicians and continued up to the time of the Meiji Restoration (1868). Along with the political, social, and cultural reforms of the Meiji Restoration, Western medicine was promoted as a national policy, and thus the way was opened for Japan's present system of modern medicine.

Introduction of Chinese Medicine

The native medicine of Japan is only fragmentarily described in chronicles such as the KOJIKI and the NIHON SHOKI, both compiled in the early 8th century. It is believed that treatment largely relied on prayer, exorcism, and primitive herbal medicine. By the 6th and 7th centuries, Chinese medicine, brought back together with Buddhism by Japanese who had studied in China, generally replaced native medicine. The YŌRŌ CODE (effective 757) included Japan's first medical code, the Ishitsuryō. Modeled after the medical system of Tang (T'ang) dynasty (618–907) China, it provided for a government office called the Ten'yakuryō (Ministry of Health), which was responsible for medical administration. The code also specified a system of medical education.

The oldest extant Japanese medical treatise is the *Ishimpō* (982), written by TAMBA YASUYORI; it consists largely of quotations from Chinese works on medicine. During the Kamakura period (1185–1333), when Buddhism was at the peak of its influence, Buddhist monks exerted a substantial influence upon medicine because they included healing as part of their religious activities. Medical books of the period include

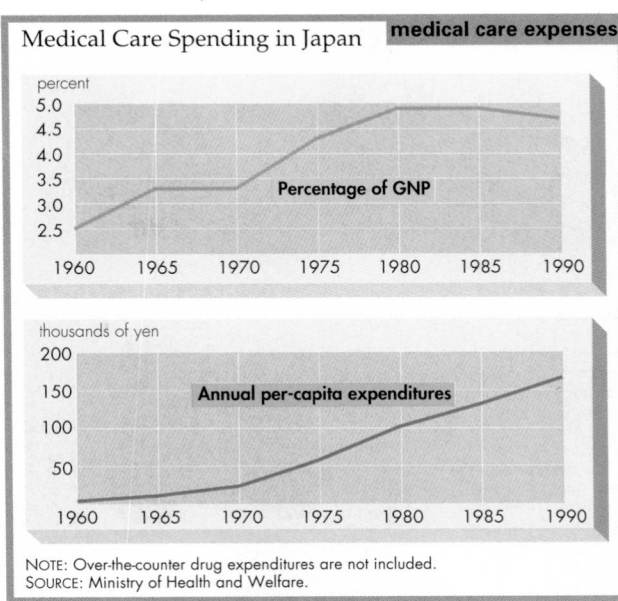

Medical Care Spending in Japan — medical care expenses

NOTE: Over-the-counter drug expenditures are not included.
SOURCE: Ministry of Health and Welfare.

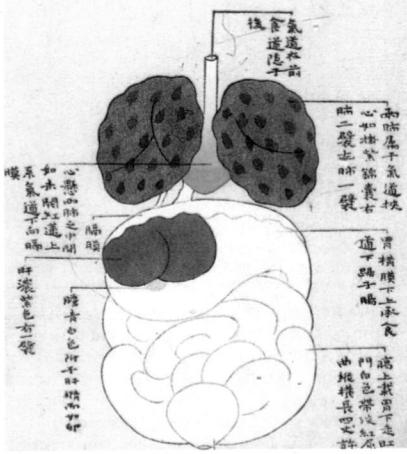

medicine
1 A detail from an Edo-period illustrated medical scroll showing a doctor treating a woman for a large boil.
2 A 19th-century medicine box.
3 This illustration of the major internal organs is from *Zōshi* (1759), the first Japanese anatomical work based on actual human dissection.

works by the monks EISAI and KAJIWARA SHŌZEN.

Latter-Day School of Medicine (16th–19th Centuries) — In China during the Jin (Chin; 1125–1234) and Yuan (Yüan; 1279–1368) dynasties, there had been major efforts to unify the traditional theories of acupuncture and moxibustion with herbal therapy. It was under the influence of this movement that the latter-day school of medicine (*goseihō* or *kōseihō*) emerged in Japan in the 16th century. Its leader was TASHIRO SANKI, a physician who studied medicine in China during the Ming dynasty (1368–1644) and settled in the Kantō region. His most prominent disciple, MANASE DŌSAN, added his own clinical experience and knowledge to the branch of Jin-Yuan medicine that is called the Li-Zhu (Li-Chu) school from the names of its two Chinese founders. Dōsan stressed the importance of simplicity and practicality in medical treatment.

The Classicist School of Medicine (17th–19th Centuries) — Criticism of the latter-day school of medicine led to the development of the so-called classicist school (*koihō*), the emergence of which marked the complete Japanization of traditional Chinese medicine. Its founder is often said to be NAGOYA GEN'I, but it is generally agreed that the real founder was GOTŌ KONZAN. Gotō concluded that *ki* (Ch: *qi* or *ch'i*), the vital energy thought to permeate the universe, served to maintain health and that all diseases occurred when this vital force became congested. KAGAWA SHŪTOKU and YAMAWAKI TŌYŌ, both pupils of Gotō, further developed thought concerning the origins of disease. Tōyō, who performed the first human dissection in Japan (1754), wrote *Zōshi*, a work based on his observations, in 1759.

YOSHIMASU TŌDŌ was the most creative and influential of the physicians belonging to the classicist school. He advocated the theory that all diseases came from one and the same poison (*mambyō ichidoku*). His theory was based on a hypothesis of the localization of pathological sites. In other words, he thought that, although all diseases had one cause, differences between them and the ne-

cessity for different treatments resulted from differences in the sites affected; hence, in treating different diseases one should first determine the site affected by the poison. His may be the only solid pathological idea among the theories of traditional Chinese medicine, which (including those of Gotō Konzan) were largely based on humoral pathology.

The basically positivist classicist school produced a number of physicians, including Nagatomi Dokushōan (1732–66), who were receptive to Western—specifically, Dutch—medicine. Based on Nagatomi's theories, HANAOKA SEISHŪ, a student of Yoshimasu Nangai (1750–1813), successfully performed an operation on breast cancer in 1805, using an anesthetic that he had invented.

Chinese Medicine and Western Medicine (16th–19th Centuries) — Western medicine, then called *namban* (southern barbarian) medicine, was first introduced to Japan by Spanish and Portuguese missionaries who arrived in the 16th century. In 1557 the first Western-style hospital was established in Funai (now the city of Ōita) by a Portuguese priest named Luis de Almeida (1525–83?). Among the notable surgeons of this period were Christovão Ferreira (1580–1652; also known as Sawano Chūan), a Portuguese naturalized in Japan, and Kurisaki Dōki (1566–1651), who studied Western medicine in the Philippines.

After the NATIONAL SECLUSION policy took effect in 1639, the Dutch were the only Westerners officially allowed to visit Japan, though a few other Europeans did manage to enter classified as Dutchmen. Dutch physicians who came to Nagasaki during the 17th century included Caspar Schambergen, who arrived in 1649 and founded a school of surgery, and Willem ten Rhijne (1647–1700), who arrived in 1674, taught medicine, and introduced the Japanese version of traditional Chinese medicine to the West. Engelbert KAEMPFER, who visited Japan in 1690, taught Western medicine there and introduced Japanese culture to Europe. Among the surgical schools founded by government interpreters at Nagasaki were the Narabayashi school, the Nishi school, and the Yoshio school. Motoki Ryōi (1628–97), an official interpreter who was influenced by Rhijne, translated a European text on anatomy and published it as the *Waran zenku naigai bungō zu* (1772, Japanese-Dutch Anatomical Atlas of the Whole Body).

An extremely important event in the history of the introduction of Western medicine was the publication in 1774 of the KAITAI SHINSHO (New Book of Anatomy) by SUGITA GEMPAKU, NAKAGAWA JUN'AN, KATSURAGAWA HOSHŪ, and other scholars of Rangaku (Dutch Learning; also known as WESTERN LEARNING). In 1771 Sugita and MAENO RYŌTAKU had observed the dissection of the body of an executed criminal and been deeply impressed by the close correspondence between the internal structure of the body and the anatomical charts found in a Dutch version of the German *Anatomische Tabellen* (1722, Anatomical Tables); the *Kaitai shinsho* was a transla-

tion of this work. It was from about this time that Western medicine, then referred to as Dutch medicine (*rampō*) due to the predominance of Dutch materials and instructors, began to rival *kampō* (Chinese medicine) in popularity.

Three generations of the Udagawa family—Udagawa Genzui (1755–97), Udagawa Genshin (1769–1834), and UDAGAWA YŌAN—made significant contributions to the development of Western medicine through their support of Rangaku and translation of Western reference works, including texts on medicine, into Japanese. Influential foreign teachers during the period of National Seclusion included Carl Peter THUNBERG, a Swedish scholar, and Philipp Franz von SIEBOLD, a German doctor. Siebold opened a school and trained many Japanese who later became eminent physicians, including TAKANO CHŌEI. In 1848 a Dutch doctor named Otto Mohnike (1814–87) successfully introduced Jennerian vaccination to Japan. In the same year OGATA KŌAN opened the Jotōkan, a smallpox clinic, in Ōsaka. In 1858 the Shutōjo, a vaccination dispensary, was established in Edo (now Tōkyō) with funds donated by Rangaku scholars; this dispensary is regarded as the forerunner of the medical faculty of Tōkyō University (see IGAKUSHO). The introduction of vaccination dealt a decisive blow to the popularity of *kampō;* however, the tradition of the latter has continued to the present day.

Modernization — In 1869 the newly established Meiji government decided that Japanese medicine was to be modeled after that of Germany. Japan's first law concerning medicine was issued in 1874 with the purpose of establishing a Westernized administrative and educational system for medical and pharmaceutical affairs. In the Meiji period (1868–1912), many German doctors, including Erwin von BÄLZ, a physician, and Julius Scriba (1848–1905), a surgeon, were engaged as professors at Japanese universities. However, foreign professors were gradually replaced by Japanese who had studied abroad, mainly in Germany. Among the Japanese sent abroad to study who returned to make important contributions to the field of medicine were KITASATO SHIBASABURŌ, HATA SAHACHIRŌ, NOGUCHI HIDEYO, TAKAMINE JŌKICHI, and SUZUKI UMETARŌ.

After World War II, German influence on Japanese medicine decreased, and further developments were heavily influenced by medical practices of the United States. The foundation for the current medical care system was laid in 1961 when a new national health insurance act, designed to achieve nationwide distribution of medical insurance, was instituted (see NATIONAL HEALTH INSURANCE). In response to a shortage of physicians, efforts were begun in 1970 to increase the number of medical schools. By 1989–90 there were approximately 183,700 practicing physicians (121,514 registered with the JAPAN MEDICAL ASSOCIATION), 80 universities with faculties of medicine, 400 national hospitals, 1,502 public hospitals, and 8,179 private hospitals. In 1988 there were 16.4 physicians per 10,000 citizens in Japan, a ratio equivalent to that of the United Kingdom and slightly lower than that of the United States.

In general, medical care, education, and research are on a par with international standards; however, a tendency to concentrate on the whole person, inherited from Chinese medicine, has acted as a brake against excessive specialization. The availability of magnetic resonance imaging (MRI) devices for diagnosis is among the highest in the world, but Japan is behind is behind in its development of organ transplant techniques, due mainly to the lack of consensus regarding the definition of BRAIN DEATH. Accomplishments of recent decades include a dramatic reduction in the incidence of tuberculosis, a decrease in mortality rates for infants and young children, and an increase in the average life expectancy. The aging of Japanese society has made the rising cost of medical care, specifically the treating of diseases that affect the elderly, such as cancer, high blood pressure, and diabetes, a major topic of discussion. There is an active program of international exchange between Japan and major research centers throughout the world. See also DISEASES; DRUGS; MEDICINE, TRADITIONAL; PUBLIC HEALTH.

medicine, traditional　　　　漢方

(kampō; literally, "Chinese medicine"). Kampō refers to the traditional Chinese herbal medicine that was dominant in Japan until the 19th century. It has been largely supplanted by Western medicine, though it continues to be practiced even today. Within the context of modern medicine, herbal remedies and traditional medical practices are often referred to as tōyō igaku ("oriental medicine"). Kampō was first brought back from China by Japanese students in the 6th and 7th centuries and, like other aspects of Chinese culture, was adopted with little modification. It was only after the 15th century, when the general public began to have access to the benefits of medicine, that efforts were made to adapt Chinese medicine to Japan's climate, environment, and people.

There are two major schools of traditional Chinese medicine in Japan, the so-called latter-day school of medicine (goseihō or kōseihō) and the classicist school of medicine (koihō). Most of the kampō schools in Japan today are based on the koihō school with some elements from goseihō.

The founder of goseihō, TASHIRO SANKI, traveled to China in 1487 and for 12 years studied the medical arts of the Li-Zhu (Li-Chu) school, a branch of the Chinese medicine that evolved during the Jin (Chin; 1125–1234) and Yuan (Yüan; 1279–1368) dynasties. After returning to Japan, he applied his knowledge to the medical treatment of the ruling military class and the general public. MANASE DŌSAN, one of Tashiro's pupils, constructed his own medical theory by combining Tashiro's teaching with his own experience. His medical treatise, the Keitekishū (1574, Enlightening Teachings), marked the development of a truly Japanese form of Chinese medicine.

The koihō school of medicine, simpler and more positivistic in its approach to medical treatment than the goseihō, became increasingly popular from the 17th century onward. It was based on a Chinese medical classic, Shang han za bing lun (Shang han tsa ping lun; Essay on Typhoid and Miscellaneous Diseases), which dealt with observed symptoms and prescribed methods of treatment that had been established after long practical experience.

The drugs used in kampō are called kampōyaku or kan'yaku. These are all crude drugs and are mostly of vegetable origin, although some are of animal or mineral origin. Drugs are mixed according to a formula (there may be as many as 10 or more ingredients), then prescribed either singly or in combination for a specific symptom. For example, there

are as many as 20 different formulas for treating the common cold, depending on the symptoms. Japanese kampō uses between 100 and 200 different drugs in its prescriptions, while the Chinese pharmacopoeia relies on as many as 500 different drugs. Japanese kampō medicines are also distinct from those of China in that they are produced from materials that are relatively easy to obtain and are usually administered in smaller doses. Drugs related to the treatment of fever-producing diseases are prescribed differently in Japanese kampō.

The pattern in which symptoms manifest themselves, known as shō, is the object of diagnosis in kampō. The investigation of shō includes the following important points. The nature of the illness is determined by observing various subjective and objective symptoms according to the doctrines of kampō. The shō is then given a name according to the drug that is to be prescribed for its treatment. The shō thus functions as prior evidence that the prescription will improve the condition. Some practitioners use the term shō in classifying the patient's physical constitution, disease characteristics, and causes of illness.

The kampō practitioner employs four methods for examining the patient: bōshin (visual examination of the patient's face, nails, and tongue for abnormalities), bunshin (examination by means of the doctor's sense of smell and hearing), monshin (questioning the patient about his or her emotional state and physical sensations), and sesshin (examination of pulse and abdominal palpation). Abdominal palpation is a unique feature of Japanese kampō that is used to evaluate the physical and mental condition of the patient. All four sensory examinations are made to evaluate the condition of the patient on the basis of diagnostic factors and to determine the appropriate treatment for the patient's shō.

medieval literature　　　　中世の文学

(chūsei no bungaku). While Japanese scholars disagree on the time frame of the term "medieval" (chūsei) as applied to Japanese literature, this article treats the medieval period as occurring roughly between 1200 and 1600. Since changes in the content and style of literature are almost never abrupt, however, some characteristics usually associated with literature of the Heian period (794–1185) continue to appear after 1200—for example, certain courtly episodes are found in the otherwise new medieval form known as GUNKI MONOGATARI (war tales), and the early stages of Edo-period (1600–1868) popular literature owe much to developments well before 1600, such as the popularization and widespread propagation of tales by itinerant performers.

Poetry and Drama——Already by the end of the Heian period the genre of court prose romances (such as the TALE OF GENJI) was in serious decline. Poetry, however, was still flourishing, and the SHIN KOKINSHŪ, the eighth imperial WAKA anthology, compiled in 1205, is in some ways the culmination of the classical poetic tradition that began with the early-10th-century KOKINSHŪ. For Fujiwara no Shunzei (FUJIWARA NO TOSHINARI; 1114–1204) and his son Fujiwara no Teika (FUJIWARA NO SADAIE; 1162–1241), one of the compilers of the Shin kokinshū, the watchword was "old words, new treatment." Shin kokinshū poets employed elaborate techniques in an attempt to give life to old and well-worn themes, and certain develop-

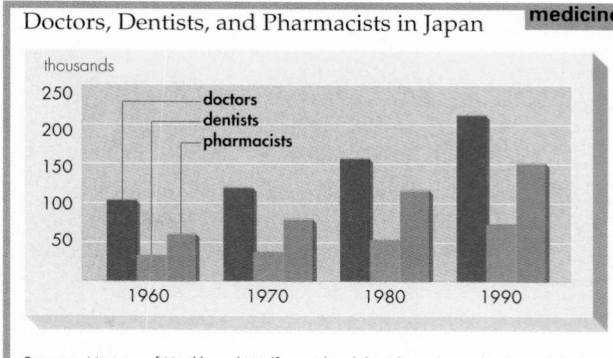

Doctors, Dentists, and Pharmacists in Japan　　medicine

thousands
- doctors
- dentists
- pharmacists

250 200 150 100 50

1960　1970　1980　1990

SOURCE: Ministry of Health and Welfare, Ishi, shika ishi, yakuzaishi chōsa, 1990.

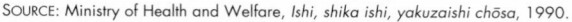

Health Insurance Coverage in Japan

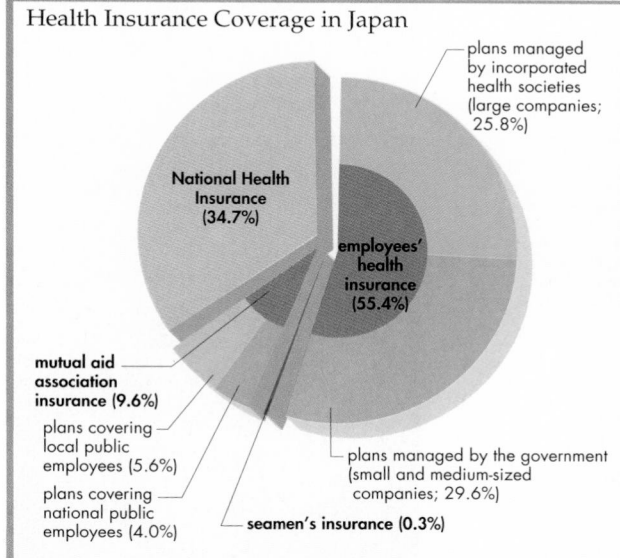

plans managed by incorporated health societies (large companies; 25.8%)

National Health Insurance (34.7%)

employees' health insurance (55.4%)

mutual aid association insurance (9.6%)

plans covering local public employees (5.6%)

plans covering national public employees (4.0%)

seamen's insurance (0.3%)

plans managed by the government (small and medium-sized companies; 29.6%)

NOTE: Figures are as of March 1991 and include both Japanese nationals and aliens resident in Japan.
SOURCE: Ministry of Health and Welfare, Kōsei hakusho (annual): 1992.

traditional medicine
A chest for storing the herbs and other ingredients used in traditional medicine. Each drawer is labeled with the name of its contents.

ments (e.g., HONKADORI, or explicit allusions to well-known poems of earlier times) contributed significantly to the range of suggestion and to the flexibility of the 31-syllable waka. Yet most critics consider that the level of poetry in the IMPERIAL ANTHOLOGIES steadily declined after the Shin kokinshū.

The way forward lay not in the waka form but in RENGA (linked verse). Courtiers in the Heian period had long delighted in capping verses, and gradually there developed a practice of stringing together a series of half poems with syllable counts of 5-7-5, 7-7, 5-7-5, 7-7, and so on. Each pair (a-b, b-c, etc) made a kind of waka poem on its own, the separate verses being linked sometimes by

ASHIKAGA YOSHIMITSU (1358–1408). The origins of Nō lie in a type of popular comic entertainment known as SARUGAKU, the direct descendants of which are still performed as KYŌGEN farces between Nō plays, as well as in plays explaining the significance of religious rites or depicting religious legends. This repertory finally came to be used outside a religious environment and to include pieces with broader artistic aims, incorporating song and dance. It was elevated by KAN'AMI (1333–84), leader of a troupe under the patronage of Yoshimitsu, and his son ZEAMI (1368–1443) into a highly serious and refined art form known as *sarugaku* Nō, which leaned heavily toward the classical aristocratic tradition of poetry. The interaction in many plays between the supernatural and the real world gives them an atmosphere of mystery; sometimes the Nō can even seem like some religious rite. One basic theme that is common to the majority of plays is the sinful nature of attachment to this world. In a typical plot, a warrior suffering torments in the afterlife is helped to lose his hatred of his former enemies and achieve salvation by the power of Buddhism and, specifically, by the grace of Buddha Amida.

Prose——The Amidist faith had in fact grown immensely in importance and popular appeal from the late Heian period. Indeed the first notable prose work of the medieval period, HŌJŌKI, is a clear assertion of the need for mankind to turn to Amida and find solace in his grace. The author, KAMO NO CHŌMEI (1156?–1216), explains his reasons for having abandoned the secular world and become a hermit, stressing tragedies arising from natural disasters rather than the terrible TAIRA-MINAMOTO WAR of his time. There is also little reflection of the war in the UJI SHŪI MONOGATARI, a collection of tales compiled about the same time as the *Hōjōki*. This collection, an example of the genre known as SETSUWA BUNGAKU ("tale" or "anecdotal literature"), contains tales about the everyday life of ordinary people of all classes, mixed with edifying religious exemplary tales. It has much in common with the KONJAKU MONOGATARI, a similar collection of the late Heian period, in which is already apparent a nostalgia for "the old days" of court culture, which becomes a prominent characteristic of later anthologies of tales. Equally nostalgic is YOSHIDA KENKŌ's (ca 1283–ca 1352) TSURE-ZUREGUSA, a collection of random jottings, or ZUIHITSU, that contains diverse anecdotes and observations on life and manners. Just as Chōmei does not comment on the Taira-Minamoto War, so Kenkō does not refer to the political troubles of his own time, the wars that resulted from the emperor GO-DAIGO's (1288–1339; r 1318–39) attempts around 1330 to restore the long-lost supremacy of imperial rule.

The Buddhist doctrine of worldly impermanence and the futility of human endeavor found frequent expression during this time. A classic statement of it is the opening lines of the HEIKE MONOGATARI, the most celebrated example of the *gunki monogatari*, which deal with the civil wars of the late 12th century and later. The most important besides the *Heike monogatari* are the HŌGEN MONOGATARI and HEIJI MONOGATARI, which recount the disturbances of 1156 and 1160, and the TAIHEIKI, dealing with the conflict between the NORTHERN AND SOUTHERN COURTS in the 14th century. Before a standard text of the *Heike monogatari* appeared in 1371, it was constantly created and re-created in the course of oral recitation by BIWA HŌSHI (literally,

"lute priests"). It tells a story that must have deeply moved its audiences by the heroic vigor and grandeur of the battle scenes, with their accounts of bravery, nobility of mind, loyalty, and self-sacrifice. The tale's most lasting effect was to glorify the image of the warrior (SAMURAI), although it contains pathos too, particularly in the fate of MINAMOTO NO YOSHITSUNE (1159–89) and in the more romantic tales. The story of the cataclysmic war in which the Heike (Taira) were finally overthrown in 1185 is told also in GEMPEI SEISUIKI, which, unlike the *Heike monogatari*, belongs to a line of written texts.

The *Heike monogatari*, at least in the early stages of its development, may have had a religious function beyond its embodiment of a moral about the Taira's inevitable fall as retribution for their arrogance. In medieval Japan the recitation of accounts of battles and the manner in which heroic figures died sometimes constituted a kind of religious ritual undertaken partly to comfort the spirits of the departed and partly to pacify them and ward off any evil and vengeful influences that they might bring to bear (see GORYŌ).

It is highly probable that early accounts of this kind about the Taira-Minamoto War contributed to the development of the *Heike monogatari*. Certainly there is ample evidence that such recitation played a major part in the genesis and growth of the SOGA MONOGATARI, the story of the revenge exacted by the Soga brothers in 1193 for the murder of their father. In the AZUMA KAGAMI, a historical account that appeared some 80 years after the brothers' deaths, one Tora Gozen appears as the actual historical mistress of the elder of the Soga brothers. Modern research suggests, however, that the name of this character almost certainly comes from a generic term for a kind of itinerant female performer of religious rituals (a type of MIKO). The mention of Tora Gozen in *Azuma kagami* suggests that this apparently documentary record uses material derived from popular tales created by narrators at the time.

It is known that the *Soga monogatari* was in the repertory of blind women called GOZE who traveled about Japan singing such tales to the accompaniment of a SHAMISEN or of a hand drum. *Etoki* (literally, "picture explainers") are also thought to have contributed to the development of the *Soga monogatari*, especially female *etoki*, known as Kumano nuns for their original association with the KUMANO SANZAN SHRINES not far from Ise. In later times these women degenerated into entertainers, but their early activities consisted of showing religious scenes and telling stories to explain the illustrations.

The Soga story inspired in audiences what is known as *soga-biiki*, sympathy for the two young men who against all odds heroically persevered in their aim of avenging the death of their father. The GIKEIKI, a 15th-century tale about Minamoto no Yoshitsune, is likewise permeated by the sentiment of *hōgan-biiki* (sympathy for Yoshitsune, *hōgan* being his title). In fact Yoshitsune was outstandingly popular as a subject of tales. Of the 50 extant KŌWAKA-MAI, a form of ballad-drama that once rivaled Nō in samurai favor, about two-fifths concern him (there are also 7 about the Soga brothers). One early tale about a fictitious love affair between Yoshitsune as a youth and a Lady Jōruri eventually developed into a distinct type of popular entertainment that ulti-

subject matter but also by word associations or wordplays. There were elaborate rules as to the intervals at which certain subjects could be mentioned or certain words repeated. Out of this unpromising game there developed by the 14th century an art that at times came to be treated with an almost religious solemnity. The attitudes of such poets as SHŌTETSU (1381–1459) and SHINKEI (1406–75) toward the composition of *renga* owed much to ZEN Buddhism; the ideal link between verses was determined as it were by intuition, not by a conscious effort to make surface links of subject matter or wording. There developed as well a genre of literature, practiced by Zen priests, that consisted principally of POETRY AND PROSE IN CHINESE (see GOZAN LITERATURE).

The influence of Zen can also be seen in the NŌ drama, which reached its perfected form during the Muromachi period (1333–1568) under the patronage of the shōgun

mately grew into the genre of puppet drama known (from the name of this story) as JŌRURI. One particularly fantastic medieval tale of Yoshitsune tells of his quest for a secret military treatise owned by a demon king; the latter's daughter falls in love with Yoshitsune and sacrifices her life to copy the treatise, which then becomes blank paper. This tale is an example of the OTOGI-ZŌSHI (companion booklets or entertainment booklets), of which some 500 are extant. Until comparatively recently they were almost entirely neglected by scholars as intended only for children or for women. It is clear, however, that they were in fact not just children's books, but appealed also to adults, including men.

Although the achievements of the medieval period in literature lie predominantly in the fields of drama and poetry, the achievements of the best among the war chronicles must also be recognized. Apart from their literary merit, these tales had a wide popular appeal, and as such they were part of the great mass of popular literature, including both chanted or recited literature (*katari-mono*) and printed books such as *otogi-zōshi*, which laid the groundwork for the development of popular prose literature in the Edo period.

Megijima
女木島

Island in the eastern Inland Sea, approximately 3 km (2 mi) north of the city of Takamatsu, Kagawa Prefecture, Shikoku. Known as the Onigashima (Island of Ogres) in the folktale of MOMOTARŌ (Peach Boy). Principal activities are coastal fishing and the cultivation of sweet potatoes and wheat. Area: 2.7 sq km (1 sq mi).

Meguro Ward
目黒区

(Meguro Ku). One of the 23 wards of Tōkyō. On the Musashino Plateau. It developed as a residential area after the Tōkyō Earthquake of 1923. Institutes of higher learning located here include the Faculty of Liberal Arts of Tōkyō University and Tōkyō Institute of Technology. Pop: 251,222.

Meiboku sendai hagi
伽羅先代萩

(The Choice Wood of a Former Era). Popular title *Sendai-hagi*. Puppet play and KABUKI play of the *jidai-mono* (historical play) category. Earliest version written by Nagawa Kamesuke in 1777. The story refers and the title alludes to a succession dispute, the DATE SŌDŌ, that disturbed the Sendai domain of the 1660s, but the setting is transposed into an earlier era, the Muromachi period (1333–1568). Two scenes remain in the kabuki repertory. In one, a group of retainers, led by the evil counselor Nikki Danjō, conspires to do away with Tsurukiyo, the young son of their incompetent lord. Nikki Danjō is exposed in the "Under the Floor" scene, where the *aragoto* ("rough business") superman Arajishi Otokonosuke tracks down a huge rat and strikes it on the head; the rat scurries away with a list of conspirators, and moments later Nikki Danjō appears in a puff of smoke, a bleeding wound on his forehead and the list clamped between his teeth.

meibutsugire
名物裂

("specialty cloth"). General name for various fabrics imported mainly from China from the Kamakura period (1185–1333) to the early Edo period (1600–1868); particularly popular among tea connoisseurs and upper-class warriors. These fabrics were used in various ways in the TEA CEREMONY. The ma-

jority are Chinese fabrics of the Song (Sung; 960–1279), Yuan (Yüan; 1279–1368), and Ming (1368–1644) dynasties, including fabrics of the types known in Japan as DONSU (damask), NISHIKI (brocade), KINRAN AND GIN-RAN (gold and silver brocade), *kantō* (woven stripes), and *inkin* (gold-leaf imprint). Others came to Japan via China from Persia, India, and Southeast Asia. Their influence on Japanese dyeing techniques and design after the Azuchi-Momoyama period (1568–1600) is historically significant.

Meidensha Corporation
[株]明電舎

(Meidensha). Manufacturer of electric machinery such as generators, dynamometers, transformers, circuit breakers, surge arresters, and robotics. Founded in 1897; joined the Sumitomo group of companies in 1966. The firm supplies equipment to electric power companies, government organizations, and private enterprise in Japan and abroad. Sales for the fiscal year ending March 1991 totaled ¥188.6 billion (US $1.4 billion), and capitalization was ¥17.0 billion (US $123.9 million). Headquarters are in Tōkyō.

Meidi-Ya Co, Ltd
[株]明治屋

(Meijiya). Food manufacturer and distributor that also operates a chain of retail stores. Established in 1885. The company supplies to the market more than 1,300 Meidi-Ya brand food items, including confections, candies, drinks, pastas, and baby foods. For the fiscal year ending February 1990, sales totaled ¥344.5 billion (US $2.4 billion) and capitalization stood at ¥270.0 million (US $1.9 million). Headquarters are in Tōkyō.

meigen
鳴弦

(resounding bowstrings). A custom that originated in the Heian period (794–1185). Chamberlains (*kurōdo*) plucked their bowstrings to make a sound that would ward off evil spirits when the emperor entered his bath, when he was ill, or upon the birth of an heir. *Meigen* is still practiced today at the birth of an imperial prince. See also HAMAYA AND HAMAYUMI.

Meigetsuki
明月記

Also known as *Shōkōki*. Diary of the courtier and noted poet FUJIWARA NO SADAIE. There are many extant manuscripts, and the number

of chapters varies; it is written in Chinese (KAMBUN) and covers 1180–1235. The text contains much discussion of the composition of poetry. Since Sadaie enjoyed the patronage of the retired Emperor GO-TOBA, taught poetics to MINAMOTO NO SANETOMO, and served as an official of the KUJŌ FAMILY, which had close ties with the Kamakura shogunate, his diary also contains important information about courtier-warrior relations early in the Kamakura period (1185–1333). Parts of *Meigetsuki* were used as a source for the AZUMA KAGAMI, the history of the Kamakura shogunate.

Meigō ōrai
明衡往来

(Akihira's Letter Writer). Earliest example of a genre called ŌRAIMONO; i.e., collections of models for letter writing. Compiled in 1040 by FUJIWARA NO AKIHIRA, an eminent scholar of Japanese and Chinese classics and history, it is also called *Meigō shōsoku*, *Unshū ōrai*, or *Unshū shōsoku*. These letters are written in HENTAI KAMBUN, a heavily Japanized form of classical Chinese. They furnish valuable material for historical linguistic study.

Meiji Canal
明治用水

(Meiji Yōsui). Irrigation canal on the Okazaki Plain, central Aichi Prefecture, central Honshū. It extends from the river Yahagigawa to Mikawa Bay. Construction of this and supporting canals was completed in the 1880s. The canal services the city of Anjō, a leading truck-gardening area, and its vicinity, irrigating about 10,000 hectares (24,700 acres) of paddy fields. Length: 52 km (32 mi); total length of branch canals: 300 km (186 mi).

Meiji Constitution → Constitution
of the Empire of Japan

Meiji, Emperor
明治天皇

(1852–1912; Meiji Tennō). The 122nd sovereign (*tennō*) in the traditional count, which includes several legendary emperors;

Emperor Meiji
1 Succeeding to the throne in 1867 at the age of 14, Emperor Meiji (shown here in a later photograph) became the symbolic focus for the movement to overthrow the Tokugawa shogunate.
2 Emperor Meiji handing the Constitution of the Empire of Japan to Prime Minister Kuroda Kiyotaka in this 1922 painting of the promulgation ceremony held 11 February 1889 at the newly built Imperial Palace.

Meiji Enlightenment
The "enlightening" impact of Westernization on early-Meiji-period Japan is lampooned in this 1873 woodblock print. The romanized legend reads "The Indecision of Enlightenment."

reigned 1867–1912. He was called Meiji posthumously from the name of the Meiji period (1868–1912). The son of Emperor KŌMEI, he became crown prince in 1860 as Mutsuhito (his personal name) and succeeded to the throne at age 14. Because of his youth, Nijō Nariyuki (1816–78) served as regent (sesshō). Emperor Meiji took as his empress Ichijō Haruko (1850–1914; later Shōken Kōtaigō or Empress Dowager Shōken). He studied calligraphy, poetry, and the principles of government with his parents. After their deaths, he received his education from his father-in-law, Tadayasu.

Historical Milestones—In the movement leading to the overthrow of the TOKUGAWA SHOGUNATE, Emperor Meiji, or rather the imperial institution, became the rallying point (see SONNŌ JŌI). With the MEIJI RESTORATION (1868), the dual system of government (under which the shōguns were de facto rulers) was destroyed, and the emperor was once more made the supreme authority. The CHARTER OATH outlining the philosophy of the new government was issued in the emperor's name, and the capital was moved from Kyōto to Tōkyō. Emperor Meiji's long reign was marked by momentous events. The IMPERIAL RESCRIPT TO SOLDIERS AND SAILORS, the CONSTITUTION OF THE EMPIRE OF JAPAN, and the IMPERIAL RESCRIPT ON EDUCATION were promulgated. The DIET was founded. Japan's industrial revolution was carried out. Important developments also occurred in foreign affairs: the extension of diplomatic relationships, the revision of the Unequal Treaties (see UNEQUAL TREATIES, REVISION OF), the signing of the ANGLO-JAPANESE ALLIANCE, the SINO-JAPANESE WAR OF 1894–1895, the RUSSO-JAPANESE WAR, and the annexation of Korea (1910).

Throughout his reign, the supreme power of the state and command of the military were increasingly concentrated in the emperor's hands. In fact, however, it is difficult to clarify to what extent policy emanated from the "direct imperial rule" of Emperor Meiji as an individual. It is likely that the emperor expressed his political views from time to time. It is known that in the 1873 controversy over a proposed invasion of Korea (see SEIKANRON) the emperor supported the policy of giving priority to internal affairs and that he fully endorsed the 1875 edict promising the establishment of a constitutional government. Yet on the whole the emperor stood above politics, a benevolent father figure rather than a stern monarch.

Emperor Meiji accepted changes that were unavoidable for diplomatic reasons, but he opposed imitation of the West and forbade discarding traditional ceremonies and rites. He also showed an interest in maintaining historical sites and other famous places.

Military Leader—As supreme commander of the military forces during the Sino-Japanese and Russo-Japanese wars, he followed closely the progress of the Japanese forces. The hard work and anxiety of the war years left him looking markedly aged. His fatal illness a few years later is said to have resulted from his exhaustion at that time.

He died on 30 July 1912 and was buried in the Momoyama Mausoleum in Fushimi, Kyōto. His death symbolically brought to an end the era of Japan's successful transformation into a modern state. See also EMPEROR.

Meiji Enlightenment　文明開化

(bummei kaika). Term applied to the movement of thought and belief during the early part of the Meiji period (1868–1912) when the Meiji government adopted a policy of modernization and began to introduce Western civilization into the country. Under the slogan A Rich Country and a Strong Military (fukoku kyōhei) the Meiji government abolished the feudal socioeconomic system, adopted modern production methods, and established universal conscription. It issued Western uniforms to the army and navy and encouraged government officials to wear Western clothes. Under the slogan Civilization and Enlightenment (bummei kaika), the government put into effect policies designed to educate the general populace. It encouraged people to eat Western foods, cut off their topknots (DAMPATSUREI), and stop wearing swords (HAITŌREI). It adopted the Gregorian calendar, implemented telegraph and postal services, started constructing railways, and established a nationwide public school system.

Independent of government initiatives, FUKUZAWA YUKICHI and others associated with the MEIROKUSHA tried to introduce Western civilization through their writings. Increased intercourse with the West stimulated the adoption of Western ideas and values such as political liberty and equality, as evidenced in the FREEDOM AND PEOPLE'S RIGHTS MOVEMENT. By 1880, in a reaction against the rising people's rights movement, the government attempted to revive conservative Confucian values and thought.

Meiji Gakuin University
明治学院大学

(Meiji Gakuin Daigaku). A private, Christian, coeducational university. Its main campus is located in Minato Ward, Tōkyō. The descendant of James Curtis HEPBURN's Eigakujuku and the Brown's School of Samuel Robbins BROWN, Meiji Gakuin was formed in 1886 and attained university status in 1949. It maintains faculties of letters, economics, sociology, law, and international studies. It has affiliated junior high and high schools. Enrollment in 1989 was 12,159.

Meiji Ishin →Meiji Restoration

Meiji Jūyonen no Seihen→
Political Crisis of 1881

Meiji literature　明治時代の文学
(Meiji jidai no bungaku). Although the Meiji period (1868–1912) was to bring sweeping changes to Japan and its literature, at the outset of the period writers of popular fiction continued to work in the traditional genre of GESAKU. Some among them, such as KANAGAKI ROBUN, satirized in witty but glib

prose the anxieties and posturings of their fellow countrymen in the face of a massive influx of Western culture (see MEIJI ENLIGHTENMENT). Interest in all things Western, actively promoted by the Meiji government, led to the appearance from the 1870s of numerous translations of European prose works. Through the introduction of new ideas and words coined to express them, these translations profoundly affected the Japanese language and laid the groundwork for a growing appreciation of the novel as a serious genre of literature.

As a consequence of the comprehensive restructuring of the social and political order under the influence of Western systems, the FREEDOM AND PEOPLE'S RIGHTS MOVEMENT arose with the aim of establishing a freely elected national assembly. In the 1880s adherents of the movement, among them YANO RYŪKEI and TŌKAI SANSHI, wrote frankly didactic SEIJI SHŌSETSU ("political novels") that illustrated democratic ideals; though their literary value is slight, their serious intent contributed to the acceptance of the novel as an important literary form. However, the watershed in the development of the novel in Japan was TSUBOUCHI SHŌYŌ's critical study *Shōsetsu shinzui* (1885–86, The Essence of the Novel), which called for a novelistic style that employed realistic characterization and avoided easy moralism. UKIGUMO (1887–89; tr in *Japan's First Modern Novel: Ukigumo of Futabatei Shimei*, 1967) by FUTABATEI SHIMEI was the first Japanese novel to be written in the colloquial language (see GEMBUN ITCHI) and in large measure it achieved the goals set forth by Tsubouchi.

Nevertheless, other more popular writers, such as OZAKI KŌYŌ and his fellow members of the KEN'YŪSHA coterie, continued to write under the influence of Edo-period (1600–1868) literature. The novels of KŌDA ROHAN, with their grandeur and nobility of content and style, stand in striking contrast to the emotional and opulent quality of Kōyō's work. Rohan often borrowed story lines from Chinese sources and wrote in a formal and spare style suggestive of the Chinese classics.

After the SINO-JAPANESE WAR OF 1894–1895, novels depicting negative aspects of Japanese society, such as the disparity between the rich and the poor, came into vogue. Both IZUMI KYŌKA and KAWAKAMI BIZAN wrote fiction in this genre, which was known as *kannen shōsetsu* ("ideological novels"), and even Kōyō reflects in KONJIKI YASHA (1897–1903; tr *The Golden Demon*, 1905) on the social implications of the spread of capitalist values. In HOTOTOGISU (1898–99; tr *Nami-ko*, 1904), which falls into a genre of fiction known as *katei shōsetsu* ("family novels"), TOKUTOMI ROKA dealt with the issues of the role of women and the nature of marriage in Meiji Japan.

KITAMURA TŌKOKU, a Christian convert and an avid reader of English romantic poets, was the most important figure in the spread of romanticism in Japan. In his critical writings, largely published in the journal BUNGAKUKAI (1893–98, The Literary World), Tōkoku dealt with such themes as freedom, God, and romantic love, for the last of which he coined the Japanese term *ren'ai. Bungakukai* also published the works of HIGUCHI ICHIYŌ, who was little noted in her time but has come to be considered one of the great writers of the Meiji period. Her most famous story, TAKEKURABE (1895–96; tr "Growing Up," 1956), describes the lives of children just outside the Yoshiwara pleasure quarter, one

of whom is destined to become a priest and another a prostitute.

In the first decade of the 20th century a new literary movement emerged. Although it arose under European influence, Japanese NATURALISM did not take the objective approach of Emile Zola. Its practitioners spoke out against idealism and technique, urging the adoption of a style based on frank confession and unflinching examination of the self. Among the most important Japanese naturalist novels are *Futon* (1907; tr *The Quilt and Other Stories*, 1981) and INAKA KYŌSHI (1909; tr *Country Teacher*, 1984) by TAYAMA KATAI, and HAKAI (1906; tr *The Broken Commandment*, 1974) and *Ie* (1910–11; tr *The Family*, 1976) by SHIMAZAKI TŌSON. By 1910 the influence of naturalism had begun to wane, but the tradition of self-reflection persisted in the confessional I-NOVEL.

Although deeply concerned with the relationship between the individual and society, NATSUME SŌSEKI was not a member of any of the literary schools of his day. Sōseki's WAGAHAI WA NEKO DE ARU (1905–06; tr *I Am a Cat*, 1961) satirizes Meiji intellectuals, and *Sorekara* (1909; tr *And Then*, 1978) describes the egoism that he perceived to be afflicting the urban middle class of Meiji Japan. MORI ŌGAI, who, with Sōseki, is considered one of the greatest writers of the period, was also not strongly associated with any literary group. Early in his career, he made translations of German romantic poetry and of Hans Christian Andersen's *Improvisatoren*, and he wrote a number of short stories that suggest affinity with the romantic school. However, in his later biographical fiction, to which he turned in the Taishō period (1912–26), he developed a deeply reserved and stately style. NAGAI KAFŪ, like Ōgai and Sōseki, was critical of Meiji Japan, and one of his early works, *Furansu monogatari* (1909, A Tale of France), was banned for its unflattering comments on Meiji society. By the end of the period, however, he had turned to fictional accounts of the Tōkyō demimonde. See also FICTION, MODERN.

During the Meiji period traditional verse forms were revitalized and a new form, SHINTAISHI, was developed under the influence of European poetry. Although several anthologies of translations of European and American poetry appeared earlier, the first great volume of native *shintaishi* was *Wakanashū* (1897, Collection of Young Herbs) by Shimazaki Tōson. The traditional poetic form WAKA was given new life by MASAOKA SHIKI and YOSANO TEKKAN and renamed TANKA. In 1900 the Shinshisha, a poetry coterie founded by Tekkan, began publication of the journal MYŌJŌ (Morning Star), which introduced the passionately romantic *tanka* of Tekkan's lover and then wife, YOSANO AKIKO. SUBARU (1909–13, Pleiades), the successor to *Myōjō*, was initially under the editorship of ISHIKAWA TAKUBOKU, considered by some to be the finest of Meiji-period *tanka* poets. Shiki and the poets who gathered about him, chief among whom were TAKAHAMA KYOSHI and KAWAHIGASHI HEKIGOTŌ, were largely responsible for developing HAIKU as a modern verse form. See also POETRY, MODERN.

Although Japan possesses a rich dramatic tradition, none of the classical genres succeeded in developing a durable form of drama that reflected contemporary concerns. It was not until the late Meiji period that a modern theater (SHINGEKI) began to develop, under the influence, most notably, of Henrik Ibsen's plays. See also DRAMA, MODERN.

In the course of the Meiji period—a mere

44 years—Japanese literature was transformed. The novel was raised from the status of second-class literature and established as the premier form of modern literary expression. At the same time, the classical forms of verse, *tanka* and haiku, were reinvigorated by the abandonment of useless conventions and a broadening of subject matter, and foundations were laid for the development of modern traditions of free verse and theater.

Meiji Milk Products Co, Ltd
明治乳業[株]

(Meiji Nyūgyō). Manufacturer of dairy and processed foods sold under the Meiji brand. Incorporated in 1917. One of the company's international activities is CP-Meiji, a joint venture with the CP group of Thailand. Continued efforts are being made to develop the company into a general food enterprise. Sales for the fiscal year ending March 1991 totaled ¥407.1 billion (US $3.0 billion), of which fluid milk products accounted for 44 percent; manufactured dairy products, 13 percent; ice cream, 14 percent; and other products, 29 percent. Capitalization stood at ¥15.8 billion (US $116.6 million) in 1991. Headquarters are in Tōkyō.

Meiji Mura
明治村

Outdoor museum in Inuyama, Aichi Prefecture. Opened in 1965 to preserve buildings and artifacts of the Meiji period (1868–1912). Among the Western- and Japanese-style structures are churches, banks, stores, hospitals, government buildings, private homes, and a prison. The homes of the Meiji-period writers MORI ŌGAI and NATSUME SŌSEKI and parts of the original Imperial Hotel of Tōkyō are preserved here, as are several running trains and trolley cars. Area: 100 hectares (247 acres).

Meiji Mura Nine structures in this open-air museum have been designated as Important Cultural Properties.
1 An aerial view of Meiji Mura.
2 The Uji-Yamada Post Office was constructed in 1870.

Meiji Mutual Life Insurance Co
明治生命保険[相]

(Meiji Seimei Hoken). Leading life insurance company and a member of the MITSUBISHI group. Founded in 1881; mutualized in 1947. It provides insurance and financial services to individuals, families, and businesses. Its domestic network extends to 94 regional offices, 10 group marketing offices, and 1,421 agency offices. It also has subsidiaries, affiliates, and offices in 15 cities around the world. The company is especially active in the fields of product development, the application of computer and communication technology, and international insurance operations. Total assets for the fiscal year ending March 1991 reached ¥11.3 trillion (US $82.4 billion). The company received premiums of ¥2.4 trillion (US $17.5 billion) in the same year. Headquarters are in Tōkyō.

Meiji period
明治時代

(1868–1912; Meiji *jidai*). The reign of Emperor MEIJI and the beginning of Japan's modern period. It started on 23 October 1868, when the 16-year-old emperor Mutsuhito selected the era name Meiji ("Enlightened Rule") for his reign; the emperor himself is therefore posthumously known as Meiji. Extended retroactively to 3 January, when the restoration of direct imperial rule (ŌSEI FUKKO) had been proclaimed, it ended with the emperor's death on 30 July 1912. The period commenced with the collapse of the TOKUGAWA SHOGUNATE and the sweeping reforms attendant upon the MEIJI RESTORATION; it was followed by the TAISHŌ PERIOD (1912–26). The Meiji period saw Japan's transformation from a feudal polity into a modern industrial state, along with its emergence from isolation into the ranks of major world powers.

The First Decade: The Abolition of Feudalism

The Meiji regime began as an alliance between Satsuma (now Kagoshima Prefecture) and Chōshū (now Yamaguchi Prefecture), two domains behind the overthrow of the Tokugawa shogunate, supported by Tosa (now Kōchi Prefecture) and Hizen (now Saga Prefecture). Though their dominance was legitimized by alliance with the emperor, Satsuma and Chōshū faced a difficult task in imposing and maintaining national unity. From January 1868 to June 1869, the nascent Meiji state fought the BOSHIN CIVIL WAR against fragmented Tokugawa forces and dissident domains. Even before the Tokugawa finally surrendered, the former shogunal capital, Edo, was renamed Tōkyō and designated as the new national capital.

As it attempted to assert control and restore order, the Meiji government sought to reassure its subjects that this new order would be one of justice and opportunity, aspirations embodied in the CHARTER OATH issued by the emperor on 6 April 1868. The Charter Oath promised, among other things, that deliberative assemblies would be established and all matters decided by public discussion and that evil customs of the past would be abandoned, this last implying a commitment to abolish feudalism. Japan's crises in the 1850s and 1860s had shown the need for a single center of power and decision making; only by controlling an integrated polity could the government build up the nation to face the West.

There were early attempts to implement the "assemblies" and "public discussion" mentioned in the Charter Oath, notably in the Constitution of 1868 (SEITAISHO), but before long the regime reverted to a more authoritarian structure dominated by the Grand Council of State (DAJŌKAN). Thereafter reform and innovation proceeded from the initiative of key Restoration leaders from Satsuma, Chōshū, Tosa, and Saga, younger *samurai* who gradually replaced the high-ranking lords and nobles who had initially filled imperial offices.

In 1869 four major *daimyō* were persuaded to relinquish their domain registers to the court (*hanseki hōkan*) and to urge that henceforth the conduct of all state affairs should repose in the imperial government. Other daimyō followed suit. All were appointed governors of their former domains by the court, and two years later the court dismissed its daimyō governors and consolidated their domains into more rationally structured prefectures.

For 18 months from 1871 to 1873, a large part of the Meiji leadership toured America and Europe as part of the IWAKURA MISSION, in fulfillment of the regime's pledge to seek wisdom throughout the world. Exposure to the West changed the priorities of many, resulting in divisions among the leadership later. The government had already combined former daimyō and court nobles into a new aristocratic elite called the *kazoku*, while also dividing samurai into gentry (SHIZOKU) and soldiers (*sotsu*) and improving the status of commoners (HEIMIN). Further reform merged *sotsu* into *shizoku* and abolished the outcaste categories of HININ and *eta* (see BURAKUMIN) by merging them with commoners. In the mission's absence, Tōkyō implemented other planned changes involving release from feudal restrictions and opportunity for commoners to participate in the new society.

Abolishing feudal domains and feudal dues necessitated a new system of taxation. After land surveys in 1873, average productivity was capitalized to produce an estimated market value of land, and the new national land tax was set at 3 percent of this assessment. The sweeping changes of the LAND TAX REFORM OF 1873–1881, often poorly understood and brusquely implemented, aroused resistance in the countryside.

The central government now had to shoulder full responsibility for education and defense, matters previously left to the individual domains. The EDUCATION ORDER OF 1872 set as its goal universal literacy, dividing the country into higher-school districts with supporting networks of middle and lower schools, all reflecting Western influence.

Samurai no longer provided an acceptable base for military strength: the social base that supported them was changing, their attachments were too often local rather than national, and their adherence to a complex system of social gradations ill-suited them for the large-scale formations of modern warfare. Observation of Western armies and experience with commoner militias (KIHEITAI) during the Restoration convinced the government of the importance of a mass army. In 1872, the government announced a system of military conscription devised by YAMAGATA ARITOMO, a Chōshū loyalist who had visited Europe earlier. The CONSCRIPTION ORDINANCE OF 1873 called for three years of active service and four years in the reserves but provided for liberal exceptions.

Deprived of its reason for being, the samurai class was phased out. Most domains had already reduced samurai stipends considerably, some to as little as one-tenth of their former amount, yet stipend payments were still viewed as a drain on the nation's resources. After the Iwakura mission's return in 1873, the government decided to begin taxing samurai stipends and ultimately to eliminate them (see CHITSUROKU SHOBUN). A progressive scale of taxation was announced; commutation for lump-sum payments was offered later. Commutation payments were made to 310,000 family heads, but inflation seriously eroded their value.

Samurai from the Restoration domains, where expectations had been highest, were bitterly disappointed. Unhappy with modernization and the government's policy toward Korea, samurai staged a series of revolts across the country from 1874 to 1876 (see SAGA REBELLION; JIMPŪREN REBELLION; AKIZUKI REBELLION OF 1876; HAGI REBELLION). The hardest test for the new government, however, came with the SATSUMA REBELLION of 1877, led by the widely admired SAIGŌ TAKAMORI.

Victory over Satsuma, though it strained governmental capacities to the utmost, firmly established the Meiji regime. But revolt, assassination, and premature death had cost it some of its early leaders, men like Saigō, ŌKUBO TOSHIMICHI, and KIDO TAKAYOSHI. Henceforth, the Meiji leadership would come from such younger Chōshū men as ITŌ HIROBUMI and Yamagata Aritomo, the Satsuma finance expert MATSUKATA MASAYOSHI, and the court nobles IWAKURA TOMOMI and SAIONJI KIMMOCHI. Though many positions were open to outsiders from other domains and even to Tokugawa veterans, the senior statesmen (GENRŌ) came from Satsuma and Chōshū.

Faced with runaway inflation incurred by printing money to cover samurai pensions, to assume debts of the old domains, and to finance military campaigns against rebels, the new government was still in a precarious position. A campaign of retrenchment began under the direction of Matsukata Masayoshi, who devoted more than 16 years of his career to Meiji finances. A new land tax and the campaign of industrialization (SHOKUSAN KŌGYŌ), management of the currency, establishment of the BANK OF JAPAN, and adherence to the gold standard were all carried out under his direction. To help put an end to inflation, Matsukata abandoned some of the government's pilot industrial projects, selling those not of strategic importance to private bidders (see KAN'EI JIGYŌ HARAISAGE). Close to government leaders and sharing their goals, these men emerged as leaders of the future ZAIBATSU industrial and financial conglomerates.

In 1884 Matsukata sponsored a study on manufactures (KŌGYŌ IKEN) that set forth a plan for increasing Japan's exports and production by intensified effort in selected markets and commodities. The MATSUKATA FISCAL POLICY, particularly of deflation, proved hard on the agrarian sector, which saw crop and land values decline in a depression that often led to forced sales and tenancies. This caused a quickening pace of protest, which contributed to the radicalization of political dissent and, in turn, to the intensification of political repression.

During the Satsuma Rebellion and the later Takahashi Insurrection of 1878, the new conscript army had shown signs of disaffection. Every effort was now bent on making the military a loyal and dependable instrument of the government's will by prohibiting military men from political participation and establishing military police to

The Westernization of Daily Life

The leaders of the new central government formed under Emperor Meiji in 1868 believed that only by imitating Western models could Japan achieve the prosperity and military strength needed to stand up to the West. First they reorganized the government bureaucracy, the military, and the educational system to create the superstructure of a unified nation-state. The leaders of this Meiji Enlightenment then turned to promoting much of the paraphernalia of Western life, urging the citizenry to adopt everything from railroads and the telegraph to Western-style haircuts, umbrellas, clothes, architecture, and food. Civilization and Enlightenment—*bummei kaika*, their slogan for this program of imposed Westernization—was largely confined to major cities.

An arc lamp with the power of 2,000 candles was lit in Tōkyō's Ginza district on 1 November 1882. For Tōkyō's citizens, the lamp potently symbolized Western scientific progress. Detail from an 1883 woodblock print.

Upper-class women sew Western clothing for themselves. Few Japanese women wore such garments before 1883, when grand balls at Japan's first Western-style social club, the Rokumeikan, fostered their popularity. Detail from an 1887 woodblock print.

Steamboats and locomotives were promoted by Meiji leaders. This boat moved people and goods on Tōkyō rivers. Detail from a woodblock print, ca 1877.

The postal system instituted by the Meiji government in 1871 aroused curiosity with its mailboxes and uniformed mailmen. The painting from which this detail was taken dates from the 1880s.

Imported goods were exhibited at the Yokohama emporium of the British firm Jardine, Matheson & Co. Detail from an 1871 woodblock print.

The introduction of Western music was encouraged by the government. Audiences came mostly from the upper class. Detail from an 1889 woodblock print.

Meiji period The commencement of the Meiji regime was symbolized by the entry of Emperor Meiji into Tōkyō (formerly Edo) on 26 November 1868, as depicted in this set of woodblock prints produced shortly after the event. With the emperor's move, the city replaced Kyōto as the national capital.

monitor political activity. But Yamagata Aritomo also introduced measures that separated the military command function (TŌSUIKEN) from routine administration, thereby strengthening the military's independent access to the throne. His protégé KATSURA TARŌ mapped out the General Staff system based on observations of the German military.

Samurai virtues of loyalty and unquestioning obedience were stressed in a campaign culminating in the IMPERIAL RESCRIPT TO SOLDIERS AND SAILORS, which was presented by the emperor in 1882. In 1900 the army minister was required to be a general and the navy minister an admiral on the active list (see GUMBU DAIJIN GEN'EKI BUKAN SEI). Even while civilian control of the military was thus being undermined, military men, as loyal and presumably nonpartisan servants, were considered eligible for nonmilitary office. Yamagata served as home minister from 1888 to 1890, overseeing the reorganization of LOCAL GOVERNMENT under central control along German lines. To mobilize the population in the national interest, Yamagata helped develop a system of reserve units (the IMPERIAL MILITARY RESERVISTS' ASSOCIATION) that attempted to integrate former soldiers, rural elites, and rural governance into a single patriotic network.

Convinced of the importance of formal constitutional structures in modern Western countries, the government in 1875 established the GENRŌIN as an experimental deliberative body. But when its recommendations seemed likely to lead to a parliament with excessive powers, the regime turned to its principal leaders for alternatives. In 1881, in response to a political crisis, the emperor made a public promise of a constitution to be completed within eight years.

The 1889 CONSTITUTION OF THE EMPIRE OF JAPAN (or Meiji Constitution) was largely the work of Itō Hirobumi, a Chōshū man who had studied abroad and accompanied the Iwakura mission. For research, Itō returned to Europe, where he was strongly influenced by German constitutional theorists, such as Rudolf GNEIST and Albert MOSSE, who argued that the parliament's powers should be limited; that the electorate should be restricted to the wealthier, therefore more responsible, sectors of society; and that the monarch should be given broad powers to ensure continuity and stability. Itō agreed. He saw the imperial house as the only possible fulcrum for a new society, believing nothing else could play the moderating and integrative role filled by religion in the West.

Itō completed his draft in 1888. Four years earlier, the government had created a new PEERAGE whose members would form an upper house that would balance the expected radicalism of the lower house. The peerage comprised former court nobles, daimyō, and government leaders; it was augmented by life peerages granted to meritorious citizens and leading taxpayers. Thus the old elite, the new plutocracy, and the new meritocracy were enlisted in support of the new order. To review and guard the constitution, a PRIVY COUNCIL was set up.

Itō and his associates regarded their countrymen as backward and ill prepared for the exercise of political rights. They also shared the conviction that radical currents in Japan must be quickly checked by a carefully weighted charter, lest they lead to civil war, a view given substance by the burgeoning FREEDOM AND PEOPLE'S RIGHTS MOVEMENT. Back in 1874, when the government made an unpopular decision against a punitive attack on Korea, many Tosa and Saga leaders had withdrawn from the Meiji regime to issue a call for an elective assembly. The government's decisions, they argued, were arbitrary and capricious: national strength required greater popular participation. Leaders of the RISSHISHA, a Tosa samurai organization, were instrumental in forming the more broadly based AIKOKUSHA, which in 1881 became the JIYŪTŌ, Japan's first national political party. The next year the RIKKEN KAISHINTŌ, a similar political organization, was founded.

Government leaders saw these groups as self-willed and irresponsible, but they could not ignore their rising popularity. The early 1880s saw a surge of interest in politics, with hundreds of discussion groups springing up across the country. Many of these prepared private draft constitutions, not a few of which were considerably more liberal than the draft produced by the government. In the countryside, agitation for political rights coincided with economic distress created by the government's policy of deflation.

In the mid-1880s, there were several unsuccessful but alarming rural outbreaks (see CHICHIBU INCIDENT; IIDA INCIDENT; KABASAN INCIDENT). By the middle of the decade, with parties temporarily disbanded, the government further restrained political activity with laws regulating the press and freedom of assembly. It also hoped that the new constitution would co-opt the dissidents permanently by granting them limited participation in government through membership in the lower house of the new IMPERIAL DIET.

The Meiji Constitution was finally promulgated in 1889 as a gift from the sovereign. The constitution invested the emperor with full sovereignty, declaring him "sacred and inviolable": he commanded the armed forces, made peace and declared war, and dissolved the lower house to call elections. Effective power lay with the executive, but executive authority was vaguely defined lest it seem to interfere with the imperial prerogative. Since the armed forces had direct and independent access to the throne, the prime minister was first among equals rather than a true head of government.

Yet the constitution marked a genuine step toward popular participation. It recognized private property as inviolate and made provision for a large number of basic rights, all circumscribed "within the limits of the law." The lower house of the Diet, elected by the approximately half-million voters who met tax qualifications, could initiate legislation, though in practice most legislation was prepared by the bureaucracy. Diet approval, however, was required to pass the budget. Should approval be denied, the previous year's budget could be used, but since the government's needs grew constantly, the Diet's budgetary control was real.

The emperor's power of appointment made the Imperial Household Ministry (see IMPERIAL HOUSEHOLD AGENCY) and lord keeper of the privy seal (see NAIDAIJIN) important bastions of power. The emperor himself reigned rather than ruled. The traditional Japanese method of indirect decision making by groups working in the emperor's name had supplanted German recommendations for an active ruler.

Although a cabinet had replaced the Dajōkan in 1885, the Yamagata cabinet, which took power after elections in 1890, was the first to experience the realities of constitutional government. From the start the lower house, dominated by the reorganized political parties, proved troublesome, taking offense at the high-handed tone of government statements and refusing to approve the government's budget. The highly collegial Meiji leadership saw itself as an embattled elite besieged by office-hungry malcontents. Yet the government was determined to make these new institutions work, for national pride, foreign approval, and political stability all depended upon their successful implementation. The first cabinets used cajolery, bribery, coercion, and imperial rescripts to try to bring the lower house into line.

From the morass of domestic politics, Meiji Japan was suddenly called to the higher ground of national unity through war with China. Although the TIANJIN (TIENTSIN) CONVENTION of 1885 supposedly governed Japanese and Chinese involvement in Korea, the two countries came to blows over Korean requests to China for help against rebels. The Japanese seized the Korean king and forced him to "request" Japan's assistance, allowing them to portray the resulting SINO-JAPANESE WAR OF 1894–1895 as an altruistic action against a "backward" China on behalf of a Korea in need of "modernization."

Japan's armies were uniformly victorious, destroying Chinese military capability in Korea and seizing the Liaodong (Liaotung) Peninsula in southern Manchuria. At the peace conference in Shimonoseki, Japan demanded the island of Taiwan, a large indemnity of 200 million taels, and the Liaodong Peninsula. But the TRIPARTITE INTERVENTION by Germany, France, and Russia forced retrocession of Liaodong in return for an additional 30 million taels in indemnification. By the Treaty of SHIMONOSEKI Japan also became heir to all privileges extracted by the West from China and gained certain additional concessions, such as the right to manufacture in treaty ports.

In yielding to the Tripartite Intervention, the Meiji government persuaded many Japanese that their country was still unequal to the West and that greater national strength was essential. This growing unanimity allowed Meiji leaders to enlist prominent party politicians in their cabinets to forge more viable parliamentary tactics. In 1898 two party leaders were even invited to form their own cabinet during a short-lived union of their parties (see ŌKUMA CABINET). When this failed, Itō Hirobumi formed his own political party, the RIKKEN SEIYŪKAI, having come to the realization that parties could no longer be excluded from the executive process. Itō's oligarchic colleagues deplored his "surrender" to political self-interest and removed him from the field by having him appointed head of the Privy Council, an imperial post theoretically above politics.

The Russo-Japanese War and the Rise to Great Power Status—Japan had chafed under the restrictions imposed by the UNEQUAL TREATIES since the 1850s. The Aoki-Kimberly treaty of 1894 with Great Britain provided for an end to extraterritoriality and the most-favored-nation clause by 1899 and for Japan's right to set its own tariffs by 1911. Similar treaties with other powers soon followed. However, the acquisition of Taiwan and the assumption of privileges in China following the Sino-Japanese War gave Japan only limited membership in the circle of Western imperialists.

The years following the Sino-Japanese War contained further reminders of Japan's second-class status. During the period of European concession grabbing in China at the end of the century, Russia appropriated the Liaodong Peninsula it had forced Japan to relinquish, while France and Germany secured ports in the south and in Shandong (Shantung), respectively. During the BOXER REBELLION of 1900, Japanese troops took part in the allied rescue of Beijing (Peking), while Russia utilized the conflict to occupy Manchuria and respond to Korean pleas for protection. With the Trans-Siberian Railway nearing completion, permanent Russian control of southern Manchuria and northern Korea seemed likely.

Britain's search for an ally in the Far East coincided with Japan's need to offset Russian power. The ANGLO-JAPANESE ALLIANCE of 1902 gave Japan the protection of the British fleet. Prime Minister Katsura Tarō's government now entered on a course of hard bargaining and eventual collision with the Russians. Early in 1904, the Japanese fleet launched an attack on the Russian Pacific squadron at PORT ARTHUR. The ensuing RUSSO-JAPANESE WAR proved immensely costly to Japan in men and money, but Japan's proximity to the fronts and indecisiveness among the Russian command brought victories at Port Arthur and in the Battle of MUKDEN, culminating in the destruction of the Russian Baltic fleet in the Battle of TSUSHIMA in 1905.

At the 1905 peace conference in PORTSMOUTH, Japan gained recognition of its paramount interests in Korea, took back the southern Manchurian leases and rights it had been denied 10 years earlier, and acquired the southern half of Sakhalin (Karafuto). The treaty, however, still disappointed the Japanese people, for they had expected more, in particular a large indemnity.

The last decade of the Meiji period was dominated by Japan's efforts to assume the role of a major imperialist power. Korea, already in Japan's orbit, was formally annexed in 1910 after a Korean patriot assassinated Itō Hirobumi (see KOREA, ANNEXATION OF). The FRANCO-JAPANESE AGREEMENT OF 1907, the RUSSO-JAPANESE AGREEMENTS OF 1907–1916, and the TAKAHIRA-ROOT AGREEMENT with the United States in 1908 brought implied or explicit recognition of Japan's sphere of hegemony in Northeast Asia. Domestic politics saw the once-troublesome political party movement drawn into the establishment, with the Seiyūkai providing parliamentary support in return for patronage.

Japan's economy was growing rapidly. By 1900 agriculture provided less than half the national product as the share of manufacturing, especially textiles, increased steadily. Industrialization concentrated labor in the cities, bringing fears of urban unrest. Worried about inroads by Western liberalism and radicalism, Meiji leaders focused on upholding Japan's traditional institutions. Emperor Meiji, now associated with success in war and always the symbol of modernization, was raised to new heights of reverence. Textbooks in the compulsory public school course in ethics (SHŪSHIN) increasingly emphasized national and military heroes as models. The family system, formally established by an 1898 supplement to the CIVIL CODE, took the samurai family as the norm for the entire nation. The commonwealth was now described as a "family state" in which political and familial loyalties reinforced rather than competed with each other.

The Home Ministry undertook to place the native cult of Shintō at the service of the government by establishing STATE SHINTŌ shrines within administrative units. Fears of subversion strengthened police surveillance and resulted in the HIGH TREASON INCIDENT OF 1910, in which an anarchist group accused of plotting against the emperor's life was arrested and executed.

The Meiji period thus left succeeding generations of Japanese with an ambiguous heritage. By the time of the emperor's death (of natural causes) in 1912, Japan stood as a model of rapid and largely successful modernization. In less than half a century it had developed from an isolated, semifeudal society into a modern state that had secured for itself a prominent place in the world community. At the same time, the rapidity of this change had left a number of difficult social problems unresolved and a tendency toward authoritarian solutions that threatened its fledgling constitutional order. Historians' interpretations of the Meiji period vary according to their assessment of the conflicting elements of the Meiji legacy; they are unanimous, however, in seeing in it the foundations of Japan's modern experience.

☞ 949

Meiji Restoration   明治維新

(Meiji Ishin). Narrowly defined, the coup d'état of 3 January 1868 in which antishogunate forces, led by the southern domains of Satsuma (now Kagoshima Prefecture) and Chōshū (now Yamaguchi Prefecture), seized the Imperial Palace in Kyōto and announced the reversion of political power from the TOKUGAWA SHOGUNATE to the emperor (see ŌSEI FUKKO). More broadly, the series of political, social, and economic changes in the latter part of the 19th century that resulted in dismemberment of the BAKUHAN SYSTEM of

shogunate and domains and Japan's rapid development into a unified modern state. The era name (NENGŌ) Meiji was chosen to indicate that the young emperor Mutsuhito (see MEIJI, EMPEROR) would institute "enlightened rule." Later the term "restoration" came into use to signify a return to direct imperial rule after eight centuries of warrior control.

Background—The Tempō era (1830–44) manifested the first clear signs of the domestic and foreign crises that led to collapse of the Tokugawa shogunate and birth of the Meiji state. The Tempō years were marked by economic dislocation and deepening fiscal problems for shogunate and domains alike. The mid-1830s brought the TEMPŌ FAMINE and increases in the frequency and magnitude of peasant rebellions (see HYAKUSHŌ IKKI), while an urban insurrection under ŌSHIO HEIHACHIRŌ laid waste to large parts of Ōsaka. Spurred by economic and social disturbances, shogunal and domainal governments embarked on the TEMPŌ REFORMS, but these met with only indifferent success.

Domestic unease was compounded by anxiety over the growing Western presence in the Far East. Russian and British efforts to end Japan's policy of NATIONAL SECLUSION had as yet achieved little, but news of China's defeat by Great Britain in the Opium War (1839–42) gave chilling confirmation of the fears of Japan's ruling elite about Western power and intentions. Concern over the Western threat was accompanied by a burgeoning interest in WESTERN LEARNING. The issue of national identity also received renewed attention with the rapid spread of the nativist teachings of KOKUGAKU (National Learning). In the Mito domain (now part of Ibaraki Prefecture), scholars blended Kokugaku nationalism with Confucianism to produce what eventually became a dominant ideology of the Restoration (see MITO SCHOOL).

The Opening of Japan and Its Consequences—It was the American flotilla under Commodore Matthew C. PERRY that finally brought about the OPENING OF JAPAN, setting off a chain of events that culminated in the Meiji Restoration. In July 1853 Perry presented his country's demand for a treaty along with a promise to return the following spring. Hoping to build a consensus and support, the shogunate circulated copies of the American letter among the *daimyō*. Their divergent responses made it clear that no stance—short of successful resistance—had much backing. Realizing that forcible resistance was impossible, the shogunate signed the KANAGAWA TREATY with the United States in March 1854.

In 1856, American diplomat Townsend HARRIS arrived in Japan to negotiate a more extensive treaty providing for trade relations, the opening of additional ports, extraterritoriality, and fixed custom rates. Though failing to secure Emperor KŌMEI's approval, the shogunate signed the HARRIS TREATY in 1858. Similar unequal treaties with other Western powers quickly followed (see ANSEI COMMERCIAL TREATIES).

The opening of Japan and the way in which it was handled seriously weakened the shogunate's position. Forced to take unpopular steps in bowing to Western demands, the shogunate had compounded its problems by seeking support from both the domains and the imperial court. Not only did the shogunate fail to build a consensus, it

Meiji Shrine An aerial view of the shrine precincts, which cover approximately 700,000 square meters and are planted with trees from all regions of Japan.

silence the Chōshū batteries. As a policy, *jōi* (Expel the Barbarians) had failed; as an incendiary slogan and long-range goal, it remained potent when yoked to *sonnō* Revere the Emperor), and ultimately subordinated to *tōbaku* (Overthrow the Shogunate).

Regional Reform — With the failure of exclusion and *kōbu gattai*, domains and shogunate alike directed their energy to regional programs combining intensified political control with military preparations. *Jōi* was hereafter translated into increasing the nation's wealth and military power (FUKOKU KYŌHEI) so that it might achieve equality with the West.

Within Chōshū, isolated now from the other domains and a haven for loyalist refugees, zealotry grew. In the HAMAGURI GOMON INCIDENT of 1864, Chōshū forces fought their way almost to the palace gates in Kyōto, only to be driven back with heavy losses. High on the staff of shogunal forces sent to punish the rebel domain in the CHŌSHŪ EXPEDITIONS, Satsuma's SAIGŌ TAKAMORI instead negotiated a settlement, fearing the destruction of Chōshū might permit a resurgence of shogunal power.

After Chōshū's agreement to its terms, the first expedition was declared a success and disbanded. Within Chōshū, however, irregular militia units (KIHEITAI) of lower-rank samurai and village leaders refused to comply, and by March 1865 important loyalists had been restored to domain office. Before a second punitive expedition could be undertaken, the domain began extensive military preparations, purchasing Western rifles and steamships, integrating irregular militia with the domain's samurai units, and drilling its forces incessantly.

Satsuma, unwilling to see total victory go to either the shogunate or a rival domain like Chōshū, took similar steps. Satsuma also began to improve relations with the more reasonable wing of the loyalist movement. With Tosa loyalists SAKAMOTO RYŌMA and NAKAOKA SHINTARŌ acting as middlemen, Saigō (acting for Satsuma) and KIDO TAKAYOSHI (acting for Chōshū) sealed the SATSUMA-CHŌSHŪ ALLIANCE in March 1866. Now the shogunate could no longer count on Satsuma's help in settling scores with recalcitrant Chōshū.

Tosa, lacking the historical antipathy to Tokugawa rule that fired Chōshū and Satsuma, was eager to prevent a full military confrontation from which it could only emerge in second place. It turned to expanding domainal income and military strength: a trading company was set up to market Tosa products in Nagasaki and Ōsaka, foreign ships and guns were bought, and military reforms brought Western-style troop formations and equipment. Tosa also reinstated exiled vassals, like Sakamoto Ryōma, who were becoming prominent in national politics.

When the shogunate again tried unsuccessfully to restore *sankin kōtai*, it became clear that Edo was no longer a national hegemon. All the powerful domains now had establishments at Kyōto as well as Edo; the shogunate could not control their channels of communication, much less impose its will upon them. By 1865, even foreign representatives gathered near Ōsaka to be closer to the court.

In 1866, better-trained and -motivated Chōshū troops defeated Tokugawa-led forces undertaking a second punitive expedition. The death of the shōgun TOKUGAWA

ended up hardening divisions and opening the political decision-making process to intervention by the daimyō and the court, two forces long held in check by the Tokugawa house but now beginning to assert their autonomy.

With the opening of Japan's ports in 1859, an influx of foreigners provoked Japanese xenophobes, while foreign trade raised the price of staples and threatened the security of the nation's currency. A wave of antiforeign sentiment (exemplified by the slogan SONNŌ JŌI or Revere the Emperor and Expel the Barbarians) swept the country. At this critical point, the shōgun Tokugawa Iesada (1824–58) died childless, creating a succession dispute that further polarized the country and made the Tokugawa regime look weak and hesitant.

Repression and Backlash — In the summer of 1858, the shogunate appointed II NAOSUKE, hereditary vassal (FUDAI) of Hikone (now part of Shiga Prefecture), as great elder (*tairō*). To reverse the flagging fortunes of the regime, Ii supervised approval of the treaties, helped resolve the succession dispute, and instituted a massive crackdown, the ANSEI PURGE, on the opposition. Several powerful daimyō were put under house arrest or ordered into retirement, court nobles unsympathetic to the Tokugawa were forced out of office, and lower-ranking dissidents from a number of domains were dismissed from their duties, exiled, or executed.

At first, Ii's policy of repression seemed effective, but ultimately it fanned the discontent stirred by treaty and succession issues. It also helped politicize lower-ranking *samurai* at the fringes of the ruling class. These were frustrated, volatile men. Anticipating a confrontation with the West and having little stake in the existing structure of inherited rank and privilege, they figured significantly in the unrest of the closing days of Tokugawa rule. Known as *shishi* (men of high purpose), these activists formed groups that acted alone or under the protection of dissident domains and court nobles and engaged in violence against shogunal officials and even foreigners. Ironically, one of their

first major victims was Ii Naosuke himself, who was cut down in front of Edo Castle in March 1860 by a band of *shishi* from Mito and Satsuma.

Proposals for "The Union of Court and Shogunate" — Ii's assassination opened a new stage in relations among the shogunate, the great domains, and the imperial court. Between 1861 and 1864, the southwestern domains of Chōshū, Satsuma, and Tosa (now Kōchi Prefecture) vied in launching reform proposals under the guise of mediating strained relations between Kyōto and Edo. Known collectively as the MOVEMENT FOR UNION OF COURT AND SHOGUNATE (*kōbu gattai*), the proposals aimed at giving the major daimyō a greater voice in national affairs. Marred by rising violence and competitiveness, the *kōbu gattai* movement failed, but not before wringing significant concessions from the shogunate, including the suspension of mandatory daimyō residence in Edo (SANKIN KŌTAI), the establishment of new posts that added a "great daimyō" element to the shogunal bureaucratic machinery, and relaxation of restrictions on ship and weapons purchases by domains.

As the shogunate weakened, the imperial court attempted to force its subordination. Late in 1862 the court sent a mission to Edo instructing the shōgun to revoke all treaties with the West and expel the foreigners. Knowing that expulsion was impossible, but facing domain extremists who favored it, the shogunate played for time. Ironically, the rising antiforeign rhetoric drove shogunal leaders to adopt a pose of seeking to revoke concessions to the West even while the shogunate was utilizing them to purchase modern arms.

A shogunal promise of expulsion, finally issued in 1863, drew quick reaction. Chōshū closed the Shimonoseki Strait and ordered its shore batteries to fire on foreign shipping. The British, aroused over the murder of an Englishman by Satsuma samurai (see RICHARDSON AFFAIR), bombarded and burned much of the town of Kagoshima. In the COUP D'ETAT OF 30 SEPTEMBER 1863, shogunal and Satsuma troops expelled Chōshū forces from Kyōto to relieve the court of antiforeign intimidation. One year later, Western forces undertook the SHIMONOSEKI BOMBARDMENT to

IEMOCHI provided a face-saving pretext for halting the battle. TOKUGAWA YOSHINOBU, who had earlier been unsuccessfully nominated for the post by reform-minded daimyō, now became shōgun, and reformist bureaucrats, many with direct experience of the West, replaced traditionalists. Using French assistance to establish the YOKOSUKA SHIPYARDS, ordering modern warships from America and Europe, and sending students and diplomatic missions abroad, the shogunate tried to strengthen itself to the point where it could once again compete effectively for national leadership.

Restoration —— Yoshinobu's reforms and his acceptability to foreigners alarmed leaders in Satsuma and Chōshū, who feared overthrow of the shogunate might become impossible. Satsuma attempted to link opening of Hyōgo (now Kōbe) as a treaty port to a shogunal pardon of Chōshū. Yoshinobu managed to force the opening of Hyōgo on lesser terms, but at the cost of convincing his rivals that strong steps would be required to unhorse him.

Tosa put forth a moderate proposal, devised by Sakamoto Ryōma, to the effect that Yoshinobu should be persuaded to resign as shōgun and recognize the authority of the emperor. The proposal also called for establishing a bicameral legislature, presumably filled with daimyō and vassals, opening the bureaucracy to "men of talent" and setting up an imperial army and navy. The three major domains laid plans to combine forces should Yoshinobu refuse.

In late 1867, about one month after the proposal had been put to him, the shōgun accepted. Satsuma remained doubtful that a voluntary resignation meant anything more than a change of titles that would leave the shōgun still powerful and able to manipulate the court. On 3 January 1868, Satsuma loyalists surrounded the Kyōto palace, securing the emperor and an imperial edict abolishing all existing offices in favor of an emergency council of imperial princes. At its first meeting, the council decided the former shōgun should surrender his lands as well as his offices. Instead, Yoshinobu moved troops toward Kyōto.

The ensuing BOSHIN CIVIL WAR ended with defeat of the last Tokugawa naval units in June 1869. In the end, the Tokugawa had remarkably few supporters. The vast majority of domains, uncertain which way to turn, chose not to act, leaving the field clear for the determined assaults of the new "Imperial Army"—created out of combined Satsuma, Chōshū, and Tosa forces—against a demoralized and disunited resistance. In 1868, even before civil war ended, the reign name was changed to Meiji and the emperor declared "restored."

The new imperial government, formed out of a coalition of samurai from the victorious domains and sympathetic members of the court nobility, proceeded cautiously to reunify the country and establish a centralized political administration. Edo, renamed Tōkyō, became the national capital, and confiscated Tokugawa lands served as the nucleus from which imperial control was extended nationwide. By 1871 the domains were rationalized in size and converted to prefectures, and the daimyō were replaced by officials appointed by the central government. With this, the system of shogunate and domains that had served as the basis for more than 250 years of Tokugawa rule was completely eliminated, clearing the path for the extensive program of reform and mod-ernization that characterized the early MEIJI PERIOD.

Meiji Seika Kaisha, Ltd   明治製菓[株]

(Meiji Seika). Confectioner principally producing food and pharmaceutical products. It is the largest company in the confectionery industry in Japan. It was incorporated in 1916 for the domestic production and export of Western-style confections. After World War II, production was temporarily curtailed because of damaged equipment and facilities and a lack of raw materials. However, mass production was resumed in 1952, and since the 1960s the firm has expanded production through emphasis on chocolate and cookies. It also started production and sales of such products as snack foods, instant foods, and health foods. In 1946 it succeeded in producing penicillin. Since then it has solidified its pharmaceutical division with the commercial production of numerous antibiotics, including streptomycin and kanamycin. It has joint-venture manufacturing companies in South Korea, Singapore, Indonesia, Thailand, and Brazil, as well as a sales company in the United States. Sales for the fiscal year ending March 1991 totaled ¥221.5 billion (US $1.6 billion), of which sales of confections and food products constituted 62 percent and pharmaceuticals 38 percent. In the same year the firm was capitalized at ¥28.3 billion (US $206.3 million). Headquarters are in Tōkyō.

Meiji Shrine   明治神宮

(Meiji Jingū). A Shintō shrine at Yoyogi, Shibuya Ward, Tōkyō; dedicated to the spirits of Emperor MEIJI (1852–1912) and his consort, Empress Shōken (1850–1914). In recognition of the great contribution made by Emperor Meiji to the modernization of Japan, the Imperial Diet passed a resolution in 1913 to build a shrine in his honor. Virtually destroyed in the air raid of 14 April 1945, the shrine was reconstructed by 1958 at a cost of ¥600 million (US $1.67 million) raised through a nationwide subscription. The annual festival is held on 3 November, Emperor Meiji's birthday, which is a national holiday (Culture Day).

Meiji University   明治大学

(Meiji Daigaku). A private, coeducational university whose main campus is located in Chiyoda Ward, Tōkyō. Its predecessor was the Meiji Hōritsu Gakkō (Meiji Law School) founded in 1881. The school was renamed Meiji University in 1903. In 1929 the women's division for the study of law and commerce was opened, the first school in Japan to offer higher education to women in these fields. The university has maintained a liberal atmosphere based on its motto "rights and freedom." It maintains faculties of law, commerce, politics and economics, letters, business management, agriculture, and engineering. It is noted for its museum of archaeology and its institutes of sciences and technology, social sciences, and cultural sciences. Enrollment was 32,909 in 1989.

Meireki Fire   明暦の大火

(Meireki no Taika). Fire in March 1657 (Meireki 3.1). It broke out at the temple Hommyōji in the Hongō section of Edo (now Tōkyō) and raged for two days, sweeping through most of the city and resulting in more than 100,000 deaths. The central tower of EDO CASTLE burned, as did daimyō residences, townsmen's houses, temples, and bridges. The Tokugawa shogunate established first-aid stations and distributed food and money to the homeless. When the city was rebuilt, houses were standardized and fire lanes were installed at various intersections. The expenses incurred contributed to the currency debasement carried out by OGIWARA SHIGEHIDE. The fire is also known as the "Furisode (young girl's *kimono*) Fire," for it was thought to have been caused by sparks from a kimono being burned in an exorcism ceremony.

Meiro   迷路

(The Maze). Novel by NOGAMI YAEKO (1885–1985) that spans the years of Japanese militarism from the FEBRUARY 26TH INCIDENT in 1936 to 1944. The author began to publish *Meiro* in 1936 but, due to the repressive climate of the times, soon suspended writing until after the war, finishing the novel in 1956. *Meiro*, a novel of over 1,000 pages written in an unadorned style, features a large and varied cast of characters. Prominent among them is Kanno Shōzō, the son of a wealthy *sake* brewer, dismissed from Tōkyō University for communist sympathies and forced to undergo the renunciation of leftist ideology known as TENKŌ. The novel follows Kanno, drafted into the army, to China, where he is shot in an attempt to desert. Other characters include Tarumi Jūta, a politician, and Masui Reizō, a businessman, both of whom grow wealthy with the war. Nogami conveys some of her sharpest criticism of the militaristic age she depicts through the figure of Ejima Munemichi, an elderly aristocrat and Nō enthusiast, who is perhaps the most skillfully drawn of all the characters. Although the work is not a uniform masterpiece, Nogami succeeded in avoiding the one-dimensionality into which many political novels of the age were prone to lapse.

Meirokusha   明六社

(Meiji 6 Society). Intellectual society proposed by the statesman MORI ARINORI in 1873, the sixth year of the Meiji period (1868–1912) and founded on 1 February 1874 for the purpose of "promoting civilization and enlightenment" (see MEIJI ENLIGHTENMENT). Through its journal, the *Meiroku zasshi*, and the public lectures delivered at its meetings, the society played a leading role in introducing and popularizing Western ideas during the early Meiji period. Its 33 members included some of Japan's most eminent educators, bureaucrats, and thinkers. Mori recruited NISHIMURA SHIGEKI and 8 others to organize a group of intellectuals to promote Western learning and establish models of ethical behavior for the Japanese. Confucian humanists such as NAKAMURA MASANAO, Nishimura, and Sakatani Shiroshi (1822–81) reasoned that Western strength

Meireki Fire This illustration from the 1661 *Musashi abumi*, a woodblock-printed book, depicts the disastrous fire of 1657.

menko

The child in the foreground hurls down his playing piece in an attempt to flip over his opponent's in a bout of this spirited game.

Pre–World War II *menko* depicting baseball players, movie stars, *sumō* wrestlers, *samurai*, and soldiers.

Modern *menko*. Although *sumō* wrestlers, *samurai*, and actors are still common *menko* illustrations, cartoon and comic-book characters are now the most popular.

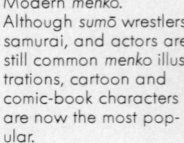

and prosperity resulted from the moral strength of its people and exhorted the Japanese to study this secret of the West's success and tread the same path. Thinkers such as KATŌ HIROYUKI, TSUDA MAMICHI, NISHI AMANE, and KANDA TAKAHIRA emphasized the organic nature of society and held that the West's strength was derived from rationally constructed and operated institutions and societies. The pragmatists, led by FUKUZAWA YUKICHI, felt that by joining the special strengths of the Japanese with successful Western values and institutions they could make their nation the Britain of the East.

Membership—The charter members of the Meirokusha were Mori Arinori, Nishimura Shigeki, Fukuzawa Yukichi, Katō Hiroyuki, MITSUKURI RINSHŌ, Mitsukuri Shūhei (1826–86), Nakamura Masanao, Nishi Amane, Sugi Kōji (1828–1917), and Tsuda Mamichi. Others joined either as regular or corresponding members during the next two years, including MAEJIMA HISOKA, William Elliott GRIFFIS, NAGAYO SENSAI, TANAKA FUJIMARO, TSUDA SEN, and ŌTSUKI FUMIHIKO. Promulgation of the PRESS ORDINANCE OF 1875 and LIBEL LAW OF 1875 led the society to cease publication of its journal; the last issue appeared in November 1875, after which the society's influence declined sharply.

Meiryō kōhan　　　　　明良洪範

(Illustrious Examples). A 40-volume collection of anecdotes about the first five Tokugawa shōguns and their vassals during the period from the 17th century to the beginning of the 18th century; written by Sanada Zōyo, a shogunal retainer. Anecdotes about schol-

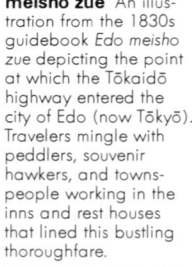

meisho zue An illustration from the 1830s guidebook *Edo meisho zue* depicting the point at which the Tōkaidō highway entered the city of Edo (now Tōkyō). Travelers mingle with peddlers, souvenir hawkers, and townspeople working in the inns and rest houses that lined this bustling thoroughfare.

ars and women and references to social customs of the period are included.

meishi →name cards

meisho zue　　　　　名所図会

Illustrated guidebooks published during the Edo period (1600–1868). The guidebooks were well illustrated and filled with detailed information on the history, legends, and special products of various temples, shrines, and famous places in Japan. Among the most famous guidebooks were the *Miyako meisho zue* (6 vols, 1780), edited by Akizato Ritō (dates unknown) and illustrated by Takehara Shunchōsai (d 1800), and the *Edo meisho zue* (7 vols, 1834–36), completed by three generations of the Saitō family from Chōshū (dates unknown) to his grandson Gesshin (1804–78) and illustrated by Hasegawa Settan (1778–1843). Other books were the *Tōkaidō meisho zue* and the *Kisoji meisho zue*, guidebooks to stops on the major highways. Guidebooks on pilgrimages to temples and shrines included the *Zenkōji meisho zue*, the *Ise sangū meisho zue*, and the *Kompira sankei meisho zue*. Guidebooks on individual provinces were also published.

Meitoku Rebellion　　　　明徳の乱

(Meitoku no Ran). Attempt in 1391–92 by Yamana Ujikiyo (1344–92) and his nephew Yamana Mitsuyuki (d 1395) to overthrow the shōgun ASHIKAGA YOSHIMITSU. Powerful descendants of a cadet branch of the ASHIKAGA FAMILY, Ujikiyo and Mitsuyuki were lords of 11 of the 66 provinces of Japan. Provoked by Yoshimitsu, they marched on Kyōto but were defeated and their lands divided among the triumphant generals. Through his victories in this and the ŌEI REBELLION, Yoshimitsu was able to consolidate shogunal dominance of Japan. A detailed record of the Meitoku Rebellion is contained in *Meitokuki* (ca 1392–93).

Meiwa Incident　　　　　明和事件

(Meiwa Jiken). Incident in 1767 (Meiwa 4) in which two scholars, YAMAGATA DAINI and Fujii Umon (1720–67), were executed by the Tokugawa shogunate for alleged subversive activities. Closely following the HŌREKI INCIDENT, in which court nobles were punished for criticizing the shogunate, this incident was another effort by the shogunate to suppress the growing proimperial (*sonnō*) movement. Yamagata was a teacher of Confu-

cianism and military science in Edo (now Tōkyō) and in 1759 had written *Ryūshi shinron*, in which he criticized the shogunate for usurping the emperor's power. To illustrate a point during a lecture on military tactics at Yamagata's school, Fujii discussed a suppositional attack on EDO CASTLE, the shogunal headquarters. The two men, with some 30 other suspects, were arrested in 1766. Despite the lack of conclusive evidence, Yamagata and Fujii were executed in 1767. The shogunate took advantage of the incident to send TAKENOUCHI SHIKIBU, a noble implicated in the Hōreki Incident, into permanent exile.

Mendenhall, Thomas Corwin
メンデンホール, T. C.

(1841–1924). Distinguished US physicist; contributor to scientific knowledge about electricity, gravity, seismology, and meteorology; popular speaker on science and able education administrator. Noted in Japan, where he served as a government-employed teacher (1878–81), for introducing the professional study of physics.

Recommended to the Japanese government by Edward S. MORSE, Mendenhall taught the first systematic course in physics at Tōkyō University, where he built the first physics laboratory, conducted studies of the earth's mass, began regular meteorological observation (later taken up by the government), and promoted the study of earthquakes. He helped found the Seismological Society of Japan.

menko　　　　　　　　　面子

Children's game originating in the Kamakura period (1185–1333). The game pieces, or *menko*, are made of circular or square pieces of clay, board, lead, or, more recently, paper. To play, one player's *menko* is placed on the ground; the opponent then attempts to flip it over by throwing his or her own *menko* at the first player's piece. During the Edo period (1600–1868) the pieces were decorated with pictures of *sumō* wrestling champions. Today they are often painted with pictures of children's favorite cartoon or comic characters.

meoto-jawan　　　　　　夫婦茶碗

(husband-and-wife cups). Pair of teacups or rice bowls, one large and one small, of the same shape and design. *Meoto-jawan* are regarded as symbolic of the steadfastness of the husband-wife relationship. Couples also use *meoto-bashi* (husband-and-wife chopsticks).

Meranoshō 米良荘

District in west-central Miyazaki Prefecture, Kyūshū, in the Kyūshū Mountains, on the upper reaches of the river Hitotsusegawa. According to legend, there was once a village here of the defeated warriors of the Kikuchi family. Today the district is greatly changed by dams and hydroelectric plants. The special local products are tea, lumber, and *shiitake* mushrooms.

merger, corporate 企業合併

(*kigyō gappei*). The joining together of two or more companies by contract to form one company. Mergers occur for various economic reasons, such as business expansion, rationalization of business operations, avoidance of competition, and market monopolization. There are two types of merger: merger by absorption, in which one company survives, absorbing the other company or companies; and merger by consolidation, in which all the companies involved are dissolved and a new company is established. The great majority of mergers in Japan are mergers by absorption.

Any company organized under Japan's COMMERCIAL CODE, whether a LIMITED PARTNERSHIP COMPANY (*gōshi kaisha*), an UNLIMITED PARTNERSHIP COMPANY (*gōmei kaisha*), a LIMITED LIABILITY COMPANY (*yūgen kaisha*), or a JOINT-STOCK COMPANY (*kabushiki kaisha*), may be a party to a merger. There are various restrictions on mergers, and the ANTIMONOPOLY LAW prohibits the merger of domestic companies if the merger substantially limits competition or constitutes an unfair trade practice.

mergers and acquisitions 企業合併と買収

(M&As; J: *kigyō gappei to baishū*). Most companies today consider mergers with or acquisitions of other firms to be an important part of their corporate strategy. M&A activity by Japanese companies increased dramatically beginning around 1985, and of the 229 M&As initiated by Japanese companies in 1988, 74.0 percent involved foreign companies. Of these, 67.8 percent took place in the United States, 8.5 percent in Australia, 4.0 percent in France, 2.8 percent in Hong Kong, 3.4 percent in the United Kingdom, and 13.5 percent in other countries. In 1989 there were approximately 600 Japanese M&As.

In the past, M&A practices have had a bad image among those supporting Japanese-style management. M&As were viewed solely as hostile takeovers and were not considered ethical management practice. However, in order to deal with such changes in the industrial structure as internationalization and the diversification of operations, steel producers, trading companies, electronics manufacturers, and other companies that are heavily dependent on their overseas operations have embraced M&A activity as legitimate business practice. As in the United States, Japanese M&As are accomplished chiefly through takeover bids or the financing technique called leveraged buyout, in which the assets of the target company serve as security for loans taken out by the acquiring company. Some banks and securities companies have established their own M&A departments and are strengthening their support services for M&A activity. In the late

1980s large-scale Japanese M&As increased, and in 1989 alone Japanese companies transacted many M&As valued at over ¥100 billion (US $724 million), such as the Sony acquisition of Columbia Pictures; the Mitsubishi Estate acquisition of the Rockefeller Group, Inc; and the Daiichi Kangyō Bank acquisition of CIT Group, a subsidiary of Manufacturers Hanover Corp.

meshi 飯

(cooked rice). The word *meshi* (more politely, *gohan*) can also mean a meal in general, which may or may not include rice. Rice is ordinarily served plain and accompanied by side dishes (*okazu*), but it can also be served with various ingredients cooked or mixed in, or as *kayu* (rice gruel). *Onigiri* (see NIGIRIMESHI), small rice balls with another ingredient in the center that are sometimes sprinkled with sesame seeds or wrapped in the dried seaweed called *nori*, are a favorite on picnics and outings. Japanese also pour green tea over a bowl of rice to make CHAZUKE (or *ochazuke*), which is often accompanied by pickled vegetables (*tsukemono*).

metalwork 金工

(*kinkō*). Bronze and iron objects were first introduced into Japan from China during the early Yayoi period (ca 300 BC–ca AD 300; see BRONZE AGE). By about 100 BC native craftsmen used these metals to produce arrowheads, swords, daggers, halberd blades, coins, mirrors, bells, and ornaments. Japan had a plentiful supply of copper. It was usually used in the form of alloys, mainly bronze, which was largely associated with ceremonial uses. Gold and silver were not often used. Iron was used widely, especially for swords and tools. The most common process in making metal objects was casting, but various metalworking techniques, such as forging, embossing, beating, chasing, engraving, damascening, and plating, were employed.

The most remarkable metal objects of the early period are the large bronze bells known as DŌTAKU. With the introduction of Buddhism in the 6th century, gilded bronze images of Buddhist deities became important to religious observances. Outstanding objects of decorative art from the 8th century, found in the SHŌSŌIN repository, include beautiful silver vessels engraved with hunting scenes, BRONZE MIRRORS in the Tang (T'ang) China style, swords, daggers, and metal utensils. During the Heian (794–1185) and Kamakura (1185–1333) periods, swords and armor were the outstanding products of metalworkers. Beginning with the Muromachi period (1333–1568), the iron teakettles used in the TEA CEREMONY played an important role. In the Azuchi-Momoyama (1568–1600) and Edo (1600–1868) periods metal was formed into firearms and clocks under European influence, as well as into ornamental door handles called *hikite*, ornamental metal coverings called *kugikakushi*, and, most significant, swords and sword guards (TSUBA). Ornamental metalwork was widespread during the late Edo and the Meiji (1868–1912) periods, with bronze jars, vases, and sculptural figures enjoying great popularity. Metalwork continues to be an important craft in contemporary Japan.

Meteorological Agency 気象庁

(Kishōchō). Government office established in 1956 as an extraministerial bureau of the Ministry of Transport. Its chief function is the careful charting of the weather, but it

metalwork A gilt-bronze pagoda-shaped Buddhist reliquary resting on a lotus pedestal borne by a tortoise. It is said to contain ashes of the Buddha that were brought to Japan by Ganjin, the temple Tōshōdaiji's founder. Heian period with later additions and repairs. Height 92 cm. Tōshōdaiji, Nara. National Treasure.

also conducts research on such related phenomena as earthquakes, volcanoes, geomagnetism, and ocean currents. This research is aimed at protecting the populace from natural disasters as well as promoting agriculture and other weather-sensitive industries. The agency administers 49 local meteorological observatories as well as the Meteorological Research Institute, the Aerological Observatory, the College of Meteorology, and the Observatory for Magnetic Phenomena.

Meteorological Research Institute 気象研究所

(Kishō Kenkyūjo). An institute engaged in research concerning meteorological, geophysical, and oceanographic phenomena. Established in 1962 in the city of Tsukuba, Ibaraki Prefecture, as a part of the Meteorological Agency. Areas of study include weather forecasting as well as climatic changes, typhoons, earthquakes and volcanoes, ocean waves, atmospherics, and weather satellites. In addition, computer simulations that predict long-range climatic trends based on global models of atmospheric and ocean currents are used in the study of environmental problems. The institute actively participates in the international cooperative research programs of the World Meteorological Organization.

Metropolitan Expressway Public Corporation 首都高速道路公団

(Shuto Kōsoku Dōro Kōdan). Public corporation whose purpose is to construct new automobile toll roads in the TŌKYŌ METROPOLITAN AREA. It was established in 1959, with half of its capital provided by the central government. When the corporation was established, its principal task was the construction of roads in preparation for the 1964

TŌKYŌ OLYMPIC GAMES. In 1990 the corporation had 25 routes extending for a total of 217.4 kilometers (135.1 mi) used by an average of a million automobiles daily. In 1990 the corporation was constructing 12 more routes; with their completion, the total network will be 326.4 kilometers (202.8 mi). See also EXPRESSWAYS.

metsuke 目付

Also known as *yokome*. Inspectors or censors. The title existed from the 15th century, when certain retainers acted as high-level spies for military rulers. The position was regularized under the TOKUGAWA SHOGUNATE (1603–1867). Just as inspectors general (ŌMETSUKE) reported to senior councillors (RŌJŪ) of the *daimyō*, *metsuke* acted as the "eyes and ears" of junior councillors (WAKADOSHIYORI) in supervising the shōgun's direct vassals (HATAMOTO and GOKENIN). *Metsuke* evaluated other shogunate officials and staff as well. They had the unusual privilege of deciding among themselves on any new appointments; all 10 were drawn from the *hatamoto*. In addition, each daimyō domain had its own autonomous system of inspectors for internal control.

Mexico and Japan メキシコと日本

(Mekishiko *to* Nihon). During the late 16th and early 17th centuries, Mexico, together with the Philippines, served as a colonial base from which the Spanish conducted relations with Japan. In 1614, however, following a shogunal edict of expulsion directed at Catholic priests, relations via Mexico ceased, and in 1624 Japan severed relations with Spain. Mexico gained independence from Spain in 1821, but it was not until 1873 that direct contacts with Japan were resumed. In 1888 Mexico signed with Japan the latter's first treaty with a Western nation that was not "unequal," a milestone in the Japanese drive for a revision of the Unequal Treaties. See UNEQUAL TREATIES, REVISION OF.

World War II severed relations between the two countries, but by the late 1950s major Japanese trading companies had established offices in Mexico City. Protectionist policies limited the importation of Japanese goods, but direct Japanese investment began on a large scale in 1960 when Nissan established an automobile assembly plant. The discovery of major petroleum reserves in Mexico in 1978 led to increased Japanese investment, and the amount of Japanese private loans swelled until the debt crisis of 1982, when President Portillo requested a rescheduling of debt payments. Japanese direct investment, however, remained quite active. By the end of 1987 there were 157 Japanese-affiliated companies in Mexico, and the total amount of investment was $1.2 billion. In 1990 Japan's imports from Mexico totaled $1.9 billion, of which crude and partly refined oil accounted for 61.6 percent. Japan's exports stood at $2.3 billion and were mainly machinery. In the late 1980s Japan had about a 5 percent share in Mexico's trade and was its second largest trade partner after the United States.

meyasubako 目安箱

Box for "appeals" (*meyasu*) posted by the shogunate during the Edo period (1600–1868). In carrying out the KYŌHŌ REFORMS, the shōgun TOKUGAWA YOSHIMUNE decided in 1721 to post a suggestion box outside one of the gates of Edo Castle for the use of townspeople and peasants. The locked box was carried to the shōgun, who personally read the contents. It was at the suggestion of a physician that a hospital, the KOISHIKAWA YŌJŌSHO, was established. The city's fire-prevention program was also based on the suggestions of Edo commoners.

mi 箕

A shallow basket shaped like the body of a coal shovel, high in back and flat in front. It is woven of bamboo strips with wisteria vine or strips of cherry bark woven in to give it strength. Formerly used by peasants as a winnowing basket.

miai 見合

The formal meeting, arranged by a NAKŌDO (go-between) of a man and a woman seeking a marriage partner. The *nakōdo* and the parents of the couple also attend the *miai*, which typically takes the form of a drive to a scenic place, dinner at a restaurant, or a theater outing. *Miai* have a strong association with pre–World War II Japanese customs, in which marriage was seen as a link between two families rather than a joining of two individuals.

The *miai* process usually begins when the *nakōdo* informally approaches one party (who has previously asked the *nakōdo*'s help in finding a marriage partner) and proposes a match. A formal written request is then made, accompanied by a photograph and a brief personal history of the prospective bride or groom. If the response is favorable, negotiations can proceed.

After the *nakōdo* has decided on a suitable place or occasion for the *miai*, all parties concerned gather for a chance to observe and assess each other. Although most *miai* are group affairs, the prospective couple are usually given a chance to talk privately at some point in the proceedings. After the *miai* both parties must decide whether or not to continue negotiations. If the man and the woman decide that they would like to see each other again, they usually date for a while. This can lead to engagement and the formal exchange of betrothal gifts (YUINŌ). However, if either party feels that the match is not right, and the *nakōdo* cannot overcome their objections, it is permissible to end negotiations after the *miai*. Many people go through a number of *miai* before finding a suitable partner, although a long history of refusals can make future meetings difficult.

Although the distinctions are not always clear-cut, a marriage initiated in the traditional style through a *miai* is known as a *miai kekkon* ("arranged marriage"); this is in contrast to the increasingly popular *ren'ai kekkon* ("love marriage"), which reflects the modern Western concept of marriage in which two people meet and fall in love without the formal intercession of a go-between. Although the post–World War II CIVIL CODE radically altered marriage laws in Japan, defining marriage as a choice between individuals, there is still considerable emphasis on the family in deciding on a suitable husband or wife, as evidenced by the continued existence of the *miai* system.

Miboro Dam 御母衣ダム

(Miboro Damu). Located on the upper reaches of the river SHŌGAWA, northwestern Gifu Prefecture, central Honshū. Completed in 1961, it was Japan's first rock-filled dam. The dam created Lake Miboro. An electric power plant, located below the dam, has a maximum output of 215,000 kilowatts. Height of embankment: 131 m (430 ft); storage capacity: 329.7 million cu m (11.5 billion cu ft).

Mibu 壬生[町]

Town in south-central Tochigi Prefecture, central Honshū. Agricultural products include *kampyō* (dried gourd shavings); a complex of toy factories was built here in 1965. There are many *kofun* (tomb mounds) in the area. Pop: 39,588.

Mibuchi Tadahiko 三淵忠彦

(1880–1950). First chief justice of the post–World War II Supreme Court. Born in Okayama Prefecture. Graduated from Kyōto University in 1905, he became judge of the Tōkyō District Court in 1907 and of the Great Court of Cassation (Daishin'in) in 1923. He concurrently taught civil law at Keiō University. He resigned from his judgeship in 1925 and worked as legal counsel to the Mitsui Trust and Banking Co. Mibuchi became the first chief justice of the Supreme Court in 1947, when the court was created under the new constitution. He strove to build a firm basis for the court's new role as the guardian of the constitution and of human rights, emphasizing in particular its power of judicial review. His writings include *Mimpō gaisetsu* (1924, Outlines of the Civil Code) and *Seken to ningen* (1950, The Public and the People).

Mibudera 壬生寺

Ranking temple of the RITSU SECT of Buddhism, located in Naka-Gyō Ward, Kyōto. According to temple tradition, Mibudera was established on the initiative of Emperor SHŌMU (r 724–749) by the monk GANJIN. In fact, however, the founder was Kaiken, a monk from the temple MIIDERA, who in 991 erected a chapel dedicated to the bodhisattva Jizō. This subsequently became the nucleus of the temple, which was finally completed in 1005. Mibudera suffered extensive damage from fires over the centuries but was restored after each disaster. Mibudera is known for a type of masked, wordless comic play known as the *Mibu kyōgen*, performed annually between 21 and 29 April.

Mibu no Tadamine 壬生忠岑

(fl ca 910). Poet and courtier, one of four compilers of the first imperial anthology of classical (WAKA) poetry, the KOKINSHŪ (ca 905, Collection from Ancient and Modern Times). One of the so-called Thirty-Six Poetic Geniuses (SANJŪROKKASEN). Some 36 of his poems are included in the *Kokinshū*. His personal collection, *Tadamineshū*, exists in two main versions; one contains 60 poems, and the other, 126. Tadamine is also the author of a very brief but important poetic document dated 945, called by later poets *Wakatei jisshu* (Ten Styles of Japanese Poetry) or *Tadamine juttei* (Tadamine's Ten Styles).

michi 道

(literally, "the Path," "the Way"). Written with a Chinese character (Ch: *dao* or *tao*) that is also pronounced *dō* in many Japanese compound words. A term used to denote the fundamental principle underlying a system of thought or belief, an art, or a skill, it is also used by extension to refer to a system of thought or belief in its entirety or to the entire body of principles and skills that constitute an art. In this latter sense it is used in Japan as part of the name of a number of traditional skills or codes of behavior, as in *chadō* or *sadō* (the Way of tea, i.e., the tea ceremony) and *bushidō* (the Way of the warrior).

In ancient China *dao*, in the sense of an ethical norm for human action, was an important concept in CONFUCIANISM, and in a more mystical sense it gave its name to the philosophy known as Taoism. In Edo-period (1600–1868) Japan the term, pronounced *michi*, became one of the central concepts of the school of Japanese Confucianism known as KOGAKU (Ancient Learning), with a meaning close to the present-day word *shinri* (truth). Such thinkers of the school as ITŌ JINSAI (1627–1705) asserted that *michi* was a road or ethical standard that human beings must follow. For OGYŪ SORAI (1666–1728), another thinker associated with the school, *michi* had a much more concrete and objective significance, referring to the institutions established by the emperors of ancient China.

Michiko, Empress 美智子皇后

(1934– ; Michiko Kōgō). Wife of Emperor AKIHITO. Eldest daughter of SHŌDA HIDESABURŌ, founder of the Nisshin Flour Milling Co, Ltd, and his wife Fumiko (d 1988). She is a graduate of the University of the Sacred Heart in Tōkyō. In April 1959 she married then crown prince Akihito. As the first imperial bride to be selected from outside the circle of the imperial family and the former peerage, her marriage to Crown Prince Akihito was broadly welcomed by the Japanese people as a symbol of the democratization of the imperial house. On 7 January 1989 she became empress upon her husband's ascension to the throne as Emperor Akihito. They have three children: Crown Prince NARUHITO, Prince AKISHINO, and Princess Sayako (b 1969). Empress Michiko maintains a lively interest in literature, arts and crafts, and music and serves as honorary president of the Japan Red Cross Society.

Midagahara 弥陀ヶ原

Highland on the western slope of TATEYAMA, eastern Toyama Prefecture, central Honshū. Said to have been created by an eruption of Tateyama, Midagahara is particularly noted for its alpine flora. Elevation: 1,500–2,000 m (5,000–6,600 ft).

Middle East and Japan 中東と日本

(Chūtō *to* Nihon). Japan's first contact with the Middle East was in the early 20th century, when Japanese scholars first traveled to the area. At that time the modern Japanese economy was in the early stages of development, and the possibilities of trade and economic relations spurred interest in the Middle East. Japan opened its first consulate in the region at Port Said in 1919, followed by others at Alexandria and Cairo, to procure the advantages offered by the Suez Canal route to Europe.

Formal relations between Japan and Middle Eastern countries were suspended during World War II but resumed relatively soon after the war. Japan steadily expanded its trade with the Middle East, and in the 1960s imports from the region reached 20 percent of total Japanese imports, while exports were 10 percent of the total, giving the Middle East a vital role in Japanese trade, next in importance after North America and Asia. Japan's industrial structure was becoming increasingly dependent on imported Middle Eastern oil, and in 1958 the ARABIAN OIL CO, LTD, of Japan signed a concession for the production of oil in the Saudi Arabian–Kuwait neutral zone. During the 1970s over half of Japan's total oil imports came from just two countries in the region—Saudi Arabia and Iran.

Japan's Middle East policy underwent a change in 1973. In response to the Arab oil strategy, adopted during the fourth Arab-Israeli war (October 1973), Japan announced a new pro-Arab policy involving support for United Nations Security Council Resolution 242 (1967), which called for Israeli withdrawal from the territories it had occupied in the Six-Day War of 1967. Also, in order to help secure Japan's oil supply lines, the Mitsui group embarked on a joint venture with the Iran Chemical Development Co, Ltd, in 1973 and formed the Iran-Japan Petrochemical Co (IJPC). The company proceeded to construct a giant petrochemical complex on the Persian Gulf coast of southern Iran, but after it sustained heavy damage during the Iran-Iraq War (1980–88) Mitsui formally withdrew from the project in 1990.

In 1980 Japan's total trade volume with the Middle East reached a peak at US $60 billion; it then began to contract owing to a slump in the price of crude oil. In 1989 trade with the region represented 3.1 percent (US $8.6 billion) of total Japanese exports and 10.9 percent (US $23.1 billion) of total imports. Seven out of the 10 countries on which Japan depended for oil were Middle Eastern nations providing 69.5 percent of Japan's crude oil requirements. In 1988 the region received 9.1 percent (US $582.5 million) of total Japanese official development assistance (ODA), with Egypt heading the list at US $172.9 million.

The Persian Gulf War of 1990–91 made it impossible for Japan to deal with Middle Eastern affairs in a simple framework of Arab-Israeli conflict. Given the dependence of the Japanese economy on Middle Eastern oil, a further revision of Japan's Middle East policy has become essential. See also EGYPT AND JAPAN; IRAN AND JAPAN; ISRAEL AND JAPAN; SAUDI ARABIA AND JAPAN; TURKEY AND JAPAN.

Middle East, economic relations with 日本中東経済関係

(Nihon Chūtō *keizai kankei*). The Middle East region, the source of nearly 70 percent of Japan's crude oil imports, is an area of great economic and strategic importance for Japan. The importation of inexpensive crude oil from this region was a major contributing factor to Japan's post–World War II economic success.

The Middle East is one of the few regions of the world that runs a consistent trade surplus with Japan. In 1988 Japan's trade deficit with this region was US $10.2 billion, with total imports from the Middle East valued at US $19.6 billion versus exports from Japan of US $9.4 billion. In 1980, the year following the second oil crisis, the Middle East accounted for 31.7 percent of Japan's total imports, but this ratio declined steadily in the 1980s. In 1988 imports from the Middle East accounted for 10.5 percent of Japan's total imports. Direct investment by Japanese firms remains at modest levels. As of 1990, cumulative Japanese investments in the Middle East stood at US $3.4 billion, or 1.3 percent of total Japanese investments worldwide.

Economic cooperation with the nations of the Middle East has increased greatly since the OIL CRISIS OF 1973, underscoring the importance of the region to Japan's economic security. Japan's official development assistance (ODA) to the Middle East accounted for 24.5 percent of total disbursements in 1977, up from only 0.8 percent in 1972. Since 1979 Japanese ODA to this region has run at approximately 10 percent of its total aid disbursements. In 1988, for example, ODA to the Middle East totaled US $580.0 million, or 9.1 percent of all disbursements. Egypt, Turkey, Jordan, Sudan, and Iraq have been the largest recipients of Japanese economic aid. Wealthy crude-oil-producing states such as Saudi Arabia have benefited mainly from technical cooperation efforts. After Iraq's invasion of Kuwait in August 1990, Japan, in compliance with UN Security Council resolutions, joined in economic sanctions against Iraq and Iraqi-occupied Kuwait and terminated all economic assistance to both countries. With the end of the Persian Gulf War in 1991, Japan's entire Middle East policy is likely to undergo revision.

middle schools 中学校

(*chūgakkō*). Schools providing the three years of compulsory secondary education required upon completion of the six-year compulsory elementary education program. In 1989 some 97 percent of Japan's middle school population attended public schools, which have no entrance examinations and are coeducational. Students attend the public school in the district where they live. Each year they are assigned to a homeroom with a maximum of 45 male and female students, with whom they take their academic classes; certain other courses, such as physical education and home economics, are segregated by gender. In addition to teaching, the homeroom teacher provides general and academic counseling, especially concerning entrance into high school. The school year runs from April through the following March and is divided into trimesters: April to July, September to December, and January to March.

Before today's middle schools were set up in 1947, *kyūsei chūgakkō* ("old-system middle schools") established under the EDUCATION ORDER OF 1872 offered secondary education mainly to male students. The five-year academic course of study offered at these elite institutions prepared students for the next stage in their academic career, a three-year college-preparatory course of study at HIGHER SCHOOLS. After World War II, most of the old-system middle schools became three-year HIGH SCHOOLS. See also SCHOOL CURRICULUM.

Midō Kampaku ki 御堂関白記

Also called *Hōjōji Nyūdō Sadaijin ki.* Diary of the court official FUJIWARA NO MICHINAGA (966–1028; also known as Midō Kampaku), who was perhaps the preeminent political figure of the entire Heian period (794–1185). The diary covers the years 998–1021 and is preserved in the library Yōmei Bunko in Kyōto. It is an important historical source for the period when the Fujiwara family reached the height of its political power. See REGENCY GOVERNMENT.

Midori → Gotō Midori

Midorikawa 緑川

River in Kumamoto Prefecture, Kyūshū, originating in the mountains on the border between Kumamoto and Miyazaki prefectures and flowing west through the Kumamoto Plain to Shimabara Bay. Several dams, including the Midorikawa Dam, and

Miho no Matsubara
This pine grove on the coast of Suruga Bay is famous for its view of Mt. Fuji.

Mie Prefecture
Location and Prefectural Crest

Mifune Toshirō The internationally acclaimed actor in Kurosawa Akira's film *Shichinin no samurai* (1954, Seven Samurai). Mifune plays the part of Kikuchiyo, a likable ruffian with *samurai* aspirations.

electric power plants are located on the river. Length: 75 km (47 mi).

Midori no Hi → holidays, national

Midway, Battle of ミッドウェー海戦

(Middouē Kaisen). Decisive battle fought between the Japanese and US fleets in the area of the island of Midway in the central Pacific, 4–6 June 1942 during WORLD WAR II. On the morning of 4 June the Japanese strike force, with a nucleus of four aircraft carriers, attacked Midway Island. The Japanese forces were surprised by attacks from US carriers and—eventually suffering the loss of all four of the aircraft carriers, one heavy cruiser, and a large number of aircraft and personnel—were forced to withdraw. This battle became the turning point of the Pacific War, as the defeat threw Japanese forces onto the defensive for the duration of the conflict.

Mie Prefecture 三重県

(Mie Ken). Located on the eastern side of the Kii Peninsula in central Honshū and bordered by Ise Bay to the east, Kumano Sea to the south, and Wakayama, Nara, Kyōto, Shiga, Gifu, and Aichi prefectures to the west and north. The northern part of the prefecture is composed of two level areas—the ISE PLAIN along the coast and the UENO BASIN further inland—that are separated by low mountains. The climate is temperate along the coast but runs to extremes in the basin area. The southern part of the prefecture is mountainous and heavily forested, with a mild climate and heavy precipitation.

Numerous remains from prehistoric settlements and tumuli (see KOFUN) attest to early habitation. Proximity to the Kyōto-Nara region and the preeminence of the ISE SHRINE led to the area's rapid development in the early historical period. Divided into the provinces of Ise, Shima, and Iga after the Taika Reform of 645, it came under the domination of a succession of feudal lords and developed a flourishing agriculture and commerce. Its present name and boundaries were established in 1876.

Rice, fruit, and vegetables are produced on the Ise Plain, while the city of MATSUSAKA is famous for its beef. Forestry is a major activity in the southern area. Heavy and chemical industries, along with the older textile and ceramics industries, center on YOKKAICHI and SUZUKA in the north. The cultured-pearl industry was first developed in TOBA.

The Ise Shrine, the principal shrine of the native cult of Shintō, brings numerous pilgrims and tourists to the prefecture annually. Other attractions include the cultured-pearl beds at Toba, the coastal scenery of ISE-SHIMA NATIONAL PARK, and the mountains of YOSHINO-KUMANO NATIONAL PARK. The cities of Matsusaka and UENO still retain vestiges of castle towns. Area: 5,778 sq km (2,231 sq mi); pop: 1,792,514; capital: TSU. Other major cit-

ies include Yokkaichi, ISE, Matsusaka, Suzuka, and KUWANA.

Mifune Kyūzō 三船久蔵

(1883–1965). *Jūdō* master who devoted himself to the spread and development of *jūdō*. Born in Iwate Prefecture. He entered the KŌDŌKAN in 1903. A man of short stature, he worked out the strategy called *kūkinage*, which enables a short man to throw a big man. In 1945 he reached the 10th or highest rank in *jūdō*. His memoirs were published as *Jūdō kaikoroku* (1953).

Mifune Toshirō 三船敏郎

(1920–). The first Japanese movie actor since HAYAKAWA SESSHŪ to achieve international star status. Born in China and repatriated to Japan after World War II with his family. He became an employee of Tōhō Co, Ltd, in 1946 and auditioned for film roles. He first appeared in director Taniguchi Senkichi's (b 1912) *Ginrei no hate* (1947, To the End of the Silver-Capped Mountains). Mifune's name and career have been firmly linked with director KUROSAWA AKIRA, with whom he did his best work. He has appeared in 16 of the director's 29 pictures, including *Yoidore tenshi* (1948, Drunken Angel), *Donzoko* (1957, The Lower Depths), and *Akahige* (1965, Red Beard). His fifth Kurosawa picture, RASHŌMON (1950), brought Mifune worldwide fame. Within Japan his popularity was based mainly upon his recreation of a familiar role—the nihilistic *samurai* hero, brought up to date in such films as *Yōjimbō* (1961) and *Tsubaki Sanjūrō* (1962, Sanjūrō).

In 1962 Mifune established his own company, Mifune Productions, and he himself directed *Gojūman no isan* (1963, The Legacy of the Five Hundred Thousand). No longer working with Kurosawa, Mifune turned increasingly to television work and to roles in foreign films. He appeared in the 1980 American television mini-series *Shōgun* and the 1989 KUMAI KEI film *Honkakubō ibun Sen no Rikyū* (Death of the Tea Master).

Migishi Kōtarō 三岸好太郎

(1903–34). Western-style painter. Born in Hokkaidō, Migishi was self-taught. In 1924 he was awarded the Shun'yōkai Prize. He participated in the establishment of the Dokuritsu Bijutsu Kyōkai (Independent Art Association) in 1930. Migishi had a unique, surrealistic style that made frequent use of shellfish and butterfly motifs. The Migishi Kōtarō Museum, devoted to his work, is located in Sapporo, Hokkaidō.

Mihara 三原[市]

City in southeastern Hiroshima Prefecture, western Honshū, on the Inland Sea. It is the center of textile, cement, and brewing industries. Ferries and passenger ships connect it with Imabari in Shikoku. Pop: 85,518.

Miharayama 三原山

Volcano in the Fuji Volcanic Zone; located on the island of ŌSHIMA, one of the Izu Islands, south of Tōkyō. Composed of basalt, it spews out smoke continuously. All of Ōshima's residents were forced to evacuate the island temporarily during an eruption of Miharayama in 1986. It attracts many tourists. Height: 764 m (2,506 ft).

Miho no Matsubara 三保ノ松原

Grove of pine trees in the southeastern part of the city of Shimizu, Shizuoka Prefecture, central Honshū. Located on a sandspit on the

coast of the Miho Peninsula in Suruga Bay, it offers a magnificent view of Mt. Fuji (Fuji-san). An ancient pine tree associated with the HAGOROMO LEGEND is in Miho Shrine.

Mihonoseki 美保関[町]

Town in northeastern Shimane Prefecture, western Honshū, on the eastern Shimane Peninsula. An important port town until the early Meiji period (1868–1912), it has many sites of historic interest, including the Miho Shrine and the temple Bukkokuji. Fishing and marine-products industries are active. It is part of the Daisen-Oki National Park. Pop: 7,788.

Miidera 三井寺

Formally known as Onjōji. Head temple of the Jimon branch of the TENDAI SECT of Buddhism, located in the city of Ōtsu, Shiga Prefecture. Founded in 686 by Prince Ōtomo no Yota, it was rescued from disrepair in the 9th century by the noted Tendai monk ENCHIN, who became its abbot. The temple had traditionally been the center of both Tendai esoteric Buddhism and SHUGENDŌ.

Although Miidera began as a branch temple of ENRYAKUJI, the head temple of the Tendai sect on nearby Mt. Hiei (HIEIZAN), the two fell into conflict as Miidera became the center of a powerful faction that nearly overshadowed its head. All followers of the Enchin line were expelled from Hieizan in 993 and Miidera buildings themselves were razed several times by WARRIOR-MONKS of Enryakuji from then through the 15th century. The temple was restored each time through the patronage of aristocratic and warrior families. Miidera's artistic treasures include its main hall, built in 1599.

Miike Coal Mines 三池炭鉱

(Miike Tankō). Coal mines located on the Ariake Sea in Kyūshū, extending over parts of Fukuoka and Kumamoto prefectures. Coal was discovered in the area in the late 15th century. In 1873 the mines were taken over by the Meiji government. From 1876 Mitsui Bussan, the trading arm of the MITSUI business group, was the sole exporter of Miike coal, and in 1888 the government sold the mines to Mitsui (see KAN'EI JIGYŌ HARAISAGE). MITSUI MINING CO, LTD, established in 1892, formed the basis of the Mitsui combine's wealth. After World War II, the Miike mines were the scene of several large-scale labor strikes, which culminated in the MIIKE STRIKE of 1960.

Miike strike 三池争議

(Miike *sōgi*). Japan's most protracted large-scale labor dispute; it began in January 1960 at the MIIKE COAL MINES, part of the MITSUI MINING CO, LTD, located near Ōmuta in Kyūshū, and continued for 282 days.

In the spring of 1959 Mitsui had called for the "voluntary" retirement of 6,000 miners in line with its policy of rationalization in the face of competition from cheap imported oil. The union rejected this proposal, and several intermittent strikes took place. In December 1959 the company issued a list of workers it wished to dismiss, which included many of the union activists.

In January 1960 management declared a lockout. Responding to the perceived threat to employment security, the union called for a full strike. Almost immediately some 4,000 miners formed a new union, allegedly with company assistance, and returned to work; but picket lines were set up and a pitched

mikan A grove of *unshū mikan*. Mikan, or Satsuma oranges, are grown on sunny slopes in areas that stay relatively warm throughout the year.

battle ensued, resulting in 1 death and about 1,750 injuries.

During the following months Mitsui received financial backing from banks and major companies, while national and local unions dispatched their members to help the strikers at the picket lines. In August 1960 the CENTRAL LABOR RELATIONS COMMISSION proposed a settlement by which the number of dismissals would be reduced to 1,200, a grace period would be offered for "voluntary" retirement with extra compensation, and training for new jobs would be provided by the company and government. Mitsui agreed immediately, and the union signed on 1 November, following the loss of about half its membership to the new union and a decline in public support for the strike.

Mikage   御影
District in the city of Kōbe, Hyōgo Prefecture, western Honshū, in the ward of Higashi Nada, facing ŌSAKA BAY. It is a wealthy residential district. Its good-quality water contributes to the excellence of the *sake* produced in the area. In the nearby Rokkō Mountains (Rokkōsan) a granite known as *mikageishi* is quarried.

Mikami Akira   三上章
(1903–71). Linguist. Born in Hiroshima Prefecture; graduate of the Tōkyō University department of engineering in 1927. Mikami studied Japanese grammar while teaching mathematics at a high school in Ōsaka, and he eventually formulated a new, creative approach to Japanese grammar. His insistence that Japanese has no true grammatical subject (*shugo*) and that the term should therefore be dropped in descriptions of the language particularly attracted attention within the field of linquistics. His works include *Gendai gohō josetsu* (1953, An Introduction to Contemporary Japanese Grammar), *Zō wa hana ga nagai* (1960, The Nose of the Elephant Is Long), *Nihongo no ronri* (1963, The Logic of Japanese), and *Nihongo no kōbun* (1963, The Syntax of Japanese).

Mikami Sanji   三上参次
(1865–1939). Historian who specialized in the Edo period (1600–1868). Born in Harima Province (now part of Hyōgo Prefecture); graduate of Tōkyō University, where he later taught Japanese history. He became chief editor of the DAI NIHON SHIRYŌ, the monumental compilation of historical sources. His own works include *Edo jidai shi* (1943–44, History of the Edo Period).

Mikami Tsugio   三上次男
(1907–87). Archaeologist and historian. Born in Kyōto. Graduate of Tōkyō University, where he was a professor from 1959 to 1967. His research centered on Jin (Chin) dynasty (1125–1234) China and the culture of ancient East Asia. He developed a system for classifying Japanese ceramics, on the basis of which he analyzed their relationship to the ceramics of the Asian continent in great detail. Mikami's works include *Tōji no michi* (1969, The Way of Ceramics) and the three-volume *Kinshi kenkyū* (1974, Research on the Jin Dynasty).

mikan   蜜柑
Tangerinelike citrus fruit grown in great quantities in Japan and the most important Japanese citrus fruit; often called Satsuma orange or, less accurately, mandarin orange. A member of the family Rutaceae. Since the late 19th century the most important variety

of *mikan* has been the *unshū mikan* (*Citrus unshiu*), which is among the most cold-resistant of all citrus trees, bears fruit abundantly, and suffers comparatively little from blight. *Mikan* fruits average about 100 grams (3.5 oz) in weight. During the Meiji period (1868–1912) new varieties of the *unshū mikan* were developed. The *mikan* now boasts the largest area under cultivation and production volume among fruit trees in Japan. In recent years, however, growers have cut back on production in response to government controls.

Mikasa   三笠[市]
City in west central Hokkaidō, on the river Ikushumbetsugawa. With the opening of the Horonai Coal Mine in 1880 and a railway line—the first in Hokkaidō—to Otaru, coal mining was for many years its principal industry. The closure of the mines has resulted in a decline in the population. Pop: 17,049.

Mikasa, Prince   三笠宮崇仁親王
(1915– ; Mikasa no Miya Takahito Shinnō). Fourth son of Emperor TAISHŌ and brother of Emperor SHŌWA (Hirohito). Graduate of the Army War College, he served in China and at Imperial General Headquarters during World War II. He turned to the study of European and Middle Eastern history in 1947 and has directed the Society for Middle Eastern Studies in Japan since 1954.

Mikata Five Lakes   三方五湖
(Mikata Goko). In western Fukui Prefecture, central Honshū. Located west of the city of Tsuruga along Wakasa Bay, this group is composed of lakes Mikata, Suigetsu, Suga, Hiruga, and Kugushi. Mikata and Suigetsu are lagoons while the others are tectonic lakes. Saltwater fish inhabit Lake Hiruga; freshwater fish inhabit Lake Mikata. The lakes form part of Wakasa Bay Quasi-National Park.

Mikatahara   三方原
Also called Mikatagahara. Diluvial upland on the eastern side of Lake Hamana, northwestern part of the city of Hamamatsu, Shizuoka Prefecture, central Honshū; an old alluvial fan of the river Tenryūgawa. Principal agricultural products are mandarin oranges and tea leaves. Many housing projects have been built here. A Japanese Self Defense Forces airfield and a motorcycle racetrack are located here. Elevation: 30–110 m (100–360 ft).

Mikatahara Canal   三方原用水
(Mikatahara Yōsui). Canal located in the city of Hamamatsu in western Shizuoka Prefecture, central Honshū. Water taken from the Akiba Dam in the upper reaches of the Tenryūgawa is channeled into Hamamatsu to expand its water supply. The main canal was completed in 1968.

Mikawa Bay   三河湾
(Mikawa Wan). Inlet of the Pacific Ocean between the Atsumi and Chita peninsulas, southern Aichi Prefecture, central Honshū. Divided into Atsumi Bay in the east and Chita Bay in the west. There is an industrial zone in the Chita Bay area.

Mikawa monogatari   三河物語
Three-volume autobiographical work by ŌKUBO HIKOZAEMON, a direct vassal (bannerman; *hatamoto*) of the Mikawa domain (now part of Aichi Prefecture); written in 1622. The first two volumes deal with the history of the TOKUGAWA FAMILY before TOKUGAWA

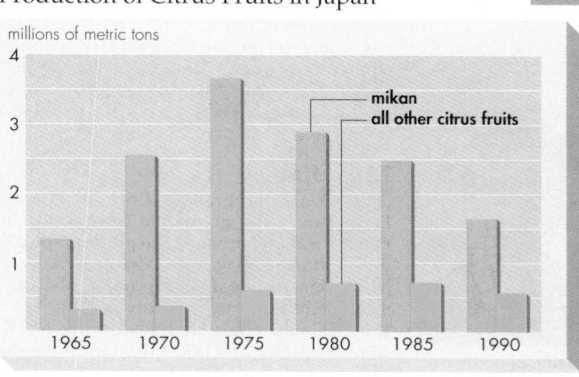

Production of Citrus Fruits in Japan

millions of metric tons

mikan
all other citrus fruits

1965 1970 1975 1980 1985 1990

SOURCE: Ministry of Agriculture, Forestry, and Fisheries, *Nōgyō hakusho fuzoku tōkeihyō* (annual): 1991.

IEYASU's unification of the country in 1600, emphasizing the achievements of Hikozaemon's ancestors. The last volume is a memoir of the author's own life in the service of Ieyasu and his successors TOKUGAWA HIDETADA and TOKUGAWA IEMITSU. In the book, Hikozaemon expresses his dissatisfaction with the inadequate rewards given to the Ōkubo family for its loyalty, while advising continued service. The *Mikawa monogatari* was widely circulated and is interesting for its examination of the lord-vassal relationship and of the *samurai* ethic during the Sengoku period (1467–1568).

Mikawa, Port of   三河港
(Mikawa Kō). Port occupying the eastern half of Atsumi Bay in southern Aichi Prefecture, central Honshū. Land reclamation is being carried out with the goal of establishing a coastal industrial zone here. Automobile and shipbuilding factories have been built on the reclaimed land, and the Port of Mikawa is known as a shipping point for automobiles.

Miki   三木[市]
City in southern Hyōgo Prefecture, western Honshū, now a residential suburb of KŌBE. A castle town from the 14th century, it has long been known for carpentry tools, knives, and rice used in brewing *sake*. Pop: 76,501.

Miki Bukichi   三木武吉
(1884–1956). Politician. Born in Kagawa Prefecture; graduate of Waseda University. He practiced law before being elected to the House of Representatives in 1917 as a candidate of the KENSEIKAI party and to the Tōkyō Municipal Assembly in 1922. After World War II, he participated in the founding of the

miko A modern-day *miko* performs a sacred dance at the grand festival held annually on 17 December at Waka-miya, a subsidiary shrine of the Kasuga Shrine in Nara.

Miki Kiyoshi This philosopher analyzed the philosophical foundations of Marxism from a humanistic perspective.

Mikimoto Kōkichi The developer of the cultured pearl. Today the name Mikimoto is synonymous with high-quality pearls.

Japan Liberal Party (Nihon Jiyūtō). In 1946 he was elected speaker of the House of Representatives but was barred from office (1946–51) during the OCCUPATION PURGE. He became secretary-general of the LIBERAL PARTY in 1953, and in 1954 formed the NIHON MINSHUTŌ (Japan Democratic Party) with HATOYAMA ICHIRŌ. Miki arranged the merger of the two conservative parties in 1955 to form the LIBERAL DEMOCRATIC PARTY.

Miki Jun   三木淳

(1919–92). Photographer. Born in Okayama Prefecture, Miki graduated from Keiō University. As a member of the photography division of the magazine *Shūkan san nyūsu*, Miki was responsible for news photography, including such events as the Tōkyō War Crimes Trials. After working for the Tōkyō bureau of Time-Life, he established himself as a freelance news photographer in 1956. *Mayaku* (1960, Drugs) and *Mekishiko* (1961, Mexico) are among his best-known works from that period. From 1981 to 1989 he was president of the Japan Professional Photographers Society. Other works include *Samba/samba/Burajiru* (1967), a collection of Miki's photographs of Brazil.

Miki Kiyoshi   三木清

(1897–1945). Philosopher. Born in Hyōgo Prefecture. After studying at Kyōto University with NISHIDA KITARŌ and HATANO SEIICHI, Miki continued his studies in Europe under Martin Heidegger and Heinrich Rickert. Returning to Japan, he became a professor at Hōsei University in 1927. Miki opened a new phase in Japanese philosophy by analyzing the philosophical foundations of Marxism from a humanistic perspective. His theory had great impact on Japanese intellectuals at the time. In 1930 he was arrested for violating the PEACE PRESERVATION LAW OF 1925 and was barred from all public offices. Seeking a new humanism that transcended nihilism, he developed what he called "the logic of creativity" (*kōsōryoku no ronri*) to encompass not only abstract logic but that of concrete human action as well. From 1938 to 1940 Miki was a leading figure in the SHŌWA KENKYŪKAI, a policy study group often characterized as a "brain trust" for Prime Minister KONOE FUMIMARO. He was imprisoned in March 1945 for harboring a communist sympathizer and died in prison a month after the end of World War II. Miki's works include the essay collection *Tetsugaku nōto* (1941, Notes on Philosophy).

Mikimoto Kōkichi   御木本幸吉

(1858–1954). Developer of the cultured pearl. Born in what is now Mie Prefecture. In 1883 he started production of PEARLS by raising pearl oysters (*akoyagai; Pinctada martensii*) in Ago Bay on Shima Peninsula in Mie

Prefecture. In 1893 he succeeded in producing a semispherical pearl and in 1898 harvested pearls from oysters that had been seeded in 1895. His cultured pearls were first introduced overseas in 1897, when he displayed semispherical specimens at an international exposition of marine products in Norway. In 1905 he finally succeeded in producing perfectly round cultured pearls, and from about 1913 he began to have appreciable harvests.

Accusations that his cultured pearls were only imitations of real pearls gained considerable publicity, but eventually it was scientifically proven that they were no different from natural pearls. Gradually the value of Mikimoto pearls was accepted throughout the world, and Mikimoto became known as the "pearl king."

Miki Rofū   三木露風

(1889–1964). Poet. Real name Miki Misao. Born in Hyōgo Prefecture. A precocious poet, he published his first collection, *Haien* (1909, The Desolate Garden), while still a student at Waseda University. First active in the movement for colloquial free verse, he soon turned to symbolist poetry. From 1920 to 1924 he was an instructor at a Trappist monastery in Hokkaidō and was baptized in 1922. His life in the monastery is reflected in many of his essays and poetry collections, which include *Shinkō no akebono* (1922, The Dawn of Faith) and *Kami to hito* (1926, God and Man). He also participated in the nursery song movement of the 1920s that was led by *Akai tori* (Red Bird), the children's magazine founded by SUZUKI MIEKICHI. "Akatombo" (Red Dragonfly) and other songs were collected in *Shinjushima* (1921, Pearl Island). In 1927 the Vatican bestowed on him the title of the Knight of the Holy Sepulcher at Jerusalem for his writings on Catholicism.

Miki Takeo   三木武夫

(1907–88). Politician; prime minister (1974–76). Born in Tokushima Prefecture. A graduate of Meiji University, he studied for several years at the University of California at Berkeley. A member of the House of Representatives for 52 years, he served as minister of communication in KATAYAMA TETSU's coalition cabinet in 1947. He joined the LIBERAL DEMOCRATIC PARTY (LDP) in 1955 and served as director-general of the Economic Planning Agency (1958) and as minister of international trade and industry (1965–66) and of foreign affairs (1966–67) in the SATŌ EISAKU cabinets. Miki headed a small LDP faction, and in a compromise between the FUKUDA TAKEO and ŌHIRA MASAYOSHI factions, he was elected president of the LDP and prime minister in 1974. As prime minister, he was confronted by a variety of problems, including the LOCKHEED SCANDAL and the recession following the OIL CRISIS OF 1973.

Miki Taku   三木卓

(1935–). Poet and novelist. Real name Tomita Miki. Born in Tōkyō; graduated from Waseda University. The basis of Miki's works is formed by tragic memories of his childhood in Manchuria and Japan's defeat in World War II. Miki's principal works include the poetry collection *Tōkyō gozen sanji* (1966, 3 AM in Tōkyō), which received the H-Shi Prize; the fairy tale *Horobita kuni no tabi* (1969, Travels in a Ruined Country); and *Hōgeki no ato de* (1973, After the Bombardment), which contains the Akutagawa Prize–winning story "Hiwa" (Finch).

Miki Tokuchika   御木徳近

(1900–1983). Religious leader and founder of the PL KYŌDAN. Born in Ehime Prefecture; son of Miki Tokuharu (1871–1938), a former Buddhist priest of the ŌBAKU SECT. Both were active members of a religion founded in 1912 by Kaneda Tokumitsu (1863–1919), called Tokumitsukyō. The Miki family continued Kaneda's work after his death, changing the sect's name to Hito no Michi Kyōdan (the Way-of-Man Organization). Under the militarist regime of the late 1930s Tokuharu and Tokuchika were imprisoned, and the group was disbanded. Tokuchika reestablished the group in 1946 under the name PL Kyōdan, modifying it to take on a Western aspect. In 1951 he helped establish the Union of New Religious Organizations.

Mikkabi   三ケ日〔町〕

Town in western Shizuoka Prefecture, central Honshū, on the northern shore of Lake HAMANA. It is known for the paleolithic human remains discovered here, the so-called Mikkabi Man. Local products include roof tiles, rushes for making *tatami* mats, mandarin oranges, and eels. Pop: 16,507.

mikkyō → esoteric Buddhism

miko   巫女

In ancient times a female shaman who played a prominent part in the early Shintō cult by acting as medium for the KAMI during his descent at the time of a ritual (*matsuri*). The term now has two meanings: (1) a woman capable of transmitting through trance the utterance of a supernatural being; (2) a female officiant at a Shintō shrine, often a young girl, who does not necessarily have psychic or shamanistic power.

In the early cult the *miko* is thought to have come to her office through election by a spiritual being, usually a *kami*. The gift was bestowed either through a dream or through sudden involuntary possession (*kamigakari*). Evidence about the early *miko* is fragmentary, but examples may be discerned in the NIHON SHOKI (720, Chronicle of Japan) in the shape of Yamato Totohi Momoso Hime and the empress Jingū. With the TAIKA REFORM of the mid-7th century the *miko* was banished from the ceremonies of the court and relegated to cults practiced outside the capital. With the advent of Buddhism her status was further reduced. The role of active summoner came to be carried out by a Buddhist priest or YAMABUSHI.

Modern counterparts of the ancient *miko* may be found among the founders of certain *shinkō shūkyō* (NEW RELIGIONS), such as NAKAYAMA MIKI, DEGUCHI NAO, and KITAMURA SAYO. Women acting as mouthpieces for gods or *hotoke* (ancestral spirits) may also still be found in many rural districts, particularly the Tōhoku (northern Honshū) area. The blind *itako* of Aomori Prefecture are rightly regarded as the remnant of a true shamanic medium tradition. See also SHAMANISM.

mikoshi   神輿

Portable Shintō shrine, basically a highly ornate palanquin-like structure that rests on two long horizontal poles. Its roof is often decorated with an elaborate gilded phoenix. Before the introduction of the *mikoshi*, a mirror with a branch of the *sakaki* tree or some other object symbolic of a divine presence was carried around, sometimes on horseback. The first recorded use of a *miko-*

shi was the transfer of the deity of the USA HACHIMAN SHRINE in Kyūshū by palanquin to Nara, where the deity was to safeguard the construction of the Great Buddha image (749) at the temple TŌDAIJI. By the 10th century it had become a common practice in Kyōto to carry the deity from a shrine through the community in a *mikoshi* on the occasion of the *ekijinsai*, a festival aimed at pacifying malevolent spirits believed to cause epidemics. Today the *mikoshi* is carried on shrine festival days through the parish, i.e., the village or ward, on the shoulders of 20 to 30 people. The procession is often raucous, with the participants pushing the *mikoshi* in zigzag fashion, first one way and then another. This tempestuous movement is commonly thought to reflect the powerful presence of the deity that is enshrined in the *mikoshi*.

mikudarihan 三行半

(literally, "three and a half lines"). Popular term for a letter of divorce used by male commoners during the Edo period (1600–1868). Whereas divorces among the *samurai* class required more elaborate proceedings, all a commoner husband needed was such a letter, handed by him to his wife or to her father or brother. A *mikudarihan* consisted of three and a half lines confirming the divorce and giving the wife permission to remarry. At that time only the husband could initiate a divorce, but, as a last resort, a discontented wife could seek refuge in a temple (see KAKEKOMIDERA).

Mikuni 三国[町]

Town at the mouth of the river Kuzuryūgawa in northern Fukui Prefecture, central Honshū. Formerly a fishing port, Mikuni has become an oil storage area with the opening of the Port of Fukui, of which it is a part. Mikuni's most famous attraction is TŌJIMBŌ, a group of rock pillars carved by the waves of the Sea of Japan. Pop: 23,492.

Mikuni Mountains 三国山脈

(Mikuni Sammyaku). Mountain range running east to west forming the boundary of Gumma and Niigata prefectures, central Honshū. The major peaks are Shirasunayama (2,140 m; 7,021 ft), TANIGAWADAKE (1,977 m; 6,486 ft), and Mikuniyama (1,636 m; 5,367 ft). Most of the peaks are part of Jōshin'etsu Kōgen National Park.

Mikuni Pass 三国峠

(Mikuni Tōge). Extends through the MIKUNI MOUNTAINS, on the border between Niigata and Gumma prefectures, central Honshū. The highway Mikuni Kaidō was important both before and during the Edo period (1600–1868), providing the area's only access to Edo (now Tōkyō). The Mikuni Tunnel of National Route No. 17 was opened in 1959. Altitude: 1,244 m (4,081 ft).

Mikuni Rentarō 三国連太郎

(1923–). Film actor. Real name Satō Masao. Born in Gumma Prefecture. Mikuni joined what is now SHŌCHIKU CO, LTD, and made his debut in KINOSHITA KEISUKE's *Zemma* (1951, The Good Fairy). A highly versatile actor, he appeared in memorable roles in such films as Shibuya Minoru's (1907–80) *Honjitsu kyūshin* (1952, No Consultations Today), UCHIDA TOMU's *Kiga kaikyō* (1964, The Straits of Hunger), IMAI TADASHI's *Echigo tsutsuishi oyashirazu* (1964, A Story from Echigo), and Yoshida Yoshishige's (b 1933) *Kaigenrei* (1973, Martial Law). His performance in the title role of TESHIGAHARA HIROSHI's *Rikyū* (1989) was widely acclaimed.

militarism 軍国主義

(*gunkoku shugi*). An ideology and a course of political action aimed at the domination of politics, culture, and all other aspects of social life by military values. War and preparation for war become so important that all else is subordinated to them. Many Japanese scholars believe that Japan was to some extent a militaristic society throughout its pre–World War II modern history. It became pervasively militaristic, they think, after the London Naval Conference Crisis of 1930 and the MANCHURIAN INCIDENT of 1931 placed Japan on the road to war in 1937 and 1941 and to disastrous defeat in 1945 (see SINO-JAPANESE WAR OF 1937–1945; WORLD WAR II).

The military was able to influence Japanese society for a number of reasons. To begin with, almost all of Japan's leaders during the Meiji period (1868–1912) were former *samurai*. Whether they served in business, the military, or the civil bureaucracy, their background and outlook were those of the martial elite. Samurai values and descendants of samurai continued to be influential after the Meiji period. Second, many of Japan's problems from the 1860s until the 1940s necessitated, or seemed to necessitate, military solutions. In fact, some scholars argue that the basic motivation for industrialization and modernization was martial and that this impetus laid the foundation for the military's power and prestige. The Meiji leaders faced armed uprisings of discontented samurai and peasants and a perceived threat from the expansionist policies of the Western powers. Since Japanese leaders did not wish their country to suffer the fate of China and become a semicolony of the Western powers, they tended to support policies that gave the development of national wealth and power (FUKOKU KYŌHEI) priority over the fostering of democracy. Third, after the SINO-JAPANESE WAR OF 1894–1895, Japan too joined the colonizers, and both the creation and the defense of its empire, which almost all leaders supported, called for a strong military.

Army leaders affiliated with the faction of Field Marshal YAMAGATA ARITOMO were among those most committed to enhancing the power of the armed forces. In January 1873 Yamagata instituted the CONSCRIPTION ORDINANCE, which, by elevating commoners, broke the samurai class's centuries-old monopoly in military matters. Revisions to this law in 1889 and 1927 were made by Yamagata's protégés, KATSURA TARŌ, TERAUCHI MASATAKE, and TANAKA GIICHI, enabling the army to increase the pool of soldiers available for war by drafting and training more men for a shorter period of time and then keeping them in the reserves for a longer period than under the original ordinance. The army could also indoctrinate thousands of men with the military-patriotic values of the emperor cult, for the IMPERIAL RESCRIPT TO SOLDIERS AND SAILORS, which Yamagata had the emperor promulgate in 1882, had made unquestioning loyalty to the emperor the basis of military training.

Also providing a basis for the growth of military power were the various freedoms from civilian restraint that the government gave the army and navy. In 1878 the army set up the ARMY GENERAL STAFF OFFICE, which was equal in authority to, and independent of, the ARMY MINISTRY; the navy later followed suit. The chiefs of the army and naval general staff offices, which were responsible for military planning and operations, reported directly to the emperor and so could act free of civilian control. Unlike the army and navy ministers, they were not cabinet members and had no responsibility to the prime minister. Thus, in military matters, the general staffs constituted a separate government. See also NAVAL GENERAL STAFF OFFICE.

According to provisions contained in the Meiji Constitution, the chief of staff of the military services, and to a lesser extent the army and navy ministers, were legally free of civilian authority, since they had the option, under certain circumstances, of reporting directly to the emperor rather than to the prime minister. Although neither the army nor the navy ever used this constitutional prerogative to circumvent the prime minister, it was still a powerful weapon in influencing the government.

The army and navy also had decisive leverage over any civilian government. Between 1898 and 1945, only officers on active duty served as army and navy ministers (see GUMBU DAIJIN GEN'EKI BUKAN SEI). Since the law required that the prime minister resign if he could not fill all cabinet posts (and he could not appoint army and navy ministers without the services' cooperation), the military could bring down or block the formation of a cabinet at any time. This power was invoked only once, in January 1937, when the army ironically prevented General UGAKI KAZUSHIGE from forming a cabinet by refusing to provide an officer for its ministerial post, but the military was able to influence the government simply by threatening to exercise this authority, especially in the late 1930s.

By the 1930s the armed forces had built powerful, independent positions from which they could exert a strong influence on Japanese society. Long-standing civilian support for military values, an unfettered legal position, and an elaborate network of paramilitary organizations—all of these factors converged in the 1930s with the sense of crisis heightened by the world depression that began in 1929 and by the imposition of trade barriers by Western powers. This led more and more Japanese leaders to believe that Japan must solve its problems by itself and that its military offered the best solutions. Those who after 1930 continued to resist military "solutions," such as Foreign Minis-

mikoshi The progression of a portable shrine through the community during a shrine festival signifies a visit of the deity to the parishioners. The ornate example pictured dates from the late Edo period.

Minakata Kumagusu
An independent scholar whose work at the turn of the century spanned the fields of biology, ethnology, and folklore.

ter SHIDEHARA KIJŪRŌ in 1930–31, were routed from government; by the mid-1930s, even some of those with impeccable patriotic credentials, such as the generals WATANABE JŌTARŌ and NAGATA TETSUZAN, fell before the accelerating patriotic-militaristic juggernaut.

The turning point in the rise of militarism was the London Naval Conference Crisis of 1930. The Minseitō government of Prime Minister HAMAGUCHI OSACHI negotiated a naval limitation treaty that many Japanese, including Naval Chief of Staff KATŌ HIROHARU, the army's leadership, members of the opposition Rikken Seiyūkai party and of the radical right, and much of the public, believed was forced on Japan by the United States and England and endangered Japan's national defense. Although Hamaguchi managed to have the treaty ratified, the tumultuous debate that occurred between its signing and ratification, including an unsuccessful attempt by Katō to invoke the right of supreme command, created the public mood for antiforeign militarism. By 1931 Hamaguchi had been shot, his government felled, and an atmosphere created in which the military was able to act with little resistance.

On 18 September 1931, two middle-level staff officers in the GUANDONG (KWANTUNG) ARMY engineered an incident in Mukden (now Shenyang) that led to their army's seizure of Manchuria. On 15 May 1932, naval cadets murdered Prime Minister INUKAI TSUYOSHI; at their trial the assassins flaunted their radical, militaristic patriotism. In 1935 the army, the radical right, and thousands of reservists, led by the president of the Imperial Veterans' Association, former chief of the Army General Staff Uzuki Sōroku (1865–1940), persecuted the respected constitutional scholar MINOBE TATSUKICHI for what they thought was the flagrant lese majesty of his "emperor-as-organ" theory (TENNŌ KIKAN SETSU). On 26 February 1936, elements of the army's First Division, led by their young platoon and company commanders, seized central Tōkyō and assassinated a number of ranking government officials (see FEBRUARY 26TH INCIDENT). In July 1937 a local clash between small units of Chinese and Japanese troops on the outskirts of Beiping (Peiping; now Beijing or Peking) grew bit by bit into the full-scale Sino-Japanese War of 1937–1945. These uprisings and assassinations demonstrated the military's freedom from outside influence, and even the general who served as prime minister at the time of the attack on Pearl Harbor in December 1941, TŌJŌ HIDEKI, had difficulty in controlling his own army.

Yet, the army and navy were never able to dominate Japanese society totally. Army efforts, beginning in 1936, to create a state-controlled economy met with stiff resistance from civil bureaucrats, party politicians, and businessmen. Political competition was also widespread. In 1942 the army failed in an attempt to wrest control of the IMPERIAL RULE ASSISTANCE ASSOCIATION from the Home Ministry. In the 1942 general election for the lower house of the Diet, the army was unsuccessful in its efforts to destroy the final vestiges of the power of the old party politicians. So, although military values pervaded every aspect of Japanese society during World War II, Japan's militarism was limited inasmuch as the army and navy could not completely dominate the nation's economic and political life.

military education in the schools
軍事教練

(*gunji kyōren*). Military training was included in the school curriculum in Japan from the Meiji period (1868–1912) until the end of World War II. It was based on a government policy expressed in the slogan *fukoku kyōhei* (Rich Country, Strong Military).

During the 1880s "infantry exercises" (*hohei sōren*) were carried out in the middle schools. (Graduates of middle schools were either exempted from regular compulsory military service or entitled to a shortened term of such duty.) In response to demands from the education minister, MORI ARINORI, "military-style calisthenics" (*heishiki taisō*) was also introduced into the teacher-training schools. After the Russo-Japanese War (1904–05) military training courses called *kyōren* became part of the curriculum for both boys and girls at the elementary and secondary school level. The emphasis on military training reached its height during World War II, when *kyōren* became mandatory even at universities. The end of the war brought about the abolition of all military training in the school system.

military factions→gumbatsu

Million Card Service Co, Ltd
[株]ミリオンカード・サービス

(Mirion Kādo Sābisu). Credit card company of the TŌKAI BANK, LTD, group. Incorporated in 1968. It entered into cooperation with Master Card International in 1968 and Visa International in 1988. It has 550,000 member shops and about 3.25 million cardholders. For the fiscal year ending March 1990, sales totaled ¥408.2 billion (US $2.7 billion) and capitalization stood at ¥1.4 billion (US $9.1 million). Headquarters are in Nagoya.

Milne, John
ミルン, J.

(1850–1913). British seismologist. Born in Liverpool. A graduate of Kings College of London University, Milne later studied at the Royal School of Mines. Upon the invitation of the Japanese government, he went to Tōkyō in 1876 to teach geology and mining at Kōbu Daigakkō (later part of Tōkyō University). Following an earthquake on 22 February 1880, with other scientists, he founded the Seismological Society of Japan and its journal, *Transactions of the Seismological Society of Japan*. Milne was awarded the Order of the Rising Sun by the Japanese government in 1895.

mimai
見舞

Traditional expressions of sympathy, consolation, or concern on occasions such as illness, death in the family, fire, or natural disaster. Usually accompanied by gifts of flowers or food, *mimai* may be in the form of a personal visit, a card or letter (*mimaijō*), or a telephone call. The custom is considered obligatory among close relatives and intimate friends. Specific types of *mimai* include *byōki mimai* (an inquiry during an illness), *kaji mimai* (an inquiry after a fire), and *jishin mimai* (an inquiry after an earthquake), among many others. *Mimai* are not limited to extraordinary circumstances. Campaigning political candidates frequently receive *mimai* of encouragement from their supporters. Another very common type of *mimai* is the *shochū mimai* or "midsummer inquiry," usually a card or letter sent sometime in July that typically fol-

lows a set pattern of comments on the summer heat and inquiry after the receiver's health. See also ON; GIRI AND NINJŌ.

Mimana→Kaya

Mimasaka
美作[町]

Town in northeastern Okayama Prefecture, western Honshū. It is mainly an agricultural district, producing tea, vegetables, and fruit. There is also dairy farming. The Yunogō Hot Spring has been known since ancient times. Pop: 13,713.

Mimikawa
耳川

River in Miyazaki Prefecture, Kyūshū, originating in the Kyūshū Mountains and flowing east to empty into the Hyūga Sea at the city of Hyūga. The river is used to generate electric power. Length: 102 km (63 mi); area of drainage basin: 880 sq km (340 sq mi).

Miminashiyama→Yamato Sanzan

Mimpō→Civil Code

mimpon shugi
民本主義

(literally, "people-as-the-base-ism"). Philosophy espoused by the political scientist YOSHINO SAKUZŌ, which served as the major theoretical underpinning of TAISHŌ DEMOCRACY, the liberal political movement of the Taishō period (1912–26). Yoshino developed this concept in a series of articles, published between 1916 and 1918 in the magazine CHŪŌ KŌRON. He chose to render "democracy" as *mimpon shugi*, rather than the more common translation *minshu shugi*, because the latter term suggested popular sovereignty, and its implicit rejection of imperial sovereignty would have caused official condemnation. In Yoshino's mind *mimpon shugi* stood for government by and for the people, but in the name of the emperor. His ideas had a profound influence on the UNIVERSAL MANHOOD SUFFRAGE MOVEMENT, but after 1925 *mimpon shugi* gradually lost influence as intellectuals and the labor movement gravitated toward more radical thought.

Min→Sōmin (Buddhist priest); Min, Queen (Korean queen)

Minabuchi no Shōan
南淵請安

(fl early 7th century). Scholar-priest of the Yamato no Aya family (see AYA FAMILY), an influential group of immigrants from Korea. After his return to Japan in 640 from 32 years of study in China, he taught Confucian texts to Prince Naka no Ōe (later Emperor TENJI) and FUJIWARA NO KAMATARI, the initiators of the TAIKA REFORM of 645, and may have influenced the shape of the reform government.

Minakami
水上[町]

Town in northern Gumma Prefecture, central Honshū, on the river TONEGAWA. Various hot springs, as well as skiing on Tenjindaira, draw visitors. It is the base for climbing TANIGAWADAKE. Pop: 7,383.

Minakami Takitarō
水上滝太郎

(1887–1940). Novelist and literary critic. Real name Abe Shōzō. Born in Tōkyō. While a student at Keiō University, he contributed poems and fiction to the literary magazines SUBARU and MITA BUNGAKU. After studying and traveling abroad, he became an executive in his father's insurance company in 1916. Combining business and writing, Minakami wrote novels about the lifestyle of white-collar workers during the 1920s and 1930s.

Principal works include *Ōsaka no yado* (1925–26), a novel, and *Kaigara tsuihō* (1918–40), a collection of essays.

Minakami Tsutomu　　　水上勉

(1919–). Novelist. Also known as Mizukami Tsutomu. Born in Fukui Prefecture. Attended Ritsumeikan University. With his autobiographical novel *Gan no tera* (1961), which received the Naoki Prize, he began to master a lyrical treatment of the sorrows of women, notably of those bound to a life of poverty in the remote Hokuriku region where he was raised. Similar novels include *Gobanchō yūgiriro* (1962) and *Echizen takeningyō* (1963). Other works are the mystery *Kiga kaikyō* (1962, The Straits of Starvation), dealing with the TŌYA MARU DISASTER; *Uno Kōji den* (1971), a biography of his mentor UNO KŌJI; and *Ryōkan* (1983), about the Zen monk RYŌKAN.

Minakata Kumagusu　　　南方熊楠

(1867–1941). Biologist, ethnologist, and folklorist. Born in Kii Province (now Wakayama Prefecture). After dropping out of the First Higher School (Daiichi Kōtō Gakkō) in 1886, he spent 15 years in Europe and the United States. His studies encompassed both the humanities and the natural sciences: he was versed in several Western languages as well as in Japanese classics, folklore, and archaeology. In the course of his scientific research he discovered many new types of fungus and slime mold. He wrote many articles for the British journal *Nature* and helped F. V. Dickens to translate the 13th-century essay collection *Hōjōki* into English. After 1910, as Japanese FOLKLORE STUDIES burgeoned through the efforts of the pioneering scholar YANAGITA KUNIO, Minakata had considerable influence. He contributed hundreds of articles to folklore journals and other magazines. One of his best-known works is *Jūnishi kō* (serialized 1914–23, On the Twelve Horary Signs).

Minakuchi　　　水口[町]

Town in southern Shiga Prefecture, central Honshū, on the river Yasugawa. In the Edo period (1600–1868) it was a castle town and a post-station town. Electrical appliances and farm machinery are produced. Tea is grown on the riverbanks. Pop: 30,683.

Minamata　　　水俣[市]

City in southern Kumamoto Prefecture, Kyūshū, on the Yatsushiro Sea. Minamata is primarily known as the site of Minamata disease, a disease of the central nervous system caused by industrial discharges from a local carbide plant; see POLLUTION-RELATED DISEASES. Yunoko and Yunotsuru hot springs are nearby. Pop: 34,594.

Minamata disease → pollution-
related diseases

Minami Ashigara　　　南足柄[市]

City in western Kanagawa Prefecture, central Honshū. A temple town (MONZEN MACHI) of the temple Saijōji, an important temple of the Sōtō Buddhist sect, it has become industrialized since the establishment of a plant by Fuji Photo Film Co, Ltd, in 1934. Pop: 42,600.

Minami Chita　　　南知多[町]

Town in Aichi Prefecture, central Honshū. Situated on the Chita Peninsula, it is a base for ocean and coastal fishing. Farming utilizes water from the AICHI CANAL. Seaweed (*nori*) is cultivated in the coastal waters.

Minami Chita is known for its good fishing, swimming, and mandarin orange groves. Pop: 25,954.

Minami Daitōjima　　　南大東島

Island approximately 350 km (220 mi) east of Okinawa; part of Okinawa Prefecture. One of the Daitō Islands. It is a coral island with steep cliffs. The cultivation of sugarcane, the chief activity, is carried out in the central lowlands. Area: 30.7 sq km (11.9 sq mi).

Minami Jirō　　　南次郎

(1874–1955). Army general. Born in Ōita Prefecture. He was made a general in 1930 and army minister in 1931. Minami was named commander of the GUANDONG (KWANTUNG) ARMY in Manchuria and ambassador to the Japanese puppet-state of MANCHUKUO in 1934. Later he was governor-general of Japanese-ruled Korea before his appointment to the Privy Council in 1942. At the WAR CRIMES TRIALS following World War II, Minami was sentenced to life imprisonment as a war criminal.

Minami Kikan　　　南機関

Japanese military intelligence organization in Burma (1941–42). Its official name was Nampō Kigyō Chōsakai (Committee for Research on Enterprises in the Southern Region). It trained 30 Burmese nationalist youths, including AUNG SAN, and helped them to organize the Burma Independence Army.

Minami Torishima　　　南鳥島

Also known as Marcus Island or Week Island. A coral island approximately 1,200 km (750 mi) southeast of the island of Chichijima. One of the Ogasawara (Bonin) Islands located south of Tōkyō. At latitude 24° 18' north and longitude 153° 58' east, it is the easternmost point in Japan. Area: 1.1 sq km (0.4 sq mi).

Minamoto family　　　源氏

(Genji). One of the four great families, including the TAIRA FAMILY, FUJIWARA FAMILY, and TACHIBANA FAMILY, that dominated court politics during the Heian period (794–1185); its descendants remained central to Japanese government until the Meiji Restoration of 1868. Like the Taira, the Minamoto family was an offshoot of the imperial family. In the Heian period, offspring of sovereigns were periodically cut off from the imperial line and given surnames (a practice known as dynastic "shedding"). This practice was held over from pre-Heian times, when shedding helped to limit succession disputes within large imperial families. In 814 Emperor SAGA (r 809–823) created the surname Minamoto for his children, and in 825 Emperor KAMMU awarded the surname Taira to his grandson Takamune. Thereafter, all members cut off from the imperial line were surnamed either Minamoto or Taira. The Minamoto family was commonly referred to as the Genji, using alternate pronunciations of the Chinese characters for Minamoto (*gen*) and *uji*, or family (*ji*). The different Genji lineages were known by the names of the emperors from whom they descended: in addition to the original "Saga Genji" there were Minamoto lineages tracing their origin to 10 of Saga's successors, most notably Seiwa (r 858–876), UDA (r 887–897), and Murakami (r 946–967). Between 1087 and 1093, as political power passed from the Fujiwara regents (see REGENCY GOVERNMENT) to the retired emperors (see INSEI), the Murakami lineage came to control many of the highest official

posts. The branch that descended from Emperor Seiwa gained greater fame in Japanese history. Minamoto no Mitsunaka (912–997) of the Seiwa Genji allied himself with the Fujiwara. His son MINAMOTO NO YORIMITSU became a protégé of the regent FUJIWARA NO MICHINAGA; another son, Yorinobu (968–1048), suppressed the rebellion of TAIRA NO TADATSUNE in 1031. Yorinobu's son Yoriyoshi (988–1075) pacified the northeast in the EARLIER NINE YEARS' WAR (1051–62), and his son MINAMOTO NO YOSHIIE completed the job in the LATER THREE YEARS' WAR (1083–87). After Yoshiie's time, however, the fortunes of the Seiwa Genji waned. His grandson Tameyoshi (1096–1156) was executed after the HŌGEN DISTURBANCE (1156). His great-grandson MINAMOTO NO YOSHITOMO was killed for his part in the HEIJI DISTURBANCE (1160), and another great-grandson, MINAMOTO NO TAMETOMO, rebelled and committed suicide in 1177. Thereafter the influence of the Genji in the capital reached a low ebb; only the elderly MINAMOTO NO YORIMASA represented the family as TAIRA NO KIYOMORI seized absolute power.

After the Heiji Disturbance, however, Kiyomori had unwisely spared the youngest sons of Yoshitomo—MINAMOTO NO YORITOMO, MINAMOTO NO YOSHITSUNE, and Minamoto no Noriyori (d 1193). In 1180 Yoritomo mounted a full-scale rebellion against Taira rule (see TAIRA-MINAMOTO WAR); within five years he had destroyed the Taira, subjugated all of eastern Japan, and established a military government (the KAMAKURA SHOGUNATE; 1192–1333). Yoritomo was succeeded as shōgun by his sons MINAMOTO NO YORIIE and MINAMOTO NO SANETOMO. With the death of the latter in 1219, the main line of the Seiwa Genji ended. Collateral lines later provided the founders of the MUROMACHI SHOGUNATE (1338–1573) and the TOKUGAWA SHOGUNATE (1603–1867). ➡ *See genealogy, next page.*

Minamoto no Raikō → Minamoto
no Yorimitsu

Minamoto no Sanetomo　　　源実朝

(1192–1219). Third shōgun (r 1203–19) of the Kamakura shogunate (1192–1333); classical (WAKA) poet. Second son of the first shōgun MINAMOTO NO YORITOMO and his wife HŌJŌ MASAKO. Sanetomo was born at Kamakura, the shogunal capital. In 1199 Yoritomo died and was succeeded as shōgun in 1202 by his eldest son, MINAMOTO NO YORIIE, a puppet in the hands of his ruthless mother, Masako, and her father, HŌJŌ TOKIMASA. In 1203 Yoriie attempted the overthrow of his mother's family and was confined at Shuzenji on the Izu Peninsula. Sanetomo was designated shōgun, and in the following year Yoriie was assassinated at the behest of his grandfather Tokimasa. Sanetomo himself was assassinated in 1219 by his nephew, the priest Kugyō, who blamed him and his uncle HŌJŌ YOSHITOKI for the murder of Kugyō's father, Yoriie.

Possessing no real political power, Sanetomo became increasingly fascinated by the traditional culture of the Heian nobility. His interests extended from the literary arts to the aristocratic game of KEMARI (kickball), but it is for his poetry that he is famous today. Sanetomo reputedly began to write classical verse when he was 14 years old. In 1209 he sent 30 of his poems for criticism to the foremost court poet, Fujiwara no Teika (FUJIWARA NO SADAIE), who seems to have pri-

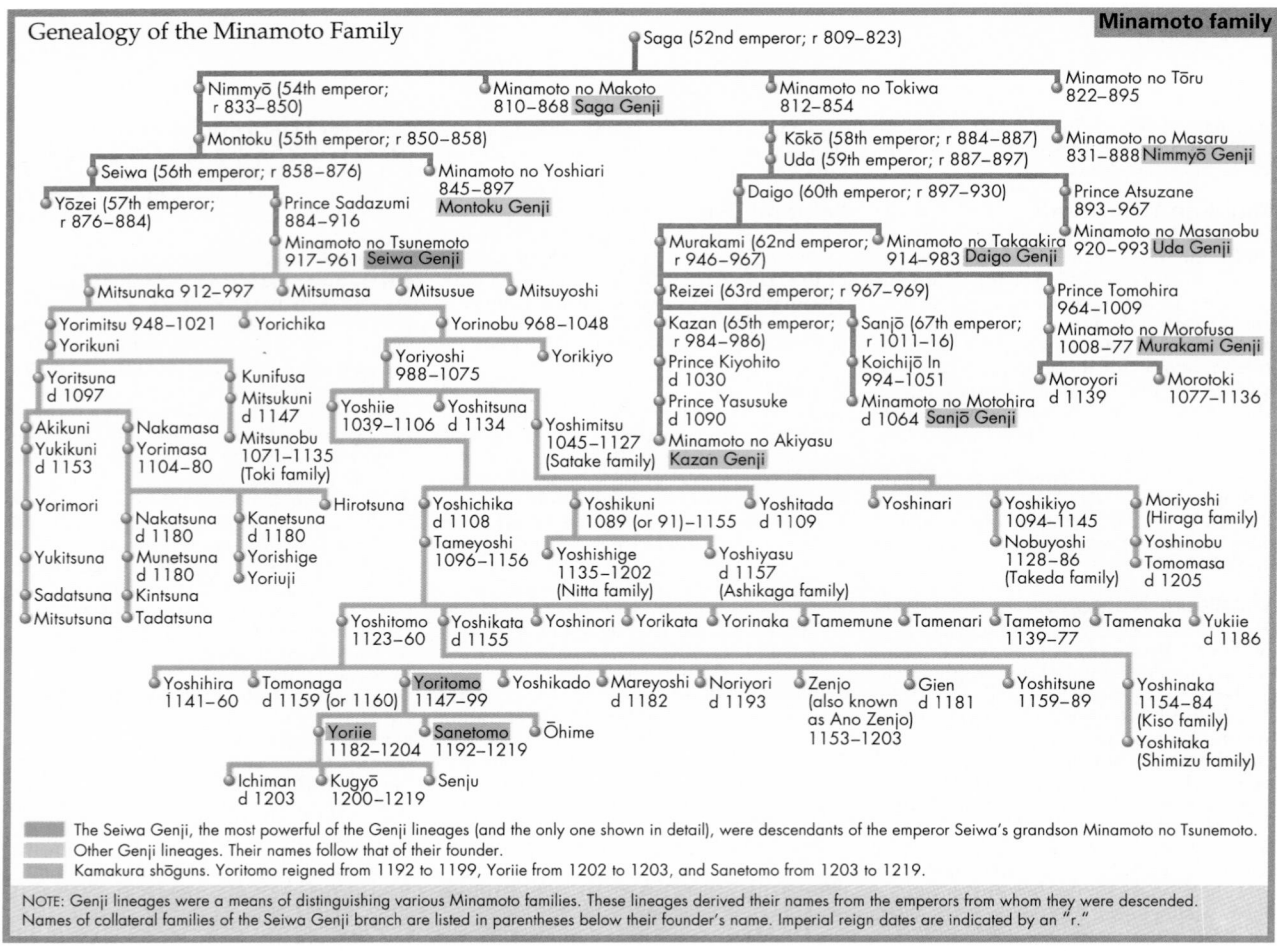

Genealogy of the Minamoto Family

The Seiwa Genji, the most powerful of the Genji lineages (and the only one shown in detail), were descendants of the emperor Seiwa's grandson Minamoto no Tsunemoto.
Other Genji lineages. Their names follow that of their founder.
Kamakura shōguns. Yoritomo reigned from 1192 to 1199, Yoriie from 1202 to 1203, and Sanetomo from 1203 to 1219.

NOTE: Genji lineages were a means of distinguishing various Minamoto families. These lineages derived their names from the emperors from whom they were descended. Names of collateral families of the Seiwa Genji branch are listed in parentheses below their founder's name. Imperial reign dates are indicated by an "r."

---

vately disapproved of the very poems for which Sanetomo is admired—his youthful, exuberant, and archaistic imitations of the 7th- and 8th-century poetry of the MAN'YŌSHŪ. Although imitation of the *Man'yōshū* was frowned upon at the time, Sanetomo composed poetry derived from it that displayed freshness and immediacy in the context of an overrefined and conventional court tradition. His best-known poems combine this mode with primitivistic imagery of almost savage power. Teika included 25 of Sanetomo's more conventional poems in the ninth imperial anthology, the *Shin chokusenshū* (ca 1234, New Imperial Collection), and an additional 66 are found in later imperial collections.

The KINKAI WAKASHŪ, Sanetomo's personal collection (commonly called the *Kinkaishū*, "The Collection of the Kamakura Minister of the Right"), exists in three main versions. The most authoritative is a copy made by Teika in his own hand (1213), which contains 663 poems. These can be supplemented from other texts and sources to constitute a total corpus of 716 poems. Owing to the Man'yōshū revival among the scholars of KOKUGAKU (National Learning) in the 17th century and later, and particularly the enthusiasm of the Meiji poet MASAOKA SHIKI, both Sanetomo and his poetry have enjoyed a revival in modern times.

Minamoto no Shitagau　源順

(911–983). Often spelled Shitagō. Major literary figure of the mid-10th century, one of the SANJŪROKKASEN (Thirty-Six Poetic Geniuses). He was also one of the so-called Five Men of the Pear Chamber (Nashitsubo no Gonin), who were chosen by Emperor Murakami (r 946–967) in 951 to compile the

second imperial anthology of Japanese poetry, the GOSEN WAKASHŪ, and also to make a scholarly study of the MAN'YŌSHŪ. He graduated as a scholar of the court university (DAIGAKURYŌ) and was a poet and scholar in both Japanese and Chinese. His works include the *Minamoto no Shitagau shū*, his personal poetry collection, and the WAMYŌ RUIJU SHŌ (Classified List of Japanese Readings), a Japanese dictionary of Chinese characters.

Minamoto no Tametomo　源為朝

(1139–77). Military leader of the late Heian period (794–1185); eighth son of Minamoto no Tameyoshi (1096–1156) and younger brother of MINAMOTO NO YOSHITOMO. At age 13 Tametomo was sent to Kyūshū, where he became a powerful warlord and defied the court; in consequence his father lost his court post and his headship of the Minamoto family. Both father and son supported the retired emperor Sutoku in the HŌGEN DISTURBANCE of 1156; Tameyoshi was put to death, but Tametomo was banished to the island of Ōshima in Izu Province (now part of Shizuoka Prefecture). There he attempted to seize local power but in 1177 was attacked by court forces and committed suicide.

Minamoto no Tameyoshi →
Hōgen Disturbance

Minamoto no Toshiyori　源俊頼

(1055?–1129?). Also known as Minamoto no Shunrai. WAKA poet; compiler of the fifth imperial anthology, KIN'YŌ WAKASHŪ (ca 1127, Collection of Golden Leaves). Son of the courtier and poet MINAMOTO NO TSUNENOBU. In 1124 the retired emperor SHIRAKAWA appointed Toshiyori, a radically innovative poet, to compile the fifth anthology of native poetry.

As a poet, Toshiyori was opposed by the arch-conservative FUJIWARA NO MOTOTOSHI. Toshiyori wrote in several styles: a convoluted, rhetorical manner; a style noted for unusual, colloquial diction (often combined with the first style); and a style distinguished by a quiet, reflective mode of natural description that he may have adopted from Tsunenobu and that was passed on to FUJIWARA NO TOSHINARI (Shunzei) and FUJIWARA NO SADAIE (Teika). More than 200 of Toshiyori's poems are included in imperial anthologies; his personal collection of 1,622 poems is *Samboku kikashū* (ca 1128, Collection of Eccentric Poems as Useless as Dead Wood). Toshiyori also wrote *Toshiyori zuinō* (ca 1115, Toshiyori's Essentials), a treatise on *waka*.

Minamoto no Tsunenobu　源経信

(1016–97). WAKA poet and high court official; credited with bringing an enhanced clarity to poetry of natural description. Like his older contemporary FUJIWARA NO KINTŌ, Tsunenobu was unusually accomplished in *waka*, music, and calligraphy—arts prized in court society. He experimented with a new mode of descriptive poetry, which led to competition with the younger but conservative FUJIWARA NO MICHITOSHI (1047–99). When Michitoshi was chosen to compile the fourth imperial anthology, the *Go shūishū* (1086, Later Collection of Gleanings), Tsunenobu responded with the first known critique of its kind, *Nan goshūi* (Failings of the *Go shūishū*). He was the father of the *waka* poet MINAMOTO NO TOSHIYORI.

Minamoto no Yoriie　源頼家

(1182–1204). Eldest son of MINAMOTO NO YORITOMO and HŌJŌ MASAKO; second shōgun of the KAMAKURA SHOGUNATE. Yoriie became head of the Minamoto house at his father's death in 1199 and shōgun in 1202. His maternal relatives, the HŌJŌ FAMILY, established a council of senior officials, leaving Yoriie essentially powerless. When he became ill in 1203, the council divided shogunal land rights between his infant son Ichiman and his younger brother MINAMOTO NO SANETOMO. Yoriie then joined his father-in-law, HIKI YOSHIKAZU, in a plot against the Hōjō. The plot failed; Yoshikazu was killed; and Yoriie, forced to abdicate, was banished. He was killed in 1204, allegedly at the order of HŌJŌ TOKIMASA.

Minamoto no Yorimasa 源頼政

(1104–80). Also known as Genzammi Nyūdō or Genzammi Yorimasa. Military aristocrat and poet of the Heian period (794–1185), best known for his role in three critical events of the 12th century. In the HŌGEN DISTURBANCE of 1156, Yorimasa allied himself with MINAMOTO NO YOSHITOMO and TAIRA NO KIYOMORI, and took the side of Emperor GO-SHIRAKAWA against the retired emperor SUTOKU's unsuccessful attempt to assert his authority. In the HEIJI DISTURBANCE of 1160, when Yoshitomo and Kiyomori clashed, Yorimasa first opposed Kiyomori, but then supported him when it became clear that Kiyomori's faction had the upper hand. As the sole remaining Minamoto of stature in a capital dominated by the Taira, he was promoted rapidly but was jealous of Kiyomori's rise to preeminence. In 1180 Yorimasa joined Go-Shirakawa's son Prince Mochihito (1151–80), who called for the overthrow of the Taira regime. Both he and Mochihito died in a skirmish at Uji near Kyōto, but their actions marked the beginning of the TAIRA-MINAMOTO WAR (1180–85), which ended in victory for the house of Minamoto, led by the future shōgun MINAMOTO NO YORITOMO.

Minamoto no Yorimitsu 源頼光

(948–1021). Military leader of the Heian period (794–1185), popularly known as Minamoto no Raikō; eldest son of Minamoto no Mitsunaka (912–997). He governed several provinces and formed a close alliance with the powerful regent FUJIWARA NO MICHINAGA. Under the leadership of Yorimitsu and his younger brother Yorinobu (968–1048), the Seiwa Genji branch of the MINAMOTO FAMILY became known as the "claws and teeth" of the Fujiwara and were generously rewarded for their services. Yorimitsu's prowess as a warrior and archer is celebrated in the KONJAKU MONOGATARI.

Minamoto no Yoritomo 源頼朝

(1147–99). Founder of the KAMAKURA SHOGUNATE (1192–1333), the first WARRIOR GOVERNMENT in Japan. Yoritomo was the third son of MINAMOTO NO YOSHITOMO. In January 1160 Yoshitomo joined an unsuccessful coup, the HEIJI DISTURBANCE, in which the rebels were routed by TAIRA NO KIYOMORI. Yoshitomo was killed, and Yoritomo was exiled to eastern Japan, where he was placed under the watchful eyes of two Taira adherents, first ITŌ SUKECHIKA and later HŌJŌ TOKIMASA. Yoritomo won the favor of Tokimasa and later married his daughter, HŌJŌ MASAKO.

In 1180 Prince Mochihito (1151–80), son of retired emperor GO-SHIRAKAWA, and MINAMOTO NO YORIMASA revolted against Taira rule. The uprising ended in a battle at Uji, in which Mochihito was killed and Yorimasa took his own life. Yoritomo used Mochihito's edict urging an uprising as a pretext for launching a rebellion. Defeated in his first major engagement, the Battle of Ishibashiyama, Yoritomo escaped and established headquarters at Kamakura.

Raising 200,000 troops, Yoritomo won the Battle of FUJIGAWA in Suruga Province (now part of Shizuoka Prefecture). He returned to Kamakura and from 1180 to 1183 built a solid political and economic foundation. He created the SAMURAI-DOKORO (Board of Retainers) in late 1180 to regularize the procedures, duties, and responsibilities in the relationship between himself and his vassals.

The final destruction of the Taira was precipitated by Yoritomo's kinsman MINAMOTO NO YOSHINAKA. When the Taira sent an army against Yoshinaka he eventually drove them out of the capital. The Taira and the young emperor ANTOKU fled westward in late 1183, leaving Yoshinaka in command of Kyōto. However, Yoshinaka and his men created havoc in the city, and Yoritomo sent his brothers Noriyori (d 1193) and MINAMOTO NO YOSHITSUNE against him in January 1184. Defeating Yoshinaka, the two immediately marched against the Taira, reducing the stronghold at Ichinotani in Settsu Province (now part of Ōsaka and Hyōgo prefectures) by March 1184. While organizing boats and supplies to pursue the Taira, Yoritomo established two more offices, the KUMONJO (Public Documents Office) and the MONCHŪJO (Board of Inquiry), to administer the expanding area under his control.

In March 1185 Yoshitsune attacked and defeated the Taira at Yashima on the island of Shikoku. Yoshitsune gathered a fleet to pursue the fleeing troops, and on 25 April the Taira and Minamoto fleets met in the Battle of DANNOURA off the southern tip of Honshū. The Taira were decisively defeated and the seven-year-old emperor Antoku drowned. See TAIRA-MINAMOTO WAR.

After his victory Yoritomo implemented various measures to consolidate his power; he had KUJŌ KANEZANE made imperial regent (sesshō, later kampaku), sympathetic nobles appointed to the Noble Council (Gisō), and his brother-in-law Ichijō Yoshiyasu (1147–97) made constable (SHUGO) of the capital. Because of disagreements over matters of vassalage, however, Yoritomo's relationship with Yoshitsune deteriorated, and Yoshitsune fled north, seeking sanctuary with the ŌSHŪ FUJIWARA FAMILY leader Fujiwara no Hidehira. To assist in apprehending Yoshitsune, Yoritomo received court approval to appoint his vassals as constables of provinces and stewards (JITŌ) of proprietary estates (SHŌEN). In 1189 Hidehira's son forced Yoshitsune to commit suicide, hoping to win Yoritomo's support, but Yoritomo led an army north and destroyed the Ōshū Fujiwara, leaving his own officials in charge of the area.

In 1192 Yoritomo was granted the title of SHŌGUN, so that in name as well as in fact he was supreme commander throughout Japan. His sons MINAMOTO NO YORIIE and MINAMOTO NO SANETOMO succeeded him as shōgun, but the shogunate then passed to the family of Yoritomo's father-in-law, Hōjō Tokimasa. Military chronicles such as the HEIKE MONOGATARI, GIKEIKI, and GEMPEI SEISUIKI portray Yoritomo as shrewd, calculating, and even ruthless; however, it was these very qualities that enabled Yoritomo to establish Japan's first warrior government, the basic structure of which would survive for nearly 700 years.

Minamoto no Yoshiie 源義家

(1039–1106). Also known as Hachiman Tarō Yoshiie. Military leader of the late Heian period (794–1185); one of the first great warriors produced by the Seiwa Genji branch of

the MINAMOTO FAMILY. He began his military career during the EARLIER NINE YEARS' WAR (1051–62) to subdue the rebellious Abe family of Mutsu Province (now Aomori, Iwate, Miyagi, and Fukushima prefectures). He was appointed governor of Mutsu (chinjufu shōgun) in 1083. Yoshiie pacified the north when the Kiyohara family rebelled in the LATER THREE YEARS' WAR (1083–87). The court considered this conflict a private matter, so Yoshiie rewarded his men with his own resources, creating a Minamoto base in northeastern Honshū.

Minamoto no Yoshinaka 源義仲

(1154–84). Better known as Kiso Yoshinaka. Warrior of the Heian period (794–1185). Yoshinaka was raised in Shinano Province (now Nagano Prefecture) by the husband of his wet nurse after his own father was killed by Minamoto no Yoshihira (1141–60). With MINAMOTO NO YORITOMO and other Minamoto warriors Yoshinaka rebelled against the rule of the TAIRA FAMILY in 1180. In 1183 he seized the capital and turned the TAIRA-MINAMOTO WAR into a triangular conflict, holding Kyōto while the Taira were in the west and Yoritomo in the east. The unruliness of his troops and his high-handed actions against the court, particularly the retired emperor GO-SHIRAKAWA, finally forced Yoritomo to dispatch his brothers MINAMOTO NO YOSHITSUNE and Minamoto no Noriyori (d 1193) to Kyōto, where they defeated Yoshinaka's forces. Yoshinaka managed to escape with his mistress, TOMOE GOZEN, but was eventually killed. His military exploits, as well as those of his mistress, have been popularized in numerous storybooks (OTOGI-ZŌSHI) and NŌ plays.

Minamoto no Yoshitomo 源義朝

(1123–60). Warrior of the Heian period (794–1185). The eldest son of Minamoto no Tameyoshi (1096–1156), he built up a power base in eastern Japan but later fell out with his father. In 1156 Yoshitomo, with TAIRA NO KIYOMORI, played a major role in Emperor GO-SHIRAKAWA's victory in the HŌGEN DISTURBANCE, which resulted in the death of many Minamoto warriors, including his father and younger brother, who fought on the losing side. Angered by Kiyomori's receipt of greater rewards, Yoshitomo launched a rebellion in 1160 (see HEIJI DISTURBANCE). He was betrayed and killed, but his sons MINAMOTO NO YORITOMO, Minamoto no Noriyori (d 1193), and MINAMOTO NO YOSHITSUNE lived to destroy Kiyomori's descendants in the TAIRA-MINAMOTO WAR (1180–85).

Minamoto no Yoshitsune　源義経

(1159–89) Warrior; principal figure in the TAIRA-MINAMOTO WAR; immortalized in legend as Japan's foremost tragic hero. The son of MINAMOTO NO YOSHITOMO and Tokiwa Gozen, he was a younger brother of MINAMOTO NO YORITOMO by a different mother. Known as Ushiwakamaru as a child, he later assumed the name Genkurō. In 1160, during the HEIJI DISTURBANCE, Yoshitomo was killed by the TAIRA FAMILY; their wife and children were captured, but their lives were spared. Yoshitsune grew to manhood intent on avenging his father's death.

In 1180, he was reunited with his brother soon after Yoritomo's victory against the Taira in the Battle of FUJIGAWA. In early 1184, as Yoritomo's deputy, Yoshitsune defeated MINAMOTO NO YOSHINAKA, who had aroused Yoritomo's suspicions by occupying Kyōto. He then defeated the Taira at Ichinotani in Settsu Province (near modern Kōbe). In 1185 Yoshitsune destroyed the Taira completely in the Battle of DANNOURA.

Yoshitsune's good relations with the former emperor GO-SHIRAKAWA once again aroused his brother's suspicions. Yoritomo's growing hostility eventually forced Yoshitsune to join with his uncle Minamoto no Yukiie (d 1186) in rebellion. In late 1185 Yoshitsune was granted a decree from Go-Shirakawa to attack Yoritomo, but the revolt failed. Yoshitsune then sought the protection of Fujiwara no Hidehira, of the ŌSHŪ FUJIWARA FAMILY in Hiraizumi, who had sheltered Yoshitsune as a youth. Hidehira died in 1187, and in 1189 his son Yasuhira (d 1189), under pressure from Yoritomo, forced Yoshitsune to commit suicide. The poignant story of Yoshitsune's life has long appealed to the Japanese. The colloquial phrase *hōganbiiki*, meaning sympathy for an underdog or an ill-fated person, derives from a military title bestowed on Yoshitsune by Go-Shirakawa. This sentiment has given rise to numerous legends about Yoshitsune (see YOSHITSUNE LEGENDS). The exploits of Yoshitsune and his faithful retainer BENKEI have been a staple of Japanese popular literature and drama since the Muromachi period (1333–1568).

Minase sangin hyakuin　水無瀬三吟百韻

(1488, One Hundred Links by Three Poets at Minase). A RENGA (linked verse) composed by SŌGI, SHŌHAKU, and SŌCHŌ and offered up at the tomb of the emperor GO-TOBA on the 250th anniversary of his death. Beginning with a link of 5-7-5 syllables by Sōgi that recalls a poem by Go-Toba, the three poets added, in turn, alternating links of 7-7 and 5-7-5 syllables to create a sequence that is distinguished by a classic grace and that has long been held a paragon of the art. The delicacy of Sōgi's strophes and the aptness of his linking are held in particularly high regard.

minasu　みなす

(fictive effect; literally, "to deem"). Device in Japanese law whereby the existence of fact A has the same legal effect as the existence of fact B (i.e., A is looked upon as B). For example, upon the issuing of a declaration of disappearance with regard to a missing person, such person is legally deemed to be dead (Civil Code, art. 31). Even if it is subsequently established that the person is still alive, the legal effects of death are not void unless the declaration of disappearance is canceled.

Minatogawa, Battle of　湊川の戦い

(Minatogawa no Tatakai). Battle between the armies of ASHIKAGA TAKAUJI and forces led by NITTA YOSHISADA and KUSUNOKI MASASHIGE on 4 July 1336 on the river Minatogawa in Settsu Province (now part of Hyōgo Prefecture), near Kōbe. Emperor GO-DAIGO overthrew the KAMAKURA SHOGUNATE (1192–1333; see also KEMMU RESTORATION), but Takauji, his general, turned against him and in the spring of 1336 arrived from Kyūshū with a new army, intent on capturing Kyōto. He was met on the banks of the Minatogawa by a detachment of loyalist warriors led by Masashige. Yoshisada, the commander-in-chief, deployed his men at Wada no Misaki. Takauji's superior forces overwhelmed Masashige, and he committed suicide. Takauji then defeated Yoshisada at Ikuta and triumphantly entered Kyōto. Enthroning Emperor Kōmyō (1322–80; r 1336–48), a member of a rival branch of the imperial house, he established the MUROMACHI SHOGUNATE (1338–1573). See also NORTHERN AND SOUTHERN COURTS.

Minato Ward　港区

(Minato Ku). One of the 23 wards of Tōkyō. A bustling business area and site of numerous foreign embassies, legations, and luxurious residences. The port of Tōkyō is located in eastern Minato Ward. The Tōgū Palace is located in the northern part of the ward. Restaurants and nightclubs abound in the AKASAKA and ROPPONGI districts. Tourist attractions include the Tōkyō Tower and the World Trade Center. Pop: 158,499.

Minazuki → calendar, dates, and time

Minchō　明兆

(1352–1431). Also known as Kichizan Minchō. ZEN monk-painter of the temple TŌFUKUJI in Kyōto. A native of the island of Awajishima (now in Hyōgo Prefecture). Early in his career he became a disciple of Daidō Ichii (d 1370), a priest of the temple Ankokuji on Awajishima, from whom he received the name Kichizan. When Daidō later moved to Tōfukuji, Minchō apparently followed and became the *densu* or superintendent in charge of the monastic buildings; thus he also became known as Chōdensu. He is considered one of the last major priest-painters to work in traditional Buddhist figure-painting styles. Although basically conservative, Minchō's works sometimes combine the traditional techniques of Buddhist painting with the new mode of landscape INK PAINTING (*suibokuga*).

Most of Minchō's extant works are in the Tōfukuji Collection. Among these are the *Shōichi Kokushi zō*, a portrait of Shōichi Kokushi (1202–80; the founder of Tōfukuji, who was also known as ENNI), and the *Dai nehanzu* (1408, Sākyamuni Entering Nirvana), the largest painting of its kind, exhibited publicly each year in February to commemorate the Buddha's death.

Mine　美祢[市]

City in western Yamaguchi Prefecture, western Honshū. It has several large lime and ce-

ment plants; some 80 percent of the marble in Japan is produced here. Pop: 19,642.

Minebea Co, Ltd　ミネベア[株]

(Minebea). Company engaged in the manufacture and sale of electronic components and devices, precision bearings, measuring instruments, fasteners, and mechanical components. Incorporated in 1951. The company is the world's leading manufacturer of miniature ball bearings and is expanding into the production of electronic equipment such as calculators and keyboards for personal computers, word processors, and typewriters. The firm has manufacturing facilities in Thailand and Singapore and has 48 subsidiaries and 12 affiliates worldwide. Sales for the fiscal year ending September 1991 totaled ¥207.9 billion (US $1.5 billion), and capitalization stood at ¥63.5 billion (US $472.2 million). Headquarters are in Tōkyō.

min'eika → privatization

mineral rights　鉱業権

(*kōgyōken*). The right to recover and use minerals, pursuant to the Mining Law (Kōgyō Hō) of 1950, under which the government has authority to grant such rights. Prospecting rights and digging rights may be granted only to Japanese citizens or Japanese juristic persons (HŌJIN).

mingei → folk crafts

mingu　民具

Traditional types of tools and other daily or ceremonial utensils used by the common people. The word *mingu* was coined by the folklorist SHIBUSAWA KEIZŌ. The 1975 CULTURAL PROPERTIES LAW (Bunkazai Hogo Hō) categorizes *mingu* as *yūkei minzoku bunkazai*, or tangible folk culture properties. The 10 subcategories described in the law are (1) utensils and objects used in daily life, including clothing and bathing and cooking equipment; (2) objects used in work, such as looms or fishing equipment; (3) objects used in transportation and communications; (4) objects used in trade; (5) objects used in societal organizations such as WAKAMONO-GUMI; (6) objects used in connection with folk beliefs; (7) objects concerned with folk knowledge, such as calendars, fortune telling, and medicine; (8) objects used in the FOLK PERFORMING ARTS; (9) objects used in family ceremonies, such as births, weddings, and funerals; and (10) objects used in annual events (NENCHŪ GYŌJI). See also FOLK CRAFTS.

miniature gardens → hakoniwa

Minidoka Relocation Center　ミニドカ収容所

(Minidoka Shūyōjo). Wartime relocation facility for Japanese Americans from the Pacific Northwest; located near Hunt, Jerome County, Idaho. In operation from 10 August 1942 until 28 October 1945, it held a maximum of 9,397 persons at any one time; a total of 13,078 persons were confined there. See also JAPANESE AMERICANS, WARTIME RELOCATION OF; WAR RELOCATION AUTHORITY.

Minimum Wage Law　最低賃金法

(Saitei Chingin Hō). Before World War II, Japan had no minimum wage law. There were minimum wage provisions in the postwar Labor Standards Law and the Labor Union Law. However, these were ineffectual, and in 1959 the Minimum Wage Law was enacted. Under this law the minimum wage differs according to industry, profession, and region. As originally enacted, the law permitted minimum wages to be based on agreements among representatives of management, on labor-management agreements, or on the recommendations of the Minimum Wage Deliberative Council, but the first of these methods was abolished by a 1968 amendment. The Ministry of Labor and the directors of local government labor-standards offices are responsible for implementing the Minimum Wage Law, in consultation with the Minimum Wage Deliberative Council. See also LABOR LAWS; LABOR STANDARDS INSPECTION OFFICES.

mining　　　　　　　　　　鉱業

(kōgyō). This article is concerned with the mining of inorganic materials; for a discussion of coal mining, see the article on COAL.

There have been three peak periods in the history of mining in Japan. During the first, from the 7th to the 9th centuries, the great image of Buddha was erected at the temple TŌDAIJI in Nara (completed 752) using copper, tin, gold, and mercury, all thought to have been mined domestically. The gathering of placer gold was the only kind of gold mining in the 7th to 9th centuries; however, lode mining of silver was carried out from the beginning. Gold mines were found mainly in eastern Japan and silver mines in western Japan. The next peak came in the 16th to 18th centuries, an age of gold and silver crowned by the erection of the lavishly decorated Azuchi Castle (1576) and Fushimi Castle (1594). Warlords of this period also encouraged gold and silver mining as a source of funds, leading to the discovery and development of many mines such as those on the island of Sado (from the 16th century; see SADO MINES). A third peak came after the Meiji Restoration of 1868. New technology was introduced from the West and great increases in production were achieved. Further modernization of equipment and techniques increased production during the late 19th and early 20th centuries.

By about 1960, however, the Japanese mining industry had depleted much of the country's mineral resources, and it soon became more cost-effective for mining companies to import minerals rather than search for new domestic sources. By 1980 many mining companies had gone out of business, and the remaining companies were concentrating on expanding mining operations abroad. In 1990 Japan mined the following percentages of its minerals domestically: zinc, 17.5 percent; lead, 14.0 percent; silver, 9.8 percent; gold, 2.9 percent; and copper, 0.4 percent. See also ASHIO COPPER MINE INCIDENT; ASHIO COPPER MINE LABOR DISPUTE; BESSHI COPPER MINE LABOR DISPUTES; NATURAL RESOURCES.

mining pollution　　　　　　鉱害

(kōgai). Mining pollution in Japan is classified by cause as follows: (1) land excavation; (2) discharge of mine pit water or wastewater; (3) dumping of waste rock, tailings, or slag; and (4) discharge of metallic smoke into the atmosphere. The development of the mining industry was a major feature of the rapid industrialization of Japan during the Meiji (1868–1912) and Taishō (1912–26) periods; a number of mine pollution cases, especially in the copper-mining industry, became serious social problems.

One of the earliest examples of mining pollution in Japan was the ASHIO COPPER MINE INCIDENT, a famous copper-poisoning case of the late 1890s. During this period another fa-

mous case resulted from smoke pollution at the Besshi Mine in Ehime Prefecture. Smoke damage from the Kosaka Mine in Akita Prefecture and the Hitachi Mine in Ibaraki Prefecture also caused great controversy. A disastrous accident occurred in 1936 at the Osarizawa Mine in Akita Prefecture, in which a tailing dam collapsed, resulting in heavy loss of life. The accident proved to be a turning point, however, as it led to the enactment of laws setting forth indemnities for injury and loss. Progress in science and technology helped prevent damage caused by mine water, wastewater, and smoke in later years. With the enactment of stronger pollution laws and technological advancements in pollution control, problems of this kind have largely disappeared. The origins of Japan's mining pollution legislation go back to the enactment in 1905 of the Mining Industry Law, which clearly held companies responsible for pollution and laid down regulations on the payment of compensation.

With the decline of the mining industry after World War II, there was a marked decrease in the number of pollution cases. A new development, however, was the emergence of itai itai (literally, "ouch-ouch") disease, the most serious case of illness in the history of Japanese mining pollution. Itai itai disease, which had been afflicting people in the basin of the river Jinzūgawa, Toyama Prefecture, was first thought to be an endemic disease. In 1957, however, a new theory suggested that it was caused by cadmium contained in wastewater flowing from the Kamioka Mine. The Ministry of Health and Welfare concluded in 1968 that the disease was indeed caused by cadmium discharged from the mine, and the company was forced to pay reparations. See also POLLUTION-RELATED DISEASES.

ministerial deliberative council
　　　　　　　　　　　　　審議会

(shingikai). A collegial or advisory body attached to a central government administrative organ that investigates and deliberates matters upon inquiry from the head of the administrative agency or, when so authorized by legislation, upon its own initiative. Deliberative councils are established under provisions of law; in May 1991 there were 246 such advisory bodies, such as the University Chartering Council (Daigaku Setchi Shingikai) of the Ministry of Education. The councils may gather information but are not empowered to determine public policy or to act as enforcement agencies. Deliberative councils are also established at the local government level.

Ministry of Agriculture, Forestry, and Fisheries　　　　　農林水産省

(Nōrin Suisan Shō). Government cabinet level ministry responsible for the administration and regulation of the agricultural, forestry, and fishing industries. Separated from the Ministry of Agriculture and Commerce (Nōshōmushō; established 1881) in 1925, it became the Ministry of Agriculture and Forestry (Nōrinshō). The name was changed again in 1978 to the present one. Its primary responsibilities are the guarantee of a stable food supply, the promotion of Japanese agriculture, and the protection of the Japanese farmer. The ministry drafts legislation for the agricultural sector and has sought to maintain agricultural subsidies and price support schemes. Other important functions of the ministry include the setting of standards and grades for farm products,

supervision of food markets and commodity exchanges, and undertaking various land reclamation and improvement projects. The ministry also has jurisdiction over the Food, Forestry, and Fisheries agencies (Shokuryō-chō, Rin'yachō, Suisanchō).

Ministry of Construction　　建設省

(Kensetsushō). Ministry of the national government, established in 1948, responsible for administration related to civil engineering and construction. The ministry has five bureaus. The Economic Affairs Bureau formulates land-use and building-development plans and adopts measures to stimulate the CONSTRUCTION INDUSTRY. The City Bureau is active in all phases of urban planning and renewal. The River Bureau administers programs concerning rivers, seacoasts, and dams, while the Road Bureau is responsible for the supervision of road projects. The Housing Bureau is in charge of housing programs. The ministry also supervises the HOUSING AND URBAN DEVELOPMENT CORPORATION, the JAPAN HIGHWAY PUBLIC CORPORATION, and the WATER RESOURCES DEVELOPMENT PUBLIC CORPORATION.

Ministry of Education　　　文部省

(Mombushō). Ministry of the national government, established in 1871, responsible for the administration of Japan's educational system and for the setting of national educational standards. The Agency for Cultural Affairs, attached to the ministry, is responsible for the promotion of cultural activities.

The ministry provides guidance, advice, and fiscal assistance to prefectural and local boards of education. It also has substantial control over the curricula, the production and content of textbooks, the training of teachers, and the standards of equipment used in schools. The ministry oversees the administration of the national universities as well as nationally established junior and technical colleges, museums, and education research institutes. The ministry is involved in numerous international educational exchange programs and is concerned with all matters pertaining to foreign students in Japan and Japanese students abroad. It provides a number of scholarships for foreign students and scholars for study and research in Japan.

Ministry of Finance　　　　大蔵省

(Ōkurashō). Government agency responsible for financial matters, including budgeting, taxes, banking, insurance, stocks and bonds, and international monetary affairs. The ministry was founded in 1869. In the early years its officials included many leading figures of the Meiji period—ŌKUBO TOSHIMICHI, INOUE KAORU, ITŌ HIROBUMI, SHIBUSAWA EIICHI, and MATSUKATA MASAYOSHI. The ministry was initially assigned broad responsibilities, overseeing not only finance but also industry, trade, agriculture, transportation, communications, and local government. However, by 1898 the basis of its present duties and organization had been established: the ministry comprised the secretariat; three main bureaus—budget, tax (including tariffs), and financial (including banking)—the mint; and local tax and customs offices. At about the same time, to preclude influence from political parties, the principle was established that all high posts, excluding only the minister and parliamentary vice-minister, must be occupied by ca-

Organization of the Ministry of Finance

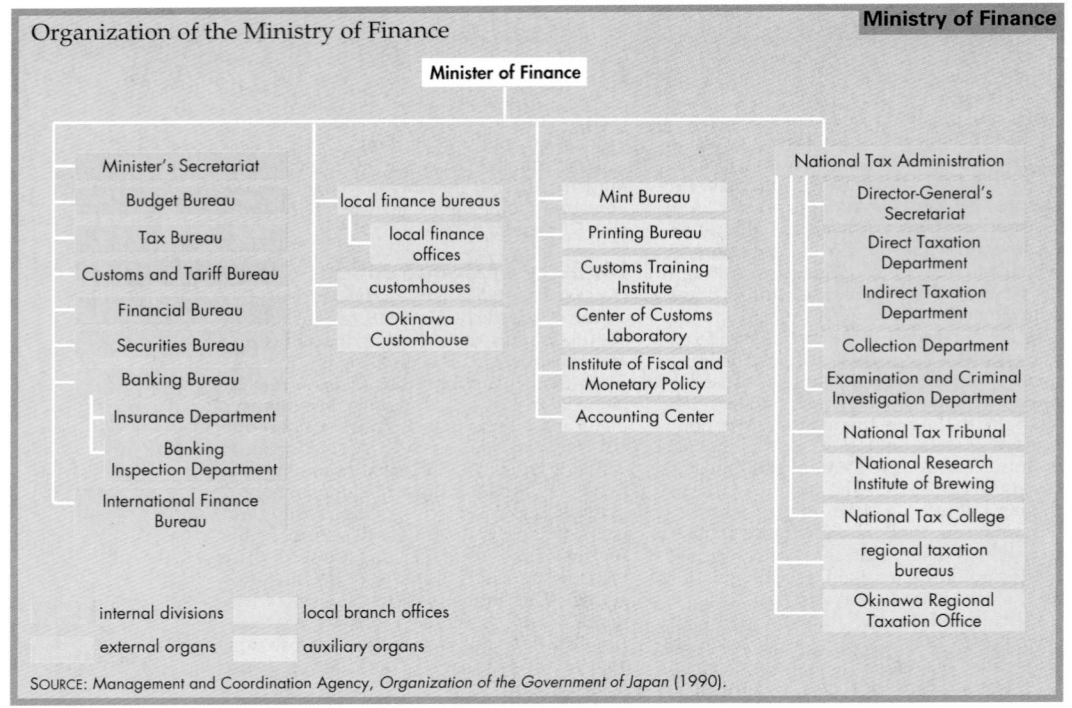

Minister of Finance

- Minister's Secretariat
- Budget Bureau
- Tax Bureau
- Customs and Tariff Bureau
- Financial Bureau
- Securities Bureau
- Banking Bureau
- Insurance Department
- Banking Inspection Department
- International Finance Bureau

- local finance bureaus
  - local finance offices
  - customhouses
  - Okinawa Customhouse

- Mint Bureau
- Printing Bureau
- Customs Training Institute
- Center of Customs Laboratory
- Institute of Fiscal and Monetary Policy
- Accounting Center

- National Tax Administration
  - Director-General's Secretariat
  - Direct Taxation Department
  - Indirect Taxation Department
  - Collection Department
  - Examination and Criminal Investigation Department
  - National Tax Tribunal
  - National Research Institute of Brewing
  - National Tax College
  - regional taxation bureaus
  - Okinawa Regional Taxation Office

internal divisions | local branch offices
external organs | auxiliary organs

SOURCE: Management and Coordination Agency, *Organization of the Government of Japan* (1990).

---

reer civil servants, a system still in force.

The impact of the Ministry of Finance in the contemporary period may be seen from two angles. Within Japan, it has usually been a restrictive, conservative force opposing the more expansionist MINISTRY OF INTERNATIONAL TRADE AND INDUSTRY (MITI), ECONOMIC PLANNING AGENCY, and ruling LIBERAL DEMOCRATIC PARTY. Viewed from outside, however, the ministry appears central to the government's dynamic growth policy.

The ministry is usually considered the most powerful and prestigious organization in the government, indeed in all Japan. Each year it enrolls 20 to 25 of the new graduates scoring highest on the government bureaucracy's employment test (a majority are from the law department of Tōkyō University); each year its retired bureaucrats move on to top jobs in business and politics (see AMAKUDARI).

Budgeting—The Finance Ministry's power stems partly from its control of the budget, since other agencies must come to it for funds. Accordingly, the Budget Bureau (Shukeikyoku) has the highest status within the ministry. Japanese budgeting is rather complicated: in addition to the general account (*ippan kaikei*), the Finance Ministry compiles 38 special accounts (*tokubetsu kaikei*), the accounts for several national enterprises, and the Fiscal Investment and Loan Program (ZAISEI TŌYŪSHI). The process begins with the preparation of ministry requests; these are submitted by 31 August, reviewed and cut by the Budget Bureau, and reported as the "Finance Ministry draft" in December or January. There follows a week of "revival negotiations" (*fukkatsu sesshō*), when the Finance Ministry responds to appeals from the ministries and the majority party. The resulting "government draft" is passed by the cabinet and sent to the Diet, where it provides the occasion for opposition party attacks on the full range of governmental policy before passage around 1 April, the beginning of the fiscal year.

Other Functions—In addition to its normal staff functions, the Minister's Secretariat (Daijin Kambō) engages in economic forecasting and other research. The Tax Bureau (Shuzeikyoku) is responsible for tax policy, revenue forecasting, and supervision of tax administration. Actual tax collections are handled by the semiautonomous NATIONAL TAX ADMINISTRATION (Kokuzeichō) through its over 500 district tax offices. The Financial Bureau (Rizaikyoku) manages the national debt, trust funds, and government-owned property and makes loans to local governments. The Banking Bureau (Ginkōkyoku) controls interest rates, licenses banks, supervises the Bank of Japan and other government financial institutions, and regulates the insurance industry. The International Finance Bureau (Kokusai Kin'yū-

kyoku) is in charge of foreign exchange, the balance of payments, and incoming and outgoing foreign investment. The functions of the Securities Bureau (Shōkenkyoku), the Customs and Tariff Bureau (Kanzeikyoku), and the external mint and printing bureaus are as indicated by their names. It is this exceptionally broad scope of responsibilities that gives the Ministry of Finance its central role in economic policy making.

Ministry of Foreign Affairs 外務省

(Gaimushō). Ministry of the national government responsible primarily for Japan's political relations with the outside world. Established in 1869 by the newly instituted Meiji government. With the exception of the 1930s and the first half of the 1940s, when the military gained ascendancy, the ministry has provided the organizational structure, channels of communication, and informed leadership necessary to plan and implement Japan's foreign policy.

The influence wielded by the ministry has varied considerably during its existence. In its early years the ministry stood at the summit of the bureaucratic hierarchy, reflecting in part the sense of urgency created by a hostile international environment and the need to establish a formalized working relationship with the Western powers (see UNEQUAL TREATIES, REVISION OF). However, as Japan's involvement in armed conflict grew in the late 19th and early 20th centuries, the ministry's monopoly on foreign policy decision making was increasingly challenged by the military. By the time of the MANCHURIAN INCIDENT of 1931 the military had clearly usurped much of the ministry's control over foreign policy. After World War II, the ministry regained some of its former power, but intraorganizational and environmental factors have worked to constrain it from assuming the preeminent position it enjoyed during the Meiji period (1868–1912).

Reflecting its rapid growth in the postwar period, economic issues have come to be the most important element of Japan's foreign relations. This has brought to the fore those government bureaucracies primarily responsible for Japan's economic well-being. For example, negotiations over exports and imports have been handled by the MINISTRY OF INTERNATIONAL TRADE AND INDUSTRY (MITI), while international monetary and financial agreements are the special preserve of the MINISTRY OF FINANCE. The Foreign Ministry is unable to assume a central role in economic or technical negotiations in part because its explicit policy of training generalists has not produced functional specialists. Furthermore, not unlike the British Foreign Office or the US State Department, the ministry's "internationalist" philosophy often clashes with the expressed desires of domestic interest groups. Finally, while the volume of its consular and diplomatic functions such as visas and passports is increasing geometrically, the ministry's financial and personnel resources are severely limited.

The ministry comprises 10 bureaus, 2 departments, and the Minister's Secretariat. Each bureau or department is headed by a director-general and contains several divisions, each led by a director. There are 63 divisions in all. Under the foreign minister, who is usually a politician with a Diet seat and who is appointed by the prime minister, are one administrative vice-minister, the senior career official of the ministry; one parliamentary vice-minister; two deputy vice-ministers; and several dozen counselors, who

---

Organization of the Ministry of Foreign Affairs

Minister of Foreign Affairs

- Minister's Secretariat
- Cultural Affairs Department
- Consular and Migration Affairs Department
- Asian Affairs Bureau
- North American Affairs Bureau
- Latin American and Caribbean Affairs Bureau
- European and Oceanic Affairs Bureau
- Middle Eastern and African Affairs Bureau
- Economic Affairs Bureau
- Economic Cooperation Bureau
- Treaties Bureau
- United Nations Bureau
- Information Analysis, Research, and Planning Bureau

- Foreign Service Training Institute

overseas establishments
embassies	165
consulates-general	65
consulates	2
permanent missions or delegations	6

internal divisions
auxiliary organs

SOURCE: Management and Coordination Agency, *Organization of the Government of Japan* (1990).

Organization of MITI

Minister of International Trade and Industry

Minister's Secretariat
- Research and Statistics Department
- International Trade Policy Bureau
- International Economic Affairs Department
- Economic Cooperation Department
- International Trade Administration Bureau
- Industrial Policy Bureau
- Industrial Location and Environmental Protection Bureau
- Basic Industries Bureau
- Machinery and Information Industries Bureau
- Consumer Goods Industries Bureau

Agency of Industrial Science and Technology
- International Trade and Industry Inspection Institute
- Research Institute of International Trade and Industry
- Weights and Measures Training Institute
- safety training institutes

- National Research Laboratory of Metrology
- Mechanical Engineering Laboratory
- National Chemical Laboratory for Industry
- Government Industrial Research Institute, Ōsaka
- Government Industrial Research Institute, Nagoya
- Fermentation Research Institute
- Research Institute for Polymers and Textiles
- Geological Survey of Japan
- Electrotechnical Laboratory
- Industrial Products Research Institute
- National Research Institute for Pollution and Resources
- Government Industrial Development Laboratory, Hokkaidō
- Government Industrial Research Institute, Kyūshū
- Government Industrial Research Institute, Shikoku
- Government Industrial Research Institute, Tōhoku
- Government Industrial Research Institute, Chūgoku

Agency of Natural Resources and Energy
- Director-General's Secretariat
- Petroleum Department
- Coal Mining Department
- Public Utilities Department
- regional bureaus of international trade and industry
- regional mine safety and inspection bureaus
- regional mine safety and inspection departments
- Naha Mine Safety and Inspection Office

Patent Office
- General Administration Department
- First Examination Department
- Second Examination Department
- Third Examination Department
- Fourth Examination Department
- Fifth Examination Department
- Department of Appeal
- Industrial Property Library
- Industrial Property Training Institute

Small and Medium Enterprise Agency
- Director-General's Secretariat
- Planning Department
- Guidance Department
- Small Enterprise Department

internal divisions
external organs
local branch offices
auxiliary organs

SOURCE: Management and Coordination Agency, *Organization of the Government of Japan* (1990).

---

rank between directors-general and directors, attached to the bureaus and departments.

Ministry of Health and Welfare 厚生省

(Kōseishō). Ministry of the national government responsible for the administration of public health and SOCIAL WELFARE programs. The ministry was formed in 1938 from two bureaus of the HOME MINISTRY and reorganized in 1948. The ministry conducts overall planning for Japan's pension, welfare, and medical systems; oversees the accreditation of doctors, nurses, and other health care personnel; administers medical facilities such as hospitals; and regulates and approves drugs and medicines. The Social Insurance Agency, an external bureau of the ministry established in 1962, has direct responsibility for the administration of the health insurance system and PENSIONS. The ministry has the largest budget of any government ministry: ¥10.8 trillion (US $82.8 billion) in 1989, 18 percent of the total general account budget. The ministry operates a network of more than 90 national hospitals, more than 150 national sanatoriums, the National Cancer Center, and other institutes. See also GOVERNMENT, EXECUTIVE BRANCH.

Ministry of Home Affairs 自治省

(Jichishō). Government cabinet-level ministry in charge of coordination and communication between the central and local governments. The ministry is also responsible for the administration of Japan's election system. Established in 1960, the ministry has assumed only a few of the functions of the powerful pre–World War II HOME MINISTRY (Naimushō). However, since it administers government grants-in-aid programs and oversees local finance, the ministry still exerts considerable influence over LOCAL GOVERNMENT. The ministry consists of three main bureaus (Local Administration Bureau, Local Finance Bureau, and Local Tax Bureau) and one agency (Fire Defense Agency).

Ministry of International Trade and Industry 通商産業省

(MITI; J: Tsūshō Sangyō Shō, abbreviated Tsūsanshō). Ministry of the national government responsible for the formulation and implementation of Japan's trade and industrial policy and the administration of patent rights and the JIS (Japanese Industrial Standard). Together with the ministries of finance, of construction, of transportation, and of agriculture, forestry, and fisheries, as well as the ECONOMIC PLANNING AGENCY, MITI occupies a central position in what the Japanese call "the economic bureaucracy."

The primary function of MITI until the early 1970s was to lead the private sector of the economy toward rapid economic growth. It was responsible for the introduction of new technology into Japan, the heavy industrialization of the economy, the rapid expansion of exports, and the import of energy and industrial raw materials. As a planning and guidance organ of the Japanese government in the context of one of the world's most vigorous open-market economies, MITI has no exact parallel with any ministry of economic affairs in other advanced capitalist nations.

Admirers hailed MITI as the leader of the Japanese "economic miracle"—the rapid postwar transformation of Japan in approximately 20 years from smoldering ruins to the world's most productive economy. Foreign rivals of Japan charged MITI with being the corporate headquarters of JAPAN INCORPO-RATED, meaning that the ministry fostered extremely close relations between government and business and worked to exclude foreign competition. Domestic critics blamed MITI for many of the pollution problems and the international economic problems that became increasingly evident during the early 1970s.

Although its origins date back to the Ministry of Agriculture and Commerce (Nōshōmushō) established in 1881, MITI was created in 1949 through the union of the Trade Agency and the Ministry of Commerce and Industry (Shōkōshō; 1925–43; 1945–49). The creation of MITI came about as part of the DODGE LINE—the basic change in US policy during the Occupation from attempts to "democratize" the Japanese economy to attempts to rehabilitate it. Throughout its first decade and a half, MITI exercised virtually total control over all imports and exports in Japan. MITI used its powers to direct imported technology, funds, and natural resources to those sectors of the economy—at first, coal, steel, shipbuilding, and electric power—that, in conjunction with business leaders, it designated as critical to Japan's rapid economic growth. MITI's overall policy was to transform Japan's economy from a light-industry, Asia-oriented one to a heavy-industry, globally oriented one. It also erected formidable barriers to protect the Japanese economy from international competition (see also INDUSTRIAL POLICY).

MITI's policies succeeded so spectacularly that by the mid-1960s Japan's foreign economic partners demanded that Japan dismantle its structure of economic controls and liberalize foreign trade and international transfers of capital to and from Japan. MITI

969

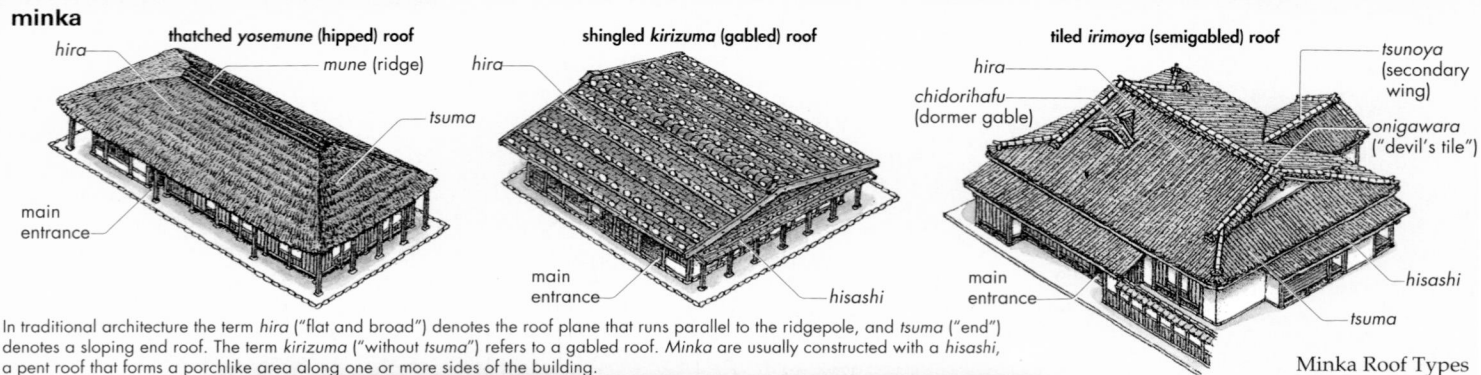

minka

thatched *yosemune* (hipped) roof

hira
— *mune* (ridge)
tsuma
main entrance

shingled *kirizuma* (gabled) roof

hira
main entrance
hisashi

tiled *irimoya* (semigabled) roof

tsunoya (secondary wing)
hira
chidorihafu (dormer gable)
onigawara ("devil's tile")
hisashi
main entrance
tsuma

In traditional architecture the term *hira* ("flat and broad") denotes the roof plane that runs parallel to the ridgepole, and *tsuma* ("end") denotes a sloping end roof. The term *kirizuma* ("without *tsuma*") refers to a gabled roof. *Minka* are usually constructed with a *hisashi*, a pent roof that forms a porchlike area along one or more sides of the building.

Minka Roof Types

This traditional townhouse in Gifu Prefecture, built in 1879, has a packed-earth entryway that opens onto a spacious dining-living area with an open hearth.

The same townhouse features a *kirizuma*-style roof.

gradually complied, but it also continued through informal ADMINISTRATIVE GUIDANCE to enhance Japan's international competitive ability. In 1973 MITI abandoned its older policies of industrial protection and guidance and reoriented its work toward developing nonpolluting, high-technology industries and toward promoting close ties with Japan's foreign customers and suppliers of raw materials.

Of the five economic ministries, MITI is the smallest in terms of personnel and budget. It has always preferred to perform its functions through the use of its extensive legislation-based licensing and approval authority and through its powers to recommend appropriate loans and investments to institutions such as the JAPAN DEVELOPMENT BANK. Much of MITI's influence derives from its extremely close ties with big business and from the fact that most of its high officials, upon "retirement" at about age 50, accept positions as executives of Japan's leading private corporations (see AMAKUDARI). The

ministry consists of the Agency of Natural Resources and Energy, the Patent Office, the Small and Medium Enterprise Agency, and the following bureaus: the minister's secretariat, international trade policy, international trade administration, industrial policy, industrial location and environmental protection, basic industries, machine and information industries, and consumer goods industries. See also FOREIGN TRADE, GOVERNMENT POLICY ON; VOLUNTARY EXPORT RESTRICTIONS.

Ministry of Justice 法務省

(Hōmushō). Government ministry in charge of administering Japan's legal system, established in 1871 and bearing its present name since 1952. Its responsibilities include the drafting of laws and ordinances relating to the judicial system, administration of the penal system, and rehabilitation of criminals. It administers registration of families, aliens, corporations, and real estate. It represents the Japanese government in litigation and is charged with the protection of civil liberties. Public prosecutor's offices (*kensatsuchō*) administratively belong to the Ministry of Justice. The public prosecutor, however, acts independently of the minister of justice. Also under the jurisdiction of the ministry are the National Bar Examination Administration Commission, the Public Security Examination Commission, and the PUBLIC SECURITY INVESTIGATION AGENCY.

Ministry of Labor 労働省

(Rōdōshō). Cabinet-level government ministry, established in 1947, responsible for the administration and implementation of labor policy on national and local levels. It dispenses unemployment compensation and worker's accident compensation, is involved

in employment and vocational training programs, and is responsible for the formation and supervision of labor standards and wage guidelines and for the improvement of working conditions for women and certain disadvantaged groups. Its CENTRAL LABOR RELATIONS COMMISSION (Chūō Rōdō Iinkai; Chūrōi) mediates or arbitrates national labor disputes in private industry.

Ministry of Posts and Telecommunications 郵政省

(Yūseishō). Government ministry that supervises Japan's mail system and approximately 20,000 post offices. It also administers postal savings, life insurance, and pension programs. The ministry controls licensing of radio and television broadcasting and exerts indirect control over the NIPPON TELEGRAPH AND TELEPHONE CORPORATION (NTT) and the International Telegram and Telephone Company (KOKUSAI DENSHIN DENWA CO, LTD; KDD).

Ministry of Transport 運輸省

(Un'yushō). Ministry of the national government, established in 1945, responsible for administering and supervising all forms of transportation in Japan and formulating national land, sea, and aviation policies (see TRANSPORTATION). The ministry is responsible for the regulation and supervision of the shipping and motor transportation industries; administration of all seaports, harbors, and major airports; inspection and registration of ships, road vehicles, and aircraft; administration of international transport and tourism; and formulation of contracts for road construction. The ministry grants licenses for ship construction and subsidizes the construction of ships. Its Maritime Safety Agency (Kaijō Hoan Chō) has police powers in coastal waters and is responsible for safeguarding navigation and assisting ships in distress. The ministry's marine-accidents inquiry agencies (*kainan shimpan chō*) investigate and judge sea casualty cases. The ministry also supervises the METEOROLOGICAL AGENCY of Japan.

Minji Soshō Hō → Civil Procedure, Code of

minka 民家

General name for traditional-style houses of the nonruling classes, usually dwellings of rather simple construction, that were built before Japanese architecture came under Western influence in the late 1800s. *Minka* in farming villages are called *nōka* (farmhouses); in cities, *machiya* (townhouses); and in fishing villages, *gyoka*.

Wood was used in the thick columns and beams of the framework, as well as for the walls, floor, ceiling, and roof. Bamboo was layered between columns as laths and plastered over with clay to form walls. Clay also was baked into ROOF TILES. Grass was used to make thatch for roofing, and straw was used for the coarse, thin *mushiro* matting and

TATAMI mats to be used on the floor. Rock was used to lay stone foundations for support but was not employed for walls.

Design Characteristics——*Minka* differed considerably in style depending on the period or region in which they were built. General design features include a skeletal framework composed of interconnecting frames, consisting of joined columns and beams. The walls were fitted between the columns and were not load bearing. On the exterior side of the house, openings were closed by a set of sliding inner lattice doors known as SHŌJI and an outer set of heavy wooden doors. Inside, the interval between columns was partitioned by paneled or lattice doors covered with heavy paper (*fusuma*). Such doors used to close off the openings are collectively called *tategu*. The interior of the house was divided into an area called the *doma*, which had a compacted earthen floor, and an area with the floor raised about 50 centimeters (20 in) off the ground. People sat directly on the raised floor, which was usually covered with *tatami* or *mushiro* mats. For cooking, a furnacelike oven (KAMADO) built of clay was installed in the *doma*. In the floored area was located an open hearth (IRORI) for burning firewood for heat, but no chimney was provided.

Roofs of *minka* are often steeply pitched, and are classified as thatched roof (*kayabuki yane*), shingle roof (*itabuki yane*), or tile roof (*kawarabuki yane*). Stones are sometimes used to keep shingles from being blown away; this type of shingle roof is also called *ishioki yane* (stone-laid roof). There are also three types of roof shapes. The first, in which planes slant down on two sides from a central ridge (*mune*), is the simplest and is called a *kirizuma* (gabled) roof. The second type, in which planes slant down to the four sides of a rectangular building, is called a *yosemune* (hipped) roof. In the third, the *irimoya* (semigabled) roof, gables are attached to the roof with four slanting planes. The roof of a farmhouse is usually thatched and in either *irimoya* or *yosemune* style, while many townhouses have tile roofs in a *kirizuma* style.

In a tile roof, tiles are also placed on the ridge, but the ends are decorated with *onigawara* (ridge-end tile with a gargoylelike design). With thatched roofs, ridge decorations (*munekazari*) are provided. In tileroofed buildings or in *minka* built where there is heavy snowfall, a hole is made and a smoke vent is built into the roof. The smoke vent may have either a small monitor roof (*koshi yane*) over the ridge or a dormer gable (*chidorihafu*).

Farmhouses (Nōka)——The arrangement of rooms in Japanese houses is called *madori*. In the standard layout of early-19th-century farmhouses, four rooms were next to the *doma;* this was called a *yomadori* (four-room arrangement). There was a large sliding plank door called the *ōdo*, giving access to the *doma* and serving as the front entrance for the building. The *doma*, which took up a third of the total floor area, was used for farming tasks and cooking. For these purposes, an earthen oven and a sink made of wood were located to the rear of the *doma*. Of the four rooms, the two closest to the *doma* were used for daily activities by the family. The room to the rear had a hearth made of hardened clay in the floor about 1 square meter (11 sq ft) in size. Here firewood was burned for warmth and light. The entire family gathered around the hearth, particularly at mealtimes, and the seating arrange-

ment was socially determined. A decorative alcove (*tokonoma*) for displaying a picture or flowers was built in the front room, which was used for receiving guests on more formal occasions; this room was called the *zashiki* or *dei*. Outside this front room was a long narrow veranda (*engawa*).

Townhouses (Machiya)——Because the width of an urban site was limited, townhouses tended to have deep, rectangular plans. Behind the main building (*omoya*) stood the storehouse (*kura* or *dozō;* see STOREHOUSES, TRADITIONAL) or a detached *zashiki*, and to provide direct access to these the *doma* penetrated to the backyard. Along this *doma* was a row of three rooms. The one closest to the road was called *mise*, and here goods were displayed or business talks held. The middle room was used as an office and also as a place where the family could receive visitors. The rear room faced an enclosed garden; this was built like a *zashiki*, complete with *tokonoma*, but was actually used for the daily activities of the family. In many cases there was a second floor. The second-floor portion, generally called *zushi*, had a low ceiling on the road side, and this area was used as storage; the side facing the backyard was used as a room.

👁 972–973

Minkan denshō　　　　民間伝承
(Oral Folklore). Journal for the study of folklore and ethnology. In 1935 Japanese ethnologists decided to found a society that would act as a national coordinating organ for the field. In September of the same year, the society, called Minkan Denshō no Kai, put out the first issue of its organ, *Minkan denshō*. The journal ceased publication in 1952, but was immediately followed by *Nihon minzokugaku* (Bulletin of the Folklore Society of Japan), the journal of the Nihon Minzoku Gakkai. Another publication by the same name, *Minkan denshō*, was put out by the Minkan Denshō Shiyūkai from 1958 to 1983.

minkatsu jigyō　　　　民活事業
The involvement of the private sector in public works projects in place of or as a supplement to national or local governments. As a means of increasing investment in public facilities without requiring massive new government bond issues, the government enacted a law (the Minkatsu Hō) in March 1986 that was designed to encourage private sector participation in projects that would otherwise have to be funded entirely by the government. This was accompanied by the removal or reduction of various regulations on the private sector participation in public projects. By 1990, 38 projects had been started under the 1986 legislation, including the TŌKYŌ BAY BRIDGE AND TUNNEL project (under the jurisdiction of the MINISTRY OF CONSTRUCTION), the New Infrastructure Improvement Project (in cooperation with the MINISTRY OF INTERNATIONAL TRADE AND INDUSTRY), harbor improvement projects (in cooperation with the MINISTRY OF TRANSPORT), and the creation of the International Telecommunications Institute for Basic Technology (under the jurisdiction of the MINISTRY OF POSTS AND TELECOMMUNICATIONS).

Mino　　　　美濃[市]
City in southern Gifu Prefecture, central Honshū, on the river NAGARAGAWA. In 1606 Mino became a castle town of the Kanamori family. It has long been known for its Mino *washi* paper, the production techniques of

which have been designated a National Treasure. Mino is also a center for machine-made paper. Pop: 26,022.

mino——▸ straw raincoats

Minobe Ryōkichi　　　　美濃部亮吉
(1904–84). Economist and politician. Born in Tōkyō, the son of the jurist MINOBE TATSUKICHI. After graduating from Tōkyō University, he taught at Hōsei University. He was arrested in 1938, along with other suspected leftists, in the so-called POPULAR FRONT INCIDENT and was removed from the university by the government. After World War II, he became a professor at the Tōkyō University of Education (now Tsukuba University). He was elected governor of Tōkyō Prefecture in 1967 with the support of the Socialist and Communist parties; he was reelected in 1971 and 1975. As governor, Minobe stressed social welfare and opposed the government's emphasis on rapid economic growth. He was elected to the House of Councillors in 1980.

Minobe Tatsukichi　　　　美濃部達吉
(1873–1948). Scholar of constitutional and administrative law. Born in Hyōgo Prefecture, he graduated from Tōkyō University in 1897 and entered the Home Ministry. From 1899 to 1902 he studied abroad, principally in Germany, and on his return became a professor at his alma mater. Minobe opposed the ultraconservative constitutional theories of HOZUMI YATSUKA and UESUGI SHINKICHI and became known as a champion of democratic constitutionalism, advocating the "emperor-as-organ-of-the-state" theory (TENNŌ KIKAN SETSU), party cabinets, and the expansion of civil liberties. Minobe was appointed to the House of Peers in 1932. In 1935 he was charged with lese majesty for expounding the emperor-as-organ theory, which was considered subversive of the national polity (KOKUTAI); he was forced to resign from the House of Peers, and some of his works were withdrawn from publication. His many writings include KEMPŌ SATSUYŌ (1923, Outline of the Constitution) and *Nihonkoku kempō genron* (1946, Principles of the Japanese Constitution). He was the father of MINOBE RYŌKICHI.

Minobu　　　　身延[町]
Town in southwestern Yamanashi Prefecture, central Honshū, on the river Fujikawa. Minobu developed as a temple town around Kuonji (see MINOBUSAN), the head temple of the Nichiren sect. Its principal industry is lumber. Pop: 9,006.

Minobusan　　　　身延山
Head temple of the NICHIREN SECT of Buddhism, located in Minami Koma District, Yamanashi Prefecture. Minobusan, the official name of which is Kuonji, was built in 1281 by Hakii Sanenaga (1222–97), a lay follower of NICHIREN, on the site of a small hermitage that Nichiren occupied after he returned from exile in 1274. In 1706 the temple was designated a *chokuganji*, i.e., a temple commissioned by the imperial family to offer prayers regularly for their well-being as well as for the prosperity of the empire. Much of Minobusan was destroyed by fire in 1875, but it has since been rebuilt.

Mino Kamo　　　　美濃加茂[市]
City in southern Gifu Prefecture, central Honshū, on the river KISOGAWA. In the Edo

Continued on page 974▸

Minobe Tatsukichi
This scholar of constitutional law was forced to resign from the House of Peers in 1935 for advocating the theory that the emperor is an organ of the state.

Minka: House of Many Faces

The sturdy dwellings of farmers, fishermen, merchants, artisans, and other commoners, *minka* were designed to suit the varied lifestyles and climates found along the Japanese archipelago. Built out of natural materials such as wood, clay, stone, bamboo, and grass, minka are characterized by exposed pillars and beams, the absence of load-bearing walls, and a high degree of adaptability.

In the Tōhoku region, for example, harsh winters and the horse's importance as a domestic animal spawned styles integrating the stable and main residence. In areas such as the Chūbu region, where cultivating silkworms was crucial to the farm economy, ingenious interior designs maximized the space available for raising them.

Although minka have gradually given way to more modern structures in most parts of Japan, some outstanding examples have been preserved for their historic significance. These simple, rugged houses thus continue to serve as vital links to life as it was lived in earlier eras.

Magariya: A Cutaway View

① Minka with L-shaped floor plans are known as *magariya*. Such houses are found throughout Iwate Prefecture, particularly in that area that once was part of the now-vanished Morioka domain. The unusual design sprang from the need to stable horses in a warm, readily accessible place. The Iwate Prefecture house shown here, built in the mid-18th century, originally had no stable; the evidence that one was added on—sturdier pillars and a lower roof—provides insight into the *magariya's* structural evolution.

Thatched roofs in this region of Japan are made from dried *susuki* (eulalia). With periodic repairs to its thatch, especially where the two sections of the L-shaped structure meet, the roof shown here will reportedly withstand even the harshest weather for 40 years or more.

The daidokoro (kitchen) encompasses the earthen-floored area called the *doma* and the wood-fueled *kamado* (oven). The sink in the corner was low enough that the house's inhabitants could work there in a squatting position.

② **This minka's floor plan** is based on the style called *chūmon-zukuri*. Although it resembles a *magariya* shown here, called a *ryōchūmon*, has its main entrance at the front of the second wing of the house. This mid-18th-century house is in Akita Prefecture.

The earthen-floored room called the *niwa* was used for threshing, milling, and other farm tasks when heavy snow or rain made working outside impossible. The portion nearest the stable housed toilet and bath facilities.

Both people and horses used the house's main door, which was built near the juncture of the two wings. To minimize drafts, the door faces southeast.

People stood on this stepping-stone to remove footwear before ascending to the porch. This entrance was primarily used by visitors.

③ **In houses** built in the *azumaya-zukuri* style, the eaves at the sides were shortened to improve ventilation and illuminate the interior. The large attic, with one section divided into two floors, provided ample space for raising silkworms. The house shown here, built in the 1870s, is located in Fukushima Prefecture.

Straw was used to line the stable's sunken floor; replaced two or three times yearly, the old straw was employed as fertilizer.

The chūnikai, or mezzanine, functioned as a storage area for seldom-used items. The room below it, known as the *nakama*, was used for silkworm cultivation, weaving, and receiving guests.

④ **For better lighting** and ventilation, roofs in the *hirakabuto-zukuri* style have a foreshortened eave in front. This minka, in Gumma Prefecture, was constructed in the late 18th century.

⑤ **Hommune-zukuri** is a style characterized by a gently sloping roof decorated with a large *suzume odori* ("sparrow dance") ornamental ridge and big, latticed bay windows. The roof shingles are held in place by heavy stones. Built in the latter half of the 19th century, this Nagano Prefecture minka was evidently the home of a wealthy farm family.

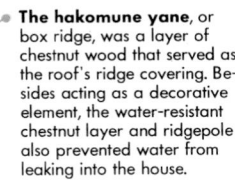

The hakomune yane, or box ridge, was a layer of chestnut wood that served as the roof's ridge covering. Besides acting as a decorative element, the water-resistant chestnut layer and ridgepole also prevented water from leaking into the house.

This sunken hearth, called the *irori*, was used for heating the house, boiling water, and cooking. Since it was the household's sole source of fire, it was always kept burning.

Reeds for repairing the roof were kept in this attic store-room; smoke rising from the hearth killed insects, thereby protecting the materials. Below the attic is the *nakanando*, or communal family bedroom.

©1989 Odo Noritsugu

The house's foundation stones helped shield its pillars and base from moisture. The pillars were cut to fit the foundation stones, which were sometimes flat and sometimes concave.

The front parlor was used as a reception area. Until the beginning of the Taishō period (1912–26), this room (now *tatami*-matted) had wood plank flooring. When guests were expected, the flooring was covered with thin reed mats called *mushiro*.

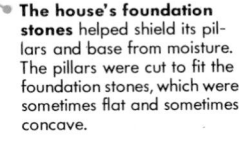

N

6 **Gasshō-zukuri** gabled roofs slope in a distinctly precipitous fashion. This home in Gifu Prefecture, built in the mid-19th century, has a tri-level attic designed for silkworm cultivation and storage. The upper floors are partially covered with bamboo lathing; the spacing between the slats allowed warm air from the first floor to heat them as well.

7 **Yamatomune-zukuri roofs** have a thatched portion tiled at both ends, tiled eaves, and a lower tiled section fitted with a covered opening that allowed smoke from the hearth to escape. Constructed in the first half of the 17th century, the minka pictured here is located in Ōsaka Prefecture.

8 **A Hyōgo Prefecture minka** built in the Muromachi period (1333–1568). Respectfully referred to as a *sennen'ya* ("thousand-year house"), it is one of Japan's oldest surviving farmhouses. The semigabled *irimoya* roof has low-hanging eaves and is supported by pillars placed symmetrically on the left and right.

9 **The family** that lived in this minka in Tokushima Prefecture was in the indigo dye business. The main house, shown here, was built in 1865. It has a distinctive hipped roof with a central thatched section surrounded by tiled eaves. This style is known as *shihōbuta-zukuri*.

10 **Of the three wings** comprising this early-19th-century farmhouse in Fukuoka Prefecture, two are directly connected at the rear, forming a "valley" between the two roofs on the right. This building style, known as *kudo-zukuri*, is found throughout the plains of northern Kyūshū.

In the Ryūkyū Islands (not shown on map), minka often had separate buildings for living and sleeping, cooking, and storage. Pictured is the *omoya* (main building) of a house built in Okinawa Prefecture in 1819.

Mino ware A teapot and teacups, representative of different types of Mino ceramics.

period (1600–1868) it flourished as a river port and a post-station town on the highway Nakasendō. Electrical-appliance and textile plants are located here. Local produce includes persimmons and pears. It is the starting point for shooting the rapids of the Kisogawa. Pop: 43,013.

Minolta Camera Co, Ltd

ミノルタカメラ[株]

(Minoruta Kamera). Manufacturer and distributor of optical products and business machines, primarily cameras and copying machines. Its Minolta brand name is well known internationally. Founded in 1928, it assumed the present company name in 1962. The company expanded into overseas markets soon after World War II. Overseas subsidiaries include two in the United States, eight in Europe, and five in Southeast Asia. Sales for the fiscal year ending March 1991 totaled ¥222.1 billion (US $1.6 billion), of which photographic goods accounted for 47 percent and business machines 53 percent. For the same year the export ratio was 76 percent, and the company was capitalized at ¥25.5 billion (US $185.9 million). Headquarters are in Ōsaka.

Mino Mikawa Kōgen

美濃三河高原

The highlands Mino Kōgen in southeastern Gifu Prefecture, central Honshū, and Mikawa Kōgen in northeastern Aichi Prefecture, central Honshū. Mino Kōgen is an abundant source of potter's clay. Mikawa Kōgen is part of Aichi Kōgen Quasi-National Park. Elevation: 100–1,000 m (328–3,280 ft).

Minomura Rizaemon

三野村利左衛門

(1821–77). Businessman. Builder of the MITSUI financial empire. Born in Shinano Province (now Nagano Prefecture), he worked for a wholesaler in Edo (now Tōkyō), where he came to the attention of OGURI TADAMASA, commissioner of finance (kanjō bugyō) in the Tokugawa shogunate (1603–1867). Through Oguri's good offices, Rizaemon was adopted as heir by the Minomura family, chief clerks of the Mitsui family business. During the BOSHIN CIVIL WAR at the time of the Meiji Restoration (1868), Minomura persuaded the Mitsui family to contribute to the imperial forces and, after the Restoration, sought preferential treatment for Mitsui in the form of lucrative government commissions (see SEISHŌ). He helped establish the Mitsui Bank

and Mitsui Trading Company, which formed the core of the Mitsui ZAIBATSU.

Minoo

箕面[市]

City in northern Ōsaka Prefecture; 16 km (10 mi) north of Ōsaka, of which it is fast becoming a residential suburb. Its northern section is part of the Meiji no Mori Minoo Quasi-National Park, which contains the TŌKAI SHIZEN HODŌ (a hiking trail). Pop: 122,120.

Mino Province

美濃国

(Mino no Kuni). Also called Nōshū. One of the eight provinces (kuni) of the Tōsandō region in central and northeastern Honshū. In 1871 it became part of GIFU PREFECTURE. In the mid-Heian period (794–1185), members of the MINAMOTO FAMILY settled here; their descendants, the TOKI FAMILY, ruled Mino as military governors (SHUGO) until they were displaced in the late Muromachi period (1333–1568). Soon afterward, ODA NOBUNAGA seized Gifu Castle and took control of the area. Strategically situated near the capital of Kyōto, Mino Province was repeatedly a battleground in civil wars. The most famous of these was the Battle of SEKIGAHARA in 1600, which made way for the TOKUGAWA FAMILY to rule Japan for 250 years. Pottery (MINO WARE) and rice paper (Mino paper) production are among the main industries.

minority groups

少数者集団

(shōsūsha shūdan). Although frequently perceived as one of the most ethnically and culturally homogenous in the world, the Japanese population includes a number of minority groups. Japan's minorities include native populations such as the BURAKUMIN and AINU, as well as groups of foreign nationals resident in Japan, the largest of which are the Koreans and the Chinese.

The 1947 CONSTITUTION OF JAPAN provides for equality under the law and prohibits discrimination in political, economic, or social relations on the basis of race, creed, sex, social status, or family origin (art. 14). Despite these provisions, minorities in Japan continue to face varying degrees of discrimination in employment, housing, marriage, and education.

The largest of Japan's minorities is the approximately 3 million burakumin living in some 6,000 communities throughout the country. Physically indistinguishable from the majority Japanese population, the burakumin have nevertheless experienced a long and painful history of discrimination that they have attempted to resist and remedy through organizations such as the Buraku Kaihō Dōmei (Buraku Liberation League).

The ancestors of the Ainu migrated to Japan in prehistoric times. Today the Ainu population of Japan is primarily to be found in Hokkaidō, where in 1986 the number of people identifying themselves as Ainu was 24,381. While blatant discrimination against the Ainu has waned and many of the younger generation are being assimilated into the general population, the Ainu tradition survives in some villages where the Ainu language, clothing, and the observance of traditional festivals are being maintained.

The Korean minority, according to 1990 alien registration statistics, has a population of 687,940, or 64 percent of all foreigners resident in Japan. A large proportion of the Korean population is concentrated in Ōsaka and the surrounding region. (See KOREANS IN JAPAN.) The Chinese minority in Japan numbered 150,339 in 1990. There are few pre-

dominantly Chinese residential areas, the thriving Chinatown in Yokohama being the exception. In addition to the sizable Korean and Chinese minorities, there is a growing, though still much smaller, number of resident foreigners from other parts of the world now living in Japan—many of them from the countries of South and Southeast Asia. See also FOREIGNERS IN JAPAN.

minority shareholders, rights of

少数株主権

(shōsū kabunushi ken). The minority shareholder in Japan is subject to the same sorts of disincentives to challenge decisions of the board of directors that confront his counterpart in other corporate systems. The situation is complicated in Japan because of the relatively high level of debt financing, which tends to diminish the importance of the shareholder. Minority shareholders have a specific right to bring an action against directors, although the imposition in most cases of a sizable advance payment as security against the costs of a successful defense by the directors operates as a significant deterrent. Reforms from 1981 give certain rights to the holder of 1 percent of the issued stock or 300 shares. See also JOINT-STOCK COMPANY; UNLIMITED PARTNERSHIP COMPANY; LIMITED PARTNERSHIP COMPANY; LIMITED LIABILITY COMPANY.

Minor Offenses Law

軽犯罪法

(Keihanzai Hō). This law, enacted in 1947, specifies 33 minor crimes that are subject to the comparatively light punishment of detention (1–30 days) or petty fine. Types of crime include (1) crimes nearly identical to those specified in the now-abolished Police Offenses Penal Regulations (Keisatsukan Shobatsu Rei) and the Law of Summary Procedures for Police Offenses (Ikeizai Sokketsu Rei), such as vagrancy, begging, mischievous interference, and carrying a concealed weapon, and (2) offenses newly created by the Minor Offenses Law: peering into such places as public baths; playing music at an inordinately loud volume; and causing a disturbance in places of public entertainment or on public transportation facilities.

minoue sōdan

身上相談

Personal advice columns in newspapers and women's magazines in the form of requests from readers and responses by specialists, scholars, and others. The first such column in Japan appeared in the magazine Jogaku zasshi in 1886. The first column permanently established in a daily newspaper was in the Yomiuri shimbun in 1914. Those requesting advice through such columns have been predominantly female. In recent years, personal advice programs have become a part of Japanese radio and television.

Mino ware

美濃焼

(mino-yaki). A general term for various styles of ceramics produced in Mino Province (now part of Gifu Prefecture), which had a long ceramic tradition. The term includes famous ceramic styles preferred for the TEA CEREMONY, such as Shino, kiseto, setoguro, and Oribe, all of which came into prominence in the Mino area during the Azuchi-Momoyama period (1568–1600).

Mino Province shared a border with Owari Province (now part of Aichi Prefecture), which included the city of SETO, the site of the most famous ceramics center in eastern Japan. Tradition has it that the national unifier ODA NOBUNAGA, then lord of Owari, annexed Mino Province in 1567 and began patronizing Mino-ware production for the TEA CEREMONY. The distribution of Mino ceramics was most probably controlled by Owari Province. Consequently, prior to the Meiji Restoration (1868), no distinction was made between the wares of the two provinces. Recent excavations, however, have yielded Mino ware of an earlier date that resembles the later tea wares.

Shino ware is noted for its nearly pure feldspathic glaze, the first white glaze in Japan. (Its forerunner is an opaque, white ash glaze, used to produce white *temmoku* teabowls.) The glaze is applied irregularly, on such vessels as teabowls and water jars, over simple iron-oxide painted decorations ranging from a reddish brown to a very dark brown. Gray and red Shino glazes were also developed, depending on the coloration of the iron slip.

Kiseto (Yellow Seto) is either plain or decorated with incisions and copper-green underglaze designs. *Setoguro* (Black Seto) is produced by removing the fired pieces from the kiln and cooling them immediately.

Oribe ware (see FURUTA ORIBE) is characterized by unconstrained application of green glaze, along with feldspathic glaze, and by a wide variety of shapes and painted decoration. Many Oribe and *kiseto* pieces consist of dishes made for use in the *chakaiseki* meal, a part of the tea ceremony, or are teabowls and other utensils for the tea ceremony.

A few potters revived the production of Oribe ware late in the Edo period (1600–1868). In 1930 ARAKAWA TOYOZŌ discovered the Mino kiln sites and was later instrumental in launching a 20th-century revival of Shino ware.

Min, Queen 閔妃

(1851–95; Kor: Min Bi; J: Bin Hi). Consort of the Korean king KOJONG (r 1864–1907), 26th ruler of the YI DYNASTY, whom she married in May 1866. "Min," though it is often so used in English, was not actually her personal name but that of her clan. The queen competed with the king's father, the grand prince (TAEWŎN'GUN), to manipulate Kojong, and the Japanese officials who directed the modernizing KABO REFORM concluded that her removal was essential to secure control of the king and the success of the reforms. The minister to Korea, MIURA GORŌ, took matters into his own hands; on 8 October 1895 he sent a Japanese military party to enter the palace and murder the queen, which they did. After her death Russia protected Kojong and became dominant in Korean affairs until the RUSSO-JAPANESE WAR of 1904–05. See also IMO MUTINY.

Minsei 民青

Abbreviation of Nihon Minshu Seinen Dōmei (Democratic Youth League of Japan); sponsored by the JAPAN COMMUNIST PARTY, it claims to have 200,000 members, mostly young workers and students. Minsei traces its origins to 1923. It became the core of the Yoyogi faction of the ZENGAKUREN (the All-Japan Federation of Student Self-Governing Associations), which dominated the postwar student movement.

Minseitō → Rikken Minseitō

minshingaku 明清楽

Urban popular songs of Chinese origin that flourished in Japan in the 18th and 19th centuries. They were of two kinds. The first date from the end of the Ming (J: Min) dynasty

(1368–1644), when a certain Wei Shuang-hou (1613?–ca 1690; J: Gi Sōkō) emigrated from China to Nagasaki and brought the musical tradition with him. In the 18th century, his descendant Wei Hao (d 1774; J: Gi Kō or Ōga Mimbu) taught and promoted these songs in Kyōto, where they gained great popularity among the court nobility. Wei Hao was said to have had over 200 songs in his repertory. The texts of 50 of these are preserved in the collection *Gishi gakufu* (1768). After his death at the end of the 18th century, interest in this art waned.

The second wave of importation of Chinese songs came during the 19th century, toward the latter part of the Qing (Ch'ing; J: Shin) dynasty (1644–1912). At that time, a handful of the earlier Ming songs were also incorporated into the Qing repertory; hence the name *minshin* (Ming-Qing) *gaku* (music). The name continued to be used even when the repertory no longer contained the Ming pieces. It was also applied to works composed in Japan after the style of the Chinese importations. The Qing-dynasty songs were brought to Japan by another Chinese immigrant, Jin Qinjiang (Chin Ch'in-chiang; J: Kin Kinkō), at the beginning of the 19th century. He taught in Nagasaki and Kyōto, where the songs became extremely popular, especially among the literati. Soon after Jin another man, Lin Dejian (Lin Te-chien; J: Rin Tokuken), also came to Nagasaki to teach this kind of Chinese song. Lin's disciples spread the art to various large cities in Japan, including Ōsaka, Edo (now Tōkyō), and Nagoya.

minshuku 民宿

A private establishment providing inexpensive lodging and meals to tourists. *Minshuku* generally offer only basic services, and guests may sometimes be asked to share a room. However, some also have tennis courts or other recreational facilities. There are approximately 25,000 *minshuku* in Japan. They are officially registered with local authorities and listed in a brochure (*Minshuku gaido: Zenkoku*) put out by the Japan Travel Bureau.

Minshutō 民主党

(Democratic Party). Political party formed in March 1947 under ASHIDA HITOSHI. Not to be confused with the NIHON MINSHUTŌ (Japan Democratic Party). The Minshutō joined with the JAPAN SOCIALIST PARTY and the People's Cooperative Party (KOKUMIN KYŌDŌTŌ) to form a coalition cabinet under KATAYAMA TETSU in May 1947. In March 1948 Ashida became prime minister, supported by the same three parties. Ashida resigned eight months later when he was implicated in the SHŌWA DENKŌ SCANDAL, and the party eventually dissolved in 1950. Some of its members joined the LIBERAL PARTY (Jiyūtō), and some merged with the Kokumin Kyōdōtō to form the People's Democratic Party (Kokumin Minshutō). See also POLITICAL PARTIES.

mintō 民党

(popular parties). A term loosely applied to the liberal parties of the early 1890s, such as the JIYŪTŌ and the RIKKEN KAISHINTŌ, that opposed the government led by the clique (HAMBATSU) from the former domains of Satsuma (now Kagoshima Prefecture) and Chōshū (now Yamaguchi Prefecture). The designation was used in contrast to the derogatory term *ritō* (bureaucrats' parties), by which the liberals referred to progovernment associations such as the KOKUMIN KYŌ-

KAI and the Taiseikai founded by TSUDA MAMICHI and other scholar-bureaucrats. The *mintō* coalition, led by the Jiyūtō and the Rikken Kaishintō, gained a majority in the first and second general elections (1890 and 1892) held under the Constitution of the Empire of Japan. The *mintō* parties persistently challenged the government's budget proposals, which included large military appropriations. See also POLITICAL PARTIES.

Minumadai Canal 見沼代用水

(Minumadai Yōsui). Irrigation canal in eastern Saitama Prefecture, central Honshū. It draws water from the river Tonegawa to irrigate approximately 15,000 hectares (37,065 acres) of farmland. Construction was completed in 1728. Length: 96 km (59 mi).

MIPRO → Manufactured Imports Promotion Organization

mirin 味醂

Type of *sake* that is used to give certain Japanese prepared foods a mildly sweet flavor. *Mirin* is made by mixing glutinous rice and malted rice with distilled liquor (SHŌCHŪ). The mixture is aged for several months and then strained. It is also used in sauces (see TERIYAKI) and stocks of simmered foods (*nimono*) to impart a sheen.

Miroku 弥勒

(Skt: Maitreya; literally, "The Benevolent One"). Bodhisattva now in the Tuṣita (J: Tosotsu) heaven who will, millions of years hence, descend to this world to attain Buddhahood and lead its inhabitants to enlightenment. Maitreya was among the first Buddhist divinities known to and worshiped by the Japanese, a stone image of Maitreya having been brought to Japan from the Korean kingdom of Paekche in 584. By the 7th century Maitreya had become one of the most important figures in the Japanese Buddhist pantheon (see KANNON; JIZŌ; AMIDA), as is attested by the many superb images dating from that period found in the temples CHŪGŪJI, KŌRYŪJI, Yachūji (in Ōsaka), and HŌRYŪJI. Maitreya continues to be worshiped today, sometimes merged with traditional veneration of high mountains (see MOUNTAINS, WORSHIP OF). Certain voluntary religious associations (KŌ) regard him as a type of messiah. His worship has been promoted by "new religion" organizations such as REIYŪKAI and the ŌMOTO.

Miruna no zashiki 見るなの座敷

(The Forbidden Room). Folktale; also known as *Uguisu no ichimon sen* (The Nightingale's Penny). A man takes lodgings in an isolated house. The beautiful mistress of the house leaves it in his charge but forbids him to look into the back room. He keeps his word and after a year is given a roll of cloth and a coin that turns out to be a treasure. His neighbor, hearing of the fortune, goes to stay at the house, but he breaks the taboo and meets disaster.

Misaki → Miura

Misasa 三朝[町]

Town in central Tottori Prefecture, western Honshū. Surrounded by mountains, Misasa chiefly produces lumber and *shiitake* mushrooms. The Misasa Hot Spring and the Institute for Study of the Earth's Interior of Okayama University are here. Other attrac-

tions include NINGYŌ PASS and Oshikakei, a gorge. Pop: 8,700.

Misato　　　　　　　三郷[市]

City in southeastern Saitama Prefecture, central Honshū. Formerly a farming district, it has become an industrial and residential area. Pop: 128,377.

Misawa　　　　　　　三沢[市]

City in eastern Aomori Prefecture, northern Honshū, on the Pacific coast. Misawa developed after World War II as a US Air Force base; the base is now shared with the Japan Air Self Defense Forces. Apart from services related to the military, its principal activity is farming. Pop: 41,342.

Misawa Homes Co, Ltd　　ミサワホーム[株]

(Misawa Hōmu). One of Japan's largest suppliers of prefabricated housing. Incorporated in 1951. The company is known for its emphasis on research and development and for its integrated housing supply system. It has conducted operations in the Antarctic and 15 countries and exported new material technology to South Korea. Company activities encompass all facets of the housing business, including research on materials and technologies, production, marketing, remodeling, land development, interior coordination, real estate, resort development, financing, and information services. Sales for the fiscal year ending March 1991 totaled ¥266.2 billion (US $1.9 billion). Capitalization stood at ¥11.0 billion (US $80.2 million) in the same year. Headquarters are in Tōkyō.

miscellaneous schools　　　各種学校

(kakushu gakkō). Category of schools in the classification established by the Ministry of Education. It includes schools outside the regular school system, most of them voca-

tional and technical training schools. In order to qualify for certification by the local municipality, the course requirements must include more than 680 hours of classroom instruction. These schools offer a certificate upon completion of the course of study.

In 1976 the Ministry of Education established a higher category of school with special requirements for certification; there were 2,520 such special training schools (SENSHŪ GAKKŌ) in 1980. After the establishment of senshū gakkō, the number of miscellaneous schools decreased drastically as they began to be recategorized. In 1980 kakushu gakkō numbered more than 5,300 and were attended by more than 724,000 students. By 1989 the number of miscellaneous schools had fallen to 3,570, and the enrollment level was down to 442,186.

Mishihase　　　　　　　粛慎

Also pronounced Shukushin. Aborigines described in the ancient chronicle Nihon shoki (720) as having lived in northern Japan; possibly a tribe of the EZO. The name Mishihase (Ch: Sushen) was earlier applied by the Chinese to a Tungusic people who lived in the Amur, Sungari, and Ussuri river basins of Manchuria from about the 8th to the 3rd centuries BC, but it is believed that the Japanese arbitrarily borrowed the name from ancient Chinese records to refer to unassimilated tribal groups in the north.

Mishima　　　　　　　三島[市]

City in eastern Shizuoka Prefecture, central Honshū, on the Izu Peninsula. In the Edo period (1600–1868) it prospered as a post-station town on the highway Tōkaidō and as a shrine town centering on Mishima Taisha. Now it is the site of several industries and the National Institute of Genetics. It is the base for trips to Mt. Fuji (Fujisan), Hakone, and Izu. Pop: 105,418.

Mishima　　　　　　　見島

Island in the Sea of Japan, approximately 45 km (28 mi) northwest of Yamaguchi Prefecture, off western Honshū. Part of Yamaguchi Prefecture. Warmed by the Tsushima Current, the island is largely agricultural and is famous for Mishima cattle. A place of exile for the Hagi domain, the island is now the site of a Self Defense Forces radar base. A group of more than 200 ancient tombs on the island has aroused much interest in recent years. Area: 7.8 sq km (3 sq mi).

Mishima Michitsune　　　三島通庸

(1835–88). Bureaucrat of the Meiji period (1868–1912). Also known as Mishima Tsūyō. Born in Satsuma domain (now Kagoshima Prefecture). After 1868, he served as governor of several prefectures. In 1882, while he was governor of Fukushima Prefecture, his high-handed methods in levying taxes incurred opposition from local residents. His ruthless suppression of an uprising (the FUKUSHIMA INCIDENT) led to the KABASAN INCIDENT two years later. In 1885 he was appointed superintendent-general of the Tōkyō Metropolitan Police; in enforcing the PEACE PRESERVATION LAW OF 1887 (Hoan Jōrei) he banished 570 members of the FREEDOM AND PEOPLE'S RIGHTS MOVEMENT from Tōkyō.

Mishima Tokushichi　　　三島徳七

(1893–1975). Physical metallurgist. Discoverer of the MK alloys, a series of powerful magnetic materials that led to the development of the Alnico V magnet used in over 90 percent of today's high-fidelity loudspeak-

ers. Born in Hyōgo Prefecture, Mishima graduated from Tōkyō University and taught there from 1920 to 1953. He is also noted for his research on stainless steel and other metals used in vacuum tube electrodes. He received the Order of Culture in 1950.

Mishima ware　　　　　三島

(mishima). General term for a type of ceramic ware initially produced during the first half of the Yi dynasty (1392–1910) on the Korean peninsula. Also known as mishima-de and hakeme. It has its roots in celadon porcelain of the Koryŏ period (935–1391). Typically in Mishima ware intricate patterns of white clay are inlaid in a gray base; the ware is then treated with a clear glaze and fired. The Mishima technique was first used to produce bowls and vessels for daily use, but when Mishima tea bowls came into vogue among connoisseurs of the TEA CEREMONY during the late Muromachi period (1333–1568), kilns all over Japan began producing versions of the ware.

Mishima Yukio　　　　三島由紀夫

(1925–70). Writer of fiction, drama, and essays. Real name Hiraoka Kimitake. Born in Tōkyō on 14 January 1925. His father, a government official, was the son of a former governor of Karafuto (southern Sakhalin). As a boy Mishima was sent to the Peers' School (now Gakushūin University). His early story "Tabako" (1946, The Cigarette) relates with what scorn he was treated by members of the rugby club when he confessed that he belonged to the school literary society. His experiences at that time are so faithfully depicted in this story and in "Shi o kaku shōnen" (1954; tr "The Boy Who Wrote Poetry," 1977) as to suggest autobiography or the I-NOVEL. But Mishima's purpose in writing these stories had little in common with the obsession for truth of the I-novelists, the facts in his stories serving mainly as points of departure for observations and analysis. "The Boy Who Wrote Poetry" describes the protagonist's fascination with words, a trait that remained with Mishima throughout his life.

The young Mishima was especially impressed with the poetry of TACHIHARA MICHIZŌ, whose influence also molded Mishima's appreciation of classical WAKA poetry. Mishima's own poems, his first publications, appeared in the literary magazine of the Peers' School. While still publishing these poems he began to write his first prose work of consequence, "Hanazakari no mori" (1941, The Forest in Full Flower). The story abounds in the metaphors and aphorisms that are typical of Mishima's later works, and the themes would also recur. The narrator describes ancestors who in some sense still live within him. They share with him various tastes, notably a love for the sea and for the sun of the south.

"Hanazakari no mori" was intended for the literary magazine of the Peers' School, but Mishima's adviser was so impressed by the manuscript that he proposed publishing it in Bungei bunka (Literary Culture), the magazine that he and other Peers' School teachers edited. The other editors decided to protect young Hiraoka Kimitake by persuading him to use a pen name of their invention, Mishima Yukio. In October 1944, "Hanazakari no mori" was published in book form. The 4,000 copies of the original printing sold out within a week.

Mishima began the story "Misaki nite no monogatari" (1945, A Story at the Cape) in

July 1945 and continued it during the chaotic months that followed Japan's defeat in World War II. In January 1946 he visited KAWABATA YASUNARI with the manuscripts of two stories, "Chūsei" (1945, The Middle Ages) and "Tabako," and in June, at Kawabata's recommendation, "Tabako" was published in *Ningen* (Humanity), a new literary magazine. At the time, Mishima was still a student in the law department of Tōkyō University. The year he completed his first full-length novel, *Tōzoku* (1946–48, The Thieves), an implausible and unsuccessful portrayal of two young members of the aristocracy who are irresistibly drawn toward suicide, was among the most productive of Mishima's career. In July he was invited to join the group that published the magazine KINDAI BUNGAKU (Modern Literature). In September he resigned from his post in the Ministry of Finance to concentrate on his writing.

In January 1949 Mishima published in *Kindai bungaku* the first of several essays on the art of Kawabata. He always professed great admiration for the older writer, but although both men were devoted to Japanese tradition, the term had different meanings for each. For Kawabata the past meant *tawayameburi*, the feminine aspects of Japanese culture; for Mishima the past was typified by *masuraoburi*, the masculine traditions of the warrior. In July 1949 Mishima published his most self-revelatory work, the novel KAMEN NO KOKUHAKU (tr *Confessions of a Mask*, 1958), which established his reputation. In it, the homosexual proclivities of the hero prevent him from feeling desire for the girl he loves. The American publishers who were first offered the translation of the novel rejected it, fearing it would "brand" Mishima, but Japanese readers have interpreted it instead as an exceptionally sensitive account of a boy's gradual self-awakening.

Mishima's writings were much sought by editors after the success of *Confessions of a Mask*, and soon he was publishing popular fiction that he would disown in later years as necessary evils. His next important work was *Ai no kawaki* (1950; tr *Thirst for Love*, 1969), the central figure of which is a widow, Etsuko, who has become the mistress of her late husband's father. The main theme is Etsuko's intense but unavowed love for a young farmer named Saburō. During the climactic scene of the novel, Etsuko, watching as Saburō cavorts at a festival, gashes his back with her nails, an echo of the sexual fantasies at the end of *Confessions of a Mask*. When Saburō, at last becoming aware of Etsuko's love, responds, she is terrified, calls for help, and kills him.

In 1952 Mishima went abroad. The high point of his journey was Greece, which had fascinated him from childhood. It made him realize that the dark pictures of life he had hitherto painted had been incomplete. The first product of this insight was the novel *Shiosai* (1954; tr *The Sound of Waves*, 1956). He drew inspiration from the ancient Greek romance *Daphnis and Chloë*, transforming the shepherd and shepherdess of the original into a fisherboy and fishergirl who live on a small island off the Ise coast.

Mishima's love for Western literature, however, did not lure him away from Japanese traditions. His modern NŌ plays, although they retain the main themes of the original works, twist the materials in a manner that intrigues or shocks contemporary audiences. His use of contemporary events was similar. Most critics believe that his finest work was the novel KINKAKUJI (1956; tr *The Temple of the Golden Pavilion*, 1959), which describes the events leading up to the burning of the famous Kyōto temple.

During the next decade Mishima produced a half dozen novels of importance, even when not wholly successful. *Kyōko no ie* (1959, Kyōko's House) failed to recapture the 1950s, as filtered through his own experiences, and became the first serious setback in his literary career. *Utage no ato* (1960; tr *After the Banquet*, 1963) was far more successful. However, this novel was based so closely on the events surrounding the campaign of the veteran politician ARITA HACHIRŌ for the governorship of Tōkyō that Arita successfully sued Mishima for invasion of privacy (see AFTER THE BANQUET CASE).

In 1962 Mishima published his most unusual novel, *Utsukushii hoshi* (The Beautiful Star), a combination of science fiction and a long dialogue on whether or not man is worthy of preservation. This was the closest Mishima ever came to writing an avant-garde novel, and its failure to attract wide attention came as another blow. In 1967 he secretly spent a month training with the SELF DEFENSE FORCES, and in 1968 he formed a private army of 100 men, the Tate no Kai (Shield Society), which was sworn to defend the emperor. For Mishima, the emperor was the abstract essence of Japan itself, not a reigning monarch. Indeed, in *Eirei no koe* (1966, The Voices of the Heroic Dead) the spirits of the *kamikaze* (see KAMIKAZE SPECIAL ATTACK FORCE) denounce the emperor for having denied his divinity: if the emperor was not a god their deaths were meaningless. His best full-length plays, *Sado kōshaku fujin* (1965; tr *Madame de Sade*, 1967) and *Waga tomo Hittorā* (1968; tr *My Friend Hitler*, 1977–78), date from this period, as does the long essay *Taiyō to tetsu* (1968; tr *Sun and Steel*, 1970), in which he deplored the emphasis given by intellectuals to the mind and insisted on the importance of the body.

The tetralogy HŌJŌ NO UMI (The Sea of Fertility), his final work, began to appear serially in September 1965. Mishima continued to produce monthly installments until the day of his death, finding the pressure of deadlines a necessary stimulus. The four volumes each bear a separate title: *Haru no yuki* (1965–67; tr *Spring Snow*, 1971), *Homba* (1967–68; tr *Runaway Horses*, 1973), *Akatsuki no tera* (1968–70; tr *The Temple of Dawn*, 1973), and *Tennin gosui* (1970–71; tr *The Decay of the Angel*, 1974). Mishima's suicide on 25 November 1970 brought worldwide attention, and the actions of the last hours of his life created widespread concern over a possible revival of Japanese militarism. His appeal for a revision of the constitution that would permit rearmament had no effect on the government, however, and Mishima's reputation rests on his literary accomplishments and not on his politics.

mishōtai   御正体

In Shintō, a sacred metal or wooden disk upon which a Buddhist or Shintō image is embossed or painted. Originally referring to the object of worship (*shintai*) in the main sanctuary (*honden*) of a shrine, the *mishōtai* ("the divine true body") is derived from the sacred mirror (*shinkyō*) used in Shintō rituals. As notions of religious syncretism took hold in the 9th century and shrines came under the influence of Buddhism, sacred mirrors were decorated with painted or embossed depictions of Buddhas (or the mysti-

cal syllables written in an Indic script that symbolized the Buddhist divinities), which were believed to represent the original Indian forms (HONJIBUTSU) of the Shintō deities (see HONJI SUIJAKU). Gradually mirrors were replaced by wooden or metal disks decorated with Buddhist images and symbols, known popularly as *kakebotoke* (hanging Buddhas). Often inscribed on the reverse with the name and vows of the donor, they were presented as offerings at Shintō shrines and Buddhist temples (see EMA) or buried in the ground in sutra mounds (*kyōzuka*).

miso   味噌

(bean paste). *Miso* is made by mixing steamed soybeans with salt and a fermenting agent (*kōji*) made of rice, wheat, or soybeans; together with soy sauce (*shōyu*), it is the basic flavoring of Japanese cuisine. *Miso* is a good source of protein, especially the amino acids lysine and threonine, but it also

miso

There are hundreds of varieties of this fermented soybean paste, a common ingredient in Japanese cooking.

▲ Most *miso* is now mass-produced commercially, but these photographs show the production of handmade farmhouse *miso*, which begins with cooking the soybeans.

◀ The beans are stirred as they cook over a wood fire in a traditional hearth.

▶ The cooked soybeans are mashed.

◀ Following inoculation with *kōji*, the fermenting agent, salt is added, and the mixture is wrapped in straw.

◀ After aging for 3 to 6 months, the *miso* is ready for consumption.

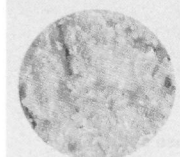

▲ A golden-yellow color is characteristic of *miso* from the Shinshū region.

Misora Hibari The phenomenally popular singer at her last major concert appearance before her death in 1989.

contains a large amount of salt, as much as 8 to 15 percent. Introduced from China in the 7th century, it became popular during the Muromachi period (1333–1568). The color, aroma, and taste of *miso* differ according to the combination of ingredients, which vary from place to place.

Miso is most commonly used for making MISO SOUP, which along with rice is an indispensable part of a Japanese-style meal. Because of its strong flavor *miso* is often used for marinating or cooking fish. It is also used as a preservative. *Miso* can be used as a dressing mixed with rice vinegar (*sumiso*), *yuzu* (citron) peel (*yuzumiso*), roasted and ground sesame seeds (*gomamiso*), or bits of bream (*taimiso*).

misogi   禊

The Shintō rite of ablution. The word *misogi* refers to the ritual cleansing of the body with water to remove both physical and spiritual defilements. Since Shintō lays great stress on purity and cleanliness, the act of cleansing the body assumes enormous importance and must be performed before any ceremony begins.

According to the *Kojiki* (712, Records of Ancient Matters) the rite of *misogi* originated with Izanagi no Mikoto (see IZANAGI AND IZANAMI), one of the divine progenitors of the Japanese islands. Izanagi descended to the netherworld (Yomi no Kuni) to search for his deceased wife. When he returned to this world he went to a river and washed away the impurities associated with decay and death.

Various types of purification rituals using water are still performed. The one most frequently observed is the rinsing of the hands and mouth before worshiping at a shrine. Before all festivals the priest is required to bathe thoroughly, in the practice known as *kessai*. *Mizugori* (literally, "removing impurities by water") entails standing virtually nude under a waterfall or pouring buckets of cold water over oneself. It differs from *misogi* in that it is basically an ascetic practice undertaken for a specified period. In many parts of Japan the ritual of *misogi* still survives in festivals. See also HARAE.

Misogikyō   禊教

One of the SECT SHINTŌ groups. Based on ideas developed during the late Edo period (1600–1868) by the Shintō priest Inoue Masakane (1790–1849), who, after studying PURE LAND BUDDHISM and other religious practices, began teaching that unity between deity and man can be attained through purification. The group advocates a purification ritual (MISOGI) and deep controlled breathing. Its doctrines emphasize faith in AMATERASU ŌMIKAMI and other Shintō deities. The sect was formally organized in 1875 and claimed some 100,000 followers in 1989.

miso soup Shown served in a lacquered bowl and garnished with Welsh onion, miso soup is one of the basic elements of a traditional Japanese meal, along with rice and pickles.

Misora Hibari   美空ひばり

(1937–89). Singer and actress. Real name Katō Kazue; born in Kanagawa Prefecture. Following her debut at the age of 12 with the song "Kappa bugiugi" (1949, Kappa Boogie-Woogie), she had a series of hits that included "Ringo oiwake" (1952, The Apple Flower Song), "Yawara" (1965, Jūdō), and "Kanashii sake" (1966, Melancholy Wine). Blessed with a natural ear and a unique talent for phrasing, Misora was a master of many genres—from the sentimental songs known as *enka* to jazz songs in English—and established an unshakable position for herself in the world of Japanese popular music. She also starred in *Izu no odoriko* (1954, The Izu Dancer) and many other films. After her death in 1989 she was given the People's Honor Award (the first awarded to a woman) for the contribution her music had made to restoring the spirits of the Japanese people in the bleak years following World War II and for the affection she had inspired throughout her career. She recorded 1,200 songs on 675 albums and singles, selling a total of 68 million copies.

miso soup   味噌汁

(*misoshiru*). An essential part of a traditional Japanese meal, *miso* soup is made with MISO (bean paste) and a soup stock (*dashi*), the customary ingredients of which are KOMBU (sea tangle), dried bonito (see KATSUOBUSHI), and dried sardine fry (*niboshi*). A powdered instant *dashi* is now commonly used. Additional ingredients may include any of a wide variety of vegetables, *tōfu*, clams, and seaweeds, such as WAKAME. *Miso* varies in texture, color, and taste according to region; some cooks use a combination of types. When the ingredients have been fully cooked in the broth, *miso* is gradually blended in. The soup should not be brought to a boil after the *miso* is added. Packaged instant *miso* soup is now widely available.

mission schools   ミッションスクール

(*misshon sukūru*). Common term for Christian-oriented educational institutions in Japan. Although they are no longer operated by foreign missionaries, many trace their origins to schools established under missionary auspices in the late 19th century, when they were centers of Western-style education. In the first half of the 20th century, mission schools grew steadily in quality and number. They often pioneered advances in educational content and method, assuming an important role in women's education. After private universities were first authorized by the government in 1918, the Christian-sponsored DŌSHISHA UNIVERSITY, RIKKYŌ UNIVERSITY, and KANSEI GAKUIN UNIVERSITY were among the few private schools to receive full accreditation (in 1920, 1922, and 1932, respectively). As of 1990 there were 38 colleges, 56 junior colleges, 100 high schools, 76 middle schools, and 31 elementary schools affiliated with Protestant churches in Japan. In 1990 there were 13 universities, 29 junior colleges, 115 high schools, 97 middle schools, and 54 elementary schools with Roman Catholic affiliations.

mission to Europe of 1582

天正遣欧使節

(Tenshō Ken'ō Shisetsu). The mission of four young Japanese boys to the courts of Philip II of Spain and Pope Gregory XIII. It was conceived by the Jesuit Alessandro VALIGNANO and organized under the auspices of three CHRISTIAN DAIMYŌ in Kyūshū—ŌTOMO SŌRIN (Francisco), ARIMA HARUNOBU (Protasio), and ŌMURA SUMITADA (Bartolomeu). The mission left Japan in February 1582 and returned in July 1590.

The arrival in Japan of Francis XAVIER in 1549 marked the beginning of the missionary work of the JESUITS in that country and particularly in Kyūshū. The Jesuits quickly formed the opinion that the exclusion of other religious orders from Japan was necessary for the proper growth of Christianity there. Father Valignano, on his first visit to Japan in 1579, realized that it would be extremely advantageous to the mission there to send a group of Japanese Christians to Rome. First of all, it would demonstrate to the Pope how the Jesuit work in East Asia could make up for the losses suffered by the Catholic Church in Europe as a result of the Reformation and thus secure the Pope's support for the Jesuit monopoly in Japan. In addition, Valignano hoped to get financial subsidies from the Pope. Another aim was to introduce Europe to the Japanese.

Its members were ITŌ MANCIO, CHIJIWA MIGUEL, NAKAURA JULIÃO, and HARA MARTINHO. They were all 12 to 13 years old and students at the Jesuit seminary in Arima. Father Valignano chose another 16 people to complete the party.

Leaving Nagasaki on 20 February 1582, the mission finally reached Portugal in August 1584. In November they were warmly received by Philip II of Spain, and they proceeded to Italy in March 1585. In Rome, Pope Gregory XIII received the young envoys, showering them with gifts, and issued a papal bull confirming that Japan was the prerogative of the Jesuits. The party later traveled elsewhere in Italy, Spain, and Portugal. The mission left Portugal in April 1586 and arrived back in Nagasaki more than four years later (July 1590). However, during the mission's absence, the military hegemon TOYOTOMI HIDEYOSHI had presented the Jesuits with his Expulsion Edict (see ANTI-CHRISTIAN EDICTS), and the four young men were able to publicize what they had learned about Europe only in their small circle in Kyūshū. Nevertheless, European interest in Japan had been greatly aroused by the mission.

Misumi   三角〔町〕

Town in west-central Kumamoto Prefecture, Kyūshū. With the construction of Misumi port in 1887 it flourished as a market town, but now it is known primarily as a stop along the tourist routes to Shimabara and the Amakusa Islands. Mandarin oranges are grown here. Pop: 11,792.

misumisō   三角草

Hepatica nobilis var. *japonica*, or *Hepatica acuta*. Also known as *yukiwarisō*. A wild perennial herb of the family Ranunculaceae that grows to a height of 5 to 10 centimeters (2–4 in) on tree-shaded hills in Honshū. The three-lobed, pointed leaves grow in clusters from the plant's base. By mid-February several flower stalks produce white or pink blossoms. A variety of *misumisō* called *suhamasō* (*H. nobilis* var. *japonica* f. *variegata*, or *Hepatica triloba*) has leaves with less pointed lobes and flowers that are white or reddish purple. The alternate name *yukiwarisō* (literally, "a plant that breaks through the snow") was originally applied to the species *Primula modesta* of the family Primulaceae (see PRIMROSES) but now also refers to the *misumisō* and *suhamasō*.

Mita bungaku   三田文学

(Mita Literature). Literary journal founded by Keiō University's Department of Letters to compete with Waseda University's WASEDA BUNGAKU; published from May 1910 to the present with numerous interruptions. Under its first editor, NAGAI KAFŪ, *Mita bungaku* joined forces with the magazines SHIN-SHICHŌ and SUBARU against the so-called Japanese NATURALISM. Its contributors included MORI ŌGAI, IZUMI KYŌKA, NOGUCHI YONEJIRŌ, YOSANO AKIKO, KITAHARA HAKUSHŪ, TANIZAKI JUN'ICHIRŌ, ABE JIRŌ, KUBOTA MANTARŌ,

MINAKAMI TAKITARŌ, SATŌ HARUO, KINOSHITA MOKUTARŌ, and HORIGUCHI DAIGAKU. Official sponsorship by Keiō University ended in 1925, after which Minakami, Kubota, and other staff members ran it as an independent journal.

The second series of *Mita bungaku* appeared from April 1926 to November 1944 and introduced HARA TAMIKI, ISHIZAKA YŌJIRŌ, SHIBATA RENZABURŌ, OKAMOTO KANOKO, and IBUSE MASUJI. Revived in 1946, it has published works by such writers as ENDŌ SHŪSAKU, ETŌ JUN, YASUOKA SHŌTARŌ, MATSUMOTO SEICHŌ, YOSHIYUKI JUNNOSUKE, ASARI KEITA, HANI SUSUMU, and MARUYA SAIICHI.

Mita Industrial Co, Ltd 三田工業[株]

(Mita Kōgyō). Major manufacturer of copiers, fax machines, and laser printers. Incorporated in 1948. Mita is known for its strength in export markets. The company has subsidiaries in 15 foreign countries and distributes its products to over 100 foreign countries. Sales for the fiscal year ending November 1991 totaled ¥123.9 billion (US $955.5 million) and capitalization stood at ¥3.3 billion (US $25.1 million). Headquarters are in Ōsaka.

Mitaka 三鷹[市]

City in east-central Tōkyō Prefecture. Farming was the principal activity until the early Shōwa period (1926–89). With the establishment of munitions plants during World War II, the population increased rapidly. It is now primarily a residential and commercial city. Attractions include Inokashira Park and the temple Zenrinji, where the graves of writers MORI ŌGAI and DAZAI OSAMU are located. The National Astronomical Observatory and International Christian University are also located here. Pop: 165,564.

Mitaka Incident 三鷹事件

(Mitaka Jiken). Controversial criminal incident of the OCCUPATION period. On 15 July 1949 an unmanned electric train with its operating handle tied down drove into the suburban Mitaka Station, west of Tōkyō, derailed, and killed six people. The government subsequently indicted 10 persons on a charge of train sabotage resulting in death, an offense that carries the death penalty in Japan. All 10 were members of the National Railroad Workers' Union (NRWU), and 9 were prominent members of the Japan Communist Party. Nine of the defendants were found innocent. The tenth, Takeuchi Keisuke, was sentenced to death, but died in prison of natural causes in 1967.

The government treated the incident as an instance of terrorism perpetrated by the communist-dominated NRWU in opposition to the efforts of government and American Occupation authorities to rehabilitate Japan economically and to end the Japan Communist Party's domination of the NRWU. The Mitaka Incident was one of three major instances of violence in 1949. See also MATSUKAWA INCIDENT; SHIMOYAMA INCIDENT.

Mita Masahiro 三田誠広

(1948–). Novelist. Born in Ōsaka Prefecture. Graduate of Waseda University. Written in a light, witty style, his novels are often self-parodying accounts of his own experiences, presented as representative of young people in the 1970s and set against the backdrop of the student movement. Mita received the Akutagawa Prize for *Bokutte nani* (1977, What Am I?). Other works include *Ryū o mita ka?* (1979, Did You See the Dragon?) and *Inochi* (1985, Life).

Mitamura Engyo 三田村鳶魚

(1870–1952). Scholar and essayist. Real name Mitamura Genryū. Born in the city of Hachiōji, Tōkyō Prefecture. He worked as a local newspaper reporter before becoming a regular contributor to the influential conservative magazine *Nihon oyobi nihonjin* (1907–45, Japan and the Japanese). He possessed a broad knowledge of the history and culture of the Edo period (1600–1868) and wrote many biographical sketches as well as essays on the manners and customs of Edo (now Tōkyō).

Mitford, Algernon ミットフォード, A.

(1837–1916). English author, linguist, and diplomat; attaché in the British legation at Edo (later Tōkyō) from 1866 to 1870. Full name, Algernon Bertram Freeman-Mitford, first Baron Redesdale (of second creation). Born in London. He is best known for his *Tales of Old Japan* (1871), one of the first popular books in English on Japanese customs and folktales.

MITI → Ministry of International Trade and Industry

Mito 水戸[市]

Capital of Ibaraki Prefecture, central Honshū, on the river Nakagawa. The city developed with the construction of a castle by the Daijō family in the Kamakura period (1185–1333). After the Battle of Sekigahara (1600), it became the castle town of Tokugawa Yorifusa (1603–61), the 11th son of the victorious hegemon TOKUGAWA IEYASU. The Mito domain flourished throughout the Edo period (1600–1868) as the base of one of the three senior collateral families (GOSANKE) of the Tokugawa and was noted for its capable *daimyō*, such as TOKUGAWA MITSUKUNI and TOKUGAWA NARIAKI. It was also the center of an emperor-oriented school of learning (MITO SCHOOL). Today Mito is primarily a commercial city. Local products include *nattō* (fermented soybeans). Of historic interest are KAIRAKUEN Park and Kōdōkan, a school established by Nariaki in 1841. Pop: 234,968.

Mito Civil War 天狗党の乱

(Tengutō no Ran). Uprising by the proimperial, antishogunate (SONNŌ JŌI) faction in the Mito domain (now part of Ibaraki Prefecture) in 1864. One of three major wars accompanying the Tokugawa shogunate's (1603–1867) disintegration (see CHŌSHŪ EXPEDITIONS and BOSHIN CIVIL WAR), it resulted in the deaths of 1,300 residents of Mito and hundreds from other domains and devastated Mito.

During the late Edo period (1600–1868), factional rivalries in Mito were reinforced by the opposing ideological viewpoints of conservative supporters of the shogunate on the one hand and of proimperial reformers on the other. In 1829 TOKUGAWA NARIAKI became *daimyō* of Mito, and his forceful reform policies generated intense political conflict between conservatives and radicals in the domain. A period of bitter quarrels followed, during which Nariaki was first forced into retirement and, in 1853, recalled to power. Tensions in Mito reached the breaking point following the repression directed against the domain by shogunate leader II NAOSUKE (see ANSEI PURGE).

Ii's murder in 1860 resulted in a brief period of calm, but, when the shogunate failed to comply with imperial court orders to expel all foreigners, Mito's proimperial Tengutō faction was strongly critical of the shogunate and in 1864 resolved to support the court's policy of expulsion. The group's subsequent actions led to armed conflict and finally to civil war in Mito. By mid-1864 the Tengutō forces under Fujita Koshirō (1842–65) had acquired hundreds of supporters including large numbers led by proimperial activist TAKEDA KŌUNSAI. The shogunate mobilized all its available forces to suppress what had now become a major insurrection against the Tokugawa regime and, with the support of daimyō forces from the Kantō region, succeeded in crushing the rebels in the autumn of 1864.

The insurgents were ruthlessly punished, but Tengutō survivors were able to exact revenge in the new situation following the Meiji Restoration of 1868. The bitterness of Mito's internal quarrels lasted for decades and still colors the interpretation of local history.

Mito domain 水戸藩

(Mito *han*). Edo-period (1600–1868) domain that extended over parts of Hitachi and Shimotsuke provinces; parts of present-day Ibaraki and Tochigi prefectures. It was granted in 1610 to Tokugawa Yorifusa (1603–61), who, as a son of TOKUGAWA IEYASU, received the status of SHIMPAN (collateral vassal). One of the three cadet houses (GOSANKE) of the Tokugawa family, Yorifusa's line produced a number of important political figures, such as TOKUGAWA MITSUKUNI and TOKUGAWA NARIAKI. OMOTEDAKA (estimated annual production of rice): 350,000 KOKU (1 *koku* = 180 liters or 5 US bushels). See also MITO SCHOOL.

Mito Kōmon → Tokugawa Mitsukuni

Mito school 水戸学

(Mitogaku). A school of thought deriving from Shintō and Confucianism whose development is usually divided into two stages. In the early Edo period (1600–1868) TOKUGAWA MITSUKUNI, lord of the Mito domain (now part of Ibaraki Prefecture), founded the Historical Research Institute, or SHŌKŌKAN, for the purpose of compiling the DAI NIHON SHI (History of Great Japan). Early Mito scholars, who had remarkably heterogenous philosophical backgrounds, included Mitsukuni and his teacher, the Chinese scholar SHU SHUNSUI, as well as KURIYAMA SEMPŌ, MIYAKE KANRAN, and ASAKA TAMPAKU. This early phase of the Mito school ended around 1720, when the major part of the *Dai Nihon shi* was presented to the shogunate.

The late Mito school began toward the end of the 18th century. Its institutional center was the Kōdōkan in Mito, founded by TOKUGAWA NARIAKI, and its activities were exemplified by scholars such as FUJITA YŪKOKU, whose *Seimeiron* (1791, On the Rectification of Names) was a pioneering work of late Mito scholarship. Together with his student AIZAWA SEISHISAI, author of the influential *Shinron* (1825, New Discourse), and his son FUJITA TŌKO, Yūkoku became a propagator of Mito *samurai* nationalism, exemplified in the famous slogan SONNŌ JŌI (Revere the Emperor, Expel the Barbarians).

In contrast to the early phase, the late Mito school had a more distinctive character and thrust as a school, combining the eclectic

misumisō This herb grows on tree-shaded hillsides and yields its white or reddish blossoms around February. Its name, literally meaning "triangular plant," comes from its trilobate leaves.

influences inherited from its predecessors in an attempt to find solutions for the internal crisis of the feudal system and the external threat posed by the Western nations. Late Mito scholars felt that the West would destroy not only Japan's social and political systems but also the true character of the Japanese nation (KOKUTAI) and its identity as the "country of the gods" (*shinkoku*). Accordingly, they focused on the clarification of the concept of *kokutai* (literally, "body of the nation"), stressing the role of the emperor as the apex of a hierarchical political and moral order and the obligations of the people to fulfill their duties and obligations within this system.

The works of the late Mito school were widely read and constituted the ideological thrust behind the proimperial movement during the last critical years before the fall of the Tokugawa shogunate (1603–1867). After the Meiji Restoration of 1868, the Mito school exerted a formative influence on the ideology of the new imperial regime and served as an important source for later nationalist thought in the period prior to World War II. See also SHUSHIGAKU; YŌMEIGAKU; KOGAKU; KOKUGAKU.

Mitsubishi   三菱

Business enterprise begun by IWASAKI YATARŌ in the early 1870s; major financial and industrial combine (ZAIBATSU) of the pre–World War II era, second in size only to MITSUI; enterprise grouping (KEIRETSU) of the postwar period.

In 1870 the new government discontinued domain-operated enterprises and the trading and shipping firm of the Tosa domain (now Kōchi Prefecture) was reorganized as a semi-public company under the management of Iwasaki Yatarō. When the government abolished the domains in 1871 (see PREFECTURAL SYSTEM, ESTABLISHMENT OF), the company received 11 ships and other facilities. In 1873 Iwasaki named it the Mitsubishi Commercial Company (Mitsubishi Shōkai).

Iwasaki profited greatly from providing marine transport during the TAIWAN EXPEDITION OF 1874, gaining 13 additional ships. In 1875 the company was renamed Mitsubishi Steamship Company (Mitsubishi Kisen Kaisha), and in 1877 it made similar gains from the suppression of the SATSUMA REBELLION in Kyūshū.

The rival Mitsui group persuaded the government in 1882 to assist it and other firms in founding a second steamship company, the Kyōdō Transport Company (Kyōdō Un'yu Kaisha). In 1885 the two shipping firms merged to form the NIPPON YŪSEN KAISHA, under de facto control of Mitsubishi.

Iwasaki Yatarō quickly diversified. He acquired the first of Mitsubishi's metal mines, the Yoshioka Copper Mine, in 1873 and the first of its coal mines, the TAKASHIMA COAL MINE, in 1881. In 1880 he established a moneylending, exchange, and warehousing operation.

Iwasaki Yanosuke (1851–1908) succeeded his older brother and added banking in 1885 when he took over the 119th National Bank. The government first leased (1884) and then sold (1887) to Mitsubishi the NAGASAKI SHIPYARDS (see KAN'EI JIGYŌ HARAISAGE). In 1887 the company added real estate to its activities by purchasing government land, which it developed into the Marunouchi business district in Tōkyō.

In 1893, when the company-law provi-

sions of the COMMERCIAL CODE went into effect, Yanosuke organized Mitsubishi, Ltd (Mitsubishi Gōshi Kaisha). The various Mitsubishi enterprises were made divisions of this limited partnership. They began to be incorporated separately again during and following World War I.

Under IWASAKI KOYATA, Mitsubishi established independent joint-stock companies, which it controlled through majority shareholding. Between 1917 and 1919 seven subsidiaries were spun off from Mitsubishi, Ltd. In the years 1919–21 two subsidiaries—Mitsubishi Internal Combustion Engine (later Mitsubishi Aircraft) and MITSUBISHI ELECTRIC CORPORATION—were set up. MITSUBISHI HEAVY INDUSTRIES, LTD, was formed in 1934, the product of a merger of Mitsubishi Shipbuilding and Engineering with Mitsubishi Aircraft. In preparation for and during World War II, the Mitsubishi companies expanded greatly, both at home and in Japan's empire, the GREATER EAST ASIAN COPROSPERITY SPHERE.

By the end of World War II, Mitsubishi, Ltd, which had been reorganized as a joint-stock company in 1937, controlled 209 companies. Between 1946 and 1950, the Mitsubishi combine was broken up by the ZAIBATSU DISSOLUTION measures of the Allied Occupation. Since the 1950s, the former Mitsubishi subsidiaries have been loosely affiliated as an enterprise grouping (*keiretsu*). The holding company has been replaced by a presidents' club (Kin'yōkai or "Friday Club"). See also CORPORATE HISTORY.

Mitsubishi Bank Foundation
三菱銀行国際財団

(Mitsubishi Ginkō Kokusai Zaidan). A foundation established in 1981 by the MITSUBISHI BANK, LTD, to promote cultural exchange and the internationalization of Japan. It provides support for international conferences and research projects and is particularly active in promoting conferences between Japanese students and students from other countries. In 1989 total assets were ¥1.8 billion (US $13.0 million). Headquarters are in Tōkyō.

Mitsubishi Bank, Ltd   [株]三菱銀行

(Mitsubishi Ginkō). One of the 12 city banks in Japan. Besides 288 domestic business offices, the bank has an overseas network of 16 branches and agencies, 21 representative offices, and 22 subsidiaries and affiliates.

The Mitsubishi Exchange Office, the predecessor of the bank, was established in 1880 by IWASAKI YATARŌ, founder of MITSUBISHI, and later became the banking division of Mitsubishi Co. In 1919 the bank was incorporated as an independent entity. Traditionally strong in corporate banking activities, the bank is now placing increased emphasis on loans to small and medium-sized companies and to individuals. In response to the rapid pace of financial deregulation, internationalization, and securitization, the bank has expanded its traditional international financing services to include a wide variety of new services, such as project financing, interest rate and currency swaps, financial advisory services, leasing, factoring, and custodian services. The bank is also active in the underwriting and trading of securities in the international capital markets.

As of March 1991, the bank had assets of ¥58.2 trillion (US $424.2 billion) and total deposits of ¥43.0 trillion (US $313.4 billion). Capitalization stood at ¥385.0 billion (US $2.8 billion) in May 1991. Headquarters are in Tōkyō.

Mitsubishi Cable Industries, Ltd
三菱電線工業[株]

(Mitsubishi Densen Kōgyō). Company engaged in the manufacture, sale, and installation of electric wire, electric cable, and O-rings. Incorporated in 1917, the company took its present name in 1986. As a member of the MITSUBISHI group, it currently is laying cables in numerous foreign countries. For the fiscal year ending March 1991, sales totaled ¥156.7 billion (US $1.1 billion) and capitalization stood at ¥15.3 billion (US $109.3 million). Headquarters are in Tōkyō.

Mitsubishi Corporation
三菱商事[株]

(Mitsubishi Shōji). Japan's largest *sōgō shōsha* (see GENERAL TRADING COMPANIES). The company originated in a shipping business founded in 1870 by IWASAKI YATARŌ and took the name Mitsubishi Gōshi Kaisha in 1911. The trading division of this company was organized as an independent entity under the name Mitsubishi Shōji Kaisha in 1918. Mitsubishi Corporation is a global enterprise engaged in general trading and diversified services. In addition to handling an enormous volume of domestic, import, export, and offshore trading transactions, the company also organizes business ventures, arranges technology transfers and resource development, and provides financing and information services. Through more than 230 offices in over 80 countries, including those of its subsidiaries, the company is expanding into new areas, such as information processing, telecommunications, biotechnology, electronics, space technology, and new materials. During the fiscal year ending March 1991, the company's total trading transactions amounted to ¥17.4 trillion (US $126.8 billion), a figure equal to about one-quarter of Japan's national budget for the same year. Capitalization stood at ¥124.8 billion (US $909.6 million) in the same year. Headquarters are in Tōkyō.

Mitsubishi Electric Corporation
三菱電機[株]

(Mitsubishi Denki). One of the leading Japanese manufacturers of electrical and electronic equipment. Incorporated in 1921. The company has 12 laboratories and 24 consolidated subsidiaries in Japan and 106 production and sales bases in 36 foreign countries. Mitsubishi Electric products include consumer electronics, information and communication systems, electronic devices, industrial products, automotive equipment, and heavy machinery. It has also developed and manufactured more than half of Japan's communication and research satellites. Sales for the fiscal year ending March 1991 totaled ¥2.6 trillion (US $19.0 billion). Capitalization stood at ¥174.6 billion (US $1.3 billion) for the same year. Headquarters are in Tōkyō.

Mitsubishi Estate Co, Ltd
三菱地所[株]

(Mitsubishi Jisho). Real estate company engaged in the leasing of land and buildings and in the sale of real estate. Founded in 1937. Mitsubishi Estate is highly diversified. In addition to managing office buildings, it engages in the design, supervision, and subcontracting of construction and public works projects; the construction and sale of houses; the dredging of ports and rivers; land reclamation; management of leisure facilities; and the purchase and sale of real estate. In 1990 Mitsubishi Estate acquired 51 percent of the stock of the Rockefeller Group Inc, which owns Rockefeller Center in New York City. In the fiscal year ending March 1991 total sales were ¥338.4 billion (US $2.5 billion). In the same year capitalization stood at ¥85.1 billion (US $620.3 million). Headquarters are in Tōkyō.

Mitsubishi Gas Chemical Co, Inc
三菱瓦斯化学[株]

(Mitsubishi Gasu Kagaku). Manufacturer of chemicals. Incorporated in 1951, it is a member of the MITSUBISHI group. Principal products include methanol, formalin, ammonia, compound fertilizer, xylenes, plasticizers, sodium hydrosulfite, and synthetic resins. In the fields of biochemistry and electronics materials the company is highly regarded for its products. Besides manufacturing and selling its products at home and abroad, it also exports its manufacturing expertise. Total sales for the fiscal year ending March 1991 were ¥225.5 billion (US $1.6 billion), and capitalization was at ¥41.8 billion (US $304.7 million). Headquarters are in Tōkyō.

Mitsubishi Heavy Industries, Ltd
三菱重工業[株]

(Mitsubishi Jūkōgyō). Also known as MHI. Japan's largest heavy machinery manufacturer. It is engaged in shipbuilding, steel structure construction, and the production of various machinery, including general and industrial machinery, plant equipment, pollution control equipment, aircraft and special vehicles, and air-conditioning and refrigeration systems. While its major products are for industrial use, MHI recently has been promoting consumer products.

MHI dates back to the 1870 establishment of Tsukumo Shōkai. In 1917 the shipbuilding division of that company (now called Mitsubishi Gōshi Kaisha) became the independent Mitsubishi Shipbuilding Co, Ltd. It took the name Mitsubishi Heavy Industries, Ltd, in 1934. A leader in its field, MHI was chosen to produce the ZERO FIGHTER and the battleship MUSASHI. In 1950 MHI, complying with Occupation policy (see ZAIBATSU DISSOLUTION), was divided into three regional companies but regrouped in 1964. In 1970 its automobile division became the separate Mitsubishi Motors Corporation. MHI maintains its operational headquarters at its main office in Tōkyō; elsewhere in Japan, it has 6 research and development centers, 7 offices, and 14 manufacturing facilities. Overseas it has 3 liaison and 7 representative offices as well as 19 affiliated companies. Consolidated sales for the fiscal year ending March 1991 reached ¥2.3 trillion (US $16.8 billion). The export ratio was 22 percent, and the company was capitalized at ¥263.2 billion (US $1.9 billion) in the same year.

Mitsubishi Kasei Corporation
三菱化成[株]

(Mitsubishi Kasei). Comprehensive chemical maker. Founded in 1934 under the name Nihon Tāru Kōgyō. One of the chief firms in the Mitsubishi group of companies. Solidly established before World War II as a chemical company manufacturing coke, tar products, dyestuffs, and fertilizers, it was incorporated as Mitsubishi Chemical Industries in 1950, and in the mid-1960s it became a comprehensive chemical firm. In Yokohama it has established the Mitsubishi-Kasei Institute of Life Sciences, one of the largest organizations of its kind in the world. In recent years it has diversified into the fields of pharmaceuticals, information-related machinery, electronics, and new materials. It has over-

seas offices in five countries, including the United States and Germany, and has engaged in joint ventures in Brazil, South Korea, Canada, and the United States. Net sales for the fiscal year ending March 1991 totaled ¥770.5 billion (US $5.6 billion), of which sales of carbon products and inorganic chemicals amounted to 29 percent; petrochemicals, 39 percent; and functional products, 32 percent. The company was capitalized at ¥108.4 billion (US $790.1 million) in the same year. Headquarters are in Tōkyō.

Mitsubishi Kasei Polytec Co
三菱化成ポリテック[株]

(Mitsubishi Kasei Poritekku). Manufacturer of styrene polymers, processed resins, compound semiconductor materials, and other chemical products. The company was established under the name Mitsubishi Monsanto Chemical Co in 1952 as a joint venture between the Mitsubishi group and Monsanto Co of the United States. The company's name changed in 1990 when it was separated from Monsanto and Mitsubishi acquired 100 percent of its stock. For fiscal year 1990, sales totaled ¥76.4 billion (US $572.1 million) and capitalization stood at ¥8.2 billion (US $61.4 million). Headquarters are in Tōkyō.

Mitsubishi Materials Corporation
三菱マテリアル[株]

(Mitsubishi Materiaru). Major producer of nonferrous metals and concrete products, created in December 1990 through the merger of Mitsubishi Metal Corporation and Mitsubishi Mining & Cement Co, Ltd, two sister companies broken up in 1950 in the course of ZAIBATSU DISSOLUTION after World War II. Nonferrous metals accounted for some 60 percent of Mitsubishi Metal's total sales in 1989, and the company ranked first in this industry in Japan. Mitsubishi Mining & Cement's sales in 1989 comprised 52 percent cement, 16 percent oil products, 12 percent construction materials, and 20 percent other products. The primary aim of the merger was to maximize economies of scale and strengthen management structure. Entry into new businesses through the pooling of the two companies' advanced technologies in metals and ceramics was also a key objective. The new company has 9,900 employees; sales for the fiscal year ending March 1991 totaled ¥761 billion (US $5.6 billion). Capitalization stood at ¥97 billion (US $706 million) in the same year. Headquarters are in Tōkyō.

Mitsubishi Motors Corporation
三菱自動車工業[株]

(Mitsubishi Jidōsha Kōgyō). Third largest automobile manufacturer in Japan. Incorporated in 1970. It is engaged in the development, design, manufacture, and sale of cars, trucks, buses, and parts. Spun off from the automobile division of Mitsubishi Heavy Industries, Ltd, Mitsubishi Motors Corporation has a manufacturing history dating to 1917. Its car models have been awarded many domestic and foreign prizes for excellence. Mitsubishi Motors has cooperative ventures with many foreign companies, especially Chrysler in the United States, Hyundai Motors in South Korea, and Mercedes-Benz in Germany. Sales for the fiscal year ending March 1991 totaled ¥2.3 trillion (US $16.8 billion), with 48 percent of sales coming from overseas markets. The company was capitalized at ¥109.5 billion (US $798.1 million) in 1991. Headquarters are in Tōkyō.

Mitsubishi Oil Co, Ltd
三菱石油[株]

(Mitsubishi Sekiyu). The oil refining and sales company of the MITSUBISHI group. Incorporated in 1931 with 50 percent of its capital provided by the Getty Oil Co of the United States. It is active in various fields, including crude imports, manufacturing and marketing of petroleum and petrochemical products, technical assistance abroad, and new non-oil businesses. The company has three oil refineries in Japan and overseas offices in New York and London. Sales for the fiscal year ending March 1991 totaled ¥1.1 trillion (US $8.0 billion). Capitalization stood at ¥34.2 billion (US $249.3 million) in the same year. Headquarters are in Tōkyō.

Mitsubishi Paper Mills, Ltd
三菱製紙[株]

(Mitsubishi Seishi). Manufacturer of pulp, paper, and photographic papers. A member of the MITSUBISHI group, the company traces its origins back to 1898. Its main products include high-grade papers (coated and thin paper) and photosensitive materials. The company has affiliated companies in New York and Düsseldorf. Sales for the fiscal year ending March 1991 totaled ¥203.3 billion (US $1.5 billion). Capitalization stood at ¥30.5 billion (US $222.3 million) in the same year. Headquarters are in Tōkyō.

Mitsubishi Petrochemical Co, Ltd
三菱油化[株]

(Mitsubishi Yuka). The largest producer of ethylene in Japan. Mitsubishi Petrochemical was incorporated in 1956 with funds invested jointly by the MITSUBISHI group and Shell Petroleum. The company constructed a petrochemical complex in Yokkaichi, Mie Prefecture, and in 1959 it began production of ethylene. It has established joint enterprises for production in Saudi Arabia, Singapore, and the United States and set up sales companies in the United States and Hong Kong. Annual sales for the fiscal year ending March 1991 were ¥434.4 billion (US $3.2 billion), and the company was capitalized at ¥53.8 billion (US $392.1 million). Headquarters are in Tōkyō.

Mitsubishi Rayon Co, Ltd
三菱レイヨン[株]

(Mitsubishi Reiyon). Company engaged in the manufacture of synthetic fibers and plastics. A member of the MITSUBISHI group, it was established in 1933. The company is now one of the largest manufacturers of acrylic fibers, acetate fibers, and MMA and MBS resins in the world. Since the 1970s the company has developed product lines which include carbon fibers, plastic optical fibers, membranes, and printed circuit boards. Mitsubishi Rayon has established joint-venture companies in the United States and the Netherlands. Sales for the fiscal year ending March 1991 totaled ¥275.4 billion (US $2.0 billion), of which exports accounted for 21 percent. The company was capitalized at ¥51.9 billion (US $378.3 million) in the same year. Headquarters are in Tōkyō.

Mitsubishi Research Institute, Inc
[株]三菱総合研究所

(Mitsubishi Sōgō Kenkyūsho). Research institute established in 1970 in commemoration of the 100th anniversary of the founding of the Mitsubishi organization. The institute is engaged in analysis and processing of in-

Mitsui This early-18th-century woodblock print depicts the dry-goods store opened in the Nihombashi district of Edo by Mitsui Takatoshi, founder of the merchant house that later became the Mitsui industrial conglomerate.

formation on social, economic, technological, and political developments for its clients, both in Japan and abroad. The institute's sales in the fiscal year ending September 1990 totaled ¥17.8 billion (US $128.1 million), of which research and systems development accounted for 87 percent and computer calculation and other services 13 percent. The institute was capitalized at ¥7.6 billion (US $54.7 million) in the same year. Headquarters are in Tōkyō.

Mitsubishi Steel Mfg Co, Ltd
三菱製鋼[株]

(Mitsubishi Seikō). Company engaged in the manufacture and sale of special steels, springs, forged and cast steel, and machinery parts. Incorporated in 1949. The company produces hot-worked springs through an integrated process. It is closely affiliated with MITSUBISHI HEAVY INDUSTRIES, LTD, and MITSUBISHI MOTORS CORPORATION. It has overseas offices in Chicago. Sales totaled ¥85.8 billion (US $625.4 million), and capitalization stood at ¥7.2 billion (US $52.5 million) in the fiscal year ending March 1991. Headquarters are in Tōkyō.

Mitsubishi Trust & Banking Corporation
三菱信託銀行[株]

(Mitsubishi Shintaku Ginkō). Leading trust bank in Japan. Incorporated in 1927. The bank makes long-term funds available to enterprises and individuals and is also active in the field of securities investment trusts and enterprise annuity trusts. In addition, the bank is expanding into land trusts and charitable trusts. As a member of the MITSUBISHI group, Mitsubishi Trust & Banking Corporation provides financial services to member companies of that group. In 1988 the bank established the MTB Investment Technology Institute, which studies portfolio theory. At the end of March 1991 the volume of the bank's funds was ¥30.1 trillion (US $219.4 billion), total assets were ¥19.5 trillion (US $124.3 billion), and capitalization stood at ¥192.6 billion (US $1.4 billion). Headquarters are in Tōkyō.

Mitsubishi Warehouse & Transportation Co, Ltd
三菱倉庫[株]

(Mitsubishi Sōko). Largest warehousing company in Japan. Incorporated in 1887. A member of the MITSUBISHI group, it is engaged in international freight forwarding, harbor transport, land transport, and real estate, in addition to warehousing. It has subsidiary firms in the United States. Sales for the fiscal year ending March 1991 totaled ¥112.5 billion (US $820.0 million); capitalization stood at ¥15.0 billion (US $109.3 million) in the same year. Headquarters are in Tōkyō.

Mitsuchi Chūzō
三土忠造

(1871–1948). Politician. Born in Kagawa Prefecture, Mitsuchi graduated from Tōkyō Higher Normal School (later Tōkyō University of Education) in 1897. He worked for the newspaper *Tōkyō nichinichi shimbun* (now *Mainichi shimbun*) before joining the political party RIKKEN SEIYŪKAI and winning election in 1908 to the first of 11 consecutive terms in the lower house of the Diet. Mitsuchi subsequently served as education and finance minister (1927–29), communications minister (1931–32), and railway minister (1932–34). In 1940 he was appointed to the Privy Council. After World War II, Mitsuchi served as home minister and transportation minister (1945–46).

mitsuda-e
密陀絵

Ancient painting technique employing oil-based pigments; often used in combination with lacquer. The medium consists of powdered pigments added to a base of perilla oil and a small amount of lead oxide (*mitsudasō*) that have been heated together. The technique, which may have originated in Persia, reached Japan via China. The earliest extant Japanese example of its use is the 7th-century Tamamushi Shrine in the temple HŌRYŪJI in Nara. During the Azuchi-Momoyama period (1568–1600) and early Edo period (1600–1868), *mitsuda-e* was used extensively in the decoration of lacquer serving trays.

Mitsuda Kensuke
光田健輔

(1876–1964). Specialist in leprosy known for his leper-relief work. Born in Yamaguchi Prefecture, Mitsuda graduated from the medical school Saisei Gakusha. He believed that leprous patients should be isolated, and succeeded in having a leprosy ward established at the Tōkyō Shi Yōikuin, a social welfare institution. In 1909 Mitsuda began work at the first public leprosarium in Japan, Tōkyō's Zensei Hospital (now the Tama Zenshōen). In 1931 he became the first president of the National Leprosarium, Nagashima Aiseien, in Okayama Prefecture. He is also known for discovering the Mitsuda reaction, a test for distinguishing types of leprosy. Mitsuda received the Order of Culture in 1951.

Mitsui
三井

Wealthiest merchant house of the Edo period (1600–1868); the largest business combine (ZAIBATSU) of the pre–World War II era; a major enterprise grouping (KEIRETSU) of the postwar period. The House of Mitsui was founded in 1673, when MITSUI TAKATOSHI established dry-goods stores in Kyōto and Edo (now Tōkyō). He later opened moneylending and exchange shops. In 1691 the Tokugawa shogunate (1603–1867) appointed two members of the Mitsui family as chartered merchants (GOYŌ SHŌNIN). To oversee its diverse enterprises, Mitsui in 1709 established a coordinating body, the Ōmotokata, in Kyōto. House rules and procedures were codified in 1722. Mitsui maintained close ties to the Tokugawa shogunate until the end of the Edo period. However, in the 1860s Mitsui's general manager, MINOMURA RIZAEMON, also established relations with the antishogunate leaders; this action made possible the company's continued favor under the new Meiji government after 1868 (see SEISHŌ). The Mitsui combine was built on three principal subsidiaries: Mitsui Banking, Mitsui Trading, and Mitsui Mining.

Banking. In February 1868 the new government delegated operational aspects of tax revenues to the three largest merchant houses: Mitsui, Ono, and Shimada. Ono and Shimada went bankrupt soon after the government in 1874 established a bond requirement equivalent to the amount on deposit. Reportedly through a leak, Mitsui was informed and thus came to enjoy exclusive use of national tax revenues until the establishment of the BANK OF JAPAN in 1882. In 1872 the government enacted the National Bank Ordinance (see NATIONAL BANKS). Mitsui was obliged to join with the ONO-GUMI in forming a bank that became the First National Bank in 1873. Three years later, following the bankruptcy of the Ono merchant house, the company was allowed to independently establish the Mitsui Bank, Ltd (see SAKURA BANK, LTD).

Trading and mining. The Mitsui Trading Company (Mitsui Bussan Kaisha) was formed in 1876, with MASUDA TAKASHI as its managing director. Masuda obtained for the company exclusive rights to the sale of coal from the MIIKE COAL MINES, and in 1888 Mitsui bought the mines outright (see KAN'EI JIGYŌ HARAISAGE). In 1892 MITSUI MINING CO, LTD, was established to manage the Miike operation, and it subsequently acquired other coal and metal mines. In 1893, when the COMMERCIAL CODE went into effect, Mitsui Trading was reorganized as an unlimited-liability partnership.

Organization. In 1892 the business was separated from family affairs and reorganized as a limited partnership; in the 1900 House Constitution this was formalized as well as the relationships among the heads of the 11 houses that made up the Household Council. Under NAKAMIGAWA HIKOJIRŌ, general manager of the combine from 1891 to 1900, Mitsui began to invest heavily in industrial enterprises, including the Shibaura Engineering Works, the ŌJI PAPER CO, LTD, and the Kanegafuchi Spinning Company. A holding company, Mitsui Gōmei Kaisha, was established in 1909 as an unlimited partnership. All Mitsui enterprises were soon reorganized as joint-stock companies, which the Mitsui families controlled through the partnership.

Mitsui was now a full-fledged *zaibatsu*, a huge financial, industrial, and commercial combine. Cooperating with the military, Mitsui continued to expand during the war years. By the end of World War II Mitsui consisted of a holding company and 273 related companies. Between 1946 and 1950, however, Mitsui was broken up through the ZAIBATSU DISSOLUTION. In the 1950s the now-independent Mitsui companies began to associate loosely in an enterprise grouping (*keiretsu*). In the Mitsui *keiretsu* the holding company has been replaced by two loosely organized presidents' clubs, the "Monday Club" and the more exclusive "Second Thursday Club," which coordinate policy. See also CORPORATE HISTORY.

Mitsui & Co, Ltd
三井物産[株]

(Mitsui Bussan). General trading company (*sōgō shōsha*). Established in 1876. By the end of World War II, it had become the largest trading firm in the nation. In 1947 it was broken up as part of the ZAIBATSU DISSOLUTION program. Several of the resulting companies were amalgamated in 1959 to form the present Mitsui & Co.

The company handles a wide range of products. Metals, machinery, oil and gas, foodstuffs, and chemicals are still major items, but business from other products, including electronics and information services, is rapidly increasing. Activities have also expanded to include telecommunications, aerospace, and biotechnology. Domestic transactions and foreign trade occupy equal parts of the firm's business, and it handles about 10 percent of Japan's entire foreign-trade volume. Mitsui & Co serves as organizer for the entire Mitsui group of companies and attempts to establish and foster new industries. It has a total of 163 overseas offices, branches, and subsidiaries. Sales for the fiscal year ending March 1991 totaled ¥18.2 trillion (US $132.7 billion), and capitalization stood at ¥175.9 billion (US $1.3 billion). Headquarters are in Tōkyō. See also GENERAL TRADING COMPANIES.

Mitsui Bank, Ltd → Sakura Bank, Ltd

Mitsui Construction Co, Ltd
三井建設[株]

(Mitsui Kensetsu). Company engaged in public works and real estate development; a member of the MITSUI group. In 1941 MITSUI REAL ESTATE DEVELOPMENT CO, LTD, purchased the forerunner of Mitsui Construction (established in 1888). The company became independent and took its current name in 1952. The company adopted computers early and introduced automatic drawing instruments and numerical control equipment to become a leader in the development of new technologies. Sales for the fiscal year ending March 1991 totaled ¥502.2 billion (US $3.7 billion); capitalization stood at ¥15.2 billion (US $110.8 million). Headquarters are in Tōkyō.

Mitsui Engineering & Shipbuilding Co, Ltd
三井造船[株]

(Mitsui Zōsen). Comprehensive heavy-industry company engaged in the manufacture and repair of ships, ocean development equipment, steel structures, chemical plants, and industrial machinery, as well as the development of new businesses, including advanced materials and products, marine systems, and aerospace systems. Established in 1917 as the shipbuilding division of MITSUI & CO, LTD, it became independent in 1937 and took its current name in 1976. It is a member of the MITSUI group. Subsidiaries have been incorporated in Hong Kong. Future plans call for the reinforcement of its land division by exporting electric power plants. Sales for the fiscal year ending March 1991 totaled ¥311.8 billion (US $2.3 billion), of which ships generated 29 percent; chemical plants and power units for land use, 32 percent; ship machinery and container cranes, 20 percent; steel structures and civil engineering, 14 percent; and others, 5 percent. The export ratio was 43 percent, and capitalization stood at ¥42.5 billion (US $310.0 million) in the same year. Headquarters are in Tōkyō.

Mitsui Home Co, Ltd
三井ホーム[株]

(Mitsui Hōmu). Construction firm specializing in house construction. Incorporated in 1974 by the MITSUI REAL ESTATE DEVELOPMENT CO, LTD, and other Mitsui group companies. Mitsui Home also supplies such services as interior design and home maintenance. The company imports materials from Canada and the United States and has an office in Vancouver. Annual sales for 1990 totaled ¥185.3 billion (US $1.2 billion), and capitalization stood at ¥8.4 billion (US $54.9 million). Headquarters are in Tōkyō.

Mitsui Marine & Fire Insurance Co, Ltd
三井海上火災保険[株]

(Mitsui Kaijō Kasai Hoken). One of the largest insurance companies in Japan and a member of the MITSUI group. Incorporated in 1918. It engages in insurance business other than life insurance both in Japan and overseas. In 1991 it had 38 overseas offices, 2 branches, and 23 subsidiaries and affiliates, as well as a total of approximately 400 claims survey and settling agents. Overseas, the company is active in various markets through direct insurance and reinsurance operations. Net premiums totaled ¥487.5 billion (US $3.6 billion) in the fiscal year ending March 1991, and the company was capitalized at ¥46.5 billion (US $338.9 million) in the same year. Headquarters are in Tōkyō.

Mitsui Mining & Smelting Co, Ltd
三井金属鉱業[株]

(Mitsui Kinzoku Kōgyō). Supplier of nonferrous metals and one of the world's largest producers of zinc. Its principal lines of business are the smelting, refining, processing, and fabricating of metals. It also produces copper foils, chemical products, and integrated circuit-related materials. Formerly the metals division of MITSUI MINING CO, LTD, the company became independent in 1950. The current name was adopted in 1952. Mines are operated in Kagoshima and Shimane prefectures and in Peru. The company has five smelting and processing plants in Japan and seven affiliated firms in Ireland, Taiwan, and the United States. Sales for the fiscal year ending March 1991 totaled ¥423.0 billion (US $3.1 billion). The company was capitalized at ¥24.4 billion (US $177.8 million) in the same year. Headquarters are in Tōkyō.

Mitsui Mining Co, Ltd
三井鉱山[株]

(Mitsui Kōzan). Company engaged in the operation of domestic coal mines, the import of foreign coal, and the sale of oil, coke, cement, and construction materials. A member of the MITSUI group, the company dates back to 1874. The present company was incorporated in 1911. It developed numerous mines and absorbed many related companies, becoming one of the largest enterprises of its kind in Japan. In order to cope with the switch from coal to oil as Japan's primary source of energy, Mitsui Mining has attempted to diversify. It established Mitsui Mining Overseas Co, Ltd, in 1977 in an effort to step up overseas activities. The company also provides consulting services. Sales for the fiscal year ending March 1991 totaled ¥289.3 billion (US $2.1 billion). Capitalization stood at ¥11.6 billion (US $84.5 million) in the same year. Headquarters are in Tōkyō.

Mitsui Mutual Life Insurance Co
三井生命保険[相]

(Mitsui Seimei Hoken). Life insurance company. Incorporated in 1927. Mitsui Life has developed its international group insurance business through a worldwide network centered on Aetna Life & Casualty Co of the United States and Assicurazioni Generali SpA of Italy. Total assets for the fiscal year ending March 1991 reached ¥7.1 trillion (US $51.7 billion). The company received total premiums of ¥1.5 trillion (US $10.9 billion) in the same year. Headquarters are in Tōkyō.

Mitsui Oil & Gas Co, Ltd
三井石油[株]

(Mitsui Sekiyu). Oil refiner and distributor and member of the Mitsui group of companies. Incorporated in 1961. Mitsui Oil distributes gasoline through 800 filling stations in Japan. For the fiscal year ending December 1991, sales totaled ¥194.0 billion (US $1.4 billion) and capitalization stood at ¥3.0 billion (US $21.9 million). Headquarters are in Tōkyō.

Mitsui O.S.K. Lines, Ltd
大阪商船三井船舶[株]

(Ōsaka Shōsen Mitsui Sempaku). One of Japan's largest shipping companies. Its origins go back more than 100 years to 1884, when the Ōsaka Shōsen company was founded. Around the same time, the trading firm Mitsui Bussan Kaisha (see MITSUI & CO, LTD) launched a coal-shipping service to Shanghai that would later become the Mitsui Steamship Co, Ltd (the Mitsui Line). In 1964 the two companies merged to form Mitsui O.S.K. Lines, Ltd.

Mitsui O.S.K. Lines is a comprehensive shipping company operating liner, tramp, and tanker services that carry food, energy, raw materials, and finished products worldwide. As of the end of fiscal year 1988, its fleet stood at 52 vessels with an aggregate 3.9 million tons deadweight. Its entire operational fleet consists of 260 vessels totaling 11.5 million tons deadweight. Mitsui O.S.K.'s 37 liner routes are the most extensive in the world and take its ships into some 300 ports in more than 100 countries. Mitsui O.S.K. Lines has diversified into real estate transactions, leasing, brokerage, computer-related services, air and ship passenger services, and advertising. For the fiscal year ending March 1991, sales totaled ¥455.8 billion (US $3.3 billion) and capitalization stood at ¥57.5 billion (US $419.1 million). Headquarters are in Tōkyō.

Mitsui Petrochemical Industries, Ltd
三井石油化学工業[株]

(Mitsui Sekiyu Kagaku Kōgyō). Integrated petrochemical company and producer of high-density polyethylene. Mitsui Petrochemical was incorporated in 1955 by seven MITSUI-affiliated firms and KŌA OIL CO, LTD. The company has constructed a petrochemical complex at Iwakuni in Yamaguchi Prefecture and also produces ethylene, polyethylene, and aromatics at a complex in Chiba Prefecture. Jointly with the Nippon Petrochemical Company, Mitsui Petrochemical established the Ukishima Petrochemical Company. In the fiscal year ending March 1991 sales totaled ¥330.8 billion (US $2.4 billion), of which synthetic resins generated 31 percent; industrial chemicals and basic raw materials, 48 percent; and specialty chemicals, 22 percent. Exports constituted 15 percent of sales, and capitalization stood at ¥32.1 billion (US $234.0 million) in the same year. Headquarters are in Tōkyō.

Mitsui Real Estate Development Co, Ltd
三井不動産[株]

(Mitsui Fudōsan). Real estate company engaged primarily in lot sales of land and houses. Originating as the real estate division of the MITSUI combine, the company became an independent enterprise in 1941. In 1969 it established the Mitsui Real Estate Sales Co. Mitsui Home Co, Ltd, was a 1974 spin-off, through which Mitsui began selling wood-frame houses. Overseas projects include the construction and sale of distribution warehouses near Los Angeles and Seattle and the development of townhouses in Saudi Arabia and Singapore. The company was in charge of the construction of Tōkyō Disneyland in conjunction with Walt Disney Co of the United States. Sales for the fiscal year ending March 1991 totaled ¥738.3 billion (US $5.4 billion). Capitalization stood at ¥130.1 billion (US $948.3 million) in the same year. Headquarters are in Tōkyō.

Mitsui Research Institute for Social and Economic History
三井文庫

(Mitsui Bunko). Library and museum of records and documents belonging to the founding family of the MITSUI financial empire. Located in Tōkyō, it ranks with the YŌMEI BUNKO of the Konoe family and the SEIKADŌ BUNKO of the Iwasaki family as one of the most outstanding private collections to survive to the present. The Mitsui library's important documents include Mitsui Takafusa's (1684–1748) CHŌNIN KŌKEN ROKU (1728), the oldest extant Mitsui literary piece.

Mitsui Sugar Co, Ltd
三井製糖[株]

(Mitsui Seitō). Japan's largest sugar refiner, producing refined, liquid, and cube sugar. Incorporated in 1947. The company has been developing a new sweetener—Palatinose, a non-tooth-decaying crystal produced by enzymes from sugar—since 1985. It has a joint-venture firm producing cane sugar in Thailand. Sales for the fiscal year ending March 1991 totaled ¥48.9 billion (US $356.4 million). It was capitalized at ¥4.2 billion (US $30.6 million) in the same year. Headquarters are in Tōkyō.

Mitsui Takatoshi
三井高利

(1622–94). Wealthy merchant of the Edo period (1600–1868) and founder of what later became the MITSUI financial and industrial conglomerate. Born in Matsusaka, Ise Province (now Mie Prefecture); fourth son of a *sake* brewer and pawnbroker. Takatoshi made his initial fortune as a rice broker and moneylender. In 1673 he opened the Echigoya *kimono* shops in Kyōto and Edo (now Tōkyō); accepting only cash and selling goods at a low profit in large quantities, these stores flourished. Takatoshi also instituted a system for the division of labor (*bungyō*) in his stores and encouraged productivity by granting bonuses. He later became the official money exchanger to the shogunate.

Mitsui Tōatsu Chemicals, Inc
三井東圧化学[株]

(Mitsui Tōatsu Kagaku). Comprehensive chemical manufacturer; a member of the Mitsui group. Founded in 1968 through the merger of Tōyō Kōatsu and Mitsui Chemical. The company's products include petrochemicals, fine chemicals, plastics, fertilizers, and pharmaceuticals. Originally specializing in fertilizers, Mitsui Tōatsu is now stressing agrichemicals and concentrating on new products such as high-function resins, electronic materials, and biotechnological materials. Sales for the fiscal year ending March 1991 totaled ¥436.6 billion (US $3.2 billion), with ¥70.8 billion (US $516.0 million) in capital. Headquarters are in Tōkyō.

Mitsui Trust & Banking Co, Ltd
三井信託銀行[株]

(Mitsui Shintaku Ginkō). Oldest trust and banking institution in Japan. A member of the MITSUI group, it was incorporated in 1924. Its major services are long-term finance and asset management. The company maintains offices in New York, Chicago, Los Angeles, London, Hong Kong, and Singapore and overseas representative offices in Toronto, São Paulo, Copenhagen, Frankfurt, Zurich, Beijing, Sydney, and Melbourne. Seven subsidiaries operate in New York, London, Brussels, Zurich, Hong Kong, Singapore, and Sydney. Total funds as of March 1991 were ¥26.1 trillion (US $190.2 billion). Capitalization stood at ¥169.3 billion (US $1.2 billion) in the same year. Headquarters are in Tōkyō.

Mitsui Warehouse Co, Ltd
三井倉庫[株]

(Mitsui Sōko). Company engaged in warehousing and port and land transportation. Incorporated in 1909 as a member of the MITSUI group. The firm is the leading container terminal operator in Japan. The company has joint-venture firms in Hong Kong, Taiwan, Korea, the Netherlands, the United States, Singapore, and Malaysia. It also operates an integrated international transportation system through tie-ups with major distributors in North America and Western Europe. Sales for the fiscal year ending March 1991 totaled ¥79.7 billion (US $580.9 million), and capitalization stood at ¥11.1 billion (US $80.9 million). Headquarters are in Tōkyō.

Mitsukaidō
水海道[市]

City in southwestern Ibaraki Prefecture, central Honshū. During the Edo period (1600–1868) it flourished as a port town on the river Kinugawa. Principal agricultural products are rice and vegetables. Several factories are located here. In recent years it has become a residential area for commuters to Tōkyō. Pop: 42,340.

Mitsuke
見附[市]

City in central Niigata Prefecture, central Honshū. Its silk-weaving industry, developed in the early 19th century, has been replaced by the manufacture of knitted goods and synthetic fabrics. Rice and tobacco are grown, and there are carp hatcheries. The Mitsuke Oil Field had one of Japan's most productive oil wells. Pop: 43,116.

Mitsukoshi, Ltd
[株]三越

(Mitsukoshi). The largest department store company in Japan. Mitsukoshi, Ltd, traces its origins to 1673, when MITSUI TAKATOSHI opened the Echigoya dry goods store in Nihombashi, Edo (now Tōkyō). This enterprise became the foundation of the MITSUI family fortune, which later launched the Mitsui ZAIBATSU, a powerful financial and industrial combine.

The name Mitsukoshi, Ltd, was adopted in 1928. In the 1930s the company opened a number of branch stores, making it the largest department store in East Asia. After World War II, Mitsukoshi fell into financial difficulties, but it managed to recover and has since surpassed its prewar peak. To counter competition from chain stores, which began the mass-merchandising of inexpensive goods in the 1960s, Mitsukoshi has placed increased emphasis on the marketing of fashionable goods and products of artistic and cultural value. The firm opened a branch in Paris in 1971 and later opened subsidiary sales companies in Rome, Düsseldorf, London, New York, and Hong Kong. In 1991 the company had a total of 14 department stores in Japan. For the fiscal year ending February 1991, sales totaled ¥866.7 billion (US $6.6 billion) and capitalization stood at ¥37.4 billion (US $286.6 million). Headquarters are in Tōkyō.

Mitsukuri Gempachi
箕作元八

(1862–1919). Historian; pioneer in the study of Western history in Japan. Born in Mimasaka Province (now part of Okayama Prefecture). Mitsukuri studied English and zoology at Tōkyō University before going to Germany in 1886 to continue his zoological studies. He later changed specialties and undertook the study of European history. In 1892 he returned to Japan to teach at the Tōkyō Higher Normal School (Tōkyō Kōtō Shihan Gakkō) and the First Higher School (Daiichi Kōtō Gakkō). He went to France in 1900 to research the French Revolution and, on his return in 1902, became a professor of Western history at Tōkyō University.

Mitsukuri Gempo
箕作阮甫

(1799–1863). Physician and scholar of WESTERN LEARNING. Born in the Tsuyama domain (now part of Okayama Prefecture), Gempo studied traditional Chinese medicine in Kyōto before succeeding his father as physician to the *daimyō* of Tsuyama in 1822. He subsequently studied Western medicine with Udagawa Shinsai (1769–1834; also known as Udagawa Genshin) in Edo (now Tōkyō). In 1839 Gempo was appointed an official interpreter in the shogunate's Office of Astronomy (Temmonkata). He was a member of the mission led by KAWAJI TOSHIAKIRA that negotiated with Russian envoy Evfimii Vasil'evich PUTIATIN at Nagasaki in 1853. The following year he participated in the talks that led to the KANAGAWA TREATY with the United States. In 1856 Gempo was named instructor in the BANSHO SHIRABESHO, the newly established shogunate center for Western studies. Gempo wrote many books on Western medicine and translated Western books on technology.

Mitsukuri Kakichi
箕作佳吉

(1858–1909). Zoologist. Born in Edo (now Tōkyō). Studied at Keiō Gijuku (now Keiō University), at Daigaku Nankō (now part of Tōkyō University), and in the United States and England. After returning to Japan, he was the first Japanese professor of zoology at Tōkyō University. He was a pioneer in the fields of taxonomy and embryology in Japan. He helped found the Misaki Marine Biological Station of Tōkyō University at Misaki in Kanagawa Prefecture and contributed to the development of biological education.

Mitsukuri Rinshō
箕作麟祥

(1846–97). Legal scholar and bureaucrat. Born in Edo (now Tōkyō), Mitsukuri pursued WESTERN LEARNING and served in the BANSHO SHIRABESHO, the translation bureau of the Tokugawa shogunate. In 1867 he accompanied a shogunate mission to the Paris Exposition and after his return became an official translator in the new Meiji government. Together with the French jurist and government adviser Gustave Emile BOISSONADE DE FONTARABIE, Mitsukuri helped draft new civil and commercial codes. As a member of the MEIROKUSHA, he was active in the Westernization movement of the 1870s. Mitsukuri later became vice-minister of justice (1888–89), a member of the House of Peers, and chief justice of the Administrative Court. He also served as president of Wafutsu Hōritsu Gakkō, predecessor of Hōsei University.

Mitsuminesan 三峰山

Mountain in western Saitama Prefecture, central Honshū. Mitsumine Shrine, which attracted many pilgrims during the Edo period (1600–1868), is located here. Height: 1,100 m (3,609 ft).

Mitsumine Shrine 三峯神社

(Mitsumine Jinja). Shintō shrine situated on the mountain Mitsumine in the Chichibu district, Saitama Prefecture; dedicated to Izanagi no Mikoto and Izanami no Mikoto, the two divine progenitors (see IZANAGI AND IZANAMI). According to tradition the shrine was founded by the legendary hero Yamatotakeru no Mikoto (see YAMATOTAKERU, PRINCE). The shrine was once a center for the practice of SHUGENDŌ, a Buddhist-Shintō syncretic cult. Annual festivals are observed on 8 April and 2 December.

Mitsunaga Hoshirō 光永星郎

(1866–1945). Founder of DENTSŪ, INC, an advertising agency. Born in Kumamoto Prefecture, he was at first a journalist. In 1901 Mitsunaga started an advertising and communications company named Nihon Kōkoku Kabushiki Kaisha. This was followed by the establishment of Dempō Tsūshinsha, which contracted with foreign news agencies to supply newspapers with domestic and foreign news. The two companies were united in 1907 as Nihon Dempō Tsūshinsha, Ltd, the predecessor of the present Dentsū.

Mitsutani Kunishirō 満谷国四郎

(1874–1936). Western-style painter. Born in Okayama Prefecture, he studied painting in Tōkyō at the Fudōsha, the art school of Koyama Shōtarō (1857–1916). In 1900 and 1901 he traveled and exhibited in France, where he studied with Jean-Paul Laurens (1838–1921); returning to Japan in 1902, he was a founder of the Pacific Painting Society (Taiheiyō Gakai). He later served as a judge at the BUNTEN, the Ministry of Education's annual exhibition. He was influenced by the French avant-garde, particularly Henri Matisse, during a second Paris sojourn (1911–14). In 1925 he was appointed to the Imperial Fine Arts Academy (Teikoku Bijutsuin).

Mitsuya plan 三矢研究

(Mitsuya Kenkyū; "Three Arrows Studies"). Series of studies concerning the deployment of the Self Defense Forces; carried out by the JOINT STAFF COUNCIL of the Self Defense Forces in 1963 and officially known as the Shōwa 38 United Defense Map Studies. The contingency plan was based on a possible military conflict on the Korean peninsula and covered various details of the mobilization of the Self Defense Forces, the cooperative strategy to be used by the United States and Japan, and requests to be made to the Diet and administrative offices. The studies were criticized from many quarters as an infringement of the principle of CIVILIAN CONTROL OF THE MILITARY, the command prerogatives of the US Forces in Japan, and the constitutional limitations on the Self Defense Forces. The affair was taken up in the Diet in 1965, and those responsible were eventually dismissed.

Miura 三浦〔市〕

City in southeastern Kanagawa Prefecture, central Honshū. Its port of Misaki is a base for deep-sea fishing, with one of the largest tuna catches in Japan. Attractions include the island of JŌGASHIMA and ABURATSUBO resort area. Pop: 52,440.

Miura Anjin → Adams, William

Miura Ayako 三浦綾子

(1922–). Novelist. Born in Hokkaidō. While fighting tuberculosis between the ages of 24 and 37, Miura converted to Christianity. Her novel Hyōten (1964–65, Freezing Point), which examines the Christian concept of original sin, won the newspaper Asahi shimbun's ¥10 million (US $27,778) prize. Other works include Tsumiki no hako (1967–68, Box of Piled Timber) and Hosokawa Garasha fujin (1975, Lady Hosokawa Gracia).

Miura Baien 三浦梅園

(1723–89). Philosopher and educator. Skeptical of conventional explanations of nature and society, he independently formulated his own epistemology and ontology. This system of thought contained a process of logical development called jōrigaku, which was remarkably similar to the dialectical method proposed by Hegel.

Born in 1723 in Bungo Province (now part of Ōita Prefecture) and educated to continue in his family's tradition of practicing medicine, Baien developed a deep interest in philosophy and immersed himself in Chinese, Indian, and Japanese philosophies, Neo-Confucianism, natural science, ethics, economics, and Dutch. He set up a private school in the home where he was born and seldom left it throughout his lifetime. Although his school drew students from throughout the country, until the Meiji period (1868–1912) his philosophic formulations attracted few followers and little interest beyond his local area.

Baien's three main works, Gengo (1775), Zeigo (ca 1786), and Kango (ca 1763), constitute one of the most thoughtful and original philosophical systems created in the Edo period (1600–1868). In Gengo he undertook to explain all phenomena in terms of a universal principle that he called jōri. Jōri is manifested as opposites, such as mind and body, spirit and matter (ki and butsu), and yin and yang (J: in and yō). Baien saw the universe grounded in the principle of oppositions, with all beings and other phenomena arising out of the interaction of sets of "dialectical" opposites. This introduction to philosophy combined what we now call epistemology and ontology.

Zeigo supplements Gengo by criticizing and synthesizing various teachings of ancient and contemporary writers in the light of Baien's theory of jōri. Kango, an introduction to ethics, applied jōri to an analysis of the ethics of human relationships and the proper display of human feelings and will.

Baien advocated that one take no book or man—even a sage or Buddha—as teacher, but rather make the universe one's teacher. In his own school he applied this philosophy, treating students as equals and questioning all ideas, even his own.

Miura Chora 三浦樗良

(1729–80). HAIKU poet. Born in Shima Province (now part of Mie Prefecture), he spent years traveling, composing verses with local poets. A friend of Yosa BUSON, he was a member of the group of poets who led the haiku revival movement of the period. His haiku collections include Chora bunshū (1786) and Chora hokkushū (1784).

Mitsumine Shrine
Pictured is the mid-17th-century worship hall of this shrine, which was once a center for the practice of Shugendō.

Miura family 三浦氏

(Miurashi). Powerful Kamakura period (1185–1333) warrior family of Sagami Province (now Kanagawa Prefecture) who claimed descent from the Kammu Heishi branch of the TAIRA FAMILY. Miura Yoshiaki (1092–1180), assistant governor of Sagami, supported the rebellion of MINAMOTO NO YORITOMO in 1180. Yoshiaki's son Yoshizumi (1127–1200) was rewarded with an appointment as military governor (shugo) of Sagami; his grandson Yoshimura (d 1239) was given important military governorships for aiding the shogunal regent (shikken) HŌJŌ YASUTOKI in the JŌKYŪ DISTURBANCE of 1221 and was appointed a member of the Council of State (HYŌJŌSHŪ). The Miura family thus became second only to the HŌJŌ FAMILY in influence in the Kamakura shogunate. Yoshimura's son Miura Yasumura (d 1247) was forced into rebellion by HŌJŌ TOKIYORI and ADACHI KAGEMORI, and the entire Miura family was destroyed and their lands confiscated in the HŌJI CONFLICT of 1247.

Miura Gorō 三浦梧楼

(1846–1926). Army officer and politician. Born in the Chōshū domain (now Yamaguchi Prefecture). After the MEIJI RESTORATION (1868) he entered the Army Ministry and supported military reform. Despite his Chōshū origins, he was a vocal opponent of the Chōshū-Satsuma monopoly of government power (HAMBATSU). Appointed minister to Korea in 1895, he was imprisoned for his part in the assassination of Queen MIN, but later released. He entered politics as a member of the KENSEI HONTŌ party and was named to the Privy Council in 1910.

Miura Hiroyuki 三浦周行

(1871–1931). Historian. Also known as Miura Kaneyuki. Born in Shimane Prefecture. He graduated from and lectured at Tōkyō University. In 1909 he was appointed to a professorship at Kyōto University, where he lectured on medieval and legal history and paleography. Miura's work on the medieval commercial city of SAKAI (Sakai Shi shi, 1931) set a standard for the compilation of local history. He was awarded the Imperial Academy Prize (Teikoku Gakushiin Shō) for his Hōseishi no kenkyū (1919, Studies in Legal History).

Miura Ken'ya 三浦乾也

(1821–89). Ceramist. Born in Edo (now Tōkyō). Ken'ya studied painting under TANI BUNCHŌ and studied MAKI-E lacquer techniques. He is best known for his pottery, mostly made in Edo, and low-temperature work with bold designs in underglaze oxides or overglaze enamels. He also made pieces in the Oribe style (see MINO WARE), but his most characteristic work was in the style of Ogata KENZAN.

Miura Kinnosuke This prominent medical scholar played an important role in the establishment of the modern science of internal medicine in Japan.

Miura Shumon This writer also served as the director-general of the Agency for Cultural Affairs in 1985–86.

Miyagi Michio The works of this performer and composer of music for the *koto* are written in a Western-influenced hybrid style.

Miura Kinnosuke 三浦謹之助

(1864–1950). Internist; founder of neurointernal medicine in Japan. Born in what is now Fukushima Prefecture. A graduate of Tōkyō University, Miura studied with Erwin von BÄLZ. He went to Europe in 1889 to pursue further studies and, upon returning home, became a professor at Tōkyō University. He carried out research on Gerlier's disease and studied *Ascaris ovis*, an intestinal nematode parasite. Miura helped found the Japanese Society of Internal Medicine and the Japanese Society of Neurology. In 1929 he became the first director of the Tōkyō Fraternity Memorial Hospital (Dōai Kinen Byōin). He received the Order of Culture in 1949.

Miura Masashi 三浦雅士

(1946–). Literary critic. Born in Aomori Prefecture; graduated from Hirosaki High School. After serving as editor of the magazines YURIIKA and *Gendai shisō*, Miura published *Watashi to iu genshō* (1981, The Phenomenon of Self). His writing on modern poetry and fiction explores the nature of criticism and artistic expression. His other works include *Shutai no hen'yō* (1982, The Metamorphosis of the Subject) and *Merankorī no suimyaku* (1984, The Vein of Melancholy).

Miura Peninsula 三浦半島

(Miura Hantō). Located in Kanagawa Prefecture, central Honshū. Extending south into the Sagami Sea, it is bounded to the east by Tōkyō Bay and the Uraga Channel and to the west by Sagami Bay. This hilly, densely populated region is a major residential and recreational area for Tōkyō. Numerous temples and shrines are here. There are some industrial areas, especially around Yokosuka, which is a large naval base. The beaches remain popular despite the pollution of Tōkyō Bay.

Miura Saku 三浦鑿

(1881–1945). Japanese journalist in Brazil. Also known as Sack Miura. Born in Ehime Prefecture, Miura emigrated to Brazil in 1908. As publisher of the newspaper *Nippaku shimbun* from 1919, he led public opinion among Japanese immigrants. He was a strong supporter of the agricultural cooperative movement. Miura was exiled to Japan as a result of a conspiracy by political enemies and was jailed there during World War II. He was discharged and died shortly after the war ended.

Miura Shumon 三浦朱門

(1926–). Author. Born in Tōkyō; graduate of Tōkyō University. In the early 1950s he wrote short stories based on ancient Chinese history, but in the late 1950s he turned to stories about the emptiness and ennui in the lives of middle-aged white-collar workers. His wife is the writer SONO AYAKO. Miura's major works include *Meifu sansuizu* (1951), *Hakoniwa* (1967), and *Musashino indian* (1982).

Miura Tetsuo 三浦哲郎

(1931–). Author. Also known as Miura Tetsurō. Born in Aomori Prefecture. Graduate of Waseda University. Affected in his youth by the suicides of two of his sisters and the disappearance of his two brothers, he was tortured by shame and despair. His mostly autobiographical works reflect his painful awareness of what he called his "cursed blood" and his wish for a fresh life. He won the Akutagawa Prize for his short story "Shinobugawa" (1960). His principal works include *Byakuya o tabisuru hitobito* (1984), a novel.

Miwada Masako 三輪田真佐子

(1843–1927). Also known as Miwata Masako. Educator. Born in Kyōto. The daughter of a scholar, she taught at her father's private school in Kyōto. In 1866 she became a tutor in the household of the court noble IWAKURA TOMOMI. In 1869 she married Miwada (or Miwata) Mototsuna (also known as Tsunaichirō; 1828–79). After his death she returned to teaching. In 1901 she helped to organize and joined the staff of Nihon Joshi Daigakkō (now JAPAN WOMEN'S UNIVERSITY). The next year she opened her own girls' school, Miwada Jogakkō (from 1903, Miwada Kōtō Jogakkō; now Miwada Gakuen).

Miwa Kyūwa 三輪休和

(1895–1981). Potter in Hagi, Yamaguchi Prefecture. Original name Miwa Kunihiro. The 10th generation of his family to become a potter in the HAGI WARE tradition, he took the name Kyūsetsu when his father retired in 1927. Following his own retirement in 1967, he was called Kyūwa, and his brother Setsuo (b 1910), also a potter, inherited the name Kyūsetsu. Recognized by the government as one of the LIVING NATIONAL TREASURES in 1970, Kyūwa was renowned for his TEA CEREMONY bowls, fresh-water jars, and sculptured figures, as well as for a thick, milky-white Korean-style glaze that he formulated.

Miwa Shissai 三輪執斎

(1669–1744). Confucian scholar of the Edo period (1600–1868). Born in Kyōto. He studied with SATŌ NAOKATA, a leading disciple of the Neo-Confucian scholar YAMAZAKI ANSAI. Shissai later converted to the Wang Yangming school (see YŌMEIGAKU), which he popularized. He eventually opened his own school, the Meirindō, in Edo (now Tōkyō).

Miwayama 三輪山

A beautiful conical mountain north of the city of Sakurai, Nara Prefecture, central Honshū. On the western slope is Japan's most ancient road, known as the Yamanobe no Michi. Miwayama serves as the SHINTAI (object of veneration) of Ōmiwa Shrine, located at the foot of the mountain's western slope. Height: 467 m (1,532 ft).

Miyabe Kingo 宮部金吾

(1860–1951). Botanist specializing in plant taxonomy and plant pathology. Born in Edo (now Tōkyō). After graduating from Sapporo Nōgakkō (now Hokkaidō University), he became a commissioner in the Hokkaidō Colonization Office and also carried on studies in plant taxonomy under the guidance of YATABE RYŌKICHI of Tōkyō University. He did research on the geographical distribution of plants in the northern region of Japan and discovered the distribution boundary in the Kuril Islands (called Miyabe's line).

Miyagawa 宮川

River in central Mie Prefecture, central Honshū, originating in the Kii Mountains and flowing northeast to enter Ise Bay at the city of Ise. The Miyagawa Dam is located on the upper reaches. The river is part of Yoshino-Kumano National Park. Length: 91 km (57 mi).

Miyagawa 宮川

River in northern Gifu Prefecture, central Honshū. The Miyagawa originates in the Hida Mountains. It flows north to join the Takaharagawa in Toyama Prefecture, becoming the JINZŪGAWA before it flows into Toyama Bay. Length: 80 km (50 mi). Area of drainage basin: 1,943 sq km (750 sq mi).

Miyagawa Chōshun 宮川長春

(1683–1753). UKIYO-E artist. Also known as Miyagawa Nagaharu or Chōzaemon. He worked exclusively as a painter and not as a designer of prints. The name Miyagawa is said to have derived from his birthplace in Owari Province (now Aichi Prefecture). He went to Edo (now Tōkyō) to learn the techniques of the TOSA SCHOOL and the KANŌ SCHOOL but was also attracted by the work of the *ukiyo-e* artists Hishikawa MORONOBU and Kaigetsudō Ando (see KAIGETSUDŌ SCHOOL). His work is mainly in the *bijin* (beautiful women) genre, and his paintings display excellent brushwork and a superb sense of color. He is the founder of the Miyagawa school of *ukiyo-e*, whose members worked primarily with paintings and not with prints.

Miyagawa Kazuo 宮川一夫

(1908–). Cinematographer. Born in Kyōto. In 1926, after graduating from Kyōto Commercial School, Miyagawa joined the Kyōto Nikkatsu studios and became a cameraman. His photography is characterized by balanced composition and unobtrusive camera handling. Miyagawa's shots, including that in which he captures the sharp play of sunlight spilling through the trees in RASHŌMON (1950, directed by KUROSAWA AKIRA), are memorable. His hand-held camera work in *Tōkyō Orimpikku* (1965, directed by ICHIKAWA KON; shown abroad as *Tokyo Olympiad*) established new methods for the documentary film.

miyage 土産

Souvenir gift that one brings back from a trip. Every locale in Japan has its specialties in food, folk art, crafts, and so forth. Japanese travelers feel a strong obligation to bring back such items as gifts to be given not only to family members but also to relatives, neighbors, and friends. If one has received a *miyage* in the recent past, one has an obligation to reciprocate. Also, when leaving for an extended trip, one often receives a farewell gift (*sembetsu*) from friends and relatives, and one is expected to present *miyage* in return.

Miyage should be distinguished from *temiyage*, a gift that one takes when visiting a friend or relative. *Temiyage* are usually sweets, fruits, or other nonstaple foods. Whereas one makes a call specifically for the purpose of delivering *miyage*, *temiyage* are given incidentally at most social calls. See also GIFT GIVING.

Miyagi Mariko 宮城まり子

(1928–). Singer, actress, and social worker. Real name Homme Mariko. Born in Tōkyō. Following the success of her 1955 hit song "Gādo shita no kutsu migaki" (The Shoeshine Boy under the Overpass), she also achieved great popularity as an actress. In 1968 she founded the Nemunoki Gakuen (Nemunoki Home for the Physically and Mentally Handicapped) in Shizuoka Prefecture at her own expense. She directed two documentary films about the children at the home, *Nemunoki no uta* (1974, Ballad of Nemunoki) and *Nemunoki no uta ga kikoeru* (1977, shown abroad as *Mariko–Mother*), which won a special award at the International Red Cross Film Festival.

Miyagi Michio　宮城道雄

(1894–1956). Composer and performer of SŌKYOKU (music for KOTO). Born in Kōbe to the supervisor of an American-owned tea warehouse, the young Miyagi was early exposed to Western music. By age seven he was completely blind; at eight he began his studies with the Ikuta school *koto* master Nakajima Kengyō II. Then, with the support of the SHAKUHACHI master Yoshida Seifū (1891–1950), he embarked on a highly successful career as a composer and as a concert and recording artist. His many compositions, which were adventurous for their day, are in a hybrid style (known as *shin* Nihon *ongaku*) that shows Western influence. They are mostly for Japanese instruments, but occasionally use Western instruments too, as in the famous piece *Haru no umi* (1929). Miyagi also invented new Japanese instruments, notably the *jūshichigen* (17-stringed *koto*).

Miyagi Prefecture　宮城県

(Miyagi Ken). Located in northern Honshū and bordered by Iwate Prefecture to the north, the Pacific Ocean to the east, Fukushima Prefecture to the south, and Akita and Yamagata prefectures to the west. The western section of the prefecture is part of the ŌU MOUNTAINS, which descend to a line of foothills and then to a coastal plain in the east. Major rivers, which include the ABUKUMAGAWA and KITAKAMIGAWA, generally flow eastward from the mountains to the Pacific. The northern coastal area is heavily indented, and the southern coast is composed of the sandy beaches of SENDAI BAY. The climate is cool with dry, clear winters. Winters in the coastal area are mild.

Archaeological discoveries suggest that the Miyagi area was fairly well developed at an early period of Japanese history. After the TAIKA REFORM of 645, it became part of the Mutsu Province. In the Heian period (794–1185) it came under the dominance of the ŌSHŪ FUJIWARA FAMILY, but it was later ruled by a succession of feudal warlords. It flourished under the rule of the DATE FAMILY in the Edo period (1600–1868), becoming the principal cultural and economic center of northeastern Honshū. Its present name was acquired in 1872, and its boundaries were established in 1876.

Agriculture and fishing remain the principal activities, with rice as the major crop. It is one of Japan's principal fishing areas, producing large quantities of sardines, tuna, and mackerel. Industrial development has increased in recent years, especially since the completion of the Tōhoku Expressway and the Tōhoku Shinkansen (a high-speed railway). Industries include metal, machine, paper, and pulp production.

The city of SENDAI continues to be the cultural and educational center of the six prefectures of the Tōhoku region (northeastern Honshū). The TANABATA FESTIVAL held there each summer is one of the most famous in Japan and attracts numerous visitors. The coastal view of MATSUSHIMA has traditionally been counted as one of Japan's most scenic areas, and other parts of the coast are included in RIKUCHŪ COAST NATIONAL PARK. There are also many hot spring resorts, among which Narugo, Tōgatta, and Sakunami are

representative. Area: 7,292 sq km (2,815 sq mi); pop: 2,248,558; capital: Sendai. Other major cities include KESENNUMA, ISHINOMAKI, FURUKAWA, and SHIOGAMA.

Miyagi Tamayo　宮城タマヨ

(1892–1960). Public official and politician who concentrated on problems of women and children. Born in Yamaguchi Prefecture; maiden name Ueda. She graduated from Nara Women's Higher Normal School (now Nara Women's University) in 1914 and joined the staff of the ŌHARA INSTITUTE FOR SOCIAL RESEARCH. She studied in the United States from 1922 to 1924, and in 1927 she became the first woman juvenile probation officer in Japan. Beginning in 1947 she served 12 years in the House of Councillors. She campaigned vigorously for the PROSTITUTION PREVENTION LAW of 1956.

Miyagi Yotoku　宮城与徳

(1903–45). Marxist artist implicated in the Richard Sorge espionage ring. Born in Okinawa, he went to California at age 16 to help on his father's farm. He graduated from the San Diego Art School in 1925. He became very active in a Japanese socialist group and joined the Workers Party of America (later the Communist Party). In 1933 he went to Japan as a Comintern agent and began to work with Sorge. He was arrested along with Sorge and other group members in 1941 and died of tuberculosis in Sugamo Prison, Tōkyō, before the completion of his trial. See also SORGE INCIDENT.

Miyaji Denzaburō　宮地伝三郎

(1901–88). Animal ecologist. Born in Hiroshima Prefecture. A graduate of Tōkyō University, Miyaji was a professor at Kyōto University from 1942 to 1964 and director of the JAPAN MONKEY CENTER from 1964 to 1976. He is credited with the founding of Japanese ecological studies. Miyaji's initial research was the study of the bottom fauna of lakes and harbors. In the post–World War II period his research centered on the fauna of rivers and streams, in particular on the AYU, or sweetfish. As director of the Japan Monkey Center he coordinated research projects conducted at Japanese universities. His chief publication is *Miyaji Denzaburō dōbutsuki* (5 vols, 1972–73, The Zoological Studies of Miyaji Denzaburō).

Miyajima → Itsukushima

Miyajima Seijirō　宮島清次郎

(1879–1963). Businessman. Born in Tochigi Prefecture. After graduating from Tōkyō University, Miyajima joined the Sumitomo group. In 1914 he rebuilt Nisshin Spinning Co, Ltd (now NISSHINBŌ INDUSTRIES, INC), into one of Japan's six most important spinning ventures. Miyajima became company president in 1919, serving in that capacity and as chairman until 1945, when SAKURADA TAKESHI took over. He helped to establish the Industrial Club of Japan in 1917 and served as its director-general from 1947 to 1963.

Miyake Issei　三宅一生

(1938–　). Fashion designer. Known abroad as Issey Miyake. Born in Hiroshima Prefecture; graduate of Tama University of Arts (Tōkyō). His fashion creations are noted for their unconventional designs. In 1976 he was invited as a participating artist to the Festival d'Automne in Paris. He was the recipient of the 1976 Mainichi Design Award. In 1988 an exhibition of Miyake's work was held at the Musée des Arts décoratifs in Paris.

Miyakejima　三宅島

Volcanic island approximately 70 km (43 mi) south of the island of Ōshima, south of the Izu Peninsula, Tōkyō Prefecture, central Honshū. It is one of the IZU ISLANDS. The highest peak on the island, Oyama (814 m; 2,670 ft), has erupted as recently as 1983. Miyakejima is part of the Fuji-Hakone-Izu National Park; air and sea routes between the island and Tōkyō have facilitated tourism. Principal activities are coastal fishing and horticulture. Area: 55 sq km (21 sq mi).

Miyake Kaho　三宅花圃

(1868–1943). Novelist, essayist, and poet; one of Japan's first modern women writers. Original name Tanabe Tatsuko. Born in Edo (now Tōkyō), oldest daughter of government official TANABE TAICHI. A graduate of Tōkyō Women's Higher School (now Ochanomizu Women's University), she also studied with woman poet Nakajima Utako (1841–1903). In 1892 she married philosopher and journalist MIYAKE SETSUREI. In 1920 Miyake and her husband published *Josei nihonjin* (Japanese Women), a magazine on women's issues.

Miyake Kanran　三宅観瀾

(1674–1718). Confucian scholar of the Edo period (1600–1868); younger brother of MIYAKE SEKIAN. Born in Kyōto, he studied with ASAMI KEISAI and KINOSHITA JUN'AN, both associated with the Zhu Xi (Chu Hsi) school of Neo-Confucianism (see SHUSHIGAKU). From 1699 Kanran served TOKUGAWA MITSU-KUNI, *daimyō* of the Mito domain (now Ibaraki Prefecture) and participated in the compilation of the history DAI NIHON SHI. He was named a Confucian adviser to the shogunate in 1711.

Miyake Sekian　三宅石庵

(1665–1730). Confucian scholar of the Edo period (1600–1868). Born in Kyōto. With his younger brother MIYAKE KANRAN, he studied under ASAMI KEISAI, a scholar of the Zhu Xi (Chu Hsi) school of Neo-Confucianism (see SHUSHIGAKU). After teaching in Edo (now Tōkyō) he went to Ōsaka, where he opened a private school. In 1724 a disciple, Nakai Shūan (1693–1758), built a school, the KAITOKUDŌ, and invited Sekian to be its head. Sekian taught a blend of the Wang Yangming (YŌMEIGAKU) and Zhu Xi schools of Neo-Confucianism.

Miyake Setsurei　三宅雪嶺

(1860–1945). Critic, philosopher, and historian. Real name Miyake Yūjirō. Born in what

Miyake Issei This fashion designer (known abroad as Issey Miyake) has won acclaim for his sophisticated reinterpretations of traditional textile designs in a variety of high-tech materials. Pictured is a 1990 exhibition at the Tōkō Museum of Contemporary Art featuring Miyake's latest experiments in fabric design.

Miyagi Prefecture Location and Prefectural Crest

Miyake Setsurei This critic of the government policy of Westernization began calling for the development of a new national consciousness in the 1880s.

miyamairi A newborn infant dressed in festive clothes is taken to a shrine, usually by both parents and the paternal grandmother, in this custom that introduces the child into the local Shintō community.

miyakogusa The name of this wildflower means "capital plant" and derives from the plant's great abundance in the ancient capital, Kyōto.

is now the city of Kanazawa, Ishikawa Prefecture; graduated from Tōkyō University in 1883. One of the leading publicists of modern Japan, he called for the development of a new national consciousness, self-reliance, and self-affirmation on the part of the Japanese at a time when the nation was diligently imitating Western models. In 1888 Miyake and several associates founded the SEIKYŌSHA (Society for Political Education) and its magazine NIHONJIN (The Japanese; renamed *Nihon oyobi nihonjin* in 1907), hoping to counter what they regarded as excessive adulation of the West. The magazine also served as a platform for criticizing the cliques (see HAM-BATSU) that dominated the politics of the time and for awakening public consciousness on such issues as the ASHIO COPPER MINE INCIDENT. Among Miyake's major writings are *Uchū* (1909, The Universe), in which he attempted to formulate a systematic philosophy synthesizing Eastern and Western thought, and the six-volume *Dōjidai shi* (1949–54), a detailed chronicle of the people and events of his time. Miyake was awarded the Order of Culture in 1943.

Miyake Shōsai   三宅尚斎

(1662–1741). Confucian scholar of the Edo period (1600–1868). Born in Harima (now part of Hyōgo Prefecture), he studied with YAMAZAKI ANSAI, a scholar of the Zhu Xi (Chu Hsi) school of Neo-Confucianism (see SHU-SHIGAKU). In 1690 Shōsai entered the service of the Oshi domain (now part of the city of Gyōda in Saitama Prefecture). He incurred the *daimyō*'s anger for his outspoken views, and was confined to Oshi Castle for three years. After his release he went to Kyōto, where he opened a school. With SATŌ NAOKATA and ASAMI KEISAI, Shōsai was considered an outstanding disciple of Ansai.

Miyake Yonekichi   三宅米吉

(1860–1929). Archaeologist and educator. Born in the Wakayama domain (now Wakayama Prefecture), Miyake studied at Keiō Gijuku (now Keiō University) but withdrew without graduating. Miyake was director of the Tōkyō Imperial Household Museum (now Tōkyō National Museum) from 1922 to 1923 and in 1929 became the first president of Tōkyō Bunrika University (successor of the Tōkyō Higher Normal School and later Tōkyō University of Education). Miyake founded the Archaeological Society (now the Archaeological Society of Nippon). His research interests included the history of the SILK ROAD and the study of ancient INSCRIPTIONS such as the KWANGGAET'O MONUMENT. His major works are collected in *Bungaku hakase Miyake Yonekichi chojutsushū* (1929).

Miyake Yoshinobu   三宅義信

(1939–   ). Featherweight-class weight lifter. Born in Miyagi Prefecture; graduate of Hōsei

University. He won a silver medal in the 1960 Rome Olympic Games, and gold medals in the 1964 TŌKYŌ OLYMPIC GAMES and the 1968 Mexico City Olympic Games. Before his retirement in 1972, he held 48 world records.

Miyako   宮古[市]

City in eastern Iwate Prefecture, northern Honshū, on the Pacific Ocean. Miyako has been a fishing port since the Edo period (1600–1868); principal catches are salmon and *samma* (saury). Miyako has numerous fertilizer, plywood, lumber, foodstuff, and electric-appliance plants. It is part of Riku-chū Coast National Park. Pop: 58,503.

miyakogusa   都草

Lotus corniculatus var. *japonicus.* A Japanese variety of the bird's-foot trefoil. Perennial herb of the pea family (Leguminosae) that grows wild along grassy roadsides or on riverbanks. The thin stem (15–30 cm [6–12 in] long) may grow either vertically or horizontally. Each alternate, compound leaf bears three obovate leaflets. In spring and summer the plant produces one to three butterfly-shaped, bright yellow flowers. The flowers of the subvariety *nishiki miyakogusa* (*Lotus corniculatus* var. *japonicus* forma *versicolor* Makino) change their color from yellow to red.

Miyako Islands   宮古諸島

(Miyako Shotō). Group of islands southwest of the main island of Okinawa, forming the eastern part of the SAKISHIMA ISLANDS. Administratively a part of Okinawa Prefecture, they consist of the island of MIYAKOJIMA and seven others. These islands are frequently ravaged by typhoons and drought. Principal activities are sugarcane cultivation and bonito fishing. Area: 226 sq km (87 sq mi).

Miyakojima   宮古島

Island approximately 300 km (185 mi) southwest of the main island of Okinawa. The main island of the Miyako Islands. A level, triangular island, Miyakojima is composed of Ryūkyū limestone; it is frequently struck by typhoons and drought. The principal activities are sugarcane cultivation and bonito fishing. Area: 159 sq km (61 sq mi).

Miyakonojō   都城[市]

City in southwestern Miyazaki Prefecture, Kyūshū. A castle town during the Edo period (1600–1868), it is now a commercial city. Agricultural products are tea, tobacco, rapeseed, and sweet potatoes. Dairy farming also flourishes. Local items include furniture and bamboo swords for KENDŌ (fencing). Ninety percent of the bows used in KYŪDŌ (Japanese archery) are made here. Pop: 130,153.

Miyakonojō Basin   都城盆地

(Miyakonojō Bonchi). In the southern Kyū-shū Mountains, in southwestern Miyazaki Prefecture, Kyūshū. Along the upper river Ōyodogawa, the basin consists of alluvial fans and uplands composed of volcanic ashes. Agriculture and dairy farming flourish here. The major city is Miyakonojō. Area: approximately 760 sq km (290 sq mi).

Miyako no Nishiki   都の錦

(1675–?). Writer of UKIYO-ZŌSHI (popular fiction). Born in Settsu (now part of Ōsaka Prefecture); a disciple of NISHIZAWA IPPŪ. His best-known work, *Genroku taiheiki* (1702), is highly original and filled with gossip about writers and their works. In 1703 he departed

for Edo (now Tōkyō), where he was apprehended for vagrancy and sent to Satsuma (now Kagoshima Prefecture) to labor in a gold mine. Pardoned in 1710, he returned to the Ōsaka-Kyōto area, but nothing is known of his subsequent life.

Miyako no Yoshika   都良香

(834–879). Courtier, scholar, and poet of Chinese; co-compiler of the *Montoku jitsuroku* (879, Chronicle of Emperor Montoku), fifth of the Six National Histories (RIKKOKU-SHI). He was appointed ambassador to the kingdom of BOHAI (Po-hai) in 872. Of his personal collection, *Toshi bunshū* (Collected Works of Master Miyako), three books (nos. 3–5) are extant.

Miyako shimbun   都新聞

Daily newspaper published in Tōkyō before World War II. Its forerunner was the evening newspaper *Konnichi shimbun*, launched in 1884. The name was changed to *Miyako shimbun* in 1888, and it became a morning theater trade paper. Fukuda Eisuke took over as company president in 1919 and turned it into a highly successful enterprise. Because of wartime pressures, in 1942 it merged with the KOKUMIN SHIMBUN to form the TŌKYŌ SHIMBUN, which continues to be an influential Tōkyō daily.

miyamairi   宮参り

(visiting the shrine). The custom, still observed today, of taking a newborn infant to the local Shintō shrine. It is observed on the 20th, 30th, 50th, or even 100th day after birth, depending on the locality. The purpose of the visit is to have the infant recognized by the local tutelary deity (UJIGAMI) as a member (*ujiko*) of the Shintō community, and the infant is often made to cry in order to ensure that the god has heard. Today the baby is usually carried by its paternal grandmother and accompanied by both parents.

Miyamoto Kenji   宮本顕治

(1908–   ). Politician and JAPAN COMMUNIST PARTY (JCP) leader. Born in Yamaguchi Prefecture; graduate of Tōkyō University. While still a student, he established a reputation when his essay on the writer AKUTAGAWA RYŪNOSUKE, "Haiboku no bungaku" (1929, The Literature of the Defeated), won first prize in a competition sponsored by *Kaizō* magazine. Miyamoto joined the JCP in 1931. He married the writer MIYAMOTO YURIKO in 1932. In 1933 he was arrested and remained in prison until the end of World War II. He joined the newly reorganized JCP immediately after his release but was purged in 1950 by Occupation authorities (see RED PURGE). In 1982 he succeeded NOSAKA SANZŌ as chairman of the Central Committee of the party. In 1989 he retired from the House of Councillors, to which he had been elected in 1977.

Miyamoto Musashi   宮本武蔵

(1584–1645). Master swordsman and painter of the Edo period (1600–1868). Known also by his artistic sobriquet, Niten. Born in either Mimasaka (now part of Okayama Prefecture) or Harima (now Hyōgo Prefecture). Like many other *samurai* whose lords had fought on the losing side in the Battle of SEKIGAHARA in 1600, Musashi was a *rōnin* (masterless samurai). He developed the *nitō-ryū* or two-sword style of fencing, and, according to his own account, he was victorious in more than 60 sword fights during his extensive travels throughout Japan. In 1637 he fought for the TOKUGAWA SHOGUNATE (1603–1867) in suppressing the SHIMABARA UPRISING, and in 1640 he became an instructor in swordsmanship for the Hosokawa *daimyō* family in Kumamoto. The book on swordsmanship *Gorin no sho* (tr *The Book of Five Rings*, 1974), which is attributed to Musashi, is considered a classic. Said to have been written in a mountain cave in 1643 and transmitted to a disciple when Musashi was on his deathbed, the book is divided into five sections—earth, water, fire, wind, and void—corresponding to the five elements that make up the Buddhist universe. Each section treats one aspect of the art of the sword; the "water" section, for example, deals with dress, posture, footwork, and other technical details, while the "fire" section presents Musashi's views on the spirit of swordsmanship.

Musashi was also a highly accomplished *suiboku* painter (see INK PAINTING) and calligrapher. His paintings of eagles, shrikes, Hotei (see SEVEN DEITIES OF GOOD FORTUNE), and Bodhidharma, the Zen Buddhist patriarch, are characterized by bold yet incisive brushwork, reflecting his training in Zen Buddhism. His most famous work, *Koboku meigeki zu* (The Shrike), may be seen at the Kubosō Memorial Museum of Arts in Ōsaka Prefecture. Musashi's exploits have been celebrated in popular literature, including a *kabuki* play by TSURUYA NAMBOKU and the novel *Miyamoto Musashi* (1935–39; tr *Musashi*, 1981) by YOSHIKAWA EIJI.

Miyamoto Musashi　宮本武蔵

(tr *Musashi*, 1981). Best-selling work of POPULAR FICTION by YOSHIKAWA EIJI (1892–1962); originally published 1935–39. Based on the life of the 17th-century master swordsman of the title, the novel depicts the many adventures he engaged in from the time he left home at age 17 until his duel with Sasaki Kojirō on the island of Ganryūjima, including his love affair with Otsū and his duel with the Yoshioka family. Yoshikawa's consistent portrayal of Musashi as a seeker of spiritual truth through mastery of the sword gained a wide audience for his work.

Miyamoto Teru　宮本輝

(1947–). Novelist and short-story writer. Real name Miyamoto Masahito. Born in Hyōgo Prefecture. Graduate of Ōtemon Gakuin University. He received the Dazai Osamu Prize for "Doro no kawa" (1977; tr "Muddy River," 1991) and the Akutagawa Prize for "Hotarugawa" (1977; tr "River of Fireflies," 1991). In a rich lyrical style, Miyamoto vividly portrays the vicissitudes of life through the unfolding of his masterful stories. His other works include *Donau no tabibito* (1985, A Traveler on the Danube) and *Yūshun* (1986, Thoroughbred).

Miyamoto Tsuneichi　宮本常一

(1907–81). Scholar of folklore studies and MINGU (traditional tools and utensils). Born in Yamaguchi Prefecture. In 1939 he was invited by YANAGITA KUNIO and SHIBUSAWA KEIZŌ to be a researcher at the Attic Museum, a predecessor of the Japanese Folk Culture Research Institute. He traveled extensively to Japan's outlying islands and remote agricultural, mountain, and fishing villages collecting oral folklore (*minkan denshō*). Miyamoto's research contributed significantly to the development of folklore studies. His publications include *Seto Naikai no kenkyū* (1965, Research on the Inland Sea Region).

Miyamoto Yuriko　宮本百合子

(1899–1951). Novelist. Born Nakajō Yuri in Tōkyō. Her first novel, *Mazushiki hitobito no mure* (A Flock of Poor People), written when she was a freshman at Japan Women's University, was published in the magazine *Chūō kōron* in September 1916. A disastrous first marriage provided the material for her first major work, NOBUKO (1924–26), an autobiographical novel.

In 1927, Yuriko left for Soviet Russia. After a three-year stay abroad, mainly in Russia, she joined the All-Japan Federation of Proletarian Arts (NAPF) in 1930 (see PROLETARIAN LITERATURE MOVEMENT). In the same year, she became the coordinator of NAPF's Women's Committee and the editor of the journal *Hataraku fujin* (Working Women). These experiences are dealt with in *Futatsu no niwa* (1947, The Two Gardens), a sequel to *Nobuko*, and in *Dōhyō* (1947–50, Road Signs).

In 1931 she joined the Japan Communist Party (JCP) and met MIYAMOTO KENJI, a young communist literary critic whom she married in 1932. From 1932 on, leftist activities were suppressed by the government with increasing severity, the publication of journals became difficult, and Yuriko's works became the target of strict censorship. She was arrested repeatedly between 1932 and 1942, spending a total of more than two years in prison; Kenji was arrested in December 1933 and remained imprisoned until 1945. Although she produced little fiction during the war period, she was prolific in essay writing.

The years between 1945 and her sudden death in 1951 were the most active and productive of her life. Reunited with her husband, she resumed full-fledged political activities. Her major works from this period include a collection of literary criticisms and essays, *Fujin to bungaku* (1947, Women and Literature); letters between her and Kenji, *Jūninen no tegami* (1950–52, The Letters of Twelve Years); *Banshū Heiya* (1946–47; tr *Banshū Plain*, 1963); and *Fūchisō* (1946, The Weathervane Plant), about her reunion with Kenji.

Yuriko's short stories, most of which are collected in *Sangatsu no daiyon nichiyō* (1940, The Fourth Sunday in March), depict working-class men and women and the growth of class consciousness. Yet her major literary achievements are clearly in her autobiographical novels, throughout which the protagonist tries to liberate herself from her own upper-middle-class background and to contribute to human welfare by fighting against war and the exploitation of the working class and women. Her novels, which mirror life in the early part of the Shōwa period (1926–89) in Japan, are widely regarded as significant achievements in modern Japanese literature. Yuriko's critical essays range from literary criticism and analyses of women writers to theoretical arguments on proletarian literature and socialist realism.

Miyanouradake　宮之浦岳

Mountain on the island of YAKUSHIMA, Kagoshima Prefecture, Kyūshū. It has beautiful forests of huge cedars (*yakusugi*). A belt of the bamboo grass known as *yakuzasa* grows near the summit, and deer and monkeys are numerous. Miyanouradake is the highest mountain in the Kyūshū region and is part of Kirishima-Yaku National Park. Height: 1,935 m (6,348 ft).

Miyamoto Musashi
An early-Edo-period portrait of this master swordsman, who developed the two-sword style of fencing. Artist unknown.

Miyao Tomiko　宮尾登美子

(1926–). Novelist. Born in Kōchi Prefecture; graduated from Takasaka Higher Girls' School. She received the Naoki Prize for *Ichigen no koto* (1978, A *Koto* with One String). Her other works include *Kai* (1972), the story of the *geisha* house where she was born; *Jo no mai* (1982), based on the life of painter UEMURA SHŌEN; and other stories depicting women's lives.

Miyatake Gaikotsu　宮武外骨

(1867–1955). Journalist and cultural historian. Born in what is now Kagawa Prefecture. Miyatake began his career as the writer-publisher of a series of satirical magazines and newspapers. These writings, of a rather scandalous nature, won him both notoriety and the displeasure of the authorities, who imprisoned him in 1889 for LESE MAJESTY after he published a parody on the promulgation of the Meiji Constitution. Altogether, Miyatake spent more than three years in prison for repeated literary indiscretions. Beginning in the Taishō period (1912–26), he devoted himself to studying the history of popular culture and of journalism. Miyatake served as the first curator of the Meiji Newspaper and Periodical Library (Meiji Shimbun Zasshi Bunko) at Tōkyō University from 1926 to 1949 and wrote more than 100 books, including *Waisetsu fūzoku shi* (1911, A History of Salacious Customs), *Tobakushi* (1923, A History of Gambling), and *Meiji enzetsu shi* (1929, A History of Public Speaking in the Meiji Period).

miyaza　宮座

Council of lay elders representing distinguished families that claimed a close association with a local shrine (see UJIGAMI). The *miyaza* presided over community religious practices. Along with the closed and privileged trade association ZA, it developed through the medieval period, especially after the 15th century, as an autonomous institution within each community. One of its members was chosen yearly to serve as the shrine official called *tōya* and to run annual village festivals. During the Edo period (1600–1868) a permanent priesthood (KANNUSHI) arose, and the *miyaza*'s privileges were gradually diminished to the organization of parishioners.

Miyazaki　宮崎[市]

Capital of Miyazaki Prefecture, Kyūshū, on the Hyūga Sea. Formerly a farming area, it developed rapidly after it was designated the prefectural capital in 1873. The outlying farming areas are noted for their rice, cucum-

Miyamoto Yuriko This novelist, literary critic, and essayist was also a political activist who joined the Japan Communist Party in 1931 after a visit to the Soviet Union.

Miyazawa Kenji
A devoted Buddhist, this poet and author of children's stories shunned the literary world, preferring a quiet rural life.

Miyazaki Prefecture
Location and Prefectural Crest

bers, tomatoes, and pumpkins. Visitors are drawn to the semitropical island of AOSHIMA, Heiwadai Park, and the Miyazaki Shrine. Miyazaki University and various cultural halls and museums are located here. Pop: 287,352.

Miyazaki Hayao   宮崎駿

(1941–   ). Animated-film director and cartoonist. Born in Tōkyō. Graduated from Gakushūin University. After working for Tōei Animation Co, Ltd, Miyazaki became an independent producer and director in 1978. His films' uninhibited humor and skillfully aimed social criticism, combined with a poetic lyricism, have made him Japan's premier modern animated-film maker. Among his major films are *Rupan Sansei: Kariosutoro no shiro* (1979, Lupin the Third: The Castle of Cagliostro), *Kaze no tani no Naushika* (1984, Nausicaä of the Valley of the Wind), and TONARI NO TOTORO (1988, My Neighbor Totoro).

Miyazaki Ichisada   宮崎市定

(1901–   ). The leading historian of China in 20th-century Japan. Born in Nagano Prefecture, he received his doctorate in 1944 from Kyōto University, where he taught from 1934 to 1965. Miyazaki's most important work is on the Song (Sung) dynasty (960–1279) and on the subsequent development of absolute monarchy in China. His major works include *Chūgokushi*, 2 vols (1977–78, a History of China).

Miyazaki Plain   宮崎平野

(Miyazaki Heiya). Coastal plain located in central Miyazaki Prefecture, Kyūshū. Mostly uplands with river terraces formed by the river Ōyodogawa. Its Pacific Ocean coast has long sand dunes. Vegetables, sweet potatoes, and mandarin oranges are cultivated on the uplands and rice on the lowlands. The major city is Miyazaki. Length: approximately 60 km (37 mi); width: approximately 20 km (12 mi).

Miyazaki Prefecture   宮崎県

(Miyazaki Ken). Located in southeastern Kyūshū and bordered by Ōita Prefecture to the north, the Pacific Ocean to the east, Kagoshima Prefecture to the southwest, and Kumamoto Prefecture to the west. The terrain is largely mountainous, and principal mountain ranges include the KYŪSHŪ MOUNTAINS in the north and the Wanitsuka Mountains in the south. The main level areas are located around the city of MIYAZAKI on the coast, along the numerous rivers that flow eastward into the Pacific, and several inland basins in the southern part. The climate is warm with heavy precipitation, especially in the form of frequent typhoons and spring gales, which are sometimes highly destructive.

Numerous archaeological excavations testify to Miyazaki's early cultural and political development. Formerly known as Hyūga Province, it was ruled by a succession of military families during the early feudal period. In the Edo period (1600–1868), it was divided into a number of small domains, with some areas under the direct rule of the Tokugawa shogunate. The present name and boundaries originated in 1873 but were not established permanently until 1883, after a period of union with the neighboring prefecture of Kagoshima.

Miyazaki has long suffered from its re-

moteness from Japan's major economic, political, and cultural centers and remains somewhat underdeveloped to this day. Agriculture is the major occupation, the principal crops being rice and sweet potatoes, although poor soil conditions and damage caused by frequent typhoons hinder productivity. Some fruit, vegetable, and dairy items are also produced for large urban markets. Industry is minimal, but the mountains in the western part of the prefecture are a rich source of hydroelectric power for the industrial areas of northern Kyūshū.

The unspoiled mountain scenery of KIRISHIMA-YAKU NATIONAL PARK, the Nichinan seacoast in the south, and places such as Takachiho that are associated with early Japanese legends attract many tourists. Area: 7,735 sq km (2,986 sq mi); pop: 1,168,907; capital: Miyazaki. Other major cities are MIYAKONOJŌ, NOBEOKA, and HYŪGA.

Miyazaki Shrine   宮崎神宮

(Miyazaki Jingū). Shintō shrine in the city of Miyazaki, Miyazaki Prefecture, Kyūshū; dedicated to the legendary first emperor, JIMMU, and his father, Ugayafukiaezu no Mikoto, and mother, Tamayorihime no Mikoto. According to tradition the shrine is situated on the original site of the Takachiho no Miya, Jimmu's palace. The annual festival is observed on 26 October.

Miyazaki Tōten   宮崎滔天

(1871–1922). Political activist and close friend of the Chinese republican revolutionary SUN YAT-SEN. Real name Miyazaki Torazō. Born in Kumamoto Prefecture. He attended the Ōe Gijuku, a school where he encountered the ideas of the FREEDOM AND PEOPLE'S RIGHTS MOVEMENT. He later attended Tōkyō Semmon Gakkō (now Waseda University). As a young man he became interested in China and was soon an ardent supporter of East Asian unity. In 1899 he was commissioned by the Foreign Ministry to gather information about revolutionary activities against the Manchu dynasty in China. After his return to Japan he met Sun Yat-sen, who was in exile there, and the two became friends. Tōten worked to secure Japanese support for Sun's cause and to raise money for the revolutionaries. Tōten went to China after the overthrow of the Manchu dynasty in 1911 and devoted himself to the revolution in China. He published an autobiography, *Sanjūsannen no yume* (tr *My Thirty-Three Years' Dream*, 1982), in 1902. See also TAIRIKU RŌNIN.

Miyazaki Yasuji   宮崎康二

(1916–   ). Olympic swimmer. Born in Shizuoka Prefecture. At the 1931 All-Japan Championship meet, Miyazaki set a new Japanese record in the 100-meter freestyle with a time of 59.2 seconds. He won the same event (58.2 seconds) at the 1932 Los Angeles Olympic Games and won a second gold medal as a member of the 800-meter relay team.

Miyazaki Yasusada   宮崎安貞

(1623–97). Agronomist of the early Edo period (1600–1868). Born in the Aki domain (now part of Hiroshima Prefecture). In 1647 he entered the service of the Fukuoka domain (now part of Fukuoka Prefecture) but resigned at 30 to become a farmer in the village of Myōbaru in Fukuoka. Miyazaki also read Chinese works on agriculture and botany and traveled extensively in western Japan, studying farming techniques. He

wrote up his findings in 1696 as the *Nōgyō zensho* (Agricultural Encyclopedia), published in 1697 with an introduction by KAIBARA EKIKEN.

Miyazawa Kenji   宮沢賢治

(1896–1933). Poet and author of children's stories. A devout Buddhist, he spent much of his life laboring to improve the material and spiritual lives of peasants in the impoverished farming communities of Iwate Prefecture in northern Japan. Miyazawa received little notice during his lifetime, but since World War II the sincerity of his work, reflecting a life of spiritual struggle, has attracted growing attention.

The eldest of five children, he was born in the rural village of Hanamaki, Iwate Prefecture, to a prosperous and pious Buddhist family of pawnbrokers. Except for brief periods in Tōkyō, he lived out his life in this bleak, snowbound region. A good student, he graduated in 1918 from the Morioka Higher Agricultural and Forestry School.

Differences with his father over religion and his repugnance for the pawnshop business were a major source of dissatisfaction in his life; he early yielded his primogenital rights of inheritance to his younger brother. Failing to convert his father from the JŌDO SHIN SECT of Buddhism to the more activist NICHIREN SECT, Miyazawa left home for Tōkyō in 1921.

After an eight-month stay in Tōkyō, during which he faithfully attended a Nichiren study group and wrote many children's stories, Miyazawa returned home to Iwate because of the illness of his sister Toshiko. In December 1921 he became a teacher at a local agricultural high school. Three years later, in 1924, he financed at considerable expense the publication of a collection of children's stories titled *Chūmon no ōi ryōriten* (title story tr "The Restaurant of Many Orders," 1972) and the first section of his most famous work of poetry, *Haru to shura* (1922–33; partial tr *Spring and Ashura*, 1973). Both books failed but brought him to the attention of the poets TAKAMURA KŌTARŌ and KUSANO SHIMPEI, who admired him greatly and introduced his work to the literary world. From 1926 until his death in 1933, Miyazawa alternated between working to improve the plight of poor farmers and bouts of pleurisy that incapacitated him for years at a time.

Miyazawa was a gifted, prolific writer; manifest in his work is a particularly acute sensitivity to the land and the people who make their living from it. Working rapidly, he wrote a large number of children's stories—many light-hearted and humorous—which he intended as an aid in moral education. His best-known children's story is "Ginga tetsudō no yoru" (1927; tr "Night Train to the Stars," 1987). Among other works of prose are a few plays written for his students, but it is his poems, evoking a simple yet strong passion for the Japanese countryside, that have attracted an international readership.

Although he wrote traditional 31-syllable verse (TANKA) and longer poems in conventional rhythms, it is *Haru to shura* (the second, third, and fourth sections of which were published posthumously), a collection of some 400 poems in free verse, dating from 1922 until his death, that represents Miyazawa's mature work. He was familiar with the work of the early modern poets who preceded him, and his abiding concern for the plight of the farmers and his sometimes perversely private imagery demonstrate his debt to the proletarian and romantic schools. See PROLETARIAN LITERATURE MOVEMENT.

One of the sources of his particular poetic tone is his lifelong struggle to submit himself to the karmic laws of his Buddhist heritage through absolute celibacy, renunciation of material values, and a life of severe self-denial and service. His poetry records with irony, pain, and passion the defeats and triumphs of his spiritual progress. Repeatedly he celebrates the renewal and joy of sky, clouds, snow, mountains, and all growing things. Or he stands mute in the thunder and rain in ruined rice fields. Takamura Kōtarō saw him not as a poet but as a man who wrote poetry. Miyazawa struggled throughout his life to help those around him overcome poverty and misery and was more a compassionate human being than a self-conscious poet. In this vein, his works still speak forcefully to the modern sensibility. The MIYAZAWA KENJI MUSEUM is located in Hanamaki, Iwate Prefecture.

Miyazawa Kenji Museum
宮沢賢治記念館

(Miyazawa Kenji Kinenkan). Museum of the life and work of the poet MIYAZAWA KENJI (1896–1933). Opened in 1982 in the city of Hanamaki, Iwate Prefecture, in anticipation of the 50th anniversary of Miyazawa's death. The few manuscripts and other autograph writings that survived the air raids on Hanamaki during World War II are displayed here, along with a collection of his photographs and personal effects.

Miyazawa Kiichi
宮沢喜一

(1919–). Politician; prime minister from November 1991. Born in Tōkyō. Miyazawa graduated from Tōkyō University in 1941 and joined the Ministry of Finance the following year. In 1953 he was elected to the House of Councillors as a candidate of the LIBERAL PARTY (NOW LIBERAL DEMOCRATIC PARTY) from Hiroshima Prefecture. In 1967 he became a member of the House of Representatives. Miyazawa has held a variety of high-ranking positions, including that of foreign minister. Implicated in the RECRUIT SCANDAL, Miyazawa resigned his post of finance minister in 1988. He succeeded KAIFU TOSHIKI as prime minister in 1991.

Miyazawa is considered an expert on both economic and foreign policy. He served three terms as director-general of the Economic Planning Agency and has often taken part in negotiations with foreign governments, including those for the SAN FRANCISCO PEACE TREATY implemented in 1952. In contrast to most of Japan's past prime ministers, Miyazawa speaks English well and is personally acquainted with many US and European politicians.

Miyazawa Toshiyoshi
宮沢俊義

(1899–1976). Scholar of constitutional law. Born in Nagano Prefecture, he graduated from Tōkyō University in 1923 and taught in its law faculty from 1925 to 1959. He was a student of MINOBE TATSUKICHI, to whose chair he succeeded in 1934, and carried on his mentor's politically liberal interpretation of the Meiji Constitution of 1889. After World War II, as a member of what was then the House of Peers, Miyazawa was appointed to a commission to discuss the draft of the new constitution that was approved by the Diet in 1946. Thereafter he was a leading defender of the constitution, organizing the CONSTITU-

TIONAL PROBLEMS STUDY GROUP in 1958 and writing many books, including the authoritative *Nihonkoku kempō* (1955, The Constitution of Japan).

Miyazu
宮津[市]

City in northern Kyōto Prefecture, central Honshū, on Miyazu Bay. The city developed as a castle town and as a port during the Edo period (1600–1868). It is now a fishing base and a trading port as well as the administrative and political center of the region. Industries include metals, processed seafood, and textiles. A chief attraction is the scenic sandbar AMANOHASHIDATE on the coast. Pop: 26,450.

Miyoshi
三次[市]

City in northern Hiroshima Prefecture, western Honshū, on the river Gōnokawa; the most important city of the northern part of the prefecture. The city thrived as a river port and castle town in the early part of the Edo period (1600–1868). It is principally known for its farming, cattle, woodworking, and food processing. Its cormorant fishing (*ukai*) is also well known. Pop: 39,465.

Miyoshi
三芳[町]

Agricultural town in southern Saitama Prefecture, central Honshū. Santome Shinden, which extends from Miyoshi to the city of Tokorozawa, is a notable example of a planned village of the Edo period (1600–1868). Potatoes, carrots, and other vegetables are grown. In recent years factories and housing developments have been built in Miyoshi. Pop: 35,067.

Miyoshi
三好[町]

Town on the western border of the city of Toyota in central Aichi Prefecture, central Honshū. Persimmons, grapes, and other fruits and vegetables are grown here. Since 1960 automobile, textile, furniture, and numerous other factories have been built. Pop: 32,241.

Miyoshi Basin
三次盆地

(Miyoshi Bonchi). In northern Hiroshima Prefecture, western Honshū. Situated between the Chūgoku Mountains and the highland Kibi Kōgen, it is at the confluence of several tributaries of the river Gōnokawa. Rice and grapes are the principal crops. The major city is Miyoshi. Length: 25 km (16 mi); width: 40 km (25 mi).

Miyoshi Jūrō
三好十郎

(1902–58). Playwright and poet. Born in Saga Prefecture. Graduate of Waseda University. In the early 1920s he was an anarchist poet, but he soon became a Marxist, participating in the PROLETARIAN LITERATURE MOVEMENT and writing plays filled with left-wing sentiment such as *Kubi o kiru no wa dare da* (1928, Who Does the Firing?) and *Tanjin* (staged in 1930, Coal Dust). Disillusioned, he underwent ideological conversion (see TENKŌ) in the mid-1930s. Later plays focused on the lives and thoughts of ordinary people. His major works are the plays *Kirare no Senta* (1934, Scar-faced Senta), *Bui* (1940, Life Buoy), and *Honoo no hito* (1951, Person of the Flames) and a collection of critical essays, *Nihon oyobi nihonjin* (1954, Japan and the Japanese).

Miyoshi Kiyoyuki
三善清行

(847–918). Scholar-official of the Heian period (794–1185). In the AKŌ INCIDENT OF 887, a power struggle centering on Fujiwara no

Mototsune's (836–891) appointment as imperial regent (*kampaku*), Kiyoyuki opposed SUGAWARA NO MICHIZANE and was said to have been partly responsible for Michizane's downfall in 901. His scholarly works included "Iken fūji jūnikajō," a memorial presented in 914 to Emperor DAIGO. It analyzed the deteriorating condition of the country and the breakdown of the RITSURYŌ SYSTEM of administration.

Miyoshi Manabu
三好学

(1861–1939). Botanist. Born in Mino Province (now Gifu Prefecture); graduated from Tōkyō University. After studying in Germany he taught at Tōkyō University and contributed to the introduction of the study of plant physiology and plant ecology in Japan. He coined the Japanese word for ecology, *seitaigaku*. He also campaigned for laws to preserve natural monuments. He played a major role in advancing the study of botany through his many publications, such as *Shokubutsugaku kōgi* (1889, Lectures on Botany).

Miyoshi Sanninshū
三好三人衆

(Miyoshi Triumvirs). Iwanari Tomomichi, Miyoshi Nagayuki, and Miyoshi Masayasu; principal captains of regional warlord Miyoshi Nagayoshi (also known as Miyoshi Chōkei; 1522–64). They killed the shōgun Ashikaga Yoshiteru (1536–65) in 1565. In 1568 they installed Ashikaga Yoshihide (1540–68) as shōgun but were checkmated by ODA NOBUNAGA, who made ASHIKAGA YOSHIAKI shōgun. In 1569 they made a surprise attack on Yoshiaki's Kyōto residence but were defeated; their action impelled Nobunaga to take harsh measures against the city of SAKAI, their supporter. The end of the Miyoshi Triumvirs came in 1573 when Iwanari Tomomichi took Yoshiaki's side in conflict with Nobunaga and was defeated and killed.

Miyoshi Tatsuji
三好達治

(1900–1964). A poet of great range and subtlety, Miyoshi is noted primarily for a large body of free verse of generally moderate length. His more involved poems portray isolation and loneliness as conditions basic to contemporary life; yet, in their highly literary diction, complex manipulation of language, and presentation of the poet as eternal traveler, these same poems hark back to certain early modern and classic periods of Japanese verse.

Born in Ōsaka, Miyoshi was the eldest son in a large family of modest means. From 1915 until 1921 he pursued a military life, first at the Ōsaka Army Cadet School and then during a brief tour in Korea. The following year he enrolled in the Third Higher School of Kyōto, where he studied literature. As early as 1914, he had begun following literary trends in Japan and composing his own HAIKU.

In 1930 he published his first major volume of free verse, *Sokuryōsen* (The Surveying Ship); thereafter his production was steady and highly varied. Miyoshi studied French literature at Tōkyō University from 1925 to 1928 and made noted translations of Baudelaire as well as several prose writers. Miyoshi was also active as an editor and critic. With Itō Shinkichi (b 1906) he arranged the definitive edition of works by the poet HAGIWARA SAKUTARŌ; Miyoshi's critical work *Hagiwara Sakutarō* (1963) is regarded as

Miyazawa Toshiyoshi This scholar of constitutional law became a leading defender of the post–World War II constitution.

Miyoshi Tatsuji This important modern poet was also active as a translator, editor, and critic.

Mizoguchi Kenji
1 This film director, who made more than 80 feature films, was revered as the dean of Japanese filmmaking.
2 Hanayagi Shōtarō (left) and Mori Kakuko in a scene from Mizoguchi's *Zangiku monogatari* (1939, The Story of the Last Chrysanthemum).

one of the finest studies of that poet. With YOSHIKAWA KŌJIRŌ he wrote a best-selling commentary on the poetry of Tang (T'ang) dynasty (618–907) China. In 1952 he published *Rakuda no kobu ni matagatte*, and in the same year he received the Japan Art Academy Award.

Miyoshi Yasunobu   三善康信

(1140–1221). Official of the KAMAKURA SHOGUNATE (1192–1333). Born into a middle-ranking courtier family, he held a post in the Empress's Office (Chūgūshiki). His mother was a sister of MINAMOTO NO YORITOMO's wet nurse, and through his connection Yasunobu became identified with the cause of the exiled Yoritomo, supplying him with news from Kyōto. Joining Yoritomo when he rebelled in 1180, Yasunobu was appointed head of the Board of Inquiry (MONCHŪJO) when Yoritomo established that body in 1184. Yasunobu made a major contribution to the organization of the shogunal government.

Mizoguchi Kenji   溝口健二

(1898–1956). World-renowned film director whose more than 80 feature films, beginning in 1922, made him the dean of Japanese directors. Born in Tōkyō. His films from the late 1930s are characterized by long takes, fluid camerawork, and beautiful mise-en-scène. Several of his films won international prizes after World War II.

Mizoguchi made his first films at a studio that was partial to stories dealing with the problems of the poor and class conflict. This tendency reflected the relatively liberal climate in Japan of the 1920s. His work in these films probably provided him with the theme he was to employ in all his major films beginning with *Nihombashi* (1929): the sacrifice (voluntary or involuntary) of a woman for a man's success or for the sake of the family. Other films in the same vein were *Tōjin Okichi* (1930, Okichi, the Foreigner's Mistress), *Taki no Shiraito* (1933, Taki no Shiraito, the Water Magician), and *Orizuru Osen* (1935, Osen's Downfall).

He directed two films in 1936 that are among the best Japanese films ever made: NANIWA EREJI (Ōsaka Elegy) and *Gion no shimai* (Sisters of the Gion). Both are set in modern Japan. In 1939 Mizoguchi directed *Zangiku monogatari* (The Story of the Last Chrysanthemum), a fine film about the life of a young KABUKI actor. In 1941, under pressure from the military government calling for national-policy films, Mizoguchi made *Genroku chūshingura* (1941–42, The Loyal Forty-Seven Rōnin of the Genroku Era).

Mizoguchi made some of his most famous films after the war: *Yoru no onnatachi* (1948, Women of the Night); *Saikaku ichidai onna* (1952, The Life of Oharu), which won a directorial prize at the Venice Film Festival; UGETSU MONOGATARI (1953, Ugetsu); *Sanshō-Dayū* (1954, Sanshō the Bailiff or The Bai-

Mizuhara Shūōshi
This *haiku* poet and founder of the haiku magazine *Ashibi* was also a practicing physician.

liff); *Chikamatsu monogatari* (1954, A Story from Chikamatsu or The Crucified Lovers); and *Akasen chitai* (1956, Street of Shame).

Mizuhara Shūōshi   水原秋桜子

(1892–1981). HAIKU poet. Real name Mizuhara Yutaka. Born in Tōkyō. Graduate of the Faculty of Medicine, Tōkyō University. Mizuhara practiced privately and also taught medicine. He studied poetry under TAKAHAMA KYOSHI, the leader of the coterie that produced the magazine HOTOTOGISU, and helped bring the group to its "golden age" in the 1920s. Later he turned from Kyoshi's objective realism to a more subjective expressionism. He founded the haiku magazine *Ashibi* in 1928, but his final break with the Hototogisu school did not occur until 1931 when he joined the *shinkō haiku* (new haiku) movement. In 1966 he became a member of the Japan Art Academy (Nihon Geijutsuin). Principal haiku collections are *Katsushika* (1930), *Shūen* (1935), and *Sōrin* (1950).

mizuhiki   水引

Decorative string used since the Muromachi period (1333–1568) to tie gift-wrapped articles and to make ornaments. A narrow strip of good quality paper made from mulberry pulp is twisted into a string, soaked in starchy water left after rinsing uncooked rice, and allowed to dry until hard. A single strand of this string may be used for tying a lock of hair or a bundle of paper. To make a *mizuhiki* for gift wrapping, several strands are laid flat side by side and glued together at the middle. Normally each half of the length is dyed a different color. For congratulatory occasions such as weddings, string dyed half in gold and half in silver is used. For other happy or neutral occasions, a red and white string is commonly used. A black and white combination is most commonly used to tie the condolence gift (*kōden*) and other gifts given in connection with funerals. Occasions of celebration (SHŪGI) require certain types of knots, while mourning or inauspicious occasions (*bushūgi*) require others.

Mizuhiki are also used to construct decorative ornaments, such as cranes, turtles, and pines, traditional symbols of good fortune that are included in a customary set of gifts exchanged between the families of the bride and the groom prior to a wedding.

Mizuho   瑞穂[町]

Town in northwestern Tōkyō Prefecture, central Honshū. During the Edo period (1600–1868) Mizuho prospered as a post-station town. The cultivation of tea flourishes here. In recent years numerous housing developments have been built for commuters to urban Tōkyō. The US Air Force's Yokota Base is located in southern Mizuho. Pop: 30,967.

Mizukami Tatsuzō   水上達三

(1903–89). Businessman; chairman of MITSUI & CO, LTD (1969–71). Born in Yamanashi Prefecture. After graduating from Tōkyō University of Commerce (now Hitotsubashi University) in 1928, he joined Mitsui & Co. He became managing director of Daiichi Bussan in 1947. Mizukami was instrumental in bringing about the grand merger of the splintered segments of the old Mitsui group of companies (one of which was Daiichi Bussan) in 1959 and served as president of the new Mitsui & Co (1961–69). He also served as president of the Japan Foreign Trade Council, Inc (1972–85).

Mizukami Tsutomu → Minakami Tsutomu

Mizuki   水城

(literally, "Water Fort"). A fortification consisting of a large earthwork with a moat. It was built across a valley near what is now the city of Dazaifu in Fukuoka Prefecture. It was completed in about 664 and served to protect DAZAIFU (the government headquarters in Kyūshū) from attack. The earthwork, originally about 14 meters (46 ft) high and 35 meters (115 ft) thick at the base, survives in two sections whose combined length is about 1.2 kilometers (0.75 mi).

Mizuki Yōko   水木洋子

(1913–). Screenwriter who has shown a sharp social consciousness in her dramatic creations. Real name Takagi Tomiko. Born in Tōkyō. Mizuki studied screenwriting under YASUMI TOSHIO and collaborated with him on many projects. Her first screenplay to be filmed was *Onna no isshō* (1949, A Woman's Life), directed by KAMEI FUMIO. Other screenplays include *Mata au hi made* (1950, Until the Day We Meet Again), directed by IMAI TADASHI; *ukigumo* (1955, Floating Clouds), directed by NARUSE MIKIO; and *Kiku to Isamu* (1959, Kiku and Isamu), directed by Imai Tadashi. Each of these three films won the Japanese best-picture award for its respective year; together they represent the best of Mizuki's writing in the 1950s. She is also known for her television screenplays, including one for the 1968 NHK drama series *Ryōma ga yuku* (Ryōma's Progress).

mizuko kuyō   水子供養

Memorial service dedicated to the bodhisattva JIZŌ that is intended to bring solace to the souls of infants who were stillborn or suffered from miscarriage, abortion, or some other accident that prevented their birth. Since the Kamakura period (1185–1333) Jizō has been regarded as the savior of children, rescuing their tormented souls at the banks of the river Sai in the realm of the dead.

Mizuko kuyō are held with increasing frequency in Japan today because of the increased number of abortions performed on young unmarried women. Because aborted fetuses and stillborn infants are not provided with graves of their own, many temples have established a monument to them in a corner of the temple precincts.

Mizumaki   水巻[町]

Town in northern Fukuoka Prefecture, Kyūshū. The coal mines that were developed here from about 1900 were among the most extensive in the CHIKUHŌ COALFIELD. After the mines were closed in 1971, housing developments were built for commuters to the city of Kita Kyūshū. The Tateyashiki archaeological site is located here. Pop: 29,756.

Mizunami   瑞浪[市]

City in southeastern Gifu Prefecture, central Honshū, on the river Tokigawa. It was the base of the Toki family, military governors (*shugo*) of this district during the Muromachi period (1333–1568). Mizunami is a center of china and pottery production, especially Western-style tableware for export. Pop: 41,006.

Mizuno Corporation   美津濃[株]

(Mizuno). Company engaged in the manufacture and sale of sporting goods and sportswear. Incorporated in 1923. It has subsidiaries in Taiwan, the United States, the United Kingdom, and Germany and manufacturing plants in Taiwan, South Korea, the United States, and Mexico. Future plans call for expansion into sports-related consulting and service industries. Sales for the fiscal year ending March 1991 totaled ¥176.8 billion (US $1.3 billion). Capitalization stood at ¥24.7 billion (US $180.0 million) in the same year. Headquarters are in Tōkyō and Ōsaka.

mizunomi-byakushō   水呑百姓

Landless peasants of the Edo period (1600–1868); literally, "water-drinking peasants," a reference to the thin, watery gruel on which they subsisted.

The lowest level of the peasant class, they earned their livelihood as tenant farmers or day laborers. Some enjoyed the right to collect fertilizer and firewood from village-owned fields and mountains (see IRIAI). Unless specified by their tenancy contracts, they did not pay the annual land tax (NENGU), but they were sometimes liable for village or other taxes such as BUYAKU and MUNABE-TSUSEN. Some industrious and fortunate *mizunomi-byakushō* were able to become landed, taxpaying peasants (HOMBYAKUSHŌ). In some regions very small landholders were also classified as *mizunomi-byakushō*.

Mizuno Rentarō   水野錬太郎

(1868–1949). Bureaucrat. Born in Tōkyō, he graduated from Tōkyō University in 1892. He was head of the Home Ministry in 1918, 1922–23, and 1924. Member of the RIKKEN SEIYŪKAI political party until 1935 and protégé of its leader, HARA TAKASHI. The quintessential bureaucrat-politician, Mizuno was also education minister 1927–28.

Mizuno Seiichi   水野清一

(1905–71). Archaeologist. Born in Hyōgo Prefecture, Mizuno graduated from Kyōto University, where he was a professor from 1949 to 1968. Much of his research centered on East Asian archaeology; he published his findings in *Unkō sekkutsu* (16 vols, 1951–55, The Stone Caves of Yungang). In excavations on the islands of Tsushima and Iki, between Korea and northwestern Kyūshū, Mizuno researched the interaction of ancient Japanese culture with that of the Asian mainland. He was also a central figure in studies of sites in Iran, Afghanistan, and Pakistan.

Mizuno Shigeo   水野成夫

(1899–1972). Businessman. Born in Shizuoka Prefecture, he was a graduate of Tōkyō University. Mizuno joined the Japan Communist Party in 1925 and was arrested in 1928. Following his release from prison in 1929 he left the party. After World War II, he played a key role in labor relations for the business-industrial community. He served as president of Nippon Cultural Broadcasting, Inc, Fuji Telecasting Co, Ltd, and Sankei Shimbun (a newspaper company). Mizuno also acted as an adviser to Prime Minister Ikeda Hayato. With SAKURADA TAKESHI, KOBAYASHI ATARU, and NAGANO SHIGEO, he was regarded as one of the most influential leaders of the business-industrial community of his day.

Mizuno Tadakuni   水野忠邦

(1794–1851). *Daimyō* of Hamamatsu domain (now part of Shizuoka Prefecture) who pursued the largely unsuccessful TEMPŌ REFORMS during the early 1840s; born in Edo (now Tōkyō), the son of Mizuno Tadamitsu, dai-

myō of the Karatsu domain (now part of Saga Prefecture) in Kyūshū. In 1812 Tadakuni became head of his branch of the Mizuno family. Three years later he was named *sōshaban* (master of shogunal ceremony). In 1817 he was promoted to JISHA BUGYŌ (commissioner of temples and shrines) and transferred to a domain at Hamamatsu. In 1825 he was appointed Ōsaka JŌDAI (keeper of Ōsaka Castle) and in 1826 he was promoted to KYŌTO SHOSHIDAI (Kyōto deputy) receiving the rank-title of Echizen no Kami, by which he was later known.

In 1828 he returned to Edo to serve as *nishinomaru rōjū* (senior councillor to the heir apparent) and guardian to the four-year-old son (Iesada) of the shogunal heir, Tokugawa Ieyoshi (1793–1853). Early in 1837 Tadakuni took the financial portfolio (*kattekata*) and assumed a preeminent role in the council of *rōjū*.

In 1841 Tadakuni had Ieyoshi announce sweeping reforms, modeled on the KYŌHŌ REFORMS and KANSEI REFORMS, that would revitalize the shogunate. Tadakuni's Tempō Reforms were carried out for two years, but several measures gained him enemies and undermined his support within the shogunate. In the fall of 1843 he resigned from office. He was recalled, but soon resigned again. His political rivals moved decisively to destroy his influence. Tadakuni was held responsible for his subordinates' corruption and mistakes and was forced to retire as daimyō in 1845. He was placed under house arrest and died six years later.

Mizusawa   水沢[市]

City in southern Iwate Prefecture, northern Honshū. Mizusawa developed as the outpost for subduing the EZO when SAKANOUE NO TAMURAMARO built a fortress (Isawajō) here in 802. It was a castle town during the Edo period (1600–1868). Local products are rice, fruits, and Nambu cast-iron goods. The Mizusawa Astrogeodynamics Observatory is here. Pop: 58,189.

Mizusawa Astrogeodynamics Observatory   国立天文台水沢観測センター

(Kokuritsu Temmondai Mizusawa Kansoku Sentā). Astronomical observatory in the city of Mizusawa, Iwate Prefecture. An adjunct of the Earth Rotation Division of the NATIONAL ASTRONOMICAL OBSERVATORY. It was founded in 1899 to cooperate with other nations in the observation of polar motion. The first head of the observatory was the astronomer KIMURA HISASHI, who discovered the Z-term, a cyclical variation in latitude. The observatory serves as the central station of a network of six observatories located at different points on the same latitude throughout the world.

Mizushima   水島

An area on the outskirts of the city of Kurashiki, Okayama Prefecture, western Honshū, facing the Inland Sea. In 1941 it became an industrial area almost overnight with the establishment of an aircraft manufacturing industry. After World War II, steel, chemical, oil-refining, and other heavy industries were established. As a result the area faces a serious water pollution problem. One of the country's largest heavy industrial complexes is located here.

Mizushima San'ichirō   水島三一郎

(1899–1983). Chemist who contributed to the understanding of the molecular structure of matter though his studies of dipole mo-

ments, infrared absorption, and the Raman effect. Born in Tōkyō, he graduated from Tōkyō University, where he later became a professor. In 1961 he received the Order of Culture. His publications include *Structure of Molecules and Internal Rotation* (1954).

Mizutani Yaeko   水谷八重子

(1905–79). Actress. Real name Matsuno Yaeko. Born in Tōkyō. She made her stage debut in 1916 as Mizutani Yaeko in the role of Sergia in *Anna Karenina*. Her first film performance was in Hatanaka Ryōha's (1877–1959) *Kantsubaki* (1921, Winter Camellia). Although she appeared in films such as Tanaka Eizō's (1886–1968) *Namiko* (1932) and SHIMAZU YASUJIRŌ's *Jōriku daiippo* (1932, First Steps Abroad), she acted primarily on stage, reviving the nearly defunct Geijutsu-za troupe and becoming Japan's leading stage actress in such roles as Nora in Ibsen's *A Doll's House* in 1924. Around 1928 Mizutani began acting in SHIMPA ("new school") dramas. She was active in the *shimpa* school through the postwar period and became the leading figure in *shimpa* following the death of star actor HANAYAGI SHŌTARŌ in 1965.

MOA Museum of Art   MOA美術館

(Emu Ō Ē Bijutsukan). Located at Atami, Shizuoka Prefecture; formerly known as the Kyūsei Atami Art Museum. This museum, opened in 1957, and its sister museum, the HAKONE MUSEUM OF ART in Hakone, belong to the SEKAI KYŪSEI KYŌ (The Religion for the Salvation of the World). The collections were assembled by the late founder of the church, OKADA MOKICHI. In January 1982 a new four-story complex was completed, and the museum was renamed in honor of Okada (MOA is an abbreviation for Mokichi Okada International Association). It houses a collection of Chinese and Japanese painting, calligraphy, ceramics, and sculpture; Chinese bronzes; Japanese lacquer, metalwork, and prints; and European art.

Mobara   茂原[市]

City in central Chiba Prefecture, central Honshū. Long a distribution center for agri-

mizuhiki
1 A craftswoman uses *mizuhiki* to fashion auspicious ornaments, such as cranes, turtles, and pines. Such objects are included in a customary set of gifts exchanged between families of the bride and groom before a wedding.
2 Tied with *mizuhiki*, the elaborate knot called *awabimusubi* decorates congratulatory gifts on such occasions as birthdays and graduations.
3 The single knot of the *musubikiri* is used for events that one hopes will occur only once, whether welcome (a wedding) or unfortunate (an illness or funeral).

Mizutani Yaeko
Although this leading stage actress also appeared in Western plays, she acted primarily in *shimpa* ("new school") dramas.

◄ On special occasions steamed rice is often pounded into *mochi* the old-fashioned way with a wooden or stone mortar and pestle.

▼ The ball of steamed rice is turned frequently during pounding to insure a smooth, even texture.

▼ To make *kirimochi*, the finished dough is rolled into a sheet, allowed to dry slightly, and cut into rectangles.

▲ The finished *mochi* may be molded into round balls for use as *kagamimochi*.

▼ Flat rectangles of rice cake, known as *kirimochi*, are either boiled or grilled before eating. Pieces of cooked *mochi* are used in soups and stews or are eaten seasoned with a little soy sauce.

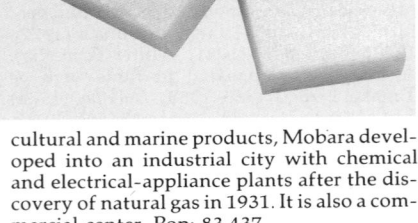

▲ *Kagamimochi*, composed of two rounds of *mochi*, is a common New Year's decoration, often presented with a piece of dried kelp and an orange.

cultural and marine products, Mobara developed into an industrial city with chemical and electrical-appliance plants after the discovery of natural gas in 1931. It is also a commercial center. Pop: 83,437.

Mobil Sekiyu KK   モービル石油[株]

(Mōbiru Sekiyu). Importer and seller of petroleum products. Incorporated in 1961. A Japanese subsidary of the American company Mobil Corporation. Mobil Sekiyu is descended from the Standard Vacuum Oil Co's Japan division, established in 1933. In 1961 that company was divided into Mobil Sekiyu KK and the present-day ESSO SEKIYU KK. Mobil Sekiyu has 12 branches and 42 storage installations in Japan. Sales for the fiscal year ending December 1990 totaled ¥696 billion (US $5.2 billion), and capitalization stood at ¥11.0 billion (US $82.4 million). Headquarters are in Tōkyō.

mochi   餅

(rice cake). A food consisting of a highly glutinous variety of rice (*mochigome*) that is steamed, kneaded by machine or, traditionally, mortar and mallet, and formed into rounds or into sheets that are then cut into squares. Fresh *mochi* may be eaten as is; grilling restores softness to dried *mochi*.

Mochi came to Japan from Southeast Asia along with rice cultivation. Long an essential offering and food at religious observances, it remains inextricably related to the annual round of Japanese rituals and festivals (see NENCHŪ GYŌJI). At New Year's, *kagamimochi* (a decoration or offering consisting of a flat-bottomed, mounded round of *mochi* placed atop a larger one) is customarily displayed in homes and religious establishments, and *mochi* is an ingredient in the celebratory soup ZŌNI. *Kashiwamochi*, with a sweet filling and wrapped in an oak leaf to impart fragrance, is eaten on CHILDREN'S DAY (5 May).

Mochi is occasionally made with millet or with other ingredients mixed in: *mamemochi* is *mochi* with soybeans, and *kusamochi* contains crushed mugwort leaves. Sweet red bean paste is often used as a filling, as in *kashiwamochi* and DAIFUKU. With the recent introduction of electric kneaders, *mochi* can easily be made; it can also be purchased in vacuum packages, convenient for storage.

Mochizuki Yūko   望月優子

(1917–77). Film actress. Real name Suzuki Mieko. Born in Tōkyō. Mochizuki appeared in several of Shibuya Minoru's (1907–80) films, including *Yonimme no shukujo* (1948, The Fourth Lady). She also appeared in KINOSHITA KEISUKE's *Nihon no higeki* (1953, A Japanese Tragedy) and *Narayama-bushi kō* (1958, The Ballad of Narayama), NARUSE MIKIO's *Bangiku* (1954, Late Chrysanthemums), IMAI TADASHI's *Kome* (1958, Rice), and YAMAMOTO SATSUO's *Niguruma no uta* (1959, The Song of the Cart). Her most effective roles were as the ideal Japanese mother, strong yet self-effacing. She ran successfully for the House of Councillors in 1971.

modern philosophy   近代哲学

(*kindai tetsugaku*). Philosophy (*tetsugaku*) as an academic discipline in the Western sense made its appearance after the Meiji Restoration of 1868. NISHI AMANE and TSUDA MAMICHI, who had been sent to Holland a few years before the restoration by the Tokugawa shogunate (1603–1867) to study philosophy and social science, had brought back mainly the utilitarianism of John Stuart Mill and the positivism of Auguste Comte, both then influential in the Dutch philosophical world. This was the start of the first real importation of Western philosophy into Japan.

Following the Meiji Restoration, Nishi and Tsuda joined with others to form the MEIROKUSHA, an organization that played a decisive role in the "civilization and enlightenment" movement of the early Meiji years (see MEIJI ENLIGHTENMENT). In 1871 NAKAE CHŌMIN introduced French theories of democratic revolution, beginning with the social philosophy of Jean-Jacques Rousseau. The democratic theories imported by Nakae served as a theoretical basis for the FREEDOM AND PEOPLE'S RIGHTS MOVEMENT.

Traditional Thought and Modern Philosophy—The third decade of the Meiji period (1868–1912) saw a decline in the influence of the Freedom and People's Rights Movement. In promulgating the CONSTITUTION OF THE EMPIRE OF JAPAN in 1889 and the IMPERIAL RESCRIPT ON EDUCATION in 1890, the government moved to erect an emperor-centered state, giving a contemporary, nationalistic guise to traditional Japanese ideas in an effort to propagate a new mass morality. Simultaneously, Japanese intellectual circles, led by NISHIMURA SHIGEKI and INOUE ENRYŌ, spawned a number of movements that employed Western philosophy to produce new treatments of Confucian and Buddhist thought.

At state-supported universities, British and French Enlightenment philosophy was already being supplanted by German idealism. INOUE TETSUJIRŌ, a professor in Tōkyō University's philosophy department, introduced the idealist philosophy of Hartmann and Hegel and criticized the Enlightenment moral philosophy taught by the previous generation of Japanese thinkers. This idealist philosophy was to serve as the foundation for a state-centered morality comprising the old virtues of loyalty and filial piety.

ŌNISHI HAJIME turned to another idealist, Kant, employing his methods of criticism to attack Inoue's anti-Enlightenment, state-centered views. Opposed to state supremacy and to Inoue's speculative metaphysics, Ōnishi attempted to develop a critical metaphysics based on epistemology and fusing Eastern and Western thought.

The Formation of Academic Philosophy—The early 20th century saw the study of German philosophy vigorously pursued in state universities, as the study of Western philosophy in Japan entered a stage of deeper understanding and original research. In particular, there was a movement to introduce idealist and personalist ethics as found in Kant, Fichte, Friedrich Paulsen, and Thomas Hill Green. Similar manifestations were the formation of the Teiyū Ethics Society and the development of religious spiritualism (see UCHIMURA KANZŌ; KIYOZAWA MANSHI; TSUNASHIMA RYŌSEN). All of these developments reflected the growth of a modern consciousness of self and the search for new ways to view human existence.

In the late Meiji and early Taishō (1912–26) periods, academia concentrated on the introduction of Neo-Kantianism, then the main current in German academic philosophy. Philosophical research became increasingly technical and specialized as scholars such as KUWAKI GEN'YOKU, TOMONAGA SANJŪRŌ, and HATANO SEIICHI carried out detailed studies of original texts. NISHIDA KITARŌ, responding to the emergence in Japan of a modern self-awareness, published *Zen no kenkyū* (1911; tr *A Study of Good*, 1960), the first truly original philosophical treatise produced in modern Japan. Nishida's creativity is seen primarily in his concept of "pure experience," a state transcending the dichotomy of subject and object; it was the state of the union of the two, a state that was, in fact, reality itself. Drawing upon his own experience in Zen meditation, Nishida took all dualities as expressive of the differentiation and development of pure experience. His was the first attempt by a Japanese to approach Western philosophy from a personal standpoint and to produce a universal philosophical system by giving logical and ontological form to traditional Japanese thought. It influenced a number of academic philosophers, including TANABE HAJIME, who used Nishida's "logic of place" (*basho no ronri*) as the starting point for his own "logic of species" (*shu no ronri*), a concept that bore elements of a doctrine of state supremacy insofar as it made an ideological absolute out of the state.

Taishō Democracy and Philosophy— Kuwaki Gen'yoku (1874–1946), head of the philosophy department at Tōkyō University, inaugurated the "Tōkyō school." Initially an adherent of the Neo-Kantian school, Kuwaki supported the Tōkyō school's position of intellectualist rationalism and contributed to the development of academic philosophy in Japan. During the high tide of TAISHŌ DEMOCRACY after World War I, he collaborated with SŌDA KIICHIRŌ as an exponent of culturalism (*bunka shugi*), one of the main trends of thought during the period, along with self-culturalism (*kyōyō shugi*), personalism (*jinkaku shugi*), and humanism (*jindō shugi*). WATSUJI TETSURŌ's "Watsuji ethics" attempted a reorganization of traditional East Asian and Japanese ethical thought in the light of culturalism and personalism.

Affiliated with the democratic inclinations of the Taishō period, these schools had their start in the reemergence of a Japanese middle class and were influenced by its nascent spirit of individualism. In one form or another, all expressed a desire to break with current ideas of state supremacy and move on to new values.

Marxist Philosophy— Socialist ideas, including Marxist ideology, entered Japan during the early Meiji years, but it was not until the SINO-JAPANESE WAR OF 1894–1895, the rapid development of industry, and the ensuing profusion of social and labor problems that these ideas began to have a real connection with Japan's social realities. Many early socialists, such as ABE ISOO and KATAYAMA SEN, were Unitarians, and they attempted to realize the ideals of their rational, Christian humanism through socialism.

The thinking of another early socialist, KŌTOKU SHŪSUI, had strong traces of idealism and humanism derived from Confucian learning. During a trip to the United States, Kōtoku came under the influence of

anarcho-syndicalist thought, abandoning the idea of obedience to the law and calling instead for direct action by the workers. His defection brought to the surface many philosophical and emotional conflicts submerged in the socialist movement, such as opposition between Christian and materialist viewpoints and between parliamentarianism and direct action. Amid these disputes, Kōtoku was executed for his involvement in the HIGH TREASON INCIDENT OF 1910, and the socialist movement entered what is known as its "winter season."

The socialist movement revived in the freer political climate following World War I. Anarcho-syndicalism, descended from the direct-action movement of the Meiji period, was espoused by ŌSUGI SAKAE, who emphasized individual freedom and opposed authority. YAMAKAWA HITOSHI and others influenced by the Russian Revolution backed Marxist-Leninism, which gradually gained ascendancy over the anarchists, resulting in the illegal formation of the JAPAN COMMUNIST PARTY. Not until the late Taishō and early Shōwa (1926–89) periods, however, did the philosophical aspects of Marxism, as opposed to its social and economic tenets, receive any serious attention. KAWAKAMI HAJIME, a pioneer in the study of Marxian economics, initially embraced Marxism as a form of idealistic humanism but later adopted a somewhat more doctrinaire version. After his Marxist studies in Europe, FUKUMOTO KAZUO exerted considerable influence on Japan's socialist movement. MIKI KIYOSHI drew upon the hermeneutics of Heidegger to interpret Marxist philosophy as a form of anthropology.

As Japanese society became increasingly fascist following the outbreak of the SINO-JAPANESE WAR OF 1937–1945, totalitarianism and Japanism (Nihon *shugi*) made inroads into intellectual circles. Members of the Materialism Study Society, including TOSAKA JUN and SAIGUSA HIROTO, continued to spread word in Japan of the development and application of Marxist philosophy in the Soviet Union, attempting to use this to oppose right-wing ideologies at home. In the face of increasing repression, however, the society was disbanded; both Miki and Tosaka died in prison in 1945.

Concomitant with the emergence of Marxist thought and Marxist movements was a growing interest in philosophical circles in historical and social problems, particularly in dialectics and Hegelian philosophy. At the same time, the climate of war and MILITARISM led to the increased influence of the totalitarian philosophies of Japanism and imperial supremacy (*kōdō shugi*) advocated by thinkers such as KIHIRA TADAYOSHI.

The Post–World War II Situation— Japan's defeat in World War II discredited the imperial-centered ideology fostered since the Meiji Restoration and revived movements aimed at political and social democracy. Many philosophical schools suppressed before or during the war reappeared. Marxism and existentialism drew particular attention, as did the concept of autonomy, the meeting point of these two approaches. Umemoto Katsumi (1912–74) was a central figure in the philosophical development of this theory of autonomy. Japan's economic resurgence in the 1950s and 1960s brought about many new developments, including the introduction of analytic philosophy and pragmatism. MARUYAMA MASAO made important contributions to the fields of political theory and the history of Japanese thought,

applying the methodology of Western political science to an analysis of Japanese society and its traditions. Yet the country's very success in achieving industrialization has brought awareness of the contradictions contained in this accomplishment, along with reassessment of Western models and of traditional Japanese thought and culture. Japanese philosophy has thus entered another stage of development, embracing the dual heritage of its own culture and that of the West.

modern prints　版画

(*hanga*). Many Japanese artists in the 20th century have worked in the print mediums with notable success. Their debt to the traditional art of woodblock printing (UKIYO-E) is undeniable, for with *ukiyo-e* prints the woodblock had been raised to dazzling heights and had become a truly Japanese medium. At the same time, there was in Japan a lingering disdain for *ukiyo-e* as a plebeian art, an attitude that transferred to all prints, no matter how far removed from *ukiyo-e* in subject and style. Thus, the modern Japanese print artist faced the challenge of discovering new possibilities in a traditional format and of creating a place for himself in the modern art world.

Japan's modern print artists divided into two schools. In general terms, one school tried to revive the *ukiyo-e* tradition, continuing its themes and designing for publishers whose artisans did the carving and printing. The other school seized on the woodblock as a native medium but used it to express a new vision born of exposure to Western art. These artists took over the whole artistic process themselves.

In the first school, KOBAYASHI KIYOCHIKA was a forerunner. HASHIGUCHI GOYŌ produced only about 15 prints, but his portraits of women rival the *ukiyo-e* masters in virtuosity. Kawase Hasui (1883–1957) designed hundreds of effective landscapes. ITŌ SHINSUI, although primarily a painter, designed both portraits of women and landscapes. YOSHIDA HIROSHI, although he is better known for his watercolors, also produced prints, which he published himself using his own carvers and printers. But it was the second school that proved to be more significant, for it brought the Japanese print into the arena of contemporary international art.

Yamamoto Kanae (1882–1946) and his friends and followers created a movement they called *sōsaku hanga* ("creative prints"). They believed that in prints, as in painting and sculpture, the artist should perform the entire creative process, carving and printing as well as designing. The *sōsaku hanga* movement gathered strength in the 1920s and 1930s and flowered after World War II when foreigners resident in Japan introduced the prints to appreciative audiences abroad.

Two artists were dominant in this period, ONCHI KŌSHIRŌ and HIRATSUKA UN'ICHI. Onchi was interested in abstract design and modified the woodblock print through his use of paper, cloth, and found objects, such as leaves. Hiratsuka used traditional techniques and often worked in black and white. MUNAKATA SHIKŌ also worked primarily in black and white, drawing on folkloric Buddhist themes. HASEGAWA KIYOSHI, HAMAGUCHI YŌZŌ, and Komai Tetsurō (1920–76) were etchers of distinction. By the close of the 1950s Japanese prints had won international

modern prints

Technical excellence and thematic innovation have made the work of contemporary Japanese printmakers eagerly sought after by collectors both in Japan and abroad.

◀ Hamaguchi Yōzō (b 1909). *Receptacle and Grapes.* 1964. Copperplate print. 26 × 53 cm. Kamakura Museum of Modern Art, Kanagawa Prefecture.

▼ Komai Tetsurō (1920–76). *A Momentary Image.* 1951. Etching. 20 × 30 cm. Machida City Museum of Graphic Arts, Tōkyō.

▲ Oda Kazuma (1882–1956). *Landscape in Tōkyō (at Kagurazaka).* 1917. Lithograph. 27 × 45 cm. National Museum of Modern Art, Tōkyō.

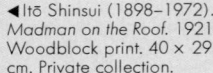

◀ Itō Shinsui (1898–1972). *Madman on the Roof.* 1921. Woodblock print. 40 × 29 cm. Private collection.

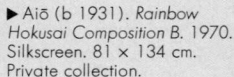

▶ Aiō (b 1931). *Rainbow Hokusai Composition B.* 1970. Silkscreen. 81 × 134 cm. Private collection.

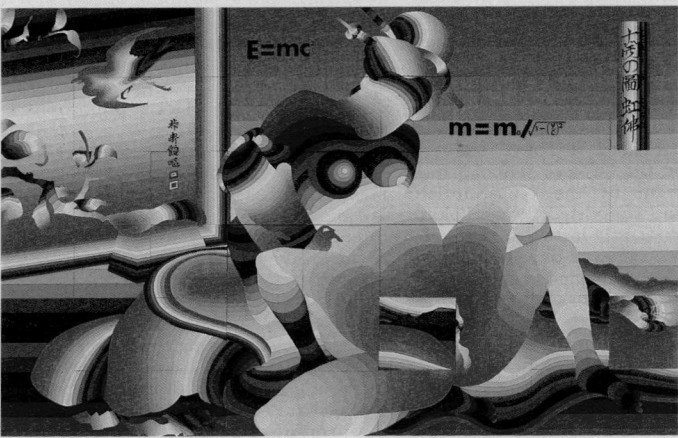

prizes, and print artists had finally achieved recognition at home.

Those Japanese printmakers who were born after 1930 and reached their prime in the 1960s and 1970s experimented with print techniques that were currently being employed by their Western counterparts and largely neglected the traditional Japanese favorite, the woodblock print. The silkscreen has been of particular interest to these Japanese artists. Aiō (known abroad as Ay-O; b 1931), with the assistance of printer Okabe Tokuzō, creates rainbow color silkscreens. His masterpiece is *Rainbow Hokusai* (1970). YOKOO TADANORI is another important silkscreen artist. Lithography is a second imported print medium in which the Japanese now excel, and Yoshihara Hideo (b 1931), ARAKAWA SHŪSAKU, and Ida Shōichi (b 1940) have become leaders of lithography today. Etching is another medium that has come into prominence in Japan. IKEDA MASUO is the prolific etcher laureate, internationally acclaimed, whose best work has been created on metal plates with color roulette, drypoint, etching, engraving, or mezzotint.

Mogamigawa   最上川

River in Yamagata Prefecture, northern Honshū, originating in the volcano Azumasan on the border between Yamagata and Fukushima prefectures and flowing north through the Yonezawa and Yamagata basins; thereafter it changes course to flow northwest through Shinjō Basin and Shōnai Plain and enters the Sea of Japan at the city of Sakata. It is known for its swift currents. Numerous electric power plants are located along the river. The water is used for irrigation, industry, and drinking. Length: 229 km (142 mi); area of drainage basin: 7,040 sq km (2,718 sq mi).

Mogami Tokunai   最上徳内

(1755–1836). Explorer of Hokkaidō, Sakhalin, and the Kuril Islands. Born in Dewa Province (now Yamagata Prefecture). In 1781 he went to Edo (now Tōkyō) and studied surveying and navigation under the mathematician HONDA TOSHIAKI. In 1785 he went on an expedition to EZO (now Hokkaidō), and in the following year he surveyed southern Sakhalin and the southern Kurils, making the earliest recorded visits by a Japanese to Etorofu (Iturup) and Uruppu (Urup) islands. An encounter with a Russian on Etorofu led Mogami to call attention to Ezo's importance for national defense. During the next two decades he conducted several surveys of Sakhalin and the Kuril Islands. An astute observer of the AINU and the Russians (he learned both their languages), Mogami illuminated through several works the ethnography as well as the geography of insular northeast Asia.

Mogi Keizaburō   茂木啓三郎

(1899–). Businessman. Born Iida Katsuji in Chiba Prefecture. Graduate of Tōkyō University of Commerce (now Hitotsubashi University). He joined Noda Shōyu (presently KIKKŌMAN CORPORATION) and was adopted by the Mogi family, the owners of the company. He ascended to the company's presidency in 1962 and chairmanship in 1974. He revolutionized the production processes and management of soy sauce manufacturing, one of the most traditional of all Japanese industries. Mogi started soy sauce production in the United States in 1973.

Moji   門司

District in the city of Kita Kyūshū in northern Fukuoka Prefecture, Kyūshū. Situated on the KAMMON STRAIT across from Honshū, Moji serves as a gateway to Kyūshū. Prior to World War II it flourished as a shipping port for rice and coal.

Mōka   真岡[市]

City in southeastern Tochigi Prefecture, central Honshū, on the river Kinugawa. Known early for its production of Mōka cotton cloth, it was shogunate territory during the Edo period (1600–1868). More recently, the establishment of several industries, notably automobile parts, machinery, and metal goods, and the construction of an industrial park have led to a population increase. Agricultural products include rice and vegetables. Pop: 61,748.

mokkan　木簡

(wooden tablets). Thin, irregular strips of wood used for writing, mainly during the 7th and 8th centuries; probably adopted from China. Japanese *mokkan* averaged 10–25 centimeters (4–10 in) in length and 2–3 centimeters (0.8–1.2 in) in width, the size generally being determined by the length of the message, which was written on both sides. It is only since 1961 that *mokkan* have been excavated in quantity. The first such excavations were at the Heijō Palace near the present-day city of Nara (see HEIJŌKYŌ). As of 1990 more than 100,000 tablets were known from some 300 different sites, including the palaces at HEIANKYŌ, ASUKA KIYOMIHARA NO MIYA, NANIWAKYŌ, FUJIWARA-KYŌ, and NAGAOKAKYŌ, as well as the military outposts of DAZAIFU and TAGAJŌ. The largest finds have been at the Heijōkyō site, where in 1987 over 30,000 *mokkan* were unearthed from the ruins of the residence of Prince Nagaya (676 or 684 to 729). The oldest *mokkan* date from the mid-7th century, although most date from the late 7th through the 8th centuries. *Mokkan* have also been excavated from medieval sites such as Ichijōdani, the stronghold of the ASAKURA FAMILY.

Mokkan were used as labels, to issue directives, for record keeping, for practicing calligraphy, or for jotting notes; some were specifically used as talismans or scroll title tags. Those used as directives mainly deal with the movement of goods and people within the palace precincts, such as requests for certain commodities, summonses, permits to enter the palace compound, and so forth. Records generally deal with the receipt and disbursement of goods and the work performance of governmental officials. *Mokkan* used to label tax goods sent in from the provinces (SO, YŌ, AND CHŌ) are of particular interest for information on the tax system of the time.

Mokkei　牧谿

(fl 13th century; Ch: Muqi or Mu-ch'i). A 13th-century Chinese Zen monk and painter. A native of Sichuan (Szechwan) Province in western China, he was a man of letters who became a Zen monk in middle age, under the master Wuzhun Shifan (Wuchun Shih-fan; d 1249). He established the temple Liutongsi (Liu-t'ung ssu) on the outskirts of Hangzhou (Hangchow) in Zhejiang (Chekiang) Province. He was accomplished in monochrome ink paintings of landscapes, figures, birds and flowers, and animals. His works were treasured in Japan, and only there have any of his paintings survived. His ability to capture the atmosphere of a particular moment and to combine telling detail with a sense of space has profoundly influenced Japanese INK PAINTING since the 14th century.

Mōko Shūrai → Mongol invasions of Japan

Mokuami　黙阿弥

(1816–93). Also known as Kawatake Mokuami. KABUKI dramatist of Edo (now Tōkyō) whose career spanned over half a century from the late Edo (1600–1868) to the early Meiji (1868–1912) periods. Real name Yoshimura Shinshichi. Other pen names include Kawatake Shinshichi II.

Noted for his *sewa-mono* (domestic plays), which pictured the lives of the ordinary townspeople of the Edo period, he first established his reputation as the creator of *shiranami-mono* (plays depicting the activities of thieves), regarded at the time as a daring departure from the typical *sewa-mono*. *Tsutamomiji Utsunoya Tōge* (1856, Bun'ya's Murder), *Kosode Soga azumi no iro-nui* (1859; tr *The Love of Izayoi and Seishin*, 1966), *Sannin Kichisa kuruwa no hatsugai* (1860, Three Men Called Kichisa), and AOTOZŌSHI HANA NO NISHIKI-E (1862, Benten the Thief) are ranked among the finest works in this category.

Soon after the Meiji Restoration (1868), Mokuami began writing *katsureki-mono* ("living history" plays), which stressed factual accuracy, literary excellence, and moral teachings. These modified versions of the traditional *jidai-mono* (historical plays) were presented largely at the insistence of Ichikawa Danjūrō IX (1838–1903), the most influential actor of this era. *Takatoki* (1884, Takatoki and the Goblins), originally part of a longer three-act play, is a rare example of a *katsureki-mono* that is still performed today.

Zangiri-mono——In the early Meiji period, the influx of Western ideas, technology, and material culture led to a profound transformation of Japanese society, described by Mokuami in *zangiri-mono* ("cropped hair" plays). Recasting the setting of the *sewa-mono* in the modern period, he presented kabuki actors in Western clothes with their hair in *zangiri*, or cropped, style—instead of the usual topknot and middle part. Those who adopted the *zangiri* haircut were openly declaring their rejection of an outmoded past. The *zangiri-mono* offered countless examples of Western exoticisms, such as European clothing, trains, steamboats, and cameras, but they also often presented topical themes, such as the plight of the ex-*samurai*, compulsory education, military conscription, and the schoolgirl—then, a novel phenomenon. However, as a rule, *zangiri-mono* failed to provide more than a superficial view of early Meiji society; the basic beliefs and attitudes expressed by the characters often merely echoed those of the bygone Edo period.

Other Works——Mokuami also wrote a number of *matsubame-mono*, adaptations of well-known plays from the NŌ theater, long identified as the exclusive entertainment of the samurai class. The kabuki versions of *Tsuchigumo* (1881, Ground Spider), *Ibaraki* (1883, Demon Ibaraki), and the like are frequently included in the current kabuki program.

Mokuami has long been recognized for his powerful lyrical passages recited by chanters to *shamisen* accompaniment, an effective device for supporting the action on the stage or for intensifying the mood of the dramatic situation. In November 1881, he announced his official retirement as an active kabuki playwright and assumed the familiar name of Mokuami; three years later he relinquished his title of Kawatake Shinshichi to one of his favorite disciples. Nevertheless, he continued to write until his death in 1893. Mokuami wrote some 360 plays during his lifetime. Nearly half of the plays in the present kabuki repertory are his.

See also ICHIKAWA DANJŪRŌ; ONOE KIKU-GORŌ.

Mokuan Reien　黙庵霊淵

(?–ca 1345). Painter-monk; the first Japanese practitioner of INK PAINTING (*suibokuga*) whose full name is known. He was a Zen monk active in the Kamakura region before he went to China as a pilgrim. The diary of GIDŌ SHŪSHIN, *Kūge nichiyō kufūshū*, reports that Mokuan's earlier name was Zeichi and that he was a disciple of Kenzan Sūki (1286?–1323). Mokuan was probably in Yuan (Yüan) dynasty (1279–1368) China as early as 1329 on a pilgrimage. He attained a high clerical position and remained in China for the rest of his life.

Six works that are generally considered to be by Mokuan are extant today. These include the *Byakui Kannon zu* (White-Robed Kannon) in ink on silk in the Ataka Collection; the paintings of the wandering monk Hotei (Ch: Budai or Pu-tai) in the MOA, Sumitomo, and Masaki collections, respectively; the *Shisuizu* (Four Sleepers) in the Maeda Ikutokukai Foundation; and another *Byakui Kannon* in ink on silk, in the Freer Gallery of Art, Washington, DC.

Mokubei → Aoki Mokubei

mokujiki　木喰

(literally, "one who eats wood"). Discipline of extreme asceticism, probably originating in Taoist ideas of sagehood, that was practiced by some Buddhist monks in Japan. The term also refers to the monks themselves and was used as a part of the names of these monks, two of whom are especially famous.

Mokujiki Ōgo (1536–1608) was a monk of the SHINGON SECT. He was born in Ōmi Province (now Shiga Prefecture) and became a priest in 1573. In 1585 Ōgo persuaded the warlord TOYOTOMI HIDEYOSHI not to destroy Shingon temples and later restored many of them and built yet more. Ōgo's collection of rules for RENGA (linked verse) composition, entitled *Mugonshō*, is a classic in this field.

Mokujiki This Thousand-Armed Kannon is one of 88 statues that Mokujiki Gogyō, a monk and follower of the Mokujiki discipline, carved for his hometown in Kai Province. 1801. Wood. Height 73 cm. Private collection.

mokkan Over 30,000 of these inscribed wooden strips have been recovered from the 8th-century residence of Prince Nagaya at the Heijō Palace, Nara. The *mokkan* at center (length 21 cm) records a gift of abalone to the prince. Nara National Research Institute of Cultural Properties.

moles
1 The *himizu*, a shrew mole with a body length of 8–10 cm, burrows under layers of fallen leaves.
2 The Azuma *mogura* has a body length of 13 cm, a short tail, and large, shovellike front paws.

Mokujiki Gogyō (1718–1810) was also a monk of the Shingon sect. He is also known as Mokujiki Myōman. Born into a peasant family in Kai Province (now Yamanashi Prefecture), he became a monk in 1739 and took the vows of a *mokujiki* in 1762. He traveled throughout Japan, carving more than 1,000 Buddhist figures, which he gave to local temples or families.

moles 土竜

(*mogura*). In Japanese, *mogura* is the general name for animals of the family Talpidae, order Insectivora; five species inhabit Honshū, Shikoku, and Kyūshū. Three of these are members of the subfamily Talpinae, the typical moles of the Old World: the Azuma *mogura* (*Mogera wogura*), found on Honshū northward from the Kantō Plain; the Kōbe *mogura* (*M. kobeae*), found south of the Kantō Plain; and the *mizuramogura* (*Euroscaptor mizura*), a relict species that inhabits subalpine and alpine zones. All three species create conspicuous mole hills.

The shrew moles *himizu* (*Urotrichus talpoides*) and *himehimizu* (*Dymecodon pilirostris*), both of the subfamily Uropsilinae, are native to Japan but closely resemble the shrew moles (genus *Neurotrichus*) of the Pacific coast of North America. Both species inhabit wooded areas but in distinct vertical distribution, with *himizu* below and *himehimizu* above elevations of 1,600 meters (5,250 ft). Both species dig tunnels under leaf litter but do not make mole hills. According to a Japanese legend the mole, dazzled by the glaring sun, contemplated shooting it down with a bow and arrow but was punished and burrowed under the ground.

Mombetsu 紋別[市]

City in northeastern Hokkaidō, on the Sea of Okhotsk. Mombetsu was developed by the Matsumae domain in the 1680s. It is a base for fishing in the northern seas, and seafood processing is the main occupation. It also has sugar-beet and dairy farming. Pop: 31,078.

Mombushō → Ministry of Education

Momijigari 紅葉狩

(Viewing Autumn Maple Leaves). NŌ play by KANZE NOBUMITSU. It is classified as a *gobammemono* ("part-five play"). A beautiful woman (the *maejite* or main character at the beginning of a play), apparently of noble birth, and her lady attendant are enjoying a banquet beneath the brilliant autumn foliage of the mountain Togakushiyama. The nobleman Taira no Koremochi (the *waki* or subordinate character) comes upon the pair and is invited to join them. Koremochi gradually becomes intoxicated with wine as he watches the lady dance, and eventually drifts into a deep sleep. She then changes into a female demon (the *nochijite* or main character at the end of a play) and bears

down upon Koremochi. However, in his sleep Koremochi has been given a sword by the god of the mountain, and he quickly vanquishes the attacking demon. This play is also performed for KABUKI.

momijigari 紅葉狩

The traditional pastime of viewing autumn foliage. Like cherry-blossom viewing (HANAMI) in the spring, it was popular among the court aristocracy of the Heian period (794–1185). The nobles went boating on ponds in the gardens around their mansions, playing music and composing poetry while viewing the fall colors, or went on excursions into the mountains to gather brightly colored leaves. In the Edo period (1600–1868) the custom spread among the common people. With the improvement of public transportation after the Meiji period (1868–1912), people began to visit distant places noted for their beautiful foliage. The tradition continues to be popular today.

Mommu, Emperor 文武天皇

(683–707; Mommu Tennō). The 42nd sovereign (*tennō*) in the traditional count (which includes several legendary emperors); reigned 697–707. His father, Prince Kusakabe, was the eldest son of Emperor TEMMU; his mother succeeded him as Empress Gemmei (661–722; r 707–715). Mommu ascended the throne on the abdication of his grandmother Empress JITŌ. He married FUJIWARA NO FUHITO's daughter Miyako and acquiesced in all of Fuhito's policies, most notably the enactment of the TAIHŌ CODE in 702.

Momotarō 桃太郎

(Peach Boy). Popular folktale recounting the adventures of the boy Momotarō. Born from a peach found by an elderly woman washing clothes on a riverbank, Momotarō is adopted by the woman and her husband. Maturing quickly, he goes off with a dog, a pheasant, and a monkey to conquer Ogre Island and returns home with treasures for his foster parents. The tale exists in many versions; its present form has been widely popular since the late Edo period (1600–1868).

Like the tales of Kaguyahime (see TAKETORI MONOGATARI), *Oyayubitarō* (The Boy as Small as a Thumb), and ISSUMBŌSHI (One-Inch Boy), *Momotarō* falls into the folktale genre *chiisako monogatari* (tales of a tiny child). *Momotarō* also falls into the category *hyōchakutan* (tales of being washed ashore), in which a child endowed with supernatural powers by gods beyond the sea or far upstream comes to confer good fortune on the human world.

Momoyama period → Azuchi-Momoyama period

mon → crests

monasticism 僧院制度

(*sōin seido*). The dominant expression of monastic life in Japan has been the Buddhist religious community, living in monasteries and nunneries (*tera*) or hermitages (*in* or *an*). When Buddhism was introduced into Japan in the 6th century, the monastic order, or *saṃgha* (J: *sōgya*), was venerated together with the Buddha and the *dharma* (J: *hō*; the Buddha's teachings) as the "Three Treasures" of Buddhism. Among the first patrons of Buddhism in Japan were members of the powerful SOGA FAMILY led by SOGA NO UMAKO, his niece Empress SUIKO, and her re-

gent, Prince SHŌTOKU. In 593 relics of the Buddha were placed in the foundation stone of the pagoda of the monastery Hōkōji (ASUKADERA) built by Umako. The monastery was completed in 596. In 606 a copper image (about 5 m [16 ft] high) of the Buddha was set in the main hall. Prince Shōtoku is credited with the foundation of SHITENNŌJI (593), Ikarugadera (HŌRYŪJI, 607), and other monastic complexes. By 623 there were in Japan 46 monasteries, 816 monks, and 569 nuns.

Secular control over monastic life and the alignment of monasteries with the state bureaucracy were enforced by the promulgation of "Regulations for Monks and Nuns" (Sōniryō) within the Taihō and Yōrō *ritsuryō* administrative codes of the early 8th century. The doctrinal studies, sutra readings, and prayer ceremonies conducted by monks and nuns were not directed at the succor or salvation of the mass of the population but at the welfare and protection of elite patrons and the secular state. The Buddhist monastic establishment was placed under the supervision of the Ministry of Civil Affairs (Jibushō). Those wishing to enter the religious life had to secure official permission, take a state-sponsored examination, and undergo the official ordination procedures.

A few monks, such as GYŌGI, were dissatisfied with the detachment, pomp, and ease of life in the official monasteries and tried to take the message of Buddhist salvation to the common people. Other monks who were dissatisfied with the ceremonious atmosphere of the official monasteries in the capital of Heijōkyō (now Nara) built mountain retreats for private study and contemplation.

The promulgation of the Sōniryō and the establishment of an ordination platform at TŌDAIJI and later at TŌSHŌDAIJI by the Chinese monk GANJIN, who came to Japan in 754 to establish the Vinaya teaching (see RITSU SECT), provided a foundation for the officially regulated Buddhist monastic life. Emperor SHŌMU ordered the building in every province of a monastery and nunnery in which prayers would constantly be offered for the welfare of the country and its ruler. The hub of this network, and a symbol of imperial authority, was the colossal bronze and gilt statue of the Buddha Vairocana in Tōdaiji. Shōmu also sponsored the building of several large monasteries in the capital and ordered the tonsuring of thousands of monks and nuns. The wave of temple building provided a massive stimulus to architecture, sculpture, painting, and the importation of Chinese culture.

Emperor KAMMU's decision in 784 to move the capital from Heijō to Heiankyō (now Kyōto) was dictated in part by his desire to remove the court and government from clerical influence. The move made it easier for him to institute monastic reform as well as overhaul the *ritsuryō* administrative and land systems.

Early in the 9th century the monks SAICHŌ and KŪKAI introduced fresh currents of Chinese Buddhism into Japan. In addition to the new TENDAI SECT and SHINGON SECT doctrines and practices, which they brought back from China, Saichō and Kūkai were advocates of strict monastic discipline and service to the nation. ENRYAKUJI, the monastic center of Tendai Buddhism, located outside the capital, was designated a center for the protection of the nation (*chingo kokka*) and, shortly after Saichō's death, was given the right to conduct ordinations.

Enryakuji, Onjōji (MIIDERA), KŌYASAN, TŌJI, and other Tendai and Shingon monasteries exerted a profound impact on the religious life of the Heian period (794–1185). They attracted large numbers of monks and held out to laypeople the promise of salvation to all who were sincere in their religious practice and performance of good works. By the 12th century, however, dissatisfaction with the prevailing forms of monastic life was becoming evident.

From the 10th century devotion to AMIDA—belief that salvation in Amida's Pure Land of the Western Paradise could be attained not only by the discipline of monastic life but also by contemplation of Amida or the invocation of his sacred title, the NEMBUTSU—had become a powerful current in Tendai monasteries. The Pure Land teaching (see PURE LAND BUDDHISM) was expressed most graphically by GENSHIN and taken out of the monastic context and carried to the common people by KŪYA, HŌNEN, SHINRAN, and IPPEN. The attitudes of Shinran in the 13th century were perpetuated among his followers in the True Pure Land school (JŌDO SHIN SECT), which grew to become the largest branch of Japanese Buddhism.

In the late 12th and 13th centuries ZEN was another powerful current in the popular upsurge of Buddhism. In their emphasis on seated meditation, *zazen*, and in their assertion that enlightenment was attainable by all, Zen pioneers shared some of the ideals of the popular movement. But Zen masters also reemphasized the monastic ideal, bringing from China Zen monastic rules (*shingi*) and the characteristic Zen monastery centered on the communal meditation hall (*sōdō*).

The challenge presented by Pure Land, Zen, and NICHIREN's Lotus teaching provoked reform in the older monastic schools of Buddhism during the 13th century. This reform was most evident in the case of the Vinaya (Ritsu) school revival under monks such as EIZON and his disciple Ninshō (1217–1303), who promoted stricter monastic discipline and concern for social problems.

Decline of Monasticism—The centuries between the 12th and 16th are often presented as a time of dissolution for monastic Buddhism, both because of the growth of the rival Pure Land, True Pure Land, and Nichiren schools and because the warrior government of this era was less protective and cooperative than the court had been. However, the older monasteries continued to flourish until the mid-16th and 17th centuries, when warrior control sapped their vitality. In their military struggles to unify the country ODA NOBUNAGA and TOYOTOMI HIDEYOSHI razed Enryakuji, reduced Honganji and Negoroji, and confiscated lands from many monasteries. TOKUGAWA IEYASU and his Tokugawa successors turned increasingly to secular Confucian scholars for advice on statecraft and diplomacy. Buddhist leadership in the intellectual domain was ended and monastic involvement in the shaping of the national political configuration was eliminated.

Between the 17th and 19th centuries Buddhist monasteries were used by the Tokugawa as centers for the registration of the local population, but little was done to promote spiritual revival. What vitality was evident in the Tokugawa period was provided by the introduction from China of ŌBAKU SECT Zen monasticism in the 17th century, the efforts of Zen monks such as HAKUIN to revitalize RINZAI SECT monastic practice and promote Zen among the common people, or the spread in urban areas of the Confucian-

ized ethical teachings of ISHIDA BAIGAN and the SHINGAKU movement. In some domains, especially those such as Mito, where the Shintō-inspired National Learning (KOKUGAKU) was strong, Buddhist monasteries were disestablished, Buddhist monks and nuns defrocked, and monastic lands confiscated.

After the MEIJI RESTORATION (1868), the new government severed the long-standing connection between Shintō and Buddhism and sought to elevate Shintō into a national ideology. This policy was interpreted by some ideologues as a license to eradicate Buddhism. In many parts of the country monasteries and temples were vandalized and monks and nuns laicized. The violence of the anti-Buddhist movement was quickly suppressed, but it served, along with the reappearance in Japan of Christian missionaries, as a salutary warning to Buddhists that reform and modernization of their religious community were required. Monks such as FUKUDA GYŌKAI and Shaku Unshō (1827–1909) led a movement to restore strict observance of the Vinaya among religious and lay people. In succeeding decades all branches of monastic Buddhism were successful in making the transition to contemporary society.

Monchūjo　　　　　　問注所

(Board of Inquiry). A judicial body of the Kamakura (1192–1333) and Muromachi (1338–1573) shogunates that adjudicated disputes between vassals (GOKENIN) over land rights as well as other property cases. It was established in 1184 by MINAMOTO NO YORITOMO, with MIYOSHI YASUNOBU as its first head (*shitsuji*). Staff members were called YORYŪDO. The office gradually became the shogunate's chief judicial arm outside Kamakura. After 1249, cases concerning shogunal vassals were under the jurisdiction of the newly created High Court (HIKITSUKE), and the Monchūjo dealt mainly with litigation concerning commercial transactions, loans, indentured servants, and goods (see ZATSUMU SATA). Under the Muromachi shogunate most of the Monchūjo's duties were taken over by the MANDOKORO, and the office was reduced to archival work.

monetary policy　　　　金融政策

(*kin'yū seisaku*). The use of official powers, primarily by the BANK OF JAPAN (Japan's central bank), to influence the amount of money in circulation, interest rates, and credit conditions, in order to achieve national goals of maintaining price stability and steady economic growth with full employment. Specific tools used by the Japanese government to implement monetary policy include manipulation of the official discount rate and reserve requirements, open-market operations, and the issuing of guidelines (*madoguchi shidō*; literally, "window guidance").

The official discount rate is the interest rate at which the Bank of Japan lends money to commercial banks, primarily the group of large banks known as city banks. A rise in the official discount rate reduces the amount of money in circulation by raising the cost of money supplied to commercial banks. As of 1989, Japan had experienced 49 changes in the official discount rate since World War II. The reserve requirement system makes it mandatory for commercial banks to maintain deposits in the central bank at a fixed ratio to their own deposit liabilities. When the reserve requirements are raised, the

banks must increase their deposits, which reduces the amount of funds they have available for loans. Open-market operations control the amount of currency in the market through the buying and selling of securities. Through *madoguchi shidō* the central bank indirectly controls the amount of currency available by instructing commercial banks and other large financial institutions on such matters as how much they are permitted to loan to customers.

Until about 1970 enterprises tended to demand more funds than commercial banks could loan, causing a chronic fund shortage at the banks that had to be covered through borrowing from the Bank of Japan. This situation increased the effectiveness of *madoguchi shidō*, specifically the unofficial regulation of the amount of loans, as an instrument of monetary policy. During the same period, the government consistently kept the official interest rate low in order to reduce the interest burden on Japanese companies. However, interest rates were sometimes forced up when rapid domestic expansion sucked in imports, causing the external trade balance and the overall balance on private current transactions to go into deficit; the central bank would then respond by adopting a tight money policy.

Following the OIL CRISIS OF 1973, government debt and its annual financing requirements increased, and the principal mechanism of government financial policy shifted to central bank open-market operations in government securities, issues of which increased considerably in the 1970s. Since the mid-1980s, a large surplus in the international balance of payments, brought about by a sharp rise in exports, has increased corporate liquidity and decreased corporate dependence on loans from commercial banks. As a result, the role played by *madoguchi shidō* has been greatly reduced, being replaced by the development of interest-rate measures and open-market operations aimed at maintaining a stable money supply and stable exchange rates.

money offerings　　　　賽銭

(*saisen*). Money offered at a Shintō shrine or Buddhist temple in repayment for the fulfillment of a petition or prayer (GANKAKE) or on the occasion of a visit for worship. At shrines and temples it is common for offering boxes to be positioned directly in front of the main hall. This feature is thought to date only from the Edo period (1600–1868), although the custom of offering newly minted coins to Shintō or Buddhist deities and gods has existed since ancient times. Prior to the spread of the custom of giving money, it was common to offer *ohineri*, a handful of rice wrapped in paper.

money, premodern　　前近代の貨幣制度

(*zenkindai no kahei seido*). Old Chinese coins have been unearthed from remains of the Yayoi period (ca 300 BC–ca AD 300) and

premodern money

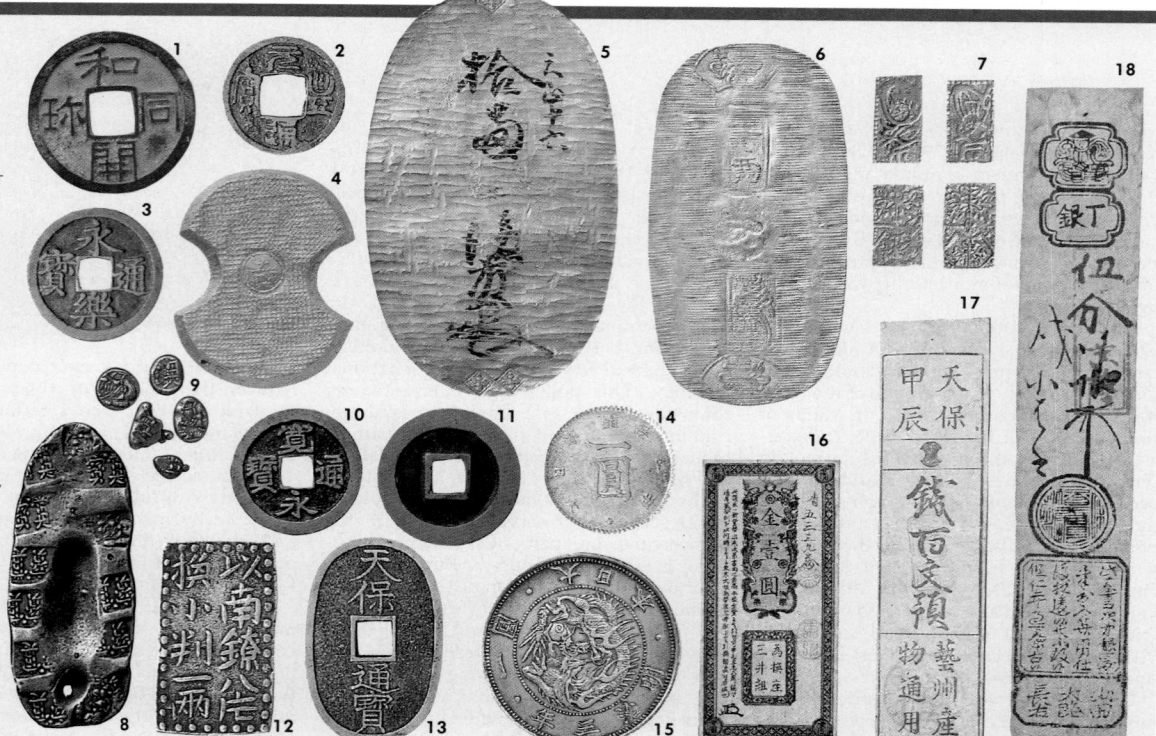

1 The early-8th-century copper and silver Wadō kaihō (copper shown here) was the first coinage minted in Japan.
2 The *bitasen*, debased coinage privately minted beginning in the Muromachi period.
3 The Eiraku *tsūhō* coin, imported from China. Circulated 15th–17th centuries.
4 The gold Taikō *fundōkin*, 16th century.
5 The Tenshō *ōban*, late 16th century. One of the largest gold coins in the world (145 × 87 mm).
6 The gold Keichō *koban*, minted beginning in 1601.
7 The gold Keichō *ichibukin*, 1601.
8 The silver Keichō *chōgin*, 1601.
9 The silver Keichō *mameitagin*, 1601.
10, 11 The copper Kan'ei *tsūhō*, minted beginning in the 17th century.
12 The silver Meiwa *nanryō nishugin* coin, first minted in 1772.
13 The brass Tempō *tsūhō* 100-mon coin, first minted in 1835.
14 A silver one-yen coin minted in 1870 for use in foreign trade.
15 A gold one-yen coin minted in 1872.
16 A yen note issued in 1871 by the Meiji government.
17 The Yamada *hagaki*, early 17th century. Considered to be Japan's first paper currency.
18 A *hansatsu* (domainal paper currency), Edo period.

tombs of the Kofun period (ca 300–710), and coins are mentioned in the NIHON SHOKI (720). However, they were probably not widely employed as currency, a function long filled by rice, cloth, and other items. The first coins minted in Japan were the silver and copper WADŌ KAIHŌ (Wadō-era coins) issued in 708 and patterned after coins of the Chinese Tang (T'ang; 618–907) dynasty. Between 760 and 958 there were at least 11 more coinages (see KŌCHŌ JŪNISEN), but barter trade continued to be the rule. In the 10th century the Bureau of the Mint (Chūsenshi) was abolished, and in 987 the use of government-minted coins was prohibited.

For nearly five centuries, until the late Muromachi period (1333–1568), the government did not mint coins but used those imported from China, Korea, Annam, and other countries. The increasing circulation of coinage led to the development of a system of cropland valuation for tax purposes that was called KANDAKA and was based on *kammon*, a unit of copper cash. As privately minted coins of poor quality came into circulation, there arose the practice called ERIZENI (coin selection), in which coins were appraised and the poorer ones devalued.

In the early Edo period (1600–1868) the shogunate established a *kinza* or gold mint (see KINZA, GINZA, AND ZENIZA) and minted ŌBAN (equivalent to 10 RYŌ), KOBAN (1 RYŌ), and *ichibukin* (one-fourth of 1 *ryō*). *Chōgin* (silver bars) and the smaller *mameitagin* were minted at *ginza* (silver mints). *Zeni*, coins with square holes made of copper, iron, or brass, were minted at various *zeniza* (*zeni* mints). In 1636 the mintage called Kan'ei *tsūhō* was designated as the official *zeni* currency, and in 1670 the use of older coinages was proscribed. With this, the premodern system of gold, silver, and *zeni* was fully established.

The various domains (*han*) issued paper currency (HANSATSU) beginning in 1661, and by the early Meiji period (1868–1912) there were 244 domains that had their own currency. The resulting confusion was eliminated in 1871 when the Shinka Jōrei (New Currency Regulation) made the YEN (equiva-

lent to 1 *ryō*) the basic unit of currency. By 1879 pre-Meiji currency had been replaced completely.

Mongaku　　　　　　　　　　　文覚

(fl late 12th century). Priest of the SHINGON SECT; secular name, Endō Moritō. Once a warrior (HOKUMEN NO BUSHI) in the service of Jōsai Mon'in (1126–89), a daughter of Emperor TOBA, he mistakenly killed a court lady whom he loved (Kesa, the wife of Minamoto no Wataru). He then renounced the world, eventually going to the temple JINGOJI on Mt. Takao (Takaosan), northwest of Kyōto. From 1173 to 1178 he was exiled to Izu Province (now part of Shizuoka Prefecture) and became a close associate of fellow exile MINAMOTO NO YORITOMO. In 1199 he was implicated in a plot against the shogunate and was exiled to the island of Sado and then to Kyūshū, where, according to legend, he died at the age of 80. His story has been recounted in *kabuki* plays and dances; his ill-fated love for Lady Kesa was fictionalized in AKUTAGAWA RYŪNOSUKE's short story "Kesa to Moritō" (1918, Kesa and Moritō), which served as the basis for the film *Jigokumon* (1953, Gate of Hell).

Mongolia and Japan　　モンゴルと日本

(Mongoru *to* Nihon). The Mongolian People's Republic (Outer Mongolia) was established in 1924. Following the invasion of Manchuria by Japan in 1931, the Mongolian People's Republic came to consider Japan a threat to its security, and in 1936 signed a mutual defense treaty with the Soviet Union. Japan set up a puppet government in Chinese Inner Mongolia in 1937, and a border clash between Mongolian People's Republic troops and forces of the Japanese GUANDONG (KWANTUNG) ARMY in 1939 led to the intervention of the Soviet army, which inflicted a crushing defeat on the Japanese (see NOMONHAN INCIDENT).

In the postwar period contact between the Mongolian People's Republic and Japan was minimal until the establishment of formal diplomatic relations in 1972. In 1974 a cultural exchange agreement was signed and in 1977 an economic cooperation agreement. Japan provided the nation with economic as-

sistance for the construction of a cashmere sweater factory—the chief source of the nation's export earnings—and has supplied language laboratory equipment to the Mongolian National University and computers to the Ministry of External Economic Relations and Supplies. Prime Minister D. Sodonom's visit to Japan in 1990 to sign the Japan-Mongolia Trade Agreement was the first by a Mongolian head of state to a capitalist country.

Mongol invasions of Japan　　　　　　　　　　　　蒙古襲来

(Mōko Shūrai; also called Genkō). Kublai Khan (1215–94), China's first Mongol emperor, twice sent naval expeditions against Japan in the late 13th century when the KAMAKURA SHOGUNATE (1192–1333) refused to acknowledge his suzerainty and send tribute to his court. In 1274 and 1281 the Mongols landed in western Japan, but each time a fortuitous storm soon forced them to withdraw. The invasions created a state of emergency in Japan that lasted for more than 30 years.

A state letter, transmitted by Korean envoys, reached Japan early in 1268. Sent by the "Emperor of Great Mongolia" to the "King of Japan," it demanded that Japan submit to a tributary relationship or face invasion. The court at Kyōto was insulted by the letter's terms, and the Japanese ignored this letter and several others.

Early in November 1274 a Mongol armada of nearly 900 vessels carrying more than 40,000 troops—Mongols, Chinese, Jurchen Tatars, and Koreans—set out from the southern tip of Korea. After devastating the islands of Tsushima and Iki, it appeared at Hakata Bay on 18 November, and the next day attacked the town of Hakata. During the night a fierce gale wrecked much of the Mongol fleet, forcing it to withdraw with heavy losses.

When Kublai renewed his demands in 1275, the Japanese beheaded his envoys. Anticipating a second attack, the shogunate reorganized the coastal defense system, extended it to the western coast of Honshū where the latest Mongol embassy had landed, and extended the military obligations of warriors. A navy of small attack ves-

Mongol invasions of Japan In this section of the 13th-century *Scrolls of the Mongol Invasion*, a Mongol firebomb explodes as Japanese warrior Takezaki Suenaga charges a band of Mongol archers.

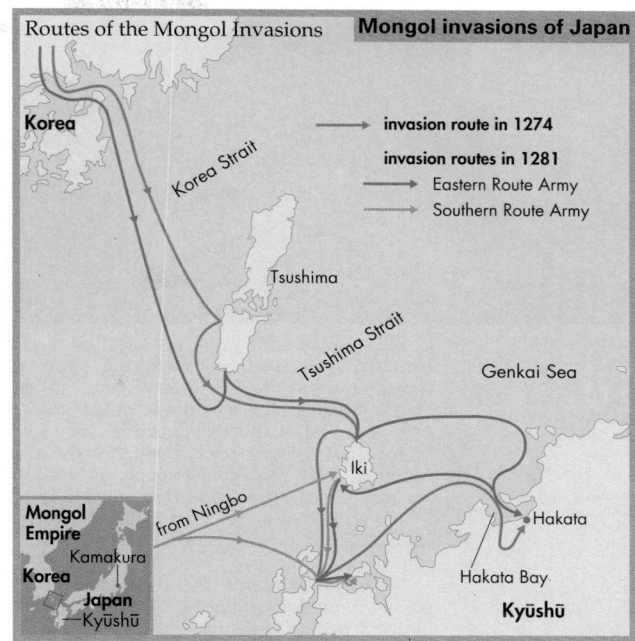

Routes of the Mongol Invasions   **Mongol invasions of Japan**

→ invasion route in 1274
invasion routes in 1281
→ Eastern Route Army
→ Southern Route Army

Korea
Korea Strait
Tsushima
Tsushima Strait
Genkai Sea
Iki
from Ningbo
from Ningbo
Hakata
Hakata Bay
Kyūshū

Mongol Empire
Kamakura
Korea
Japan
Kyūshū

sels was formed and Kyūshū warriors constructed an earth-and-stone wall around Hakata Bay.

Kublai's final embassy (1279) was beheaded like the previous one. In June 1281 two Mongol fleets—a total of 4,400 warships bearing 140,000 men—set out from Korea and from South China. The Eastern Route Army from Korea, after again laying waste Tsushima and Iki, arrived first at Hakata on 23 June. The Japanese defenders, aided by the wall at Hakata, held it off for weeks, while the small Japanese attack vessels harassed the enemy. When the Southern Route Army from China belatedly arrived, a typhoon on 16 August destroyed most of the Mongol fleet, forcing the remainder to withdraw.

To the Japanese, whose belief that their land was protected by the gods and whose faith had been deepened by the "divine wind" (KAMIKAZE) of a few years before, this second storm was a confirmation of divine favor. The western coast, however, remained on military alert for nearly 20 years. To improve military control, Kamakura appointed shogunal deputies (TANDAI) in Kyūshū and in western Honshū; and, to coordinate the war effort more efficiently, the regent HŌJŌ FAMILY concentrated the most important posts in their own hands. The cost of this defensive alert was enormous, with the shogunate and its vassals suffering great economic distress. Disaffection among the warrior class, caused ultimately by the Mongol invasions, contributed to the fall of the Kamakura shogunate.

Mongol invasions of Korea

モンゴルの高麗侵入

(Mongoru no Kōrai shinnyū). Mongol armies first invaded Korea in 1231. The KORYŎ dynasty (918–1392) quickly submitted, but once the Mongols had withdrawn, the court moved to Kanghwa Island off Korea's west coast and was able to defy the Mongols for

some 25 years, while the latter continually invaded and devastated the peninsula. By 1259, however, Korean resistance was crushed and its kings became puppets who had no choice but to cooperate fully in the MONGOL INVASIONS OF JAPAN, though the Koreans kept the Japanese informed of Mongol intentions. Mongol rule in Korea was weakened in 1356 by revolts that coincided with uprisings in China; it ended with the fall of the Mongols' Yuan (Yüan) dynasty (1279–1368) in China in 1368. The Koryŏ dynasty fell with the Yuan, and Korea remained in chaos until the founding of the YI DYNASTY in 1392.

monkeys

猿

(saru). *Macaca fuscata*. The Japanese macaque is a medium-sized monkey with a short tail. The head and body measure about 60 centimeters (24 in) in length and the tail about 7 centimeters (3 in). The fur is burnt umber, and the exposed skin of the face and buttock pads is red. Monkeys are relatively common in Japan: in 1962, the last time a survey was taken, their number was estimated to be nearly 30,000. They are found in Honshū, Shikoku, and Kyūshū, in troops of 20 to 150 individuals organized in strict hierarchy. About 100 monkeys in 6 troops inhabit the Shimokita Peninsula at the northern end of Honshū, the northernmost habitat of any primate in the world.

Japanese myth contains mention of a monkey deity, Sarutahiko, and some Shintō shrines treat the monkey as a divine messenger. A superstition that monkeys had the power to keep diseases away from horses gave rise to the custom of keeping a monkey tied to a post in stables. This superstition

survived until modern times. Monkey shows (sarumawashi) were once a common STREET ENTERTAINMENT in Japan.

Monnō

文雄

(1700–1763). Philologist and Buddhist priest of the Edo period (1600–1868). Born in the Kuwada district of Tamba (now part of Kyōto Prefecture), he studied the phonetics of Chinese characters (KANJI). In particular, his study of the yunjing (yün-ching; J: inkyō), the tables of Chinese syllables, was an epoch-making achievement. His works include *Makō inkyō* (2 vols, 1744) and *San'on seika* (2 vols, 1752).

monogatari bungaku

物語文学

(narrative literature). Various prose works of the 9th through the 14th century, ranging from long romances to historical accounts and collections of short anecdotes. Distinguished from WAKA *bungaku* (poetry), NIKKI BUNGAKU (journals or diaries), and ZUIHITSU *bungaku* (essays or random notes).

Individual *monogatari* are written primarily in prose and in a narrative mode, but they usually contain a significant number of poems. The origin of much Japanese prose writing is in the creation of stories around poems, a practice that gave rise to and is exemplified in the *uta monogatari* (stories about poems, or poem tales). The other major source of early prose writing is the retelling of folktales and fantasies, often derived from Chinese examples.

monkeys
1 The Japanese macaque lives in deciduous forests and eats leaves, berries, and insects. The male (right), at up to 18 kg in weight, is twice as heavy as the female.
2 A female macaque and young immersed in the Jigokudani Hot Spring in Nagano Prefecture, where monkeys have learned to weather the cold winters by taking to the waters.

1

2

monzen machi The approach to the temple Zenkōji in the city of Nagano, lined with inns and stores, is a well-known example of one of these urban communities that sprang up around major religious institutions.

Monogatari literally means "talk of things" and developed from the popular pastime of storytelling among court ladies. In the broadest sense of the term the varieties that eventually developed include *uta monogatari, tsukuri monogatari* (courtly romances), GIKO MONOGATARI (pseudoclassical tales), *rekishi monogatari* (historical tales), GUNKI MONOGATARI (military tales), and *setsuwashū* (collections of orally transmitted tales).

Uta Monogatari—*Uta monogatari* consist of a number of tales or chapters formed around poems with prose parts ranging in length from one line to several pages and represent an early phase in the development of a Japanese narrative tradition. The early-10th-century ISE MONOGATARI (Tales of Ise) contains 125 tales. YAMATO MONOGATARI (ca 951; tr *Tales of Yamato*, 1980) contains 173 tales, and HEICHŪ MONOGATARI (ca 960, Tales of Heichū) is composed of tales that recount the love affairs of one historical figure.

Tsukuri Monogatari—The earliest of these full-fledged narratives is TAKETORI MONOGATARI (tr *Tale of the Bamboo Cutter*, 1956) from the early 10th century. Other examples are UTSUBO MONOGATARI (Tale of the Hollow Tree) and OCHIKUBO MONOGATARI (Tale of the Lower Room), both from the late 10th century. The development of *tsukuri monogatari* reaches its climax in the unrivaled masterpiece TALE OF GENJI (*Genji monogatari*) of the early 11th century.

The most important romances of the late Heian period (794–1185)—all strongly influenced by, but lacking the narrative power of, *Genji monogatari*—are HAMAMATSU CHŪNAGON MONOGATARI (11th century, Tale of Middle Counselor Hamamatsu), SAGOROMO MONOGATARI (ca 1075, Tale of Sagoromo), and YORU NO NEZAME (mid-11th-century, Nights of Fitful Waking). An important collection of short stories is TSUTSUMI CHŪNAGON MONOGATARI.

Giko Monogatari—Considerable numbers of romances called *giko monogatari* were written through the 14th century, including SUMIYOSHI MONOGATARI (Tale of Sumiyoshi) and *Iwashimizu monogatari* (ca 1270, Tale of Iwashimizu). These works are largely abridged imitations of the great prose works of the 11th century, in particular *Genji monogatari* and *Sagoromo monogatari*.

Rekishi Monogatari—In the late 11th century, the EIGA MONOGATARI (tr *A Tale of Flowering Fortunes*, 1980) appeared, the first of eight historical narratives, successors to the RIKKOKUSHI (Six National Histories). Although their historical content is generally accurate, they tend to concentrate on personal aspects of courtiers' lives, emphasizing emotional and aesthetic values. ŌKAGAMI (late 11th or early 12th century; tr *Okagami: The Great Mirror*, 1980), IMAKAGAMI (ca 1170, Mirror of the Present), *Mizukagami* (12th century, Water Mirror), and MASUKAGAMI (1338–76, Enlarged Mirror) are other examples.

Gunki Monogatari—These appeared following the wars of the late 12th century, which are the subjects of several of the tales. Examples are HŌGEN MONOGATARI (Tale of Hōgen) and HEIJI MONOGATARI (Tale of Heiji), both early 13th century; HEIKE MONOGATARI (Tale of the Heike), early 13th to late 14th century; GEMPEI SEISUIKI (The Rise and Fall of the Genji and the Heike), mid-13th to 14th century; and TAIHEIKI (Chronicle of Great Peace), mid-14th century.

Setsuwashū—Often treated as a separate genre under the heading SETSUWA BUNGAKU (tale literature), these consist of collections of brief anecdotes. While the origins of this form are in Buddhist miracle tales, orally transmitted secular tales were later set down in a similar format. Their chief value is in their depiction of the practical, even earthy, side of life as a complement to the idealized courtly romances. The best of these collections are KONJAKU MONOGATARI (ca 1120; partial tr *Tales of Times Now Past*, 1979), UJI SHŪI MONOGATARI (ca 1200; tr *A Collection of Tales from Uji*, 1970), and KOKON CHOMONJŪ (1254, Collection of Things Heard Past and Present).

mono no aware   もののあわれ

A literary and aesthetic ideal cultivated during the Heian period (794–1185). At its core is a deep, empathetic appreciation of the ephemeral beauty manifest in nature and human life, and it is therefore usually tinged with a hint of sadness; under certain circumstances it can be accompanied by admiration, awe, or even joy. The word was revived as part of the vocabulary of Japanese literary criticism through the writings of MOTOORI NORINAGA (1730–1801).

According to Norinaga, the word *aware* (or *ahare* in traditional orthography) is a combination of two interjections, *a* and *hare*, each of which was uttered spontaneously when one's heart was profoundly moved. The Heian court nobility toned down the emotional intensity and limited the meaning of *aware* so as to stress elegant beauty, gentle melancholy, and the Buddhist sense of ephemerality. The word gradually lost its happier connotations, however, and by Norinaga's time *aware* referred almost exclusively to pathos, sorrow, or grief.

From his study of the TALE OF GENJI, Norinaga was the first scholar to notice that *aware* was an important aesthetic ideal pervading all Heian literature, prose and poetry alike. In order to distinguish this ideal from the ordinary *aware* of pathos or grief used in his own time, he called it *mono no aware*—literally, "a deep feeling over things." But, explaining the connotations of "things," Norinaga pointed out that the word *mono* was used to speak in broad general terms. *Mono*, in other words, universalizes the meaning of *aware*. A sad thing is sad to any man of cultivation and breeding; if there is anyone who fails to feel sad, he is heartless or, in Norinaga's idiom, he does not know *mono no aware*. In Norinaga's view, then, *mono no aware* is a purified and exalted feeling, close to the innermost heart of man and nature. Theoretically the meaning of *mono no aware* is as comprehensive as the whole range of human emotions and can be viewed as a humanistic value, but in its actual usage it tends to focus on the beauty of impermanence and on the sensitive heart capable of appreciating that beauty.

Mononobe family   物部氏

(Mononobeshi). Powerful family of the YAMATO COURT (ca 4th century–ca mid-7th century). Together with the ŌTOMO FAMILY, the Mononobe had hereditary charge of military affairs, and during the 5th century the heads of both families shared the important hereditary post of ōmuraji (great *muraji;* see UJI-KABANE SYSTEM). In the 6th century, however, with Mononobe no Arakabi's (d 536) suppression of the Rebellion of IWAI and then ŌTOMO NO KANAMURA's failure to protect the Japanese enclave of KAYA from Korean encroachment, the office of ōmuraji became the prerogative of the Mononobe. Through their numerous branch families, the Mononobe also held considerable power in the provinces. They later joined the Nakatomi in opposing the pro-Buddhist policies of the newly ascendant SOGA FAMILY. The conflict came to a head over the question of imperial succession; in 587 MONONOBE NO MORIYA was killed in a battle mounted by the Soga, and the family was all but annihilated.

Mononobe no Moriya   物部守屋

(?–587). Official of the YAMATO COURT; son of Mononobe no Okoshi, who as ōmuraji (chief minister) competed with members of the ŌTOMO FAMILY for power in the court. Succeeding his father, Moriya served as ōmuraji under the emperors Bidatsu (r 572–585) and Yōmei (r 585–587). During the reign of the former, the Mononobe family opposed the spread of Buddhism under the sponsorship of SOGA NO UMAKO. After the death of Emperor Yōmei, Moriya conspired to raise Prince Anahobe, a son of Emperor KIMMEI, to the throne. Moriya and his family were killed by an army led by Umako, and power fell into the hands of the Soga.

mononoke   物の怪

Vagrant spirits of the living or the dead believed to possess a person and to cause death or illness. *Mononoke* are associated mainly with the Heian period (794–1185). A person's spirit was believed to detach itself from the body permanently at death, or temporarily during times of emotional stress. Such a spirit was termed *mononoke* when it possessed another person either from anger, jealousy, or vengeful resentment. See also GORYŌ; EXORCISM.

monopoly and oligopoly   独占と寡占

(*dokusen to kasen*). The ANTIMONOPOLY LAW (1947) prohibits private monopolies in Japan. Since regulations exist for the partitioning of private companies with market monopolies, monopolies can be found only in public works businesses such as electricity, water, gas, and communications companies. Salt and tobacco are considered monopoly products, but even though the company involved is private (see JAPAN TOBACCO, INC), there is no monopolistic control of pricing, which is based on administrative guidance and authorization from the government. In the case of tobacco, there is competition from foreign tobacco.

The oligopoly structure in which a small number of suppliers control a market can be seen in several places in the Japanese domestic marketplace. A highly oligopolistic industry in which one company dominates is called a Gulliver oligopoly. An international example of this is IBM. Domestic examples are KIRIN BREWERY CO, LTD, in the beer market; BRIDGESTONE CORPORATION in the tire market; and ASAHI GLASS CO, LTD, in the plate-glass market.

Privatized in 1985, NIPPON TELEGRAPH AND TELEPHONE CORPORATION (NTT) inherited a communications market monopoly from its predecessor, a public corporation. However, with the strong entry of such telecommunications companies as Daini Denden, Inc, this market is moving toward becoming a Gulliver oligopoly.

Montblanc, Charles, Comte des Cantons de モンブラン, C.

(1832–93). Belgian aristocrat and adventurer; European agent for the Satsuma domain (now Kagoshima Prefecture). Montblanc first visited Japan in 1861–62. He later gained the confidence of some Satsuma students in London and signed an agreement with them to serve as Satsuma's agent in the formation of a joint French-Satsuma trading company and the development of Satsuma's natural resources in return for European arms and manufactured goods. He also arranged for Satsuma's independent participation in the Paris Exposition of 1867. In late 1867 and early 1868 he accompanied Satsuma's leaders to Kyōto, where he provided valuable diplomatic advice during the early weeks of the new Meiji government. As reward for his service Montblanc was named Japan's minister and consul general in Paris, a post he held until an embassy was established late in 1870.

monzen machi 門前町

(temple town). Literally, "a town in front of the gate," referring to a built-up area located near the entryway to a Buddhist temple or a Shintō shrine. *Monzen machi* were commercial districts that developed along the roads to popular temples or shrines and sold religious objects, offered food and lodging to visitors, and sometimes formed the nuclei for substantial urban communities.

During the 13th to 16th centuries religious organizations often provided the security and the concentration of resources essential for the formation of marketing centers (see MARKET TOWNS) or cities. Shrines and temples were also linked to trading activities by their long experience in financial management—a heritage of their SHŌEN (landed estate) property rights and revenues—and by the pilgrims they attracted, who required the services of an embryonic tourist industry. However, community vitality rarely rested solely on these factors, frequently depending also on the popularity of the recently established periodic market or on the acquisition of a post station (see POST-STATION TOWNS). During the Edo period (1600–1868) temples and shrines were often reestablished near the periphery of the city and exerted little impact on city-building forces. Genuine *monzen machi* persisted as outlying settlements with small-scale commerce. Today *monzen machi* are valued primarily as historic and religious sites. See also PILGRIMAGES.

moon viewing 月見

(*tsukimi*). Moon viewing has long been a popular pastime in Japan, especially on Jūgoya, the night of the full moon of the eighth month, which was the 15th night (*jūgoya*) of the month in the old lunar calendar. The Japanese adopted the Chinese custom of setting out melons, green soybeans, and fruits in the garden as offerings to the moon on this day. Jūgoya is considered to be the "harvest moon" and is an occasion for thanksgiving and partying. Sprays of *susuki* (eulalia) are displayed on the veranda and tiny skewered dumplings (*dango*) and vegetables are offered to the moon. Because new

sweet potatoes (*satsumaimo*) are offered, the full moon on Jūgoya is also known as the "sweet potato moon" (*imo meigetsu*). A repeat viewing of the "harvest moon" is held on the 13th day of the ninth lunar month.

Moon viewing is a common theme in Japanese poetry, particularly in WAKA and HAIKU. It ranks with SNOW VIEWING and HANAMI (cherry-blossom viewing) as one of the three most favored settings for declarations of love and poetic outpourings of the soul.

Moraes, Wenceslau de モラエス, W.

(1854–1929). Portuguese naval officer, diplomat, and writer. As a naval officer he was stationed in the Portuguese colony of Mozambique and later Macao. In 1889 he made the first of several visits to Japan. He was deeply attracted by Japan and its people and left the navy in 1898 to seek a permanent home there. With the formal establishment of a Portuguese consulate in Ōsaka in 1899, he was appointed vice-consul. In 1913 he retired from public service and spent his remaining years in Tokushima on the island of Shikoku, writing essays and stories. His writings on Japan are collected in *Teihon Moraesu zenshū* (5 vols, 1969).

moral education 道徳教育

(*dōtoku kyōiku*). Moral education in Japanese schools—particularly public schools—is of a secular rather than a religious nature. Before World War II, moral training took on an excessively nationalistic and authoritarian bias (see SHŪSHIN), but the postwar emphasis has been on preparation for life in a democratic society. Since 1958 one hour a week has been set aside for moral education in elementary and middle schools. Moral values in everyday life and one's obligations in personal relationships, the family, and the society are discussed in the classroom. In recent years there has been conservative sentiment calling for a greater stress on national values; as a result, it has now become a requirement to sing the national anthem and display the flag at major school ceremonies.

morality 道徳

(*dōtoku*). In the West the concept of morality is based on custom and tradition, as can be seen in the derivation of the word morality from the Latin *mores*. This is not the case in China and Japan, where the corresponding word, pronounced *dōtoku* in Japanese, is written with two Chinese characters, the first of which means "the Way." Confucius expounded the Way thus: "In the morning hear the Way; in the evening die without regrets" (*Analects* 4:8). The idea of *logos* and the Way of sainthood are both represented in this idea of the Way. As is implied in Lao Tzu's saying that "the Way which can be named is not the true Way," morality is a universal principle hidden in the inner part of man that governs his thinking and acting.

Morality in the East is thus not merely a system of ethics, that is, an act of human society, a model for living. It consists of the attitude of man toward absolute being (religion), other human beings (ethics), and other creatures and things (technology).

Japanese morality at present is going through a process of transition similar to what is taking place elsewhere as it seeks to come to terms with problems occasioned by the impact of technology on human life, e.g., problems of the environment, se euthanasia. See also ETHICS, EAST

Morgan, Yuki モルガン雪

(1881–1963). Maiden name Katō; born in Kyōto. She was a *geisha* in the Gion section of Kyōto from the age of 14. In 1904 she accepted an offer of marriage from the American George Dennison Morgan, nephew of the financier J. P. Morgan. Their marriage created a journalistic sensation in both Japan and the United States, and they eventually chose to settle in France. After her husband's death in 1915, Morgan remained in France; she lived in the home of the linguist S. Tandart (1877–1931) and helped with the posthumous publication of his *Dictionnaire cambodgien-français* (1935). She was drawn to the Catholic faith and supported church activities with her wealth. Returning to Japan in 1938, she lived modestly in Kyōto. Her life has been the subject of a musical play and several novels and biographies.

Mori Arimasa 森有正

(1911–76). Philosopher. Born in Tōkyō, Mori graduated from Tōkyō University in 1938. After teaching there, he taught Japanese language and literature at the University of Paris from 1950 until his death. Mori's great interest in the essential natures of the cultures of Japan and Europe was in part due to his desire to explore a new direction for Japan in the aftermath of World War II. Central to his philosophy is the concept of "experience" (*keiken*), through which abstract words and concepts come alive. His writings include *Pasukaru no hōhō* (1938, Pascal's Method) and *Babiron no nagare no hotori nite* (1957, By the Waters of Babylon).

Mori Arinori 森有礼

(1847–89). Prominent educational statesman, diplomat, and outspoken proponent of Western thought and social practices early in the Meiji period (1868–1912). As the first minister of education (1885–89) he imposed much of the elitist, statist, and utilitarian structure and tone of pre–World War II Japanese education. Mori was born in the Satsuma domain (now Kagoshima Prefecture). Educated at the Zōshikan (a *samurai* school) and at the Kaiseijo (School for Western Learning) in Kagoshima, in 1865 he went to Britain, where he studied naval surveying, mathematics, and physics. He returned to Japan in 1868 to join the new Meiji government, taking a variety of administrative posts. As Japan's first envoy to Washington (1871–73), Mori cultivated US political and intellectual leaders and surveyed US educational and social institutions. He organized Japan's first modern intellectual society, the MEIROKUSHA, in 1873.

As a member of the MEIJI ENLIGHTENMENT movement of the 1870s, Mori advocated reli-

Mori Hanae This internationally renowned fashion designer began her career in 1951 in Tōkyō.

gious freedom and secular education in *Religious Freedom in Japan* (1872); adoption of a modern school system in *Education in Japan* (1873); abandoning the Japanese language in favor of English; the social, but not political, emancipation of women; and the adherence of all nations to *jōri* (reason) and the principles of international law. Mori advocated a strong, stable state and an educational system that would support it; ITŌ HIROBUMI took Mori into his first cabinet in 1885. During Mori's tenure as Japan's first education minister, the training of an elite class was assured by the multiple tracking of secondary schools, the creation of the privileged HIGHER SCHOOLS (*kōtō gakkō*), and the redesignation of Tōkyō University as "Imperial." See IMPERIAL UNIVERSITIES.

Although denounced by progressives after World War II as a reactionary, he grated on his own generation of Japanese as an outspoken, heavily Anglicized harbinger of change. Mori was assassinated by a Shintoist fanatic on 11 February 1889.

Mōri family   毛利氏

(Mōrishi). Warrior family and later *daimyō* of southwest Honshū from the Kamakura period (1185–1333) until 1868. Proud of their ties with the imperial court since the Heian period (794–1185), the Mōri encouraged a high level of culture in their domain. Their direct ancestor was ŌE NO HIROMOTO (1148–1225). His son Suemitsu adopted the surname Mōri. The family's power base shifted to Aki Province (now part of Hiroshima Prefecture) when Mōri Tokichika was appointed estate steward (JITŌ) there in 1336. MŌRI MOTONARI greatly expanded the family domain, beginning with his victory over the AMAKO FAMILY in 1540; he came to control as many as 10 provinces in southwestern Honshū. After his grandson Mōri Terumoto (1553–1625), ally of TOYOTOMI HIDEYOSHI, was defeated by TOKUGAWA IEYASU at the Battle of SEKIGAHARA in 1600, the family's domain was reduced to the two provinces of Suō and Nagato, commonly known as Chōshū (now Yamaguchi Prefecture). Chōshū's last daimyō, Mōri Yoshichika, allowed his domain to become a center for the movement that overthrew the Tokugawa shogunate in 1867–68 (see MEIJI RESTORATION).

Moriguchi   守口[市]

City in central Ōsaka Prefecture, bordering the city of Ōsaka to the southwest. Moriguchi thrived as a post-station town during the Edo period (1600–1868). It is the site of factories for the Matsushita Electric Industrial Co, Ltd, and the San'yō Electric Co, Ltd. Pop: 157,372.

Mori Hanae   森英恵

(1926–). Fashion designer. Born in Shimane Prefecture; graduated from Tōkyō Women's Christian University. Her striking designs with their oriental flavor have won her international fame. Well known in Paris fashion circles, Mori has also designed uniforms for public officials in the People's Republic of China. She is a recipient of the Neiman Marcus Award.

Mori Kaku   森恪

(1882–1932). Entrepreneur and politician. Also known as Mori Tsutomu. A native of Ōsaka. Upon graduation from the Tōkyō Middle School of Commerce and Industry

(Tōkyō Shōkō Chūgakko) in 1901, he was sent by the MITSUI company to China as a trainee and formally entered the company's Shanghai branch in 1905. During assignments to various Mitsui branches in China he established the China Enterprise Company (Chūgoku Kōgyō Kaisha), later renamed the China-Japan Enterprise Company (Chūnichi Jitsugyō Kaisha), to facilitate Japanese investments in China. Retiring from Mitsui in 1920, Mori joined the RIKKEN SEIYŪKAI political party and was elected to the Imperial Diet five times. As a leader in the Seiyūkai, he advocated an expansionist policy on the Asian continent.

Mori Kansai   森寛斎

(1814–94). MARUYAMA-SHIJŌ SCHOOL painter. Born in the castle town of Hagi, Chōshū domain (now Yamaguchi Prefecture). He went to Ōsaka in 1835 and received his most important training from Mori Tetsuzan (1775–1841), whose daughter he married and whose name he took upon adoption into the family. He traveled widely and finally settled in Kyōto. There he succeeded Shiokawa Bunrin (1808–77) upon his death as head of the Jōunsha, an organization that mounted exhibitions of paintings. His painting on the theme *Red Cliff* won a silver medal at the first Domestic Painting Competitive Exhibition (Naikoku Kaiga Kyōshinkai) in 1882. He was appointed imperial household artist (*teishitsu gigeiin*) in 1890. He taught at the Kyōto Prefectural Painting School (Kyōto Fu Gagakkō) from its beginning in 1880, and he also opened his own painting school. He painted without preliminary sketches and rarely repeated subject matter. His style, like that of MARUYAMA ŌKYO, relies more on wash, shading, and color than on line.

Morikawa Kyoroku   森川許六

(1656–1715). *Haiku* poet of the Edo period (1600–1868); one of the 10 principal disciples of BASHŌ and a systematic interpreter of his poetics. Also known as Morikawa Kyoriku. He taught himself from works of Bashō, apparently with such success that when he finally met Bashō in Edo (now Tōkyō) in 1692, the master immediately felt a spiritual kinship with him. *Haikai mondo* (1697–98), a record of his debates with MUKAI KYORAI, illustrates his critical acumen with regard to the central issues of Bashō's poetics. He is probably best remembered as the compiler of the influential *Fūzoku monzen* (1706; also known as the *Honchō monzen*), the first extensive collection of the HAIBUN prose writings of the Bashō school.

Mori Masayuki   森雅之

(1911–73). Actor. Real name Arishima Ikumitsu. Born in Sapporo, Hokkaidō, the eldest son of the novelist ARISHIMA TAKEO. He studied at Kyōto University but left to become a popular stage actor. He made his film debut in SHIMAZU YASUJIRŌ's *Haha no chizu* (1942, Mother's Map). Although he continued to act on stage, Mori was increasingly in demand for films, in which he became known for his sensitive interpretations of inner torment. He appeared in such masterpieces as YOSHIMURA KŌZABURŌ's *Anjoke no butōkai* (1947, A Ball at the Anjō House), KUROSAWA AKIRA's RASHŌMON (1950) and *Hakuchi* (1951, The Idiot), and NARUSE MIKIO's UKIGUMO (1955, Floating Clouds).

Morimoto Kaoru   森本薫

(1912–46). Playwright. Born in Ōsaka; graduate of Kyōto University. Early plays include

Migoto na onna (1934), *Hanabanashiki ichizoku* (1935), and *Taikutsu na jikan* (1937). In 1941 he joined the BUNGAKUZA (Literary Theater), a theater company organized by KISHIDA KUNIO. His *Tomishima Matsugorō den* (1942), a historical drama based on a novel by Iwashita Shunsaku (1906–80), scored a hit in 1942 and was later made into a movie. In 1945 he wrote *Onna no isshō* (1945; tr *A Woman's Life*, 1961–62) for actress SUGIMURA HARUKO, which became another Bungakuza hit. In 1960 Sugimura performed this play in China, and it was later staged in Russia. Morimoto wrote radio dramas and other scenarios and translated Thornton Wilder's play *Our Town* into Japanese.

Mōri Motonari   毛利元就

(1497–1571). SENGOKU DAIMYŌ in western Honshū. The second son of Mōri Hiromoto, Motonari became head of the MŌRI FAMILY of Aki Province (now part of Hiroshima Prefecture) in 1523. To maintain their independence during the chaos of the Sengoku period (1467–1568), the Mōri had allied themselves first with the neighboring AMAKO FAMILY and later with the ŌUCHI FAMILY.

With the help of the Ōuchi, Motonari defeated the Amako in 1540. When his ally ŌUCHI YOSHITAKA was murdered by Sue Harukata (1521–55) in 1551, Motonari made war on Sue, defeating him in a 1555 battle on the island of Itsukushima. Motonari then occupied the lands of the Ōuchi and in Kyūshū challenged the ŌTOMO FAMILY. His successes continued, and by his death he controlled numerous provinces in western Honshū and in parts of Kyūshū.

Morimoto Rokuji   森本六爾

(1903–36). Archaeologist. Born in Nara Prefecture. A graduate of Unebi Middle School in Nara, Morimoto studied archaeology with MIYAKE YONEKICHI and also studied in France. In 1929 he founded the Tōkyō Archaeological Society (Tōkyō Kōko Gakkai) and became editor of its journal, *Kōkogaku* (Archaeology). Morimoto's interests centered on the wet-rice agricultural technology of the Yayoi period (ca 300 BC–ca AD 300) and on the mounded tombs (KOFUN) of ancient Japan. His works include *Nihon kōkogaku kenkyū* (1943, Studies on Japanese Archaeology).

Morimura Seiichi   森村誠一

(1933–). Mystery writer. Born in Saitama Prefecture. Graduate of Aoyama Gakuin University. Morimura began his career with *Kōsō no shikaku* (1969, Dead Angles of a High-Rise), a locked-room mystery for which he won the Edogawa Rampo Prize. He received the Award of the Mystery Writers' Association of Japan for *Fushoku no kōzō* (1972, The Structure of Decay). Morimura is the author of the controversial *Akuma no hōshoku* (1981, The Devil's Gluttony), an investigation into the activities of the 731st Regiment of Japan's Guandong (Kwantung) Army in Manchuria during World War II, which exposed its use of biological weapons. He is also known for his "Shōmei" (Evidence) series, which includes *Ningen no shōmei* (1976, Evidence of Humanity).

Morinaga & Co, Ltd   森永製菓[株]

(Morinaga Seika). The largest confectioner in Japan. Established in 1899, it took its current name in 1912. Utilizing modern advertising and promotion and mechanized production, Morinaga became one of the leading confectionery and packaged food companies in Japan. In order to become self-sufficient in raw materials, the company founded the predecessor of MORINAGA MILK INDUSTRY CO, LTD, in 1917. The company is affiliated with the Sunkist Growers, Inc, of the United States, whose soft drinks and other products are sold on the domestic market. Sales for the fiscal year ending March 1991 totaled ¥142.6 billion (US $1.0 billion), and capitalization stood at ¥18.3 billion (US $133.4 million). Headquarters are in Tōkyō.

Morinaga Milk Industry Co, Ltd

森永乳業[株]

(Morinaga Nyūgyō). Company engaged in the manufacture and sale of milk, dairy products, soft drinks, and foodstuffs. Morinaga Milk Industry's predecessor was the milk division of MORINAGA & CO, LTD. Becoming independent in 1949, it expanded operations to produce butter, cheese, and casein. It is a pioneer in exporting technology and currently has three joint-venture firms incorporated overseas, as well as offices in the United States, Europe, and Taiwan. Sales for the fiscal year ending March 1991 totaled ¥343.5 billion (US $2.5 billion); the company was capitalized at ¥20.9 billion (US $152.3 million) in the same year. Headquarters are in Tōkyō.

Morinaga Powdered Milk Incident

森永ヒ素ミルク事件

(Morinaga Hiso Miruku Jiken). A major case of food poisoning in 1955 that affected about 12,000 infants, with more than 130 deaths. Throughout western Japan newborn children suffered from appetite loss, fever, rashes, diarrhea, dark spotting of the skin, and convulsions that sometimes ended in death. The first victims began appearing in June 1955. In August a professor at the Okayama University School of Medicine identified the causative agent as arsenic in powdered milk produced by the MORINAGA MILK INDUSTRY CO, LTD.

The Morinaga poisoning case was initially resolved in December 1955 by a five-man committee of medical specialists appointed by the minister of health and welfare. The committee announced that the poisoning had no aftereffects and recommended that deaths be compensated by payments of ¥250,000 (US $694) and all other injuries by ¥10,000 (US $27). Fourteen years later, the first follow-up study demonstrated that there were serious aftereffects, including a high incidence of cerebral palsy and brain damage.

The Morinaga case had a long legal history. In 1955 in the Tokushima District Court, the local prosecutor's office filed criminal charges against a Morinaga production manager and factory superintendent for professional negligence. They were acquitted after an eight-year trial, but a retrial was ordered. On 28 November 1973 the Tokushima District Court sentenced the production manager to three years in prison. Based on this decision, in December 1973 Morinaga, the Ministry of Health and Welfare, and a patients' association signed an agreement providing the poisoning victims with assistance for the duration of their lives.

Morinaga, Prince

護良親王

(1308–35; Morinaga Shinnō). Also known as Prince Moriyoshi or Ōto no Miya; son of Emperor GO-DAIGO. Morinaga entered the Buddhist priesthood at an early age and was made chief priest of the TENDAI SECT in 1327. When Go-Daigo attempted to overthrow the KAMAKURA SHOGUNATE in 1331 (see GENKŌ INCIDENT) Morinaga fought on his father's side. The prince raised forces in support of the imperial cause, eventually leaving the priesthood. When his father succeeded in restoring direct imperial rule in 1333 (see KEMMU RESTORATION) Morinaga was appointed supreme military commander. ASHIKAGA TAKAUJI overthrew Go-Daigo's government in 1336. Morinaga was killed in exile at Kamakura by Takauji's brother ASHIKAGA TADAYOSHI.

Mori Nobuteru

森矗昶

(1884–1941). Businessman and politician. Founder of the Mori Kontserun (from the German *Konzern*), a financial and industrial combine. Born in Chiba Prefecture. After operating a family iodine production venture, he became a prominent businessman with the strong support of the Suzuki family of AJINOMOTO CO, INC, fame. By 1937 Mori had formed his own industrial combine centered on electrochemical and metallurgical manufacturing. The Mori Kōgyō holding company controlled 14 direct subsidiaries, including SHŌWA DENKŌ KK. Mori also served four terms as a member of the House of Representatives beginning in 1924.

Mori Ōgai

森鷗外

(1862–1922). Novelist, critic, and medical scientist. Real name Mori Rintarō. Born in Tsuwano, Iwami Province (now part of Shimane Prefecture). The Mori family, founded in the mid-17th century, were hereditary domain physicians in the service of the *daimyō* of Tsuwano, the Kamei family.

Education——The early education of Ōgai, the eldest son, was predicated on the assumption that he would succeed his father as domain doctor. Starting at the age of seven, he attended classes in the Confucian classics at the domain school and took private lessons in Dutch, the language of Western medical studies in the Edo period (1600–1868).

In 1872, following the abolition of the daimyō domains the previous year, the Mori family moved to Tōkyō. Ōgai temporarily boarded at the house of the eminent scholar-official from Tsuwano, NISHI AMANE, and attended a private school to receive instruction in German, which had replaced Dutch as the language for medical studies in the Meiji period (1868–1912). In January 1874 Ōgai was admitted to the government medical school, which developed into the Tōkyō University Medical School after 1877. He graduated from the school in 1881 at the age of 19.

During his early years at medical school, Ōgai developed a taste for literature, reading extensively the late-Edo-period vernacular novels (see GESAKU) of BAKIN, TAMENAGA SHUNSUI, and SANTŌ KYŌDEN and taking lessons in classical Chinese composition from the writer Yoda Gakkai (1833–1909). Later he studied Chinese poetry and Chinese medicine with Satō Genchō (1818–97), a former professor of the shogunate's School of Oriental Medicine.

Early Career——After graduation, he entered the army and began his career as a medical officer, choosing military medical administration and hygiene as his special fields. In 1884 he was sent by the army to Germany, where he studied for four years. During his years in Germany, Ōgai read extensively in European literature.

Returning to Japan in 1888, he campaigned for the development of scientific medical research in Japan, publishing a medical journal on his own and introducing among other subjects Richard Krafft-Ebing's writings on sexual psychology. Outside his career in the army, he waged a campaign for the creation of a modern Japanese literature, publishing his own literary journal, the SHIGARAMI SŌSHI (The Weir, 1889–94), and a volume of lyric poetry, *Omokage* (1889). He was a staunch "antirealist" in literature. Leaving the study of reality to medicine and history, he assigned literature to the spiritual and emotional domain of life. He opposed the modern materialism that leads to the reckless pursuit of the gratification of desires. Opposing TSUBOUCHI SHŌYŌ's theory of realism, he insisted on the necessity of ideals in literary works. Materializing his theory in his work, Ōgai published three original short stories: "Maihime" (1890, The Dancing Girl), "Utakata no ki" (1890, The Mirage), and "Fumizukai" (1891, The Letter Carrier). In the last piece of the trilogy, he advocated Goethe's spirit of "labor and renunciation," which he regarded as akin to the traditional East Asian faith in the way of heaven.

Later Career——In 1889 he married Akamatsu Toshiko, the daughter of Vice Admiral Akamatsu Noriyoshi (1841–1920), an old friend of Nishi Amane, but divorced her the following year. The divorce irreparably damaged his relationship with Nishi Amane. He remained a bachelor until 1902 when, at the age of 40, he married Araki Shigeko, 18 years his junior, at the express wish of his mother. At the outbreak of the Sino-Japanese War of 1894–95, he was sent to Manchuria and, after Japan's victory the following year, to Taiwan. In 1899 he was appointed head of the medical corps in Kokura in Kyūshū and, as he put it, was in "exile" for 3 years. In 1902 he returned to Tōkyō, having been appointed head of the medical corps there. During the Russo-Japanese War of 1904–05, he was again sent to Manchuria. In 1907 he was promoted to surgeon general and was appointed head of the medical division of the Army Ministry, the highest post within the medical corps. He held these posts for 9 years until his retirement in 1916.

Literary Works——During the 17 years between 1892 and 1909, Ōgai did not publish much fiction, though he did found and edit a second magazine of literature and criticism, *Mezamashi-gusa* (1896–1902). His significant works from this period are *Sokkyō shijin* (1892–94; 1897–1901), a masterful translation of Hans Christian Andersen's novel *Improvisatoren*, and *Doitsu nikki* (German Diary), which he rewrote from the original Chinese diary kept during his years in Germany into the present classical Japanese. In 1909 Ōgai resumed activity as a novelist. For the remaining 13 years of his life, he wrote

Mori Ōgai A 1905 photograph taken during the Russo-Japanese War, when Ōgai was stationed in Manchuria. During his middle years, Ōgai devoted himself to his medical career, but after 1909 he began to write again, producing both historical fiction and more introspective works.

Morishige Hisaya The actor in one of his 900 stage appearances as Tevye in *Fiddler on the Roof*. A witty and versatile performer, Morishige has shown equal facility in film and television.

Morishita Yōko Known for the speed, precision, and expressiveness of her dance, Morishita is one of Japan's finest ballerinas.

Morita Akio The cofounder of Sony Corporation had his first international marketing success in 1955, when he introduced Sony's miniature transistor radio to the world market.

and published energetically. His works in these years may be divided into three groups. From 1909 to 1912 he wrote fiction based on his own experiences, such as the short stories "Hannichi" (1909, A Half Day), "Shokudō" (1910, Office Restaurant), "Mōsō" (1911, Fantasy), "Hyaku monogatari" (1911, One Hundred Tales), "Kano yō ni" (1912, As if . . .), and the novels *Wita sekusuarisu* (1909, Vita Sexualis), *Seinen* (1910–11, A Youth), GAN (1911–13, Wild Goose), and *Kaijin* (1911–12, Ruins), the last incomplete.

Deeply impressed by the suicide of General NOGI MARESUKE following the death of Emperor Meiji in 1912, Ōgai wrote "Okitsu Yagoemon no isho" (The Death Note of Okitsu Yagoemon), in which he depicted the psychology of a *samurai* who commits ceremonial suicide following his master's death. In the following four years, he wrote a series of historical stories, such as "Abe ichizoku" (1913, The Abe Family), "Gojiin ga hara no katakiuchi" (1913, The Vendetta at Gojiin ga hara), "Ōshio Heihachirō" (1914), "Sakai jiken" (1914, The Sakai Incident), "Sanshō-Dayū" (1915), and "Takasebune" (1916, The Takase Boat). In these stories he dealt with the problem of the anarchic impulse for destruction and self-annihilation and presented various examples of the conversion of that impulse into constructive emotions such as patriotic sentiment and readiness for self-sacrifice.

In 1916 he turned to biographies of doctors of Chinese medicine in the late Edo period: *Shibue Chūsai* (1916), *Izawa Ranken* (1916–17), and *Hōjō Katei* (1917–21). Ōgai regarded them as his major work.

After his retirement from the army, Ōgai was appointed in 1917 the head of the ZU-SHORYŌ and the Tōkyō Imperial Household Museum. He remained in both posts until his death.

Morioka   盛岡[市]

Capital of Iwate Prefecture, northern Honshū, on the river Kitakamigawa. Morioka developed as a castle town of the Nambu family during the Edo period (1600–1868). It has long been known for its traditional Nambu ironware. Iwate University is located here. A parade of colorfully caparisoned horses in June is a popular tourist attraction. Also of interest are the remains of Morioka Castle and the home of the politician HARA TAKASHI. Pop: 235,434.

Mori Rammaru   森蘭丸

(1565?–82). Also known as Mori Naritoshi. A page of the presence (*koshō*) at the court of ODA NOBUNAGA. Son of Mori Yoshinari (1523–70) and brother of Mori Katsuzō (1558–84), distinguished captains of Nobunaga's forces. The SHINCHŌ KŌ KI and Nobunaga's letters make it clear that Rammaru was Nobunaga's intermediary with other notables and a member of his secretariat. Rammaru's notoriety derives from fiction, which portrays him as Nobunaga's minion. Rammaru and his two younger brothers, Bōmaru and Rikimaru, also Nobunaga's pages, died alongside their lord in the HONNŌJI INCIDENT of 1582.

Morisada mankō   守貞漫稿

A book on customs of the Edo period (1600–1868) written by Kitagawa Morisada (b 1810). Although completed in 1853, the manuscript was unpublished until 1908,

when it appeared as the *Ruijū kinsei fūzoku shi*. In the book, begun in 1837, the author set down what he had heard and observed about local mores and customs. For facts predating the Bunka-Bunsei eras (1804–30), he relied on written sources. The information is divided into sections on housing, trades and occupations, currency, food and drink, clothing, houses of prostitution, theaters, and other categories. Of special interest are his comparisons of the different customs of Kyōto, Ōsaka, and Edo. The book is an invaluable source for late Edo customs and folkways, particularly about the artisans of that period.

Mori Shigefumi   森重文

(1951–). Mathematician. Born in Aichi Prefecture. Graduate of Kyōto University and a professor there from 1990. He first achieved academic notice in 1978 for his solution to Hartshorne's conjecture and thereafter contributed to the study of higher dimensional algebraic variety. In 1986 he proved the existence of minimal models, which play a very important role in solving problems of the classification of three-dimensional algebraic varieties, a central issue in algebraic geometry. He received the Fields Medal in 1990.

Morishige Hisaya   森繁久弥

(1913–). Actor known for his comic roles. Born in Ōsaka Prefecture; attended Waseda University. In his early career he performed onstage and in radio and vaudeville. His motion pictures, in which he often played an unreliable ladies' man, include *Koshinuke nitōryū* (1950, Chicken Swordsman); *Santō jūyaku* (1952, Third-Class Executive); the *Shachō* (Company President) series (1956–71); *Meoto zenzai* (1955, Marital Relations or Love Is Shared like Sweets); *Neko to Shōzō to futari no onna* (1956, A Cat, Shōzo, and Two Women); and *Ekimae ryokan* (1958, Station Hotel), which developed into the *Ekimae* series (1958–69). He performed in the stage version of the musical *Yane no ue no baiorin-hiki* (1967–86, Fiddler on the Roof) 900 times. Morishige is also a popular singer known for his "*morishige-bushi*" style. He received the Order of Culture in 1991.

Morishima Michio   森嶋通夫

(1923–). Economist. Born in Ōsaka Prefecture. A graduate of Kyōto University, he became a professor at Kyōto and Ōsaka universities and the London School of Economics. He elevated Japan's scholastic standards in economics, and his mathematical approaches to Marxist economics gained international distinction. He won the Order of Culture in 1976. Morishima's works (he wrote in both Japanese and English) include *Dōgakuteki keizai riron* (1950), an attempt to synthesize John R. Hicks's and Paul Samuelson's theories of stabilization conditions; *Theory of Economic Growth* (1973); and *Marx's Economics* (1973).

Morishita Yōko   森下洋子

(1948–). Ballerina. Real name Shimizu Yōko. Born in Hiroshima Prefecture. Morishita, who began learning ballet at the age of three, studied under Tachibana Akiko (1907–71), Matsuyama Mikiko (b 1923), and Marika Besobrasova (b 1918). She was the first Japanese to win a gold medal in the International Ballet Concours at Varna, Bulgaria (1974). Morishita is active as a leader of the Matsuyama Ballet Company, which she

joined in 1971, as is her husband, the ballet dancer Shimizu Tetsutarō (b 1948), who is the son of Matsuyama. She has made many appearances abroad, and her performances with Rudolf Nureyev won enthusiastic reviews. Her specialties include *Giselle*, *Swan Lake*, and *Don Quixote*. In 1985 she received the Japan Art Academy Prize and a Laurence Olivier Award.

Mori Sosen   森狙仙

(1747–1821). Painter. Real name Mori Shushō. He lived in Ōsaka from his youth and was trained in the KANŌ SCHOOL of painting. Sosen became famous for his paintings of monkeys. His first paintings were of tame monkeys, but later he went to the mountains and spent three years observing and sketching wild animals, developing a remarkable skill based on direct observation and detailed sketches from life. Sosen shared this approach with the artists of the MARUYAMA-SHIJŌ SCHOOL and is sometimes considered an unofficial adherent of the school. He was also adept at painting deer and other animals.

Morita Akio   盛田昭夫

(1921–). Businessman and cofounder of SONY CORPORATION. Born in Aichi Prefecture, he graduated from Ōsaka University. Together with IBUKA MASARU, Morita established Tōkyō Tsūshin Kōgyō (later Sony Corporation) in 1946, becoming president in 1971 and chairman in 1976. Morita handled the financial and business matters of the company, marketing Sony products all over the world. He had his first international triumph when he introduced the world's smallest transistor radio to the world market in 1955. He led Sony to great success by "Americanizing" it through the establishment of a plant in San Diego, California, and by establishing an importing business through Sony Trading Corporation. Morita had Sony's stock listed on the New York Stock Exchange in 1970 (the first Japanese corporation to do so) and contributed to the company's internationalization in many other ways. As a member of the Japan–United States Economic Relations Group, he has been active in efforts to ease trade friction between Japan and the United States.

Morita Kan'ya   守田勘弥

Well-known family line of KABUKI actors that began with Morita Kan'ya I (d 1679?), an actor who was also the owner (*zamoto*) of the Moritaza, founded in 1660, one of the three principal kabuki theaters in the city of Edo (now Tōkyō). Kan'ya II (1676–1734), Kan'ya III (d 1722), and Kan'ya IV (d 1743) were all notable performers. Other outstanding artists of this family acting tradition were Kan'ya VI (1724–80), who was both a *tachiyaku* (performer of leading male roles) and an ONNAGATA (female impersonator); Kan'ya VIII (1759–1814), a superb dancer; and Kan'ya XI (1800–63), a gifted *tachiyaku* and dancer.

Kan'ya XII (1846–97) distinguished himself as a theater manager who initiated such Western-style developments as seats and gaslights. He also worked to improve the social status of kabuki theater. Kan'ya XIII (1885–1932) performed best in *wagoto* (male romantic leads); he also worked actively through his own theater troupe to promote newly written kabuki plays and Western dramas in translation. Kan'ya XIV (1907–75), the nephew of Kan'ya XIII, excelled in male romantic roles.

Morita Sōhei   森田草平

(1881–1949). Novelist and translator of Western literature. Real name Morita Yonematsu. Born in Gifu Prefecture, he graduated from Tōkyō University. A follower of novelist NATSUME SŌSEKI, he won acclaim when his novel *Baien* (1909, Smoke) was serialized. Highly autobiographical, the novel is based on Sōhei's unsatisfying marriage and his subsequent meeting with Haruko, later known as the major feminist leader HIRATSUKA RAICHŌ, and their unsuccessful attempt to commit double suicide. From 1920 to 1930, he taught at Hōsei University. Besides a two-volume biography of Natsume Sōseki, his other works include the novels *Rinne* (1923–25, Reincarnation) and *Hosokawa Garashiya fujin* (1949–50) based on the life of the 16th-century Christian HOSOKAWA GRACIA.

Morita therapy   森田療法

(Morita *ryōhō*). A form of psychotherapy named after its originator, Morita Masatake (also known as Morita Shōma; 1874–1938), to treat a cluster of neuroses termed *shinkeishitsu*. Morita graduated from Tōkyō University and was familiar with European medicine, psychiatry, and psychotherapy, as well as Buddhist philosophy, particularly ZEN. Jikei University School of Medicine in Tōkyō, where Morita taught, is the academic center of Morita therapy.

Shinkeishitsu as defined by Morita therapy stems from a hypochondriacal temperament characterized by excessive introversion, self-consciousness, and hypersensitivity to one's physical or mental condition. The central tenet of Morita therapy is to "accept things as they are" (*aru ga mama ni*). Patients are directed to abandon their compulsive desire for self-control and to concentrate on immediate and concrete experience rather than verbal exchange, speculation, and conjecture. Treatment on an outpatient basis is possible, but hospitalization for about 40 days is preferred. Therapy is divided into two distinct stages: bed rest and work. Bed rest, roughly for a week, in seclusion and without diversion, encourages the patients to live with their problems, reenact their suffering, and eventually endure. The subsequent work stage generally takes the form of contributing to the hospital's maintenance, such as laundry and meal preparation.

Morito Incident   森戸事件

(Morito Jiken). The prosecution of MORITO TATSUO for publishing in January 1920 a scholarly article on the Russian radical Peter Alekseevich Kropotkin (1842–1921). Morito's long trial, which involved the issues of academic freedom and free speech, set justice officials to thinking about measures to suppress what they saw as dangerous ideologies and prompted Prosecutor-General HIRANUMA KIICHIRŌ to create semiofficial groups to stamp out subversive thought.

Morito, an assistant professor of economics at Tōkyō University, published an article entitled "Study on the Social Thought of Kropotkin" ("Kuropotokin no shakai shisō no kenkyū") in the first issue of *Keizaigaku kenkyū*, a journal of economics. Prime Minister HARA TAKASHI and other officials, eager to express their displeasure with radical university professors, decided to prosecute Professor Morito and Professor ŌUCHI HYŌE, the journal's editor. Morito and Ōuchi were charged with sedition under the PRESS LAW OF 1909. The court found Morito guilty of a lesser charge, but the prosecution appealed, and the new court convicted Morito and Ōuchi on the original charges, imposing fines and short jail sentences on both men. The Great Court of Cassation upheld the decision of the appeals court. This court decision not only set new limits for publication and speech, but publicly demonstrated the government's interest in promoting traditional ideologies.

Morito Tatsuo   森戸辰男

(1888–1984). Economist, educator, and politician. Born in Hiroshima Prefecture. After graduation from Tōkyō University, Morito became an assistant professor in its Department of Economics. In 1920 he was dismissed from the university and briefly jailed for publishing a controversial article on the Russian anarchist P. A. Kropotkin (see MORITO INCIDENT). On his release he joined the ŌHARA INSTITUTE FOR SOCIAL RESEARCH. After World War II, Morito was elected three times to the House of Representatives as a member of the Japan Socialist Party. He worked for important educational reforms as minister of education in the cabinets of KATAYAMA TETSU and ASHIDA HITOSHI from May 1947 to October 1948. He later served as president of Hiroshima University, chairman of the Japan Scholarship Foundation, and chairman of the CENTRAL COUNCIL FOR EDUCATION.

Moriyama   守山[市]

City in southwestern Shiga Prefecture, central Honshū, on the eastern shore of Lake Biwa. In the Edo period (1600–1868) Moriyama developed as a post-station town. Long a center of rice production and pearl cultivation, it has also developed textile and chemical industries. Pop: 58,561.

Moriyama Takichirō   森山多吉郎

(1820–71). Interpreter. Born to a family of hereditary interpreters of Dutch (ORANDA TSŪJI) in Nagasaki, he studied English with Ranald MACDONALD. When Russian admiral E. V. PUTIATIN came to Nagasaki in 1853 and Commodore Matthew C. PERRY in 1854, Moriyama acted as chief interpreter. He also helped in the compilation of *Egeresugo jisho wage*, an English-Japanese dictionary. In 1862 Moriyama accompanied the overseas mission led by TAKENOUCHI YASUNORI (see SHOGUNATE MISSIONS TO THE WEST).

Mori Yōko   森瑤子

(1940–　). Novelist. Real name Itō Masayo. Born in Shizuoka Prefecture; graduated from Tōkyō University of Fine Arts and Music. She is known for her intensely depicted love stories and urbane essays. Her works include *Jōji* (1978, The Affair), *Kizu* (1981, The Wound), and *Onna-zakari* (1984, The Prime of Womanhood).

morning glories   朝顔

(*asagao*). *Pharbitis nil* or *Ipomoea nil*. One of the commonest garden plants in Japan, grown since ancient times. This annual, twining herb of the family Convolvulaceae has alternate, usually three-lobed, pointed leaves with long leafstalks. In summer large funnel-shaped flowers open in early morning and close by mid-morning. They are usually bluish purple but are sometimes white, red, purple, or variegated.

The 10th-century collection of regulations ENGI SHIKI records that morning glories were brought to Japan for medicinal use, the seeds serving as a laxative and diuretic as they do still. Another Japanese species of morning glory is the wild *noasagao* (*I. indica*) with heart-shaped leaves and blue flowers, found from the southern coastal areas of Honshū south.

Morning glories have been extensively cultivated since the Heian period (794–1185). Some are prized for the size of their blossoms, which may be over 20 centimeters (8 in) in diameter, and some for their form. The large-flowered types are the most commonly cultivated. See also MORNING GLORY FAIR.

morning glory fair   朝顔市

(*asagaoichi*). Annual event held in early July around the temple Kishibojin in the Iriya district of Tōkyō. Until the end of the 1920s, morning glory vendors were a common sight in the streets of Tōkyō, and the morning glories sold in the compound of the Kishibojin became especially famous. Since the blossoms close early in the day, customers often arrive before daybreak. Similar fairs are held in other areas. See also MORNING GLORIES.

Morohashi Tetsuji   諸橋轍次

(1883–1982). Sinologist, philosopher, literary scholar, and lexicographer; best known for his compilation of the 13-volume DAI KANWA JITEN (1955–60, Great Chinese-Japanese Character Dictionary). This work is

morning glory fair This annual display and sale of morning glories, held each July in Tōkyō's Iriya district, had its origins in the Edo period (1600–1868).

Morohashi Tetsuji This scholar and lexicographer compiled what is generally considered the most authoritative and exhaustive Chinese-Japanese character dictionary.

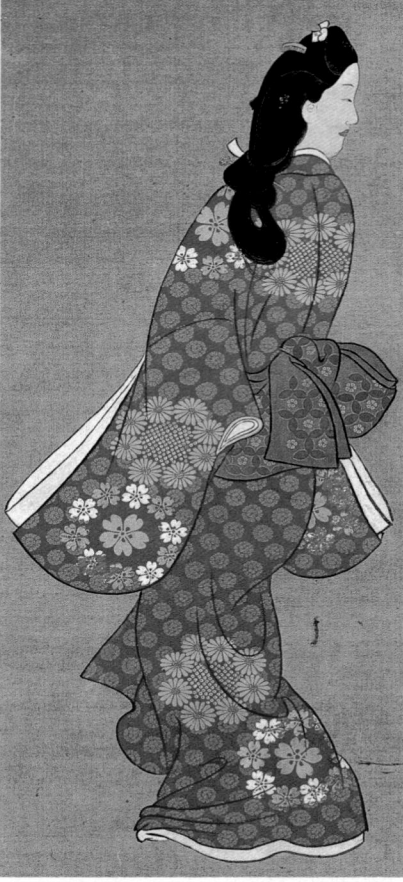

universally accepted as the most authoritative and exhaustive dictionary of the Chinese language and Chinese characters as used in China and Japan throughout written history. Born in Niigata Prefecture, he studied in the department of Chinese and Japanese in Tōkyō Higher Normal School (1904–08) and, later, the graduate department of the same school (1909–10). He taught at Tōkyō Higher Normal School (1910–45) and Tōkyō University of Literature and Science (1929–45). Morohashi completed the *Dai kanwa jiten* despite the destruction in a 1945 air raid of all the data he had compiled in over 15 years of effort. All Morohashi's publications, excluding dictionaries, are contained in the 10-volume *Morohashi Tetsuji chosakushū* (1975–77). See also DICTIONARIES.

Moroi Ken   諸井虔
(1928–   ). Businessman; chairman of CHICHIBU CEMENT CO, LTD (1986–   ). Born in Tōkyō. After graduating from Tōkyō University in 1953, he entered the INDUSTRIAL BANK OF JAPAN, LTD. He joined Chichibu Cement Co, Ltd, in 1967, becoming its president in 1976. He diversified the company by expanding into fields such as ceramics and real estate. Moroi also served as vice-chairman of the JAPAN ASSOCIATION OF CORPORATE EXECUTIVES (1981–88).

Moromoriki   師守記
Diary of the 14th-century courtier and senior secretary (*daigeki*), Nakahara Moromori. The diary, in some 50 chapters, covers 1339–68, as well as parts of 1371 and 1374 in some copies. The work is a valuable document for understanding various problems that led to the division of the imperial house into the NORTHERN AND SOUTHERN COURTS. Also known as *Moroshigeki*, the diary was once mistakenly attributed to Moromori's brother. Another *Moromoriki*, by Oshikōji

Moromori (1714–44), covers the years 1729–37 and 1740.

Moronobu   師宣
(?–1694). The most prominent of the early UKIYO-E artists. Full name Hishikawa Moronobu. Born at Hota (in what is now Chiba Prefecture), son of the noted brocade artisan Hishikawa Kichizaemon. Several years after his father's death in 1662 he went to nearby Edo (now Tōkyō) and became an *ukiyo-e* artist, possibly under the tutelage of the KAMBUN MASTER. Moronobu's first signed and dated works are the illustrated book *Buke hyakunin isshu* (One Hundred Verses by Warriors) and sections of a painted handscroll depicting YOSHIWARA pleasure-quarter scenes (in the collection of the Tōkyō National Museum), both from the spring of 1672.

With the death or retirement of the Kambun Master around 1673, Moronobu became the preeminent *ukiyo-e* artist of Edo, a position he was to maintain until his death. Moronobu's illustrated books and albums number at least 150, including novels, verse anthologies, guidebooks, JŌRURI plays, courtesan and actor critiques, *kimono* pattern books, SHUNGA (erotica) texts and albums, and *ukiyo-e* picture books. Moronobu's importance lay in his effective consolidation of the ephemeral styles of early genre painting and illustration. His style, one of controlled, powerful brush strokes and solid, dynamic figures, provided the groundwork for the *ukiyo-e* masters of the following two centuries.

Morrison Incident   モリソン号事件
(*Morison gō Jiken*). An incident in 1837 in which an American merchant ship, the *Morrison*, attempted to approach the Japanese coast and was fired upon in accordance with the Tokugawa shogunate's order forbidding foreign vessels to enter Japanese waters (see GAIKOKUSEN UCHIHARAI REI).

The *Morrison's* ostensible purpose in coming to Japan was to repatriate seven shipwrecked Japanese sailors. The American trading firm of Olyphant and Co, owners of the ship, and the American Board of Foreign Missions saw this as an opportunity to break Japan's NATIONAL SECLUSION and to initiate trade and Christian proselytizing. It was the shogunate's decision to repel the *Morrison* that inspired the WESTERN LEARNING scholars WATANABE KAZAN and TAKANO CHŌEI to write tracts critical of the seclusion policy. Their action resulted in severe repression of Western Learning and its proponents (see BANSHA NO GOKU).

Morse, Edward Sylvester
                                                モース, E. S.
(1838–1925). US zoologist and director of the Peabody Museum in Salem, Massachusetts, an outstanding early collector of Japanese artifacts, and author of works on a wide variety of subjects concerning Japan. Born in Portland, Maine, he studied conchology at Harvard University and taught at Bowdoin College, Maine, from 1871 to 1874. In 1877 he traveled to Japan at his own expense to study Pacific Ocean brachiopods. He established a marine biology laboratory at Enoshima in Kanagawa Prefecture and shortly thereafter was invited to teach zoology at the new Tōkyō University. From 1877 until he returned to the United States in 1880, Morse organized the university's zoology department and was instrumental in establishing the Japanese Imperial Museum. Morse

helped introduce modern scientific methods to the study of zoology and biology in Japan, introduced and popularized Darwinian theories, and discovered the ŌMORI SHELL MOUNDS in what is now the southwestern part of Tōkyō.

mortgage → hypothec

Mosse, Albert   モッセ, A.
(1846–1925). German legal adviser to the Japanese government in the late 1880s. Born in Grätz (now Poznan), Mosse studied law under Rudolph von GNEIST at the University of Berlin. In 1882, at the request of the German government, he and Gneist gave lectures on constitutional law to ITŌ HIROBUMI and his group, who were then touring Europe to study constitutional systems. Like his teacher, Mosse advised that a Prussian-style monarchical constitutionalism was best suited to Japan. In 1886 he was invited to Japan as a legal adviser. He assisted Itō and INOUE KOWASHI in drafting the 1889 Meiji Constitution. As an adviser to the Home Ministry, he also helped YAMAGATA ARITOMO draft laws for local government. Returning to Germany in 1890, Mosse became a judge in Königsberg and taught law at its university.

mosses   苔類
(*kokerui*). Small plants of the division Bryophyta. The Japanese archipelago, whose climate ranges from cool temperate to subtropical, is home to about 2,000 of the approximately 25,000 species of known bryophytes. The same species that inhabit the subarctic zones of North America and Europe are found in Hokkaidō and in the high mountains of northern Honshū, while those inhabiting tropical East Asia are also found in southwestern Japan. Mosses growing in deciduous, broad-leaved forest areas of Japan resemble those of the Himalayas and the Appalachian Mountains of North America.

The Japanese have developed distinctive styles of moss horticulture. The best known is the moss garden (*kokeniwa*), in which the ground is covered by mosses interspersed with deciduous trees and rocks. Many examples of these gardens are found in temple precincts in Kyōto and in private homes. The other style is the moss tray garden (*koke bonkei*), a miniature landscape created with mosses in a shallow bowl.

MOSS talks   市場分野別協議
(Market-Oriented Sector-Selective talks; J: *shijō bun'yabetsu kyōgi*). Discussions opened in February 1985 between the United States and Japan on the opening of the Japanese market. The talks included investigation of various Japanese markets, the location of possible barriers to market entry, and discussion of possible remedial measures. The MOSS talks, modeled after the Japan–United States Group on Yen-Dollar Issues, were superseded in 1989 by the Structural Impediments Initiative.

mother-of-pearl inlay   螺鈿
(*raden*). Decorative technique used in Japan mainly with wood and LACQUER WARE. The technique originated in the Near East and was introduced to Japan via Tang (T'ang; 618–907) China around the 8th century. In the 11th century mother-of-pearl inlay was used with the MAKI-E lacquer technique, a Japanese innovation. Among the finest examples of Japanese *raden* are the interior of

the Konjikidō (Golden Hall) of the temple CHŪSONJI in Iwate Prefecture and a lacquered cosmetics box with a design of wheels floating in water (Tōkyō National Museum). In the 17th century the inlay technique was used in many works of the RIMPA school. The method using abalone shells, sometimes referred to as *aogai*, became popular from the Muromachi period (1333–1568).

Motion Picture Code Committee
映倫管理委員会

(Eirin Kanri Iinkai). A voluntary control organization of the Japanese motion picture industry formed to oversee and impose censorship standards on the depiction of sex and violence. The committee was originally established under an order issued by the American Occupation forces in 1949 to screen for films inconsistent with Occupation guidelines. It took its current name in 1957. It implements and supervises application of the Motion Picture Code of Ethics (Eiga Rinri Kitei) established by Eiren (abbreviation of Nihon Eiga Rengōkai), a united federation of Japan's major motion picture companies. Movies that have not obtained the approval of the Motion Picture Code Committee cannot be shown to the public. It also specifies which films should be restricted to viewers 18 years and over.

Motobu
本部[町]

Town on the island of Okinawa, Okinawa Prefecture. Motobu was the site of the Okinawa International Ocean Exposition in 1975. Principal products are pineapples, sugarcane, bonito, and tuna. Pop: 15,043.

Motoda Nagazane
元田永孚

(1818–91). Confucian scholar and educational theorist of the Meiji period. Also known as Motoda Eifu. Born in the Kumamoto domain (now Kumamoto Prefecture), he studied at the domainal school under YOKOI SHŌNAN, who introduced him to the pragmatic or realist (*jitsugaku*) school of Neo-Confucianism. In 1871, on the recommendation of ŌKUBO TOSHIMICHI and others, Motoda entered the Imperial Household Agency as tutor (*jidoku*) to Emperor Meiji. He became a court adviser in 1886 and a member of the Privy Council (Sūmitsuin) in 1888. As a leader of the conservative faction in the court, he helped establish an educational ideology for the Meiji government centered on patriotism and reverence for the emperor. He also took part in the drafting of the IMPERIAL RESCRIPT ON EDUCATION, promulgated in 1890. His writings include *Kyōgaku taishi* (1879, Outline of Learning) and *Yōgaku kōyō* (1882, Essentials for the Education of Youth).

Motonobu→Kanō Motonobu

Motoori Haruniwa
本居春庭

(1763–1828). Scholar of Japanese language and literature. Born in Ise (now Mie Prefecture), the eldest son of MOTOORI NORINAGA. He lost his sight in his early thirties. Supporting himself as an acupuncturist, he trained students and wrote two books on Japanese grammar. In his *Kotoba no yachimata* (2 vols, 1806–08) and *Kotoba no kayoiji* (3 vols, 1828) he classified Japanese verbs into seven conjugations and studied transitive and intransitive verbs by dividing them into six types.

Motoori Norinaga
本居宣長

(1730–1801). Classical scholar of the Edo period (1600–1868) who was largely responsi-

ble for bringing the KOKUGAKU (National Learning) movement to its culmination. Literary name Suzunoya. Born at Matsusaka in Ise Province (now Mie Prefecture). His works total more than 90 titles and 260 volumes and are characterized by a rigorous philological approach, a recognition of the emotional nature of man, and a profound sense of reverence for Shintō mythology. His aim was to discern the identity of Japanese culture through an intensive study of the ancient classics, especially the KOJIKI (712, Record of Ancient Matters).

In 1752 he was sent to Kyōto for medical studies, and as a student of Chinese medicine there he read many Chinese classics under the tutelage of Hori Keizan (1688–1757). Norinaga became familiar with the works of KEICHŪ, a founder of the Kokugaku movement, and of OGYŪ SORAI, an influential Confucian scholar. He also became a student of well-known WAKA (classical Japanese poetry) masters. He drafted his first major work, *Ashiwake obune*, toward the end of his six-year sojourn in Kyōto. The book expounded his concept of *waka* and touched on the nature, history, and art of poetry. Norinaga saw verse writing as the instinctive act of a person moved by intense emotion, an act totally independent of political and moral purposes.

Early Works in Literary Criticism— Norinaga returned to Matsusaka in 1757 and immediately began practicing medicine. He also began to offer informal lectures on the Japanese classics at his residence. By 1763 he had completed two works on Japanese literature. The first, *Shibun yōryō*, was a general study of the *Genji monogatari* (TALE OF GENJI). Norinaga interpreted the tale in light of a literary ideal he termed MONO NO AWARE, defining this as an empathetic appreciation of human feeling. In *Isonokami sasamegoto*, he made *mono no aware* the focus of his discussion of *waka* theory and practice.

From Literary Scholar to Classicist— From his one meeting with the aging Kokugaku scholar KAMO NO MABUCHI in 1763, Norinaga learned the paramount significance of the time before the Heian period (794–1185) in studying Japanese civilization. He was made to realize the urgent need to go beyond the *Genji monogatari* to the earliest of all Japanese classics, the *Kojiki*. The following year he began writing *Kojiki den*, a detailed study of that Shintō classic, which was to become his lifework.

By 1771 Norinaga had written *Naobi no mitama*, an outline of his interpretation of ancient Japanese mythology. He saw the image of ideal society in Japanese antiquity where the land had been in perfect order under the reign of emperors, descendants of the Shintō deities. The same nationalistic belief prompted Norinaga to write *Gyojū gaigen* (or *Karaosame no uretamigoto*) six years later, this time focusing on the history of Japan's foreign relations.

Several philological works, including *Himokagami* (1771) and *Kotoba no tama no o* (1779), represent his attempts to examine the use of grammatical particles in the classics. *Kanji san'on kō*, completed in the early 1770s, was a study in Sino-Japanese phonology. In his *Jion kana zukai* (1775), Norinaga tried to establish a proper correlation between Chinese ideograms and Japanese phonetic symbols.

Achievements of Later Years— By 1787 he had written *Tamakushige* in an effort to relate his Shintō ideas more closely to political philosophy. His work *Kakaika* re-

mother-of-pearl inlay This 12th-century box is considered one of the finest examples of this decorative technique. Tōkyō National Museum. National Treasure.

plied to UEDA AKINARI, who had attacked some of his contentions in philology and classical studies. In 1789 he wrote *Kamiyo no masagoto*, retelling ancient myths in a more contemporary language. During the 1790s he completed several studies of the Japanese classics. The most notable was *Genji monogatari tama no ogushi* (1796), an exhaustive study of the massive tale.

His lifework, *Kojiki den*, was finally completed in 1798, 34 years after it had been begun. The 44-volume work was the first comprehensive study of the *Kojiki* ever attempted. In addition to *Kojiki den*, two

Motoori Norinaga A 1790 self-portrait by this prolific scholar and proponent of the National Learning movement.

works stand out among Norinaga's later writings: *Tamakatsuma*, a collection of over 1,000 essays on miscellaneous topics, and *Uiyamabumi*, which lucidly expounds the aim and method of classical studies. By 1798 he had compiled *Suzunoyashū*, an anthology of his own literary writings, which includes over 2,500 *waka*.

Norinaga's writings had a considerable impact on later ages. His method provided a model for many later scholars, including BAN NOBUTOMO. Norinaga's interpretation of Shintō was further elaborated by HIRATA ATSUTANE and became part of an ideology that eventually brought about the Meiji Restoration of 1868; the same ideology was later used by militarists to promote nationalism before World War II. Norinaga's life and thought have been studied by such eminent intellectuals as KOBAYASHI HIDEO and YO-SHIKAWA KŌJIRŌ.

Motoori Ōhira 本居大平

(1756–1833). KOKUGAKU (National Learning) scholar and disciple of MOTOORI NORINAGA. Born in Ise (now part of Mie Prefecture). Adopted by Norinaga, Ōhira transmitted Norinaga's poetic and scholarly traditions to more than a thousand students. His works include *Kagurauta shinshaku* (1827) and *Kogakuyō* (1809). See also JAPANESE LANGUAGE STUDIES, HISTORY OF.

Motosu, Lake → Fuji Five Lakes

Motoyakushiji remains 本薬師寺跡

(Motoyakushiji *ato*). Site of a late-7th-century temple in Kidono, the city of Kashihara, Nara Prefecture. The temple was built in 680–698 to fulfill a pledge by Emperor TEMMU, who had prayed to the Buddha Yakushi (see NYORAI) for the recovery of his consort (later Empress JITŌ). Because of the removal of the capital from FUJIWARAKYŌ to HEIJŌKYŌ in 710, the temple was relocated in 718 (see YAKUSHIJI). The original temple survived until the mid-11th century. According to *Yakushiji engi*, a Heian-period (794–1185) document on the origins of the Yakushiji, the building plans for both temples were the same—the so-called Yakushiji style, consisting of a square compound occupied by two pagodas (one at each of the south corners), with the main hall in the center and a lecture hall to the north. The arrangement of the surviving foundation stones confirms this. See also BUDDHIST ARCHITECTURE.

Motoyama Hikoichi 本山彦一

(1853–1932). President of the national newspaper MAINICHI SHIMBUN. Born in what is now Kumamoto Prefecture, he became an adviser to the *Ōsaka mainichi shimbun* in 1889 and its president in 1903. Under his leadership the paper became a rival of the *Ōsaka asahi shimbun* (see ASAHI SHIMBUN). In 1911 Motoyama bought out the *Tōkyō nichinichi shimbun*, successfully establishing a foothold in the Tōkyō market. He is credited with transforming the Japanese newspaper industry into a modern enterprise.

Mōtsuji 毛越寺

Temple of the TENDAI SECT of Buddhism. Located in the town of Hiraizumi, Iwate Prefecture. Said to have been founded in 850 by the priest ENNIN. Its central hall once held a statue of the Buddha Yakushi (Skt: Bhaiṣajyaguru). Originally services were conducted here for the protection of the country. Destroyed during wars between factions of the nobility, the temple was rebuilt in the early 12th century. Along with CHŪSONJI, Mōtsuji reflected the prosperity of what is called Hiraizumi culture. A new main hall built within the grounds (on a different site from the previous main hall) in 1899 replaced buildings razed by fires. During an annual festival held in the first month of the lunar calendar, a ritual dance (ENNEN) is performed that has been designated an Intangi-

ble Cultural Asset. The temple houses many important art objects. See also MŌTSUJI REMAINS.

Mōtsuji remains 毛越寺跡

(Mōtsuji *ato*). Site of the original compound of the temple MŌTSUJI, founded by Ennin in 850, in the town of Hiraizumi, Iwate Prefecture. Archaeological excavations since 1930 have revealed the basic outlines of the temple compound. The main hall faced south, and corridors on either side connected it to the drum and bell towers. South of the main hall was a large pond with a central island positioned on the axis formed by the main hall and the south gate, a plan that was adopted by many Jōdo sect temples late in the Heian period (794–1185).

mountaineering 登山

(*tozan*). Since 85 percent of Japan's land mass is composed of mountainous terrain, mountain climbing for pilgrimage, pleasure, or research has always been popular. From ancient times the Japanese people have regarded mountains with awe, looking upon them as dwelling places of the gods (KAMI) and in some cases as deities in their own right (see MOUNTAINS, WORSHIP OF). Mountain locations were often chosen as sites for both Shintō shrines and Buddhist temples. See also SHUGENDŌ.

With the Meiji period (1868–1912) came the first significant achievements in modern mountain climbing, notably those of SHIGA SHIGETAKA and the Englishman Walter WESTON, who helped found the Japan Alpine Club in 1905. MAKI ARITSUNE's ascent of the east ridge of Mt. Eiger in the Bernese Alps in 1921 sparked interest in rock and ice climbing. The Japan Alpine Club succeeded in scaling Mt. Manaslu in the central Himalayas in 1956. Their achievements brought a "mountaineering boom" to Japan. Japanese climbers such as TABEI JUNKO and UEMURA NAOMI have successfully conquered the most difficult peaks in the world.

mountains, worship of 山岳信仰

(*sangaku shinkō*; literally, "mountain beliefs"). *Sangaku shinkō* began as a form of nature worship centered upon mountains, volcanoes, or mountain ranges. The belief that spirits and gods (KAMI) lived in mountains developed gradually. Hunters in the mountains revered mountain *kami* (YAMA NO KAMI), and farmers in villages climbed mountains in early spring to welcome the *kami* to the village and pray for a good harvest. Japanese also thought of mountains as the dwelling place of ancestral spirits (see AFTERLIFE). The ancestral spirit was called a mountain *kami* and was thought to remain there. Folk belief held that the *kami* spent the winter in the mountain, descended to the rice paddy in early spring to protect farming endeavors, and returned to the mountain after harvest (see TA NO KAMI). Shrines were built in villages, and the spring and autumn festivals were dedicated to these *kami* (see FESTIVALS: matsuri). During the Heian period (794–1185) the Buddhist monks SAICHŌ and KŪKAI advocated a religious life in the mountains. At the same time, a form of religion called SHUGENDŌ developed, the goal of which was to develop supernatural powers through mountain asceticism. In modern times, the worship of mountains has continued to be practiced along with Shugendō in certain shrines and temples on sacred mountains. See also ON-TAKE.

Mt. Ikoma Space Science Museum　生駒山宇宙科学館

(Ikomayama Uchū Kagakukan). Science museum and planetarium on the summit of Mt. Ikoma in Nara Prefecture. The museum was established in 1951 and renovated in 1969. Its exhibits include model rockets and satellites.

mourning　喪

(mo). The observance of mourning in Japan was originally connected to the belief that exposure to death constituted a form of ritual impurity (KEGARE), which called for taboos surrounding relatives of the deceased. The period of mourning thus varied according to the closeness of one's relation to the deceased: in some regions there were set periods of mourning of 100 days for a parent or child, 49 days for a sibling, and 7 days for a cousin. Mourning consisted of remaining at home in seclusion, abstaining from fish and meat and the performance of one's usual occupation, and, above all, avoiding contact with Shintō deities. Heavy mourning (ki) was observed during the first 7 days following a death, light mourning (fuku) until 49 days after a death. The practice of not exchanging New Year's greetings on the year following the death of a parent or sibling is still observed.

Movement for Union of Court and Shogunate　公武合体運動

(Kōbu Gattai Undō). A political movement of the 1860s that attempted to strengthen Japan by forging a more unified leadership embracing the imperial court in Kyōto, the Tokugawa shogunate in Edo (now Tōkyō), and the leaders of the major domains.

From about 1857, members of the court began to participate actively in state affairs, meeting in Kyōto with officials of the shogunate and several domains. During 1858 the shogunate leader II NAOSUKE tried to terminate this court-daimyō association by a policy of harsh repression (see ANSEI PURGE) and by forging closer ties between the court and the shogunate. Subsequently he arranged a marriage between the new shōgun, TOKUGAWA IEMOCHI, and the emperor's sister, Princess KAZU (the marriage took place in 1862).

After Ii was assassinated in 1860, his successors ANDŌ NOBUMASA and KUZE HIRO-CHIKA continued this policy of kōbu gattai (court-shogunate unity), but after Andō was wounded by assassins, the dynamic leader of the SATSUMA DOMAIN (now Kagoshima Prefecture), SHIMAZU HISAMITSU, succeeded in replacing court-shogunate unity with court-daimyō unity. During the next four years the shogunate and the great domains vied for control of the court.

While the various leaders were attempting to realign the central relationships of the political elite, efforts were under way by proponents of the SONNŌ JŌI (Revere the Emperor, Expel the Barbarians) movement to restore political authority to the emperor and the court (see COUP D'ETAT OF 30 SEPTEMBER 1863). As such developments began to render kōbu gattai obsolete, many saw the forceful unification of the country as the only solution.

During 1867 these two strands of thought (imperial restoration and unification by force) coalesced into a powerful political movement that pitted leaders of the shogunate against leaders of the Satsuma domain and the CHŌSHŪ DOMAIN (now Yamaguchi Prefecture). In this context the kōbu gattai

movement was reduced to a conservative compromise strategy that was most fully articulated in late 1867 (see KŌGI SEITAI RON). It would have left intact both the decentralized feudal structure and the class hierarchy of the Tokugawa system. But that, too, failed, and the kōbu gattai movement became an anachronism that was swept aside in the BOSHIN CIVIL WAR of the MEIJI RESTORATION of 1868.

Movement to Protect Constitutional Government　憲政擁護運動

(Kensei Yōgo Undō). Name adopted by two separate political movements, the first during the TAISHŌ POLITICAL CRISIS of 1912–13 and the second in 1924, both of which aimed to secure party control of the cabinet.

1. When the second SAIONJI KIMMOCHI cabinet fell, the retired elder statesmen (GENRŌ) in December 1912 designated KATSURA TARŌ as prime minister. Members of the political parties RIKKEN SEIYŪKAI and RIKKEN KOKUMINTŌ decided to challenge the political dominance of cliques from the former Satsuma (now Kagoshima Prefecture) and Chōshū (now Yamaguchi Prefecture) domains (known as HAMBATSU) and the military's power to interfere in government. They organized an extremely successful popular protest movement "to protect constitutional government." Katsura resigned in February 1913. The Seiyūkai did not immediately gain control of the government, but the way was opened for Seiyūkai leader HARA TAKASHI to form Japan's first party-dominated cabinet in 1918.

2. In 1924 liberal factions of the political parties Seiyūkai, KENSEIKAI, and KAKUSHIN KURABU joined forces in a second movement to protest the resurgence of "transcendental" (i.e., non-party) cabinets. A coalition cabinet was formed, headed by the Kenseikai leader KATŌ TAKAAKI (see GOKEN SAMPA NAIKAKU). Internal dissension forced the resignation of the coalition cabinet in July 1925. See also TAISHŌ DEMOCRACY.

moxa treatment　灸

(kyū). Moxibustion. Traditional East Asian medical treatment in which cones of moxa or a similar substance are applied on the skin at specific points (keiketsu) and then ignited. The vital energy essential for life is believed to circulate through the body, and disease occurs when this flow is obstructed at crucial points. Moxa treatment consists of identifying these points and stimulating them through moxibustion. It is believed that the resulting heat makes the body react and adjust any physical irregularities.

Moxa is a combustible substance made of the densely matted fine hairs on the undersurface of the leaves of yomogi (mugwort; Artemisia vulgaris var. indica). As moxa cones burn on the skin for two or more minutes, a sensation of intense but bearable heat is felt, which turns into a pleasant feeling as the body adapts to the heat.

Moyoro shell mound　モヨロ貝塚

(Moyoro kaizuka). Archaeological site located on a sand dune at the mouth of the Abashiri River in the city of Abashiri, Hokkaidō; composed of deposits from the Final (ca 1000 BC–ca 300 BC) and Continuing (ca 300 BC–AD 700) JŌMON CULTURE and the OKHOTSK CULTURE (8th–12th centuries), with some AINU burials in the upper strata. Moyoro is an Ainu word for "bay." Near the shell mound are Jōmon and Okhotsk dwellings, the latter including some 10 PIT HOUSES with

moxa treatment Treatment for digestive disorders involves placing salt on the navel and burning moxa on top of it, a procedure that thoroughly warms the abdomen.

interior hearths and niches for the ritual deposit of bear and other animal skulls. Several hundred FLEXED BURIALS have been found in the Okhotsk stratum, some with pots covering the heads. Ainu burials are in the straight position. The investigations and collections of Yonemura Kioe (1892–1981) at this site are well known.

Mozume Takami　物集高見

(1847–1928). Japanese-language scholar. Born in Bungo Province (now Ōita Prefecture). Trained in KOKUGAKU (National Learning), Chinese classics, and WESTERN LEARNING, he worked for the Imperial Household Ministry and taught at Tōkyō University. He is noted chiefly as a lexicographer, having compiled the dictionary Kotoba no hayashi (1888) and Kōbunko (1916–18), a 20-volume compendium of writings from Japanese and Chinese classics and Buddhist scriptures.

mu → nothingness

mube　郁子

Stauntonia hexaphylla. Climbing evergreen shrub of the family Lardizabalaceae that grows wild in mountain areas of Kyūshū, Shikoku, and Honshū west from the Kantō region; also planted in gardens. Although similar to the deciduous AKEBI, the mube is an evergreen; hence its alternate name tokiwa akebi (evergreen akebi). It has a long leafstalk and palmate, compound leaves. Around May it produces three to seven long-stemmed unisexual flowers, white outside and pale reddish purple inside. The sweet white pulp of the purple, egg-shaped fruits was used as a flavoring before sugar became common. The mube is considered an auspicious plant in Japan because its palmate leaves grow in clusters of three, then five, and finally seven leaflets, thus corresponding to a traditionally lucky numerical series. The mube was exported to Western countries as an ornamental in the 19th century.

Muika　六日[町]

Town in southern Niigata Prefecture, central Honshū. Also known as Muikamachi. Situated on the river Uonogawa, during the Edo period (1600–1868) Muika developed as a castle town and a post-station town on the highway Mikuni Kaidō. A hot spring and several ski resorts are located in the town. Pop: 29,212.

mujin　無尽

(literally, "inexhaustible"). Traditional associations (KŌ) for pooling members' funds. Also called tanomoshi. They first appeared during the Kamakura period (1185–1333) as mutual financial aid societies for poor farmers. Members (usually 10 to 20) were required to pay in specific sums of money on

mube This climbing evergreen shrub is grown as a hedge and is also used in ikebana (flower arrangement).
1 Mube flowers have six sepals and no petals.
2 The fruit of the mube has a sweet pulp, which was used as a flavoring before sugar became common in Japan.

Munakata Shikō
1 *Three Women Rising.* 1953. Woodblock print. 99 × 111 cm. Munakata Museum, Kamakura.
2 *Sarasvati, Goddess of Fortune.* 1965. Woodblock print. 27 × 22 cm. Munakata Museum, Kamakura.

Mukōda Kuniko
A critically acclaimed scriptwriter and essayist whose career was cut short by an airplane crash in 1981.

a regular basis. After a certain reserve had accumulated, they were entitled to take turns drawing cash to pay for livestock, farming implements, and other major expenses. An association was dissolved when the funds were used up. *Mujin* have existed up through the modern period. In 1951 some of them, which had taken on the structure of companies, became mutual financing banks (*sōgo ginkō*). Informal *mujin* of the traditional type can still be found.

mujō　　　無常

(impermanence, transience, mutability; Skt: *anitya*). Originally a Buddhist term expressing the doctrine that everything that is born must die and that nothing remains unchanged. The phrase *shogyō mujō* (all the various realms of being are transient) is the first of the Three Laws of Buddhism. Japanese have traditionally been keenly aware of the impermanence of things, and the sense of *mujō* has been a major theme in literature. Works of the medieval period (mid-12th–16th centuries), such as the *Hōjōki* (The Ten-Foot-Square Hut) of KAMO NO CHŌMEI, the *Tsurezuregusa* (Essays in Idleness) of YOSHIDA KENKŌ, and the *Heike monogatari* (The Tale of the Heike), are especially noted for this essentially Buddhist view of life.

Mujū Ichien → Shasekishū

Mukai Kyorai　　　向井去来

(1651–1704). HAIKU poet of the Edo period (1600–1868); one of the 10 principal disciples of BASHŌ. Real name Mukai Kanetoki; son of a Confucian physician in Nagasaki. He excelled in the martial arts but at age 23 decided to go to Kyōto to study poetry. In 1686 he went to visit Bashō, who was living in Ise, and his unpretentious sincerity immediately won him the master's trust and affection. Whenever Bashō visited Kyōto thereafter, he stayed at Rakushisha, Kyorai's country cottage in Saga; Bashō's diary *Saga nikki* is a record of his stay there in 1691. With NOZAWA BONCHŌ, Kyorai edited the SARUMINO (1691), an anthology of the Bashō school. His lasting reputation is based upon his authorship of the *Kyoraishō* (1702–04). Principally a record of the conversations of Bashō and his disciples on haiku, it includes discussion of the important concepts of *fueki ryūkō* ("permanence and change"), *sabi* (lonely, austere beauty), and *shiori* (an indefinable quality of pathos).

Mukai Tadaharu　　　向井忠晴

(1885–1982). Businessman. Important figure in the MITSUI *zaibatsu* (financial and industrial combine) in the early 1940s. Born in Tōkyō. After graduating from Tōkyō Higher Commercial School (now Hitotsubashi University) in 1904, Mukai joined MITSUI & CO, LTD. He later became its chairman as well as managing director of Mitsui Gōmei Kaisha, a holding company of the Mitsui *zaibatsu*, in 1939. He reorganized this *zaibatsu* in 1940. After a dispute with the military, Mukai retired from the business world in 1943. He was finance minister in 1952.

mukashi-banashi → folktales

Mukawa　　　鵡川

River in south-central Hokkaidō, originating in the northern part of the Hidaka Mountains and flowing southwest to enter the Pacific Ocean at the town of Mukawa. Regions along the river are covered with coniferous forests. The water is used for irrigation. Length: 135 km (84 mi); area of drainage basin: 1,270 sq km (490 sq mi).

Mukden, Battle of　　　奉天会戦

(Hōten Kaisen). Last and fiercest land battle of the RUSSO-JAPANESE WAR; fought in March 1905. The Russians had gathered a huge force of 320,000 near the strategic city of Mukden (Fengtian or Feng-t'ien; now Shen-yang) in Manchuria, in northeast China. Moving from the west were Japanese forces, totaling 250,000. The Japanese forces captured Mukden on 10 March 1905, after 10 days, but the Russian army was able to escape. Until 1945, 10 March was celebrated as Army Day (Rikugun Kinembi).

Mukō　　　向日[市]

City in southern Kyōto Prefecture, central Honshū. Mukō is a residential suburb of Kyōto and Osaka. It has machine, textile, and foodstuff industries. The western section is noted for its bamboo shoots. Eggplants are also grown. Pop: 52,928.

Mukōda Kuniko　　　向田邦子

(1929–81). Television scriptwriter; essayist; novelist. Born in Tōkyō; graduated from Jissen Women's University. Her works include *Terauchi Kantarō ikka* (1975, Terauchi Kantarō's Family; televised in 1974 and 1975) and *Ashura no gotoku* (1981, Berserk; televised in 1979 and 1980). In addition to her television scenarios, which won wide acclaim for their superb dialogue, she also published essays, including *Chichi no wabijō*

(1978, Father's Letter of Apology). In 1980 she received the Naoki Prize for *Omoide torampu* (Card Game of Memories).

Mukōgaoka shell mound　　　向ケ岡貝塚

(Mukōgaoka *kaizuka*). A shell mound dating mainly from the Latest or Final Jōmon period (ca 1000 BC–ca 300 BC) in which the first YAYOI POTTERY was discovered in 1884 by Arisaka Shōzō, TSUBOI SHŌGORŌ, and others; located in Yayoi Chō in the Hongō district of Tōkyō. Originally regarded as merely transitional ware from the earlier JŌMON POTTERY, Yayoi pottery was not named until later, and the YAYOI CULTURE was not formally introduced to the academic world until 1923.

Mukogawa　　　武庫川

River in eastern Hyōgo Prefecture, western Honshū, originating in the Tamba Mountains and flowing through the western part of the Ōsaka Plain to enter Ōsaka Bay between the cities of Amagasaki and Nishinomiya. The middle reaches are noted for scenic gorges and hot springs. The water is used by the cities of Kōbe, Nishinomiya, and Amagasaki for drinking and industry. Length: 66 km (41 mi); area of drainage basin: 496 sq km (192 sq mi).

mukoirikon　　　婿入婚

Also called *shōseikon*. Matrilocal marriage. The couple often come from the same locale and meet at the house of the wife's parents during courtship. Wedding ceremonies are sponsored by the wife's family and are less elaborate than in the case of patrilocal marriages (YOMEIRIKON). The practice of *mukoirikon* begins with a preliminary stage of courtship initiated at the discretion of the couple involved and with little interference from the family heads. The future bridegroom then makes a formal visit to his bride and her family, which is called *hatsumukoiri* (bridegroom's first visit). He exchanges cups of *sake* and drinks with his future in-laws. The groom continues to visit the bride at her home for a specified interval, after which the couple chooses to remain or move to a separate residence. *Mukoirikon* developed in the Nara (710–794) and Heian (794–1185) periods but diminished with the rise of the warrior class. The practice has continued to the present among a few communities of traditional laborers, such as fishermen.

Mukyōkai　　　無教会

(Nonchurch Christianity). An indigenous Japanese Christian movement that developed out of a Bible study group around the turn of the 20th century and was led by UCHIMURA KANZŌ. The Mukyōkai Christians reject church denominations as materialistic, formalistic, sectarian, exclusivist, intolerant, Western in nature, and inappropriate for Japanese. Consequently they reject dogma, liturgy, and church institutions. The movement consists of independent Bible-study groups, each led by a teacher and informally integrated through the mutual exchange of published literature and occasional common activities. Each group is reorganized upon the death or retirement of its leader. Spiritually the movement emphasizes personal religious experience and an ethic of hard work, duty, and honesty. It attempts to synthesize the spiritual tradition of Japan with the Christian gospel as interpreted in the puritan manner. During the World War II era the Mukyōkai strongly opposed Shintō nationalism and Japanese imperialism; current nonchurch Christians are critical of conservative government policies. The movement has actively participated in the debate of social issues since its inception.

Mumyō-zōshi　　　　　無名草子

(The Nameless Booklet). Also pronounced *Mumyō sōshi*. Kamakura-period (1185–1333) work of criticism of Heian-period (794–1185) fiction (see MONOGATARI BUNGAKU). The unknown author adopts the KANA orthography and narrative framework of the historical work ŌKAGAMI, positing a fictional setting in which the narrator, an 83-year-old nun, and several aristocratic ladies discuss "things cherished in this world": the moon, letter writing, dreams, tears, the NEMBUTSU, and the LOTUS SUTRA. The work discusses in detail the TALE OF GENJI (earlier works are dismissed as lacking in sophistication), and gives short critical pronouncements upon extant works such as SAGOROMO MONOGATARI, YORU NO NEZAME, and HAMAMATSU CHŪNAGON MONOGATARI and upon lost works—concerning which it is an invaluable source—such as *Kakuremino, Asakure, Iwa utsu nami,* and *Hatsuyuki*. There are also analyses of poetry anthologies (see IMPERIAL ANTHOLOGIES; SHIKASHŪ) and brief remarks on the poetic gifts of literary ladies such as ONO NO KOMACHI, SEI SHŌNAGON, IZUMI SHIKIBU, and MURASAKI SHIKIBU and of several empresses.

munabetsusen　　　　　棟別銭

(house tax). Tax imposed on each household during the Kamakura (1185–1333) and Muromachi (1333–1568) periods. Also called *munabechisen, munebetsusen,* and *muneyaku*. At first *munabetsusen* was levied occasionally to pay for extraordinary court or temple and shrine expenses. In the Muromachi period, however, when shogunate and estate (SHŌEN) proprietors lost the ability to collect land taxes from military governors (SHUGO) and land stewards (JITŌ), *munabetsusen* became permanent. Some warlords of the 16th century resorted to similar taxation, but the practice died out by the 17th century when the HONTO MONONARI and other taxes were established.

Munakata　　　　　宗像[市]

City in northern Fukuoka Prefecture, Kyūshū. In earlier times it flourished as a post-station town and market town. Located between the cities of Fukuoka and Kita Kyūshū, Munakata now serves as a commuter suburb for both. Pop: 68,265.

Munakata Shikō　　　　　棟方志功

(1903–75). Woodcut artist. Born in the city of Aomori, the son of a poor blacksmith and the third of 15 children. Munakata became the best-known artist of his day and through his work brought about the general acceptance in Japan of printmaking as one of the fine arts. Although he had only an elementary school education, he had a passion for art from early childhood. In 1924 he decided to become a full-time painter in oils and moved to Tōkyō. He submitted his work without success to the annual imperial art exhibition (Teiten), until in 1928 one of his oil paintings was finally accepted. The same year, he turned to woodcuts and became a pupil of HIRATSUKA UN'ICHI. His house and most of his woodblocks were destroyed in the Tōkyō air raids of May 1945.

After the war he produced countless woodcuts, paintings in watercolor and oil, calligraphic scrolls, and illustrated books.

His work is in many institutional and private collections in Japan, the United States, and Europe, and three Japanese museums are named after him. He received many Japanese and international awards, including the First Prize, Print Division, São Paulo Bienal (1955); the Grand Prix, Venice Biennale (1956); and the Order of Culture (1970). Munakata's huge output shows a variety of influences, Japanese and Western, but at all times overflows with the driving vigor of his dynamic personality.

Munakata Shrines　　　　　宗像大社

(Munakata Taisha). One of the principal Shintō shrine complexes of northern Kyūshū; located in the coastal town of Genkai, Fukuoka Prefecture, and on two islands of the Genkai Sea. Dedicated to three female sea-deities, the shrines are located near the points of embarkation for official diplomatic missions to China and Korea between the 4th and 9th centuries. They attained national political significance during this period as sites of religious observances to pray for safe passage on these dangerous voyages to the Asian mainland. The Munakata Shrine complex consists of three separate shrines: the Hetsumiya, dedicated to the deity Ichikishimahime and located on the mainland of Kyūshū; the Nakatsumiya, dedicated to Takitsuhime (Tagitsuhime) and located on the island of Ōshima; and the Okitsumiya, dedicated to Tagorihime and located on the island of OKINOSHIMA.

Thousands of ritual relics have been excavated at the Okitsumiya Shrine in recent years (see OKINOSHIMA SITE). Many of them have been designated national treasures and are preserved in a museum at the Munakata Hetsumiya Shrine. Festivals are held each year on 1–2 April and 1–3 October.

Munenaga, Prince　　　　　宗良親王

(1311–85; Munenaga Shinnō). Also known as Muneyoshi Shinnō. Son of Emperor GO-DAIGO. In 1330 Munenaga succeeded his half-brother Prince MORINAGA as chief priest of the TENDAI SECT of Buddhism. He supported his father against the KAMAKURA SHOGUNATE (see GENKŌ INCIDENT) and backed the KEMMU RESTORATION of 1333. Leaving the priesthood in 1337, Munenaga fought the turncoat general ASHIKAGA TAKAUJI. In 1374 he retired to the Southern Court at Yoshino (see NORTHERN AND SOUTHERN COURTS), where he compiled the poetic anthology *Shin'yō wakashū* (1381, Collection of New Leaves).

Munetaka, Prince　　　　　宗尊親王

(1242–74; Munetaka Shinnō). First son of Emperor GO-SAGA and sixth shōgun of the KAMAKURA SHOGUNATE (1192–1333). The first imperial prince to serve as shōgun, he was selected in 1252 by the shogunal regent (*shikken*) HŌJŌ TOKIYORI, who retained power. Munetaka was deposed in 1266 and entered the Buddhist priesthood in 1272. His *waka* are collected in such volumes as *Keigyoku wakashū* (Collection of Precious Gems) and *Ryūyō wakashū* (Collection of Willow Leaves).

Muqi (Mu-ch'i) →Mokkei

mura　　　　　むら

(village). Smallest unit of LOCAL GOVERNMENT; also, the "natural" village, specifically the self-contained agricultural community. The word *mura* is believed to be derived from *mure* (group) and *muragaru* (to cluster) and to be closely related to Korean *mul*

Munakata Shrines
1 The main building of the Hetsumiya, the main shrine of the Munakata Shrine complex, was rebuilt in 1578.
2 This Kofun-period (ca 300–710) bronze mirror was excavated at the Okitsumiya Shrine, another of the Munakata Shrines, on the island Okinoshima. Diameter 27 cm. National Treasure.

(district) and *maïl* (village).

With the establishment of the RITSURYŌ SYSTEM of government in the late 7th century, a new village unit, the RI (renamed GŌ in 715), consisting of 50 households (*ko*), replaced the *mura* as the basic administrative unit (see GŌRI SYSTEM; KOKUGUN SYSTEM). In the mid-Heian period (794–1185) the *mura* emerged once more as the basic administrative unit. Physically, a *mura* consisted of as many as 20 houses enclosed by a fence (*kaito* or *kakiuchi*) and inhabited largely by extended families or groups of related families who collectively managed nearby woods and meadowlands (see IRIAI), as well as water resources. By the mid-1300s, many of these *mura* formed their own organs of self-government, with wealthier peasants (HYAKUSHŌ) serving as headmen. See GŌSON SYSTEM.

In the 1580s the *mura* were clearly demarcated as units in the great cadastral survey (KENCHI), and during the Edo period (1600–1868) the *mura* headed by a SHŌYA or *nanushi* remained the primary unit of administration. After the Meiji Restoration (1868) the government combined the villages into new and larger *mura* and *machi* (towns). The original, "natural" *mura* were renamed *ōaza*, which survive today as the basic neighborhood communities in rural areas.

Muragaki Norimasa　　　　　村垣範正

(1813–80). Official of the Tokugawa shogunate. Born in Edo (now Tōkyō). In 1854 he was appointed a shogunate comptroller (KANJŌ GIMMIYAKU) and assisted in treaty negotiations with Russian envoy E. V. PUTIATIN. In 1860 he was named vice ambassador of the shogunal mission to the United States to ratify the HARRIS TREATY (see UNITED STATES, MISSION OF 1860 TO).

murahachibu　　　　　村八分

Loosely, village (*mura*) ostracism. The practice of barring a household from full participation in the social and economic life of the rural community. Because the break was partial, *hachibu* (eight parts) is said to refer

Murakami won the Gunzō Prize for New Talent in 1979 for *Kaze no uta o kike* (tr *Hear the Wind Sing*, 1987). He followed this with *1973 nen no pimbōru* (tr *Pinball, 1973*, 1985), published in 1980, and *Hitsuji o meguru bōken* (tr *A Wild Sheep Chase*, 1989), a fanciful and humorous suspense story published in 1982. Together these works form a trilogy. Murakami's novels often have an episodic quality: his characters move through life in a desultory fashion, frequenting bars, recalling lyrics from songs, encountering and losing touch with each other. His writings have been immensely popular with younger readers. Other works include *Sekai no owari to hādoboirudo wandārando* (tr *Hard-Boiled Wonderland and the End of the World*, 1991), a highly imaginative work that borders on science fiction, published in 1985; *Noruuē no mori* (tr *Norwegian Wood*, 1989), a novel published in 1987 that sold more than 3 million copies; and *Dansu dansu dansu* (Dance, Dance, Dance), published in 1988, also a best seller. Murakami is also known for his translations of works by American writers such as F. Scott Fitzgerald and Raymond Carver.

Murakami Kagaku   村上華岳

(1888–1939). Japanese-style painter. Real name Murakami Shin'ichi. Born in Ōsaka. He studied art at the Kyōto Shiritsu Bijutsu Kōgei Gakkō and later studied painting at the Kyōto Shiritsu Kaiga Semmon Gakkō (now Kyōto City University of Arts), from which he graduated in 1911. With TSUCHIDA BAKUSEN, Ono Chikkyō (1889–1979), and others, he helped establish the Kokuga Sōsaku Kyōkai, an association of artists dedicated to modern Japanese-style painting (see NIHONGA). His earlier works are predominantly paintings of mountains, and his later ones are of Buddhist subjects, executed in an introspective lyrical style.

Murakami Kijō   村上鬼城

(1865–1938). HAIKU poet. Real name Murakami Shōtarō. Born in Edo (now Tōkyō), the son of a *samurai*. His worsening deafness made impossible the military and judicial career to which he had aspired, and he ended up working as a scribe in the city of Takasaki. Under the tutelage of MASAOKA SHIKI and later TAKAHAMA KYOSHI, he came to be a major poet of the HOTOTOGISU school, which emphasized photographic description (*shasei*) in haiku. Because of his impoverished life and his touching verses about animals and insects, he has been compared with the poet Kobayashi ISSA. His main collections are *Kijō kushū* (1917), *Teihon Kijō kushū* (1940), and *Kijō haiku hairon shū* (1947).

Murakami Namiroku   村上浪六

(1865–1944). Novelist. Born Murakami Makoto in Sakai, in what is now Ōsaka Prefecture. He began to work for the newspaper *Hōchi shimbun* in 1890. The next year he published *Mikazuki*, a novel about a swordsman, in which he reaffirmed traditional virtues. It was an immediate success. Murakami wrote popular historical novels and essays until about 1920, after which he became a businessman.

Murakami Naojirō   村上直次郎

(1868–1966). Historian. Born in what is now Ōita Prefecture. A graduate of Tōkyō University, he traveled to Europe in 1899 to research Japan's relations with Europe during its period of NATIONAL SECLUSION (1639–1854). Murakami taught at various schools

before accepting a professorship at Jōchi (Sophia) University. He was named president of the university in 1945. Murakami is best known for his translations of correspondence and reports by Jesuits in Japan during the 16th century and of the records kept by Dutch merchants in Nagasaki.

Murakami Ryū   村上龍

(1952–). Novelist. Real name Murakami Ryūnosuke. Born in Nagasaki Prefecture. Murakami studied at Musashino Art University. He won the Gunzō Prize for New Talent and the Akutagawa Prize for *Kagiri naku tōmei ni chikai burū* (1976; tr *Almost Transparent Blue*, 1977). Set against the backdrop of a US military base, the novel depicts the lives of young people immersed in drugs, sex, and rock music. Other works include *Koin rokkā beibīzu* (1980, Coin Locker Babies), a story of the uproar that ensues when two baby boys are abandoned in a coin locker, and *69* (1987), a tale of adolescence.

Murakami Takejirō   村上武次郎

(1882–1969). Metallurgist who contributed to the advancement of Japanese metallurgy with his research on special metal alloys and arc welding. Born in Kyōto Prefecture, he graduated from Kyōto University. In 1922 he became a professor at Tōhoku University and later served as director of its Research Institute for Iron, Steel, and Other Metals. He received the Order of Culture in 1956.

mural painting—→ screen and wall painting

Muramatsu Shōfū   村松梢風

(1889–1961). Novelist. Real name Muramatsu Giichi. Born in Shizuoka Prefecture. Attended Keiō University. His 1917 story "Kotohime monogatari" is based on his youthful experiences in a Tōkyō brothel district. Although he produced numerous popular romantic novels, he is better known for his biographical novels. Works include *Shōden Shimizu Jirochō* (1926–28), about a 19th-century gambler, *Honchō gajin den* (1940–43), and *Kinsei meishōbu monogatari* (1952–61).

Muramatsu Takeshi   村松剛

(1929–). Critic and scholar of French literature. Born in Tōkyō; graduated from Tōkyō University. Muramatsu writes literary, political, and social criticism from a broad perspective grounded in his considerable knowledge of European culture. His works include *Hyōden Andore Marurō* (1972, A Critical Biography of André Malraux) and *Sameta honoo* (1979–87, The Awakened Flame; winner of the Kikuchi Kan Prize), which focuses on the life of KIDO TAKAYOSHI in depicting the events surrounding the Meiji Restoration of 1868.

Muramatsu Tomomi   村松友視

(1940–). Novelist. Born in Tōkyō; graduated from Keiō University. Grandson of MURAMATSU SHŌFŪ. Muramatsu won the Naoki Prize for *Jidaiya no nyōbo* (1982, The Antique Shop Owner's Wife). His other works include *Namidabashi* (1983, Bridge of Tears) and *Shanhai rarabai* (1984, Shanghai Lullaby).

Murano Shirō   村野四郎

(1901–75). Poet and critic. Born in Tōkyō. Almost all of his poetry is free verse in the modern colloquial language, and much of it

to the parts of normal relationships that were suspended. Another possible origin of *hachibu* is a corruption of *hajiku* (to reject or repel). The ostracized household is itself also called *murahachibu*.

Until the recent past the Japanese hamlet acted as a corporate entity whose member households regularly performed communal religious rites and exchanged mutual aid and labor, particularly for the purpose of rice production and irrigation. Conduct such as cutting firewood in the communal forests without permission or revealing illegal or shameful village actions to the police or outsiders was cause for a charge of wrongdoing to be brought against the household at a hamlet council meeting. If it was unanimously agreed that the charges were valid, an official notification of ostracism was delivered to the household. As urban employment replaces farming, the power of the hamlet and incidence of ostracism have steadily diminished.

Murakami   村上[市]

City in northern Niigata Prefecture, central Honshū. A castle town from the 16th century, it has long been known for its tea, salmon, and *tsuishu* (a kind of red lacquer ware). The Senami Hot Spring is located nearby. Pop: 32,171.

Murakami Genzō   村上元三

(1910–). Novelist. Born in Korea, the son of a Japanese government official. After completing middle school in Tōkyō, he worked as a playwright for a small theater. Receiving the Naoki Prize in 1940 for *Kazusa fudoki*, he became known for popular historical novels. His best seller, *Sasaki Kojirō* (1949–50), dealt with the rivalry between the swordsmen Sasaki Kojirō and MIYAMOTO MUSASHI. Murakami's other major works include *Minamoto no Yoshitsune* (1951–55) and *Mito Kōmon* (1956–62).

Murakami Haruki   村上春樹

(1949–). Novelist. Born in Kyōto Prefecture. Graduate of Waseda University.

Murakami Haruki A novelist whose stories of wayward youth have been very popular with younger readers, Murakami also translates American fiction.

Murakami Ryū This writer's debut novel, *Almost Transparent Blue*, caused a sensation when it was published because of its graphic treatment of sex, drugs, and teenage aimlessness.

has a prose-like stylistic quality. However, a startling use of imagery and an uncompromising existentialism give a unique cast to most of his poems.

Murano underwent an apprenticeship in the composition of HAIKU when he was a schoolboy, but chose to study economics and German at Keiō University. He saw these studies as a means of countering the sentimentality to which, in his judgment, the composition of Japanese verse so readily led. After graduating from Keiō, Murano began a lifelong and successful career in business. While in his twenties Murano was part of the group behind the modernist journal *Bungaku*, and later he performed important editorial work for the poetry journal *Mugen* (Infinity).

After World War II, Murano continued to write poetry with a hard, objectively rendered surface. But, in volumes like *Jitsuzai no kishibe* (1952, The Shore of Reality), *Bōyōki* (1959, A Record of Lost Sheep), and *Sōhaku na kikō* (1963, Pale Journey), critics such as Ayukawa Nobuo (1920–86) see an attempt to render starkly the condition of a psyche beset by existential anxieties.

Murano Tōgo   村野藤吾

(1891–1984). Architect. Born in Saga Prefecture; graduate of Waseda University. He is noted for his thorough professionalism and mastery of a wide range of styles. Highlights of his long career include the starkly modern Sogō Department Store in Ōsaka (1936), the Nippon Life Insurance Hibiya Building with its art nouveau theater interior (1963), and numerous houses in the SUKIYA-ZUKURI style. Other impressive structures are the Ube Civic Hall (1937), the World Peace Memorial Cathedral (1953), the Japan Lutheran Theological Seminary (1970), and the New Takanawa Prince Hotel (1982), his final work. He was awarded the Order of Culture in 1967.

Muraoka Hanako   村岡花子

(1893–1968). Writer and translator of children's literature; social commentator. Born Yasunaka Hana in Yamanashi Prefecture, she graduated in 1913 from Tōyō Eiwa School for Women. From 1932 to 1941 she was widely known as the producer and announcer of a children's news hour on the radio. Her works after World War II include translations of L. M. Montgomery's series beginning with *Anne of Green Gables* (1908; tr *Akage no An*, 1952).

Muraoka Iheiji   村岡伊平治

(1867–1942). A notorious procurer of KARAYUKI SAN, Japanese prostitutes who were sent overseas from the Meiji period (1868–1912) to the end of World War II. His autobiography is one of the few informative records concerning illegal Japanese migration to the Asian continent and Pacific Islands, although its reliability has recently been questioned. Born in the Shimabara domain (now part of Nagasaki Prefecture), Muraoka went to Hong Kong at age 18 and engaged in a variety of disreputable occupations throughout China and Southeast Asia. His life was full of illegal activities, but his rather simple, energetic patriotism earned him a reputation that provoked both admiration and hatred.

murasaki   紫

Lithospermum erythrorhizon. Perennial herb of the family Boraginaceae that grows in sunny mountain areas throughout Japan; also found in Korea and China. The hairy stem (30–60 cm; 12–24 in) has alternate narrow, hairy leaves. White flowers bloom in summer; the fruits are hard and glossy. The dark purple root grows thick and straight and reaches 5–10 centimeters (2–4 in) in length. This root was formerly important as a source of purple dye, especially in the Nara period (710–794), when the plant was cultivated in gardens called *murasakien.* This purple (*murasaki*) was regarded as the noblest color during the Heian period (794–1185). Since the Meiji period (1868–1912) synthetic dyes have replaced the *murasaki* root. However, its elegant color has recently been rediscovered and is favored by some connoisseurs.

Murasaki Shikibu   紫式部

(fl ca 1000). Celebrated court lady and author who wrote a large part, if not all, of the *Genji monogatari* (TALE OF GENJI), the supreme classic of Japanese literature. The work known as the *Murasaki Shikibu nikki* (Diary of Murasaki Shikibu; tr *Murasaki Shikibu: Her Diary and Poetic Memoirs,* 1982) is also attributed to her, as are most of the poems in the collection *Murasaki Shikibu shū.* She is generally held to be the greatest author of narrative prose in the history of Japanese literature.

Name, Lineage, Early Life——Of her life, almost nothing can be said with certainty. Although she was known during her lifetime as Tō no Shikibu, the sobriquet by which she is known today has prevailed since the late Heian period (794–1185). Tō, the Sino-Japanese reading for the character *fuji* or "wisteria," clearly designates the FUJIWARA FAMILY, to a cadet branch of which she was born. Shikibu refers to the Shikibushō or Ministry of Rites, in which both her father and her brother held office. Two theories have been advanced to explain the Murasaki element: that because it means "purple" it refers to the wisteria of her family name and it derives from the name of Genji's great love in the *Genji monogatari.*

The SOMPI BUMMYAKU (a collection of genealogical tables) of the Muromachi period (1333–1568) gives her a common ancestor in the male line with FUJIWARA NO MICHINAGA, the most powerful statesman of her time, and makes them fifth cousins. By perhaps her grandfather's generation, Murasaki's branch of the family had slipped to the second level of the clan hierarchy. It is conjectured that she was born sometime in the eighth decade of the 10th century and that, from what is known of her father's career, she spent her early years in the imperial capital of Heiankyō (now Kyōto). In 996 her father was posted as governor to Echizen (now part of Fukui Prefecture), which bordered the Sea of Japan, and it is believed that Murasaki accompanied him.

Middle Years——Very late in the 10th century she was married to a fourth cousin, Fujiwara Nobutaka. She had one daughter and was widowed in 1001. Sometime in the first decade of the 11th century she was summoned to court as a lady-in-waiting to the empress Akiko (also known as Fujiwara no Shōshi; see JŌTŌ MON'IN), daughter of Fujiwara no Michinaga. The likelihood is that she began writing the *Genji monogatari* in the early years of her widowhood and that because of it she attracted Michinaga's notice and was invited into the service of his most important daughter. Murasaki's knowledge of the early historical chronicle *Nihon shoki* (720), which was written in Chinese, led to her being called "the chronicle woman" (*Nihongi no tsubone*), the *nikki* tells us, and, among other duties, she gave the young empress instruction in the verse of the Chinese poet Bo Juyi (Po Chü-i). Remarks in the *Genji monogatari* about painting, calligraphy, and the polite arts establish that her learning was not merely academic, and from her collected poems it is apparent that she was adept at the *koto,* or zither. A famous passage in the *nikki* in which she comments upon the inclinations and endowments of other court ladies suggests that she may have been a rather tart and cross-grained woman.

Late Years——Murasaki Shikibu was apparently still in Akiko's service in 1013, but the implicit evidence in the *Genji monogatari* itself perhaps tells us as much about her life as does any explicit evidence. It argues for single authorship over a lengthy period of years, with the possibility of later additions and revisions. The *Genji monogatari* grows and develops just as an author might be expected to grow and at the end suggests a serene rejection of the world such as comes with age and experience. The reasonable conclusion is that an aging Murasaki Shikibu wrote the last chapters. If she lived approximately as long as Genji, then she lived about 50 years and died in the third decade of the 11th century.

Place in Literature——In the late Heian period and after, there were imitations of the *Genji,* but their authors fell short of the qualities that account for Murasaki Shikibu's excellence—her interest in the complexities of the human spirit and her ability to create the illusion of individual life upon the written page. She was a dramatic writer in the sense of achieving her effects and conveying her messages through the mediation of character rather than through simile and metaphor, the rhetorical devices that characterize the largely lyrical tradition of Japanese literature. Murasaki Shikibu is generally placed beside SEI SHŌNAGON at the pinnacle of premodern prose literature; however, the writings of Sei Shōnagon are much less boldly original and much nearer the main lyrical tradition. In the middle ages (mid-12th–16th centuries) Murasaki became an almost mythological figure. In the Nō play *Genji kuyō,* for instance, she is revealed to be an incarnation of KANNON, patron deity of ISHIYAMADERA, a temple not far from Kyōto where, tradition has it, she began writing the *Genji monogatari.* In the millennium since it appeared, the reputation of the *Genji* has never flagged, and its author is still held in the greatest esteem.

murasaki shikibu   紫式部

(Japanese beauty-berry). *Callicarpa japonica.* Deciduous shrub of the family Verbenaceae that grows wild in mountain areas and on hills in Honshū, Shikoku, Kyūshū, and

Murasaki Shikibu This 17th-century painting depicts the celebrated Heian author at work on her masterpiece, the *Tale of Genji.*

murasaki The root of this perennial herb was used as a source of high-quality purple dye from ancient times. During the Edo period (1600–1868) the cultivation of *murasaki* roots was monopolized by the feudal domains.

murasaki shikibu The *komurasaki* (pictured), the cultivated variety of this deciduous shrub, is often planted in parks and gardens.

southern Hokkaidō. It reaches a height of around 2–3 meters (7–10 ft) and has toothed oval leaves. In June and July it produces clusters of small pale purplish flowers, which ripen into small round purple fruits. The plant was named after MURASAKI SHIKIBU, the author of the TALE OF GENJI.

Murata Harumi　村田春海

(1746–1811). KOKUGAKU (National Learning) scholar and WAKA poet of the late Edo period (1600–1868). Born in Edo (now Tōkyō). He studied under KAMO NO MABUCHI and succeeded him as a mainstay of the Kokugaku school. Together with KATŌ CHIKAGE, Harumi was a leading figure of the Edo school of *waka*. Disagreeing with the anti-Confucian views of the eminent Kokugaku scholar MOTOORI NORINAGA, Harumi infused his work with a broad appreciation of both the Japanese and the Chinese literary traditions. He is noted for his rediscovery of the long-lost SHINSEN JIKYŌ (late 9th or early 10th century), the oldest extant Chinese-Japanese dictionary.

Murata Mfg Co, Ltd　[株]村田製作所

(Murata Seisakusho). Manufacturer of electronic components. Incorporateed in 1950. The company is well known for its ceramic capacitors and ceramic filters. Murata has 17 overseas subsidiaries and branches in 13 countries. Sales for the fiscal year ending March 1991 totaled ¥236.4 billion (US $1.7 billion), and the company was capitalized at ¥50.5 billion (US $368.1 million) in the same year. Headquarters are in Kyōto.

Murata Minoru　村田実

(1894–1937). Film director. A pioneer of early Japanese cinema, he is remembered for making one of the first Japanese masterpieces, *Rojō no reikon* (1921, Souls on the Road). Murata came to cinema from a career in SHINGEKI theater. In 1920 he joined what is now SHŌCHIKU CO, LTD, where he teamed with OSANAI KAORU to make *Rojō no reikon*. Murata went on to make many successful pictures, all of which expressed an interest in the sanctity of the individual and humane social conventions. Many of his films were drawn from European dramas and carefully adapted to fit Japanese situations. Murata's contributions to early Japanese cinema were in his promotion of dramas about contemporary life at a time when period films held sway and in his concern for character and atmosphere over story.

Murata Seifū　村田清風

(1783–1855). Also called Murata Kiyokaze. Leading official of the Chōshū domain (now Yamaguchi Prefecture) and architect of its reform program of 1838–45. Educated at the Meirinkan, the domainal academy. In 1838 he was appointed director of a temporary reform ministry to meet the domain's enormous debt and to solve problems caused by drought, famine, and peasant uprisings.

Murata devised a system of repayment of *samurai* debts to merchant creditors. Besides enforcing the usual sumptuary regulations, Murata in 1840 took the unprecedented step of publishing the domain's budget and soliciting suggestions. He sold domainal monopolies to merchant guilds and increased the domain's gold and silver holdings by taking these metals in payment for Chōshū products while forbidding their use in payments to other domains. During his administration educational opportunities for samurai were expanded. In 1845 merchant opponents forced Murata's resignation; he was reinstated in 1855 but died shortly afterward.

Murata Shōzō　村田省蔵

(1878–1957). Businessman. Born in Tōkyō, he was a graduate of Tōkyō Higher Commercial School (now Hitotsubashi University). Murata joined Ōsaka Shōsen Kaisha Co (now MITSUI O.S.K. LINES, LTD) and built it into a major shipping company. He served as company president from 1934 to 1940. He also served as postal and communications minister in 1940 and 1941 and as ambassador plenipotentiary to the Philippines in 1943. In 1954 Murata became president of the Japan Association for the Promotion of International Trade (Nihon Kokusai Bōeki Sokushin Kyōkai), working for the normalization of Japan-China relations and promotion of trade between the two countries.

mura yakunin　村役人

General term for village officials during the Edo period (1600–1868). Villages were under the authority of *samurai* administrators known as DAIKAN or GUNDAI (intendants), but their internal affairs were handled by the *mura yakunin*, officials of rural commoner status who were chosen locally by election, appointment, or heredity. There were four main types of *mura yakunin*. The highest ranking were the *ōjōya*, who represented the interests of several villages and sometimes acquired quasi-samurai status (see MYŌJI TAITŌ). The other three types—known collectively as *murakata san'yaku*—were SHŌYA, *kumigashira*, and *hyakushōdai*. *Shōya* were the village headmen and directly responsible to the higher authorities for all village affairs, including collection of taxes. *Kumigashira* were the spokesmen for the neighborhood groups called GONINGUMI. *Hyakushōdai* served as representatives of the landowning members of the village community in the settlement of disputes, allocation of the tax burden, and other collective matters. Together these officials constituted the link between the samurai rulers of Japan and the rural populace.

Murayama　村山[市]

City in central Yamagata Prefecture, northern Honshū. A castle town until the Edo period (1600–1868), Murayama developed as a market and post-station town on the highway Ushū Kaidō. Today it is an administrative and commercial center. Its principal occupation is the processing of dairy products

and meat; rice and sericulture also figure prominently. It is the birthplace of MOGAMI TOKUNAI, an early explorer of Ezo (now Hokkaidō). Pop: 31,589.

Murayama Kaita　村山槐多

(1896–1919). Western-style painter and poet. Born in Yokohama. Influenced by his cousin, the Western-style painter Yamamoto Kanae (1882–1946), Murayama studied Western painting at the Japan Fine Arts Academy (Nihon Bijutsuin). He received the academy's award at its exhibition (Inten) in 1915. His subject matter was the sorrow of youth, with fauvism as the stylistic keynote. A collection of his poetry, *Kaita no utaeru* (1928, Kaita Sings), was published after his death at the age of 22.

Murayama Ryōhei　村山竜平

(1850–1933). Newspaperman; longtime president and owner of the newspaper ASAHI SHIMBUN. Born in Ise Province (now Mie Prefecture). Murayama opened a variety store in Ōsaka in 1871, and in 1879 became titular owner of the newspaper *Ōsaka shimbun*, which his friend Kimura Heihachi and Kimura's son Noboru had founded. Murayama bought the *Asahi* in 1881, and in two years his astute management secured for it the largest circulation in the country. He began publication of the *Tōkyō asahi shimbun* in 1888. He continued to expand the newspaper firm and set a precedent for other large newspapers by sponsoring various events such as middle-school baseball tournaments and cultural exhibits.

Murayama Tomoyoshi　村山知義

(1901–77). Playwright and producer. Born in Tōkyō. He attended Tōkyō University and studied painting in Germany. He was influential in introducing expressionist and constructivist art to Japan, and then became a leading figure in the proletarian theater movement of the 1920s (see PROLETARIAN LITERATURE MOVEMENT). After World War II, Murayama headed the Tōkyō Geijutsuza (Tōkyō Art Troupe), and in 1960 he led it on a visit to China. His works include the short story "Byakuya" (1934) and a two-volume collection of plays, *Murayama Tomoyoshi gikyokushū* (1971).

Murdoch, James　マードック, J.

(1856–1921). Educator and journalist; author of the first major English-language history of Japan. Born in 1856 near Aberdeen, Scotland, he won a fellowship to Aberdeen University and subsequent study at Oxford, Göttingen, and the University of Paris. His brilliance in foreign languages earned him an assistant professorship at the age of 24, which he soon resigned to emigrate to Australia. There he taught and worked as a journalist until he moved to Japan in 1889. With the exception of a short stay in a socialist community in Paraguay during 1893, he taught in Japanese-government higher schools until 1917. He then returned to Australia to found a Japanese studies program at the University of Sydney. Among the students Murdoch taught in Japan were the writer NATSUME SŌSEKI and the scholar of English Yamagata Isoo (1869–1959). Yamagata was Murdoch's research associate for his three-volume *History of Japan*, written between 1903 and 1917 but not published as a unit until 1926.

Murōji　室生寺

Head temple of the Murōji branch of the SHINGON SECT of Buddhism. Murōji was founded in the late 8th century in the village of Murō, Nara Prefecture. It houses a number of excellent sculptures carved during the Heian period (794–1185). SEE BUDDHIST SCULPTURE.

Although the precise origin of Murōji is unknown, its site has been regarded as sacred since ancient times. It has long been associated with monks who left worldly city temples to devote themselves to ascetic and magical practices in the mountains. One of many legends about Murōji tells of the wandering ascetic and miracle worker EN NO GYŌJA, who founded a temple there in 681 on behalf of Emperor Temmu (r 672–686). According to another tradition, Murōji was founded by the monk Kenkei (d 793) of the temple Kōfukuji.

Because Murōji admitted women as visitors and participants in esoteric rituals, which Mt. Kōya (Kōyasan), the center of the Shingon sect, did not, Murōji was popularly called "the women's Mt. Kōya" (nyonin Kōya). Murōji's oldest structure, a five-storied pagoda, was built either in the late 8th or early 9th century. It is the smallest in Japan and has been designated a National Treasure. The kondō (main hall) also dates from the 9th century, as does an outstanding image of a seated Buddha Śākyamuni carved from a single block of cedar.

Muro Kyūsō   室鳩巣

(1658–1734). Neo-Confucian scholar of the Edo period (1600–1868). Real name Muro Naokiyo. In 1672 he entered the service of MAEDA TSUNANORI, the enlightened daimyō of the Kanazawa domain (now Ishikawa Prefecture). He was subsequently sent by the domain to study in Kyōto with KINOSHITA JUN'AN, the Neo-Confucian scholar. At the recommendation of the scholar-statesman ARAI HAKUSEKI, he was appointed Confucian scholar to the shogunate in 1711. When the eighth shōgun TOKUGAWA YOSHIMUNE, dissatisfied with the formalistic teaching of Confucian doctrine at the shogunal academy (SHŌHEIKŌ), set up a separate school (Takakura Yashiki) in 1719, Kyūsō was named to its staff. From 1722 until his death, he was private tutor to the shōgun. Unlike many other Confucianists of his time, he refused the Japanization of Neo-Confucianism and maintained the strict orthodoxy of the Zhu Xi (Chu Hsi) doctrine (see SHUSHIGAKU). His works include Akō gijin roku (1703, rev 1709), a defense of the perpetrators of the FORTY-SEVEN RŌNIN INCIDENT, and Sundai zatsuwa (1732), a collection of discourses that take the form of lectures to his students.

Muromachi period   室町時代

(1333–1568; Muromachi jidai). A period of cultural achievement and social disorder, lasting from 1333, when forces led by ASHIKAGA TAKAUJI destroyed the KAMAKURA SHOGUNATE, until 1568, when the hegemon ODA NOBUNAGA captured the capital of Kyōto. Named for the district of Kyōto in which the shogunal residence was situated, it is also commonly known as the Ashikaga period, after the family that held the position of SHŌGUN from 1338 to 1573.

The dates for the Muromachi period adopted by this encyclopedia are, however, open to dispute. Some historians date both the founding of the MUROMACHI SHOGUNATE and the period itself from 1336, when Takauji captured Kyōto, ending the short-lived KEMMU RESTORATION of Emperor GO-DAIGO. Other scholars contend that

Takauji's assumption in 1338 of the title seii tai shōgun—following the precedent set by MINAMOTO NO YORITOMO and thus providing himself with rank and office to cloak his usurpation of power—marks the beginning of the period. Similarly, some scholars assign the termination of the period to 1573, when Nobunaga expelled the 15th shōgun, ASHIKAGA YOSHIAKI, from Kyōto, and others to 1588, when the exiled Yoshiaki resigned and thus ended the legal existence of his family's shogunate. Furthermore, some scholars view the years 1337–92, during which Go-Daigo and his scions maintained a separate court in Yoshino south of Kyōto to rival the court of the child emperor Kōmyō (1322–80; r 1336–48) set up by Takauji, as constituting a distinct period (see NORTHERN AND SOUTHERN COURTS); and many historians argue that the authority of the shogunate had so declined after the ŌNIN WAR (1467–77) that the succeeding century, the Warring States or SENGOKU PERIOD, should be considered a distinct historical era.

Political Developments: Central Government—In establishing the Muromachi shogunate, Ashikaga Takauji borrowed personnel and institutions from the Kamakura shogunate. He and the warriors who helped him draft the statement of legal and political principles known as the KEMMU SHIKIMOKU (1336) had been vassals of the HŌJŌ FAMILY, the regents who effectively ruled the Kamakura shogunate, and the Kemmu Shikimoku was a reaffirmation of the principles of the Kamakura warrior code, the GOSEIBAI SHIKIMOKU (1232). The chief offices of central and local warrior government, the Board of Retainers (SAMURAI-DOKORO), the Administrative Board (MANDOKORO), the Board of Inquiry (MONCHŪJO), and the provincial posts of military governor (SHUGO) and military land steward (JITŌ), had all been developed under the Kamakura shogunate and were now staffed by Ashikaga vassals.

However, unlike the Kamakura regime, under which the Hōjō regents had kept their vassals tightly in rein until the aftermath of the MONGOL INVASIONS OF JAPAN (1274 and 1281), Ashikaga control over the vassals they appointed as shugo was from the outset weak. Shugo families, many of whom were as powerful militarily as the Ashikaga shōguns, were well entrenched in the provinces and able to take advantage of the disturbances of the 13th and 14th centuries to extend their local authority. Moreover, powerful shugo families such as the SHIBA FAMILY, the HOSOKAWA FAMILY, and the HATAKEYAMA FAMILY were able to monopolize the important office of shogunal deputy (KANREI) and to dominate the senior councils of the shogunate. Several of the earlier Ashikaga rulers were able to impose their authority, but later shōguns were much less successful in managing the coalition of shugo.

The Muromachi shogunate got off to a troubled start. Takauji allowed considerable administrative and judicial responsibility to his younger brother, ASHIKAGA TADAYOSHI, while reserving for himself authority over the Samurai-dokoro and Onshō-gata (Office of Rewards), which together regulated the affairs of vassals and other warriors. The division of authority resolved into a breach between the brothers that hampered both the conduct of campaigns against the Southern Court loyalists and containment of the local aggrandizements of shugo. The death of Emperor Go-Daigo and the assassination of Tadayoshi left Takauji in a stronger posi-

tion, yet Ashikaga control was far from secure at his death in 1358.

His successors Ashikaga Yoshiakira (1330–67; r 1359–67) and ASHIKAGA YOSHIMITSU were able, with the support of the general Sasaki Dōyo (1306–73) and the shogunal deputies (kanrei) Hosokawa Yoriyuki (1329–92) and Shiba Yoshimasa (1350–1410), to increase shogunal authority over the country. Appointed shōgun in 1369 at the age of 11, Yoshimitsu, under the secular tutelage of Hosokawa Yoriyuki and the religious and cultural guidance of the ZEN monk GIDŌ SHŪSHIN, grew into a vigorous, cultivated ruler. Although Yoshimitsu relished the life of the courtier—he gave lavish entertainments for emperors and nobles and in 1395 was granted the highest court office, dajō daijin (grand minister of state)—he did not neglect his responsibilities as the warrior ruler of the country. He took the lead in organizing vassals in western Japan to crush uprisings by the TOKI FAMILY in 1390, the YAMANA FAMILY in 1391 (see MEITOKU REBELLION), and the ŌUCHI FAMILY in 1399–1400 (see ŌEI REBELLION). He commanded sufficient authority to oblige most shugo to establish residences in Kyōto and to remain fairly constantly in attendance at court. The only important area of the country that remained outside the full scope of his control was eastern Japan, where the governor-general of the Kantō region (Kantō KUBŌ), a cadet member of the Ashikaga house, exercised autonomous regional control from Kamakura, the site of the first shogunate.

Yoshimitsu surrounded himself with such arbiters of taste and literary style as the NŌ dramatists KAN'AMI and ZEAMI, the courtier-poet NIJŌ YOSHIMOTO, and the Zen master ZEKKAI CHŪSHIN and patronized Nō, poetry, painting, and garden design. His "Palace of Flowers" (Hana no Gosho) and his Kitayama villa (see KINKAKUJI) in northwestern Kyōto became vital cultural and intellectual centers (see KITAYAMA CULTURE). Yoshimitsu encouraged the entrance into court of lowborn but talented individuals, resulting in the transformation of elements of popular culture into high culture (see also DŌBŌSHŪ).

In 1401, in order to obtain Chinese art objects and cash to offset the relative paucity of shogunal landholdings, Yoshimitsu initiated the TALLY TRADE with Ming dynasty (1368–1644) China. During a period of 10 years, eight embassies completed the voyage, and,

Murōji This five-story pagoda, built in the late 8th or early 9th century, is the temple Murōji's oldest building, and, at 16 meters high, the smallest pagoda in Japan.

as a single embassy might yield as much as 10,000 *kammon* (10 million coins), they became an important source of revenue.

The power and prestige of the shogunate declined under Yoshimitsu's son Yoshimochi (1386–1428; r 1395–1423). Although he succeeded in putting down a revolt in the Kantō in 1417 (see UESUGI ZENSHŪ, REBELLION OF), his commitment to government was erratic. Shogunal authority was reasserted briefly by the despotic sixth shōgun, ASHIKAGA YOSHINORI, who put down a revolt by Ashikaga Mochiuji (1398–1439) in the east, and in the west brought the ŌTOMO FAMILY and the Ōuchi family to heel. He also reopened the China trade, which Yoshimochi had broken off, and worked to offset the influence of the *kanrei* and *shugo* by making greater use of the corps of hereditary bureaucrats, the *bugyōninshū*, and his palace guards, the *hōkōshū*, both of which were drawn from lower-ranking warrior families close to the Ashikaga. Yoshinori's policies briefly strengthened the shogunate, but his brutal methods antagonized courtiers and *shugo*, and his assassination in 1441 by AKAMATSU MITSUSUKE, one of his own vassals, marked the beginning of the disintegration of Ashikaga authority, accompanied by its increasing inability to protect its lands and its gradual exclusion from the Ming trade by the Hosokawa and Ōuchi families.

Under the eighth shōgun, ASHIKAGA YOSHIMASA, shogunal influence over the country all but collapsed. *Shugo* family succession disputes festered, encouraging warriors to take sides in unstable alliances. Responding to demands by indebted warriors and peasants, Yoshimasa issued "acts of virtuous government" (TOKUSEI), canceling debts owed moneylenders, merchants, and temples. These debt moratoriums threw the markets into confusion and Yoshimasa's vacillating attempts to revoke them provoked riots and pillaging. His construction of an elegant villa, the GINKAKUJI (Silver Pavilion; see also HIGASHIYAMA CULTURE), depleted already-straitened shogunal coffers, and his change of mind over a successor at the insistence of his consort HINO TOMIKO created a dispute that drew into its vortex rival leagues of *shugo* led by the Hosokawa and Yamana, thus commencing the Ōnin War. When efforts to halt the conflict proved futile, Yoshimasa retreated to his hillside villa, and the contesting armies reduced Kyōto to

ashes. The authority of succeeding shōguns was limited to the environs of the capital, and they were appointed and deposed almost at will by the Hosokawa family, which monopolized the post of *kanrei*.

Political Developments: Local Government—Under the Ashikaga the imperial institutions of local control (see KOKUSHI) withered completely. Provinces, with their scattered estates (SHŌEN) held by absentee noble proprietors or by temples or shrines, as well as lands held by resident local warriors (*kokujin*), were assigned to the administrative and judicial authority of *shugo*. In the mid-14th century the shogunate was often too weak to control the *shugo*. Making full use of their powers to grant as prizes lands seized in war, to adjudicate disputes, to bestow rights to half the tax yield (HANZEI) of local estates, and to impose local levies (HYŌRŌMAI), the *shugo* invaded private estates (*shōen*) and organized the powerful *kokujin* as their feudal subordinates. *Shugo* who by these means succeeded in aggrandizing themselves are referred to by historians as SHUGO DAIMYŌ. None was able to convert his territories into fully feudal domains over which he exerted exclusive proprietary control (ICHIEN CHIGYŌ). Some, however, like the Ōuchi and the Hosokawa, exerted tight control over several provinces.

With the consolidation of shogunal authority by Yoshimitsu, the *shugo* were put on a shorter leash and obliged to reside more or less permanently in Kyōto (or Kamakura in the case of eastern *shugo*). Entrusted to deputies (*shugodai*), their provinces were racked by power struggles between the *shugodai* and *kokujin*; peasant uprisings increased and tax income often failed to reach the *shugo* (see KUNI IKKI). The majority of *shugo* houses, bereft of the support of strong central authority after the mid-15th century, outmaneuvered by their deputies, starved of income, and torn by succession disputes, were toppled in the late 15th century and their regional domains carved up into more compact units under the control of warlords (SENGOKU DAIMYŌ), most of whom had emerged from the *kokujin*.

The Sengoku daimyō were a very different breed from the *shugo* daimyō. Indifferent to shogunal authority, they lived in their domains, devoting their energies to improving their own military, political, and economic strength. They promulgated law codes (BUNKOKUHŌ), built CASTLE TOWNS, conducted land surveys (KENCHI), broke up

shōen, crushed peasant uprisings, and brought villages under close supervision. It was this fragmented political order, free of central guidance or uniformity, that the Portuguese found upon their arrival in Japan in the 1540s.

Economy and Society—Warfare and instability in the Muromachi period did not prevent major advances in agriculture, commerce, transportation, village organization, and urban development. The demands of warrior leaders for arms and provisions, the growth of local power centers, dismemberment of *shōen*, and the loosening of the old political order, which had been dominated by the nobility of the capital, spurred the economy and encouraged social mobility and diversification. The Muromachi period witnessed a quantum leap forward in economic activity and the emergence of two powerful social forces, a self-conscious mercantile group and an increasingly restive and market-oriented peasantry.

Double-cropping of rice and barley, begun in western Japan, had by the Muromachi period spread into the eastern part of the country. Irrigation systems were improved and more extensive use made of draft animals, contributing to the increasing availability of crops from all parts of Japan. Mines were pushed deeper to satisfy demands for weapons, coins, and gilded decorations, and the building of massive CASTLES, around which towns developed, stimulated haulage and forestry. Increases in agricultural output, the growth of crafts, and demands for payment of taxes and levies in cash instead of in rice or cloth contributed to the spread of local markets, to greater specialization among merchants, and to more sophisticated exchange facilities. Copper cash, imported from China in small quantities during the Kamakura period (see SŌSEN), came in much greater quantities during the Muromachi (see KŌBUSEN; EIRAKUSEN), and monetization of the economy increased markedly. In return for the payment of dues (UTOKUSEN) to the shogunate, warehouse owners (DOSŌ) and *sake* brewers (SAKAYA) were permitted to engage in usury. Shogunal and *shugo* levies on land under cultivation (see TANSEN AND TAMMAI) and on households (MUNABETSUSEN) were collected in cash, and some among the Sengoku daimyō developed a system of administration whereby landholdings, grants of fief, and military service were expressed in cash units (see KANDAKA). The need for peasants to convert part of their crops into cash to pay taxes and levies contributed to the formation of a market economy.

MARKETS (*ichi*) were held regularly on six days of the month. Produce from villages was bought by traveling merchants, transported by packhorse haulers (BASHAKU) over an extended system of roads, and sold at market stalls by retailers. Merchants and craftsmen organized themselves in guildlike associations known as ZA, some 40 of which were based in Kyōto and more than 80 in Nara. *Za* were sponsored by nobles or temples to which dues were paid for the protection of monopoly rights and exemption from barrier-station fees (SEKISEN). Although membership in *za* was restricted, some of them, such as the *za* of oil traders in Ōyamazaki, had as many as 300 members, whose activities spread over a dozen provinces. *Za* served to maintain high standards among members, contributed to small-scale accumulation of capital, and brought order to the growing commercial activity. However, they also sought to block participation by provincial merchants and craftsmen, and from the mid-16th century Sengoku daimyō issued a spate of edicts freeing markets (see RAKUICHI AND RAKUZA).

The growth of commerce, the China trade, the diffusion of Buddhism, a vogue for pilgrimages, and the deliberate policies of the Sengoku daimyō contributed to urbanization and the growth of entirely new types of towns. Castles, which had formerly been built on craggy peaks, were erected on the plains by Sengoku daimyō and quickly grew into urban centers. New towns sprang up at ports, market sites, and transportation nodes. Ōminato, Obama, Tsuruga, Mikuni, Yodo, Sakamoto, and Ōtsu all developed during this period. Sakai, Hakata, and Hyōgo grew rich on the overseas trade. Sakamoto developed as the supply point for the temple ENRYAKUJI, Uji-Yamada benefited from the influx of pilgrims to ISE SHRINE, and the towns of Ishiyama and Yoshizaki were the commercial centers for the powerful HONGANJI Buddhist communities.

Daimyō exercised autocratic control over their castle towns. In other towns, however, self-governing civic communities emerged. Thirty-six leading citizens in Sakai formed a council known as the EGOSHŪ, which governed the city. A similar council existed in Hakata, and in Kyōto groups of townsmen (MACHISHŪ) were responsible for governance of the districts (*machi*) in which they resided. Although tightly controlled by Sengoku daimyō, villages also organized councils (YORIAI) to regulate common land and irrigation, to enforce village codes, and to resist excessive claims for taxes (see SŌ). Many villages won the right to collect and forward annual taxes (HYAKUSHŌUKE) and to mete out justice to local miscreants, thus laying the basis for the village system (GŌSON SYSTEM) of the Edo period (1600–1868).

Religion and Culture⸻Zen Buddhism, which was introduced from China in the 13th century, developed rapidly under the patronage of the Ashikaga shōguns and their vassals. The GOZAN network of the RINZAI SECT, the head temples of which were in Kyōto and Kamakura, covered Japan and gave training in meditation and the arts to the sons of provincial warriors. Chinese priests, such as Yishan (I-shan; J: ISSAN ICHINEI), introduced to Japan not only Zen practices and Buddhist texts, but Neo-Confucian political thought (SHUSHIGAKU) and Chinese poetry and painting. Zen monas-

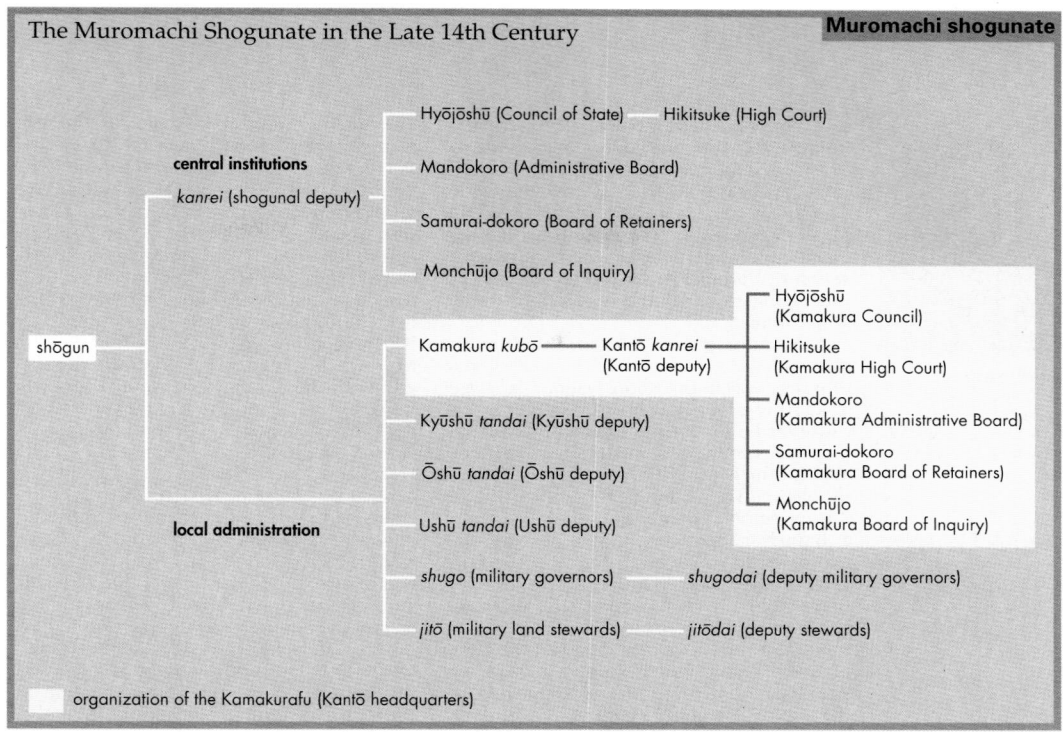

The Muromachi Shogunate in the Late 14th Century

teries were centers for the development of new styles of architecture, the design of GARDENS, the TEA CEREMONY, and FLOWER ARRANGEMENT. By the mid-Muromachi period, arts inspired by Zen were spreading from monasteries into secular society. Song (Sung) dynasty (960–1279) styles of Chinese ink painting, mastered by the Japanese monk-painters MINCHŌ, JOSETSU, and SHŪBUN, were transformed and carried outside Zen cloisters by SESSHŪ TŌYŌ. Under the early KANŌ SCHOOL masters KANŌ MASANOBU and KANŌ MOTONOBU, the Chinese style of ink painting developed by Shūbun and Sesshū was blended with the techniques of Japanese-style painting (YAMATO-E). A similar secularization and diffusion took place in the development of the tea ceremony, in garden design, and in the art of flower arrangment.

The influence of other sects of Buddhism also spread widely during the Muromachi period. The NICHIREN SECT attracted many *samurai* followers in the Kantō region and put down deep roots among the townspeople of Kyōto. Adherents of the JŌDO SHIN SECT, organized under the leadership of the temple Honganji by RENNYO in the 15th century, included samurai and peasants, and their devotion and militancy enabled them to mount large-scale uprisings (IKKŌ IKKI) against the Sengoku daimyō. With the arrival of Francis XAVIER in 1549, CHRISTIANITY was also introduced to Japan.

Muromachi culture was an intricate blending of elite and popular elements to which all sectors of society contributed and from which all derived stimulus and enjoyment. Emperors and courtiers shared with high-ranking warriors an interest in Nō and *kyōgen* and in the historical chronicles and war tales of the age, JINNŌ SHŌTŌ KI, BAISHŌRON, MASUKAGAMI, and TAIHEIKI, and both shared with commoners a passion for the short tales known as OTOGI-ZŌSHI, dance and mime (DENGAKU), and linked verse (RENGA). SŌGI and SŌCHŌ, two of the finest *renga* poets of the age, were of low birth but through their mastery of their art were able to mix with the highest in the land. Indeed some of the most characteristic arts of the period, including Nō and *kyōgen*, had their origins among the common people before being elevated through the genius of

artists such as Zeami into entertainments for the elite.

Muromachi shogunate　室町幕府

(1338–1573; Muromachi *bakufu*). The second of Japan's three military regimes (see WARRIOR GOVERNMENT), falling between the KAMAKURA SHOGUNATE (1192–1333) and the TOKUGAWA SHOGUNATE (1603–1867). Established by ASHIKAGA TAKAUJI, its name derives from the Muromachi district of Kyōto, the seat of the shogunate after 1378. It is also known as the Ashikaga shogunate after the name of its ruling house. Under the ASHIKAGA FAMILY, the shōguns greatly expanded the scope of military rule, asserting authority over most of Japan's political and military affairs, including the conduct of foreign relations, leaving to the emperors little more than a ritualized residual sovereignty.

Shōgun and Shugo⸻In extending its influence beyond its headquarters at Kamakura, the Kamakura shogunate had relied on its network of military land stewards (JITŌ) and provincial constables (SHUGO) chosen from among its own vassals (GOKENIN). Under the Muromachi shogunate, the *shugo* added to their military powers those previously held by the civil provincial governors (KOKUSHI), thereby becoming military governors. Neither shōguns nor *shugo* acquired independent power to exercise fully the authority they claimed. Even the shōguns never commanded a private army that could hold its own against the strongest of their major vassals, let alone against a combination of *shugo*. Most of the area of any given province was occupied by the estates of court nobles, religious organizations, and local military proprietors (KOKUJIN), some of whom might be direct vassals (*gokenin*) of the shōgun. *Shugo*, especially those brought in from outside by the Ashikaga shōguns, had to compete with these absentee and local proprietors for land and manpower. *Shugo* had the authority to levy certain imposts (TANSEN AND TAMMAI) for special purposes and to award half-tax (HANZEI) rights to local warrior families.

During the 15th century, as some *shugo* and *kokujin* became more powerful and lo-

Muroo Saisei The strong lyricism that characterizes this writer's poetry is equally present in his novels.

cally entrenched, they were able to assemble unitary domains, becoming SHUGO DAIMYŌ. The shogunal connection became increasingly less useful in the local power struggle. The shogunate, for its part, tried to keep the *shugo* dependent on the shōgun by juggling *shugo* appointments, by using its provincial *gokenin* to protect its local interests, and by interfering in the household affairs of its *shugo* houses.

Maintaining the Power of the Shogunate——Despite the fact that his family's base of power was in the Kantō region, Ashikaga Takauji was obliged to settle in Kyōto because his hold over the capital area was too precarious to leave it unattended. This created for the Muromachi shogunate a "Kantō problem." To maintain a presence in the Kantō region, Takauji created at Kamakura a branch shogunate, known as the Kamakurafu, to which he posted his second son with the title KANTŌ KANREI (Kantō deputy). Before long the head of the Kantō Ashikaga house adopted the style of KUBŌ (a title reserved for the shōgun) and passed the office of *kanrei* to the UESUGI FAMILY. In 1439 the Ashikaga Kantō line was extinguished by the sixth shōgun, ASHIKAGA YOSHINORI. Thereafter the Uesugi family, serving as *kanrei*, became the highest officials at Kamakura.

Kyūshū presented the Ashikaga in Kyōto with similar problems of control. In the southern island most of the provinces had long been subordinated to entrenched military houses such as the SHIMAZU FAMILY, ŌTOMO FAMILY, SHŌNI FAMILY, and ŌUCHI FAMILY. As a regional representative of the shogunate in Kyōto, however, the Ashikaga shōguns kept in northern Kyūshū, usually at Hakata, the head of an influential branch family with the title of Kyūshū TANDAI (Kyūshū deputy). Of these IMAGAWA SADAYO, who served in the post from 1371 to 1395, was outstanding for his ability to bring the Kyūshū *shugo* to the support of the Muromachi shogunate. But Kyōto's ability to control the west, so critical to the TALLY TRADE with Korea and China, was never direct or complete.

The third shōgun, ASHIKAGA YOSHIMITSU, had great success in sending out coalition armies against threats to the shogunate posed by aggressive *shugo* houses. However, the eighth shōgun, ASHIKAGA YOSHIMASA, proved unable to maintain the balance of power. The result was the ŌNIN WAR (1467–77), which brought to an end the shogunate's ability to influence affairs beyond the capital city.

Of course the shōgun's powers were not limited to the use of military force. The post of shōgun was an imperial appointment and with it eventually came high court status and assimilation into the high court nobility with attendant prestige. The Ashikaga demonstrated their attainment of aristocratic status through conscious patronage of the arts. Beginning with the shogunal residences—the so-called Hana no Gosho (Palace of Flowers), the KINKAKUJI (Golden Pavilion), and the GINKAKUJI (Silver Pavilion)—the Ashikaga house gave expression to the values of a new elite culture, which fused the traditional style of the civil nobility with the dynamism of the warrior aristocracy (see KITAYAMA CULTURE; HIGASHIYAMA CULTURE).

Machinery of Government——Two men are credited with giving shape to the machinery of Muromachi government. Ashikaga Takauji, the military organizer and strategist, was concerned primarily with the balance of power (the "feudal" dimension), while his younger brother ASHIKAGA TADAYOSHI devoted himself to establishing the administrative organs of government (the "bureaucratic" dimension). The promulgation of the KEMMU SHIKIMOKU (Kemmu Code) in 1336 demonstrated the Ashikaga's intent to follow the Kamakura model for military rule. For the first few years after its founding the Muromachi shogunate was run by the shōgun with the aid of a general manager (*shitsuji*). In 1362 that office was renamed KANREI or "deputy shōgun." The post was passed around in succession among the Shiba, Hosokawa, and Hatakeyama families. A council of *shugo* (*yoriai*) consisting of the heads of the three *kanrei* houses and other powerful *shugo* houses, such as the YAMANA FAMILY, Isshiki family, and Imagawa family, worked well up to the time of the sixth shōgun, Yoshinori, who tried to bypass the *kanrei* and *yoriai* and to rule directly through his inner staff of hereditary administrators (*bugyōnin*). This put the *shugo* at odds with the shōgun. Yoshinori's assassination in 1441 by a disgruntled *shugo* put an end to strong shogunal rule.

In the Kamakura shogunate the HYŌJŌSHŪ (Council of State) established in 1226 had developed into the primary deliberative council under the HŌJŌ FAMILY regency. Ashikaga Takauji set up a Hyōjōshū in Kyōto. Another important office adopted from Kamakura was the SAMURAI-DOKORO (Board of Retainers), used by Takauji as his war council. Its head, known as the *shoshi*, was selected from among a group of four important *shugo* houses, the Yamana family, AKAMATSU FAMILY, Isshiki family, and KYŌGOKU FAMILY. The most influential and durable body in the Muromachi shogunate was the MANDOKORO, or Administrative Board.

Decline and Demise——By the 16th century the provinces were in the hands not of centrally appointed *shugo* but of self-made SENGOKU DAIMYŌ—powerful military lords of *shugo* and *kokujin* origin who were rapidly extending both their territorial grasp and their autonomy from central authority. The shogunate declined, and in 1573 ODA NOBUNAGA ousted the last Ashikaga shōgun, ASHIKAGA YOSHIAKI, from Kyōto. Yoshiaki formally resigned in 1588.

Muroo Saisei　　　　室生犀星

(1889–1962). Poet, novelist, and essayist. Born Obata Terumichi in Kanazawa, Ishikawa Prefecture, he was an illegitimate child adopted into the Muroo family. In his youth he worked as a page at a district court. His superior, who taught HAIKU on the side, introduced him to literature. In 1910 he left Kanazawa for Tōkyō and, through his contributions to the journal *Zamboa* (Shaddock), came to know KITAHARA HAKUSHŪ (1885–1942) and HAGIWARA SAKUTARŌ (1886–1942). Quickly becoming recognized as a born lyricist, he wrote short poems in a free style and slightly unorthodox classical language. His collections include *Ai no shishū* (1918, Poems of Love) and *Jojō shōkyokushū* (1918, Short Lyrical Songs).

After he married in 1918, Muroo associated with novelist AKUTAGAWA RYŪNOSUKE and began writing lyrical autobiographical novels. His first work in prose was *Yōnen jidai* (My Childhood), which was followed by *Sei ni mezameru koro* (As I Was Awakened to Sex) and *Aru shōjo no shi made* (The Death of a Certain Girl), all in 1919. However, as Japanese writers cultivated new ideas and techniques in their literature and expanded their vision and sought to deepen their introspection, he was somewhat isolated from the main current.

His longest novel, *Anzukko* (1956–57, Apricot Child), was awarded the Yomiuri Literary Prize in 1958. He won the Noma Literary Prize for *Kagerō no nikki ibun* (1958–59, A Supplement to *The Gossamer Years*), a long novel based on the famous Heian-period (794–1185) diary KAGERŌ NIKKI. Muroo also composed haiku and published several collections. In 1960 he established the Muroo Saisei Poetry Prize.

Muroran　　　　室蘭［市］

City in southwestern Hokkaidō, on Uchiura Bay. Its port, opened in 1872, developed as a shipping center for coal from the Ishikari Coalfield. A steel plant constructed at the end of the Meiji period (1868–1912) led to the city's industrialization; today there are large cement factories, steel mills, oil refineries, and shipyards clustered around the port. Pop: 117,855.

Muroto　　　　室戸［市］

City in southeastern Kōchi Prefecture, Shikoku. It is a base for fishing fleets; the principal catch is bonito and tuna. The processing of marine products is consequently the major industry. Vegetables and fruits are grown in the coastal areas. The cape of MUROTOZAKI, the most scenic feature of the Muroto-Anan Coast Quasi-National Park, is located here. Pop: 23,308.

Murotozaki　　　　室戸岬

Cape in Kōchi Prefecture, southeastern Shikoku. Famous for its rocky coast, subtropical plants and trees, and lighthouse. Typhoons cause much damage every year. Hotsumisakiji, one of the 88 pilgrimage temples of Shikoku, is located here. Murotozaki is part of the Muroto-Anan Coast Quasi-National Park.

Murray, David　　　　マレー, D.

(1830–1905). US educator. One of the FOREIGN EMPLOYEES OF THE MEIJI PERIOD who served as an adviser to the Ministry of Education. Murray graduated from Union College, New York, in 1852 and later taught at Rutgers College. In 1872, when MORI ARINORI, the Japanese chargé d'affaires and acting minister to the United States at the time, sought the opinions of five prominent US educators about what Japanese education should be like, Murray submitted a written opinion. As a result he was invited to Japan in 1873. As top-ranking foreign adviser to the Ministry of Education, he directed the implementation of the EDUCATION ORDER OF 1872. On his advice the government founded the Tōkyō Women's Normal School (now OCHANOMIZU WOMEN'S UNIVERSITY). He took particular interest in the establishment of TŌKYŌ UNIVERSITY, drawing up plans and seeing to the adoption of a system of university degrees and graduation modeled on that of American and British universities. He returned to the United States in January 1879.

musasabi → flying squirrels

Musashi　　　　武蔵

Battleship of the Imperial Japanese Navy of the YAMATO class. With a displacement of 64,000 tons, the *Musashi* was 250 meters (820 ft) long, 39 meters (128 ft) wide, and mounted with a main battery of nine 46-centimeter (18-in) guns. The *Musashi*, the flagship of the Combined Fleet from February 1943, was sunk on 24 October 1944 at the Battle of LEYTE GULF.

Musashi→Miyamoto Musashi

Musashi Murayama　武蔵村山［市］

City in north-central Tōkyō Prefecture. Long a farming village, the city underwent rapid urbanization after the establishment of several automobile plants in 1961 and the construction of an enormous housing complex in 1966. There are also electrical-machinery and precision-instrument factories. Pop: 65,562.

Musashino　武蔵野［市］

City in east-central Tōkyō Prefecture. Formerly an agricultural district, it became a residential suburb after the Tōkyō Earthquake of 1923. The central shopping area of Kichijōji and Inokashira Park are popular. Seikei University is located here. Pop: 139,077.

Musashino Art University
武蔵野美術大学

(Musashino Bijutsu Daigaku). A coeducational private university in the city of Kodaira, Tōkyō Prefecture. Originally the Teikoku Bijutsu Gakkō (the Imperial Art School), which was established in 1929, it became a four-year university in 1962. Its only academic division is its college of art and design. Enrollment in 1989 was 2,403.

Musashino College of Music
武蔵野音楽大学

(Musashino Ongaku Daigaku). A coeducational private college whose main campus is located in Nerima Ward, Tōkyō. Originally the Musashino Ongaku Gakkō (Musashino Music School), which was established in 1929, it became a university in 1949. Its only academic division is its School of Music. Enrollment in 1989 was 3,992.

Musashino Plateau　武蔵野台地

(Musashino Daichi). Diluvial upland; extends from Tōkyō to Saitama Prefecture, southwestern Kantō Plain, central Honshū. Surrounded by the rivers Tamagawa, Irumagawa, and Arakawa and by Tōkyō Bay, it is elevated from the Tamagawa's diluvial fan. The woodland and cultivated land formerly typical of the Musashino Plateau are now replaced by housing projects, factories, and other urban facilities. Elevation: 20–180 m (70–590 ft).

Musashi Province　武蔵国

(Musashi no Kuni; also called Bushū). One of the 15 PROVINCES (*kuni*) of the Tōkaidō region of central Japan established in 646 at the time of TAIKA REFORM; now Tōkyō, Saitama, and eastern Kanagawa prefectures. Naturalized Koreans (KIKAJIN) were early settlers there. From the 12th century on, Musashi Province was ruled successively by the MINAMOTO FAMILY, HŌJŌ FAMILY, UESUGI FAMILY, and "Later Hōjō" family (see HŌJŌ SŌUN). The Later Hōjō were destroyed by TOYOTOMI HIDEYOSHI in the ODAWARA CAMPAIGN of 1590. In 1603 Edo (now Tōkyō) became the political center of Japan, and most of Musashi was administered directly by the shōguns until the Meiji Restoration of 1868.

Musashi Shichitō　武蔵七党

(Seven Bands of Musashi). Major warrior bands (BUSHIDAN) that were active from about the 10th century in the Musashi area, primarily in what is now Saitama Prefecture. The bands' origins are unclear, but they were apparently descended from court nobles who had been sent out as provincial governors. Each band was held together by real and fictive ties of kinship and by shared military ambitions. Although it is not clear which families constituted the seven bands at any given time, the best known are the Yokoyama, Kodama, and Inomata. All of them became vassals of the MINAMOTO FAMILY, but they retained their identity down through the 14th century.

Museum of Kyōto　京都文化博物館

(Kyōto Bunka Hakubutsukan). Museum in Naka-Gyō Ward, Kyōto. Established in 1988, the museum presents historical exhibits designed to educate visitors about the city's traditional culture, exhibits of arts and crafts produced by resident artists, and a reconstruction of two streets lined with shops as they appeared in the city in the late Edo period (1600–1868). The shops sell traditional crafts and foods. The building housing the museum, a section of the former Kyōto branch of the Bank of Japan, has been designated an Important Cultural Property.

Museum of Modern Japanese Literature　日本近代文学館

(Nihon Kindai Bungakukan). Library facility for modern Japanese literature in Komaba Park, Tōkyō, combining the features of a museum and a literary center. Through the efforts of writers such as TAKAMI JUN (later the first director of the museum) and ITŌ SEI and of various scholars, support from donors was received in 1962 for a collection of modern literature, begun at Ueno Library in 1964. In April 1967 the collection was moved to its present location. Holdings include the works and papers of novelists Takami Jun and AKUTAGAWA RYŪNOSUKE and of the socialist politician SUZUKI MOSABURŌ. The noncirculating collection totaled more than 954,130 items in 1989, including periodicals, books, and manuscripts. Many publishers contribute two copies of each new literary work to the museum.

Museum of Oriental Ceramics, Ōsaka　大阪市立東洋陶磁美術館

(Ōsaka Shiritsu Tōyō Tōji Bijutsukan). Municipal museum in the city of Ōsaka. Opened in 1982, the museum was established to accommodate the Ataka Collection, which was donated to the city by the 21 companies of the Sumitomo group. The collection contains approximately 1,300 ceramic works from China and Korea, including 2 pieces classified as National Treasures, and is one of the finest collections of oriental ceramics in the world.

museums　博物館

(*hakubutsukan*). Western-style museums first appeared in the Meiji period (1868–1912), against the background of the Meiji government's attempts to import Western culture and educational systems. When the Mombushō Hakubutsukan (Museum of the Ministry of Education) staged Japan's first exhibition in Tōkyō in 1872, it launched an era of intense museum development. The Ministry of Education's facility was followed by the Kyōiku Hakubutsukan (Museum of Education) in 1877, which featured displays devoted to physics, chemistry, zoology, geology, and other sciences. In 1895 the institution now known as the NARA NATIONAL MUSEUM opened its doors, followed in 1897 by what is today the KYŌTO NATIONAL MUSEUM. The trend also led to the establishment of private museums. The ŌKURA SHŪKOKAN MUSEUM was built in 1917 to house ŌKURA KIHACHIRŌ's collection. The ŌHARA MUSEUM OF ART, established by ŌHARA MAGOSABURŌ in 1930, was the first Japanese museum devoted to Western painting.

As the Sino-Japanese War of 1937–45 and World War II commenced, museum-related activities stagnated. When the war ended in 1945, there were 150 museums in Japan. The Kyōiku Hakubutsukan became the Kokuritsu Kagaku Hakubutsukan (NATIONAL SCIENCE MUSEUM) in 1949, and the former Mombushō Hakubutsukan became the Tōkyō Kokuritsu Hakubutsukan (TŌKYŌ NATIONAL MUSEUM) in 1952; both renewed their activities within new organizational frameworks. The government also became active in art museum development, opening the Tōkyō Kokuritsu Kindai Bijutsukan (NATIONAL MUSEUM OF MODERN ART, TŌKYŌ), which is devoted to both Japanese and foreign art, in 1952 and the Kokuritsu Seiyō Bijutsukan (NATIONAL MUSEUM OF WESTERN ART) in 1959. The latter is centered on the modern French paintings and sculptures collected by Matsukata Kōjirō (1865–1950), which were sent to Japan from France after the war. In 1966 the YAMATANE MUSEUM OF ART and the IDEMITSU ART GALLERY, both private museums built around superb individual collections, were established.

In the 1970s a movement calling for greater emphasis on prefectural and other local governmental units led to the founding of art museums and museums devoted to the traditions or commerce of individual communities. An ethnology museum, the Kokuritsu Minzoku Hakubutsukan (NATIONAL MUSEUM OF ETHNOLOGY) was established in 1974 and opened its doors to the general public in 1977. In 1983 the Kokuritsu Rekishi Minzoku Hakubutsukan (NATIONAL MUSEUM OF JAPANESE HISTORY) was established. The 1980s saw a national boom in new art museum development, with some 90 new facilities constructed in 1988 alone. Most were established by local governments. Museums devoted to particular industries were also founded, among them the Denryokukan (Electric Energy Museum, 1984) and the Chikatetsu Hakubutsukan (Subway Museum, 1986). In 1988, of the 2,622 Japanese facilities large enough to be truly called museums, nearly 60 percent were public institutions. Those devoted to history or to local cultural tradition made up the majority; art was the next largest category.

Musha Incident　霧社事件

(Musha Jiken). Insurrection in October–November 1930 against the Japanese colonial governor-general by members of the aboriginal Takasago tribe in the village of Wushe (J: Musha), Taiwan. The Musha region suffered from police repression, delayed payment of wages, and abuse of native women. On 27 October some 300 tribesmen stormed the local police office and killed 134 Japanese who were attending a school sports event. The colonial administration retaliated, leaving more than 500 (some estimates say 1,000) Taiwanese dead. The governor-general, Ishizuka Eizō (1866–1942), resigned, and the colonial government tightened its control of aborigines.

Mushanokōji Saneatsu
武者小路実篤

(1885–1976). Novelist, playwright, poet, and painter. Born in Tōkyō. Attended Tōkyō University. Although Mushanokōji's writing has frequently been criticized as pompous and naive, critics agree that he played a pivotal role in the literary coterie Shirakaba (White Birch; see SHIRAKABA SCHOOL).

In his youth Mushanokōji was rather weak and sickly and could not compete successfully in physical activities at school. To compensate for this he became a skilled debater. He also began to do some writing on his own and was encouraged in this decision by his uncle Kadenokōji Sukekoto, who introduced him to the Bible and to the works of Tolstoy. In 1907 he left Tōkyō University to form a literary group called the Jūyokkakai with SHIGA NAOYA, KINOSHITA RIGEN, and Ōgimachi Kinkazu (1881–1960). This became the nucleus of the Shirakaba school. The group circulated a handwritten magazine called *Bōya* (Perspective) and met every week to discuss literature and to comment on each other's writings. In 1910 Mushanokōji helped organize several groups, including the Jūyokkakai, into the literary coterie Shirakaba. The group published the first issue of its magazine, *Shirakaba*, in April 1910, the same year Mushanokōji published one of his most important works, *Omedetaki hito* (Good-Natured Person). Through the Shirakaba school, Mushanokōji was proposing a philosophical and artistic alternative to NATURALISM, and yet he preserved some of the elements that were central to the naturalist philosophy. In particular, he retained the ultraindividualism of the earlier writers. But he saw man as controlling his own destiny by the assertion of his will, in contrast to the naturalists, who saw the individual as alienated and desperate.

In 1918 Mushanokōji went to Hyūga in Kyūshū to establish a utopian commune called Atarashiki Mura (New Village). He still occasionally contributed to *Shirakaba*, but most of his energy went into his utopian community, his new magazine, *Atarashiki mura*, and a long work called *Aru otoko* (1921–23, A Certain Man), which was serialized in the magazine KAIZŌ. From the time of the founding of *Atarashiki mura* until the Great Earthquake of 1923, Mushanokōji wrote prolifically, producing such works as the novel *Yūjō* (1920, Friendship) and the play *Ningen banzai* (1922, Long Live Human Beings). From 1929 he was active as a painter and art gallery owner.

After World War II, as a result of his uncritical acceptance of the war, he was removed from public office under the OCCUPATION PURGE (he had been a member of the House of Peers), but he made a comeback in the literary world with his novel *Shinri sensei* (1949–50, Teacher of Truth). He received the Order of Culture in 1951 and became a member of the Japan Art Academy in 1952.

Mushanokōji Senke
武者小路千家

A school of the TEA CEREMONY, begun by Sen no Sōshu (1593–1675), the second son of Sen no Sōtan (1578–1658), grandson of the Azuchi-Momoyama-period (1568–1600) tea master SEN NO RIKYŪ, when Sōshu established the tea hut Kankyūan in what is now Kami-Gyō Ward in Kyōto. Sen Sōshu (b 1945) became the eleventh-generation head of the

school in 1989. Mushanokōji Senke prizes quiet, simple refinement (WABI).

mushi
虫

(literally, "worm" or "bug"). The word *mushi* is used in a number of idioms to describe certain emotions or feelings. When one is depressed, one is said to be "possessed by the worm of depression" (*fusagi no mushi*). When a person is in a bad temper, "the worm is in the wrong place" (*mushi no idokoro ga warui*). When a person persists in anger, it is because "the worm in his abdomen has not calmed down" (*hara no mushi ga osamaranai*). When a man is suddenly tempted to have an extramarital affair, it may be explained as the result of "the worm of fickleness" (*uwaki no mushi*). If a child has violent temper tantrums, the mother may take the child to a shrine to have "the worm of tantrum (*kan no mushi*) sealed off" (see MUSHIFŪJI). It might be that the Japanese, in their traditional reluctance to hold an individual responsible for impulsive behavior, attribute such behavior to an external agent, the "worm," which has made its way into his body. The *mushi* can always be "sealed off," and the "victim" can return to the community without too much guilt. See also KŌSHIN.

mushifūji
虫封じ

(literally, "sealing up of a worm or insect"). Kind of exorcism formerly used on sick children, usually employing spells, prayers, and talismans. Disorders were sometimes attributed to a MUSHI, or worm, that was believed to inhabit the child's body. To exorcise the *mushi*, one could give the child a folk medicine or take the child to a shrine or temple, have special prayers recited, and have the name of a Shintō deity written on the palms of his or her hands or the characters for the fifth day of the fifth month (Children's Day) written on the soles of the child's feet. Another method was to affix a paper talisman to the front doorway or to the Shintō family altar. See also EXORCISM.

mushin
無心

(literally, "lacking heart or depth of feeling"). A term used in both literary aesthetics and Buddhism with quite different meanings. Used in opposition to USHIN ("having heart, feeling"). As an aesthetic term *mushin* refers to the absence of elegance and refinement in concept or literary expression; on occasion it may mean a positive attempt to be amusing or even vulgar. In Buddhism the term *mushin* denotes one who is free from mundane desires or attachments, i.e., one who is enlightened. In the same sense an innocent or guileless child is also described as *mushin.*

The native Japanese equivalent of this borrowed Chinese term is *kokoronashi*, which was originally used to mean without discretion and good judgment or lacking sensitivity; it could also mean lacking an understanding of artistry or human sentiment or being devoid of good taste. The famous line by the poet-priest SAIGYŌ, "*kokoronaki mi ni mo aware wa shirarekeri*," if interpreted in this sense, would mean "Even an insensitive man can feel sadness." However, when Saigyō and others like him (priests) described themselves as *kokoronaki mi* ("a person without a heart"), they were using the phrase in the Buddhist sense of detachment from the ordinary passions and attractions: "Even a person without a heart can know deep feeling."

mushrooms
茸

(*kinoko*). Approximately 4,000 species of mushroom grow in Japan, a number equal to or exceeding that in the whole of Europe, which is about 12 times as large as Japan. This is owing to the climatic variety of the regions of Japan. Mushroom gathering is one of the Japanese people's pleasures in fall, with the *Tricholoma matsutake* (MATSUTAKE in Japanese) and *Lyophyllum shimeji* (*honshimeji*) the most highly valued species. *Matsutake* grows mainly in Japanese red pine forests and *honshimeji* in mixed forests. These two wild mushrooms, however, are mycorrhizal fungi, so they cannot be cultivated.

The most common cultivated mushrooms in Japan generally belong to the wood-rot fungi. Among them, *Lentinus edodes* (SHIITAKE) has the greatest production and economic value. Besides *shiitake*, *Flammulina velutipes* (*enokitake*; winter mushroom), *Pleurotus ostreatus* (*hiratake*; oyster mushroom), and *Pholiota nameko* (*nameko*; a Japanese endemic mushroom) are very popular.

musical instruments
楽器

(*gakki*). Although many different instruments have been used in traditional Japanese music, the most characteristic and most favored sounds are those produced by plucked strings, flutes, and percussion. For convenience, Japanese musical instruments are here considered in terms of the standard Sachs-Hornbostel classification.

Idiophones—This group includes bells, gongs, metallophones, percussion sticks, plaques and tubes, and vessel rattles. Among bronze bells (*kane*) are prehistoric bell-shaped objects (*dōtaku*) and various Buddhist bells: the large bells (*bonshō, kane*), suspended and struck from the outside; the large resting bell (*kin*); and the small handbells (*rin*). Gongs include the small gong (*shōko*) of court music; metallophones include the Buddhist *dora* and *kei;* percussion sticks include the wooden clappers (*shakubyōshi*) of court music; percussion plaques include the Buddhist "fish board" (*gyoban*); percussion tubes include the Buddhist "wooden fish" (*mokugyo*); and vessel rattles include bronze pellet bells (*suzu*), usually multiple. Many of these and other idiophones are used in KABUKI MUSIC.

Membranophones—The majority of Japanese drums have two membranes, which may be nailed or laced, and are usually struck with sticks. Nailed drums include the large drum (TAIKO) of court and festival music. Laced drums with hourglass shapes include the three drums (*kotsuzumi, ōtsuzumi, taiko*) of Nō drama. These and other drums appear in kabuki music. There are also rattle drums (*furitsuzumi*). The most general Japanese word for drum, TSUZUMI, derives from the Sanskrit *dundubhi.*

Chordophones—Japanese stringed instruments include zithers, long and short lutes, and an angular harp (the *kugo* of 8th-century court music) now obsolete. The zithers include the classical 13-stringed zither (KOTO) and the modern 17-stringed zither (*jūshichigen*). These are plucked, usually with a plectrum. Long lutes include various kinds of SHAMISEN and the bowed KOKYŪ. Short lutes comprise various kinds of BIWA, and the "moon lute" (*gekkin*) of popular Sino-Japanese music.

Aerophones—Most Japanese aerophones are end- or side-blown flutes, but there is also the free-reed mouth organ (SHŌ)

Mushanokōji Saneatsu This early-20th-century novelist and playwright was a central figure in the literary coterie Shirakaba.

and a cylindrical oboe (HICHIRIKI), both used on special occasions. End-blown flutes (*tate-bue*) include the bamboo SHAKUHACHI and the obsolete *hitoyogiri*. Side-blown flutes (*yoko-bue*) include those of court music (*ryūteki, komabue, kagurabue*), the Nō flute (*nōkan*), and the flute of festival and other popular music (*shinobue*).

music, religious   宗教音楽

(*shūkyō ongaku*). Japanese religious music may be taken to comprise not only liturgical chant and its instrumental accompaniment but also various kinds of secular music that are performed in the context of a religious ceremony or that are imbued with the spirit or teachings of organized religion, especially of Shintō or Buddhism. The tendency to syncretism that is characteristic of the Japanese approach to religious belief and practice makes it hard sometimes to draw a sharp distinction between the sacred and the profane. The two most important kinds of purely religious music are Shintō and Buddhist. Christian music has a history that goes back to the 16th century.

Shintō Music——The oldest description of Japanese music and dance is preserved in the legend that the goddess Ame no Uzume no Mikoto performed an obscene dance before the Rock-Cave of Heaven, and so enticed the sun goddess from hiding. This dance is the first known KAGURA, "music of the gods," or Shintō music. *Mikagura*, as a branch of court music (GAGAKU), has existed in organized form for some 1,500 years, and at present consists of a long ritual song cycle (apparently formalized in the 11th century), which is performed once a year on the night of 15 December. Distinct from this is the so-called *sato kagura* ("village *kagura*"), comprising a great variety of local music, usually associated with particular shrines, towns, or regions.

Buddhist Music——The earliest documented Buddhist music to reach Japan was the masked dance-drama known as *gigaku*, which was introduced from Korea in 612 but probably derived from Kuqa (Kucha) in Central Asia. Its 10 dances, which had no words, were accompanied by an ensemble of transverse flute (*kagurabue*), narrow cylindrical drum, and small bronze gong. Buddhism itself reached Japan in 538 or even earlier, and some form of liturgical chant (SHŌMYŌ) may be assumed to have come with it. However, the oldest document referring to chant is a decree of 720. The Eye-Opening Ceremony for the Great Buddha of Tōdaiji in 752 included performances of *shō-myō* as well as various kinds of court music and dance. Today the major remnant of Nara-period (710–794) Buddhist chant is the *omizutori* ceremony performed annually at the Nigatsudō of Tōdaiji.

In general, Japanese Buddhist chant since the Heian period (794–1185) divides into two great streams, Tendai and Shingon. The three schools of Zen Buddhism (Rinzai, Sōtō, and Ōbaku) introduced some new elements from Song (Sung) and Ming liturgical music, but their influence can be seen more in secular music. The evangelical schools (Jōdoshū, Nichirenshū, Jishū, etc) have on the whole followed Tendai models but have been less conservative, so that modern music of Jōdo Shinshū, for example, includes harmonized hymns in the style of many Protestant Christian sects.

Christian Music——The Gregorian chant was introduced to Japan by the first Jesuit missionaries, and by 1563 they could boast that 1,000 converts performed a *Laudate Dominum*. A Japanese mass had been compiled in 1553, and by the early 17th century pipe organs were being made in Kyūshū. All this activity was brought to an abrupt halt by the persecutions of the 1620s and later, though some hymns were preserved down to the Meiji period (1868–1912) among crypto-Christian groups. See also MUSIC, TRADITIONAL.

music, traditional   邦楽

(*hōgaku*). Term applied to the varieties of music performed in Japan in premodern times and to forms of such music that are played today. Although archaeological materials and Chinese documents provide evidence of music in Japan as far back as the 3rd century BC, the traditional history of Japanese music normally starts with the Nara period (710–794). Japanese music had its roots in the music of Buddhism and the vibrant traditions of Tang (T'ang) dynasty (618–907) China.

History——Buddhism was established as an official court religion by the 6th century, and its sounds and music theories became influential in Japan. Chinese and Korean courts or monasteries were the sources and models of most of the music in courts and temples but, because of the international dynamism of continental Asia from the 7th through the 10th century, influences from South and Southeast Asia can be found as well. The fact that Japan seemed to be "at the end of the line" in this cultural diffusion is of particular interest, for many traditions remained in Japan long after they had disappeared in the lands of their origins. The instrumental and dance repertoires of the court, generically known as GAGAKU, reflect such origins in their classification into two categories: *tōgaku*, pieces derived from Chinese or Indian sources, and *komagaku*, music from Korea and Manchuria.

Although the ancient musical traditions of Japan have carried on to modern times, each period produced other styles of music that better suited its own needs and tastes. During the turbulent change from a court-dominated to a military-dominated culture at the end of the 12th century, more theatrical genres of music became popular. The BIWA (lute) of the court became the accompaniment not only of itinerant priests and evangelists but also of chanters who recited long historical tales, particularly the HEIKE MONOGATARI (see HEIKYOKU). Pantomime theatricals at Buddhist temples and Shintō shrines gradually combined in the 14th century with the rich heritage of folk theatricals to produce a new form known as NŌ drama. The 13-stringed KOTO (zither) tradition is one of the few types of ancient courtly solo and chamber music that continued to develop in the 16th century, primarily in the mansions of the rich or in temples. At first there were remnants of older traditions, but by the 17th century quite different *koto* pieces appeared, particularly in the new Ikuta school. The founding of the Yamada school in the 18th century further enriched the repertoire. Both these schools have continued to the present day, and their solo and chamber music form the basis of what most Japanese would consider to be their "classical" music. The end-blown SHAKUHACHI (bamboo flute) also developed new schools of performance and repertory during this period, but it is the three-stringed plucked lute (SHAMISEN) that best represents the new musical styles and new audiences of the 16th through the 19th century. By the 18th century the narrative tradition of the puppet theater (known generically as JŌRURI) had become a major source of literature, which was performed by skilled chanters (*tayū*) with *shamisen* accompaniment. The KABUKI theater adopted some of this material for its own plays, but it also developed a combination of other genres of *shamisen* music plus the percussion and flute ensemble (*hayashi*) of the Nō, along with an eclectic assortment of folk and religious instruments. A logical outgrowth of an economically and socially supported theater music was the creation in the 19th century of compositions using theatrical genres and instruments but intended for dance recital or purely concert performances. The *shamisen* genre called NAGAUTA was particularly active in this new field. Such concerts were originally held in private mansions but, by the end of the century, actual concert halls for such music were common.

Musical Characteristics——Although Japanese traditional music and the classical music of the West have equally long histories, the two musical traditions have very different theoretical bases. Most Japanese music shares with its East Asian counterparts a general tendency to be word-oriented. Except for the variation (*dammono*) pieces for the *koto*, Japanese traditional music has either a vocal part with text or a title that evokes some image. Instrumental genres differ widely in Japanese music, but the general concept of the Western chamber-music sound ideal seems to apply to almost all Japanese traditional ensembles over the past 1,200 years. No matter how large or small an ensemble may be, the tone color of the instruments combined is such that the sounds do not "melt" into a single experience as they do in some Western orchestral music.

Another important feature of Japanese traditional music is the general lack of interest in the type of vertical sound units known in the West as chords or harmony. Two factors supersede any need for chords. One is the careful use of "pillar tones," central pitches in changing tone systems that are used as points of resolution from pitches just above or below them. The other major factor is rhythm. If only a single vocalist and one accompanying instrument are performing, they seldom coincide in entrances unless the tempo is quite fast or cadence occurs. This aspect serves two functions: it allows the listener to hear the text "between" the sounds of the accompaniment, and it creates some sonic tension that will be resolved at the cadence. If a percussion ensemble is used, as in Nō and kabuki, another important Japanese concept is evident: the use of named stereotyped rhythmic patterns. These patterns tend to appear in progressions and thus, like Western traditional harmony, play a vital role in giving music a sense of progression in time.

Perhaps the most difficult aspect of traditional music for the inexperienced listener is that it is generally through-composed. It does not state a theme and then develop it as in the standard Western classical tradition. Instead it moves on to new musical ideas. What gives it a sense of logical progression is its conventions of form, which are stated most generally by the terms *jo*, *ha*, and *kyū* (introduction, scattering, rushing toward the finale). In much of Japanese classical music there is a general goal of creating the maximum effect with a minimum of material. After becoming used to the music's reduced volume and activity, it is possible to begin to appreciate the artistry of "less action—more meaning." The challenge is to the flexibility of the listener, not the composer or performer. See also FOLK SONG; SŌKYOKU; DENGAKU; SHŌMYŌ; GIDAYŪ-BUSHI; NANIWA-BUSHI.

music, Western   洋楽

(yōgaku). The story of Western music in Japan (i.e., of music in the West European tradition) begins with the arrival of Portuguese missionaries in the 16th century. The first pipe organs were brought to Japan in 1579 by the Italian Jesuit Alessandro VALIGNANO, and Western stringed instruments, namely viols and rebecs, were widely used even earlier for both religious and secular music. In 1591 a Portuguese ensemble played before TOYOTOMI HIDEYOSHI on clavier, harp, lute, and rebec. There is little doubt that European music and musical instruments appealed to the Japanese, and one Japanese instrument, the KOKYŪ, was partly inspired by the rebec. However, the expulsion of the missionaries in 1613 put an end to this activity.

The profound social upheavals of the Meiji period (1868–1912) had great effects on music, not least because Japanese official attitudes were still strongly influenced by Confucianism, which maintained that correct ritual and music were important for good government. The old imperial court music was revived, NŌ drama, which had been the official entertainment of the old regime, was discouraged, and Western music was actively promoted.

In conformity with Confucianism, vulgar music was excluded, and, since Japanese acquaintance with Western music was still limited, only two genres, military music and children's educational music, were regarded as wholesome. In 1869 an Englishman, John William Fenton, began teaching in Yokohama 30 bandsmen from the Satsuma domain (now Kagoshima Prefecture). This was the first brass band in Japan, and Fenton was the first of many foreign music teachers.

Meanwhile, a series of educational reforms was passed, providing for the teaching of Western music. In 1879 IZAWA SHŪJI organized the Music Study Committee (Ongaku Torishirabe-Gakari), Japan's first official school of Western music. In 1881 it was renamed the Tōkyō Music School (Tōkyō Ongaku Gakkō; now Tōkyō University of Fine Arts and Music). Although Izawa advocated a blend of the new Western music and traditional Japanese music, the relationship between the two was still problematic. Attempts were made to harmonize SHAMISEN music, and the songs of TAKI RENTARŌ (1879–1903) showed that Japanese could compose successfully in a Western idiom, but the immensely popular GUNKA (military songs) came closest to satisfying Izawa's prescription.

The 20th Century—At the turn of the century other organizations for Western music came into being: the Meiji Music Society (Meiji Ongaku Kai) in 1898, the Imperial Music Society (Teikoku Ongaku Kai) in 1907, and the Tōkyō Philharmonic Society in 1914. At the same time several other Western music schools were started, all in Tōkyō. As a result of World War I and also of the Russian Revolution, numerous refugee musicians passed through Japan on their way to the United States. From 1917 onward a series of recitals and concert tours was given by foreign artists, mainly White Russian or Italian, and in the 1920s various Western artists were invited to perform in Japan.

The only regular symphony orchestra then was that of the Tōkyō Music School. In 1922 the Tōkyō Symphony Orchestra was formed but the Tōkyō Earthquake in September 1923 put an end to its activities. In 1925 the Japan Symphony Association began giving concerts in western Japan and Tōkyō.

Meanwhile, the procession of foreign guest artists and music teachers continued, and standards of Japanese performance gradually improved. Audiences too were becoming more appreciative, not least because of the gramophone. By 1937, Japan had become the largest market in the world for classical records.

Despite all this activity, composition under Western influence lagged behind. On the other hand, the Taishō period (1912–26) saw the flowering of a new genre of popular songs (RYŪKŌKA) in which there was a strong Western element. In the late 1920s and early 1930s there also developed a budding interest in Western opera, and in 1934 the tenor Fujiwara Yoshie (1898–1976) formed his own opera company (Fujiwara Kagekidan). After 1941 the orchestra of the Japan Symphony Association, which had a broadcasting contract, was mainly responsible for keeping Western music alive for the Japanese and even in 1945 it continued to give concerts.

During the American OCCUPATION foreign influence on music was naturally very strong and is seen above all in ryūkōka. However, interest in serious Western music was quickly revived. The old Tōkyō Symphony Orchestra had been dissolved in 1945, but its name was adopted in 1951 by the Tōhō Symphony (formed 1945). The Japan Symphony (originally founded in 1927 as the New Symphony Orchestra) became the NHK SYMPHONY ORCHESTRA, and several other symphony orchestras were founded between 1947 and 1956. Opera was presented by Fujiwara Yoshie's company and by the NIKI-KAI organization, formed in 1952 for the study and performance of Western opera. Composition, which had been slow to develop, was fostered by a number of groups, notably the Japan Contemporary Music Association (Nihon Gendai Ongaku Kyōkai), which from 1950 promoted an annual festival. Foreign performers began to visit Japan again from 1950 and foreign orchestras from 1955. Meanwhile, Japanese musicians were going abroad to study and perform; and since the 1960s some of them, such as the conductor OZAWA SEIJI, have established worldwide reputations.

Today Western music flourishes in Japan. In quantity and quality of composition, performance, music education, instrument making, musicology, and music journalism, Japan bears comparison with Europe and North America. All types of Western music—Renaissance, baroque, romantic, modern, jazz, folk, and the various kinds of popular music—are now heard. Most Japanese are strangely ignorant of Japanese traditional music, but somehow it too has managed to survive and to influence modern Japanese composers of varying musical sympathies. The old opposition between national and Western music persists, however. Most record companies distinguish between hōgaku (national music), a category that includes such disparate forms as children's songs, film scores, and Japanese rock, and yōgaku (Western music), which includes classical, popular, folk, and various other kinds of Western music.

Musō Soseki   夢窓疎石

(1275–1351). The most prominent and influential Zen master of the GOZAN (Five Temples) system of Zen monasteries of the RINZAI SECT of Buddhism and spiritual mentor to emperors and military rulers (including HŌJŌ TAKATOKI, GO-DAIGO, ASHIKAGA TAKAUJI, and ASHIKAGA TADAYOSHI) of the Muromachi period (1333–1568). Born in Ise Province (now part of Mie Prefecture), he was raised in Kai Province (now Yamanashi Prefecture). At KENCHŌJI, one of the chief Rinzai-sect temples in Kamakura, he received instruction from the Chinese master Yishan Yining (I-shan I-ning; 1247–1317; J: ISSAN ICHINEI). He also studied with the renowned Rinzai master Kōhō Kennichi (1241–1316) and in 1305 attained enlightenment. He became abbot of NANZENJI in Kyōto in 1325 and again in 1334 after a sojourn in Kamakura. In 1339 Soseki converted the Pure Land temple SAIHŌJI into a Zen monastery. The temple TENRYŪJI was built with profits from a trading vessel sent to China (see TENRYŪJI-BUNE) by the Ashikaga at his suggestion. He was instrumental in the establishment of the Gozan system and, aided by his political associations, contributed to the spread of Rinzai-sect Zen throughout Japan.

Mutai Risaku   務台理作

(1890–1974). Philosopher. Born in Nagano Prefecture. After graduating from Kyōto University in 1918, Mutai served as NISHIDA KITARŌ's assistant and traveled to Germany and France in 1926 and studied phenomenology with Husserl. Subsequently he taught at the University of Taipei, Tōkyō University of Education, and Keiō University. In his search to grasp man as a socio-existential entity, Mutai attempted to synthesize the methodology of phenomenology, Hegel's philosophy of history, and Nishida's philosophy with the concept of "spatial, contradictory self-identity" (bashoteki mujunteki jiko dōitsu). He wrote Daisan hyūmanizumu to heiwa ron (1951, The Third Humanism and Peace). See also MODERN PHILOSOPHY.

Mutō Akira   武藤章

(1892–1948). Army officer. Born in Kumamoto Prefecture; graduated from the Army War College in 1920. As a staff officer in the GUANDONG (KWANTUNG) ARMY in 1936 and chief of operations on the General Staff in 1937, he helped formulate the army's Manchurian policy. In 1939 he was appointed chief of the Military Affairs Bureau. A central figure within the wartime army leadership, Mutō became head of the Imperial Guard Division in 1942 and chief of staff for Japanese forces in the Philippines in 1944. He was executed in 1948 as a class A war criminal.

Mutō Kiyoshi   武藤清

(1903–89). Structural engineer. Born in Ibaraki Prefecture. Graduate of Tōkyō University. Mutō taught at Tōkyō University from 1927, becoming professor emeritus in 1963. He perfected a method of aseismic calculation by which the effect of earthquake forces on the structure of buildings could be determined. He was involved in the construction of many of Japan's high-rise buildings, including the 36-story Kasumigaseki Building, the first such building in Japan (Tōkyō, 1968, 147 m or 482 ft), and the 60-story Sunshine Building (Tōkyō, 1978, 240 m or 787 ft). He was the head of the Architectural Institute of Japan from 1955 to 1957 and the head of the International Association for Earthquake Engineering from 1963 to 1965. He received the Architectural Institute of Japan Award in 1970 and the Order of Culture in 1983.

Mutō Sanji 武藤山治

(1867–1934). Businessman and politician. Born in Gifu Prefecture, he studied at Keiō Gijuku (now Keiō University). After a stay in the United States, Mutō joined Mitsui Bank in 1893. In 1894 he moved to a Mitsui subsidiary, Kanegafuchi Spinning Company (now KANEBŌ, LTD), becoming its president in 1921. Mutō was widely known for his family-style corporate management. He formed the JITSUGYŌ DŌSHIKAI political party in 1923 and was elected to the House of Representatives in 1924. He strongly criticized collusion between politicians and business executives. After retiring from politics in 1932, Mutō became president of Jiji Shimpō Sha, a newspaper company.

Mutsu むつ[市]

City in northeastern Aomori Prefecture, northern Honshū, on Ōminato Bay. Facilities of the Japanese Maritime Self Defense Force are located here. It was formerly the home port of Japan's first nuclear-powered ship, the *Mutsu*. Principal industries are farming and fishing. Pop: 48,470.

Mutsu 陸奥

Battleship of the Imperial Japanese Navy. A sister ship of the NAGATO, it was built as part of the so-called HACHIHACHI KANTAI (Eight Eight Fleet) building program. Completed in 1921, it had a displacement of 43,000 tons, a top speed of 25 knots, and a main battery of eight 40-centimeter (16-in) guns. The *Mutsu*, which participated in the Battle of MIDWAY during World War II, sank on 8 June 1943 in Hiroshima Bay after an accidental explosion.

Mutsu むつ

Japan's first nuclear-powered ship. Built for the Japan Nuclear Ship Development Agency by ISHIKAWAJIMA-HARIMA HEAVY INDUSTRIES CO, LTD. Launched in Tōkyō, June 1969; length: 130 meters (426 ft); speed: 16.5 knots; tonnage: 8,242 tons. Following its completion, the ship was based in the port of Ōminato in the city of Mutsu, Aomori Prefecture. A leak was discovered in the nuclear reactor during a test run using conventional supplementary engines on 1 September 1974, and the local government refused to allow the ship to reenter port. The ship was repaired at Sasebo in Kyūshū and later based in the port of Sekinehama in Mutsu. The first nuclear-powered test runs were not made until 1990. The ship was scheduled to be decommissioned after 1991.

Mutsu Bay 陸奥湾

(Mutsu Wan). Large bay on the northern coast of Aomori Prefecture, northern Honshū. It extends from the Shimokita Peninsula on the east to the Tsugaru Peninsula on the west and opens into the Tsugaru Strait on the northwest.

Mutsuki → calendar, dates, and time

Mutsu Munemitsu 陸奥宗光

(1844–97). Foreign minister from 1892 to 1896. Born in Wakayama domain (now Wakayama Prefecture). He was best known for ridding Japan of the "unequal treaties" imposed by the Western powers and for his diplomacy during the SINO-JAPANESE WAR OF 1894–1895.

From early 1868 Mutsu held a variety of posts: Foreign Office bureaucrat, government official in the Kansai area, governor of Kanagawa Prefecture, head of the Finance Ministry office in charge of the LAND TAX REFORM OF 1873–1881, and member of the GENRŌIN (Chamber of Elders) from 1875 to 1878. Implication in an antigovernment plot landed him in prison from 1878 to 1883, when he was pardoned and swiftly rehabilitated. In 1884 he went to Europe to study and in 1886 returned to a post in the Foreign Ministry (Gaimushō), where he began efforts to revise the "unequal" ANSEI COMMERCIAL TREATIES of 1858.

Mutsu became ambassador to the United States from 1888 to 1890 and during that time concluded a Treaty of Amity and Commerce with Mexico and a revised treaty of commerce with the United States. He returned to Japan in 1890 to become minister of agriculture and commerce. In 1892 he was made foreign minister, the zenith of his career. In this capacity, he concluded the ANGLO-JAPANESE COMMERCIAL TREATY OF 1894, which finally placed Japan's relations with Britain on an equal footing.

The Sino-Japanese War broke out after Japan intervened in the TONGHAK REBELLION in 1894. Mutsu represented Japan at the peace negotiations, concluding the Treaty of SHIMONOSEKI with China on 17 April 1895. Only six days later, the TRIPARTITE INTERVENTION by Russia, Germany, and France reversed Mutsu's triumph and forced Japan to return the Liaodong (Liaotung) Peninsula, which it had gained as part of the peace settlement. The outraged Japanese public vented its rage on Mutsu, who resigned the following year. He died in 1897, soon after completing *Kenkenroku* (A Record of Suffering), his personal account of the diplomacy of the Sino-Japanese War. See also UNEQUAL TREATIES, REVISION OF.

Mutsu Province 陸奥国

(Mutsu no Kuni). Originally called Michinoku no Kuni (Province of the Farthest Region); also known as Ōshū or Rikushū. One of the eight provinces of the Tōsandō (Eastern Mountain Circuit) in central and northeastern Japan; established under the KOKUGUN SYSTEM early in the 8th century, it included what are now Fukushima, Miyagi, Iwate, Aomori, and a small part of Akita prefectures. Mutsu was originally an undeveloped frontier region, inhabited by the aboriginal EZO people. In 801–802, SAKANOUE NO TAMURAMARO succeeded in subduing the Ezo. The ŌSHŪ FUJIWARA FAMILY secured control over all of Mutsu in the mid-Heian period (794–1185). The family stronghold of HIRAIZUMI flourished as the military, political, and cultural center of northern Japan. In the late Muromachi period (1333–1568) the province came under the control of the DATE FAMILY in the south and the Nambu family in the north. Under the Tokugawa shogunate (1603–1867) the territory of the province was divided among some 20 *daimyō* domains (HAN), of which Aizu and Sendai were the most powerful.

mutual aid association pensions 共済年金

(*kyōsai nenkin*). A part of Japan's public pension system. Mutual aid association pensions cover local and national public service employees, schoolteachers, and employees in agriculture, forestry, and fishery organizations. The costs of the program are met by equal contributions from employers and employees, with contributions determined as a percentage of the employee's basic salary. Since 1986 mutual aid association pensions have supplemented the basic benefits provided by the NATIONAL PENSION. As of 1988 there were 5.9 million people enrolled in mutual aid association pension programs; in March 1989 the average monthly benefit of this pension program (including the portion provided by the National Pension) was ¥177,500 (US $1,362).

mutual company 相互会社

(*sōgo kaisha*). Also called a mutual insurance company (*sōgo hoken kaisha*); an incorporated juristic person (see HŌJIN) organized for the purpose of providing mutual insurance. Although mutual companies are not companies under the Commercial Code, but rather under the Insurance Business Law (Hokengyō Hō), a great many provisions of the former are applied to mutual companies as well. Mutual insurance refers to insurance offered by an association whose members insure each other. In order to establish a mutual company, the association must have at least 100 members and at least ¥30 million in funds. An association must receive the license of the minister of finance in order to conduct a mutual insurance business.

Mutual Security Assistance MSA援助

(Emu Esu Ē *enjo*). Also referred to as Mutual Security Agreement (both abbreviated MSA). A general term used to describe US military and economic assistance to friendly nations after World War II. The United States enacted the Mutual Defense Assistance Act in 1949 and the Mutual Security Act in 1951 and has provided large amounts of military equipment and other forms of military assistance to cooperating nations, including Japan. See UNITED STATES–JAPAN MUTUAL DEFENSE ASSISTANCE AGREEMENT.

Myanmar and Japan → Burma and Japan

Myōe 明恵

(1173–1232). Also known as Kōben. Buddhist monk of the KEGON SECT who criticized the PURE LAND BUDDHISM of HŌNEN and advocated a revival of Nara and Heian Buddhism in the early Kamakura period (1185–1333). Born in Kii Province (now Wakayama Prefecture); placed at age eight in the care of his uncle, a SHINGON SECT priest at the temple JINGOJI on the outskirts of Kyōto. After completing his training under MONGAKU, Myōe left Jingoji and thereafter lived alternately in seclusion in the mountains of Kii and at the temple Kōzanji (in Kyōto), which the retired emperor GO-TOBA granted him in 1206. In translating Kegon philosophy into religious experience, Myōe relied primarily on Shingon methods and on the ideas of Li Tongxuan (Li T'ung-hsüan; 635–730), a Chinese lay advocate of the Huayan (Hua-yen;

Mutsu Munemitsu
Foreign minister at the time of the Sino-Japanese War of 1894–95, Mutsu represented Japan at the peace negotiations. His personal account of the diplomacy of the period, *Kenkenroku* (1896), remains a valuable source for historians.

myōō A wooden statue of Fudō Myōō, a fierce incarnation of the cosmic Buddha whose task is to bring salvation to beings resistant to the Buddhist teaching. Sculpted in 1203 by Kaikei. Daigoji, Kyōto.

J: Kegon) school. Myōe borrowed freely from all schools. His career is notable for remarkable meditative experiences and rigorous defense of traditional methods for attaining altered states of consciousness. His writings include Buddhist technical treatises and commentaries, meditation manuals, poetry, rituals, criticism, aphorisms, and a journal of his dreams recorded over a 40-year period.

Myōen   明円

(?–1199). Buddhist sculptor active in Kyōto during the late Heian period (794–1185) and early Kamakura period (1185–1333). Myōen is known primarily as an important member of the EN SCHOOL of sculpture, which flourished through the 13th century. Among his known masterpieces are the Five Wisdom Kings (1176, Go Dai Myōō) in the temple Daikakuji in Kyōto.

myōgakin   冥加金

(literally, "offertory money"). Tax imposed during the Edo period (1600–1868) by the shogunate and domain administrators on merchants, artisans, fishermen, and other tradesmen who did not pay regular land taxes. Initially requisitioned as a one-time payment for the privilege of operating a trade or business, in time *myōgakin* became a fixed annual tax, much like the UNJŌ tax. Payment was usually in cash, although goods or labor could be substituted. *Myōgakin* were of two kinds, those assessed on individuals, such as *sake* or soy-sauce brewers and owners of inns or pawnshops, and those levied on KABUNAKAMA, or merchant monopoly associations.

Myōgisan   妙義山

Mountain in western Gumma Prefecture, central Honshū. It has three peaks: Kondō-zan, the highest (1,104 m; 3,622 ft); Hakuunzan; and Kinkeizan. Weathering and erosion have created striking rock formations and cliffs. Myōgi Shrine is located here. It is part of Myōgi-Arafune-Saku Kōgen Quasi-National Park.

Myōjinshō   明神礁

Underwater volcano about 130 km (80 mi) south of the island of HACHIJŌJIMA in the Izu Islands, south of the Izu Peninsula, central Honshū. Active from 1928 with periodic eruptions. In 1952 an eruption sank an observation boat; there were no survivors. There was another eruption in 1970.

myōji taitō   苗字帯刀

(literally, "surname and girded sword"). The official practice in the Edo period (1600–1868) of restricting the use of a surname (*myōji*) and the right to bear a sword (*taitō*) to families of *samurai* and noble (KUGE) status. Surnames had gradually spread beyond the aristocracy and were widely adopted by warriors from the 12th to the 16th century. After it came to power, the TOKUGAWA SHOGUNATE sought to halt further diffusion of sword carrying and surname usage. Although the shogunate did grant the privilege of sword carrying and surnames to a few commoners (either for one generation or in perpetuity) as a reward for meritorious service, this honor did not affect their official status. On the other hand, samurai sometimes surrendered or were stripped of their status and thus obliged to give up the right to *myōji taitō*. See also SWORD HUNT.

Myōjō   明星

(Bright Star; also translated as Morning Star or Evening Star). Innovative and influential literary journal launched in 1900 by YOSANO TEKKAN as the organ of the Shinshisha (New Poetry Society), the society he founded in November 1899. It appeared in three separate series with long lapses in between. The first series was published from April 1900 to November 1908. *Myōjō* was known for its sensual romanticism, epitomized by the poetry of Tekkan's wife, YOSANO AKIKO. Members included Akiko, HAGIWARA SAKUTARŌ, ISHIKAWA TAKUBOKU, IWANO HŌMEI, KITAHARA HAKUSHŪ, KINOSHITA MOKUTARŌ, and SATŌ HARUO. Advisers were MORI ŌGAI, UEDA BIN, and BABA KOCHŌ. *Myōjō* evolved into a sophisticated, sumptuously laid-out journal stressing the visual arts, TANKA, and Western-style poetry. The innovative brilliance of the *Myōjō* poets was a formative influence in the development of modern Japanese poetry. After internal dissension caused *Myōjō* to cease publication, its members helped found the poetry journal SUBARU. *Myōjō* was later revived from 1921 to 1927 and again from 1947 to 1949.

Myōkensan   妙見山

Hill on the border between Ōsaka and Hyōgo prefectures, central Honshū. On the summit is Myōkendō, a temple of the NICHIREN SECT of Buddhism. Height: 660 m (2,165 ft).

myōkōnin   妙好人

(Ch: *miaohaoren* or *miao-hao-jen*). Term used by the Chinese Pure Land monk Shandao (Shan-tao; J: Zendō; 613–681) in the work known in Japanese as *Kangyōsho* (a commentary on the *Amitāyurdhyāna-sūtra*) to praise those known for their devotional practice of recitation of AMIDA's name (J: NEMBUTSU). In the JŌDO SHIN SECT it has come to indicate the lay *nembutsu* practitioner who has attained faith in the Buddha Amida. The profound experiential understanding of the workings of Amida displayed by a number of these *myōkōnin* has led such modern thinkers as Daisetz T.

SUZUKI to emphasize their importance in Japanese religious history.

Myōkōsan   妙高山

Volcano in the Fuji Volcanic Zone, southwestern Niigata Prefecture, central Honshū. It is the central cone of a double volcano. The lower slopes of the mountain provide excellent skiing. It is a part of Jōshin'etsu Kōgen National Park. Height: 2,454 m (8,051 ft).

myōō   明王

(Skt: *vidyārāja;* kings of light or wisdom). The third-ranking category in Japanese Buddhist iconography, the first two being NYORAI (Buddhas) and *bosatsu* (see BODHISATTVA) and the fourth, TEMBU (Skt: *deva*). *Myōō* were originally non-Buddhist Hindu deities who were adopted into the pantheon of ESOTERIC BUDDHISM. They are considered to be incarnations of the cosmic Buddha who proselytize and save nonbelievers with the power of sacred words. Most of them are represented with fierce visages: hair aflame, face contorted, and weapons in hand. The best known of the *myōō* are Fudō Myōō (Skt: Acalanātha), Gōzanze Myōō (Trailokyavijaya), Gundari Myōō (Kuṇḍalī), Daiitoku Myōō (Yamāntaka), Kongōyasha Myōō (Vajrayakṣa), Aizen Myōō (Rāgarāja), and Kujaku Myōō (Mahāmayūrī). The last expresses compassion, unlike the other fearful *myōō*. The first five are usually grouped together as the Go Dai Myōō (Five Wisdom Kings), as exemplified in the statuary at the temple TŌJI in Kyōto. The most popular of the *myōō* is Fudō; the temple Shinshōji (Naritasan) in Chiba Prefecture is the center of the Fudō cult.

Myōshinji   妙心寺

Head temple of the Myōshinji branch of the RINZAI SECT of Buddhism, located in Ukyō Ward, Kyōto. Myōshinji was founded in 1337 by the retired emperor Hanazono (r 1308–18), who practiced Zen under the distinguished master SŌHŌ MYŌCHŌ. At one point, under the control of the powerful NANZENJI, the temple entered a period of decline. Myōshinji regained its independence and became a center for Zen practice. Completely destroyed during the Ōnin War (1467–77), the temple was restored by its ninth abbot, Sekkō Sōjin (1408–86). Myōshinji contains 57 subtemples and chapels, many of which are attached to tombs of *daimyō* patrons, and has 3,423 affiliated temples. The Myōshinji complex is noted for its many art objects, its superb gardens, and its temple bell, the oldest in Japan.

myōshu   名主

Local landholders from about the 10th through the 16th century, generally under the private estate system (see SHŌEN). *Myōshu* were designated by estate proprietors or managers (RYŌSHU). By the 10th century, land parcels under *myōshu* control were called "name fields" (*myōden* or *myō*), a system that later spread to the remaining public lands (*kokugaryō*). From the 12th to the 13th century, many cultivators gained land privileges as new *myōshu* (*shimmyō*), in contrast to the original *myōshu* (*hommyō*). From the 14th century the term applied to any person or religious institution holding *myōshu shiki* (the right to receive income from *myōden*).

Myōshu living on their lands were classed as commoners (*shōmin*). They were responsible for taxes and labor services of their own families, tenants, and subordinate families (see GENIN). Some with "*samurai* equivalent status" (*samuraibun*) came to be called JIZAMURAI (local landholding warriors). As the estate system eroded, powerful landholders tended to become either armed vassals of provincial barons (KOKUJIN) and of emerging *daimyō*, or headmen (OTONA) of autonomous groups of cultivators (SŌ).

mystery stories 推理小説

(*suiri shōsetsu*). Although the popular literature and drama of the Edo period (1600–1868) featured both outlaws and the supernatural, the true mystery or detective story appeared in Japan only in the Meiji period (1868–1912), when the tradition started by Edgar Allan Poe was imported from abroad. Early in the Meiji period, court trial novels and accounts of criminal investigations were already being introduced from the West to Japan, where they appeared alongside such Edo-style pieces as Kawatake MOKUAMI's outlaw plays and KANAGAKI ROBUN's tales of evil women. In 1887 translations of Anna Katherine Green's *XYZ* and Poe's "The Murders in the Rue Morgue" were published. In the following year KUROIWA RUIKŌ became active as a translator and went on to publish versions of more than 30 European works. Kuroiwa and other translators adapted these works freely to make them more acceptable to Japanese readers. Arthur Conan Doyle's *Adventures of Sherlock Holmes* (1891) was introduced to Japan in 1899. As for original writing, Kuroiwa's "Muzan" (1889) became a model for later short stories of the riddle-solving type. The writers of the KEN'YŪSHA group produced a number of works imitative of Western mystery writers. From about 1918 writers such as TANIZAKI JUN'ICHIRŌ and SATŌ HARUO were also publishing mysteries and bizarre stories.

Prewar Mystery Writing—The mystery magazine *Shin seinen*, which was first published in 1920, promoted mystery stories from abroad. Inspired by these imported works, EDOGAWA RAMPO published his own "Nisen dōka" in 1923. Mystery writing became an established profession, with its own literary circles and with *Shin seinen* as the most important medium of publication.

Mystery writers separated into two groups: an orthodox group, which emphasized stories of logic and deduction, and an innovative group, which encompassed the bizarre, fantasy, crime, mental perversion, adventure, and science fiction. Among the members of the former group were Edogawa Rampo, Kōga Saburō (1893–1945), Tsunoda Kikuo (b 1906), HIRABAYASHI HATSUNOSUKE, and Hamao Shirō (1896–1935); among the latter were Kozakai Fuboku (1890–1929), Ōshita Udaru (1896–1966), Mizutani Jun (b 1904), YOKOMIZO SEISHI, Jō Masayuki (1904–76), YUMENO KYŪSAKU, and Unno Jūza (1897–1949). When mystery novels began to be carried in magazines for the general public, they took on more and more the character of thrillers, with an aura of eroticism. Writers such as OGURI MUSHITARŌ, Kigi Takatarō (1897–1969), and HISAO JŪRAN, who made their debut around 1933, tried to raise literary standards. As World War II approached, mystery stories were suppressed, and writers could produce only spy and adventure stories and science fiction.

Postwar Writers—With the end of World War II, Japanese mystery writers turned to lengthy, logically constructed novels. Yokomizo Seishi's *Honjin satsujin jiken* (1946), SAKAGUCHI ANGO's *Furenzoku satsujin jiken* (1947–48), Tsunoda Kikuo's *Takagike no sangeki* (1947), and Takagi Akimitsu's

(b 1920) *Shisei satsujin jiken* (1948) are examples of this trend. An influx of new literary styles, led by the "hard-boiled" school, began to add variety to the Japanese mystery scene. YAMADA FŪTARŌ, Hikage Jōkichi (b 1908), and Ōtsubo Sunao (1904–65) made their appearance at this time.

With his *Ten to sen* (1957–58; tr *Points and Lines*, 1970) and *Me no kabe* (1957), MATSUMOTO SEICHŌ established a style that had both social and human interest, and he was followed by such writers as MINAKAMI TSUTOMU, KUROIWA JŪGO, and KAJIYAMA TOSHIYUKI. The works of Yokomizo Seishi, which combined logical structure with romantic coloration, sold more than 4 million copies in paperback. Other popular writers include Ayukawa Tetsuya (b 1915), NIKI ETSUKO, SASAZAWA SAHO, and Sano Yō (b 1928) of the orthodox school; among those who write in a variety of styles are Takigawa Kyō (b 1920), YŪKI SHŌJI, CHIN SHUNSHIN (Ch: Chen Shunchen or Ch'en Shun-ch'en), and Miyoshi Tōru (b 1931). MORIMURA SEIICHI and other newer writers have attempted to combine orthodox detective fiction with social consciousness.

Recent Trends—In the 1980s, mysteries began to handle an even broader range of themes. AKAGAWA JIRŌ's lighthearted and humorous tales, Nishimura Jukō's (b 1930) violent thrillers, and Nishimura Kyōtarō's (b 1930) travel mysteries have all won large and enthusiastic followings. Women writers such as TOGAWA MASAKO, Natsuki Shizuko (b 1938), and Yamamura Misa (b 1934) have made impressive contributions to the genre. A number of new literary prizes for mystery fiction have been established.

mythology 神話

(*shinwa*). Japanese mythology is a composite of native themes and continental imports mainly under the aegis of Buddhism and Taoism. Japanese myths are generally rather gentle. There is a trickster deity, but no divinity embodies evil. Compromise rather than confrontation is the touchstone of Japanese mythology.

THE MYTHS OF THE KOJIKI AND NIHON SHOKI

The chief literary sources for Japanese myths are the KOJIKI (712, Records of Ancient Matters) and the NIHON SHOKI (720, Chronicle of Japan; also known as *Nihongi*). These works were assembled at imperial command from a wide assortment of no longer extant texts compiled by the Yamato line of rulers and other powerful family lines, over whom the Yamato kings had only in the 7th century fully established their ascendancy. Other sources include the KOGO SHŪI (807, Gleanings from Ancient Stories) by Imbe no Hironari, which contains myths and legends handed down in the Imbe family; the FUDOKI (provincial gazetteers), of which the most important one—and the only one that is complete—is the *Izumo no Kuni fudoki* (733); the *Shoku nihongi* (797, Chronicle of Japan, Continued); the 8th-century anthology of poetry MAN'YŌSHŪ (Collection for Ten Thousand Generations or Collection of Ten Thousand Leaves); and the NORITO, court religious liturgies collected at the end of the 10th century in the ENGI SHIKI (Procedures of the Engi Era).

The myths recounted in the *Kojiki* and the *Nihon shoki* can be divided into three major cycles: the cycle of Takamagahara (High Plain of Heaven), where the gods of generation appear at the time of the formation of

heaven and earth (Takamagahara is given in trust to the goddess AMATERASU ŌMIKAMI); the cycle of Izumo (now Shimane Prefecture), the land to which the god SUSANOO NO MIKOTO descends from Takamagahara (his descendant ŌKUNINUSHI NO MIKOTO takes control of this land, later yielding it to Amaterasu Ōmikami); and the cycle of Tsukushi (now Kyūshū), the land to which NINIGI NO MIKOTO, grandson of Amaterasu Ōmikami, descends to establish his rule over Ashihara no Nakatsukuni (the lands of Japan; also referred to as Utsushi no Kuni or the Revealed Land) and from which Ninigi's great-grandson, the legendary first emperor JIMMU, departs for Yamato (now Nara Prefecture). As the Takamagahara cycle and the Tsukushi cycle represent an unbroken line from the gods of generation, through Amaterasu, to the emperor Jimmu, they are sometimes referred to together as the Yamato cycle. The version of the myths related below derives from the *Kojiki*.

The Takamagahara Cycle—When the heavens and the earth first open apart, three gods of generation, Ame no Minakanushi no Kami, Takamimusubi no Kami, and Kamimusubi no Kami, appear and then hide themselves. While the land is yet young, floating like oil, drifting like a jellyfish, two more gods appear: Umashiashi Kabihikoji no Kami and Ame no Tokotachi no Kami, who also hide themselves. These five primal gods (*kotoamatsukami*) remain alone, keeping to themselves. Next Kuni no Kototachi no Kami and then Toyokumono no Kami appear, and they too are alone. Then five pairs of deities appear. The final pair, Izanagi no Mikoto and Izanami no Mikoto (see IZANAGI AND IZANAMI), are commanded by the five primal gods to make the land and fix it in place. Receiving from them the Heavenly Jeweled Spear (Ame no Nuboko), Izanagi and Izanami stand upon the Floating Bridge of Heaven (Ame no Ukihashi) and thrust the spear into the sea. After churning and churning, they raise the spear. From its tip fall drops of brine that gather and grow to become the Self-Curdling Island (Onogorojima).

The two descend to the land. They see a good pillar and erect it. They also erect a great mansion. Izanagi asks Izanami, "How is your body formed?" and she says, "My body was formed, but there is a part that is not done forming." Izanagi responds, "My body was formed, but there is a part that was formed too much. I think I'll take this part that was formed too much and fill your part that is not done forming and make the land. What do you think?" She agrees and they circle the pillar, she to the right and he to the left. When they meet she cries, "Ah, my good man!" He replies that it is wrong for a woman to speak first. Nevertheless, they have intercourse and the infant Hiruko is born, but they send it away in a reed boat. The island Awashima is born, but neither it nor Hiruko is numbered among their children.

They return to Takamagahara and are told by the five primal gods that they should again circle the pillar and that when they meet Izanagi should speak first. This is done, and the gods that comprise the Land of the Eight Great Islands (Ōyashimaguni) are born, and, following them, the gods of the sea, river, mountain, field, tree, stone, and fire. Izanami is burned in giving birth to the fire god, but as she dies the gods of metal,

1027
mythology

earth, water, and youthful production are born of her vomit and excreta. Izanagi cuts off the head of the fire god, and from the blood that drips from his sword eight gods are born. From the fire god's body spring eight more.

Izanami has gone to Yomi no Kuni, the land of the dead, and Izanagi follows to urge her return. She agrees to consult with the gods of Yomi, but adjures him not to look at her as she does. Impatient for her return, he enters the palace of the gods of Yomi, only to see her corpse teeming with maggots. He flees, and she, having been shamed, sends the minions of Yomi after him. At the Level Slope of Yomi (Yomotsu Hirasaka) on the border of the region, he discovers three peaches, which he flings at his pursuers, dispersing them. Izanami herself then pursues him, but he blocks the entrance with a huge boulder, across which he announces their divorce. She declares that every day she will strangle 1,000 people in the land of the living, and he replies that he will each day erect 1,500 parturition huts, bringing about the birth of 1,500 children.

Defiled by his passage into Yomi, Izanagi goes to Tsukushi to purify himself by bathing (MISOGI). From each piece of clothing he casts off springs a god; from the filth washed from his body spring two polluting deities. Two purifying deities (see NAOBI NO KAMI) are generated and then 10 other deities, the last 3 of which are Amaterasu Ōmikami (goddess of the sun), born from his left eye when he cleanses it; Tsukuyomi no Mikoto (god of the moon), born from his right eye; and Susanoo no Mikoto (god of storms), born from his nose. Izanagi charges Amaterasu with the rule of the High Plain of Heaven, Tsukuyomi with the Realm of Night, and Susanoo with the Plain of the Seas. But Susanoo weeps copiously. When asked the reason for his tears, Susanoo replies that he wishes to see his mother. Angered, his father banishes him.

Susanoo ascends to the High Plain of Heaven to speak with Amaterasu; the mountains and rivers rumble, the lands tremble. Suspecting that he comes to usurp the heavens, Amaterasu strings her bow and girds herself for battle, but Susanoo swears that he has come only to tell her of his banishment and offers to make children with her. His sister produces three girls from his sword and he five boys from the jewels in her hair. Flushed with victory because the girls are fine maidens, he breaks through the berms between Amaterasu's rice paddies, fills in the irrigation ditches, and besmirches with excrement her Palace of First Fruits. These offenses she forgives, but he then breaks a hole in the roof of her weaving hall and casts in a heavenly dappled colt that he has flayed backward, tail to head.

Amaterasu is horrified and hides herself behind the Heavenly Cave Door (Ame no Iwaya To). Darkness descends upon Takamagahara and Ashihara no Nakatsukuni (the lands of Japan; elsewhere referred to as Utsushi no Kuni or the Revealed World), and the darkness persists. The gods assemble and are counseled by Omoikane no Kami, child of Takamimusubi no Kami, to bring from the mountain Amanokaguyama (see YAMATO SANZAN) a SAKAKI tree on which are hung 500 jewels, a great mirror, and sacred cloth. Ame no Uzume no Mikoto begins a thunderous dance on an overturned tub. Divinely possessed, she exposes her breasts

and lowers her skirt to her genitals, provoking uproarious laughter among the gods. Amaterasu opens the door of her cave a little and asks why Uzume dances and why the gods are laughing. Uzume replies that a god has come who is greater than Amaterasu, and the great mirror is shown to her. She opens the door further in order to see, and a god of great strength grasps her hand and pulls her out. Light returns to the two realms. Susanoo is made to submit vast quantities of goods in atonement (see HARAE), his hair is cut and his fingernails and toenails pulled off, and he is banished. Susanoo asks for food, which is brought forth from the nose, mouth, and fundament of Ōketsuhime no Kami. Susanoo takes the manner of his meal's production ill and slays Ōketsuhime. However, from the orifices of her body appear silkworms, rice, millet, red beans, wheat, and broad beans.

The Izumo Cycle — Susanoo descends to the mountain Torikamiyama in Izumo, where he comes upon an old couple weeping beside their daughter. The man says that he is a god of the land (kunitsukami) and that each year the eight-headed, eight-tailed serpent YAMATA NO OROCHI has devoured one of his daughters and that the time has come for him to claim the last. Susanoo transforms the girl, Kushinada Hime, into a comb, which he puts in his hair, and orders that a special wine be brewed and barrels of it placed along a fence with eight apertures. When the serpent drinks the potion and falls into a drunken sleep, Susanoo severs each of the heads with his sword. In one of the tails he discovers a sword, which he presents to Amaterasu. This is the sword that is later known as Kusanagi (Mower of Grass). It is given to Ninigi no Mikoto by Amaterasu as one of the three symbols of his authority over Ashihara no Nakatsukuni (see IMPERIAL REGALIA).

Ōkuninushi is a sixth-generation descendant of Susanoo and Kushinada Hime. He has many older brothers, all of whom wish to marry a maiden named Yagami Hime. They set off to win her, followed by Ōkuninushi, who is brought along to carry their baggage. The brothers torment a hare that has lost its pelt, but when Ōkuninushi arrives he helps it restore its fur, and the rabbit foresees that Ōkuninushi will win the girl. Indeed, she announces her decision to marry Ōkuninushi. Twice the brothers kill Ōkuninushi, but each time his mother brings him back to life. In the hope that his ancestor Susanoo can help him, he goes to the Netherworld (Ne no Katasu no Kuni), where he meets and falls in love with Susanoo's daughter Suseribime. Susanoo puts Ōkuninushi to a series of tests intended to cause his death, but the latter is saved each time by Suseribime. Eventually, while Susanoo sleeps, Ōkuninushi takes from him his great bow, his great sword, and the zither that he uses when enunciating oracles and flees with Suseribime. Susanoo pursues but fails to catch them. From the Level Slope of Yomi, Susanoo commands Ōkuninushi to use the sword, bow, and zither to become lord of the land. Ōkuninushi defeats his brothers and, with the tiny deity Sukunabikona no Kami, extends his mastery over the land. He makes Suseribime his principal wife, much to the displeasure of Yagami Hime.

Amaterasu determines that the lands of Ashihara no Nakatsukuni must now be ruled by her descendants and sends a series of emissaries to persuade Ōkuninushi to yield them. Ōkuninushi leaves the matter to two

of his sons, Kotoshironushi no Kami, who is for yielding, and Takemina no Kami, who is not. The two do battle, and Kotoshironushi is the victor. Ōkuninushi gives up the land.

The Tsukushi Cycle — Accompanied by eight gods and led by the kunitsukami Sarutabiko no Kami, Ninigi no Mikoto, the infant grandson of Amaterasu, descends with the imperial regalia to the mountain Takachihonomine in Tsukushi (Kyūshū). He builds a palace and takes as wife Konohanasakuya Hime, with whom he has three children, Hoderi no Mikoto, Hosuseri no Mikoto, and Hoori no Mikoto. Hoderi has the luck of the sea and Hoori the luck of the land. The latter suggests that they exchange their luck and his brother reluctantly agrees. Not only does Hoori catch no fish, he loses his brother's fishhook. Although Hoori breaks up his sword and makes 500 hooks, Hoderi remains adamant that the original hook be restored. As Hoori laments by the seashore, a deity appears and sends him to sea in a boat, which takes him to the palace of Wadatsumi (also called Watatsumi), the god of the sea. Hoori falls in love with the deity's daughter Toyotama Hime and lives happily with her for three years. One day Hoori tells Wadatsumi of his brother's fishhook, and the god succeeds in effecting its recovery. He gives Hoori, who desires to return to his own land, a tide-raising jewel and a tide-ebbing jewel with which Hoori is able to bring Hoderi into submission.

The sea deity's daughter comes to the shore to give birth. As she must revert to her original form to deliver, she warns Hoori not to look at her during delivery. Unable to restrain his curiosity, Hoori looks at her and discovers that she is a crocodile. Shamed, she abandons her child and returns to the sea, sending her younger sister to serve as wet nurse. When the child grows up he marries his aunt, and they have four children, the last of whom, Kamuyamato Iwarebiko no Mikoto, later becomes Emperor Jimmu.

JAPANESE MYTHOLOGY AND THE MYTHS OF OTHER CULTURES
Evidence of a multiplicity of influences upon the formation of Japanese myths is readily found in the numerous correspondences with myths of other cultures. In cosmogonic myths of northern Asia and North America, a creator, often assisted by another, dives for land in the primal ocean, and the helper of the earth-diver often becomes an archrival; the myth of Izanami and Izanagi can be seen as a variant of this type. However, the origin of death described in this myth appears to be a variant of the banana myth of Indonesia, in which an argument between a stone and a banana plant results in the establishment of the death and birth of human beings. The myth of the pillar or tree at the center of the world that connects heaven and earth is of nearly universal occurrence. The explanation of the origin of sex given in the Nihon shoki—a wagtail alights beside Izanami and Izanagi and wags its tail feathers up and down and they imitate it—has exact correspondents in myths of Okinawa and Taiwan. Correspondents can be found throughout the world of the myth of the fertility deity Ōketsuhime, who is killed by Susanoo and from whose body grain and beans are obtained. Similarly, the story of Susanoo, who vanquishes the serpent and wins the maiden, and the account of the trials of Ōkuninushi in the Netherworld have parallels in the myths and legends of many other cultures. See also FOLKTALES.

N

Nabari　名張[市]

City in western Mie Prefecture, central Honshū. During the Edo period (1600–1868) it developed as a castle town and post-station town on the route to the Ise Shrine. Farming and industry are active, but many of Nabari's residents commute to Ōsaka. Nearby attractions include the gorge called Kōchidani and the 48 Waterfalls of Akame. Pop: 68,933.

Nabeshima family　鍋島氏

(Nabeshimashi). Warrior family and *daimyō* of Saga in Hizen Province (now Saga and Nagasaki prefectures). Nabeshima Naoshige (1538–1618) was steward from 1584 for the RYŪZŌJI FAMILY, lords of Saga, and it was not until 1607 that his line was given formal title to the domain. Naoshige fought in TOYOTOMI HIDEYOSHI's Korean expeditions (see INVASIONS OF KOREA IN 1592 AND 1597) and brought back Korean potters as captives, thus laying the foundations for the pottery tradition known as NABESHIMA WARE. His son Katsushige (1580–1657) fought for the Toyotomi in the Battle of SEKIGAHARA (1600), but the Nabeshima soon afterward swore fealty to TOKUGAWA IEYASU, who confirmed them in their domains. Three collateral branches of the family were enfeoffed as lesser daimyō in Hizen; in 1648 the main branch was granted honorary use of the shogunal family name Matsudaira. In the late Edo period (1600–1868), NABESHIMA KANSŌ pioneered modern industries in Saga.

Nabeshima Kansō　鍋島閑叟

(1814–71). Also called Nabeshima Naomasa. *Daimyō* of the Saga domain (now Saga Prefecture). Kansō instituted land reforms, allowed capable lower *samurai* to fill positions of leadership, and took steps to stimulate commercial trade with other domains. The accumulated capital was used to modernize the domain's military and associated industries. He was a supporter of the MOVEMENT FOR UNION OF COURT AND SHOGUNATE. After the MEIJI RESTORATION of 1868, he served the new government briefly as a councillor (*gijō*) and as head of the Hokkaidō Colonization Office (KAITAKUSHI).

Nabeshima ware　鍋島焼

(*nabeshima-yaki*). Blue and white, celadon, and polychrome porcelain ware made in or near Arita, Hizen Province (now Saga Prefecture), Kyūshū, from 1628 to the present. From 1675 to 1871 production was under the patronage of the NABESHIMA FAMILY, lords of the Hizen domain; the finest work, of a technical perfection unrivaled by other Edo-period (1600–1868) porcelain, was done in the late 17th and early 18th centuries. Production was carefully supervised, technical secrets were carefully guarded, and defective pieces were destroyed. Nabeshima designs were outlined in soft, pale, dull underglaze blue or (if polychrome) finished in strong, transparent, thinly applied red, yellow, and bluish green overglaze enamels. After 1696 designs with a central white area derived from Imari porcelains (see ARITA WARE) became characteristic, the backs of dishes underglazed with blue decorative motifs of flowers, scrolls, or jewels. Starting with Soeda Kizaemon (d 1654), the kilns were managed for many generations by the Soeda family. Today Soeda Imaemon XIII (b 1926) carries on the family tradition.

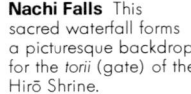

Nachi Falls This sacred waterfall forms a picturesque backdrop for the *torii* (gate) of the Hirō Shrine.

Nachi Falls　那智滝

(Nachi no Taki). Located on the upper reaches of the river Nachigawa, southeastern Wakayama Prefecture, central Honshū. This sacred falls of the Kumano Nachi Shrine is located within Yoshino-Kumano National Park. Height: 133 m (436 ft).

Nachi-Fujikoshi Corporation　[株]不二越

(Fujikoshi). Manufacturer of tools, bearings, machine tools, hydraulic equipment, industrial robots, and specialty steels. Incorporated in 1928, it is the largest producer of cutting tools in Japan. The company's overseas operations consist of seven manufacturing plants, nine sales companies, and a laboratory, which support international business and technical services. Sales for the fiscal year ending November 1990 totaled ¥160.3 billion (US $1.2 billion); capitalization stood at ¥13.3 billion (US $103.0 million). Headquarters are in Toyama, Toyama Prefecture.

Nachi-Katsuura　那智勝浦[町]

Town in southeastern Wakayama Prefecture, central Honshū, on the Kumano Sea. Formed in 1951 by the merger of the towns of Nachi and Katsuura. Katsuura has the prefecture's largest fishing port. Hot springs on the coast, the Kumano Nachi Shrine (one of the KUMANO SANZAN SHRINES), and NACHI FALLS attract visitors. Pop: 20,610.

Nachisan　那智山

Mountain group in southeastern Wakayama Prefecture, central Honshū. It includes Ōkumodorisan (966 m; 3,169 ft), Eboshiyama (909 m; 2,982 ft), and Myōhōsan (749 m; 2,457 ft). The area has many shrines and temples. The NACHI FALLS, in the headwaters of the river Nachigawa, is one of Japan's highest (133 m; 436 ft).

Nada　灘

District in the city of Kōbe, Hyōgo Prefecture, western Honshū, along the northern part of Ōsaka Bay. The name Nada is associated with fine-quality *sake*. The coastal

Nagai Kafū This writer, a master stylist, is known for the nostalgic, evocative beauty of his depictions of a fading urban past.

part of the district is industrializing rapidly, and its interior is an affluent residential area.

Naebasan 苗場山

Also called Naebayama. Shield volcano in the Nasu Volcanic Zone, on the border between Niigata and Nagano prefectures, central Honshū. On the summit is Ime Shrine. It is a well-known ski area. Height: 2,145 m (7,037 ft).

Nagahama 長浜[市]

City in northeastern Shiga Prefecture, central Honshū, situated on Lake Biwa. Nagahama had its origins in 1573, when TOYOTOMI HIDEYOSHI built a castle here. From the Edo period (1600–1868) it prospered as the temple town of Daitsūji and as a port. After World War II, machine and resin industries were introduced. The remains of Nagahama Castle and the site of the Battle of ANEGAWA are of interest. Pop: 55,485.

Nagai 長井[市]

City in southern Yamagata Prefecture, northern Honshū. It produces capacitors, knitted goods, and Nagai *tsumugi* (pongee). Rice is the main agricultural product. There are several parks noted for their flowers; the autumn foliage along the gorge of the river Nogawa also attracts visitors. Pop: 33,260.

Nagai Kafū 永井荷風

(1879–1959). Novelist and essayist, noted for his lyrical portrayals of the rapidly vanishing remnants of late-Edo-period (1600–1868) and Meiji-period (1868–1912) urban culture. Real name Nagai Sōkichi. Born in Tōkyō, the eldest son of a high-ranking bureaucrat. He was taught classical Chinese as a child but felt drawn to the world of Edo-period literature and arts under the influence of his mother. Although he entered the Chinese Language Department of the Tōkyō School of Foreign Languages (now Tōkyō University of Foreign Studies), he rarely attended classes and eventually left school. By then he had become immersed in the lifestyle of a typical urban dilettante, frequenting the pleasure quarters, the KABUKI theater, and other popular entertainments. He took SHAKUHACHI (flute) and SHAMISEN (lute) lessons, was for a short time the pupil of a RAKUGO (storyteller) performer, and worked briefly as an apprentice kabuki playwright.

In September 1898 he took a short story to the then-popular writer HIROTSU RYŪRŌ and was accepted as a protégé. Like many aspiring writers at that time, he had exposed himself to Western literature, both in Japanese and English translation, and was strongly attracted to French literature. He became one of the leading advocates of Zola and "naturalism," a phase in his life that he later renounced, but that nonetheless left a deep imprint on his entire career.

Kafū's father sent him to the United States in 1903, and he spent four years there, first in Tacoma, Washington, and then at

Kalamazoo College in Michigan. Later he became a clerk in a Japanese bank in New York City. In July 1907, he was transferred to the bank's branch in Lyons, France. He left this job after eight months and spent two months in Paris before returning to Japan. He was never to go overseas again. His collection of short stories and essays written in the United States was published under the title *Amerika monogatari* (1908, American Stories). Its highly lyrical and vivid style caught the imagination of the Japanese reading public, and he became a popular writer, producing short novels, stories, and essays in quick succession. Some of them, most notably *Furansu monogatari* (1909, French Stories) and *Kanraku* (1909; tr *Pleasure*, 1961), were banned by the government, allegedly because they contained highly critical and irreverent comments on Japanese society and its moral codes.

In 1910 he was appointed professor of literature at Keiō Gijuku (later Keiō University), where he founded and edited the literary journal MITA BUNGAKU. Two years later he married Saitō Yone, primarily to please his parents, but divorced her in less than five months, shortly after his father's death. He then married his mistress, Uchida Yae, a former *geisha*, who, however, soon left him because of his frequent affairs with other women. In 1916, he quit both his teaching and editing positions.

Later Works—Subsequently, he published several novels, stories, and essays, including *Udekurabe* (1916–17; tr *Geisha in Rivalry*, 1963), *Okamezasa* (1918, Dwarf Bamboo), and *Ame shōshō* (1922; tr *Quiet Rain*, 1964), all of which dealt with various aspects of life in the Tōkyō demimonde. After a decade of relative inactivity, Kafū's *Tsuyu no atosaki* (1931, During the Rainy Season) heralded his return to the literary scene. This work was followed by BOKUTŌ KIDAN (1937; tr *A Strange Tale from East of the River*, 1958), which is widely regarded as his masterpiece. Although quite popular after World War II, he never regained his previous level of creativity.

Kafū was one of the first modern Japanese writers who, upon direct contact with the Western world, managed to create a literature that was rooted in tradition (in his case primarily that of the late Edo period) and at the same time marked by universalism. His grasp of Western literature was limited but this was compensated for by an unusual sensibility. His principal theme was the ever-changing city of Tōkyō and its pleasure quarters. While he is frequently condemned as a writer who felt nostalgia for a past that he misrepresented, he managed to preserve in his works many aspects of Tōkyō life that disappeared after the Tōkyō Earthquake of 1923, the wartime destruction, and the postwar rebuilding. Critics who confuse the artist's life with his works tend to label Kafū's writings as dilettantish, if not downright insincere, but there have been few modern Japanese writers who tried harder, with occasional success, to create a world of fiction that was neither provincial nor superficially Westernized. He received the Order of Culture in 1952.

Nagai Nagayoshi 長井長義

(1845–1929). Organic chemist and pharmacologist. Born in Awa Province (now Tokushima Prefecture); graduate of the Daigaku Nankō (now Tōkyō University). One of the first doctors of pharmacy in Japan. Nagai went to Europe as a government scholar and served as an assistant to Professor August Wilhelm von Hofmann of the University of Berlin. He studied the chemical compositions of various Japanese and Chinese herbal remedies and, most notably, isolated the alkaloid ephedrine from *maō* (*Ephedra sinica*). He served as a professor at Tōkyō University.

Nagai Ryūtarō 永井柳太郎

(1881–1944). Politician, educator, and journalist. Born in Ishikawa Prefecture. Graduated from Waseda University in 1905. He attended Manchester College, Oxford University, from 1906 to 1909. Upon his return from England, he taught social and colonial policy at Waseda and edited *Shin Nippon* (New Japan), a leading liberal journal of the day. In 1917 Nagai left Waseda to launch a career in politics. In 1920 he was elected to a seat in the lower house of the Diet, which he retained until his death. He soon became one of the most conspicuous "democrats" of the era of TAISHŌ DEMOCRACY.

With his progressive stance and eloquence, Nagai rose to fame in the 1920s as a "champion of the masses" and by 1931 had become a leader of the RIKKEN MINSEITŌ. But by the late 1920s, he had become disillusioned with the established parties as well as with Japan's cooperative stance toward the Anglo-American bloc, and his politics began to swerve to the right. During the 1930s he served at the ministerial level in several nonparty cabinets, including an appointment as minister of communications in the first KONOE FUMIMARO cabinet. He was active in both Konoe's NEW ORDER MOVEMENT and the IMPERIAL RULE ASSISTANCE ASSOCIATION and during World War II served as an official in the Greater East Asia Ministry. He died shortly before Japan's defeat.

Nagai Tatsuo 永井龍男

(1904–90). Author. Born in Tōkyō. His first literary success came when his short story "Kappan'ya no hanashi" (1920, Tale of a Printer's Shop) was praised by the well-known author KIKUCHI KAN. After 1927 he served as an editor of Kikuchi's literary magazine *Bungei shunjū*, going to Manchuria in 1942 to open a branch office and returning in 1944 to the Tōkyō home office as executive director. His most active period as a writer came after his release in 1947 from restrictions imposed under the US OCCUPATION PURGE for his role as a journalist during World War II. "Asagiri" (1949; tr "Morning Mist," 1962) and other short stories exhibit a *haiku*-like clarity and lightness. His 1965 story collection *Ikko sono ta* (One and Others) received both the Noma Literary Prize and the Japan Art Academy Literary Prize that year. He was elected to the Japan Academy in 1968 and was awarded the Order of Culture in 1981. Other major works include the story "Kuroi gohan" (1923, Black Rice) and the novel *Kaze futatabi* (1951, The Wind Again).

Nagai Uta 長井雅楽

(1819–63). Official of the Chōshū domain (now Yamaguchi Prefecture). In 1861 he recommended that Chōshū accept the controversial ANSEI COMMERCIAL TREATIES and work as a mediator to resolve the differences that had sprung up between the imperial court and the shogunate over the treaty issue; this marked Chōshū's entrance into the arena of national politics. However, in 1862 the Chōshū domain suddenly adopted the antiforeign imperial-loyalist position advocated by

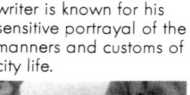

Nagai Tatsuo This writer is known for his sensitive portrayal of the manners and customs of city life.

KUSAKA GENZUI and other radicals. This undercut Nagai's efforts, and the court soon approved an alternative plan from the Satsuma domain (now Kagoshima Prefecture). Nagai abandoned his attempts at mediation and returned to Chōshū; the next year he was ordered to commit suicide to atone for Chōshū's loss of national influence.

Nagaizumi 長泉[町]

Town in the northern part of the Izu Peninsula, eastern Shizuoka Prefecture, central Honshū. The town is rapidly becoming industrialized, and chemical fiber mills and machinery factories have been established here. Nagaizumi is a commuter suburb of the cities of Numazu and Mishima. Pop: 33,101.

Nagako, Empress Dowager

良子皇太后

(1903– ; Nagako Kōtaigō). Consort of Emperor SHŌWA. Eldest daughter of Kuni no Miya Kuniyoshi (Prince Kuni) and Princess Chikako. Educated at the Gakushūin Girls' School, she married Crown Prince Hirohito (later Emperor Shōwa) in January 1924 and became empress upon his ascension to the throne in December 1926. Together they had seven children, including Emperor AKIHITO. She is known for her Japanese-style paintings, done under the name Tōen. Two collections of her work have been published: *Tōen gashū* (1967) and *Kimpōshū* (1969). She became empress dowager on 7 January 1989 upon the death of Emperor Shōwa.

Nagakubo Sekisui 長久保赤水

(1717–1801). Geographer and cartographer whose *Nihon yochi rotei zenzu* (completed 1775, revised 1779) was the first Japanese-published map of Japan to incorporate the Western system of longitudinal-latitudinal notation. Nagakubo was born in Hitachi Province (now Ibaraki Prefecture). He was a Confucian scholar and geographer, and he also helped in the compilation of the DAI NIHON SHI.

nagamochi 長持

An oblong, legless wooden chest used for storing clothing and household utensils. Until the early 20th century, the *nagamochi* was an indispensable part of a bride's dowry; it was slung from a long pole resting on the shoulders of two bearers and carried in the bridal procession. The number of *nagamochi* a bride brought with her reflected the wealth of her family. Bearers traditionally sang a wedding song known as *nagamochi uta*.

Nagano 長野[市]

Capital of Nagano Prefecture, central Honshū. Nagano was established in the Kamakura period (1185–1333) as the temple town (MONZEN MACHI) of ZENKŌJI, an early 7th-century temple. During the Edo period (1600–1868) it developed as a market and one of the post-station towns on the highway Hokkoku Kaidō. Today it is a commercial center with electrical-machinery, foodstuff, publishing, and printing industries. Nagano is known for its apples and Chinese yams. Shinshū University is located here. Zenkōji attracts more than 4 million visitors yearly; other attractions are the site of the Battles of KAWANAKAJIMA and the former castle town of MATSUSHIRO. It is the gateway to the western part of the JŌSHIN'ETSU KŌGEN NATIONAL PARK. The 18th Winter Olympic Games are scheduled to be held in Nagano in 1998. Pop: 347,026.

Nagano Basin 長野盆地

(Nagano Bonchi). Also known as the Zenkōjidaira. In northern Nagano Prefecture, central Honshū. Consisting mainly of alluvial fans below the fault scarp and the floodplain of the river Chikumagawa, this long, narrow basin is known for the cultivation of rice, apples, and apricots. It is the political and commercial center of Nagano Prefecture. The major city is Nagano. Area: approximately 270 sq km (105 sq mi).

Nagano Osami 永野修身

(1880–1947). Fleet admiral. Born in Kōchi Prefecture. Nagano graduated from the Naval Academy in 1900 and from the Naval War College in 1910. He became vice-chief of the Naval General Staff Office in 1930. Promoted to admiral in 1934, he represented Japan at the second of the LONDON NAVAL CONFERENCES in 1935. He was named navy minister in 1936, commander in chief of the Combined Fleet in 1937, and chief of the Naval General Staff Office in 1941. At the onset of World War II, he was head of the Supreme Command of the Imperial Japanese Navy and an advocate of war with the United States. He became a fleet admiral in 1943. Charged as a class A war criminal at the WAR CRIMES TRIALS, he died in prison.

Nagano Prefecture 長野県

(Nagano Ken). Located in central Honshū and bordered by the prefectures of Niigata, Gumma, Saitama, Yamanashi, Shizuoka, Aichi, Gifu, and Toyama. The terrain is largely mountainous, and major ranges include the Hida, Kiso, and Akaishi (see JAPANESE ALPS), as well as the Mikuni Mountains. Numerous rivers, including the CHIKUMAGAWA, Himekawa, KISOGAWA, and TENRYŪGAWA, flow between the mountains. Because of its mountainous terrain and distance from the sea, the climate is generally cooler and drier than that of surrounding prefectures. The extreme northern and southern areas, however, receive more precipitation.

Known after the TAIKA REFORM of 645 as Shinano Province, the Nagano area was crossed by several major highways linking eastern and western Japan, including the NAKASENDŌ, which was then called the Tōsandō. The area came under the rule of contending warlords such as the Uesugi and Takeda during the ascendancy of warrior rule and was divided into small domains during the Edo period (1600–1868). The present name dates from 1871, and the present boundaries were established in 1876.

Agriculture is a major occupation, rice being the main crop. Dairy cattle are also bred there. The silk industry flourished before World War II, but more recently the precision-machinery industry has become highly developed. Other industries include machinery, metals, food processing, and woodworking.

Nagano's mountains, lakes, and hot springs make it a favorite tourist area. Parts of the four national parks of Jōshin'etsu Kōgen, Chichibu-Tama, Chūbu Sangaku, and the Southern Alps are located in the prefecture, and it also has three quasi-national parks. Area: 13,585 sq km (5,245 sq mi); pop: 2,156,627; capital: NAGANO. Other major cities include MATSUMOTO, UEDA, and IIDA.

Nagano Shigeo 永野重雄

(1900–1984). Businessman. Born in Shimane Prefecture, he graduated from Tōkyō University. In 1925 he became manager of a bankrupt firm, Fuji Iron, which he revitalized and which subsequently merged into the Nippon Steel Co. Nippon Steel split in 1950 into the Yawata and Fuji steel concerns, then the companies merged in 1970 as the NIPPON STEEL CORPORATION, of which Nagano became chairman. After World War II, he served as vice-director of the ECONOMIC STABILIZATION BOARD. An important leader of the business-industrial community, Nagano became chairman of the JAPAN CHAMBER OF COMMERCE AND INDUSTRY in 1969. Together with KOBAYASHI ATARU, SAKURADA TAKESHI, and MIZUNO SHIGEO, he was recognized as one of the major powers in the postwar Japanese political and economic world.

Nagano Takeshi 永野健

(1923–). Business leader. Born in Hiroshima. Graduated from Tōkyō University. Upon graduation in 1945 he joined the predecessor company to Mitsubishi Metal Corporation. In 1982 he became president of Mitsubishi Metal. During his term as president he orchestrated the merger of the company with Mitsubishi Mining & Cement Co. The new company began operations in December 1990 as MITSUBISHI MATERIALS CORPORATION, with Nagano as chairman. In May 1991 he became chairman of NIKKEIREN (Japan Federation of Employers' Associations).

Naganuma case 長沼訴訟

(Naganuma *soshō*). Controversial legal case in postwar Japan, centering on the question of the constitutionality of the SELF DEFENSE FORCES (SDF), established in 1954. The suit, initiated in July 1969, alleged that the SDF violated article 9 of the 1947 constitution of Japan, which contains an explicit RENUNCIATION OF WAR and prohibits the maintenance of military forces. The Naganuma case arose when the SDF began construction of a Nike antiaircraft missile launching site in the town of Naganuma in Hokkaidō. Some 270 residents filed suit to halt construction on the grounds that the very existence of the SDF was unconstitutional.

In 1973 the Sapporo District Court agreed that the SDF was unconstitutional and barred construction. In 1976 the Sapporo High Court reversed the decision on appeal. The reversal was upheld by the Supreme Court in 1982. See also SUNAGAWA CASE; NATIONAL POLICE RESERVE CASE; CONSTITUTION, DISPUTE OVER REVISION OF.

Nagaoka 長岡[市]

City in central Niigata Prefecture, central Honshū. Located on the river Shinanogawa, Nagaoka developed as a port and castle town in the Edo period (1600–1868). With the opening of the oil fields here, machine and chemical industries developed. In 1983 it was designated for development as a TECHNOPOLIS (planned industrial, academic, and residential complex). The fireworks display at the Nagaoka festival (early August) attracts visitors. Pop: 185,938.

nagamochi Although rare today, the custom of carrying *nagamochi* in a bridal procession is occasionally practiced in rural areas, as here in Iwate Prefecture.

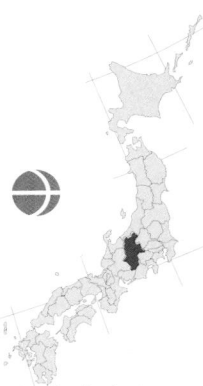

Nagano Prefecture Location and Prefectural Crest

Nagaoka Hantarō　　　長岡半太郎

(1865–1950). Japan's most eminent physicist before the age of quantum mechanics. Born in Nagasaki; a graduate of Tōkyō University. His research included work in the fields of electromagnetism, spectroscopy, and geophysics. He is known especially for his theory of atomic models, advanced in 1903. Nagaoka taught at Tōkyō University, became the first president of Ōsaka University in 1931, and served as president of the Japan Academy from 1939 to 1948. He was awarded the Order of Culture in 1937, the year of its inception.

Nagaokakyō　　　長岡京[市]

City in southern Kyōto Prefecture, central Honshū. The site of NAGAOKAKYŌ, the imperial capital from 784 to 794. Located between the cities of Ōsaka and Kyōto, it is undergoing rapid urbanization. Principal industries are machinery and electrical apppliances. There are excavated remains of the ancient capital and Kōmyōji, a temple as-

sociated with HŌNEN, the founder of the Jōdo Buddhist sect. Pop: 77,191.

Nagaokakyō　　　長岡京

Imperial capital from 784 to 794. In 784 the emperor KAMMU decided to move the capital from HEIJŌKYŌ (now Nara) to Nagaokakyō (now in Kyōto Prefecture). The new site, proposed by Fujiwara no Tanetsugu, was more convenient for transportation. After several misfortunes took place, including the assassination of Tanetsugu by jealous rivals in 785, it was decided to move the capital to HEIANKYŌ (now Kyōto) in 794. Excavations in Nagaokakyō since 1955 have yielded the remains of several government buildings.

Nagaoka Shūsei　　　長岡秀星

(1936–　　). Illustrator. Real name Nagaoka Shūzō. Born in Nagasaki Prefecture. Attended Musashino Art University. In 1970, after serving as chief of design for the Sumitomo Pavilion at Expo '70 in Ōsaka, Nagaoka moved to Los Angeles to pursue a career as a graphic designer and mechanical illustrator. He is known for scientific and space illustrations characterized by precise rendering and a surrealistic use of color. He currently lives and works in the United States.

Nagaragawa　　　長良川

River in central Gifu Prefecture, central Honshū. It originates in the mountain Dainichidake in the northwestern part of the prefecture, flows through the Nōbi Plain past the cities of Mino and Gifu, and enters Ise Bay. Together with the IBIGAWA and KISOGAWA, it is known for numerous floods. Numerous WAJŪ (farming settlements protected by circular embankments) are found along the lower reaches. The water is used for irrigation. CORMORANT FISHING (*ukai*), a popular tourist attraction, takes place from May to October. Length: about 140 km (87 mi).

Nagareyama　　　流山[市]

City in northwestern Chiba Prefecture, central Honshū, on the river EDOGAWA. *Mirin* (a sweet *sake*) is its main product. The construction of large housing complexes has made it a suburb of Tōkyō. Pop: 140,059.

Nagasaki　　　長崎[市]

Capital of Nagasaki Prefecture, Kyūshū. Its importance as a port dates from 1571, when it was opened to foreign trade at the request of the Portuguese. During the 200-year-long period of NATIONAL SECLUSION, the island of DEJIMA, constructed in Nagasaki Bay in 1634–36, was the only port opened to foreign trade (see NAGASAKI TRADE). In 1855–61, Japan's first modern shipbuilding yard, the NAGASAKI SHIPYARDS, was constructed here. On 9 August 1945 an ATOMIC BOMB was dropped on Nagasaki; destruction was almost total. The city has recovered since then as a center of shipbuilding and other industries. The port also serves as a base for deep-sea fishing. The Urakami district, where Christianity was secretly practiced in defiance of the Tokugawa shogunate's bans (see KAKURE KIRISHITAN), is the site of the Urakami Catholic Church, Peace Park, International Cultural Hall, and Nagasaki University. The Ōura district contains the Glover Mansion, the residence of the English merchant Thomas Blake GLOVER. Area: 241.8 sq km (93.4 sq mi); pop: 444,599.

Nagasakibana　　　長崎鼻

Cape on southern Satsuma Peninsula, Kagoshima Prefecture, Kyūshū; part of Kirishima-Yaku National Park. Composed of volcanic rock. It offers a view of the mountain Kaimondake and the islands dotting the sea to the south. The Ryūgū Shrine is located here.

Nagasaki Flag Incident　　　長崎国旗事件

(Nagasaki Kokki Jiken). One of the most serious diplomatic issues between Japan and the People's Republic of China in the period before Japan's formal recognition of the latter. On 2 May 1958 a Japanese man took down the national flag of the People's Republic of China at an exhibition of Chinese postage stamps and paper cuttings sponsored by the Japan-China Friendship Association (Nitchū Yūkō Kyōkai) at the Hamaya department store in Nagasaki. The culprit was arrested but was soon released. Shortly before this incident, the Japanese government had stated that since Japan had no formal diplomatic relations with the People's Republic, the Chinese flag was not protected by Japanese law. The incident underlined the fact that Japan had not yet officially recognized the People's Republic of China. After the Nagasaki incident, the People's Republic broke off trade negotiations as well as cultural and friendship exchanges, and it was more than two years before another trade delegation came to Japan.

Nagasaki Holland Village–Huis Ten Bosch　　　長崎オランダ村ハウステンボス

(Nagasaki Oranda Mura–Hausu Ten Bosu). A replica of an old Dutch town, opened in 1992 in the city of Sasebo, Nagasaki Prefecture. Operated by the Nagasaki Holland Village Co, Ltd, the 152-hectare (376-acre) town commemorates the early days of Japanese-Dutch relations with examples of row houses, a 6-kilometer (3.7-mi) canal, and a replica of a Dutch ship. Other features include such symbols of the Netherlands as tulip gardens and windmills as well as a folk

art museum, an amusement park, and an assortment of street entertainers from around the world.

Nagasaki Kaisho 長崎会所

(Nagasaki Meeting Place). Semiofficial merchant organization that monopolized overseas trade during the Edo period (1600–1868) when foreign trade was limited to the port of Nagasaki under the NATIONAL SECLUSION policy of the Tokugawa shogunate. Formed in 1604 by merchants who were granted monopoly rights in the raw-silk trade (see ITOWAPPU), it was later enlarged. It was known first as the Shōnin Kaisho, then as the Gokasho Shōnin Kaisho, and from 1698 as the Nagasaki Kaisho. By that year it not only controlled all goods brought by Chinese and Dutch traders—the only foreigners allowed to enter Japan—but also supervised the flow of gold and silver in foreign exchange and the financial administration of Nagasaki. In return for its privileges, the organization paid taxes (UNJŌ) to the shogunate and donated part of its profits to the residents of Nagasaki. Although it was nominally under the jurisdiction of the city commissioners (*machi bugyō*) of Nagasaki, the Kaisho operated as a self-governing organ until it was dissolved in 1867. See also NAGASAKI TRADE.

Nagasaki Prefecture 長崎県

(Nagasaki Ken). Located in northwestern Kyūshū and bounded on the north by the Genkai Sea and Tsushima Strait, on the east by Saga Prefecture and the Ariake Sea, on the south by the Amakusa Sea, and on the west by the East China Sea. The prefecture is composed of four hilly peninsulas (Kita Matsuura, Nishi Sonogi, Nagasaki, and Shimabara) and many offshore islands that include TSUSHIMA, HIRADOSHIMA, and the Iki and Gotō groups. The climate is generally mild because of the prefecture's southerly location and warm ocean currents.

Because of its proximity to the Asian mainland, the Nagasaki area has long served as one of Japan's most important contact points with foreign cultures. After the TAIKA REFORM of 645 the islands of Iki and Tsushima were made into island provinces, and the peninsular area was part of Hizen Province. Following St. Francis XAVIER's arrival at the port of Hirado in 1550, the area was visited by numerous European missionaries and traders. A major uprising occurred on the Shimabara Peninsula in 1637 (see SHIMABARA UPRISING) following the suppression of Christianity by the Tokugawa shogunate. For most of the Edo period (1600–1868) the city of NAGASAKI was the only port open to foreign commerce. The present boundaries were established in 1883 after the Meiji Restoration. In 1945 Nagasaki was the second city, after Hiroshima, to suffer an atomic bomb attack.

The main agricultural products of the prefecture are potatoes and sweet potatoes. Cattle are bred on Hiradoshima and the Gotō Islands. In fishing it is second only to Hokkaidō. Pearl and seaweed culture is also carried out. Coal began to be mined in the 18th century and flourished in the Meiji period (1868–1912), but most of the mines have been shut down. Manufactured products include machinery, transportation equipment, and processed foods.

Tourist attractions include Unzen-Amakusa and Saikai national parks; the remains of the Dutch trading post on the island of Dejima; and the Chinese temple Sōfuku-ji, in the city of Nagasaki. There are also sites associated with Christianity, such as the ruins of Hara Castle, the scene of the Shimabara Uprising. Area: 4,113 sq km (1,588 sq mi); pop: 1,562,959; capital: Nagasaki. Other major cities include SASEBO, ISAHAYA, and ŌMURA.

Nagasaki school 長崎派

(Nagasakiha). School of artists active in Nagasaki from the 17th through the 19th century. Nagasaki was the only port open to foreigners during most of the Edo period (1600–1868). Consequently, Nagasaki artists tended to concentrate on foreign subjects, such as the Dutch and Chinese residents of the city, sometimes borrowing technical and stylistic innovations from European or Chinese painting. Their art may be divided into four main categories: woodblock prints created for the local tourist trade; official pictures painted by government artists to illustrate foreign objects imported into Japan; BIRD-AND-FLOWER PAINTING inspired by the Chinese artist SHEN NANPIN (Shen Nan-p'in; J: Chin Nampin), who taught in Nagasaki from 1731 to 1733; and works by individualist artists, often with Western techniques of shading and perspective. In addition, other types of art prevalent in Nagasaki included ŌBAKU SECT Zen paintings, *kanga* (Chinese painting), and BUNJINGA (literati painting). By the end of the Edo period, international treaties between Japan and the United States (1854), Britain (1854), and Russia (1855) opened other ports to foreign trade, and Nagasaki lost its prominence. The mystique of the foreigner, which had nurtured and sustained the tradition of the Nagasaki school, faded with the greater visibility of foreigners. See also WESTERN-STYLE PICTURES, EARLY.

Nagasaki Shipyards 長崎造船所

(Nagasaki Zōsenjo). Shipyard in the city of Nagasaki, Kyūshū. Built in 1855–61 by the Tokugawa shogunate (1603–1867) with Dutch help, it was taken over by the Meiji government (see GOVERNMENT-OPERATED FACTORIES, MEIJI PERIOD). The shipyard was leased to IWASAKI YATARŌ in 1884 and sold to his firm, the Mitsubishi Trading Co, in 1887 (see KAN'EI JIGYŌ HARAISAGE). Renamed the Mitsubishi Nagasaki Zōsenjo in 1893, it is now part of MITSUBISHI HEAVY INDUSTRIES, LTD.

Nagasaki trade 長崎貿易

(Nagasaki *bōeki*). Overseas trade centered in the port of Nagasaki from the first arrival of Portuguese ships in 1571 until the opening of Japan late in the Edo period (1600–1868). In a narrower sense the term refers to foreign trade after Japan was closed in 1639 by the NATIONAL SECLUSION policy of the Tokugawa shogunate. This policy permitted only the Chinese and the Dutch to trade at DEJIMA, an artificial island in Nagasaki Harbor (see also DUTCH FACTORY; DUTCH TRADE). The shogunate also kept the city under its direct control and stationed a commissioner (Nagasaki *bugyō*) there to oversee the trade. For the next 200 years the administration of commerce was left largely to the NAGASAKI KAISHO, a semiofficial merchant organization that enjoyed exclusive rights to the Chinese raw-silk trade (see ITOWAPPU). Besides raw silk, the principal imports were silk fabric, herbs, sugar, and spices; exports included silver, copper, camphor, sulfur, and swords. With the signing of the ANSEI COMMERCIAL TREATIES in 1858 and the rescinding of the seclusion policy, Nagasaki lost its position as Japan's only international seaport.

Nagasaki University 長崎大学

(Nagasaki Daigaku). A coeducational national university located in the city of Nagasaki, Nagasaki Prefecture. Founded in 1949, the university maintains faculties of education, economics, medicine, dentistry, pharmaceutical sciences, engineering, and fisheries. Nagasaki University also has an institute for tropical medicine and an atomic disease institute. Enrollment in 1989 was 6,661.

Nagasakiya Co, Ltd [株]長崎屋

(Nagasakiya). Chain store operator concentrating on retail sales of clothing, foods, and household goods. Incorporated in 1948. The company has chain stores nationwide and is enlarging its network of convenience stores in Tōkyō, Sendai, and Sapporo. The company also supplies clothing and other merchandise to a franchised regional supermarket chain. Sales for the fiscal year ending February 1991 totaled ¥409.2 billion (US $3.1 billion), and capitalization was ¥10.8 billion (US $82.8 million). Headquarters are in Tōkyō.

Nagasawa, Kanaye 長沢鼎

(1853–1934). California winemaker. Real name Isonaga Hikosuke. His career illustrates the Westernization of a *samurai* from the Satsuma domain (now Kagoshima Prefecture) late in the Edo period (1600–1868). He was born in Kagoshima, the son of Isonaga Magoshirō, superintendent of a gunpowder factory. Renamed Nagasawa, he arrived in Great Britain in 1865, attended two years of school in Aberdeen, Scotland, and went to London. Through Laurence OLIPHANT, Nagasawa met Thomas Lake HARRIS, an American mystic who invited him to the state of New York in 1867. As Harris's secretary, he rose to prominence in the Brotherhood of the New Life, Harris's utopian community. Nagasawa became manager of 2,000 acres near Santa Rosa when the group moved to California in 1875. Eventually inheriting the estate as sole owner, Nagasawa continued to run the community's winemaking ventures.

Nagasawa Rosetsu → Rosetsu

Nagase & Co, Ltd 長瀬産業[株]

(Nagase Sangyō). Trading firm specializing in chemical products. Incorporated in 1917. It

Nagasaki Prefecture Location and Prefectural Crest

naginata During the Edo period (1600–1868) *samurai* women as well as men were trained in the use of this weapon. The modern art of *naginata* is primarily a women's sport, with tournaments such as that shown here.

Nagashima Shigeo Superior batting by "Mr. Giants," as this baseball player is known to his fans, helped the Yomiuri Giants to nine successive championships, from 1965 to 1973.

Nagatsuka Takashi Known as well for his *tanka* poems, Nagatsuka wrote the novel *Tsuchi* (1910, The Earth), a masterpiece of "agrarian literature."

has tie-up arrangements with General Electric Co of the United States and CIBA-Geigy A.G. of Switzerland. It maintains three offices and eight local companies overseas. Sales for the fiscal year ending March 1991 totaled ¥543.4 billion (US $4.0 billion), and the company was capitalized at ¥9.7 billion (US $70.7 million). Headquarters are in Ōsaka and Tōkyō.

Nagashima Shigeo   長嶋茂雄

(1936–). Professional baseball player. Born in Chiba Prefecture. While playing for Rikkyō University, he twice posted the highest batting average in the Tōkyō Big Six University Baseball League. Joining the Yomiuri Giants in 1958, he won the Rookie of the Year Award, leading the league in home runs and batting average. Known thereafter as "Mr. Giants," Nagashima and teammate Ō SADAHARU led the Giants to nine successive championships (1965–73) before Nagashima retired as a player in 1974. He then managed the Giants from 1975 to 1980 and has been active as a commentator.

Nagashino, Battle of   長篠の戦い

(Nagashino no Tatakai). One of the decisive military encounters in the process of Japan's reunification in the late 16th century. On 29 June 1575 the forces of ODA NOBUNAGA and TOKUGAWA IEYASU routed TAKEDA KATSUYORI, *daimyō* of Kai, Shinano, and Suruga provinces (now Yamanashi, Nagano, and part of Shizuoka prefectures), who had laid siege to Ieyasu's fort at Nagashino in Mikawa Province (now Hōrai Chō, Aichi Prefecture). Katsuyori's defeat removed a threat from Nobunaga's eastern flank, freed him to mount a campaign against the adherents of the Buddhist JŌDO SHIN SECT (see IKKŌ IKKI) in Echizen (now part of Fukui Prefecture) three months later, and helped him consolidate control over central Japan. Nobunaga's victory was due in great part to 3,000 musketeers (*teppō ashigaru*) who inflicted severe damage on Katsuyori's mounted knights, indicating a shift from medieval to modern warfare (see FIREARMS, INTRODUCTION OF).

Nagasue Eiichi   永末英一

(1918–). Politician. Born in Fukuoka Prefecture, Nagasue graduated from Tōkyō University. He was first elected to the House of Councillors in 1959 as a Japan Socialist Party (JSP) candidate. In 1963 he was elected to the House of Representatives as a candidate from the DEMOCRATIC SOCIALIST PARTY (DSP), formerly a faction of the JSP. In February 1989 he succeeded TSUKAMOTO SABURŌ as chairman of the DSP. He resigned in April 1990, accepting responsibility for the party's defeat in the House of Representatives that February.

Nagata Masaichi   永田雅一

(1906–85). Film producer and owner of a professional baseball team. Born in Kyōto.

Nagata began to work for the Kyōto film studio Nikkatsu Productions (see NIKKATSU CORPORATION) in 1925. He produced several masterpieces directed by MIZOGUCHI KENJI, such as NANIWA EREJI (1936, Ōsaka Elegy) and *Gion no shimai* (1936, Sisters of the Gion). As president of DAIEI CO, LTD, Nagata also produced KUROSAWA AKIRA's RASHŌMON (1950) and Misumi Kenji's (1921–75) *Shaka* (1961, Buddha).

Nagata Takeshi   永田武

(1913–91). Geophysicist. Born in Aichi Prefecture. Graduate of Tōkyō University and professor there from 1952. Nagata's research spans the entire field of geomagnetics; he is particularly acclaimed for his work in clarifying the relationship between the thermoremanence of volcanic rock and long-period changes in the earth's magnetic field. He also led three expeditions to the South Pole between 1956 and 1959 and was the first director of the National Institute of Polar Research, which was established in 1973. He received the Order of Culture in 1974.

Nagata Teiryū   永田貞柳

(1654–1734). Also known as Taiya Teiryū or Yuensai. KYŌKA poet; elder brother of JŌRURI playwright KI NO KAION. He became the first professional *kyōka* poet, training numerous disciples. His *kyōka*, a skillful blend of the literary and the colloquial, are both amusing and delicate. Main collections are *Kyōka iezuto* (1729) and *Yuensai okimiyage* (1734).

Nagata Tetsuzan   永田鉄山

(1884–1935). Lieutenant general of the Imperial Japanese Army and architect of the army's long-range military and industrial preparation for war. Born in Nagano Prefecture. He graduated from the Army Academy in 1904 and the Army War College in 1911. He was attached to several Japanese legations in Europe during and immediately after World War I. He was the first to articulate the concept of national defense mobilization, designed to put the Japanese army and nation on a total war footing in times of national emergency.

Promoted to major general in 1932 and appointed chief of the Military Affairs Bureau (Gummukyoku) in 1934, Nagata was identified with the more pragmatic faction of the army, the TŌSEIHA ("Control" faction). His national planning ideas earned him the violent animosity of the KŌDŌHA ("Imperial Way" faction). On 12 August 1935 he was assassinated by a Kōdōha officer, Lieutenant Colonel Aizawa Saburō (1889–1936).

Nagata Tokuhon   永田徳本

(?–ca 1630). Physician. Also known as Kai no Tokuhon. Birthplace unknown. Nagata traveled throughout the country, treating the public at a nominal fee. He was the first in Japan to practice the basic medical treatments prescribed in the ancient Chinese medical book *Shang han lun* (ca 3rd century), such as inducing sweating and vomiting and using cathartic treatments.

Nagato   長門[市]

City in northwestern Yamaguchi Prefecture, western Honshū. Nagato developed as a fishing port and market town during the Edo period (1600–1868). Fishing is still its chief industry. The island of Ōmijima off the coast is one of the most scenic spots in the Kita Nagato Coast Quasi-National Park. Pop: 26,110.

Nagato   長門

Battleship of the Imperial Japanese Navy. Completed in 1920 as part of the so-called HACHIHACHI KANTAI (Eight Eight Fleet) program, it was the first battleship in the world to mount a 40-centimeter (16-in) main battery. The *Nagato* took part in the battles of MIDWAY, the PHILIPPINE SEA, and LEYTE GULF.

Nagatoro   長瀞

Gorge on the middle reaches of the river ARAKAWA, western Saitama Prefecture, central Honshū. It is characterized by exposed crystalline schist terraces. Part of the Nagatoro-Tamayodo Prefectural Natural Park, it is approximately 4 km (2.5 mi) in length.

Nagatsuka Takashi   長塚節

(1879–1915). TANKA poet and novelist. Born in Ibaraki Prefecture. He became a disciple of the poet MASAOKA SHIKI and strove to attain his ideal of objective photographic description (*shasei*). He helped to fund the *tanka* magazine *Ashibi* in 1903 with ITŌ SACHIO. He also wrote treatises on poetic theory. His *tanka* reveal a delicate sensibility, finely tuned to the seasonal progression of nature. His masterpiece, the long novel *Tsuchi* (1910, The Earth), depicts the poverty-stricken life of tenant farmers in his native village. Highly praised by novelist NATSUME SŌSEKI, *Tsuchi* is considered a classic of the "agrarian literature" (*nōmin bungaku*) of the early 20th century. His works are collected in *Nagatsuka Takashi zenshū* (1976–78).

Nagatsuki → calendar, dates, and time

nagauta   長唄

(literally, "long song"). A major form of lyrical song (*utai-mono*) accompanied by SHAMISEN music, common in KABUKI theater and in concerts. The earliest direct reference to *nagauta* is in the *Matsu no ha*, a 1703 collection of lyrics for *shamisen* songs. Though the term originally referred to music of the Kyōto-Ōsaka (Kamigata) area, *nagauta* developed primarily in the city of Edo (now Tōkyō) as kabuki dance music.

The standard *nagauta* ensemble today consists of several *shamisen* and singers plus hand drums (*ōtsuzumi* and *kotsuzumi*), the *taiko* stick drum, and either the NŌ-drama flute (*nōkan*) or a bamboo flute (*takebue* or *shinobue*). The drums and flute are known collectively as the *hayashi*. The basic *nagauta* repertory contains over 100 pieces in both the dance and concert traditions. The kabuki dance form (*odoriji*) is basic to the structure of *nagauta* pieces, although, like the sonata form in Western music, it serves only as a frame of reference upon which very different compositions can be created. See also KABUKI MUSIC.

nagaya   長屋

(literally, "long roof"). A type of wood-frame, one-story row house most closely identified with the Edo period (1600–1868), although *nagaya*-type structures have been common throughout the post–World War II period. *Nagaya* in the Edo period were divided into separate dwellings, each with its own doorway, and housed up to 10 families. Temples built *nagaya*-type dwellings to house their priests, and low-ranking retainers of *samurai* also lived in *nagaya*. The most common image of *nagaya*, however, is that of the slumlike back-alley tenements where the lower strata of Edo-period city dwellers lived.

Many *nagaya* were built in Edo (now Tōkyō) after about 1700 as the population increased. There were two main types: the *omote* (front) *nagaya*, which faced a main street, and the *ura* (back) *nagaya*, which faced an inner alley. Most dwelling units within *nagaya* were 9.9 square meters (106.5 sq ft) and had only a small earth-floored kitchen (*doma*) and one *tatami*-floored room. There was no running water, and residents shared a well and toilet facilities. Although *nagaya* could still be found in the postwar period along with types of accommodation such as apartments and high-rise low-cost condominiums, by the mid-1970s they were gradually disappearing amid calls for more efficient use of land and a general improvement in the standard of rented accommodation.

Nagaya no Ō, Rebellion of　　長屋王の変

(Nagaya no Ō no Hen). Political incident of the Nara period (710–794). Since the reign of Emperor TEMMU (r 672–686), members of the imperial family had moved steadily toward political ascendance at court. By the time of Emperor SHŌMU (r 724–749), Prince Nagaya (684–729), a grandson of Temmu and descended from Emperor TENJI (r 661–672) on his mother's side, had come to rival the influence of the FUJIWARA FAMILY. In 729 a minor official of the Fujiwara faction falsely informed the emperor that the prince was plotting a rebellion. The emperor had his residence surrounded, and the prince and his family were obliged to commit suicide.

Nagayo Sensai　　長与専斎

(1838–1902). Medical administrator. Born to a family of physicians in Hizen (now Nagasaki Prefecture). At age 16 he went to Ōsaka and became a pupil of OGATA KŌAN. After serving as president of the Nagasaki Igakkō, a medical school, he visited Europe and the United States as a member of the IWAKURA MISSION (1871–73). Upon his return he was responsible for the establishment of the Medical Affairs Bureau in the Ministry of Education, for the promulgation of the Vaccination Law, and for the drafting of a comprehensive medical law, the so-called Medical Order (Isei). He helped set up the Tōkyō Igakkō, a predecessor of the medical faculty of Tōkyō University. He served as its president from 1875 to 1878.

Nagayo Yoshirō　　長与善郎

(1888–1961). Novelist and playwright. Born in Tōkyō. Studied at Tōkyō University. He participated in SHIRAKABA, a coterie magazine founded in 1910 by MUSHANOKŌJI SANEATSU and other Peers' School (see GAKUSHŪIN UNIVERSITY) alumni. He was a typical spokesman for the liberal and humanistic philosophy of the group (see SHIRAKABA SCHOOL). Also known as a critic, Nagayo maintained his humanistic stance in the face of proletarian literature's popularity in the 1920s and the coming of World War II. His works include the play *Kōu to Ryūhō* (1916–17); *Indara no ko* (1921), a collection of plays; the novel *Takezawa sensei to iu hito* (1924–25); and his autobiography, *Waga kokoro no henreki* (1957–59).

nagegane　　投銀

(literally, "invested silver"). Speculative investments in overseas trade made by wealthy early Edo period (1600–1868) merchants from the seaports of Hakata (now Fukuoka) and Nagasaki. They lent large sums of money to Portuguese and Chinese merchants, as well as to owners of Japanese ships engaged in the VERMILION SEAL SHIP TRADE, charging interest rates ranging from 35 to 110 percent for a term of six months.

naginata　　薙刀

A weapon with a wooden shaft approximately 1.2 to 2.4 meters (4–8 ft) in length and a curved blade usually 30 to 60 centimeters (1–2 ft) in length. The *naginata* was the principal weapon of foot soldiers from the 11th century until well into the 15th century and was the favorite weapon of Buddhist WARRIOR-MONKS. From the 17th century onward, the techniques of its use became established as one of the MARTIAL ARTS, and several different schools emerged. *Samurai* women were also trained in its use.

During the Meiji period (1868–1912), the art of *naginata* came to be practiced principally by women. After World War II, it sank into a brief decline, but in 1955 the All Japan Naginata Federation was formed, and the art has survived to the present day as a women's sport.

Nago　　名護[市]

City on the island of Okinawa, Okinawa Prefecture. Principal products are pineapples, sugarcane, rice, beer, and cement. Attractions include Nago Bay, Todoroki Falls, and the remains of Nago Castle. Pop: 51,154.

nago　　名子

Low-status peasants dependent on specific landowners. Variously known as *myōshi, tsukurigo, hikan,* FUDAI, or *jige.* During the medieval period (mid-12th–16th centuries), *nago* were serf-like peasants who worked for such local landholders as MYŌSHU. During the Edo period (1600–1868) they were tenant cultivators in hereditary subordination to landowners called HOMBYAKUSHŌ. In return for their labor, *nago* received use of land, separate dwellings, and common village property. *Nago* were often listed in temple registers (*shūmonchō*) as members of their master's household. The master assured their livelihood, and they were required to obtain his permission to marry and to conduct funeral services. With development of a money economy, their numbers declined. Some became tenant farmers (MIZUNOMI-BYAKUSHŌ); others chose to remain *nago* to evade official responsibilities. Until recently the term *nago* continued to be used for hired help or menials in farming communities. See also OYAKATA AND HIKAN.

Nago Bay　　名護湾

(Nago Wan). Inlet of the East China Sea, on the western coast of the main island of Okinawa, Okinawa Prefecture. The city of Nago is on this bay, which is part of the Okinawa Coast Quasi-National Park.

nagoshi　　夏越

Annual rite of purification (HARAE) held at Shintō shrines on the last day of the sixth month according to the lunar calendar. It is also called *minatsuki-barae,* borrowing the poetic synonym for the lunar sixth month, Minatsuki. Along with *ōharae* (grand *harae*) on New Year's Eve, *nagoshi* is one of two purificatory rites, observed by the imperial court since ancient times, which divides the year into equal segments. Today the rite of *nagoshi* takes different forms in various

Nagoya This city's chief tourist attraction, Nagoya Castle, was originally built in 1610–14.

locales. A common practice is the rite of *chinowa,* in which the source of disease and defilement is believed to be eliminated by passing through a circle made of reeds. See also KEGARE; MISOGI.

Nagoya　　名古屋[市]

Capital of Aichi Prefecture, central Honshū, on Ise Bay. The political, financial, and cultural center of the Pacific coastal area between TŌKYŌ and ŌSAKA and the center of the CHŪKYŌ INDUSTRIAL ZONE, it is the fourth largest city in Japan.

Nagoya was settled early on; several mounded tombs (KOFUN) are here. Toward the end of the medieval period (13th–16th centuries) it prospered as the seat of ATSUTA SHRINE. With the construction of a castle in 1610–14, Nagoya became the base of the Owari domain, one of the three successor houses (GOSANKE) of the Tokugawa family. It suffered considerable destruction during World War II.

Nagoya is preeminently a business and industrial city, with about 40 satellite cities within a 40-km (25-mi) radius. Principal industries are transportation machinery, chemicals, steel, textiles, foodstuffs, and ceramic ware for export. Its port facilities are among the largest in the country.

Nagoya Castle, rebuilt in 1959, is the chief tourist attraction. Educational institutions include Nagoya University. Area: 327.9 sq km (126.6 sq mi); pop: 2,154,793.

Nagoya Castle　　名古屋城

(Nagoyajō). Castle located in the city of Nagoya; originally built in 1610–14 by TOKUGAWA IEYASU, on the site of a smaller abandoned castle once occupied by ODA NOBUNAGA, to ensure the security of the Tōkai region in central Japan. It served as the residence of Ieyasu's ninth son, Tokugawa Yoshinao (1600–1650), whose descendants (see GOSANKE) maintained control of the castle until the Meiji Restoration of 1868. The city of Nagoya grew up around the castle, which is considered an excellent example of late Momoyama architecture. The five-story donjon was destroyed during World War II but has since been reconstructed, and replicas of its famous pair of golden *shachi* (dolphinlike sea creatures), almost 3 meters (10 ft) high, rise from the ends of the rooftree of the new ferroconcrete main keep. Three original corner turrets, three gatehouses, and the stone foundation walls survived the war and have been designated Important Cultural Properties.

Nagoya domain → Owari domain

Nagoya Gen'i　　名古屋玄医

(1628–96). Physician. Also known as Nagoya Tansuishi. Regarded by many as the founder

Naitō Konan This influential scholar of Chinese history helped build Kyōto University's strong tradition in East Asian studies during the early 20th century.

of *koihō*, the classicist school of traditional Chinese-style medicine. A native of Kyōto, Nagoya advocated a return to classical Chinese medicine and rejected the Chinese Jin-Yuan (Chin-Yüan) medicine on which the "latter-day school" of Chinese medicine in Japan (*goseihō*) was based. See also MEDICINE.

Nagoya Institute of Technology
名古屋工業大学

(Nagoya Kōgyō Daigaku). A coeducational national university located in the city of Nagoya, Aichi Prefecture. Founded in 1949, it traces its origins to the Nagoya Higher Technical School, founded in 1905. The university's only academic department is its faculty of engineering. Enrollment in 1989 was 5,249.

Nagoya Railroad Co, Ltd
名古屋鉄道[株]

(Nagoya Tetsudō). Private railway company. It has the second longest railway lines among private railway companies in Japan. Founded in 1894 as a streetcar company in the city of Nagoya, it extended its lines to the suburbs and absorbed other smaller lines in Aichi and Gifu prefectures to create a unified rail network in the Nagoya area. After World War II, it diversified its activities by creating subsidiary companies in the fields of bus transportation, department stores, housing development, and leisure. It is now the mainstay of the Meitetsu (Nagoya Railway) group, which numbers 270 companies in all. In 1989 the total length of its railway tracks was 539.8 kilometers (337.4 mi). At the end of March 1991, annual revenue totaled ¥137.2 billion (US $1.0 billion), and the company was capitalized at ¥65.9 billion (US $480.3 million). Headquarters are in Nagoya.

Nagoya University
名古屋大学

(Nagoya Daigaku). A national, coeducational university located in Nagoya. Founded as Nagoya Imperial University in 1939, it became Nagoya University in 1949. It has faculties of letters, education, law, economics, science, medicine, engineering, and agriculture. Nagoya University also has research institutes in environmental medicine, atmospherics, water research, and plasma physics. Enrollment in 1989 was 8,640.

Nagumo Chūichi
南雲忠一

(1887–1944). Admiral. Born in Yamagata Prefecture, he graduated from the Naval Academy in 1908. In 1941 Nagumo became the commander-in-chief of the Imperial Navy's First Carrier Fleet. He led the attack on Pearl Harbor later that year, although he personally thought it to be a risky gamble. Nagumo was also commander of the Japanese forces in the decisive Battle of MIDWAY in 1942, suffering a defeat which marked a turning point in the war. Nagumo took his own life during the unsuccessful defense of Saipan in 1944.

Naha
那覇[市]

Capital of Okinawa Prefecture, on the island of OKINAWA. A trading port of the kingdom of Ryūkyū from early times, it served as a transit port for trade. It became the prefectural capital in 1879, when Okinawa was incorporated into the Japanese prefectural system. Completely destroyed in World War II, Naha was under American military administration until 1972. Industries include tourism and small businesses. Local products are traditional Okinawan handicrafts such as por-

celain, lacquer ware, *bingata* fabrics (see OKINAWAN TEXTILES), and *awamori* liquor. Of interest are the gate called Shurei no Mon, the graves of the kings of Ryūkyū, and the stone pavement at Kanagusuku. Pop: 304,836.

naichi zakkyo
内地雑居

(mixed residence in the interior). A term used during the Meiji period (1868–1912) in reference to the opening of Japan to foreign residence. This was one of the most important and emotional issues connected with the revision of the so-called Unequal Treaties (see UNEQUAL TREATIES, REVISION OF).

Under the terms of the ANSEI COMMERCIAL TREATIES of the 1850s, by which Japan ended 200 years of NATIONAL SECLUSION, foreigners were allowed to reside in their own enclaves, usually in cities and towns where legations and consulates were established (see KYORYŪCHI). Within these enclaves they enjoyed rights of extraterritoriality, so that all litigation concerning them was conducted in consular, rather than Japanese, courts.

The foreigners pressed for *naichi zakkyo*, wishing to escape the limits of their communities and to enjoy similar freedoms throughout the country. They were, however, reluctant to surrender their privileges, fearing that their rights would not be protected under Japanese law. But as the Meiji government promulgated new civil and criminal codes modeled on Western examples, foreign reluctance abated.

The Japanese viewed extraterritoriality as evidence that Westerners considered them an inferior nation, and though they wished to end these prerogatives, most Japanese were adamant against mixed residence, fearing the contamination of aliens in Japan, "the land of the gods." Other Japanese, however, saw opening the country as a necessity if Japanese were to be treated as Westerners' equals.

New treaties signed in 1894 (see ANGLO-JAPANESE COMMERCIAL TREATY OF 1894) and subsequent years terminated extraterritoriality, and Japan was opened to foreign residence and commerce in 1899—a development that brought capital and technology from abroad and contributed to the economic transformation of the country.

naidaijin
内大臣

1. (inner minister). In ancient times, an auxiliary government post (RYŌGE NO KAN), not prescribed by the TAIHŌ CODE (701) as part of the RITSURYŌ SYSTEM. FUJIWARA NO KAMATARI was the first to hold the post in 669. After the appointment of Fujiwara no Michitaka (953–995) in 989, the post became permanent, directly under the ministers of the right and left (*udaijin* and *sadaijin*).

2. (lord keeper of the privy seal). A post established in 1885, as a separate administrative office not of cabinet rank. The first *naidaijin* was SANJŌ SANETOMI. With the passing of the Meiji oligarchs (GENRŌ), the holders of the post gradually gained influence. In 1907 the Naidaijin Fu (Office of the Lord Keeper of the Privy Seal) was established. After the death of the last *genrō*, SAIONJI KIMMOCHI, in 1940, *naidaijin* KIDO KŌICHI chose the prime ministers. The post was abolished in November 1945.

Naimushō→Home Ministry

naishinsho
内申書

("confidential report"). Report on each student, prepared by the principals of elemen-

tary, middle, and high schools for use as a reference for admission to a higher school. Based on the CUMULATIVE GUIDANCE RECORD, the *naishinsho* contains academic and attendance records as well as information on personality, conduct, and participation in extracurricular activities. *Naishinsho* play a particularly important role in the competition to gain admission to the best high schools. Critics of Japan's school admissions system have pointed out that ENTRANCE EXAMINATIONS—which an applicant takes only once for a given school, under extreme pressure—are often the sole criterion, and they have argued that the *naishinsho*, as a record of sustained academic performance, should be given more weight. Others contend that the *naishinsho*'s fairness and objectivity are questionable.

Naitō Jōsō
内藤丈草

(1662–1704). HAIKU poet of the early Edo period (1600–1868); one of BASHŌ's 10 principal disciples. His poetry is considered the finest expression of SABI, a concept of beauty that occupies a central place in Bashō's poetics. Some of his verses may be found in the anthology *Sarumino* (1691) and his personal collection, *Jōsō hokkushū* (1774).

Naitō Konan
内藤湖南

(1866–1934). Scholar of Chinese history. Real name Naitō Torajirō. Born in what is now Akita Prefecture, Naitō graduated from Akita Normal School in 1885. Deciding to become a journalist, in 1887 he went to Tōkyō and worked for the *Meikyō shinshi* (Journal of Enlightened Teaching) and for the newspapers YOROZU CHŌHŌ and *Ōsaka asahi shimbun*. In 1899 Naitō made the first of many trips to China; in 1907 he joined the newly established seminar on Chinese history at Kyōto University and became a professor there in 1909. From then until 1926, Naitō trained many scholars and helped build the university's strong tradition in East Asian studies. His interests in Chinese history ranged from ancient times through the Qing (Ch'ing) dynasty (1644–1912), and he formulated a new theory of periodization analogous to that used for Europe. The Naitō historiography (Naitō *shigaku*) was influential among non-Marxist scholars and is still a principal feature of the "Kyōto school" of Asian studies.

Nakabayashi Chikutō
中林竹洞

(1776–1853). Artist in the BUNJINGA (literati painting) tradition. Born in Nagoya, the son of a physician. When Chikutō was 20, he took up residence in a local temple and established a studio. At age 27 he went to Kyōto with fellow painter YAMAMOTO BAIITSU, and there he joined the literati circle of the calligrapher and historian RAI SAN'YŌ.

Chikutō professed strict adherence to Chinese literati theories and brush methods. His paintings utilize restrained brushwork and are formal and academic rather than overtly expressive, in harmony with his quiet, retiring nature. He is best known for his landscapes but also painted the "Four Gentlemen" (SHIKUNSHI) and birds and flowers. In addition, he published a number of painting manuals.

Nakadai Tatsuya
仲代達矢

(1932–). Actor. Real name Nakadai Motohisa. Born in Tōkyō. He joined the Haiyūza actors' training school in 1952 and performed his first stage role in 1954. A truly versatile film actor, he has starred in Inoue Umetsugu's (b 1923) *Hi no tori* (1956, Firebird); ICHIKAWA KON's *Enjō* (1958, Conflagration); KOBAYASHI MASAKI's NINGEN NO JŌKEN (1959–61, The Human Condition), SEPPUKU (1962, Harakiri), and *Kaidan* (1964, KWAIDAN); and KUROSAWA AKIRA's *Yōjimbō* (1961), *Tsubaki Sanjūrō* (1962, Sanjuro), *Kagemusha* (1980, The Shadow Warrior), and RAN (1985). On the stage he has starred in *Hamlet* (1964), *Othello* (1970), and *Richard III* (1974). Nakadai and his wife, scriptwriter Ryū Tomoe (b 1931), founded Mumeijuku, a free school to train young actors, in 1979.

Nakada Kaoru   中田薫

(1877–1967). Scholar of the history of law. Born in Yamanashi Prefecture. A 1900 graduate of Tōkyō University, where he studied legal institutions of the Kamakura period (1185–1333), he joined its faculty in 1902 and became a full professor in 1911. Known primarily as the founder of the modern discipline of legal history in Japan, his interests extended to Chinese and European legal systems as well, but from 1925 onward he devoted most of his research to Japanese legal institutions of the premodern and early modern periods. He received the Order of Culture (Bunka Kunshō) in 1946. His writings include *Ōchō jidai no shōen* (1906, Shōen during the Late Heian Period) and *Meiji shonen no iraiken* (1928, Commonage in the Early Meiji Period).

Nakae Chōmin   中江兆民

(1847–1901). Materialist philosopher, political theoretician, and popular-rights advocate of the Meiji period (1868–1912). Real name Nakae Tokusuke. Born in the Tosa domain (now Kōchi Prefecture). Chōmin went to France in 1871 to study history, philosophy, and literature. Returning to Japan in 1874, he headed the Tōkyō Foreign Language School and was secretary of the GENROIN (Chamber of Elders).

Chōmin became known as one of the leading liberals of his day—a major spokesman for the radical wing of the FREEDOM AND PEOPLE'S RIGHTS MOVEMENT. In 1881 he helped found the *Tōyō jiyū shimbun* (Oriental Free Press), which urged adoption of parliamentary government and proclaimed the rights of the people. With the demise of this paper in 1882 under government pressure, Chōmin began to publish his own magazine, *Seiri sōdan* (Anecdotes of Statecraft), including in it his own translation of Rousseau's *Social Contract*. After he was expelled from Tōkyō under the PEACE PRESERVATION LAW OF 1887 (Hoan Jōrei) as a supporter of and writer for the Liberal Party (JIYŪTŌ), Chōmin moved to Ōsaka and founded the *Shinonome shimbun* (Dawn News). KŌTOKU SHŪSUI became his student at this time.

With the promulgation of the Meiji Constitution in 1889, Chōmin decided to enter politics. He was elected to the first national DIET in 1890. His political goals were to form a united front of the popular parties against the government in order to fight for greater public rights. When his allies in the Liberal Party gave way to government bribery, however, he resigned. His next 10 years were spent in a variety of unsuccessful commercial ventures. His attempt to reenter politics in 1898 with a new political party, the Kokumintō (National People's Party), also met with failure.

Chōmin was nevertheless a prolific writer on political and philosophical subjects. His major political treatise, *Sansuijin keirin mondō* (1887; tr *A Discourse by Three Drunkards on Government*, 1984), was an attempt to stimulate popular interest in sovereignty, parliamentarianism, and other questions of government. His most important philosophical works, *Ichinen yūhan* (A Year and a Half) and *Zoku ichinen yūhan* (A Year and a Half, Continued), were written after his doctors told him in 1901 that he had only a short time to live. The latter, subtitled *No God, No Spirit* and completed a few days before his death in 1901, constitutes what many scholars regard as the most important statement on Meiji materialism. Chōmin's brand of philosophy is often seen as a link between the Japanese intellectual tradition and modern doctrines such as socialism and Marxism, to which his disciple Kōtoku Shūsui was subsequently attracted.

Nakae Tōju   中江藤樹

(1608–48). Confucian scholar; founder of the Wang Yangming school (YŌMEIGAKU) of Confucianism in Japan. He was born in Ōmi (now Shiga Prefecture) but raised and educated by his grandfather in Iyo (now Ehime Prefecture) in Shikoku. Tōju later returned to Ōmi and started a private Confucian academy; he came to be known as the Sage of Ōmi.

Tōju began his Confucian studies with the philosophy of Zhu Xi (Chu Hsi; see SHUSHIGAKU) but in his mid-thirties turned to the teachings of Wang Yangming. Zhu Xi taught that *li* (J: *ri*), the principle of all things, emanates from an objective, timeless Supreme Ultimate (*taiji* or *t'ai chi;* J: *taikyoku*). In contrast, Wang Yangming believed that *li* exists in the mind a priori and is known intuitively. The two schools came into conflict, the Zhu Xi school being officially endorsed by the Tokugawa shogunate (1603–1867), but Tōju continued to admire both philosophers.

Tōju's chief concerns were moral conduct and the pursuit of justice. Tōju emphasized unity of thought and action. His philosophy, therefore, tended to foster activism and influenced many important thinkers and political leaders in Tokugawa Japan. The most prominent of Tōju's disciples was KUMAZAWA BANZAN. *Okina mondō* (1641, Dialogues with an Old Man) is Tōju's best-known work.

Nakagami Kenji   中上健次

(1946–92). Novelist. Born in Shingū, a coastal city on the Kii Peninsula in Wakayama Prefecture. Soon after graduating from high school, he moved to Tōkyō where he began his career in writing. Nakagami won the Akutagawa Prize in 1975 for *Misaki* (The Cape), a novella that depicts the "alley" (*roji*), a BURAKUMIN ghetto. The alley reappears in Nakagami's subsequent fiction such as *Karekinada* (1977, The Kareki Sea) and *Chi no hate, shijō no toki* (1983, End of the Earth, Supreme Time). Blood ties in this community, incestuous at times, assume an important role in Nakagami's writing. He also draws on the myths and legends of the Kumano district, a region south of Nara, reputed as a mysterious and mystical place since ancient times. The influence of Kumano lore is evident in *Sennen no yuraku* (The Joy of a Thousand Years), a novel published in 1982, and *Kumanoshū*, a collection of short stories published in 1984. Nakagami is also the author of *Nichirin no tsubasa* (1984, The Wings of the Sun) and *Sanka* (1990, Songs of Praise).

Nakagawa   那珂川

River in Tochigi and Ibaraki prefectures, central Honshū, originating in the volcano NASUDAKE and flowing southeast past the city of Mito to enter the Pacific Ocean at the city of Nakaminato. The water is utilized by Mito for drinking and by the city of Katsuta for industry and irrigation. Length: 150 km (93 mi); area of drainage basin: 3,270 sq km (1,263 sq mi).

Nakagawa   那賀川

River in eastern Tokushima Prefecture, Shikoku, originating in the mountain Tsurugisan on the border between Tokushima and Kōchi prefectures and flowing east into Kii Channel at the city of Anan. Cedar afforestation is in progress on the upper reaches, and dams and electric power plants have been constructed. Length: 125 km (78 mi); area of drainage basin: 874 sq km (337 sq mi).

Nakagawa Gorōji   中川五郎治

(1768–1848). Introducer of smallpox vaccination techniques into Japan. While serving as a guard-interpreter in the southern Kuril Islands in 1807, he was captured by Russian raiders and taken to Siberia, where he observed the immunizing effects of smallpox vaccine. He was brought back to Japan in 1812 to be exchanged for Captain V. M. GOLOVNIN.

Nakagawa Jun'an   中川淳庵

(1739–86). Physician and scholar of WESTERN LEARNING. Born to a family of physicians in the Obama domain (now part of Fukui Prefecture), he developed an interest in botany and mineralogy, and in 1764, with HIRAGA GENNAI, he invented a kind of asbestos cloth. After studying the Dutch language with the physician Yasutomi Kiseki, he joined with MAENO RYŌTAKU, SUGITA GEMPAKU, and others in translating into Japanese the *Ontleedkundige Tafelen* (1734, Anatomical Tables), a Dutch version of a German work. Published in 1774 as KAITAI SHINSHO (New Book of Anatomy), this work laid the foundation for study of European medical science in Japan. Jun'an also studied with Dutch physician Carl Peter THUNBERG and became friendly with Izaak TITSINGH.

Nakagawa Kazumasa   中川一政

(1893–1991). Painter. Born in Tōkyō. Self-taught, Nakagawa won the prize of the painters' society Nikakai in 1921. In 1922 he helped found the Western-style painters' society Shun'yōkai. Influenced by TOMIOKA TESSAI, he also created Japanese-style paintings

Nakahama Manjirō
Manjirō was cast away on a Pacific island at the age of 14 in 1841. His rescue by an American whaler led to a career as a diplomatic interpreter and teacher of English.

Nakahara Chūya
Initially a *tanka* poet, Nakahara later adopted the techniques of French symbolist poetry.

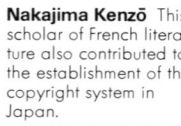

Nakajima Kenzō This scholar of French literature also contributed to the establishment of the copyright system in Japan.

(NIHONGA). His mature style was suggestive of 18th- and 19th-century BUNJINGA (literati painting). He was the author of *Mienai sekai* (1954, Unseen World). He received the Order of Culture in 1975.

Nakagawa Yoichi 中河与一

(1897–). Novelist and poet. Born in Kagawa Prefecture; studied at Waseda University. Nakagawa began as a TANKA poet, in 1924 joining *Bungei jidai*, a coterie magazine that gave birth to the SHINKANKAKU SCHOOL. Nakagawa's *Ten no yūgao* (1938), a love story, was very popular just before World War II. His postwar novels include *Shitsuraku no niwa* (1950) and *Tambi no yoru* (1956–59).

Nakagawa Zennosuke 中川善之助

(1897–1975). Legal scholar. Born in Tōkyō, he graduated from Tōkyō University in 1921. The following year he was appointed to the law faculty of Tōhoku University, where he remained until his retirement in 1961. Thereafter he served as a professor at Gakushūin University and as president of Kanazawa University. A protégé of HOZUMI SHIGETŌ, Nakagawa made important contributions to the field of family law, and he played a leading role in the revision of the CIVIL CODE after World War II. His writings include *Mibunhō no kiso riron* (1939, Basic Theory of the Law of Domestic Relations), *Nihon shinzokuhō* (1942, Family Law in Japan), *Shinzokuhō* (1958, Family Law), and *Sōzokuhō* (1964, Inheritance Law).

Nakahama Manjirō 中浜万次郎

(1827–98). Also known as John Manjirō or John Mung. Fisherman from Tosa Province (now Kōchi Prefecture) who lived in the United States for several years and later became an official of the Tokugawa shogunate and the Meiji government. In 1841 Manjirō and others were shipwrecked on a deserted island south of Edo (now Tōkyō). Rescued by an American whaling ship, the others went to Hawaii, but Manjirō was invited to go to the United States by the captain, who had been impressed by Manjirō's intelligence. He studied at a school in Fairhaven, Massachusetts, traveled, and worked at various jobs before returning to Japan in 1851. Because of the shogunate's NATIONAL SECLUSION policy, Manjirō was first interrogated before being allowed to return to his home province, where he was employed by the *daimyō*.

When Commodore PERRY arrived in Japan in 1853, Manjirō was called into service as a translator. In 1855 he was made an instructor at the Nagasaki Naval Training Center (KAIGUN DENSHŪJO). In 1859, after Japan had opened its ports to trade with the United States, he published *Eibei taiwa shōkei* (Shortcut to Anglo-American Conversation), the first English-language phrase book. Manjirō acted as chief interpreter for the shogunate embassy to the United States to ratify the HARRIS TREATY of 1858 (see UNITED STATES, MISSION OF 1860 TO). After the Meiji Restoration of 1868, he was appointed an instructor at the Kaisei Gakkō (now Tōkyō University).

Nakahara Chūya 中原中也

(1907–37). Poet. Born in Yamaguchi Prefecture. Graduated from Tōkyō University of Foreign Studies. Initially a TANKA poet, he was later attracted to the free-form poetry of

the dadaist TAKAHASHI SHINKICHI. In 1924, he went to Tōkyō, became friends with the critic KOBAYASHI HIDEO, and was introduced to the poetry of French symbolists Verlaine and Rimbaud. He subsequently employed symbolist technique in the writing of his own verse. His poetry collections include *Yagi no uta* (1934) and *Arishi hi no uta* (1938).

Nakai Hideo 中井英夫

(1922–). Novelist. Born in Tōkyō; attended Tōkyō University. Nakai began his career as editor of a TANKA poetry magazine and a proponent of the avant-garde *tanka* movement. Later he published *Kyomu e no kumotsu* (1964, Offering to Nothingness) under the name Tō Akio. Nakai established himself with fantasy novels that depict a world of refined beauty. His works include *Gensō hakubutsukan* (1972, Museum of Fantasy) and *Akumu no karuta* (1973, Nightmare Card Game).

Nakai Riken 中井履軒

(1732–1817). Neo-Confucian scholar. Born in Ōsaka. Son of Nakai Shūan (1693–1758), a founder of the KAITOKUDŌ, a school for commoners. After his father's death, he and his brother Chikuzan (1730–1804) took over the school. Riken later founded his own school, the Suisaikan, but eventually returned to the Kaitokudō. His teachings synthesized elements from different intellectual traditions.

Nakajima Atsushi 中島敦

(1909–42). Novelist. Born in Tōkyō. Graduate of Tōkyō University. During a year (1941–42) he spent in Palau, Western Caroline Islands (at that time under Japanese mandate), he wrote *Kotan* (1942), a set of stories published in *Bungakukai*. His next work was *Hikari to kaze to yume* (1942), an account of Robert Louis Stevenson's final years in Samoa, which gained him further recognition. The novel *Riryō* (1943), published posthumously, was set in China during the early Han dynasty (206 BC–AD 8) and perhaps best exemplifies Nakajima's elegance of language, erudition, and pessimism.

Nakajima Chikuhei 中島知久平

(1884–1949). Businessman and politician who was a pioneer of Japan's aircraft industry. Born in Gumma Prefecture, he was a graduate of the Naval Engineering School. He served in the navy, resigning in 1917 to establish the Airplane Research Institute, later to become Nakajima Aircraft Co, manufacturer of military airplanes and engines for the ZERO FIGHTER. Nakajima was elected to the House of Representatives in 1930, becoming leader of one of the factions of the RIKKEN SEIYŪKAI in 1939. He served as railways minister (1937–39) and commerce and industry minister (1945). In 1950 Nakajima Aircraft Co was split into 12 independent companies, 5 of which later merged to establish FUJI HEAVY INDUSTRIES, LTD, an automobile company that now makes Subaru.

Nakajima Kenzō 中島健蔵

(1903–79). Literary critic; scholar of French literature. Born in Tōkyō; graduated from Tōkyō University. Translator of Paul Valéry and other French writers. Nakajima received the Kikuchi Kan Prize in 1954 for his contributions to the establishment of the copyright system in Japan. He was awarded the Noma Literary Prize for *Kaisō no bungaku* (1977, Literary Memoirs), a five-volume personal history of Japanese literature from the be-

ginning of the Shōwa period (1926–89) to the end of World War II. Nakajima's other works include *Kaisō no sengo bungaku* (1979, Memoirs of Postwar Literature).

Nakajima Nobuyuki 中島信行

(1846–99). Politician. Born in Tosa Province (now Kōchi Prefecture). An antishogunate activist in the 1860s, after the Meiji Restoration (1868) he became governor of Kanagawa Prefecture (1874) and then a member of the GENRŌIN (Chamber of Elders). His sympathies with the FREEDOM AND PEOPLE'S RIGHTS MOVEMENT eventually alienated Nakajima from the government, however, and he joined the JIYŪTŌ (Liberal Party) in 1881. The following year he left to become president of the Rikken Seitō (Constitutional Government Party). He was banished from Tōkyō under the PEACE PRESERVATION LAW OF 1887 (Hoan Jōrei) for his political activities, but in the first Diet elections (1890) he was elected to the House of Representatives as a member of the Rikken Jiyūtō (later the Jiyūtō) and became the first speaker of the House. He left the Jiyūtō in 1892, was appointed ambassador to Italy the same year, and was made a member of the House of Peers two years later. His wife was KISHIDA TOSHIKO, an early feminist.

Nakajima Shōen → Kishida Toshiko

Nakajō 中条[町]

Town in northern Niigata Prefecture, central Honshū. Nakajō developed as a market town and post-station town in the Edo period (1600–1868). With the discovery of natural gas, a chemical industry has developed. Agriculture is also active. Pop: 28,910.

Naka Kansuke 中勘助

(1885–1965). Novelist and poet. Born in Tōkyō. Graduate of Tōkyō University, where he was a student of NATSUME SŌSEKI. His novel *Gin no saji* (1913, 1915; tr *The Silver Spoon*, 1976) was based on his own experiences as an introverted child of poor health who is fascinated with beauty and hungry for love. At Sōseki's recommendation, it was serialized in the newspaper *Asahi shimbun* (April–June 1913; April–June 1915). Throughout his life, Naka remained outside the main literary currents, writing essays and short stories that reflected his stoic, reclusive life. Other works include the novel *Inu* (1922, The Dog) and *Rōkan* (1935), a collection of poems.

Nakama 中間[市]

City in northern Fukuoka Prefecture, Kyūshū, on the river Ongagawa. Formerly a farming village, Nakama developed rapidly in the mid-Meiji period (1868–1912) with the opening of the CHIKUHŌ COALFIELD. Since the closing of the mines in 1964, machinery and electrical-appliance industries have been introduced. Housing projects have made it a satellite city of KITA KYŪSHŪ. Habu Park is noted for its 86 images depicting the disciples of Buddha. Pop: 49,216.

Naka Michiyo 那珂通世

(1851–1908). Historian. Born in the Morioka domain (now Iwate Prefecture). After graduating from Keiō Gijuku (now Keiō University), he taught East Asian history and Chinese classics. Naka is remembered for having proven that the traditional date (660 BC) for the accession of JIMMU, the legendary first emperor of Japan, was historically invalid (see KIGEN).

Nakamigawa Hikojirō　中上川彦次郎

(1854–1901). Businessman who laid the foundation of the MITSUI industrial and financial conglomerate (ZAIBATSU). Born in the Nakatsu domain (now part of Ōita Prefecture), Nakamigawa was a nephew of FUKUZAWA YUKICHI, the outstanding propagator of Western knowledge during the Meiji period (1868–1912). After studying at Keiō Gijuku (now Keiō University) and in England, he entered government service in 1878 but resigned his post in the POLITICAL CRISIS OF 1881. In 1882 he began publishing the newspaper JIJI SHIMPŌ for Fukuzawa.

As president of the San'yō Railway Company from 1887 to 1891, Nakamigawa introduced radical and innovative management policies. In 1891 he was appointed director of the Mitsui Bank and entrusted with reorganizing the Mitsui combine. Serving until his death as leader of the entire Mitsui *zaibatsu* during its formative years, Nakamigawa carried out major reforms, modernizing Mitsui's management, abandoning its dependence on government patronage, and expanding its investment in modern industry.

Nakaminato　那珂湊[市]

City in eastern Ibaraki Prefecture, central Honshū, on the Pacific. The city flourished as a transit port during the Edo period (1600–1868). It is a base for deep-sea fishing for bonito, mackerel, and tuna, and has an active seafood-processing industry. The beach at Ajigaura is popular with swimmers. Pop: 32,577.

Nakamura　中村[市]

City in southwestern Kōchi Prefecture, Shikoku. Situated on the river Shimantogawa, Nakamura developed under the courtier Ichijō Norifusa (1423–80), who fled here with his followers from Kyōto during the ŌNIN WAR. Rice, vegetables, fruit, lumber, and marine products are produced. Pop: 35,816.

Nakamura Chōhachi　中村長八

(1865–1940). Roman Catholic priest active in the Japanese immigrant community in Brazil. Born in Nagasaki Prefecture and christened Domingos, Nakamura was assigned to Brazil as a missionary in 1923. He spent the rest of his life in the difficult task of evangelizing in remote areas and gained great respect among Japanese immigrants and native Brazilians alike.

Nakamura Fusetsu　中村不折

(1866–1943). Western-style painter and calligrapher. Real name Nakamura Sakutarō. Born in Tōkyō, he studied there with Koyama Shōtarō (1857–1916) and then in France with Jean-Paul Laurens. Upon his return to Japan in 1905 he joined the Taiheiyō Gakai (Pacific Painting Society). He often painted historical subjects, particularly from Chinese history, in a European academic style. He was an accomplished calligrapher. In 1936 Nakamura established the Calligraphy Museum (Shodō Hakubutsukan) in Tōkyō.

Nakamura Gakuryō　中村岳陵

(1890–1969). Japanese-style painter. Real name Nakamura Tsunekichi. Born in Shizuoka Prefecture, he studied traditional TOSA SCHOOL painting with Kawabe Mitate (1837–1905). In 1912 he graduated from the Tōkyō Bijutsu Gakkō (now Tōkyō University of Fine Arts and Music). Later he became a member of the reorganized Nihon Bijutsuin (see JAPAN FINE ARTS ACADEMY) artist group. He is chiefly remembered for his copies of the wall paintings in the temple HŌRYŪJI in Nara and for his murals in the main hall of the SHI-TENNŌJI in Ōsaka. He received the Order of Culture in 1962 and was made a member of the Japan Art Academy (Nihon Geijutsuin).

Nakamura Hajime　中村元

(1912–). Scholar of Indian philosophy and Buddhism. Born in Matsue, Shimane Prefecture, he graduated from Tōkyō University in 1936 and taught there from 1954 to 1973. He has produced a large number of works in the field of the comparative study of ideas and promoted cultural exchange between Japan and other nations. His best-known work is *Tōyōjin no shii hōhō* (1948–49; tr *Ways of Thinking of Eastern Peoples: India, China, Tibet, Japan*, 1962–63). In 1974 he completed a three-volume dictionary of Buddhist terms, *Bukkyōgo daijiten.* He received the Order of Culture in 1977.

Nakamura Kanzaburō　中村勘三郎

Professional name used by a family of KABUKI actors starting with Kanzaburō I (1598–1658), founder of an Edo (now Tōkyō) kabuki theater and troupe called the Nakamuraza. For many generations the stage name Kanzaburō was held by successive heads of the troupe, but the theater met with hard times over a long period starting from the mid-19th century, and the leadership of the Nakamuraza was turned over to Nakamura Nakazō II (1809–86) in 1875. The name Kanzaburō was not used again until 1950, when Kanzaburō XVII (1909–88), who had made his debut in 1916, revived it. Inheriting the acting styles of his older brother, Nakamura Kichiemon I (1866–1954; see NAKAMURA KICHIEMON), and his father-in-law, Onoe Kikugorō VI (1885–1949; see ONOE KIKUGORŌ), Kanzaburō XVII became known for his wide range of roles and rich power of expression. In 1975 he was designated a Living National Treasure and in 1980 he was awarded the Order of Culture.

Nakamura Kenkichi　中村憲吉

(1889–1934). TANKA poet. Born in Hiroshima Prefecture; graduate of Tōkyō University. From around 1909 he contributed to *Araragi*, the *tanka* poetry magazine, to which he submitted naturalist-style poems colored by a youthful romanticism. He later shifted to a more subjective and meditative style. His principal collections are *Rinsenshū* (1916) and *Keiraishū* (1931).

Nakamura Kichiemon　中村吉右衛門

Professional name of a series of KABUKI actors. Nakamura Kichiemon I (1886–1954) first appeared onstage under that name in 1897. "The Kiku-Kichi Era," during which both he and the great actor Onoe Kikugorō VI (see ONOE KIKUGORŌ) performed at the Ichimuraza theater, is considered one of the golden ages of kabuki. He was the leading kabuki actor of the Shōwa period (1926–89) in *jidaimono* (historical plays) and received the Order of Culture in 1951. His grandson (b 1944) took the name Kichiemon II in 1966. Along with his father, Matsumoto Kōshirō VIII (see MATSUMOTO KŌSHIRŌ), Kichiemon II worked briefly for the TŌHŌ CO, LTD, appearing more frequently in motion pictures and popular theater than in kabuki, but in the 1970s kabuki once again became his major occupation. His acting as the *tachiyaku*, or male

Nakamura Kanzaburō
A scene from the *kabuki* play *Kanadehon chūshingura* (The Treasury of Loyal Retainers), with actor Nakamura Kanzaburō XVII in the role of Hayano Kampei.

lead, retained the flavor of the *jidaimono* style. He is especially noted for his technical mastery of elocution.

Nakamura Kiyoo　中村精男

(1855–1930). Meteorologist. Born in Nagato Province (now part of Yamaguchi Prefecture). A graduate of Tōkyō University, Nakamura studied in Germany from 1886 to 1889. Employed by the Central Meteorological Observatory (Chūō Kishōdai), he did research on the duration of meteorological conditions and developed a standard chart for plotting weather changes. He was director of the observatory from 1895 to 1923. Nakamura assisted in the foundation of the Tōkyō School of Science (now Science University of Tōkyō) in 1881 and served as its chancellor from 1896 until his death.

Nakamura Kusatao　中村草田男

(1901–83). HAIKU poet. Real name Nakamura Seiichirō. Born in Fujian (Fukien), China, where his father was a diplomat. Graduate of Tōkyō University. From 1933 he associated with the haiku coterie at the periodical HOTOTOGISU. Later, disenchanted with the group's emphasis on nature, he left to establish his own magazine, *Banryoku*, in 1946. In his later works, he attempted to evoke the whole of human existence. Principal collections are *Chōshi* (1936) and *Banryoku* (1941).

Nakamura Masanao　中村正直

(1832–91). Confucian scholar; best known for translations of Samuel Smiles's *Self Help* (1859; tr *Saigoku risshi hen*, 1871) and John Stuart Mill's *On Liberty* (1859; tr *Jiyū no kotowari*, 1872). Also known by his pen name, Nakamura Keiu. Born in Edo (now Tōkyō). Nakamura was a prominent educator and thinker. He founded the Dōjinsha school in 1873, later headed what was to become Ochanomizu Women's University, and taught at Tōkyō University.

Nakamura Kichiemon
Nakamura Kichiemon II, grandson of the first *kabuki* actor to assume this professional name, in the historical play *Yoshitsune sembon-zakura* (The Thousand Cherry Trees of Yoshitsune).

Nakamura Utaemon
Utaemon VI (right), a leading *onnagata* (female impersonator), in a performance of *Kanadehon chūshingura* (The Treasury of Loyal Retainers).

The first prominent Meiji figure to become a Christian, Nakamura's humanism and belief that God's laws are inscribed upon each man's conscience can be traced to his background as a Confucian scholar. In search of the moral foundation for the West's strength, Nakamura concluded it was Christianity. Equating the Confucian concept of *tendō* (the "Way of heaven") with the Christian concept of the "Laws of God," Nakamura maintained that Japan would become a strong nation if individual Japanese listened to God's voice within them and acted accordingly. Nakamura took the lead in the MEIROKUSHA, Japan's leading society of modernizers, in advocating moral development as the necessary prelude to institutional change.

Nakamura Mitsuo　　中村光夫

(1911–88). Literary critic. Real name Koba Ichirō. Born in Tōkyō. Graduate of Tōkyō University. He began writing literary essays in his early twenties and gained recognition for *Futabatei Shimei ron* (1936), a critical study of modern novelist FUTABATEI SHIMEI. His 1950 book *Fūzoku shōsetsu ron* asserted that modern Japanese novels were "distorted," tending to be no more than fictionalized autobiographies lacking in meaningful social criticism. Most of Nakamura's works are critical biographies of writers that emphasize their intellectual development. He received the Yomiuri Literary Prize in 1958 for his *Futabatei Shimei den* and again in 1964 for the play *Kiteki issei*. His other works include the critical studies *Tanizaki Jun'ichirō ron* (1954) and *Shiga Naoya ron* (1954) as well as *Nihon no kindai shōsetsu* (1954; tr *Modern Japanese Fiction*, 1968), and *Nihon no gendai shōsetsu* (1968; tr *Contemporary Japanese Fiction*, 1969).

Nakamura Shin'ichirō　　中村真一郎

(1918–　). Novelist, poet, and literary critic. Born in Tōkyō. Graduate of Tōkyō University. He was a member of the group Matinée Poétique, formed in 1942, which made a great contribution after World War II to new forms of poetry. He published a set of five novels that begins with *Shi no kage no moto ni* (1946–47, In the Shadow of Death) and ends with *Nagai tabi no owari* (1952, The End of a Long Journey). Nakamura also wrote essays on 20th-century European literature. His principal works are *Kaiten mokuba* (1957, Merry-go-round) and *Kūchū teien* (1963, Space Garden), both novels, and *Rai San'yō to sono jidai* (1971), a critical biography of the early-19th-century scholar RAI SAN'YŌ.

Nakamura Tekisai　　中村惕斎

(1629–1702). Neo-Confucian scholar of the early Edo period (1600–1868). Born in Kyōto,

Nakamura Mitsuo
One of the most prominent literary biographers and critics of post–World War II Japan.

Nakamura Tsune *Portrait of Vasilii Yaroshenko.* 1920. Oil on canvas. 47 × 46 cm. National Museum of Modern Art, Tōkyō.

he led a reclusive life devoted to the Neo-Confucian ideal of the "investigation of things and penetration of principle" (*kakubutsu kyūri*), conducting research in areas ranging from heavenly bodies to plants, animals, and weights and measures. He and ITŌ JINSAI were considered the most prominent scholars of their time. See SHUSHIGAKU.

Nakamura Tsune　　中村彝

(1887–1924). Western-style painter. Born in Ibaraki Prefecture. Nakamura studied under artists of the painters' societies Hakubakai and Taiheiyō Gakai, among them Nakamura Fusetsu (1866–1943) and Mizutani Kunishirō (1874–1936). Although influenced by Renoir, Cézanne, and Rembrandt, he developed his own style. He was especially adept at portraits, one of which won the highest award at the 1916 Teiten (Exhibition of the Imperial Fine Arts Academy).

Nakamura Utaemon　　中村歌右衛門

Well-known family line of KABUKI actors, originally from the Kyōto-Ōsaka area. Utaemon I (1714–91) was famous for his *jitsuaku* (villainous *samurai*) roles. Utaemon III (1778–1838) became one of the greatest actors of his time, covering the entire range of male and ONNAGATA (female impersonator) roles. He was also a gifted dancer. Utaemon IV (1798–1852) also was remarkably versatile, capable of playing any role in the kabuki repertory.

Throughout his long and distinguished career, Utaemon V (1865–1940) remained primarily an *onnagata*. His son, Utaemon VI (b 1917), is a leading *onnagata* of the contemporary kabuki stage and has a concern for the preservation of the classical style in the kabuki theater. He also performs in the revival of those important kabuki plays that are rarely presented. Utaemon VI was awarded the Order of Culture in 1979.

Nakano　　中野[市]

City in northeastern Nagano Prefecture, central Honshū. Fruits, mainly apples, grapes, and peaches, are grown. Nakano is Japan's leading producer of *enokidake*, a kind of mushroom. It is also known for its handicrafts made of willow, akebia (*akebi*), and wood. Pop: 40,996.

Nakano Kōji　　中野孝次

(1925–　). Novelist and scholar of German literature. Born in Chiba Prefecture; graduated from Tōkyō University. Nakano has translated Franz Kafka and Hans Erich Nossack, among others, and has written extensively on contemporary literature. His works include *Buryūgeru e no tabi* (1976, Traveling to Bruegel), a collection of essays, and the autobiographical trilogy *Mugi ururu hi ni* (1978, When the Wheat Ripens), *Nigai natsu* (1979, Bitter Summer), and *Kisetsu no owari* (1980, The End of the Season).

Naka no Ōe, Prince —→ Tenji, Emperor

Nakano School　　陸軍中野学校

(Rikugun Nakano Gakkō). Popular name given to the secret sabotage, propaganda, and intelligence program conducted by the Imperial Japanese Army during World War II. Formed under the auspices of the Army Ministry's Military Service Bureau in 1938, the program took the cover name Kōhō Kimmu Yōin Yōseijo (Rear Service Personnel Training Center) and was loosely called a school by its members. It was first located in the Kudan district of Tōkyō. Moved to the western Tōkyō suburb of Nakano in 1940, the Rikugun Nakano Gakkō was assigned a commanding officer of the rank of major general. Students, selected from intellectually astute junior officers, followed an ambitious curriculum that included foreign languages, foreign cultures, cryptography, and radio engineering. Between 1938 and 1945, some 3,000 graduates took assignments in several countries.

Nakano Seigō　　中野正剛

(1886–1943). Journalist and politician. Born in Fukuoka, he graduated from Waseda University in 1909 and joined the newspaper *Tōkyō asahi shimbun*. He consistently advocated the importance of "popular nationalism" and criticized the dominance of politics by elites. Nakano joined the political party movement and, beginning in 1920, was elected eight times to the lower house of the Diet. He joined the KENSEIKAI party and in 1927 its successor, the RIKKEN MINSEITŌ. Later, as vice-minister of communications in the HAMAGUCHI OSACHI cabinet, he submitted legislation to establish government ownership of the telephone system. But Nakano's political career was destined to end in frustration. His idealistic populism and individualism could not be actualized within Diet politics, and he found himself increasingly isolated from the major factional alignments in the Rikken Minseitō. In 1932 he joined a splinter group called the National Alliance (Kokumin Dōmei), and in 1936, the TŌHŌKAI, serving as president. Believing that Diet politics was hopelessly corrupt, Nakano was briefly attracted to what he believed to be an "idealistic individualism" in Hitler and Mussolini. Moreover, on the basis of this popular nationalism, which held that all societies in Asia had the right to develop their own distinctive cultural identities, Nakano endorsed the "liberation of Asia."

Nakano openly criticized the government headed by TŌJŌ HIDEKI during World War II. He denounced the IMPERIAL RULE ASSISTANCE ASSOCIATION and condemned the government-controlled elections of 1942. In October 1943, suspected of plotting the overthrow of Tōjō, Nakano was arrested and jailed. A month later, while under house arrest, he took his own life.

Nakano Shigeharu　　中野重治

(1902–79). Poet, critic, and novelist. Born in Takaboko, Fukui Prefecture. His first literary works were *tanka* (31-syllable WAKA poems in the classical 5-line form), composed while in secondary school. In 1924 Nakano entered Tōkyō University, and in 1925 he was admitted to the SHINJINKAI (New Man Society), Japan's first Marxist student organization. His poems and an important essay on the *tanka* poet ISHIKAWA TAKUBOKU in the magazine *Roba* (Donkey) organized by

Marxist students under the aegis of the poet MUROO SAISEI, won him praise from AKUTAGAWA RYŪNOSUKE. After graduating in 1927, he devoted himself full time to the PROLETARIAN LITERATURE MOVEMENT.

In the summer of 1931 Nakano joined the underground organization of the Japan Communist Party. In April 1932 he was arrested and imprisoned for nearly two years. He was released with a commuted sentence after making a statement of ideological conversion (TENKŌ) in which he promised to resign from the party. In 1935 he published his first collection of poetry, *Nakano Shigeharu shishū*, and in 1939 the autobiographical novel *Uta no wakare* (Farewell to Song).

After World War II, Nakano rejoined the Communist Party. He worked in party cultural activities throughout the 1950s and early 1960s while writing novels and numerous essays. The novel *Muragimo* (1954, Gut Feelings) captures Nakano's years at Tōkyō University, his Shinjinkai experience, and the conflicting demands of art and political commmitment. *Nashi no hana* (1957–58, Pear Blossoms), based on Nakano's rural childhood, won the Yomiuri Literary Prize in 1959. In 1964 Nakano was purged from the Communist Party along with other dissidents. His long novel *Kō, otsu, hei, tei* (1965–69, A, B, C, D) is a retrospective examination of his relationship with the party.

Nakanoshima Kin'ichi   中能島欣一

(1904–84). Composer, performer, and scholar of sōkyoku *koto* music. Born in Tōkyō. His father, a SHAKUHACHI player, was the eldest son of the Yamada-school KOTO musician Nakanoshima Shōsei (1838–94); his own earliest studies were with his mother, who died when he was 10. After studies in *koto*, NAGAUTA, and *itchū-bushi* with various other teachers, he became head of the Nakanoshima line, and in 1937 was appointed a professor at the Tōkyō Music School (now Tōkyō University of Fine Arts and Music), where he remained throughout his professional career.

Representative of his many works are the *koto* solo *Mittsu no danshō* (1942) and the SHAMISEN solo *Banshikichō* (1941). He frequently performed with his wife, Keiko (1912–88), daughter of the Yamada-school musician Imai Keishō (1871–1947). Nakanoshima also edited all the classical Yamada-school works.

Nakano Tomonori   中野友礼

(1887–1965). Businessman. Born in Fukushima Prefecture; graduate of Kyōto University. As an assistant there he developed the Nakano cell for brine electrolysis. He established the NIPPON SODA CO, LTD, to make commercial use of the new technology. He later diversified and in 1937 developed a financial and industrial combine known as Nissō Kontserun (from the German *Konzern*). After World War II, however, Nakano's business empire was forced to break up.

Nakano Vinegar Co, Ltd

[株]中埜酢店

(Nakano Sumise). Manufacturer of vinegar. Founded in 1804. As a result of its acquisition of American Industries Co, Inc, in 1981, the firm has eight manufacturing plants in the United States. It entered into cooperative agreements with Sunkist Growers, Inc, in 1971, Douwe Egberts France (Mayolande) in 1986, and Campbell Soup Co in 1988. For the fiscal year ending November 1990, sales totaled ¥138.0 billion (US $1.1 billion) and

capitalization stood at ¥600.0 million (US $4.6 million). Headquarters are in Handa, Aichi Prefecture.

Nakano Ward   中野区

(Nakano Ku). One of the 23 wards of Tōkyō. A residential community on the Musashino Plateau. A number of railway stations in the ward are surrounded by shopping centers. Pop: 319,687.

Nakano Yoshio   中野好夫

(1903–85). Scholar of English literature and literary critic. Born in Ehime Prefecture. Graduate of Tōkyō University, where he later taught Elizabethan drama. His translations of English works include *The Merchant of Venice*, *Gulliver's Travels*, and *The Moon and Sixpence.* Other works are *Erizabesu chō engeki kōwa* (1947), lectures on Elizabethan drama, and *Roka Tokutomi Kenjirō* (1972–74), a voluminous critical biography of novelist TOKUTOMI ROKA.

Nakaoka Shintarō   中岡慎太郎

(1838–67). Antishogunate activist from the Tosa domain (now Kōchi Prefecture). The eldest son of a high-ranking village official, he became interested in the SONNŌ JŌI (Revere the Emperor, Expel the Barbarians) movement. In 1862 he went to Kyōto to join proimperial activists. After the COUP D'ETAT OF 30 SEPTEMBER 1863 expelled the radical loyalists from Kyōto, however, Tosa rejected extremism in favor of the more moderate MOVEMENT FOR UNION OF COURT AND SHOGUNATE. Nakaoka was obliged to quit his domain and join other activists in Chōshū (now Yamaguchi Prefecture). In 1864 he participated in the unsuccessful attempt to reestablish Chōshū's influence at the court (see HAMAGURI GOMON INCIDENT). In 1866 he and SAKAMOTO RYŌMA, another Tosa activist, negotiated the SATSUMA-CHŌSHŪ ALLIANCE. Allowed to return to Tosa, he organized a 50-man squad (the RIKUENTAI) to engage in antishogunate activities in Kyōto. In December 1867 he and Sakamoto were killed by members of the Mimawari-gumi, a shogunate patrol squad in Kyōto. See also MEIJI RESTORATION.

Nakao Kumaki   中尾熊喜

(1900–1975). A leader of the Japanese immigrant community in Brazil. Born in Kumamoto Prefecture, Nakao emigrated to Brazil at the age of 14. He helped found the Cotia Cooperative Society (1927) and later established the Jaguaré Fertilizer Co. He was the second president of the Japanese Culture Society of Brazil (Sociedade Brasileira de Cultura Japonesa) and the founder and director of the Center for Japanese-Brazilian Studies (Centro de Estudos Nipo-Brasileiros).

Nakarai Bokuyō   半井卜養

(1607–78). Physician and poet of *haikai* (see HAIKU) and KYŌKA. Born in Sakai, in what is now Ōsaka Prefecture; studied *haikai* under MATSUNAGA TEITOKU, founder of the Teimon school. He was called to Edo (now Tōkyō) to serve as physician to the shōgun's family. The sharp wit of his extemporaneously composed *kyōka* gained him considerable respect among a circle of prominent shogunate officials and their wives. Nakarai is noted chiefly for the posthumous collection *Bokuyō kyōkashū*.

Nakasendai Rebellion   中先代の乱

(Nakasendai no Ran). Unsuccessful rebellion led by Hōjō Tokiyuki (d 1353) against Em-

Nakano Shigeharu
A poet, critic, and novelist, Nakano was also a political activist and longtime Communist Party member.

peror GO-DAIGO and his KEMMU RESTORATION government in 1335; an attempt to restore the KAMAKURA SHOGUNATE, which had fallen in 1333. Remnants of the HŌJŌ FAMILY raised an army with the aid of the Suwa family of Shinano Province (now Nagano Prefecture). They occupied Kamakura briefly but were defeated by ASHIKAGA TAKAUJI. Tokiyuki was later killed in battle by Takauji in 1353. The term *nakasendai* ("middle generation") refers to Tokiyuki. His father, HŌJŌ TAKATOKI, the last Kamakura regent, was called *sendai* ("previous generation"), in contrast to Ashikaga Takauji, who was called *kōdai* ("later generation").

Nakasendō   中山道

Also known as Kiso Kaidō or Kisoji. One of the five main highways (GOKAIDŌ) directly controlled by the Tokugawa shogunate during the Edo period (1600–1868). With 67 post stations along its 500-kilometer (310-mi) route, this road started at Nihombashi, the bridge in Edo (now Tōkyō) where all highways converged, passed through the mountains of central Japan, and ended slightly east of Kyōtō at Kusatsu (in present Shiga Prefecture) where it joined the TŌKAIDŌ. In contrast to the heavily traveled Tōkaidō, the mountainous Nakasendō had little traffic.

Nakashibetsu   中標津[町]

Town in eastern Hokkaidō on the KONSEN HIGHLANDS along the upper and middle reaches of the river Shibetsugawa. Dairy farming is the principal industry here; sugar beets and potatoes are grown. Nakashibetsu is home to the Yōrōushi Hot Spring. Pop: 21,900.

Nakasone Yasuhiro   中曽根康弘

(1918–). Politician and prime minister (1982–87). Born in Gumma Prefecture; graduate of Tōkyō University. Nakasone was elected to the House of Representatives in 1947 and was returned to office in all subsequent elections. He was appointed directorgeneral of the Science and Technology Agency in 1959 and headed the Ministry of International Trade and Industry from 1972 to 1974. In 1982 Nakasone was elected president of the Liberal Democratic Party (LDP) and given the post of prime minister. Domestic policy during his term of office was characterized by administrative reform, fiscal and budgetary stringency, privatization of government-run monopolies such as the national railways and the telephone system, and deregulation of Japan's financial markets. In foreign policy Nakasone attached great importance to Japan's relations with the United States, particularly in areas such as policy toward the Soviet Union and trade issues. Suspicion surrounding the RECRUIT SCANDAL, which implicated numerous politicians in influence peddling, brought Nakasone's official withdrawal from the LDP in 1989.

Nakatomi no Kamatari → Fujiwara no Kamatari

Nakatsu   中津[市]

City in northern Ōita Prefecture, Kyūshū, on the Suō Sea. Nakatsu flourished as a castle town in the Edo period (1600–1868). Industrial products include steel tubes and porcelain ware. It is the birthplace of the scholar FUKUZAWA YUKICHI. The Taigadō is a hall that houses the paintings of IKE NO TAIGA. Naka-

Nakayama Ichirō This economist's views were influential during Japan's post–World War II period of recovery and growth.

tsu is the gateway to the gorge YABAKEI. Pop: 66,388.

Nakatsugawa 中津川[市]

City on the river Kisogawa in southeastern Gifu Prefecture, central Honshū. In the Edo period (1600–1868) Nakatsugawa was an important post-station town. A major railway line and highway pass through the city, and industry and commerce thrive. To the southeast lie Enakyō and Enasan prefectural parks. Pop: 53,722.

Nakatsuka Ippekirō 中塚一碧楼

(1887–1946). HAIKU poet. Real name Nakatsuka Naozō. Born in Okayama Prefecture; attended Waseda University. Nakatsuka participated in KAWAHIGASHI HEKIGOTŌ's Shinkeikō (New Trend) haiku movement and became a leading writer of free-verse haiku. In 1913 he published the haiku collection *Hakagura.* Beginning in 1915 Nakatsuka participated in the publication of the magazine *Kaikō* and eventually became its editor. The style of his early poems was decadent but gradually grew more refreshing and lyrical.

Nakatsukasa no Naishi nikki

中務内侍日記

(Diary of Nakatsukasa no Naishi). The diary of a woman in service at the imperial court; late 13th century. The work is attributed to a daughter of Fujiwara no Nagatsune, an attendant to the heir apparent who later became Emperor FUSHIMI. There are about 150 WAKA poems in the diary, which chronicles the years 1280 to 1292. The work is one of the last in the tradition of poetic diaries by court ladies. See also NIKKI BUNGAKU.

Nakatsu Keikoku 中津渓谷

Gorge on the upper reaches of the river Nakatsugawa (tributary of the SAGAMIGAWA), northern Kanagawa Prefecture, central Honshū. It is noted for huge rugged rocks, spring foliage, and crimson autumn leaves. Length: approximately 4 km (2.5 mi).

Nakatsukyō 中津峡

Gorge on the upper reaches of the Nakatsugawa (a tributary of the ARAKAWA), western Saitama Prefecture, central Honshū. Located within Chichibu-Tama National Park. Sheer cliffs of the Chichibu Paleolithic bed soar up on both banks. Length: 6 km (3.7 mi).

Nakauchi Isao 中内功

(1922–). Businessman and chairman of DAIEI, INC (1982–). Born in Hyōgo Prefecture. After graduating from Kōbe University of Commerce in 1941, he joined Nichimen Co, Ltd. In 1957 he established Daiei Pharmaceutical Industries and entered the discount retail business by opening a store in Ōsaka specifically aimed at housewives. Since then he has opened a succession of supermarkets nationwide. By 1980 Daiei had annual sales of more than ¥1 trillion (US $4.4 billion). The Daiei group comprised 190 stores in 1990. In 1988 Nakauchi became the owner of a professional baseball team, the Fukuoka Daiei Hawks.

Nakaumi 中海

Also called Nakanoumi. Saltwater lagoon located between Tottori and Shimane prefectures, western Honshū. Prawn and eel culture flourish. A project to reclaim 28 sq km (11 sq mi) of land for agricultural and in-

dustrial use is under way. Area: 98 sq km (38 sq mi); circumference: 183 km (114 mi); depth: 17 m (56 ft).

Nakaura Julião 中浦ジュリアン

(ca 1570–1633). One of the envoys sent by the CHRISTIAN DAIMYŌ of Kyūshū on the MISSION TO EUROPE OF 1582. Born in Nakaura in the Ōmura domain (now part of Nagasaki Prefecture), he studied at the Jesuit seminary in Arima. The mission left Japan in 1582 and returned in 1590. Nakaura entered the Society of Jesus in 1591 and was ordained in 1608. Even when the Tokugawa shogunate intensified its persecution of Christianity after 1612, he continued his missionary activities. He died a martyr in October 1633.

Nakayama Gishū 中山義秀

(1900–1969). Novelist. Real name Nakayama Yoshihide. Born in Fukushima Prefecture. Graduate of Waseda University. Nakayama's novelette *Atsumonozaki* won the 1938 Akutagawa Prize. His experience as a war reporter during World War II resulted in the short story "Teniyan no matsujitsu" (1948), a eulogistic account of two young intellectuals who died on the Pacific island of Tinian toward the end of the war. After 1950 he wrote historical novels. He often took as subjects historical figures who fought for lost causes. Other works include "Ishibumi" (1939), a short story based on his grandfather, and *Shōan* (1963–64), a novel about the 16th-century warrior AKECHI MITSUHIDE, which was awarded the Noma Literary Prize.

Nakayama Ichirō 中山伊知郎

(1898–1980). Economist. Born in Mie Prefecture. After graduating from the Tōkyō University of Commerce (now Hitotsubashi University) in 1923, he studied under J. A. Schumpeter in Germany. Nakayama later became a professor at his alma mater and taught economic theory. In 1949 he began a seven-year term as president of Hitotsubashi. He served from 1946 as member and later as chairman of the Central Labor Relations Commission. Nakayama helped popularize the general equilibrium theory of economics in Japan and contributed to the development of an econometric analysis of the Japanese economy. He trained a number of young economists, and his policies were important to Japan's postwar recovery and growth. Nakayama's major works on economics are found in *Nakayama Ichirō zenshū* (1972–81).

Nakayama Iwata 中山岩太

(1895–1949). Photographer. Born in Fukuoka Prefecture. After graduating from Tōkyō Bijutsu Gakkō (now Tōkyō University of Fine Arts and Music) in 1918, Nakayama opened a photography studio in New York. In 1927 he returned to Japan and became a pillar of the avant-garde photography movement. Nakayama made illusionistic photomontages combining elements such as nudes and seashells.

Nakayama Miki 中山みき

(1798–1887). Founder of TENRIKYŌ. Born in Sammaiden, Yamato Province (now the city of Tenri, Nara Prefecture). Her outlook on life was influenced by the pessimism of her family, devout followers of PURE LAND BUDDHISM. At her parents' urging she abandoned plans to become a nun and was married in 1810 at the age of 13. Nakayama was her married name. Out of a desire to ease the lot of humankind she began to devote herself to the worship of Shintō deities and to acts of

compassion. At about age 40 she claimed to have received a revelation from the deity Tenri Ō no Mikoto and to have become the "Shrine of God." She decided to give away her belongings to the needy, and her family suffered great poverty. Some 20 years later Miki began to work miracles of healing, gaining many followers and remaining firm in her purpose despite persecution and imprisonment. She wrote the *Mikagura uta* (Songs for the Sacred Dance) and the *Ofudesaki* (Tip of the Divine Writing Brush), both considered the scriptures of Tenrikyō. Her followers believe that she eternally resides in the world, extending protection.

Nakayama Shichiri 中山七里

Gorge on the upper reaches of the river Hidagawa, central Gifu Prefecture, central Honshū. Located between Gero Hot Spring and the town of Kanayama, it is a part of Hida-Kisogawa Quasi-National Park. Length: approximately 23 km (14 mi).

Nakayama Shimpei 中山晋平

(1887–1952). Composer. Born in Nagano Prefecture; educated at the Tōkyō School of Music (now Tōkyō University of Fine Arts and Music). He gained fame with his song "Kachūsha no uta" (1914), as performed by MATSUI SUMAKO in a drama based on Tolstoy's last novel, *Voskresenie* (1899, Resurrection). However, he became best known for his many melodies in the style of Japanese folk songs, festival music, *kouta* chamber songs, and children's songs; his "new folk songs" (*shimmin'yō*) were an important influence on popular commercial music (RYŪKŌKA) in the 1920s. Their lyrics were often by well-known poets, notably NOGUCHI UJŌ (1882–1945), KITAHARA HAKUSHŪ (1885–1942), and SAIJŌ YASO (1892–1970). His songs, which are still widely sung today, include "Sendō kouta" (1922), "Habu no minato" (1928), and "Tōkyō ondo" (1933).

Nakayama Sohei 中山素平

(1906–). Banker. Born in Tōkyō. After graduating from Tōkyō University of Commerce (now Hitotsubashi University), Nakayama joined the INDUSTRIAL BANK OF JAPAN, LTD, in 1929 and became chairman in 1968 after serving as vice-president and president. He concurrently served as director of the JAPAN DEVELOPMENT BANK and the JAPAN ASSOCIATION OF CORPORATE EXECUTIVES (Keizai Dōyūkai). One of Japan's leading bankers, he played an important role in reorganizing the shipping industry and rescuing the Yamaichi Securities Co, Ltd, from bankruptcy.

Nakayama Steel Works, Ltd

[株]中山製鋼所

(Nakayama Seikōsho). Company engaged in the manufacture and sale of steel and secondary steel products. Incorporated in 1923. Under the brand name Three Stars, the company sells such products as galvanized and corrugated sheets. Progress is being made in developing new products and engineering. Sales for the fiscal year ending March 1991 totaled ¥153.9 billion (US $1.1 billion), and the company was capitalized at ¥12.9 billion (US $94.0 million). Headquarters are in Ōsaka.

Nakayama Tadamitsu 中山忠光

(1845–65). Court noble and activist in the movement to overthrow the Tokugawa shogunate and restore direct imperial rule. In 1863 he joined loyalists in the TENCHŪGUMI

REBELLION, an attack on shogunate officials in Yamato Province (now Nara Prefecture). The following year he was murdered by opponents. See MEIJI RESTORATION.

Nakaya Ukichirō   中谷宇吉郎

(1900–1962). Physicist. Known internationally for his research on snow. Born in Kaga, Ishikawa Prefecture, he graduated from Tōkyō University in 1925. He became interested in snow while a professor at Hokkaidō University and in 1938 produced the first laboratory-synthesized snow crystals in the world. He served as director of Hokkaidō University's Institute of Low Temperature Science. He was also a noted essayist, whose works included *Fuyu no hana* (1938, Flowers of Winter). His *Snow Crystals: Natural and Artificial* was published in 1954.

Nakazato Kaizan   中里介山

(1885–1944). Popular writer and author of the highly acclaimed multivolume novel DAIBOSATSU TŌGE (1913–41). Born Nakazato Yanosuke in Hamura, Kanagawa Prefecture (now part of suburban Tōkyō), Nakazato was very poor as a youth and was drawn to the FREEDOM AND PEOPLE'S RIGHTS MOVEMENT (Jiyū Minken Undō) and the ideas of UCHIMURA KANZŌ and other Christian thinkers. He was also a student of Buddhist philosophy and came to be known as an outspoken pacifist poet. By the time he joined the staff of the newspaper MIYAKO SHIMBUN in 1906, he had decided on writing as a career.

The first installment of *Daibosatsu Tōge*, his masterpiece and perhaps the most successful work of POPULAR FICTION in Japan, appeared in the *Miyako shimbun* in 1913; however, only with the appearance of a new series in 1925 in the *Tōkyō nichinichi* and other newspapers did it win nationwide popular acclaim. The series was left uncompleted after the publication of the 32nd volume in 1941. *Daibosatsu Tōge* (tr *Dai-Bosatsu Toge: Great Boddhisattva Pass*, 1929) is set against the turbulent political events of the 1850s and 1860s leading up to the MEIJI RESTORATION of 1868. In this panoramic sweep one figure stands out, the master swordsman Tsukue Ryūnosuke, who was the first character in popular Japanese literature to emerge as a fascinating individual.

The work lacks a unifying plot; it is instead a series of episodes, each bearing on the human cycle of life, suffering, death, and man's stubborn blindness to truth. At the same time, by exploring the meaning of events like peasant uprisings, the author brings a historical depth to his work. An important reason for the immense popularity of the *Daibosatsu Tōge* series during the 1920s may have been its timeliness: readers suffering from the post–World War I economic depression and the social unrest that followed the great Tōkyō Earthquake of 1923 felt that they could somehow identify with its amoral, nihilistic antihero.

In 1920 Nakazato resigned from the *Miyako shimbun*. He settled in his home town of Hamura, founded a school based on agrarianist principles, and traveled in Japan, Korea, China, and the United States. During World War II, he chose not to abandon his pacifist principles and, unlike many of his colleagues, refused to contribute his talents as a writer to the war effort.

Nakazato Tsuneko   中里恒子

(1909–87). Novelist. Real name Nakazato Tsune. Born in Kanagawa Prefecture. Na-kazato graduated from Kanagawa Girls' Higher School. She established herself as a writer with the encouragement of the novelist YOKOMITSU RIICHI (1898–1947). In 1938, with her short story "Noriai basha," she became the first woman to win the Akutagawa Prize. After World War II, she wrote a number of novels describing international marriages, including *Mariannu monogatari* (1946; title later changed to *Bochi no haru*) and *Kusari* (1959), which deals with her daughter's marriage to an American. In her works of the 1970s and 1980s she moved from a refined description of the inner workings of human life to a more symbolic style of writing, as in *Utamakura* (1973; winner of the Yomiuri Literary Prize in the same year). In 1974 Nakazato received the Japan Art Academy Prize, and she became a member of the academy in 1983.

Nakazawa Dōni   中沢道二

(1725–1803). Teacher and propagator of SHINGAKU, the school of ethics directed at commoners. Born in Kyōto into a family of textile weavers. He succeeded to the family business, but in middle age became a student of TESHIMA TOAN, a disciple of ISHIDA BAIGAN. At Toan's behest in 1779 he went to Edo (now Tōkyō) to spread Shingaku teachings and to establish a school. He lectured widely in eastern Japan and was given permission by MATSUDAIRA SADANOBU to lecture shogunal retainers. Dōni's success was largely due to his informal lecturing style and his advice that the study of life itself was the highest form of learning. His major work is *Dōni ō dōwa* (1795–1810), a collection of talks.

Nakijin Castle remains   今帰仁城跡

(Nakijinjō *ato*). Late-14th-century castle site at Nakijin, Okinawa Prefecture. Belonging to the kings of Hokuzan, the northernmost of the three medieval Ryukyuan kingdoms (see OKINAWA), Nakijin Castle flourished for nearly a century. After Hokuzan was subdued in 1416 (or 1422) by Shō Hashi (see CHŪZAN'Ō), unifier of the Ryūkyūs, Nakijin Castle functioned (until the 17th century) as an administrative base for the northern Ryūkyūs. See also GUSUKU.

nakōdo   仲人

(go-between). A person who arranges marriages. The *nakōdo*'s duties and level of involvement with the couple vary, but the traditional role includes introducing the parties, acting as an intermediary in the preliminary negotiations, presiding over the MARRIAGE ceremonies, and maintaining a long-term relationship with the couple. The *nakōdo*'s spouse usually assists in these duties. Most *nakōdo* are not "professionals"— more frequently they are people who command respect and who can lend an air of authority and legitimacy to the marriage negotiations, such as one party's teacher, superior at work, or elder relative. The institution of the *nakōdo* has a strong association with the traditional Japanese custom of *miai kekkon*, or "arranged marriage," but even couples who meet and decide to marry on their own what is known as a *ren'ai kekkon*, or "love marriage," almost always ask an honorary *nakōdo* to be present at their wedding ceremony for form's sake.

A *nakōdo*'s role in marriage negotiations typically begins with a request for assistance from a man or woman interested in finding a suitable marriage partner (the request may also come from the person's family). The *nakōdo* decides on a match from among other requests on hand or through informal personal connections, with particular attention to three areas: (1) family background; (2) the earning potential of the man, since he will have primary responsibility for supporting the family; and (3) personal characteristics. After informally approaching one party the *nakōdo* proposes the match to the other, usually by means of a written request that includes a photograph and brief personal history of the future bride or groom. If the response is favorable, each party will refrain from considering another offer until the proceedings are completed (successfully or not) as a sign of good faith.

The *nakōdo*'s next responsibility is the arrangement of the MIAI, or first formal meeting of the prospective bride and groom and their parents. The role of the *nakōdo* at the *miai* is to facilitate conversation and to ensure that the two parties create a favorable impression upon one another. If the *miai* is successful and the two principals express a desire to see each other again, the *nakōdo* communicates these sentiments to the respective families. If, on the other hand, one of the parties feels that the pairing is not suitable, and attempts at negotiation are unsuccessful, it is the job of the *nakōdo* to relay the refusal with tact and grace so as to avoid any loss of face to either party.

When the couple become engaged to marry, the *nakōdo* officiates at the YUINŌ, or ritual exchange of betrothal gifts. The *nakōdo* and spouse also officiate at the wedding, and, if the *nakōdo* is a woman, her husband may be asked to make a speech wishing the newlyweds a long and happy marriage. However, this important role is sometimes assumed by another respected or prestigious person who may or may not have been part of the prior negotiations.

In most cases the *nakōdo*'s responsibilities do not end with the wedding ceremony. A *nakōdo* may be called upon to mediate in the event of marital discord, or, in extreme cases, even to arrange for divorce. Newlyweds are generally expected to acknowledge the relationship with their *nakōdo* throughout their marriage. See also WEDDINGS.

Nakoku   奴国

Small state in northern Kyūshū during the 2nd and 3rd centuries. Nakoku has been identified with Wa no Nakoku (the country of Na in Wa) mentioned in the Chinese *Hou Han shu* (History of the Later Han Dynasty [25–220]) and with the inscription on a gold seal (KAN NO WA NO NA NO KOKUŌ NO IN) discovered near Fukuoka in 1784. The seal was thought to have been bestowed on the ruler of Nakoku by the first emperor of that dynasty. Nakoku is thought to be identical with Nanoagata or Nanotsu, places mentioned in the chronicle NIHON SHOKI (720), located near Hakata, now the city of Fukuoka.

Nakoso no Seki   勿来関

(Barrier of Nakoso). Originally called Kikuta no Seki, it was known as Nakoso (literally, "do not come") no Seki by the beginning of the Heian period (794–1185). Located in what is now the city of Iwaki in Fukushima Prefecture, it was one of the three ancient fortified barriers (the others were SHIRAKAWA NO SEKI and Nezu no Seki) built in northeastern Honshū in the 8th century to prevent southward incursions by the aboriginal EZO people. Nakoso no Seki is one of the stock

Nakaya Ukichirō This 20th-century physicist is known for his research on snow crystals.

Nakazato Kaizan This writer's multivolume, episodic novel *Daibosatsu Tōge* (1913–41) is considered one of the masterpieces of Japanese popular fiction.

place names known as UTA MAKURA and evokes the loneliness and desolation of military service or exile on a distant frontier.

namahage 生剝

Custom in which visitors, costumed as gods or demons called *namahage*, make the rounds of local households on the eve of Koshōgatsu (the 15th of the first month in the old lunar calendar; 15 January in the present calendar). Although the custom is found widely in Japan, its observance on the OGA PENINSULA in Akita Prefecture is especially famous and has become a tourist attraction. Two or three young men in the village, wearing fierce-looking masks and covered with straw capes, visit each house and ask whether there is a disobedient child or lazy person in the family. They are then plied with food and drink and sent away with money and rice cakes.

namako → sea cucumbers

Namamugi Jiken → Richardson Affair

Namba 難波

Busy commercial and transportation district straddling the border between the Chūō and Minami wards of the city of Ōsaka, extending from the Dōtombori district on the north to the area around Namba Station on the south. The development of the district began with the opening of the Nankai Electric Railway in 1884, and it accelerated rapidly with the opening of many department stores and subways. Today, Namba, also called Mina-

mi, or "south," is one of Ōsaka's two busiest districts, the other being the Kita, or "north," district around Ōsaka Station (see UMEDA).

Namba Daisuke → Toranomon Incident

namban 南蛮

(literally, "southern barbarian"). Term applied principally to the Iberian and Italian missionaries, merchants, and sailors in Japan in the 16th and 17th centuries and to European customs and products. The term originated in China, where all foreigners were regarded as barbarians. Hence "southern barbarians" referred to the inhabitants of countries to the south of China. Similarly, the Japanese used the term in reference to the peoples of Siam (now Thailand), Java, and the Philippines.

The Portuguese and Spaniards had sailed from the south, either from Macao or the Philippines, and so by extension the term *nambanjin*, or "southern barbarian men," came to be applied to them as well (in distinction to the word *kōmōjin*, or "red-haired men," used in connection with the Dutch and English).

namban art 南蛮美術

(*namban bijutsu*; "Southern barbarian" art). Art connected in any way with the European missionaries and merchants in Japan during the 16th and 17th centuries. This broad definition allows the inclusion of not only the works of Japanese artists painting in Western style, to which the term is often restricted, but also European imported art and traditionally executed Japanese screens depicting Europeans. Most of the *namban* art produced in Japan can be dated between 1590, when interest in things European reached its peak, and 1614, when missionaries were expelled from the country.

The Jesuits imported from Europe a large number of religious paintings to decorate their churches and to use as gifts. Only a few are now extant. These paintings also served as models for Japanese artists. The arrival of the Italian Jesuit Giovanni Niccolo in 1583 enabled the Jesuits to organize courses on Western painting and engraving at their boys' school in Kyūshū. The paintings produced by these students and other Japanese artists were for the most part copies of Western pictures and were often religious in theme.

The majority of extant *namban* paintings produced by Japanese, however, are secular in theme, many of them probably inspired by the portraits, atlases, and illustrated books known to have been brought back from Europe by the youthful envoys of the

Christian *daimyō* of Kyūshū (see MISSION TO EUROPE OF 1582) on their return to Japan in 1590. Prominent among such works are the large sixfold screens portraying idyllic pastoral scenes with languid Western figures, often playing musical instruments in the foreground, and with lakes and mountains in the background. Another type of painting inspired by imported European works is seen in screens depicting either maps of the world or bird's-eye views of Western cities.

In its broadest sense, the term *namban* art includes works that, although executed in traditional Japanese style, take Europeans as their principal theme. Of these, the best-known examples are the *namban* screens. Usually produced in pairs, about 60 of these six-panel screens have been cataloged. Most of the screens appear to have been painted by lesser members of the KANŌ SCHOOL. The copperplate illustrations found in some of the books published by the JESUIT MISSION PRESS can also be included in the wider definition of *namban* art.

Nambanji 南蛮寺

(Southern Barbarian Temple). A Jesuit church built in Kyōto in 1576. The church was dedicated to the Assumption of Our Lady, and the official inauguration took place at Christmas 1576. The building was destroyed in 1588 on the orders of TOYOTOMI HIDEYOSHI. A contemporary fan painting by Kanō Motohide depicts the church as a three-story building in Japanese style. A metal European-style bell bearing the Jesuit IHS monogram and the date 1577, preserved in the temple Myōshinji in Kyōto, is thought to have belonged to the church.

namban trade 南蛮貿易

(*namban bōeki*; literally, "southern barbarian" trade). Trade conducted by Iberian merchants in Japan during the 16th and 17th centuries. It was carried on mainly by the Portuguese, who utilized their spacious carracks and their Macao entrepôt to supply the Japanese with Chinese silk in exchange for silver. A small trade was also conducted by Spanish merchants until 1624, when Spaniards were expelled from the country.

The first Europeans to reach Japan were three Portuguese traders who landed on Tanegashima, an island south of Kyūshū, in 1543. European merchants were subsequently allowed to enter the country freely and trade with little or no restriction. After experimenting with various Kyūshū ports, in 1570 the Portuguese sounded the Bay of Nagasaki, and this fine natural harbor became the headquarters of their commerce in Japan. The Ming dynasty (1368–1644) had forbidden direct commerce between China and Japan, so the Portuguese were able to monopolize the Sino-Japanese trade. The official carrack carrying silk to Nagasaki was limited to one a year and was placed under the command of a *capitão-mor* (captain major), a crown appointment. A system called the *armação* was developed by which Macao citizens were able to purchase a share in the trading venture. From the beginning of the 17th century the silk was sold in bulk to a consortium of Japanese merchants; this system was called *pancada* in Portuguese and ITOWAPPU in Japanese. The end to the *namban* trade was occasioned by the SHIMABARA UPRISING of 1637–38, which made the shogunal government apprehensive about the threat of Christianity and the possibility of intervention by European colonial powers. As a result, in 1639 the Portuguese were ordered to leave Japan.

Nambara Shigeru 南原繁

(1889–1974). Political scientist and educator. Born in Kagawa Prefecture. While a student at Tōkyō University, he was drawn to Christianity, in particular to the MUKYŌKAI (nonchurch) movement of UCHIMURA KANZŌ. He began his teaching career in 1921 at his alma mater. During World War II, as a Christian and a liberal, he spoke out against the militarist government. After the war, as president of Tōkyō University (1945–51) and a member of several government committees on educational reform, he vigorously defended academic freedom; he also criticized the policies of Prime Minister YOSHIDA SHIGERU and opposed revision of the 1947 constitution. His works are collected in the six-volume *Nambara Shigeru chosakushū* (1972–73).

Nambokuchō period → Northern and Southern Courts

Nambokuchō seijun ron 南北朝正閏論

Historical debate (*ron*) over the question of imperial legitimacy (*seijun*) during the period of the NORTHERN AND SOUTHERN COURTS (1337–92). Although the Northern Court at Kyōto was supported by the MUROMACHI SHOGUNATE (1338–1573), KITABATAKE CHIKAFUSA, an early leader of the Southern Court at Yoshino, argued for that court's legitimacy in his historical tract JINNŌ SHŌTŌ KI (1339–43, Chronicle of the Direct Descent of Divine Sovereigns). Long after the Southern Court itself had ceased to exist, the case for its legitimacy was renewed during the Edo period (1600–1868), especially by scholars of the MITO SCHOOL, who argued that Emperor GO-DAIGO (r 1318–39) and his successors (southern rulers) had retained possession of the IMPERIAL REGALIA (mirror, sword, and jewels), the unchallengeable symbols of imperial rank.

In 1911 the government of Prime Minister KATSURA TARŌ became embroiled in a debate over the presentation of the Northern and Southern Courts in history textbooks. It was argued that there could be no division of imperial sovereignty as suggested by the simultaneous existence of two courts. The Katsura government, after consulting Emperor MEIJI (a descendant of the Northern Court), decided in favor of southern legitimacy, decreeing that school texts should deal with the years 1337–92 as "The Period of the Yoshino Court" (Yoshino *jidai*).

Nambu Chūhei 南部忠平

(1904–). Track and field athlete in the long and triple jumps. Born in Hokkaidō; gradu-

ate of Waseda University. Professor at Kyōto Industrial University. He set a world record of 7.98 meters (26.18 ft) in the long jump in 1931, which remained an unbroken Japanese record for 39 years. He won the gold medal in the triple jump in the 1932 Los Angeles Olympic Games.

Nambu Yōichirō 南部陽一郎

(1921–). Theoretical physicist. A US citizen since 1970, he was born in Fukui Prefecture and graduated from Tōkyō University. He became a professor at Ōsaka City University in 1950 and at the University of Chicago in 1958. In 1965 he proposed a three-color quark model, laying the groundwork for research in quantum chromodynamics and contributing greatly to the advancement of unified field theory. He received the Order of Culture in 1978.

name cards 名刺

(*meishi*). Card printed with a person's name; place of employment, title, address, and telephone number are usually included. In Japan such cards are exchanged during introductory greetings at business and social occasions. Name cards with a person's name handwritten on Japanese paper were first used in Japan around the beginning of the 19th century. Western-style printed name cards were probably first used in the final years of the Tokugawa shogunate (1603–1867) by government officials who came into contact with foreigners at the time of the opening of Japan. During the Meiji period (1868–1912) various types of name cards came into common use. Businessmen who meet often with foreigners generally use cards with the information printed on one side in English. Japanese customarily exchange name cards at their first meeting to establish relative status.

Namerikawa 滑川[市]

City in north central Toyama Prefecture, central Honshū, on Toyama Bay. Its proximity to the city of Toyama has made it an industrial and residential suburb. Machine, electrical, and pharmaceutical plants are located here. Stock farming and the cultivation of rice and tulips are also important. Pop: 30,923.

names 名前

(*namae*). Proper names in Japan present a problem since virtually all Chinese characters used in names have a multiplicity of readings—both ON READINGS, based on Chinese pronunciation, and KUN READINGS, based on native Japanese words. Moreover, since most names are written with two or more characters, it is often impossible to be sure of the combination of readings needed in any particular case without having personal knowledge. Conversely, the same name element usually can be found written with a number of different characters. In the case of personal names, for example, more than 130 characters have 10 or more possible name readings, and the common name elements *taka* and *nori* are found written with 168 and 225 different characters, respectively. Since some characters and readings are much more common in names than others, it usually is possible to arrive at the likely reading of a name, and the number of characters available for use when registering the personal names of children is now limited by law. However, since there is no restriction on the readings that can be given to these characters, many uncertainties remain in all types of names.

People's Names——In Japanese usage the family name comes before the personal name, but otherwise the treatment of names is much the same as in the West. A Japanese has a family name and an official personal name; artistic or professional names also are often used. Suffixes equivalent to titles such as Mr. or Mrs. (san) or Dr (sensei) are used after the family name in formal reference, and within the family or among intimates the familiar ending chan is used after personal names, often in abbreviated form, very much as -y is used in diminutives such as Willy or Lizzy.

Group (Clan and Family) Names——Up to the end of the 8th century, the two main types of group names within society were UJI, to indicate lineage groups or clans, and KABANE, hereditary titles of nobility granted to *uji* and individuals. In the case of an individual, the *kabane* was used between the name of the *uji* and the personal name; for example, Nakatomi no Muraji Kamako indicates one Kamako of the Nakatomi clan who had the rank of *muraji*.

During the Heian period (794–1185), clans such as the Ariwara, Minamoto, and Taira, which were related to the imperial line and had been granted their names by the court, increased in size so much that subdivisions became necessary. These smaller groups usually were distinguished by their locations. Groups within the great Fujiwara clan, for example, called themselves either by the place within the capital of Kyōto where they had their residence (e.g., Ichijō [First Avenue]) or, if they were based in an outlying area, by a new group name that combined one character denoting the locality with one character of the clan name (e.g., Itō was the name of the clan based in Izu, *tō* being the *on* reading of the character for *fuji*).

From the 13th century on, military families in rural areas distinguished themselves from others of the same clan by using as their standard family name the name of their locality, and all types of group names had become wholly fixed by the early 17th cen-

tury. With a few exceptions, the use of family names remained limited to the upper classes of society, with the lower orders generally being referred to only by their personal names or, where necessary, by prefixes indicative of their trade or location.

Two years after the Meiji Restoration of 1868, however, everyone was allowed to take a family name, and in 1875 family names were made compulsory. Certain names came to be adopted more generally in some areas than others, but the whole process led to the appearance of family names of every conceivable kind, and the frequent mistakes made in writing the characters for newly acquired names have in some cases survived to add to the present confusion of Japanese name readings.

At the present time, the names Satō and Suzuki each account for more than 1.5 percent of the population, and other common family names are Tanaka, Yamamoto, Watanabe, Kobayashi, Saitō, Tamura, Itō, and Takahashi. In the case of family names, native Japanese readings are more frequent than *on* readings.

Personal Names—As in many societies, it was the custom in ancient times in Japan not to call people, especially superiors, by their true names but to refer to them by their titles or similar indirect terms. It was felt that the name was so intimately associated with the person that knowledge or use of it took something away from the individual concerned. In ancient court circles, for example, for a man to ask a woman's true name was equivalent to a proposal of marriage, and for her to give it indicated acceptance. Court ladies of the time therefore would be known generally by the court titles of male relatives or other sobriquets (e.g., MURASAKI SHIKIBU, SEI SHŌNAGON). Even today most countries usually refer to their dignitaries by title rather than by name, and in Japan the personal name of the emperor, for example, is never used.

Various considerations may apply in the naming of children in modern Japan—seniority in the case of brothers, for example, or the advice of fortune-tellers in choosing characters deemed appropriate to the family name. In nearly all cases, though, names and characters are chosen primarily for their auspicious meanings and happy associations, that is, as talismans of good fortune.

The choice of characters permitted for use in personal names was first limited in 1948 and was restricted as of 1990 to the 1,945 JŌYŌ KANJI and the 284 characters selected for use only in personal names.

Men's Names—Until late in the 8th century, men's personal names usually ended in *-maro* or *-ko*, but thereafter they most often took the form of four-syllable Japanese readings of two-character combinations (e.g., Michi-naga) or, less often, three-syllable Japanese readings of only one character (e.g., Susumu). The custom also arose of demonstrating a link between two people (as in brothers) by their having one character of their names in common. A father might give his son one of the characters in his own name. Similarly, a military lord or the dignitary in charge of the coming-of-age ceremony (GEMPUKU) might grant the use of a character from his name when a young man was given his adult name. A teacher often granted a pupil the use of a character on the latter's attainment of fully accredited status, a practice still continued today in the art world.

In premodern Japan men of the upper ranks of society could have a variety of personal names. The main categories were as follows: (1) *Yōmyō* or *dōmyō* (child name). Often ending in *-waka*, *-maru*, *-maro*, or *-ō* (e.g., Ushiwaka), a name of this type was customarily given to a boy on or by the seventh day after birth (SHICHIYA) and generally was used until superseded by other names at *gempuku* when he was about 15. Men of the lower classes normally used these child names throughout their lives. (2) *Tsūshō* or *yobina, zokumyō, kemyō* (current name). This name was given to a male at *gempuku* together with his *jitsumyō* (see below) and was the one by which he generally was known (e.g., Tarō). Some of these names could take prefixes to indicate a particular generation (Kotarō for Tarō II) or lineage (Heitarō for a member of the Heike [i.e., Taira] clan). (3) *Jitsumyō* or *nanori* (true name). This was a formal adult name used in association with the clan name (Minamoto no Shitagau [also spelled Shitagō] for Shitagau of the Minamoto clan) and so closely associated with the individual that other people would use it of him very rarely or never at all if he was their superior. Upon the death of a dignitary, his *jitsumyō* would be used as his *imina* (posthumous name).

Many other types of name were, and still are, used in special circumstances. Nicknames (*adana*) were not uncommon, used either alone or in conjunction with a *tsūshō*—for example, Nossori Jūbei ("Plodder" Jūbei). More current are the YAGŌ (house names) traditionally associated with *kabuki* actors and families, which are shouted out by members of the audience during performances.

More widespread are names consisting of two Chinese characters, always appropriately pronounced in their *on* readings. It is natural that Buddhist names and the vast majority of artistic, literary, and other assumed names are read with *on* readings of the characters because of the cultural heritage from China and because of the formal, classical associations of such readings. Names of this kind include *azana* (formal literary names), adopted by classical scholars and the like; *hōmyō* (Buddhist names), taken upon entry into the priesthood; and *kaimyō* (precept names), for use as posthumous titles of exalted personages and, in the case of emperors in modern times, also for their reign period while they are still alive (e.g., Meiji, Taishō, Shōwa). Also to be included here is a host of *gō* (pseudonyms) and *gagō* (elegant pseudonyms), used by writers and artists, often in bewildering succession. Hokusai, for example, was only one of more than 30 *gō* used by the same artist. Particular types of *gō* include *haimyō*, or names taken by *haiku* poets, and the *geimei* (artistic names) used by actors and other kinds of entertainers.

Sometimes men's personal names also are read in the *on* even though they are officially registered in their *kun* readings. Hence, the novelists Itō Hitoshi and Kikuchi Hiroshi are universally known as Itō Sei and Kikuchi Kan, respectively. On occasion this is done to make the name sound more formal or academic, but more often it is simply for brevity.

Women's Names—Before the 9th century most women's names seem to have ended in *-me*, *-iratsume*, or *-toji*, as in Shimame. From then on, high-ranking court ladies had formal personal names consisting of one character followed by the suffix *-ko*—for example, Sadako—but the taboos against the general use of such *jitsumyō* led also to the wide use of *yōmyō, tsūshō* (e.g., Murasaki Shikibu), and, later, to the use of various elegant names, many of them derived from the TALE OF GENJI. Among humbler women the *-ko* suffix was never used, but the 16th century saw the introduction of the prefix *o-*, as in Oichi. This practice spread during the Edo period (1600–1868), when most women had two-syllable names, often written in KANA (phonetic syllabic characters) and a woman's status was immediately evident from her name.

The changes brought about by the Meiji Restoration, however, led to a vast increase in the use of Chinese characters. The employment of the formerly aristocratic suffix *-ko* grew steadily from about 3 percent in the mid-1880s to 80 percent in 1935. Today women follow the ancient court practice of having two-syllable names plus *-ko* or having elegant three-syllable names such as Harue with no suffix.

Place Names—Accounts of the origins of place names are a common feature of the earliest written works in Japan, especially those known as FUDOKI, but many of their etymologies are still uncertain. In general, though, they can be said to derive from natural features or historical causes.

The names of geographical origin generally refer to such obvious features of the land as a river, mountain, valley, plain, moor, ford, or beach. These designations often are combined with prefixes describing such aspects as size, length, depth, or direction, such as Nagasaki (long cape), Yokohama (side beach), or Hiroshima (broad island).

History-based names include some derived from the AINU, most typically those ending in *-betsu* or *-nai* in northern parts of Japan. Names such as Shinden (new rice fields) indicate the development of an area, while others show religious associations by the use of such components as *kami* (god), *miya* (shrine), and *tera* (temple). Also, Edo was renamed Tōkyō (eastern capital) in 1868 in contrast to its predecessor Kyōto (capital metropolis).

As well as specific administrative areas such as *ken* (prefecture), *shi* (city), and *gun* (rural district), more extensive regions may also have names. For example, in addition to Kinai (the prefectures around Kyōto), there are eight *dō* (roads, circuits) covering the rest of the country, the best known being the Tōkaidō (eastern sea road) and Hokkaidō (northern sea road). Also, names for an area covering two adjacent places are sometimes coined by combining one character from each name; Keihin, for example, is used for the Tōkyō (*kei* = *kyō*) and Yokohama (*hin* = *hama*) area.

Nametoko Keikoku 滑床渓谷

Gorge on the upper reaches of the river Megurogawa, a tributary of the SHIMANTOGAWA, southern Ehime Prefecture, Shikoku. Surrounded by primeval forests, in which wild monkeys roam. It abounds with deep pools and waterfalls, including Yukinowanotaki, and is part of Ashizuri-Uwakai National Park.

Namiki Gohei 並木五瓶

The name of a succession of major dramatists in the KABUKI theater. Gohei I (1747–1808), a pupil of Namiki Shōzō I (1730–73), was already the foremost dramatist of the Kyōto-Ōsaka area by the age of 40 but later moved to Edo (now Tōkyō). His plays are noted for their masterful blending of realistic characters and the logical consistency of their plots, elements then lacking in the Edo kabuki but generally adopted soon after his arrival. His works include *Kimmon gosan no kiri* (1778, Thief Goemon on the Temple Gate), *Kanjin kammon tekuda no hajimari* (1789, The Murder of a Foreign Emissary), and *Tomigaoka koi no yamabiraki* (1798, The Two Shimbei).

Gohei II (1768–1819) died about two years after assuming this name and is better remembered as Shinoda Kinji I. Gohei III (1790–1855) is celebrated as the writer of the dialogue for Ichikawa Danjūrō VII's KANJIN-CHŌ, one of the greatest masterpieces in the kabuki repertory.

Namiki Shōzō 並木正三

The name of two important figures in the KABUKI theater. Shōzō I (1730–73), a dramatist from the Kyōto-Ōsaka area, is best remembered as the inventor of the revolving stage. He wrote some 100 works, mostly *jidai-mono* (historical plays). These include *Keisei ama no hagoromo* (1753, The Feathery Garment from Heaven), *Sanjikkoku yobune no hajimari* (1758, The Beginning of Heavy Cargo Ships on the Yodo River), and *Sanzen-sekai yarikuri ōrai* (1772, Kin'emon, the Notorious Pirate). Shōzō II (d 1807), a relative of Shōzō I, might be the author of *Kezairoku* (or *Gezairoku*, 1801), a manual for kabuki play writing that is a rare and valuable source on this subject.

Namiki Sōsuke 並木宗輔

(1695–1751?). Also known as Namiki Senryū. Dramatist of the PUPPET THEATER who wrote over 40 JŌRURI plays. He often collaborated with other playwrights, including Takeda Izumo I (d 1747; see TAKEDA IZUMO), Izumo II (1691–1756), and Miyoshi Shōraku (1696?–1772?). He worked at both the Takemotoza and Toyotakeza playhouses in Ōsaka. His collaborations associated with the Takemotoza include *Natsumatsuri Naniwa kagami* (1745, The Summer Festival in Naniwa), *Sugawara denju tenarai kagami* (1746, The Secrets of Sugawara's Calligraphy), YOSHITSUNE SEMBON-ZAKURA (1747, The Thousand Cherry Blossoms of Yoshitsune), and KANADEHON CHŪSHINGURA (1748; tr *Chūshingura: The Treasury of Loyal Retainers*, 1971). He died while writing *Ichinotani futaba gunki* (1751, The Chronicle of the Battle of Ichinotani), which was completed by his collaborators.

Nampo Jōmyō 南浦紹明

(1235–1308). Also known as Nampo Jōmin, Nampo Shōmyō, or Entsū Daiō Kokushi. Monk of the RINZAI SECT of Zen Buddhism. Born in Suruga Province (now part of Shizuoka Prefecture). He studied at the temple KENCHŌJI in Kamakura under the Chinese monk RANKEI DŌRYŪ. In 1272 after some 8 years of study in China and a term of service as librarian at Kenchōji, he moved to Sōfukuji in Dazaifu and devoted himself to proselytizing in northern Kyūshū. He became abbot of Kenchōji in 1307. Nampo laid the foundation for the subsequent rise of the Rinzai sect, and among his disciples were many notable monks, including SŌHŌ MYŌ-CHŌ. The Daiō subsect of the Rinzai sect began with Nampo. He wrote a book called *Goroku* (Record of Sayings).

Namu Amida Butsu 南無阿弥陀仏

Also known as the formula of the NEMBUTSU, this phrase literally means "I take my refuge in the Buddha AMIDA." The recitation of *Namu Amida Butsu* is the fundamental practice in PURE LAND BUDDHISM and, along with faith in the Buddha Amida, is the essential key to ensuring birth in the Pure Land where attainment of Buddhahood is assured. As its recitation is easy to perform, it is considered by the Pure Land sects to be the practice most suited for the dull-witted people of an age far removed from the time of the historical Buddha, Śākyamuni (see ESCHATOLOGY).

Namu Myōhō renge kyō 南無妙法蓮華経

Also known as *daimoku. Namu Myōhō renge kyō* is a phrase meaning "I take my refuge in the LOTUS SUTRA." Its recitation is the basic practice of the NICHIREN SECT. Not only is *Myōhō renge kyō* the title of the Lotus Sutra, but it is held to be the essence of the reality that the sutra reveals. The recitation of *Namu Myōhō renge kyō* is considered to lead a person to Buddhahood and to be the practice most suitable for followers of the Lotus Sutra during the degenerate age of *mappō* (see ESCHATOLOGY). Along with the *honzon* (object of worship) and the *kaidan* (ordination platform), it is one of the "three great secret doctrines" (*sandai hihō*) of the Nichiren sect.

nanakamado 七竈

(mountain ash). *Sorbus commixta.* Deciduous tree of the family Rosaceae that grows wild in mountainous areas all over Japan and is known for its beautiful fall foliage and red fruit. It grows 7–10 meters (23–33 ft) high and has a diameter of 0.3 meters (1 ft). The dark brown, rough bark has a peculiar smell. Alternate compound leaves carry five to seven pairs of oblong, serrated leaflets. In July white florets on compound flower stalks appear. The berries that follow the flowers are round and become red as they ripen.

The tree's name derives from the saying that even after putting its hard wood into a stove (*kamado*) seven (*nana*) times, it remains unburned. Related species found in Japan include the *sabiba nanakamado* (*S. commixta* var. *rufo-ferruginea*); the *urajiro nanakamado* (*S. matsumurana*); the *takane nanakamado* (*S. sambucifolia*); and the *nankin nanakamado* (*S. gracilis*).

nanakusa 七草

("the seven herbs"). *Nanakusa* refers to either of two sets of seven herbs: one consisting of the seven spring herbs (*haru no nanakusa*) and one consisting of the seven autumn herbs (*aki no nanakusa*).

The seven spring herbs are *seri* (dropwort; Japanese parsley), *nazuna* (shepherd's purse), *gogyō* (cottonweed), *hakobera* (chickweed), *hotokenoza* (henbit), *suzuna* (turnip), and *suzushiro* (Japanese radish; *daikon*). In ancient Japan, people customarily gathered herbs in the spring and ate them as an expression of their wish for good health. Beginning in the Muromachi period (1333–1568), the seven spring herbs were added to a gruel to make *nanakusagayu* ("seven-herb gruel"), which was eaten on 7 January. This practice continues today.

The autumn herbs are HAGI (Japanese bush clover), SUSUKI (eulalia), KUZU (kudzu vine), *nadeshiko* (fringed pink), OMINAESHI (a perennial herb of the family Valerianaceae), *fujibakama* (boneset), and *asagao* (the equivalent of the KIKYŌ of today, which is the balloonflower or Chinese bellflower). The autumn herbs are used as decorative flowers at the time of the BON FESTIVAL (a Buddhist observance honoring the souls of one's ancestors) and at moon-viewing festivities.

Nanao 七尾[市]

City in northern Ishikawa Prefecture, central Honshū, on Nanao Bay. A busy port from the Edo period (1600–1868), Nanao is today one of the major trading ports on the Sea of Japan. Lumber processing and brick and cement industries flourish. Wakura Hot Spring is located here. Pop: 50,103.

Nanatsugama 七ツ釜

Sea caves in the city of Karatsu, northern Saga Prefecture, northwestern Kyūshū. Located along the Genkai Sea, they consist of seven basaltic caves in jointed columnar cliffs on the sea. Part of the Genkai Quasi-National Park.

nanga 南画

("Southern painting"). Term used to refer to BUNJINGA, Japanese literati painting of the 18th and 19th centuries. The term originated with the Chinese expression *nanzonghua* (*nan-tsung-hua*), meaning "Southern-school painting," which is pronounced *nanshūga* in Japanese. *Nanga* is an abbreviation of *nanshūga* and has no counterpart in Chinese.

The term *nanzonghua* was first used by the Chinese painter-critic Dong Qichang (Tung Ch'i-ch'ang; 1555–1636). He traced the aesthetic lineage of literati painters of his day from the 8th-century painter-poet Wang Wei down through such artists as Dong Yuan (Tung Yüan) of the Five Dynasties (907–960), Mi Fu of the Northern Song (Sung) dynasty (960–1126), and Huang Gongwang (Huang Kungwang) of the Yuan (Yüan) dynasty (1279–1368), to Wen Zhengming (Wen Cheng-ming) of the Ming dynasty (1368–1644). Japanese literati painters, who were mainly influenced by the landscape styles of the Chinese literati, were not well informed of the subtleties of this genealogy when they adopted the term *nanga.*

Nangakuha 南学派

("Southern Learning" school). A branch of Neo-Confucian studies (SHUSHIGAKU) founded in Tosa (now Kōchi Prefecture) around 1548 by a ZEN Buddhist priest, Minamimura Baiken. It was later led by TANI JICHŪ, who secularized the movement and counted among his disciples NONAKA KENZAN and YAMAZAKI ANSAI. The Tosa school placed special emphasis on translating theory into action and on defining the proper relationship of the emperor to the people (*taigi meibun*). It influenced the antishogunate restorationist (SONNŌ JŌI) movement of the late Edo period (1600–1868).

naniwa-bushi 浪花節

Also commonly known as *rōkyoku.* A type of narrative ballad rhythmically intoned by a solo chanter/narrator to the accompaniment of a single SHAMISEN player. The repertory of this popular stage entertainment consisted of embellished narratives taken largely from accounts of actual historical events, widely known stories, and traditional tales (*monogatari*).

An early form of STREET ENTERTAINMENT, with affinities to religio-secular chants of the 13th and 14th centuries, *naniwa-bushi* first developed in the Kansai (Ōsaka-Kyōto) re-

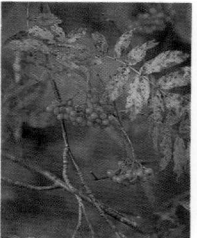

nanakamado The ripe red fruit and autumn foliage of the mountain ash.

gion during the Edo period (1600–1868). It was originally performed by street musicians, who gradually moved indoors to small huts set up on the grounds of temples and shrines. By the late 1870s *naniwa-bushi* came to be a feature attraction in hundreds of small YOSE (variety or vaudeville) halls and larger theaters. The influence of the phonograph record in the early 1900s helped foster a "golden age" of *rōkyoku*, but with the advent of motion pictures in the late 1920s, its popularity declined. In the 1930s nationalistic fervor helped revive these ballads, but they declined again after World War II and are rarely broadcast today.

Naniwa erejī 浪華悲歌

(Ōsaka Elegy). A 1936 film directed by MIZOGUCHI KENJI, starring YAMADA ISUZU. In the film, a young telephone operator becomes the mistress of her boss in order to pay off a debt incurred by her father when he embezzled money. Arrested for immoral behavior, she is acquitted but upon returning home meets a hostile reception and leaves. The process by which she achieves spiritual independence is depicted with unprecedented realism, making the film a milestone in the history of Japanese cinema.

Naniwakyō 難波京

First established as a capital city in 645 by Emperor Kōtoku (r 645–654), it was the site of a series of palaces; located in what is now Hōenzaka Chō in the city of Ōsaka. The first large palace there was built by Emperor TEMMU (r 672–686) in 679. It was destroyed by fire in 686, but Empress JITŌ (r 686–697) rebuilt it, at least in part, and Emperor MOMMU (r 697–707) and Empress Genshō (r 715–724) both resided there. Emperor SHŌMU (r 724–749) began a new palace at Naniwakyō in 726. It was completed in 732, but the capital was located there only from March 744 to February 745 before it was moved to SHIGARAKI NO MIYA.

Temmu probably laid out the city in a grid pattern of squares with the palace at the north. It was largely unoccupied until the 8th century. It has been conjectured that the grid pattern was composed of 16 broad blocks running north–south (these were called *bō*) and 12 blocks running east–west (these were called *jō*); however, this hypothesis has not yet been supported by archaeological evidence. The outer dimensions of Naniwakyō in its earliest form were probably about 4 by 3 kilometers (2.5 by 1.9 mi). Shōmu expanded the city in 734.

Naniwa miyage 難波土産

Book in five volumes on the puppet plays (JŌRURI) of CHIKAMATSU MONZAEMON, written by Miki Sadanari and published in 1738. Although Miki was a Confucian scholar and a disciple of ITŌ TŌGAI, he is best remembered for this work, which provides commentary on the titles, difficult passages, and organization of nine of Chikamatsu's *jōruri*. The work is especially remarkable in that it begins with the only extant record in his own words of Chikamatsu's views on *jōruri*. In a passage, thought to have been recorded by his friend Hozumi Ikan (1692–1769), Chikamatsu declares that the art of *jōruri* "resides in the realm between fact and fiction." The title *Naniwa miyage* (Souvenir of Naniwa) refers to the birthplace, Naniwa (or Ōsaka), of the *jōruri* genre.

Nanjing (Nanking) Incident 南京事件

(J: Nankin Jiken). Clash between Chinese Nationalist (Guomindang; Kuomintang) soldiers and foreigners at Nanjing on 24 March 1927. The Nationalist army, attempting to suppress warlordism and unify China under the Nationalist Party (see CHIANG KAI-SHEK), occupied Nanjing on 23 March. Nationalist soldiers thereupon assaulted foreigners, looted foreign businesses and residences, and attacked the Japanese, US, and British consulates. The incident was the climax of xenophobia in the Nationalist Revolution and appears to have occurred spontaneously. The Western powers and Japan demanded an apology, indemnities, and punishment for the perpetrators of the incident. In May 1929 China and Japan reached an agreement on this issue.

Nanjing (Nanking) Massacre 南京虐殺事件

(J: Nankin Gyakusatsu Jiken). Sometimes known as the Rape of Nanking. Atrocities committed by the Japanese army against the civilian population of Nanjing and vicinity from December 1937 to January 1938, early in the SINO-JAPANESE WAR OF 1937–1945. Upon entering Nanjing on 13 December 1937 after a few days of fighting, the Japanese army began a wholesale murder of Chinese men on the pretext that they were Chinese soldiers trying to escape in civilian clothes. As discipline broke down among the Japanese troops, they began to kill civilians indiscriminately. According to estimates made at the Tōkyō WAR CRIMES TRIALS, about 42,000 civilians, mostly women and children, were killed in Nanjing, and over 100,000 civilians and prisoners of war in the vicinity of the city over the next six weeks. The massacre was accompanied by rape, looting, and arson; a third of the city was destroyed by fire. The incident, committed with the sanction of officers, was the worst atrocity committed by Japanese military forces during World War II. The commander of the Japanese troops at Nanjing, Matsui Iwane (1878–1948), was sentenced to death for war crimes in 1948.

Nanjō Bun'yū 南条文雄

(1849–1927). Eminent Buddhologist and Sanskrit scholar. Born in Mino Province (now part of Gifu Prefecture). Ordained a priest of the Ōtani branch of the JŌDO SHIN SECT, he went to England in 1876 to study Sanskrit Buddhist texts. Returning to Japan in 1884, he taught at Tōkyō University and later served as president of Shinshū (now Ōtani) University. The most famous of his many publications is a *Catalogue of the Chinese Translation of the Buddhist Tripitaka* (1883), commonly known as the Nanjō Catalogue.

Nankai Electric Railway Co, Ltd 南海電気鉄道[株]

(Nankai Denki Tetsudō). Private railway company with operations centered in southern Ōsaka and northern Wakayama prefectures. Founded in 1885 as a local railway company. The company is planning to build a rail line connecting Ōsaka and the new Kansai International Airport. Sales for the fiscal year ending March 1991 totaled ¥105.2 billion (US $766.8 million), and capitalization stood at ¥41.3 billion (US $301.0 million). Headquarters are in Ōsaka.

Nanki Bunko 南葵文庫

(Nanki Library). Collection of some 100,000 volumes assembled by successive generations of the Ki (Wakayama) branch of the Tokugawa family (see GOSANKE). Today it is one of the special collections of the Tōkyō University Library; it was the first important gift of books after the library's destruction in the Tōkyō Earthquake of 1923. The Nanki Bunko was donated by Tokugawa Yorimichi. It contains histories, literary works, and maps, as well as works on Japanese aesthetics, theater, art, music, flower arrangement, and the tea ceremony.

Nankoku 南国[市]

Also known as Nangoku. City in central Kōchi Prefecture, Shikoku. The prefecture's granary since ancient times, Nankoku produces rice, vegetables, and tobacco. It is known for its *onagadori* (a long-tailed Japanese fowl). Pop: 46,823.

Nansei Islands →Ryūkyū Islands

nanshinron →southern expansion doctrine

Nansō Satomi hakkenden 南総里見八犬伝

(Satomi and the Eight "Dogs"). Illustrated historical romance published 1814–42 by the GESAKU fiction writer Takizawa BAKIN. Organized in 9 sections and 181 chapters, *Nansō Satomi hakkenden* describes how the fortunes of a warrior family, defeated in the Kakitsu Rebellion (1441), are revived with the aid of eight "dog" warriors (each of their surnames begins with the Japanese word for dog) and a host of other loyal retainers. An epic work, it may be divided into three parts: the establishment of the Satomi family in Kazusa, now part of Chiba Prefecture (chapters 1–14); the assembly of the eight "dog" warriors under the Satomi banner (chapters 15–131); and the struggles of the Satomi against the combined forces of the shōgun's deputies in the Kantō (eastern Honshū) region (chapters 132–81). After a Satomi victory the eight warrior heroes and a family embassy go to Kyōto to pay respects to the emperor and shōgun and ask that Fusehime, the daughter of Satomi patriarch Yoshizane, be recognized as a deity and that a shrine be constructed in her honor because of the many miracles she has performed. Each of the eight "dogs" is married to one of Satomi Yoshinari's eight daughters, and the Satomi clan flourishes in peace for generations thereafter. *Nansō Satomi hakkenden* is classified as a YOMIHON ("reading book"). In form and structure *Hakkenden* is historical romance of an allegorical nature. Good and evil are incarnated in characters who serve as emblems. Bakin's basic theme is restoration, with morality as its foundation and fate the force ensuring that morality prevails.

Nantaisan 男体山

Also called Futarasan and Kurokamiyama. Conical volcano in the Nasu Volcanic Zone, northwestern Tochigi Prefecture, central Honshū, dominating the northern shore of Lake Chūzenji. Composed of andesite, it has highly developed radial drainages. Once a center for religious exercises of the SHUGENDŌ sect, the inner sanctuary of Futarasan Shrine is still situated on its summit. Height: 2,484 m (8,150 ft).

nanten 南天

(nandin). *Nandina domestica.* Evergreen shrub of the family Berberidaceae, found in mountainous areas of Kyūshū, Shikoku, and western Honshū, as well as in central China and India. In Japan it is widely cultivated as an ornamental. Its dark brown trunks grow in clusters from 2–3 meters (7–10 ft) high. Large alternate pinnate leaves bear leathery leaflets; small white flowers appear in June, followed by clusters of bright red berries. Numerous horticultural varieties have been developed, including *shiromi nanten,* distinguished by its white berries; *fujinanten,* with lavender berries; and *kinshi nanten,* which has threadlike leaves.

Because its name suggests the expression *nan o tenzuru* (to overturn misfortune or adversity), *nanten* has traditionally been regarded as an auspicious plant. Warriors of old put its leaves in their armor to ensure victory. *Nanten* was also used as an alcove ornament for coming-of-age ceremonies (GEMPUKU), and pregnant women were known to place sprays of *nanten* under their coverlets to ensure a safe delivery.

nanushi → shōya

Nan'yō 南陽[市]

City in southern Yamagata Prefecture, northern Honshū. Grapes are cultivated in the city's hills. The principal products are wine and switchboards. The Akayu Hot Spring attracts visitors. Pop: 36,977.

Nanzan University 南山大学

(Nanzan Daigaku). A private, Catholic, coeducational university located in Nagoya. Its predecessor was Nanzan Foreign Language School, established in 1946. It was granted university status in 1949 and maintains faculties of letters, foreign languages, economics, business management, and law. It also has affiliated junior high schools, high schools, and a two-year women's junior college. Enrollment in 1989 was 5,371.

Nanzenji 南禅寺

Head temple of the Nanzenji branch of the RINZAI SECT of ZEN Buddhism; located in Sakyō Ward, Kyōto. Nanzenji was originally the detached palace (or villa) of the retired emperor KAMEYAMA. In 1291 he converted it to a Zen temple. In 1334 Emperor GO-DAIGO ranked Nanzenji first among the Five Temples (GOZAN) and installed as chief priest MUSŌ SOSEKI. In 1386 the shōgun ASHIKAGA YOSHIMITSU elevated Nanzenji to a special rank above five newly designated Gozan temples. The temple was largely destroyed by fires in 1447 and 1467. During and after the Azuchi-Momoyama period (1568–1600), with the support of the imperial court, TOYOTOMI HIDEYOSHI, and the Tokugawa shōguns, Nanzenji was again reconstructed. In 1876 it became the head temple of the Nanzenji branch of the Rinzai Zen sect.

The well-known main gate, known as Tenka Ryūmon (Dragon Gate of the World), was constructed in 1628 by TŌDŌ TAKATORA in the Zen style. On the ceiling of the sanctum of the main gate are drawings of Chinese phoenixes and celestial nymphs ascribed to KANŌ TAN'YŪ. The two *hōjō* (abbot's living quarters) have been designated National Treasures. The larger contains paintings and murals ascribed to KANŌ MOTONOBU, KANŌ SANRAKU, KANŌ EITOKU, and KANŌ MITSUNOBU; the smaller is thought to have been brought from FUSHIMI CASTLE and is well known for its

three Tora no Ma (Tiger Chambers) famous for paintings of tigers ascribed to Kanō Tan'yū. Nanzenji is also noted for its gardens, one of which is thought to have been designed by KOBORI ENSHŪ. The garden of Nanzen'in, a subsidiary temple, is preserved in the Kamakura style and is one of the most noted gardens in Kyōto today.

Naobi no Kami 直日神

(The Rectifying Deities). A divine couple, Kamu Naobi no Kami and Ō Naobi no Kami, who appear in a myth on the origin of evil and purification in the two early chronicles KOJIKI (712) and NIHON SHOKI (720). When the deity Izanagi no Mikoto (see IZANAGI AND IZANAMI) returned from the Land of the Dead (Yomi no Kuni), he bathed in a river (or the sea) to purify himself of the pollution he had incurred there and gave birth to a series of deities, among them the Makatsuhi no Kami, a divine couple born of the dust and filth of the underworld. He then gave birth to the two Naobi no Kami, whose function was to rectify the disorder and pollution connected with the two Makatsuhi no Kami.

Naoetsu → Jōetsu

Naoki Prize 直木賞

(Naoki Shō). A literary prize awarded twice annually, for works of POPULAR FICTION. The prize was established in 1935 by BUNGEI SHUNJŪ, LTD, at the suggestion of KIKUCHI KAN, to commemorate the writer NAOKI SANJŪGO. The AKUTAGAWA PRIZE, which was established by Bungei Shunjū in the same year, is generally intended for works by new writers, while the Naoki Prize is for works by more established ones. Until 1938 the Naoki Prize was awarded by Bungei Shunjū; since then it has been awarded by the Society for the Promotion of Japanese Literature (Nihon Bungaku Shinkōkai). The prize was not awarded from 1945 to 1948. The winning works are published in the magazine *Ōru yomimono.* See also LITERARY PRIZES.

Naoki Sanjūgo 直木三十五

(1891–1934). Novelist. Born Uemura Sōichi in Ōsaka. Attended Waseda University. He was an eccentric, as illustrated by his choice of pen name, which he changed four times between the ages of 31 and 35 to reflect his age (he finally settled on Sanjūgo or "thirty-five"). He first became known as a columnist for the magazine BUNGEI SHUNJŪ, writing scathing critical gossip about contemporary literary figures. After this he started writing historical fiction and popular novels. The year after Naoki's death, his friend KIKUCHI KAN established in his honor the NAOKI PRIZE, one of Japan's most prestigious literary awards. His works include *Nangoku taiheiki* (1930–31), a historical novel.

naorai 直会

(communion). SHINTŌ ceremony of communion between a god (KAMI) and human worshipers in which the participants share *sake,* rice, fish, and vegetables previously offered to and sanctified by the god. In the ancient past *naorai* formed a central part of a Shintō rite. All participants—parishioners and priests alike—were required to purify themselves through abstinence and to observe various taboos prior to the rite. Food offerings were prepared with a purified fire and subsequently eaten by participants in front of the altar as a form of a common meal with the god. In modern practice, however, the rules of abstinence are generally no longer observed, and the *naorai* feast is held, often

Nanzenji The main gate of this Kyōto temple was rebuilt in the two-story Zen style in 1628 as a memorial to the warriors killed in the 1615 siege of Ōsaka Castle.

in another room, after the food offerings have been removed from the altar area. *Naorai* thus now forms not the central but last stage of the rite before the return to daily life in the community. See also SHINTŌ RITES.

Naoshima Islands 直島諸島

(Naoshima Shotō). Group of islands in the central Inland Sea, off the city of Tamano, Okayama Prefecture, western Honshū. Administratively a part of Kagawa Prefecture. The group consists of 27 islands centering on Naoshima, the main island, which has a copper-smelting plant. Sea bream and *hamachi* (young yellowtail) are cultivated.

Nara 奈良[市]

City located in the northern part of Nara Prefecture, central Honshū. The capital of Japan from 710 to 784, Nara is today the seat of the prefectural government. Spared from destruction in World War II, it still preserves a large number of cultural relics. Constructed in 710 and patterned after the Tang (T'ang) dynasty capital of Chang'an (Ch'ang-an; modern Xi'an or Sian), the original city (HEIJŌKYŌ) at one time boasted a population of 200,000. Heijōkyō was later expanded to the east, where the KASUGA SHRINE and the temples KŌFUKUJI and TŌDAIJI were situated.

With the transfer of the capital to NAGAOKAKYŌ in 784, Heijōkyō fell into decline. However, the temples of Kōfukuji and Tōdaiji continued to wield power, especially in the Heian period (794–1185), operating large-scale manors (SHŌEN). Their powerful warrior-monks came into conflict with the TAIRA FAMILY, who set fire to Nara in 1180. In the Kamakura period (1185–1333) the city recovered its prosperity and achieved a larger population and size than ever before.

The making of *sumi* (india ink), begun in the Heian period, and calligraphic brushes are the two most important industries today, with Nara supplying over 90 percent of the country's *sumi.* National highways and railway lines now link Nara with Ōsaka, giving rise to residential development and new industries, such as plastics. Agriculture and animal husbandry still remain popular.

Nara Park, famed for its tame deer and set against the rolling hills of WAKAKUSAYAMA and KASUGAYAMA, is a favorite tourist spot. Many shrines and temples are scattered throughout the city. Institutions of note include the NARA NATIONAL MUSEUM, the NARA NATIONAL RESEARCH INSTITUTE OF CULTURAL PROPERTIES, and the YAMATO BUNKAKAN (a museum). Pop: 349,349. — *See map, next page; photos, page 1051.*

nara → oaks

Nara Basin 奈良盆地

(Nara Bonchi). Also known as the Yamato Basin. In northern Nara Prefecture, central Honshū. One of several fault basins in the central Kinki (Kyōto-Nara-Ōsaka) region. Flanked by the Kasagi, Ikoma, and Kongō

nanten The white flower and the berry cluster of the evergreen shrub *nanten.* Cherished for its colorful beauty and regarded as auspicious, it is often cultivated in gardens.

Naoki Sanjūgo A year after this novelist's death the prestigious Naoki Prize for literature was established in his honor.

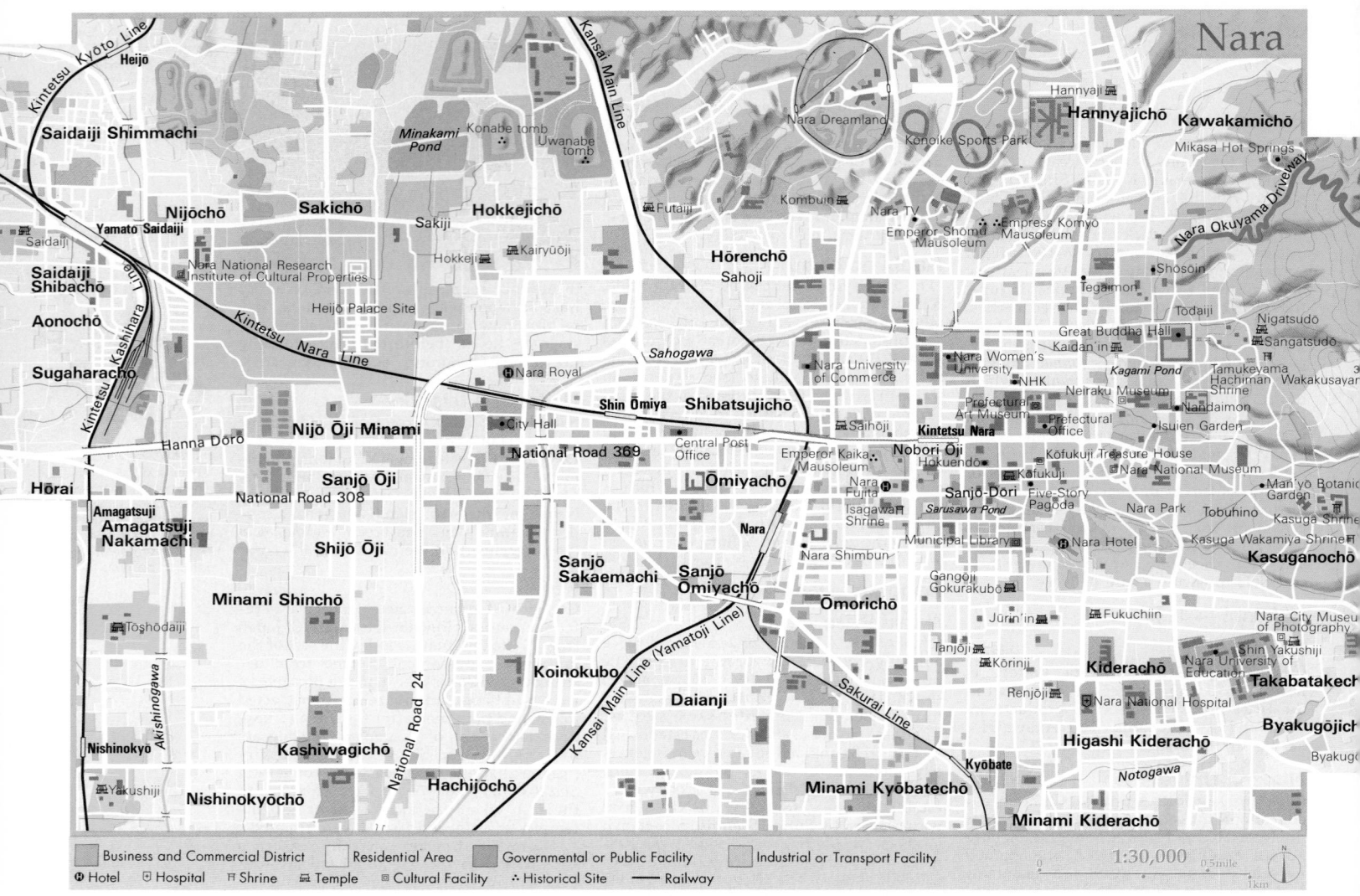

mountains, it consists of the floodplain of the river Yamatogawa and alluvial fans in the lower regions. The principal crops are rice, strawberries, and watermelons. A center of ancient culture, it has many historical tombs, palace sites, and temples, including HŌRYŪJI. Today it is a residential area, and industries are developing. The major cities are Nara, Tenri, and Kashihara. Area: approximately 300 sq km (115 sq mi).

Narabayashi Chinzan　　楢林鎮山

(1649–1711). Dutch interpreter and physician. Born in Hizen Province (now Nagasaki Prefecture). Narabayashi studied Dutch at Dejima, the Dutch trading outpost in Nagasaki, and achieved the rank of chief interpreter (ōtsūji) in 1686. At that time he also began to study medicine, and in 1698 he turned his full attention to the practice of medicine. He was the founder of the Narabayashi school of surgery. In 1706 Narabayashi compiled the *Kōi geka sōden* for Japanese students of Dutch medicine. The book was based on a Dutch translation of a surgery manual written by the French surgeon Ambroise Paré (1510–90), supplemented by medical information Narabayashi had directly gained from the Dutch in Nagasaki.

Nara Buddhism　　南都六宗

(Nanto Rokushū). A term referring to the six Buddhist sects officially recognized during the Nara period (710–794). They were introduced into Japan in the following approxi-

mate order: Sanron, Jōjitsu, Hossō, Kusha, Kegon, and Ritsu (see articles on the individual sects). The Kusha and the Jōjitsu were not truly independent sects but rather "text schools" concerned with the exegesis of the *Kusharon* (*Abhidharmakośa*) and the *Jōjitsuron*. Only three of the original Nara sects survive today as religious bodies: the Hossō with its headquarters at the temples YAKU-SHIJI and KŌFUKUJI, the Ritsu with its headquarters at TŌSHŌDAIJI, and the Kegon with its headquarters at TŌDAIJI. The Sanron sect, which was the major Buddhist school in the pre-Nara and early Nara periods, declined rapidly after the 9th century and disappeared entirely as an independent lineage in the 14th century. There are 139 temples currently affiliated with one or another of the three surviving Nara sects.

Nara ehon　　奈良絵本

("Nara picture book"). Type of manuscript book, consisting of a short story accompanied by illustrations, produced from the late Muromachi period (1333–1568) to the mid-Edo period (1600–1868). The term Nara *ehon* derived from the fact that they are thought to have originated among priest-painters of the Nara area. The front cover and flyleaf are often richly decorated with gold and silver leaf. Most of the pictures are done in a naive style although some, apparently influenced by the TOSA SCHOOL, feature more ornate detail. Bright colors predominate. Many of the short medieval tales known as OTOGI-ZŌSHI were mass-produced in the form of Nara *ehon* and circulated widely among the general public.

Narai　　奈良井

District in the village of Narakawa, southwestern Nagano Prefecture, central Honshū. During the Edo period (1600–1868) Narai prospered as a post-station town; today its Edo-period atmosphere attracts many visitors.

Nara National Museum

奈良国立博物館

(Nara Kokuritsu Hakubutsukan). Museum in Nara noted for its collection of Buddhist art; established in 1889 as the Nara Teikoku Hakubutsukan (Nara Imperial Museum) and known by its present name since 1952. In addition to the Buddhist images and altar articles owned by the museum itself, there are on exhibit various Buddhist art objects entrusted to the museum by ancient shrines and temples throughout Japan. Each autumn a special exhibition is held of imperial properties normally kept in the SHŌSŌIN art repository. In the museum's collection is a 12th-century handscroll of the type known as JIGOKU-ZŌSHI. The museum's old main building, a representative Western-style building of the Meiji period (1868–1912), has been designated an Important Cultural Property. Also at the museum is the Hassōan, a tea ceremony house.

Nara National Research Institute of Cultural Properties

奈良国立文化財研究所

(Nara Kokuritsu Bunkazai Kenkyūjo). One of two national research institutes attached to the Agency for Cultural Affairs under the

Nara

The capital of Japan for most of the 8th century, this city is known today for its temples, works of art, and historical sites.

▶ The twin pagodas at the temple Yakushiji. The East Pagoda (foreground) dates from the 8th century; the West Pagoda is a reconstruction.

▼ Nara Park on a winter morning with one of the park's numerous tame deer making its way over the frost-covered grass.

▲ A stone-paved path inside the spacious grounds of the temple Tōdaiji.

▶ Tōdaiji's Great Buddha Hall, the largest wooden building in the world. The building dates from 1709 but was extensively renovated in the 1970s. National Treasure.

◀ One of the entrances to the main compound of the Kasuga Shrine.

▶ Sarusawa Pond in Nara Park. In the background is the five-story pagoda of the temple Kōfukuji.

Ministry of Education; established in 1972. Located in the city of Nara, with branches in the city of Kashiwara and the village of Asuka, all in Nara Prefecture. The institute comprises departments for the excavation and restoration of HEIJŌKYŌ, FUJIWARAKYŌ, and other sites, and for the study of documents from Japan's early historical and Nara (710–794) periods. See also TŌKYŌ NATIONAL RESEARCH INSTITUTE OF CULTURAL PROPERTIES.

Nara Park   奈良公園

(Nara Kōen). Prefectural park located in the eastern part of the city of Nara in Nara Prefecture, central Honshū. The rolling hills WAKAKUSAYAMA and Mikasayama are part of the park, which is one of Japan's most popular tourist attractions. The temples KŌFUKUJI and TŌDAIJI are located in Nara Park, as is KASUGA SHRINE, the NARA NATIONAL MUSEUM, and the Man'yō Botanical Garden. The many tame deer that graze in the park provide an additional attraction. Area: 528 ha (1,304 acres).

Nara period   奈良時代

(710–794; Nara *jidai*). The period during which the seat of government was at HEIJŌKYŌ (now the city of Nara) in YAMATO (now Nara Prefecture). Strictly speaking, the Nara period began in 710, when the imperial capital was moved from FUJIWARAKYŌ, and ended in 784 with the transfer of the capital to NAGAOKAKYŌ, excluding temporary removals to KUNI NO MIYA, NANIWAKYŌ, and SHIGARAKI NO MIYA. Dates for the period are usually given as 710–794, however, to include the 10 years during which the capital was in

Nagaoka. The period was characterized by the full implementation of the RITSURYŌ SYSTEM of government; the establishment of Buddhism as the religion of the court and, by extension, of the state; and new heights in intellectual and cultural achievement, as exemplified in the building of the Great Hall of the temple TŌDAIJI. Early in the period the central administration was able to exercise close control over the country, but during the middle of the period a power struggle broke out among the court nobility. Modifications in the land tenure system, and the absconding from state lands of peasants overburdened by taxes, contributed to the breakdown of central authority.

Political Developments——The political history of the Nara period may be seen as a series of struggles for power that pitted the FUJIWARA FAMILY against factions composed of, among others, members of the Tachibana and Ōtomo families in association with disaffected members of the imperial family. The leader of the government at the beginning of the Nara period was FUJIWARA NO FUHITO. His daughter Kyūshi was a consort of Emperor MOMMU (r 697–707), and Fuhito succeeded in establishing her son Obito as crown prince. He further arranged for another daughter, Asukabehime (see KŌMYŌ, EMPRESS), to become Prince Obito's consort, thus assuring the continuing influence of the Fujiwara family.

However, when Fuhito died in 720 the political situation underwent drastic change, and the princess Toneri Shinnō and Nagaya no Ō formed a faction to oppose the Fujiwara ascendancy. After Prince Obito began his

reign as Emperor Shōmu (r 724–749), a crisis developed over recognition of Asukabehime as Shōmu's empress. Nagaya no Ō was forced to commit suicide (see NAGAYA NO Ō, REBELLION OF), and Asukabehime became Empress Kōmyō. Fuhito's sons, Muchimaro, Fusasaki, Umakai, and Maro, took control of the government, and it appeared that the era of a Fujiwara dispensation had begun. In 737, however, Fuhito's four sons died in a smallpox epidemic.

The center of power now shifted to TACHIBANA NO MOROE and Prince Suzuka no Ō (brother of Nagaya no Ō), who were advised by the priest GEMBŌ and KIBI NO MAKIBI, former members of an embassy to China. They attempted to reform the administration by disbanding the provincial militia (the KONDEI system) and reducing the number of district

Nara ehon An early-Edo-period example of this type of manuscript book celebrates the divine favors bestowed by Daikokuten, the god of wealth. Hōsa Library, Nagoya.

1 From 710 to 784, Heijōkyō (now Nara) was the capital of Japan. This model of the original city shows its checkerboard plan, a layout based on the Chinese Tang-dynasty capital.

2 A detail from a 13th-century handscroll shows Kibi no Makibi (in black), a minister from Nara Japan to China, playing go with a Chinese master.

officials (*gunji*), but turmoil in the provinces weakened their position. See FUJIWARA NO HIROTSUGU, REBELLION OF.

Emperor Shōmu was deeply disturbed by this course of events, and, in the hope that the powers of Buddha would bring an end to epidemic disease and social ills, in 741 he ordered the construction of temples and nunneries (KOKUBUNJI) in every province. This undertaking was completed only after many years. In 743 he also ordered the construction of a gigantic statue of the Buddha Vairocana so that the blessings of the Buddha would extend over the entire country. Completed in 752 at enormous expense, it was known as the Great Buddha (DAIBUTSU) of Tōdaiji.

Emperor Shōmu abdicated in 749 and was replaced by his daughter Empress KŌKEN (r 749–758). An office (Shibichūdai) was established for the empress dowager Kōmyō, and FUJIWARA NO NAKAMARO appeared in the political arena as administrator of her palace affairs. Nakamaro disposed of his principal rival, Tachibana no Moroe, in 756 on a charge of sedition. Emperor Shōmu's zeal in spreading Buddhism had imposed an intolerable burden on the peasantry, and, under the pretext of ameliorating their lot, Moroe's son Naramaro attempted a coup in 757. Nakamaro foiled the coup, but, realizing that the plot had profited from peasant distress, he immediately reduced by half the most burdensome of the taxes, the *zōyō* (see YŌEKI), which called for 60 days of labor each year. He also commuted the interest on all debts accumulated through the previous year. In 758 Nakamaro dispatched officials (*momikushi*) throughout the country to listen to the peasants' grievances and to give relief to the indigent. Within officialdom he encouraged the observance of filial piety and

renamed official ranks and ministries in the Chinese manner. He publicly commended his grandfather Fuhito for his work in drawing up the TAIHŌ CODE (701) and the YŌRŌ CODE (718), and he belatedly enforced the latter in 757. The government, which had been dominated by Buddhism, now took on a more Confucian aspect.

However, the former reigning empress Kōken, who by 762 had gained ascendancy over her successor, Emperor Junnin (r 757–764), was displeased with the new measures; she dismissed Nakamaro and instead relied heavily on the priest DŌKYŌ, who she believed had cured her of an illness. In 764 Nakamaro instigated a rebellion but was captured and killed. Dōkyō was elevated to the rank of *dajō daijin zenji* (priestly grand minister of state) and given the title of *hōō* (priestly retired sovereign). With the appointment of his fellow monks as religious councillors (*hōsangi*), court politics was monopolized by the Buddhist clergy. Previous policies were reversed and Buddhism once again became supreme. Finally, on the basis of an oracle he claimed to have received at the Usa Hachiman Shrine, Dōkyō tried to have himself enthroned. He was thwarted by Fujiwara no Momokawa, WAKE NO KIYOMARO, and others. The empress Shōtoku (the name taken by Empress Kōken when she reascended the throne in 764) died without issue in 770, and Dōkyō was banished.

After the death of Shōtoku, Fujiwara no Momokawa and his followers successfully countered the attempts of Kibi no Makibi to enthrone the grandson of Emperor TEMMU (r 672–686) and installed instead the grandson of Emperor TENJI (r 661–672), 62-year-old Prince Shirakabe. As Emperor Kōnin (r 770–781), he was the last sovereign whose reign fell completely within the Nara period. His rule was distinguished by efforts to reduce national expenditures, to discipline officials and monks, and to rebuild farming villages. Government offices founded for the construction of religious edifices were reduced in size or abolished altogether. Sinecures established outside the *ritsuryō* administrative framework to provide income for officials were eliminated. In 780 the staffs of all government offices were reduced, and men conscripted from the provinces to work in the bureaucracy were allowed to return home. In order to encourage the return of dispossessed peasants who had left their homes to escape debts, a limit was set on the interest on borrowed seed rice (SUIKO). Tax payments to the national coffers continued to decrease, however, and the decay of the central government's authority was felt as far away as northeastern Japan, where the EZO tribes rose in rebellion. The rebellion spread to other areas and posed a grave problem for years afterward. In 781 Emperor Kōnin's crown prince acceded to the throne as Emperor KAMMU (r 781–806), and it was he who was instrumental in moving the capital to Heiankyō in 794.

Society and Economy——The social structure in the Nara period conformed to the *ritsuryō* system, as set forth in the Taihō Code. The central government was headed by the Dajōkan (Grand Council of State), which presided over eight ministries, and the country was divided into provinces (*kuni* or *koku*), which in turn were divided into districts (*gun*), villages (*gō*), and hamlets (*ri*). An early-Nara-period document lists 67 provinces, comprising 555 districts, 4,012 villages, and 12,036 hamlets. The provinces were administered by governors (KOKUSHI), who were sent out from the capital. All the people were considered the emperor's subjects and were expected to obey officials who acted in his name. See also KOKUGUN SYSTEM; GŌRI SYSTEM.

All rice land was declared public domain. Under the HANDEN SHŪJU SYSTEM the land was redistributed every six years to all males and females over six years of age (five in Western reckoning). Men received 2 *tan* (1 *tan* = 0.12 hectare or 0.3 acre), women two-thirds that amount. In order to ensure proper allocation of rice land, the census register was updated every six years. The authority of the imperial court at the time extended as far south as the islands off the coast of Kyūshū and as far north as AKITAJŌ in what is now Akita Prefecture. The population within this area is estimated to have been about 5 to 6 million and the acreage of rice land about 601,000 *chō* (721,200 hectares or 1.8 million acres; 1 *chō* = 10 *tan*); it is clear that even after taking into consideration the ratio of men to women, there was not enough arable land. Judging from historical materials, however, the *handen* system and the census registration seem to have been implemented throughout the country with little resistance. Holders of allotted rice land (*kubunden*) were liable to corvée (*zōyō*), a rice tax (*so*), and a handicraft or local products tax (*chō*). There was also a handicraft or local products tax (*yō*) in lieu of labor (see SO, YŌ, AND CHŌ). To strengthen administrative and military communications with the provinces and to facilitate the payment of taxes, the government established a network of post stations (EKISEI) on the public roads connecting the capital and provincial seats of government. The rice and produce taxes that had hitherto been paid to local chieftains were now sent directly to the central government.

A faithful imitation of the Chinese system of government was bound to have negative side effects, for it was unsuited to Japan's agricultural reality. According to a document of 730, in the province of Awa (now part of Chiba Prefecture) 412 out of 414 households were listed as being at the bare subsistence level. The figures for Echizen Province (now part of Fukui Prefecture) in that year tell the same story: of 1,019 households, 996 were found to be poverty stricken. The tax burden fell most heavily on the peasants, and the number of those who absconded increased at an alarming rate.

At the same time, as a means of increasing

revenue, there was a demand for an expansion of acreage under cultivation through the reclamation of land. This plan was to be implemented chiefly by provincial governors and district officials and would require a large-scale mobilization of peasant labor. Since the early 8th century, however, members of the royal family, the aristocracy, the great temples, local magnates, and, to a lesser extent, the peasants themselves had set about gaining control of uncultivated lands. It is believed that a large number of vagrant peasants supplied the labor for these private endeavors. The reclaimed lands were not subject to taxation under the *handen* system, but, as there was no clear title attaching to them, there were cases of reclaimed land being summarily placed by governors in the *handen* pool of rice lands.

In 723 the government issued the SANZE ISSHIN NO HŌ, a law declaring that reclaimed lands could be held in private hands for up to three generations, but that thenceforth they must be given over to the *handen* system. This law proved to be ineffective, however, and in 743, through the KONDEN EISEI SHIZAI HŌ, the government permitted the privatization of reclaimed lands in perpetuity. As a consequence the aristocracy, the great temples, and local magnates naturally redoubled their efforts to reclaim land. Although the reclaimed lands were, in fact, subject to taxation, their loss to the public domain had grievous effects upon the *handen* system. Furthermore, the influence of members of the central power structure acting as private citizens was brought to bear upon the provincial populace through the medium of lands subject to reclamation. The fact that a large number of peasants were thus organized outside of the *ritsuryō* system into a labor force to develop land was a decisive factor in the evolution of society during and after the Nara period, for it created the basis for the formation of privately owned estates (SHŌEN).

Diplomacy——Embassies to Tang (T'ang; 618–907) China, which had been interrupted for some 30 years after the defeat of Japan by the combined armies of China and the Korean state SILLA (J: Shiragi) in the Battle of HAKUSUKINOE, were revived in 702, the year in which the Taihō Code came into effect. During the Nara period eight embassies, six of which actually reached the continent, were commissioned. The purpose of sending embassies to China was, first, to profit from trade and absorb the culture, knowledge, and methods of an advanced society. Second, through the establishment of diplomatic relations the Japanese court hoped to gain a closer relationship with China than that enjoyed by other nations. Among students who accompanied these embassies, each of which numbered as many as 500 to 600 men, were Kibi no Makibi and the priest Gembō. Gembō returned with over 5,000 sutras, while Kibi no Makibi, who had studied Confucianism, military science, and ceremonial rites in China, set up an educational program for future government officials.

On their homeward journeys from China the missions were joined by numerous non-Japanese, and these men too had great influence upon the politics and culture of the time. Notable among them was the Chinese monk GANJIN, transmitter of the teachings of the RITSU SECT, who established the Ordination Hall (Kaidan'in) at the temple Tōdaiji and founded the temple TŌSHŌDAIJI. There were also members of embassies who, because of their talents and facility with the Chinese language, were retained by the Tang court to serve as administrators. Among these was ABE NO NAKAMARO. See also SUI AND TANG (T'ANG) CHINA, EMBASSIES TO.

Relations with Silla were not so felicitous. The Japanese insisted that Silla was a subject nation and referred to its embassies as tribute missions. However Silla, which had unified the Korean peninsula in the late 7th century, demanded that its dealings with Japan be conducted on a basis of equality. In 753, at a banquet held by the Tang imperial court, the embassies of Japan and Silla argued over which should sit closest to the representatives of the host nation. Relations deteriorated, and Fujiwara no Nakamaro urged that a punitive force be dispatched to the peninsula. Before the plan was carried out, Nakamaro was removed from his position of power, but relations with Silla remained troubled throughout the Nara period.

In 727 an embassy from BOHAI (Po-hai), a nation situated north of the Korean peninsula, arrived in Japan. Bohai's diplomatic relations with both Silla and China were unstable, and it was anxious to form an alliance with Japan. Japan reciprocated Bohai's visit the following year, and, treating it as a tributary nation, permitted it a lucrative trade. For the Japanese, Bohai was a convenient window through which to follow events on the continent. It was in this way that Japan learned of the An Lushan (An Lu-shan) Rebellion (755) in China. More than 30 missions were exchanged by the two nations before Bohai lost its sovereignty in the 10th century.

Culture——The ripening of TEMPYŌ CULTURE, so termed after the era name (*nengō*) for the years 729–749, owed much to the resumption of relations with Tang China. Visitors came to Japan from as far away as Central and West Asia, Indonesia, Vietnam, Malaysia, and India, contributing to the culture's vigor and diversity.

As receptive as Japan was to foreign influence, however, the culture of the period remained uniquely Japanese. The process of domestication of foreign influences is readily apparent in the development of a native writing system, for until Chinese characters were imported Japan had no letters of its own. The NIHON SHOKI (720, Chronicles of Japan) was actually written in Chinese (*kambun*), whereas the KOJIKI (712, Record of Ancient Matters) and the poetic anthology MAN'YŌSHŪ (mid-8th century) employed various devices, among them the use of Chinese characters to represent similar-sounding Japanese syllables, to enable a concatenation of Chinese characters to be read in Japanese. This development was the result of a phenomenal increase in the production of manuscripts and books in Chinese during the 8th century. Contributing to this growth were the flourishing of Buddhism, which was accompanied by the copying of sutras and the writing of exegetic works, and the activities of the *ritsuryō* state itself, which relied chiefly on the use of Chinese characters to transmit information.

Influenced by the import of foreign cultural artifacts and the growth of Buddhism, an aristocratic culture flourished, characterized by impressive developments in the fine arts. Emperor Shōmu was the great patron of Tempyō culture, and objects made for his personal use, such as goblets, musical instruments, and other items, compose the heart of the collection of treasures at SHŌSŌIN. Employing materials gathered throughout Asia and applying technology that often required

specialization of labor, a large number of these treasures were fabricated in Japan by immigrant artisans and by craftsmen assembled under the administration of the *ritsuryō* system. For the construction of each temple a special government bureau, such as the Zō-Tōdaiji-Shi (Bureau for the Erection of Tōdaiji), was formed in order to direct the huge labor required.

The Nara period marked the culmination, largely through state sponsorships, of the first great flowering of Japanese literature and the fine arts, supplying the foundation upon which the pervasive domestication of continental culture was achieved in the Heian period (794–1185).

Nara Prefectural Folk Museum
奈良県立民俗博物館

(Nara Kenritsu Minzoku Hakubutsukan). Museum of folk culture established in 1974 in the city of Yamato Kōriyama, Nara Prefecture. The exhibits include a restored farmhouse (MINKA) and traditional tools and equipment used in rice cultivation, weaving, indigo dyeing, and forestry.

Nara Prefecture   奈良県

(Nara Ken). Located in the central part of the Kinki region in central Honshū, Nara Prefecture is landlocked and borders Kyōto Prefecture to the north, Mie Prefecture to the east, and Ōsaka and Wakayama prefectures to the west and south.

Geography and Climate——Apart from the NARA BASIN in the northern part, the prefecture is generally mountainous. The Median Tectonic Line runs through the central part of the prefecture to the east and west along the river Yoshinogawa. To the north of this line, graben basins and horst mountains alternately run north to south. From the west are located, respectively, the Ikoma and Kongō mountains, the Nara Basin, and the highland called Yamato Kōgen. To the south of the line are found steep young mountain ranges such as the KII MOUNTAINS. The principal rivers of the prefecture are, besides the Yoshinogawa, the YAMATOGAWA and TOTSUKAWA. Reflecting the complicated topography, the climate of Nara Prefecture varies greatly. The Nara Basin to the north is generally warm with low precipitation, hot summers, and cold winters, while the temperature is low and precipitation heavy in the southern mountainous district.

History——As the site of the YAMATO COURT, which unified Japan from the 4th to the 7th centuries, the area flourished as the political center of ancient Japan; it was designated as Yamato Province in the ancient provincial system (KOKUGUN SYSTEM). The city of Nara was the country's capital and religious and cultural center during the Nara period (710–794), when it was known as HEIJŌKYŌ. After the capital was moved to NAGAOKAKYŌ in 784 and then HEIANKYŌ in 794, Nara was only briefly at the center of political events in the period of Northern and Southern Courts (1337–92). The present boundaries of Nara Prefecture were established in 1887.

Industries, Tourism, and Culture——As evidenced by Jōmon (ca 10,000 BC–ca 300 BC) and Yayoi (ca 300 BC–ca AD 300) artifacts, farming in the Nara Basin dates back more than 2,000 years. Agriculture and forestry centering on the mountainous Yoshino district are the two main industries in the prefecture. The Nara Basin is noted for its rice and vegetables. Tea is grown on the Yamato

Narita More than 10 million people flock to Narita each year to visit the temple Shinshōji, a center for worship of the deity Fudō Myōō. Shown here is the concrete main hall, rebuilt in 1968.

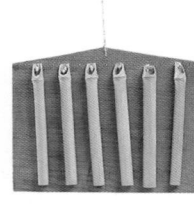

naruko The "bird rattle," a type of scarecrow, is hung from a long rope tied between two poles; the rope may be pulled from a distance in order to create a racket that frightens away animals and birds.

Kōgen and persimmons in the valleys of the Yoshinogawa. The woodworking industry centers on the cities of SAKURAI and GOJŌ. Modern industries such as spinning, plastics, rubber, and electrical machinery are located in Nara, YAMATO KŌRIYAMA, and YAMATO TAKADA. Traditional products include lacquer ware, *sumi* (india ink), brushes, *chasen* (bamboo whisks), *sōmen* (a kind of noodles), and Japanese paper (WASHI).

The prefecture has many historical sites and scenic views. The temples TŌDAIJI, KŌFUKUJI, KASUGA SHRINE, Heijō Palace site, and Nara Park are found in the city of Nara. The temples HŌRYŪJI, YAKUSHIJI, and TŌSHŌDAIJI are located in neighboring towns. The TAKAMATSUZUKA TOMB is located in the village of ASUKA. The oldest road in Japan, the Yamanobe no Michi, is located in the eastern part of the Nara Basin. YOSHINO-KUMANO NATIONAL PARK attracts many visitors with such outstanding mountains and gorges as YOSHINOYAMA, ŌDAIGAHARASAN, ŌMINESAN, and DOROKYŌ. Area: 3,692 sq km (1,425 sq mi); pop: 1,375,481; capital: NARA. Other major cities include KASHIHARA, Yamato Kōriyama, Yamato Takada, IKOMA, and TENRI.

Narashino 習志野[市]

City in northwestern Chiba Prefecture. A military base in World War II, it has become a residential suburb of Tōkyō. Chiba Institute of Technology and Nihon University are here. Pop: 151,471.

Nara Women's University 奈良女子大学

(Nara Joshi Daigaku). A national women's university located in the city of Nara, Nara Prefecture. Established in 1908 as the Nara Women's Higher Normal School, it attained its present status in 1949 and is now one of two national women's universities, along with OCHANOMIZU WOMEN'S UNIVERSITY. It has faculties of letters, science, and home economics. Enrollment was 1,809 in 1989.

Narayama-bushi kō 楢山節考

(tr *The Songs of Oak Mountain*, 1961). Novella by FUKAZAWA SHICHIRŌ (1914–87) dealing with the OBASUTE legend, in which the elderly are said to have been abandoned in the mountains in premodern Japan; published in 1956. In Fukazawa's rendition, poor families from a village in the province

of Shinshū (now Nagano Prefecture) leave their elderly to die on the mountain Narayama when they reach age 70. Orin, the central figure, believes it is her responsibility to die before she becomes a burden to her family and has long anticipated her journey to the mountain. She urges her son, Tatsuhei, to help her; Tatsuhei sorrowfully complies, carrying the old woman up the mountain on his back. Fukazawa depicts the custom with gentle humor, but the story's subject matter shocked modern readers with its presentation of a world view so different from their own. KINOSHITA KEISUKE and IMAMURA SHŌHEI have both directed film versions of the story, in 1958 and 1983, respectively.

Naraya Mozaemon 奈良屋茂左衛門

Name of successive heads of a merchant family of Edo (now Tōkyō) during the Edo period (1600–1868). The second Naraya Mozaemon was a laborer for a lumber merchant, but Mozaemon IV (d 1714) amassed a great fortune, stemming from profits made from rebuilding the Tokugawa family shrine, the Tōshōgū at Nikkō, after an earthquake in 1683. He became official lumber purveyor to the shogunate and was reputed to be one of Japan's wealthiest merchants. His son Mozaemon V (1695–1725; nicknamed Naramo) was known for extravagance, spending vast sums in the theater district and the YOSHIWARA pleasure quarter. When his favorite courtesan, Tamagiku, died, he spent lavishly to honor her memory. The family business survived until the end of the Edo period.

Narcotics Control Law 麻薬取締法

(Mayaku Torishimari Hō). Law enacted in 1953 to control the import, export, manufacture, compounding, distribution, receipt, and possession of narcotics in order to prevent injury to health arising from the use of narcotics for purposes other than medicinal or research and to provide measures to assist in the medical treatment of drug addicts. As a measure to treat drug addicts, the law provides that, by order of the governor, drug addicts may be medically examined by psychiatrists and may be compulsorily hospitalized.

The use of opium and related derivatives is controlled through the Opium Law (Ahen Hō) of 1954. The use of stimulant drugs is controlled through the Stimulant Drug Control Law (Kakuseizai Torishimari Hō) of 1951. The use of poisons and deleterious substances is controlled by the Poisons and Deleterious Substances Control Law (Dokubutsu oyobi Gekibutsu Torishimari Hō) of 1950.

Narita 成田[市]

City in northern Chiba Prefecture, central Honshū. Narita developed as the temple town (MONZEN MACHI) of Shinshōji. The construction of the NEW TŌKYŌ INTERNATIONAL AIRPORT (popularly called Narita Airport) in the Sanrizuka district has led to the creation of new housing and industrial complexes. Pop: 86,708.

Narita Airport → New Tōkyō International Airport

Narita Tomomi 成田知巳

(1912–79). Politician. Born in Kagawa Prefecture; graduate of Tōkyō University. Narita worked for what is now Mitsui Tōatsu Chemicals, Inc, but resigned to pursue a political career. In 1947 he was elected

to the House of Representatives as a member of the JAPAN SOCIALIST PARTY. Aligned with its left wing, he became party secretary (1962) and then party chairman (1968–77).

Naruhito, Crown Prince 徳仁皇太子

(1960– ; Naruhito Kōtaishi). Princely title Hiro no Miya. Eldest son of Emperor AKIHITO and Empress MICHIKO. The crown prince graduated from Gakushūin University in 1982 and completed his initial coursework for the doctorate in history there in 1988. From 1983 to 1985 he studied at Merton College, Oxford University, where he conducted research into the sea trade routes and port cities of medieval Europe. In October 1987, when Emperor SHŌWA was incapacitated by illness, and then crown prince Akihito was away on a visit to the United States, Prince Naruhito acted on the emperor's behalf in the conduct of affairs of state, welcoming foreign dignitaries to Japan and attending various official functions. On 7 January 1989 he became crown prince when his father ascended to the throne as Emperor Akihito. He enjoys sports and music and during his college days played viola with his university orchestra.

Narukami 鳴神

KABUKI play; one of the 18 celebrated kabuki plays known as the KABUKI JŪHACHIBAN. A *jidai-mono* (historical play) by Tsuuchi Hanjūrō, Yasuda Abun, and Nakada Mansuke, it was first performed in 1742. Originally it was act 4 of a longer play entitled *Narukami fudō kitayama-zakura*. In it, a Buddhist monk called Narukami (literally, "Thunder God"), incensed at the emperor for withholding from him the privilege of performing rites of ordination, decides to retaliate. Through supernatural powers, he imprisons the rain-causing dragon, and a severe drought follows. The distressed emperor then sends a beautiful court lady to the monk's hermitage deep in the mountains to seduce him. She succeeds, releases the dragon, and flees.

Naruko 鳴子[町]

Also known as Narugo. Town in northwestern Miyagi Prefecture, northern Honshū. Onikōbe and Narugo hot springs, Narugo Gorge, and ski resorts attract tourists. It is known for its Narugo *kokeshi* (dolls) and *narugo-nuri* lacquer ware. Pop: 10,791.

naruko 鳴子

("bird rattles"). Type of KAKASHI or scarecrow used to frighten birds and animals away from crops. In premodern times they were also called "pulling boards" (*hikiita*). A series of small wooden boards with bamboo sticks attached are suspended from a long rope tied between two poles and fixed so that one end can be pulled from a distance to create a racket that scares away animals and birds.

Naruse Jinzō 成瀬仁蔵

(1858–1919). Educator. A pioneer in higher education for women in Japan. Founder of JAPAN WOMEN'S UNIVERSITY (Nihon Joshi Daigaku). Born in what is now Yamaguchi Prefecture. After working in several posts there, he became a Christian and engaged in missionary work in Kōriyama, Nara Prefecture, and Niigata. In 1890 he went to the United States to do research on education for women. After returning to Japan in 1894, he became principal of Baika Jogakkō (Baika Girls' School) in Ōsaka. In 1901 he founded Nihon Joshi Daigakkō, which later became Japan Women's University.

Naruse Mikio 成瀬巳喜男

(1905–69). Film director. Born in Tōkyō. His career extended from the latter part of the silent film era in the early 1930s to the 1960s. One of his most consistent themes is the entrapment of his characters, especially women, through their internalization of Japanese social values.

Naruse began working at what is now SHŌCHIKU CO, LTD, and became a director, eventually moving to a small studio named PCL (later part of TŌHŌ CO, LTD). His film *Tsuma yo bara no yō ni* (1935, Wife! Be Like a Rose!) was an international success. *Meshi* (1951, Repast) was based on a novel by HAYASHI FUMIKO. With more adaptations of Hayashi's work Naruse found his element, and success: *Inazuma* (1952, Lightning), *Bangiku* (1954, Late Chrysanthemums), *Hōrōki* (1962, A Wanderer's Notebook, or Lonely Lane), and the phenomenally successful UKIGUMO (1955, Floating Clouds).

Naruse's cinematic style was simple, usually set in confined working-class Japanese houses, requiring minimal camera movement. Naruse was primarily concerned with character revelation through slow, almost dramaless stories; hence the actors and the script were of prime importance.

Narushima Ryūhoku 成島柳北

(1837–84). Journalist, essayist, and critic. Real name Narushima Korehiro. Born in Edo (now Tōkyō). In 1859–60, while serving as an official of the Tokugawa shogunate (1603–1867), he wrote the first part of his major work *Ryūkyō shinshi*, set in Edo's Yanagiboshi red-light district. After the Meiji Restoration (1868) he traveled to Europe (1872–73), returning to become editor in chief of *Chōya shimbun*, an antigovernment newspaper. He treated with a sharp sense of irony the social and psychological changes wrought by the Meiji Restoration in the second part of *Ryūkyō shinshi*, completed in 1874. The third part was censored by the government, and only its preface survives. His other works include *Kōsei nichijō* (1881–84), a travel diary of his European tour.

Naruto 鳴門〔市〕

City in northeastern Tokushima Prefecture, Shikoku, on the Naruto Strait. In ancient times Naruto developed as a port linking Shikoku with Ōsaka and Kyōto. Today it has pharmaceutical and chemical industries, seabream fishing, and *wakame* (seaweed) cultivation. Ferry service connects the city with the Ōsaka-Kōbe area, and in 1985 a bridge linking Naruto to the island of Awaji was completed, the first of two bridges that will link Naruto to the city of Akashi in Honshū. Pop: 64,575.

Naruto Strait 鳴門海峡

(Naruto Kaikyō). Narrow strait between the island of AWAJISHIMA and the city of Naruto, Tokushima Prefecture, northeastern Shikoku, connecting the eastern Inland Sea and the Kii Channel. Well known for the many whirlpools created by its rapid tidal currents and the resulting differences in water level. One section of a bridge system connecting Honshū with Shikoku (HONSHŪ-SHIKOKU BRIDGES) was built over the strait. Width: 1,300 m (4,265 ft); deepest point: 85 m (280 ft).

Nasu 那須〔町〕

Town in northern Tochigi Prefecture, central Honshū, between the mountains Nasudake

and Yamizo. Principal industries are lumbering, woodworking, dairy farming, and stone quarrying. Hot springs, golf courses, and skiing are tourist attractions. Pop: 26,670.

Nasudake 那須岳

Also called Chausudake. Composite volcano in the NASU VOLCANIC ZONE, northern Tochigi Prefecture, central Honshū. It is composed of andesite, and gas rises from its crater. Nasu Hot Springs is on its slopes. Climbing and skiing are available. It is part of Nikkō National Park. Height: 1,915 m (6,282 ft).

Nasu Hot Springs 那須温泉郷

(Nasu Onsenkyō). Group of more than ten hot springs scattered along the southeastern slopes of NASUDAKE, northeastern Tochigi Prefecture, central Honshū. Many of the springs are found on an upland with an elevation of over 1,000 m (3,280 ft) There are both simple thermal and sulfur springs; water temperature 40°–76°C (104°–169°F).

Nasu Kōgen 那須高原

Highland on the southeastern slope of the mountain NASUDAKE, northern Tochigi Prefecture, central Honshū; part of the Nikkō National Park. This resort area is known for rice cultivation and dairy farming. Numerous villas have been built here, and a toll road leads up to the highland. Hot springs include Nasu Yumoto, Shin Nasu, and Ōmaru. Elevation: 300–1,260 m (1,000–4,100 ft).

Nasunogahara 那須野原

Upland extending from the Nasu Mountains toward the KANTŌ PLAIN in northern Tochigi Prefecture, central Honshū. Also called Nasuno. Wetland rice farming and dairy farming are mainstays of the local economy; however, the region is now being industrialized. Area: 400 sq km (154 sq mi).

Nasu no Yoichi 那須与一

(fl late 12th century). Warrior on the side of the Minamoto in the TAIRA-MINAMOTO WAR (1180–85). He is known for a feat of archery recounted in the 13th-century war chronicle HEIKE MONOGATARI: during the Battle of Yashima (1185), the Taira tied a fan to a boat's mast and challenged the Minamoto on the beach to shoot it down. Nasu no Yoichi succeeded with his first arrow. This story is a favorite subject in performing arts, notably in HEIKYOKU recitation.

Nasu Volcanic Zone 那須火山帯

(Nasu Kazantai). Volcanic zone running from the southeast coast of Sakhalin through western Hokkaidō, the central Tōhoku region, and northern Kantō region, Honshū, ending at ASAMAYAMA on the border between Gumma and Nagano prefectures—more than 1,000 km (600 mi). Major volcanoes include YŌTEIZAN, HAKKŌDASAN, IWATESAN, ZAŌ-ZAN, BANDAISAN, NASUDAKE, NANTAISAN, and AKAGISAN. The zone includes the great caldera lakes of Shikotsu, Tōya, Towada, and Tazawa and has many hot-spring spas.

National Aerospace Laboratory 航空宇宙技術研究所

(Kōkū Uchū Gijutsu Kenkyūjo). Government research center administered by the SCIENCE & TECHNOLOGY AGENCY. Located in the city of Chōfu, Tōkyō Prefecture. Established in 1955, it conducts a wide range of research in technology for aircraft, rockets, and aerospace in general. It publishes the *Technical Report of the National Aerospace*

"Kimigayo"

♩=69

Words: Anonymous
Music: Hayashi Hiromori

ki mi ga – yo – wa   chi yo ni – – ya chi yo ni

sa za re   i shi no   i wa o to   na ri te

ko ke no   mu – su – ma – – de

Laboratory and the *Technical Memorandum of the National Aerospace Laboratory.*

national anthem 国歌

(*kokka*). The de facto Japanese national anthem is "Kimigayo" (His Majesty's Reign). Basil H. Chamberlain (1850–1935), author of *Things Japanese* (1890), translated the anthem as follows:

*Kimi ga yo wa
Chiyo ni yachiyo ni
Sazare ishi no
Iwao to nari te
Koke no musu made*

Thousands of years of happy reign be thine;
Rule on, my lord, till what are pebbles now
By age united to mighty rocks shall grow
Whose venerable sides the moss doth line.

The words of the song are from a WAKA in the 10th-century anthology KOKINSHŪ. The author is unknown. The tune was composed by Hayashi Hiromori (1831–96) in 1880. In 1893 the Ministry of Education made it the ceremonial song to be sung in elementary schools on national holidays. Soon it was sung at state ceremonies and sports events. Although popularly identified as the national anthem for many years, "Kimigayo" has never been officially adopted as such.

National Archives 国立公文書館

(Kokuritsu Kōbunshokan). Official depository for records of the Japanese government; opened in 1971. The National Archives concerns itself with the gathering, preserving, processing, organizing, and servicing of the official documents, both domestic and foreign, that had previously been maintained by the CABINET LIBRARY (Naikaku Bunko) and by each government ministry since the Meiji Restoration (1868). Housed in a building located in the Kitanomaru Park area of the Imperial Palace grounds in Tōkyō, the Kōbunshokan presently holds and administers the 530,000 items of the Cabinet Library (which still retains its name). In addition, the Kōbunshokan contains the archival documents of the Prime Minister's Office.

National Association of Commercial Broadcasting in Japan 日本民間放送連盟

(Nihon Minkan Hōsō Remmei). A nationwide organization of commercial radio and television stations. Founded in July 1951. By

Japan's Defense-Related Expenditures

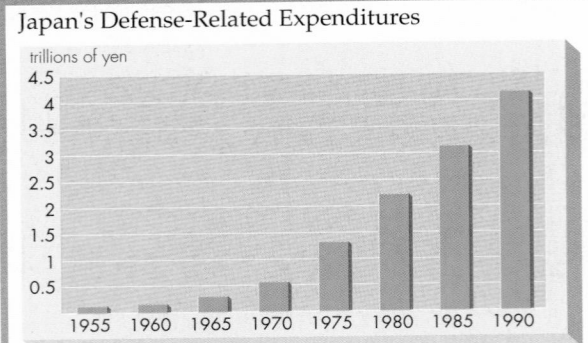

trillions of yen

(bar chart showing values from 1955 to 1990)

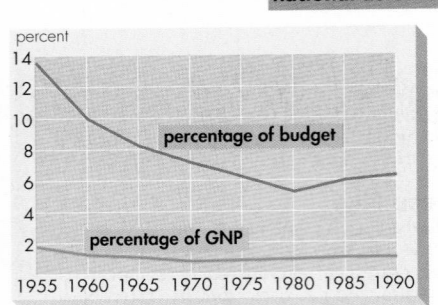

percent

(line chart showing "percentage of budget" and "percentage of GNP" from 1955 to 1990)

SOURCE: Defense Agency, *Bōei hakusho* (annual): 1990.

Countries with the Highest Military Spending, 1988

Country	Total (billions of US dollars)	Per capita (US dollars)	Percent of GNP
United States	307.70	1,250	6.3
Soviet Union	299.80	1,047	11.9
France	35.95	644	3.9
West Germany	35.10	576	2.9
United Kingdom	34.68	609	4.3
Japan	28.87	235	1.0
China	21.27	20	3.9
Italy	20.43	356	2.6
Poland	15.66	413	8.7
East Germany	14.32	863	7.7

SOURCE: US Arms Control and Disarmament Agency, *World Military Expenditures and Arms Transfers* (annual): 1989.

1991 there were 162 affiliates. The association engages in the promotion of broadcast ethics in accordance with existing broadcast codes, research in broadcast technology and operations, overseeing the proper handling of materials under copyright, and handling public relations concerning commercial broadcasting.

National Astronomical Observatory
国立天文台

(Kokuritsu Temmondai). Interuniversity astronomical research institute. Located in the city of Mitaka, Tōkyō Prefecture. Established in 1878 as part of the Tōkyō University science department, the institute was reorganized in 1888 as the Tōkyō Astronomical Observatory. It took its present name in 1988, after merging with the Latitude Observation Center. The National Astronomical Observatory conducts various types of astronomical observation and research, including astrophysics and radio astronomy. It also maintains atomic clocks for precise time measurement and compiles a calendar and ephemeris. The observatory maintains five affiliated observatories in Japan, including the Mizusawa Astrogeodynamics Observatory, the Okayama Astrophysical Observatory, and the Nobeyama Radio Observatory.

National Atlas of Japan
日本国勢地図帳

(Nihon kokusei chizuchō). First published by the GEOGRAPHICAL SURVEY INSTITUTE in 1977. Contains information concerning Japan's

National Bunraku Theater This Ōsaka theater was established by the Japanese government to preserve, promote, and stage performances of traditional Japanese puppet theater.

natural resources, society, economy, and culture provided by government departments, universities, and research institutes. It is the first full-scale atlas compiled and published by a Japanese government agency and follows the format found in the national atlases of other nations. There are Japanese and English editions.

national banks
国立銀行

(*kokuritsu ginkō*). Private banking facilities established in accordance with the National Bank Ordinance (Kokuritsu Ginkō Jōrei) of 1872 and converted into ordinary commercial banks between 1883 and 1899. Patterned after the US National Bank Act, the National Bank Ordinance called for the issue of convertible national bank notes to replace nonconvertible government notes (DAJŌKAN SATSU) and to supply capital for industrial development (see SHOKUSAN KŌGYŌ). However, only four national banks were established under these regulations. The Meiji government revised the ordinance in 1876, authorizing the use of the pension bonds (KINROKU KŌSAI) that had been issued for compulsory commutation of *samurai* stipends (CHITSUROKU SHOBUN) as banking capital and abolishing the specie reserve requirement. As a result, many new national banks were established. After the establishment of the BANK OF JAPAN under the MATSUKATA FISCAL POLICY, the government in 1883 again revised the National Bank Ordinance, and the national banks were gradually converted into ordinary commercial banks.

National Bunraku Theater
国立文楽劇場

(Kokuritsu Bunraku Gekijō). Theater established by the government for the performance of Japan's traditional puppet theater (BUNRAKU). Opened in 1984, the theater is in the Nippombashi district of Chūō Ward, Ōsaka, and seats 753 people. It was established in Ōsaka because of the city's history as the birthplace of bunraku. It is dedicated to the preservation, promotion, and spread of bunraku as well as to the training of new performers. Regular performances are scheduled six times a year. In addition to the main theater, there is a smaller hall (159 seats), which doubles as a place for rehearsals and training. The main theater, also used for KABUKI and other traditional performing arts, has a revolving stage and removable HANAMI-CHI (ramp through the audience).

National Cancer Center
国立がんセンター

(Kokuritsu Gan Sentā). Japan's leading facility for cancer research, diagnosis, and treatment. Established in 1962, it is located in Chūō Ward, Tōkyō. The center maintains a research laboratory and a hospital. The laboratory engages in a wide variety of activities, from clinical and diagnostic studies to research in molecular biology and carcinogenic materials. The center is also an important

training facility for physicians and medical technicians from Japan and abroad. It maintains an extensive library of documents on cancer and related fields.

National Center for Science Information Systems
学術情報センター

(Gakujutsu Jōhō Sentā). A facility established by the Ministry of Education in 1986 to maintain academic data bases for scholars and bibliographers from colleges and universities throughout Japan. Located in Bunkyō Ward, Tōkyō.

The center employs the NACSIS-IR computer system to access foreign data bases such as the Life Science Collection, MathSci, COMPENDEX, Harvard Business Review, ISTP&B, SciSearch, Social SciSearch, A&H Search, and JCMARC, as well as Japanese data bases, including the Outline of Scientific Research Funding and Results, the Index of Academic Theses and Dissertations, JPMARC (a bibliographical data base), and JSCAT (an index of scholarly periodicals). The center also maintains facilities for computer networking and electronic mail between key participating universities.

National Christian Council in Japan
日本キリスト教協議会

(Nihon Kirisutokyō Kyōgikai). Association formed in 1948 to promote cooperative activities among Japan's major Protestant denominations and organizations. The group's forerunner was the Nihon Kirisutokyō Remmei, which was founded in 1923 and banned during World War II. The council has 14 member organizations and 20 associated groups. In addition to its domestic activities, it is active in the world ecumenical movement.

national defense
国防

(*kokubō*). The Japanese term *kokubō* encompasses the maintenance of military forces as well as such nonmilitary aspects of a nation's security as economic strength, political stability, and the international environment. It is less specifically military in connotation than *bōei*, the word that normally stands for "defense" in such phrases as DEFENSE AGENCY (Bōeichō).

The international environment has changed profoundly since the end of World War II, bringing Japan to realize that the increasing complexity and diversity of threats to world and regional peace call for keener attention to questions of national defense. Instead of relying solely on its own forces to maintain peace, Japan has emphasized the UNITED STATES–JAPAN SECURITY TREATIES, peaceful diplomacy, economic relations of mutual interdependence, and cultural exchange with other nations.

Evolving Attitudes—It is said that General Douglas MacArthur, the supreme commander of the Allied forces (see SCAP) occupying Japan after World War II, intended to dismantle completely the old military forces and military industries and to transform Japan into "the Switzerland of the Far East" (see OCCUPATION). But in 1950, after the outbreak of war in Korea and hardening of the cold war, a NATIONAL POLICE RESERVE of 75,000 men was formed. In the early days of the cold war, as the United States requested a considerable degree of Japanese rearmament, Prime Minister YOSHIDA SHIGERU resisted on grounds that such action would "suppress the economy and make for domestic instability." In 1952, with Japan's independence restored and the United States–Japan Security Treaty

National Diet Library
1 The library maintains a collection of some 5.1 million volumes and also provides other information services. **2** An aerial view of the library (the two buildings in the foreground).

in effect, the National Police Reserve, adding maritime and air branches, became the NA-TIONAL SAFETY FORCES, later reorganized as the SELF DEFENSE FORCES (SDF).

This combination of the relatively small Self Defense Forces with a bilateral security treaty with the United States remains the core of Japan's national defense. Japan has pursued Yoshida's policy of "inexpensive defense" and achieved economic development by favoring peaceful coexistence and promoting an international environment favorable to free trade, engaging in economic exchanges with both China and the former Soviet Union.

National Defense Policy—The Japanese government's basic policy for national defense, enunciated by its National Defense Council (now SECURITY COUNCIL) in 1957, sets forth the objectives of preserving Japan's peace and independence, deterring direct or indirect aggression, and repelling any assaults. International cooperation, stabilization of public welfare, a gradual increase in defense capabilities, and reliance on the security treaties were among the original means to achieving those objectives. Since then, a few new principles have been added. These include the HIKAKU SANGENSOKU (the three nonnuclear principles of not manufacturing, possessing, or introducing into Japanese territory nuclear weapons, as approved by the Diet in 1972), a prohibition on the dispatch of troops overseas, a prohibition against conscription, the three principles regarding the export of arms (see ARMS EXPORT, THREE PRINCIPLES OF), and the maintenance of a "strictly defensive posture" (*senshu bōei*), a peculiarly Japanese term signifying a passive defense strategy. The strategy, elaborated as defense policy in the 1970 defense white papers, centered on the concept of keeping military capabilities to a minimum level necessary for self-defense. The NATIONAL DEFENSE PROGRAM OUTLINE adopted in 1976 called for a limited attack into Japanese territory to be repelled by Japan's own defensive forces, with assistance from the United States should these prove to be inadequate. When this outline was adopted, the MIKI TAKEO cabinet also enunciated a policy of limiting defense spending to 1 percent or less of Japan's gross national product (see ONE-PERCENT DEFENSE CEILING), a precedent followed by succeeding governments.

National Defense Policies of the Major Political Parties—In contrast to Western nations, where, since World War II, ruling and opposition parties have often argued bitterly about domestic policy while agreeing broadly on foreign relations and national defense issues, Japan has seen relatively little difference among its political parties on domestic policy, but sharp disagreements over diplomacy and defense. Thus opposition parties such as the JAPAN SOCIALIST PARTY and the JAPAN COMMUNIST PARTY considered the SDF unconstitutional.

By the early 1980s, however, most opposition parties supported the constitutionality of the SDF and accepted the security treaties. The ruling LIBERAL DEMOCRATIC PARTY, echoing a private consulting group formed by Prime Minister NAKASONE YASUHIRO, called for the abolition of the 1-percent limit on defense spending and reliance on public opinion as a brake on excessive military spending. According to public opinion surveys conducted in the 1980s, the Self Defense Forces were accepted by over 80 percent of the Japanese people. A somewhat smaller figure supported the security treaties with the United

States, but a large majority believed that defense expenditures should remain within the limit of 1 percent of GNP.

National Defense Academy 防衛大学校

(Bōei Daigakkō). School to train officers of the SELF DEFENSE FORCES; located in Yokosuka, Kanagawa Prefecture. Begun as the National Safety Academy (Hoan Daigakkō) under the jurisdiction of the Safety Agency, it assumed its present name in 1954, when the Safety Agency became the Defense Agency. It offers a four-year university-level program in the natural sciences, engineering, liberal arts, and social science. Postgraduate courses have been given since 1964. About 500 students are admitted each year. After graduation they receive about a year of military cadet education, together with ordinary university graduates, at the military cadet schools of the Ground, Air, and Maritime Self Defense Forces.

National Defense Program Outline 防衛計画の大綱

(Bōei Keikaku no Taikō). A policy guideline stipulating minimal defense levels required in peacetime and how to build, maintain, and organize them. Established by the MIKI TAKEO cabinet in 1976, it has been the fundamental policy for the buildup of defense strength since 1977. It states that the objective of the buildup program is to achieve and maintain the capacity to deal with a limited attack without external aid. Strength levels deemed necessary are specified in an appendix to the outline. See also NATIONAL DEFENSE.

National Diet Library 国立国会図書館

(NDL; J: Kokuritsu Kokkai Toshokan). Japan's largest library; situated next to the National Diet Building in Chiyoda Ward, Tōkyō. The NDL is under the jurisdiction of the Diet and is open to anyone over age 20. As of 1990 it housed 5.1 million books. It was formed in 1948 by combining the former Imperial Library with the libraries of the House of Peers and the House of Representatives of the former Imperial Diet. Modeled after the US Library of Congress and the Congressional Research Service, the NDL's primary function is to serve the informational needs of the national legislators. Upon request its research bureau provides drafts, analyses, and evaluations of proposed legislation. The secondary purposes of the library lie in the extension of services to scholars and the general citizenry of Japan. As a result of legal provisions for mandatory deposit in the library of all Japanese publications and the receipt of foreign publications through purchase, gift, and exchange, the public has access to a wide range of informational resources. The NDL also fulfills an important role as a bibliographic center and as a central library for the preparation of cataloging records for use by other libraries in Japan and abroad.

National Enterprise Labor Relations Law 国営企業労働関係法

(Kokuei Kigyō Rōdō Kankei Hō). Name given to the former Public Corporations and Government Enterprises Labor Relations Law when it was revised in 1986. There are four national enterprises covered by the law: the postal service, the national forestry and agricultural service, the government printing office, and the national mint. The principal contents of the law are special restrictions regarding the right of public employees to organize and bargain collectively, a provision (art. 8) exempting management and administrative affairs from collective bargaining, and a complete prohibition of strike actions (art. 17). The revised law also reorganized the Public Corporations and Government Enterprises Labor Relations Commission as the CENTRAL LABOR RELATIONS COMMISSION, which assumed authority for the resolution of labor disputes. There is debate over the issue of whether the prohibition of strikes contained in this law is in violation of article 28 of the constitution, which guarantees fundamental labor rights. See also LABOR LAWS; PUBLIC EMPLOYEES.

National Federation of Regional Women's Organizations→Chifuren

national flag 国旗

(kokki). The national flag of Japan has a crimson disc, symbolizing the sun, in the center of a white field. It is popularly known as the Hinomaru (literally, "sun disc"). It is said that at the time of the MONGOL INVASIONS OF JAPAN (1274 and 1281) the priest NICHIREN presented a sun flag to the shōgun. The Tokugawa shogunate (1603–1867) adopted the flag for its ships in the early 1600s. In the mid-19th century the shogunate decreed that all Japanese ships fly flags with the sun on a white field. In 1870 the Meiji government officially designated it for use on Japanese merchant and naval ships. It has never been officially designated as the national flag; however, it has become so by customary use. The "rising-sun" flag with 16 rays used by the former Japanese navy and by the present Maritime Self Defense Forces is

---

Hinomaru: The Japanese National Flag   **national flag**

The design and proportions of Japan's national flag were fixed in 1870 by the Meiji government. The vertical to horizontal ratio was set at 2:3, the disc was to be placed at the exact center, and the diameter of the disc was to equal three-fifths of the vertical measurement of the flag.

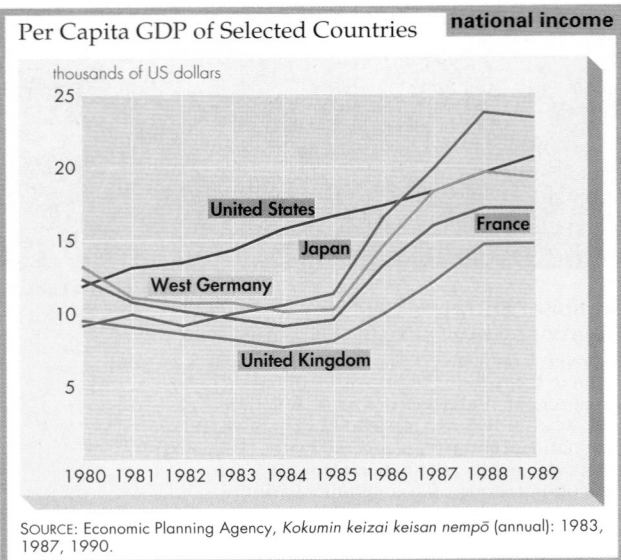

Per Capita GDP of Selected Countries · national income

thousands of US dollars

United States
Japan
West Germany
United Kingdom
France

1980 1981 1982 1983 1984 1985 1986 1987 1988 1989

SOURCE: Economic Planning Agency, *Kokumin keizai keisan nempō* (annual): 1983, 1987, 1990.

a military service flag and should not be confused with the national flag.

National Health Insurance
国民健康保険

(Kokumin Kenkō Hoken). Major component of Japan's medical care security system, providing local-government-sponsored health insurance for Japanese citizens and resident aliens. It covers the self-employed and their dependents, retired persons, and various other categories of individuals ineligible for EMPLOYEES' HEALTH INSURANCE or any of the other MEDICAL AND HEALTH INSURANCE plans. Under the first National Health Insurance Law, passed in 1938, health insurance unions established voluntarily by local communities oversaw the system. In 1958 a new law gave that responsibility to local governments. Under the present system premiums are paid solely by the insured; they consist of a fixed portion and a means-proportional portion. The amount of the premium varies from one municipality to another. The system also receives financial assistance from the national treasury. The insurance covers 70 percent of medical costs incurred by the principal insured or the principal's dependents (the rate is 80 percent for an insured retiree). As of 1989 there were 44.6 million people enrolled in National Health Insurance plans.

National House Industrial Co, Ltd
ナショナル住宅産業[株]

(Nashonaru Jūtaku Sangyō). Housing division of the Matsushita group, specializing in the development of high-quality homes under the brand name of National Pana Home. Incorporated in 1950. Sales for the fiscal year ending March 1991 totaled ¥211.8 billion (US $1.5 billion), of which prefabricated housing components accounted for 66 percent; houses, 18 percent; and residential lots, 16 percent. The company was capitalized at ¥27.1 billion (US $197.5 million) at the end of March 1991. Headquarters are in Toyonaka, Ōsaka Prefecture.

national income
国民所得

(*kokumin shotoku*). The value of goods and services produced in a nation over a specified period of time. The national income measures used in international comparisons are gross national product (GNP) and gross domestic product (GDP). Japan's GDP in 1990 was ¥434.2 trillion (US $3.0 trillion), making it the second largest market economy in the world. In the same year per capita income was ¥2.8 million (US $19,242), comparable with that of Western European nations and the United States after adjusting for Japan's high cost of housing and other goods. This high economic scale was achieved largely due to high economic growth from 1955 to the late 1960s, during which period the nation's average annual growth rate was around 10 percent, about double those of Western nations. Although this rate then showed a temporary decline at the time of the OIL CRISIS OF 1973, it has remained higher than those of most other industrialized nations up to the present time.

Structure of National Income—The Japanese economy that has evolved through this process can be understood by examining three aspects of the national income: production, distribution, and disposition. Regarding production, primary industry (agriculture, forestry, and fishing), which accounted for 26.0 percent of the GDP in 1950, shortly after the war, fell to 2.4 percent in 1990, while the share of secondary industry (manufacturing) rose from 31.8 percent to 36.9 percent, and tertiary industry (services) rose from 42.3 percent to 60.7 percent in the same years. In recent years, the share of secondary industry appears to have reached a ceiling, and that of tertiary industry has continued to develop, creating a service-oriented economy (see INDUSTRIAL STRUCTURE).

As for distribution, the proportion of employee compensation has increased, keeping pace with the development of the secondary and tertiary industries, whereas that of income from private unincorporated and private unincorporated entrepreneurial income has decreased. In 1950, employee compensation stood at 41.8 percent, while private unincorporated entrepreneurial income was 45.6 percent. In 1990, these figures were 69.0 percent and 9.1 percent, respectively, percentages equivalent to those of other industrialized nations.

When expenditures, or disposition of national income, are broken down into consumption and savings, the share of savings in national disposable income steadily increased from about 20 percent in the 1950s, peaking at 30.3 percent in 1970. It then fell to an average of 21.1 percent in the 1980s. Even now, however, this figure is higher than that of other advanced nations. See also ECONOMY, CONTEMPORARY.

National Industrial Exhibition
内国勧業博覧会

(Naikoku Kangyō Hakurankai). Name of a series of five exhibitions of domestic products, sponsored by the Meiji government between 1877 and 1903 as part of its SHOKUSAN KŌGYŌ (Increase Production and Promote Industry) policy. Although the first exhibition displayed mostly industrial crafts, such as textiles, paper, and china, successive exhibitions increasingly included machines. Along with the prefecture-sponsored *kyōshinkai* (competitive exhibitions) begun in 1879, the National Industrial Exhibitions helped develop and propagate industrial technology.

National Institute for Basic Biology
基礎生物学研究所

(Kiso Seibutsugaku Kenkyūjo). Interuniversity research facility for basic biological re-

search. Located in the city of Okazaki, Aichi Prefecture, the institute was founded under the auspices of the Ministry of Education in 1977 and conducts research in 13 areas within the 3 main fields of cell biology, embryology, and bodily control mechanisms.

National Institute for Defense Studies
防衛研究所

(Bōei Kenkyūsho). Institution for advanced officers' training and research on national security problems. Located in Meguro Ward, Tōkyō. Founded in 1952 as the National Safety College (Hoan Kenshūsho), it was renamed the National Defense College (Bōei Kenshūsho) in 1954. It assumed its present name in 1986. Two-thirds of the students are uniformed men of the rank of colonel, and the rest are civilians drawn from the Defense Agency and other ministries and agencies of the Japanese government. The institute has three departments: education, research, and military history.

National Institute for Molecular Science
分子科学研究所

(Bunshi Kagaku Kenkyūjo). Interuniversity research facility for molecular science. Established in 1975, it is located in the city of Okazaki, Aichi Prefecture. The institute consists of six departments—theory, molecular structure, electron structure, molecular grouping, correlation domain, and extreme ultraviolet sciences—accommodated by seven research facilities. The institute analyzes material composition and properties at the molecular level and studies chemical response and properties that produce molecular correlation. The National Institute for Molecular Science, the NATIONAL INSTITUTE FOR PHYSIOLOGICAL SCIENCES, and the NATIONAL INSTITUTE FOR BASIC BIOLOGY form the group known as the Okazaki National Research Institutes.

National Institute for Physiological Sciences
生理学研究所

(Seirigaku Kenkyūjo). Interuniversity physiological research facility. Located in the city of Okazaki, Aichi Prefecture, the institute was founded in 1977 and conducts research in 13 areas within such fields as molecular physiology and study of the body's regulatory and information-processing mechanisms.

National Institute for Research Advancement
総合研究開発機構

(Sōgō Kenkyū Kaihatsu Kikō). Commonly known as NIRA. Located in Shinjuku Ward, Tōkyō. NIRA performs a variety of activities focusing primarily on the advancement of research or social policy. This encompasses disseminating research findings through publications, seminars, and symposia; providing information on policy research; and engaging in exchanges with other research organizations in Japan and abroad. NIRA was established in 1974 by a special act of the Diet. As a joint public-private organization, NIRA's founding resulted from the initiatives of representatives from government, business, labor, and the academic community. Its endowment was ¥25.2 billion (US $164.6 million) at the end of March 1990.

National Institute for Resources and Environment
公害資源研究所

(Kōgai Shigen Kenkyūjo). Research institute attached to the Agency of Industrial Science and Technology within the MINISTRY OF IN-

TERNATIONAL TRADE AND INDUSTRY (MITI). Located in the city of Tsukuba, Ibaraki Prefecture, the institute was founded in 1920. It conducts research on the effective utilization of natural resources, such as the liquefaction of coal, and on the prevention of industrial pollution.

National Institute of Genetics
国立遺伝学研究所

(Kokuritsu Idengaku Kenkyūjo). Interuniversity institute for genetic research. Located in the city of Mishima, Shizuoka Prefecture. Founded in 1949, the institute conducts research in such fields as molecular genetics, population genetics, and cytogenetics. It also maintains the DNA Data Bank of Japan, a computer data base.

National Institute of Health
国立予防衛生研究所

(Kokuritsu Yobō Eisei Kenkyūjo). General research facility for the prevention and treatment of contagious disease. Founded in Tōkyō in 1947 by the Ministry of Health and Welfare, the institute engages in the development of new vaccines and conducts pure and clinical research on contagious diseases.

National Institute of Industrial Health
産業医学総合研究所

(Sangyō Igaku Sōgō Kenkyūjo). Research institute established in 1956 to investigate the causes, diagnosis, and prevention of occupational diseases and the maintenance and improvement of workers' health. Located in the city of Kawasaki, Kanagawa Prefecture. The institute conducts research in a number of areas, including the work environment and its relation to workers' health.

National Institute of Polar Research
国立極地研究所

(Kokuritsu Kyokuchi Kenkyūjo). Research institute conducting studies and observations of the polar regions. Founded in 1973, it is located in Itabashi Ward, Tōkyō. The institute coordinates Japan's antarctic observation activities and operates the Shōwa Station, Mizuho Station, and Asuka Camp in Antarctica. It also collects, analyzes, and publishes data derived from polar research. Its staff is involved in international exchanges.

nationalism
国家主義・民族主義

(kokka shugi; minzoku shugi). Since early times the Japanese have been conscious of their own distinctiveness in relation to their East Asian neighbors. The chief components of this separateness have included Japan's geographic isolation, its monolingual culture, its ethnic homogeneity, its people's strong ties to the soil, common beliefs in the gods of Shintō, and an EMPEROR who simultaneously propitiated the gods, legitimized the state, and symbolized the people. Nevertheless, no clear conception of nation or of the commonweal emerged before Japanese feudalism began to weaken in the late 18th century, when there was an upwelling of nativist thought, especially among scholars of National Learning (KOKUGAKU), of whom MOTOORI NORINAGA was the most important.

Nationalism in the Meiji Period (1868–1912)—Following the opening of Japan to the outside world in the mid-19th century, Japanese society underwent a radical change from a feudal social structure to a more open status hierarchy based on vertically organized interests of wealth and talent. After the MEIJI RESTORATION of 1868, internally hierar-

chical groups such as joint-stock companies, small manufacturing enterprises, early agricultural producers' cooperatives, and even nascent political parties after 1868 began to compete for places on a status ladder presuming inequality but also mobility. When these vertically arranged groups vied with one another for predominance, they naturally trumpeted their own partisan interests for political and economic advantage. In response Japanese patriots began to speak out on behalf of the whole society, trying to surmount private, selfish advantage by directing attention to the shared interests of all the nation's people.

The agents that catalyzed Japanese patriotism in the mid-19th century included strong military, diplomatic, and economic pressures from Europe and America and discontent with the Tokugawa shogunate's treatment of the throne and its passive attitude toward the foreign powers. While scholars such as AIZAWA SEISHISAI and YOSHIDA SHŌIN had flaunted the xenophobic slogan Revere the Emperor, Expel the Barbarians (SONNŌ JŌI) during the 1850s, patriotic loyalties expressed by a few farsighted statesmen helped to sanction new leaders and reform programs after the Meiji Restoration. In their drive to enrich the country and strengthen the army (FUKOKU KYŌHEI), government officials erected a stong, efficient state. The integration of Japanese society after 1868 through the development of media, education, and a single national market helped every adult Japanese to understand the common national interest as determined by the government.

As society grew more integrated in the late 19th century, nationalist feelings took two main forms. One was statist nationalism (kokka shugi), which demanded that all Japanese subjects obey and serve the state as the highest object of their allegiance. The other main form was popular nationalism (minzoku shugi) with allegiance centering on the Japanese as a people and upon their history, traditions, and customs.

Statist Nationalism, 1890–1945—In the late 1880s ITŌ HIROBUMI and others created for the Meiji government a full-dress constitution (see CONSTITUTION OF THE EMPIRE OF JAPAN) and defined allegiance to the state as the citizen's highest duty. The IMPERIAL RESCRIPT ON EDUCATION, issued in 1890, was the sacred scripture of this new statism. Government-sponsored Shintō festivals, ceremonies honoring the emperor, and homiletic ethics texts in the schools after 1903 helped to spread the statist version of nationalism to every family. This indoctrination took place just as the Meiji hierarchy of competing interests began to give way to the social relations of enterprise capitalism, particularly during and after World War I. New formulations of nationalism stressing myths of social harmony and Japanese uniqueness appeared, now that Japan was growing more like other modern societies and experiencing similar internal stresses. Political leaders such as TANAKA GIICHI and patriot-scholars such as ŌKAWA SHŪMEI elaborated these doctrines of state loyalism while Japan lapsed into economic and diplomatic peril in the 1920s and 1930s. Statism was magnified into ultranationalist dogmas once politics fell under strong military influence in the late 1930s. The government handbook KOKUTAI NO HONGI (Cardinal Principles of the National Essence), published in 1937, announced that the "individual is an existence belonging to a State" and "is fundamentally one body with

it." Such doctrines evaporated with defeat in August 1945.

Popular Nationalism, 1890–1945—Equally strong in the late 19th century were sentiments focused on the nation as a people (minzoku shugi). The antigovernment FREEDOM AND PEOPLE'S RIGHTS MOVEMENT of the 1870s was followed in 1887 by the Nihon dōtoku ron (Discourse on Japanese Morality) of NISHIMURA SHIGEKI, who wrote not to praise the state but to build character among the people.

Popular nationalists with conservative predilections attacked the government for its halfhearted attempts to revise the Unequal Treaties after 1887 (see UNEQUAL TREATIES, REVISION OF). The nationalist dreams of those involved in such movements as PAN-ASIANISM and Japanism (NIHON SHUGI), such as the influential GEN'YŌSHA and the AMUR RIVER SOCIETY, embraced a far more aggressive policy abroad than the state intended. The SINO-JAPANESE WAR OF 1894–1895 and the RUSSO-JAPANESE WAR a decade later helped to disseminate nonofficial nationalism of this conservative sort to citizens who believed that their state was not standing up to the Western powers.

Popular nationalists on the left such as the socialist leader KŌTOKU SHŪSUI felt no less loyal to the nation for all their stiff opposition to the government ruling them. Indeed, except for anarchists and certain communists, nearly all modern Japanese political thinkers have been nationalists in that they have felt deep emotional attachment to their countrymen.

Whereas for statists the emperor's exalted role was in good part a modern political and legal function specified in constitutional writ, most popular nationalists venerated the emperor because of his unique historical role as chief priest of Shintō and intercessor with the gods on behalf of his people. It seems very likely that the country's capacity for national mobilization in the late 1930s and early 1940s was enhanced because the state fitted itself to the ethnopsychological inclinations of common Japanese to identify with one another as a people under a sacerdotal throne, rather than because the state extracted unyielding popular devotion to itself as sovereign.

Postwar Nationalism—Because of the defeat in World War II loyalties to the state have been muted, but affinities with fellow Japanese remain strong and meaningful. The main framework for discussing Japanese nationalism has been the extraordinary internationalization of cultural life since 1945. Japanese nationalism has had to compete with other claims on the individual's loyalty, both transnational (sports, jazz, art, world peace) and subnational (company, school, family). Literature and the arts have grown so cosmopolitan, and with them styles and tastes in the marketplace, that some critics have found it hard to separate modernity from Japaneseness.

Yet few Japanese, however free from provincial prejudices, forget that their distinctive social structure makes them still feel remarkably different from other peoples. According to some critics, statist nationalism's potential for future mischief in some worldwide economic or military crisis is reinforced by the persistence of the imperial throne as a rallying point of loyalties. As the country moves into the 21st century new definitions of Japanese nationalism will have

National Museum of Western Art Statues by Rodin, including *The Thinker* (right) and *The Burghers of Calais* (left), are displayed in the courtyard before the main building, which was designed by Le Corbusier.

to be developed to accommodate the nation's continuing need for psychic security amid constant change.

Nationality Law → Japanese nationality

National Land Agency 国土庁

(Kokudochō). Cabinet-level agency attached to the Prime Minister's Office, established in 1974 in conjunction with the enactment of the National Land Use Planning Law (Kokudo Riyō Keikaku Hō). The agency is empowered to formulate basic land-use plans, while coordinating water resources management, regional land development, and countermeasures against future large-scale earthquake disasters. See also LAND PROBLEM.

National Language Research Institute 国立国語研究所

(Kokuritsu Kokugo Kenkyūjo). National institute for scientific research on all matters concerning the Japanese language. Located in Kita Ward, Tōkyō, the institute was established on 20 December 1948 for the scientific study of the Japanese language and of the linguistic life of the Japanese people. It carries out research in the areas of linguistics and language education, and it publishes KOKUGO NENKAN, a yearbook offering a comprehensive bibliography of works published in Japan and abroad that are related to the Japanese language. It has also published the *Nihon gengo chizu* (1966–74, 6 vols, Linguistic Atlas of Japan). In 1976 the Center for Teaching of Japanese as a Foreign Language was established in this institute.

National Mobilization Law 国家総動員法

(Kokka Sōdōin Hō). Legislation for mobilizing Japan's civilian society and economy during World War II. It was drafted by the Planning Board of the first KONOE FUMIMARO cabinet soon after Japan went to war with China in July 1937 (see SINO-JAPANESE WAR OF 1937–1945). The bill was attacked as unconstitutional when it was introduced to the 73rd Diet in January 1938. Under pressure from the military, legislators finally approved the law without amendment on 24 March 1938. It was officially promulgated on 1 April and took effect on 5 May.

Twenty-five of its 50 articles provided for controls on civilian organizations, labor, industrial and consumer commodities, corporations, contracts, prices, and the news media. The law empowered the government to subsidize war production and indemnify manufacturers for losses caused by mobilization. It also contained 18 articles setting penalties for violations.

The full authority of the Kokka Sōdōin Hō was brought to bear on the society as well as the economy between 1942 and 1945. The mobilization foundered because of incomplete integration, growing scarcity of natural resources, and the fact that Japan was losing World War II. The law was formally abolished on 20 December 1945.

National Museum of Art, Ōsaka 国立国際美術館

(Kokuritsu Kokusai Bijutsukan). Museum in the city of Suita, Ōsaka Prefecture. Opened in 1977. The collection includes works by Picasso, Miró, Giacomo Manzù, and SAEKI YŪZŌ. The museum presents exhibitions focusing on the connection between Japanese and international art from early to modern times. Current acquisition efforts are focused on obtaining works by contemporary artists worldwide.

National Museum of Ethnology 国立民族学博物館

(Kokuritsu Minzokugaku Hakubutsukan). Located in the city of Suita, Ōsaka Prefecture, the museum was established in 1974 and opened to the public in 1977. It offers up-to-date ethnographic information, based upon field research, on the world's peoples and societies. The museum's collection includes articles of daily life as well as materials related to religion and art. Exhibits are divided into geographical areas corresponding to Oceania, the Americas, Europe, Africa, West Asia, Southeast Asia, and East Asia. Special cross-cultural exhibits deal with overall themes such as music and linguistics. The museum features a Videoteque, consisting of audiovisual equipment that automatically selects, presents, and returns video cassette tapes upon request of the viewer.

National Museum of Japanese History 国立歴史民俗博物館

(Kokuritsu Rekishi Minzoku Hakubutsukan). A museum of history and folk culture that opened in March 1983 in the city of Sakura, Chiba Prefecture. It collects and preserves Japanese historical, archaeological, and folk material and data and exhibits them to the public. It also conducts surveys and studies in the fields of history, archaeology, and folklore and assists scholars engaged in research in these fields. Its exhibitions emphasize the history of the life of the common people instead of a general display of material. The first president of the museum was Inoue Mitsusada (1916–83), a historian. The museum also operates a nationwide information network. The site of the museum occupies approximately 130,000 square meters (1,400,000 sq ft).

National Museum of Modern Art, Kyōto 京都国立近代美術館

(Kyōto Kokuritsu Kindai Bijutsukan). Institution in Sakyō Ward, Kyōto. Founded in 1963 as the Kyōto Annex Museum of the National Museum of Modern Art in Tōkyō, it became the National Museum of Modern Art, Kyōto, in 1967. The museum presents numerous exhibitions of both domestic and international art and handicrafts. Among its holdings are some 420 ceramic pieces by KAWAI KANJIRŌ, 181 copperplate prints by HASEGAWA KIYOSHI, and paintings by TAKEUCHI SEIHŌ and UMEHARA RYŪZABURŌ. The museum also houses a collection of over 1,000 photographs by Western photographers.

National Museum of Modern Art, Tōkyō 東京国立近代美術館

(Tōkyō Kokuritsu Kindai Bijutsukan). Located in Kitanomaru Park, Chiyoda Ward, Tōkyō, the museum collects, preserves, and exhibits outstanding works of modern art and related reference materials. The museum was first opened in 1952 in the Kyōbashi section of Tōkyō under the auspices of the Ministry of Education. In 1969 it was moved to its present building, designed by TANIGUCHI YOSHIRŌ and donated by ISHIBASHI SHŌJIRŌ. The Film Center, Japan's only national film institute, was opened in 1970 in the original building in Kyōbashi. The museum has a collection of some 4,000 works in the fields of Western-style painting, Japanese-style painting, sculpture, prints, and crafts.

National Museum of Western Art 国立西洋美術館

(Kokuritsu Seiyō Bijutsukan). Located in Ueno Park in Tōkyō. A collection of European art, the basis of which is the large group (over 400 items) of French paintings and sculpture of the 19th and 20th centuries collected by Matsukata Kōjirō (1865–1950). Since its opening in 1959 the museum has broadened its collection to include works of earlier centuries by artists from Italy, Holland, Flanders, Spain, and England. The museum's main building was designed by Le Corbusier; the annex, which opened in 1979, was designed by MAEKAWA KUNIO. See also MUSEUMS.

National Nō Theater 国立能楽堂

(Kokuritsu Nōgakudō; formal name Kokuritsu Gekijō Nōgakudō). Theater dedicated to the performance of the traditional Japanese dramatic forms of NŌ and KYŌGEN. Located in the Sendagaya district of Tōkyō, the theater opened in 1983. On the first floor it seats 591 people. A separate theater on the second floor, intended for training, accommodates 200 people. There are about 50 scheduled performances per year. The primary goals of the National Nō Theater are the performance and preservation of the art of Nō, the training of actors and musicians, and Nō study and research.

national parks and quasi-national parks 国立公園と国定公園

(*kokuritsu kōen to kokutei kōen*). These terms denote scenic land declared public property by the Japanese government with a view to preservation and development for purposes of recreation and culture. National parks (*kokuritsu kōen*) are administered by the Environment Agency of the Prime Minister's Office, and quasi-national parks (*kokutei kōen*) are administered by the prefectural governments under the supervision of the Environment Agency. These parks represent a concerted effort to protect Japan's environment, which began in the 1930s and gained momentum in the 1950s. The first national parks were the Inland Sea and the Unzen (now Unzen-Amakusa) national parks, established in 1934. Attempts are being made to protect and preserve a wide variety of land as well as wildlife. In 1991 there were 28 national parks and 55 quasi-national parks. National parks are generally much larger than other parks.

National Pension 国民年金

(Kokumin Nenkin). Japan's basic public pension program. Introduced in 1959, the National Pension was originally designed for those not covered by other existing pension programs, especially farmers and the self-employed. Since reform of the pension system in 1986, the National Pension has provided a basic, mandatory pension to all Japanese citizens between the ages of 20 and 60, regardless of employment or marital status. Employed persons also receive addi-

Japan's National Parks and Quasi-National Parks in 1991

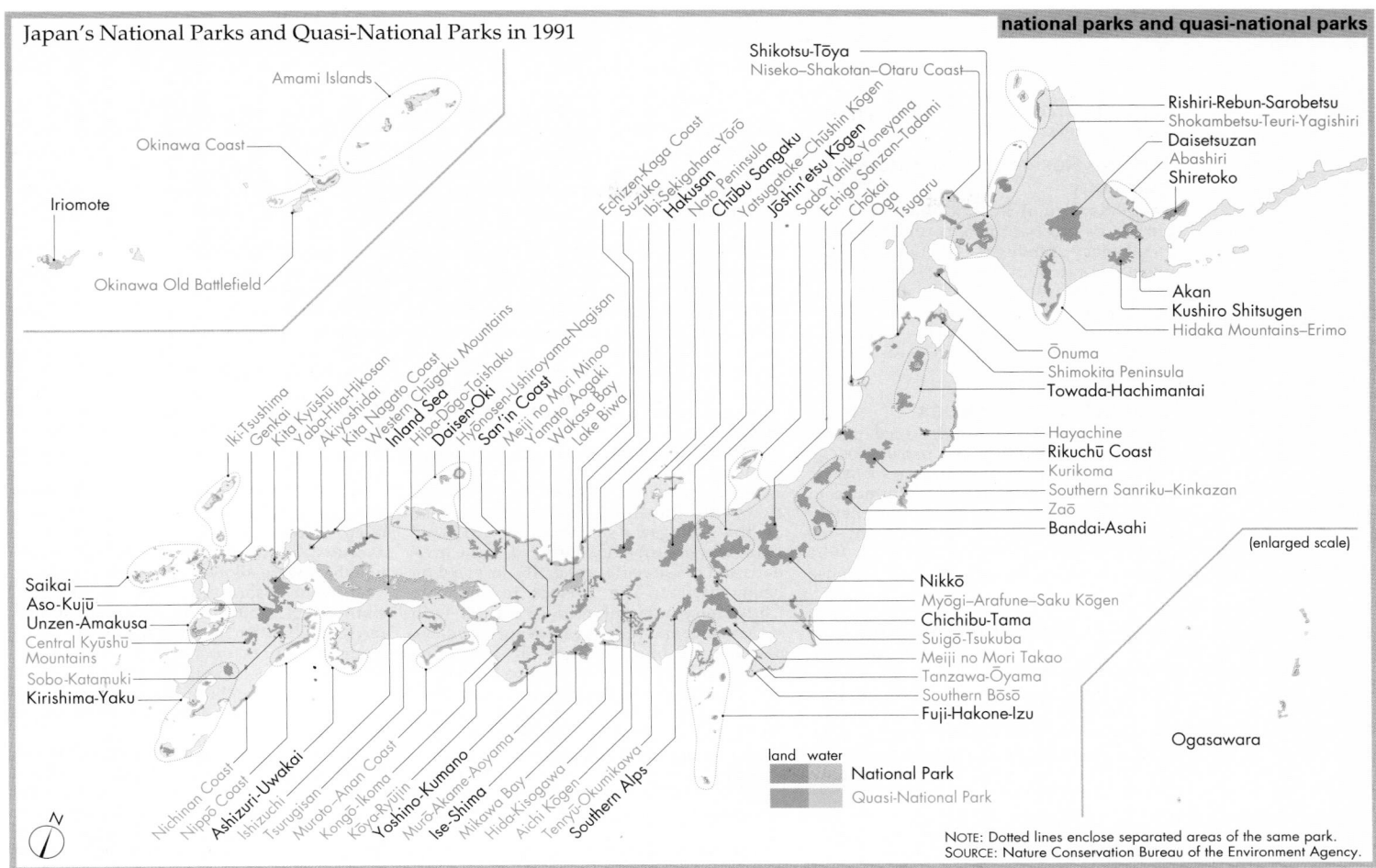

NOTE: Dotted lines enclose separated areas of the same park.
SOURCE: Nature Conservation Bureau of the Environment Agency.

tional benefits from EMPLOYEES' PENSION INSURANCE or MUTUAL AID ASSOCIATION PENSIONS. In 1988, 64.9 million people were covered under the National Pension system. Of these, 30.0 million received their sole pension coverage from this program.

The National Pension consists of three components: a basic old-age pension, a disability pension, and a basic survivor's pension. Contributions from insured persons and employers cover two-thirds of the cost of National Pension benefits, with the remainder paid by the national treasury. In 1989 the monthly payment required of all individual contributors to the National Pension system was ¥7,700 (US $55.80). The basic old-age pension of ¥55,500 (US $402) per month (as of 1989) is paid to people aged 65 and over who have fulfilled the minimum contributory requirement of 25 years. See also PENSIONS.

National Personnel Authority
人事院

(Jinjiin). Independent agency of the Japanese government responsible for the administration of the national civil service. It was established in 1947 under the National Civil Service Law (Kokka Kōmuin Hō) at the recommendation of the supreme commander for the Allied powers (SCAP) as a part of the democratization of the bureaucracy and improvement of personnel management. First called Rinji Jinji Iinkai, it was renamed the Jinjiin in 1948. It acts as a board of equity, ensuring that recruitment is done impartially based on merit and that disciplinary actions are fair. It advises the government and the Diet on setting wages for civil servants, who are restricted in their right to engage in collective bargaining and to strike; its annual recommendations are based on comparative wage surveys.

National Police Reserve
警察予備隊

(Keisatsu Yobitai). Post–World War II armed organization; forerunner of the SELF DEFENSE FORCES. When the Korean War began in June 1950, the supreme commander for the Allied powers, Douglas MACARTHUR, ordered the Japanese government to form a National Police Reserve of 75,000 men. From the time the order was issued on 8 July 1950 to the end of the year, the National Police Reserve gradually took over from US forces the job of maintaining public peace and order. In 1952 the reserve was reorganized into the NATIONAL SAFETY FORCES, which later became the Self Defense Forces.

National Police Reserve case
警察予備隊訴訟

(Keisatsu Yobitai soshō). A legal case filed by SUZUKI MOSABURŌ, chairman of the Left Faction (Saha) of the Japan Socialist Party, challenging the constitutionality of the NATIONAL POLICE RESERVE. It resulted in the landmark decision of 8 October 1952, in which the Japanese SUPREME COURT asserted its power of JUDICIAL REVIEW for the first time. While exercising its power of review, the court declined to issue a judgment on the abstract issue of whether the National Police Reserve, which was more heavily armed than the police force, indeed possessed "war potential" and was thus illegal under article 9 of the CONSTITUTION OF JAPAN (see RENUNCIATION OF WAR). However, it did rule that the National Police Reserve had been established not for mobilization in wartime, but to support the police in maintaining domestic order. It left unresolved the apparent conflict—exacerbated by the subsequent establishment of the SELF DEFENSE FORCES—between Japan's 1947 constitution and the presence of potential instruments of war.

National Public Safety Commission
国家公安委員会

(Kokka Kōan Iinkai). Government body, attached to the Prime Minister's Office, that is responsible for the administration and coordination of police activities throughout Japan and for the supervision of Japan's law enforcement agency, the National Police Agency (Keisatsuchō). The commission is comprised of a chairman who holds the rank of minister of state and five members, all of whom are appointed by the prime minister. It was established in 1947 specifically to guarantee the neutrality of the police in politics and to prevent government misuse of police powers. It was to do this by insulating the police from political pressure and by ensuring the maintenance of democratic methods of administration within the police forces. At the same time a public safety commission (kōan iinkai) was established in each prefecture to supervise its police. Prefectural public safety commission members are appointed by the governor with the consent of the prefectural assembly. They are independent from the National Public Safety Commission. See POLICE SYSTEM.

National Research Institute for Earth Science and Disaster Prevention
防災科学技術研究所

(Bōsai Kagaku Gijutsu Kenkyūjo). Center for research on disaster prevention technologies in the city of Tsukuba, Ibaraki Prefecture. Affiliated with the Science and Technology Agency, the institute was founded in 1963. It studies methods for predicting earthquakes and conducts basic research on prevention of and response to disasters due

National Research Laboratory of Metrology 計量研究所

(Keiryō Kenkyūjo). Research institute of the MINISTRY OF INTERNATIONAL TRADE AND INDUSTRY's Agency of Industrial Science and Technology. Located in the city of Tsukuba, Ibaraki Prefecture. The institute was founded in 1903 to establish official standards for fundamental and derived units and also to conduct research in measurement technology.

National Safety Forces 保安隊

(Hoantai). Post–World War II armed organization; forerunner of the SELF DEFENSE FORCES. In August 1952 the NATIONAL POLICE RESERVE, together with a maritime force founded in April 1952, was put under the newly founded National Safety Agency and renamed the National Safety Forces. In 1954 the organization became the Self Defense Forces.

National Salvation Association 中国人民救国会

(Chūgoku Jimmin Kyūkoku Kai; Ch: Zhongguo Renmin Jiuguo Hui or Chung-kuo Jen-min Chiu-kuo Hui). Part of the growing Chinese protest against Japan's aggression in North China, the All-China Federation of National Salvation Associations, commonly referred to as the National Salvation Association, was founded in Shanghai in June 1936 by noncommunist intellectuals and politicians who opposed the Guomindang (Kuomintang; Nationalist Party) government's policy of fighting Chinese communists instead of the Japanese. The association became the leader of the National Salvation Movement, a proliferation of organizations and demonstrations sparked by the DECEMBER NINTH MOVEMENT (1935) in Beiping (Peiping; now Beijing [Peking]).

Communist support for the association's aims was one of the pretexts used by the Guomindang to arrest seven prominent leaders of the association in November 1936. After the arrests, pressure increased on CHIANG KAI-SHEK, leader of the Guomindang, to adopt a policy of resistance to Japan. The National Salvation Movement achieved its aim by July 1937, when Chiang implemented a united front policy against Japanese aggression (see SINO-JAPANESE WAR OF 1937–1945) and also released the association leaders.

National Science Museum 国立科学博物館

(Kokuritsu Kagaku Hakubutsukan). Museum in Ueno, Taitō Ward, Tōkyō, in which materials concerning natural science are studied, collected, and displayed. In addition to carrying out educational activities, it functions as a research center for the study of the natural history of the Japanese archipelago. Started in 1877 as the Kyōiku Hakubutsukan, it acquired its present name in 1949. Educational and research programs on conservation and ecology are carried out at the museum's nature study park in Minato Ward, Tōkyō.

National Seclusion 鎖国

(Sakoku). Policy (1639–1854) adopted by the Tokugawa shogunate (1603–1867) in an effort to legitimize and strengthen its authority, both domestically and in East Asia. The main elements of the policy were the exclusion of Roman Catholic missionaries and traders, the proscription of Christianity in Japan (see ANTI-CHRISTIAN EDICTS), and the prohibition of foreign travel by Japanese. The seclusion was not total, because Dutch, Chinese, and Koreans were permitted access to Japan. Moreover, designated officials and traders from the domains of Satsuma (now Kagoshima Prefecture) and Tsushima (now part of Nagasaki Prefecture) were allowed to go to the Ryūkyūs and to Korea, respectively. The Korean trade in Japan, however, was confined to Tsushima, and the only Japanese port open to the Dutch and Chinese was Nagasaki.

The movement toward seclusion began with the first edict prohibiting Christianity issued by TOYOTOMI HIDEYOSHI in 1587. This, along with the anti-Christian edicts issued by the Tokugawa shogunate in 1612 and 1614, was occasionally enforced, but Christians and missionaries generally survived by being discreet. The attempt to eliminate Christianity was enforced in earnest with surveillance and torture following TOKUGAWA IEMITSU's becoming shōgun in 1623. The shogunate may also have seen seclusion as a way of securing the benefits of foreign trade for itself and preventing the *daimyō* of the southwest from using independent trade with foreign countries to build their own strength. Though the prime motive is debated, it is clear that the tendency toward seclusion began before it became official policy.

The official seclusion policy was enunciated in five directives issued by the shogunate's senior councillors (RŌJŪ) in Edo (now Tōkyō) to its two commissioners (BUGYŌ) in Nagasaki between 1633 and 1639. The term Sakoku (literally, "Closed Country") did not come into use until early in the 19th century, when it was coined by a Japanese scholar of WESTERN LEARNING.

The first Sakoku edict was issued in 1633. The 17-article directive covered the coming and going of Japanese overseas, the search for Christian converts and missionaries, and the regulation of foreign trade. All ships and Japanese subjects were forbidden to leave Japan for a foreign country without a license (see HŌSHOSEN); all Japanese living abroad were to be put to death if they tried to return to Japan, except for those who had resided abroad for less than five years and had been unavoidably detained. The Nagasaki commissioners were to investigate all those suspected of being Christians, and a reward was offered to any informer who revealed the location of a BATEREN (foreign priest). When a foreign ship arrived, it was to be guarded while a report was sent to Edo. Any foreigner who helped a *bateren* or any other proscribed foreigner was to be imprisoned at Ōmura (now part of Nagasaki Prefecture), and, finally, a strict search was to be made for *bateren* on all ships entering Japan. The last section dealt with foreign trade, more specifically with the operation of the ITOWAPPU system (a raw-silk monopoly system) in Nagasaki.

The second edict (1634) and the third edict (1635) were similar to the first directive, but the 1635 edict was more specific in its prohibitions. The dispatching of ships abroad was absolutely forbidden. Moreover, if a Japanese was caught trying to leave or return to Japan, he was to be executed, and both the ship and its captain were to be detained pending charges.

The fourth edict (1636) contained 19 articles. The offspring of "southern barbarians" (Portuguese and Spanish) were not allowed to remain in Japan, upon the threat of execution, and Japanese who had adopted such offspring were to be handed over, together with the children, to the Portuguese for deportation. The reward for informing on a *bateren* was increased, and foreign trade regulations were explained in greater detail, with a few minor changes made as to how and when raw silk could be sold.

The last of the Sakoku edicts, issued in 1639 in the aftermath of the SHIMABARA UPRISING, stated that Portuguese ships would no longer be allowed to enter Japanese ports. Any ship disobeying this order was to be destroyed, and its crew and passengers were to be executed.

In 1640 the shogunate arrested 74 people who sailed from Macao to Nagasaki to reopen relations with Japan. Sixty-one were executed, but the remaining 13 Chinese crew members were allowed to return to Macao.

In what is sometimes referred to as the sixth Sakoku edict, the shogunate transferred the Dutch from Hirado to the manmade island of DEJIMA in Nagasaki Harbor in 1641. After this, apart from the Ryukyuan and Korean trade, the only foreign trade permitted was that of the Dutch and Chinese at Nagasaki.

The PHAETON INCIDENT of 1808, in which a British warship sailed into Nagasaki Harbor in defiance of shogunate orders, demonstrated that, after nearly 200 years of unsuccessful attempts by foreign interests to alter the seclusion policy, regulations had become quite lax (see also GAIKOKUSEN UCHIHARAI REI). Although the shogunate temporarily attempted to strengthen National Seclusion in 1825, it relaxed the policy again in 1842. On the theoretical level, it continued to be championed by scholars of the nationalistic MITO SCHOOL, but with the arrival of Commodore Matthew C. PERRY in 1853 the shogunate was forced to abandon its seclusion policy. National Seclusion was formally brought to an end by the KANAGAWA TREATY of 1854 and the ANSEI COMMERCIAL TREATIES of 1858.

National Service Draft Ordinance 国民徴用令

(Kokumin Chōyō Rei). Imperial ordinance promulgated in July 1939 on the authority of the NATIONAL MOBILIZATION LAW to draft the civilian population to ensure an adequate supply of labor for strategic industries during wartime. Enforcement was left to the minister of welfare. Exemptions were allowed only in cases of illness or physical handicap. Under the ordinance 1,610,000 men and women were drafted, and 4,500,000 workers were reclassified as draftees. The ordinance was subsumed under the more comprehensive Kokumin Kinrō Dōin Rei (National Labor Service Mobilization Law) of March 1945 (abolished in October 1945).

National Space Development Agency of Japan 宇宙開発事業団

(Uchū Kaihatsu Jigyōdan). Government agency established in 1969 to develop a space exploration program. Headquarters are in Tōkyō. The agency operates a rocket launching site on the island of Tanegashima, south of Kyūshū, and carries out the development and testing of satellites. The Tsukuba Space Center in Ibaraki Prefecture, which tracks the flight of satellites after launching, is also under its supervision. Following the successful launching in 1975 of Engineering Test Satellite I (nicknamed *Kiku*), the agency has continued the development and launching of satellites for various purposes. See also SPACE TECHNOLOGY.

National Spiritual Mobilization Movement　国民精神総動員運動

(Kokumin Seishin Sōdōin Undō). Movement formed in 1937 as a part of the National Mobilization (Kokka Sōdōin) Movement to rally the nation for an all-out effort for victory in the war against China (see SINO-JAPANESE WAR OF 1937–1945). Representatives from 74 national organizations assembled at Prime Minister KONOE FUMIMARO's official residence in October 1937 and were incorporated as the Central League of the Spiritual Mobilization Movement. Under the direction of Admiral Arima Ryōkitsu (1861–1944), the organization had few concrete programs and simply appealed to the masses for patriotic support. To bolster the movement, Konoe added 19 organizations to the league.

The HIRANUMA KIICHIRŌ cabinet, which took office in January 1939, reorganized the movement under ARAKI SADAO. The Spiritual Mobilization Movement reached the masses through public rallies, radio programs, and printed information, and through neighborhood associations called TONARIGUMI.

National Sports Festival　国民体育大会

(Kokumin Taiiku Taikai, commonly referred to as Kokutai). Begun in 1946. One of the representative amateur sports events in Japan jointly sponsored by the JAPAN AMATEUR SPORTS ASSOCIATION, the Ministry of Education, and the local government of the prefecture where the festival takes place. The site is selected annually. The festival consists of three seasonal meets (winter, summer, and fall). The games are played in two major divisions, one for adults and the other for those under age 18, with athletes representing each prefecture competing. The festival covers some 39 different sports, including traditional martial arts.

national stadiums　国立競技場

(*kokuritsu kyōgijō*). A collective term used to refer to three sports complexes located in Tōkyō: Kasumigaoka National Stadium in Shinjuku Ward, which includes a track and field stadium, a rugby field, and an indoor swimming pool; Yoyogi National Stadium in Shibuya Ward, which includes a gymnasium and tennis courts; and Nishigaoka National Stadium in Kita Ward, which includes a soccer field and an indoor pool. Most commonly, however, the term is used to refer to the Kasumigaoka National Stadium, which was the site of the opening and closing ceremonies of the Olympic Games held in Tōkyō in 1964. The National Stadium and School Health Center of Japan, a special corporation funded by the Japanese government, administers the three complexes.

National Tax Administration　国税庁

(Kokuzeichō). Agency primarily responsible for the assessment and collection of national taxes. Established in 1949. The agency is attached to the MINISTRY OF FINANCE, whose Tax Bureau (Shuzeikyoku) is responsible for the overall planning and formulation of tax policy. The agency gives guidance and direction to a network of 12 regional taxation bureaus (*kokuzeikyoku*) and 517 district tax offices (*zeimusho*) engaged in the actual collection process. It has a staff of 53,000.

National Tax Tribunal　国税不服審判所

(Kokuzei Fufuku Shimpanjo). Adminstrative tribunal that reviews and rules on requests for review of dispositions based on the laws concerning national taxes under article 78 of the National Tax Common Provisions Law (Kokuzei Tsūsoku Hō). The National Tax Tribunal is affiliated with the NATIONAL TAX ADMINISTRATION. The president of the tribunal is appointed by the director of the agency subject to the approval of the minister of finance, but he is given independence in the exercise of his authority. In addition to the main tribunal office in Tōkyō, there are 13 branch offices, 1 each in Tōkyō, in Ōsaka, and in the other regional national tax office jurisdictions.

Most requests for review that come to the tribunal concern dispositions (rectifications, decrees, and delinquency dispositions) made by a head of a district tax office. In general, requests for review of other dispositions cannot be made without first declaring an objection to the head of the district tax office. The direct request for review must be made within two months of learning of the disposition, and then the actual review must be requested within one month of receiving approval to proceed. See also TAX LAW.

National Theater　国立劇場

(Kokuritsu Gekijō). Theater established by the Japanese government to promote and preserve Japan's traditional performing arts. Opened in November 1966, the National Theater is located in the Miyakezaka district of Tōkyō. The building houses a large theater (seating 1,746) and a small theater (seating 630); the former is primarily used for KABUKI performances and the latter mainly for BUNRAKU. In addition to the regularly scheduled performances of these two genres sponsored by the National Theater itself, performance space is made available for privately sponsored performances in a variety of other traditional genres, including dance and JŌRURI. The National Theater also fosters the development and training of performing artists and sponsors research, exhibitions, and films on subjects related to the traditional performing arts.

National Treasures　国宝

(Kokuhō). Designation given by the Japanese government to objects of exceptional historical and artistic importance in order to ensure their preservation. National Treasures were originally given recognition under the Preservation of Ancient Shrines and Temples Law (Koshaji Hozon Hō), which was passed in 1897. The Preservation of National Treasures Law (Kokuhō Hozon Hō), passed in 1929, took the place of the older law and expanded the definition of National Treasures. When a fire in 1949 destroyed many of the early-8th-century Buddhist wall paintings at the temple HŌRYŪJI in Nara, the Diet took the disaster as an occasion to enact the Law for the Protection of Cultural Assets (Bunkazai Hogo Hō; see CULTURAL PROPERTIES LAW). Under this 1950 law (revised in 1954 and 1975) all items previously known as National Treasures were designated Important Cultural Properties (Jūyō Bunkazai). The law stipulated that Important Cultural Properties could be advanced to the now more-exclusive status of National Treasure only after a lengthy, quasi-legislative selection process involving the Ministry of Education and the Committee for the Protection of Cultural Assets.

The cultural properties of special historical and artistic value listed in the cultural assets legislation include tangible objects—such as buildings, paintings, decorative art, sculpture, calligraphy, books, and old documents—and Intangible Cultural Assets, which are traditional skills and techniques in areas such as theater, music, weaving, dyeing, and the ceramic arts. The practitioners of these skills and techniques have come to be known popularly as LIVING NATIONAL TREASURES (Ningen Kokuhō). As of January 1989 Important Cultural Properties numbered 11,476 and National Treasures numbered 1,034.

national universities　国立大学

(*kokuritsu daigaku*). Universities established, managed, and funded by the national government. Each prefecture has at least one national university. In 1989 there were 96 such schools, with a total enrollment of 560,000 in undergraduate and graduate programs. Admission and tuition fees for these schools are roughly half those at private universities. The fees for 1988–89 at national universities were ¥206,000 (US $1,580) for admission and ¥339,000 (US $2,605) for tuition. National universities were established as part of the EDUCATIONAL REFORMS OF 1947. Their predecessors were the 7 imperial universities and numerous higher and normal schools, all of which were reorganized into 70 national universities in 1950.

national vacation villages　国民休暇村

(*kokumin kyūka mura*). A type of public recreation area established in Japan's national and quasi-national parks and other natural environments to assure access to low-cost, wholesome recreation for all citizens. The villages are furnished with sports and recreation facilities, campgrounds, and lodgings of various types. Staff provide instruction in hiking, tennis, skiing, and other sports. The first of these villages was created in 1961, and by 1990 there were 32 of them nationwide.

national wealth　国富

(*kokufu*). A country's total tangible fixed assets such as buildings and structures (roads, harbors, and other facilities), machinery and apparatus, vessels, rolling stock and transportation equipment, tools and accessories, and plants and animals; inventories of raw materials, finished and unfinished work, and merchandise; and NET EXTERNAL ASSETS (foreign assets minus foreign liabilities). Financial assets are not included. At the end of 1988 Japan's national wealth was assessed at US $21.9 trillion, or 7.6 times its gross national product (GNP) of US $2.9 trillion.

Natsume Sōseki The author and scholar in the study of his Tōkyō home in 1914.

This was a considerable increase over 1978, when national wealth, at US $4.7 trillion, was 4.8 times the GNP.

This rapid increase in national wealth in recent years has been caused primarily by sharp increases in the price of land. In 1988 land represented 67.5 percent of Japan's national wealth, compared to 28.2 percent in the United States. The rise in land asset values is producing serious problems, including the pricing of most families out of the housing market and the increasing inequality of INCOME DISTRIBUTION as those who own land are able to generate large capital gains (see LAND PROBLEM).

Net external assets have also increased greatly over the last two decades, although, at US $288.7 billion in 1988, they were still only 1.3 percent of Japan's national wealth.

Natori   名取[市]

City in central Miyagi Prefecture, northern Honshū. Natori developed as a post-station town on the highway Ōshū Kaidō. Today it is one of the satellite cities of Sendai. Fishing and farming are its principal occupations. The largest mounded tomb (KOFUN) in northeastern Japan, the Raijin'yama Tomb, and several other *kofun* attest to early settlement of the area. Pop: 53,732.

Natori Reiji   名取礼二

(1912–). Physiologist. Born in Tōkyō. Graduate of Jikei University School of Medicine, where he served as a professor from 1949 to 1976 and as president from 1975 to 1982. In 1949 he extracted myofibrils, the basic units of muscle contraction, from the skeletal muscles of frogs, thus contributing greatly to the clarification of how muscles contract. He received the Order of Culture in 1986.

Natori Yōnosuke   名取洋之助

(1910–62). Photographer; a pioneer of Japanese photojournalism. Born in Tōkyō. In 1933 he founded Nihon Kōbō, a journalistic and commercial photo production studio, and then launched the photo magazine *NIPPON* (1934–44), printed in four languages, to introduce Japanese culture to the world. After World War II he was editor in chief of the Iwanami Photo Library (Iwanami Shashin Bunko), a popular series of photo-illustrated books.

Natsuigawa   夏井川

River in eastern Fukushima Prefecture, northern Honshū, originating in the Abukuma Mountains and flowing southeast to enter the Pacific Ocean at the city of Iwaki. Length: 67 km (42 mi).

Natsume Seibi   夏目成美

(1749–1816). HAIKU poet and wealthy merchant of the late Edo period (1600–1868). Real name Natsume Kaneyoshi. Seibi is well known as a patron of the haiku poet ISSA. His own poems have a refined, sensuous, elegant subtlety. Seibi's haiku collections include *Seibi kashū* (1816). He was also a haiku scholar whose published research includes *Zuisai kaiwa* (1819).

Natsume Sōseki   夏目漱石

(1867–1916). Novelist and scholar of English literature. Real name Natsume Kinnosuke. Born in Tōkyō. Sōseki scrutinized Japan's "civilization" and the psychology of intellectuals who experience the contradictions of life in a backward country during modern times. At first his style was florid and pedantic, combining the traditional *haibun* (essay style employed by HAIKU poets, usually studded with haiku) and *kambun* (Chinese prose) styles with European modes of expression. Eventually he developed a more colloquial and flexible prose style better suited to examining the depths of human psychology. Sōseki ranks with MORI ŌGAI as a major figure in modern Japanese literature.

Biography——The eighth and last child of Natsume Kohyōe Naokatsu and his wife, Chie, Sōseki was sent to a foster home immediately after birth. He was to go back and forth between the two houses throughout his childhood. The death of his mother in 1881, when he was 14, and of his two oldest brothers in 1887 intensified his sense of insecurity. His early education included intensive studies in classical Chinese. By the time he entered the English department of Tōkyō University, he had already decided to become a scholar of English literature. There he began to compose haiku under the influence of MASAOKA SHIKI. In 1895 he taught at Matsuyama Middle School, Ehime Prefecture, and in the following year at the Fifth Higher School in Kumamoto Prefecture.

Sōseki went to England as a government student in 1900. There he suffered serious bouts of depression as a result of solitude and poverty, but these torments became the basis for his work *Bungakuron* (1907, Literary Theory). On returning home in 1903, he replaced Lafcadio HEARN at the First Higher School and at Tōkyō University and lectured on literary theory and literary criticism.

During that period Sōseki continued to contribute haiku, *renku* (haiku-style linked poetry), *haitaishi* (poetry similar to *renku* but with a set theme), and *shaseibun* (literary sketches) to the haiku periodical HOTOTOGISU, founded by his friend Masaoka Shiki and later headed by TAKAHAMA KYOSHI. In the meantime, the first part of his novel WAGAHAI WA NEKO DE ARU (1905–06; tr *I Am a Cat*, 1961), completed in December 1904, was well received by members of *Hototogisu* and printed in its January issue. Sōseki also wrote short stories, including "Rondon tō" (1905, Tower of London). His 1906 works *Botchan* (Little Master; tr *Botchan*, 1972) and *Kusamakura* (Grass Pillow; tr *The Three-Cornered World*, 1965) established his reputation as a novelist. In 1907 he quit all his teaching jobs and joined the newspaper *Asahi shimbun*. During the time he worked for the *Asahi*, he wrote approximately one full-length novel per year.

In the summer of 1910, while at Shuzenji spa, he vomited blood from a gastric ulcer and remained bedridden until the following year. During his illness he wrote *Omoidasu koto nado* (Things I Recall, Etc), which probes his experiences on the brink of death. He took a strong interest in the new literary generation and supported the members of the SHIRAKABA SCHOOL and SHINSHICHŌ group.

In Sōseki's later years AKUTAGAWA RYŪNOSUKE, KUME MASAO, Matsuoka Yuzuru (1891–1969), and others became staunch followers of his literary principles. They created a literary circle called "the Sōseki mountain range" by later generations.

Works——*I Am a Cat*, a humorous narrative written from the viewpoint of a cat, is a biting satire on human lives distorted by a "civilized" society. While *I Am a Cat* was being published in installments, Sōseki wrote the seven short stories collected in *Yōkyoshū* (1906). These are mostly fantasies in a restrained and elegant style. *Uzurakago* (1906, Quail Basket), the collection of fictional works after *Yōkyoshū*, includes *Botchan*, *Kusamakura*, and *Nihyakutōka* (The Typhoon; tr *Nihyakutoka*, 1918). Journeys and idealized main characters are themes common to these works.

Sōseki's major literary interests began to develop in the works published in installments by the *Asahi shimbun*. The first installment novel, *Gubijinsō* (1907; tr *Red Poppy*, 1918), criticizes modern civilization through its portrayal of various types of youths. This motif is continued in *Sanshirō* (1908; tr *Sanshirō*, 1977) and *Sorekara* (1909; tr *And Then*, 1978). In *Sanshirō*, Sōseki utilized the "stream of consciousness" technique, with which he had already experimented in *Kōfu* (1908, tr *The Miner*, 1988). It depicts the shifting psychological state of the main character, Sanshirō, and his relationships with intellectuals of different ages in a modern city. The bitterness of lost love that the modern youth Sanshirō tastes contrasts with the absurdity of the youthful experiences recalled by his mentor Hirota, demonstrating Sōseki's understanding of the changing times.

Sōseki's middle period also includes *Mon* (1910, The Gate; tr *Mon*, 1972) and a group of short pieces on dreams and psychology. These include "Bunchō" (1908; tr "The Paddy Bird," 1951), "Yumejūya" (1908; tr "Ten Nights of Dreams," 1961), and "Eijitsu shōhin" (1910, Spring Day's Small Pieces). In these, Sōseki's style became even more polished and versatile.

The serious illness at Shuzenji marked the beginning of Sōseki's late period. In such characters as Sunaga Ichizō in *Higansugi made* (1912, Until after the Equinox), Nagano Ichirō in *Kōjin* (1912–13; tr *The Wayfarer*, 1967), and Sensei in KOKORO (1914, The Heart; tr *Kokoro*, 1957), Sōseki intensifies his examination of the solitary, intense, and even occasionally demented mind. His next work, *Michikusa* (1915; tr *Grass on the Wayside*, 1969), further develops the theme of an intellectual's sufferings in the context of changing human relationships. This novel contains striking autobiographical elements.

The shifting between a subjective examination of the self and an objective view of others is further developed in Sōseki's final and unfinished work, *Meian* (1916; tr *Light and Darkness*, 1971). With its grand scope *Meian* demonstrates the potential of the Meiji-period novel for analyzing the state of society. While working on *Meian*, Sōseki composed a poem in classical Chinese every day. It is said that these poems express the idea of *sokuten kyoshi* ("become one with heaven, liberated from the self"), for which he longed in his later years.

nattō   納豆

Food product made by fermenting steamed soybeans with the bacillus known as *nattō* for several days. The bacillus breaks up the protein in the soybeans, leaving them soft, sticky, and brown. A valuable source of protein, vitamin B_2, and enzymes, *nattō* was first made in the late Edo period (1600–1868). It is usually eaten mixed with minced scallions (*negi*), mustard, raw egg, and soy sauce as a side dish for rice. Being easily digested, *nattō* is also used as a baby food.

natural disasters 自然災害

(*shizen saigai*). The most destructive of natural disasters in Japan are EARTHQUAKES. The TŌKYŌ EARTHQUAKE OF 1923 alone left more than 140,000 dead or missing and 100,000 injured. In Japan's recorded history there have been 17 earthquakes that caused at least 1,000 deaths each and 7 that caused more than 5,000 deaths. In most of these cases the major destruction was caused by fires or tidal waves (TSUNAMI) that followed the tremors. The most destructive natural disasters, after earthquakes, are the numerous autumn TYPHOONS. The typhoon that struck Ise bay on the Pacific coast of western Honshū in 1959 left more than 5,000 people dead or missing. Where terrain has been altered by excessive housing construction the incidence of posttorrent mudslide and landslide damage has increased. There were no large-scale disasters in the 1970s or 1980s, although the eruption in 1986 of the Miharayama volcano, on the island of Ōshima, forced residents to evacuate for nearly a month. The large number of active VOLCANOES in Japan is a continuing source of concern. In 1991 more than 35 people died in the eruption of UNZENDAKE (Mt. Unzen) in Kyūshū. In 1962 the government passed the Basic Disasters Prevention Law (Saigai Taisaku Kihon Hō) and in 1969 established the Coordinating Committee for Earthquake Prediction to conduct research on the likelihood of severe (up to 8.0 on the Richter scale) earthquakes in heavily populated regions.

naturalism 自然主義

(*shizen shugi*). Significant Japanese literary movement begun around 1906 and lasting through the 1920s. Strongly influenced by its late-19th-century European model, naturalism in Japan stood in opposition to subjectivism, imaginative escapism, and classicistic posturing by earlier Meiji-period (1868–1912) writers and sought to depict modern society and the lives of the men and women who composed it as objectively and truthfully as the subject matter of science is studied and presented.

TAYAMA KATAI's *Futon* (1907, The Quilt) and SHIMAZAKI TŌSON's *Hakai* (1906; tr *The Broken Commandment*, 1974) are regarded as the first and most important works of Japanese naturalism. IWANO HŌMEI, TOKUDA SHŪSEI, KOSUGI TENGAI, NAGAI KAFŪ, OGURI FŪYŌ, and KUNIKIDA DOPPO wrote novels and short stories that adhered, at least in part, to the principles formulated by their European forerunners, most notably Zola. In these works there is a pervading sense of the deterministic control exerted over the actions and destinies of the characters by impersonal social, economic, and biological forces. In time, owing to the confessional nature of these and similar works, Japanese naturalist fiction went the way of the *watakushi shōsetsu* or I-NOVEL.

naturalization 帰化

(*kika*). Process whereby one who is not a Japanese citizen acquires Japanese citizenship. The permission of the minister of justice must be obtained for naturalization. Application for citizenship can be made through the district legal affairs bureau (*chihō hōmukyoku*) that has jurisdiction over the area in which the applicant resides. The application requires submission of documents certifying that the applicant meets certain qualifications for naturalization. When application is made on behalf of an alien under 15 years of age by a legal representative, documents that certify the applicant's competency must also be submitted.

Requirements—Under the provisions of the Nationality Law (Kokuseki Hō) of 1950, as revised in 1984, an alien who desires to be naturalized must fulfill the following requirements: he or she must have maintained a domicile (*jūsho*) in Japan for five or more consecutive years, be at least 20 years old and legally competent according to the law of his or her native country, be of good character, have sufficient means to support himself or herself, have no other citizenship or surrender any other citizenship upon acquiring Japanese citizenship, and never have plotted or advocated the overthrow of the constitution or government of Japan and never have formed or belonged to a party or other organization that has plotted or advocated the overthrow of the constitution or government of Japan.

Special Circumstances—The minister of justice is authorized to grant naturalization to a foreign spouse of a Japanese national on condition that he or she has been married to the Japanese national for three years or more and has had a domicile in Japan for at least one full year. The minister may also permit naturalization if the alien is unable, despite his or her intention, to divest himself or herself of his or her current nationality and if the minister finds exceptional circumstances.

The minister of justice, with the approval of the Diet, may also grant citizenship to an alien who does not fulfill any of the above requirements if that person has rendered especially meritorious service to Japan. The minister of justice informs the applicant by public notice in the OFFICIAL GAZETTE (*Kampō*) when citizenship has been granted. The citizenship is effective from the date of issue of the public notice. See also FOREIGNERS, LEGAL STATUS OF.

natural monuments and protected species 天然記念物

(*tennen kinembutsu*). The Japanese term *tennen kinembutsu*, usually translated as "natural monument," has a wider range of meaning than any one English equivalent. In the strict sense it refers to natural objects and phenomena (including species of animals and plants) characteristic of or peculiar to Japan that have been designated for preservation under the CULTURAL PROPERTIES LAW of 1950 or similar local laws. These include certain geologic or mineral formations and areas (other than national parks) of special historic, scenic, or scientific interest, as well as certain species of animals and plants found only in specific areas of Japan. Natural monuments and protected species are classified into two categories: those designated for preservation by the national government under the Cultural Properties Law (953 in 1992, including 75 classified as "special natural monuments") and those set aside for protection by the laws of local public bodies such as prefectures, cities, towns, and villages.

Protected Areas—Areas of specific interest that have been set aside as *tennen kinembutsu* are classified under a number of official designations such as Nature Protection District, Primeval Forest, and Shrine Forest. Nature Protection Districts include Lake TOWADA; the river OIRASEGAWA; the Kurobe gorge (see KUROBE KYŌKOKU); the Oze, Torishima, and Kushiro bogs; and the island of Minami Iōjima (see IŌ ISLANDS). Primeval Forests include the Daisetsuzan area in Hokkaidō, the SARUGAWA Headwaters Primeval Forest, the Maruyama Primeval Forest, the Kasugayama Primeval Forest in Nara, and the Aso Kitamukidani Primeval Forest. One Shrine Forest is the Miyazaki Kashima Forest in Toyama Prefecture.

Animals—Indigenous species of Japanese wildlife designated as *tennen kinembutsu* include the Amami *no kurousagi* (see RABBITS), the *meguro* (Bonin honeyeater), and the giant salamander (*ō sanshōuo*; see SALAMANDERS). Although not indigenous species, the Japanese crested ibis, the short-tailed albatross, the Japanese crane, and the Japanese stork are limited in distribution to certain areas. Other *tennen kinembutsu* include cranes and their migration grounds in Kagoshima Prefecture, the natural habitat of SEA BREAM in the waters of Tainoura in Chiba Prefecture, and the breeding grounds of the HORSESHOE CRAB in the waters near Kasaoka, Okayama Prefecture. Naturalized species include the magpie, the turtledove and domestic birds and animals (such as certain varieties of fowl), the *misaki* horse (*misaki uma*; see HORSES), Mishima cattle (Mishima *ushi*; see CATTLE), and the long-tailed cock (*onagadori*; see CHICKEN, JAPANESE).

Plants—Certain rock-zone flora found in specific locations and the boundary zones of distribution of certain plants found only in limited areas are also classified as *tennen kinembutsu*. A great number of very old or very large individual trees have also been designated as natural monuments.

Geologic formations that have been designated as natural monuments include the group of cirques (deep, steep-walled basins) at YAKUSHIDAKE, the limestone cave known as AKIYOSHIDŌ in Yamaguchi Prefecture, and the upthrust coasts of Kisakata in Akita Prefecture. A number of unique mineral formations and fossil sites have also been designated. ☎ *1066–1067*

natural resources 天然資源

(*tennen shigen*). Japan's industrial complex is built on one of the world's weakest resource bases, being poor in conventional energy resources and in almost all of the major materials needed for modern industry. Although in variety Japan's resources are surprisingly rich, their amount, availability, and quality limit domestic production to a fraction of the country's needs.

The degree of Japan's dependence on imported raw materials is illustrated by the following import figures from 1989: petroleum,

Continued on page 1068 ▶

Found only in Japan, the *kamoshika,* or Japanese serow (*Capricornis crispus*), dwells in the mountainous areas of Honshū, Shikoku, and Kyūshū. Just 1 meter from head to tail, it resembles a small mountain goat.

The giant salamander, or ō *sanshōuo* (*Megalobatrachus japonicus*), found in rivers in Honshū, Shikoku, and Kyūshū, is the largest amphibian in the world, with specimens measuring up to 1.2 meters in length, although the usual size is about 60 cm. The salamanders can live as long as 100 years.

Preserving Japan's Natural Treasures

Efforts to preserve and protect important natural resources began in Japan in the early 20th century in response to the environmental strain of rapid industrialization. Inspired by the German *Naturdenkmal* ("Natural Monument") movement, the Japanese government enacted the first of several preservation laws in 1919.

Under the provisions of an all-encompassing Cultural Properties Law passed in 1950, the Japanese Ministry of Education designates as "natural monuments" rare natural phenomena, endangered plant and animal species (and/or their habitats), species endemic to Japan, and certain geological or mineral formations.

As of 1992, there were 953 legally designated natural monuments, 75 of which were further distinguished as "special natural monuments." These photographs offer a sampling of some of Japan's special natural monuments.

The mikado ageha butterfly (*Graphium doson*), found in various locations in East and Southeast Asia, is legally protected in the city of Kōchi, Kōchi Prefecture, its northernmost habitat in Japan.

The Japanese crane, or *tanchō* (*Grus japonensis*), concentrated mainly in Hokkaidō, is a popular symbol of longevity. Shown here is an elegant mating dance. Cranes pair in winter and lay their eggs in April; a little more than a month later, their offspring are hatched.

The alpine vegetation of the Shirouma mountain group in Nagano Prefecture includes many species that have disappeared from more heavily traveled mountain areas. Pictured here is a field of summer flowers blooming in the lingering snow.

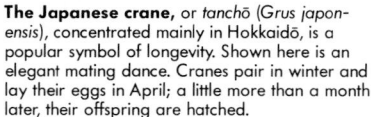

Kyūshū

Kōchi Prefecture
Shikoku

An unusual species of algae called *marimo* (*Cladophora sauteri*), at Lake Akan, Hokkaidō. Individual organisms join to form balls up to 25 cm in diameter.

Daisetsuzan, a group of volcanic mountains in central Hokkaidō, forms the core of Japan's largest national park. Beautiful alpine meadows, such as this one, are found throughout the park.

Two ancient cedar trees, each more than 1,000 years old, on the grounds of the Yasaka Shrine in the town of Ōtoyo, Kōchi Prefecture. The tree in the foreground is 20 meters in circumference at the base and 60 meters tall.

Daisetsuzan •
Hokkaidō   • Lake Akan

Niigata Prefecture
**Shirouma
ountain group**   Fukushima Prefecture
●   ● **Oze moor**
agano Prefecture   **Gumma Prefecture**

Japanese Alps

Honshū

N

A year-round mountain resident, the ptarmigan, or *raichō* (*Lagopus mutus*), breeds in the Japanese Alps. Brown in spring and summer, its plumage turns white in winter, providing camouflage.

The Oze moor, Japan's largest, is located at the intersection of Niigata, Fukushima, and Gumma prefectures and is part of Nikkō National Park. Rare and important wetland plants and animals make Oze a valuable resource for biological study.

99.7 percent; coal, 91.4 percent; bauxite, 100 percent; nickel, 100 percent; iron ore, 99.8 percent; copper, 98.4 percent; and lead, 90.0 percent. Japan also relies on outside sources for 100 percent of its raw cotton, wool, and rubber, as well as large and growing amounts of forest products, agricultural commodities, and seafood. In almost all cases, domestic resources were at best barely adequate before the Japanese economy began expanding; the country's exceptionally high rate of economic and industrial growth since the 1960s has resulted in ever greater reliance on foreign sources. In many cases, imported raw materials are of better quality and cheaper than the domestic products. Even coal, one resource in relative abundance, has seen domestic production drop precipitously because of high costs and low quality.

Resources, especially sources of energy, have also been strained by the rising affluence of Japanese society. In addition to industrial growth rates of 20 percent or better during some years, the purchase of major household appliances by Japanese families has greatly increased the demand for energy. Periodic shortages along with sharp rises in production costs have given the energy industries top priority in government planning.

Coal—Japan's coal reserves were estimated at about 7 billion metric tons (7.7 billion short tons) in 1990, but the largest and most productive fields are poorly located at opposite ends of the country in Hokkaidō and Kyūshū, far from the industrial heartland, adding transportation fees to relatively high production costs.

Japanese coal is generally low-grade bituminous of inferior heating value. High-grade coking coal supplies are negligible, so virtually all of the nation's needs must be imported. Coal seams are generally thin, deep below the surface, badly broken, steeply inclined, and plagued by inflammable gases, all of which make mechanization difficult and work hazardous. High production costs, bitter labor-management strife, dangerous operations, and competition from oil and other energy sources have led to a sharp drop in output and in the number of mines and miners. Production in the 1950s and 1960s averaged 50 to 55 million metric tons (55 to 60.5 million short tons) annually; by 1990 it had dropped to 8.3 million metric tons (9.1 million short tons). Coal-mining labor has similarly declined from a force of roughly 244,000 in 1960 to about 5,000 in 1990, and the number of operating mines has dropped from 682 to 26, partly under a rationalization program that closed marginal mines. Despite greatly improved productivity, the domestic coal industry has a doubtful future, notwithstanding government subsidies and the higher cost of petroleum. Any major endeavor to replace oil with coal would add enormous costs to the economy, while the increased production necessary to satisfy such a demand would soon exhaust Japan's reserves.

Petroleum and Natural Gas—Japan's petroleum-refining industry is the third largest in the world, but virtually all crude oil must be imported from China, Indonesia, and especially the Middle East. A trickle of domestic oil comes from the Niigata fields along the northwest coast of Honshū, with smaller fields scattered through northern Honshū and Hokkaidō.

Small natural gas fields and wells are also

scattered, with the largest concentrations in Hokkaidō, northern Honshū, and Chiba Prefecture near the huge Tōkyō metropolitan markets. But as with coal, most of Japan's increased demand for petroleum and liquefied gas will have to be met by foreign sources, often through joint development projects with countries having surplus energy resources.

Hydroelectric Power—Rugged terrain, abundant precipitation, and fast-flowing streams have made it possible for Japan to develop one of the world's largest hydroelectric industries. Numerous small hydroelectric plants once produced the largest share of Japan's electricity, but in 1991 they accounted for only a little over 20 percent, while thermal power supplies almost 80 percent. While possibly half of the country's hydroelectric power is yet undeveloped, the remaining sites are in marginal locations, where construction and transmission costs would be much higher than for those sites already developed.

Nuclear Power and Alternative Energy Sources—Although the country lacks uranium ore and must import its nuclear fuel, Japan is among the world leaders in the development of nuclear power plants. Despite growing concern and an increasingly vigorous anti-nuclear-energy movement, the government has pressed ahead with its nuclear power program. By 1990, 39 atomic reactors had been built, and Japan was the world's fourth largest producer of nuclear power, supplying 25.8 percent of its total electrical power output through nuclear generation. Japanese electrical power producers have signed agreements with suppliers in Canada, the United Kingdom, Australia, and Niger to secure reserves of unprocessed uranium amounting to a total of 200,000 metric tons (220,000 short tons).

Only a small fraction of the nation's energy is currently supplied by alternative sources, but research and development proceed in such areas as solar and geothermal power, gasification and liquefaction of coal, and the separation of hydrogen from seawater.

Metal and Minerals—Japan's metal resources have become almost totally inadequate for such a large industrial complex. In 1991 it ranked third in steel production, just behind the USSR and the United States, but produced more on a per capita basis than either nation. Japan also has the world's third largest aluminum industry. The small size of Japan's deposits of metal ores, coupled with the scale of production for both export and domestic consumption, makes it impossible to reduce the nation's dependence on overseas supplies. Even with a slower rate of industrial growth than in the past, Japan's need for imported metals will only grow.

In the steel industry, for example, Japan imported 99.8 percent of its iron ore requirements in 1989, mainly from Australia and Brazil; it also imports 99.5 percent of the coking coal essential to steel production. The bulk of raw materials for the ferroalloys used in the steel industry also come from abroad.

Similarly, though more than 3 million metric tons (3.3 million short tons) of aluminum is produced annually in Japan, production is totally dependent on imported bauxite, mainly from Australia. Japan was once self-sufficient in copper and zinc, but in 1989 imported 98.4 percent of the materials used in making copper and 82.2 percent of those used by the zinc industry. Domestic supplies of lead meet only 10.0 percent of the de-

mand. In other minerals, Japan is virtually wholly dependent on foreign sources.

Wood and Pulp—Even though Japan's forests cover about 60 percent of the land, lumber supplies have grown tight, forcing Japan to look to outside sources for over half of its present lumber. Nor are domestic supplies adequate for one of the world's largest producers of pulp, paper, rayon, and other wood products; pulp imports now constitute roughly 20 percent of consumption.

With the growth of affluence and tourism, Japan's forest lands have become increasingly valuable as parks. But heavy demands on the forests have led to overcutting, especially in Hokkaidō. Any further expansion of domestic wood and pulp production would result in heavy environmental damage to Japan.

Future Outlook—Without continued access to foreign resources, Japan has no chance for economic survival, for Japan's resource base is pitifully weak. Virtually all its natural resources are of such small quantities as to make it impossible to expand production without quickly exhausting them. In addition to the problems posed by escalating costs and diminishing supplies of the few key materials still supplied domestically, Japan also faces the challenges of increasing international competition for resources and rising global concern over ecological issues—factors that are likely to have a significant impact on Japan's resource policies in the years to come.

natural sciences 自然科学

(*shizen kagaku*). Natural science in Japan faced a critical time of change in the latter half of the 19th century, particularly after the MEIJI RESTORATION of 1868. Before 1868, under the NATIONAL SECLUSION policy of the Tokugawa shogunate (1603–1867), the development of traditional science as well as WESTERN LEARNING followed what may be called an indigenous pattern. It was only with the opening of the entire country to foreign influences following 1868 that science developed more freely and began to parallel modern Western science in content and quality.

Premodern Science—Natural science as it now is understood in the West did not exist in Japan prior to the 7th century. It was only with the introduction of Chinese thought and culture, first brought to Japan by immigrants from the Korean states and China (see KIKAJIN), that science in its present sense came into being. The continental immigrants brought with them Chinese science, including mathematics, ASTRONOMY, metallurgy, and medicine. As in many other ancient societies, medicine and astronomy were usually associated with fortune-telling and magic and covered a broader range of subjects than what is considered to be science today (see OMMYŌDŌ). Toward the close of the 9th century, the Japanese decided to stop sending embassies to China (see SUI AND TANG [T'ANG] CHINA, EMBASSIES TO). The Chinese system remained in form only, and astronomy, mathematics, and other studies, as well as the offices connected with them, became the hereditary prerogatives of certain families.

Parallel to the development of Chinese-style scientific studies was the introduction of Indian medical, astronomical, and cosmological thought in conjunction with the transmission of Buddhism from the Korean penninsula and China to Japan during the mid-6th century. The Buddhist influence on natural science predominated until the end of the medieval period (mid-12th–16th centuries). Studies that were distinct from Chinese court culture were introduced through the Buddhist scriptures (sutras), many of which were composed within the sphere of Indian cultural influence. Monks from the continent used their knowledge of medicine, herbs, calendrical science, and astronomy to gain influence and to further the spread of Buddhism in Japan. In medicine, for example, the notable doctors were Buddhist monks, and in astronomy and calendrical science, monks made horoscopes according to Indian astronomical illustrations contained in the Chinese text *Xiuyaojing* (*Hsiu-yao-ching*).

Early Modern Science—The scientific knowledge introduced in the 16th century by Jesuit missionaries did not have a great impact in Japan. Western astronomy was not much more advanced than Chinese or Japanese astronomy, but it nevertheless had some influence, especially in navigational astronomy. In medicine, Western methods of surgery were introduced, although 16th-century surgery was concerned mainly with stanching bleeding and stemming infection.

During the early Edo period (1600–1868), a second wave of Chinese influence accompanied a renewed interest in Confucianism. The Shoushi (Shou-shih) calendar of the Yuan (Yüan) dynasty (1279–1368) of China, in slightly modified form, was adopted in 1684, effective 1685. Although solar and lunar eclipses were predicted according to Japanese methods of calculation, calendrical science relied heavily on Chinese astronomy through the first half of the Edo period. Chinese therapeutic medical techniques also were widely used until the 18th century, when more clinically centered medicine began to be practiced.

In the late 17th and early 18th centuries a Japanese mathematics (WASAN) was developed by such men as SEKI TAKAKAZU, who created their own schools. Going beyond practical mathematics, these scholars solved geometric problems using algebraic formulas. *Wasan* attracted many who enjoyed mathematics simply as an intellectual game, especially in the 19th century.

With the establishment of a Dutch trading outpost in DEJIMA and regular trade contacts with the Dutch in the early 17th century, the Dutch language became the main medium for the entry of Western Learning, the successor to the scientific and cultural teachings introduced by the Jesuits, into Japan. The influx of new information concerning such diverse fields as medicine, mathematics, chemistry, and military science provided a major stimulus to the growth of natural science in Edo Japan.

It was against this background that Western astronomy became the focus of interest, and many Japanese scholars who had regarded China as their model became convinced of the superiority of Western science. During this period the theories of Copernicus, Galileo, Kepler, and Newton were introduced into Japan. In both China and Japan, where the universe was viewed in more relative terms than in the West (see NATURE, CONCEPT OF), the Copernican theory was accepted without much opposition; it was simply a shift in emphasis (see also SHIZUKI TADAO). In contrast, Newtonianism, which tried to reduce everything to particles and their motion, was too reductionist and heterogeneous to be grasped within the scope of traditional East Asian scholarship.

At the same time, however, the reductionist method of Newtonianism was useful in explaining individual phenomena. There existed in it a hierarchy of theory and application, and this hierarchical view was to be taken up by later scholars of Western studies, especially professional physicians. Physicians, unlike astronomers and translators in government, were relatively free agents. In Japan, as a group they were the only scientific professionals. The kinds of modern scientists and technologists that were emerging in the West were completely unknown in 18th- and 19th-century Japan. Among the physicians were many translators of books on modern science. In their translations, especially in the prefaces, they emphasized that physics was the basis of all science, including medicine, and explained the relationship between theory and application; that is, they explained that physics was the basis of physiology, that physiology was the foundation of medicine, and that the knowledge of practical cures was based on them all. Actually, for all practical purposes what physicians practicing Western medicine needed was enough knowledge of physics and chemistry to prepare medicinal compounds.

From the point of view of natural history, Western studies did not strongly impress the Japanese; natural history was merely a matter of certain differences between East and West. However, the emphasis of natural philosophy on hierarchy, universality, and methodology was welcomed as something that had not existed in traditional science. The scholars of Dutch Learning gave it the name *kyūri* (Ch: *qiongli* or *ch'iung-li;* "to understand the principle"), indicating that they correctly understood the idea of natural philosophy in Western science, but the existence of the term in the vocabulary of Zhu Xi (Chu Hsi) philosophy also suggests that they wanted to take part in the respect and authority enjoyed by the Zhu Xi school. See also SHUSHIGAKU.

After the mid-18th century, physicians led the way in the study of Western science, looking first to anatomy. In Chinese medicine, physiology and pathology were explained in terms of *ki* (Ch: *qi*), the energy that permeated the universe. Traditionally, there was no need for an accurate science of anatomy, and there was no materialist tradition. However, in the *koihō* or classicist school of medicine in Japan, the necessity for taking a materialist approach was perceived and autopsies were carried out. In 1774 SUGITA GEMPAKU published a translation of a Dutch textbook of anatomy, but it was more to advertise the superiority of Western medicine than for practical application.

Scientific learning, then, was primarily concerned with medicine. But in the mid-19th century, as foreign ships approached Japanese shores and the necessity for national defense increased, the emphasis shifted to military technology.

Science after the Meiji Restoration—At the outset of the Meiji period (1868–1912) Japan embarked on a program of Westernization. The idea of modernizing science and technology had already been present in Western Learning, but its application had not been systematic. Science education was now institutionally organized. *Kagaku* replaced *kyūri* as the term for science. Unlike *kyūri*, which was a cognitive term, *kagaku* was an institutional one and reflected well the Meiji government's policy. The government stopped supporting traditional studies

such as astronomy, *wasan*, and Chinese medicine (*kampō;* see MEDICINE, TRADITIONAL). It invited Western lecturers, sent students abroad, and had them teach specialized courses when they returned to Japan. Until 1880 basic projects were initiated by the government, mainly to meet the requirements of a modern nation. While Western science during the 18th and 19th centuries had been accepted by scholars of Western Learning as a form of natural philosophy, for Meiji policy makers, who were much more interested in its specific applications, it was a means to an end.

In Japan, as in the United States, during the two world wars scientific research was carried out by universities, companies, and government. Of these only the laboratories at national universities enjoyed high prestige. The INSTITUTE OF PHYSICAL AND CHEMICAL RESEARCH, founded in 1917, is still considered an excellent research institution. During World War II, science in Japan suffered from being cut off from foreign sources of information. The Japanese military and government, which had previously relied on foreign technology, had to depend solely on Japanese scientists and technologists. Research funds were increased, and in a sense for the first time the Japanese scientific community was given an opportunity to express its identity as a group. However, as Japan's war position deteriorated, scientific research came to a virtual standstill.

Science in the Postwar Era—Under the Allied OCCUPATION, the SCIENCE COUNCIL OF JAPAN was established. Members elected from the scientific community at large sat on the council. However, the Japanese scientific world, which remained inactive long after the war, started to recover only in the late 1950s. In the 1960s, stimulated by technological innovation abroad and rapid economic growth at home, the Japanese scientific community expanded greatly.

One characteristic of scientific research in Japan today is that research funds come mostly from private investment. This is because companies were reorganized and expanded greatly after the war, and military research was forbidden under the 1947 constitution. After the 1973 oil crisis, research investment by private companies temporarily decreased, but investment by the public sector has steadily increased. The opinion that scientific research should not be left in the hands of the private sector and that a comprehensive science policy should be thought out is gaining support. See also BIOLOGY; CHEMISTRY; EARTH SCIENCES; MATHEMATICS, MODERN; PHYSICS.

nature, concept of 自然観

(*shizenkan*). The basic, etymological meaning of the Japanese word *shizen*, which is used to translate the English word "nature," is the power of spontaneous self-development and what results from that power. The Chinese characters for the Japanese term *shizen* literally mean "from itself thus it is," expressing a mode of being rather than the existence of a natural order.

The term *shizen* as a general expression for nature is not found in ancient Japanese. The ancient Japanese people recognized every phenomenon as a manifestation of the KAMI (god or gods). Such terms as *ametsuchi* (heaven and earth) and *ikitoshi ikerumono* (living things) were the closest to a comprehensive word for nature in their literature.

Nebuta Festival One of the spectacular floats from the Nebuta Festival in the city of Aomori. The floats sometimes require as many as 30 bearers.

In the mythology of the NIHON SHOKI (720) the first offspring of the primordial couple Izanagi and Izanami were neither *kami* nor human but islands and landmasses. Thus human beings were not considered to be superior or opposed to nature, as in Western thought, but related as if in one family.

Later, attempts were made to understand nature according to laws. YAMAGA SOKŌ (1622–85) wrote of the inevitability of nature, by which he meant that the universe, by necessity, is as it is. MIURA BAIEN (1723–89) and ANDŌ SHŌEKI (1703?–62) tried to describe the logic of the universe, but this was not yet a conception in abstract terms. Not until the Meiji period (1868–1912) did the Western concept of nature signifying the natural order come to be attached to the term *shizen.*

Naumann, Edmund   ナウマン, E.
(1854–1927). German geologist; known as the father of Japanese geology. One of the first teachers of geology at Tōkyō University (1875–85), Naumann conducted geological surveys in many parts of Japan. He is famous for his identification of the FOSSA MAGNA (Great Fissure Zone), which vertically divides the main island of Honshū southwest to northeast. At Naumann's suggestion, the Ministry of Agriculture and Commerce in 1878 established a geology department (now the GEOLOGICAL SURVEY OF JAPAN). Entering its employment, he created the basis for geological mapmaking in Japan. His major work was *Geologische Arbeiten in Japan* (1901).

Naval Academy   海軍兵学校
(Kaigun Heigakkō). School to train officers of the Imperial Japanese Navy. Founded in Tsukiji, Tōkyō, in 1869 and moved to Etajima in Hiroshima Prefecture in 1888. The academy was closed in 1945 when the navy was disbanded after World War II. Students studied for three or four years. Upon graduation they became midshipmen, candidates for the rank of ensign, attaining that rank after a period of active duty and an overseas cruise.

Naval General Staff Office   軍令部
(Gunreibu). Highest military organization of the Imperial Japanese Navy. Established in 1893. The chief of the Naval General Staff Office was directly subordinate to the emperor and was in charge of the planning of national defense and strategy. See also ARMED FORCES, IMPERIAL JAPANESE.

Navix Line, Ltd   ナビックス ライン[株]
(Nabikkusu Rain). One of Japan's leading tanker operators. Formed in 1989 through a merger of the Yamashita-Shinnihon Steamship Co, Ltd, and Japan Line, Ltd. Business operations include tramp-steamer, specialcarrier, and tanker services. The company operates 216 vessels totaling 16 million deadweight tons, making it the largest Japanese shipping firm in terms of tramp and tanker ownership. It has subsidiaries in New York, London, Hong Kong, and Panama.

Operating revenues for the fiscal year ending March 1991 totaled ¥191.8 billion (US $1.4 billion), and capitalization stood at ¥19.6 billion (US $142.9 million). Headquarters are in Tōkyō.

Navy Ministry   海軍省
(Kaigunshō). Cabinet ministry from 1872 to 1945. The Navy Ministry and the ARMY MINISTRY (Rikugunshō) were established in April 1872 under the DAJŌKAN system of government to replace the Ministry of Military Affairs (Hyōbushō). Initially the ministry was in charge of both administration and command of the navy, but in May 1893, when the Naval General Staff (Kaigun Gunreibu) was established as a separate organ of command, the ministry was left with only administrative functions. It was abolished in November 1945 and replaced by the temporary Demobilization Ministry (Fukuinshō). See also ARMED FORCES, IMPERIAL JAPANESE.

nawabari   縄張り
(literally, "rope stretching"). A figurative term meaning domain, territory, or sphere of influence. It is derived from the folk custom of land demarcation by stretching a straw rope along boundaries to delineate an area that was supposed to be a sacred area of the gods.

From the Kamakura period (1185–1333) onward, *nawabari* signified the location of a military camp or the area in which a castle was to be built. *Nawabari*—along with other terms such as *shima* (island) and *niwaba* (garden)—has been used since the Edo period (1600–1868) by YAKUZA (gangsters) and gamblers to refer to their territory. The concept of *nawabari* is also important in business and bureaucratic organizations.

Nawa Nagatoshi   名和長年
(?–1336). Warrior of Hōki Province (now part of Tottori Prefecture). One of the heroes of the KEMMU RESTORATION and a paradigm of loyalty to the emperor in pre–World War II Japanese historical writing. In 1333, when Emperor GO-DAIGO escaped from exile on Oki Island and landed in Hōki, Nagatoshi organized forces that helped to destroy the regime of the HŌJŌ FAMILY. Nagatoshi was appointed to important posts in the Records Office (Kirokusho) and the Office of Imperial Guards (Musha-dokoro) in Go-Daigo's restoration government. When ASHIKAGA TAKAUJI turned against Go-Daigo and attacked Kyōto in 1336, Nagatoshi was one of the loyalist generals who chased him to Kyūshū; when Takauji returned later in the year, Nagatoshi lost his life in defense of the emperor. The Nawa Shrine in Tottori Prefecture was built in his honor. He is also memorialized in KŌDA ROHAN's play *Nawa Nagatoshi* (1913).

Naya Sukezaemon → Ruson Sukezaemon

Nayoro   名寄[市]
City in northern Hokkaidō. One of the most important cities of the Nayoro Basin. Dairy products, potatoes, and medicinal herbs are produced here. Other industries include paper and lumber. Pop: 30,776.

nayosechō   名寄帳
Land register used in premodern Japan. In the Kamakura (1185–1333) and Muromachi (1333–1568) periods, *nayosechō* were tax collection ledgers prepared by estate (SHŌEN) proprietors. Based on land surveys conducted by these proprietors, the *nayosechō*

documented, under the names of local landholders (MYŌSHU), the types and sizes of fields and the amounts of tax to be levied. In the Edo period (1600–1868) the term came to refer to basic ledgers used to assign the annual tax to the farmers within a village.

Naze   名瀬[市]
City on the island of Amami Ōshima in the Amami Islands. A part of Kagoshima Prefecture, Kyūshū, it is the administrative, economic, and cultural center for the Amami Islands. Its subtropical climate is suited for growing bananas, papayas, and pineapples. Ōshima *tsumugi,* a silk weave, is a local product. Pop: 46,306.

nazo nazo → riddles

NCR Japan, Ltd   日本エヌ・シー・アール[株]
(Nippon Enu Shī Āru). Company engaged in the manufacture and sale of cash registers and other business machines. Incorporated in 1920. It also imports computers made by NCR Corporation of the United States, which holds 70 percent of its stock. The company began to diversify its business during the 1960s to include accounting machines, adding machines, and data processing equipment. Sales for the fiscal year ending November 1990 totaled ¥119.5 billion (US $925.8 million). In the same year the company was capitalized at ¥11.0 billion (US $85.2 million). Headquarters are in Tōkyō.

Nebuta Festival   ねぶた祭
(Nebuta Matsuri; also called Neputa Matsuri). One of many festivals held during the BON FESTIVAL season. The most famous Nebuta festivals are held in the cities of Aomori and Hirosaki in Aomori Prefecture. Between 1 August and 7 August large floats are carried or rolled on wheels through the city in the evening, with singing, dancing, and music. The floats have enormous paper images of popular or legendary characters lit from the inside, making them glow in the dark. After the procession the floats are thrown into a river or the sea. The festival originated in a purification rite in which paper images of human beings, straw boats, paper lanterns, or other objects were cast away on a river as a means of sending away illness or bad fortune (see TANABATA FESTIVAL). Such festivals, found all over Japan, are called *nemurinagashi* (literally, "floating away sleep").

NEC Corporation   日本電気[株]
(Nippon Denki). NEC Corporation is a world leader in communications, computers, semiconductors, and home electronics products. NEC was incorporated in 1899 as Nippon Electric Co, Ltd, to manufacture telephone sets and switching equipment. The company is now one of the world's foremost electronics manufacturers. In Japan, NEC operates 53 manufacturing plants and over 200 sales offices. International operations include 25 manufacturing affiliates with 25 plants in 14 countries; 37 marketing, service, and research firms in 20 countries; and 25 liaison offices in 23 countries. The NEC group of companies has 158,000 employees worldwide.

NEC invests over 10 percent of its consolidated sales revenue in research and development and engineering projects. This investment has created a huge development base of advanced technologies, which the company applies in manufacturing more than 15,000 products. Total sales for the fiscal year ending March 1991 were ¥3.0 trillion (US $21.9 billion). The company was capitalized at ¥188.1 billion (US $1.4 billion) in the same year. Headquarters are in Tōkyō.

NEC Home Electronics, Ltd
日本電気ホームエレクトロニクス[株]

(Nippon Denki Hōmu Erekutoronikusu). Manufacturer of home electrical appliances; subsidiary of NEC CORPORATION. Incorporated in 1953. It specializes in the creation of new media products, adapting NEC's computer and telecommunications techniques for home electrical appliances. The firm also commands more than a 50 percent share of the personal computer market. Following its global managerial strategy, it has manufacturing plants in many countries. Sales for the fiscal year ending March 1990 totaled ¥386.0 billion (US $2.5 billion), and capitalization stood at ¥20.5 billion (US $133.9 million). Headquarters are in Tōkyō.

negi →Welsh onion

negoro-nuri
根来塗

(Negoro lacquer). A type of LACQUER WARE characterized by a red lacquer surface rubbed to reveal an underlying layer of black. The term *negoro-nuri* is derived from lacquer ware made and utilized from the end of the 13th century onward by the priests of Negoroji, a temple in Kii Province (now Wakayama Prefecture). These were originally monochrome lacquer wares, but with repeated handling the surface layer of red was worn away in uneven patches, producing a striking contrast of red and black lacquer. The term *negoro-nuri* has been extended to include lacquer ware in which this surface effect is deliberately rather than accidentally achieved. Wares of a similar type were made before the founding of the temple in 1140 and after its destruction in 1585. There are few surviving lacquer-ware pieces from the Negoroji itself.

nehan
涅槃

A transliteration of the Sanskrit term *nirvāṇa*, which literally means the extinction of a flame. It refers to the state of enlightenment that is achieved, either in life or in death, when one attains wisdom and eliminates the flames of craving. It is paradoxically described as being beyond life and death, being and nonbeing. In Theravāda Buddhism, *nirvāṇa* is rather clearly opposed to *saṃsāra* (the endless round of suffering in transmigration; see RINNE), understood as a release from *saṃsāra* and rebirth and limited primarily to members of the monastic community. Mahāyāna Buddhism, to which Japanese Buddhism belongs, posited the paradoxical notion of the final identity of *nirvāṇa* and *saṃsāra* through the development of notions such as EMPTINESS (Skt: *śūnyatā*; J: *kū*), which embrace the two. This was accompanied by a belief in the Buddha nature within all beings, an extension of the possibility of attaining enlightenment to all, and an emphasis on the BODHISATTVA (*bosatsu*) who has achieved enlightenment but chooses to stay in *saṃsāra* to help others. The contribution of Japanese Buddhism to these developments is usually seen to lie in pushing the equation between *saṃsāra* and *nirvāṇa* even further. At the popular, devotional level, *nirvāṇa* is often understood as a rebirth in a Buddha's Pure Land (see PURE LAND BUDDHISM), which is similar in some re-

spects to the notion of heaven in Western religious traditions.

neighborhood associations
近隣集団

(*kinrin shūdan*). Informal, quasi-governmental, or mandatory neighborhood associations have played an important role in Japanese society at various times in its history. GONINGUMI (literally, "five-man groups") were established throughout the country during the Edo period (1600–1868). First utilized as a mechanism for social control, they later developed into vehicles for local self-help and self-governance. The *goningumi* lost their legal status after the Meiji Restoration (1868), but informal ties remained. New neighborhood associations called CHŌNAIKAI emerged after 1920. These were made mandatory by the government in 1940. At the same time, smaller groups called TONARIGUMI (neighbor groups) were also established. Both were used for social control, mobilization, and such functions as rationing. Both *tonarigumi* and *chōnaikai* were abolished by Occupation authorities after World War II, but unofficial associations have been revived in many areas. See also KUMI.

nekki
根っ木

Children's game for two or more players. A tree branch or bamboo root is cut to a length of about 30 centimeters (1 ft). One end is sharpened and driven into the ground. Players attempt to knock down the stick by tossing their own sticks against it. Iron spikes are also used. This game is said to have originated from the practice of driving into the earth the *nekki*, the piece of wood used to support the traditional New Year's pine and bamboo decoration (*kadomatsu*).

nemawashi
根回し

(prior consultation). A technique used in Japan to avoid conflicts and obtain a consensus in decision making. The literal meaning of *nemawashi* is to dig around the roots of a tree prior to transplanting, thus making the uprooting and movement much easier. But the term is used much more widely in a

figurative sense to describe maneuvering behind the scenes to reach a consensus and obtain certain objectives, especially in politics and business. When various interests are potentially in conflict, reaching a consensus and attaining political objectives are very difficult through direct, public confrontation. Instead, in Japanese politics and business the practice is to discuss decisions in advance with various interested parties and to incorporate their views, wherever possible, into any final proposals. Much of the groundwork for decisions is therefore laid well in advance of meetings where final decisions are made, and, if the *nemawashi* is successful, conflicts can be avoided in public discussion. As with decision making in general in Japan, the process involved in *nemawashi* is time-consuming, but final decisions and their implementation generally go much more smoothly than when decisions are made through confrontation or are imposed from above. See also CONFLICT RESOLUTION.

nembutsu
念仏

The invocation NAMU AMIDA BUTSU (I take my refuge in the Buddha AMIDA [Skt: Amitābha]), uttered in the hope of rebirth into Amida's Pure Land. This modern conception of *nembutsu*, popularized by HŌNEN in the 12th century, describes but one form of what was once a varied practice. In addition to this invocational *nembutsu* (*shōmyō nembutsu*), there were also contemplative *nembutsu* (*kannen nembutsu*) and meditative *nembutsu* (*okunen nembutsu* or *rikan*). By the 9th century, Pure Land devotion and the cultivation of all varieties of *nembutsu* flourished in China and were imported into Japan by the founders of the TENDAI SECT. In 985 the most comprehensive treatment of *nembutsu* in Buddhist literature, the ŌJŌYŌSHŪ (Essentials of Pure Land Rebirth), was composed by the Tendai monk GENSHIN. In 1175 Hōnen asserted the independence of the Pure Land movement and taught that

nembutsu odori *Dai nembutsu kembai*, a local variety of *nembutsu odori* folk dancing, is performed in the city of Morioka, Iwate Prefecture. The men dressed in black (center) sing and accompany the dancers on flutes.

the simple utterance of the Buddha's name was the best path to salvation. The JŌDO SECT and the JŌDO SHIN SECT founded by SHINRAN took *nembutsu* as their primary religious exercise.

nembutsu odori   念仏踊

Folk dance expressing the joyfulness of those whose faith assures them salvation, through the chanting or singing of the Buddha AMIDA's name (see NEMBUTSU) or the Buddhist hymns (WASAN). Reputedly started by the monk KŪYA (903–972), the *nembutsu odori* spread widely during the Kamakura period (1185–1333) through the efforts of IPPEN (1239–89), the founder of the JI SECT OF PURE LAND BUDDHISM. This dancing has also been performed to pacify the spirits of the dead at the BON FESTIVAL or to ward off evil. Its impact on Japanese traditional dance and FOLK PERFORMING ARTS in general is significant.

Nemuro   根室〔市〕

City in eastern Hokkaidō. It was developed in the early Meiji period (1868–1912) by colonist militia (TONDENHEI). A base for fishing in the northern seas, it has large catches of salmon, trout, and crab. Dairy farming is a more recent development. Pop: 36,912.

Nemuro Peninsula   根室半島

(Nemuro Hantō). Located in eastern Hokkaidō. Extending northeast into the Pacific Ocean, it has a hilly terrain with extensive grazing grounds. The surrounding waters are rich with salmon. NOSAPPUMISAKI, a cape at the eastern tip of the peninsula, offers excellent views of the HABOMAI ISLANDS.

Nemuro Strait   根室海峡

(Nemuro Kaikyō). Strait between eastern Hokkaidō and the island of Kunashiri. Its narrowest section, the Notsuke Channel (narrowest point 16 km or 10 mi), is shallow and unfit for navigation by large ships. Parts of the strait freeze over during the winter. Length: approximately 120 km (75 mi).

nenchū gyōji   年中行事

(annual events). As opposed to *matsuri* (festivals), which are essentially Japanese festivals of Shintō origin, *nenchū gyōji* are annual and seasonal observances, many of Chinese or Buddhist origin. *Nenchū gyōji* are arranged seasonally to form an annual calendar of events and tend to be observed by families or communities throughout Japan at about the same time. The term *nenchū gyōji* or *nenjū gyōji* was first used in the Heian period (794–1185) to refer to the imperial court calendar, a schedule of recurring annual activities greatly influenced by Chinese court schedules and astrology. Until 1873 this schedule of events was ordered on

the basis of the Chinese calendar, some events being reckoned by the ancient solar calendar, others by the lunar year (see CALENDAR, DATES, AND TIME). Today the term refers both to this ancient schedule of events as a historical phenomenon and to the body of annual events (including national holidays and international events) that are observed by contemporary Japanese society in general. See also FESTIVALS; HOLIDAYS, NATIONAL.

Influences on the formation of the *nenchū gyōji* include on the one hand native AGRICULTURAL RITES and rites of communion with gods and ancestors and on the other hand traditions absorbed from the Asian continent. Japan's political and cultural history was accompanied by a continual process of revision of the *nenchū gyōji* and a proliferation of specialized schedules of annual events meeting the needs of such occupations as agriculture, commerce, fishing, and government.

Sources——The first use of the term *nenchū gyōji* was in 885 in connection with the dedication at court of a wall screen on which over 200 court events were inscribed—48 for the first month alone. However, the oldest extant list of such events is contained in the 10th-century collection of administrative and ceremonial codes known as the ENGI SHIKI. Various martial observances introduced into the *nenchū gyōji* during the Kamakura (1185–1333) and Muromachi (1333–1568) periods are described in the records of the OGASAWARA SCHOOL OF ETIQUETTE. For the Edo period (1600–1868) important sources of information are the SAIJIKI, compendiums of words indicating the season for use in composing *haiku*, and (particularly for events in the provinces) YASHIRO HIROKATA'S *Shokoku fūzoku toijō kotae*, a collection of answers to questionnaires sent out in 1813 concerning provincial customs.

Pre-Heian Antecedents of the Nenchū Gyōji——Although there is little documentary evidence of Japanese religious practices before the Nara period (710–794), it can be speculated that with the prehistoric development of an agricultural society based on the cultivation of rice there arose a distinct pattern of feasts and observances related to seasonal and lunar cycles (see also MOON VIEWING). The annual cycle, perceived in terms of the planting and harvesting of rice (the word for "year," *toshi*, originally meant "rice"), was marked by celebrations in the spring before transplanting seedlings to paddies and celebrations of thanksgiving in autumn when the rice was harvested.

The chief annual observances of the protohistoric period were joined with practices introduced from the continent and regularized to agree with the Chinese calendar, which was adopted in 604. Under the influence of Taoism and *yin-yang* astrology (see OMMYŌDŌ), various superstitions became connected with certain conjunctions of the traditional solar and lunar calendric systems and many of them (for example, the one called KŌSHIN) were adopted as observances by the Japanese. The system became so closely connected with farm life that, in spite of the adoption of the Gregorian calendar in 1873, a survey conducted by the government following World War II showed that 60 percent of farm villages still conducted daily affairs and celebrated annual events in accordance with the old calendar.

Nenchū Gyōji of the Heian Period——The performance of certain court events shortly before and after the Taika Reform of

645 (which marked a concerted effort to order the operation of government after the Chinese model) is recorded in the chronicles NIHON SHOKI (720) and *Shoku nihongi* (797). Most of these ceremonies were not yet conducted on a regular basis; however, among them were some that are still performed though their rituals have undergone change. The initial ceremony of the New Year, celebrated first in 642 and regularly from the reign of Emperor Saga (r 809–823) until today, was the Shihōhai (Obeisance in Four Directions). Following the casting out of evil influences (Ōharae) and before the sun rose on the first day of the New Year, the emperor offered up prayers to his birth star among the seven stars of the Big Dipper (Shichiyōsei) and in the direction of the graves of his mother and father, made obeisances in the four cardinal directions, and uttered a propitiatory incantation for peace in the land.

Many Heian-period annual events of Chinese origin developed into folk traditions and are still observed today. Chief among these are the five SEKKU: Jinjitsu (Day of Mankind) no Sekku on 7 January (modern calendar), the chief observance of which is the preparation of a seven-herb gruel (*nanakusagayu*); Jōshi no Sekku (see DOLL FESTIVAL) on 3 March; Tango no Sekku (see CHILDREN'S DAY) on 5 May; Tanabata (TANABATA FESTIVAL) on 7 July; and Chōyō no Sekku (CHRYSANTHEMUM FESTIVAL) on 9 September. Some regions of Japan also celebrate the Buddha's birthday on 8 April as HANA MATSURI.

Post–Heian Period Observances——After the assumption of governmental powers by the Kamakura shogunate in 1192, the court suffered a gradual diminution of its economic resources, reaching a low point during and after the ŌNIN WAR of 1467–77, which ravaged Kyōto. The court therefore lost the means to celebrate *nenchū gyōji* in the former fashion. However, many of its ceremonies had passed into popular usage and were joined by new events manifesting values of the warrior class as well as folk practices, which continued to filter upward. Thus a heterogeneous body of *nenchū gyōji*, modified and expanded in the practice of the Edo-period townsmen (CHŌNIN), has been transmitted to the present day. An example is the observance known as SHICHIGOSAN (Seven-Five-Three), which derives from court observances in which rites of passage were performed for boys of three and five years and girls of three and seven years. Another court observance still practiced today is HATSUUMA, a celebration related to belief in the god of rice Uka no Mitama (see INARI).

In addition to such general observances as New Year's, SETSUBUN, the BON FESTIVAL, and HIGAN, numerous regional annual observances, festivities of shrines and temples, and agricultural rituals are still performed today. A few traditional events have now become national holidays: the celebrations of the equinoxes and Children's Day are of ancient provenance; Labor Thanksgiving Day is celebrated on 23 November, the day on which, from the Meiji period until the end of World War II, the Niinamesai (tasting of first fruits) was held. The most recent introductions into this patchwork of observances are certain Western or international events: labor groups celebrate May Day; many families, irrespective of actual religious beliefs, have a party and give presents to their children at Christmas; and on Valentine's Day, it is customary for women to give gifts of chocolate to the men they favor.   ▶▶ *1074–1075*

nengajō→New Year's cards

nengō 年号

(era names). Also called *gengō*. Official names or slogans, usually of good omen, applied to reigns or parts of reigns in China and the East Asian countries that adopted its writing and calendrical systems. The use of era names in Japan began with the Taika period (645–650) and has continued down to the present Heisei period (1989–). Japan is now the sole country employing this system of reckoning time.

Before the Meiji period (1868–1912), *nengō* might be changed upon the accession of a new emperor, the occurrence of auspicious or malign events, or at certain points in the traditional 60-year calendrical cycle. The right to alter the era name resided with the emperor, but in practice such changes were made after deliberation by groups of court officials. In the long period of warrior government from the late 12th to the mid-19th century, successive shogunates also exerted considerable influence in the selection of *nengō*, which served as a symbolic expression of the political unity of the Japanese islands even in periods of conflict.

With the Meiji Restoration of 1868, the present system of using one era name for each imperial reign (*issei ichigen*) was adopted; since that times era names have changed only on the death of an emperor and the accession of his heir to the throne. As before, passages in the Chinese classics have been selected for use as era names: Meiji (1868–1912; "Enlightened Rule"), Taishō (1912–26; "Great Righteousness"), Shōwa (1926–89; "Enlightened Peace"), and Heisei (1989– ; "Attaining Peace"). Emperors are referred to posthumously by the era name of their reign (e.g., Emperor Hirohito now being known as Emperor Shōwa).

The legal basis for the era name system was established by the Imperial Household Law of 1889 and the Tōkyokurei of 1909, which called for a new era name to be established on the day of an emperor's death. However, the post–World War II revisions of the Imperial Household Law and the Japanese constitution made no provisions for changes in era name, and the custom lost its formal legal standing. This situation continued until 1979, when a new Era Name Law (Gengōhō) passed the Diet in the face of fairly strong opposition. The continued use of era names and the *issei ichigen* system remains a controversial issue in Japan, with dissenters arguing for abandonment of the practice on the grounds that it is incompatible with modern international usage and the symbolic role of the emperor in contemporary Japan. However, upon the death of the emperor Shōwa in January 1989 the name Heisei was adopted for the era then beginning, in accordance with the provisions set down in the Era Name Law of 1979.

nengu 年貢

(literally, "annual tribute"). The basic land tax collected from the peasantry by the proprietors of estates from the late Heian period (794–1185), and later by feudal lords (*daimyō*) during the period of warrior rule (1185–1868). With the gradual breakdown of the RITSURYŌ SYSTEM of administration and the rise of large private estates (SHŌEN) in the 10th century, the statutory taxes on grain, textiles, and labor (SO, YŌ, AND CHŌ) were diverted from the central government. The

grain tax (*so*) came to be called *nengu*. It was appropriated in whole or in part first by estate proprietors (RYŌSHU), then by land stewards (JITŌ) or military governors (SHUGO), and later by daimyō.

Nengu was in principle collected from all MYŌSHU, the peasant-cultivators with certain rights to land. *Nengu* was usually paid in the form of rice (from wet fields) or barley (from dry), but in later centuries it was sometimes paid in money.

nenki 年季

In legal history a term generally meaning period or era, a person's age, or a period of time from a certain point in the past until the present. From the last of these senses it took on—from the late Heian (794–1185) through the Muromachi (1333–1568) periods—the more specific meaning of a period of limitation of rights regarding real estate. Also known as *nenjo*, this period of limitations was fixed at 20 years by the GOSEIBAI SHIKIMOKU, the fundamental code of the Kamakura shogunate (1192–1333).

Nenki also refers to a land trade system in use from the Kamakura (1185–1333) through the Edo (1600–1868) periods, also called *nenki uri* and *nenki kokyaku*. Under this system a piece of land was purchased for a fixed number of years, at the end of which it was automatically returned to the seller. A similar system was *honsen-gaeshi* (or *hommono-gaeshi*), in which the land sold did not return to the seller unless he bought it back. The two systems were often used as methods of establishing collateral for credit.

nenkō joretsu→seniority system

Neo-Confucianism→Confucianism; Shushigaku

neolithic period 新石器時代

(*shinsekki jidai*). The Jōmon period (ca 10,000 BC–ca 300 BC) is considered to be Japan's neolithic period because it possessed at least two artifacts common to other neolithic cultures: pottery (see JŌMON POTTERY) and polished STONE TOOLS. However, the Jōmon period was characterized by a hunting and gathering way of life, rather than the agricultural village life typical of other neolithic cultures. See also JŌMON CULTURE.

Nepal and Japan ネパールと日本

(Nepāru to Nihon). Nepal and Japan have traditionally maintained friendly ties despite the absence of formal treaty relations. There have been frequent contacts by officials of the two governments, as well as by members of the Nepalese royal family and the Japanese imperial family. King Berendora (r 1972–), for instance, studied at Tōkyō University. Currently the main areas of contact between the two countries are in trade, economic cooperation, and tourism. The volume of trade between the two countries averaged US $66 million between 1988 and 1990. Although Japan is one of Nepal's largest overall trading partners, Nepal's annual exports to Japan in this period averaged less than US $2 million. Japan's official development assistance (ODA) to Nepal has gone largely toward improving the transportation and communications infrastructure and toward meeting basic human needs such as medical care. Japanese assistance to Nepal exceeded US $77 million in 1989, making it the country's largest foreign aid donor. Tourism is a rapidly expanding sector of the Nepalese economy. In 1990 more than

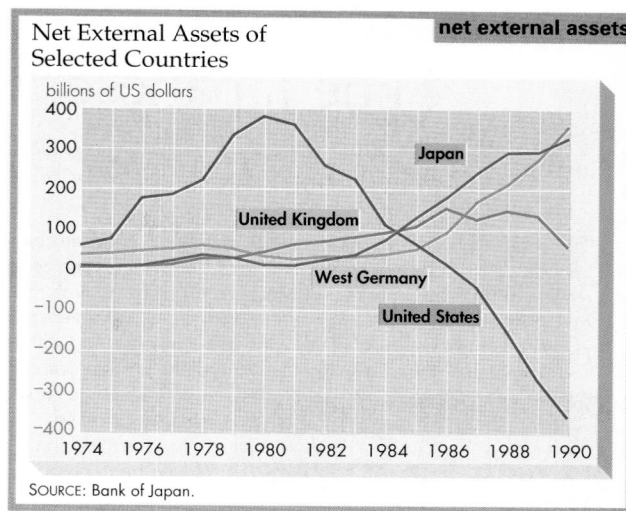

net external assets

Net External Assets of Selected Countries

SOURCE: Bank of Japan.

19,000 Japanese tourists visited Nepal, particularly the Kathmandu area.

Nerima Ward 練馬区

(Nerima Ku). One of the 23 wards of Tōkyō. Residential district whose recreational facilities include Shakujii Park and Toshimaen Amusement Park. Pop: 618,663.

Nestlé KK ネッスル[株]

(Nessuru). Company engaged in production and wholesale of foods and beverages. Founded in 1913 as a subsidiary of Nestlé SA (Switzerland). A comprehensive food manufacturer, its products include milk products, chocolates, and coffee. Sales for the fiscal year ending December 1990 totaled ¥191.1 billion (US $1.4 billion), and the company was capitalized at ¥35.0 billion (US $261.1 million). Headquarters are in Kōbe.

net external assets 対外純資産

(*taigai junshisan*). Japan lost most of its external assets (such as direct foreign investments, international loans, and portfolio investments) following its defeat in World War II. As the result of borrowing from the International Bank for Reconstruction and Development (IBRD; see WORLD BANK), Japan was a net debtor nation until 1967. Since 1968 Japan has been a net creditor and consistently has maintained a positive external account, although its surplus declined during the two oil crises. Because Japan's current account surplus has widened since the mid-1980s, its net external assets have also accumulated rapidly. At the end of 1990 Japan's external assets of US $1,857.9 billion, compared to external liabilities of US $1,529.8 billion, gave it net external assets of US $328.1 billion, the second largest in the world. In this same period United States net external assets fell to a negative US $360.6 billion. The ratio of Japan's net external assets to its gross national product stood at 11 percent at the end of 1990.

There are three chief features of the recent increase in Japan's net external assets. First is the desire by Japanese investors to raise short-term capital and to engage in long-term investments overseas. Second, a large part of the increase in Japan's net external assets is accounted for by investments in foreign securities and, more recently, direct foreign investments. The third factor is the high ratio of short-term capital flow, especially liquid capital, relative to both external assets and liabilities. The internationalization of Japanese banking operations is a major factor in this development.

The Japanese Year: Cycles of Renewal

From the tolling of the temple bells on New Year's Eve to the opening of the All-Japan High School Baseball Championship in summer, the country's annual events reflect the national spirit.

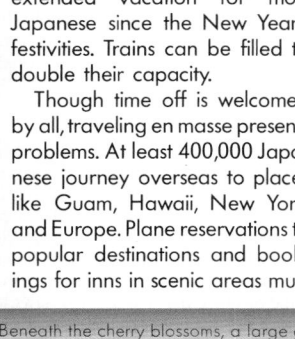

Traditionally, the Japanese divided their year in accordance with nature, observing seasonal celebrations and the rice-growing cycle. The annual rhythm of planting and reaping was punctuated by festivals to ensure fertility and to celebrate harvests. But over the centuries, as farmers moved from the paddies to the cities, their rituals were transformed along with their lifestyles. Today, echoes of the past meld with events of the present, and ancient ceremonies are commemorated while new ones are created.

To the Japanese, who have always been absorbed with the distinctive beauty and moods of the months, each season evokes an awareness of the pathos of human life. The famous 10th-century writer Sei Shōnagon captures the essence in her classic work, *Makura no sōshi* (The Pillow Book): "In spring it is the dawn . . . in summer the nights . . . in autumn the evening . . . in winter, the early morning."

Vestiges of these seasonal sensibilities still abound. Every *haiku*, for example, has its seasonal word, and hanging scrolls in tearooms depict cherry blossoms in the spring and chrysanthemums in the fall. Desk calendars often list, along with national holidays, appropriate seasonal greetings for letters and the prime times for flowers and foods. But today work, school, and leisure time shape the course of Japanese life.

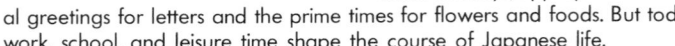

Children proudly display their *kakizome*, the first calligraphy of the new year.

The New Year Begins

At midnight on New Year's Eve, temple bells across Japan toll *joya no kane*, 108 strokes to cleanse away the 108 delusions of mankind, a purifying Buddhist ritual. Renewal is a basic element of Shintō, too, thus the importance of the "firsts" of the year: *hatsumōde*, the first visit, often in *kimono*, to a shrine or a temple; *kakizome*, the first calligraphy of the year; and *shigoto hajime*, the return to work after the holidays.

Many Japanese like to do their renewing in the mountains or on the beach. The recent trend has been for tens of thousands of tourists to take off for Hawaii, Australia, Thailand, and other vacation spots, bidding farewell to the old year with champagne or *mai tais* instead of New Year's *sake*.

Some women wear their kimono on the first day back to the office, laughing that they get more attention that day than any other.

Coming-of-Age Day on 15 January honors those who have reached voting age—20 years. Young men dress up in suits, and women don kimono for ceremonies held by the local ward office.

On 3 February, the last day of winter on the old Japanese calendar, roasted soybeans are scattered inside and outside people's homes while family members chant, "Out with the demons, in with good luck!" Afterward, everyone eats one soybean for each year of his or her age. This is known as Setsubun, a remnant of an exorcism rite which was meant to start the year off on a good note and prepare the rice fields for planting.

For high school seniors, the middle of February is a time of great importance because that is when they must take the notoriously competitive university entrance exams. The tests are said to determine the rest of a teenager's life: graduating from one of the top universities leads to job offers from the best companies, lifetime employment, and social status. Studying for the exams is the focus of most students' existence for years before the fateful testing day. More than a third of the one-million-plus students attempting to get into colleges and universities fail and become *rōnin*, "masterless

samurai," who must prepare to take the test again the following year.

Valentine's Day is a relatively new holiday, introduced to Japan in the late 1960s by astute retailers. But there's a twist to this traditional day of romance. Instead of mutual declarations of love, or flowers and poems for ladies, women give chocolate to men—more than 25,000 metric tons of it! Secretaries bestow *giri choko*, chocolate given out of obligation, not adoration, on an average of 10 colleagues. Men return the favor a month later on White Day, 14 March, another boon for confectioners.

Hina Matsuri, or the Doll Festival, is celebrated on 3 March. *Hina* dolls, which represent the emperor, empress, court attendants, and musicians in ancient court attire, are displayed in the home. It is customary for the parents or grandparents of a little girl to give her a set of *hina* dolls when she is born or on her first birthday. The dolls are given along with a wish for future domestic happiness. In Japan, Hina Matsuri heralds the beginning of spring.

March is an extremely busy time in both the public and private sectors because the Japanese fiscal year closes at the end of the month. Sessions of the Diet, Japan's parliamentary body, run late into the night as politicians rush to pass bills and settle on a new budget for the year. Companies reshuffle and reassign personnel and announce profits or declare losses.

The academic year also runs from April to March, so March is the time for graduation ceremonies.

Spring

The undisputed harbinger of spring in Japan is the cherry blossom. Symbol of evanescence and fragile beauty, the cherry blossom has been a classic image in haiku and literature for more than a millennium. But the blossom's beauty is a fleeting pleasure, lasting only a few days. After the first bud opens on the southern island of Kyūshū, the wave of blossoms moves north like a warm front, at the rate of about 30 kilometers (19 mi) a day. Tōkyō trees usually bloom by the end of March, but Hokkaidō isn't blessed until early May.

When the trees transform into ethereal puffs of pink flowers, people flock to local parks for *hanami*. Literally translated as "flower viewing," it more accurately means drinking lots of *sake* and beer on plastic tarps underneath the cherry trees. Oftentimes families or groups of company employees set up elaborate picnics amidst the blossoms.

Appropriately, spring, the season of beginnings, is the time for starting school and entering companies. *Shinnyū shain*, or new company employees, begin training programs. April is also the time for the *shuntō*, or annual spring labor offensive, when unions demand higher wages.

Golden Week is a series of holidays, beginning on 29 April with Greenery Day, which commemorates the birthday of the late emperor Shōwa (Hirohito). On May Day, organized labor shows solidarity with workers around the world. Constitution Memorial Day is marked on 3 May, and on 5 May, Children's Day, families fly carp banners for their sons' good health. Recently, the government added an extra holiday to Golden Week on 4 May.

These stepping-stone holidays, bracketed by weekends, make up the first extended vacation for most Japanese since the New Year's festivities. Trains can be filled to double their capacity.

Though time off is welcomed by all, traveling en masse presents problems. At least 400,000 Japanese journey overseas to places like Guam, Hawaii, New York, and Europe. Plane reservations to popular destinations and bookings for inns in scenic areas must

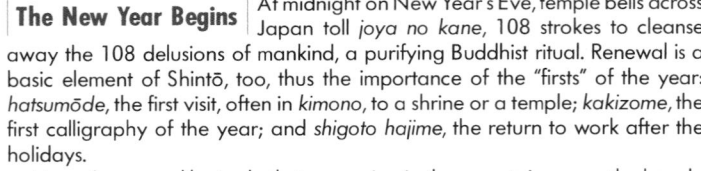

Beneath the cherry blossoms, a large group gathers to eat, drink, and make merry.

Summer crowds enjoy the pools and water slides at an amusement park near Tōkyō.

be made up to a year in advance. Returning from vacation can also prove troublesome. Television news helicopters film 80-kilometer (50-mi) traffic jams on the worst-hit highways on the Sunday before work resumes.

June marks the beginning of the rainy season and is the time when rice is planted. On the few fair-weather days, people air *futon* (bedding) and hang wash out.

Summer | Following on the heels of the June bonus for salaried workers is *chūgen*, one of two times in the year when gifts are given to pay back favors or create goodwill. During *chūgen*, special gift packs make up 20 percent of department-store sales. Some of the most popular gifts include towels, ham, canned fruit, beer, *sake*, whiskey, and even taxi coupons.

On 7 July, during the Tanabata Festival—when legendary lovers Vega and Altair are said to be reunited on a bridge of magpies across the Milky Way—children write wishes on streamers and hang them on bamboo branches.

Beginning around 20 July, students get a summer vacation of about five or six weeks, which many spend in cram schools or summer camps.

The Day of the Ox in the old lunar calendar, which falls on or around 23 July depending on the year, is considered the peak of summer. People traditionally eat eel on that day for extra stamina. Other typical warm weather foods include cold barley tea, cold noodles, watermelon, and boiled green soybeans in their pods. During the summer, the Japanese drink enough beer to fill the Tōkyō Dome stadium nearly two times.

Fireworks are a hallmark of the season—the display over the river Sumida-gawa is reputedly Japan's biggest and most beautiful. More than a million people gather on riverbanks and rooftops in Tōkyō's Asakusa district on the last Saturday in July for the three-hour spectacular.

Summer is also time for *matsuri* (festivals). Many were originally held to appease the gods and stave off crop-threatening pests and drought. The most enduring event is the Bon Festival, or the Festival of the Dead, which is observed in either mid-July or mid-August, depending on the region of Japan. Families visit cemeteries to greet returning ancestral spirits and lead them back home. The streets are crowded with townspeople dressed in bright cotton summer kimono, and parks and empty schoolyards are used to stage traditional Bon dances. On the last night, in some areas lanterns are set adrift on the water to guide the spirits back across the sea.

Ghosts are not the only ones returning home; in August most living Japanese try to make it back to their hometowns too. During the August Bon season, Japan Railways adds several thousand trains to its schedule to cope with the millions of passengers using the rails. Airlines transport more than 7 million people during this period, many of whom are traveling not to their hometowns, but overseas. On the highways, traffic jams are a problem, but as one driver commented, "At least you can listen to the high school baseball tournament while you're waiting."

Baseball is a national obsession in Japan, but the All-Japan High School Baseball Championship, held every August, pushes it to feverish heights. Electric companies report a sharp increase in power usage during the two weeks of the tournament as enthusiasts turn on air conditioners and television sets and settle in to watch 49 teams battle for the championship in Kōshien Stadium near Ōsaka. The combination of nostalgia and team loyalty, along with the excitement of watching young men give it their all, makes the tournament appeal to more than the usual audience of baseball fans. The

end of the tournament signals that summer will soon be over.

Autumn | With September comes the beginning of the rice harvest—the climax of the traditional Japanese agricultural cycle. While farmers reap the national staple, the rest of the country goes about business as usual. The month is highlighted by two national holidays. Respect-for-the-Aged Day is 15 September, and 23 September commemorates the Autumnal Equinox.

During late summer and early autumn there can be typhoons, which usually hit the southeastern seacoast. The cyclonic winds can cause great destruction, but as Sei Shōnagon wrote, the day after a typhoon is the most beautiful.

October begins to look and feel like autumn, as a slight chill enters the air and leaves turn brilliant shades of orange and red. Families make pilgrimages to places like Kamakura and Kyōto to see temples backdropped by crimson maple trees. Fall foods like mackerel, apples, or persimmons top off the trip.

Boys and girls aged 7, 5, and 3 celebrate the Shichi-gosan Festival with the comic-book hero Ultraman.

Sports Day, a holiday instituted in 1964 when Japan hosted the Tōkyō Olympic Games, is held on 10 October. It is observed with athletic competitions in schools and with vigorous rounds of golf by businessmen.

Culture Day is 3 November. The Order of Culture, the most prestigious award given to outstanding people in the arts and sciences, is presented on this day. Many colleges and universities also stage exhibitions of pop culture and have festivals.

On 15 November, known as Shichigosan, or the Seven-Five-Three Festival, young boys and girls of those ages get a dose of traditional culture. Girls are dressed in tiny kimono, and boys are dressed in miniature men's kimono with *haori* and *hakama*. The children are then taken to a shrine, where a priest prays for their health and success. Afterward, they receive *chitose-ame*, a stick-type candy, and are permitted to ring the big shrine bell.

Labor Thanksgiving Day is observed on 23 November. This holiday was established to thank the workers behind Japan's economic success.

December is bonus season, a time for employers to show their appreciation to workers in a tangible fashion. Employees' year-end envelopes are usually fattened by two to six months' extra salary. Some of that bonus money is spent on *seibo*, year-end gifts to repay social debts and maintain good relationships.

Christmas is a secular commercial holiday, without a hint of its religious origins. Department stores hang extravagant three-story-high wreaths and pipe "Jingle Bells" in Japanese continuously for weeks. Skinny Santas, their false beards hanging loose, sell Christmas cakes on the street. Young people look forward to Christmas Eve, a night considered the most romantic of the year. On Christmas, a regular work day, more business cards are exchanged than presents.

The end of December is spent preparing for the biggest holiday of the year—the New Year's celebration. Housewives spend hours preparing *osechi ryōri*, special holiday foods. More and more, however, these foods are being bought ready-made. People often set aside 30 December for cleaning the house in anticipation of New Year's visitors. A pair of *kadomatsu*, bamboo and pine decorations, is placed in front of the entrance. On New Year's Eve, families flock to local shrines and temples. At the stroke of midnight, temple bells begin their 108 tolls to dispel the evils of mankind. Afterward, people throw coins over the heads of the crowd into the offering box and pray for a fruitful new year. Then the cycle begins anew.

Maggie Farley

A Christmas advertisement on a department store in Tōkyō's Shibuya district.

Netherlands and Japan

オランダと日本

(Oranda *to* Nihon). The history of relations between Japan and the Netherlands began in 1600, when the Dutch ship LIEFDE drifted ashore in Bungo Province (now Ōita Prefecture). Trade formally began with the establishment of a trading house (see DUTCH FACTORY) in Hirado (near Nagasaki) in 1609. The trading post was moved to DEJIMA, an artificial island in Nagasaki Harbor, in 1641 under the terms of the Tokugawa shogunate's (1603–1867) NATIONAL SECLUSION policy. The Dutch conducted trade from Dejima until 1860. During that time more than 600 Dutch ships came to Japan, bringing such items as raw silk, textiles, leather, and dyes. Japanese exports to the Netherlands consisted of bullion, coins, camphor, and other products (see DUTCH TRADE).

Because of the policy of National Seclusion during the Edo period (1600–1868), Western civilization entered Japan primarily through the medium of the Dutch language, and the study of Western culture became known as Rangaku or "Dutch studies" (see WESTERN LEARNING). The well-known pioneer Japanologist Philipp Franz von SIEBOLD worked as a physician at the Dutch Factory in the 1820s and established a boarding school near Nagasaki where he taught Western medicine and treated Japanese patients.

Soon after Commodore Matthew PERRY's fleet pressured the Tokugawa shogunate into opening Japan to intercourse with the United States in 1854, the Dutch followed in the footsteps of the other Western powers by signing a treaty of amity with the Japanese in 1856 and a treaty of amity and commerce in 1858. The Tokugawa shogunate sent NISHI AMANE, TSUDA MAMICHI, ENOMOTO TAKEAKI, and others to the Netherlands in 1862 to study. They were to contribute significantly to the politics, education, and military affairs of Japan in the years to follow.

During the Meiji period (1868–1912), the Dutch contributed greatly to the modernization of Japan in medicine and other fields. Trade relations between the two nations, however, were gradually overwhelmed by commerce from other nations, and by the 1880s the Netherlands Trading Company (founded in 1824) in Kōbe had virtually suspended its activities.

From the end of the Meiji period relations between Japan and the Netherlands became complicated by the existence of the Dutch colonial empire in Southeast Asia and Dutch fears of Japanese economic and territorial expansion. Following the world economic crisis of 1929, relations between the two nations rapidly deteriorated because of the unfavorable trade balance and, after the occupation of the Netherlands by Nazi Germany, because of Japanese designs on the oil, rubber, and other strategic resources of the Dutch East Indies.

After the Japanese attack on Pearl Harbor in 1941, the Netherlands government-in-exile declared war upon Japan, while Japan embarked on its "southern advance," occupying Dutch-ruled Indonesia in 1942 in order to obtain the supplies necessary for its war effort (see INDONESIA AND JAPAN). At that time many Dutch nationals were placed in internment camps, where the harsh treatment they received gave rise to anti-Japanese feelings that have persisted until the present among a significant portion of the Dutch population.

After the war diplomatic relations were resumed with the conclusion of the SAN FRANCISCO PEACE TREATY in 1951, and the Japanese government immediately established a foreign affairs office in the Netherlands. In the following year, the office was elevated to the status of an embassy. In 1953 an aviation agreement was concluded and in 1960, a trade agreement.

The Japanese trade surplus with the Netherlands has been one of the dominant concerns of recent discussions between leaders of the two nations. In 1990 the total amount of Japanese exports was US $6.2 billion, in contrast to an import total of only $1.2 billion. The primary export from Japan to the Netherlands is automobiles. Other important items include television cameras, computers, copying machines, facsimile machines, and recording tape. The leading Japanese imports from the Netherlands, in order of importance, are chemicals, cut flowers, cheese, and fresh fish. The Japanese corporate presence in the Netherlands is also considerable, totaling about 250 companies in 1989; in the same year the value of Japanese investment in the Netherlands reached $4.6 billion, representing, after Great Britain, the highest figure for Japanese investment in a European nation.

A cultural agreement between the two countries was concluded in 1980, and exchange in this area is lively as well. The Japan-Netherlands Association maintains offices in both countries, and the Society for the Study of Historical Relations between Japan and the Netherlands (Nichiran Kōshōshi Kenkyūkai) and the Japan-Netherlands Institute (Nichiran Gakkai) are also active in promoting cultural relations.

netsuke

根付

A piece of sculptured wood or ivory used to secure a cord carrying personal belongings to the sash (*obi*) that acts as a belt on traditional Japanese dress. Traditional Japanese dress for men and women had very few places in which to keep small personal objects. Women kept things in their sleeves, but men had no equivalent in which to carry essentials such as seal cases (INRŌ), tobacco pouches, purses, pipes in cases, and small writing kits, known as *yatate.* Things like this were called *sagemono* ("hanging objects"), and the logical place to hang these things was from the sash. To hold the cord in place, a toggle called a *netsuke* was fitted at the other end. *Netsuke* were produced in the greatest numbers during the Edo period (1600–1868).

Two developments were of seminal importance to the growing use of *netsuke:* the widespread acceptance and use of tobacco and an increasing interest in Chinese carved toggles and seals. Tobacco smokers needed a place to keep their smoking paraphernalia. The Chinese influence is apparent both in the themes and the materials that appear in the *netsuke* of this period, notably in an increased fashion for ivory, which had not been much used in Japan until then, especially for carving.

The earliest *netsuke* carvers appear to have been amateurs. Painting of *netsuke* remained a comparative rarity except in the rather folklike pieces resembling simple dolls made at Nara and other provincial centers. The preference was always for natural, polished wood or ivory, which gained softness and patina from rubbing against the clothing.

Early *netsuke* tended to be unsigned, reflecting the Japanese tradition of anonymity in arts and crafts. However, by the early 19th century it was becoming usual rather than exceptional for *netsuke* to be signed. The great age of *netsuke* in terms of production, quality, and artistic achievement was the first half of the 19th century. *Netsuke* became more humorous, and there was more variation in both subjects and materials. The characteristics of *netsuke* of this period are small size, intricacy, and compactness. There is an emphasis on native subjects of all kinds, such as craftsmen, entertainers, legendary figures from Japanese history, mythical creatures, animals and birds, and even representations of objects, such as tiles, tea bowls, or hanging paintings. Perhaps the most highly skilled of all the carvers was Kaigyokusai of Ōsaka (1813–92), who specialized almost entirely in ivory.

The end of Japan's NATIONAL SECLUSION in the 1850s had negative results for *netsuke*. *Netsuke* became very popular among foreigners, being both amusing and easy to transport. To meet this new demand, large amounts of inferior *netsuke* were produced for the undiscriminating foreign buyer, usually in ivory or cheap substitutes, and this practice has continued. Moreover, the market that had existed for high quality *netsuke* was affected by changes in Japanese dress. Dress codes disappeared with the abolition of the official class system by the Meiji government, and Western clothes became increasingly popular. However, there was a continued, if small, demand for fine *netsuke* in the Meiji period (1868–1912). During this period *netsuke* carvers also started making *okimono* (ornaments), which tended to be larger, naturalistic works in ivory very much slanted toward the Western market.

The *netsuke* tradition still produces masterpieces of miniature carving, but these *netsuke* have become an art form in themselves and do not have the same feeling as those made for use. Within the last 20 years several American and European carvers have begun making them.

Physical Characteristics—To carry out *netsuke*'s practical function, there were definite limits to their possible size, which ranged from 2.5 to 15 centimeters (1 to 6 in). *Netsuke* were generally three-dimensional carvings (*katabori*) of a mask, a human being, a deity, a mythical creature, an apparition, an animal, a plant, or an architectural fantasy. The holes for the cord were either bored into a flat back or created by such aspects of the design as limbs or branches.

Some *netsuke* had a practical use in addition to securing the cord to the sash. The earliest of these were seals and flint and tinder sets, but later on small knives, ashtrays, watches, sundials, and tea ceremony utensils were made as *netsuke.*

The materials used in *netsuke* varied a great deal and included wood, ivory, lacquer, and other organic materials, such as nuts, antler, horn, amber, and corals such as the black coral called *umimatsu.* Eyes were often inlaid with tortoiseshell, glass, amber, metal, horn, or ebony.

Nevskii, Nikolai Aleksandrovich

ネフスキー, N. A.

(1892–1945). Russian philologist who specialized in Japanese, Ainu, and Ryukyuan languages and cultures. Born in Yaroslavl, he graduated from the Oriental Languages Department of St. Petersburg University. Nev-

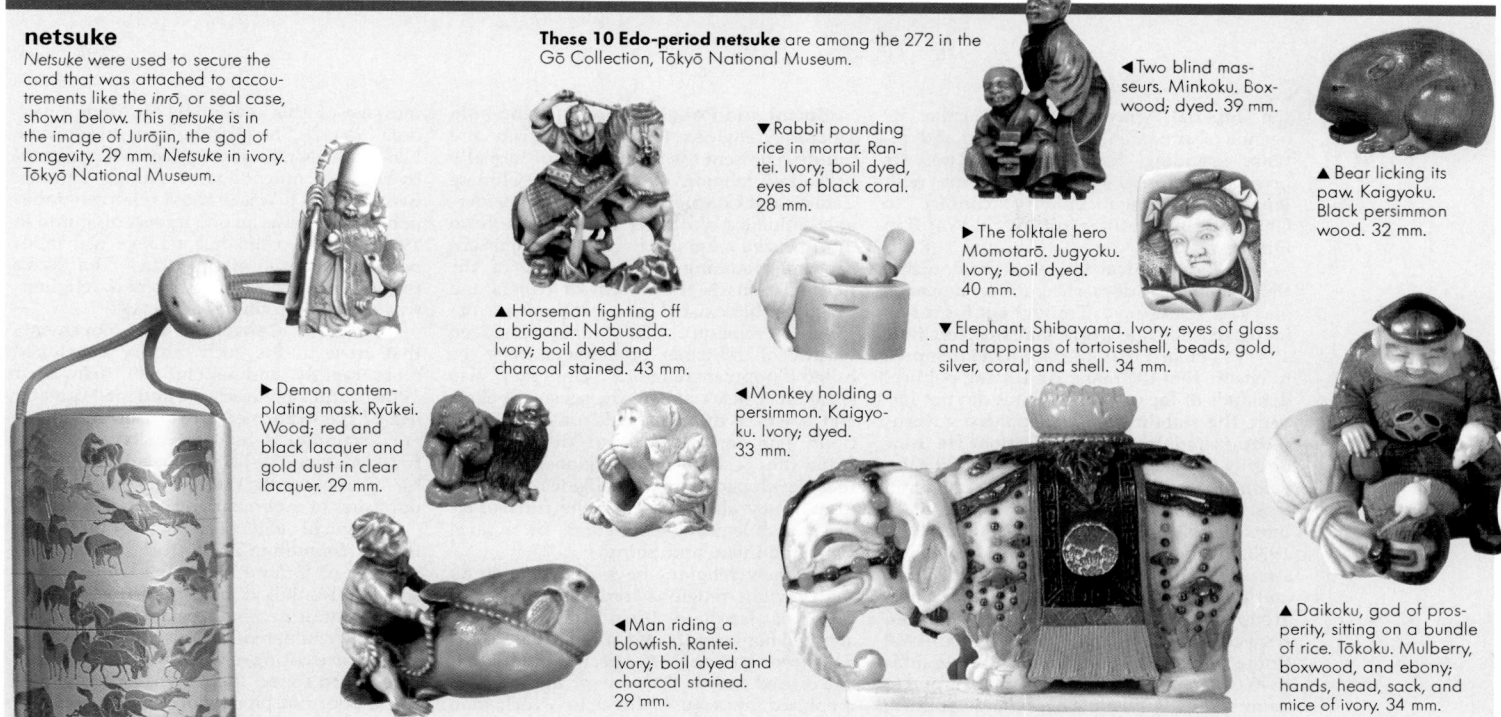

netsuke

Netsuke were used to secure the cord that was attached to accoutrements like the *inrō*, or seal case, shown below. This *netsuke* is in the image of Jurōjin, the god of longevity. 29 mm. *Netsuke* in ivory. Tōkyō National Museum.

These 10 Edo-period netsuke are among the 272 in the Gō Collection, Tōkyō National Museum.

▶ Demon contemplating mask. Ryūkei. Wood; red and black lacquer and gold dust in clear lacquer. 29 mm.

▲ Horseman fighting off a brigand. Nobusada. Ivory; boil dyed and charcoal stained. 43 mm.

▼ Rabbit pounding rice in mortar. Rantei. Ivory; boil dyed, eyes of black coral. 28 mm.

◀ Monkey holding a persimmon. Kaigyoku. Ivory; dyed. 33 mm.

◀ Man riding a blowfish. Rantei. Ivory; boil dyed and charcoal stained. 29 mm.

◀ Two blind masseurs. Minkoku. Boxwood; dyed. 39 mm.

▶ The folktale hero Momotarō. Jugyoku. Ivory; boil dyed. 40 mm.

▼ Elephant. Shibayama. Ivory; eyes of glass and trappings of tortoiseshell, beads, gold, silver, coral, and shell. 34 mm.

▲ Bear licking its paw. Kaigyoku. Black persimmon wood. 32 mm.

▲ Daikoku, god of prosperity, sitting on a bundle of rice. Tōkoku. Mulberry, boxwood, and ebony; hands, head, sack, and mice of ivory. 34 mm.

---

skii came to Japan in 1915 and studied under the folklorists YANAGITA KUNIO, ORIKUCHI SHINOBU, and KINDAICHI KYŌSUKE. For the next 14 years, while supporting himself as a Russian language instructor, he conducted ethnographic surveys throughout Japan and Taiwan and collected material on Tangut sources in Peking. In 1929 he returned to Russia, leaving behind a Japanese wife and daughter. With the help of a successful classmate, Nikolai KONRAD, he became an instructor of Japanese at Leningrad University and continued his Tangut research at the Oriental Institute and Hermitage Museum. In 1937, at the height of Stalin's purges, Nevskii and his wife (who had rejoined him) were arrested as spies. They both died in 1945 at separate prison camps.

New Business Conference

ニュービジネス協議会

(NBC; J: Nyū Bijinesu Kyōgikai). The New Business Conference is Japan's sole incorporated association devoted to new business and service ventures. It was founded in September 1985 by top management personnel from companies actively engaged in developing new business fields.

NBC membership consisted of more than 300 business executives from throughout Japan as of May 1989. Its main objective is to move society and the economic structure in directions favorable to emerging new businesses. NBC's activities include organizing local and international seminars, symposia, and conferences; compiling information, statistics, and research results about emerging new businesses; informing the public of social and economic problems that new business corporations might have; and assisting new business ventures.

new glass materials

ニューガラス

(*nyū garasu*). The new generation of glass materials used in electrical, magnetic, mechanical, and chemical applications. Japanese government and business organizations have targeted new glass as an industry for intensive development. In 1986 the MINISTRY OF INTERNATIONAL TRADE AND INDUSTRY (MITI) formed the New Glass Study Group (Nyū Garasu Kihon Mondai Kondankai), and in 1988 a group of 93 Japanese glass manufac-

turers established the New Glass Forum (Nyū Garasu Fōramu), which by 1991 had increased its membership to 161 companies. In 1989 Japan's new-glass domestic shipments were approximately ¥400 billion (US $2.9 billion).

Optical fiber (quartz glass fiber), a major product of new-glass research, is widely used in telecommunications cables. In 1991 Japan produced some 41,800 kilometers (26,000 mi) of optical fiber, more than any other country. Other developments in Japanese new-glass research include the production of glass for use in lasers and the increased use of new glass in liquid crystal displays, electroluminescent displays, optical and magnetic disks, and solar cells.

new industrial cities

新産業都市

(*shin sangyō toshi*). Areas designated according to the 1962 Act for the Development of New Industrial Cities. The areas were chosen in order to promote local industry and to check the concentration of people and industries in large cities. The 15 designated zones are Dōō (central Hokkaidō), Hachinohe, Sendai Bay, Jōban-Kōriyama, Niigata, Matsumoto-Suwa, Toyama-Takaoka, Okayama Kennan (southern Okayama Prefecture), Tokushima, Tōyo (eastern Ehime Prefecture), Shiranui-Ariake-Ōmuta, Ōita, Hyūga-Nobeoka, Akita Bay, and Nakaumi. Public funds were used to improve basic facilities and to introduce new industries, but the results have not been as good as anticipated, creating pollution, among other problems.

New Japan Philharmonic

新日本フィルハーモニー交響楽団

(Shin Nihon Firuhāmonī Kōkyō Gakudan). Orchestra originating in Tōkyō in July 1972 as an independent alliance of musicians. In September of that year the group gave its inaugural concert under the direction of its principal conductor, OZAWA SEIJI, who still serves in that role. The New Japan Philharmonic is known for its tremendously varied, innovative programs.

New Japan Securities Co, Ltd

新日本証券[株]

(Shin Nihon Shōken). Comprehensive securities company. Established in 1967 through

the merger of three securities companies, the firm is affiliated with the INDUSTRIAL BANK OF JAPAN, LTD. The company founded an investment information service company jointly with Wakō Securities and Okasan Securities. It has overseas representative offices in Sydney, Seoul, Beijing, Singapore, Frankfurt, and Paris and subsidiaries in Hong Kong, Zurich, Geneva, London, and New York. Midterm sales for the fiscal year ending March 1991 totaled ¥154.2 billion (US $1.1 billion); and capitalization stood at ¥59.0 billion (US $430.0 million). Headquarters are in Tōkyō.

"New Order in East Asia" → Tōa Shinchitsujo

New Order Movement

新体制運動

(Shin Taisei Undō). A generic term popularized in 1940 and 1941 to describe a series of domestic reform proposals in Japan. Although the term was used loosely to refer to a wide range of reforms, it was most widely used in the context of political reform plans.

The calls for a new political order (*seiji shin taisei*) in one sense reflected more than a quarter century of attacks on the efficacy and morality of the early-20th-century political system under the Meiji Constitution. In fact, however, the major forces active in the movement in 1940 merely constituted a conglomeration of conventional interest groups.

Various groups saw the creation of a new political party as the way to realize their goals. Members of major parties within the Diet—the RIKKEN SEIYŪKAI and RIKKEN MINSEITŌ—hoped to regain influence lost in the 1930s. Minor parties and factions hoped to gain political power that had hitherto eluded them. Reformist groups outside the Diet wished to replace existing members with a reformist coalition. Some political leaders wished to enhance the influence of vocational and agrarian guilds that had lost ground to big business. The Home Ministry hoped to establish stronger administrative controls over small towns and villages, and the Imperial Army wished to further its agenda of armaments' development and defense spending. Each group declared its proposed reforms essential to cope with Japan's protracted military conflict in China and the outbreak of World War II in Europe.

The key political figure in harmonizing these conflicting domestic political demands was KONOE FUMIMARO. Throughout his career (and particularly as prime minister from June 1937 to January 1939), Konoe had attempted to ensure that the many conflicting political demands of Japan's ruling elites did not impede the stability of the Japanese government or its international position. He drew heavily upon the "reformist" ideas being developed by the SHŌWA KENKYŪKAI "brain trust," an organization of intellectuals, bureaucrats, and journalists established in 1933. Konoe's principal goals were to strengthen the prime minister's prerogatives and to create a new mass political support group for his domestic and foreign policies. Between late August and early October 1940 Prime Minister Konoe met with representatives of each major political interest group to hammer out the details of the new political order. On 12 October 1940 the new popular organization was officially launched as the IMPERIAL RULE ASSISTANCE ASSOCIATION (Taisei Yokusankai).

However, the New Order Movement encountered three serious barriers. First, although many groups assumed a positive attitude toward Konoe's reform program, none of them was willing to surrender any of its prerogatives. Second, the proposed reforms were perceived by many conservatives, such as HIRANUMA KIICHIRŌ, as violating the spirit of the Meiji Constitution and giving an excess of state power to one man and his political support group. Finally, as the promise of an early diplomatic settlement of the war with China proved to be illusory, Konoe himself became increasingly reluctant to provoke a major political upheaval through forceful implementation of his new order program. By 1941 the Imperial Rule Assistance Association had been converted from a vanguard of political reform to the status of a nonpartisan, nationwide organization for promoting citizen backing for established government programs. The failure of the new order movement to "reform" the political system revealed the vitality and strength of existing political forces in Japan.

New Ōtani Co, Ltd

[株]ホテルニューオータニ

(Hoteru Nyū Ōtani). One of the most prestigious hotels in Japan. Incorporated in 1963. It now operates 19 chain hotels, 5 of them abroad in Los Angeles, Honolulu, Singapore, Beijing (Peking), and Sophia. For the fiscal year ending March 1990, sales totaled ¥58.0 billion (US $378.9 million) and capitalization stood at ¥3.5 billion (US $22.9 million). Headquarters are in Tōkyō.

new religions   新宗教

(shin shūkyō; an abbreviation of the term shinkō shūkyō or newly arisen religions). Although often used disparagingly to refer to pseudoreligious and even to fraudulent groups, the term new religions will be used here to describe the various religious movements outside organized SHINTŌ and BUDDHISM that have arisen in Japan since the 19th century.

Social and Religious Background—In Japanese religious history Buddhism and Shintō represent the mainstream of formally organized religion (kisei shūkyō). Chinese Taoism and Confucianism exerted considerable influence but rarely assumed the form of organized religions. Even more important for understanding the background of the new religions is the wealth of beliefs and practices that existed informally outside organized religions. This unsystematized wealth of religious phenomena may be called "popular religion." One may also speak of FOLK RELIGION in the sense of beliefs and practices that emerged from folk traditions. The new religions are distinguished from the "established religions" because they developed new socioreligious organizations. They also claimed to be fully organized and legitimate religions, on a level with Buddhism and Shintō.

The new religions have drawn upon all the previous religious traditions. One element of Japanese Buddhism frequently adopted has been the memorial ritual for the dead (see REIYŪKAI). An aspect of Shintō that has carried over is the view of the world as inhabited by KAMI (deities) to which man should be responsive; this is the indirect source of the "revelations" received by many founders of new religions. The popular teachings of Neo-Confucianism, with their emphasis on family stability and social responsibility as a kind of cosmic obligation, have penetrated the teachings of a number of new religions. Even Taoism provided a host of cosmological notions from which some new religions have drawn (see KONKŌKYŌ). Probably the best example of popular religion's influence upon the new religions is the widespread faith in the Lotus Sutra and the practice of reciting its title. This faith and practice is central to such new religions as Reiyūkai, RISSHŌ KŌSEIKAI, and SŌKA GAKKAI. Folk practices such as shamanism also exerted tremendous influence upon the new religions.

In the Edo period (1600–1868) a family took care of its ancestors with the help of Buddhism, sought tutelary help for its residence through Shintō, made special requests at particular shrines and temples, and accepted many of the moral ideas of Neo-Confucianism. At the same time, families and individuals believed in and practiced many aspects of popular and folk religion. During the same period, however, the social fabric that supported this complex religious worldview began to change, and ties to local Buddhist temples and Shintō shrines were weakened. By the 16th and 17th centuries, pilgrimages had become popular among the common people. Pilgrim associations and similar grass-roots organizations (KŌ) were ways in which local people could draw together for social and religious communion. The kō were a form of transition from family and village units of participation in religion to the pattern of nationwide participation eventually seen in the new religions.

Early Development—The first identifiable new religion, Nyoraikyō, was founded in 1802, followed by KUROZUMIKYŌ in 1814, TENRIKYŌ in 1838, and others throughout the 19th century. The development of Tenrikyō is typical of 19th-century new religions. Its founder, NAKAYAMA MIKI, was a pious and hardworking farm wife who received a divine revelation in the form of "permanent" possession by a kami who claimed to be the true original kami. This new divinity, Tenri Ō no Mikoto, ordered her to spread the

message of this revelation of "divine wisdom" (tenri). She quickly gained followers. Nakayama Miki's success led to harassment by the government and even imprisonment. Even though it was granted relatively independent status as an official sect of Shintō in 1908, Tenrikyō did not achieve real independence until after 1945. Tenrikyō's founder, like those of other new religions, was seen as a living god (IKIGAMI).

The 20th Century—The movements that arose in the 20th century developed more rapidly and extensively than their 19th-century predecessors and made greater use of the mass media to recruit members. For example, TANIGUCHI MASAHARU, who founded SEICHŌ NO IE in 1930, gained support for his movement through his success as a publisher of a popular spiritual magazine.

Taniguchi had been active in ŌMOTO before founding Seichō no Ie, and the founder of Ōmoto, DEGUCHI NAO, had been active in Konkōkyō before starting her own movement. It became a frequent pattern for spiritually talented persons to gain experience in an existing new religion before being inspired to found their own. Deguchi Nao was a poor but pious woman who received her revelation through possession by a kami in 1892. Leaving Konkōkyō, she ministered to the sick and spiritually troubled through her own mixture of elements borrowed from Konkōkyō and folk religious practices. Deguchi Nao's son-in-law, Deguchi Onisaburō (1871–1948), expanded Nao's rather utopian vision into a more highly organized and intellectually phrased message. The movement attracted large numbers of followers and at the same time came under suspicion from the state. The authorities twice prosecuted Ōmoto, alleging that it was engaging in treasonous activities. In spite of government oppression, the 19th-century movements held their own or grew in influence while other movements arose, such as Reiyūkai (1923) and Seichō no Ie (1930). After World War II, with the end of government religious oppression, religious movements could develop any teachings and form any organizational ties they wished. In 1951 many new religions formed the UNION OF NEW RELIGIOUS ORGANIZATIONS OF JAPAN to facilitate cooperation on such issues as the promotion of freedom of religion.

Two new religions that experienced some of the most remarkable growth in the postwar period, Risshō Kōseikai and Sōka Gakkai, have their roots in the Nichiren tradition of Buddhism. Risshō Kōseikai is famous for its success with the hōza system of gathering small groups of people under leaders to discuss religious issues and problems in daily life. Sōka Gakkai, officially a lay movement of the Nichiren Shōshū Buddhist sect, is the largest contemporary new religion, claiming more than 8 million households in 1990. This movement, which had its formal beginnings in 1930, was fairly small through World War II, when it was persecuted by the government for refusing to participate in Shintō support for the war effort. After the war, the general director, Toda Jōsei (1900–1958), had to rebuild the organization almost from scratch. Sōka Gakkai entered the political arena, and in 1964 it formed a political party, KŌMEITŌ (the Clean Government Party). It also established a number of its own schools and Sōka University.

By the 1970s, new religions founded during the 19th century had achieved an institutional and bureaucratic development equivalent to that of established religions. The trend has been for newly emerging religions to assume more quickly a complex institutional structure. Recently developed new religions have also seen the maturation of small, yet stable, overseas branches that include Japanese as well as non-Japanese members. Since the 1970s new religions with a decidedly magical character—such as Agonshū, Mahikari, and Shinnyoen—have come to prominence. Despite earlier predictions that interest in new religions would level off or decline, the success of these magical movements, particularly among the young, is an indication of the continued strength and appeal of new religions in Japan. See also HOLY SPIRIT ASSOCIATION FOR THE UNIFICATION OF WORLD CHRISTIANITY; MISOGIKYŌ; PL KYŌDAN; SEKAI KYŪSEI KYŌ.

news agencies 通信社

(tsūshinsha). Japan's first contact with a foreign news agency took place in 1871 when Denmark's Great Northern Telegraph completed a telegraphic line via Shanghai to Nagasaki. The first news agency in Japan, the Jiji Tsūshinsha (no connection with the present Jiji Tsūshinsha or JIJI PRESS), was established in 1888 by Mitsui & Co upon the urging of the Japanese government. About this time newspapers began to concentrate more on news reportage and less on opinion statements, a trend that served to increase the importance of news agencies. Many new agencies appeared in the ensuing years, and by 1926 the news agencies based in Tōkyō alone numbered 33.

As World War II approached, the Japanese government, to control speech, made plans to create a single government news agency, and in 1936 the Japan Telegraphic News Agency (Nihon Dempō Tsūshinsha) and the Japan Associated Press (Nihon Shimbun Rengōsha) were combined to form the DŌMEI TSŪSHINSHA (Dōmei News Agency). All other news agencies were disbanded. Following the war, the staff of the Dōmei agency created the KYŌDŌ NEWS SERVICE (Kyōdō Tsūshinsha) and the Jiji Press. These two firms are the largest news agencies in Japan. Also active are the Radio Press (RP), which translates important news from foreign shortwave broadcasts, and many specialized agencies, which distribute news in particular fields. See also INTERNATIONAL COMMUNICATIONS.

newspapers 新聞

(shimbun). The modern Japanese newspaper industry reflects the character of Japanese business as a whole: in the vanguard are several colossal national newspaper organizations that are, in effect, media corporations in the broadest sense and that publish either morning or evening editions of their newspapers or both morning and evening editions. In addition to these major national media companies publishing general news-oriented papers, there is a host of local and special-interest newspapers that also help cater to the diverse interests of the world's most literate readership.

History—The first modern newspaper was the *Nagasaki Shipping List and Advertiser*, published twice a week beginning in 1861 by the Englishman A. W. Hansard in Nagasaki. In 1862 the Tokugawa shogunate (1603–1867) began publishing the KAMPAN BATABIYA SHIMBUN, a translated and re-edited edition of *Javasche Courant*, the organ of the Dutch government in Indonesia. These two papers contained only foreign news. Newspapers covering domestic news were first started by the Japanese in Edo (now Tōkyō), Ōsaka, Kyōto, and Nagasaki in 1868. YANAGAWA SHUNSAN's *Chūgai shimbun*, typical of early papers and a model for later papers, carried domestic news as well as abridged translations from foreign papers. The first Japanese daily paper, the YOKOHAMA MAINICHI SHIMBUN, was launched in 1871. The *Tōkyō nichinichi shimbun* (predecessor of the MAINICHI SHIMBUN), the YŪBIN HŌCHI SHIMBUN (predecessor of the HŌCHI SHIMBUN), and the oldest existing local newspaper, the *Kōchū shimbun* (predecessor of the *Yamanashi nichinichi shimbun*), were all begun in 1872.

Most papers published at this time were referred to as "political forums" because they demanded the establishment of a national Diet and printed political opinions at the time of the FREEDOM AND PEOPLE'S RIGHTS MOVEMENT (Jiyū Minken Undō). However, after the establishment of the Diet, the newspapers virtually became organs of the newly formed political parties. These newspapers were called *ōshimbun* (large newspapers). *Koshimbun* (small newspapers) were popular newspapers containing local news, human interest stories, and light fiction. The YOMIURI SHIMBUN, which began publishing in 1874, is a typical example. Partially because strong government pressure caused the *ōshimbun* to fail, new newspapers printing impartial news started springing up around 1880. The ASAHI SHIMBUN was launched in 1879 in Ōsaka, and the JIJI SHIMPŌ in 1882 in Tōkyō. Around 1892 NEWS AGENCIES were formed. The sudden increase in circulation made possible in the 1890s by the widespread use of rotary presses and the growth of advertising turned Japanese newspapers into large business enterprises.

When the TŌKYŌ EARTHQUAKE OF 1923 destroyed much of Tōkyō, the Ōsaka-based *Asahi* and *Mainichi* became the two largest national newspapers overnight, virtually dominating the Japanese newspaper industry. The *Asahi* has maintained its prominent position to this day. The opinion-shaping activity of Japanese newspapers gradually declined as the papers became interested in profits and had to respond to a broader readership. The heavy pressures from the government and the military authorities weakened the papers' capacity for strong editorial policy.

The press was placed under complete government control from the outbreak of the Sino-Japanese War in 1937 (see SINO-JAPANESE WAR OF 1937–1945) until the end of World War II in 1945. Newsprint was rationed, and many newspapers were forced to merge. The number of newspapers dropped from 848 in 1939 to 54 in 1942.

Free competition among newspapers revived after the abolition of wartime regulations by the Allied OCCUPATION and the lifting of controls on newsprint in 1951. The system of morning and evening editions of the same paper, which had been suspended, also revived, and major papers started printing local editions, adding to the already severe competition. When weekly magazines, comic magazines, and television became popular after World War II, most general newspapers began to concentrate on news and advertising. As in other countries, progress in broadcast media such as radio and television deprived the newspapers of their edge in prompt reporting, which forced the press to turn to in-depth articles and news commentary. In the late 1970s and 1980s Japanese newspapers greatly increased the efficiency of their operations by moving to full computerization of all aspects of their work—reporting, editing, typesetting, and printing—and by utilizing satellite communications.

Circulation—According to statistics of the JAPAN NEWSPAPER PUBLISHERS AND EDITORS ASSOCIATION, the total circulation of daily papers as of 1991 was 52,026,372, or an average of 1.24 newspapers per Japanese household. General papers accounted for 88.5 percent and sports papers for 11.5 percent. Morning papers accounted for 57 percent, evening papers 4 percent, and papers publishing both morning and evening editions 39 percent.

The five major daily general papers in order of their circulation are: *Yomiuri shimbun*, *Asahi shimbun*, *Mainichi shimbun*, NIHON KEIZAI SHIMBUN, and SANKEI SHIMBUN. Maintaining their own nationwide home-delivery networks, they account for 52.6 percent of the entire circulation of daily general papers. The two leading newspapers, the *Yomiuri* and the *Asahi*, had circulations of 9,764,551 and 8,255,902, respectively, in 1991 (morning editions). The readers of these national papers are concentrated in and around large cities such as Tōkyō and Ōsaka, where publishing offices are located. Many prefectural papers enjoy more than 50 percent of the newspaper circulation in their areas.

Monopoly Dealership—At first, newspapers were sold on consignment to bookstores, but the *Tōkyō nichinichi shimbun* initiated a home delivery system that was soon followed by other papers. The *Hōchi shimbun* started exclusive dealerships in 1903 to distribute only its own papers nationwide. The dealers not only were responsible for delivery but also acted as subscription salesmen. News of the increase in circulation for the *Hōchi* prompted other papers to set up their own news dealerships, and the system of monopoly newspaper dealerships peculiar to Japan was created in 1930.

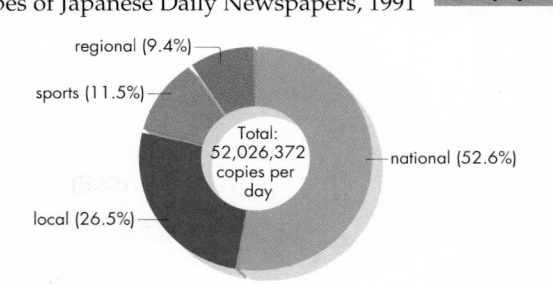

Types of Japanese Daily Newspapers, 1991

regional (9.4%)
sports (11.5%)
Total: 52,026,372 copies per day
national (52.6%)
local (26.5%)

NOTE: English-language and specialist newspapers are included in the local category.
SOURCE: Japan Newspaper Publishers and Editors Association.

Circulation of Daily Newspapers

Year	Circulation in millions[1]	Copies per household	Copies per thousand people	Number of dailies[2]
1980	46.39	1.29	570	125
1981	47.26	1.30	575	125
1982	47.99	1.30	579	125
1983	47.04	1.26	563	125
1984	47.52	1.25	565	125
1985	48.23	1.25	569	124
1986	48.57	1.25	569	124
1987	49.83	1.26	578	124
1988	50.60	1.26	584	124
1989	51.06	1.26	584	124
1990	51.91	1.26	591	125
1991	52.03	1.24	589	124

[1] When morning and evening editions of the same paper are published, a purchase of both is counted as one purchase.
[2] Papers that publish both a morning and an evening edition are counted as one.
SOURCE: Japan Newspaper Publishers and Editors Association.

New Year

The observance of the New Year (Shōgatsu) is the most important and elaborate of Japan's annual events.

▶ The *kagamimochi*, an offering of rice cakes to the deity of the New Year, is a common sight from late December to early January.

▲ An elaborate lacquered set for serving *toso*, a ceremonial spiced *sake*, which is sipped from the shallow cups to celebrate the New Year.

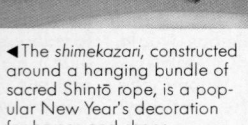

◀ The *shimekazari*, constructed around a hanging bundle of sacred Shintō rope, is a popular New Year's decoration for homes and shops.

▲ *Hatsumōde*, or the first shrine or temple visit of the New Year, is central to the New Year observances of most Japanese.

Journalists—Would-be journalists in Japan are selected from among new university graduates through examinations conducted by the individual newspaper companies. The examinations are notoriously difficult, and hundreds of applicants may compete for a single job. Once accepted, however, they can look forward to lifetime employment. Japanese companies more often than not shift the journalists to administrative positions by the time they become senior reporters, leaving actual reporting and editing activities to subordinates. PRESS CLUBS are a significant characteristic of Japanese journalism. They function both as social clubs for journalists and as locations for important press interviews and political announcements. It is widely recognized that there exists the danger of such clubs' becoming too closely associated with the government and other public bodies to which nonmembers have difficulty gaining access. See also FREEDOM OF SPEECH, REGULATION OF; INTERNATIONAL COMMUNICATIONS; NEWSPAPERS, LOCAL; NEWSPAPERS, NATIONWIDE.

New Year's cards At the bottom of this government-issued card (left) is a lottery number that may enable the recipient to win a prize; on the reverse (right) is the New Year's greeting.

newspapers, local　　　地方紙

(*chihōshi*). Local newspapers in Japan consist primarily of prefectural and regional pa-

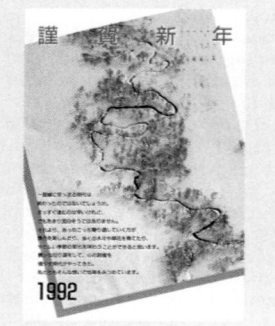
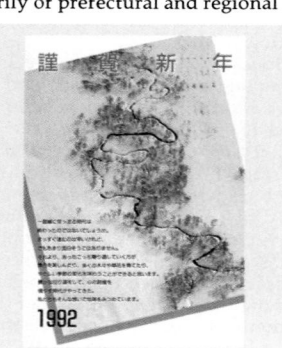

pers. The majority of these newspapers started during the political and social movements of the Meiji (1868–1912) and Taishō (1912–26) periods. Most of the present prefectural papers came into existence with the system established by the government in 1942 of one paper to a prefecture. Regional papers such as the HOKKAIDŌ SHIMBUN, CHŪNICHI SHIMBUN, and the NISHI NIPPON SHIMBUN have sales territories that extend over several prefectures. The largest of these papers, such as the *Chūnichi*, have two million or more readers, while most of the prefectural papers generally have between 100,000 and 300,000 subscribers. Since the late 1960s national newspapers began making advances into the territory of local and regional papers, and the market is rapidly changing. On the other hand, local newspapers have been strong in their coverage of such issues as local environmental problems and movements to revive local culture.

newspapers, nationwide　　全国紙

(*zenkokushi*). A general term for the five major national dailies, the ASAHI SHIMBUN, YOMIURI SHIMBUN, MAINICHI SHIMBUN, SANKEI SHIMBUN, and NIHON KEIZAI SHIMBUN, all of which have nationwide distribution. The *Asahi*, *Yomiuri*, and *Mainichi* started in Ōsaka in the 1870s and 1880s, offering entertainment features and news to the masses as so-called small newspapers (*koshimbun;* see NEWSPAPERS) in contrast to the so-called large newspapers (*ōshimbun*), which concentrated on political issues. The great TŌKYŌ EARTHQUAKE OF 1923 dealt a destructive blow to Tōkyō-based newspapers and allowed the Ōsaka-based dailies to become national newspapers with large nationwide circulations.

From their very first editions, the *Asahi*, *Yomiuri*, and *Mainichi* offered feature articles, serial novels by well-known writers of the day, sensational news reportage, and sports coverage. They also devoted space to items on hobbies, women's topics, and family columns, thus creating a content with mass appeal. In recent years the big national dailies have expanded their operations to include radio and television programming and have begun making inroads into local newspaper markets.

New Tōkyō International Airport　　新東京国際空港

(Shin Tōkyō Kokusai Kūkō). Also known as Narita Airport. International airport located some 66 kilometers (41 mi) east of Tōkyō in the city of Narita, Chiba Prefecture. It opened in May 1978 and replaced TŌKYŌ INTERNATIONAL AIRPORT (Haneda Airport) as Tōkyō's chief international airport. Haneda had registered a sharp increase in passengers and freight in the early 1960s and was judged inadequate to serve the volume of traffic pro-

jected for the near future. In 1966 the New Tōkyō International Airport Authority was established and charged with the construction, management, and operation of a new airport at Narita. Construction work on the airport began in 1969, but its completion was delayed from 1971 to 1975 and its opening until 1978 because of fierce opposition from a coalition of local inhabitants and radical students.

The New Tōkyō International Airport is served by two railways, the Narita line and the Keisei line. An extension of the Narita line into the airport area was completed in March 1991, considerably shortening commuting time to 56 minutes from Tōkyō Station. There is also limousine bus service to the airport from various points in the city. Check-in procedures for most flights can be performed at Tōkyō City Air Terminal, located in Hakozaki, Chūō Ward, from which buses are dispatched to the airport.

The New Tōkyō International Airport's main runway measures 4,000 meters (13,120 ft) in length. Under a second-stage construction program, begun in 1987, a 2,500-meter (8,200-ft) parallel runway and a 3,200-meter (10,496-ft) crosswind runway are being built. Upon completion (projected for autumn 1992) the area of the airport will double in size to 1,065 hectares (2,631 acres). As of March 1991, 52 airlines of 38 countries utilized the airport, with approximately 325 flights landing and departing daily. The airport annually handles some 20.6 million passengers and 1.4 million metric tons (1.5 million short tons) of air freight.

New Woman's Association→

Shin Fujin Kyōkai

New Year　　正月

(Shōgatsu). New Year observances are the most important and most elaborate of Japan's annual events. Although local customs differ, at this time homes are decorated and the holidays are celebrated by family gatherings, visits to shrines or temples, and formal calls on relatives and friends. In recent years the New Year festivities have been officially observed from 1 January through 3 January, during which time all government offices and most companies are closed.

Preparations for seeing in the New Year were originally undertaken to greet the TOSHIGAMI, or deity of the incoming year. These began on 13 December, when the house was given a thorough cleaning; the date is usually nearer the end of the month now. The house is then decorated in the traditional fashion: A sacred rope of straw (*shimenawa*) with dangling white paper strips (*shide*) is hung over the front door to demarcate the temporary abode of the *toshigami* and to prevent malevolent spirits from entering. It is also customary to place KADOMATSU, an arrangement of tree sprigs, beside the entrance way. A special altar, known as a *toshidana* (literally, "year shelf"), is piled high with *kagamimochi* (flat, round rice cakes), *sake* (rice wine), persimmons, and other foods in honor of the *toshigami*. The night before New Year's is called Ōmisoka. Many people visit Buddhist temples to hear the temple bells rung 108 times at midnight (JOYA NO KANE) to dispel the evils of the past year. It is also customary to eat TOSHIKOSHI SOBA (literally, "year-crossing noodles") in the hope that one's family fortunes will extend like the long noodles.

New Year's Days—The first day of the year (*ganjitsu*) is usually spent with members of the family. People also throng to Buddhist temples and Shintō shrines (see HATSUMŌDE). In the Imperial Palace at dawn or early on the morning of 1 January, the emperor performs the rite of *shihōhai* (worship of the four quarters), in which he does reverence in the directions of various shrines and imperial tombs and offers prayers for the well-being of the nation. On 2 January the public is allowed to enter the inner palace grounds; the only other day this is possible is the emperor's birthday. On the second and third days of the New Year holidays, friends and business acquaintances visit one another to extend greetings (*nenshi*) and sip *toso*, a spiced rice wine.

Ōshōgatsu and Koshōgatsu—Shōgatsu refers to the first month of the year as well as to the period of the New Year's holidays. The events described above concern what is commonly referred to as Ōshōgatsu (literally, "Big New Year"). There is, however, another traditional New Year called Koshōgatsu (literally, "Small New Year"). The former follows the date calculated by the Gregorian calendar, and the latter is set according to the lunar calendar. Koshōgatsu thus starts with the first full moon of the year or more commonly on about 15 January and is largely observed in the rural areas of Japan, where the *toshigami* have been traditionally considered as agricultural deities. In some areas visits by the *toshigami* are enacted by costumed performers who do the pony dance (*harukoma-mai*) or the lion dance (SHISHI-MAI) or who masquerade as gods or demons (see NAMAHAGE). The main events of Koshōgatsu are rites and practices praying for a bountiful harvest. *Niwataue* and *taasobi* are rites in which the entire rice-growing cycle from planting to harvest is symbolically acted out. Several games played at New Year's, such as SUGOROKU (a kind of parcheesi), *karuta* (see PLAYING CARDS), and HANETSUKI (shuttlecock and battledore), are also sometimes augural in nature. See also NEW YEAR'S CARDS; ENKAI; OTOSHIDAMA.

New Year's cards   年賀状

(*nengajō*). Japanese send NEW YEAR's greeting cards to virtually all of their relatives, friends, and acquaintances, while businesses send out cards to their customers. The Japanese New Year's card fulfills much the same function as the Western Christmas card, but the Japanese send out New Year's cards in much greater quantities, the average family mailing being about 100. The customary New Year's card is a government-issued postcard printed with lottery numbers, which may enable the recipient to win a prize. Many families design their own postcards and have them printed. Cards posted between 15 and around 25 December are held by the post office and delivered together on 1 January. The government also issues special New Year's picture postcards

sold, in 1990, at five yen above the regular price, part of the extra money going to charity. New Year's cards delivered in Japan in 1990 numbered 3.8 billion.

New Zealand and Japan
ニュージーランドと日本

(Nyūjīrando *to* Nihon). Relations between New Zealand and Japan were limited prior to World War II. During the war Japan's military expansion in the Pacific threatened New Zealand, but direct military conflict was minimal. A bilateral relationship developed quickly in the postwar period. New Zealand was a strong supporter of Japan's admission to the United Nations. In September 1958 the two nations signed a treaty of commerce, and in 1962 New Zealand became the first of Japan's wartime enemies to grant it most-favored-nation status. In the subsequent decade annual trade significantly expanded. Bilateral relations during this period were relatively smooth, as trade was based on complementary needs, with New Zealand exporting agricultural and forestry products and Japan exporting manufactured goods. In the 1970s, however, economic relations were marked by friction, first over the lingering protection of agriculture in Japan and then over Japan's access to fishing rights in New Zealand's waters.

Since the mid-1970s, Japan has been one of New Zealand's most important economic partners. In 1990 New Zealand exported products valued at US $1.7 billion to Japan and imported goods worth US $1.2 billion. Its major exports were aluminum, kiwi fruit, and wool, while its main imports were automobiles and textile products. Japan's investments in New Zealand have been minimal, representing less than 1 percent of global Japanese investments, but they have grown in recent years. In 1989 Japanese investments there totaled US $101.0 million, making Japan New Zealand's second largest investor. Both governments have advocated greater cooperation among the nations of the Pacific and are strong supporters of the PACIFIC BASIN ECONOMIC COUNCIL.

Neyagawa   寝屋川［市］

City in northeastern Ōsaka Prefecture, central Honshū, on the river Yodogawa. The area was formerly known for its rice and lotus roots (*renkon*); however, the establishment of machine, textile, and chemical factories and the growth of residential areas have made it a satellite city of Ōsaka. Of interest are archaeological sites and a branch temple of the Narita Fudōsan (SHINSHŌJI). Pop: 256,524.

Nezame monogatari emaki
寝覚物語絵巻

(Tale of Nezame Scroll). Illustrated handscroll (EMAKIMONO) in the brightly colored *tsukuri-e* style; dated to the second half of the 12th century. It illustrates the 11th-cen-

tury novel *Nezame monogatari* (The Tale of Nezame), better known as YORU NO NEZAME. The single surviving scroll, measuring 25.6 by 508.3 centimeters (10 by 200 in), in the collection of the Yamato Bunkakan in Nara, contains four pictures with four garbled and fragmentary sections of text.

The main elements of the plot of *Nezame monogatari* are the unhappy love affair of the heroine, Nezame, with her sister's husband; Nezame's flight from an infatuated emperor; and, finally, the romantic adventures of her son Masako no Kimi and the emperor's daughter. All existing texts are lacking much of the third part of the story. Since this is the portion covered by the surviving fragments of the *emaki*, the scroll has literary as well as artistic importance.

Nezamenotoko   寝覚ノ床

Scenic gorge on the river KISOGAWA, Nagano Prefecture, central Honshū. It consists of huge granite rocks that have been eroded into strange shapes. The area is claimed to be associated with the legend of URASHIMA TARŌ, a fisherman who visited a palace in the sea and returned after an absence of many years.

Nezu Art Museum   根津美術館

(Nezu Bijutsukan). Located in Tōkyō. The collection of NEZU KAICHIRŌ, it opened to the public in 1940 but was evacuated during World War II and escaped the destruction suffered by the estate property in the bombing of May 1945. Its exhibits are now shown in a building erected in 1955 and an annex that opened in 1990. The Japanese section includes paintings, calligraphy, ceramics, lacquer, and metalwork; the Chinese section has bronzes, paintings, sculpture, lacquer, and ceramics. Among the best-known Japanese paintings in the collection are the 13th- or early-14th-century *Nachi no taki* (Nachi Waterfall) and a KŌRIN masterpiece—the famous pair of sixfold screens with irises on a gold ground.

Nezu Kaichirō   根津嘉一郎

(1860–1940). Businessman and politician. Born in Yamanashi Prefecture. He became president of TŌBU RAILWAY CO, LTD, in 1905 and brought prosperity to the company by extending the line to Nikkō and Kinugawa. He was elected to the House of Representatives in 1904 and later served in the House of Peers. He established several academic and cultural institutions, including the Musashi Higher School (now Musashi University). His large art collection served as the basis for the NEZU ART MUSEUM in Tōkyō.

nezumi→rats and mice

nezumimochi   鼠黐

(Japanese privet). *Ligustrum japonicum.* Evergreen shrub of the olive family (Olea-

Nezame monogatari emaki In this fragment from the single surviving scroll, three children are playing flutes in the garden while two ladies in the house sit listening. 12th century. Colors on paper. Yamato Bunkakan, Nara. National Treasure.

NHK NHK Hall (left), home of the NHK Symphony Orchestra, and NHK Broadcasting Center (right) are located in Tōkyō's Shibuya Ward.

nezumimochi The Japanese privet is a wild highland species that produces flowers around June and fruit toward November. Pollution resistant, it is sometimes planted alongside public highways.

ceae) that grows wild in mountainous areas of central and western Honshū; it is also planted as a hedge. About 2 meters (7 ft) high, it has elliptical, opposite, glossy leaves. Conical flower stalks produce dense clusters of small white blossoms in summer, followed by oblong, purplish black fruits.

NGK Insulators, Ltd   日本碍子[株]

(Nippon Gaishi). Manufacturer and distributor of electrical insulators, environmental control equipment, corrosion-resistant chemical equipment, automotive and engine ceramics, beryllium-copper products, and electronic components. Incorporated in 1919. It exports insulators to more than 110 countries and has sales and service centers in the United States, Canada, and Belgium. Locke Insulators, Inc, NGK's insulator production base in North America, was established in 1974 jointly by NGK and the General Electric Co, USA. In 1977 NGK-Baudour, SA, was established in Belgium. For production of automotive ceramics it established NGK Ceramics Europe, SA, in Belgium in 1985 and NGK Ceramics, USA, in North Carolina in 1988. NGK Metals Corporation in Pennsylvania produces and sells beryllium-copper products. Sales for the fiscal year ending March 1991 totaled ¥206.6 billion (US $1.5 billion). In the same year the company was capitalized at ¥32.2 billion (US $234.7 million). Headquarters are in Nagoya.

NGK Spark Plug Co, Ltd
日本特殊陶業[株]

(Nippon Tokushu Tōgyō). Manufacturer of automotive spark plugs. Incorporated in 1936. Its new ceramics business has applications in diversified industries, including electronics, electrical appliances, machinery, automobiles, nuclear power, aircraft, space development, and ocean development. The company has overseas subsidiaries in the United States and Brazil. Sales for the fiscal year ending March 1991 totaled ¥106.0 billion (US $772.6 million), and capitalization stood at ¥22.8 billion (US $116.2 million). Headquarters are in Nagoya.

NHK   日本放送協会

(Nippon Hōsō Kyōkai; Japan Broadcasting Corporation). The public broadcasting system in Japan. In contrast to commercial broadcasting, which operates on advertising revenue, NHK receives 98 percent of its financing from reception fees paid by television set owners. Radio broadcasting in Japan began in 1925 with the Tōkyō Broadcasting Station. This station and two others in Ōsaka and Nagoya were combined in 1926 to form Nippon Hōsō Kyōkai, forerunner of the present NHK and sole broadcaster in Japan until the end of World War II. Enacted in 1950, the BROADCASTING LAW included provisions for commercial broadcasting (which began in 1951), stripping NHK of its status as Japan's sole broadcasting station. Regular television programming commenced in 1953.

At present NHK conducts nationwide and local broadcasts through two television, one FM radio, and two AM radio channels. In 1987, NHK began 24-hour satellite broadcasting and in 1989 started another 24-hour satellite channel. As of 1990, NHK was received by 1.7 million households. It also conducts international broadcasts (RADIO JAPAN) in 22 languages throughout the world for a composite total of nearly 49 hours a day. NHK employs some 15,000 people, making it by far the country's largest broadcasting organization. See also BROADCASTING, COMMERCIAL.

NHK Broadcast Museum
NHK放送博物館

(Enu Eichi Kē Hōsō Hakubutsukan). Located in Minato Ward, Tōkyō. Affiliated with NHK (Japan Broadcasting Corporation). Established in 1956, the museum chronicles the history of radio and television broadcasting by means of exhibits, audiovisual presentations, and lectures. Its library, which is open to the public, houses a collection of 8,000 books. The museum also offers summer courses on broadcasting for senior-high-school students.

NHK Science and Technical Research Laboratories
日本放送協会総合技術研究所

(Nippon Hōsō Kyōkai Sōgō Gijutsu Kenkyūjo). Institute in Setagaya Ward, Tōkyō, maintained by NHK (Japan Broadcasting Corporation) for research and development in broadcasting technology. Founded in 1930, the institute develops state-of-the-art broadcasting equipment as well as technology for satellite broadcasting and high-definition television.

NHK Spring Co, Ltd   日本発条[株]

(Nippon Hatsujō). Producer of springs and related products. Incorporated in 1939. One of the world's largest spring manufacturers, the company has 9 branches and 27 affiliated companies domestically. In the overseas market it has manufacturing bases or sales companies in 7 countries, and it supplies technical assistance to 17 licensees. Eighty percent of its production is related to the automotive industry. The company is actively promoting its overseas business. Sales for the fiscal year ending March 1991 totaled ¥149.2 billion (US $1.1 billion), and capitalization was ¥16.8 billion (US $122.4 million) in the same year. Headquarters are in Yokohama.

NHK Symphony Orchestra
NHK交響楽団

(Enu Eichi Kē Kōkyō Gakudan). Japan's oldest symphony orchestra; formed as the New Symphony Orchestra in Tōkyō in 1926 with partial backing from NHK (Japan Broadcasting Corporation). Under the baton of its first conductor, Konoe Hidemaro (1898–1973), it began giving performances in 1927. The orchestra's name was changed to the Japan Symphony Orchestra in 1942; it adopted its present name in 1951, when it began receiving all of its support from NHK. Konoe's successors have included Joseph Rosenstock (1895–1985) of Poland and Wolfgang Sawallisch (b 1923) of Germany. The NHK Symphony Orchestra is considered Japan's leading symphony orchestra.

Nichias Corporation   ニチアス[株]

(Nichiasu). A leading manufacturer of ceramic building materials, thermal insulating materials, fluoropolymer products, industrial and automotive sealants, and flooring systems. Incorporated in 1896. Sales for the fiscal year ending March 1991 totaled ¥107.9 billion (US $786.4 million), and capitalization stood at ¥7.8 billion (US $56.9 million). Headquarters are in Tōkyō.

Nichibei Kyōiku Iinkai→Japan–
United States Educational Commission

Nichibei Shūkō Tsūshō Jōyaku
→Harris Treaty

Nichibei Washin Jōyaku→
Kanagawa Treaty

Nichidō Fire & Marine Insurance Co, Ltd   自動火災海上保険[株]

(Nichidō Kasai Kaijō Hoken). Insurance company. Established in 1898. The company underwrites insurance and reinsurance of all classes except life. It has business tie-ups with AIG, Inc, operating at over 130 locations worldwide. For the fiscal year ending March 1991, the company had annual net premiums of ¥325.9 billion (US $2.4 billion), and capitalization was ¥50.1 billion (US $365.2 million). Headquarters are in Tōkyō.

Nichidokui Sangoku Bōkyō Kyōtei
→Anti-Comintern Pact

Nichidokui Sangoku Dōmei→
Tripartite Pact

Nichiei Dōmei→Anglo-Japanese
Alliance

Nichii Co, Ltd   [株]ニチイ

(Nichii). Major retailer in the Japanese supermarket industry. Established in 1963 through the merger of four clothing companies, Nichii has diversified its sales to include foodstuffs, sundry goods, and housewares. Sales totaled ¥708.1 billion (US $5.4 billion) in the fiscal year ending February 1991, with 44 percent generated by clothing, 18 percent by household items, 28 percent by foodstuffs, and 9 percent by other products. The company was capitalized at ¥48.3 billion (US $352.0 million) in the same year. Headquarters are in Ōsaka.

Nichimen Corporation   ニチメン[株]

(Nichimen). General trading company (*sōgō shōsha*) engaged in exports and imports, domestic wholesaling, plant engineering and construction, and real estate. One of the nine leading Japanese trading firms, it is a principal member of the SANWA BANK, LTD, group. Nichimen's predecessor, Nippon Menka Kaisha (Japan Cotton Trading Company), was incorporated in 1892 and changed its name to Nichimen Jitsugyō in 1957. The company took its current name in 1982. It has approximately 80 branches and liaison offices overseas, all linked by a computerized communications system. The company is also involved in some 100 joint ventures overseas. Sales for the fiscal year ending March 1991 totaled ¥6.2 trillion (US $45.2 billion). Capitalization stood at ¥52.2 billion (US $380.5 million) in the same year. Headquarters are in Tōkyō and Ōsaka.

Nichinan   日南[市]

City in southern Miyazaki Prefecture, Kyūshū, on the Hyūga Sea. A former castle town, the city is noted for early harvest rice, vegetables, and mandarin oranges. It is also a fishing base for bonito and tuna. Its pulp industry utilizes the cedars that grow in the city. Nichinan is a part of the Nichinan Coast Quasi-National Park. Pop: 49,178.

Nichinan Coast 日南海岸

(Nichinan Kaigan). Area on the Pacific coast of southern Miyazaki Prefecture, Kyūshū, extending from the island of Aoshima to the city of Kushima. Its heavily indented shoreline is characterized by spectacularly eroded rock formations. Subtropical plants grow naturally here. Length: 50 km (31 mi).

Nichiō 日奥

(1565–1630). Buddhist priest of the NICHIREN SECT and founder of the FUJU FUSE SECT. Born in Kyōto. Nichiō became a monk at the temple Myōkakuji, and in 1592 its abbot. In 1595 he objected to the Nichiren sect's participation in an interdenominational Buddhist service proposed by the hegemon TOYOTOMI HIDEYOSHI. His objection was based mainly on the Nichiren tradition that a believer in the LOTUS SUTRA as interpreted by NICHIREN should neither receive offerings from nonbelievers, such as Hideyoshi, nor give to them (*fuju fuse*; literally, "not giving, not receiving"). Nichiō's intransigence created a division among Nichiren sectarians, and in 1599 the future shōgun TOKUGAWA IEYASU summoned both parties for a debate, which resulted in Nichiō's exile. He returned to Kyōto in 1612 and continued to criticize compromisers in the sect. In 1691 the Fuju Fuse sectarians were outlawed by the shogunate; they survived as a clandestine group until 1876, when the ban was lifted.

Nichirei Corporation [株]ニチレイ

(Nichirei). Integrated processed-food company, engaged in production, refrigeration, distribution, trade, and marketing of food products. Incorporated in 1942. Nichirei's operations comprise 4 food-manufacturing plants, 2 processing plants, 66 refrigerated warehouses, 24 sales offices, 10 overseas representative offices, and 17 major overseas affiliates. Its products are sold under the brand name Nichirei. Sales for the fiscal year ending March 1991 totaled ¥386.1 billion (US $2.8 billion), and the company was capitalized at ¥30.1 billion (US $219.4 million). Headquarters are in Tōkyō.

Nichiren 日蓮

(1222–82). Buddhist monk. Founder of the NICHIREN SECT (also known as the Hokke or Lotus sect) of Buddhism. Nichiren was born in the village of Kominato in Awa Province (now part of Chiba Prefecture). Sent at the age of 12 to be educated at a nearby TENDAI SECT temple, Kiyosumidera, Nichiren underwent a crisis stemming from doubts about the efficacy of Pure Land (Jōdo) beliefs (see PURE LAND BUDDHISM). Ordained at the age of 16 as Zeshōbō Renchō, he studied at the major centers of Buddhist learning in the Kansai area. His early works show a devotion to esoteric Tendai and SHINGON SECT teachings (see also ESOTERIC BUDDHISM) as well as to theories of absolute monism derived from Tendai HONGAKU (original enlightenment) ideas, a growing faith in the LOTUS SUTRA (Skt: *Saddharmapuṇḍarīka-sūtra*; J: *Myōhō renge kyō* or *Hokekyō*), and a strong dislike for Pure Land Buddhism.

On 26 May 1253, Nichiren preached against the Jōdo and ZEN sects at Kiyosumidera. A subsequent quarrel with the local magnate Tōjō Kagenobu, a Pure Land devotee, led to Nichiren's expulsion from Awa the following year. Settling in Kamakura, Nichiren developed faith in the supremacy of the Lotus Sutra with its doctrine of universal salvation and the eternal Buddha

Śākyamuni. Nichiren evolved a belief in the practice called *daimoku* (title), a chanting recitation of the phrase NAMU MYŌHŌ RENGE KYŌ ("I take my refuge in the Lotus Sutra") as an invocation affirming the devotee's belief and conferring salvation. He also developed his early idea of "blasphemy" (heresy, unbelief in the Lotus Sutra). Based on this idea, Nichiren completed in 1260 his RISSHŌ ANKOKU RON (A Treatise on Pacifying the State by Establishing Orthodoxy). Presented to Hōjō Tokiyori (1227–63), the de facto head of the Kamakura shogunate, it led to attacks on Nichiren and his exile to Izu in 1261.

Nichiren's life in Izu is not well documented. His surviving works show increasing doubts about esoteric Buddhism. The organization of his so-called five principles (*gogi*), which provide the rationale behind Nichiren's turn toward the Lotus Sutra, are also found in his writings from this period. From this period Nichiren felt a growing sense of his mission as the persecuted ascetic (*gyōja*) of the Lotus Sutra, the messenger of the Buddha in the latter days (*mappō*; see ESCHATOLOGY).

Released from exile in 1263, he returned to Kamakura. His expanded denunciations of the Jōdo, Shingon, and other sects and of prominent monks embroiled him in lawsuits, while his aggressive behavior and the arming of his followers led to his arrest in September 1271. Nichiren was banished to the island of Sado. The most notable of his apologetic works from this time is the *Kaimoku shō* (1272, Opening the Eyes). Nichiren also began to compose his distinctive MANDALA (written in Chinese characters), which arrange Buddhas, bodhisattvas, and other deities around the *daimoku* of the Lotus Sutra. He wrote the *Kanjin honzon shō* (The Object of Worship in Contemplation) for his inner circle of disciples in the spring of 1273.

A movement to secure Nichiren's release finally succeeded, and he left Sado on 21 April 1274. Nichiren settled at Minobu in Kai Province (now Yamanashi Prefecture), where he remained for eight years. Repeatedly ill from 1278, Nichiren left Minobu in 1282 to visit a hot spring but died before reaching it.

His religion, a fusion of several elements of old and new Buddhism, was upheld by his magnetic personality and clearly filled a need among lower-level warriors, from whom he drew many of his followers and who saw in him a master not unlike their military leaders. His frequently intemperate language and reputation as a fanatic must be balanced against his scholarship and his genuine concern for his followers.

Nichiren sect 日蓮宗

(Nichirenshū). Also known as the Hokke or Lotus sect. One of the new Buddhist sects of the Kamakura period (1185–1333), founded in 1253 by the Tendai monk NICHIREN. Based on faith in the LOTUS SUTRA (Skt: *Saddharmapuṇḍarīka-sūtra*), a Mahāyāna Buddhist scripture known in Japan as the *Myōhō renge kyō* or *Hokekyō*, this sect is noted for its practice of chanting as an invocation the *daimoku* (title) of that scripture, NAMU MYŌHŌ RENGE KYŌ ("I take my refuge in the Lotus Sutra").

The Nichiren movement is so sharply divided into various branches that a common statement of belief is not easy to formulate; certain doctrines are common to most sects, but the sects frequently interpret them in different ways.

In common with certain aspects of TENDAI

Nichiren This detail from a late-13th-century painting shows the founder of the Lotus sect of Buddhism seated in a chair draped with fabric bearing a lotus-root pattern.

SECT teachings, the Lotus Sutra is declared to be the supreme scripture of the Buddha. The first half of the scripture (the *shakumon* or "manifestation doctrine") reveals the attainment of Buddhahood by all beings; the second half (the *hommon* or "fundamental aspect") reveals the eternal nature of the Buddha. For the Nichiren sect the *hommon* is the more important. The metaphysical teaching of the Lotus Sutra is the Tendai monistic concept of "3,000 realms in one thought" (*ichinen sanzen*); this is contained in the *daimoku* of the Lotus Sutra, which, when chanted with faith, yields all the merits of Buddhahood to even the simplest believer.

The Lotus Sutra is to have its true meaning revealed only in the current age on the basis of "five principles" (*gogi*): (1) its teaching is the highest; (2) the faculties of beings are now lowly and therefore need this highest teaching; (3) the "time" is *mappō* (see ESCHATOLOGY), the third and most degenerate age of Buddhism starting in 1052; (4) the "country," namely Japan, will be the center of propagation; and (5) the "order of propagation" or later the "teacher," namely the bodhisattva Jōgyō (Skt: Viśiṣṭacaritra), is a disciple of the eternal Buddha, whose reincarnation is Nichiren. The essence of the Lotus Sutra is thought to be manifested in "three great secret doctrines" (*sandai hihō*): (1) the *honzon* (object of worship), the nature of which is most commonly a mandala in Chinese characters with the names of Buddhas, bodhisattvas, and other deities arranged around either the *daimoku* or a statue of the Buddha Śākyamuni attended by Jōgyō and three other companion bodhisattvas; (2) the *kaidan* ("ordination platform"), meant as a replacement for the Tendai center at Mt. Hiei (see HIEIZAN); and (3) the title (*daimoku*).

Faith in the Lotus Sutra is to be shown by the aggressive refutation of other beliefs (*shakubuku*; "break and subdue"), a practice that deliberately courts persecution to expiate past sins. This is known as "reading the Lotus Sutra with one's body" (*shikidoku*). Salvation is variously characterized as "becoming a Buddha in one's present body" (SOKUSHIN JŌBUTSU) or rebirth in the Pure Land of the eternal Buddha (Ryōzen Jōdo; "the Pure Land of the Spiritual Mountain").

History since Nichiren——Just before his death in 1282, Nichiren chose six senior monks as his spiritual heirs: Nichiji (b 1250), Nitchō (1252–1317), Nikō (1253–1314), Nikkō (1246–1333), Nichirō (1245–1320),

and Nisshō (1236–1323). Except for Nichiji (who went to the Asian mainland in 1295), these monks, with Nichiren's old warrior disciple Toki Tsunenobu (known as Nichijō; 1216–99), founded the original lineages in the Kantō region.

The lack of a single leader, the ambiguities of Nichiren's teachings and the early lack of a complete standard canon of his writings, the influx of Tendai ideas, the tendency to create exclusive secret doctrines or "oral transmissions" supposedly from Nichiren himself, and temperamental differences among the disciples made schisms almost inevitable. Schisms in the movement developed in two phases, first in the Kantō area and then in Kyōto.

The Nichiren sect counted about half the populace of Kyōto as adherents in 1469 and became an autonomous power in the region until 1536, when monk armies from Mt. Hiei destroyed the Nichiren establishments in Kyōto. Even after the sect was allowed to rebuild its temples, it never regained its former power. Its general decline in the Kansai region was hastened by persecutions under military dictator ODA NOBUNAGA.

The real power of the Nichiren movement shifted in modern times to lay-oriented movements largely outside the traditional sects and generally labeled "Nichirenism" (Nichiren *shugi*). Popular religious organizations arose, characterized by faith healing and the promise of benefit in this life, shamanistic practices (in many cases ancestor worship), strong group-consciousness, and more or less aggressive proselytization. These groups are represented now by the REIYŪKAI, founded in 1925; its offshoot, the RISSHŌ KŌSEIKAI, founded in 1938; and the SŌKA GAKKAI, founded in 1930. Its turbulent history has left the Nichiren movement sharply divided yet has also endowed it with a range of thought that has allowed it to appeal to wide segments of Japanese society and thus to expand beyond traditional sectarian institutions in a way unparalleled by any other Buddhist sect.

Nichiro Corporation [株]ニチロ

(Nichiro). Company engaged primarily in fishing and fish processing. Incorporated in 1907. A pioneer in whaling and fishing in northern waters, Nichiro is now a comprehensive food company, processing and producing canned foods and frozen and refrigerated foods under the brand name Day Break. Main seafood product lines include salmon, trout, crab, tuna, octopus, squid, and shrimp; the company also sells canned bamboo shoots and asparagus. It has more than 30 overseas subsidiaries, purchasing organizations, and representative offices worldwide, including production facilities in Chile, Indonesia, and the United States. Sales for the fiscal year ending March 1991 totaled ¥222.5 billion (US $1.6 billion), and capitalization stood at ¥8.2 billion (US $59.8 million). Headquarters are in Tōkyō.

Nichiro Sensō → Russo-Japanese War

nigirimeshi 握り飯

(rice balls). Also called *onigiri*. A food consisting of boiled rice (MESHI) that is molded with the hands, which are dampened to prevent the rice from sticking to them, into round, triangular, or cylindrical shapes. A small amount of another ingredient is often placed in the center of a rice ball, most commonly an UMEBOSHI (pickled plum), some TSUKUDANI (delicacies simmered in soy sauce), small pieces of salted salmon, or bonito flakes flavored with soy sauce. Rice balls are often wrapped in NORI (a kind of dried seaweed) and sometimes sprinkled with sesame seeds. Rice balls are often made for picnics and packed in lunch boxes.

Nihombashi 日本橋

District in the northern part of Chūō Ward, Tōkyō. The area takes its name from a bridge, the Nihombashi, first built here in 1603. As the starting point for the Tōkaidō and other highways leading out of the shogunal capital, the bridge served as the symbolic center of Japan during the Edo period (1600–1868), and the district flourished as a commercial center. Today it is a major shopping area, with many department stores clustered around the bridge; to the west is a financial center where the Bank of Japan is located; to the east is the Kabutochō district, home of the Tōkyō Stock Exchange and many securities firms.

nihommachi 日本町

Japanese communities in Southeast Asia in the 16th and 17th centuries. The VERMILION SEAL SHIP TRADE, especially in the first half of the 17th century, took Japanese to almost every part of Southeast Asia. Various edicts against Christianity, beginning in 1585, caused the exodus of many Japanese Christians. The earliest Japanese settlement overseas was in Dilao (now part of Manila) in the Philippines, where early-17th-century documents record a Japanese population of some 3,000, the largest known. The second largest appears to have been in Ayuthia (now Ayutthaya, Thailand); the Japanese settlers there were active in trade under the leadership of YAMADA NAGAMASA. Other *nihommachi* were in San Miguel (now part of Manila); Tourane (now Da Nang) and Faifo, in Vietnam; and Phnom Penh and Ponhealu, in Cambodia. Many Japanese were also residents in Tainan, Taiwan; Batavia (now Jakarta, Indonesia); and Macao. With the implementation of the NATIONAL SECLUSION policy in the 1630s, these communities lost contact with Japan and gradually lost their identity.

Nihommatsu 二本松[市]

City in central Fukushima Prefecture, northern Honshū. It developed as a castle town in the Muromachi period (1333–1568) and later became a post-station town. A once prosperous silk-reeling industry is being replaced by the furniture industry. Attractions are the site of the old castle; Adachigahara Plateau, supposedly the site of the devil's den mentioned in a Nō play by the same name; and chrysanthemum and lantern festivals, both in October. The mountain ADATARASAN and the DAKE HOT SPRING are nearby. Pop: 34,927.

Nihon 日本

Influential Meiji-period (1868–1912) newspaper launched by KUGA KATSUNAN in 1889. It championed NIHON SHUGI (literally, "Japanism"), the term for a kind of Japanese nationalism that sprang up in the late 19th century in reaction to the growing tide of Westernization that followed the Meiji Restoration. Stressing the importance of native Japanese traditions, it advocated democracy by means of a people-oriented constitutional system. *Nihon* ceased publication in 1914.

Nihon Bungaku Hōkokukai 日本文学報国会

(Patriotic Association for Japanese Literature). Society created in 1942 (during World War II) to mobilize Japanese writers and to propagate a Japan-centered view of the world. Organized with the aid of the government's intelligence bureau, it had more than 3,000 members, led by such writers as TOKUTOMI SOHŌ, KUME MASAO, Nakamura Murao (1886–1949), YOSHIKAWA EIJI, and KIKUCHI KAN. It published a newsletter, *Bungaku hōkoku* (Serving the Country through Literature), and held two annual Great Asian literary congresses. It also sponsored anthologies of nationalistic poems and war novels. The society was disbanded after Japan's defeat in 1945.

Nihon Bungeika Kyōkai 日本文芸家協会

(Japan Writers' Association). A professional organization, originally founded in 1926 as Bungeika Kyōkai (Writers' Association) for the protection of the rights of writers and for their mutual aid. The association adopted its present name in 1946. It has published the *Bungei nenkan* (Literary Almanac) annually since 1928. In 1989 there were 1,643 members.

Nihon Cement Co, Ltd 日本セメント[株]

(Nihon Semento). Formerly known as Asano Cement. Major cement manufacturer. The company originated in a government-built cement factory bought by ASANO SŌICHIRŌ in 1884. Besides various types of cement, the product line includes building and construction materials, steel, and industrial equipment. Sales for the fiscal year ending March 1991 totaled ¥212.9 billion (US $1.6 billion). The company was capitalized at ¥43.5 billion (US $317.1 million) in the same year. Headquarters are in Tōkyō.

Nihon Chiri Gakkai → Association of Japanese Geographers

Nihon daijisho 日本大辞書

Japanese-language dictionary compiled by the novelist YAMADA BIMYŌ and published in 1892–93 in 12 volumes. With ŌTSUKI FUMIHIKO's *Genkai* (1889–91), it was the first Japanese-language dictionary to employ a modern format. Despite the uneven quality of its definitions, its indication of word accents was innovative.

Nihondaira 日本平

Upland between the cities of Shimizu and Shizuoka, central Shizuoka Prefecture, central Honshū. Near the top of Udosan (307 m; 1,007 ft), it is known for its panoramic view of Mt. Fuji (Fujisan). This popular recreation and resort area is covered largely by tea plantations and is the center of Nihondaira Prefectural Natural Park.

Nihon eihō → swimming

Nihon Fukushi University 日本福祉大学

(Nihon Fukushi Daigaku). A coeducational private university in Chita District, Aichi

Prefecture. It was established in 1953 as the Chūbu Shakai Jigyō Daigaku (Chūbu Junior College of Social Work). In 1957 the school became a four-year university and took its present name. It maintains faculties of social welfare and economics. Enrollment in 1989 was 5,531.

nihonga 日本画

(Japanese-style painting). Paintings that have been executed in accordance with traditional Japanese conventions and techniques, and using traditional materials, and that do not display the strong influence of Western painting styles and techniques. The term *nihonga* was introduced in the Meiji period (1868–1912) to distinguish works executed in this manner from Western-style painting (YŌGA).

Nihonga are painted on WASHI (Japanese paper) or silk in monochrome or polychrome, using brushes of a wide range of sizes. Monochrome paintings are normally done with *sumi*, or Chinese ink, which is made of soot from burned wood or oil mixed with *nikawa* (hide or fishbone glue). Pigments for polychrome paintings are derived from natural substances, such as minerals, insects, shells, or plants, that are prepared, ground to a powder, and bound in a medium of *nikawa* and water. In the past, most *nihonga* were mounted on hanging scrolls (see KAKEMONO), hand scrolls (see EMAKIMONO), or sliding or folding screens (see SCREEN AND WALL PAINTING), but today many are framed.

The expressive power of monochrome *nihonga* derives from modulation of ink tones in the drawing of lines and from shading of pigments in polychrome works. As a consequence of the fundamental importance placed on line, *mokkotsu*—painting forms without outlines—developed as a contrasting technique, and it has often been used in depictions of birds and flowers. Other devices are application of areas of gold or silver foil, scattering of small pieces of foil over a painting, and layering of pigment over a portion of still damp paint of another color to achieve a contingent effect (TARASHIKOMI).

The influence of Western painting has led to the introduction of methods such as impasto and to the abandonment of outline in polychrome paintings. In recent years it has become increasingly difficult to clearly distinguish, on the basis of painterly technique and the surfaces and pigments used, between *yōga* and *nihonga*. Nevertheless, at the annual Nitten exhibition paintings are classified according to these categories, and at the Inten only *nihonga* are exhibited.

Nihon Gakushiin→Japan Academy

Nihongi→Nihon shoki

Nihongo kyōiku jiten 日本語教育事典

(Encyclopedia of Japanese Language Education). One-volume encyclopedia compiled by the Society for Teaching Japanese as a Foreign Language and published in 1982. This compilation of new information about the teaching of Japanese to non-native speakers is intended for use by both language instructors and interested laypeople. The encyclopedia is grouped into sections dealing with pronunciation, grammar, vocabulary and diction, usage, the Japanese writing system, language skills, methods of instruction, and audiovisual education. Lists of organizations, researchers, and educators in the field of Japanese language teaching are also included.

Nihonjin 日本人

(The Japanese). Magazine of criticism. First published in April 1888 by MIYAKE SETSUREI, SHIGA SHIGETAKA, and the other organizers of the group known as the SEIKYŌSHA. The title of the magazine, *Nihonjin*, indicates the traditionalism of the editors, who were against the uncritical Westernization popular during the early Meiji period (1868–1912). The magazine not only stressed traditionalism by declaring the inherent value of the state itself, but called for the autonomous reform of Japanese society without slavishly imitating the West; it also criticized the social ills produced under the capitalist system. Because of its strong criticism of the government, publication of the magazine was frequently prohibited, and there were two periods in which it changed its name to *Ajia* (Asia). In 1907 the magazine changed its name to *Nihon oyobi nihonjin* (Japan and the Japanese) when reporters from the newspaper *Nihon* (Japan) joined the staff. It ceased publication on 1 September 1923.

Nihonkai Kaisen→Tsushima, Battle of

Nihon keizai shimbun 日本経済新聞

Japan's largest financial and business trade newspaper with a nationwide circulation. In 1876 MASUDA TAKASHI, general manager of Mitsui Bussan (MITSUI & CO, LTD), launched a business weekly, the *Chūgai bukka shimpō*, which became a daily in 1885. In 1889 its name was changed to *Chūgai shōgyō shimpō*. It was divested from Mitsui and came under a privately managed partnership. In 1911 the Chūgai Shōgyō Shimpōsha was organized as a company to run the paper. In 1942 it absorbed two other business papers, including the *Nikkan kōgyō shimbun*, along with a handful of trade journals to form the *Nihon sangyō keizai shimbun*. The *Nikkan kōgyō* became independent again in 1945, and in 1946 the company (Chūgai Shōgyō Shimpōsha) and paper (*Nihon sangyō keizai shimbun*) took the present name of *Nihon keizai shimbun*. The company also publishes magazines and books. Circulation was 3.0 million in 1991.

Nihon kiryaku 日本紀略

(Outline Record of Japan). Also known as *Nihon kirui* and *Hennen kiryaku*. A history of Japan, of unknown authorship, compiled late in the Heian period (794–1185). Its 34 chapters cover the mythological age of the gods and historical times to the reign of Emperor Go-Ichijō (1016–36). The mythological section is taken from the NIHON SHOKI (720).

Nihon kokugo daijiten 日本国語大辞典

(Dictionary of the Japanese Language). Twenty-volume Japanese-language dictionary compiled by the Nihon Daijiten Kankōkai and published by Shōgakukan, Inc, in 1972–76. The dictionary, based on earlier dictionaries such as the DAI NIHON KOKUGO JITEN but incorporating a range of new materials, contains approximately 500,000 entries. One of the most important features of the dictionary is its attention to etymology and history of usage of the words listed. It also contains more definitions of words dating from postmedieval Japan than many of its predecessors and more illustrative source citations than any other dictionary currently available.

Nihon Minka Shūraku Hakubutsukan Old farmhouses are arranged in a village-like exhibit at this outdoor museum in Ōsaka Prefecture. The L-shaped building pictured here was transported from northern Japan.

Nihonkoku Kempō→Constitution of Japan

Nihon kokusei chizuchō→ National Atlas of Japan

Nihon Kyōsantō→Japan Communist Party

Nihon Minka Shūraku Hakubutsukan 日本民家集落博物館

(Open-Air Museum of Old Japanese Farmhouses). Outdoor museum established in 1960 in the city of Toyonaka, Ōsaka Prefecture. On exhibit are 11 structures, the majority of which are traditional farm buildings brought to the museum site from around Japan and rebuilt. Traditional farm tools and items used in the home are also on display. Three of the farmhouses on exhibit have been designated Important Cultural Properties.

Nihon Minshutō 日本民主党

(Japan Democratic Party). Conservative political party formed in November 1954. Not to be confused with the MINSHUTŌ (Democratic Party). The party drew its 140 members in the Diet from three conservative groups: the Japan Reform Party (Nihon Kaishintō), the Japan Liberal Party (Nihon Jiyūtō), and a faction of the LIBERAL PARTY (Jiyūtō) opposed to prime minister YOSHIDA SHIGERU. HATOYAMA ICHIRŌ was president, SHIGEMITSU MAMORU vice-president, and KISHI NOBUSUKE party secretary. With the resignation of the Yoshida cabinet in December 1954, Hatoyama formed his first cabinet. In the general election of February 1955 the Nihon Minshutō became the dominant party, and Hatoyama formed his second cabinet. In November 1955 the Nihon Minshutō merged with the Liberal Party in the so-called *hoshu gōdō* (conservative merger) to form the LIBERAL DEMOCRATIC PARTY (Jiyū Minshutō). See also POLITICAL PARTIES.

Nihon Montoku Tennō jitsuroku →Rikkokushi

Nihon Musantō 日本無産党

(Japan Proletarian Party). Left-wing political party formed in March 1937 with Katō Kanjū (1892–1978) as chairman and SUZUKI MOSABURŌ as secretary general; made up mainly of labor union members. Katō won a seat in the lower house of the Diet in the general election held in April 1937. The party failed in its effort to create a popular front against the government's militaristic and inflationary policies. In December 1937 the government arrested the leaders of the Nihon Musantō in the POPULAR FRONT INCIDENT, and the party was disbanded.

Nihon Nōsan Kōgyō KK

日本農産工業[株]

(Nihon Nōsan Kōgyō). Formula-feed manufacturer; also produces pork and poultry products. Incorporated in 1931, it doubled its business by merging with the feed companies of the Mitsubishi and Tōkyū groups in 1971. For the fiscal year ending March 1991, sales totaled ¥106.0 billion (US $772.6 million), and capitalization was ¥7.4 billion (US $53.9 million). Headquarters are in Yokohama.

Nihon rettō kaizō ron   日本列島改造論

(plan for the remodeling of the Japanese archipelago). An economic plan promoting decentralized development that was proposed in 1972 by Prime Minister TANAKA KAKUEI. The proposal was initially put forth in Tanaka's best-selling book by the same name, published a month before he became prime minister. The goal of the plan was to deconcentrate industry from the heavily populated and polluted Tōkyō-Ōsaka industrial belt to form regional industrial centers linked by superhighways and high-speed trains.

Critics argued that the plan would spread pollution throughout the country, undermine agricultural production, and increase Japanese dependence on imported raw materials and food. Real estate speculation based on the plan pushed land prices to unprecedented levels. The recession following the OIL CRISIS OF 1973 led to the scuttling of the plan. See also COMPREHENSIVE NATIONAL LAND DEVELOPMENT PLAN.

Nihon Rōmanha   日本浪曼派

(Japanese Romantic school). Nationalistic literary movement active in the mid-1930s through World War II; also the name of the magazine published by the same group. It advocated patriotism and sought to instill pride in the native literary tradition. The movement's principal organizers were YASUDA YOJŪRŌ, Nakatani Takao (b 1901), and KAMEI KATSUICHIRŌ.

The Nihon Rōmanha grew out of an earlier literary movement centered around the magazine *Kogito*, first published in 1932. The magazine *Nihon rōmanha* was published from 1935 to 1938 as a forum for young authors interested in bringing about a revival of Japanese classical literature. By 1938 more than 50 noted writers had joined the movement, including DAZAI OSAMU, SATŌ HARUO, DAN KAZUO, ITŌ SHIZUO, NAKAGAWA YOICHI, and HAGIWARA SAKUTARŌ. The movement had a great impact on young intellectuals during the war years, offering them a kind of solace in the face of political uncertainty and the threat of violent death. Following Japan's defeat in World War II, the Nihon Rōmanha movement was criticized for its support of Japanese militarism through literature. However, in 1979 a new magazine, *Rōmanha*, was begun, promising to carry out the movement's original mission of looking to the Japanese classics as a source for a new literature.

Nihon Rōnōtō   日本労農党

(Japan Labor-Farmer Party; also called Nichirōtō). "Proletarian" party founded by the moderate wing of the RŌDŌ NŌMINTŌ in December 1926.While trying throughout 1927 to organize a united noncommunist front of left-wing parties, the Nihon Rōnōtō campaigned for tenant rights, reduction of utility rates, and Japan's noninvolvement on the China mainland. This program won it only one seat in the 1928 election. Later in 1928 it attempted to expand its power by creating a new party for leftists who had survived the government's banning of the Rōdō Nōmintō and mass arrest of communists in the MARCH 15TH INCIDENT. The resulting merger of the Nihon Rōnōtō with the Nihon Nōmintō (Japan Farmers' Party), some local labor parties, and the remnants of the Rōdō Nōmintō led to the formation of the Nihon Taishūtō (Japan Masses Party) in December 1928.

Nihon ryōiki   日本霊異記

Also called *Nihon reiiki.* The earliest Japanese collection of *setsuwa* (Buddhist moral tales; see SETSUWA BUNGAKU). Compiled around 822 by Kyōkai (also known as Keikai), a Buddhist priest of the temple YAKUSHIJI in Nara. The 116 tales depict intervention in human affairs by supernatural elements. The Buddhist message of cause and effect is the shared theme and the major source of unity in the work.

The *Ryōiki* is written entirely in the hybrid form of Chinese known as HENTAI KAMBUN. The simple stories generally fit into two categories: Buddhist stories, such as those about men reborn as cows or sent to the Land of the Dead because they violated the Buddhist law, and non-Buddhist stories. The *Ryōiki* was inspired by such Chinese writings as the *Meihōki* (Ch: *Mingbaoji* or *Ming-pao-chi*). It had an extensive influence on later *setsuwa* collections, such as the *Konjaku monogatari* (ca 1120), as well as on other genres.

Nihon sandai jitsuroku→
Rikkokushi

Nihon Sankei   日本三景

(The Three Views of Japan). This refers to the three most famous scenic spots in Japan: MATSUSHIMA, a group of islands in Miyagi Prefecture; AMANOHASHIDATE, a pine-tree-covered sandbar in Kyōto Prefecture; and ITSUKUSHIMA, an island in Hiroshima Prefecture.

Nihon Shakai Shugi Dōmei
日本社会主義同盟

(Japan Socialist League). Confederation of socialist organizations formed in December 1920 by YAMAKAWA HITOSHI, SAKAI TOSHIHIKO, and other leftist leaders; Japan's first alliance of socialist, anarchist, and labor groups. The SHINJINKAI and other left-wing intellectual groups called for an all-encompassing union of labor and socialist organizations. With 3,000 members, the resulting Japan Socialist League organized groups and lecture meetings throughout the country. However, the organization suffered from a lack of ideological unity and an inability to go beyond mere propaganda because of the heterogeneous character of its membership. The alliance was also subject to heavy government suppression and was forced to disband in May 1921. After its dissolution, communists and anarchists began to break away from the socialist movement.

Nihon Shakaitō→Japan Socialist
Party

Nihon shihon shugi hattatsu shi kōza   日本資本主義発達史講座

(Lectures on the History of the Development of Japanese Capitalism). Landmark collection of works by Marxist scholars who supported the JAPAN COMMUNIST PARTY; published in seven volumes by Iwanami Shoten in 1932–33. The authors, under the direction of NORO EITARŌ, HIRANO YOSHITARŌ, YAMADA MORITARŌ, and Ōtsuka Kinnosuke (1892–1977), analyzed various aspects of Japanese capitalism to clarify the revolution they believed was imminent in Japan in view of the worldwide economic crisis. They sought to prove that the revolution would be a "bourgeois-democratic" upheaval by pointing out the feudal elements remaining within Japanese capitalism. From the title of this collection, the coterie of scholars who subscribed to this viewpoint came to be known as the KŌZAHA ("Lectures" faction). Publication of the work intensified the continuing dispute over revolutionary strategy between supporters of the Communist Party and its opponents, the so-called RŌNŌHA, who argued that the impending revolution would be a socialist one. See NIHON SHIHON SHUGI RONSŌ.

Nihon shihon shugi ronsō
日本資本主義論争

(the debate on Japanese capitalism). Pre–World War II debate among Japanese Marxist economists concerning the nature and degree of capitalist development in Japan. Although certain parts of this debate began in the early 1920s and continued well into the postwar period, the full-scale debate can be said to extend roughly from 1927 to 1937, from the establishment of the journal *Rōnō* (Labor-Farmer) to the mass arrests of Marxist university professors between 1936 and 1938. The debate divided Marxist economists into two schools of thought: the KŌZAHA ("Lectures" faction) and RŌNŌHA (Labor-Farmer faction), so called because of publications associated with each group. The Kōzaha stressed what it considered to be the essentially feudal or "semifeudal" aspects of post-Meiji Japan, while the Rōnōha stressed the characteristics Japan shared with the more advanced capitalist nations.

Central Issues of the Debate—The main question addressed by the debate was whether to characterize Japan's economic development as purely capitalist in nature or as a kind of partial capitalist development resting on, and in some sense being determined by, a feudal or semifeudal base. To Kōzaha writers the MEIJI RESTORATION of 1868 had simply brought about a reconstitution of the feudal land system under an absolutist monarchy supported by a sociopolitical stratum of feudal landlords and capitalists. As a result of this analysis, they argued that socialist revolution in Japan must have as its prelude a bourgeois-democratic upheaval that would clear away these feudal and absolutist obstacles. The Rōnōha, on the other hand, saw the Meiji Restoration as marking the end of feudalism in Japan and as the beginning of full-scale capitalist development; accordingly, they believed that Japan was poised for immediate transformation by socialist revolution.

Because of the highly politicized nature of the academic world during this period, the course of the debate was often influenced by political affiliation and external pressures. Indeed, the debate was intimately tied to changes within the JAPAN COMMUNIST PARTY (JCP). By 1924 the JCP had divided into two opposing groups, whose different analyses of the level of Japan's political development were direct forerunners of the arguments expanded in the debate on Japanese capitalism. Writings supporting the JCP position were collected in the 1932–33 NIHON SHIHON SHUGI HATTATSU SHI KŌZA (Lectures on the History of the Development of Japanese Capitalism), the seven-volume lecture series (*kōza*) by which this school of thought came to be known. See also COMINTERN 1927 THESIS and COMINTERN 1932 THESIS.

The Kōza position came to be exemplified in the works of such scholars as NORO EITARŌ, HATTORI SHISŌ, YAMADA MORITARŌ, and HIRANO YOSHITARŌ and in the aforementioned lecture series that they and others edited. Representative writers of the Rōnōha came to include KUSHIDA TAMIZŌ, SAKISAKA ITSURŌ, TSUCHIYA TAKAO, and other authors whose articles appeared in the journal *Rōnō* edited by ARAHATA KANSON, INOMATA TSUNAO, SUZUKI MOSABURŌ, YAMAKAWA HITOSHI, and others.

Postwar Debates—The immediate postwar period brought a renewed interest in Marxist economics, and with this came a variety of attempts to analyze Japan's new economic circumstances. Initially these were outgrowths of the prewar positions, but both Rōnō and Kōza positions subsequently underwent considerable change. The proliferation of individual studies and lines of argument within Marxist economics since the 1950s stands in sharp contrast to the unified schools of the prewar years. However, the fact that postwar studies are able to be conducted at a more sophisticated level is in large part due to the earlier research and discussion. Above all, the arguments of the prewar Rōnō and Kōza schools are suggestive interpretations of important historical and theoretical issues regarding the analyses of the uneven development of capitalism in Japan, as well as in other countries.

Nihon shoki 日本書紀

(Chronicle of Japan). Oldest official history of Japan covering events from the mythical age of the gods up to the reign of the empress JITŌ (r 686–697). The *Nihon shoki* was completed on 1 July 720. The *Nihon shoki*'s 30 volumes plus 1 volume of genealogical charts are the work of many people, including Prince TONERI, a son of Emperor TEMMU, and possibly FUJIWARA NO FUHITO, a powerful figure in the government. Although the official name of the work was *Nihongi*, other early documents refer to it as *Nihon shoki*.

Compilation—The process of compilation may be said to have begun in the 10th year of the reign of Temmu (681), when Prince Kawashima (657–691), a son of the former emperor TENJI, and 11 others were ordered to draw up an official copy of the genealogy of the imperial family (see TEIKI) and various other ancient records. In 714 Ki no Kiyohito (d 753) and Miyake no Fujimaro (dates unknown) were added to the team.

Of the 30 volumes, written in classical Chinese, the first and second deal with mythical times and are known as "Jindaiki." Volumes 3 to 30 cover events from the reign of Emperor JIMMU until that of Jitō. The *Nihon shoki* differs from the earlier KOJIKI in that it includes sections from the Chinese historical work WEI ZHI (*Wei chih*) and the Korean works *Paekche ki*, *Paekche pon'gi*, and *Paekche sinch'an* (see PAEKCHE). It also includes quotations from the IKI NO MURAJI HAKATOKO NO FUMI, an account by an official who visited Tang (T'ang) China, and the *Ilbon segi* (J: *Nihon seiki*), a history by the Korean

monk Tohyŏn (J: Dōken) from the kingdom of Koguryŏ. From volume 14 onward the accounts become increasingly detailed. Unlike the *Kojiki* the focus is on recent rather than mythical events.

Commentaries—The *Nihon shoki* was read and studied widely by government officials and intellectuals. *Hizen no Kuni fudoki* and *Bungo no Kuni fudoki*, gazetteers from the mid-8th century, both contain sections based on passages from the work. In addition the *Koki* (ca 738), a commentary on the TAIHŌ CODE, and annotations in the MAN'YŌSHŪ include quotations from the *Nihon shoki*. The genealogical work SHINSEN SHŌJIROKU (815) makes special mention of whether its information agrees with the *Nihon shoki*.

Several ancient manuscript copies of the *Nihon shoki* survive from the Nara (710–794) and Heian (794–1185) periods. Commentaries include the SHAKU NIHONGI, compiled in the late 13th century. Beginning in the Kamakura period (1185–1333) the *Nihon shoki* came to be viewed as a Shintō sacred text; commentaries from these times include Imbe no Masamichi's *Nihon shoki kuketsu* and ICHIJŌ KANEYOSHI's *Nihon shoki sanso*. In the Edo period (1600–1868) academic research appeared, notably *Nihon shoki tsūshō* by TANIGAWA KOTOSUGA; *Shoki shikkai* (or *Shoki shūge*) by Kawamura Hidene (1723–92) and his son Masune; SUZUKI SHIGETANE's commentary on the mythical sections, *Nihon shoki den*; and BAN NOBUTOMO's exegesis of volume 28, *Nagara no yamakaze*. See also RIKKOKUSHI.

Nihon Short-Wave Broadcasting Co, Ltd [株]日本短波放送

(Nihon Tampa Hōsō). Popularly known as Rajio Tampa. Japan's only private short-wave broadcasting station. The station was established in 1955, primarily with the support of the newspaper *Nihon keizai shimbun*. The station operates two separate channels, which are transmitted to all parts of Japan. Among its most popular shows are "Tōkyō Stock Market Conditions" and "Economic Report." The station also offers live broadcasts of horse racing. News broadcasts represent roughly half of the station's programming.

Nihon shugi 日本主義

(Japanism). A nationalistic ideology that emerged in the late 1880s; it opposed Western concepts and sought to preserve traditional Japanese values and institutions. It was originally advocated by intellectuals such as INOUE TETSUJIRŌ and TAKAYAMA CHOGYŪ in reaction to the policy of Westernization the government had pursued since the MEIJI RESTORATION of 1868. Stressing the uniqueness of Japan's national polity (KOKUTAI) and the supremacy of the state, Japanism was part of a conservative backlash that found its definitive expression in the IMPERIAL RESCRIPT ON EDUCATION of 1890. After being temporarily eclipsed by liberal currents in the Taishō period (1912–26), it reemerged during the upsurge of ultranationalism in the 1930s.

Nihon Shuruihanbai Co, Ltd 日本酒類販売[株]

(Nihon Shurui Hambai). Wholesaler of liquor and foods. Specializes in sales of Scotch whiskey and French and German wines. Incorporated in 1949. The company is the largest of its type in terms of quantity of liquor handled. Its strong buying and selling networks consist of 12 branches and 50 sales offices nationwide. Sales for the fiscal year

ending March 1990 totaled ¥348.7 billion (US $2.3 billion), and capitalization stood at ¥400.0 million (US $2.6 million). Headquarters are in Tōkyō.

Nihon Tetsudō Kaisha 日本鉄道会社

(Japan Railway Company; became Nihon Tetsudō Kabushiki Kaisha in 1893). The first and, until its nationalization in November 1906, the largest private railway company in Japan; founded in November 1881 by a group of nobles and former *samurai* led by IWAKURA TOMOMI with funds from the Fifteenth National Bank or "peers' bank." See also RAILWAYS.

Nihon Unisys, Ltd 日本ユニシス[株]

(Nihon Yunishisu). Firm engaged in the selling, leasing, and maintenance of electronic computer systems. Incorporated in 1958 as a joint venture of the then Sperry Rand Corporation of the United States and Mitsui & Co, Ltd. In April 1988 the company was merged with Burroughs Co, Ltd, and renamed Nihon Unisys, Ltd. The company acts as a systems integrator combining systems development and application engineering services with products ranging from mainframe computers to microcomputers. Sales for the fiscal year ending March 1991 totaled ¥324.6 billion (US $2.4 billion), and capitalization stood at ¥5.5 billion (US $40.1 million). Headquarters are in Tōkyō.

Nihon University 日本大学

(Nihon Daigaku). A private, coeducational university with central administrative offices in Chiyoda Ward, Tōkyō. It was founded as Nihon Hōritsu Gakkō (Nihon Law School) in 1889 by Yamada Akiyoshi (1844–92). In 1903 the school was reorganized and adopted its present name, and in 1920 it received university status. Since World War II, it has expanded its faculties and campuses throughout Japan and is now the largest private university in the country. There are faculties of law, arts and sciences, political science and economics, commerce, fine arts, science and technology, engineering, industrial engineering, medicine, dentistry, pharmaceutical science, agriculture and veterinary medicine, and international relations. University affiliates include a correspondence division, a two-year junior college, and 21 research institutes. Enrollment was 67,891 in 1989.

Niichi Suto → General Strike of 1947

Niigata 新潟[市]

Capital of Niigata Prefecture, central Honshū. It is the largest city on the Sea of Japan coast. During the Edo period (1600–1868) it was a prosperous port. With the signing of the ANSEI COMMERCIAL TREATIES (1858), it was opened to foreign trade. Still the largest port in the Hokuriku region, it has chemical, oil-refining, machinery, textile, and lumber industries. Pop: 486,097.

Niigata Engineering Co, Ltd [株]新潟鉄工所

(Niigata Tekkōsho). Manufacturer of ship engines, industrial machine tools, and rolling stock. It was established in 1895 as an iron works, producing and repairing oil-drilling equipment for the NIPPON OIL CO, LTD. The company later began production of railway cars and gasoline motors, becoming independent of Nippon Oil in 1910. After World War II, Niigata Engineering became a com-

Niigata Plain The river Shinanogawa flows across the plain, one of Japan's major rice-producing regions.

Niigata Prefecture Location and Prefectural Crest

Niijima Jō The first Japanese ordained as a Protestant minister, Niijima contributed greatly to the spread of Christian education in 19th-century Japan.

prehensive machinery maker. The company exports oil and chemical plants to the Middle and Near East, Latin America, Southeast Asia, and Africa. Sales for the fiscal year ending March 1991 totaled ¥165.1 billion (US $1.2 billion), and capitalization stood at ¥16.7 billion (US $121.7 million). Headquarters are in Tōkyō.

Niigata Plain   新潟平野

(Niigata Heiya). Also known as Echigo Plain. Located in central Niigata Prefecture, central Honshū. This floodplain with deltas of the rivers SHINANOGAWA and AGANOGAWA borders the Sea of Japan. The long, flat, and low coast has sand dunes and sand banks, while the interior of the plain is marshy. In 1924 a project to shorten the course of the Shinanogawa was completed. This plain yields the richest harvest of rice in Japan, and tulip bulbs and pears are now also grown. The region is also a source of natural gas. Most of the cities in the prefecture are located on the plain, the largest being NIIGATA. Area: approximately 2,000 sq km (800 sq mi).

Niigata Prefecture   新潟県

(Niigata Ken). Located in central Honshū and bounded on the north by the Sea of Japan and Yamagata Prefecture; on the east by Fukushima and Gumma prefectures; on the south by Nagano Prefecture; and on the west by Toyama Prefecture. The border areas are all covered by mountain ranges, and foothills and plateau areas cover most of the interior section. The major level areas are located along the coast. The island of SADO in the Sea of Japan is administratively a part of Niigata and one of the largest of Japan's offshore islands. The climate is noted for its heavy snowfall, especially in the interior mountain valleys.

Parts of the Niigata region were occupied by EZO tribesmen as late as the 7th century, but they were gradually conquered or pushed farther north by the advancing forces of the central government. The mainland portion of Niigata constituted Echigo Province after the TAIKA REFORM of 645, while Sado was designated a separate province. The Echigo area fell under the rule of various warlords, including the Uesugi family, after the Heian period (794–1185) and was divided into numerous domains in the Edo period (1600–1868). The discovery of gold deposits on Sado led the Tokugawa shogunate to take direct control over the island. The prefecture's present name dates from 1871; the current boundaries were established in 1886.

Niigata remains one of Japan's major rice-producers; forestry is also important. Large-scale industries, which include chemicals, machine production, and oil refining, are of recent development. The *sake*, textile, and furniture industries are active. The country's largest reserves of petroleum and natural gas are located here.

Sado's rugged scenery and distinctive folk culture attract visitors. The mountains of Niigata proper belong to the Jōshin'etsu Kōgen, Chūbu Sangaku, Bandai-Asahi, and Nikkō national parks. Well-known hot-spring resorts include Echigo Yuzawa, Myō-kō, Akakura, and Tsubame. Area: 12,579 sq km (4,857 sq mi); pop: 2,474,583; capital: Niigata. Other major cities include NAGAOKA, JŌETSU, SANJŌ, and KASHIWAZAKI.

Niigata University   新潟大学

(Niigata Daigaku). A coeducational national university located in the city of Niigata, Niigata Prefecture. Founded in 1949, the university maintains faculties of humanities, education, law, economics, science, engineering, and agriculture as well as schools of medicine and dentistry. Being located in the "snow belt" of Japan, Niigata University is also noted for its Research Institute for Hazards in Snowy Areas. Enrollment in 1989 was 9,407.

Niihama   新居浜[市]

City in eastern Ehime Prefecture, Shikoku, on an inlet of the Inland Sea. From the 17th century Niihama prospered as a port for shipping ore from the Besshi Copper Mine (closed in 1973; see BESSHI COPPER MINE LABOR DISPUTES). In the early part of the Meiji period (1868–1912) chemical, metal, and machine industries affiliated with the Sumitomo ZAI-BATSU developed here. More recently, a petrochemical complex has been constructed. Pop: 129,149.

Niijima Jō   新島襄

(1843–90) Also known as Joseph Hardy Neesima. The first ordained Protestant Japanese Christian; founder of Dōshisha (now DŌSHISHA UNIVERSITY). Born in Edo (now Tōkyō).

A desire to travel grew out of his extensive reading, and in 1864 he secretly departed without government permission for the United States. Niijima was baptized at Andover, Massachusetts, in 1866; graduated from Amherst College in 1870 (the first Japanese recipient of a degree from a Western college); and attended Andover Theological Seminary. In 1872 he became interpreter to the IWAKURA MISSION to the United States and Europe. At the 65th annual meeting of the Congregational mission board at Rutland, Vermont, in October 1874 he made a successful appeal for funds to start a Christian school in Japan. Founded in 1875 in Kyō-to, the new school, named Dōshisha, grew rapidly and became a university in 1912. The year before his death Amherst College honored Niijima with a Doctor of Laws degree, the first given a Japanese. He died in Ōiso and was buried on Nyakōji, a hill in eastern Kyōto.

Niimi   新見[市]

City in northwestern Okayama Prefecture, western Honshū. Niimi is an important railway center. Limestone quarrying and cement making are its principal industries. Farm products include tobacco, vegetables, and beef. Pop: 27,291.

Niinamesai   新嘗祭

(Festival for the New Tasting). Also called the Shinjōsai. An annual rite performed from ancient times in the 11th month, in which the emperor makes an offering of the newly harvested rice to the deities of heaven and earth (*tenjin chigi*). He expresses his gratitude to them for having protected the crops and then partakes of the offering in communion with the deities. The rite was supposedly first performed by the divine imperial ancestress, the sun goddess AMATERASU ŌMIKAMI, using rice newly harvested from the sacred fields in heaven. The Niinamesai is similar to the DAIJŌSAI in that it is an offering from the new harvest to all the deities of heaven and earth, but differs from the latter in that it is an annual rite, whereas the Daijōsai is held only at the accession of a new emperor. Hence the Niinamesai is omitted during the year that a Daijōsai is held. The observance of the Niinamesai was discontinued during the Ōnin War (1467–77) and was not formally resumed until 1739.

The basic ritual consists of the presentation by the emperor of the new rice and other offerings at a special hall (Shinkaden) in the palace; it is repeated the next morning and is then followed by a feast called Toyo no Akari no Sechie. The day on which the Niinamesai has been observed since 1873, 23 November, was chosen in 1948 as the date of a new national holiday, Labor Thanksgiving Day (Kinrō Kansha no Hi). See also KAN-NAMESAI.

Niitsu   新津[市]

City in central Niigata Prefecture, central Honshū. During the Edo period (1600–1868) Niitsu prospered as a market town. Its oil fields have been depleted, and it now grows rice and vegetables. Pop: 63,999.

Niiza   新座[市]

City in southern Saitama Prefecture, central Honshū. A copper-rolling center since the Edo period (1600–1868), Niiza began developing other industries from 1960. It is rapidly becoming a residential suburb of Tōkyō. Pop: 138,919.

Niji no Matsubara   虹ノ松原

Pine grove located in the city of Karatsu, Saga Prefecture, Kyūshū. Facing Karatsu Bay, the area is famous for its sand and beautiful pine trees, which are reputed to have been planted by the lord of Karatsu Castle in the early Edo period (1600–1868). Length: approximately 5 km (3 mi).

Nijō Castle   二条城

(Nijōjō). Residential castle located in the city of Kyōto. Construction was begun in 1569 by the warlord ODA NOBUNAGA and was completed by TOKUGAWA IEYASU, the founder of the Tokugawa shogunate (1603–1867). It served as a residence for shōguns during visits to Kyōto. Rectangular in layout, its main compound (*hommaru*) is distinctive in that it is built on a slightly raised earth bank. The main keep was brought from FUSHIMI CASTLE between 1624 and 1626, but it was destroyed by fire in 1750. The mansion-style buildings of the Ninomaru Palace in the secondary compound (*ninomaru*) have been designated a National Treasure. Nijō Castle is famous for its creaking floorboards, which are said to chirp like nightingales to warn of intruders. It is also known for the elegant design of its garden.

Nijōgawara no rakusho   二条河原落書

(Nijōgawara Scribblings or Nijōgawara Lampoons). A set of 88 lines of satirical verse posted by an anonymous author at the intersection of Nijō (Second Avenue) and the

Kamogawa riverbed (*kawara*) in Kyōto in September 1334. Although brief, the lampoons are an invaluable commentary on the state of confusion and social flux into which Kyōto was thrown after the destruction of the KAMAKURA SHOGUNATE (1192–1333) and during the effort of Emperor GO-DAIGO to restore imperial rule (see KEMMU RESTORATION). Lawlessness was rife, and both courtiers and warriors made spectacles of themselves as they sought to ape each other's ways. Above all, according to the lampoons, the old social statuses and distinctions were being rudely upset, especially by the rough *samurai* parvenus from the Kantō region intruding so conspicuously upon the traditional world of courtier elegance and privilege. The lampoons are contained in the chronicle KEMMU NENKAN KI. An English translation may be found in David John Lu, ed, *Sources of Japanese History*, vol 1 (1974).

Nijō Tameyo   二条為世

(1250?–1338). WAKA poet and leader of the dominant conservative Nijō poetic faction at court. Tameyo succeeded his father Fujiwara no Tameuji (1222–86) as head of the senior Nijō branch of the Mikohidari family of court poets and critics descended from FUJIWARA NO SADAIE (Fujiwara no Teika; 1162–1241). He compiled two imperial poetry anthologies, the *Shin gosenshū* (1303, New Later Collection) and the *Shoku senzaishū* (ca 1320, Collection of a Thousand Years, Continued).

Nijō Yoshimoto   二条良基

(1320–88). Courtier and statesman; scholar and authority on traditional customs and practices; poet and theoretician, particularly of RENGA (linked verse). Son of the regent Nijō Michihira (1288–1335), he served at court first under Emperor GO-DAIGO (r 1318–39) and later under several other emperors. He became head of the Fujiwara family and was four times regent. During the period of dynastic schism between the NORTHERN AND SOUTHERN COURTS, Yoshimoto stood out as a scholar and authority ranking in importance with ICHIJŌ KANEYOSHI and SANJŌNISHI SANETAKA as a custodian and transmitter of traditional aristocratic culture.

He was a pupil of the conservative poet TON'A and of the *renga* master GUSAI. Yoshimoto compiled the TSUKUBASHŪ, a collection of superior *renga* verses, and in 1372 a set of rules for linked verse known as *Renga shinshiki* (New Rules of *Renga*) or *Ōan shinshiki* (New Rules of the Ōan Era).

Nijūshikumi-doiya   二十四組問屋

(Twenty-Four Groups of Wholesalers; also pronounced Nijūyokumi-don'ya). A merchant association of wholesale suppliers (TOIYA) and shipping agents in the Ōsaka area during the Edo period (1600–1868). They supplied commercial goods to the TOKUMI-DOIYA, an association of 10 wholesale houses in Edo (now Tōkyō), shipping their goods in cargo vessels called KAISEN. Monopolizing freight transport between the two cities, the Ōsaka and Edo wholesalers formed a kind of exclusive shipping trade. The association was formed in 1694 with 10 groups; 14 others were added during the next 30 years. Each group specialized in one or several commodities. In 1784 the association was recognized by the Tokugawa shogunate as an official merchant guild (KABUNAKAMA). Abolished in 1841 under the TEMPŌ REFORMS, it was reorganized in 1851 and lasted until the Meiji Restoration (1868).

Nijūshi no hitomi   二十四の瞳

(Twenty-Four Eyes). A 1954 film written and directed by KINOSHITA KEISUKE. Considered Kinoshita's best work, *Nijūshi no hitomi* is a close adaptation of a short novel of the same title by TSUBOI SAKAE. In 1928 a young woman teacher (played by TAKAMINE HIDEKO) just out of normal school comes to a small village school on the Inland Sea island of SHŌDOSHIMA. She is assigned to a first-grade class of 12 boys and girls. She is later transferred to a less isolated consolidated school where her first pupils eventually show up as fifth graders. Teacher and pupils become friends for life. In two-and-a-half hours, the film covers three decades as they endure the hardships of economic depression, the militarism of the 1930s, and the tragedies of World War II and the immediate postwar period. Their individual fates become a microcosm that reveals the emotional history of the nation. Kinoshita, Takamine, and the film, which was a popular and critical success, received all of the major prizes for motion picture excellence in 1954.

Nikaidō family   二階堂氏

(Nikaidōshi). Family descended from the Southern Branch of the FUJIWARA FAMILY; founded by Fujiwara no Yukimasa. Yukimasa worked with MINAMOTO NO YORITOMO during establishment of the Kamakura shogunate (1192–1333) and was appointed to a position on the Administrative Board (MANDOKORO). He took his family name from the Nikaidō area of Kamakura, where he lived. The Nikaidō subsequently played an important role in the Mandokoro, the High Court (HIKITSUKE), and the Council of State (HYŌJŌSHŪ). The family was influential in the KEMMU RESTORATION government (1333–36) and in the Muromachi shogunate (1338–1573); they remained influential provincial lords throughout the medieval age (mid-12th–16th centuries).

Niki Etsuko   仁木悦子

(1928–86). Mystery writer. Real name Futsukaichi Mie. Born in Tōkyō. Afflicted with a degenerative bone disease at the age of four, she was tutored at home by her older brother. Her first work, *Neko wa shitte ita* (1957, The Cat Knew), won the Edogawa Rampo Prize. Niki achieved fame as the first woman in Japan to become a professional mystery writer. Her other works include the short story "Akai neko" (1980, Red Cat).

Nikikai   二期会

(Nikikai Opera Foundation). The largest opera company in Japan. Nikikai was founded in 1952 by four singers: Miyake Harue (b 1918), Kawasaki Shizuko (1919–82), Shibata Mutsumu (1913–88), and Nakayama Teiichi (b 1920), all graduates of Tōkyō Music School (now Tōkyō University of Fine Arts and Music). Its first production was Puccini's *La Bohème*. In 1966 Nikikai mounted a successful production of Wagner's *Tannhäuser*. The company went on to establish itself as a talented producer of German operas by staging many of Wagner's operas.

Nikkatsu Corporation   [株]にっかつ

(Nikkatsu). One of Japan's five major motion picture companies. Incorporated in 1912 as Nippon Katsudō Shashin, it is the oldest movie company in Japan. The company was forced to curtail production in 1971 due to financial difficulties. It also started producing

a series of so-called ROMAN PORUNO (soft-core pornography) films. However, in 1988 Nikkatsu returned to ordinary film production. The company is planning diversification into areas such as video software sales, new electronic media, and golf club management. Sales totaled ¥11.5 billion (US $61.3 million) for the fiscal year ending January 1991; capitalization stood at ¥14.5 billion (US $105.7 million) in the same year. Headquarters are in Tōkyō.

Nikka Whisky Distilling Co, Ltd

ニッカウヰスキー[株]

(Nikka Uisukī). Company engaged in the production, sale, export, and import of whiskey, brandy, gin, vodka, liqueurs, and wine; second largest whiskey maker in Japan. Established in 1934 by Taketsuru Masataka (1894–1979). The company operates malt whiskey distilleries in Yoichi (Hokkaidō) and Sendai and a grain whiskey distillery in Nishinomiya (near Ōsaka). Overseas offices are located in Los Angeles, New York, and London. Sales for the fiscal year ending December 1990 totaled ¥97.7 billion (US $731.6 million); the company was capitalized at ¥11.8 billion (US $88.4 million) in the same year. Headquarters are in Tōkyō.

Nikkeiren   日経連

(abbreviation of Nihon Keieisha Dantai Remmei; Japan Federation of Employers' Associations). Nationwide organization of managers of business corporations. Established in 1948. It serves as the employers' counterpart to the labor unions of the employees. Aiming for the promotion of healthy labor-management relations, it determines management policy in labor disputes and collective bargaining and provides guidance to member organizations. The federation also submits proposals to the government on labor policies and is the official voice of Japanese employers at the International Labor Organization (ILO).

With the removal of restrictions on the labor movement by the Allied Occupation Forces after World War II, many labor unions were organized. In order to cope with this new situation, the Kantō Employers' Society was established for the Tōkyō area in 1946, followed by the organization of similar bodies in the Kyūshū, Hokkaidō, Chūbu, and Kansai regions. As of 1990 Nikkeiren was composed of 47 such regional bodies and 57 industrywide groups such as the Japan Iron and Steel Federation.

Shortly after Nikkeiren's founding, the organization gave its full support to management during the TŌHŌ STRIKE and, in 1960, gained a reputation as "fighting Nikkeiren" for its support of management during the MIIKE STRIKE. During the Japanese economy's period of high growth, Nikkeiren provided employers with guidelines to follow when labor unions made their wage demands in the annual spring labor offensive (SHUNTŌ). Its general policy has been to urge wage increases appropriate to Japan's economic growth rate. See also KEIDANREN; LABOR.

Nikkō

1 Yōmeimon, the elaborately carved and decorated gate at Tōshōgū, the famous shrine at Nikkō dedicated to the shōgun Tokugawa Ieyasu. National Treasure.

2 Shinkyō, the bridge formerly crossed by visitors to Tōshōgū. Today, the bridge is used only during festivals and other special occasions.

nikki bungaku 日記文学

(diary literature). Literary genre consisting of diaries or tales in the form of diaries. Early examples were modeled after diaries of Chinese government officials who recorded the sayings and actions of the emperor. With the establishment in Japan of the Chinese-style RITSURYŌ SYSTEM of government in the 7th century, these developed into official annals recorded in Chinese. From the Heian period (794–1185), government officials began to keep private diaries written in Chinese or a Japanized form of Chinese (see KAMBUN).

The first diary of literary value was the TOSA NIKKI (935; tr The Tosa Diary, 1969) by KI NO TSURAYUKI, a government official. To be free from the constraints of his position, he adopted the persona of a woman and used KANA, the Japanese syllabary used mainly by women.

Many diaries by court ladies appeared in the 10th and 11th centuries. These were not daily records but later recollections. While the diaries are distinguished by their candid self-expression, their narrative devices, such as the use of the third person, often make them seem like works of fiction. The KAGERŌ NIKKI (974; tr The Gossamer Years, 1964) by FUJIWARA NO MICHITSUNA NO HAHA records the unhappy life of a married woman; it influenced later women writers. Other notable examples from the Heian period include the IZUMI SHIKIBU NIKKI (ca 1010; tr The Izumi Shikibu Diary, 1969), said to be by IZUMI SHIKIBU, although some scholars attribute the work to another woman; the Murasaki Shikibu nikki (ca 1010) by MURASAKI SHIKIBU, the author of the Genji monogatari (TALE OF GENJI); the SARASHINA NIKKI (ca 1060; tr As I Crossed a Bridge of Dreams, 1971) by Sugawara no Takasue no Musume; and the SANUKI NO SUKE NO NIKKI (ca 1108; tr Sanuki no Suke Nikki, 1977) by Sanuki no Suke.

Diaries of later periods include the Kenshun Mon'in no Chūnagon nikki (ca 1219) by Kenshun Mon'in no Chūnagon (b 1157), the Ben no Naishi nikki (1246–52) by Go-Fukakusa In Ben no Naishi (13th century), and the IZAYOI NIKKI (1280; tr The Izayoi Nikki, 1951) by ABUTSU NI. The number of travel diaries, such as KAIDŌKI (ca 1223) and TŌKAN KIKŌ (ca 1242), increased dramatically at this time. Of note is the TOWAZUGATARI (ca 1307; tr The Confessions of Lady Nijō, 1973) by Go-Fukakusa In no Nijō. OKU NO HOSOMICHI (1694; tr The Narrow Road to the Deep North, 1966) by the poet BASHŌ and Chichi no shūen nikki (1801) by the poet ISSA are also classified as diaries.

In the modern age, confessional diaries appeared, including Ichiyō nikki (1912) by HIGUCHI ICHIYŌ, Azamukazaru no ki (1893–97) by KUNIKIDA DOPPO, the diaries of NATSUME SŌSEKI—a section of his Shuzenji monogatari—and Danchōtei nichijō (1946–47) by NAGAI KAFŪ.

Nikkō 日光[市]

City in northwestern Tochigi Prefecture, central Honshū. It has flourished as a religious center since 782, when the priest Shōdō (735–817) founded a temple there. In the Edo period (1600–1868) it became the site of TŌSHŌGŪ, a shrine containing the mausoleum of TOKUGAWA IEYASU, the founder of the Tokugawa shogunate. Nikkō has a metal industry and a more traditional woodworking industry. It is the center of NIKKŌ NATIONAL PARK, which offers such scenic spots as Lake Chūzenji and KEGON FALLS, as well as numerous temples and shrines. A samurai procession is held annually in May and October at Tōshōgū. Nikkō has about 7 million visitors annually. Pop: 20,128.

Nikkō Kyōdō Co, Ltd [株]日鉱共石

(Nikkō Kyōseki). One of the largest nonferrous metal producers in Japan. Directly and through a subsidiary, it produces copper, zinc, gold, silver, sulfuric acid, and certain minor metals. The company's operations began in 1905; it was incorporated under the name Nippon Mining Co, Ltd, in 1929 and took its present name in 1992. The company is also a major refiner of crude oil in Japan, producing various petroleum products. The company has 14 subsidiaries, and among its major affiliates is KYŌDŌ OIL CO, LTD, the fifth largest distributor of petroleum products in Japan. Overseas activities include the design, development, and manufacture of computers, electronic systems, and related products and materials, including semiconductors and copper foil, used in information processing, industrial automation, engineering, and scientific applications. Sales for the fiscal year ending March 1991 were ¥989.9 billion (US $7.2 billion). The company was capitalized at ¥77.0 billion (US $561.2 million) in the same year. Headquarters are in Tōkyō.

Nikkō National Park 日光国立公園

(Nikkō Kokuritsu Kōen). Situated in Fukushima, Tochigi, Gumma, and Niigata prefectures. This popular park and pilgrimage center is set in rugged mountain terrain with volcanoes, waterfalls, lakes, and temples and shrines. Northwest of the city of NIKKŌ, in the southern part of the park, the terrain rises steeply to Lake CHŪZENJI, dominated by the extinct volcano NANTAISAN. On the lake's eastern shore are the KEGON FALLS, to the northwest lies the mountain SHIRANESAN, and further west is the desolate marshland of OZE.

Two famous resorts are Shiobara Hot Spring, northeast of Nikkō, and Nasu Hot Spring, on the slopes of the volcano NASUDAKE. Nikkō is celebrated for its numerous Shintō shrines, including the TŌSHŌGŪ, and Buddhist temples, including Rinnōji, a temple of the Tendai sect. Among the park's chief attractions are the maples, firs, and giant cryptomerias (sugi) that line the mountain roads around Nikkō. Area: 1,402 sq km (541 sq mi).

Nikkō Securities Co, Ltd 日興証券[株]

(Nikkō Shōken). One of the "Big Four" securities firms in Japan. Incorporated in 1944. Traditionally strong in the handling of bonds, Nikkō Securities was the first in Japan to introduce quantitative investment methods from the United States. In 1965 Nikkō Securities Co International, Inc, was established in New York and was appointed a primary dealer in US government securities in 1987. There are 14 other subsidiaries and 8 representative offices in 17 countries. Affiliated companies include Nikkō Research Center, Ltd, Nikkō International Capital Management Co, Ltd, and Nikkō Securities Investment Trust & Management Co, Ltd. Revenue for the fiscal year ending March 1991 totaled ¥376.6 billion (US $2.7 billion), with capitalization at ¥122.3 billion (US $891.4 million). Headquarters are in Tōkyō.

Nikkyōso 日教組

(abbreviation of Nihon Kyōshokuin Kumiai; Japan Teachers' Union). National organization of teachers' unions. Consisting mainly of prefectural unions of primary and junior high school teachers, Nikkyōso was formed in 1947 and was affiliated with SŌHYŌ (General Council of Trade Unions of Japan). In 1950 high school teachers seceded to form an independent organization, but about half returned to the union in the 1970s. Though teachers are forbidden to strike or to engage in collective bargaining by the Local Civil Service Law (Chihō Kōmuin Hō), Nikkyōso has adopted various legal and illegal tactics to achieve its goals. When Sōhyō disbanded in 1989, Nikkyōso joined RENGŌ (Japanese Trade Union Confederation). At that time some Japan Communist Party supporters who opposed joining Rengō left Nikkyōso and formed a new organization, the Zen Nihon Kyōshokuin Kumiai Kyōgikai (All-Japan Council of Teachers' and Staffs' Unions). In 1989 Nikkyōso had 655,000 members.

Nikō Jiken →Nikolaevsk Incident

Nikolaevsk Incident 尼港事件

(Nikō Jiken). Controversial series of events from February to May 1920, during the Russian Civil War, in which several hundred Japanese were annihilated by Russian partisans at a town called Nikolaevsk. Located near the mouth of the Amur River some 640 kilometers (400 mi) from Khabarovsk, Nikolaevsk at this time had a Japanese community of about 450 civilians and a garrison of 350 (see SIBERIAN INTERVENTION). In January 1920 Nikolaevsk was encircled by partisans under Yakov Triapitsyn, who was loosely cooperating with the Bolsheviks. Without any immediate prospects of reinforcements, the Japanese garrison commander agreed to a truce that allowed Triapitsyn's forces to enter Nikolaevsk. When Triapitsyn, in violation of the truce, began shooting White Russian prisoners, the garrison launched a

surprise attack on 12 March that miscarried and resulted in the slaughter of all but 122 Japanese. As a Japanese relief expedition approached in late May, Triapitsyn liquidated all surviving prisoners. The Bolsheviks executed Triapitsyn, but Tōkyō reacted by occupying northern (Russian) SAKHALIN and demanding compensation. The Nikolaevsk affair prolonged the Siberian intervention and delayed Japan's recognition of the Soviet regime until 1925.

Nikolai   ニコライ

(1836–1912). Preordination name Ioann Dmitrievich Kasatkin. Archbishop of the Russian Orthodox Church in Japan. A graduate of the theological academy in St. Petersburg, Nikolai went to Japan in 1861 as a monk. He spent the first seven years of his stay in intensive study of the language, literature, thought, and customs of Japan.

Nikolai was named head of a Russian Orthodox mission that was established in Japan in 1870. In 1872 he moved to Tōkyō and built a seminary, a school for catechists, a theological school for women, and the Byzantine Cathedral of the Resurrection, popularly known in his honor as Nikorai-dō, or Nikolai Cathedral. Elevated to the bishopric of Japan in 1880, Nikolai remained in Tōkyō until his death. He stressed the national character of the Orthodox Church of Japan. He recruited a native clergy and insisted at the time of the RUSSO-JAPANESE WAR (1904–05) that the political loyalty of his flock must be to the Japanese emperor, not to the tsar.

Nikon Corporation   [株]ニコン

(Nikon). Manufacturer of Nikon cameras and other optical equipment, including steppers (machines used in computer chip manufacture), eyeglasses, microscopes, measuring instruments, telescopes, and surveying instruments. A member of the MITSUBISHI group, it was established in 1917 through the merger of the optical division of Tōkyō Keiki Seisakujo and the reflex mirror division of Iwaki Garasu Seizōjo. In 1948 it brought out its Nikon-I camera; in the 1950s it began to win a reputation among photographers overseas, leading to a rapid growth in sales volume. In 1953 a subsidiary, Nikon, Inc, was established in New York, followed by subsidiaries in Switzerland, the Netherlands, Germany, Canada, the United Kingdom, and Hong Kong. The Nikon F camera, introduced in 1959, was popular among professionals as well as amateurs. Nikon started selling step-

pers in 1980, and they have become one of the company's largest-selling products. Sales for the fiscal year ending March 1991 totaled ¥254.6 billion (US $1.9 billion), of which cameras accounted for 42 percent; steppers and semiconductor-related equipment, 32 percent; eyeglasses, 8 percent; microscopes, 7 percent; surveying instruments, 6 percent; telescopes, 4 percent; and other products, 1 percent. In the same year the company was capitalized at ¥36.6 billion (US $266.8 million). Headquarters are in Tōkyō.

nimbetsu aratame   人別改

Population censuses conducted during the Edo period (1600–1868); compiled in registers known as *nimbetsuchō*. During the 16th century the *daimyō* had begun counting the people in their domains, and during the Edo period censuses became common. In 1644 the Tokugawa shogunate conducted a census of its own domains (*tenryō*). The censuses were usually prepared by village and town officials upon instruction from district and town administrators (DAIKAN; GUNDAI; and MACHI BUGYŌ). After 1671 they were carried out in conjunction with religious registration (see SHŪMON ARATAME). They were not made regularly until after 1726, when national surveys were scheduled every six years. The censuses did not count *samurai* or court nobles, and they sometimes omitted children and marginal social groups. Although imperfect records, they are valuable sources for demographic, economic, and social patterns of early modern Japan.

Ninagawa Torazō   蜷川虎三

(1897–1981). Scholar; seven times elected governor of Kyōto (1950–78). Born in Tōkyō, he studied at Kyōto University, published a book on economic statistics, and became a full professor at the university in 1939. Ninagawa was head of the newly established Small and Medium Enterprise Agency (1948–50) but left this position following a dispute with the conservative YOSHIDA SHIGERU cabinet. Backed by a leftist united-front coalition, he then ran successfully for the governorship of Kyōto Prefecture. During the 1960s Ninagawa consistently opposed government policies favoring large industry and centrally directed rapid economic growth, emphasizing instead local policies, such as large-scale loans without collateral, that developed small and medium and rural enterprises. After 1966 Ninagawa moved closer to the Japan Communist Party,

which gradually became the mainstay of his reelection campaigns. Ninagawa retired in 1978.

Ninagawa Yukio   蜷川幸雄

(1935–). Stage producer. Born in Saitama Prefecture. Ninagawa started his career with the Seihai theater group. In 1969 he established a troupe called the Gendaijin Gekijō (Theater of Contemporary Man). The troupe's productions received critical acclaim, but it disbanded in 1971. With his 1974 production of *Romeo and Juliet*, Ninagawa made the commercial theater the center of his activities. His reputation continued to grow with his productions of *Medea* (1978) and AKIMOTO MATSUYO's *Chikamatsu shinjū monogatari* (1979). Ninagawa specializes in shifting the setting of classic Western plays to Japan, as he did in 1981 with *Macbeth* and in 1987 with *The Tempest*. In 1984 he established a theater company that is now known as the Young Ninagawa Company.

Nin'ami Dōhachi   仁阿弥道八

(1783–1855). Ceramist. Real name Takahashi Mitsutoki; also known as Takahashi Dōhachi. A disciple of OKUDA EISEN, Dōhachi is most famous for his excellent imitations. Along with AOKI MOKUBEI and EIRAKU HOZEN, he was considered one of the three master potters of KYŌTO CERAMICS in the late Edo period (1600–1868). Dōhachi specialized in TEA CEREMONY wares that included incense boxes in the form of figures. His imitations of the work of NONOMURA NINSEI and Ogata KENZAN as well as of Korean styles and RAKU WARE were accurate and lively. Among his finest works are his enameled wares with cherry-blossom and maple-leaf designs.

Nine-Power Treaty   九ヵ国条約

(Kyūkakoku Jōyaku). A treaty concerning China concluded among the United States,

Nikkō National Park
1 Kegon Falls, a renowned feature of the park, viewed from the Akechidaira observatory. Lake Chūzenji, the source of the falls, appears in the distance.
2 Mist rises from Lake Chūzenji, its shores colored by autumn foliage.
3 The Odashirogahara plain is surrounded by forest. Here it is seen early in the morning.

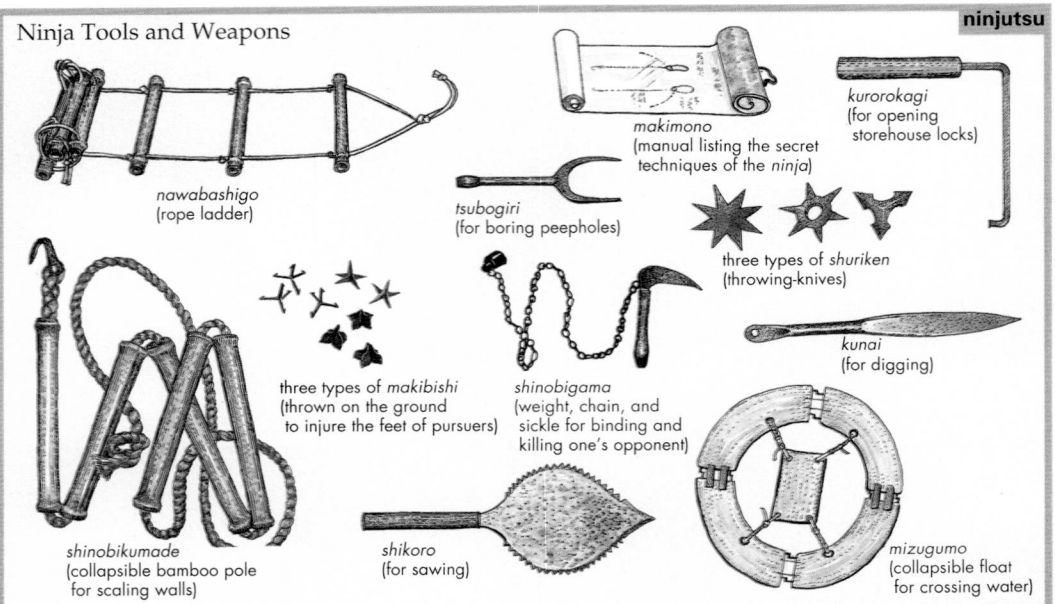

Ninja Tools and Weapons

nawabashigo
(rope ladder)

makimono
(manual listing the secret
techniques of the ninja)

kurorokagi
(for opening
storehouse locks)

tsubogiri
(for boring peepholes)

three types of shuriken
(throwing-knives)

kunai
(for digging)

three types of makibishi
(thrown on the ground
to injure the feet of pursuers)

shinobigama
(weight, chain, and
sickle for binding and
killing one's opponent)

shinobikumade
(collapsible bamboo pole
for scaling walls)

shikoro
(for sawing)

mizugumo
(collapsible float
for crossing water)

Great Britain, France, Italy, the Netherlands, Belgium, Portugal, China, and Japan at the WASHINGTON CONFERENCE on 6 February 1922. The treaty prescribed respect for the national sovereignty and territorial integrity of China and maintenance of the "open door," ensuring equal opportunity in commerce and industry for foreign nations there. Because of the treaty's conclusion, the LANSING-ISHII AGREEMENT approving the special interests of Japan in China was abrogated in April 1923, and the Nine-Power Treaty came into full effect in August 1925. Through this treaty the United States hoped to stop Japan's advance into China. Beginning with the MANCHURIAN INCIDENT of 1931, however, Japan continually ignored the treaty, which was in effect nullified with Japan's entry into World War II in 1941.

Nine Principles for Economic Stabilization　経済安定九原則

(Keizai Antei Kyū Gensoku). A package of economic measures imposed on the YOSHIDA SHIGERU cabinet by the US government on 18 December 1948 to control the inflation that had plagued Japan during the early years of the Allied Occupation, following World War II. They were one manifestation of the general shift in Occupation policies away from punishment and reform toward recovery and rehabilitation. See ECONOMIC HISTORY.

The program required the Japanese government to balance its budget; to improve tax collections; to limit credit extension; to establish a program for wage stability; to strengthen price controls; to improve foreign trade controls, the rationing system, and the food collection program; and to increase production of raw materials and manufactured goods.

Joseph Dodge, General Douglas MACARTHUR's financial adviser, headed a special economic mission to ensure the plan's implementation (see DODGE LINE). Along with the tax reforms proposed by the SHOUP MISSION, the program is generally credited with reducing inflation and stabilizing the Japanese government's finances, though some critics maintain that it was unnecessarily severe.

Ningen no jōken　人間の条件

(The Human Condition). A film in six parts (often shown in three parts) made by director KOBAYASHI MASAKI from 1959 to 1961, starring NAKADAI TATSUYA and Aratama Michiyo (b 1930). Set in Manchuria, it tells of a young man who struggles to survive World War II with his spirit intact. Punished harshly by the Japanese army for refusing to assimilate its values, he is then captured by the Soviet forces as the war ends. Interned as a war criminal, he escapes only to die, but maintains his humanity to the end. Depicting the repulsive nature of the military and the war and the abuses visited on those who refused to renounce their convictions, Ningen no jōken is one of the most powerful Japanese antiwar films ever made. Its total running time is 9 hours, 38 minutes.

Ningen shikkaku　人間失格

(tr No Longer Human, 1958). Novel by DAZAI OSAMU (1909–48); published 1948. Ningen shikkaku consists mainly of notes written by Ōba Yōzō, a young man born into a wealthy family in northern Japan. Ōba grows up with a terror and distrust of people; a sense of alienation and difference plagues him. Sent to Tōkyō for his education, he tries desperately to hide his fears, performing lighthearted antics and affecting a carefree attitude toward life. His inability to understand the emotions of others, however, leaves him in a state of desolation. After two unsuccessful suicide attempts and an addiction to morphine, he is confined to a mental hospital. Ōba eventually returns to his hometown a broken man, dominated by a sense that he is unfit to be called human. Ningen shikkaku, written in the style of the I-NOVEL genre, is widely considered the crowning achievement of the author's career.

Ningyō Pass　人形峠

(Ningyō Tōge). Located on the border of the town of Misasa in Tottori Prefecture and the village of Kami Saibara in Okayama Prefecture, western Honshū. It became famous with the discovery of uranium ores. National Route No. 179 runs through the pass, and the highland Ombara Kōgen has a hiking course and good skiing. Altitude: 739 m (2,425 ft).

Ninigi no Mikoto　瓊瓊杵尊

An important figure in Japanese mythology. His father was Ame no Oshihomimi no Mikoto, the son of the sun goddess AMATERASU ŌMIKAMI. His mother was Takuhata Chijihime, the daughter of Takamimusubi no Kami, the god of creation in the Yamato myth cycle (see MYTHOLOGY).

He was sent by Amaterasu and Takamimusubi to pacify the islands of Japan and rule over them. He was given symbols of his power and functions that became the three IMPERIAL REGALIA: the mirror, the sword, and the curved jewels (magatama). He then set out to conquer the land. He married Konohana no Sakuyahime (whose name symbolizes a blooming flower) instead of Iwanagahime (whose name symbolizes the eternity of rocks) against the wishes of the father of both goddesses, Ōyamatsumi no Kami, with the ultimate result of shortening the lives of future emperors. His great-grandson was to become the person Japanese mythology considers the first emperor, JIMMU. Ninigi no Mikoto is today worshiped at the Kirishima Shrine in Kagoshima Prefecture.

Niniroku Jiken →February 26th Incident

ninja →ninjutsu

ninjōbon　人情本

(literally, "books about human feelings"). Genre of late-Edo-period (1600–1868) fiction that derives historically from the SHAREBON of the late 18th century. In form, both rely heavily on dialogue and deal with contemporary life in the pleasure quarters of Edo (now Tōkyō). Early sharebon illustrated the ideal behavior of the tōrimono or tsū, the accomplished connoisseur of the ways of the licensed quarter. SANTŌ KYŌDEN, however, in works such as Keiseikai shijūhatte (1790, Forty-Eight Tricks to Buying a Courtesan) and Nishiki no ura (1791, The Underside of the Brocade), began to shift the attention of the sharebon toward the human relationships that underlay the ritualized formalities of life in the quarter. A new kind of sharebon that dealt with emotional and psychological relationships between courtesan and customer came to be called nakihon, "weeping books." A name often associated with the nakihon is Umebori Kokuga (1750–1821).

The ninjōbon descended from the nakihon of the late 1790s and early 1800s, with the possible addition of themes and plot devices borrowed from the tragedies of the JŌRURI puppet theater. Its greatest practitioner, TAMENAGA SHUNSUI, is known for his dialogue. Shunsui's Shunshoku umegoyomi (1832–33, Spring Love: A Plum-Blossom Almanac) was the prototype of later ninjōbon and the first work to be formally styled ninjōbon in its subtitle. Shunsui produced several other ninjōbon of note, including Shunshoku tatsumi no sono (1833–35, The Tatsumi Quarter), which was a sequel to Umegoyomi, and Harutsugedori (1837, Bush Warbler). Shunsui's pupil Shōtei Kinsui (1795–1862) achieved considerable prominence as a ninjōbon writer. Other writers such as Hanasanjin (1790–1858) and Kyokusanjin (d 1836) also developed the genre.

What sets the mature ninjōbon apart from the sharebon and other writing about the pleasure quarters, both licensed (principally the YOSHIWARA in Edo) and unlicensed (the so-called okabasho), is its sympathetic treatment of its characters. See also GESAKU.

ninjutsu　忍術

Also called shinobi. One of the Japanese MARTIAL ARTS. Concerned with what might today be called spycraft, ninjutsu involved the clandestine penetration of the enemy's territory or organizations to observe their movement, to obtain secret information, or to engage in assassination or commando raids.

Ninjutsu evolved a complex repertoire of artifice, strategy, and camouflage techniques designed to deceive the enemy and avoid detection, supported by a variety of specialized tools and weapons. Masters of these techniques were known as *ninja.*

There are legends tracing the origins of *ninjutsu* back to Japanese antiquity, but in fact it was the expansion of warfare during the medieval period (mid-12th–16th centuries) that made it an indispensable part of military operations. The full-scale civil wars of the Sengoku period (1467–1568) brought *ninjutsu* to its peak, and gave rise to famous bands of *ninja* such as the Iga school (from what is now Mie Prefecture) and the Kōga school (from what is now Shiga Prefecture).

In the Edo period (1600–1868), the advent of peace under Tokugawa rule threatened to make *ninjutsu* and its practitioners obsolete. To counter this threat, *ninjutsu* was systematized as a martial art and its techniques, tools, and weapons were codified in written texts, rather than being handed down by secret oral transmission as in the past. One of the best known of these manuals of the craft was the *Mansen shūkai* (1676), compiled by Fujibayashi Samuji, which served as a compendium of traditions and techniques of the Iga and Kōga schools.

Beginning in the late Edo period, the *ninja* entered into popular culture through an exaggerated depiction as a kind of superhero in storybooks and drama—a trend that has continued into the 20th century as novels, films, television shows, and comics centered on the romantic figure of the *ninja* have stirred imaginations both in Japan and abroad.

Ninnaji   仁和寺

Head temple of the Omuro branch of the SHINGON SECT of Buddhism; located in Ukyō Ward, Kyōto. Its construction was begun in 886 at the initiative of Emperor Kōkō (r 884–887) and completed two years later by his son, Emperor UDA. Until the Meiji period (1868–1912) Ninnaji customarily chose its abbot from tonsured members of the imperial family; hence it is known also as Omuro Gosho, or Omuro Palace. (Temples so associated with aristocracy were called *monzeki.*) Ninnaji was burned to the ground during the Ōnin War (1467–77) and was virtually defunct until the third Tokugawa shōgun, TOKUGAWA IEMITSU, sponsored its restoration in 1634. In 1903 Ninnaji declared its independence from the main body of the Shingon sect controlled by KONGŌBUJI.

Ninohe   二戸〔市〕

City in northern Iwate Prefecture, northern Honshū. Principal activities are dairy farming and the cultivation of apples, tobacco, and hops. There are also foodstuff-processing plants. Pop: 28,858.

Ninomiya Sontoku   二宮尊徳

(1787–1856). Farm technologist and the leading agricultural philosopher of the late Edo period (1600–1868). Real name Ninomiya Kinjirō. His practical and moral teachings, which urged cultivators to raise output and pay their taxes, helped strengthen the economic basis of Tokugawa rule. For this he was later praised as a paragon of virtue in the national ethics textbooks of the 1930s, and a statue of the young Ninomiya was a familiar sight in every elementary school.

Born in Sagami Province (now Kanagawa Prefecture) and orphaned at age 16, Ninomiya lived briefly with an uncle and then returned home to scrape out a living for himself and his younger brothers. In time his thrift and perseverance revived his family's fortunes, leading to employment as an agricultural technologist in the Odawara domain (in what is now Kanagawa Prefecture). His success amid the ravages of economic depression in the Tempō era (1830–44) caught the attention of the shogunal reformer MIZUNO TADAKUNI, and Ninomiya soon became engaged in the Imbanuma lake drainage project (see IMBANUMA) in Shimōsa Province (now part of Chiba Prefecture). His work in the Sōma domain (now part of Fukushima Prefecture) included supervising road building, housing construction, bridge repairs, aqueduct mending, and bookkeeping. Within 30 years farmers in some 100 villages under his direction grew so much more rice than before that the shogunate eventually placed him in charge of land development in 89 villages under Tokugawa administration at Nikkō. He died before completing the task.

Ninomiya's method involved precise calculations of irrigation and fertilizer requirements in relation to weather and maximum land yields. Furthermore, Ninomiya taught farmers to improve themselves through *hōtoku* ("repaying virtue"), the idea that benefits received from heaven, man, and earth should be repaid, and that doing so would create a "true society" of peacefulness and prosperity. To the familiar Confucian virtues of sincerity, diligence, and thrift, Ninomiya added cooperation with others to his code of ethics.

The *hōtoku* movement founded by his followers became the basis for both popular and official agrarianism after the Meiji Restoration of 1868. In no sense, however, was Ninomiya a rural leveler. He accepted and supported the hierarchy of Tokugawa society, advocating frugality and hard work within the feudal structure. See also NŌHON SHUGI.

Ninsei → Nonomura Ninsei

ninsoku yoseba   人足寄場

(literally, "laborers' camp"). Premodern form of prison, originally designed to provide lodging and rehabilitation assistance to vagrants, beggars, and banished criminals. *Ninsoku yoseba* were instituted in 1790 by MATSUDAIRA SADANOBU as part of the KANSEI REFORMS, mainly to ease social unrest caused by the TEMMEI FAMINE (1782–87). The Tokugawa shogunate hoped to rehabilitate transients by teaching them vocational skills, offering them work, and in some cases providing them with homes. The first *ninsoku yoseba* was located in Edo (now Tōkyō). The shogunate later built camps in other places, and various *daimyō* established similar facilities. By the end of the Edo period (1600–1868), *ninsoku yoseba* served essentially as prison camps. Following the MEIJI RESTORATION (1868) they were replaced by modern prisons.

Nintendō Co, Ltd   任天堂〔株〕

(Nintendō). Manufacturer of consumer electronic games, amusement machines, and playing cards. Incorporated in 1947. The company has profited from the sharp growth of home video games and has a 90 percent share of the domestic market. It established Nintendō of America, Inc, in 1980. Sales for the fiscal year ending August 1991 totaled

¥451.0 billion (US $3.3 billion), and capitalization stood at ¥10.1 billion (US $73.6 million). Headquarters are in Kyōto.

Nintoku, Emperor   仁徳天皇

(first half of the 5th century; Nintoku Tennō). The 16th sovereign (*tennō*) in the traditional count (which includes several legendary emperors). According to the chronicle NIHON SHOKI (720) he reigned 313–399, although modern scholars reject these dates. The *Nihon shoki* and the chronicle KOJIKI (712) state that he was the fourth son of Emperor ŌJIN and ascended the throne only after the death of a younger half-brother to whom he had yielded his position as crown prince. The chronicles describe him as a benevolent ruler. Nintoku is said to have established his capital at Naniwa (now Ōsaka), then the gateway to trade with the continent. The largest of Japan's keyhole-shaped grave mounds, in the city of Sakai, Ōsaka Prefecture, is said to be his resting place (see NINTOKU MAUSOLEUM). It has been speculated that Nintoku was one of the FIVE KINGS OF WA mentioned in the Chinese history *Song (Sung) shu* (History of the Liu-Song Dynasty [420–479]).

Nintoku Mausoleum   仁徳天皇陵

(Nintoku Tennōryō). An early-5th-century mounded tomb (KOFUN) located on a high riverine terrace in the city of Sakai, Ōsaka Prefecture. Identified as the grave of Emperor NINTOKU (first half of the 5th century) by a document in the 10th-century collection ENGI SHIKI, this tomb is the largest in Japan. The central keyhole-shaped mound, 486 meters (1,594 ft) in length, is alternately surrounded by three moats and two greenbelts and altogether occupies 32.3 hectares (80 acres). Protected and preserved by the Imperial Household Agency, the tomb has never been excavated. In 1872, however, part of the front mound collapsed and a pit-style stone burial chamber was exposed. Some iron armor and weapons, gilt-bronze ornaments, a glass bowl from ancient Persia, and a stone coffin were recovered, but they are not thought to be part of the main burial. See also ŌJIN MAUSOLEUM.

Nippon Budōkan
Although primarily used for martial arts competitions, this Tōkyō arena is also the site for numerous concerts.

Nippara Shōnyūdō   日原鍾乳洞

Limestone caves on the river Nipparagawa (a tributary of the Tamagawa), northwestern Tōkyō Prefecture. A natural monument and part of the Chichibu-Tama National Park. The largest of the caves has a depth of 527 m (1,729 ft).

Nippo jisho   日葡辞書

Japanese name for *Vocabulario da Lingoa de Iapam com a declaração em Portugues.* Japanese-Portuguese dictionary compiled by Jesuit missionaries in the 17th century; mistakenly attributed to João RODRIGUES. Published in 1603–04 by the Jesuit collegium in Nagasaki, it remains an indispensable source for the study of Japanese during the Muromachi period (1333–1568), containing entries on nearly 33,000 words. It was translated into Spanish by J. Esquivél (1630, *Vocabulario de Iapon*) and into French by the diplomat Léon PAGÈS (1868, *Dictionnaire japonais-français*). A modern edition with Japanese translations of the Portuguese explanations was published in 1980. See also JESUIT MISSION PRESS.

Nippon Beet Sugar Mfg Co, Ltd   日本甜菜製糖[株]

(Nippon Tensai Seitō). Largest beet sugar manufacturer in Japan. Also refines imported raw sugar. The company was incorporated in 1919. It prospered as a result of government protection of beet growers. Sales for the fiscal year ending September 1991 totaled ¥65.5 billion (US $477.4 million); capitalization stood at ¥8.3 billion (US $64.5 million). Headquarters are in Tōkyō.

Nippon Broadcasting System, Inc   [株]ニッポン放送

(Nippon Hōsō). A Tōkyō-based commercial AM radio broadcasting station serving the greater Kantō area of eastern Honshū. It was established in 1954 with backing from the Tōkyō financial world. In recent years it has been first among Japanese radio stations in number of listeners. It pioneered late-night radio broadcasting in Japan (see BROADCASTS, LATE-NIGHT).

Nippon Budōkan   日本武道館

MARTIAL ARTS arena, also used as a concert hall, located in Kitanomaru Park, Chiyoda Ward, Tōkyō. Nippon Budōkan was constructed in 1964 and served as the site for the *jūdō* competition of the Tōkyō Olympics held that same year. The arena comprises a large hall, which holds 14,000, and two smaller ones. Modeled after the Yumedono ("Dream Hall") of the temple Hōryūji, the outside of the structure is Japanese-style and octagonal in shape. Each year the national championship matches of the various martial arts are held here, as are many concerts.

Nippon College of Physical Education   日本体育大学

(Nippon Taiiku Daigaku). A coeducational private college in Setagaya Ward, Tōkyō. The college traces its origins to the Nippon Taiiku Semmon Gakkō (Nippon School of Physical Education), which was established in 1941, and ultimately to the Taiikukai (Physical Education Association), which was founded in 1891 by Hidaka Tōkichirō (1856–1932). It became a college in 1949. Its only academic department is its faculty of physical education. Enrollment in 1989 was 5,832.

Nippon Columbia Co, Ltd   日本コロムビア[株]

(Nippon Korombia). Manufacturer of phonograph records and acoustic equipment. It was incorporated in 1910 by F. W. Horn, an American, under the name Nipponophone Co, Ltd. In 1927 the Columbia companies of the United States and Great Britain invested in Nipponophone, but they abandoned their ties in the 1930s. The company took its present name in 1946. Its phonograph records, compact discs, and acoustic equipment are exported under the brand name Denon. In 1969 the company came under the control of HITACHI, LTD. Sales for the fiscal year ending March 1991 totaled ¥102.0 billion (US $743.4 million). Capitalization stood at ¥6.8 billion (US $49.6 million) in the same year. Headquarters are in Tōkyō.

Nippon Credit Bank, Ltd   [株]日本債券信用銀行

(Nippon Saiken Shin'yō Ginkō). Long-term credit bank incorporated in 1957 under the Long-Term Credit Bank Law. It was called Nippon Fudōsan Ginkō (Japan Real Estate Bank) until 1977. The bank makes long-term loans, raising funds by issuing its own financial debentures. The bank is well known in the fields of project finance, mergers and acquisitions, and the development of new financial products. The bank has 18 domestic offices as well as 13 branches and representative offices and 6 subsidiaries abroad. Its total assets for the fiscal year ending March 1991 reached ¥18.4 trillion (US $134.1 billion), deposits were ¥14.3 trillion (US $104.2 billion), and capitalization stood at ¥152.2 billion (US $1.1 billion) in the same year. Headquarters are in Tōkyō. See INDUSTRIAL BANK OF JAPAN, LTD; LONG-TERM CREDIT BANK OF JAPAN, LTD.

Nippon Cultural Broadcasting, Inc   [株]文化放送

(Bunka Hōsō). Tōkyō-based commercial radio station serving the greater Kantō (eastern Honshū) area. It began operation in 1952 as the Nippon Bunka Hōsō Kyōkai (Nippon Cultural Broadcasting Corporation). Programs were cultural in nature, usually classical music and radio drama, aiming at wholesome family entertainment. Funding problems soon arose, however, and in 1956 the firm became a shareholding company under the present name. The station now broadcasts mostly variety shows that offer a combination of news and entertainment.

Nippon Dantai Life Insurance Co, Ltd   日本団体生命保険[株]

(Nihon Dantai Seimei Hoken). Life insurance company specializing in group life insurance, particularly nondividend term life insurance. Incorporated in 1934. Nippon Dantai provides insurance for 20 million workers and their families. For the fiscal year ending March 1990, the company had an annual premium income of ¥1.0 trillion (US $6.5 billion), total assets were ¥2.5 trillion (US $16.3 billion), and capitalization stood at ¥30.0 million (US $196,000). Headquarters are in Tōkyō.

Nippondensō Co, Ltd   日本電装[株]

(Nippon Densō). Japan's largest manufacturer of automotive components; a member of the Toyota group. Incorporated in 1949, when it became independent from Toyota Motor Co, Ltd (now known as Toyota Motor Corporation). The company has 9 domestic plants and 26 overseas manufacturing and sales companies in 14 countries. It produces a wide range of automotive products, such as heaters, air conditioners, and electrical equipment. It has developed electronic-fuel-injection, suspension-control, and cathode-ray-tube systems. Consolidated sales for the fiscal year ending December 1990 totaled ¥1.4 trillion (US $10.5 billion), and capitalization stood at ¥83.5 billion (US $625.2 million). Headquarters are in the city of Kariya, Aichi Prefecture.

Nippon Dream Kankō Co, Ltd   日本ドリーム観光[株]

(Nippon Dorīmu Kankō). Comprehensive leisure service company. Incorporated in 1913. It manages the Shin Kabukiza theater in Ōsaka and recreational lands in Nara and Yokohama through affiliated companies. Sales for the fiscal year ending January 1991 totaled ¥4.8 billion (US $35.9 million), and the company was capitalized at ¥7.6 billion (US $56.8 million). Headquarters are in Ōsaka.

Nippon Electric Glass Co, Ltd   日本電気硝子[株]

(Nippon Denki Garasu). Manufacturer of specialty glass products, especially cathode-ray tubes. Affiliated with NEC CORPORATION, it was incorporated in 1944. The company's other products include tubing glass, powdered glass, and glass fibers. The company also manufactures glassmaking machinery and equipment and has a capital and technology tie-up with Owens-Illinois of the United States. Sales for the fiscal year ending March 1991 totaled ¥203.4 billion (US $1.5 billion), and capitalization stood at ¥18.4 billion (US $134.1 million). Headquarters are in Ōtsu, Shiga Prefecture.

Nippon Express Co, Ltd   日本通運[株]

(Nippon Tsūun; also known as Nittsū). Company engaged in forwarding, trucking, sea and port transport, air transport, warehousing, and heavy haulage. The largest nationwide transport company in Japan, it was incorporated in 1937 as a semipublic corporation. In 1950, Nippon Express became a completely private company. In 1953 it concluded contracts with the International Air Transportation Association (IATA) and rapidly expanded overseas. In 1962 Nippon Express USA, Inc, was established, and since then 26 other overseas subsidiaries have been created. In the fiscal year ending March 1991 revenue totaled ¥1.2 trillion (US $8.7 billion), of which trucking accounted for 46 percent; air transport, 11 percent; sea transport, 10 percent; warehousing, 7 percent; express service, 5 percent; and other categories, 21 percent. That same year the company was capitalized at ¥69.9 billion (US $509.5 million). Headquarters are in Tōkyō.

Nippon Fire & Marine Insurance Co, Ltd
日本火災海上保険[株]

(Nihon Kasai Kaijō Hoken). Japanese nonlife insurance company. Established in 1892. It has a broad overseas sales network of 20 representative offices, along with 400 branch offices in Japan. The firm is independent of any financial clique. Total assets at the end of May 1991 reached ¥1.8 trillion (US $13.0 billion). The company received net premiums of ¥360.1 billion (US $2.6 billion) for the fiscal year ending March 1991. Headquarters are in Tōkyō.

Nippon Flour Mills Co, Ltd
日本製粉[株]

(Nippon Seifun). Manufacturer of flour and flour products. Incorporated in 1896, the company is Japan's oldest Western-style flour mill. Beginning in 1927 the company consigned the sale of its products to MITSUI & CO, LTD, and since then has been a member of the Mitsui group. Since World War II, company growth has been helped by changes in Japanese dietary habits and increased demand for flour. For the fiscal year ending March 1991 sales totaled ¥140.5 billion (US $1.0 billion), and the company was capitalized at ¥10.6 billion (US $77.3 million). Headquarters are in Tōkyō.

Nippon Formula Feed Mfg Co, Ltd
日本配合飼料[株]

(Nihon Haigō Shiryō). Company producing all types of feed for poultry, hogs, cattle, pets, and fish farming. It was incorporated in 1929 under the leadership of MITSUI & CO, LTD; the companies still have strong ties in material supply and product sales. The firm has 12 feed plants throughout Japan and has built a research center. It joined with Hendrix Feed of the Netherlands to import technical know-how for livestock farming. Sales for the fiscal year ending March 1991 totaled ¥70.7 billion (US $515.3 million), and capitalization was ¥6.6 billion (US $48.1 million). Headquarters are in Yokohama.

Nippon Hodō Co, Ltd
日本鋪道[株]

(Nihon Hodō). Largest road-paving enterprise in Japan. Incorporated in 1934. New business operations include architecture and sports and leisure facilities. Sales for the fiscal year ending March 1991 totaled ¥283.6 billion (US $2.1 billion). Capitalization stood at ¥14.8 billion (US $107.9 million) in the same year. Headquarters are in Tōkyō.

Nippon Housing Loan Co, Ltd
日本住宅金融[株]

(Nihon Jūtaku Kin'yū). Leading housing-loan institution. Incorporated in 1971. The firm provides general housing loans, rental and mortgage loans, and loans for replacement purchases; it is also involved in real-estate rental and securities transactions. It was the first specialized housing-loan company with backing from major Japanese banks. It maintains subsidiaries in New York and London. Revenue for the fiscal year ending March 1990 totaled ¥139.2 billion (US $909.3 million), and capitalization stood at ¥31.2 billion (US $203.8 million). Headquarters are in Tōkyō.

Nippon hyōron
日本評論

(Japan Review). General-interest magazine. It began in 1926 as a financial journal, *Keizai ōrai*. Its name was changed to *Nippon hyōron* in 1935. Following the lead of CHŪŌ KŌRON and KAIZŌ, it became a general-interest mag-azine. In 1951 it was suppressed by the authorities as a result of articles criticizing OCCUPATION policies. It resumed publication in 1956 but failed after putting out two issues.

Nippon Kayaku Co, Ltd
日本化薬[株]

(Nihon Kayaku). Leading manufacturer of chemical products. Incorporated in 1916 as the Nippon Explosives Manufacturing Co. The company is well known for its emphasis on research and development of anticancer drugs. Sales for the fiscal year ending May 1990 totaled ¥110.2 billion (US $717.8 million), of which pharmaceuticals accounted for 46 percent; dyestuffs, 23 percent; agrochemicals, 8 percent; resins, polymers, and related products, 15 percent; and explosives, 8 percent. In the same year the company was capitalized at ¥14.7 billion (US $96.0 million). Headquarters are in Tōkyō.

Nippon Life Insurance Co
日本生命保険[相]

(Nihon Seimei Hoken). Firm engaged in the sale of life insurance and reinsurance. Incorporated in 1889. Nippon Life is the world's largest life insurance company in terms of total assets, the value of new insurance policies issued annually, the total value of policies in force, and revenue from premiums. It was the first insurer to use a mortality table based strictly on the causes of death found among the Japanese people and also the first in Japan to issue dividends to policyholders. In 1972 it concluded a group insurance tie-up with the Travelers Corporation of the United States, followed by a tie-up with the investment bank Shearson Lehman Hutton, Inc. Overseas offices have been established in nine countries. Total assets for the fiscal year ending March 1991 reached ¥27.4 trillion (US $199.7 billion). In 1990 revenue from premiums totaled ¥5.1 trillion (US $37.2 billion). Headquarters are in Ōsaka.

Nippon Life Insurance Foundation
日本生命財団

(Nihon Seimei Zaidan). A foundation established in 1979 by the NIPPON LIFE INSURANCE CO. It provides support for research on environmental problems, programs to improve the health and welfare of the elderly, infant and child development programs, and publication of educational materials and scholarly research. The foundation also provides financial assistance to graduate students from other Asian countries attending Japanese universities. In 1989 total assets were ¥10.5 billion (US $76.1 million). Headquarters are in Ōsaka.

Nippon Light Metal Co, Ltd
日本軽金属[株]

(NLM; J: Nippon Keikinzoku). Major aluminum producer. NLM was incorporated in 1939. Its operations include the fabrication of aluminum, aluminum alloys, and nonaluminum materials into semifabricated and finished products; the distribution and marketing of aluminum and nonaluminum products; and, in connection with its aluminum operations, the production and sale of industrial chemicals. In 1952 Alcan of Canada, one of the biggest aluminum companies in the world, purchased 50 percent of the outstanding NLM shares, although NLM maintains a large degree of autonomy. Sales for the fiscal year ending March 1991 totaled ¥291.9 billion (US $2.1 billion), and capitalization was ¥45.2 billion (US $329.4 million). Headquarters are in Tōkyō.

Nippon Meat Packers, Inc
日本ハム[株]

(Nippon Hamu). One of Japan's largest meat and food processing companies. Incorporated in 1949. A fully integrated meat packer, it is involved in activities ranging from livestock breeding to production and distribution of a wide spectrum of fresh meat, processed meat, and processed food products. Products are generally sold and distributed in Japan under the NMP brand directly through its network of 700 sales offices. In addition, it operates restaurants and owns the Nippon Ham Fighters, a professional baseball team. NMP has 11 overseas offices in the United States, the United Kingdom, Australia, and other countries. Sales for the fiscal year ending March 1991 were ¥504.2 billion (US $3.7 billion), and capitalization was ¥23.0 billion (US $167.6 million). Headquarters are in Ōsaka.

Nippon Medical School
日本医科大学

(Nippon Ika Daigaku). A coeducational private college located in Bunkyō Ward, Tōkyō. Officially recognized as a medical college in 1926, it traces its origins to the Saiseigakusha, established in 1876. In addition to the faculty of medicine and four affiliated hospitals, Nippon Medical School also maintains an Institute for the Study of Geriatric Diseases and an Institute for the Study of Vaccines. Enrollment in 1989 was 627.

Nippon Menard Cosmetic Co, Ltd
日本メナード化粧品[株]

(Nihon Menādo Keshōhin). Manufacturer and distributor of cosmetics and health food. Incorporated in 1959. The firm has a domestic network of 12,000 sales agents and 160,000 saleswomen. Nippon Menard has a joint-venture company in Taiwan and manufacturing companies in Malaysia, South Korea, and Indonesia. For the fiscal year ending March 1990, sales totaled ¥112.6 billion (US $735.6 million), and capitalization stood at ¥74.2 million (US $48,340). Headquarters are in Nagoya.

Nippon Metal Industry Co, Ltd
日本金属工業[株]

(Nippon Kinzoku Kōgyō). Firm engaged in the manufacture and sale of stainless steel sheets, wire, pipes, and secondary processed products; currently the leading manufacturer specializing in stainless steel products. Incorporated in 1932. It was the first in Japan to introduce the argon oxygen decarburization (AOD) refining furnace. The company has overseas offices in New York, Düsseldorf, and Singapore. Sales for the fiscal year ending March 1991 totaled ¥101.4 billion (US $739.1 million), of which exports constituted 16 percent; capitalization stood at ¥12.0 billion (US $87.5 million). Headquarters are in Tōkyō.

Nippon Oil & Fats Co, Ltd
日本油脂[株]

(Nihon Yushi). Company engaged in the manufacture and sale of oil-based and specialty chemicals, edible oils and fats, industrial coatings, and explosives and propellants. The company also has diversified into areas such as ceramics, medical products, and welding materials. It is a member of the Fuyō group and was incorporated in 1949. The company has established overseas subsidiaries and joint ventures, with offices located in New York, London, Düsseldorf, and Singa-

Niseko Skiers come from all over Japan for the many excellent ski slopes near this small Hokkaidō town. Across the valley is the volcano Yōteizan, the "Mt. Fuji" of Hokkaidō.

pore. Sales for the fiscal year ending March 1991 totaled ¥137.4 billion (US $1.0 billion), and capitalization stood at ¥15.8 billion (US $115.2 million). Headquarters are in Tōkyō.

Nippon Oil Co, Ltd   日本石油[株]

(Nihon Sekiyu). Japan's largest and oldest oil company. Incorporated in 1888. While the company itself is engaged principally in the sale of oil, it has subsidiaries and affiliated firms engaged in oil exploration, transportation, refining, and storage, as well as petrochemical projects. The company was founded to produce and refine indigenous crude oil, expanding in the mid-1920s to include the refining of imported crude oil. In 1949 the company concluded an agreement with Caltex Petroleum Corporation, a joint-venture company established by Texaco, Inc, and Standard Oil Company of California (now called Chevron Corporation). Nippon Oil, its subsidiaries, and Nippon Petroleum Refining Co, Ltd, a 50-50 joint venture established in 1951 between the company and Caltex, together form the largest distributor in Japan of petroleum products. Since that time the company has established tanker, exploration, and other related enterprises. The company currently owns a controlling interest in about 20 affiliated companies. Sales for the fiscal year ending March 1991 totaled ¥2.2 trillion (US $16.0 billion). In the same year the company was capitalized at ¥123.6 billion (US $900.9 million). Headquarters are in Tōkyō.

Nippon Otis Elevator Co
日本オーチス・エレベータ[株]

(Nippon Ōchisu Erebēta). Elevator manufacturer. Incorporated in 1932 as a joint venture of Otis Elevator Co (US) and Mitsui & Co. The company developed the world's first linear motor elevator in cooperation with Otis Elevator and Ascinter Otis (France). For the fiscal year ending November 1990, it had sales of ¥55.7 billion (US $431.5 million) and capitalization of ¥4.4 billion (US $34.1 million). Headquarters are in Tōkyō.

Nippon Paint Co, Ltd   日本ペイント[株]

(Nippon Peinto). Manufacturer of synthetic resin paints, thinners, lacquers, and other surface-treatment agents. Established in 1881. It is the second largest paint manufacturer in Japan after KANSAI PAINT CO, LTD. The company expanded overseas in the 1960s and is now involved in joint ventures or technical collaboration with firms in 12 countries. Sales for the fiscal year ending March 1991 totaled ¥160.2 billion (US $1.2 billion), and capitalization stood at ¥27.6 billion (US $201.2 million). Headquarters are in Ōsaka.

Nippon Road Co, Ltd   日本道路[株]

(Nippon Dōro). Road paver. Affiliated with Shimizu Corporation. Incorporated in 1929.

It has overseas offices in Malaysia, Thailand, Indonesia, and Taiwan. Sales for the fiscal year ending March 1991 totaled ¥147.7 billion (US $1.1 billion), of which road paving accounted for 68 percent; paving materials, 15 percent; and civil engineering, 17 percent. The company was capitalized at ¥12.2 billion (US $89.0 million) in the same year. Headquarters are in Tōkyō.

Nippon Roche KK   日本ロシュ[株]

(Nippon Roshu). Pharmaceutical manufacturer. Incorporated in 1932 as an affiliate of F. Hoffmann-La Roche, Ltd, Switzerland. In 1988 the firm introduced to the Japanese market Roferon A, a genetically engineered alpha-interferon drug. For the fiscal year ending December 1990, sales totaled ¥57.1 billion (US $427.6 million) and capitalization stood at ¥8.8 billion (US $65.9 million). Headquarters are in Tōkyō.

Nippon Sanso Corporation
日本酸素[株]

(Nippon Sanso). Firm engaged in the production and sale of industrial gases and gas-manufacturing plants. Incorporated in 1918. Sales for the fiscal year ending March 1991 were ¥179.3 billion (US $1.3 billion), of which sales of oxygen and nitrogen were 28 percent; gas-related equipment, 19 percent; specialty gases, 12 percent; foodstuffs, 8 percent; argon gas, 7 percent; and other products, 26 percent. In the same year capitalization stood at ¥26.9 billion (US $196.1 million). Headquarters are in Tōkyō.

Nippon Sharyō, Ltd   日本車輛製造[株]

(Nippon Sharyō Seizō). Firm producing chiefly rolling stock but also construction machinery and bridges. Incorporated in 1896, it is the oldest Japanese manufacturer of rolling stock. It is known for its technologically advanced railway cars, of which one example is the high-speed "bullet train" (see SHINKANSEN). Its products are exported throughout the world. Sales for the fiscal year ending March 1991 were ¥103.4 billion (US $753.6 million), and capitalization was ¥11.6 billion (US $84.5 million). Headquarters are in Nagoya.

Nippon Sheet Glass Co, Ltd
日本板硝子[株]

(Nihon Itagarasu). Second largest manufacturer of flat glass in Japan. Incorporated in 1918. It possesses outstanding technologies in the manufacture of flat glass, safety glass, and optical fibers. Affiliated with the Sumitomo group, it has joint ventures in the United States, Mexico, Taiwan, Korea, and Malaysia. Sales for the fiscal year ending March 1991 were ¥249.3 billion (US $1.8 billion), and capitalization stood at ¥40.8 billion (US $297.4 million) in the same year. Headquarters are in Ōsaka.

Nippon Shinpan Co, Ltd
日本信販[株]

(Nippon Shimpan). Firm engaged in consumer credit. Incorporated in 1951. Nippon Shinpan initiated an installment credit purchase system and soon after became the first in Japan to offer mortgage loans and to market condominiums. The company introduced a credit card system in the 1960s. Nippon Shinpan is also engaged in personal loans, mortgage loans, and leasing, as well as real estate development. Nippon Shinpan is expanding in Japan and overseas. Agreements with both Visa International and

MasterCard International, Inc, have allowed Nippon Shinpan cards to be used internationally. The company has also built an extensive network of member stores overseas. Total sales for the fiscal year ending March 1991 were ¥331.2 billion (US $2.4 billion), and capitalization was ¥36.6 billion (US $266.8 million). Headquarters are in Tōkyō.

Nippon Shokubai Co, Ltd
[株]日本触媒

(Nippon Shokubai). Manufacturer of chemicals, synthetic resins, and catalysts. Incorporated in 1941. In 1991 its technology for ethylene oxide and ethylene glycol was licensed to the Soviet Union and North Korea, and its technology for acrylic acid and esters to the United States, France, China, Taiwan, the Soviet Union, South Korea, and Mexico. The company has established joint-venture firms in the United States and Germany. Sales for the fiscal year ending November 1990 were ¥137.5 billion (US $1.1 billion), of which export sales were 24 percent; capitalization stood at ¥16.5 billion (US $127.8 million). Headquarters are in Ōsaka.

Nippon Soda Co, Ltd   日本曹達[株]

(Nihon Sōda). Manufacturer of industrial chemicals, fine chemicals, agricultural chemicals, and other chemical products. Incorporated in 1920. In its early years it produced caustic soda through the diaphragm cell process. Since World War II, it has concentrated on producing industrial chemicals and fine chemicals. Sales for the fiscal year ending March 1991 totaled ¥92.3 billion (US $672.7 million). In the same year the export ratio was 27 percent, and the company was capitalized at ¥4.7 billion (US $34.3 million). Headquarters are in Tōkyō.

Nippon Stainless Steel Co, Ltd
日本ステンレス[株]

(Nihon Sutenresu). Manufacturer of stainless steel products. Established in 1934. Using its advanced stainless steel technology, the company produces a wide range of other products, including titanium, high-density alloys, and shape memory alloys. Sales for the fiscal year ending March 1991 totaled ¥104.1 billion (US $758.7 million), of which stainless steel sheets accounted for 72 percent; stainless steel bars, 11 percent; castings, 3 percent; and other products, 14 percent. The company was capitalized at ¥9.5 billion (US $48.3 million) in the same year. Headquarters are in Tōkyō.

Nippon Steel Chemical Co, Ltd
新日鉄化学[株]

(Shin Nittetsu Kagaku). Largest producer of coal-based chemicals in Japan. Incorporated in 1956 as a subsidiary of Nippon Steel Corporation. Its main products are coking coal and a variety of coal tar derivatives. In 1989 its subsidiary, Nippon Steel Chemical Co of America, merged with the American plastic compounder Thermofil, Inc. Sales for the fiscal year ending March 1991 totaled ¥306.1 billion (US $2.2 billion); capitalization stood at ¥21.0 billion (US $153.1 million). Headquarters are in Tōkyō.

Nippon Steel Corporation
新日本製鉄[株]

(Shin Nippon Seitetsu). Largest steelmaker in the world. Its forerunner was Nippon Steel Co, established in 1934. By World War II, Nippon Steel had become an enormous steelmaker. In 1950 it was divided into two companies, Yawata Seitetsu and Fuji Seitetsu, under a law to eliminate excess economic concentration. The two merged in 1970 to form the present Nippon Steel Corporation.

Through the adoption of an integrated steel-manufacturing system, basic oxygen furnaces, reduced coke ratios to lower energy costs, and the computerization of all manufacturing processes, the corporation has come to employ the world's most advanced steel-manufacturing technology. It enables the company to provide technical assistance to steel manufacturers in 35 countries throughout the world. There are 9 mills in Japan and 11 overseas offices. Sales for the 1991 fiscal year totaled ¥2.6 trillion (US $19.0 billion), of which steel products comprised 87 percent; pig iron and steel ingots, 1 percent; and other categories, 12 percent. In the same year the export ratio of steel was 20 percent, and the company was capitalized at ¥419.0 billion (US $2.5 billion). Headquarters are in Tōkyō.

Nippon Suisan Kaisha, Ltd
日本水産[株]

(Nippon Suisan). Fishery company, ranked first in Japan in the volume of fish caught. Founded in 1908. The company specializes in Antarctic krill fishing and other marine products. It has been diversifying from fishing into the production of frozen and canned foods under the Nissui brand name, and into pharmaceutical products. The company is also involved in the building of large fishing ships. The firm has subsidiaries in the United States, South America, Europe, Oceania, and Asia. It is expanding worldwide through 105 affiliates, both domestic and overseas. Sales for the fiscal year ending March 1991 totaled ¥460.7 billion (US $3.4 billion), and capitalization stood at ¥23.5 billion (US $171.3 million). Headquarters are in Tōkyō.

Nippon Telegraph and Telephone Corporation
日本電信電話[株]

(NTT; J: Nippon Denshin Denwa). Largest operator of domestic telephone networks in Japan. The company's predecessor was Nippon Telegraph and Telephone Public Corporation, a government enterprise that monopolized public telecommunications businesses in Japan. The public corporation completed nationwide microwave networks in 1958 and completely automated telephone services in 1979. It inaugurated telex services in 1956, data communications services in 1968, telefacsimile services in 1973, and mobile telecommunications services in 1979. It also played a pioneering role in the fields of microwaves, optical communications, semiconductors, and other high-technology fields. In April 1985 the public corporation was privatized and turned into Japan's largest joint-stock company, capitalized at ¥780.0 billion (US $3.3 billion) and having assets totaling ¥10.0 trillion (US $41.9 billion).

Of NTT's sales in fiscal 1991, 95.0 percent were from domestic telecommunications services (85.0 percent, telephone services; 1.3 percent, telegraph services; 1.5 percent, wireless paging services; and 7.2 percent, other services) and 5.0 percent were from related businesses.

The company's sales for the fiscal year ending March 1991 stood at ¥6.0 trillion (US $43.7 billion), while capitalization stood at ¥780.0 billion (US $5.7 billion) in the same year. Headquarters are in Tōkyō.

Nippon Television Network Corporation (NTV)
日本テレビ放送網[株]

(Nippon Terebi Hōsōmō). A Tōkyō-based commercial broadcasting company serving the Kantō (eastern Honshū) area. SHŌRIKI MATSUTARŌ, an early advocate of the Japanese television industry, founded the company in 1952 as the first commercial broadcasting company to operate a television station. It is closely allied with the YOMIURI SHIMBUN, one of Japan's large national daily newspapers. NTV is a key station in the Nippon News Network (NNN), which includes 30 stations nationwide (1992). It concentrates on mass entertainment, including professional baseball telecasts and variety shows.

Nippon Travel Agency Co, Ltd
[株]日本旅行

(Nihon Ryokō). Travel agency. Founded in 1905. The company has an on-line system for booking the services of hotels, trains, and airlines and is one of the few agents appointed to sell the Japan Rail Pass to foreign tourists. Twenty-five sales offices are located overseas and 320 throughout Japan. Sales revenue in 1990 totaled ¥554.8 billion (US $4.2 billion). Capitalization reached ¥1.0 billion (US $7.5 million) in the same year. Headquarters are in Tōkyō.

Nippon Yakin Kōgyō Co, Ltd
日本冶金工業[株]

(Nippon Yakin Kōgyō). Integrated steel manufacturer, specializing in producing high-grade stainless steel. Incorporated in 1925. Its subsidiaries produce processed stainless steel products such as pipes, wire, kitchen equipment, bathtubs, and storage tanks. Sales for the fiscal year ending March 1991 totaled ¥103.7 billion (US $755.8 million), of which stainless steel sheets accounted for 83 percent; cast and forged stainless steel, 4 percent; and other products, 13 percent. The company was capitalized at ¥20.9 billion (US $152.3 million) in the same year. Headquarters are in Tōkyō.

Nippon Yūsen Kaisha
日本郵船[株]

(Nippon Yūsen). Known around the world as the NYK Line. First modern maritime shipping company in Japan. Nippon Yūsen was originally part of the Mitsubishi Co, established in 1870 by IWASAKI YATARŌ. NYK's direct predecessor was the Mitsubishi Mail Steamship Co. In 1885 the Mitsubishi Mail Steamship Co merged with Kyōdō Un'yu to become Nippon Yūsen. In 1893 NYK opened the first of its long-distance routes, the Bombay line. In 1896 NYK opened routes to Europe, the United States, and Australia. Then in 1916, via the Panama Canal, NYK finally achieved its goal of opening an around-the-world route. In 1989 NYK's fleet consisted of 322 ships, 59 of which were NYK's own ships. NYK offers both container and conventional services. The company is restructuring its operations to provide a full range of sea, land, and air transportation and logistics services. Sales for the fiscal year ending March 1991 totaled ¥532.7 billion (US $3.9 billion). The company was capitalized at ¥74.7 billion (US $544.5 million) in the same year. Headquarters are in Tōkyō.

Nippon Zeon Co, Ltd
日本ゼオン[株]

(Nippon Zeon). Manufacturer of synthetic rubber, synthetic latex, polyvinyl chloride, and C5 hydrocarbon resin. It was incorporated in 1950 as a joint venture of the Furukawa group and Goodrich Chemical of the United States, although the latter withdrew its shares in 1970. The company has developed a unique process of butadiene extraction, which it has licensed in 16 countries worldwide. Sales for the fiscal year ending March 1991 totaled ¥129.4 billion (US $943.1 million), and the company was capitalized at ¥18.6 billion (US $135.6 million). Headquarters are in Tōkyō.

NIRA → National Institute for Research Advancement

Nirasaki
韮崎[市]

City in northwestern Yamanashi Prefecture, central Honshū. Situated on the river Kamanashigawa, in the Edo period (1600–1868) Nirasaki prospered as a post-station town and a terminus for transportation on the river Fujikawa. Main products are rice, fruits, and vegetables. Sericulture is also important. Of note are the Takeda Hachiman Shrine and the Sakai archaeological site. Nirasaki is the gateway to the Southern Japanese Alps (AKAISHI MOUNTAINS). Pop: 29,766.

Nireke no hitobito
楡家の人びと

(tr *The House of Nire*, 1984–85). A saga of a Japanese family, written by KITA MORIO (b 1927); published 1964. The story revolves around Nire Hospital, a mental institution established by Nire Kiichirō, the head of the first of the three generations portrayed. The work spans the Meiji (1868–1912), Taishō (1912–26), and Shōwa (1926–89) periods, ending with the destruction of the hospital during World War II. The novel has a sophisticated sense of humor and many well-drawn and uncommon characters, of which Kiichirō is the prime example. Born Kanesawa Jinsaku, the son of a farmer, Kiichirō fled his hometown, became a doctor, and adopted the unheard-of name of Nire. He builds a reputation and a flourishing practice despite his unorthodox method of examination—looking in the ear of the patient to see the brain. *Nireke no hitobito* stands out among postwar Japanese novels for its intricate characterization, comic flair, and wide-ranging plot. Tetsukichi, the head of the second generation, and Shūji, his son, are based on the author's father, the poet-psychiatrist SAITŌ MOKICHI, and on the author himself.

nirvana → nehan

Niseko
ニセコ[町]

Town in southwestern Hokkaidō; formerly called Kaributo. Principal agricultural products are rice, potatoes, beans, and sugar beets. Dairy farming is also active. Niseko Annupuri, a mountain in Niseko–Shakotan–Otaru Coast Quasi-National Park, is known for its excellent skiing and for its numerous hot springs. Pop: 4,511.

Nishi Amane
西周

(1829–97). Educator and government official; one of the first to assert that Western civilization should be a model for Japan's national reforms in the late 19th century. Nishi adapted European positivism and utilitarianism to the Japanese intellectual tradition.

Nishi was born in the Tsuwano domain (now part of Shimane Prefecture), the son of a *samurai* physician. He grew fascinated with the practical social thought of OGYŪ

Nishi Amane This 19th-century educator and government official advocated European positivism and utilitarianism as superior to Confucian values.

Nishi Honganji This temple's Imperial Messenger's Gate, built in the early 17th century, is an example of the arched gateway called *karamon*, a style that dates back to the 12th century. It has been designated a National Treasure.

Nishida Kitarō Japan's most influential 20th-century philosopher, Nishida attempted a fusion of Western method with the traditions of Buddhist thought.

SORAI (1666–1728). After studying in Holland he transmitted the principles of positivism and utilitarianism through lectures, writings, and Japan's first academic association, the MEIROKUSHA, which was established in 1874. He became a leading figure in the movement to "civilize and enlighten" (*bummei kaika*) the nation.

Nishi introduced the full spectrum of European arts and sciences in *Hyakugaku renkan* (1870, Encyclopedia), which was patterned after the works of Auguste Comte (1798–1857). He also advocated the inductive logic developed by John Stuart Mill (1806–73) as the best approach to learning and denounced the deductive method of Confucians as unscientific. His scholarly *Hyakuichi shinron* (1874, New Theory of the Hundred and One) dismissed Confucian social ethics as no longer appropriate for Japan. However, he avoided rejecting the Chinese and Japanese heritage as useless, reinterpreting these traditions in a progressive, non-Confucian manner so as to justify radical changes. In *Jinsei sampō setsu* (1875, Theory of the Three Human Treasures) Nishi urged all Japanese to seek the goals of health, knowledge, and wealth, stressed by utilitarian philosophers, in place of the Confucian virtues of subservience and frugality.

As a bureaucrat in the Ministry of Military Affairs, he wrote the CONSCRIPTION ORDINANCE OF 1873 (Chōheirei), perhaps the most portentous reform of the new Meiji government. In lectures to young military officers, he emphasized discipline and obedience over the Confucian ideas of hierarchy. He incorporated these ideas in a draft of the IMPERIAL RESCRIPT TO SOLDIERS AND SAILORS (Gunjin Chokuyu) in 1882. Although subsequent intellectuals found Nishi's thought somewhat static, he was a major figure in his country's successful effort to reconcile history with change, imported thought with native ideas, and tradition with modernism.

Nishibiwajima　　　　西枇杷島［町］

Town on the northwestern border of the city of Nagoya in northwestern Aichi Prefecture,

central Honshū. Principal industries include machinery and textile manufacture. Pop: 17,116.

Nishibori Eizaburō　　　　西堀栄三郎

(1903–89). Chemist, specialist in vacuum tube production technology, and mountaineer. Born in Kyōto. Graduated from Kyōto University, where he became a professor in 1956. Also in 1956 Nishibori headed the first Japanese observation team to winter in Antarctica. From 1965 to 1969 he was a trustee of the Japan Nuclear Ship Research and Development Agency and headed the construction project for the nuclear-powered ship MUTSU. In 1980 he served as the leader of the Japan Mountaineering Club's Mt. Everest climb.

Nishida Kitarō　　　　西田幾多郎

(1870–1945). The most important philosopher of modern Japan. Nishida's active life spans some 40 years, during which he strove to assimilate Western philosophy and methodology and to create his own distinctive philosophy based largely upon the eastern religious, especially Buddhist, tradition.

Born in 1870 near the city of Kanazawa in Ishikawa Prefecture to a prominent family, Nishida studied privately under several teachers, including the mathematician Hōjō Tokiyoshi (1859–1929). After entering the Fourth Higher School in 1886, he formed a circle of friends, including the prominent philosopher and exponent of Zen Buddhism D. T. SUZUKI, as well as the educator Yamamoto Ryōkichi (1871–1942). He maintained a close relationship with these two men throughout his life. Nishida left the Fourth Higher School in 1890 to study on his own and in 1891 entered Tōkyō University as a special student. Despite loneliness and unhappiness he performed brilliantly in his course work, producing philosophical essays of considerable distinction. He graduated in 1894.

Because of his irregular academic background, Nishida encountered difficulties in finding employment, but eventually obtained a position at a middle school on the remote Noto Peninsula, enabling him to marry his first cousin, Tokuda Kotomi, and to support a family. Financial hardship and family responsibility prompted him to begin Zen meditation when he returned to Kanazawa in 1896 to take a teaching position at the Fourth Higher School.

For ten years (1899–1909) he taught at the Fourth Higher School, and through his lectures in psychology, logic, and ethics he developed the material that came to constitute his maiden work, ZEN NO KENKYŪ (1911; tr *A Study of Good*, 1960). This work presents Nishida's formulation of the concept of "pure experience," which he saw as prior to and underlying all oppositions, such as those of subject and object, body and mind, and spirit and matter.

Nishida taught at Kyōto University from 1910 until his retirement in 1928. All his works between *Zen no kenkyū* and his retirement emerged through his extensive research and philosophical speculation in conjunction with his position as a professor of philosophy. His second major work, *Jikaku ni okeru chokkan to hansei* (1917, Intuition and Reflection in Self-Consciousness), shows the influence of the French philosopher Henri Bergson and a range of Neo-Kantian philosophers. Nishida strove to eliminate psychologism from his thinking, arriving at a position close to mysticism, which he termed "absolute free will." His

Hataraku mono kara miru mono e (1927, From the Acting to the Seeing) is widely viewed as a unique breakthrough to a realm of reality corresponding to his own mystical experience. In this work he articulated his new concept of *basho*, the "place" of "absolute Nothingness" wherein the "true self" is revealed. In accordance with Buddhist tradition he sought to derive the individual reality of everything, whether a thing or a self, from the self-identity of "absolute Nothingness."

After his retirement from Kyōto University, Nishida produced a succession of essays collected in the following volumes: *Ippansha no jikakuteki taikei* (1930, The Self-Conscious System of the Universal), *Mu no jikakuteki gentei* (1932, The Self-Conscious Determination of Nothingness), *Tetsugaku no kompon mondai* (2 vols, 1933–34; tr *Fundamental Problems of Philosophy*, 1970), and *Tetsugaku rombunshū* (7 vols, 1937–46, Philosophical Essays).

Concerned by the rise of militarism in the 1930s, Nishida was profoundly distressed as World War II progressed, yet he continued his philosophical writings at his home in Kamakura. He died suddenly in early June 1945, just two months before Japan's surrender. Despite criticism from Marxists and other antimetaphysical thinkers, Nishida's work is recognized as constituting the first genuinely original Japanese philosophy of the modern period. A number of the leading philosophers of present-day Japan were either his students or directly influenced by his thought. Since the late 1950s Nishida's work has begun to be introduced and evaluated in the West, where it has been favorably received among those looking toward the establishment of a truly universal philosophy transcending traditional Eastern and Western categories of thought.

Nishida Mitsugi　　　　西田税

(1901–37). A right-wing activist. Also known as Nishida Mitsugu or Nishida Zei. Born in Tottori Prefecture. After graduating from the Military Preparatory School in Hiroshima, he entered the Army Academy, where he organized a group of cadets to discuss political affairs. In 1922 Nishida graduated from the Army Academy, but in 1925 he resigned from active service.

Thereafter he devoted himself to political activity, becoming a disciple of the right-wing thinker KITA IKKI and working to convert young army officers to the cause of helping to establish a new Japan that would replace the old regime dominated by corrupt politicians. In 1927 Nishida tried to organize his followers into the clandestine Heavenly Swords Party (Tenkentō) but gave up when it was discovered by the military police. Although not formally organized, Nishida's disciples in the army started calling themselves the Young Officers' Movement (Seinen Shōkō Undō). Through Nishida they established links with right-wing organizations.

When the Young Officers staged a coup d'état on 26 February 1936 (see FEBRUARY 26TH INCIDENT), in which central Tōkyō was seized and several government officials killed, Nishida stayed behind the scenes. The rebellion was quickly suppressed, and Nishida was executed by a firing squad on 19 August 1937.

Nishihara loans　　　　西原借款

(Nishihara *shakkan*). Financial loans made by the Japanese government to China's DUAN

QIRUI (Tuan Ch'i-jui) government during World War I; named after Nishihara Kamezō (1873–1954), who, as the personal representative of Prime Minister TERAUCHI MASATAKE, negotiated eight loans to China from January 1917 to September 1918 totaling ¥145 million. Ostensibly these loans were made by private Japanese banks for the economic development of China, with the exception of the War Participation Loan. In reality the funds came from the Japanese government for the support of Duan's corrupt government and for financing the civil war against his rivals. In return Japan received confirmation of its claims in Shandong (Shantung) Province (having already acquired German rights in that area at the outbreak of World War I) and more privileges in Manchuria. The Beijing (Peking) government was violently attacked by the Chinese public for making traitorous deals with the Japanese, and the disclosure of the Shandong railway agreement, one of the Nishihara loan agreements, sparked the MAY FOURTH MOVEMENT in 1919.

Nishiharu　　　　　西春[町]

Town in northwestern Aichi Prefecture, central Honshū. Formerly a farming community, Nishiharu now has machinery factories and textile mills and has become a commuter suburb of Nagoya. Situated near the Ichinomiya interchange of the Meishin Expressway, it is also a transportation and warehousing center. Pop: 32,972.

Nishi Honganji　　　　　西本願寺

The head temple of the Jōdo Shinshū Honganji branch of the Buddhist True Pure Land sect (Jōdo Shinshū; see JŌDO SHIN SECT); located in Shimogyō Ward, Kyōto, since 1591, when the site was granted by TOYOTOMI HIDEYOSHI (1537–98) to Kennyo Kōsa (1543–92), the HONGANJI's 11th abbot (hossu). As headquarters of the sect, the temple replaced the ISHIYAMA HONGANJI, which had been destroyed in 1580. The name Nishi (western) Honganji distinguishes this temple from the Higashi (eastern) Honganji situated a few blocks to the east, founded in a succession dispute between Kennyo's sons Kyōnyo Kōju (1558–1614) and Junnyo Kōshō (1577–1631). Junnyo, whom Hideyoshi recognized as abbot in 1593, retained the Nishi Honganji, and Kyōnyo built the Higashi Honganji in 1603. The TOKUGAWA SHOGUNATE (1603–1867) recognized the two rival Honganji as independent establishments of the Jōdo Shin sect.

The Nishi Honganji was devastated by an earthquake in 1596 and a fire in January 1618; the present temple complex postdates these events. Nevertheless, the complex contains a number of important architectural and artistic features, including an outdoor Nō stage said to be the oldest in existence, the three-story Hiunkaku (Flying Cloud Pavilion), and decorative paintings by members of the KANŌ SCHOOL. The Nishi Honganji is the headquarters of a religious organization that as of 1989 had 6,921,908 members and 10,364 branch temples and maintained missions in the United States, Canada, Brazil, Great Britain, Switzerland, and Taiwan. See also HIGASHI HONGANJI.

nishijin-ori　　　　　西陣織

General term for high-quality silk fabrics produced in the Nishijin weaving district of Kyōto. The Kyōto weaving industry dates back to the foundation of the city in 794. During the ŌNIN WAR (1467–77) weavers as well as other townspeople left Kyōto for outlying areas, and upon their return organized themselves into work groups in the Nishijin district. In the late Edo period (1600–1868) a number of other textile production centers arose and began to compete with the Nishijin district. Nishijin maintained its primacy, especially after it imported the jacquard loom (1874) and made other technical improvements. Today Nishijin weavers produce wools and synthetic fabrics, in addition to high-quality silks such as KARA-ORI.

Nishikawa Joken　　　　　西川如見

(1648–1724). Astronomer of the mid-Edo period (1600–1868). Real name Nishikawa Tadahide. Born in Hizen Province (now Nagasaki and Saga prefectures). Nishikawa studied astronomy under Kobayashi Yoshinobu (1600–1683) and Confucianism under Nambu Sōju. A man of wide interests, he was invited in 1719 by the shōgun TOKUGAWA YOSHIMUNE to discuss astronomy and Western learning in general. Nishikawa wrote many books on astronomy and geography, as well as a book of practical advice to merchants entitled Chōnin-bukuro (1719, Merchant's Satchel).

Nishikawa Kōjirō → Nishikawa Mitsujirō

Nishikawa Mitsujirō　　　　　西川光二郎

(1876–1940). Socialist. Also known as Nishikawa Kōjirō. Born in Hyōgo Prefecture, Nishikawa became a Christian while in middle school, and at Sapporo Agricultural College (now Hokkaidō University) he came under the influence of NITOBE INAZŌ. Transferring to Tōkyō Semmon Gakkō (now Waseda University), he became interested in socialism and collaborated with the socialist KATAYAMA SEN in publishing a labor magazine called Rōdō sekai (Labor World) and in founding the Socialist Democratic Party (SHAKAI MINSHUTŌ) in 1901. In 1903 he joined the socialist-pacifist organization HEIMINSHA (Society of Commoners) and wrote for its weekly, the Heimin shimbun. A charter member of the JAPAN SOCIALIST PARTY (Nihon Shakaitō), Nishikawa was jailed in 1908 for organizing a demonstration against fare increases in the Tōkyō streetcar system. Upon his release in 1910, he withdrew from politics altogether.

Nishikawa Shōji　　　　　西川正治

(1884–1952). Physicist who pioneered the use of X-ray diffraction in the analysis of atomic structures of complex crystals. Born in the city of Hachiōji, Tōkyō Prefecture. Nishikawa graduated in 1910 from Tōkyō University, where he taught from 1915 until his retirement in 1945. In 1917 he became associated with the INSTITUTE OF PHYSICAL AND CHEMICAL RESEARCH. Through his work he helped raise the level of Japanese research on X-ray and electromagnetic diffraction to the highest international standards. He received the Order of Culture in 1951.

Nishikawa Sukenobu　　　　　西川祐信

(1671–1750). Leading Kyōto UKIYO-E artist. Studied first under the traditional masters Kanō Einō (ca 1631–97) and Tosa Mitsusuke (dates unknown). From about 1699 he turned from classical subjects and styles to genre depictions of the current world, soon developing his own style of ukiyo-e—strongly influenced by Hishikawa MORONOBU. Sukenobu first illustrated novels and kabuki texts, particularly for the noted Kyōto publisher Hachimonjiya Jishō (d

1745; see HACHIMONJIYA-BON), producing a total of about 60 such books during the period 1699–1745. Sukenobu's best-known works are his picture books depicting the life and legends of old Japan; these, too, comprise at least 60 separate works and date from 1718 to 1750. In addition, he did several volumes of kimono designs, as well as some two dozen or more SHUNGA (erotica) books. Though genuine works by him are rare today, Sukenobu was also a leading painter of the time.

Nishikawa Yasushi　　　　　西川寧

(1902–89). Calligrapher. Professional name Nishikawa Seian. Born in Tōkyō. Graduated from Keiō University. Nishikawa was the son of the calligrapher Nishikawa Shundō, and he studied calligraphy under his father. As a student in Beijing (Peking) in 1940, he studied Chinese literature and ancient Chinese bronze and stone inscriptions. Nishikawa became a leading figure in contemporary Japanese calligraphy, both as a scholar of Chinese calligraphy and for his own work. He received the Japan Art Academy Prize in 1955 and became a member of the academy in 1969. In 1985 he was awarded the Order of Culture. His books include Sho no hensō (1960, The Changing Face of Calligraphy).

nishiki　　　　　錦

(brocade). Term loosely applied to multicolored cloth. Today it suggests silk of brocade weave with supplementary weft patterns in thick, glossy silk or gold or silver thread, appearing much like embroidery. The earliest reference to nishiki was in the 3rd century and describes a multicolored, plain-weave cloth known as wakin or imon zatsukin. In the 7th and 8th centuries, warp brocade (keikin) with repetitive patterns of Persian and Chinese origin was popular among the aristocracy. By the 9th century the art of warp brocade lost favor to the more flexible weft brocade (ikin). The length of the pattern floats gradually increased, especially after the introduction in the 14th and 15th centuries of extra warp threads intended to catch the reserved weft on the back of the cloth. Types of nishiki include KARA-ORI, ATSUITA, ungen nishiki, Ezo nishiki, toji nishiki, KINRAN AND GINRAN, and tsuzure nishiki (see TSUZURE-ORI). These brocades are used for garments such as OBI, KIMONO, hats, and shoes, or for bags or scroll mountings.

Nishimatsu Construction Co, Ltd　　　　　西松建設[株]

(Nishimatsu Kensetsu). Company engaged in civil engineering and architectural construction. Incorporated in 1937. The company operates in more than 10 countries, in-

nishijin-ori
1 A chain of perforated cards (at left in photo) controls the warp threads of a jacquard loom, one of a variety of looms used by the weavers of the Nishijin district.
2 A detail of an obi sash richly brocaded in the style known as karaori on the loom of a Nishijin weaver.

cluding Hong Kong, Thailand, Singapore, the United States, and the United Kingdom. Sales for the fiscal year ending March 1991 totaled ¥552.1 billion (US $4.0 billion), of which construction accounted for 58 percent and civil engineering and other work, 42 percent. In the same year the firm was capitalized at ¥22.3 billion (US $162.5 million). Headquarters are in Tōkyō.

Nishimura Eiichi　　西村栄一

(1904–71). Politician. Born in Nara Prefecture. Nishimura graduated from a French high school in Shanghai. He was elected to the House of Representatives as a candidate for the JAPAN SOCIALIST PARTY in 1946. He participated in the formation of the DEMOCRATIC SOCIALIST PARTY in 1960, became its secretary-general in 1962, and its chairman in 1967.

Nishimura Shigeki　　西村茂樹

Nishimura Shigeki This Meiji-period educator worked to teach the public about Western civilization and to promote moral reform as a prerequisite for Japan's modernization.

(1828–1902). Educator and moralist of the early Meiji period (1868–1912) and author of more than 130 books and 200 articles. Pen name Nishimura Hakuō. Born in the Sakura domain (now part of Chiba Prefecture). Nishimura's early education was based on the Confucian classics but included WESTERN LEARNING as well.

Nishimura did not support the MEIJI RESTORATION of 1868, yet he later entered the new imperial government and became a major figure in the movement to educate the Japanese on the essentials of Western civilization. He became a charter member of the MEIROKUSHA (Meiji 6 Society), a short-lived intellectual group organized in 1873–74 by Japan's former diplomatic representative to the United States, MORI ARINORI. In their well-known journal, the *Meiroku zasshi*, published in 43 issues between spring 1874 and fall 1875, Nishimura wrote on subjects such as free trade, world political systems, the relevance of ethics to government, and changes occurring in Japanese society.

In 1876 Nishimura founded in Tōkyō a society for ethical training, reorganized in 1887 as the Nihon Kōdōkai (Japan Society for the Expansion of the Way). This reflected his belief that a reassertion of moral values was necessary for Japan's entry into the modern world. The society was a remarkable success. In 1890 he was selected as an imperial appointee to the House of Peers. His most popular works are *Nihon dōtoku ron* (1887, Discourse on Japanese Morality) and *Fujo kagami* (1887, A Mirror for Women). *Hakuō Nishimura Shigeki den* (1933) is his official biography.

nishin ⟶ herring

Nishina Yoshio　　仁科芳雄

(1890–1951). Physicist. Father of Japanese nuclear physics. Born in Okayama Prefecture, he graduated from Tōkyō University in 1918. His laboratory at the INSTITUTE OF PHYSICAL AND CHEMICAL RESEARCH became the center for the study of nuclear physics in Japan. He served as mentor to YUKAWA HIDEKI, TOMONAGA SHIN'ICHIRŌ, SAKATA SHŌICHI, and many other internationally known physicists. In 1937 Nishina became the first to measure the mass of the Yukawa meson, narrowly missing being its discoverer. He received the Order of Culture in 1946.

Nishi-Nippon Railroad Co, Ltd
西日本鉄道[株]

(Nishi Nippon Tetsudō). Company engaged in railway and bus transportation as well as

leasing. Incorporated in 1908. Its bus division is the largest in the nation. The company has business offices in 22 overseas cities, including New York. Revenues for the fiscal year ending March 1991 totaled ¥140.0 billion (US $1.0 billion), and the company was capitalized at ¥25.9 billion (US $188.8 million) in the same year. Headquarters are in the city of Fukuoka, Fukuoka Prefecture.

Nishi Nippon shimbun　　西日本新聞

A leading Kyūshū daily newspaper published in the city of Fukuoka. The paper began publication in 1877 as the *Tsukushi shimbun;* in 1880 its name was changed to *Fukuoka nichinichi shimbun.* In 1942 the *Fukuoka nichinichi* merged with another daily, the *Kyūshū nippō,* under the present name. Today the *Nishi Nippon shimbun* is an influential voice among Kyūshū news media. Circulation: 817,000 (1990).

Nishinomiya　　西宮[市]

City in southeastern Hyōgo Prefecture, western Honshū, on ŌSAKA BAY. It developed early as a market town as well as a shrine town. Known for its *sake*-brewing industry since the 17th century, it has steel and food-processing factories. The city is a residential satellite city of Ōsaka and Kōbe. KŌSHIEN STADIUM (a baseball stadium) is located here. Pop: 426,909.

Nishinoomote　　西之表[市]

City on the island of Tanegashima; administratively a part of Kagoshima Prefecture, Kyūshū. A castle town of the Tanegashima family beginning in the Kamakura period (1185–1333), it is now the island's commercial, administrative, and cultural center, known for fishing, dairy farming, sweet potatoes, sugarcane, and vegetables. Pop: 20,952.

Nishio　　西尾[市]

City in south-central Aichi Prefecture, central Honshū. It has been known for its cotton textiles and tea since the Edo period (1600–1868), when it was a castle town of the Matsudaira family. Pop: 95,197.

Nishio Suehiro　　西尾末広

(1891–1981). Labor leader and politician. Born in Kagawa Prefecture. Nishio began working in a factory at age 14 and joined the fledgling labor organization YŪAIKAI in 1919. He rose quickly in the labor movement and was chosen chairman of the SŌDŌMEI central committee in 1924. In 1926 he led the withdrawal of the Sōdōmei from the RŌDŌ NŌMINTŌ party and was instrumental in forming the SHAKAI MINSHŪTŌ. In the first election (1928) held after the enactment of universal manhood suffrage, he was elected to the Diet for the first of 15 terms. In November 1945, with KATAYAMA TETSU and others, Nishio formed the JAPAN SOCIALIST PARTY. He was named head of the cabinet secretariat in 1947 and deputy prime minister in 1948. Opposed to any form of cooperation with communists, he and his supporters formed the Minshu Shakaitō (DEMOCRATIC SOCIALIST PARTY) in January 1960. He stepped down as party chairman in 1967 and retired in 1972.

Nishi-Rosen Agreement
西・ローゼン協定

(Nishi-Rōzen Kyōtei). Accord between Japan and Russia concerning Korea; signed in Tōkyō on 25 April 1898 by Russian Minister Roman Romanovich Rosen (1847–1922) and Foreign Minister Nishi Tokujirō (1847–

1912). Japan and Russia had been vying for influence in the Korean peninsula, especially since Japan's victory in the SINO-JAPANESE WAR OF 1894–1895 and the ensuing TRIPARTITE INTERVENTION. Under the terms of the agreement the two nations would refrain from intervention in Korean domestic politics and would seek prior approval from each other before sending military or financial advisers at Korea's request. Russia also pledged not to obstruct Japanese commercial and industrial development in Korea. Russia explicitly recognized Japan's special position in Korea, while Japan implicitly recognized Russia's sphere of influence in Manchuria. See also YAMAGATA-LOBANOV AGREEMENT.

Nishi Sonogi Peninsula　　西彼杵半島

(Nishi Sonogi Hantō). Located in northwestern Nagasaki Prefecture, northwestern Kyūshū, bounded by Ōmura Bay to the east and by the Gotō Sea to the west. Sweet potatoes, watermelons, and mandarin oranges are grown. Pearl culture flourishes. The Saikai Bridge connects the northern tip with the mainland.

Nishi Takeichi　　西竹一

(1902–45). Equestrian and military man. Born in Tōkyō. Graduate of the Army Academy. He won the gold medal in equestrian jumping in the 1932 Los Angeles Olympic Games. Died in the Battle of Iōjima (Iwojima) in 1945.

Nishitani Keiji　　西谷啓治

(1900–1990). Philosopher. Born in Ishikawa Prefecture, he graduated from Kyōto University and became a professor there in 1943. His primary concern was the fundamental relation between human existence and religion. He compared "nothingness" and "detachment" in the mysticism of Meister Eckhart (ca 1260–1327) with the Buddhist notion of "emptiness" (*kū*), finding a common transcendental or absolute stance. He developed a philosophy of absolute nothingness as the religious realization of a self located in a bottomless abyss. This new kind of nihilism serves to synthesize Eastern and Western thought. His major works include *Kami to zettaimu* (1948) and *Shūkyō to wa nani ka* (1961; tr *Religion and Nothingness,* 1982).

Nishiwaki　　西脇[市]

City in central Hyōgo Prefecture, western Honshū, on the river KAKOGAWA. The city is famous for its textiles, known collectively as *banshū-ori.* These include ginghams and broadcloths, which presently are exported worldwide. Pop: 38,230.

Nishiwaki Junzaburō　　西脇順三郎

(1894–1982). One of Japan's outstanding contemporary poets and an influential literary critic. Born in Niigata Prefecture. His major collections of verse, written between 1933 and 1970, reveal an astonishing range of intellectual accomplishment and bear comparison with the work of Western poets Nishiwaki most admired, notably Ezra Pound, T. S. Eliot, and the French surrealists. Nishiwaki was strongly attracted to literature while a student at Keiō University. In 1922 he left Japan to study in England. His first volume of poems, *Spectrum,* was written in English and published in London in 1925. Soon afterward, Nishiwaki returned to Japan and in 1926 became a professor of English literature at Keiō University.

Inspired by the artistic and linguistic accomplishments of HAGIWARA SAKUTARŌ (1886–1942), the finest poet of his period, Nishiwaki began to compose poetry in Japanese, creating new techniques for writing contemporary poetry. These experiments were grouped together and published in 1933 as *Ambarvalia*, a collection that remains influential. Another major collection, *Tabibito kaerazu* (No Traveler Returns), was published in 1947.

In 1952 Nishiwaki published his much-admired translation of T. S. Eliot's *The Wasteland*. In 1953 he published his poetry collection *Kindai no gūwa* (Modern Fables), the first in what was to remain his mature style. In addition to poetry, Nishiwaki continued his multiple career as a teacher (until his retirement from Keiō in 1962), scholar, critic, and translator (notably of Eliot's *Four Quartets*, Shakespeare's sonnets, a lengthy collection of Mallarmé, and Joyce's *Chamber Music*).

Nishiyama Sōin　西山宗因

(1605–82). RENGA (linked verse) and *haikai* (see HAIKU) poet. Born in Yatsushiro, Higo Province (now Kumamoto Prefecture). While a teenager he entered the service of Katō Masakata (1580–1648), master of Yatsushiro Castle and chief retainer of Katō Tadahiro (1601–53), the Higo *daimyō*. Masakata introduced Sōin to the art of *renga* and sent him to Kyōto in 1621 to study with Satomura Shōtaku, official *renga* master to the shogunate. Sōin reached the height of his career in 1647, when he was appointed master of the Ōsaka Temmangū shrine *renga* office. He did not become active in *haikai* circles until after 1670. When he had already retired and taken the tonsure, he became the leader of a radical movement of young *haikai* poets (the DANRIN SCHOOL) in Ōsaka. The successive publication of his *haikai* verses—first with *Saiō toppyakuin* (Sōin's Ten 100-Verse Sequences; composed between 1661 and 1670) in 1673 and then his visit to Edo (now Tōkyō) in 1675, which occasioned the *Danrin toppyakuin* (Ten 100-Verse Sequences of the Danrin School)—established the new group under his reputable leadership.

Nishiyama Suishō　西山翠嶂

(1879–1958). Japanese-style (NIHONGA) painter, who specialized in figure paintings, landscapes, and historical subjects. Real name Nishiyama Usaburō. Born in Kyōto. He studied with TAKEUCHI SEIHŌ and graduated from the Kyōto Municipal School of Fine Arts and Crafts in 1899. He won third prize in the government exhibition, the BUNTEN, in 1907. He subsequently received special awards for three consecutive years (1916–18) and was also invited to serve as a judge in official exhibits. In 1929 he was elected to the Imperial Fine Arts Academy (Teikoku Bijutsuin). Nishiyama received the Order of Culture in 1957.

Nishizawa Ippū　西沢一風

(1665–1731). Writer and publisher of the mid-Edo period (1600–1868). Born in Ōsaka; owner of a small publishing business and author of 20 popular novels (UKIYO-ZŌSHI). He was the central *ukiyo-zōshi* writer in the Kyōto-Ōsaka area following the death of SAIKAKU. He later became interested in JŌRURI puppet plays and coauthored approximately 10 of these. After retiring he wrote books on the history of *jōruri*, such as *Imamukashi ayatsuri nendaiki* (1727). His best-known *ukiyozōshi* is *Gozen gikeiki* (1700).

Nishizawa Jun'ichi　西沢潤一

(1926–). Physicist. Born in Miyagi Prefecture. Nishizawa graduated from Tōhoku University, becoming a professor there in 1962 and president of the university in 1990. He is one of Japan's pioneers in the field of semiconductor research. He gained international attention for a 1955 paper outlining the basic principles of fiber optics and for his invention in 1970 of the static induction transistor. He received the Order of Culture in 1989.

Nishizuka Yasutomi　西塚泰美

(1932–). Biochemist. Born in Hyōgo Prefecture. Graduate of Kyōto University, Nishizuka became a professor at Kōbe University in 1969. He is known for his discovery of protein C kinase, a protein kinase (phosphate enzyme) that responds sharply to external stimuli. In 1986 Nishizuka published a dissertation on the role of calcium ions in cellular signal transfer that became well known throughout the scientific world. He received the Order of Culture in 1988.

Nissan Chemical Industries, Ltd　日産化学工業[株]

(Nissan Kagaku Kōgyō). Chemical company engaged in the manufacture of chemical products, fine chemicals, fertilizers, agrochemicals, and pharmaceuticals. Incorporated in 1927. In 1937 it joined with the Nissan group and took its present name. Sales for the fiscal year ending March 1991 were ¥88.1 billion (US $642.1 million), with an export ratio of 19 percent. The company was capitalized at ¥11.8 billion (US $86.0 million) in the same year. Headquarters are in Tōkyō.

Nissan Diesel Motor Co, Ltd　日産ディーゼル工業[株]

(Nissan Dīzeru Kōgyō). Manufacturer and seller of diesel engines, trucks, and buses. An affiliate of the Nissan Motor group. Nissan Diesel's predecessor was a company established in 1935 to manufacture two-cycle diesel engines under license from Krupp Junkers AG, Germany. Since then, Nissan Diesel has expanded its product line to include trucks, buses, and industrial and marine engines. The firm started exporting its products in 1960, and more than 270,000 vehicles have been exported to overseas markets. In the fiscal year ending March 1991 sales totaled ¥393.8 billion (US $2.9 billion), of which exports constituted 21 percent, and the company was capitalized at ¥11.6 billion (US $84.5 million). Headquarters are in Ageo, Saitama Prefecture.

Nissan Motor Co, Ltd　日産自動車[株]

(Nissan Jidōsha). Automotive manufacturer, ranked second in the number of cars produced in Japan. Passenger cars occupy the bulk of the company's sales, but the firm also manufactures trucks, automobile parts, forklift trucks, textile machinery, aerospace components, and boats. The forerunner of the company was the Jidōsha Seizō Co, established by AIKAWA YOSHISUKE in 1933; it took its current name the following year. The company completed a new plant in Yokohama in 1934 and started mass production of small cars. After World War II it began to produce passenger cars again and increased production capacity by a series of investments in production facilities and equipment, developing a high level of automation as early as 1956. It currently has 250 dealers in Japan and 181 distributors with more than 6,300 dealers in 149 foreign countries. In the 1980s the company developed numerous overseas local manufacturing facilities and as of 1989 managed 24 assembly factories in 21 countries, including the United States, the United Kingdom, Spain, Mexico, and Australia. Sales for the fiscal year ending March 1991 totaled ¥4.2 trillion (US $30.6 billion), and the company's capitalization stood at ¥203.3 billion (US $1.5 billion). Headquarters are in Tōkyō.

Nissan Shatai Co, Ltd　日産車体[株]

(Nissan Shatai). Company engaged chiefly in the development and assembly of passenger cars, small commercial vans, and sports cars for the NISSAN MOTOR CO, LTD. Its predecessor was Nippon Kokusai Kōkū Kōgyō, established in 1941 as an aircraft manufacturer. In 1951 it affiliated with the Nissan Motor Co and engaged in the production of car bodies. Sales for the fiscal year ending March 1991 totaled ¥528.8 billion (US $3.9 billion), and capitalization stood at ¥7.9 billion (US $57.6 million). Approximately 43 percent of the capital of the company was provided by the Nissan Motor Co. Headquarters are in the city of Hiratsuka, Kanagawa Prefecture.

Nisshinbō Industries, Inc　日清紡績[株]

(Nisshin Bōseki). Cotton-spinning, weaving, and processing company. It also produces chemical and synthetic fibers, automobile brakes, machine tools, and polyurethane foam, as well as manufacturing paper and printing labels. Incorporated in 1907, it has subsidiary firms in Brazil, the United States, and the Netherlands. Sales for the fiscal year ending March 1991 totaled ¥204.2 billion (US $1.5 billion), with an export ratio of 11 percent. The company was capitalized at ¥27.1 billion (US $197.5 million) in the same year. Headquarters are in Tōkyō.

Nisshin Flour Milling Co, Ltd　日清製粉[株]

(Nisshin Seifun). Largest flour-milling company in Japan, producing wheat flour, processed foods, and pharmaceuticals. The company was established in 1900 as the Tatebayashi Flour Milling Co and took its current name in 1907. The company concentrated solely on flour milling until 1961, when it started production of feeds and processed foods. It has four affiliated feed and livestock companies and two affiliated food firms, as well as subsidiary companies in the fine chemicals and engineering sectors. Sales for the fiscal year ending March 1991 totaled ¥317.4 billion (US $2.3 billion), and the company was capitalized at ¥15.5 billion (US $113.0 million) in the same year. Corporate headquarters are in Tōkyō.

Nisshin Oil Mills, Ltd　日清製油[株]

(Nisshin Seiyu). Manufacturer of edible oil and fats. Incorporated in 1907. The first company to produce salad oil in Japan. The company imports raw materials, including soybeans from the United States and Canada, and provides technological assistance to oil mills in Canada, South Korea, and China. The firm operates oil mills as joint ventures in Canada and China. It is also involved in the development of chemical products, such as raw materials for pharmaceuticals and cosmetics. Sales for the fiscal year ending March 1991 totaled ¥128.2 billion (US $934.4 million), and capitalization stood at ¥13.7

Nishiwaki Junzaburō This outstanding contemporary poet had a powerful influence on the development of avant-garde Japanese poetry.

Nitobe Inazō The author, teacher, and diplomat during a 1932 visit to the United States.

Nitta Jirō Many of this novelist's works have harsh mountain settings, drawn from his experience as a technician at the meteorological station on Mt. Fuji.

billion (US $99.9 million). Headquarters are in Tōkyō.

Nisshin Senso → Sino-Japanese War of 1894–1895

Nisshin Steel Co, Ltd
日新製鋼[株]

(Nisshin Seikō). Sixth largest integrated steel producer in Japan, with an annual crude steel production capacity of 3.3 million metric tons (3.6 million short tons). Incorporated in 1928. Nisshin's products include surface-treated steel, stainless steel, hot- and cold-rolled ordinary steel, and specialty steel. The company is active in export markets and maintains offices in New York, Düsseldorf, and Singapore. Sales for the fiscal year ending March 1991 were ¥429.2 billion (US $3.1 billion), with an export ratio of 14 percent; the company was capitalized at ¥80.0 billion (US $583.1 million) in the same year. Headquarters are in Tōkyō.

Nisshō Iwai Corporation
日商岩井[株]

(Nisshō Iwai). General trading company (*sōgō shōsha*); member of the SANWA BANK, LTD, group. Established in 1968 through the merger of Nisshō Co, Ltd, and Iwai & Co, Ltd. The firm is involved in the trading of a variety of commodities, including metal and steel products, machinery (including aircraft, ships, and rolling stock), and energy-related materials such as liquefied natural gas. The company has 20 overseas subsidiaries and affiliates and 153 representative offices worldwide. Sales for the fiscal year ending March 1991 totaled ¥13.3 trillion (US $96.9 billion), with ¥79.9 billion (US $582.4 million) in capital. Headquarters are in Ōsaka.

Nissin Food Products Co, Ltd
日清食品[株]

(Nisshin Shokuhin). Manufacturer of instant noodles. Incorporated in 1948. Its products are marketed abroad under the brand names Cup o' Noodles, Oodles of Noodles, and Top Ramen. It has subsidiaries in the United States, Singapore, Brazil, and Hong Kong, and it provides technology to six companies overseas. Sales for the fiscal year ending March 1991 totaled ¥171.2 billion (US $1.3 billion). The company was capitalized at ¥24.8 billion (US $180.8 million) in the same year. Headquarters are in Ōsaka.

Nissin Sugar Mfg Co, Ltd
日新製糖[株]

(Nisshin Seitō). Sugar manufacturer. Established in 1950. For the fiscal year ending March 1991, sales totaled ¥48.2 billion (US $351.3 million), of which sugar accounted for 86 percent and sports club operation and other businesses 14 percent. Capitalization stood at ¥7.0 billion (US $51.0 million) in the same year. Headquarters are in Tōkyō.

Nitchū Senso → Sino-Japanese War of 1937–1945

Nitobe Inazō
新渡戸稲造

(1862–1933). Educator, cultural interpreter, and civil servant. He spent his early years in the northern Honshū city of Morioka. He studied agricultural economics at the new Sapporo Agricultural College (now Hokkaidō University), became a Christian, and in 1883 entered Tōkyō University for further instruction in English literature and economics. Desiring to become a "bridge" between

Japan and the West, he studied in the United States for three years and in Germany for another three years. By the time he returned to Japan he had published one book each in English and German and had earned the first of five doctoral degrees (two of them honorary).

As a professor at his alma mater in Sapporo, Nitobe lectured widely, reorganized the curriculum, and helped administer two private schools. In 1897 he resigned because of poor health and went with his American wife to the United States, where he wrote his famous *Bushido: The Soul of Japan* (1899). He was head of the First Higher School in Tōkyō from 1906 to 1913, when he became a professor of colonial policy at Tōkyō University. In 1918 he attended the Versailles Peace Conference and remained in Geneva as the under-secretary-general of the League of Nations. He returned to Japan in 1926 and became chairman of the Japan Council of the INSTITUTE OF PACIFIC RELATIONS.

Nitobe's numerous writings in English made him the best-known Japanese writer in the West during his lifetime. He also wrote widely on individual moral cultivation, the subject of his work *Shūyō* (1911, Self-Cultivation).

Nitta family
新田氏

(Nittashi). Warrior family founded by MINAMOTO NO YOSHIIE's grandson Yoshishige (1135–1202), whose lands were in the Nitta district of Kōzuke Province (now Gumma Prefecture). He supported MINAMOTO NO YORITOMO against the TAIRA FAMILY in 1180 in the Battle of Ishibashiyama. In 1333 NITTA YOSHISADA espoused the cause of Emperor GO-DAIGO and was a leader in the destruction of the HŌJŌ FAMILY in Kamakura. After the KEMMU RESTORATION (1333–36) Yoshisada fell out with ASHIKAGA TAKAUJI. When Takauji turned against the emperor, the Nitta remained loyal to Go-Daigo's Southern Court (see NORTHERN AND SOUTHERN COURTS), fighting against Ashikaga forces and eventually being destroyed. A branch family, the Iwamatsu, joined the Ashikaga, took over the Nitta lands, and revived the name.

Nitta Isamu
仁田勇

(1899–1984). Chemist noted for his use of X-ray diffraction techniques to determine the lattice structure of organic compounds. He is also known for his detailed analysis of tetrodotoxin, a powerful poison found in certain kinds of globefish. Born in Tōkyō, he graduated from Tōkyō University in 1923. After working at the INSTITUTE OF PHYSICAL AND CHEMICAL RESEARCH, he moved to Ōsaka University, where he served as professor from 1933 to 1960. He received the Order of Culture in 1966.

Nitta Jirō
新田次郎

(1912–80). Novelist. Real name Fujiwara Hiroto. Born in Nagano Prefecture. Nitta received the Naoki Prize for *Gōrikiden* (1951, The Story of a Mountain Guide). He was a prolific writer in many genres, with period novels and novels set in the mountains prominent among them. A common element throughout Nitta's works is his vigorous depiction of man's struggles with the harshness of nature. Nitta's works include *Hakkōdasan shi no hōkō* (1971, Death on Mt. Hakkōda) and *Takeda Shingen* (1969–73).

Nitta Yoshisada
新田義貞

(1301–38). Warrior of the late Kamakura (1185–1333) and early Muromachi (1333–

1568) periods. The NITTA FAMILY, a branch of the MINAMOTO FAMILY, originated in the Nitta district of Kōzuke Province (now Gumma Prefecture). Yoshisada was dispatched by the HŌJŌ FAMILY, regents of the KAMAKURA SHOGUNATE, to suppress a revolt by Emperor GO-DAIGO in 1331. Instead of attacking Go-Daigo, Yoshisada embraced the emperor's cause, captured Kamakura, and destroyed the shogunate in 1333 (see GENKŌ INCIDENT; KEMMU RESTORATION). When ASHIKAGA TAKAUJI revolted against Go-Daigo in 1335, Yoshisada led imperial forces against him at Takenoshita in Hakone but was defeated. In the following year he tried to check Takauji's advance on Kyōto. Takauji, however, cut him off from his ally KUSUNOKI MASASHIGE, destroyed Masashige at the Battle of MINATOGAWA, and chased Yoshisada from the field. Yoshisada was killed in 1338 in an engagement with Takauji's ally Shiba Takatsune (1305–67) in Echizen (now part of Fukui Prefecture).

Nittetsu Mining Co, Ltd
日鉄鉱業[株]

(Nittetsu Kōgyō). Company primarily engaged in limestone mining. Formerly the mining division of Japan Iron & Steel Co, Ltd (now NIPPON STEEL CORPORATION), the company became independent in 1939 and is now diversifying into civil-engineering and mining machinery and chemical products, including coagulants and inorganic paper items. For the fiscal year ending March 1991, sales totaled ¥72.8 billion (US $530.6 million) and capitalization stood at ¥3.8 billion (US $27.7 million). Headquarters are in Tōkyō.

Nittetsu Shōji Co, Ltd
日鉄商事[株]

(Nittetsu Shōji). Trading company specializing in steel. Incorporated in 1977 as a subsidiary of NIPPON STEEL CORPORATION. For the fiscal year ending March 1991, sales totaled ¥1.3 trillion (US $9.4 billion) and capitalization stood at ¥9.0 billion (US $65.6 million). Headquarters are in Tōkyō.

Nittō Bōseki Co, Ltd
日東紡績[株]

(Nittō Bōseki). Textile company; also Japan's largest producer of glass fibers and rock wool. Nittō Bōseki was incorporated in 1918 as Fukushima Seiren Seishi and changed its name to Fukushima Bōshoku in 1919. In 1923 it purchased Iwashiro Bōsekisho from Katakura Seishi Bōseki Co and assumed its present name. Sales for the fiscal year ending April 1991 totaled ¥141.2 billion (US $1.0 billion). In the same year the company was capitalized at ¥20.0 billion (US $145.8 million). Headquarters are in Tōkyō.

Nittō Chemical Industry Co, Ltd
日東化学工業[株]

(Nittō Kagaku Kōgyō). Manufacturer of industrial chemicals, acrylonitrile, and unique fine chemicals such as chemical grouts and polyelectrolytes. Incorporated in 1937. The company does business in more than 20 countries. Sales for the fiscal year ending March 1991 were ¥40.4 billion (US $294.5 million), the export ratio was 11 percent, and the company was capitalized at ¥8.6 billion (US $62.7 million). Headquarters are in Tōkyō.

Nittō Denkō Corporation
日東電工[株]

(Nittō Denkō). Manufacturer of high-polymer industrial materials. Incorporated in 1918. Nittō Denkō manufactures more than 4,000 different products, including adhesive tape (for electrical insulation, surface protection, and packaging), electronic materials (encapsulating resins for semiconductors and integrated circuits; polarizing films for flexible printed circuits), membranes and modules, and medical and health-care products. The company has more than 1,300 employees overseas. Sales for the fiscal year ending March 1991 totaled ¥160.0 billion (US $1.2 billion), and capitalization stood at ¥11.1 billion (US $80.9 million). Headquarters are in the city of Ibaraki, Ōsaka Prefecture.

niwaban   庭番

(literally, "garden guard"). Shogunal attendants who supervised maintenance of the EDO CASTLE gardens and escorted the shōgun around the gardens; often used as secret agents (OMMITSU). The shōgun TOKUGAWA YOSHIMUNE established the office in 1716. The niwaban later consisted of two supervisors (shihaigashira) and a number of hereditary subordinates under the authority of junior councillors (wakadoshiyori).

Niwa Fumio   丹羽文雄

(1904–). Novelist. Born in Mie Prefecture. Graduate of Waseda University. Niwa succeeded his father as a Buddhist priest but left his temple in 1932 for Tōkyō, where he became a well-known writer of FŪZOKU SHŌSETSU (novels dealing with modern urban life). In 1956 he became executive director of the Japan Professional Writers' Guild and in 1965 was elected to the Japan Art Academy. Niwa's writings include "Iyagarase no nenrei" (1947; tr "The Hateful Age," 1956), Bodaiju (1955–56; tr The Buddha Tree, 1968), and Shinran (1965–69). His works are collected in the 28-volume Niwa Fumio bungaku zenshū (1974–76).

Niwano Nikkyō   庭野日敬

(1906–). Founder and president of the RISSHŌ KŌSEIKAI, one of Japan's NEW RELIGIONS. Born in Niigata Prefecture, he moved to Tōkyō in 1923. Upon hearing lectures on the LOTUS SUTRA delivered by a follower of a new religion known as the REIYŪKAI in 1934, he became an active member of that group. Niwano and one of his converts, Naganuma Myōkō (1889–1957), avidly spread the Reiyūkai's teachings until 1938, when doctrinal differences with the group's leadership led the two men to form the Risshō Kōseikai. Niwano was an active administrator and public speaker and the author of numerous books. He also served as honorary president of the international committee of the World Conference on Religion and Peace and as chairman of its Japanese committee, as vice-president of the International Association for Religious Freedom, and as chairman of the board of directors of the UNION OF NEW RELIGIOUS ORGANIZATIONS OF JAPAN. In 1979 he was awarded the Templeton Foundation Prize for Progress in Religion.

Niwa Yasujirō   丹羽保次郎

(1893–1975). Electrical engineer. Inventor of the NE-type telephotographic system, on which modern-day global picture transmission systems are based. Born in Mie Prefecture, he graduated from Tōkyō University in 1916. He joined Nippon Electric Co, Ltd, in 1923 and in 1925 went to study at Bell Laboratories in the United States. In 1936 he used his NE-type telephotographic system to transmit photographs of the Berlin Olympics over 8,000 kilometers (about 5,000 mi) from Berlin to Tōkyō, a record distance for

that time. After his retirement, he served as president of TŌKYŌ DENKI UNIVERSITY from 1949 to 1974. He received the Order of Culture in 1959.

Nixon shocks   ニクソン・ショック

(Nikuson shokku). Popular designation for a number of policy changes announced in the summer of 1971 by US President Richard Nixon without prior notification to the Japanese government. The first "shock" occurred in July 1971 when Nixon announced his plan to visit the People's Republic of China. The second "shock" came a month later when Nixon announced his New Economic Program, which included the abandonment of the gold standard. This move resulted in the replacement of the fixed exchange rate between the dollar and the yen with a floating rate system, bringing a major increase in the international value of the yen. The incidents signaled the beginning of a new stage in US-Japan relations, with the United States indicating that Japan could no longer expect to receive preferential treatment and Japan embarking on a more independent foreign policy. See also UNITED STATES AND JAPAN.

Niyodogawa   仁淀川

River in central Kōchi Prefecture, Shikoku, originating in Ishizuchiyama, Ehime Prefecture, the highest peak in Shikoku, and flowing southeast to enter Tosa Bay at the western fringe of the Kōchi Plain. It has created numerous gorges where it transects the Shikoku Mountains. The gorge known as OMOGOKEI is a part of the Ishizuchi Quasi-National Park. WASHI (Japanese paper) and lumber are produced. Length: 124 km (77 mi); area of drainage basin: 1,560 sq km (600 sq mi).

NKK Corporation   日本鋼管[株]

(Nippon Kōkan). Integrated steelmaker; also a major engineering, construction, and shipbuilding company. Established in 1912 by Shiraishi Motojirō as Japan's first private steelmaker. With the onset of World War I, it grew into an integrated steel manufacturer, producing steel plates, sheets, bars, shapes, and alloys. With its merger with Tsurumi Seitetsu Zōsen in 1940, NKK entered the shipbuilding field. NKK's Fukuyama facility became the largest steel mill in the world with the completion of the fifth blast furnace there in 1973; the facility has an annual production capacity of 16 million metric tons of crude steel. In 1984 NKK bought 50 percent of National Steel Corporation, the seventh largest US steelmaker, to further promote the company's internationalization. NKK is now rapidly diversifying into advanced materials, electronics, and urban development. Sales for the fiscal year ending March 1991 totaled ¥1.3 trillion (US $9.5 billion), of which steel products accounted for 80 percent and engineering, construction, and shipbuilding 20 percent. In the same year the company was capitalized at ¥233.7 billion (US $1.7 billion). Headquarters are in Tōkyō.

Nō   能

The oldest extant professional theater; a form of musical dance-drama originating in the 14th century. Nō preserves what all other important contemporary theater has lost: its origin in ritual, reflecting an essentially Buddhist view of existence. The performance looks and sounds more like solemn observance than life. The actors are hieratic, playing their ancient roles of intermediaries be-

tween the worlds of gods and men. To the bare stage come soberly dressed instrumentalists, the six-or-eight-member chorus, then the supporting character (waki), handsomely robed, often as a priest. Finally, out of the darkness at the end of the long passageway leading to the stage proper, evoked by drums and flute, the resplendently caparisoned (usually masked) leading character (shite) materializes. In strict rhythms, out of music, voice, and movement rather than the artifice of stagecraft, time and space are created and destroyed. Language is largely poetic. Costumes are rich and heavy, movement, even in dance, deliberate. The shite seeks intercession by the waki and, having attained it at the end, returns to the darkness freed of karma.

Origins——At the middle of the 14th century professional theater was based in Kyōto and Nara, and the actors organized into troupes under the patronage of Shintō shrines and Buddhist temples. They raised money, piously and commercially, with subscription Nō (kanjin Nō), their performances at religious festivals serving both to propagate doctrine and to entertain.

Some troupes presented dengaku Nō, others sarugaku Nō (see DENGAKU; SARUGAKU). At this time little distinguished the two kinds, for both had a common theatrical inheritance. Their masks had origins in the ancient dance-drama called GIGAKU. Their music came from Shintō ritual dance (KAGURA), the Buddhist liturgy (SHŌMYŌ), popular 10th-century songs (imayō), and 13th-century "party music" (ENKYOKU). Their dance was influenced by 7th-century dance music (bugaku; see GAGAKU); by FURYŪ, an 11th-century dramatic dance accompanied by flute and drum; and by SHIRABYŌSHI, a type of 12th-century song-and-dance performance. Their plots were drawn from legend, history, literature, and contemporary events, given some literary refinement by the influence of ennen Nō (see ENNEN). The players distinguished between comic and serious materials, the comic pieces, KYŌGEN, being played as interludes between serious ones. In spite of their similarities, however, sarugaku eventually emerged as dominant, replacing dengaku in popularity.

The transformation of sarugaku into Nō, in basically the same form it has today, was accomplished by KAN'AMI and his son ZEAMI, both prodigious actor-dancers and playwrights of the Muromachi period (1333–1568). Kan'ami concentrated on "realistic" character portrayal; subtle, mysterious expression of beauty (YŪGEN); and immediate, total rapport with his audience. Most important, he emphasized the rhythmic accompaniment of the plays and changed their structure by adopting elements from kusemai, a popular entertainment in which the performer simultaneously mimed, danced, and sang.

In 1374 Kan'ami and Zeami performed before the shōgun ASHIKAGA YOSHIMITSU, who, greatly taken by the performance and by Zeami, thereafter sponsored the troupe. Never before had actors attained such social esteem. Kan'ami's troupe, the KANZE SCHOOL, was preeminent, and three other troupes that now survive, the KOMPARU SCHOOL, the HŌSHŌ SCHOOL, and the KONGŌ SCHOOL, adopted the Kanze style of performance. It was on the ZEN artistic principles of restraint, economy of expression, and suggestion rather than statement that Zeami fashioned his 40 or so plays,

Niwa Fumio Buddhism is a major theme in the more recent work of this writer who established his reputation through novels concerning the problems of modern urban life.

Niwa Yasujirō This pioneering electrical engineer is remembered for his accomplishments in the transmission of graphic images.

Nō

The Stage The Nō stage provides two acting areas: a long passageway (the *hashigakari*)—also used for entrances and exits by actors and musicians—and the stage proper—shared by actors, musicians, and a chorus of six or eight.

◄ A view from the side of the stage: the chorus sits on the *wakiza* (rear of photo); musicians are on the *atoza* (left of photo).

▲ Music is central to Nō performances. *From left:* the large floor drum, large hand drum, small hand drum, and flute.

Costumes Nō costumes, multiple layers of brilliantly colored stiff brocades, serve both to create a sense of elegance and to make the actors larger than life.

▲ Embroidery and gold leaf decorate this Edo-period costume.

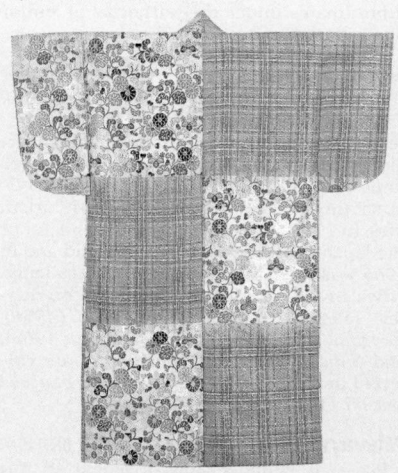

▲ Blocks of plaid brocade alternate with blocks of brocade decorated with chrysanthemums and paulownia blossoms in this bold design from the Azuchi-Momoyama period.

The Nō Stage

- *kyōgen-* or *kōken-bashira* (comedian's or stage assistant's pillar)
- *shite-bashira* (principal actor's pillar)
- *agemaku* (curtain)
- *hashigakari* (bridge)
- *san no matsu* (third pine)
- *ni no matsu* (second pine)
- *ichi no matsu* (first pine)
- *metsuke-bashira* (eye-fixing pillar)
- *kagamiita* (mirror board, acoustic)
- *kijinguchi* (nobleman's entrance; once used by actors portraying nobility)
- *kirido* (sliding door)
- *fue-bashira* (flute pillar)
- *atoza* (rear stage)
- *wakiza* or *jiutaiza* (side stage)
- *waki-bashira* (subordinate actor's pillar)
- *butai* (main stage)
- *shirasu* (strip of pebbles)
- *kizahashi* (steps; once used by actors to receive tribute from a *daimyō* or other man of rank)

his acting, and his productions. His ideas on every aspect of the theater were set down in a series of essays that remain the essential documents of the Nō.

Evolution—A civil war, the ŌNIN WAR, started in 1467 and was fought in and around Kyōto until 1477, when the battles shifted to the provinces. By the end of the century the entire country was engaged in a period of conflict known as the Sengoku, or Warring States, period, which lasted until 1568. The shogunate had little time for Nō, but for others the war whetted the desire for entertainment and culture. Toward 1500, amateur performances became widely popular. The study of Nō music and dance spread not only among aristocrats but also among priests, soldiers, and commoners, who wanted professional instruction, which the troupes gladly gave them for a fee. Written copies of the songs and chants (*utaibon*) of the Kanze and Komparu troupes appeared in 1512. By disseminating the performances throughout the country, civil war made Nō an increasingly integral part of the culture.

Nō returned to the center of political power when in 1571 the Kanze troupe was summoned to the military headquarters of TOKUGAWA IEYASU. But it found its most enthusiastic support when TOYOTOMI HIDEYOSHI

came to power in 1582. Hideyoshi bolstered his soldiers' morale by having all four troupes perform for them, and he commissioned 10 plays written about himself, in which he played the lead. When Tokugawa Ieyasu became shōgun in 1603 he celebrated the occasion with Nō performances, and in 1609 he employed all of Hideyoshi's performers and established them in Edo (now Tōkyō). The KITA SCHOOL, which still exists today, was added to the original four in 1618. Nō became the official property and ceremonial art of the Tokugawa line. In 1647 TOKUGAWA IEMITSU issued regulations for its governance, as stringent as those by which he ran the country: tradition must be maintained, the troupe leader brooking no deviations. Over more than two centuries Nō became more and more codified, even surpassing Zeami's refined art in solemnity. Performances that took half an hour in Zeami's day take an hour and a half or more today.

During the Edo period (1600–1868) favored commoners were invited to performances at the shōgun's castle on auspicious occasions. They were forbidden to learn Nō music and dance, but they did nonetheless. As the economic life of the military class worsened in the 19th century, that of many commoners improved, and they were able to pay well for Nō instruction. Large numbers

of them also became attracted to the popular KABUKI theater. When the shogunate fell in 1867 and government subsidy of Nō stopped, some of the nobility kept Nō alive. Their support ended with the end of World War II, however, and the public became Nō's sole sponsor. Today Nō has a small but dedicated following, many members of which belong to Nō study groups.

Stage—Tokugawa formalization of Nō also standardized the stage, and today that architecture is requisite for the correct performance of the plays. Although the stage is now usually inside a concrete building, it retains its original appearance as an exterior structure. The elaborate, carved, cypress-bark-covered roof of Shintō shrine architecture extends over the main stage (*butai*), which measures 6 by 6 meters (19.7 by 19.7 ft), as well as the side stage (*wakiza*), the rear stage (*atoza*), and the bridge (*hashigakari*). The bridge joins the main stage at an oblique angle, connecting it with the "mirror room" (*kagami no ma*), the actors' dressing room. Musicians (*hayashikata*) and actors enter and exit on the bridge. The only other entrance to the stage is a 1 meter (39 in) high sliding door (*kirido*), upstage left on the main stage, used by stage assistants (*kōken*) and the members of the chorus (*jiutai*).

Along the front of the entire structure, at audience level, is a strip of pebbles. In front

Plays There are basically two types of Nō plays: those dealing with "real people" and those portraying supernatural beings.

▼ The spirit of the ground spider (*tsuchigumo*) spins a web in this scene from *Tsuchigumo*.

▲ In this scene from *Momijigari* (Viewing Autumn Maple Leaves), a beautiful young woman performs a dance.

◄ In the play *Takasago*, an aged couple (standing center and left) reveal themselves to be the spirits of two pine trees.

Masks In Nō, masks are worn only by the *shite*, or leading character. Masks fall into general categories, including holy old man, god, demon, man, and woman.

▲ Ōtobide ("large protruding eyes") is a god or demon mask.

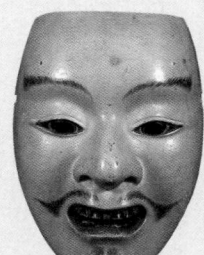

▲ A male mask known as *heita*, used for warrior roles.

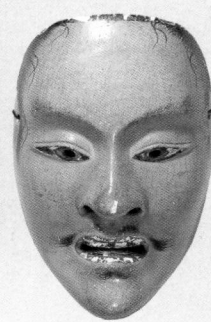

▲ The *shintai* mask portrays a warrior's angry spirit.

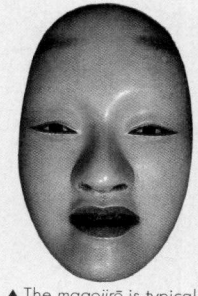

▲ The *magojirō* is typically used for young female roles in the Kongō school of Nō actors.

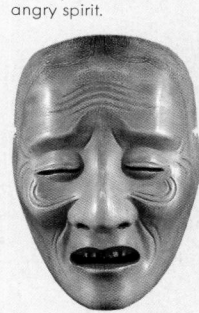

▲ A *rōjo* (old woman) mask reveals the character's karma and a beauty long faded. This variation suggests blindness.

of the bridge in this area are three equidistantly placed pine trees. A stylized pine tree, the only scenic background, is painted on the back wall (*kagamiita*) of the main stage. The entire structure is built of polished Japanese cypress (*hinoki*).

Five pillars supporting the roof govern the actors' movements. Upstage at the point where bridge and rear stage join is the comedian's pillar (*kyōgen-bashira*), for the comic actor sits there if he is to appear in the interlude of a serious play. Directly downstage of it is the principal actor's pillar (*shite-bashira*), for beside it the principal actor (*shite*) stops after his entrance on the bridge. At the downstage-right corner of the main stage is the "eye-fixing" pillar (*metsuke-bashira*), from which the principal actor, masked and unable to see clearly, takes his bearing. Opposite it, at stage left, is the *waki-bashira*, the pillar of the subordinate actor, who sits here during most of the play. Upstage from it is the "flute" pillar (*fue-bashira*), near which the flute player sits. All areas on the stage have their designations—"at the first pine tree," "in front of the drum players," "in front of the chorus"—used to describe movement and choreography. The actor's place on the stage at a given moment defines, for the audience, the progression of the play. In the absence of scenic indications, place is established by the words of

actor or chorus. Characters standing at either side of the main stage may be separated by a province at one moment but in the same room the next. (Time can similarly be speeded up, slowed, or stopped.) Specific places may also be indicated by *tsukurimono*, usually a lightweight construction consisting of a bamboo framework wrapped in strips of white cloth, suggesting the outline of a real object.

Performers—All performers are male, and their organization is that established in the Edo period. Each of the five schools of Nō, mentioned earlier, trains its own *shite*, his "companion" (*tsure*), the child actor (*kokata*), the chorus, and the stage assistants. The *waki* and his "companion" have their own separate schools, such as Fukuō and Takayasu. Each instrument—the flute, small and large hand drums (see TSUZUMI), and the large drum standing on the floor (see TAIKO)—is taught in a number of different schools.

The actors' children, trained in the traditional manner beginning at the age of seven, appear in performance in children's roles. Training is strictly by rote, vocally and physically. Each unit of movement, including the Nō style of walking in which the heel never leaves the floor, is called a *kata* ("form"). Some 200 *kata* exist, each having a name, but only about 30 are commonly

used. A given *kata* varies little from one school to another. The *kata* for weeping, for example—no movement but the head slightly bowed, the left hand raised toward the forehead—is not subject to the individual actor's interpretation; it is the fixed way of illustrating the words of the text.

Properties, Masks, and Costumes—The expressiveness of the *shite* and the *waki* is enhanced by hand properties, among them letters, umbrellas, rosaries, and the bamboo branch signifying derangement, but most of all by the folding fan (*chūkei*). Closed, partly closed, or open, it may represent any object suggested by its shape and handling—dagger, lantern, rising moon. In other *kata* it represents not objects but actions—listening, moon viewing, sleeping. The abstract or pictorial design painted on the fan is conventionally associated with a type of character such as a ghost, old woman, or demon. Only the *shite* and *waki* use them. The other actors and the chorus carry fans (*ōgi*) bearing the crest of the school. The chorus place their fans, always closed, on the floor in front of them and pick them up to signal the beginning of a chant.

Only the *shite* and his companions wear masks, carved of wood and painted, though

Continued on page 1108 ►

The Expressive Power of Nō

1 The first character onstage is a court official, who explains the circumstances of Lady Aoi's illness and calls upon a medium to divine its source.

O f all the plays in the Nō repertoire, none is performed more often than *Aoi no Ue* (Lady Aoi), which is based on events in Murasaki Shikibu's great early-11th-century novel the *Tale of Genji*. This drama's power stems from both its theme—the bitterness of a neglected lover—and the gravity and elegance of its staging.

Lady Aoi is pregnant with the child of her husband, the

2 The medium performs a ritual of divination to call forth the wandering spirit that attacks Lady Aoi.

3 The spirit of Lady Rokujō approaches, seen only by the medium. A *deigan* mask is used to suggest the barely contained anger of her tormented spirit.

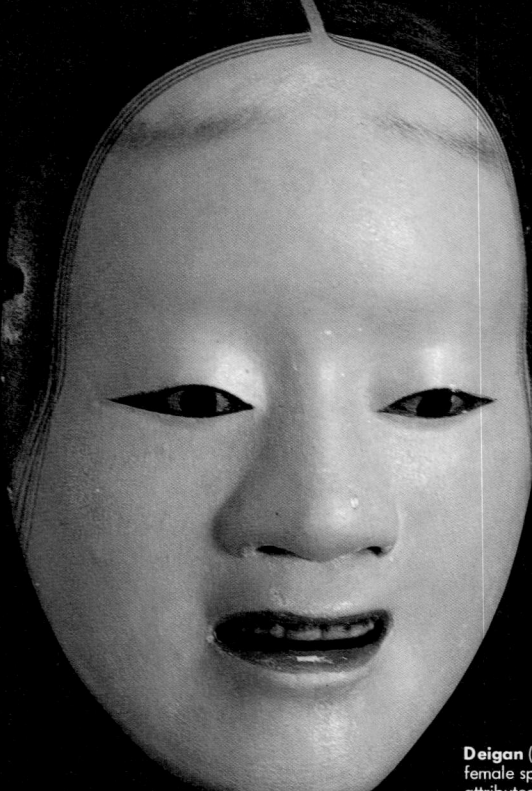

Deigan (malevolent female spirit) mask attributed to Himi. Late 15th century.

4 Kneeling before the prostrate figure of Lady Aoi, represented by the spread-out robe, the spirit of Lady Rokujō proclaims the reasons for her hatred. At the back of the stage is the full complement of Nō musicians.

court noble Genji. When she is suddenly taken ill, possession by an evil spirit is suspected, and a medium is summoned to divine its identity. The spirit is soon revealed as that of the jealous Lady Rokujō, who was once Genji's lover. Lady Rokujō's bitterness and regret over the fading of Genji's affections and her anger at Lady Aoi over a recent slight become so intense that Lady Rokujō's spirit leaves her body and attacks that of her rival.

When Lady Aoi's condition worsens, a Buddhist mountain ascetic is summoned to perform an exorcism of Lady Rokujō's spirit, which now appears in terrifying demon form and attacks him. Invoking the names of Buddhist deities, he succeeds in quelling the angry spirit, and Lady Aoi is saved—an ending that diverges from the *Tale of Genji* itself, in which the lady dies soon after giving birth to Genji's son.

Masuda Shōzō

Photographs by Masuda Shōzō

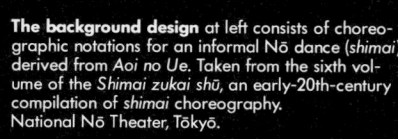

The background design at left consists of choreographic notations for an informal Nō dance (*shimai*) derived from *Aoi no Ue*. Taken from the sixth volume of the *Shimai zukai shū*, an early-20th-century compilation of *shimai* choreography. National Nō Theater, Tōkyō.

6 A Buddhist mountain ascetic attempts to exorcise the angry spirit, who crouches behind him, covered by her robe.

7 Her demonic nature now revealed by a *hannya* mask, the vengeful spirit of Lady Rokujō reappears from beneath the concealing robe.

Hannya (female demon) mask by Tōsui. 17th century.

5 Brandishing her fan, a symbol of the fires of jealousy and rage, Lady Rokujō's spirit moves to strike her rival.

8 Wielding a demon wand, the spirit battles the prayers of the priest. The drama ends with the pacification of Lady Rokujō's spirit through the power of Buddhist law.

not in plays in which the characters they portray are living men. Each mask is a variation on a general type—holy old men, gods, demons or spirits, men, women—and in many plays the *shite* changes masks midway through the play, the second mask revealing the character's true being. The *shite* chooses the mask he prefers for the role, and his choice determines, by association and custom, his costume.

Many of the costumes (*shōzoku*) used today were constructed in the 18th and 19th centuries when the patterns, colors, and materials to be worn by a given character were systematized. Costume creates an effect of luxurious elegance but also a bulky, massive figure, that of the *shite* looming largest. This is effected by at least five layers of clothing, the outermost richly figured damask, brocade, or embroidered silk gauze. No garment completely conceals the one beneath it; surfaces and textures are multiple. Wigs, hats, and headdresses heighten the figure.

Plays—*Okina*, the oldest item in the repertory, consists principally of three dances extant in the 10th century that are prayers for peace, fertility (the basis of Shintō), and longevity. Scarcely a play, it is performed only on ceremonial occasions and always first on the program. The usual program today consists of two or three Nō plays with half-hour comic pieces, KYŌGEN, between them.

The other 240 or so plays now performed, most dating from the 15th century, are grouped into five categories, corresponding to the five parts of the traditional Nō program called *goban-date*. *Shobamme-mono* (part-one plays) are sometimes called *wakinō-mono* or *kami* (god) plays. *Nibamme-mono* (part-two plays), or *shura-mono*, are often about men or warriors. *Sambamme-mono* (part-three plays) are also called *katsura-mono* ("wig" plays) and are usually about women. *Yobamme-mono* (part-four plays) are also called *zō-mono* ("miscellaneous Nō") or "madwoman" plays. Some of these are referred to as "present-day" or "realistic" plays. *Gobamme-mono* (part-five plays) are also called "demon" plays, or *kirinō-mono* ("final Nō").

Parts of the script are prose (*kotoba*) but most are poetry (*utai*). The prose is 14th-century upper-class Japanese; the poetry is taken from classical Chinese and Japanese collections, along with quotations from Buddhist texts. After choosing a subject, the playwright would then assemble his script out of appropriate pieces of ready-made poetry. The instrumental and vocal forms are also traditional. The plays embody the Buddhist concept that life is a continuum; thus the *shite* may be an ancient poetess, a dead warrior, a butterfly, wisteria, or may undergo transformations during the play (from woman to serpent, man to spider).

Performance—The basic aesthetic theory of Japanese music is that it must have three parts: *jo*, introduction; *ha*, exposition; and *kyū*, a rapid finale. The theory was in Zeami's time applied both to the entire performance, a series of five Nō plays, and to the individual play, the *jo* having one section (*dan*), the *ha* three sections, and the *kyū* one. Although the plays are not identical in structure, the basic arrangement of "transformation" plays, in which the *shite* is a different character on his second appearance, is as follows:

With the three or four musicians seated at the rear of the main stage and the six, sometimes eight, members of the chorus seated in two rows at the stage-left side of the main stage, the *waki*, often a priest, enters on the bridge and moves slowly to the main stage. There he pauses and identifies himself (*nanori*). Then, as he moves toward stage left, he sings a description of his travel (*michiyuki*). He reaches the down-left corner of the stage, announces arrival at his destination, and sits down beside the *waki*'s pillar, marking the end of the *jo* movement.

The curtain at the end of the bridge is lifted from the bottom and the *shite* enters. He advances toward the main stage singing of the landscape or the season, about who or what he is, and stops at the *shite*'s pillar. The second section of the *ha* movement begins with declaimed prose dialogue (*mondō*) between *shite* and *waki*. The latter, a stranger to this place, questions the *shite* about its significance and the event that happened here. In the third section the *waki* asks questions about the identity of the *shite*, either in prose or in a sung exchange (*rongi* or "discussion"). The *shite* is evasive, but pleads for the *waki*'s prayers in a dance, his thoughts expressed by the chanting chorus (*kuse*). The *shite* moves onto the bridge and exits, while the chorus concludes the *ha* movement and the first half of the play with a chant (*nakairi*).

An actor from the *kyōgen* troupe who has been sitting to the right of the comedian's pillar comes forward onto the main stage and in colloquial prose explains, sometimes in dialogue with the *waki*, the subject of the play for the benefit of those unable to understand the ancient poetry. This passage is called AIKYŌGEN (intermission *kyōgen*).

The *kyōgen* actor retires, and the *kyū* movement begins with the *waki* singing of his willingness to pray for the deliverance of the *shite*. Having changed costume and mask, the "after" *shite* (*nochijite*) reappears in his true being, identifying himself in song. He then dances out, in another *kuse*, the event that binds him to existence, or sometimes he sits motionless while the chorus describes it. A short, quick dance may follow. The *shite* goes to his pillar, sings the final lines of the play (*kiri*), and stamps his foot, indicating that the play has ended. He makes a slow, silent exit on the bridge, and the silent audience watches him return to the darkness from which he came.

For synopses of individual Nō plays see AOI NO UE; ATAKA; ATSUMORI; AYA NO TSUZUMI; HAGOROMO; IZUTSU; KAMO; KANTAN; KIYOTSUNE; MATSUKAZE; MOMIJIGARI; SAIGYŌ-ZAKURA; SHAKKYŌ; SUMIDAGAWA; TAKASAGO; TOMOE; UTOU; YASHIMA; YUYA. ☎1106–1107

Nōami 能阿弥

(1397–1471). Best known of the early DŌBŌSHŪ, connoisseur-painter-curators attached to the household of the Ashikaga shōgun, and a figure who, to some extent, set the course for the roles of later AMI SCHOOL painters. He was most skillful in painting and in connoisseurship, mounting, and ceremonial display of the Chinese paintings in the shōgun's collection. He prepared the curator's manual of the shōgun's collection, *Gyomotsu on'e mokuroku*, and he has also been associated with the early compilation of the *Kundaikan sō chōki*, the records of painters represented in the shōgun's collection, and with the preparation of labels for these works. His painting styles appear to have included a Muqi (Mu-ch'i; J: MOKKEI) style for figures, an academy style (Ma Lin) for BIRD-AND-FLOWER PAINTING, a literati-oriented style for bamboo and rocks (see BUNJINGA), and a Ma-Xia (Ma-Hsia) style for landscapes (see INK PAINTING). See also GEIAMI; SŌAMI.

Nobeoka 延岡[市]

City in northeastern Miyazaki Prefecture, Kyūshū, on the Hyūga Sea. It developed as a castle town during the Edo period (1600–1868). Since the establishment in 1923 of a fertilizer factory by Nippon Chisso Hiryō (now ASAHI CHEMICAL INDUSTRY CO, LTD), the city has become a center for the pharmaceutical, synthetic-fiber, foodstuff, and plastic industries. There are yellowtail hatcheries as well as offshore fishing for sardines. Pop: 130,624.

Nobeyama 野辺山

District in the village of Minami Maki, southeastern Nagano Prefecture, central Honshū, on the eastern slopes of the mountain YATSUGATAKE. Dairy farming and the cultivation of cabbage and other highland vegetables flourish. The Nobeyama Railway Station has the highest elevation (1,346 m; 4,416 ft above sea level) of all stations of the JR (Japan Railways) lines.

Nobi 野火

(tr *Fires on the Plain*, 1957). Novel by ŌOKA SHŌHEI (1909–88); published 1952. Set on the Philippine island of Leyte near the end of World War II, the novel is narrated by a soldier named Tamura, who, suffering from a lung ailment, is abandoned by his platoon and left to wander by himself. Tamura falls into increasingly hallucinatory reflections—on his tropical surroundings, impending death, and the nature of God. Nagamatsu, a comrade, discovers Tamura on the verge of collapse and nourishes him back to life on "monkey meat." When Tamura learns that he has actually been eating human flesh, he shoots Nagamatsu and then loses consciousness. The final chapter takes the form of Tamura's diary as a patient in a Tōkyō mental hospital, where, still questioning God and the meaning of existence, he is haunted by images of fires on the plain, a sight that meant Filipinos and the threat of attack were near. With its profound ethical questions and graphic depiction of the atrocities of war, *Nobi* is one of the most powerful of Japanese war novels.

Nōbi Plain 濃尾平野

(Nōbi Heiya). Located in Aichi and Gifu prefectures, central Honshū. The largest plain in the Tōkai region. Bordering Ise Bay on the Pacific seaboard, this plain is composed mostly of the deltas of the rivers KISOGAWA, NAGARAGAWA, and IBIGAWA, with an alluvial fan on the foothills of the Yōrō Mountains. The principal agricultural products are rice and vegetables, and the principal industrial products are textiles, iron and steel products, and machinery. The major city is NAGOYA. Land reclamation projects have encouraged industrialization on the coast, while the hilly areas are becoming more residential. Area: 1,800 sq km (695 sq mi).

nobori →flags and banners

Noboribetsu 登別[市]

City in southwestern Hokkaidō, on the Pacific Ocean. The city has numerous spas. Ceramics, chemical, and food-processing industries, as well as rice cultivation and dairy farming, are active. Lake Kuttara is known for its clear waters and good fishing. The city is a part of the SHIKOTSU-TŌYA NATIONAL PARK. Pop: 55,571.

Nobuko 伸子

Autobiographical novel by MIYAMOTO YURIKO (1899–1951); serialized 1924–26, published 1928 in book form. The novel opens in 1918 in New York City, where 19-year-old Sasa Nobuko and her father have recently arrived. Nobuko enrolls in a university and there enters into a romantic relationship with Tsukuda Ichirō, a scholar of dubious academic and social repute. Despite warnings from family and friends, Nobuko marries him. She returns to Japan soon thereafter, slightly ahead of her husband, and meets the full force of her family's disapproval. The situation worsens after Tsukuda arrives: Nobuko is aware of her husband's social inadequacies and pettiness but is also inclined to protect him from her family. The couple are thrown out of the household and their life together degenerates into a series of quarrels and disappointments as Tsukuda's manipulative nature reveals itself. Amid continuous tension, Nobuko befriends the Russian literature scholar Yoshimi Motoko, whose amiability becomes a catalyst for Nobuko's decision to divorce her husband and move out of his home. *Nobuko* is significant for questioning the institution of marriage, probing the relations between the sexes, and portraying a woman's move toward greater freedom.

Nobunaga Kō ki → Shinchō Kō ki

nobushi 野伏

Armed bands of farmers or unemployed *samurai* who waylaid and robbed stray or fallen soldiers in the period from the 14th to the 16th centuries. During the Sengoku period (1467–1568) they were often employed by warlords as spies or guerrillas to harass the enemy's rear guard. The most famous *nobushi* leaders were Hachisuka Koroku (1526–86) and Ishikawa Goemon, whose adventures as a spy and a thief are glorified in several KABUKI dramas.

Noda 野田[市]

City in northwestern Chiba Prefecture, central Honshū, between the rivers EDOGAWA and TONEGAWA. Noda is primarily known for its *shōyu* (soy sauce), first produced here in the Muromachi period (1333–1568) and still the most important local product. The city is now developing into a residential suburb of Tōkyō. Pop: 114,475.

Noda Hideki 野田秀樹

(1955–). Playwright. Born in Nagasaki Prefecture. Attended Tōkyō University. After he founded the theatrical troupe Yume no Yūminsha in 1976, Noda established himself as an important force in contemporary theater. He received the 1983 Kishida Drama Award for *Nokemono kitarite* (1982, Descent of the Beasts). His other works include his 1985 Valkyrie trilogy: *Byakuya no Warukyūre* (Valkyries in the Midnight Sun), *Suisei no Jīkufurīto* (Siegfried the Comet), and *Waruhara jōhatsu* (Valhalla Evaporates).

Noda Kōgo 野田高梧

(1893–1968). Screenwriter. Born in Hokkaidō, he graduated from Waseda University. In 1924 he joined the scriptwriting department of Shōchiku Kinema Co (see SHŌCHIKU CO, LTD). Noda contributed much to the development of screenwriting techniques in Japan. He turned out numerous screenplays, writing both comedy and serious drama, but his strong suit was melodrama. One of his early representative screenplays was the script for OZU YASUJIRŌ's *Zange no yaiba* (1927, The Sword of Penitence). Other memorable Ozu films for which Noda was screenwriter include BANSHUN (1949, Late Spring), *Bakushū* (1951, Early Summer), and TŌKYŌ MONOGATARI (1953, Tōkyō Story).

Nogami Yaeko 野上弥生子

(1885–1985). Novelist. Born Kotegawa Yae in Ōita Prefecture; daughter of a wealthy *sake* brewer. She studied Chinese and Japanese classics privately with the scholar Kubo Kaizō and composed TANKA as the only child member of Kubo's poetry circle. In Tōkyō, Yaeko met the novelist KINOSHITA NAOE, who persuaded her to enter Meiji Jogakkō, a Christian-oriented girls' school known for progressive scholarship. While there, Yaeko came to know Nogami Toyoichirō (1883–1950), a student of English literature and Nō drama, whom she married in 1906.

In the 1910s Yaeko wrote for such magazines as *Chūō kōron*, *Shinchō*, and the feminist magazine *Seitō* (see SEITŌSHA). She was a well-established author when she shocked her readers with *Kaijin maru* (1922; tr *The Neptune*, 1957). Partially based on a real event involving the four-man crew of a fishing boat, the story explores the choice between starvation or cannibalism.

Her works include the historical novel *Ōishi Yoshio* (1926), about the FORTY-SEVEN RŌNIN INCIDENT. In *Machiko* (1928–30), she stresses that human liberation is impossible without individual striving toward moral perfection. The themes of morality and social activism again appear in her first major postwar work, MEIRO (1948–56, Maze). The relationship between artist and patron is the main theme in her outstanding historical novel *Hideyoshi to Rikyū* (1962–63). Other important works include the short story "Wakai musuko" (1932, Young Son), *Kitsune* (1946; tr *The Foxes*, 1957), the autobiographical *Mori* (1972–85, Woods), and the essay collection *Hana* (1977, Flowers). Although her own life had few dramatic incidents, she is noteworthy for her 70 years of constant exploration of new horizons in her writing.

Nōgata 直方[市]

City in northern Fukuoka Prefecture, Kyūshū, on the river Ongagawa. The city developed as a castle town and river port during the Edo period (1600–1868). From the early Meiji period (1868–1912) it prospered as a coal-mining town, but with the closure of the mines efforts have been made to encourage new industries. Many residents commute to KITA KYŪSHŪ. Pop: 62,530.

Nogawa site 野川遺跡

(Nogawa *iseki*). Archaeological type site for the paleolithic period in Japan (pre-10,000 BC); located on a Pleistocene terrace of the river Nogawa in the city of Chōfu, Tōkyō Prefecture. This was the first paleolithic site discovered to have vertically stratified cultural deposits. Excavations from 1968 to 1970 revealed nine successive occupation layers spanning about 25,000 years, as indicated by the presence of STONE TOOLS, workshop debris, and clusters of cobble-size stones. The tool sequence ranged from the earliest utilized flakes and pebble hand axes

of amorphous character to scrapers and backed blades and, finally, to small points including bifacials. See also PALEOLITHIC CULTURE.

Nogi Maresuke 乃木希典

(1849–1912). Army general and war hero. Born in Edo (now Tōkyō) as the son of a retainer of the Chōshū domain (now Yamaguchi Prefecture). Commissioned a major in the newly formed Japanese army in 1871 and given command of the 14th Infantry Regiment at Kokura in 1873, he took part in quelling antigovernment rebellions in Hagi, Yamaguchi Prefecture (see HAGI REBELLION), in 1876. Given a brigade command in 1878, he was promoted to major general in 1885.

During the SINO-JAPANESE WAR OF 1894–1895, Nogi, commanding the First Infantry Brigade, gained fame in the rapid conquest of the Liaodong (Liaotung) Peninsula and its major military base, PORT ARTHUR (Ch: Lüshun, now part of Lüda). His victorious campaign brought him a divisional command, promotion to lieutenant general, and the title of baron. Nogi took part in the final pacification of Taiwan and served as governor-general of the colony from 1896 to 1898. At the outbreak of the RUSSO-JAPANESE WAR in 1904, Nogi was promoted to general and given command of the Third Army for the assault on Port Arthur. (Japan had been forced by the TRIPARTITE INTERVENTION of 1895 to return the Liaodong Peninsula to China, which had then leased it to Russia; Japan was now trying to recover it.) Nogi's relentless, bloody, and futile assaults resulted in 56,000 Japanese casualties—a failure of strategy for which he felt personally responsible.

Nogi's stoic acceptance of the death in combat of his two sons—both infantry officers—won him the admiration of the Japanese public. Elevated to count in 1907, Nogi was that year made director of the Peers' School (now Gakushūin University). The ritual suicide of Nogi and his wife on the evening of the funeral of the Emperor Meiji (13 September 1912) created a sensation because it supposedly reflected Nogi's ultimate protest against the luxury and profligacy of contemporary Japan, although it may have been as much an act of atonement for the mistakes of his military career. Nogi's self-destruction had a particularly profound impact on Japanese intellectuals and writers, including NATSUME SŌSEKI and MORI ŌGAI. For the public at large, Nogi became an object of veneration and a symbol of loyalty and sacrifice. Among the Japanese military, his professional reputation was always marginal.

Noguchi Fujio 野口冨士男

(1911–). Author. Real name Hirai Fujio. Born in Tōkyō. Attended Keiō University. Noguchi made his literary debut with the publication of *Kaze no keifu* (1940, Genealogy of the Wind), which depicts the pathos of the lives of the common people. His *Tokuda Shūsei den* (1965, Biography of Tokuda Shūsei) is an important work in the field of literary biography. Noguchi's other works include *Kurai yoru no watashi* (1969, Myself on a Dark Night), about the literary world of the late 1920s and early 1930s; *Waga Kafū* (1975, My Kafū), a biography of NAGAI KAFŪ that won the Yomiuri Literary Prize; and *Kanshokuteki Shōwa bundan shi* (1986, An Impressionistic History of Shōwa Literature). In 1981 he received the Japan Art Academy Prize.

Nogami Yaeko Morality and social activism are recurring themes in this novelist's works.

Nogi Maresuke The ritual suicide of this army general following the death of Emperor Meiji was viewed by the general public as a symbol of loyalty and sacrifice.

Isamu Noguchi The sculptor standing before the Horace E. Dodge Fountain (1972–79), designed by Noguchi for the Detroit Civic Center, Michigan.

Noguchi Hideyo
野口英世

(1876–1928). Bacteriologist who isolated the spirochete that causes syphilis. Original name Noguchi Seisaku. Born in Fukushima Prefecture. As a youth he studied medicine by living in the home of a doctor, and, after attending Seiseigakusha in Tōkyō, he passed the government medical examinations in 1897. He began his bacteriological studies at the Epidemiological Research Institute (Densembyō Kenkyūjo). In 1900 he went to the United States, where he worked as a research assistant at various institutes before receiving an appointment at the Rockefeller Institute for Medical Research in 1904. It was here that he succeeded in cultivating *Treponema pallidum*, the causative agent of syphilis. In 1918 he went to Central and South America to do research on a vaccine for yellow fever. He then went to Africa in 1927 to confirm his findings but contracted yellow fever and died. Noguchi also did work on Oroya fever, poliomyelitis, and trachoma.

Noguchi Hideyo This pioneering bacteriologist gave his life to science, dying of yellow fever contracted in his search for a serum to combat the disease.

Noguchi, Isamu
野口イサム

(1904–88). American sculptor and designer. Born in Los Angeles. His father was the poet NOGUCHI YONEJIRŌ, but he was raised by his American mother. He spent his early years in Japan, returning to the United States to attend high school and then Columbia University. In 1927 he won a Guggenheim fellowship and went to Paris. After his return to New York, Noguchi made a living by doing portrait sculpture but at the same time developed his own abstract style. During World War II, he was interned voluntarily for seven months in a war relocation camp for Japanese Americans in Arizona. After World War II, he made frequent visits to Japan.

His abstract sculptures in stone, terracotta, cement, or wood often reflect Japanese influence. He created fountains, gardens, and other architectural projects throughout the world; his major works include the Detroit Civic Center. He also designed furniture, lighting equipment, and stage sets, especially for the Martha Graham Dance Company.

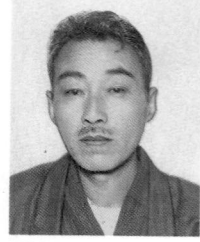

Noguchi Ujō During the 1920s this poet wrote the lyrics for a number of children's songs that are still popular today.

Noguchi Shitagau
野口遵

(1873–1944). Businessman. Born in Ishikawa Prefecture, he was a graduate of Tōkyō University. In 1908 Noguchi established Nippon Nitrogen Fertilizers, becoming the first in Japan to manufacture ammonium sulphate. After World War I, he successfully applied the Casale process of synthetic ammonia production for commercial purposes. He later built an industrial complex in Korea that used electrochemical technology and formed a financial and industrial combine, known as Nitchitsu Kontserun (from the German *Konzern*), in Japan and Korea.

Noguchi Takehiko
野口武彦

(1937–). Critic. Born in Tōkyō. Graduate of both Waseda and Tōkyō universities. Noguchi established a reputation when his *Ishikawa Jun ron* (1963–66, On Ishikawa Jun) was serialized in *Tōdai bungaku*. His principal works include *Mishima Yukio no sekai* (1968, The World of Mishima Yukio) and *Tanizaki Jun'ichirō ron* (1973, On Tanizaki Jun'ichirō).

Noguchi Ujō
野口雨情

(1882–1945). Poet. Real name Noguchi Eikichi. Born in Ibaraki Prefecture; studied at Waseda University. Noted as a lyricist of *dōyō* (see CHILDREN'S SONGS) and folk songs. Taking advantage of the rising popularity of *dōyō* and folk songs in the 1920s, he composed numerous, often sentimental, lyrics. His "Sendō kouta" (1918, Boatman's Song), "Habu no minato" (1924, Habu Harbor), "Nanatsu no ko" (1921, Seven Little Crows), and "Aoi me no ningyō" (1921, The Blue-Eyed Doll) are still widely read and sung today. Most of his lyrics were set to music by NAKAYAMA SHIMPEI.

Noguchi Yonejirō
野口米次郎

(1875–1947). Poet. Pen name Yone Noguchi. Born in Aichi Prefecture. In 1893 he went to the United States and in 1895 became a reporter for a Japanese-language newspaper in San Francisco. There he became acquainted with the poet Joaquin Miller, under whose influence he turned to poetry. He began writing poems in the manner of Poe and the 17th-century *haiku* poet BASHŌ. His first collection of English poetry, *Seen and Unseen*, which won critical acclaim in 1896, was followed by a second volume of poems, *The Voice of the Valley* (1897). After his return to Japan, he became professor of English at Keiō University. He continued to write poems and essays in Japanese. *Nijū kokuseki-sha no shi* (1921, Poems of a Dual National) is the best-known collection of his Japanese poems. He is also known for his studies of UKIYO-E (woodblock prints) and other aspects of Japanese art. His son was the sculptor and artist Isamu NOGUCHI.

Nōgyō zensho
農業全書

(Agricultural Encyclopedia). Book on agriculture by the agronomist MIYAZAKI YASUSADA (1623–97); published in 1697. Patterned after a Chinese book of the Ming period (1368–1644), the *Nōgyō zensho* deals with methods of cultivation and techniques of animal husbandry. The first systematic work of its kind, the book was long regarded as a model for writings on agriculture. A preface to the 10-volume work was contributed by the Confucian scholar Kaibara Ekiken, and an appendix was compiled by Kaibara Rakuken (d 1702), who had been a consultant to the author.

nōhon shugi
農本主義

(agrarianism; agrarian nationalism). A set of farm-centered beliefs current from the 1890s to the end of World War II that stressed the economic and social benefits of agriculture. As a reaction to industrialization, urbanization, and centralized rule, this agrarianism made village farming the basis of its ideal political and social order.

One main form was bureaucratic agrarianism, designed to increase the farm productivity that was needed to pay for industrialization. Such major officials as SHINAGAWA YAJIRŌ and HIRATA TŌSUKE extolled the small cultivator as the backbone of the nation.

The other chief form was popular *nōhon shugi*, which overshadowed bureaucratic agrarianism after World War I. Spokesmen such as GONDŌ SEIKYŌ and TACHIBANA KŌZABURŌ, glossing over landlord-tenant conflicts (see LANDLORDISM), expressed instead the antipathy of all rural classes toward industry, urban society, centralized government, and foreign culture. Young military officers who attempted coups d'état in the 1930s were influenced by the teachings of Gondō and Tachibana, without completely sharing their brand of romantic rural communalism. Although it rejected the powerful centralized state of the late 1930s and early 1940s, agrarian nationalism shared with Japan's wartime leaders a faith in industriousness, social solidarity, the uniqueness of Japan, and the emperor as the embodiment of public loyalties. See also NINOMIYA SONTOKU; FARMERS' MOVEMENT.

noibara → wild roses

Nōin
能因

(988–?). Classical (WAKA) poet, scholar-critic, and Buddhist priest. Lay name Tachibana no Nagayasu. He studied under Fujiwara no Nagatō, establishing the precedent of the master-disciple relationship in Japanese poetry. He took holy orders around 1013 and thereafter led an itinerant life, thus contributing to the tradition of the wandering poet-priest, later to be epitomized by SAIGYŌ (1118–90). Out of his poetic travels, Nōin produced *Nōin utamakura* (Nōin's Poetic Places), a handbook giving brief notes and examples of the treatment in poetry of various scenic places, natural phenomena, and seasonal topics. His *Gengenshū* (ca 1046, Collection of Profundity upon Profundity) is an anthology of 167 poems by 92 poets covering the 59 years from 987 to 1045. His personal anthology of 257 poems, *Nōinshū* (Collection of Nōin), is believed to have been compiled by him between 1044 and 1049. The *Goshūishū* (1086, Collection of Gleanings, Continued), the fourth imperial anthology, contains 31 of his poems, and some 34 more are included in subsequent imperial collections.

Nojimazaki
野島崎

Cape on the southern tip of the Bōsō Peninsula in Chiba Prefecture, central Honshū. Originally a small island, Nojimazaki became part of the mainland in 1703 after a major earthquake. The Nojimazaki Lighthouse was built here in 1868. The cape is the center of Minami Bōsō Quasi-National Park.

Nojiri, Lake
野尻湖

(Nojiriko). Lake in northern Nagano Prefecture, central Honshū. Its water is used by the city of Nagano for irrigation and drinking. With many villas located on its southern shore, it is also a popular vacation spot among foreigners resident in Japan. Area: 4 sq km (1.5 sq mi); circumference: 16 km (10 mi); depth: 38 m (125 ft); altitude: 654 m (2,146 ft).

nōka → minka

Nokogiriyama   鋸山

Hill in the Bōsō Hills, southern Chiba Prefecture, central Honshū. It faces the Uraga Channel. Composed of sandy tuff, it is characterized by its saw-toothed ridges. At its summit there is a panoramic view of Tōkyō Bay, Mt. Fuji (Fujisan), and the Miura and Izu peninsulas. Height 329 m (1,079 ft).

nōkyō → agricultural cooperative associations

Noma Hiroshi   野間宏

(1915–91). Novelist. Born in Kōbe, Hyōgo Prefecture. Noma entered the French literature department of Kyōto University in April 1935, becoming increasingly involved with the left-wing movement. After graduating in 1938, Noma was employed by the Ōsaka City Welfare Department to work with outcaste (BURAKUMIN) communities. In the summer of 1943, he was arrested for being a pacifist and was imprisoned for six months. In February 1944 he married Fuji Mitsuko.

Shortly after World War II, Noma began work on his first novel, *Kurai e* (Dark Painting), published serially between April and October 1946. This novel, with its innovative sections of turgid stream-of-consciousness prose, was called "the first voice of postwar literature" by critics. In 1947 Noma published the first installment of the multivolume *Seinen no wa* (Ring of Youth), completed in 1971. This novel, which builds on Noma's experiences with *burakumin* and the *buraku* liberation movement, won the Tanizaki Prize in 1971.

Noma was active in Communist Party cultural activities from 1947 until his expulsion from the party in 1964. In 1952 he published *Shinkū chitai* (tr *Zone of Emptiness*, 1956), a compelling depiction of corruption and brutality in the army. Noma's detailed report on the trial of a *buraku* youth, *Sayama saiban* (1975, The Sayama Trial), is indicative of his continued intense involvement with the *buraku* cause.

Noma Institute of Educational Research   野間教育研究所

(Noma Kyōiku Kenkyūjo). Private research institute established in 1946 in accordance with the will of NOMA SEIJI, founder of KŌDANSHA, LTD. An incorporated foundation, the Noma Institute conducts and publishes basic scientific research in the field of education. The institute comprises three research departments: History of Japanese Education, Community Education, and Educational Psychology. *Kindai Nihon kyōiku seido shiryō* (1956), a 35-volume set of works on the history of Japan's modern education system compiled and edited by the Noma Institute, is regarded as the major source for material on the history of Japanese education.

Noma Koremichi   野間惟道

(1937–87). Publisher; fifth president of KŌDANSHA, LTD. Born in Tōkyō; son of former army minister ANAMI KORECHIKA. He graduated from the law department of Tōkyō University in 1962 and entered Mitsubishi Electric Corporation. In 1965 he married Noma Sawako (b 1943; president of Kōdansha, Ltd,

from 1987), daughter of Kōdansha's fourth president, NOMA SHŌICHI, and was adopted into the family. In the same year he entered Kōdansha and became a director. In October 1975 he started the daily magazine *Nikkan gendai*. In 1981 he became president of the company and strengthened the magazine division by launching a series of innovative new publications. He also endeavored to expand the book-publishing division and promoted a variety of international cultural projects such as the *Kodansha Encyclopedia of Japan* and the JAPAN FORUM.

Noma Literary Prize   野間文芸賞

(Noma Bungei Shō). Literary prize established in 1941 in memory of NOMA SEIJI, the first president of KŌDANSHA, LTD. Awarded annually (except for the period 1947–52) by the Noma Hōkō Kai (Noma Memorial Society). The prize is given to the author of an outstanding work of popular or serious fiction, nonfiction, drama, criticism, or other genre of writing.

Noma Seiji   野間清治

(1878–1938). Publisher; founder of KŌDANSHA, LTD. Born in Gumma Prefecture. In 1909, while employed by Tōkyō University, Noma helped establish the law school's Midori Kai Benron Bu, an oratory club. He also helped to publish the speeches made at the opening ceremony of the club and in 1910 published the magazine *Yūben* (Oratory). In 1911 he founded Kōdansha and began publishing the magazine *Kōdan kurabu*. Later, he published the following magazines: SHŌNEN KURABU (1914), *Omoshiro kurabu* (1916), *Gendai* and *Fujin kurabu* (both in 1920), *Shōjo kurabu* (1923), KINGU (1925), and *Yōnen kurabu* (1926). With the publication of *Kingu*, Japan's first magazine to attain a circulation of 1 million, Noma changed the name of his publishing firm to Dai Nippon Yūben Kai Kōdansha (it was renamed Kōdansha, Ltd, in 1958). Kōdansha's nine magazines accounted for 70 percent of the entire magazine circulation in Japan in the 1930s.

Noma Shōichi   野間省一

(1911–84). Publisher; fourth president of KŌDANSHA, LTD. Born in Shizuoka Prefecture. Graduate of Tōkyō University. Noma joined Kōdansha in 1941 as a director, having been adopted by the Noma family. In the early post–World War II period the JAPAN BOOK PUBLISHERS ASSOCIATION and others demanded that Kōdansha be investigated for its role in the war effort. Noma, who became president of Kōdansha in 1945, was purged from public office by an OCCUPATION directive in 1946. By the time he was rehabilitated in 1949, Kōdansha's business had deteriorated drastically, but after his return to management the company launched a series of modernizing and streamlining programs that restored and expanded its position in Japanese publishing. Under Noma's leadership the company also entered the field of international publishing with the establishment of Kōdansha International, Ltd, in 1963. Until his retirement in 1981, Noma played an influential role in maintaining Kōdansha as one of the largest publishing houses in Japan.

Nōmijima   能美島

Island in the central Inland Sea, approximately 14 km (8.5 mi) southwest of the city of Hiroshima; part of Hiroshima Prefecture. It is divided into Higashi Nōmijima (East Nōmijima) and Nishi Nōmijima (West Nōmijima) by an isthmus. It is connected to

Nōgyō zensho This illustration from the pioneering Edo-period book on agriculture depicts the harvesting, threshing, and drying of rice plants.

the island of Etajima by land and to the island of Kurahashijima by bridge. Principal activities are seaweed (*nori*) and oyster culture and the growing of flowers. Area: 61.5 sq km (23.7 sq mi).

Nomonhan Incident   ノモンハン事件

(Nomonhan Jiken). Military conflict from May to September 1939 between Japanese and Soviet forces near the village of Nomonhan on the border between northwestern Manchuria and Outer Mongolia. The incident began on 12 May, when Soviet troops came to the aid of the People's Republic of Mongolia after a border clash between Mongolian troops and the GUANDONG (KWANTUNG) ARMY of Japan. The superiority of the Soviet mechanized units commanded by Georgi K. Zhukov (1896–1974) resulted in repeated reversals for the Japanese, culminating in the complete rout of the Guandong Army's 23rd Division in late August (Japanese casualties included 17,450 dead or missing in action). With the signing on 23 August of a nonaggression pact between Germany (Japan's ally) and the Soviet Union and the resignation of the HIRANUMA KIICHIRŌ cabinet five days later, this defeat prompted the Japanese to sue for a cease-fire, signed in Moscow on 15 September. Japan's defeat at Nomonhan was a setback for those in the army who advocated military confrontation with the Soviet Union rather than the United States.

Noma Hiroshi This award-winning novelist was known for his deep involvement in the problems of Japan's *burakumin* minority group.

Nomugi Pass   野麦峠

(Nomugi Tōge). Located south of the mountain NORIKURADAKE in the southern Hida Mountains, on the border of Nagano and Gifu prefectures, central Honshū. An important route connecting Takayama with Matsumoto once ran through the pass. Altitude: 1,672 m (5,486 ft).

Nomura Kichisaburō   野村吉三郎

(1877–1964). Naval officer and diplomat. Born in Wakayama Prefecture; graduated from the Naval Academy in 1898. He served in a variety of naval posts, including a position as naval attaché at the Japanese embassy in Washington, DC, during World War I. He was promoted to the rank of admiral in 1933 and served as director of the Peers' School (see GAKUSHŪIN UNIVERSITY) in 1937. Appointed foreign minister in the ABE NOBUYUKI cabinet in 1939, he carried on discussions with US Ambassador Joseph GREW to improve Japan's seriously strained relations with the United States. In 1941 he was sent as ambassador extraordinary and plenipotentiary to the United States, but his efforts to avert war through negotiations with Secretary of State Cordell HULL ultimately proved ineffective. He recorded his experiences as ambassador in *Beikoku ni tsukaishite* (1946, As Envoy to the United States). After

Noma Seiji Founder of the publishing company Kōdansha and pioneer in the field of mass-market periodicals.

Nomura Kichisaburō

Nonomura Ninsei
Tea-leaf storage jar with mountain and cherry-blossom design. Late 17th century. Glazed stoneware. Height 36 cm. Fukuoka Art Museum, Fukuoka Prefecture.

World War II, he was twice elected to the House of Councillors.

Nomura Kodō   野村胡堂

(1882–1963). Novelist and music critic. Real name Nomura Osakazu. Born in Iwate Prefecture. Studied at Tōkyō University but left to work for *Hōchi shimbun*, a Tōkyō-based newspaper. He worked for the paper until it merged with *Yomiuri shimbun* in 1942. A writer of popular historical novels, he is noted for his series of period detective stories *Zenigata Heiji torimono hikae* (1931–58), in which he created the Edo-period (1600–1868) characters Heiji, a detective, and his underling Hachigorō (modeled on Sherlock Holmes and Watson) and which won the Kikuchi Kan Prize in 1958.

Nomura Manzō VI   野村万蔵6世

(1898–1978). A KYŌGEN actor of the Izumi school. Born in Tōkyō. The eldest son of Manzō V (later known as Mansai), he made his stage debut in 1903. His acting style won him many admirers and raised public interest in *kyōgen*. He was also a talented NŌ mask maker. He was designated a Living National Treasure in 1967. His three sons, Mannojō (b 1930), Mansaku (b 1931), and Mannosuke (b 1939), are also *kyōgen* actors, as was his brother Miyake Tōkurō IX (1901–90).

Nomura Motoni   野村望東尼

(1806–67). WAKA poet. Also known as Nomura Bōtōni. Given name Moto; also known as Kōryō. After her *samurai* husband's death in 1859, she became a nun. A student of ŌKUMA KOTOMICHI, she wrote poetry supporting the imperial loyalist movement. She was an associate of TAKASUGI SHINSAKU. Her main collection of poetry is *Kōryōshū* (1863).

Nomura Research Institute, Ltd
[株]野村総合研究所

(Nomura Sōgō Kenkyūsho). Japan's largest think tank. Incorporated in 1966, the institute merged with Nomura Computer Systems Co in 1988. It provides research, con-

sulting, and system integration services. Its researchers and employees number 2,400. The institute has overseas offices in New York, Washington, London, Hong Kong, Singapore, and Sydney. Sales for the fiscal year ending March 1990 totaled ¥109.6 billion (US $716.0 million), and capitalization stood at ¥10.1 billion (US $66.0 million). Headquarters are in Tōkyō.

Nomura Securities Co, Ltd
野村証券[株]

(Nomura Shōken). Largest securities firm in Japan. It was incorporated in 1925 when the securities division of the Ōsaka Nomura Bank (now DAIWA BANK, LTD) became independent. It initially engaged in the bond business, expanding into stocks in 1938. In 1941 Nomura became the first in Japan to start investment trust operations. During the period of rapid economic growth in the 1960s, it emphasized the underwriting of newly issued stocks and debentures. In 1961 it underwrote Sony Corporation's American depositary receipts (ADRs) and other debentures of Japanese firms issued in the United States. In 1969 it established Nomura Securities International, Inc, in the United States, followed by Nomura Europe, N.V. in Amsterdam in 1972. It has 141 branches in Japan and 46 overseas branches and subsidiaries. Revenue for the fiscal year ending March 1991 totaled ¥688.3 billion (US $5.0 billion), of which commissions constituted 48 percent; underwriting and distribution, 19 percent; net gain on trading, 14 percent; interest and dividends, 18 percent; and other sources, 1 percent. In the same year the company was capitalized at ¥181.7 billion (US $1.3 billion). Japan's largest think tank, the NOMURA RESEARCH INSTITUTE, LTD, was established in 1965 as a subsidiary of the firm. Headquarters are in Tōkyō.

Nonaka Kenzan   野中兼山

(1615–63). Scholar-administrator. Born in Harima Province (now part of Hyōgo Prefecture); adopted by a prominent retainer of the Tosa domain (now Kōchi Prefecture). Kenzan studied with the Neo-Confucianist TANI JICHŪ. As chief retainer of the *daimyō* of Tosa for 27 years he carried out land reclamation, initiated water control and harbor development projects, established domain monopoly of certain products, and resettled *samurai* in rural areas (see GŌSHI). His projects caused hardship to peasants, earned the enmity of several colleagues, and led to his downfall.

Nonchurch Movement→
Mukyōkai

nonlife insurance   損害保険

(*songai hoken*). "Nonlife insurance" is a term used to refer to all types of casualty and property insurance; that is, all forms of insurance other than life insurance. Marine insurance and fire insurance were made available in Japan in 1879 and 1888, respectively, with companies as the main clients. Other types of nonlife insurance soon followed. The recent focus of new insurance products has been the individual client, as seen in the development of savings insurance and automobile insurance. In addition, nonlife insurance companies have become active institutional investors, utilizing the stock market to gain short-term profits. In 1988 there were 23 nonlife companies licensed to operate under the Insurance Business Law; in the same year they listed total assets of ¥17.7

trillion (US $138.8 billion), over half of which was invested in stocks and bonds.

Nonoguchi Ryūho   野々口立圃

(1595–1669). *Haikai* (see HAIKU) poet of the early Edo period (1600–1868). A wealthy merchant from Kyōto, he was a disciple of the *haikai* master MATSUNAGA TEITOKU but later broke with the Teitoku school. His prose pieces are precursors of the poetic prose style called HAIBUN. Among his works are an anthology, *Haikai hokkuchō* (1633), and a critical work, *Kawabune tokumanzai* (1653).

Nonoichi   野々市[町]

Town on the southwest border of the city of Kanazawa in southern Ishikawa Prefecture, central Honshū. Nonoichi developed as a post-station town during the Edo period (1600–1868). Having become rapidly urbanized after World War II, Nonoichi is now part of the Kanazawa metropolitan area. Pop: 39,769.

Nonomura Ninsei   野々村仁清

(fl mid-17th century). Real name Nonomura Seiemon. Leading ceramic artist in Kyōto in the mid-17th century. Ninsei probably came from the village of Nonomura in Tamba (now part of Kyōto Prefecture). He set up a kiln at the Kyōto temple NINNAJI, and the work he produced there is known as Omuro ware. Many of Ninsei's pieces show the influence of Kanamori Sōwa (1584–1656), a leading tea master who may have been Ninsei's sponsor. The most famous of Ninsei's works are highly decorated in enamels of many colors, including silver and gold. His work ranges from simple tea caddies in the style of SETO WARE and rough vases in the style of SHIGARAKI WARE to elegantly decorated bowls, water jars, and four-lugged vases. His pieces were almost entirely for the TEA CEREMONY or related meals (*chakaiseki ryōri*). The tradition passed to Ogata KENZAN, who is said to have been one of Ninsei's pupils.

nonrecognition policy   不承認政策

(*fushōnin seisaku*). US policy, commonly known as the Stimson or Hoover-Stimson Doctrine, announced at the time of the MANCHURIAN INCIDENT (1931) by Secretary of State Henry Lewis STIMSON. It constituted a refusal to recognize any changes brought about by Japanese aggression in violation of the KELLOGG-BRIAND PACT and the NINE-POWER TREATY.

The Japanese GUANDONG (KWANTUNG) ARMY, stationed in Manchuria, began to take over Manchuria in September 1931. China immediately appealed to the League of Nations and the United States to intervene, and on 10 December the league resolved to set up the LYTTON COMMISSION to look into the Manchurian situation. On 6 January 1932 the Japanese army reached Shanhaiguan (Shanhaikwan) at the Great Wall. On 7 January Stimson sent an identical note to Japan and China, stating that his government would not recognize any treaty, agreement, or situation impairing US rights or any gains made in violation of the Kellogg-Briand Pact and that the OPEN DOOR POLICY would be maintained.

After Japan attacked Shanghai in late January, Stimson extended the nonrecognition doctrine to cover violations of the Nine-Power Treaty. His policy was endorsed by the Assembly of the League of Nations on 11 March, and most league members refused to recognize the new puppet state of MANCHUKUO. Japan withdrew from the league in

Nomura Kodō This writer is best known for a series of stories about an Edo-period detective and his assistant.

▲ The noren of a silk wholesaler in the city of Tango, north of Kyōto.

▶ Some noren are brown, like this one over the door of an ankō (anglerfish) restaurant.

noren

A noren is a type of split curtain, often with a distinctive logo, that is displayed to indicate that an establishment is open for business. The most common color is navy blue.

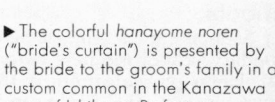

▶ The colorful hanayome noren ("bride's curtain") is presented by the bride to the groom's family in a custom common in the Kanazawa area of Ishikawa Prefecture.

▲ A typical noren in navy blue with the restaurant's specialty in white.

▼ An apprentice geisha emerges from between the panels of the noren of a geisha house in Kyōto.

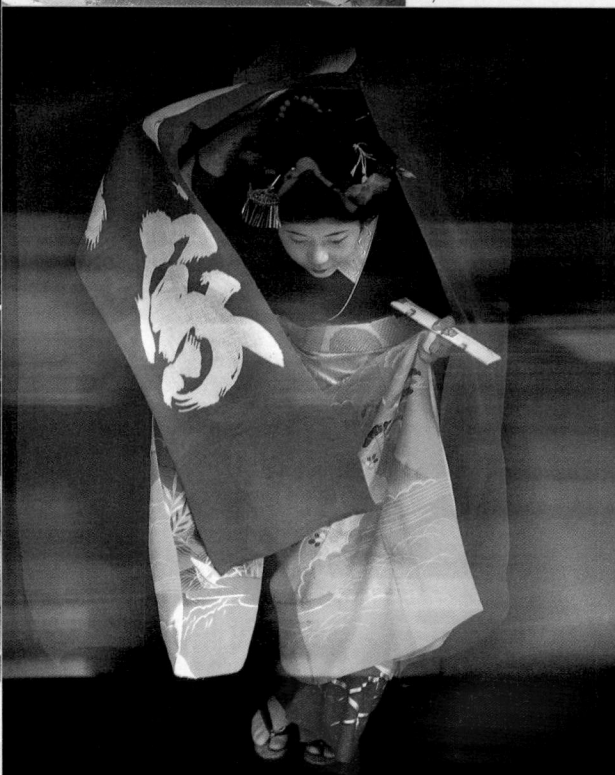

March 1933 and began a new military campaign in China.

nonsmokers' rights 嫌煙権

(ken'enken). In Japan, as elsewhere, the right of nonsmokers to be free from the health hazards of tobacco smoke generated by those around them has been an important social issue since the 1970s. In 1978 a citizens' action group called the Japan Action for Nonsmokers' Rights was formed. One of its demands was that at least half the passenger cars on the Japanese National Railways (JNR; now Japan Railways) be designated as no-smoking cars, and in 1980 it initiated a lawsuit to force the railroad to comply. JNR responded by agreeing to designate one no-smoking car on each of its Shinkansen trains, and to follow this up with no-smoking cars on its other trains. Over the last decade, the concept of nonsmokers' rights has made considerable progress. In 1991, 30 to 40 percent of Shinkansen cars were reserved for nonsmokers, and no-smoking cars on other routes have increased as well. Smoking has been banned in the waiting rooms of public hospitals and since 1988 in all stations of the Tōkyō subway system. The principal umbrella organization of nonsmokers' rights groups is now known as Japan Action on Smoking and Health.

nonverbal communication
非言語コミュニケーション

(higengo komyunikēshon). In the highly homogeneous society of Japan, both consciously learned and unconsciously absorbed ETIQUETTE and GESTURES account for a significant portion of the communication between individuals. Functioning as nonverbal cues, they activate underlying behavior patterns that condition the import of verbal communication. Across a broad range of human relationships, beginning with that implied by the shared culture of Japan and extending to that of members of a profession, workplace, or family, essential information for the interpretation of a conversa-

tion is supplied by the silences and ellipses that link individual utterances. This aspect of language is by no means unique to Japanese; however, Japanese does offer particularly fertile ground for its study.

Social Background——Inculcation of silence as a means of communication begins with the relationship of mother and child. Comparison with samples taken in the United States indicates that Japanese mothers place greater importance on nonverbal communication with their children. It is in the relationship between mother and child that is fostered the virtue of SUNAO (trust in the intentions and silent compliance with the decisions of others). Physical closeness, such as bathing together and sleeping in the same room even when greater privacy is possible, is the norm, and early striving for independence is discouraged, largely by nonverbal means. Bonding of the child to the mother is customarily reinforced by feelings of guilt induced by the mother's silent suffering.

In the larger social frame there are complex and interacting behavioral patterns, such as the concepts of ON (indebtedness) and giri (duty or obligation; see GIRI AND NINJŌ), that condition communication between individuals. The social convention of avoidance of confrontation, manifested in the radical bifurcation of public and personal opinion (see TATEMAE AND HONNE), encourages silence or even concurrence in opinions contrary to one's true feelings.

Nonverbal Cues——In Japan the bow (ojigi) serves the same purpose as a handshake, but it can also, depending on its depth, signify a hierarchy between two or more persons. The smile, besides displaying pleasure, is also used to hide feelings of antagonism or deep unhappiness, and laughter can display commiseration with the embarrassment which others are assumed to feel when they meet with some sudden con-

Egerton Herbert Norman A Canadian historian and diplomat who examined the roots of modern Japan in his influential writings.

tretemps, such as tripping and falling down. Eye contact during a conversation is much less frequent than in Western countries and, if excessive, may be construed as threatening. An expressionless face can indicate a range of feeling from indifference to scorn, and is commonly used when addressing an adversary. Silence concerning a matter may convey concern about it, and apparently blithe remarks, deep feeling. Silences during a conversation are often felt to be a pleasant interval during which a shared atmosphere is savored.

In Japanese there are several levels of HONORIFIC LANGUAGE, and, when addressing a stranger, a judgment, often on the basis of dress, is made as to which level of speech one should adopt. The need to know a person's social position in order to introduce into one's speech the proper level of deference has led to the nearly universal use of calling cards (*meishi*) that indicate one's place of work and position and that are invariably exchanged at a formal first meeting.

noren 暖簾

Split curtains originally hung in front of a shop door to keep out the sun and dust. Decorated with the shop's name (*yagō*) and house insignia, *noren* also served as the shop's sign. They were hung as shades in front of houses from the Heian (794–1185) to Kamakura (1185–1333) periods. With the development of large shops during the Muromachi period (1333–1568), *noren* were installed in place of doors to allow customers to enter and exit easily. At about the same time *noren* began to be dyed navy blue, with the shop's name or business in white. When an apprentice or employee of a shop with a highly esteemed *noren* opened his own shop, it was an honor to be allowed to use his master's *noren*. *Noren* were used extensively until the Taishō period (1912–26) but began to fall into disuse as shop layouts were Westernized. However, some shops, especially Japanese-style restaurants, still hang out *noren* to indicate that they are open for business. *Noren* made of hanging strands of twisted rope (*nawa noren*) are peculiar to cheaper drinking establishments. *Noren* are often used in private homes as space dividers or decorations. ► *See photos, previous page.*

nori 海苔

(laver). The word *nori* is used in Japan both as a general term for seaweed and as a name for a species of red algae (*Porphyra tenera*) that is commonly used as a foodstuff and is also known as *asakusanori*. *Asakusanori* is harvested, cut, and spread out thin on boards to dry until it resembles brittle paper. The dried product, called *hoshinori*, is a blackish purple color, but it turns a lustrous dark green and gives off a unique aroma when passed quickly over a flame. It is used for making *makizushi* (rolled SUSHI), NIGIRIMESHI (rice balls), CHAZUKE (rice with green tea), and numerous other dishes. See also SEAWEED CULTIVATION.

Norikuradake 乗鞍岳

Stratovolcano on the border between Nagano and Gifu prefectures, central Honshū. On the summit are many peaks, including Kengamine (the highest). In the bottom of its two great craters are several lakes. Near the summit, aside from alpine flora and snowy ravines, are a corona observatory and

a cosmic ray observatory. Hirayu and Shirahone hot springs are located in the foothills. It is part of Chūbu Sangaku National Park. Height: 3,026 m (9,928 ft).

Norikura Volcanic Zone 乗鞍火山帯

(Norikura Kazantai). Volcanic zone on the border between Gifu and Nagano prefectures, central Honshū. It encompasses the southern half of the HIDA MOUNTAINS. The major volcanic peaks are YAKEDAKE, NORIKURADAKE, and ONTAKESAN. Many of the zone's volcanoes are included in Chūbu Sangaku National Park.

Nōrin Chūkin Bank 農林中央金庫

(Nōrin Chūō Kinko; literally, Central Bank for Agriculture and Forestry). Financial institution that regulates the flow of funds within the cooperative organizations in farming, forestry, and fishing. It is maintained jointly by the approximately 9,800 primary-sector cooperatives throughout the country and their federations. Nōrin Chūkin was established in 1923 by special legislation. In 1990 some 65 percent of its funds came from deposits by the cooperatives. In recent years, it has been expanding its international business by investing its funds overseas and supporting its customers' overseas activities. In the fiscal year ending March 1990 the bank had total assets of ¥35.4 trillion (US $231.3 billion). Headquarters are in Tōkyō. See also AGRICULTURAL CO-OPERATIVE ASSOCIATIONS.

Nōrin Suisan Shō → Ministry of Agriculture, Forestry, and Fisheries

Noritake Co, Ltd

[株]ノリタケカンパニーリミテド
(Noritake Kampanī Rimitedo). Japan's leading manufacturer of ceramic tableware and whetstones; also manufactures grinding machines, industrial ceramics, and other industrial materials. Incorporated in 1917. Noritake was the first Japanese manufacturer and exporter of hard-glazed white porcelain dinnerware. Since World War II, the company has successfully diversified into industrial ceramics and related fields. Noritake's various subsidiary companies (which include TOTO, LTD; NGK INSULATORS, LTD; NGK SPARK PLUG CO, LTD; and INAX CORPORATION) are referred to as the Morimura group. Noritake has both sales outlets and manufacturing affiliates throughout the world. Sales for the fiscal year ending March 1991 totaled ¥107.9 billion (US $786.4 million), and capitalization stood at ¥10.3 billion (US $75.1 million). Headquarters are in Nagoya.

norito 祝詞

A formulaic statement in the classical language addressed to the deities present at a Shintō ceremony. Reflecting the early Japanese view that a spirit resides in words (see KOTODAMA), *norito* are considered a particularly sacred form of speech originating in mythical times. There are various types of *norito*: those expressing thanksgiving, those seeking the blessings or protection of the deities, those commemorating a particular legendary or historical event in the religious calendar, and those making specific prayers for individuals. The earliest surviving collection of *norito* is found in the ENGI SHIKI (927; tr *Procedures of the Engi Era*, 1970–72).

Norito texts employ a peculiar orthography called *semmyōgaki*, in which particles, verb endings, and other lexical elements

normally written in the KANA syllabary appear in Chinese characters of reduced size, indicating that they are to be read phonetically and not semantically as ideographs. Although *norito* were freely composed by priests over the centuries, after the establishment of STATE SHINTŌ at the beginning of the Meiji period (1868–1912) all shrine rituals, including the texts of *norito*, were standardized by government decree and published in official compendia. Priests today generally follow the *norito* collections.

Nōritz Corporation [株]ノーリツ

(Nōritsu). Manufacturer of household water heaters and distributor of other related products. Incorporated in 1951. Sales for fiscal year ending December 1990 totaled ¥89.3 billion (US $668.7 million), of which gas-fueled bathwater heaters accounted for 51 percent; gas-fueled water heaters, 20 percent; oil-fueled water heaters, 12 percent; and system equipment and other products, 17 percent. The company was capitalized at ¥17.6 billion (US $131.8 million) in the same year. Headquarters are in Kōbe.

normal schools 師範学校

(*shihan gakkō*). Schools for training elementary and secondary school teachers before World War II. Upon promulgation of the EDUCATION ORDER OF 1872, the first normal school (later Tōkyō University of Education; now TSUKUBA UNIVERSITY) was founded in Tōkyō. In the following years, national normal schools were established in the cities of Ōsaka, Sendai, Nagoya, Hiroshima, Nagasaki, and Niigata. The Women's Normal School (now Ochanomizu Women's University) was opened in 1874. The Normal School Order of 1886 established a national system comprised of one higher normal school (*kōtō shihan gakkō*) located in Tōkyō to train secondary school teachers and a normal school in each prefecture (*jinjō shihan gakkō*) to train elementary school teachers. Higher normal schools were later founded in Hiroshima (1902), Nara (1908), and other cities. Some higher normal schools became universities after the war. See also TEACHERS.

Norman, Egerton Herbert

ノーマン, E. H.
(1909–57). Canadian diplomat and historian whose writings on the rise of modern Japan have influenced Western and Japanese scholars. Born in Karuizawa, Nagano Prefecture, of Canadian missionary parents, he studied East Asian history at Harvard and Columbia universities. In 1938 he joined the research staff of the INSTITUTE OF PACIFIC RELATIONS, for which he produced his first book, *Japan's Emergence as a Modern State* (1940). In 1939 he entered the Canadian diplomatic service, working in Japan as a language officer until the outbreak of war forced him home in 1942.

Over the next 15 years he continued his historical studies. In *Soldier and Peasant in Japan* (1943) and *Feudal Background of Japanese Politics* (1945) he examined the roots of the militarism that had led to Japan's involvement in World War II. With the coming of peace he turned to the search for an indigenous democratic tradition in *Andō Shōeki and the Anatomy of Japanese Feudalism* (1949; see ANDŌ SHŌEKI).

His criticism of OCCUPATION policy and alleged left-wing connections resulted in investigations by Canadian and US government agencies. Although he was exonerated in Canada, the pressure affected him deeply, and he committed suicide in 1957.

Normanton Incident

ノルマントン号事件

(*Normanton gō Jiken*). Diplomatic controversy in 1886 surrounding the sinking of the British freighter *Normanton*. On 24 October 1886 the *Normanton* sank off the coast of Wakayama Prefecture. The captain, John William Drake, and his English crew escaped safely, but all 23 of the abandoned Japanese passengers drowned. At a hearing at the British consulate in Kōbe in November, the captain was declared innocent. Public outcry was such that the trial was moved to the consulate in Yokohama, and on 8 December, Captain Drake was given a sentence of three months' imprisonment. No compensations were made. The incident convinced the Japanese public of the urgency of revising treaties with Western nations and abolishing extraterritoriality (see UNEQUAL TREATIES, REVISION OF; NAICHI ZAKKYO).

Noro Eitarō

野呂栄太郎

(1900–1934). Marxist economist and important theoretician of the JAPAN COMMUNIST PARTY (JCP) in the early 1930s. Born in Hokkaidō, he graduated from Keiō University. While at Keiō he was influenced by NOSAKA SANZŌ, later a leader of the JCP. Noro later studied Japanese economics at the Sangyō Rōdō Chōsajo (Industrial Labor Research Institute) and at the Puroretaria Kagaku Kenkyūjo (Proletarian Science Research Institute). His writings stressed the bourgeois revolutionary character of the MEIJI RESTORATION of 1868 and later focused on the semifeudal character of rural society as the basic determinant of the character of Japanese capitalism. Noro edited NIHON SHIHON SHUGI HATTATSU SHI KŌZA (1932–33) with YAMADA MORITARŌ, HIRANO YOSHITARŌ, and Ōtsuka Kinnosuke (1892–1977). This publication provided a focus for the ideological controversy between the KŌZAHA and the RŌNŌHA factions (see also NIHON SHIHON SHUGI RONSŌ). Noro's major work was the essay collection *Nihon shihon shugi hattatsu shi* (1930). He was arrested in 1933 and died while under police detention.

Noro Genjō

野呂元丈

(1693–1761). Herbal botanist and scholar of WESTERN LEARNING. Born in Ise Province (now part of Mie Prefecture), he went to Kyōto to study medical science and herbal medicine, the latter under INŌ JAKUSUI. In 1739 Noro was appointed physician to the shōgun TOKUGAWA YOSHIMUNE. With AOKI KON'YŌ, he was ordered by Yoshimune to study Dutch in 1740. Noro subsequently translated a Dutch *materia medica*, the *Cruydeboeck* (or *Herbarius*, 1554) by Rembert Dodoens (1517–85), and published it as *Oranda honzō wage* (A Dutch Herbal Translated).

Noro Kageyoshi

野呂景義

(1854–1923). Metallurgist. Pioneer in Japanese metallurgy. Born in what is now Aichi Prefecture, he graduated from Tōkyō University. He studied in England and Germany from 1885 to 1889 and became a professor at Tōkyō University upon his return. He instituted and taught Japan's first courses in metallurgy and was an important force behind the establishment of the YAWATA IRON AND STEEL WORKS and the Japan Iron and Steel Federation.

Northern Alps → Hida Mountains

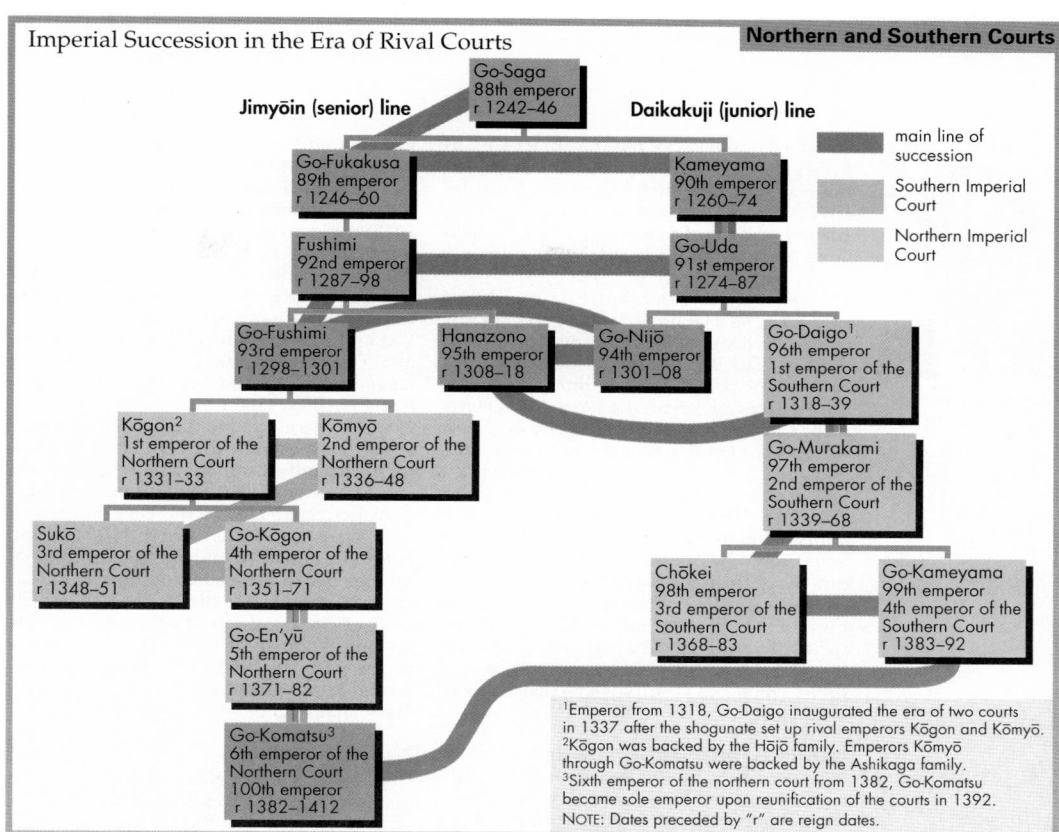

Imperial Succession in the Era of Rival Courts

[1]Emperor from 1318, Go-Daigo inaugurated the era of two courts in 1337 after the shogunate set up rival emperors Kōgon and Kōmyō.
[2]Kōgon was backed by the Hōjō family. Emperors Kōmyō through Go-Komatsu were backed by the Ashikaga family.
[3]Sixth emperor of the northern court from 1382, Go-Komatsu became sole emperor upon reunification of the courts in 1392.
NOTE: Dates preceded by "r" are reign dates.

Northern and Southern Courts

南北朝

(Nambokuchō). The two rival imperial courts that existed in Japan between 1337 and 1392, each claiming the legitimate right to rule. The period during which they were in conflict is known as the period of the Northern and Southern Courts (Nambokuchō *jidai*). The Nambokuchō schism raised questions about imperial legitimacy that were revived in the EDO PERIOD (1600–1868) and in modern times.

The conflict originated when the imperial house at Kyōto split into two rival lines, the Jimyōin (senior) line descended from Emperor GO-FUKAKUSA (r 1246–60), and the Daikakuji (junior) line descended from his younger brother Emperor KAMEYAMA (r 1260–74). They were in constant competition for the throne, the position of senior retired emperor (see INSEI), and control of imperial estates. The KAMAKURA SHOGUNATE (1192–1333) imposed a compromise whereby members of the two lines would succeed in alternation. When Emperor GO-DAIGO (r 1318–39) of the junior line became emperor, he resolved to keep the succession in his own line and restore direct imperial rule. In 1331 Go-Daigo attempted a coup d'état against the shogunate (see GENKŌ INCIDENT); it failed and he was exiled to the island of Oki in southwestern Japan. Go-Daigo's supporters, however, continued to resist the shogunate. They gradually gained in strength, and the balance of power tipped in their favor when the Kamakura vassals ASHIKAGA TAKAUJI and NITTA YOSHISADA embraced the imperial cause. They destroyed the Kamakura shogunate in 1333.

Go-Daigo returned to Kyōto and attempted to reestablish imperial rule through a series of reform measures (see KEMMU RESTORATION), but the attempt ended in complete failure. Takauji turned against Go-Daigo in 1335, and his armies defeated the imperial forces at the Battle of MINATOGAWA in 1336. Takauji forced the emperor to abdicate in favor of the second son of the former emperor Go-Fushimi (r 1298–1301); a member

of the senior line, he ascended the throne as Emperor Kōmyō (r 1336–48). Go-Daigo escaped to Yoshino (in what is now Nara Prefecture), where he established the rival Southern Court in January 1337. Takauji formed a new military government in Kyōto that soon became the MUROMACHI SHOGUNATE (1338–1573). The two courts were reconciled in 1392, when Emperor GO-KOMATSU (r 1382–1412) of the Northern Court was accepted as sole sovereign in a compromise arranged by the shogunate whereby the rival imperial lines would once more alternate. This promise was not kept, and the southern line vanished from history.

Several centuries later the schism was still an issue. Many Confucian and KOKUGAKU (National Learning) scholars of the Edo period sided with the Southern Court, as seen in the writings of YAMAZAKI ANSAI, RAI SAN'YŌ, and various scholars of the MITO SCHOOL of historical studies who participated in the compilation of the DAI NIHON SHI (History of Great Japan). The controversy over imperial legitimacy was revived again late in the MEIJI PERIOD (1868–1912). The KATSURA TARŌ government persuaded Emperor MEIJI (r 1867–1912) to issue a decree recognizing the Southern Court as the rightful claimant (see NAMBOKUCHŌ SEIJUN RON) at the time of the schism. This politically inspired statement, however, did not threaten the status of the imperial line.

Northern Territories issue

北方領土問題

(Hoppō Ryōdo *mondai*). Dispute concerning Japan's Northern Territories, which consist of Kunashiri, Etorofu, Shikotan, and the Habomai Islands, occupied by the Soviet Union since 1945 and still occupied by the Russian Federation in late 1992. The Japanese government maintains that the Russian occupation is illegal and demands the return of these islands.

After Japan's defeat in World War II, it signed the SAN FRANCISCO PEACE TREATY with

Nosaka Akiyuki This writer's most powerful works reflect his traumatic childhood experiences of Japan's defeat in World War II and subsequent occupation.

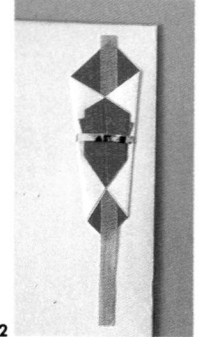

48 Allied nations (but not the Soviet Union) in September 1951. In the treaty Japan renounced all rights and title to the Kuril Islands, but the text did not stipulate which islands made up the Kuril chain nor which government was to exercise sovereignty over them.

Asserting that Kunashiri, Etorofu, Shikotan, and the Habomai Islands are not included in the term "Kuril Islands" as used in the San Francisco treaty and that they have historically constituted an integral part of the territory of Japan, the Japanese government sought their return. The Soviet Union refused, contending that the territorial issue had already been resolved. Then during Soviet president Mikhail Gorbachev's visit to Tōkyō in 1991, both sides confirmed in a joint communiqué that final resolution of the issue would be carried out as a part of a future peace treaty between the two countries. However, the Soviet Union was dissolved at the end of that year, and, as of late 1992, the issue still remained to be negotiated between Japan and the Russian Federation. See also SOVIET UNION AND JAPAN; SOVIET-JAPANESE JOINT DECLARATION.

Norway and Japan　ノルウェーと日本

(Norué to Nihon). Diplomatic relations between Japan and Norway (then part of Denmark) were initiated in 1868 with the signing of a treaty of amity and commerce. Following a hiatus during and after World War II, relations were resumed in 1952 when the SAN FRANCISCO PEACE TREATY went into effect. The two nations concluded a treaty of commerce and navigation in 1957 and have held yearly trade talks since 1962. King Olav V of Norway visited Japan in 1983, as did Crown Prince Harald (King Harald V since 1991) in 1978, 1989, and 1990; Prime Minister Gro Harlem Brundtland attended a meeting of the United Nations Special Committee on the Environment in Tōkyō in 1987. Japanese foreign minister Abe Shintarō (1924–91) and Crown Prince (now Emperor) AKIHITO visited Norway in 1985.

Norway's shipping industry brings in substantial freight income from Japan, but the balance of trade between the two nations has been consistently in favor of Japan. Norway's deficit expanded in 1990 when Japan's exports to Norway increased by 38 percent from the previous year to US $831 million even though its imports, chief among which were fish and shellfish, rose 11 percent to $623 million.

Nosaka Akiyuki　野坂昭如

(1930–). Novelist. Born in Kanagawa Prefecture. After attending Waseda University he worked as a copywriter for television commercials. In 1963 he made his debut as a novelist with *Erogotoshitachi* (tr *The Pornographers*, 1968). He received the Naoki Prize for "Amerika hijiki" (1967; tr "American Hijiki," 1977) and "Hotaru no haka" (1967; tr "A Grave of Fireflies," 1978). In 1972, as the editor of the magazine *Omoshiro hambun*, he printed a story attributed to NAGAI KAFŪ, which resulted in a major obscenity trial (see YOJŌHAN FUSUMA NO SHITABARI TRIAL). Other works include *Ninshō daimeishi* (1985, Personal Pronoun).

Nosaka Sanzō　野坂参三

(1892–). Politician and a leader of the JAPAN COMMUNIST PARTY (JCP). Born in Yamaguchi Prefecture; graduate of Keiō University.

While a student, he joined the YŪAIKAI, a labor organization formed by SUZUKI BUNJI, and he joined the Communist Party soon after its founding in 1922. He was arrested in 1923 and again in 1928 during mass arrests of communists (see MARCH 15TH INCIDENT). In 1931 he went to the Soviet Union as the JCP representative to the Comintern. He went to China in 1940 and spent the war years in Yan'an (Yenan) with the Chinese Communist Party, indoctrinating and organizing Japanese soldiers taken prisoner by communist guerrillas. Upon his return to Japan in 1946, he was elected to the Central Committee of the reestablished JCP. Nosaka called for a "friendly Communist Party" and advocated a nonviolent revolution. The same year, he was elected to the Diet. Purged by the Occupation authorities in 1950 (see RED PURGE), he remained underground until 1955. By then one of the leaders of the JCP, he was elected a member of the House of Councillors in 1956, a position he held until 1977. He became chairman of the Central Committee of the party in 1958. In 1982 he was succeeded by MIYAMOTO KENJI and became honorary chairman of the Central Committee.

Nosappumisaki　納沙布岬

Cape on the eastern Nemuro Peninsula. The easternmost tip of Hokkaidō (145°49′14″ E), separating Nemuro Bay from the Pacific Ocean. It is famous for its clear view of the HABOMAI ISLANDS, the nearest of which is only 4 km (2.5 mi) away.

Noshappumisaki　野寒布岬

Cape in northern Hokkaidō. Extending north into the Sōya Strait, it is the northernmost point of Hokkaidō (45°27′). The city of Wakkanai, a major fishing port, is in the southeastern part.

noshi　熨斗

Decoratively folded paper with a strip of dried abalone inside; an element of formal gift wrapping that symbolizes a happy occasion. *Noshi* is an abbreviation of *noshiawabi*, meaning stretched-out or flattened-out abalone. Its origin lies in the Buddhist injunction against consumption of flesh at inauspicious times. Attaching a strip of abalone thus signifies an auspicious occasion. A gift is wrapped with heavy white paper (*hōshogami*) and tied with a special string called MIZUHIKI. The *noshi* is glued onto the paper at the upper right-hand corner. Today, a strip of yellow paper often substitutes for abalone. For a less formal gift, the *noshi* and *mizuhiki* are printed on cheaper wrapping paper. One may also write the word *noshi* in *hiragana* script.

Noshiro　能代[市]

City in northwestern Akita Prefecture, northern Honshū, on the Sea of Japan. Known as a lumber port during the Edo period (1600–1868), Noshiro has prosperous lumber, plywood manufacturing, and furniture manufacturing industries. Pop: 55,915.

Noshiro Plain　能代平野

(Noshiro Heiya). Located in northwestern Akita Prefecture, northern Honshū. With high sand dunes along the Sea of Japan coast, this floodplain of the river YONESHIROGAWA consists of fan-shaped deltas in the uplands and an alluvial plain. The principal agricultural products are rice, pears, and vegetables. The major city is NOSHIRO. Area: approximately 220 sq km (85 sq mi).

Nōshōmushō　農商務省

(Ministry of Agriculture and Commerce). Government ministry during the Meiji (1868–1912) and Taishō (1912–26) periods that handled matters connected with agriculture, forestry, commerce, and industry. Established in 1881, it took over the responsibilities that had previously been discharged by the HOME MINISTRY, the MINISTRY OF FINANCE, and the Ministry of Public Works (Kōbushō). After adoption of the cabinet system in 1885, responsibilities for posts and telegraphs, railways, and sea-lanes were transferred to the newly established Ministry of Communications (Teishinshō). At the same time, the responsibilities for mines and factories that had belonged to the now-defunct Ministry of Public Works came under the Nōshōmushō's jurisdiction. On 1 April 1925 responsibilities for these matters were divided between two newly established organs, the Ministry of Agriculture and Forestry (Nōrinshō) and the Ministry of Commerce and Industry (Shōkōshō).

notary public　公証人

(*kōshōnin*). In Japan a notary public is a legal specialist whose function is to certify officially matters related to the public's legal affairs. A notary drafts notarial deeds regarding juristic acts, acknowledgments of articles of association, wills under notarial deed, and other publicly certified documents.

nothingness　無

(J: *mu;* Ch: *wu*). Fundamental Chinese Taoist concept; the term for absolute nonexistence, from which all existence arises and to which mankind ultimately returns. The idea of nothingness transcending ethics and politics was developed by Taoists critical of the Confucian preoccupation with ethical and political problems. This philosophy of nothingness merged with the Indian Buddhist philosophy of EMPTINESS (*kū*) in Chinese and Japanese Buddhism, especially ZEN Buddhism. As defined by Buddhism, however, nothingness is seen not as a state of nonexistence as opposed to existence but as an absolute, transcending the opposition of existence and nonexistence, or as an ideal and absolute human state identical to religious enlightenment (*satori*).

Noto Peninsula　能登半島

(Noto Hantō). Located in northern Ishikawa Prefecture, central Honshū. It extends northeast into the Sea of Japan. Bounded by Toyama Bay to the east and by the Sea of Japan to the west, it is a desolate, mountainous region, with many cliffs on the western coast and numerous indentations and inlets on the eastern coast. The peninsula is famous for its many hot springs, beautiful stretches of coastline, and Tsukumo Bay. Nanao, the largest city, is an important fishing port. The principal products are lacquer ware, cultured pearls, and oysters. Parts of the peninsula are included in the Noto Peninsula Quasi-National Park.

Notoro, Lake　能取湖

(Notoroko). Lagoon in the western part of the city of Abashiri, northeastern Hokkaidō. Hills extend on the east and west of the lake; the northern part faces the Sea of Okhotsk. Shrimp and flatfish are found in the lake. Area: 58 sq km (22 sq mi); circumference: 35 km (22 mi); depth: 23.1 m (75.8 ft).

Notsukezaki　　　　野付崎

Sand spit in eastern Hokkaidō. Shaped like a fishhook, it extends 28 km (17 mi) into the Nemuro Bay, making it Japan's largest recurved spit. Principal activities are prawn fishing and cattle raising. It is famous as a resting place for hundreds of swans from October to April as well as for Todowara, a forest of dead trees.

November Incident　　　　十一月事件

(Jūichigatsu Jiken; also known as the Shikan Gakkō Jiken or Army Academy Incident). The arrest in November 1934 of young army officers of the KŌDŌHA (Imperial Way faction) and cadets at the Army Academy for plotting a coup d'état. The officers were suspended for six months; the cadets were expelled. The Kōdōha accused its rival, the TŌSEIHA (Control faction), of having fabricated the affair to discredit MAZAKI JINZABURŌ, inspector general of military education. The incident led to the dismissal of Mazaki; the murder of his successor NAGATA TETSUZAN by a Kōdōha officer; and, indirectly, the FEBRUARY 26TH INCIDENT, a 1936 mutiny.

Nozawa Bonchō　　　　野沢凡兆

(?–1714). HAIKU poet of the early Edo period (1600–1868). Born in Kaga Province (now Ishikawa Prefecture). A physician in Kyōto, he became a disciple of BASHŌ and collaborated with MUKAI KYORAI in compiling the SARUMINO (1691), an anthology of the Bashō school. His own haiku in this collection, produced under the direct guidance of Bashō, are his best work, excelling in their objectivity and clarity of image. After he drifted away from Bashō, Bonchō's work became mediocre.

Nozawa Hot Spring　　　　野沢温泉

(Nozawa Onsen). Located on a plateau in northern Nagano Prefecture, central Honshū; said to have been discovered by the Buddhist priest GYŌGI in the 8th century. Known for its therapeutic facilities and ski grounds. A hydrogen sulfide spring; water temperature 40°–90°C (104°–194°F).

Nozoe Tetsuo　　　　野副鉄男

(1902–). Chemist. He extracted a substance known as *hinokichiōru* from the Taiwanese *hinoki* tree (a variety of cypress). He identified the substance as tropolone, a nonbenzenoid aromatic compound, and later synthesized it. Born in Miyagi Prefecture, he graduated from Tōhoku University. In 1937 he became a professor at Taipei University (now Taiwan National University), where he did his work on tropolone. He returned to Tōhoku University in 1948 as a professor. He received the Order of Culture in 1958.

NSK, Ltd　　　　日本精工[株]

(Nippon Seikō). Manufacturer of ball and roller bearings, automotive steering gears, ball screws, precision grinding spindles, and car belts. Incorporated in 1916. Its products are known worldwide under the brand name NSK. It has sales subsidiaries and affiliates in 12 countries and representative offices in 5 countries. Sales for the fiscal year ending March 1991 totaled ¥368.6 billion (US $2.7 billion). In the same year the company was capitalized at ¥65.2 billion (US $475.2 million). Headquarters are in Tōkyō.

NTN Corporation　　　　エヌティエヌ[株]

(Enu Tī Enu). Manufacturer of bearings. Incorporated in 1934. It is second in size only to

NSK, LTD, and it dominates the Japanese market for constant-velocity universal ball joints for use in automobiles. It has manufacturing and sales subsidiaries in 33 countries, including the United States, Britain, France, Germany, and Canada. In the fiscal year ending March 1991 sales totaled ¥293.9 billion (US $2.1 billion). In the same year the company was capitalized at ¥39.6 billion (US $288.6 million). Headquarters are in Ōsaka.

NTT → Nippon Telegraph and Telephone Corporation

nuclear family　　　　核家族

(*kaku kazoku*). The nuclear family has become far more common in Japan with the changes in industrial structure and increased urbanization of the country in the years since World War II. Traditionally, the usual pattern in Japan was that of the extended family (see IE), in which the head of the household (*kachō*) lived not only with his wife and children but with his parents, grandparents, and occasionally other relations as well. After the end of the war the *ie* concept and the legal system supporting it gradually lost their power, and the nuclear family has come to predominate. The shift away from primary industries such as farming and fishing, which involved the labor of all family members, toward secondary and tertiary industries in which the husband became the sole breadwinner has also accelerated this trend. In 1955 nuclear families constituted 45.3 percent of all households, a figure that rose to 59.6 percent by 1991. See also FAMILY.

nuclear power plants　　　　原子力発電所

(*genshiryoku hatsudensho*). As of December 1990 there were 16 commercial nuclear power plants operating in Japan, with a total of 21 boiling water reactors, 17 pressurized water reactors, and 1 advanced thermal reactor; total electrical capacity was 31.48 million kilowatts. In 1990 Japan was the world's fourth largest producer of nuclear power, following the United States, France, and the Soviet Union. With 181.9 billion kilowatt-hours produced (25.8 percent of the nation's total output), atomic energy was Japan's single largest source of electrical power, and 2 additional nuclear power plants were in the planning stage or under construction. The average rate of operation of the nation's nuclear power plants in 1990 was 72.7 percent, the highest in the world.

Although Japan had long been dependent on the light-water-reactor technology of the United States, by the early 1980s construction and maintenance were performed by Japanese. However, Japan still depended on Britain, the United States, and France for all of the enriched uranium used as fuel. In 1991 Japan Nuclear Fuel Industries, Inc, completed construction of Japan's first nuclear fuel plant in the village of Rokkasho, Aomori Prefecture. The plant is expected to begin operations in 1992, meeting a portion of Japan's demand for enriched uranium.

Following the catastrophe in 1986 at the Chernobyl nuclear power plant in the So-

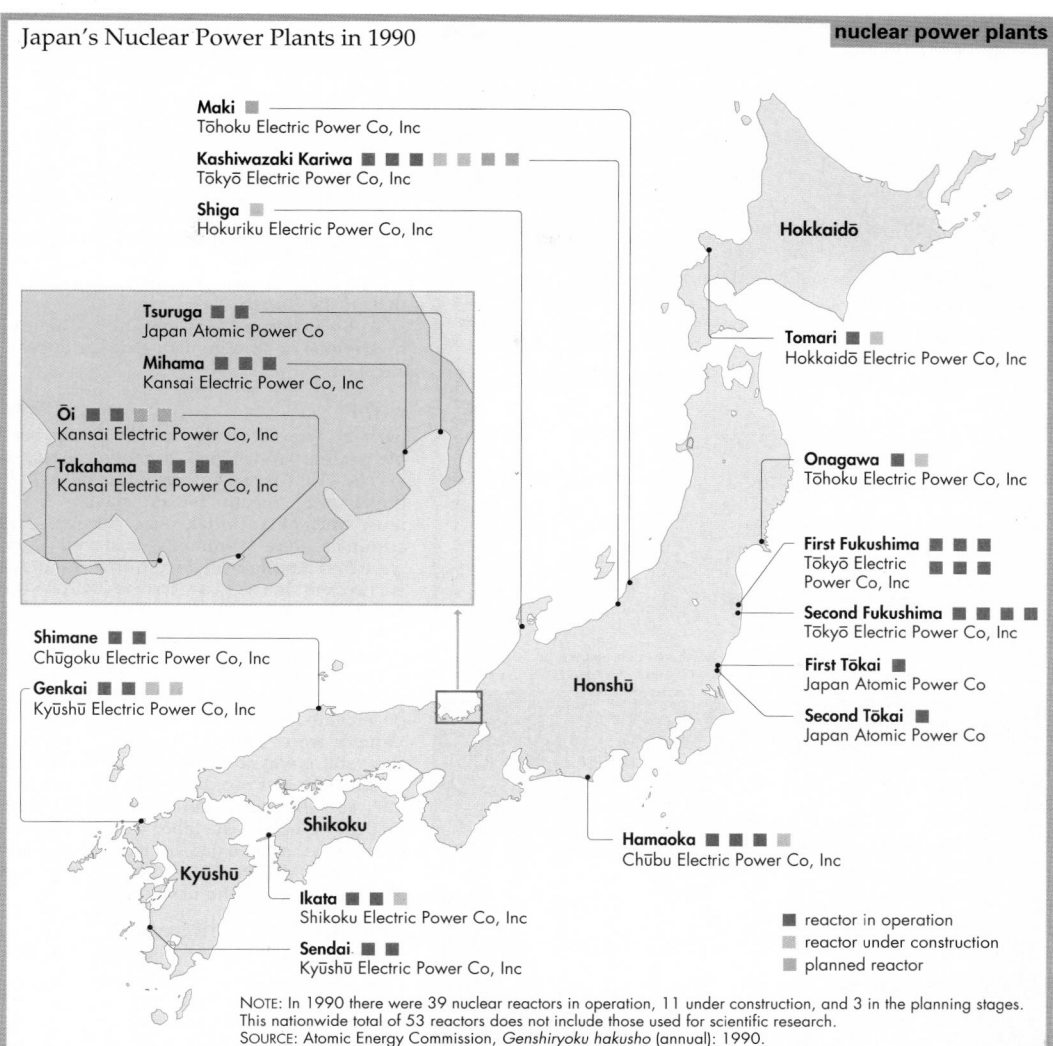

Japan's Nuclear Power Plants in 1990

Maki ■
Tōhoku Electric Power Co, Inc

Kashiwazaki Kariwa ■ ■ ■ ■ ■
Tōkyō Electric Power Co, Inc

Shiga ■
Hokuriku Electric Power Co, Inc

Tsuruga ■ ■
Japan Atomic Power Co

Mihama ■ ■ ■
Kansai Electric Power Co, Inc

Ōi ■ ■ ■ ■
Kansai Electric Power Co, Inc

Takahama ■ ■ ■ ■
Kansai Electric Power Co, Inc

Hokkaidō

Tomari ■ ■
Hokkaidō Electric Power Co, Inc

Onagawa ■ ■
Tōhoku Electric Power Co, Inc

First Fukushima ■ ■ ■ ■ ■
Tōkyō Electric Power Co, Inc

Second Fukushima ■ ■ ■ ■
Tōkyō Electric Power Co, Inc

First Tōkai ■
Japan Atomic Power Co

Second Tōkai ■
Japan Atomic Power Co

Honshū

Shimane ■ ■
Chūgoku Electric Power Co, Inc

Genkai ■ ■ ■ ■
Kyūshū Electric Power Co, Inc

Shikoku

Kyūshū

Ikata ■ ■ ■
Shikoku Electric Power Co, Inc

Sendai ■ ■
Kyūshū Electric Power Co, Inc

Hamaoka ■ ■ ■ ■
Chūbu Electric Power Co, Inc

■ reactor in operation
■ reactor under construction
■ planned reactor

NOTE: In 1990 there were 39 nuclear reactors in operation, 11 under construction, and 3 in the planning stages. This nationwide total of 53 reactors does not include those used for scientific research.
SOURCE: Atomic Energy Commission, *Genshiryoku hakusho* (annual): 1990.

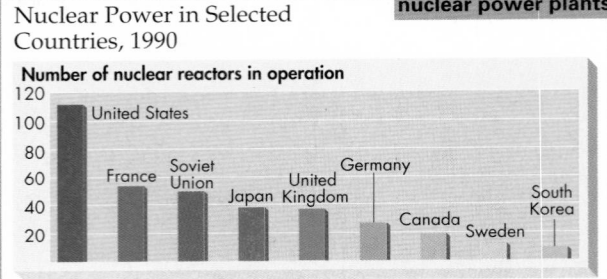

Nuclear Power in Selected Countries, 1990

Number of nuclear reactors in operation

United States, France, Soviet Union, Japan, United Kingdom, Germany, Canada, Sweden, South Korea

SOURCE: Adapted from the Energy Conservation Center, Japan, *Shō enerugī binran* (annual): 1990.

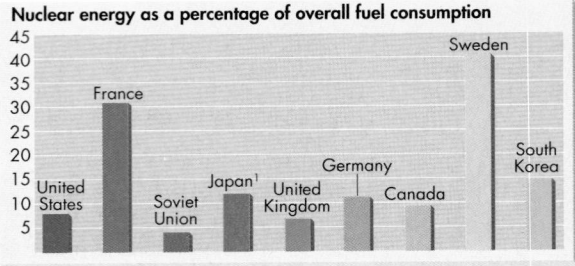

Nuclear energy as a percentage of overall fuel consumption

Sweden, France, United States, Soviet Union, Japan[1], United Kingdom, Germany, Canada, South Korea

[1]Method of calculation differs from that used elsewhere in this encyclopedia.
SOURCE: British Petroleum Company, *BP Statistical Review of World Energy* (1992).

nuclear power plants The four nuclear reactors of Tōkyō Electric Power Co's Second Fukushima Plant in the town of Naraha, Fukushima Prefecture, generate a combined total of 1.1 million kilowatts of electricity.

viet Union, many Japanese expressed concern over the safety of such facilities. Although the Japanese government revised its safety inspection standards and established a public information bureau, it made no general policy changes concerning the nuclear generation of electricity. It is estimated that by the year 2010 the demand for electricity in Japan will require the expansion of nuclear power output to 72.5 million kilowatts. See also ATOMIC ENERGY COMMISSION; ATOMIC ENERGY RESEARCH INSTITUTE, JAPAN; NUCLEAR SAFETY COMMISSION; POWER REACTOR AND NUCLEAR FUEL DEVELOPMENT CORPORATION; RADIOACTIVE WASTE.

Nuclear Safety Commission
原子力安全委員会

(Genshiryoku Anzen Iinkai). Committee in charge of safety regulations governing the use of nuclear power in Japan. Founded in October 1978 through a partial revision of the Basic Law on Atomic Energy (Genshiryoku Kihon Hō) whereby responsibility for nuclear safety was moved from the ATOMIC ENERGY COMMISSION to the newly formed commission. The Nuclear Safety Commission consists of five members who are appointed by the prime minister, subject to approval of the Diet. The commission publishes the *Genshiryoku anzen hakusho* (Annual Report on Nuclear Safety in Japan).

nue
鵺

1. Another name for the thrush, *toratsugumi* (*Turdus dauma toratsugumi*). Since it cries at night, it is considered a bearer of bad luck.

2. Legendary monster with the head of a monkey, the body of a raccoon dog, the tail of a serpent, the legs of a tiger, and a cry like that of the thrush.

3. By extension, any person or thing of mysterious or ambiguous nature or appearance.

nuhi
奴婢

(slaves). The lowest class of "lowborn" people (SEMMIN) under the 7th-century RITSURYŌ SYSTEM. *Nu* (or YAKKO) meant male and *hi* (*menoyakko*) meant female slaves. As in most ancient societies, war captives and criminals were commonly enslaved. *Nuhi* were first distinguished from free commoners (RYŌMIN) in the TAIKA REFORM (645). In the TAIHŌ CODE of 701, the *semmin* were divided into five classes, of which the lowest were *kunuhi* or *kannuhi* (public slaves owned by the government) and *shinuhi* (private slaves owned by individuals). While *kunuhi* could be elevated to higher status by amnesty, *shinuhi* were private property. Although slave status was abolished by law in the Engi Kyaku (Penal Procedures of the Engi Era, 907; see ENGI SHIKI), effective in 909, *nuhi* made up much of the labor force of the private landed estates (SHŌEN) through the late Heian period (794–1185), and they gradually merged with the GENIN (serfs).

Nukatabe no Omi sword inscriptions
額田部臣の鉄刀銘文

(Nukatabe no Omi *no tettō meibun*). Inscriptions on the blade of an iron long-sword found in 1915 in Okadayama Tomb Number One in the city of Matsue, Shimane Prefecture. The sword was badly rusted, but in 1983 X-ray studies revealed an inscription of 10 or more characters in silver inlay on the blade of the sword. The first 4 characters, Nukatabe no Omi, are either a family name or a hereditary title. They also appear in the *Izumo fudoki* (compiled in 733) before the names of two district officials (GUNJI). This discovery is expected to be valuable for future studies of the relationship between the YAMATO COURT and the Izumo region in the late 6th century.

Nukata no Ōkimi
額田王

(ca 630–after 690; Princess Nukata). Poet. Daughter of Prince Kagami; consort of Emperor TEMMU (r 672–686); probably born in Yamato Province (now Nara Prefecture) in the village of Nukata, whence she derived her name. Her maternal family was a powerful clan of the Izumo group. She was married first to Prince Ōama (the future Emperor Temmu) and later, perhaps around 658, to Prince Naka no Ōe (the future Emperor TENJI; r 661–672). The most outstanding woman poet of her generation, Princess Nukata was in the forefront of the transition from a primitive milieu of oral literature and song to a sophisticated literary society. Her 12 surviving poems are preserved in the MAN'YŌSHŪ (ca 759, Collection for Ten Thousand Generations or Collection of Ten Thousand Leaves). Her most famous poem is a *chōka* (long poem) on the rival beauties of spring and autumn.

Nukina Kaioku
貫名海屋

(1778–1863). Confucian scholar, calligrapher, and painter of the NANGA style. Born

Nukina Shigeru into a *samurai* family in Awa (now Tokushima Prefecture) on Shikoku, he studied calligraphy, Kanō-style painting (see KANŌ SCHOOL), and Chinese literati painting, as well as Buddhism and Confucianism. Kaioku opened a successful Confucian school in Kyōto while writing and painting; he came to be considered Kyōto's finest calligrapher. He was a member of an artistic circle that included the painters NAKABAYASHI CHIKUTŌ and YAMAMOTO BAIITSU. Kaioku's painting followed the conservative Chinese literati tradition; he enjoyed wet brushwork, often on satin, in the manner of the Mi family of Song (Sung) dynasty (960–1279) China. Kaioku based his calligraphy primarily upon Chinese Tang (T'ang) dynasty (618–907) masters, using firm, forceful, and dynamic brushwork.

Numa Morikazu
沼間守一

(1844–90). Politician and journalist. Born in Edo (now Tōkyō). Numa studied Western military science in Nagasaki and Yokohama. He fought on the side of the Tokugawa shogunate in the BOSHIN CIVIL WAR, which accompanied the Meiji Restoration of 1868, but joined the new government after a brief imprisonment. Numa came to disagree with government policies on freedom of speech, and in 1879 he resigned his post in the GENRŌIN (Chamber of Elders) to devote himself to the FREEDOM AND PEOPLE'S RIGHTS MOVEMENT. As publisher of the newspaper *Tōkyō Yokohama mainichi shimbun*, he called for the establishment of a parliament. Numa participated in the founding of the JIYŪTŌ (Liberal Party) in 1881 but later left to join Ōkuma Shigenobu's RIKKEN KAISHINTŌ (Constitutional Reform Party). He also served as the chairman of the Tōkyō Prefectural Assembly.

Numata
沼田[市]

City in north-central Gumma Prefecture, central Honshū. Numata flourished as a castle town from the early 16th century. It is a distribution center for raw silk, tobacco, and timber. Lumber and woodwork industries are active. Numata is a gateway to such recreational areas as OZE and the SHIGA KŌGEN highland. Pop: 46,854.

Numazu
沼津[市]

City in eastern Shizuoka Prefecture, central Honshū, on Suruga Bay. It developed as a post-station town on the highway TŌKAIDŌ during the Edo period (1600–1868). Machinery, printing, and seafood-processing industries flourish. Agricultural products include mandarin oranges, tea, and flowers. Its port is a base for offshore and deep-sea fishing. Points of interest are the Sembon Matsubara (a stand of pines), beaches, and an aquarium. Pop: 211,732.

No. 18 Fujisan maru Incident
第18富士山丸事件

(*Daijūhachi Fujisan maru* Jiken). In November 1983 a North Korean soldier smuggled himself onto the Japanese freighter *No. 18 Fujisan maru* and was arrested and detained by the Japanese Coast Guard. When the freighter returned to North Korea, officials there arrested the ship's captain, Beniko Isamu, and one crew member, demanding the extradition of the soldier to North Korea for trial in return for the release of the two Japanese seamen. In 1987 the Japanese government paroled the soldier, but this did not satisfy North Korea's demands, and the Japanese seamen were sentenced to 15 years' imprisonment. After much negotiation the issue was finally resolved in September 1990, when North Korean president KIM IL-SŎNG announced the release of the seamen, who were returned home the next month.

nursing homes　老人ホーム

(rōjin hōmu). Three types of nursing home for elderly people unable to live at home were established under the provisions of the 1963 OLD-AGE WELFARE LAW (Rōjin Fukushi Hō): keihi rōjin hōmu (low-cost nursing homes), for healthy people aged 60 and over who have no relatives or whose family circumstances make it difficult for them to remain at home; yōgo rōjin hōmu (low-income nursing homes), for people aged 65 and over whose incomes are low and whose physical or mental health requires professional care; and, finally, tokubetsu yōgo rōjin hōmu (special nursing homes), for people aged 65 and over who require regular special care, such as those who are bedridden or whose intellectual faculties have deteriorated.

Traditionally, elderly people in Japan lived with, or near, their children or relatives and were cared for by them; in recent years, however, Japanese society has been aging rapidly, resulting in a growing demand for nursing homes, particularly the special nursing homes, as increasing numbers of elderly people become bedridden or suffer from senile dementia. In 1988 there were 1,995 special nursing homes caring for 144,000 residents, as well as 945 low-cost nursing homes with 68,000 residents and 288 low-income nursing homes with 17,000 residents. Every year about 100 new special nursing homes take in some 8,000 new residents. The three types of nursing home are established and maintained by the local municipal authorities. Applications for residence at special and low-income nursing homes are made to local welfare offices, while applications for residence at low-cost nursing homes are subject to contracts between the applicants and those in charge of the home. Residents in all these three types of home are charged according to their ability to pay. Recently, however, there have appeared a number of private nursing homes that offer residents a range of services to meet their personal needs but that receive no public assistance and therefore charge their residents full price.

Nutari no ki　淳足柵

Stockade (SAKU) erected in 647 by the YAMATO COURT in the vicinity of the modern city of Niigata in Niigata Prefecture in order to consolidate political control and to serve as an outpost for further military expeditions against the aboriginal EZO tribesmen. By the early 8th century, colonists had pushed farther north along the coast of the Sea of Japan. It is thought that the stockade, with IWAFUNE NO KI, another fortification in the same area, fell into disuse sometime around 708. No trace of the settlement at Nutari has yet been found.

Nu, U　ウー・ヌ

(1907–). Burmese statesman. He studied law at Rangoon University. In 1936, together with AUNG SAN, he led a student strike against the British educational system. Arrested and imprisoned in 1940, he was released after the Japanese invaded Burma, and he served in the Japanese-sponsored wartime cabinet under BA MAW. In 1948 he became the first prime minister of the independent Republic of Burma and, except for two brief periods in the late 1950s, continued in office until his overthrow in a coup d'état in 1962. See also BURMA AND JAPAN.

nyōbō hōsho　女房奉書

Type of document conveying the wishes of the sovereign; issued by ladies-in-waiting. A variation of the naishisen, documents written by Heian-period (794–1168) court ladies in a similar capacity, nyōbō hōsho originated in the Kamakura period (1185–1333), flourished during the Muromachi period (1333–1568), and were used for some time even after the Meiji Restoration (1868). They closely resembled RINJI (imperial orders), but usually concerned more private matters. The documents were written in the kana syllabary, occasionally by the emperor himself, but always in the manner of women's private letters. The name of the sender was not written on the letter, but the word gyō (imperial command) was written on an outside corner.

nyōbō kotoba　女房詞

(language of the court ladies). A group of special feminine words originally created and used by court ladies (nyōbō) of the imperial household in the Muromachi period (1333–1568) to achieve a certain euphemistic elegance when discussing food and other mundane matters among themselves. Some of the approximately 1,000 vocabulary items now identified as nyōbō kotoba have seeped into contemporary FEMININE LANGUAGE as well as the standard Japanese used by men and women alike.

By 1420 the nyōbō use of their own terms for food and utensils had become sufficiently prominent to warrant inclusion in the Ama no mokuzu, a document of manners and customs from the mid-Kamakura (1185–1333) to early Muromachi periods, compiled by Emyōin Nobumori.

However, nyōbō kotoba did not long remain the exclusive property of imperial court ladies. Drawn by the cultural prestige of the imperial court and by the elegance of the words, high-ranking women outside court circles began imitating the example of the nyōbō. By the Edo period (1600–1868), nyōbō kotoba had come to be regarded as an inseparable part of every upper-class woman's cultural education. The vocabulary later extended beyond the original terms for food and personal belongings to include words for clothing, plants, animals, and parts of the body. In modern Japanese, the use of the polite prefix o-, go-, and mi-, and the suffix -moji can be attributed to the influence of nyōbō kotoba.

Nyohōsan　女峰山

Stratovolcano in the Nasu Volcanic Zone, northwestern Tochigi Prefecture, central Honshū. It has well-developed radial drainages. On the southern slopes are two shrines, Futarayama and TŌSHŌGŪ. Nyohōsan is part of Nikkō National Park. Height: 2,483 m (8,146 ft).

Nyonin geijutsu　女人芸術

(Women's Arts). Monthly literary magazine, published from July 1928 to June 1932 by Nyonin Geijutsu Sha. It was founded by the playwright Hasegawa Shigure (1879–1941) as a general-interest magazine for women which was to be managed, written, edited, and illustrated by women. Heavily influenced by the PROLETARIAN LITERATURE MOVEMENT of the time, Nyonin geijutsu de-

nyorai Dainichi Nyorai as portrayed in the *Diamond Realm Mandala*, one of the Mandalas of the Two Realms.

voted much of its editorial content to the lives and opinions of working women. The journal provided a springboard for many important woman novelists and critics, including HAYASHI FUMIKO, ENCHI FUMIKO, SATA INEKO, and MIYAMOTO YURIKO.

nyonin kinzei　女人禁制

("no women allowed"). The exclusion of women from sacred places or events, because of their supposed impurity. Although the position of women in ancient Japanese religion was high (see MIKO; SHAMANISM), it is thought that Buddhism reinforced certain indigenous taboos against the blood associated with menstruation and childbirth. The mountains HIEIZAN, KŌYASAN, ŌMINESAN, and ONTAKESAN, all sacred to Shintō or Buddhism, were known for their strict prohibition of women. Fishermen also banned women from their boats, for the boat spirit (FUNADAMA) was thought to be averse to them. Today such practices have virtually disappeared.

nyorai　如来

One of the epithets for the Buddha. Literal translation of Sanskrit tathāgata ("thus-come" or "thus-gone"), meaning one who has come from, or gone to, truth. Among the best-known examples of this word's use are the terms Shaka Nyorai (the historical Buddha Śākyamuni), Amida Nyorai, Yakushi Nyorai (healing Buddha; Skt: Bhaiṣajyaguru), and Dainichi Nyorai (the great sun Buddha; Skt: Mahāvairocana). In Buddhist art, portrayals of the nyorai manifestation (usually a monk either seated or standing) have few or no ornaments but have the physical signs of Buddhahood.

Nyūtōzan　乳頭山

Also called Eboshidake. Volcano in the Nasu Volcanic Zone, on the border between Akita and Iwate prefectures, northern Honshū. At its foot are the Nyūtō Hot Springs. Height: 1,478 m (4,849 ft).

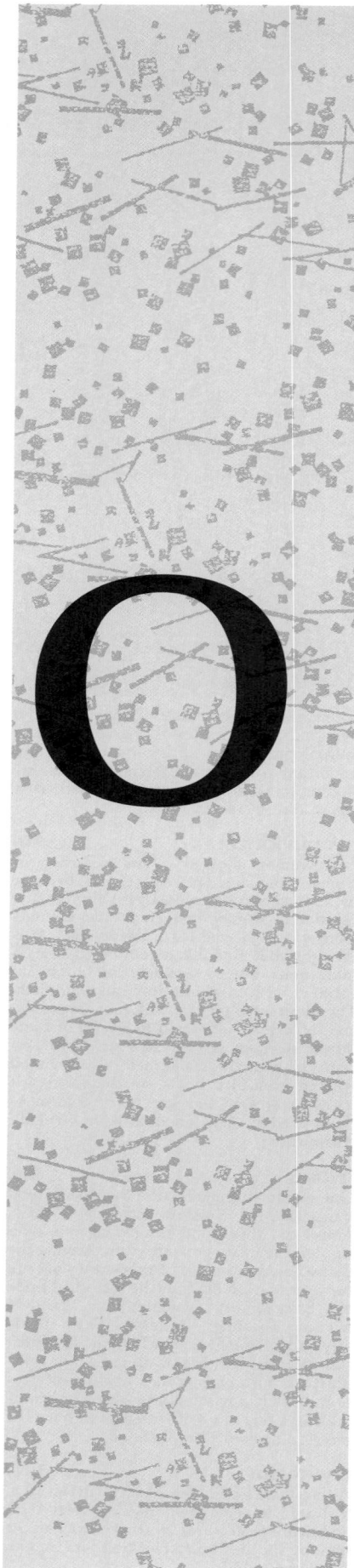

Oakandake 雄阿寒岳

Conical volcano in the Chishima Volcanic Zone, eastern Hokkaidō. The entire mountain is covered with forests of Yeddo spruce (*ezomatsu*) and Sakhalin fir (*todomatsu*). Alpine flora grow at elevations above 1,000 m (3,300 ft). In its foothills are located Lake Akan and the Panketō and Penketō swamps. It is part of Akan National Park. Height: 1,371 m (4,498 ft).

oaks 樫・楢

(*kashi; nara*). *Quercus* spp. Any of a number of broad-leaved trees of the family Fagaceae. Evergreen oaks (*kashi*) grow wild in the mountains of Honshū, Shikoku, and Kyūshū. They are also cultivated. The leaves are leathery and alternate. In late spring through early summer male and female flowers appear on separate catkins. Acorns are called *donguri* in Japanese. Species planted around houses include *shirakashi* (*Q. myrsinaefolia*), which has whitish wood; *akagashi* (*Q. acuta*), with reddish wood; *arakashi* (*Q. glauca*), with rough, hard branches and leaves; and *tsukubanegashi* (*Q. paucidentata*), indigenous to Japan, which has dark grayish brown branches. *Kashi* wood is widely used for shipbuilding and wheel making.

The principal deciduous oak in Japan is the *nara* (*Q. serrata*), sometimes called *konara*, which grows throughout the country. Some trees reach 17 meters (56 ft) in height and about 0.6 meters (2 ft) in diameter. The leaves are obovate with serrated edges. In May yellowish brown florets hang from the branches like tails.

Ōama, Prince → Temmu, Emperor

Ōarai 大洗[町]

Town in eastern Ibaraki Prefecture, central Honshū. A fishing port and tourist center on the Pacific, it is known for its swimming resorts and coastal scenery. Pop: 20,745.

Ōba Iwao 大場磐雄

(1899–1975). Archaeologist. Born in Tōkyō. Graduate of Kokugakuin University, where he became a professor in 1949. Ōba studied Shintō ritual sites and artifacts of the Jōmon (ca 10,000 BC–ca 300 BC) and later periods in an attempt to establish the nature of early religious beliefs. He is credited with establishing Shintō archaeology as a branch of archaeological studies. His principal works include *Matsuri* (1967, Festivals) and *Saishi iseki: Shintō kōkogaku no kisoteki kenkyū* (1970, Ritual Sites: Basic Research in Shintō Archaeology).

Ōbaku sect 黄檗宗

(Ōbakushū). Third largest Zen sect in Japan after the RINZAI SECT and SŌTŌ SECT. Originally brought to Japan by Chinese monks in the mid-17th century. In 1654 the Zen patriarch INGEN left his native China to visit Japan. Near Kyōto, with the shōgun TOKUGAWA IETSUNA's permission, he built the temple Mampukuji on the mountain he named Ōbakusan. Ōbaku Zen reached the height of its popularity about 50 years later and has declined somewhat since then.

Ōbaku Zen, like late-Ming-dynasty Buddhism, added elements of PURE LAND BUDDHISM and the esoteric sects to Zen practice. The use of *nembutsu* (chanting Buddha's name) was widespread in Ōbaku. The monks greatly influenced Japanese literati artists and scholars, especially in the art of calligraphy, the Ōbaku style of which was broad, fluent, and supple. The so-called Three Brushes of Ōbaku were Ingen and his pupils Mokuan (1611–84) and Sokuhi (1616–71).

Obama 小浜[市]

City in western Fukui Prefecture, central Honshū, on WAKASA BAY. The city developed in the Edo period (1600–1868) as a castle town and fishing port. Local products are *wakasa-nuri* (lacquer ware) and agate products. It has such scenic attractions as the Sotomo Coast and the former site of Obama Castle. Mantokuji, Myōrakuji, Chōgenji, and several other shrines and temples possess important examples of medieval religious art. Pop: 33,774.

Obama 小浜[町]

Town in southeastern Nagasaki Prefecture, Kyūshū. It is within Unzen-Amakusa National Park and is known for its hot springs, Unzen and Obama. Pop: 13,149.

Ōba Minako 大庭みな子

(1930–). Novelist. Born in Tōkyō; lived with her family in Alaska for 11 years. Graduated from Tsuda College. In 1968 Ōba won the Akutagawa Prize for *Sambiki no kani* (Three Crabs), which depicts loneliness and death experienced abroad. Ōba writes poetically of loneliness and the barrenness of love. Her works include *Funakuimushi* (1969, Shipworms), *Katachi mo naku* (1982, Loneliness), and *Naku tori no* (1985, Bird's Cry), which won the Noma Literary Prize.

ōban 大判

Gold coins in use from the Muromachi (1333–1568) through the Edo (1600–1868) periods but issued only sporadically before the 17th century. *Ōban* were elliptical, ranging in size up to 10 by 15 centimeters (about 4 by 6 in), weighing about 44 *momme* (165 gm, or about 6 oz). They bore a face value of 10 RYŌ and had the mark of the Gotō family, traditional masters of the mint. *Ōban* were used on special occasions as offerings, gifts, or awards. The first officially minted *ōban* were produced by Gotō Tokujō (1547–1631) in 1588 at the behest of TOYOTOMI HIDEYOSHI. In 1601 TOKUGAWA IEYASU issued identical coins as the basis of a standardized national currency. These *ōban*, produced by GOTŌ MITSUTSUGU, were 68 percent pure (16 kt). The coins were recalled and reissued four times during the Edo period, their gold content diminishing each time. See also KINZA, GINZA, AND ZENIZA.

Obanazawa 尾花沢[市]

City in northeastern Yamagata Prefecture, northern Honshū. Obanazawa developed as a post-station town on the highway Ushū Kaidō and is the site of the Nobesawa Ginzan, once a flourishing silver mine. Principal activities are sericulture and the cultivation of vegetables and rice. Ginzan Hot Spring is located here. Pop: 23,909.

Obara Kuniyoshi 小原国芳

(1887–1977). Educator. Born in Kagoshima Prefecture. Graduate of Hiroshima Higher Normal School (now HIROSHIMA UNIVERSITY) and Kyōto University. In 1919 he became the director of the private Seijō Elementary School at the request of SAWAYANAGI MASATARŌ, its founder, and made it one of the leading forces in the progressive education movement in Japan (see SHIN KYŌIKU UNDŌ). He established Tamagawa Gakuen (now

Examples of women's formal brocade *obi*. All are of brocade made in the Nishijin weaving district of Kyōto.

A side view of an *obi* made of gold brocade tied in the common *otaiko* manner.

Bunko, a festive knot used for *obi* worn by young women.

In this stylish variation of an everyday knot, the fabric at one end of the *obi* is reversed out.

The *kakuobi*, a stiff silk *obi* worn by men, is generally tied in a half-bow. The knot shown here is called *kainokuchi* ("shell mouth").

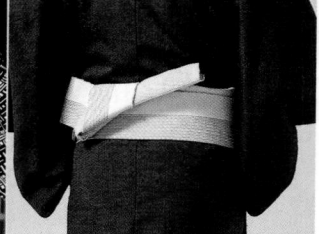

A man's *obi* tied in a variation of the *kainokuchi* half-bow.

TAMAGAWA UNIVERSITY) in 1929, where he put into practice the doctrine of education for the whole person (*zenjin kyōiku*). His written works have been collected in 46 volumes.

obasute
姨捨

(literally, "abandoning old women"). Also called *ubasute*, or sometimes *oyasute* ("abandoning parents"). The practice of abandoning the aged, usually in the mountains, is the subject of legends throughout Japan, but it does not seem ever to have been a common custom, considering the valued economic and social role of older people even in the poorest peasant families (see FILIAL PIETY). In one group of such legends, apparently imported from India via China, a young man secretly defies an official order to dispose of his aged parents, and they subsequently save their area with wise advice. Another type describes the agony of the decision to abandon an elderly relative. In these legends it is usually a wife who forces the decision on her husband; he deeply regrets it and generally changes his mind. The legends are particularly associated with the mountain OBASUTEYAMA in Nagano Prefecture. See also NARAYAMA-BUSHI KŌ.

Obasuteyama
姨捨山

Also known as Ubasuteyama and Kamurikiyama. Mountain in central Nagano Prefecture, central Honshū. Rugged and triangular-shaped, it is covered with forests. The mountain is associated with the legend of OBASUTE (or *ubasute;* abandoning the aged) as told in such collections as YAMATO MONOGATARI and KONJAKU MONOGATARI. Height: 1,252 m (4,108 ft).

Ōbayashi Corporation
[株]大林組

(Ōbayashi-Gumi). One of the "Big Five" general construction firms in Japan. Incorporated in 1936. Ōbayashi is engaged in construction and civil engineering. It has undertaken a number of Japan's most famous projects, including Tōkyō Station, Kōshien Stadium, and large-scale restoration work on the Katsura Detached Palace (Katsura Rikyū). In recent years it has participated in projects such as the Honshū-Shikoku Bridges and Seikan Tunnel. It was one of the first construction companies to expand its activities abroad and is now doing business in Southeast Asia, the United States, Australia, China, and Europe. Sales for the fiscal year ending March 1991 totaled ¥1.3 trillion (US $750.7 billion), and capitalization stood at ¥57.7 billion (US $420.6 million) in the same year. Headquarters are in Ōsaka.

obi
帯

The long sash worn with traditional Japanese KIMONO. Until the early 8th century people wore loose, one-piece robes or upper garments (*kinu*) with wide trousers (HAKAMA) for men and pleated skirts (*mo*) for women, secured by a narrow *obi*. With the introduction of new weaving techniques from Korea and China during the Nara period (710–794), *obi* became more elegant. In the Heian period (794–1185) gems and other stones were used to adorn men's leather *obi* (*kakutai*), but the court ladies did not wear *obi*. Clothing styles did not call for *obi* again until the end of the 15th century through the Edo period (1600–1868).

Men's *obi* have changed little over the centuries. The *obi* worn by men today are either stiff, about 9 centimeters (3.5 in) wide, and tied in a half-bow (*kakuobi*), or of soft gray or black silk that is often tie-dyed (*hekoobi*). The latter is at least 50 centimeters (20 in) wide; when folded over it forms a narrow band that is worn tied or tucked in just under the waist.

Early in the Edo period women's *obi* measured approximately 30 centimeters (1 ft) in width and 2 meters (6.6 ft) in length, eventually reaching their present length of about 3–4 meters (10–13 ft). Women's *obi* were usually made of silk, generally twill (*aya*), satin (*shusu*), figured satin (*rinzu*), or gold and silver brocade (KINRAN AND GINRAN). Girls and unmarried women tied their *obi* at the back, while married women tied them in front.

Today most women, married or single, wear their *obi* tied in back in a square-shaped bow (*otaiko*). The season of the year and the nature of the occasion usually determine what kind of *obi* a woman wears. Formal *obi* are made of brocade (NISHIKI) or figured brocade (TSUZURE-ORI); daily-wear *obi* are made of figured satin, *habutae* silk, or synthetic fabrics. The *obi* is often considered a more important element of dress than the kimono, and a good one may cost several times as much as a kimono.

Obihiro
帯広[市]

City in southeastern Hokkaidō. First settled in 1883, it developed into a market center for farm products. Processing agricultural, dairy, and lumber products are its chief industries. Pop: 167,384.

Obihiro University of Agriculture and Veterinary Medicine
帯広畜産大学

(Obihiro Chikusan Daigaku). A coeducational national university located in the city of Obihiro, Hokkaidō. The school was established in 1941 as the Obihiro Kōtō Jūi Gakkō (Obihiro Higher Technical School of Veterinary Medicine); it became a university in 1949. The school maintains a faculty of agriculture and veterinary medicine and operates a veterinary hospital and a university farm. Enrollment in 1989 was 1,173.

obi iwai
帯祝

The custom according to which a woman in the fifth month of pregnancy ties a special cloth, called *iwata obi*, around her waist to ensure a safe and painless delivery. It is done on a particular day of the zodiacal cycle (see JIKKAN JŪNISHI) called *inu no hi* (day of the dog) because of the belief that dogs enjoy a relatively painless delivery. It is customary for the woman's parents to send the *obi*.

obligation
債権・債務

(*saiken; saimu*). In Japanese law, an obligatory right (*saiken*) is the right of one party, the obligee (*saikensha*), to demand the performance of a specific act from a second party, the obligor (*saimusha*); an obligatory duty (*saimu*) is the duty of one party, the obligor, to perform a specific act for the benefit of a second party, the obligee. In the event that the obligor does not voluntarily perform the obligatory duty, the obligee may initiate a lawsuit seeking a court order directing the obligor to perform. Based on such an order, the obligee may seek compul-

oaks The acorns of the *konara* (bottom), one of the most common deciduous oaks in Japan, are an important food source for animals.

Ōboke The cliffs of this gorge rise above the river Yoshinogawa as it flows through the Shikoku Mountains.

sory execution or claim compensation for damages. See OBLIGATIONS, DEFAULT OF.

obligations, default of   債務不履行

(*saimu furikō*). Failure of an obligor to perform a duty established by contract; the term is defined in the Civil Code (art. 415). When an obligor fails to perform a duty, the obligee may exercise the following rights: (1) The right to demand specific performance (art. 414): when the obligor fails to perform a duty, even though performance is possible, the obligee may petition a court to force the obligor to perform his or her duty. (2) The right to demand compensatory damages (art. 416): when specific performance of the duty is not possible because of the nature of the obligation or when it is no longer possible to perform the duty, the obligee may demand compensation for damages. (3) The right to rescind the contract (arts. 541–543): the obligee may rescind the contract, avoiding liability thereunder, and claim compensation for damages against the obligor. To exercise this right, there are three conditions that must be satisfied: the obligor was responsible for nonperformance; the obligee gave notice to the obligor to perform within a reasonable period of time; and the obligor did not perform within that period of time after notice.

Ōboke   大歩危

Gorge in western Tokushima Prefecture, Shikoku. Created by the river YOSHINOGAWA when it carved through the Shikoku Mountains. Together with the gorge called Koboke along the river's lower reaches, it is famous for its precipitous cliffs, strangely shaped rocks, and huge stones. The stretch of rapids called Adonose is noted for *ayu* (sweetfish) fishing. Ōboke is part of Tsurugisan Quasi-National Park. Length: approximately 4 km (2.5 mi).

obscenity   猥褻

(*waisetsu*). Obscenity is regulated by law and society as offensive public display or description of sex in such media as print and film. Although earlier relevant regulatory systems existed, the Japanese term *waisetsu* ("obscenity") first appeared in article 259 of the Penal Code of 1880 (see CRIMINAL LAW). Article 175 of the 1907 revised Penal Code remains the primary legal provision concerning obscenity, changed only by the 1947 addition of imprisonment to fines as possible penalties.

It has been a well-established rule that obscenity falls short of the guarantees of the FREEDOM OF SPEECH, press, or any other form of expression enshrined in article 21 of the CONSTITUTION OF JAPAN (1947), and the Japanese courts have repeatedly upheld the validity of

the Penal Code, which penalizes the sale, distribution, or public exhibition of obscene materials. The Supreme Court in 1957 defined obscene writings as writings that "wantonly arouse and stimulate sexual desire, offend the normal sense of shame and run counter to proper concepts of sexual morality," and reserved for the courts a "clinical role" in the event society's moral sense should become dulled (see LADY CHATTERLEY'S LOVER CASE). In the DE SADE CASE of 1969, the majority of the court emphasized artistry and intellectual values as a counterbalance to eroticism.

These two decisions continue to be the most important sources of judicially applicable standards of obscenity. On the whole, Japanese law and society have been relatively tolerant of erotic material, and, although in recent decades official and parental concern for young people has increased, obscenity in Japan is primarily regulated not by judicial decisions, but by an elaborate combination of governmental and nongovernmental mechanisms, such as self-imposed industry codes administered by trade associations or industry ethics committees. The MOTION PICTURE CODE COMMITTEE (Eiga Rinri Kitei Kanri Iinkai, or Eirin), for instance, is a nongovernmental body organized by and among the major motion picture producers and distributors and is responsible for the enforcement of its own ethical code. The video and magazine industries have also established similar bodies.

Apart from the Penal Code, other statutory provisions regulating obscene materials include the Customs Standards Law (Kanzei Teiritsu Hō), the Entertainment Facilities Law (Kōgyōjō Hō), the Law Regulating Businesses Affecting Public Morals (Fūzoku Eigyō Torishimari Hō), the Healthy Environment Law (Kankyō Eisei Hō), the Radio Law (Dempa Hō), the BROADCASTING LAW (Hōsō Hō), and various youth protection ordinances enacted by local authorities. These statutory provisions, as well as the self-imposed media industry codes of ethics, often include regulations relating not only to obscene matters but also to materials that are extremely cruel, vulgar, or harmful to a child's sense of dignity or that cause "abnormal horror" among ordinary citizens.

Ōbu   大府［市］

City in western Aichi Prefecture, central Honshū. Formerly a farming village, it has become industrialized since 1960. Machine manufacturing is the city's chief industry. Pop: 69,720.

Ōbunsha Publishing Co, Ltd
    ［株］旺文社

(Ōbunsha). Publisher, mainly of school reference books; founded in 1931 by Akao Yoshio (1907–85). Ōbunsha was the first company to introduce and market a correspondence course designed to aid students in their preparation for school entrance examinations. This program was later put into magazine format under the title *Keisetsu jidai*. After World War II, the company broadened its readership to include students from high-school down to elementary-school levels. It also publishes a number of different types of periodicals.

Occupation   占領政策

(*senryō seisaku*). The period of military and political control of Japan by the United States and its allies following World War II; a period that technically lasted from Japan's

formal acceptance of the POTSDAM DECLARATION on 14 August 1945 to the implementation on 28 April 1952 of the SAN FRANCISCO PEACE TREATY. For more than six and a half years, Japan was subject to the authority of the supreme commander for the Allied powers (SCAP), a term that referred both to the holder of the title—General Douglas MACARTHUR and his successor, General Matthew Ridgway—and to the supporting bureaucracy. In late 1945 the 11- (later 13-) nation FAR EASTERN COMMISSION and the 4-power ALLIED COUNCIL FOR JAPAN were established to give guidance and supervision to SCAP, but these bodies could not act effectively without the concurrence of the United States and were therefore limited in their power. The Occupation, while officially an Allied effort, was primarily directed and staffed by the United States. Unlike Germany, Japan was to have no separate zones of Occupation, and there was to be no real chance for the Soviet Union or the other Allies to make policy decisions.

The Occupation may be roughly divided into three major phases: (1) a period from 1945 to 1947 when extensive political, social, and economic reforms were instituted under heavy American pressure; (2) a period between 1947 and 1950, sometimes known as the "reverse course," when US policy makers shifted their major concern from reform to the economic rehabilitation of Japan; and (3) a period from 1950 to 1952 when discussion focused most sharply upon preparing for the restoration of Japanese sovereignty and on the nation's post-Occupation security requirements.

Occupation Policy and Structure—Basic policy for the Occupation was spelled out in the "United States Initial Post-Surrender Policy for Japan" of 29 August 1945. SCAP was to work through the existing Japanese government to disarm Japan, to eliminate institutions that had supported its militarism and aggression, and to encourage the democratization of the Japanese polity and society.

To accomplish this, SCAP had at its command a contingent of about 150,000 troops and some 5,500 bureaucrats. In the absence of any real security problems, it was the latter group that was by far more important. Divided into a number of functional sections (Government, Intelligence, Economic and Scientific, etc) often engaged in bitter competition with one another, the SCAP bureaucrats engineered a sweeping set of social, political, and economic reforms—using a relatively unified group of conservative Japanese civilian politicians as the medium for their implementation. Chief among these was the veteran diplomat YOSHIDA SHIGERU, who served as foreign minister from September 1945 to May 1946, and as prime minister from May 1946 to May 1947 and again from October 1948 to December 1954. Though his relations with SCAP were cool at first, he greatly influenced the course of the Occupation reforms and the character of postwar Japanese politics.

Political Reforms—As promised in the Potsdam Declaration, the Occupation moved quickly to dismantle Japan's empire and war machine. Japan lost all its overseas colonies, its armed forces, and its right to conduct an independent foreign policy. Over 6 million soldiers and civilians were forcibly repatriated from overseas outposts to the home islands. WAR CRIMES TRIALS convicted close to 4,000 lower-ranking war criminals, and 28 representatives of Japan's wartime leadership were tried in Tōkyō as class A war criminals, charged with crimes against peace and humanity. Over 200,000 other key military, political, and business leaders were barred from public office and corporate positions (see OCCUPATION PURGE).

Intensive efforts were made to reform Japan's political structure. Beginning in October 1945 a series of directives guaranteed the Japanese people fundamental civil liberties such as freedom of speech, press, and assembly, and set about dismantling the prewar and wartime institutions of police surveillance and control. A new CONSTITUTION OF JAPAN was promulgated on 3 November 1946 and went into effect on 3 May 1947. Based on a SCAP draft given minor revisions by the Japanese government, it reduced the emperor's status to that of a symbol of the Japanese state and people, established a British-style system of parliamentary government headed by a cabinet, protected civil rights, separated religion from state, forbade gender discrimination, and in article 9 renounced war as an instrument of national policy. Supplementary legislation gave women the vote, defined new election procedures, established a reformed judiciary, and revised the legal codes to lessen the authority that the family head had enjoyed under Japan's traditional patriarchal family system.

Some of the reforms of this period were eventually subjected to change or reinterpretation. For example, efforts to decentralize the police and provide for the local election of school board officials were later diluted by Yoshida Shigeru's conservative government, and General MacArthur's July 1950 decision to permit the establishment of what would eventually become the SELF DEFENSE FORCES appeared to many to change the meaning of article 9 of the constitution. But the significance of the constitutional and other reforms was great, for the Japanese people vigorously enjoyed their new political freedoms.

Economic Reforms——Conscious that political reforms would fail unless accompanied by economic changes, SCAP instituted the LAND REFORMS OF 1946, under which the percentage of cultivator-owned paddy land increased from 55.7 percent in 1947 to 88.9 percent in 1949. The Labor Union Law of December 1945 guaranteed the right to organize and bargain collectively, touching off an explosive growth of LABOR UNIONS, whose membership reached 4.8 million by 1946. The Labor Standards Law of April 1947 (see LABOR LAWS) set minimum wage, overtime, and work conditions. Meanwhile, Japan's ZAIBATSU or financial combines were forced to dissolve their interlocking holding companies, offer stock more broadly to the general public, and regulate some of their monopolistic activities (see ZAIBATSU DISSOLUTION).

In the economic realm, as in the political, the high tide of reform peaked fairly quickly. SCAP's ban on the GENERAL STRIKE OF 1947, its reluctance to reform Japanese banks, the abandonment of earlier ambitious plans to "deconcentrate" key industries, and the generally conservative policies of SCAP financial adviser Joseph M. Dodge in the later years of the Occupation (see DODGE LINE) were welcomed by conservatives in both the United States and Japan, who were more concerned with the reconstruction and stabilization of Japan's battered and disorganized economy than with idealistic schemes for economic democratization.

The Last Phase——The outbreak of the KOREAN WAR on 25 June 1950 marked the be-

ginning of the final phase of the Occupation of Japan. The entrance of United States and United Nations forces into the Korean conflict greatly stimulated the Japanese economy through special procurements (TOKUJU) of goods and services to support the war effort, and production gradually increased to meet and surpass prewar levels.

The Korean War also serves as a convenient symbol of the growing hostility between SCAP and the Japanese left. Although in fact the so-called RED PURGE directed by SCAP against Japan Communist Party activists commenced on 6 June 1950, before the fighting in Korea began, the cold war and its hotter manifestation in Korea began to inspire a fundamental change in US thinking about Japan's defense policy. After the outbreak of the Korean conflict, SCAP permitted the formation of a 75,000-man NATIONAL POLICE RESERVE that would eventually evolve into the present Self Defense Forces, and began to move rapidly to negotiate a peace settlement that would restore Japan's sovereignty while at the same time effectively preserving the influence and military presence of the United States. The result was the San Francisco Peace Treaty between Japan and 48 noncommunist Allied nations, signed on 8 September 1951. The same day, Japan also concluded a mutual security treaty with the United States (see UNITED STATES–JAPAN SECURITY TREATIES), allowing US troops to use bases in Japan to protect the Asian security interests of both nations and in effect committing Japan to support the cold war policies of the United States. In return, Japan was able to regain its standing within the international community and end its status as a defeated nation subject to foreign domination.

The shifting nature of Occupation policy has been the subject of much debate, both in Japan and abroad. Most observers see it as the period in which the foundations for Japan's current prosperity and stability were laid down; critics tend to emphasize the "reverse course" and regret that fundamental reforms were not pursued more aggressively and thoroughly. What is clear, however, is that Japan was a very different nation in 1952 than it had been in 1945, and that the Occupation years witnessed the restoration of a war-shattered nation to domestic health and international recognition.

occupational diseases 職業病

(*shokugyōbyō*). Occupational diseases such as silicosis and sunstroke among mine and quarry workers have been known in Japan since the premodern period. For many years most occupational diseases were accepted as inevitable. After World War II, however, preventive measures, checkups, and compensation payments by employers became obligatory under the Labor Standards Law (Rōdō Kijun Hō, 1947). In recent years the variety of occupational diseases has grown rapidly because of the industrial use of chemicals, high-pressure and high-temperature processes, and radioactive materials. Occupational diseases that have gained attention recently include Raynaud's disease (caused by machine vibration) and cancer caused by harmful chemicals. The number of cases of stress-related mental illness and death from overwork (*karōshi*) has also increased greatly. To counteract the growing diversity of these diseases, the MINISTRY OF LABOR established the Industrial Medical Research Center (Sangyō Igaku Sōgō Kenkyūjo) to study the causes and diagnosis of occupational diseases and to develop prevention and rehabilitation methods.

Occupation Purge 公職追放

(Kōshoku Tsuihō). Official English name, "Removal and Exclusion of Undesirable Personnel from Public Office." The removal of about 200,000 Japanese military, government, and business leaders from their wartime positions and their exclusion from public office by the authorities of the Allied OCCUPATION (1945–52) of Japan following World War II. This program was based on paragraph 6 of the POTSDAM DECLARATION (July 1945): "There must be eliminated for all time the authority and influence of those who have deceived and misled the people of Japan into embarking on world conquest, for we insist that a new order of peace, security, and justice will be impossible until irresponsible militarism is driven from the world."

Officials of SCAP (Supreme Commander for the Allied Powers; headquarters of the Occupation of Japan) refined orders from Washington in two directives issued to the Japanese government on 4 January 1946. SCAPIN (SCAP Directive) 548, "Abolition of Certain Political Parties, Associations, Societies, and Other Organizations," ordered the dissolution of specific militarist, terrorist, and ultranationalist groups. Its companion, SCAPIN 550—the Purge Directive itself—detailed seven removal and exclusion categories: war criminals, career army and navy personnel, leaders of ultranationalist and terrorist societies, influential persons in the IMPERIAL RULE ASSISTANCE ASSOCIATION and affiliated organizations, officers of financial and development organizations involved in Japanese expansion, governors of former Japanese colonies and occupied territories, and a catchall label, "additional militarists and ultranationalists." In turn, Japanese government bureaucrats translated these directives into a series of imperial and cabinet orders. The emperor was not purged, primarily because SCAP officials feared political destabilization and also because they believed that he had not exercised any real power.

Occupation
1 General Douglas MacArthur arrives at Atsugi Air Base near Tōkyō on 30 August 1945 to command the Allied Occupation of Japan.
2 After the US Army entered Tōkyō on 8 September 1945, romanized street signs were put up at major intersections throughout the city.

1123

However, in the spring of 1946 SCAP did remove Prime Minister–elect HATOYAMA ICHIRŌ, replacing him with YOSHIDA SHIGERU as prime minister and president of the Japan Liberal Party. Although uneven in its impact, the purge did remove much of Japan's political elite, career military establishment, and industrial and publishing magnates from power, allowing a new generation of business and political leaders to emerge. See also RED PURGE.

ocean resource development
海洋開発

(*kaiyō kaihatsu*). The effort to tap the mineral, biological, chemical, and energy resources of the sea. Japanese government policy on ocean development is formulated by the Council for Ocean Development (Kaiyō Kaihatsu Shingikai), an advisory body to the prime minister. In 1979 the council published a 10-year plan that focused on the following areas of potential development: the cultivation of the biological resources of the sea; the development of technologies for the exploitation of sea minerals and metals, especially the recovery of uranium from seawater and the mining of manganese from the seabed; the generation of electricity from thermal sources, waves, and ocean currents; and the utilization of ocean areas for industrial projects, airports, and recreation. Japan has joined with 19 other nations, including China and Australia, in a cooperative effort (called WEST-PAC) to study the western Pacific Ocean in order to make predictions regarding global changes in climate and marine food resources.

One step in guaranteeing the preservation of Japan's ocean resources was taken in 1970 with the passage of legislation setting up MARINE PARKS. Other development projects involve altering the natural state of the ocean. One Japanese proposal, for instance, foresees the building of man-made islands for recreational purposes. Man-made headlands and the anchoring of floating structures have been suggested as ways of controlling currents along the shore, so that nutrient-rich seawater would be carried to offshore fisheries. Saturation diving, which enables divers to remain submerged for long periods of time, may lead to the establishment of a deep-sea operating base. Today emphasis in government planning has shifted from ocean resource development to development of land reclaimed from the sea as living areas for people.

Ochanomizu Women's University
お茶の水女子大学

(Ochanomizu Joshi Daigaku, usually referred to in English as Ochanomizu University). National university for women located in Bunkyō Ward, Tōkyō. Founded in 1874 as the Women's Normal School, it was Japan's first institution of higher education for women. It was renamed Women's Higher Normal School in 1890 and Tōkyō Women's Higher Normal School in 1908. It adopted its present name in 1949. In 1963 a graduate school was established; there are departments of literature and education, science, and home economics. Enrollment was 2,015 in 1989.

Ochiai Eiji
落合英二

(1898–1974). Pharmaceutical chemist. Born in Chiba Prefecture. Ochiai graduated from the pharmaceutical division of the Faculty of Medicine of Tōkyō University in 1922 and received a doctorate in pharmacy in 1928. He studied in Germany from 1930 to 1932 and taught at Tōkyō University from 1938 to 1959. He published over 470 papers on plant alkaloids, including sinomenine and matrine. In 1944 he was awarded an Imperial Academy Prize for his paper on aromatic heterocyclic bases. He was appointed an honorary member of the Pharmaceutical Academy of the United States in 1963 and awarded the Order of Culture in 1969.

Ochiai Naobumi
落合直文

(1861–1903). TANKA poet and scholar of Japanese literature. Pen name Haginoya. Born in Rikuzen Province (now Miyagi Prefecture). He founded ASAKASHA, a coterie of *tanka* poets, in 1893; devoted himself to the renovation of the traditional WAKA style; and encouraged modern *tanka* poets, including YOSANO TEKKAN and ONOE SAISHŪ. His works include *Shinsen katen* (1891), a textbook of *tanka* poetry, and *Haginoya ikō* (1904), a collection of essays and *tanka* poetry.

Ochi Etsujin
越智越人

(1656–1735?). HAIKU poet of the early Edo period (1600–1868); believed to have been born in Echigo Province (now Niigata Prefecture). One of the 10 principal disciples of BASHŌ. His verses appear in the Bashō-school anthologies *Haru no hi* (1686), *Arano* (1689), and *Sarumino* (1691), and he compiled the anthology *Shakubikan* (1717). He debated with KAGAMI SHIKŌ about Bashō's teachings.

Ochikubo monogatari
落窪物語

("The Tale of the Lower Room"; tr *Ochikubo monogatari, or The Tale of the Lady Ochikubo*, 1970). Late-10th-century fictional tale. Immediately popular in its own time and widely read as late as the Edo period (1600–1868). Scholars now believe that it was composed in the 960s or 970s. It may not have been written by MINAMOTO NO SHITAGAU (911–983), to whom it has often been attributed. In the story a high official has three sons and five daughters. Four of the daughters are children of the principal wife; the second youngest, however, is the daughter of a secondary wife who has died. The author is careful to point out that this daughter's mother was herself of high birth. The daughter has been taken into her father's house to be raised. The principal events of the story are her persecution by her stepmother, who forces her to live in a room on a lower level than the other daughters (the *ochikubo* or "lower room" of the title); her secret marriage to a desirable husband with the aid of a devoted maid; her physical escape from the house where she has been persecuted; the various acts of revenge through which the husband chastises those who would have injured her; and finally the favors and blessings that he eventually bestows on them at her urgent pleading—they are, after all, her family. *Ochikubo monogatari* is the earliest surviving example of a fictional story on the *mamako ijime* (stepchild persecution) theme.

ochiudo legends
落人伝説

(*ochiudo densetsu*). Legends of "fallen people," usually disgraced nobles or defeated warriors who fled to remote areas. Such stories, especially those associated with the TAIRA FAMILY, which was expelled from Kyōto in 1183, often explain place names or the origin of villages. In fact, over 100 places are said to have given refuge to, or to have been founded by, fugitive Taira, and so are known as "Taira family valleys" (*heike-dani*). The tragic story of the Taira, as told in the HEIKE MONOGATARI and spread by traveling performers (BIWA HŌSHI), greatly appealed to people in isolated areas seeking links with national history or mythology. Thus the legends are not only in the tradition of HERO WORSHIP but are also related to stories of divine visitors (MAREBITO).

October Incident
十月事件

(Jūgatsu Jiken; also known as the Kinki Kakumei Jiken or Imperial Flag Revolution Incident). Abortive coup d'état by military extremists in October 1931. Having failed in the MARCH INCIDENT to establish a military government, Lieutenant Colonel HASHIMOTO KINGORŌ, other members of the SAKURAKAI (a society of ultranationalist field-grade officers), and such rightist civilians as ŌKAWA SHŪMEI conspired to carry out a coup on 21 October. Their aim was to overthrow the government and install a cabinet headed by General ARAKI SADAO, to eliminate parliamentary parties, and to consolidate the territorial gains made in the MANCHURIAN INCIDENT. They planned to kill Prime Minister WAKATSUKI REIJIRŌ and his cabinet, take over the Tōkyō Metropolitan Police Department, and have martial law declared. On 17 October the army officers were arrested after their plans became known. Army Minister MINAMI JIRŌ excused the participants on the grounds that they had acted in an excess of patriotic fervor; Hashimoto was sentenced to 20 days' house arrest and Ōkawa was not even arrested. This incident set the stage for increased military intervention in politics.

octopuses
蛸

(*tako*). In Japanese, *tako* is the common name for members of the order Octopoda, class Cephalopoda. About 50 species live in Japan, of which the most common, the *madako* (common octopus; *Octopus vulgaris*), is also distributed extensively in Europe and off the East Coast of the United States. The *mizudako* (Pacific octopus; *O. dofleini*) is the world's largest octopus, with a body over 3 meters (10 ft) long, and is found off northern Japan and also off the West Coast of North America. The *iidako* (*O. ocellatus*) is a small species. These three species are important in the Japanese fishing industry because they are used for food. Other species found off Japan include the *aoigai* (paper nautilus; *Argonauta argo*) and the flat-shaped *mendako* (*Opisthoteuthis depressa*), which lives in deep-sea waters.

The first Japanese reference to the octopus is in the *Honzō wamyō* (completed in 918), the oldest Japanese dictionary of natural history.

Ōda
大田[市]

City in central Shimane Prefecture, western Honshū, on the Sea of Japan. Situated in a mainly agricultural and dairy farming area, it is a market center for timber and agricultural products. The site of the once-flourishing IWAMI SILVER MINE, the mountain Sambesan, and the Sambe Hot Spring draw tourists. Pop: 36,922.

Oda family
織田氏

(Odashi). Military house of the Muromachi (1333–1568), Azuchi-Momoyama (1568–1600), and Edo (1600–1868) periods; attained national prominence with the rise of ODA NOBUNAGA to control over central Japan. The family's provenance was Oda no Shō, Echizen Province (now Ota Chō, Fukui Prefecture), where the Oda were resident estate managers (SHŌKAN) and priests of the Shintō shrine Oda Tsurugi Jinja. Members of the Oda family served as deputy military governors (*shugodai*) of Owari (now part of Aichi Prefecture) into the 16th century. The Oda were embroiled in the succession struggle within the SHIBA FAMILY that was one of the causes of the ŌNIN WAR (1467–77), and Owari became the scene of decades of violent conflict between the rival lineages of Oda. A sublineage produced the winners of that conflict in Oda Nobuhide (1510–51) and his son Nobunaga. Nobuhide in the 1540s emerged as a SENGOKU DAIMYŌ. Nobunaga became hegemon of central Japan.

The Oda family suffered a decline after Nobunaga's spectacular career ended in the HONNŌJI INCIDENT in 1582. However, descendants of Nobunaga's son Nobukatsu (also called Nobuo; 1558–1630) and younger brother Nagamasu (better known as ODA URAKU) were *daimyō* until the end of the Edo period.

Odagiri Hideo 小田切秀雄

(1916–). Literary critic. Born in Tōkyō. Graduate of and later professor at Hōsei University. In 1946 he participated in the founding of *Kindai bungaku*, a progressive literary magazine that launched the first major wave of post–World War II writers. He became established as a literary critic while writing for this magazine and is considered a leader in the postwar Marxist literary movement. His principal works are *Minshu shugi bungaku ron* (1948), *Nippon kindai bungaku no shisō to jōkyō* (1965), *Gendai bungaku shi* (1975), and *Watakushi no mita Shōwa no shisō to bungaku no gojūnen* (1983–87), all of which treat the relationship linking literature, politics, and thought in modern Japan.

Ōdaigaharazan 大台ケ原山

Mountain on the border of Nara and Mie prefectures, central Honshū; highest peak in the Daikō Mountains. The eastern slope is a forest-covered gorge; the southern slopes are steep cliffs. The area has Japan's greatest precipitation, and Ōdaigaharazan is known for its variety of alpine flora and its primeval forests. Height: 1,695 m (5,560 ft).

Odaira Namihei 小平浪平

(1874–1951). Businessman and founder of HITACHI, LTD. Born in Tochigi Prefecture; graduate of Tōkyō University. Odaira joined the Hitachi Mine of Kuhara Kōgyōsho in 1906. He soon started electric machinery production, hoping to make the mine's operations self-sufficient domestically. In 1920 he established Hitachi, Ltd, by separating the mine's repair and manufacturing divisions. As president of Hitachi from 1929 to 1947, Odaira turned the company into one of Japan's leading general electric machinery firms.

Odaka Tomoo 尾高朝雄

(1899–1956). Legal scholar. Born in Seoul, Korea. On his graduation from Tōkyō University in 1923, Odaka entered the philosophy department of Kyōto University and studied under NISHIDA KITARŌ. From 1928 to 1932 he studied in Germany and Austria. In 1928 he was named assistant professor (later full professor) at Keijō Imperial (now Seoul National) University. From 1944 onward he was a professor at Tōkyō University. With the promulgation of the new constitution

after World War II, he engaged in a debate with MIYAZAWA TOSHIYOSHI on the question whether the KOKUTAI (Japan's national polity or state structure as embodied in the imperial institution) had fundamentally changed. Odaka maintained that the *kokutai* was a principle derived not from power but from prevailing law or custom, and he concluded that the *kokutai* was not changed even by the relegation of the emperor to symbolic status. His writings include *Kokka kōzō ron* (1936, Structure of the State) and *Hōtetsugaku gairon* (1953, Outline of Legal Philosophy).

Odakyū Electric Railway Co, Ltd 小田急電鉄[株]

(Odakyū Dentetsu). Railway company; also operates real estate enterprises, amusement facilities, and travel agencies. Incorporated in 1948, it is the core company of the Odakyū group. The number of passengers per day reached 1.8 million in the fiscal year 1987. In 1989 the company opened an overseas representative office in London and acquired a condominium hotel in Hawaii. Sales for the fiscal year ending March 1991 totaled ¥135.0 billion (US $984.0 million), and the company was capitalized at ¥58.6 billion (US $427.1 million). Headquarters are in Tōkyō.

Oda Makoto 小田実

(1932–). Novelist and literary critic. Born in Ōsaka Prefecture. Graduate of Tōkyō University. After studying in the United States, he published a best-selling account of his travels, *Nandemo mite yarō* (1961, I'll See It All), and novels such as *Amerika* (1962), which presents a picture of racial discrimination in America as experienced by a Japanese student. An outspoken critic of the establishment, he was the founder and leader of the pacifist PEACE FOR VIETNAM COMMITTEE. His principal works include *Sengo o hiraku shisō* (1965, Thought in the Postwar Era), *Hiroshima* (1981), and *Betonamu kara tōku hanarete* (1980–89, Far from Vietnam).

Oda Mikio 織田幹雄

(1905–). Triple jumper. Born in Hiroshima Prefecture; graduate and professor emeritus of Waseda University. He became Japan's first Olympic gold medal holder by winning the triple jump competition at the 1928 Amsterdam Olympic Games. He set a world triple jump record of 15.58 meters (51.12 ft) in a domestic meet in 1931. He also coached triple jumpers NAMBU CHŪHEI and TAJIMA NAOTO, who won gold medals in later Olympic Games.

Odani no Kata 小谷の方

(1547?–83). Also known by her personal name, Oichi no Kata. A noblewoman of great beauty, Oichi was the younger sister of ODA NOBUNAGA, who sent her to marry the *daimyō*

ASAI NAGAMASA; she was called Odani no Kata (the Lady of Odani) after the name of her husband's castle in Ōmi Province (now Shiga Prefecture). In 1570 Nagamasa turned against Nobunaga and was destroyed three years later. While Nobunaga spared his sister and her three small daughters, he ordered the death of her two infant sons. In 1582, after Nobunaga's assassination, her nephew Oda Nobutaka (1558–83) ordered Oichi to marry his ally, SHIBATA KATSUIE. A year later TOYOTOMI HIDEYOSHI attacked her new husband. She chose to die with her husband, but her three daughters were again spared.

Oda Nobunaga 織田信長

(1534–82). The prime mover of Japan's 16th-century reunification after a hundred years of strife. The Sengoku period (1467–1568) ended and the Azuchi-Momoyama period (1568–1600) began with his advent to power.

Rising from modest beginnings, Nobunaga subjected central Japan to one governing authority, with himself as the supreme hegemon. At the time of his violent death the realm (*tenka*) united under his rule comprised over a third of the 16th-century Japanese empire. The rigorous system of government he left behind—later called the SHOKUHŌ SEIKEN (Shokuhō regime)—was the foundation for the work of the other two of the "Three Heroes" of Japan's unification, his sometime vassals TOYOTOMI HIDEYOSHI and TOKUGAWA IEYASU. Nobunaga, who dealt ruthlessly with his enemies, deserves his reputation as a brutal warlord, but he was also an enthusiastic patron of the arts and a powerful stimulus for the brilliant culture of the Azuchi-Momoyama period.

Provenance and Early Career—Nobunaga's family was a sublineage of a *shugodai* (deputy military governor) house that settled in Owari Province (now part of Aichi Prefecture) since about 1400. His father, Nobuhide (1510–51), nominally a vassal of the Kiyosu branch of the Oda, who were *shugodai* of Owari's "lower four districts," was actually a SENGOKU DAIMYŌ in his own right. After his father's death in 1551 Nobunaga, his heir, first consolidated his position as the lord of Nagoya Castle and then began his campaign of military expansion. In 1555 Nobunaga seized Kiyosu, killed the *shugodai*, Oda Hikogorō, and moved from Nagoya into the castle there. After a protracted campaign, he succeeded in 1559 in reducing the fortress of Iwakura, the seat of the *shugodai* of Owari's "upper four districts," gaining control of all of Owari. In 1560 Nobunaga's position was challenged by IMAGAWA YOSHIMOTO of Mikawa Province (now part of Aichi Prefecture). Nobunaga surprised and routed Imagawa's vastly su-

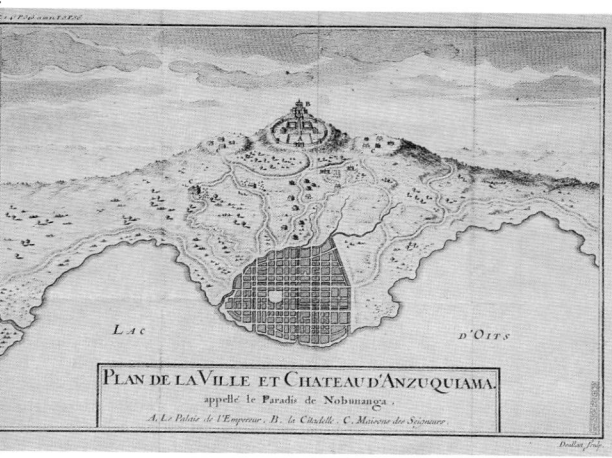

Oda Nobunaga
1 Nobunaga in semiformal attire. Detail of a posthumous portrait from 1583.
2 This 1736 map showing Nobunaga's castle at Azuchi in Ōmi Province was printed in France, based on a 16th-century report sent by a missionary living in Azuchi.

PLAN DE LA VILLE ET CHATEAU D'ANZUQUIAMA,
appellé le Paradis de Nobunanga.
A, Le Palais de l'Empereur. B, la Citadelle. C, Maisons des Seigneurs.

LAC D'OITS

Oda Mikio Winner of the gold medal in the triple jump at the 1928 Amsterdam Olympic Games, Japan's first Olympic gold medal.

perior army at the Battle of OKEHAZAMA (now the city of Toyoake, Aichi Prefecture) the same year. By 1562 he had entered into an alliance with Imagawa's Mikawa vassal Matsudaira Motoyasu (the future shōgun Tokugawa Ieyasu), thus securing his eastern flank.

In 1567, after repeated invasions of Mino, the domain of Saitō Tatsuoki (1548–73), Nobunaga seized Saitō's Inokuchi Castle. He renamed the castle Gifu and declared its marketplace, Kanō, a duty-free market (see RAKUICHI AND RAKUZA). By the spring of 1568 Nobunaga had subdued much of northern Ise Province (now part of Mie Prefecture).

In the fall of 1568 Nobunaga marched on Kyōto, swept aside armed opposition from Rokkaku Yoshikata (1521–98) and his son Yoshiharu (1545–1612) of Ōmi Province (now Shiga Prefecture) and from the Miyoshi Triumvirs (MIYOSHI SANNINSHŪ), and installed ASHIKAGA YOSHIAKI as shōgun. However, he forced the new shōgun to acknowledge Nobunaga's primacy in the realm's affairs. Nobunaga's successes continued unimpeded through 1569, when he gained control over the merchant city and firearms manufacturing center of SAKAI and expanded into southern Ise. In Ise Nobunaga decreed the abolition of toll barriers (SEKISHO) restricting the free flow of commerce and ordered the destruction of the rural gentry's forts.

By 1570 Nobunaga's steady advance brought into being a coalition of daimyō intent on stopping him. Nobunaga tossed down the gauntlet to them in the late spring of 1570 by invading Echizen (now part of Fukui Prefecture), the domain of ASAKURA YOSHIKAGE. Nobunaga had to retreat when ASAI NAGAMASA, the daimyō of Odani in northern Ōmi, attacked his rear; he barely managed to return to Gifu when the remnants of Rokkaku Yoshikata's party rose again in southern Ōmi, cutting Nobunaga's communications with his home base. That summer Nobunaga and Tokugawa Ieyasu defeated Asai's and Asakura's forces at the Battle of ANEGAWA, but it was not a decisive victory: within 10 weeks Asai and Asakura had recuperated enough to advance into the vicinity of Kyōto. They entered into an alliance with Kennyo Kōsa (1543–92), the pontiff of HONGANJI in Ōsaka. Nobunaga neutralized Asai's and Asakura's threat to Kyōto, scattering their troops on Mt. Hiei (HIEIZAN), where their collaborators in Enryakuji, the headquarters of the Buddhist TENDAI SECT, gave them shelter. The next year Nobunaga burned Enryakuji in retaliation (see ENRYAKUJI, BURNING OF).

Honganji, head temple of the major branch of the JŌDO SHIN SECT, proved a far more formidable opponent. Kennyo and the armed leagues (IKKŌ IKKI) of his sectarians (monto) fought Nobunaga in a war that lasted with a few interruptions from 1570 to 1580. The year 1570 ended with a massive rising of the Ikkō ikki of Nagashima in Ise. Nobunaga was to invade Nagashima unsuccessfully twice before he finally managed to subdue this Ikkō ikki in 1574 through wholesale slaughter.

By 1572 Nobunaga and the coalition ranged against him were stalemated. Nobunaga's enemies sought to break the deadlock by persuading the powerful eastern daimyō TAKEDA SHINGEN to join their league. On 6 January 1573 Shingen defeated Tokugawa Ieyasu's and Nobunaga's allied

army at the Battle of Mikatagahara in Tōtōmi (now the city of Hamamatsu, Shizuoka Prefecture). Two months later he took Noda Castle in Mikawa (now the city of Shinshiro, Aichi Prefecture), penetrating deeply into Ieyasu's territory. The news of Shingen's successes enticed the shōgun, Yoshiaki, to take up arms against Nobunaga, who assumed a conciliatory attitude until news of Shingen's death reached him. At the beginning of May 1573 Nobunaga surrounded Kyōto and methodically put its periphery to the torch, forcing Yoshiaki into surrender. When the shōgun rose again in July, Nobunaga chased him into exile. De jure, the Muromachi shogunate (1338–1573) continued to exist until Yoshiaki's abdication in 1588; de facto, Nobunaga's hegemony had replaced it.

In September 1573 Nobunaga attacked Asai Nagamasa; when Asakura Yoshikage came to his ally's relief, Nobunaga defeated him and forced him to commit suicide. Having thereby conquered Echizen, Nobunaga eliminated Asai and assigned his domains in northern Ōmi to Hashiba Hideyoshi (the future Toyotomi Hideyoshi). Nobunaga's triumph was tarnished, however, by a rebellion that swept Echizen in early 1574. Honganji reopened hostilities on the Ōsaka front, and the Takeda, led by Shingen's son TAKEDA KATSUYORI, again invaded Ieyasu's territories. Nobunaga recovered this lost ground in 1575 by a spectacular victory over Takeda Katsuyori at the Battle of NAGASHINO in Mikawa (now Hōrai Chō, Aichi Prefecture) and by another gruesome slaughter of the Honganji's sectarians, this time in Echizen.

Nobunaga now dominated Kyōto and the five provinces of the Kinki area around it; he held Owari, Mino, Ise, Ōmi, Wakasa (now part of Fukui Prefecture), and Echizen; his "tenka" (realm) included Mikawa and Tōtōmi, the domains of Tokugawa Ieyasu, who acknowledged Nobunaga's primacy. By 1577 SHIBATA KATSUIE, Nobunaga's appointee to the governorship of Echizen, had implemented there the policies that became the identifying features of the Shokuhō regime: the SWORD HUNT (katanagari; confiscation of weapons from the populace), the separation of the agricultural and military classes (heinō bunri), and the provincial land survey (KENCHI).

Climax and Abrupt End of Career——In 1576 Nobunaga began building a residential castle at Azuchi in Ōmi Province (now Azuchi Chō, Shiga Prefecture). AZUCHI CASTLE, whose central donjon (tenshu) became Nobunaga's official residence in 1579, contributed its name to the Azuchi-Momoyama period, which is fittingly called an age of grandeur.

In 1576 a second coalition formed against Nobunaga: the diplomatic efforts of the exiled shōgun Yoshiaki and Kennyo Kōsa of Honganji incited Mōri Terumoto (1553–1625), the lord of Aki Province (now part of Hiroshima Prefecture) and vast other territories in the Chūgoku region, and UESUGI KENSHIN (1530–78), the daimyō of Echigo (now part of Niigata Prefecture), into joining the effort to stop Nobunaga. A fleet sent by Mōri broke through Nobunaga's blockade of ISHIYAMA HONGANJI, Kennyo's temple fortress in Ōsaka. On the southwest of his "realm," Nobunaga campaigned in the spring of 1577 against the Ikkō ikki of Saiga in Kii Province (now the city of Wakayama). On the south, Matsunaga Hisahide (1510–77) of Yamato (now Nara Prefecture) took up arms against Nobunaga but was destroyed, his province

conquered by Nobunaga's eldest son Nobutada (1557–82) and his generals AKECHI MITSUHIDE, HOSOKAWA YŪSAI, and TSUTSUI JUNKEI. The colossal struggle with the Mōri of the northwest and the west of the "Tenka" was to be the major military effort of Nobunaga's last years, but remained unfinished at his death.

The situation eased for Nobunaga in 1578 with the sudden death of his formidable enemy Kenshin, which was followed by a succession struggle in the Uesugi family. Nobunaga and his generals, including Hideyoshi, gradually reduced the defenses of the Mōri by early 1580. Honganji itself was isolated, and Kennyo Kōsa entered into peace negotiations. The surrender of the Ōsaka Honganji in 1580 was Nobunaga's greatest victory. The victory was completed late that year with the conquest of the part of Kaga that was still held by monto, and the religious monarchy of the Jōdo Shin sect accordingly ceased to exist. One of the greatest symbols of the Japanese middle ages had fallen.

In the spring of 1582, Nobunaga celebrated another great triumph: the destruction of Takeda Katsuyori and the incorporation of four more provinces—Suruga (now part of Shizuoka Prefecture), Kai (now Yamanashi Prefecture), Shinano (now Nagano Prefecture), and Kōzuke (now Gumma Prefecture)—into his realm. The imperial court then offered to make him shōgun or "appoint him to any rank at all," but Nobunaga evaded replying to this offer.

In June 1582 an army commanded by Nobunaga's son Kambe Nobutaka (1558–83) assembled in the area of Ōsaka and Sakai and stood poised to invade Shikoku. Another large force was encircling KONGŌBUJI, the great monastery of the Buddhist Shingon sect on Mt. Kōya (Kōyasan) in Kii Province. On the San'indō front in western Honshū, Mōri Terumoto's major fortress, Tottori, had fallen to Hideyoshi in 1581; Hideyoshi had turned to the San'yōdō front and was besieging Takamatsu in Bitchū Province (now part of the city of Okayama), the fort of Mōri's vassal SHIMIZU MUNEHARU. At the news that Mōri's main force had come to the relief of Takamatsu, Nobunaga himself planned to join the campaign. He ordered Akechi Mitsuhide to lead a force in the expedition's van.

On 19 June Nobunaga arrived in Kyōto on his way to the front and took up his habitual quarters at Honnōji, a temple of the Buddhist Nichiren sect. In the early morning of 21 June Akechi attacked Honnōji, catching Nobunaga completely by surprise. According to the chronicle Shinchō Kō ki, Nobunaga realized that all was lost but defended himself until he was wounded. He then made sure that all women abandoned the temple, which was in flames, withdrew into the depths of the building, locked himself in a service room to keep the enemy from witnessing his end, and there disemboweled himself. See also HONNŌJI INCIDENT.

Odano Naotake   小田野直武

(1749–80). AKITA SCHOOL painter. Born in Kakunodate in what is now Akita Prefecture to a samurai family. Naotake first studied the KANŌ SCHOOL style of painting. In 1773 he met HIRAGA GENNAI, who taught him the theory and techniques of Western-style painting. In December of that year Naotake moved to Edo (now Tōkyō) and took up residence in Gennai's home. He achieved rapid artistic success, and in 1774 he was chosen to illustrate SUGITA GEMPAKU'S KAITAI SHINSHO (New Book of Anatomy). Naotake's extant works cover a broad range of subjects, including flowers, birds, animals, figures, and landscapes, rendered through Western naturalistic techniques.

Oda Sakunosuke 織田作之助

(1913–47). Novelist. Born in Ōsaka Prefecture. Attended the Third Higher School (now part of Kyōto University). In works such as *Meoto zenzai* (1940) he depicted the lives of ordinary citizens of Ōsaka. He is remembered with DAZAI OSAMU and SAKAGUCHI ANGO as a writer of the "decadent" school. His principal works include the critical essay "Kanōsei no bungaku" (1946), which advocated liberation from the I-NOVEL (*watakushi shōsetsu*) tradition of Japanese fiction, and the novel *Doyō fujin* (1946–47), unfinished at the time of his death.

Oda Shigeru 小田滋

(1924–). Judge of the United Nations International Court of Justice and scholar of international law. Born in Hokkaidō, Oda graduated from Tōkyō University in 1947, received an LLD from Yale University in 1953, and became a professor at Tōhoku University in 1959. In 1968 he served as defense counsel for West Germany in a case submitted to the International Court of Justice concerning territorial rights of West Germany, Denmark, and the Netherlands on the continental shelf in the North Sea. Oda became an associate member of the Institute for International Law in 1969, honorary member of the American Institute of International Law in 1975, and, following TANAKA KŌTARŌ, in 1976 he became the second Japanese to serve as a judge on the International Court of Justice. Oda is the author of numerous publications dealing with the law of the sea, including *International Control of the Resources of the Sea* (1979).

Ōdate 大館[市]

City in northeastern Akita Prefecture, northern Honshū, on the river YONESHIROGAWA. The city developed as a castle town of the SATAKE FAMILY. Lumber and woodwork industries flourish. The Akita *inu*, an indigenous dog, was originally bred here. Pop: 68,195.

Ōdate Basin 大館盆地

(Ōdate Bonchi). In northern Akita Prefecture, northern Honshū. This triangular-shaped basin is situated along the upper reaches of the river YONESHIROGAWA, bounded by the Ōu and Dewa mountain ranges. Thick forests of the Japanese cedar called Akita *sugi* surround the basin, and a lumber industry flourishes. The major city is Ōdate. Area: approximately 230 sq km (90 sq mi).

Oda Uraku 織田有楽

(1547–1621). *Daimyō* and master of the TEA CEREMONY; youngest brother of ODA NOBUNAGA. Born Oda Nagamasu, he used the name Uraku in his role as a tea master. After Nobunaga's death he transferred allegiance to TOYOTOMI HIDEYOSHI. After Hideyoshi's death he fought on the side of TOKUGAWA IEYASU at the Battle of SEKIGAHARA in 1600. In 1614, during the first siege of Ōsaka Castle, he fought for TOYOTOMI HIDEYORI and tried to mediate between the Tokugawa and Toyotomi camps. With the second siege in 1615 (see ŌSAKA CASTLE, SIEGES OF), he retired to Higashiyama, near Kyōto. A disciple of the tea master SEN NO RIKYŪ and a friend of Sen no Sōtan (1578–1658), he designed tea utensils,

teahouses, and tea gardens, establishing the Uraku school.

Odawara 小田原[市]

City in southwestern Kanagawa Prefecture, central Honshū, on Sagami Bay. It grew up around Odawara Castle, built around the end of the 12th century, and was a castle town of the Ōkubo family during the Edo period (1600–1868). It also developed as one of the post-station towns on the highway TŌKAIDŌ. The city produces photographic materials, electrical appliances, and cosmetics. Local products include mandarin oranges and *kamaboko* (fish paste). Of interest are the castle and a museum and shrine in honor of the agriculturalist-philosopher NINOMIYA SONTOKU. Pop: 193,417.

Odawara Campaign 小田原征伐

(Odawara Seibatsu). The defeat of the Later Hōjō family (see HŌJŌ FAMILY), who controlled the strategic Kantō region, by TOYOTOMI HIDEYOSHI in 1590. When Hōjō Ujimasa (1538–90) and his son Ujinao (1562–91) refused to submit to him, Hideyoshi besieged their castle at Odawara (in what is now Kanagawa Prefecture) and forced its surrender after 100 days. Hideyoshi assigned the Hōjō domain to his most powerful vassal (and former rival), TOKUGAWA IEYASU. The fall of Odawara in effect completed the military phase of Hideyoshi's unification of Japan.

oden 御田

Dish consisting of several ingredients simmered in a pot; usually eaten during the winter months. *Oden* is customarily served on a shallow dish with a splash of broth and a bit of hot mustard. Common ingredients are KONNYAKU, a jellylike food made from the root of a bulbous herb of the same name; shelled hard-boiled eggs; thick slices of *daikon*, or Japanese white radish; *gammodoki*, or dehydrated *tōfu* mixed with vegetables and deep-fried; and *chikuwa*, a hollow tube of grilled fish paste. *Oden* is often sold at street stalls specializing in the dish.

OECD 経済協力開発機構

(Organization for Economic Cooperation and Development; J: Keizai Kyōryoku Kaihatsu Kikō). Japan joined the OECD in 1964. Prior to this, it had been a member of the Development Assistance Group, which was the predecessor of the OECD's Development Assistance Committee (DAC). Upon becoming a full member of the OECD, Japan committed itself to a rapid liberalization of its international transactions. In addition to the liberalization of tariff and trade regulations required by the GATT and the IMF, which Japan joined during the same period, the OECD required the removal of restrictions on current invisible transactions and on capital movements.

At the outset, Japanese trade restrictions were far more severe than those of other OECD members. But in response to the repeated requests of the OECD and its member nations, in 1973 the Japanese government committed itself to complete trade liberalization. A meeting of the OECD Council was held in Tōkyō in 1989 on the occasion of the 25th anniversary of Japan's joining the OECD.

OECF → Overseas Economic Cooperation Fund

Ōei Invasion 応永の外寇

(Ōei no Gaikō). Attack by a Korean force on the island of Tsushima (now part of

Nagasaki Prefecture) in 1419 (Ōei 26). Tsushima had become a base for Japanese pirates (WAKŌ), who regularly pillaged Korean coastal towns. King T'aejong, third ruler of the Yi dynasty (1392–1910), resolved to capture the pirates' stronghold in their absence and destroy them on their return. In July 1419 T'aejong dispatched a fleet of more than 200 ships and landed some 17,000 troops on Tsushima. Sō Sadamori (1385–1452; see SŌ FAMILY), the lord of Tsushima, retaliated and, warning of the coming typhoons, induced them to withdraw.

Ōei Rebellion 応永の乱

(Ōei no Ran). Revolt of November 1399 (Ōei 6.10) to January 1400 (Ōei 6.12) against the MUROMACHI SHOGUNATE (1338–1573) by Ōuchi Yoshihiro (1356–1400). Yoshihiro was military governor (SHUGO) of six western provinces and was considered a threat to the shogunate by the third Muromachi shōgun, ASHIKAGA YOSHIMITSU, who was determined to curb his power. Provoked by heavy exactions, rescision of several governorships, and other signs of shogunal hostility, Yoshihiro gained the support of the governor-general for the Kantō area (the Kamakura *kubō*), Ashikaga Mitsukane (1378–1409), and revolted. He was defeated and slain after a two-month siege. The shogunate thus strengthened its control over provincial military lords (SHUGO DAIMYŌ). See also MEITOKU REBELLION.

Ōe Kenzaburō 大江健三郎

(1935–). Novelist, short-story writer, and essayist. Born in Ehime Prefecture on the island of Shikoku. Ōe graduated from Tōkyō University in 1959. He won the Akutagawa Prize in 1958 for "Shiiku" (tr "The Catch," 1959), a story that depicts a young boy in an isolated village during World War II. Ōe's first full-length novel, *Memushiri kouchi* (1958, Pluck the Buds, Shoot the Kids), which also portrays a rural world inhabited by children, established him in the forefront of the new writers of the day.

Ōe's fiction quickly moved toward an increasing preoccupation with social and political issues and was often written in a scathing manner that created a rift between him and some of his contemporaries. His novel *Warera no jidai* (1959, Our Age) was attacked from many quarters. In the turmoil surrounding the protests against the revision of the United States–Japan Security Treaty in 1960, Ōe, strongly opposed to the revision, became overtly political and aggressive in his writing. "Sebuntīn" (Seventeen) and its sequel "Seiji shōnen shisu" (The Death of a Political Youth), both published in 1961 and based on the murder of Chairman ASANUMA INEJIRŌ of the Japan Socialist Party by a right-wing youth in 1960, provoked vicious attacks by right-wing organizations. The novel *Okurete kita seinen* (1962, A Youth Who Came Too Late) and the short-story collec-

oden *Oden*, which is often accompanied by hot sake, makes a warming meal popular during the winter months.

Oda Sakunosuke This 20th-century novelist also wrote a famous essay criticizing the I-novel tradition of Japanese fiction.

Ōe Kenzaburō This postwar novelist and critic, shown here in a 1986 photograph, described the spiritual confusion of Japanese youth of the sixties and seventies in many of his politically controversial works.

ōendan A high school ōendan, or cheering section, encourages its team during the annual high school baseball tournament. Cheerleaders, usually male, wear school uniforms while leading their classmates in cheers that include hand clapping and whistling.

tion *Seiteki ningen* (1963, Sexual Beings) portray characters who often turn to violent and oppressive behavior out of a sense of frustration with life in an affluent and apathetic postwar Japan.

Two events in Ōe's own life acted as catalysts in bringing about new developments in his work—the birth in 1963 of a son with a congenital abnormality of the skull and a visit to Hiroshima to investigate the aftereffects of the atomic bomb. The first of these experiences is reflected in his novel of 1964, KOJINTEKI NA TAIKEN (tr *A Personal Matter*, 1968), in which the birth of a child with severe brain damage places a frighteningly burdensome responsibility on a young father. This was followed by works dealing with the threat of nuclear annihilation. One of these, *Kōzui wa waga tamashii ni oyobi* (1973, The Floodwaters Reach My Soul), ends in a scene of destruction as wrecking crews demolish the nuclear shelter in which the protagonist remains trapped.

Although Ōe's writing left behind the innocence of his very first fiction, it often clung to the rural landscape and mythical tenor of those works. Over the years, Ōe drew and redrew a village community with a distinct geography and collection of residents. The village appears in a number of works, including MAN'EN GANNEN NO FUTTOBŌRU (1967; tr *The Silent Cry*, 1974). It emerges full-blown in *Dōjidai gēmu* (1979, The Game of Contemporaneity), which uses a village as a microcosm of Japanese society.

Ōe's fiction of the 1980s and 1990s, which includes *Rein tsurī o kiku onnatachi* (1982; partial tr "The Clever Rain Tree," 1985), *Natsukashii toshi e no tegami* (1987, A Letter to a Fondly Remembered Year), and *Shizuka na seikatsu* (1990, A Quiet Life), took on a more reflective tone. The last of the three draws heavily upon the author's own life to paint a subdued portrait of a family. In *Saigo no shōsetsu* (The Last Novel), a collection of essays published in 1988, Ōe deals with issues that have distinguished him from postmodern authors and have reaffirmed his connections to an older generation of politically oriented postwar novelists.

ōendan 応援団

(cheering section). The custom of group cheering and cheerleading was imported along with certain sports from the West during the Meiji period (1868–1912) and after. From the 1890s, students used flags and streamers to encourage their teams in baseball games and boat races. Almost every university in Japan has a male cheerleading club. Members profess an unswerving allegiance to their schools, and relations between junior and senior members are rigidly formal (see SEMPAI-KŌHAI). Cheerleaders wear standard black school uniforms, and their gestures in leading the cheering of their fellow students are based on the stylized poses native to KABUKI and SUMŌ. In recent years women have

become involved through the introduction of US-style cheerleading.

Ōe no Hiromoto 大江広元

(1148–1225). Adviser to MINAMOTO NO YORITOMO, founder of the KAMAKURA SHOGUNATE. A great-grandson of ŌE NO MASAFUSA, Hiromoto served as a drafter of documents at the imperial court. In 1184 he went to Kamakura to head the KUMONJO (Public Documents Office) and in 1185 advised Yoritomo to appoint JITŌ (land stewards) and SHUGO (provincial constables or military governors) to consolidate control over outlying provinces. Hiromoto became the first head (*bettō*) of the MANDOKORO (Administrative Board) in 1191. After Yoritomo's death in 1199 he helped Yoritomo's widow, HŌJŌ MASAKO, put down dissidents such as WADA YOSHIMORI and HIKI YOSHIKAZU and establish the HŌJŌ FAMILY's regency. After taking Buddhist orders in 1217 he continued to aid the Hōjō and contributed to the swift suppression of the JŌKYŪ DISTURBANCE.

Ōe no Masafusa 大江匡房

(1041–1111). Court official, scholar of Chinese, author, and poet. Masafusa's family, the Ōe, was with the Sugawara one of the two most important court families with a hereditary expertise and specialization in Chinese studies. Masafusa was the author of *Gōke shidai* (1111, Ceremonial Usages According to the Ōe House), of which 19 of an original 21 books are extant. He produced collections of anecdotes and tales of the strange and marvelous. These include *Gōdanshō* (ca 1104–11; Tales of Master Ōe), *Kobi ki* (1101, Record of Seductive Fox Spirits), *Honchō shinsen den* (ca 1098, Lives of Japanese Wonder Workers), and *Zoku honchō ōjō den* (1099–1104, Lives of Japanese Buddhist Saints, Continued), a sequel to a late-10th-century work by YOSHISHIGE NO YASUTANE (d 1002). A total of 121 of Masafusa's poems are included in various imperial anthologies. His personal collection is *Gō no Sochi shū* (Collection of the Ōe Viceroy).

Ōe Taku 大江卓

(1847–1921). Politician, businessman, and social reformer. Born in Tosa Province (now Kōchi Prefecture). He was convicted of complicity in the SATSUMA REBELLION of 1877 and sentenced to prison. In 1890 he was elected to the Diet, but, defeated in the election of 1892, he abandoned politics and became president of the Tōkyō Stock Exchange. He took Buddhist holy orders in 1914 and devoted the rest of his life to ending discrimination against outcasts.

Ōeyama 大江山

Mountain in northwestern Kyōto Prefecture, central Honshū; highest peak in the Tango Mountains. The mountain is famous for its association with the legend of Shuten Dōji, an ogre who devoured women and children but was eventually killed by MINAMOTO NO YORIMITSU. The mountain is mentioned in a poem in the popular collection HYAKUNIN ISSHU. Height: 833 m (2,733 ft).

Official Gazette 官報

(*Kampō*). The Japanese government's official daily journal. It contains such material as newly enacted laws, official notices, budgetary matters, texts of treaties, important personnel actions relating to government officials, and items relating to the Diet and government offices. Publication of laws and

regulations in the *Official Gazette* has the force of their official proclamation. The modern version first appeared in 1868, although the Tokugawa shogunate (1603–1867) had issued similar publications before this.

Ōfunato 大船渡〔市〕

City in southeastern Iwate Prefecture, northern Honshū. Situated on a natural fishing harbor. Oysters and *nori* (a type of seaweed) are cultivated in the bay. Its coastal industrial district has seafood-processing and cement factories. The city is the southern gate to Rikuchū Coast National Park. Pop: 37,853.

ofuregaki 御触書

(literally, "matters to be announced"). General proclamations issued by the Tokugawa shogunate (1603–1867) to guide the conduct of selected segments of the populace. They consisted of ethical admonitions, explicit prohibitions, administrative stipulations, and practical advice. In 1615 TOKUGAWA IEYASU issued the first Laws for the Court and Nobility (KINCHŪ NARABI NI KUGE SHOHATTO) and the first Laws for the Military Houses (BUKE SHOHATTO). Subsequently these *hatto* or laws were revised and others were issued for *samurai* in general, as well as for specific temples and shrines. In 1649 the third shōgun, TOKUGAWA IEMITSU, issued the KEIAN NO OFUREGAKI, 32 admonitory guidelines for villagers. It was distributed to villages throughout the shogunate's domains (*tenryō*) and was also adapted for use in many *daimyō* domains (*han*). Major *hatto* were issued by the shōgun, but less general administrative notices (*kakitsuke*) were often sent by senior councillors (*rōjū*) to subordinate administrators. Notices that were directed to only a few persons were known as *tasshi*, while those addressed to a wide audience were known as *ofuregaki* or *ofuregoto*. Over the years the quantity of *ofuregaki* grew unmanageable, and in 1744 the first of several compilations (OFUREGAKI SHŪSEI) was made in an attempt to systematize regulations.

Ofuregaki Shūsei 御触書集成

Collective name for four official compilations of proclamations (OFUREGAKI) of the Tokugawa shogunate (1603–1867). The eighth shōgun, TOKUGAWA YOSHIMUNE, undertook to systematize the immense body of laws, administrative regulations, and proclamations. In 1742 he had orders of a judicial nature codified as the KUJIKATA OSADAMEGAKI. He then ordered compiled the regulations and announcements issued between 1615 and 1743 that were in the archival collections of the secretaries (YŪHITSU), commissioners of finance (KANJŌ BUGYŌ), and inspectors (METSUKE). These were published in 50 *kan* (volumes) as the Ofuregaki Kampō Shūsei.

This major compilation proved so useful that it was supplemented periodically. In 1762 (Hōreki 12) the *ofuregaki* issued between 1744 and 1760 were published in 33 *kan* as the Ofuregaki Hōreki Shūsei. The proclamations issued between 1761 and 1787 were compiled in 1787 (Temmei 7) in 51 *kan* as the Ofuregaki Temmei Shūsei. Finally in 1841 (Tempō 12) the *ofuregaki* issued between 1788 and 1837 were compiled in 107 *kan* as the Ofuregaki Tempō Shūsei.

Oga 男鹿〔市〕

City in western Akita Prefecture, northern Honshū. The recent construction of large lumber factories has led to its rapid industrialization. It is part of Oga Quasi-National Park, with several scenic spots, including the mountain KAMPŪZAN. The NAMAHAGE festival, in which young men dress up as demons and scare children, is held here at New Year's Eve. Pop: 34,291.

Ōgaki　大垣[市]

City in western Gifu Prefecture, central Honshū, on the river Ibigawa. During the Battle of SEKIGAHARA (1600) Ōgaki Castle served as a base for the forces of ISHIDA MITSUNARI. A castle town of the Toda family during the Edo period (1600–1868), it prospered as a river port and post-station town. Principal industries are textiles, chemicals, and machinery. It is the center of the Ibi-Sekigahara-Yōrō Quasi-National Park. Pop: 148,281.

Oga Peninsula　男鹿半島

(Oga Hantō). Located in Akita Prefecture, northern Honshū. It is linked with the mainland by two sandbars. Extending west into the Sea of Japan, the peninsula is known for its spectacular coastal scenery, the volcano KAMPŪZAN and some small volcanic lakes. Several sections of the peninsula are part of Oga Quasi-National Park. Area: 224 sq km (86 sq mi).

Ogasawara family　小笠原氏

(Ogasawarashi). Warrior family of the Kamakura (1185–1333) and Edo (1600–1868) periods. The Ogasawara descended from the Kagami family, an offshoot of the MINAMOTO FAMILY, in Kai Province (now Yamanashi Prefecture). As a reward for service during the JŌKYŪ DISTURBANCE (1221), Ogasawara Nagakiyo was appointed military governor (SHUGO) of Awa Province (now Tokushima Prefecture). Successive members of the family were appointed *shugo* of Shinano Province (now Nagano Prefecture). In the latter Muromachi period (1333–1568) the family split into the Fuchū and Matsuo lines. The Fuchū Ogasawara were *daimyō* of Akashi in Harima Province (now Hyōgo Prefecture) from 1617 to 1632 and were then granted Kokura in Buzen Province (now part of Fukuoka Prefecture), with an income of 150,000 *koku* (see KOKUDAKA). Members of the collateral Matsuo line were daimyō of Katsuyama in Echizen Province (now part of Fukui Prefecture), with 22,000 *koku*. The Ogasawara originated the OGASAWARA SCHOOL OF ETIQUETTE.

Ogasawara Islands　小笠原諸島

(Ogasawara Shotō). A small group of mountainous islands, also known as the Bonin Islands, located approximately 1,000 km (620 mi) south of Tōkyō. Administratively part of Tōkyō Prefecture, the group includes the nearby IŌ ISLANDS (known internationally as the Volcano Islands). Believed to have been discovered in 1593, the islands remained sparsely inhabited until their rediscovery in the 1820s and 1830s by British and American seamen, who established small settlements. In 1853 Commodore Matthew PERRY raised the American flag, but Japan laid claim in 1862, and in 1876 the Meiji government formally annexed the islands. They were considered strategically important in World War II as sites for naval and airplane bases. With the deterioration of Japan's position, all the inhabitants were evacuated. The islands were captured by US military forces in 1945 and were under US administration until they were restored to Japanese control in 1968.

The inhabitants, who engage mainly in farming, now number over 2,000.

Ogasawara National Park　小笠原国立公園

(Ogasawara Kokuritsu Kōen). Japan's smallest national park, some 1,000 km (620 mi) south of Tōkyō. It comprises the OGASAWARA ISLANDS proper and Kita Iōjima, one of the IŌ ISLANDS. The Ogasawara Islands are a group of some 30 volcanic islands with dense semitropical forests. Tourism is developed on CHICHIJIMA, the largest island, noted for its white-sand beaches, and Hahajima, whose chief feature is the sheer cliffs at Ōkuzure Bay. Among the semitropical plants that thrive on the islands are the hibiscus, Ogasawara palm (*birō*), screw pine (*takonoki*), and white popinac (*ginnemu*). Coral, various species of tropical fish, and the Ogasawara limpet (*kasagai*) are found in the surrounding waters. Area: 61 sq km (23.5 sq mi).

Ogasawara school of etiquette　小笠原流礼法

(Ogasawararyū *reihō*). Traditional manners used among the warrior class. The code was compiled early in the Muromachi period (1333–1568) by Ogasawara Sadamune (1294–1347), whose family had preserved certain formalities and rules of etiquette related to the practice of archery and horsemanship in martial sports such as INUOUMONO, KASAGAKE, and YABUSAME. Later in the Muromachi period, descendants of Sadamune wrote books on etiquette that dealt with the coming of age of a *samurai* (see GEMPUKU), marriage, and other ceremonial events. In the Edo period (1600–1868) the shogunate established the school's prescriptions as its code of manners. Because of its origins in the warrior class, it is distinguished by an emphasis on unadorned grace and persists today as the basis for conventional etiquette. "Ogasawararyū" has become a synonym for good manners.

Ōgata　大潟[村]

Village in northwestern Akita Prefecture, northern Honshū, created through the reclamation of the lagoon HACHIRŌGATA. Known for the use of large-scale agricultural methods, the farms here average 15 hectares (37 acres), more than 10 times the national average. Pop: 3,286.

Ogata Ken　緒形拳

(1937–). Actor. Born in Tōkyō. Ogata joined the SHINKOKUGEKI (New National Theater) as a stage actor in 1958 but left in 1960.

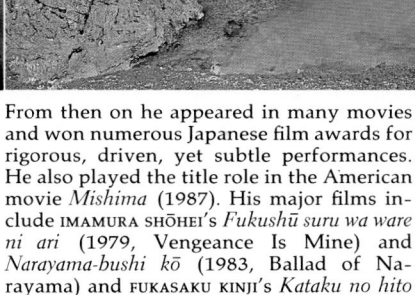

From then on he appeared in many movies and won numerous Japanese film awards for rigorous, driven, yet subtle performances. He also played the title role in the American movie *Mishima* (1987). His major films include IMAMURA SHŌHEI's *Fukushū suru wa ware ni ari* (1979, Vengeance Is Mine) and *Narayama-bushi kō* (1983, Ballad of Narayama) and FUKASAKU KINJI's *Kataku no hito* (1986, Man in a Burning House).

Ogata Kenzan → Kenzan

Ogata Kōan　緒方洪庵

(1810–63). Physician and teacher of European medicine and Dutch Learning (Rangaku; see WESTERN LEARNING). Born in Bitchū Province (now part of Okayama Prefecture), he first studied medicine in Ōsaka and in 1831 moved to Edo (now Tōkyō), where he studied Dutch, basic science, and medicine. In 1836 Ogata went to Nagasaki for study with a Dutch doctor, and in 1838 he opened a school of medicine and Dutch Learning in Ōsaka, the Tekijuku (or Tekitekisaijuku), which was immediately successful. FUKUZAWA YUKICHI, ŌMURA MASUJIRŌ, SANO TSUNETAMI, ŌTORI KEISUKE, and others who played important roles in Japanese society after the Meiji Restoration of 1868 studied at the Tekijuku.

Ogata's *Fushi keiken ikun*, a translation of a German text on internal medicine, was widely circulated in handwritten copies. Ogata directed an effort against smallpox, and his findings from research during the 1858 cholera epidemic were published as *Korori chijun*. In 1862 he was appointed physician to the shōgun and head of the Tokugawa shogunate's institute of Western medicine (later named the IGAKUSHO).

Ogata Koreyoshi　緒方惟準

(1843–1909). Physician who contributed to medical education and the establishment of the army medical system. Born in Ōsaka as the second son of the scholar OGATA KŌAN. He went to the Netherlands to study at the University of Utrecht. Returning to Japan in 1868, he served in the Imperial Household Ministry. He was later made responsible for army medical affairs and served as president of the Army Medical School. Ogata also founded the Ogata Hospital and the Ōsaka Jikei Hospital. Among his publications is *Eisei shinron* (1872, New Theory of Hygiene).

Ogata Kōrin → Kōrin

Ogasawara National Park
1 The park's beautiful coral formations, abundance of tropical fish, and crystal-clear waters make it a popular destination among divers.
2 The Ōgiike Inlet on Minamijima, a tiny (0.3 sq km) coral islet that is part of the Ogasawara Islands.

Ogawa Usen *Suimi tawamuru* (Water Spirits). 1923. Hanging scroll. Ink and colors on paper. 63 × 95 cm. Museum of Modern Art, Ibaraki. Mito, Ibaraki Prefecture.

Ogata Tomosaburō
A pathologist at Tōkyō University, Ogata proved the essential role played by the parotid gland hormone in the growth of the bones and teeth.

Ogawa Mimei Known for the warmth and imagination of his stories, Ogawa was one of Japan's most important writers of children's literature.

Ogata Taketora
緒方竹虎

(1888–1956). Journalist and statesman; born in Yamagata Prefecture and brought up in Fukuoka. Upon graduating from Waseda University, Ogata joined the newspaper *Tōkyō asahi shimbun* in 1911, eventually becoming managing editor (1925) and editor in chief (1934). As a liberal he confronted the rise of militarism in the 1930s, including the attack on the newspaper's office by military insurgents in the FEBRUARY 26TH INCIDENT of 1936. As state minister and head of the Information Bureau in the wartime KOISO KUNIAKI cabinet, Ogata attempted to negotiate a separate peace with the Chiang Kaishek government in China. Immediately after Japan's surrender (1945), he played a crucial role as state minister and chief cabinet secretary of Prince HIGASHIKUNI NARUHIKO's cabinet in arranging for the peaceful arrival of the Allied Occupation forces in Japan.

After being barred from public activities for a period in the OCCUPATION PURGE, he was elected to the House of Representatives (1952) and served as deputy prime minister (1952–54). He became president of the LIBERAL PARTY (Jiyūtō) in 1954. He served as one of the four deputies of the newly formed (1955) LIBERAL DEMOCRATIC PARTY (Jiyū Minshutō).

Ogata Tomosaburō
緒方知三郎

(1883–1973). Pathologist. Born in Tōkyō as the third son of OGATA KOREYOSHI. Graduate of Tōkyō University. He proved that the parotid gland hormone was essential to the growth of the bones and teeth. With SHIMAZONO JUNJIRŌ he was coauthor of a series of works on vitamin B$_1$ deficiency (1926). Ogata taught at Tōkyō University from 1913 until 1943 and served as president of Tōkyō Medical College from 1946 to 1954. A member of the Japan Academy from 1946, he received the Order of Culture in 1957.

Ogawa
小川[町]

Town in central Saitama Prefecture, central Honshū; noted since ancient times for its *washi* (handmade paper). Silk textiles, woodwork, *sake* (rice wine), and vegetables are also produced here. Pop: 33,709.

Ogawa Heikichi
小川平吉

(1870–1942). Politician. Born in Nagano Prefecture; graduate of Tōkyō University. In 1901 he joined KONOE ATSUMARO's Kokumin Dōmeikai, a nationalist organization calling for war with Russia, after having helped Konoe found the TŌA DŌBUNKAI, a Sino-Japanese cultural and educational organization. Deciding on a career in politics, Ogawa joined the RIKKEN SEIYŪKAI party in 1900. He rose rapidly in the party (then under HARA TAKASHI's leadership) and was elected to the Diet 10 times. He was named justice minister in the first KATŌ TAKAAKI cabinet (1924–25) and railway minister in the TANAKA GIICHI cabinet (1927–29). Indicted in 1929 for his part in a bribery scandal involving private railroad companies, he was sentenced in 1936 to two years in prison.

Ogawa Kunio
小川国夫

(1927–). Novelist. Born in Shizuoka Prefecture. Graduate of Tōkyō University. He studied in France for two years and then, in 1957, he published his first work, *Aporon no shima*, a collection of literary sketches from his trip to the Mediterranean islands. He gained recognition eight years later when this book was praised by the leading writer SHIMAO TOSHIO. Later works include the novels *Kokoromi no kishi* (1970), *Kare no kokyō* (1971), and *Afurika no shi* (1980).

Ogawa Mimei
小川未明

(1882–1961). Novelist and children's story writer. Real name Ogawa Kensaku. Born in Niigata Prefecture. Graduate of Waseda University. His early works, mostly poetic fantasies such as "Bara to miko" (1911; tr "Rose and Witch," 1925), include some children's stories. He was drawn to the socialist movement and later joined an anarchist writers' group. From the late 1920s, Ogawa devoted himself entirely to writing the imaginative and humane tales that made him one of Japan's most important writers of children's stories. His principal works include *Rodon na neko* (1912, Stupid Cat), an autobiographical novel, and the children's stories "Akai rōsoku to ningyo" (1921; tr "The Red Candle and the Mermaid," 1957) and "Tsukiyo to megane" (1922, The Moonlit Night and the Eyeglasses). He became a member of the Japan Art Academy (Nihon Geijutsuin) in 1953.

Ogawa Shinsuke
小川紳介

(1935–92). Film director. Born in Gifu Prefecture. He joined Iwanami Productions, Inc, as an assistant director in 1965. Ogawa's internationally respected documentaries focus on farmers' traditional ways of thinking and their lives and customs, which center on rice cultivation. His major films include *Sanrizuka no natsu* (1968, Summer in Narita), about the opposition to the annexation of farmland for the New Tōkyō International Airport, and *Nipponkoku Furuyashiki Mura* (1982, A Japanese Village—Furuyashiki Mura).

Ogawa Takuji
小川琢治

(1870–1941). Geologist and geographer. Born in Wakayama Prefecture. After graduating from Tōkyō University in 1896, he carried out geological surveys. In 1908 he was appointed to the newly founded chair of geography at Kyōto University. Ogawa was the father of YUKAWA HIDEKI, a Nobel laureate in physics; Ogawa Tamaki (b 1910), a scholar of Chinese literature; and KAIZUKA SHIGEKI, a historian of China.

Ogawa Usen
小川芋銭

(1868–1938). Japanese-style painter. Real name Ogawa Mokichi; born in Tōkyō to an impoverished *samurai* family from the village of Ushiku in Ibaraki Prefecture. As a child, he studied Western-style painting at a private school while teaching himself traditional literati painting (BUNJINGA). In 1888 he became associated with *Chōya shimbun*, a liberal newspaper to which he contributed satirical political cartoons. In 1896 he married and returned to his hometown in Ibaraki Prefecture. The quiet, rural environment that he loved led him to establish his own style of ink painting, a blend of landscape and airy imagination. He was a member of the Japan Fine Arts Academy (Nihon Bijutsuin) from 1917.

Ogidō shell mound
荻堂貝塚

(Ogidō *kaizuka*). Prehistoric site in Ogidō, the village of Kita Nakagusuku, Okinawa Prefecture; contemporaneous with the Late Jōmon period (ca 2500 BC–ca 1000 BC; also dated as ca 2000 BC–ca 1000 BC) culture in Japan proper. The deposit, 1 meter (3.3 ft) thick, was excavated in 1919 and yielded a wide variety of shells, fish and animal bones, STONE TOOLS, BONE ARTICLES, and pottery. The shell mound is the type site for Ogidō ware—deep, flat-bottomed pots with projections and semicircular punctuate patterns on the upper body. Ogidō ware is considered a regional variation of Late JŌMON POTTERY.

Ogino Ginko
荻野吟子

(1851–1913). First Japanese woman licensed to practice Western medicine in Japan. Born in what is now Saitama Prefecture. Following a divorce from her first husband, Ogino resolved to become a physician. After graduating from the Women's Normal School (now Ochanomizu Women's University) she entered Kōjuin, a private medical school for men, graduating in 1882. In 1885 she was finally allowed to take the medical qualifying examination and established an obstetrics and gynecology practice in Tōkyō. She also served as physician for the Meiji Girls' School and contributed to the magazine JOGAKU ZASSHI. She was remarried to a younger Christian activist named Shikata Yukiyoshi and in 1894 went with him to Hokkaidō, returning to Tōkyō after his death.

Ogino Kyūsaku
荻野久作

(1882–1975). Physician and researcher in reproductive physiology. Born in Aichi Prefecture. After graduating from Tōkyō University in 1909, he worked at Takeyama Hospital in the city of Niigata and later served as its head from 1936 to 1957. In 1924 he published a theory that human ovulation is independent of the total length of the menstrual cycle, occurring 12 to 16 days before the next period is due. (This theory was later applied in the rhythm method of birth control, known in Japan as the Ogino method.) Working independently in Austria, Herman Knaus (1892–1970) reached approximately the same conclusion as Ogino; their findings were unified in 1934 as the Ogino-Knaus theory. See also FAMILY PLANNING.

Ogisu Takanori
荻須高徳

(1901–86). Western-style painter. Also known as Oguiss. Born in Aichi Prefecture. After graduating from Tōkyō Bijutsu Gakkō (now Tōkyō University of Fine Arts and Music), Ogisu went to France. Influenced by the Japanese Western-style painter SAEKI YŪZŌ and by Maurice Utrillo (1883–1955), Ogisu produced richly poetic paintings of streets and buildings in Paris. Oguiss Memorial Museum is in the city of Inazawa, Aichi Prefecture. He received the Legion of Honor from France in 1956 and the Order of Culture in 1986.

Ogiwara Morie 荻原守衛

(1879–1910). Western-style sculptor. Artist name Ogiwara Rokuzan. A pioneer in the modernization of Japanese sculpture, he is noted primarily for introducing the style of Auguste Rodin to Japan. Born in Nagano Prefecture, he went to Tōkyō in 1899 and studied painting at the Fudōsha, the art school of Koyama Shōtarō (1857–1916). From 1901 to 1904 he traveled in the United States. From there he went to France, where he studied briefly with Jean-Paul Laurens (1838–1921) at the Académie Julian. Profoundly impressed by Rodin, he turned to sculpture in 1906. Returning to Japan in 1908, he exhibited at the second and third BUNTEN, the annual Ministry of Education art exhibitions, where his Rodinesque works caused a sensation. His last sculpture was the epoch-making work *Onna* (1910, Woman).

Ogiwara Seisensui 荻原井泉水

(1884–1976). HAIKU poet. Real name Ogiwara Tōkichi. Born in Tōkyō. Graduate of Tōkyō University. He founded the coterie magazine *Sōun* in 1911 with KAWAHIGASHI HEKIGOTŌ. Ogiwara's haiku disregard the traditional season words and the 5-7-5 syllable pattern. In the critical work *Haiku teishō* (1917) Ogiwara urged on his readers the writing of such free-verse haiku. In 1965 he became a member of the Japan Art Academy (Nihon Geijutsuin). Principal collections of his works include *Wakiizuru mono* (1920) and *Chōryū* (1964).

Ogiwara Shigehide 荻原重秀

(1658–1713). Commissioner of finance (KANJŌ BUGYŌ) for the Tokugawa shogunate (1603–1867). He began in the Finance Office (Kanjōsho) and advanced under the shōgun TOKUGAWA TSUNAYOSHI to its highest office in 1696. To meet the shogunate's financial crisis, Ogiwara carried out debasements of the coinage between 1695 and 1711, but the relief was only temporary and led to economic confusion and higher prices. Ogiwara was suspected of having used his office for personal profit. ARAI HAKUSEKI, adviser to Tsunayoshi's successor, TOKUGAWA IENOBU, petitioned repeatedly for Ogiwara's removal from office, and Ogiwara was finally forced to resign in 1712. Hakuseki gives an account of this episode in his memoirs, *Oritaku shiba no ki* (ca 1716).

Ogōchi Dam 小河内ダム

(Ogōchi Damu). Located on the upper reaches of the river TAMAGAWA, western Tōkyō, central Honshū. Completed in 1957, the dam created Lake Oku Tama, which is one of the sources of drinking water for the Tōkyō Metropolitan Area. Height: 149 m (489 ft); width: 535 m (1,755 ft); storage capacity: 185 million cu m (6.5 billion cu ft).

Ogōri 小郡[市]

City in central Fukuoka Prefecture, Kyūshū. Its principal activity is rice cultivation; saplings, poultry, and hogs are also raised. A Japanese Self Defense Forces base is located here. Pop: 47,116.

Ogōri 小郡[町]

Town in southwestern Yamaguchi Prefecture, western Honshū. The terminus of several railways and major highways, it is

known for its rice, lotus roots (*renkon*), furniture, and farming equipment. Pop: 21,772.

ōgosho 大御所

An honorific term most commonly used to designate a retired shōgun. First applied to the residence of the shōgun's father in the 13th century, it was later used as a title of respect for retired Ashikaga and Tokugawa shōguns, including TOKUGAWA IEYASU during the period 1605–16. The term *ōgosho jidai*, "age of the retired shōgun," refers specifically to the years 1837–41, when TOKUGAWA IENARI lived in retirement but retained firm control of state affairs.

Oguma Hideo 小熊秀雄

(1901–40). Poet. Born in Hokkaidō. He began writing poetry while working as a newspaper reporter in Hokkaidō. In the late 1920s he moved to Tōkyō and contributed to the proletarian poetry magazine *Shiseishin*. Principal works include the epic poem *Tobu sori* (1935) and the poetry collection *Ryūmin shishū* (1947).

Ogura Kinnosuke 小倉金之助

(1885–1962). Mathematician; noted for his achievements in the teaching of mathematics and research in the history of mathematics. Born in Yamagata Prefecture. Graduate of Tōkyō Butsuri Gakkō (now Science University of Tōkyō). He played a leading role in Japan in the reform movement in the teaching of mathematics that flourished internationally from the late 19th to the early 20th century. He also advocated closer ties between natural scientists and social scientists, participating in the establishment in 1932 of the Yuibutsuron Kenkyūkai (Association for the Study of Materialism) with TOSAKA JUN and others. In the postwar period he served as president of the Democratic Scientists Association and of the Japan Society for the History of Science. His works include *Sūgaku kyōiku no kompon mondai* (1924) and *Ogura Kinnosuke chosakushū* (1973–75).

Ogura Masatsune 小倉正恒

(1875–1961). Businessman; leader of the SUMITOMO *zaibatsu* (financial and industrial combine). He was born in Ishikawa Prefecture and graduated from Tōkyō University. After serving in the Home Ministry, Ogura switched to Sumitomo in 1899. After becoming general director of Sumitomo, Ltd, in 1930, Ogura vigorously promoted the *zaibatsu*'s modernization by turning its various business divisions into independent corporations. He became state minister and finance minister in 1941. He was also president of the Wartime Finance Corporation.

Ogura Shimpei 小倉進平

(1882–1944). Philologist and noted Korean language specialist. He laid the foundation for the study of the Korean language in Japan. Born in Sendai, Miyagi Prefecture, Ogura graduated from and later taught at Tōkyō University. For his invaluable contribution to the study of ancient Korean language and culture in Japan, he was awarded the Imperial Prize in 1935. His important published works include *Kyōka oyobi ritō no kenkyū* (1929), a study of *hyangga* (Korean poems of the Silla period) and *idu* (Chinese characters used as Korean phonetic signs); *Chōsengo ni okeru kenjōhō, sonkeihō no jodōshi* (1938), a study of humble and honorific Korean verb forms; and *Zōtei chōsen-*

gogaku shi (1920; rev ed 1940), an enlarged and revised history of the study of the Korean language.

Ogurayama 小倉山

Hill in northwestern Kyōto on the northern bank of the river Hozugawa. A major landmark in one of Kyōto's most historic areas, it has often been mentioned in novels and poetry. It gives its name to the *Ogura hyakunin isshu* (or HYAKUNIN ISSHU), a collection of 100 poems compiled by FUJIWARA NO SADAIE (1162–1241). Tourist attractions include temples, cherry blossoms, and autumn foliage. Height: 295 m (958 ft).

Ogura Yuki 小倉遊亀

(1895–). Japanese-style (NIHONGA) painter specializing in graceful family scenes and pictures of women. Born in Shiga Prefecture (her maiden name was Mizogami Yuki). Ogura graduated from Nara Women's Higher Normal School. In 1920, while working as a teacher, she began studying painting under YASUDA YUKIHIKO. Her painting *Kyūri* (Cucumbers) was selected for an Inten exhibition (see JAPAN FINE ARTS ACADEMY) in 1926, and afterward she showed paintings at Inten exhibitions regularly. In 1976 she became a member of the JAPAN ART ACADEMY. She received the Order of Culture in 1980. Her best-known works include *Yuami onna* (1938, Bathing Women), *Oyako* (1961, Mother and Child), which won the Japan Art Academy Prize in 1962, and *Maiko* (1969, Apprentice Geisha).

Oguri Fūyō 小栗風葉

(1875–1926). Novelist. Best known as a follower of OZAKI KŌYŌ and as an early Japanese experimenter with naturalism. Real name Oguri Isoo. Born in Aichi Prefecture. In 1891 he became a member of the KEN'YŪSHA. Fūyō's first success came in 1896–97 with a series of family-focused romantic melodramas laced with love, sex, and suicide. After 1900 he became interested in naturalism, producing more realistic works. *Seishun* (1905–06, Youth), an imitation of Turgenev's *Rudin*, is considered Fūyō's best work. Fūyō remains noteworthy for his vivid style and pioneering efforts in the development of the modern Japanese novel.

Oguri Kōhei 小栗康平

(1945–). Film director. Born in Gumma Prefecture; graduated from Waseda University. After working as a freelance assistant to directors such as SHINODA MASAHIRO and Urayama Kirio (1930–85), Oguri made his directorial debut in 1981. His work portrays the lives of the poor and discrimination faced by the Korean community in Japan with a frank and humanistic realism. His major films include *Doro no kawa* (1981, Muddy River) and *Kayako no tame ni* (1984, For Kayako). He won the Grand Prix at the 1990 Cannes Film Festival for *Shi no toge* (1990, The Sting of Death).

Oguri Mushitarō 小栗虫太郎

(1901–46). Novelist. Real name Oguri Eijirō. Born in Tōkyō. He gained prominence with his mystery novel *Kanzen hanzai* (1933). Among his other works are exotic horror stories (which he called neogothic romances), such as *Tekkamen no shita* (1935) and *Nijisseiki tekkamen* (1936), and nonfiction pieces based upon obscure European legends, such as *Yūbijin* (1944).

Ogino Ginko In 1885 Ogino became the first female physician licensed to practice Western medicine in Japan.

Ogino Kyūsaku This physician's early research on human ovulation was applied in the rhythm method of birth control, which in Japan is known as the Ogino method.

Ogura Kinnosuke This mathematician made considerable contributions to mathematics education and to research in the history of the field.

ohajiki Flicked across a flat surface during play, the pieces used in this children's game are usually flat and round, like the colorful glass ones shown here.

Oguri Sōtan 小栗宗湛

(1413–81). ZEN monk-painter. Born Oguri Sukeshige, he took the name Sōtan when he was ordained at age 30 at the temple SHŌKOKUJI in Kyōto. Sōtan was known in his lifetime for his INK PAINTING (*suibokuga*) and also for his polychrome BIRD-AND-FLOWER PAINTING (*kachōga*). That he particularly admired the Chinese painter-priest Muqi (Mu-ch'i; fl 13th century; J: MOKKEI) is evidenced by his art name, Jiboku (literally, "himself a Muqi"). Sōtan was the pupil and successor of the Shōkokuji monk-painter SHŪBUN. In 1463, according to a precedent established with Shūbun, the shōgun ASHIKAGA YOSHIMASA appointed Sōtan painter-in-attendance and awarded him an annual stipend. Unfortunately, no surviving works can be assigned definitely to Sōtan.

Oguri Tadamasa 小栗忠順

(1827–68). Official of the Tokugawa shogunate. Born in Edo (now Tōkyō). He directed military and financial reforms and the expansion of foreign relations (1864–68). An advocate of eliminating the *daimyō* domains (HAN) and creating a centralized Tokugawa state with French aid, he was the only important shogunate official to be executed in the MEIJI RESTORATION (1868).

A high-ranking HATAMOTO (direct vassal), Oguri began as a *metsuke* (inspector) on a mission to the United States (see UNITED STATES, MISSION OF 1860 TO). As KANJŌ BUGYŌ (commissioner of finance) from 1865 to 1868, his purpose was to strengthen and modernize Tokugawa power, crush the major domains, and establish a unified nation. Oguri played a key role in the development of a special relationship between the shogunate and Léon ROCHES, the French minister, that was to provide French military and financial support for these objectives. Oguri also established the Yokohama and YOKOSUKA SHIPYARDS, formed companies to expand and monopolize foreign trade, directed Western-style army and navy reforms, and devised a plan to finance a standing army with monetary levies. A proponent of war against the imperial government in Kyōto, Oguri was dismissed from office by the shōgun TOKUGAWA YOSHINOBU in early 1868. Arrested by imperial agents after leaving Edo, he was executed on 27 May.

Ogyū Sorai 荻生徂徠

(1666–1728). Leading Confucian thinker of the Edo period (1600–1868). An adviser to two shōguns, he had an even greater impact on the world of letters and ideas. Thanks in part to the studies of MARUYAMA MASAO, Sorai has come to be recognized as a significant figure in the intellectual history of Japan.

Sorai was born in Edo (now Tōkyō), scion of a *samurai* family that specialized in medicine. His father had served as physician to the shōgun TOKUGAWA TSUNAYOSHI, but in 1679 he incurred official displeasure and was exiled to Kazusa (now part of Chiba Prefecture). The years in exile were important in Sorai's development and the hardships would shape his thinking.

Sorai left medicine to his elder brother and struck out on his own in Confucian studies. Upon his return to Edo in 1690, he set himself up as a Confucian teacher. In 1696 he entered the service of YANAGISAWA YOSHIYASU, a leading adviser of Tsunayoshi, and re-

mained until shortly after Tsunayoshi's death in 1709. Sorai's interests included poetry and music, politics and military science, linguistics and philosophy. He annotated the Chinese classics, composed his own poetry (over 600 poems), and wrote hundreds of letters that have been preserved.

From his philological and literary concern with classical Chinese, Sorai developed his interpretation of CONFUCIANISM. Most noteworthy is his attack on the entire Neo-Confucian tradition, for he insisted upon returning to the Chinese originals of the Six Classics—i.e., the Five Classics (see FOUR BOOKS AND FIVE CLASSICS) plus the *Zhou li* (*Chou li*; Rituals of Chou). According to Sorai, the language of the Neo-Confucianists differed sharply from that of the classics, and the Neo-Confucianists seemed unaware of the difference; they used "today's words to read the ancient words" and did "not know the old words." This difference in interpretation of language led him to attack the very foundations of Neo-Confucianism. The Way, he contended, was not innate; rather it had been "established" by the sages. He thus stressed the need for faith in the creator-sages even in instances when their teachings conflicted with one's own reason. For Maruyama Masao, writing in the late 1930s, Sorai represented the "irrationalism" that paved the way for "modern rationalism" in Japanese thought. Although Maruyama later modified this view, the brilliance of his original argument has made Sorai a focus of contemporary concern, both in Japan and in the West. Among his major works are *Gakusoku* (1711–17; tr *Instructions for Students*, 1976), *Bemmei* (1717?, Distinguishing Names), and *Rongochō* (1718?, Commentaries on the Analects). See also KOGAKU; KOBUNJIGAKU.

ohagi 御萩

Also called *botamochi*. A confection made with steamed *mochi-gome* (glutinous rice). The *mochi-gome* is formed into balls and covered with *an* (sweet bean paste) or *kinako* (sweetened soybean powder). *Ohagi* was traditionally made during the spring and autumn equinoxes. The term *ohagi* comes from the autumn flower *hagi* (bush clover), while *botamochi* comes from the spring flower *botan* (peony).

ohaguro 御歯黒

Tooth blackening, also known as *kane*. Until the late 19th century the custom was believed to enhance sex appeal and help maintain healthy teeth. The mixture used was made by soaking iron or nails in tea, *sake*, and other ingredients to produce a liquid blackened by the metal's oxidation. Until about the 12th century tooth blackening was a sign of a girl's coming of age. During the 12th century the custom spread to male nobility and *samurai*. By the 18th century it was again confined to women and was fairly universal. Later, however, it was used by married women only, and the custom continued until the end of the 19th century, when Western influences rendered it obsolete.

ohajiki 御弾き

A children's game played with shells, pebbles, coin-shaped glass pieces, or other small, flat objects. The name derives from the Japanese verb *hajiku*, meaning "to flick." The game is played by scattering pieces on a flat surface, such as a *tatami* matted floor; players then take turns claiming them by hitting

one piece against another piece with the flick of a finger. The player with the most pieces wins. *Ohajiki* derived originally from *dangi*, a game introduced into Japan from China in the 8th century. It was played at court and by the nobility. In ancient times it was called *ishihajiki* ("pebble flicking") because it was played with small pebbles.

Ōhara 大原［町］

Town in southeastern Chiba Prefecture, central Honshū, on the Pacific Ocean. It is the second largest fishing port in the prefecture after CHŌSHI. Sea-bream fishing is a popular local sport. Pop: 21,271.

Ōhara 大原

District in the northeastern part of the city of Kyōto. A mountain village in the Heian period (794–1185), it produced charcoal and firewood that women peddlers called OHARAME sold in the city. Today Ōhara is a tourist area; attractions include the temple SANZEN'IN and the convent JAKKŌIN.

Ōhara Institute for Social Research 大原社会問題研究所

(Ōhara Shakai Mondai Kenkyūjo). Research institute founded in Ōsaka by business magnate ŌHARA MAGOSABURŌ in 1919. Statistician TAKANO IWASABURŌ was its first head. It pioneered social studies in Japan, attracting such scholars as KUSHIDA TAMIZŌ and HOSOKAWA KAROKU, and has published reports on Japanese labor conditions and social problems. The institute moved to Tōkyō in 1937 and became affiliated with Hōsei University in 1949. Its main publication is the annual *Nihon rōdō nenkan* (since 1920).

Ōhara Magosaburō 大原孫三郎

(1880–1943). Entrepreneur. Born in Okayama Prefecture. After studying at Tōkyō Semmon Gakkō (now Waseda University), Ōhara took over his father's business and served as president of Kurashiki Spinning, Kurashiki Silk Weaving (Kurashiki Kenshoku; now KURARAY CO, LTD), and the Chūgoku Bank. Ōhara believed that the basis of good management was the promotion of the welfare of the worker. His many contributions in the social and educational fields include the establishment of the ŌHARA INSTITUTE FOR SOCIAL RESEARCH (now at Hōsei University), the ŌHARA MUSEUM OF ART, a library, and a hospital.

oharame 大原女

Woman peddlers from Ōhara, Yase, Takano, and other outlying areas of the city of Kyōto. They have sold their wares—firewood, flowers, pickles, and the like—in the streets of Kyōto since the late Heian period (794–1185) and may be recognized by their distinctive costume, which includes an apron, black handcovers, and white leggings. They often carry their wares on their heads. Some are employed to clean the grounds of imperial gardens.

Ōhara Museum of Art 大原美術館

(Ōhara Bijutsukan). The first Japanese museum of modern Western art. Located in the city of Kurashiki, Okayama Prefecture. Opened in 1930. The collection was assembled by the artist Kojima Torajirō (1881–1929) at the request of industrialist ŌHARA MAGOSABURŌ. With El Greco's *Annunciation* as its centerpiece, the collection is further enhanced by works of such artists as Renoir, Gauguin, Matisse, and Rodin. Among the museum's several annexes are a modern art gallery with works by Kandinsky and Pollock; a handicraft wing containing ceramics, woodblock prints, and dyed textiles; and an Oriental wing containing ancient Chinese art. Of the approximately 2,700 items in the museum and annex collections, roughly 600 are paintings.

Ohara school 小原流

(Ohararyū). A school of FLOWER ARRANGEMENT (*ikebana*), established by Ohara Unshin (1861–1916) when he broke with the IKENOBŌ school in the mid-Meiji period (1868–1912). Ohara's introduction of *moribana*, which makes use of flat, shallow vases, later led to the development of styles based on natural landscape and traditional RIMPA painting. Although its emphasis is on *moribana*, the school also incorporates *heika*, a type of *ikebana* that makes use of tall, slender vases. The school's main offices are in Tōkyō and Kōbe, with 160 chapters around Japan. In addition to the Ohara Center in New York, there are 51 other chapters overseas. The third-generation head of the school is Ohara Hōun (b 1908).

Ōhara Sōichiro 大原総一郎

(1909–68). Business executive. Born in Okayama Prefecture, he was a graduate of Tōkyō University. Ōhara joined Kurashiki Silk Weaving (now KURARAY CO, LTD), managed by his father, ŌHARA MAGOSABURŌ, and became its president in 1939. He was concurrently president of Kurabō Industries in 1941. Successfully expanding all of his father's businesses, Ōhara succeeded in developing vinylon with Kuraray's own technology after World War II and started its commercial production in 1950.

Ōhara Tomie 大原富枝

(1912–). Novelist. Born in Kōchi Prefecture; attended Kōchi Women's Normal School. Her *Sutomai tsumbo* (1956, Streptomycin Deafness) describes her experiences as a tuberculosis patient. Ōhara won the Noma Literary Prize for *En to iu onna* (1960, A Woman Called En), the story of the life of Nonaka En (1660–1725), the celebrated Edo-period (1600–1868) physician who was under house arrest for 40 years as the daughter of a political criminal. In 1976 Ōhara converted to Catholicism. Her other works include *Aburahamu no makuya* (1981, Abraham's Tent).

Ōhara Yūgaku 大原幽学

(1797–1858). Teacher and moralist who worked to revitalize the peasant economy. A native of Nagoya, he left home in 1814 and traveled widely in western Japan, acquiring knowledge of Confucianism, Buddhism, Shintō, poetry, farming, and augury. He later traveled for 20 years throughout the Kantō region, depending on the hospitality of rural families. In 1850 he opened a school, the Kaishinrō, in Shimōsa Province (now part of Chiba Prefecture), where he lectured on farming techniques, land reclamation, and land use. He also exhorted peasants to practice thrift and frugality and to form mutual savings funds. His activities came into conflict with the policies of the shogunate, and he was placed under house arrest. Even after receiving a pardon, he was overwhelmed by the expenses of the judicial proceedings, and, also ashamed of the immoral behavior of several disciples, he committed suicide.

Ōhashi Sahei 大橋佐平

(1836–1901). Founder of the publishing house HAKUBUNKAN. Born in what is now Niigata Prefecture. In 1887, together with his son Ōhashi Shintarō (1862–1944), he founded Hakubunkan. Within a little more than two years Hakubunkan established 13 different magazines and later began to publish books. By the turn of the century it had established the enormously influential magazines TAIYŌ, BUNGEI KURABU, and *Shōnen sekai*.

Ōhira 大平[町]

Town in southern Tochigi Prefecture, central Honshū. Although located in an agricultural zone and famous for its strawberries, Ōhira has in recent years become the home of electronics and automobile factories. Pop: 27,782.

Ōhira Masayoshi 大平正芳

(1910–80) Politician and prime minister (1978–80). Born in Kagawa Prefecture. A graduate of Tōkyō Shōka Daigaku (now Hitotsubashi University), Ōhira pursued a career in the Ministry of Finance and in 1949 became private secretary to Finance Minister IKEDA HAYATO. He was elected to the House of Representatives in 1952 as a member of the LIBERAL PARTY (Jiyūtō) and later served as foreign minister and minister of finance. He became secretary-general of the LIBERAL DEMOCRATIC PARTY in 1976 and party president and prime minister in 1978. In the summer of 1980 he dissolved the House of Representatives after a no-confidence vote against his cabinet and died 10 days before the ensuing election.

Ōhiroma 大広間

(Great Hall). A chamber in the Omote (Exterior or "public") section of the central enclosure (*hommaru*) of EDO CASTLE during the Edo period (1600–1868). It was the chamber in which some 20 of the most distinguished TOZAMA *daimyō* (known as *kunimochi daimyō* because their domains covered one or more *kuni* or provinces) assembled for formal audiences (see SANKIN KŌTAI) with the Tokugawa shōgun. The Ōhiroma and other chambers were also used to receive foreign emissaries, groups of lesser shogunal vassals, and shogunate officials. Other Omote rooms served as administrative offices.

Ōi 大井[町]

Town in southern Saitama Prefecture, central Honshū. An important truck-farming area for the Tōkyō market, Ōi is known for its carrots, burdock, and watermelons. In recent years there has been a notable increase in factory and residential construction. Pop: 39,213.

oie sōdō 御家騒動

(domainal disturbances). Factional struggles within a domain (HAN) in which one group of retainers was pitted against another over a variety of matters that affected the well-being of the domain and its members. *Oie sōdō* were a principal form of political disorder during the Edo period (1600–1868). The best known are the Kuroda Sōdō of the 1620s in the Fukuoka domain (now part of Fukuoka Prefecture), the DATE SŌDŌ of the 1660s in the Sendai domain (now Miyagi Prefecture), and the Kaga Sōdō of the 1750s in the domain ruled by the MAEDA FAMILY.

One of the chief reasons for the frequency of *oie sōdō* was the fact that in the

Ōhara school Lotus, water hyacinth, and arrowhead in a *moribana* composition employing a flat, shallow vase—a style characteristic of this school of flower arrangement.

Tokugawa political system (BAKUHAN SYSTEM) real administrative authority in the domain resided with the domainal government. Since the decisions of domainal governments affected domain members, retainers formed groups or factions to advance their own interests. Factional leaders tried to influence affairs by taking sides in daimyō succession disputes or by supporting one group or another of high officials within the domainal government.

The *sōdō* of the 1630s resulted in the reduction, transfer, or confiscation (KAIEKI) of domains and the proliferation of masterless *samurai* (RŌNIN). The period of greatest turbulence was around 1640, when disturbances ruined the Ikoma family at Takamatsu (now part of Kagawa Prefecture), the Katō family at Aizu (now part of Fukushima Prefecture), and the Ikeda family at Yamazaki in Harima Province (now part of Hyōgo Prefecture).

Ōigawa 大井川

River in northern and central Shizuoka Prefecture, central Honshū, originating in the Akaishi Mountains and emptying into the western part of Suruga Bay. There are deep valleys and gorges in the upper reaches, the middle reaches form terraces and meanders, and the lower reaches form the Ōigawa Plain. The upper reaches are important sources of lumber and electric power. Length: 160 km (99 mi); area of drainage basin: 1,280 sq km (495 sq mi).

Oikawa Heiji 及川平治

(1875–1939). Educator. Born in Miyagi Prefecture. From 1907 to 1936 Oikawa was active as the director of the elementary school attached to the Akashi Women's Normal School in Hyōgo Prefecture. He advocated a German theory of group instruction, stressed the value of the child's experiences, and put into practice an educational method emphasizing activity on the part of the students. These reflected the progressive education movement then underway in Japan. See SHIN KYŌIKU UNDŌ.

Ōi Kentarō 大井憲太郎

(1843–1922). Politician and one of the leading figures of the FREEDOM AND PEOPLE'S RIGHTS MOVEMENT of the 1870s and 1880s. Born in what is now Ōita Prefecture. In his youth he went to Edo (now Tōkyō) to study political theory, law, and economics. He became famous for his debate with the scholar-bureaucrat KATŌ HIROYUKI over the establishment of a national assembly. In 1882 Ōi joined the JIYŪTŌ (Liberal Party), becoming a spokesman for its extremist wing. In 1885 he was arrested in a plot to establish a reform government in Korea (see ŌSAKA INCIDENT)

Ōhira Masayoshi A Liberal Democratic Party member who served as prime minister from 1978 until his death in 1980.

oiran At the Jidai Festival held in the Asakusa district of Tōkyō, a woman dressed as an oiran helps recreate the oiran dōchū, a customary procession of high-class prostitutes of the Edo period.

and sentenced to nine years in jail. Released in 1889, Ōi campaigned for universal manhood suffrage. In 1892 he decided to form his own party, the TŌYŌ JIYŪTŌ (Oriental Liberal Party). The party, which called for universal male suffrage, a strong foreign policy, and the protection of laborers and tenant farmers, was dissolved after two months. Even after retiring from politics, Ōi continued to work for the poor.

oil crisis of 1973   石油危機
(sekiyu kiki). Often referred to as the "oil shock" (sekiyu shokku); the economic and political crisis resulting from oil export restrictions adopted by Arab countries toward pro-Israeli governments during the 1973 Middle East war. The quadrupling of oil prices by the Organization of Petroleum Exporting Countries (OPEC) caused an economic recession in Japan and prompted a major revision of the nation's Middle East policy and the adoption of measures to reduce dependence on oil. On 22 November, the cabinet adopted a new set of policies toward the Middle East, including the recognition of the rights of the Palestinian people, and pledged to review all of its relations with Israel, which prior to this time had been quite close.

The revision of Japan's foreign policy brought the short-term crisis to an end, but the impact of higher oil prices continued to be felt. Inflation continued at unprecedented rates and in 1974, for the first time since the postwar recovery, the gross national product declined. The international balance of payments was also thrown into deficit. The oil crisis is considered by many to have been a watershed, marking the end of the period of rapid growth in the Japanese economy. In the ensuing years, government policy emphasized stable growth (antei seichō) at a moderate level. See also MIDDLE EAST AND JAPAN.

oiran   花魁
A type of high-class prostitute of the Edo period (1600–1868). The word oiran refers to a certain class of YŪJO (licensed prostitute) in the YOSHIWARA brothel and entertainment district of Edo (now Tōkyō). Oiran enter-

tained their clients in well-appointed zashiki (sitting rooms) and often had several attendants to see to their personal needs. A common sight in Yoshiwara was the oiran dōchū, a public procession of oiran clad in their finest kimono and accompanied by their attendants.

Oirasegawa   奥入瀬川
River in southeastern Aomori Prefecture, northern Honshū, originating in Lake Towada and flowing east into the Pacific Ocean. The 14-km (9-mi) stretch below the river's source is known as the Oirase Gorge and is noted for forests and ravines. Length: 67 km (42 mi).

Ōishi Kuranosuke→Ōishi Yoshio

Ōishi Yoshio   大石良雄
(1659–1703). Also known as Ōishi Kuranosuke. Samurai of the Akō domain (now part of Hyōgo Prefecture) and leader of the band of warriors who avenged the death of their lord, Asano Naganori (1665–1701), in the FORTY-SEVEN RŌNIN INCIDENT. Ōishi studied military science under YAMAGA SOKŌ and Confucianism under ITŌ JINSAI. In 1679 he succeeded his grandfather as chief retainer to Asano. In 1701 Asano was deprived of his domain and ordered to commit suicide for having drawn his sword in Edo Castle against KIRA YOSHINAKA, a Tokugawa shogunate official who had caused him humiliation. For two years Ōishi and his followers plotted revenge, and on 31 January 1703 they succeeded in killing Kira. Soon afterward Ōishi and the others were ordered to commit suicide. The men were widely acclaimed for their loyalty and heroism and immediately celebrated in popular literature.

Ōiso   大磯[町]
Town in south-central Kanagawa Prefecture, central Honshū, on Sagami Bay. Ōiso was a post-station town on the TŌKAIDŌ highway during the Edo period (1600–1868). Favored by a mild climate and convenient to Tōkyō, it is primarily a residential town for the well-to-do. Pop: 31,599.

Ōita   大分[市]
Capital of Ōita Prefecture, Kyūshū, on BEPPU BAY. The seat (kokufu) of a provincial government in the ancient period, it flourished in the 16th century under the rule of ŌTOMO SŌRIN, who traded with the Portuguese and invited Christian missionaries. Industries include oil refining, petrochemicals, metallurgy, pulp, and food processing. Mandarin oranges and loquats are grown. Ōita is a major transportation center. The mountain TAKASAKIYAMA is known for its colony of wild monkeys. Pop: 408,501.

Ōita Plain   大分平野
(Ōita Heiya). Alluvial plain located in central Ōita Prefecture, Kyūshū, bordering the Inland Sea. Composed of the deltas of the rivers Ōnogawa and Ōitagawa, the coastal region is an industrial zone with oil refining and steel works. The major city is Ōita. Length: 10 km (6 mi); width: 20 km (12 mi).

Ōita Prefecture   大分県
(Ōita Ken). Located in northeastern Kyūshū and bordered to the north and east by the Inland Sea, to the south by Miyazaki Prefecture, and to the west by Kumamoto and Fukuoka prefectures. Its terrain is largely mountainous, with the southern part of the

prefecture occupied by part of the KYŪSHŪ MOUNTAINS and the northern part by a chain of volcanic mountains. Level areas are concentrated along the coast. The climate is generally mild, with heavy precipitation along the east coast.

Archaeological excavations have yielded numerous artifacts of the Jōmon (ca 10,000 BC–ca 300 BC) and Yayoi (ca 300 BC–ca AD 300) periods. The area was originally known as Toyo Province and later divided into two parts, Buzen and Bungo, under the ancient provincial system. It was further divided into numerous small domains during the feudal period. The present name was adopted in 1871, and the present prefectural boundaries were established in 1876.

Ōita remains primarily agricultural. The principal crops are rice, mandarin oranges, and vegetables. Cattle breeding, forestry, and fishing are also important. Industry has been limited to small-scale local enterprises, although heavy and chemical industries in the coastal districts have been developed.

Attractions include Aso Kujū National Park and the Inland Sea National Park, several quasi-national and prefectural parks, the gorge YABAKEI, the mountain Yufudake, the highland Kijima Kōgen, and the KUNISAKI PENINSULA. The Kunisaki and Usuki areas contain ancient Buddhist statues carved from large rocks. Ōita has numerous hot-spring resorts, including the popular BEPPU. Area: 6,338 sq km (2,447 sq mi); pop: 1,236,942; capital: ŌITA. Other major cities include Beppu, NAKATSU, HITA, and SAIKI.

Ōizumi   大泉[町]
Town on the northern bank of the river Tonegawa in southeastern Gumma Prefecture, central Honshū. Ōizumi is an industrial area, manufacturing electrical machinery and appliances. Pop: 39,232.

ojigi→bowing

Ōjin, Emperor   応神天皇
(late 4th to early 5th century; Ōjin Tennō). The 15th sovereign (tennō) in the traditional count (which includes several legendary emperors). Personal name Homutawake no Mikoto. He is said to have been the fourth son of the legendary emperor Chūai and the legendary empress JINGŪ. Native as well as contemporary Chinese and Korean sources report that it was during Ōjin's reign that immigrants (KIKAJIN) such as YUZUKI NO KIMI and WANI came to Japan from the Korean peninsula. It is generally agreed that Ōjin was an historical figure and that his reign was marked by growing imperial power. He received tribute from the aboriginal EZO people of northern Honshū and dispatched TAKENOUCHI NO SUKUNE to subdue Kyūshū. Ōjin's imposing tomb (ŌJIN MAUSOLEUM) is at Habikino, Ōsaka Prefecture.

Ōjin Mausoleum   応神天皇陵
(Ōjin Tennōryō). An early-5th-century keyhole-shaped mounded tomb (KOFUN) in the city of Habikino, Ōsaka Prefecture. Believed to be the mausoleum of Emperor ŌJIN, the tomb measures 415 meters (1,362 ft) in length and is second in size only to the NINTOKU MAUSOLEUM. It is built in three tiers and surrounded by two moats and two dikes. Although the tomb has not been excavated, HANIWA funerary sculptures in the form of houses, waterfowl, and ceremonial sunshades have been recovered from its edge and inner dike. The tomb's monumental size attests to the power of the 5th-century rulers

Ōita Prefecture
Location and
Prefectural Crest

of the YAMATO COURT (ca 4th century–ca mid-7th century) and the opulence of Middle Kofun period culture. The tomb is mentioned in both the NIHON SHOKI (720) and the 10th-century ENGI SHIKI.

Ōji Paper Co, Ltd 王子製紙[株]

(Ōji Seishi). Firm engaged in the manufacture of paper, paperboard, and paper converted products, as well as the purchase and sale of timber. Established in 1873 by SHIBUSAWA EIICHI, it is the oldest joint-stock company in Japan and is closely tied to the Mitsui group. After World War II, Ōji Paper was divided into three companies (Ōji, JŪJŌ PAPER CO, LTD, and HONSHŪ PAPER CO, LTD) in accordance with the ANTIMONOPOLY LAW. Ōji produces a wide range of paper (newsprint; printing, packaging, and specialty papers; and tissue) and white paperboard. More than 50 percent of its wood resources come from overseas, mainly from North America. Joint ventures for pulp and paper production have been formed in New Zealand, Brazil, and Canada. Sales for the fiscal year ending March 1991 totaled ¥482.0 billion (US $3.5 billion). In the same year capitalization stood at ¥46.1 billion (US $336.0 million). Headquarters are in Tōkyō.

Ojiya 小千谷[市]

City in central Niigata Prefecture, central Honshū. Situated on the valley mouth of the river Shinanogawa, Ojiya developed as a river port. It was long known for its Ojiya *chijimi* (a crinkled linen fabric), the weaving of which has been designated an Intangible Cultural Property. The city is also noted for its beautiful *nishikigoi* (colored carp). Pop: 43,437.

Ōjōyōshū 往生要集

(The Essentials of Pure Land Rebirth). A compendium of important passages from the Chinese Buddhist canon on the Pure Land of the Buddha AMIDA and the means, principally the NEMBUTSU, to achieve rebirth there; compiled by the Tendai priest GENSHIN and completed in 985. One of the most widely read works of Japanese Buddhist literature. Its 10 chapters discuss in great depth the bondage of karmic transmigration as a painful alternative to Pure Land rebirth; the pleasures and superiority of Amida's Pure Land; the concept, practice, and rewards of *nembutsu;* and various doctrinal problems. The *Ōjōyōshū* strongly influenced the teachings of PURE LAND BUDDHISM, and its vivid descriptions terrified and beguiled generations of common folk. The *Ōjōyōshū* takes the position that while the simple utterance of the name of Amida is inferior to the *nembutsu-zammai* (Skt: *samādhi;* concentration of mind) of TENDAI SECT teachings, it is the most practical way to salvation for the average person.

Oka Asajirō 丘浅次郎

(1868–1944). Biologist. Born in what is now Shizuoka Prefecture. After studying in Germany, where he received a degree for his research on leeches, Oka became known as an authority on the comparative morphology of marine animals. However, it was his numerous writings applying Darwin's theory of evolution to social problems that won him fame. Examining society through the theory of natural selection, he hoped to arrive at a formulation of the ideal society. Critical of all forms of dogmatism, he advocated the scientific method (i.e., empirical verification) in social science.

Okabe Kinjirō 岡部金治郎

(1896–1984). Electrical engineer; known for his development of the split-anode magnetron, which made possible a practical microwave-frequency communication system and laid the groundwork for the development of radar. His work on several types of magnetrons has had a profound influence on worldwide research in the field. Born in Nagoya, Okabe graduated from Tōhoku University in 1922. He taught at Ōsaka University from 1935 to 1956 and received the Order of Culture in 1944.

Okada Beisanjin 岡田米山人

(1744–1820). A leader of the BUNJINGA (literati painting) movement in Ōsaka. A self-taught artist, he turned to painting in middle age and was regarded as an eccentric in his lifetime, along with his friend URAGAMI GYOKUDŌ. In general Beisanjin's compositions are large, expansive, and generously endowed with bold, symbolic forms. His brushwork was studied, rather awkward, and plain. His figure paintings, often comic, have an appealing eccentricity. A few of his extant paintings were done with his son, OKADA HANKŌ.

In 1775 Beisanjin was living in Ōsaka as a grain merchant, and some time in the 1790s he was hired by the Tōdō family in Ise Province (now part of Mie Prefecture) to serve at their Ōsaka rice storehouses. Retiring from his position with the Tōdō family around 1809, Beisanjin moved to a place nearby, although his family continued to operate its small grain business. After his wife died in 1818, he devoted himself to painting, becoming a model of the literati artist in his style and his manner of living.

Okada Eiji 岡田英次

(1920–   ). Film actor who has appeared in Japanese, French, and American motion pictures. Born in Chiba Prefecture, he attended Keiō University. In 1946 he joined the Shinkyō Theater Group (Shinkyō Gekidan) and three years later made his film debut in Shibuya Minoru's (1907–80) *Hana no sugao* (1949, Face of a Flower). In IMAI TADASHI's *Mata au hi made* (1950, Until the Day We Meet Again), Okada performed in the first kissing scene in a Japanese film; it was shot with a glass window between the two. He also appeared in Shibuya's *Seidō no Kirisuto* (1955, The Bronze Christ), Alain Resnais's

Hiroshima mon amour (1959), and TESHIGAHARA HIROSHI's award-winning *Suna no onna* (1964, Woman in the Dunes).

Okada Hankō 岡田半江

(1782–1846). Literati painter from Ōsaka; son of OKADA BEISANJIN. At home he learned from the painters, scholars, and literary figures who were members of his father's circle. His early efforts in painting and calligraphy, often signed Shōbei (Little Bei), were in his father's style. By 1809 he was working for the Tōdō family, probably at his father's old post at the Tōdō rice storehouse in Ōsaka. On his father's death in 1820 he inherited the family business.

By 1832 he had resigned from the Tōdō post and built a studio home on the banks of the river Yodogawa near Temma Bridge. During a short-lived rebellion in 1837 led by his friend ŌSHIO HEIHACHIRŌ, it is believed that Hankō's studio burned down in the fire that devastated much of Ōsaka. Hankō withdrew to Sumiyoshi, down the coast from Ōsaka, where he seems to have spent the remainder of his life. He painted little for two or three years after he left Ōsaka, but when he took up his brush again, he created a flood of landscape paintings in the BUNJINGA (literati painting) style. His style in full maturity can be characterized as mellow in color, delicate in handling, and often atmospheric in depiction, related to the work of AOKI MOKUBEI and TANOMURA CHIKUDEN.

Okada Keisuke 岡田啓介

(1868–1952). Admiral and prime minister (1934–36). Born in what is now Fukui Prefecture; a graduate of the Naval Academy and the Naval War College. Okada served in both the Sino-Japanese (1894–95) and Russo-Japanese (1904–05) wars and was promoted to admiral in 1924. In 1927 he was named navy minister. As a military councillor (*gunji sangikan*), he worked for the ratification of the disarmament treaty resulting from the London Naval Conference of 1930 (see LONDON NAVAL CONFERENCES). In July 1934 he was named prime minister. Okada narrowly escaped death at the hands of extremist military officers in the FEBRUARY 26TH INCIDENT (1936). His entire cabinet resigned on 27 February when it mistakenly assumed that he had been killed. Okada himself re-

Okada Keisuke

okage mairi These spontaneous "thanksgiving" pilgrimages attracted millions of people. The 1830 mass pilgrimage is depicted in this late-Edo-period handscroll.

Okakura Kakuzō Noted for his efforts to preserve traditional Japanese art forms, Okakura also advanced the understanding of Asian culture in the West.

Okame and Hyottoko The chubby, smiling Okame and the purse-lipped Hyottoko are often paired in masked comic dances at village festivals and in folk plays.

signed on February 28th. Okada then served as a *jūshin* (senior statesman) and played a leading role in overthrowing the TŌJŌ HIDEKI cabinet (1941–44) near the end of World War II.

Okada Mokichi   岡田茂吉

(1882–1955). Founder of SEKAI KYŪSEI KYŌ, one of Japan's NEW RELIGIONS. Born in Tōkyō, Okada was an active member of ŌMOTO before establishing his own organization in 1935. This group underwent several name changes, finally being renamed the Sekai Kyūsei Kyō (Religion for the Salvation of the World). Okada's followers believed him to have divine healing powers. He claimed that the god of creation appointed him his messiah during a revelation in 1926, asking him to create a paradise on earth by eliminating human suffering.

Okada Saburōsuke   岡田三郎助

(1869–1939). Western-style painter. Born in what is now Saga Prefecture. He first studied privately with Soyama Yukihiko (1859–92) and then with KUME KEIICHIRŌ and KURODA SEIKI in Tōkyō. In 1896 he helped to found the artists' group HAKUBAKAI and taught in the newly opened Department of Western Arts of the Tōkyō Bijutsu Gakkō (now Tōkyō University of Fine Arts and Music). In 1902 he succeeded to Kuroda's post at the Tōkyō Bijutsu Gakkō. With FUJISHIMA TAKEJI, he established the Hongō Kaiga Kenkyūjo (Hongō Institute of Painting) in 1912. His paintings are in the delicate plein-air manner; he is best known for his landscapes and his portraits of women, which reflect a decorative, traditional Japanese style. He received the Order of Culture in 1937.

Okada Takematsu   岡田武松

(1874–1956). Meteorologist who contributed greatly to the advancement of practical meteorology in Japan through his numerous technical and administrative innovations. Born in Chiba Prefecture, he graduated from Tōkyō University in 1899 with a degree in physics. In 1930 he became president of the Japan Meteorological Society. He instituted important innovations (such as airborne weather observation) and received the Order of Culture in 1949. His publications include *Kishōgaku kōwa* (1908, A Discourse on Meteorology) and *Kishōgaku* (1927, Meteorology).

Okada Yoshio   岡田善雄

(1928–). Cell biologist. Born in Hiroshima Prefecture. Graduate of Ōsaka University. In 1972 Okada became a professor at the Institute for Molecular and Cellular Biology at Ōsaka University and in 1982 was appointed chairman of the institute. He pioneered a technique of artificially inducing cell fusion by infecting animal cells with viruses (notably the hemagglutinin virus of Japan or HVJ, also known as the "Sendai virus") and established a procedure for bringing about cell fusion outside a living body. The results of his research have played a leading role in the development of bioscience and biotechnology. He received the Order of Culture in 1987.

Okadera   岡寺

(formally known as Ryūgaiji). Temple in Asuka Mura in the Takaichi district of Nara Prefecture belonging to the Buzan branch (see HASEDERA) of the SHINGON SECT of Buddhism. Okadera was established in 663 by Emperor Tenji (r 661–672). The temple was turned into a center of esoteric Buddhism by KŪKAI (774–835), founder of the Shingon sect and supposed sculptor of Okadera's main object of worship, the image of the bodhisattva Nyoirin Kannon (Cintāmaṇicakra Avalokiteśvara). Other temple sculptures date from the 7th and 8th centuries. Okadera is the 7th stopping place for pilgrims touring the 33 holy places dedicated to Kannon in western Japan.

Ōkagami   大鏡

(tr *Ōkagami: The Great Mirror*, 1980). Second of eight "historical tales" (*rekishi monogatari*; see MONOGATARI BUNGAKU) written in Japanese, so called in contrast to the RIKKOKUSHI (Six National Histories) and other historical sources written in classical Chinese. Compiled by an unknown hand in the late 11th or early 12th century, it covers the years 850 to 1025, concentrating on the lives and families of the Fujiwara regents and chancellors, particularly FUJIWARA NO MICHINAGA. It duplicates much of the material of its predecessor, EIGA MONOGATARI (tr *A Tale of Flowering Fortunes*, 1980). *Ōkagami* consists of biographical sketches and anecdotes and uses a language close to the common speech of the time. *Ōkagami* can be divided into three basic sections: biographical sketches of emperors from Montoku (r 850–858) to GO-ICHIJŌ (r 1016–36), emphasizing their ties with the Fujiwara family; accounts of Fujiwara noblemen and their offspring, with an account of the family from its founding by FUJIWARA NO KAMATARI up to the time of Michinaga; and miscellaneous tales of courtiers and court life.

okage mairi   御蔭参り

(literally, "thanksgiving pilgrimage"). Spontaneous, periodic mass pilgrimages to the ISE SHRINE in the Edo period (1600–1868). Although access to the shrine was originally severely restricted, the Ise Shrine began to draw increasingly large numbers of pilgrims from all levels of society after the 10th century. By the late Muromachi period (1333–1568) it was commonly believed that each Japanese should visit the shrine at least once during his lifetime. Pilgrims thronged to Ise, especially during the *okagedoshi* ("thanksgiving year"), the year following the reconstruction of the shrine sanctuary, which was supposed to take place every 20 years in order to preserve the purity of the shrine.

The *okage mairi* differed from the regular pilgrimages in that they were frenzied, spontaneous events occurring at intervals of roughly 60 years and involving millions of people, who would occupy the roads to Ise for several months. In all there were four major *okage mairi* in the Edo period: 1650, 1705, 1771, and 1830. These mass pilgrimages typically were touched off by a rumor that in a certain district of Ise, amulets (GOFU) miraculously fell from heaven. For some the mass pilgrimage was a profound religious experience and a unique chance to receive the special blessings of AMATERASU ŌMIKAMI; for others it provided an outlet for pent-up emotions, with wild dancing (*okage odori*), singing, and cavorting taking place en route. See also EEJANAIKA.

Oka Kiyoshi   岡潔

(1901–78). Mathematician known for his work with analytical functions of several variables. Oka proved Runge's theorem in general and was the first to solve the problems of the domain of holomorphy and the difficult Cousin problems. Born in Ōsaka Prefecture, he graduated from Kyōto University and studied in France for three years. He taught successively at Kyōto University, Hiroshima University, and Nara Women's University. He was also noted as a conservative social critic and published many highly regarded essays and social commentaries. In 1960 he received the Order of Culture.

Okakura Kakuzō   岡倉覚三

(1862–1913). Art critic, philosopher, and interpreter of the East to the Western world; known primarily for his attempts to protect and restore traditional Japanese art forms. More commonly known by his pen name, Okakura Tenshin. Born in Yokohama, Okakura began studying English when he was 9; at 11 he entered the Tōkyō School of Foreign Languages (Tōkyō Gaikokugo Gakkō) and at 15 the newly created Tōkyō University, where he studied under Ernest F. FENOLLOSA. After graduation he worked in the art administration section of the Ministry of Education.

In 1886 Okakura traveled to Europe and America to study Western art and art education. He was one of the founders of Japan's first official art academy, Tōkyō Bijutsu Gakkō (now TŌKYŌ UNIVERSITY OF FINE ARTS AND MUSIC), which opened in 1889. He was curator of the Imperial Household Museum (now the TŌKYŌ NATIONAL MUSEUM) and was also involved in the publication of Japan's first art magazine, KOKKA (National Essence), and the organization of art exhibits to introduce works of younger artists. Upon his resignation from the Ministry of Education, he helped form the Nihon Bijutsuin (JAPAN FINE ARTS ACADEMY) to synthesize Japanese and Western art forms. He also lectured and traveled in the United States and Europe as part of an effort to educate the West about Asian culture. His books include *The Ideals of the East* (1903), *The Awakening of Japan* (1904), and *The Book of Tea* (1906). In 1905 Okakura became adviser and later assistant curator to the Chinese and Japanese Department of the Boston Museum of Fine Arts. In the last years of his life he commuted often between Boston and Japan.

Okakura Tenshin → Okakura Kakuzō

Okame and Hyottoko
おかめとひょっとこ

(Okame *to* Hyottoko). Two comic masks often worn in theatricals or displayed in houses and shops. Okame, also known as Otafuku, is a plump, rosy-cheeked, laughing maiden's face, whose well-fed look symbolizes prosperity. A modification of the KYŌGEN Oto mask, it is often worn in folk plays (see KAGURA) or KABUKI dances. Hyottoko is the face of a man whose pursed protruding lips are skewed to one side. It is thought to derive either from the *kyōgen* Usobuki mask or from the face of a man trying to kindle a fire. Hyottoko and Okame are often paired in comic dances during village agricultural festivals.

Okamoto Ayako
岡本綾子

(1951–). Professional golfer. Born in Hiroshima Prefecture. In 1979 she won the Japan Ladies' Professional Golf Championship by scoring an astonishing 17 under par for three rounds, and this won her a place in *The Guinness Book of World Records*. In 1981 she acquired her US tour license and went on to win 14 tournaments on the US women's golf tour over the next nine years. In 1987 she was the top earner on the US women's tour and won the Ladies' Professional Golf Association Player of the Year Award.

Okamoto Ippei
岡本一平

(1886–1948). Cartoonist. Born in Hokkaidō. Graduate of Tōkyō Bijutsu Gakkō (now Tōkyō University of Fine Arts and Music). Okamoto studied under the Western-style painter FUJISHIMA TAKEJI. He began to draw cartoons for the daily newspaper *Asahi shimbun* in 1912 and became the leading cartoonist of the Taishō period (1912–26). He enjoyed widespread popularity for his un-

conventional drawing style, his sharp wit, and his resistance to authority. He was married to the novelist OKAMOTO KANOKO; their son is the artist OKAMOTO TARŌ. Okamoto was a forerunner of today's political cartoonists and helped to establish cartooning as a popular art form.

Okamoto Kanoko
岡本かの子

(1889–1939). Poet and novelist. Born Ōnuki Kano in Tōkyō. Influenced by her older brother Shōsen and his classmate TANIZAKI JUN'ICHIRŌ, at age 17 she started contributing TANKA (31-syllable poems) and Western-style poems to magazines, including MYŌJŌ. The first of her five *tanka* anthologies was *Karoki netami* (1912).

In 1910 Kanoko married OKAMOTO IPPEI. The first decade of the marriage was troubled, but eventually Ippei came to accept and support her pursuit of a writing career. She became interested in the Buddhist prophet SHINRAN, a development that led to her fame as a writer on Buddhism. Her first critically acknowledged fiction was *Tsuru wa yamiki* (1936, The Dying Crane), a novelette about the last days of the writer AKUTAGAWA RYŪNOSUKE. Her short stories and novels repeatedly treat the weight of a family's ancestral influences on individuals, as in "Karei" (1939, Ancestral Spirits), and the primordial power of woman, as in "Hana wa mijikashi" (1937, The Brief Life of Flowers), "Rōgishō" (1938, The Aging Geisha), and *Shōjō ruten* (1939, Metempsychosis). Kanoko has been criticized for her "uncontrolled passion," narcissism, and excessive literary flourishes, yet she is at the same time admired for the richness of her language.

Okamoto Kansuke
岡本監輔

(1839–1904). Explorer, government official, and schoolteacher, who promoted Japan's northern expansion during the late 19th century. Born in Awa Province (now Tokushima Prefecture), Okamoto grew concerned, while still quite young, about Russia's looming proximity to Japan. Between 1863 and 1865 he made three trips to SAKHALIN as a surveyor. He repeatedly urged authorities to occupy and take over all of Sakhalin, regardless of Russian reactions. His views conflicted with those of KURODA KIYOTAKA, a leading figure in the Hokkaidō Colonization Office (KAITAKU-SHI). In protest Okamoto resigned as chief of the Karafuto (Sakhalin) Colonial Office in 1870. Five years later Japan relinquished Sakhalin to Russia, in return for the central and northern Kuril Islands. During the 1880s and 1890s Okamoto tried to organize a group to colonize the northern Kurils, but his efforts met with little direct success.

Okamoto Kidō
岡本綺堂

(1872–1939). Playwright and novelist. Real name Okamoto Keiji. Born in Tōkyō. While working as a reporter for a series of Tōkyō newspapers he wrote KABUKI plays, including *Shuzenji monogatari* (produced in 1911). He collaborated with actor Ichikawa Sadanji II (1880–1940) to develop a "new kabuki" that combined the nostalgic mood of traditional kabuki with the innovations of SHINGEKI drama. He is also known for *Hanshichi torimonochō* (1917–36), his popular detective stories set in the Edo period (1600–1868). His other plays include *Toribeyama shinjū* (1915) and *Gonza to Sukejū* (1926).

Okamoto Kihachi
岡本喜八

(1924–). Film director. Born in Tottori Prefecture, he graduated from Meiji University.

Okamoto Tarō Injured Arm. 1936. Oil on canvas. 114 × 162 cm. Private collection.

In 1943 he joined the TŌHŌ CO, LTD, as an assistant director. Promoted to director in 1958, he showed a talent for fast-moving action pictures and comedies and greatly influenced the form popular entertainment movies would take. Among his major films are *Dokuritsu gurentai* (1959, Street Gang on Its Own) and *Nihon no ichiban nagai hi* (1967, Japan's Longest Day).

Okamoto Tadanari
岡本忠成

(1932–90). Animator. Born in Ōsaka Prefecture. Okamoto studied filmmaking at Nihon University and started his own animation production company in 1964. As both producer and director, he created a wide variety of individualized short features in both cartoon and 3-D (puppet) animation, adapting puppet designs and painting techniques to his subject matter. His themes ranged from folk and fairy tales to social satire and science fiction. His well-known works include "Mochimochi no ki" (1972, The Mochimochi Tree) and "Okon jōruri" (1982, The Puppet Story Okon).

Okamoto Ayako
Known for her smooth form and precision, Okamoto won 17 tournaments on the US women's golf tour from 1982 to 1990.

Okamoto Tarō
岡本太郎

(1911–). Artist and essayist. Born in Tōkyō. Son of the cartoonist OKAMOTO IPPEI and the novelist OKAMOTO KANOKO. In 1929 he went to France and participated in the abstract art movement. After graduating from the University of Paris, he returned to Japan in 1940 and became a leader in the Japanese avant-garde art movement after World War II. He has painted murals and designed stage sets. The huge structure *Taiyō no tō* (Sun Tower), symbol of Expo '70, was designed by Okamoto. He wrote *Wasurerareta Nihon* (1961, Forgotten Japan), a study of the culture of Okinawa.

Okamoto Toyohiko
岡本豊彦

(1773–1845). Painter of the Shijō school. Born in Bitchū Province (now Okayama Prefecture). He studied painting in Bitchū under Kuroda Ryōzan (1757?–1814), an artist of the BUNJINGA (literati painting) style. The growing fame of the MARUYAMA-SHIJŌ SCHOOL brought him to Kyōto to study under MATSUMURA GOSHUN. He eventually became, with MATSUMURA KEIBUN, one of Goshun's most important pupils. His knowledge of, and respect for, Chinese culture, part of his early *bunjinga* training, was reflected in his works throughout his life. His finest work was in landscapes. Although his paintings lack Keibun's accessibility and bright colors, they have an astringent quality and an appealing lyricism.

Okamoto Kanoko
This writer, who published her first volume of verse in 1912, later gained renown for her impassioned novels.

Ōkawa Shūmei
A right-wing ideologue
influential in the 1920s
and 1930s, Ōkawa was
a lifelong opponent of
European colonialism
in Asia.

Okamura Corporation

[株]岡村製作所

(Okamura Seisakusho). Manufacturer and distributor of steel office furniture. Incorporated in 1946. The firm developed integrated office systems, including partition walls with built-in air conditioners and under-floor wiring systems. It also produces store furniture such as shelving, display fixtures, and refrigerated showcases. The company has eight factories, including one in Thailand, as well as technical tie-ups with 18 companies in the United States, Germany, the United Kingdom, Italy, Finland, Denmark, Canada, Korea, and Australia. Sales for the fiscal year ending March 1991 totaled ¥181.9 billion (US $1.3 billion), and capitalization stood at ¥17.6 billion (US $128.3 million). Headquarters are in Yokohama.

Okanishi Ichū

岡西惟中

(1639–1711). HAIKU poet and scholar of the early Edo period (1600–1868). Known as the principal theoretician and spokesman of NISHIYAMA SŌIN's school of haiku, the DANRIN SCHOOL, whose iconoclastic stance he defended during heated debates with the rival Teimon school. Born in Inaba Province (now part of Tottori Prefecture), he lived for a time in Okayama and from middle age settled in Ōsaka. From around the age of 40, his activities within haiku circles diminished as his interests shifted to composing RENGA (linked verse) and classical Chinese poetry. His main works include *Haikai mōgyū* (1675) and *Kinrai haikai fūtai shō* (1679).

Okano Keijirō

岡野敬次郎

(1865–1925). Legal scholar and government minister. Born in Kōzuke Province (now Gumma Prefecture). A graduate of Tōkyō University (1886), he taught commercial law there from 1895 to 1922. He also served as director general of the government's Legislative Bureau (Hōseikyoku) and chief judge of the ADMINISTRATIVE COURT. In 1922 he was named minister of justice in the KATŌ TOMOSABURŌ cabinet. In the succeeding YAMAMOTO GONNOHYŌE cabinet he served simultaneously as minister of education and as minister of agriculture and commerce. He was later named head of the Imperial Academy (now the Japan Academy) and vice president of the PRIVY COUNCIL. Okano is generally regarded as having laid the foundation for modern commercial law in Japan. His writings include *Nihon tegata hō* (1905, The Bills and Notes Law of Japan) and *Kaisha hō* (1929, Company Law).

okashi

おかし

An aesthetic sensibility cultivated especially during the Heian period (794–1185). The basic meaning of the term is "delightful" or "charming," referring to a more detached, light-hearted response to scenes and events than *aware* (see MONO NO AWARE), the other principal aesthetic ideal of premodern Japan. Yet in actual usage, the delight it designates encompassed several different types, ranging from enjoyment of graceful, courtly beauty to laughter at the ludicrous.

In general the meaning of *okashi* leaned toward an appreciation of elegant beauty in the literature of the Heian period. In SEI SHŌNAGON's MAKURA NO SŌSHI (996–1012; tr *The Pillow Book of Sei Shōnagon*, 1967) the word appears 466 times and is used to describe such scenes as a spring dawn, pussy willows in bud, and chirping autumn insects.

From the Kamakura period (1185–1333) onward the meaning of *okashi* steadily shifted toward amusement with the ludicrous. Even the NŌ actor ZEAMI (1363–1443), an ardent admirer of Heian culture, broadly defined *okashi* as "that which people laugh at." Inevitably the term came to be associated with comic literature, such as KYŌGEN, early RENGA, and SENRYŪ. With the popularization of the term, *okashi* in time lost its aesthetic implications and became a plain adjective meaning "laughable" or "amusing," the sense in which it is used in modern Japanese.

Oka Shigeki

岡繁樹

(1878–1959). Journalist and social activist. Born in Kōchi Prefecture, he became a reporter for the newspaper YOROZU CHŌHŌ and associated with socialists and anarchists, including SAKAI TOSHIHIKO and KŌTOKU SHŪSUI. He was dismissed from the newspaper as a "troublemaker" and went to San Francisco in 1902. In Oakland in 1906 he helped to form a group of 50 Japanese socialists, called the Shakai Kakumeitō (Social Revolutionary Party). He opposed the Japanese military regime during World War II and volunteered to serve with a British Army propaganda unit in India. He published several newspapers and operated Japanese printing shops in San Francisco, Sacramento, and Los Angeles.

Oka Shikanosuke

岡鹿之助

(1898–1978) Western-style painter. Born in Tōkyō. After studying under OKADA SABURŌSUKE he attended classes at Tōkyō Bijutsu Gakkō (now Tōkyō University of Fine Arts and Music). He went to France in 1924 and joined the Salon d'Automne. Returning to Japan in 1939 he joined the artists' group Shun'yōkai. Oka used a pointillistic technique to create his tranquil, illusionistic style. He received the Order of Culture in 1972.

Okauchi Hideo

岡内英夫

(1908–). Businessman; leading figure in SHISEIDŌ CO, LTD, a major cosmetics firm. Born in Kagawa Prefecture. After graduating from Takamatsu Higher Commercial School (now Kagawa University), Okauchi joined Shiseidō, became president in 1967, and served as chairman from 1975 to 1978. He developed Shiseidō into the largest cosmetics company in Japan and established overseas markets for its products.

Ōkawa

大川[市]

City in southwestern Fukuoka Prefecture, Kyūshū, at the mouth of the river Chikugogawa. It originally flourished as a river port, but since the 16th century it has been the center of a woodcraft industry. Other activities are the cultivation and processing of *igusa* (rush used to make the outer covering for *tatami* mats), the raising of goldfish and carp, and the cultivation of *nori* (a type of seaweed) in the Ariake Sea. Pop: 45,704.

Ōkawa Heizaburō

大川平三郎

(1860–1936). Businessman. Born in what is now Saitama Prefecture. Nephew of SHIBUSAWA EIICHI, business leader of the Meiji period (1868–1912). Ōkawa joined ŌJI PAPER CO, LTD, at age 16. He later received training in the United States and Europe, establishing himself as a leading papermaking expert in Japan. He left Ōji Paper in 1903 to become independent. Establishing his own paper company (Karafuto Kōgyō) in 1913, he turned it into the third-ranking paper manufacturer in Japan. The company merged with Ōji Paper in 1933.

Ōkawa Kazushi

大川一司

(1908–). Economist. Born in Shizuoka Prefecture. After graduating from Tōkyō University in 1933, he became a professor at Utsunomiya University. After World War II, he worked on the staff of the ECONOMIC STABILIZATION BOARD and served as a professor at Hitotsubashi University from 1950 to 1972. He has long been engaged in the compilation and analysis of long-term economic statistics in Japan and in the theoretical and historical study of the nation's economic development. Ōkawa was the first director-general of the Economic Research Institute of the ECONOMIC PLANNING AGENCY (1958–61).

Ōkawa Shūmei

大川周明

(1886–1957). Ideologue of the civilian RIGHT WING from 1920 to 1945. With KITA IKKI and others, he founded nationalistic societies designed to encourage the preservation of traditional Japanese values. In the 1930s he was involved in a number of antigovernment plots and eventually jailed. After his release his books were widely published and read during World War II.

Born in Yamagata Prefecture, his education was a mixture of the Confucian classics and modern foreign languages. After graduation from Tōkyō University in 1911, he remained in Tōkyō, doing translation work for the Army General Staff. After years of interest in foreign philosophies, he came to find more and more aspects of the Japanese tradition that seemed relevant to the needs of the nation as he perceived them. He soon became convinced that Japan's salvation from the social tensions of the day lay in the revitalization of its own traditions.

In 1918 he began work with the SOUTH MANCHURIA RAILWAY as a member of its East Asian Economic Research Bureau. He, Kita, and others founded a discussion group and political club, the YŪZONSHA. From the early 1920s Ōkawa was involved in the creation of student study groups at several universities, including Takushoku University, where he became an instructor in history and colonial policy in 1920. Ōkawa founded the Kōchisha, a rightist organization, in 1925, and the Daigakuryō, a nationalist educational institute.

In 1926 Ōkawa published *Nihon oyobi nihonjin no michi* (Japan and the Way of the Japanese), which by the end of World War II had gone through 46 printings. He became involved in various coups planned by members of the military and in 1932 was arrested in the MAY 15TH INCIDENT. Sentenced in 1935 to five years in prison, he was released after serving less than two years. He rejoined the South Manchurian Research Bureau and in 1939 joined the faculty of Hōsei University. In the years that followed he published numerous books and articles.

Ōkawa helped to popularize such ideas as the inevitability of a military clash between Asia and the West, in which Japan would act as champion of the East and do battle with the United States. After World War II, he was arrested as a propagandist and put on trial in the WAR CRIMES TRIALS but was declared unfit to stand trial by reason of insanity. After his recovery, he continued to write and published an autobiography, *Anraku no mon* (1951, The Gate of Tranquillity).

Okaya 岡谷[市]

City in central Nagano Prefecture, central Honshū, on Lake Suwa. Okaya was one of the country's most prosperous silk-reeling towns during the Meiji period (1868–1912). It has precision-instrument (watches and cameras) and automotive-parts industries. A municipal silk museum exhibits machinery and historical materials illustrating the development of the silk industry. Pop: 59,849.

Okayama 岡山[市]

Capital of Okayama Prefecture, western Honshū, on the Inland Sea. Okayama developed as a castle town in the Sengoku period (1467–1568). Rice is grown on reclaimed land on Kojima Bay; nearby Okayama Plain is also rich agricultural farmland. Principal industries are rubber, textiles, and the manufacture of agricultural implements. There are also developing heavy and chemical industries. The garden KŌRAKUEN, Okayama Castle, Okayama Fine Arts Museum, and the so-called Naked Festival at the temple Saidaiji attract visitors. Pop: 593,730.

Okayama domain 岡山藩

(Okayama han). Edo-period (1600–1868) domain that extended over Bizen Province and part of Bitchū Province; part of present-day Okayama Prefecture. In 1602 Ikeda Tadatsugu (1599–1615), son of the lord of Himeji domain, IKEDA TERUMASA, was installed as lord of Okayama Castle with the status of TOZAMA (outside vassal). In 1632, the domain passed into the hands of IKEDA MITSUMASA, a grandson of Terumasa, whose descendants ruled the domain until the end of the Edo period. OMOTEDAKA (estimated annual production of rice): 315,200 KOKU (1 koku = 180 liters or 5 US bushels).

Okayama Plain 岡山平野

(Okayama Heiya). Located in Okayama Prefecture, western Honshū. Bordering the Inland Sea, this alluvial plain is on the lower reaches of the rivers Yoshiigawa, Asahigawa, and Takahashigawa. The Mizushima Coastal Industrial Region is located on reclaimed land in Kojima Bay. The farmers grow rice and hothouse grapes and peaches. The major cities on the plain are Okayama and Kurashiki. Area: approximately 250 sq km (97 sq mi).

Okayama Prefecture 岡山県

(Okayama Ken). Located in western Honshū and bounded by Tottori Prefecture to the north, Hyōgo Prefecture to the east, the Inland Sea to the south, and Hiroshima Prefecture to the west. The prefecture is separated into three distinct zones: the plains area along the coast, the highland Kibi Kōgen in the center, and the mountainous area in the north. Several small basins and plains are also interspersed in the central and northern areas. The climate is mild, with moderate rainfall.

Archaeological excavations in the area have yielded numerous Yayoi-period (ca 300 BC–ca AD 300) artifacts. Divided after the TAIKA REFORM of 645 into the three provinces of Bizen, Bitchū, and Mimasaka, it came under the rule of a succession of feudal warlords from the late Heian period (794–1185) until the Edo period (1600–1868). The present name dates from 1871 after the Meiji Restoration, and the present boundaries were established in 1876.

Agriculture, although declining in importance, remains a major occupation. Crops include rice, tobacco, fruits, and igusa, used to make tatami mats. Light industry developed before World War II, while the postwar period has seen a rapid development of steel, petrochemical, and machinery industries in the southern littoral area.

Tourist attractions include the view of the Inland Sea from the hill WASHŪZAN and the highland Hiruzen Kōgen in DAISEN-OKI NATIONAL PARK. The city of KURASHIKI, with its Edo-period warehouses and modern- and folk-art museums, as well as the KŌRAKUEN garden in the city of OKAYAMA, are also popular. Area: 7,092 sq km (2,738 sq mi); pop: 1,925,877; capital: Okayama. Other major cities are Kurashiki, TSUYAMA, and TAMANO.

Okayama University 岡山大学

(Okayama Daigaku). A coeducational national university located in the city of Okayama, Okayama Prefecture. Founded in 1949, the university maintains faculties of letters, education, law, economics, science, medicine, dentistry, pharmaceutical sciences, engineering, and agriculture. Okayama University strongly advocates international exchange, enrolling foreign students from over 25 countries and offering research and technical aid to developing countries. Enrollment in 1989 was 9,777.

Okaya Silk Museum 岡谷蚕糸博物館

(Okaya Sanshi Hakubutsukan). Museum of silk reeling in the city of Okaya, Nagano Prefecture. Established in 1964. Okaya was the center of Japan's silk-reeling industry during the Meiji period (1868–1912). The museum's exhibits illustrate the entire silk-reeling process, from the moth larvae stage to the use of reels to manufacture raw silk thread from cocoons. Also on display is the French-made reeling machine that was used at the TOMIOKA SILK-REELING MILL, the only extant machine of its kind.

Okazaki 岡崎[市]

City in central Aichi Prefecture, central Honshū. Now a satellite city of NAGOYA, it prospered in the Edo period (1600–1868) as a castle town and a post-station town. Its development as a commercial and textile manufacturing city dates from the Meiji period (1868–1912). More recently, chemical and machinery industries have been established. Of interest are the remains of Okazaki Castle, where the military ruler TOKUGAWA IEYASU was born; the temple Takiyamadera; and Okazaki Park, famed for its cherry blossoms and wisteria. Pop: 306,822.

Okazaki Katsuo 岡崎勝男

(1897–1965). Diplomat and politician. Born in Tōkyō; graduate of Tōkyō University. Okazaki joined the Ministry of Foreign Affairs in 1922 and on Japan's defeat in 1945 was appointed director of the Shūsen Renraku Jimukyoku, the liaison office set up to negotiate between the cabinet and the OCCUPATION authorities. From 1947 to 1948 he served as vice-minister of foreign affairs under YOSHIDA SHIGERU and ASHIDA HITOSHI. In 1949 he was elected to the first of three terms in the House of Representatives. He was ambassador to the United Nations from 1961 to 1963.

Okazaki Kunisuke 岡崎邦輔

(1854–1936). Politician. Born in what is now Wakayama Prefecture. Beginning in 1891 he was elected 10 times to the House of Repre-

sentatives. As a leader of the RIKKEN SEIYŪKAI political party, Okazaki took a leading role in the MOVEMENT TO PROTECT CONSTITUTIONAL GOVERNMENT.

oke 桶

A general term for traditional wooden bucketlike or tublike containers. Originally oke were made from thin sheets of cypress (hinoki) curved or bent into a cylinder or oval, fitted with a bottom, and sealed with bark. During the Muromachi period (1333–1568), they came to be made of wooden staves bound together with a hoop of split bamboo or, later, wire. Types include the furooke (a large oke used as a bathtub), the tomeoke (for use at the public bath), the kometogioke (for washing rice), the bandai (used in fish markets), the kaibaoke (for feeding animals), and the tsurubeoke (used to draw well water).

Okegawa 桶川[市]

City in east-central Saitama Prefecture, central Honshū; about 40 km (25 mi) north of Tōkyō. In the Edo period (1600–1868) Okegawa prospered as a post-station town on the highway Nakasendō and as a market center for agricultural products. Its proximity to Tōkyō has made it a desirable site for industry and housing. The temple Sempukuji dates from the 9th century. Pop: 69,029.

Okehazama, Battle of 桶狭間の戦い

(Okehazama no Tatakai). The first major strategic victory in the career of ODA NOBUNAGA; fought on 12 June 1560. The young Nobunaga had barely established his dominance over Owari Province (now part of Aichi Prefecture) when he was faced by an expedition mounted by his eastern neighbor IMAGAWA YOSHIMOTO, daimyō of Mikawa (now part of Aichi Prefecture), Suruga, and Tōtōmi (the latter two both now part of Shizuoka Prefecture). Nobunaga could muster only 2,000 or 3,000 troops against Yoshimoto's 25,000, but under the cover of a violent rainstorm he succeeded in surrounding and surprising the enemy encamped in a ravine called Dengaku Hazama. This site, located on the border between the present-day cities of Nagoya and Toyoake, is about 2 kilometers (1.2 mi) north of Okehazama. In the ensuing rout Yoshimoto lost his life; his vassal Matsudaira Motoyasu (the future shōgun TOKUGAWA IEYASU) obtained freedom of action. By 1562 Nobunaga and Motoyasu had formed an enduring alliance, and the path to national hegemony lay open before them.

okera 朮

Atractylis ovata. Formerly known as ukera. Perennial herb of the family Compositae

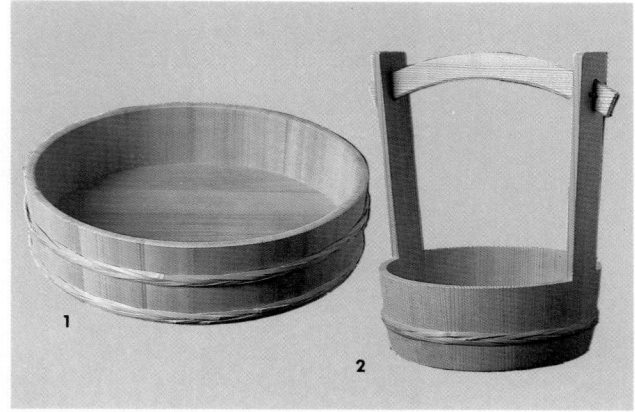

oke Old-style wooden buckets and tubs are still used for a variety of purposes in Japan.
1 The hangiri tub is a must for mixing sushi rice—wood absorbs excess water from cooked rice in a way that plastic or metal cannot.
2 Low-sided buckets such as the one pictured are used for carrying food and sometimes do double duty as tabletop servers.

Okayama Prefecture Location and Prefectural Crest

okera A traditional method of purging the body of illness and "noxious vapors" calls for burning okera as incense and allowing the smoke to waft about the afflicted person.

that grows in sunny, dry areas in mountainous regions of Honshū, Shikoku, and Kyūshū, as well as in Korea and northeastern China. It is dioecious. New shoots appear from the rhizomes each spring and develop into hard cylindrical stems about 30–60 centimeters (1–2 ft) high. The alternate leaves are pinnate on the lower stem and elliptical on the upper stem. In autumn a white head appears at the top of the stem, with bracts resembling fishbones concealing the flowers.

The young shoots used to be eaten, and the dried rhizomes were valued as an aromatic digestive and diuretic; the herb remains in use as a gourmet delicacy and traditional medicine. *Okera*, along with other herbs and spices, is used in the preparation of TOSO, a spiced *sake* traditionally drunk on New Year's Day.

Oketani Hideaki　桶谷秀昭

(1932–). Literary critic. Born in Tōkyō; graduated from Hitotsubashi University. Oketani's works examine the thought and spiritual struggle of modern Japanese intellectuals such as KITAMURA TŌKOKU, NATSUME SŌSEKI, YASUDA YOJŪRŌ, and KITA IKKI. He is the author of *Dochaku to jōkyō* (1967, Indigenous Culture and Its Situation), *Kindai no naraku* (1968, The Abyss of Modernity), *Natsume Sōseki ron* (1972), and *Yasuda Yojūrō* (1983).

Okhotsk culture　オホーツク文化

(Ohōtsuku *bunka*). Deep-sea fishing and hunting culture that flourished during the 8th through 12th centuries in the coastal areas of southern Sakhalin, northeastern Hokkaidō, and the southern Kuril Islands bordering on the Sea of Okhotsk. The Okhotsk culture, judged to have been more closely related to Siberian cultures than to those of the prehistoric Japanese or the aboriginal AINU people, was contemporaneous with the SATSUMON CULTURE of southern Hokkaidō and northernmost Honshū. Okhotsk pottery, BONE ARTICLES such as harpoon toggles, STONE TOOLS, and Japanese-made iron implements have been found in abundance at such sites as the MOYORO SHELL MOUND. Within the pentagonal or hexagonal PIT HOUSES characteristic of Okhotsk culture, there were central hearths and special niches where animal bones were placed for ceremonial purposes.

Okhotsk, Sea of　オホーツク海

(Ohōtsukukai). Arm of the northwestern Pacific Ocean, separated from the Pacific Ocean by the Kamchatka Peninsula and the Kuril Islands and from the Sea of Japan by

Sakhalin and Hokkaidō. Its northern section has a continental shelf (depth 100–150 m; 328–492 ft) abundant in cold-water fish. Annual negotiations have been held between Japan and the Soviet Union to determine the limits on salmon and trout catches as well as the boundaries of fishing areas. Area: 1,590,000 sq km (614,000 sq mi).

okibumi　置文

(testamentary document). A medieval documentary form, in use during the Kamakura (1185–1333) and Muromachi (1333–1568) periods, that apparently evolved from a narrative codicil attached to a will into an independent statement. There are two broad categories of *okibumi*: determinate statements regulating matters of inheritance, composed in connection with a conveyance of property (*yuzurijō*); and hortatory statements elaborating on what the author considers significant for his successors to observe so that the integrity of his family (or religious institution), its holdings, and its traditions may be preserved. *Okibumi* vary in length. Since the family's continuity is at the heart of their concern, *okibumi* resemble KAKUN (family precepts) in nature; the latter documentary form, however, tends to be more elaborate and diffuse.

Oki Electric Industry Co, Ltd　沖電気工業[株]

(Oki Denki Kōgyō). Company engaged in the manufacture and sale of telecommunications systems, information processing systems, and electronic devices. It ranks as one of Japan's leading electronics manufacturers. Founded in 1881, it expanded with production of such communications equipment as telephone exchanges. After World War II, it moved into electronic products and is now concentrating on developing sophisticated integrated circuits and expanding production of on-line data terminal equipment. It has 11 overseas offices and 8 subsidiaries throughout the world, including North America, Europe, and Asia. Sales for the fiscal year ending March 1991 totaled ¥582.2 billion (US $4.2 billion), distributed as follows: information processing systems, 47 percent; telecommunications systems, 29 percent; electronic devices, 22 percent; and others, 2 percent. Paid-in capital was ¥67.5 billion (US $492.0 million) in fiscal 1991. Headquarters are in Tōkyō.

Oki Islands　隠岐諸島

(Oki Shotō). Group of islands in the Sea of Japan, approximately 50–90 km (30–55 mi) north of the Shimane Peninsula, western Honshū; part of Shimane Prefecture. It con-

sists of the Dōzen and Dōgo islands and some 180 smaller islands. Fishing is the main activity. Garden-plot farming and cattle and horse raising are carried on. The islands, formerly used as places of exile for political prisoners, have many historical remains, including those related to Emperor GO-DAIGO. The islands are part of the Daisen-Oki National Park. Area: 348 sq km (134 sq mi).

Okinaka Shigeo　沖中重雄

(1902–92). Internist and neuroscientist. Born in Ishikawa Prefecture. Graduate of and professor at Tōkyō University. He is known for his extensive studies on the mechanism of body fluid regulation, clinopathological evaluations on cerebral vascular disturbances, and the autonomic nervous system of various visceral organs. Okinaka worked with his teacher KURE KEN to establish the anatomical pathway of the spinal parasympathetic nervous system (the vagus nerve system). Okinaka carried out a large number of autopsies for comparison with clinical findings. He was director of the Toranomon Hospital and received the Order of Culture in 1970.

Okinawa　沖縄

The islands of the Ryūkyū (Ch: Liuqiu or Liu-ch'iu) archipelago south of the Amami group, centering on the island of Okinawa, constitute Okinawa Prefecture. Being geographically separated from the rest of Japan, Okinawans developed their own distinct dialect and cultural traditions. Archaeological, linguistic, folkloric, and historical evidence points to early ethnic and cultural ties to southern Kyūshū.

　The Ryūkyū Kingdom——Until the establishment of Okinawa Prefecture in 1879 the Ryūkyū archipelago was the domain of the Ryūkyū Kingdom. Beginning in the late 12th century, regional petty rulers gradually gained ascendance over their neighbors, and by the 14th century the island of Okinawa was divided among three kingdoms. In 1429 the second king of the first Shō dynasty, Shō Hashi (1372–1439), unified the island. The second Shō dynasty was founded in 1470 and continued for four centuries. However, Okinawa nominally compromised its independence by sending tribute missions to the court of the Chinese emperor and by receiving Chinese investiture missions to legitimize each royal successor. Initiated in 1372 by the regional king Satto (1321–95) and continued for five centuries thereafter, the missions brought the kingdom under the influence of Chinese culture, and the tribute trade enriched it.

　The king's independence was further restricted when the Japanese domain of Satsuma (now Kagoshima Prefecture) conquered the islands in 1609. The king, who was taken hostage, agreed to a treaty in 1611 that preserved the kingdom's independence but placed it under the overlordship of Satsuma. This relationship was concealed from China because Ryūkyū's "independence" was necessary to preserve its tribute trade, now a monopoly of Satsuma.

　British and French warships made separate appearances in Okinawa in 1816 and 1844, respectively, demanding trade relations with the kingdom. China, recently overcome by the British in the Opium War, had no intention of defending Ryūkyū. Although Japan's policy of NATIONAL SECLUSION had been imposed on the kingdom, Satsuma received the shogunate's tacit agreement to concede limited trade if diplomatic resistance proved futile. It was a tactic designed to forestall a direct approach by the Western ships to Japan's main islands. However, Commodore Matthew C. PERRY was successful in forcing Edo (now Tōkyō) in 1853–54 to open ports in Japan, and this event diminished Western interest in Ryūkyū.

Okinawa Prefecture——The establishment of the Meiji government (see MEIJI RESTORATION) in 1868 marked the end of Satsuma as a domain. Japan's new government asserted its authority over Ryūkyū in 1874 and ordered Ryūkyū to discontinue its tribute relationship with China in 1875. Finally, in 1879 the kingdom was abolished and Okinawa Prefecture became an administrative unit of the Japanese government.

Prefectural status did not immediately bring Okinawa into the Japanese political mainstream, nor did it dissolve loyalty to the former ruling house. The local assembly was weaker and the tax burden heavier than for other Japanese prefectures. Participation in national parliamentary politics was delayed until 1919. However, lingering questions about retaining the old China connection were expunged by Japan's victory in the SINO-JAPANESE WAR OF 1894–1895, and shortly thereafter Okinawans were given the responsibility of Japanese citizenship under the universal military conscription law.

World War II to the Present——Okinawans suffered greatly in the Pacific War, especially in the defense of Okinawa against the full onslaught of the Allied invasion, which began 1 April 1945. The 82-day battle cost 12,500 American lives, 37,000 American wounded, and a quarter-million Japanese lives, in addition to the destruction of cities and the ruination of the economy.

Postwar Okinawa again found itself under two sovereign powers, one de facto, the other nominal. On the one hand, Okinawa was controlled by the US military, and on the other, Japan's "residual sovereignty" over Okinawa was recognized in the SAN FRANCISCO PEACE TREATY of September 1951. Okinawans had no direct voice either in Congress or in the Japanese Diet.

The American military interlude contributed substantial benefits. The military need for workers, supplies, and services; the buildup of a transportation network; and the infusion of dollars into the local economy greatly shortened the period of economic recovery in Okinawa. Scholarships were provided to Okinawan youths to study in the United States, and the University of Ryūkyū was established in 1950 with US government funds.

However, three issues generated friction between the local populace and the US military. (1) The bulldozing of village homes and agricultural land to expand military facilities sparked popular resistance, which proved futile. The farmers refused lump-sum compensatory payments, but finally in 1958 the US government promised larger rental payments stretched out over a long period of time. (2) Although legislative, judicial, and executive institutions were permitted, the military government, known after 5 December 1950 as the United States Civil Administration of the Ryūkyū Islands (USCAR), retained the power to override their decisions and to nullify the results of elections. The chief executive for the Government of the Ryūkyū Islands (GRI) until 1967 was an appointee of the commanding general of Ryūkyū. (3) The issue of Okinawa's "reversion" to Japanese administration became more pressing after the Allied OCCUPATION of Japan

ended in 1952. On 8 November 1968 President Lyndon Johnson announced the intention of the United States to effect the reversion of the Ryūkyū Islands. Okinawa was permitted to hold an election in November 1970 to select seven representatives to the Japanese Diet, and it was reunited with Japan on 15 May 1972. Yet for many Okinawans a major issue remains: the removal of nuclear weapons and the reduction of American bases on their islands.

Okinawa   沖縄[市]

City on the island of Okinawa, Okinawa Prefecture. It was created in 1974 by a merger of the city of Koza and the village of Misato. The second largest city in the prefecture after Naha, part of it is still occupied by the Kadena US Air Force Base. A recreational park called Okinawa Children's Land is located here. Pop: 105,845.

Okinawa Development Agency
沖縄開発庁

(Okinawa Kaihatsu Chō). Agency of the national government responsible for development planning in Okinawa. Established in 1972 upon the return of Okinawa to Japanese sovereignty, it operates as an external organ of the Prime Minister's Office and is headed by a cabinet minister. It is involved in the formulation and implementation of plans for the construction and maintenance of cities, roads, houses, and sewerage facilities, as well as the development of industries, traffic and construction facilities, and water resources. It also administers the Okinawa Development Finance Corporation.

Okinawa Islands   沖縄諸島

(Okinawa Shotō). Group of islands southwest of Kyūshū, between the Amami Islands and the Sakishima Islands; part of Okinawa Prefecture. It includes the main island of Okinawa as well as KUMEJIMA, Kudakajima, the KERAMA ISLANDS, and the Yokatsu Islands. The principal activities are the cultivation of sugarcane and industry related to US military bases on the main island. The Okinawa Old Battlefield National Park is on the island of Okinawa. Area: 1,388 sq km (536 sq mi). See also OKINAWA PREFECTURE; OKINAWA.

Okinawa Memorial Park National Aquarium   国営沖縄記念公園水族館

(Kokuei Okinawa Kinen Kōen Suizokukan). A nationally administered aquarium in the town of Motobu, Okinawa Prefecture. Opened in 1976 in commemoration of the Okinawa International Ocean Exposition (EXPO '75), which was held the year before. It is the only aquarium in Japan located in the

subtropics. The main attractions of the aquarium are exhibits of subtropical ocean life peculiar to the region surrounding the main island of Okinawa. The Okinawa aquarium was the first in the world to keep what may be the largest fish in captivity, the whale shark.

Okinawan textiles   沖縄の染織

(Okinawa no senshoku). Handwoven and dyed fabrics made in OKINAWA PREFECTURE. After an invasion in 1609 by the daimyō of Satsuma (now Kagoshima Prefecture), the fruits of Okinawa's extensive foreign trade were given up as tribute to the daimyō and Okinawans had to develop local alternatives to foreign products, including textiles.

The first Okinawan textile was probably abaca cloth (bashōfu), which, along with other bast-fiber cloth such as ramie and sisal, was worn by commoners. Cotton and silk were reserved for the nobility. Colors were from natural dyestuffs, such as plants (INDIGO blue), tree barks (yellow, black, brown), certain woods (brown, red), and ferruginous mud (brown, black). For surface-dyed fabrics, mineral and organic pigments, such as cochineal, were used. Before the introduction of the treadle loom used today, a backstrap-frame loom was used.

Most Okinawan textiles are of plain weave. The main patterning techniques are warp or weft stripping and warp or weft ikat (KASURI). A method, originally Chinese, of stenciling resist paste onto fabric and richly coloring the unresisted areas by hand is utilized in the production of bingata, Okinawa's famous surface-dyed textile. The same method, using only shades of indigo blue, produces ēgata. Okinawan woven textile designs are mostly geometric, reflecting the structure of the weave. Within Okinawa there are distinctive fabrics, developed partly as a result of the distances between the islands that make up the prefecture. The city of Naha is known for bingata, the island Kumejima for kasuri-patterned handspun silk cloth in deep brown and yellow patterns, and the Miyako Islands for indigo-dyed ramie cloth (jōfu) with a kasuri pattern of tiny crosses that form larger designs.

Okinawa Prefectural Museum
沖縄県立博物館

(Okinawa Kenritsu Hakubutsukan). Museum established in 1946 in the city of Naha, Okinawa Prefecture. The museum was established by a group of US military personnel and interested Okinawans who were anxious to preserve what remained of the area's cultural properties after the majority

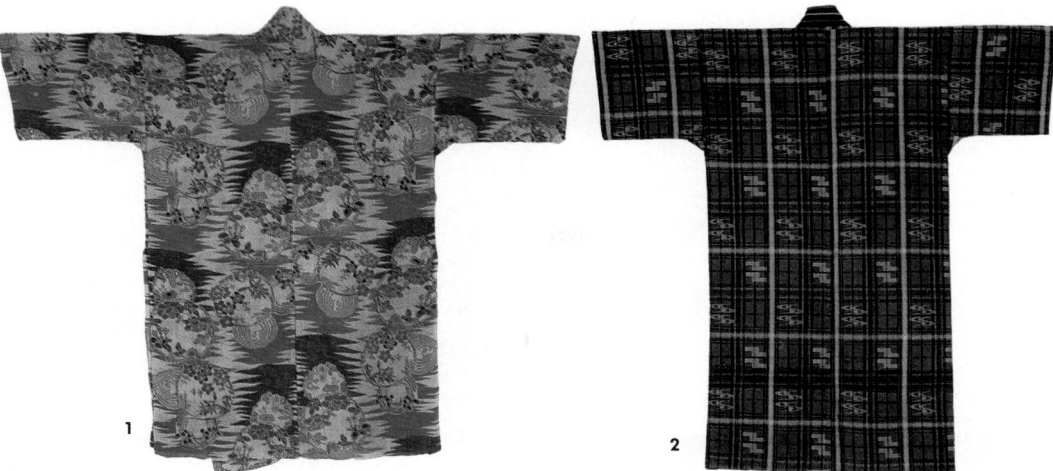

Okinawan textiles
1 A traditional garment dyed using the bingata method, which may involve cut stencils or hand coloring.
2 A kasuri-style garment. The kasuri weaving and dyeing techniques developed in Okinawa provided the basis for later kasuri weaving in the main islands of Japan.

Okinawa Prefecture

▶ Bougainvillea adorning a coral fence. Over 20 varieties of bougainvillea are grown in subtropical Okinawa Prefecture.

◀ Zampa beach on the west coast of the island of Okinawa.

▼ Statues of *shīsā* (an imaginary beast resembling a lion) are placed on roofs and gates to ward off evil.

▼ Kūkō-Dōri, a street near the US air base at Kadena, reveals the continuing presence of the US military in Okinawa.

50%~80% OFF
CASUAL WEAR BLUE WAY

▼ Memorial in the city of Itoman to the Himeyuri Butai, a unit of nurses, many of whom committed suicide in 1945 as Japan's defeat neared.

▲ The Shurei no Mon on the outskirts of the city of Naha is believed to have been built in the early 16th century as one of the gates of Shuri Castle. The present gate is a reconstruction completed in 1958, the original having been destroyed during World War II.

▲ These dancers wear traditional Okinawan textiles and carry bamboo castanets to perform the dance *odoriko hadesa*.

Okinawa Prefecture
Location and Prefectural Crest

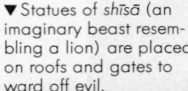

of them were destroyed in the Battle of Okinawa during World War II. The museum's exhibitions are divided into four sections: regional history; the plants and animals of the region; arts and crafts, including OKINAWAN TEXTILES and pottery; and folklore, featuring the essential implements of traditional Okinawan life.

Okinawa Prefectural Peace Memorial Museum

沖縄県立平和祈念資料館

(Okinawa Kenritsu Heiwa Kinen Shiryōkan). Museum opened in 1975 in the city of Itoman, Okinawa Prefecture. Established to commemorate the experiences of the prefecture's citizens during the Battle of Okinawa in World War II, thus laying a foundation for lasting peace. In addition to the personal belongings, memoirs, photographs, and documents of those who were involved in the fighting, the museum features exhibits detailing the chronology of the battle and the experiences of civilian residents at the time.

Okinawa Prefecture   沖縄県

(Okinawa Ken). Composed of a chain of some 60 islands generally referred to as the

RYŪKYŪ ISLANDS; located south of Kyūshū and surrounded by the East China Sea and the Pacific Ocean. The islands are generally subdivided into the OKINAWA, Miyako, Yaeyama, and Senkaku groups. Okinawa, the main island of the Okinawa group, is by far the largest in terms of both size and population and is the prefecture's economic, administrative, and cultural center. With the exception of the northern portion of the main island, most of the terrain is fairly level. The climate is subtropical, with abundant rainfall; typhoons are frequent.

While the people of Okinawa are of the same ethnic strain as those of mainland Japan, they have developed outside the framework of the Japanese state for much of their history. By the 12th century numerous small local rulers known as *anji* or *aji* had emerged, but their domains were gradually consolidated by conquest. In the 15th century the Ryūkyūs developed into a unified kingdom, whose ruler paid tribute to the Chinese emperor. In 1609 the kingdom was conquered by the SHIMAZU FAMILY of the Satsuma domain (now Kagoshima Prefecture), which exploited its strategic location and freedom from shogunal supervision to profit from commerce with China. However, tribute missions continued to be sent to China.

After the Meiji Restoration (1868) the Japanese government claimed formal sovereignty over the Ryūkyūs and incorporated them as Okinawa Prefecture. This was not recognized by the Chinese until the conclusion of the Sino-Japanese War in 1895. The invasion of Okinawa by American troops in 1945 resulted in some of the bloodiest fighting in World War II, with great loss of life among the civilian population. The islands were administered by the American military from 1945 until 1972, at which time they were returned to Japan.

Economic development has been made difficult by the fact that much of Okinawa, including prime agricultural land, has been occupied by American military bases. Remoteness from mainland Japan and lack of fresh water have also hindered progress. Agricultural activity is limited to sugarcane, pineapples, and vegetables. Manufacturing also lags. Tourism is the primary source of revenue.

Okinawa's warm climate, subtropical vegetation, and beaches, as well as its unique arts and handicrafts, attract visitors. The island of IRIOMOTEJIMA has been designated as the IRIOMOTE NATIONAL PARK, and the entire west coast of the main island of Okinawa has been designated as a quasi-national park.

The International Ocean Exposition was held here in 1975. Area: 2,256 sq km (871 sq mi); pop: 1,222,398; capital: NAHA. Other major cities include OKINAWA, GINOWAN, and URASOE. See also OKINAWAN TEXTILES; RYŪKYŪ MUSIC.

Okinoerabujima   沖永良部島

Coral island between Kyūshū and Okinawa. One of the AMAMI ISLANDS. It has numerous stalactite grottoes. The principal products are sugarcane and lily bulbs. The latter are shipped to the United States and Europe and to all parts of Japan. Area: 95 sq km (37 sq mi).

Okinoshima   沖ノ島

Small island in the Genkai Sea, midway between the island of TSUSHIMA and the northern tip of Fukuoka Prefecture, northern Kyūshū; administratively part of Fukuoka Prefecture. The island is composed of basalt and covered with virgin forests of subtropical trees. Sea bream and other fish are plentiful. One of the MUNAKATA SHRINES is located on the island. Area: 1 sq km (0.4 sq mi).

Okinoshima site   沖ノ島遺跡

(Okinoshima iseki). The island of Okinoshima, Fukuoka Prefecture, located in the Genkai Sea, contains some two dozen archaeological sites that have yielded ceremonial offerings deposited between the 4th and 9th centuries by voyagers between Japan and the Asian continent. Six investigations since 1954 have discovered 23 offering places under natural rock overhangs, on rock outcroppings, and in level areas. The offerings include bronze mirrors, ancient beads, horse trappings, armor, swords and daggers, three-color pottery, metal fetish-figures, and gilt-bronze dragons' heads—artifacts generally associated with the Kofun (ca 300–710) and Nara (710–794) periods. See also MUNAKATA SHRINES.

Okinotorishima   沖ノ鳥島

Also known as Douglas Reef. Coral island, about 700 km (430 mi) southwest of the island of Iōjima of the Ogasawara Islands, southeast of Tōkyō; part of Tōkyō Prefecture. The southernmost point in Japan, at latitude 20°25′ north and longitude 136°05′ east. The island was temporarily under US jurisdiction after World War II. It is uninhabited but important in meteorological observation. Width: approximately 5 km (3 mi); length: approximately 1.7 km (1.1 mi).

Ōki Takatō   大木喬任

(1832–99). Politician of the Meiji period (1868–1912). Born in what is now Saga Prefecture. He supported the imperial cause in the Meiji Restoration (1868), supervised the transfer of the imperial capital from Kyōto to Edo (now Tōkyō), and was appointed governor of Tōkyō. As minister of justice, in 1876 he suppressed several antigovernment uprisings (see HAGI REBELLION; JIMPŪREN REBELLION). In 1885 he became chairman of the GENRŌIN and in 1889 president of the PRIVY COUNCIL.

Ōkita Saburō   大来佐武郎

(1914–93). Government official and economist. Born in Dalian (Ta-lien; now part of Lüda); graduate of Tōkyō University. After World War II, he drew up economic and regional development plans at the Economic Stabilization Board and then at its successor, the ECONOMIC PLANNING AGENCY. Among the plans he developed was the INCOME-DOUBLING PLAN (1960). Okita became chairman of the

Overseas Economic Cooperation Fund in 1973 and foreign minister in 1979. He also was the first president of the International University of Japan from 1982 to 1987.

Ōkōchi Denjirō   大河内伝次郎

(1898–1962). Actor both in films and on the stage. Real name Ōbe Masuo. Born in Fukuoka Prefecture, he attended the Shin Minshūgeki drama school. His first role in films was in KINUGASA TEINOSUKE's Wakaki hi no Chūji: Midagahara no satsujin (1925, Young Chūji: Showdown at Midagahara), the script of which he originally wrote for the stage. He gained recognition in ITŌ DAISUKE's Chōkon (1926, Lingering Resentment) and continued to work with Itō, starring in the three-part series entitled Chūji tabi nikki (1927, Chūji's Travels). Other films were Chikemuri Takatanobaba (1928, Bloodshed at Takatanobaba) and Shimpan Ōoka seidan (1928, A New Version of Ōoka's Cases). His forte was playing villains.

Ōkōchi Kazuo   大河内一男

(1905–84). Economist and president (1963–68) of Tōkyō University. Born in Tōkyō. After graduating from Tōkyō University in 1929, he became a researcher there and was a leading student of social policy under KAWAI EIJIRŌ. During World War II, Ōkōchi established social policy theory as a branch of economics. His theory, later known as the Ōkōchi Theory, argued that effective social policy was essential to the process of capitalist reproduction, since productive capacity could be maintained and expanded only by guaranteeing a stable livelihood to the work force. He became a professor in 1945, and at the university's Institute of Social Science he distinguished himself in the study of social policy and labor problems. His collected works are contained in the Ōkōchi Kazuo zenshū (8 vols, 1980–81).

Ōkōchi Masatoshi   大河内正敏

(1878–1952). Scientist, industrialist, and author. Born in Tōkyō, Ōkōchi graduated from Tōkyō University in 1903. He joined its faculty and, after study in Europe from 1908 to 1911, was appointed full professor. He received his doctorate in 1914. Ōkōchi was a cofounder of the INSTITUTE OF PHYSICAL AND CHEMICAL RESEARCH (Rikagaku Kenkyūjo; often abbreviated as Riken) and served as director from 1921 to 1946. In 1927 he founded Riken Industries, a commercial offshoot of the institute. Aided by military contracts, the conglomerate expanded rapidly during the 1930s in the metals, machinery, and chemical industries. By 1945 it comprised more than 60 companies. In 1942 Ōkōchi resigned as Riken's president to head the Industrial Machinery Control Association and also served until 1945 as cabinet adviser on ordnance production.

Ōkōchi is best known for his promotion of "scientific industry." To modernize Japanese industry he advocated technical training, creative entrepreneurship, and industrial application of research in physics and chemistry. His many publications include Kōgyō keiei sōron (1936, General Theory of Industrial Management) and Moteru kuni Nihon (1939, Japan, The Have Nation).

okonomiyaki   お好み焼き

Pancakelike food eaten as a light meal. To make it, a batter of flour, eggs, and water is poured on a hot griddle; shredded cabbage and one or more of a variety of other ingredients, such as meat, shrimp, or cuttlefish, are

added. The pancake is cooked on both sides and usually topped with a Japanese version of Worcestershire sauce and sometimes mayonnaise and chopped ginger as well.

Ōkubo Hikozaemon   大久保彦左衛門

(1560–1639). Personal name Tadataka; warrior of the Azuchi-Momoyama period (1568–1600) and early Edo period (1600–1868); author of the memoir MIKAWA MONOGATARI. Five generations of Hikozaemon's forefathers had served the house of Matsudaira (named Tokugawa from 1566) of Mikawa Province (now part of Aichi Prefecture), and he himself served the first three Tokugawa shōguns, TOKUGAWA IEYASU, TOKUGAWA HIDETADA, and TOKUGAWA IEMITSU. Hikozaemon fought with distinction in Ieyasu's campaigns from 1576 and was made his direct retainer (jikisan) in 1614. However, he attained only modest rank as a commander of the shōgun's color guard (hata bugyō; appointed 1632) and resented newcomers who attained high office through administrative expertise. Hikozaemon figures in the Edo period's JITSUROKUMONO (historical fiction) and moralistic KŌDAN tales as the very image of a cross-grained but straight-speaking old war-horse.

Ōkubo Nagayasu   大久保長安

(1545–1613). Commissioner of mines and shogunate adviser of the early Edo period (1600–1868). Born into a family of SARUGAKU performers in Kai Province (now Yamanashi Prefecture). When his family's patrons, the TAKEDA FAMILY, were destroyed in 1582, Nagayasu entered the service of Ōkubo Tadachika (1553–1628), lord of Sagami Province (now Kanagawa Prefecture), who gave him the Ōkubo surname and commended him to TOKUGAWA IEYASU. Appointed commissioner of the Iwami silver mines in 1601, he greatly increased their output. He was subsequently appointed head of the SADO MINES in 1603 and of the IZU GOLD MINE in 1606. He was given a fief assessed at 30,000 koku (see KOKUDAKA). He showed great administrative ability but was suspected of having embezzled public funds, and after his death his fief was confiscated and his children were ordered to commit suicide.

Ōkubo Toshimichi   大久保利通

(1830–78). One of the most able of the men who guided Japan during the MEIJI RESTORATION (1868). After a successful career as an official in the Satsuma domain (now Kagoshima Prefecture), Ōkubo participated actively in the proimperial movement leading to the Restoration. He subsequently became a progressive driving force behind the new government.

Born in the castle town of Kagoshima, Ōkubo was the son of Ōkubo Jūemon, a low-ranking retainer of the daimyō Shimazu Narioki (1791–1859). In 1846 Ōkubo was given a position as an aide to the domainal archivist. The new daimyō, SHIMAZU NARIAKIRA, recognized Ōkubo's talents; in 1858 he was appointed a tax administrator. Nariakira, who had opposed the Tokugawa shogunate's policy of opening Japan to foreign intercourse, died in 1858, and Ōkubo took up the anti-Tokugawa proimperial cause. By 1862 Ōkubo called for specific shogunate reforms and advocated kōbu gattai (see MOVEMENT FOR UNION OF COURT AND SHOGUNATE), a policy less extreme than

Ōkōchi Denjirō Known for his work on stage and screen, Ōkōchi achieved renown in the film Chōkon (1926, Lingering Resentment) under the direction of Itō Daisuke.

okonomiyaki This Japanese pancake is often cooked in front of the diner. Here it is topped with sauce, aonori (green seaweed), and katsuobushi (dried bonito) flakes.

Ōkubo Toshimichi A skillful and single-minded leader of the Meiji Restoration, Ōkubo is regarded as one of the founders of modern Japan.

Okumura Dogyū
Maelstrom. 1959. Colors on paper. 128 × 161 cm. Yamatane Museum of Art, Tōkyō.

SONNŌ JŌI (Revere the Emperor, Expel the Barbarians).

Satsuma's defeat in its clash with England (1863; see KAGOSHIMA BOMBARDMENT) precipitated by the RICHARDSON AFFAIR, along with the COUP D'ETAT OF 30 SEPTEMBER 1863 in Kyōto, were key factors in convincing Ōkubo and others that *kōbu gattai* was hopeless and that the shogunate should be overthrown. In 1866, together with SAIGŌ TAKAMORI, another loyalist *samurai* from Satsuma, Ōkubo met KIDO TAKAYOSHI of Chōshū (now Yamaguchi Prefecture), an anti-Tokugawa domain at the western tip of Honshū, and agreed to form a secret SATSUMA-CHŌSHŪ ALLIANCE against the shogunate.

On 3 January 1868 Satsuma and Chōshū forces seized the palace in Kyōto and proclaimed an "imperial restoration" (see ŌSEI FUKKO). With the Meiji Restoration, the triumvirate of the movement—Ōkubo, Saigō, and Kido—laid the groundwork for the new Japanese state, instituting a number of administrative reforms. The government that took shape was authoritarian. Ōkubo became minister of finance in 1871; he brought about the LAND TAX REFORM OF 1873–1881, the prohibition of wearing swords (HAITŌREI), and the abolition of official discrimination against outcastes.

In foreign relations, Ōkubo sought to renegotiate the so-called Unequal Treaties of 1858 (see UNEQUAL TREATIES, REVISION OF). He also joined the IWAKURA MISSION of 1871–73, which toured the United States and Europe. On returning to Japan, he opposed those advocating an invasion of Korea (see SEIKANRON). When it was decided not to attack Korea, Saigō, ITAGAKI TAISUKE, and other government leaders resigned in protest.

As head of the newly established HOME MINISTRY (Naimushō), Ōkubo exercised civil control through its police bureau and encouraged industrial growth (SHOKUSAN KŌGYŌ) through its industrial promotion bureau. He virtually wielded the power of a prime minister (the office of premier was not established until 1885), and he joined in the so-called ŌSAKA CONFERENCE OF 1875 to seek an accommodation with the opposition.

In January 1877 the SATSUMA REBELLION—the last serious attempt by the samurai to gain influence in the government—erupted under the leadership of Saigō. The rebels were defeated by the well-organized government conscript army under Home Minister Ōkubo's command. Ōkubo was now considered a traitor by his own domain and fellow samurai. On 14 May 1878 Ōkubo was assassinated by six samurai conspirators from Satsuma.

Through competence and single-mindedness, Ōkubo had become, in the years

Ōkuma Shigenobu An important politician of the Meiji and Taishō periods and founder of Waseda University, Ōkuma led Japan's first party cabinet in 1898.

preceding his death, the strongest man in the government. He made enemies, but he also won the respect of his colleagues. He was a devout loyalist and nationalist and as such symbolized the growing concept of nationalism in Japan, which he helped to nurture. Ōkubo held power relatively briefly, but by the time of his death Japan's basic policies had been established, and the country was sufficiently far along the road to economic and political maturity so that succeeding leaders could continue what he had begun.

Ōkuchi   大口［市］
City in northern Kagoshima Prefecture, Kyūshū. Once a flourishing gold-mining town, it has become primarily a rice-growing area, with some forestry. The Sogi Falls and Tsuruda Dam are part of a prefectural natural park. Pop: 25,700.

Oku Chichibu   奥秩父
Mountain group extending through Saitama, Yamanashi, Gumma, and Nagano prefectures, central Honshū. It consists of the highest peaks in the Chichibu Mountains, including those of KIMPUSAN, KOBUSHIGADAKE, Kumotoriyama, MITSUMINESAN, and Kita Okusenjōdake (2,601 m; 8,534 ft), the highest peak. The mountains are a central feature of the Chichibu-Tama National Park.

Okuda Eisen   奥田穎川
(1753–1811). Amateur Kyōto ceramist. Real name Okuda Yōtoku. His designs are considered among the best of the KYŌTO CERAMICS. He is said to have introduced porcelain making to Kyōto. Many of his pieces in underglaze blue or overglaze enamels imitate the late Ming (1368–1644) and early Qing (Ch'ing; 1644–1912) Chinese styles fashionable at the time. His work is thick-bodied and characterized by free, quick brushwork; flowers, birds, dragons, or typical Chinese scenes predominate. The glazes are very thick and a "pinhole" effect is often seen. Among his many students were AOKI MOKUBEI and NIN'AMI DŌHACHI.

Okuda Gensō   奥田元宋
(1912–). Japanese-style (NIHONGA) painter. Real name Okuda Genzō. Born in Hiroshima Prefecture. A specialist in landscapes in an original style blending the ink painting tradition of China and Japan with the color expression of Western painting. After graduating from middle school, he studied painting with Kodama Kibō (1898–1971). His painting *Sannin no josei* (Three Women) was selected for the BUNTEN exhibition in 1936. He became a member of the Japan Art Academy in 1974 and received the Order of Culture in 1984.

Ōkuma cabinet   大隈内閣
(Ōkuma *naikaku*). Either of two cabinets headed by ŌKUMA SHIGENOBU. The first, the so-called Waihan cabinet, Japan's first party cabinet, was formed in 1898 by members of the KENSEITŌ (Constitutional Party) and lasted barely four months. The second Ōkuma cabinet succeeded that of YAMAMOTO GONNOHYŌE in April 1914 and lasted until October 1916. Five of its ministers were members of the RIKKEN DŌSHIKAI (Constitutional Association of Friends). It dealt with two important foreign policy issues, Japan's entry into World War I and the TWENTY-ONE DEMANDS to the government of China.

Ōkuma Kotomichi   大隈言道
(1798–1868). WAKA poet. Born into a merchant's family in Chikuzen Province (now

Fukuoka Prefecture). He wrote most actively in his middle and later years. In his essay on *waka*, "Hitorigochi" (1857), he maintained that poetry should be composed in a language and style peculiar to the poet's place and time. His own poems are written in a simple and direct style and employ words and phrases from his native dialect. Among his followers was the poet NOMURA MOTONI. His most important collection is *Sōkeishū* (1863).

Ōkuma Shigenobu   大隈重信
(1838–1922). Politician of the Meiji (1868–1912) and Taishō (1912–26) periods; prime minister, cabinet minister, political party leader, and founder of Tōkyō Semmon Gakkō (now WASEDA UNIVERSITY). Born in the Saga, or Hizen, domain (now Saga Prefecture). Ōkuma's first appointment in government was in 1868, just after the Meiji Restoration, as a diplomatic and commercial official in Nagasaki. His financial expertise and his friendship with the restoration leader INOUE KAORU led to his initial appointments in the central government in Tōkyō as *san'yo* (junior councillor) and later as *sangi* (councillor).

Following his appointment as minister of finance in 1873, Ōkuma directed his attention to unifying the currency system, establishing a national mint, and creating a ministry of industry. He wielded considerable political power as the head of the finance ministry, and this aroused the suspicions of the small group of men from the domains of Satsuma (now Kagoshima Prefecture) and Chōshū (now Yamaguchi Prefecture) that had dominated government from the beginning of the Meiji period (see HAMBATSU). Unlike these men, Ōkuma lacked a domainal base of political support and had to seek other alliances.

A series of political blunders confirmed Ōkuma's outsider status in the Satsuma-Chōshū oligarchy. In 1880 Ōkuma offended conservative government leaders by suggesting that an overseas loan of ¥50 million be raised to redeem the paper money issued during the SATSUMA REBELLION in 1877. In 1881 he presented a memorial for the speedy drafting of a constitution on the British model, a plan at variance with the views of other councillors. Finally Ōkuma made public the proposal of a Satsuma councillor that government assets in Hokkaidō be sold to a consortium of businessmen headed by former officials from Satsuma and Chōshū (see HOKKAIDŌ COLONIZATION OFFICE SCANDAL OF 1881). In August 1881 senior councillors demanded Ōkuma's removal from office. He resigned in October and, soon after, a dozen of his followers resigned or were dismissed (see POLITICAL CRISIS OF 1881). Ōkuma remained politically active, however, and in 1882 formed Japan's second major political party, the RIKKEN KAISHINTŌ (Constitutional Reform Party). He founded Tōkyō Semmon Gakkō the same year.

Ōkuma returned to political office in 1888 as foreign minister and reopened negotiations with the Western powers in an attempt to revise the Unequal Treaties (see UNEQUAL TREATIES, REVISION OF). The treaty he drafted was conciliatory toward the Western powers and brought a strong negative response from the Japanese public. In 1889 Ōkuma was seriously injured in an assassination attempt by a member of the ultranationalist GEN'YŌSHA (Dark Ocean Society). His injuries forced him into a temporary retirement from government.

In 1896 Ōkuma returned to politics, reorganizing the Kaishintō into a new party, the SHIMPOTŌ (Progressive Party), which he led. That same year he served again as foreign minister, and in 1897 he also took the post of minister of agriculture and commerce. In 1898 he merged the Shimpotō with ITAGAKI TAISUKE's Jiyūtō to form the KENSEITŌ (Constitutional Party). A few days later Ōkuma and Itagaki were ordered to form a party cabinet, the first in Japan (see ŌKUMA CABINET). Itagaki was appointed home minister, while Ōkuma served concurrently as foreign minister and prime minister. Internal dissension led to the dissolution of the cabinet within four months. In 1900 Ōkuma became head of the KENSEI HONTŌ, a splinter group of the Kenseitō. He resigned in 1907 to become president of Waseda University and withdrew from public affairs.

In 1914 Ōkuma was appointed prime minister by the GENRŌ (elder statesmen). His cabinet was notable for presenting the TWENTY-ONE DEMANDS to China and for an election scandal in 1915 that led to the resignation of several members of the cabinet. In 1916 he resigned as prime minister and retired from politics permanently.

Ōkuma was an iconoclast and modernizer who was constantly fighting the arbitrary exercise of power by the Satsuma and Chōshū *hambatsu*. He preferred to appeal to popular opinion, believing that all men were entitled to share in the business of government. In many ways he was a precursor of Japan's post–World War II democracy.

Okumiya Takeyuki　　奥宮健之

(1857–1911). Social activist of the Meiji period (1868–1912); also known as Okumiya Kenshi. Born in Tosa Province (now Kōchi Prefecture). He joined the JIYŪTŌ (Liberal Party) at the time of its formation in 1881. In 1884 Okumiya became involved in the Nagoya Incident, an antigovernment uprising organized by Jiyūtō members in Aichi Prefecture. Okumiya was sentenced to life imprisonment on the charge of having assaulted a police officer, but was released in 1897 after repeated petitions by Jiyūtō politicians. He later claimed that during his 12 years in prison he had drawn support from the writings of Thomas Carlyle and Ralph Waldo Emerson and from the Bible. From 1900 to 1902 he traveled in Europe and the United States. On his return to Japan he embraced socialism and joined KŌTOKU SHŪSUI's organization, the HEIMINSHA. With Kōtoku and others, Okumiya was arrested in the HIGH TREASON INCIDENT OF 1910, an alleged plot to assassinate the emperor. He steadfastly maintained his innocence but was executed the following year.

Oku Mumeo　　奥むめお

(1895–). Feminist and consumer activist. Born in Fukui Prefecture; maiden name Wada. A graduate of Japan Women's University in 1916, she soon became involved with current social problems, associating with radicals such as ŌSUGI SAKAE. She helped found the women's rights group SHIN FUJIN KYŌKAI in 1920 and led it in 1922. She then published a magazine called *Shokugyō fujin* (Working Women; later *Fujin undō*, or Women's Movement). She also started settlements, child-care centers, and a lecture series for working women with the help of ABE ISOO and Seki Akiko (1899–1973). Beginning in 1947 she was elected to three terms in the House of Councillors. In 1948 she founded and began her leadership of the

consumer group Shufu Rengōkai (SHUFUREN). See also CONSUMER MOVEMENT.

Okumura Corporation　　［株］奥村組

(Okumura-Gumi). General contractor, known for its construction of railways, highways, sewage and water tunnels, and dams. Incorporated in 1938. The firm is recognized for its high technological standards and for its shield tunneling methods. Sales for the fiscal year ending March 1991 amounted to ¥340.1 billion (US $2.5 billion), and capitalization stood at ¥19.8 billion (US $144.3 million). Headquarters are in Ōsaka.

Okumura Dogyū　　奥村土牛

(1889–1990). Japanese-style (NIHONGA) painter. Real name Okumura Yoshizō. Born in Tōkyō; studied *nihonga* under KOBAYASHI KOKEI. Okumura's work was first shown at the 1927 Inten (Exhibition of the Japan Fine Arts Academy). He developed a distinctive style based on contemplation of nature. In 1947 he became a member of the Japan Art Academy (Nihon Geijutsuin). He received the Order of Culture in 1962.

Okumura Ioko　　奥村五百子

(1845–1907). Founder and leader of the AIKOKU FUJINKAI (Patriotic Women's Association), which offered aid and comfort to Japanese soldiers and their families. Born in Karatsu, Hizen Province (now Saga Prefecture), the daughter of a Buddhist abbot. A supporter of SAIGŌ TAKAMORI's proposal to send a military expedition to Korea (see SEIKANRON), she had a strong interest in Korea and China from early on. She made several trips to Korea, founding a trade school in Kwangju in 1896. During the Boxer Rebellion (1900) Ioko went to China and joined a group organized to help wounded Japanese soldiers. She returned to Japan and in 1901 founded the Aikoku Fujinkai, which soon grew to be a nationwide organization.

Okumura Masanobu　　奥村政信

(1686–1764). UKIYO-E artist and publisher; founder of the Okumura school of *ukiyo-e*. He is credited with the introduction of perspective prints (*uki-e*) and pillar prints (*ha-*

shira-e). Real name Okumura Shimmyō. A self-taught artist, Masanobu's earliest prints showed the influence of TORII KIYONOBU I and Hishikawa MORONOBU. He designed many actor prints, often substituting pink (*beni*) for orange (*tan*) in accordance with the current trend. He soon added glossy black lacquer prints (*urushi-e*) to his repertoire, and around 1736 his first prints employing Western perspective appeared, a style that was rapidly adopted by his contemporaries. In the Kampō era (1741–44) he began to produce long, narrow, vertical prints and signed them Hashira-e Kongen (literally, "the originator of the pillar print"). During the last 20 years of his life he experimented with *benizuri-e* and other color-printing techniques, producing many actor prints and genre prints.

Okuni　　阿国

(fl 1600). Also known as Izumo no Okuni. The supposed founder of the KABUKI theater. According to popular accounts, she acquired nationwide acclaim as the leader of a women's theatrical troupe. In 1603 her company achieved outstanding success in performances held at the Kitano Shrine and on the Shijō-Gawara (Fourth Street Dry Riverbed) of the river Kamogawa, both located in Kyōto; in fact, this date (1603) is generally regarded as the beginning of the kabuki tradition.

The sensational presentations of her troupe, which combined singing, dancing, music, tantalizing erotic themes, and short dramatic sketches, became known as "Okuni kabuki." Early records indicate that Okuni kabuki employed popular and timely themes derived from the culture of the newly prosperous townspeople and strongly accentuated the sensual element. In 1629, the Tokugawa shogunate officially banned all women from the stage on the grounds that they had a corrupting influence on public morals. There is strong disagreement over the accuracy of the various fragmentary accounts of Okuni's life. Thus any effort to distinguish clearly the specific elements of

Okuni The life of the woman regarded as the founder of *kabuki* theater is shrouded in mystery. This early-17th-century painting presents an idealized image of Okuni (right, on stage) performing.

Oku Mumeo The founding of the Shufuren consumer rights group in 1948 is among the achievements of this pioneering feminist and consumer advocate.

Okuni kabuki, which may have influenced the later kabuki tradition, must remain highly speculative. See also KAWARAMONO.

Ōkuninushi no Mikoto　　大国主命

A Shintō deity, also known as Ōkuninushi no Kami or as Ōnamuchi no Kami, said to be either the son or a descendant of SUSANOO NO MIKOTO. Originally a major local deity of Izumo Province (now part of Shimane Prefecture), Ōkuninushi no Kami ("The Deity Who Is the Great Lord of the Land") was incorporated into the national Shintō pantheon by the time of the compilation of the KOJIKI (712, Records of Ancient Matters), in which he figures prominently. Ōkuninushi is portrayed as a benevolent, heroic, and civilizing deity who cannot be deflected from his noble tasks by adversity. When his brothers torment a hare, Ōkuninushi comes to its rescue and hears from it the prophecy that he will win the hand of the beautiful Yagamihime.

Ōkuninushi was viewed in Izumo not merely as the guardian deity of that province but as the creator of the world and as an agricultural deity. As a purveyor of civilization he is reputed to have taught the people farming, irrigation, sericulture, pest control, and medicine. He is also venerated for his military prowess under the name Yachihoko no Kami ("Deity of 8,000 Spears"). In popular belief Ōkuninushi was often identified with the Buddhist guardian deity DAIKOKUTEN (Mahākāla), who was counted among the SEVEN DEITIES OF GOOD FORTUNE. The chief shrine to Ōkuninushi is the Izumo Taisha (IZUMO SHRINE), one of Japan's oldest shrines, located in the town of Taisha, Shimane Prefecture, reputed to be the original site of Ōkuninushi's palace. At another old shrine, ŌMIWA SHRINE in Nara Prefecture, the chief deity, Ōmononushi no Kami, is considered to be the nigimitama (harmonious spirit; see TAMA) of Ōkuninushi.

Ōkuni Takamasa　　大国隆正

(1792–1871). Scholar of KOKUGAKU (National Learning). Born to a samurai family of the Tsuwano domain in Iwami (now Shimane Prefecture), as a youth he studied with the noted Kokugaku scholar HIRATA ATSUTANE. He also studied Confucianism with Koga Seiri (1750–1817) and WESTERN LEARNING at Nagasaki. Ōkuni opened schools in the Kyōto-Ōsaka area devoted to Kokugaku but later returned to Tsuwano to teach at the domainal school. Calling ·his school of thought Honkyō or Hongaku, he conceived of a world presided over by the Shintō goddess AMATERASU ŌMIKAMI, in which people diligently pursued their callings and helped one another. Following the Meiji Restoration (1868) he served the new government but resigned when he could not accomplish his goal of promoting Shintō.

Oku no hosomichi　　奥の細道

(tr The Narrow Road to the Deep North, 1966). Travel diary written by Matsuo BASHŌ (1644–94) in 1694 in an allusive poetic prose (see HAIBUN). The verses that punctuate the text, hokku, the antecedent of the modern HAIKU, are some of Bashō's most celebrated. The best-known work of the famous Edo-period (1600–1868) poet, Oku no hosomichi was the result of a 156-day, 1,500-mile journey into the rugged regions of northern Honshū. Leaving Edo late in the spring of 1689, Bashō traveled northward up the Pacific coast, across the inland mountains to the Japan Sea coast, south along that coast, and then again across the island. As Bashō, in the tradition of wandering poet-priests such as SAIGYŌ, visits the great poetic places of Japanese literature (see UTA MAKURA), the work takes on a spiritual tone. Although the diary has its refined side—indeed, it is a web of allusions to the classics of Chinese and Japanese literature and makes frequent use of the aesthetic concept of SABI—it also has its lighter moments, incorporating such lowly images as fleas, lice, prostitutes, and filth. The journal as a whole is modeled on a RENGA (linked verse) sequence, interspersing scenes of high emotional content with more reserved ones. The careful literary structure of events departed from the truth. The more factually correct journal kept by his companion KAWAI SORA (1649–1710) provides a very different account of the journey. Some of the more memorable sections include the introduction and the entries for Matsushima, Hiraizumi, and Kisakata.

Ōkunojima　　大久野島

Island in the central Inland Sea, approximately 2 km (1 mi) south of the city of Takehara, Hiroshima Prefecture. One of the GEIYO ISLANDS. Poison gas was made on the island during World War II; this resulted in long-term health problems for the workers in that industry. Area: 0.7 sq km (0.3 sq mi).

Okuno Takeo　　奥野健男

(1926–). Critic. Born in Tōkyō. Graduate of Tōkyō Institute of Technology. His first important publication was Dazai Osamu ron (1952, On Dazai Osamu). Okuno's critical study Bungaku ni okeru genfūkei (1972, The Primal Landscape in Literature) centers on the question of setting, which he argues is fundamental to modern literature. He develops his thesis further in "Ma" no kōzō (1983, The Structure of Ma).

Ōkura & Co, Ltd　　大倉商事[株]

(Ōkura Shōji). Medium-scale trading company (sōgō shōsha; see GENERAL TRADING COMPANIES) formerly under the control of the Ōkura ZAIBATSU. Incorporated in 1911. Ōkura is now especially active in high-technology fields such as aerospace, communications, electronics, and biotechnology. Sales for the fiscal year ending March 1991 totaled ¥518.6 billion (US $3.8 billion). The company was capitalized at ¥6.4 billion (US $46.6 million) in the same year. Headquarters are in Tōkyō.

Ōkura Kihachirō　　大倉喜八郎

(1837–1928). Entrepreneur and founder of the Ōkura zaibatsu (financial and industrial combine). Born in what is now Niigata Prefecture, Ōkura opened a gun shop following the Meiji Restoration (1868). He later established the Ōkura-Gumi Shōkai (1873), a general trading company, amassing great riches as a trader with the military. He financed a number of Japanese corporations, including Tōkyō Electric Lighting (now TŌKYŌ ELECTRIC POWER CO, INC) and the Imperial Hotel. He also started a variety of businesses in China and Korea. In 1911 Ōkura created a huge industrial combine headed by Ōkura-Gumi, comprising direct subsidiaries like Ōkura Shōji (see ŌKURA & CO, LTD), Ōkura Doboku (see TAISEI CORPORATION), and Ōkura Kōgyō. Ōkura also established the Ōkura Commercial School (now Tōkyō University of Economics) and the ŌKURA SHŪKOKAN MUSEUM.

Ōkura Nagatsune　　大蔵永常

(1768–?). Agronomist of the Edo period (1600–1868). Born in Bungo Province (now Ōita Prefecture) to a rural family. As a young man Ōkura traveled widely in Kyūshū. He then went to Ōsaka, teaching and writing on farming techniques. In 1825 he went to Edo (now Tōkyō) and continued to teach, write, and travel in the Kantō region, frequently serving as a consultant to various daimyō. His best-known work, Kōeki kokusan kō (1842–59, On Increasing Profits and Productivity), was one of the most influential books on farming in premodern Japan. Ōkura believed that the prosperity of individual farming households was directly linked to the wealth of the nation as a whole, and unlike more conservative agricultural writers of the time, he urged the cultivation of cash crops such as sugar, cotton, herbs, dyes, and fruits and discussed not only cultivation techniques but improvements in soil and farming implements.

Ōkura school　　大蔵流

(Ōkuraryū). One of the three main schools of KYŌGEN. The school was once part of the Komparu school of NŌ. The founder is said to have been the priest Gen'e Hōin of Mt. Hiei (Hieizan), but Komparu Shirojirō (late Muromachi period, 1333–1568) was more likely its actual founder. The three branch families, the Yasōemon, Hachiemon, and Yadayū, had little success after the MEIJI RESTORATION of 1868, and two other families of the school, the Yamamoto and the Shigeyama, took over the leadership. In 1942 the second son of Zenchiku Yagorō (1883–1965), a member of the Shigeyama family, was adopted by the Ōkura family and took the name of Ōkura Yatarō (b 1912), becoming the 24th head of the Ōkura school.

Ōkurashō →Ministry of Finance

Ōkura Shūkokan Museum　　大倉集古館

(Ōkura Shūkokan). Art museum located in Minato Ward, Tōkyō. The first private art museum in Japan. Opened in 1917 by the entrepreneur ŌKURA KIHACHIRŌ. The collection includes 1,700 representative Japanese artworks from ancient to modern times (including paintings, Buddhist figures, and ceramics) as well as approximately 35,500 books. Among the holdings are three National Treasures, including the Zuishin teiki emaki (Imperial Guards Cavalry Scroll) from the Kamakura period (1185–1333).

Okushiri　　奥尻

Island approximately 18 km (11 mi) west of the Oshima Peninsula, southwestern Hokkaidō; administratively part of Hokkaidō. The principal activity on the island is fishing. Ships run regularly between the island and Esashi on Hokkaidō. The highest point is the mountain Kamuiyama (585 m; 1,919 ft). Area: 143 sq km (55 sq mi).

Oku Tadami Dam　　奥只見ダム

(Oku Tadami Damu). Located on the upper river TADAMIGAWA, between western Fukushima Prefecture and eastern Niigata Prefecture, northern Honshū. Completed in 1961, the dam created Lake Oku Tadami (area: 11.5 sq km; 4.6 sq mi) in Ginzandaira. An electric power plant, located directly below the dam, has a maximum output of 360,000 kilowatts. Height: 157 m (515.1 ft); length of embankment: 475 m (1,558.4 ft); storage capacity: 458 million cu m (16.2 billion cu ft).

Oku Tama 奥多摩

Mountainous region in western Tōkyō Prefecture, central Honshū. It contains the headwaters of the river Tamagawa and surrounds Lake Oku Tama. The highest peak is Kumotoriyama (2,018 m; 6,621 ft). It is noted for the rugged peaks and spectacular gorges along the Tamagawa.

Oku Tama, Lake →Ogōchi Dam

Ōkyo →Maruyama Ōkyo

Old-Age Welfare Law 老人福祉法

(Rōjin Fukushi Hō). This law was enacted in 1963 to create the facilities necessary for the financial security and the mental and physical health of the elderly. The law provides for social welfare officers in local public welfare offices who carry out special duties and supply technical guidance relating to the welfare of the elderly. In addition, social welfare offices and health centers, among others, offer necessary investigatory and advisory services.

A yearly health checkup is provided for persons 65 and over, and a fixed percentage of the medical expenses of persons 70 and over is paid. Also, persons over 65 can be placed in NURSING HOMES for the elderly free of charge or at low cost. In addition, the law promotes the dispatch of helpers to the homes of the elderly and provides for recreation and clubs.

Oliphant, Laurence オリファント, L.

(1829–88). British journalist, novelist, explorer, diplomat, utopian, and spiritualist. Born in Capetown, South Africa. He traveled to North America in 1855 and to India, China, and Japan in 1857–61. First Secretary of the British legation in 1861, Oliphant was wounded during an attack by a group of xenophobic *samurai* on the embassy in Edo (now Tōkyō), one of many such incidents at the time. In 1865 he wrote a novel, *Piccadilly*, and ran for Parliament. He gave up his seat in 1867 to join Thomas Lake HARRIS's Brotherhood of the New Life in New York State. He initially took six Japanese students from the Satsuma domain (now Kagoshima Prefecture) with him and later induced other Japanese to join the brotherhood. In 1881 Oliphant broke with Harris to form his own community in Palestine.

Olympus Optical Co, Ltd

オリンパス光学工業[株]

(Orimpasu Kōgaku Kōgyō). Known chiefly as a manufacturer of cameras and microscopes, Olympus also produces and sells medical equipment, photometric instruments, and communications equipment. The company was incorporated in 1919 to manufacture microscopes. Olympus's overseas operations are handled by its international offices, and affiliates are maintained in the United States and Europe. Sales for the fiscal year ending March 1991 totaled ¥173.0 billion (US $1.3 billion), of which 68 percent was exports, and capitalization stood at ¥19.9 billion (US $145.0 million). Headquarters are in Tōkyō.

Ōmachi 大町[市]

City in northern Nagano Prefecture, central Honshū. Ōmachi developed as a market town in the Edo period (1600–1868). Chief products are aluminum, cotton thread, and rice. A base camp for visitors to the Northern Alps (Hida Mountains), Ōmachi is also the starting point of the so-called Alpine Route to the group of mountains called TATEYAMA and to the KUROBE DAM. Pop: 31,597.

Ōmachi Alpine Museum

大町山岳博物館

(Ōmachi Sangaku Hakubutsukan). Located in the city of Ōmachi, Nagano Prefecture, the gateway to Japan's Northern Alps (the HIDA MOUNTAINS). Established in 1951. Among the museum's exhibits are items related to the natural history of the Northern Alps, materials tracing the development of mountain climbing in Japan, and photographs and documents concerning the history and folklore of the area.

Omaezaki 御前崎

Cape on western Suruga Bay, southern Shizuoka Prefecture, central Honshū. Separating Suruga Bay from the Enshū Sea, it is famous for its coastal scenery, which includes towering cliffs, jagged rocks, and sand dunes. Coastal fishing and tourism are the main industries.

Ōmagari 大曲[市]

City in southeastern Akita Prefecture, northern Honshū, on the river Omonogawa. It has been a rice production center since the Edo period (1600–1868). The fireworks festival in August attracts visitors. Pop: 40,429.

Ōmama 大間々[町]

Town on the river Watarasegawa in eastern Gumma Prefecture, central Honshū. Ōmama's principal products are rice and vegetables. Pop: 23,417.

omamori →gofu

Ōmazaki 大間崎

Cape on the northern Shimokita Peninsula, northeastern Aomori Prefecture. Projecting into Tsugaru Strait, it is the northernmost point of Honshū (41°32′ N). The cape, which is only about 20 kilometers (12 mi) distant from Shiokubimisaki, a cape on the island of Hokkaidō, is famous for its reefs, rocky beaches, and lighthouse.

ombin 音便

(literally, "convenient sound"). A term used in traditional Japanese linguistics to cover a wide range of sound changes that sometimes occur in Japanese verb and adjective inflections and in word compounding. *Ombin* are usually divided into four classes: *i ombin, u ombin, hatsu ombin* (mora-formative nasal *ombin*), and *soku ombin* (geminate consonant *ombin*). In the following examples *ombin* occurs when the inflectional suffix *-te* is added to the continuative form (*ren'yōkei*) of verbs and adjectives to form the gerundive: (1) *i ombin: kaku* "write" > *kaki* (continuative) + *te* > *kaite* "writing"; (2) *u ombin: samui* "cold" > *samuku* + *te* > *samūte* "being cold" (now considered dialectal); (3) *hatsu ombin: shinu* "die" > *shini* + *te* > *shinde* "being dead"; and (4) *soku ombin: toru* "take" > *tori* + *te* > *totte* "taking." Occurrences of *i ombin* and *u ombin* became frequent in the Heian period (794–1185), although they can already be observed in documents of the Nara period (710–794). It is generally accepted that *hatsu ombin* and *soku ombin* developed in the Kamakura (1185–1333) and Muromachi (1333–1568) periods.

Ombin can be considered diachronically as a historical process of sound change (e.g., the evolution of *kaite* "writing" from the earlier *kakite* and of *otōto* [*oto-u-to*] "younger brother" from the compound word *otohito*) or synchronically as sound transposition that arises from inflectional contingency (e.g., *kaki* + *-masu* > *kakimasu*, whereas *kaki* + *te* > *kaite*).

ombu 負んぶ

Child's word for being carried on someone's back; from the verb *obuu*, to carry a baby strapped on the back. Also used in the sense of a piggyback ride. In Japan a special sash is used to tie the baby securely to the mother's back. Although the custom has been discouraged because it restricts circulation in the limbs, this method of carrying children is still favored. It not only enables the mother to pursue her household tasks but also gives her child warmth and a sense of security. In winter a special cotton-filled robe (*nenneko*), which enwraps both mother and child, is worn to provide extra warmth.

Ōme 青梅[市]

City in northwestern Tōkyō Prefecture, on the river Tamagawa. It first developed as a post-station town but has long been known for its cotton textiles, principally bedding and towels. In recent years machinery manufacturing plants have been set up. Attractions include the Mitake Shrine, a grove of ancient Japanese plum trees at Yoshino, and the Ōme Railway Museum Park. Pop: 125,960.

ōmetsuke 大目付

(inspectors general). Officials of the Tokugawa shogunate (1603–1867). In 1632 the third shōgun, TOKUGAWA IEMITSU, designated four of his trusted officials as inspectors general (*sōmetsuke;* the title was later changed to *ōmetsuke*), thereby distinguishing them from the regular inspectors (METSUKE). *Ōmetsuke* were drawn from bannerman (HATAMOTO) families of relatively high rank and often were older, more experienced officials with substantial political influence in the government. Formally responsible to the senior councillors (RŌJŪ), they exercised surveillance over the highway system, various suspect sects such as Christianity, and the *daimyō*. In the event of turbulence, hardship, misbehavior, or malfeasance in a daimyō domain, *ōmetsuke* conducted an investigation and made recommendations to the *rōjū* for corrective action.

Ōmi 青海[町]

Town on the coast of the Sea of Japan in southwestern Niigata Prefecture, central Honshū. During the Edo period (1600–1868) Ōmi developed as a post-station town on the highway Hokurikudō. The nearby section of coast called OYASHIRAZU was famous as the most difficult stretch on that highway. With an abundant supply of limestone, Ōmi is the site of cement and chemical factories and is Japan's top producer of lime nitrogen. Pop: 10,704.

Ōmi Basin 近江盆地

(Ōmi Bonchi). South and east of Lake Biwa, central Shiga Prefecture, central Honshū. This fault basin is bounded by the Ibuki, Suzuka, and Hira mountains. The alluvial plain formed by the rivers Yasugawa and Echigawa forms the southeast shore of the lake. A rich rice-producing area, in recent years it has become a residential area, and industries are developing rapidly. The

Ōmi Hakkei
1 The Ukimidō, Buddha hall of the temple Mangetsuji, on the waters of Lake Biwa. The temple's picturesque setting led to its inclusion in one of the Eight Views of Ōmi: *Katata no rakugan* (Descending Geese at Katata).
2 Andō Hiroshige's woodblock print *Descending Geese at Katata* (1830). The Ukimidō is at left.

omikuji New Year's visitors to the Heian Shrine in Kyōto tie their paper fortunes, obtained by drawing lots, to a tree.

major cities are Hikone and Ōtsu. Area: approximately 300 sq km (115 sq mi).

Ōmi Code 近江令

(Ōmiryō). Legal code compiled under Emperor TENJI in 668. Although the text no longer survives, it is believed to have been Japan's first legal formulary. According to the legal compendium *Kōnin kyakushiki jō* (820), 22 chapters of administrative statutes (*ryō*) were drawn up in 668, and the biography of FUJIWARA NO KAMATARI in the TŌSHI KADEN states that Kamatari helped Tenji codify both penal and administrative statutes (*ritsu* and *ryō*) at that time. The NIHON SHOKI (720), however, makes no mention of a code in its section on Emperor Tenji. Many scholars doubt that the Ōmi Code ever existed and claim that the ASUKA KIYOMIHARA CODE of Emperor TEMMU (drawn up in 681 and promulgated in 689) was Japan's earliest. It is theorized that the Ōmi Code may have been an informal collection of miscellaneous regulations.

Ōmi Hachiman 近江八幡[市]

City in central Shiga Prefecture, central Honshū, on the eastern shore of Lake Biwa. Ōmi Hachiman developed as the castle town of TOYOTOMI HIDETSUGU. It was long known for its enterprising Ōmi merchants, who peddled mosquito nets, jute yarn, household medicine, and *kimono* throughout the country. It is also a famous rice-producing area. Of interest are the ruins of the castle, the

Ōmiwa Shrine This shrine is one of the oldest in Japan, but the relatively new oratory pictured here was constructed in 1664.

temple Chōmeiji, and the Himure Hachiman Shrine. Pop: 66,066.

Ōmi Hakkei 近江八景

(Eight Views of Ōmi). Eight famous scenic spots on the shores of Lake Biwa in Ōmi Province (now Shiga Prefecture), a Japanese version of the SHŌSHŌ HAKKEI, or Eight Views of Xiao and Xiang (Hsiao and Hsiang) in China. The Ōmi views were praised in a poem composed in 1500 by Konoe Masaie (1444–1505) and his son Naomichi. The scenes are *Hira no bosetsu* (Evening Snow on Mount Hira), *Katata no rakugan* (Descending Geese at Katata), *Karasaki no yau* (Evening Rain at Karasaki), *Mii no banshō* (Evening Bell from Miidera), *Seta no sekishō* (Sunset Glow over Seta), *Awazu no seiran* (Clearing Mist at Awazu), *Yabase no kihan* (Sails Returning to Yabase), and *Ishiyama no shūgetsu* (Autumn Moon over Ishiyamadera).

Ōmikenshi Co, Ltd オーミケンシ[株]

(Ōmikenshi). Spinner and manufacturer of fiber and chemical products. Incorporated in 1917. The company also is engaged in the production of electronic products and health foods. For the fiscal year ending March 1991, sales totaled ¥68.9 billion (US $502.2 million), of which exports accounted for 16 percent, and capitalization stood at ¥3.0 billion (US $21.9 million). Headquarters are in Ōsaka.

omikuji 御神籤

A method of fortune-telling available at Japanese shrines and temples; it is practiced by drawing lots (*omikuji*). The custom was imported from China in ancient times. The usual method consists of drawing sticks from a container, which are exchanged for paper fortunes—typically with passages from the Chinese *Book of Changes* (*Yi jing* or *I ching*). Japanese people have traditionally consulted the gods via *omikuji* on such important occasions as marriage and business transactions. If the fortune is unfavorable, the piece of paper is often tied to a nearby tree within the shrine or temple grounds in the hope that it will not come true.

ominaeshi 女郎花

Patrinia scabiosaefolia. Perennial herb of the family Valerianaceae that grows in sunny fields and on mountains throughout Japan and is also found in Korea, China, and eastern Siberia. Erect stems (about 1 m; 3 ft) have opposite, deeply lobed, pinnate leaves. In late summer and autumn numerous small yellow flowers appear on branching stems. It is one of the "seven flowers of autumn." Because of its gentle appearance it was lik-

ened to a beautiful woman in ancient Japanese literature.

Ōminesan 大峰山

Also called Sanjōgatake. Mountain in southern Nara Prefecture, central Honshū. From ancient times the mountain has been a sacred place for mountain-dwelling ascetics (see SHUGENDŌ). Until 1960 women were prohibited from climbing Ōminesan. Height: 1,719 m (5,640 ft).

Ōmi no Mifune 淡海三船

(722–785). Scholar and official of the Nara period (710–794); with ISONOKAMI NO YAKATSUGU, regarded as the most important literary figure of his time. A great-grandson of Emperor KŌBUN. He was an editor of the historical chronicle *Shoku nihongi* (see RIKKOKUSHI) and may have compiled the Chinese verse anthology KAIFŪSŌ. His Chinese poetry appears in the KEIKOKUSHŪ.

Ōmi Ōtsu no Miya → Ōtsu no Miya

Ōmi Province 近江国

(Ōmi no Kuni). Present-day Shiga Prefecture. Established at the time of the TAIKA REFORM (645), it is contiguous with YAMASHIRO PROVINCE and located on the route between the four (later five) capital provinces (KINAI) and the eastern provinces. Within its borders were three important barrier stations (SEKISHO): Arachi, Fuwa, and SUZUKA. During the Heian period (794–1185) the temple ENRYAKUJI, which gained control of extensive estate lands (SHŌEN), was erected on the mountain HIEIZAN in Ōmi. In the ensuing Kamakura period (1185–1333) the province was torn by a territorial struggle between Enryakuji and the Sasaki family, who had been appointed hereditary provincial constables (SHUGO) by the Kamakura shogunate. ODA NOBUNAGA erected AZUCHI CASTLE to the east of Lake Biwa in 1576. In the Edo period (1600–1868), many areas became shogunal lands (TENRYŌ), and several small domains, among them the HIKONE DOMAIN, were established.

Ōmishima 大三島

Island in the central Inland Sea, off the northeastern coast of Ehime Prefecture, Shikoku. The largest of the GEIYO ISLANDS and midpoint on a series of planned bridges, which, when completed, will connect Honshū and Shikoku. Its principal product is mandarin oranges. Ōyamatsumi Shrine on the island holds some 80 percent of the armor and helmets designated as National Treasures, including those of MINAMOTO NO YOSHITSUNE. Area: 64 sq km (25 sq mi).

Ōmishima 青海島

Island in the Sea of Japan, off the city of Nagato, Yamaguchi Prefecture, western Honshū. It is connected with the Senzaki district of Nagato by a bridge. The northern coast of the island is made up of rugged cliffs. Sea bream and yellowtail culture are important activities. It is part of the Kita Nagato Coast Quasi-National Park. Area: 14.6 sq km (5.6 sq mi).

Ōmi Shrine 近江神宮

(Ōmi Jingū). Shintō shrine in the city of Ōtsu, Shiga Prefecture; dedicated to the spirit of Emperor TENJI (626–672; r 661–672), who as Crown Prince Naka no Ōe helped carry out the TAIKA REFORM in 645. He was also responsible for moving the capital from Asuka to Ōtsu in 667. Construction of the shrine was completed in 1940. The annual festival is held on 20 April.

Ōmiwa Shrine 大神神社

(Ōmiwa Jinja). A Shintō shrine in the city of Sakurai, Nara Prefecture; dedicated to the deity Ōmononushi no Kami (see ŌKUNINUSHI NO MIKOTO). One of the oldest shrines in Japan, Ōmiwa Jinja does not have a main sanctuary (honden) in which the sacred object (SHINTAI) of the shrine normally reposes. Instead, the Ōmiwa Shrine venerates the exposed peak of Mt. Miwa (MIWAYAMA) as its shintai. This veneration of an exposed natural object such as a mountain is thought to represent one of the earliest forms of Shintō worship. In the medieval period (mid-12th–16th centuries) the shrine was a center of the Miwa school of Shintō, a syncretic theology based on Shingon Buddhist doctrines (see RYŌBU SHINTŌ). The annual festival is observed on 9 April.

Ōmiya 大宮[市]

City in southeastern Saitama Prefecture, central Honshū. Ōmiya first developed as a so-called shrine town and later prospered as a post-station town in the Edo period (1600–1868). With the opening of the Tōhoku Main Line of the Japanese National Railways (now JR; Japan Railways) in the Meiji period (1868–1912), commerce and industry grew. It is fast becoming a satellite city of Tōkyō. Points of interest include the Hikawa Shrine; Ōmiya Park; and Bonsai Village, Japan's largest producer of BONSAI. Pop: 403,776.

Omizutori 御水取

(literally, "water-drawing"). Also known as Otaimatsu ("torch"). A central rite of the shunie (literally, "rite observed in February") held at the Nigatsudō Hall of the Buddhist temple Tōdaiji in Nara Prefecture. The entire shunie, now held from 1 to 14 March (according to the solar calendar), is sometimes called Omizutori, but the term properly applies only to the events held from the late hours of 12 March into the early hours of the 13th. Said to date from 752, the rite begins with the waving of torches from the hall's veranda, sprinkling sparks over the crowd below. Next, the monks go down to draw water from the nearby well and offer it to the image of the 11-faced Kannon, the central divinity of the hall around which this rite takes place. One of the most important rites in the Kansai area, it symbolizes the arrival of spring.

ommitsu 隠密

A general term for various categories of secret agents of the TOKUGAWA SHOGUNATE (1603–1867) such as ninja (see NINJUTSU), kakushi metsuke, shinobi metsuke, and NIWABAN. Ommitsu were used as early as the late Kamakura period (1185–1333) and came into systematic use in the Edo period (1600–1868). In the early Edo period they traditionally came from Kōga (now part of Shiga Prefecture) and Iga (now part of Mie Prefecture) and were sometimes known as kōgamono and igamono. The Tokugawa shogunate used these spies (who often disguised themselves as merchants, priests, or fortune-tellers) to gather information on conditions in daimyō domains and to keep government officials and household members under surveillance. Daimyō also used ommitsu.

Ommyōdō 陰陽道

(literally, "The Way of Yin and Yang"). Also known as On'yōdō. A system of belief based on the ancient Chinese theories of yin and yang and of the five elements (Ch: wuxing or wu-hsing), and the magical practices that developed after their importation into Japan. Ommyōdō originally referred to the world view and practices found in the ancient Chinese Yi jing (I ching) or Book of Changes. In this work the two essences of yin and yang are said to stem from taikyoku, the source of the universe. The ebb and flow of yin and yang bring about the changes observed in the world. In the Han dynasty (206 BC–AD 220) the theory dividing all things into five elements (wood, fire, earth, gold, and water) combined with the theory of change. Direction and position, the five colors, and the guardian animals were also related to this five-element theory. In 7th-century Japan the central government established the OMMYŌRYŌ, or Bureau of Yin and Yang, to study the stars to make a calendar and to foretell the future. Many popular beliefs today, such as the auspiciousness of certain days, lucky and unlucky directions, and prediction of a person's fate through his name, stem from Ommyōdō. See also CALENDAR, DATES, AND TIME; JIKKAN JŪNISHI.

Ommyōryō 陰陽寮

(Bureau of Yin and Yang). Also known as On'yōryō. Government bureau established under the TAIHŌ CODE of 701–702, attached to the Ministry of Central Imperial Affairs (Nakatsukasashō) and engaged in astrology, astronomy, calendar making, timekeeping, and divination (see OMMYŌDŌ). From the 10th century, the bureau was headed by members of the ABE FAMILY and Kamo family, and later by the Tsuchimikado family, descendants of the Abe.

Omogokei 面河渓

Gorge on the upper reaches of the river Niyodogawa, central Ehime Prefecture, Shikoku. Landscape consists of caves, waterfalls, towering cliffs, and rapids. Surrounded by dense forests famous for their spring verdure and brilliant autumn foliage, Omogokei is located within Ishizuchi Quasi-National Park. Length: 10 km (6.2 mi).

Omonogawa 雄物川

River in Akita Prefecture, northern Honshū, originating in southern Akita Prefecture and flowing through the Yokote Basin and the Akita Plain to enter the Sea of Japan at the city of Akita. It is a major water source for Akita Prefecture. The port of Akita is at the mouth of the Omonogawa. Length: 133 km (83 mi); area of drainage basin: 4,710 sq km (1,818 sq mi).

Ōmori Fusakichi 大森房吉

(1868–1923). Seismologist who laid the foundations for seismological research in Japan. Born in Fukui Prefecture. Graduate, and later a professor, of Tōkyō University. Among his numerous accomplishments are historical surveys of earthquakes in Japan, designs of seismometers, and a formula for determining epicentral distance by measuring the duration of the preliminary tremors at the point of observation. See also EARTH SCIENCES.

Ōmori shell mounds 大森貝塚

(Ōmori kaizuka). A series of Late Jōmon-period (ca 2500 BC–ca 1000 BC; also dated as ca 2000 BC–ca 1000 BC) and Latest or Final Jōmon-period (ca 1000 BC–ca 300 BC) SHELL MOUNDS, extending over 80 meters (262 ft), located in Ōta and Shinagawa wards, Tōkyō; site of the first modern archaeological excavation in Japan, undertaken by Edward S. MORSE in 1877. The excavated JŌMON POTTERY, STONE TOOLS, BONE ARTICLES, and skeletal remains are now preserved at Tō-

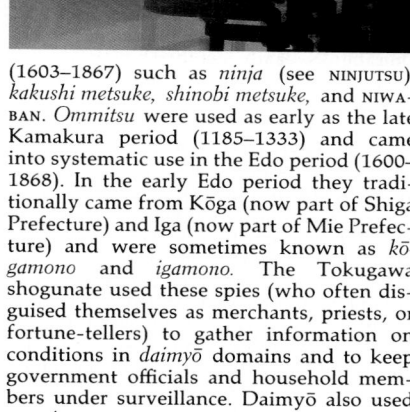

Omizutori In this time exposure, a single large torch is waved along the veranda of the Nigatsudō hall of the temple Tōdaiji as part of the ceremony of purification by fire that opens the Omizutori rite.

ominaeshi The upper sections of the stem of this perennial herb branch out in the late summer and early autumn to form small, delicate flowers.

omoto The beautifully colored leaves and fruit of this evergreen herb make it popular as a New Year's decoration.

kyō University. Nothing now remains of the mounds, but two monuments commemorate the site.

Ōmori Shōzō 大森荘蔵

(1921–). Philosopher. Born in Okayama Prefecture, he graduated from Tōkyō University, where he became a professor in 1965. From an analytic point of view, he has explored problems over a wide area including science, language, perception, logic, time, and religion. Demolishing the dualisms of being and consciousness, things and representations, body and mind, and subject and object, he views the world monistically. Physical and mental phenomena are taken as double aspects—perceptual and conceptual—of the same world, both being considered as superimpositions. His works include *Gengo, chikaku, sekai* (1971) and *Shin shikaku shinron* (1982).

omotedaka 表高

The officially designated putative yield of a domain during the Edo period (1600–1868), whether that of a *daimyō*, HATAMOTO, shrine, temple, or other landholder. The *omotedaka* figure is arrived at by a land survey (KEN-CHI) and was used in determining military obligations (GUN'YAKU) and the value of land being transferred. Because of technological improvements and reclamation of land, the actual yield of most domains came to exceed the *omotedaka* figures. Real productivity was more accurately reflected in internal domainal figures known as *uchidaka* (internal yield) or *jitsudaka* (true yield). See also KOKUDAKA.

Omote Senke 表千家

A major school of the TEA CEREMONY. Founded when Sen no Sōsa (1619–72) took over as master of the Fushin'an tea hut in what is now Kami-Gyō Ward, Kyōto. Sen no Sōsa was the third son of Sen no Sōtan (1578–1658) and the great-grandson of the Azuchi-Momoyama-period (1568–1600) tea master SEN NO RIKYŪ. The school upholds the tradition of Sen no Rikyū, who stressed spiritual richness in simplicity. The 14th-generation head of Omote Senke is Sen Sōsa (b 1938). There are 53 Omote Senke chapters in Japan and 3 abroad. See also URA SENKE.

omoto 万年青

Rhodea japonica. Perennial evergreen herb of the family Liliaceae that grows wild in warm, wooded places in Shikoku, Kyūshū, and western Honshū, as well as in China. It is also cultivated as an ornamental. Large subterranean stems bear fibrous roots and clustered green leaves (30–50 cm; 12–20 in) on top. In spring a thick flower stalk carries a spike of light yellow flowers. The sap fruits turn red or occasionally yellow when ripe.

The plant is said to have been brought into favor by TOKUGAWA IEYASU (1543–1616). The *omoto*'s popularity has fluctuated widely over the years. Its high point was the Tempō era (1830–44). The varieties now may number over 200, and the rarer species command high prices from fanciers. The *omoto* was introduced to the West for the first time in 1783. The rhizome of the *omoto* is useful as a cardiac medicine and diuretic.

Ōmoto 大本

One of Japan's NEW RELIGIONS. Founded in 1892 by DEGUCHI NAO. Ōmoto centers on its

god, Ushitora no Konjin (probably related to Konjin, the deity of the KONKŌKYŌ religion), whom Deguchi Nao claimed to have seen in a vision in 1892. The god informed her that he would send a messiah to save mankind and that a "Kingdom of Heaven" would be established after judgment day. Ōmoto teaches that man's purpose in life is to help achieve the Kingdom of Heaven by realizing that man and god are interdependent and one. Ōmoto advocates world peace and universal brotherhood.

Ōmoto's phenomenal growth started around 1898, when Deguchi Nao met Ueda Kisaburō (1871–1948), later named DEGUCHI ONISABURŌ, who eventually emerged as the religion's chief organizer and leader. He was recognized by many members as the messiah. Ōmoto attracted members from all walks of life and spread abroad in the 1920s. In 1923 ESPERANTO was introduced into the religion. Ōmoto experienced severe government repression during the 1920s and 1930s, when it reached its peak membership of about 2 million, and in 1935 Onisaburō and other Ōmoto leaders were imprisoned. After Onisaburō's death membership in Ōmoto declined. In 1989 it claimed only 180,000 followers.

Omron Corporation オムロン[株]

(Omuron). Manufacturer of electronic control components, information systems, electronic funds transfer systems, banking systems, office automation systems, and health and medical equipment. Incorporated in 1948. After 1965 the company developed a cybernetic technology to produce electronic controls. Omron is active in overseas markets, with 26 sales companies in Canada, Brazil, the United States, the Netherlands, Australia, Germany, and Singapore. The company operates manufacturing plants in Malaysia. Sales for the fiscal year ending March 1991 totaled ¥376.5 billion (US $2.7 billion). Capitalization stood at ¥38.6 billion (US $281.3 million) in the same year. Headquarters are in Kyōto and Tōkyō.

Ōmura 大村[市]

City on Ōmura Bay in central Nagasaki Prefecture, Kyūshū. It was once the castle town of the Ōmura family. From the Meiji period (1868–1912), it was a military base. The principal industrial product is refractory bricks. Dairy and poultry farming, as well as pearl culture in Ōmura Bay, are active. Nagasaki Airport is located here. Ōmura Castle is noted for its cherry blossoms. Pop: 73,435.

Ōmura Bay 大村湾

(Ōmura Wan). Bay bounded by the Nishi Sonogi, Nagasaki, and Hizen peninsulas, Nagasaki Prefecture, Kyūshū. The island of Hariojima is located at the mouth of the bay, and Nagasaki Airport is on a small island in the eastern section.

Ōmura Masujirō 大村益次郎

(1824–69). Military expert from the Chōshū domain (now Yamaguchi Prefecture); creator of Japan's modern military system. Ōmura was interested in medicine and WESTERN LEARNING. He studied at the Tekijuku, OGATA KŌAN's school in Ōsaka, and with Philipp Franz von SIEBOLD in Nagasaki. Ōmura became interested in Western military technology in the early 1850s. From 1853 he taught military studies in the Uwajima domain (now part of Ehime Prefecture) and from

1857 he taught at the military academy, the Kōbusho, in Edo (now Tōkyō).

Early in 1862 Ōmura was ordered to return to Chōshū; he taught at the domain school and directed military reforms. His reputation as a brilliant tactician was established when he routed Tokugawa troops sent against Chōshū in the second of the CHŌSHŪ EXPEDITIONS in 1866. He distinguished himself again in the BOSHIN CIVIL WAR. After the MEIJI RESTORATION (1868), he served as vice-minister of military affairs. His proposals for universal conscription were very unpopular because they would have abolished the privileges of the *samurai* class. In October 1869 he was attacked and seriously wounded in Kyōto by a group of reactionaries. He died the next month. Ōmura's plan to create a modern army was later carried out by YAMAGATA ARITOMO.

Ōmura Sumitada 大村純忠

(1533–87). The first of the CHRISTIAN DAIMYŌ; baptized in 1563, he took the Christian name Bartolomeu. Sumitada, a son of the *daimyō* Arima Haruzumi (1483–1566), was adopted into the Ōmura family of Hizen Province (now part of Nagasaki Prefecture) in 1538, becoming its head in 1551. Sumitada sought to strengthen his authority by forming ties with Portuguese traders and Jesuit missionaries. In 1562 Sumitada made concessions to the Jesuits in his port of Yokoseura; in turn they diverted the annual Portuguese trading vessel (see NAMBAN TRADE) to that harbor. The next year Yokoseura was destroyed by Sumitada's own vassals, but Portuguese vessels continued to call at his other ports, Fukuda and (from 1571) Nagasaki. On 9 June 1580 Sumitada ceded Nagasaki "in perpetuity" to the Society of Jesus. This cession was rendered illusory in 1584, when the SHIMAZU FAMILY occupied Nagasaki, and was nullified in 1587, the year of Sumitada's death, when TOYOTOMI HIDEYOSHI defeated the Shimazu, absorbed Nagasaki, and issued his ANTI-CHRISTIAN EDICTS. Sumitada was a sponsor of the MISSION TO EUROPE OF 1582.

Ōmuta 大牟田[市]

City in southern Fukuoka Prefecture, Kyūshū, on the Ariake Sea. The city developed rapidly after the Mitsui Company took over the government-run MIIKE COAL MINES in 1889. Chemical, metal, and machinery industries flourished, but because of the general decline in coal consumption from the 1960s, the population has decreased. The coal-mine and other Mitsui-affiliated enterprises are still in operation. Pop: 150,453.

on 恩

(favor; indebtedness). The social and psychological debt one incurs upon receiving a favor or gift of major proportions. *On* occupies a central place among the values that maintain the Japanese social order, in which human relations are bound in a network of reciprocal obligations.

In feudal Japan, *on* referred to the debt a warrior incurred in receiving land and protection from his lord and carried the obligation to serve in battle. Similarly, one receives *on* from the parents and ancestors who have given one life. This is repaid with FILIAL PIETY (*kō*). Others who may be *onjin* (a person to whom one owes *on*) include a teacher, an employer, or someone who has saved one's life.

On is intimately linked to *giri*, the Japanese concept that one is required to return a favor (see GIRI AND NINJŌ), and one who fails

Ōmura Masujirō This military expert played a seminal role in the creation of the modern Japanese army following the Meiji Restoration.

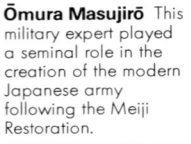

to repay *on* is called *on shirazu* (one who does not know *on*), one of the worst insults a Japanese can receive. At the same time *on* is so profound that one can never fully repay it, which puts the *on*-receiver in a relationship of permanent subordination to the *on*-giver.

Onagawa
女川[町]

Town in eastern Miyagi Prefecture, northern Honshū; gateway to the Oshika Peninsula. Onagawa is a base for coastal and deep-sea fishing and has a seafood-processing industry. Onagawa is the site of an atomic power plant. Pop: 14,018.

Ōnakatomi no Yoshinobu
大中臣能宣

(921–991). Poet, courtier, and Shintō priest. He was a compiler of the second imperial anthology of classical (WAKA) poetry, the GOSEN WAKASHŪ or *Gosenshū* (completed ca 955–966), and one of the Thirty-Six Poetic Geniuses (SANJŪROKKASEN). In 951 he was appointed one of the five fellows (YORYŪDO) of the Bureau of Poetry. His personal collection is entitled *Yoshinobushū*.

Onchi Kōshirō
恩地孝四郎

(1891–1955). Printmaker, poet, book designer, and theorist on art; one of Japan's earliest nonrepresentational artists. Born in Tōkyō, he entered the Tōkyō Bijutsu Gakkō (now Tōkyō University of Fine Arts and Music) in 1910 in the oil painting curriculum but left without graduating. Under the influence of TAKEHISA YUMEJI, he received his first commission as a book designer in 1911. With his classmates Tanaka Kyōkichi (1892–1915) and Fujimori Shizuo (1891–1943) he launched the early poetry and print magazine *Tsukubae* (Moonglow) in 1914. He began the poetry magazine *Kanjō* (Sentiment) with his friends MUROO SAISEI and HAGIWARA SAKUTARŌ in 1916. Onchi designed the first edition of Hagiwara's 1917 book of poems, *Tsuki ni hoeru* (Howling at the Moon), which he and Tanaka Kyōkichi had illustrated. Onchi made his greatest contribution as a maker of the single-sheet print. He was one of the founders of the *sōsaku hanga* (creative print) movement (see MODERN PRINTS). Using motifs drawn from the vocabulary of international modernism, Onchi's elegant and elusive work seems linked to the Japanese tradition of rich and subtle color and decorative design.

Onda Moku
恩田木工

(1717–62). Also known as Onda Takumi. Financial reformer of the Matsushiro domain (now part of Nagano Prefecture). Onda was responsible for restoring depleted domain funds. He issued sumptuary laws, encouraged land reclamation and cultivation of cash crops, and instituted a budget system. His innovative tax system featured partial payments in cash in addition to the usual payments in rice. His *Higurashi suzuri* (Daylong Jottings) is a record of his administrative experiences.

Ondo Strait
音戸ノ瀬戸

(Ondo no Seto). Narrow strait between the town of Ondo on the island of Kurahashijima and the city of Kure, southern Hiroshima Prefecture, western Honshū. This important shipping route is spanned by a bridge completed in 1961. Legend says the strait was created by TAIRA NO KIYOMORI in the 12th century. Width: 90 m (295 ft).

one-percent defense ceiling
防衛費GNP1％枠

(*bōeihi jī enu pī ichi pāsento waku*). A government policy limiting Japan's defense spending during any year to 1 percent of the nation's gross national product (GNP) for that year.

In October 1976, when the DEFENSE AGENCY adopted the NATIONAL DEFENSE PROGRAM OUTLINE establishing defense strength levels to be attained, the cabinet of Prime Minister MIKI TAKEO decided to "aim" at keeping defense spending within 1 percent of the GNP "for the present." By 1985 it appeared that this ceiling might soon be exceeded, and the question of whether this should be permitted became an important political issue. Some segments of the LIBERAL DEMOCRATIC PARTY, as well as certain other groups, advocated abolishing the limit altogether. In December 1986 defense-related expenses for the following year were for the first time budgeted at more than 1 percent of the GNP. However, in January 1987 the cabinet of Prime Minister NAKASONE YASUHIRO agreed on new standards designed to limit defense spending and, specifically, to "honor the spirit" of the 1 percent ceiling during the period covered by the Five-Year Defense Program (1986–91).

One Village, One Product Movement
一村一品運動

(Isson Ippin Undō). A plan for the revitalization of local industry that was promoted by Hiramatsu Morihiko (b 1924), the governor of Ōita Prefecture. The slogan One Village, One Product was first used in November 1979. Each town or village in the prefecture was to choose a local product (typically an agricultural product) to be promoted on the national market, resulting in the revitalization of local industry and further development of the towns and villages themselves. Similar plans were adopted in other parts of Japan, including Okinawa and Fukushima prefectures and Hokkaidō. In 1984 the Small and Medium Enterprise Agency of the central government's Ministry of International Trade and Industry began an attempt to spread this plan even further under the slogan Village Vitalization Enterprise (*mura okoshi jigyō*). This effort of the central government focused on the development of unused resources and the reevaluation of traditional Japanese industries to stimulate employment in sparsely populated areas.

Ongagawa
遠賀川

River in northern Fukuoka Prefecture, Kyūshū, originating in the Tsukushi Mountains and flowing north through the Nōgata Plain to enter the Hibiki Sea at the town of Ashiya. It is the largest source of water for the city of Kita Kyūshū. Length: 61 km (38 mi); area of drainage basin: 1,030 sq km (398 sq mi).

oni
鬼

Horned, ferocious, scarlet-faced figure usually equated in folktales, proverbs, and common parlance with a demon or ogre. His true nature, however, is more complex and ambivalent, in that he has a benevolent, tutelary face as well as a demonic one. The demonic side of the *oni* was strengthened by the connotations of the Chinese character with which the word is written and by the *oni*'s association with the demon torturers of various Buddhist hells. Evidence of the *oni*'s ancient benevolent role, however, may still be seen in a number of festivals or rituals (*matsuri*), in which he marches at the head of the procession, sweeping away evil influences.

Certain families and villages claim descent from *oni*. These include the village of Zenki at the foot of Mt. Ōmine (Ōminesan) in Nara Prefecture and the Yase district near Kyōto. See also SETSUBUN.

Onigashima → Megijima

onigiri → nigirimeshi

Ōnin War
応仁の乱

(Ōnin no Ran). A war fought mainly in Kyōto from 1467 until 1477; named for the Ōnin era (1467–69), in which it began. It brought to an end the hegemony over the central and western provinces of Japan, previously established as a balance of power between the MUROMACHI SHOGUNATE and its provincial military governors, the SHUGO. The Ōnin War ushered in a century known as the SENGOKU PERIOD, or the Age of Warring States (1467–1568).

In order to extend their authority outward from Kyōto, the Ashikaga shōguns (see ASHIKAGA TAKAUJI) were obliged to acknowledge the de facto acquisition of territorial powers by the *shugo* and to grant additional such powers. By the end of the 14th century there had emerged an identifiable group of

oni Humans suffer torments at the hands of *oni* in hell, as depicted in the 16th-century scroll *Legend of the Temple Yatadera Jizō.*

Ōnin War This scene from the 16th-century handscroll *Legends of Shinnyodō Temple* depicts one of the war's battles, fought in 1468.

shugo, called SHUGO DAIMYŌ, who enjoyed considerable autonomy. However, the balance of power between shōgun and *shugo daimyō* deteriorated due chiefly to the precipitous decline in shogunal leadership after the assassination of ASHIKAGA YOSHINORI in 1441 and to dissension within *shugo daimyō* families, who required strong shogunal support to effect orderly succession in the face of disaffected family members and fractious vassals.

The proximate cause for war was contention in the mid-1460s over succession to the headship of the Ashikaga shogunal house. Discouraged by the failure of his wife, HINO TOMIKO, to produce an heir and anxious to unburden himself of the responsibility of public duty, ASHIKAGA YOSHIMASA in 1464 persuaded his brother Yoshimi (1439–91) to relinquish his status as a Buddhist priest and to stand in line as successor to the office of shōgun. Within a year, however, Tomiko gave birth to a male child, Yoshihisa (1465–89), and insisted that he be made the next shōgun. The lines for a major struggle were drawn when HOSOKAWA KATSUMOTO, head of the KANREI (shogunal deputy) HOSOKAWA FAMILY, backed Yoshimi's candidacy, and YAMANA SŌZEN (Katsumoto's father-in-law and the *shugo daimyō* of a great western domain) gave his support to Tomiko and the infant Yoshihisa.

The war began in Kyōto in 1467 with a clash between the allies of the Hosokawa, known as the Eastern Army, and the Yamana and their backers, known as the Western Army. Contending factions within great *shugo daimyō* houses such as the HATAKEYAMA FAMILY and SHIBA FAMILY sought to use the Ōnin War to continue their intrafamily struggles and to this end allied themselves with the Eastern and Western armies.

The commanders of the two armies, Hosokawa Katsumoto and Yamana Sōzen, both died in 1473, and, although the fighting continued in Kyōto for four more years, the last half of the Ōnin War was a stalemate. The issue of the Ashikaga succession was quietly settled, also in 1473, with Yoshihisa's appointment as shōgun. The war had become an insane exercise in mutual destruction that neither side saw any compelling reason to terminate. When the last troops were finally withdrawn from Kyōto in 1477, they left not only a devastated city but also a shattered structure of military rule. Henceforth the Muromachi shogunate, although it continued until 1573, was a central government in name only, and those *shugo*

daimyō houses still intact soon joined the others in decline. An age of disunity was begun that would continue for more than a hundred years, until a more thorough and enduring military hegemony was imposed by TOKUGAWA IEYASU, the last of the great national unifiers.

Onioshidashi 鬼押出

Series of lava beds on the northern slopes of ASAMAYAMA in western Gumma Prefecture, central Honshū. Formed by a great lava flow following a disastrous eruption of Asamayama in 1783, it is an area full of fantastically shaped rocks. Elevation: 1,200–2,100 m (4,000–6,900 ft).

Ōnishi Hajime 大西祝

(1864–1900). Philosopher of the Meiji period (1868–1912). Born in what is now Okayama Prefecture. Graduate of the theology department of Dōshisha University and the philosophy department of Tōkyō University. He taught philosophy and ethics at Tōkyō Semmon Gakkō (now Waseda University) and the Tōkyō Higher Normal School (later Tōkyō University of Education) and helped edit the influential Christian journal *Rikugō zasshi* (The Universe). In addition, he participated in the founding of the Teiyū Ethics Society (Teiyū Rinrikai) in 1896.

Ōnishi's critical writings reveal an idealistic stand, reflecting the influence of Kant. INOUE TETSUJIRŌ and other nationalist scholars saw Christianity as being opposed to the spirit of loyalty and patriotism as articulated in the IMPERIAL RESCRIPT ON EDUCATION, but Ōnishi saw religion as transcending the state. He called for protection of freedom of thought and speech and propounded the "necessity for socialism." His writings are collected in *Ōnishi hakase zenshū* (1903–04).

Ōnishi Kyojin 大西巨人

(1919–). Novelist. Real name Ōnishi Norito. Born in Fukuoka Prefecture; studied at Kyūshū University. Through his writings, Ōnishi examines political movements, state authority, and the moral responsibility of the writer in time of war. His *Shinsei kigeki* (Divine Comedy), which was serialized 1960–80, is a profound study of a man's rebellion against the power structure of the army. Ōnishi's other works include the two-volume *Ōnishi Kyojin bungei ronsō* (1982–85, Collected Criticism of Ōnishi Kyojin).

Onjōji → Miidera

Onjuku 御宿 [町]

Town in southeastern Chiba Prefecture, central Honshū, on the Pacific. A fishing town whose main catches are sardine and saurel, Onjuku is also an important tourist center with fine swimming beaches. The area is noted for its AMA (female divers). Pop: 7,939.

Onkō → Jiun Onkō

Onna daigaku 女大学

(The Great Learning for Women). A manual of ethics and proper behavior for women that was widely used in the late Edo period (1600–1868); published in 1716. Its title makes clear its Confucian standpoint, *Daigaku* being the Japanese for the Chinese classic *Da xue* (*Ta hsüeh*; Great Learning). It reflects the manner in which women were regarded in *samurai* families and to some extent in other social classes. Although its authorship is not certain, the work is commonly attributed to KAIBARA EKIKEN.

The book, which consists of 19 chapters, states general principles for the education of women and prescribes a specific code of behavior. A woman was expected to be obedient and respectful at all times: her place was at home. Its values persisted well into the 20th century.

onnagata 女形

Also called *oyama*. Technical term for a female impersonator in the KABUKI theater. The term *onnagata* was first used in registration documents introduced after 1652 to ensure that the government's 1629 ban against employing women on the stage was not contravened. The roles played by female impersonators are subdivided into representative types to meet the needs of a repertoire dependent on archetypal characterization. Important examples are a maiden, *musume;* an attractive young woman, *waka oyama;* a matron, *kashagata;* an aged woman, *babayaku;* a lady of high *samurai* rank, *katahazushi;* and a high-class courtesan, *tayū*. The senior female impersonator in a kabuki troupe is called *tate oyama* and is accorded equal professional status with his counterpart in the male roles.

The government-imposed need to develop the female impersonator's skills permanently affected the formulation of aesthetic principles and acting styles. Dance, for example, became central to the accomplishments of the female impersonators, who contributed to the growth of *shosagoto*, a dance-drama form of kabuki performance. Actors skillfully exploited deportment, speech, styles of clothing, and hairdressing in devising forms that would provide a symbolic concept of femininity while retaining theatrical credibility. The early female impersonators dressed like women and retained their theatrical deportment and mannerisms in public and in private life.

The social ferment that followed the Meiji Restoration of 1868, however, induced deep change in the kabuki world. The geographical isolation of playhouses was abolished, actors were accorded their place in normal society, and a more positive public image was promulgated. Today the female impersonator lives, dresses, and takes his recreation like any ordinary citizen. One of the more prominent *onnagata* active today is BANDŌ TAMASABURŌ V, who is renowned for the grace and delicacy of his performances.

The female impersonator's craft was developed through time in answer to an absolute theatrical need. The stylized form was deliberately designed to be symbolic rather than mimetic. That form is so intrinsically related to kabuki dramatic structure that, so long as the old theater serves a public demand, it seems likely that the *onnagata* actor will remain essential to performance.

Onnazaka   女坂

(tr *The Waiting Years*, 1971). Novel by ENCHI FUMIKO (1905–86), published 1949–57, depicting the married life of Shirakawa Tomo, a woman of Meiji-period (1868–1912) Japan. Tomo's marriage begins in a spirit of devotion to her husband, Yukitomo, and his household (see IE), but this palls when she is forced to procure other women to become live-in concubines for him. The novel describes Yukitomo's sexual avarice with composed objectivity, Tomo's slowly developing sense of injustice with pity and understanding. Tomo's deathbed message to her husband—to dump her body in the ocean without a funeral—blazes with the resentment that has smoldered inside her throughout her married life; it is a final, outright rejection of the patriarchal *ie* system, which has both oppressed her and involved her in the oppression of other women. The novel remains a favorite among Enchi's works.

Ono   小野[市]

City in southern Hyōgo Prefecture, western Honshū. It is the largest producer of the *soroban* (abacus) in Japan and is also famous for its sickles and kitchen knives. The temple Jōdoji has several important works of art dating from the 12th century. Pop: 46,007.

Ōno   大野[市]

City in northeastern Fukui Prefecture, central Honshū. It developed as a castle town in the late 16th century. Industries include textiles, lumber processing, and the manufacturing of skis and furniture. Hot springs and ski resorts are located here. Pop: 40,991.

Ono Azusa   小野梓

(1852–86). Scholar and government official of the early Meiji period (1868–1912). Born in the domain of Tosa (now Kōchi Prefecture). In 1871 he went to the United States to study law and then to London to study the British banking and political systems. Returning to Japan in 1874, he founded the Kyōzon Dōshū (Coexistence Association), consisting mainly of students who had studied abroad, to spread the principles of liberalism and constitutionalism in Japan. In 1876 Ono became a government official but resigned in the aftermath of the POLITICAL CRISIS OF 1881 together with ŌKUMA SHIGENOBU, his friend and mentor. With Ōkuma he helped found the RIKKEN KAISHINTŌ (Constitutional

Reform Party). He also helped Ōkuma establish the Tōkyō Semmon Gakkō (now Waseda University). His works include *Kokken hanron* (1882–85, Outline of the National Constitution), a constitutional draft, and *Mimpō no hone* (1883, Essence of Civil Law).

Ōno Bamboku   大野伴睦

(1890–1964). Politician. Born in Gifu Prefecture; attended Meiji University. He was elected to the Tōkyō Municipal Assembly in 1923 and as a candidate of the RIKKEN SEIYŪKAI party to the House of Representatives in 1930. After World War II, he helped form the Japan Liberal Party (Nihon Jiyūtō; see LIBERAL PARTY), becoming secretary-general. Implicated in the SHŌWA DENKŌ SCANDAL in 1948, he resigned but was acquitted in 1951. He served as speaker of the House of Representatives in 1952, as state minister in 1953, and as vice-president of the LIBERAL DEMOCRATIC PARTY (Jiyū Minshutō) until his death.

Ono Chikukyō   小野竹喬

(1889–1979). Japanese-style (NIHONGA) painter. Born Ono Eikichi in Okayama Prefecture, he studied under the *nihonga* painter TAKEUCHI SEIHŌ and at the Kyōto Shiritsu Kaiga Semmon Gakkō (now Kyōto City University of Arts). While in Europe during 1921–22, he began to take a strong interest in traditional Japanese painting. Thereafter, he painted richly lyrical landscapes. His most important work is *Fuyubichō* (1928, Winter Diary). He received the Order of Culture in 1976.

Onoda   小野田[市]

City in southwestern Yamaguchi Prefecture, western Honshū. A coal-mining center from the 18th century until the early 1960s, it was also the site of Japan's first privately owned cement and chemical plants. Drugs and petrochemicals are also produced. Pop: 46,491.

Onoda Cement Co, Ltd

小野田セメント[株]

(Onoda Semento). Manufacturer of cement. The first private cement company in Japan. Incorporated in 1881. Onoda's Dragon-brand cement is now exported to almost 50 countries. The company has progressively diversified into concrete products, cement additives, building materials, soil-stabilizing materials, fertilizers, and various kinds of chemicals. Sales for the fiscal year ending March 1991 totaled ¥219.0 billion (US $1.6 billion), of which cement constituted 72 percent and limestone and other products 28 percent. The export ratio was 4 percent, and the company was capitalized at ¥29.1 billion (US $212.1 million) in the same year. Headquarters are in Onoda, Yamaguchi Prefecture.

Onoe Baikō   尾上梅幸

One of the most distinguished names among the traditional acting families in the KABUKI theater. From Baikō I through Baikō V, the name Baikō alternated with the name ONOE KIKUGORŌ from father to son. Onoe Baikō VI (1870–1934), an ONNAGATA (female impersonator) was the adopted son of Onoe Kikugorō V (1844–1903). Baikō VII (b 1915) began his training in early childhood under his adoptive father, the great actor Onoe Kikugorō VI (1885–1949), making his stage debut at the age of six. He succeeded to the name Baikō VII in 1947. He helped found the Kikugorō acting troupe, named for his late adoptive father, and became its leading on-

nagata. He primarily specializes in portrayals of noble and refined female characters, but he is also skilled at *tachiyaku*, or leading male roles. Also an accomplished dancer, Baikō VII was made a Living National Treasure in 1968.

Onoe Kikugorō   尾上菊五郎

One of the most distinguished names among the traditional acting families in the KABUKI theater. Kikugorō I (1717–83) began as an ONNAGATA (female impersonator) in Kyōto but later excelled in heroic *samurai* roles. His son Kikugorō II (1769–87), also an *onnagata*, died young.

Because of his enormously wide range in executing both masculine and feminine roles, Kikugorō III (1784–1849) earned the title of "Kaneru" ("Versatile One"). In 1855 the son-in-law of Kikugorō III, an *onnagata*, became Kikugorō IV (1808–60), but he held this name only briefly. Along with Ichikawa Danjūrō IX (1838–1903; see ICHIKAWA DANJŪRŌ), Kikugorō V (1844–1903) is considered one of the two finest actors of the Meiji kabuki theater.

Experimenting constantly with fresh ideas—including those from abroad—Kikugorō VI (1885–1949) tried to promote the further development of kabuki in the 20th century. He was an actor of extremely broad scope and versatility and was an expert dancer. Kikugorō VII (b 1942) is the son of Onoe Baikō VII (b 1915), who had been adopted by Kikugorō VI, and like his father is an *onnagata*. He assumed his present name in 1973.

Onoe Matsunosuke   尾上松之助

(1875–1926). Actor and director. Real name Nakamura Tsuruzō. Born in Okayama Prefecture. He first appeared on the KABUKI stage at age five. He made his movie debut in *Goban Tadanobu* (1909), produced by Yokota Shōkai (a precursor of the NIKKATSU CORPORATION). For his ability to roll his eyeballs, he came to be known as Medama no Matchan (Eyeball Matchan), "Matchan" being an affectionate abbreviation of Matsunosuke. At the peak of his career he was making nine films per month. His 1,000th movie, Ikeda Tomiyasu's (1892–1968) *Araki Mataemon* (1925), was the biggest success in the history of Nikkatsu. He himself directed several films, most notably *Yūkoku no shishi* (1924, *The Noble Patriot*). He served as head of Nikkatsu's studios between 1921 and 1923 and became a director of the company in 1923.

Onoe Saishū   尾上柴舟

(1876–1957). TANKA poet, calligrapher, and scholar of Japanese literature. Real name Onoe Hachirō. Born in Okayama Prefecture. Graduate of Tōkyō University. A disciple of the poet OCHIAI NAOBUMI, in 1902 he collaborated with KANEKO KUN'EN on the classical

Onoe Shōroku
Shōroku II was the better known of the two *kabuki* actors who used the name Onoe Shōroku. Here, holding a staff, he plays the role of Benkei in a pivotal scene from the play *Kanjinchō* (The Subscription List).

poetry collection *Jokeishi*. As a calligrapher and scholar he specialized in the 12th-century *sōsho* (cursive) style (see CALLIGRAPHY). In 1937 he was elected to the Japan Art Academy (Nihon Geijutsuin). From 1949 until his death, he judged the annual imperial *tanka* contest (see IMPERIAL NEW YEAR'S POETRY READING). His *tanka* collections include *Nikki no hashi yori* (1913) and *Shiroki michi* (1914).

Onoe Shōroku   尾上松緑

Professional name used by two KABUKI actors active in different eras. In 1809, Onoe Matsusuke I (1744–1815) changed his name to Shōroku I. Shōroku II (1913–89), the third son of Matsumoto Kōshirō VII (1870–1949; see MATSUMOTO KŌSHIRŌ), received his acting training studying under the great actor Onoe Kikugorō VI (1885–1949; see ONOE KIKUGORŌ). He inherited the name Shōroku II in 1935. In 1949 he helped found the Kikugorō theater troupe, named for his late teacher, and served as *tachiyaku* (leading male actor) for it. He was especially noted for his mastery of the *aragoto* ("rough business") style, *sewamono* (domestic plays), and dance. He was designated a Living National Treasure in 1972. In 1984 he was awarded the Order of Culture. He succeeded to the position of head master of the Fujima school of Japanese-style dance under the name Fujima Kansai.

Ōnogawa   大野川

River in Ōita Prefecture, Kyūshū, originating in the mountain Sobosan and flowing through the Ōita Plain into Beppu Bay. It is the largest river in Ōita Prefecture. The water is utilized for irrigation, electric power, and industry. Length: 107 km (66 mi); area of drainage basin: 1,460 sq km (564 sq mi).

Ono-Gumi   小野組

(House of Ono). Merchant house that flourished in the early Meiji period (1868–1912). The Ono-Gumi began as a silk importer in Kyōto in the late 17th century. It was then appointed one of several official money-changing houses by the Tokugawa shogunate (1603–1867). After the Meiji Restoration (1868), it was appointed an official purveyor and financial agent (see SEISHŌ). In 1872 the government persuaded the houses of Ono and MITSUI to join together in founding a bank, later called the First National Bank (Daiichi Kokuritsu Ginkō). The House of Ono went bankrupt when in 1874 the government suddenly demanded collateral for its loans.

Ōno Harunaga   大野治長

(?–1615). A vassal of the national unifier TOYOTOMI HIDEYOSHI and of his son TOYOTOMI HIDEYORI and a favorite of the latter's mother, YODOGIMI; also known as Shuri no Suke. An anti-Tokugawa hothead, he led the defense

of Ōsaka Castle against the shogunate in 1614–15. In June 1615, as the castle fell to the Tokugawa, Hideyori and Yodogimi committed suicide, and Harunaga followed them into death. See also ŌSAKA CASTLE, SIEGES OF.

Ōnojō   大野城[市]

City in northwestern Fukuoka Prefecture, Kyūshū. A large munitions plant set up here during World War II later became the site of an American military base. With the expansion of the neighboring city of FUKUOKA, Ōnojō has become a satellite city. The remains of Japan's oldest mountain fort, Ōnojō Castle, are found here. Pop: 75,214.

Ōno Kazuo   大野一雄

(1906–   ). BUTŌ dancer. Born in Hokkaidō, he studied modern dance with Eguchi Takaya (1900–1977). In 1929 he saw the Spanish dancer La Argentina (1888–1936) perform in Japan and was deeply moved and inspired by her work. From 1952 to 1959 he performed a series of dances, such as *Tango*, *Machikado* (Street Corner), and *Rōjin to umi* (Old Man and the Sea). This was followed by a hiatus in creative activity which lasted until 1977, when he returned to the stage with *Ra Aruhenchīna shō* (Eulogy for La Argentina). Always absorbing and reacting to the spirit of the times, he has stayed in the forefront of the *butō* movement. Among his other works is *Watashi no okāsan* (1981, My Mother).

onomatopoeia   擬声語・擬態語

(*giseigo; gitaigo*). Japanese has a much larger vocabulary of onomatopoetic words than English. A recent dictionary lists close to 1,000 such words, with many more if variants are counted. Japanese terminology makes a distinction between two types of onomatopoeia: *giseigo* (also called *giongo*) are words that imitate sounds as do the English cackle, hiss, and sizzle; *gitaigo* are words that use sound to express an abstract quality or condition, the manner in which something is done, or a subjective feeling as do the English drizzle, waddle, flutter, flash, and tingle. However, in common usage the term *giseigo* is often used to refer to both types. Onomatopoetic words are usually written in the *katakana* syllabary (see KANA). They are normally used adverbially (often followed by the quotative particle *to*) or verbalized by the verb *suru* (to do).

Onomichi   尾道[市]

City in southeastern Hiroshima Prefecture, western Honshū. Situated on the Inland Sea, it has been a commercial port since the 12th century. Shipbuilding is its main industry. Sights of interest include the temple Jōdoji. In 1990 an island-hopping chain of bridges was under construction that would link Onomichi with Imabari on the island of Shikoku. See HONSHŪ-SHIKOKU BRIDGES. Pop: 97,103.

Ono no Imoko   小野妹子

(fl early 7th century). Court official and diplomat during the reign of Empress SUIKO (r 593–628). In 607 Prince SHŌTOKU appointed Ono to lead an embassy to the Sui dynasty (589–618) in China, where he delivered the famous letter addressed by "the Son of Heaven in the land where the sun rises" to "the Son of Heaven in the land where the sun sets," greatly offending the Chinese emperor. In 608 he returned to Japan, but later that year went back to China as the head of an embassy that included TAKAMUKO NO

KUROMARO, MINABUCHI NO SHŌAN, and the priest SŌMIN, whom Shōtoku sent to study Chinese culture and institutions. Ono's missions established formal trade relations and informal cultural exchanges with China; the students who accompanied the missions had a far-reaching influence on Japanese culture and became leaders of the Chinese-inspired TAIKA REFORM of 645. See also SUI AND TANG (T'ANG) CHINA, EMBASSIES TO.

Ono no Komachi   小野小町

(fl mid-9th century). WAKA poet. One of Japan's most famous poets. KI NO TSURAYUKI, compiler of the first official anthology of poetry, the KOKINSHŪ (ca 905), ranked her among the Six Poetic Geniuses (ROKKASEN). Komachi was probably born in the northern provinces in the first decades of the 9th century.

Of some 100 poems preserved under her name in various official anthologies and in the *Komachishū* (also known as the *Ono no Komachi kashū*), a collection compiled (ca 1108) by an unknown hand, about 80 can be considered genuine. Nearly all of her poems are about unhappy or unrequited love, separation, or the infidelity of men.

A number of romantic legends that arose due to her reputation for beauty, wit, and passion have inspired literary works ranging from the *Tamatsukuri Komachi sōsui sho* (Book of the Grandeur and Decadence of Tamatsukuri Komachi), an 11th-century Buddhist treatise on the impermanence of worldly things, to MISHIMA YUKIO's modern NŌ play *Sotoba Komachi*. The most important literary treatments of the legend of Komachi are five 14th- to 15th-century plays by the great masters of Nō, KAN'AMI Kiyotsugu and ZEAMI Motokiyo: *Sōshi arai Komachi* (Komachi Washing the Manuscript), *Sekidera Komachi* (Komachi at Sekidera), *Ōmu Komachi* (Komachi Answering Yukiie), *Sotoba Komachi* (Komachi at the Stupa), and *Kayoi Komachi* (Visiting Komachi). During the Edo period (1600–1868), "Komachi" came to be used as a suffix with place names to refer to some especially beautiful woman of a locality, a practice that continues even today.

Ono no Takamura   小野篁

(802–853). Courtier, poet, scholar, and writer of Chinese poetry and prose. Numerous apocryphal anecdotes and legends about Takamura are found in old tale collections. An account pieced together from various sources indicates that as a child he lived for a time in the wild northeastern province of Mutsu, where his father was governor. He became an imperial adviser (*sangi*) and the foremost Chinese litterateur of his generation. Only a few of Takamura's Chinese writings are preserved in the old anthologies. Some of his more famous verses were appropriated as lyrics for songs to accompany formal court music and dance performances and survive by this means. Of his poems in Japanese, 12 are preserved in imperial anthologies, beginning with 6 in the KOKINSHŪ (ca 905). His so-called personal collection, known variously as *Takamurashū*, *Ono no Takamura shū*, *Takamura nikki*, and *Takamura monogatari*, contains 32 poems attributed to him, but probably few if any are actually his. It is believed that the work was actually written as late as the mid-11th century.

Ono no Tōfū   小野道風

(894–966). Also known as Ono no Michikaze. Calligrapher of the Heian period

(794–1185) and grandson of courtier-poet ONO NO TAKAMURA. One of the so-called San-seki (Three Brush Traces), with FUJIWARA NO SUKEMASA and FUJIWARA NO YUKINARI. Tōfū is considered the founder of Japanese-style calligraphy, a major stylistic transformation from the Chinese-influenced calligraphy exemplified by the 9th-century monk KŪKAI, Emperor SAGA, and others.

Ono Pharmaceutical Co, Ltd
小野薬品工業[株]

(Ono Yakuhin Kōgyō). Pharmaceutical manufacturer and distributor. Incorporated in 1947. The company conducts intensive research and development activities in prostaglandins and in enzyme inhibitors. Ono grants licenses to May & Baker (the United Kingdom), Schwarz (Germany), Sereno (Italy), Lepetit (Italy), and Esteve (Spain), among others. Sales for the fiscal year ending November 1991 totaled ¥75.0 billion (US $546.6 million), and capitalization stood at ¥17.3 billion (US $126.1 million). Headquarters are in Ōsaka.

Ono Ranzan
小野蘭山

(1729–1810). Specialist in honzōgaku (traditional pharmacognosy) who perfected the study of descriptive pharmacology in Japan. Born in Kyōto, he studied under MATSUOKA JOAN. He studied the Bencao gangmu (Pents'ao kang-mu; J: Honzō kōmoku), an important pharmacognosy book from China, and in 1803 published Honzō kōmoku keimō, a 48-volume compilation of honzōgaku studies in Japan. From age 72 to 78 he collected medicinal plants throughout the Kantō and Chūbu regions under the orders of the Tokugawa shogunate (1603–1867).

Ono Seiichirō
小野清一郎

(1891–1986). Jurist and prominent specialist of criminal law, criminal procedure, and legal theory. Born in Morioka, Iwate Prefecture, Ono graduated from the law department of Tōkyō University in 1917. He served for a time as a public prosecutor, later becoming a professor at Tōkyō University. Ono was one of the first scholars in Japan to specialize in the study of CRIMINAL PROCEDURE. His early book Keiji soshohō kōgi (1924, Lectures in Criminal Procedure) was the first comprehensive discussion of this branch of legal science in Japan. Ono's theory of criminal law is stamped with a strong ethical bias; it is based on a theory of moral responsibility grounded in philosophy, particularly Buddhist philosophy. In 1938 he succeeded his mentor, MAKINO EIICHI, on his retirement, as professor of criminal law at Tōkyō University. His drafts of the Revised Penal Code, although criticized for authoritarian bias, influenced postwar revision of Japan's penal code. He was awarded the Order of Culture in 1972.

Ono Tōzaburō
小野十三郎

(1903–). Poet. Born in Ōsaka Prefecture. Studied at Tōyō University. He participated in the anarchist poetry movement in the 1920s and in 1926 published his first collection of poems, Hambun hiraita mado (The Half-Opened Window). He established himself as a realist poet with his collections Ōsaka (1939) and Fūkeishi shō (1943) and published a collection of essays titled Shiron (1947, Essays on Poetry), which rejected as valueless traditional Japanese lyricism such as that of the WAKA and stressed the importance of realism and social criticism in po-

etry. His poetry collections include Jūyu Fuji (1956).

Ō no Yasumaro
太安万侶

(?–723). Scholar-official of the Nara period (710–794). In 711, at the command of Empress Gemmei (661–721; r 707–715), Yasumaro transcribed the imperial genealogy (see TEIKI) and ancient myths (see KYŪJI) as recited by the blind oral historian HIEDA NO ARE. These records formed the KOJIKI (712), now Japan's oldest surviving written history. Yasumaro is also credited with having compiled the later history NIHON SHOKI (720) in collaboration with Prince TONERI. In January 1979 the site of Yasumaro's grave was ascertained when a bronze funerary plaque inscribed with his name and date of death was discovered in a tea field in the Tawara district, Nara Prefecture.

Ono Yōko
オノ・ヨーコ

(1933–). Artist and musician, known for joint works with her husband, the musician John Lennon (1940–80). Born in Tōkyō; attended Sarah Lawrence College. Ono is a creator of avant-garde music, paintings, films, and "events" designed to stimulate the imagination and clarify perception. In 1956 she married Japanese composer Ichiyanagi Toshi (b 1933); she later married American artist Anthony Cox. Her third marriage, in 1969, was to Beatle John Lennon. The two drew worldwide attention for their unconventional lifestyle, open sexuality, and support for the peace movement. After Lennon was killed by a deranged fan in 1980, she recorded the album Seasons of Glass (1981) in his memory.

on readings
音読み

(on yomi). One of the two basic types of pronunciation of Chinese characters (KANJI) as they are used in the Japanese writing system, the other being KUN READINGS. On readings are Japanese approximations of the Chinese pronunciations of the characters, and they occur when characters are used to write words of Chinese origin. Kun readings are native Japanese words that translate the meaning of the characters. A single character may have more than one pronunciation of either type, selection among them being determined by the context in which the character is used.

A character's various on readings reflect Chinese pronunciations that differ according to the historical period or region of China. These pronunciations, which often differ markedly from each other, have been classified into three major categories: GO ON, KAN ON, and TŌ ON.

Go on (the Wu pronunciations) are pronunciations introduced in the 5th and 6th centuries along with the Chinese writing system. Kan on (the Han pronunciations), which were introduced in the 7th and 8th centuries, approximate the contemporary pronunciations of the Tang (T'ang) dynasty (618–907) capital in North China. Tō on (the Tang pronunciations), despite the name, represent still later pronunciations, most of which were brought into Japan by Zen Buddhist monks during the Song (Sung; 960–1279), Yuan (Yüan; 1279–1368), and Ming (1368–1644) dynasties.

onryō → goryō

onsen → hot springs

Ontake
御岳

Also pronounced Otake or Mitake. A name given to a number of mountains throughout Japan, the best known of which are Ontake-san, a mountain in the Kiso district of Nagano Prefecture, and the mountain known as Mitakesan in the Oku Tama area of Tōkyō Prefecture. At the foot of Ontake-san and the summit of Mitakesan are shrines respectively known as Ontake Shrine and Mitake Shrine. Both shrines are sites of mountain worship (sangaku shinkō; see MOUNTAINS, WORSHIP OF) where practioners of the eclectic SHUGENDŌ order form groups to climb the mountains and engage in ascetic discipline. In the Edo period (1600–1868), KŌ or fraternal religious groups were organized around the mountains bearing this name. Ontakesan, in particular, is the chief sacred site of the Ontakekyō sect, one of the SECT SHINTŌ religious orders. Local farmers regard such mountains as holy places where the gods dwell and select a day in early spring to worship there.

Ontakesan
御岳山

Also called Kiso Ontake. Composite stratovolcano on the border between Nagano and Gifu prefectures, central Honshū; it is composed of andesite. The mountain has five peaks, and there are two lakes on or near the summit. White-robed pilgrims climb to Ontake Shrine on the summit. One of the lakes, Ni no Ike, is the highest mountain lake in Japan. Ontakesan is noted for its beautiful cypress (hinoki) forests and alpine flora such as the Japanese black fritillary (kuroyuri). The folk song "Kisobushi" has made the mountain famous throughout Japan. The volcano erupted in 1979 for the first time in recorded history. The highest peak is Ken-gamine (3,067 m; 10,062 ft).

Onta ware
小鹿田焼

(onta-yaki). Also known as Onda ware (onda-yaki). Pottery made in Sarayama in Ōita Prefecture. Production began in 1705. Pots traditionally were made for and sold to the local farming populace. Some small pots such as pitchers and teapots were also made. These were often partially slipped before being glazed in transparent or translucent honey glazes. Green and yellow were often used as overglazes. The techniques of tobiganna chattering (in which a series of raindrop-size chips are cut into the leather-hard slipped body of a pot), slip trailing (nagashigake) or splashing (uchikake), and slip brushing (hakebiki and hakeme) are all now hallmarks of Onta ware. Dug locally and high in iron content, the clay fires a deep gray black that contrasts with the white slip and gives Onta ware its distinctive beauty. The local clay is so hard that its preparation averages about a month and thus limits production. Because of its traditional production techniques, Onta ware was designated a Mukei Bunkazai (Intangible Cultural Property) in 1970.

Ōnuma
大沼

Lake in southern Oshima Peninsula, southwestern Hokkaidō. Located on the southern slopes of Komagatake within Ōnuma Quasi-National Park. Created when the river Oritogawa was dammed by an eruption of Komagatake. Landslides during the eruption created several islands. Area: 5.3 sq km (2.0

Ono Yōko An avant-garde artist and musician, Ono collaborated on several albums with her third husband, former Beatle John Lennon.

Ōoka Shōhei This novelist's best-known works draw upon his wartime experiences in the Philippines.

sq mi); circumference: 26 km (16 mi); depth: 11.6 m (38 ft); altitude: 130 m (426 ft).

Ōnuma Chinzan　　　　大沼枕山

(1818–91). Writer of Chinese poetry (*kanshi*). Born in Edo (now Tōkyō), the son of a minor provincial official. He received instruction in Chinese poetry from YANAGAWA SEIGAN among others and later opened his own school, the Shitaya Ginsha. A master of the Song (Sung) style, he was for over three decades the most prominent writer of Chinese poetry in Edo. His chief collection was the *Chinzan shishō* (1859–67). The modern novelist NAGAI KAFŪ was related to the Ōnuma family on the maternal side.

Onward Kashiyama Co, Ltd

[株]オンワード樫山

(Onwādo Kashiyama). Manufacturer and wholesaler of ready-made garments. Incorporated in 1947. Its clothes bear the trade name Onward. The leading domestic producer of ready-made men's wear, it also produces clothing in the native Japanese style. In addition, it handles fine arts and jewelry. In 1985 Kashiyama entered into the marine leisure business. It has subsidiary firms in New York, Paris, Milan, and Hong Kong and has concluded numerous technology exchange agreements. Sales for the fiscal year ending February 1991 totaled ¥208.2 billion (US $1.6 billion), and capitalization stood at ¥16.6 billion (US $121.0 million). Headquarters are in Tōkyō.

Ōoka Makoto　　　　大岡信

(1931–). Poet and literary critic. Born in Shizuoka Prefecture. Graduate of Tōkyō University. His *Kioku to genzai* (1956, Memory and the Present) is a volume of poems rich in intellectual lyricism. Among his other writings are *Tōji no kakei* (1969, Lineage of a Profligate); *Ki no Tsurayuki* (1971), a study of the poet who compiled the KOKINSHŪ poetic anthology; and *Nihon shiika kikō* (1978, Travels through Japanese Poetry). Ōoka has published a number of volumes of *Oriori no uta* (1979– , Poems for All Occasions).

Ōoka Shōhei　　　　大岡昇平

(1909–88). Novelist and literary critic. Born in Tōkyō; graduated from Kyōto University. He published critical studies of Stendhal and other European writers before being drafted into the army in 1944. After World War II, he gained prominence with the autobiographical short story "Furyoki" (1948; tr "Prisoner of War," 1967) and the novel NOBI (1951; tr *Fires on the Plain*, 1957), which won the Yomiuri Literary Prize in 1951. The latter, one of the most important Japanese novels of the postwar period, explores the meaning of human existence through the struggle for survival of men who are driven by starvation to cannibalism. Ōoka's other works include *Musashino fujin* (1950), a psychological novel in the manner of Stendhal; *Reite senki* (1967–69), a semidocumentary account of the battle for Leyte; and the novel *Kaei* (1958–59), which won the Shinchōsha Prize in 1961.

Ōoka Tadasuke　　　　大岡忠相

(1677–1751). Edo city commissioner (EDO MACHI BUGYŌ), 1717–36, whose reputation for just decisions made him a legend. As commissioner of Yamada in Ise Province (now Mie Prefecture) Ōoka impressed TOKUGAWA

YOSHIMUNE, then *daimyō* of Kii (now Wakayama Prefecture), when he decided a boundary dispute against Kii despite that domain's power. When Yoshimune became the eighth Tokugawa shōgun he appointed Ōoka commissioner of Edo (now Tōkyō). The book *Ōoka seidan*, purportedly a record of the legal cases over which Ōoka presided, actually includes judgments of other magistrates, retellings of tales from abroad, and complete fabrications. Ōoka's journal has been published as *Ōoka Echizen no Kami Tadasuke nikki* (1972–75).

Ōoku　　　　大奥

(Great Interior). Large separate living quarters in the central compound (*hommaru*) of EDO CASTLE for the women who served the Tokugawa shōguns during the Edo period (1600–1868). Women connected with the former shōgun or the current shōgun's heir were generally housed elsewhere, in the western enclosure (*nishinomaru*). The Ōoku had more than 60 principal rooms, most of which were designated for specific people (for example, the shōgun's official wife) and purposes. The Ōoku was connected with the Exterior (Omote) section of the castle by a single "bell-door" (*suzu-guchi*), where the ringing of a bell signaled entrances and exits.

The Ōoku's organization was formalized in the 1620s under the third shōgun, TOKUGAWA IEMITSU, and his influential former nurse, KASUGA NO TSUBONE. Since entrance to the Ōoku was generally barred to all men except the shōgun, the women there administered their own affairs. Some 200 women held posts in the Ōoku hierarchy, and each had several personal attendants, so that the total employed in the Ōoku is said to have been about 3,000.

The elaborate Ōoku hierarchy was theoretically headed by the official wife but was in fact controlled by the most powerful women or groups within the Ōoku, commonly the wife's advisers (*jōrō*) or the "elders" (*otoshiyori*). High-ranking women left the Ōoku only on rare occasions, but despite all precautions, scandalous outside liaisons were not unknown (see EJIMA INCIDENT).

The women of the Ōoku sometimes exerted indirect political influence in advancing the careers of male relatives or promoting certain projects such as the construction of Buddhist temples. The organization and customs of the shōgun's Ōoku provided a general pattern for the women's quarters (*oku*) in the homes of other wealthy members of the warrior class, although such "interiors" were much smaller and simpler.

Open Door policy　　　　門戸開放政策

(Monko Kaihō *seisaku*). The principle of the Open Door originated in the concept of equality of commercial opportunity for nations trading with China, a traditional British policy. The United States first espoused this principle in the Open Door Notes (September–November 1899) and Circular (July 1900) of Secretary of State John M. Hay. In addition to commercial equality, the Circular championed the preservation of China's political and territorial integrity.

The nations involved in China acknowledged the Open Door principle and made reference to it in treaties made after 1900, but the competition for spheres of influence in China (concessions, railway and mining rights, and loans) continued. In the Nine-Power Treaty (1922), which emerged from the WASHINGTON CONFERENCE, the powers reaffirmed the Open Door policy but failed

to include enforcement regulations. The United States continued to advocate the policy during the 1930s, when Japan violated China's integrity, but only belatedly backed its statements with economic sanctions. See also NONRECOGNITION POLICY.

Opening of Japan　　　　開国

(Kaikoku). The process by which the TOKUGAWA SHOGUNATE (1603–1867) discarded its policy of NATIONAL SECLUSION and resumed trade and diplomatic relations with the West in the 1850s and 1860s. Specifically the term refers to the opening of Japanese ports to Western countries under the KANAGAWA TREATY of 1854 and the ANSEI COMMERCIAL TREATIES of 1858.

Since the institution of the seclusion policy in 1639, the Tokugawa shogunate had maintained trade relations with only the Netherlands and China. By the beginning of the 19th century, however, Russian, British, and US ships had begun to frequent Japanese waters. Demands for trade and other relations soon followed, but the shogunate resisted. In 1825 it issued the GAIKOKUSEN UCHIHARAI REI, an edict ordering the bombardment of all foreign ships entering Japanese waters. Japanese intellectuals such as SATŌ NOBUHIRO, TAKANO CHŌEI, and WATANABE KAZAN began calling for improved coastal defenses and the opening of Japanese ports to foreign ships; Takano and Watanabe were arrested in 1837 as a result of their criticism of shogunal policies (see BANSHA NO GOKU).

Awareness of the foreign threat increased when China lost the Opium War and concluded the Treaty of Nanking with Britain in 1842. Then, in 1853, Commodore Matthew PERRY arrived in Uraga with the ships of his East India Squadron and a request from the US president for trade. The following year the shogunate grudgingly concluded the Kanagawa Treaty, opening two ports to US ships; they were soon opened to Russia, France, and Britain as well.

In 1858 the US consul general Townsend HARRIS concluded a commercial treaty (see HARRIS TREATY) between Japan and the United States. This, the first of the Ansei treaties, was followed by similar treaties with the Netherlands, Russia, Britain, and France. Although the shogunate had obtained imperial approval for the earlier Kanagawa Treaty, it failed to secure this approval for the commercial treaties, and friction between the shogunate and its critics increased. Chief Councillor II NAOSUKE pushed the treaties through and suppressed his opponents (see ANSEI PURGE), but he was assassinated in the spring of 1860 by discontented *samurai* (see SAKURADAMONGAI INCIDENT).

The Ansei agreements are often referred to as unequal treaties since they granted Western nations extraterritorial rights in Japan and denied Japan tariff autonomy (see UNEQUAL TREATIES, REVISION OF). Trade with foreign countries began in 1859, but the immediate result was an outflow of gold from Japan, disruption of traditional markets, rises in commodity prices, and other economic fluctuations. These in turn triggered popular unrest and uprisings (see IKKI; UCHIKOWASHI).

Discontent over trade relationships and treaties also intensified the antishogunate SONNŌ JŌI (Revere the Emperor, Expel the Barbarians) movement and spurred a series of antiforeign incidents such as the RICHARDSON AFFAIR. On the other hand, men such as SAKUMA SHŌZAN, YOKOI SHŌNAN, and KATSU KAISHŪ supported the opening of Japan and pressed for shogunal reform. But the unrest stirred up by the foreign crisis had severely shaken the Tokugawa shogunate, and it was overthrown in 1867. After the MEIJI RESTORATION in 1868 the new government maintained existing relations with foreign countries and worked to better Japan's international position.

Operation Number One　一号作戦

(Ichigō Sakusen). Largest offensive carried out by the Japanese army in China during WORLD WAR II. Launched in April 1944, the operation continued until February 1945. Deploying 500,000 troops, the Japanese army extended itself along a vertical line 1,500 kilometers (900 mi) long in South and North China with the aim of destroying the US air bases that were being used by Maj. Gen. Claire L. Chennault to stage bombing raids on the Japanese mainland. Initially effective, the offensive gradually lost momentum after Japanese forces lost command of the air.

Operation Victory　捷一号作戦

(Shō Ichigō Sakusen). Military campaign conducted in the summer of 1944 by the imperial Japanese armed forces against the Allied forces advancing toward the Philippines in WORLD WAR II. Despite the heroic efforts of front-line troops, supported by Kamikaze units (see KAMIKAZE SPECIAL ATTACK FORCE), a series of blunders—including a miscalculation of the outcome of an air battle off the coast of Taiwan and of the strategic importance of the island of Leyte—contributed to the Allied victory. Japanese military forces lost their capacity for sustained operations and were ultimately defeated.

Oppler, Alfred Christian
オプラー, A. C.

(1893–1982). Scholar of law and principal architect of the legal and judicial reforms during the OCCUPATION. Born in Alsace-Lorraine, he studied law in Germany and served in the German army during World War I. In 1918 he settled in Berlin, where he became an associate justice of the Supreme Administrative Court and vice-president of the Supreme Disciplinary Court. He emigrated to the United States in March 1939. In 1944 he joined the Foreign Economic Administration in Washington, DC.

In 1946 he accepted an assignment to General MacArthur's headquarters in Tōkyō, where he became chief of the Courts and Law Division of the Government Section (renamed Legislation and Justice Division in May 1948). Oppler oversaw reorganization of the Japanese legal and judicial systems, influencing their modernization and democratization. In 1976 he published *Legal Reform in Occupied Japan: A Participant Looks Back*, an account of his Far Eastern activities.

Oraga haru　おらが春

(1820; tr *The Year of My Life*, 1972). A HAIBUN narrative written by HAIKU poet Kobayashi ISSA (1763–1827). The birth and death of Issa's second child, Sato, was the inspiration for the work, which became his best known. It is primarily a biographical account of the year during which this sad event took place, but also includes sketches of thoughts and experiences from other years and areas of his life. The work successfully combines the traditional gravity of haiku with unexpectedly intimate, unconventional (and at times comic) glimpses of Issa's daily experiences.

ōraimono　往来物

(letter writers). Classical textbooks for letter writing; later all sorts of textbooks for social common sense came to be classified in this category. The word ōrai ("go and come") originally meant correspondence. The first ōraimono was MEIGŌ ŌRAI (1040, Akihira's Letter Writer). The ōraimono texts are important linguistic materials for investigating the development of SŌRŌBUN (the epistolary style).

During the Kamakura (1185–1333) and Muromachi (1333–1568) periods many letter-writing books were produced, including TEIKIN ŌRAI (before 1350?, Household-Precept Letter Writer), one of the best-known examples of the ōraimono genre. In the Edo period (1600–1868), use of the word ōrai was extended to beginning textbooks in various fields, as in *Shōbai ōrai* (A Guide to Commerce) and *Hyakushō ōrai* (A Guide for Farmers). All textbooks used at TERAKOYA (village schools) were called ōraimono. Altogether, over two thousand kinds of ōraimono were produced. Some were still being published at the beginning of the Meiji period (1868–1912) but were soon replaced by Western-style textbooks.

Oranda fūsetsugaki　オランダ風説書

(Dutch reports). News of foreign events brought by the Dutch trading ships that visited Nagasaki regularly during the Edo period (1600–1868). When the Tokugawa shogunate adopted a policy of strict NATIONAL SECLUSION in 1639, the Dutch were the only Europeans authorized to trade with Japan (see NAGASAKI TRADE). They were also charged with informing the shogunate of events overseas, particularly the activities of Spanish and Portuguese missionaries. The news was translated by interpreters (ORANDA TSŪJI) and forwarded to the shogunate by the commissioners (*bugyō*) of Nagasaki. The oldest extant fūsetsugaki dates from 1641. After the termination of the seclusion policy in 1854, the fūsetsugaki were replaced by translations of newspapers from the Netherlands and from Batavia (now Jakarta, Indonesia), the headquarters of the Dutch East India Company.

Oranda Shōgatsu　オランダ正月

(Dutch New Year). Celebrations of the Western New Year held by the physician and Rangaku (Dutch Learning; see WESTERN LEARNING) scholar ŌTSUKI GENTAKU at his residence in Kyōbashi, Edo (now Tōkyō). Ōtsuki held a Western-style celebration in place of traditional midwinter festivities that practitioners of Chinese medicine held in honor of Shinnō (Ch: Shennong or Shennung), a mythical Chinese hero. The first Oranda Shōgatsu took place on 1 January 1795. Ōtsuki invited friends, colleagues, and students, displayed a picture of Hippocrates, and served Western food and drink. A painting of this gathering by Ichikawa Gakusan shows one guest wearing Western clothing and seated on a chair. After Ōtsuki's death the observance was maintained by his son Genkan until 1837.

Oranda tsūji　オランダ通詞

(Dutch-language interpreters). Japanese interpreters and customs officers stationed by the Tokugawa shogunate (1603–1867) in Nagasaki during the Edo period (1600–1868). In addition to acting as interpreters for the Dutch (the only Western traders allowed to

Opening of Japan The landing at Kanagawa of Commodore Matthew Perry on 8 March 1854 with an armed force of sailors and marines. Black-and-white reproduction of a color original by Wilhelm Heine, an artist who accompanied Perry's mission.

enter Japan under the terms of the NATIONAL SECLUSION policy), these officials took charge of various matters related to trade, such as the inspection of Dutch ships on their arrival and departure and the translation of freight inventories. The chief interpreter (*ōtsūji*) had a staff of assistants in several ranks, who numbered some 140 by the last years of the shogunate. The post was hereditary in specially designated families, of whom the Nishi, the Baba, and the Shizuki are the best known. Many tsūji mastered other foreign languages and became versed in WESTERN LEARNING, as the study of European science and culture was called at the time. A Dutch-Japanese dictionary known as the *Nagasaki wage* (see HARUMA WAGE) was compiled by younger tsūji in the early 19th century.

Orange War　オレンジ戦略案

(Orenji *senryakuan*; literally, "Orange plan"). Code name for the contingency plan for a possible war between the United States and Japan in the Pacific area. It was developed by US military strategists in the period of growing tension before World War II. The plan, which placed Japan before Europe on a list of priorities, formed the basis of US naval planning until 1939, when it was replaced by the RAINBOW PLAN.

Order of Culture　文化勲章

(Bunka Kunshō). Official decoration awarded annually to honor individuals who have made a significant contribution to the developments of the arts and sciences. The Order of Culture does not have rankings. Recipients usually number four or five each year, in fields of endeavor ranging from the natural sciences and medicine to literature, the fine arts, music, drama, architecture, and scholarly research. The Order of Culture was first established in 1937, in an effort to encourage and foster greater originality and creativity in the cultural sphere. Since 1949 it has been awarded annually on Culture Day (3 November). Recipients of the award are selected by the cabinet from among a list of persons of cultural merit (*bunka kōrōsha*) chosen by the minister of education and recommended to the prime minister.

organ transplants　臓器移植

(*zōki ishoku*). Organ transplants are now a widely recognized treatment for incurable diseases of vital organs such as the heart, liver, and kidney, but Japan has been comparatively slow to adopt them as a standard medical procedure. In 1990 the number of kidney transplants performed in Japan (757) was less than one-tenth the number performed in the United States, although there were 35 kidney banks nationwide, registering a total of 293,069 individuals who have agreed to donate their kidneys after death and 15,925 potential recipients awaiting transplants.

Crane

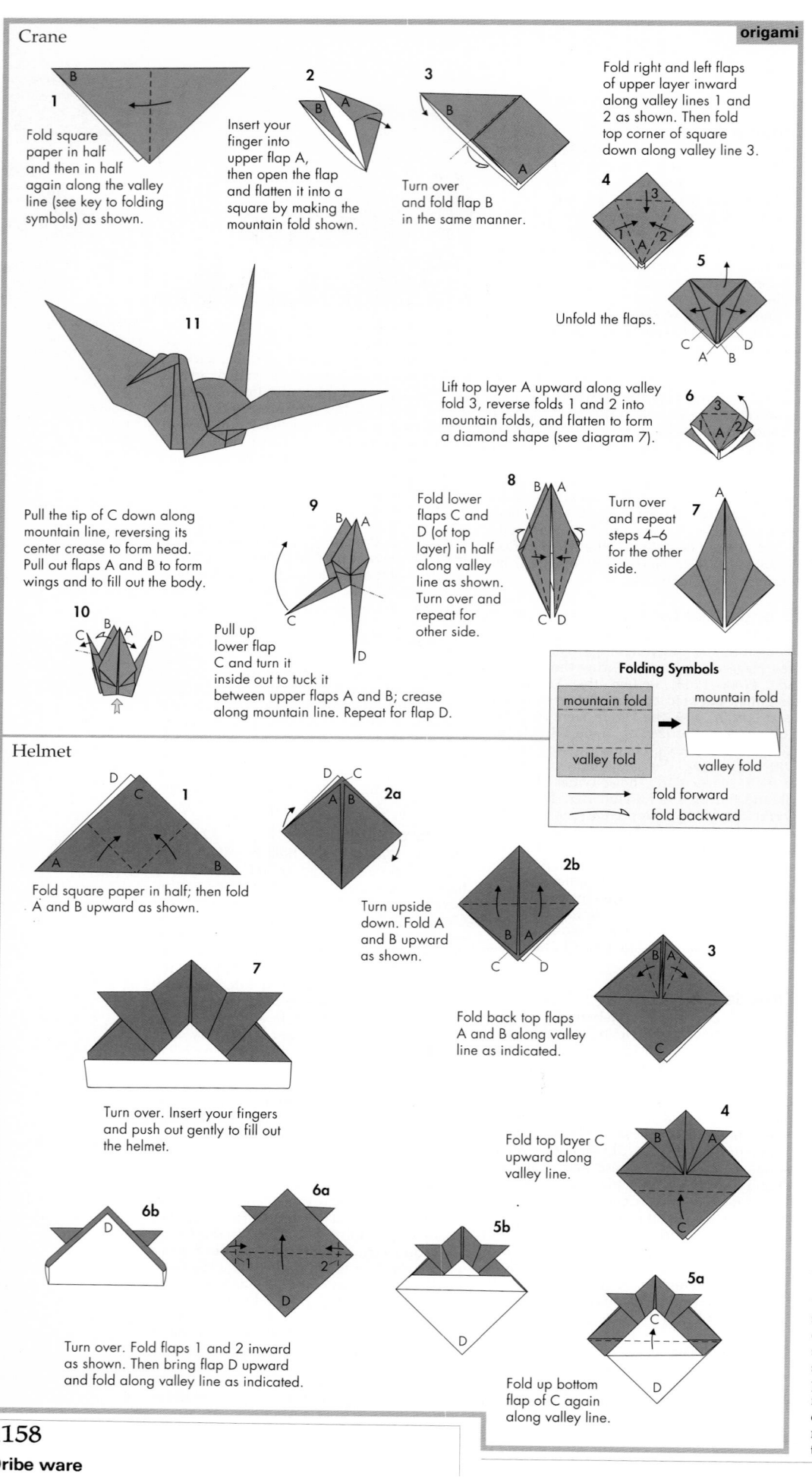

1 Fold square paper in half and then in half again along the valley line (see key to folding symbols) as shown.

2 Insert your finger into upper flap A, then open the flap and flatten it into a square by making the mountain fold shown.

3 Turn over and fold flap B in the same manner.

Fold right and left flaps of upper layer inward along valley lines 1 and 2 as shown. Then fold top corner of square down along valley line 3.

4

5 Unfold the flaps.

Lift top layer A upward along valley fold 3, reverse folds 1 and 2 into mountain folds, and flatten to form a diamond shape (see diagram 7).

6

7

8 Fold lower flaps C and D (of top layer) in half along valley line as shown. Turn over and repeat for other side.

Turn over and repeat steps 4–6 for the other side.

9 Pull up lower flap C and turn it inside out to tuck it between upper flaps A and B; crease along mountain line. Repeat for flap D.

10

11 Pull the tip of C down along mountain line, reversing its center crease to form head. Pull out flaps A and B to form wings and to fill out the body.

Helmet

1 Fold square paper in half; then fold A and B upward as shown.

2a Turn upside down. Fold A and B upward as shown.

2b Fold back top flaps A and B along valley line as indicated.

3 Fold top layer C upward along valley line.

4

5a Fold up bottom flap of C again along valley line.

5b

6a Turn over. Fold flaps 1 and 2 inward as shown. Then bring flap D upward and fold along valley line as indicated.

6b

7 Turn over. Insert your fingers and push out gently to fill out the helmet.

Folding Symbols

mountain fold	mountain fold
valley fold	valley fold

→ fold forward
⤳ fold backward

The first and (as of 1991) last heart transplant performed in Japan took place in 1968, and the patient died after 83 days. The operation created such a controversy that heart transplants have since been treated as taboo by the Japanese medical community. At issue was the use of a brain-dead patient as the organ donor, because the concept of BRAIN DEATH has been slow in winning acceptance in Japan and many people still feel uneasy about the removal of organs—particularly the heart—from donors whose brains are dead but whose bodies are still functioning.

Partial liver transplants from healthy, living donors commenced in 1989, and by June 1991 a total of 28 of these operations had been performed. All donors were relatives of the recipients. There is a strong movement to establish a consensus of brain death that would increase the pool of potential donors and the number and type of organ transplants that can be performed, but as of 1991 full acceptance of this standard had not yet been achieved.

Oribe ware → Mino ware

Oriental Land Co, Ltd

[株]オリエンタルランド

(Orientaru Rando). Company operating recreational facilities. Incorporated in 1960. It is the owner and operator of TŌKYŌ DISNEYLAND, under license from the Walt Disney Co of the United States. Built on 82.6 hectares (204 acres) of reclaimed land in the city of Urayasu, Chiba Prefecture, Tōkyō Disneyland opened in 1983. The number of visitors during its first six years of operation totaled 70 million. Sales for the fiscal year ending March 1990 totaled ¥132.9 billion (US $868.2 million), and capitalization stood at ¥3.3 billion (US $21.6 million). Headquarters are in Urayasu.

origami

折紙

Folded paper; also the art of folding paper to form shaped figures and ornamental objects. *Origami* ranges from a simple form of child's play to a complex art form. It is used in certain Japanese ceremonies and rituals, as well as for practical, educational, and entertainment purposes.

Background—*Origami* as a form of entertainment was not practiced during ancient times when paper was scarce and hence very valuable; it probably began during the Heian period (794–1185). *Origami* with only folding and no cutting developed first in the Muromachi period (1333–1568). In the Edo period (1600–1868) other techniques of folding, cutting, and dyeing paper were developed. By the Taishō period (1912–26) patterns for some 150 different kinds of *origami* figures had been established. Contemporary *origami* is distinguished from paper cutting, paper sculpture, and *kumigami* (paper assembling). The new art of creative *origami* does not, generally speaking, use cutting or coloring techniques, and the main pattern of expression is cubic.

Uses for Origami—The oldest known use of *origami* in Japan is found in the KATASHIRO, used from ancient times in Shintō ceremonies at the Ise Shrine. The *katashiro* is a symbolic representation of a deity cut from special paper called *jingū yōshi* (shrine paper). Vestiges of *katashiro* can still be found in the paper cutouts of human figures currently used in various purification ceremonies and in the paper dolls displayed on the occasion of the DOLL FESTIVAL in March

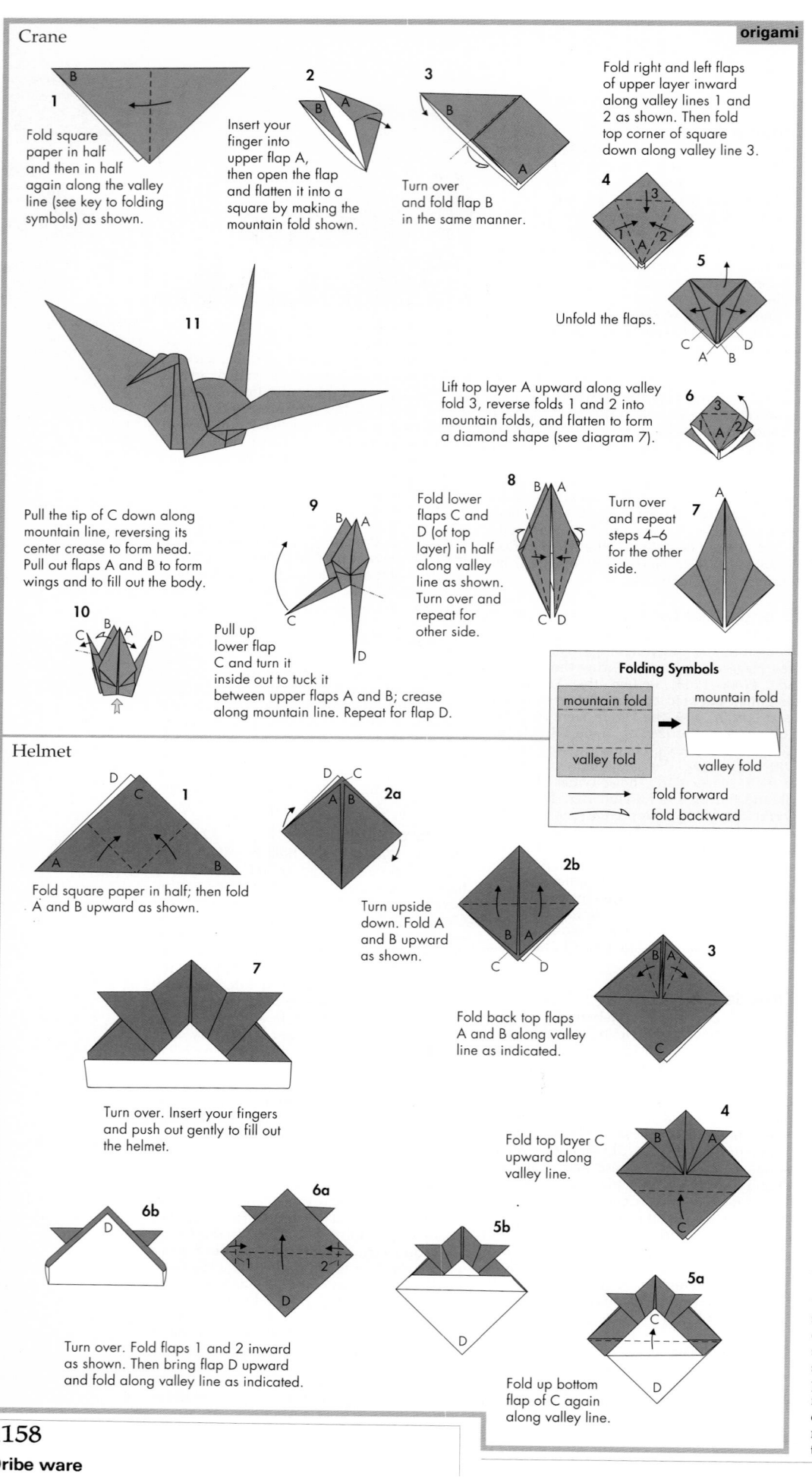

(see also DOLLS). The GOHEI, or *shide*, an implement used in Shintō purificatory rituals, is made of paper that has been specially cut and folded.

Origami also plays an important part in formal etiquette. There are many different ways to fold wrapping paper for gifts presented on ceremonial occasions or on special days in the cycle of annual events. Weddings and funerals, in particular, require elaborate folded paper ornaments such as the male and female butterflies that adorn *sake* bottles. Paper folding has an important part of Japanese folk ritual as well; for example, it is used in making NOSHI, a kind of traditional ornament attached to gifts, and *tatō*, a kind of paper billfold or case carried in the breast fold of the *kimono*.

During the late Meiji period (1868–1912) and the Taishō period, *origami* was used as a teaching device in kindergartens and primary schools. In the beginning of the Shōwa period (1926–89), creativity came to be emphasized in Japanese education, and *origami* was criticized because children were required to handle the paper in standardized ways. Recently, however, *origami* has come to be appreciated once again as an educational technique. In particular, it is used to teach such concepts as the relationship between a plane and a solid.

Origami in the World   There are a few examples of early paper folding to be found in other parts of the world. Some folded paper considered Asian in origin was brought to Europe by the Moors in the 8th century. There is evidence that the Japanese *origami* for *inu* (dog) was imitated in Spain, England, and France in the form of a bird, horse, or hen.

The number of devotees of *origami* and *origami* associations in Japan and abroad has rapidly increased in recent years. Origami associations are maintained in 14 foreign countries, including the United States, England, Italy, the Netherlands, and Peru.

☎ 1160–1161

Orikuchi Shinobu   折口信夫

(1887–1953). Scholar of Japanese literature and folklore and TANKA poet. Literary name Shaku Chōku. Born in Ōsaka Prefecture. Having graduated from Kokugakuin University in Tōkyō, he became professor there in 1922. In 1928 he was appointed professor at Keiō Gijuku University (now Keiō University). As well as being a scholar, Orikuchi was a serious poet, participating in the ARARAGI poetry group from about 1917 to 1921.

Orikuchi's most original accomplishment was his establishment of a folkloric approach to studying the development of Japanese literature. In 1913 Orikuchi began work with YANAGITA KUNIO, the pioneer and leader of Japanese Folklore Studies, an association he continued until his death. Orikuchi advocated the study of "ancient times" (*kodai*) to discover the basic traits of the Japanese psyche; he traveled throughout Japan, including Okinawa, in search of its traces. His poems are based largely on these journeys. His major works include KODAI KENKYŪ (3 vols, 1929–30, The Study of Ancient Times) and collections of *tanka* poetry titled *Umi yama no aida* (1925, Between Mountains and Sea) and *Kodai kannai shū* (1947, Poems Inspired by Ancient Times). See also FOLKLORE STUDIES.

Orix Corporation   オリックス[株]

(Orikkusu). Japanese leasing firm; formerly called Orient Leasing. Incorporated in 1964.

Orix offers a diversified range of financial services, including housing and mortgage security loans, consumer credit, and security brokerage. It also provides services in the real estate and leisure industries. Orix has 228 offices in Japan and 76 offices abroad in 19 countries. In 1989 Orix bought the Hankyū Braves professional baseball team, which is now known as the Orix BlueWave. In fiscal 1991 annual revenues were ¥620.0 billion (US $4.5 billion), and capitalization stood at ¥20.2 billion (US $147.2 million); total assets were ¥3.6 trillion (US $26.2 billion). Headquarters are in Tōkyō.

ornamented tombs   装飾古墳

(*sōshoku kofun*). Protohistoric tombs with painted or carved designs on the interior walls of the burial chamber, stone coffins, entrance barrier, or other surfaces. The elaborate ornamentation of mounded tombs (KOFUN) with corridor-style stone chambers was especially abundant during the 5th and 6th centuries in northern Kyūshū. However, simple incised line drawings and decoration are also found in the mounded tombs and burial caverns (YOKOANA) in eastern Japan. On the Asian continent these kinds of tomb are called wall mural tombs. In Japan the TAKAMATSUZUKA TOMB is the only ornamented tomb that has wall murals reflecting direct continental influence. Most others are decorated with such geometric designs as CHOKKOMON, concentric circles, triangles, FERN FROND DESIGN, and other abstract motifs, or with representations of military accoutrements, or with people, horses, dogs, birds, boats, and wave patterns. Colors used for wall murals were red, white, blue, yellow, and black, all of which were derived from mineral substances.

Orthodox Church → Holy Orthodox Church

Ōru yomimono   オール読物

(All Stories). Monthly fiction magazine published by BUNGEI SHUNJŪ, LTD, since April 1931. The magazine, which publishes mostly popular and "middlebrow" fiction (CHŪKAN SHŌSETSU), has made a major contribution to the development of popular literature as a genre. Contributors have included SHIRAI KYŌJI, KAWAGUCHI MATSUTARŌ, YAMAMOTO SHŪGORŌ, and IKENAMI SHŌTARŌ. NOMURA KODŌ's long-running historical detective series *Zenigata Heiji torimono hikae* (1931–58) is a work representative of the magazine's style both before and after World War II.

ōryōshi   押領使

Local military command position in charge of maintaining local order, principally in the Heian period (794–1185). Before this time, *ōryōshi* were commanders temporarily appointed by the central government to supervise soldiers such as SAKIMORI (border guards) en route to their posts. In the Heian period, the title was given to temporary auxiliary officers (*ryōge no kan*). After the mid-10th century, *ōryōshi* became a permanent position in provincial government offices. Holding this position was a powerful advantage for local landholders seeking to expand their power. In the Kamakura period (1185–1333), the post of *ōryōshi* gradually disappeared.

osabyakushō   長百姓

Influential farmers comprising upper levels of village society during the EDO PERIOD

(1600–1868). Also called *otonabyakushō* or *chōbyakushō*. These farmers, usually the largest landholders, enjoyed privileged positions in religious ceremonies and other social functions. Village officials (MURA YAKUNIN) were generally chosen from this group. In many cases their ancestors had founded the village by financing the reclamation of the community's farmland (see SHINDEN KAIHATSU). See also HYAKUSHŌ.

Ō Sadaharu   王貞治

(1940–). Usually spelled Oh Sadaharu. Professional baseball player. Born in Tōkyō. Ō was a pitcher for the Waseda Jitsugyō High School team that won the National Invitational Senior High School Baseball Tournament in 1957. He joined the Yomiuri Giants in 1959 and for 19 consecutive years hit more than 30 home runs a year (55 in 1964). His 868 career home runs far surpass the previous world record of 755 home runs achieved by Henry (Hank) Aaron. He also won the triple crown in 1973 and 1974. Ō retired in 1980 and became manager of the Giants from 1984 to 1988. He received the People's Honor Award in 1977.

Osada Hiroshi   長田弘

(1939–). Poet and critic. Born in Fukushima Prefecture. Graduate of Waseda University. In college Osada published a literary magazine called *Tori*. Profoundly influenced by the events of the 1960s, he explores through his work the sensitive inner life of youth at that time. His works include the poetry collection *Warera shinsen na tabibito* (1965, We Are Fresh Travelers) and the essay collections *Jojō no henkaku* (1965, Lyrical Revolution) and *Nijū no shikō* (1969, Duplicitous Thoughts).

Ōsaka   大阪[市]

Capital of Ōsaka Prefecture, central Honshū. The third largest city in Japan after Tōkyō and Yokohama, it is the financial center of western Japan. In the 7th and 8th centuries Ōsaka was a port for trade with China and the site of several imperial residences. In the 16th century it was the site of ISHIYAMA HONGANJI, a powerful religious and secular organization. After the destruction of the organization in 1580, the national unifier TOYOTOMI HIDEYOSHI built ŌSAKA CASTLE on the site of its headquarters in 1583. In the Edo period (1600–1868) Ōsaka served as the entrepôt for

Continued on page 1162►

ornamented tombs Geometric patterns decorate this corridor-style stone chamber of the Hinooka tomb in the town of Yoshii, Fukuoka Prefecture. Early 6th century. Length of interior wall 2 meters.

Orikuchi Shinobu The scholar and poet in 1935. His unique views on the study of folklore and literature are reflected in his research, essays, and poetry.

Ō Sadaharu Early in his career, this baseball player mastered the powerful one-legged batting stance that he used to break one batting record after another.

Origami Unfolded

A few folding techniques and a little inspiration are all you need to recreate the wonders of nature from a single sheet of paper. The butterfly, frog, and swan illustrated here are examples of *sōsaku origami*, or free-style paper folding. Compared to traditional origami, these pieces incorporate more intermediate folds and allow for greater latitude in the folding process, resulting in lifelike origami compositions. Practice the following patterns until you feel comfortable with the basic folding process—but don't stop there. Make slight alterations in the folding lines to enlarge the frog's eyes or adjust the curve of the swan's neck. Or select an unusual paper texture to reproduce the fragile beauty of a butterfly's wings. The only limit is your imagination.

Yoshizawa Akira

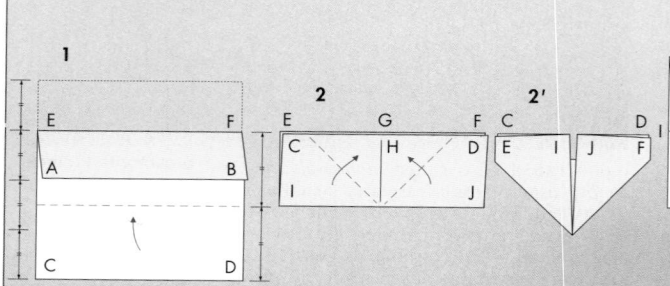
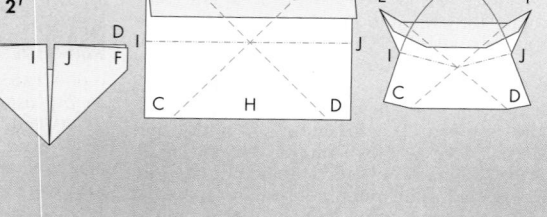
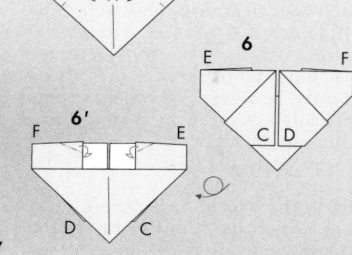
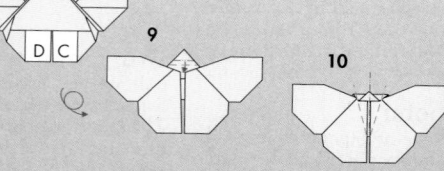
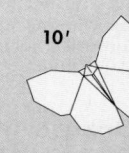

BUTTERFLY

1 Fold down top quarter of sheet. Align CD with EF; crease.
2–2' Fold flaps I and J toward center. Unfold as in step 3.
3 Refold creases along mountain and valley lines (see key to folding symbols) as indicated.
4 Push in sides so points I and J come together in the middle. Flatten to form shape in step 5.
5 Fold C and D downward.
6–6' Turn over. Fold under corners of front flaps.
7 Fold rear flaps 1 and 2 down over front flaps. Fold up lower flap along valley line 3.
8–8' Fold down rear flaps C and D, pushing in outer corners to flatten.
9 Turn over. Fold top flap down and up again to hook it over body.
10–10' Fold body in half along mountain line; then tilt wings upward along valley lines.

JUMPING FROG

1 Make mountain and valley folds as indicated. Bring together A and C, and B and D.
2 Fold back flaps AC and BD.
3 Fold F and G inward. Unfold AC and BD; bring out to dotted line.
4 Fold flaps A and B inward.
5 Bring flap B over to left side.
6 Fold D along mountain and valley lines to form bottom leg.
7 Bring A and B over to right side; fold C in same manner as D.
8 Bring A back to left side. Fold up bottom flap H; turn over.
9 Make mountain and valley folds; open up to form eyes.
10 From point X, slide finger down back to make frog jump.

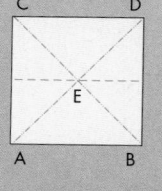
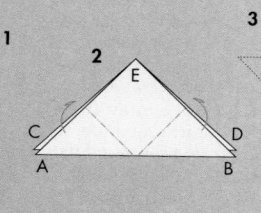
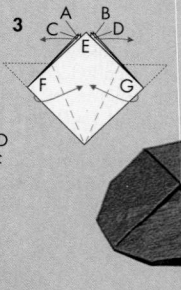
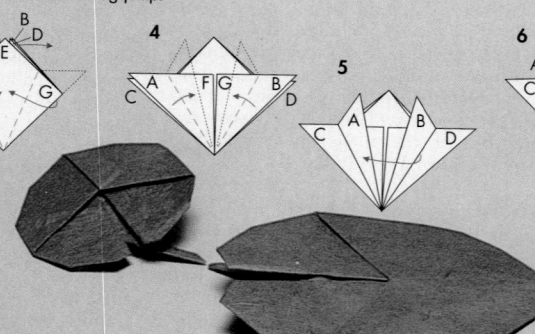
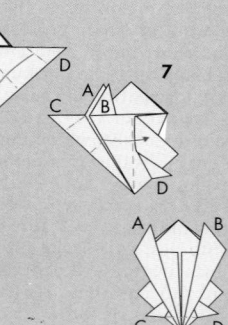
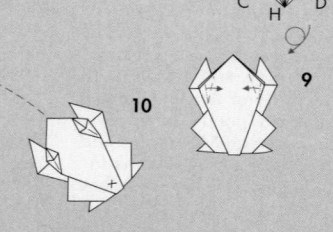

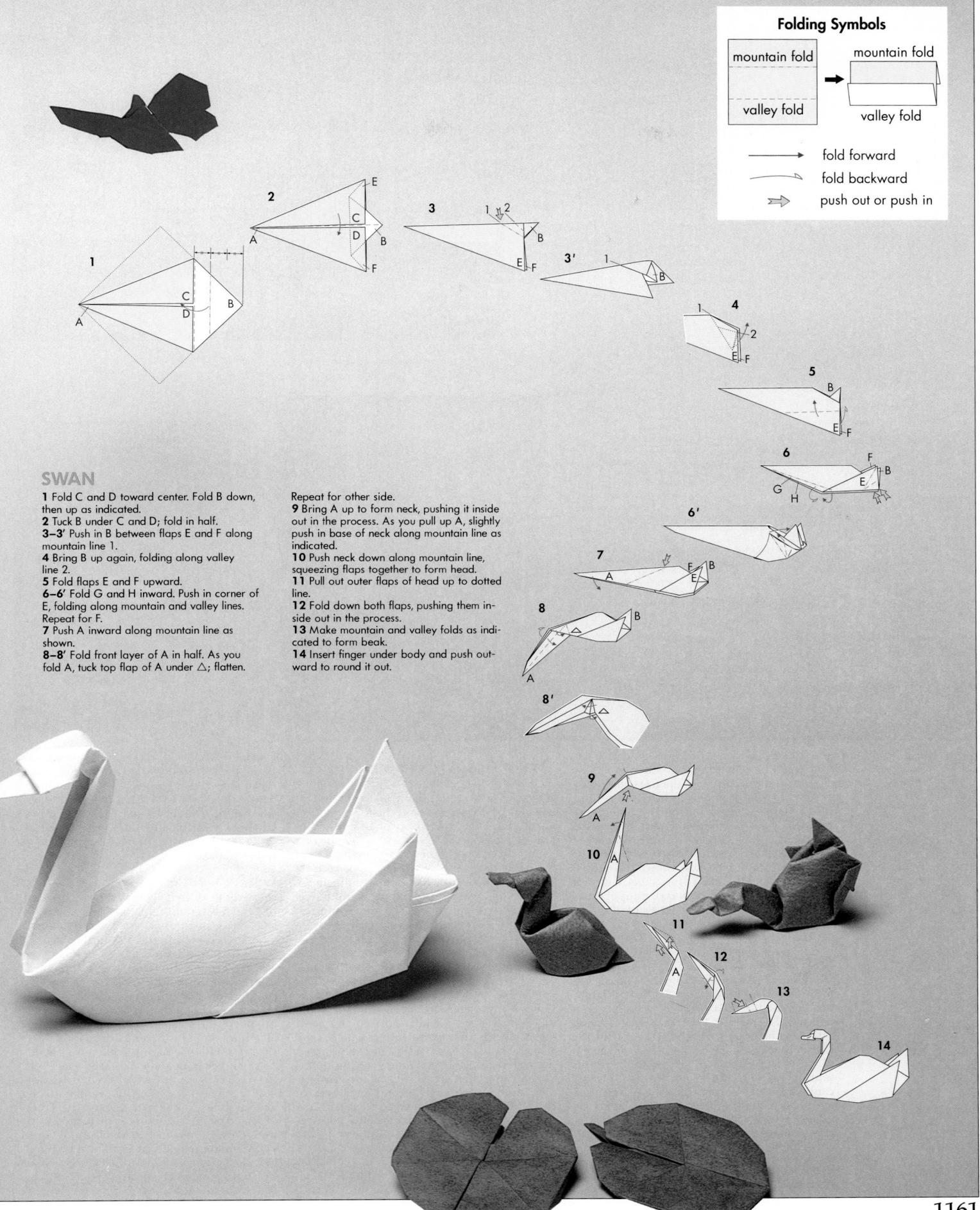

Folding Symbols

mountain fold

valley fold

→ mountain fold / valley fold

→ fold forward

fold backward

push out or push in

SWAN

1 Fold C and D toward center. Fold B down, then up as indicated.

2 Tuck B under C and D; fold in half.

3–3' Push in B between flaps E and F along mountain line 1.

4 Bring B up again, folding along valley line 2.

5 Fold flaps E and F upward.

6–6' Fold G and H inward. Push in corner of E, folding along mountain and valley lines. Repeat for F.

7 Push A inward along mountain line as shown.

8–8' Fold front layer of A in half. As you fold A, tuck top flap of A under △; flatten.

Repeat for other side.

9 Bring A up to form neck, pushing it inside out in the process. As you pull up A, slightly push in base of neck along mountain line as indicated.

10 Push neck down along mountain line, squeezing flaps together to form head.

11 Pull out outer flaps of head up to dotted line.

12 Fold down both flaps, pushing them inside out in the process.

13 Make mountain and valley folds as indicated to form beak.

14 Insert finger under body and push outward to round it out.

Ōsaka

► Nakanoshima, a narrow island in one of the city's many rivers, is home to Ōsaka's city administration and a variety of businesses.

▼ Ōsaka Castle, with the towers of the Twin 21 buildings behind. In the last several years, the area near the castle has become a new business center.

▲ The historic Dōtombori entertainment district in central Ōsaka is named for the canal along which it is located.

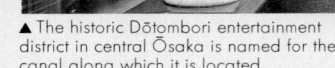

◄ The 103-meter Tsūtenkaku Tower, built in 1956 and modeled after the Eiffel Tower, is the symbol of the surrounding Shinsekai ("New World") amusement district.

▼ Located at the junction of several rail lines, Umeda, in Kita Ward, is a busy shopping and amusement center. Pictured is the Hankyū Sambangai shopping mall.

goods, especially tax rice, for the entire nation and was called Japan's "kitchen."

Ōsaka is the center of the HANSHIN INDUSTRIAL ZONE. Its principal industries are textiles, chemicals, steel, machinery, and metal. Besides Ōsaka Castle, attractions include the ŌSAKA MUSEUM OF NATURAL HISTORY, ŌSAKA MUNICIPAL MUSEUM OF FINE ARTS, the remains of the ancient capital of NANIWAKYŌ, the temple SHITENNŌJI, and the SUMIYOSHI SHRINE. Cultural attractions include the BUNRAKU puppet theater as well as *kabuki*. Area: 220 sq km (85 sq mi); pop: 2,623,801. — *See map, pages 1164 and 1165.*

Ōsaka Aquarium   海遊館

(Kaiyūkan). A privately owned aquarium located in the city of Ōsaka, Ōsaka Prefecture; opened in 1990. At 9 meters (30 ft) in depth and 34 meters (112 ft) across at its widest, the central tank, symbolizing the Pacific Ocean in the scheme of the aquarium, is one of the world's largest. Thirteen tanks representing regions of the circum-Pacific volcanic zone (see VOLCANOES) are arranged around the central tank. In total, approximately 16,000 animals representing 300 species, including mammals and amphibians, are displayed in the aquarium in tanks corresponding to their natural habitats.

Ōsaka Asahi Hikka Incident
大阪朝日筆禍事件

(Ōsaka Asahi Hikka Jiken). Also known as the Hakkō Hikka Incident. Incident in 1918 surrounding an article published by the liberal newspaper *Ōsaka asahi shimbun* (see ASAHI SHIMBUN). The newspaper, whose staff included HASEGAWA NYOZEKAN, ŌYAMA IKUO, and KUSHIDA TAMIZŌ, had consistently taken a critical stance toward the government of General TERAUCHI MASATAKE (prime minister 1916–18), particularly regarding suppression of news coverage of the RICE RIOTS OF 1918. In an article of 26 August the newspaper quoted a classical Chinese phrase (literally, "a white rainbow [*hakkō*] has pierced the sun") that could have been construed as an oblique reference to imminent rebellion. Home Ministry officials indicted the company under the PRESS LAW OF 1909, and MURAYAMA RYŌHEI, president of the newspaper, was assaulted by members of the RŌNINKAI and the AMUR RIVER SOCIETY, ultranationalist groups. He and several members of the editorial staff resigned in October, and the paper was allowed to continue publication.

Ōsaka Bay   大阪湾

(Ōsaka Wan). Inlet of the Pacific Ocean on the coast of Hyōgo and Ōsaka prefectures,

central Honshū. Bounded by the Ōsaka Plain, the Izumi Mountains, and the island of Awajishima, it is connected with the Inland Sea on the west by the Akashi Strait and with the Pacific Ocean on the south by the Kii Channel. It is the site of the ports of Ōsaka and Kōbe and forms the heart of the Hanshin Industrial Zone.

Ōsaka Castle   大坂城

(Ōsakajō). Castle located in the city of Ōsaka, Ōsaka Prefecture. It was built by the national unifier TOYOTOMI HIDEYOSHI. Construction began in 1583 at the site of the headquarters of the ISHIYAMA HONGANJI sect and took some three years to complete. Of impressive scale, the castle measured approximately 3.3 kilometers (2.0 mi) east and west and approximately 2.4 kilometers (1.5 mi) north and south. It was considered virtually impregnable. After Hideyoshi's death, the castle fell to invading Tokugawa forces in 1615 and was heavily damaged (see ŌSAKA CASTLE, SIEGES OF). It was restored in 1620 as a seat for the Ōsaka *jōdai*, the shogunate deputy of the Tokugawa shogunate (1603–1867). Among surviving structures are the Inui Tower, Sengan Tower, Tamon Tower, and Ōtemon (Main Gate), all of which have been designated Important Cultural Properties. The present tower keep is a 1931 concrete reconstruction.

Ōsaka Castle, Sieges of 大坂の陣

(Ōsaka no Jin). Two campaigns in 1614 and 1615 in which TOKUGAWA IEYASU destroyed TOYOTOMI HIDEYORI, the son of TOYOTOMI HIDEYOSHI, thereby eliminating the most serious potential challenge to the shogunate Ieyasu had established in 1603.

Hideyori was *daimyō* of a large domain centered on ŌSAKA CASTLE. Ieyasu found in the SHŌMEI INCIDENT of 1614 a pretext to denounce Hideyori for subversive behavior. Hideyori's mother, YODOGIMI, called upon daimyō to rally to the Toyotomi cause, but none did. Toyotomi vassals, notably ŌNO HARUNAGA, and large numbers of unemployed *samurai* (RŌNIN), like SANADA YUKIMURA, saw an opportunity to improve their fortunes, and some 100,000 fighting men assembled in Ōsaka Castle. Late in 1614 Ieyasu and his son, the shōgun TOKUGAWA HIDETADA, led armies totaling some 200,000 men to surround the fortress, which proved impregnable. On 19 January 1615 Ieyasu agreed to a settlement permitting him to fill in the outer moats, and the winter's seige (*fuyu no jin*) ended. Ieyasu withdrew, and crews began to fill in the inner moats as well as the outer ones. When Hideyori protested, Ieyasu gave him the choice of dispersing the *rōnin* under him or leaving Ōsaka Castle for another province. Hideyori refused and Ieyasu mobilized another army of 200,000. Because the castle was now vulnerable, Toyotomi forces took to the field, where their detachments were crushed in scattered battles in the Kyōto-Ōsaka region. On 3 June 1615 the castle fell, ending the summer campaign (*natsu no jin*). The next day Hideyori and Yodogimi committed suicide.

Ōsaka Cement Co, Ltd
大阪セメント[株]

(Ōsaka Semento). Cement manufacturer. Incorporated in 1926. The company maintains sales networks throughout eastern and western Japan. It has recently focused its efforts on the development of new construction materials and industrial ceramics. Sales for the fiscal year ending March 1991 totaled ¥65.6 billion (US $478.1 million), and capitalization stood at ¥9.5 billion (US $69.2 million). Headquarters are in Ōsaka.

Ōsaka City University 大阪市立大学

(Ōsaka Shiritsu Daigaku). A coeducational public university located in the city of Ōsaka, Ōsaka Prefecture. Founded in 1949, the university has faculties of business, economics, law, letters, science, engineering, medicine, and home economics. Enrollment in 1989 was 6,430.

Ōsaka Conference of 1875
大阪会議

(Ōsaka Kaigi). The meeting of government leaders ŌKUBO TOSHIMICHI, ITŌ HIROBUMI, and INOUE KAORU with KIDO TAKAYOSHI and ITAGAKI TAISUKE at Ōsaka, in January-February 1875, to discuss the establishment of a representative assembly. In 1873 Itagaki had resigned from his position as *sangi* (councillor) over the question of whether to attack Korea and, as a leader of the FREEDOM AND PEOPLE'S RIGHTS MOVEMENT, had worked actively for the establishment of a parliamentary institution. The next year Kido resigned from the government in protest over the punitive TAIWAN EXPEDITION OF 1874. Itō, Ōkubo, and Inoue were left vulnerable to popular opposition, and in January and February 1875 they met with Kido and Itagaki to resolve political

differences and to persuade them to rejoin the government. As concessions to Kido and Itagaki decisions were made to establish a senate (GENRŌIN), a GREAT COURT OF CASSATION, and an ASSEMBLY OF PREFECTURAL GOVERNORS and to separate the functions of the *sangi* and the ministers within the government. Kido and Itagaki returned to the government, and the decisions were formally promulgated by an imperial proclamation in April 1875. Although the oligarchs appeared to be sanctioning representative government, the reality was different, for implementation of the decisions was left to conservative bureaucrats. Moreover, that same year the government issued new press and publication laws designed to thwart the people's rights movement.

Ōsaka Elegy → Naniwa erejī

Ōsaka Gas Co, Ltd 大阪瓦斯[株]

(Ōsaka Gasu). Company concentrating on the manufacture and supply of natural gas. Incorporated in 1897, the company began to supply gas in the Ōsaka area in 1905. By 1989 it was supplying gas to over 5 million homes, offices, and factories in Ōsaka, Kyōto, Nara, Shiga, Wakayama, and Hyōgo prefectures. In 1972 Ōsaka Gas began importing liquefied natural gas, and it began supplying natural gas in 1975. Sales for the fiscal year ending March 1991 totaled ¥591.0 billion (US $4.3 billion). Capitalization stood at ¥132.0 billion (US $962.1 million) in the same year. Headquarters are in Ōsaka.

Ōsaka Incident 大阪事件

(Ōsaka Jiken). The arrest and trial of liberal politicians who plotted a military expedition to Korea in 1885, exemplifying the distinctive combination of nationalism and liberalism in the FREEDOM AND PEOPLE'S RIGHTS MOVEMENT of the Meiji period (1868–1912). The incident occurred in the wake of the KAPSIN POLITICAL COUP of December 1884, in which Japanese activists and members of a Korean reform party had conspired to overthrow the Korean government. With Chinese assistance Korean authorities crushed this revolt, though KIM OK-KYUN and other Korean rebel leaders were rescued by their Japanese supporters. Official Japanese policy was cautious, aimed at averting conflict with China over Korea.

Frustrated by what they saw as the Japanese government's abandonment of the Korean reformist cause and its despotism at home, members of the Japanese liberal movement looked to Korea as the best place to strike a blow for the cause of "progress and liberty." ŌI KENTARŌ, a leader of the JIYŪTŌ (Liberal Party), plotted with other activists to raise an armed force to invade Korea and install Kim Ok-kyun and his reformers in power. They reasoned that a victory for democracy in Korea might in turn speed its development in Japan. Police uncovered the plot, however, and arrested some 130 suspects in Ōsaka and Nagasaki; 31 were convicted, including Ōi and FUKUDA HIDEKO. See also KOREA AND JAPAN.

Ōsaka Municipal Museum of Fine Arts 大阪市立美術館

(Ōsaka Shiritsu Bijutsukan). Large collection of Japanese, Chinese, and Korean art; opened in Ōsaka in 1936. The Japanese items include archaeological material from the Jōmon period (ca 10,000 BC–ca 300 BC) through the Kofun period (ca 300–710);

sculpture, generally on extended loan from various local temples; and ceramics. The museum is best known for the more than 200 Chinese paintings of the Abe Collection, the most famous item of which is a small scroll with a portrait of the Chinese scholar Fu Sheng, thought to be of the 9th century.

Ōsaka Museum of Natural History 大阪市立自然史博物館

(Ōsaka Shiritsu Shizenshi Hakubutsukan). Museum opened in 1974 in Higashi Sumiyoshi Ward, Ōsaka. The topics of the four exhibition rooms are nature in Ōsaka, the history of the earth and life, evolution and the diverse forms of life, and the use and conservation of nature. The museum also conducts outdoor nature studies and issues a variety of publications.

Ōsaka no Jin → Ōsaka Castle, Sieges of

Ōsaka Philharmonic Orchestra
大阪フィルハーモニー交響楽団

(Ōsaka Firuhāmonī Kōkyō Gakudan). Orchestra established in 1947 in the city of Ōsaka as the Kansai Philharmonic Orchestra by a group of musicians led by Asahina Takashi (b 1908). The orchestra adopted its present name in 1960. The orchestra's principal conductor from the time of its establishment, Asahina served as its general music director from 1976.

Ōsaka Plain 大阪平野

(Ōsaka Heiya). Located in Ōsaka and Hyōgo prefectures, central Honshū. This low-lying region beside Ōsaka Bay, formed by deltas of the rivers Yodogawa and Yamatogawa, is the center of both the Kinki (Kyōto-Nara-Ōsaka) region and western Japan. The Hanshin Industrial Zone, where heavy and chemical industries are concentrated, dominates the coastal area from Amagasaki in the north to Sakai in the south. The largest city is ŌSAKA. Area: approximately 1,600 sq km (620 sq mi).

Ōsaka Prefectural University
大阪府立大学

(Ōsaka Furitsu Daigaku). A coeducational public university located in the city of Sakai, Ōsaka Prefecture. Founded in 1949 as Naniwa University, it became Ōsaka Prefectural University in 1955. The university maintains faculties of engineering, agriculture, economics, arts and sciences, and social welfare. Enrollment in 1989 was 4,493.

Ōsaka Prefecture 大阪府

(Ōsaka Fu). Located centrally in the Kinki region in central Honshū, Ōsaka Prefecture borders the prefectures of Kyōto to the north, Nara to the east, Wakayama to the south, and Hyōgo to the west. Facing Ōsaka Bay, it has long prospered as a center of land and marine transportation. Its capital, the city of ŌSAKA (pop: 2,623,801), is the third largest city in Japan. Other cities include SAKAI, HIGASHI ŌSAKA, TOYONAKA, HIRAKATA, TAKATSUKI, and SUITA. Although the area of the prefecture is 1,869 sq km (722 sq mi), the smallest in the country, its population is 8,734,516, second only to that of Tōkyō Prefecture.

The prefecture is surrounded on three sides by mountains: the Hokusetsu Mountains to the north, the Ikoma and Kongō

Continued on page 1166 ←

Ōsaka Prefecture
Location and Prefectural Crest

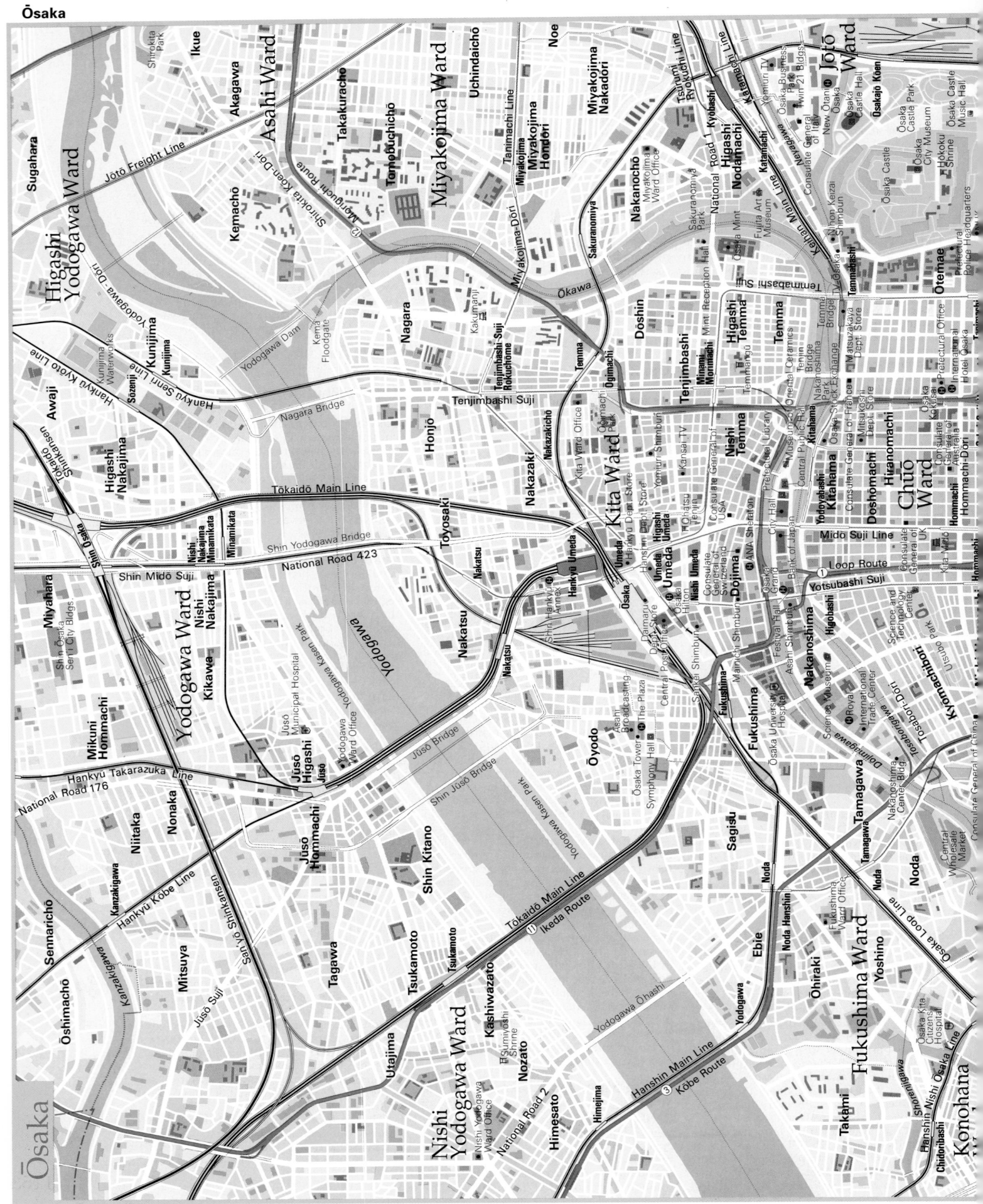

Shinrokita Park
Ikue
Akagawa
Sugahara
Asahi Ward
Takakuracho
Tomobuchicho
Uchindaicho
Noe
Miyakojima Ward
Miyakojima Nakadōri
Miyakojima Nakadōri
Jōtō Ward
Higashi Yodogawa Ward
Higashi Yodogawa-Dōri
Jōtō Freight Line
Shiriokita Kōen-Dōri
Moriguchi Route
Kemachō
Miyakojima-Dōri
Miyakojima Hondōri
Tanimachi Line
Tsurumi Ryokuchi Line
Katamachi Line
New Ōtani
Ōsaka Business Park
Twin 21 Bldgs.
Ōsaka Castle Park
Ōsaka Castle Hall
Ōsaka Castle Music Hall
Consulate General of Italy
Ōsaka Castle
Kyōbashi
Ōsaka City Museum
Hōkoku Shrine
Nagara
Kakumanji
Kemā Floodgate
Yodogawa Dam
Ōkawa
Nakanochō
Miyakojima Ward Office
Sakuranomiya
Sakuranomiya Park
Ōsaka Mint
Fujita Art Museum
Mint Reception Hall
National Road
Higashi Nodamachi
Temmabashi
Ōsaka Shop Keizai Shimbun
Temmabashi
Ōtemae
Prefectural Police Headquarters
Hankyu Kyoto Line
Hankyu Senri Line
Shinkansen
Shinkaidō Line
Awaji
Kunijima
Kunijima Waterworks
Sōzenji
Nagara Bridge
Honjō
Tenjinbashi Suji
Nakazakichō
Nakazaki
Tenjinbashi-Suji Rokuchōme
Tenma
Tenma
Doshin
Tenjimbashi
Higashi Temma
Tenmangū
Temma
Temma Bridge
Nakanoshima Park
Ōjimachi
Ōjimachi Park
Kita Ward Office
Nishi Temma
Minami Morimachi
Tenjin Bridge
Nakanoshima
Tennin Ceramics
Ōsaka Stock Exchange
Matsuzakaya Dept. Store
Consulate General of France
Museum of Oriental Ceramics
Osaka Kaikan
Consulate General of UK
Consulate General of Australia
International Hotel Ōsaka
Prefectural Office
Hommachi-Dōri
Higashi Nakajima
Higashi Nakajima
Tōkaidō Main Line
Toyosaki
Nakatsu
Central Public Hall
City Hall
Nishi Temma
Kitahama
Kita-Ōji
Dōshōmachi
Hiranomachi
Hommachi
Mido Suji Line
Chūō Ward
Shin Ōsaka
Miyahara
Shin Ōsaka Senri City Bldgs.
Shin Mido Suji
Nishi Nakajima Minamikata
Minamikata
Minamikata
Shin Yodogawa Bridge
National Road 423
Nakatsu
Nakatsu
Hankyu Umeda
Shin Hankyu Annex
Umeda
Hanshin Dept. Store
Hankyu Dept. Store
Umeda
Higashi Umeda
Umeda
Nishi Umeda
ANA Sheraton
Ōhatsu Tenjin
Consulate General of USA
Consulate General of Switzerland
Dōjima
Ōsaka Grand
Bank of Japan
Loop Route
Yotsubashi Suji
Higobashi
Science and Technology Center
Ōsaka Hilton
Hommachi
Yodoyabashi
Nishi Nakajima
Kikawa
Yodogawa Kasen Park
Yodogawa Municipal Hospital
Shin Yodogawa Bridge
Jūsō Higashi
Jūsō
Jūsō
Yodogawa Ward Office
Ōyodo
Asahi Broadcasting
The Plaza
Daimaru Dept. Store
Ōsaka Hilton
Central Post Office
Saikei Shimbun
Mainichi Shimbun
Festival Hall
Asahi Shimbun
Royal
Ōsaka University Hospital
Science Museum
International Trade Center
Nakanoshima Center Bldg.
Consulate General of China
Central Wholesale Market
Dojimagawa
Tosabori-Dōri
Tosabori-Dōri
Tosaborigawa
Utsubo Park
Kyōmachibori
Nakanoshima
Yodogawa Ward
Mikuni Hommachi
Mikuni
Hommachi
Hankyu Takarazuka Line
National Road 176
Nonaka
Niitaka
Jūsō Bridge
Jūsō Hommachi
Jūsō Hommachi
Shin Kitano
Ōsaka Tower
Symphony Hall
Sagisu
Noda
Tamagawa
Tamagawa
Sennarichō
Kanzakigawa
Hankyū Kōbe Line
Mitsuya
Tagawa
Tōkaidō Main Line
Ikeda Route
Noda
Noda Hanshin
Fukushima
Fukushima Ward Office
Noda
Noda
Fukushima Ward
Ōsaka Loop Line
Oshimachō
Kanzakigawa
San'yō Shinkansen
Jūsō Suji
Tsukamoto
Tsukamoto
Ebie
Yoshino
Fukushima
Ōshimachō
Nitaka
Mitsuya
Utajima
Kashiwazato
Kashiwazato
Sumiyoshi Shrine
Nozato
Himesato
Himejima
Yodogawa Ōhashi
Yodogawa
Ōhiraki
Takami
Ōsaka Kita Citizens' Hospital
Nishi Yodogawa Ward
Nishi Yodogawa Ward Office
National Road 2
Hanshin Main Line
Kōbe Route
Hanshin Nishi Ōsaka Line
Chidoribashi
Konohana
Shotenjigawa

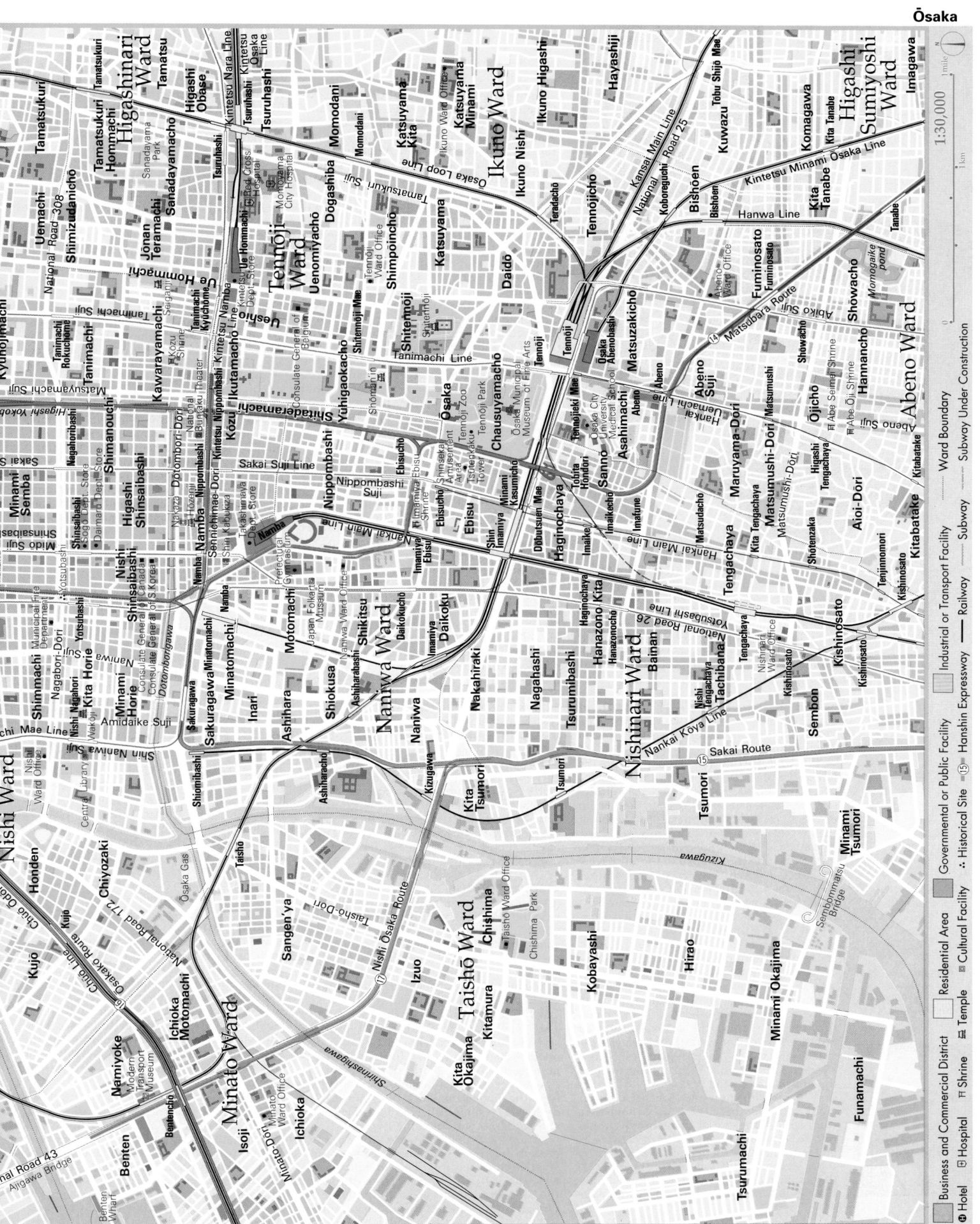

Ōsaka

1:30,000

Higashinari Ward

Tamatsukuri
Tamatsukuri
Tamatsu
Tamatsu
Higashi Obase
Higashi Obase
Hommachi
Sanadayama Park
Uemachi
Shimizudanichō
National Road 308
Jōnan Teramachi
Ue Hommachi
Tamatsukuri Suji

Ikuno Ward
Ikuno Higashi
Hayashiji
Ikuno Nishi
Ikuno Minami
Katsuyama Kita
Katsuyama Minami
Momodani
Momodani
Dōgashiba
Ōsaka Loop Line
Kintetsu Nara Line
Tsuruhashi
Tsuruhashi
Tsuruhashi
Kintetsu Ōsaka Line
Red Cross Hospital
Momoyama City Hospital
Uenomiyachō
Tamatsukuri Suji
Katsuyama

Kintetsu Minami Ōsaka Line
Kansai Main Line
Teradachō
Tennōjichō
National Road 25
Koboreguchi
Bishōen
Bishōen
Kuwazu
Tōbu Shijō Mae
Komagawa
Kita Tanabe
Kita Tanabe
Tanabe
Hanwa Line

Higashi Sumiyoshi Ward
Imagawa

Tennōji Ward
Tennōji Ward Office
Tennōji
Shitennōji
Shitennōji
Shitennōji
Shimpōinchō
Katsuyama
Daidō
Tennōjichō
Tennōji
Tanimachi Line
Shōman-in
Ōsaka Municipal Museum of Fine Arts
Tennōji Zoo
Tennōji Park

Ōsaka Abenobashi
Matsuzakichō
Matsubara Route
Abeno
Abeno
Abeno Suji
Matsuzakichō
Fuminosato
Fuminosato
Shōwachō
Shōwachō
Momogaike pond
Hannanchō
Abeno Ward

Kyūhōjimachi
Tanimachi Suji
Matsuyamachi Suji
Tanimachi Rokuchōme
Tanimachi
Tanimachi Kyūchōme
Sakai Suji
Nagahoribashi
Higashi Yokobori

Kawaramachi
Kōzu Shrine
Segawa

Kōzu
Shitaderamachi
Yuhigaokachō
Shōman-in

Ōsaka University
Tennōeki Mae
Ōsaka City University Medical School
Tobita Hondōri
Sanno
Abeno
Imaikechō
Imabune
Asahimachi
Matsudachō
Maruyama-Dōri
Kita Tengachaya
Matsumushi-Dōri
Matsumushi
Matsumushi-Dōri
Matsumushi
Ōjichō
Ōjichō
Higashi Tengachaya
Abe Seimei Shrine
Abe Ōji Shrine
Tenjinnomori
Kitabatake
Kitabatake
Aioi-Dōri

Kyōbashi Mae Line
Nishi Nagahori
Kita Horie
Minami Horie
Amidaike Suji
Shinsaibashi
Sogo Dept. Store
Daimaru Dept. Store
Nakaza
Hōzenji
Dōtombori-Dōri
Sakai Suji Line
Takashimaya Dept. Store
Namba
Nippombashi Suji
Nippombashi Suji
Nippombashi
Ebisuchō
Ebisuchō
Shinsekai Amusement Area
Tsūtenkaku
Tsūtenkaku Tower
Shin Sekai
Ebisuchō
Imamiya Ebisu
Imamiya Ebisu Shrine
Ebisu
Minami Kasumichō
Haginochaya
Haginochaya
Haginochaya Kita
Hanazono Kita
Hanazono
Hanazomonochō
Tengachaya
Tengachaya
Nishi Tengachaya Tachibana
Sembon
Hankai Main Line
Nishinari Ward Office
Kishinosato
Kishinosato
Kishinosato
Kishinosato
Tenjinnomori
Kishinosato

Nishi Ward
Nishi Ward Office
Central Library
Ōsaka Gas
Chiyozaki
Chūō Dōri
Chūō Line
Kujō
Kujō
Kujō
Ōsaka Route
National Road 172
Honden
Shin Naniwa Suji

Naniwa Ward
Japan Folkart Museum
Naniwa Ward Office
Motomachi
Motomachi
Daikokuchō
Daikoku
Imamiya
Imamiya
Nakahiraki
Nagahashi
Tsurumibashi
National Road 26
Yotsubashi Line
Bainan

Nishinari Ward

Prefectural Gymnasium
Consulate General of Canada
Consulate General of S. Korea
Dōtombori
Dōtomborigawa
Shimmachi
Municipal Fire Department
Nagabori-Dōri
Yotsubashi
Nishi Nagahori
Yotsubashi

Shiokusa
Ashiharabashi
Shikitsu
Shioku
Shinsaibashi
Minami Semba
Thailand
Mido Suji
Sakai Suji
Consulate General of Belgium
Shitennōji
National Bunraku Theater
Shin Kabukiza
Namba
Namba

Ashihara
Inari

Sakuragawa
Minatomachi
Sakuragawa

Shin Naniwa Suji

Kizugawa
Kita Tsumori
Tsumori
Tsumori
Tsumori
Nankai Kōya Line
Sakai Route
Tsumori
Tsumori
Minami Tsumori
Minami Tsumori
Sembonmatsu Bridge

Nishi Osaka Route
Taishō Ward Office
Taishō
Sangen'ya
Taishō-Dōri
Kitamura
Izuo
Kitamura
Chishima
Chishima
Chishima Park

Taishō Ward

Kobayashi
Hirao

Kizugawa

Minato Ward
Minato-Dōri
Minato Ward Office
Ichioka Motomachi
Ichioka
Ichioka

Namiyoke
Modern Transport Museum
Benten
Bentenchō
Isoji

Kita Okajima
Kita Okajima
Minami Okajima

Funamachi

Shinhashigawa

National Road 43
Ajigawa Bridge
Benten Wharf

Tsurumachi

1165

Business and Commercial District   Residential Area   Governmental or Public Facility   Industrial or Transport Facility   — Ward Boundary

Hotel   Hospital   Temple   Shrine   Cultural Facility   Historical Site   ⑮ Hanshin Expressway   Railway   Subway   Subway Under Construction

osechi ryōri Each of the traditional New Year's foods served in these ornate lacquer boxes symbolizes, usually through wordplay involving their names, wishes for good health and prosperity in the year ahead.

Osaragi Jirō This popular writer established his reputation with the "Kurama Tengu" series of historical novels.

mountains to the east, and the Izumi Mountains to the south. In the center of the prefecture is the ŌSAKA PLAIN, and to the west is Ōsaka Bay. There are vast tracts of diluvial land along the fringes of the plain, particularly near the hills called Senriyama and Kasen. The principal rivers flowing through the Ōsaka Plain are the YODOGAWA, which has its origin in Lake Biwa and flows into Ōsaka Bay, and the YAMATOGAWA, which flows from Nara Basin into Ōsaka Bay. The climate of the prefecture is mild. In the district facing Ōsaka Bay, strong westerly winds blow in summer and winter.

The wide distribution of remains from the Jōmon (ca 10,000 BC–ca 300 BC) and Yayoi (ca 300 BC–ca AD 300) periods and paleolithic-style stone utensils attest to early settlement of the prefecture. With the consolidation of the YAMATO COURT's power in the 5th century, a number of large tombs, including the ŌJIN MAUSOLEUM and the NINTOKU MAUSOLEUM, were constructed. From the 6th to 8th centuries Naniwazu was the port of departure for traffic between Japan and the East Asian continent. It was during this period that Buddhism and continental culture and technology were brought to Japan by Korean and Chinese immigrants (KIKAJIN). The development of the Ōsaka Plain also proceeded steadily, as witnessed by the digging of the Sayama Pond, the oldest artificial pond in Japan, and numerous other ponds and irrigation systems. Under the ancient system of provinces (KOKUGUN SYSTEM) the area was divided into the three provinces of Settsu, Kawachi, and Izumi. A decline set in from the mid-Heian period (794–1185) to the period of the Northern and Southern Courts (1337–92), but the city of SAKAI flourished from around the end of the Muromachi period (1333–1568) as a center of foreign trade, and with the construction of ŌSAKA CASTLE by the hegemon TOYOTOMI HIDEYOSHI in 1583, Ōsaka once more prospered. In the Edo period (1600–1868) Ōsaka and Sakai were

put under the direct control of the Tokugawa shogunate. Warehouses of various domains were constructed in Ōsaka, and the city became the entrepôt of rice and other products from throughout the nation. After the establishment of the modern prefectural system in 1871, the boundaries of Ōsaka Prefecture were defined in 1887.

The prefecture is a major center of commerce and industry. Its importance as a commercial center was solidified during the Edo period, and its modern industries, mainly spinning, developed during the Meiji period (1868–1912). After World War II, the metal, machinery, and chemical industries witnessed a dramatic growth, and some 70 percent of the prefecture's total production is occupied by the heavy and chemical industries. The industrial center, known as the HANSHIN INDUSTRIAL ZONE, is located along the lower reaches of the river Yodogawa; more recently, iron and steel, shipbuilding, oil, and lumber industrial complexes have been constructed on land reclaimed from Ōsaka Bay. Farming, chiefly vegetables and flowers, is carried out in the rural districts.

During the Edo period the city of Ōsaka, drawing on the wealth of its merchants, developed a culture that contrasted sharply with that of Edo (now Tōkyō), the shogunal capital. Representative figures of the so-called Kamigata culture were the *haiku* poet NISHIYAMA SŌIN, the novelist Ihara SAIKAKU, and the playwright CHIKAMATSU MONZAEMON. Among renowned scholars were KEICHŪ, TOMINAGA NAKAMOTO, YAMAGATA BANTŌ, and OGATA KŌAN. Places of interest are Ōsaka Castle in the city of Ōsaka, the Naniwa palace site (see NANIWAKYŌ), the temple SHITENNŌJI, and SUMIYOSHI SHRINE. Located in the northern part of the prefecture is Meiji no Mori Minoo Quasi-National Park, and in the eastern part is Kongō-Ikoma Quasi-National Park. To the north of Senriyama is Expo Memorial Park (see EXPO '70). The NINTOKU MAUSOLEUM, the largest mounded tomb (KOFUN) in Japan, is in Sakai.

Ōsaka Sayama   大阪狭山[市]

City in southeastern Ōsaka Prefecture; formerly a castle town of the HŌJŌ FAMILY. Rice, vegetables, and mandarin oranges are grown, and there are numerous suburban housing developments, such as Sayama New Town. Sayama Pond, one of Japan's oldest irrigation reservoirs, is located here. Pop: 54,319.

Ōsaka school   大坂派

(Ōsakaha). A descriptive term applied to woodblock prints, paintings, and illustrated books in the UKIYO-E style, mostly related in some way to the KABUKI theater, produced in the city of Ōsaka between the middle of the 18th century and the end of the 19th century. Originally, styles developed in the Kyōto-Ōsaka area were adopted in Edo (now Tōkyō), but by the end of the 18th century Taga Ryūkōsai, the founder of the Ōsaka style, followed precedents set by Edo artists of the Katsukawa school. In the decade beginning in 1810 the works of the Edo artists UTAGAWA KUNISADA and UTAGAWA TOYOKUNI were the models on which the young Ōsaka designers Ashikuni, Ashiyuki, Hokushū, and Kunihiro patterned their work.

After the 1840s a new type of print appeared that portrayed large heads or full-length figures of actors. The outstanding artist in this style was Konishi Hirosada (active to 1863). Other prints were also published in Ōsaka, notably the beautiful SURIMONO of the MARUYAMA-SHIJŌ SCHOOL, which appeared

from the 1820s until the end of the century. In the Meiji period (1868–1912) many views and historical prints were published, but stylistically they conformed to the conventions of Tōkyō.

Ōsaka Spinning Mill   大阪紡績会社

(Ōsaka Bōseki Kaisha). Established in Ōsaka Prefecture by SHIBUSAWA EIICHI in 1882. Using the latest technology from England, it was the first large-scale cotton mill in Japan and became a model for subsequent mills. In 1914 it merged with the Mie Bōseki Kaisha to become the TŌYŌBŌ CO, LTD.

Ōsaka University   大阪大学

(Ōsaka Daigaku). National, coeducational university; main campus located in the city of Suita, Ōsaka Prefecture. Its predecessor was the Tekijuku, a private academy for "Dutch Learning" (WESTERN LEARNING) founded in 1838 by OGATA KŌAN. It became Ōsaka Imperial University in 1931 and Ōsaka University in 1949. It maintains faculties of letters, human sciences, law, economics, science, medicine, dentistry, pharmacology, engineering science, and engineering. The university is known for its institutes for research on proteins, welding, microbial diseases, science and industry, and society and economics. Enrollment was 11,148 in 1989.

Ōsaka University of Foreign Studies   大阪外国語大学

(Ōsaka Gaikokugo Daigaku). A national, coeducational university in the city of Minoo, Ōsaka Prefecture. Established in 1921 as the Ōsaka School of Foreign Languages, it became a university in 1949. The university emphasizes the languages and cultures of Asian countries. It offers courses in 18 languages, including 10 Asian languages such as Mongolian, Korean, Hindi, Thai, and Indonesian. Enrollment was 4,004 in 1989.

Ōsaka Uoichiba Co, Ltd   大阪魚市場[株]

(Ōsaka Uoichiba). Wholesaler of marine products, operating in the Ōsaka Central Wholesale Market. Incorporated in 1946. Sales for the fiscal year ending March 1991 totaled ¥365.1 billion (US $2.7 billion), of which fresh fish accounted for 31 percent; frozen fish, 43 percent; and salted and dried fish, 26 percent. The company was capitalized at ¥5.7 billion (US $41.5 million) in the same year. Headquarters are in Ōsaka.

Ōsakayama   逢坂山

Hill on the border between Shiga and Kyōto prefectures, central Honshū. A check station called Ōsaka no Seki was located in a pass in these foothills during the Heian period (794–1185). The pass, often mentioned in classic poems, was a vital transportation link in ancient days. Today, National Route No. 1 and the Meishin Expressway run through the pass, while a railroad tunnel passes under the hill. Height: 325 m (1,066 ft).

Osanai Kaoru   小山内薫

(1881–1928). Theatrical impresario, playwright, and director; a vital force in creating and sustaining the movement for a modern theater (SHINGEKI) in the early 20th century. Born in Hiroshima Prefecture. Graduate of Tōkyō University. Excited by his reading of modern Western drama, Osanai began in 1909 the first professional company for modern drama in Japan, the Jiyū Gekijō (Free

Theater), which continued until 1919. In 1924 Osanai opened a new company, the Tsukiji Shōgekijō (Tsukiji Little Theater), which he designed to serve as a laboratory for the development of Japanese actors, writers, directors, and stage designers. The company was dissolved after Osanai's death in 1928. His vitality, enthusiasm, and profound belief in the modern theater make him a major figure in Japanese cultural history. His works include the novel *Ōkawabata* (1911) and the plays *Daiichi no sekai* (1921) and *Musuko* (1922).

Osaragi Jirō 大仏次郎

(1897–1973). Novelist. Real name Nojiri Kiyohiko. Born in Yokohama. Graduate of Tōkyō University. Studying with the liberal scholar of political science YOSHINO SAKUZŌ, he formed democratic and antiauthoritarian views. He entered the Foreign Ministry in 1922, but, following the great Tōkyō Earthquake of 1923, he resolved to devote himself to writing as a full-time occupation. In 1924 he published his first piece of popular fiction, *Hayabusa no Genji*. Immediately after World War II, he served for two months in the cabinet of Prince HIGASHIKUNI NARUHIKO as cabinet councillor.

Osaragi won lasting fame with the historical novels in his "Kurama Tengu" series (1924–59). Other POPULAR FICTION by Osaragi includes *Teru hi kumoru hi* (1926–27, Sunny Days, Cloudy Days) and *Akō rōshi* (1927–28). Many of his novels were serialized for newspapers (see SHIMBUN SHŌSETSU).

Novels with more contemporary settings also gained popular acclaim, including *Kikyō* (1948; tr *Homecoming*, 1954) and two other novels that portray the anguish of Japanese intellectuals under the militarist regime. Osaragi also wrote about several European historical incidents and published several plays. His ambitious *Tennō no seiki* (1967–73, Century of Emperors) is a broad assessment of the intellectual and spiritual history of Japan from the MEIJI RESTORATION (1868) to the present. He died before its completion.

osechi ryōri お節料理

In Japanese cooking, an assortment of specialty foods served at New Year's. Originally, during the Heian period (794–1185), the term denoted the food served at *sechie*, banquets given by the imperial court to celebrate changes of season.

Today, *osechi ryōri* is typically eaten after a celebratory toast with TOSO (spiced *sake*) and accompanied by ZŌNI (a soup containing rice cakes and vegetables). The foods, which are prepared in advance, are highly preservable, thus eliminating the need for cooking during the first three days of the New Year. They are often stored and served in multitiered lacquered boxes known as JŪBAKO. The dishes served vary from region to region but traditionally include *kuromame* (stewed black soybeans), *kazunoko* (salted herring roe), *tazukuri* (dried sardines cooked in soy sauce), a salad of carrot and white radish (*daikon*) dressed with vinegar, cooked burdock (*gobō*) marinated in vinegar, KAMABOKO (broiled fish paste), *datemaki* (sweet omelet squares), broiled shrimp and sea bream, and vegetables such as lotus root and carrot simmered in seasoned broth.

Traditionally, all dishes were prepared in the home, but today most are also sold ready-made in stores. In addition, new types of food, chiefly Western and Chinese, have been introduced to the repertoire.

Ōseidasaresho 被仰出書

(formally, Gakuji Shōrei ni kansuru Ōseidasaresho; Proclamation concerning the Encouragement of Education). A document issued by the DAJŌKAN, the central organ of the new Meiji government, to explain to the Japanese public the basic content of the EDUCATION ORDER OF 1872. It elucidated the modern doctrine of education and called on all citizens to study the practical arts and sciences. It emphasized that the function of schools was to create independent individuals and criticized the feudal education system that was intended only for the *samurai* class. These concepts had a great similarity to the arguments in FUKUZAWA YUKICHI'S GAKUMON NO SUSUME.

Ōsei Fukko 王政復古

(Restoration of Imperial Rule). Coup d'état of 3 January 1868 that formally abolished the Tokugawa shogunate (1603–1867) and restored direct rule by the emperor. This action marked the beginning of the MEIJI RESTORATION. On 9 November 1867 the shōgun TOKUGAWA YOSHINOBU attempted to shore up his regime by surrendering much of his authority to the imperial court (see TAISEI HŌKAN). Although the offer was accepted (leading some scholars to accept this date as the end of the Tokugawa shogunate), opponents were determined to exclude the Tokugawa family from power.

On 3 January 1868 troops from five domains seized the gates of the palace in Kyōto. An assembly that included sympathetic *daimyō* and court officials discussed plans for a new political structure: some envisioned the restoration of the old DAJŌKAN system; others saw the restoration as the first step toward the creation of a new Western-style imperial state. In any case, they issued an edict restoring imperial rule (Ōsei Fukko no Dai Gōrei), and the shogunate was abolished. Resistance by some supporters of the shogunate led to the brief BOSHIN CIVIL WAR.

Ōse Jintarō 大瀬甚太郎

(1865–1944). Educator. Born in Fukui Prefecture. Graduate of Tōkyō University. From 1893 to 1897 Ōse studied in Germany and France and was particularly influenced by German pedagogical theory. After returning to Japan, he worked in teacher training and educational research at various schools, including Tōkyō Higher Normal School (later Tōkyō University of Education; now TSUKUBA UNIVERSITY).

Osenkorogashi おせんころがし

Sea cliffs southwest of the city of Katsuura, southern Chiba Prefecture, central Honshū. A railway line and a road ascend these rugged and majestic cliffs on the Pacific Ocean. The name is derived from a story concerning the filial piety of a young woman named Osen, who fell to her death from the cliffs.

ōsetsuma 応接間

(parlor; reception room). Western-style room set aside especially for the reception of guests. In place of the *kyakuma* (literally, "guest room") that is found in traditional Japanese-style homes, both Japanese- and Western-style houses from the Meiji period (1868–1912) to the present have included such a room for receiving visitors. It was commonly a room without *tatami* mats, adjacent to the entrance, furnished in Western style with tables and chairs. In recent years there has been a growing tendency to dispense with the *ōsetsuma* and to entertain guests in the living room (*ima*).

oshi 御師

A term of Buddhist origin that came to be used in syncretic SHUGENDŌ and Shintō contexts. *Oshi* (literally, "master") designated masters of exorcism and others with certain religious or magical powers. They functioned as agents between shrines and devotees, transmitting amulets from shrines and supplications from followers and guiding and accommodating pilgrims. They grew in importance as pilgrimages to famous shrines and temples became popular and had a key role in the popularization of religion. Their status was abolished in 1871.

oshibori 御紋り

A small towel moistened with hot or cold water and provided to guests in private homes and at many restaurants and coffee shops for use in wiping the hands and face. Cold *oshibori* are used most commonly in summer and hot ones in winter. In public eating and drinking establishments *oshibori* often come sterilized and individually wrapped; there are many companies that specialize in providing the food-service industry with clean *oshibori*. In Japanese-style restaurants *oshibori* are usually brought to patrons on a long, narrow tray as soon as they sit down. In recent years, disposable paper towels have come to be used as *oshibori* with increasing frequency.

oshidashibutsu 押出仏

Also known as *tsuikibutsu*. Type of Buddhist relief image formed by hammering a thin copper sheet against a cast copper core, resulting in a relief in the form of the cast image. Fine details were then chiseled into the relief, which received a final coating of gold leaf or gold plate. This sculptural technique, which allowed the mass production of an image, was imported from China and popularized in Japan in the 7th and 8th centuries. The AMIDA triad of the temple HŌRYŪJI is a representative example of *oshidashibutsu*, and molds for the production of sculptures by this technique are found among the treasures of the SHŌSŌIN. See BUDDHIST SCULPTURE.

Oshika Peninsula 牡鹿半島

(Oshika Hantō). Located in the eastern part of Ishinomaki Bay, eastern Miyagi Prefecture, northern Honshū. It is an extension of the heavily indented Sanriku coastline. *Nori* (a kind of seaweed) and oyster cultivation flourish in the bay, as well as coastal fishing for abalone and kelp (*kombu*). The ports of Onagawa and Ayukawa are bases for deep-sea fishing. The island of KINKAZAN, located

off the peninsula, is a noted tourist attraction.

Ōshikōchi no Mitsune　凡河内躬恒

(fl ca 900). Courtier and poet; one of the four compilers of the first imperial anthology (*chokusenshū*) of Japanese classical poetry, the KOKINSHŪ (ca 905, Collection from Ancient and Modern Times); one of the Thirty-Six Poetic Geniuses (SANJŪROKKASEN). Next to KI NO TSURAYUKI, Mitsune was perhaps the most outstanding poet of his generation. More than 190 of his poems are included in imperial anthologies from the *Kokinshū* on. His personal collection, *Mitsuneshū*, exists in several different versions containing 140 to 482 poems. Some of the more extensive versions also contain selections of his Chinese verse and a few poems by friends and correspondents.

Ōshima　大島

Also known as Suō Ōshima and Yashirojima. Island in the western Inland Sea, off the city of Yanai, eastern Yamaguchi Prefecture; part of Yamaguchi Prefecture. Much of the arable land has been planted with fruit trees, especially mandarin oranges. Coastal fishing is an important activity. Since the late 19th century many inhabitants of Ōshima have emigrated to Hawaii. Area: 130 sq km (50 sq mi).

Ōshima　大島

Also known as Izu Ōshima. Volcanic island approximately 40 km (25 mi) east of the Izu Peninsula; northernmost and largest of the IZU ISLANDS. Administratively part of Tōkyō Prefecture. The active volcano MIHARAYAMA (758 m; 2,487 ft) makes up most of the island; there were eruptions in 1986, 1987, and 1988. The KUROSHIO (Japan Current) acts to produce a temperate climate; camellias bloom even during winter. Part of the Fuji-Hakone-Izu National Park, the island has an active tourist industry and numerous hot springs. The special product of the island is camellia oil. Area: 91 sq km (35 sq mi).

Ōshima　大島

Also known as Kii Ōshima. Island off the Kii Peninsula, southern Wakayama Prefecture, central Honshū. It is connected by ferry to Kushimoto on the mainland. The island is part of Yoshino-Kumano National Park and the site of a botanical garden housing tropical plants. Area: 9.9 sq km (3.8 sq mi).

Ōshima Hiroshi　大島浩

(1886–1975). General and diplomat. Born in Gifu Prefecture. Graduate of the Army Academy (1905) and the Army War College (1915). Noted as a German specialist, Ōshima was appointed military attaché to Germany in 1934. With Foreign Minister Joachim von Ribbentrop (1893–1946) he brought about the ANTI-COMINTERN PACT. In 1938 he was appointed ambassador to Germany. In that capacity he worked to strengthen the Axis alliance by the conclusion of the TRIPARTITE PACT. At the WAR CRIMES TRIALS after the war, he was designated a class A war criminal and sentenced to life imprisonment. He was released, however, in 1955.

Ōshima Nagisa　大島渚

(1932–). Film director. Leader of the French-inspired, leftist, so-called Shōchiku New Wave (Nūberu Bāgu; i.e., *nouvelle vague*) of young directors in the 1960s. Born in Kyōto, he graduated from Kyōto University.

Hired by what is now SHŌCHIKU CO, LTD, in 1954 as an assistant director, he also wrote film criticism that stressed the importance of self-assertion, spontaneity, and freedom of expression and attacked the established commercialism of American and Japanese films. In his films Ōshima has addressed the psychological dilemmas and social injustices of modern Japan. These include the dilemma of youth without ideals, the impotence of the organized Left, and the suffering of the oppressed. Many of Ōshima's protagonists are outsiders or criminals, as seen in *Seishun zankoku monogatari* (1960, Cruel Story of Youth or Naked Youth: A Story of Cruelty).

Ōshima left Shōchiku in 1961 after widely publicized differences with the company. By 1965 he was producing films through his own independent company, Sōzōsha, including SHŌNEN (1969, Boy) and *Gishiki* (1971, The Ceremony). He had to seek a French producer to deal with the forbidden subject of sexual obsession in *Ai no korīda* (1976, IN THE REALM OF THE SENSES). He won the Best Director award in 1978 at the Cannes Film Festival for its sequel, *Ai no bōrei* (Empire of Passion). In 1983 Ōshima directed the joint Japanese-British production *Merry Christmas, Mr. Lawrence*.

Oshima Peninsula　渡島半島

(Oshima Hantō). Located in southwestern Hokkaidō; part of the Ōnuma Quasi-National Park. Its hilly terrain is scattered with farming and fishing villages. The city of Hakodate and numerous volcanoes and hot springs are located in the southern part of the peninsula.

Ōshima Ryōta　大島蓼太

(1718–87). HAIKU poet. He disapproved of the recondite wit and urbanity of the Edoza school of TAKARAI KIKAKU and urged a return to the original precepts of the BASHŌ school. An energetic teacher and traveler, he was said to have had 2,000 disciples. His main works include *Bashō kukai* (1757) and *Haikai jūsanjō* (1767). Particularly noteworthy are his critical editions of Bashō's works.

Ōshima Sadamasu　大島貞益

(1845–1914). Economist. Born in Hyōgo Prefecture. In 1856 Ōshima moved to Edo (now Tōkyō), hoping to pursue Western studies. He became a participant in the SONNŌ JŌI (Revere the Emperor, Expel the Barbarians) movement and in 1868 started working as a translator for the new Meiji government. Ōshima introduced the social policy studies of Wilhelm Roscher and other Western scholars and made a great contribution to the study of labor and social questions in Japan. Ōshima's published works on economics include *Keizai sanron* (1900, Essays on Economics) and translations such as *Rishi keizairon* (1889; from *The National System of Political Economy* by Friedrich List).

Ōshima Takatō　大島高任

(1826–1901). Mining engineer and metallurgist. Ōshima worked to develop, expand, and modernize mining, processing, and manufacturing methods in the Japanese metal industry. Born in what is now Morioka, Iwate Prefecture, he studied WESTERN LEARNING, especially gunnery and mining, in Nagasaki. In 1858 he built Japan's first Western-style blast furnace at what is now Kamaishi, Iwate Prefecture. In Mito (now part of Ibaraki Prefecture) he manufactured the first modern Japanese-made Western-style rifle. Later he began development of numerous metal ore deposits throughout Japan.

Ōshio Heihachirō　大塩平八郎

(1793–1837). Idealistic Confucian philosopher and teacher of the Wang Yangming school (see YŌMEIGAKU) who led a rebellion in Ōsaka in 1837 (known as the Tempō Uprising) against the Tokugawa shogunate (1603–1867). Also known as Ōshio Chūsai. Ōshio's family origin is obscure. As a youth Ōshio entered training to become a constable under the shogunate and began the study of Neo-Confucianism, eventually concentrating on the ideas of Wang Yangming, which shaped his moral commitment to act in the name of popular justice. In 1830 he resigned his position and founded a school, the Senshindō, to teach the ideas of Wang Yangming. He compiled and published his lectures as the *Senshindō satsuki* (1833). Ōshio's theme was that injustice was caused by men of wealth and rank who did not act in concord with the timeless ideal of a goodness that cut through social distinctions.

In 1835 and 1836 famine spread throughout the Kansai region as a result of crop failure (see TEMPŌ FAMINE). After pleading futilely for government assistance, Ōshio called on the peasantry and the downtrodden to rise up against injustice and oppression. On 19 February 1837 Ōshio attacked the shogunate's administrative offices and set fire to parts of the city of Ōsaka, hoping to trigger popular peasant uprisings in the neighboring areas. One-fourth of Ōsaka, including the shogunate's storehouse, was destroyed in two days of confusion and fire. The rebellion was crushed, and Ōshio, surrounded by superior shogunate troops, took his own life.

Ōshū Fujiwara family　奥州藤原氏

(Ōshū Fujiwarashi). Also known as the Mutsu or Hiraizumi Fujiwara family. Warrior family, based in the city of HIRAIZUMI (now in Iwate Prefecture), that ruled northeastern Japan virtually as an independent kingdom during the late Heian period (794–1185). The name Ōshū refers to the ancient provinces comprising the entire northeastern region of Honshū.

By the end of the Heian period the family of Fujiwara no Tsunekiyo was accepted as descendants of the Hidesato branch of the FUJIWARA FAMILY of Kyōto. Tsunekiyo was a son-in-law and leading vassal of ABE NO YORITOKI (d 1057), whose family dominated the Ōshū region from the 9th century until they were crushed in the EARLIER NINE YEARS' WAR (1051–62) and replaced by the Kiyohara family. Tsunekiyo's son Fujiwara no Kiyohira (1056–1128) gained control of the Kiyohara domains in the LATER THREE YEARS' WAR (1083–87) and dominated northern Japan for 35 years. Kiyohira's son Motohira (d 1157) and grandson Hidehira (1096–1187) maintained this regional hegemony. Hiraizumi became the political and economic capital of the north and was perhaps the most advanced cultural center in Japan outside of Kyōto. After the Minamoto victory in 1185 (see TAIRA-MINAMOTO WAR), MINAMOTO NO YORITOMO (1147–99) controlled all Japan except the Ōshū region. His brother MINAMOTO NO YOSHITSUNE (1159–89), forced into an unsuccessful revolt by Yoritomo's jealousy and suspicion, fled to Hiraizumi and was sheltered by Hidehira. After Hidehira's death in 1187, his son Yasuhira (1155–89) forced Yoshitsune (1155–89) to commit suicide in 1189, but Yoritomo, unappeased, led troops into Hiraizumi. The Ōshū Fujiwara were destroyed and their domains came under the control of the Kamakura shogunate (1192–1333).

Osorezan 恐山

Also called Osoreyama. Composite volcano in the Nasu Volcanic Zone, Shimokita Peninsula, northeastern Aomori Prefecture, northern Honshū. In the caldera is Lake Usoriyama. Entsūji, a temple said to have been founded by ENNIN in the 9th century, stands on the banks of the lake. The mountain is sacred to Japanese shamans (see SHAMANISM) and, during the annual gathering held 20–24 July, mediums called *itako* communicate with the deceased when requested. Osorezan is part of the Shimokita Peninsula Quasi-National Park. Height: 879 m (2,884 ft).

osso 越訴

Appeal for retrial in premodern times; or, in a broader sense, direct remonstrance to higher authorities, bypassing official channels. Attempts to circumvent proper procedures in bringing suit were strictly forbidden in the penal codes (*ritsu*) of the Nara period (710–794) and their supplements (*kyaku*) of the Heian period (794–1185). The Kamakura shogunate (1192–1333) also prohibited appeals without proper endorsements. Appeals procedures were institutionalized when HŌJŌ TOKIMUNE in 1264 established the office of *osso bugyō* (commissioner of appeals). This institution was incorporated in the table of organization of the Muromachi shogunate (1338–1573) but was not retained by the Tokugawa shogunate (1603–1867), which forbade direct appeals. See also JIKISO.

Ōsuga Otsuji 大須賀乙字

(1881–1920). HAIKU poet. Real name Ōsuga Isao. Born in Fukushima Prefecture. Graduate of Tōkyō University. A disciple of the haiku poet KAWAHIGASHI HEKIGOTŌ, he became a haiku poetry editor of the newspaper *Tōkyō nichinichi shimbun* and wrote critical essays championing free verse but later reverted to a more traditional approach. In his highly regarded essays on haiku theory, he argued that even the objective photographic description of nature (*shasei*) called for by the HOTOTOGISU school should embody something of the poet's subjective feelings (*i*); for this he coined the term *sha-i*. He also argued that the traditional obligatory "season words" (*kidai* or KIGO) should be raised to the level of symbols. His main works include *Otsuji kushū* (1921), *Otsuji haironshū* (1921), and *Otsuji shokanshū* (1922).

Ōsugi Sakae 大杉栄

(1885–1923). Foremost Japanese anarchist of the Taishō period (1912–26) and prominent leftist leader. Ōsugi was born in Marugame,

Kagawa Prefecture, the first child of a middle-ranking army officer. At age 14 he entered Nagoya Cadet School (Nagoya Yōnen Gakkō), but in 1901 he was expelled for insubordination. He resumed his education in Tōkyō, where he encountered the leftist ideas of KŌTOKU SHŪSUI and SAKAI TOSHIHIKO. In 1906 he joined a protest movement against increases in Tōkyō trolley fares and was arrested and imprisoned for rioting.

Ōsugi spent most of the years between 1906 and 1910 in and out of jail and read extensively about anarchism. Imprisoned for his role in the RED FLAG INCIDENT OF 1908, he escaped implication in the HIGH TREASON INCIDENT OF 1910. In 1912 Ōsugi and ARAHATA KANSON began to publish *Kindai shisō* (Modern Thought), the first of seven journals that served as vehicles for anarchist philosophy. In 1915–16, while married to Hori Yasuko, Ōsugi became romantically involved with KAMICHIKA ICHIKO and ITŌ NOE, both prominent in the women's movement. Kamichika stabbed him, Hori divorced him, and Itō married him. The scandal led his leftist colleagues to shun him, but after the 1917 Russian Revolution he again became an active essayist and labor leader.

In December 1922 Ōsugi traveled to France. He was arrested and deported to Japan the following year, arriving just before the TŌKYŌ EARTHQUAKE OF 1923. On 16 September, in the confused aftermath of the disaster, Ōsugi, Itō Noe, and a nephew were arrested and beaten to death by military police. The killings, known as the Amakasu Incident (after the police captain in charge), together with the killings of 10 radical labor union leaders by civil police in the 4 September KAMEIDO INCIDENT, are assumed by many to have been ordered by high authorities.

Ōsu Incident 大須事件

(Ōsu Jiken). One of a number of political riots that occurred soon after the SAN FRANCISCO PEACE TREATY became effective on 28 April 1952, all of which resulted from opposition to the conservative administration left in power when the Allied OCCUPATION ended as well as to the United States–Japan Security Treaty of 1952 and the Korean War. The riot broke out at a political rally at Ōsu Stadium in Nagoya on 7 July 1952. Participants in the rally clashed with police outside the stadium. One demonstrator was killed and over 80 people were injured. A total of 150 demonstrators were convicted of sedition (*sōjōzai*). See also MAY DAY INCIDENT; SUITA INCIDENT.

Ōsumi Peninsula 大隅半島

(Ōsumi Hantō). Located in southeastern Kagoshima Prefecture, southern Kyūshū. Extending southwest into the Pacific Ocean, it is bounded to the west by Kagoshima Bay and to the east by Shibushi Bay and the Pacific Ocean. Consisting mainly of plateaus and mountains, it is largely an agricultural and forest region. Sections of the peninsula are part of Kirishima-Yaku National Park and Nichinan Coast Quasi-National Park. Area: 2,000 sq km (775 sq mi).

Ōsumi Strait 大隅海峡

(Ōsumi Kaikyō). Strait between the Ōsumi Peninsula in southern Kagoshima Prefecture, southern Kyūshū, and the island Tanegashima. The KUROSHIO (Japan Current) flows through the strait, which is an excellent fishing grounds. Depth: 100–250 m (328–820 ft).

Ōta 太田[市]

City in southeastern Gumma Prefecture, central Honshū. It was a market and post-station town on the highway to NIKKŌ in the Edo period (1600–1868). The aircraft factories of World War II have been succeeded by automobile plants. Other industries are plastics, electrical appliances, and machinery. Pop: 139,801.

ōtabumi 大田文

Land registers in the Kamakura (1185–1333) and Muromachi (1333–1568) periods that recorded the size of landholdings and information on land ownership in each province. Assembled from *kenchūchō*, individual registers of private estates (SHŌEN) and public lands (*kokugaryō*), they were used to apportion taxes. There were two kinds of *ōtabumi*. One, initiated by the shogunate, included not only the size of each cultivated area but also details of history of ownership; the second, commissioned by provincial headquarters (*kokuga*), simply recorded the area of each landholding. Several are extant and show graphically how landholding patterns were shifting in a period when warriors were taking over estates owned by court nobles and religious institutions.

Ōta Dōkan 太田道灌

(1432–86). Warrior of the Muromachi period (1333–1568). Vassal of the Ōgigayatsu branch of the UESUGI FAMILY. In 1457 Dōkan built a castle at EDO (now Tōkyō) that, expanded by TOKUGAWA IEYASU after 1590, became the headquarters of the Tokugawa shogunate (1603–1867) and, after 1868, the imperial palace. During an armed conflict between branches of the Uesugi, he was falsely accused of disloyalty to his lord and was killed. Highly reputed as a military tactician (see ASHIGARU), Dōkan was also skilled in the composition of WAKA poetry.

Ōtagaki Rengetsu 大田垣蓮月

(1791–1875). WAKA poet, calligrapher, potter, and painter. Probably born in Kyōto, she adopted the Buddhist name Rengetsu ("Lotus Moon") in 1823, after the death of her husband. An admirer of OZAWA ROAN, she

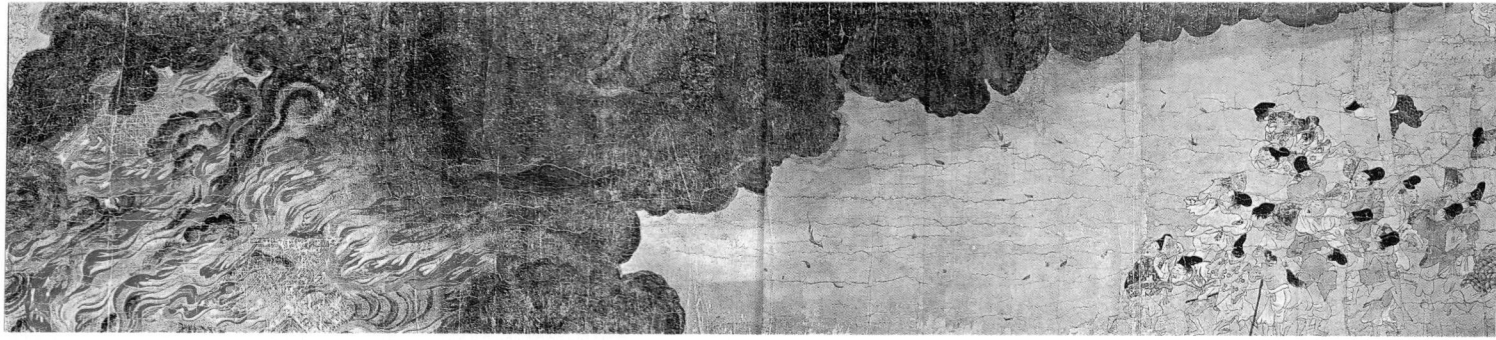

studied with the poet Mutobe Yoshika (d 1862) and the author UEDA AKINARI, and later taught poetry to TOMIOKA TESSAI. Her poems are notable for their use of mundane imagery drawn from everyday life.

Ōtagawa 太田川

River in western Hiroshima Prefecture, western Honshū, originating in the mountain Kammuriyama, flowing through the Hiroshima Plain, where it creates deltas, and emptying into Hiroshima Bay in the Inland Sea. The water is used for drinking and industry by the cities of Hiroshima and Kure. Length: 103 km (64 mi); area of drainage basin: 1,700 sq km (655 sq mi).

Ōta Kaoru 太田薫

(1912–). Leader of the Japanese labor movement; chairman of SŌHYŌ (General Council of Trade Unions of Japan) from 1958 to 1966. Graduate of Ōsaka University. In 1950 he became chairman of Gōka Rōren (Japan Federation of Synthetic Chemical Workers' Unions). He helped organize the SHUNTŌ, an annual nationwide labor offensive.

Ōtake 大竹[市]

City in southwestern Hiroshima Prefecture, western Honshū. Long known for its *washi* or handmade Japanese paper, it also has rayon and pulp factories. The construction of a petrochemical plant has led to water- and air-pollution problems. Pop: 33,236.

Ōtakineyama 大滝根山

Mountain in eastern Fukushima Prefecture, northern Honshū; the tallest peak in the Abukuma Mountains. In its foothills is a limestone plateau whose stalactite grottoes are designated as natural monuments. Height: 1,193 m (3,914 ft).

Ōta Memorial Museum of Art 太田記念美術館

(Ōta Kinen Bijutsukan). Institution in Shibuya Ward, Tōkyō. Established in 1980 to house the UKIYO-E collection of Ōta Seizō (1893–1977), former chairman of the Tōhō Mutual Life Insurance Co. The museum's 12,000 prints and paintings span the Edo period (1600–1868) and chronicle the development of *ukiyo-e*. Among its holdings are prints by artists such as SHARAKU, HARUNOBU, UTAMARO, and HOKUSAI.

Ōta Mizuho 太田水穂

(1876–1955). Poet and scholar of Japanese literature. Real name Ōta Teiichi. Born in Nagano Prefecture; graduated from Nagano Normal School (now Shinshū University). In 1915 he launched the TANKA magazine *Chōon*. Ōta advocated a type of Japanese symbolism as opposed to the realism of the poets associated with the magazine ARARAGI. Ōta's poetry collections include *Unchō* (1922, Cloud Bird), *Fuyuna* (1927,

Winter Greenery), *Sagi u* (1933, Heron and Cormorant), and *Raden* (1940, Mother-of-Pearl Inlay). His poetic style continues the lyric tradition of WAKA (classical Japanese poetry). Ōta's scholarly works include *Nihon wakashi ron* (1949 and 1954, On the History of Waka).

Ōta Nampo 大田南畝

(1749–1823). KYŌKA and *kyōshi* poet and writer of popular fiction of the Edo period (1600–1868). Real name Ōta Tan. Other pen names include Kyōkaen, Yomo no Akara, and Shokusanjin. Born in Edo (now Tōkyō), Nampo began as a student of Chinese literature, publishing a study of Ming poetry at the age of 17. Under the influence of satirist and playwright HIRAGA GENNAI, he used the medium of comic Chinese verse, *kyōshi* (see KYŌSHI AND KYŌBUN), in his first collection, *Neboke sensei bunshū* (1767, Literary Works of Master Groggy), a humorous look at the foibles of Edo society. Nampo also wrote *kyōka* (comic verses in WAKA form), KOKKEIBON, KIBYŌSHI, and SHAREBON. *Manzai kyōkashū* (1783), a collection of *kyōka* edited by Nampo, established him as the central figure of the Edo literary scene. His works include the *kyōka* collection *Shokusan hyakushu* (1818) and the essay collection *Ichiwa ichigen* (1775–1820).

Ōtani Takejirō 大谷竹次郎

(1877–1969). Entertainment entrepreneur. Ōtani founded SHŌCHIKU CO, LTD, with his twin brother Shirai Matsujirō (1877–1951) in 1902. In 1913 he took over management of the Kabukiza theater in Tōkyō, and before long built an entertainment empire that gave him managerial control over the majority of KABUKI, SHIMPA, and BUNRAKU theaters and performers. In 1920 he entered the film industry with the formation of Shōchiku Kinema Co, a subsidiary consolidated with the parent company in 1937. Ōtani contributed to both the preservation of the kabuki tradition and the development of modern Japanese film. He was awarded the Order of Culture in 1955.

Ōtani University 大谷大学

(Ōtani Daigaku). A private, Buddhist, coeducational university located in Kyōto. Founded by KIYOZAWA MANSHI in 1901 under the name Shinshū Daigaku, its origins date back to its establishment in 1655 as a seminary of the temple HIGASHI HONGANJI. Shinshū Daigaku achieved university status in 1922 and adopted the name Ōtani Daigaku in the same year. The university has a faculty of letters, emphasizing Buddhist studies, and an affiliated two-year junior college. Enrollment was 2,482 in 1989.

Otaru 小樽[市]

City in western Hokkaidō, on Ishikari Bay. It flourished from the beginning of the Meiji period (1868–1912) as a port town for shipping coal from the Ishikari Coalfields and as a base for fishing. In 1880 the first railway in

Hokkaidō was built, connecting Otaru and Sapporo. Now a center of commerce, it has seafood processing, ski equipment, furniture, rubber products, and foodstuff factories. There is skiing on nearby mountains. Pop: 163,211.

Otaru University of Commerce 小樽商科大学

(Otaru Shōka Daigaku). A coeducational national university located in the city of Otaru, Hokkaidō. Founded in 1910 as the Otaru Higher School of Commerce, it achieved university status in 1949. The college's only academic department is its faculty of commerce. Enrollment in 1989 was 1,772.

Ōtawara 大田原[市]

City in northern Tochigi Prefecture, central Honshū; named after the Ōtawara family, which built a castle here in 1545. It flourished as a castle town and post-station town. Principal industries are rice cultivation, dairy farming, and electrical-appliance manufacture. Pop: 52,547.

Ōta Ward 大田区

(Ōta Ku). One of the 23 wards of Tōkyō. Site of numerous factories producing metal, machinery, and foodstuffs. The eastern part of Ōta Ward faces Tōkyō Bay and is part of the Keihin Industrial Zone. Western Ōta Ward, on the Musashino Plateau, is principally a residential area. Also located within Ōta Ward are Haneda Airport (TŌKYŌ INTERNATIONAL AIRPORT) and the ŌMORI SHELL MOUNDS. Pop: 647,914.

otedama → beanbag

Ōtemachi 大手町

Business district in the eastern part of Chiyoda Ward, Tōkyō. It takes its name from its location in front of the Ōtemon, one of the Imperial Palace gates. During the Edo period (1600–1868), many *daimyō* mansions were located here. Today, the headquarters of major corporations, newspapers, communications companies, and government agencies are found in Ōtemachi, which is Japan's largest business center. The area also serves as a hub of Tōkyō's subway network.

Ōtemmon Conspiracy 応天門の変

(Ōtemmon no Hen). An incident associated with the burning of the Ōtemmon, one of the gates of the Imperial Palace in Kyōto, in 866; well known from the painted scroll BAN DAINAGON EMAKI. Ban (Tomo no) Yoshio (809–868), a descendant of the ŌTOMO FAMILY, accused his political rival Minamoto no Makoto (810–868) of having started the fire. Makoto had the support of the grand minister of state (*dajō daijin*) FUJIWARA NO YOSHIFUSA, however, and was cleared. Later, accused by an alleged eyewitness, Yoshio, his son, and several kinsmen, as well as members of the illustrious KI FAMILY, were convicted and exiled.

Ōte Takuji　大手拓次

(1887–1934). Poet. Born in Gumma Prefecture; graduate of Waseda University. A student of the poet KITAHARA HAKUSHŪ. During his twenties, he published poems in such magazines as *Zamboa* and *Ars*. Posthumously published poetry collections include *Ai iro no hiki* (1936, An Indigo Toad), *Hebi no hanayome* (1940, Snake's Bride), and *Ōte Takuji shishū* (1948).

Othello game　オセロ

(Osero). "Othello" is the trademarked name of a Japanese board game that originated in 1972, based on a similar English board game. The board is divided into 64 squares arranged in eight vertical and eight horizontal rows. Two players, designated "black" and "white," alternate moves of one chip. Chips are black on one side and white on the other. To begin, two white and two black chips are placed diagonally across from each other in the exact center of the board. Black moves first. Each player places his chip so as to enclose on two opposing sides one or more of his opponent's. Enclosed chips are turned over, exposing the capturing player's color. If a player is unable to enclose any of his opponent's chips, he must pass. The game ends when all 64 squares are filled with chips. The winner is the player whose chips outnumber his opponent's. The Japan Othello Game Association was formed in 1973, and the International Othello Championship has been held annually since 1977.

otogishū　御伽衆

Men who served their masters as conversational partners; also known as *ohanashishū* and *odampan*. The *daimyō* began to employ such attendants during the Sengoku period (1467–1568), and the practice continued into the Edo period (1600–1868). *Otogishū* were expected to entertain daimyō between battles, but later became personal advisers, helping in the management of the daimyō's domains. Some *otogishū*, such as Ōmura Yūko (d 1596), the author of Nō plays celebrating his master TOYOTOMI HIDEYOSHI and the chronicler of his deeds, were men of genuine literary accomplishment. *Otogishū* lost their importance in the mid-Edo period, and their function changed to that of professional jesters. From the mid-17th century, the term *otogishū* was used for pages (KOSHŌ) who served as companions to children of daimyō families.

otogi-zōshi　御伽草子

(companion stories). Term first used in the 18th century as an appellation for *Otogi bunko* (The Companion Library), a set of 23 medieval stories collected and printed around 1700 by the Ōsaka publisher Shibukawa Seiemon. It was used anachronistically by scholars beginning in the late 19th century as a generic label for the whole body of short tales produced during the late Kamakura period (1185–1333) and the Muromachi period (1333–1568). More recently, the term has become confused with *otogi-banashi* (fairy tales for children).

The original body of medieval short tales from which Shibukawa drew his selection covered such subjects as tragic love and suicide, jealousy, insanity, murder, brutal agonies suffered by men and women before they are reborn as deities, homosexual love between priests and young acolytes, and travels through hell. About 500 short tales from

the 13th to the 17th centuries, almost all of them anonymous, have been recovered and ascribed to the *otogi-zōshi* genre. Scholars today refer to them as *chūsei shōsetsu* (medieval novellas) or *Muromachi jidai tampen shōsetsu* (short stories of the Muromachi period). Themes and sometimes text are drawn directly from religious *setsuwa* (see SETSUWA BUNGAKU), GUNKI MONOGATARI (war tales), and other narrative genres. Medieval jongleurs—such as the blind lute-playing chanters known as BIWA HŌSHI, the blind hand-drum-playing (see TSUZUMI) female chanters called GOZE, and the proselytizing nuns referred to as Kumano *bikuni*—played key roles in the creation of medieval short stories, drawing materials from temple sermons and epics such as HEIKE MONOGATARI (The Tale of the Heike) and SOGA MONOGATARI (The Tale of the Soga Brothers).

Short medieval tales come down to us in three forms. First, there are the *emaki*, or horizontal handscrolls, which combine alternating sections of calligraphic text and painting. Second, there are hand-painted and calligraphically handwritten books known as Nara *ehon* (picture books drawn in styles ranging from the naive to highly professional, some of which may have originated among temple artists of the Nara area). Third, there are *shahon*, or "copies," hand-calligraphed books or scrolls that reproduce the text only.

Most medieval short fiction served nonliterary ends; the tales often conclude with instructions to read their pages daily as a substitute for religious pilgrimages or other acts of piety.

Otoko wa tsurai yo → Tora san

Ōtomo family　大伴氏

(Ōtomoshi). Powerful family (UJI) of the YAMATO COURT. The Ōtomo, like the rival MONONOBE FAMILY, were the military arm of the *uji* that eventually became the imperial house. In the first half of the 6th century ŌTOMO NO KANAMURA held supreme power; he fell because of the failure of his policies in KAYA, the Japanese enclave in Korea. The fortunes of the family revived when Emperor KŌTOKU appointed Ōtomo no Nagatoko (d 651) minister of the right (*udaijin*), and the Ōtomo enjoyed imperial favor

after supporting the future emperor TEMMU in the JINSHIN DISTURBANCE of 672. During the Nara period (710–794) the Ōtomo produced many officials and poets, including ŌTOMO NO TABITO, ŌTOMO NO SAKANOUE NO IRATSUME, and ŌTOMO NO YAKAMOCHI. In 823 they changed their name to Tomo. In the early Heian period (794–1185) the Ōtomo came into conflict with the ascendant FUJIWARA FAMILY. After Tomo no Yoshio (809–868) was implicated in the ŌTEMMON CONSPIRACY (866) and banished, the Ōtomo never regained their lost influence.

Ōtomo family　大友氏

(Ōtomoshi). Prominent warrior family of northern Kyūshū. Ōtomo Yoshinao (1172–1223), the family's founder, was appointed military governor (SHUGO) of Bungo Province (now part of Ōita Prefecture) at the end of the 12th century. The family gradually extended its power by establishing branch families throughout Kyūshū. Early in the civil war between the NORTHERN AND SOUTHERN COURTS (1337–92), Ōtomo Ujiyasu (dates unknown) fought for ASHIKAGA TAKAUJI and was rewarded with the governorship of several provinces. By the time of ŌTOMO SŌRIN (1530–87), the family held sway over a third of Kyūshū and had amassed enormous wealth through foreign trade. In 1578 Sōrin was defeated by the rival SHIMAZU FAMILY. The Ōtomo were saved by the national hegemon TOYOTOMI HIDEYOSHI in 1587 and retained only Bungo as their domain. After Sōrin's son Yoshimune (1558–1605) showed timidity in the first of Hideyoshi's INVASIONS OF KOREA IN 1592 AND 1597, the family was stripped of its possessions. Its descendants later served the Tokugawa shogunate (1603–1867) as hereditary masters of shogunal court ceremony (KŌKE).

Ōtomo no Kanamura　大伴金村

(fl ca 495–540). Military leader and statesman of the Yamato court (ca 4th century–ca mid-7th century). Scion of the military ŌTOMO FAMILY, hereditary protectors of the imperial house. On the death of Emperor Ninken, he overthrew the grand minister (*ōomi*) Heguri no Matori and secured the succession of Emperor Buretsu, who ap-

otogi-zōshi A detail from the Muromachi-period handscroll *Nezumi no sōshi* (Storybook of Rats), an example of this genre of medieval short tales.

Ōtomo Sōrin Depicted in this 1587 portrait in the garb of a Buddhist lay monk, Sōrin converted to Christianity in 1578, perhaps motivated as much by desire for foreign-trade profits as by religious feelings.

pointed him minister of state (*ōmuraji*). When Buretsu died without an heir, Kanamura discovered an alleged fifth-generation descendant of Emperor ŌJIN and installed him as Emperor KEITAI. Kanamura managed affairs of state throughout the reigns of Keitai, Ankan, and Senka. He suppressed the Rebellion of IWAI (527–528). The accession of Emperor KIMMEI in 531 (or 539), with the support of Ōtomo rival Mononobe no Okoshi (see MONONOBE FAMILY), brought Kanamura's long official career to an abrupt end. His downfall resulted from his involvement in a Korean diplomatic crisis many years before, when Kanamura had agreed to the cession of the Japanese enclave on the Korean peninsula. The Ōtomo fell into relative obscurity until the mid-7th century.

Ōtomo no Sakanoue no Iratsume
大伴坂上郎女

(fl ca 728–746; Lady Ōtomo of Sakanoue). Poet and matriarch of the Ōtomo clan. The MAN'YŌSHŪ (ca 759, Collection for Ten Thousand Generations or Collection for Ten Thousand Leaves), the first and largest anthology of Japanese vernacular poetry, contains 84 of her poems—more than any other woman poet. This is probably because of her closeness to ŌTOMO NO YAKAMOCHI, the dominant poet of the period and a compiler of the anthology. As a young woman, Lady Ōtomo was evidently a favorite of Prince Hozumi, fifth son of Emperor Temmu (d 686; r 672–686). On his death in 715 she formed a relationship with Fujiwara no Maro (695–737) but later married her elder half-brother Ōtomo no Sukunamaro and bore him two daughters. She ultimately became a kind of clan matriarch. Some of her verses are fashionably clever and elegant, showing the influence of Chinese modes and techniques of wit and intellectual ingenuity. Others are more traditional, employing the forms and techniques of older poetry and preliterate song.

Ōtomo no Tabito
大伴旅人

(665–731). Courtier, official, military commander, and poet. A member of the Ōtomo family of hereditary warriors, palace guards, and military commanders for the imperial family, Tabito became middle counselor (*chūnagon*) in 718. In 727 or 728 he was appointed viceroy of the government headquarters at Dazaifu in northwestern Kyūshū. In 730 he was promoted to great counselor (*dainagon*) and returned to Nara, but he died the following year.

Tabito is better known as a poet and literary man than as an official. It is believed that his influence encouraged his half-sister

ŌTOMO NO SAKANOUE NO IRATSUME, his son ŌTOMO NO YAKAMOCHI, and other relatives to become their generation's most prominent poets. Tabito's Chinese studies and poetic activities were stimulated by the priest Manzei and Tabito's friend YAMANOUE NO OKURA. A record of the plum blossom feast held by Tabito in 730 and some poems composed by the participants are preserved in book 5 of the MAN'YŌSHŪ (ca 759). The *Man'yōshū* also contains nearly all of Tabito's surviving poems. His characteristic poetic mode is a rather uncomplicated, direct declaration of feeling. Most famous of all his works is a set of 13 poems celebrating wine and the pleasure of drunkenness.

Ōtomo no Yakamochi
大伴家持

(718?–785). The last major poet in and reputed compiler of the MAN'YŌSHŪ, the earliest extant anthology of Japanese verse. Yakamochi is the outstanding poet of the final period represented in the *Man'yōshū* (ca 733–759). His 479 poems compose some 10 percent of the entire collection, and its last four books consist of his poetic diary.

Yakamochi grew up in a very literary circle of the nobility. His father, ŌTOMO NO TABITO, was an important poet, as was Tabito's friend YAMANOUE NO OKURA. After his father's death, Yakamochi was left in the care of his aunt ŌTOMO NO SAKANOUE NO IRATSUME, another noted poet. As a fashionable young man at court, Yakamochi exchanged skillful, but slight, love poems with numerous women, including his cousin, Lady Sakanoue's daughter Ōiratsume, whom he eventually married. Under the protection of the period's most powerful minister, TACHIBANA NO MOROE, Yakamochi's future looked bright.

By age 30, Yakamochi was the governor of Etchū Province (now Toyama Prefecture). In that isolated outpost, he and a small group of other provincial officials diverted themselves with excursions to scenic places, parties, and writing poetry, including some unique CHŌKA (long poems). These poems from his years in Etchū comprise most of books 17 to 19 of the *Man'yōshū* and much of Yakamochi's extant work. Usually considered Yakamochi's supreme accomplishment are his poems in book 19 from his final years in Etchū and shortly thereafter. These works often involve delicate depictions of nature that subtly reflect the poet's emotion.

After his return to the capital in Nara, Yakamochi served in the Ministry of Military Affairs, where he collected poems from the drafted frontier guards. He was embroiled in political intrigue for the rest of his life, and either he wrote little during the next quarter century or his poetry does not survive. Yakamochi used traditional—at times even old-fashioned—styles, forms, and language. His vast-ranging work also had new qualities that became characteristic of Japanese poetry in later centuries—sophisticated wit, sensitivity to delicate nuances of feeling, and a narrowed focus on man as the center of a restricted world.

Ōtomo, Prince → Kōbun, Emperor

Ōtomo Sōrin
大友宗麟

(1530–87). *Daimyō* of the Sengoku period (1467–1568) and the Azuchi-Momoyama period (1568–1600). Also known as Ōtomo Yoshishige. He took the name Sōrin after becoming a Buddhist lay monk (*nyūdō*) in 1562. In 1578 he was baptized and took the Christian name Francisco. The ŌTOMO FAMILY

had been prominent in Kyūshū since the early 13th century; Sōrin's predecessors had served the Kamakura shogunate (1192–1333) as military governors (SHUGO), and Sōrin's father was *shugo* of Bungo Province (now part of Ōita Prefecture) and of Higo Province (now Kumamoto Prefecture). On inheriting his father's posts in 1550, Sōrin contended for power in northern Kyūshū with the ŌUCHI FAMILY, the Mōri family, and others, gaining numerous military and political victories. In 1559, the shōgun Ashikaga Yoshiteru (1536–65) invested him with the title of Kyūshū *tandai*, the shogunal deputy in that island.

Sōrin retired in 1576 in favor of his son Yoshimune but remained involved in religious affairs. His long flirtation with Christianity, which began in 1551 with his welcome of Francis XAVIER, was consummated in 1578 with his baptism and the massive destruction of Buddhist temples. As a result of warfare with the Shimazu family of southern Kyūshū, the Ōtomo had lost much power by 1587 and were saved only by TOYOTOMI HIDEYOSHI's invasion of Kyūshū, which Sōrin had solicited. Sōrin died on 28 June 1587. His son Ōtomo Yoshimune was confirmed by Hideyoshi as daimyō of Bungo; in 1593 he was disenfeoffed for unsatisfactory performance in Hideyoshi's first invasion of Korea (see INVASIONS OF KOREA IN 1592 AND 1597).

otona
乙名

(elders). Village headmen in self-ruled organizations of the Muromachi (1333–1568) and Azuchi-Momoyama (1568–1600) periods. *Otona* originally referred to leaders of Shintō ritual guilds (MIYAZA) in the Kyōto-Ōsaka area during the Kamakura period (1185–1333). With the decline of the private estate (SHŌEN) system in the 13th century and formation of autonomous village organizations known as sō, the title was applied to landowning farmers (MYŌSHU) who led village government and served as officials in the *miyaza*. Elected by the villagers, *otona* assumed responsibility for collection of taxes (NENGU), labor service, and water control. Later *otona* received exemption from such taxes as the MUNABETSUSEN and other privileges from local proprietary lords (RYŌSHU) and eventually evolved into the official village elders (MURA YAKUNIN) of the Edo period (1600–1868). See also HYAKUSHŌ; GŌSON SYSTEM.

Ōtori Keisuke
大鳥圭介

(1833–1911). Retainer of the Tokugawa shogunate and later a Meiji government official. Born in Harima Province (now part of Hyōgo Prefecture). After studying with the WESTERN LEARNING scholar OGATA KŌAN in Ōsaka, he studied military science with EGAWA TARŌZAEMON in Edo (now Tōkyō). At the time of the MEIJI RESTORATION (1868) he fought against the imperial forces in northeastern Japan and later joined ENOMOTO TAKEAKI's forces in the Battle of GORYŌKAKU. He was imprisoned after their surrender but was pardoned in 1872 and subsequently named principal of the Peers' School (now Gakushūin University). Ōtori was appointed minister to China in 1889 and concurrently envoy to Korea in 1893, playing an important diplomatic role before the SINO-JAPANESE WAR OF 1894–1895.

otoshidama
御年玉

(New Year's gift; literally, "gem of the year"). In the past, *otoshidama* were ex-

otoshidama Colorful envelopes such as this one are used when giving New Year's gifts, usually in the form of cash, to children.

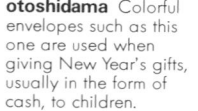

changed between families in the form of food and sundries. Also, offerings that had been made to deities were distributed at New Year's by Shintō shrines or Buddhist temples as *otoshidama* to their parishioners. At present, however, *otoshidama* have largely lost their religious meaning. They are almost always given to children in the form of cash by parents, grandparents, and other close relatives or by neighbors. *Otoshidama* differ from other traditional types of Japanese gifts in that, rather than being given to a family as a unit, they are given to a specific individual, either in one's own family or another's, and usually from a superior to an inferior.

Ōtoshi no kyaku　　　大歳の客

(The New Year's Eve Visitor). Group of folktales on the theme that a visitor welcomed on New Year's Eve will bring great fortune. In some versions a poor old couple gives shelter to a traveler; the following morning they discover that his body has turned into gold. In other versions, a maidservant in search of coals to relight the hearth fire is asked to take charge of a stranger's coffin, which is later found to be filled with gold. These tales are based on the belief that divine beings (TOSHIGAMI) visit households at the NEW YEAR. See also KASA JIZŌ.

Ototake Iwazō　　　乙竹岩造

(1876–1953). Educator. Born in Mie Prefecture. Graduate of Tōkyō Higher Normal School. He was one of the editors of the pre–World War II state-compiled "ethics" textbook (see SHŪSHIN). From 1904 to 1907 he studied ethics and education in Europe and the United States, and then introduced new educational theories to Japan. He became a professor at Tōkyō Higher Normal School and Tōkyō Bunrika Daigaku (later combined as TSUKUBA UNIVERSITY). He wrote *Nihon shomin kyōikushi* (3 vols; 1929), a history of popular education in Japan.

Otowa Nobuko　　　乙羽信子

(1924–). Film actress. Real name Shindō (née Kaji) Nobuko. Born in Tottori Prefecture. After first working with director SHINDŌ KANETO in the leading role as the wife in his *Aisai monogatari* (1951, Story of a Beloved Wife), she became a regularly featured actress in Shindō's films. She is particularly known for her understated portrayals of the gloom and sadness or the strength of women. She gave a highly acclaimed performance in Shindō's HADAKA NO SHIMA (1960, Naked Island or The Island), which was awarded the Grand Prix at the 1961 Moscow Film Festival. She and Shindō were married in 1978. In 1979 Otowa received the award for best actress at the Venice Film Festival for her role in Shindō's *Kōsatsu* (1979, Strangulation).

Ōtsu　　　大津［市］

Capital of Shiga Prefecture, central Honshū, on the southwestern shore of Lake Biwa. The site of an imperial residence (ŌTSU NO MIYA) in the 7th century, it later developed as a lake port, a post-station town on the highway TŌKAIDŌ, and as the seat of the temple MIIDERA. After World War II, Ōtsu became the center of the industrial zone south of Lake Biwa; large electrical-industry plants and textile mills are located here. Of interest are the remains of Ōtsu no Miya; Zeze Castle; the temples ISHIYAMADERA, Miidera,

and ENRYAKUJI; and the HIE SHRINE. Pop: 260,018.

ōtsu-e　　　大津絵

(Ōtsu pictures). Also known as *oiwake-e* (Oiwake pictures). Folk pictures sold at roadside stands in Oiwake near ŌTSU from the Kan'ei era (1624–44). They were popular mementos for pilgrims to the nearby temple MIIDERA as well as for other travelers along the TŌKAIDŌ, the main highway between Kyōto and Edo (now Tōkyō) during the Edo period (1600–1868). *Ōtsu-e* were roughly drawn in ink and plain colors and often displayed a naive humor. Religious themes reflecting the faith of the common people were typical; popular folktales were also represented. Later *ōtsu-e* were influenced by UKIYO-E woodblock prints. During the Meiji period (1868–1912) their quality and variety declined and production dwindled. See also FOLK CRAFTS.

Ōtsu Incident　　　大津事件

(Ōtsu Jiken). Assassination attempt on Russian Crown Prince Nicholas Alexandrovitch (1868–1918; later Tsar Nicholas II) on 11 May 1891 in the city of Ōtsu, Shiga Prefecture. The prince, who was visiting Japan on a pleasure trip, was slightly wounded by an escort policeman, Tsuda Sanzō (1854–91). Anxious lest the incident worsen relations with Russia, Prime Minister MATSUKATA MASAYOSHI advised Emperor Meiji to go immediately to Kyōto to visit the recuperating prince. The government put pressure on the GREAT COURT OF CASSATION to apply article 116 of the Criminal Code, which prescribed the death penalty for acts against the emperor, the empress, and the crown prince. Chief Justice KOJIMA IKEN, however, ruled that it did not apply in this case and on 27 May sentenced Tsuda to life imprisonment for attempted homicide. Accepting responsibility for the incident, Home Minister SAIGŌ TSUGUMICHI and Foreign Minister AOKI SHŪZŌ resigned, and the Russian government expressed full satisfaction. At the time, Kojima's decision was cited as an example of the independence of the judiciary in Japan and used as an argument for abolishing the extraterritorial privileges of the Western nations (see UNEQUAL TREATIES, REVISION OF).

Otsuji Katsuhiko　　　尾辻克彦

(1937–). Novelist and illustrator. Real name Akasegawa Katsuhiko. Born in Kanagawa Prefecture. Attended Musashino Art University. Otsuji received the Akutagawa Prize for *Chichi ga kieta* (1981, My Father Disappeared). He specializes in short stories that depict the minute changes in the psychology of everyday life. His works include *Tōkyō rojō tanken ki* (1986, An Exploration of the Streets of Tōkyō).

Ōtsuka Hisao　　　大塚久雄

(1907–). Scholar of Western economic history. Born in Kyōto Prefecture, he graduated from the economics department of Tōkyō University in 1930. He taught at Hōsei, Tōkyō, and International Christian universities. In *Kindai Ōshū keizaishi josetsu* (1944, Introduction to Modern European Economic History), Ōtsuka argued that middle-class producers are the nucleus of modern society, an idea central to his theory of history. Other books and articles by Ōtsuka include *Kabushiki kaisha hasseishi ron* (1938, Studies on the Origin of Joint Stock Companies) and *Kindai shihon shugi no keifu* (1946, Development of Modern Capitalism).

Ōtsuka Pharmaceutical Co, Ltd

大塚製薬［株］

(Ōtsuka Seiyaku). Producer of Pharmaceuticals and nutrition products. Incorporated in 1964. The company operates overseas research and manufacturing bases predominantly in the Pacific Rim countries, including the United States, Korea, China, and Taiwan, and also in Egypt, Spain, and Pakistan. Sales for the fiscal year ending March 1990 totaled ¥290.3 billion (US $1.9 billion), and capitalization stood at ¥6.0 billion (US $39.2 million). Headquarters are in Tōkyō.

Ōtsuki　　　大月［市］

City in eastern Yamanashi Prefecture, central Honshū, on the river Katsuragawa. Formerly known for its fine silk, it now has a thriving synthetic-fiber industry. It is a gateway to Mt. Fuji (FUJISAN) and the FUJI FIVE LAKES. The strangely shaped bridge called Saruhashi is a tourist attraction. Pop: 34,941.

Ōtsuki Bumpei　　　大槻文平

(1903–92). Businessman; president of Mitsubishi Mining & Cement Co (now MITSUBISHI MATERIALS CORPORATION; 1976–86); president of NIKKEIREN (Japan Federation of Employers' Associations; 1979–87). Born in Miyagi Prefecture. After graduating from Tōkyō University in 1928, Ōtsuki entered Mitsubishi Mining Co, becoming its president in 1963. In 1973 the firm merged with Mitsubishi Cement Co and Hōkoku Cement Co to form Mitsubishi Mining & Cement Co. Ōtsuki also served from 1987 to 1990 as chairman of the Provisional Council for Promotion of Administrative Reform, a government advisory board.

Ōtsuki Fumihiko　　　大槻文彦

(1847–1928). Linguist, philologist, and lexicographer. Pioneer scholar in the grammatical study of the contemporary Japanese language. He is especially well known for his compilation of *Genkai* (1889–91, Sea of Words), the first comprehensive dictionary of contemporary Japanese arranged in the order of the KANA syllabary.

Ōtsuki studied Western linguistics at Tōkyō University. In 1872 he entered the Ministry of Education, where his assignments included the compilation of *Eiwa taiyaku jiten* (1872, English-Japanese Translation Dictionary) and of *Genkai*. The special attention to the systematization of semantic and grammatical categories, the interpretations and explanations of word meanings, and the usage examples in Ōtsuki's *Genkai* were all new features in Japanese dictionary making. His *Kō Nihon bunten* (1897, Comprehensive Grammar of Japanese) and *Kōgohō* (1916, Grammar of Spoken Japanese) were also highly influential in shaping the way contemporary standard Japanese was taught and spoken. See also DICTIONARIES.

Ōtsuki Gentaku　　　大槻玄沢

(1757–1827). Scholar of Rangaku (Dutch Learning; see WESTERN LEARNING). The son of a physician in the Ichinoseki domain (now part of Iwate Prefecture). Ōtsuki went to Edo (now Tōkyō) in 1778 to study Western medicine under SUGITA GEMPAKU. He also studied Dutch under MAENO RYŌTAKU and made a trip to Nagasaki in 1785 to study with Motoki Yoshinaga (1735–94), a shogunal interpreter at the Dutch trading post on DEJIMA. In 1786

Ōuchi Hyōe The Marxist economist in a photograph taken during his tenure as president of Hōsei University from 1950 to 1959.

he was appointed physician to the Sendai domainal residence in Edo and opened a school, the Shirandō; among his students were INAMURA SAMPAKU, Udagawa Genzui (1755–97), and Udagawa Genshin (1769–1834). His textbook, *Rangaku kaitei* (1788, A Ladder to Dutch Learning), was widely read. The Western New Year's celebrations (ORANDA SHŌGATSU) held at his school were attended by leading Rangaku scholars. In 1811 Ōtsuki was appointed *bansho wage goyō-gakari* (literally, "translator of foreign works") for an annotated translation of a Dutch version of a French encyclopedic work (see KŌSEI SHIMPEN).

Ōtsuki Joden 大槻如電

(1845–1931). Literary scholar. Also known as Nyoden. Born in the Sendai domain (now Miyagi Prefecture). He was the son of Ōtsuki Bankei (1801–78), a Confucian scholar, and grandson of ŌTSUKI GENTAKU, a scholar of Western Learning. He worked for the Ministry of Education, helping compile the dictionary *Shinsen jisho* (1872). He also wrote several works on traditional Japanese music, including *Zokkyoku no yurai* and *Bugaku zusetsu* (1927), and compiled a historical chronology of Western Learning in Japan, *Shinsen yōgaku nempyō* (1927).

Ōtsuma Women's University 大妻女子大学

(Ōtsuma Joshi Daigaku). A private university for women in Chiyoda Ward, Tōkyō. Founded as the Ōtsuma Women's College in 1942, it became a university in 1949. The institution developed around its faculty of domestic science, which seeks to train students to be "good wives and wise mothers." The university also maintains a faculty of literature, which was established in 1967. Enrollment in 1989 was 2,498.

Ōtsu no Miko 大津皇子

(663–686). Poet of Japanese and Chinese verse and third son of Emperor TEMMU. Four of his poems were anthologized in the MAN'YŌSHŪ (759) and four in the KAIFŪSŌ (751). After his father's death Ōtsu no Miko was arrested for treason and executed. The classical Japanese and Chinese poems he wrote on the eve of his death are emotionally charged masterpieces. Biographies of him appear in both the *Kaifūsō* and the *Nihon shoki* (720, Chronicle of Japan).

Ōtsu no Miya 大津宮

Imperial palace 667–672; located at Ōtsu in Ōmi Province (now Shiga Prefecture). In 667 Prince Naka no Ōe moved the capital from Asuka to Ōmi and the following year was enthroned as Emperor TENJI. He died in 672, and his successor, Emperor TEMMU, moved the capital to ASUKA KIYOMIHARA NO MIYA. Tenji's move to Ōmi and his subsequent enforcement of a census registration (KŌGONENJAKU) and codification of COURT RANKS are regarded by historians as significant steps toward the establishment of the RITSURYŌ SYSTEM of government. Recent excavations have found the site of the palace near Nishikōri Chō in the city of Ōtsu.

Ottama, U ウー・オッタマ

(1879–1939). Politically influential Burmese monk. In the early 20th century he traveled widely in various Asian countries, including Japan. Inspired by the Indian National Congress, he returned to Burma and began to de-

nounce the British domination of his country. He was arrested in 1922 and imprisoned from 1924 to 1927 and again from 1928 until his death. He published the book *Japan* in 1914. See also BURMA AND JAPAN.

otter → kawauso

Ott, Eugen オット、E.

(1889–1976). German general and diplomat. Sent to Japan by the German army in 1933, Ott was named military attaché at the German embassy the following year. He was appointed ambassador to Japan in 1938 but was dismissed in 1942 in the aftermath of the SORGE INCIDENT.

Ōuchi family 大内氏

(Ōuchishi). Territorial warlord (SENGOKU DAIMYŌ) family who controlled the western part of the Chūgoku region from the 14th through 16th centuries. Said to be descendants of an immigrant who came from the Korean state of PAEKCHE in the 7th century, the family adopted the village name of Ōuchi and eventually appropriated the office of acting assistant governor (*gon no suke*) of Suō. Ōuchi Hiroyo (d 1380) entered the service of the ASHIKAGA FAMILY and established his headquarters at Yamaguchi. His son Yoshihiro (1356–1400) was appointed military governor (SHUGO) of six provinces. In 1399–1400 Yoshihiro revolted against the MUROMACHI SHOGUNATE in the ŌEI REBELLION. Despite his death, the Ōuchi recovered and amassed wealth through trade with China (see TALLY TRADE). They were patrons of the painter SESSHŪ TŌYŌ and the poet SŌGI. In the early 16th century ŌUCHI YOSHITAKA ruled as *shugo* of seven provinces; he supported Francis XAVIER and welcomed Western culture. In 1551 Yoshitaka was overthrown by his vassal Sue Harukata (1521–55), and the Ōuchi line was soon extinguished. The ŌUCHIKE KABEGAKI is one of the earliest domainal codes.

Ōuchi Hyōe 大内兵衛

(1888–1980). Marxist economist. Born in Hyōgo Prefecture. After working for the Ministry of Finance, he joined the Tōkyō University faculty in 1919. He was involved in the 1920 MORITO INCIDENT and from 1921 to 1923 studied in Germany, deepening his knowledge of Marxist economics. In 1938 he left Tōkyō University because of a government crackdown on leftists but returned after World War II and retired in 1949. From 1950 to 1959 he served as president of Hōsei University. He also served as chairman of the Statistics Council of Japan (Naikaku Tōkei Iinkai) and of the ADVISORY COUNCIL ON SOCIAL SECURITY (Shakai Hoshō Seido Shingikai). He collaborated with SAKISAKA ITSURŌ and YAMAKAWA HITOSHI in establishing the Socialist Association (Shakai Shugi Kyōkai) and was an ideological leader for the leftist faction of the JAPAN SOCIALIST PARTY. His main works include *Zaiseigaku taikō* (1930–31, Principles of Public Finance) and *Nihon infurēshon no kenkyū* (1946, A Study of Japanese Inflation).

Ōuchi Keigo 大内啓伍

(1930–). Politician. Born in Tōkyō, Ōuchi graduated from Waseda University. In 1953 he joined the staff of the Japan Socialist Party; in 1960 he became a founding member of the DEMOCRATIC SOCIALIST PARTY, eventually serving as chairman of its Central Executive

Committee. In 1976 he was elected to the House of Representatives. He became the party's secretary-general in 1985 and its seventh chairman in April 1990.

Ōuchike Kabegaki 大内家壁書

A domainal law code (BUNKOKUHŌ) of the Sengoku period (1467–1568); enacted by heads of the ŌUCHI FAMILY, *daimyō* of Suō (now part of Yamaguchi Prefecture) between 1459 and 1495. Compiled over three generations, it included 50 articles by the 16th century. Most clauses are injunctions to vassals and subjects and provisions concerning domainal government, taxation, and commercial regulations.

Ōuchi Yoshitaka 大内義隆

(1507–51). SENGOKU DAIMYŌ; son of Ōuchi Yoshioki (1477–1529; see ŌUCHI FAMILY), the military governor (SHUGO) of six provinces in southwestern Honshū and northern Kyūshū. Succeeding his father in this vast domain, Yoshitaka sought to expand and defend it against the ŌTOMO FAMILY and the AMAKO FAMILY. His success in doing so was due in part to his control of Japan's trade with China (see TALLY TRADE) and Korea. Under Yoshitaka's rule, Yamaguchi became a flourishing commercial and cultural center. His benevolent interest in the Jesuit Francis XAVIER, the first Christian missionary in Japan, inspired Jesuits to spread the fame of Yoshitaka, "King of Yamaguchi," as far as Europe. In 1551 Yoshitaka's vassal Sue Harukata (1521–55) rebelled and forced him to commit suicide.

Ōuetsu Reppan Dōmei 奥羽越列藩同盟

Alliance of proshogunate domains in northeastern Japan during the BOSHIN CIVIL WAR (1868–69). The term Ōuetsu refers to the provinces Dewa, Mutsu, and Echigo, where the 31 allied domains were located. In the spring of 1868 the new imperial government sent an order to the *daimyō* of Sendai to dispatch troops against the Aizu (now part of Fukushima Prefecture) and Shōnai (now part of Yamagata Prefecture) domains, which refused to surrender to the new government. The daimyō of Sendai, sympathetic to Aizu and Shōnai, led 14 northeastern domains in requesting lenient treatment for them. The request was rejected, and on 10 June Sendai *samurai* assassinated a government representative. An antigovernment alliance then formed, its ranks swelling to 31 domains. In the summer of 1868 the imperial army drove northward against them; Aizu, the last to fall, surrendered on 6 November. Many of these domains were reduced in size and their leaders punished. See also BYAKKOTAI.

Ōu Mountains 奥羽山脈

(Ōu Sammyaku). Mountain range running north to south through the center of the Tōhoku region to the northern corner of the Kantō region, northern Honshū. About 500 km (300 mi) long, it is the longest mountain range in Japan. Overlapping the NASU VOLCANIC ZONE, it contains several volcanoes in the 2,000 m (6,500 ft) range, including IWATESAN and AZUMASAN. The range separates the Pacific side of northern Honshū from the Sea of Japan side. The latter receives heavy snowfalls. Mineral resources include copper, lead, and zinc. The three national parks of Towada-Hachimantai, Bandai-Asahi, and Nikkō are located here.

Ōura Kanetake　大浦兼武

(1850–1918). Government official and conservative politician. Born in the Satsuma domain (now Kagoshima Prefecture). In 1893 he was appointed governor of Shimane Prefecture and later served as governor of several other prefectures. In 1898 he was named superintendent-general of police (*keishi sōkan*). Ōura subsequently served in several cabinet posts, including that of home minister, resigning in 1915 amid a bribery scandal.

Ōu region → Tōhoku region

overseas direct investment
海外直接投資

(*kaigai chokusetsu tōshi*). Post–World War II investment by Japanese firms to acquire existing firms or to establish new concerns in foreign countries began in 1951. The level of investments abroad remained low for the next two decades but began to intensify in the 1970s. Most of these investments were undertaken by Japanese manufacturing firms motivated by the appreciation of the yen and a desire to stabilize the supply of resources from the developing countries.

Japanese foreign direct investment surged again in the 1980s. The primary factors in this expansion were the amendment of the Foreign Exchange and Foreign Trade Control Law, the internationalization of Japanese financial institutions, a large increase in the value of the yen, and the rising threat of protectionism in foreign countries. Japan's foreign investments in fiscal year 1988 totaled US $47.0 billion, representing an increase over 1985 of 380 percent. Japan's cumulative foreign investments stood at US $110.8 billion at the end of 1988. (The cumulative figure for the United States was US $326.9 billion.) Regionally, more than 40 percent of Japan's investments are concentrated in North America, followed by the rest of Asia, Europe, and Latin America, each of which accounts for 16–17 percent of total Japanese investments.

Foreign direct investment generally results in useful technology transfers and employment increases, but it has also been a source of friction in host countries. Those enterprises that have successfully extended their business overseas have found it necessary to increase the local character of their operations to ensure that they are accepted in communities abroad.

Overseas Economic Cooperation Fund
海外経済協力基金

(OECF; J: Kaigai Keizai Kyōryoku Kikin). Special public corporation that provides financial assistance to developing countries. The OECF is the principal agency administering Japanese official development assistance (ODA), managing about 40 percent of the net disbursements of ODA funds. It was established in 1961 under the provisions of the Overseas Economic Cooperation Fund Law.

The OECF's main functions fall into two categories. First, it provides loans to governments and government agencies in developing countries. Loans outstanding as of August 1989 totaled ¥4.9 trillion (US $34.7 billion). Approximately 80 percent of all loans in this category have gone to countries in Asia, mostly for the development of infrastructure facilities (transportation, electric power, gas, etc) and for the purchase of commodities. Second, the OECF extends loans to, or makes equity investments in, Japanese

corporations involved in overseas development projects. Loans and investments in this category totaled ¥173.0 billion (US $1.2 billion) as of August 1989.

The ECONOMIC PLANNING AGENCY directs the activities of the OECF, acting in conjunction with the Ministry of Foreign Affairs, the Ministry of Finance, and the Ministry of International Trade and Industry (MITI). The OECF has its head office in Tōkyō and maintained 16 overseas offices as of 1992.

overseas financing　海外資本調達

(*kaigai shihon chōtatsu*). With globalization and the creation of more multinational companies, overseas fund-raising by Japanese firms has increased sharply. In 1975 Japanese companies listed on the Tōkyō Stock Exchange raised only some 16 percent of their funds in overseas markets, but, with the beginning of the DEREGULATION of Japanese financial markets in the early 1980s, the figure had risen to 48 percent by 1984 (see also CAPITAL MARKETS). An unprecedented stock-market boom followed in 1986–87, along with a rapid rise in the amount of funds raised through equity issues and Eurobonds. Japanese companies had raised over ¥11 trillion (US $83.1 billion) in overseas financial markets in 1989, but, with the sharp downturn in the Tōkyō Stock Market the following year, the figure fell to just over ¥5 trillion (US $37.3 billion). The reasons for the growth of overseas financing in the 1980s include the following: First, it became necessary to raise foreign currency funds as a risk hedge for assets denominated in foreign currency. Second, the Japanese corporate bond market is restricted, and foreign markets, Europe in particular, are superior with respect to cost and mobility. Third, yen assets (Euro-yen) are now becoming more common overseas, and Japanese companies can therefore raise funds without foreign exchange risks and without being subject to foreign domestic regulations. Despite the 1990 decline in the stock market, the long-term trend toward overseas financing is likely to continue and is underpinned by the development of new financial instruments such as swaps (where one security is exchanged for another) and by the growth of the cash markets and futures markets.

Ōwakudani　大涌谷

Also called Ōwakidani. Valley in southwestern Kanagawa Prefecture, central Honshū. Located in the HAKONEYAMA volcano group. A mixture of steam and sulfurous gas gushes from numerous fumaroles to hot springs such as Gōra and Sengokuhara.

Ōwani　大鰐[町]

Town in southwestern Aomori Prefecture, northern Honshū. Principal products are rice, apples, and lumber. The Ōwani Hot Spring, discovered in the 12th century, is part of a prefectural park. Pop: 14,751.

Owari Asahi　尾張旭[市]

City in northwestern Aichi Prefecture, central Honshū, some 13 km (8 mi) northeast of Nagoya. It produces SETO WARE and has a growing machine and metal industry. Shinrin Prefectural Park is located in the hills of its northern section. Pop: 65,675.

Owari domain　尾張藩

(Owari *han*). Edo-period (1600–1868) domain that extended over OWARI PROVINCE and parts of MINO PROVINCE and Shinano Province; parts of present-day Aichi, Gifu, and

Nagano prefectures. Also known as the Nagoya domain, its administrative center was NAGOYA CASTLE. It was granted in 1616 to Tokugawa Yoshinao (1600–1650), who, as a son of TOKUGAWA IEYASU, received the status of SHIMPAN (collateral vassal). Yoshinao's line became the leader among the three cadet houses of the Tokugawa family (GO-SANKE). The sixth lord, Tokugawa Muneharu (1696–1764), adopted fiscal policies that made Nagoya a flourishing commercial center. OMOTEDAKA (estimated annual production of rice): 619,500 KOKU (1 *koku* = 180 liters or 5 US bushels).

Owari Province　尾張国

(Owari no Kuni; also called Bishū). One of the 15 provinces (*kuni*) of the Tōkaidō (Eastern Sea Circuit); established under the KOKUGUN SYSTEM in 646, comprising what is now the western half of Aichi Prefecture. It developed in early times as the site of the ATSUTA SHRINE. From the 12th century onward the province came under the domination of such military-governor (SHUGO) families as the HATAKEYAMA FAMILY, the IMAGAWA FAMILY, the SHIBA FAMILY, and the ODA FAMILY. ODA NOBUNAGA came to dominate the region and most of the country; his successor as military hegemon, TOYOTOMI HIDEYOSHI, also came from Owari. One of the sons of TOKUGAWA IEYASU, founder of the Tokugawa shogunate (1603–1867), established his headquarters in Owari at NAGOYA CASTLE. Nagoya and its hinterland flourished as a major commercial and agricultural center, known for its rice, cotton, *sake*, and ceramics (see SETO WARE). With the establishment of the prefectural system in 1871, Owari was combined with Mikawa Province to form AICHI PREFECTURE.

Owase　尾鷲[市]

City in southern Mie Prefecture, central Honshū, on the Kumano Sea. The area has the highest annual rainfall (4,000 mm; 160 in) in Japan. In addition to the processing of marine products, there is an active lumber industry, which draws on nearby forests. A thermoelectric generating plant is located here. Pop: 27,114.

owls　梟

(*fukurō*). In Japanese, *fukurō* is the general name for birds of the family Strigidae. Species inhabiting Japan include the *fukurō* (Ural owl; *Strix uralensis*), the *shimafukurō* (Blakiston's fish owl; *Ketupa blakistoni*), the *aobazuku* (brown hawk owl; *Ninox scutulata*), the *konohazuku* (Japanese scops owl; *Otus scops*), and the *ō konohazuku* (collared scops owl; *Otus bakkamoena*). These and other species are found throughout the mountainous and forested regions of Japan from northern Hokkaidō to Kyūshū; however, recent deforestation has brought a decrease in the numbers of some species. In 1971 the Ezo *shimafukurō* (a subspecies of the *shimafukurō*), found in eastern Hokkaidō, was designated a natural monument (see NATURAL MONUMENTS AND PROTECTED SPECIES).

In ancient China the hooting of an owl at night was feared as the omen of a blood relative's death and it was thought that the owl was a depraved animal that ate its mother. Japanese attitudes toward the owl were strongly influenced by Chinese beliefs and in the Edo period (1600–1868) owls living near homes were feared as inauspicious animals.

owls The nocturnal *fukurō* (Ural owl), which is often found nesting in large trees in areas populated by humans, attains a length of 50 cm and preys on mice, insects, and small birds.

Ōyama Ikuo Opposed to Japan's militarist expansion, this scholar and political activist worked steadily for more than three decades to promote democratic ideas.

ownership rights　　所有権

(*shoyūken*). The rights of a person freely to produce profits from and to dispose of property; specified in the Japanese CIVIL CODE, article 206. The constitution guarantees the PROPERTY RIGHTS of the people (art. 29), the basis of which is ownership. The Civil Code recognizes real rights such as hypothecs and superficies that limit the rights of ownership, but within these limits ownership confers complete control over the property.

The constitution also provides that, upon just compensation to the owner, property can be used for the public welfare. Recently, ownership rights have been restricted by such laws as the Land Expropriation Law (Tochi Shūyōhō), the URBAN PLANNING LAW, and the ARCHITECTURAL STANDARDS LAW. There are also many restrictions on the exercise of ownership rights under the principle of prohibiting the ABUSE OF RIGHT. Owners of land and buildings will often arrange to have other parties use a property through lease contracts. See LEASED LAND RIGHTS; LEASED HOUSE RIGHTS.

ōya　　大家

Also called *yanushi* or *yamori*. Realtors for large landholders (*iemochi*) in Edo (now Tōkyō) during the Edo period (1600–1868). Accorded a legal status one rank higher than that of Edo commoners, they made a living renting out houses, apartments, and land in Edo. Their close relations with tenants (*tanako*) created a lore of humorous situations that formed a major genre of RAKUGO comic expositions. Today the owners of houses and apartments for rent are known as *ōya*.

Oyabe　　小矢部［市］

City in western Toyama Prefecture, central Honshū, on the river Oyabegawa. During the Edo period (1600–1868) central Oyabe developed as a post-station town, and south Oyabe developed as a river-port town. Clothing, paper, rubber, and ceramic industries are active. The Battle of KURIKARA PASS (1183), in which MINAMOTO NO YOSHINAKA defeated Taira forces, took place in nearby Kurikara Pass. Pop: 36,374.

oyabun-kobun　　親分・子分

(literally, "parent role-child role"). Also called *oyakata-kokata*. A relationship between a fictive parent (*oyabun* or *oyakata*) and child (*kobun* or *kokata*) established for mutual economic benefit or social support. *Oyabun-kobun* ties have traditionally been the backbone of small-scale cooperative organizations and are still common in the less modernized sectors of Japanese society. The bond may be between individuals or extend to groups, such as households. The *oyabun-kobun* relationship dates far back in Japanese history, reaching into many areas of society. It reflects the powerful influence of the family system (see IE) as a model and metaphor for close relationships that develop between persons outside the fixed patterns of kinship.

The basis of the relationship is the greater economic, political, or social power of the *oyabun*. He assumes responsibility for the welfare, behavior, and guidance of the *kobun*. The *kobun* accepts the authority of the *oyabun* and is thus obligated to obedience, LOYALTY, and certain services as repayment for the benefits he receives. The inci-

Ōya Sōichi This acerbic social commentator was known for his critical views of contemporary social trends and the mass media.

dence of *oyabun-kobun* relations has declined radically during the last century, but the terms *oyabun* and *kobun* themselves are still heard quite frequently today in reference to relationships that resemble the traditional pattern. A classic example of *oyabun-kobun* patterns can be seen in gangster groups. Powerful individuals in any sphere may be jokingly referred to as *oyabun*. The *oyabun-kobun* relationship has been a popular theme in Japanese dramas and movies. The conflict between personal feelings, such as affection for a parent or lover, and loyalty to an *oyabun* and his group often provides the tragedy for these stories. See also VERTICAL SOCIETY; GIRI AND NINJŌ; PATERNALISM.

oyakata and hikan　　御館と被官

(*oyakata to hikan*). Well-to-do landowners (*oyakata*) and their tenant-laborers (*hikan*) bound together in a master-servant relationship; a characteristic feature of village society, particularly in Shinano Province (now Nagano Prefecture) during the Edo period (1600–1868). *Hikan* were also known as NAGO OR FUDAI. The *oyakata* granted protection and hereditary rights to work a plot of his land, use his tools and seed rice, rent a dwelling, gather fodder, and so forth. In return the *hikan* was obliged to provide labor and other services at specified times; he was also required to receive permission for marriage and other important decisions. In some cases the *hikan* was treated as chattel that could be pawned or otherwise transferred to another at his master's will. Through the generosity of the *oyakata* or in return for money, he could become an independent farmer.

oyako domburi　　親子丼

One-dish meal consisting of a bowl of rice topped with a mixture of chicken and egg. To make it, pieces of chicken and onions or scallion are simmered in a broth seasoned with soy sauce and sugar. Beaten eggs are added and the mixture is cooked until the egg is almost set, then placed atop the cooked rice in the bowl.

Oyama　　小山［市］

City in southern Tochigi Prefecture, central Honshū. A castle town in the 16th century, it was subsequently set up as a post-station town on the highway Ōshū Kaidō. Foodstuffs, textile, machinery, electrical-appliance, and metal industries flourish. Yūki *tsumugi* (a silk fabric) is produced in the farming areas to the east. Pop: 142,262.

Ōyama　　大山

Also known as Afurisan. Mountain in the Tanzawa Mountains, west-central Kanagawa Prefecture, central Honshū. Afuri Shrine, on the summit, has attracted a large number of worshipers since the Edo period (1600–1868). Height: 1,246 m (4,088 ft).

Ōyama Ikuo　　大山郁夫

(1880–1955). Scholar, politician, and writer during the Taishō (1912–26) and Shōwa (1926–89) periods. Born in Hyōgo Prefecture. He graduated from Waseda University in 1905 and pursued graduate studies in sociology and political science at the University of Chicago and the University of Munich from 1910 through 1914. Upon his return to Japan he was appointed professor at Waseda.

In 1917 he left Waseda to write editorials for the *Ōsaka asahi shimbun*. He regarded it as his mission to educate the masses concerning the importance of establishing dem-

ocratic institutions in Japan. In 1918 he joined YOSHINO SAKUZŌ and others in forming an organization called REIMEIKAI to promote democratic ideas. Ōyama also began publishing a magazine called *Warera*.

In 1920 Ōyama returned to Waseda University, where the students made him their symbol of opposition to government policies. In 1926 he became chairman of the Labor-Farmer Party (RŌDŌ NŌMINTŌ; often abbreviated as Rōnōtō), which the authorities disbanded in 1928. Ōyama reestablished the party in 1929 and won a seat in the House of Representatives in 1930. His opposition to Japan's militarist expansion incurred the enmity of right-wing organizations. Fearing possible attempts on his life, he left Japan to live in the United States from 1932 to 1947. After the war he returned to Waseda University, became active in the peace movement, was elected to the Diet, and in 1951 received the International Stalin Peace Prize.

Ōyama Iwao　　大山巌

(1842–1916). General and field marshal. One of the GENRŌ (elder statesman) of the Meiji period (1868–1912). Born in the Satsuma domain (now Kagoshima Prefecture). He studied gunnery at the school founded by EGAWA TARŌZAEMON and invented a gun known as the *yasukehō*. He participated in the BOSHIN CIVIL WAR. After serving as army minister (*rikugunkyō*) in the DAJŌKAN in 1880, Ōyama was named army minister in the first modern cabinet of 1885. He commanded the Second Army in the SINO-JAPANESE WAR OF 1894–1895 and became chief of the Army General Staff Office in 1899. In the RUSSO-JAPANESE WAR of 1904–05, he was in command of the armies in Manchuria.

Ōyamazaki　　大山崎［町］

Town in southwestern Kyōto Prefecture, central Honshū. Ōyamazaki is situated in a narrow alluvial flatland; three rivers meet here and it has long been an important center for transportation by water and, more recently, by railway and highway. Much of the land has been developed for residential and industrial use. The Battle of YAMAZAKI took place here in 1582. Pop: 16,152.

Ōya Shinzō　　大屋晋三

(1894–1980). Businessman and politician; president of TEIJIN, LTD (1945–48; 1956–80). Born in Gumma Prefecture. After graduating from Hitotsubashi University in 1918, Ōya entered the trading firm Suzuki Shōten. He later was transferred to the textile company Teikoku Jinzō Kenshi Co (now Teijin, Ltd) and became its president. He ran successfully on the Japan Liberal Party ticket in the first elections for the House of Councillors in 1947 and served in several cabinet posts. He returned to Teijin, Ltd, in 1956, quickly restoring the faltering company to its former leading position.

Oyashio　　親潮

Also known as the Okhotsk Current or Kuril Current (Chishima Kairyū). Major cold ocean current that flows southwestward along the eastern side of the Kuril Islands and southward along the east coast of Hokkaidō and northeastern Honshū. The current meets the warm waters of the KUROSHIO or Japan Current off the SANRIKU COAST of northeastern Honshū, where it forms a huge front known as the "Oyashio front," providing excellent fishing grounds.

Oyashirazu 親不知

Cliffs in the town of Oumi, western Niigata Prefecture, central Honshū. Located at the end of the Hida Mountains, these steep cliffs fall directly into the Sea of Japan. The name Oyashirazu literally means "not knowing one's parents," because with the ferocity of the waves that buffet the road along the cliffs, even parents and children might be separated. Length: 10 km (6 mi).

Ōya Sōichi 大宅壮一

(1900–1970). Social commentator. Born in Ōsaka; studied at Tōkyō University. He was influenced by socialist thought in his youth but later became more conservative, making sharp commentaries on social trends and the mass media. He coined such phrases as *ichioku sōhakuchika* (the "moronization" of a hundred million—i.e., Japan), which was his appraisal of the age of television. The ŌYA SŌICHI LIBRARY, founded in 1971, is based on his personal collection of 200,000 magazines.

Ōya Sōichi Library 大宅壮一文庫

(Ōya Sōichi Bunko). Library consisting chiefly of a collection of magazines assembled by the social commentator ŌYA SŌICHI (1900–1970). Located in Setagaya Ward, Tōkyō. Founded as the Ōya Library in 1971, the name was changed in 1978. There are approximately 6,500 titles and 240,000 individual issues in the collection, which includes magazines from the Meiji period (1868–1912) to the present.

oyatoi gaikokujin → foreign

employees of the Meiji period

Ōya Tōru 大矢透

(1850–1928). Japanese-language scholar. Born in what is now Niigata Prefecture, Ōya graduated from Niigata Normal School (now Niigata University). He was a member of the Research Committee on the Japanese Language and was awarded an Imperial Prize in recognition of his contribution to the study of Japanese. He was a pioneer in the systematic study of *kunten*, marks used in reading classical Chinese texts as if they were Japanese (see KAMBUN). His numerous published works include *Kanazukai oyobi kana jitai enkaku shiryō* (1909)—materials on the historical development of *kana* orthography and *kana* forms—and "Kogen eeben hokō," a work on the distinction between *e* and *je* in ancient Japanese, which was completed in 1907 and published as *Kogen eeben shōho* in 1932.

Ōyodogawa 大淀川

River in southern Miyazaki Prefecture, Kyūshū, originating in the southern part of the Miyakonojō Basin and flowing east into the Hyūga Sea. It is the largest river in Miyazaki Prefecture. Length: 107 km (66 mi); area of drainage basin: 2,230 sq km (860 sq mi).

Ōyu stone circles 大湯環状列石

(Ōyu *kanjō resseki*). Stone constructions from the Late Jōmon period (ca 2500 BC–ca 1000 BC; also dated as ca 2000 BC–ca 1000 BC) in the Ōyu district of the city of Kazuno, Akita Prefecture. Discovered in 1931, they were systematically excavated in 1951–52. Two circles—one with a diameter of about 46 meters (151 ft) and the other of about 40 meters (131 ft)—lie about 90 meters (295 ft) apart. Each consists of two concentric rings of stones. Between the outer and inner rings

of each circle is a standing stone from which smaller stones radiate outward. The discovery of pitlike cavities underneath the stones has led some to think that the site was a burial ground. Similar stone circles are found throughout Japan.

Ozaki Hōsai 尾崎放哉

(1885–1926). HAIKU poet. Real name Ozaki Hideo. Born in Tottori prefecture. Graduated from Tōkyō University. While attending the First Higher School in Tōkyō, he was influenced by OGIWARA SEISENSUI, a pioneer of free-verse haiku and editor of the poetry magazine *Sōun*.

After working for over a decade in the insurance business, he became a lay mendicant at a Buddhist training center. Eight months before his death, he settled on the island of Shōdoshima in Kagawa Prefecture. He was given the tenancy of Nangōan, the inner sanctum of the temple Saikōji, and, amid great poverty, began seriously composing haiku. His only haiku anthology, *Taikū* (1926, Big Sky), published posthumously, contains poems that treat of the solitary life of his last years.

Ozaki Hotsuki 尾崎秀樹

(1928–). Literary critic. Born in Taipei, Taiwan. He completed his secondary education in Taiwan, where he studied the Chinese classics. A critic of popular literature, he has written such essays as *Taishū bungaku* (1964, Popular Literature) and *Taishū bungaku ron* (1965, Theory of Popular Literature). His *Ikite iru Yuda* (1959, The Living Judas) was about the SORGE INCIDENT, as a result of which his brother OZAKI HOTSUMI had been executed (1944) for espionage. In 1980 he published a biography of the novelist NAKAZATO KAIZAN.

Ozaki Hotsumi 尾崎秀実

(1901–44). Journalist and writer on Chinese affairs. Born in Tōkyō, he attended Tōkyō University. Sent to Shanghai as a correspondent for the newspaper *Asahi shimbun* in 1928, he associated with local left-wing elements, including the Comintern agent Richard Sorge. Ozaki returned to Japan in 1932. He continued writing and served as an adviser on Chinese affairs to the first KONOE FUMIMARO cabinet. He also renewed his connection with Sorge, who was involved in espionage activities at the German embassy in Tōkyō. In 1941 Ozaki was arrested along with Sorge; both were executed as Soviet agents in 1944 (see SORGE INCIDENT).

Ozaki Kazuo 尾崎一雄

(1899–1983). Novelist. Born in Mie Prefecture; graduate of Waseda University. Inspired and encouraged by the noted writer SHIGA NAOYA. "Nonki megane" (1933), a short story that won the 1937 Akutagawa Prize, established him as a writer. His writing, in the traditional autobiographical style (see I-NOVEL), is characterized by humor and philosophical insight. *Maboroshi no ki* (1961, Illusory Writings) was awarded the Noma Literary Prize. Another notable work is "Mushi no iroiro" (1948; tr "Various Kinds of Bugs," 1958). He received the Order of Culture in 1978.

Ozaki Kōyō 尾崎紅葉

(1868–1903). Novelist and poet. In the age of transition between Edo-period (1600–1868) feudalism and Meiji-period (1868–1912) modernism, Ozaki Kōyō was instrumental in turning the once disreputable pursuit of fic-

tion writing into a respectable and profitable career. Influenced in his early writings by the Edo-period (1600–1868) writers SHIKITEI SAMBA and JIPPENSHA IKKU, and in a later period by Ihara SAIKAKU, the work of his final years shows a turn to extensive psychological description. As leader of KEN'YŪSHA, Japan's first modern literary coterie, Ozaki was a major influence on early modern Japanese literature.

Born in the Shiba district of Edo (now Tōkyō) as Ozaki Tokutarō, he later adopted the pen name Kōyō (autumn leaves). He was a student in a preparatory school for Tōkyō University in 1885 when he formed Ken'yūsha with three student friends and began to circulate their works in its organ, *Garakuta bunko* (Library of Odds and Ends), Japan's first coterie journal of modern fiction. In 1889 Kōyō joined YOMIURI SHIMBUN and soon was given the management of the newspaper's prestigious literary section, which was to carry most of his masterpieces. Concurrently, he played an active role in the revitalization of HAIKU poetry.

Kōyō helped to launch many prominent writers, including IZUMI KYŌKA, OGURI FŪYŌ, Yanagawa Shun'yō (1877–1918), and TOKUDA SHŪSEI. Kōyō died of cancer in 1903, leaving behind a legacy of best sellers that were ambitious experiments in thematic content and literary technique.

Kōyō's most notable works include *Ninin bikuni irozange* (1889, Love Confessions of Two Nuns), *Kyara makura* (1890, Aloeswood Pillow), *Ninin nyōbō* (1891, Two Wives), and *Sanninzuma* (1892, Three Wives), all of which show the strong influence of Edo-period realist writers. His last and best work is KONJIKI YASHA (1897–1902; tr *The Golden Demon*, 1905), perhaps the most popular Meiji novel, which generated plays, movies, and songs. Preceding the advent of NATURALISM, which cast a long shadow across modern Japanese literature, Kōyō left a unique body of romantic fiction rich in imaginative plotting and characterization.

Ozaki Masashi 尾崎将司

(1947–). Professional golfer. Born in Tokushima Prefecture. Ozaki was a star pitcher in high school and played baseball professionally from 1965 to 1967. He began to play golf professionally in 1970. He won the Japan Pro Golf Championship in 1971 and 1974 and the Japan Open Golf Championship in 1972. He had the highest earnings of any Japanese golfer in 1973, 1974, 1977, 1988, and 1990. In 1989 he became the first Japanese player ever to win every weekly match at the Japan Open for three straight weeks. Ozaki's power (he can drive the ball over 300 yards) and effortless delivery have earned him the nickname "Jumbo."

Ōyu stone circles There are two stone circles, lined up on a north-south axis. Pictured is the "sundial" arrangement of stones within the northern circle.

Ozaki Hotsumi A journalist and adviser on Chinese affairs to the first Konoe Fumimaro cabinet, Ozaki was executed in 1944 after being found guilty of serving as a Soviet agent.

Ozaki Kōyō This Meiji-period novelist and poet was a major influence on early modern Japanese literature.

Ozawa Seiji Ozawa is Japan's first orchestra conductor to achieve wide recognition in Europe and the United States. In recent years, he has increasingly turned his talents to opera.

Ozu Yasujirō
1 Ozu, whose spare directing and editing techniques and low camera placement contributed to his reputation as a definitively "Japanese" filmmaker.
2 Sugawara Hideo (left) and Aoki Tomio in a scene from *Umarete wa mita keredo* (1932, I Was Born, but . . .), the first of Ozu's many films dealing with Japanese family life.

1

Ozaki Shirō

Ozaki Shirō   尾崎士郎

(1898–1964). Novelist. Born in Aichi Prefecture. Studied at Waseda University. Although some of his early works reflect an interest in the socialist movement, he became a nationalist during World War II. After the war he was banned from publishing between 1948 and 1950 during the OCCUPATION PURGE. His seven-volume novel JINSEI GEKIJŌ (1933–59) is a *Bildungsroman* set in the politically stormy decades preceding World War II. Other works include *Kagaribi* (1941, Beacon) and *Tennō kikan setsu* (1951, On the Emperor System).

Ozaki Yukio   尾崎行雄

(1858–1954). Pen name Gakudō. Liberal politician, elected 25 times to the House of Representatives. Born in Sagami Province (now part of Kanagawa Prefecture). He studied at Keiō Gijuku (now Keiō University) and Kōgakuryō, an engineering academy.

Ozaki assisted ŌKUMA SHIGENOBU in the formation of the political party RIKKEN KAISHINTŌ in 1882. Elected to the Diet in 1890, he vigorously supported Japan's imperialistic advances during the SINO-JAPANESE WAR OF 1894–1895, but domestically he advocated certain democratic principles. Ozaki helped establish the RIKKEN SEIYŪKAI in 1900.

While mayor of Tōkyō (1903–12), Ozaki sent 3,000 cherry-tree seedlings to Washington, DC. During the TAISHŌ POLITICAL CRISIS of 1912–13, he and INUKAI TSUYOSHI led the opposition against the government. He campaigned on behalf of the UNIVERSAL MANHOOD SUFFRAGE MOVEMENT until this right was granted in 1925; he even advocated WOMEN'S SUFFRAGE. During the 1930s he became increasingly isolated from party politics and criticized the growing influence of the military. Thus he was understandably hailed again as a political hero after World War II. The Ozaki Memorial Hall in Tōkyō commemorates his contributions to the development of constitutional government in Japan.

Ozawa Roan   小沢蘆庵

(1723–1801). WAKA poet and theorist of the late Edo period (1600–1868). Born in Owari (now part of Aichi Prefecture), he received his early training in the conservative Dōjō school of *waka*, which was aristocratic in nature and emphasized adherence to the poetics of the KOKINSHŪ. He later broke away and developed his own concept of poetry, *tadagoto uta* (poetry employing the diction of ordinary speech), which stressed the direct, simple expression of the poet's feelings in everyday language with a minimum of embellishment. His major works include the *waka* collection *Rokujō eisō* (1811) and an essay on poetics, *Furu no nakamichi* (1800).

Ozawa Seiji   小沢征爾

(1935–). Conductor. Born in Shenyang, China; studied under the conductor SAITŌ HIDEO (1902–74) at the Tōhō Gakuen School of Music. In 1959 Ozawa won first prize in the International Competition of Orchestra Conductors at Besançon, France, and went on to serve as assistant conductor of the New York Philharmonic and music director of the Toronto Symphony Orchestra. Ozawa was conductor and music director of the San Francisco Symphony Orchestra from 1970 to 1976. He was named music director of the Boston Symphony Orchestra in 1973.

Oze   尾瀬

High moor, at junction of Gumma, Fukushima, and Niigata prefectures, central Honshū, part of Nikkō National Park. It includes Ozenuma, a lake, and Ozegahara, a marshy moor. Ozegahara (elevation: about 1,400 m [4,600 ft]; area: 8 sq km [3 sq mi]) is the largest high moor in Japan. Ozenuma, surrounded by several towering peaks, is famous for its natural scenery. Wildflowers and birds abound at Oze.

Ōzu   大洲［市］

City in western Ehime Prefecture, Shikoku, on the river Hijikawa. Ōzu developed as a castle town in the Edo period (1600–1868). Principal activities are dairy and vegetable farming; raw silk is also produced. Attractions include the residence of NAKAE TŌJU, Ōzu Castle, and cormorant fishing (*ukai*). Pop: 39,850.

Ōzuka tomb   王塚古墳

(*Ōzuka kofun*). A keyhole-shaped mounded tomb (KOFUN) in Keisen Machi, Fukuoka

2

Prefecture. Discovered in 1934, the stone burial chamber is believed to have been built in the mid-6th century. It is noted for its wall paintings of horses, quivers, shields, and swords, as well as triangular and fern frond designs, all brilliantly executed in red, green, yellow, and black. Burial goods include bronze mirrors, beads, gold ear ornaments, horse trappings, armor, and weapons. See also ORNAMENTED TOMBS.

Ozu Yasujirō   小津安二郎

(1903–63). Film director, noted for his works on contemporary Japanese family life. Born in Tōkyō. At age 10 he and his mother and brothers were sent to his father's ancestral hometown of Matsusaka, where he was brought up for the most part without his father, whose work kept him in Tōkyō. Ozu spent much of his youth in movie theaters. In 1923 he became an assistant cameraman with Shōchiku (see SHŌCHIKU CO, LTD), one of Japan's most important film companies. He became an assistant director in 1926 and a full-fledged director a year later.

Ozu first made numerous short comedies before turning to more somber themes in the 1930s. His subject matter eventually narrowed to a concern for the activities and problems of the Japanese family, a social unit that he saw disintegrating under the pressures of modern life, as in UMARETE WA MITA KEREDO (1932, I Was Born, but . . .), a comedy with serious overtones about growing up. It is widely regarded as the first great work of social criticism in Japanese cinema and as the first of Ozu's great films. Ozu at first scorned new film technologies, and he did not make his first talkie, *Hitori musuko* (The Only Son), until 1936. He disdained color films until the late 1950s when Shōchiku insisted that *Higambana* (1958, Equinox Flower) be made with a newly developed Japanese color-film process.

An apparent parallel between his life and art became clear in the autobiographical *Chichi ariki* (1942, There Was a Father), which describes the subdued yet strong bond of affection between a man and his son that endures despite years of separation. Following World War II, Ozu took a stern view of the corrupting influence of postwar society on the institution of the family. TŌKYŌ MONOGATARI (1953, Tōkyō Story), his most famous film, expresses this view and another common element in Ozu's cinema: several peripheral characters are negligent relatives who do not meet their obligations to the family. Ozu listed this film as one of his personal favorites, along with *Chichi ariki* and BANSHUN (1949, Late Spring).

In his last films, Ozu's outlook was one of gentle resignation to the ways of the world. His characters face the same problems but bear their disappointments with wistful good humor. His last six films, though his most conservative both socially and stylistically, are the most lighthearted since his very early work.

Ozu refined a singular technique that has come to be regarded as the essence of the Japanese cinema aesthetic. It is characterized by low camera placement, static compositions that proceed in leisurely and well-ordered transitions punctuated only by simple cuts, and laconic dialogue with the plain ring of everyday conversation. His films are characterized by an elegant simplicity. Although they are rooted in the particular experience of Japanese life, they touch upon the universal desire for a secure and happy home life and familial affection.

P

Pabst, Jean Charles パブスト, J. C.

(1873–1942). Dutch military man and diplomat. In 1910 he was sent to Japan as a military attaché to the Dutch ministry and to study the Japanese military system. He was named minister in 1923 and worked to improve Dutch-Japanese relations until the outbreak of World War II. He died in Tōkyō.

pachinko パチンコ

Japan's most popular arcade game; a variety of pinball. First played commercially in Nagoya in 1948, it rapidly became popular throughout the country. It has been estimated that more than 30 million Japanese play the game on a regular basis. *Pachinko* is played in brightly lit, gaudy parlors. A player buys a number of steel balls, loads them into a *pachinko* machine, and (in one of the original mechanical models) flips a lever in order to propel a ball to the top of the machine. The ball then bounces down through a maze of pegs, either falling into a winning hole on the way down or becoming lost in a hole at the bottom of the machine. When the ball enters a winning hole, the machine discharges additional balls, which can be fed back into the machine or redeemed for prizes (which are sometimes illegally exchanged for cash). Today, mechanical *pachinko* machines have been completely replaced by computer-controlled machines in which a knob is turned and the balls are propelled automatically. Some newer types of *pachinko* machines have number displays similar to those of slot machines. A winning combination earns the player bonus points. The illegal use of certain types of these machines for gambling has led to their regulation.

Pacific Basin Economic Council 太平洋経済委員会

(PBEC; J: Taiheiyō Keizai Iinkai). Organization of business and professional leaders from nations of the Pacific Rim, formed in 1968. Membership was originally limited to Australia, Canada, Japan, New Zealand, and the United States but was extended to include a Pacific Region Committee representing Hong Kong, Malaysia, Peru, South Korea, Taiwan, Chile, and Mexico. The purpose of the council is to facilitate and improve economic and trade relations among member states. The council helped to found the Private Investment Company for Asia (PICA), a multinational corporation designed to make and facilitate capital investments in the developing countries of Asia. The council's annual International General Meeting was held in Tōkyō in 1990. See also JAPAN–AUSTRALIA BUSINESS CO-OPERATION COMMITTEE.

Pacific Coastal Belt 太平洋ベルト地帯

(Taiheiyō Beruto Chitai). Official designation for an industrial zone extending from the KANTŌ REGION through the TŌKAI and KINKI regions to northern Kyūshū. Japan's major cities and 70 to 80 percent of its population are concentrated in this area. The industrial belt was created when the KEIYŌ, Tōkai, and INLAND SEA regions became heavily industrialized, thus linking Japan's existing four major industrial zones (the KEIHIN, CHŪKYŌ, HANSHIN, and KITA KYŪSHŪ industrial zones). Other factors were the development of a transportation network that includes the high-speed Tōkaidō and San'yō Shinkansen railways and the Tōmei and Meishin expressways.

Pacific Economic Cooperation Conference 太平洋経済協力会議

(PECC; J: Taiheiyō Keizai Kyōryoku Kaigi). A series of international conferences that is one of the two main private forums for the promotion of economic cooperation in the Pacific region (the PACIFIC BASIN ECONOMIC COUNCIL is the other). Participants in the PECC come from the political, economic, and academic spheres. The first conference was held in Australia in 1980 on the basis of an agreement between Prime Ministers ŌHIRA MASAYOSHI of Japan and Malcolm Fraser of Australia. The sixth conference, held in 1988, was the first convened in Japan. In 1991, countries participating in the conference included Japan, the United States, Canada, Australia, South Korea, and China.

Pacific Islands and Japan 太平洋諸島と日本

(Taiheiyō Shotō *to* Nihon). Japan's interest in the islands of the South Pacific began in the late 19th century when the Germans established colonies in the Caroline, Marshall, and Mariana islands. As soon as WORLD WAR I broke out, Japan occupied the German possessions in the Pacific Islands and after 1922 governed them under mandates granted by the League of Nations. During WORLD WAR II, Japan went on to invade and occupy many more of the Pacific Islands, and at the height of its military dominance controlled a vast area of the central Pacific. After the war, most of the Pacific Islands were placed under United Nations trusteeships, which continued until they gained their independence in the 1970s. Economic ties with Japan in terms of trade, investment, and aid have been small, but as Japan's economic strength has increased, there has been growing interest among the Pacific nations in deepening the economic relationship. For instance, the South Pacific Forum in 1985 advocated the strengthening of relations with

pachinko
1 A *pachinko* parlor's lively neon lights beckon customers.
2 A recent model of *pachinko* machine, incorporating a slot machine in the center of the pinball board. If certain numbers on the slot machine come into alignment, more holes on the board open up, allowing the player to win more balls.
3 Players sit mesmerized before rows of *pachinko* machines.

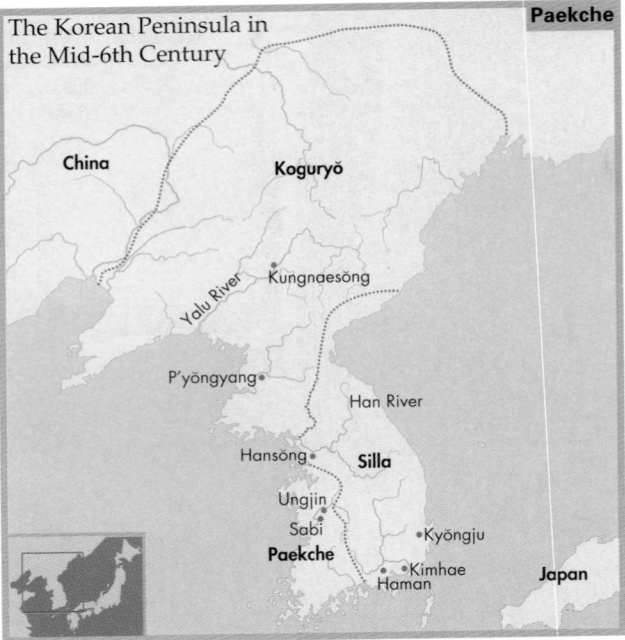

The Korean Peninsula in the Mid-6th Century

China
Koguryŏ
Yalu River
Kungnaesŏng
P'yŏngyang
Han River
Hansŏng
Silla
Ungjin
Sabi
Paekche
Kyŏngju
Kimhae
Haman
Japan
Paekche

Japan. Since 1986, high officials from Fiji, Tuvalu, Western Samoa, Papua New Guinea, and other Pacific island nations have visited Japan. Japan has also shown a growing interest in the islands, as demonstrated by official visits to the area by Prime Minister NAKASONE YASUHIRO in 1985 and by Foreign Minister Kuranari Tadashi (b 1918) in 1987.

Pacific War→World War II

pacifism 平和主義
(*heiwa shugi*). The roots of pacifism in Japan go back to the mid-Meiji period (1868–1912), when the Western concepts of nonviolence and nonaggression were first introduced. Its development falls into two periods: the first covering events up to the end of World War II, during which time pacifism was almost unknown to the general public and was feared by the government because of its supposed socialist implications, and the second coming after World War II, when pacifism became, in a sense, quasi-official policy and a potent political ideology.

The missionaries who brought pacifism to Japan in the late 19th century introduced an idea that had quite different connotations in Japan than it did in the Western world. In the West, pacifism developed from early Christian thought and flourished as a result of the increasingly destructive wars between rival nation-states. Japan, on the other hand, had been through only two minor civil wars in the preceding two centuries, so that the Japanese as a whole had no recent experience of war. The message of the pacifists therefore came as an entirely new concept, part of the Western tradition that excited the interest of restless Japanese youths.

Early Development—Two young writers first dealt with pacifist ideas: KITAMURA TŌKOKU and KINOSHITA NAOE. Both young men became Protestants under the influence of evangelical Christian thought and embraced the New Testament term "peace." Kitamura founded Japan's first pacifist journal, *Heiwa* (Peace), in 1892, and Kinoshita decried the impending Russo-Japanese War of 1904–05, but both became discouraged by the general indifference to their arguments.

Even before this, other thinkers had started to form the core of the pacifist tradition as it would exist until 1945. They were

moved to their convictions by events in the society around them. The Sino-Japanese War of 1894–95 had ended in a stunning victory for Japan. Very few thinkers opposed the war at the time, but the number increased as war with tsarist Russia appeared probable in the early 1900s. Among these emerging pacifists were KŌTOKU SHŪSUI and UCHIMURA KANZŌ, who resigned from the influential newspaper YOROZU CHŌHŌ when its owner ordered his editors to support the Japanese government position. Uchimura thereupon began in 1900 to publish *Seisho no kenkyū* (Biblical Studies), using the rhetoric of the Bible to deplore war. Kōtoku, whose pacifism had been influenced by Leo Tolstoy's philosophy, established with a number of fellow socialists the HEIMIN SHIMBUN (Commoner's News) in 1903. The authorities quickly censored it. Kōtoku, disillusioned that his rational pleas for peace met with so little understanding, became increasingly radical, in the end dying on the gallows in 1911 convicted, probably wrongly, of an attempt to assassinate the Meiji emperor.

One of Kōtoku's associates on the *Heimin shimbun* was ABE ISOO, a clergyman who, though always critical of government policies, phrased his criticism so that he could continue his unobtrusive protest against war until his death in 1949. Another individual who gained recognition as a pacifist after World War I was KAGAWA TOYOHIKO, who became known for his Christian social work in the slums of Kōbe and later as a best-selling novelist and labor leader. His works demonstrated an inclination toward pacifism, but caution kept him from fully developing his ideas.

In contrast to numerous such pacifists was the outspoken YANAIHARA TADAO, a fervent believer in the Christian pacifism espoused by his teacher Uchimura Kanzō. Yanaihara held the chair of Colonial Policy at Tōkyō University when the Japanese invaded Manchuria in 1931. Having satisfied himself that Japan was the aggressor, he repeatedly criticized government policy. Forced to resign his university post, he continued to protest throughout the war, privately publishing his own monthly magazine, *Kashin* (Good News). Less courageous colleagues took heart from his opposition, seeing in it a sign that a more rational view of the world would return. After Japan's defeat in World War II, Yanaihara was elected president of Tōkyō University and became one of the architects of the postwar democratic education system. Yanaihara's belated recognition and elevation to a position of national prominence demonstrate how what had been anathema suddenly became not only accepted but also meritorious.

Postwar Trends—In the immediate postwar confusion of 1945, the Japanese voluntarily repudiated the ultranationalism of their leaders. The weary public had developed a strong revulsion against war in general and atomic weapons in particular. Thus article 9 of the new constitution of 1947 states that the "Japanese people forever renounce war," to which end they will never maintain "land, sea, and air forces, as well as other war potential" (see RENUNCIATION OF WAR). Rapidly changing conditions in East Asia soon challenged the idealism of this so-called peace clause. The invasion of South Korea by North Korea in 1950 drew the Allied garrison troops out of Japan and led Supreme Commander General Douglas MACARTHUR to request that the Japanese develop a "police reserve force" to replace them. In

1951 when Japan signed the peace treaty and concomitant security treaty with most of its former adversaries, the "police force" became the SELF DEFENSE FORCES.

Concurrently, a number of individuals and groups started to look into the theoretical problems connected with the maintenance of peace. At first their interests were shaped by memories of wartime defeat, but with continuing warfare in Korea and Vietnam their attention turned more and more to causes and effects of war in the late 20th century. Scholars first generalized on the basis of specific examples of international violence that occurred either in Japan or proximate areas of Asia, then, increasingly, they began to link Japanese peace research to similar work in Europe and North America. In 1966 a number of researchers, including Hosoya Chihiro (b 1920) and Ishida Takeshi (b 1923), formed the Nihon Heiwa Kenkyū Kondan Kai (Japan Peace Research Group), which published the English-language *Peace Research in Japan*. In 1973 these same scholars established the Nihon Heiwa Gakkai (Peace Studies Association of Japan), an academic society with open membership and affiliations with similar organizations throughout the world.

The history of pacifism in Japan demonstrates how, in a closely controlled and warless society, the ideas of peace seemed at first more relevant to individual psychic needs than to international relations. Only after World War II did a war-weary generation begin to build on the foundations of earlier pacifist thought. Contemporary peace researchers in Japan have begun to contribute to the body of international peace scholarship with insights based upon their own experience in East Asia. See also PEACE MOVEMENT.

Paekche 百済
(J: Kudara). One of the Three Kingdoms of early Korean history, the other two being SILLA and KOGURYŎ. Paekche (ca 350–663) occupied the southwestern quarter of the peninsula and was responsible for the introduction of numerous features of continental civilization, including Buddhism, to Japan.

The earliest Korean historical text, the SAMGUK SAGI, avers that Paekche was established in 18 BC by King Onjo (trad 18 BC–AD 23), the leader of a band of immigrants from the eastern Manchurian state of Fuyü (Kor: Puyŏ). Chinese sources contain no references to the kingdom predating the middle of the 4th century.

The presence of three independent states produced constant strife on the peninsula. During the first two centuries of Paekche's existence, it was almost incessantly on the defensive against Koguryŏ, the kingdom to the north, and for safety moved its capital from Hansŏng (located near present-day Seoul) south to Ungjin (present-day Kongju) in 475 and yet farther south to Sabi (present-day Puyŏ) in 538.

Late in the 5th century, Paekche and Silla, the neighboring kingdom to the east, formed an alliance, but in 553 Silla seized the strategic Han River valley, and thereafter Paekche regarded Silla as its primary enemy. Early in the 7th century, Silla sought Chinese assistance. The emperors of the contemporary Tang (T'ang) dynasty (618–907) sent a large Chinese army in 660; acting in conjunction with Silla troops, they easily captured the capital and the reigning king. Paekche loyalists, with Japanese support, mounted a war of restoration against the Tang-Silla occupation, but this effort was crushed in 663 following the destruction of a Japanese naval force (see HAKUSUKINOE, BATTLE OF).

Paekche seems to have assumed the role of the subordinate in its recurrent dealings with Japan between the mid-4th and the mid-7th centuries, but both benefited from the relationship. Paekche provided Japan with many of the personnel needed for its adoption of continental civilization, including scholars, monks, and artisans (see also KIKAJIN). Japan in return supplied Paekche with military assistance.

Paekche's King Sŏng (523–554) sent the delegation that formally introduced Buddhism to the Japanese court. He seems to have been the first Paekche ruler to espouse the religion ardently, and by the beginning of the 7th century Buddhism had become a virtual state religion.

Pagès, Léon パジェス, L.

(1814–86). French diplomat, scholar, and writer who specialized in the early history of CHRISTIANITY in Japan. Born in Paris, he was attached to the French embassy in China from 1847 to 1851. His stay in Asia aroused his interest in Japanese history, and he subsequently published in France a number of widely read books. Among them are *Essai de grammaire japonaise* (1861), a translation of DONKER CURTIUS's *Proeve eener Japansche spraakkunst* (1857); *Dictionnaire japonais-français* (1862–68), a French version of *Vocabulario da Lingoa de Iapam* (1603–04; NIPPO JISHO); and *Histoire de la religion chrétienne au Japon, 1598–1651* (1869–70).

In 1873, on the occasion of the visit of the IWAKURA MISSION to France, Pagès published *La persécution des chrétiens au Japon et l'ambassade japonaise en Europe* as part of the successful foreign campaign to obtain religious freedom for Japanese Christians. Christianity had been officially proscribed in Japan since 1614.

pagoda 塔

(*tō;* literally, "tower"). In Japanese BUDDHIST ARCHITECTURE, a multistoried, towerlike structure, usually made of wood or stone with a square, circular, or polygonal configuration, used for enshrining sacred remains or relics of the Buddha, celebrating mass, and storing sutras. The Japanese pagoda, which derives in design and function from the ancient Indian stupa, was a major religious architectural form and generally occupied a prominent place in the ground plan of a monastic compound.

Originating in ancient India, the stupa was transformed into a tall, wooden structure in China. From there it was introduced into Japan following the transmission of Buddhism to Japan in the early 6th century. The first pagoda in Japan is said to have been built in 585. Among the earliest known pagodas were the ones built at ASUKADERA (between 593 and 596), SHITENNŌJI, HŌRYŪJI (site of the oldest surviving pagoda in Japan), YAKUSHIJI, KŌFUKUJI, and TŌDAIJI.

Most pagodas are three bays square at the base, and the upper stories that rise above this base, each with extended, upward-curving roofs, gradually diminish in size as they move topward. Odd numbers of stories were preferred. There is a central pillar (*shimbashira*) running through the core of the structure, in which the Buddha's relics are installed. The multistoried pagoda is capped by a spire (*sōrin*) at the top. This is a modification of the mast or disk capping the stupa.

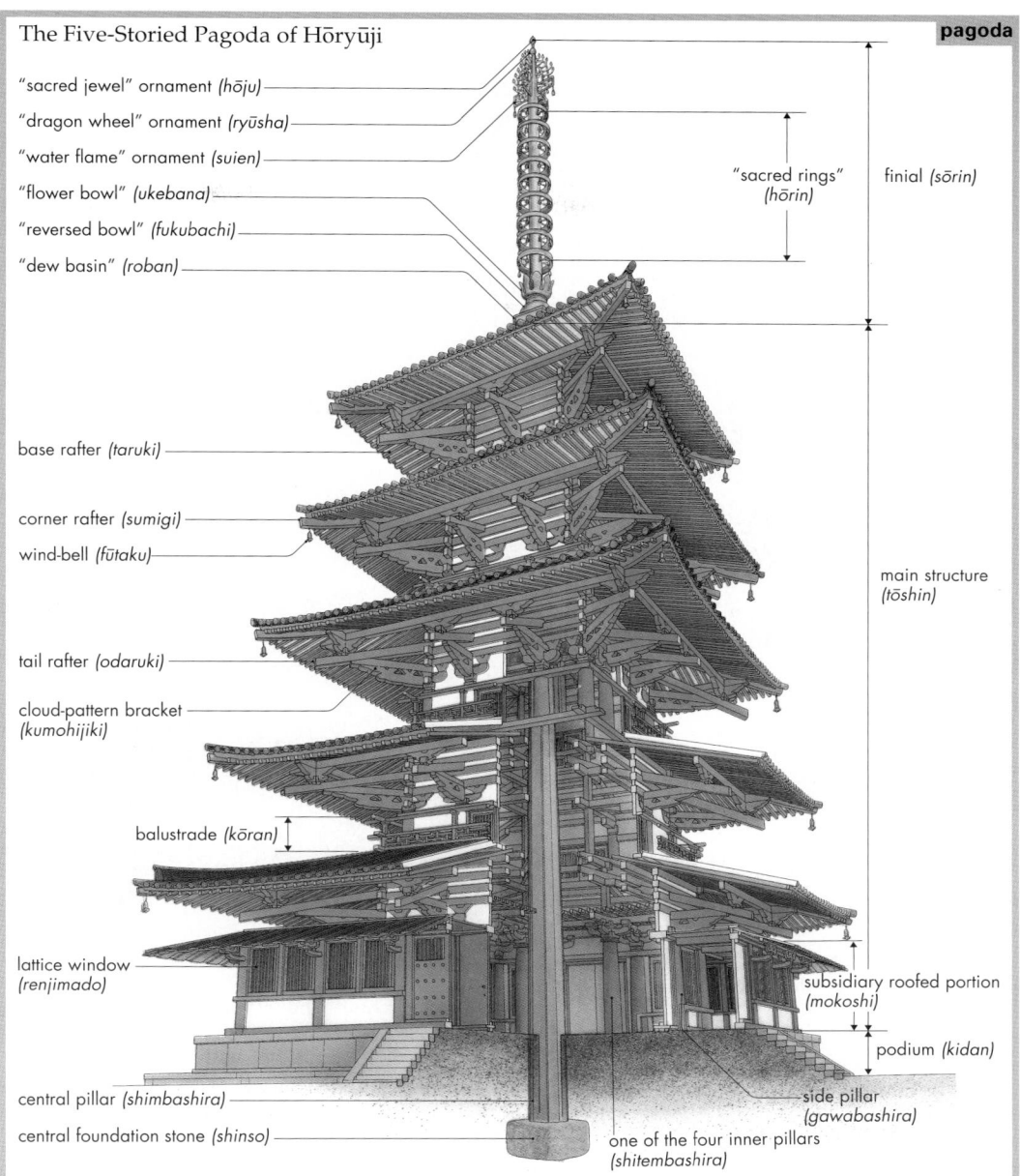

The Five-Storied Pagoda of Hōryūji

"sacred jewel" ornament (*hōju*)
"dragon wheel" ornament (*ryūsha*)
"water flame" ornament (*suien*)
"flower bowl" (*ukebana*)
"reversed bowl" (*fukubachi*)
"dew basin" (*roban*)
"sacred rings" (*hōrin*)
finial (*sōrin*)
base rafter (*taruki*)
corner rafter (*sumigi*)
wind-bell (*fūtaku*)
tail rafter (*odaruki*)
cloud-pattern bracket (*kumohijiki*)
main structure (*tōshin*)
balustrade (*kōran*)
lattice window (*renjimado*)
subsidiary roofed portion (*mokoshi*)
podium (*kidan*)
central pillar (*shimbashira*)
side pillar (*gawabashira*)
central foundation stone (*shinso*)
one of the four inner pillars (*shitembashira*)

painting 絵画

(*kaiga*). Japanese painting is characterized by a wide range of styles in a wide array of formats, from horizontal and hanging scrolls to album leaves, fans, walls, and free-standing and sliding screens. Like the history of Japanese art in general, Japanese painting has been dominated by two components, continental and indigenous, in the development of style and technique.

PREMODERN PAINTING

Until the 19th century, China was the principal source of innovation. Much of the history of painting in premodern Japan can be described as a dialogue between Chinese and native styles.

Painting through the Nara Period (710–794)—The origins of painting in Japan can be traced to the simple stick figures found on Yayoi-period (ca 300 BC–ca AD 300) bells (see DŌTAKU) and the murals, both geometric and figural, on the inner walls of Kofun-period (ca 300–710) tombs (see ORNAMENTED TOMBS). With the introduction of Buddhism and Buddhist culture from Korea and China in the 6th century, painting began to flourish as the production of Buddhist art and architecture became a

major concern of the ruling class.

A number of paintings from the late 7th and early 8th centuries are preserved at the temple HŌRYŪJI. In Hōryūji's museum a votive shrine called the Tamamushi Shrine, or "Beetle-Wing Shrine," bears a series of 7th-century paintings on its panels, whose bronze filigree frames were backed originally by the iridescent wings of the *tamamushi* beetle. These paintings illustrate episodes from the life of the Buddha as well as depicting figures of bodhisattvas and other deities. Their style of execution is reminiscent of painting styles in late-Six-Dynasties (222–589) China.

By the close of the 7th century, a new style in painting—that of Tang (T'ang; 618–907) China—was in vogue. The *kondō* (main hall) at Hōryūji contains a set of wall paintings of Buddhist paradises rendered in this new continental format (the paintings today are restorations of the original late-7th-century works, which were largely destroyed in a fire in 1949). Another group of important early wall paintings is located at the TAKAMATSUZUKA TOMB, which dates to approximately 700. See also HŌRYŪJI GREAT TREASURE HOUSE; HŌRYŪJI, TREASURES OF.

▶ One of the painted panels of the Tamamushi Shrine—thought to be a depiction of a memorial ceremony for the Buddha. Visible at the bottom of the photo is part of the stand on which the shrine rests. Mid-7th century. Red, light brown, yellow, and green oil pigments on lacquered wood. Height of panel approximately 65 cm. Hōryūji, Nara. National Treasure.

▼ Detail from the *E inga kyō* (Illustrated Sutra of Cause and Effect). This scroll pictorializes a sutra that describes events in the life of the historical Buddha. Nara period. Colors on paper. 27 × 1,095 cm. Tōkyō University of Fine Arts and Music. National Treasure.

▲ Three hanging scrolls form the triptych *Descent of Amida and His Host*, depicting the Buddha as he descends to save a believer's soul. 12th century. Colors on silk. Size of left and right scrolls: each 211 × 106 cm; central scroll 210 × 211 cm. Yūshi Hachimankō Jūhakkain, Kōyasan, Wakayama Prefecture. National Treasure.

◀ This example of 12th-century portrait painting by Fujiwara no Takanobu is thought to be of the warrior and statesman Taira no Shigemori. Colors on silk. 143 × 112 cm. Jingoji, Kyōto Prefecture. National Treasure.

A number of paintings produced in the Nara period and exhibiting mature Tang influence are found in the SHŌSŌIN storehouse, originally part of the TŌDAIJI complex. These include the banner-painting known as *Sumi-e bosatsu zō* (Bodhisattva Seated on a Cloud) and a six-panel screen depicting the motif known as JUKA BIJIN (Beauties beneath Trees).

Painting of the Heian (794–1185) and Kamakura (1185–1333) Periods—With the rise in the early 9th century of esoteric Buddhism as developed by the SHINGON SECT and the TENDAI SECT, the painted MANDALA emerged into prominence. Important examples of this genre are the Diamond Realm (KONGŌKAI) and Womb Realm (TAIZŌKAI) mandalas, dated 824–833, at the temple JINGOJI, and the 11th-century *Kojima Mandala* at Kojimadera in Nara. The five-story pagoda at DAIGOJI, constructed in 952, contains a number of murals depicting various esoteric deities in a mandala format.

After the 10th century, the influence of Pure Land Buddhism—popularized by the JŌDO SECT and its predecessors—became increasingly apparent in painting. An important new genre was the RAIGŌZU, a depiction of the Buddha Amida arriving to welcome the dying to paradise. Examples of *raigōzu* are seen in the Phoenix Hall (Hōōdō) at BYŌDŌIN, dating to 1053, and in the mid-12th-century triptych called *Amida shōju raigōzu* (Descent of Amida and the Heavenly Multitude), which is now housed on Mt. Kōya but originally belonged to the temple ENRYAKUJI on Mt. Hiei (Hieizan).

By the mid-Heian period, Chinese modes of painting (KARA-E) had begun to give way to a distinctly indigenous style known as YAMATO-E. The earliest paintings in this style were sliding screens and folding screens. Two new painting formats evolved as the native style was developed: the album leaf (*sōshi*) and the illuminated handscroll (*EMAKIMONO*).

The earliest example of the illuminated handscroll format is the fragmentary GENJI MONOGATARI EMAKI (*Tale of Genji* Scrolls), which date from the early 12th century. The graceful and restrained style of these works is called *onna-e*, "painting in the feminine mode," a term derived from 12th-century literature. "Painting in the masculine mode," *otoko-e*, flourished after the late 12th century and reflected a more popular vein, especially in illustrated handscrolls. An important example in this category is SHIGISAN ENGI EMAKI (The Legends of Mt. Shigi). Other key works in the *emakimono* format include BAN DAINAGON EMAKI (Story of the Courtier Ban Dainagon); *Nenchū gyōji emaki* (Scrolls of Annual Rites and Ceremonies), which is attributed to Tokiwa Mitsunaga (fl ca 1173); and HEIJI MONOGATARI EMAKI (Tale of Heiji Scrolls). Early handscrolls with a religious theme include the CHŌJŪ GIGA (Scrolls of Frolicking Animals) and JIGOKU-ZŌSHI (Scrolls of Hells).

Painting of the Muromachi Period (1333–1568)—During the 14th century, scroll painting declined as *suibokuga*, or INK PAINTING, took hold in the great ZEN monasteries of Kamakura and Kyōto. An austere monochrome style, introduced from Song (Sung; 960–1279) and Yuan (Yüan; 1279–1368) China, was favored by Zen painters and their patrons. The styles of the Chinese monk-painters Muqi (Mu-ch'i; J: MOKKEI; fl ca 1250) and Liang Kai (Liang K'ai; 1140?–1210?) were particularly influential. Although numerous polychrome portraits called *chinsō* (see PORTRAIT PAINTING) were also produced by Zen painters, such as the painting of MUSŌ SOSEKI (1275–1351) by his disciple Mutō Shūi (dates unknown), ink painting was the favored medium. Important artists in the early development of this tradition were MOKUAN REIEN (d ca 1345) and KAŌ NINGA (fl early 14th century).

By the end of the 14th century, a monochrome landscape painting genre (see SANSUIGA) had emerged as the preferred medium among Zen painters and their ASHIKAGA FAMILY patrons in Kyōto. Artists whose works helped form the landscape genre include MINCHŌ (1352–1431) and JOSETSU (early 15th century). During the 15th century, Tenshō SHŪBUN (d ca 1460) and SESSHŪ TŌYŌ (1420–1506) developed the Chinese-inspired monochrome landscape style into a fully Japanese format. A key work by Sesshū is *Amanohashidate* (ca 1501, Kyōto National Museum), which depicts the famous scenic spot of that name.

In the last years of Ashikaga rule, a new genre of ink painting was developed largely outside the Zen community by artists of the AMI SCHOOL and the KANŌ SCHOOL. The Kanō school was initiated by the layman painter KANŌ MASANOBU (1434–1530) and continued by his son KANŌ MOTONOBU (1476–1559). Although Chinese styles and themes remained their model, Kanō-school artists introduced a more decorative and plastic sensibility that would come to dominate the landscape painting of the succeeding centuries.

Painting of the Azuchi-Momoyama (1568–1600) and Edo (1600–1868) Periods—The Kanō school, promoted by ODA NOBUNAGA (1534–82), TOYOTOMI HIDEYOSHI (1537–98), and other powerful patrons, dominated painting in the late 16th century and developed a grandiose polychromed style for SCREEN AND WALL PAINTING. KANŌ EITOKU (1543–90) was commissioned by Nobunaga to decorate AZUCHI CASTLE (1576–79; destroyed 1582) near Lake Biwa and by Hideyoshi to decorate Jurakudai Palace (1587; destroyed 1595) in Kyōto. Eitoku is believed to be the first painter to have introduced the dramatic use of fields of gold leaf in large mural compositions. Eitoku's pupil and adopted son KANŌ SANRAKU (1559–1635) continued this style into the early Edo period. By the time that Eitoku's grandson KANŌ

▲ This detail from a scroll painting illustrating stories about the warrior Obusuma Saburō exhibits the aerial perspective common in scroll paintings. Late 13th century. Colors on paper. 29 × 1,270 cm. Tōkyō National Museum.

◀Detail of *Four Elders on Mt. Shang,* one of a pair of six-panel folding screens by Kanō Moto-nobu. 16th century. Ink on paper. Each screen 153 × 360 cm. Tōkyō National Museum.

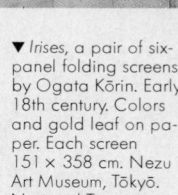

▼ *Irises,* a pair of six-panel folding screens by Ogata Kōrin. Early 18th century. Colors and gold leaf on paper. Each screen 151 × 358 cm. Nezu Art Museum, Tōkyō. National Treasure.

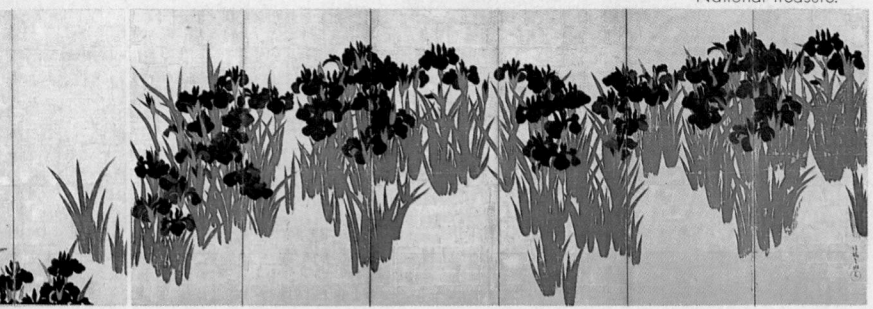

TAN'YŪ (1602–74) was active, the Kanō school was firmly established as the painting academy of the Tokugawa shogunate (1603–1867).

A number of artists outside the Kanō school adapted Chinese themes and styles to the contemporary decorative sensibility. Among such painters were HASEGAWA TŌHAKU (1539–1610) and KAIHŌ YŪSHŌ (1533–1615). Another genre, one belonging to the *yamato-e* tradition, was developed by painters of the TOSA SCHOOL, whose small-scale works often illustrated the literary classics of earlier generations. The *yamato-e* tradition also gave rise to the decorative painters of the group called RIMPA. The principal artists of this school were Tawaraya SŌTATSU (d 1643?) and Ogata KŌRIN (1658–1716), whose works—taking classical styles and themes and presenting them in a new, boldly decorative format—have come to symbolize the lavish tastes of Edo (now Tōkyō) society in the 17th and 18th centuries.

FŪZOKUGA, or genre paintings, became popular in the late 16th century and gave rise to UKIYO-E, "paintings of the floating world," which captured the transient experiences of the pleasure quarters of Edo and other urban centers. The woodblock print as a significant Edo-period medium emerged out of this tradition.

The late Edo period was one of eclecticism in painting. The influence of European painting, earlier represented by the "southern barbarian" NAMBAN ART of the late 16th century, was increasingly apparent. The port city of Nagasaki acted as the conduit for both Chinese and Western influence in painting (see NAGASAKI SCHOOL; WESTERN-STYLE PICTURES, EARLY.) Major artists of this period include MARUYAMA ŌKYO (1733–95) and MATSUMU-

RA GOSHUN (1752–1811), founders of the MARUYAMA-SHIJŌ SCHOOL, and ITŌ JAKUCHŪ (1716–1800). The works of these painters show a mixture of Japanese, Chinese, and Western elements and often evidence a heightened concern with naturalistic depiction.

Another major trend in late-Edo-period painting was that of BUNJINGA, "literati painting," whose artists took their inspiration from a tradition of Chinese scholar–amateur painters who, since the Yuan dynasty, had worked in a style called NANGA ("Southern painting"). This style entered Japan in the 18th century via Nagasaki, where it was introduced by Chinese immigrant painters and described in Chinese painting manuals. The first literati painters, among them GION NANKAI (1677–1751), SAKAKI HYAKUSEN (1697–1752), and YANAGISAWA KIEN (1704–58), tended to imitate rather than innovate. The second generation of *bunjinga* artists is represented by IKE NO TAIGA (1723–76), who was able to render Chinese and Japanese landscapes in a variety of modes, and Yosa BUSON (1716–83), who painted intimate images of great lyricism. Important later *bunjinga* artists include URAGAMI GYOKUDŌ (1745–1820), OKADA BEISANJIN (1744–1820), TANOMURA CHIKUDEN (1777–1835), YAMAMOTO BAIITSU (1783–1856), and TOMIOKA TESSAI (1836–1924).

MODERN PAINTING

During the Meiji period (1868–1912), political and social change was effected in the course of a modernization campaign by the new government. Western-style painting (YŌGA) was promoted officially, and a number of painters such as HARADA NAOJIRŌ (1863–99), YAMAMOTO HŌSUI (1850–1906), and

ASAI CHŪ (1856–1907) traveled abroad for study under government auspices. However, the initial burst of enthusiasm for Western art soon yielded to renewed appreciation of traditional Japanese art, promoted by the art critic OKAKURA KAKUZŌ (1862–1913) and the American educator Ernest FENOLLOSA (1853–1908). Japanese-style painting (NIHONGA) rose to prominence as its conservative advocates gained control of art institutions. By the 1880s, Western-style painters were barred from exhibitions and widely criticized.

Actively supported by Okakura and Fenollosa, the painters KANŌ HŌGAI (1828–88) and HASHIMOTO GAHŌ (1835–1908) developed their work into a "new *nihonga*" much affected by European Pre-Raphaelite romanticism. The Kyōto-based Maruyama-Shijō school represented the only dominant *nihonga* group not altogether influenced by Okakura.

Confronted by the resurgence of traditionalism, Western-style painters formed the Meiji Bijutsukai (Meiji Fine Arts Society) and began to hold their own exhibitions. Prominent among these painters was KURODA SEIKI (also known as Kuroda Kiyoteru; 1866–1924), who introduced pleinairism and established the influential White Horse Society (HAKUBAKAI). Among Kuroda's many students who became major figures in Western-style painting were WADA EISAKU (1874–1959), OKADA SABURŌSUKE (1869–1939), SAKAMOTO HANJIRŌ (1882–1969), AOKI SHIGERU (1882–1911), and FUJISHIMA TAKEJI (1867–1943).

By 1907, with the institution of the BUNTEN (Mombushō Bijutsu Tenrankai; Ministry of Education Fine Arts Exhibition), *yōga* and *nihonga* artists began to appear in the same exhibitions and competitions. The first Bunten set a precedent for peaceful coexistence among these groups and even mutual stylistic influence.

Painting of the Taishō Period (1912–1926)—The Taishō period saw burgeoning Western influence in the arts. After long stays in Europe the painters Yamashita Shintarō (1881–1966), Saitō Yori (1885–1959), and Arishima Ikuma (1882–1974) introduced impressionism and early features of the post-impressionist movement to Japan; YASUI SŌTARŌ (1888–1955) and UMEHARA RYŪZABURŌ (1888–1986), whose careers would span the modern period, returned to promote the styles of Camille Pissarro, Paul Cézanne, and Pierre Auguste Renoir. The eclecticism that informed Taishō-period painting came as a direct result of the rapid infusion of the full

▼ Detail from *Chinese Lions*, a six-panel folding screen by Kanō Eitoku. Colors on a gold ground. Late 16th century. 225 × 460 cm. Imperial Household Agency.

▲ A courtesan is depicted in this example of *ukiyo-e* painting by Miyagawa Chōshun. 1752. Colors on silk. 88 × 37 cm. Tōkyō National Museum.

▶ *Scenes Sketched from a Boat Window*, one leaf of a six-leaf album by *bunjinga* artist Tanomura Chikuden, based on a boat trip the artist made in 1829. Shown are octopus vendors in a boat. Ink and colors on paper. 21 × 13 cm. Private collection.

▲ *Shinobazu Pond*, a Western-style painting by Odano Naotake. Late 18th century. Colors on silk. 99 × 133 cm. Akita Prefectural Museum.

range of contemporary European styles.

A manifestation of Taishō eclecticism was the proliferation of dissident painters' circles. The Fusain Society (Fyūzankai), formed in 1912 by KISHIDA RYŪSEI (1891–1929) and YOROZU TETSUGORŌ (1885–1927), emphasized styles derivative of postimpressionism, especially fauvism. In 1914 the Nika Society (Nikakai; Second Division Society), headed by Umehara and Yasui, emerged to oppose that year's Bunten. By 1915 Kishida had turned from postimpressionism to a severe realism, founding the Sōdosha (Grass and Earth Society) and promoting a style much influenced by Cézanne.

Although on a limited scale, Japanese-style painting too was affected by European styles, especially neoclassicism and, later, postimpressionism. Modernizing trends first appeared among second-generation *nihonga* members of the JAPAN FINE ARTS ACADEMY (Nihon Bijutsuin), which had been reorganized in 1914 to compete with the Bunten. Its founding members, YOKOYAMA TAIKAN (1868–1958), SHIMOMURA KANZAN (1873–1930), and HISHIDA SHUNSŌ (1874–1911), all to some degree adopted Western-style atmospheric treatment of space and light, for which they were called the Mōrōha ("Dim and Hazy school"). The second wave of academy painters, while emphasizing *yamato-e* traditions, embraced certain features of postimpressionism. Representative second-generation painters were KOBAYASHI KOKEI (1883–1957), MAEDA SEISON (1885–1977), IMAMURA SHIKŌ (1880–1916), YASUDA YUKIHIKO (1884–1978), TOMITA KEISEN (1879–1936), HAYAMI GYOSHŪ (1894–1935), and KAWABATA RYŪSHI (1885–1966).

Another forum for European influence in Japanese-style painting was the Kokuga Sōsaku Kyōkai (National Creative Painting Association) of 1918. Formed by students of TAKEUCHI SEIHŌ (1864–1942), the group adapted the Maruyama-Shijō tradition to the various formal styles of postimpressionism. Prominent members were TSUCHIDA BAKUSEN (1887–1936) and MURAKAMI KAGAKU (1888–1939).

Painting of the Shōwa Period (1926–1989)—The painters Yasui Sōtarō and Umehara Ryūzaburō stood at the forefront of pre–World War II Shōwa painting. In recognition of their importance, the period 1925–40 is termed the "Yasui-Umehara era." While incorporating notions of pure art and abstraction, both succeeded in surmounting the heretofore largely derivative character of Western-style painting in Japan. Umehara in particular brought aspects of the *nihonga* tradition to his work and launched Western-

style painting on a more interpretative path. However, neither artist completely dominated Western-style painting of the 1930s. A far more international contemporary of Yasui and Umehara was FUJITA TSUGUHARU (also known as Fujita Tsuguji, Léonard Foujita; 1886–1968). The Nika Society widened its sphere of influence by absorbing surrealism and abstractionism, and the essentially fauvist Dokuritsu Bijutsu Kyōkai (Independent Art Association) was formed in 1931.

Japanese-style painting of the 1930s continued to modernize under the leadership of Yasuda Yukihiko and Kobayashi Kokei, and the period is referred to as the "Yukihiko-Kokei era" of *nihonga.* Also, painters such as Kawabata Ryūshi, who established the Seiryūsha (Blue Dragon Society), sought to broaden the appeal of Japanese-style painting through popular subject matter and more frequent exhibitions.

The tide of war stopped all but nominal activity for most painters and painters' groups. After 1940 there was only one choice of subject matter: war. The many paintings chronicling the war, especially those of Fujita Tsuguharu and Yasuda Yukihiko, deserve closer scrutiny; a critical evaluation has yet to be made.

Prominent painters' circles formed during the late Taishō and early Shōwa periods, such as the Nika Society, weathered the war years to emerge as leading interests among painters today. The government-subsidized JAPAN ART ACADEMY (Nihon Geijutsuin) was formed in 1947 and contains both *yōga* and *nihonga* divisions. Government-sponsored art exhibitions like the Bunten have disappeared, replaced by privately sponsored exhibitions on a large scale. The Nitten (Nihon Bijutsu Tenrankai; Japan Art Exhibition) in

particular has functioned as the modern counterpart of the Bunten. Initially the exhibition of the Japan Art Academy, the Nitten since 1958 has been run by a corporation, Nitten, Inc. Exhibition of works in the Nitten can lead to membership in the Japan Art Academy and, for a few, decoration with the Order of Culture. Only a handful of non-Nitten artists have received this award, among them MUNAKATA SHIKŌ (1903–75).

Today Japanese artists are active members of a worldwide artistic community. By the 1960s, avant-garde notions of art had been embraced, and an internationalization of Japanese art followed. Indeed, a number of modern Japanese painters have worked almost exclusively abroad, among them ARAKAWA SHŪSAKU (b 1936), Okada Kenzō (1902–82), Sugai Kumi (b 1919), OGISU TAKANORI (1901–86), and Migishi Setsuko (b 1905). Postwar trends in the West have been taken up rapidly in Japan, from the abstract expressionism of the 1950s to later developments such as the antiart movement, assemblage, pop and op art, primary structure, minimal art, and kinetic art. After a largely derivative past, modern Japanese painters have emerged as significant contributors to international movements in art.

painting subjects　　画題

(*gadai*). Following Chinese precedent, the Japanese broadly classify painting subjects into figure painting (*jimbutsuga*), landscape painting (*sansuiga*), and BIRD-AND-FLOWER PAINTING (*kachōga*). Most orthodox Buddhist painting (*butsuga;* see BUDDHIST ART) can be classified as figure painting, as can YAMATO-E painting, including EMAKIMONO handscrolls and *koji jimbutsuga* dealing with themes from Chinese historical tradition. *Dōshakuga,* de-

Osorezan Lake Usoriyama fills the caldera of the volcano Osorezan. Small stones are piled here by parents who come to pray for the souls of children who died young. In the foreground, center, a small stone Buddhist image.

Ōsugi Sakae The stormy life of this Taishō-period anarchist and labor leader ended with a savage beating at the hands of military police in the aftermath of the Tōkyō Earthquake of 1923.

Ozawa Seiji Ozawa is Japan's first orchestra conductor to achieve wide recognition in Europe and the United States. In recent years, he has increasingly turned his talents to opera.

Ozu Yasujirō
1 Ozu, whose spare directing and editing techniques and low camera placement contributed to his reputation as a definitively "Japanese" filmmaker.
2 Sugawara Hideo (left) and Aoki Tomio in a scene from *Umarete wa mita keredo* (1932, I Was Born, but . . .), the first of Ozu's many films dealing with Japanese family life.

(1898–1964). Novelist. Born in Aichi Prefecture. Studied at Waseda University. Although some of his early works reflect an interest in the socialist movement, he became a nationalist during World War II. After the war he was banned from publishing between 1948 and 1950 during the OCCUPATION PURGE. His seven-volume novel JINSEI GEKIJŌ (1933–59) is a *Bildungsroman* set in the politically stormy decades preceding World War II. Other works include *Kagaribi* (1941, Beacon) and *Tennō kikan setsu* (1951, On the Emperor System).

(1858–1954). Pen name Gakudō. Liberal politician, elected 25 times to the House of Representatives. Born in Sagami Province (now part of Kanagawa Prefecture). He studied at Keiō Gijuku (now Keiō University) and Kōgakuryō, an engineering academy.

Ozaki assisted ŌKUMA SHIGENOBU in the formation of the political party RIKKEN KAISHINTŌ in 1882. Elected to the Diet in 1890, he vigorously supported Japan's imperialistic advances during the SINO-JAPANESE WAR OF 1894–1895, but domestically he advocated certain democratic principles. Ozaki helped establish the RIKKEN SEIYŪKAI in 1900.

While mayor of Tōkyō (1903–12), Ozaki sent 3,000 cherry-tree seedlings to Washington, DC. During the TAISHŌ POLITICAL CRISIS of 1912–13, he and INUKAI TSUYOSHI led the opposition against the government. He campaigned on behalf of the UNIVERSAL MANHOOD SUFFRAGE MOVEMENT until this right was granted in 1925; he even advocated WOMEN'S SUFFRAGE. During the 1930s he became increasingly isolated from party politics and criticized the growing influence of the military. Thus he was understandably hailed again as a political hero after World War II. The Ozaki Memorial Hall in Tōkyō commemorates his contributions to the development of constitutional government in Japan.

(1723–1801). WAKA poet and theorist of the late Edo period (1600–1868). Born in Owari (now part of Aichi Prefecture), he received his early training in the conservative Dōjō school of *waka*, which was aristocratic in nature and emphasized adherence to the poetics of the KOKINSHŪ. He later broke away and developed his own concept of poetry, *tadagoto uta* (poetry employing the diction of ordinary speech), which stressed the direct, simple expression of the poet's feelings in everyday language with a minimum of embellishment. His major works include the *waka* collection *Rokujō eisō* (1811) and an essay on poetics, *Furu no nakamichi* (1800).

(1935–). Conductor. Born in Shenyang, China; studied under the conductor SAITŌ HIDEO (1902–74) at the Tōhō Gakuen School of Music. In 1959 Ozawa won first prize in the International Competition of Orchestra Conductors at Besançon, France, and went on to serve as assistant conductor of the New York Philharmonic and music director of the Toronto Symphony Orchestra. Ozawa was conductor and music director of the San Francisco Symphony Orchestra from 1970 to 1976. He was named music director of the Boston Symphony Orchestra in 1973.

High moor, at junction of Gumma, Fukushima, and Niigata prefectures, central Honshū, part of Nikkō National Park. It includes Ozenuma, a lake, and Ozegahara, a marshy moor. Ozegahara (elevation: about 1,400 m [4,600 ft]; area: 8 sq km [3 sq mi]) is the largest high moor in Japan. Ozenuma, surrounded by several towering peaks, is famous for its natural scenery. Wildflowers and birds abound at Oze.

City in western Ehime Prefecture, Shikoku, on the river Hijikawa. Ōzu developed as a castle town in the Edo period (1600–1868). Principal activities are dairy and vegetable farming; raw silk is also produced. Attractions include the residence of NAKAE TŌJU, Ōzu Castle, and cormorant fishing (*ukai*). Pop: 39,850.

(Ōzuka *kofun*). A keyhole-shaped mounded tomb (KOFUN) in Keisen Machi, Fukuoka

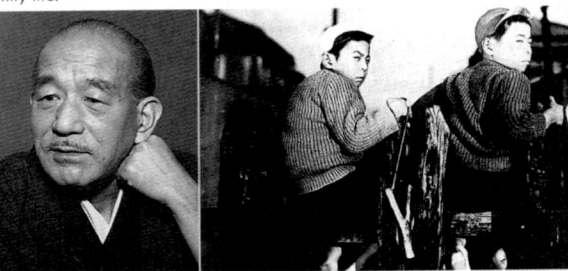

▲ In this *ukiyo-e* painting by Hokusai, *Five Beauties*, five women discuss material for a *kimono*. Edo period. Colors on silk. 41 × 80 cm. Private collection.

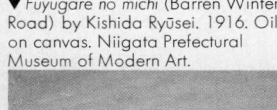

▼ *Fuyugare no michi* (Barren Winter Road) by Kishida Ryūsei. 1916. Oil on canvas. Niigata Prefectural Museum of Modern Art.

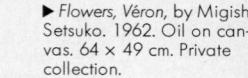

▶ *Flowers, Véron*, by Migishi Setsuko. 1962. Oil on canvas. 64 × 49 cm. Private collection.

◀ *Maiko* (Apprentice Geisha) by Kuroda Seiki. 1893. Oil on canvas. 81 × 65 cm. Tōkyō National Museum.

▼ Section of the *Seisei ruten* (Wheel of Life) scroll by Yokoyama Taikan. 1923. Ink on silk. 55 × 4,060 cm. National Museum of Modern Art, Tōkyō.

pictions of Taoist and Buddhist religious figures, are associated with the ZEN sect. FŪZOKU-GA (genre painting), fashionable stylizations of beautiful women (*bijinga*) and actors (*yakusha-e*) created by UKIYO-E designers, and PORTRAIT PAINTING are also in this category.

SANSUIGA refers to the philosophical ink landscapes (*suiboku sansuiga*) stimulated by Chinese art in the 15th century and to the Japanese literati landscapes (*nanga sansuiga*) initiated in the 18th century by awareness of the Chinese scholar-painting tradition (see BUNJINGA). *Kachōga* (bird-and-flower painting) and monochromes in the Chinese literati tradition were sketched from the 14th century, and polychrome scrolls appeared in the 15th century.

Pak Chŏng-hŭi   朴正熙

(1917–79; J: Boku Seiki). President of the Republic of Korea (ROK), 1963–79. Often spelled Park Chung-hee. Born in Sŏnsan, North Kyŏngsang Province, he graduated from Taegu Normal School in 1937 and from Japan's Manchurian Army Officers Academy and the Japanese ARMY ACADEMY (Rikugun Shikan Gakkō) in Tōkyō. Commissioned in 1944, he was stationed in Manchuria until the end of World War II. He joined the army in South Korea in 1946 and rose rapidly through the officers' ranks during the Korean War.

Pak joined the military junta that seized control of the government on 16 May 1961. By August 1961 he was chairman of the Supreme Council for National Reconstruction (the junta's official name); he was elected president in October 1963. Reelected in May 1967 and April 1971, he proclaimed himself president for life in November 1972. An authoritarian ruler, Pak treated political opponents harshly, intensifying resistance to his

rule. However, normalization of relations with Japan in 1965 and close cooperation with the US military intervention in Vietnam brought economic assistance that helped to set the stage for rapid industrialization and the establishment of a burgeoning export trade. Pak was assassinated by the director of the Korean Central Intelligence Agency in November 1979.

Pakistan and Japan   パキスタンと日本

(Pakisutan *to* Nihon). During World War II, Pakistan, then a part of India and a member of the British Commonwealth, fought against Japan. Pakistan gained its independence in 1947 and subsequently signed a peace treaty with Japan in 1951 and a treaty of commerce and friendship in 1960. The bilateral economic relationship expanded considerably during the 1980s. Bilateral trade in 1990 totaled US $1.5 billion, with Japan exporting US $1.0 billion to Pakistan and importing US $536.7 million. The sizable trade imbalance was the result of the structure of trade: Japanese exports consisted of machinery and vehicles, while its imports were mainly cotton and textile products. After the Soviet invasion of Afghanistan in 1979, Japanese official development assistance (ODA) to Pakistan increased dramatically, reaching a peak of US $302.2 million in 1988. In 1990 aid to Pakistan totaled US $193.6 million, the eighth largest sum among recipients of Japanese aid and 2.8 percent of Japan's total foreign aid disbursements. Japanese direct investments in Pakistan have been limited and today remain negligible compared to investments by British and US companies. A growing number of Pakistanis have come to Japan to work, some illegally, particularly since the late 1980s.

Pak Yŏl   朴烈

(1902–74; J: Boku Retsu). Also named Pak Chun-sik (J: Boku Junshoku). Korean anarchist convicted of plotting to assassinate Emperor Taishō and Crown Prince Hirohito in 1923. Convicted on circumstantial evidence and a confession obtained under intensive interrogation, Pak and his wife Kaneko received a death sentence, commuted to life imprisonment. Pak was released after World War II and returned to Korea in 1948.

Pak Yŏng-hyo   朴泳孝

(1861–1939; J: Boku Eikō). Prominent Korean government official; leading advocate of Korean Westernization; journalist. As a young man Pak joined the KAEHWAP'A (Enlightenment Faction), a political clique that sought Westernization and autonomy from Chinese influence for Korea, and was a leader in the unsuccessful KAPSIN POLITICAL COUP of 1884, after which he fled Korea for Japan and the United States. After the KABO REFORM of 1894, instituted in Korea at Japan's insistence, he returned to Korea and served as minister of home affairs until July 1895, when he was driven out of the country during a crackdown on pro-Japanese leaders. Once again he fled to Japan. In 1907, having returned to Korea, Pak was appointed minister of palace affairs, but was arrested and exiled, this time for opposing the Japanese-enforced abdication of King KOJONG. Despite this, in 1910 he was made a member of the peerage created by Japan for Koreans following the Japanese annexation of Korea. In 1920, Pak became the founding editor of the newspaper *Tong'a ilbo*, famous for its criti-

Major Paleolithic Sites

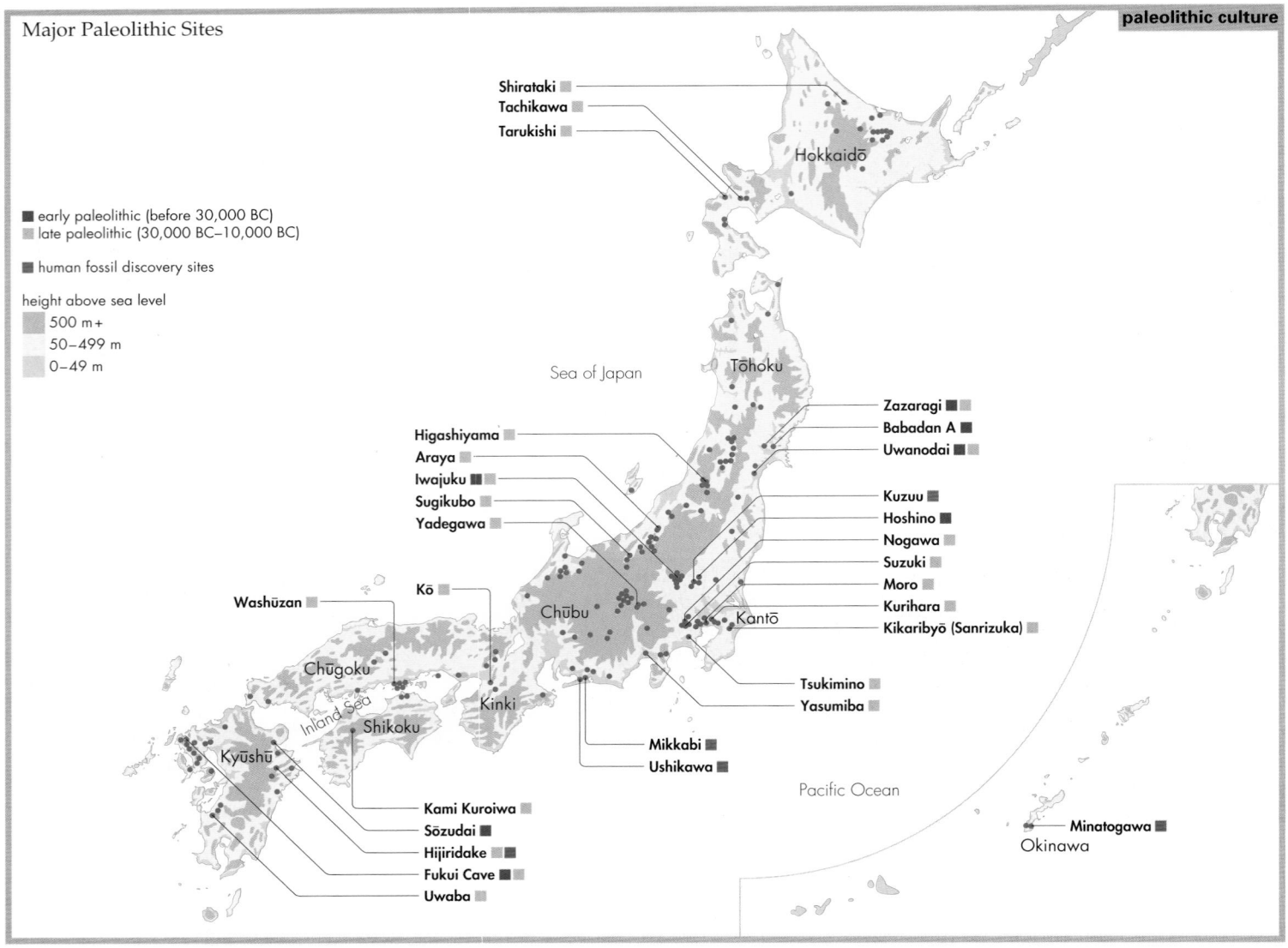

■ early paleolithic (before 30,000 BC)
■ late paleolithic (30,000 BC–10,000 BC)

■ human fossil discovery sites

height above sea level
█ 500 m+
░ 50–499 m
░ 0–49 m

Shirataki ■
Tachikawa ■
Tarukishi ■

Hokkaidō

Sea of Japan

Tōhoku

Zazaragi ■ ■
Babadan A ■ ■
Uwanodai ■ ■

Higashiyama ■
Araya ■
Iwajuku ■ ■
Sugikubo ■
Yadegawa ■

Kuzuu ■
Hoshino ■
Nogawa ■
Suzuki ■
Moro ■
Kurihara ■
Kikaribyō (Sanrizuka) ■

Washūzan ■

Kō ■

Chūbu

Kantō

Chūgoku

Inland Sea

Kinki

Shikoku

Tsukimino ■
Yasumiba ■

Mikkabi ■
Ushikawa ■

Pacific Ocean

Kyūshū

Kami Kuroiwa ■
Sōzudai ■
Hijiridake ■ ■
Fukui Cave ■ ■
Uwaba ■

Minatogawa ■
Okinawa

---

cism of the Japanese colonial administration of Korea.

paleolithic culture   旧石器文化

(*kyūsekki bunka*). The material culture of the paleolithic period (pre-10,000 BC), consisting mainly of STONE TOOLS. Other artifacts—BONE ARTICLES and bamboo or wooden objects— and remains of plant and animal food of this period are rarely recovered by archaeologists because of destruction by the high acidity of Japanese volcanic soils. Traces of hearths, dwellings, and skeletal remains, however, are sometimes discovered at paleolithic open-air or cave sites.

The stone tools of the early paleolithic period (more than 30,000 years ago) are of two kinds: hand axes or choppers and flakes of stone whose sharp edges were used without being shaped into regular, recognizable forms. Between 30,000 and 25,000 years ago, two important technological innovations in stone-tool manufacture occurred: the grinding of stone axes to produce more durable working edges, and a technique of chipping stones in a methodical manner to produce large numbers of slender, regularly shaped blades. More than 90 percent of paleolithic-period sites in Japan date from between 30,000 and 12,000 years ago, when new stoneworking techniques included a method of making leaf-shaped spearpoints. Pottery making began 12,500 years ago (see JŌMON POTTERY). The people of the paleolithic period

(see JAPANESE PEOPLE, ORIGIN OF) probably were ancestors of the Jōmon people because some of their cultural traditions continued into the earliest phase of the Jōmon period. See also FUKUI CAVE; HOSHINO SITE; IWAJUKU SITE; NOGAWA SITE.

paleolithic period   旧石器時代

(*kyūsekki jidai*). In Japan the paleolithic period is also sometimes referred to as the "preceramic" (*sendoki*) period; it includes all of the cultures that existed in Japan before 10,000 BC. Since Japan was connected to the Asian mainland for much of this period, Japanese paleolithic cultures are similar to contemporaneous cultures known in other parts of East Asia. Paleolithic artifacts were first discovered in Japan in 1946, and since then more than 4,500 sites dating from the Pleistocene epoch, or Ice Age, have been located throughout the country. Most paleolithic sites are small and preserve only stone tools, so relatively little is known about the lifestyles of this period.

"Early paleolithic" is the name given to a small number of stone tool assemblages that date from before 30,000 BC. These assemblages have been controversial because the crudity of the stone choppers and other coarse tools raises doubts about whether their origins are human. Support for the use of the term early paleolithic has strengthened in recent years, however, and a great many archaeologists agree that paleolithic cultures of the type known from Zhoukoudian (Chou-k'ou-tien) and other sites in

China and East Asia were carried over to Japan.

Between 30,000 and 10,000 BC Japan was occupied by cultures that are designated as "late paleolithic." About 90 percent of the known paleolithic sites date from this period. Late paleolithic sites have been found from Hokkaidō to southern Kyūshū. Paleolithic peoples probably occupied the wide expanses of coastal shelves exposed by lowered sea levels during the terminal Pleistocene. However, modern sea levels have inundated these areas, limiting our knowledge to the small sites surviving in the present coastal, plain, and hilly upland zones. Late paleolithic tool kits included finely made blade tools that are generally similar to tools made by known paleolithic groups from Siberia and the rest of Eurasia. Ground stone axes also appeared in Japan at this time.

palmistry   手相

(*tesō*). Palmistry as traditionally practiced in Japan is similar in principle, though not in detail, to that of Europe. It is said to have come to Japan from China, where it had appeared by the start of the Christian era. A Chinese book on palmistry, *Shenxiang quanbian* (*Shen-hsiang chüan-pien;* ca 1400), had great influence in Japan, and by the Edo period (1600–1868), professional palmists, many of them unemployed *samurai*, had begun to appear. Palmists can still be seen in busy urban districts; they usually combine palmistry with *Yi jing* (*I ching;* J: *Ekikyō*) divination. See also PHYSIOGNOMY.

pan-Asianism 汎アジア主義

(*han Ajia shugi*). A concept that stresses the alleged uniqueness of Asia vis-à-vis the rest of the world, and particularly contrasts Asia with the West. The concept has played an important role in modern Japanese history. Arguing that it was foolish or even dangerous to pretend that close identification with Western nations would solve national problems, pan-Asianists held that the Japanese should learn to identify with Asians and pay more attention to their collective future. There were, however, variations on these ideas.

TARUI TŌKICHI (1850–1922), an early exponent of Asian unity, was primarily interested in political and economic union with China, whereas OKAKURA KAKUZŌ (1862–1913), Japan's first pan-Asian ideologue, emphasized the distinctive essences of East and West in his writings, published at the turn of the 20th century, which promulgated the doctrine that "Asia is one." During the next few decades pan-Asianism became bound up with a policy debate on China. Pan-Asianism appealed to those, like SUN YAT-SEN and his Japanese supporter MIYAZAKI TŌTEN, who were convinced that the two nations' salvation lay in close political, economic, and cultural cooperation. Paradoxically, pan-Asianism also provided the ideological justification for Japanese military expansionism in the 1930s, when Japan was ostracized by Western nations for its aggressive acts in China. Writers came to call the Chinese war, and ultimately the war against the United States and Britain, cultural warfare, a struggle of East against West, which would reawaken Asia to its true destiny. Although the war was a national disaster, some of these ideas survived and even today seem to affect Japanese thinking.

Panay Incident パネー号事件

(*Panē gō Jiken*). Diplomatic incident surrounding the 12 December 1937 attack by Japanese naval planes on the American gunboat *Panay* and other American craft on the Yangzi (Yangtze) River near Nanjing (Nanking), China. The attack took place five months into the SINO-JAPANESE WAR OF 1937–1945. The Japanese planes sank the *Panay* and damaged the other vessels, all of which were flying the American flag, during a bombing raid on Nanjing. The Japanese government paid an indemnity of more than $2 million in March 1938. See also LADYBIRD INCIDENT.

Pan no Kai パンの会

(The Pan Society). Group of writers and artists organized in late 1908 and continuing until 1911 or 1912; named for the Greek god of woods, fields, and shepherds. In contrast to the then-dominant naturalists (see NATURALISM), the members of the society subscribed to various forms of aestheticism, romanticism, and idealism, scorning the bare, factual, quasi-scientific manner of the naturalists as inartistic.

The founding members included KINOSHITA MOKUTARŌ, Nagata Hideo (1885–1949), and KITAHARA HAKUSHŪ, all members of the group associated with the literary magazine *Okujō teien*, as well as the Western-style painters Ishii Hakutei (1882–1958), Yamamoto Kanae (1882–1946), and Morita Tsunetomo (1881–1933), who were connected with the magazine *Hōsun.* Later, YOSHII ISAMU, TAKAMURA KŌTARŌ, and other members of the SUBARU group joined, as did

the young TANIZAKI JUN'ICHIRŌ. NAGAI KAFŪ and other members of the MITA BUNGAKU group associated with Keio University also entered the society. The group as a whole regarded the Kyōto University literary scholar and author UEDA BIN as its mentor. The Pan no Kai included, then, most of the promising young writers in Tōkyō at that time, numbering over 40 regular members at its height. For the brief period of its existence, it became one of the major forces in the literary and artistic life of Japan.

paperback books 文庫本・新書

(*bunkobon; shinsho*). Most Japanese paperbacks fall into two standardized formats. *Bunkobon* ("bunko books," *bunko* meaning "library" in the sense of a publisher's series) are 10.5 by 14.8 centimeters (4.1 by 5.8 in) in size and typically present Japanese literature or foreign literature in Japanese translation. *Shinsho* (literally, "new books") are 10.6 by 17.3 centimeters (4.1 by 6.8 in) and emphasize nonfiction, including history, biography, social issues, and current affairs, and popular introductions to technical subjects.

The series TACHIKAWA BUNKO pioneered the *bunkobon* beginning in 1911, but perhaps the most famous venture employing this format was the Iwanami Bunko of IWANAMI SHOTEN, PUBLISHERS, modeled on the German publisher Reclam's Universal-Bibliothek, which began publication in 1927 and continues to the present. The first *shinsho* series was the Iwanami Shinsho, which commenced in 1938 and was modeled on the English series Penguin Books. Since the late 1950s paperback books have come to occupy an essential place in Japanese publishing, with sales exceeding 125 million *bunkobon* and 55 million *shinsho* annually.

paper balloons 紙風船

(*kami fūsen*). A toy made from thin colored paper cut into the shape of flower petals and pasted together to form a balloon; also called *kami temari* (paper handball). *Kami fūsen* first appeared in the 1890s. They are enjoyed for the sound they make when bounced on the hand. Paper balloons with bells inside appeared later.

paper, handmade → washi

parcel delivery service 宅配便

(*takuhaibin*). Door-to-door transportation of small packages by truck—primarily for individual consumers—has become a very popular service industry in Japan. In fiscal year 1989, about 1.03 billion packages were handled by such truck parcel delivery services.

Packages are picked up at the individual's home upon a request by telephone, or they can be left at a designated pickup point, typically a rice shop or a convenience store in the customer's neighborhood. This kind of parcel service was introduced to Japan in 1974. After the YAMATO TRANSPORT CO, LTD, entered the field in 1976, using the trade name Takkyūbin, parcel delivery services grew rapidly. Large terminals in major Japanese cities are equipped with automatic machines to facilitate sorting. There is radio communication with the trucks, and the number of days required for delivery (usually one or two) is stated clearly. The fee schedule is simple, being determined by the number of packages, the distance involved, and the weight of the packages.

The convenience of door-to-door parcel delivery has not only convinced people to

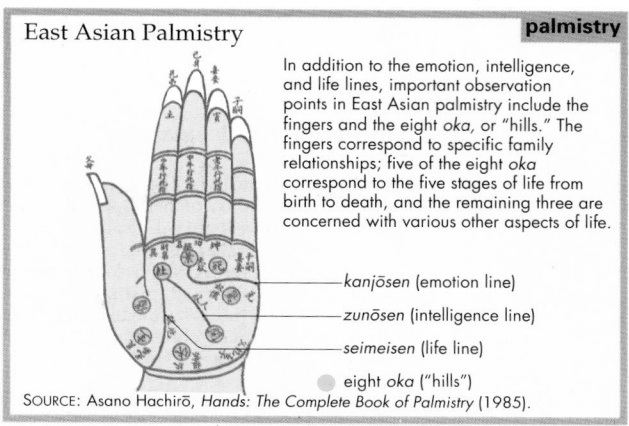

East Asian Palmistry   **palmistry**

In addition to the emotion, intelligence, and life lines, important observation points in East Asian palmistry include the fingers and the eight *oka*, or "hills." The fingers correspond to specific family relationships; five of the eight *oka* correspond to the five stages of life from birth to death, and the remaining three are concerned with various other aspects of life.

—— *kanjōsen* (emotion line)

—— *zunōsen* (intelligence line)

—— *seimeisen* (life line)

● eight *oka* ("hills")

SOURCE: Asano Hachirō, *Hands: The Complete Book of Palmistry* (1985).

shift their patronage from parcel post and the parcel service of the JR rail lines to parcel delivery by truck, it has also helped to create an increased demand for the transport of small packages. Consumers' rights in this field are enforced by the Ministry of Transport.

pardon 恩赦

(*onsha*). Absolution of crimes or nullification or reduction of criminal convictions or sentences (or their legal effects) by the executive branch of the government. In Japan a pardon frequently has been granted as an act of imperial mercy since ancient times. The constitution of 1947 grants the cabinet pardoning power, subject to attestation by the emperor (arts. 7[vi], 73[vii]). A pardon may be granted to mark the celebration of national events, to correct wrong convictions, or to rehabilitate offenders.

While pardons of all persons who have committed certain categories of crimes (*taisha*) have been declining, commutation of punishment (*genkei*) and restoration of rights to individuals (*fukken*) have been increasingly employed to promote the rehabilitation of convicted offenders. In 1989, on the occasion of the death of Emperor SHŌWA (Hirohito), *taisha* and *fukken* were granted to certain categories of offenders; special pardons (*tokusha*) and *fukken* were also granted at the time of Emperor AKIHITO's enthronement in November 1990. See also CABINET ORDER; CRIMINAL LAW.

parental power 親権

(*shinken*). Legal term referring to the rights and duties of a parent held for the benefit of a minor child prescribed in the CIVIL CODE (arts. 818–837). In the past, parental power derived from the absolute authority of the head of the household and resided with the father. Under the present Civil Code, father and mother are accorded equal status. If the parents are married, they jointly exercise parental power. If the parents are divorced or if the child is illegitimate, parental power will be vested in one of the parents. The family court, if it deems it necessary for the benefit of the child, may transfer parental power from one parent to the other on the application of any relative of the child.

The functions of a person exercising parental power fall into two general categories: those powers related to the custody and education of the child and those related to the management of the child's property. If a person abuses parental power or is guilty of gross misconduct, the family court may, on the application of any of the child's relatives or the public prosecutor, declare a forfeiture of such person's authority. If there is no one to exercise parental power over a minor, a guardianship commences (art. 838). See also KŌKENNIN.

paperback books
A *bunkobon* paperback in the Kōdansha Bungei Bunko (Kōdansha Literary Library) with a Penguin paperback behind it for comparison.

parent and child, legal definition of 親子(法律上の)

(*oyako, hōritsujō no*). In the existing Civil Code only two kinds of legal parent-child relationships are recognized: *jisshinshi* (natural parent–child relationships) and *yōshinshi* (adoptive parent–child relationships). Natural parent–child relationships are now divided into (1) the relationship between parents and legitimate children, and (2) the relationship between parents and illegitimate children.

In cases of illegitimacy, there is a difference between father-child relationships and mother-child relationships. The father-child relationship is based on registration of the child's acknowledgment by the father or on a paternity decision ordered by a court as claimed by the child or by the child's legal representatives (usually the mother) on the child's behalf. The mother-child relationship is based on the fact of childbirth, acknowledgment not being necessary. In the case of a parent–illegitimate child relationship, the full effects of a parent-child relationship are in force, although the illegitimate child's share of intestate succession is only one-half of the legitimate child's.

An adoptive parent–child relationship is based on the registration of an ADOPTION by both the adoptive parents and the adoptive child; it has the same effect as a parent–legitimate child relationship. There are two types of adoption, general and special. Under general adoption the adopted person maintains a legal relationship with his or her natural parents, and there is no age restriction so even an adult can be adopted. In contrast, under the SPECIAL ADOPTION SYSTEM only children up to age six can be adopted, and all legal ties with the natural parents are severed.

parenticide 尊属殺人

(*sonzoku satsujin*). In Japanese feudal law it was a general principle that the status relationship between perpetrator and victim determined the punishment for various criminal acts. Thus especially severe punishments were provided for the killing of one's lord or of one's parents, considered respectively as transgressions against the virtues of LOYALTY and FILIAL PIETY. The first modern Criminal Code of 1880 prescribed only the death penalty for the killing of ascendants. The Criminal Code of 1907 also provided for a more severe punishment for the killing of one's ascendants or of those of one's spouse than for other homicides. In a 1950 case the constitutional question arose as to whether the provision of the Criminal Code regarding parenticide violated the equality clause of the 1947 constitution. According to the majority decison in that case, the equality clause did not prevent individual laws from establishing different standards of treatment for criminals. In a 1973 decision in a similar case, the Supreme Court found that aggravation of punishment for killing ascendants was not necessarily a constitutional violation in itself but was unconstitutional when it was unreasonably extreme.

Parkes, Sir Harry Smith
パークス, H. S.

(1828–85). British minister plenipotentiary to Japan from 1865 to 1883. Parkes was the second person to hold the post after the signing of the ANSEI COMMERCIAL TREATIES of 1858, which opened Japan to trade with the West. Born in the English Midlands, he was orphaned at an early age and went to live in Macao with a cousin's family. At 14 he began to study Chinese. After diplomatic service in China as an interpreter and consul, he was knighted in 1862 and afterwards appointed British minister to Japan.

The British government's main concerns were the expansion of trade to the limits of the Ansei treaties, the protection of British nationals, and a united front among the Western powers in Japan. By the close of 1865, Parkes had secured the assent of the imperial court to the treaties of 1858, which until then had received only shogunal approval. With the Tariff Convention of 1866 (see KAIZEI YAKUSHO), he also achieved reforms for trade and foreign shipping.

In Japan's domestic politics he maintained a consistent neutrality, urging all parties to work out some form of government that would give the emperor, the shōgun, and the *daimyō* a fair share of power. The overthrow of the Tokugawa shogunate in January 1868 came as a surprise to the British, and, during the ensuing BOSHIN CIVIL WAR, Parkes ordered all British subjects to remain neutral in the civil conflict. On 22 May 1868 Parkes presented his credentials to the emperor, becoming the first representative of any foreign power to recognize the new imperial government.

Parkes assisted the Japanese in obtaining British officers to train the Japanese navy and in having British engineers build lighthouses, the telegraph, and the first railway between Tōkyō and Yokohama. He was recognized as a true friend of the Japanese people and was honored by the emperor. In 1883 he left Japan to become minister plenipotentiary to China, where he died.

particle accelerator → TRISTAN

partnership 組合

(*kumiai*). Important form of contractual relationship constituted under the CIVIL CODE. Several incorporated variants exist under the COMMERCIAL CODE. In legal terminology the term *kumiai* refers exclusively to an association established under the law by several persons to carry out common purposes, of a business or nonbusiness nature. The members are, in principle, entitled both to an equal vote in the association's policy decisions and, in proportion to the amount of their investment in the association, to receive any profit accruing from the association's activities. They are also responsible jointly and without limit for every outcome of the association's activities. A typical example is the *gomei kaisha* (UNLIMITED PARTNERSHIP COMPANY).

The term *kumiai* in layperson's usage simply means a partnership, group, union, or association of people banded together for a common purpose and refers to a wide variety of organizations such as *rōdō kumiai* (labor unions), *shin'yō kumiai* (credit unions), *shōhi seikatsu kyōdō kumiai* (consumers' cooperative associations), or *nōgyō kyōdō kumiai* (agricultural cooperative associations).

passports 旅券

(*ryoken*). Japanese passports are of three types: diplomatic, official, and ordinary. Ordinary passports are valid for a five-year period and allow the bearer to leave and re-enter the country an unlimited number of times. The number of passports issued annually increased markedly in the 1970s and 1980s. It was about 4.2 million in 1989.

Patent Law 特許法

(Tokkyo Hō). A 1959 law that is designed to protect as inventions those highly advanced creations or technical ideas that utilize the laws of nature. Along with the UTILITY-MODEL LAW, which protects devices that are not as advanced as inventions, the DESIGN LAW, and the TRADEMARK LAW, the Patent Law is called an INDUSTRIAL PROPERTY law. Japan's first patent law was enacted in 1871 but was suspended the following year because of difficulties in application. A second patent law, enacted in 1885, has been superseded many times, the latest being the Patent Law of 1959.

Patent rights accrue to a person (or his or her successors) who has made a novel invention capable of industrial use and who makes a patent application. Patent rights are property rights by which one has exclusive control of an invention for a fixed period of time. Inventions include both products and processes. Patents of products grant exclusive rights to produce, use, sell, and import the product, while patents of processes grant the exclusive right to use that process as well as to use, sell, and import the product manufactured by that process. Patentees may assign the patent or grant licenses of the patent. If another party engages in behavior covered by the patent without either the consent of the patentee or statutory authorization, the patentee can seek protection against and a cessation of the injurious behavior. The patentee can also seek compensation for damages or, in the case of intentional violations, criminal liability.

A patent right is established by registration with the Patent Office, an external bureau of the Ministry of International Trade and Industry. It continues for 15 years from the day of the publication of the application (and in no case longer than 20 years from the date of application). In Japan one must pay gradually increasing patent fees every year. If these payments are neglected, the patent right is terminated. Japanese courts are not permitted to determine the validity of a patent in civil proceedings, such as patent infringement cases. Only the Patent Office can conduct a trial for the invalidation of a patent.

paternalism 温情主義

(*onjō shugi*). An unequal relationship between two people or between one person and a relatively small group, in which the superordinate person patterns his behavior on or invokes the authority of the father. The Japanese have a number of terms to denote paternalistic relationships; the most common of these is OYABUN-KOBUN (literally, "parent role-child role").

Feudal societies throughout the world were characterized by such relationships, and it is widely assumed that paternalism remains prevalent in Japan because of its comparatively recent emergence from feudalism. The degree to which paternalism persists in Japan is, however, a matter of dispute. Some analysts discern feudalistic paternalism persisting in the hierarchical organization of GROUPS, in the cliques (BATSU) of the political world, in the application of the concept of household (IE) to various social organizations, and in the benefits extended to employees under the company welfare system. They argue that the Japanese people have a cultural predisposition to hierarchical organization and authority, a perspective summed up in the term VERTICAL SOCIETY. Other analysts cite nonhierarchical traditions in Japan (see, for example, KUMI) and trends in modern society toward egalitarian relationships, contractual rights, and individualism as evidence of movement away from paternalism.

PATOLIS → JAPIO

Patriotic Women's Association
→ Aikoku Fujinkai

patriotism   愛国心

(*aikokushin*). Prior to the rise of Meiji-period Japan (1868–1912) as a modern nation-state, there was no proper mental or emotional setting for patriotism to grow among the Japanese. The Japanese word *kuni* ("country") in phrases corresponding to "my beloved country" or "from the same country" referred to the speaker's domain (*han*) or home province within Japan, where the members of the province's upper class demanded *chūgi* (loyalty) of those in the lower. In order to establish a centralized political structure the leaders of the new government after the Meiji Restoration, skillfully making use of public education, transmuted the sense of feudalistic loyalty that had long been nurtured among the Japanese into the notion of loyalty to the emperor and the nation as a whole. Such ideas as "nation as family" and "society as organic entity" came into use, and the Japanese were required in the name of patriotism to submit unconditionally to the emperor, the nation, and the powers that be.

patterns, traditional decorative
文様

(*mon'yō*). The most widely used decorative patterns in prehistoric Japan were geometric, as can be seen in pottery from the Jōmon (ca 10,000 BC–ca 300 BC) and Yayoi (ca 300 BC–ca AD 300) periods. The DŌTAKU (bronze bells) produced during the Yayoi period also display geometric patterns using motifs known as *kesadasuki* ("square block") and *ryūsui* ("flowing water").

Along with the introduction of Buddhism and continental Asian culture to Japan during the Asuka (593–710) and Nara (710–794) periods came a variety of patterns of Chinese, Korean, and Indian origin. *Nindō* (palmette motif) and *hōsōge* (peonylike floral motif) patterns decorated Buddhist images, architecture, and handicrafts. *Nindō* patterns are found on many of the objects stored at the HŌRYŪJI GREAT TREASURE HOUSE, and floral patterns predominate on objects in the SHŌSŌIN art repository.

In the Heian period (794–1185) Japan stopped sending embassies to China and the culture borrowed up until then was gradually assimilated. New Japanese-style patterns that made use of delicate motifs incorporating shapes from nature became popular. The bronze mirrors of this period are elegantly ornamented in relief with flower, bird, and flowing-water motifs. The *katawaguruma* motif, which depicts the ancient practice of soaking wooden cartwheels in a river to prevent them from drying out and cracking, was a favorite pattern for gold-inlaid *maki-e* lacquer ware. *Ashide-e* painting (see ASHIDE) combined the depiction of flowers, reeds, and other subjects from nature with calligraphy.

As the culture of Zen Buddhism flourished in the Kamakura (1185–1333) and Muromachi (1333–1568) periods, nature

came to be viewed as a spiritual realm, and artists turned increasingly to nature for decorative and ornamental themes. Among the most popular were the chrysanthemum, sandbar-with-plovers, and scattered-fan motifs.

During the Azuchi-Momoyama period (1568–1600) trade with Spain and Portugal brought exotic items from the West, and the *namban karakusa* (arabesque or foliage-scroll) motif entered the design vocabulary. Western influences led to the making of the highly ornamental KŌDAIJI MAKI-E lacquer, known for its decoration with representations of autumnal flowers and grasses.

With the flourishing of urban culture during the Edo period (1600–1868), motifs broke away from traditional themes of nature and began to reflect the city dweller's sense of style. The continuous patterns that were developed during this time decorated such everyday objects as fans, umbrellas, *sake* decanters and cups, and even farm tools. Fabric patterns favored by commoners of the Edo period are distinguished by their use of stripes and KASURI (dyed-in-the-yarn) designs. The stripes, crosses, and checkered patterns inherent to fabric woven on the loom were developed into infinite varieties of patterns. The rich tradition of patterns and decorative motifs has exerted a deep and lasting influence on many aspects of contemporary Japanese design.
☎ 1190–1191

Pauley, Edwin Wendell
ポーレー, E. W.

(1903–81). US oil corporation executive and World War II reparations expert. He headed the US reparations mission to Japan (the Pauley mission), which in November 1946 recommended removal of all equipment from Japanese war industries and drastic reduction of capacity in defense-related industries. These recommendations, however, were never carried out. Born in Indianapolis, Indiana, and educated at the University of California, he spent most of his career in the oil business, serving as a wartime petroleum expert.

paulownia   桐

(*kiri*). *Paulownia tomentosa.* Also called princess tree. Deciduous tree of the family Scrophulariaceae widely planted in various parts of Japan but not found growing in the wild. The trunk grows as high as 10 meters (33 ft). The opposite, hairy leaves (20–30 cm; 8–12 in) are broadly ovate with pointed tips. In early summer numerous purple flowers develop. The large oval fruits are used for flower arrangements. The original habitat of the paulownia is not known, but it seems to have been introduced to Japan from China or Korea in very early times. Paulownia wood is very light, fine-grained, soft, and warp-resistant and is used for chests, boxes, and clogs (*geta*). The wood is burned to make charcoal for sketching and powder for fireworks, the bark is made into a dye, and the leaves are used in vermicide preparations.

Peace for Vietnam Committee
ベ平連

(Beheiren; full name Betonamu ni Heiwa o Shimin Rengō, or "People's Organization for Peace in Vietnam"). An anti-Vietnam War organization founded in Japan in 1965 when American forces started bombing North Vietnam. Novelists ODA MAKOTO and KAIKŌ KEN and social scientist Tsurumi Shunsuke (b

1922) were among its organizers. The members held teach-ins and encouraged and supported US army deserters. They publicized their cause in various ways, at one time placing a full-page advertisement in the *New York Times.* Among their publications was the weekly magazine *Shūkan ampo.* The organization disbanded in January 1974, the first anniversary of the Paris Peace Treaty.

peace movement   平和運動

(*heiwa undō*). Antiwar citizens' movement active since the end of World War II. (For the prewar movement, see PACIFISM.) Advocating nonviolence and nonalignment, it has sought to maintain peace in Japan, abolish nuclear weapons worldwide, and support article 9 of the 1947 Japanese constitution, which calls for the RENUNCIATION OF WAR by Japan.

Led mainly by leftist political parties, labor unions, peace and international friendship organizations, student organizations, and citizens' groups, peace movement activities have been numerous and varied, but three stand out because of their scale and duration: the anti-nuclear-bomb movement, the movement opposing the United States–Japan Security Treaty, and the movement opposing the Vietnam War and calling for the return of Okinawa.

The Anti-Nuclear-Bomb Movement—
The movement to ban nuclear bombs, initiated shortly after World War II, received tremendous impetus from the LUCKY DRAGON INCIDENT of March 1954, in which the crew of a Japanese fishing boat was showered with fallout from a nuclear bomb test. In 1955 the Japan Council against Atomic and Hydrogen Bombs (Gensuibaku Kinshi Nihon Kyōgikai; also called Gensuikyō) was organized. Its world conferences grew in size every year, including at one time representatives from 30 nations.

In 1961 a rival organization, the National Council for Peace and against Nuclear Weapons (Kakuheiki Kinshi Heiwa Kensetsu Kokumin Kaigi; also called Kakkin Kaigi or Kakkin), was formed by members of the LIBERAL DEMOCRATIC PARTY (LDP), the DEMOCRATIC SOCIALIST PARTY, and the Japanese Confederation of Labor (Zen Nihon Rōdō Sōdōmei). The Gensuikyō split into two camps in 1965 when its JAPAN SOCIALIST PARTY members broke away to form the Japan Conference against Atomic and Hydrogen Bombs (Gensuibaku Kinshi Nihon Kokumin Kaigi; also called Gensuikin). Divided into three organizations, the movement lost its original vigor and broad social base. See also ATOMIC WEAPONS, MOVEMENT TO BAN.

Anti-Security-Treaty Movement—
The United States–Japan Security Treaty, signed together with the SAN FRANCISCO PEACE

Continued on page 1192 ►

paulownia As a fast-growing source of high-quality wood for furniture, this tree was traditionally planted at the birth of a daughter to be later used for her wedding trousseau chest. At top, early summer blooms.

Classic Design Motifs

Traditional Japanese patterns are recognized throughout the world for their simplicity, elegance, and economy of design. Plants, animals, man-made objects, natural and celestial phenomena, and geometric patterns have all been employed as motifs, and the names of specific patterns—often acquired after the design has been in existence for some time—can have deep significance. Names symbolizing luck and happiness are particularly popular. An example is the geometric pattern known as *matsukawabishi*, or "pine-bark diamonds": the pine's associations with joy and fortune make this a recurring motif on wedding *kimono* and other items of a celebratory nature. The *kikkō* pattern—interlocking hexagons depicting tortoise shells—has equally auspicious associations.

Given the importance of design to the Japanese aesthetic, even everyday objects can be as lavishly adorned as those that are meant purely for decoration. The way patterns are used in Japanese arts and crafts—as revealed in the textile samples displayed here—shows a sensitive eye for detail, a genius for presentation, and a lively appreciation of nature.

Plants

1 A *shidarezakura*, or weeping cherry. The cherry blossom is Japan's national flower. **2** Pine trees—signs of good fortune. **3** Bamboo symbolizes vitality. **4** Plum branches and blossoms. *Shōchikubai*—a traditional fusion of pine, bamboo, and plum blossoms—represents happiness. **5** *Kiku* (chrysanthemums) are a symbol of elegance and refinement. **6** The *hyōtan* (gourd) is a favorite image because its plentiful seeds suggest abundant offspring. **7** The *kakitsubata* (rabbit-ear iris), combined here with a geometric pattern representing woven bamboo baskets, heralds the coming of summer.

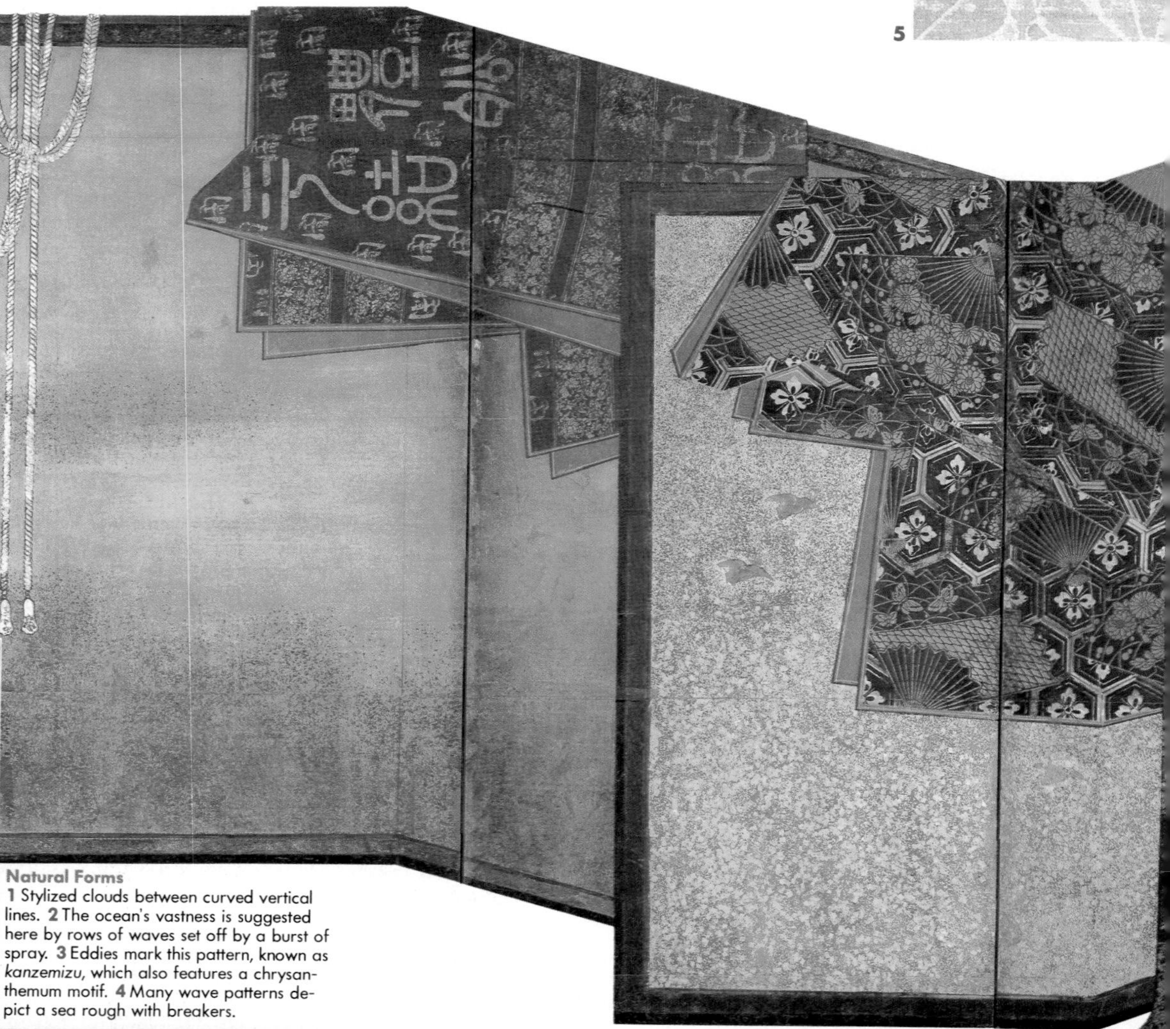

Natural Forms

1 Stylized clouds between curved vertical lines. **2** The ocean's vastness is suggested here by rows of waves set off by a burst of spray. **3** Eddies mark this pattern, known as *kanzemizu*, which also features a chrysanthemum motif. **4** Many wave patterns depict a sea rough with breakers.

Man-Made Objects

1 An opening fan is a symbol of increasing good fortune. **2** The pattern called *genjiguruma*, which features the wheels of an ox-drawn cart, takes its name from the 11th-century novel *Genji monogatari* (Tale of Genji). **3** The *takara-zukushi* ("collection of treasures") is a collection of various items with lucky associations.

Geometric Forms

1 A design resembling stylized fish scales, called *uroko*, this pattern was favored by Nō and *kabuki* actors portraying characters transformed into snakes or demons. **2** In this pattern, six diamonds combine to form a six-pointed star that resembles the leaf of the hemp plant. **3** Four elliptical flower petals set inside interlocking circles—a popular pattern known as *shippōtsunagi*. **4** Arrow feathers alternating positive and negative. **5** This design, called *ichimatsu*, was popularized by a famous Edo-period kabuki actor. **6** The *matsukawabishi* ("pine-bark diamonds") pattern gained its name because of its resemblance to the way pine bark splits. **7** The wavy lines shown here resemble a fishnet. **8** Tortoise shells are represented in the abstract by interlocking hexagons; this pattern is often graced with tortoises or, as in the example given here, flowers.

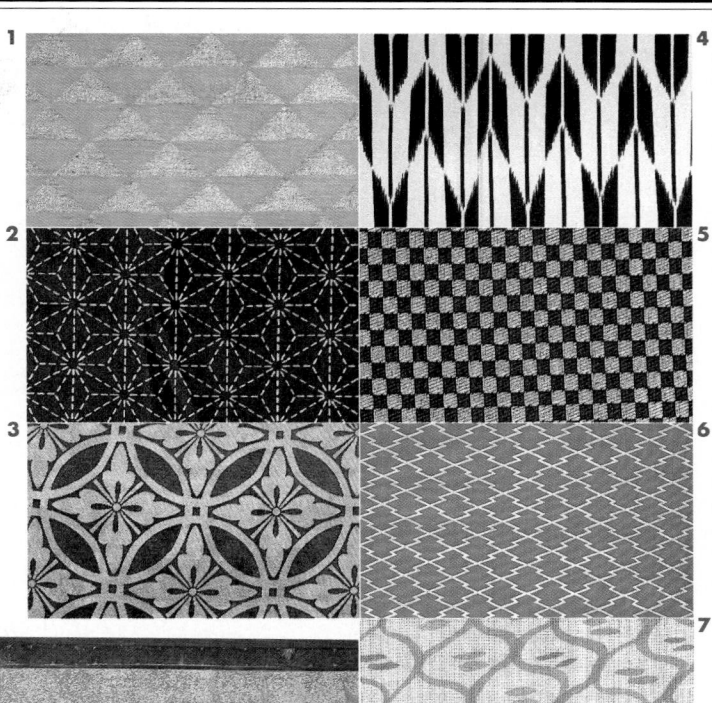

Detail of an Edo-period six-fold screen painting of the Kanō school. One of a genre that features the design motifs of women's kimono shown as draped over a decorated folding screen. Gold and color on paper. 151 × 353 cm. Courtesy of the Freer Gallery of Art, Smithsonian Institution, Washington, DC.

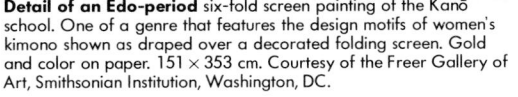

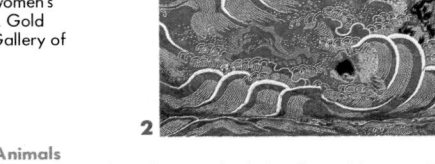

Animals

1 Butterflies such as these *agehachō* (swallowtails) are symbols of rebirth. **2** Carp are renowned for their strength and perseverance; the motif of carp fighting their way up a waterfall originated in China. **3** The combination of deer and maple leaves is highly suggestive of the autumn season. **4** The crane has been regarded since ancient times as a mystical bird because of the elegant simplicity of its form. Cranes, here surrounded by other birds, are often found on wedding decorations and signify long life and happiness.

TREATY in September 1951, gave the United States the right to station military forces in Japan for an indefinite length of time. Members of the peace movement realized that a revised treaty would further strengthen the United States–Japan military alliance and possibly involve Japan automatically and unconditionally in US military action. In March 1959 the Japan Socialist Party, the JAPAN COMMUNIST PARTY, SŌHYŌ (General Council of Trade Unions of Japan), and 134 other groups organized the People's Council to Prevent the Security Treaty Revision and held mass rallies throughout the country. In January 1960 a new security treaty, the Treaty of Mutual Cooperation and Security between Japan and the United States, was signed in Washington. The opposition activities of the People's Council intensified both inside and outside the Diet.

The People's Council, however, was unable to block the new security treaty. On 19 June it was ratified despite rallies, protests, and strikes by as many as 7 million workers, constituting the largest popular movement in postwar Japan. See UNITED STATES–JAPAN SECURITY TREATIES.

Vietnam and Okinawa Movement— Members of the peace movement considered the US bombing of North Vietnam to be aggression, and they organized strikes and protests against it. During the same period (1965–73), the peace movement took up the issue of the return to Japan of OKINAWA, which had been under US administrative authority since the end of World War II. In November 1969 Prime Minister SATŌ EISAKU and President Nixon agreed in Washington that

the administration of Okinawa should be returned to Japan. Harboring deep suspicions about the terms of the agreement, the peace movement worked to ensure that the US military bases and nuclear weapons would be removed and that full sovereignty would be returned to Japan.

At the same time the peace movement sought the abolition of the US–Japan treaty upon its expiration on 22 June 1970 in order to end the military alliance. Its three objectives—termination of the Vietnam War, return of Okinawa to Japan, and abolition of the security treaty—were in fact interrelated. The US bases in Japan and Okinawa functioned as supply or attack bases for the Vietnam War, which the peace movement hoped would be hindered by the cessation of the security treaty and the return of Okinawa. After the security treaty was automatically extended on 23 June 1970, administrative authority over Okinawa returned to Japan in May 1972, and the truce in Vietnam signed in January 1973, the activities of the peace movement declined.

In the early 1980s, aggravated by the increasingly tense nuclear arms race between the Soviet Union and the United States, a movement arose in opposition to the arming of US Navy ships with nuclear cruise missiles. With the waning of the cold war in the early 1990s, the peace movement became concerned with the issue of Third World poverty and economic development.

Peace Preservation Law of 1887
保安条例

(Hoan Jōrei). An ordinance issued on 25 December 1887 (Imperial Ordinance No. 67). Its purpose was to contain the FREEDOM AND

PEOPLE'S RIGHTS MOVEMENT, and it was the most drastic of the many criminal laws enacted after 1875 to control antigovernment political activities by the stringent regulation of public meetings, speeches, and the press.

Article 4, the heart of the ordinance, authorized the chief of the metropolitan police, with the approval of the home minister, to expel for three years any person residing or sojourning within a seven and a half mile radius of the Imperial Palace who was judged to be inciting disturbances or scheming to disrupt public order. Within three days of its issuance, and under conditions resembling martial law, 570 prominent figures in the people's rights movement, including HOSHI TŌRU, OZAKI YUKIO, and NAKAE CHŌMIN, were arrested and expelled from Tōkyō. The law, drawn up by Home Minister YAMAGATA ARITOMO, was repealed in 1898, but it was to be replaced by other equally stringent legislation (see PUBLIC ORDER AND POLICE LAW OF 1900).

Peace Preservation Law of 1925
治安維持法

(Chian Iji Hō). A law enacted on 12 May 1925 to control communists and anarchists; one of the most significant laws enacted in prewar Japan. Many bureaucrats and politicians supported the idea of a strict law to control leftist radicals, but the main force behind this measure was HIRANUMA KIICHIRŌ and his followers in the Ministry of Justice. Twice amended before Japan's defeat in World War II, this law was the central pillar of the system of ideological control established in the prewar period and served as the framework for the creation of special techniques for handling "thought criminals" (shisōhan).

The bill passed the Diet with overwhelming support after its introduction by the KATŌ TAKAAKI cabinet; there was little significant public protest against it. The main thrust of the law was presented in article 1, which read: "Anyone who has formed an association with the objective of altering the kokutai or the system of private property, and anyone who has joined such an association with full knowledge of its object, shall be liable to imprisonment with or without hard labor for a term not exceeding 10 years." By the use of the highly enigmatic and emotional term KOKUTAI—the political system, regarded as unique to Japan, embodied in the imperial line and the institutions supporting it—the Hiranuma clique blended politics and ethics in a traditional manner, turning dissent into a moral as well as a legal issue and undermining the liberal interpretation of the CONSTITUTION OF THE EMPIRE OF JAPAN.

By 1925 some members of a radical national student organization, the Student Federation of Social Science (Gakusei Shakai Kagaku Rengōkai, or Gakuren), had vowed to support Marxism-Leninism and to cooperate with the communists. On 16 December law enforcement officials met in Tōkyō and decided to destroy the Gakuren. A series of arrests began in mid-January 1926, resulting in charges against 38 students for violating the Peace Preservation Law. That same year the Justice Ministry created the "Thought Section" to deal with "thought criminals." In mid-May the Tōkyō District Court created a special section to deal exclusively with "thought crimes" (shisō hanzai).

Renewed activity by the Japan Communist Party prompted the government to carry out a mass roundup of suspected commu-

1 The Hakuhō variety is almost perfectly round.
2 The Ōkubo variety can weigh as much as 260 grams each.

3 The Hakutō variety is light with pink spots and white flesh.
4 A peach grove in Nagano Prefecture with peaks of the Hida Mountains in the background.

1 The pearl-culturing process begins with the insertion of a tiny round bead of mother-of-pearl into an oyster.
2 A worker balances on one of the large rafts used in culturing pearls in Ago Bay, Mie Prefecture. He tends bags of oysters that are suspended in the sea while pearls form.
3 After harvesting, pearls are separated and graded according to such qualities as size, color, and luster.

nists on 15 March 1928 in which about 1,600 were arrested (see MARCH 15TH INCIDENT). The strongly anticommunist government of TANAKA GIICHI struck out at radical leftists in a number of ways, including a revision of the Peace Preservation Law through an emergency imperial ordinance (later approved by the Diet). Leaders and organizers of groups attempting to overturn the *kokutai* now faced a possible death sentence; even non-members could be charged with "furthering the aims" of illegal groups.

In the Ministry of Education, a Student Section was created to watch and report on radicals. "Thought police" under the control of the Home Ministry were assigned throughout the country, and agents were sent abroad. The most significant change in the Ministry of Justice was the assignment of "thought prosecutors" (*shisō kenji*) to the Great Court of Cassation, 7 appeals courts, and 10 district courts. They had orders to seek out and prosecute "thought criminals."

Officials developed techniques that would encourage TENKŌ (conversion). Authorities deliberately created an organization to supervise the step-by-step reintegration of each offender; the *tenkō* system was institutionalized, and each graduate who was certified as "cured" was welcomed back into society.

As Japan slipped into a period of crisis after the MANCHURIAN INCIDENT (1931), dissent was tolerated less and officials demanded greater conformity and harmony. The seemingly endless conflict in China and the drift toward war in the Pacific provided the background for the final revision of the Peace Preservation Law. Early in February 1941 the House of Representatives received a 65-article bill that was actually a complete rewriting rather than a revision of the law. The purpose of this "revision" was to destroy all support for the Japan Communist Party within the framework of legal organizations by stretching the definition of illegal activities. Religious groups that ventured into politics were included. "Thought prosecutors" were given wide powers, defense lawyers were to be chosen by the Ministry of Justice, the appeals court step was removed, and other civil liberties were sacrificed. Incorrigi-

ble "thought offenders" were to receive open-ended sentences. The new Peace Preservation Law was passed by the Diet and became effective on 15 May 1941. Between 1925 and 1945 nearly 70,000 people were arrested as suspected violations of the law. However, only about ten percent of these cases went to trial (including the preliminary examination). This law's death penalty was never used in Japan proper or in Korea. Following Japan's defeat in World War II, the Peace Preservation Law was abolished on 15 October 1945.

peaches 桃

(*momo*). *Prunus persica.* The majority of Japan's peaches developed from chance seedlings of varieties introduced from China in 1872 and 1873; varieties belonging to the southern European group are not suited to cultivation in Japan because of the large amount of rainfall. The flesh of the Japanese peach is generally white and soft. Many varieties, including Ōkubo, Hakutō, and Hakuhō, are grown throughout the country, but production is centered in Yamanashi, Yamagata, Fukushima, Nagano, and Okayama prefectures. A variety with yellow and firm flesh has been developed by crossing Japanese strains with European strains and is grown commercially. Japanese peaches are used mainly as fresh fruit and secondarily (about 30 percent) for canning and juice.

Pearl Harbor, attack on 真珠湾攻撃

(Shinjuwan *kōgeki*). Surprise attack on the US Pacific Fleet in Pearl Harbor, Hawaii, by Japanese carrier-based planes. Planned by Admiral YAMAMOTO ISOROKU and carried out early in the morning on 7 December (8 December, Japanese time) 1941, the raid touched off the Pacific War. Four battleships and 2 other vessels were sunk; 4 battleships and 12 other ships were severely damaged; 188 aircraft were destroyed; and some 3,700 men were killed or wounded. The loss to the attackers was 29 aircraft, 5 special submarines, and 64 killed in action. The attack, which took place while negotiations were still going on with Japanese representatives in Washington, had the effect of uniting the American people into an all-out effort to defeat Japan. See also WORLD WAR II.

pearls 真珠

(*shinju*). Pearls are solid, usually lustrous, spherical objects formed of nacre generated within the shell of many species of mollusk. They develop naturally when an irritating object inside the shellfish is isolated in layers of nacre secretions from the shell mantle.

In the late 19th century, MIKIMOTO KŌKICHI succeeded in producing the first artificially cultured pearl. Mikimoto's method involves inserting a tiny round bead of mother-of-pearl into the gonad of a pearl oyster, which is then left submerged in the sea for a period of time while the oyster's nacre accumulates in layers on the pearl nucleus. The method was developed along the Pacific coast of Mie Prefecture. Today the majority of Japan's pearls are produced in Ehime and Mie prefectures.

Until recently, immature pearl oysters were collected from natural seabeds to be used for culturing, but oysters are now bred specially for the purpose. The formation of pearls takes from six months to a year for nuclei of less than 7 millimeters (0.28 in) and one to two years for nuclei of more than 7 millimeters. Host shells in lots of 20 to 40 are then placed in metallic mesh bags and suspended from rafts in the sea at a depth of 0.5 to 1.0 meters (1.6–3.3 ft), 60 to 120 bags per raft. The shell exteriors are cleaned periodically during the year, and the shells are removed to warm waters when the water temperature drops below 15°C (60°F) in the winter. The optimum harvesting time is believed to be the month of November. Fresh-

pears A round shape and grainy skin distinguish Japanese pears from Western pears.
1 The flowers of the Japanese pear are white and appear in April; here a pear tree in full bloom frames the Hida Mountains in Nagano Prefecture.
2 The Nijisseiki ("Twentieth-Century") pear is considered the best among Japanese varieties because of its fine-textured, juicy flesh and perfectly round shape.
3 Although the flesh of the Chōjūrō has a coarse texture, this pear is very juicy and the trees are hardy.

peiron boat race
In Nagasaki, oarsmen sitting in a double row face the bow of the boat, which juts up in a sharp point, and move the boat along at very high speeds. This form of racing originated in southern China.

water pearl culture is conducted on a small scale in KASUMIGAURA and Lake BIWA.

pears   梨

(*nashi*). The three major species of pear cultivated in Japan are the Japanese pear or Nihon *nashi* (*Pyrus serotina* var. *culta*), Western pear (*P. communis* var. *sativa*), and Chinese pear (*P. sinensis*). The Japanese pear has been improved over a long period of time from varieties that grew wild from the central part of Honshū southward. The two main orchard varieties, Nijisseiki and Chōjūrō, are grown from the southern part of Hokkaidō to Kyūshū. The Japanese pear, called the sand pear in the West because of the rather rough texture of the pulp, has larger and more numerous stone cells in the fruit than the Western pear and is produced in large quantities. Varieties developed after World War II have a sweeter taste and better-quality pulp. The pear is used mainly as a table fruit, but the consumption of its juice has increased in recent years. Western and Chinese pears were introduced in the Meiji period (1868–1912) and are produced only in limited quantities; because of Japan's heavy rainfall, there are few areas suitable for growing these species.

peasant uprisings → hyakushō ikki

peerage   華族

(*kazoku*). The Japanese term *kazoku* is applied collectively and individually to the pre–World War II hereditary aristocracy. It was adopted in 1869 to apply specifically to 427 families of former *kuge* (court nobles) and former *daimyō*, comprising a class of nobility distinct from the other social classes designated after the 1868 MEIJI RESTORATION: former *samurai* (SHIZOKU) and commoners (HEIMIN). After 1884 the term *kazoku* was applied to an expanding aristocracy, which was augmented first by the elite of the feudal military aristocracy (*buke kazoku*), and later by certain outstanding individuals of nonaristocratic background (*kunkō kazoku*). The aristocracy reached a peak of 1,016 families in 1944 before it was abolished in 1947 by the new constitution.

The aristocratic elite had its origins in influential families of the YAMATO COURT (ca 4th century–ca mid-7th century). In the middle of the Heian period (794–1185) and through the Kamakura period (1185–1333), the FUJIWARA FAMILY dominated the government and, with the MINAMOTO FAMILY, provided the framework for court nobility for several centuries. Court nobility was eclipsed from the 11th century with the rise of the provincial military, including the TAIRA FAMILY and certain branches of the Minamoto family.

With the Meiji Restoration (1868) the court nobility regained some of its lost status. Several court nobles played key roles in the restoration of direct imperial rule, and in the first Meiji government, all seven administrative departments were headed by court nobles or royal princes. But within a few years court nobles were displaced from all but a handful of government offices, and the daimyō too were deprived of their domains by stages. On 25 July 1869 a new social system was adopted under which the traditional Confucian divisions of society (SHI-NŌ-KŌ-SHŌ) were replaced by four classes: imperial family (*kōzoku*), nobles (*kazoku*), former samurai (*shizoku*), and commoners (*heimin*). At the same time, the old titles of *kuge* and daimyō were abolished, and 427 families were merged into a single hereditary nobility to be called *kazoku*.

All families accorded the title of *kazoku* but not given provincial office were ordered to reside in Tōkyō. By the end of 1869 a pension system was adopted for former *kuge* and former daimyō, but eventually the stipends were replaced by bonds (see CHITSU-ROKU SHOBUN).

The fortunes of the nobility were altered dramatically by the Peerage Act of 7 July 1884. Under the terms of this act new hereditary titles were established in five ranks: prince (*kōshaku*), marquis (also *kōshaku*, but written with a different first character), count (*hakushaku*), viscount (*shishaku*), and baron (*danshaku*); they were conferred by the emperor on 508 family heads. The new peerage system followed European models, but the terms used for the five ranks were taken from ancient China. The striking departure of the 1884 Peerage Act was the addition of members from nonaristocratic backgrounds who were rewarded for distinguished service to the nation. All ranks received hereditary financial awards. The nobility could become members of the HOUSE OF PEERS, which was conceived of as a balance to the elected lower house of the new Diet.

The peerage system was abolished when the new constitution came into effect in 1947. Today, former aristocrats are to be found in many professions and occupations, the majority of them wealthy and successful, and informally organized into a "Peers Club."

peiron boat race   ペーロン

(*peiron*). Races in boats propelled either by sculling or rowing; *peiron* is derived from the Chinese word for dragon (*palong* or *p'a-lung*). Boat races using sculls have been known in Japan since ancient times. Variously called *oshifune* or *funaguro*, this type of boat racing is observed as a religious event in some areas. In contrast, boat racing using oars or paddles was introduced from southern China and is popular in the coastal area from Nagasaki to Okinawa. In the city of Nagasaki, along with the Okunchi Festival (the October harvest festival) and kite flying (in April), the *peiron* boat race held on the last Sunday in July is one of the three main events of the year.

Teams of 36 men board boats about 12 meters (40 ft) long that are especially designated for the race. Also on board are a coxswain, a drummer, and a man with gongs. There are races for youths and for older men.

Penal Code → criminal law

penal system   刑罰

(*keibatsu*). Early Japanese society was characterized by an indigenous law that was not yet separated from religion. Acts corresponding to crimes were called sins (TSUMI). In a legal code dating from the beginning of the 9th century, a sin is defined as that which the gods find defiling and despicable. Sickness and accidents were included as sins. People who committed sins were required to placate the gods by HARAE (purification). The sinner made an atonement offering (*haraetsumono*), or a MISOGI might be conducted, in which the offender stripped and immersed himself in water to wash away impurities.

Toward the end of the protohistoric period, under the influence of Chinese laws, the idea of earthly sanctions developed; these were at times combined with religious purification. During the Nara (710–794) and early Heian (794–1185) periods, a criminal code adapted from the Chinese was used. The objective of the sanctions in the penal laws (*ritsu*) was the punishment of criminals and the reformation of their lives in accordance with Confucian teaching. The maintenance of social order was given serious attention. The five sanctions of whipping, caning, penal servitude, banishment, and death were taken from the Chinese practice and used as penalties (see RITSURYŌ SYSTEM). From the beginning of the 9th century a trend toward lighter punishments appeared, and for a period of about 350 years the death penalty was abolished. About the mid-14th century a principle appeared that considered both sides in a dispute at fault (KENKA RYŌSEI-BAI). During the Sengoku period (1467–1568) punishments were severe and very often meted out even to a criminal's relatives and members of his village (see ENZA; RENZA). In the early Edo period (1600–1868) punishments continued to be relatively severe, and cases of sanctions based on family relationships were numerous. The KUJIKATA OSADAMEGAKI (Official Provisions), a legal code enacted in 1742 by the shōgun TOKUGAWA YOSHIMUNE, eased the severity of punishment. From 1791 facilities called NIN-SOKU YOSEBA (literally, "laborers' camps") were established for people who had been given minor punishments and also for non-criminal vagrants. During this period, when Japan was divided into some 270 feudal domains (HAN), there were many cases of punishment by banishment to other domains. Generally the punishments of the various domains were more severe than those of the shogunate.

After the Meiji Restoration of 1868, the influence of European and American law became predominant. Early in the period, however, a carryover from the past, the SHINRITSU KŌRYŌ (New Legal Principles), a system of penal servitude derived from Chinese legal codes, was enacted (1870; revised 1873). In 1882 a criminal code based largely on the French criminal code was enacted. Differences in punishment based on social position were abolished, but the varieties of punishment were complicated. In 1872 a prison system was established, and the present prison law was finally adopted in 1907. In 1908 the present penal code was enacted on the model of the German code.

The Contemporary System — In 1989 the number of Penal Code offenses on police records was 2,261,076; of these, 587,808 were traffic related. The number of offenses per 100,000 population has steadily decreased from 2,644 in 1950 to 1,834 in 1989.

All offenders under 20 years of age are considered juveniles and are first sent to the FAMILY COURT. Under article 248 of the Code of CRIMINAL PROCEDURE, public prosecutors have discretionary power not to prosecute adult offenders, but plea bargaining is explicitly prohibited by the code (art. 319[3]). In 1989, 94.3 percent of all Penal Code offenses were punished by fines. The Penal Code prescribes a fairly wide range of terms of imprisonment for each offense. Punishments for intentional homicide, for example, range from imprisonment for three years to the death penalty. A district court, composed of three judges in serious cases and one judge in other cases—there is no jury system in Japan—awards a determinate sentence within this broad statutory range. Appeal against all sentences to high courts and, in serious cases, to the Supreme Court is permitted. The rate of acquittal is very low. In 1989 only 89 accused persons, 0.17 percent of the total, were acquitted. Prison terms are relatively short. Among offenders imprisoned in 1989, 33.1 percent received sentences of one year or less, and 95.8 percent sentences of three years or less. Execution of a sentence of imprisonment may be suspended by the court if the sentence is for not more than three years. By a decision of a parole board, prisoners may be paroled after serving one-third of their prison terms. In fact, most paroles are granted only at a relatively late stage in the term of imprisonment. See also CRIMINAL LAW; CAPITAL PUNISHMENT; JUVENILE CRIME; PRISONS; JUDICIAL SYSTEM.

penshon
ペンション

(from the French *pension*). A small-scale lodging facility, normally operated by a private owner, which provides bed and board to travelers at lower cost than a hotel. The buildings are Occidental in style, with an average of 10 twin-bed rooms. In recent years, however, there has been an increase in *penshon* with some Japanese-style rooms, which are more convenient for groups and families. As a rule, guests provide their own towels, toothbrushes, and sleepwear. Often the meals, served by the proprietor and his family, are the specialty of the establishment. There are about 2,500 *penshon* in Japan.

Japan's Pension System in 1990
pensions

Type of pension	Insured person	Insurer	Number of insured persons (in millions)	Number of persons now eligible for pension benefits (in millions)	Average monthly pension benefits (in yen)
National Pension (basic)	Self-employed workers	Nation	18.16	7.58	31,000
	Spouses of salaried workers	Nation	11.79		
	All salaried workers	Nation	35.73	3.93	—*
	Total		65.68	11.51	—
Supplemental pensions received by salaried workers					
Employees' Pension Insurance	Private-sector salaried workers	Nation	29.92	4.51	138,000
Mutual aid association pensions (MAAs)	Public employees and employees of groups that have MAAs	MAA	5.81	2.08	142,000 to 201,000†
	Total		35.73	6.59	—

*Salaried workers' National Pension benefits are included in the figures given below for Employees' Pension Insurance and mutual aid association pensions.
†This is a range of averages for seven different associations.
SOURCE: Ministry of Health and Welfare, *Kōsei hakusho* (annual): 1991.

pensions
年金

(*nenkin*). The Japanese pension system centers on public pensions administered by the national government, providing old-age, disability, and survivor benefits. Public pensions are supplemented by individual pension plans provided by private enterprises. By law, all Japanese citizens of working age must subscribe to a public pension plan. Pensions are an important part of Japan's system of SOCIAL WELFARE.

Japanese pensions started in 1875 with the *onkyū* system for retired army and navy servicemen. This system was later expanded to cover government officials, schoolteachers, and policemen. In 1939 the first pension program for private-sector employees, the Seamen's Insurance Law, was enacted. From 1942 Laborers' Pension Insurance provided coverage for general workers; this was the precursor to the current EMPLOYEES' PENSION INSURANCE. In 1959 the National Pension Law was passed; it covers farmers, the self-employed, housewives, and other categories of people who had been excluded from employees' pensions.

The pension system was greatly simplified in 1986. The reform was intended to provide a more stable financial base for the pension system, a pressing national concern in light of the aging of Japan's population. Public pensions were reorganized into a two-tiered system. The NATIONAL PENSION was extended to provide basic, mandatory pension coverage to all Japanese citizens. Spouses of employees' pension subscribers are now required to enroll in the National Pension program (previously enrollment was voluntary for spouses). As of 1990, 65.7 million citizens were enrolled in this program, 30.0 million of whom depended on it as their sole pension coverage. Two supplemental programs provide additional coverage and benefits. The Employees' Pension Insurance program provides coverage for 29.9 million private-sector employees. MUTUAL AID ASSOCIATION PENSIONS enroll an additional 5.8 million public employees and teachers. A declining number (now under 3.0 million) still receive *onkyū* pensions. Additional coverage for employees of certain companies is provided by privately funded corporate pensions.

The National Pension and Employees' Pension Insurance are administered by the MINISTRY OF HEALTH AND WELFARE. The smaller mutual-aid-association programs are administered by the relevant associations and are under the jurisdiction of various ministries. One-third of the costs of contributory National Pension benefits are provided by the national treasury, with the rest supplied by contributions from the insured and from other pension plans. The costs of employee insurance are usually covered by equal contributions of employer and employee proportionate to the employee's wage rate.

Penta-Ocean Construction Co, Ltd
五洋建設[株]

(Goyō Kensetsu). Construction company founded in 1888 under the name Mizuno-Gumi and incorporated under its present name in 1950. In 1961 the company successfully bid for a Suez Canal repair project and since then has received additional orders for Suez-related projects. Penta-Ocean has become best known as a leader in marine engineering, but the company's operations are not limited to this field. Recent overseas projects include a comprehensive building complex in Singapore and a desalinization plant in Saudi Arabia. Sales for the fiscal year ending March 1991 totaled ¥439.1 billion (US $3.2 billion). The company was capitalized at ¥15.1 billion (US $109.8 million) in the same year. Corporate headquarters are located in Tōkyō.

peonies
牡丹・芍薬

(*botan; shakuyaku*). *Paeonia* spp. The main peony species cultivated in Japan are the *botan*, or tree peony (*Paeonia suffruticosa*), and the *shakuyaku* (*Paeonia albiflora* f. *hortensis*), one of the herbaceous peonies. Both types are members of the buttercup family (Ranunculaceae). The tree peony has a straight trunk, usually about 1 meter (3 ft) in height. The leaves are pale green and either biternate or bipinnate compound. Flowers, averaging 15 centimeters (6 in) across, bloom in early summer. Single-flowered varieties have seven to nine petals per flower; double-flowered varieties have many more.

The tree peony, which has become one of East Asia's most celebrated flowers, was introduced to Japan from China during the Heian period (794–1185). Many new varieties were introduced during the Edo period (1600–1868), with a wide range of flower shapes and colors. Peony-root extract is a traditional remedy for stomachache, arthritis, headache, and fever.

peonies

The two main species of Japanese peony, the *botan* (tree peony) and the *shakuyaku* (herbaceous peony), were introduced from China as medicinal plants.

► *Botan* at Hasedera, a temple in Sakurai, Nara Prefecture.

▲ Peonies are a common element in Japanese design, as in this mirror back with *botan* carved in *kamakura-bori*-style lacquer.

► An Edo-period Nō theater costume embroidered with a pattern of peonies and young pine trees.

▼ A common double-flowered type of *shakuyaku*.

The herbaceous peony was introduced from China as a medicinal plant even earlier than the tree peony. By the Genroku era (1688–1704) over 100 varieties were recorded. In spring the *shakuyaku* grows several stems (60 cm; 24 in) from a rhizome. The leaves are alternate and biternately compound in the lower part. In early summer large red, white, or parti-color flowers appear.

People's Finance Corporation
国民金融公庫

(Kokumin Kin'yū Kōko). Government-funded financial institution providing low-interest loans for small businesses having difficulty borrowing money from private financial institutions. Established in 1949 entirely by government capital. Since 1973 the corporation has offered regular loans to small businesses using pension accounts or government bonds as collateral, and since 1979 it has provided education loans to high school and college students. The number of loans to small businesses in March 1989 reached 1.6 million, which is one-quarter of the total number of small businesses nationwide. The ceiling on a general loan to a small business is ¥35.0 million (US $268,000) for a maximum term of 10 years. Outstanding loans for March 1990 totaled ¥6.3 trillion (US $41.2 billion). The bank had ¥37.3 billion (US $243.7 million) in capital in the same year. Headquarters are in Tōkyō.

People's Honor Award
国民栄誉賞

(Kokumin Eiyo Shō). Official prime ministerial commendation established at the suggestion of former prime minister FUKUDA TAKEO in 1977; awarded irregularly to persons "widely loved and respected by the Japanese people." Most recipients have been active in fields such as sports and entertainment, and include baseball player Ō SADAHARU, popular composer KOGA MASAO, actor HASEGAWA KAZUO, and singer MISORA HIBARI, who in 1989 became the first woman to receive the award.

periodization
時代区分

(*jidai kubun*). In the course of their long history the Japanese have employed a number of methods of designating a year for purposes of historical dating. As in any dynastic political system, histories were first written and documents dated by reference to the year of the sovereign's reign. Reign dating was practiced throughout Japanese history, and, for official purposes, what can be called the imperial era name (NENGŌ) was adopted. This was a practice developed in China whereby a year was identified by number from the start of the era in which it fell. Eras were named by the imperial court and were not of any specific duration. They were frequently changed, often for political reasons, either in hopes of bringing about a change of fortune for the country or to mark a change of power alignment around the throne. The first official use of a *nengō* in Japan came after the coup d'état of 645 that established the primacy of what we now recognize as the main line of the house of Yamato. It was to commemorate this event that the era name Taika (Great Reform) was adopted beginning in 645 (see TAIKA REFORM).

Another commonly used dating device, also adopted from China, was the practice of identifying years in 60-year cycles. Two sets of Chinese characters, 10 "stems" and 12 "branches," were used to form a set of 60 two-character combinations, one of which was assigned to each year (see JIKKAN JŪNISHI). There was an established series of 60-year cycles whereby years could be numbered both backward and forward in time. But since this method had no internal device for locating a given 60-year cycle within the broader span of history, other data such as the *nengō* had to be known to make identification complete.

A year could also be identified by number within the reign of a given sovereign. This practice was in use in Japan prior to the adoption of *nengō* in 645. Thereafter the *nengō* became the preferred method, although historians and particularly court writers referred to reigns of past emperors as a general way of locating events. Beginning in 1868, however, the government adopted the practice of making reign and era names coextensive, so that after 1868 *nengō* could well be translated as "reign name." A few remnants of the imperial dating terminology can still be found in the writings of contemporary historians. This is because such terms refer to relatively short blocks of years and have come to carry useful historical connotations or because they have become identified with some particularly significant event.

Premodern Japanese historians did not devise a simple method of counting years forward from a distant epochal starting point and perhaps for that reason did not form the habit of thinking in terms of centuries or decades. However, following the MEIJI RESTORATION of 1868, the government did conceive of the idea of a "national era" that would start with the founding of the imperial dynasty (see KIGEN), set by tradition at 660 BC. This chronology was used sporadically as a way of dating that could compete with the Christian and Islamic calendars. As such it had its greatest play in 1940 when the government celebrated what it proclaimed to be the 2,600th anniversary of the founding of the Japanese state. This dating practice is now abandoned. For the purpose of consecutive historical counting, therefore, modern Japanese have tended increasingly to use the Christian calendar to identify historical and contemporary dates. Nevertheless the use of the *nengō* persists either as the sole means of dating or in combination with the Western system. In 1979 (Shōwa 54) the Diet adopted legislation making the use of the *nengō* mandatory for official purposes. See CALENDAR, DATES, AND TIME.

Periodization in the historiographical sense differs from dating, in that periods or blocks of time are identified and named to give meaning to the historical process. Premodern historians did this by using era and reign names as units to which they attached certain historical meanings.

The Jidai—The system of periodization most commonly used by Japanese historians is based on the concept of *jidai* (epoch, age, period). This system was devised and popularized during the late 19th century by Japan's first generation of modern historians. The method utilized two separate sets of terms: the names of the successive locations of centers of dominant political authority and power, and the names of the families other than the imperial house that successively held dominant political power. The first category of names includes, in chronological order, Yamato, Nara, Heian, Kamakura, Muromachi, Azuchi, Momoyama, and Edo. Among the second set, the main families to give their names to *jidai* were the Fujiwara, Ashikaga, Oda, Toyotomi, and Tokugawa.

Since the naming of *jidai* was the work of historians, it is natural that there should be differences of opinion over matters of definition and usage. It is characteristic of the *jidai* system of periodization that the units are defined by specific dates of certain events that are considered significant as transition points, chiefly in the political sphere. Thus a selected number of historical events are raised to special prominence as period markers. The pioneering work of KUROITA KATSUMI (1874–1946), which meticulously appraised the significance of such events, began but did not end the debate over periodization by Japanese historians.

Other Systems of Periodization——The standard *jidai* system of periodization, being both passive in its reference to historical change and arbitrary in its selection of "significant events," has not served sufficiently the needs of historians for a method of periodization that carries with it a sense of "explanation." Modern historians have devised a number of controlling ideas as a basis for periodization. Kuroita, for instance, superimposed on the finely calibrated *jidai* divisions a more broadly conceived scheme of explanatory periodization based on his attempt to link together political and social currents of change. The result was a four-part division of Japanese history: the age of clans (*uji*), before 645; the age of the aristocratic houses (*kuge*), 592–1167; the age of the military houses (*buke*), 1156–1867; and the modern age, beginning in 1867. This four-part periodization has served as a sort of commonsense scheme of division for many modern historians. Kuroita retained the breakpoints of the *jidai* and simply clustered the *jidai* into four: Yamato; Nara and Heian; Kamakura, Muromachi, and Edo; and Meiji.

The fact that Japanese history can be made to fit into a five- or six-part scheme of periodization has invited the application of concepts of periodization emerging out of the study of European history. Western historiographical practice has provided Japan with two models. One is the common sixfold division of history proper (see also PREHISTORY) into protohistoric, ancient, medieval, early modern, modern, and contemporary. The Japanese terms that respectively conform to these divisions are *genshi, kodai, chūsei, kinsei, kindai*, and *gendai*. This method of division is now in almost universal use.

The second model is the Marxist, which sees Japanese history as passing through the socioeconomic stages of primitive communalism, ancient slave society, feudal serf society, and modern capitalist society. This makes for a basic four-part division, but Marxist historians also have recognized the need to break the feudal and modern ages into two parts each, making an overall six-part system. The importance of the Marxist system for modern Japanese historians has been the explanations it provides for historical change and the rationale it gives for the selection of major historical turning points. Thus, although Japanese historians were from the time of Kuroita tending on their own toward the six-part division, justification of these divisions and arguments over selection of transition points have been based most often on Marxist theory.

The literature on periodization generated by contemporary Japanese historians focuses on two main problems: that of defining the

Major Periods of Japanese History

Western calendar	Commonly used periods (*jidai*)	Major era names (*nengō*)	Western periodization
10,000 BC —	Paleolithic (pre-10,000 BC)		Prehistoric (*senshi*)
300 BC —	Jōmon (ca 10,000 BC–ca 300 BC)		
AD 300 —	Yayoi (ca 300 BC–ca AD 300)		
400 —	Kofun (Yamato; ca 300–710)		Protohistoric (*genshi*)
500 —			
600 —	Asuka (593–710)	Taika (645–650)	
700 —		Taihō (701–704)	
800 —	Nara (710–794)	Tempyō (729–749)	
	Heian (794–1185)		
900 —		Jōgan (859–877)	Ancient (*kodai*)
1000 —		Engi (901–923)	
1100 —	Fujiwara (894–1185)		
		Hōgen (1156–59)	
1200 —		Heiji (1159–60)	
	Kamakura (1185–1333)	Jōkyū (1219–22)	
1300 —			
1400 —	Muromachi (Ashikaga; 1333–1568)	Kemmu (1334–36)	Medieval (*chūsei*)
	Northern and Southern Courts (1337–92)	Ōnin (1467–69)	
1500 —	Sengoku (1467–1568)		
	Azuchi-Momoyama (Oda-Toyotomi or Shokuhō; 1568–1600)	Bunroku (1593–96)	
1600 —			
1700 —	Edo (Tokugawa; 1600–1868)	Genroku (1688–1704)	Early modern (*kinsei*)
1800 —		Bunka (1804–18)	
		Bunsei (1818–31)	
1900 —	Meiji (1868–1912)	Meiji (1868–1912)	Modern (*kindai*)
	Taishō (1912–26)	Taishō (1912–26)	
	Shōwa (1926–89)	Shōwa (1926–89)	
	Heisei (1989–)	Heisei (1989–)	Contemporary (*gendai*)

"nature" of each major period and that of probing the "meaning" of transition points. The many arguments on these subjects give evidence of the still dynamic nature of periodization as interpreted by historians of Japan.

Perry, Matthew Calbraith

ペリー, M. C.

(1794–1858). US naval officer who reopened Japan to the Western world after more than 200 years of NATIONAL SECLUSION. A veteran of the Mexican War, Perry was selected in 1852 to lead an expedition to open diplomatic and commercial relations between the United States and Japan. Perry set sail late in 1852 and arrived on 8 July 1853 in Edo Bay (now Tōkyō Bay), subsequently delivering his credentials and his president's letter with great pomp and ceremony. In February 1854 he returned for an official answer and demanded that negotiations be held at Kanagawa (now part of Yokohama), close to Edo (now Tōkyō). Perry displayed great skill as a diplomat but also benefited from internal dissension in Japan over foreign relations and was able to secure the KANAGAWA TREATY on 31 March 1854. The main provisions were hospitality for shipwrecked Americans, most-favored-nation treatment, the opening of two ports (Shimoda and Hakodate) as supply stations, and the right of the United States to station a consular official at Shimoda after 18 months. The treaty was the model for agreements Japan made with Britain, Russia, and the Netherlands in 1854–56.

persecutions at Urakami 浦上崩れ

(Urakami *kuzure*). Recurrent persecutions carried out between 1790 and 1873 against Christians hiding in Urakami, now a suburb of Nagasaki. In the first (1790–95) and sec-

ond (1842) instances no one was executed, but in the third persecution (1859) more than 10 people died under torture. The fourth and most extensive persecution was carried out between 1867 and 1873.

With the opening of the treaty ports in the 1850s, Catholic missionaries settled in Nagasaki. Numerous Japanese embraced Christianity, but the Tokugawa shogunate's ANTI-CHRISTIAN EDICTS were still in force. In 1867, 64 Christians were arrested in Urakami, and in nearby Ōmura 110 were jailed under such harsh conditions that 60 died of exposure. The MEIJI RESTORATION (1868) brought no relief. In January 1870, 2,810 adherents in Urakami were shipped to other provinces. After international protest, the government finally issued a decree on 14 March 1873 withdrawing sanctions and allowing the exiles to return to their homes. A total of 4,010 Christians had been uprooted; of the 3,404 deported from Urakami, no fewer than 660 died in exile. See also CHRISTIANITY; KAKURE KIRISHITAN.

Matthew Calbraith Perry This US naval officer led the 1853–54 expedition that reopened Japan's diplomatic and commercial relations with the Western world.
1 The Black Ship Festival is held every May in the city of Shimoda, Shizuoka Prefecture, to commemorate the arrival of Perry's "black ships" (*kurofune*).
2 A photograph of Perry taken on his return from Japan to the United States.

persimmons
1 The fruit of the sweet variety Fuyū ripens between early November and December.
2 Hachiya persimmons are oblong and slightly pointed, with astringent flesh that is suitable for drying.
3 Astringent persimmons, inedible when fresh, are often peeled and sun-dried, as shown here.

persimmons 柿

(*kaki*). The oriental persimmon (*Diospyros kaki*), a member of the family Ebenaceae, is one of the major fruit trees of Japan, grown throughout the country except for Hokkaidō. It is divided into nonastringent (*amagaki*) and astringent (*shibugaki*) types. The predominant nonastringent variety is Fuyū, followed by Jirō, Gosho, and others, which are grown in warm places. The principal astringent variety, Hiratanenashi, is distributed widely, but there are special local varieties such as the Aizu Mishirazu of Fukushima Prefecture. The persimmon has a long history of cultivation and is now grown

more in home gardens than in orchards. The harvest season is September through November. Fruits of the nonastringent variety are eaten as is when ripe, but those of the astringent variety can be eaten only after their tannin content has been made insoluble by treatment with warm water, alcohol, and carbon dioxide, or when they are very ripe or dried. The white powder on dried persimmons (*hoshigaki*) is composed of fructose and glucose. Persimmon wood is used for making utensils.

personal computers パソコン

(*pasokon*). Japanese computers do not differ from the products of Europe and the United States in terms of the basic structure of their microprocessors and operating systems. Much of their software was developed in the United States, and until the early 1980s Japanese computer users were dependent on English-language software or Japanese-language software in either romanized or *katakana* (a type of Japanese phonetic script; see KANA) format. Since then, advances in both software and hardware design have made it possible for Japanese computer users to process data using the full Japanese orthography, which includes a mixture of *kana* and KANJI (Chinese characters; see WORD PROCESSORS, JAPANESE-LANGUAGE).

Personal computers were introduced to the Japanese market in 1979. The availability of low-cost computers, intended for personal enjoyment as well as for business, stimulated the market, and sales grew rapidly, from 111,000 in 1980 to about 1.87 million in 1984. Thereafter, sales leveled off at about 2 million units yearly until 1987, reflecting deepening United States–Japan trade friction and a stagnation in technical developments. Sales began to grow again in 1988, due to increased data-processing speed and the appearance of easy-to-carry laptop computers. In 1990 still smaller and lower-priced notebook-size computers appeared. These greatly boosted the demand, and sales reached 2.66 million units, of which 22 percent were exported and 78 percent went to the domestic market. The major issue facing Japanese personal computer makers is that their operating systems and data are frequently incompatible with other systems, both domestic and foreign, unlike the world market, where IBM-compatible models hold the principal share. Some Japanese manufacturers have sought to remedy this disadvantage by bringing out their own IBM-compatible models, but development is also proceeding to establish specifications that emphasize compatibility between machines produced by different manufacturers (see TRON). See also COMPUTER INDUSTRY; SOFTWARE INDUSTRY.

personnel assignment 人事配置

(*jinji haichi*). Japanese firms regularly rotate staff to different departments and sections so that employees can gain experience in various areas of company operation and, while doing so, can prepare themselves for possible future management positions. Wages are largely determined by length of service and are usually unaffected by the transfers. Employees place a high value on stability of employment with the company, and there is relatively little of the resistance to transfers that can be seen in some Western nations.

Nevertheless, for many white-collar workers in large corporations with plants

and offices throughout the country and abroad, transfers often involve a lengthy separation from their families (see WORK AWAY FROM FAMILY). Recently, some companies have introduced new career categories for employees who wish to avoid such transfers, but these employees must accept severely reduced promotion opportunities.

person without capacity 無能力者

(*munōryokusha*). Japanese legal term that refers to persons lacking the ability or legal qualification to perform complete juristic acts autonomously. The CIVIL CODE denies full legal autonomy to minors, incompetents (*kinchisansha*), and quasi incompetents (*jun kinchisansha*). Formerly, wives were also deemed to be persons without legal capacity, but this disability was abolished in 1947 when the Civil Code was substantially revised. This system is intended to protect persons who are deemed to have insufficient judgmental capacity. Accordingly, a parent, guardian, or custodian is appointed to protect and supervise such persons. In general, a juristic act performed by a person without capacity can be cancelled. See also CAPACITY TO ACT.

Peru and Japan ペルーと日本

(*Perū to Nihon*). The MARIA LUZ INCIDENT of 1872 led to the conclusion of a friendship treaty between Peru and Japan in the following year, marking the first formal relations between Japan and a Latin American nation. In 1899, 790 Japanese farmers sailed to Peru to work on sugar farms. The number of Japanese immigrants to Peru before World War II was over 33,000. There was serious friction between the Peruvian and Japanese communities, most notably an anti-Japanese riot in 1940. Diplomatic relations, which had been severed in 1942, were restored in 1952 by the San Francisco Peace Treaty.

With the end of large-scale emigration, the Japanese community in Peru has increasingly become integrated into Peruvian society. Trade and investment are important aspects of contemporary Peruvian-Japanese relations. Generally, Japan imports raw materials and metals from Peru while Peru purchases machinery and tools from Japan. The balance of trade has been regularly in Peru's favor. In 1990 Japan's exports to Peru were valued at $75.9 million, with imports from Peru valued at $572.0 million. Japanese investment in Peru has fluctuated, depending on political and economic conditions; due to the Peruvian debt problem, there has been a decrease in Japanese investment in Peru in recent years. The election in 1990 of a second-generation Japanese Peruvian, Alberto Fujimori (b 1938), as president of Peru gave both countries a new appreciation of their mutual relations.

PETA Army ジャワ郷土防衛義勇軍

(J: Jawa Kyōdo Bōei Giyūgun). Abbreviation of Pembela Tanah Air (National Defense Forces), a military force of Indonesians created by the Japanese in October 1943 and disbanded in August 1945. Although initially reluctant to give military training to Indonesians, the Japanese military authorities were forced by the worsening war situation (see WORLD WAR II) to use them as auxiliary troops. The army's strength reached a total of about 47,000 in August 1945 and formed the core of the Indonesian national army

Japanese Personal Computer Sales — personal computers

Value of Sales

billions of yen

Year	1982	1983	1984	1985	1986	1987	1988	1989	1990

(lines: total, domestic, export; scale 200–1,400)

Sales in Units

millions

Year	1982	1983	1984	1985	1986	1987	1988	1989	1990

(lines: total, domestic, export; scale 0.5–3.0)

NOTE: Figures for value of sales include both computers and peripheral equipment.
SOURCE: Japan Electronic Industry Development Association.

through the subsequent struggle for independence. See also INDONESIA AND JAPAN.

petrochemical industry

石油化学工業

(*sekiyu kagaku kōgyō*). Japan's petrochemical industry began in the late 1950s. Under the guidance of the Ministry of International Trade and Industry (MITI) and based on the First-Stage Petrochemical Plan for fiscal years 1958 and 1959, four companies constructed naphtha-refining centers with annual production capacities of 20,000 tons of ethylene each. Following this, the Second-Stage Petrochemical Plan (1962–64) provided for an expansion in ethylene production capacity to 80,000 tons annually at the four original plants and the establishing of five new naphtha centers with production capacities in the 40,000-ton range. By the end of the 1960s, naphtha centers had been approved and built in 17 locations. In 1991 there were 14 petrochemical complexes run by 11 companies in Japan. These complexes were almost all located in the industrial belt on the Pacific coast, and each had a yearly ethylene production capacity of 300,000–600,000 tons.

petroleum

石油

(*sekiyu*). Petroleum is indispensable to Japan's economy, but since Japan lacks significant resources of its own, it has had to depend on imported petroleum to meet the growing demand for energy. Compared with that of other major industrialized nations, Japan's degree of dependence on petroleum imports is very high. In 1990, of some 239 million kiloliters (1.5 billion barrels) of oil supplied to domestic consumers, 99.7 percent was imported.

In response to repeated petroleum price increases and the difficulty of maintaining stable sources of supply (see OIL CRISIS OF 1973), the government has embarked on a program to create a petroleum stockpile, which in 1990 was 82.6 million kiloliters (519.6 million barrels). Japan is also seeking to develop new sources of energy, diversify its sources of petroleum supply, and increase energy conservation.

Until the 1950s exploration of crude oil in Japan was limited to three prefectures in northern Honshū facing the Sea of Japan. Production averaged from 4,000 to 8,000 barrels a day. In 1955 the semigovernmental Japan Petroleum Exploration Co, Ltd (JAPEX), invested capital and introduced new technology from abroad to concentrate on prospecting for domestic petroleum. Since 1965 the Mining Law (Kōgyō Hō) has been extended to the outer continental shelf, and, as a result, claims for petroleum mining rights have been issued for a wide offshore area. In 1990 wells chiefly in Niigata and Akita prefectures and wells off the shore of Niigata produced 655,000 kiloliters (4.1 million barrels) of crude oil. A more promising area, centering on the Senkaku Islands in the East China Sea to the west of Kyūshū, has not yet been explored because of a boundary dispute with Taiwan and China.

Domestic oil prospecting and exploitation are now conducted by TEIKOKU OIL CO, LTD, and JAPEX. Overseas, ARABIAN OIL CO, LTD, obtained a concession in Saudi Arabia in 1957. In 1967 the Japan National Oil Corporation (JNOC) was established to support oil prospecting overseas by Japanese companies. In order to forge closer relations with oil-producing nations, secure a steady supply of oil, and pay off international debts arising

from Japan's oil consumption, some 80 Japanese overseas oil-development projects were under way in 1991.

Pfizer Pharmaceuticals, Inc

ファイザー製薬[株]

(Faizā Seiyaku). Manufacturer of pharmaceuticals, animal health products, and medical equipment. Incorporated in 1955 through a joint venture with TAITŌ CO, LTD, and the American company Pfizer, Inc. Became a wholly owned subsidiary of Pfizer, Inc, in 1983. Pfizer Pharmaceuticals is known for its production of third-generation antibiotics. Sales for the fiscal year ending November 1990 totaled ¥72.1 billion (US $558.6 million), and capitalization stood at ¥17.1 billion (US $132.5 million). Headquarters are in Tōkyō.

Phaeton Incident

フェートン号事件

(*Fēton gō Jiken*). An incident in August 1808 in which a British frigate, the *Phaeton*, succeeded in entering Nagasaki Harbor by flying the Dutch flag. At the time Britain and France were at war, and because Napoleon's armies had conquered Holland, the Dutch settlement at DEJIMA in Nagasaki Harbor was an object of British attack. The *Phaeton* seized several Dutch traders, who were ransomed, before leaving Dejima two days later. The commissioner of Nagasaki, Matsudaira Yasuhide (d 1808), assumed responsibility for the incident and committed suicide, and the *daimyō* of Hizen, whose domain included the port, was placed under temporary house arrest. This violation of the NATIONAL SECLUSION policy led to more stringent measures against the intrusion of foreign ships (see GAIKOKUSEN UCHIHARAI REI).

Phan Boi Chau

ファン・ボイ・チャウ

(1867–1940). The most prominent nationalist leader of early-20th-century Vietnam. In 1904 Phan founded the nationalist organization Vietnam Duy Tan Hoi (Vietnam Reformation Society), appointing CUONG DE as its head. In 1905 Phan went to Japan to request military aid for the organization, but, failing to receive it, he instead started the Dong Du (Visit the East) movement to promote study in Japan by Vietnamese youths. The number of Vietnamese students in Japan reached its peak at 200 in 1908. By early 1909, when Phan was expelled from Japan, first the French and then the Japanese had acted to suppress the movement. In 1912 he organized the Vietnam Quang Phuc Hoi (Vietnam Restoration Society) in Guangzhou (Canton). He was captured in Shanghai by French police in 1925, extradited to Hanoi, and kept in confinement in Hue until his death.

pharmaceutical industry

医薬品工業

(*iyakuhin kōgyō*). Before World War II, the Japanese pharmaceutical industry was made up of subsidiaries of major US and European manufacturers and of traditional Japanese drug makers that had adopted Western methods. Domestic firms were small and lacked the capacity to develop new products. After World War II, however, the industry enjoyed remarkable growth, thanks in part to the introduction of pharmaceutical technologies from the West, strong demand for prescription drugs stemming from the MEDICAL AND HEALTH INSURANCE system, and brisk sales of over-the-counter drugs. The Japanese pharmaceutical industry is now the world's second largest, after that of the United States. In 1988 production totaled

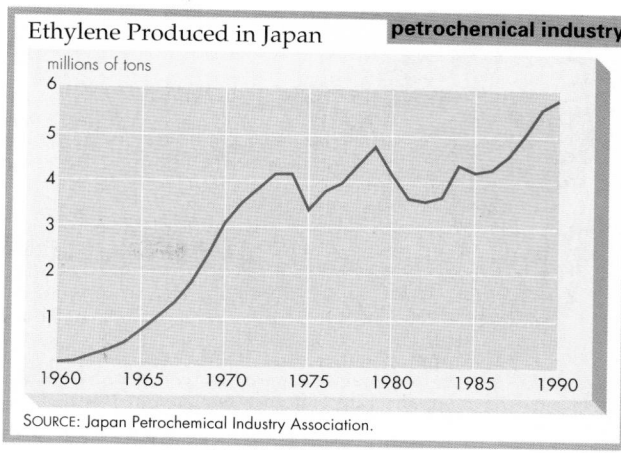

Ethylene Produced in Japan — petrochemical industry

millions of tons

SOURCE: Japan Petrochemical Industry Association.

¥5.1 trillion (US $39.8 billion). Recently, the industry's capacity to develop new drugs has come to rank among the most sophisticated in the world. The Japanese industry is especially strong in antibiotics and in biotechnology applications using fermentation technology. The aggressive entry of foreign corporations and large domestic food and chemical firms has intensified competition in the pharmaceutical industry. As a result, a major reorganization of the industry is now in progress.

Pharmacopoeia of Japan

日本薬局方

(*Nihon yakkyokuhō*). A book issued by the Japanese government to provide standards of quality, strength, and purity for medicines and basic preparations in general use. The first edition was published in 1886. It is

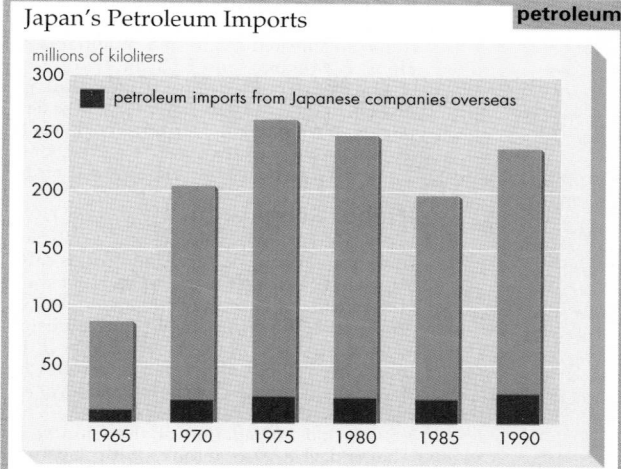

Japan's Petroleum Imports — petroleum

millions of kiloliters

■ petroleum imports from Japanese companies overseas

SOURCE: Agency of Natural Resources and Energy, *Sekiyu kaihatsu shiryō* (annual): 1992.

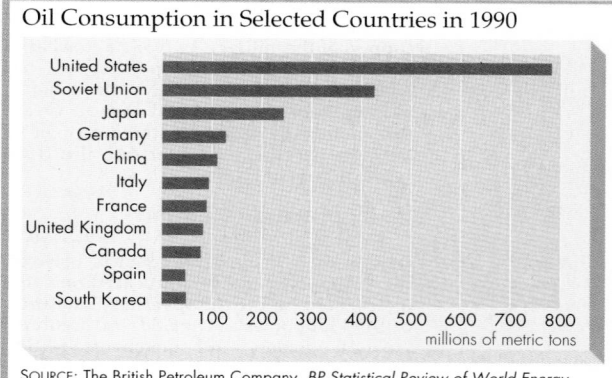

Oil Consumption in Selected Countries in 1990

United States
Soviet Union
Japan
Germany
China
Italy
France
United Kingdom
Canada
Spain
South Korea

100 200 300 400 500 600 700 800
millions of metric tons

SOURCE: The British Petroleum Company, *BP Statistical Review of World Energy* (annual): 1992.

pheasants The *kiji* (common pheasant) is one of two major species to be found in Japan. At top are the male (left) and female (right) of the Nihon *kiji* (green pheasant), a subspecies peculiar to Japan. Below them are the male (left) and female (right) of the *yamadori* (copper pheasant), the other major Japanese species. Five basic types of *yamadori* have been identified.

now revised approximately every five years; the 12th edition was issued in 1991.

pheasants

雉・山鳥

(*kiji; yamadori*). The two major species of pheasant (family Phasianidae) in Japan are the *kiji* (common pheasant; *Phasianus colchicus*) and the *yamadori* (copper pheasant; *P. soemmerringii*). The *kiji* is the smaller of the two, with the male measuring about 80 centimeters (31 in) and the female about 60 centimeters (24 in). The Nihon *kiji* (green pheasant; *P. c. versicolor*), a subspecies peculiar to Japan, is found in Honshū, Shikoku, and Kyūshū. The male's neck, breast, and abdomen are a blackish green, and its forehead is red. The female is yellow brown. Another subspecies, the *kōraikiji* (ring-necked pheasant) is found in Hokkaidō and Tsushima. It is brown from throat to breast, with a white ring at the throat.

The *yamadori* is native to Japan. The male measures about 125 centimeters (49 in); it is reddish brown with white striations on its long tail. The female is about 55 centimeters (22 in) and has a white-tipped tail. It is found in forested plains and mountains on Honshū, Shikoku, and Kyūshū.

Long prized in Japan for its beautiful appearance and its unique call, the *kiji* was designated the national bird after World War II. The *yamadori* was regarded as sacred. Both *kiji* and *yamadori* are prized as game birds.

Phibul Songkhram

ピブン

(1897–1964). Thai soldier and politician. Born in Bangkok. He served in various cabinet posts following the coup d'état that abolished Thailand's absolute monarchy in 1932, and in 1938 he was named prime minister. During the early years of World War II, he reluctantly allied with Japan and followed nationalistic policies for the expansion of armaments, spiritual integration of the Thai nation, and assimilation of the Chinese in Thailand. He also retook, with Japanese help, border territories lost to the French and British. Soon after the war, he was arrested as a war criminal but was later released and in 1948 he was again named premier with the support of the military. In 1955 he concluded a pact with Japan for the repayment of Thai government expenses on behalf of the Japanese military during World War II. Overthrown in a 1957 coup, he went into exile in Japan in 1958 and died there. See also THAILAND AND JAPAN.

Philippines and Japan

フィリピンと日本

(Firipin *to* Nihon). Early contacts between the Philippines and Japan focused on commerce. Long before the Spanish colonization of the Philippines in the mid-16th century, Japanese traders and merchants settled around Manila, which became the focal point of early bilateral trade. In 1593 Spanish authorities in Manila sent to Japan four Franciscan priests who, despite official Japanese distrust of missionary activity, were able to preach and build a church near Kyōto. However, in 1597 TOYOTOMI HIDEYOSHI ordered their sudden execution, together with other missionaries and their Japanese converts (see TWENTY-SIX MARTYRS). By the mid-17th century the Japanese government had banned overseas trade, and all Spanish priests and traders had been expelled from Japan. More than two centuries passed before contact between the two nations was renewed with the opening of Japan in 1854.

Relations before World War II—— In 1896 a revolution against Spanish colonial rule broke out, and in 1898, during the Spanish-American War, the Filipino revolutionary government sought assistance from Japan. Japanese supporters of the Filipino cause attempted to send arms aboard the *Nunobiki maru*, but the ship sank before reaching Manila. On an official level, however, no Japanese diplomatic, military, or financial aid was offered to the Filipinos, and Japan acquiesced in the American annexation of the former Spanish colony.

Japan's relations with the Philippines during the American colonial period were marked by expanding economic ties and a growing Japanese immigrant presence. In 1899 Japan was the fifth largest trading partner of the Philippines, and by 1929 commerce had expanded to make Japan the colony's second largest trading partner after the United States. Japanese investments were most significant in real estate, including residential and business properties, and in the development of agricultural and natural resources. By 1935 the Japanese had come to control 35 percent of all retail trade in the islands. Minerals were another important sector of trade, particularly iron ore, copper, manganese, and chrome; in 1940 base metals made up some 40 percent of the value of Philippine exports to Japan.

The American annexation of the Philippines in 1898 was followed by an influx of Japanese immigrants, composed mainly of merchants, construction workers, gardeners, and prostitutes (known as KARAYUKI SAN). By 1918 Japanese settlers outnumbered Americans in the Philippines. A main center of Japanese migration was the hemp-producing province of Davao on the island of Mindanao, which by 1941 was the home of over 20,000 Japanese.

Japanese Occupation—— Japan attacked the Philippines hours after the bombing of Pearl Harbor in 1941 and swiftly defeated the American miliary forces stationed there. Japanese conquest of the islands was a significant event in World War II because it prevented American bases in the Philippines from being used for a counterattack against Japan. The puppet government that Japan established in 1943 was composed of members of the Filipino oligarchy who had maintained their prewar business or other contacts with the Japanese. Japan's brutal conduct during the war, in which an estimated 1 million Filipinos died, gave rise to very strong anti-Japanese sentiments. The HUKBALAHAP (People's Anti-Japanese Army) was formed in 1942 as an armed guerrilla or-

photography

Introduced into Japan in the 1850s, photography soon developed as an art form.

Portrait of the statesman Saionji Kimmochi (1849–1940). Ueno Hikoma. Ca 1878.

ganization; it eventually became the nucleus of the Communist Party of the Philippines.

Postwar Relations—— The Philippines was granted independence from the United States in 1946. In 1951 it joined 47 other nations in signing the SAN FRANCISCO PEACE TREATY with Japan. However, diplomatic relations with Japan were not restored until 1956, when a reparations agreement was concluded. The Philippines had originally demanded US $8 billion for losses incurred during the war, but, after prolonged negotiations and pressures from the United States, Japan was required to pay only US $550 million in goods and services over a period of 20 years. This agreement ushered in a new era in bilateral economic relations and led to the revival of contacts between Japanese businessmen and the Filipino elite. By the end of the 1950s, Japanese corporations and investors had moved back into the Philippines.

The two countries signed a treaty of amity, commerce, and navigation in 1960, but only the Japanese side ratified it. The treaty did not go into effect until 1973, when President Ferdinand Marcos, who had abolished the Philippine legislature under martial law the previous year, ratified the treaty 10 days before the visit of Prime Minister TANAKA KAKUEI. By 1975 Japanese investments had outstripped American investments in the country, due in part to the Marcos regime's encouragement of joint ventures between Japanese conglomerates and the Filipino economic elite. Even industries that were known sources of pollution in Japan, such as iron-ore sintering, were encouraged to set up plants in the Philippines. However, it was only after the Marcos government had been overthrown in 1986 that systematic bribery by Japanese corporations, including the misuse of reparations funds, came to light.

Official development assistance (ODA) from the Japanese government has grown in tandem with Japanese private investments in the Philippines. In 1986–90, under the new administration of President Corazon Aquino, Japan provided US $2.4 billion in ODA funds. These funds have gone to support development projects involving roads, irrigation, and power plants. Since the early 1970s, Japan has replaced the United States as the largest donor of foreign aid to the Philippines. Japan's 1990 exports to the Philippines totaled US $2.5 billion, while its imports from that nation totaled US $2.2 billion.

Following a Marcos government campaign to boost tourism in the early 1970s,

Woman Combing Her Hair.
Nojima Yasuzō. 1914.

Sakhalin Cat. Photographer
unknown. Late Meiji period
(1868–1912).

Autumn. Fukuhara
Shinzō. 1925.

Japanese tourism has been a principal source of foreign exchange for the Philippines. On the other hand, the growing labor shortage in Japan has led to an influx of Filipino workers to fill gaps in the construction, service, and entertainment sectors of Japan's economy.

Growing economic activity between the Philippines and Japan has also intensified political interaction between the two countries. Cultural, academic, and educational interaction remains relatively neglected but has begun to receive more attention lately. Although frustrations and frictions have occurred in contacts between the two countries, overall relations remain cordial with an outlook to improved economic and political cooperation. See also SOUTHEAST ASIA AND JAPAN.

Philippine Sea, Battle of
マリアナ沖海戦

(Mariana Oki Kaisen). Known in Japan as the Battle of the Marianas. World War II naval engagement between the Japanese and US fleets west of the Mariana Islands, 19–20 June 1944. The US carrier force under Admiral Raymond A. Spruance bombed Saipan and Tinian preparatory to a landing on Saipan on 15 June. The Japanese fleet, under the command of Vice Admiral Ozawa Jisaburō (1886–1966), advanced from its base at Tawitawi and attacked the US fleet on 19 June. The Japanese suffered heavy losses and withdrew. Saipan was subsequently used as a base for air raids on Japan proper.

photography
写真

(shashin). Photographic techniques were introduced into Japan soon after their development in the West, and by the end of the 19th century photography had established itself as an art.

The first datable photographs taken in Japan are those done by Eliphalet Brown, Jr, a daguerreotypist who accompanied Commodore Matthew PERRY's expedition to Japan in 1853–54. The oldest surviving daguerreotype made by a Japanese is one of SHIMAZU NARIAKIRA, daimyō of the Satsuma domain (now Kagoshima Prefecture), taken in 1857.

The first professional Japanese photographer was Shimooka Renjō (1823–1914), who set up a studio in Yokohama in the early 1860s. Two other notable photographers were UENO HIKOMA and Uchida Kuichi (1844–75). Ueno opened a commercial studio in Nagasaki in 1862 that was active until his death in 1904. Uchida made a celebrated

photograph of Emperor Meiji in 1872, but his promising career was cut short by his untimely death at age 30.

Many other Japanese photographers set up studios during the 1860s. In 1867 the *Photographic News* (London) reported that in Ōsaka alone—then a city of some 300,000 inhabitants—there were no fewer than 40 professional photographers at work. However, not all photographers remained in their studios. Starting in 1871 the Hokkaidō Colonization Office employed Tamoto Kenzō (1831–1912) and other photographers to produce more than 1,000 documentary photographs of Hokkaidō. In 1876 Yokoyama Matsusaburō (1838–84) was appointed lecturer in photography at the Japanese Military Academy, and in the 1880s and 1890s the military maintained large photographic units that produced extensive documentation of the SINO-JAPANESE WAR OF 1894–1895 and the RUSSO-JAPANESE WAR (1904–05).

European photographers such as Felix Beato (1825–1906) and Baron von Stillfried studied the composition and line of UKIYO-E prints and later transmitted their vision of Japan to Japanese photographers. Beato, who began the tradition of coloring photographs by hand, employed Japanese artisans who had formerly colored *ukiyo-e* prints. The most prominent photographer in Asia during the 19th century, Beato took the oldest surviving photographs of the Japanese landscape. Beato's carefully composed photographs of such occupational types as grooms and priests tended to emphasize the appearance of the subject, whereas the work of Baron von Stillfried and his protégé Kusakabe Kinnosuke (1841–1934) concentrated on individuality and personality. Ogawa Kazumasa (1860–1929) ran a printing establishment that between 1890 and 1910 issued over 36 photographically illustrated books printed on the first collotype press in Japan.

Many amateur photographic groups were established and exhibitions held in Japan from the beginning of the 20th century. Photography at this time was influenced by the work of Henry Peach Robinson (1830–1901), the English pioneer of art photography, and was marked by efforts to achieve pictorial effects. The leader of this new movement in Japan was Akiyama Tetsusuke (1880–1944), who introduced the gum bichromate process and other pigment prints that became popular for aesthetic photography. A particularly Japanese visual sense is manifested in the ideas of the photographer Fukuhara Shinzō (1883–1948), who compared photography to

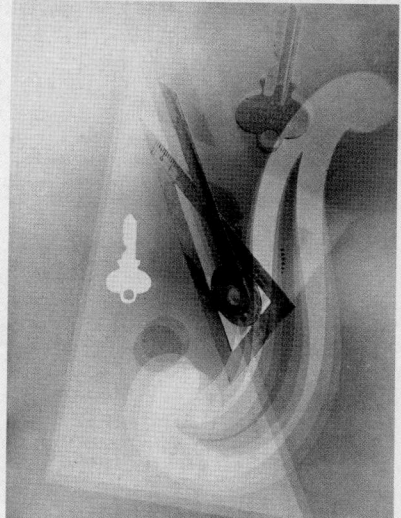

Photogram (a photograph made by direct exposure of light-sensitive paper).
Nakayama Iwata. 1932.

HAIKU in his *Hikari to sono kaichō* (1923, Light and Its Harmony).

In the 1930s the various art movements that had spread through Europe after World War I, including functional, objectivist, and surrealist trends, strongly influenced both art and documentary photography in Japan. During this period NAKAYAMA IWATA and Kanamaru Shigene (1900–1977) were active in commercial photography, while KIMURA IHEI, DOMON KEN, Watanabe Yoshio (b 1907), and NATORI YŌNOSUKE were noted for their photojournalism.

From the outbreak of the SINO-JAPANESE WAR OF 1937–1945 until the end of World War II, photography in Japan went through a dormant period with the exception of documentary photography for the war effort. However, the photography equipment and supply industry, unable to depend on imports, made strides that were to form the basis for rapid recovery after World War II. In reaction to wartime oppression, photographers began to pursue a wide range of subjects. By the 1960s Japanese society was more pluralistic, and photography became more politically oriented and concerned with social realities rather than with beauty for its own sake. Pop art was also influential, and the period was characterized by a concern with individualistic expression, the por-

Continued on page 1204 ►

Currents in Postwar Japanese Photography

In the immediate aftermath of Japan's defeat in 1945, gravure photo spreads in cheaply produced pulp magazines provided virtually the sole means by which photographers could reach their public. Domon Ken (shown at left) was prominent among those who turned their cameras on the harsh conditions of that time, and by the 1950s Realist Photography, the first coherent postwar movement, had coalesced around him. Tōmatsu Shōmei and Kawada Kikuji, who cofounded the photographers' agency VIVO in 1959, shared Domon's emphasis on social themes, but Tōmatsu's desire to assert his own individuality can be seen in the stress he put on presenting a topic "as I saw it."

The dizzying economic growth of the 1960s pushed Japan's visual media into a new age of documentary and commercial photography devoted to depicting the changes in Japanese society. A group calling itself PROVOKE used photographs to convey the profound distrust of establishment values then being openly expressed by youth around the world.

With the explicitly documentary orientation of the immediate postwar period fading into a memory by the 1970s, photographers clearly felt there was leeway to conceive of their work either in terms of self-expression (so-called Personal Photos) or as an expression of the times (the "Contemporary Photography" genre). The move away from human subjects in the late 1970s and a growing preoccupation with technique in the 1980s carried postwar photography even further from its documentary roots.

Nishii Kazuo

Yagishita Hiroshi

The photographs displayed on these pages are not arranged in strict chronological order. The date at the end of each caption indicates when the photograph was taken.

Hayashi Tadahiko (1918–90). *Furōji* (Waifs). Part of a photograph series published soon after the war in a cheaply produced magazine. (1946)

Ueda Shōji (1913–   ). *Kogitsune tōjō* (The Arrival of the Little Fox). This photographer, who lived in Tottori Prefecture, far from the rush of contemporary events, is a representative of the amateur tradition in Japanese photography. (1948)

Hamaya Hiroshi (1915–   ). *Awara no taue* (Rice Planting in Deep Mud). Long attracted to folk-life subjects, Hamaya recorded the rugged land and people of the Sea of Japan coast. (1955)

Kimura Ihei (1901–74). *Hei* (Wall). Kimura possessed an urban sensitivity like that of Cartier-Bresson, whose concept of the "decisive moment" influenced him. The shot shows the city of Akita in the remote Tōhoku region. (1953)

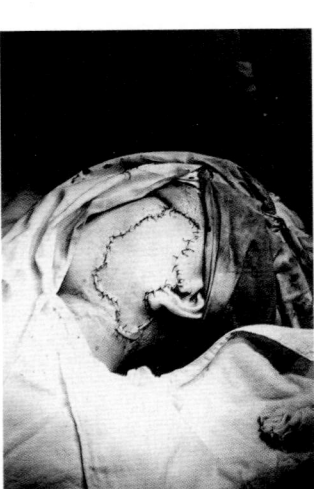

Domon Ken (1909–90). *Hidari gammen shūkei hankon shokuhi shujutsu* (Skin Graft to Remove an Unsightly Lesion on the Left Side of the Face). Domon advocated "completely unstaged, candid shots." (1957)

Tōmatsu Shōmei (1930–   ). *Ie* (Household). A cofounder of the VIVO agency, Tōmatsu is noted for his treatment of Japan's Occupation period. This kitchen sink in a farmhouse is presented as a symbol of a vanishing Japan. (1960)

Kawada Kikuji (1933–　). From *Chizu* (Map). This cofounder of the VIVO agency comments on postwar Japanese society through sardonic images, like this one of the national flag in the mud. (1962)

Ishimoto Yasuhiro (1921–　). From *Chicago, Chicago*. Born in San Francisco, this frequent visitor to the United States approached his work with a cool professionalism that brought a breath of fresh air to Japanese photography. (1960)

Tomiyama Haruo (1935–　). *Kamitsu* (Overcrowding). People wait at a cramped streetcar stop in the middle of the street in this example of the 1960s "visual documentary" style. (1964)

Shinoyama Kishin (1940–　). From *Tanjō* (Birth). A leading exponent of the new commercial photography of the 1960s, Shinoyama fascinated the public with his semiscandalous visual fantasies. (1968)

Takanashi Yutaka (1935–　). From *Tōkyōjin* (Tokyoites). A member of the PROVOKE group, Takanashi coolly recorded the changes that occurred in his native Tōkyō following the 1964 Olympics. (1966)

Moriyama Daidō (1938–　). *Norainu* (Stray Dog). To evoke the feeling of a mysterious dream seen in broad daylight, this member of the PROVOKE group distorted images by using blurred focus, coarse grain, and camera movement. (1971)

Naitō Masatoshi (1938–　). *Baba bakuhatsu* (An Explosion of Hags). Strobe lighting is used to capture the earthy energy of a group of old women gathered at a Shintō shrine in Aomori Prefecture to honor a deity of the rice harvest. (1970)

Araki Nobuyoshi (1940–　). From *Senchimentaru na tabi* (Sentimental Journey). This photograph of Araki's wife Yōko, which is from a collection made during the couple's honeymoon, exemplifies the photographer's advocacy of the "Personal Photo." (1970)

Suzuki Kiyoshi (1943–　). *Onna* (Woman). The genre called "Contemporary Photography" originated with Suzuki. In this example, false eyelashes float in a washbasin on the *tatami* floor of an apartment room. (1971)

Yamazaki Hiroshi (1946–　). From *Heliography*. The photographic pioneer Joseph Niepce described photography as "pictures drawn by the sun." In this time-exposure image of the trajectory of the rising sun, Yamazaki attempts a symbolic return to the beginnings of the art. (1978)

Shibata Toshio (1949–　). From *Nihon tenkei* (Quintessence of Japan). Cold, severe photographs in high-quality prints document a landscape scarred by the artificial works of man. (1990)

Satō Tokihiro (1957–　). From *Breath-graph*. The photographer left the lens open and exposed it to light reflected from mirrors and penlights that he manipulated. In the protracted time exposure, his own figure in motion formed no lasting image. (1990)

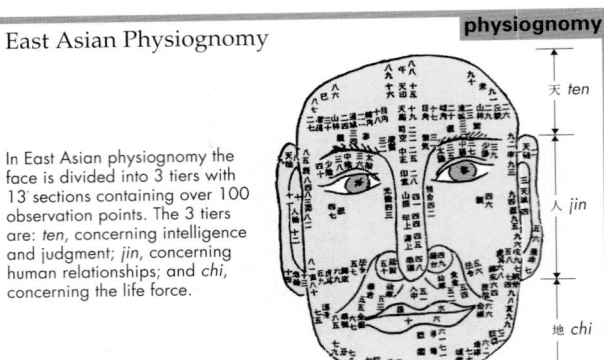
trayal of mental images, and the meaning and nature of photography itself.

A new generation of photographers emerged, including HAMAYA HIROSHI, AKIYAMA SHŌTARŌ, Hayashi Tadahiko (1918–90), Irie Taikichi (b 1905), Ishimoto Yasuhiro (b 1921), Narahara Ikkō (b 1931), Tōmatsu Shōmei (b 1930), and Hosoe Eikō (b 1933). Okamura Akihiko (b 1929) and Sawada Kyōichi (1936–70) were widely acclaimed for their photojournalism during the Vietnam War. In the 1970s new photographers frequently utilized filmmaking, television, printmaking, and computer graphic techniques, stressing the search for an ever more personal image (*eizō*).

In the latter half of the 1980s Japanese photography entered a new phase, with emphasis on constructed photography and topographic photography, yet the traditional empathy for and identification with nature still remain strong elements.

Interest in collecting original photographic prints has spread rapidly, and in 1990 the Tōkyō Shashin Bijutsukan (Tōkyō Metropolitan Museum of Photography) was opened in Shibuya Ward, Tōkyō. Photography in Japan today is characterized by large numbers of amateur photographers, the influential role played by many camera magazines, and the high quality of Japanese camera, video, and computer equipment. Photography has become an indispensable part of journalism, advertising, and publishing.

The diversity of current photography is represented by the experimental photographs of Shinoyama Kishin (b 1940), who has consciously set out to create vivid mass-media images with his studies of women in the entertainment world; the photo essays of Fujiwara Shin'ya (b 1944), with their keen social commentary on Tōkyō life in the 1980s; and the intimately personal and subjective work of Araki Nobuyoshi (b 1940), which was a reaction against a grandiose style of photography that had excluded people's private lives. Araki's work had a great impact on Japanese photography in the 1970s and 1980s. ☎ 1202–1203

Physically Handicapped Welfare Law
身体障害者福祉法

(Shintai Shōgaisha Fukushi Hō). Law enacted in 1949 to assist in the rehabilitation and training of the physically handicapped. Under this law, a physically handicapped person is defined as a person over the age of 18 who has a specific visual handicap, hearing disorder, or impairment of equilibrium, impairment of vocal or language facilities, or a form of paralysis and who has been issued a physically handicapped person's identification card by the prefectural governor.

The Advisory Council on the Welfare of the Physically Handicapped (Shintai Shōgaisha Fukushi Shingikai) investigates matters relating to the welfare of the physically handicapped. Offices of welfare for the physically handicapped function as part of the welfare offices of the local governments and provide special technical guidance and services to welfare officers. Rehabilitation counseling offices operate in each prefecture to provide medical, psychological, and occupational counseling. The law provides for the commissioning of qualified counselors. See also SOCIAL SECURITY LEGISLATION; SPECIAL EDUCATION.

physics
物理学

(*butsurigaku*). The study of modern physics in Japan began in the late Edo period (1600–1868). A few books on physics written in Dutch were brought by traders from the Netherlands to the Dutch factory at DEJIMA, the only window open to the outside world during the period of NATIONAL SECLUSION. Translations of several of these, along with such Japanese secondary works as *Kyūritsū* (1836, Physics) by HOASHI BANRI, a noted scholar of Rangaku or "Dutch Learning" (see WESTERN LEARNING), were read only by a small group of Japanese scholars thirsting for information on scientific matters and did not lead to formal study of modern physics, because no system of modern scientific research existed.

During the two decades after the Meiji Restoration of 1868, a number of Western physicists, technicians, and engineers contributed to the development of physics in Japan. William Edward AYRTON, an Englishman, helped develop the study of electrical engineering. Thomas Corwin MENDENHALL, an American known for his measurements of gravity at the summit of Mt. Fuji (Fujisan), laid the foundations for studies in physics and seismology.

In 1873 YAMAKAWA KENJIRŌ, who had studied at Yale University in the United States, instituted a lecture course in physics at Tōkyō University. This was followed by similar programs at other major universities. Original research by Japanese scholars of modern physics began to bear fruit after 1887. Particularly outstanding were the study of elementary particles carried out by NAGAOKA HANTARŌ and the developmental study of magnetic material started by HONDA KŌTARŌ. The award of the Nobel Prize for Physics went to YUKAWA HIDEKI in 1949 for his meson theory and to TOMONAGA SHIN'ICHIRŌ in 1965 for the super-many-time theory and the renormalization theory. In 1973 the physicist ESAKI REONA received the Nobel Prize for his tunnel-diode research. Contemporary developments in Japanese physics include the TRISTAN particle accelerator project. See also NATURAL SCIENCES.

physiognomy
人相

(*ninsō*). The art of physiognomy, particularly as practiced in China and Japan, is characterized by the adoption of divination techniques related to the diagnosis of disease. It has its roots in ancient China and especially in the OMMYŌDŌ school of cosmology. Although physiognomy was practiced in rudimentary form in early Japan, the first attempt at a systematization appears to have been the Muromachi-period (1333–1568) work *Senten sōhō*, written by a priest of the Tendai sect of Buddhism. In the Edo period (1600–1868), Japan produced many physiognomists.

The commonest method involves the study of a series of fixed observation points on the face and body, with a final judgment as to a person's character and temperament resting on a complex synthesis of these observations in accordance with Ommyōdō theory. Although not as popular as it once was, *ninsō* still has its practitioners in contemporary Japan.

pickles
漬物

(*tsukemono*). Japanese pickles are generally made from vegetables, although seafood or meat may also be used. The pickling base (*tsukedoko*) is made from salt, rice bran (*nuka*), MISO (fermented bean paste), or vinegar. The innumerable varieties of *tsukemono* are classified according to the main ingredient, the pickling base, and the duration of pickling time. *Tsukemono* are regarded as an essential part of a meal. They are eaten with boiled rice, with tea, or as an accompaniment to *sake* or beer.

Nukamisozuke, or vegetables pickled in rice bran paste, are unique to Japan. The ingredients are put into a pickling base of rice bran and salt water kneaded together to the consistency of *miso*. When the vegetables have acquired the proper flavor, consistency, and color, the pickling base is washed away and the vegetables are sliced and eaten alone or with soy sauce.

Foods may be pickled in salt (*shiozuke*) from two to three hours, as in the case of *asazuke* (lightly pickled radish), or for a long time, as in the case of UMEBOSHI (pickled plums). They may also be pickled in *miso* flavored with soy sauce or *mirin* (sweet *sake*), in mustard, or in *sake* lees.

picture brides
写真花嫁

(*shashin hanayome*). Popular term for Japanese women in the early 20th century who married in absentia Japanese immigrants, mainly to the United States and Canada, after an exchange of photographs and then went to join their new husbands. Picture brides emerged as a result of the GENTLEMEN'S AGREEMENT of 1907–08, in which the Japanese government agreed to issue passports only to immigrants already established in the United States and to the parents, wives, and children of such immigrants. Picture bride marriages were recognized by US immigration officials, but they were made an issue by forces calling for the exclusion of Japanese immigrants. In an attempt to avoid the complete exclusion of Japanese immigrants, the Japanese government voluntarily stopped issuing passports to picture brides for the continental United States in 1920–21, although passports continued to be issued for Hawaii, then a US territory. Nevertheless, the Immigration Act of 1924 excluded new Japanese immigrants from the continental United States and Hawaii, preventing many Japanese immigrants already resident in the United States from marrying Japanese wives. Naturalization of Japanese immigrants and the entry of close relatives of naturalized Japanese were not permitted until a new immigration act was passed in 1952 (see UNITED STATES IMMIGRATION ACTS OF 1924, 1952, AND 1965). See also JAPANESE AMERICANS; JAPANESE AMERICANS IN HAWAII.

Piggott, Francis Stewart
ピゴット，F. S.

(1883–1966). British army officer. Piggott served as military attaché at the British embassy in Japan on three tours over a period of 13 years. In the late 1930s he worked to ease tension between Britain and Japan over the

▲ *Sugukina*, a kind of turnip, is pickled in a well-known Kyōto style popular since the Edo period (1600–1868). Layers of the vegetable, with its leaves attached, are alternated with layers of salt in wooden tubs for the first "rough pressing."

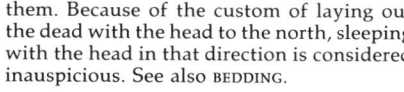

pickles

◄ The center for the type of pickling shown in the three photos at left is the area around the Kami-Gamo Shrine in Kyōto, where the weighted pickling tubs are a common sight in late November. After being compressed for 10 days, the pickles are aged for a week before being packaged.

◄ After 24 hours, the *sugukina* are washed and again layered with salt, this time in smaller wooden tubs.

► The pickles of Kyōto are famous for their color, taste, and variety. Among the pickled vegetables shown here are *sugukina* (right top) as well as eggplant, cucumber, and radish.

question of extraterritorial Western concessions in China. After World War II, Piggott became president of the Japan Society in London. His autobiography, *Broken Thread* (1950), recounts his experiences in Japan.

pilgrimages 巡礼

(*junrei*). In Japan pilgrimages can be divided into two general types. The first is the type exemplified by the "Pilgrimage to the 33 Holy Places of KANNON in the Western Provinces" and the "Pilgrimage to the 88 Temples of Shikoku," in which one makes a circuit of a series of temples or holy places, sometimes separated by great distances, in a set order. The order of visitation is an important feature of this type of pilgrimage. The second type is a journey to one particular holy place. Pilgrimages to the KUMANO SANZAN SHRINES and ISE SHRINE, as well as to certain holy mountains, belong to this type (see also OKAGE MAIRI). In common usage the term *junrei* usually refers to the first type only.

It is thought that pilgrimages were first undertaken in the Nara period (710–794), although the custom did not become popular until the Heian period (794–1185). Kumano, in southern Wakayama Prefecture, became a large center for adherents of the SHUGENDŌ sect. HASEDERA, SHITENNŌJI, KŌYASAN, and KIMPUSENJI were also popular pilgrimage sites. In the Edo period (1600–1868) the number of pilgrims who made journeys to the western provinces, Shikoku, KOTOHIRA SHRINE, ZENKŌJI, Ise, Kiso Ontake, and Mt. Fuji increased rapidly. Travel since the Meiji period (1868–1912) has basically preserved the Edo-period pattern of pilgrimage. Behind this phenomenon, perhaps lies a nostalgia for the past, a resurging interest in religion, and a desire for temporary escape from urban centers. See also TRAVEL.

pillows 枕

(*makura*). Stone pillows, which have been discovered in ancient tombs, were probably the first pillows used in Japan. Later, wooden pillows (*komakura*) and pillows made from bundles of grass (*kusamakura*) came into general use. When a style of coiffure called *keppatsu* became popular in the Edo period (1600–1868), wooden pillows were replaced by raised pillows supported by a boxlike frame (*hakomakura*). Stuffed pillows (*kukurimakura*), made of cotton and filled with buckwheat chaff or tea grounds, replaced grass pillows. Today most pillows are stuffed with buckwheat chaff, kapok, or down.

There are a number of popular superstitions connected with pillows. In ancient times it was thought that during sleep the spirit left the body and dwelt in the pillow. As a result, many Japanese still have an aver-

sion to stepping over pillows or throwing them. Because of the custom of laying out the dead with the head to the north, sleeping with the head in that direction is considered inauspicious. See also BEDDING.

pines 松

(*matsu*). *Pinus* spp. *Matsu* is the common name for evergreen trees of the family Pinaceae, genus *Pinus*, which are found throughout Japan, both wild and cultivated. Among the best-known native Japanese pines are the following:

The *akamatsu* (*P. densiflora*), or Japanese red pine, is found in the interiors of Honshū, Shikoku, and Kyūshū and is also planted extensively as timber. The most common ornamental pine, it reaches a height of 40 meters (130 ft). Its name is derived from the reddish hue of its bark. The *akamatsu* is also known as the *mematsu* (female pine) for its graceful shape.

The *kuromatsu* (*P. thunbergii*), or Japanese black pine, is distributed in the same areas as the *akamatsu*, but it is found more generally in coastal areas. It grows to as much as 40 meters in height. It is used as a windbreak as well as for erosion control, landscaping, and BONSAI. Its blackish bark gives it its name. It is also known as the *omatsu* (male pine), being more burly in appearance than the *akamatsu*.

The *goyōmatsu* (*P. parviflora*), or "five-leafed pine," is found throughout Japan. Its needles grow in clusters of five, hence its name. It grows to a height of 18 meters (59 ft). It is used for building, furniture, and *bonsai*.

In ancient times the pine was considered a sacred tree, and it is still used today in the New Year's decoration known as KADOMATSU.
— *See photos, next page.*

Pioneer Electronic Corporation パイオニア[株]

(*Paionia*). A major manufacturer of audio and video products. The company was established in 1938 to produce loudspeakers and took its current name in 1961. More than 50 percent of its sales are derived from overseas markets. It has a total of some 20 production and sales subsidiaries in North America and Europe. The company launched the first laser videodisk in Japan and is the current leader in that market. The worldwide consolidated sales for the fiscal year ending March 1991 totaled ¥396.4 billion (US $2.9 billion). The company was capitalized at ¥48.4 billion (US $352.8 million) in the same year. Headquarters are in Tōkyō.

pit houses 竪穴住居

(*tateana jūkyo*). Semisubterranean, single-room dwellings used throughout the Japanese prehistoric periods and into the early

historic periods. They consisted of square, round, or oval pits dug up to 0.5 meter (1.6 ft) below the existing ground surface, with cone-shaped superstructures built of posts, beams, and leaning poles, and thatched with grass (miscanthus), reeds, or bark. These primitive houses were eventually replaced by surface and raised-floor buildings developed in later centuries. Features such as fireplaces or hearths, drainage ditches, storage pits, and bed platforms changed along with the size and construction of the pit houses throughout the various periods.

Few pit houses have been discovered for the earliest phases of the Jōmon period (ca 10,000 BC–ca 300 BC). Known examples were first rounded then squarish in shape, about 4 by 4 meters (13 by 13 ft) in size, with an irregular number of posts. In contrast, Middle Jōmon (ca 3500 BC–ca 2500 BC; also dated as ca 3500 BC–ca 2000 BC) pit houses were generally

pilgrimages Pilgrims praying at Shimabuji, the first stop on the popular circuit of 33 Kannon temples in the Chichibu district of Saitama Prefecture. Pilgrims typically wear white clothes and sedge hats and carry staffs.

pines

▶ A pine tree on the coast of Tottori Prefecture. "Ocean, rock, and pine" is a favorite theme in traditional Japanese art.

Left: the mature cone of the red pine. *Above:* two twigs showing pollen-bearing male cones (top) and immature female cones.

◀ The image of the pine has long played an important part in Japanese art and culture. Here, a Nō costume of the late Edo period (1600–1868) decorated with a stylized, woven pine motif.

▶ The red pine is planted extensively for its timber. Red pine forests are also the best place to find the *matsutake* mushroom, a Japanese delicacy.

round, averaging 5–6 meters (16.4–19.7 ft) in diameter, with roofs supported by 5 or 6 posts around a central interior fireplace. Most of the houses of the Yayoi period (ca 300 BC–ca AD 300) were built over shallow oval-shaped pits averaging 6 by 8 meters (19.7 by 26.2 ft) and supported by 4 posts. Those of the Kofun period (ca 300–710) also had 4 posts and were strictly rectangular, with a clay or stone hearth along one wall.

Planning Board Incident
企画院事件

(Kikakuin Jiken). World War II incident involving the arrest of members of the Kikakuin (Planning Board), a government agency created by Prime Minister KONOE FUMIMARO in October 1937 to formulate plans for rationalizing Japan's wartime economy. Submitted in November 1940, the board's plans called for the separation of capital and management, equitable distribution of profits, extensive land reform, and strict bureaucratic control of the economy. The plans encountered strong opposition from Japanese business interests and conservative bureaucrats led by HIRANUMA KIICHIRŌ. The latter group, on the pretext that Kikakuin bureaucrats were secretly working toward the same goals as the Japan Communist Party, arranged for the arrest in early 1941 of 10 Planning Board members and former members. The accused, who included Wada Hiroo (1903–67), Inaba Hidezō (b 1907), and Katsumata Seiichi (1908–89), were charged with violating the PEACE PRESERVATION LAW OF 1925 and sentenced to prison. In September 1945, after the conclusion of World War II, the 10 men were vindicated and returned to office.

plant crops
農作物

(nōsakumotsu). More than 400 species of crop plant are cultivated in Japan; of these more than half are food crops and the rest are industrial and forage crops. Japan's food crops are notably rich in variety, partially

due to Japan's wide range of CLIMATE. A more important reason is that the Japanese have, for more than 2,000 years, introduced many foreign food crops. Although Japan has an abundance of common flora, indigenous crops are few. They include FUKI (butterbur) and *wasabi* (Japanese horseradish) among vegetables, *kuri* (Japanese chestnut) and *kaki* (persimmon) among fruits, and *hakka* (mint) and *mitsumata* (*Edgeworthia papyrifera*) among industrial crops.

The most important of all crops in Japan is RICE, the nation's staple food. Of the total area of 5.2 million hectares (12.8 million acres) under cultivation in Japan as of 1990, paddies occupied 2.8 million hectares (6.9 million acres) and produced 10,499,000 metric tons (11,549,000 short tons) of unpolished rice. The cultivation of WHEAT AND BARLEY as secondary crops in paddies has largely been discontinued. Corn is rarely grown as a grain crop. About 455,000 metric tons (500,500 short tons) of pulses were produced in 1989, of which SOYBEANS accounted for about 169,000 metric tons (185,900 short tons), satisfying only 6 percent of the domestic demand. As with cereal crops other than rice, pulse cultivation was in a state of decline; one exception was the AZUKI bean.

Among vegetables, RADISHES (*daikon*) are produced in greatest abundance, followed by Chinese cabbage. Numerous leaf and root vegetables are grown for pickling purposes and are important elements in traditional Japanese meals. As the habit of eating Western food has become widespread, the cultivation of cabbage, onions, cucumbers, tomatoes, lettuce, and cauliflower has increased.

In 1990 fruit trees were being grown on about 475,000 hectares (1,174,000 acres) throughout the country. The mandarin orange (MIKAN) and the apple, both introduced from abroad, are Japan's most important fruits. Next in importance, in terms of area under cultivation, are the indigenous chestnut, persimmon, and Japanese sand pear. Most fruits, including GRAPES and PEACHES, are produced mainly for eating fresh.

MUSHROOMS such as *shiitake*, *enokitake*, *hiratake*, and *nameko* are cultivated artificially and are in much demand. White mushrooms introduced from Europe are also grown. Green TEA is grown, as is rush, used in making TATAMI (floor mats). Konjak tuber (KONNYAKU) to be processed for food is cultivated. TOBACCO, sugar beets, and sugarcane are also grown, but production is decreasing, as is production of such industrial crops as sesame, rape, and flax. Industrial plants indigenous to Japan include *urushi* (the Japanese LACQUER TREE) and *kōzo* (paper mulberry; *Broussonetia kazinoki*), used for making Japanese paper. Many medicinal herbs are also grown, including ginseng (Chōsen *ninjin*), digitalis, Chinese bellflower (KIKYŌ), rhubarb, senega, and PEONIES. The Japanese INDIGO plant (*tadeai*) is grown for traditional dyes, and dyer's saffron (*benibana*) is produced in small amounts for traditional cosmetics. Mulberry trees for silk production are still grown, but silk is now declining gradually. Corn is the feed crop grown in most quantity, followed by sorghum and sunflowers.

plant hopper
浮塵子

(*unka*). A general term for insects of the family Delphacidae and including the superfamily Fulgoroidea and the superfamily Cicadelloidea. The *himetobi-unka* (smaller brown plant hopper; *Laodelphax striatellus*), *sejiro-unka* (white-backed plant hopper; *Sogatella furcifera*), and *tobiiro-unka* (brown plant hopper; *Nilaparvata lugens*) are the three species most harmful to the rice plant. The insect resembles a cicada in shape, is about 5 millimeters (0.2 in) long, and feeds on the sap of growing rice. It is occasionally recorded as a cause of rice crop failure.

plants
植物

(*shokubutsu*). Extending north to south for some 3,500 kilometers (2,175 mi), the Japanese archipelago has a great diversity of climate and vegetation. Botanists estimate that there are 5,000 to 6,000 native species

1206

Planning Board Incident

of plant. This article deals chiefly with certain seed plants (spermatophytes) that are of particular importance to the Japanese people.

Types of Plants in Japan——In terms of plant distribution, Japan is included in the East Asian temperate zone and may be roughly subdivided into the following five zones:

1. The subtropical zone, which includes the Ryūkyū and Ogasawara island groups. Characteristic plants are the *gajumaru* (*Ficus microcarpa*) of the Ryūkyūs and the *hime-tsubaki* (*Schima wallichii*) of the Ogasawaras.

2. The warm-temperate zone of broad-leaved evergreen forests, which covers the greater part of southern Honshū, Shikoku, and Kyūshū. The *yabutsubaki* (*Camellia japonica*), the *shiinoki* (*Castanopsis sieboldii*), and the *kusu* (*Cinnamomum camphora*) are among its characteristic plants.

3. The cool-temperate zone of broad-leaved deciduous forests, which covers central and northern Honshū and the southwestern part of Hokkaidō. Characteristic plants include the *konara* (*Quercus serrata*) and the *buna* (*Fagus crenata*).

4. The subalpine zone, which includes central and northern Hokkaidō. Characteristic plants include the *kokemomo* (*Vaccinium vitis-idaea*) and the *tōhi* (*Picea jezoensis*).

5. The alpine zone, which covers the highlands of central Honshū and the central part of Hokkaidō, with the *haimatsu* (*Pinus pumila*) and *komakusa* (*Dicentra peregrina*) among the characteristic plants.

The more prominent native species are treated in separate entries in this encyclopedia and are listed at the end of this article. Particularly rare species include the *yakkosō* (*Mitrastemon yamamotoi*), a parasitic plant of the family Rafflesiaceae, without chlorophyll and thus all white, growing only in parts of Shikoku and Kyūshū on the roots of the *shiinoki;* the *kōshinsō* (*Pinguicula ramosa*), an insectivorous perennial of the family Lentibulariaceae, growing on rock walls in the high mountains near Nikkō; the *shakujōsō* (*Monotropa hypopithys*), a perennial saprophyte of the family Pyrolaceae, growing in the shade of mountain trees; the *tsuchitorimochi* (*Balanophora japonica*), a parasitic perennial of the family Balanophoraceae, growing under trees in warm places; the *kawagokesō* (*Cladopus japonicus*), a perennial of the family Podostemonaceae, resembling moss, growing on rocks along the rivers in the mountains of Kagoshima Prefecture; the *togakushi shōma* (*Ranzania japonica*), a perennial of the family Berberidaceae, growing under trees in the deep mountains northward from central Honshū, with light purple flowers in spring; the *shiraitosō* (*Chinographis japonica*), a perennial of the family Liliaceae, growing in the mountains and under trees southward from central Honshū, bearing white flowers in spikes; and the *kan'aoi* (*Asarum nipponicum*), an evergreen perennial of the family Aristolochiaceae, growing under trees in the mountains of central Honshū, bearing dark purple flowers in late autumn.

Although some plants came to Japan very early in the nation's history, most of the naturalized plants were introduced in rapid succession after the beginning of the Meiji period (1868–1912). The number of naturalized plants is said to be between 200 and 500. Although most came from Europe, the United States has in recent years become a major source.

In the mid-Edo period (1600–1868) Japa-nese floriculture began to develop. As few flowering plants were imported during the age of NATIONAL SECLUSION (1639–1854), many excellent garden plants were developed from wild species. Arbores developed include the *sakura* (flowering cherry), the *tsubaki* (camellia), and the *kaede* (maple); arborets include the *tsutsuji* (azalea).

Floriculture plants developed in China and introduced to Japan by the Edo period include the *suisen* (narcissus), the *kiku* (chrysanthemum), the *ume* (Japanese plum), the *momo* (peach), and the *boke* (Japanese quince). These were greatly improved, and many excellent floricultural varieties were produced in the Edo period.

Uses of Plants in Japan——Throughout their recorded history, the Japanese have utilized plants for food and for countless other purposes, including clothing, medicines, dyes, oils, tools, roofing, sculpture, paper, matting, hats, ropes, baskets, and fuel. Most plants now being put to such uses are indigenous to Japan, but the majority of edible plants are thought to have been introduced from the Asian continent. These include rice, wheat, barley, beans, corn, buckwheat, sweet potatoes, potatoes, radishes, and cabbage. Flax and cotton for clothing, medicinal plants, and plants for dyes also came from foreign countries in ancient times. Of the edible plants indigenous to Japan, *seri* (water dropwort; *Oenanthe javanica*), *udo* (*Aralia cordata*), *fuki* (*Petasites japonicus*), *mitsuba* (*Cryptotaenia japonica*), and *wasabi* (*Wasabia japonica*) have been domesticated from wild plants and are still used in cooking.

Plants in Literature——The beauty of nature, embodied in the term *kachō fūgetsu* ("flowers, birds, wind, and moon"), has been a principal theme in Japanese literature, especially WAKA and HAIKU. The fact that flowers have been given first place in this phrase does not seem to be coincidental. The TALE OF GENJI, written about the year 1000 and noted for its superb descriptions of nature, makes reference to 101 kinds of plants. Frequent use of trees and plants in similes is often considered one of the characteristics of Japanese literature.

For the Japanese, nature has not only been an object of aesthetic appreciation but also an agent evoking intense poetic sentiments. They have loved flowers not so much for their fragrance and color as for their form and emotional import. The special significance Japanese have attached to the seasons in their poetry is an expression of their close observation of and affection for plants as signs of the ever-vanishing, ever-perpetuating pattern of nature. An understanding of this attitude is essential to the appreciation of traditional Japanese literature.

Plants in the Visual Arts——Pictorial and other arts in Japan have also traditionally relied heavily on the artist's sensitivity to nature and have generally tended toward the simple, compact, and sparely graceful. Traditional Japanese renditions of landscapes do not display the wide range of color seen in Western-style oil paintings. In sculpture, too, works are in general delicately carved and small in scale. Plants, flowers, and birds or their patterns are frequently reproduced in lifelike colors on fabric, lacquer ware, and ceramic ware. A love of natural form and an eagerness to express it ideally have been primary motives in the development of traditional Japanese arts, such as FLOWER ARRANGEMENT, the TEA CEREMONY, tray landscapes (*bonkei;* see BONKEI AND BONSEKI), BONSAI, and landscape gardening.

Plants and Folklore——In the hope of avoiding natural disasters, early people formulated sacred rites of exorcism, ablution, and divination. These mystico-religious activities and an awe of nature in general led people to see symbols of the divine in trees and flowers. An excellent example is the once widely practiced worship of primeval evergreen trees—pines (*matsu*), cedars (*sugi*), cypresses (*hinoki*), and camphor trees (*kusunoki*)—which the early Japanese believed offered habitation (*yorishiro*) to deities who descended from heaven. The practice of decorating the gates of houses with pine branches (KADOMATSU) on New Year's Day derives from the belief that this was a means of welcoming deities.

Spirits were also thought to abide in flowers, and "flower divination" was conducted to forecast each year's harvest. When the *sakura* (flowering cherry), *utsugi* (deutzia), *tsutsuji* (azalea), and *asebi* (Japanese andromeda) bloomed profusely, people believed it meant a year of abundance; when the blossoms fell early, they believed that the harvest would be poor. The practice of offering to the dead selected flowers at the height of their bloom is based on the folk belief that the soul can pass through living flowers. Linked to Buddhism, it represented an attempt to call back the soul of the dead. It was also thought that the deities who caused epidemics roamed abroad when spring blossoms fell. In the hope of controlling such epidemics, a rite called Chinkasai (Soothing of the Flowers) was held; it is still celebrated today in several places in Japan.

Another folk custom involving flowers, the flower-viewing party (*hanami*), also dates back to antiquity. Originally an event closely related to agricultural rites, it later became a purely recreational activity. The most popular flower for viewing has been the *sakura.* An annual cherry-viewing party sponsored by the imperial court became an established custom in the Heian period (794–1185). During the Edo period the practice of holding annual flower-viewing parties spread among the common people. Besides the *sakura,* the *ume* (Japanese plum), *fuji* (wisteria), *kiku* (chrysanthemum), and *hasu* (lotus) are common objects of viewing. The Japanese also play games of *hana-awase* (making comparisons of flowers for beauty). Each prefecture now has its own official tree and flower.

Plants and Religion——The early Japanese worshiped nature as divine. They believed that natural features such as mountains, rivers, stones, and plants all had spirits and offered prayers to and sought salvation from them. For religious festivals, evergreen trees such as pines and *sakaki* (*Cleyera japonica*) were used because they were thought to be dwellings of gods, and marine products (seaweed, fish, and shellfish) and fresh farm vegetables were offered to the deities instead of animal flesh. These traditions survive in present-day SHINTŌ (see also FESTIVALS). Buddhism, which was introduced to Japan in about the 6th century, banned the destruction of living creatures, so flowers and plants were used for its rituals, a practice that is still followed.

Plants in Modern Japan——During the Meiji period, the Japanese became preoccupied with modern and Western values and much less concerned with nature. At one time this change was generally regarded as a

playing cards *Unsun karuta*, shown with the card box (left), were used during the Edo period for gambling.

sign of progress, but a major consequence of Japan's rapid industrialization (especially since World War II) has been the indiscriminate exploitation of nature, including reckless deforestation. This in turn has led to widespread pollution that has affected every element of Japanese society. People have recently come to realize that the "progress" they once believed to be entirely beneficial is not necessarily so and that conservation and rehabilitation of the natural environment should be a major priority. Many Japanese now feel strongly that their country's great wealth of plant life should be protected and reconsidered in light of old values.

This encyclopedia contains entries on the following plants and plant groups:

Ornamental Trees and Shrubs—AOKI; ASEBI; AZALEAS; CAMELLIAS; CHERRY, FLOWERING; CHINABERRY; GARDENIA; HYDRANGEA, JAPANESE; ICHII; KOBUSHI; MANRYŌ; MAPLES; NANTEN; PAULOWNIA; PEACHES; PLUM, JAPANESE; QUINCE, DWARF JAPANESE; RHODODENDRONS; SAZANKA; SENRYŌ; SHIMOTSUKE; SOTETSU; TOBERA; TOSA MIZUKI; UMEMODOKI; UTSUGI; WILLOWS; WISTERIA, JAPANESE; WITCH HAZEL; YABUKŌJI; YAMABUKI; YATSUDE.

Other Trees and Shrubs—AKEBI; BUNA; CAMPHOR TREE; CYPRESSES; EGONOKI; GINKGO; HAGI; HŌNOKI; HORSE CHESTNUT, JAPANESE; KATSURA TREE; KUROMOJI; LARCH, JAPANESE; MUBE; MURASAKI SHIKIBU; NANAKAMADO; NEZUMIMOCHI; OAKS; PINES; SAKAKI; SHIKIMI; SUGI; TARANOKI; TSUGE; WILD ROSES; YAMABŌSHI; ZELKOVA.

Chiefly Garden Flowers—ANEMONE, JAPANESE; BENIBANA; CHRYSANTHEMUMS; EBINE; FUKKISŌ; HECHIMA; HOTOTOGISU; IRISES; JOCHŪGIKU; KIKYŌ; LILIES; MORNING GLORIES; PEONIES; PRIMROSES; SAGISŌ; SHIRAN; SHUNRAN; SUISEN; TSUWABUKI.

Chiefly Wild Flowers—ASHI; DAY LILIES; FRINGED PINK; FUKI; FUKUJUSŌ; GENTIANS; HAMAYŪ; HIGAMBANA; HIRUGAO; HITORISHIZUKA; HONEYSUCKLE, JAPANESE; ICHIRINSŌ; ITADORI; KANAMUGURA; KATAKURI; KUMAGAISŌ; KUZU; MATSUMUSHISŌ; MISUMISŌ; MIYAKOGUSA; MURASAKI; OKERA; OMINAESHI; OMOTO; RENGESŌ; RYŪNŌGIKU; SEMBURI; SHŌBU; SUSUKI; THISTLES; TSURIGANE NINJIN; TSUYUKUSA; VIOLETS; YAMABUKISŌ; YAMA TORIKABUTO; YOMENA; YOMOGI.

Other Plants—BAMBOO; CHLORELLA; FERNS; LOTUS; MATSUTAKE; MOSSES; MUSHROOMS; SEAWEED; SHIITAKE; WATER LILY.

playing cards カルタ

(*karuta*; from Portuguese *carta*, "card"). Rectangular cards inscribed with numbers, pictures, or writing, used in playing Western and Japanese card games. Card playing was introduced to Japan in the early 16th century, and eventually GAMBLING became so rampant that ordinances were issued by the Tokugawa shogunate (1603–1867) banning

card games and other forms of gambling. The earliest Western-style card games, *tenshō karuta* (named after the Tenshō era, 1573–92) and *unsun karuta* (from the Portuguese *um* "one" and *summo* "highest"), were both associated with gambling. Today *karuta* usually refers to HANAFUDA ("flower cards"), *uta karuta* ("poem cards"), and IROHA KARUTA ("ABC cards"), favorite games at New Year's festivities. Western-style playing cards are now called *torampu*.

Uta karuta developed in the early Edo period (1600–1868) out of traditional Japanese games of matching halves of decorated clamshells (KAI-AWASE). In *uta karuta*, two sets of 100 cards are used. One set has the entire text of a WAKA poem—usually one from the HYAKUNIN ISSHU (ca 1235, Single Poems by 100 Poets) anthology—on each card, and the other, the last two lines only. One person, chosen as reader, reads the first three lines of a poem from the first set of cards, and the players try to pick out the matching card from the second set, which is spread out before them.

Plaza Accord プラザ合意

(*Puraza Gōi*). Agreement reached at the financial conference held at the Plaza Hotel in New York in September 1985 by members of the Group of Five, or G5 (see G5, G7). The main purpose of the meeting was to halt the excessive rise of the US dollar in an attempt to correct chronic trade imbalances that were seen as a source of growing protectionist pressures. It was agreed to reduce the dollar's value by 10–20 percent of its then-current exchange rate through coordinated central bank intervention by the G5 members. It was also agreed that the United States should reduce its fiscal deficit by 1 percent of its gross national product annually and that Japan and Germany should expand domestic demand. The Plaza Accord was important as an attempt at international cooperation in the management of economic policies of the major industrialized nations.

PL Kyōdan PL教団

(Pī Eru Kyōdan; The Church of Perfect Liberty). Religious organization founded in 1946. Its origins lie in the Tokumitsukyō, founded in 1912 by Kaneda Tokumitsu (1863–1919). Kaneda attracted many followers through his faith healing and teachings on prosperity. MIKI TOKUCHIKA and his father, Miki Tokuharu (1871–1938), took over Tokumitsukyō after Kaneda's death and changed its name in 1931 to Hito no Michi Kyōdan (the Way-of-Man Organization). Despite its conformist views and positions, which included the adoption of the IMPERIAL RESCRIPT ON EDUCATION, the group was dissolved by the militarist government during World War II. In 1946 Tokuchika reestablished and modified it, choosing an English name, Perfect Liberty. Stating "Life Is Art" as the first of 21 mottoes, the teachings emphasize that man's divine nature should be expressed creatively. In 1974 the name was officially changed to Pāfekuto Ribatī Kyōdan. The group, which claimed over 1.8 million adherents in 1989, holds its annual festival on 1 August.

plovers 千鳥

(*chidori*). Small shorebirds of the family Charadriidae, with long legs, round heads, short bills, and large eyes. Twelve species are found in Japan. Among them are the *munaguro* (American golden plover; *Pluvialis dominica*), *daizen* (grey plover; *P. squataro-*

la), the *kochidori* (little ringed plover; *Charadrius dubius*), *ikaru chidori* (long-billed ringed plover; *C. placidus*), *shirochidori* (Kentish plover; *C. alexandrinus*), *medai chidori* (Mongolian plover; *C. mongolus*), *ōmedai chidori* (greater sand plover; *C. leschenaultii*), *keri* (gray-headed lapwing; *Microsarcops cinereus*), and the *tageri* (lapwing; *Vanellus vanellus*).

The spectacle of flocks of *chidori* feeding on the seashore has been celebrated since ancient times by Japanese poets. The "plover and wave" pattern (*chidorigata*) is widely used as a decoration for *kimono* and sliding-panel doors.

plum, Japanese 梅

(*ume*). *Prunus mume*. Also known as Japanese apricot. Deciduous tree of the family Rosaceae, grown as a garden and orchard plant in Japan and bearing deep and varied associations with traditional Japanese culture. Its fruits are smaller and less sweet than those of European plums (*sumomo*) or European apricots (*anzu*).

The *ume* reaches a height of about 6 meters (20 ft). The five-petaled blossoms appear in early spring before the leaves and give off a distinctive fragrance. Unripened, the fruit is used to make wine, vinegar, and pickled plums (UMEBOSHI). In the past the fruit was used for dyeing, and the ripe yellow fruit is still used for a confection called *noshiume*, in which the pulp is mixed with sugar and agar-agar and rolled out in strips.

The *ume* fruit has long been valued for medicinal purposes. It is picked before ripening and smoke-cured or cooked in ashes to be used as a remedy for vomiting, intestinal worms, fevers, coughing, and colds. The bark of the tree is also used as a dye, and the wood is used for fine woodwork.

The original home of the *ume* was China. From references in the 8th-century poetry collection, the MAN'YŌSHŪ, its arrival in Japan can be placed before or during the Nara period (710–794), when it became a favorite theme in Japanese court poetry (WAKA). The first plants imported from China had single white blossoms (*hakubai*), but during the Heian period (794–1185) a red-blossomed variety (*kōbai*) made its appearance. By the Edo period (1600–1868) the demand for *ume* extract as a color fixative in cosmetics and for *umeboshi* as an emergency food item encouraged the cultivation of *ume* orchards. At the same time the cultivation of the *ume* as a garden plant became highly popular and resulted in the development of many hybrid varieties. It was also during the Edo period that the combined decorative motif known as SHŌCHIKUBAI (pine, bamboo, plum) came into use in Japan for the celebration of auspicious occasions.

There is only one species of *ume*. However, more than 300 named varieties within this single species have been developed. Variations occur in the color, shape, and size of the flowers and in the size of the fruit.

poetry and prose in Chinese 漢文学

(*kambungaku*). The term *kambungaku* is used in Japan to refer to all types of literary works written in classical Chinese by both Chinese and non-Chinese authors. The term *kanshi* is used to refer specifically to poetry in Chinese. *Kambungaku* is read in Japan by the method called *kundoku*: interlinear symbols (*kaeriten*) indicate to the reader changes in word order and syntax that enable translation into Japanese directly from the original Chinese text (see KAMBUN).

Introduction of Chinese Writing—It is thought that Chinese writing, or *kambun*, was brought to Japan, which was still preliterate, from the Korean peninsula in the 4th century. Methods of adapting Chinese characters to record the sounds of Japanese evolved only gradually, and initially all writing—chiefly government documents—was in Chinese. The earliest scribes were immigrants from Korea and their immediate descendants, but from the 7th century they were joined by Japanese. The SEVENTEEN-ARTICLE CONSTITUTION (604), drafted by Prince SHŌTOKU, regent to Empress SUIKO, displays a firm grasp of Chinese rhetorical devices. After the TAIKA REFORM of 645, a system of schools was instituted and education in the Chinese classics was promoted. Even after it became possible to write in Japanese by using Chinese characters to represent the sounds of Japanese syllables, the prestige of Chinese civilization was such that not only government documents but also private correspondence and works of literature were written in Chinese.

Development of a Native Literary Corpus in Chinese—Beginning in 600 and continuing through the Nara period (710–794) and the first century of the Heian period (794–1185), numerous official missions were sent to China to gather knowledge about its culture (see SUI AND TANG [T'ANG] CHINA, EMBASSIES TO). Chinese was the language of learning, and the Japanese believed the study of Chinese poetry and belletristic prose to be second in importance only to that of the Chinese classics themselves. An educated man of the time was expected to be able to express conventional sentiments correctly rhymed in Chinese verse. The books that provided models for such versifiers were imported from China by members of the embassies. Especially well known in Japan was the *Wenxuan* (*Wen-hsüan*; J: *Monzen*). Compiled during the Liang dynasty (502–557), it was a monumental anthology of ornate prose and verse. Another important work was *Bunkyō hifuron* (early 9th century), a systematic explication of the poetics of Chinese verse by the Japanese monk KŪKAI.

The first extant collection of Chinese verse composed by Japanese, KAIFŪSŌ (751), was followed in the early 9th century by three more native anthologies, *Ryōunshū*, BUNKA SHŪREISHŪ, and KEIKOKUSHŪ. Although Japanese tastes in Chinese literature generally reflected cultural developments in China a century earlier, an exception was the poetry of Bo Juyi (Po Chü-i; J: Haku Kyoi or Haku Rakuten; 772–846), which became popular in Japan in the poet's lifetime, in part because couplets extracted from it were used as song texts. His collected works, *Boshi wenji* (*Po-shih wen-chi*; J: *Hakushi monjū*), and the *Wenxuan*, the two most revered models for composition in Chinese, exerted an influence not only on poetry in Chinese but also on Japanese poetry (WAKA) and prose. A quarter of the verse in WAKAN RŌEISHŪ, an anthology of Japanese and Chinese poetry assembled early in the 11th century, consists of couplets from poems by Bo Juyi.

During the first half of the Heian period, the study and composition of Chinese literature flourished at court and among the professors of the state academy; however, the second half of the period was marked by the predominance of native literary forms. In the Kamakura period (1185–1333) and especially

in the Muromachi period (1333–1568), a renaissance occurred, due largely to ZEN monks, the new bearers of Chinese culture. Many of these monks traveled to the continent and brought back with them the poetry and prose of the Song (Sung) dynasty (960–1279). Their own poetry in Chinese displayed linguistic skills superior to those of their Japanese predecessors. See GOZAN LITERATURE.

Chinese Literature in the Edo Period and in Modern Japan—Throughout the Edo period (1600–1868) the Tokugawa shogunate encouraged learning, and the study of Kangaku (Chinese Learning) flourished to an extent surpassing that of the Heian period. Scholars were no longer primarily Zen monks, as in the Muromachi period, but members of the military class, and even commoners. There appeared a number of scholars who eschewed official posts and devoted themselves to the education of disciples. Endorsed by the shogunate, SHUSHIGAKU, the Neo-Confucian exegesis of the classics as taught by Zhu Xi (Chu Hsi; 1130–1200), was the most esteemed form of Chinese learning. Opposed to it was YŌMEIGAKU, which advocated the theories of the Ming philosopher Wang Yangming (1472–1529).

In 1790 the government prohibited the teaching of any interpretation of Confucianism other than Shushigaku; however, in the domain schools (HANKŌ) Kangaku continued to flourish. An unexpected consequence of the prohibition was a general increase in the popularity of Chinese poetry, and in the 19th century the tradition of Chinese literature written by Japanese reached its high-water mark with the appearance of such great poets as KAN SAZAN and YANAGAWA SEIGAN. After the Meiji Restoration of 1868, Japan hastened to adopt Western technology, and Chinese studies lost favor accordingly. China's defeat in the Sino-Japanese War of 1894–95 was the decisive factor in the decline of *kambungaku* as a mode of literary expression used by Japanese.

poetry, modern　　　現代詩

(*gendaishi*). Modern Japanese poetry, called *shi* to distinguish it from traditional TANKA and HAIKU, has a relatively short history, but it has played a leading role in the development of modern Japanese literature, introducing new language, movements, and ideas. Although some feel that modern poetry has alienated the Japanese public due to its abstruseness, there are still numerous journals and little magazines publishing

contemporary poetry and a readership that is limited but devoted.

Historical Background—When the major importation of Western ideas began after 1868, no poet of distinction was writing. *Tanka* and haiku were saddled with antiquated diction, hackneyed imagery, and repetitious themes. As Western culture and thought penetrated all areas of life, writers felt the need for new forms and styles in which to express themselves.

The first important book of modern poetry was *Shintaishi shō* (1882, Collection of New Style Poetry), an anthology consisting mainly of translations of English and American poems. It introduced lineation and stanzas, both of which were new to the Japanese, while retaining the centuries-old practice of alternating metrical units of five and seven syllables. The collection provided Japanese with a renewed awareness of poetry as a serious expression of man's consciousness. The term *shintaishi* came to be used for all new poetry in this form and style.

MORI ŌGAI (1862–1922) introduced European romanticism in his translations of Goethe, Heine, and other poets. SHIMAZAKI TŌSON (1872–1943) integrated stylistic influences from the European romantics with the classical Japanese ideal that poetry arises from a spontaneous overflowing of the heart, bringing *shintaishi* to a new level of maturity. UEDA BIN's (1874–1916) *Kaichōon* (1905, Sound of the Tide) introduced French symbolist techniques, while NAGAI KAFŪ's (1879–1959) *Sangoshū* (1913, Coral Collection), which contained translations from Baudelaire, Verlaine, and others, was instrumental in furthering the symbolist aesthetic. Symbolist free verse, although mostly written in classical Japanese, appealed to Japanese readers' preference for suggestiveness and their familiarity with the ambiguous character of their language. The use of colloquial language in poetry began with KITAHARA HAKUSHŪ's (1885–1942) *Jashūmon* (1909, Heretics) and TAKAMURA KŌTARŌ's (1883–1956) *Dōtei* (1914, The Journey), but it was HAGIWARA SAKUTARŌ (1886–1942) who was most successful in using it to produce a truly modern poetic vision. In his *Tsuki ni hoeru* (1917; tr *Howling at the Moon*, 1978), Hagiwara wedded his innate lyricism with symbolism to create free verse of an almost neurotic, haunted beauty.

HORIGUCHI DAIGAKU's (1892–1981) collec-

Japanese plum

▶ Stylized representations of the *ume* blossom are a favorite element of traditional Japanese design. This jar is by the Edo-period artist Nonomura Ninsei.

▼ A branch of *ume* in flower. Though not as celebrated as those of cherry blossoms, groves of the fragrant *ume* are popular sights for flower viewing.

▼ The taste of the *umeboshi*, or pickled plum, is typically salty-sour; it is made by salt-curing and then slightly sun-drying the fruit of the *ume*.

▶ The fruit of the *ume* ripens during the rainy season (*tsuyu*) in early summer. This has given rise to the alternative name for the rainy season, *baiu*, or "plum rains."

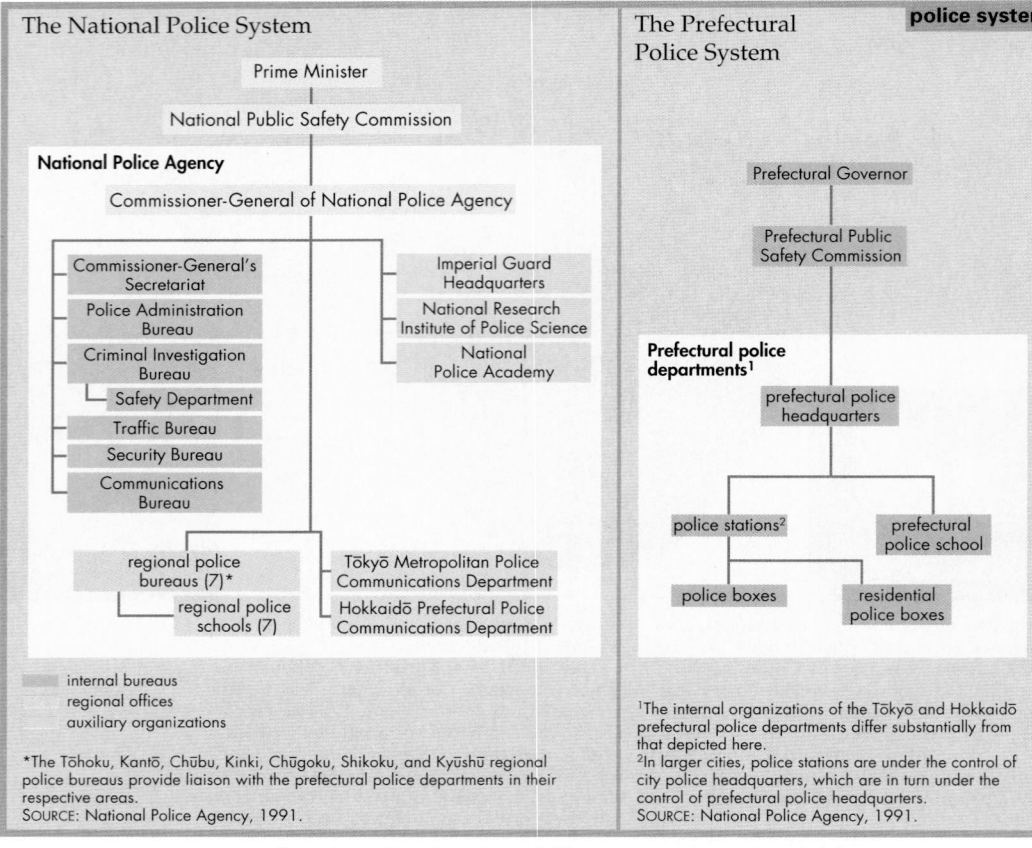

The National Police System

```
Prime Minister
    │
National Public Safety Commission
    │
National Police Agency
    │
Commissioner-General of National Police Agency
```

- Commissioner-General's Secretariat
- Police Administration Bureau
- Criminal Investigation Bureau
  - Safety Department
- Traffic Bureau
- Security Bureau
- Communications Bureau

- Imperial Guard Headquarters
- National Research Institute of Police Science
- National Police Academy

- regional police bureaus (7)*
  - regional police schools (7)
- Tōkyō Metropolitan Police Communications Department
- Hokkaidō Prefectural Police Communications Department

internal bureaus
regional offices
auxiliary organizations

*The Tōhoku, Kantō, Chūbu, Kinki, Chūgoku, Shikoku, and Kyūshū regional police bureaus provide liaison with the prefectural police departments in their respective areas.
SOURCE: National Police Agency, 1991.

The Prefectural Police System

```
Prefectural Governor
    │
Prefectural Public Safety Commission
    │
Prefectural police departments¹
    │
prefectural police headquarters
```

- police stations²
  - police boxes
  - residential police boxes
- prefectural police school

¹The internal organizations of the Tōkyō and Hokkaidō prefectural police departments differ substantially from that depicted here.
²In larger cities, police stations are under the control of city police headquarters, which are in turn under the control of prefectural police headquarters.
SOURCE: National Police Agency, 1991.

---

tion of modern French poets, *Gekka no ichigun* (1925), introduced surrealist tendencies which greatly influenced poetry circles of the mid-1920s and early 1930s, perhaps reaching their peak of expression in NISHIWAKI JUNZABURŌ's (1894–1982) *Ambarvalia* (1933), a collection that remains influential today. In addition, the quarterly SHI TO SHIRON (1929–31, Poetry and Poetics) played an instrumental role in introducing various of the other currents of European modernism.

Other significant poetry journals were SHIKI (Four Seasons), founded in 1934 by MIYOSHI TATSUJI (1900–1964), with contributors such as Hagiwara, HORI TATSUO (1904–53), TACHIHARA MICHIZŌ (1914–39), and NAKAHARA CHŪYA (1907–37), and REKITEI (Historical Course), which commenced publication in 1935 under Takamura Kōtarō's guidance, continued in the postwar era with KUSANO SHIMPEI (1903–88) as its central figure, and remains today an important forum for contemporary poetry. Isolated in a northern farming region far from these urban literary circles, MIYAZAWA KENJI (1896–1933) wrote brilliant poems of religious conviction and humanity.

In the 1930s, as military control over the government increased and censorship spread, some poets moved further into surrealism, while others published propaganda to support the country's war effort. Many became reticent, but few resisted authority. A handful, like KANEKO MITSUHARU (1895–1975), continued writing poetry that expressed their convictions and dissent, but did not publish until after the war ended.

Postwar Poetry—For several years after World War II, poets who wrote out of their war experience dominated the scene even as some of them sank into despair. Some poets empathized with the spiritual vacuum and sense of futility of T. S. Eliot's *The Waste Land* and formed the ARECHI (Waste Land) group, with TAMURA RYŪICHI (b

1923) as its central figure.

A new generation of poets later emerged, many of whom broke with the dark and heavy lyricism that characterized Arechi poetry. Prominent among these were TANIKAWA SHUNTARŌ (b 1931), ŌOKA MAKOTO (b 1931), and SHIRAISHI KAZUKO (b 1931). Tanikawa made a stunning debut with his *Nijūokunen no kodoku* (1952, Two Billion Light Years of Solitude), and Ōoka became one of the leading members of a study group that helped reintroduce surrealism to Japanese poetry in the 1950s. Shiraishi is best known for her use of jazz-influenced sensibility in her long narrative poems.

Poetry of the 1960s was characterized by both the eruption of contemporary social and economic issues into poetic discourse and by its radical concern with language itself, as embodied in the work of AMAZAWA TAIJIRŌ (b 1936). The poetry of the 1970s and 1980s saw a retreat from concern with larger events and greater focus on personal experience and the events of daily life. At the same time, as in the West, the overall context of poetic production—decreasing publishing opportunities, falling sales, and a decline in the number of serious readers—has conspired to make the pursuit of poetic self-expression more difficult as the 20th century draws to a close.

Pola Cosmetics, Inc

[株]ポーラ化粧品本舗

(Pōra Keshōhin Hompo). Cosmetics sales company, ranking first in direct sales in Japan. Incorporated in 1946. The company also deals in jewelry and apparel. For the fiscal year ending December 1990, sales totaled ¥221.6 billion (US $1.7 billion) and capitalization stood at ¥800.0 million (US $6.0 million). Headquarters are in Tōkyō.

police box → kōban

police system
警察制度

(*keisatsu seido*). Japan's approximately 220,000 police officers are organized into

prefectural forces coordinated and partially controlled by the National Police Agency in Tōkyō. They enjoy wide community support and respect.

Historical Development—Until 1600, social control was performed essentially by the military and by groups of citizens organized for mutual defense. During the Edo period (1600–1868), the Tokugawa shogunate developed an elaborate police system based on town magistrates, who held *samurai* status and served as chiefs of police, prosecutors, and criminal judges. The system was augmented by citizens' groups such as the GONINGUMI (five-family associations), composed of neighbors collectively liable to the government for the activities of their membership.

After the MEIJI RESTORATION (1868), the HOME MINISTRY was established in 1873. With jurisdiction over the Police Bureau, it effectively controlled the police even though routine management was handled at the prefectural level. This new, centralized police system had wide-ranging responsibilities, including the authority to issue ordinances and handle quasi-judicial functions. It also regulated public health, factories, construction, and businesses and issued permits, licenses, and orders. To help control proscribed political activities, the SPECIAL HIGHER POLICE were established in 1928. With the outbreak of the SINO-JAPANESE WAR OF 1937–1945, the police were given the added responsibilities of regulating business activities for the war effort, mobilizing labor, and controlling transportation. Even fire fighting came under police direction, as did the regulation of publications, motion pictures, political meetings, and election campaigns.

After World War II, leaders of the Allied OCCUPATION (1945–52) required the Diet to enact a new Police Law. This 1947 law abolished the Home Ministry and relieved the police of their fire protection, public health, and other administrative duties as well as their authority to issue ordinances and adjudicate minor offenses. It also decentralized the system by establishing about 1,600 independent municipal police forces in all cities and towns with populations of over 5,000. Smaller communities would be served by the National Rural Police, which was prefecturally based. Popular control of the police was to be ensured by the establishment of politically neutral, civilian public safety commissions.

This attempt at decentralization was unsuccessful. In June 1951, the Police Law was amended to allow smaller communities to merge their police forces with the National Rural Police. Eighty percent of the communities with autonomous forces did so. The system was further centralized with passage of a new Police Law in 1954.

Present Structure—Today the Japanese police system is based on prefectural units that are autonomous in daily operations yet are linked nationwide under the National Police Agency, which supervises police education and training programs, procures equipment, compiles crime statistics, furnishes criminal identification services, and coordinates interprefectural activities.

Prefectural police headquarters, including the Tōkyō Metropolitan Police Department, control everyday police operations in each prefecture. In effect, the prefectures pay for the patrolman on the beat, traffic control, criminal investigation, and other routine functions but have little control over domestic security units, which are funded by the national government, as are the salaries of senior national and prefectural police officials.

Prefectures are divided into districts, each with its own police station under direct control of prefectural police headquarters rather than linked administratively to the government of the town or city in which it is located. There are about 1,250 of these police stations nationwide. Districts are further subdivided into jurisdictions of urban KŌBAN (police boxes) and rural *chūzaisho* (residential police boxes).

The mainstay of the Japanese police system is the uniformed patrol officer (*omawari san*). The patrol officers man the police boxes and patrol cars and comprise 40 percent of all officers. They are the generalists who usually respond first to all incidents and crimes and then funnel them to the specialized units for further investigation. Theirs is also the training ground for all officers prior to specialization in such areas as administration, criminal investigation, crime prevention, and traffic.

The scope of police responsibilities remains broad, though considerably narrowed from the prewar period. Besides solving ordinary crimes, criminal investigators establish the causes of fires and industrial accidents. Crime prevention police bear added responsibility for juveniles, businesses such as bars and Mah-Jongg parlors, and the enforcement of "special laws" regulating gun and sword ownership, drugs, smuggling, prostitution, pornography, and industrial pollution. Public safety commissions usually defer to police decisions and have proven less effective than public opinion in serving as a check on police power.

Although popular attitudes toward the police are generally favorable, they reflect the conflict between prewar authoritarianism and postwar egalitarianism. Contact with the community is augmented by the requirement that *kōban*-based police visit every home in their jurisdiction twice a year to gather information, pass on suggestions regarding crime prevention, and hear complaints. Neighborhood crime prevention and traffic safety associations provide another link between police and community, further promoting extensive public involvement in law and order. See also NATIONAL PUBLIC SAFETY COMMISSION.

political asylum   亡命

(*bōmei*). Permission given by a nation for an alien political refugee to remain in that nation, often as a permanent resident. Since 1 January 1982, Japan has been a party to the 1951 Convention relating to the Status of Refugees and to the 1967 Protocol relating to the Status of Refugees (hereafter referred to as the Refugee Treaties). The Refugee Treaties define "refugee" as a person who is likely to be persecuted in his or her own country for reasons of race, religion, political views, and so on and stipulate various protection measures for such persons. Political refugees are distinguished from other aliens, migrants, stateless persons, and nonpolitical refugees.

An alien in Japan who feels that he or she falls under the definition of "refugee" in the Refugee Treaties is entitled to apply to the minister of justice for recognition of refugee status. Aliens abroad are not eligible to apply for refugee status, however. The period for application for recognition of refugee status starts from the date of landing in Japan and runs for 60 days. If an event that makes an

alien a refugee takes place while the alien is in Japan, the period runs for 60 days from the day the alien becomes aware of such an event.

An alien recognized as a refugee is issued a certificate of refugee status and a refugee travel document, which enables the holder to leave and enter Japan freely. A refugee may be granted permission for permanent residence, at the discretion of the minister of justice. A refugee who is granted such permission is entitled to the same treatment as a Japanese national in instances stipulated in the Refugee Treaties, such as residence, primary education, public relief, social security benefits, national health insurance, and so forth.

political corruption   政治腐敗

(*seiji fuhai*). The types and concept of political corruption in Japan have changed in accordance with the stages of Japan's economic development and the changes in modes of governmental intervention. At present, four major types of corruption can be identified. The first is administrative corruption, in which lower-level government officials and private individuals are involved in small-scale malfeasance. Immediately after World War II, there were several thousand cases of this type annually in Japan. Since the 1960s, the number of arrests and indictments has remained almost constant at about 1,000 a year. Among those arrested, about 80 percent are local government officials, 10 percent national government officials, and 10 percent private individuals. Among the reported cases of arrest, about 36 percent have been connected with construction and public works, 18 percent licensing and sanctioning, and 11 percent examination and inspection.

The second type is small-scale scandal, in which high-level government officials, businessmen, or intermediaries are involved in secret collusion.

The third is institutionalized corruption, in which powerful political leaders and business interests try to divert the wealth to their own interests through close relationships with bureaucrats. This is done in a sophisticated manner that is largely immune to legal sanctions.

International corruption, the fourth type, is committed by politicians, businessmen, and their agents in collusion with government officials from both donor and recipient countries. These four types of corruption can, of course, coexist both on the national and on the international level.

Postwar Corruption — After World War II, the Japanese government developed numerous programs to promote economic development. Government intervention in the economy included such measures as sanctioning loans at subsidized rates; providing tax exemptions, grants, and subsidies to developing industries; investing in public utilities; and purchasing private sector goods. The government also instituted protective measures to bolster certain industries (e.g., steel, coal mining, and shipbuilding). A side effect of these programs was the spawning of political corruption.

Since competition for markets remains severe, businesses try to win favorable treatment from the government by strengthening their ties with bureaucrats and politicians. The principal means of doing this have included hiring cooperative bureaucrats for attractive corporate posts upon their retirement from government service (AMAKUDARI)

as well as giving donations to politicians and bribes to bureaucrats in return for the drafting and application of laws beneficial to particular corporations.

Politicians require these donations from corporations to help cover the huge expenses incurred in electoral campaigns and in the provision of services to their constituents. In Japan, political donations by corporations, individuals, and other organizations are legal under certain conditions. This was upheld by the Supreme Court of Japan in 1970 in the Yawata Iron and Steel Company Political Donation Case. Corporations now have few reservations, apart from internal financial considerations, in making political contributions, and this has no doubt encouraged further collusion between the donor corporations and the political parties. Thus, businesses require the assistance of politicians to promote their interests, while politicians need corporate backing to collect political funds. See also POLITICAL FUNDING.

Almost all important political corruption cases are directly or indirectly related to political donations, which can give rise to the arbitrary or unfair use of political power or influence the disposal of rights and interests in return for these donations. Public financing of electoral campaigns and the employment of public representatives such as ombudsmen will have to be seriously utilized if this type of corruption is to be brought under control. Among the prominent political bribery cases since 1945 are the SHŌWA DENKŌ SCANDAL (1948), the Kyōwa Seitō Affair (1966), Tanaka Political Fund Case (1974), the LOCKHEED SCANDAL (1976), the Nisshō Iwai Case (1979), the KDD Case (1979), and the RECRUIT SCANDAL (1988).

Political Crisis of 1881
                                明治十四年の政変

(Meiji Jūyonen no Seihen). Political crisis surrounding the expulsion of ŌKUMA SHIGENOBU from the government; it resulted in a new solidarity among the councillors from the former domains of Satsuma and Chōshū and the promise of a constitution within 10 years.

In mid-1878 Home Minister ŌKUBO TOSHIMICHI was murdered by a group of *samurai* who opposed his policies and seeming monopoly of power. Ōkubo was from Satsuma (now Kagoshima Prefecture) but had singled out ITŌ HIROBUMI of Chōshū (now Yamaguchi Prefecture) as his special protégé, and Itō now succeeded him as home minister. But, as finance minister, Ōkuma Shigenobu of Hizen (now Saga Prefecture) had built up a strong following, and Ōkubo's Satsuma colleagues also had claims to a role in government leadership.

The pressure of events revealed that this competition for leadership could not be left unresolved. On the economic front, large sums of paper money were issued at the time of the SATSUMA REBELLION; this caused a rapid inflation that virtually halved the government's income. The FREEDOM AND PEOPLE'S RIGHTS MOVEMENT swept the country in 1880, and massive delegations arrived in Tōkyō to press petitions for the promulgation of a constitution and the formation of a national legislature.

Ōkuma in 1880 had offended conservative government leaders by suggesting an overseas loan of ¥50 million be raised to redeem the paper currency. Then in March 1881 Ōkuma presented a memorial for the speedy drafting of a constitution on the English model, a plan at variance with the views of the other councillors. Finally, Ōkuma refused to approve the proposal of a Satsuma councillor that government assets in Hokkaidō be sold to a consortium of businessmen headed by former officials from Satsuma and Chōshū (see HOKKAIDŌ COLONIZATION OFFICE SCANDAL OF 1881).

Faced with this challenge, the Satsuma and Chōshū councillors met in August 1881 and agreed to demand the expulsion of Ōkuma and his followers from the government. Ōkuma resigned in October and more than a dozen officials regarded as Ōkuma's followers either resigned or were dismissed.

The Satsuma and Chōshū councillors announced that a constitution would be granted by the emperor within the next decade. They also agreed that Itō should draft this constitution, taking Prussia as his model rather than England or the United States. At the same time, the Satsuma councillor MATSUKATA MASAYOSHI was appointed finance minister. Matsukata set out to solve the government's financial problems through a policy of ruthless retrenchment and deflation, while exercising strict control over the national economy through the new BANK OF JAPAN (see MATSUKATA FISCAL POLICY).

Ōkuma and his followers threw in their lot with the Freedom and People's Rights Movement, setting up their own political party, the RIKKEN KAISHINTŌ (Constitutional Reform Party), early in 1882. With the rival JIYŪTŌ (Liberal Party), Ōkuma's Kaishintō was one of the two national political parties demanding constitutional progress on democratic lines. These two parties won an increasing share in the government under the constitution that was promulgated in 1889. Ōkuma returned to office as foreign minister from 1888 to 1889, then was prime minister in 1898 and again from 1914 to 1916.

political funding 政治資金

(seiji shikin). Funding for politicians and political parties in Japan is obtained from a variety of sources: corporations, business associations, industrial organizations, labor unions, supporters' groups (kōenkai), and individual contributors. Fund-raising parties have also become a common method employed by individual politicians in recent years.

The Political Funding Control Law was enacted in 1948 to ensure the equitable management of political revenues. This law has been revised periodically, with the most sweeping reforms coming in 1975, when limitations on monetary contributions and procedures for their public disclosure were written into it. However, these regulations contain certain loopholes, such as the fact that the names of contributors of less than ¥1 million (US $7,700) annually are not required to be reported to the election administration committees: as a result, the full picture with regard to political contributions remains unclear. Under the law, contributions linked to the solicitation of specific favors or which might involve conflict of interest on the part of the recipient are subject to allegations of bribery—but the criteria used to determine this are subtle and complex, as both the LOCKHEED SCANDAL and the RECRUIT SCANDAL have demonstrated (see POLITICAL CORRUPTION).

In 1987 political contributions totaling

¥144.2 billion (US $997.0 million) were reported to the minister of home affairs; ¥134.2 billion (US $927.8 million) in contributions was reported to prefectural election administration committees. The actual sums involved, however, are rumored to be several times larger than the officially reported figures.

political parties 政党

(seitō). Political parties emerged in Japan after the MEIJI RESTORATION (1868), gained increasing influence with the opening of the IMPERIAL DIET (1890), and attained temporary political ascendancy following World War I. Outmaneuvered by the military, they declined in the 1930s and were dissolved and absorbed by the IMPERIAL RULE ASSISTANCE ASSOCIATION in 1940. Political parties were revived under the Allied OCCUPATION in the wake of World War II, and since 1952, when Japan regained its independence, they have been the primary force in national and local politics.

Parties in the Making—"Political associations" (seisha), which arose in the 1870s and were usually groups of disgruntled former samurai, rural landowners, and urban intellectuals, were the precursors of political parties and spearheaded the FREEDOM AND PEOPLE'S RIGHTS MOVEMENT for representative government. Their demands for a popularly elected national assembly brought them into confrontation with the Meiji oligarchs or GENRŌ (see also HAMBATSU), who held tight rein on the government and reacted by promulgating repressive laws to control publications, political libel, and public assemblies (see PRESS ORDINANCE OF 1875; LIBEL LAW OF 1875; SHŪKAI JŌREI).

The two major party builders of the early Meiji period (1868–1912) were ITAGAKI TAISUKE and ŌKUMA SHIGENOBU. Itagaki had joined the government in 1869 but resigned in 1873 and recruited former samurai and rural elites from the southwestern provinces to found in Tōkyō the first protoparty, the AIKOKU KŌTŌ (Public Party of Patriots), which memorialized the government on the need to institute an elected assembly. Itagaki and his compatriots also established a regional group in Ōsaka called the AIKOKUSHA (Society of Patriots), which was the basis for the founding in 1881 of Japan's first national party, the JIYŪTŌ (Liberal Party). Many emulators among disaffected former samurai set up similar parties and between 1882 and 1886 mounted armed revolts (see FUKUSHIMA INCIDENT) against the government, whose reaction was swift and ruthless and was accompanied by the enactment of the PEACE PRESERVATION LAW OF 1887, which tightened restrictions on political activity. The Liberal Party was disbanded in 1884 but was reformed after the promulgation of the CONSTITUTION OF THE EMPIRE OF JAPAN in 1889.

Ōkuma resigned from the government in 1881 (see POLITICAL CRISIS OF 1881) and in 1882 formed the RIKKEN KAISHINTŌ (Constitutional Reform Party), which drew its membership mainly from the fledgling urban intelligentsia. Although Ōkuma dissociated himself from the party in 1884, it remained active until 1896. More conservative parties, such as the RIKKEN TEISEITŌ (Constitutional Imperial Rule Party; 1882), represented themselves as defenders of the oligarchic government, but their memberships were much smaller than those of either the Liberal Party or the Constitutional Reform Party.

Parties in the Diet—Parliamentary politics in the Diet, which opened in November

1890, was marked by an intense rivalry between the oligarchic government, which reserved the right to appoint cabinets (see "TRANSCENDENTAL" CABINETS; PRIME MINISTER AND CABINET), and the Liberal and Constitutional Reform parties, which were defiant but largely ineffectual because of their inability to unite and control the elected lower house. The Constitutional Reform Party, which was initially overshadowed by the Liberal Party and even by some of the pro-oligarchy groups, such as the KOKUMIN KYŌKAI (Nationalist Association; 1892), was reconstituted as the SHIMPOTŌ (Progressive Party) in 1896 and consolidated its position as the second party. In common parlance the Liberal and Progressive parties were termed MINTŌ (popular parties), while groups of supporters of the oligarchic bureaucracy, which denigrated the parties yet clearly functioned as such themselves, were referred to as ritō (bureaucrats' parties). Neither of the popular parties had representation in the hereditary and appointive HOUSE OF PEERS, nor did they control local politics, for key local officials were appointed by the central government. Yet despite the popular parties' intransigent opposition to the fiscal and antiparty policies of the oligarchs, the mintō platforms reflected the interests of the rural elite—some 60 percent of mintō members were former local assemblymen—and were no less conservative and nationalistic than the pronouncements of the oligarchs.

The Politics of Compromise—Rapprochement between parties and oligarchs was spurred in 1898 when Prime Minister ITŌ HIROBUMI, who was a genrō and had been the first head of the PRIVY COUNCIL, dissolved the Diet due to opposition by the popular parties to his proposal for extra land taxes. The Liberal and Progressive parties merged to form the KENSEITŌ (Constitutional Party), which won a majority in the Diet in the succeeding election. Itō resigned and invited Ōkuma and Itagaki to form a cabinet, Japan's first party cabinet, which was led by Ōkuma as prime minister and Itagaki as home minister (see ŌKUMA CABINET). The alliance collapsed within months and the Progressive Party faction reorganized as the KENSEI HONTŌ (True Constitutional Party; 1898) and later as the RIKKEN KOKUMINTŌ (Constitutional Nationalist Party; 1910). However, in 1900 Itō formed the RIKKEN SEIYŪKAI (Friends of Constitutional Government Party; commonly called Seiyūkai), a coalition of former Jiyūtō members and bureaucrats that won a majority in the Diet, marking the forthright entrance of oligarchs and bureaucrats into party politics on a basis of compromise with conservative factions of the popular parties. In 1913 General KATSURA TARŌ, protégé of the authoritarian oligarch YAMAGATA ARITOMO, formed the RIKKEN DŌSHIKAI (Constitutional Association of Friends), absorbing the wealthier half of the Rikken Kokumintō; in 1916 it was reconstituted as the KENSEIKAI (Constitutional Association) and temporarily wrested the majority from the Seiyūkai. From 1922 onward, rivalry between the Kenseikai and the Seiyūkai, rather than between parties and oligarchs, became the dominant pattern.

With the increasing incidence of cabinets formed by parties during the first quarter of the 20th century, the practice of appointing governors and key local officials began to work to the advantage of the parties. Party control of local assemblies was achieved even more swiftly than in the Diet, and by

1910 some 90 percent of prefectural assemblymen were affiliated with one of the two major parties.

In the late 19th and early 20th centuries a number of proletarian parties appeared, but they evoked hostile reactions from the leaders of the major parties as well as the oligarchs, and many were banned soon after their formation by the invocation of such repressive laws as the PUBLIC ORDER AND POLICE LAW OF 1900. Following the Bolshevik Revolution of 1917 and the emergence of LABOR UNIONS, renewed efforts were made to form proletarian parties and the NIHON SHAKAI SHUGI DŌMEI (Japan Socialist League) was established in 1920 and the JAPAN COMMUNIST PARTY (JCP; Nihon Kyōsantō) in 1922. The chief threat to the major parties was not the proletarian parties, popular support of which was limited, but the military. An 1899 rule restricted eligibility for appointment to head the service ministries to generals and admirals on active duty, who were responsible only to their supreme commander, the emperor (see GUMBU DAIJIN GEN'EKI BUKAN SEI; TŌSUIKEN). The political power of the military was made clear in 1912 when the army minister UEHARA YŪSAKU resigned to protest the government's decision not to provide funds for two new army divisions. The army's refusal to name a successor to Uehara brought down the cabinet.

Ascendancy of Parties and the Military Takeover——The cabinet formed in 1918 by HARA TAKASHI, made up of members of the Seiyūkai (except for the army, navy, and foreign ministers), was the first viable party cabinet, and from then until 1922 and from 1924 until 1932, the premiership was held by the leaders of major parties. Nevertheless, the selection of prime ministers and cabinets, though it reflected public support of individual political parties, was not a democratic process; candidates for the premiership were nominated by the *genrō* and their protégés and appointed by the emperor, while ministers, except for those of the army and navy, were chosen by prime ministers in consultation with imperial advisers and confirmed by the emperor.

A coalition cabinet was formed in 1924 by the Kenseikai, the Seiyūkai, and the KAKUSHIN KURABU (Reform Club), which had together organized the second MOVEMENT TO PROTECT CONSTITUTIONAL GOVERNMENT and brought down the last of the nonparty "transcendental cabinets." Thereafter the two major parties, the Kenseikai (reorganized in 1927 as the RIKKEN MINSEITŌ) and the Seiyūkai, alternated in power until the assassination in 1932 of INUKAI TSUYOSHI, Seiyūkai president and prime minister (see MAY 15TH INCIDENT). Although prime ministers throughout the period were nominally designated by SAIONJI KIMMOCHI, protégé of ITŌ HIROBUMI, it was the influence of parties upon the formation of cabinets that distinguished this brief era of TAISHŌ DEMOCRACY.

Party hegemony did not, however, diminish persistent acrimony in the House of Representatives or government repression of proletarian groups. By the early 1930s there had emerged two legal noncommunist proletarian parties, which united in 1932 to form the SHAKAI TAISHUTŌ (Socialist Masses Party), a party that soon began to compromise step by step with the emergent forces of militarist authoritarianism. The JCP, which had been dissolved under government pressure in 1924, was reestablished underground in 1926 and remained active until about 1935, by which time arrests had decimated

its membership.

The number of voters quadrupled with passage of the Universal Manhood Suffrage Law in 1925 and political campaigns became vastly more expensive. The industrial and financial combines MITSUI and MITSUBISHI, the two largest ZAIBATSU, funded the Seiyūkai and the Rikken Minseitō, respectively, but both parties tapped additional sources, legal and illegal, and well-publicized malfeasance and corruption among politicians made it easier for the military to denounce party politicians. Although the military made sporadic attempts to wrest control from the parties, it was Inukai's death in 1932 at the hands of young naval officers that signaled the end of party cabinets. From that point until the end of World War II, there was a succession of "national unity" cabinets led by military men or their collaborators. In 1940 all political parties were absorbed by the Imperial Rule Assistance Association.

The Postwar Period——With the conclusion of hostilities in August 1945 efforts were made to resuscitate the major prewar parties, and by November all had reappeared, most under new names. The abolition of the Privy Council and the military and the replacement of the House of Peers with an elected HOUSE OF COUNCILLORS left the civil bureaucracy as the only major institutional rival of the parties, while the new CONSTITUTION OF JAPAN made the National DIET the "highest organ of government" and provided for control of the cabinet by the Diet.

The OCCUPATION PURGE, which began in 1946, had a debilitating effect on the postwar conservative parties and leadership passed from prewar party leaders to former Ministry of Foreign Affairs bureaucrats. The purge also removed many local leaders from positions of influence, requiring all of the parties to rebuild their bases of local power. Revision of the election laws lowered the voting age, granted suffrage to women, and increased the number of members elected from constituencies. This encouraged the participation of independents and minor parties and provoked fierce competition among the major parties, leading to unstable cabinets and frequent stalemates until February 1949, when YOSHIDA SHIGERU of the Minshu Jiyūtō (successor of the prewar Seiyūkai; reorganized in 1950 as the LIBERAL PARTY) formed a stable cabinet that endured until October 1952. The LAND REFORMS OF 1946 eliminated large landed estates and vested title in former tenants, removing an important stimulus to radicalism in rural areas and creating an electorate that became a dependable source of support for the conservatives. The leftist parties, on the other hand, benefited from the Occupation's labor policies, which led to unionization of many of the nation's industrial workers. In some important respects, however, the Occupation had little effect on Japanese party politics. POLITICAL CORRUPTION, particularly "money politics," was as common as before the war. Moreover, all parties remained ridden with the factionalism that had afflicted their forebears.

By 1952 the percentage of conservative party Diet members who were former local assemblymen had fallen to 30 percent and the number of businessmen had increased proportionately. However, the most striking change was a dramatic increase from 1949, especially in the Minshu Jiyūtō, of conservative members who were retired government bureaucrats. The entry of former senior bureaucrats into party politics became a permanent pattern, and while it testified to the

new influence and prestige of the Diet, it also brought about an increasingly cozy relationship between the conservative parties and the upper levels of the administrative bureaucracy.

The 1955 Status Quo——Following the restoration of Japan's independence in 1952, division among the conservatives made it impossible for either the Liberal Party or the NIHON MINSHUTŌ (Japan Democratic Party; successor of the prewar Rikken Minseitō) to form a stable majority in the Diet, while the JAPAN SOCIALIST PARTY (JSP) had split in 1951 into parties of the Left and the Right. In 1955, however, the JSP reunited and a month later the conservatives merged to form the LIBERAL DEMOCRATIC PARTY (LDP), thus giving birth to the "1955 status quo" (*gojūgonen taisei*), with the LDP controlling both Houses, the JSP holding roughly half the number of LDP seats in each, and the LDP mounting a series of one-party cabinets.

During the late 1950s the LDP took controversial stands in favor of the revision of the new constitution (not achieved as of 1991), the augmentation of police powers, the mandatory performance evaluation of public-school teachers, and the revision of the United States–Japan Security Treaty. When the last of these was settled in 1960 after considerable turmoil, the government turned to the problems of economic growth and foreign trade, and in these areas its policies were in general popular. The only serious threat to the ruling party's security and power came from internal factional feuding, but this mainly concerned the allocation of party posts and could periodically be accommodated.

By the late 1960s, however, the 1955 status quo was showing strain. LDP popularity waned due to a series of political scandals and the party's failure to deal satisfactorily with social and economic issues, such as a housing shortage, environmental pollution, and rising land prices. By the end of the decade the 1955 status quo had disintegrated. With the JSP racked by factionalism, the power vacuum was filled by splinter groups, such as the DEMOCRATIC SOCIALIST PARTY (DSP; Minshu Shakaitō), founded in 1960 by right-wing members of the JSP, and newcomers such as the KŌMEITŌ (Clean Government Party), which, with the support of members of the religious organization SŌKA GAKKAI, gained an increasing number of seats in the Diet in the 1960s. In 1967 the LDP failed for the first time since 1955 to receive a majority of the popular vote, and its share continued to decline, as did that of the JSP, until the late 1970s.

From the late 1960s the Kōmeitō, the DSP, and the JCP gained increasing support among residents of cities, and beginning with the 1969 elections for the House of Representatives they consistently controlled a third of all votes cast. The formation of a multiparty system was further spurred by the establishment of splinter parties: in 1976 critics of the LDP's "money politics" broke away to found the Shin Jiyū Kurabu (New Liberal Club), while in 1977 a group of right-wing members of the JSP founded the Shakai Shimin Rengō (Social Citizens' League; now UNITED SOCIAL DEMOCRATIC PARTY). Continuing corruption and factionalism contributed to diminishing popular support of the LDP, and in the periods 1976–80 and 1983–86 the party failed to win a majority of seats in the House

Continued on page 1216——

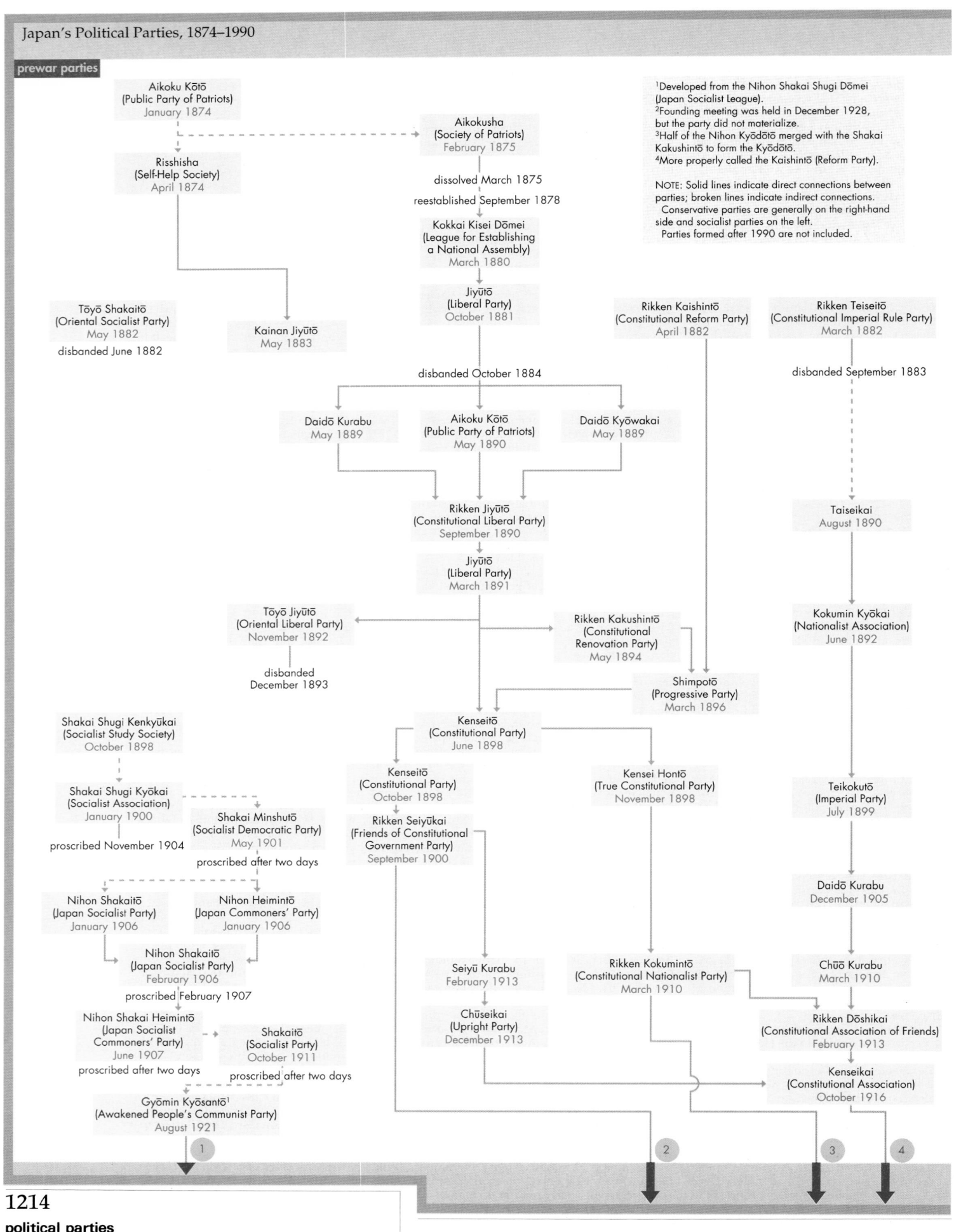

prewar parties

Aikoku Kōtō
(Public Party of Patriots)
January 1874

Risshisha
(Self-Help Society)
April 1874

Aikokusha
(Society of Patriots)
February 1875

dissolved March 1875
reestablished September 1878

Kokkai Kisei Dōmei
(League for Establishing
a National Assembly)
March 1880

Jiyūtō
(Liberal Party)
October 1881

Tōyō Shakaitō
(Oriental Socialist Party)
May 1882
disbanded June 1882

Kainan Jiyūtō
May 1883

Rikken Kaishintō
(Constitutional Reform Party)
April 1882

Rikken Teiseitō
(Constitutional Imperial Rule Party)
March 1882

disbanded September 1883

¹Developed from the Nihon Shakai Shugi Dōmei
(Japan Socialist League).
²Founding meeting was held in December 1928,
but the party did not materialize.
³Half of the Nihon Kyōdōtō merged with the Shakai
Kakushintō to form the Kyōdōtō.
⁴More properly called the Kaishintō (Reform Party).

NOTE: Solid lines indicate direct connections between
parties; broken lines indicate indirect connections.
   Conservative parties are generally on the right-hand
side and socialist parties on the left.
   Parties formed after 1990 are not included.

disbanded October 1884

Daidō Kurabu
May 1889

Aikoku Kōtō
(Public Party of Patriots)
May 1890

Daidō Kyōwakai
May 1889

Rikken Jiyūtō
(Constitutional Liberal Party)
September 1890

Jiyūtō
(Liberal Party)
March 1891

Tōyō Jiyūtō
(Oriental Liberal Party)
November 1892

disbanded
December 1893

Rikken Kakushintō
(Constitutional
Renovation Party)
May 1894

Taiseikai
August 1890

Kokumin Kyōkai
(Nationalist Association)
June 1892

Shimpotō
(Progressive Party)
March 1896

Shakai Shugi Kenkyūkai
(Socialist Study Society)
October 1898

Kenseitō
(Constitutional Party)
June 1898

Shakai Shugi Kyōkai
(Socialist Association)
January 1900

proscribed November 1904

Shakai Minshutō
(Socialist Democratic Party)
May 1901
proscribed after two days

Kenseitō
(Constitutional Party)
October 1898

Rikken Seiyūkai
(Friends of Constitutional
Government Party)
September 1900

Kensei Hontō
(True Constitutional Party)
November 1898

Teikokutō
(Imperial Party)
July 1899

Nihon Shakaitō
(Japan Socialist Party)
January 1906

Nihon Heimintō
(Japan Commoners' Party)
January 1906

Nihon Shakaitō
(Japan Socialist Party)
February 1906

proscribed February 1907

Nihon Shakai Heimintō
(Japan Socialist
Commoners' Party)
June 1907
proscribed after two days

Shakaitō
(Socialist Party)
October 1911
proscribed after two days

Seiyū Kurabu
February 1913

Chūseikai
(Upright Party)
December 1913

Rikken Kokumintō
(Constitutional Nationalist Party)
March 1910

Daidō Kurabu
December 1905

Chūō Kurabu
March 1910

Rikken Dōshikai
(Constitutional Association of Friends)
February 1913

Gyōmin Kyōsantō¹
(Awakened People's Communist Party)
August 1921

Kenseikai
(Constitutional Association)
October 1916

1   2   3   4

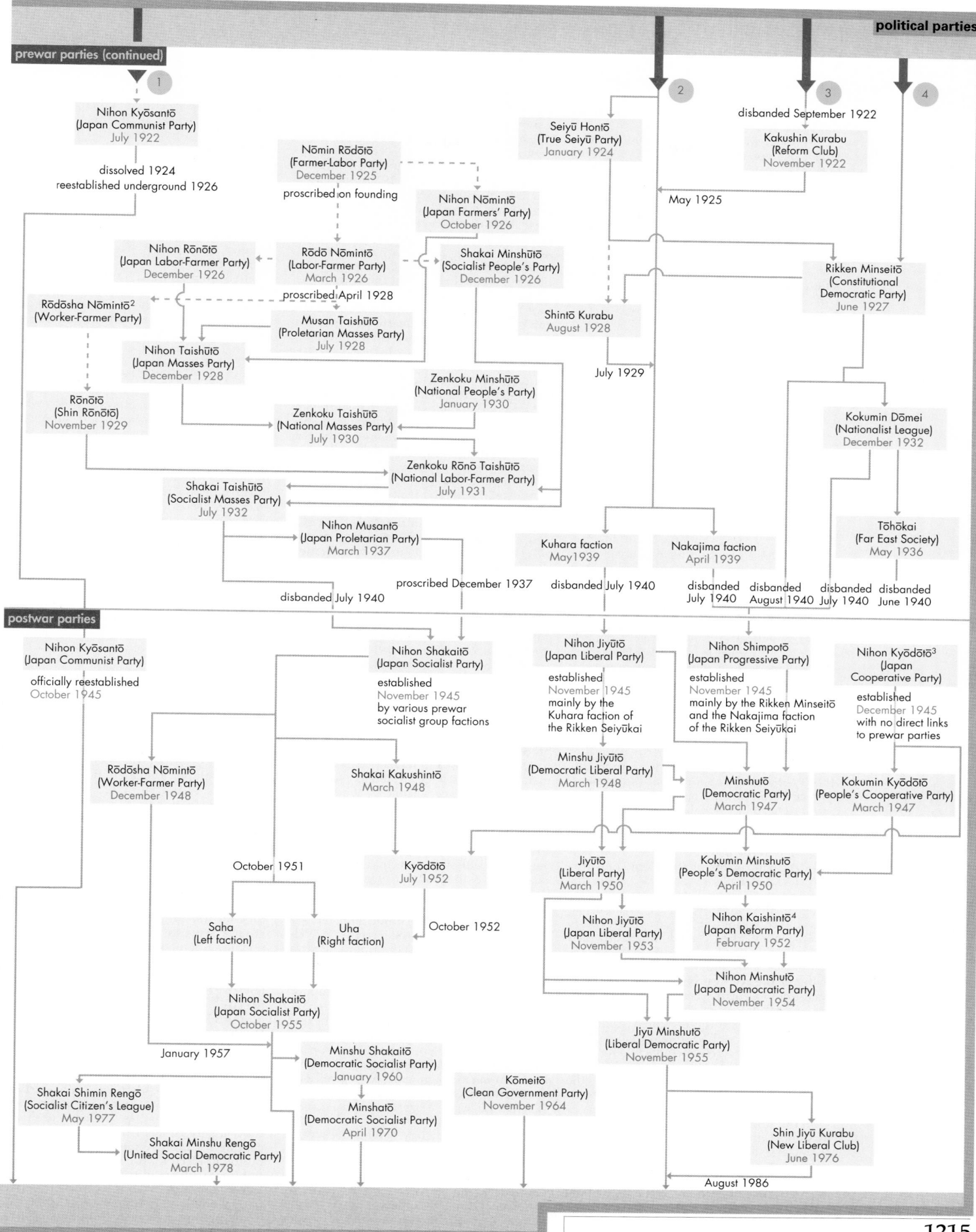

prewar parties (continued)

① Nihon Kyōsantō
(Japan Communist Party)
July 1922

dissolved 1924
reestablished underground 1926

Nōmin Rōdōtō
(Farmer-Labor Party)
December 1925

proscribed on founding

Nihon Nōmintō
(Japan Farmers' Party)
October 1926

Nihon Rōnōtō
(Japan Labor-Farmer Party)
December 1926

Rōdō Nōmintō
(Labor-Farmer Party)
March 1926

Shakai Minshūtō
(Socialist People's Party)
December 1926

Rōdōsha Nōmintō²
(Worker-Farmer Party)

proscribed April 1928

Musan Taishūtō
(Proletarian Masses Party)
July 1928

Nihon Taishūtō
(Japan Masses Party)
December 1928

Rōnōtō
(Shin Rōnōtō)
November 1929

Zenkoku Minshūtō
(National People's Party)
January 1930

Zenkoku Taishūtō
(National Masses Party)
July 1930

Zenkoku Rōnō Taishūtō
(National Labor-Farmer Party)
July 1931

Shakai Taishūtō
(Socialist Masses Party)
July 1932

Nihon Musantō
(Japan Proletarian Party)
March 1937

proscribed December 1937

disbanded July 1940

Seiyū Hontō
(True Seiyū Party)
January 1924

② disbanded September 1922

Kakushin Kurabu
(Reform Club)
November 1922

③

④

May 1925

Rikken Minseitō
(Constitutional Democratic Party)
June 1927

Shintō Kurabu
August 1928

July 1929

Kokumin Dōmei
(Nationalist League)
December 1932

Kuhara faction
May 1939

Nakajima faction
April 1939

Tōhōkai
(Far East Society)
May 1936

disbanded July 1940

disbanded July 1940

disbanded August 1940

disbanded July 1940

disbanded June 1940

postwar parties

Nihon Kyōsantō
(Japan Communist Party)

officially reestablished
October 1945

Nihon Shakaitō
(Japan Socialist Party)

established
November 1945
by various prewar
socialist group factions

Nihon Jiyūtō
(Japan Liberal Party)

established
November 1945
mainly by the
Kuhara faction of
the Rikken Seiyūkai

Nihon Shimpotō
(Japan Progressive Party)

established
November 1945
mainly by the Rikken Minseitō
and the Nakajima faction
of the Rikken Seiyūkai

Nihon Kyōdōtō³
(Japan Cooperative Party)

established
December 1945
with no direct links
to prewar parties

Rōdōsha Nōmintō
(Worker-Farmer Party)
December 1948

Shakai Kakushintō
March 1948

Minshu Jiyūtō
(Democratic Liberal Party)
March 1948

Minshutō
(Democratic Party)
March 1947

Kokumin Kyōdōtō
(People's Cooperative Party)
March 1947

October 1951

Kyōdōtō
July 1952

Jiyūtō
(Liberal Party)
March 1950

Kokumin Minshutō
(People's Democratic Party)
April 1950

Saha
(Left faction)

Uha
(Right faction)

October 1952

Nihon Jiyūtō
(Japan Liberal Party)
November 1953

Nihon Kaishintō⁴
(Japan Reform Party)
February 1952

Nihon Shakaitō
(Japan Socialist Party)
October 1955

Nihon Minshutō
(Japan Democratic Party)
November 1954

January 1957

Minshu Shakaitō
(Democratic Socialist Party)
January 1960

Kōmeitō
(Clean Government Party)
November 1964

Jiyū Minshutō
(Liberal Democratic Party)
November 1955

Shakai Shimin Rengō
(Socialist Citizen's League)
May 1977

Minshatō
(Democratic Socialist Party)
April 1970

Shakai Minshu Rengō
(United Social Democratic Party)
March 1978

Shin Jiyū Kurabu
(New Liberal Club)
June 1976

August 1986

of Representatives, while the JSP, which in the 1960s had held some 30 percent of House seats, found its share reduced to 20 percent in the 1970s and 1980s.

However, in the 1986 elections for the House of Representatives the LDP won 300 of the 512 seats, and in the wake of the election the dissident Shin Jiyū Kurabu returned to the fold. The LDP lost its majority in the House of Councillors in 1989, but in the 1990 elections it did well, retaining a solid majority in the House of Representatives. The JSP also gained a sizable number of new seats in this election; the losers were the other opposition parties such as the Kōmeitō, JCP, and DSP. Between them the LDP and JSP occupied 80 percent of the lower-house seats, leading to speculation that a return to the 1955 status quo might be a distinct possibility. However, in the 1991 local elections the LDP won a massive victory and the JSP suffered unprecedented losses. In sum, as of the early 1990s the LDP's nearly 40-year monopoly on government remained intact, and it is still unclear if the 1990s will simply see a continuation of LDP dominance or the gradual emergence of a system in which power is shared or traded between two or more parties.

political system　　　　政治制度

(*seiji seido*). The development of the contemporary Japanese political system has been influenced by two main sources. One has been the principles embodied in the CONSTITUTION OF JAPAN, largely authored by US government advisers early in the post–World War II OCCUPATION of Japan. The other has been the remnants of the prewar Japanese political system, which owed much to 19th-century German and British parliamentary models and which was governed by the CONSTITUTION OF THE EMPIRE OF JAPAN (the Meiji Constitution of 1889).

The Prewar Political System—The writers of the Meiji Constitution sought to provide the popularly elected HOUSE OF REPRESENTATIVES with as little access to real political power as possible, allowing it no more authority than the appointive HOUSE OF PEERS. The emperor, not the people, was to be the fountainhead of sovereignty, and his ministers were supposed to be individually responsible to him rather than collectively responsible to the DIET.

In the early years of the Meiji Constitution, the real locus of practical power lay with the GENRŌ (elders), a group of senior advisers to the emperor, most of whom had played leading roles in the MEIJI RESTORATION (1868). When they ceased to occupy their pivotal positions because of death or advanced age, a vacuum opened up at the very center of the political system; the *genrō* had been able to ensure that factional rivalries did not get out of hand and had controlled those other institutions which, independently of the Diet, had sought to exert their influence on government policy. These included the Imperial Household Ministry (now the IMPERIAL HOUSEHOLD AGENCY), the PRIVY COUNCIL, the BUREAUCRACY, and the chiefs of staff of the army and navy.

In the absence of the *genrō*, Japanese politics under the Meiji Constitution came to be characterized by constant jockeying for power between rival factions using various institutions to further their own ends. During the "liberal" period of the 1920s and early 1930s (see TAISHŌ DEMOCRACY), the

broadening scope of political participation followed rather closely the increase in the numbers of those involved in the modern economy and the spread of education; in 1925 all men who had attained the age of 25 were granted the vote. Nevertheless, factionalism remained a disturbing element in Japanese politics, and the 1920s were a period of frequent cabinet changes. The executive remained weak; indeed, it was not always clear who the executive was supposed to be. In the early 1930s various factors began to tip the balance of the system in favor of other political forces, notably the military. A convention that the army minister had to be a serving general and the navy minister an admiral meant that the chiefs of staff could sabotage a government they disliked by withdrawing their own ministers, a practice they resorted to increasingly (see GUMBU DAIJIN GEN'EKI BUKAN SEI). As the decade wore on, the parties mostly abandoned their relative liberalism for the nationalistic and totalitarian philosophies that were coming into vogue. Structurally, however, the political system retained many of the features inherited from the experience of earlier governments under the Meiji Constitution—in particular, the lack of clear lines of responsibility for the making of policy.

Postwar Political Structure—The system that emerged from the Allied Occupation was based on clarification of responsibility and extended political participation. Women received the vote for the first time, the voting age was reduced from 25 to 20 for all, and controls were taken off left-wing political movements (at least in the early years of the Occupation; a gradual retreat from this policy of toleration for the left culminated in the RED PURGE of the early 1950s). The postwar system was also designed to prevent the emergence of institutional rivals to the power of the Diet.

The 1947 constitution proclaimed the Diet "the highest organ of state power" and "the sole law-making authority of the State." The Diet was divided into a House of Representatives, or lower chamber, the members of which are elected to a four-year term, and an upper chamber, the HOUSE OF COUNCILLORS, the members of which are elected to a six-year term (half are elected every three years). The House of Councillors has the power to delay and reject pending legislation, although its veto can be overridden by a two-thirds majority in the House of Representatives.

Executive power is vested in the cabinet, the head of which is the prime minister, who is chosen, in effect, by the lower house. The only constitutional restraint upon the prime minister in selecting cabinet members is that a majority must be members of the Diet (cabinet ministers without a Diet seat are rare); all must be civilians. The prime minister may dismiss cabinet ministers at will, but in practice he is bound in both selection and dismissal by the internal politics of his own party. The cabinet is collectively responsible to the Diet and must resign upon passage of a no-confidence resolution in the lower house. See also GOVERNMENT, EXECUTIVE BRANCH; PRIME MINISTER AND CABINET.

The highest judiciary body is the SUPREME COURT; its members are appointed by the cabinet (with the exception of the chief justice, who, according to the constitution, is appointed by the emperor "as designated by the cabinet"). Judges of lower courts are appointed by the cabinet from a list of persons nominated by the Supreme Court. Though

the cabinet is given the power of appointment, the constitution forbids any organ or agency of the executive branch to be given final judicial power and grants the Supreme Court the "power to determine the constitutionality of any law, order, regulation, or official act," although this power has been used sparingly. See JUDICIAL SYSTEM.

Postwar Politics: Centralization and Participation—Japanese politics since 1945 has been characterized by countervailing tendencies toward centralization and popular participation. The single most important factor has been the dominant electoral position attained by the LIBERAL DEMOCRATIC PARTY (LDP) since its formation in 1955. Reasons for the electoral supremacy of the LDP include the satisfaction of material demands through rapid economic growth, relative moderation on ideologically sensitive issues, better organization and internal party cohesion than in the opposition parties, an electoral system grossly imbalanced in favor of rural areas which support the LDP, financial superiority brought about by close connections with wealthy interest groups, an effective bureaucracy, and an opposition incapable either of staying together or of producing political programs that are appealing to the electorate (see ELECTIONS).

While power has been concentrated in the center, relatively autonomous popular interest groups have come to play a more significant part in the political system. The best-known examples have been the CITIZENS' MOVEMENTS that began to appear in the late 1960s to protest against environmental pollution and that later included a host of other single-issue campaigns, such as the CONSUMER MOVEMENT, the anti-nuclear-arms and anti-nuclear-power movements, and the ecological movement (see ATOMIC WEAPONS, MOVEMENT TO BAN; PEACE MOVEMENT; UNITED STATES–JAPAN SECURITY TREATIES). The public is more prepared to organize in defense of its own interests than used to be the case, and the high nonvoting rates, especially in urban areas, suggest that the electorate, disillusioned with party politics and frequent corruption scandals, turns to such PRESSURE GROUPS as functional substitutes for political parties. The worth of a rural Diet member to his electors often seems to be measured largely in terms of his ability to deliver roads, bridges, and other amenities to the constituency, or material favors to the individual elector. The more urbanized electorate, excluded from long-established party channels to government, tends to turn to interest groups that can establish new channels of pressure upon government.

Another factor that has appeared to contradict the trend toward centralization of power has been the continuing strong propensity for Japanese organizations to divide into leader-centered factions (see BATSU). While the opposition parties' own liability to factionalism has gravely weakened their capacity to attack the government, the LDP itself is so affected by factionalism that some regard it as a coalition of "mini-parties." However, LDP factions do not primarily represent contrasting policy positions; they largely concern themselves with bargaining for cabinet and party office, distribution of electoral funds, and the organization of party presidential elections. Faction leaders are those who are capable of effective manipulation of the party machine and of the appropriate marshaling of financial resources.

Cabinet reshuffles since 1955 have been frequent, because prime ministers have been under pressure from the various factions to give their senior members a turn in the cabinet. Changes in prime minister, which have also occurred frequently, invariably mean a completely new cabinet, and since cabinet ministers' tenure of office is usually short (on average, two years), bureaucratic power is consequently enhanced, though it is in turn affected by interministerial rivalries. All of these factors have tended to make for uncertainty and lack of focus in policy making. They have also led, both at home and abroad, to frequent accusations of POLITICAL CORRUPTION and have contributed to the electorate's disillusionment with party politics as a whole.

Nevertheless, since the Occupation, the core institutions of Japanese politics have been greatly strengthened, to the point that the system's capacity for authoritative action in key fields can be impressive. On the other hand, despite the fact that since 1955 Japan has had, in effect, one-party government, effective campaigns by the media and various pressure groups attest to the fact that pluralist democracy has put down firm roots; popular and media pressure brought down two successive LDP cabinets in 1989 (see TAKESHITA NOBORU; UNO SŌSUKE). Currently, fundamental demographic shifts, combined with popular disaffection with LDP money politics and US pressure for Japan to open its agricultural sector to foreign imports—a move that would antagonize the LDP's traditional rural supporters—are all factors forcing the government to consider changes in the boundary rules of the electoral system to enable the LDP to become more of a broadly based urban party and thus enable it to continue to win elections and stay in power. Meanwhile, the major opposition parties, such as the Social Democratic Party of Japan (SDPJ; the former JAPAN SOCIALIST PARTY) and the KŌMEITŌ, have in recent years been seeking to modify their policies and strategy in order to appeal to a broader segment of the electorate and convince voters that they are capable of effectively wielding political power at the national level. A new pragmatism—including experimentation with various concepts of coalition government—now informs their continuing struggle to break or dilute the monopoly on national government that the LDP has enjoyed for nearly 40 years. As Japan enters the last decade of the 20th century, there are signs of increasing fluidity and potential for change within the political system as a whole that neither the ruling party nor the opposition can afford to ignore.

Polivanov, Evgenij Dmitrievich
ポリワーノフ, E. D.

(1891–1938). Soviet scholar of linguistics and phonetics. Polivanov is known for his pioneering studies on accents in Japanese dialects and his meticulous research on Chinese, Turkic, and other Asian languages. He graduated from the University of St. Petersburg and taught there. In 1914 and 1915 he visited Japan. Polivanov came under government censure for opposing N. Marr's Marxist interpretation of language and was imprisoned. He died in jail.

Pollution Countermeasures Basic Law
公害対策基本法

(Kōgai Taisaku Kihon Hō). Law enacted in 1967 providing for the protection of the people's health and the conservation of the environment. It prescribes antipollution measures for air, water, soil, noise, vibration, ground subsidence, and offensive odors. It also sets up the Environmental Pollution Countermeasures Council. It originally embodied a clause, at the insistence of industry, that the law's aims should be pursued in "harmony between the protection of the environment and economic development." The law was amended in 1970, the harmony clause being deleted after a heated debate in the Diet.

pollution litigation
公害訴訟

(kōgai soshō). Legal proceedings brought against industries by victims of various forms of industrial pollution. After World War II, Japan concentrated on industrial expansion without consideration of the environment, leading to the development during the 1950s and 1960s of POLLUTION-RELATED DISEASES among the general public. Toward the end of the 1960s, because of the refusal by polluting companies to take any responsibility and because of inaction on the part of the government, groups of victims sought redress in the courts. Important legal precedents were established as a result of decisions in four major cases, all found in favor of the plaintiffs: companies dealing with toxic chemicals are required to exercise a high degree of care; companies must prove that their discharge of pollutants has not caused the plaintiff's disease; and several companies operating in an industrial area may be held jointly liable for health injuries caused by their air pollution. The Pollution-Related Health Vitiation Compensation Law (1973, Kōgai Kenkō Higai Hoshō Hō) provided for facilities where victims were treated, but a revision of the law in 1987 resulted in the closing of the facilities and termination of official recognition of and compensation to new applicants.

pollution-related diseases
公害病

(kōgaibyō). As elsewhere in the world, industrialization in Japan has generated many pollution-related diseases. The Japanese word kōgai, commonly translated as "pollution," literally means "public injury" and is often used more broadly than the English term "environmental pollution." Environmental pollution in Japan was at its worst between about 1965 and 1975. During this time improper disposal of industrial waste, coupled with other polluting practices, led to the contamination of various areas of the environment and the appearance of various pollution-related diseases. Calls for government and industry to take responsibility led to the passage in 1967 of the POLLUTION COUNTERMEASURES BASIC LAW, which prescribed a number of antipollution measures.

Air Pollution Cases—*Respiratory disorders.* Urban industrialization has been accompanied by a rise in the number of cases of such occlusive respiratory disorders as chronic bronchitis, bronchial asthma, asthmatic bronchitis, and pulmonary emphysema. Their symptoms include chronic cough, increased sputum, and asthmatic attacks, and although various causes (including cigarette smoking) may exist, air pollution is known to be a significant factor. Many respiratory disorders were formerly named after the area where they most frequently occurred, such as Kawasaki asthma or Yokkaichi asthma, but such designations can no longer be used because these disorders are now known to be common to all industrial areas. Sulfur oxides and nitrogen oxides released into the atmosphere by combustion of organic materials are the principal causal agents in respiratory disorders.

With the enactment of various measures, such as the desulfurization of fuel oil and exhaust smoke, stricter environmental standards, and the promotion of low-sulfur oil imports, the atmospheric concentration of sulfur oxides was halved between 1966 and 1976. As for nitrogen oxides, it is very difficult to establish control measures, since they are always produced in any kind of combustion; the atmospheric concentration of nitrogen oxides has remained relatively unchanged since the 1970s.

Photochemical smog. In the suburbs of large cities such as Tōkyō and Ōsaka, photochemical smog causes irritation of the eyes and of the pharyngolaryngeal mucosa. Even though the atmospheric concentration of nitrogen oxides and hydrocarbons remains unchanged, photochemical smog has been less prevalent in recent years.

Water Pollution Cases—A disease similar to acute anterior poliomyelitis appeared in Japan between 1953 and 1960. Since cases centered in the city of Minamata, Kumamoto Prefecture, Kyūshū, the illness was named Minamata disease. By December 1979 the number of officially designated patients totaled 1,293, with another 305 dead. In addition, 6,009 patients filed applications for recognition as Minamata disease patients. (The legally required early designation of patients for compensation is one remaining problem concerning this disease.) The blame was fixed on organomercury compounds, which had polluted the local fish population via the effluent waters of the acetaldehyde-synthesizing plant of the CHISSO CORPORATION (then Nippon Chisso Hiryō) in the city of Minamata.

Symptoms of Minamata disease include numbness of the extremities, perioral numbness, centripetal constriction of the visual field, loss of hearing, clumsiness of minute movements, articulation disorders, tremor, and ataxia; mental disorders are observed in serious cases, and mentally retarded children are especially common in cases of congenital Minamata disease. The pathology of this disease is characterized by the degeneration of nerve cells.

Niigata mercury poisoning incident. Patients with symptoms similar to those of Minamata disease appeared in a fishing and farming district of the city of Niigata on the estuary of the river Aganogawa in 1964–65. By December 1979 there were 610 officially designated surviving patients, 73 dead, and 119 applicants for official designation. The symptoms and pathology are the same as in Minamata disease, causing the illness to be called the second Minamata disease. As in Minamata, mercury was found to be responsible, more particularly the mercury in

pollution-related diseases The tragedy of Minamata disease is captured in this scene of a mother bathing her stricken child, photographed by W. Eugene Smith in 1972.

such river fish as *nigoi* (*Hemibarbus barbus*). As in Minamata, there was a plant nearby synthesizing acetaldehyde; the Kanose plant of SHŌWA DENKŌ KK 60 kilometers (37 mi) upstream was found to have polluted the entire river basin. Eventually the company agreed to pay compensation allowances based on those accorded Minamata disease victims.

Land Pollution Cases—*Itai itai disease.* The *itai itai*, or "ouch-ouch," disease appeared mainly in the town of Fuchū on the lower Jinzūgawa in Toyama Prefecture in central Japan. The overwhelming majority of victims were women aged 35 or over who had had two or three pregnancies; a few men suffered mild symptoms. The disease is said to have been present since the Taishō period (1912–26), but there have been no new cases since 1946.

In this disease, spontaneous pain occurs in the inguinal region, lower back, back, and joints, with muscular movement easily causing bone fractures. Steppage gait and hunchback are characteristic, and X rays reveal existing or healed fractures. Cadmium accumulates in the renal tubules of the kidneys; there is cellular degeneration, and the reabsorption of necessary urinary elements by the renal tubules is impaired. Cadmium poisoning is the generally accepted cause of *itai itai* disease. In this case, the liquid wastes of the Kamioka mine of the MITSUI MINING & SMELTING CO, LTD, were incriminated as the source of cadmium.

Chronic arsenic poisoning. Many patients thought to be chronic arsenic poisoning cases appeared in the Sasagatani district in Shimane Prefecture in 1970 and in the Toroku district in Miyazaki Prefecture in 1972. Symptoms included perforation of the nasal septum, cutaneous pigmentation, and polyneuritis. The victims worked in, or resided in the vicinity of, active arsenic mines, and high concentrations of arsenic were found in the settled dust of the area. The mines have now been closed, and relief for the patients is being dispensed under the Pollution-Related Health Damage Compensation Law. In December 1979 the officially designated patients in the two districts totaled 121, with another 19 dead.

Food Poisoning Cases—*Rice oil poisoning (PCB).* A series of patients with complaints of an acnelike rash, edema of the knees, and pigmentation of the lips and nails appeared in the second half of 1968 in western Japan, particularly northern Kyūshū. These ailments struck males and females, with many cases coming from the same families. Named *yushō* (oily skin disease), this disorder has affected a total of 1,858 persons. Rice bran oil manufactured by the Kanemi Sōko Co in the city of Kita Kyūshū came under suspicion as the causative agent because it was a dietary product common to all patients, and its analysis revealed contamination with 2,000 parts per million of polychlorobiphenyl (PCB). See KANEMI OIL POISONING INCIDENT.

Since pollution of the fish population is a major problem in Japan, a fish-eating nation, the Ministry of Health and Welfare provisionally set standards for PCB levels in foodstuffs in 1972. Measures taken included suspending the domestic production of PCB and recovering all liquids, small condensers, noncarbon copying paper, and so forth.

Dried milk poisoning (arsenic). Many cases of a strange and often fatal disorder striking infants appeared in the Chūgoku region, especially Okayama, Shikoku, and the Kinki region, between June and October 1955. There were a total of 7,864 officially designated victims (unofficial estimates are much higher), of whom 130 died. Symptoms included sullenness, paleness, sleeplessness, emaciation, coughing, diarrhea, fever, cutaneous pigmentation, hypertrophy of the liver, and leukopoenia; aftereffects included underdevelopment and oligophrenia. The causal agent was found to be the arsenic-contaminated dried milk manufactured by MORINAGA MILK INDUSTRY CO, LTD. See also MORINAGA POWDERED MILK INCIDENT.

Pollution-Related Health Damage Compensation Law—In order to protect against, and provide compensation for, health damage resulting from the effects of air and water pollution, the various programs theretofore covered by prefectural or municipal regional ordinances were made into a national law in 1973. This Pollution-Related Health Damage Compensation Law applies (1) to widespread health damage that stems from unspecified pollution sources, entails unspecific symptoms (respiratory disorders and so forth), and occurs in industrial districts throughout the country, as in air pollution, and (2) to characteristic health damage, such as Minamata disease or *itai itai* disease, that results from specified pollution sources (e.g., liquid wastes).

Compensation benefits include medical care allowances, compensation for handicaps, compensation payments to survivors, child compensation allowances, and funeral expenses, with polluting companies paying levies proportional to the amount of pollutants released. Part of the tax levied on vehicles is also used for compensation, since automobiles are another major source of pollution.

Pompe van Meerdervoort, Johannes Lydius Catherinus

ポンペ・ファン・メーテルフォールト, J. L. C. (1829–1908). Dutch naval medical officer invited in 1857 by the Tokugawa shogunate (1603–1867) to teach medicine at the naval training school KAIGUN DENSHŪJO in Nagasaki. He almost single-handedly taught the entire medical curriculum to the 133 students. Japan's first modern Western-style hospital and medical school, the Nagasaki Yōjōsho, was built in 1861 at his suggestion. Pompe van Meerdervoort returned home in 1862 accompanied by two of his students, the first Japanese medical students to study abroad. Selected chapters of his diary *Vijf jaren in Japan* (1857–63, Five Years in Japan) are translated in Elizabeth P. Wittermans and John Z. Bowers, tr and ed, *Doctor on Desima* (1970).

Poporo Players case   ポポロ劇団事件

(Poporo Gekidan *jiken*). Legal case in which ACADEMIC FREEDOM, police power, and UNIVERSITY AUTONOMY were at issue. While a student theatrical group named the Poporo Players was performing on the Tōkyō University campus on 20 February 1952, two plainclothesmen in the audience were assaulted by students. One of the students involved, Chida Kenzō (b 1931), was later charged with intimidation but was acquitted by the Tōkyō District Court and by the Tōkyō High Court. Upon appeal, the Supreme Court reversed the lower court's decision on 22 May 1963 and remanded the case.

Convicting Chida, the Tōkyō District Court ruled that the intrusion by the police had not gone beyond the limits of acceptable police activities on university campuses and had not violated the students' freedom of assembly.

popular fiction   大衆文学

(*taishū bungaku*). Modern Japanese popular literature, written primarily as entertainment. It includes *jidai shōsetsu* (historical fiction), *tsūzoku shōsetsu* (fiction of social manners and problems), and, more generally, adventure stories, humorous books, MYSTERY STORIES, tales of the supernatural, and SCIENCE FICTION.

History—The materials and forms of popular literature have their origins in oral storytelling traditions, such as the *kōshaku* (historical narratives; see KŌDAN) and *ninjōbanashi* (a type of sentimental anecdote; see RAKUGO) as well as the various genres of GESAKU, or popular literature of the Edo period (1600–1868). The fusion of Western influences with traditional elements during the Meiji period (1868–1912) led to the birth of this new genre.

In the years after 1885, younger Japanese writers began to criticize traditional literature for its heavy didacticism and dreary moralism. Using Western concepts and techniques, these authors made possible the creation of modern literature in Japan, but this was a literature written by and for the intellectual elite. As a consequence, the reading public was split in two, and popular works written in the traditional manner were relegated to a lower position. However, in the mid-Meiji period, novels describing domestic life, such as those of OZAKI KŌYŌ and TOKUTOMI ROKA, gained a broad readership despite their tendency to retain certain of the moralistic elements of earlier fiction. Their popularity was further enhanced when they were adapted for the stage by the SHIMPA theater movement.

In the Taishō period (1912–26) a distinction came to be made between pure literature (*jumbungaku*), which was characterized by intellectual depth and sophisticated expression, and popular literature, which emphasized storytelling and entertainment. With the appearance of large publishing houses and new mass-circulation newspapers and magazines, some writers previously associated with "pure literature," such as KIKUCHI KAN and KUME MASAO, began to write for the general public. At the same time the writers of historical fiction NAKAZATO KAIZAN and YOSHIKAWA EIJI broke new ground in popular fiction.

In 1925 popular fiction writers organized a society called the Nijūichinichi Kai, which published the journal *Taishū bungei* (Popular Literature). Two years later they participated in the editing of *Gendai taishū bungaku zenshū*, a major collection of popular fiction. Having established *taishū bungaku* as an acceptable genre, these same writers, among them HASEGAWA SHIN and OSARAGI JIRŌ, went on to create the popular literature of the Shōwa period (1926–89).

Postwar Fiction—After World War II came the rise of the FŪZOKU SHŌSETSU (novels of modern urban life) and the growth in popularity of erotic literature. The postwar years also saw the publication of new mass-circulation popular fiction magazines. In the 1950s so-called CHŪKAN SHŌSETSU ("in-between" fiction), neither wholly pure nor wholly popular, began to appear, somewhat blurring the boundary between these two

Distribution of Japanese Population by Age

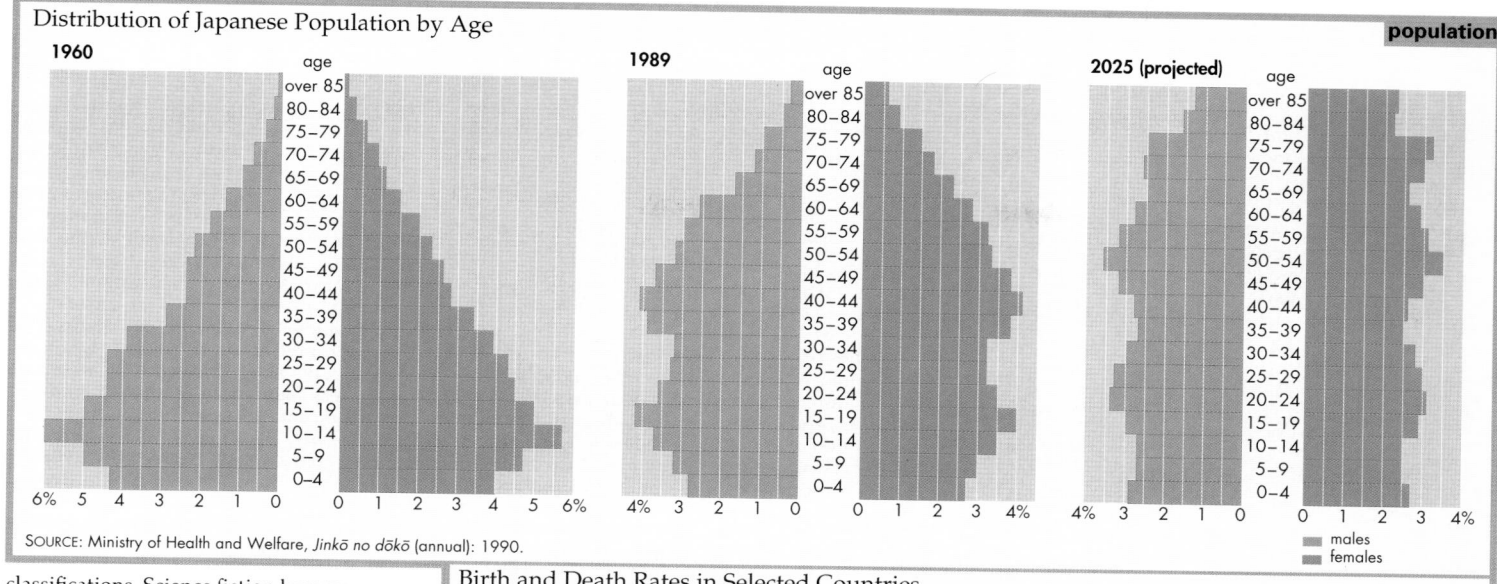

1960   **1989**   **2025 (projected)**

SOURCE: Ministry of Health and Welfare, *Jinkō no dōkō* (annual): 1990.

■ males
■ females

classifications. Science fiction became prominent, with HOSHI SHIN'ICHI and KOMATSU SAKYŌ showing particular originality. Mystery stories by YOKOMIZO SEISHI and MATSUMOTO SEICHŌ also broke away from the traditional format developed by such earlier writers as EDOGAWA RAMPO. With an increasing emphasis on the contradictions and problems of contemporary society, the main themes of popular fiction have now become those of literature as a whole.

Popular Front Incident 人民戦線事件

(Jimmin Sensen Jiken). Wide-scale repression of liberals and leftists in December 1937 and February 1938, soon after the outbreak of the SINO-JAPANESE WAR OF 1937–1945. On 15 December the government arrested left-wing socialists SUZUKI MOSABURŌ, ARAHATA KANSON, YAMAKAWA HITOSHI, and approximately 400 others, alleging that they were obstructing the war effort and organizing Japanese leftists at the behest of the seventh Comintern (Communist International). A week later the NIHON MUSANTŌ (Japan Proletarian Party) and the Nihon Rōdō Kumiai Zenkoku Hyōgikai (All-Japan Council of Labor Unions) were dissolved. The following February a second series of arrests was carried out, this time concentrating on intellectuals and university professors such as AONO SUEKICHI, MINOBE RYŌKICHI, and ŌUCHI HYŌE. Many of those arrested were jailed until the end of World War II.

popular sovereignty 国民主権

(kokumin shuken). The people's power to make the final decision about the way the state should function. The 1947 CONSTITUTION OF JAPAN stipulates that sovereign power resides with the people. Based on this principle, the constitution calls for the adoption of a representative democratic system (preamble) and the establishment of the National Diet composed of elected members, representative of all the people, making it the highest organ of state power (arts. 41 and 43). Choosing and dismissing public officials, recognized as the people's inalienable rights (art. 15, para. 1), and universal adult suffrage, guaranteed with regard to the election of public officials (art. 15, para. 3), are based on this principle. Certain procedures of direct democracy have been incorporated into the constitution, including the popular vote necessary for amendment of the constitution (art. 96, para. 1), the people's review of the appointments of Supreme Court justices (art. 79, paras. 2 and 3), and local citizens' voting on special Diet leg-

Birth and Death Rates in Selected Countries

births per 1,000 population

Japan
United States
France
United Kingdom
West Germany

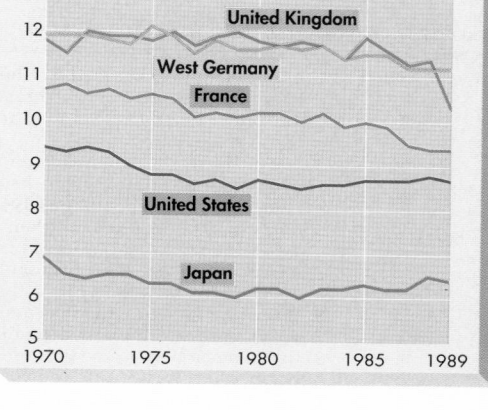

deaths per 1,000 population

United Kingdom
West Germany
France
United States
Japan

NOTE: Figures for Japan after 1972 include Okinawa.
SOURCE: OECD, *Labour Force Statistics 1969–1989* (1991).

islation applicable only to one local entity (art. 95).

population 人口

(jinkō). Japan's population of 123,612,000 people (1990) is the seventh largest in the world. Fairly accurate statistics have existed concerning the Japanese population since the mid-Edo period (1600–1868). The eighth shōgun, Tokugawa Yoshimune (1684–1751), ordered a national survey of all households in the 1720s. From the mid-18th to the mid-19th century, the population maintained a level of approximately 30–32 million. However, beginning with the shift from a feudal to a modern society that took place in the Meiji period (1868–1912), the Japanese population increased steadily. The only exception to this rise occurred during 1944 and 1945, the latter part of World War II, when the population declined by about 2.3 million. The population of 38.7 million in 1887 increased by a factor of 3.2 during the next century.

Because premodern societies in general have both a high birthrate and a high death rate, the population is stable and the age structure can be represented as a pyramid with a wide base. As a society modernizes it passes through a stage in which the population rises quickly, because the death rate drops sharply while the birthrate falls slowly. Finally, the society reaches a stable, mature population level with both low birthrates and low death rates. The age structure of Japan's population has resulted in

several problems for the society. Because of the low birthrate, the average family size is shrinking, and there is a shortage of young people entering the work force. In addition, since the Japanese have the longest average life span in the world, the percentage of elderly in the population is increasing rapidly. In recent years the rate of population growth has been decreasing an average of 0.5 percent per year, and it is predicted that the growth rate will continue to decrease. According to a forecast by the Ministry of Health and Welfare's Institute of Population Problems, Japan's population will continue increasing until 2013, when it will peak at 136 million and then begin to decline. Although Japan will not reach a fully stable population level until far into the future, the country is entering a stage of population maturity with low birthrates and death rates.

Falling Birthrate——The falling birthrate in Japan has become a cause for much concern because of its relationship to problems such as the shortage of young workers, the unbalanced age structure aggravated by the increasing size of the elderly population, and the problems in family life and personality development for children with no brothers and sisters. From the early Meiji period to the mid-Taishō period (1912–26), the birthrate tended to increase. This was primarily due to the decree prohibiting abortion issued by the Meiji government and to an improvement in the nutrition level of the Japanese diet. How-

Japan's Population Growth, 1872–1990

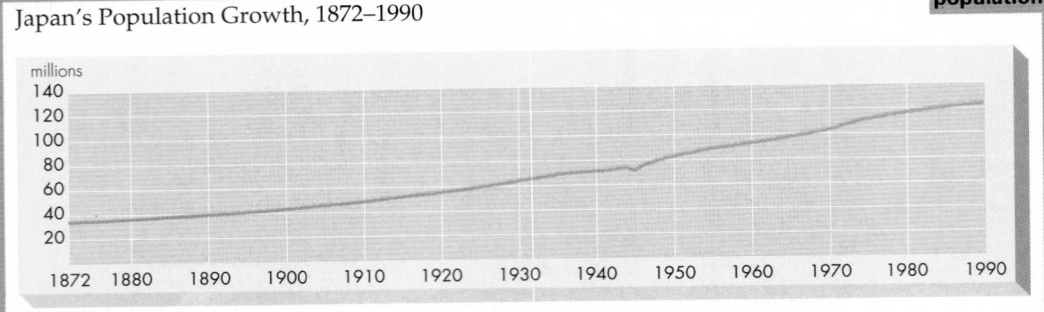

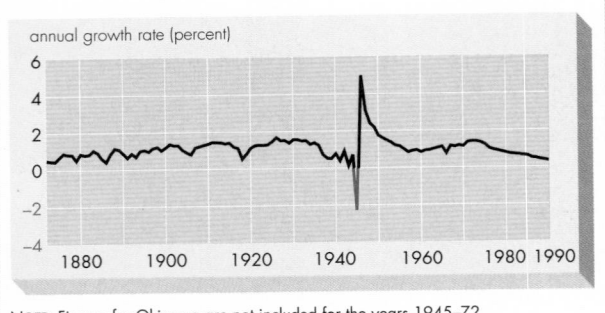

NOTE: Figures for Okinawa are not included for the years 1945–72.
SOURCE: Ministry of Health and Welfare, *Jinkō no dōkō* (annual): 1991.

ever, beginning in the late Taishō period and continuing to today, the birthrate has gradually fallen, mostly as a result of an increase in the average marriage age.

An interesting phenomenon occurred in 1966. The birthrate, which had been 18.6 (births per 1,000 people) in 1965, fell suddenly to 13.7 in 1966 and then returned to 19.4 in 1967. Based on the old Japanese calendar, which was derived from the Chinese zodiac, 1966 was the year of the HINOE UMA (fire-*yang* horse), which occurs once every 60 years. Since there is a traditional belief that women born in the year of the fire-*yang* horse bring misfortune, birth control was strictly practiced in 1966. While it is surprising that so many people in modern Japan still pay attention to this superstition, another significant aspect of this phenomenon is the evidence it provides that Japanese couples are able to control their fertility.

After the jump in the birthrate to 19.4 in 1967, the trend toward lower birthrates continued, and in 1990 the birthrate was 10.0. The drop in the birthrate in recent years is certainly related to the rise in the average marriage age of women, accompanying recent changes in lifestyle and the progress of women in the workplace. However, another factor is that women in the marriage and childbearing age group simply represent a lower percentage of the overall population than they used to. It is predicted that the birthrate will continue at a low level in the future.

Death Rate—The average life expectancy in the last decade of the 19th century appears to have been about 43 years for men and 44 years for women. By 1947 this had risen to 50 years for men and 54 years for women. In the 43 years from 1947 to 1990, the average life expectancy jumped to 75.9 years for men and 81.9 for women, giving the Japanese the longest average life span in the world for both men and women.

From the early Meiji period until World War II, increases in average life expectancy were caused primarily by a drop in infant mortality. Infant mortality due to infectious diseases such as pneumonia, bronchitis, and gastroenteritis began decreasing in the Meiji period because of an increase in the standard of living and improvements in public sanitation. This trend continued after World War II, and in addition the widespread introduction of antibiotics resulted in a dramatic decrease in death from tuberculosis among adolescents. By 1955 infectious diseases had been replaced by cancer, heart disease, and cerebrovascular disease as major causes of death. Although average life expectancy has increased, since the percentage of elderly in the population has also increased, the average death rate has changed little since 1955.

Aging of Society—As the percentage of young people in the population is decreasing and the average life expectancy is increasing, Japanese society is aging. Even so, the percentage of the population over 65, 12 percent in 1990, is not necessarily high compared with the United States and Europe. The major problem associated with the aging of Japanese society is the extreme speed at which it is proceeding. Although the percentage of the population over 65 reached 14 percent in Sweden in 1975, it had already reached the 7 percent level in 1890 and took 85 years to double. The actual or predicted time period required for the percentage of elderly to double from 7 percent to 14 percent is 70 years for the United States, 45 years for Great Britain, and 130 years for France (from United Nations data). In contrast Japan reached the 7 percent level in 1970 and is predicted to hit the 14 percent level by 1995, a span of 25 years. This rapid expansion of the elderly population is causing increasingly serious problems, including a lag in social welfare services and a mounting social security burden on the working population. The percentage of elderly in the Japanese population is forecast as follows: year 2000, 17 percent; 2015, 24 percent; and 2030, 26 percent. By the early 21st century, Japan will have one of the world's oldest populations. Major social policy issues for the future include finding ways to increase the quality of life, maintain people's purpose in life throughout their 80-year existence, make the most of the elderly work force, and sustain the vitality of the society.

population redistribution

過疎・過密

(*kaso; kamitsu*). Continuing a trend already well established in the Edo period (1600–1868), Japan has seen rapid population growth in urban areas in its modern period, while many rural areas have experienced population declines. This shift has been especially extreme since World War II ended.

About 60 percent of the total Japanese population resides in a little more than 3 percent of the total land area of the country. Together the densely populated areas in and around the cities of TŌKYŌ, ŌSAKA, and NAGOYA account for nearly half of Japan's population. As a result, these areas are confronted with a variety of issues related to overcrowding, including environmental problems and HOUSING PROBLEMS.

In the course of Japan's postwar recovery and period of high economic growth since the 1960s, there have been major employment shifts away from primary industries toward secondary and tertiary industries. These changes were accompanied by a massive concentration of the population in urban areas: between 1955 and 1975 the population of the three largest regions rose steeply, from 30 million to 50 million. As the economy entered a period of slower and more stable growth in the mid-1970s, this trend appeared to reverse itself slightly. In the 1980s, however, there was a renewed, although less vigorous, flow of population into the urban centers—especially Tōkyō.

Concerned by these developments, the national government decided in 1988 to begin relocation of certain administrative functions from Tōkyō to other regions. This decision followed the 1986 announcement of the FOURTH COMPREHENSIVE NATIONAL LAND DEVELOPMENT PLAN, which extended the concept of "Established Zones for Habitation," a program designed under the 1972 Third Plan to encourage development and population growth in certain outlying regions. These plans are intended to resolve some of the serious underpopulation problems that have developed in the countryside as a result of the large shifts since the end of World War II. With the systematic rearrangement of living and working environments as its basic goal, the development plans proposed the creation of new settlement zones throughout the country in areas of reduced population density. An underpopulated region is an area where, due to a sudden and large-scale population decrease, it becomes difficult for the community to continue to function and its people become unable to maintain an acceptable standard of living. According to 1984 government statistics, such underpopulated communities accounted for 45.8 percent of the country's total land area and 35.4 percent of all municipalities.

In recent years, attempts to revitalize local industries (such as the One Village, One Product Movement [Isson Ippin Undō] in Ōita Prefecture) have had some success in attracting young people back to depopulated, rural areas from the big cities. Yet the disproportionately high number of elderly people in these regions remains a serious and deepening problem, especially in terms of the rising demand it is creating for welfare services, health insurance, and medical care.

Poroshiridake
幌尻岳

Also called Horoshiridake. Mountain in southern Hokkaidō; highest peak in the Hidaka Mountains. There is a cirque group near the summit dating back to the glacial age. Height: 2,052 m (6,732 ft).

Port Arthur
旅順

English name for the Chinese city of Lüshun (J: Ryojun), a strategic railway terminus and ice-free port located 37 kilometers (about 23 mi) southwest of Dalian (Ta-lien; J: Dairen) on the tip of the Liaodong (Liaotung) Peninsula in southern Manchuria. Briefly occupied by the British in 1858, it was fortified by the Chinese during the 1880s. During the SINO-JAPANESE WAR OF 1894–1895, Japan captured Port Arthur but was obliged to relinquish it in 1895 as a result of the TRIPARTITE INTERVENTION. Russia acquired a leasehold there in 1898. On 2 January 1905, at the height of the RUSSO-JAPANESE WAR (1904–05), the Japanese captured Port Arthur. Receiving the lease on the tip of the Liaodong Peninsula, including Port Arthur, the Japanese developed the city as a naval base and made it the capital of the leased Guandong (Kwantung) Territory until 1934 and headquarters of the GUANDONG (KWANTUNG) ARMY until 1931. Soviet paratroopers occupied Port Arthur on 22 August 1945, after agreeing with the Chinese to use it jointly as a military base; Soviet forces were withdrawn in 1955.

Portman, Anton L. C.

ポートマン, A. L. C.

(fl late 19th century). American diplomat stationed in Japan during the late Edo (1600–1868) and early Meiji (1868–1912) periods. He came to Japan in 1853 as a Dutch interpreter for Commodore Matthew C. PERRY and assisted in the 1854 KANAGAWA TREATY. He returned to Japan in 1861 as secretary to the American legation and from 1865 to 1866 served as chargé d'affaires, returning to his position as secretary in 1866. In 1869 he was involved in a dispute with the newly formed Meiji government over the construction of a Tōkyō-Yokohama rail line; over American protests the line was built with British financial and technical assistance.

portrait painting

肖像画

(shōzōga). Japanese portrait painting stretches back to the 7th century and comprises two broad categories: portraits of famous Buddhist monks and secular portraiture. Stylistically, Japanese portraiture has vacillated between periods of Chinese (and later Western) influence, when efforts were made to create the illusion of volume, and periods of internalization, when the native taste for flat and more decorative surfaces asserted itself.

Early Portraiture——The earliest portraits in Japan followed Tang (T'ang dynasty; 618–907) Chinese prototypes in both subject matter and style. The famous 7th-century portrait of Prince SHŌTOKU (Tōkyō National Museum, Imperial Household Collection), showing the prince flanked by two sons, is clearly derived from the Tang imperial portrait type. The earliest surviving religious portraits of the Heian period (794–1185), the *Seven Shingon Patriarchs,* arrived in Japan when KŪKAI returned from Tang China in 806 to found the Shingon sect of esoteric Buddhism in Japan. He brought with him five portraits of Indian and Chinese patriarchs of the sect. In 821 he had portraits done of two other patriarchs to complete the set. The Chinese portraits convey emotional intensity and a sense of physical volume, whereas the two Japanese portraits are less intense and more brightly colored.

Kamakura-Period (1185–1333) Portraiture——A shift in attention to the earthly realm that accompanied the collapse of the court aristocracy and the rise of the military class in the late 12th century led to an emphasis on secular portraiture, often with documentary intent. The portraits of TAIRA NO SHIGEMORI and his rival, MINAMOTO NO YORITOMO, traditionally attributed to FUJIWARA NO TAKANOBU, are done in a naturalistic style known as nise-e ("likeness pictures"). The soft brushwork and exceptional detail of the faces are in brilliant contrast to the stark, almost geometric shapes of the costumes. A new development in Kamakura portrait painting was the introduction from China of CHINSŌ, or portraits of Zen masters, bestowed on a favored pupil to certify his progress or attainment of enlightenment. There are two stylistic streams in chinsō painting; both are derived from Southern

Song dynasty (Southern Sung; 1127–1279) modes. One is polychrome and minutely detailed; the other is monochrome or in muted colors and even more precisely rendered. Two exceptionally fine chinsō are the 1349 portrait of MUSŌ SOSEKI, the founder of Tenryūji, and the late-15th-century portrait of IKKYŪ Sōjun, the controversial abbot of the temple Daitokuji.

Muromachi (1333–1568) and Azuchi-Momoyama (1568–1600) Portraiture—— In the 14th century subject matter in secular portraiture was expanded to include powerful members of the warrior class, and later still their wives and children. The TOSA SCHOOL of artists dominated portraiture at this time: to the traditional courtier pose, they added the equestrian pose of a fully armed warrior, called *shutsujin'ei* ("departure-for-the-battlefield pictures").

Edo and Modern Portraiture——In the Edo period (1600–1868), Western painting came to Japan's attention and occasionally influenced portraiture. At the outset of the 17th century, before the ban on Christianity, portraits based on European models were done under the tutelage of missionaries (see NAMBAN ART). In the mid-17th century, a group of ŌBAKU SECT Zen monks emigrated from China and brought with them an updated, Ming-dynasty (1368–1644) version of the chinsō format. These portraits are remarkable for their manneristic, rather hard-edged shading of flesh tones. However, more important was the influence of European prints and paintings upon scholars of WESTERN LEARNING. WATANABE KAZAN, one of the artists in this circle, forged his own synthesis between Western and Japanese traditions. His portrait of his teacher, TAKAMI SENSEKI, displays a blend of careful observation and the use of softened chiaroscuro in the face, with a loosely drawn rendering of the robes.

Japanese portraiture since the Meiji period (1868–1912) has reflected the large schism between YŌGA (Western-style painting) and NIHONGA (Japanese-style painting). *Yōga* artists have been heavily influenced by contemporary Western styles, typically working in oil on canvas, while *nihonga* artists have preferred traditional Japanese media—ink and water-based pigment on paper or silk—and a style of portraiture that has its roots in the work of late-Edo-period artists like Watanabe Kazan.

Portsmouth, Treaty of

ポーツマス条約

(Pōtsumasu Jōyaku). Treaty concluding the RUSSO-JAPANESE WAR; signed on 5 September 1905 in Portsmouth, New Hampshire, by KOMURA JUTARŌ of Japan and Sergei WITTE of Russia. When war broke out in February 1904, Japanese forces were unexpectedly successful at first, but their material and human resources had become seriously depleted by the Battle of MUKDEN (March 1905). Therefore, following the naval victory in the Battle of TSUSHIMA (27–28 May 1905), the Japanese government requested that American president Theodore Roosevelt mediate between the two countries.

After difficult negotiations, which saw Japan accept the southern half of Sakhalin Island rather than hold to its demand for all of the island plus large indemnities, an agreement was signed. The Japanese public, which had been led to believe that victory was imminent, reacted negatively to the treaty in such outbursts as the HIBIYA INCENDIARY INCIDENT. To government leaders, however, the

treaty signified a step forward in enlarging Japan's influence in Korea and southern Manchuria. First, the treaty assured Japan's preeminence in Korea (clause 2). Having successfully fought for Korea's independence in the SINO-JAPANESE WAR OF 1894–1895, Japan was now able to claim it as a protectorate (and eventually to annex it in 1910). Second, on the condition of Chinese consent, the treaty gave Japan the Russian leaseholds of PORT ARTHUR and Dalian (Ta-lien; J: Dairen) on the Liaodong (Liaotung) Peninsula and railway rights in Manchuria south of Changchun (clauses 5 and 6).

port towns

港町

(minato machi). Trading centers that prospered around seaports from the Nara (710–794) through the Edo (1600–1868) periods. Some of the earliest port towns were ANOTSU and BŌ NO TSU. Several, such as ONOMICHI on the Inland Sea and TSURUGA and OBAMA on the Sea of Japan, later became commercial harbors. With the development of the money economy and the expansion of overseas trade during the Sengoku period (1467–1568), many cities, such as Hakata (see HAKATA MERCHANTS), SAKAI, NAGASAKI, and Hyōgo, flourished as trading ports. Although trade with other countries was restricted by the NATIONAL SECLUSION policy of the Tokugawa shogunate (1603–1867), domestic trade continued at port towns, such as ŌSAKA, SHIMONOSEKI, NIIGATA, and other sites on major sea lanes. See also KAISEN.

Portugal and Japan

ポルトガルと日本

(Porutogaru to Nihon). The initial period of intercourse between Portugal and Japan lasted from 1543 until the adoption of the NATIONAL SECLUSION policy by the Japanese in 1639. The Portuguese who came to Tanegashima, an island near Kyūshū, in 1543 brought with them firearms (see FIREARMS, INTRODUCTION OF). This changed traditional tactics and fortification at a time when such warlords as ODA NOBUNAGA were trying to establish national hegemony. Although himself a Spaniard, Francis XAVIER went to Japan with Portuguese Jesuits at the request of King João III of Portugal in 1549 and began proselytizing. The Jesuits brought with them European sciences such as medicine and astronomy, as well as European philosophy, literature, and other cultural attainments. They studied the Japanese language and culture systematically so as to better carry out their missionary work (see CHRISTIANITY), and a dictionary they compiled, the *Vocabulario da Lingoa de Iapam com a declaração em Portugues* (NIPPO JISHO), is today considered indispensable for the study of the history of the Japanese language.

Portugal competed for Japanese trade with Spain, the Netherlands, and England in the early Edo period (1600–1868), but with the adoption of the seclusion policy, all foreigners, with the exception of the Dutch and Chinese, were forbidden entry (see also NAMBAN TRADE). Relations were resumed after the Meiji Restoration of 1868, and Portuguese diplomat Wenceslau de MORAES dedicated much time and effort to introducing Japanese culture to his countrymen. Diplomatic relations were severed temporarily as a result of World War II, but they were restored in October 1953. Trade between the two countries is increasing. In 1990, the volume of exports from Japan to Portugal was US $560.1 mil-

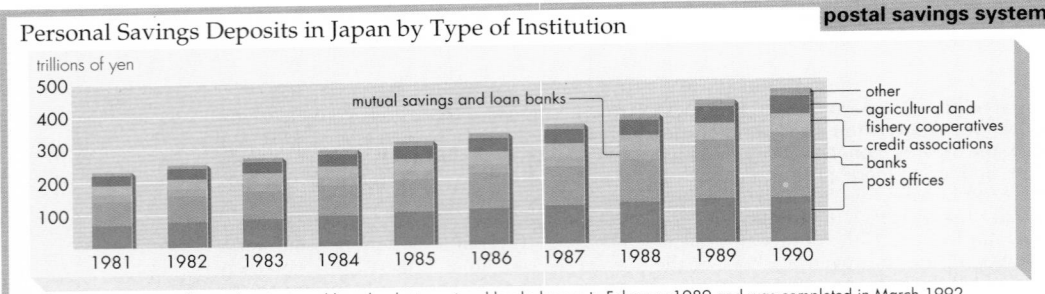

Personal Savings Deposits in Japan by Type of Institution

trillions of yen

NOTE: The conversion of mutual savings and loan banks to regional banks began in February 1989 and was completed in March 1992. Beginning in 1989, deposits in mutual savings and loan banks are thus included in the category "banks." "Other" includes credit cooperatives and labor credit associations.
SOURCE: Bank of Japan, *Keizai tōkei nempō* (annual): 1991.

lion and imports totaled US $215.4 million. Exports to the Portuguese colony of Macao totaled US $60.0 million, while imports registered US $88.1 million.

postal savings system　郵便貯金制度

(*yūbin chokin seido*). Postal savings—a system in which the post office as a government enterprise handles the personal savings of individuals—was introduced in Japan in 1875. The present system is based on the Postal Savings Law (Yūbin Chokin Hō) of 1947. Originally intended for small savers, the system had limits on the amounts that could be deposited, and interest payments were tax exempt. The tax reform of April 1988 introduced a separate tax rate of 20 percent on interest (for the handicapped and those aged 65 and over, interest payments on deposits of up to ¥3.0 million [US $24,000] remain tax free). At the same time, the ceiling on deposits was raised from ¥3.0 million to ¥5.0 million (US $40,000). In May 1991 the ceiling was raised again to ¥10.0 million (US $72,000). Drawn by a national network of somé 24,000 post offices, savings at the end of fiscal year 1990 amounted to ¥136.3 trillion (US $993.3 billion), or 29 percent of the total savings invested with all Japanese financial institutions. Until recently, the total amount was placed with the Trust Fund Bureau and used for fiscal loans and investment, but since June 1987 a certain amount has been invested independently.

postal service　郵便

(*yūbin*). The Japanese postal service efficiently handles one of the largest volumes of mail in the world. Founded in 1871, the cur-

rent system has its roots in an ancient system of post horses and stations.

History——In 646 a post-horse system modeled after the post-horse relay system in Tang (T'ang) China (618–907) was established in several provinces in what is now the Kyōto-Ōsaka region (see EKISEI). In 718 a system of post stations was set up in various other provinces to facilitate communication with the capital, HEIJŌKYŌ (now Nara). With the establishment of the Kamakura shogunate (1192–1333), the use of couriers on foot was added to the existing post-horse relay stations. The distance between Kyōto and Kamakura was covered in five days.

Following the unification of the country carried out by TOYOTOMI HIDEYOSHI and TOKUGAWA IEYASU from the end of the 16th to the beginning of the 17th century, postal systems were expanded. Post horses, relay couriers, and foot messengers were maintained by the powerful institutions of the time—the shōgun, the *daimyō*, and various religious orders—to serve their particular needs. Communication links between Edo (now Tōkyō) and each daimyō's domain were established, but they were exclusively for military and official use. The forerunner of the postal system for use by private persons was the "three-times" courier system for *samurai* family communications. Begun in 1615, this consisted of three round trips each month between Ōsaka, Kyōto, and Edo. See also HIKYAKU.

The modern public postal system began in the Meiji period (1868–1912). Following the establishment of the Meiji government in 1868, a new government-run postal system between Tōkyō and Ōsaka was put into effect on 20 April 1871. This system was developed by the superintendent of postal services, MAEJIMA HISOKA, known in Japan as "the father of the post." It was based on the British and other postal systems that Maejima had studied in Europe. Postal service was extended throughout the country in July 1872. In 1873 the postal service was declared a government monopoly, and a nationwide system of uniform postal rates adopted. Postage stamps were introduced, the speed of mail delivery was increased, and postal charges were reduced. In 1877 Japan joined the Universal Postal Union.

The Contemporary Postal System

The postal system in Japan is a government monopoly operated as a profit-making business to provide postal service as cheaply as possible. It has an independent profit structure in which income from postal fees is applied to expenditures. Administered by the MINISTRY OF POSTS AND TELECOMMUNICATIONS, the postal service maintains 24,000 post offices throughout the nation. Apart from regular postal operations, it operates a savings and money-transfer service.

In the 1960s a program of modernization and rationalization of postal operations was begun. The unification of standards for envelope sizes was implemented, and in 1966 a

system was established in which first-class mail (mainly letters) was classified into standard size and nonstandard size. A postal code address system was adopted in 1968 whereby postal code numbers could be machine-read for sorting standard-size first-class mail and second-class mail (postcards). This was the first practical application in the world of a machine that could sort mail by automatic reading of postal code numbers. Today the postal system uses a linked system of automatic separating and culling machines, facing and stamping machines, and postal-code-reading machines.

The annual volume of mail handled in Japan has increased dramatically with the development of the economy. The increase in business correspondence is particularly striking: in 1991 some 80 percent of all mail in Japan was business mail.

Poston Relocation Center　ポストン収容所

(Posuton Shūyōjo). Wartime relocation facility for Japanese Americans from California and Arizona; located on the Colorado River Indian Reservation, Arizona. In operation from 8 May 1942 until 28 November 1945, it held a maximum of 17,814 inmates at any one time; in all 19,534 persons were confined there. It was one of two such camps located on Indian reservations. See also JAPANESE AMERICANS, WARTIME RELOCATION OF.

post-station towns　宿場町

(*shukuba machi*; also called *shukueki*). Officially regulated settlements catering to travelers along major roadways. The development of *shukuba machi* from the Nara (710–794) through the Edo (1600–1868) periods facilitated national integration through speedy and safe official communications, monopolies over military deployment, control over the movement of citizens and individuals traveling for official purposes, and control of the circulation of goods, including tax revenues. Until the system was abolished in 1870, residents in these locations operated under regulations stipulating the number of transport workers and horses they were required to provide.

During the Edo period five radial roads (GOKAIDŌ) extended from the shogunal capital of Edo (now Tōkyō). Along the two main roads, the TŌKAIDŌ and the NAKASENDŌ respectively, 53 and 67 *shukuba machi*, spaced roughly 3 to 10 miles (10–17 km) apart, welcomed travelers. *Daimyō* and their retainers stopped in special inns (HONJIN) enroute to fulfilling their obligation of alternate-year residence (see SANKIN KŌTAI) in Edo. The Tokugawa shogunate assumed direct oversight of these settlements, imposing a form of corvée (SUKEGŌ) that extended to neighboring villages. *Shukuba machi* included tiny post stations along mountain passes where service-related employment in inns and eating places prevailed, relatively small agriculturally based stations, large *shukuba machi* with services for transport and commerce (see MARKET TOWNS), and large CASTLE TOWNS. *Shukuba machi* might best be thought of as links in a chain that crisscrossed central Japan and beyond. The relatively large number of *shukuba machi* stands as a tribute to the high degree of integration achieved in communications, the exchange of goods, and the circulation of people, especially during the Edo period.

postwar literature→Shōwa literature

postal service

1 Letter carriers in Japan usually deliver the mail by motorcycle or bicycle.
2 A city mailbox. One slot is for local mail, the other for long-distance mail. The T-shaped mark is the Japanese postal symbol.
3 A mail truck. The Japanese postal service accepts mail addressed either in Japanese writing or in the Roman alphabet.

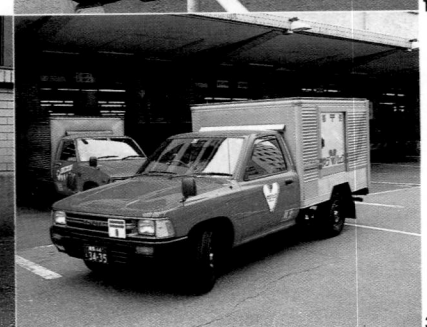

potatoes and yams 芋類

(*imorui*). Japanese tuber crops include common white potatoes (*jagaimo*), sweet potatoes (*satsumaimo*), taros (*satoimo*), Chinese yams (*nagaimo*), and Japanese yams (*yamatoimo*). Common potatoes were introduced to Japan in 1601 and sweet potatoes in 1605, and their value as emergency crops in times of scarcity led to their widespread cultivation. In 1990 production of white potatoes (*Solanum tuberosum*), the most intensively cultivated tuber crop, totaled 3,552,000 metric tons (3,907,000 short tons). The main production center is Hokkaidō; however, the white potato can be harvested twice a year, in spring and late autumn, in warm areas such as Kyūshū.

The sweet potato (*Ipomoea batatas*) is cultivated in warm places from the Kantō Plain southward. Production reached about 7,200,000 metric tons (7,920,000 short tons) a year in the immediate post–World War II period, but in 1990 it was only 1,400,000 metric tons (1,540,000 short tons).

The *satoimo* (*Colocasia antiquorum* var. *esculenta*) is a kind of taro introduced to Japan in ancient times from the southwest Pacific region. It is cultivated in moist fields or paddies. Although it was well known in traditional Japanese life, present consumption is small. The Chinese yam (*Dioscorea batatas*) was introduced to Japan from China several centuries ago. In 1990 production reached 363,000 metric tons (400,000 short tons). The old custom of digging and eating wild yams (*D. japonica*) in the autumn is still practiced in Japan.

Potsdam Declaration ポツダム宣言

(Potsudamu Sengen). Declaration defining the terms for Japanese surrender; issued on 26 July 1945 at the last Allied conference held during WORLD WAR II, from 17 July to 2 August 1945, in Potsdam (near Berlin). The United States, the Soviet Union, and Great Britain were represented by Truman, Stalin, and Churchill (the latter being replaced by his successor as prime minister, Clement Attlee, during the conference). The declaration itself was issued in the names of Truman, Churchill, and Chiang Kai-shek, whose approval was obtained by telephone; the Soviet Union had not yet declared war against Japan and endorsed the declaration later. It called on Japan to surrender unconditionally or face utter destruction, and to rid itself of its militarist leaders and establish a new political order. It further stated that its military forces would be disarmed but allowed to return home, that Japanese sovereignty would be limited to the territorial borders established at the beginning of the Meiji period (1868–1912), and that Japan would be occupied by Allied forces until it had set up a democratic government. Japan substantially agreed to the terms on 10 August, two days after the Soviet Union had declared war against Japan and one day after a second ATOMIC BOMB was dropped on Japan by the United States. It formally accepted the terms on 14 August. Japan's surrender was formally announced to the Japanese people on 15 August.

potter's wheels →rokuro

Power Reactor and Nuclear Fuel Development Corporation
動力炉・核燃料開発事業団

(Dōryokuro-Kakunenryō Kaihatsu Jigyōdan). Special-status corporation founded in 1967 to succeed the Atomic Fuel Corporation. The successor corporation promotes the development of technology for fast breeder reactors, advanced thermal converter reactors, and the mining, refining, processing, and reprocessing of nuclear fuels. It has constructed a number of prototype fast breeder reactors and is researching the centrifugation process for enriching uranium. The corporation operates a nuclear fuel reprocessing plant in the village of Tōkai, Ibaraki Prefecture, and is also studying new technology for storing high-level radioactive waste that involves mixing liquid waste with molten glass and hardening the resulting mixture within stainless steel canisters—a process called glassification.

Pozdneev, Dmitrii Matveevich
ポズネーエフ, D. M.

(1865–1942). Russian orientalist who made important contributions to Japanese studies. Born the son of a priest in Orel, he graduated from a seminary in Kiev and in 1893 entered the Faculty of Oriental Languages at the University of St. Petersburg, where he studied Chinese, Manchu, and Mongol. After spending six years in China, he took up residence in Japan in 1905 and wrote the monumental *Material on the History of Northern Japan and Her Relations with the Asian Continent and Russia*, published in Yokohama in 1909. From 1910 until 1917 he directed the Oriental Institute at Vladivostok. Following the revolution, he worked at the Oriental Institute in Leningrad and authored several volumes on Japanese politics and economics.

pragmatism プラグマティズム

(*puragumatizumu*). The philosophical concept of pragmatism was introduced to Japan in 1888 by Motora Yūjirō (1858–1912) in an article on the psychological theories of John Dewey. In addition to the American schools represented by Charles Peirce, William James, and Dewey, such philosophers as Ferdinand Schiller and Henry Sturt became well known in Japan as English proponents of pragmatism.

Before 1945 pragmatism received only marginal recognition among Japanese academic philosophers. The influential KUWAKI GEN'YOKU (1874–1946) effectively ended academic interest in pragmatism at imperial universities and government schools by calling it a "*Pseudophilosophie*" that debased philosophy by seeking usefulness in it. In his *Zen no kenkyū* (1911; tr *A Study of Good*, 1960), however, NISHIDA KITARŌ (1870–1945) attempted to incorporate James's "radical empiricism" into rationalist epistemology. The writers of the Japanese naturalist school (see NATURALISM) claimed that they, like the pragmatists, studied the scientific truth of life. Some opponents of naturalism also accepted pragmatism, notably the novelist NATSUME SŌSEKI (1867–1916). In political philosophy, TANAKA ŌDŌ (1867–1932), with his call for "radical individualism," was the strongest advocate of pragmatism.

Japan's defeat in 1945 created the most favorable political and intellectual situation that pragmatism had ever enjoyed in Japan. Some scholars viewed Japan's defeat as the defeat of Japanese thought and behavior at the hand of the "philosophy of American democracy" and began debating the nature of this philosophy. Its power seemed to lie in the individual's sense of self and critical intelligence—qualities fostered by empirical thinking. Major figures in this postwar resurgence of pragmatism are MARUYAMA MASAO (b 1914), Tsurumi Shunsuke (b 1922), and the group of writers and scholars associated with the monthly journal SHISŌ NO KAGAKU (Science of Thought).

Of the Japanese who developed pragmatist methods and modes of thought outside the direct influence of foreign philosophies, the most important figure was FUKUZAWA YUKICHI (1835–1901). Fukuzawa, a contemporary of William James, formulated many ideas—including an empiricism of both method and the theory of reality—that closely resembled James's thought.

prayer 祈り

(*inori*). As the dialogue between humans and the divine, prayer has played an important part in all Japanese religions. In both SHINTŌ and BUDDHISM there were many prayers for the welfare of the community and the nation. The texts of these kinds of prayer were closely tied to ceremony and extremely formalized. With the introduction of the Buddhist idea that one's actions will result in future rewards, individuals began to recite prayers for their own benefit. Personal prayer sometimes took the form of 100 visits to a shrine for worship (*hyakudo mairi*). The magical element was strong in indigenous forms of prayer from primitive days. This element was further developed by ESOTERIC BUDDHISM. Importance was placed on the meaning and content expressed by the words of ordinary prayers, but, in the case of incantations, a magic power was thought to reside in the words themselves. The *shingon* (MANTRA) employed in the prayer for grace (*kaji kitō*) in esoteric Buddhism is an example of this.

preceramic period 先土器時代

(*sendoki jidai*). This pre–10,000 BC period, more generally known as the PALEOLITHIC PERIOD, begins with the arrival from the Asian continent of the first paleolithic inhabitants

post-station towns
1 This Edo-period print by Keisai Eisen, part of the *Sixty-Nine Stations of the Kiso Road* series, depicts a shop in the post-station town of Narai, located on the Kiso section of the highway Nakasendō.
2 Narai has preserved much of its traditional flavor and has been designated a historical landmark. Iseya, the Narai inn pictured here, began as a stable for cattle and horses.

of Japan and lasts until their invention of pottery and their adaptation to a new post-glacial climate in the succeeding JŌMON PERIOD (ca 10,000 BC–ca 300 BC).

precision machinery industry
精密機械産業

(*seimitsu kikai sangyō*). Japan's precision machinery industry is best known for its watches and cameras, but it also produces precision instruments, measuring equipment, medical equipment, sewing machines, and optical equipment. Japan's experience in producing *wadokei* (classic Japanese-style clocks), which dates back to the 17th century, provided a springboard for the development of the modern chronometer industry. Japan started to produce Western-style watches and clocks in the early Meiji period (1868–1912), and by the 1920s exports had exceeded imports. See also CLOCKS AND WATCHES.

Japanese cameras were of very poor quality until after World War II. By the 1950s, however, manufacturers had raised the quality of their products to world standards, dramatically expanded production, and carved out a considerable share of the international market. Japan now ranks first in the world in production of cameras (16.6 million units in 1988) and is second only to Hong Kong in timepieces (350.0 million units in 1988). As the two industries depend heavily on exports, they have been hurt by the recent appreciation of the yen. They are also facing growing competition from the newly industrializing economies (NIEs). However, in many cases Japan exports crucial high-technology parts to producers in the NIEs for final assembly with locally produced parts. As Japan's camera production is not likely to increase in the future, camera manufacturers are diversifying into the production of office automation equipment such as copying machines and facsimile machines, as well as medical equipment.

prefectural system, establishment of
廃藩置県

(*haihan chiken*). The abolition of feudal domains (*han*) and the establishment of a centralized prefectural (*ken*) system by the Meiji government in 1871. The decree marked the culmination of a movement underway since the MEIJI RESTORATION of 1868 to give the central government full authority over local administration. The *daimyō* accepted the order with barely a murmur of protest.

Political centralization was implicit in the concept of imperial restoration, and the Meiji leaders implemented it by gradual stages. The first step, in 1868, was the establishment of centrally controlled prefectures in the lands confiscated from the Tokugawa family and their allies in the BOSHIN CIVIL WAR of 1868–69. About one-fourth of the nation was affected. The second step was the surrender in 1869 of the domain registers (*hanseki hōkan*), whereby the imperial government asserted title to the remainder of Japan. Feudal lords became national officers known as *hanchiji*, or domain governors, but for the time retained some of their military and fiscal authority. The final step, *haihan chiken*, extinguished even this residual autonomy by dissolving domain armies along with the domains and replacing the former hereditary daimyō with appointed prefectural governors.

Hanseki Hōkan——KIDO TAKAYOSHI of the Chōshū domain (now Yamaguchi Prefecture) initiated debate on the issue. With the approval of the heads of the new government, SANJŌ SANETOMI and IWAKURA TOMOMI, he succeeded in persuading the daimyō of his own domain and of Satsuma (now Kagoshima Prefecture) to petition the emperor to accept the cession of their lands. Most other daimyō, fearing that their loyalty would be questioned, followed suit. Between 25 July and 2 August 1869 the central government took possession of the registers of lands and people from 262 domains. It also ordered 14 others that had not petitioned to surrender theirs. A change of title had now been effected.

In principle, the daimyō became imperial officials, having surrendered the autonomy their ancestors had long enjoyed. They received nonhereditary titles as domain governors and were allotted generous stipends amounting to one-tenth of the tax revenues of their domains, to be based on actual rice production (*jitsudaka*), a greater amount than the nominal production (OMOTEDAKA).

Domain governors could name their subordinates, but national regulations specified the names and qualifications for local office. Ability replaced rank as the controlling criterion. By imperial decree the complex status system for *samurai* was replaced by a uniform and simplified system providing for only two categories, SHIZOKU (upper samurai) and *sotsu* (or *sotsuzoku;* lower samurai). Their hereditary stipends (which were reduced) were paid by the domain office (*hanchō*) in the name of the government, not the daimyō, thus severing another tie in the traditional lord-retainer relationship. The domain heads themselves lost the title of daimyō in July 1869 and were merged with the *kuge* (court nobles) to form a single category of nobility called *kazoku* (see PEERAGE). Customary veneration for former daimyō continued, however, and Japan remained a half-feudal nation.

Abolition of Domains——These and other sweeping changes were bound to bring unrest. The rising tide of civil disorder led central government leaders Iwakura Tomomi and ŌKUBO TOSHIMICHI to draft a plan for the dissolution of all domains in November 1870. As always, support from the Satsuma and Chōshū domains was essential. SHIMAZU HISAMITSU, the powerful former regent of Satsuma, refused to go to the capital. The real power in Satsuma, however, rested with SAIGŌ TAKAMORI. Saigō led a contingent of Satsuma troops to the capital in June 1871, joining with forces from Chōshū and Tosa, to form an imperial force of 10,000 men. On 24 August 1871 Saigō, Kido, Ōkubo, and YAMAGATA ARITOMO, the vice-minister of military affairs, decided to force the issue by imperial decree, and Saigō announced that he would crush all opposition with his imperial forces. An edict was issued five days later.

The abolition of domains and the establishment of prefectures amounted to a coup against the daimyō. Two hundred sixty-one domains—a small number of domains had already requested incorporation into neighboring prefectures—were turned into a total (adding existing prefectures) of 3 urban prefectures (*fu*) and 302 prefectures. Realignment of boundaries in January 1872 resulted in 3 urban prefectures and 72 prefectures.

The domain governors retained their handsome house stipends, and the central government assumed domain debts (greater in amount than the Meiji government's annual budget). It also promised to convert the HANSATSU, depreciated domain currency, into the money of the new government. As *kazoku*, the domain governors' social status remained high. Only *shizoku*, whose stipends shrank to less than 50 percent of their former income, remained to challenge the stability of the regime in the late 1870s.

prehistory
先史時代

(*senshi jidai*). Japanese archaeologists traditionally divide the country's prehistoric past into several periods, each of which is marked by a distinctive cultural assemblage and different social and economic patterns.

The earliest occupation of Japan occurred during the PALEOLITHIC PERIOD (*kyūsekki jidai*), which dates from the late Pleistocene epoch. At that time Japan was still connected to the Asian mainland. Early paleolithic (pre-30,000 BC) cultures are poorly known, but associated with crude stone tools. Late paleolithic (ca 30,000 BC–ca 10,000 BC) Japan was occupied by cultures that made fine stone tools and other artifacts that have much in common with those of other north Eurasian hunting peoples.

The JŌMON PERIOD (ca 10,000 BC–ca 300 BC) is marked by several dynamic pottery-making traditions. The cord markings (*jōmon*) that decorate much of the pottery of this time give the period its name. Jōmon cultures were based on hunting-and-gathering economies and made efficient use of the wild plants and animals of Japan's forests and coasts.

Wet-rice agriculture and metalworking became established in Japan during the YAYOI PERIOD (ca 300 BC–ca AD 300), when rice-farming villages spread from Kyūshū to northern Honshū. The Late Yayoi period (ca 100–ca 300) saw the regional development of relatively complex political communities. The protohistoric KOFUN PERIOD (ca 300–710) marked the end of Japan's prehistory; it was a time of transition during which Japan developed a unified state, a strong central government, and a vital civilization that began to leave written records of its existence. The political and social stratification of this period is indicated by the construction of the large tomb mounds (KOFUN) that give it its name. See also ARCHAEOLOGY.

preschool education
就学前教育

(*shūgakuzen kyōiku*). Childhood education prior to elementary school; conducted through kindergartens and day-care centers. Japanese kindergartens are classified as educational institutions for children three to five years of age under the SCHOOL EDUCATION LAW OF 1947 and day-care centers as welfare institutions under the CHILD WELFARE LAW.

The first kindergarten in Japan was established in affiliation with Tōkyō Women's Normal School (now Ochanomizu Women's University) in 1876. Public kindergartens were established throughout Japan by the mid-Meiji period (1868–1912). Day-care centers were first instituted after the turn of the 20th century. By 1926, when the kindergarten system was formally established, the number of kindergartens exceeded 1,000 and was increasing annually. Meanwhile, day-care centers were also steadily developing, and in 1938, in accordance with the Social Service Law (Shakai Jigyō Hō), they were designated as social service institutions. In 1989 kindergartens numbered 15,080, of which nearly 58.3 percent were privately run, and 64.0 percent of all five-year-old children attended kindergarten.

prescriptive period 時効

(jikō). A span of time during which certain legal rights are established or extinguished. In the Japanese CIVIL CODE, there are two types of prescription: acquisitive prescription (shutoku jikō) and extinctive prescription (shōmetsu jikō).

In *acquisitive prescription*, a person who continuously possesses property owned by another for a certain period of time is permitted to acquire ownership of that property. The situation must continue for 10 years in the case of a person who believes in good faith that he owns the property in question and for 20 years in the case of a person who knows that he does not.

In *extinctive prescription*, a person loses a right because of nonexercise of such right for a certain period of time. Extinctive prescription applies to all property rights except ownership but is most often applied to rights involving obligations (saiken). The length of time resulting in such forfeiture is usually 10 years, but in the case of some types of obligatory right the period may be as short as 1 year.

press clubs 記者クラブ

(kisha kurabu). Groups of newspaper and broadcast journalists assigned to gather news from government departments and the police; the term also refers to the rooms provided for these groups. There are more than 1,000 such clubs throughout Japan. The first press club was the Gikai Deiri Kishadan (Diet Journalists Club), formed by newspaper journalists who campaigned for the right to cover the proceedings of the first session of the Diet in 1890. Today important announcements and press interviews routinely take place in the clubs. As a consequence, Japanese newspapers tend to carry similar articles because news gathering has been customarily done solely through the press clubs.

Press Law of 1909 新聞紙法

(Shimbunshi Hō). Law enacted to regulate newspapers and other periodical publications; it replaced the PRESS ORDINANCE OF 1875. Along with the PUBLICATION LAW OF 1893, it served as the basic law for restricting freedom of the press in Japan until the end of World War II. For example, it gave the home minister the authority to prohibit at will the sale and distribution of periodicals and granted the army, navy, and foreign ministers the power to ban the publication of certain articles and stories in periodicals. In 1945 Occupation forces nullified this law, and it was officially repealed in 1949. See also FREEDOM OF SPEECH, REGULATION OF.

Press Ordinance of 1875 新聞紙条例

(Shimbunshi Jōrei). Ordinance issued by the Meiji government in June 1875 to control the press in the face of growing criticism from the FREEDOM AND PEOPLE'S RIGHTS MOVEMENT and the newspapers associated with it. The ordinance and amendments added in 1876 and 1880 empowered the home minister to suspend or ban any newspaper that published articles considered injurious to public order or the security of the state. Although the home minister's powers were limited in a revision of 1897, the ordinance was replaced by the even more stringent PRESS LAW OF 1909, which remained in effect until the end of World War II. See also LIBEL LAW OF 1875; CENSORSHIP.

pressure groups 圧力団体

(atsuryoku dantai). Voluntary associations that try to influence the making and administering of public policy favorable to their interests. They participate directly in the political process by making demands on appropriate organs of government.

History——Although some pressure groups existed in Japan before World War II, their effectiveness was hampered by uncongenial political values. Not until new values were introduced under the Allied OCCUPATION (1945–52) did pressure groups appear in strength across the political spectrum. Today they are numerous and specialized, representing an array of interests ranging from those of the large and small businessman, worker, and farmer to those of the doctor, teacher, and environmentalist.

Interaction with Government——Since the main purpose of pressure groups is to influence public policy, their ability to gain access to key points in the decision-making process of public policy is crucial. In Japan public policy is formulated almost exclusively in the executive, not the legislative, branch of government. Given this reality, the prime targets of pressure groups are the BUREAUCRACY and the ruling party, not the Diet (parliament).

For pressure groups, particularly business groups, that support the ruling LIBERAL DEMOCRATIC PARTY (LDP) and its ideology, access to government is relatively easy. Positive interaction occurs. Regular access to key government bodies at appropriate times in the decision-making process is the norm for most such groups. For pressure groups, particularly LABOR UNIONS, that historically have opposed the LDP, access is more difficult. Less direct interaction occurs, although the unification of the labor movement in the 1980s brought improvement.

Methods of Exerting Influence——An important tactic is to provide information to appropriate government bodies. Because pressure groups represent particular interests, they possess more complete information concerning these interests than do ministries, the LDP, or Diet committees. Information supplied by pressure groups is therefore indispensable to the making of public policy.

Meetings between leaders of pressure groups and government and party officials are also a crucial means of influencing policy decisions. The fact that leaders of the most powerful business pressure groups in Japan are often linked by marriage and other family ties to high-level party and bureaucratic officials only reinforces the effectiveness of formal meetings and at the same time provides important avenues for the flow of influence and persuasion through informal channels.

Pressure groups also attempt to influence public policy by transferring large sums of money to political parties. It is typical for a pressure group to contribute funds on a large scale to only one party while contributing far less to other parties. Election of pressure group leaders to the Diet is an additional means of attempting to influence public policy. This tactic has been used in Japan primarily by groups—such as the Japan Teachers' Union (NIKKYŌSO) and the JAPAN MEDICAL ASSOCIATION (Nihon Ishikai)—that have a membership large enough to elect their own leaders to the Diet without relying on the votes of nonmembers. Another highly effective means is the employment by business

preschool education
preschool education
A group of kindergartners in blue uniforms line up in their school yard.

groups of retired bureaucrats. See AMAKUDARI.

CITIZENS' MOVEMENTS, or pressure groups of ordinary citizens, have turned to the courts as a means of influencing public policy. These groups mushroomed in the late 1960s and early 1970s, demanding compensation for loss of life and damage to health and property resulting from severe environmental pollution. Victims of POLLUTION-RELATED DISEASES—such as Minamata disease, itai itai disease, and Yokkaichi asthma—brought suits to the courts for damages against specific companies. The courts, in a series of precedent-shattering decisions, repeatedly placed the blame for pollution diseases squarely on specific firms and forced the government to strengthen its environmental protection policies.

Major Pressure Groups——The most influential pressure groups in Japan are business associations. The most powerful is the Federation of Economic Organizations (KEIDANREN, founded in 1946), a national federation of leading industrial, commercial, financial, and trade associations that serves to express the views of business to the government. It is difficult to overestimate the power of Keidanren since its membership includes associations of all major industries, from construction, oil refining, iron and steel, electricity, automobiles, shipbuilding, and chemicals to city banks, securities, life insurance, and beer. Another influential business pressure group is the Japan Federation of Employers' Associations (NIKKEIREN, founded in 1948), whose purpose is to develop rational labor policies and promote cooperation between labor and management. Also important is the JAPAN CHAMBER OF COMMERCE AND INDUSTRY (founded in 1922), a federation of local chambers of commerce, whose chief interests are the promotion of foreign trade, the strengthening of small and medium-sized enterprises, and the development of local and regional industries. The JAPAN ASSOCIATION OF CORPORATE EXECUTIVES (Keizai Dōyūkai, founded in 1946 as the Japan Committee for Economic Development), the most liberal of the national economic associations, is made up of individual members who use their influence to modernize industry, liberalize trade, and increase production efficiency. The Japanese Political League of Small and Medium Enterprises (Chūseiren) is widely regarded as the most influential pressure group representing small businesses.

Pressure groups also represent labor, but they are less influential than business groups. The largest labor group is the Japanese Trade Union Confederation or RENGŌ, founded in 1987. Rengō was the result of a labor unification movement begun in 1978 by private sector unions. The first step comprised the joining of two private sector labor organizations into a loose parent federation, the National Federation of Unions in Japan (Sōrengō). Envisioning a huge single national labor confederation that would include both private and public sector unions, leaders of Sōrengō then worked to persuade the giant General Council of Trade Unions of Japan (SŌHYŌ), consisting predominantly of left-wing public sector unions closely tied to the JAPAN SOCIALIST PARTY (JSP) and the JAPAN COMMUNIST PARTY (JCP), to join the unification movement. Step by step this was accomplished, and in 1989 Sōhyō, minus a few member unions closely tied to the JCP, joined Rengō.

In the agriculture sector the most powerful pressure groups are the AGRICULTURAL CO-OPERATIVE ASSOCIATIONS (nōkyō), which support the LDP and use their influence to shape government policies favorable to farmers. Such influence is crucial as the government has the authority to fix the price of rice and determine support for agricultural research. The government and LDP are sympathetic to the demands of the nōkyō because a disproportionately large number of LDP Diet representatives come from rural areas where the agricultural unions can muster strong support for conservative candidates.

As might be expected, a host of other pressure groups exist at all levels of the society to protect specialized interests. The JAPAN MEDICAL ASSOCIATION (Nihon Ishikai) represents 75 percent of all medical practitioners. Important to local and rural interests are the National Association of Towns and Villages (Zenkoku Chōsonkai) and the National Association of Chairmen of Town and Village Assemblies (Zenkoku Chōson Gichōkai). Similar organizations represent the city and prefectural levels. Pressure groups in cities are well organized and have clearly defined political interests and programs. Particularly active are such groups as the Japan Housewives Association (SHUFUREN), the Red Cross Service Organization (Nisseki Hōshidan), and the National Veterans' Association (Gōyūren); the list is very long and includes groups of restaurant, cabaret, bathhouse, and barbershop owners as well as many others.

Price Control Order of 1946
物価統制令

(Bukka Tōsei Rei). An emergency imperial order (kinkyū chokurei) put into effect at the behest of Allied OCCUPATION authorities on 3 March 1946 to mitigate the impact of severe postwar inflation on the Japanese public. The order established price controls, and both buyer and seller were held responsible for violations of them. The number of items controlled under the order rose sharply in 1948, reaching a peak in March 1949 with 2,129 published notices covering 10,716 items. There was a gradual reduction of economic controls following the success of the 1949 DODGE LINE stabilization program, and the number of items affected by the Price Control Order was gradually decreased.

Pridi Phanomyong
プリディ

(1900–1983). Thai politician and lawyer. Also known as Pradit Manudham. Before World War II, he was instrumental in estab-

lishing a constitutional government in Thailand. When the war began, Pridi, then serving as finance minister, stated that, although Thailand had no choice but to grant military bases to the Japanese, it should offer no economic support. Prime Minister PHIBUL SONGKHRAM insisted that it should do both, and Pridi resigned from the cabinet. During the war he acted as the king's regent and led the anti-Japanese FREE THAI MOVEMENT, which supplied information to the Allies on Japanese military forces in Thailand. Pridi was appointed prime minister in 1946 and promoted constitutional democracy in Thailand, but he was ousted in the military coup of 1947. See also THAILAND AND JAPAN.

priesthood
聖職

(seishoku). The term seishoku refers to the organization of religious functionaries within SHINTŌ, BUDDHISM, and some NEW RELIGIONS.

Shintō—The general term for Shinto priest is KANNUSHI. Rankings within the priesthood include gūji (head priest of a shrine), negi (senior priest), and gonnegi (junior priest). Until the Meiji period (1868–1912) the Shintō priesthood was generally a hereditary office. In 1871 the Meiji government decreed public Shintō shrines to be places for the observance of "national rites" (kokka no saishi), required the shrine priests to perform these rites, and replaced the hereditary priesthood with one selected by government appointment (see STATE SHINTŌ). During the Meiji period, the government also recognized 13 independent denominations of SECT SHINTŌ that were not considered to be affiliated with public shrines. The clerical structure of Sect Shintō differed from sect to sect, but in most cases the position of head priest was hereditary. After World War II, government control over Shintō was abolished and independent organizations were formed to fulfill organizational and supervisory functions (see SECT SHINTŌ, ASSOCIATION OF; SHINTŌ SHRINES, ASSOCIATION OF). Since then, the various denominations of Sect Shintō have become increasingly splintered and their clerical composition has grown correspondingly varied.

Buddhism—After Buddhism entered Japan in the 6th century, the government incorporated the Buddhist order into an administrative structure, establishing the office of sōgō (chief administrator of monks). In the 7th century a clerical hierarchy consisting of the ranks (in descending order) of sōjō, sōzu, and risshi was created. A system by which the emperor awarded ranks (sōi) to monks in recognition of their erudition, saintliness, or years of service was established in the 8th century. In the 9th century the three ranks of hōin daikashō-i, hōgen kashō-i, and hokkyō shōnin-i were established. The sōgō and sōi titles lost their specific priestly applications from the late part of the Heian period (794–1185) and were conferred upon laymen, such as artists and sculptors of Buddhist images. During the Muromachi period (1333–1568) the Ashikaga shogunate instituted the office of sōroku for the administration of Zen monks at the chief Zen temples (the GOZAN) and other temples. This system was abolished in 1615. After the Meiji government abolished the system of giving titles to Buddhist priests and artists in 1872, titles were awarded privately by the sects themselves. See also MONASTICISM.

New Religions—New religions are characterized by the centralization of au-

thority in a founder or leader and by the existence of small lay groups, such as kō (religious associations) and hōza (religious meetings). In these groups, lay members with some training assume the role of priest. The priesthood of all believers, wherein each member is a disseminator, is also practiced among the new religions. Within some new religions, however, a specialized priesthood with a format similar to that of the established religions has developed.

Prima Meat Packers, Ltd
プリマハム[株]

(Purima Hamu). Manufacturer of ham, sausages, and processed and fresh meat. Established in 1931, it took its present name in 1948. Affiliated with ITŌCHŪ CORPORATION. Prima has a subsidiary in the United States. Sales for the fiscal year ending March 1991 totaled ¥265.0 billion (US $1.9 billion), and capitalization stood at ¥14.8 billion (US $107.9 million). Headquarters are in Tōkyō.

Primate Research Institute
京都大学霊長類研究所

(Kyōto Daigaku Reichōrui Kenkyūjo). Research organ of Kyōto University. Established in 1967; located in Inuyama, Aichi Prefecture. A large staff in nine departments conducts PRIMATE STUDIES in morphology, neurophysiology, psychology, sociology, variation, ecology, physiology, biochemistry, and systematics and phylogeny. A laboratory at Inuyama maintains monkeys for experimental studies, while research on monkeys in their native habitat is conducted at five affiliated field laboratories. The institute publishes Annual Reports of the Primate Research Institute, Kyōto University.

primate studies
霊長類研究

(reichōrui kenkyū). Since the late 1950s Japanese ethologists, notably the late IMANISHI KINJI of Kyōto University, have played an important role in the revival of field studies of primate behavior. Their work has drawn considerable attention outside Japan.

Japanese primatologists took as their first and principal object of study a primate species indigenous to their own country, Macaca fuscata (the common Japanese monkey). Observers enticed the monkeys to come regularly to a feeding place set up within the home range of a particular troop. This method, known as provisioning, made possible the individual identification of all adult members of a troop with minimum outside interference, thus enabling the determination of kinship ties and dominance relationships.

Continuous observation of a number of troops for over 20 years has made possible the study of changes in the social organization and habits of each troop. This has resulted in a type of analysis that includes such factors as the influence of particular leaders, the incidence of group fissioning, and the adjustment of a given troop to modifications in the environment. The parallel intensive study of several troops has also revealed the existence of numerous intertroop behavioral differences. Feeding habits, degrees of sexual tolerance, patterns of child care, and sharpness of ranking order have been found to vary from group to group. Behavioral variability among individual animals had been recognized before, but this analysis offered proof that members of a group tend to be more similar to each other than to animals in another group.

By drawing attention to analogies with

human society, Japanese primatologists have helped cultural anthropologists to refine their definition of culture. Anthropologists had noted that a set of behavioral patterns was proper to a given group rather than to an animal species as a whole. This similarity to humans could also be seen in the influence exerted on social configuration by the personalities of dominant individuals and environmental changes. Such observations have led to the conclusion that, if interpreted solely as a form of social heredity, culture can no longer be considered the exclusive prerogative of the human species. See also PRIMATE RESEARCH INSTITUTE.

prime minister and cabinet
首相と内閣

(*shushō to naikaku*). The chief executive officer of the Japanese government and his cabinet. The cabinet system was adopted in Japan in 1885 and has continued without interruption until the present. There have, however, been a number of fundamental changes in the powers, functions, and composition of the cabinet, particularly when the prewar cabinet system under the Meiji Constitution is compared with the postwar cabinet system under the 1947 constitution. The postwar system is based on the British model; that is, the constitution vests supreme executive authority in the cabinet, which is responsible to the legislature. In the prewar system the cabinet was not responsible to the legislature and the legislature had no power either to select a prime minister or dissolve a cabinet. In addition, prewar cabinets shared executive power with a number of other more or less coequal offices and institutions.

The Prewar Cabinet System — Following the MEIJI RESTORATION, a Grand Council of State (DAJŌKAN) made up of 26 councillors was established in 1868 as the supreme political authority. However, the system evolved into a central deliberative body consisting of three state ministers who had direct access to the emperor and seven councillors, or SANGI. Heads of the various government ministries often served as *sangi* as well, so that by the end of 1881 real power was in the hands of a virtual oligarchy.

The change to the cabinet system in 1885 appears to have been motivated by the desire to gain Western acceptance and by the effort to strengthen the executive branch in the face of the projected establishment of an independent legislative branch with a popularly elected lower house (see IMPERIAL DIET). The prime minister and the various cabinet ministers were made responsible only to the emperor, not to the Diet. Moreover, upon the promulgation of the constitution in 1889, the oligarchs announced their intention to remain aloof from party politics by adhering to the principle of nonparty or "TRANSCENDENTAL" CABINETS (*chōzen naikaku*).

For the seven cabinets between 1885 and 1898 the prime ministership was rotated among the oligarchs (see HAMBATSU). As the oligarchs retired from the day-to-day administration of cabinet affairs they assumed the role of elder statesmen (GENRŌ), particularly after the inauguration of the first KATSURA TARŌ cabinet in 1901.

The prewar prime minister was perhaps the single most important person in the government. His duties included supervising the cabinet, directing the Tōkyō Metropolitan Police Department and the prefectural governors, and advising the emperor on administrative matters. He also enjoyed extensive

appointment powers, including the appointment of cabinet ministers and vice-ministers, judges, prosecutors, directors of government bureaus, and prefectural governors. Nevertheless, the prime minister was not a strong chief executive but rather had to share the right to advise the throne with the *genrō*, the officers of the imperial household, the privy councillors, and the military chiefs of staff. Even within the cabinet the prime minister's powers were limited, as each minister was directly and individually responsible to the emperor and, once appointed, a cabinet minister could not be removed by the prime minister.

Until the TAISHŌ POLITICAL CRISIS of 1912–13, the oligarchs coordinated the decision-making process behind the scenes through the vehicle of the informal, extraconstitutional *genrō* council and through their position on the PRIVY COUNCIL. Following World War I, this single dominant coordinating oligarchy was gradually replaced by a much larger and more diverse set of institutional elites, composed of the parties, the military, the bureaucracy, the peerage, and the court. Much of the political history of the 1918–45 period can be viewed as a competition among these institutional elites for control of the government. From the mid-1930s the military dominated the cabinet until Japan's defeat in World War II.

Postwar Changes in the Cabinet System — The postwar constitution introduced two major kinds of change in the cabinet system. First, executive power was vested solely in the prime minister and his cabinet. All real executive authority was removed from the emperor, and the throne became a purely symbolic and ceremonial institution. The prime minister is now empowered to appoint and remove all cabinet members at his own discretion. Moreover, to ensure civilian control of the military, the DEFENSE AGENCY has formally been made a subordinate part of the Prime Minister's Office. As a further check against a military resurgence, the constitution requires that all cabinet members be civilians. See GOVERNMENT, EXECUTIVE BRANCH.

The second major change was the clear establishment of cabinet responsibility to the elected representatives of the people. The prime minister is elected by the Diet, and he and his cabinet ministers must, when requested, attend the sessions of both houses

and their committees to reply to questions on government policy. In addition, either house of the Diet may adopt a resolution of impeachment against any individual cabinet member. Moreover, if the lower house passes a nonconfidence resolution, rejects a confidence resolution, or, in effect, fails to support any major cabinet bill, the cabinet must resign en masse within 10 days or dissolve the lower house, call an election, and resign following the opening of the new Diet. Finally, the constitution requires that the prime minister and the majority of all cabinet members be elected members of the Diet.

The Making of the Prime Minister and His Cabinet — The prime minister is selected by a majority vote in each House of the Diet and is formally appointed by the emperor. If the two Houses disagree on their selection or the upper house fails to act within 10 days after the lower house has voted, the choice of the lower house stands as the decision of the Diet. Since the LIBERAL DEMOCRATIC PARTY (LDP) has maintained majority control of both houses of the Diet from its inception in 1955, the president of the LDP has routinely been installed as prime minister. The LDP president is elected to a two-year term at the party convention on the basis of factional politics. New official cabinets come into being following the selection of a new prime minister and after each election of the House of Representatives. In practice, cabinet posts are reshuffled much more frequently, with virtually annual major reconstructions of the cabinet in which over half its personnel are changed. The reasons for this frequent turnover are based on factional politics. The prime minister must reward those factions that support him while not totally shutting out his intraparty opponents. Continuity is maintained by the Conference of Administrative Vice-Ministers, composed of the highest civil-service career officers in each ministry. Most policy matters are in effect decided at this level and forwarded to the cabinet for fairly routine approval.

Cabinet Powers and Organizations — The prime minister and his cabinet have important judicial and legislative powers as well as executive responsibilities. In the judi-

prime minister and cabinet Yoshida Shigeru (front row, center) poses in this 1946 photograph with the members of his first cabinet. A crusty career diplomat who served five terms as prime minister, Yoshida dominated Japanese politics during the first decade following World War II.

Prime Ministers and Cabinets, 1885–1991

Prime minister	Cabinet number	Cabinet term
1. Itō Hirobumi	1st	22 December 1885–30 April 1888
2. Kuroda Kiyotaka		30 April 1888–24 December 1889
3. Yamagata Aritomo	1st	24 December 1889–6 May 1891
4. Matsukata Masayoshi	1st	6 May 1891–8 August 1892
5. Itō Hirobumi	2nd	8 August 1892–18 September 1896
6. Matsukata Masayoshi	2nd	18 September 1896–12 January 1898
7. Itō Hirobumi	3rd	12 January 1898–30 June 1898
8. Ōkuma Shigenobu	1st	30 June 1898–8 November 1898
9. Yamagata Aritomo	2nd	8 November 1898–19 October 1900
10. Itō Hirobumi	4th	19 October 1900–2 June 1901
11. Katsura Tarō	1st	2 June 1901–7 January 1906
12. Saionji Kimmochi	1st	7 January 1906–14 July 1908
13. Katsura Tarō	2nd	14 July 1908–30 August 1911
14. Saionji Kimmochi	2nd	30 August 1911–21 December 1912
15. Katsura Tarō	3rd	21 December 1912–20 February 1913
16. Yamamoto Gonnohyōe	1st	20 February 1913–16 April 1914
17. Ōkuma Shigenobu	2nd	16 April 1914–9 October 1916
18. Terauchi Masatake		9 October 1916–29 September 1918
19. Hara Takashi		29 September 1918–13 November 1921
20. Takahashi Korekiyo		13 November 1921–12 June 1922
21. Katō Tomosaburō		12 June 1922–2 September 1923
22. Yamamoto Gonnohyōe	2nd	2 September 1923–7 January 1924
23. Kiyoura Keigo		7 January 1924–11 June 1924
24. Katō Takaaki		11 June 1924–30 January 1926
25. Wakatsuki Reijirō	1st	30 January 1926–20 April 1927
26. Tanaka Giichi		20 April 1927–2 July 1929
27. Hamaguchi Osachi		2 July 1929–14 April 1931
28. Wakatsuki Reijirō	2nd	14 April 1931–13 December 1931
29. Inukai Tsuyoshi		13 December 1931–26 May 1932
30. Saitō Makoto		26 May 1932–8 July 1934
31. Okada Keisuke		8 July 1934–9 March 1936
32. Hirota Kōki		9 March 1936–2 February 1937
33. Hayashi Senjūrō		2 February 1937–4 June 1937
34. Konoe Fumimaro	1st	4 June 1937–5 January 1939
35. Hiranuma Kiichirō		5 January 1939–30 August 1939
36. Abe Nobuyuki		30 August 1939–16 January 1940
37. Yonai Mitsumasa		16 January 1940–22 July 1940
38. Konoe Fumimaro	2nd	22 July 1940–18 July 1941
39. Konoe Fumimaro	3rd	18 July 1941–18 October 1941
40. Tōjō Hideki		18 October 1941–22 July 1944
41. Koiso Kuniaki		22 July 1944–7 April 1945
42. Suzuki Kantarō		7 April 1945–17 August 1945
43. Higashikuni Naruhiko		17 August 1945–9 October 1945
44. Shidehara Kijūrō		9 October 1945–22 May 1946
45. Yoshida Shigeru	1st	22 May 1946–24 May 1947
46. Katayama Tetsu		24 May 1947–10 March 1948
47. Ashida Hitoshi		10 March 1948–15 October 1948
48. Yoshida Shigeru	2nd	15 October 1948–16 February 1949
49. Yoshida Shigeru	3rd	16 February 1949–30 October 1952
50. Yoshida Shigeru	4th	30 October 1952–21 May 1953
51. Yoshida Shigeru	5th	21 May 1953–10 December 1954
52. Hatoyama Ichirō	1st	10 December 1954–19 March 1955
53. Hatoyama Ichirō	2nd	19 March 1955–22 November 1955
54. Hatoyama Ichirō	3rd	22 November 1955–23 December 1956
55. Ishibashi Tanzan		23 December 1956–25 February 1957
56. Kishi Nobusuke	1st	25 February 1957–12 June 1958
57. Kishi Nobusuke	2nd	12 June 1958–19 July 1960
58. Ikeda Hayato	1st	19 July 1960–8 December 1960
59. Ikeda Hayato	2nd	8 December 1960–9 December 1963
60. Ikeda Hayato	3rd	9 December 1963–9 November 1964
61. Satō Eisaku	1st	9 November 1964–17 February 1967
62. Satō Eisaku	2nd	17 February 1967–14 January 1970
63. Satō Eisaku	3rd	14 January 1970–7 July 1972
64. Tanaka Kakuei	1st	7 July 1972–22 December 1972
65. Tanaka Kakuei	2nd	22 December 1972–9 December 1974
66. Miki Takeo		9 December 1974–24 December 1976
67. Fukuda Takeo		24 December 1976–7 December 1978
68. Ōhira Masayoshi	1st	7 December 1978–9 November 1979
69. Ōhira Masayoshi	2nd	9 November 1979–17 July 1980
70. Suzuki Zenkō		17 July 1980–27 November 1982
71. Nakasone Yasuhiro	1st	27 November 1982–27 December 1983
72. Nakasone Yasuhiro	2nd	27 December 1983–22 July 1986
73. Nakasone Yasuhiro	3rd	22 July 1986–6 November 1987
74. Takeshita Noboru		6 November 1987–3 June 1989
75. Uno Sōsuke		3 June 1989–10 August 1989
76. Kaifu Toshiki	1st	10 August 1989–28 February 1990
77. Kaifu Toshiki	2nd	28 February 1990–5 November 1991
78. Miyazawa Kiichi		5 November 1991–

NOTE: The numbering system used here is the one used by the Prime Minister's Office. Many Japanese academics, however, consider Katō Takaaki to have led two separate cabinets (11 June 1924–2 August 1925; 2 August 1925–30 January 1926), bringing the total number of cabinets as of November 1992 to 79 rather than 78.

Cabinet terms begin on the date the cabinet takes office and end on the date the succeeding cabinet takes office. They do not necessarily coincide with the prime minister's tenure in office.

cial area they are empowered to select the chief justice and the other judges of the Supreme Court and to appoint lower-court judges from a list nominated by the Supreme Court. The cabinet may also grant pardons and amnesty. In the legislative area the cabinet determines the convocation of extraordinary sessions of the Diet, enacts cabinet orders to execute the provisions of the constitution and Diet laws, and, perhaps most important, prepares and submits bills to the Diet. The various cabinet staff offices and government ministries and agencies assist the cabinet in the exercise of this extensive concentration of powers.

As of 1990 the cabinet was composed of the prime minister and the heads of the 12 ministries: Justice; Foreign Affairs; Finance; Education; Health and Welfare; Agriculture, Forestry, and Fisheries; International Trade and Industry; Transport; Posts and Telecommunications; Labor; Construction; and Home Affairs (Jichishō). Another 8 ministers of state without portfolios head other important executive offices and agencies such as the Cabinet Secretariat, the Defense Agency, the ECONOMIC PLANNING AGENCY, and the SCIENCE AND TECHNOLOGY AGENCY. See also separate articles on the individual ministries.

Prime Minister's Office   総理府

(Sōrifu). Executive body under the direct administration of the prime minister. Established in 1947, it took on its present name in 1949. Although under direct administration of the prime minister, it is distinct from the various ministries; however, the position of director-general of the Prime Minister's Office is of ministerial rank. The responsibilities of the Prime Minister's Office include the awarding of official government decorations (kunshō), overall coordination of the policies and affairs of other executive agencies, and administrative affairs not within the purview of any other executive agency. The office consists of 2 relatively small internal bureaus—the Secretariat and the Decoration Bureau—and 12 external agencies, including the MANAGEMENT AND COORDINATION AGENCY, NATIONAL PUBLIC SAFETY COMMISSION, DEFENSE AGENCY, OKINAWA DEVELOPMENT AGENCY, and ECONOMIC PLANNING AGENCY. Also administered by the Prime Minister's Office are the NATIONAL ARCHIVES, SCIENCE COUNCIL OF JAPAN, and AKASAKA DETACHED PALACE, which functions as a state guesthouse. See also GOVERNMENT, EXECUTIVE BRANCH.

primogeniture   長子相続

(chōshi sōzoku). In Japanese legal history, the system of sole inheritance by the eldest son. From early times, there were two categories of inheritance in Japan: household headship inheritance and property inheritance. Under the TAIHŌ CODE of 701 household headship could be inherited only by the eldest son. In the Kamakura (1185–1333) and Muromachi (1333–1568) periods, if the eldest son was incapable, the testator designated another heir. Property inheritance in early times was divided among sons, and sometimes daughters were included as well, but by the mid-Muromachi period property inheritance by the eldest son alone had become the norm. The CIVIL CODE of 1898 prescribed that the inheritance of katoku (the household headship and all property) must accord with primogeniture. After World War II, the Civil Code was revised in accordance with the equal protection clause of the 1947 constitution, and primogeniture was abolished.

primroses   桜草

(sakurasō). Primula spp. Perennial herbs of the family Primulaceae, popular for their attractive flowers. They are known collectively in Japan as sakurasō, but this name is also used to denote a particularly well-known species, P. sieboldii, which grows wild in Kyūshū, Honshū, and southern Hokkaidō and is also widely cultivated. It has several oval leaves with shallow lobes growing from the base of the plant on long fuzzy stems; a flower stalk produces several reddish purple flowers with corollas deeply lobed into five sections. Over 200 variations in the color or shape of the flower have been developed.

Some other species of the genus Primula in Japan are the kurinsō (P. japonica), which grows wild in the damp mountain valleys of Hokkaidō, Honshū, and Shikoku and has dark purple (or occasionally pink or white) flowers that bloom in several whorled layers; the ōsakurasō (P. jesoana), which grows wild on high mountains in Hokkaidō and northern Honshū and has reddish purple flowers; and the koiwazakura (P. reinii), which grows among the rocks on and around Mt. Fuji and also has reddish purple flowers.

Prince Hotels, Inc   [株]プリンスホテル

(Purinsu Hoteru). Hotel chain. Incorporated in 1971. A prominent member of the Seibu group, the principal company of which is the SEIBU RAILWAY CO, LTD. Prince Hotels operates 17 hotels in Japan and 6 overseas in Hawaii, Singapore, Australia, and Canada. The company was capitalized at ¥1.0 billion (US $7.3 million) in 1991. Headquarters are in Tōkyō.

principle of changed circumstances   事情変更の原則

(jijō henkō no gensoku). A Japanese legal term referring to the common contractual clause "where conditions remain as is." The principle is that contracts or agreements may lose their validity if conditions change. The principle was first recognized in court decisions involving rent increases for land and house leases; it was later codified in the Leased House Law (Shakuya Hō) and the Leased Land Law (Shakuchi Hō).

principle of fidelity and good faith   信義誠実の原則

(shingi seijitsu no gensoku). A private law principle to the effect that all people, as members of one community, should act in good faith so as not to betray mutual confidence. Also referred to as shingisoku (principle of fidelity), this principle is stated in article 1, section 2, of the CIVIL CODE. Both the performance of obligations and the exercise of rights must be made pursuant to this rule. That is, the performance of an obligation may be found invalid if inconsistent with this principle of good faith. See also KŌJO RYŌZOKU.

printing, modern   近代印刷

(kindai insatsu). Book publishing and printing played a significant role in Japan's development as a modern nation from the time of the Meiji Restoration (1868). The introduction of advanced foreign techniques and machines, as well as a rapidly increasing demand for printed materials, resulted in the fast-paced growth of printing.

Motoki Shōzō (1824–75) is regarded as

the founder of the modern printing industry in Japan. In 1851 he designed molded types and later studied printing techniques with Dutch and American printers living in Japan. Motoki eventually established printing factories in Ōsaka and Tōkyō. The old art of woodblock printing was soon replaced by modern printing, and hand printing eventually gave way to mechanical printing. Traditional handmade paper (WASHI) was replaced by machine-produced Western paper, and bookbinding took on a Western format.

In 1867 the first Japanese magazine, *Seiyō zasshi* (The Western Magazine), published by Yanagawa Shunsan (1832–70), appeared, followed by the first daily newspaper, the YOKOHAMA MAINICHI SHIMBUN, in 1871. As the government promoted the spread of education, more newspapers and magazines began to be published; about 200 magazines were in print by 1877.

In 1872 an Editing Section and a Translation Section were established within the Ministry of Education and many translations of Western works, as well as new school textbooks, were published. The ministry also set up its own printing office, which in effect stimulated the development of private printing and publishing. In the same year the DAJŌKAN (Grand Council of State) established the Printing Bureau, which was in charge of printing the *Dajōkan nisshi* (Records of the Grand Council of State) as well as official proclamations. In 1875 the Printing Bureau was combined with the Shiheiryō (Paper Currency Office), which had been set up in 1871 within the Ministry of Finance to print paper money.

By the end of the 19th century typographic and offset printing techniques brought about rapid changes, such as more efficient gas and electric printing presses, the rotary press, photo copperplate, and photogravure printing. Major publishing firms established at this time included HAKUBUNKAN (1887), Jitsugyō no Nihonsha (1897), and Dai Nippon Yūben Kai (1909; now KŌDANSHA, LTD). By 1920 Japan had become the second largest book-publishing nation in the world.

Today the application of printing technology has expanded to areas not directly related to printing, such as the production of parts for color television sets, electronic computers, cameras, and medical equipment. Computerized methods have been used increasingly, accelerating the conversion from surface printing to offset printing.

The total production of the commercial printing industry in 1988 was estimated at US $34.0 billion, which represents 60 percent of the total estimated value of overall publishing output (including newspapers, bookbinding, etc) for that year. This constituted a threefold increase over 1978. In 1988 there were 48,877 commercial printing companies with four or more employees.

The largest commercial printing companies in Japan today are DAI NIPPON PRINTING CO, LTD; TOPPAN PRINTING CO, LTD; and Kyōdō Printing Company, Ltd. The three major printers' and bookbinders' organizations are the Insatsu Kōgyō Kai (Japan Printers' Association), the Zen Nihon Insatsu Kōgyō Kumiai Rengōkai (All-Japan Printing Association), and the Zen Nihon Seihon Kōgyō Kumiai Rengōkai (All-Japan Bookbinding Association). The Japanese printing and publishing industry is primarily under the supervision of the MINISTRY OF INTERNATIONAL TRADE AND INDUSTRY (MITI). See also PUBLISHING.

printing, premodern 前近代の印刷

(*zenkindai no insatsu*). Printing in Japan up to the 1870s was almost entirely a product of the engraved woodblock, varied only in the late 16th and early 17th centuries by the brief use of movable type. Originating in Buddhist monasteries, printing later passed into the hands of commercial publishers and became in the period from the 17th to the 19th century a powerful force for popular instruction and entertainment. The use of engraved woodblocks for making monochrome and polychrome illustrations in books and sheet prints resulted in a degree of technical perfection and aesthetic quality unsurpassed in the world.

The Legacy from China—Ancient Japan, having developed no writing system of its own, adopted the Chinese written language and script. Chinese writing probably penetrated to Japan around the turn of the Christian era, but it was not until the end of the 5th century that a considerable number of Japanese could read and write Chinese with some fluency and the systematic copying of imported manuscripts and the composition of original written works began. By far the most important factor in the spread of literacy and the making of books in Japan was the introduction of Buddhism in the mid-6th century. The new doctrines were avidly studied and inspired the reverent copying of scriptural texts.

Early Japanese Printing—Between the years 764 and 770 the empress Shōtoku (see KŌKEN, EMPRESS) ordered the printing of one million Buddhist charms or mantras (*dhāraṇī*), each to be placed in a miniature wooden pagoda and distributed among 10 of the leading monasteries of the land. Many of these printed texts are still extant and appear to be the oldest datable printed documents yet discovered.

The next oldest dated example of Japanese printing still surviving is a 10-roll copy of the *Jōyuishiki ron* (Treatise on the Establishment of the Doctrine of Conciousness Only; see HOSSŌ SECT) bearing the printed date 1088. From the late Heian period (794–1185) until the last years of the 16th century, printing in Japan was carried on almost exclusively in Buddhist monasteries.

Woodblock-Printing Technique—The engraved wooden block was the principal medium of printing in Japan until about 1870. The technique of block printing scarcely changed in all that time and employed the same basic methods for printing both text matter and illustrations. First a page of text was handwritten by a calligrapher, or a design was drawn by an artist, on a sheet of thin paper. This was pasted facedown on a prepared block of seasoned wood, and when dry, the paper was oiled to enable the engraver (i.e., the block cutter) to see the text or the picture more clearly. Next came the delicate task of cutting away those parts of the block that were not required to print, leaving the engraved characters or the outlines and shaded areas of the design standing out in relief, but in reversed image. After cleaning off surplus paper, the engraved block (*mokuhan*) was ready for printing. The printer applied ink (*sumi*) to the block with a brush and placed a sheet of dampened paper on top of the block to receive the impression. Pressure was applied to the paper with a rubbing block (*baren*), and when the inked impression had been transferred, the printed page was removed, dried, and eventually bound into a book.

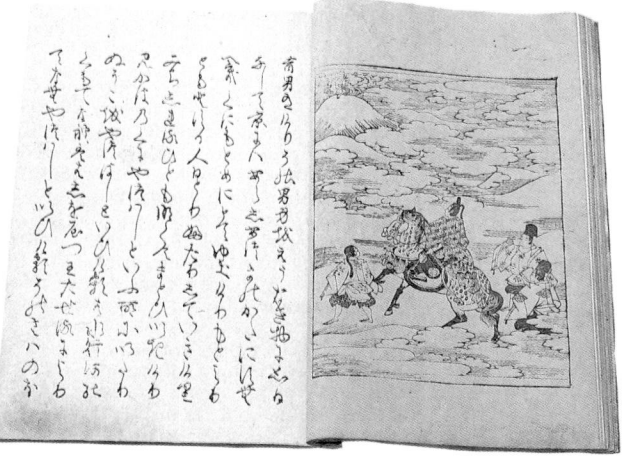

Book Illustration—Book illustration began in Japan with decorated frontispieces and interspersed pictures in Buddhist manuscripts. This practice spread to printed texts, and woodcut illustrations began to appear in a few Japanese Buddhist works from the Kamakura period (1185–1333) onward. From the 17th century, woodblock illustrations appeared in works of fiction, such as the UKIYO-ZŌSHI novels. During the late 18th and early 19th centuries, the quality of book illustration reached its highest level technically and artistically in books of pure illustration (*ehon*), reproducing sketches in color and monochrome by artists of NANGA (*bunjinga*), the MARUYAMA-SHIJŌ SCHOOL, and UKIYO-E.

Printing with Movable Type—During the 60 years from 1590 to 1650 the introduction of movable type from Korea revolutionized Japanese printing. Its use was short-lived, for its technology ultimately proved to be less suited to Japan's needs than the traditional method of printing from woodblocks, but it led to final liberation from the Buddhist yoke and to the first printing of nearly all the great classics of Japanese literature. By 1650 printing from movable type had all but ceased. It was rarely used again in Japan until the Meiji period (1868–1912).

Luxury Printing—A special place in the field of fine printing must be given to the *sagabon*. This is the name given to a group of luxury editions of Japanese literary works printed, largely with movable type, at the so-called Saga press of HON'AMI KŌETSU (1558–1637) and Suminokura Soan (1571–1632). Each book was a harmonious blend of fine-quality paper and ink, with tasteful covers often ornamented with stenciled patterns in powdered mica, and above all, a sensitively designed font of type modeled on the hand of a good calligrapher. Most of the 13 recognized *sagabon* were printed in the Keichō era between 1608 and 1615. They included the exquisite edition of 100 texts of the Kanze school of NŌ and the illustrated ISE MONOGATARI editions of 1608 and 1610.

Printing and Publishing—17th to 19th Century—The Edo period (1600–1868) was a time of change and development in Japanese society that significantly affected the production of books and the classes of readers for whom they were intended. It was an age when general literacy rose to a figure approaching 40 percent of the population, when the growing number of town dwellers created a huge demand for reading matter, and when commercial publishing became a profitable proposition for the first time. It was in book illustration that the greatest

premodern printing
In the early 17th century, *sagabon*, the first printed versions of a number of Japanese classics, were produced using movable wooden type. The 1608 edition of *Ise monogatari* is shown here.

primroses Hundreds of indigenous and imported varieties of primrose are cultivated. *Primula sieboldii* (pictured) grows wild throughout Japan.

strides were made in Edo-period printing, and by the end of the 18th century the cooperative endeavors of artist, engraver, and printer were producing polychrome woodblock illustrations of astonishing beauty.

At this time, the publisher was responsible for all operations, from preparing the author's manuscript, block cutting, printing, and binding, to selling and distributing the book. Most publishing houses were small family concerns, located near a temple or shrine.

Commercial publishers of the Edo period began to issue printed editions of almost all the works of Japanese literature that had hitherto existed only in manuscript—poetical anthologies, novels, diaries, essays, and short stories. At the same time, new creative works unrelated to Buddhism began to be printed and published soon after they were written. In addition to works of pure literature, books on a wide range of other subjects were written and published during the Edo period. The woodblock medium was supplanted by the Western-style printing press soon after the Meiji Restoration (1868).

prints → ukiyo-e; modern prints

priority production program
傾斜生産方式

(*keisha seisan hōshiki*). The Japanese government's post–World War II economic program to concentrate available capital and labor on key industries in an immediate effort to revitalize the shattered economy. Adopted by the cabinet in December 1946, it was in force for a year and a half. The program's strategy was to allocate imported oil and coal to steel production; use the increased steel output to repair coal mines, thereby increasing coal output; and allocate the increased outputs of steel and coal to other industries to bring about an overall recovery. The program did lead to gradual recoveries in coal and industrial production, but since these increases resulted from government subsidies and financing through the RECONSTRUCTION FINANCE BANK, they did not represent an actual overall economic recovery.

prisons
刑務所

(*keimusho*). As of 1990 there were 59 prisons (including 8 for young prisoners, 5 for women, and 4 for those in need of medical care), 8 branch prisons for convicted prisoners, 7 detention houses, and 109 branch detention houses for unconvicted prisoners in Japan. All are centrally administered by the Ministry of Justice through the Corrections Bureau. In 1989 the average daily prison population (including individuals awaiting trial) was 51,658, of which 2,236 were women.

The main objective in the treatment of convicted prisoners is rehabilitation. Work in prisons is compulsory for prisoners sentenced to imprisonment with forced labor (*chōeki*) and voluntary for those sentenced to imprisonment without forced labor (*kinko*).

Prisoners may be released on parole by regional parole boards, after serving one-third of their term of imprisonment (10 years in the case of life imprisonment). In practice, however, parole has not been greatly used, probably because prison terms tend

to be short. See also CRIMINAL LAW; CRIMINOLOGY.

privacy, right to
プライバシーの権利

(*puraibashī no kenri*). The constitutional right of an individual to be free from intrusion into his or her private affairs; related, as a right of the person (*jinkakuken*), to the right of a good name or freedom from defamation. Drawn from the concept in US law of "the right to be let alone," the idea of privacy in Japanese law has been expanded to include constitutional safeguards against state intervention in private life; the right to self-determination, including the right to abortion; and the right to control private information.

In group-oriented Japan, the value of privacy has been traditionally less honored than the right of the family, group, or community to know about and intervene in an individual's affairs, and indeed the general right to privacy is nowhere mentioned in Japanese law. Moreover, expanded FREEDOM OF THE PRESS under the 1947 CONSTITUTION OF JAPAN occasioned increased journalistic excursions into the personal lives of public and private figures. It was not until 1964 that the right to privacy in its original sense (the right to be let alone) was first recognized in Japanese law, in the form of the ruling of the Tōkyō District Court in the AFTER THE BANQUET CASE that a novel by MISHIMA YUKIO had violated the privacy rights of the plaintiff, politician ARITA HACHIRŌ.

Japanese courts found statutory basis for the concept of the right to privacy in the constitutional requirement (art. 13) that "all of the people shall be respected as individuals," and two articles of the CIVIL CODE, which read as follows:

"Article 709. A person who violates intentionally or negligently the right of another is bound to make compensation for the damage arising therefrom.

"Article 710. A person who is liable in compensation for damages in accordance with the preceding Article shall make compensation therefor even in respect of a nonpecuniary damage, irrespective of whether such injury was to the person, liberty, or reputation of another or his or her property rights."

Other Aspects of Privacy—Article 21(2) of the constitution guarantees "the secrecy of any means of communication." This constitutional provision was implemented in article 9 of the Postal Law, which specifically protects the secrecy of the mails, while articles 133 and 134 of the Penal Code prohibit the opening of sealed letters or the disclosure of professional secrets.

The privacy of the individual home is protected by article 235 of the Civil Code, and Peeping Toms are penalized by the MINOR OFFENSES LAW of 1948.

In 1969 the Supreme Court of Japan recognized the right to likeness (*shōzōken*; the right not to be photographed without one's consent) as an ingredient of the constitutional right to privacy.

With rapid development of modern computer and data-processing technologies, new means for the protection of the right to privacy are being explored. A number of personal information protection ordinances (*kojin jōhō hogo hōrei*) have been enacted by local legislative bodies to protect the individual's right to privacy vis-à-vis governmental storage and utilization of computerized personal data. At the national level, the Law concerning the Protection of Personal

Information Registered in the Government Computer System was passed in 1988.

private international law
国際私法

(*kokusai shihō*). In Japanese law the term "private international law" is used in its narrow sense to refer to what Anglo-American lawyers would call choice-of-law rules, i.e., rules for determining which national law will govern a legal transaction that involves non-Japanese parties or acts occurring outside Japan. In its broader sense the term also includes issues relating to international civil procedure (*kokusai minji soshō hō*), such as the standing of a foreign litigant to sue or be sued in Japan and the recognition and enforcement of foreign judgments in Japan.

CHOICE-OF-LAW RULES

The primary source for Japanese choice-of-law rules is the Hōrei (sometimes translated as the Law on the Applicability of Laws). Special choice-of-law rules for promissory notes and bills of exchange are found in the laws governing these instruments. See COMMERCIAL PAPER.

General Rules—1. *Personal status. Legal capacity* (*kōi nōryoku*) to perform legal acts (e.g., the age of majority) is determined by the individual's national law (Hōrei, art. 3[1]), provided that the foreign individual's capacity to perform legal acts in Japan is governed by Japanese law (CIVIL CODE, arts. 3–6) if his or her national law is more restrictive than Japanese law (Hōrei, art. 3[2]).

Legal incompetency (*kinchisan*) is determined on the basis of the individual's national law, and the effect of a decree of incompetency is determined by the law of the place where such a decree was issued (Hōrei, art. 4[1]). A foreigner with a domicile (*jūsho*) or residence (*kyosho*) in Japan may be declared legally incompetent by a Japanese court only if the grounds for such a decree are recognized in both Japanese law (Civil Code, art. 7) and the foreigner's national law (Hōrei, art. 4[2]).

2. *Legal acts and contracts*. The validity and effect of a *legal act* (*hōritsu kōi*), such as entering into a contract, is determined by the law chosen by the parties to govern their legal relationship (Hōrei, art. 7[1]). If the parties fail to make an express choice of the governing law, most Japanese courts will attempt to determine which law the parties had intended to govern. If this is impossible, then the governing law will be the law of the place where the legal act was performed (Hōrei, art. 7[2]).

3. *Legally imposed obligations*. Obligations arising from TORTS (*fuhō kōi*), unjust enrichment (*futō ritoku*), and VOLUNTEER MANAGEMENT OF AFFAIRS (*jimu kanri*) are governed by the law of the place where the act or acts giving rise to the obligation took place (Hōrei, art. 11[1]).

Special Rules—The Hōrei contains several special rules governing the determination of the *national law* (*hongokuhō*) of a person. If a person is a citizen of more than one country, the national law of that person is the law of the country where the person regularly resides or to which the person most closely relates; if one of the countries of which the person is a citizen is Japan, however, that person's national law is Japanese law in all cases (Hōrei, art. 28[1]). The Hōrei prohibits the application of a foreign law that is repugnant to Japanese concepts of "public order and good morals" (KŌJO RYŌZOKU; Hōrei, art. 30).

INTERNATIONAL CIVIL PROCEDURE

1. *Standing to sue.* A foreign corporation can bring an action in Japan regardless of whether it has complied with the registration requirements set forth in article 481 of the COMMERCIAL CODE. A foreign individual can bring suit if he or she is legally competent to do so under Japanese law even when the person is legally incompetent under his or her national law (Hōrei, art. 3[2]).

2. *Jurisdiction over foreigners.* The Japanese Code of Civil Procedure contains various "venue" (or domestic jurisdiction) rules in articles 1 through 29, which define the territorial competence of the district courts of Japan (see CIVIL PROCEDURE, CODE OF). Since Japanese law contains no explicit rules for determining the existence of "international jurisdiction," the Japanese courts in order to accept international litigation have resorted in general to adapting the domestic venue rules to such litigation.

3. *Recognition and enforcement of foreign judgments.* The requirements that a foreign judgment must satisfy in order to be recognized as a conclusive judgment on the merits by a Japanese court are set forth in article 200 of the Code of Civil Procedure. These requirements, as generally interpreted by the Japanese courts and legal scholars, are that the foreign judgment is final (i.e., cannot be appealed under local procedural rules); the foreign court had proper grounds to exercise international jurisdiction according to Japanese concepts of jurisdiction; if judgment was in favor of the plaintiff and the defendant is Japanese, the defendant received adequate notice of the action; the foreign judgment does not offend Japanese concepts of public order and good morals; and reciprocity exists between Japan and the country in which the foreign judgment was rendered. If the foreign judgment meets these requirements, the Japanese court would be barred by the principle of *res judicata* (*kihanryoku*) from making a new determination of the merits of the case. The most difficult of these recognition requirements have usually been those of adequate jurisdiction (art. 200[1]) and reciprocity (art. 200[4]).

private law → public law

private schools 私立学校

(*shiritsu gakkō*). Any school founded by a school-related juristic person acting under the Private School Law (Shiritsu Gakkō Hō, 1949). Private schools are characterized by their independence and originality. Some private schools emphasize preparatory education for entrance to a higher school; others stress vocational education, building character, cultivating moral sentiments, sports, club activities, or particular religious approaches. Since Japanese private schools are administered as part of the public education system, however, they are not totally independent of government supervision.

At the time of the EDUCATION ORDER OF 1872, which marked the beginning of modern education in Japan, private schools were strictly supervised and even suppressed. Even so, under the name *semmon gakkō* (professional school), the forerunners of private institutions, such as WASEDA UNIVERSITY, founded by ŌKUMA SHIGENOBU; KEIŌ UNIVERSITY, founded by FUKUZAWA YUKICHI; and DŌSHISHA UNIVERSITY, founded by NIIJIMA JŌ, offered excellent higher education.

Since World War II, private education has flourished in Japan. As of 1989 some 72.9 percent of the nation's universities, 83.9 percent of the junior colleges, and 58.3 percent of the kindergartens were private. See also UNIVERSITIES AND COLLEGES.

private universities 私立大学

(*shiritsu daigaku*). Universities established under the Private School Law of 1949; licensing is by the minister of education. Administration and operation of these universities are carried out by boards of directors and trustees. The establishment of private universities was first authorized in Japan in 1918 under the Daigaku Rei (University Order). After World War II, the number of private universities increased rapidly; in 1989 they numbered 364. The operation of these universities is dependent upon student tuition. In 1970, to alleviate the cost differential with national universities, the government began offering financial aid to private universities. Associations of private universities include the ASSOCIATION OF PRIVATE UNIVERSITIES IN JAPAN, the JAPAN ASSOCIATION OF PRIVATE COLLEGES AND UNIVERSITIES, and the Japan Association of Private Junior Colleges (Nihon Shiritsu Tanki Daigaku Kyōkai). See also UNIVERSITIES AND COLLEGES.

privatization 民営化

(*min'eika*). The SECOND PROVISIONAL COMMISSION FOR ADMINISTRATIVE REFORM in May 1982 proposed that the three major public corporations be privatized as part of a broad national effort to restore fiscal balance. Consequently, in April 1985 Nippon Telegraph and Telephone Public Corporation and Japan Tobacco and Salt Public Corporation were privatized as NIPPON TELEGRAPH AND TELEPHONE CORPORATION (NTT) and JAPAN TOBACCO, INC, respectively. At that time NTT became the largest private corporation in Japan. The JAPANESE NATIONAL RAILWAYS (JNR) was partitioned and a new private Japan Railways (JR) group was created in April 1987, composed of six passenger railway companies, a freight company, the Shinkansen Holding Corporation, and the JNR Settlement Corporation. All three former public corporations appear to be stable and profitable.

Privy Council 枢密院

(*Sūmitsuin*). A senior consultative body to the emperor and the government. The Privy Council's organization, procedures, and functions were defined in an imperial ordinance of 30 April 1888. It was established mainly to ratify the Meiji Constitution, in which it received constitutional status. It went out of existence in 1947 after the ratification of the present constitution. The establishment of the council was inspired by ITŌ HIROBUMI, the principal architect of the constitutional system, who saw the need for a supracabinet organ able to settle disputes that might arise between the cabinet and the legislature.

The Privy Council consisted of a president, vice-president, and 12 (later expanded to 24) councillors, all over 40 years of age and appointed for life by the emperor, as well as a secretary-general and other secretaries. Cabinet ministers were members by virtue of their office and were given the right to vote. The president had extraordinary power because he called and controlled the meetings, which were held in secret at the palace with the emperor in attendance on important occasions. Matters on which the council would deliberate included interpretations of the constitution, laws, and questions related to the budget; amendments to the constitution; international treaties and plans of administrative organizations; and all matters, fiscal and administrative, on which the emperor desired an opinion.

Assessments of the importance of the Privy Council have varied from claims that it was the most powerful single agency in the government—probably true both legally and theoretically—to judgments that it was comparatively insignificant in national politics, which appears to have been true in practice. During its early years, from 1888 to 1922, the council exercised modest influence. Many of the same men who dominated the government presided over it, including Itō Hirobumi, KURODA KIYOTAKA, and YAMAGATA ARITOMO. During the 1920s the staunchly conservative council clashed repeatedly with party-led governments, rejecting several government decisions and asserting its power to advise on foreign policy. In the 1930s and 1940s the council became less active and important politically; it was ignored in Japan's decision to go to war in 1941. After the war it approved the new constitution, which made no provision for its continuance.

product liability 製造物責任

(*seizōbutsu sekinin*). An aggregate of substantive legal theories and procedural rules that determine who bears ultimate financial responsibility for physical or other damage caused by defects in products placed on the market. It was only after the occurrence of such tragedies as SMON DISEASE and the KANEMI OIL POISONING INCIDENT in the 1960s that the issue of product liability became a major concern.

Article 709 of the Japanese CIVIL CODE states, "A person who intentionally or negligently violates the right of another is bound to make compensation for damage arising therefrom" (see TORTS). It has thus been left to the courts to determine on a case-by-case basis which persons in the distribution chain (manufacturer, wholesaler, retailer, lessor, licensor) are liable and which persons in the consumption chain are entitled to relief (purchaser, household member, guest, lessee, licensee). In most cases, manufacturers and retailers are required to exercise "ordinary care," that is, the care an ordinary person would take when handling the product under similar circumstances. Those who handle products that are dangerous in themselves or that may become dangerous if defective are held responsible for a high degree of care.

Under notions of STRICT LIABILITY, a manufacturer or other person may be held liable for defects in his products even in the absence of negligence. The reasons for this are that modern distribution processes rarely afford the consumer the opportunity to inspect products adequately; that, in most cases, the consumer does not have the technical knowledge to detect defects; and that the manufacturer or distributor, as the receiver of benefits from a profitable activity, is in the best position to assume the costs of legal liability for all his customers. Japanese jurists, while attracted to strict liability theory, have been reluctant to apply it to cases unless specifically authorized by statute. Some judges have utilized article 717 of the Civil Code, which provides for strict liability in cases of articles attached to the ground (buildings, bridges, roads, walls, gas pipes,

proletarian literature movement Cover of the October 1921 issue of *Tane maku hito* (The Sowers), the leftist literary monthly credited with starting this movement.

utility poles), as the basis for imposing liability, but its usefulness is limited in regard to most consumer products. However, a large body of scholarly opinion holds that shifting the burden of proof to the manufacturer, as was done in the Kanemi case, which was found against the manufacturer of a cooking oil into which PCBs had leaked and caused 51 deaths, is equivalent in substance to the imposition of a strict liability standard. It remains to be seen whether the decision will provide a precedent for cases in which defective products do not possess such a high degree of danger.

proletarian literature movement
プロレタリア文学運動

(*puroretaria bungaku undō*). "Proletarian literature," in Japan, refers to a body of literature emerging between the end of World War I and the early 1930s from a literary movement that was part of a larger sociopolitical effort by socialist writers to improve the position of the working class.

Activist literature in Japan has its roots in political novels of the FREEDOM AND PEOPLE'S RIGHTS MOVEMENT (Jiyū Minken Undō) of the early Meiji period (1868–1912). In the 1890s and early 1900s, this body of literature evolved into the Christianity-inspired "socialist novel" (*shakai shugi shōsetsu*) of the kind represented by KINOSHITA NAOE's *Hi no hashira* (1904; tr *Pillar of Fire*, 1972). During the same period such writers as SAKAI TOSHIHIKO, KŌTOKU SHŪSUI, ISHIKAWA TAKUBOKU, Shirayanagi Shūko (1884–1950), and ŌSUGI SAKAE laid the groundwork for the proletarian literary movement of the 1920s and early 1930s.

Widespread unrest among the masses in the depression following World War I, an active labor union movement, a series of strikes, rice riots (see RICE RIOTS OF 1918), agrarian discontent, and the success of the Russian Revolution in 1917 influenced the movement, generally recognized to have started with the establishment of the magazine TANE MAKU HITO (The Sowers) in February 1921. The stimulus for the founding of *Tane maku hito* came from the formation of the Japan Socialist League (NIHON SHAKAI SHUGI DŌMEI) in December 1920. Contributors comprised a broad spectrum of left-wing sentiment. The leaders, headed by Komaki Ōmi (1894–1978) and Kaneko Yōbun (1894–1985), proclaimed their intention to work for modernity, revolution, and internationalism. The leading theorist for *Tane maku hito* was HIRABAYASHI HATSUNOSUKE. In the destruction following the Tōkyō Earthquake of 1923, *Tane maku hito* was forced to cease publication, but former members of the magazine such as AONO SUEKICHI, Kaneko Yōbun, and Komaki Ōmi were quick to revive the literary movement with the publication of *Bungei sensen* (Literary Battlefront), its first issue appearing in June 1924. *Bungei sensen* was instrumental in bringing about the formation on 6 December 1925 of the Japan Proletarian Literary Arts League (Nihon Puroretaria Bungei Remmei).

The push toward Marxism evident in Aono's work was accelerated by youthful members of the Society for the Study of Marxist Arts (Marukusu Shugi Geijutsu Kenkyūkai), a student organization at Tōkyō University that included HAYASHI FUSAO, NAKANO SHIGEHARU, and KAMEI KATSUICHIRŌ. They ousted the non-Marxists from the league in November 1926 and renamed and reorganized it into the Japan Proletarian Arts League (Nihon Puroretaria Geijutsu Remmei).

Further schisms divided the path of the proletarian literary movement. The Marxist FUKUMOTO KAZUO's political theory insisted on a thoroughgoing knowledge of Marxist theory for participants in the proletarian movement, in contrast to socialist YAMAKAWA HITOSHI's older and more pragmatic theory. The rift caused Hayashi and Aono, together with KURAHARA KOREHITO, to leave the Japan Proletarian Arts League to form the Worker Farmer Artists League (Rōnō Geijutsuka Remmei) in June 1927, which continued *Bungei sensen*, while the former brought out its official organ, *Puroretaria geijutsu* (Proletarian Arts). The Worker Farmer Artists League split, with some former members establishing the Vanguard Artists League (Zen'ei Geijutsuka Dōmei), which began publishing *Zen'ei* (Vanguard).

During the *Bungei sensen* period those who made their mark as fiction writers included KUROSHIMA DENJI, HIRABAYASHI TAIKO, SATA INEKO, and HAYAMA YOSHIKI, whose *Umi ni ikuru hitobito* (People Who Live On the Sea), published in 1926, has been called Japan's first true proletarian literary work because it introduces consciously revolutionary characters.

From 1920 to 1934 a progressive theater movement, called *puroretaria engeki*, paralleled the development of proletarian literature. In 1934 all proletarian theater groups were forced by government pressure to disband.

NAPF–KOPF Period, 1928–1934——In January 1928 the Japan Proletarian Arts League and the Vanguard Artists League merged and in late March created the All-Japan Federation of Proletarian Arts (Zen Nihon Musansha Geijutsu Remmei), commonly known as NAPF after the initials of its Esperanto name Nippona Artista Proleta Federacio. It began publishing *Senki* (Battle Flag), and the proletarian arts movement assumed a strong communist direction. A reorganization in 1931 included renaming the federation the Japan Proletarian Culture Federation (Nihon Puroretaria Bunka Remmei), ordinarily referred to as KOPF, from the Esperanto name Federacio de Proletaj Kultur-organizoj Japanaj. *Puroretaria bunka* (Proletarian Culture) replaced *Senki* as its official organ.

The early years of the NAPF–KOPF period produced the finest works of the entire proletarian literary movement. Rising to prominence were such writers as KATAOKA TEPPEI, TOKUNAGA SUNAO, and KOBAYASHI TAKIJI. Mounting government oppression of leftists and internal dissension led KOPF to dissolve itself in 1934.

The heyday of the proletarian literary movement lasted only about six years at most, and although it gave birth to few literary monuments, it left a number of legacies. In its depiction of the working class plight, for instance, proletarian literature contributed a new dimension, and, more importantly, it brought to modern Japanese literature a social and political consciousness hitherto unexplored.

property rights
財産権

(*zaisanken*). Article 29 of the CONSTITUTION OF JAPAN provides that "the right to own or to hold property is inviolable" and also that "[p]roperty rights shall be defined by law, in conformity with the public welfare." The second provision is the basis upon which numerous restrictions have been placed on property rights in order to benefit society as a whole.

Property rights, except for some legal claims, can be transferred. When property rights are transferred, there is public notification to third parties. If anyone violates property rights without justifiable cause, criminal or civil liability must be borne.

prosecution review commissions
検察審査会

(*kensatsu shinsakai*). Commissions to review the propriety of decisions by PUBLIC PROSECUTORS not to prosecute criminal cases. In Japan, public prosecutors have the discretionary power of nonprosecution. *Kensatsu shinsakai*, based on the US grand jury system, were first instituted in July 1948. A commission is composed of 11 laypersons chosen by lot from among those qualified to vote in House of Representatives elections; commission members serve for six months. A commission is empowered to examine all evidence produced by public prosecutors, summon witnesses, inspect the scene of a crime, request public prosecutors to appear before it and comment on a case, and hear advisory opinions of qualified experts. A commission considers only those cases in which public prosecutors already have decided not to institute public prosecution. If more than 8 members concur, a commission recommends that the case be reinvestigated and prosecution instituted.

prostitution
売春

(*baishun*). Until after World War II, the sale of extramarital sex was highly institutionalized in Japan; government officials legally recognized and attempted to supervise brothels from the 12th century on. Another characteristic of Japanese prostitution was its association with various popular arts, especially during the flowering of urban culture in the Edo period (1600–1868). But today prostitution is illegal in Japan, where it has become informal and more or less clandestine.

Premodern——Some scholars trace the origins of prostitution in Japan to UNEME, women sent to serve at the YAMATO COURT from at least the 6th century. Others believe prostitution was begun by the early shamanesses (MIKO). Women entertainers called SHIRABYŌSHI became popular with the ruling warrior class. Male prostitutes were fairly common from the 12th century on (see HOMOSEXUALITY).

Brothels began to develop from the 12th century. As early as 1193, the Kamakura shogunate (1182–1333) began to supervise and tax brothels. From the late 16th century, designated areas were licensed by the Tokugawa shogunate (1603–1867) as "pleasure quarters" (*yūkaku*). The most famous of the licensed quarters was YOSHIWARA in Edo (now Tōkyō), with over 2,000 prostitutes. This and other major brothel districts provided inspiration for well-known literary and artistic works (notably in the genre known as UKIYO-E). Alongside the hierarchy of licensed prostitutes (*yūjo* or *shōgi*), there emerged another group called GEISHA, who specialized in musical and dancing skills. In addition, there were many unlicensed prostitutes (*shishō*), working outside the enclosed brothel districts.

Meiji to Present——In 1872, when the MARIA LUZ INCIDENT caused concern over the actual or de facto sale of persons, the new

Meiji government issued what was known as the "antislavery law" (*jinshin baibai kinshi rei*) or the "prostitute liberation law" (*shōgi kaihō rei*). In 1900 the government's highest court again tried to end the indenture system, and the Home Ministry banned the prostitution of girls under age 18. But the Meiji government, like the former shogunates, eventually began licensing and supervising brothels as a means of social control. In the 1930s the antiprostitution campaign died, and the army itself encouraged recruitment of prostitutes (called *jūgun ianfu*) to serve the soldiers overseas.

In the first week after Japan's surrender at the end of World War II, the Home Ministry moved to recruit prostitutes to serve the expected OCCUPATION troops. But early in 1946 the Occupation authorities officially recommended the abolition of licensed brothels. As a compromise, brothels were relabeled with such names as "special eating and drinking shops" (*tokushu inshokuten*). They continued operating much as before in designated "red-line districts" (*akasen chitai*; areas for informal prostitution were known as "blue-line districts," or *aosen chitai*). By 1955 the total number of prostitutes in Japan may have been as many as 500,000.

Yet open prostitution came to be considered "undemocratic," and, although brothelkeepers put up determined resistance, the Diet at last passed the PROSTITUTION PREVENTION LAW in 1956, to take effect beginning in 1957–58. This ended the official tolerance of brothel districts.

However, the law is aimed mainly at discouraging formal brothels and open solicitation. Informal prostitution continues, mainly within the entertainment, lodging, and restaurant business (*mizu shōbai*). In recent years the number of prostitutes who have come from overseas to work in Japan has increased. Over 40 percent of the men convicted as pimps (*pombiki*) are thought to be connected with organized gangs (see YAKUZA), and some prostitution is still more or less involuntary. See also KARAYUKI SAN.

Prostitution Prevention Law
売春防止法

(Baishun Bōshi Hō). Law enacted in 1956 to prevent PROSTITUTION. Formerly, under the CONSTITUTION OF THE EMPIRE OF JAPAN (1889), police regulations recognized the existence of licensed prostitution. However, on the basis of the 1947 CONSTITUTION OF JAPAN, which declares respect for human rights and equality of the sexes, prostitution is now prohibited. The 1956 law places criminal sanctions on the act of a prostitute's enticing a customer and on other activities that promote prostitution. It also provides corrective guidance measures for prostitutes and protective guidance for young women likely to become involved in prostitution. The heaviest penalty is a maximum of 10 years' penal servitude or a fine of up to ¥300,000. For a prostitute's open enticement of customers, the penalty is a maximum of six months' penal servitude or a fine of up to ¥10,000. When these activities are carried out by an organization, both penalty provisions are to be applied. Women's guidance institutions, focusing on rehabilitative guidance rather than incarceration, were also established under this law.

protection of computer software
ソフトウエアの保護

(*sofutouea no hogo*). Under the COPYRIGHT LAW (Law No. 48, 1970), computer programs are works of authorship in the scientific domain (art. 2[1] i), and ROM (read only memory) chips or floppy disks that contain computer programs are reproductions or copies of such programs. The law broadly defines "reproduction" (*fukusei*) as "to reproduce (*saisei*) in a tangible form by means of printing, photography, copying (*fukusha*), sound recording, visual recording or other method" (art. 2[1] xv).

The Copyright Law was amended in 1985 to make it more suitable to protect computer programs. The essence of the revision is as follows: (1) the word *puroguramu* (computer program) is defined as "an expression of combined instructions given to a computer so as to make it function and obtain a certain result" (art. 2[1] x-ii); (2) *puroguramu no chosakubutsu* (program work) is added to the list of works of authorship (art. 10[1]); (3) copyright protection does not extend to any programming language, rule, or algorithm used for making computer programs (art. 10[3]); (4) the authorship of a program that, at the initiative of a juristic person (HŌJIN), is made by an employee in the course of his duties is attributed to the juristic person unless otherwise stipulated in a contract or work regulations (art. 15[2]); and (5) exceptions to an author's right to the integrity of his work are provided to facilitate the use of computer programs by allowing necessary modifications (art. 20[2] iii) and to allow owners of copies of programs to make copies or adaptations to the extent necessary for use in their computers (art. 47-2).

Protestant missionaries
プロテスタント宣教師

(Purotesutanto *senkyōshi*). The earliest Christian missionaries in Japan were Catholics, who arrived in the mid-16th century. They had made an estimated 300,000 converts before the mid-17th century, when Christianity was proscribed and the policy of NATIONAL SECLUSION was adopted (see CHRISTIANITY; CATHOLIC MISSIONARIES). Protestant activity came only with the reopening of the country to commerce with Western nations in the mid-19th century, as missionaries accompanied American and European trade expansion into the Pacific. In 1858 the HARRIS TREATY allowed religious establishments in foreign concessions, and in 1859 seven American Protestants arrived. Between 1859 and 1870, 15 Protestant missionaries arrived in Japan, among them the first missionaries from the British Isles.

A continuing prohibition against proselytizing, combined with increased demand for training in English and other European languages, led to a growing missionary emphasis on education. The present Meiji Gakuin University evolved from a co-educational school opened by Clara Hepburn, wife of James C. HEPBURN, a medical missionary. The American-trained former *samurai* NIIJIMA JŌ (Joseph Hardy Neesima) founded a school that became DŌSHISHA UNIVERSITY. The relaxation of the prohibition in 1873 was followed by the founding of many mission schools.

From 1872 the number of missionaries in Japan began to increase, with representatives of European and Canadian societies joining the Americans and British. By 1908 an estimated 960 Protestant missionaries had arrived. Japanese converts played a prominent role in missionary activity. Even more important were the members of the various "bands," groups of autonomous young converts mainly of samurai origin who pledged to propagate their newfound faith. Many of these men left a lasting mark on Christianity in Japan: UEMURA MASAHISA, EBINA DANJŌ, KOZAKI HIROMICHI, UKITA KAZUTAMI, TOKUTOMI SOHŌ, UCHIMURA KANZŌ, and NITOBE INAZŌ.

The number of missionaries from abroad continued to increase. As nationalism and militarism made the foreign presence difficult in the years before World War II, indigenous clergy and workers took over. After the war ended foreign missionaries flocked back to Japan. Between 1956 and 1960, missionaries of the older Protestant denominations gradually began to leave, so that by 1970 the number of Protestant foreigners had declined.

proverbs
諺

(*kotowaza*; literally, "verbal skill"). In ancient Japan the words of a god conveyed through an oracle were called *kotowaza*. Later the word came to signify aphorisms or succinct expressions of folk wisdom. During the Edo period (1600–1868) proverbs were published in collections such as *Kefukigusa* (1645), which increased their popularity and currency. Besides the frequent didactic element, many *kotowaza* are jocular, often containing puns, or are designed as insults or criticisms. Some examples of Japanese proverbs:

Kiite gokuraku mite jigoku. ("Sounds like paradise, but hell when you see it," or "Imagination goes a long way.")

Saru mo ki kara ochiru. ("Even monkeys fall out of trees," or "Even Homer sometimes nods.")

Chiri mo tsumoreba yama to naru. ("Dust accumulated makes a mountain.")

Kawaii ko ni wa tabi o saseyo. ("If you love your children, send them on a journey"; i.e., expose them to the hardships of travel.)

Neko ni koban. ("Gold coins to a cat," or "Pearls before swine.")

provinces
国

(*kuni* or *koku*). Administrative units established under the KOKUGUN SYSTEM, following the TAIKA REFORM of 645. Fifty-eight *kuni* and 3 island provinces were established, and provincial governors (KOKUSHI) and district officials (GUNJI) were appointed. From time to time changes were made in the system in response to local developments and governmental needs. In 824 the administrative system was reorganized to comprise 66 *kuni* and 2 island provinces, a division that survived until the MEIJI RESTORATION of 1868. The provinces were abolished in 1871 (see PREFECTURAL SYSTEM, ESTABLISHMENT OF). ▬ *See map, next page.*

provincial capitals→kokufu

Provisional Council on Educational Reform
臨時教育審議会

(Rinji Kyōiku Shingikai). Advisory council set up by the cabinet in 1984 to make recommendations on basic policies for the reform of Japan's educational system. The council was made up of 25 members supported by a staff of 20 specialists and was chaired by Okamoto Michio (b 1913), former president of Kyōto University. The council submitted four reports; all four stressed the principle of respect for and encouragement of individuality as a fundamental goal of education. Among the proposals put forward were (1) a restructuring of systems for adult and continuing education; (2) the replacement of the

The Traditional Provinces and the Modern Prefectures

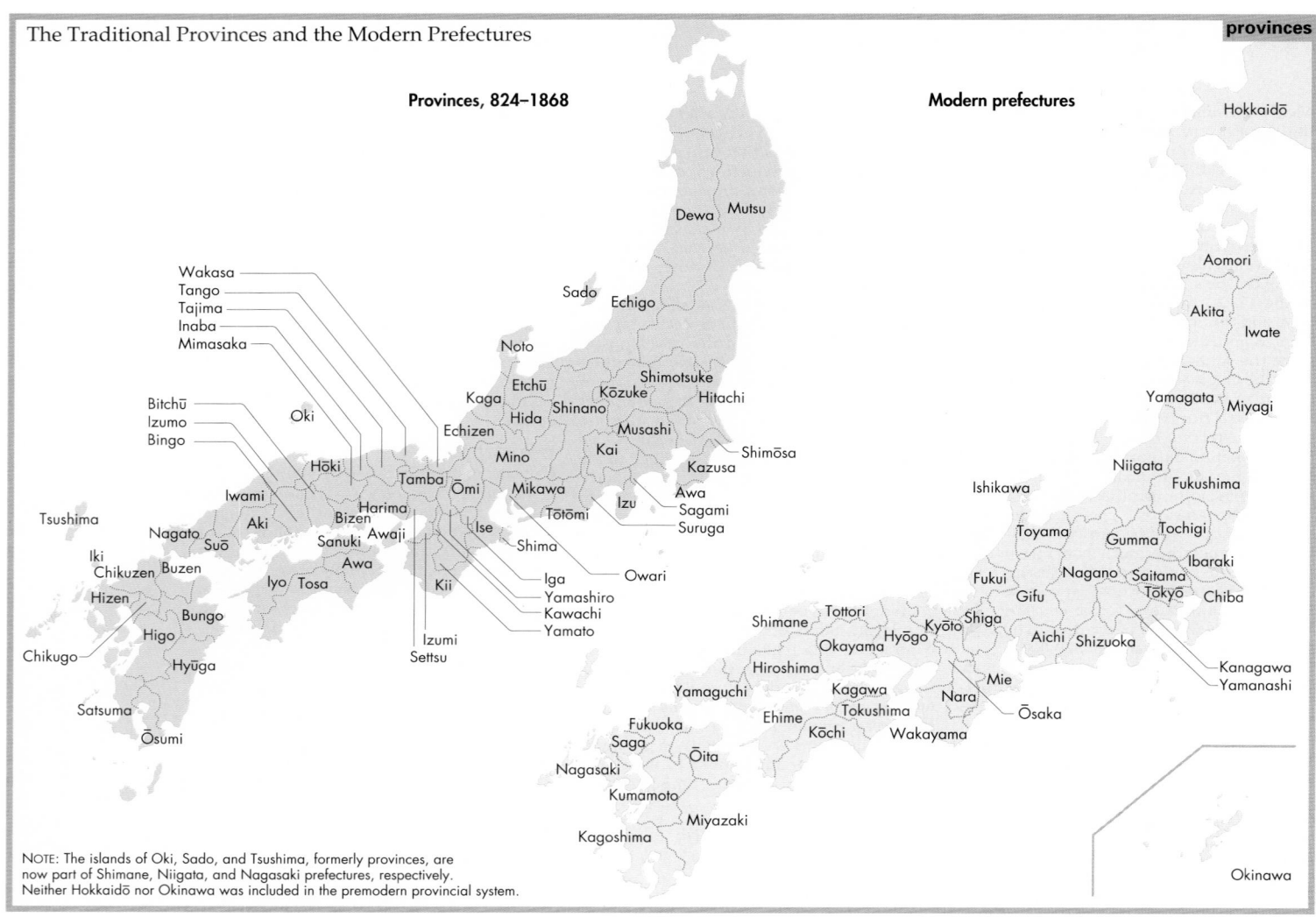

Provinces, 824–1868

Modern prefectures

NOTE: The islands of Oki, Sado, and Tsushima, formerly provinces, are now part of Shimane, Niigata, and Nagasaki prefectures, respectively. Neither Hokkaidō nor Okinawa was included in the premodern provincial system.

Joint First-Stage Achievement Test for entrance to national and public universities with the UNIVERSITY ENTRANCE EXAMINATION CENTER TESTS, which would be open to use by private universities as well; (3) the creation of a six-year secondary school system that would combine the existing three-year middle- and high-school systems; (4) the adoption of an elective system for high schools that would allow graduation upon completion of a certain number of credits and fulfillment of the mandatory three-year attendance requirement; and (5) the establishment of a training program for teachers during their first year of employment. The Ministry of Education began implementing a number of these proposals in April 1988 and the teacher training program in 1990.

provisional disposition 仮処分

(*kari shobun;* temporary injunction). Provisional remedy under the Code of Civil Procedure and the Civil Execution Law (Minji Shikkō Hō; Law concerning the Execution of Judgment) to preserve the status quo or to permit the status quo to be changed to avoid an immediate danger to the applicant. For example, the court may order an employer to pay wages to the applicant worker who claims his or her discharge to be void and is under financial difficulty. The procedure is so designed that the remedy is given speedily. The measure is merely provisional in that a final determination of the applicant's claim must be made through a principal action that must be brought by the applicant.

Provisional Government of Free India 自由インド仮政府

(*Jiyū Indo Kariseifu*). Indian anti-British government in exile, in existence from October 1943 to August 1945. It was headed by Subhas Chandra BOSE and based in Singapore and Japan. Both the Provisional Government and the INDIAN NATIONAL ARMY were sponsored by the Japanese military. See also INDIA AND JAPAN.

Provisional Government of Korea 大韓民国臨時政府

(Kor: Taehan Minguk Imsi Chŏngbu; J: Daikan Minkoku Rinji Seifu). Organized as the legitimate government-in-exile of Korea on 9 April 1919 in Shanghai. Its most important figures included KIM GU, Syngman RHEE (Yi Sŭng-man), and Yi Tong-hwi. They hoped to end Japanese rule of Korea, but the group ceased to be a cohesive entity by 1921. Japan's 1931 conquest of Manchuria and Kim Gu's subsequent alliance with Chiang Kai-shek revived interest in the organization. By 1941 it had formed a division of Korean soldiers to fight with Chinese forces against Japan. The Korean provisional government was disbanded by Soviet and US Occupation forces in 1945, when they formed their own military governments in Korea.

Provisional Government of the Republic of China 中華民国臨時政府

(Ch: Zhonghua Minguo Linshi Zhengfu or Chung-hua Min-kuo Lin-shih Cheng-fu; J: Chūka Minkoku Rinji Seifu). Government sponsored by political agents of Japan's North China Area Army. Inaugurated in Beiping (Peiping; now Beijing [Peking]) on 14 December 1937, it lasted until March 1940. This collaborationist regime was the outgrowth of Japanese efforts to create an autonomous North China and link it to Japan and its puppet state MANCHUKUO. The first chief executive of the Provisional Government was WANG KEMIN (Wang K'o-min). The Provisional Government was equipped with an official state philosophy—the "kingly way" (Ch: *wang dao* or *wang tao;* J: *ōdō*), or rule by benevolent example. This ideal was to combat SUN YAT-SEN's "three principles of the people," and its propagation became a major function of the Provisional Government and its XINMIN HUI (Hsin-min Hui; New People's Society). In March 1940 the Provisional Government was dissolved and supplanted by the REORGANIZED NATIONAL GOVERNMENT OF THE REPUBLIC OF CHINA.

ptarmigan 雷鳥

(*raichō*). *Lagopus mutus.* A bird of the family Tetraonidae; it is a year-round inhabitant of high mountain regions. The ptarmigan measures about 37 centimeters (15 in) in length. Its plumage changes seasonally, being brown in the summer and white in the winter; however, its wings remain white and the tail remains black year round. Found in the Japan Alps in central Honshū as well as in northern Europe, Canada, and Alaska, it does not descend to the lowlands even in winter. In early summer the *raichō* nests under the *haimatsu* (*Pinus pumila*), a low creeping pine, and produces 5–10 eggs.

PTAs
父母と教師の会

(*fubo to kyōshi no kai*). US Occupation authorities introduced the parent-teacher association to Japan after World War II in order to promote the democratization of education. The primary purpose of the PTA was to help provide financial support for school equipment and activities; in many cases the PTA replaced prewar parent-support organizations called *hogosha kai.* The PTA in Japan has not developed into a democratic group that reflects the minds of the people on educational issues; like its predecessors it tends to function as a support group for the school. Since most parents automatically become members when their children enroll in school and withdraw when the children graduate, they do not develop a deep sense of identification with the organization. Attempts are being made to induce members to devote more attention to the study of educational issues within PTAs and to develop relationships with other citizens' groups.

public assistance
生活保護

(*seikatsu hogo*). Public assistance programs are designed to assure a subsistence-level income to all citizens, in accordance with article 25 of the CONSTITUTION OF JAPAN, which guarantees "the right to maintain the minimum standards of wholesome and cultured living." Antipoverty programs in Japan originated with the Poor Relief Regulation of 1874 and the Poor Relief Law of 1929. Today, public assistance is codified in the 1950 LIVELIHOOD PROTECTION LAW. Poverty in postwar Japan has largely been eradicated, and in 1987 only 1.04 percent of the population received such assistance. (The definition of poverty depends on a variety of factors, but as an illustration, the income level defining poverty was set at ¥140,674 (US $888) per month for a three-member family in the most expensive area of Tōkyō in 1990.) Seventy-five percent of the costs of public assistance are covered by the national government, with local governments providing the remainder. Assistance is provided in seven areas—subsistence, medical, educational, housing, maternity, vocational, and funeral expenses. Of these, medical benefits accounted for 64.4 percent of all public assistance in 1986. See SOCIAL WELFARE.

Publication Law of 1893
出版法

(Shuppan Hō). One of the fundamental laws controlling publishing before World War II. It was promulgated in April 1893 and abolished in May 1949. Under this law all published materials were to be registered with the government and a copy submitted to the Home Ministry for official inspection. Firms and individuals responsible for publications that were found to obstruct peace and order, or to be morally corrupt, were subject to severe restraints on operations and harsh penalties.

Publication Ordinance of 1869
出版条例

(Shuppan Jōrei). Originally issued to serve as a copyright law, this ordinance became primarily a means of checking criticism of the government by supporters of the FREEDOM AND PEOPLE'S RIGHTS MOVEMENT. In accordance with the revisions of 1872, all publications except newspapers had to be submitted for CENSORSHIP to the Ministry of Education. The final revision of the ordinance was issued in 1875, shortly before the PRESS ORDINANCE OF 1875

and the LIBEL LAW OF 1875. The 1875 version placed the Home Ministry in charge of censorship. It was supplanted by the even more repressive PUBLICATION LAW OF 1893.

public auction
競売

(*keibai*). Auction held by the court under the Civil Execution Law (Minji Shikkō Hō) of 1979. It provides for three occasions to hold an auction: (1) to sell an attached property in a civil execution proceeding to enforce obligations embodied in a judgment or other documents given executory force; (2) to sell the collateral of a lien, contractual or otherwise, in a proceeding to foreclose such lien; and (3) to sell a property for other purposes as provided for by laws (for example, in connection with the partition of a jointly owned property). Public auction is conducted by a bailiff of the court. Usually it takes place orally with open bids, but it can be conducted through closed bids. A minimum bidding price is set by the court on the basis of an appraisal. The purchaser at a public auction obtains the title to the property, when he or she pays the price, free of liens. Lienholders are paid fully with the proceeds.

public baths→bath

public deposit→kyōtaku

public employees
公務員

(*kōmuin*). General term referring to employees of both central and local governments. The Japanese civil service system is broadly divided into the national civil service, governed by the National Civil Service Law (Kokka Kōmuin Hō, Law No. 120, 1947) and related special legislation and regulations, and local public employees, under the Local Civil Service Law (Chihō Kōmuin Hō, Law No. 261, 1950). These basic statutes further classify all public officials as either special (*tokubetsu*) or general (*ippan*) officials. At the national level special officials include the prime minister, ministers of state, their confidential secretaries and parliamentary vice-ministers, members of the NATIONAL PERSONNEL AUTHORITY, the BOARD OF AUDIT, the head of the Cabinet Legislation Bureau, certain members of the DEFENSE AGENCY, all judges, members of other special commissions, and, as a rule, other officials whose appointments require consent by one or more houses of the Diet (National Civil Service Law, art. 2). The general civil service comprises most public employees engaged in the regular administrative operations of government. As of 1991 there were an estimated 1.2 million general public employees at the national level and 3.2 million local general public employees.

public employment security offices
公共職業安定所

(*kōkyō shokugyō anteisho*). Public offices for employment referral established by the EMPLOYMENT SECURITY LAW OF 1947 (Shokugyō Antei Hō). The 631 existing offices are under the direction and supervision of prefectural governors, but the national government also influences personnel selection.

A public employment referral service began with the Employment Referral Law (Shokugyō Shōkai Hō) of 1921, and in 1938 the service came under national administration. During World War II, the offices were renamed labor mobilization agencies (*kinrō dōinsho*), carrying out labor conscription for government projects. After Japan's defeat Occupation authorities ordered their reor-

ganization along present lines.

The aim of the offices is to regulate labor supply and demand while preventing unemployment. The offices provide employment referrals, offer job counseling, distribute unemployment insurance benefits, and verify working standards established by the Labor Standards Law of 1947.

In recent years the function of providing information on available positions to job candidates has largely been taken over by several new magazines specializing in classified advertisements and personnel recruiting information. As a result, the public employment security offices are concentrating on special problem areas such as jobs for older workers and the handicapped.

public health
公衆衛生

(*kōshū eisei*). Rapid economic growth in recent years has brought about a marked improvement in Japan's standard of living, and as a concomitant to this, remarkable progress has been made in all aspects of public health.

At the national level, the MINISTRY OF HEALTH AND WELFARE is responsible for the general administration of public health, social welfare, and social security programs. In addition to the Minister's Secretariat, the Ministry of Health and Welfare consists of nine bureaus, including those of public health, environmental sanitation, and medical affairs. Affiliated institutions include national research institutes and hospitals and quarantine stations at certain ports of entry. Other administrative bodies concerned with public health include the ENVIRONMENT AGENCY, the MINISTRY OF LABOR, and the MINISTRY OF EDUCATION. Locally, a department or bureau of health is found in each of the 47 prefectures, and, as of 1 April 1991, 850 health centers (*hokenjo*) were in existence throughout the country. Municipalities also have offices in charge of public health. See also MEDICAL AND HEALTH INSURANCE.

The age structure of the population is probably the single most important element in the consideration of public health needs. Both the birth rate and the death rate decreased drastically in the decade after World War II, and they have since remained low, leading to a longer life expectancy and to an increase in the number of the aged. See also AGING POPULATION.

Death Trends——The total number of deaths in 1988 was approximately 793,000, a death rate of 6.5 per 1,000 population. The infant mortality rate in Japan decreased from 30.7 per 1,000 live births in 1960 to 4.6 in 1989, placing Japan among those countries with low infant mortality rates. In 1935, infectious diseases caused 43.5 percent of the total number of deaths, while adult diseases such as CANCER, cerebral apoplexy, and heart disease caused only 24.7 percent. By 1988, the former accounted for 1.4 percent, and the latter, 61.9 percent of total deaths.

The discovery of effective antibiotics and the development of new and better preventive and treatment methods have led to a marked decrease in the incidence of acute and chronic infections. While vaccines have dramatically reduced the incidence of such diseases as poliomyelitis and tuberculosis, there have been some serious incidents of harmful side effects from preventive vaccination, particularly the smallpox vaccine. To cope with this problem, inoculation of the smallpox vaccine is given to people in specific areas, and only when there is danger of an epidemic.

For many years, government agencies responsible for public health in Japan have been concerned mainly with the prevention and treatment of diseases. Recently, however, increasing importance has been given to the promotion and maintenance of general health at both local and national levels.

Despite significant improvements in the quality and diversity of medical care, many serious health problems remain unsolved. These include chronic degenerative diseases; mental disorders; diseases from environmental pollution, food and drug additives and agricultural insecticides and fungicides (see POLLUTION-RELATED DISEASES); various iatrogenic disorders; and so-called intractable diseases with "unidentifiable causes."

public law   公法

(*kōhō*). The Japanese legal system, traditionally under the influence of German and French law, has come to distinguish between private and public law. The CIVIL CODE, the COMMERCIAL CODE, and similar regulations that govern relations between private persons constitute the private law system. By contrast, public law is the legal system governing relations between the state and private persons, particularly between government administrative organs and private persons. Public law is a system of law that recognizes the special legal treatment to be accorded to administrative organs. In other words, public law recognizes the privileges granted to administrative authorities as opposed to those afforded to private persons.

Under the Meiji constitution of 1889, the judicial courts had jurisdiction over criminal cases and civil cases, and an independent ADMINISTRATIVE COURT was established with sole jurisdiction over administrative cases. The rights and liberties of citizens received scant protection against the power of state and administrative authorities. Under the CONSTITUTION OF JAPAN (1947), the administrative court has been abolished and the judicial system unified. Moreover, the constitution guarantees the right to resort to judicial adjudication as a fundamental human right.

public opinion surveys   世論調査

(*yoron chōsa* or *seron chōsa*). Although the techniques of public opinion surveys were not unknown in Japan before World War II, they were first used extensively by the postwar Occupation and became especially popular in the postwar years. In 1949 a Public Opinion Survey Department was created in the Diet, but it was discontinued in 1954 and public opinion surveys were taken over by the Prime Minister's Office. Surveys by newspapers and broadcasting companies and, later, by private research institutes followed. Local autonomy, local administrations, national politics, elections, education, and· problems of the younger generation were among the most common themes of the surveys. The respondents were selected through careful random samplings, a highly developed technique in Japan. The principal methods employed were personal interviews or mail surveys; telephone surveys have not been used often. Comparative time series showing transitions in public opinion are a favorite Japanese technique, and the comparison of Japanese surveys with those of other countries is a recent trend.

public order and good morals→   kōjo ryōzoku

Public Order and Police Law of 1900   治安警察法

(Chian Keisatsu Hō). Law promulgated by the YAMAGATA ARITOMO cabinet in March 1900 to restrict the freedom of assembly, association, and speech. An extension of the existing Assembly and Political Association Law (Shūkai oyobi Seisha Hō), it was specifically intended to check organized labor movements. Articles 17 and 30, restricting the rights of workers to organize and strike, were deleted in 1926, although a similar provision later appeared as an amendment to the PEACE PRESERVATION LAW OF 1925 (Chian Iji Hō). The provisions prohibiting women from joining political associations were deleted in 1922. The Police Law remained in effect until after World War II, when it was abolished (November 1945) by order of the OCCUPATION authorities.

public prosecutors   検察

(*kensatsu*). Career government officials in charge of prosecution, crime investigation, and other matters related to the execution of judgments rendered by courts; public prosecutors also represent the public interest in civil, family, and other legal disputes as provided by law. *Kensatsu* as a class include *kenji* (prosecutors) and *fukukenji* (assistant prosecutors). *Kenji*, all of whom have legal educations, are classified hierarchically into (1) the prosecutor-general; (2) the vice-prosecutor-general and superintending prosecutors, all of whom are appointed by the cabinet and whose nomination ceremony is held in the presence of the emperor; and (3) prosecutors, who are appointed by the minister of justice. *Fukukenji* also are appointed by the minister from among persons with extended experience as assistants to public prosecutors, senior police officials, etc, who have passed a Ministry of Justice examination. *Kenji* are assigned to the Supreme Public Prosecutor's Office (headed by the prosecutor-general); to 8 high prosecutor's offices (each headed by a superintending prosecutor); and 6 branch offices; and to 50 district public prosecutor's offices (each directed by a chief prosecutor) and 201 branch offices. *Fukukenji* are posted to each of the 452 local public prosecutor's offices. The number and duties of these offices correspond to the number and functions of the courts—Supreme Court, high courts, district and family courts, and summary courts—established under the Japanese JUDICIAL SYSTEM.

Public Security Investigation Agency   公安調査庁

(Kōan Chōsa Chō). Agency of the national government attached to the MINISTRY OF JUSTICE. Formed in 1952, its main function is the investigation of subversive groups based on the provisions of the SUBVERSIVE ACTIVITIES PREVENTION LAW of 1952. The agency has no direct legal enforcement powers, but it can make recommendations concerning the restriction of activities by subversive groups or the dissolution of organizations involved in such activities to the Public Security Examination Commission (Kōan Shinsa Iinkai), also attached to the Ministry of Justice.

public universities   公立大学

(*kōritsu daigaku*). Term used in Japan to refer to universities established, managed, and funded by prefectural or city governments, as opposed to NATIONAL UNIVERSITIES or PRIVATE UNIVERSITIES. Before public universities were authorized by the University Order (Daigaku Rei), promulgated in 1918, the university system consisted solely of the imperial universities (which would later become national universities). The first public university, the Kyōto Prefectural University of Medicine, opened in 1921. There were 2 public universities in operation at the end of World War II, but in 1950, following the EDUCATIONAL REFORMS OF 1947, 26 SEMMON GAKKŌ (professional schools) achieved public university status. In 1988 there were 38 public universities with a total enrollment of about 60,000 in undergraduate and graduate schools.

public utilities   公益事業

(*kōeki jigyō*). The first public utilities in Japan were transportaion and communications facilities developed by the government in the 1880s. Local public utilities, including transportation and energy supply systems, followed after the turn of the century. There has been a notable tendency toward denationalization of Japanese utilities; many public operations were developed by the government and later transferred to private enterprise.

Nine privately owned regional power companies supply electric power to the nation. Energy resource development is assisted by the quasi-governmental ELECTRIC POWER DEVELOPMENT CO, LTD. The regional divisions used for the electric power companies also serve to define the geographical limits for the organization of regional economic and political interest groups, and the power companies often play an important role in these matters. See also TŌKYŌ ELECTRIC POWER CO, INC; ELECTRIC POWER.

Gas is a less important source of energy in Japan. The largest gas companies are in large cities and include the TŌKYŌ GAS CO, LTD, and the ŌSAKA GAS CO, LTD. Nuclear power generation has grown in importance in recent years, with the government providing development assistance and regulation.

Water is generally provided to private homes by the municipality, while industries receive water from utilities operated by the prefecture. Sewage disposal and garbage collection, where provided, are operated by the local government.

Transportation systems operate on a mixed public and private basis. Since the restructuring of the JAPANESE NATIONAL RAILWAYS (JNR) in 1987, national passenger lines have been operated by six privately managed, regionally based rail companies known collectively as JR. Urban SUBWAYS exist in Tōkyō, Ōsaka, Sapporo, Nagoya, Yokohama, Kōbe, Kyōto, Fukuoka, and Sendai; there are both public and private lines. Bus lines are operated both by municipalities and private companies. See also RAILWAYS; ROADS; TRANSPORTATION.

TELECOMMUNICATIONS SYSTEMS are operated by the NIPPON TELEGRAPH AND TELEPHONE CORPORATION, the national POSTAL SERVICE, and the international communications company KOKUSAI DENSHIN DENWA CO, LTD.

Regulation of the energy industries is handled by the Public Utilities Department of the MINISTRY OF INTERNATIONAL TRADE AND INDUSTRY. The central government controls rates for energy, telephone and telegraph services, and transportation. Local governments set rates for water and locally controlled transportation operations.

public utility rates 公共料金

(*kōkyō ryōkin*). Commodity prices and service charges determined by, or subject to approval by, the Japanese central government or local governments. Regulated charges include electricity, gas, telephone, railroad, and taxi rates, as well as fees for medical care. Public utility rates constitute 40 of the items used for the consumer price index compiled by the Management and Coordination Agency and accounted for 15.6 percent of consumer expenditures in 1985. With the addition of the prices of rice, tobacco, and salt (which are termed public utility rates in the broad sense), the proportion of regulated charges rose to 19.1 percent of consumer expenditures. At the time of the 1973 oil crisis strong controls on public utility rates prevented price increases, but rates were later raised substantially. Since 1985 the high value of the yen and low oil prices have brought major cost reductions and profit increases to some utility companies. However, lower costs have been passed on to customers only in rather limited rate reductions, and Japanese utility rates are still some of the highest in the world. This has led to calls for an end to government protection of utilities from competition.

public welfare 公共の福祉

(*kōkyō no fukushi*). Four provisions of the 1947 CONSTITUTION OF JAPAN (arts. 12, 13, 22, and 29) are the principal basis in general law for limiting individual rights and freedoms. In articles 12 and 13 the comprehensive principle that human rights shall be the supreme consideration in legislation and in other governmental affairs is qualified by the requirement that rights not be abused but exercised for and within the parameters of the public welfare. PROPERTY RIGHTS (art. 29) and the rights to choose one's occupation and place of residence (art. 22) are expressly qualified by public welfare clauses.

A 1949 Supreme Court decision, later used as precedent, invoked the public welfare as a positive law doctrine for regulating rights and freedoms. In a 1950 decision the same court defined the public welfare as follows: "The maintenance of order and respect for the fundamental human rights—it is precisely these things which constitute the content of the public welfare." No right is put in a preferred position in relation to the public welfare, but the spirit of the constitution rules out any notion of the public welfare antithetical to the primacy of human rights.

public works 公共事業

(*kōkyō jigyō*). Government-sponsored projects to construct or improve public facilities and infrastructures. The "public works expenditures" figure in the general account budget is usually taken to be the total spending for public works in Japan. However, another measurement is the sum of investments made by the national and local governments, public corporations, and government agencies that appear in the national income statistics.

Public works expenditures accounted for about 10 percent of total general account outlays in 1989. Spending for road improvements has consistently been the largest budget item since World War II. However, recent changes in the economy and in patterns of national demand have led to gradually increasing expenditures for the improvement of housing and public facilities. Most public works expenses are covered by governmen-

tal subsidies given to local public bodies, with projects administered and carried out by those local bodies.

Public Works Research Institute 土木研究所

(Doboku Kenkyūjo). Organ of the Ministry of Construction in charge of basic research covering all aspects of public works. Located in the city of Tsukuba, Ibaraki Prefecture. Established in 1922, it initially carried out experiments on roads; test facilities for waterway and harbor improvements were added in 1925. It regularly issues the *Doboku kenkyūjo hōkoku* (Report of the Public Works Research Institute) and the *Journal of Research, Public Works Research Institute.*

publishing 出版

(*shuppan*). The history of modern Japanese publishing covers a period of only a little over a century starting from the Meiji Restoration (1868), but the history of printing in Japan is much older. (See PRINTING, PREMODERN.) From the mid-Edo period (1600–1868), private commercial publishing enterprises flourished with the development of townsmen (CHŌNIN) culture.

Development of Modern Publishing— As in the case of the majority of institutions in Japan, newspapers, magazines, and books underwent a process of Westernization after the Meiji Restoration. Following the practice in Europe and the United States at that time, the Japanese press and newspapers formed their own unique sphere from the beginning. The rest of the printed media, such as books and magazines, formed a separate world of publishing. This division has exercised a great influence on the formation of the character of Japanese journalism.

Before World War II, FREEDOM OF THE PRESS was greatly restricted by the Publications Law, the Newspaper Law, the Peace Preservation Law, and other repressive laws and regulations. A large number of publishers, editors, scholars, and writers were punished and imprisoned under these laws. After World War II, however, the situation rapidly improved. Article 21 of the 1947 constitution guarantees freedom of speech and the press, prohibits censorship, and abolishes all the laws and regulations that had controlled the press.

Contemporary book publishing. In 1990 Japan published 38,680 new book titles. As of 1989 Japan ranked second in the world behind the United States in the consumption of printing and writing paper.

Magazine publishing. Until 1955 weeklies had been put out by newspaper companies, but beginning with *Shūkan shinchō* (1956), publishing companies began to issue their own weeklies, and by 1960 they were dominating the field of weekly magazines. With government, scholarly, and corporate publications included, the total number of magazine titles in Japan is estimated to be over 10,000. Magazine sales for 1990 totaled ¥1.26 trillion (US $8.73 billion).

The Publishing Industry— As in the publishing industry throughout the world, the majority of Japanese publishers operate on a small scale. According to the 1990 edition of *The Almanac of Publishing*, the total number of publishers in Japan was 4,282, of which publishers with capital of less than ¥5 million (US $38,910)—or whose capital was not known—numbered 2,763 (64.5%) and those with 10 employees or fewer (or with unknown numbers) totaled 2,929 (68.4%). According to the same source, more than half

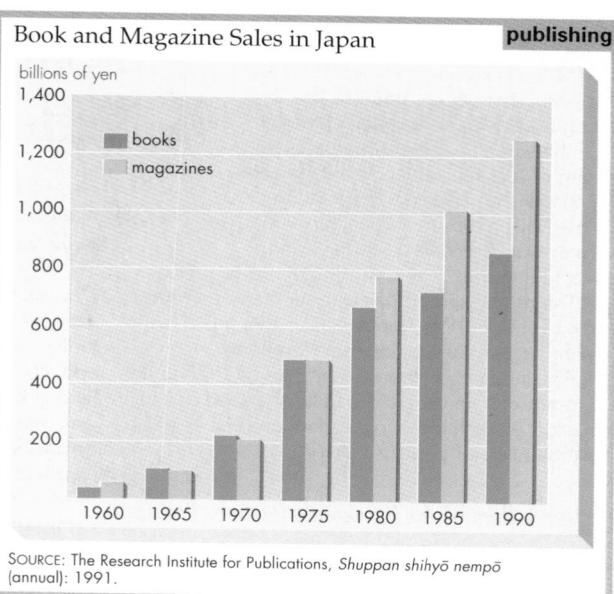

Book and Magazine Sales in Japan

billions of yen

legend: books / magazines

years: 1960 1965 1970 1975 1980 1985 1990

SOURCE: The Research Institute for Publications, *Shuppan shihyō nempō* (annual): 1991.

of the new titles in Japan were published by 120 publishers. In other words, less than 3 percent of all publishers accounted for more than half of all publishing activities. This oligopolistic situation was even more clearly reflected in the respective share of sales.

Top-ranking publishers have been moving into nonprint media such as radio, television, and motion pictures, and newspaper and broadcasting companies have also been active in publishing activities.

Distribution system. The framework of the distribution system for publications in Japan had already been formed by the beginning of the 20th century. The basic route of this distribution was from publisher to agent to bookstore. The basis of the sales system was fixed-price sales and consignment sales. These channels were called the regular route, by which the majority of publications have been traded.

As of 1990 about 12,556 bookstores belonged to the Association of Booksellers; when nonmember stores are added, the total number exceeds 20,000. A distribution agent connects a bookstore with a publisher and handles the distribution and return of books. Books and magazines traded by this route are considered to account for 50 percent of the total; about 70 percent are handled by the two major agencies, Tōkyō Shuppan Hambai (abbreviated Tōhan) and Nippon Shuppan Hambai (abbreviated Nippan). Distribution agencies are said to be the most centralized aspect of the Japanese publishing industry.

Buying and selling. The buying and selling of published material by the so-called regular route has been characterized since the 1920s by strict observance of fixed retail prices and consignment sales. An antitrust law prohibits producers from compelling agents or retailers to sell at fixed prices. From its inception, however, this law exempted so-called cultural items and daily necessities and in 1953 extended exemptions to include published material as well. As a result, published materials in Japan have been sold according to price maintenance agreements. The Japanese Fair Trade Commission has begun reviewing the price maintenance system because of growing consumer pressure.

Postwar Reforms— In prewar Japanese publishing circles, a clear line was drawn between publications for intellectuals and those for the masses. Since the end of the

Continued on page 1240

Japanese Best Sellers: A Reflection of the Times

The tastes of Japan's reading public have kept pace with the nation's transition from postwar confusion through economic boom into the information age.

After World War II, the history of the Japanese best seller can be divided into three phases. The first began in 1945, in the chaotic aftermath of the war, and lasted until the beginning of Japan's high economic growth period in the mid-1960s. For most Japanese, this upturn in the country's fortunes was dramatized by Tōkyō's hosting role in the 1964 Olympics.

During the second phase, from the mid-1960s to the oil crisis of 1973, popular culture flourished along with the burgeoning Japanese economy.

The third phase, from the oil crisis of 1973 to the present, can be characterized by the flood of information unleashed by computers and the resulting pluralization of popular culture.

Best Sellers of the Immediate Postwar Period

On 15 September 1945, just one month after Japan's surrender, the first postwar best seller was published. *Nichibei kaiwa techō* (Anglo-Japanese Conversation Manual) sold an unprecedented 3.6 million copies. A mere 32-page booklet, 9×13 centimeters (3.5×5.0 in) and printed on rough straw paper, the manual contained 80 practice dialogues with a vocabulary of only 170 words. Nonetheless, in the days of continuing wartime shortages, the manual was enthusiastically received.

Its publisher was Ogawa Kikumatsu, founder of Seibundō Shinkōsha Publishing Co, Ltd. Ogawa was in Chiba when he heard the emperor's broadcast of 15 August 1945 announcing Japan's surrender. On the train ride back to Tōkyō, the idea suddenly came to Ogawa that an English-Japanese conversation manual would be a success. Working around the clock, he proceeded to put the book, which was written by Itakura Katsumasa, on the market. Just as Ogawa had anticipated, the manual was quickly consumed by a public seeking to cooperate with the Allied Occupation forces.

The next major best seller was *Sempū nijūnen* (The Twenty-Year Upheaval). Part one was rushed to publication in December 1945; part two followed in the spring. Together they sold about 800,000 copies.

Sempū nijūnen was the first book to reveal the truth about World War II to the Japanese people, who had been kept in the dark by the military's propaganda and suppression of information. It provoked a wave of publications debunking the war and Japan's role in it. Beginning with the assassination of the Chinese warlord Zhang Zuolin by the Japanese military in 1928, the book traced the course of the "15-year war" that led through Japan's attacks on China in 1937, developed into the wider Pacific conflict, and ended ultimately with the signing of the surrender document on board the USS *Missouri*. The book was based on a series of formerly top-secret documents. Researched by a team of journalists from the newspaper *Mainichi shimbun*, under the direction of coordinating editor Mori Shōzō, the material was written up as a history of the period. Although it reflected the new mood of liberation from wartime censorship, the book was itself subject to censorship by the Occupation authorities: references to President Harry S. Truman's atomic bomb tests had to be cut from the revised edition.

Four or five years after the end of the war, when Japanese society had become more settled, best sellers began to appear that contained serious reflections on the war and the period that produced it.

One such book, which continues to sell well even today, was *Kike wadatsumi no koe* (1949; tr *Hearken to the Ocean's Voice!*, 1968), a collection of letters and other writings of students from prestigious Japanese colleges and universities who had died in the war. Determined that a similar tragedy never happen again, some surviving students banded together and launched a nationwide appeal to the families of those who had been killed. They asked for letters and diaries written by the fallen soldiers. Of the 319 such writings that were received from bereaved families, 75 were chosen to be included in the book.

The letters and diaries are strikingly poignant, full of the inner pain and distress caused by receiving a death sentence—for to serve in the armed forces of Imperial Japan meant to die. None of the letters and diaries show any bitterness toward the enemy or any belief in the justice of Japan's cause. Rather, they reveal only too vividly the anguished states of mind of the young students who desperately sought a meaning for their certain deaths. The heartrending search for truth evoked a tremendous wave of public sentiment, and every subsequent collection of the students' writings also became a best seller.

The spiritual or moral quest has been a consistent theme in modern Japanese literature. Popular novelist Yoshikawa Eiji enjoyed great success with two works of historical fiction. His *Miyamoto Musashi* was originally published as a newspaper serial from 1935 to 1939. When the serialization was completed, it was published in book form and became a big best seller. Ten years later, after World War II, the book was re-released and became a best seller again. To date the novel has sold nearly 10 million copies. *Shinran* (1935–36) had a similar history and enjoyed best-seller status upon its original publication and its re-release in 1948. The book sold well over a million copies. Both novels featured heroes struggling after the truth by following, respectively, "the Way of the sword" and "the Way of the Buddha." It was Yoshikawa's belief that one could attain spiritual fulfillment only by fighting off selfish desires.

Toward the end of the first phase of the postwar period, another theme—a different kind of search for the truth—began to emerge. Representative of the new trend was *Ningen no jōken* (1956–58, The Human Condition), a novel by Gomikawa Jumpei. *Ningen no jōken* portrayed a man's struggle to retain his humanity amid the hell that was Manchuria after the Soviet entry into World War II. But what the public found most appealing was the realistic depiction of the 15-year war—the collusion of political and business circles and the corruption of the military. The six-volume novel sold 2.4 million copies and turned its previously unknown author into a literary star.

Another successful author of this new genre of socially conscious writing was Matsumoto Seichō, whose books were imbued with a sense of social injustice and sympathy for the victims of the Japanese meritocracy. Matsumoto's novels depicted the structures of power and self-interest that those in authority kept hidden from the eyes of ordinary people. Read-

ers began to show an appetite for novels that provided insight into such matters.

Matsumoto's best-selling mystery novels *Ten to sen* (1957–58; tr *Points and Lines*, 1970) and *Me no kabe* (1957, Beyond the Wall) also portrayed the corruption of the political and business worlds and sparked off a boom in mysteries with social and political themes.

In the early 1960s, as anticipation mounted over the Tōkyō Olympics, a new blockbuster was born. *Eigo ni tsuyoku naru hon* (1961, Strength in English) by Iwata Kazuo sold more than a million copies in its first month. Written in an amusing style, the book capitalized on the public's renewed interest in learning English. The publisher was Kanki Haruo, president of the Kōbunsha Publishing Co, Ltd, who was widely known as "the best-seller king." It was Kanki who conceived of Kappa Books, a line of paperback pocket editions that included *Eigo ni tsuyoku naru hon* and was very popular during the high-growth period.

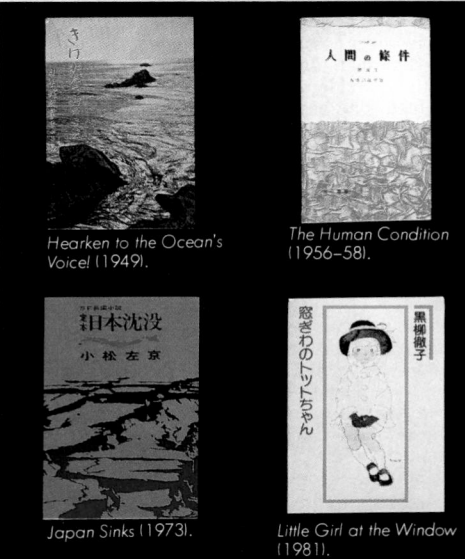

Hearken to the Ocean's Voice! (1949).

The Human Condition (1956–58).

Japan Sinks (1973).

Little Girl at the Window (1981).

Best Sellers of the Economic Boom

A book that heralded the arrival of the economic growth phase was *Maikā* (1961, My Car) by the technology analyst Hoshino Yoshirō. At a time when owning high-quality consumer goods was seen as a sign of status, Hoshino's book was instrumental in turning the automobile into the ultimate status symbol.

Maikā was a "how-to" book that explained all aspects of automobile mechanics, maintenance, and running costs, as well as providing purchasing information (on Japanese-made cars). It was the first Japanese book to be written entirely from the consumer's viewpoint. The author test-drove each vehicle himself and subjected them all to intensive analysis and merciless criticism. Readers flocked to buy *Maikā*, and it became a huge best seller. Its Japanized-English title quickly established itself as a household name for the family automobile. In the wake of the book's success, a market for other consumer-oriented titles soon developed.

Books aimed at businessmen also became popular at this time. *Abunai kaisha* (1963, Companies in Danger) by Urabe Kuniyoshi analyzed the finances of a number of firms and indicated several that were in danger of bankruptcy. *Higeki no keieisha* (1964, Managers of Tragedy), by the economic analyst Miki

Yōnosuke, focused on the human aspects of management. Miki was thought to have a finger on the pulse of the business community. Both books were widely read by businessmen who wished to know what managers and corporate leaders were thinking and who were eager for information about other firms.

Coinciding with Japan's entrance into a period of dynamic economic growth was the emergence of a new best-selling genre—sports books that emphasized a "fighting spirit." Typical of the genre were *Ore ni tsuite koi!* (1963, Follow Me!) and *Naseba naru* (1964, If There's a Will, There's a Way). The author of these books, Daimatsu Hirofumi, had coached the Japanese women's volleyball team to victory in the Tōkyō Olympics.

Another best-selling genre of the economic expansion era was the period novel. Especially popular among businessmen and managers, period novels were read as much for their historical content as for their entertainment value. Yamaoka Sōhachi's 26-volume *Tokugawa Ieyasu* (1950–67; a best seller from 1962 to 1965) sold 15 million copies. It was the

My Car (1961).

Clouds over the Hills (1969–72).

Norwegian Wood (1987).

Tsugumi (1988–89).

epic life story of the man who founded the Tokugawa shogunate at the beginning of the 17th century, completed the transformation of Japan into a feudal society, and laid the foundations for a 250-year peace. The novel reflected the mood of recovery, peace, and prosperity in Japan in the 1960s and early 1970s.

A peculiarly Japanese phenomenon was the way many businessmen saw parallels between their own lives and those of the *samurai* characters in historical sagas. Businessmen viewed their companies as the modern equivalent of feudal domains, with themselves in the role of samurai serving their lords. The irony is that most office workers' ancestors were not samurai but peasants. After all, during the Tokugawa shogunate more than 90 percent of the population had been peasants.

The historical novels read by businessmen always featured heroes and characters who belonged to an organization—something that had not been true of historical novels up to that point. By the late 1960s the concept of groupthink had become firmly established in Japanese corporations and labor relations. As Japan's economic strength grew to equal that of other advanced nations, many Japanese began to feel that the collective organizational path represented the only way forward.

Shiba Ryōtarō's best-selling novel *Saka no ue no kumo* (1969–72, Clouds over the Hills) depicted another organization—the Japanese military, during the Sino-Japanese War of 1894–95 and the Russo-Japanese War of 1904–05. The novel focused on the behavior and lifestyles of staff officers rather than those at the top of the military hierarchy. Many Japanese had come to believe that responsibility for the maintenance and collective dynamic of an organization lay more with the staff than the higher-ups.

As its economic strength grew, Japan's confidence revived. A renewed appreciation of Japanese culture and values produced a fresh crop of best sellers. Some concentrated on traditional themes, while others compared the culture of Japan with the cultures of other nations, reflecting Japan's desire to understand its place in the wider world.

Best sellers with traditional themes included *Kankon sōsai nyūmon* (1970, A Guide to Etiquette and Ceremonial Occasions), by Shiotsuki Yaeko, and *Onna no ko no shitsukekata* (1972, The Upbringing of Young Girls), by Hamao Minoru, former chamberlain to the crown prince.

The most celebrated of the comparative culture books was *Nihonjin to yudayajin* (1970; tr *The Japanese and the Jews*, 1972), by "Isaiah Ben-Dasan," a pseudonym used by Yamamoto Shichihei. The mystery surrounding the identity of the book's author excited the media for some time, as did Yamamoto's acerbic characterization of the Japanese.

Best Sellers of the Information Age

The oil crisis of 1973 brought a halt to the period of unbridled economic growth, but many people had already begun to feel that if Japan were to continue its economic acceleration indefinitely, it would wind up in ruins.

This anxiety was reflected in a number of popular novels. For example, *Nihon chimbotsu* (1973; tr *Japan Sinks*, 1976), by the science-fiction writer Komatsu Sakyō, describes efforts to control an enormous crisis—a massive fissure that opened up under the volcanic Japanese archipelago threatening to sink the entire country.

The novel *Kōkotsu no hito* (1972; tr *The Twilight Years*, 1984), by a prominent woman writer, Ariyoshi Sawako, describes with graphic realism the story of an elderly man suffering from Alzheimer's disease. *Fukugō osen* (1974–75, Compound Pollution), also by Ariyoshi, is built around the theme of industrial pollution. The depiction of social problems and possible solutions is a feature of this type of novel—one which has proved attractive to the public.

Another popular woman writer of this period is Yamazaki Toyoko. Yamazaki is the author of *Fumō chitai* (1973–78; tr *The Barren Zone*, 1985), the story of a trading company employee involved in petroleum development in Iran, and *Daichi no ko* (1988–90, Children of the Continent), which portrays the plight of Japanese children left behind in China after World War II.

Throughout the 1980s and into the 1990s, the media-dominated culture gave rise to the phenomenon of "telly sellers"—best sellers written by media personalities. The popularity of "telly sellers" has been attributed in large part to the status accorded television stars, who are looked up to as prototypes of successful individuals.

Two "telly sellers" of the previous decade were *Aoi toki* (1980, Green Days), by the singer and actress Yamaguchi Momoe, and *Madogiwa no Totto chan* (1981; tr *Little Girl at the Window*, 1982), by television

hostess Kuroyanagi Tetsuko. Both Yamaguchi, whose family was poor, and Kuroyanagi, whose parents held unorthodox views on education, became successful without the benefit of a standard high school education. *Madogiwa no Totto chan*, Kuroyanagi's story of the free and informal education she received as a child, won great popular acclaim and sold more than 7 million copies.

Television-related memoirs remained popular into the 1990s, sometimes becoming number-one best sellers. Some examples include *Aisareru riyū* (1990, The Reason to Be Loved), by actress Nitani Yurie, and *Mukatsukuze!* (1991, I'm Sick of It!) by Muroi Shigeru. The success of these authors stemmed from their ability to capture the spirit of the times.

Books on astrology and health have also found favor in recent years. Publishers have tried to get as much mileage as possible out of these categories, which tend to sell well whenever there is widespread anxiety about the future. Astrological guides have centered mainly on ancient Chinese methods such as *shichū suimei* and *sammei senseigaku*, both based on one's birth date, and *tenchūsatsu*, based on cycles of good and ill fortune. Books about the prophecies of the 16th-century French seer Nostradamus have also sold well. Among the health-related titles, many have been on folk remedies such as *kōcha kinoko* (mushroom tea) and garlic diets.

A number of books by foreign futurologists and international relations specialists have also been best sellers in Japan as well as in their own countries. Examples include Alvin Toffler's *The Third Wave* (1980; tr *Daisan no nami*, 1981); *The Age of Uncertainty* (1977; tr *Fukakujitsusei no jidai*, 1978), by John Kenneth Galbraith; and *Megatrends* (1982; tr *Megatorendo*, 1983), by John Naisbitt.

Also conspicuous in recent years are best sellers reflecting international tensions, such as *"No" to ieru Nihon* (1989; tr *The Japan That Can Say No*, 1991) by Ishihara Shintarō and Morita Akio. The thesis of the book was that Japan should be more forthright in expressing its views and standing up for its global interests, particularly as concerns the United States. An unauthorized English translation caused a stir in US political circles. The 1991 authorized translation was based on a revised version and was published only under Ishihara's name.

During the 1980s a new generation of writers made a tremendous splash on the Japanese literary scene. Murakami Haruki, a highly acclaimed author and translator, wrote a wry, provocative novel about college students searching for love in an impersonal age. Entitled *Noruuē no mori* (1987; tr *Norwegian Wood*, 1989), the novel sold an impressive 4.4 million copies. A collection of *tanka* poems by a 26-year-old schoolteacher, Tawara Machi, was also a runaway best seller: *Sarada kinembi* (1987; tr *Salad Anniversary*, 1988) sold 2.6 million copies. And Yoshimoto Banana, a young writer who says she is inspired by Japanese *manga* (comics), topped the best-seller list with *Tsugumi* (1988–89), a coming-of-age story about a beautiful, self-centered young woman. The novel sold 1.7 million copies. The thematic thread that runs through all of these works is the isolation, disaffection, and longings experienced by contemporary Japanese youth.

As the 20th century draws to a close and Japan's literary mantle passes to the next generation, it will be interesting to note the course of Japanese literature and the parallels in social and political history.

Kida Jun'ichirō

war, the movement toward a mass society has been symbolized by television, as well as the numerous weekly magazines created by publishing companies. However, the so-called masses that brought about postwar booms in these areas are no longer distinguished from the intellectual elite in the prewar sense. After 1950 best-seller fiction was neither infraliterature nor subliterature but books of quality intended for the masses. Equality of the sexes, improvement of labor conditions, and an increase and leveling in income (all conditions of postwar democratization) also stimulated the creation of a new class of readers.

What played the decisive role for the postwar publishing boom, however, was the spread of secondary-school and university education. Only 3 percent of all youths attended universities in 1940, while in 1975, 30 percent attended a university or junior college. There may be other causes to explain the phenomenon, however, and the influence of mass media other than publishing cannot be overlooked.

When the conditions for the development of the publishing business in Japan are reviewed, it may be concluded that favorable growth as a whole may be expected for some time to come. But it cannot be denied that the conditions that hitherto supported the publishing business may turn into brakes: the growth of the economy has slowed since the 1970s, the proportion of students wishing to go on to universities has peaked, individual households have been hard pressed economically, and the growth of female readership has declined. Furthermore, the full-scale arrival of the television age and the revival of motion pictures are contributing to a departure from the written media. Yet there are also signs that these visual media are forcing written media forms to undergo a kind of transformation, including the popularization of "cassette books" since 1987 and the fact that one-third of all types of magazines in Japan are comics. This revolution within the publishing industry will in all probability continue for some time.

▶▶*1238–1239*

P'u-i→ Puyi (P'u-i)

punctuation marks　　　句読点

(*kutōten*). The major punctuation marks used in Japanese are the mark 、 (called *ten* or *tōten*), which is similar in form and use to the comma in English, and the small circle 。(called *maru* or *kuten*), which is used like a period; together these are referred to as *kutōten*, a word that is also used to refer to punctuation marks in general. A solid, centered dot ・ (called *nakaten* or *nakaguro*) is used like the comma or slash in English between listed or alternate items. Marks like corner brackets 「 」(called *kagi* or *kagikakko*), which function as quotation marks, are placed in the upper right and lower left corners of a word or words when lines are written vertically from top to bottom in the normal Japanese way. The question mark (*gimonfu*), exclamation point (*kantanfu*), parentheses (*kakko*), dash (*dasshu*), and ellipsis (*tenten*) are used as in English. For emphasis, dots called *wakiten* are placed to the right of individual characters (when written vertically; they are placed above or underneath when characters are written horizontally). Ancient Japanese texts contain no punctuation.

puppet theater　　　人形劇

(*ningyōgeki*). The earliest extant reference to Japanese puppet performances is in the 11th-century *Kairaishi ki* (Account of Kairaishi [a type of puppeteer]) by ŌE NO MASAFUSA (1041–1111), which describes wandering communities whose men gave puppet performances. Around 1560, centered on the shrine at Nishinomiya near Ōsaka, a group of puppeteers known as *ebisukaki* or *ebisumawashi* emerged. Sometime after 1600 they collaborated with chanters and players of SHAMISEN, a popular three-stringed instrument recently imported from Okinawa, to produce the first three-part (voice, *shamisen*, and puppet) performance. This combination of dramatic elements provided the basis from which BUNRAKU developed. Genre paintings of the 17th century show street performers who used portable stages with puppets worked from below.

It was in the mid-17th century that the puppet drama known as *ningyō jōruri*, and later as bunraku, began to take form, and by the end of the century the *jōruri* puppet had come into use; it was held above the manipulator's head with both hands and worked from below behind a curtain, the top of which formed the imaginary floor on which the puppets maneuvered. Later developments in the standard puppets included complicated devices, such as legs for male dolls, rolling eyes, and grasping hands. The entry for the manipulator's hand was shifted to an aperture in the doll's back. By 1734, three-man manipulation was practiced, and by 1750 the dolls had reached more or less their present form, in which principal male dolls might have faces with movable features, jointed limbs, and a wide range of hand and even finger movements. Costumes fit the doll's role and may be richly ornate. Special heads are used for certain effects, such as a woman turned into a fox, and to simulate wounds. Simple dolls operated by one man are used for supporting roles.

Local groups have maintained or developed puppetry on their own; however, most dolls are derivatives of bunraku puppets. Centers of regional puppet performance today are the islands of Sado and Awaji, the Chichibu area north of Tōkyō, and the district of Kitabaru in Ōita Prefecture. Another tradition still alive is that of marionettes, the use of which dates back to the early 17th century.

Pure Land Buddhism　　　浄土教

(*Jōdokyō*). Form of Buddhism that seeks rebirth for its believers into the Buddha AMIDA's Western Paradise, known as the Pure Land. Introduced into Japan from China in the 6th century, it became popular among the Japanese aristocracy in the middle of the Heian period (794–1185). From the 7th century Pure Land faith flourished in China, where it retained its form as an amorphous folk faith or subordinate monastic cult. In Japan there was a great surge of popular Pure Land faith from the 12th century, and under HŌNEN (1133–1212) and his disciples Pure Land Buddhism established its independence from the TENDAI SECT of Buddhism.

A new conception of Buddhahood—in which there were a multitude of "Buddhaworlds," each the realm of a Buddha—developed in early Mahāyāna Buddhism. It was believed that by means of their wisdom, compassion, and skill these Buddhas could bring sentient beings to rebirth in their lands and from there guide them to enlightenment and Buddhahood. Amida became the most popular of the Buddhas possessing a purified Buddha-land (J: Jōdo).

Pure Land scriptures emphasize that NEMBUTSU, the recitation of the Buddha Amida's name, is the way to express one's reliance on Amida, and those who call upon Amida with great sincerity and devotion will be welcomed into the Pure Land. Pure Land Buddhism also teaches that Amida especially wishes to save those who are sinful, destitute, and have no other means of salvation, and that Pure Land Buddhism is therefore a genuine means of universal salvation. Contemporary denominations include the JŌDO SECT, the JŌDO SHIN SECT, the JI SECT, and the YŪZŪ NEMBUTSU SECT.

purification──→misogi

Putiatin, Evfimii Vasil'evich
プチャーチン, E. V.

(1803–83). Russian naval officer who competed with American Commodore Matthew C. PERRY in the opening of Japan (see RUSSIA AND JAPAN). Vice Admiral Putiatin was appointed commander of the Russian Japan Expedition of 1852–55 and envoy to Japan.

Arriving at Nagasaki on 21 August 1853, Putiatin negotiated the Russo-Japanese Treaty of Amity (Nichiro Washin Jōyaku), concluded on 7 February 1855. It provided for recognition of the Kuril Islands south of Iturup (J: Etorofu) as Japanese and the Kuril Islands north of Urup (J: Uruppu) as Russian; Sakhalin (J: Karafuto) remained in common possession. The treaty opened Shimoda, Hakodate, and Nagasaki to Russian vessels for repairs and supplies.

Putiatin and his countrymen were later shipwrecked in the wake of an earthquake that leveled Shimoda. They were moved to Heda, where they built a Western-style schooner. Putiatin and 40 men left Japan on this vessel on 8 May 1855 and reached Russia two weeks later. He returned to conclude the first Russo-Japanese Treaty of Friendship and Commerce at Edo (now Tōkyō) on 19 August 1858 (see ANSEI COMMERCIAL TREATIES). In 1861 Putiatin was appointed minister of education and soon thereafter councillor of state.

Puyi (P'u-i)　　　溥儀

(1906–67; J: Fugi). The last Manchu emperor in China, reigning as the Xuantong (Hsüant'ung) emperor; later the figurehead of the Japanese puppet state of MANCHUKUO in Manchuria. Also known as Henry Pu-yi. An infant when he succeeded to the throne in 1908, Puyi was only six when he was forced to abdicate in February 1912, bringing an end to the Qing (Ch'ing) dynasty (1644–1912) in China.

After the MANCHURIAN INCIDENT of September 1931, DOIHARA KENJI of Japan's GUANDONG (KWANTUNG) ARMY went to Tianjin (Tientsin) to negotiate Puyi's participation in the creation of a Japanese-sponsored state in Manchuria. On 9 March 1932 Puyi was formally installed as chief executive of Manchukuo, and on 15 September 1932 the Tōkyō government recognized the new state.

Surrounded by Japanese advisers, Puyi's position as head of state was purely ceremonial. In August 1945, after Japan's defeat, Puyi was arrested by Soviet troops. In August 1950 Puyi was sent to China, where he remained in prison until 4 December 1959. After his release he held minor posts in Beijing (Peking).

Q

QC circles   QC運動

(quality control circles; J: *kyūshī undō*). Small, in-plant discussion groups held by workers to examine and assess company products and their own methods of working in order to improve product quality and customer service. The concept of QC circles was introduced into Japan by W. Edwards Deming (b 1900), an American, in 1950 and was first applied in the steel industry. At first QC circles were established in production departments in order to meet standards of quality for export goods set by the Allied OCCUPATION, but from 1962 they became more widespread and were aimed at increasing productivity and reducing industrial accidents. Large numbers of workers became involved, and the success of the idea led to its adoption in all industries. In Japan today the QC circle concept is being developed further by the Japan Union of Scientists and Engineers to include managerial and clerical staff in an effort to achieve total quality control (TQC).

Qingdao (Tsingtao)   青島

(Chintao). Port and summer resort on Jiaozhou (Kiaochow) Bay in Shandong (Shantung) Province, China. It is also an industrial city built up by Germany and Japan in the early 20th century. Qingdao was forcibly leased by Germany as a naval base for 99 years in 1898. At the outbreak of World War I, Japan took Qingdao and other German holdings in Shandong and succeeded in 1919 in claiming former German rights through the provisions of the Treaty of Versailles. This decision touched off massive anti-Japanese student demonstrations in China, especially in May 1919 (see MAY FOURTH MOVEMENT). As a result, Chinese delegates in Paris refused to sign the peace treaty. Subsequently, bilateral negotiations between China and Japan in 1921–22, at the time of the WASHINGTON CONFERENCE, reached a solution to the SHANDONG (SHANTUNG) QUESTION. Even after the restoration of Qingdao to Chinese administration, however, Japanese economic and cultural influence remained strong. Japan reoccupied the city during the SINO-JAPANESE WAR OF 1937–1945. Today, Qingdao remains a major port and industrial center.

Q. P. Corporation   キユーピー[株]

(Kyū Pī). Manufacturer and distributor of food products including mayonnaise and salad dressings, canned foods, and egg products. Incorporated in 1919. Sales for the fiscal year ending November 1990 totaled ¥188.9 billion (US $1.5 billion), and the company was capitalized at ¥23.7 billion (US $183.6 million). Headquarters are in Tōkyō.

quality control   品質管理

(*hinshitsu kanri*). Activities undertaken as part of a manufacturing process, such as design analysis and the statistical monitoring of production defects, with the goal of eliminating the production of defective goods.

Quality control methods were introduced into Japan during the Allied OCCUPATION. Following the recommendations of US experts, a quality control seminar was held in 1948 under the cosponsorship of the Telecommunications Ministry (Denki Tsūshin Shō) and the telecommunications industry association. The seminar had a large impact on Japanese industry. Organizations such as the Japan Union of Scientists and Engineers (JUSE) worked to spread the practices throughout the country. In 1950 W. Edwards Deming (b 1900), an expert on statistical quality control in the United States, was invited to Japan to speak at a JUSE seminar. The following year the Deming Prize was established, to be awarded annually to the enterprise demonstrating the most effective use of quality control techniques.

In 1949 the Industrial Standards Law (Kōgyō Hyōjunka Hō) was passed, and only products meeting established quality standards were allowed to display the JIS (Japanese Industrial Standard) mark. The adoption of some form of quality control was made a precondition for such authorization, and it resulted in the rapid spread of the practice.

The goal of quality control is to produce goods without defects, and many Japanese manufacturers have attained standards of production at which defect rates are expressed in parts per million rather than in percentages. Since the solution of quality problems involves every aspect of the production system, participation by all members of the enterprise is important. In Japan, quality control circles (see QC CIRCLES), small work groups at various levels of the enterprise, have been utilized for this function. By some counts, more than 321,000 registered circles, with a total membership of over 2.5 million, existed at the end of 1990.

Quezon, Manuel Luis   ケソン, M. L.

(1878–1944). Philippine national leader during the period of dominion by the United States (1898–1945). Born in Baler, Tayabas, he studied law at the University of Santo Tomás but left to fight with Emilio AGUINALDO's Philippine Revolutionary Army from 1899 to 1901. After serving in Washington, DC, as resident commissioner to the United States (1909–16), Quezon was elected president of the Philippines senate upon its founding in 1916 and presided over that body until 1935, when he was elected the first president of the Philippines, a post he held until his death. In 1937 he negotiated with the Japanese government for recognition of the Philippines as a neutral territory. He also spoke out against the opposition of Filipinos to acquisition and development of land by the Japanese community on Mindanao. Shortly after the Japanese attack on the islands in December 1941, Quezon retreated to Corregidor and then to the United States, where he presided over a government-in-exile. See also PHILIPPINES AND JAPAN.

quince, dwarf Japanese   草木瓜

(*kusaboke*). *Chaenomeles japonica.* Deciduous shrub of the rose family (Rosaceae) that grows wild in hilly regions of Honshū and Kyūshū but also is raised as an ornamental. It is the only indigenous Japanese species of its genus. It grows to a height of 30–60 centimeters (1–2 ft). The stems have spines, and the leaves are obovate with serrated edges. In early spring before leaves have sprouted, it opens scarlet five-petaled flowers about 2.5 centimeters (1 in) across. The yellow, sour fruits may be pickled and eaten or used as a diuretic.

The species that is commonly known as *boke* in Japan (Japanese quince; *C. speciosa*) is native to China. It was imported to Japan in early times and includes varieties that bear pink, crimson, or white flowers.

dwarf Japanese quince A deciduous shrub indigenous to Japan. Growing in sunny mountain locales, it bears scarlet, five-petaled flowers in early spring.

rabbits 兎

(*usagi*). In Japanese, *usagi* is the general name for animals of the order Lagomorpha. The *nakiusagi* (pika; *Ochotona hyperborea*) is found in the mountainous districts of Hokkaidō; the *yukiusagi* (snow hare; *Lepus timidus*) in Hokkaidō; the *nousagi* (*L. brachyurus*) in Honshū, Shikoku, and Kyūshū; and the Amami *no kurousagi* (*Pentalagus furnessi*) on the islands of Amami Ōshima and Tokunoshima. The species most commonly seen are the *yukiusagi* and *nousagi*. The *yukiusagi* has a head-and-body length of 55 centimeters (22 in) and a tail length of 6 centimeters (2 in). The *nousagi* is slightly smaller. In snowy areas the *nousagi* turns white in winter. The Amami *no kurousagi* is a rabbit of a primitive type; it has a blackish brown body and lives in forests of broadleaf *shii* (genus *Shiia*) evergreen trees.

The rabbit has traditionally been regarded as a cunning animal and is a familiar trickster figure in folktales. A traditional belief holds that a rabbit pounding rice can be seen in the full moon.

raden → mother-of-pearl inlay

radio ラジオ放送

(*rajio hōsō*). As of April 1991 Japan had 84 radio stations, most of which broadcast special-interest programs aimed at specific listening audiences. These programs include news, music, traffic reports, domestic variety programs for women, talk shows for young people, and live sports broadcasts.

Japan's first AM broadcasts began on NHK radio in 1925. The first commercial AM radio stations started in Nagoya and Ōsaka in 1951, and by the mid-1950s commercial radio stations were broadcasting throughout the country. Radio soon became Japan's most popular source of family entertainment with its broadcasts of dramatic presentations, comedy and variety programs, live sporting events, and educational programs.

With the rapid expansion of television in the late 1950s, radio stations were confronted with a decline in listener interest. In order to recapture their audience, radio stations developed live general-interest programs and call-in programs that took advantage of radio's characteristic immediacy, mobility, and coverage of fast-breaking events. By the late 1960s, radio made a strong comeback with the development of "audience segmentation." Programs began to be designed for specific listening audiences as a response to prevailing trends away from family or group listening and toward more personal enjoyment; examples of this include late-night programs for young people. This laid the foundation for the radio programming format that continues to be used today.

FM radio stations began broadcasting in 1969 with programming focused mainly on youth-oriented music programs that could take advantage of the superior sound quality and stereo broadcast capability of the new format. At the beginning of the 1990s, radio broadcasters were contemplating increasing the number of FM stations and employing digital pulse-code-modulation (PCM) satellite broadcasting and multiplex broadcasting. See also BROADCASTS, LATE-NIGHT; BROADCASTING, COMMERCIAL.

radioactive waste 放射性廃棄物

(*hōshasei haikibutsu*). Most of Japan's radioactive waste consists of low-level waste products resulting from the operation of nuclear reactors and from the use of radioactive isotopes. Gaseous radioactive waste and low-level liquid radioactive waste from nuclear power stations are released into the air or the ocean after being processed to a level of radioactivity that is low enough to meet the standards required by Japanese law. Other radioactive waste is concentrated and solidified. Solid waste such as filters and waste paper used in cleaning is reduced in volume by incineration, placed in drums, encased in asphalt or concrete, and then stored at nuclear power facilities. As of the end of March 1988, the volume of Japan's stored radioactive waste was equivalent to 710,000 drums with a capacity of 2,001 liters (528.7 gal) each.

Both land and ocean sites have been considered for the ultimate disposal of low-level solid waste. Construction of a facility for disposal of low-level radioactive waste was completed in 1992 by Japan Nuclear Fuels, Ltd, in the village of Rokkasho in Aomori Prefecture. The storage facility is composed of 40 concrete pits constructed on the bedrock 10 meters (32.8 ft) beneath the ground. Five thousand drums of waste material will be placed in each pit and then covered with earth.

Ocean disposal would take place in stages according to a plan that includes initial environmental assessment, test disposal, safety evaluation of test results, and finally full-scale disposal. Japan must conduct ocean disposal under international supervision and in accordance with international agreements to which it is a signatory, including the OECD/NEA (Organization for Economic Cooperation and Development/Nuclear Energy Agency) agreements pertaining to the ocean disposal of radioactive waste material. Approval must also be obtained from Japan's domestic fisheries industry and other nations of the Pacific region.

High-level radioactive waste from reprocessing plants in Japan, which amounted to roughly 321 cubic meters (11,334.5 cu ft) as of the end of March 1988, is stored under strictly controlled conditions. Although the volume of this waste is small, it is highly radioactive and possesses a long half-life. For this reason the waste liquid first is incorporated into glass and hardened into a more stable form. It then is stored in 100-liter (26.4-gal) stainless-steel containers and "cooled" for between 30 and 50 years. Eventually the containers of waste will be buried several hundred meters beneath the earth's surface.

radio drama ラジオドラマ

(*rajio dorama*). Drama was first heard on radio in Japan when—a few weeks after stations in Tōkyō, Ōsaka, and Nagoya began to broadcast in early 1925—KABUKI, SHIMPA, and SHINKOKUGEKI actors came to the studios to perform short excerpts from their respective repertoires. Within a year, remote pickups

Daikon hung to dry in the sun, the first step in preparing *takuan-zuke,* probably the most popular type of pickled radish.

radishes

Miyashige *daikon,* a variety used grated or in soups.

Moriguchi *daikon,* more than a meter in length, are often pickled with *sake* lees.

Huge Sakurajima *daikon*—which can weigh more than 15 kg—are grown in the ashy soil of the volcanic island Sakurajima, across the bay from the city of Kagoshima, Kyūshū.

Miura *daikon* are named for the region where they are cultivated, the Miura Peninsula in Kanagawa Prefecture.

of regular performances directly from theaters became a source of ready-made dramatic programming. Today, both radio and television continue to carry direct broadcasts of theatrical performances.

In August 1925 the Tōkyō station produced the first drama especially written for radio, and, beginning in 1927, the newly organized national public monopoly Nippon Hōsō Kyōkai (NHK; Japan Broadcasting Corporation) commissioned original radio dramas from KIKUCHI KAN, SATOMI TON, KISHIDA KUNIO, and other major playwrights. For several years after 1947, NHK produced the acclaimed experimental *Rajio shōgekijō* (Radio Little Theater) with scripts from leading authors such as IIZAWA TADASU and KIKUTA KAZUO. After NHK lost its monopoly status in 1951, new commercial radio stations emerged as competitive producers of drama and broadened the scope of drama programs during radio's golden age.

Most radio dramas were presented complete in a single broadcast until 1946, when the daily or weekly series format became dominant. Soon the "home drama" serial, with its focus on everyday family life, emerged as the primary genre.

Until the 1950s, broadcasts of NANIWA-BUSHI (*rōkyoku*), RAKUGO, and KŌDAN performers outnumbered standard radio drama programs. These traditional aural narrative arts also influenced the development of distinctive radio storytelling forms during the 1930s, such as the *rajio monogatari* (radio story) and *rajio shōsetsu* (radio novel). In the former, a solo performer narrated and acted out a story written especially for radio. The latter, a mixture of *rajio monogatari* and dramatic forms, was performed by two or more actors.

After 1960 radio drama declined with the rise of television. Today it occupies only a minor place in schedules dominated by music and talk shows (see also TELEVISION DRAMA).

Radio Japan   ラジオ・ジャパン

(Rajio Japan). Japan's only internationally broadcast multilingual shortwave radio service, produced by Nihon Hōsō Kyōkai (NHK; Japan Broadcasting Corporation). Radio Japan broadcasts daily 49 hours of programming in 22 languages, including Chinese and Arabic, with its main emphasis on broadcasts in Japanese and English. Programming includes international and domestic news, and introductions to Japanese life, culture, politics, economics, and social trends. Radio Japan also airs commentary and public opinion concerning current international issues.

Radio Tōkyō, the forerunner of Radio Japan, began broadcasting in 1935 and was terminated in 1945 at the end of World War II. Broadcasting resumed in 1952 under the name Radio Japan.

radishes   大根

(*daikon*). The principal radish grown in Japan is *daikon* (*Raphanus sativus* var. *acanthiformis*), a biennial root vegetable that leads all other Japanese vegetable crops in both area under cultivation and quantity of production. Since its introduction in ancient times from China, many new varieties have been developed. The color is usually white, although some have a reddish tinge. Compared with foreign varieties, the Japanese radish is larger in size, weighing on the average 2–3 kilograms (4–7 lb). Smaller Western-style radishes, known as *hatsuka daikon,* are grown in much smaller quantities.

Daikon is produced all the year round, with certain varieties suitable for specific seasons. Among its many uses, pickling is the most important (see PICKLES). It is pickled in rice-bran paste (*nuka*), salt, rice malt (*kōji*), or bean paste (*miso*). When dried and pickled in salt and rice bran it is called TAKUAN-ZUKE. *Daikon* can also be used as an ingredient for MISO SOUP and other dishes or eaten raw, either grated or finely chopped.

Ragusa, Vincenzo   ラグーザ, V.

(1841–1927). Italian sculptor who lived in Japan from 1876 to 1882. Born in Palermo. He launched Western-style sculpture in Japan by introducing European techniques in bronze casting and new methods such as modeling from life, wire armature, and the use of clay and plaster of paris.

In 1876 Ragusa accepted a contract from the Japanese government to teach at the short-lived Technical Fine Arts School (Kōbu Bijutsu Gakkō) in Tōkyō. He made a lasting impression on pioneer Meiji-period (1868–1912) sculptors and teachers such as Ōkuma Ujihiro, Naganuma Moriyoshi, Fujita Bunzō, Sano Shō, Kikuchi Chūtarō, Ogura Sōjirō, and TAKEUCHI KYŪICHI and the potter Terauchi Shin'ichi.

Returning to Italy in 1882, Ragusa sculpted and taught for the rest of his life in Palermo. Examples of his work in Japan are a plaster bust of his wife (the painter Kiyohara Tama; 1861–1939), a bronze bust of the statesman ŌKUBO TOSHIMICHI, and a bronze of the *kabuki* actor Ichikawa Danjūrō IX (see ICHIKAWA DANJŪRŌ) in the role of Sukeroku.

raigōzu   来迎図

More formally, *shōju raigōzu.* Also known as *gōshō mandara* (mandalas of the welcoming) or *gōshō hensō* (illustrations of the welcoming). *Raigōzu* (literally, "welcoming pictures") are pictorial representations of the idea that the Buddha AMIDA (Skt: Amitābha) and bodhisattvas descend to welcome the dying faithful into the Pure Land of the Blessed (see PURE LAND BUDDHISM). They be-

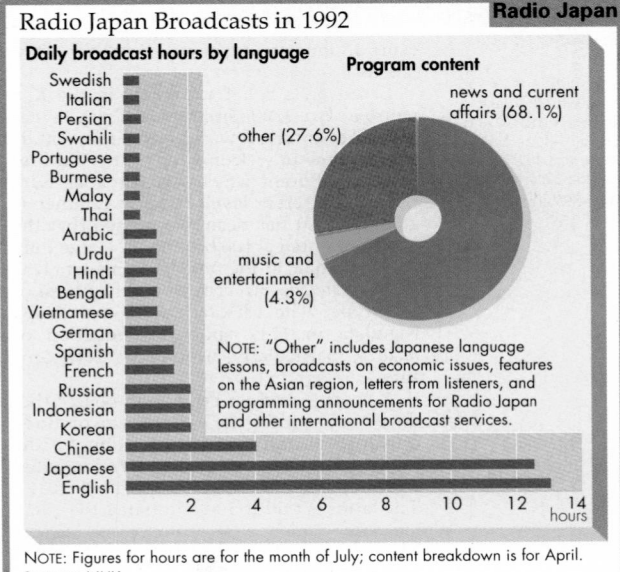

Radio Japan

Radio Japan Broadcasts in 1992

Daily broadcast hours by language

Language	hours
Swedish	
Italian	
Persian	
Swahili	
Portuguese	
Burmese	
Malay	
Thai	
Arabic	
Urdu	
Hindi	
Bengali	
Vietnamese	
German	
Spanish	
French	
Russian	
Indonesian	
Korean	
Chinese	
Japanese	
English	

2   4   6   8   10   12   14 hours

Program content

news and current affairs (68.1%)

other (27.6%)

music and entertainment (4.3%)

NOTE: "Other" includes Japanese language lessons, broadcasts on economic issues, features on the Asian region, letters from listeners, and programming announcements for Radio Japan and other international broadcast services.

NOTE: Figures for hours are for the month of July; content breakdown is for April. SOURCE: NHK.

raigōzu *Descent of Amida and Twenty-Five Bodhisattvas. Late 13th century. Colors on silk. 145 × 155 cm. Chion'in, Kyōto. National Treasure.*

rails Most rails are secretive, living close to the ground in thick vegetation; the flightless Yambaru *kuina* (Okinawan rail) eluded discovery until 1981, making it the only new bird discovered in Japan in the 20th century.

came an important genre of Buddhist art in Japan.

Based on a belief expressed in the *Kan muryōju kyō* (*Amitāyurdhyāna-sūtra*), a canonical scripture, it was thought that Amida would come to welcome (*raigō*) the faithful in nine different ways in accordance with the nine different levels of their commendable deeds. It has been maintained that the *raigōzu* painted at the bottom of a large Pure Land mandala at the temple Taimadera (the *Taima mandara;* 8th century) is the oldest of this type. The restoration of the Taima Mandala in 1217 spurred production of *raigōzu,* particularly around the 14th century.

Raigōzu based on Pure Land beliefs that developed within the TENDAI SECT of Buddhism were introduced from China by the monk ENNIN (794–864) and were promoted and popularized by Genshin (942–1017). The latter is said to have initiated the *gōshō mandara,* which is a prototypical *raigōzu.* Masterpieces of this tradition produced toward the end of the Heian period (794–1185) include those at the Phoenix Hall of BYŌ-

DŌIN, at the temple HOKKEJI in Nara, and at Mt. Kōya (KŌYASAN).

Raigōzu were the principal images in the rite for the dying. Some *raigōzu* depicted Amida and his retinue bending forward as if they were hastening to welcome the dead (*hayaraigō,* literally, "swift welcome"). In others a length of thread links the hand of Amida to that of the dying. Divine figures other than Amida were also depicted in *raigōzu* during the Kamakura period (1185–1333): the bodhisattva MIROKU (Skt: Maitreya), the bodhisattva KANNON with eleven heads, the bodhisattva JIZŌ (Skt: Kṣitigarbha), and the Buddha Śākyamuni.

rails   水鶏

(*kuina*). Migratory marsh birds of the order Grues and the family Rallidae. The most common species in Japan is the *kuina* or water rail (*Rallus aquaticus*). It has a brown body (29 cm [12 in] in length) with black and white stripes across the belly. After breeding in northern Japan it migrates to warmer areas in winter. The species is widely distributed throughout north central Eurasia.

Several other kinds of rail are found in Japan: the *hikuina* (ruddy crake; *Porzana fusca*), the *himekuina* (Baillon's crake; *P. pusilla*), the *shimakuina* (Swinhoe's yellow rail; *P. exquisita*), the *ōkuina* (banded crake; *Rallina eurizonoides*), and the *shiroharakuina* (white-breasted water hen; *Amaurornis phoenicurus*). Since the chirping of the *kuina*—or, more precisely, the *hikuina*—sounds like a light knock on a wooden door, Japanese writers since the Heian period (794–1185) have used the expression *tataku kuina* (tapping rail) to evoke a sense of solitude.

railways   鉄道

(*tetsudō*). Railways in Japan date from 1872, only four years into the country's modern

period, but almost four decades from the time that railways first appeared in Europe and the United States. Japan's relatively late entry into the railway era brought both benefits and disadvantages in the development of a national system. The early technological breakthroughs had already taken place, and equipment was available from abroad. Planning could proceed in the light of difficulties already experienced elsewhere, and a unified national system took shape from the outset. On the other hand, domestic technical expertise was nil, and the need to import both equipment and technicians placed formidable demands upon a nation rushing to modernize in many spheres at the same time. Progress was rapid after the late start, however, and in the 20th century Japan's railways have compared favorably with those of any other nation in the world. In the post–World War II period, and especially since the development of the SHIN-KANSEN "bullet train," Japan has been at the forefront of railway technology.

History and Early Development—The first railway equipment to be seen in Japan arrived with a Russian squadron led by Admiral E. V. PUTIATIN in 1853, but no concrete plans for a Japanese railway system took shape during the late Edo period (1600–1868), and it remained for the new Meiji period (1868–1912) government to take the first action in this field. The first line, begun in 1870 and completed in 1872, was of modest proportions, running 28 kilometers (17.4 mi) from Shinagawa in Tōkyō to Yokohama. Construction and operation were undertaken entirely by the government during the 1870s, and it was not until the next decade that any private building took place. Financing for the first state lines was obtained partly by floating bonds on the London money market, and British technicians and technology figured prominently in the early construction of both public and private railways. Domestication of technical expertise and equipment was relatively rapid and thorough, and one of the few lasting reminders of British influence is that Japanese trains run on the left, a practice that has carried over to highway traffic control.

In the KINKI REGION, a state-constructed line between Kōbe and Ōsaka was opened in 1874. Initial government plans had called for a trunk line between Tōkyō and Kyōto, and in 1886 a coastal route, the TŌKAIDŌ, was decided upon as the route of this first trunk line. Famous throughout Japanese history, and today running through one of the world's most concentrated areas of industry and population, the Tōkaidō was first spanned by rails in 1893. The first Japanese steam locomotive was built in 1893, and two years later the nation's first electric railway began operating in Kyōto. By 1901 tracks had been laid the entire length of the main island of HONSHŪ, and, although early building was concentrated on Honshū, each of the other three main islands also had some trackage by this time. Gaps in the system were filled in gradually in the 1890s and in the early years of the 20th century, so that, in effect, a nationwide network was in place by the eve of nationalization in 1906–07. Further extensions and gap filling went on until World War II—the first subway opened in Tōkyō in 1927—but the system laid down in the late 19th and early 20th centuries is basically the same one that exists today.

Nationalization—Although the earliest lines had been constructed by the government, and the first private railway had been launched (1881) only with private support, after about 1885 the apparent profitability of railways was sufficient to attract a flood of private entrepreneurs into the field, and most of the major trunk lines were private efforts. During the period prior to nationalization, however, the wars with China (1894–95) and Russia (1904–05) raised the question of the desirability of private control of such a key national resource. The importance of foreign loans in financing railway development after the turn of the century was thought to raise the specter of foreign control of the private lines, and this possibility was a key element in arguments in favor of nationalization. Sympathy for the idea of nationalization built up gradually over a period of about 15 years, and the measure was finally put into effect in 1906–07. The resulting system was known as the JAPANESE NATIONAL RAILWAYS from 1949 until denationalization took place in 1987.

Postwar Developments—Destruction of railway facilities by Allied bombing during World War II was widespread; the end of the war saw the system badly overused and in need of repair. Much of the early postwar period was necessarily devoted to restoring the system to late prewar levels, to upgrading existing routes, and to planning for the future.

The extension of urban commuter systems, including subways, has been a major accomplishment of the postwar period, but the most spectacular development has been the routes of the world-famed Shinkansen "bullet trains" and the infrastructure that has been created to extend these routes throughout Japan. The original section of the Shinkansen was opened in 1964 as a route between Tōkyō and Ōsaka, perhaps the most heavily traveled intercity corridor in the world. Since then, extensions have opened to Okayama (Okayama Prefecture) in 1972 and Hakata (Fukuoka Prefecture) in 1975, the latter upon completion of a new railway tunnel under the Kammon Strait between Honshū and Kyūshū. Two more new lines, connecting Tōkyō with northern Japan, were put into operation in 1982: the Jōetsu Shinkansen, from Tōkyō to Niigata (Niigata Prefecture), and the Tōhoku Shinkansen, from Tōkyō to Morioka (Iwate Prefecture). The latter is expected to be extended to Aomori (Aomori Prefecture), and the intention is to take it on further to Hokkaidō through the new SEIKAN TUNNEL, completed in 1985, under the Tsugaru Strait between Honshū and Hokkaidō. Conventional passenger and freight rail traffic has been using the tunnel since 1988. New Shinkansen routes are planned for other parts of the country as well. Since it began operating in 1964, the Shinkansen has become famous throughout the world for its technology, speed, and maintenance, and also for its service, comfort, and punctuality. It has been estimated that about 94 percent of the traffic between Tōkyō and Ōsaka is now by train, 1 percent by air, and the rest by road.

Many overnight trains with sleeping car service are available on non-Shinkansen routes. The older system has by no means been supplanted by the Shinkansen. Approximately 2,300 limited express and ordinary express trains operate on principal lines every day, along with about 23,300 local trains. A wide variety of service is available to virtually any populated place in Japan, while remote areas and islands can usually be reached by bus or boat.

Since most of the major cities in Japan are seaports, goods that do not need to be moved rapidly between them can most easily go by water. Thus, coastal shipping has been a formidable competitor with railway freight traffic, and, unlike those in many countries, the Japanese rail system can be characterized as passenger oriented, at least with regard to the trunk lines. While the pattern of urban inland settlement owes little to the rail network, having been dictated by the mountainous geography of Japan, suburban residential patterns have been dependent on the spread of commuter railways. Land values for lots within walking distance of stations are correspondingly higher, and only recently has the automobile caused the kinds of changes found in suburban areas in the United States.

Denationalization—The basic form of the railway system remained the same from nationalization in 1906–07 until 1987, when the Japanese National Railways was privatized and broken up into six regional private passenger services and one rail freight company, known collectively as the JR (Japan Railways) group. The JNR had been suffering an increasing burden of debt and operating deficits since the 1960s. Most of the new JR companies returned to profitability within two to three years of privatization by cutting staff, by reducing services on loss-making lines or abolishing them altogether, and by buying into service industries such as restaurants and hotels.

In addition to the main JR network—20,175 kilometers (12,535 mi) of track—and the private local lines, subway systems serve the main cities of Japan, including Tōkyō, Yokohama, Ōsaka, Nagoya, and Sapporo. In these densely populated urban centers, the subways provide important feeder services to the aboveground rail lines without their space requirements. As crowding increases even further, SUBWAYS should become an even more important component of the urban transportation system.

Railway Technical Research Institute　　鉄道総合技術研究所

(Tetsudō Sōgō Gijutsu Kenkyūjo). Research foundation located in Kokubunji, Tōkyō Prefecture. Founded in 1986 and subsidized by the companies that constitute the nationwide rail network, JR (Japan Railways), the institute conducts research at the request of individual companies as well as pursuing projects beneficial to the industry as a whole. It operates a linear motorcar experimental facility in Miyazaki Prefecture.

Rainbow plan　　レインボー戦略案

(Reimbō senryakuan). Code name for a contingency plan drawn up by US military strategists in 1939 on the assumption that, if war broke out, it would be in both the Atlantic and Pacific areas and would be against Germany, Italy, and Japan. One of five plans drafted in 1939, it was ultimately adopted as a replacement for the ORANGE WAR plan. The Rainbow plan called for defeating the enemy first in Europe and then in Asia.

raingear, traditional　　雨具

(amagu). Japan, with its long rainy season, has a wide variety of traditional raingear, including rain hats (kasa; see HEADGEAR), STRAW RAINCOATS, and so forth. The Heian-period (794–1185) elite wore amaginu, garments of oiled silk. In the mid-16th century the Portuguese introduced their rain capes (Port: capa; J: kappa). Early kappa were mainly made of wool and were favored by the military elite; the lower classes used kappa of handmade paper (WASHI) treated with paulownia-seed oil. Cotton kappa appeared during the Edo period (1600–1868), when umbrellas also came into general use (see UMBRELLAS, TRADITIONAL). Footgear included ashida, a kind of high-platform clog with attached toe covers (see GETA). Rainwear has gradually become Westernized.

rain, rituals for　　雨乞

(amagoi). Since Japan is dependent upon wet-rice agriculture, there were in the past many rites and prayers for rain. These include formal prayers offered by villagers while in seclusion at a shrine, a group rain dance, the ceremonial journey to receive water from shrines or certain specified places, and the throwing of dirty objects into a body of water or other acts in an attempt to anger the water god, thus causing rain. Rain dances (amagoi odori) survive as one of the FOLK PERFORMING ARTS. See also AGRICULTURAL RITES.

Rai San'yō　　頼山陽

(1781–1832). Historian and poet, chiefly famous for writing the Nihon gaishi, the most popular history of Japan during the 19th century. Born in Ōsaka, where his father, Rai Shunsui (1746–1816), had gone to study, then to teach Confucianism and Chinese literature. In 1797 San'yō went with his uncle Rai Kyōhei (1756–1834), a Confucian scholar of the Aki domain (now part of Hiroshima Prefecture), to Edo (now Tōkyō), where San'yō studied for a year at the offi-

Volume of Railway Traffic in Selected Countries				railways
Passengers transported				
Country	1960	1970	1980	1990
(in billions of passenger-kilometers)				
Japan	180.9	288.1	313.3	383.7
Soviet Union	170.8	265.4	332.1	417.4
France	31.7	41.1	54.5	63.6
Italy	30.7	32.5	39.6	45.5
United Kingdom	34.7	35.6	31.7	34.1
United States	34.3	17.3	17.7	9.9*

Net freight transported				
Country	1960	1970	1980	1990
(in billions of metric ton–kilometers)				
Japan	53.4	62.7	39.3	26.7
Soviet Union	1,504.4	2,494.7	3,439.9	3,717.0
United States	840.0	1,116.6	1,341.7	1,513.8
France	56.9	70.4	70.9	51.5
Italy	15.9	18.1	18.4	21.3
United Kingdom	30.5	26.8	17.6	15.8

*1990 US passenger figures exclude commuter railroads.
SOURCES: United Nations, Monthly Bulletin of Statistics: December 1991; Statistical Yearbook: 1963 and 1981.

rakkan

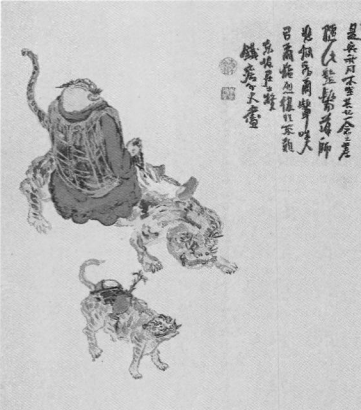

► Here, an inscription accompanies the signature and two seals of the late-18th-century *haiku* poet and painter Buson.

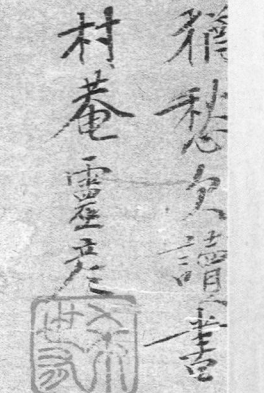

▼ The signature and seal of a 15th-century Zen monk.

▲ The signature and two seals of the artist Tomioka Tessai can be seen to the left of the poem in this 1905 painting. Seals may be carved with the artist's name, sobriquet, or studio name.

▲ The signature and seal of the 15th-century ink painter Sesshū Tōyō.

cial shogunal academy, the SHŌHEIKŌ. In 1800 he ran away from home—and from the Aki domain, a serious offense under feudal law. He was apprehended in Kyōto and taken back to Aki, where he was placed under house arrest for three years. During this confinement he began his most important work, the *Nihon gaishi* (Unofficial History of Japan). This work would occupy him for 25 years and would be seen by many as predicting the fall of the TOKUGAWA SHOGUNATE, since it traced the cycles of ascent and decline of military families, beginning with the TAIRA FAMILY, which prevailed in the closing years of the Heian period (794–1185) and ending with the founding of the Tokugawa shogunate (1603–1867). An important representative of the imperial loyalist (*kinnō*) tradition of Japanese historiography, the *Nihon gaishi* was taken up by participants in the movement that culminated in the MEIJI RESTORATION (1868). Published in 1844, it went through 15 editions by 1887.

Disinherited by his father in 1804, San'yō found employment as an assistant to KAN SAZAN, who had opened a school at Kanname in Bingo (now part of Hiroshima Prefecture) in 1810 and under whose tutelage he studied *kanshi* (Chinese poetry). In 1811 San'yō set out for Kyōto, where he spent the remainder of his life writing and teaching.

rajio taisō   ラジオ体操

(radio calisthenics). Program of exercises broadcast daily over the radio by NHK (Japan Broadcasting Corporation). Radio calisthenics were initiated in 1928, soon after radio programming was introduced to Japan. The

rajio taisō   Elementary school students keeping fit during summer vacation through "radio calisthenics" in a local park.

broadcasts, which last for about half an hour, begin at 6:30 AM and are repeated three more times during the course of the day. Sponsored in part by the Ministry of Education, they have been incorporated into school curricula, especially in the elementary schools, and as a result are familiar to nearly all Japanese.

rakan   羅漢

(literally, "worthy one"). Also called *arakan* (Skt: *arhat;* Ch: *aluohan* [*a-lo-han*] or *luohan* [*lo-han*]). Used originally as an epithet for the Buddha, and later as the term in Theravāda Buddhism for a Buddhist who attained the highest rank of religious wisdom equal to the Buddha's. Paintings of these figures became popular in China during the Song (Sung; 960–1279) and Yuan (Yüan; 1279–1368) dynasties, and these were copied in Japan. There are also many sets of *rakan* statues, such as those at the temple Rakanji in Ōita Prefecture and at the temple Gohyaku Rakanji in Meguro Ward, Tōkyō.

rakkan   落款

Signatures and seals on works of art. A practice initiated under Chinese influence and gradually established in Japan between the 12th and 16th centuries. An artist's signature and personal seal or SEALS affixed to a painting or calligraphy are invaluable for establishing the authorship and historical context of a work of art. In addition to a name or sobriquet, the artist's inscription may include one or more of the following: the date of execution of the work in the sexagenary cycle (JIKKAN JŪNISHI) or *nengō* (era-name) form, the artist's age on that date, the place or circumstances of execution of the work, or the artist's official or honorary titles. Rarely, seals may denote ownership rather than authorship of a work. The KAŌ (cipher), a unique abbreviated written form of an individual's name, occasionally appears in lieu of a conventional signature or stamped seal, especially as a mark of ownership on certificates or other documents.

Japanese seals were made by carving the characters of an artist's name or sobriquet, usually in the archaic Chinese seal script (*tensho*), into a hard material. The mark of the seal was imprinted using red ink.

rakugo   落語

Popular form of comic monologue in which a storyteller (*rakugoka*) creates an imaginary

drama through episodic narration and skillful use of vocal and facial expressions to portray various characters. Typically, the storyteller uses no scenery; the only musical accompaniment is the *debayashi*, a brief flourish of drum, *shamisen*, and bamboo flute that marks his entrance and exit. The storyteller, dressed in a plain *kimono*, crosses to stage center and seats himself on a cushion before his audience, with a hand towel and a fan as his only props. There he remains until he has delivered his final line, usually a punning punch line (*ochi;* literally, "the drop"). This is the characteristic ending from which the term *rakugo* was coined, the word being written with two Chinese characters meaning "drop" (J: *raku*, also pronounced *ochi*) and "word" (*go*).

In a *rakugo* performance the interplay between performer and audience is extremely important. Since the repertory of classic *rakugo* is small, aficionados have heard the basic story many times. They delight in the storyteller's particular version, his arrangement of familiar episodes, and appreciate his timing and the verisimilitude of the details he adds, such as the sound of *sake* as he pours it into his imaginary cup. The introduction to the story proper must be completely original. The plots of the stories are never as important as the characterizations in them, for *rakugo* pokes fun at all manner of human foibles.

The antecedents of *rakugo* can be traced to the end of the 16th century, when professional entertainers, or OTOGISHŪ, were regularly employed in the retinues of warlords to provide companionship and distraction for them during military campaigns. The publication in 1628 of *Seisuishō*, an edition of stories that had been performed by the storyteller ANRAKUAN SAKUDEN, stirred interest in the genre and prompted publication of other anthologies. By the early 1670s professional performers called *hanashika* had emerged. Tsuyu no Gorobei (1643–1703) from Kyōto and Yonezawa Hikohachi (d 1714) from Ōsaka are regarded as the forefathers of Kamigata (Kyōto-Ōsaka) *rakugo*, while Shikano Buzaemon (1649–99) is credited with founding the Edo *rakugo* tradition, later perfected by SAN'YŪTEI ENCHŌ.

A regular entertainment feature at roadside shows, private banquets, and makeshift stages set up at restaurants during off-hours, this vagabond art found a home in 1791 when the first permanent Japanese-style vaudeville theater, or YOSE, was opened in Edo (now Tōkyō). Soon afterward the popularity of *yose* spread to Kyōto and Ōsaka. By 1842 there were 200 *yose* in Edo, and between 1854 and 1860 as many as 392. Between then and 1912 the number of *yose* stabilized at around 80, approximately one for each of the city's neighborhoods. The admission fee to these accessible and intimate theaters, which accommodated about 100 people for a three-hour performance, was an extremely reasonable 36 *mon*, or the equivalent of a few pennies.

After surviving the challenge of cinema in the 1920s and 1930s, which significantly reduced *yose* attendance, *rakugo* performers met with increasing official disapproval during World War II, because they did not adapt their material to complement national ideology.

With the resumption of civilian broadcasting at the end of World War II, *rakugo* recovered its popularity. Although the proliferation of new entertainment media has greatly reduced the number of *yose*, the

1246
rajio taisō

adaptability of *rakugo* to both radio and television has ensured its survival. There are still four traditional *yose* in Tōkyō, along with *rakugo* halls, larger and more expensive, where all-*rakugo* programs are presented for devotees, often on a monthly basis. Many universities also sponsor *rakugo* clubs whose members study and perform *rakugo* for their own entertainment. See also KŌDAN; NANIWA-BUSHI.

rakuichi and rakuza 楽市楽座

(*rakuichi to rakuza*; free markets and open guilds). The abolition of market taxes and monopolistic privileges of guildlike trade associations (ZA) during the 16th century. The policy was adopted by regional warlords (SENGOKU DAIMYŌ) who sought to increase local wealth and production. The earliest such "free market" on record is that established for the sale of paper in 1549 by the ROKKAKU FAMILY, based in Ōmi Province (now Shiga Prefecture). The revocation of exclusive *za* rights that had gradually accrued under religious and aristocratic patronage had a more dramatic effect on freeing the market. The earliest record of *rakuza* was in 1576, when SHIBATA KATSUIE abolished all *za* privileges in the area of Echizen Province (now part of Fukui Prefecture) under his control. ODA NOBUNAGA espoused the policy of *rakuichi* and *rakuza*, and his successor, TOYOTOMI HIDEYOSHI, extended the policy to the whole country. They were not always consistent, however, making exceptions when they saw fit, and their actions did not necessarily result in a market free of all restrictions. Rather, the policy produced a new configuration of the market economy, one that centered on castle towns instead of noble houses and religious establishments.

Raku ware 楽焼

(*raku-yaki*). A soft, low-fired, lead-glazed ware primarily for use in the TEA CEREMONY. Teabowls are most common, but incense containers, tea jars, flower vases, and water jars are also made in the Raku tradition. Raku ware is said to have been started in Kyōto during the Azuchi-Momoyama period (1568–1600) by a tilemaker named CHŌJIRŌ. According to tradition, Chōjirō's tiles caught the eye of the famed teamaster SEN NO RIKYŪ, who invited Chōjirō to make tea-ceremony utensils for him, especially teabowls. Introduced around 1577–80, the name Raku for the new ware can be traced to TOYOTOMI HIDEYOSHI, who presented Chōjirō's son Jōkei (d 1635?) with a gold seal inscribed with the character *raku* ("pleasure").

Raku bowls have always been handmade and expressive of the potter's individuality. The teabowls are rounded with a slightly constricted rim. A subtly colored or transparent lead glaze is applied in many thin layers, and parts of the body are often exposed. The bowls are usually red (with transparent glaze), black, or sometimes white.

Chōjirō's son Jōkei and grandson Nonkō (also known as Dōnyū; 1599–1656) made wares for Sen no Rikyū. The Raku family line has continued to make teabowls down to the present day. Currently, the name *raku-yaki* is also used in Japan to denote any quick, low-fired ware.

rāmen ラーメン

Chinese noodles made mainly of wheat flour and seasoned to suit the Japanese palate; the name is thought to be a corruption of *la mian* (*la mien*), the Chinese word for "stretched noodle," so called because the noodles are pulled out by hand into a thin thread. The noodles are eaten with a broth seasoned with soy sauce or MISO (fermented bean paste) and garnished with thin slices of roast pork, bean sprouts, Chinese bamboo shoots, and other ingredients. Restaurants specializing in *rāmen* are found all over Japan. Dehydrated and packaged "instant *rāmen*" is also popular.

Ran 乱

A film directed by KUROSAWA AKIRA, released in 1985. Set in the strife-torn Sengoku period (1457–1568), the film—whose title means war or insurrection—is loosely based on Shakespeare's *King Lear*, with an aging warlord (played by NAKADAI TATSUYA) and his three contentious sons taking the place of Lear and his three daughters. A tragic spectacle on a grand scale, it displays Kurosawa's painterly visual sense and his skill as a film craftsman. Jointly financed by Japanese and French producers, it won a 1986 Academy Award for its costumes, which were designed by WADA EMI.

Rangaku → Western Learning

Rangaku kaitei 蘭学階梯

(A Ladder to Dutch Learning). A two-volume introduction to Rangaku ("Dutch Learning"), as WESTERN LEARNING was known during the Edo period (1600–1868). Written by the physician and scholar ŌTSUKI GENTAKU, it was published in 1788. Volume 1 presents a brief discussion of the history and significance of Rangaku; volume 2 is a basic primer of the Dutch language, the first of its kind in Japan.

Rangaku kotohajime 蘭学事始

(The Beginning of Dutch Learning). Book completed in 1815 by SUGITA GEMPAKU; also known as *Rantō kotohajime* or *Oranda kotohajime*. It begins with a short history of the development of Rangaku (Dutch Learning), as WESTERN LEARNING was called at the time. This is followed by a long account of Sugita's monumental effort, in collaboration with other scholars, in the preparation of KAITAI SHINSHO (1774, New Book of Anatomy), a translation from the Dutch that was the first European medical work to be rendered into the Japanese language. The final section describes the activities of ŌTSUKI GENTAKU and other scholars of Western Learning.

Rankei Dōryū 蘭渓道隆

(1213–78; Ch: Lanqi Daolong or Lan-ch'i Tao-lung). Chinese ZEN Buddhist monk born in Sichuan (Szechwan) Province. Eager to promote Zen in Japan where it was not yet solidly established, he set out on a journey which brought him to Kyūshū in 1246. At the request of Kamakura regent HŌJŌ TOKIYORI he established the RINZAI SECT temple KENCHŌJI. From there he went to KENNINJI and then to Zenkōji. He was twice banished because of slanderous rumors. The conferral of the title Daikaku Zenji (Master of Great Enlightenment) on Rankei was the first bestowal of the title *zenji* (master of Zen) in Japan.

Rashōmon 羅生門

(tr "Rashōmon," 1930). Short story by AKUTAGAWA RYŪNOSUKE (1892–1927); published 1915. Set in 12th-century Kyōto, the story tells of a servant recently discharged from his master's house. Contemplating a

life of thievery, the man, with nothing better to occupy his time, climbs the great gate at the southern entrance to the capital. At the top he spies a poor old woman pulling hair from a corpse (abandoned in an epidemic) to fashion a wig for sale. The former servant is enraged, forgetting that only moments before he himself considered becoming a thief. The old woman says she must do this to survive and the man, apparently persuaded by her logic, steals her clothes and disappears. In this work Akutagawa, who often explores psychological extremes, describes the egoism that drives individuals to desperate measures in desperate times. The title, which refers to the gate, and the story line derive from the late-Heian-period (794–1185) literary work KONJAKU MONOGATARI. "Rashōmon" is an early example of Akutagawa's highly creative historical stories, a genre that constituted about one-quarter of his fiction.

Rashōmon 羅生門

KUROSAWA AKIRA's 1950 film, one of the most famous Japanese motion pictures ever made. Based on two stories of AKUTAGAWA RYŪNOSUKE ("Yabu no naka" and, peripherally, "Rashōmon") and written by HASHIMOTO SHINOBU and Kurosawa himself, it is about a rape and a murder near Kyōto toward the end of the Heian period (794–1185). A *samurai* (played by MORI MASAYUKI) has been killed, apparently by a bandit (MIFUNE TOSHIRŌ), and his wife (KYŌ MACHIKO) raped. The film consists of a recounting of this story, presented a number of times by characters in the film in a number of different ways. All versions of the story are given as flashbacks, leaving the spectator unconvinced of the veracity of the storyteller. Thus truth is revealed as relative and reality itself is questioned.

The *Rashōmon* murder mystery is never solved. In the Akutagawa stories the author is content to question all moral values. In the Kurosawa film, however, there is the suggestion that men are incapable of judging reality, much less truth, and that they must continually deceive themselves if they are to remain true to their necessary ideas of themselves. The appeal of *Rashōmon* to the West—it has always been less popular in Japan—lay perhaps in its questioning of accepted values at the very time when the West itself was beginning to do so. Well acted, beautifully photographed by MIYAGAWA KAZUO, and splendidly edited by the director himself, *Rashōmon* won first prize at the 1951 Venice Film Festival.

Rastvorov Incident ラストボロフ事件

(Rasutoborofu Jiken). Events surrounding the defection of a Soviet spy in Japan. On 24 January 1954 Yuri Rastvorov, a lieutenant colonel in the Soviet Ministry of Internal Affairs (MVD), sought the protection of US

military authorities in Tōkyō, who secretly flew him to the United States. Moscow claimed that the Americans had abducted him. Washington confidentially informed Tōkyō of what had transpired (while denying it publicly), and the Japanese government protested to Washington the breach in diplomatic procedure. Some of Rastvorov's Japanese agents came to the Tōkyō Metropolitan Police and made confessions implicating three Japanese Foreign Ministry officials in espionage. By 14 August, when Tōkyō made a formal announcement concerning the incident, the three officials had been arrested. One committed suicide, and the other two were imprisoned.

ratification of treaties 批准

(*hijun*). In Japan, the procedures for the ratification of a treaty are as follows. The cabinet, upon concluding a treaty, obtains either prior or subsequent approval of the DIET and then ratifies the treaty (constitution, art. 73[iii]). With the advice and approval of the cabinet, the emperor attests the instrument of ratification (art. 7[viii]). The instrument of ratification requires the signatures of the prime minister and the foreign minister and the emperor's attestation. The ratification procedure is complete when the instrument of ratification is exchanged or deposited with the other nation or nations party to the treaty. See also TREATIES.

rats and mice 鼠

(*nezumi*). In Japanese, *nezumi* is the general name for the animals of the suborder Myomorpha, order Rodentia. There are no Japanese words corresponding to the English "mouse," "rat," and "vole," all of which are called *nezumi*. The most common distinction is their habitats: *ienezumi* inhabit human environments (houses), while *nonezumi* inhabit natural environments (including farms). The *ienezumi* category includes three species, *kumanezumi* (roof rat; *Rattus rattus*), *dobunezumi* (Norway rat; *R. norvegicus*), and *hatsukanezumi* (house mouse; *Mus musculus*). These are presumed to have entered Japan from the Asian continent via human traffic routes in ancient times. Most numerous in urban areas is the *dobunezumi*, but as high-rise buildings have

increased, the *kumanezumi*, which excels in tree climbing and depends less on sewage systems, has also become common. Field mice (*Apodemus speciosus* and *A. argenteus*), found throughout the country, and the vole (*Microtus montebelli*), inhabiting Honshū and Kyūshū, are the most common *nonezumi*.

The *nezumi* has always been viewed ambiguously by the Japanese. Detested as a pest, it has also been held in high esteem as the messenger of Daikokuten, one of the Seven Deities of Good Fortune, who bestows and protects wealth.

Rausudake 羅臼岳

Conical volcano in the Chishima Volcanic Zone, central Shiretoko Peninsula, eastern Hokkaidō. It is the peninsula's highest peak. It has numerous alpine flora and snowy ravines and is part of Shiretoko National Park. Height: 1,661 m (5,449 ft).

Raymond, Antonin レイモンド, A.

(1888–1976). Progressive American architect who helped pioneer modern architecture in Japan. Born in Czechoslovakia, Raymond graduated from the Polytechnic College in Prague and went to the United States in 1910. In 1919 he accompanied Frank Lloyd WRIGHT to Japan to work on the Imperial Hotel in Tōkyō, staying on until 1937. He trained Japanese architects, including MAEKAWA KUNIO and YOSHIMURA JUNZŌ. He returned to Japan in 1948 and designed a number of foreign embassies and houses. Representative works include his Tōkyō home in Reinanzaka (1924), the library and chapel of Tōkyō Women's Christian University (1931 and 1935), and St. Alban's Church (1959).

reapportionment issue 議員定数是正問題

(*giin teisū zesei mondai*). During the 1970s and 1980s the problem of inequalities in the apportionment of seats in the national Diet among election districts became a serious constitutional issue in Japan. Shifts of population from rural to urban districts had resulted in apportionment inequalities between the two. Numerous Supreme Court decisions between 1976 and 1988 declared disproportionate votes for national candidates between particular districts to be un-

constitutional. Having received the Supreme Court's judgment of unconstitutionality, the Diet, in May 1986, passed an amendment to the Election Law that would reduce the greatest disparity to approximately 3 to 1. However, partly because of the differing opinions and tactics of the various political parties, the Diet was unable to agree on the changes that were necessary if the principle of equality of the vote, which is the basis of democracy, was to be maintained.

Rebun 礼文

Island in the Sea of Japan, approximately 50 km (30 mi) west of Wakkanai, northern Hokkaidō; administratively part of Hokkaidō. Funadomari in the north and Kafuka in the south are the main fishing centers. Marine products include kelp and sea urchins. Together with the neighboring island of RISHIRI, it is part of the RISHIRI-REBUN-SAROBETSU NATIONAL PARK. Area: 82 sq km (32 sq mi).

Reconstruction Finance Bank 復興金融金庫

(Fukkō Kin'yū Kinko). Bank established by the Japanese government following World War II to aid private financial institutions in rebuilding Japan's shattered economy. Three-quarters of the funds provided by the bank were for plant and equipment for such basic industries as coal, steel, and electric power (see PRIORITY PRODUCTION PROGRAM).

Outstanding loans from the bank at the end of March 1949, immediately before the suspension of its activity, amounted to about ¥132 billion (US $366.7 million), equal to 30 percent of the outstanding loans of all national banks. The bulk of the funds was raised through reconstruction finance bonds, but 60 percent of the bonds were not sold in the market and had to be purchased by the BANK OF JAPAN. Together with the government's budget deficit, these bonds contributed to severe postwar inflation. Under the 1949 Dodge stabilization program (see DODGE LINE), new loans from the bank were suspended. In January 1952 the bank was disbanded, transferring its claims and obligations to the JAPAN DEVELOPMENT BANK.

Recruit Scandal リクルート事件

(Rikurūto Jiken). POLITICAL CORRUPTION scandal. In 1986 Recruit Co, Ltd, a large information-industry company, distributed shares of a subsidiary's stock that were not yet available on the market to many powerful politicians, bureaucrats, and businessmen. Those who received the shares reaped large profits the following month when the subsidiary's stock was officially offered to the public. When this came to light in 1988, in most cases the direct blame fell on the staffs of the politicians implicated (a group that included Prime Minister NAKASONE YASUHIRO and the future prime minister TAKESHITA NOBORU) rather than on the politicians themselves, who claimed that they had no knowledge of the transaction. Seventeen people, including two politicians, had been indicted on charges of corruption by 1989.

Red Army faction 赤軍派

(Sekigunha). Radical student group. Formed in 1969 within the student-dominated Japanese New Left Movement, it has advocated world revolution through armed violence. Throughout the 1970s the group gained worldwide attention for acts of terrorism and violence both within Japan and abroad.

The Red Army faction was formed in September 1969 by dissident members of the Kansai faction of the Communist League (Kyōsan Shugisha Dōmei), who had failed to rally mass support for the removal of US forces from Okinawa. The group began attacking police boxes in Ōsaka and Tōkyō, but in November 53 members were arrested and a large arms cache found. Looking abroad for targets, the group hijacked a Japan Air Lines jetliner in 1970. Throughout 1971 bombings and robberies occurred in Japan. That same year the group merged with another to form the Rengō Sekigun (United Red Army). In February 1972 eight members were arrested and the remaining members, with a hostage, were besieged by police at a lodge in Karuizawa, Nagano Prefecture. The lodge was taken after two policemen were killed. Interrogations revealed that over the previous winter the Rengō Sekigun members had tortured and killed 14 of their own comrades on grounds of ideological deviation and buried them in shallow graves in the mountains.

Meanwhile, in 1971 the Red Army faction cadre Shigenobu Fusako (b 1945) had traveled to Europe and contacted the Popular Front for the Liberation of Palestine (PFLP). Believed to be based in Lebanon, she became the mastermind of the foreign-based group that calls itself the Japanese Red Army (Nihon Sekigun). This group used machine guns and grenades in a May 1972 attack that killed 24 people at Lod Airport in Tel Aviv, Israel. Throughout the remainder of the 1970s the Japanese Red Army engaged in various international terrorist activities, including a number of hijackings as well as the seizure of the French embassy in the Netherlands (1974) and the US consulate in Malaysia (1975). The Japanese Red Army fired mortar rounds in 1986 at the embassies of Japan, Canada, and the United States in Jakarta and in 1987 at the embassies of the United Kingdom and the United States in Rome. In 1989 the Japanese government requested that foreign governments arrest 11 members of the group. See also STUDENT MOVEMENT.

Red Data Book   レッドデータブック
(*Reddo dēta bukku*). The *Reddo dēta bukku* is the Japanese domestic edition of a worldwide data book that provides information on the habitats and other conditions of animals that are in danger of becoming extinct. The worldwide *Red Data Book* was first published by the International Union for Conservation of Nature and Natural Resources (IUCN) in 1966. Separate editions are published in each country. The Japanese edition, released by the Environment Agency in 1991, covers Japan's vertebrate species, of which 20 are extinct, 49 are endangered, 50 are vulnerable, and 139 are rare. An additional 25 local populations are considered in need of protection. A future volume is planned for Japan's invertebrate species.

Red Flag Incident of 1908   赤旗事件
(Akahata Jiken). Also known as the Kinkikan Incident. A police crackdown on socialist groups on 22 June 1908. The socialists, who were split among those favoring parliamentary tactics and those favoring direct action (violence), had agreed to ignore their differences and gather at a meeting to commemorate the release of their colleague Yamaguchi Gizō (1882–1920), from prison. At the close of the 22 June meeting, held at the Kinkikan, a hall in the Kanda section of Tōkyō, several

advocates of direct action, led by ŌSUGI SAKAE and ARAHATA KANSON, raised red flags inscribed with the words "anarchism" and "anarcho-communism." A fight broke out with the police over the flags. Ōsugi, Arahata, and 14 others, among them SAKAI TOSHIHIKO and YAMAKAWA HITOSHI, who had sought to prevent the clash, were arrested. The incident signaled the increased harassment of socialists that would culminate in the HIGH TREASON INCIDENT OF 1910.

Red Purge   レッドパージ
(Reddo Pāji). The dismissal of JAPAN COMMUNIST PARTY (JCP) members and suspected sympathizers from their jobs between May and December 1950. On 3 May General Douglas MACARTHUR, supreme commander for the Allied powers (SCAP), denounced the JCP. On 6–7 June all 24 members of the party's central committee (including NOSAKA SANZŌ and TOKUDA KYŪICHI) and 17 members of the editorial board of the party organ AKAHATA were removed from their posts. Following the outbreak of the Korean War on 25 June, the OCCUPATION authorities redoubled their efforts. On 28 July JCP members were banned from the newspaper, broadcasting, communications, and motion-picture industries; in September similar action was taken against workers in the coal and steel industries. In all, 1,177 teachers and other government employees and 10,972 workers in the private sector were dismissed. The purge greatly diminished the influence of the JCP in the labor movement.

reed warblers   葦切
(*yoshikiri*). In Japanese, *yoshikiri* is the common name for two bird species of the family Muscicapidae. Both are brown with white feathers around the eyes. The *ōyoshikiri* or *gyōgyōshi* (great reed warbler; *Acrocephalus arundinaceus*) measures about 18 centimeters (7 in).

The *koyoshikiri* (black-browed reed warbler; *A. bistrigiceps*) is about 13 centimeters (5 in) long. It builds its nest between tall reeds or in the top branches of bushes. See also BUSH WARBLER.

The call of the *yoshikiri* has been celebrated by many poets, most notably BASHŌ (1644–94). The *yoshikiri* was also known as the *yoshiwara suzume* (literally, "sparrow of the reed plains"), a name that by the late 17th century had come to mean a garrulous person; in the 19th century it was also applied to the vocally seductive prostitutes of the YOSHIWARA pleasure quarters.

Reform Government of the Republic of China   中華民国維新政府
(Ch: Zhonghua Minguo Weixin Zhengfu or Chung-hua Min-kuo Wei-hsin Cheng-fu; J: Chūka Minkoku Ishin Seifu). Also referred to as the Restored Government of the Republic of China. Puppet regime created by Japan in Nanjing (Nanking) in March 1938, four months after the retreat of CHIANG KAI-SHEK's government from that city. The regime was to administer Central and South China, North China having already been placed under a separate government, the PROVISIONAL GOVERNMENT OF THE REPUBLIC OF CHINA, in December 1937. The activities of the Reform Government were carefully prescribed and overseen by Japanese army "advisers." On 30 March 1940 the Reform Government was dissolved, and its functions were absorbed by the REORGANIZED NATIONAL GOVERNMENT OF THE REPUBLIC OF CHINA. See also SINO-JAPANESE WAR OF 1937–1945.

reed warblers The great reed warbler builds a cup-shaped nest from the stems of the reeds that are its main habitat.

refugees   難民
(*nammin*). Japan's first real encounter with political refugees was in the mid-1970s, when refugees from Indochina ("boat people") began landing in Japan. At that time the Japanese government was extremely reluctant to allow political refugees into the country, but growing numbers of refugees from Vietnam, Cambodia, and Laos forced the government to liberalize its rigid and closed policy. The first step was a series of cabinet decrees permitting unconditional temporary disembarkation in Japan of boat people rescued by Japanese or foreign vessels and the establishment of a cumulative quota of 3,000 refugees to be accepted for permanent resettlement in Japan. In 1981 Japan became a signatory to the 1951 UN Convention and the 1967 UN Protocol relating to the Status of Refugees, and in the same year Japan passed the Immigration Control and Refugee Recognition Act (Shutsunyūkoku Kanri oyobi Nammin Nintei Hō). By 1985 the government had raised the cumulative quota for permanent resettlement of Indochinese refugees to 10,000, and by mid-1989 more than 6,300 refugees had been granted permission to remain in Japan. However, about half of the nearly 2,000 boat people who landed in Kyūshū and Okinawa in the summer of 1989 were refused entry into Japan because the government classed them as "economic refugees"—that is, people simply looking for work in Japan—rather than true political refugees.

refusal to be fingerprinted
指紋押捺拒否問題
(*shimon ōnatsu kyohi mondai*). All foreigners aged 16 or above who have been granted residence status in Japan for a term of one year or more are required by the Alien Registration Law of 1952 (see ALIEN REGISTRATION) to register as aliens within 90 days of the beginning of their term of residence and to renew their registration every five years. Until 1993 it was mandatory that a print of their left forefinger be placed on several documents at the time of registration.

During the 1980s opposition to this requirement was expressed by an increasing number of individuals, especially among Japan's large population of Korean residents, many of whom were born in Japan but who are still required, as foreign nationals, to register as aliens. Objections centered on the argument that fingerprinting is discriminatory, demeaning, and an invasion of privacy. By December 1991, 156 registrants had simply refused to be fingerprinted, and a number of cases had been prosecuted in the courts. In each case, lower courts ruled that the practice was constitutional on the grounds that a fingerprint was not private information and that fingerprinting is a reliable method of verifying the identity of aliens.

The two cases that had been brought before the Supreme Court on appeal were both dismissed in 1989 as a part of the general amnesty that accompanied the death of the Emperor SHŌWA, and in January 1991 the governments of Japan and the Republic of Korea agreed that the fingerprinting requirement for Korean permanent residents would be abolished as of January 1993. The requirement was later abolished for all permanent residents as of that date, but it remained in force for nonpermanent residents.

regency government 摂関政治

(*sekkan seiji*). A phase of Heian-period (794–1185) government lasting from 967 to 1068, when members of the FUJIWARA FAMILY continuously held the post of imperial regent (*sesshō* if regent for an underage sovereign; *kampaku* for an adult sovereign). The Fujiwara perpetuated the post in their family through extensive intermarriage with the imperial line. The frequent practice of abdication brought to the throne many very young emperors, chosen by the Fujiwara and easily manipulated by the regents, who were also their maternal uncles or grandfathers.

The regency was not a Fujiwara invention but developed as a guardianship for female sovereigns in the late 6th and early 7th centuries. Regents were always members of the imperial house before the Fujiwara gained these positions. During the 8th and 9th centuries, however, the Fujiwara came to enjoy a special status that made their regency possible. Under a 793 law governing marriages between the great families and the royal house, the Fujiwara were allowed to marry princesses only two generations (or collateral degrees) removed from a reigning emperor, while other nobles were restricted to three generations (or collateral degrees).

In 866 FUJIWARA NO YOSHIFUSA was appointed regent (*sesshō*) for his grandson, the minor emperor Seiwa (850–881; r 858–876). Seiwa was the first child emperor and the first male ruler to have a regent; Yoshifusa was the first regent not of royal blood. In 876 Yoshifusa's adopted son Mototsune (836–891) became *sesshō* to Emperor Yōzei (869–949; r 876–884), and in 887 Mototsune became the first Fujiwara *kampaku*, serving as regent to two adult emperors.

After Mototsune's death in 891, however, the post remained vacant for 40 years, although the Fujiwara continued to control the government. Emperor UDA (r 887–897), exceptionally, was not born of a Fujiwara mother and refused to appoint a regent (see AKŌ INCIDENT OF 887). He favored members of rival families, including the famous scholar SUGAWARA NO MICHIZANE. Uda's abdication in favor of DAIGO (r 897–930) gave the Fujiwara the opportunity to banish Michizane to Kyūshū.

In 930 the regency was revived in the person of Fujiwara no Tadahira (880–949), a son of Mototsune, and after another interruption between 949 and 967, revived again by Tadahira's son Saneyori (see ANNA INCIDENT). From 967 onward the regency was essentially a permanent hereditary prerogative of the head of the Fujiwara family.

It became established that a *sesshō* governed for a minor sovereign while a *kampaku* ruled under an adult sovereign by virtue of his control of the Grand Council of State (DAJŌKAN). A *kampaku* could advise the emperor but in theory could not, like a *sesshō*, act in his stead. The distinction became clear in the regency of Tadahira, who served as *sesshō* during Emperor Suzaku's (923–952; r 930–946) minority (from 930) and then as *kampaku* when the emperor came of age (941). After 967 the head of the Fujiwara family alternated between the two titles in accord with the age of the reigning emperor (usually his grandson).

The regency government reached its apogee in the late 10th and early 11th centuries under FUJIWARA NO MICHINAGA and his son FUJIWARA NO YORIMICHI. Michinaga dominated the court from 995 to his death in 1028. Four of his daughters were married to emperors and three of his grandsons became emperors.

The heads of the Fujiwara family continued to hold the post of regent for the rest of the Heian period (and indeed until the MEIJI RESTORATION of 1868, except for a brief period in the late 16th century when the title of *kampaku* was assumed by TOYOTOMI HIDEYOSHI and his son TOYOTOMI HIDETSUGU), but the regents were virtually powerless after the accession of Emperor GO-SANJŌ in 1068. Go-Sanjō devised a system whereby an emperor could abdicate and remove himself from the Fujiwara-dominated court but continue to rule from retirement. Called cloister government (INSEI) by historians, this system (which was fully instituted by Go-Sanjō's son, Emperor SHIRAKAWA) allowed the retired emperor to guide his successor and protect him from Fujiwara influence.

regional geographies 地誌

(*chishi*). The history of topography in Japan goes back to the Nara-period (710–794) FUDOKI—reports on land conditions, products, and local traditions—sent by provincial governments to the central government. Regional gazetteers were published in the Edo period (1600–1868). Many of these, such as *Shimpen Musashi fudoki kō* (1830, New Edition of Musashi Fudoki), are extant today. Since the Meiji period (1868–1912), topographical-historical accounts of each prefecture, county, city, town, and village have been printed.

The first full-scale topographical work dealing with Japan as a whole was the *Dai Nihon chishi* by YAMASAKI NAOMASA and Satō Denzō (10 vols, 1903–15). There is also a complete geographical dictionary, the *Dai Nihon chimei jisho* (11 vols, 1900–1907) by Yoshida Tōgo (1864–1918). *Kyōdo shinshu* (32 vols since 1949) and *Nihon chishi* (21 vols, 1963–80) are noted for their high scholarly standards. Western language topographical studies include *Japan* by G. T. Trewartha (1945, 1965), *Japan* by R. B. Hall (1963), and *Das Japanische Inselreich* by M. Schwindt (1967, 1981).

registration of property 財産登記

(*zaisan tōki*). Japan has systems of registration for immovable property, businesses, marital property contracts, etc. However, the most important of these is registration of real property, which includes land and buildings. If a person does not register variations or changes in his immovable property rights in buildings and land, he cannot assert those rights against a third-party purchase. For example, when a buyer fails to register the transfer of OWNERSHIP RIGHTS, he will be unable to assert ownership rights against a third party should the original seller subsequently sell the same immovable property to the third party. If the transfer of owner-ship rights from the seller to the second buyer is registered, the second buyer will be able to assert ownership rights against the original buyer and all other persons.

If immovable property owned by one person is for some reason registered as belonging to a second, and the first person not only knows of the fact but has expressly or implicitly approved of it, a third party who purchases the immovable property from the second person, believing him to be the owner of that immovable property, can acquire rights of ownership.

rei 礼

(rites, propriety, decorum; Ch: *li*). An important ethical and social concept in Chinese Confucianism. Its classical formulation is found in the *Li ji* (*Li chi*; J: *Raiki*), which describes *li* as proper conduct in rituals and ceremonies and in etiquette, as well as the laws and regulations of the state. *Li*, believed to be an expression of the Heavenly Principle, was internalized by Mencius, while Xunzi (Hsün-tzu; J: *Junshi*) interpreted it as man-made rules that guided man and society. In Japan OGYŪ SORAI (1666–1728) took a position similar to Xunzi's, viewing the social order and *li* or *rei* as man-made. His ideas are considered by some to have prepared the way for the ready acceptance of Western political and social institutions by the Japanese after the Meiji Restoration of 1868. To most Japanese (as to the Chinese) *rei*, or its compound form *reigi*, means a socially established pattern of conduct conforming to tradition, especially in the sense of proper manners and etiquette.

Reimeikai 黎明会

("Dawn Society"). Educational society of the Taishō period (1912–26). Formed in 1918 by YOSHINO SAKUZŌ, FUKUDA TOKUZŌ, and other liberal thinkers who, in the wake of government repression of the newspaper *Ōsaka asahi shimbun* (see ŌSAKA ASAHI HIKKA INCIDENT), saw the need for an organization to propagate democratic ideas. Members included NITOBE INAZŌ, MORITO TATSUO, and ŌYAMA IKUO. The Reimeikai called for universal manhood suffrage and abolition of two articles of the PUBLIC ORDER AND POLICE LAW OF 1900 restricting the right of workers to strike or form associations. Dissension among members led to dissolution in 1920.

Reischauer, August Karl

ライシャワー, A. K.

(1879–1971). Presbyterian missionary and scholar; a founder of Tōkyō Joshi Daigaku (Tōkyō Women's Christian College; now Tōkyō Women's Christian University) in 1918 and, with his wife, of Nihon Rōwa Gakkō (Japan Deaf Oral School) in 1920. Born in Jonesboro, Illinois, he graduated from Hanover College in 1902 and from McCormick Theological Seminary in 1905 before he went to Japan. His interest in the relationship of Christianity to other religions led to his *Studies in Japanese Buddhism* (1917). He also worked to eliminate duplication of Protestant missionary efforts in Japan and to consolidate denominational seminaries. Leaving Japan in 1941, he taught comparative religion at Union Theological Seminary for several years. His works include *The Task in Japan: A Study in Modern Missionary Imperatives* (1926) and *Ōjō yōshū: Collected Essays on Birth into Paradise* (1930). His second son, Edwin O. REISCHAUER, was a well-known Japanologist who served as ambassador to Japan from 1961 to 1966.

Reischauer, Edwin Oldfather

ライシャワー, E. O.

(1910–90). US scholar and diplomat. By force of his writings on Japanese history and current affairs, his teaching, and his able performance as US ambassador to Japan (1961–66), Reischauer made great contributions to mutual understanding between Japanese and Americans. Born in Tōkyō, Reischauer graduated in 1927 from the American School in Japan and from Oberlin College in 1931. He began his studies of early Japanese and Chinese history at Harvard University under the tutelage of Serge ELISSÉEFF and then spent five years studying in Paris, Tōkyō, Kyōto, and Beijing (Peking). After completing his doctoral dissertation on the travels in 9th-century China of the Japanese Buddhist monk ENNIN, in 1938 he joined the Harvard faculty. Together with the China historian John King Fairbank (1907–91), he was a pioneer in introducing East Asian studies to the American college curriculum.

Between 1941 and 1946 Reischauer served in the Department of War, the Department of State, and the US Army. President John F. Kennedy named him ambassador to Japan in 1961. He sought to restore what he called the "broken dialogue" between the two countries, and his diplomacy paved the way for the return of Okinawa to Japan.

Returning to the Harvard faculty in 1966, Reischauer also served as chairman of the Board of Trustees of the Harvard-Yenching Institute. His published works include *Japan, Past and Present* (1946; rev ed 1963); *Japan: The Story of a Nation* (1970; rev ed 1981); *The Japanese* (1977); and *My Life between Japan and America* (1986).

Reiyūkai

霊友会

One of Japan's largest lay religious organizations. Its doctrines stress ancestor veneration, the Japanese family system, and the Buddhist tradition as embodied in the LOTUS SUTRA, although there is no formal affiliation with any Buddhist sect. The group was founded in 1925 by Kubo Kakutarō (1892–1944), his brother Kotani Yasukichi (1885–1929), and Kotani's wife, Kimi (1901–71). Kubo developed the idea of ancestor veneration as the key to national salvation and social harmony and devised an ancestral ritual to be performed twice daily. Faith healing also is practiced. After World War II the Reiyūkai called for a revival of the prewar extended family system and traditional morality. *Hōza*, a small group meeting in which members consult with a lay leader on personal problems and receive religious instruction, also became important. The organization claimed about 3 million adherents in 1989.

Reizei Family Shiguretei Museum

冷泉家時雨亭文庫

(Reizeike Shiguretei Bunko). Museum in Kyōto, built by the Reizei family. Established in April 1981. The purposes of the museum are to preserve the Reizei family residence, a unique example of a Japanese noble-family mansion built in 1790; to preserve books and documents handed down by the family; and to preserve the traditions of flower arrangement and other ceremonial observances that had been in the family for hundreds of years. The Reizei family documents had remained unopened for 800 years by imperial order until 1980. The overwhelming majority of the approximately

20,000 items are literary materials, including collections of WAKA poetry (a specialty of the Reizei family) and related materials. Three of the items, including a copy, in the handwriting of FUJIWARA NO SADAIE (1162–1241), of the 10th-century *waka* anthology KOKINSHŪ, are classified as National Treasures.

Reizei Tamechika

令泉為恭

(1823–64). Painter in the classical Japanese YAMATO-E style. Also known as Okada Tamechika. Born in Kyōto, the son of a KANŌ SCHOOL painter. However, he did not follow the Kanō style but studied the paintings of the Nara (710–794) and Heian (794–1185) periods instead. Taking Buddhist themes and court life as his subject matter, he sought to revive the ancient *yamato-e* style (see FUKKO YAMATO-E SCHOOL). He even adopted the aristocratic surname Reizei. His fervent proimperial stance led to his assassination by a *rōnin*, or masterless *samurai*, in the political chaos of the late Edo period (1600–1868).

Reizei Tamesuke

冷泉為相

(1263–1328). Classical (WAKA) poet and courtier. Tamesuke was the son of FUJIWARA NO TAMEIE—heir of FUJIWARA NO SADAIE (Fujiwara no Teika)—and Tameie's second wife, ABUTSU NI. Tamesuke was the founder of the Reizei family, one of the three poetic houses into which Teika's descendants were divided (the other two were the Nijō and Kyōgoku lines). Some 65 of Tamesuke's poems are included in IMPERIAL ANTHOLOGIES. Much of his verse has a quality of flatness—an effect of his pursuit of realism in natural and psychological description.

Rekitei

歴程

(The Traveled Path). Monthly poetry magazine. Published by Rekiteisha, it ran for a total of 26 issues after its inauguration in May 1935. The magazine was revived in July 1947 and remains an important forum for contemporary poetry in Japan. Its original group of contributors included KUSANO SHIMPEI, TAKAHASHI SHINKICHI, and NAKAHARA CHŪYA. *Rekitei* avoids any specific ideology or aesthetic position, preferring instead to give free rein to the creative talents of its contributing poets.

religion

宗教

(*shūkyō*). Religious life in Japan is rich and varied, with a long history of interaction among a number of religious traditions. Most of the individual features of Japanese religion are not unique; the distinctiveness of Japanese religion lies in the total pattern of interacting traditions.

Many traditional Japanese beliefs and practices hark back to prehistoric customs, and most of these form the core of SHINTŌ, the only major religion indigenous to Japan. Indian Buddhism, the Chinese contributions of Confucianism and Taoism (transmitted first through the cultural bridge of Korea) and, much later, Christianity were introduced to Japan from outside. All these foreign traditions have undergone significant transformations in a process of mutual influence with the native tradition.

The Historical Formation of Japanese Religion In Judaism and Christianity religion entails faith in one supreme deity; revelation of the will of this deity in a sacred book; concern with sin as disobedience to the deity; relation of man to divinity through a conscious decision or act of faith; specific ecclesiastical organizations, involving regular

attendance and worship; and ethical behavior linked directly to this religious commitment.

Japanese religion differs significantly on each of the aforementioned points: there are not one but many deities; there is no one sacred book, but many religious scriptures; rather than emphasis on sin as disobedience to the deity there is a concern with ritual impurity and purification; one person usually participates in more than one religious tradition; there is no regular worship day comparable to the Sabbath but many seasonal festivals; and ethical codes are more closely related to family life and philosophy than to organized religion, while ethical shortcomings are not linked directly to divine will but are considered in terms of human imperfection.

In early Japan religious life was closely related to rice agriculture. Religious rites focused on seasonal celebrations anticipating and giving thanks for agricultural fertility and on venerating ancestral spirits who were considered directly responsible for fertility. From about 500 BC to AD 500, southwest Japan was developing into a centralized kingdom headed by an imperial family. From about AD 500, the high culture of China—including written language—entered Japan and immediately became a major influence upon the elite class and eventually upon the common people. The tendency in Japanese history has not been "either-or" exclusivity, but rather "both-and" inclusivity, in adopting foreign cultural elements. Therefore, instead of rejecting Buddhism, the Japanese eventually incorporated it into the life of the family, making Buddhist memorial rites central to the veneration of family ancestors and directly linking Buddhist divinities to Shintō gods (see HONJI SUIJAKU). Confucian notions were adopted to encourage loyalty to the emperor.

By the 8th century, local myths and traditions were largely unified around one account of creation and the descent of the emperor from the gods as seen in the KOJIKI (712) and NIHON SHOKI (720), the two earliest Japanese historical chronicles. Partly in reaction to the highly organized Buddhist religion, Japanese rituals and practice came to be organized as Shintō, "the Way of the gods." From this time on, Buddhism and Shintō were the major organized religions and gradually penetrated more into the lives of ordinary people. Many Shintō shrines that originated as family institutions developed into territorial shrines and eventually expanded to include branch shrines in other locales. Buddhist temples for the common people also gradually arose to fulfill the need for funerary and memorial services. From about 800 to 1400, various Buddhist sects and Shintō schools developed. In the Edo period (1600–1868) Buddhist temples became closely allied with the power of the state, and families were required to belong to a specific temple (see TERAUKE); at about the same time, Confucian thought became important for providing the rationale for the state. With the Meiji Restoration of 1868, however, Shintō became prominent in justifying and maintaining the new nation-state under its emperor and was influential even in education.

The Major Features of Traditional Japanese Religion The seven major features that characterized Japanese religion until about 1900 overlapped and interlocked to form the general pattern of what is now con-

Edwin Oldfather Reischauer One of the pioneers in the introduction of East Asian studies to the American college curriculum, Reischauer is best remembered by the Japanese for his able performance as US ambassador to Japan from 1961 to 1966.

rendai A two-passenger *hirarendai* portrayed in a fan-type woodblock print by Hiroshige. The scene is a crossing on the river Ōigawa along the Tōkaidō.

sidered traditional Japanese religion. These features can be identified briefly as follows:

Mutual interaction among several religious traditions. Typical of religious history in Japan is both a plurality of religious traditions and simultaneous or alternate participation by one person (or family). In recent times a person might be married in a Shintō shrine, live his life according to Confucian social teachings, hold some Taoistic beliefs about "lucky" and "unlucky" phenomena, participate in folk festivals, and have his funeral conducted by a Buddhist temple.

Intimate relationship between man and the gods and the sacredness of nature. In Japan the relationship between man and the sacred (*kami*) is very close. In addition to the specific deities represented in mythology, natural phenomena and emperors and other special human beings were also considered to be sacred or *kami.* The spirits of the dead of each family, as revered ancestors, were termed either *hotoke* (Buddhas) or *kami.* In Japanese religion *kami* and Buddhas are not conceived as being in another world so much as they are thought to exist within the world of nature and in the lives of human beings.

The religious significance of the family and ancestors. The ancient Japanese emphasis on lineage or family carried with it devotion to clan *kami* (UJIGAMI), and CONFUCIANISM, with its insistence on FILIAL PIETY and social harmony, provided a philosophical rationale for strong family ties. The home was always a center of religious practice, and this became more formalized during the Edo period, when it became customary for most homes to possess both SHINTŌ FAMILY ALTARS (*kamidana*) and Buddhist altars (BUTSUDAN) for venerating ancestors. Traditional Japanese religious life was conducted by family participation rather than by individual choice.

Purification as a basic principle of religious life. Notions of purity and impurity (KEGARE) and procedures of ritual purification (HARAE; MISOGI) in Japan have assumed an extraordinary importance and have pervaded the culture as a whole. The Japanese people have not conceptualized sin (TSUMI) as a violation of divine commandments, but they have had a clear sense of the impurity or defilement that separates one from one's fellowmen and especially from the *kami.* The traditional observance at a Shintō shrine is to rinse the hands and mouth ceremonially as a symbolic act of purification before coming into contact with the *kami.* In Japan no one tradition dominates ethical concerns; rather each tradition contributes its concepts of ideal behavior: for Shintō, ritual purity and sincerity; for Buddhism, compassion and liberation from desire; for Confucianism,

loyalty to superiors and benevolence toward inferiors.

Festivals as the major means of religious celebration. The pattern of religious activities was determined by each religious institution observing its own special festival days, in addition to annual festivals celebrated by families and the nation as a whole. Festivals at shrines and temples often celebrate the particular *kami* or Buddhist divinities enshrined there, but more often festivals are part of a seasonal drama reenacted every year. Shrines usually have both a spring festival and fall festival roughly coinciding with the transplanting and harvesting of rice. The time surrounding the NEW YEAR is a long festival period marked by large crowds visiting both Shintō shrines and Buddhist temples. The summer BON FESTIVAL in honor of the returning spirits of the dead is observed in most Japanese homes. See also FESTIVALS.

Religion in daily life. In traditional Japan, religion was not an organization apart from everyday life but closely related to every aspect of economic and social life. Rituals followed a person throughout life, from birth to marriage and death (see LIFE CYCLE). Aesthetic pursuits such as the tea ceremony and flower arranging also embodied religious notions concerning veneration of the forces of nature.

Close relationship between religion and state. In Japan the general rule has been for religious authority to be subservient to political power. From the beginnings of Japanese history, myth has sanctioned the unity of ritual and government (*saisei itchi*) through the notion that the *kami* created the Japanese islands as a sacred land to be ruled by a sacred emperor who was a descendant of the supreme *kami,* the sun goddess AMATERASU ŌMIKAMI. Cultural influence from China, especially Confucianism and Buddhism, strengthened and modified this basic pattern.

Religion in Modern Japan—Religion has undergone gradual and significant change throughout Japanese history. After the remarkable changes in national life of the late 19th and early 20th centuries, religion changed even more drastically.

During the Edo period, both Shintō and especially Buddhism became more highly formalized, and the still vital folk traditions tended to attract more of the attention and enthusiastic participation of the people. In the 19th century, popular movements formed around pilgrimage associations (KŌ) and charismatic leaders. Such groups often expanded to form the so-called NEW RELIGIONS (*shinkō shūkyō*). Until 1945 the government controlled religion closely, but new religious movements continued to arise and expand, and after 1945 they became the most conspicuous development of the religious scene. With urbanization and centralization, folk customs generally and FOLK RELIGION in particular declined. Social mobility, especially immigration to cities, tended to weaken both local ties and family relationships, in turn impinging upon organized religion.

A significant event for religion during the Allied Occupation of Japan (1945–52) was the enactment of complete religious freedom. Technically, there had been freedom of religion since the CONSTITUTION OF THE EMPIRE OF JAPAN of 1889, but in actuality government control was so stringent that it had been almost impossible to organize religious groups and propagate religious teachings freely. Complete religious freedom meant that any religious group could now organize indepen-

dently under its own auspices and be exempt from taxes. This resulted in the proliferation of hundreds of new religions and the splintering of many religious organizations, especially Buddhist denominations. See also CHRISTIANITY.

religious education   宗教教育
(*shūkyō kyōiku*). Following the Meiji Restoration of 1868, the new government initiated a campaign to establish Shintō as the state religion (see HAIBUTSU KISHAKU). The 1889 Meiji constitution guaranteed freedom of religion, but stressed the duty of subjects toward the emperor, a Shintō concept that was reinforced in the IMPERIAL RESCRIPT ON EDUCATION (1890). The ideals of state Shintō and imperial rule were incorporated into elementary school subjects such as moral training (SHŪSHIN) and national history (*kokushi*), but the government, apprehensive of Christianity's spread, prohibited formal religious education in all government and public schools, as well as in private schools. Following a brief relaxation of the prohibition, article 20 of the postwar CONSTITUTION OF JAPAN stipulated that neither the state nor its organs could engage in religious education or activities. The Fundamental Law on Education (1947; see EDUCATION, FUNDAMENTAL LAW OF) was more explicit, prohibiting state and public schools from conducting education on specific religions. However, approximately 2 percent of all schools in Japan are private schools affiliated with some religious organizations. Of this group, two-thirds are private Christian schools.

rendai   輦台
Litter used to carry passengers across river fords during the Edo period (1600–1868). Along with boats (*watashibune*) *rendai* were widely used because the shogunate prohibited the construction of bridges along principal highways. The *rendai* consisted of a platform attached to two long poles that were shouldered by bearers. They ranged from the single-passenger *hirarendai* (carried by 4 men) to the *daikōran* (carried by about 20). See also KOSHI.

rendaku   連濁
(sequential voicing). A phonological phenomenon, common in most dialects of the Japanese language, in which a voiceless consonant at the beginning of a word is sometimes replaced by the corresponding voiced consonant when the word occurs noninitially in a compound. This alteration can affect the initial sounds of words of Chinese origin as well as those of native origin but is frequent only with the latter.

The following are the consonant correspondences involved in *rendaku.*

Voiceless	Voiced
h, f	b
t	d
s, ts	z
sh, ch	j
k	g

There are no known rules that completely predict the occurrence of *rendaku,* although in certain circumstances it never occurs. Many words begin compounds that exhibit *rendaku,* but the occurrence of these words does not necessarily predict it; e.g., *hana* "nose" gives *hanaji* "nosebleed" with *chi* "blood," but *hanasaki* "tip of the nose" with *saki* "end." Similarly, the initial voiceless consonants of many words are affected by rendaku in some compounds but not in others; e.g., kana "Japanese syllabic orthography" is affected in hiragana "cursive kana" but not in katakana "angular kana." Indeed, doublets such as the names Nakata and Nakada, both from naka "middle" + ta "rice paddy," are not uncommon. In modern standard Japanese, the initial voiceless consonant of a word that already contains b, d, z, j, or g is never subject to rendaku; e.g., hana "flower" + fuda "card" yields hanafuda "Japanese playing cards," but hana + fusa "cluster" yields hanabusa "corolla" or "flower cluster." Reduplicative compounds typically display rendaku unless they are giseigo or gitaigo (often called idiophonic, mimetic, or onomatopoetic expressions); e.g., tokidoki "sometimes" (reduplication of toki "time"), but katakata "clattering."

renga 連歌

(linked verse). Form of poetry that flourished chiefly from the 13th through the 16th century and that culminated in the late 15th century in such 100-stanza (hyakuin) masterpieces as MINASE SANGIN HYAKUIN (1488, One Hundred Links by Three Poets at Minase). The origin of renga, however, is in tan renga (short renga), a 31-syllable poem (WAKA) composed in two units: a three-line unit of 5, 7, and 5 syllables by one poet, followed by a unit of two 7-syllable lines by another. Out of this tradition arose chō renga (long renga), or kusari renga (chain renga), an extended sequence of alternating 5-7-5 and 7-7 units composed by one or, more commonly, multiple poets. The term renga refers primarily to this latter type, which represents the culmination of a collaborative art form foreshadowed by the tan renga.

History—An exchange of three-line poems (katauta) between the legendary hero Prince YAMATOTAKERU and an old man that is recorded in the 8th-century chronicle NIHON SHOKI is considered the ancestor of the renga tradition. Because the initial poem contains a reference to Mt. Tsukuba, the art of renga is sometimes called Tsukuba no Michi (the Way of Tsukuba).

A linked verse of 5-7-5 and 7-7 syllable units attributed to ŌTOMO NO YAKAMOCHI and a nun, which appears in book 8 of the MAN'YŌSHŪ (ca mid-8th century), is the oldest known example of tan renga. The writing of tan renga flourished in the latter half of the Heian period (794–1185), and many were included in anthologies. Chō renga came into existence toward the end of the Heian period and were widely composed during the early Kamakura period (1185–1333) by poets such as Emperor GO-TOBA, FUJIWARA NO SADAIE, and FUJIWARA NO IETAKA. As the form matured, the literary quality of renga improved, and the 100-stanza sequence of alternate 5-7-5 and 7-7 stanzas became the established form. Renga were categorized as either ushin ("having heart"), serious in intent and elegant in style, or mushin ("lacking heart"), comical. Ushin renga eventually became the dominant form.

Toward the end of the Kamakura period, rules for the composition of renga (shikimoku) were established, and poets who devoted their creative efforts chiefly to renga appeared. NIJŌ YOSHIMOTO collaborated with his teacher GUSAI to compile the first anthology of renga, TSUKUBASHŪ (1356). The two also collaborated on Renga shinshiki (1372), a codification of the rules of renga. Renga developed rapidly during this period, becoming independent of waka and achieving equality with it as a genre of verse.

Thereafter the art languished for a period but was revitalized by renga masters such as TAKAYAMA SŌZEI and SHINKEI. In SASAMEGOTO (1463), a treatise on renga, Shinkei emphasized the importance of the aesthetic ideals ushin (elegant and mysterious beauty). Ushin renga was brought to fulfillment by Shinkei's successors, a group of poets led by SŌGI that included INAWASHIRO KENSAI, SHŌHAKU, and SŌCHŌ. The 100-stanza sequence Minase sangin hyakuin, by Sōgi, Shōhaku, and Sōchō, is considered one of the great achievements of the genre, and the anthology SHINSEN TSUKUBASHŪ (1495), compiled by Sōgi and Kensai, is regarded as the classic statement of the aesthetic concepts ushin and yūgen. After Sōgi's death ushin renga fell into decline and haikai no renga (or haikai; see HAIKU) came into vogue. Emerging from the mushin renga tradition of wit and humor, haikai was less closely oriented toward the classical literary tradition.

Composition—Gatherings at which renga are composed jointly are referred to as za or kaiseki; contributing poets are collectively called renjū. A group of seven or eight people is considered ideal for composing renga. A sequence created by a group of three is called a sangin, one composed by two people, a ryōgin, and a renga by one person, a dokugin. The basic form is the 100-stanza sequence. The first stanza is called hokku; the second, wakiku; the third, daisan; the fourth through the penultimate, hiraku; and the last, ageku. The renga is recorded on folded sheets of paper (kaishi) by one of the poets. When contributing to a renga it is important to consider not only how a new link meshes with the stanza preceding it, but also the effect it will have on the form and tone of the sequence as a whole. For this reason there arose many rules for renga, stipulating the manner of linking and the distribution, in set positions throughout the sequence, of stanzas that must evoke traditional themes, such as the progress of the seasons, cherry blossoms, the full moon, and love.

rengesō 蓮華草

(Chinese milk vetch). Astragalus sinicus. A perennial herb of the family Leguminosae that grows in paddy fields, on plains, and along roadsides from central Honshū southward. The stem is 10–30 centimeters (3.9–11.8 in) high, and the leaves are alternate and pinnate. From April to June, the 10–30 centimeter flower stalk bears about seven butterfly-shaped reddish purple flowers. The plant is cultivated as pasture, green manure, and as a source of honey nectar. It is also used in folk remedies.

Rengetsu → Ōtagaki Rengetsu

Rengō 連合

(abbreviation of Nihon Rōdō Kumiai Sōrengōkai; Japanese Trade Union Confederation). Japan's largest federation of labor unions. Formed in November 1987 through the unification of Zen Nihon Minkan Rōdō Kumiai Kyōgikai (All-Japan Council of Private-Sector Unions), Chūritsu Rōren (Federation of Independent Unions), and Dōmei (Japanese Federation of Labor). Shinsambetsu (National Federation of Industrial Labor Organizations) joined in 1988. Private-sector unions affiliated with SŌHYŌ (General Council of Trade Unions of Japan) also joined Rengō, against strong opposition from Sōhyō's public-sector affiliates. However, the public-sector unions were weakened by the privatization of leading public-sector in-

dustries, and, when Sōhyō was disbanded in 1989, many of its remaining unions joined Rengō. At the same time those Sōhyō unions under the influence of the JAPAN COMMUNIST PARTY refused to join and formed their own national labor federation, ZENROREN, in opposition to Rengō. As of 1990, Rengō had 78 union affiliates and a membership of 7.61 million.

Rengō Co, Ltd レンゴー[株]

(Rengō). Company engaged in the manufacture and sale of corrugated paper products. Incorporated in 1920. It was Japan's first manufacturer of corrugated board. Since its inception, Rengō has specialized in packaging materials; it exports many of its technological innovations. Sales for the fiscal year ending March 1991 totaled ¥235.2 billion (US $1.7 billion); the company was capitalized at ¥19.9 billion (US $145.0 million) in the same year. Headquarters are in Ōsaka.

Rengō Kantai → Combined Fleet, Imperial Japanese Navy

renju 連珠

Also called gomoku narabe. Board game that is thought to be an offshoot of GO. Black and white stones are alternately placed on any of the intersecting points of 15 vertical and 15 horizontal lines; the first player to connect a vertical, horizontal, or diagonal line of five stones wins the game. Variously known as gomoku narabe, kakugo, or kyōgo, it became a popular pastime during the 17th century, but it was not until 1899 that the game was called renju by KUROIWA RUIKŌ. In 1906 the Tōkyō Renju Sha (Renju Society) was organized, and a grade (dan) system was established after the manner of go. In 1936 the third master Takagi Rakuzan introduced a renju game board of 15 by 15 squares to replace the go game board of 19 by 19 squares, which had previously been used. Besides Japan, the main countries in which renju is played are the former USSR, Sweden, the Netherlands, and France. The Renju International Federation (Renju Kokusai Remmei) was founded in 1988, and the first world renju championship was held in August 1989 in Kyōto.

Rennyo 蓮如

(1415–99). Also known as Rennyo Kenju. Buddhist priest and eighth hossu (head abbot) of the temple HONGANJI. Under his leadership Honganji grew to become the unchallenged center of Shinshū (the JŌDO SHIN SECT) and the largest, most powerful religious organization in late medieval Japan. Within the Shinshū tradition Rennyo's status is second only to that of its founder, SHINRAN. As hossu, Rennyo concentrated his

rengesō This perennial herb is often raised in rice paddies for use as green manure.
1 Fields of rengesō in flower in Nara Prefecture. The hutlike structures are frames for drying rice stalks.
2 The rengesō germinates in autumn. The stems trail along the ground as it grows, and flowers are produced in spring.

rensha This illustration from a set of early-14th-century handscrolls depicts a *rensha* carrying a noblewoman on a religious pilgrimage.

missionary activity in the central provinces, particularly Ōmi (present Shiga Prefecture). Alarmed by Rennyo's success, the TENDAI SECT headquarters of ENRYAKUJI on Mt. Hiei (HIEIZAN), which considered Ōmi its own preserve, sent armed forces of monk-warriors to destroy Honganji in 1465. Rennyo sought temporary refuge in various locations, including Enryakuji's traditional Tendai rival, the MIIDERA in Ōmi. Finally, in 1471, Rennyo moved his base to Yoshizaki (in what is now Fukui Prefecture). During the next four years Rennyo perfected and disseminated the *ofumi* (epistle), his principal contribution to Shinshū literature. In concise, easily understandable vernacular language, Rennyo set forth the essence of Shinran's teaching of salvation through faith in the Buddha AMIDA and vigorously attacked the various heresies he encountered. Rennyo devoted his remaining years to rebuilding the temple Honganji and to organizing Honganji's ever-increasing following into a cohesive sect.

Renown, Inc   [株]レナウン

(Renaun). Largest comprehensive apparel manufacturer in Japan. Its primary product lines include menswear, women's and children's coats, stockings, and underwear. Prior to World War II, the company produced and sold knitted goods under the name Sasaki Eigyōbu Co, Ltd. Reincorporated in 1947, it changed its name to Renown (the firm's major brand) in 1955. In affiliation with overseas companies, the firm markets Arnold Palmer brand sportswear, Addenda and Cacharel brand women's apparel, and Vassarette brand women's underwear. Annual sales for the fiscal year ending December 1990 totaled ¥231.8 billion (US $1.7 billion), and the company was capitalized at ¥48.9 billion (US $366.2 million). Headquarters are in Tōkyō.

rensha   輦車

A small enclosed carriage with two wheels, propelled by four or more men by means of long poles that extended from the front and back of the vehicle on either side. During the Heian period (794–1185) it was used within the palace grounds by members of the imperial family, their regents or advisers, and others with imperial permission. GISSHA (oxcarts) were used outside the palace grounds.

rensho   連署

(cosigner). A subordinate to the regent (SHIKKEN) in the KAMAKURA SHOGUNATE (1192–1333). The *rensho* put his signature next to that of the *shikken* on official directives such as KUDASHIBUMI, *migyōsho*, and *gejijō*. In 1225 HŌJŌ YASUTOKI appointed his uncle Tokifusa (1175–1240) as the first *rensho;* thereafter it was a prerogative of the HŌJŌ FAMILY. In a broader sense, *rensho* (or *rempan*) refers to the placement of two or more signatures, or to a document so signed.

rentai saimu   連帯債務

(joint and several obligation). An obligatory relationship in which several parties (obligors) assume equal responsibility for the discharge or payment of contractual debts or obligations jointly entered into with a third party (the obligee). In a joint and several obligation, the obligee may demand performance of all or part of the contracted obligatory duty of one or several of the obligors either simultaneously or in succession. If one of the obligors discharges the obligation, the others are severally relieved of their obligation (CIVIL CODE, art. 432). See also SURETYSHIP.

rental deposit   敷金

(*shikikin*). Payment by the lessee (tenant) of a specified sum of money to the lessor (landlord) at the commencement of a lease agreement for land or a structure as a deposit to be returned to the lessee upon the expiration of the lease. The deposit system in Japan is based on the traditional landlord-tenant relationship and does not have a legal basis. Although whether a lessee is required to pay a deposit is left to the lease agreement, there are very few instances in which a lessee can avoid paying. Similarly, there is no law regulating the amount of the deposit, which is therefore determined by the intent of the parties. The amount of the deposit is usually several months' rent. Upon the lease's expiration, the lessor must return the deposit, although he or she may deduct a sum in compensation for damages to the leased structure or for rent charges. See also KEY MONEY.

renunciation of war   戦争の放棄

(*sensō no hōki*). Doctrine arising out of article 9, the most famous and most controversial article, of the CONSTITUTION OF JAPAN (1947). Article 9 reads as follows:

"Aspiring sincerely to an international peace based on justice and order, the Japanese people forever renounce war as a sovereign right of the nation and the threat or use of force as a means of settling international disputes.

"In order to accomplish the aim of the preceding paragraph, land, sea, and air forces, as well as other war potential, will never be maintained. The right of belligerency of the state will not be recognized."

The SAN FRANCISCO PEACE TREATY of September 1951 specifically stated that the Allied powers "recognize that Japan as a sovereign nation possesses the inherent right of individual or collective self-defense." With that provision as the basis, the Diet in 1954 passed a law creating the SELF DEFENSE FORCES (SDF). The twin questions of the development of the SDF and the possible violation of article 9 have been highly controversial issues in Japanese politics.

The Supreme Court of Japan has ruled several times on possible violations of article 9. However, it has not dealt directly with the constitutionality of the SDF, only on the constitutionality of the UNITED STATES–JAPAN SECURITY TREATIES that permit US bases in Japan, which, according to some, constitute war potential. However, the court has refused to declare such bases unconstitutional, arguing that matters relating to national security are by their nature political and must therefore be decided by the sovereign people, who can express political judgments on security matters by exercising their suffrage in free elections. See also ENIWA CASE; NA-

TIONAL POLICE RESERVE CASE; SUNAGAWA CASE; NAGANUMA CASE.

renza   連坐

The principle of group responsibility and liability; a part of Japanese legal practice from the Heian (794–1185) through the Edo (1600–1868) periods. Specifics varied, but as a general rule group liability was applied to kinsmen (in which case it was called *enza*), neighbors, or colleagues of the suspect. The policy was based on the belief that the threat of group punishment would prompt the group to restrain troublesome people. A broadened principle of village and community responsibility was developed by regional barons (SENGOKU DAIMYŌ) during the 16th century and later codified in the KUJIKATA OSADAMEGAKI of the Tokugawa shogunate (1603–1867). Crime-specific punishments were prescribed for the guilty person and for members of his mutual-responsibility group (GONINGUMI) and officials of his village or town (MURA YAKUNIN and MACHI YAKUNIN). The *renza* system was abolished after the Meiji Restoration of 1868.

Reorganization Loan   善後借款

(Ch: Shanhou Jiekuan or Shan-hou Chieh-k'uan; J: Zengo Shakkan). Financial loan of £25 million made in April 1913 to the new Chinese republic under President YUAN SHIKAI (Yüan Shih-k'ai) by an international consortium consisting of England, France, Germany, Russia, and Japan. The foreign powers sought, by means of the consortium, to support a regime that would maintain stability and protect foreign interests in China. The United States, initially part of this consortium, withdrew, explaining that the consortium's demand to administer and collect China's salt taxes, as security for the loan, was a threat to China's administrative integrity and the OPEN DOOR POLICY. Despite its onerous terms, Yuan Shikai was eager to obtain the loan to finance his government and armies. The signing of the loan on 26 April 1913, without the approval of the National Assembly, contributed to the abortive second revolution against Yuan in the summer of 1913. See also NISHIHARA LOANS.

Reorganized National Government of the Republic of China   南京政府

(Nankin *seifu;* literally, "Nanjing government"). Collaborationist government in China headed by WANG JINGWEI (Wang Ching-wei) and sponsored by Japan in an attempt to govern the areas of China occupied during the SINO-JAPANESE WAR OF 1937–1945; inaugurated on 30 March 1940 in Nanjing (Nanking). The new "national government" replaced the puppet PROVISIONAL GOVERNMENT OF THE REPUBLIC OF CHINA and the REFORM GOVERNMENT OF THE REPUBLIC OF CHINA. It did not receive formal Japanese recognition until 30 November 1940, when Japan gave up hope that its threat of recognition would force CHIANG KAI-SHEK's Nationalist government in Chongqing (Chungking) to a negotiated peace. In an attempt to rival the government in Chongqing, Wang adopted the Guomindang (Kuomintang; Nationalist Party) government structure, flag, and ideology, emphasizing SUN YAT-SEN's perception of China and Japan as natural friends. After SHIGEMITSU MAMORU, the former ambassador to Nanjing, became Japan's foreign minister, a new treaty, signed on 30 October 1943, gave Wang's government some recognition as an ally. On 10 November 1944, Wang died, and his death destroyed Japan's last hope of using the Nanjing regime to persuade Chongqing to collaborate against the Chinese communists instead of continuing resistance to Japan.

reparations for Southeast Asia
東南アジア賠償問題

(Tōnan Ajia baishō mondai). Payments Japan made to Southeast Asian nations victimized by Japanese aggression in World War II. Demands for reparations were first made by the Allied powers. The first US plan, formulated by Edwin W. PAULEY and made public in April 1946, recommended transferring to the devastated nations of Asia all Japanese industrial equipment beyond that needed to maintain prewar living standards in Japan. The Japanese considered the plan harsh and impractical. General Douglas MACARTHUR agreed, and the US War Department reduced demands by two-thirds. Then in May 1949 the United States, which had come to envision an economically powerful and friendly Japan as the cornerstone of its postwar Asian policy, unilaterally dropped all demands for reparations payments.

Strong opposition from the Philippines, however, led to an article in the 1951 SAN FRANCISCO PEACE TREATY providing that Japan negotiate and pay reparations in goods and services to any former enemy demanding them. The governments of the Philippines, Burma, Indonesia, and South Vietnam (after the division of Vietnam in 1954) all insisted on reparations. Although negotiations were prolonged by controversy in Japan over alleged government-business collusion in awarding reparations contracts, separate agreements were finally reached with all four countries. The payments totaled $1.15 billion. Most of the reparations were paid in the form of capital goods, with the recipient country providing Japan with necessary raw materials. Thus through the payments Japan regained access to markets and sources of raw materials in Southeast Asia.

report cards
通信簿

(tsūshimbo). At the end of each term Japanese schools issue report cards to parents recording the school performance, conduct, attendance, and physical condition of each student. These reports are not regulated by the Ministry of Education, as is the CUMULATIVE GUIDANCE RECORD, and their form is left up to the individual school. In the past, report cards followed a five-grade, norm-referenced evaluation system as used in the cumulative records, but an increasing number of schools have adopted a different evaluation method, using written evaluations or specific content-referenced criteria.

reptiles
爬虫類

(hachūrui). About 73 species of reptiles inhabit Japan. Of the reptiles, 14 species are marine, inhabiting the sea along the coasts of the Ryūkyū and Ogasawara islands. Five species of marine turtles are found, including the taimai (hawksbill turtle) and the osagame (leatherback turtle; Dermochelys coriacea). Only the akaumigame (ridley) and aoumigame (green turtle) land on Japanese beaches and lay eggs. The green turtle lives on seaweeds; its meat and eggs are edible. Other marine reptiles are sea snakes that prefer warm seas: the Erabu umihebi (sea krait) is found as far north as the coast of the mainland, and the seguro umihebi (yellow-bellied sea snake; Pelamis platurus) farther north to the coast of Hokkaidō.

Of the land reptiles, about half the species

are endemic to Japan. The ishigame (pond turtle), the TOKAGE (skink), the kana hebi (lizard), 4 species of rat snakes (genus Elaphe), and the shiromadara (colubrid snake; Dinodon orientalis), which is marked with black and white, are all endemic and inhabit the mainland. Unlike the mammals and resident birds, many of these live as far north as Hokkaidō. Among the reptiles in the Ryūkyū Islands, 19 species are endemic, including the Kishinoue tokage (Kishinoue's skink; Eumeces kishinouyei), which often grows to a length of 33 centimeters (13 in) and is the largest of all lizards in Japan, and the Kuroiwa tokagemodoki (panther gecko; Eublepharis kuroiwae), a skinklike gecko. Endemic species of snakes include the arboreal, big-eyed Iwasaki sedakahebi (snail eater; Pareas iwasakii), said to live exclusively on snails, and the deadly poisonous, aggressive habu (Okinawa habu). The mamushi (Haly's viper) is the only poisonous snake in the mainland and is far smaller, slower in motion, and less dangerous than the Okinawa habu. The Haly's viper is distributed extensively on the Asian continent in addition to mainland Japan and Hokkaidō. The Takachiho hebi (Japanese xenodermin snake; Achalinus spinalis), which lives on earthworms and is nocturnal, is a relict that is distributed intermittently in the mainland and the eastern part of China; the Amami Takachiho hebi (A. werneri) is endemic to the Ryūkyū Islands. See also SNAKES; TURTLES.

research and development
研究開発

(R&D; J: kenkyū kaihatsu). A popular term in the post–World War II period used to describe a wide range of applied and basic research for the development of industrial and military technology.

History—Japan's modern R&D efforts have important prewar roots. Among the most significant were the science and technology training capabilities established in the Meiji-period (1868–1912) system of higher education, notably at TŌKYŌ UNIVERSITY's faculty of engineering. The government played a prominent role throughout the prewar period in fostering technological development. Most university-trained engineers entered government service, where they served in government enterprises, schools, and laboratories or as advisers to and inspectors of private industry. The proportion of graduates from IMPERIAL UNIVERSITIES employed in government service before World War II never seems to have fallen below 50 percent.

The goal of military strength provided an important source of motivation for the government's role in promoting research and development, but industrial technology was also regarded as a legitimate government concern. Before World War II it was rare for a government to become directly concerned with technological development to the degree that Japan's did. While the government usually provided the impetus, however, most prewar R&D efforts in Japan exhibited a high degree of cooperation among the academic, private, and government sectors. A noteworthy example of this kind of cooperation was the INSTITUTE OF PHYSICAL AND CHEMICAL RESEARCH (Rikagaku Kenkyūjo, often called Riken), founded in 1917 and funded by private and public money. Because the facilities were better than those available in universities or private companies, much of the basic and applied research in Japan during the 1930s and 1940s was done at Riken.

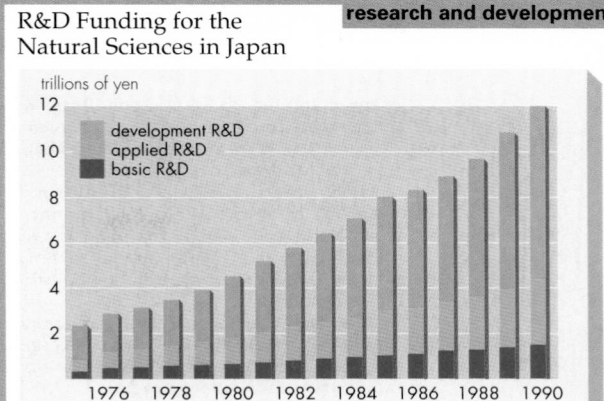

R&D Funding for the Natural Sciences in Japan

trillions of yen

development R&D
applied R&D
basic R&D

1976 1978 1980 1982 1984 1986 1988 1990

SOURCE: Management and Coordination Agency, Kagaku gijutsu kenkyū chōsa hōkoku (annual): 1991.

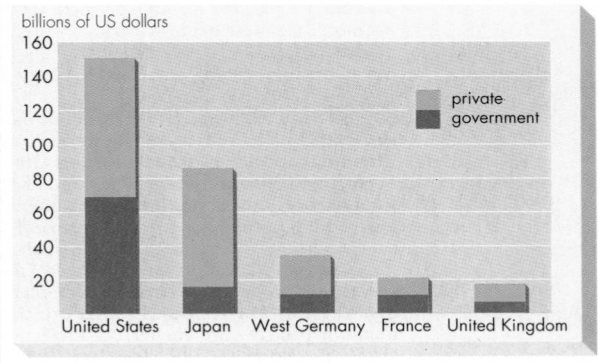

R&D Funding in Selected Countries

billions of US dollars

private
government

United States   Japan   West Germany   France   United Kingdom

NOTE: Figures include funding for the social sciences as well as the natural sciences. Support from private corporations, universities, and research organizations is included in the category of private funding. Figures for the United States and Japan are for 1990, West Germany for 1989, and France and the United Kingdom for 1988.
SOURCE: Science and Technology Agency, Kagaku gijutsu hakusho (annual): 1991.

Probably the single largest research-related project undertaken by the Japanese government in the prewar period was the establishment of the predecessor of the JAPAN SOCIETY FOR THE PROMOTION OF SCIENCE (Gakujutsu Shinkōkai, commonly called Gakushin) under the Ministry of Education in December 1932. Mainly a research-funding agency, Gakushin dispensed over ¥26 million (approximately US $13 million at the prewar rate of exchange) in research funds for basic and applied research from 1933 to 1946, when it was dissolved by the Allied OCCUPATION authorities. Although research had become increasingly related to the war effort in the late 1930s, the work done under the aegis of Gakushin provided an important base for the postwar development of many fields of Japanese industry, including chemicals, optics, electronics, metallurgy, medicine, and agriculture.

Postwar R&D Efforts—In contrast to the prewar period, when funds, initiative, and manpower came from the government, R&D in the postwar period has been concentrated in private industry. This trend has intensified in recent years. In 1975, for example, 27.5 percent of R&D in Japan was financed by government. A decade later, in 1985, the figure had fallen to 19.4 percent, and by 1990, 18.6 percent of R&D was financed by public funds. One major factor accounting for this is the comparatively low level of defense expenditures in Japan and, accordingly, the low level of defense-related R&D. In 1990, for example, 46.1 percent of all R&D expenditures in the United States came from the government and 59.4 percent of the government's R&D expenditures were for defense. In contrast, only 4.6 percent of the Japanese government's R&D expenditure was for defense.

Government R&D in Japan——In the second half of the 1980s the amount allocated to R&D in Japan's national and local budgets grew at an average annual rate of 4.4 percent. By 1990 it amounted to ¥2.0 trillion (US $13.7 billion).

The two most important government R&D agencies are the SCIENCE AND TECHNOLOGY AGENCY (STA) and the AGENCY OF INDUSTRIAL SCIENCE AND TECHNOLOGY (AIST). AIST is attached to the MINISTRY OF INTERNATIONAL TRADE AND INDUSTRY (MITI) and commands the largest single share of budget and personnel of any branch of MITI. Its main task is the funding, organization, and execution of industrial-related research projects; it thus promotes Japanese exports by improving the quality of Japanese goods and advancing the development of indigenous technology to replace imported products.

The STA was established to administer government R&D efforts of a more basic nature. Attached to the Prime Minister's Office, the agency commands over 40 percent of the total science and technology promotion budget, although it employs only 11 percent of the government's research staff. Much of its research is actually commissioned from private firms, quasi-governmental research institutes, or universities. Its two principal ongoing projects are nuclear research and space development. Nuclear research is mainly focused on developing nuclear-energy sources, such as fast breeder reactors.

Universities and R&D——One function of universities that has deteriorated in the postwar period is their contribution to national research efforts. The academic sector's share of total research expenditures fell steadily from 40.6 percent in 1952 to 18 percent in 1989, while the share of private industry climbed from 30 percent to about 70 percent. The trend is accounted for by a number of factors. First, the largest share of research expenditures now originates in the private sector, where there is ample talent available and therefore less need to depend on universities for research. Second, research has become increasingly expensive in the past 46 years because of the use of sophisticated equipment. Third, partly in reaction to the involvement of academics in the war effort, a strong preference for disinterested academic pursuits and an antiestablishment ethic have emerged in universities during the postwar period, trends which incline Japanese academics to distance themselves from the private sector.

R&D in the Private Sector——Japanese private industry provided 72.3 percent of national R&D funds in 1990, as against government and academic contributions of 18.6 percent and 8.4 percent, respectively. This is in sharp contrast to the United States, where the respective shares stood at 49.5 percent, 46.1 percent, and 2.9 percent. The ratio of R&D expenditure to corporate sales stands at 2.8 percent for all industries in Japan. By industry, the ratio is highest in pharmaceuticals (8.0 percent), followed by electronics (6.1 percent), electric machinery (5.9 percent), and chemicals (4.9 percent). All of these are considered future growth industries.

In postwar Japan the private sector has played an important role in importing for-

eign technology through licensing agreements. With technology exports of ¥358.9 billion (US $2.5 billion) in 1990 as against technological imports of ¥874.4 billion (US $6.0 billion), the ratio of exports to imports was 0.41, a considerable improvement over the situation in 1970, when the ratio was a mere 0.13. Nevertheless, it is often asked why Japanese technological imports remain relatively high, given the mature stage that Japan's economy has reached. Part of the answer is that technology imports are a function of capital formation and the industrial maturation process; that is, as an industrial system develops it becomes more able to absorb technology, and therefore imports tend to increase.

The nature of Japanese technology transfer is also affected by researchers' career patterns. Despite a certain trend in recent years toward increasing labor mobility among industrial researchers, they still tend to follow traditional Japanese career patterns—permanent employment, promotion according to seniority, and a high degree of loyalty to the firm (see EMPLOYMENT SYSTEM, MODERN). Japanese firms are less tolerant than Western firms of long-range basic research unrelated to immediate product lines; Japanese management looks for quick, sure results. Perhaps one reason why technological imports still remain comparatively high is that it is easier to buy technology from abroad than to hire seasoned manpower—and there is a greater chance of success.

Summary——In Japan the share of research conducted by private corporations is increasing and those of universities and government research institutes are on a decline, while in the United States the share of private corporations is leveling off, that of universities is rising, and that of government institutes is on the decline. As a result of the increasing share of private sector research in Japan, applied and development R&D related to industrial products has grown, while basic-science R&D has declined. It is important to note that the shares of the three R&D categories—basic (13 percent of total national R&D), applied (24 percent), and development (63 percent)—are already about the same as in the United States. Also, unique and original projects can be found in the development sector just as in the basic R&D field. Considering that Japan's R&D expenditure accounted for only 1.3 percent of the gross national product (GNP) in 1965, as compared with more than 2 percent in the United States, Germany, Britain, and France, the Japanese achievement of a 2.8 percent figure in 1990, roughly equivalent to those of Western countries, is a truly significant improvement.

Research Institute for Nuclear Medicine and Biology, Hiroshima University　広島大学原爆放射能医学研究所

(Hiroshima Daigaku Gembaku Hōshanō Igaku Kenkyūjo). Institute that investigates the effects of nuclear radiation on the human body. Founded in 1961 in Hiroshima Prefecture. The institute conducts medical research aimed at helping the victims of the atomic bombing of Hiroshima and also performs a broad array of basic research on the physiological effects of nuclear radiation.

research institutes　研究所

(kenkyūjo). Research institutes in Japan achieved their full growth in the post–World War II period, although their foundations reach back into the late 19th century,

when institutions specifically for research, such as the ELECTROTECHNICAL LABORATORY and Tōkyō University's Institute for Infectious Diseases, began to appear. The establishment in 1917 of the Rikagaku Kenkyūjo (INSTITUTE OF PHYSICAL AND CHEMICAL RESEARCH), the birthplace of scientific and technological research in Japan, marked the starting point for the establishment of government and industrial research centers. The ŌHARA INSTITUTE FOR SOCIAL RESEARCH, established in 1919, was the first research center devoted to the social sciences. Institutions specializing in the physical sciences and engineering were established in the period following World War I. Beginning about 1959, long-range research and development centers were established by large industrial concerns.

In addition, institutes attached to the national universities were established, such as the YUKAWA INSTITUTE FOR THEORETICAL PHYSICS, Kyōto University, and the Institute for Nuclear Studies, Tōkyō University. Other such national institutes—for example, the NATIONAL MUSEUM OF ETHNOLOGY—were not attached to a specific university. See also RESEARCH AND DEVELOPMENT.

Resident General in Korea, Office of　韓国統監府

(Kankoku Tōkan Fu). Office to administer Korea's foreign affairs; established in Seoul in February 1906 by the Japanese government in accordance with the KOREAN-JAPANESE CONVENTION OF 1905. A July 1907 agreement gave the office administrative authority over the Korean judiciary, military, and police. ITŌ HIROBUMI was appointed the first resident general. After Japan's annexation of Korea in August 1910 the Resident General's Office was replaced by the Government-General of Korea, with TERAUCHI MASATAKE as first governor-general. See also KOREA AND JAPAN.

resident registration　住民登録

(jūmin tōroku). A system by which Japanese nationals are required to register their name, their birthdate, their address, their household, and other information prescribed by law with the municipal authority (city, town, ward, or village) in which they live. Each local authority then compiles this information in a Residents' Basic Register (Jūmin Kihon Daichō).

resident's lawsuit → jūmin soshō

residual import restrictions　残存輸入制限

(zanson yunyū seigen). When Japan joined the General Agreement on Tariffs and Trade (GATT) in 1963, it agreed, in principle, to remove all quantitative import restrictions. However, Japan, like other industrialized nations, in practice retained a number of import quotas. In January 1971 more than 80 items were covered by such import restrictions. The number of protected items dropped to 30 in 1975. By 1986, with the lifting of quotas on leather and shoe imports, all residual quantitative restrictions on manufactured goods had been removed. As of 1992, however, Japan maintained import quotas on 14 agricultural and marine products. Some of these remaining restrictions were in politically sensitive sectors, particularly rice. In continuing negotiations for the removal of the remaining barriers, the United States indicated a preference for direct bilateral negotiations with Japan.

Japan, on the other hand, preferred to use the multilateral international talks of the URUGUAY ROUND.

restaurants 飲食店

(*inshokuten*). Restaurants serving complete meals developed in Japan from the late 18th century. The emergence of a class of wealthy townsmen led to the establishment, particularly in Edo (now Tōkyō), of elegant restaurants called *ryōri-jaya* that had private rooms and lush gardens and provided elaborate meals. Restaurants that served Western foods appeared in Yokohama and Nagasaki in the mid-19th century, but were patronized chiefly by Westerners.

Today among the more than 1 million restaurants in Japan there are many that offer foreign cuisines. Chief among these are restaurants that specialize in Chinese, Korean, French, or Italian cooking, and recently Southeast Asian cuisines, such as Thailand's, have enjoyed particular popularity.

Restaurants serving Japanese cooking range from elegant *ryōtei*, which provide elaborate multicourse meals (see KAISEKI RYŌRI), to simple eating houses. Many restaurants specialize in one type of Japanese food, such as SUSHI, TEMPURA, SUKIYAKI, broiled eel (*unagi*), deep-fried pork cutlets (TONKATSU), grilled chicken (YAKITORI), simmered foods (ODEN), pancakes containing vegetables (OKONOMIYAKI), or TŌFU. There are also restaurants that serve regional cuisine, such as that of Okinawa Prefecture or Akita Prefecture, as well as locally brewed brands of SAKE.

One of the more popular noon meals consists of Japanese noodles (SOBA; UDON), which are served at restaurants known as *sobaya*. Many such restaurants also serve *domburimono*, a bowl of rice topped with any of a variety of ingredients (see KATSUDON; TENDON; OYAKO DOMBURI). RĀMEN, a Japanese version of Chinese-style noodles, is also a common lunchtime repast. *Rāmen'ya*, the Chinese restaurants that specialize in it, serve other simple Chinese dishes as well, such as fried rice (*chāhan*) and fried or steamed pork dumplings (*gyōza*). *Yōshokuya*, which specialize in Japanese variations of Western dishes, offer such foods as sautéed pork cutlets, spaghetti, and beef stew.

On their way home office workers often stop at drinking houses (*nomiya* or *izakaya*) that serve a variety of foods such as *yakitori*, grilled fish (*yakizakana*), raw fish (SASHIMI), chilled *tōfu*, and PICKLES (*tsukemono*) to go along with beer, *sake*, or the distilled liquor known as SHŌCHŪ. Young people in particular have acquired a taste for Western-style fast foods, and a number of franchise chains have established restaurants throughout the country. There is also a type of large restaurant known as a *famirī resutoran* (family restaurant) that serves a wide range of Western foods from club sandwiches to steak and to which parents often take their children.

▶▶*1258–1259*

Restoration of Imperial Rule→
Ōsei Fukko

Restoration Shintō 復古神道

(Fukko Shintō; "Shintō Returned to Its Ancient State"). Also known in English as Revival Shintō, Renaissance Shintō, and Pure Shintō. Fukko Shintō refers to a major movement among scholars, beginning in the 17th century and culminating in the 19th century, that sought to determine the true form of Shintō in ancient Japan before the introduc-

tion of Buddhism, Confucianism, and Taoism. The movement began as a reaction against medieval Shintō schools that had incorporated Buddhist ideas and Chinese philosophies. Fukko Shintō thinkers held that these "alien" ideologies had distorted and corrupted the real meaning of Shintō. The Fukko Shintō movement, especially in its later phase, turned violently against Buddhism and Chinese thought, advocating a return to *kodō* (the ancient way), i.e., pre-Buddhist Japan, seen as a golden age.

Among the foremost advocates of the Fukko Shintō movement were MOTOORI NORINAGA (1730–1801) and HIRATA ATSUTANE (1776–1843). The ideology of Fukko Shintō provided the political and theoretical basis for the establishment of STATE SHINTŌ. See also BAN NOBUTOMO; FUKUBA BISEI; ŌKUNI TAKAMASA; SUZUKI SHIGETANE.

retail industry 小売産業

(*kouri sangyō*). The Japanese retail industry can be divided overall into department stores, supermarkets, specialty stores, and small, family-owned stores. Department stores include those such as MITSUKOSHI, LTD, and MATSUZAKAYA CO, LTD, which have their roots in the dry goods stores of the Edo period (1600–1868), and stores, such as HANKYŪ DEPARTMENT STORES, INC, which were started by private railway companies beginning in the 1930s. Following World War II, department stores expanded in size, opened branches in smaller cities, and formed store groups. In addition, Japanese department stores have opened 70 overseas branches in 11 countries.

Seeking an economy of scale by establishing many branches, supermarkets expanded rapidly in the 1960s. In the second half of the 1960s, supermarkets achieved overall sales on the same level as department stores. In 1973 industry reorganization took place when the LARGE-SCALE RETAIL STORES LAW replaced the Department Store Law and restricted the opening of new branches. Large supermarkets formed affiliated store groups with unprofitable small and medium-sized supermarkets and regional department stores, and they achieved growth by opening specialty store chains, restaurant chains, and discount stores.

Convenience stores, which grew rapidly beginning in the late 1970s, have enjoyed a yearly sales growth of 20–30 percent since 1978. Large-scale specialty stores are polarizing into expensive high-class boutiques and inexpensive discount stores. However, by far the largest number of retail stores are small, family-run stores, which handle fresh foods and daily necessities.

As of 1988 there were 1,620,000 retail and 430,000 wholesale stores in Japan. Sales for 1988 totaled ¥446.4 trillion (US $3.5 trillion) for wholesale and ¥114.8 trillion (US $901.9 billion) for retail. There were 11,182,000 employees in the industry. See also DISTRIBUTION SYSTEM.

retirement 退職

(*taishoku*). The ideal pattern of employment in Japan is a long-term relationship between employer and employee in which the latter joins the company immediately upon graduation and continues to work for that same company until retirement. In recent years, however, there has been a great deal of mobility among young workers, especially those unable to get positions in larger, prestigious companies. Many middle-aged workers have also had to leave their firms

before the retirement age owing to companies' needs to reduce personnel levels or make room for younger employees. Those who have worked for a certain number of years receive a retirement allowance when they leave, and for many the amount is increased if their departure is dictated by the company.

A retirement system based on the practice of lifetime employment has been the norm in Japan since the 1930s. The effect of this system, combined with the seniority wage system, was that older workers' wages continued to rise even though their efficiency might be declining. Workers were therefore required to resign at a certain age in return for being guaranteed a job until that age. Until recently the average age for retirement was 55, but the increasing life expectancy of the Japanese has created a large number of people capable of productive work far beyond that age. The government encouraged extending the age of retirement, and in 1988, 76.7 percent of Japanese firms were retiring their employees at the age of 60. However, retirement does not necessarily mean the end of working life, and most workers do in fact have to find another job, usually for lower pay, in order to support themselves. The minimum age at which most are currently retiring from work altogether is 65. See also ELDERLY WORKERS; EMPLOYMENT SYSTEM, MODERN.

retrial 再審

(*saishin*). The English term "retrial" normally refers to an upper-court order to hold a new hearing at the original court of adjudication. Retrial in this sense obtains in the Japanese judicial process as well. In addition, *saishin* refers to a special procedure under which, upon application to the original court, proceedings are reopened and the final judgment in a criminal case is reviewed. The procedures for *saishin* are set forth in the Code of Criminal Procedure. A convicted person may file a motion for retrial after every ordinary means of remedy has been exhausted. There must, however, be new evidence that is manifestly sufficient to overturn the judgment in question, and because of this restriction most motions have in the past been dismissed. But in 1975 the Supreme Court lowered the barrier in some measure by ruling that a retrial could be initiated if there was evidence to support a rational demonstration that "the final judgment was questionable." This ruling has resulted in a sharp increase in instances of retrial. See also CRIMINAL PROCEDURE.

Rezanov, Nikolai Petrovich
レザノフ, N. P.

(1764–1807). Russian nobleman and majority stockholder of the Russian American Company. Tsar Alexander I sent Rezanov to Japan as an official Russian envoy on the occasion of an around-the-world expedition. Rezanov reached Nagasaki on the merchant ship *Nadezhda* in October 1804. He brought with him a number of Japanese castaways and various gifts. When after several months of waiting and talking the demands and gifts of his government were rejected, Rezanov was outraged. To avenge the imagined slight to Russia, the tsar, and himself, and to frighten the Japanese into the establishment of commercial relations, Rezanov, without the knowledge or permission of his

Continued on page 1260◄

Nikolai Petrovich Rezanov An advocate of trade with Japan, Rezanov negotiated unsuccessfully at Nagasaki in 1804 for the establishment of commercial relations beween Russia and Japan.

Japanese Restaurants: Behind the Noren

Once you master the conventions of dining out in Japan, you will be able to enjoy any type of restaurant—even if you only speak a few phrases of Japanese.

Although Japanese food has become widely available throughout the Western world, it is only in Japan that one can experience the delectable variety of the national cuisine. There are a dozen distinctly different styles of Japanese cooking, each with its own tradition, dispersed among the nation's roughly one million eateries.

While Japanese restaurants in the West often serve several types of cuisine in the same establishment—such as *sushi, tempura, yakitori,* and *soba*—restaurants in Japan specialize to an amazing extent. If you are in the mood for anglerfish stew, for example, you go to a restaurant that for the past hundred years or so has been perfecting its anglerfish stew to the exclusion of any other dish.

The only problem is accessibility to foreigners, who may have little or no knowledge of the language and of the protocol involved in dining out in Japan. I have agonizing memories of my own first forays into Tōkyō's Japanese restaurants. I remember wandering into an exquisite little place in Roppongi. Speaking almost no Japanese and being unable to read the menu—which had been written with a brush on a paper-thin strip of Japanese cedar—I pointed to

three selections at random. A solemn waitress duly brought me, in succession, three marvelously delicate soups. I wrote the names of those soups down in a notebook I still have and, at that moment, began my Japanese culinary education.

As I discovered, there is a certain protocol to dining out in Japan—phrases to be uttered, expectations to be fulfilled—which if adhered to will put everyone at ease. Once you know the routine, you should be able to make your way in any eating establishment without a detailed grasp of the language. Let us look, then, behind the *noren*—the split curtain that hangs across the threshold of traditional Japanese restaurants.

Ryōtei Starting at the top, there are *ryōtei* restaurants, which serve *kaiseki ryōri,* Japanese haute cuisine. It is easy to have a memorable meal without trauma at a *ryōtei* because everything is taken care of. The only difficulty you may encounter is in making a reservation, because the most exclusive *ryōtei* are reluctant to reserve a room for you unless they know you or you have been introduced to them. For this reason, it will be necessary to go with knowledgeable Japanese friends.

The style of *ryōtei* dining is derived from the tea ceremony, which is highly formal in its etiquette but relaxed within the form. You might go for a walk in the garden between courses. During the meal, your waitress will spend much of her time by the table, simply to be with you. You will quickly adjust to the tempo; conversation is low and measured, and the

meal, which can consist of a dozen or more courses (some just a mouthful or two), is eaten at a contemplative pace. *Kaiseki* is labor-intensive and thus very expensive, but it is an experience not to be missed.

Izakaya and Nomiya At the opposite end of the spectrum are little restaurants called *izakaya* ("a place to drink while seated") and *nomiya* ("drinking shop"), which are interchangeable terms. They can be identified by the red paper lanterns (*akachōchin*) that hang outside their doors and by the guffaws and happy commotion inside. It is here that a large percentage of Tōkyō's population spends an hour or two each evening between leaving work and boarding a train for the long commute home.

The menus in *izakaya* and *nomiya* are a good deal more sophisticated than those in Western bars or pubs and may include anything from pan-fried clams to crab eggs to a stew of pork and vegetables. The food is cheap and the protocol in this type of establishment is minimal. Simply enter, sit down anywhere, request a beaker of *nihonshu* (Japanese for Japanese *sake, sake* being the generic word for alcoholic beverages), and specify whether it is to be brought *kan* (warmed) or *hiya* (chilled). By the time you have been brought your *sake* and *otsumami,* a little dish of something to nibble on, the people sitting next to you will probably have engaged you in conversation with gestures and bits of English sentences memorized long ago. You can order along with them. "*Onaji mono, onegai shimasu*" ("Same thing for me, please").

Skewers of *yakitori,* a popular snack of charcoal-broiled chicken.

Yakitoriya and Yatai Even more informal than *izakaya* and *nomiya* are *yakitoriya*—the battered, smoky, and pleasantly rowdy places that serve charcoal-broiled chicken pieces on bamboo skewers and *sake* in bistro glasses.

Yatai are street carts, found mostly near train stations. They serve up bowls of hot noodles or *oden,* a Japanese stew of many ingredients. Just point to the items in the pan of simmering broth that you'd like to try. Most *yatai* serve *sake* too.

At such places you will find that Tōkyō has a heart of gold and that your lack of fluency in the language matters not a jot.

Noodles Noodle shops deserve a few words of their own, for they provide an inexpensive way to eat and can be elegant in their simplicity.

Late-night diners gather inside the colorful *noren* of a street cart serving *rāmen* noodles and *sake*.

There are three kinds of noodles: *soba* (buckwheat), *udon* (wheat flour), and *rāmen* (Chinese-style noodles). *Soba* enjoys something of a mystique, with connoisseurs holding forth on the necessity of split-second timing in preparing the dough, water of a heavenly purity, and a deft wrist action while cutting the noodles. In a *soba* shop, order *mori* if you'd like plain noodles, *zaru* if you'd like them sprinkled with slivers of seaweed called *nori*, or *tempura soba* if you'd like a bowl of buckwheat noodles in broth topped with a shrimp deep-fried in batter.

You may also be able to order *udon* in a *soba* shop, but *rāmen* can only be had at shops that serve that dish. *Rāmen* is punchier than *soba* or *udon* and is often jazzed up with spicy red pepper oil. In the Japanese scheme of things, *rāmen* is considered more down-to-earth than *soba* or *udon*, more a dish for the common man. *Chāshūmen* is *rāmen* with slices of roast pork on top. A side order of *gyōza*, Chinese fried dumplings, is a common accompaniment to a bowl of *rāmen*.

Sushi

Although *sushi* has its own special vocabulary, it is easy to negotiate a meal. Simply take a place at a table and ask for *ichinimmae* (an order for one) or *ninimmae* (orders for two), and you'll be brought the most basic set course. Another strategy is to sit at the counter and point to what you want, but be warned that this can be significantly more expensive. Note that you cannot tell just by looking at a *sushi* shop whether it will be expensive or not. The *sushi* shops inside Tōkyō's Tsukiji fish market look ordinary, but because they cater to experts they are excellent—and pricey.

Tempura

There's exquisite *tempura*, which is expensive, and there's run-of-the-mill *tempura*, which is not. The ordinary stuff is eaten by Japanese much as corned beef on rye is eaten by New Yorkers.

Tempura restaurants usually offer three courses, most often designated *ume* ("plum"), *take* ("bamboo"), and *matsu* ("pine"), in ascending order of price and complexity. The *ume* course offers good value, and even if the place doesn't have an *ume* course as such, you will be understood if you say, "*Ume kōsu, onegai shimasu*" ("The plum course, please").

Sukiyaki and Shabushabu

Sukiyaki—thin slices of beef and vegetables cooked in a broth flavored with soy sauce and sugar—is prepared right at your table and is something of a treat. Still, it's a simple dish of peasant origins and is often prepared at home or partaken *en famille* in a *sukiyaki* restaurant.

Shabushabu consists of thinner slices of beef that are eaten after being dipped in a copper cauldron of boiling stock.

There's not much sense in paying a lot of money for *sukiyaki* or *shabushabu* at a fancy place in the Ginza. You can find perfectly good restaurants on the top floors of large department stores, and the prices are calculated to put shoppers in an agreeable mood.

Teppan'yaki and Okonomiyaki

In *teppan'yaki* restaurants, steak, seafood, and vegetables are cooked before you on a large iron hotplate. *Teppan'yaki* has its origins in the countryside, as it was an efficient way to feed an extended farm family. Urban adaptations are mostly upscale and self-conscious.

An attractive, downscale variation is *okonomiyaki*, a cook-it-yourself Japanese-style pancake affair. *Okonomiyaki* literally means "grilled whatever-you-like," and you order according to the kind of ingredients you want—*ika* (squid), *tako* (octopus), *ebi* (shrimp), and so on. This is all eaten with a generous helping of thick, sweetish sauce. *Okonomiyaki* places are informal, noisy, cheap, and great fun.

Tonkatsu

Tonkatsu refers to deep-fried breaded pork cutlets, which are invariably served with a mound of shredded cabbage and liberally doused with a thick, sweet sauce. It is an utterly basic dish, far removed from the sublime sense-play of *kaiseki*. Nevertheless, *tonkatsu* has a place in the Japanese soul roughly equivalent to hamburger in the American.

Order *tonkatsu* by specifying *hire*—Japanese for "filet," the best cut.

Nabe

Nabe restaurants offer all manner of things cooked in ceramic pots or in iron cauldrons, often over charcoal. The distinguishing characteristic of this dish is its main ingredient—seafood, chicken, or pork—and you should specify your preference when you order. *Sukiyaki* and *shabushabu*, which were described earlier, are also considered types of *nabe*.

Chankonabe, the hearty stew favored by *sumō* wrestlers, is available at specialty *chanko* restaurants. This dish features pork, chicken, beef, seafood, and vegetables of a sort you have never imagined (chrysanthemum leaves, for instance) and will dispel forever any suspicions you may have had that Japanese cuisine consists only of pretty, dainty tidbits. This is food for lumberjacks.

Unagi

Unagi means "eel," and when charcoal-broiled it is rich and filling, like foie gras. The old *unagi* emporia are traditional places, comfortably worn, where you will be served in your own private *tatami*-matted room by your own waitress, just as in a *ryōtei*. There probably won't be a menu, just a choice of three courses, the cheapest being the most popular. Personally, I find *unagi* the single dish

that most fully characterizes the delights of dining out in Japan.

Fugu

Fugu is "blowfish," the famous Japanese gourmet treat that can be poisonous if not prepared properly. (By law, only licensed chefs can do the job.)

Fugu is eaten raw, in paper-thin slices, or cooked in a *nabe*, called *fuguchiri*. There will be a choice of courses. The taste of *fugu* is delicate to the point of ineffability.

In the Ginza district in Tōkyō, *fugu* can cost a small fortune, but in an Asakusa back alley it will be more affordable.

Some Phrases to Remember

In restaurants that offer a confusing variety of dishes, such as a *nomiya*, you could ask, "*Osusume wa?*" ("What do you recommend?"). In a *sushi* bar, where a meal is essentially variations on a single dish, you might say, "*Omakase shimasu*" ("I'll leave it up to you"). No one will consider this a cop-out by someone who hasn't done his homework. It is a perfectly respectable way of ordering *sushi* that is used by many Japanese. After all, who knows what is especially good on a given day? Other phrases you may find useful are:

Kekkō desu.
      That's enough. No more for me, thanks.
Okanjō onegai shimasu.
      May I have the check, please?
Gochisōsama deshita.
      Many thanks for a fine meal.

A Final Tip

It is true that tipping is not required or expected; you will only cause confusion if you try to tip. Just relax, eschew English in favor of winningly inventive gestures, show yourself to be curious and appreciative, and you cannot fail to have a memorable meal.

Rick Kennedy

Sushi chefs at work in a typical *sushi* bar.

government, induced two young naval officers in the service of the Russian American Company, Nikolai Aleksandrovich Khvostov and Gavriil Ivanovich Davydov, to raid Japanese settlements on the islands of ETOROFU and SAKHALIN.

Rhee line　　　　　　　　李承晩ライン

(J: Ri Shōban *rain*). Artificial line established by the Korean president Syngman RHEE (Yi Sŭng-man; J: Ri Shōban) on 18 January 1952, claiming a larger area of international waters for Korea than that demarcated by the so-called MacArthur line (1945; revised in 1949). The Japanese government strongly protested. Several incidents involving Japanese fishermen occurred. The disagreement was settled by the signing of a Korean-Japanese fishing agreement in 1965 (see KOREAJAPAN TREATY OF 1965, SUPPLEMENTARY AGREEMENTS).

Rhee, Syngman　　　　　　　李承晩

(1875–1965; Yi Sŭng-man; J: Ri Shōban). President of the Republic of Korea (ROK; South Korea), 1948–60. In 1904 he traveled to the United States, where he received a PhD from Princeton University in 1910. A brief stay in Korea between 1910 and 1912 convinced him that he should devote himself to the cause of freeing Korea from Japanese domination, and in the following years he lectured about Korea throughout the United States. Prominent overseas Koreans, who organized the PROVISIONAL GOVERNMENT OF KOREA in Shanghai, elected him its first president in 1919. Replaced in 1925, he retired from politics and settled in Hawaii.

Rhee continued to agitate for Korean independence and diplomatic recognition of the exiled Korean government during World War II. After Korea was liberated from the Japanese in 1945, the US government supported Rhee as a leader; with the partition of the peninsula between north and south, he became president of the ROK in 1948.

South Koreans respected him for his determination to reunite Korea during the KOREAN WAR and his refusal to normalize relations with Japan. However, inefficiency and corruption in his administration led to a mas-

rhododendrons
1 *Hon shakunage*, a common garden variety closely related to *tsukushi shakunage*, at the temple Murōji in Nara. The blooms appear in late April or early May.
2 The species *hakusan shakunage* is distributed in subalpine regions throughout Japan, excluding Kyūshū. It blooms in July or early August in clusters of 5 to 15 blossoms.

sive student uprising in April 1960, and Rhee was forced to resign.

rhododendrons　　　　　　　石楠花

(*shakunage*). *Rhododendron* spp. A group of mostly evergreen shrubs of the heath family (Ericaceae), which grow wild in mountainous areas of Japan; also cultivated as ornamentals. The Japanese species best known abroad is the *tsukushi shakunage* (*R. metternichii*), which occurs mostly in warm areas and has seven-lobed, reddish purple blossoms. Other Japanese rhododendrons include the *azuma shakunage* (*R. degronianum* or *R. metternichii* var. *pentamerum*), which grows wild from central Honshū eastward and has five-lobed pink blossoms, the alpine *kibana shakunage* (*R. aureum*), with pale yellow flowers, and the subalpine *hakusan shakunage* (*R. brachycarpum*), with white or pink flowers. Ornamental species with large flowers grown in Japan are mostly of foreign origin. See also AZALEAS.

ri　　　　　　　　　　　　　　里

1. (village or hamlet). The smallest unit of local administration outside Kyōto under the RITSURYŌ SYSTEM established in the late 7th century. Sometimes called *sato*. Each *ri* comprised 50 households under a village headman or *richō* (see KOKUGUN SYSTEM). In 715 the GŌRI SYSTEM was enacted, whereby the preexisting *ri* were renamed GŌ (townships or villages), each comprising two or three new *ri* (hamlets). The *gōri* system was never fully established, and in 740 the new *ri* were abolished.

2. Unit of square measure. In the JŌRI SYSTEM of land division initiated in the mid-7th century a *ri* was a tract of land 6 *chō* (0.65 km or 0.41 mi) square; its area was thus 42.8 hectares or 105.7 acres.

3. Unit of linear measure. Under the *ritsuryō* system a *ri* was defined as 6 *chō* (0.65 km or 0.41 mi). From the Heian period (794–1185) onward, the *ri* was commonly 36 *chō* (3.93 km or 2.44 mi).

ri　　　　　　　　　　　　　　理

(law; principle). The basic metaphysical principle of the Zhu Xi (Chu Hsi) school of Confucianism (see SHUSHIGAKU). *Ri* (Ch: *li*) means the source of being of the universe,

underlying all existence within it, as well as the natural law and social norms that govern the universe. *Ri*, in this philosophical system, is considered an independent and self-sufficient absolute principle, formless and motionless. All things in the universe are produced through the interaction of this quiescent principle and *ki* (Ch: *qi* or *ch'i*; "vital breath"), the creative source of the universe.

In Japan the concept of *ri* was understood in different ways, depending on whether its aspect as absolute principle or as natural and moral law was emphasized. In the Edo period (1600–1868) the KOGAKU (Ancient Learning) school denied the ontological aspect of *ri* and limited its meaning to natural and social law. Later, this school further distinguished between natural law and social norms and limited *ri* to the former meaning.

Riccar Art Museum　　　リッカー美術館

(Rikkā Bijutsukan). Located in Tōkyō. This museum, opened in 1972 and devoted exclusively to UKIYO-E prints, concentrates on showing parts of Hiraki Shinji's (1910–71) well-known collection of some 6,000 prints. Also exhibited are prints by HIROSHIGE, UTAMARO, and HARUNOBU as well as prints by foreign artists. The museum also has a library for *ukiyo-e* studies.

rice　　　　　　　　　　　　　米

(*kome*). Principal Japanese staple crop; an annual marshland plant of tropical origin; introduced into Japan in the Yayoi period (ca 300 BC– ca AD 300), either from China or the Korean peninsula. Rice cultivation was traditionally regarded as a religious act—an invoking of the *inadama* or spirit of the rice plant (see TA NO KAMI). Supplications to the deity survive today in various forms of FOLK PERFORMING ARTS. Many festivals in honor of tutelary deities are also harvest festivals (see also AGRICULTURAL RITES). It is generally agreed that the Japanese extended family (IE) system evolved within the context of the rice culture, which required intensive farming, a sophisticated system of water control, and communal cooperation (see YUI). In this sense rice may be said to have determined the very contours of Japanese society.

The common agricultural species is *Oryza sativa*. Like other plants of the family Gramineae, it has leaves with parallel venation; they sprout from the upper nodes of the stem, and the roots from the lower nodes. From the base of the main stem grow tillers (offshoots), and from these grow more tillers. Each tiller has leaves and roots, is virtually self-sustaining, and forms a panicle at its tip. Rice grows best in warm temperatures; the lowest temperature for germination is about 8°–10°C (46°–50°F), and the ideal temperature for growth is 26°–31°C (79°–88°F). High temperature and short days hasten heading. Since rice plants have a system for conducting oxygen from the air to the roots, they are resistant to severe oxygen shortage. They cannot withstand drought and flourish best in irrigated paddies. With proper fertilization and burning of stubble after harvest, there are no ill effects from repeated cultivation of the same field.

O. sativa is divided into three general types according to form, ecotype, and hereditary characteristics: *indica, japonica,* and *javanica. Japonica*-type rice contains less amylose and more amylopectin than other types of rice, giving it the greater glutinousness and special texture favored by the Japanese. Both *mochi* (glutinous rice), which becomes sticky when cooked, and the less starchy *uruchi* (regular rice) strains are found in all three types. Varieties classified according to area of cultivation are paddy or wet rice, suited for paddy fields; upland or dry rice, for dry fields; and floating rice, for flood-prone areas. In Japan, paddy rice accounts for 99.7 percent of the total production.

More than 100,000 varieties of rice are grown in more than 100 countries, with several thousand in Japan alone. In Japan, improvement of rice plants on an institutionalized and modern scientific basis was started in 1904 with hybridization experiments; pure line selection and, later, radiation breeding have also been utilized. These experiments have resulted in improved productivity, early maturity, and resistance to disease, cold weather, and lodging (stalk collapse). Koshihikari and Sasanishiki, both grown in the northeast, are among the most popular types of Japanese rice and command a high price. Since World War II, with land improvement, breeding of varieties responsive to fertilizers, improvement of fertilizing techniques, and the development of chemical fertilizers, herbicides, and insecticides, average yields have increased to more than 4.0 metric tons per hectare (1.8 short tons per acre). Since the beginning of the 1960s agricultural machinery has largely replaced human and animal labor, and threshing and hulling as well as transplanting of seedlings are now done by machines. At the same time, because of herbicides, there has been a reduction in the work load.

Typhoons pose the greatest hazard to rice plants in Japan, but in northern Japan considerable damage can be done if there is unseasonably cool weather during the inflorescence stage. Growing use of fertilizers has led to an increase in such diseases as RICE BLIGHT (*imochibyō*), which causes the greatest damage of all crop diseases. Insects such as rice-stem borers, paddy borers, and plant hoppers cause considerable damage. Preventive measures have included the planting of insect-resistant varieties and, until recently, the application of various herbicides and insecticides. Because of restrictions on the use of environmentally unsafe chemicals, the employment of natural enemies has been encouraged.

Rice consumption has decreased dramatically in Japan since the early 1960s. This phenomenon may be explained by the increased consumption of bread and animal food products. Rice contains somewhat less protein than wheat, but the quality of the protein is superior. Although customarily boiled and eaten plain, rice can be processed in many ways. Cooked glutinous rice is pounded into a kind of dough called MOCHI, which is then prepared in various ways. It may also be thinly sliced and then dried, roasted, and flavored with soy sauce to be made into a variety of rice crackers called *arare*. Rice confections, such as DANGO, are made from rice flour, as are the type of rice crackers known as SEMBEI. Rice is also brewed as rice wine (SAKE), rice vinegar, and cooking wine (MIRIN), and by adding *kōji*, a fermenting agent, is made into a sweet, fermented rice drink (*amazake*) or used as a pickling base.

Despite the decrease in rice consumption, rice is still considered a staple, and rice production and supply is a key element in agricultural policy. The present policy regarding rice production is based on the 1942 Foodstuff Control Law (see FOODSTUFF CONTROL SYSTEM), which put the pricing and distribu-

Today, rice seedlings are generally planted with the help of machines, but the traditional method may be glimpsed in this ritual connected with the Fushimi Inari Shrine in Kyōto.

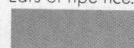

A rice plant in flower.

Production and Consumption of Rice

Year	Production		Consumption	
	Tonnage (1,000 metric tons)	Area (1,000 ha)	Total (1,000 metric tons)	Per capita (kg)
1960	12,858	3,308	12,618	114.9
1962	13,009	3,285	13,315	118.3
1964	12,584	3,260	13,361	115.8
1966	12,745	3,254	12,503	105.8
1968	14,449	3,280	12,251	100.2
1970	12,689	2,923	11,948	95.1
1972	11,897	2,640	11,948	91.7
1974	12,292	2,724	12,033	89.7
1976	11,772	2,779	11,819	86.2
1978	12,589	2,548	11,364	81.6
1980	9,751	2,377	11,209	78.9
1982	10,270	2,257	11,817	76.4
1984	11,878	2,315	10,948	75.2
1986	11,647	2,303	10,871	73.4
1988	9,935	2,110	10,584	71.0
1990	10,499	2,074	10,484	70.0

NOTE: Production and total consumption figures refer to unpolished rice. Per capita consumption figures refer to white rice.
SOURCES: Ministry of Agriculture, Forestry, and Fisheries, *Poketto nōrin suisan tōkei* (annual): 1982, 1989, 1991; *Sakumotsu tōkei* (annual): 1989; *Shokuryō jukyū hyō* (annual): 1975, 1991; *Shokuryō juyō ni kansuru kiso tōkei* (1976).

Ears of ripe rice.

After rice is cut, it is bundled and dried on racks.

tion of rice under government control (see RICE PRICE CONTROLS). The import of rice, which has also been strictly controlled by the government, was permitted early in the postwar era when Japanese domestic production was unable to meet demand. As domestic production increased, imports were curtailed, and since 1983 the import of rice for table use has been prohibited. The chief issues being debated in the early 1990s concerning Japanese rice policy included chronic overproduction, consumer demands for high-quality rice, and the price differential between domestically produced and imported rice. The relaxation of governmental distribution restrictions and the introduction of free-market principles were also being

pursued. In addition, Japan was under strong pressure from the United States and other countries to open its rice market to imports. See also TRADE FRICTION; URUGUAY ROUND.

🖙 1262

rice blight　　　　稲熱病

(*imochibyō*). A rice plant disease; one of the most destructive to Japanese farming. *Pyricularia oryzae* is its pathogen. The disease can break out in any stage of the rice plant's growing season, from the seedling stage through harvesting. It attacks all of the rice plant above the ground, especially the leaves, culms, and roots of ears. The disease

This maiko, or apprentice *geisha,* has her hair done up with rice buds, a New Year's custom for *maiko.* The rice symbolizes an abundant harvest and good fortune.

A "Hinomaru lunch." The pickled plum (*umeboshi*) on its bed of white rice is said to resemble the Japanese flag (Hinomaru).

Rice and the Japanese

Wet rice farming demands intensive labor and extensive irrigation, as the Japanese learned 2,000 years ago when the required techniques were introduced from the Asian mainland. Highly cooperative farm villages developed to maximize rice production, and their customs have had a shaping influence on Japanese life and politics. Until the modern era, the rice crop also served as the principal index for allocating and managing the land and taxing the populace. The proportion of Japan's population engaged in agriculture has now declined to 14 percent, but the values and customs adhered to by rice-farming villagers for centuries remain a powerful, if not always obvious, influence on the society as a whole. Japan's folk culture, for example, continues to reflect the respect, fear, and awe the rice farmer feels toward the natural environment.

A rice-bag pull, part of a harvest festival. At the center of this ritual tug-of-war is a huge *tawara,* or bag for storing rice. Town of Aizu Takada, Fukushima Prefecture.

The transplanting of seedlings to the paddies has been transformed into a festival ritual that includes prayers for a bountiful harvest. Town of Chiyoda, Hiroshima Prefecture.

A family crest using a stylized form of the Chinese character for rice.

Costumed villagers enact a wedding between foxes, messengers of Inari, god of the rice harvest, in the Inaho ("ear of rice") Festival. Fukutoku Inari Shrine, city of Kudamatsu, Yamaguchi Prefecture.

The doburoku, or unrefined *sake,* that is offered to the gods is being served to villagers at the Doburoku Festival. Shirakawa Hachiman Shrine, village of Shirakawa, Gifu Prefecture.

changes the color of the infected part, destroys the tissue, and causes a large decrease in production. Rice blight occurs most frequently during unusually cool summers when the temperature is low and sunny days are few; it thus aggravates cool-weather damage. The excessive use of nitrogen fertilizer tends to generate rice blight. For prevention of the disease, the use of agricultural chemicals and propagation of varieties with a strong innate resistance to rice blight are being studied.

rice price controls 米価

(*beika*). Rice prices in Japan have been directly controlled by the national government since the early 1930s. Although free marketing of a certain portion of the rice crop has been allowed since 1969, farmers remain obliged to sell most of their rice only to the government at a price determined by the government. The rice is then distributed to authorized retailers, who sell it to consumers at a price established by the government. Thus, rice prices in Japan have been principally determined not by free-market forces but by political considerations, because the government feels that it must protect both farmers and consumers.

Government interference in price formation began in 1921, when the Rice Law (Beikoku Hō) was enacted following unprecedented price fluctuations during and after World War I. It was amended in 1931 to authorize official buying and selling operations to help keep prices within a fixed range. The Rice Control Law (Beikoku Tōsei Hō) of 1933 empowered the government to establish purchase and sale prices, and the Rice Distribution Law (Beikoku Haikyū Tōsei Hō) of 1939 greatly increased the government's control over rice distribution. By 1939 a period of scarcity was beginning, and the shortage of rice intensified dramatically during World War II. The Foodstuff Control Law (Shokuryō Kanri Hō) of 1942 terminated free trade in rice and other staple foods.

Stiff controls on most staple foods were removed when agricultural production recovered in 1949, but rice remained directly controlled because of uncertain international conditions and scarcity at home. Throughout most of the 1950s, year-to-year price fluctuations were remarkably narrow, and official deficits remained modest. Strict rationing of rice became unnecessary.

Adoption of the "cost-of-production and income-compensation" pricing formula in 1960 ended the stable relationship between rice prices and general prices. Costs connected with price support and stockpiling pushed government deficits to record levels. See FOODSTUFF CONTROL SPECIAL ACCOUNT.

The government has been taking measures to cope with a rice surplus since 1968. Producer prices were frozen in 1969 and 1970, and an "autonomous" market was inaugurated to introduce free-market forces. Nonetheless, in 1978 Japan still had a rice surplus, deficits in buying and selling operations were substantial, and prices remained high by international standards. In the latter half of the 1980s rice, the import of which is prohibited, became a symbol of Japan's closed market and the object of criticism from foreign countries, in particular the United States.

rice riots of 1918 米騒動

(*kome sōdō*). A series of popular disturbances that erupted throughout Japan from late July to mid-September 1918. Unparalleled in modern Japanese history in their magnitude, diffusion, and violent intensity, they brought about the collapse of the TERAUCHI MASATAKE cabinet (1916–18). The outbreak of the rice riots coincided with the peak of an inflationary price spiral that affected rents, consumer goods, and especially rice. This precipitous rise in rice prices caused economic hardship and engendered popular hostility toward rice merchants and toward government officials, who failed to intervene with remedial action.

The protests broke out in the small fishing village of Uozu in Toyama Prefecture on 23 July and spread throughout Japan during August, escalating from peaceful petitioning of officials to riots, strikes, looting, incendiarism, and armed clashes. By the middle of September, when rioting finally ceased, the country had witnessed 623 separate disturbances. Estimates of total participation range from one to two million people in 38 cities, 153 towns, and 177 villages. Almost 25,000 persons were arrested and about 8,250 of these were prosecuted for riot-related crimes, with penalties for those convicted ranging from small fines to the death sentence. In the aftermath of the riots the Terauchi cabinet collapsed and the political powers acquiesced to the selection of HARA TAKASHI as premier and to the formation of the first party cabinet in Japanese history in which the prime minister was the head of the majority party in the lower house.

Richardson Affair 生麦事件

(Namamugi Jiken). Antiforeign incident in which British subjects were attacked by retainers of SHIMAZU HISAMITSU, *daimyō* of Satsuma (now Kagoshima Prefecture), in the village of Namamugi near Yokohama. The incident occurred on 14 September 1862, when British merchant Charles Richardson and three companions rode across the path of Hisamitsu's procession, an action regarded as offensive. Richardson was killed and two of his companions injured. The British demanded an apology and an indemnity from the Tokugawa shogunate; from Satsuma they demanded an indemnity and the executions of the murderers. The shogunate complied the following year, but Satsuma refused, and on 15 August the British bombarded Kagoshima, the domainal capital. See KAGOSHIMA BOMBARDMENT.

rickshaw 人力車

(*jinrikisha*). Small two-wheeled vehicle for transporting people, drawn by a man; hence its name, *jinriki* (man power), *sha* (vehicle). Said to be invented by three Japanese who claimed inspiration from the horse-drawn carriage, which had been newly introduced from abroad, the rickshaw was produced on a large scale after government permission was obtained in 1870. Because of its speed and mobility, it quickly replaced the palanquin (KAGO). It was at first a primitive structure, consisting of four poles and a canopy mounted on a wagon. A folding cover was later added to the body of the carriage, which became increasingly elaborate with lacquer and gold ornamentation. The carriages were later uniformly black. Although initially built to accommodate two passengers, the structure was modified from about 1887 to a one-passenger vehicle. Gradually displaced by the automobile after the Tōkyō Earthquake of 1923, the rickshaw virtually disappeared; it survives only as a tourist attraction.

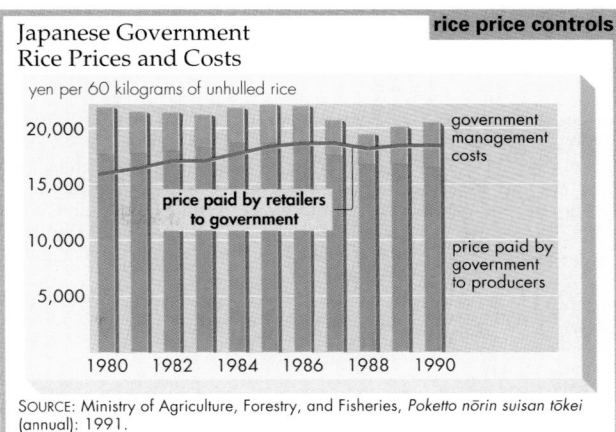

SOURCE: Ministry of Agriculture, Forestry, and Fisheries, *Poketto nōrin suisan tōkei* (annual): 1991.

Japanese Government Rice Prices and Costs

yen per 60 kilograms of unhulled rice

government management costs

price paid by retailers to government

price paid by government to producers

rice price controls

rice riots of 1918
A mounted police officer stands guard over a crowd in Nagoya during a lull in the confusion and violence that wracked Japan in the summer of 1918. At the root of the rioting was a sharp increase in rice prices.

Ricoh Co, Ltd 〔株〕リコー

(Rikō). Company engaged in the manufacture and sale of cameras and office automation equipment (copiers, facsimiles, data processing systems, etc). Incorporated in 1936 as Riken Kankōshi, it took its present name in 1963. With the development of its plain-paper copier in the 1970s, Ricoh became one of the two largest copying machine manufacturers in Japan. It has concentrated its efforts in recent years on the development and mass production of facsimile machines. It has five overseas manufacturing subsidiaries and affiliates and nine overseas sales firms. Sales for the fiscal year ending March 1991 were ¥677.4 billion (US $4.9 billion). The company was capitalized at ¥79.3 billion (US $578.0 million) in the same year. Headquarters are in Tōkyō.

riddles 謎謎

(*nazo nazo*). The Japanese word for riddle comes from the question *nanzo*, or "what is it?" It is believed that the *nazo nazo* was originally a religious exercise related somewhat to KŌAN in Zen Buddhism. Later, the religious aspect gave way to humor. In the Heian period (794–1185), *nazo nazo* became a favorite pastime of the nobility, played along with such games as poetry contests and shell-matching. During the Edo period

rickshaw Detail of an 1872 woodblock-print triptych by Hiroshige III depicting a rickshaw in use. Soon after its invention, the rickshaw was exported to Shanghai, Hong Kong, and other Southeast Asian cities.

Matthew Bunker Ridgway Upon the recall in 1951 of General Douglas MacArthur, General Ridgway was appointed supreme commander for the Allied powers (SCAP) in Japan.

(1600–1868) riddling became extremely popular, and itinerant entertainers called "riddle priests" stood on street corners and challenged passersby with humorous *nazo nazo.* In more recent times, there have been radio and television quiz programs that feature riddles. An example of the typical modern riddle is:

Q: What is one thing that can't be grasped with the right hand?

A: The right hand.

See also WORD GAMES.

Ridgway, Matthew Bunker

リッジウェイ, M. B.

(1895–). US general who served from 1951 to 1952 as supreme commander for the Allied powers (SCAP) in Japan and as commander in chief of the US FAR EAST COMMAND (FEC). Born in Fort Monroe, Virginia, and educated at West Point, he had a distinguished combat record in Europe during World War II. Six months after the outbreak of the Korean War in June 1950, he succeeded to the command of the United States Eighth Army and United Nations ground forces. After the recall of General Douglas MACARTHUR in April 1951, Ridgway succeeded him as the head of SCAP and FEC. In July of that year the UN Command, under his leadership, entered into negotiations for a Korean armistice. He became supreme allied commander in Europe in 1952 and chief of staff of the US Army in 1953, serving until he retired in 1955. His success in Korea and Japan markedly buttressed the military and diplomatic position of the United States in the Far East.

Riess, Ludwig

リース, L.

(1861–1928). German historian. Riess studied under Leopold von Ranke at the University of Berlin. At the invitation of the Japanese government, he came to Japan in 1887 and taught Western history at Tōkyō University. He played a leading role in the establishment of the Shigakukai (Historical Society of Japan) and the founding of its journal *Shigaku zasshi* (Historical Journal), both in 1889. He returned to Germany in 1902.

Rigen shūran

俚言集覧

A Japanese-language dictionary compiled in the late Edo period (1600–1868) comprising 26 fascicles in nine volumes. In contrast to the GAGEN SHŪRAN, a dictionary of classical vocabulary on which it is modeled, the *Rigen shūran* focuses on the spoken language, including dialect and slang. The work is an expanded and revised version of the *Gen'en,* compiled by Ōta Zensai (1759–1829). The *Rigen shūran* ranks with the BUTSURUI SHŌKO as one of the two great Edo studies on spoken Japanese and far exceeds the latter in number of entries. All entries are listed in a variant arrangement of the 50-symbol (*gojūon*) Japanese phonetic syllabary, in wider use today is the *Zōho rigen shūran,* a revised three-volume edition dating from 1900, which arranges the entries in the traditional order of the phonetic syllabary.

rights in rem

物権

(*bukken*). The right to control property directly and exclusively. In contrast to obligatory rights, such as loan obligatory rights, which allow one person to demand payment in a fixed amount from another, rights *in rem,* like OWNERSHIP RIGHTS, are rights to control property. In Japan, the CIVIL CODE (art. 175) proscribes the recognition of such

rights other than those defined by the Civil Code or other statutes. Rights *in rem* include (1) ownership rights, (2) usufruct rights, (3) security rights, and (4) rights of possession. See PROPERTY RIGHTS.

right to live → seizonken

right to organize labor unions

団結権

(*danketsuken*). One of the three FUNDAMENTAL LABOR RIGHTS guaranteed by article 28 of the CONSTITUTION OF JAPAN. The Labor Union Law (Rōdō Kumiai Hō) of 1949, which was enacted pursuant to the constitutional provision, prohibits the government from imposing criminal penalties on workers engaged in legitimate labor union activities. It also prohibits employers from engaging in the following activities, which constitute UNFAIR LABOR PRACTICES: discharge or adverse treatment of an employee for organizing or joining a union or for engaging in legitimate union activity, control of organization or operation of a union, or interference with union activities. Japan also has passed measures to ratify International Labor Organization conventions guaranteeing the right to organize unions. See also COLLECTIVE BARGAINING RIGHT; LABOR LAWS; RIGHT TO STRIKE.

right to remain silent

黙秘権

(*mokuhiken*). Prohibition in the 1947 constitution (art. 38[1]) against the compulsion to give a disadvantageous statement (*nambito mo, jiko ni furieki na kyōjutsu o kyōyō sarenai;* no one can be compelled to make a disadvantageous statement or declaration). Before 1947, suspects and defendants were required to answer incriminating inquiries by investigating judges and courts. Article 38(1), patterned on the fifth amendment to the US Constitution, was intended to change prior law.

Witnesses in criminal prosecutions (Code of Crim. Proc., art. 146) and civil proceedings (Code of Civil Proc., art. 280) may decline to answer incriminating questions (*shōgen kyozetsuken*). There is no waiver doctrine like that in American constitutional law. Juristic persons (HŌJIN) are not protected by the constitution or codes.

Although the constitution does not require it, both the Code of Criminal Procedure (art. 147) and the Code of Civil Procedure (art. 280) allow witnesses to withhold responses incriminating to those in specified close relationships, such as a spouse or near blood relative. The Criminal Procedure rules (art. 121[1]) provide that witnesses and suspects be warned about privilege.

right to strike

争議権

(*sōgiken*). One of the three FUNDAMENTAL LABOR RIGHTS guaranteed by article 28 of the CONSTITUTION OF JAPAN. The constitution guarantees "the right of workers to . . . act collectively," and the Labor Union Law (Rōdō Kumiai Hō) protects "legitimate dispute activities." Labor's dispute-related actions are thus not limited to strikes and other traditional forms; rather, they encompass a multitude of acts that interfere with the operation of an enterprise.

The legal effect of the right to strike is to guarantee the worker freedom from adverse treatment by the employer. The dispute activity, however, must be recognized as "proper" (*seitō*), both with respect to its purpose and the means employed. See also COLLECTIVE BARGAINING RIGHT; RIGHT TO ORGANIZE LABOR UNIONS; LABOR DISPUTES; LABOR DIS-

PUTE RESOLUTION PROCEDURES; LABOR LAWS; STRIKES AND OTHER FORMS OF LABOR DISPUTE.

right to sunshine

日照権

(*nisshōken*). A legal right to receive a certain amount of daily sunshine on residential property. With the increase in high-rise buildings in the 1960s, residences began to lose sunlight for a substantial number of hours each day, and access to sunlight became a serious social problem. The development of the right to sunshine began in the 1960s and was confirmed in a 1972 Supreme Court decision (*Mitamura* v *Suzuki*). Most sunlight suits seek prior injunctive relief, which may mean a design change. By 1976 more than 300 local public entities had some form of sunlight restrictions on new construction. In October 1976 the Diet established national standards by amending the ARCHITECTURAL STANDARDS LAW (Kenchiku Kijun Hō).

right wing

右翼

(*uyoku*). In Japan the term generally refers to individuals or groups publicly advocating NATIONALISM or ultranationalism and opposing socialism, communism, and other leftist ideologies.

The Meiji Period (1868–1912)—The right-wing movement had its origin in the discontented *samurai* class, who opposed the new Meiji government's policy of divesting them of their privileges. In 1877 dispossessed samurai of the former Fukuoka domain (now part of Fukuoka Prefecture) participated in the SATSUMA REBELLION. After their defeat, TŌYAMA MITSURU and others formed a group called the Kōyōsha.

Aligning themselves with the FREEDOM AND PEOPLE'S RIGHTS MOVEMENT, they pressed for the early establishment of a national legislature. In 1881 the name of the group was changed to the GEN'YŌSHA. Collaborating with the IMPERIAL JAPANESE ARMY, the Gen'yōsha organized its own paramilitary force and played a major role in rousing popular domestic fervor for the SINO-JAPANESE WAR OF 1894–1895 and the RUSSO-JAPANESE WAR (1904–05). In 1901 the AMUR RIVER SOCIETY (Kokuryūkai) was organized under the leadership of UCHIDA RYŌHEI. It conducted secret intelligence operations against Russia. Both the Gen'yōsha and the Amur River Society strongly favored the centrality of the imperial system in Japanese politics and simultaneously advocated PAN-ASIANISM against the Western powers and supported the military's invasion of the Asian continent.

The Taishō Period (1912–1926)—Particularly after the RICE RIOTS OF 1918, a large number of new right-wing groups, including the DAI NIPPON KOKUSUIKAI (Great Japan National Essence Society, 1919), took direct and violent measures to suppress socialist movements.

At this time right-wing political theories were formulated by ŌKAWA SHŪMEI and KITA IKKI and were propagated by the Rōsōkai (1918), the YŪZONSHA (1919), and other groups. The KOKUHONSHA, begun in 1924 by Minister of Justice HIRANUMA KIICHIRŌ, gained the support of influential members of the bureaucratic, military, financial, and intellectual elite.

The 1930s and 1940s—In the period between the depression of 1930 and the FEBRUARY 26TH INCIDENT in 1936, the power of the right wing reached its peak. Right-wing army and navy officers and civilians directly intervened in domestic politics in a series of bloody incidents. Prime Minister HAMAGUCHI

OSACHI was shot by a right-wing youth. Soon afterward a circle of key army officers formed a secret organization called the SAKURAKAI (Cherry Blossom Society), which in 1931 caused the MARCH INCIDENT as well as attempting a coup d'état (OCTOBER INCIDENT). Later that year the MANCHURIAN INCIDENT triggered the onset of war in Asia. Right-wing army and navy members instigated the MAY 15TH INCIDENT of 1932, the Military Academy Incident of 1934, the slaying of Director of Military Affairs NAGATA TETSUZAN in 1935, the February 26th Incident in 1936, and other acts of terror. Some right-wing civilians also took the law into their own hands on several occasions (see LEAGUE OF BLOOD INCIDENT; SHIMPEITAI INCIDENT). They participated in all aspects of the 1935 "National Polity Debate" (KOKUTAI DEBATE) and actively denounced MINOBE TATSUKICHI's emperor-as-organ theory (TENNŌ KIKAN SETSU). Nonetheless, the right-wing movement lacked a broad popular base.

After the February 26th Incident of 1936, the right-wing movement fell under the control of the government and the military and was used by them to promote their policies. The 1940 NEW ORDER MOVEMENT hastened the consolidation of right-wing factions, and the TŌJŌ HIDEKI cabinet pressured reluctant rightwing and other groups to enter a single organization, the Kōa Dōmei (League to Invigorate Asia).

The Postwar Era——The defeat of Japan on 15 August 1945 dealt a great blow to the right-wing movement. The OCCUPATION further undermined the social base of rightwing power through its total disarmament of the Japanese military and its systematic democratization of the political system. From about the time of the Korean War, the right wing regained some of its previous vigor. The late 1950s saw a heated debate over the issue of renewing the United States–Japan Security Treaty (see UNITED STATES–JAPAN SECURITY TREATIES). Right-wing activities again increased, culminating in the assassination of ASANUMA INEJIRŌ by a right-wing youth in October 1960.

Since then there have been sporadic acts of right-wing violence in connection with the US–Japan Security Treaty and the return of Okinawa. Although the postwar rightwing movement has advocated rearmament and constitutional revision rather than overseas expansion, in basic orientation and tactics for political change it still closely resembles its prewar predecessor. However, because of the outmoded political orientation of its leadership and lack of a solid financial base, the right wing now falls far short of attaining the power and influence it wielded before the war.

Ri Kaisei → Lee Hwe-song

Rikken Dōshikai 立憲同志会

(Constitutional Association of Friends). Also known as the Dōshikai. Political party founded in 1913 by KATSURA TARŌ. In 1912 the MOVEMENT TO PROTECT CONSTITUTIONAL GOVERNMENT led by INUKAI TSUYOSHI and OZAKI YUKIO won support of the Diet's majority party, the RIKKEN SEIYŪKAI. Katsura then formed a political party to support his cabinet against Seiyūkai criticism. Some 90 Diet members joined, including all 30 members of the Chūō Kurabu, half of the RIKKEN KOKUMINTŌ, and some key former bureaucrats. The party survived Katsura's death in October 1913. Choosing KATŌ TAKAAKI as its first leader, the Dōshikai placed five ministers in the second

ŌKUMA SHIGENOBU cabinet of 1914–16 and became the Diet's largest party after the 1915 election. After dissolution of the Ōkuma cabinet the Dōshikai decided to merge with the CHŪSEIKAI, the Kōyū Kurabu, and other small Diet factions to form the KENSEIKAI in October 1916. See also POLITICAL PARTIES; TAISHŌ POLITICAL CRISIS.

Rikken Kaishintō 立憲改進党

(Constitutional Reform Party). Also known as the Kaishintō. Political party formed by ŌKUMA SHIGENOBU in April 1882 after the POLITICAL CRISIS OF 1881. Members included popular-rights advocates YANO RYŪKEI, INUKAI TSUYOSHI, and OZAKI YUKIO. Support came from urban intellectuals and businessmen, including IWASAKI YATARŌ, founder of the Mitsubishi financial empire. The Kaishintō's moderate program called for a British-style parliamentary democracy with a constitutional monarch, which enabled it to survive the government's suppression of the FREEDOM AND PEOPLE'S RIGHTS MOVEMENT in 1883–84. In the first elections to the House of Representatives, held in 1890, the Kaishintō won 46 seats, becoming the second largest party in the Diet after the JIYŪTŌ. The Kaishintō advocated an increasingly nationalistic foreign policy, and in March 1896 the party merged with several small nationalist parties to form the SHIMPOTŌ. See also POLITICAL PARTIES.

Rikken Kokumintō 立憲国民党

(Constitutional Nationalist Party). Political party formed in March 1910 through a merger of the KENSEI HONTŌ with the Yūshinkai, Mumeikai, and several other minor Diet groups. This party called for constitutional government, universal suffrage for men 20 years and older, and naval armament. The dominant faction under INUKAI TSUYOSHI opposed any compromise with the oligarchs, while the faction under Ōishi Masami (1855–1935) considered such an alliance essential for electoral victory over the RIKKEN SEIYŪKAI. In January 1913 Ōishi and four other party leaders defected to the RIKKEN DŌSHIKAI, recently established by the oligarch KATSURA TARŌ. About half the Rikken Kokumintō's Diet members joined them. In the 1920 general election the party won only 29 seats. In September 1922 it disbanded to form the core of the KAKUSHIN KURABU. See also POLITICAL PARTIES.

Rikken Minseitō 立憲民政党

(Constitutional Democratic Party). Also known as the Minseitō. Together with the RIKKEN SEIYŪKAI, one of the two major political parties of the early Shōwa period (1926–89). Founded on 1 June 1927 through a merger of the KENSEIKAI and the SEIYŪ HONTŌ, the party elected HAMAGUCHI OSACHI as its president. In the 1928 election it won 216 of the Diet's 464 seats. In July 1929 Hamaguchi became prime minister, and in the 1930 election the party gained its first absolute Diet majority with 273 seats. Its cabinet advocated fiscal restraint, lifted the gold embargo, and acceded to the naval limitations imposed on Japan by the London Naval Conference of 1930 (see LONDON NAVAL CONFERENCES). The party politicians' domination of the military during this heyday of party rule and conciliatory foreign policy abruptly ended in 1930, when Hamaguchi was shot by a right-wing fanatic. His cabinet hobbled on for five more months under SHIDEHARA KIJŪRŌ. The succeeding Minseitō cabinet under WAKATSUKI REIJIRŌ tried in vain to limit the militaristic repercussions of the MANCHURIAN INCIDENT and was

overthrown in 1931. In the 1932 election the party lost its Diet majority, which it again secured in the 1936 and 1937 elections. However, its resistance to army policies gradually weakened, and the party eventually contained a promilitary faction led by NAGAI RYŪTARŌ. The party dissolved on 15 August 1940 and was absorbed into the IMPERIAL RULE ASSISTANCE ASSOCIATION. Two post–World War II parties, the Nihon Shimpotō (Japan Progressive Party) and the MINSHUTŌ, derived from the Minseitō. See also POLITICAL PARTIES.

Rikken Seiyūkai 立憲政友会

(Friends of Constitutional Government Party). Usually called the Seiyūkai. One of the leading political parties from 1900 to 1940. The party was formed in September 1900 by ITŌ HIROBUMI as a progovernment alliance of bureaucrats and former members of the dissolved KENSEITŌ party. The Seiyūkai came into power in October 1900 when Itō formed his fourth cabinet.

Under its second president, SAIONJI KIMMOCHI, the Seiyūkai participated in the MOVEMENT TO PROTECT CONSTITUTIONAL GOVERNMENT from 1912 to 1913. It became the ruling party with the YAMAMOTO GONNOHYŌE cabinet (1913–14). TAKAHASHI KOREKIYO, a minister in the cabinet with extensive experience in banking, became a party member at this time, reinforcing its ties with business and financial circles. HARA TAKASHI became the third party president in June 1914. When he formed a cabinet in September 1918, all the ministerial portfolios, except for the army, navy, and foreign ministry, were taken by Seiyūkai members, and it is considered the first party cabinet. He led the party to its peak of popularity in the 1920 general elections but was assassinated in November 1921. In 1924 members of the majority bureaucratic faction within the party, including TOKONAMI TAKEJIRŌ, seceded over the issue of party participation in the second Movement to Protect Constitutional Government and formed the SEIYŪ HONTŌ.

The cabinet formed by General TANAKA GIICHI in 1927 sent a military expedition to Shandong (Shantung) that same year, under the pretext of protecting Japanese nationals, and in 1928 passed a retrogressive revision of the PEACE PRESERVATION LAW OF 1925 (Chian Iji Hō). When the RIKKEN MINSEITŌ cabinet of HAMAGUCHI OSACHI approved the London Naval Treaty in 1930, restricting the number of Japanese warships, the Seiyūkai attacked the cabinet as encroaching upon the concept of supreme command (TŌSUIKEN). The party's action is said to have opened the way for military dominance in the government.

INUKAI TSUYOSHI, the sixth party president, formed a cabinet in 1931 but was assassinated in the MAY 15TH INCIDENT of 1932. During the spring of 1939 intraparty struggle intensified, and the Seiyūkai split into the KUHARA FUSANOSUKE and NAKAJIMA CHIKUHEI factions. In July 1940 the party voted to dissolve itself. See also POLITICAL PARTIES.

Rikken Teiseitō 立憲帝政党

(Constitutional Imperial Rule Party). Political party formed in March 1882 by FUKUCHI GEN'ICHIRŌ, Maruyama Sakura (1840–99), and other journalists to support the government. Its manifesto advocated a constitution decreed by the emperor, an electoral franchise limited to property holders, and restrictions on freedom of speech and assembly. It criticized the recently formed people's rights parties, the JIYŪTŌ and the RIKKEN KAISHINTŌ. The party disbanded in September 1883. See also POLITICAL PARTIES.

Rikkokushi 六国史

(Six National Histories). A general term for the NIHON SHOKI, *Shoku nihongi, Nihon kōki, Shoku Nihon kōki, Nihon Montoku Tennō jitsuroku,* and *Nihon sandai jitsuroku.* Compiled in the Nara (710–794) and early Heian (794–1185) periods, these histories cover the mythology and history of Japan from the earliest times to AD 887. The term *kokushi* for "national history" was used in the Nara period, but the name *Rikkokushi* did not appear until the Muromachi period (1333–1568).

The *Rikkokushi* are all official histories (*seishi*), compiled by court functionaries at the emperor's command. Such histories were modeled on the annalistic form (*hennentai*) of Chinese historical writing. The *Rikkokushi* are arranged in the order of the imperial reigns, each section normally beginning with genealogical and biographical notes on an emperor before his enthronement (*sokui zenki*). The historical narrative is written in classical Chinese (*kambun*); Chinese characters are also used to render imperial edicts (SEMMYŌ) and lyrical passages or poetry originally written in Japanese. They include many biographies of high officials, mostly inserted in the form of an obituary. Natural phenomena, unusual customs, political events, and religious ceremonies are noted.

1. The *Nihon shoki* (Chronicle of Japan; also called *Nihongi*), the oldest official history of Japan, was compiled by Prince TONERI, among others. Compilation began in 681 in the reign of Emperor TEMMU (r 672–686) and was finished in 720 under Emperor Genshō (r 715–724). After the consolidation of the monarchy and the establishment of a centralized state by the TAIKA REFORM of 645, the court felt it necessary to produce a history of the YAMATO COURT (ca 4th century–ca mid-7th century) to demonstrate the legitimacy of imperial rule. Source material included records of the imperial house and the noble families, mostly of a genealogical nature; early administrative documents; old records of Shintō shrines and Buddhist temples; ancient Korean chronicles; and legends from the oral tradition. The first two volumes of the *Nihon shoki* cover the mythological period, and the 3rd through 30th volumes are devoted to the reigns of the sovereigns from the legendary emperor JIMMU through the historical empress JITŌ (r 686–697). In contrast to the KOJIKI of 712, the 30-volume *Nihon shoki* is arranged in a strict chronology. However, this chronology is fictitious for the legendary period and is antedated by two sexagenary cycles (120 years) in the protohistorical period; it offers reliable dates only from the 6th century onward.

2. The *Shoku nihongi* (Chronicle of Japan, Continued; also called *Shokki*) is the second official history of Japan. This chronicle includes events from the first year of Emperor MOMMU's (r 697–707) reign to Emperor KAMMU's (r 781–806) reign up to 791. It was revised several times, taking its final form in 797. It has survived intact. The *Shoku nihongi* is the best primary source for the Nara period. A valuable historical and literary feature of the work is the inclusion of 62 imperial decrees written in *semmyōgaki*

(Chinese characters used to signify Japanese phonetic equivalents).

3. The *Nihon kōki* (Later Chronicle of Japan) was begun in 819, progressed under several committees of compilers, and was completed in 840. The *Nihon kōki* covers the reigns of the emperors Kammu (from 792), Heizei (r 806–809), SAGA (r 809–823), and Junna (r 823–833), ending in 833. It is a valuable source for the history of the early Heian period, but only 10 of the original 40 volumes survive. However, many citations from the lost portion of the text appear in the RUIJŪ KOKUSHI and NIHON KIRYAKU (see below).

4. The *Shoku Nihon kōki* (Later Chronicle of Japan, Continued) was begun by order of Emperor Montoku (r 850–858) and completed under Emperor Seiwa (r 858–876), to whom the work was presented in 869. The 20 volumes deal with the reign of Emperor Nimmyō (r 833–850), from his enthronement in 833 to his death in 850. This chronicle survives intact. It is the most comprehensive chronicle of one emperor's reign in early Japanese history.

5. The *Nihon Montoku Tennō jitsuroku* (Veritable Record of Emperor Montoku of Japan; also called *Montoku jitsuroku*) was begun in 871. It was completed in 10 volumes under Emperor Yōzei (r 876–884) and presented in 879. It covers the reign of Montoku (r 850–858). This chronicle has survived intact.

6. The *Nihon sandai jitsuroku* (Veritable Record of Three Generations [of Emperors] of Japan; also called *Sandai jitsuroku*) was begun at the command of Emperor UDA (r 887–897) in 892 and completed under Emperor DAIGO (r 897–930) in 901. Compiled by SUGAWARA NO MICHIZANE and others, it covers the reigns of the emperors Seiwa, Yōzei, and Kōkō (r 884–887), from 858, the year of Seiwa's accession, to 887, the year of Kōkō's death. All 50 volumes have survived. The *Sandai jitsuroku* provides copious citation from official documents and detailed accounts of court ceremonies and folk festivals. Natural phenomena, including 293 earthquakes, are scrupulously noted. It is a mature and trustworthy compilation.

The tradition of compiling national histories (*kokushi*) continued after the *Sandai jitsuroku.* The bibliography HONCHŌ SHOJAKU MOKUROKU (late 13th century) mentions a SHINKOKUSHI (New National History) in 40 volumes, covering the reigns of Uda and Daigo; the encyclopedia *Shūgaishō* (13th century?) records a *Shoku sandai jitsuroku* (Veritable Record of Three Generations, Continued) in 50 volumes, which probably covered the reigns of Uda, Daigo, and Suzaku (r 930–946). Neither work has survived, and it is not known whether they were partly identical.

During the compilation of the *Sandai jitsuroku,* Sugawara no Michizane composed the *Ruijū kokushi* (Classified National History), completed in 892. This work arranged important records from the *Rikkokushi* in categories (Shintō, the imperial house, law, music, Buddhism, etc) in 200 volumes, 61 of which survive as a valuable supplement to the *Rikkokushi.* Also extant is the *Nihon kiryaku* (Outline History of Japan), an annalistic summary of the *Rikkokushi* and later historical sources up to the reign of Emperor Go-Ichijō (r 1016–36).

Rikkyō University 立教大学

(Rikkyō Daigaku). A private, coeducational university located in Toshima Ward, Tōkyō.

Founded in 1874 in Tsukiji, Tōkyō, as St. Paul's School by the Episcopal missionary Channing Moore Williams, the school moved to its present location in 1918 and in 1922 was granted university status. Its goal is academic freedom in accordance with Christian teachings. The university has five faculties: letters, economics, law, sociology, and science. The department of tourism and hotel management was established in 1967, the first such program in Japan. It has affiliated elementary, junior high, and high schools and a two-year women's junior college. Enrollment was 12,018 in 1989.

Ri Kōran → Yamaguchi Yoshiko

Rikuchū Coast National Park
陸中海岸国立公園

(Rikuchū Kaigan Kokuritsu Kōen). Situated in northern Honshū, in Iwate and Miyagi prefectures. This narrow park stretches about 180 km (110 mi) along the Pacific coast. The entire coast is famed for spectacular examples of sea erosion, rock pillars, and grottoes. The northern coastline has sheer sea cliffs; the southern coastline consists of numerous small bays and coves. The popular beach at JŌDOGAHAMA is located about halfway along the coast, outside the city of MIYAKO. Red pines (*akamatsu*) and rhododendrons thrive in the area, which is inhabited by several bird species, among them the black-tailed gull (*umineko*) and the shearwater (*ōmizunagidori*). Land area: 123.5 sq km (47.5 sq mi).

Rikuentai 陸援隊

(Army Commandos). A small military brigade organized in 1867 by the activist NAKAOKA SHINTARŌ of the Tosa domain (now Kōchi Prefecture) in support of the movement to overthrow the Tokugawa shogunate. Nakaoka gathered more than 50 antishogunate *samurai* from all parts of Japan. Although Nakaoka was assassinated late in 1867, the Rikuentai continued its anti-Tokugawa activities under TANAKA MITSUAKI. When the brigade was disbanded in 1868, its members were enlisted into the newly formed Imperial Army.

Rikugien Garden 六義園

(Rikugien). Municipal park in Bunkyō Ward, Tōkyō. Completed in the early 18th century by shogunal official YANAGISAWA YOSHIYASU, it is representative of the *kaiyū* ("many-pleasure") style landscape gardens of the Edo period (1600–1868). The garden includes a large pond with an island and a hill with a dense grove of ancient trees. It was donated to Tōkyō in 1938. Area: 10 hectares (25 acres).

Rikuzen Takata 陸前高田[市]

City in southeastern Iwate Prefecture, northern Honshū, on the Pacific Ocean. Rikuzen Takata is a fishing base for tuna and bonito; *wakame* (a type of seaweed) and oysters are also cultivated. Part of Rikuchū Coast National Park, Rikuzen Takata has many beaches. The nearby island of Tsubakishima is a breeding place for black-tailed gulls. Pop: 27,242.

Rimpa 琳派

School of painting started around 1600 by SŌTATSU; also associated with his contemporary HON'AMI KŌETSU. Not a tradition monopolized by a single family, it was revived in the early 18th century by KŌRIN and again in the early 19th century by SAKAI

HŌITSU. Works by members of this school embody the classical Japanese sense for decorativeness, delicate coloring, and abstraction, combined with a keen study of the visible world. Rimpa works typically employed precious materials, such as gold and silver, together with colors on folding screens, albums, fans, and so on. Subject matter was taken from medieval literature as well as from nature. Although the Rimpa school did not survive past the Edo period (1600–1868), its traditional, strong design and purely Japanese qualities influenced 20th-century Japanese painting.

The word "Rimpa" is a compound of the last syllable in Kōrin's name (rin) and the word for school (ha). The true founder of Rimpa, Sōtatsu, was long overshadowed by Kōetsu and Kōetsu's follower Kōrin. In the 18th and 19th centuries the school was also known as the Kōetsu school, the Kōrin school, and the Sōtatsu-Kōrin school.

Sōtatsu's workshop originally made decorated writing paper and fans, but later expanded to include illustrative subjects in the YAMATO-E tradition and ink painting. Sōtatsu's sliding wall panels and screens adapted the yamato-e style, hitherto used in small-scale formats, to the modern taste for monumental size and splendor.

Sōtatsu's successor, Nonomura Sōsetsu (fl 1639–50), specialized in paintings of flowers and grasses, as did his successor, Kitagawa Sōsetsu (mid-17th century). The illustrative genre was neglected until its revival in the early 18th century by Ogata Kōrin. With his brother KENZAN, Kōrin created a new style in the decoration of ceramics. Kōrin's students included Fukae Roshū (1699–1757) and WATANABE SHIKŌ and TATEBAYASHI KAGEI in Edo (now Tōkyō).

Sakai Hōitsu, whose family had been one of Kōrin's sponsors, published 100 woodcuts after paintings of Kōrin (Kōrin hyakuzu). Hōitsu's pupils SUZUKI KIITSU, Sakai Ōho (1808–41), and Tanaka Hōji (1813–85) transmitted the Rimpa style into the late 19th century. Rimpa was rediscovered once more in the early 20th century by painters of the JAPAN FINE ARTS ACADEMY (Nihon Bijutsu-in) under the leadership of OKAKURA KAKUZŌ.

rindō → gentians

ringi system   稟議制度

(ringi seido). A process of decision making by the use of circular letters (ringisho) that is commonly used in Japanese companies and bureaucratic organizations. The antecedents of the system date back to the administration of the Tokugawa shogunate during the Edo period (1600–1868). The ringi system is above all a group-oriented, from-the-bottom-up, consensus-seeking process that is often initiated by middle management personnel and their juniors rather than by senior executives. All groups that will be affected by the decision that is to be made, as well as those that must implement it, are able to participate in the decision-making process as the circular letter bearing the proposal for decision slowly makes its way around the various departments and sections of the organization. Possible complaints and objections are dealt with through bargaining, compromise, or accommodation at each step of the process. Thus the final decision that emerges from this process has a high likelihood of being effectively implemented, since it has resulted from a process of group interaction, rather than being made explicitly by an individual

who occupies the formal leadership role. See also MANAGEMENT.

rinji   綸旨

A type of private imperial edict issued by the KURŌDO-DOKORO (Bureau of Archivists or Chamberlains' Office) at the emperor's command. The first known rinji dates from 1028, during the reign of Emperor GO-ICHIJŌ. They eventually replaced the more formal and complicated imperial edicts, or SENJI. Rinji were most frequently used during the KEMMU RESTORATION (1333–36) of Emperor GO-DAIGO.

Rinji Kyōiku Kaigi   臨時教育会議

(Extraordinary Council on Education). An advisory organ to the prime minister on educational policy; in existence between 1917 and 1919. It was established to make a fundamental reassessment of government modernization policies since the 1870s. The focus of discussion was on reform of the higher schools and universities. The committee recommended a seven-year higher education system and a government policy to approve establishment of private, municipal, and prefectural universities in addition to the then-existing government schools. It set up a system whereby the government would fund compulsory education and also called for a strong emphasis on "moral education" (SHŪSHIN). The council thus set the course for educational policy up to World War II.

Rinnai Corporation   リンナイ[株]

(Rinnai). Gas appliance manufacturer. Established in 1920 as Rinnai Shōkai. Its product lines include gas-related kitchen appliances, home heating equipment, and industrial burners and furnaces. It also produces home security equipment. The firm has nine overseas factories. Sales for the fiscal year ending March 1991 totaled ¥109.8 billion (US $800.3 million), and capitalization stood at ¥6.4 billion (US $46.6 million). Headquarters are in Nagoya.

rinne   輪廻

(Skt: samsāra, "wandering through [the cycle of birth and death]"). A Buddhist term denoting the process of transmigration and rebirth. According to Buddhist belief, all

sentient beings undergo rebirth after death. Whether they are reborn in a pleasant environment or one of torment depends upon the moral nature of the acts (karma) they committed during their lifetime. Buddhism holds that rebirth takes place in one of six realms, which, in ascending order, are the undesirable realms of hell, hungry spirits (J: gaki), and animals, and the favorable realms of bellicose spirits (J: ashura), man, and the heavens. Since there is always the possibility, depending on one's actions, of falling from a higher to a lower realm whenever rebirth occurs, the Buddhist seeks ultimately to escape from this cycle of transmigration, which can be accomplished only by attaining Buddhahood or entering the Pure Land of a Buddha such as AMIDA. See also JIGOKU-ZŌSHI; PURE LAND BUDDHISM; HEAVEN; HELL.

Rinzai sect   臨済宗

(Rinzaishū). One of the two major sects of ZEN Buddhism in Japan, the other being the SŌTŌ SECT. The Rinzai school of Zen Buddhism takes its name from the Chinese Chan (Ch'an; J: Zen) master Linji Yixuan (Lin-chi I-hsüan; J: Rinzai Gigen; d 867). The so-called Southern school of Chan to which Linji belonged emphasized "sudden enlightenment," as opposed to the "gradual enlightenment" of the Northern school, and stressed the possibility of direct perception of one's own Buddha nature through intense meditation, in mind-to-mind encounter with a truly enlightened master, and during even the most commonplace everyday activities. Linji even resorted to slaps and shouts to encourage monks and laymen who sought his guidance to strive harder for their own direct and spontaneous experience with reality. Vigorous meditation, sharp verbal exchanges between master and student, and the use of blows with a rod (J: bō) and shouts (katsu) have remained integral to Rinzai Zen practice. Chan emphasized the study of gongan (kung-an; J: KŌAN), or "public cases," used to discourage students of Zen from rationalization and to drive them toward a direct perception of self and reality.

Rishiri-Rebun-Sarobetsu National Park

1 Day lilies cover the fields near the volcano Rishirizan in July and August.

2 *Kombu,* a variety of kelp, is harvested from the sea near the island of Rishiri.

Rinzai Zen, as practiced in the great Song-dynasty (960–1279) Buddhist monasteries of the Hangzhou (Hangchow) region, was first brought to Japan by Japanese and Chinese monks during the late 12th and 13th centuries. Of the 24 major Zen lineages that took root in Japan, 21 were Rinzai. The Japanese monk EISAI (or Yōsai; 1141–1215) is generally regarded as the founder of Rinzai Zen in Japan. From 1187, on the second of two journeys to China, Eisai studied for four years under the Chan master Xu'an Huaichang (Hsü-an Huai-ch'ang). Eisai and other Zen pioneers introduced Zen meditation and the Zen emphasis on monastic rules (*shingi*) and precepts (Skt: *vinaya*). Eisai's activities aroused the opposition of the established Buddhist schools, especially Tendai monks from the temple ENRYAKUJI. To counter their attacks he wrote *Kōzen gokoku ron* (1198, The Propagation of Zen for the Protection of the Nation), in which he argued that Zen practice would reinvigorate Tendai Buddhism and contribute to the welfare and security of the country. Eisai eventually won the favor of the shōgun and established the monastery KENNINJI in Kyōto. Eisai's immediate followers included the monk ENNI, who returned from six years of Chan training in China to found the monastery of TŌFUKUJI in Kyōto.

Japanese understanding of Rinzai Zen practice was greatly enhanced by Chinese émigré masters who began to come to Japan after the mid-13th century. With the support of the political elite and under the stern direction of these Chinese masters, Rinzai Zen in Japan began to assume sectarian independence and institutional cohesion. The Rinzai monasteries were linked by the shogunate into an officially sponsored and carefully regulated network headed by five great metropolitan monasteries in Kamakura and five in Kyōto (see GOZAN). Sponsorship of metropolitan Rinzai Zen was continued en-

thusiastically by the Ashikaga shōguns during the 14th and 15th centuries. Under the leadership of monks such as MUSŌ SOSEKI and GIDŌ SHŪSHIN, the 300 or so monasteries in the Gozan network reached their apogee of religious, political, cultural, and economic influence.

Some Rinzai monks, however, were critical of the material prosperity, bureaucratization, and secular cultural tone of the Gozan monasteries. Shūhō Myōchō (1282–1337; see SŌHŌ MYŌCHŌ), the founder-abbot of the temple DAITOKUJI, and Kanzan Egen (1277–1360), his disciple and founder-abbot of the temple MYŌSHINJI, both insisted upon a more Spartan monastic life. These two monasteries and their branch temples remained outside the Gozan network. In the 15th century the irreverent monk IKKYŪ of Daitokuji excoriated the formalism, luxury, and complacency of Gozan monks and monasteries. With the erosion of shogunate authority in the wars of the late 15th and early 16th centuries, Gozan monasteries suffered loss of social and political influence.

Japanese Rinzai Zen was roused from this torpor during the 17th and 18th centuries by two powerful stimuli, one from outside Japan and one from within. In 1654 the Chinese monk Yinyuan Longji (Yin-yüan Lung-chi; J: INGEN Ryūki; 1592–1673) and a dozen disciples from the monastery of Wanfusi (Wan-fu-ssu) in Fujian (Fukien) Province arrived in Japan (see ŌBAKU SECT). Yinyuan secured the patronage of the Tokugawa shōguns and members of the imperial court who encouraged him to remain in Japan as head of the newly established monastery MAMPUKUJI (the Japanese pronunciation of Wanfusi), near Kyōto.

More important for the reinvigoration of Rinzai Zen in Japan, however, was the contribution made by the monk HAKUIN of the Myōshinji lineage, one of a small but influential group of Edo period (1600–1868) Zen masters, including SUZUKI SHŌSAN, SHIDŌ BUNAN, and BANKEI YŌTAKU, who sought to make Zen more accessible to the common people of Japan. Hakuin spent much of his time wandering as he carried his advocacy of Zen to warriors, townsmen, and farmers. To farmers Hakuin offered a simplified Zen practice that left room for prayers, moral fables, and invocations from the sutras. For monks and *samurai* he urged an unremitting *zazen* (meditation) and *kōan* practice. Hakuin restructured traditional Rinzai *kōan* practice by giving greater prominence to the *wu* (nothingness) *kōan* and devising his own *kōan,* "What is the sound of a single hand clapping?"

Hakuin attracted many disciples. Through them, his prolific writings, collected in *Hakuin Oshō zenshū* (8 vols), and his brilliant ink paintings, he had a profound impact on the subsequent development of Rinzai Zen. In the 14 surviving branches of Japanese Rinzai Zen, all masters trace their lineage to Hakuin. Moreover, the Rinzai teachings introduced to the West by D. T. SUZUKI and other Japanese scholars and Zen masters also bear the stamp of Hakuin's determined spirit.

Riot Police　　　　　機動隊

(Kidōtai). Mobile task force of the Tōkyō Metropolitan Police Department (Keishi-chō) and other prefectural police agencies. Its functions are to control crowds and violent civil disorders, perform rescue operations, and assist local police officers through group patrolling and criminal investigation. The

Kidōtai was first established in 1948 in Tōkyō.

Ri Sampei　　　　　李参平

(1579–1655). Also known as Kanegae Sampei or Sambei (Kor: Yi Sam-p'yong). A Korean potter who discovered kaolin clay for porcelain production in the Arita area, Kyūshū, in 1616. Ri Sampei came to Japan in 1598 from Korea. Before his discovery of the kaolin deposits Ri Sampei set up several kilns in Kyūshū where he made household wares in the style of KARATSU WARE. Until he discovered the proper clay he could not produce the type of porcelain being made in Korea at that time. He set up a kiln with 18 other Korean potters at Tengudani, and the wares they produced were a continuation of the Korean Yi-dynasty (1392–1910) plain white, as well as underglaze blue, porcelains. Later pieces show the influence of Chinese Ming (1368–1644) and Qing (Ch'ing; 1644–1912) wares. The discovery of the clay spurred a revolution in Japanese ceramics and changed the Arita area into a major porcelain-producing area, which it remains today. See also ARITA WARE.

Rishiri　　　　　利尻

Island in the Sea of Japan, 19 km (12 mi) west of the northern tip of Hokkaidō; administratively part of Hokkaidō. It is separated from Hokkaidō by the Rishiri Channel. The volcano Rishirizan (altitude: 1,721 m; 5,646 ft) makes up a large part of the island. Kutsugata is the leading fishing port. Marine products include kelp, sea urchins, and Atka mackerel. Together with the neighboring island of REBUN, it is part of the RISHIRI-REBUN-SAROBETSU NATIONAL PARK. Area: 183 sq km (71 sq mi).

Rishiri-Rebun-Sarobetsu National Park　　　利尻礼文サロベツ国立公園

(Rishiri-Rebun-Sarobetsu Kokuritsu Kōen). Situated at the northern tip of Hokkaidō. This subarctic park comprises a marshy coastal strip, 27 km (17 mi) long, called the SAROBETSU PLAIN, and the two islands of RISHIRI and REBUN in the Sea of Japan to the west. Rishiri, dominated by the volcano Rishirizan, is separated by a 10 km (6 mi) stretch of water from Rebun, which has the much lower peak, Rebundake. Both islands are rich in alpine flora. The flowers of the Sarobetsu Plain—lilies, rhododendrons, irises—are also a major tourist attraction in the summer. The surrounding coastal waters abound in kelp (*kombu*) and are excellent fishing grounds. Area: 212 sq km (82 sq mi).

Risshakuji　　　　　立石寺

Also called Yamadera. Temple of the TENDAI SECT of Buddhism located near the foot of the mountain Hōjusan in the city of Yamagata, Yamagata Prefecture; subsidiary temple (*betsuin*) of ENRYAKUJI. Risshakuji, likely founded by the monk ENNIN (reportedly buried in a cave behind the temple) in 860, became the major Heian-period (794–1185) temple for rural Dewa Province (now Yamagata and Akita prefectures). Destroyed during years of local wars in the early 16th century, the temple was rebuilt in 1543. The present Kompon Chūdō (Main Hall) houses a Heian-period wood image of the Buddha Bhaiṣajyaguru (J: Yakushi). Within Risshakuji's precincts are numerous Shintō shrines. The temple is a popular site for viewing cherry blossoms and autumn foliage.

Risshisha 立志社

(Self-Help Society). Political association active in the FREEDOM AND PEOPLE'S RIGHTS MOVEMENT of the 1870s and 1880s. Formed in Kōchi Prefecture (the former Tosa domain) in April 1874 by ITAGAKI TAISUKE and others, the association derived its name from the Japanese title of the 1870 translation of Samuel Smiles's (1812–1904) *Self-Help* (see SAIGOKU RISSHI HEN). The Risshisha originally concerned itself with local issues in Kōchi, but through its advocacy of a national assembly, land-tax reduction, and revision of foreign treaties, it soon became involved primarily with national issues and established branches throughout the country. The leaders of popular-rights associations such as the AIKOKUSHA and JIYŪTŌ were usually Risshisha members. In 1883 it changed its name to Kainan Jiyūtō. See also POLITICAL PARTIES.

Risshō ankoku ron 立正安国論

(A Treatise on Pacifying the State by Establishing Orthodoxy). A famous polemical dialogue by the Buddhist monk NICHIREN against the PURE LAND BUDDHISM of HŌNEN begun in 1258 and presented on 31 August 1260 to HŌJŌ TOKIYORI, the de facto head of the Kamakura shogunate (1192–1333). Using Buddhist scriptural citations, the work attributes a series of natural disasters plaguing Japan from 1258 to the departure of the guardian deities of Japan, whose spiritual sustenance, orthodox Buddhism, was being replaced by Hōnen's "blasphemous" doctrine. The proposed solution to this problem was the suppression of Hōnen's movements by withholding economic support; execution of the heretics, however, was rejected. Nichiren maintained that, according to scriptural prophecy, failure to suppress the movement would lead to further disasters such as foreign invasions and rebellions. He believed the MONGOL INVASIONS OF JAPAN fulfilled this prediction. Nichiren's proposals were not adopted, and he was exiled in 1261.

Risshō Kōseikai 立正佼成会

One of Japan's largest popular Buddhist organizations, founded by NIWANO NIKKYŌ (b 1906) and Naganuma Myōkō (1889–1957) in 1938. Niwano, born in Niigata Prefecture, joined REIYŪKAI, one of the NEW RELIGIONS, which led him to an understanding of the LOTUS SUTRA. He and Naganuma later withdrew from that group and founded Risshō Kōseikai (Society for Establishment of Righteousness and Personal Perfection through Fellowship). A laymen's organization inspired by the NICHIREN Buddhist tradition, it has no clergy and no formal affiliation with any Nichiren sect. Niwano made the doctrines of the Lotus Sutra easy to understand. The concepts of social harmony and the interdependence of all persons and things in the universe are emphasized, as is ancestor veneration. Each member family has in its home a Buddhist altar (BUTSUDAN) before which selections from the Lotus Sutra are recited twice a day.

One of the organization's main activities is *hōza*, in which small groups meet daily for personal exchange between members and leaders. This has proved an effective means of attracting new members, teaching them Buddhist doctrine, and providing a sense of belonging to people alienated by industrialized society. Participation in rallies and special festivals is also important, as are the promotion of world peace and interreligious

cooperation. In 1990 the organization claimed some 6.7 million members.

Risshō University 立正大学

(Risshō Daigaku). A coeducational private university located in Shinagawa Ward, Tōkyō. Originally established as the Nichiren Buddhist College in 1904, it achieved university status in 1924. Its aim is to foster the spirit of the teachings of the 13th-century monk NICHIREN. It maintains faculties of law, economics, business administration, letters, and Buddhism. Enrollment in 1989 was 9,205.

ritō 吏党

("bureaucrats' parties"). A pejorative term referring to the progovernment parties of the period immediately following formation of the Diet in 1890. It was coined by the MINTŌ ("popular parties") such as the JIYŪTŌ and the RIKKEN KAISHINTŌ that grew out of the FREEDOM AND PEOPLE'S RIGHTS MOVEMENT of the 1880s. Both the Taiseikai (1890) and its successor, the KOKUMIN KYŌKAI (1892), were described by this term.

Ritsumeikan University 立命館大学

(Ritsumeikan Daigaku). A private, coeducational university located in Kinugasa, Kita Ward, Kyōto. Founded in 1900 as the Kyōto Hōsei Gakkō (Kyōto School of Law and Politics) by Nakagawa Kojūrō (1866–1944), a secretary to the minister of education. University status was granted in 1922. The university first specialized in law and economics. It now has faculties of law, economics, business administration, science and engineering, letters, industrial sociology, and international relations. It also has affiliated junior high and high schools. Enrollment was 20,679 in 1989.

Ritsurin Park 栗林公園

(Ritsurin Kōen). In Takamatsu, Kagawa Prefecture, Shikoku. Located at the foot of the hill known as Shiunzan and consisting of artificial ponds and hillocks, it harmonizes with the surrounding scenery. Formerly in the possession of the Matsudaira family, it was opened to the public in 1875. Area: 75 hectares (185 acres).

ritsuryō system 律令制度

(*ritsuryō seido*). System of centralized autocracy, derived from a Chinese model, that

Risshakuji The precincts of this temple encompass the entire mountain Hōjusan and are especially popular for cherry blossom and autumn foliage viewing.

was structured by comprehensive legal codes called *ritsuryō* (Ch: *lü-ling*), and that prevailed in Japan from the late 7th century to the late 10th century. The *ritsuryō* state was characterized by a ruling aristocracy organized as a hierarchical bureaucracy in the service of the throne. The common people were subjected to a uniform system of per capita taxation both in labor and in kind, and rice fields were allotted to them following a general census held every six years. Designed to maximize the sovereign ruler's economic and social control over the subject population, the administrative order prescribed by *ritsuryō* law imposed a wide variety of duties on both officials and commoners without conferring corresponding rights. Although protection was extended to property, inheritance, and certain contracts, violations of rules were always treated as crimes rather than civil wrongs, and injured parties were not awarded compensatory damages. The ruler was presumed to be at the apex of a compulsory system of economic distribution. Each taxable household, for example, was required to prepare its own parcel of tax commodities, to be duly labeled and delivered to the capital, with no intermediate trading allowed. The system's hierarchy of officials was viewed as merely the means by which the ruler exercised his power over both land and people.

General Principles of Ritsuryō Law — *Ritsuryō* law, based on the assumption that all rightful power derived from a sovereign who was himself above the law, was, for the rulers of late-7th-century Japan, a new and ideal instrument for the consolidation and maintenance of political authority by the royal court. The laws were most meticulous in defining the duties of office, regimenting the officials, and strictly limiting their discretionary powers. This emphasis on rational marshaling of power on the sovereign's behalf was somewhat mollified, but ultimately reinforced, by the further assumption that the principal function of the ruler and his officials was to maintain the necessary moral order, as exemplars of virtue more than as enforcers of rules. The legal system itself incorporated this ideology, and its fundamental distinction between coercive sanction and moral instruction appeared as the division between *ritsu* (Ch: *lü*),

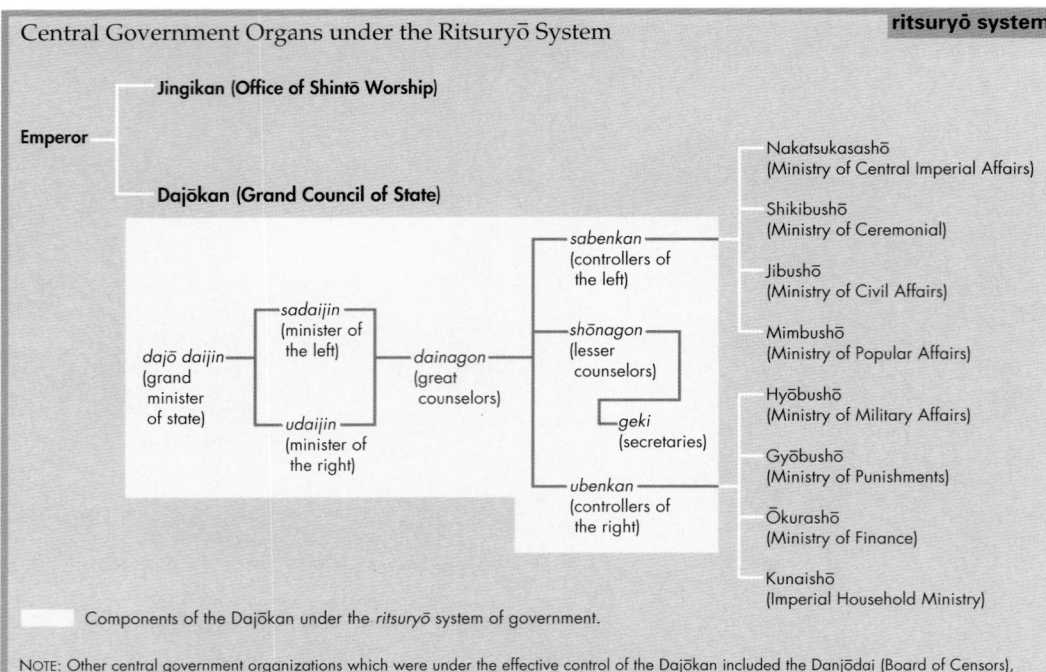

Emperor

Jingikan (Office of Shintō Worship)

Dajōkan (Grand Council of State)

dajō daijin (grand minister of state) — sadaijin (minister of the left) / udaijin (minister of the right) — dainagon (great counselors) — sabenkan (controllers of the left) / shōnagon (lesser counselors) — geki (secretaries) / ubenkan (controllers of the right)

Nakatsukasashō (Ministry of Central Imperial Affairs)
Shikibushō (Ministry of Ceremonial)
Jibushō (Ministry of Civil Affairs)
Mimbushō (Ministry of Popular Affairs)
Hyōbushō (Ministry of Military Affairs)
Gyōbushō (Ministry of Punishments)
Ōkurashō (Ministry of Finance)
Kunaishō (Imperial Household Ministry)

▭ Components of the Dajōkan under the *ritsuryō* system of government.

NOTE: Other central government organizations which were under the effective control of the Dajōkan included the Danjōdai (Board of Censors), Emonfu (Headquarters of the Gate Guards), Ejifu (Headquarters of the Palace Guards), and Hyōefu (Headquarters of the Military Guards).

the penal code, and *ryō* (Ch: *ling*), the code of civil and administrative rules. The underlying assumption here was that, as one writer put it, "*ritsu* rely on deterrent sanction, and *ryō*, on moral instruction." The provisions of *ritsu* and *ryō* interlocked at many points and, in theory at least, made up an internally consistent organic whole.

Administrative precedent sometimes had the force of law, but, in this system of jurisprudence, "law" always meant written law, promulgated by sovereign authority. There were, in addition to *ritsu* and *ryō*, two other major categories of law: *kyaku* (Ch: *ke* or *k'o*), rulings promulgated from time to time to meet "occasional" circumstances, and *shiki* (Ch: *shi* or *shih*), rulings on matters of procedure and form, such as local place names, deemed too particularistic for inclusion in *ritsu* or *ryō*. *Kyaku* were ordinances addressing particular issues already covered by *ritsu* or *ryō*, sometimes supplementing preexisting rules but more often revising them substantially. Regarded as adaptations to present necessity and intended for immediate enforcement, *kyaku* were seen as more coercive than instructive, and hence analogous to the penal rules of *ritsu*. Viewed as expedients rather than principles, *kyaku* could not repeal the rules of *ritsu* and *ryō*, but suspended their operation, sometimes for a very long time.

Most *shiki* were interpretative regulations, elaborations of rules already established by *ritsu*, *ryō*, or *kyaku*. Many were mere confirmations of preexisting official custom, and some, most notably those dealing with official ceremonies and Shintō ritual, were remarkable for their minute detail. Although *shiki* were generally supplementary rules, some were of great substantive importance.

The Ritsu — Much of the *ritsu* penal code prescribed the precise punishment merited by each of the hundreds of narrowly defined crimes. A homicide committed during a sporting contest not involving dangerous weapons, for example, was less serious, by 2 degrees of punishment, than a homicide committed during a fight. There were in all 20 "degrees" of punishment, 5 degrees of beating with the light rod (depending on number of strokes), 5 degrees of the heavy rod, 5 degrees of penal servitude (from one to three years), 3 degrees of exile (near, medium, and distant), and 2 degrees of death (strangulation and beheading). The rules regarding crime and punishment illustrate the marked tendency of the entire legal system to quantify and calibrate wherever possible.

Status as an official, or as a Buddhist monk or nun, usually enabled an offender to avoid corporal punishment. In all but the most extreme cases, high-ranking persons were exempted from public execution and judicial torture. The *ritsu*, moreover, provided a table of equivalencies allowing the forfeiture of grades of rank and office to substitute for the infliction of degrees of punishment. Officials and their close kin were also usually permitted to escape punishment by making a payment of copper in an amount stipulated by *ritsu* rules. Among other advantages made available to the upper strata were provisions for special clemency for people of very high rank or royal kindred, whose cases, if not involving one of the "Eight Outrages" (HACHIGYAKU), were to be specially "deliberated." They were thus assured of a reduced sentence and given the chance for an imperial pardon.

In the many rules for the calculation of penalties, great weight was given to familial relationships, so that injuries inflicted on children by parents were of little or no gravity, while any offense against parents or grandparents would merit very severe punishment. Family relationships could also result in criminal liability without personal fault, and in extreme cases, such as treason or sedition, the penalty was "family extermination." High crimes such as these were among the Eight Outrages and hence beyond the reach of amnesties. Among the "outrages," however, were acts such as the profanation of a shrine, a crime not serious enough to merit death but nevertheless intrinsically unforgivable. Penal deterrence in the service of absolute power, as embodied in the *ritsu*, had the concurrent purpose of reinforcing Confucian morality.

The Ryō — The hierarchically structured political and social order that moral propriety required was a central concern of the *ryō*. The many specific rules for the administrative constitution of the state were, more-over, especially detailed about the selection of officials and the prerogatives of official rank status. By these rules, entry into the corps of officials was almost completely restricted to descendants of officeholders, with the advantages precisely graded according to the ancestor's rank. Although the rules of the *ryō* made room for the advancement of officials of merit and ability, the integration of family organization into the apparatus of state authority was of paramount importance. The numerous provisions on succession to "family headship" and the mourning of deceased kin were essential elements of the political order spelled out in the *ryō*.

With 30 chapters and over 900 articles, the *ryō* text promulgated in 757, which may be taken as typical, was about twice the length of the *ritsu*. It set forth, in detail, the organization of each government bureau, including the numbers, ranks, and specific functions of personnel involved. The *ritsuryō* state was thus the only premodern Japanese polity to have a legally enacted constitutional structure. At the core stood about 500 officials who headed every important bureau and provincial headquarters. At the apex stood the Grand Council of State, or DAJŌKAN, staffed by officials of the highest rank. *Ryō* rules on official procedure made the issuing of imperial edicts without the assent of this council impossible. On the next lower level were eight ministries, each with a specific function, and numerous subordinate bureaus. The staff officers of all these bureaus, including the governing boards of the provinces, were, by the operation of *ryō* rules on hereditary rank prerogative and selection and placement of officials, all drawn from the same pool of aristocrats residing in the capital. The officials of local and central bureaus were divided into four levels, but only the top two levels were endowed with discretionary powers (see SHITŌKAN). *Ryō* provisions aimed at rewarding virtue and ability were not intended to broaden opportunities for enrollment into the official class so much as to provide internal discipline for those already enrolled. With considerably less indirection, the *ryō* provided for the prerogatives of a separate regional elite, principally by establishing provincial subdivisions called *gun* (see KOKUGUN SYSTEM), whose officers, recruited locally, shared administrative and fiscal responsibilities with the provincial headquarters. *Gun* magistrates held their offices for life.

In addition to the conduct of state functions such as tax collecting (see SO, YŌ, AND CHŌ) and military administration, the subject matter of the *ryō* included property, domestic relations, and other areas of what would now be considered private law. The *ryō*, however, offered no truly civil remedies to aggrieved persons but simply provided an impeachment procedure by which an offended person could initiate criminal process against the offender. Contrasted as they were to the morally instructive forces of law, legal sanctions meant penal sanctions.

History — The *ritsuryō* state and its legal system were the culmination of the massive assimilation of Chinese political culture that took place in 7th-century Japan. Major landmarks in this process were the ranking system (KAN'I JŪNIKAI) and other innovations of Prince SHŌTOKU during the first decade, the TAIKA REFORM of the 640s, and the ASUKA KIYOMIHARA CODE, Japan's first complete *ryō*, put into effect during the 680s. The expanding power of China under the Sui (589–618) and Tang (T'ang; 618–907) dynasties intensified preexisting Chinese influence throughout East Asia, stimulating the rulers of emergent states such as Japan to consolidate their power by deliberately applying Chinese methods of rule at home. The culmination of this process in Japan was the study of Tang *lü-ling* codes and their replication, reedited and modified, as *ritsuryō*. The first fully implemented *ritsuryō* was the TAIHŌ CODE, put into effect in 702. The second and last complete *ritsuryō* was the YŌRŌ CODE, fully drafted by about 718 but not put into effect until 757. *Ritsuryō* law and the *ritsuryō* state were at their peak during the first 60 years of the 8th century but slowly declined thereafter.

Ritsuryō administration in Japan retained its vitality for about the same period of time as its Chinese counterpart. Periodic land allotment, one of the system's most demanding features, was in fact carried out fairly regularly throughout the 8th century. Yet the implied consensus between regional and national officialdoms was increasingly strained by conflicts over local revenues and lands, and a general trend toward estate building led repeatedly to extralegal fiscal transactions between local magnates and capital nobles, weakening bureaucratic centrality. By the mid-9th century, decision-making power in the capital had largely shifted from the ministries instituted by the *ryō* to a series of newly established boards and councils, some of which developed legal traditions of their own. The growth of customary law was never actually regarded as a repudiation of the *ritsuryō*, and provisions of *ritsu*, *ryō*, *kyaku*, or *shiki* were always cited, as the *ritsu* requires, to justify legal decisions. Custom became the major source of law as legal traditions established what rules from the written law corpus would apply to a given case. The Yōrō Ritsuryō, never effectively revised, became obscured by *kyaku* and *shiki*, and large compilations of these materials were made and enacted as law in 820 and 871. A third collection was completed in 907, but the *shiki* portion, combined with the two earlier *shiki* collections into codified form, became law only in 967. This, the ENGI SHIKI, was the last codification made in ancient Japan.

Ritsu sect 律宗

(Risshū). A Buddhist school that emphasizes ascetic discipline (J: *ritsu*; Skt: *vinaya*). One of the six sects of NARA BUDDHISM, it was introduced by GANJIN, a Chinese monk who came to Japan in 754. Stationed first at the temple TŌDAIJI in Nara, he established the *kaidan'in* (ordination-hall platform) from which he conferred bodhisattva precepts. In 759 he founded the temple TŌSHŌDAIJI in Nara. Two more *kaidan'in* were installed, at Yakushiji in Shimotsuke Province (now Tochigi Prefecture) and at Kanzeonji in Tsukushi (northern Kyūshū), and every monk or nun was required to receive precepts at one of the three platforms. The school, having declined in the late Heian period (794–1185), was revived by Shunjō (1166–1227), Kakujō (1194–1249), EIZON, and Ninshō (1217–1303). Today the Ritsu sect is centered at Tōshōdaiji, with a score of affiliated temples.

Rittō 栗東[町]

Town in southern Shiga Prefecture, central Honshū. Formerly a rice-growing village, Rittō now has chemical, machinery, and metalworking plants that developed after a Meishin expressway interchange opened here in 1963. Pop: 45,049.

roads 道路

(*dōro*). Railroads provided the primary means of land transportation in Japan prior to World War II because most roads were unpaved, narrow, and winding, and thus inadequate for motor vehicle transportation. It was not until the 1950s that comprehensive planning for road construction began. In 1953 funds for road construction were set aside from gasoline taxes; the first five-year plan for construction was initiated in 1954; and in 1956 the JAPAN HIGHWAY PUBLIC CORPORATION was established. These provisions laid the groundwork for modern highway development in Japan. Although the quality and capacity of highways have increased dramatically, it has been impossible to adequately accommodate the explosive increase in the number of automobiles (from 2 million in 1960 to 60 million in 1990), and traffic congestion is a nationwide problem.

Roads in Japan are under the jurisdiction of the MINISTRY OF CONSTRUCTION, and are classified as national EXPRESSWAYS (total mileage in March 1991 was 4,869 km or 3,025 mi), national highways (47,000 km or 29,201 mi), prefectural roads (129,040 km or 80,173 mi), and local roads (939,552 km or 583,744 mi). Virtually all national highways are paved, and 93 percent of prefectural roads and 66 percent of local roads are paved.

Road construction and management is financed through a special road improvement account, which is primarily funded by taxes on gasoline, the oil trade, automobile sales, and automobile weight. Road construction is also financed by the national budget (see BUDGET, NATIONAL) and public investment funds (ZAISEI TŌYŪSHI). Total expenditure in 1990 was about ¥9.0 trillion (US $65.2 billion), or approximately 3.2 percent of the gross national product.

Road Traffic Law 道路交通法

(Dōro Kōtsū Hō). The basic law regulating road traffic. Enacted in 1960, it has been revised frequently. Its purpose is to ensure the smooth and safe flow of traffic and to prevent undue air pollution, noise, vibrations, and other harm resulting from road traffic.

Motor vehicles were first imported to Japan in 1900. Shortly thereafter, each prefecture established its own traffic regulations. The first national regulations, the Road Traffic Control Order, were enacted in 1920 and replaced by the Road Traffic Control Law after World War II. Until that time, both pedestrians and vehicles had kept to the left-hand side of the road; under the new law, pedestrians began to use the right-hand side, and motor vehicles continued to drive on the left. The Road Traffic Law was enacted in 1960 in response to a great increase in motor traffic; it applies to all public roads and other places open to general traffic. In general, specific traffic regulations are established by metropolitan and prefectural public safety commissions. Penalties are provided for violations, ranging from fines and loss of DRIVERS' LICENSES to jail for drunken drivers.

ro and sha 絽と紗

(*ro to sha*; leno gauze weaving). Types of gauze weaving in which the warp threads are twisted in groups of two, creating an open-mesh effect in the finished fabric. A weft thread is passed through the "eye" of the twisted threads and holds the twist in place. *Sha* is the technique that uses one weft thread through each row of twisting warp threads. For *ro*, each row of twisted warp threads may be followed by several weft threads and then another row of twisting warp. By varying the number of weft threads and the arrangement of the twists, complex patterns can be created. These techniques were formerly used for imperial coronation garments and priests' robes. More recently, *ro* and *sha* have come to be used in the weaving of KIMONO, HAORI, and OBI for summer wear.

Rōben 良弁

(689–773). Also known as Ryōben. Monk of the KEGON SECT (Ch: Huayan or Hua-yen) of Buddhism. Born in Sagami Province (now part of Kanagawa Prefecture). He first studied Hossō (Ch: Faxiang or Fa-hsiang; see HOSSŌ SECT) teachings under Gien (d 728), who, together with such disciples as GYŌGI and Rōben, cemented the foundations of Buddhism in Japan. Emperor Shōmu (701–756; r 724–749) established the temple Kinshōji on Rōben's behalf. Rōben is the second patriarch of the Kegon sect in Japan after Shinjō. He contributed to the construction of the Great Buddha at the temple TŌDAIJI and is regarded as the temple's founder.

robots ロボット

(*robotto*). At the beginning of the 1990s Japan led the world in the development of robot technology—approximately half the world's total number of robots of all types were then operating in Japan—but the Japanese robot industry itself dates back only to the late 1960s; Unimation and AFM of the United States exported the first advanced robot technology to Japan in 1967. Against the background of the rapid economic growth of that period and the consequent severe shortages of skilled labor, the appearance of robots had a great impact in Japan. KAWASAKI HEAVY INDUSTRIES, LTD, started production of robots using Unimation technology in 1968, and in the same year ISHIKAWAJIMA-HARIMA HEAVY INDUSTRIES CO, LTD, and YASKAWA ELECTRIC CORPORATION began selling robot systems based on Japanese technology. The first industrial robot conference, which was held just three years later, was attended by 35 companies, and by 1978 some 10,000 robot systems were being produced domestically each year, a figure that had doubled by 1980.

While the 1970s were a decade of development and application, the 1980s witnessed a shift from factory automation for mass production to smaller-scale diverse-product manufacturing, which called for greater sophistication in object recognition and handling. In 1990 the Advanced Robot Technology Research Association completed an eight-year plan under the auspices of the MINISTRY OF INTERNATIONAL TRADE AND INDUSTRY (MITI) aimed at expanding robot technology beyond the industrial robot field to applications in nuclear power generation, offshore development, disaster prevention, and other areas in which remote-controlled robot systems could perform their functions quickly and accurately under difficult or dangerous conditions.

In 1981 it was estimated that there were 67,435 industrial robots in operation in Japan, or about 70 percent of the world total. By 1990 European and American systems had reduced the Japanese share to about 50

robots

▼ A robot designed for tasks in hostile environments. In a radioactive area, for example, it is capable of taking measurements, moving objects, and making simple repairs.

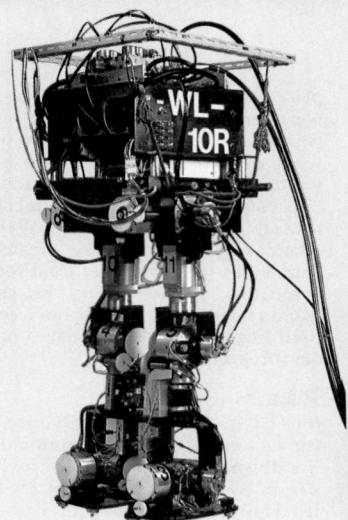

▲ The inventors of the WL-10 dynamic walker claim it has a speed of 1.3 seconds per step.

▼ A manipulation robot replicates the movements of the person at right.

▶ Sensors for attachment to human hands are a basic component of manipulation research, which seeks to develop robots able to respond to very subtle hand movements.

▼ Equipped with two video camera "eyes," this intelligent robot can analyze a three-dimensional structure like a pile of blocks and make an identical pile with its "arms."

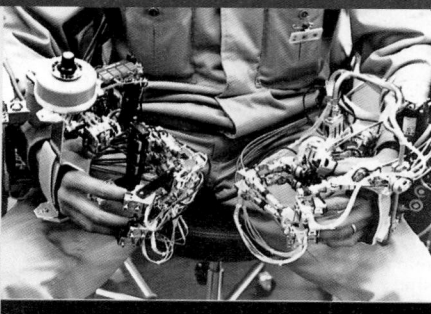

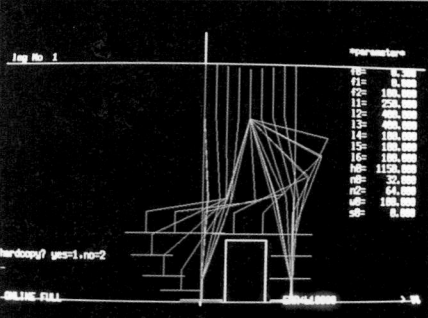

▲ Computer analysis of an obstacle in a robot's path.

▶ A multipurpose industrial robot for automated factories. Jointed in five places, it can move in complex ways.

▼ The "hands" of a manipulation robot can make the delicate movements necessary to screw a nut onto a bolt.

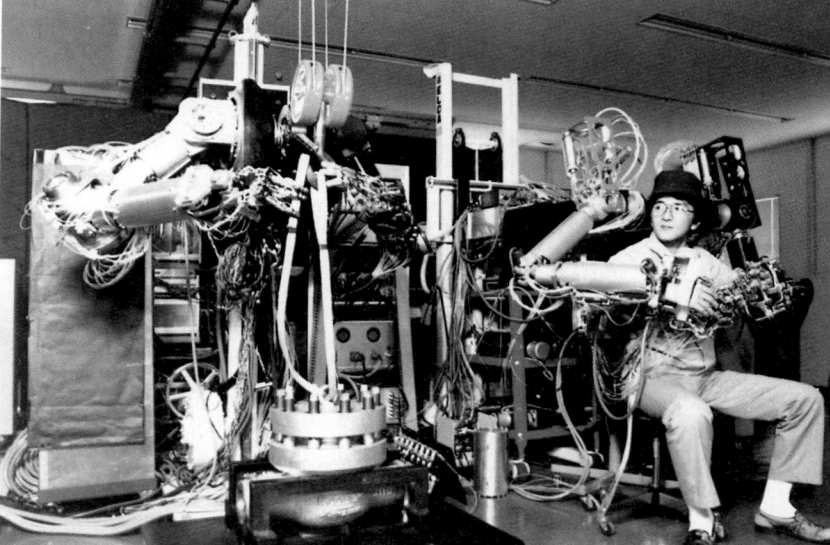

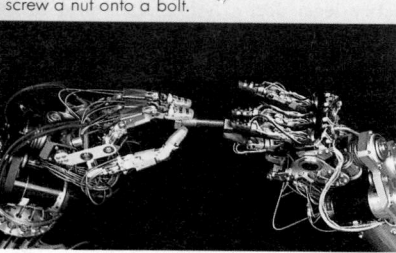

percent, although Japan continued to play a leading role in robot development. The highest concentrations of robot use in the early 1980s were in electronic machinery manufacturing and automobile manufacturing, but by 1990 robots were being used for such diversified functions as finishing concrete, painting tall buildings, and even medical care.

The economic and social role of robots is likely to expand considerably in the future, as they make possible greater improvements in industrial productivity and product quality. Robots contribute to the humanization of work life by releasing human beings from heavy, dangerous, and monotonous work; they also facilitate the development of new industries and contribute to the conservation of resources and energy.

Roches, Léon   ロッシュ, L.

(1809–1901). French diplomat and minister plenipotentiary to Japan in the years immediately preceding the MEIJI RESTORATION (1868). An experienced diplomat, he used his influence with the Tokugawa shogunate (1603–1867) to promote French commercial interests in Japan. Upon arriving in Japan in

1864, he joined other foreign powers in protesting Japan's refusal to honor its treaty obligations (see ANSEI COMMERCIAL TREATIES) and its harassment of foreign nationals. He supported the Western military expedition against the Chōshū domain (now Yamaguchi Prefecture) in 1864 (see SHIMONOSEKI BOMBARDMENT).

After this incident Roches pursued a policy of supporting the shogunate in its efforts to modernize, thus ensuring French industry a part in Japan's economy (see OGURI TADAMASA). He recommended changes that would have brought greater centralized control to Japan. Some proposals were implemented: construction of the YOKOSUKA SHIPYARDS was begun in 1865, and in 1867 a French military mission arrived in Japan (see CHANOINE, CHARLES SULPICE JULES).

Roches's downfall started before the collapse of the shogunate. Complaints by foreign traders over his commercial activities made his position precarious. Moreover, he failed to understand the significance of the emerging anti-Tokugawa forces in Japan. After the overthrow of the shogunate, he was recalled in 1868 and retired from the foreign service.

rockets → space technology

Rōdō Kumiai Kiseikai → Shokkō
Giyūkai

Rōdō Nōmintō   労働農民党

(Labor-Farmer Party; also known as Rōnōtō). Political party formed on 5 March 1926. Its goal was to improve the standard of living of the working classes through parliamentary means; its membership comprised moderate socialists and members of labor groups. More radical socialists and communists soon demanded entry, and with the defection of the moderates to form the NIHON RŌNŌTŌ and the SHAKAI MINSHŪTŌ late in 1926, the party was reorganized along leftist lines. Under ŌYAMA IKUO it adopted more aggressive tactics. In the first election held under universal manhood suffrage in February 1928, two of its candidates were elected. The party was banned in April 1928 following the MARCH 15TH INCIDENT but was reorganized in 1929 under the abbreviated name Rōnōtō.

Rōdōsha Nōmintō   労働者農民党

(Worker-Farmer Party). Also known as Rōnōtō.

1. Planned pre–World War II leftist political party that did not materialize because of factional infighting. After the outlawed RŌDŌ

NŌMINTŌ (Labor-Farmer Party) disbanded in April 1928, ŌYAMA IKUO and other leftists, with guidance from the JAPAN COMMUNIST PARTY, began preparations to found a new party. However, the communists shifted their policy line to one of opposition, and the new party was never formed.

2. Post–World War II party organized in December 1948 by KURODA HISAO, Kimura Kihachirō (1901–75), and others who had left the JAPAN SOCIALIST PARTY (JSP). The new party hoped to be the nucleus of a united front bringing together the left and right wings of the JSP with the Japan Communist Party. It was dissolved in 1957, its members returning to the reunited JSP.

Rōdōshō → Ministry of Labor

Rodrigues, João   ロドリゲス, J.

(1561?–1633). Portuguese Jesuit; interpreter and commercial agent for TOYOTOMI HIDEYOSHI and TOKUGAWA IEYASU, he also compiled two grammars of spoken Japanese. Born in Sernancelhe, Rodrigues arrived in Japan as a youth in 1577 and entered the Society of Jesus three years later. His renowned fluency in Japanese earned him the sobriquet of Tçuzzu, or Interpreter. He first met Hideyoshi in 1591 and often negotiated with him, and, later, Ieyasu about Portuguese trade and mission affairs. But commercial jealousy in Nagasaki, where Rodrigues wielded much influence, led to the Jesuit's expulsion from Japan in 1610. Rodrigues spent the rest of his life in China.

In 1608 Rodrigues published at Nagasaki his celebrated *Arte da Lingoa de Iapam*. In it he describes not only Japanese grammar but also history, poetry, and etiquette; in 1620 he brought out at Macao a heavily revised and briefer edition titled *Arte Breve da Lingoa Iapoa*.

Roesler, Karl Friedrich Hermann
ロエスレル, K. F. H.

(1834–94). German scholar of public law and an adviser to the Japanese government during the Meiji period (1868–1912); he participated in the drafting of the COMMERCIAL CODE (1899) and the Meiji Constitution (1889), Japan's first modern constitution. The son of a lawyer, Roesler studied law and political science at the universities of Erlangen and Munich. He became a professor at the University of Rostock in 1861. In 1878 he accepted an invitation to work for the Japanese government. Serving first in the Ministry of Foreign Affairs, in 1884 he became a legal adviser to the cabinet. At the behest of ITŌ HIROBUMI, Roesler assisted INOUE KOWASHI in preparing drafts that became the basis of the Meiji Constitution. Roesler's contributions reflected his preference for a strong monarchical system.

Rohm Co, Ltd   ロ一ム[株]

(Rōmu). Manufacturer of custom linear integrated circuits. Rohm also produces semiconductor devices such as diodes and transistors for videocassette recorders and other consumer electronic products. Incorporated in 1958. The company began as a manufacturer of resistors and developed much of its own technology. Manufacturing facilities are located in the United States, Brazil, Malaysia, Korea, and Thailand. Sales for the fiscal year ending March 1991 totaled ¥165.7 billion (US $1.2 billion), and capitalization stood at ¥59.2 billion (US $431.5 million). Headquarters are in Kyōto.

Rohwer Relocation Center
ローワー収容所

(Rōwā Shūyōjo). Wartime relocation facility for Japanese Americans from California; located near Rohwer, Desha County, Arkansas. In operation from 18 September 1942 until 30 November 1945, it held a maximum of 8,745 persons at any one time; a total of 11,928 persons were confined there. See also JAPANESE AMERICANS, WARTIME RELOCATION OF; WAR RELOCATION AUTHORITY.

rōjū   老中

(senior councillors). Senior officials of the TOKUGAWA SHOGUNATE (1603–1867); also called TOSHIYORI. The post took form in the 1620s and was usually held by four or five men, the senior being chief senior councillor (rōjū shuseki or shuza). The post was usually occupied by men of middle-level FUDAI daimyō status. Its occupants alternated duty at monthly intervals (tsukibansei) but dealt with important matters in conciliar fashion. They were responsible for most shogunate officials and through them supervised foreign affairs, the imperial court and nobility, daimyō, the shogunal household, religious establishments, Tokugawa vassals, and all people, lands, towns, and cities in the shogunate's own domains. Before being promoted to the post, men usually served as commissioner of temples and shrines (JISHA BUGYŌ), master of shogunal ceremony (sōshaban), keeper of Ōsaka Castle (Ōsaka JŌDAI), Kyōto deputy (KYŌTO SHOSHIDAI), or senior councillor to the heir apparent (nishinomaru rōjū). Senior councillors in domainal governments were known as KARŌ.

rōketsu → wax-resist dyeing

Rokkaku family   六角氏

(Rokkakushi). Military governors (SHUGO) from the Kamakura period (1185–1333) through the Sengoku period (1467–1568). Founded by Rokkaku Yasutsuna, a son of Sasaki Nobutsuna (1180–1242), the family controlled the southern half of Ōmi Province (now Shiga Prefecture) from the early 13th century; they took their surname from the location of their Kyōto residence. Yasutsuna's great-grandson Ujiyori served ASHIKAGA TAKAUJI and adopted one of Takauji's younger brothers, assuring the family's prominence in the MUROMACHI SHOGUNATE (1338–1573); his fifth-generation descendant Sadayori (1495–1552) served as shogunal deputy (KANREI). After the ŌNIN WAR (1467–77), the Rokkaku remained close to the shogunate and shared in its decline. Rokkaku Yoshiharu (1545–1612) is remembered for the domainal law code YOSHIHARU SHIKIMOKU. In 1568 the Rokkaku resisted ODA NOBUNAGA; they were defeated and faded from historical significance.

Rokkakushi Shikimoku →
Yoshiharu Shikimoku

Rokkaku Shisui   六角紫水

(1867–1950). Lacquer craftsman. Real name Rokkaku Chūtarō. Born in Ōgaki, Hiroshima Prefecture. Graduate of Tōkyō Bijutsu Gakkō (now Tōkyō University of Fine Arts and Music). After returning to Japan from a tour of Europe and the United States with OKAKURA KAKUZŌ, he studied ancient Oriental lacquer techniques. He taught at Tōkyō Bijutsu Gakkō and contributed to the modernization of the lacquer ware craft, invent-

ing the new techniques of *shiro-urushi* (white lacquer) and *iro-urushi* (color lacquer).

Rokkasen   六歌仙

(The Six Poetic Geniuses). Six Heian-period (794–1185) poets given the appellation "genius" because they are mentioned by name in the two prefaces to the KOKINSHŪ, the first imperial anthology of Japanese poetry, compiled in 905. Of the six, ARIWARA NO NARIHIRA and ONO NO KOMACHI are two of Japan's greatest poets. The remaining four are Bishop HENJŌ, Fun'ya no Yasuhide (Bun'ya no Yasuhide; d 885), Ōtomo no Kuronushi (dates unknown), and the monk Kisen (dates unknown). Although considered second rate, they are representative of the mid-to-late 9th century, when Japanese poetry began to achieve acceptance and status comparable with that of poetry in Chinese. Their styles are the direct precursors of the mature *Kokinshū* style. The number of Rokkasen was no doubt fixed to coincide with the six styles of Japanese poetry. The Rokkasen as a group was more of a symbol and a revered presence than a direct influence on poetry from the *Kokinshū* onward. See also SANJŪROKKASEN.

Rokkōsan   六甲山

Mountain in the northeastern part of the city of Kōbe, Hyōgo Prefecture, western Honshū; also a general term for the entire Rokkō Mountains. The Rokkō Mountains' highest peak, it is a recreational area. The summit, reached by cable car and road, provides a night view of Kōbe and the Ōsaka Bay area. It is part of Inland Sea National Park. Height: 931 m (3,054 ft).

Rokōkyō Jiken → Marco Polo Bridge
Incident

Rokuharamitsuji   六波羅蜜寺

A temple in Higashiyama Ward, Kyōto, belonging to the Chizan branch (see CHISHAKUIN) of the Shingon sect of Buddhism. The temple, originally named Saikōji, was founded in 963 by the itinerant preacher KŪYA to house an eleven-headed image of the bodhisattva KANNON that he had carved. At first affiliated with the Tendai sect, Rokuharamitsuji (named so at the time of Chūshin, the second abbot) became a temple of the Shingon sect around 1600. During the Meiji period (1868–1912) the government confiscated most of its land. Today the temple is reduced to what had been the main hall and several smaller buildings. Its most noted sculpture is a statue of Kūya. Rokuharamitsuji is the 17th station for pilgrims touring the 33 holy places dedicated to Kannon in western Japan.

Rokuhara tandai   六波羅探題

(Rokuhara deputies). Also known as Rokuhara *shugo*. Shogunal deputies (TANDAI) stationed at Rokuhara in southeastern Kyōto by the KAMAKURA SHOGUNATE (1192–1333). Their duties included supervision of the political, military, and judicial affairs of the southwestern half of Japan (the area west and south of what is now Aichi Prefecture). The post was established in 1221 after Emperor GO-TOBA attempted a coup d'état in the JŌKYŪ DISTURBANCE. The *tandai* took over the duties of the former Kyōto *shugo* (military governors of Kyōto), appointed in the earliest days of the shogunate. The post was held concurrently by two men, both chosen

Léon Roches
Appointed French minister plenipotentiary to Japan in 1864, Roches was recalled in 1868 following the collapse of the Tokugawa shogunate.

Rokumeikan The Rokumeikan, built in 1883, provides the backdrop for a stylish couple in this painting of the period.

1. *Senshō.* The morning is auspicious, but the afternoon will bring bad luck. On this type of day, everything should be done expeditiously. It is a good day for urgent business and litigation.

2. *Tomobiki.* Except for noontime, the day is auspicious. It is bad luck to hold funerals and Buddhist services on this day. To hold a funeral on this day is said to be inviting another death.

3. *Sempu.* Urgent business and controversy should be avoided on this day. It is a good day for going about all activities in a serene manner. The afternoon is auspicious.

4. *Butsumetsu.* This day is bad luck in all respects. It is best to avoid scheduling auspicious events and opening a business on this day.

5. *Taian.* This day is auspicious in all respects. A good day for scheduling celebrations, such as weddings and shrine visits (MIYAMAIRI).

6. *Shakku.* This day is bad luck in all respects; the only auspicious time is noon.

rōkyoku→ naniwa-bushi

romanization of Japanese ローマ字

(*rōmaji*). The romanization of Japanese is the use of roman (Latin) script, or *rōmaji*, to transliterate the Japanese language, which in its usual written form is a mixture of Chinese characters (called KANJI in Japanese) and two KANA syllabaries (indigenous phonetic spellings derived from these characters). The system of romanization most commonly used since the early Meiji period (1868–1912) is the modified Hepburn (J: Hebon) system, also known as the Hyōjun (or Standard) system. Another widely used system, especially in Japan, is the Kunrei system.

Disagreement continues, however, both in Japan and abroad, over which *rōmaji* system is best for which purposes and whether or not, or to what extent, Japan should convert to romanization in place of the currently accepted writing system. Writing in an alphabet, instead of *kana* and thousands of *kanji* that have to be memorized, reduces learning time to a fraction and simplifies typewriting and printing. But the cultural, psychological, and practical barriers to any large-scale conversion to romanization are formidable.

The first romanization system, developed in the 16th century by Jesuit missionaries, including Francis XAVIER, was based on Portuguese and was initially used in printing in 1591 by Alessandro VALIGNANO. In 1885 the Rōmajikwai (as it was spelled) brought together interested Japanese and foreigners to develop a new system of romanization and to promote it as a replacement for the existing system of mixed *kanji* and *kana*. An adviser to the group, the American missionary and physician James Curtis HEPBURN, adopted its recommended system for the third edition (1886) of the popular Japanese-English dictionary he published. The system came to bear his name, although it had been developed collaboratively by a group composed of Japanese and foreigners. Its supporters formed the Rōmaji Hiromekai in 1905 and regrouped in 1938 as the Hyōjun Rōmaji Kai, which remains active to the present.

The Kunrei system, the main alternative to the Hepburn system, likewise dates back to the 1880s. Its origins are in the Nippon style, a system developed by TANAKADATE AIKITSU, a physicist and professor at Tōkyō University.

rokuro The potter's wheel was used in Japan as early as the 9th century.

from members of the regent HŌJŌ FAMILY; their administrative system was modeled on that of Kamakura. The last Rokuhara *tandai* were deposed by ASHIKAGA TAKAUJI in 1333.

Rokumeikan   鹿鳴館

(Deer Cry Pavilion). A two-story brick building built in 1883 in the Hibiya section of Tōkyō near the present location of the Imperial Hotel; its architect was Josiah CONDER. The site of numerous balls and other social events attended by prominent Japanese and foreigners, it came to symbolize the period of rapid Westernization during the early Meiji period (the so-called Rokumeikan era). A reaction against Westernization set in after Foreign Minister INOUE KAORU's attempts to revise the so-called Unequal Treaties (see UNEQUAL TREATIES, REVISION OF) ended in failure, and the Rokumeikan was redesignated the Kazoku Kaikan (Peers' Hall) in 1890. The building was razed in 1941.

Rokuonji→ Kinkakuji

Rokuon nichiroku   鹿苑日録

Journal kept by supervisory priests (*sōroku*) of Rokuon'in, a subtemple of the ZEN Buddhist temple SHŌKOKUJI in Kyōto. The 78-volume journal, which covers the period 1487–1651 and includes drafts of letters and excerpts from poetry anthologies, is valuable for its insights on politics and society in Kyōto and the clerical organization of Zen.

rokuro   轆轤

1. (lathe). That lathes were used in Japan as early as the Yayoi period (ca 300 BC–ca AD 300) is indicated by pedestaled wooden bowls excavated from the KARAKO SITE in Nara Prefecture. These lathes were manually operated by alternately pulling the left and right ends of a rope wound around the horizontal bar of the tool. Foot-driven lathes were subsequently devised, and these were eventually replaced by those powered by water.

2. (potter's wheel). The earliest evidence for the use of the potter's wheel is found in the string-cut bases on SUE WARE bowls dating from the 9th century. Until then, as evidenced by Yayoi pottery and HAJI WARE, a turntable was employed for applying designs, shaping, and finishing rims. See CERAMICS.

rokuyō   六曜

("six days"). Also called *rokki.* Designations or fortunes added to Japanese calendars indicating whether or not a given date is auspicious. In the old Japanese solar calendar, six different fortunes—*senshō, tomobiki, sempu, butsumetsu, taian,* and *shakku*—were applied in continuous six-day cycles. This custom was imported from China in the 14th century and was practiced in Japan from the mid-Edo period (1600–1868). These fortunes still appear on many Japanese calendars and are observed to some extent in everyday life in Japan. For example, when one is selecting a wedding date, the *butsumetsu* designation is avoided and *taian* is regarded as most desirable. Funerals are customarily not scheduled on dates with the *tomobiki* designation. The following is a glossary of the six designations.

The Kunrei system remains in use for grade school textbooks and the National Diet Library, among others, while the Foreign Ministry and most Japanese-English dictionaries continue to use the Hyōjun system. Requests have been made by the International Organization for Standardization (ISO) for a clear stand by the Japanese government, but as of the early 1990s the issue had not been resolved.

The romanization system used in this encyclopedia is the Hyōjun or Hepburn system. This book differs from many recent publications in maintaining the older spelling of *m* (rather than *n*) before *b*, *m*, or *p*.

roman poruno   ロマンポルノ

(literally, "romantic pornography"). Low-cost narrative films turned out by NIKKATSU CORPORATION between 1971 and 1988 that accent the erotic. *Roman poruno* occasionally display artistic ambition and achievement, especially when handled by directors of the caliber of KUMASHIRO TATSUMI, Fujita Toshita (b 1932), or Tanaka Noboru (b 1937). Noteworthy examples include Fujita's *Hachigatsu no nureta suna* (1971, Wet Sand of August), Kumashiro's *Ichijō Sayuri: Nureta yokujō* (1972, Ichijō Sayuri: Wet Desire), and Tanaka's *Jitsuroku Abe Sada* (1975, The True Story of Abe Sada). Production of *roman poruno* films slowed and finally stopped during the 1980s, largely due to the rising popularity of pornographic videos.

rōnin   浪人

(literally, "floating men"). The term *rōnin* is most familiar as a label for the masterless SAMURAI of the Edo period (1600–1868), but in early Japan it referred to peasants who left their land to work elsewhere. They formed an element of most armies and readily transferred from one commander to another or returned to the land.

From the Muromachi period (1333–1568), the term came to refer to samurai who had lost their commanders and their stipends. The Battle of SEKIGAHARA (1600) and the ensuing defeat of many commanders and redistribution of fiefs saw an increase in the number of *rōnin* to an estimated 400,000. Some 100,000 joined TOYOTOMI HIDEYORI's forces at Ōsaka Castle (1614–15; see ŌSAKA CASTLE, SIEGES OF); many also fought for his adversary, TOKUGAWA IEYASU.

After Ieyasu's victory at Ōsaka many *rōnin* sought employment in castle towns or entered new professions in the developing cities. The marginal position of those who remained *rōnin* in the early Edo period bred considerable discontent among them, and there was an abortive *rōnin* uprising (the KEIAN INCIDENT) in 1651. The shogunate took measures to encourage their employment. Gradually many *rōnin* families died out or abandoned their samurai status. Small numbers of samurai continued to enter the ranks of *rōnin* by absconding, confiscation of fiefs (KAIEKI), criminal activities, and the like. One famous absconder was the poet Matsuo BASHŌ. In 1703, in the famous FORTY-SEVEN RŌNIN INCIDENT, a group of *rōnin* avenged their lord's death and then were forced to commit suicide.

During the period leading up to the MEIJI RESTORATION of 1868, a new sort of *rōnin*, those who left their lords in order to support the imperial cause, appeared; some became leaders in the efforts to overthrow the Tokugawa shogunate. With the abolition of the Edo-period social system after the Meiji Restoration, the *rōnin* ceased to exist as a social category. However, from the late 19th century to the end of World War II the term lived on in expressions such as Shina *rōnin*, Manshū *rōnin*, and TAIRIKU RŌNIN, all labels for Japanese nationalists and adventurers active in China and Manchuria. Today it refers to high school graduates unable to enter the university of their choice on their first attempt, who live "masterless" until successful in later attempts.

Rōninkai   浪人会

(Society of Masterless Samurai). Nationalist society formed by TŌYAMA MITSURU, MIURA GORŌ, and others in 1908. With its parent organizations the GEN'YŌSHA and the AMUR RIVER SOCIETY, the Rōninkai engaged in covert political activities to promote Japan's imperialist interests on the Asian continent. See also ŌSAKA ASAHI HIKKA INCIDENT.

rōnō   老農

("master farmers"). A term used mainly in the Edo (1600–1868) and Meiji (1868–1912) periods to refer to model farmers recognized for their agricultural expertise as well as for a wide range of general knowledge and culture. For instance, the Tsushima domain (now part of Nagasaki Prefecture) published *Rōnō ruigo* (1722), a collection of the opinions of 53 *rōnō* living in the domain, and used it as a textbook on farming. After the Meiji Restoration (1868), the government sought to modernize Japanese agriculture by introducing seeds, agricultural implements, and specialists from Europe and the United States. But it still continued to attach importance to the methods advocated by the experienced *rōnō*. Toward the end of the Meiji period, however, as new scientific ideas gradually took root, *rōnō* farming methods were replaced by more modern techniques.

Rōnōha   労農派

(Labor-Farmer faction). Group of Marxist theorists centering on the journal *Rōnō* (Labor-Farmer) who opposed the JAPAN COMMUNIST PARTY (JCP) line in the late 1920s and 1930s. The Rōnōha engaged in a famous dispute over revolutionary strategy with the KŌZAHA, a rival group of Marxist theorists affiliated with the JCP. In contrast to the Kōzaha, which stressed the feudal character of Japanese capitalism and held that Japan's impending revolution would be a "bourgeois-democratic" one, the Rōnōha argued that feudalism had essentially disappeared from Japan, that the bourgeoisie had already come to power, and that the coming revolution would be a socialist upheaval aimed at overthrowing the bourgeoisie. Proponents of the Rōnōha viewpoint included YAMAKAWA HITOSHI, INOMATA TSUNAO, ARAHATA KANSON, KUSHIDA TAMIZŌ, TSUCHIYA TAKAO, and ŌUCHI HYŌE. Rōnōha activities effectively came to an end when many of its members were arrested in 1937. After World War II, the Rōnōha resumed its debate with the Kōzaha, publishing journals such as *Zenshin*. See also NIHON SHIHON SHUGI RONSŌ.

Rōnōtō → Rōdō Nōmintō; Rōdōsha Nōmintō

roof tiles   瓦

(*kawara*). Although used for such diverse purposes as floor surfacing (*kawara-jiki*), wall insulation (*kawara shitomi*), wall decoration (*namako-bei*), and daub wall strengthening (*kawara-bei*), tiles have been most frequently employed in Japan as roofing (*kawara yane*).

Romanization Systems

Kana (hiragana)	Phonetic transcription	Modified Hepburn/Hyōjun	Kunrei	Nippon
か	ka	ka	ka	ka; kwa
が	ga	ga	ga	ga; gwa
し	ʃi	shi	si	si
じ	dʒi	ji	zi	zi
ち	tʃi	chi	ti	ti
ぢ	dʒi	ji	zi	di
つ	tsu	tsu	tu	tu
づ	zu	zu	zu	du
ふ	Φu	fu	hu	hu
を	o	o	o	wo
しゃ	ʃa	sha	sya	sya
しゅ	ʃu	shu	syu	syu
しょ	ʃo	sho	syo	syo
じゃ	dʒa	ja	zya	zya
じゅ	dʒu	ju	zyu	zyu
じょ	dʒo	jo	zyo	zyo
ちゃ	tʃa	cha	tya	tya
ちゅ	tʃu	chu	tyu	tyu
ちょ	tʃo	cho	tyo	tyo
ぢゃ	dʒa	ja	zya	dya
ぢゅ	dʒu	ju	zyu	dyu
ぢょ	dʒo	jo	zyo	dyo

NOTE: This table includes only those syllables for which the romanization systems differ. For a complete table of the Japanese syllabary as romanized in the Hepburn system see KANA.

Both fireproof and water-resistant, they are also easy to position on the roof frame. The weight of roof-tiling in traditional buildings was considerable and necessitated a complex roof truss with cantilevers and eaves bracketing to carry it.

Along with other technical knowledge related to temple construction, tiles were introduced to Japan from the continent during the 6th century. The tiling system adopted as the standard was *hongawara-buki*, a term meaning "normal" or "orthodox" tiling. It consisted of pan-tiles (*hiragawara*) laid in parallel rows running from the roof ridge to the eaves and semicylindrical cover-tiles (*marugawara*) positioned over the interstices between the rows to make the roof waterproof. Eave-end tiles with lotus-flower motifs adorned the roof edges.

During the latter half of the 17th century an entirely new composite tiling was devised by combining the pan- and cover-tiles of *hongawara-buki*. The new form, known as *sangawara-buki*, was much lighter and simpler to manufacture and position on the roof. *Sangawara* could be placed directly on the roof by hooking lugs on the underside of the tile over purlins and tile battens, thereby eliminating the weighty clay bed into which tiles had been inserted in the *hongawara-buki* system.

During the Edo period (1600–1868) the shogunate enforced the conversion of straw-thatched (*warabuki*) and reed-thatched (*kayabuki*) roofs to tiled roofs as one of several major fire-prevention measures, and the use of the new tiling technique spread rapidly. In the 20th century the term *sangawara* became synonymous with the word *kawara* itself.

Various types of decorative tiles were placed at the ends of ridge courses: in the Asuka (593–710) and Nara (710–794) periods there were plumelike *shibi*, which curved back toward the center of the ridge; from around the 10th century, grotesque, often amusing *onigawara* or "devil's tiles"; and from the end of the Muromachi period (1333–1568), *shachihoko* ("dolphin tiles"), which were similar in form to *shibi*. *Karakusa-gawara*, eave pan-tiles decorated with foliage motifs, were used extensively

Roof Tiles in the Hongawara-buki Style

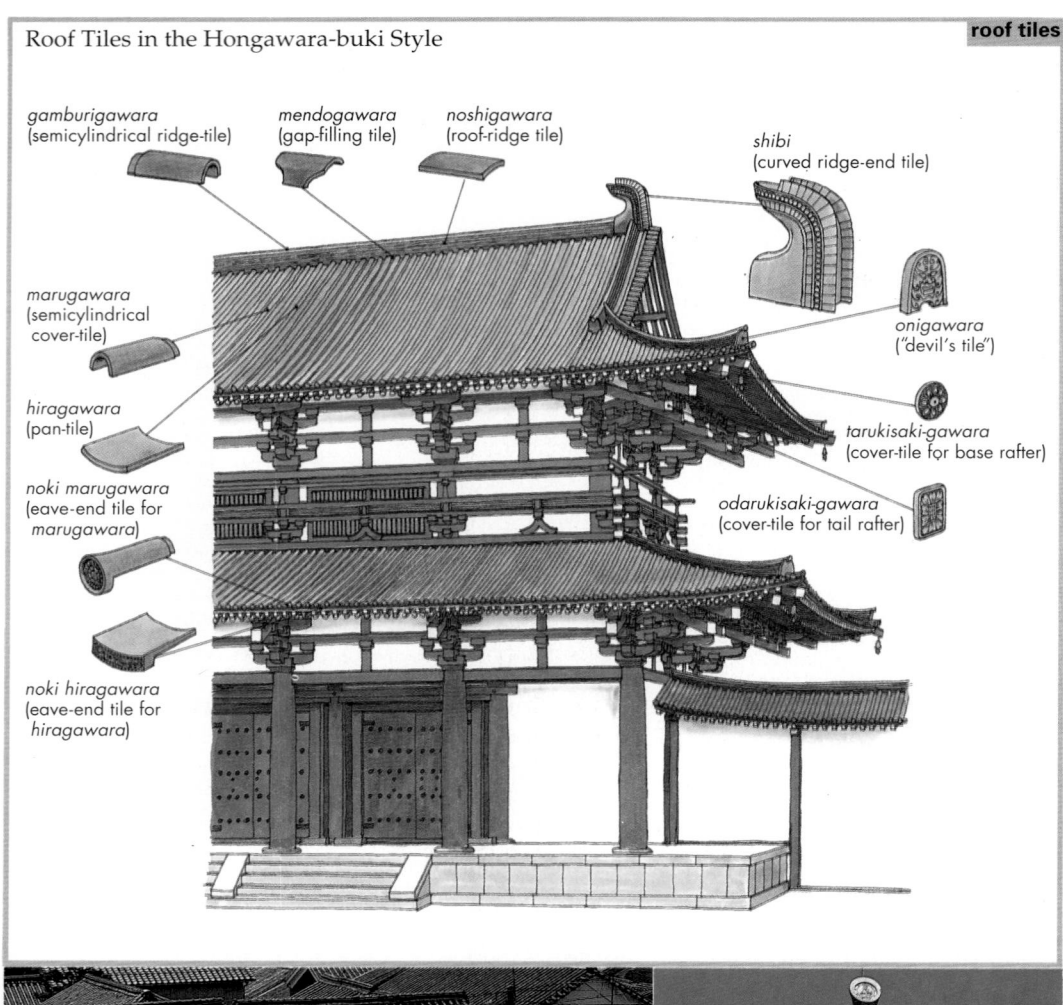

gamburigawara
(semicylindrical ridge-tile)

mendogawara
(gap-filling tile)

noshigawara
(roof-ridge tile)

shibi
(curved ridge-end tile)

marugawara
(semicylindrical
cover-tile)

hiragawara
(pan-tile)

noki marugawara
(eave-end tile for
marugawara)

noki hiragawara
(eave-end tile for
hiragawara)

onigawara
("devil's tile")

tarukisaki-gawara
(cover-tile for base rafter)

odarukisaki-gawara
(cover-tile for tail rafter)

roof tiles
1 These dwellings in Kurashiki, Okayama Prefecture, use the two principal tile-roofing styles: the flat tile roof in the foreground is an example of *sangawara-buki*; the others of *hongawara-buki*.
2 The use of *onigawara*, ridge-course end tiles cast in the shape of a devil, became widespread in Japan from the 10th century.

during the early stages of the tiled roof in Japan.

Until the Meiji period (1868–1912) the profession of tiler (*kawaraya*) had included the whole process from the making of tiles to their placement. Tile-making, however, became a separate enterprise at the end of the 19th century in response to the accelerating technical complexity of tile-making and increasing demand for tiled roofs. With the introduction of mechanization and technological improvements, tile-making today is a modern industry.

Roosevelt, Franklin Delano
ルーズベルト, F. D.
(1882–1945). US statesman and 32nd president of the United States. After holding the positions of assistant secretary of the navy and governor of New York, Roosevelt, a

Democrat, was elected president in 1932 and was reelected in 1936, 1940, and 1944. Despite the growing tension in Europe and Asia, Roosevelt generally maintained a neutral foreign policy. After the Japanese attack on Pearl Harbor on 7 December 1941 (see PEARL HARBOR, ATTACK ON), however, at his request, Congress declared war on Japan and, a few days later, on Germany and Italy. He guided the mobilization of the country's economy and deliberated wartime policies with other world leaders in a series of conferences. At one of these, the YALTA CONFERENCE in February 1945, he, Churchill, and Stalin discussed plans for the surrender and occupation of Germany and for Soviet participation in the war against Japan.

Roosevelt, Theodore
ルーズベルト, T.
(1858–1919). US politician and 26th president of the United States. Elected vice-president in 1900, Roosevelt became president

after the assassination of William McKinley in 1901. He was elected president in 1904. He supported Secretary of State John Hay's OPEN DOOR POLICY in regard to China. He was awarded the Nobel Peace Prize in 1906 for mediating the end of the RUSSO-JAPANESE WAR (1904–05). In 1908 he concluded the GENTLEMEN'S AGREEMENT with Japan, restricting immigration of Japanese laborers to the United States.

Roppongi
六本木
Amusement and residential district in the center of Minato Ward, Tōkyō. From the Meiji period (1868–1912) onward, it was home to high-level bureaucrats and wealthy entrepreneurs; two regiments of the Imperial Japanese Army were also stationed here. During the Allied Occupation of Japan, the old regimental headquarters became a US Army base, and a variety of entertainment establishments catering to American military personnel sprang up in the area—the predecessors of the restaurants, cafes, bars, and discos which today make Roppongi one of the liveliest nightspots in Tōkyō. Asahi National Broadcasting Co, Ltd (TV Asahi), and the Haiyūza Theater are located in Roppongi, as are the embassies of Spain and Sweden. In recent years it has once again become a fashionable and expensive residential area.

Rosanjin → Kitaōji Rosanjin

Rosetsu
蘆雪
(1754–99). Also known as Nagasawa Rosetsu; real name Nagasawa Masakatsu. Painter known for his original and eccentric style. Rosetsu's father was a *samurai* of low rank. He studied under MARUYAMA ŌKYO, founder of the Maruyama school of painting (see MARUYAMA-SHIJŌ SCHOOL). Rosetsu received much encouragement from his friend Minagawa Kien (1734–1807), a well-known painter and calligrapher. Kien organized Japan's first public art exhibitions, and Rosetsu often participated. His work is characterized by vital and expressive brushwork; insightful representations of people, animals, and birds; and good-natured humor. He did numerous screen and wall paintings for temples.

Rosny, Léon Louis Lucien Prunol de
ロニー, L. L. L. P.
(1837–1916). French scholar and author. A student at the École des Langues Orientales (School for Oriental Languages), Rosny wrote numerous books and articles on Japan, China, and Korea. He could read, write, and speak Japanese, and although he never set foot in Japan, he strove to live in Japanese fashion. He was even paid by the Tokugawa shogunate to send news reports on European affairs to Edo (now Tōkyō). In 1868 he became professor of Japanese at the École des Langues Orientales and founded a Japanese-language newspaper, *Yo no uwasa* (Talk of Society). Rosny also established the Society for American and Oriental Ethnography (1858) and the International Congress of Orientalists (1873).

Rotary Club
ロータリー・クラブ
(Rōtarī Kurabu). Rotary Club activities in Japan began in 1920 when the Tōkyō chapter was founded by Yoneyama Umekichi of the Mitsui Bank. In 1940, however, war forced the Japanese branch to withdraw from international membership; it was reinstated in

1949. The Rotary Club, whose membership includes businesspeople and professionals, promotes international fellowship and ethical conduct in business and community services. As of 1990, 1,921 chapters existed throughout Japan, with a membership totaling 115,942.

rotary engine　　　ロータリーエンジン
(*rōtarī enjin*). Also known as the Wankel engine. Internal combustion engine in which a rotary-piston device is used instead of conventional cylinders with reciprocating pistons. Rotary engines were put on the market in Japan by MAZDA MOTOR CORPORATION in 1967 and have since been mass-produced as automobile engines. The engines are also manufactured by several companies for outboard motorboats, chainsaws, and motorcycles in limited quantities.

Royal Co, Ltd　　　ロイヤル[株]
(Roiyaru). Suburban restaurant chain operator. Incorporated in 1956. It operates 304 "Royal Host" outlets nationwide and also manufactures and sells cold dessert items and operates an in-flight catering service. Royal launched overseas operations in 1986. Sales for the fiscal year ending December 1990 totaled ¥82.0 billion (US $614.0 million), and capitalization stood at ¥13.7 billion (US $102.6 million). Headquarters are in Fukuoka.

Royal Hotel, Ltd　　　[株]ロイヤルホテル
(Roiyaru Hoteru). Operator of hotels. Incorporated in 1932. Sales for the fiscal year ending March 1991 totaled ¥43.2 billion (US $314.9 million), of which banquets accounted for 36 percent; room charges, 17 percent; and restaurant and other revenues, 47 percent. Headquarters are in Ōsaka.

Ruijū kokushi　　　類聚国史
(Classified National History). Historical work completed in 892 by the court scholar SUGAWARA NO MICHIZANE. He took information from the Six National Histories (RIKKOKUSHI), divided it into categories, and arranged it in chronological order. Besides some 200 volumes of text, the work contained a two-volume index and a three-volume genealogy of the imperial house. Although only 61 volumes survive, it is useful for the study of ancient history because it complements, and facilitates use of, the Six National Histories.

Ruiju myōgi shō　　　類聚名義抄
A Chinese-Japanese character dictionary of unknown authorship compiled in the early 12th century; it is believed by some to be the work of one or more Buddhist monks. The contents are divided according to the conventional Buddhist classification of Buddha, dharma, and *saṃgha* (J: Buppōsō, from Butsu, *hō*, and *sōgya*; the Buddha, the doctrine, and the priesthood) into three broad groupings of Chinese characters (KANJI) and then further subdivided according to character radical, supplying the character form, Chinese pronunciation (see ON READINGS), and Japanese pronunciation (see KUN READINGS). The *Ruiju myōgi shō* is one of the oldest extant Chinese-Japanese dictionaries known to scholars and an important document for research into the ancient Japanese language. The Kanchiin and Zushoryō editions, in particular, have played an important role in determining the history of accent patterns in Japanese. See also ACCENT IN THE JAPANESE LANGUAGE.

rukei　　　流刑
(exile, banishment). Criminal penalty imposed from the 6th century until the late Meiji period (1868–1912). Of the "five punishments" prescribed in the penal code of the RITSURYŌ SYSTEM, enacted late in the 7th century, only death was considered more severe than *rukei*. There were three degrees of exile: *onru* (distant exile) to a distance of 1,500 *ri* (1 *ri* = 3.93 km); *chūru* (moderate exile) to a distance of 560 *ri*; and *konru* (nearby exile) to a distance of 300 *ri*. Exile as a penalty was retained, with variations, over the centuries, and disappeared only with the enactment of the current Penal Code in 1908.

rules of court　　　裁判所規則
(*saibansho kisoku*). Rules regulating certain procedural matters and activities of the courts, bar, procuracy, and other court officials as determined by the SUPREME COURT under the rule-making power granted it pursuant to article 77 of the CONSTITUTION OF JAPAN. One reason for granting the Supreme Court this power is to secure judicial independence from the other branches of government. Public prosecutors, practicing attorneys, and all other parties involved in litigation in a court of law are subject to these rules. It is, however, generally accepted that laws enacted by the Diet take priority over rules determined by the Supreme Court, although there exists no provision in the constitution to regulate the relationship between laws and rules.

In its exercise of this power, the Supreme Court acts upon the resolutions of the Judicial Conference, which is made up of all 15 justices. Since its establishment in 1947, the Supreme Court has adopted more than 100 rules, including the Rules of Civil Procedure (Minji Soshō Kisoku) and the Rules of Criminal Procedure (Keiji Soshō Kisoku).

Rumoi　　　留萌[市]
City in northwestern Hokkaidō, on the Sea of Japan. Its principal occupation is fishing. Seafood processing thrives as an industry. The port handles lumber and oil. Pop: 32,429.

Ruson Sukezaemon　　　呂宋助左衛門
Legendary overseas trader of the Azuchi-Momoyama period (1568–1600); also known as Naya Sukezaemon. Sukezaemon is said to have been a native of the merchant city of SAKAI who made his fortune from a voyage to Luzon in the Philippines, returning in 1594 with 50 ceramic jars (*matsubo* or Ruson *tsubo*) that were admired by TOYOTOMI HIDEYOSHI and sold at high prices in Ōsaka Castle. The story's source, the *Taikōki* (Life of Hideyoshi; preface dated 1617) by Oze Hoan (1564–1640), is generally unreliable and in this instance clearly mistaken, for the tea master SEN NO RIKYŪ, said to have appraised the pots in 1594, had died three years earlier. Hence Sukezaemon's historicity is doubtful; however, it is true that large jars of Luzon ware (actually Chinese ware of the Song [Sung; 960–1279] and Yuan [Yüan; 1279–1368] dynasties, used as burial items in the Philippines) were highly esteemed by Japanese votaries of the TEA CEREMONY.

Russia and Japan　　　ロシアと日本
(Roshia to Nihon). The first contacts between Russians and Japanese occurred in the late 17th century; in the mid-19th century, Russia, along with the United States,

Roppongi A view down Roppongi's Gaienhigashi-Dōri; Tōkyō Tower appears in the distance.

was one of the earliest Western nations to press Japan to open its ports to foreign trade. Following the Meiji Restoration of 1868, Russia and Japan competed—and occasionally cooperated—in their efforts to establish influence in northern Asia. Russia became a republic of the Soviet Union following the Bolshevik Revolution of 1917, but, with the demise of the Soviet Union in 1991 and the establishment of the Russian Federation, Russo-Japanese relations entered a new era.

Early Relations—Tradition holds that intercourse between Japan and Russia began in 1697, when the Russian explorer Vladimir Vasil'evich Atlasov (d 1711) met Dembei, a Japanese whose vessel had been cast ashore at Kamchatka. During the early 18th century Russian Cossacks, hunters, and government officials explored the northernmost islands of the Kuril Archipelago, attempting to reach Japan. Russian explorers and settlers penetrated to the island of Etorofu in the 1760s and to Hokkaidō in 1778 and asked for the establishment of commercial relations. Since Japan was still committed to its policy of NATIONAL SECLUSION, the *daimyō* of the Matsumae domain on Hokkaidō declared that the Russians must not come again to Hokkaidō, Kunashiri, or Etorofu. Rather, permission to trade could be sought at Nagasaki, the only port open to foreigners.

In 1792 an expedition sent by Catherine the Great and commanded by Adam Erikovich LAXMAN arrived in Nemuro Bay, Hokkaidō, under the pretext of returning DAIKOKUYA KŌDAYŪ and several other Japanese castaways. The underlying motive of the expedition was to establish commercial relations. The shogunate reaffirmed the seclusion policy and reiterated that the question of trade could be determined only at Nagasaki. It was not until October 1804, however, that another expedition reached Nagasaki. When the shogunate continued to resist the establishment of commercial relations, Nikolai Petrovich REZANOV, representing Alexander I as official envoy, decided to force the Japanese into commercial relations by military intimidation. At his instigation two young naval officers led an attack on Japanese settlements on Etorofu and SAKHALIN (Karafuto) and harassed Japanese shipping off Hokkaidō.

These raids led to the July 1811 capture of Lieutenant Commander Vasilii Mikhailovich GOLOVNIN and several subordinates on Kunashiri Island. In turn the Russian side seized a Japanese merchant, TAKATAYA KAHEI, took him to Russia, and with his help eventually arranged for an exchange of prisoners. Surprisingly, the capture of Golovnin and Takataya had a salutary effect on Russo-Japanese relations.

In 1843, as Great Britain encroached on the privileged position that Russia had enjoyed in China, Nicholas I decided to send Vice Admiral Evfimii Vasil'evich PUTIATIN to Japan in another attempt to open the country. Putiatin reached Nagasaki on 21 August 1853. His visit to Japan overlapped with that of Commodore Matthew Calbraith PERRY, who had arrived a month earlier. Although Perry rejected Putiatin's offer to join forces, the presence of the Russian squadron no doubt contributed to the decision of the shogunate to reopen the doors of Japan. On 7 February 1855 Putiatin succeeded in concluding the Russo-Japanese Treaty of Amity, which went beyond the KANAGAWA TREATY obtained by Perry in that it stipulated the opening of three ports (Shimoda, Hakodate, and Nagasaki) rather than just two, authorized the posting of consuls at Hakodate or Shimoda, provided for reciprocal extraterritoriality, and delineated the Russo-Japanese frontier. The Treaty of Friendship and Commerce, concluded three years later at Edo, provided for the exchange of ministers and for the establishment of trade. Russo-Japanese relations following the Meiji Restoration in 1868 were generally amicable. An exception was the ŌTSU INCIDENT OF 1891, in which the Russian crown prince was the target of an assassination attempt while visiting Japan.

The Korean Question——The relative harmony in Russo-Japanese relations was shattered as Russian and Japanese interests clashed on the Asian continent. In the 1880s the tsarist government resisted the temptation to become involved in the rivalry between China and Japan over control of the Korean peninsula. Desirable as the acquisition of an ice-free port in Korea might have been, Russia was unwilling to alienate either China or Japan until its own position in East Asia had been strengthened by the construction of the Trans-Siberian Railway. It was only after the dramatic victory of Japan over China in the SINO-JAPANESE WAR OF 1894-1895 that Russia finally realized that Japan had suddenly emerged as a modern military power on the threshold of Russia's weakly defended possessions.

The Tripartite Intervention——A treaty concluded between ITŌ HIROBUMI and the Chinese plenipotentiary LI HONGZHANG (Li Hung-chang) in 1895 (see SHIMONOSEKI, TREATY OF) provided for the cession of the Liaodong (Liaotung) Peninsula in southern Manchuria, including PORT ARTHUR and Dalian (Ta-lien; J: Dairen) to Japan. This would have given Japan a foothold on the continent and, in the eyes of the tsarist government, a base of operations against China, Korea, and Russian territory. When Ger-

many and France agreed to join in blocking Japanese entrenchment on the mainland, Russia joined them in the TRIPARTITE INTERVENTION, "advising" Japan to restore the Liaodong Peninsula to China in return for an increased war indemnity. Exhausted by the war, Japan gave in.

The Russo-Japanese Entente——Having intervened on behalf of China, Russia obtained a shortcut for its trans-Siberian line through Manchuria, the so-called CHINESE EASTERN RAILWAY. In exchange, Russia agreed in a secret alliance made on 3 June 1896 to defend China in case of renewed attack by Japan. The possibility of a collision between Russia and Japan arose when the Korean king KOJONG took refuge in the tsarist legation in Seoul and ruled from there. The St. Petersburg Protocol (known also as the YAMAGATA-LOBANOV AGREEMENT), concluded on 9 June 1896, ensured the Korean government's freedom to create and maintain its own army and police force. Neither Japan nor Russia was to send troops to the peninsula without prior consultation with the other.

Russo-Japanese relations worsened again in 1898, when Germany occupied Jiaozhou (Kiaochow) in retaliation for the murder of German nationals, and Russia then obtained from China a lease of the Liaodong Peninsula, the very territory that had been denied Japan three years earlier. Nevertheless, a détente of sorts was achieved by a convention signed on 25 April 1898. See NISHI-ROSEN AGREEMENT.

The Russo-Japanese War——It was the BOXER REBELLION (1900) in China that propelled Russia deeper into Manchuria and ultimately precipitated the RUSSO-JAPANESE WAR of 1904-05. As the insurgents ripped up the track of the Chinese Eastern Railway and killed Russian construction personnel and their families, the tsarist government sent troops into Manchuria. Once in Manchuria, however, the Russians demanded exclusive political and economic privileges as a condition for withdrawal. Negotiations between Premier Itō Hirobumi and Foreign Minister Vladimir Nikolaevich Lamsdorf in November and December 1901 failed to achieve an equitable division of Russian and Japanese interests. Unable to come to an agreement with Russia, Japan in January 1902 concluded the ANGLO-JAPANESE ALLIANCE with Russia's major rival, Great Britain.

Alarmed by what it saw as growing Russian power in East Asia, Japan began to believe that war between the two powers was inevitable. On 8 February 1904 the Japanese launched a surprise attack on the Russian fleet at Port Arthur. The war was fought primarily in Korea and Manchuria. Although the Japanese outfought the Russians, the Russians played a waiting game, trading space for time. The sinking of the Russian Baltic fleet, which had sailed around Africa, by Admiral TŌGŌ HEIHACHIRŌ in the Tsushima Strait in May 1905 spelled the end of the war. By the Treaty of PORTSMOUTH, concluded on 5 September 1905 through the mediation of US president Theodore ROOSEVELT, Russia ceded to Japan its Liaodong leasehold, the SOUTH MANCHURIA RAILWAY (the branch line of the Chinese Eastern Railway running from Changchun to Port Arthur), and the southern half of Sakhalin Island. It also recognized the independence of Korea and Japan's paramount political, military, and economic interests in that country.

The Russo-Japanese Alliance——By conventions concluded in 1907 and 1910, Russia and Japan agreed to respect the integrity of

each other's territory and to defend the maintenance of the status quo by peaceful means. Following the Chinese Revolution of 1911, Russia and Japan delineated their spheres of influence in Mongolia by a secret convention in July 1912. World War I led to the transformation of the Russo-Japanese entente into a full-fledged alliance, since the tsarist government desperately required Japanese ammunition and supplies. (See RUSSO-JAPANESE AGREEMENTS OF 1907-1916.) After the Bolshevik Revolution of 1917, however, the new Soviet government declared these secret agreements void. For a discussion of Soviet-Japanese relations, see SOVIET UNION AND JAPAN.

In 1991 the dissolution of the Soviet Union was followed by the establishment of the Russian Federation, which Japan recognized. The first issue addressed by Japan upon the establishment of diplomatic relations was that of aid to the Russian Federation, which faced a grave economic crisis. It remained for Japan and Russia to work out a peace treaty formally terminating the hostilities of World War II and to resolve the issue of the Northern Territories, former Japanese possessions occupied by the Soviet Union at the close of the war, the return of which continued to be demanded by Japan. See also NORTHERN TERRITORIES ISSUE.

Russo-Japanese agreements of 1907–1916　　　　日露協約

(Nichiro *kyōyaku*). Agreements between Japan and Russia following the RUSSO-JAPANESE WAR (1904–05) concerning spheres of economic and military influence in East Asia. With the ANGLO-JAPANESE ALLIANCE of 1902, these agreements became a pivot of Japanese diplomacy before and during World War I. The 1907 agreement called for maintenance of the status quo in East Asia and included OPEN DOOR POLICY pledges to respect the independence and territorial integrity of China. In a secret convention Russia and Japan recognized each other's special interests in East Asia and agreed to partition Manchuria into spheres of interest. The 1910 agreement provided for cooperation in securing railway concessions from China, and a 1912 pact stipulated the division of Inner Mongolia into Russian and Japanese spheres of influence. In 1916 Japan and Russia agreed to prevent the encroachment upon Chinese territory of any nation hostile to either of them, to offer assistance to one another toward that end, and, further, not to treat for peace independently with such a nation. After the 1917 Bolshevik Revolution, the Soviet government declared the secret agreements null and void. See also RUSSIA AND JAPAN.

Russo-Japanese fisheries
　　　　　　　　日ソ・日露漁業問題

(Nisso, Nichiro *gyogyō mondai*). The fisheries of the Kuril (Chishima) Islands, Sakhalin (Karafuto), and the coasts of Kamchatka are vital to both Japan and Russia. Utilization and development of these fishing grounds have been subject to negotiation between the two nations since 1875, when Japan exchanged its territorial rights to southern Sakhalin for title to the northern Kuril Islands. Japanese worked Sakhalin fishing grounds under leases until obtaining southern Sakhalin and all of its fisheries as a result of victory in the RUSSO-JAPANESE WAR of 1904–05. The Fishery Convention of 1907 gave Japanese subjects equal rights with Russians in bidding for fishing lots along the coasts of the Russian possessions in the Japan, Okhotsk, and Bering seas. With the necessary capital, experienced fishermen, and cheaper equipment, the Japanese soon gained a dominant position.

When the Bolsheviks seized power in November 1917, they refused to honor commitments made by the tsarist government. The Japanese continued to fish without any firm agreement until the 1928 fishery convention gave Japan fishing rights in Russian waters and the lease of lots by public auction. This agreement also authorized the establishment and operation of canning factories, although corporate fishing giants later circumvented Soviet restrictions by utilizing floating canneries. The convention was periodically renewed, but Japanese operations were drastically reduced and restricted for the duration of World War II.

With the return of southern Sakhalin and the loss of the entire Kuril Archipelago and the HABOMAI ISLANDS to the USSR following the war, Japan became more dependent than ever on Russian fishing grounds. Yet once again the break in diplomatic relations had left the country without a fishery convention. Japanese fishermen braved capture as they ventured into Russian waters in the absence of an agreement.

With normalization of relations, the Fishery Convention of 1956, concluded for a period of 10 years, regulated the catch of salmon, herring, flatfish, and crab on the open seas in the northwestern part of the Pacific Ocean between Japan and the USSR. It set up a Northwest Pacific Fisheries Commission, which was to meet every year alternately in Tōkyō and in Moscow to limit the annual catch of the types of fish listed above and recommend measures for the conservation and growth of fishery resources. Subsequent agreements sought to alleviate disputes arising from the operation of Russian and Japanese fishermen in each other's open waters and to foster collaboration in the breeding of salmon at Sakhalin.

The 200-mile exclusive fishery zones established by Russia and Japan nullified previous agreements in 1977. They were replaced by interim agreements for rights to operate within each other's zones, concluded twice each year. In 1984 the Japan-USSR Agreement on Offshore Fisheries recognized the right of each country's vessels to enter the other country's economic zone and to oversee the operation of fisheries in the area. Negotiations widened in 1987 to cover new systems of licensed fisheries and fish deliveries at sea in place of fixed-quota hauls. Salmon fishing in the open sea was regulated by the 1978 Cooperative Fishery Agreement. Another agreement covering fishing outside the 200-mile zones, signed in 1985, resulted in recognizing Soviet control over trout and salmon caught by Japanese vessels outside the Russian 200-mile zone because those fish were dependent on the rivers of the USSR for spawning. Total hauls were subject to agreement between the two nations, and Japan agreed to bear part of the financial burden of protecting stocks of these fish. After the dissolution of the USSR in 1991, negotiations continued between the Japanese and Russian governments.

Russo-Japanese War 日露戦争

(Nichiro Sensō). War between Japan and Russia from 8 February 1904 to 5 September 1905 for control over Korea and Manchuria. Japan had earlier fought the SINO-JAPANESE WAR OF 1894–1895 and had succeeded in ending Chinese suzerainty over Korea, but was prevented from establishing its own control over the Korean peninsula when the TRIPARTITE INTERVENTION by Russia, Germany, and France forced it to return the Liaodong (Liaotung) Peninsula to China. Japan's ambitions in the peninsula were further blocked by growing Russian influence.

Russia concluded an anti-Japanese military alliance with LI HONGZHANG (Li Hungchang) and gained the right to build the CHINESE EASTERN RAILWAY in Manchuria. In 1898 Russia obtained leases in PORT ARTHUR and Dalian (Talien; J: Dairen); Germany in Jiaozhou (Kiaochow) Bay; France in Guangzhou (Kwangchow) Harbor; and England in Weihaiwei and the Jiulong (Kowloon) Peninsula. The United States enunciated the OPEN DOOR POLICY to guarantee its interests in China. The Russian move into the Liaodong Peninsula, taking place barely three years after the Tripartite Intervention, stimulated strong nationalist feeling in Japan. Japan signed a treaty with China that recognized only Japan's special interests in Fujian (Fukien) Province and, at the same time, concluded the NISHI-ROSEN AGREEMENT of 1898 in which Russia promised not to obstruct the development of Japanese commerce and industry in Korea.

In 1900 Russia took advantage of the BOXER REBELLION in northern China to send a large army into Manchuria and then secured Chinese permission to maintain its troops in the area. In response Britain and Germany concluded the so-called Yangzi (Yangtze) River Agreement asserting the inviolability of Chinese territory; Japan also signed this agreement.

Within the Japanese government ITŌ HIROBUMI, INOUE KAORU, and others advocated exchanging Japanese interests in Manchuria for Russian recognition of Japan's special position in Korea, but Prime Minister KATSURA TARŌ and others insisted on an alliance with Britain. When Russia rejected a "Manchuria-Korea exchange" (Mankan kōkan), the ANGLO-JAPANESE ALLIANCE of 1902 was concluded, enabling Japan to oppose Russia without fear of intervention by European powers. Two months later Russia promised to withdraw all troops from Manchuria but did not comply. Moreover, Russia pressed China for a monopoly of rights in Manchuria. The Russians were rebuffed by China, which was joined by Japan, the United States, and other powers, but Russian troops remained in Manchuria.

Public opinion in Japan overwhelmingly supported taking a hard line toward Russia. KONOE ATSUMARO, president of the House of Peers, formed the TAIRO DŌSHIKAI (Anti-Russia League) in August 1903, and seven university professors made known their anti-Russian views and criticized the government for its vacillation (see SHICHIHAKASE JIKEN). Japan continued to negotiate while preparing for war. In October Russia refused Japan's request for recognition of its exclusive rights in Korean military affairs, and in January 1904 Japan resolved to go to war. On 6 February Japan broke off diplomatic relations with Russia; on the 8th the navy attacked and trapped the Russian fleet at Port Arthur; war was declared on the 10th.

The first Japanese troops landed on the Korean peninsula in February and March, reached Manchuria in May, and moved to attack Liaoyang. At about the same time the second army landed on the Liaodong Peninsula and occupied Nanshan and Dalian. In August the third army, under General NOGI

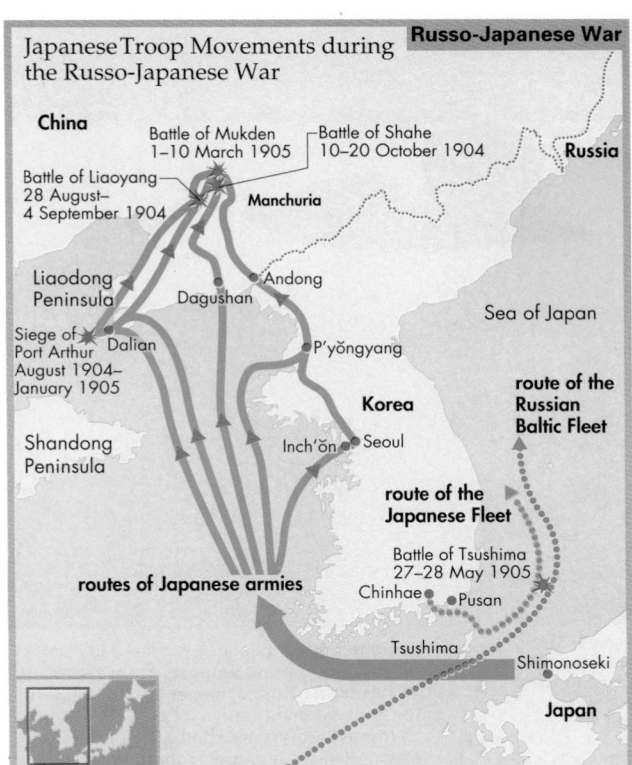

Japanese Troop Movements during the Russo-Japanese War

China
Battle of Mukden 1–10 March 1905
Battle of Shahe 10–20 October 1904
Russia
Battle of Liaoyang 28 August–4 September 1904
Manchuria
Liaodong Peninsula
Andong
Dagushan
Sea of Japan
Siege of Port Arthur August 1904–January 1905
Dalian
P'yŏngyang
route of the Russian Baltic Fleet
Korea
Shandong Peninsula
Inch'ŏn
Seoul
route of the Japanese Fleet
routes of Japanese armies
Battle of Tsushima 27–28 May 1905
Chinhae
Pusan
Tsushima
Shimonoseki
Japan

Russo-Japanese War
1 A view from the deck of an Imperial Japanese Navy vessel, photographed just before the Battle of Tsushima, during which the Japanese Combined Fleet destroyed Russia's Baltic Fleet.
2 Imperial Army forces fire on Port Arthur. This strategic stronghold fell to the Japanese Third Army on 2 January 1905 after a six-month siege and 60,000 Japanese casualties.

MARESUKE, launched an attack on Port Arthur, which finally fell in January 1905. The Japanese army also won the battles of Liaoyang and Shahe (Shaho). In March the Japanese tried unsuccessfully to crush the principal Russian force in the Battle of MUKDEN, although they captured the city itself after 10 days of fighting. Despite these victories the Japanese were unable to rout the Russian forces completely. Japan's ability to wage war had reached its limit; it had lost a large number of officers, and the need for arms

Ryōanji The temple's celebrated Zen-style dry landscape garden. Surrounded by a low wall on three sides, it consists of only 15 oddly shaped rocks of varying sizes placed on a bed of white sand.

could no longer be met by increased domestic production and imports from Germany and Britain. Russia began to revitalize its forces in Manchuria.

Immediately after the Battle of Mukden, ŌYAMA IWAO, supreme commander of the Manchurian army, urged the government to open peace negotiations. In April 1905 the Katsura cabinet decided to negotiate. Taking advantage of its destruction of the Russian Baltic Fleet in the Battle of TSUSHIMA in late May, Japan secretly asked US President Theodore Roosevelt to mediate. Roosevelt, seeking a settlement that would give neither side a decisive victory, began his mediation in June. Although Russia still had considerable military power, it feared that the war might aggravate the revolutionary movement within the country and so responded positively to Roosevelt's overtures.

Negotiations were held in August at Portsmouth, New Hampshire, and the Treaty of PORTSMOUTH was signed on 5 September. Japan won Russian acceptance of its exclusive rights in Korea and territorial rights to Sakhalin south of the 50th parallel. It also gained, subject to Chinese approval, Russia's leases in Port Arthur and Dalian, and control of the SOUTH MANCHURIA RAILWAY. However, it received no indemnity. At the Beijing (Peking) Conference held at the end of 1905, Japan secured even greater rights in Manchuria than those designated in the treaty. Japan had mobilized a force of over 1 million, and lost nearly 90,000. Military expenses had amounted to over ¥1.5 billion, and more than half of it had been raised through foreign loans from England and the United States. Throughout the war only a tiny minority (notably the members of the socialist HEIMINSHA) opposed it. Most Japanese wholeheartedly supported the war effort and reacted to the peace terms with outrage (see HIBIYA INCENDIARY INCIDENT), believing that the terms did not reflect the completeness of Japan's victory. However, Japan had established itself as an imperialist state in East Asia and entered into competition with the European imperialist powers in the region. Japan suppressed the emerging Chinese and Korean nationalist movements, but its relationship with the United States became strained.

To the Japanese the Russo-Japanese War embodied the achievement of national independence that had been the nation's goal since the MEIJI RESTORATION. Until the end of World War II, Japan celebrated the anniversary of the Battle of Mukden as Army Day and that of the Battle of Tsushima as Navy Day; even today the war stands for some as the symbol of "the glory of Meiji Japan."

rusui 留守居

(caretaker or keeper). An official post of the Edo period (1600–1868). In *daimyō* domains the *rusui* was a vassal of a daimyō who officially represented the lord in his domain or in Edo whenever he was away from either on alternate attendance service (SANKIN KŌTAI). In the Tokugawa shogunal government *rusui* were a group of four to six officials of HATAMOTO (bannerman) rank responsible for supervising EDO CASTLE. The post was analogous to that of JŌDAI (castellan).

ryō 両

1. A unit of weight established under the RITSURYŌ SYSTEM. Standards were modeled after those of the Chinese Tang (T'ang; 618–907) dynasty; units were *shu*, *ryō*, and *kin*. One *shu* was the weight of 100 grains of millet (*kibi*), or approximately 0.52 gram (0.018 oz); 24 *shu* constituted 1 *ryō*; 16 *ryō* equaled 1 *kin*.

2. A unit of weight employed during the medieval period (mid-12th–16th centuries) to weigh gold, silver, medicine, and incense. In Kyōto 1 *ryō* of gold usually equaled 4.5 *momme* (1 *momme* = 3.75 g or 0.132 oz) and in the provinces between 4 and 5 *momme*.

3. A unit of currency adopted in the late 16th century. The standard gold coin of the TOKUGAWA SHOGUNATE (1603–1867), the KOBAN, was equivalent to 1 *ryō*. The ŌBAN was originally 10 *ryō* but later declined in value. The standard weight of a 1-*ryō koban* was 4.76 *momme*. In 1871, under the Meiji government's New Currency Regulation, 1 *ryō* became 1 yen. See also MONEY, PREMODERN.

Ryōanji 竜安寺

Temple in Ukyō Ward, Kyōto, belonging to the Myōshinji branch of the RINZAI SECT of ZEN Buddhism. Ryōanji was built in 1450 by the general HOSOKAWA KATSUMOTO, who, hoping to revive the declining fortunes of the temple Myōshinji, invited its fifth abbot, Giten Genshō (1393–1462), to take up residence there. During the following century many well-known Zen monks stayed at Ryōanji. Among its patrons were the HOSOKAWA FAMILY; TOYOTOMI HIDEYOSHI, who frequently visited and endowed it with land; and TOKUGAWA IEYASU. Ryōanji entered a period of decline after 1797, when a disastrous fire claimed many of its subtemples, halls, and chapels. The temple, which is now much reduced in size, is particularly noted for its Zen-style rock garden executed in the *karesansui* ("dry landscape") mode, reportedly the work of the artist Sōami (ca 1455–1525).

Ryōben → Rōben

Ryōbu Mandara 両部曼荼羅

(Paired Mandalas). Also known as the Ryōkai Mandara (Mandalas of the Two Realms). Collective name for two mandalas that are the most fundamental of those used by the SHINGON SECT of ESOTERIC BUDDHISM (see MANDALA). They are the *Taizō mandara* (Womb or Matrix Mandala; Skt: *Garbha-maṇḍala*) and the *Kongōkai mandara* (Diamond or Thunderbolt Realm Mandala; Skt: *Vajradhātu-maṇḍala*). The *Taizō mandara*, also known as the *Taizōkai mandara*, is based on a sutra called the *Dainichikyō* (Skt: *Mahāvairocana-sūtra*); the first part of another sutra, the *Kongōchō-gyō* (Skt: *Vajraśekhara-sūtra*), is the source for the *Kongōkai mandara*. See TAIZŌKAI; KONGŌKAI.

The two mandalas, along with the two lines of esoteric Buddhism that they represent, were introduced to Japan from China by the priest KŪKAI early in the 9th century and were preserved and transmitted in their original form. The best-known examples are those in the temple TŌJI in Kyōto.

The *Taizō mandara* has 12 sections or "halls" (*jūnidaiin*). (1) In the center of the *Chūdai hachiyō in* (hall of the central eight petals) sits the Buddha DAINICHI, the chief deity of the Shingon sect, who symbolizes the DHARMA realm itself. Surrounding Dainichi are four Buddhas and four bodhisattvas, the former symbolizing aspects of attained wisdom and the latter the means to attainment. (2) In *Jimyō in* (hall of the *vidyādhara*) are represented deities who realize universal knowledge. (3) In the center of *Henchi in* (hall of universal knowledge) is a triangle that symbolizes the three aspects of the wisdom of emancipation. The above three halls, joined by (4) *Kongōshu in* (hall of Vajrapāṇi) and (5) *Kannon in* (hall of Avalokiteśvara), describe the basic tranquillity of enlightenment. Halls 6 through 8 describe the process toward enlightenment (the center hall) and halls 9 through 11 the compassion toward beings that arises from enlightenment. (12) In *Saige in* (the exterior hall) are depicted guardian deities of esoteric Buddhist teachings and the mandala.

The *Kongōkai mandara* consists of nine assemblies (J: *kue*) or mandalas forming equal rectangles. (1) In *Kompon jōshin e* (assembly of Buddhahood) are five lunar disks, each with a figure of Buddha. The five Buddhas represent the five dimensions of wisdom of the Ultimate Reality. (2) *Sammaya e* (assembly of coming together; from Skt: *samaya*) represents the joining of the Buddha's enlightenment with the vow to save all beings. (3) *Misai e* (assembly of subtlety) is a mandala that symbolizes the Buddha's wisdom as indivisible, subtle, and, like the *vajra* (see BUDDHIST RITUAL IMPLEMENTS), indestructible. (4) The mandala *Kuyō e* (assembly of veneration) describes the working of mutual veneration; all divinities except the five Buddhas are drawn as female figures. Mandalas 5 through 7 represent simple summaries of the first four mandalas. Mandalas 8 and 9 represent the fierce deities who conquer evil.

Although the *Taizō mandara* and the *Kongōkai mandara* are sometimes viewed as a dichotomy, they do not exist only in relation to one another or present contrasting or opposing doctrines. Each of the mandalas is independent and complete in itself, and they are both insights into a single all-embracing truth. — *See photos and illustrations, next two pages.*

Ryōbu Shintō   両部神道

("Dual Shintō"). A syncretic Buddhist-Shintō school that sought to harmonize the teachings of the Buddhist SHINGON SECT with worship at the Ise shrine.

The beginnings of an Ise-centered syncretism go back at least to the 11th century, when it was first claimed that AMATERASU ŌMIKAMI (the sun goddess) was a Japanese manifestation of Dainichi Nyorai (Mahāvairocana), the "Great Sun Buddha." Despite opposition by shrine authorities, the next three centuries saw the appearance of a score of works by Buddhist monks that identified the Inner and Outer Shrines of Ise and their respective deities (Amaterasu Ōmikami and Toyouke no Ōkami) with two aspects of Dainichi that are depicted iconographically in a pair of Shingon mandalas known as the RYŌBU MANDARA.

Ryōbu Shintō eventually split into four or five subschools, each centering around an esoteric tradition transmitted within a particular Shingon temple. It developed its own secret consecration rituals. Ryōbu Shintō greatly influenced the Shintō schools of the 13th to the 16th centuries, particularly YOSHIDA SHINTŌ, but came under attack by proponents of RESTORATION SHINTŌ in the 18th and 19th centuries, after which time it virtually disappeared as a religious movement.

Ryōgae nendaiki   両替年代記

(Chronological Records of the Money-Changing Houses). A two-volume collection of important records kept by the major money-changing houses (*honryōgae;* see RYŌGAESHŌ) of Edo (now Tōkyō) between 1657 and 1845. Compilation of the work was begun in 1832 and completed in 1845. The work is an invaluable record of money-changing practices after the great MEIREKI FIRE of 1657.

ryōgaeshō   両替商

(money changers). Merchants of the Edo period (1600–1868) who engaged in money changing and financial transactions. Originating in the 13th century money changers called *ryōgae*, they prospered in urban cen-

ters from the 17th century. Since there were three different kinds of currency (gold, silver, and copper), with daily value fluctuations and different circulation systems, the services of *ryōgaeshō* were indispensable. With the development of a commercial economy these merchants branched out, establishing credit markets and drawing drafts. *Honryōgae,* who dealt mainly in gold and silver coins, and the more numerous *wakiryōgae,* who handled copper coins, organized guilds. After the Meiji Restoration (1868) most *ryōgaeshō* went out of business, but some wealthier ones, such as the MITSUI, Kōnoike, and SUMITOMO, established modern banks. See also DAIMYŌ LOANS.

Ryōgen   良源

(912–985). Monk of the TENDAI SECT of Buddhism who, as chief abbot (966–985), brought the sect to the height of its prosperity. Born in Ōmi Province (now Shiga Prefecture). He sought to restore the moral standards of the monks of Mt. Hiei (Hieizan) by reviving academic studies of Buddhist doctrines, and in 970 he issued a set of regulations in an attempt to control the violent *sōhei* (WARRIOR-MONKS). He also wrote the *Gokuraku Jōdo kubon ōjō gi* (On the Nine Grades of People Attaining Rebirth in the Pure Land of Bliss), the first Pure Land treatise written by a Japanese Tendai monk. Ryōgen is also noted as the teacher of GENSHIN.

ryōge no kan   令外官

(extrastatutory or auxiliary posts). Offices, bureaus, or departments created in addition to those stipulated under the RITSURYŌ SYSTEM of government (late 7th–10th century). Extrastatutory positions included inner minister (NAIDAIJIN), middle counselor (*chūnagon*), councillor (SANGI), and the powerful post of regent (SESSHŌ or KAMPAKU). During the Heian period (794–1185) several extrastatutory offices such as the Bureau of Archivists (KURŌDO-DOKORO) and the imperial police (KEBIISHI) began to take over most of the duties of the offices established under the *ritsuryō* codes.

Ryōjin hishō   梁塵秘抄

(Secret Selection of Rafter Dust). Collection of popular *imayō* songs of the late Heian period (794–1185). Compiled with an introduction by the retired emperor GO-SHIRAKAWA around 1169. *Imayō* consist of folk songs and religious hymns recast in a contemporary style and a flexible verse form, usually four lines, each containing a 7-5 syllable pattern. Popularized by prostitutes, puppeteers, and dancing girls, *imayō* achieved greatest favor with the court nobles during the early 12th century. By the time of *Ryōjin hishō,* however, the *imayō* had lost so much of their popularity that Go-Shirakawa felt compelled to revitalize the tradition by collecting the songs in one work. Although the collection originally consisted of 20 volumes, only 2 of these are extant. More than 500 songs survive. Marked by a freshness of imagery and a simplicity of rhythm, they have inspired modern poets such as SAITŌ MOKICHI and KITAHARA HAKUSHŪ.

ryokan →inns

Ryōkan   良寛

(1758–1831). Zen monk of the Sōtō sect; poet and calligrapher. Ryōkan was the eldest son of Yamamoto Yasuo, a village headman and Shintō priest of Echigo Province (now

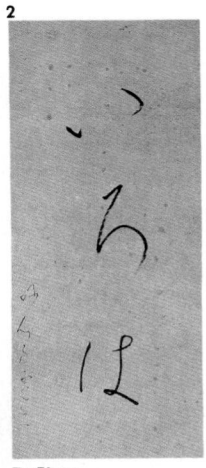

Niigata Prefecture). At 17 he became a novice at Kōshōji, a nearby temple of the Sōtō branch of Zen. At 21 he took his vows under a Zen priest named Kokusen (d 1791) and returned with him to Kokusen's temple, Entsūji, in Bitchū Province (now part of Okayama Prefecture). After Kokusen's death he began a long series of wanderings about western Japan. In 1826 Ryōkan met the nun Teishin, a young widow of 29. A record of their companionship and affection was preserved by Teishin (who lived until 1872) in a work entitled *Hachisu no tsuyu* (1835, Dew on the Lotus).

Ryōkan composed poetry in both Chinese and Japanese and is celebrated in Japan for his calligraphy. His poems in Chinese number about 450. Some 1,400 of his Japanese poems are preserved in several different versions of his personal collection. Of these, most are in the standard 31-syllable *tanka* (short poem) form, but there are also 90 CHŌKA (long poems) and 20 others in various nonstandard, shorter forms. His poetry grows from the largely unremarkable incidents of his daily life, and his plain, direct style has an effect of immediacy and true-to-life realism for which he has been extolled in modern times.

Ryokufūkai   緑風会

(Green Breeze Society). Group of independent members of the House of Councillors organized in May 1947 by YAMAMOTO YŪZŌ and others to reaffirm the House of Councillors' nonpartisan role. At the time of its inception, the Ryokufūkai constituted the largest group in the house. Contrary to its original goal, however, the Ryokufūkai lost its claimed neutrality and became more like an ordinary party with a political agenda. It lost influence as members left its ranks to join the LIBERAL DEMOCRATIC PARTY. After several name changes it was dissolved in 1965. See also DIET.

ryōmin   良民

(literally, "good people"; also known as *kōmin*). The free people of ancient Japan. Under the Chinese-inspired RITSURYŌ SYSTEM adopted in the late 7th century, people were designated either *semmin* ("lowborn") or *ryōmin,* the latter including the aristocracy (other than the imperial house) as well as farmers and other free commoners. *Ryōmin* formed independent households, were duly entered in HOUSEHOLD REGISTERS, received field allotments, and were responsible for taxes (SO, YŌ, AND CHŌ). Intermarriage be-

Ryōkan
1 Portrait scroll of the Zen monk, poet, and calligrapher Ryōkan.
2 Ryōkan's rendering of the *kana* syllables *i ro ha* is regarded as a masterpiece of Japanese calligraphy.

Taizō Mandara

The *Taizō mandara* and *Kongōkai mandara*, known together as the Ryōbu Mandara (The Paired Mandalas), are considered essential tools in the transmission of esoteric Buddhism as it is practiced in the Shingon sect, and together they represent the entire Buddhist cosmos. Both mandalas are divided into ordered units, as seen in the two diagrams below, each representing different aspects of esoteric Buddhist doctrine. (Late 9th century. Colors on silk. Each 183 × 154 cm. Tōji, Kyōto. National Treasures.)

The *Taizō mandara* (left) represents the Taizōkai (Matrix or Womb Realm), a manifestation of the ever-present, dynamic enlightenment of the Buddha Dainichi. It is divided into 12 sections or "halls." In the central hall (the *Chūdai hachiyō in*) four Buddhas and four bodhisattvas form a circle around Dainichi, who sits at the center of an eight-petaled lotus. The four Buddhas symbolize aspects of attained wisdom, the four bodhisattvas the means to attainment.

The first 5 halls of the *Taizō mandara* form the first major division of the mandala, and as a whole describe the fundamental tranquillity of enlightenment. The second and third divisions, consisting of halls 6 through 8 and 9 through 11, respectively, describe the progress toward enlightenment and the compassion extended to other beings from the enlightened state. The 12th hall consists of the outer margins of the mandala, in which are depicted guardian deities protecting esoteric Buddhist teachings and the mandala itself.

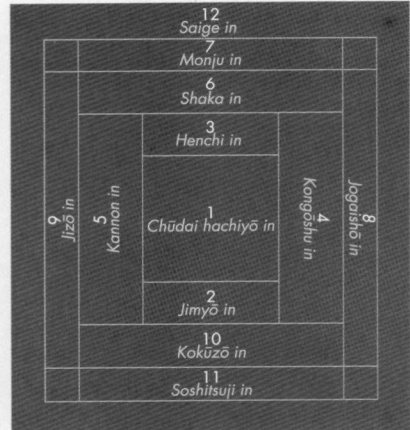

The Twelve Halls of the Taizō Mandara

tween *ryōmin* and *semmin* was forbidden by law, but it did occur. The distinction gradually lost its meaning and about 900 was abolished.

Ryōnin 良忍

(1073–1132). Founder of the YŪZŪ NEMBUTSU SECT. Born in Owari Province (now part of Aichi Prefecture), he studied at Mt. Hiei (Hieizan) and later moved to Ōhara in Kyōto. According to legend, in 1117 Ryōnin learned from the Buddha AMIDA the significance of *yūzū nembutsu*, a form of NEMBUTSU (chanting of the name Amida) in which one "interfuses" (*yūzū*) with other practitioners, enabling the salvation of all mankind. Ryōnin propagated this knowledge throughout the area surrounding Kyōto. At the former emperor TOBA's behest, he built the temple Dainembutsuji in 1127. Ryōnin is also known as the reviver and systematizer of the Tendai SHŌMYŌ (Tendai sect tradition of musical recitation of sutras). See also PURE LAND BUDDHISM.

Ryō no gige 令義解

(Exposition of the Administrative Laws). Compiled by a committee of 12 headed by the courtier-official Kiyohara no Natsuno

(782–837), these 10 volumes of commentary on the administrative section (*ryō*) of the YŌRŌ CODE (drafted in 718 and applied from 757) were completed in 833 and themselves enacted into law in 834. The work consists of a brief preface and 30 chapters, corresponding to the 30 chapters of the Yōrō Code. The text of the code is reiterated, with interpretative comments included for particular terms or phrases. The work has survived almost complete and is the principal source of information on the original code, which is lost. See also RITSURYŌ SYSTEM.

Ryō no shūge 令集解

(Collected Interpretations of the Administrative Laws). This work, privately compiled during the years 859–884 by the legal scholar Koremune no Naomoto (fl 859–930), was essentially an annotated edition of the administrative section (*ryō*) of the YŌRŌ CODE with annotations culled from earlier works. Only 35 of the original 50 chapters survive. *Ryō no shūge* is a valuable source on the RITSURYŌ SYSTEM, as the works it quotes from are, with the exception of the RYŌ NO GIGE, completely lost. *Ryō no shūge* sometimes quotes provisions of Chinese Tang (T'ang) dynasty (618–907) codes, as well as Japanese *ritsu*, *kyaku*, and *shiki*, that are not preserved elsewhere. Its quotations from the "old com-

ments," or *koki*, written during the period 737–740, when the TAIHŌ CODE was still in force, are now the best source on the content of Taihō *ryō* provisions.

Ryōshoku, Ltd [株]菱食

(Ryōshoku). Food trader. Incorporated in 1925. The company has a product and technology exchange agreement with Fleming, Inc, of the United States. For the fiscal year ending December 1990, sales totaled ¥430.0 billion (US $3.2 billion) and capitalization stood at ¥1.6 billion (US $12.0 million). Headquarters are in Tōkyō.

Ryoshū 旅愁

(A Traveler's Sadness). Novel by YOKOMITSU RIICHI (1898–1947) left unfinished at his death; published 1937–46. The novel is divided into two parts: the first part takes place in Europe and describes the activities of a group of Japanese intellectuals who met on the ship on the way there, and the second half concerns the decision to marry and the engagement of two members of the group, Yashiro Kōichirō and Usami Chizuko. Through his portrayal of discussions between Yashiro, a Japanese nationalist, and Kuji, a Western-style rationalist, and of the relationship between Chizuko, a Catholic, and Yashiro, a Shintō believer, Yokomitsu

The *Kongōkai mandara* (right) represents the Kongōkai (Diamond or Thunderbolt Realm), an expression of Dainichi's boundless and infinite wisdom, indestructible as diamond. It is made up of nine smaller mandalas, or "assemblies," each representing different aspects of Dainichi's wisdom.

The central mandala, known as the *Kompon jōshin e* (assembly of Buddhahood), expresses the core teachings of the mandala. It contains five "lunar disks" (called wheels of liberation) in which sit the "Five Buddhas," representing the five dimensions of wisdom of the Ultimate Reality. In the central disk, Dainichi is surrounded by four *haramitsu* ("perfection") bodhisattvas. The other four Buddhas in the disks surrounding Dainichi are in turn surrounded by four bodhisattvas each; together they comprise the "Sixteen Bodhisattvas," symbolizing the 16 stages of spiritual exercises for the Shingon practitioner.

The three concentric squares enclosing the five lunar disks contain still more deities, each representative of different aspects of the divine truth. In total, over 1,000 deities are represented in the *Kompon jōshin e*, and their interrelation and interaction comprise the teachings of the mandala. The eight other assemblies of the *Kongōkai mandara*, like this one, purport to express in different modes the basic doctrines of esoteric Buddhism—truth being revealed in the relationship of the parts to the whole.

Though each of the *Ryōbu Mandara* is independent and complete in itself, they are both insights into a single, all-embracing truth.

Kongōkai Mandara

5 *Shiin e*	6 *Ichiin e*	7 *Rishu e*
4 *Kuyō e*	1 *Kompon jōshin e*	8 *Gōzanze katsuma e*
3 *Misai e*	2 *Sammaya e*	9 *Gōzanze sammaya e*

The Nine Assemblies of the Kongōkai Mandara

---

lays bare his own painful confrontation with an inability to resolve the conflict between East and West, tradition and science, and ancient Shintō and Catholicism.

ryōshu   領主

(proprietary lords). General term for individuals or families that actually or nominally held landed estates (SHŌEN) as private property (*shiryō*) and exercised fiscal and administrative control over them, either directly or through appointed managers. Under the RITSURYŌ SYSTEM, established at the end of the 7th century, the central government owned most cultivable land and allocated it to farmers (see HANDEN SHŪJU SYSTEM). However, by the 10th century nobles and large temples called estate proprietary lords (*shōen ryōshu*) or central proprietors (*ryōke*) had, chiefly through large-scale enclosure and reclamation of wild lands, gained considerable holdings, which they administered through resident managers (SHŌKAN). A second class of estate owners were the local proprietary lords (*zaichi ryōshu*), local magnates who personally managed the estates they developed; they often commended these lands to powerful *shōen ryōshu* in the capital, who as nominal owners guaranteed protection in exchange for a share of the income. The creation by

the Kamakura shogunate (1192–1333) of military estate stewards (JITŌ) and military governors (SHUGO) greatly diminished the wealth and authority of both *shōen ryōshu* and *zaichi ryōshu*, and, as military control of land increased under the Muromachi shogunate (1338–1573), many *ryōshu* were dispossessed altogether. By the early Edo period (1600–1868) the *shōen* system was replaced by the BAKUHAN SYSTEM (shogunate-domain system), under which *ryōshu* became a general term for feudal lords and domainal retainers. See also DAIMYŌ; HATAMOTO.

Ryōsō Canal   両総用水

(Ryōsō Yōsui). Government-managed canal in eastern Chiba Prefecture, central Honshū; completed in 1967. The canal diverts water from the river TONEGAWA at the city of Sahara, carries it across the Ryōsō Plateau to the city of Mobara, and empties into the river Ichinomiyagawa. Length: 80 km (49.6 mi).

Ryōtsu   両津[市]

City in Niigata Prefecture, on the island of Sado. The island's only city, Ryōtsu prospered from early times as a fishing port. The opening of regular boat service to the city of Niigata in 1885 led to further development. Yellowtail fishing and oyster cultivation are active. Pop: 19,432.

Ryōzen   霊山

Mountain in the northern part of the Abukuma Mountains, northeastern Fukushima Prefecture, northern Honshū. A holy mountain with the remains of a castle built by KITABATAKE AKIIE in 1337. The remains of Ryōzen Shrine are on the summit. Ryōzen is known for its strangely shaped peak of agglomerate rock. Height: 825 m (2,706 ft).

Ryū Chishū   笠智衆

(1904–93). Actor; best known for his performances in supporting roles, usually as the kindly, warm-hearted father. Born in Kumamoto Prefecture, Ryū entered the studio acting school of what is now SHŌCHIKU CO, LTD, in 1925. For 11 years he pursued his acting career without notable success, finding only bit parts or work as an extra. The turning point came in 1936 when he appeared in OZU YASUJIRŌ's *Daigaku yoi toko* (College Is a Nice Place) and followed this with performances in such Ozu classics as *Chichi ariki* (1942, There Was a Father), BANSHUN (1949, Late Spring), and TŌKYŌ MONOGATARI (1953, Tōkyō Story). Ryū has also appeared in many of the films of KINOSHITA KEISUKE, including the hit *Karumen kokyō ni kaeru* (1951,

Ryū Chishū In Ozu Yasujirō's film *Samma no aji* (1962, The Flavor of Mackerel), the actor played a widower who is uneasy about his daughter's approaching marriage.

Okinawan and Miyako Dialects

Selected syllables in standard Japanese

a	ka	sa	ta	na	ha	ma	ya	ra	wa	ga	za	da	ba	pa
i	ki	shi	chi	ni	hi	mi		ri	i	gi	ji	ji	bi	pi
u	ku	su	tsu	nu	fu	mu	yu	ru		gu	zu	zu	bu	pu
e	ke	se	te	ne	he	me		re	e	ge	ze	de	be	pe
o	ko	so	to	no	ho	mo	yo	ro	o	go	zo	do	bo	po

Corresponding syllables in Okinawan (Shuri)

a	ka	sa	ta	na	ha	ma	ya	ra	wa	ga	za	da	ba	pa
i	chi	shi	chi	ni	fi	mi		i	wi	ji	ji	ji	bi	pi
u	ku	si	tsi	nu	fu	mu	yu	ru		gu	zi	zi	bu	pu
i	ki	shi	ti	ni	fi	mi		ri	wi	gi	ji	di	bi	pi
u	ku	su	tu	nu	fu	mu	yu	ru	wu	gu	zu	du	bu	pu

Corresponding syllables in Miyako (Hirara)

a	ka	sa	ta	na	pa	ma	ya	ra	ba	ga	dza	da	ba	pa
i	ksz	sz	tsz	n	psz	m		z	bz	gz	dz	dz	bz	psz
u	f(u)	sz	tsz	n	fu	m	yu	z		v	dz	dz	v	pu
i	ki	shi	ti	ni	pi	mi		ri	bi	gi	ji	di	bi	pi
u	ku	su	tu	nu	pu	mu	yu	ru	bu	gu	dzu	du	bu	pu

NOTE: Standard Japanese is transliterated according to the Hepburn system of romanization used in this encyclopedia. Okinawan and Miyako are transliterated according to an adaptation of this system.

Some Okinawan Grammatical Elements and Their Counterparts in Standard Japanese

Verb endings

Meaning	Okinawan	Standard Japanese
Nonpast positive informal	-(y)un	-(r)u
Past positive informal	-tan	-ta/-da
Nonpast negative informal	-(r)an	-(a/e)nai
Past negative informal	(r)antan	-(a/e)nakatta
Nonpast positive formal	-(ya)bīn	-(i/e)masu
Past positive formal	-(ya)bitan	-(i/e)mashita
Nonpast negative formal	-(ya)biran	-(i/e)masen
Past negative formal	-(ya)birantan	-(i/e)masen deshita

Adjective endings

Meaning	Okinawan	Standard Japanese
Nonpast positive informal	-san	-i
Past positive informal	-satan	-katta
Nonpast negative informal	-kō nēn	-ku nai
Past negative informal	-kō nēntan	-ku nakatta
Nonpast positive formal	-saibīn	-i desu
Past positive formal	-saibītan	-katta desu
Nonpast negative formal	-kō nēbiran	-ku arimasen
Past negative formal	-kō nēbirantan	-ku arimasen deshita

Postpositive particles

Meaning/Function	Okinawan	Standard Japanese
agent marker (human agent)	-ga	ga
of (a human)	-ga	no
from	-kara	kara
until	-madi	made
also	-n	mo
at, to	-nkai	ni, e
agent marker	-nu	ga
of	-nu	no
with (instrumental)	-sāni	de
and, with	-tu	to
at	-uti	de
topic marker	-(y)a	wa
compared to	-yaka	yori
direct object marker	—	o

Carmen Comes Home), the first Japanese color film. He has appeared in all of the movies in YAMADA YŌJI's TORA SAN series (it began in 1969) and has acted in numerous television dramas.

Ryūgadō 竜河洞

Limestone cave in the town of Tosa Yamada, eastern Kōchi Prefecture, Shikoku. The cave consists of many chambers, with stalagmites and pillars and several tiny streams formed by water dripping from the ceiling. Remains of clay pots thought to be prehistoric have been excavated. About 2 km (1.2 mi) is open to the public. The total length is about 4 km (2.5 mi).

Ryūgasaki 竜ヶ崎[市]

City in southern Ibaraki Prefecture, central Honshū, on the river Tonegawa. Rice cultivation is its chief activity. The site of several factories, Ryūgasaki has become a commuter suburb of Tōkyō. Pop: 57,238.

Ryūjōkō Jiken →Liutiaogou

(Liu-t'iao-kou) Incident

ryūkōgo 流行語

Japanese term used to refer to words or phrases that come into fashion and are widely used during a particular period. *Ryūkōgo* may be newly coined phrases, words borrowed from foreign languages, or already existing words that become popular because they fit some new situation. With the spread of the mass media, expressions used by entertainers, social commentators, politicians, or in television commercials become a major type of *ryūkōgo*. As they reflect popular interests, *ryūkōgo* can be valuable clues to the life and manners of an age. For example, the expressions *moga-mobo* (modern girl and modern boy), *daigaku wa deta keredo* (I graduated from college but . . .), and *ero-guro-nansensu* (eroticism, the grotesque, nonsense) reflect the social and economic changes and confusion of the late 1920s and early 1930s. The coming of war in the late 1930s and early 1940s can be seen in such phrases as *zeitaku wa teki da* (extravagance is the enemy) and *ichioku isshin* (100 million with one heart). The changes of the 1950s are reflected in such expressions as *gyaku kōsu* (reverse course) referring to the Cold War reversal of early Allied OCCUPATION policies, *taiyōzoku* (sun tribe) for the new generation of nihilistic youth, and *ichioku sōhakuchika* (the making of 100 million into idiots) referring to the growing television addiction of the Japanese people. More recent *ryūkōgo* include *hapuningu* (happening), *haijakku* (hijack), and *okaruto* (occult). See also INGO.

ryūkōka 流行歌

Popular urban songs, especially those influenced by Western music and composed between the Meiji Restoration (1868) and the end of World War II. The history of popular song in Japan can be traced back at least to the *imayō* of the Heian period (794–1185), which were based on court and religious music. During the Kamakura (1185–1333) and Muromachi (1333–1568) periods, various other forms of popular song developed, especially *kouta*, "short song." The forms of popular songs after the Muromachi period used a variety of 7-5 syllabic meters, but the music itself is lost.

In the Edo period (1600–1868), *ryūkōka* were usually known as *hayari uta*, a term written with the same characters, and many new kinds appeared. The old *kouta* had been sung unaccompanied, but most of the Edo forms were performed to the accompaniment of the SHAMISEN. Some of them were actually regional folk songs (*min'yō*); some were influenced by JŌRURI, the narrative chant of the puppet and *kabuki* theaters; others originated in the entertainment districts of the three great cities of Edo (now Tōkyō), Kyōto, and Ōsaka.

During the Meiji period (1868–1912), although native traditions continued to flourish, *ryūkōka* started to come under the influence of Western music (see MUSIC, WESTERN); many new strophic songs appeared with a four-square melodic shape, while others were modeled on Western-style military music (GUNKA) or educational chorus songs (*shōka*).

Before the days of phonograph recording, an important role in the creation and dissemination of new songs was played by the *enkashi*, itinerant musicians who sang to the accompaniment of the violin and who were the successors of the wandering balladsingers of the Edo period who had accompanied themselves on the Japanese fiddle (KOKYŪ) or the *shamisen*. The first and most famous *enkashi* was Soeda Azembō (1872–1944), the popular composer of many songs of the late Meiji period. Many *enkashi* songs popularized Western democratic ideals, and some made political statements.

The Taishō (1912–26) and early Shōwa (1926–89) periods produced a new crop of songs in which the Western influence was even stronger; some included English words or were drawn from or even set to Western tunes. Soeda Azembō continued to be the most popular composer in the Taishō period. Many new educational chorus songs and children's songs (*dōyō*) were produced with texts by well-known poets, and both forms have continued to be important genres of popular music down to the present day. As urbanization proceeded apace, folk song, often nostalgic in nature, enjoyed a renewed popularity. A new type of lyric song, *jojōka*, started to develop during the 1920s and came to dominate the popular market. There were also new political and "labor songs" (*rōdōka*) that were inspired by the Russian Revolution. The earliest commercial phonograph records in Japan date from 1907, and during the 1920s an increasing amount of popular music was put out in this form. From about 1928 all successful *ryūkōka* were recorded, and the number of composers, singers, and hit songs multiplied. The composer KOGA MASAO (1904–78) burst on the scene in 1931 and went on to dominate Japanese popular music for over 20 years.

Many songs of the 1930s reflect the Japanese occupation of Manchuria, and whereas the *gunka* (military songs) texts urge sacrifice for one's country, the *ryūkōka* spoke of loneliness and separation on the Russian frontier. The majority of other songs dealt with domestic events and situations, especially the parting of lovers. By this time the hybrid musical style of *ryūkōka* had been perfected. Western instruments were now widely used, either exclusively or in combination with native instruments. Texts were no longer in 7-5 meter, the length of lines now being dictated by the melody, underpinned by a simple regular two- or four- (and occasionally three-) beat structure that had been derived at first from Meiji military and educational music but increasingly from jazz, which was introduced to Japan as early as 1912. Although *ryūkōka* were usually harmonized, their tonality was, as is still largely the case with many Japanese popular songs, minor—in keeping with the *in* scale of traditional Japanese music. In the 1920s the term *kayōkyoku* gradually came to be used as an alternative to *ryūkōka*.

After 1941 there were comparatively few new *ryūkōka*, and in the postwar period the term itself largely passed out of common usage as the world of Japanese popular music was inundated by wave after wave of different genres of Western pop music. It is these that now define the terminology of popular music, and it is no longer possible to describe modern popular music with one single all-embracing term such as *ryūkōka*. The kind of bittersweet nostalgic songs of lost love and hometown that formed the bulk of *ryūkōka* in the prewar period have continued under the name of *enka*, but their audience is slowly declining, as the nature of Japanese society changes and young people's tastes become ever more Westernized.

▶▶1286–1287

Ryūkoku University 竜谷大学

(Ryūkoku Daigaku). A coeducational private university located in the city of Kyōto. Founded in 1922. It traces its origins back to a 17th-century seminary for the Nishi Honganji branch of the Jōdo Shin sect of Buddhism. Ryūkoku University maintains faculties of letters, economics, business administration, law, science and technology, and sociology. Research facilities include the Institute of Buddhist Cultural Studies. Enrollment in 1989 was 9,534.

Ryūkyū → Okinawa

Ryūkyū dialects 琉球語

(*ryūkyūgo*). The dialects of the RYŪKYŪ ISLANDS, including Okinawan (Shuri), exhibit considerable variation, the dialects of AMAMI ŌSHIMA in the north being unintelligible to the people of OKINAWA, as are the dialects of the SAKISHIMA ISLANDS (the Miyako and Yaeyama islands) in the south. Although the Ryukyuan dialects are closely related to Japanese, none of them is intelligible to speakers of standard Japanese or of any dialects spoken in the main islands of Japan.

History——The archaeological evidence indicates that the Ryūkyūs were already settled by the third millennium BC. From Okinawa to the north there were connections with Japan, while the Sakishima Islands had connections with Taiwan. Around the 2nd century AD a new type of settlement pattern appeared from Okinawa northward. This may be when an early form of Japanese was introduced.

In the 15th century the Okinawan state of Chūzan, with its capital at Shuri, conquered all of Okinawa and subjugated the islands to the north as far as Amami Ōshima and the Sakishima Islands to the south as well. Throughout the Ryūkyūs the educated classes became fluent in the Shuri dialect. Local dialects continued in use, but they were increasingly influenced by the speech of Shuri.

In the 17th century the Ryūkyūs were subjugated by the SHIMAZU FAMILY, *daimyō* of Satsuma in western Kyūshū. The Shimazu *daimyō* attached the islands north of Okinawa directly to Satsuma, but they controlled the rest of the Ryūkyūs through the Shuri government, so that the speech of Shuri remained the language of the Ryūkyūs until the Meiji period (1868–1912).

Early in the Meiji period the Ryūkyūs were detached from Satsuma, and Okinawa Prefecture was established. Although Naha (of which Shuri is today a suburb) became the capital of the prefecture, standard Japa-

nese (with a Ryukyuan accent) soon replaced the speech of Shuri as the standard language of the Ryūkyūs. Through universal public education and the modern communications media, all classes of Ryukyuans have become fluent in standard Japanese. The local dialects are still in common use, but the percentage of the population that is familiar with the speech of Shuri has declined steadily.

According to tradition, Okinawan was first written in the 13th century—using the Japanese phonetic syllabary (KANA). The oldest records in Okinawan date from the 16th century, when the sacred literature of part of Amami Ōshima and all of Okinawa, which had been handed down orally, was recorded in a document called the *Omoro sōshi*.

Phonology——The phonological differences between Okinawan and standard Japanese are usually described in terms of differences in pronunciation of syllables in the standard *kana* syllabary. In the following examples, Japanese syllables are in the standard Hepburn romanization and their Okinawan equivalents are given in an adaptation based on the Hepburn romanization.

The *e* and *o* of standard Japanese become *i* and *u* in Okinawan. Examples: *yumi* "bride" (J: *yome*), *ukiti* "receiving" (J: *ukete*), and *tukuru* "place" (J: *tokoro*).

Japanese *ki* and *gi* become *chi* and *ji* in Okinawan, so that Okinawan *ki* and *gi* correspond to Japanese *ke* and *ge* but not to Japanese *ki* and *gi*. Examples: *chiki* "listen" (J: *kike*) and *yanaji* "willow" (J: *yanagi*), but *isugu* "hurry" (J: *isoge*).

Japanese *ri* becomes *i* in Okinawan, so that Okinawan *ri* corresponds to Japanese *re* and not to *ri*. Examples: *tui* "bird" (J: *tori*), but *ari* "that" (J: *are*).

Japanese *su*, *tsu*, and *zu* become *si*, *tsi*, and *zi*, so that Okinawan *su* and *zu* correspond to Japanese *so* and *zo* but not to Japanese *su* and *zu*. Examples: *titsi* "iron" (J: *tetsu*), *sina* "sand" (J: *suna*), and *kazi* "number" (J: *kazu*).

The above examples, which by no means cover all the phonological differences between Okinawan and standard Japanese, represent the conservative upper-class pronunciation of Shuri. Today most people in Naha substitute, for example, *shi* for *si*, *chi* for *tsi*, and *ji* for *zi*. Japanese short vowels are sometimes lengthened in Okinawan. The Okinawan words shown above as beginning with a vowel actually have a glottal stop before the vowel.

Morphology and Syntax——Okinawan sentence structure very closely resembles that of standard Japanese. The predicate stands at the end of the clause and has numerous suffixes marking tenses, moods, styles, conjunctions, etc, though the suffixes themselves differ markedly from those of standard Japanese. Okinawan retains a feature that has been lost in modern spoken Japanese—the distinction between predicative and attributive verb forms. Unlike Japanese, Okinawan marks yes-no questions differently from interrogative-word questions. Adjectives in Okinawan, like those of Japanese, are conjugated in much the same way as verbs. The relationships between nouns and other words in a sentence are marked by suffixes that correspond fairly closely to Japanese postpositions. There is nothing corresponding to the Japanese direct object marker *o*, the object being unmarked in Okinawan.

Dialects of the Outer Islands——Unlike Okinawan, the major dialects of Sakishima and Amami Ōshima have maintained a contrast between earlier *i* and *e* (though not be-

tween earlier *o* and *u*). In each case there are four vowels: *a*, *i*, *u*, and *ï* (this last being an unrounded high back vowel), but whereas in Amami Ōshima *ï* corresponds to Japanese *e*, in Sakishima it corresponds to Japanese *i*, while *i* corresponds to Japanese *e*. The Miyako dialects probably differ from standard Okinawan more than any other Ryukyuan dialects. A striking development in Miyako is the change of *ku* and *gu* into *f(u)* and *v*. These are labio-dental *f* and *v*, just as in English, and are unique among the dialects of Japan.

Ryūkyū Islands 琉球諸島

(Ryūkyū Shotō). In the broad sense a chain of islands extending southwest from Kyūshū in an arc 1,200 km (746 mi) long; in this sense usually called the Nansei Islands (Nansei Shotō) in Japanese. In the narrow sense, and in general Japanese usage, the Ryūkyū Islands take in the main group of the OKINAWA ISLANDS and islands to the southwest, all of which are administered as OKINAWA PREFECTURE. These include the MIYAKO ISLANDS and the YAEYAMA ISLANDS, which are often referred to together as the SAKISHIMA ISLANDS. In the broader sense the Ryūkyū or Nansei Islands include the SATSUNAN ISLANDS northeast of the Okinawa group, all of which are part of Kagoshima Prefecture. In either sense the Ryūkyū Islands are almost all in the subtropical zone and are surrounded by coral reefs. They are often struck by typhoons, and although rainfall is usually plentiful, they sometimes suffer from drought as well. Many of the islands are noted for their beauty, and tourism is becoming increasingly important.

Ryūkyū kizoku mondai 琉球帰属問題

(Ryūkyū territorial question). Controversy in the early Meiji period (1868–1912) between Japan and China over possession of the Ryūkyū Islands (Ch: Liuqiu or Liuch'iu). Since the 14th century, the kings of the Ryūkyūs had paid tribute to China, but following a successful invasion by the *daimyō* of Satsuma (now Kagoshima Prefecture) in 1609, they also became vassals of Satsuma. Four years after the Meiji Restoration of 1868, the Japanese government designated the Ryūkyūs a daimyō domain and notified Western nations that it would henceforth assume responsibility for all treaties. As a result of the TAIWAN EXPEDITION OF 1874, in which Japanese forces were sent to Taiwan in retaliation for the massacre of 54 shipwrecked Ryukyuans by Taiwanese aborigines, China tacitly acknowledged Japanese claims to the islands by paying indemnities. In 1879 the Ryūkyūs were designated Okinawa Prefecture as part of the new prefectural system. The Qing (Ch'ing) dynasty (1644–1912) in China strongly objected to this move. It was only with the signing of the Treaty of SHIMONOSEKI, concluding the Sino-Japanese War of 1894–95, that Japan gained undisputed control of the islands. See also OKINAWA.

Ryūkyū music 琉球音楽

(Ryūkyū *ongaku*). The traditional folk and court music of the RYŪKYŪ ISLANDS, frequently accompanied by a three-stringed plucked lute, known as the *sanshin* (also called *jamisen* or *jabisen*), with a snakeskin soundboard head.

Ryūkyū music comprises two musically distinct spheres: the Amami Islands, and the

Continued on page 1288 ▶

Ryūkyū music
A *sanshin*, one of the instruments employed in the traditional music of the Ryūkyū Islands. This example has the typical snakeskin soundboard.

Popular Music in Japan

Japan's enormous appetite for popular music has fueled a lucrative music market and attracted artists from around the globe.

Claiming the second-largest domestic record market in the world and an expanding portfolio of music properties, Japan has become an international music center. Major artists are just as likely to appear in Tōkyō as they are in London or New York, and many musicians ranging from Madonna to little-known British punk bands have their own loyal followings in Japan.

The flow of music has always been one-sided, however. While a number of ambitious Japanese musicians have tried to break into US and European markets, their overall batting average has been dismal, leaving many Westerners with the impression that the bulk of Japanese pop is unimaginative, uninspired, and imitative of their own music. But there have been some promising new developments on Japan's domestic music scene. A glimpse into this self-contained world reveals a wide range of native artists—from teen idols to serious jazz musicians—as well as a profitable music industry with some unique features of its own.

Western Influences

Foreign music was first introduced to Japan after the Meiji Restoration of 1868 as part of the government's move towards modernization. But it was not until the Allied Occupation following World War II that Western, especially American, music caught on.

While General MacArthur was determined to convey the grand ideals of democracy and Christian morality, the Japanese more easily embraced the simple pleasures of blue jeans, hamburgers, jitterbugging, and popular music. The songs that resulted from filtering various types of American music through Japanese sensibilities formed the beginnings of Japan's contemporary popular music scene.

In the 1950s Elvis Presley made a splash in Japan with his movies, especially *Blue Hawaii*. His music inspired a rockabilly cult that continues to this day. Young '50s-style dancers dressed like Elvis still gather in Yoyogi Park in Tōkyō on weekends and have become quite a tourist attraction. Modern-day rockabilly bands such as the Stray Cats from the United States do a very strong business in Japan and tour there often.

The Beatles played at the renowned martial arts stadium Nippon Budōkan in 1966. Their appearance helped kick off the *gurūpu saunzu* ("group sounds") movement that paralleled the "British Invasion" in the United States. Leading groups included the Tigers, Spyders, Blue Comets, Ox, and Tempters. Jazz music became popular around this time as well, spawning jazz bars and coffee shops that turned into hangouts for members of the leftist student movement.

A folk-music counterculture also developed in the 1960s. Protest songs and odes documenting the difficulties of life were written and sung in a Bob Dylan vein. This acoustic folk music eventually went electric in the 1970s, following the "West Coast sound" of artists such as Jackson Browne, the Eagles, and Little Feat.

Growing access to information about international trends gave Japanese fans of the 1980s and early 1990s an expanded view of the music scene. Television programs and music magazines, along with a boom in overseas travel, helped to expose many Japanese to the latest musical developments abroad. A diverse range of imported genres—heavy metal, funk, rap, ethnic music, jazz, and reggae—now make up a significant share of the Japanese market.

Enka

Not all of Japan's postwar music has come from overseas. *Enka*, a genre that has been popular for decades, claims indigenous roots. While there are some who maintain that *enka* has Korean influences, most people trace its origins to older, traditional Japanese strains of popular music known collectively as *ryūkōka*. What gives *enka* its unique sound is the *kobushi*, the slow vibrato in which the melodies are sung. Some compare *enka* to blues or soul, though it is probably more analogous to country-and-western music. Like country and western, *enka* songs often have sentimental themes: reminiscences about hometowns and the good old days, the pains of lost love, and drinking away one's sorrows.

Enka's appeal is limited primarily to the older generation, as younger Japanese tend to favor trendier, more Westernized pop music. But because *enka* is less susceptible to changing fads, an *enka* singer may enjoy a relatively long career after just one or two hits. Misora Hibari, the undisputed queen of *enka*, boasted a career that spanned four decades until it was ended by her greatly mourned death in 1989.

"Idol Singers"

The *aidoru*, or "idol singer," occupies another unique niche in the world of Japanese popular music. Certainly other countries have their own pop idols, but the extent to which Japanese idols have dominated record and CD sales and have generated media exposure distinguishes them from their Western counterparts.

Matsuda Seiko was not only the reigning idol of the 1980s, but the overall best-selling artist in Japanese music history, with more than $500 million in sales, 16 number-one albums, and 25 number-one singles. But pop idols do not only sing songs—they model for advertisements, act in movies, and appear on television shows and commercials. The TV commercials made in the early 1990s by one top idol, Koizumi Kyōko, had the impact of hit videos, and are even believed to have had a favorable effect on a company's stock price.

Usually, a prospective pop idol is recruited in his or her teen years by talent scouts. Often chosen on the basis of looks alone, the candidate is put through various screenings. If successful, he or she is sent to one of Japan's "production companies," talent management agencies which nurture the careers of potential stars. These agencies train young hopefuls in singing, dancing, and all other aspects of their carefully crafted public persona. They also put great effort into promoting and marketing their clients.

The faces of pop idols appear in a variety of media: newspaper and magazine advertisements, billboards, train placards, and television commercials. The talent agencies also put out a wide array of idol-related products—from calendars and posters to notebooks and buttons. Since the popularity of idols usually lasts just a few years, agencies try to capitalize on their demand to the greatest extent possible.

Though there are a few male singing idols, the most popular idols are usually female. Their repertoire typically consists of innocuous tunes patterned after prevailing pop music fads. Actual musical ability is of minor significance—even top-selling record artist Matsuda Seiko can claim little talent as a singer. Yet she and other singing idols are able to sell records primarily on the appeal of their public image. Many of Matsuda's fans, for example, are drawn to her girl-next-door beauty and her sentimental nature, which she exhibits frequently with dramatic crying bouts.

The trend in recent times has been toward a bolder, sexier image, as seen in pop stars like Miyazawa Rie, who originally gained fame as a model and actress. Her debut single hit the charts at number one—and she had never even performed live as a singer!

Kayōkyoku

Idol music falls into a larger category of music called *kayōkyoku* (popular song). While *kayōkyoku* was once used as a general term for Western-style popular music, it now refers to a wide variety of trendy pop music that thrives primarily on television publicity.

The word *kayōkyoku* connotes music with little substance. The types of singers can range from lip-synching, flavor-of-the-week teen idols to the all-female rock band Princess Princess, which was formed on its own and writes its own music but became popular largely through appearances on television shows and commercials.

"New Music"

Not all Japanese musicians are mass-produced, made-for-TV pop stars. In the 1970s, a genre called "new music" (*nyū myūjikku*) emerged, which in the West might be defined simply as popular music by singer-songwriters. Until this time, singers who wrote their own songs were considered rather bold in a world of manufactured stars. Though stylistically influenced by the folk-music movement of the late 1960s, which also produced some independent singer-songwriters, new music had brighter themes than folk and more sophisticated instrumentation and arrangement.

Though the label "new music" is now considered passé, this broad category of independent singer-songwriters continues to occupy a large niche in the pop-music market. The most famous purveyors of new music—Matsutōya Yumi (known as "Yuming"), Yamashita Tatsurō, and the band Southern All-Stars—are still extremely popular today. In contrast to *kayōkyoku* stars, they do not bind themselves to prevailing fads and rarely make appearances on television talk shows and variety programs. And while *kayōkyoku* stars are often in a subservient position to their production companies, new music stars have reversed this relationship in order to maintain their artistic integrity.

Developing alongside new music are a number of more specialized strains of Western-influenced Japanese rock that lie outside the *kayōkyoku* world. Japanese adaptations of everything from heavy metal to funk, punk, glam-rock, reggae, and even rap can be heard today. Black music in the style of Bobby Brown and Janet Jackson has become particularly fashionable, spawning a copycat genre called *burakon*, the Japanese abbreviation for black contemporary music. Many of these stars not only copy the music but also go to great lengths to imitate the looks and stage manner of the stars they idolize. For instance, the success of one *burakon* singer, Kubota Toshinobu, owes much to his painstaking

The popular female rock group Princess Princess on stage at Tōkyō's Nippon Budōkan.

imitation of the dance moves, clothes, and hairstyles of black American pop musicians, as well as their singing styles.

Jazz

One Western genre that has firmly established itself within the Japanese music scene is jazz. Japan is home to an important and highly profitable market for jazz, boasting numerous clubs, some of the best jazz magazines in the world, and a steady core of avid fans. Major international jazz figures play extensively in Japan's clubs and concert halls. This flourishing scene has also produced native musicians like saxophonist Watanabe Sadao, regarded as the patriarch of Japanese jazz, Hino Terumasa, and Watanabe Kazumi, and jazz fusion groups Casiopea and T Square. Yet while many of Japan's jazz artists display marvelous technical ability, few display any real originality.

The Struggle to Break into the West

A number of Japanese musicians have tried to translate their success at home into success overseas, but their record so far has not been impressive. Some of the problems they face stem from a fundamental difference in Japanese and Western attitudes toward music. For many Japanese, imitating a recognized master to perfection is a respectable thing to do—it is like returning to the source. So in Japan, it is not uncommon for musicians to pattern themselves after others. For example, there is a group that models its appearance almost entirely on the rock band Kiss; a singer whose stage manner mimics Madonna's; and a jazz guitarist who plays exactly like Wes Montgomery.

Westerners, however, seek an exotic or original element in Japanese music, something to set it apart from the average pop fare that already abounds at home. The Japanese musicians who have proved most popular abroad are those who have successfully incorporated Asian elements into their music. One example is New Age synthesizer player Kitarō. Many of his Western fans seem to be attracted to an Oriental element in his music, an otherworldly effect that is often intensified by the extravagant stagings for his live performances.

The most famous example is Sakamoto Ryūichi, former member of the Japanese supergroup Yellow Magic Orchestra, whose soundtracks to the films *Merry Christmas, Mr. Lawrence* and *The Last Emperor* both received prestigious international awards. Like Kitarō, much of Sakamoto's appeal abroad seems to stem from what Westerners perceive as an Oriental feel to his music.

Although a number of Japanese groups seem contrived and quick to jump on the latest musical bandwagon, a noteworthy exception is the group Shōnen Knife, a band consisting of three young women from Ōsaka. Their simple yet imaginative rock sound became an underground sensation in the United States and Europe, despite the fact that their records were hard to come by. Fame spread mostly through word of mouth and fanzines. Shōnen Knife was largely ignored in the band's own country for nearly 10 years, and they did not release an album on a major label until 1992. In recent times they have attained more mainstream acceptance in Japan, and their fanatic international following continues to grow as the band tours increasingly overseas.

But the majority of Japanese musicians today lack the originality or exoticism that Westerners seek. Even the more sophisticated pop sound of domestic artists like Matsutōya Yumi and Yamashita Tatsurō would probably not seem terribly original to Westerners, who may find Matsutōya's material akin to that of singer-songwriters like Carole King or Joni Mitchell, and Yamashita's music similar to that of Beach Boys' mastermind Brian Wilson.

The first and only Japanese song to become a genuine international hit came about as a remarkable fluke. Sung entirely in Japanese, Sakamoto Kyū's 1963 hit "Sukiyaki" managed to become number one in the United States and number six in Great Britain, a surprising feat that to this day no other Japanese artist has been able to match.

The Japanese Music Industry

But of course, success abroad is not everything. In the self-contained Japanese music market, it is possible to sell as many as two million albums without any overseas sales. Indeed, despite all the fanfare accorded Western musicians, in actual fact Japanese artists control 70 percent of the domestic market—which is today the second-largest market in the world following that of the United States.

The giant industry that sustains these artists has developed a few unique characteristics of its own. Radio, for instance, has a relatively minor impact on record sales. Strict broadcasting regulations tend to inhibit competition among radio stations, resulting in programming that is usually bland and predictable. Magazines, on the other hand, are a vital medium for the music industry. A variety of high-quality music and lifestyle magazines are widely read and are excellent sources of information on the latest developments in the music world.

Television also plays an important role in Japan's music industry. While there is still no 24-hour music video channel to match America's MTV, the "tie-up" with television commercials often provides a profitable link to record sales. Songs by popular musicians are used as music tracks for the commercials, and many of these songs turn into hit singles. The trade magazine *Music Labo* even has a "tie-up" chart listing the top TV commercial songs for the week.

In the United States, writing or performing songs for television commercials may imply a compromise in artistic standards. In Japan, however, there is no similar stigma. Even respected Japanese musicians like Sakamoto Ryūichi and international stars like Sting have made commercial tracks. Television advertising campaigns are often coordinated with scheduled concert performances. In 1991, for example, Frank Sinatra appeared and sang in a commercial for All Nippon Airways. The commercial aired right before his concert tour in Japan.

A similar "tie-up" strategy is used with prime-time television drama series that have high viewer ratings among younger audiences. Songs by popular musicians are often used as theme tracks for these series, and many make their way onto the pop charts. A recent "tie-up" hit was Eric Clapton's *Wonderful Tonight*, which was used as the theme song for the drama series *Shiawase no ketsudan*.

Expanding Markets

Japanese music industry giants are attuned to the fact that there is much more to the music business than selling records and concert tickets. Several of the corporations that own Japanese record labels, such as Sony, Matsushita, Tōshiba, and Pioneer, are also manufacturers of electronics goods. Controlling rights to the music of popular artists can provide a profitable link to sales of these expensive hardware items. With Sony's acquisition of CBS in 1987 and Matsushita's purchase of MCA in 1990, the Japanese now own the contracts of many of the world's top recording artists.

Although Japanese popular music has yet to make waves on an international level, Japan has secured for itself an important place in the global music industry and is likely to play a significant role in determining future trends.

Keith Cahoon

ryūnōgiku The *ryūnōgiku* blooms in October and November. In some varieties, the outer ray flowers, which are usually white, turn slightly red as they mature.

Ryū Shintarō
A newspaperman and prominent figure in pre–World War II political and intellectual circles, Ryū also played a leading role in the postwar Japanese press.

Okinawa, Miyako, and Yaeyama islands, represented by Okinawa proper. Okinawa's centrality in East Asian trading routes (see RYŪKYŪ TRADE) resulted in influence from various musical traditions, primarily Chinese and Japanese. The *sanshin*, direct ancestor of the Japanese SHAMISEN, is a modification of the Chinese *san xian (san hsien)*; however, its music apparently owes almost nothing to China. The other essential instrument in Okinawan music is the Japanese-style stick drum (see TAIKO). In classical song the Japanese KOTO (a 13-stringed, zitherlike instrument), a Chinese transverse flute, and the *kūchō*, an upright 3-stringed fiddle of complex origins (the Ryūkyū version of the KOKYŪ), may accompany the *sanshin*. Other instruments are used for particular music of limited distribution. There is no solo instrumental tradition to speak of.

Traditional rural musical activities of Chinese origin included the lion dance (SHISHIMAI), the STICK DANCE, and the flower-drum song. From Japan came the Buddhist dance tradition of NEMBUTSU ODORI, which developed into the *eisā* dance of the BON FESTIVAL. Indigenous work, religious, and dance songs flourished.

Ryukyuan song texts were first recorded in the *Omoro sōshi*, a collection of over 1,000 court and regional songs edited in three installments between 1532 and 1623 under court supervision. The texts are very diverse in content, but the collection was intended for ritual use.

The dominant native poetic form known as *ryūka* (Ryūkyū song), consisting of three lines of eight syllables followed by one six-syllable line, seems to have emerged in the 17th century (although songs with eight-syllable lines are not uncommon in the *Omoro sōshi*). *Ryūka* meter predominates in Okinawan classical and folk song, although Miyako and Yaeyama folk songs are more often in lines of five and four syllables.

Ryūkyū trade   琉球貿易

(Ryūkyū *bōeki*). Ryukyuans were the primary carriers in trade among Southeast Asian and East Asian countries from the early 15th to the mid-16th century. The rise of Ryūkyū (see OKINAWA) as a trade center was made possible by conditions in neighboring Japan and China that restricted their participation in international trade. In 1429 the three principalities of the Ryūkyū Archipelago—Hokuzan, Chūzan, and Nanzan—were united into one kingdom under the ruler of Chūzan (see CHŪZAN'Ō). The kingdom prospered, carrying from one country to another Japanese swords and copper, Chinese raw silk, silk textiles, and ceramics, and Southeast Asian pepper, sappanwood, tumeric, sugar, and other local products. From 1380 to the late 16th century Ryūkyū dispatched over 200 missions to Southeast Asian countries, including Java, Palembang, and Malacca. The end of Ryūkyū commercial dominance came with the appearance of European, Chinese, and Japanese competitors in the late 16th century. Japanese merchants were particularly aggressive, establishing several Japanese communities (NIHOMMACHI) near Southeast Asian ports. Portuguese and Spaniards also pushed out from their Southeast Asian bases to explore the markets in China and Japan.

Trade with Korea was established during the reign of the Ryukyuan king Satto (r 1350–95), but neither country showed strong interest in commercial relations. The Ryukyuans found it difficult to compete in the Korean market against such Japanese *daimyō* as the SŌ FAMILY, the ŌUCHI FAMILY, the Matsura, and the SHIMAZU FAMILY of Satsuma Province (now part of Kagoshima Prefecture).

Ryūkyū's tributary relationship with China, which began in the late 14th century and lasted five centuries, was of great political, economic, and cultural significance to the island kingdom, leading to many cultural importations. After the 1609 invasion of Ryūkyū by the Shimazu family of Satsuma, Satsuma allowed the kingdom to maintain a facade of independence. Since China refused to have official relations with the Japanese after TOYOTOMI HIDEYOSHI's military campaigns against Korea, Satsuma encouraged "independent" Ryūkyū to send tribute missions to China to obtain high-quality silk. The Satsuma-Ryūkyū trade in Chinese goods was a monopoly granted by the Tokugawa shogunate (1603–1867) to the Shimazu. Ryūkyū remained under the domination of Satsuma until the end of the Edo period in 1868, and in 1879 it was incorporated into the Japanese prefectural system as Okinawa.

Ryūkyū University   琉球大学

(Ryūkyū Daigaku). A national university located in the town of Nishihara, Okinawa Prefecture. It was established in 1950. Its predecessors were the Bunkyō School and the Gaikokugo Gakkō (School of Foreign Languages), both established in 1947. In 1966 the university came to be administered by the Ryūkyū government under the Law for the Establishment and Management of Ryūkyū University. In 1972, with the return of the Ryūkyū Islands to Japan, it became a national university. It maintains faculties of medicine, law and letters, education, science, engineering, and agriculture. Enrollment was 5,394 in 1989.

ryūnōgiku   竜脳菊

Dendranthema japonicum. Perennial herb of the family Compositae found on low sunny hills in Kyūshū, Shikoku, and central and western Honshū. The volatile oil taken from its stem and leaves is scented like refined Borneo camphor (*ryūnō*). It has a long slim rhizome and a narrow stem (30–60 cm; 12–24 in) from which a head inflorescence develops in autumn. The head consists of white ray flowers outside and yellow disk flowers inside. The leaves are alternate, oval, and trilobed like the chrysanthemum's, whose ancestor this plant may be.

Ryūsendō   竜泉洞

Limestone caves in the town of Iwaizumi, eastern Iwate Prefecture, northern Honshū. The caves and the bats called *usagikōmori* (*Plecotus auritus*) inhabiting them have been designated natural monuments. Measurable length: 2,500 m (8,200 ft); number of branch caves: 35; depth of cave-bottom lake: 120 m (394 ft).

Ryū Shintarō   笠信太郎

(1900–1967). Journalist. Born in Fukuoka Prefecture; graduated from Hitotsubashi University. After serving as a researcher at the Ōhara Institute for Social Research, Ryū went to work at the newspaper *Tōkyō asahi shimbun* (now ASAHI SHIMBUN) in 1936. His positions there included that of editorial writer and European correspondent. He was also a member of the SHŌWA KENKYŪKAI, a

political study group popularly known as the "brain trust" for Prime Minister KONOE FUMIMARO. He became chairman of the *Asahi*'s editorial board in 1948 and was an influential leader of the Japanese press. In 1950 his *Mono no mikata ni tsuite*, a book comparing the peoples and philosophies of all of the European countries, became a best seller. Ryū's works are collected in *Ryū Shintarō zenshū* (1968–69).

Ryūtei Rijō   滝亭鯉丈

(?–1841). Author of popular fiction. Real name Ikeda Yaemon. Born in Edo (now Tōkyō). He was said to be the older brother of NINJŌBON writer TAMENAGA SHUNSUI, with whom he wrote *Akegarasu nochi no masayume* (1821–24). He was the author of 12 serialized KOKKEIBON and a successor to the *kokkeibon* writers JIPPENSHA IKKU and SHIKITEI SAMBA. His stories depict the frivolous and decadent lifestyle of the merchant class of Edo in a light and amusing fashion. Among the most famous are *Hanagoyomi hasshōjin* (1820–49) and *Kokkei wagōjin* (1823–44), both of which were completed by other writers after his death.

Ryūtei Tanehiko   柳亭種彦

(1783–1842). A writer of light fiction (GESAKU) of the late Edo period (1600–1868). Real name Takaya Hikoshirō. Born in Edo (now Tōkyō). He was influenced by plebeian authors of the Genroku era (1688–1704), such as Ihara SAIKAKU and EJIMA KISEKI, as well as by the JŌRURI plays of CHIKAMATSU MONZAEMON and other playwrights of the puppet and KABUKI theaters.

Tanehiko began writing historical novels (YOMIHON) but turned to GŌKAN, a light fiction characterized by the close relationship of the text to illustrations that appear on every page. He was a literary scholar as well, and published essays on bibliographic studies of Edo literature, the best known of which is "Sukikaeshi" (1826, Recycled Paper). His extensive library of Genroku-era books has been preserved and constitutes a valuable resource for studies of that era's literature.

Tanehiko's fame today rests largely on his *gōkan*, *Nise Murasaki inaka Genji* (1829–42, Bogus Murasaki, Bumpkin Genji), a popular parody of the classic TALE OF GENJI. Tanehiko set his story in the 15th century, but many believed he based his work on contemporary society, in particular the intrigues within the harem of the shōgun TOKUGAWA IENARI, which included over 900 women. With illustrations by UTAGAWA KUNISADA, the novel was published serially from 1829 to 1842 and was suppressed during the TEMPŌ REFORMS of 1842.

Ryūzōji family   竜造寺氏

(Ryūzōjishi). Provincial leaders, later *daimyō*, in western Kyūshū from the 12th through 16th centuries. In 1186 Fujiwara no Sueie took the name Ryūzōji when he was appointed JITŌ (estate steward) of the lands surrounding the temple Ryūzōji in Hizen Province (now Saga and Nagasaki prefectures). In 1336 the family allied itself with ASHIKAGA TAKAUJI. It was long subordinate to the SHŌNI FAMILY, but in 1559 Ryūzōji Takanobu (1529–84) defeated the Shōni. He came into conflict with the ŌTOMO FAMILY and the SHIMAZU FAMILY and was killed in battle with the Shimazu in 1584. His heir, Masaie (1566–1607), could not maintain control, and the Ryūzōji domain was taken over by its former vassals, the NABESHIMA FAMILY.

S

saba━━▶mackerel

Sabae
鯖江[市]

City in northern Fukui Prefecture, central Honshū. In the 13th century it developed as a JŌDO SHIN SECT temple town and, in the 18th century, as castle town of the Sabae domain. In the Meiji period (1868–1912) a textile industry was established. Today Sabae produces 80 percent of Japan's eyeglass frames. Other important industries are synthetic-fiber and lacquer ware production. Pop: 62,283.

sabi
寂

Poetic ideal fostered by BASHŌ (1644–94) and his followers in *haikai* (see HAIKU), though the germ of the concept and the term existed long before them. *Sabi* points toward a medieval aesthetic combining elements of old age, loneliness, resignation, and tranquillity, yet the colorful and plebeian qualities of Edo-period (1600–1868) culture are also present. At times *sabi* is used synonymously or in conjunction with WABI, an aesthetic ideal of the TEA CEREMONY.

FUJIWARA NO TOSHINARI (1114–1204), the first major poet to employ a *sabi*-related word (the verb *sabu*) in literary criticism, stressed its connotations of loneliness and desolation, pointing to such images as frost-withered reeds on the seashore. With later medieval artists such as ZEAMI (1363–1443), Zenchiku (1405–68), and SHINKEI (1406–75), the implications of *sabi* focused so heavily on desolation that the emerging beauty seemed almost cold. Underlying this aesthetic was the cosmic view typical of medieval Buddhists, who recognized the existential loneliness of all men and tried to resign themselves to, or even find beauty in, that loneliness.

Bashō himself wrote little on *sabi*, but from his disciples' writings it can be inferred that his concept of *sabi* was a considerably modified version of the medieval ideal. Bashō is said to have found *sabi* in this haiku of his disciple MUKAI KYORAI:

> Two blossom-watchmen
> With their white heads together
> Having a chat.

Such a synthesis of conflicting aesthetic values—the gorgeous beauty of the white cherry blossoms and the "colorless" beauty of white-haired old men—elevates loneliness to a higher level of meaning. A person awakened to the essential mutability of life does not dread physical waning or loneliness; rather, he or she accepts these sad facts with quiet resignation and even finds in them a source of enjoyment.

sacred, the
聖

(*sei*). The concept of the sacred in Japan is fundamentally based on native SHINTŌ beliefs that were influenced by BUDDHISM introduced from China in the 6th century, with some overlay of Western beliefs. The Shintō concept of *kami*, the Shintō-Buddhist concept of *kami-hotoke*, and the Shintō concepts of *ke, hare,* and *kegare* are the most important components of the overall concept of the sacred.

Kami——In Japan sacred beings or objects are known as KAMI. After conducting a study of the KOJIKI (712, Records of Ancient Matters), MOTOORI NORINAGA (1730–1801) defined *kami* as "the deities of heaven and earth who appear in the ancient texts and the gods enshrined in the shrines; any being which possesses some eminent quality out of the ordinary and is awe-inspiring, including not only human beings but also such objects as birds, beasts, trees, grass, seas, and mountains." It is apparent, then, that there is in the concept of *kami* no quality of "the wholly other," which is characteristic of God in the Judeo-Christian tradition, and no definite division between human beings and *kami*.

TAMA (spirits) can also be *kami*. Just as human beings (*hito*) have a soul, or *hitodama*, other entities have a *tama*. It was believed that the souls of humans became ancestor gods when the descendants performed the *tomuraiage*, the last memorial service that was performed on the 33rd or 50th anniversary of death. The spirits of the dead who did not have descendants to conduct these memorial services became ghosts and haunted the living, and the souls of those who, abused by others, met their deaths with hatred in their hearts became evil spirits called *onryō* or GORYŌ and tormented the living.

The *kami* of Japan are collectively known as *yaoyorozu no kami* (literally, "the 8 million deities"). Ultimately *kami* and human beings are seen as merging together through the ideal of each human being achieving a cheerful, pure, honest, and true heart; in fact, Shintō may be defined as the belief that the realization of this ideal is the ultimate goal for human beings.

Kami-hotoke——After Buddhism was introduced into polytheistic Japan, a Shintō-Buddhist fusion took place, resulting in the theory of HONJI SUIJAKU. According to this theory, Buddhist deities (*hotoke*) sometimes took the form of Shintō *kami*. The common people were not interested in theological views and simply believed that *kami* and *hotoke* were one and the same; that is, *kami-hotoke*. After the Meiji Restoration in 1868 the concept of *kami* underwent further change with the introduction of Western beliefs. Used as a translation for *theos, deus,* or God, *kami* took on the additional meaning of an abstract deity or of a unique, absolute being.

Ke, Hare, and Kegare——The concept of the sacred in Japan is characterized by an absence of the dichotomy between the sacred and the profane. Western-oriented ethnologists in Japan distinguish the two elements of *ke* and *hare*, defined respectively as profane ordinariness and the sacred extraordinariness of the *matsuri* (Shintō ceremonies and festivals). The third element is *kegare* (defilement). In extraordinary actions *hare* and *kegare* are paradoxically both in direct opposition and merged, as illustrated in the Shintō ceremonies and festival events of the *matsuri*.

The first step in a *matsuri* is the preparation of a sacred order through abstinence and purification (*imi*) before the ceremonies. In this way the body and mind increase in energy and vitality, leading to a pure sacred state of *hare*. The second step is the performance of Shintō ceremonies, which include the NAORAI, a feast at which the *sake* and food offered to the *kami* are consumed as an act of communion with the *kami*, helping to achieve the manifestation of the sacred in the world. In the third step of the *matsuri* joyous celebrations are held. The celebration marks a return from the *hare* of the *matsuri* to the *ke* of ordinary life. When this *ke*, or profane energy, has been con-

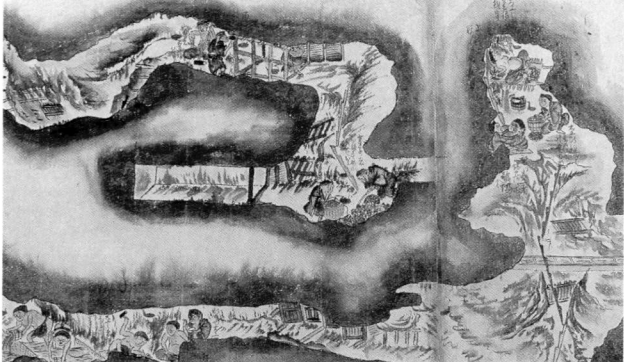

Sado mines
1 This detail from an 18th-century handscroll illustrating work at the Sado mines shows the production of iron mining tools (top) and the cleaning and grading of gold ore (bottom), the latter done primarily by women.
2 Operations inside the Sado mines are illustrated in another detail from the same scroll.

Sada Keiji This film actor's cool, intellectual demeanor won him a huge following among movie fans in the 1940s and 1950s.

sumed in ordinary life, resulting in a decline to a state of *kegare* (impure sacredness; literally, "*ke* exhausted"), the functioning of ordinary life is impaired. Thus, after a year, the *hare* (pure sacred) events of the *matsuri* are once again carried out. See also FESTIVALS.

sacrifice 供儀

(*kugi*). Offerings of food, drink, plants, animals, or other precious substances to a deity or ancestral spirit that form a part of both Shintō and Buddhist ceremony. Chief offerings in Shintō ceremonies consist of rice, *sake*, fish, and vegetables. Meat offerings have been rare because of the influence of the Buddhist prohibition against the killing of animals. Shintō offerings may also consist of cloth, paper (GOHEI), jewels, weapons, and money. After the ceremony participants take part in a communion (NAORAI), in which they consume the food offered to the deity. Buddhist offerings consist of food, incense, and flowers. Blood offerings were rare in Japan, but there are legends telling of human sacrifices to mountain and river deities when a castle or bridge was to be built.

Sada Keiji 佐田啓二

(1926–64). Film actor who rose to stardom during the heyday of the Japanese motion picture industry in the early 1950s. Real name Nakai Hiroshi. Born in Kyōto, he graduated from Waseda University and joined the studios of SHŌCHIKU CO, LTD. He debuted in the lead role in KINOSHITA KEISUKE's *Fushichō* (1947, Phoenix), followed by Kinoshita's *Ojōsan kampai* (1949, A Toast to the Young Miss), Ōba Hideo's (b 1910) KIMI NO

NA WA (1953–54, What's Your Name?), and OZU YASUJIRŌ's *Higambana* (1958, Equinox Flower). His cool intellectual demeanor appealed to the public. His career was cut short by his death in an automobile accident.

Sadamisaki Peninsula 佐田岬半島

(Sadamisaki Hantō). Located in western Ehime Prefecture, Shikoku. One of the narrowest peninsulas in Japan, it has numerous sea cliffs and little level ground. The town of Mitsukue is known as the training site for the Japanese submarines that attacked Pearl Harbor on 7 December 1941. The tip of the peninsula is part of the Inland Sea National Park. Length: 40 km (25 mi).

Sado 佐渡

Also known as Sadogashima. The largest island in the Sea of Japan, 35 km (22 mi) from the city of Niigata, central Honshū. Administratively part of Niigata Prefecture. It consists of three regions: the northern region with the Ōsado Mountains, the southern region with the Kosado Hills, and the Kuninaka Plain in between. The island has two major bays, Ryōtsu Bay in the northeast and Mano Bay in the southwest. Sado was an independent province from 702 until 1876 and a place of criminal exile during the medieval period (mid-12th–16th centuries). When gold and silver mines opened in 1601 (see SADO MINES), Sado prospered. Gold production has dwindled, however, and today rice, cuttlefish, and yellowtail are major products. Sado's attractions include its scenic coasts, various historical sites, and traditional songs and dances such as the Sado *okesa*. It is also the home of the endangered *toki* (Japanese crested ibis; *Nipponia nippon*). Area: 857 sq km (331 sq mi); pop: 78,061.

sadō → tea ceremony

Sado bugyō 佐渡奉行

(commissioner of Sado). Title held by the official or officials of the Tokugawa shogunate (1603–1867) responsible for the island of Sado in the Sea of Japan, valuable for its gold and silver deposits. In 1601 it was placed under direct shogunate control by TOKUGAWA IEYASU. Referred to as the Sado *daikan* (intendant of Sado) until about 1618, the post of Sado *bugyō* was routinely occupied by one or two officials of HATAMOTO (bannerman) status, assisted by civil servants and about 100 YORIKI AND DŌSHIN as constabulary,

along with various other subordinate officials. See also SADO MINES.

Sado mines 佐渡金山

(Sado *kinzan*). Precious-metal mines near the village of Aikawa on the island of Sado in the Sea of Japan. By the 12th century it was known that there was gold in surface waters on Sado. Intensive mining of the region dates from the opening of the Aikawa mines in 1601. Two years later TOKUGAWA IEYASU designated ŌKUBO NAGAYASU as the first Sado commissioner (SADO BUGYŌ). Under his supervision, production of both gold and silver increased dramatically, annually yielding an estimated 66–100 tons of gold and silver during the years 1618–27 and becoming a major source of income for the Tokugawa shogunate. Flooding disrupted production, and the richest veins were quickly exhausted. After the 1730s annual production was frequently less than a ton of precious metal, almost entirely silver. After the Meiji Restoration (1868) production expanded. In 1896 the mines were turned over to private (MITSUBISHI) interests. Though mining has ceased, the mines now serve as a tourist attraction.

Sado Strait 佐渡海峡

(Sado Kaikyō). Strait between the mainland of central Honshū and the island of SADO. It is an excellent fishery for squid and walleyed pollack. Ferries linking Honshū with Sado cross the strait. Narrowest point: 31 km (19 mi).

Saegusa Kazuko 三枝和子

(1929–). Novelist. Born in Hyōgo Prefecture; graduated from Kansei Gakuin University. Saegusa's novels show considerable aesthetic influences from both the Greek classics and the NŌ drama. Her major works include the antirealist *Shokei ga okonawarete iru* (1969, The Execution Proceeds); *Oni-domo no yoru wa fukai* (1983, Deep Is the Night of Demons), which combines dark wartime memories with the customs and folklore of rural communities; and *Sono hi no natsu* (1986, Summer in a Day) and *Sono fuyu no shi* (1988, Death That Winter), which explore the events of World War II from a woman's perspective.

Saeki Kiichi 佐伯喜一

(1913–). Economist and president of NOMURA RESEARCH INSTITUTE, LTD (1965–78). Born in Hiroshima Prefecture. After graduating from Tōkyō University in 1936, he joined the research department of the South Manchuria Railway. After World War II, he joined the ECONOMIC STABILIZATION BOARD, which planned the restoration of the Japanese economy. He moved to the National Defense Agency in 1953 and became president of the Nomura Research Institute in 1965. He has been vice-president of the International Institute for Global Peace since 1988.

Saeki Shōichi 佐伯彰一

(1922–). Critic and scholar of American literature. Born in Tōkyō; graduated from Tōkyō University. Saeki reexamines Japanese literature and culture from an international perspective. He received the Yomiuri Literary Prize for *Monogatari geijutsu ron* (1979, The Art of the Narrative). Saeki's other works include *Jiden no seiki* (1985, The Autobiographical Century). He received the Japan Art Academy Prize in 1982.

Saeki Yūzō 佐伯祐三

(1898–1928). Western-style painter. Born in Ōsaka. After graduating from Tōkyō Bijutsu Gakkō (now Tōkyō University of Fine Arts and Music) he traveled to France. Influenced by Maurice de Vlaminck (1876–1958) and Maurice Utrillo (1883–1955), he painted in a starkly expressionistic style, depicting the melancholy back streets of Paris. One of his paintings won a prize at the Salon d'Automne in 1925. He died in Paris at the age of 30.

Saga 佐賀[市]

Capital of Saga Prefecture, Kyūshū. A castle town in the Edo period (1600–1868), it is now a distribution center for regional products, such as rice, dairy products, vegetables, and mandarin oranges. Foodstuffs, electrical-appliance, textile, brewing, and paper industries are located here. Saga is the birthplace of the Meiji-period (1868–1912) government leader ŌKUMA SHIGENOBU. Pop: 169,963.

Saga domain → Hizen domain

Sagae 寒河江[市]

City in central Yamagata Prefecture, northern Honshū. Formerly a castle town. Main agricultural products are rice, apples, pears, and cherries. It is a base camp for climbing the mountains GASSAN, HAGUROSAN, and YUDONOSAN. Sagae Hot Spring is located here. Pop: 42,076.

Saga, Emperor 嵯峨天皇

(786–842; Saga Tennō). The 52nd sovereign (tennō) in the traditional count (which includes several legendary emperors); reigned 809–823. Second son of Emperor KAMMU. At his accession, the court was divided between Saga's supporters and those of his brother, the former emperor Heizei (r 806–809). Saga defeated his rivals in 810 (see KUSUKO INCIDENT). Striving to strengthen imperial power, he established the KURŌDO-DOKORO (Bureau of Archivists) in 810 and the KEBIISHI (imperial police) in 816. He was known as a talented poet and as one of the three great early calligraphers (Sampitsu; see CALLIGRAPHY). He sponsored collections of Chinese verse—the *Ryōunshū* (814) and the BUNKA SHŪREISHŪ (818)—as well as the completion of the lineage record SHINSEN SHŌJIROKU (815) and the compilation of the edicts and regulations known as Kōnin Kyakushiki (820).

Sagami Bay 相模湾

(Sagami Wan). Inlet of the Pacific Ocean in southern Kanagawa Prefecture, central Honshū. Extends from the Miura Peninsula on the east to the northeastern coast of the Izu Peninsula on the west. The bay is a major fishing area. The coast of the bay includes the Shōnan Coast, a residential and resort area. Cities include Zushi, Kamakura, Fujisawa, Chigasaki, Hiratsuka, and Odawara.

Sagamigawa 相模川

River in Yamanashi and Kanagawa prefectures, central Honshū, originating in Lake Yamanaka and flowing east into Kanagawa Prefecture to enter Sagami Bay east of the city of Hiratsuka. The upper reaches in Yamanashi are known as Katsuragawa. Numerous dams are located on the river. The water is utilized for drinking, irrigation, and industry. Length: 109 km (68 mi); area of drainage basin: 1,680 sq km (649 sq mi).

Sagamihara 相模原[市]

City in northern Kanagawa Prefecture, central Honshū. An army base during World War II, it has been industrialized since 1958 and is now a satellite city of Tōkyō. Pop: 531,542.

Sagamihara 相模原

Upland between the rivers Sagamigawa and Sakaigawa, northern Kanagawa Prefecture, central Honshū; formed by an upheaval of the Sagamigawa's diluvial fan. After World War II, industrial and housing complexes were constructed in and around the city of SAGAMIHARA. Average elevation: 125 m (400 ft).

Sagami, Lake 相模湖

(Sagamiko). Artificial lake in northern Kanagawa Prefecture, central Honshū. Created by damming the river Sagamigawa, a project completed in 1947. The water is utilized for electric power, drinking, and irrigation. The lake is a popular recreational center easily accessible by car and train. Area: 2.6 sq km (1 sq mi); storage capacity: 48.2 million cu m (1.7 billion cu ft).

Sagami Province 相模国

(Sagami no Kuni). Comprising the major part of present-day Kanagawa Prefecture, this province was established at the time of the TAIKA REFORM (645). During the Heian period 794–1185), a number of large estates (SHŌEN) came under the control of local magnates, around whom bands of warriors formed. These magnates and their followers played an important role in the founding of the Kamakura shogunate in 1192 by MINAMOTO NO YORITOMO. The shogunal government was situated at Kamakura in Sagami, and the province flourished as an economic and cultural center. During the succeeding Muromachi period (1333–1568), when the capital was removed to Kyōto, Kamakura became the administrative center for 10 eastern provinces, and Sagami continued to thrive. During the Sengoku (Warring States) period (1467–1568) the SENGOKU DAIMYŌ of the Go-Hōjō Family (see HŌJŌ FAMILY) established their headquarters at Odawara in Sagami. In the Edo period (1600–1868) most of the province came under the direct control of the shogunate.

Sagami Railway Co, Ltd 相模鉄道[株]

(Sagami Tetsudō). Private railway company. Incorporated in 1918. Its main business lines are rail transportation, bus transportation, and real estate. Sales for the fiscal year ending March 1991 totaled ¥125.0 billion (US $911.1 million), and capitalization stood at ¥27.4 billion (US $199.7 million) in the same year. Headquarters are in Yokohama.

Sagano 嵯峨野

District in the western part of the city of Kyōto. The river Katsuragawa separates this district from the hill ARASHIYAMA. It was a recreational area for Kyōto nobility and the imperial family, many of whom built villas here during the Heian period (794–1185). It flourished in the Edo period (1600–1868) as a collection center for lumber. Today Sagano is a tourist area; attractions include the temples Daikakuji, Tenryūji, and Seiryōji, as well as Hirosawa Pond.

Saeki Yūzō *Streetlight and Posters.* 1927. Oil on canvas. 65 × 100 cm. National Museum of Modern Art, Tōkyō.

Saganoseki 佐賀関[町]

Town in eastern Ōita Prefecture, Kyūshū; located at the tip of a peninsula that faces Shikoku across the BUNGO CHANNEL. From ancient times Saganoseki was an important stronghold at the entrance to the Inland Sea. In 1916 Japan's largest copper refinery was established here. Pop: 15,775.

Saga Prefecture 佐賀県

(Saga Ken). Located in northwestern Kyūshū and bordered by the Genkai Sea to the north, Fukuoka Prefecture to the east, ARIAKE SEA to the south, and Nagasaki Prefecture to the west. The western portion of the prefecture consists of low hills, with occasional basin areas. The SEFURI MOUNTAINS separate Saga from Fukuoka Prefecture to the northeast, and south of the mountains lies the broad Saga Plain, which fills most of the eastern portion of the prefecture. The climate is generally mild.

Formerly known as Hizen Province, Saga was ruled by various warlords until the Edo period (1600–1868), when the Nabeshima family took control over most of the area. The present name and boundaries were established in 1883, after the Meiji Restoration.

Saga developed in the modern period as an agricultural and coal-mining area, but many coal mines have been shut down. Agriculture is centered on rice production, with secondary crops including vegetables and mandarin oranges. Dairy farming is currently expanding. Fishing and pearl cultivation are major industries on the northern coast, and the Ariake Sea is famous for its *nori* (a type of seaweed) cultivation. Industrial development has been hampered by the area's remoteness from major economic and population centers, but in recent years food-processing, ceramics, and electrical machinery industries have emerged.

The heavily indented coast of the Genkai Sea is the location of many scenic areas, including one of Japan's largest coastal pine forests. It has been designated a quasi-national park. The cities of KARATSU in the north and ARITA in the south have long been known for their pottery (see ARITA WARE; KARATSU WARE). Area: 2,440 sq km (942 sq mi); pop: 877,851; capital: SAGA. Other major cities are Karatsu, IMARI, and TOSU.

Sagara Morio 相良守峯

(1895–1989). Scholar of German literature. Born in Yamagata Prefecture; graduated from Tōkyō University, where he taught from 1933 until his retirement. He helped found the Japanese Society for German Literature in 1947 and served as its chairman from 1947 to 1957. His most important works include *Doitsu chūsei jojishi kenkyū* (1948) and a translation of the *Nibelungen-*

Saga Prefecture Location and Prefectural Crest

Saichō The Buddhist monk who transmitted the teachings of the Tendai sect to Japan from China is shown seated in meditation in this detail of an 11th-century scroll.

sagisō Resembling egrets in flight, the flowers of this perennial herb bloom from late July to early August.

lied (1955). He translated many works of German literature into Japanese. He was awarded the Order of Culture in 1985.

Sagara Sōzō 相楽総三

(1839–68). *Samurai* and proimperial activist of the late Edo period (1600–1868). Born in Edo (now Tōkyō). In 1864 he joined Fujita Koshirō (1842–65) in an unsuccessful anti-shogunate rebellion in Mito (now part of Ibaraki Prefecture). With imperial approval he formed his own battalion, which he led toward Edo. The fickle imperial court declared Sagara's army illegitimate, and he was executed.

Saga Rebellion 佐賀の乱

(Saga no Ran). *Samurai* insurrection of 1874 led by ETŌ SHIMPEI and Shima Yoshitake (1822–74) in their native domain of Saga (now Saga Prefecture) against the Meiji government. Etō resigned as councillor (*sangi*) in 1873 to protest the government's refusal to launch a punitive expedition against Korea (see SEIKANRON). Etō then helped ITAGAKI TAISUKE to organize the AIKOKU KŌTŌ party and compose the Tosa Memorial, a sharp critique of government policies. In January 1874, frustrated by the government's rejection of these efforts, Etō returned to Saga to gather the necessary funds and followers. Of his 3,000 Saga supporters, two-thirds belonged to his group Seikantō advocating the invasion of Korea, while the other third belonged to a local group demanding a return to the feudal order. When the insurgents attacked a bank and government offices in Saga in February, Home Minister ŌKUBO TOSHIMICHI dispatched troops to suppress the rebellion. Etō and Shima were tried and executed two months later.

sagi → herons

sagisō 鷺草

Habenaria or *Pecteilis radiata*. Perennial herb of the family Orchidaceae that grows wild in sunny bogs in Honshū, Shikoku, and Kyūshū and is also cultivated as an ornamental. It grows from a corm 1 centimeter (0.4 in) in diameter. The leaves are alternate and broadly linear, with pointed tips. To-

ward August it produces a stalk bearing one to four pure white flowers, each about 3 centimeters (1.2 in) across. The flowers have a distinctive shape, resembling egrets on the wing, which explains the plant's name, *sagisō*, literally, "egret plant."

Sagoromo monogatari 狭衣物語

(Tale of Sagoromo). Work of prose fiction thought to have been written between 1069 and 1081; authorship uncertain, although generally attributed to Seji (d 1092), a lady-in-waiting to the imperial princess Baishi (1039–96). It tells the story of Sagoromo, a handsome but irresolute aristocrat, whose unrequited love for his cousin and adopted sister, Genji no Miya, causes him to vacillate between periods of melancholy, when he yearns to enter the priesthood, and passionate dalliances with a succession of charming ladies. The novel concludes with Sagoromo being made emperor by an oracular decree ascribed to the goddess Amaterasu Ōmikami. Strongly influenced by the Uji chapters of the TALE OF GENJI, it is noted for its intricate plot, fine prose, and graceful WAKA poems.

Sahogawa 佐保川

River in northern Nara Prefecture, central Honshū, originating in the Kasugayama Mountains and flowing through the city of Nara to join the YAMATOGAWA. Length: 15 km (9 mi).

saibara 催馬楽

Type of song widely sung at the imperial court during the Heian period (794–1185). Derived from folk songs, primarily of the Kyōto and Nara region, and set to GAGAKU melodies, *saibara* were sung to an accompaniment of reed pipes, KOTO, and BIWA. Their subject matter was the feelings of ordinary people, particularly love, expressed openly and directly. *Saibara* were commonly sung as songs of celebration at court gatherings; such scenes appear frequently in the TALE OF GENJI, which has the titles of *saibara* songs as several of its chapter headings. Toward the end of the Heian period, *saibara* were surpassed in popularity by the more contemporary popular songs known as *imayō* and virtually disappeared. See also KAGURA UTA.

Saichō 最澄

(767–822). Founder of the TENDAI SECT of Buddhism in Japan; he succeeded in winning institutional autonomy for the sect and altered the character of Buddhist monasticism by replacing the traditional precepts for monks with the simpler Mahāyāna bodhisattva precepts. Personal name Hirono. Born in Ōmi Province (now Shiga Prefecture), he began instruction in Buddhism at age 12; two years later, he took the clerical name Saichō when he received initial ordination at Nara. After final ordination in 785, he built himself a thatched hut on Mt. Hiei (HIEIZAN), northeast of the present-day city of Kyōto, intending a life of meditation and prayer. This hermitage later became the Tendai headquarters monastery of ENRYAKUJI. His decision to leave Nara was prompted by his dissatisfaction with the priests of the great temples who, in spite of their lofty philosophical ideals, were preoccupied with rituals performed for the protection of the state.

Sometime before 797, he began to study the texts of the Chinese Tiantai (T'ien-t'ai; J: Tendai) sect and lecture on its doctrines. Emperor KAMMU (r 781–806) supported Saichō's

new movement, probably as a counterweight to the influence of the Nara temples. Receiving permission in 802 to study under a Chinese Tiantai master, Saichō left for China in 804. After his return in 805, Kammu gave official recognition to the Tendai sect, stipulating that it include the practices of ESOTERIC BUDDHISM. However, the state-regulated system of ordination required that all novice monks go to Nara to be tested and to receive final ordination. Between 818 and 819 Saichō petitioned the court in three works, known collectively as the *Sange gakushō shiki* (Regulations for Student-Monks of Mt. Hiei), for permission to set up an independent ordination hall on Mt. Hiei. This proposal aroused strong opposition from the Nara monks, and the court withheld its reply. Seven days after Saichō's death in 822, the Tendai sect was granted the right to ordain its monks, thus establishing the institutional autonomy of the sect. In 866 Saichō was honored by the court with the posthumous title of Dengyō Daishi ("Great Teacher Who Transmits the Teachings"), the name by which he is best known in Japan.

Saidaiji 西大寺

The headquarters of the Shingon Ritsu sect of Buddhism, located in the city of Nara. Saidaiji ("West Great Temple") is said to have been built in 765 by order of Empress Shōtoku (see KŌKEN, EMPRESS) on a scale comparable to that of Nara's TŌDAIJI (East Great Temple). The priest EIZON (1201–90) made Saidaiji the chief monastery of his newly founded Shingon Ritsu sect. Many Buddhist texts edited in the monastery during the Muromachi period (1333–1568) survive as Saidaijihan ("Saidaiji editions"). Also here are early-Heian-period (794–1185) paintings of the Twelve Deva that have been declared National Treasures. Saidaiji is also known for Ōchamori, a tea ceremony, now performed in January, April, and October, in which very large bowls and whisks are used.

saifu 割符

(bill of exchange). A promissory note developed in the Kamakura (1185–1333) and Muromachi (1333–1568) periods as part of the KAEZENI system of payment. *Saifu* were originally used in lieu of the annual tax rice (NENGU) or its money equivalent that was paid by landed estates (SHŌEN) to their lords. Ordinary merchants also began to deal in *saifu*, and brokers called *saifuya* or *kaezeniya* appeared in major towns and business centers. The form and conditions of payment of these notes became standardized in the Edo period (1600–1868).

Saigawa 犀川

River in northern Nagano Prefecture, central Honshū. It originates at the confluence of the Azusagawa and Naraigawa in the city of Matsumoto and flows into the CHIKUMAGAWA in the city of Nagano. There are numerous dams and power plants along the course of the river. Length: 158 km (98 mi).

Saigawa 犀川

River in central Ishikawa Prefecture, central Honshū, originating in Daimon'yama, a mountain on the border of Toyama and Ishikawa prefectures, and flowing through the city of Kanazawa to enter the Sea of Japan. Length: 34 km (21 mi).

Saigoku risshi hen 西国立志編

(Self-Improvement in Western Nations). Japanese translation (1871) by NAKAMURA

MASANAO of Samuel Smiles's *Self-Help* (1859). *Saigoku risshi hen* was widely read; it came to be regarded as a guide for aspiring young men and exerted a profound influence during the early Meiji period (1868–1912).

Saigō Takamori   西郷隆盛

(1827–77). A leader in the overthrow of the Tokugawa shogunate and the establishment of the Meiji government in 1867–68. Born in the Satsuma domain (now Kagoshima Prefecture). For 10 years he served as a minor provincial official. He left for Edo (now Tōkyō) in 1854 to attend his lord SHIMAZU NARIAKIRA, who appointed Saigō as his principal agent for promoting closer ties between the shogunate and the imperial court (see MOVEMENT FOR UNION OF COURT AND SHOGUNATE).

National Career—Saigō's activities in Edo ended in 1858, when II NAOSUKE began purging those who encroached on shogunate prerogatives (see ANSEI PURGE). Nariakira died unexpectedly before he could be punished. Saigō escaped to Satsuma but was soon banished to the island of Amami Ōshima. He was recalled from exile in late 1861, only to be exiled again by SHIMAZU HISAMITSU. Hisamitsu pardoned Saigō in 1864 and sent him to Kyōto to take charge of domainal policy in national affairs.

As a commander of Satsuma troops in Kyōto, Saigō joined with *samurai* from the Aizu domain (now part of Fukushima Prefecture) against the Chōshū domain (now Yamaguchi Prefecture) extremists who had attacked the imperial gates in a struggle to regain their influence at court (see HAMAGURI GOMON INCIDENT). In August 1864 Saigō was one of the leaders of the expeditionary force assembled by the shogunate to chastise Chōshū, but he negotiated an agreement that ultimately paved the way for a SATSUMA-CHŌSHŪ ALLIANCE against the shogunate. When the shogunate attacked Chōshū a second time, in 1866, Satsuma maintained neutrality while Chōshū turned back shogunate troops on every front (see CHŌSHŪ EXPEDITIONS).

End of Shogunate Rule—In November 1867 the shōgun, TOKUGAWA YOSHINOBU, resigned, returning political power to the emperor. But Saigō's demand that the Tokugawa be expropriated forced the shogunate into military action. Saigō defeated the shogunal forces at Toba and Fushimi and then led an imperial-loyalist army toward Edo (see BOSHIN CIVIL WAR). At Edo, he negotiated with shogunate representative KATSU KAISHŪ the terms for a peaceful transfer of power to Emperor MEIJI (see MEIJI RESTORATION).

Although ŌKUBO TOSHIMICHI and others took the initiative in organizing the new Meiji government, Saigō's cooperation was essential for the success of such difficult programs as the reversion of *daimyō* territory to the emperor and the establishment of a conscript army. In 1871 the departure of the IWAKURA MISSION abroad left Saigō head of a caretaker government. However, in 1873 an argument erupted over the alleged insult of Japan by Korea (see SEIKANRON). Saigō obtained government approval for a personal diplomatic mission to Korea, but when the Iwakura mission returned, the decision was reversed, causing Saigō's resignation. He returned to Kagoshima with thousands of his former-samurai adherents.

Satsuma Rebellion—To provide these disaffected warriors with useful occupations,

Saigō and his friends established a network of military-oriented "private" schools called the Shigakkō; these soon came to dominate the Kagoshima government. Fearing a rebellion, the government dispatched a naval unit to remove weapons from the Kagoshima arsenal. Shigakkō students thwarted this move, and open conflict began in 1877. Though greatly dismayed by the action of his spirited "followers," Saigō resigned himself to leading a Satsuma army to Tōkyō to challenge the government (see SATSUMA REBELLION). Only after months of sporadic fighting and Saigō's suicide on 24 September 1877 did the rebellion end.

Although he ended his life as a rebel, his popularity soared, for many saw him as a protester against arbitrary government, while others admired him as a paragon of traditional virtues. Saigō was posthumously pardoned in 1891.

Saigō Tsugumichi   西郷従道

(1843–1902). Admiral and politician. Born in the Satsuma domain (now Kagoshima Prefecture). A younger brother of SAIGŌ TAKAMORI, a leader of the Meiji Restoration (1868), he took part in the BOSHIN CIVIL WAR. In 1869 he accompanied YAMAGATA ARITOMO to Europe to study military systems. Early in his military career he commanded the TAIWAN EXPEDITION OF 1874. In the SATSUMA REBELLION of 1877 he refused to side with his rebel brother and served instead as commander of the imperial guards. He served as navy minister as well as home minister in several cabinets and was later appointed to the PRIVY COUNCIL. Closely identified with the Satsuma-Chōshū clique (see HAMBATSU) that monopolized the government, he was known as a conservative. Together with SHINAGAWA YAJIRŌ he founded the KOKUMIN KYŌKAI, a progovernment political party, in 1892.

Saigusa Hiroto   三枝博音

(1892–1963). Philosopher. Born in Hiroshima Prefecture. Graduate of Tōkyō University. He made important contributions to the histories of philosophy, scientific thought, and technology. Beginning with studies on Kant, Hegel, and Dilthey, he gradually came to take a materialist position. Following study in Germany (1931–32), he established the Association for the Study of Materialism (Yuibutsuron Kenkyūkai) in 1932 with TOSAKA JUN and Oka Kunio (1890–1971). In 1946 Saigusa founded a private school, later known as Kamakura Academia. From 1952 he served on the faculty of Yokohama City University, later becoming its president. His major writings include *Miura Baien no tetsugaku* (1941), a study of the Edo-period (1600–1868) philosopher MIURA BAIEN; *Gijutsu no tetsugaku* (1951), on the philosophy of technology; and *Nihon no yuibutsuronsha* (1956), on several important Japanese materialists. His collected works are found in *Saigusa Hiroto chosakushū* (12 vols, 1972–73).

Saigyō   西行

(1118–90). WAKA poet and Buddhist priest of the SHINGON SECT. His lay name was Satō Norikiyo, and his official Buddhist name was En'i, but he was commonly known as Saigyō. The Japanese prototype of the poet-monk, Saigyō is famous for his semireclusive life, which combined Buddhist asceticism and a deep love of beauty.

The modern image of Saigyō was largely

Saigyō A portrait, painted by Kanō Tan'yū in the 17th century, of the 12th-century Buddhist priest who is one of Japan's most revered classical poets.

shaped by apocryphal accounts of his life and wanderings. Such medieval works as *Saigyō monogatari* (Tales of Saigyō) popularized a pseudobiographical, pietistic image of the man and poet, which has been perpetuated by modern enthusiasts. Saigyō was one of the most important poets of the late 12th century—poetically, an exceptionally brilliant age. He should probably be ranked with KAKINOMOTO NO HITOMARO and BASHŌ as one of Japan's foremost poets.

Life—He was born into a *samurai* family in Kyōto. In his younger years, Saigyō served as one of the palace guards of the retired emperor TOBA (r 1107–23) and later knew the former emperor SUTOKU (r 1123–42) as a friend and patron. He entered the priesthood at 22 and soon after composed a sequence of 100 poems whose strong autobiographical element already distinguished his characteristic stance from the more impersonal manner of the court poets. Among the important relationships Saigyō formed in this period was a friendship with the great poet FUJIWARA NO TOSHINARI (Shunzei).

His center of activities shifted from Kyōto to the relatively isolated Shingon Buddhist monastery on Mt. Kōya (Kōyasan). Saigyō's visit around 1147 (at age 29) to the remote province of Mutsu in northeastern Honshū was the first of a long series of walking tours to pilgrimage centers and scenic spots all over Japan, during which he composed many poems about his lonely existence and his aesthetic and emotional response to the unfolding scenes of nature. As he grew older, he grew in both poetic and priestly prestige. During the 1160s and 1170s, while generally remaining in residence on Mt. Kōya, he was in contact with powerful nobles and military leaders as well as with his old friend Shunzei, the latter's son FUJIWARA NO SADAIE (Teika), and other court poets.

In the decade preceding his death in 1190, Saigyō was surrounded by an admiring group of young Shintō priests of the Ise shrines and by others who sought poetic instruction from him. A record of his discourses on poetry was written down by one of his students. Known as *Saigyō shōnin danshō* (Notes on the Discourses of the Venerable Saigyō; alternative title *Saikō danshō*), it is the only existing account of Saigyō's critical views and comments on poetry.

Works—Saigyō's personal collection is entitled *Sankashū* (The Mountain Hermitage) and contains over 1,500 poems of the more than 2,000 attributed to him. *Kikigakishū* (Collection Written Down as Heard) and *Kikigaki zanshū* (Supplement to the Collection Written Down as Heard) are two small selections of Saigyō's poems that were rediscovered only in modern times. They are of uncertain date, but both may be considered supplements to the *Sankashū* because they contain no duplicates of its poems. The

Saigō Takamori Posthumous portrait of Saigō, a key figure in the Meiji Restoration who later led the last major rebellion against the modern centralized state he had helped to bring into being.

Saikai National Park
This maritime park includes the Minami Kujūkushima island chain, here seen from the city of Sasebo.

Ihon sankashū (Variant Sankashū), also known as *Saigyō hōshi kashū* and *Saigyō shō-nin kashū*, duplicates 428 of the poems in the main collection, supplemented by 16 poems from *Kikigakishū* and 2 from *Kikigaki zanshū*. In addition, the text contains 139 poems not found elsewhere. The text is thought to have been put together personally by Saigyō and to have been used as a source by the compilers of the SHIN KOKINSHŪ.

Saigyō's place in Japanese literary history is unique—perhaps comparable only to that of the great *haikai* poet Bashō, whom he profoundly influenced. The rich evocativeness and deep feeling, yet breathtaking simplicity, of his best poems are unmatched and were appreciated as much in his own time as by later generations.

Saigyō is preeminently a poet of SABI (lonely, austere beauty), the spirit of lyric melancholy, which was cultivated as an aesthetic ideal by the poets of his time. Some 262 of Saigyō's poems are included in imperial anthologies from the 6th, the *Shikashū* (ca 1151–54), through the 21st, the *Shin zoku kokinshū* (1439). The 8th imperial anthology, the great *Shin kokinshū* (ca 1205), includes 94 of Saigyō's poems, more than any other poet.

Saigyō-zakura 西行桜

(Saigyō's Cherry Blossoms). NŌ play by ZEAMI. It is classified as a *sambamme-mono* ("part-three play"). The cherry trees around the hut of the poet SAIGYŌ (the *waki* or subordinate character) in the Nishiyama district of Kyōto are in full bloom. As Saigyō peacefully contemplates the blossoms at dusk, the silence is suddenly broken by boisterous cherry-blossom viewers (other *waki*, and *tsure* or "companion" characters) from the city. Irritated, Saigyō composes and reads aloud a poem that censures the crowd-pleasing cherry blossoms. The spirit of the cherry trees then appears in the form of an old man (the *shite* or main character) who emerges from the trunk of a nearby cherry tree and tells Saigyō that it is the human heart, not the cherry blossom, that is at fault.

Saihōji 西芳寺

Temple in Ukyō Ward, Kyōto, belonging to the Tenryūji branch of the RINZAI SECT of Zen Buddhism. According to tradition, Saihōji was founded in the Tempyō era (729–749) by GYŌGI. KŪKAI, 9th-century founder of the Shingon sect, and HŌNEN, 12th-century founder of the Jōdo sect, are said to have lived here. Saihōji's affiliation with the Rinzai Zen sect dates from 1339, when the great Zen master MUSŌ SOSEKI took up residence in the temple. The Saihōji is known for its exquisite teahouse, the Shōnantei, and for its moss garden, from which comes the popular name of the temple, Kokedera (Moss Temple).

Saiiki monogatari 西域物語

(Tales of the West). Also known as *Seiiki monogatari*. Three-volume tract on government by the political economist HONDA TOSHIAKI; completed in 1798. The author introduces Western customs and geography, and, basing his position on what might be called a Malthusian theory of population, he advocates foreign trade and colonization, especially of EZO (now Hokkaidō), to alleviate shogunate financial difficulties and the misery of the peasants. His other important work, *Keisei hisaku* (1798, A Secret Plan for Governing the Country), advanced similar mercantilist views.

saijiki 歳時記

Also known as *kiyose*. Glossaries of words with seasonal connotations (KIGO) used in the writing of HAIKU; organized in four seasonal sections with an additional section for the New Year season. In many cases the words are accompanied by definitions and sample poems. *Saijiki* was first employed as a specific term of reference for such glossaries by Kyokutei BAKIN in *Haikai saijiki* (1803). Initially *saijiki* were appended to textbooks on the compositional conventions of RENGA (linked verse), but early in the Edo period (1600–1868) they were introduced as a feature of handbooks published for the specific use of haiku poets. First among these was *Hanahigusa* (ca 1636), assembled by NONOGUCHI RYŪHO, which was followed by MATSUE SHIGEYORI's *Kefukigusa* (1645), Saitō Tokugen's (1559–1647) *Haikai shogaku shō* (1641), and Kitamura Kigin's (1624–1705) *Yama no i* (1648). The most complete premodern compilation, Rantei Seiran's (dates unknown) *Zōho kaisei haikai saijiki shiorigusa* (1851), categorized over 3,420 seasonal words. During the modern era revised compilations of *saijiki* have regularly appeared, introducing into the vocabulary of haiku new seasonal words that reflect the culture of the time of their publication.

Saijō 西条[市]

City in eastern Ehime Prefecture, Shikoku, on the Inland Sea. Saijō developed as a castle town in the Edo period (1600–1868). Electrical-machinery, paper-making, textile, and dyeing industries utilize its abundant underground water supply. *Nori* (a seaweed) is cultivated in coastal areas. Saijō is the base camp for climbing ISHIZUCHISAN (1,982 m; 6,503 ft), Shikoku's highest peak. Pop: 56,821.

Saijō Yaso 西条八十

(1892–1970). Poet. Born in Tōkyō. Graduate of Waseda University. His first collection of poems was *Sakin* (1919, Gold Dust). In the 1920s he began writing for *Akai tori* (Red Bird), the influential children's magazine begun by SUZUKI MIEKICHI, and with KITAHARA HAKUSHŪ and NOGUCHI UJŌ became a major contributor of children's song lyrics. He studied in France from 1924 to 1926, where he associated with French symbolist poets, becoming friends with Valéry and writing symbolist poems himself. From the 1930s, and particularly in his later years, he wrote the lyrics of numerous popular songs for recording companies. Another poetry collection is *Rōningyō* (1922, Wax Doll).

Saikai National Park 西海国立公園

(Saikai Kokuritsu Kōen). Situated in northwestern Kyūshū, in Nagasaki Prefecture. This maritime park consists of coastal regions of the Kita Matsuura Peninsula close to the city of SASEBO, as well as hundreds of small islands lying off the western coast of Kyūshū. The park's mild climate has resulted in subtropical vegetation that is rare in Japan. Both Kujūkushima (literally, "Ninety-Nine Islands"), which comprises over 200 small islands lying to the west, and hilly HIRADOSHIMA, still further west, are noted for their heavily indented coastlines with numerous small bays and islets. Lying to the far west are the GOTŌ ISLANDS.

The most characteristic trees in the park are fig trees and tree ferns (*onihego*). The offshore waters provide rich fishing grounds. Within the park there are numerous historical sites related to trade with the Dutch and to Christianity. The city of HIRADO, on the northern tip of Hiradoshima, was the first Japanese port opened to European trading vessels. Area: 247 sq km (95 sq mi).

Saikaku 西鶴

(1642–93). Poet and writer of popular fiction whose novels and stories are now ranked among the classics of Japanese literature. Also known as Ihara Saikaku. Saikaku is a literary name adopted in his early thirties; before that he used the name Ihara Kakuei; his original name is said to have been Hirayama Tōgo. He was born in Ōsaka. After the death of his young wife in 1675 he devoted himself to his flourishing career as a poet of *haikai* (comic linked verse; see HAIKU), traveling widely and continuing to frequent theaters and pleasure quarters. At 40, Saikaku published his first work of prose fiction, KŌSHOKU ICHIDAI OTOKO (1682; tr *The Life of an Amorous Man*, 1964). Its great success made him a hardworking professional writer, the author of some two dozen books during the last decade of his life.

Early Works—Saikaku began writing *haikai* in his teens and soon became an established teacher and critic (*tenja*). In 1673 he participated in a 12-day mass poetry gathering held at Ōsaka's Ikutama Shrine, where 156 poets produced a grand total of 10,000 verses. From these Saikaku edited a selection of 300, with a preface in which he disparaged the *haikai* orthodoxy of the school of MATSUNAGA TEITOKU. Under the nominal leadership of NISHIYAMA SŌIN, Saikaku and his friends went far beyond their master in creating the fresh new style of Sōin's DANRIN SCHOOL. Saikaku himself carried its narrative and descriptive tendencies, its colloquial freedom, and its spontaneity farthest of all.

In 1677 Saikaku gave the first marathon performance of what he proudly called "arrow-counting" (*yakazu*) *haikai* in emulation of a kind of archery endurance contest then popular among *samurai*. On this occasion, Saikaku extemporized a series of 1,600 verses in a day and a night; in 1680 he managed to compose 4,000 verses in a similar 24-hour session. In 1684 he outdid his own record by improvising the astounding number of 23,500 verses in 24 hours, a performance attested to by witnesses though too rapid for the scribes to do more than tally the number of verses.

Later Works—*Kōshoku ichidai otoko*, published in 1682, with illustrations by Saikaku himself, was the brilliant beginning of a genre of fiction later to be defined by his works and called UKIYO-ZŌSHI. Besides reflecting *haikai* influence in its kaleidoscopic poetic style, *Ichidai otoko* tells its picaresque tale with the formal balance and wayward

Saijō Yaso This poet studied in France and associated with French symbolist poets, including Valéry.

irreverence of a linked-verse sequence; its division into 54 chapters implies a burlesque parallel to the classic *Genji monogatari* (TALE OF GENJI), and Saikaku's ridiculously amorous hero Yonosuke is clearly a modern-day Prince Genji. Two years later Saikaku published *Shoen.ōkagami* (The Great Mirror of the Beauties), subtitled *Kōshoku nidai otoko* (Son of the Amorous Man). But Saikaku confines his "sequel" to the barest frame story, setting off a further collection of comic anecdotes of the pleasure quarters. The following year he produced *Saikaku shokokubanashi* (Saikaku's Stories from the Provinces), presumably gathered in the course of his travels but always deftly recast.

Saikaku's fascination with the theater, and with the scandalous incidents that were the source of many of its plays, was also evident in *Kōshoku gonin onna* (tr *Five Women Who Loved Love*, 1956), which appeared in 1686. Superficially more dramatic than his other works, these five masterly tales of adultery and start-crossed love were based on actual events. Pathos and farce are interwoven within each tale as Saikaku shifts from one mood to another, exploring his great theme of the uncertainty of life. Another major work of the same year is *Kōshoku ichidai onna* (tr *The Life of an Amorous Woman*, 1963). Like Yonosuke in her appetite for sex, this nameless heroine pursues an equally active career but along a steep downward path. She tells her own improbable story, a bizarre confession that amounts to a burlesque of earlier Buddhist confessional literature. Her Boccaccian account of a stay at a monastery is merely one highlight of her harlot's progress, which ends with a dubious conversion to pious retirement.

Saikaku also wrote stories about samurai. Whether he shared the ideals praised in such important collections of stories as *Budō denraiki* (1687, Traditions of the Way of Samurai) and *Buke giri monogatari* (1688, Tales of Samurai Honor) remains unclear. Saikaku tells his stories from the viewpoint of a detached observer, but his samurai are usually paragons of virtue who seem immune to satrical attack. Not so the merchants caricatured in *Nippon eitaigura* (1688; tr *The Japanese Family Storehouse*, 1959), whose success or failure can be succinctly conveyed in an entertaining anecdotal style. The wit seems even greater in SEKEN MUNESAN'YŌ (1692; tr *Worldly Mental Calculations*, 1976).

Saikaku continued his furious rate of production through 1688 with the aid of apprentices. He continued to publish until his death in 1693. Five of Saikaku's books were published posthumously. All are uneven works, edited and no doubt partly written by his faithful disciple HŌJŌ DANSUI.

Saiki　　　　　　　　　佐伯[市]

City in southeastern Ōita Prefecture, Kyūshū, on the Bungo Channel. It developed as a castle town in the Edo period (1600–1868). There are pulp-manufacturing, cement, and lumber industries. Pop: 52,323.

Saikontan　　　　　　　菜根譚

(Vegetable-Root Discourses). Japanese translation of the Chinese collection of popular philosophical sayings *Caigen tan* (*Ts'ai-ken t'an*) by Hong Yingming (Hung Ying-ming), who was active during the Wanli era (1573–1620) of the Ming dynasty. The work is in two chapters, containing 222 (225 in some versions) and 134 aphorisms respectively. A thoroughgoing eclectic, Hong drew on Con-

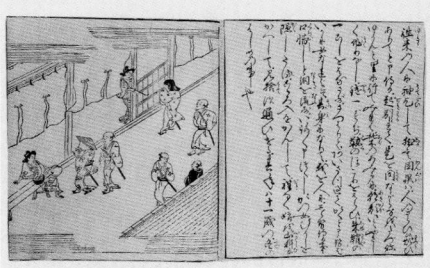

fucian, Taoist, and Buddhist (especially Zen) sources. Since its first Japanese edition (1822) it has enjoyed enormous popularity as a convenient epitome of traditional Chinese wisdom. More than 40 annotated editions have appeared in this century alone.

Sai, Lake　→ Fuji Five Lakes

Saimei, Empress　　　斉明天皇

(594–661; Saimei Tennō). Also known as Empress Kōgyoku. The 35th and 37th sovereign (*tennō*) in the traditional count (which includes several legendary emperors); official consort of Emperor Jomei; mother of emperors TENJI and TEMMU. She reigned as Kōgyoku from 642 to 645, and as Saimei from 655 to 661.

St. Andrew's University
　　　　　　　　　　　桃山学院大学

(Momoyama Gakuin Daigaku). A coeducational private university located in the city of Sakai, Ōsaka Prefecture. The university traces its origins to an English-language school for boys founded by the Church Missionary Society of England in 1884. The university itself was established in 1959 in commemoration of the centennial of the Anglican Mission in Japan. It maintains faculties of economics, business administration, sociology, and letters. Enrollment in 1988 was 5,818.

St. Petersburg, Treaty of
　　　　　　　　　樺太千島交換条約

(Karafuto-Chishima Kōkan Jōyaku; literally, "Sakhalin–Kuril Islands Exchange Treaty"). Treaty concluded on 7 May 1875 between Russia and Japan. In earlier treaties, the Kuril Islands from Iturup (J: Etorofu) south had been designated Japanese, and the islands from Urup (J: Uruppu) north, Russian; the status of Sakhalin (J: Karafuto) had been left open. After a year of negotiations between ENOMOTO TAKEAKI and the tsarist government, a new treaty was signed at St. Petersburg. Japan gave up claims to Sakhalin in exchange for the Kurils, Japanese residents of Sakhalin were compensated for their property, and most-favored-nation treatment for Japanese fishing boats in the Sea of Okhotsk, with 10 years' free use of Russian ports in the area, was granted. See also RUSSIA AND JAPAN.

Saionji family　　　　　西園寺家

(Saionjike). Family of the Kan'in house of the Northern Branch (Hokke) of the FUJIWARA FAMILY; descended from the courtier Fujiwara no Michisue (1089–1128). As one of the original seven families of the Seiga group (Seigake; see PEERAGE), the Saionji ranked just below the Five Regents' Houses (GOSEKKE). Michisue's great-grandson SAIONJI KINTSUNE, who married a niece of MINAMOTO NO YORITOMO, was grand minister of state (*dajō daijin*) after the JŌKYŪ DISTURBANCE (1221) and enjoyed more power than the imperial regent (KAMPAKU). The family name comes from his villa in northwest Kyōto. The Saionji were virtually exterminated during the KEMMU RESTORATION (1333–36),

when Saionji Kimmune (1310–35) plotted with the HŌJŌ FAMILY, but the line was later revived. After the Meiji Restoration (1868), the Saionji were given the rank of prince (*kōshaku*). SAIONJI KIMMOCHI was twice prime minister (1906–08; 1911–12) and the most influential of the elder statesmen (GENRŌ) before World War II.

Saionji Kimmochi　　　西園寺公望

(1849–1940). Statesman and prime minister (1906–08; 1911–12). One of the most influential figures of modern Japan. Born in Kyōto, the second son of the court noble Tokudaiji Kin'ito (1821–83), he was adopted at the age of two into the SAIONJI FAMILY. Both his own and adopted families are branches of the ancient and influential FUJIWARA FAMILY.

In 1867, at age 18, Saionji was appointed *san'yo* (junior councillor), and in 1868, during the BOSHIN CIVIL WAR accompanying the MEIJI RESTORATION, he took part in various battles as an imperial representative. Saionji then went to France, where he studied European institutions and law between 1871 and 1880. In 1881 he founded Meiji Hōritsu Gakkō (Meiji Law School, later MEIJI UNIVERSITY) and was made president of the antigovernment newspaper *Tōyō jiyū shimbun* (Oriental Free Press) but resigned under imperial order. In 1882 Saionji accompanied the constitutional investigations group of ITŌ HIROBUMI to Europe. After this trip, he was appointed minister to Austria and then Germany.

After his return to Japan, Saionji became a member of the PRIVY COUNCIL and served as vice-president of the HOUSE OF PEERS. As minister of education in Itō's second and third cabinets (1892–96 and 1898), he advocated and worked for an international standard for Japanese education. When the RIKKEN SEIYŪKAI political party was formed in 1900, Saionji was a member of the organizing committee. In 1900 Saionji succeeded Itō as president of the Privy Council, and in 1903 he became president of the Seiyūkai.

From 1901 until 1913, KATSURA TARŌ and Saionji alternated as prime minister. In 1906 Saionji formed his first cabinet and in 1911 his second, which was brought down by the army in 1912. On Saionji's resignation, the emperor accorded him treatment as a GENRŌ (elder statesman). In 1918 HARA TAKASHI became prime minister, with Saionji's support. Saionji was appointed Japanese plenipotentiary to the Paris Peace Conference (see VERSAILLES, TREATY OF) and was raised in the peerage from marquis to prince.

As *genrō*, with his major function to nominate prime ministers, Saionji favored the political parties only when he thought they could form effective governments and accordingly recommended nonparty governments in 1913, 1923, and 1924. After the outbreak of promilitarist violence in the MAY

Saitobaru tomb cluster An aerial view of the cluster area. Several of the keyhole-shaped mounds can be seen on the hill in the foreground.

Saitama Prefecture Location and Prefectural Crest

Saitō Hideo A cellist and conductor, Saitō was largely responsible for the development of the Tōhō Gakuen School of Music, which has trained many of Japan's great classical musicians in the period since World War II.

15TH INCIDENT of 1932, Saionji again chose "neutral" nonparty cabinets, attempting to restrain the military's growing power. Saionji's last exercise of a significant role in recommending a prime minister was in 1937, when he supported General HAYASHI SENJŪRŌ. Saionji died in 1940 at the age of 91.

In the 1930s he was doubtless the most liberal of the emperor's close advisers, but he quickly accepted defeat whenever the emperor's private desires for peace and moderation seemed impractical or risky. However, Saionji favored harmonious relations with Britain and America, and by mediating among the various political leaders, so often at odds, he was able to exert some influence for moderation.

Saionji Kintsune   西園寺公経

(1171–1244). Court noble of the Kamakura period (1185–1333). Born in Kyōto. A scion of the FUJIWARA FAMILY, he was married to a niece of MINAMOTO NO YORITOMO. In 1221 he was arrested by proimperial forces for warning the Kamakura shogunate of a planned coup (see JŌKYŪ DISTURBANCE). Later his grandson Kujō Yoritsune (1218–56) was named fourth Kamakura shōgun, and Kintsune was promoted to grand minister of state (*dajō daijin*); he created for himself the post of shogunal liaison (Kantō *mōshitsugi*) and exercised great political power. In 1225 Kintsune built Saionji temple, from which he derived the family name.

Saison Foundation   セゾン文化財団

(Sezon Bunka Zaidan). A foundation established in 1987 by TSUTSUMI SEIJI, chairman of the Saison Corporation. The foundation's objective is support of the arts and the promotion of international cultural exchange. It provides grants and awards to persons engaged in the arts and supports performances and exhibitions. In 1989 total assets were ¥9.3 billion (US $67.4 million). Headquarters are in Tōkyō.

Saitama Prefecture   埼玉県

(Saitama Ken). Located in central Honshū and bounded on the north by Gumma and Tochigi prefectures, on the east by Ibaraki and Chiba prefectures, on the south by Tōkyō, and on the west by Yamanashi and Nagano prefectures. Situated in the northern portion of the KANTŌ PLAIN, Saitama is among the least mountainous of Japan's prefectures, with only a few high peaks belonging to the KANTŌ MOUNTAINS in the west. The flat eastern

section is traversed by several rivers, including the TONEGAWA, the third longest in Japan, and the ARAKAWA. The climate is distinguished by hot, rainy summers and cool, dry winters.

Numerous remains from the Jōmon (ca 10,000 BC–ca 300 BC) and Yayoi (ca 300 BC–ca AD 300) periods have been excavated in the prefecture. After the Taika Reform in 645 the area was designated part of Musashi Province, and from the Heian period (794–1185) on, it fell under the control of contending warlords. In the Edo period (1600–1868) several districts came under the direct control of the Tokugawa shogunate, which developed several highways to link Edo (now Tōkyō) with the provinces of northern and central Honshū. The present boundaries and name were established in 1876.

Saitama remained predominantly agricultural until relatively recently, with major crops including rice and vegetables. Livestock breeding, mostly for the Tōkyō market, is active, and industries, including machinery, food processing, chemicals, steel, and nonferrous metals, are growing rapidly. The eastern area has taken on the characteristics of a residential suburb of Tōkyō, with a rapidly expanding population.

Portions of CHICHIBU-TAMA NATIONAL PARK lie within Saitama and attract hikers and campers from the nearby Tōkyō-Yokohama area. Area: 3,799 sq km (1,467 sq mi); pop: 6,405,319; capital: URAWA. Other major cities include KAWAGUCHI, ŌMIYA, KAWAGOE, and TOKOROZAWA.

Saito   西都〔市〕

City in central Miyazaki Prefecture, Kyūshū. Principal activities are farming and forestry. Main agricultural products are green peppers and sweet potatoes. It is becoming a residential suburb of nearby Miyazaki. The SAITOBARU TOMB CLUSTER, dating from the Kofun period (ca 300–710), is one of the largest of its kind in Japan. Pop: 37,218.

Saitobaru tomb cluster

西都原古墳群

(Saitobaru *kofungun*). A group of 311 late 5th- and 6th-century mounded tombs (KOFUN) located on the Saitobaru Plateau overlooking the river Hitotsusegawa in the city of Saito, Miyazaki Prefecture. Most of the mounds are round (278), some are keyhole shaped (32), and one is square. Thirty-one of these tombs were excavated between 1912 and 1917 by the Imperial Household Agency, the Tōkyō Imperial Museum, Tōkyō University, and Kyōto University. Weapons, armor, horse trappings (see HORSE TRAPPINGS, ANCIENT), and unusual HANIWA funerary sculptures were recovered.

Saitō Dōsan   斎藤道三

(1494?–1556). Also known as Saitō Toshimasa. *Daimyō* of the Sengoku period (1467–1568); considered an example of GEKOKUJŌ ("those below overthrowing their superiors"). Dōsan rose from the status of rear vassal of Toki Yorinari (1502–82)—SHUGO (military governor) of Mino Province (now part of Gifu Prefecture)—to overlordship of that province. Later chronicles describe Dōsan as a renegade Buddhist priest turned oil peddler who gained entry into a Mino *samurai* household, ruthlessly exterminated his benefactors, overthrew the Toki, and set himself up as daimyō. These chronicles are not trustworthy; however, it is clear that Dōsan's road to power was

paved with murders, including that of Toki Yorinari's son Jirō; in 1542 he forced Yorinari to flee Mino and seek the protection of Oda Nobuhide (1510–51). Dōsan married his daughter to Nobuhide's son, the future hegemon ODA NOBUNAGA, in 1548. When Dōsan's son Yoshitatsu (1527–61) turned against him in 1555, few provincial barons (KOKUJIN) supported Dōsan, and he was killed in 1556.

Saitō Eishirō   斎藤英四郎

(1911–). Businessman; chairman of NIPPON STEEL CORPORATION (1981–87). Born in Niigata Prefecture. After graduating from Tōkyō University in 1935, he joined Mitsubishi Mining Co, and in 1941 he moved to Nippon Steel Co (now Nippon Steel Corporation). He became its president in 1977, contributing to the development of the steel industry during a period of low economic growth. He served as president of the International Iron and Steel Institute (1977–79) and of the Japan Iron and Steel Federation (1979–84) and as chairman of KEIDANREN (Federation of Economic Organizations; 1986–90).

Saitō Gesshin   斎藤月岑

(1804–78). Writer. Born in Edo (now Tōkyō). He was a student of Chinese classics, KOKUGAKU (National Learning), and painting. He completed *Edo meisho zue*, a 20-volume gazetteer about Edo, which had been started by his grandfather and continued by his father; as well as *Seikyoku ruisan*, a history of popular songs of the Edo period (1600–1868); and *Bukō nempyō*, a chronicle dealing with everyday life in Edo.

Saitō Hideo   斎藤秀雄

(1902–74). Cellist, conductor, and music educator. Born in Tōkyō. He studied cello at the Leipzig Conservatory from 1923 to 1927 and at the Berlin Academy of Music from 1930 to 1932. He played first cello for what is now the NHK Symphony Orchestra from 1927 to 1941. In 1948 he started his "Music Classroom for Children," which grew over the years into TŌHŌ GAKUEN SCHOOL OF MUSIC, fostering such budding musicians as conductor OZAWA SEIJI and cellist Tsutsumi Tsuyoshi (b 1942). In 1984, Ozawa gathered together a group of Saitō's former pupils to form the Saitō Memorial Orchestra.

Saitō Hiroshi   斎藤博

(1886–1939). Diplomat; ambassador to the United States (1934–39) during the critical years immediately preceding World War II. Born in Niigata Prefecture. A graduate of Tōkyō University, Saitō began his diplomatic career in 1910. He served as consul general in New York (1923–28), Foreign Office spokesman (1929), delegate to the LONDON NAVAL CONFERENCES of 1930, and minister to The Hague (1933). Saitō was a staunch advocate of amity with the democratic nations at a time when rising right-wing political forces in Japan were working toward alliance with Nazi Germany and Fascist Italy. In 1934 he was sent as ambassador to the United States in an attempt to improve Japanese-US relations, which had begun to deteriorate after the MANCHURIAN INCIDENT of September 1931. He died in Washington and his ashes were returned to Japan on board the US Navy cruiser *Astoria*, with full honors, by order of President Franklin D. Roosevelt in appreciation of Saitō's courageous commitment to peace. A great lover of literature, Saitō translated English poetry in a posthumously published collection called *Ishokurin* (1948, The Transplanted Forest).

Saitō Makoto 斎藤実

(1858–1936). Navy admiral and prime minister (1932–34). Born in what is now Iwate Prefecture, he was a graduate of the Naval Academy. Saitō served as naval vice-minister during the RUSSO-JAPANESE WAR of 1904–05. As navy minister from 1906 to 1914, he worked for expansion and modernization of the navy and in 1912 was promoted to admiral. Appointed governor-general of Korea (1919–27) following the SAMIL INDEPENDENCE MOVEMENT there, he inaugurated a moderate and less exploitative period of Japanese rule. In 1932 Saitō was named prime minister after the assassination of Prime Minister INUKAI TSUYOSHI in the MAY 15TH INCIDENT. In defiance of world opinion, his government formally recognized the puppet state of MANCHUKUO in Japanese-occupied Manchuria and withdrew from the League of Nations. The Saitō cabinet resigned in July 1934, following the TEIJIN INCIDENT, a corruption scandal in which high officials were implicated. In 1935 he was named land keeper of the privy seal (NAIDAI-JIN), but his policies were considered too conciliatory toward Western nations by ultranationalists, and he was assassinated by army officers in the FEBRUARY 26TH INCIDENT of 1936.

Saitō Mokichi 斎藤茂吉

(1882–1953). Psychiatrist, TANKA poet, critic, and essayist. Saitō was born Moriya Mokichi, the third son in a farming family in Yamagata Prefecture. In 1896 he went to live in Tōkyō with a relative, Saitō Kiichi, who did not have a son. Later he was adopted by Saitō in order to continue the family line and the practice of medicine. While in a premedical program, Saitō began writing *tanka*. In this he was inspired by MASAOKA SHIKI, a *tanka* reformer who advocated precise observation. Saitō published his *tanka* in *Ashibi*, a magazine edited by Shiki's follower, ITŌ SACHIO. Before he graduated from Tōkyō University Medical School in 1910, he had been recognized as a promising poet. Saitō pursued a dual career in medicine and literature. While working as a doctor at a psychiatric institution, he also served on the editorial staff of a new *tanka* poetry magazine, ARARAGI. In 1913 he published his first collection of *tanka* poems, titled *Shakkō* (Red Radiance).

In 1917 Saitō became a professor of psychiatry at a medical school in Nagasaki. Although he was sickly in those years, he managed to publish *Aratama* (1921), his second collection of *tanka* and important critical essays. In 1921 he was sent by the government to Germany and Austria to further his study of amnesia. While returning to Japan in 1925, he learned of the destruction by fire of his foster father's hospital. Back in Japan, he helped to rebuild the hospital and soon became its director; at the same time he was also an energetic poet, argumentative critic, and skillful editor of *Araragi*. He was instrumental in reviving the long tradition of *tanka* as a major genre in literature. Before World War II began, he completed a number of books, including his critical work on the great MAN'YŌSHŪ poet KAKINOMOTO NO HITO-MARO in five volumes (1934–40, *Kakinomoto Hitomaro*), which is still considered a standard reference source. During the war he wrote a considerable number of *tanka* in support of the war effort. He was awarded the Order of Culture in 1951. He was the father of the novelist KITA MORIO.

Saitō Ryokuu 斎藤緑雨

(1867–1904). Novelist and essayist. Real name Saitō Masaru. Other pen name Shōjiki Shōdayū. Born in Ise Province (now part of Mie Prefecture). In the 1890s, he wrote satirical essays and parodies of contemporary writers for a newspaper. Once established as an eccentric critic, he went on to write fiction such as *Abura jigoku* (1891, Hell of Boiling Oil) and "Kakurembo" (1891, Hide and Seek). Imitating the farcical style of the early 19th century (see GESAKU), he wrote scathing criticisms of contemporary society. His principal work is *Amagaeru* (1897), a collection of critical essays.

Saitō Sanemori 斎藤実盛

(?–1183). Warrior who fought for the Taira during the TAIRA-MINAMOTO WAR (1180–85), although having earlier served MINAMOTO NO YOSHITOMO. He was killed in battle against Yoshitomo's nephew MINAMOTO NO YO-SHINAKA. The HEIKE MONOGATARI relates that when Sanemori's head was presented to Yoshinaka it could not be identified. The hair was black, whereas Sanemori had had white hair. It was discovered that Sanemori had dyed his hair lest he be thought too old to fight. Depending on the source of information, Sanemori was either 57 or over 60 at his death.

Saitō Setsudō 斎藤拙堂

(1797–1865). Confucian scholar and long-time headmaster of the Yūzōkan, the school of the Tsu domain (now part of Mie Prefecture); also known as Saitō Tekkan. Born in Edo (now Tōkyō), he studied under Koga Seiri (1750–1817) at the SHŌHEIKŌ. In 1820 Saitō was appointed lecturer at the Yūzōkan, becoming its headmaster in 1844 and introducing WESTERN LEARNING into its curriculum.

Saji Keizō 佐治敬三

(1919–). Businessman. Born in Ōsaka, the second son of TORII SHINJIRŌ, the founder of Torii Shōten (later Kotobukiya, Ltd; now SUNTORY, LTD). After graduating from Ōsaka University, Saji joined the company in 1945 and was its president from 1961 to 1990. Saji started mass production and sales of Torys brand whiskey in 1950 and was instrumental in bringing about a whiskey boom in Japan. In 1963 the company entered the beer market through a tie-up with a Danish brewer. A member of the Kansai Association of Corporate Executives (Kansai Keizai Dōyūkai) since 1972, Saji became chairman of the Ōsaka Chamber of Commerce (Ōsaka Shōkō Kaigisho) in 1985. He became chairman of Suntory, Ltd, in 1990. Saji established the SUNTORY MUSEUM OF ART (1961) and the Suntory Music Foundation (1969) in Tōkyō.

Sakado 坂戸[市]

City in southern Saitama Prefecture, central Honshū. Because of the city's proximity to Tōkyō, many industrial plants and housing complexes have been built here recently. Pop: 95,740.

Sakagami Hiroshi 坂上弘

(1936–). Author. Born in Tōkyō; graduate of Keiō University. He was a nominee for the Akutagawa Prize with his short story "Musuko to koibito" (1955, A Son and a Lover). Other works include "Aru aki no dekigoto" (1959, It Happened One Autumn) and *Hajime no ai* (1980, First Love). His works concentrate on urban, middle-class domestic scenes.

Sakaguchi Ango 坂口安吾

(1906–55). Writer known mainly for his short stories and essays. Real name Sakaguchi Heigo. Along with his contemporaries DAZAI OSAMU and ODA SAKUNOSUKE, he was among the first serious authors in Japan to emerge as a popular cultural figure.

Ango was born in the city of Niigata. After failing in his third year at Niigata Middle School, he was sent by his family to Tōkyō, where he entered Tōyō University in 1926 and began the study of Sanskrit, Pali, and Tibetan in order to read Buddhist scriptures. He also studied French at the Tōkyō Athénée Français.

Among his most notable early works were the stories "Kaze hakase" (1931, Doctor Wind), an imaginative farce, and "Kurodani Mura" (1931, Kurodani Village), a more serious work juxtaposing the Buddhist search for enlightenment with the power of carnal desires. These two stories received enthusiastic praise from such prominent authors as SHIMAZAKI TŌSON and MAKINO SHIN'ICHI, and Ango suddenly found himself regarded as a promising new voice in the Japanese literary world. This recognition seems to have come too soon for his own good, and he lapsed into a long period marked by literary frustration and personal problems.

Japan's defeat in 1945 brought a new age of free expression and an uneasy groping for new values to replace those shattered by the national collapse. These conditions proved ideal for Ango. In stories such as "Hakuchi" (1946; tr "The Idiot," 1962) and essays such as "Darakuron"(1946, On Falling), he urged the Japanese people to abandon the discredited, restrictive customs of the past and seek their salvation in a rediscovery of the basics of human nature.

The years 1946 to 1949 stand out as the peak period of Ango's career. While continuing to publish first-rate serious fiction such as "Sakura no mori no mankai no shita" (1947, Beneath the Blossoming Cherry Trees), the persistent demands of popularity caused him to turn to mystery stories, travelogues, historical tales, and journalism. This pressure led him into a heavy reliance on alcohol and drugs, causing the gradual collapse of his personal life, but his excesses only served to make him a greater celebrity in the public eye. After a breakdown in 1949, his final years were more tranquil. Although he failed to regain the immense popularity he had enjoyed in the immediate postwar years, his role as one of the principal shapers of postwar Japanese literature has won him a permanent place in literary history, and the originality and boldness of his best writing have sparked a revival of interest in his work in recent years.

Saitō Mokichi Shown here in a 1950 photograph, Saitō, trained as a psychiatrist, was one of the greatest *tanka* poets of the 20th century.

Sakaguchi Ango This writer was one of the seminal figures in Japanese literature in the period immediately after World War II.

Sakaguchi Kin'ichirō 坂口謹一郎

(1897–). Microbiologist. Born in Niigata Prefecture. Graduate of the Department of Agricultural Chemistry at Tōkyō University, he was later a professor at that university and the first director of its Institute of Applied Microbiology. He contributed to the study of the rice-fermenting fungus *Aspergillus oryzae* (J: *kōji*) and other fermentative microorganisms and developed procedures for manufacturing the nucleic-acid artificial flavors inosinic acid and guanylic acid. Apart from academic works, he published essays on alcoholic beverages as well as a volume of poetry, *Hakkō* (Fermentation). He

received the Japan Academy Prize in 1950 and in 1967 was awarded the Order of Culture.

Sakai 堺[市]

Important port and commercial city of the mid-14th to mid-17th century on the eastern end of the Inland Sea; now a city within Ōsaka Prefecture. Sakai grew up haphazardly, serving as a way station for pilgrims and as a center for transshipment of estate rents and other goods. Its fine harbor made it a major port.

Sakai reached the peak of its premodern development in the mid-1500s, when its powerful merchants made it a center of trade with China, Korea, the Ryūkyū Islands, and, later, with Western nations. Besides trade its major industries included ironwork, printing, brewing, and the production of damask and bleached cotton. Sakai also gave rise to many RENGA poets; the tea-ceremony master SEN NO RIKYŪ lived here. Sakai's merchants governed the city unofficially through the EGŌSHŪ council. Despite defensive towers and a moat, sponsored by the merchants, the city was conquered by ODA NOBUNAGA in 1569. Many Sakai craftsmen moved to Ōsaka when TOYOTOMI HIDEYOSHI made that city his base, but Sakai remained prosperous during the early years of the Tokugawa shogunate (1603–1867), having been granted rights to the raw-silk trade (ITOWAPPU) with China. The city's importance waned because of the decline of overseas trade following the institution of the NATIONAL SECLUSION policy in 1639 and because of a change in the course of the river Yamatogawa that damaged Sakai's harbor in the early 1700s.

Sakai was made a municipality (*shi*) in 1889, and it has since developed into an important modern port and industrial center, with metallurgy, electric-appliance, chemical, petrochemical, steel, and textile industries. Pop: 807,765.

Sakaida Kakiemon → Kakiemon ware

Sakaide 坂出[市]

City in northern Kagawa Prefecture, Shikoku. Situated on the Inland Sea, Sakaide had been an important salt producer since 1602. The former salt fields have been converted to land for housing and for shipbuild-

ing, oil refining, and chemical plants. The city is now connected by bridges to Kojima in Honshū. Pop: 63,876.

Sakai, Frankie フランキー堺

(1929–). Film and television actor, noted as a comedian. Real name Sakai Masatoshi. Born in Kagoshima Prefecture. His first major success as a comic actor was in Kawashima Yūzō's (1918–63) *Bakumatsu taiyō den* (1957, Sun Legend of the Last Days of the Shogunate). Sakai became the first comedian to receive the prestigious Blue Ribbon awarded by newspaper film critics and the Leading Actor Award given by the film journal *Kinema jumpō*. He played comic roles in such films as TOYODA SHIRŌ's *Ekimae ryokan* (1958, Station Hotel) and others of the so-called Ekimae series (1958–69), and in Matsubayashi Shūe's (b 1920) *Shachō* series (1956–71). He received an acting award for his brilliant performance in the television drama *Watashi wa kai ni naritai* (1958, A Clam Is What I Want to Be).

Sakai Hōitsu 酒井抱一

(1761–1829). RIMPA painter. Real name Sakai Tadanao. Born in Edo (now Tōkyō) into a wealthy *samurai* family. Early on, Hōitsu experimented with a wide variety of styles, finally taking up the Rimpa style. In 1797 Hōitsu took Buddhist vows at the temple Nishi Honganji in Kyōto. He returned to Edo in 1809 and established a painting studio, calling it the Ukaan (Rain Flower Hermitage). Hōitsu's devotion to KŌRIN (1658–1716), an earlier Rimpa master, was strong; in 1815 he published two books, the *Kōrin hyakuzu* (One Hundred Paintings of Kōrin) and *Ogataryū ryaku impu* (Seals of the Ogata School). Like all later Rimpa masters, Hōitsu was greatest as a painter of nature, primarily flowers and plants.

Sakai merchants 堺商人

(Sakai *shōnin*). Wealthy merchants of the city of SAKAI (in what is now Ōsaka Prefecture) who flourished from the mid-Muromachi period (1333–1568) to the early Edo period (1600–1868). In the late 15th century Sakai replaced Hyōgo (now Kōbe) as the main port for Japan's TALLY TRADE with Ming China and for trade with Korea and the Ryūkyū Islands. During the civil wars of the Warring States, or Sengoku period (1467–1568), Sakai became a free city and the mer-

chants set up the EGŌSHŪ to administer city government. ODA NOBUNAGA held Sakai under direct control, as did his successor TOYOTOMI HIDEYOSHI. The Tokugawa shogunate (1603–1867) designated the city as shogunal domain (TENRYŌ), to be administered by the Sakai commissioners (Sakai *bugyō*), and granted monopoly privileges to its raw-silk-importing guild (see ITOWAPPU). After the implementation of the NATIONAL SECLUSION policy in 1639, Sakai was eclipsed as a trading center by Nagasaki and Ōsaka. Sakai merchants were known for their patronage of the arts. The tea masters SEN NO RIKYŪ, TSUDA SŌGYŪ, and IMAI SŌKYŪ were originally based in Sakai.

Sakaiminato 境港[市]

City in northwestern Tottori Prefecture, western Honshū. Located on the Sea of Japan, Sakaiminato has long been a seaport and, since World War II, a fishing base for western Japan. Marine-food-processing and woodworking industries are prominent. Yonago Airport is located in the south. Pop: 37,282.

Sakai Spinning Mill 堺紡績所

(Sakai Bōsekisho). Japan's second Western-style cotton-spinning mill, built in 1869–70 in the city of Sakai, Ōsaka Prefecture. In 1872 it was taken over by the government, which operated the mill as a model to encourage private enterprise (see GOVERNMENT-OPERATED FACTORIES, MEIJI PERIOD). Privatized in 1889, the mill became part of the Senshū Spinning Company, which continued operating until 1933.

Sakai Tadakiyo 酒井忠清

(1624–81). Senior councillor (RŌJŪ) and great elder (TAIRŌ) under TOKUGAWA IETSUNA, the fourth Tokugawa shōgun (r 1651–80). *Daimyō* of the Umayabashi domain in Kōzuke Province (now Gumma Prefecture). As the most powerful man in the shogunate under Ietsuna, Tadakiyo was nicknamed Geba Shōgun (Hitching-Post Shōgun) because he had his residence opposite the hitching post at the Ōte gate to Edo Castle. When Ietsuna died without an heir, Tadakiyo is said to have proposed the adoption of an imperial prince as heir. However, Ietsuna's younger brother, TOKUGAWA TSUNAYOSHI, became shōgun in 1680 and Tadakiyo resigned as *tairō* the following year.

Sakai Toshihiko 堺利彦

(1871–1933). Journalist and socialist leader. Pen name Sakai Kosen. Born in Fukuoka Prefecture, he left the First Higher School (Daiichi Kōtō Gakkō) in 1889. In 1899 he joined the newspaper YOROZU CHŌHŌ, where he became attracted to socialism. In 1903 he and KŌTOKU SHŪSUI left the *Yorozu chōhō* to form the HEIMINSHA (Society of Commoners), an organization that propagated socialist ideas and opposed the RUSSO-JAPANESE WAR of 1904–05 through its newspaper, the HEIMIN SHIMBUN.

Sakai helped found the JAPAN SOCIALIST PARTY (Nihon Shakaitō) in 1906. Imprisoned for his part in the RED FLAG INCIDENT OF 1908, he was released in 1910. In 1922, with YAMAKAWA HITOSHI and ARAHATA KANSON, he founded the JAPAN COMMUNIST PARTY (Nihon Kyōsantō); he was arrested the following year. After his release he joined Yamakawa and others in founding the influential journal *Rōnō* (Labor-Farmer; see RŌNŌHA). He helped organize the Nihon Taishūtō (Japan Masses Party), a coalition of noncommunist leftist groups, and was elected to the Tōkyō Metropolitan Assembly in 1929. Two years later he joined the Zenkoku Rōnō Taishūtō (National Labor-Farmer Masses Party). Until his death he continued to play an important role in unifying various socialist and antiwar groups.

Sakaiya Taichi 堺屋太一

(1935–). Writer and social critic. Real name Ikeguchi Kotarō. Born in Ōsaka; graduated from Tōkyō University. From 1960 to 1978 he served in the Ministry of International Trade and Industry (MITI), participating in the planning of Expo '70 in Ōsaka, Expo '75 in Okinawa, and MITI's Sunshine Project for the development of alternative energy sources. His debut as a writer came with the publication of *Yudan* (1975, The Slipup), a novel depicting Japan's panic during the oil crisis of 1973. He is also the author of *Dankai no sedai* (1976, Baby Boomers), whose title became the standard Japanese phrase used to refer to the postwar baby-boom generation, and *Chika kakumei* (1985; tr *The Knowledge-Value Revolution*, 1991).

sakaki 榊

Cleyera japonica. Low evergreen tree of the tea family (Theaceae) that grows wild in mountain woods in warm areas of Kyūshū, Shikoku, and central and southern Honshū, as well as in Korea, northeastern China, and northern Taiwan. The trunk reaches a height of about 10 meters (33 ft). The glossy, unserrated leaves are obovate-elliptical and 7–8 centimeters (about 3 in) long. In early summer it produces cream white, five-petaled flowers that droop from long stalks. The sap fruit is black and globular and contains many seeds.

The name *sakaki* is thought to mean "prospering tree," and the ancient idea that gods dwell in evergreen trees led to the use of this tree to demarcate sacred space or to make an offering to the deities in SHINTŌ rituals. In places where the *sakaki* is scarce, the *hisakaki* (*Eurya japonica*), a similar but smaller tree, is used as a substitute.

Sakakibara Yasumasa 榊原康政

(1548–1606). General of the Azuchi-Momoyama period (1568–1600). Together with Sakai Tadatsugu (1527–96), Honda Tadakatsu (1548–1610), and II NAOMASA, he was renowned as one of the "Four Guardian Deities" (Tokugawa Shitennō) of TOKUGAWA IEYASU. Yasumasa fought at the Battle of ANEGAWA in 1570 and played a key role in the victory over TOYOTOMI HIDEYOSHI at Nagakute in the KOMAKI NAGAKUTE CAMPAIGN in 1584; in 1585 he played a major role in the reorganization of Ieyasu's army. After Ieyasu's victory in the Battle of SEKIGAHARA in 1600, Yasumasa played a major role in the massive redistribution of domains but thereafter faded away from the center of power.

Sakaki Hyakusen 彭城百川

(1697–1752). Pioneer master in NANGA ("Southern painting") or BUNJINGA (literati painting). Real name Sakahi Shin'en. Born in Nagoya into a druggist family that was probably of Chinese descent, Hyakusen was active first as a HAIKU poet in the Ise region, then as a painter in Kyōto from around 1726. His work included *haiga*, the sketchy drawings done to accompany haiku poems; he was probably the outstanding master of *haiga* before BUSON.

Hyakusen's major works are based on Chinese painting of the late Ming and early Qing (Ch'ing) dynasties (17th century), which he copied and imitated assiduously. He, more than any other early *bunjinga* artist, is to be credited with introducing to Japan these Chinese styles, especially those of the late Ming masters of Suzhou (Soochow). His finest paintings, such as *Li Bo (Li Po) Gazing at a Waterfall* (ca 1745), depict figures in landscapes. He was followed by IKE NO TAIGA and Buson, who brought the *bunjinga* school to maturity.

Sakakura Junzō 坂倉準三

(1901–69). Architect. Born in Gifu Prefecture. After graduating from Tōkyō University he studied for two years in Paris. From 1931 to 1936 he worked for the French architect Le Corbusier. His design for the Japan Pavilion at the Paris World Exposition (1937) brought him international recognition for his skillful blending of modern materials and forms evoking native traditions. His notable works include the KAMAKURA MUSEUM OF MODERN ART (1951), Kure City Hall (1962), and Shinjuku Station Square (1966).

Sakamoto Hanjirō 坂本繁二郎

(1882–1969). Western-style painter whose work is influenced by the French impressionists. Born in Kurume, Fukuoka Prefecture. In 1902 he went to Tōkyō where, with his primary-school friend AOKI SHIGERU, he studied under Koyama Shōtarō (1857–1916) at the Fudōsha School. In 1914 he helped found the Nikakai artists' group, an association of Western-oriented artists opposed to the conservative tendencies of the BUNTEN. From 1921 to 1924 he lived in France. Many of his later paintings are of animals and still lifes. In 1956 he received the Order of Culture.

Sakamoto Ryōma 坂本竜馬

(1836–67). Proimperial activist in the period that preceded the Meiji Restoration of 1868. Born in the castle town of Kōchi in the Tosa domain (now Kōchi Prefecture). Sakamoto was in Edo (now Tōkyō) when Commodore Matthew PERRY's ships arrived in 1853. He participated in the flurry of martial activity that Perry precipitated.

The ANSEI PURGE conducted by II NAOSUKE in 1858 swept Sakamoto into national politics, imperial loyalism, and extremism. TAKECHI ZUIZAN, antishogunate leader of the Tosa domain, enrolled Sakamoto in his Tosa Loyalist Party. However, before the loyalists gained influence in Tosa, Sakamoto fled to take up the life of a masterless *samurai* (*rōnin*). During this period, Sakamoto plotted to assassinate KATSU KAISHŪ, a highly placed shogunal official and modernizer, but instead was persuaded by Katsu of the necessity of a long-range program to build up national strength, and ended up working as Katsu's assistant.

By 1864, however, the shogunate began to take a harder line against the loyalist cause, and Sakamoto sought shelter in Satsuma (now Kagoshima Prefecture), which was emerging as the center of the anti-Tokugawa movement. In March 1866 he was an agent in the SATSUMA-CHŌSHŪ ALLIANCE, a pact that guaranteed the survival of Chōshū (now Yamaguchi Prefecture) in the hostilities with Tokugawa armies. Chōshū's victory in the summer war of 1866 and the impending Tokugawa collapse made Sakamoto's politics and contacts of increasing interest to his former superiors in Tosa. He was welcomed back as a Tosa retainer. Tosa authorities were anxious to thwart the plans of Satsuma and Chōshū to overthrow the shogunate by force with a negotiated settlement of their own that would prevent a new monopoly of power by a rival domain. Sakamoto was a central figure in these efforts and participated in formulating the proposal that led to the resignation of the last shōgun, TOKUGAWA YOSHINOBU. He continued to work for new political forms until he was murdered in 1867 by a member of one of the *rōnin* companies the shogunate had organized to maintain public order.

Sakamoto Ryūichi 坂本龍一

(1952–). Composer and musician. Born in Tōkyō, he graduated from Tōkyō University of Fine Arts and Music. He has shown himself to be remarkably multifaceted, working as a pianist, composer, arranger, and producer. In 1978 he formed the group Yellow Magic Orchestra (YMO) with Hosono Haruomi (b 1947) and Takahashi Yukihiro (b 1952). His mastery of the synthesizer gained him attention in the area of electronic music. In 1983 he composed the soundtrack for and starred in ŌSHIMA NAGISA's film, *Merry Christmas, Mr. Lawrence*. He became the first Japanese to win the Academy Award for Best Soundtrack, for the film *The Last Emperor* (1988).

Sakamoto Tarō 坂本太郎

(1901–87). Historian. Born in Shizuoka Prefecture. Graduate of Tōkyō University, where he became a professor. Sakamoto is noted for his positivistic studies of ancient Japanese history based on the actual record, particularly his close examination of such basic materials as the 8th- and 9th-century chronicles called the RIKKOKUSHI and the 7th- and 8th-century legal codifications called

sakaki
1 The leaves, flower, and fruit of the *sakaki*.
2 Branches of this evergreen tree are often used in Shintō rituals like this one at the Izumo Shrine, Shimane Prefecture.

Sakamoto Ryōma
Born to a rural *samurai* family, Sakamoto was active in the pro-imperial movement that preceded the Meiji Restoration. He was murdered by shogunate assassins in 1867.

Sakamoto Ryūichi
This classically trained composer and musician has gained international recognition for his imaginative synthesizer work.

Sakata Shōichi In his later years this theoretical physicist campaigned tirelessly for the peaceful use of atomic energy.

ritsuryō. In addition to the editing and revision of the *Shintei zōho kokushi taikei* (see KOKUSHI TAIKEI), his works include *Nihon kodaishi no kiso kenkyū* (2 vols, 1964; Basic Studies of Ancient Japanese History) and *Shōtoku Taishi* (1979). He was awarded the Order of Culture in 1982.

Sakanishi Shiho 坂西志保

(1896–1976). Social critic, essayist, and translator. Also known as Sakanishi Shio. Born in Tōkyō. She went to the United States in 1922, worked her way through Wheaton College in Massachusetts, and then earned a PhD at the University of Michigan. From 1930 to 1942 she served as head of the Asian section in the US Library of Congress but was forced to return to Japan after the outbreak of World War II. After the war she worked to promote democratic reforms as a member of many advisory committees for the Japanese government.

Sakanoue family 坂上氏

(Sakanoueshi). Military and administrative family from the 5th to the 14th century. The Sakanoue were the most distinguished branch of the AYA FAMILY of immigrant (KIKA-JIN) descent. Sakanoue no Okina served Prince Ōama (later Emperor TEMMU) in the JINSHIN DISTURBANCE of 672. SAKANOUE NO TAMURAMARO (758–811) was named *seii tai shōgun* (barbarian-subduing generalissimo; see SHŌGUN). Later members of the family were distinguished as poets, scholars, and legal experts.

Sakanoue no Tamuramaro 坂上田村麻呂

(758–811). Military leader of the early Heian period (794–1185). The SAKANOUE FAMILY were hereditary court generals from the 7th century. Tamuramaro's father, Karitamaro (728–786), helped suppress the rebellions of Tachibana no Naramaro (757; see TACHIBANA NO MOROE) and FUJIWARA NO NAKAMARO (764). In 791 Tamuramaro was commissioned by Emperor KAMMU to lead an expedition against the aboriginal EZO people of northeastern Honshū, and he subsequently served as governor and military commander of that region. In 797 he was named "barbarian-subduing generalissimo" (*seii tai shōgun;* see SHŌGUN), becoming the first recipient of the title shōgun. In 801–802 he again fought in the north, establishing fortresses at Izawa (see IZAWAJŌ) and Shiwa (both in what is now Iwate Prefecture). In 810 he helped suppress an attempt to restore retired emperor Heizei (774–824; r 806–809) to the throne (see KUSUKO INCIDENT). Tamuramaro is traditionally said to have sponsored the construction of the temple KIYOMIZUDERA in Kyōto.

Sakashitamongai Incident 坂下門外の変

(Sakashitamongai no Hen). An assassination attempt on 13 February 1862 by antishogunate activists against ANDŌ NOBUMASA, senior councillor (*rōjū*) in the Tokugawa shogunate. The incident is named for the Sakashita Gate (Sakashitamon) of Edo Castle, close to where it occurred. Andō had hoped to strengthen the shogunate by encouraging an alliance between it and the imperial court in Kyōto (see MOVEMENT FOR UNION OF COURT AND SHOGUNATE). To that end he arranged the marriage of the imperial princess KAZU to the shōgun TOKUGAWA IEMOCHI. This, and rumors

that Andō was plotting to depose Emperor KŌMEI, inflamed imperial loyalists. Six assailants managed only to wound their victim before they were cut down. Andō was nonetheless unable to continue in office, and the attempt to strengthen the shogunate faltered.

Sakata 酒田[市]

City in northwestern Yamagata Prefecture, northern Honshū, at the mouth of the river Mogamigawa. It developed as a port for transshipping rice during the 1700s and still functions as a distribution center. Food-processing and chemical plants are located here. Pop: 100,811.

Sakata Hiroo 阪田寛夫

(1925–). Poet and novelist. Born in Ōsaka Prefecture. Graduate of Tōkyō University. Sakata's works include the poetry collection *Watashi no dōbutsuen* (1965, My Zoo) and the nursery rhyme collections *Ûtae banban* (1973) and *Satchan* (1975). Sakata won the Akutagawa Prize for *Tsuchi no utsuwa* (1974, Clay Vessel), the story of a Christian household at the time of the mother's death. He is also the author of *Kaidō tōsei* (1986, East across the Seas).

Sakata Seed Corporation [株]サカタのタネ

(Sakata no Tane). Seed wholesaler. Incorporated in 1942. The company wholesales vegetable seeds, flower seeds, flower bulbs, and horticultural supplies. It has a subsidiary company in the United States, Sakata Seed America, Inc. For the fiscal year ending May 1991, the company had annual sales of ¥32.2 billion (US $234.9 million), and capitalization stood at ¥13.5 billion (US $98.5 million). Headquarters are in Yokohama.

Sakata Shōichi 坂田昌一

(1911–70). Theoretical physicist, known for his two-meson theory (1942) and for the Sakata model of atomic structure (1956), which predated and is considered to be more encompassing than the Murray Gell-Mann theory that won the Nobel Prize in 1969. Born in Tōkyō, he graduated from Kyōto University in 1933. Along with YUKAWA HIDEKI, TOMONAGA SHIN'ICHIRŌ, and many other nuclear physicists throughout the world, Sakata campaigned tirelessly for the peaceful use of atomic energy. His publications include *Butsurigaku to hōhō* (1951, Physics and Its Techniques).

Sakata Tōjūrō I 坂田藤十郎1世

(1647–1709). One of the greatest figures among the KABUKI actors of the Kyōto-Ōsaka area during the Genroku era (1688–1704). His realistic acting style was especially evident in his *yatsushigoto* (the "downtrodden") roles, in which he played gentle, romantic, upper-class characters temporarily reduced to humble circumstances by unscrupulous enemies. He elevated kabuki acting to an unprecedented level of excellence through the subtlety with which he conveyed to the audience the fine breeding and the purity of heart that lay beneath the outwardly wretched appearance of the "downtrodden" characters he depicted.

In the early 1690s he began performing in kabuki plays written by CHIKAMATSU MONZAEMON. By the time Tōjūrō I starred in *Keisei Hotoke no Hara* (1699, The Hotoke Field) and *Keisei Mibu dainembutsu* (1702, The Mibu Kyōgen), both celebrated Chikamatsu plays, he was the foremost *wagotoshi* (per-

former of romantic male leads) in the Kyōto-Ōsaka area.

Sakawagawa 酒匂川

River in Kanagawa Prefecture, central Honshū, originating on the eastern slopes of Mt. Fuji (FUJISAN) and the Tanzawa Mountains and emptying into Sagami Bay at the city of Odawara. Dam construction has resulted in the creation of artificial lakes such as Lake Tanzawa. The water is utilized for drinking. The river is known for *ayu* (sweetfish) fishing. Length: 45 km (28 mi).

sakaya 酒屋

SAKE brewers and dealers. *Sake* brewing had originally been confined to temples and monasteries, but during the KAMAKURA PERIOD (1185–1333) professionals entered the business. *Sake* brewers and dealers of the MUROMACHI PERIOD (1333–1568) also engaged in money lending. By the early 15th century there were some 340 *sakaya* in Kyōto alone. From about 1400, *sakaya* paid the MUROMACHI SHOGUNATE an annual brewing tax (*sakaya yaku*) in return for monopoly rights and official protection. With the tax on DOSŌ (pawnshop owners), it became an important source of government revenue. *Sakaya* and *dosō* were often targets of peasant uprisings (TSUCHI IKKI).

Sakaya Kaigi 酒屋会議

(Conference of *Sake* Brewers). Meetings held by representatives of the *sake* (rice wine) industry in 1882 to demand reductions in taxes imposed on materials used for brewing *sake*. Local *sake* brewers allied themselves with the FREEDOM AND PEOPLE'S RIGHTS MOVEMENT in order to seek redress, enlisting the support of UEKI EMORI. Ueki composed a manifesto demanding free enterprise and an end to unfair taxation. Although unsuccessful the meetings suggested that political action might be used to secure economic goals.

sakazuki 杯

Also called *choko*. Small thimblelike cup, usually ceramic, from which *sake* is sipped. The average capacity of the *sakazuki* is 30 cubic centimeters (1 fl oz); larger ones that look like shot glasses are called *guinomi*. *Sakazuki* made of gold or silver or wood lacquered red are used for ceremonial purposes, such as weddings. Most *sakazuki* come in sets that include a TOKURI, or *sake* vessel.

sake 酒

A brewed alcoholic beverage made from fermented rice. *Sake* is also used as a generic term for all alcoholic drinks. The formal name for refined *sake*, the kind most commonly drunk in Japan, is *seishu;* it is often referred to as *nihonshu* to distinguish it from Western liquors (*yōshu*). The other traditional Japanese alcoholic beverage is a distilled spirit called SHŌCHŪ. Malted rice (*kōji*) is the fermenting agent in both refined *sake* and *shōchū.*

The manufacture of *sake* from rice came to Japan sometime after the introduction of wet rice cultivation in 300 BC, and the first written record of *sake* in Japan dates from the 3rd century AD. In ancient Japan *sake* was made primarily by the imperial court or by large temples and shrines, and it was often associated with religious agricultural festivals. The general populace began brewing *sake* around the end of the 12th century. Although laws against drinking or making *sake* were promulgated from time to time, none of them had much effect.

Today there are about 3,000 manufacturers of refined *sake* in Japan. The chief producing districts are Kyōto and Hyōgo prefectures. A few national brands are also produced in places such as Akita and Hiroshima prefectures. *Jizake* (local brands) are numerous and are produced all over Japan.

Sake is made with a yeast of rice, malted rice, and water. This is placed in a vat, additional amounts of the three yeast ingredients are added, and the mixture is left to ferment for 20 days (the drained solids of the mixture, called *sakekasu* or dregs, are used in cooking and in the preparation of *tsukemono* or PICKLES). After fermentation the mixture is ready for pressing, filtration, and blending. The *sake* is then pasteurized, bottled, and stored. The alcohol content of crude *sake* is about 40 proof; *sake* on the market is about 32 proof. A good-quality *sake* has a subtle blend of the so-called five flavors (sweetness, sourness, pungency, bitterness, and astringency) and a mellow fragrance. Older *sake* has a soft, mellow taste, but *sake* is rarely stored for more than a year. There are also carbonated, sweet, dry, hard, and aged types. Unrefined *sake* is called *nigorizake*. A sweet *sake* called *mirin* is made especially for cooking.

Sake is customarily served hot in a small earthenware bottle known as a *tokkuri*. Traditionally, the *tokkuri* is placed in hot water until the *sake* reaches the proper temperature (about 50°C [122°F]), although many people now use microwave ovens. The *sake* is then drunk from small cups known as *sakazuki*. A special type of *sake* is brewed for drinking cold or on ice. Although beer and whiskey (and more recently wine) have been popular among the Japanese for some time, it is still a popular Japanese custom to drink *sake* while appreciating the beauty of nature, especially during the flowering of the *sakura* (cherry tree).

☎ 1302–1303

sake → salmons

Sakhalin　　　　　　　　サハリン

(Saharin). An elongated island north of Hokkaidō, separated from the continent by a narrow strait; traditionally called Karafuto in Japanese. Originally inhabited by AINU and Gilyaks (a Paleosiberian people).

In 1855 the Treaty of Shimoda provided for Sakhalin's joint occupation by Russia and Japan, a formula that led to escalating friction during the 1860s and early 1870s. Attempts by the Tokugawa shogunate and, after 1868, by the Meiji government to partition or buy the island failed. In the Treaty of ST. PETERSBURG signed 7 May 1875, Japan exchanged its rights in Sakhalin for the central and northern Kuril Islands.

In the final stages of the RUSSO-JAPANESE WAR (1904–05), Japanese forces seized all of Sakhalin, but the Treaty of PORTSMOUTH of 5 September 1905 entitled Japan to keep only that portion south of the 50th parallel. In the spring of 1920 Japan occupied northern Sakhalin (see NIKOLAEVSK INCIDENT). Japanese forces were withdrawn from the north in 1925 when Japan and the Soviet Union established diplomatic relations; however, Japan retained oil and coal concessions in northern Sakhalin until 1944. In 1942 Karafuto ceased to be a colony and was made an integral part of Japan. Soviet forces invaded Karafuto on 11 August 1945. Southern Sakhalin was formally incorporated into the USSR in 1947 and remains part of the Russian Federation.

sakimori　　　　　　　　防人

Soldiers in ancient Japan charged with the defense of Kyūshū. The chronicle NIHON SHOKI (720) states that *sakimori* were sent to Kyūshū after the fall of the Japanese enclave of KAYA on the Korean peninsula in the mid-6th century. The term was first used in the imperial edict of 646 proclaiming the TAIKA REFORM. Under the RITSURYŌ SYSTEM soldiers were conscripted from all over the country and sent to Kyūshū on a three-year rotational basis. In addition to performing military duties, they were expected to grow their own food. After 730, however, only those from the eastern provinces of Honshū were sent.

There was a special office (Sakimori no Tsukasa) in DAZAIFU, the government headquarters in northern Kyūshū, for matters related to *sakimori*. The *sakimori* system was abolished in 795; nevertheless, recruitment continued well into the 10th century. The 8th-century poetry anthology MAN'YŌSHŪ includes about 100 poems by *sakimori* (SAKIMORI UTA).

sakimori uta　　　　　　防人歌

(Poems of the Frontier Guards). Poems by young peasants from eastern Japan who were sent for military guard duty on the southern island of Kyūshū and on offshore islands in the 7th and 8th centuries. Called *sakimori*, these young soldiers and the families they left suffered great hardship.

All extant poems of the frontier guards and their families are preserved in the MAN'YŌSHŪ (ca 759): a group of 5 in Book 14; a series of 93 in Book 20; one *chōka* and one *tanka*, said to be by wives of frontier guards, in Book 13; and one *tanka* in Book 7. ŌTOMO NO YAKAMOCHI is thought to have gathered the majority of these poems. Except for two *chōka* ("long poems"), the poems are all 31-syllable *tanka* ("short poems"), suggesting that they may have been revised and metrically regularized by court poets, who may also have composed some of them in the guise of frontier guards. Thematically, the poems fall into two main types: declarations of fealty to the sovereign and willingness to die in his service; and laments at parting, expressions of concern about the fate of those left behind, and dread of the loneliness to come. Sometimes the two types were combined. They are among the most moving poems that survive from Japan's early literary period.

Sakisaka Itsurō　　　　　　向坂逸郎

(1897–1985). Marxist economist and theoretician. Born in Fukuoka Prefecture, he graduated from Tōkyō University. After studying Marxist theories in Germany from 1922 to 1925, he returned to Japan and joined the faculty of Kyūshū University, from which he was dismissed in 1928 during a government crackdown on leftists (see MARCH 15TH INCIDENT). In the same year he joined *Rōnō*, a scholarly Marxist periodical under the editorship of YAMAKAWA HITOSHI, and became a leading spokesman for the RŌNŌHA group of Marxist theoreticians during their ideological debates with the rival KŌZAHA group (see also NIHON SHIHON SHUGI RONSŌ). Sakisaka was imprisoned from 1937 through 1939 as a result of the POPULAR FRONT INCIDENT but returned to Kyūshū University in 1945. After his retirement in 1960 he exerted strong ideological influence on the JAPAN SOCIALIST PARTY and on SŌHYŌ (General Council of Trade Unions of Japan). Sakisaka

was a translator and biographer of Marx and editor of the first Japanese edition of the complete works of Marx and Engels. His original works include *Keizaigaku hōhō ron* (1950, The Methodology of Economics).

Sakishima Islands　　　　先島諸島

(Sakishima Shotō). Group of islands southwest of the main island of Okinawa; made up of the MIYAKO ISLANDS and YAEYAMA ISLANDS, and administratively a part of Okinawa Prefecture. The principal products are sugarcane and pineapple. Area: 817 sq km (315 sq mi).

Sakoku → National Seclusion

Saku　　　　　　　　　　佐久〔市〕

City in eastern Nagano Prefecture, central Honshū, on the river Chikumagawa. Saku is noted for its rice, electronics industry, and carp hatcheries. Pop: 62,003.

saku　　　　　　　　　　柵

(stockades or palisades). Also pronounced *ki*. Fortresses in frontier regions built at the command of the imperial court. Most were constructed in northeastern Honshū between the 7th and 9th centuries for defense against the aboriginal EZO tribesmen and for administration of the surrounding countryside. Among the most famous were TAGAJŌ, IZAWAJŌ, and AKITAJŌ. See also NUTARI NO KI; IWAFUNE NO KI.

Saku Basin　　　　　　　佐久盆地

(Saku Bonchi). In eastern Nagano Prefecture, central Honshū. Situated along the upper reaches of the river Shinanogawa, this basin consists of the floodplain of the river Chikumagawa in the south and uplands covered with mudflows and volcanic ash in the north. Apples, highland vegetables, and rice are cultivated. The basin is also known for carp breeding. The major cities are Komoro and Saku. Area: approximately 300 sq km (115 sq mi).

Sakuma Dam　　　　　　佐久間ダム

(Sakuma Damu). Gravity dam located on the middle reaches of the river TENRYŪGAWA, between Aichi Prefecture and Shizuoka Prefecture, central Honshū. One of Japan's largest dams. Completed in 1956, it created Lake Sakuma. The dam is utilized for electric power generation with a maximum output of 350,000 kilowatts. Height of embankment: 155.5 m (510.2 ft); storage capacity: 200 million cu m (7 billion cu ft).

Sakuma Kanae　　　　　佐久間鼎

(1888–1970). Linguist and psychologist. Born in Chiba Prefecture and graduate of Tōkyō University. He was a professor at Kyūshū and Tōyō universities and a member of the JAPAN ACADEMY. He is noted for the introduction into Japan of Gestalt psychology and his research on the grammar of modern spoken Japanese. His chief works include *Nihon onseigaku* (1929), a study of the phonetics of Japanese; and *Gendai nihongo no hyōgen to gohō* (1936), an investigation of contemporary expression and usage.

Sakuma Shōzan　　　　　佐久間象山

(1811–64). Progressive *samurai* intellectual of the late Edo period (1600–1868). Also called Sakuma Zōzan. Born in Matsushiro, the castle town of the Matsushiro domain (now Nagano Prefecture), Shōzan studied Chinese learning under his father, a scholar-

Sakisaka Itsurō An influential Marxist economist, Sakisaka edited the first Japanese version of the complete works of Marx and Engels.

Continued on page 1304 ►

Brewing Sake the Old-Fashioned Way

The process of manufacturing *sake* has changed very little in the last 400 years. Although major manufacturers today rely largely on computer-controlled operations, *sake* was originally produced by hand under the direction of an experienced brewmaster. Even now, many small brewers maintain the old traditions.

Sake, like wine made from grapes, is a living thing; slight variations in taste depend on the quality of its basic ingredients (rice and water), the quality of the yeast, weather conditions at the time of brewing, the brewing temperatures used, and the skill of each worker involved. The decisive element in the success of the brewing process, however, is the experience and subtle intuition of the veteran brewmaster. Those *sake* connoisseurs who prefer local brews (*jizake*) over the well-known national brands fully appreciate such proficiency.

Sake is brewed at the very coldest time of winter with rice harvested in the autumn. In April the brewing process is complete and the new *sake* is ready for the critical first quality check, conducted by brewmasters and brewery owners with the same sense of expectancy and anxiety that attends the birth of a child. While the new *sake* may have great vigor, its taste and aroma still have a certain harshness, and so it is left to mellow and mature throughout the summer before being bottled in autumn and readied for sale.

Unrefined sake flows from the spigot of a *sake* press, called a *fune*, during the brewing process.

Steamed rice is removed from a steaming tub. Good quality rice is an absolute precondition for fine *sake*.

Cedarwood casks, displaying the brewer's unique logo, were most often used to hold finished *sake* in the days before bottling.

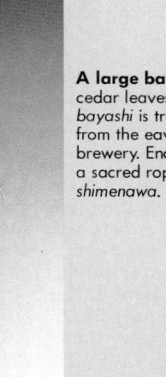

Sake aficionados meet regularly to sample the breweries' new offerings.

A large ball of Japanese cedar leaves called a *saka-bayashi* is traditionally hung from the eaves of a *sake* brewery. Encircling this one is a sacred rope known as a *shimenawa*.

An earthenware serving vessel (*tokkuri*) and cup (*sakazuki*), typical vessels used for drinking *sake*.

During festivals and other auspicious events, the lid of a *sake* cask is smashed open with wooden mallets in a merry ritual.

The Traditional Brewing Process

1 Dehulled, polished rice is first washed by hand in well water, then soaked and made ready for steaming.

2 The soaked rice is steamed in large wooden tubs, then spread on straw mats for cooling. In a special room (below) part of it is mixed with spores of a mold called *kōji*.

3 The *kōji* converts starch to sugar. The resulting "*kōji* rice" is combined with steamed rice, water, and yeast to make the basic mash, or *moto*.

4 More water, *kōji* rice, and steamed rice are added to produce the final mash, which continues to ferment for 20–30 days and is then filtered.

5 The filtered mash is pressed in the *fune*, producing cloudy, unrefined *sake*. After settling in vats, the resulting clear, refined *sake* is finally pasteurized and aged.

Sakurajima The city of Kagoshima with Kagoshima Bay and the active volcano Sakurajima beyond. Volcanic ash often blows across the bay, dusting the city.

administrator of the domain, and SATŌ ISSAI, a professor at Shōheikō (the Confucian school of the Tokugawa shogunate) in Edo (now Tōkyō). Shōzan was awakened to the danger from the West as illustrated by China's humiliation in the Opium War (1839–42). He studied under many scholars of WESTERN LEARNING (Yōgaku), including EGAWA TARŌZAEMON. In 1850 he opened his own private school of Western gunnery in Edo. Among his students were YOSHIDA SHŌIN, SAKAMOTO RYŌMA, and HASHIMOTO SANAI.

By mid-1853, when Commodore Matthew PERRY's ships entered Edo Bay (now Tōkyō Bay), Shōzan had come to believe in the necessity of sending talented observers to the West. His attempts to smuggle one of his disciples abroad earned him an eight-year confinement for violation of the NATIONAL SECLUSION policy. During this house arrest he wrote his famous *Seikenroku* (Reflections on My Errors). Much of the work, written in Chinese (*kambun*), consists of a criticism of the general ignorance of Western science on the part of Confucian scholars and the ineptness of the shogunate in dealing with Perry.

Despite his critical stance, Shōzan was an advocate of reform and modernization within the existing framework of shogunal rule. In 1864 he was made an adviser to the shogunate and sent to Kyōto, apparently to win the SONNŌ JŌI (Revere the Emperor, Expel the Barbarians) faction over to the MOVEMENT FOR UNION OF COURT AND SHOGUNATE, but before he could exert much influence on policy, he was assassinated by *sonnō jōi* adherents.

Shōzan is best remembered for his motto "Eastern ethics and Western technique" (see WAKON YŌSAI). After studying Western technology and science and comparing it with Neo-Confucianism (see SHUSHIGAKU), he concluded that each was indispensable but that Eastern ethics, with its greater spirituality, was more exalted. The motto foreshadowed the blending of the old and new, the East and West, that has been characteristic of the transformation of modern Japan since the mid-19th century.

Sakunami Hot Spring　作並温泉

(Sakunami Onsen). Located near the upper reaches of the river Hirosegawa, west of the city of Sendai, central western Miyagi Prefecture, northern Honshū. An alkaline, saline, gypsum spring; water temperature is approximately 60°C (140°F).

Sakura　佐倉[市]

City in northern Chiba Prefecture, central Honshū; south of the lake IMBANUMA. It prospered during the Edo period (1600–1868) as the site of Sakura Castle, built by DOI TOSHIKATSU. With many thriving industries, it is rapidly becoming a satellite city of Tōkyō. The area around Imbanuma has hiking and fishing. Pop: 144,688.

sakura → cherry, flowering

Sakura Bank, Ltd　[株]さくら銀行

(Sakura Ginkō). World's second largest bank in terms of deposits, surpassed only by DAI-ICHI KANGYŌ BANK, LTD. The bank was formed in April 1990 through a merger between Mitsui Bank, Ltd, and Taiyō Kōbe Bank, Ltd; it was initially known as Mitsui Taiyō Kōbe Bank, Ltd, and changed its name to Sakura Bank, Ltd, in 1992.

Before the merger, in September 1989, Mitsui Bank had deposits totaling ¥22.3 trillion (US $153.7 billion), 245 business offices, and 10,978 employees. Its capital stood at ¥208.4 billion (US $1.4 billion) as of February 1990. Although a long-established ZAIBATSU bank, Mitsui had ranked only seventh in total deposits, following Tōkai Bank, Ltd.

Taiyō Kōbe Bank, established in 1973 through the merger of the Bank of Kōbe and Taiyō Bank, had, in September 1989, deposits totaling ¥20.1 trillion (US $138.6 billion), 374 business offices, and 13,139 employees. Its capital stood at ¥199.9 billion (US $1.4 billion) as of February 1990. Although the bank had enough business offices to rival leading city banks, it trailed them seriously in both deposits and profits.

As of September 1991, Sakura Bank employed 23,282 people and had 652 business offices in Japan and abroad. Assets at that time totaled ¥60.2 trillion (US $447.0 billion), and capitalization stood at ¥423.1 billion (US $3.1 billion). The bank's headquarters are in Tōkyō.

Sakurada Ichirō　桜田一郎

(1904–86). Chemist. Noted for his work involving the viscosity of high polymers and X-ray analyses of their structures, he was also a part of the three-man team that succeeded in the first Japanese production of synthetic fibers in 1939. Born in Kyōto Prefecture, he graduated from Kyōto University in 1926. He became professor there in 1935 and dean of engineering in 1965. He retired in 1967 to become professor at Dōshisha University. He received the Order of Culture in 1977.

Sakurada Jisuke　桜田治助

Name of a succession of major dramatists in the KABUKI theater. Jisuke I (1734–1806) wrote over 120 *jidai-mono* (historical plays) and *sewa-mono* (domestic plays) and more than 100 *shosagoto* (dance pieces). Although his full-length works are no longer performed, his shorter *shosagoto* pieces, such as *Oshiegusa Yoshiwara suzume* (1768, Birds of Yoshiwara) and *Modorikago iro ni aikata* (1788, A Returning Palanquin), are still frequently presented. His disciple, Jisuke II (1768–1829), excelled in the *shosagoto*. Jisuke III (1802–77), a pupil of Jisuke II, achieved some prominence but was soon overshadowed by Kawatake MOKUAMI, the dominant kabuki playwright after the mid-1850s. Jisuke IV (dates unknown), who had once worked under Jisuke III, abandoned his 30-year playwriting career to become a journalist.

Sakuradamongai Incident　桜田門外の変

(Sakuradamongai no Hen). The assassination of the shogunal great elder (*tairō*) II NAOSUKE outside the Sakurada Gate (Sakuradamon) of Edo Castle on 24 March 1860 (Man'en 1.3.3) by a group of 18 antiforeign, proimperial activists from the Mito domain

(now part of Ibaraki Prefecture) and the Satsuma domain (now Kagoshima Prefecture). Ii had incensed the activists when he signed the ANSEI COMMERCIAL TREATIES without imperial sanction. His ruthless suppression of political dissent following the 1858 shogunal succession dispute (see ANSEI PURGE) further alienated him from the progressive *daimyō*, who sought reconciliation between the court and the Tokugawa shogunate (see MOVEMENT FOR UNION OF COURT AND SHOGUNATE). The assassins claimed they had punished Ii for capitulating to the Western powers and defying the imperial will. His murder thoroughly discredited Tokugawa absolutism and set the stage for further antishogunate, proimperial activities.

Sakuradamon Incident　桜田門事件

(Sakuradamon Jiken). A political assassination attempt on Emperor SHŌWA (Hirohito) on 8 January 1932. A hand grenade was thrown at the emperor's procession near the Sakurada Gate (Sakuradamon) of the palace, causing minor damage. Prime Minister INUKAI TSUYOSHI took responsibility for the incident and immediately submitted his resignation, which was not accepted by the emperor. The Korean suspect was executed after he was convicted in a secret trial.

Sakurada Takeshi　桜田武

(1904–85). Businessman. Born in Hiroshima Prefecture and a graduate of Tōkyō University. Sakurada joined NISSHINBŌ INDUSTRIES, INC, in 1926, becoming president in 1945 and chairman in 1964. He helped create NIKKEIREN (Japan Federation of Employers' Associations) and served as its executive director and permanent executive secretary, as well as its chairman from 1974 to 1979. A leader in the business-industrial community, he was counted among the "big four" of the business world during the premiership of IKEDA HAYATO and continued to wield strong influence in later years.

Sakurai　桜井[市]

City in northern Nara Prefecture, central Honshū. One of the post-station towns during the Edo period (1600–1868). After the opening of a railroad line in the late 19th century it became a distribution center for lumber. Sakurai is known for its *sōmen* noodles. Attractions include Ōmiwa Shrine and the temple Hasedera. Pop: 60,262.

Sakurai Jōji　桜井錠二

(1858–1939). Organic chemist. Born in what is now Ishikawa Prefecture. Attended Tōkyō University but left midway through his education to study in England, where he graduated from the University of London in 1881. From 1882 to 1919 he served as a professor at Tōkyō University. He is credited with having introduced modern chemistry to Japan. His achievements included research on the molecular structure of organic substances and developing the Japanese-language lexicon of chemistry. He was also a science administrator in the Meiji-period (1868–1912) government and worked to promote the development of science in Japan.

Sakurajima　桜島

Volcanic island connected to the Ōsumi Peninsula on the Kyūshū mainland, Kagoshima Bay, central Kagoshima Prefecture, southern Kyūshū. An active stratovolcano composed of the peaks Kitadake, Nakadake, and Minamidake. As a result of a large eruption in 1914, the island became fused with the Ōsumi Peninsula. Even today large quantities of smoke and ash are sometimes emitted by the volcano. Sakurajima forms part of the Kirishima-Yaku National Park, and the hardened lava flows are a tourist attraction. It is the site of numerous hot springs as well. The special product of the island is Sakurajima *daikon* (a large white radish). Area: 77 sq km (30 sq mi).

Sakurakai 桜会

(Cherry Blossom Society). Secret society established by young army officers advocating national reform; organized in September 1930 by Lieutenant Colonel HASHIMOTO KINGORŌ, then chief of the Russian Section of the Army General Staff. The society claimed it would resort to military force to achieve reorganization of the state on totalitarian, militaristic lines. The Sakurakai began with a membership of about 10, mostly field-grade officers from the General Staff and the Army Ministry. Later company-grade regimental officers joined the society; by February 1931 membership totaled more than 50. Twice in 1931 (see MARCH INCIDENT; OCTOBER INCIDENT) Sakurakai members and ultranationalist civilian elements tried to topple the government and set up a military cabinet. With the arrest of 12 members, including Hashimoto, after the October Incident, the Sakurakai was dissolved.

sakurasō → primroses

Sakura Sōgorō 佐倉惣五郎

(mid-17th century). Also known as Sakura Sōgo or Kiuchi Sōgorō. Farmer and folk hero of the early Edo period (1600–1868). As a village headman (SHŌYA) in the Sakura domain in Shimōsa Province (now part of Chiba Prefecture), Sōgorō is said to have petitioned the *daimyō* of Sakura to reduce the extremely heavy taxes under which the peasants of the area were suffering. Legend has it that Sōgorō, unsuccessful in his plea, presented a direct appeal (JIKISO) to the shōgun, an action usually punishable by death. It is said that his request was granted, but that he and his family were executed nonetheless. It is difficult to separate fact from fictional accounts of Sōgorō in popular literature, of which the *kabuki* play *Sakura gimin den* by MOKUAMI is particularly well known. See also HYAKUSHŌ IKKI.

sakushiki 作職

(cultivators' rights). Rights of cultivation and livelihood, held by farmers (*sakunin*) over land rented from the proprietary lords (RYŌSHU) of estates (SHŌEN) in the Kamakura (1185–1333) and Muromachi (1333–1568) periods. Cultivators' rights were subordinate to *myōshushiki* (rights of the landholder, or MYŌSHU), which were subordinate to *ryōshushiki* (rights of the proprietary lord). There were three kinds of tenure: (1) indefinite, so long as the holder paid annual rent and labor service; (2) revocable at the proprietary lord's discretion; and (3) limited to the term of one year. The first was the most common. *Sakushiki,* together with the *shōen* system, were officially abolished at the time of the nationwide land survey (KENCHI) ordered by the national unifier TOYOTOMI HIDEYOSHI in the 1580s.

salamanders 山椒魚

(*sanshōuo*). In Japanese, *sanshōuo* is the general name for amphibians of the order Urodela, family Salamandridae, with the exception of newts (IMORI). Some 13 species are found in Japan; most common are the Hakone *sanshōuo* (*Onychodactylus japonicus*) and *kasumi sanshōuo* (*Hynobius nebulosus*), which hide under rocks and fallen trees in forests by day—except during the breeding season when they swarm about stagnant pools—and move about at night to prey on insects and earthworms. The *ō sanshōuo* (*Megalobatrachus japonicus*), the world's largest amphibian, is usually 60–70 centimeters long (24–28 in), but sometimes reaches a length of more than 120 centimeters (50 in). Inhabiting streams or rivers in mountainous areas of southern Honshū and northern Kyūshū, it digs holes 2–3 meters (7–10 ft) deep in riverbanks, coming out only at night to hunt.

salmons 鮭・鱒

(*sake; masu*). In Japanese, *sake* and *masu* are the common names for various species of anadromous fish of the family Salmonidae. *Sake* refers chiefly to fish of the genus *Oncorhynchus*, and *masu* to certain, usually sea-running, fish of the genera *Oncorhynchus, Salmo,* and *Salvelinus.*

Sake refers specifically to the dog salmon (*Oncorhynchus keta*), the most important Japanese salmon. This fish, which grows to a length of about 1 meter (3 ft), is distributed in the northern Pacific Ocean and adjoining seas, as well as the rivers emptying into them. Salted *sake* is highly favored by the Japanese. The roe is also considered a delicacy; *sujiko* is the term for the whole roe and *ikura* for the loose salmon eggs or caviar.

The word *masu* is often translated into English as "trout"; however, the only trout of any importance in Japan is the rainbow trout or *nijimasu* (*Salmo gairdneri*), which was introduced from the United States in 1877. *Masu* is also the general commercial name for such fish as the Karafuto *masu* or *sepparimasu* (pink salmon; *Oncorhynchus gorbuscha*). Various *masu,* including rainbow trout, are raised by fish-farming in ponds throughout Japan.

Salvation Army 救世軍

(Kyūseigun). Japanese branch of the international Christian evangelical and charitable organization; headquartered in Tōkyō. It carries out missionary work among the poor as well as various welfare programs for the less fortunate. The Salvation Army was first organized in Japan under Colonel Edward Wright in 1895, about 30 years after its founding in London.

Among the founding Japanese members, YAMAMURO GUMPEI was prominent for his work as a missionary, social worker, and author and was promoted to the rank of commander of the Salvation Army in Japan in 1926. The organization now operates various welfare facilities, including low-cost dormitories for day laborers and students, nurseries for working mothers, sanatoriums, and job-training centers for the handicapped. The members and baptized followers of the Salvation Army in Japan totaled 6,645 in 1989.

Sambesan 三瓶山

Double volcano in the Hakusan Volcanic Zone, central Shimane Prefecture, western Honshū; composed of granite-based quartz amphibole and biotite andesite. It is part of Daisen-Oki National Park. Height: 1,126 m (3,694 ft).

Sambetsu Kaigi 産別会議

(abbreviation of Zen Nihon Sangyōbetsu Rōdō Kumiai Kaigi; Congress of Industrial Labor Unions of Japan). Labor federation organized in August 1946. Initially it had 21 affiliated unions with a total membership of 1,630,000, comprising 44 percent of the organized labor force. It had strong ties with the JAPAN COMMUNIST PARTY and led political struggles such as the GENERAL STRIKE OF 1947. Divisions within the Sambetsu Kaigi led to the formation of SŌHYŌ (General Council of Trade Unions of Japan) in 1950. It was also under outside attack through the RED PURGE of the Occupation authorities. As a result Sambetsu Kaigi quickly lost both influence and membership, disbanding in 1958.

Sambugyō 三奉行

(the Three Commissioners). Sambugyō refers to the three most important administrative offices of the Tokugawa shogunate (1603–1867): the EDO MACHI BUGYŌ, who were in charge of the commoners of Edo (now Tōkyō); the KANJŌ BUGYŌ, who handled shogunal finances and rural lands; and the JISHA BUGYŌ, who oversaw religious establishments. See also BUGYŌ.

Sameura Dam 早明浦ダム

(Sameura Damu). Multipurpose dam located on the upper reaches of the river Yoshinogawa in northern Kōchi Prefecture, Shikoku. Completed in 1973, the Sameura Dam provides water for industrial, agricultural, and urban use to Shikoku's four prefectures. Height: 106 m (348 ft); storage capacity: 289 million cu m (10.2 billion cu ft).

Samguk sagi 三国史記

(History of the Three Kingdoms; J: *Sangoku shiki*). The oldest extant history of the Korean Three Kingdoms period, compiled about 1145 under the supervision of the Koryŏ-dynasty scholar Kim Pu-sik (1075–1151). The work resembles a Chinese dynastic history in that coverage extends from the legendary origins of the three kingdoms to Silla's demise in 935. The *Samguk sagi* also contains information on the relationship between the Japanese and Korean languages.

Samguk yusa 三国遺事

(Memorabilia of the Three Kingdoms; J: *Sangoku iji*). A medieval Korean work written in Chinese by the Koryŏ-dynasty Buddhist

monk Iryŏn (1206–89). Compiled about 1285, it contains Buddhist lore and other anecdotal materials concerning the KOREAN THREE KINGDOMS PERIOD. Its Buddhist perspective complements the Confucian orientation of the SAMGUK SAGI.

Samil Independence Movement
三・一独立運動

(J: San'ichi Dokuritsu Undō). Also known as the March First (Samil) Movement after the day in 1919 when the Koreans launched their most determined attempt to gain independence from Japan (see KOREA, ANNEXATION OF). The sudden death of former Korean king KOJONG (r 1864–1907) in January 1919 provided the immediate catalyst for the movement.

On 1 March, posters appeared, claiming that the king had been assassinated by poisoning and explaining the principle of self-determination advocated by US president Woodrow Wilson at the Paris Peace Conference. Students gathered in Seoul's Pagoda Park to read a declaration of independence; people filled the streets chanting *manse* (J: *banzai*), the movement's rallying cry. Similar noisy but nonviolent demonstrations occurred throughout Korea on that day.

The Japanese government responded with brutal force, fanning Korean emotions into a rage; order was not fully restored until the spring of 1920. The Japanese attempted to conceal the extent of the movement and the ferocity of their repression of it; however, a tabulation made by the PROVISIONAL GOVERNMENT OF KOREA in Shanghai indicated that between 1 March and 31 May 1919 more than 2 million Koreans participated, some 7,500 of whom were killed and some 47,000 of whom were arrested. There were very few Japanese casualties. The movement failed to restore Korea's independence, but it did force the Japanese to reform their colonial administration somewhat. These measures stabilized the situation, at least until the KWANGJU STUDENT RESISTANCE MOVEMENT of 1929. See also KOREA AND JAPAN.

samma
秋刀魚

(saury). *Cololabis saira*. A littoral and pelagic migratory fish of the family Scombresocidae, order Atheriniformes, class Osteichthyes. It reaches 40 centimeters (16 in) and is distributed in the temperate and subarctic zones of the northern Pacific Ocean and adjoining waters. Unlike the fish of the same family living in the Atlantic Ocean, the *samma* has short upper and lower jaws. The annual haul in Japan ranges from 200,000 to 600,000 metric tons (220,000–660,000 short tons). As a food it is broiled with salt and canned. It is also used as bait for tuna.

Samp'o Incident
三浦の乱

(J: Sampo no Ran). A 1510 uprising by Japanese merchants and residents in three southeastern Korean ports (*samp'o*). Regulated trade between Japan and Korea had been established in 1426 at Naeip'o (now Chep'o, in Ungch'ŏn district), Pusanp'o (now Pusan, in Tongnae district), and Yŏmp'o (in Ulsan district). Korean government attempts to limit the trade to 50 Japanese ships calling at each port per year led to the uprising, after which the Japanese were expelled. Relations were renewed in 1512, but only Naeip'o was reopened and trade ships were limited to 25 per year. Pusanp'o was reopened in 1521; except for periodic disruptions in Korean-Japanese relations it remained the center of intercourse until the 1876 Treaty of KANGHWA. See also WAEGWAN.

Samukawa
寒川［町］

Town on the river Sagamigawa in south-central Kanagawa Prefecture, central Honshū. Samukawa grew up around the Samukawa Shrine, said to date to the 8th century. The area was agricultural until the end of World War II, after which it became a residential and industrial district. Tires, chemicals, and other products are manufactured here. Pop: 44,532.

samurai
侍

(literally, "one who serves"). Also known as *bushi* ("military gentry"). Term designating the warrior elite of premodern Japan that emerged in the provinces from at least the early 10th century and became the ruling class of the country from the late 12th century until the MEIJI RESTORATION of 1868.

Origins of the Samurai——The main reason for the rise of the *samurai* class was the failure of the central government in Kyōto, controlled by courtiers in the emperor's service, to maintain adequate administration of the provinces. Samurai became active as lesser officials to whom the management in charge of provincial governments was often delegated and also as functionaries in the SHŌEN or private estates of courtiers and religious institutions.

The first BUSHIDAN, or warrior bands, were family organizations, military units recruited by chieftains from among their kinsmen. By the 11th century, however, *bushidan* had developed into more permanent entities structured on lord-vassal ties between fighting men not necessarily related by blood, perpetuated generationally in the families of both lords and vassals and conceived of in fictive kinship terms. Vassals were typically designated as KENIN (housemen) or *ienoko* (children of the house; see IENOKO AND RŌTŌ), and lords were looked upon as fathers.

Leadership of the samurai class was assumed chiefly by men who were descended from the imperial family. Surplus progeny of the polygamous emperors were deprived of royal status and given the surnames Taira or Minamoto (see TAIRA FAMILY; MINAMOTO FAMILY). Some of these imperial kinsmen accepted appointments to the provinces and eventually settled there. Branches of the Taira began appearing in the Kantō from about 900, and in the 10th and 11th centuries the Minamoto established influence both in Kantō and the northern provinces of Honshū.

The Medieval Period——In the HŌGEN DISTURBANCE of 1156 there were Taira and Minamoto on both sides of the fighting, but in the HEIJI DISTURBANCE (1160) the Taira were solidly aligned against the Minamoto. A

Taira victory enabled the clan to become the new aristocracy at court from 1160 until the early 1180s. In 1180 Minamoto chieftains rose in the provinces to precipitate a war (TAIRA-MINAMOTO WAR) that led to the defeat of the Taira in 1185.

The main victor in the Taira-Minamoto War was MINAMOTO NO YORITOMO, who in 1192 established the first true WARRIOR GOVERNMENT in Japanese history, the KAMAKURA SHOGUNATE (1192–1333). In 1192 Yoritomo received court appointment as *seii tai shōgun*, or "barbarian-subduing generalissimo," the title that in ensuing centuries symbolized military overlordship of Japan. See SHŌGUN.

The Kamakura shogunate, overthrown in 1333, was succeeded by the MUROMACHI SHOGUNATE (1338–1573). In a society similar to the feudalistic one of medieval Europe, peasants were bound as serfs to the land and paid harvest rent to samurai, who held superior proprietary rights in the form of fiefs (CHIGYŌ). The samurai themselves were organized into lord-vassal hierarchies. See also FEUDALISM.

The last century of the Muromachi period, beginning with the ŌNIN WAR (1467–77), was a time of civil strife known as the SENGOKU PERIOD, or Warring States period. Gradually, during the first half of the 16th century, a new class of samurai, DAIMYŌ, established territorial domains throughout Japan; and competition began among the leading daimyō to unify the entire country. Unification was finally achieved by three successive leaders, ODA NOBUNAGA, TOYOTOMI HIDEYOSHI, and TOKUGAWA IEYASU.

Samurai warfare expanded markedly during the 16th century. In addition to the traditional samurai cavalrymen, infantry (ASHIGARU) recruited from the peasantry became a standard part of armies. After the arrival in 1543 of the Portuguese as the first Europeans to visit Japan, Western-style rifles and cannon were used. (See FIREARMS, INTRODUCTION OF.) Toward the close of the 16th century samurai were increasingly compelled to take up residence in castle towns and peasants were forbidden to leave the countryside, thus effecting a greater separation of samurai and peasants.

Edo and Early Meiji Periods——The TOKUGAWA SHOGUNATE (1603–1867) brought peace, which posed problems for the ruling samurai class. Some samurai were employed in government, but many more became idle stipendaries. In response to these problems of the samurai during the peaceful Edo period (1600–1868), intellectuals formulated the code of BUSHIDŌ, or the "Way of the warrior." *Bushidō* romanticized the Japanese warrior tradition and enjoined samurai to maintain military preparedness.

The visit to Japan in 1853 of a squadron of ships commanded by Commodore Matthew Perry of the United States brought Japan's National seclusion policy to an end. During the next decade and a half, owing to its inability to deal effectively with foreign relations, the shogunate was increasingly criticized and attacked, especially by samurai opponents within those domains, including Satsuma (now Kagoshima Prefecture) and Chōshū (now Yamaguchi Prefecture), that had never been permitted to participate directly in central government affairs. Ultimately there arose in the mid-1860s an imperial-loyalist movement, led by lower-level samurai from Satsuma, Chōshū, and other domains, which branded the shogunate an unworthy government and led to the MEIJI RESTORATION of 1868.

The Meiji government, however, could ill

afford to continue payment of the hereditary samurai stipends; moreover, continuance of the samurai's elite warrior status was incompatible with the building of a modern conscript army. Dissolution of the samurai class was carried out between 1873 and 1876 in a series of measures collectively called CHITSUROKU SHOBUN. Some samurai leaders undertook armed rebellions, the last of which—the SATSUMA REBELLION—was put down in 1877; others founded Western-style political parties and launched a movement for representative government (see FREEDOM AND PEOPLE'S RIGHTS MOVEMENT). See also SHIZOKU.

Samurai-dokoro　侍所

(Board of Retainers). Office of the Kamakura (1192–1333) and Muromachi (1338–1573) shogunates, established in 1180 by MINAMOTO NO YORITOMO as a bureau to control his vassals (GOKENIN). With the KUMONJO (Public Documents Office, later absorbed into the MANDOKORO or Administrative Board) and the MONCHŪJO (Board of Inquiry), it was a central organ of Yoritomo's government. WADA YOSHIMORI served as first administrative director (bettō), but, after 1213, the post was held by the HŌJŌ FAMILY regent. Duties included supervision of the police authority (KENDAN) of estate stewards (JITŌ).

Throughout the Muromachi shogunate, members of the YAMANA FAMILY, AKAMATSU FAMILY, Isshiki family, and KYŌGOKU FAMILY acted in rotation as its director (now called shoshi). The Samurai-dokoro became responsible for guarding Kyōto and overseeing property owned by the shogunate and religious institutions. The office was abolished during the Bummei era (1469–87). The Samurai-dokoro sata hen, compiled late in the Muromachi period (1333–1568), spells out the functions of the office and contains examples of its rulings.

Sanada Yukimura　真田幸村

(1567–1615). More properly Sanada Nobushige. Warrior of the Azuchi-Momoyama (1568–1600) and early Edo (1600–1868) periods. Son of Sanada Masayuki (1545–1609), the lord of Ueda in Shinano (now Nagano Prefecture). In 1585, when his father was involved in a conflict with TOKUGAWA IEYASU, Yukimura sought the backing of UESUGI KAGEKATSU, daimyō of Echigo (now part of Niigata Prefecture), and was granted a fief by him. By 1587, however, he had switched his allegiance to TOYOTOMI HIDEYOSHI, whom he served in the ODAWARA CAMPAIGN of 1590 and the invasion of Korea in 1592 (see INVASIONS OF KOREA IN 1592 AND 1597). In the great conflict that led to the Battle of SEKIGAHARA in 1600 Yukimura initially joined Ieyasu's expedition against Uesugi Kagekatsu but then adhered to the "Western Army" of ISHIDA MITSUNARI; his brother Nobuyuki (1566–1658) remained loyal to the Tokugawa. The lives of Masayuki and Yukimura were spared after the Tokugawa victory. In the Ōsaka campaigns of 1614–15 (see ŌSAKA CASTLE, SIEGES OF), he fought with TOYOTOMI HIDEYORI and fell in battle on 3 June 1615, the day the castle fell.

Sanage　猿投

Ceramic production area in Aichi Prefecture near the present-day city of Nagoya that began making SUE WARE during the late 5th century. Sanage later developed the first intentionally ash-glazed ceramics in Japan, which made it the country's largest ceramic production site from the late 8th century. These wares were produced until the end of the 12th century. Sanage is particularly fa-

mous for the green ash-glazed stonewares known as shiki (or, more recently, as shirashi), which were produced from about the mid-8th century. Numerous vase and bottle forms were made, the most notable being multispouted bottles (tashihei), long-necked bottles (suibyō), and some long-necked bottles with spouts (jōhei). Sets of drinking cups and jugs and a range of plates and stemmed serving dishes were also produced. In general the body of this ware is light buff, which shows off the rich transparent green ash glaze to good advantage. Methods of decoration include incising, perforation, and underglaze painting in iron salts, the painted motif showing up as darker passages of green. See CERAMICS.

Sanda　三田[市]

City in southeastern Hyōgo Prefecture, western Honshū. Sanda developed as a castle town during the Edo period (1600–1868). Known for rice and cattle, it is becoming a residential suburb of Ōsaka and Kōbe. Of interest are the temples Konshinji and Yōtakuji. Pop: 64,560.

Sandai Jiken Kempaku Movement　三大事件建白運動

(Sandai Jiken Kempaku Undō; Movement to Memorialize Three Important Items). An 1887 antigovernment political movement led by members of the FREEDOM AND PEOPLE'S RIGHTS MOVEMENT. In 1886, Foreign Minister INOUE KAORU submitted a program for nominal revision of the so-called Unequal Treaties (see UNEQUAL TREATIES, REVISION OF). In June 1887 Inoue's program was inadvertently made public. Gustave Emile BOISSONADE DE FONTARABIE and TANI KANJŌ submitted memorials denouncing Inoue's plans as too accommodating to Westerners; their statements were also leaked to the press, causing a political crisis that forced Inoue to resign. In September 1887 HOSHI TŌRU, another popular-rights activist, addressed a mass political rally in Tōkyō and called for treaty revision, reduction of the land tax, and freedom of speech and assembly. A month later KATAOKA KENKICHI forwarded a petition to the GENRŌIN requesting approval of these three demands. The government suppressed this political agitation on 25 December by issuing the PEACE PRESERVATION LAW OF 1887 (Hoan Jōrei). See also DAIDŌ DANKETSU MOVEMENT.

Sandankyō　三段峡

Gorge located on the upper reaches of the river Shibakigawa, a tributary of the Ōtagawa, in northwestern Hiroshima Prefecture, western Honshū. The gorge is noted for its many waterfalls and deep pools. Upstream of the gorge is the man-made lake Hijiriko. Length: 16 km (10 mi).

S&B Shokuhin Co, Ltd　エスビー食品[株]

(Esu Bī Shokuhin). Manufacturer of spices, seasonings, and instant foods. Incorporated in 1940. It has the largest domestic share in the spice market. It is diversifying into snack food, and it operates a chain of take-out lunch shops through a subsidiary. Sales for the fiscal year ending March 1991 totaled ¥66.9 billion (US $487.6 million). The company was capitalized at ¥1.6 billion (US $11.7 million) in the same year. Headquarters are in Tōkyō.

Sanden Corporation　サンデン[株]

(Sanden). Manufacturer of automobile air-conditioning systems and air-conditioner

compressors and clutches. Incorporated in 1943. The company also manufactures automatic vending machines. For the fiscal year ending March 1991, sales totaled ¥100.8 billion (US $734.7 million) and capitalization stood at ¥11.0 billion (US $80.2 million). Headquarters are in the city of Isesaki, Gumma Prefecture.

Sanetaka Kō ki　実隆公記

Diary of courtier SANJŌNISHI SANETAKA (1455–1537). Sanetaka served emperors GO-HANAZONO (r 1428–64), Go-Tsuchimikado (r 1464–1500), and Go-Kashiwabara (r 1500–1526), and became inner minister (naidaijin) in 1506. He was a noted scholar, poet, and compiler of court ceremonial. His diary covers 1474–1536 and is a basic source for the late Muromachi period (1333–1568). Besides containing information concerning his own family, the diary is rich in details of courtier culture and its penetration into the provinces, and the social and political upheavals of the day. Moreover, the diary is written on the backs of letters received by Sanetaka, which are themselves valuable historical documents.

San Felipe Incident　サン・フェリペ号事件

(San Feripe gō Jiken). The confiscation of the Spanish galleon San Felipe by TOYOTOMI HIDEYOSHI in December 1596, inaugurating his persecution of Catholic missionaries. Bound from Manila to Acapulco, the San Felipe was dismasted in a typhoon and stranded at Urado, Tosa Province (now Kōchi Prefecture), on 7 December 1596. Hideyoshi ordered the confiscation of the rich cargo of the San Felipe and in February 1597 executed 6 Spanish Franciscan missionary friars, 3 JESUITS, and 17 laymen on the grounds that they were subversive (see TWENTY-SIX MARTYRS). Many of the Spanish survivors considered that Hideyoshi had been provoked by the intrigues of the Portuguese Jesuit missionaries in Japan. Hideyoshi made it clear to the governor of the Philippines, when the latter protested, that he could no more tolerate the propagation of Christianity in Japan than would the king of Spain and Portugal allow Shintō or Buddhist missionaries in his realms. See CHRISTIANITY; ANTI-CHRISTIAN EDICTS.

San Francisco Peace Treaty　サンフランシスコ平和条約

(San Furanshisuko Heiwa Jōyaku). Name commonly given to the treaty of peace signed by Japan and 48 other nations at San Francisco on 8 September 1951 and formally implemented on 28 April 1952 (its formal name in English is Treaty of Peace with Japan). Negotiations for a postwar peace settlement became a public issue at least as early as 17 March 1947, when General Douglas MACAR-

San Francisco Peace Treaty　With the Japanese negotiating team looking on, Prime Minister Yoshida Shigeru signs the treaty that formally ended the state of war between Japan and the Allied powers.

San'in Coast National Park A deeply indented section of the pine-topped volcanic tuff coastline at Uradome in Tottori Prefecture.

Margaret Sanger In 1922 Sanger, an early advocate of birth control, made the first of a number of visits to Japan to lecture on family planning.

THUR, the supreme commander of the Allied OCCUPATION forces, held a news conference to urge the quick conclusion of a peace treaty with Japan. What was necessary now, he thought, was for Japan to regain a spirit of independence so that its economy could grow without excessive reliance on US aid.

MacArthur's comments helped to set off a fierce debate about the kind of treaty that should be written. On the one hand, the British Commonwealth countries, China, and many of the Southeast Asian nations that had suffered most at the hands of the Japanese argued that the treaty should be tough, with provisions for reparations and demilitarization under close international supervision. Advocates of a softer peace treaty put primary emphasis upon a treaty that the ruling Japanese government could regard without humiliation. Advocates of this view rapidly gained influence in the United States.

Faced with concerns over Japan's postwar security and disagreements with its allies, the United States began its "piecemeal peace" program of restoring as much national sovereignty to the Japanese government as possible and at the same time hinted that it would conclude peace with the Japanese whether or not the other Allies agreed. Also important was the appointment by President Harry S. Truman, supported by Secretary of State Dean Acheson, of Republican John Foster DULLES as foreign policy adviser to the secretary of state. Dulles was expected to bring badly needed bipartisan support to this exceedingly complex issue. Dulles embarked upon a series of bilateral negotiations designed to complete the treaty. British Commonwealth objections were met by including some British suggestions in the final text and by making the United Kingdom cosponsor of the actual peace conference. Moreover, the signing of the ANZUS treaty of defense by Australia, New Zealand, and the United States tended to dispel fears of revived Japanese militarism. Intense Philippine objections were met by the promise of US aid and by the Philippine defense pact signed on 31 August 1951. Disputes over China were settled by inviting neither the People's Republic of China nor the Republic of China to the conference and by asking Japan to negotiate the problem of Chinese relations separately.

At the conference itself, the United States and Britain quickly asserted control over procedure. The Soviet Union, Poland, and Czechoslovakia, the only communist countries represented, had little hope of influencing the outcome and soon walked out without signing a treaty. A peace treaty with the Soviet Union and the fate of various northern territories such as the HABOMAI ISLANDS would continue to be major problems for Japanese diplomacy throughout the postwar period (see NORTHERN TERRITORIES ISSUE).

The treaty was reasonably generous in its terms. Japan was deprived of all of its territories seized since 1895, including Taiwan, Korea, southern Sakhalin, and subsidiary islands. US trusteeship of the RYŪKYŪ ISLANDS including OKINAWA was permitted indefinitely, although a 1972 treaty later returned these islands to Japan. Japan renounced all claims to property in its former colonies and occupied territories and agreed to pay reparations for war damage, but, in a major victory for the "soft peace" advocates, it was clearly stated in the treaty that Japan's fragile economic position would have to be respected. Japan and 48 other nations signed this document at San Francisco on 8 September 1951.

Ensuring US ratification then became the principal task for the US and Japanese negotiators. Warned by Dulles, then visiting Japan as a special envoy, that any dealings with the People's Republic of China would jeopardize US Senate approval of the treaty, the Japanese prime minister, YOSHIDA SHIGERU, in a 24 December 1951 letter to Dulles, promised to deal only with the Nationalists. Accordingly, on 28 April 1952 a peace treaty was signed with Nationalist China. More important, the United States–Japan Security Treaty (see UNITED STATES–JAPAN SECURITY TREATIES), signed two hours after the peace treaty, assured the continued presence of US forces and military bases in Japan. Ratification was achieved, and the peace treaty went into effect on 28 April 1952.

In the legal sense, the peace treaty ended the state of war between Japan and most of the Allied powers. It is notable chiefly for its relatively generous terms with regard to reparations, "war guilt," and the like. In a larger sense, however, the treaty is an example of the way in which the Dulles-Acheson coalition replaced the Occupation of Japan with a network of US security alliances extending beyond Japan to the other nations of South and East Asia. The treaty and its accompanying entanglements actually set the stage for a new relationship between Japan and the United States that would become a major source of political contention in Japan.

sangaku shinkō → mountains, worship of

Sanger, Margaret サンガー, M.

(1883–1966). Leader of the birth control movement in the United States. Born in Corning, New York. In June 1921 an article by Sanger appeared in the Japanese magazine *Kaizō*, and in March 1922 at the invitation of the publisher she arrived in Japan to give a series of lectures. Although closely watched by police, who confiscated most of her pamphlets and contraceptives, she was able to give eight lectures in Tōkyō and Yokohama. Sanger's activities aroused much interest, and she is considered the initiator of the birth control movement in Japan. Her tract, *Family Limitation*, was translated and privately published by YAMAMOTO SENJI. In 1954 she again went to Tōkyō to attend the founding ceremony of the Nihon Kazoku Keikaku Remmei (Family Planning Federation of Japan). See also FAMILY PLANNING.

Sangetsu Co, Ltd [株]サンゲツ

(Sangetsu). Company engaged in the sale of wallpaper and other wall materials, curtains, and carpets. Incorporated in 1953. It has overseas offices in Hamburg, Germany, and in Hong Kong. Sales for the fiscal year ending March 1991 totaled ¥101.8 billion (US $742.0 million), and capitalization stood at ¥12.2 billion (US $88.9 million) in the same year. Headquarters are in Nagoya.

sangi 参議

(councillor). 1. An extrastatutory post (RYŌGE NO KAN), that is, one not prescribed by the TAIHŌ CODE (701) and YŌRŌ CODE (effective 757) as part of the RITSURYŌ SYSTEM of government. Created in 731. From the 9th century onward there were eight *sangi*, who worked with the Grand Council of State (DAJŌKAN).

2. A post in the Meiji Dajōkan (the early Meiji government, 1868–85) established in August 1869. The first to hold it were ŌKUBO TOSHIMICHI and others from the domains that had led the Meiji Restoration. Until 1871 the role of the *sangi* was to assist the ministers of the left and right (sadaijin and udaijin) and the great councillors (dainagon). After the reorganization of 13 September 1871, the *sangi*, the grand minister of state (dajō daijin), and the ministers of the left and the right formed the Seiin, the new government's central deliberative body. Generally, *sangi* served concurrently as heads of the ministries. The post ceased to exist when the cabinet system was created in 1885.

Sangoku Kanshō → Tripartite Intervention

Sangyō gisho 三経義疏

The three oldest Japanese commentaries on Buddhist sutras, presumably by Prince SHŌTOKU, under whose patronage Buddhism became fully established in Japan in the early 7th century. The three commentaries are the *Shōmangyō gisho* (on the *Śrīmālādevī-siṃhanāda-sūtra*), the *Yuimagyō gisho* (on the

Vimala-kīrti-nirdeśa-sūtra), and the *Hokke gisho* (on the LOTUS SUTRA), all probably composed between 609 and 615. They show a remarkable grasp of Buddhist philosophy and manifest deep religious feeling.

San'in Coast National Park
山陰海岸国立公園

(San'in Kaigan Kokuritsu Kōen). A long, narrow park, situated in western Honshū, in Kyōto, Hyōgo, and Tottori prefectures, stretching 77 km (48 mi) along the Sea of Japan coast. The park is characterized by small bays and islets, strangely shaped rock formations, and gentle hills. Kinosaki Hot Spring, in the park's eastern end near the town of KINOSAKI, is a popular resort. The coasts around Kasumi, in the center, and at Uradome, in the west, are noted for their rock islands and caves. At the western tip of the park are the TOTTORI SAND DUNES, the largest in Japan. Notable among the plant and animal life are the black pine (*kuromatsu*), the Japanese martin (*iwatsubame*), and the black-tailed gull (*umineko*). Area: 90 sq km (35 sq mi).

San'in region
山陰地方

(San'in *chihō*). Region in western Honshū along the Sea of Japan encompassing Tottori, Shimane, and Yamaguchi prefectures, as well as the northern portions of Kyōto and Hyōgo prefectures. The region corresponds to the San'indō of the old GOKI SHICHIDŌ system of administrative units in Japan. Located on the northern side of the Chūgoku Mountains, it has few large plains and receives much snow and rain in the winter months. Industrial development in the region has been slow, for it is located far from the cultural and economic heartland of Japan. Tourist attractions include the Daisen-Oki National Park, the San'in Coast National Park, and numerous hot springs.

Sanja Festival
三社祭

(Sanja Matsuri). Annual festival of the Asakusa Shrine (also known as Sanja Gongen) in Taitō Ward, Tōkyō. One of the major festivals of Edo (now Tōkyō) along with the KANDA FESTIVAL and the SANNŌ FESTIVAL. High points of the festival include the parading of about 100 portable shrines (MIKOSHI), the dance called *binzasara no mai*, and *tekomai*, a dance performed by *geisha*. It is held on the third weekend in May.

Sanja Matsuri
三社祭

(Sanja Festival). KABUKI dance piece. Narrative written by Segawa Jokō II (1757–1833). Formal title *Yayoi no hana Asakusa Matsuri* (Asakusa Festival, Spring Flowers). The piece was first performed in 1832 at the time of the SANJA FESTIVAL of the ASAKUSA SHRINE in Edo (now Tōkyō), and it includes material based on the legend of the shrine's origin, hence its popular title. It is one of the liveliest of all kabuki dances. Successive segments reflecting life in old Edo (notably one in which two fishermen are possessed by good and evil spirits) are danced to the rhythmic KIYOMOTO-BUSHI accompaniment.

sanjo
散所

(literally, "scattered places"). A medieval type of "lowborn" people (see SEMMIN; RYŌMIN). The term originated in the late Heian period (794–1185) and was used to denote scattered possessions of aristocratic SHŌEN (landed estate). The service population grouped together in such places, originally called *sanjo zōshiki* or *sanjo meshitsugi*, by extension also became known as *sanjo*. Their provenance was among people who sought to escape various exactions by subordinating themselves to powerful individuals or institutions for whom they performed miscellaneous specialized services. As early as 1072, *sanjo zōshiki* exempt from public duties are mentioned in official documents along with analogous groups such as JINNIN.

In response to discrimination, *sanjo* formed their own communities, and some of those in Kyōto became powerful enough to form guilds (ZA) under aristocratic protection. These and similar settlements are regarded by some historians as the antecedents of the *hisabetsu buraku* ("communities that suffer discrimination"; see BURAKUMIN) of the Edo (1600–1868) and modern periods.

Sanjō
三条〔市〕

City in central Niigata Prefecture, central Honshū. Located on the river Shinanogawa, Sanjō developed as a post-station town during the Edo period (1600–1868). Its ironware industry is especially known for its carpenter's tools, scissors, and knives. Of note are the temple Honjōji, founded in the 13th century, and a branch of Kyōto's temple HIGASHI HONGANJI. Pop: 85,823.

Sanjō, Emperor
三条天皇

(976–1017; Sanjō Tennō). The 67th sovereign (*tennō*) in the traditional count (which includes several legendary emperors); reigned 1011–16. Second son of Emperor Reizei (950–1011; r 967–969); his mother was a sister of FUJIWARA NO MICHINAGA and one of his consorts was Michinaga's daughter. Chafing under the domination of the powerful Michinaga, and suffering from an eye ailment, Sanjō relinquished the throne after five years.

Sanjōnishi Sanetaka
三条西実隆

(1455–1537). Courtier, poet, and polymath of the Sengoku period (1467–1568). The son of the *naidaijin* (inner minister) Sanjōnishi (Fujiwara) Kin'yasu (d 1460), Sanetaka was himself appointed *naidaijin* in 1506. His fame is based on his maintenance and transmission of the highest cultural standards in an age that he described as "unspeakable" and a time of "war, contention, and brute force." Sanetaka studied with SŌGI, whom he assisted in compiling the RENGA (linked-verse) collection SHINSEN TSUKUBASHŪ and by whom he was initiated into the secret traditions (see KOKIN DENJU) of the KOKINSHŪ poetry anthology. Sanetaka was a WAKA and *renga* poet; the author of at least one NŌ play, *Sagoromo*; an authority on classical Japanese literature, notably the TALE OF GENJI; a student of Chinese history; an expert on etiquette and ceremonial matters (YŪSOKU KOJITSU); a renowned calligrapher; and a master of SHŌGI (Japanese chess). His diary, SANETAKA KŌ KI, which covers the years 1474–1536, is an indispensable source for the history of his age.

Sanjō Sanetomi
三条実美

(1837–91). Court noble and political leader at the time of the MEIJI RESTORATION of 1868. Born in Kyōto. Sanjō became a supporter of the anti-Western, antishogunate SONNŌ JŌI (Revere the Emperor, Expel the Barbarians) movement. In 1863 he was appointed *kokuji goyō-gakari* (commissioner of state affairs) at the imperial court in Kyōto. When the COUP D'ETAT OF 30 SEPTEMBER 1863 brought to power the more moderate Aizu (now part of Fuku-

Sanja Festival Participants in this annual festival carry a portable shrine as they thread their way through crowds of spectators. At right are banners announcing the festival.

shima Prefecture) and Satsuma (now Kagoshima Prefecture) domains, Sanjō fled to Chōshū (see SHICHIKYŌ OCHI). He returned to Kyōto after TOKUGAWA YOSHINOBU returned government powers to the emperor (see TAISEI HŌKAN) in 1867.

Named to the Gijō (Office of Administration; see SANSHOKU) in 1868, he became a central figure in the new government. In 1869 he was appointed *udaijin* (minister of the right), and two years later he became *dajō daijin* (grand minister of state). He remained in the post until 1885, when the cabinet system was introduced.

Sanjūrokkasen
三十六歌仙

(The Thirty-Six Poetic Geniuses). List of outstanding Japanese poets from the time of the poetry anthology *Man'yōshū* (759) to the end of the 10th century. It was based on an anthology, which no longer exists, known as the *Sanjūrokunin sen* (Selection of Thirty-Six Poets), compiled in the early 11th century by FUJIWARA NO KINTŌ and inspired by the earlier group of the Six Poetic Geniuses (ROKKASEN). The list includes such poets as ARIWARA NO NARIHIRA, Bishop HENJŌ, FUJIWARA NO KANESUKE, KI NO TSURAYUKI, ONO NO KOMACHI, ŌTOMO NO YAKAMOCHI, and YAMABE NO AKAHITO. The chief importance of the list is that it led in the mid-11th century to the making or remaking of personal poetry collections (SHIKASHŪ) for all of the 36 poets, thus helping to preserve their work.

Kintō chose about 150 poems, 3 to 5 of the finest poems of each poet, probably with the intention of comparing them in an imaginary poetry contest. The sumptuous 12th-century Nishi Honganji version of the anthology of the type known as the *Sanjūrokuninshū* (Anthologies of the Thirty-Six Poets) comprises the vastly expanded complete collections of the works of each poet. Paintings of the 36 as a group (KASEN-E) were made by many artists.

Sanjūsangendō
三十三間堂

The main hall (*hondō*), and only building, of the Rengeōin, a small Buddhist temple affiliated with the Myōhōin, a TENDAI SECT temple located in Higashiyama Ward, Kyōto. The Sanjūsangendō is so named because the inner sanctum is made up of 33 (*sanjūsan*) bays (*ken*) separated by evenly spaced pillars. The Rengeōin, built in 1164 by warrior ruler TAIRA NO KIYOMORI, was destroyed by fire in 1249. By 1266 its *hondō* had been rebuilt by the retired emperor GOSAGA; it is this structure that is now known as Rengeōin or Sanjūsangendō. Its sculpture includes 1,001 "Thousand-Armed Kannon" (Senju Kannon) statues carved by TANKEI, Kōen (b 1207), and others. The 16th-century *nandaimon* (south main gate) and *tsuijibei* (*tsuiji* fence) are Important Cultural Properties. During the Edo period (1600–1868) the

Sanjūsangendō
The 33 bays of this small Buddhist temple in Kyōto contain 1,001 figures of the "Thousand-Armed Kannon." The statues were carved in the 12th and 13th centuries in the belief that the people of this degenerate latter age of Buddha's law (*mappō*) could win salvation only by repeated acts of devotion.

Sanjūsangendō was the site of popular archery contests known as *tōshiya*.

sanka   山窩

(literally, "mountain cave"). Term referring to a type of people who formerly maintained a migratory way of life in the mountains of Japan. Typically traveling in family units and living in tents pitched along mountain streams, they made their living by selling the fish they caught or the winnows, baskets, and brooms they produced. They moved south in the winter and north in the summer. Nothing definite is known about their origins. Their number diminished drastically during and after World War II. *Sanka* are one type of *yamabito* ("mountain people"). Such people have always been treated as strange and different by the rest of Japanese society.

Sankai Juku   山海塾

BUTŌ (avant-garde dance) group founded in 1975 under the leadership of Amagatsu Ushio (b 1949). With smoothly shaved heads and bodies painted white, the dancers seem to portray the flesh reduced to its essence and have become popular for their highly refined performances. They attracted notice at the 1980 Nancy Theater Festival in France, afterward making Paris, in addition to Tōkyō, a base from which they tour all over the world. At the 1982 Belgrade International Theater Festival they won the Grand Prix for *Kinkan shōnen* (The Kumquat Seed). Other works include *Jōmonshō* (1982, Homage to Prehistory) and *Unetsu* (1986, The Egg Stands Out of Curiosity).

sankechi   三纈

(literally, "three press-dyes"). Three resist-dyeing techniques of *kyōkechi*, *rōkechi*, and *kōkechi*; also referred to as Tempyō *no sankechi* (*sankechi* of the Tempyō era [729–749]).

In the 6th century continental dyeing techniques were imported from China. The details of *kyōkechi*, a block-resist technique, remain a mystery of the Nara period (710–794). In *rōkechi*, a technique similar to batik, the cloth was stamped with wax (*rō*) or other resin by a printing block, then dyed. Multicolored pieces of cloth were made by repeating these steps (see also WAX-RESIST DYEING). *Kōkechi* is single-color TIE-DYEING including white-spotted or dapple tie-dyeing, stitched tie-dyeing, and folded or pressed tie-dyeing. *Kōkechi* alone has survived to the present.

Sankeien   三渓園

Garden in Naka Ward, Yokohama, Kanagawa Prefecture; built by Hara Tomitarō, a wealthy businessman, and opened to the public in 1906. It consists of several ponds and many varieties of flowering trees. An old farmhouse from Gifu Prefecture, a tea-ceremony house, and other historic buildings have been brought here. Area: 20 hectares (49 acres).

Sankei shimbun   産経新聞

A large, national daily newspaper. It was first launched in Ōsaka in 1933 by Maeda Hisakichi as a financial trade paper called *Nihon kōgyō shimbun*. In 1942 the name was changed to *Sangyō keizai shimbun*. The paper began a Tōkyō edition in 1950, and the business news format was dropped in favor of more general news coverage. In 1955 it merged with the JIJI SHIMPŌ to form the *Sankei jiji*. This enterprise did not prosper, and in 1958 it took the name *Sankei shimbun* under businessman MIZUNO SHIGEO. It was rapidly modernized, and in 1967 it joined with FUJI TELECASTING CO, LTD, NIPPON CULTURAL BROADCASTING, INC, and NIPPON BROADCASTING SYSTEM, INC, in forming the Fuji-Sankei group, a large newspaper, radio, and television concern. Circulation was 2.1 million in 1991.

Sanken Electric Co, Ltd
サンケン電気[株]
(Sanken Denki). Specialized manufacturer of semiconductor devices. Incorporated in 1946. Sanken also manufactures power supply equipment for computer and communication systems. Sales for the fiscal year ending March 1990 totaled ¥107.4 billion (US $701.1 million), and capitalization stood at ¥14.4 billion (US $94.1 million). Headquarters are in Niiza, Saitama Prefecture.

Sanki Engineering Co, Ltd
三機工業[株]
(Sanki Kōgyō). Company mainly engaged in the installation of equipment for air-conditioning, water supply, drainage, electricity, and other systems in construction projects. Incorporated in 1949. A member of the MITSUI group, it supplies equipment to the mining and chemical industries. It is active in introducing foreign technology. Sales for the fiscal year ending March 1991 totaled ¥238.6 billion (US $1.7 billion), and the company was capitalized at ¥8.0 billion (US $58.3 million). Headquarters are in Tōkyō.

sankin kōtai   参勤交代

(alternate attendance). A rule of the TOKUGAWA SHOGUNATE (1603–1867), whereby *daimyō*, or territorial lords, were required to reside in alternate years at Edo (now Tōkyō) in attendance on the shōgun. The *sankin kōtai* system was a device to maintain control over the more than 260 daimyō who were the virtually autonomous feudal rulers of four-fifths of the country. The term referred to the obligation of the daimyō to attend the shogunal court in Edo at fixed intervals, dividing their time equally between the capital and their domains. This service—actually a polite form of hostageship—was performed in alternating groups. To perform this obligation the daimyō had to maintain *yashiki* (residential estates) in

Edo, where their wives and children were permanently detained by the shogunate. Between 1635 and 1642 *sankin kōtai* was regularized and made compulsory under the third shōgun, TOKUGAWA IEMITSU. The typical daimyō traveled to the capital every other year and returned to his domain after a year's service. He traveled with a retinue of 150 to 300 or more (see DAIMYŌ PROCESSIONS), using the main highways, which were all under shogunal control (see GOKAIDŌ). The journeys and the upkeep of a daimyō's Edo estates consumed about 70 to 80 percent of his income. The system endured with little change until it was terminated in 1862.

Sankyō Aluminium Industry Co, Ltd

三協アルミニウム工業[株]

(Sankyō Aruminiumu Kōgyō). Manufacturer of aluminum sashes, fixtures, and kitchenware. Incorporated in 1960. Sankyō is the largest sashmaker in Japan. Recently the company has turned its attention to automated products for use in the home, such as home security systems. Sales for the fiscal year ending May 1991 totaled ¥256.8 billion (US $1.9 billion), and the company was capitalized at ¥26.4 billion (US $192.7 million). Headquarters are in Toyama Prefecture.

Sankyō Co, Ltd

三共[株]

(Sankyō). Manufacturer of pharmaceuticals, agricultural chemicals, food additives, and chemical products. Incorporated in 1899. It has technical and business ties with companies in the United States and Europe and joint-venture companies in India and Taiwan. Sales for the fiscal year ending March 1991 totaled ¥336.3 billion (US $2.5 billion), and the company was capitalized at ¥34.4 billion (US $250.7 million) in the same year. Headquarters are in Tōkyō.

Sankyō Seiki Mfg Co, Ltd

[株]三協精機製作所

(Sankyō Seiki Seisakusho). Manufacturer of electronic, information, and control equipment as well as music boxes. Incorporated in 1947. The company has diversified into audio systems, micromotors for videocassette recorders, and magnetic heads. The firm has manufacturing and sales subsidiaries in the United States, Germany, Switzerland, Hong Kong, Singapore, Malaysia, Taiwan, and Korea. Sales for the fiscal year ending March 1991 totaled ¥108.9 billion (US $793.7 million), and capitalization stood at ¥15.6 billion (US $113.7 million). Headquarters are in Tōkyō.

Sankyō Seikō Co, Ltd

三共生興[株]

(Sankyō Seikō). Trader in fabrics, fashion apparel, interior decorating materials, and electrical and industrial machinery; also a leading importer and licensed producer of famous American and European brands of fashion apparel. Incorporated in 1938. It has three overseas subsidiaries and is participating in a joint venture overseas. Sales for the fiscal year ending March 1991 totaled ¥103.3 billion (US $752.9 million), and the company was capitalized at ¥3.0 billion (US $21.9 million). Headquarters are in Ōsaka.

Sankyū, Inc

山九[株]

(Sankyū). Transport company engaged mainly in transportation and distribution of steel-related materials and equipment. Incorporated in 1917. The firm is also engaged in plant construction and installation and plant services. It has nine overseas subsidiaries and representative offices in the United

States, Singapore, Hong Kong, Indonesia, Thailand, Brazil, Malaysia, China, and the Republic of Korea. Sales for the fiscal year ending March 1991 totaled ¥241.2 billion (US $1.8 billion), and the company was capitalized at ¥13.1 billion (US $95.5 million). Headquarters are in Tōkyō.

Sannō Festival

山王祭

(Sannō Matsuri). Major Shintō festival of the HIE SHRINE (popularly called Sannōsama) in Tōkyō; celebrated in recent times from 7 to 16 June. During the Edo period (1600–1868) the deity Sannō Gongen, associated with the shrine, was designated a tutelary deity of the Tokugawa family, and Hie Shrine was granted shogunal patronage. The extravagant Sannō Festival was held (as it is today) every other year, alternating with the KANDA FESTIVAL. Neighborhood groups carried portable shrines (MIKOSHI) and paraded floats (DASHI) of their own design into Edo Castle.

Sannō Festival refers as well to the annual festival of the original Hie Shrine (Hiyoshi Taisha) in the city of Ōtsu, Shiga Prefecture. Also called Hie Matsuri, it is held from 12 April to 15 April; the highlight is a flotilla of *mikoshi* on Lake Biwa on 14 April.

Sannō Ichijitsu Shintō

山王一実神道

A syncretic Buddhist-Shintō school that sought to harmonize the teachings of the Buddhist TENDAI SECT with the cult of the Hie Shrine on Mt. Hiei (Hieizan), whose chief deity was given the name Sannō (Mountain King). The school arose in the 13th century under the influence of RYŌBU SHINTŌ. Based on the prevailing belief that Shintō deities were Japanese manifestations of Buddhist divinities (see HONJI SUIJAKU), Sannō Shintō held that the deities of the Hie and Ise shrines corresponded, respectively, to the Buddhas Shaka (Skt: Sākyamuni) and Dainichi (Skt: Mahāvairocana). Just as Shaka and Dainichi were ultimately identical in the view of Japanese Tendai, so too were the deities Sannō Gongen of the Hie Shrine and AMATERASU ŌMIKAMI of the Ise Shrine. Sannō Shintō was further developed by the Tendai monk Tenkai (1536–1643). Tenkai taught a doctrine known as Sannō Ichijitsu Shintō (Shintō That Reveals the One Truth of Sannō) which maintained that Amaterasu, while being the Shintō counterpart of Dainichi, is the ultimate source from which all Buddhist and Shintō deities spring. After 1867, with the collapse of the Tokugawa shogunate (1603–1867), Sannō Ichijitsu Shintō virtually disappeared as a religious movement. See also ICHIJITSU SHINTŌ KI.

Sannō Pass

山王峠

(Sannō Tōge). Pass in the northwestern part of the city of Nikkō in Tochigi Prefecture, central Honshū. It is traversed by the Oku Kinu road linking Senjōgahara in Oku Nikkō to the Oku Kinu Hot Springs. Elevation: 1,739 m (5,705 ft).

Sano

佐野[市]

City in southwestern Tochigi Prefecture, central Honshū. Sano developed in the Edo period (1600–1868) as a post-station town on the highway to NIKKŌ. Principal industries are textiles and clothing, although precision-instrument, automobile-parts, and plastic industries have developed recently. Pop: 83,484.

Sano Manabu

佐野学

(1892–1953). Economist and social activist. Born in Ōita Prefecture. As a student at Tōkyō University, Sano became interested in the socialist movement and helped found the study group SHINJINKAI. He was appointed an economics lecturer at Waseda University in 1920. In 1922 he joined the newly established Japan Communist Party (JCP). The JCP sent him to the Soviet Union in 1923, where he served as a representative to the Comintern. He returned to Japan in 1925 and in 1927 became chairman of the JCP's central committee. In 1928 he again went to the Soviet Union just before the first mass arrests of suspected communists (see MARCH 15TH INCIDENT). In June 1929 Sano was arrested by Japanese authorities in Shanghai and sentenced by the Tōkyō District Court to life imprisonment. In June 1933 he repudiated communism; his act inspired recantations by fellow communists (see TENKŌ). His prison term was reduced to 15 years, and he was released in 1943. He returned to Waseda University after World War II.

Sano no Chigami no Otome

狭野茅上娘子

(fl early 8th century; "The Maiden Sano no Chigami"). Also called Sano no Otogami no Otome. A poet and palace attendant of low rank, she served in the Bureau of the High Priestess of the Great Shrine at Ise. In spite of the taboo prohibiting men from entering the palace of the priestess, she had a clandestine affair with Nakatomi no Yakamori, who was exiled when the lovers were discovered. Book 15 of the MAN'YŌSHŪ (ca 759) contains a series of 63 love poems exchanged by

Sankai Juku This avant-garde *butō* dance troupe has won acclaim around the world for its thought-provoking, visually striking performances.
1 The piece *Unetsu* (The Egg Stands Out of Curiosity) takes death as its theme. Thin columns of sand and water stream onto the stage from above.
2 *Kinkan shōnen* (The Kumquat Seed), the work that propelled the group to fame in the late 1970s, explores the unconscious hopes, fears, and eroticism of childhood.

Chigami and Yakamori; 23 of them are by Chigami.

Sano Tsunetami 佐野常民

(1822–1902). Politician who founded the Red Cross in Japan. Born in the Saga domain (now part of Saga Prefecture), Sano studied WESTERN LEARNING under Hirose Mototaka, OGATA KŌAN, ITŌ GEMBOKU, and others. He played a leading role in founding a naval force in his domain. After the Meiji Restoration (1868) he helped establish the Japanese navy. In 1877 he founded a relief organization called the Hakuaisha to treat soldiers wounded in the SATSUMA REBELLION. This organization became the JAPANESE RED CROSS SOCIETY in 1887; Sano served as its first president. Sano served in the GENRŌIN and in various government posts.

Sanraku → Kanō Sanraku

Sanriku Coast 三陸海岸

(Sanriku Kaigan). Coastal area that extends from Samekaku in the city of Hachinohe, Aomori Prefecture, to KINKAZAN off the Oshika Peninsula in Miyagi Prefecture, northern Honshū. It is noted for its narrow beaches and heavily indented coastline. Much of it is included in the RIKUCHŪ COAST NATIONAL PARK. The area is known for its earthquakes and tidal waves. Length: 600 km (370 mi).

Sanrio Co, Ltd [株]サンリオ

(Sanrio). Designer and merchandiser of gift items and greeting cards. Incorporated in 1960. The company has overseas subsidiaries in the United States, Germany, Switzerland, and Brazil. Sales for the fiscal year ending March 1991 totaled ¥116.9 billion (US $852.0 million), of which gift merchandise accounted for 88 percent. The company was capitalized at ¥36.8 billion (US $268.2 million) in the same year. Headquarters are in Tōkyō.

Sanrizuka 三里塚

District in the southeastern part of the city of NARITA, northern Chiba Prefecture, central

Honshū. Until recently a farm owned by the imperial family to produce dairy goods for its own use was here. Sanrizuka is the site of the NEW TŌKYŌ INTERNATIONAL AIRPORT.

Sanron school 三論宗

(Sanronshū; School of the Three Treatises). Buddhist school that employed three philosophical treatises as its basic texts: the *Chū-ron* (Skt: *Mādhyamika-śāstra;* Treatise of the Middle Way) and the *Jūnimonron* (Skt: *Dvādaśamukha-śāstra;* Treatise of the Twelve Gates)—both by the Indian Buddhist monk-philosopher Nāgārjuna (J: Ryūju; ca AD 150–ca AD 250)—and the *Hyakuron* (Skt: *Śata-śāstra;* One Hundred Treatises) by Āryadeva (J: Daiba; fl 3rd century), Nāgārjuna's disciple. Their central theme is EMPTINESS (J: *kū*) and the relativity of the philosophical positions of various Buddhist sutras. The school taught that the true path lies in the middle way. Ekan (Kor: Ekwan) of the Korean kingdom of KOGURYŎ brought the school to Japan in 625. It was the first of the so-called Six Schools of the Southern Capital (Nanto Rokushū; see NARA BUDDHISM) to reach Japan. The school had its centers at the temples GANGŌJI and DAIANJI and at a subtemple of TŌDAIJI. The school continued until the Edo period (1600–1868).

Sanshimpō 三新法

(Three New Laws). Laws defining the first comprehensive system for local administration devised by the Meiji government; drawn up as a result of the second meeting of the ASSEMBLY OF PREFECTURAL GOVERNORS and promulgated on 22 July 1878. The Three Laws regulated, respectively, prefectural administrative organization (Gun-ku-chō-son Hensei Hō), elected metropolitan and prefectural assemblies (Fukenkai Kisoku) and local taxation (Chihōzei Kisoku). As a departure from the completely autocratic centralization that had previously existed, the Sanshimpō were at the time considered a victory for the FREEDOM AND PEOPLE'S RIGHTS MOVEMENT. Although often revised, they remained in force until the implementation of a new local autonomy system in 1888 and 1890.

Sanshō-Dayū 山椒太夫

The name of a legendary wealthy resident of Tango Province (now Kyōto Prefecture) who appears as a character in stories featuring a sister and brother named Anju Hime and Zushi Ō, respectively. As the siblings are traveling with their mother to Tsukushi (northern Kyūshū) to visit their father, who has been exiled on false charges, they fall into the hands of slave traders. The mother is sent to the island of Sado and the brother and sister are sold to Sanshō-Dayū, at whose hands they suffer much cruelty. Later Zushi Ō avenges himself against Sanshō-Dayū. The moral of the story is that those who flaunt their prosperity will meet with destruction, thus making the legend a vehicle

for the masses' condemnation of the rich. The Sanshō-Dayū legend has been a frequent theme of the dramatic narrative chanting known as JŌRURI and is the subject of MORI ŌGAI's story of that name as well as a 1954 film version by MIZOGUCHI KENJI.

Sanshoku 三職

(Three Offices). The first administrative organs of the Meiji government; established 3 January 1868. They were the Office of the President (Sōsai), the Office of Administration (Gijō), and the Office of Councillors (San'yo). These and subsidiary departments were abolished on 11 June when the SEITAISHO (Constitution of 1868) established the DAJŌKAN (Grand Council of State).

sanshōuo → salamanders

sanshu no jingi → imperial regalia

Sansom, George Bailey サンソム, G. B.

(1883–1965). Diplomat, historian, and doyen of Japanese studies in the West. Born in Kent, England, Sansom was educated in France and entered the British consular service at age 19. He was sent to the Far East in 1904 and began a career in Japan that lasted until World War II.

Sansom's years in Japan were filled with intense activity both as a career diplomat and as a scholar who had established himself by the early 1930s as the leading Western student of Japanese language, culture, and history. In 1928 he published *An Historical Grammar of Japanese* and, in 1931, *Japan: A Short Cultural History.* It was the latter that first brought fame to Sansom as a scholar and remains one of the classics of the Western literature on Japan.

Sansom was knighted in 1935 and served on the FAR EASTERN COMMISSION in Washington after World War II. In 1947 he became the first director of the East Asian Institute at Columbia University, where he wrote *The Western World and Japan* (1951). An appointment to Stanford University enabled Sansom to undertake his major scholarly work, the three-volume *A History of Japan* (1958–63).

Sansui Electric Co, Ltd 山水電気[株]

(Sansui Denki). Specialized manufacturer of electronic products for consumer and industrial uses. Incorporated in 1947. Sansui is well known for its quality audio components. In 1990, 51 percent of its shares were acquired by Polly Peck International (PPI), a multinational conglomerate headquartered in the United Kingdom. Sales for the fiscal year ending October 1991 totaled ¥20.5 billion (US $160.0 million), with an export ratio of 69 percent. The company was capitalized at ¥50.8 billion (US $396.7 million) in the same year. Headquarters are in Tōkyō.

sansuiga 山水画

(landscape painting). One of three broad categories of East Asian art, the other two being *jimbutsuga* (figure painting) and *kachōga* (BIRD-AND-FLOWER PAINTING). By the 5th century scholar-painters in China had laid the foundations for landscape as a subject for expressing philosophical principles as well as for interpreting natural beauty, but realization of this idea in painting was a phenomenon of the Song (Sung) dynasty (960–1279). During this time the basic compositional types were established, and techniques were developed for handling trees, structuring mountains, and suggesting rock textures. Solutions devised by celebrated Song artists in the 10th century became the basis for the so-called Southern school of Chinese literati painters (see NANGA), traceable through various schools into the Ming dynasty (1368–1644).

Landscapes with the philosophical significance of Chinese *sansuiga* were not painted in Japan until the 15th century. The importation of Song and Yuan (Yüan; 1279–1368) period culture that accompanied the development of ZEN Buddhism brought scores of Chinese paintings. Early Japanese landscapists, such as the 15th-century Shōkokuji priest-painter SHŪBUN, used motifs from the paintings of Chinese priests or academic court artists to create evocative, idealized landscapes. Shūbun's follower, SESSHŪ TŌYŌ, magnified the forces of nature into a style of dramatic grandeur. The 16th-century demand for wall paintings brought about a uniquely Japanese transformation of landscape painting on large-scale surfaces, notably in the creative synthesis achieved by KANŌ MOTONOBU. In the 18th century heightened awareness of the Chinese Southern school tradition generated a revitalization of landscape painting in the hands of *nanga* artists such as IKE NO TAIGA and Yosa BUSON. Increasing interest in sketching from nature among such masters as TANI BUNCHŌ, MARUYAMA ŌKYO, and HOKUSAI led away from conceptual *sansuiga* to realistic scenic views referred to as *fūkeiga*.

Santō Kyōden 山東京伝

(1761–1816). Leading writer of popular fiction (GESAKU) in late-18th-century Edo (now Tōkyō). He was also an illustrator, *ukiyo-e* artist, poet, antiquarian, and shopkeeper. As an artist he used the name Kitao Masanobu. His work was most prolific in the KIBYŌSHI and the SHAREBON, but he also wrote KOKKEIBON, *hanashibon*, GŌKAN, and YOMIHON, all genres of popular fiction.

Born Iwase Samuru, Kyōden lived in Edo all his life. In about 1775 he began studying *ukiyo-e* under KITAO SHIGEMASA, and from about 1780 until 1806 he wrote and illustrated some 130 *kibyōshi*. Kyōden was fined for his illustrations of Ishibe Kinkō's *Kokubyaku mizukagami* (1789), whose sharp satire incurred the wrath of the authorities. His most famous *kibyōshi* was *Edo umare uwaki no kabayaki* (1785). He was still writing *kibyōshi* in 1808, but from 1809 to 1816 he deserted them entirely for *gōkan*.

In 1785 Kyōden began to write *sharebon*. The finest of these is *Tsūgen sōmagaki* (1787), which exemplifies his technical mastery and the realism and warmth with which he portrays the pleasure quarters. In 1790 the shogunate had issued edicts severely restricting the publication of fiction, which had frequently been used as a vehicle of satire. In 1791, possibly at the urging of his publisher Tsutaya Jūzaburō (1750–97), Kyōden produced three lively *sharebon: Shōgi kinuburui, Nishiki no ura,* and *Shikake bunko.* Kyōden was obliged to spend 50 days in manacles and Tsutaya was fined, but the three *sharebon* were immensely popular. In the spring of 1790 Kyōden's first work in the form of a *yomihon, Tsūzoku daiseiden* (A Popular Biography of Confucius), was published. From 1799 until 1813 Kyōden published 10 *yomihon*, most notably *Sakurahime zenden akebonozōshi* (1805) and *Mukashigatari inazuma-byōshi* (1806). Kyōden's *yomihon* owe much to the popular theater, as well as to the Chinese vernacular fiction that was popular in 18th-century Japan. Takizawa BAKIN, Kyōden's former pupil and arch rival in literature, was his most eloquent critic.

Santō Shuppei → Shandong
(Shantung) Expeditions

Sanuki Mountains 讃岐山脈

(Sanuki Sammyaku). Also called Asan Mountains. Mountain range that runs east to west, forming the border between Kagawa and Tokushima prefectures, northern Shikoku. The highest peak is Ryūōzan (1,060 m; 3,478 ft). The gently sloping northern side has numerous dams and lakes. Villages are mainly concentrated on the steep southern side, with its well-developed terraces.

Sanuki no Suke no nikki 讃岐典侍日記

(The Diary of Lady Sanuki). Account of a brief period in the life of Fujiwara no Nagako, who, under the official title Lady Sanuki, was lady-in-waiting to Emperor Horikawa (1079–1107; r 1087–1107) and later to his son Emperor TOBA. She probably was born in 1079, the same year as Horikawa, and is occasionally referred to as his foster sister. Nominally she was one of his personal attendants, having entered court service around 1100, but the relationship seems to have been a deep and complex one, having the character both of a love affair and of a simple brother-sister intimacy.

The diary is divided into two volumes and seems originally to have had a middle volume, now lost. Volume 1 describes in a vivid but factual style the last illness of Horikawa, concluding with the shock of Lady Sanuki and others following his death. Volume 2 begins with her unexpected recall to court service to attend the boy emperor Toba in the autumn of 1107 and ends with the last night of 1108. The work derives much of its charm from the latter volume, in which Lady Sanuki gives lyrical expression to her feelings and offers many recollections of the dead Horikawa.

Sanuki Plain 讃岐平野

(Sanuki Heiya). Located in northern Kagawa Prefecture, Shikoku. Consisting of alluvial fans, as well as floodplains and deltas, of the rivers Gōtōgawa, Dokigawa, and Saitagawa, it is bounded by the fault scarps of the Sanuki Mountains in the south and the Inland Sea in the north. It is a rice-producing region and the focus of industrial development. The major city is Takamatsu. Area: approximately 410 sq km (160 sq mi).

Sanwa Bank, Ltd [株]三和銀行

(Sanwa Ginkō). One of Japan's leading city banks. Incorporated in 1933, through the merger of three banks. It has a well-balanced domestic network and a strong network in international financial markets. Sanwa has foreign investment banking subsidiaries in London, Frankfurt, and other cities. In Japan, the bank provides a wide spectrum of financial services through domestic affiliates.

In the fiscal year ending March 1991 the bank's total deposits stood at ¥20.6 trillion (US $150.1 billion). At the fiscal year end, the bank's total assets were ¥58.1 trillion (US $423.5 billion), and capitalization stood at ¥464.5 billion (US $3.4 billion). The bank's head office is located in Ōsaka. Its principal operational headquarters are in Tōkyō.

Sanwa Shutter Corporation
三和シヤッター工業[株]

(Sanwa Shattā Kōgyō). Manufacturer of shutters and steel doors. Incorporated in

Sanrizuka The site of the New Tōkyō International Airport, this district in the city of Narita was the center for demonstrations protesting the airport's opening in 1978.

Sapporo Ōdōri Park, a boulevard running east and west through central Sapporo, is the stage for the Snow Festival held every February.

Sanzen'in The gardens of this Kyōto temple are famous for their striking autumn foliage. Visible through the trees is the main hall, Ōjō Gokurakuin, believed to have been built in 1148.

1948. The company has overseas sales subsidiaries in Hong Kong and Singapore and a manufacturing and sales subsidiary in Taiwan. Sales for the fiscal year ending March 1991 totaled ¥203.4 billion (US $1.5 billion). The company was capitalized at ¥22.5 billion (US $164.0 million) in the same year. Headquarters are in Tōkyō.

San'yō Electric Co, Ltd   三洋電機[株]

(San'yō Denki). Consolidated manufacturer and distributor of household appliances, consumer electronics, cold-chain electrical equipment, information/communications systems, semiconductors, batteries, and solar energy generation systems. Established as San'yō Denki Seisakusho in 1947, the firm was incorporated in 1950 as San'yō Electric Co, Ltd. It has 93 affiliates, including 55 manufacturing and 31 sales companies in 27 countries. Annual sales for the fiscal year ending November 1990 totaled ¥1.1 trillion (US $8.5 billion), and capitalization in the same year stood at ¥167.5 billion (US $1.3 billion). Headquarters are in the city of Moriguchi, Ōsaka Prefecture.

San'yō-Kokusaku Pulp Co, Ltd
山陽国策パルプ[株]

(San'yō-Kokusaku Parupu). One of the leading paper and pulp manufacturers in Japan. Incorporated in 1946. The company imports wood chips primarily from Australia and the United States. Sales for the fiscal year ending March 1991 totaled ¥317.7 billion (US $2.3 billion), of which paper accounted for 61 percent; pulp, 9 percent; chemicals, 5 percent; building materials, 12 percent; and other products, 13 percent. The company was capitalized at ¥55.2 billion (US $402.3 million) in the same year. Headquarters are in Tōkyō.

San'yō region   山陽地方

(San'yō chihō). Region on the Inland Sea in western Honshū encompassing the four prefectures of Hyōgo, Okayama, Hiroshima, and Yamaguchi. The region had its origins as the San'yōdō, one of the administrative units in the old GOKI SHICHIDŌ system. It developed during ancient times along an important sea route. Located on the south side of the Chūgoku Mountains, the San'yō region has a mild climate, with light rainfall. Because the region is well-suited for land reclamation and convenient to marine transport, many coastal industrial cities have been established here.

San'yō Shōkai, Ltd   [株]三陽商会

(San'yō Shōkai). Apparel manufacturer with more than 60 well-known brand names on its production roster. Incorporated in 1943. The company has licensing agreements with Burberrys, Yves Saint-Laurent, Bill Blass, and Krizia. For the fiscal year ending December 1990, sales totaled ¥134.9 billion (US $1.0 billion) and capitalization stood at ¥15.0 billion (US $112.3 million). Headquarters are in Tōkyō.

San'yūtei Enchō   三遊亭円朝

(1839–1900). RAKUGO (comic monologue) storyteller, noted for his masterful presentation of tales of human compassion (ninjō-banashi) drawn from everyday life. Real name Izubuchi Jirokichi. Born in Edo (now Tōkyō), he was apprenticed to master storyteller San'yūtei Enshō II (1806–62) and took the name Koenta. In 1855 he changed his name to Enchō and began making regular stage appearances. By age 21 he was a leading rakugo performer who wrote his own monologues and excelled in the presentation of stories accompanied by music or told before painted scenes. Stenographic records were made of his performances, and several KABUKI plays were written based on his tales. His works are collected in the eight-volume Enchō zenshū (1976).

San'yūtei Enshō VI   三遊亭円生6代

(1900–1979). RAKUGO (comic monologue) storyteller. Born in Ōsaka Prefecture. He performed GIDAYŪ-BUSHI (narrative ballads) from the age of 6, then began to study rakugo with Tachibana Enzō IV (1864–1922) in Tōkyō at the age of 10. Adopted by San'yūtei Enshō V (1884–1940), he assumed the name San'yūtei Enshō VI in 1941. He was known for the size and versatility of his repertory and was adept at both shibai-banashi (anecdotes related to the theater) and kuruwa-banashi (stories set in the pleasure quarters). In 1978 he withdrew from the Rakugo Kyōkai (Rakugo Association) in protest over what he considered the excessive awarding of shin'uchi, certificates of rakugo expertise.

Sanze Isshin no Hō   三世一身の法

(Law of Three Generations or a Lifetime). A law of 723 designed to encourage cultivation of wasteland. Under the land distribution system (HANDEN SHŪJU SYSTEM) of the 7th-century RITSURYŌ SYSTEM, all land belonged to the state, and individuals were granted only the right to use a prescribed amount of land during their productive years. A need arose to expand available tillage. The Sanze Isshin no Hō granted private ownership for three generations (sanze) to those who reclaimed land by constructing new irrigation systems, and for one generation (isshin) to those who reclaimed land by extending existing systems. In 743 the KONDEN EISEI SHIZAI HŌ was enacted, granting the land in perpetuity. Under both laws, wealthy magnates and temples—those with the means to open new land—were able to amass large tracts. This practice led to the breakdown of the public ownership and control of land and the development of the SHŌEN system of private landholding.

Sanzen'in   三千院

Temple of the Enryakuji branch of the TENDAI SECT of Buddhism; located in the Ōhara district, Sakyō Ward, Kyōto. In 860 in the Tōtō section of Mt. Hiei (see HIEIZAN) the monk Shōun rebuilt a Buddhist hall (founded by SAICHŌ) as a chokuganji, a temple that offers prayers for the country and the emperor. A statue of the Buddha of healing, Yakushi (Skt: Bhaiṣajyaguru), made by Saichō, was installed in a building named Sanzen'in En'yūbō. In 1086 the main sanctuary was moved to a new temple in the village of Sakamoto (now in the city of Ōtsu). The worship of AMIDA became central to its practices. The temple was moved several times; after the ŌNIN WAR (1467–77) it was moved to its present site.

Sanzen'in's main hall (kondō), called Ōjō Gokurakuin, has been designated an Important Cultural Property. Its ceiling, shaped like the inside of a ship's hull, is the oldest of its kind. The doors of the guest hall (kyakuden) are adorned with the art of TAKEUCHI SEIHŌ and others. To the east of the kondō is the Raigōin subdivision of Sanzen'in. Raigōin is the birthplace of Tendai chanting and singing in praise of the Buddha.

sanzonzō   三尊像

(images of Buddhist trinities). Sculptural or pictorial representations of Buddhist trinities or triads in which a large central image of the Buddha is flanked by two smaller attendant bodhisattvas. The convention spread to Japan from China. The earliest surviving sanzonzō in Japan is a bronze sculptural group attributed to KURATSUKURI NO TORI in the 7th-century Nara temple HŌRYŪJI. Other examples of Buddhist trinities include AMIDA (Skt: Amitābha) flanked by KANNON (Skt: Avalokiteśvara) and Seishi (Skt: Mahāsthāmaprāpta) and Yakushi (Skt: Bhaiṣajyaguru) flanked by Nikkō (Skt: Sūryaprabha) and Gakkō (Skt: Candraprabha).

saotome   早乙女

Women who traditionally transplanted seedlings into paddies at rice-planting time. It was thought that their participation in the task was vital, serving as a sort of ritual honoring the god of the paddy fields (TA NO KAMI) to ensure a good harvest. In modern times the word is also used as an epithet for women or girls from other villages hired to help with rice transplanting.

Sapporo   札幌[市]

Capital of Hokkaidō. Located in the southwestern part of ISHIKARI PLAIN in western Hokkaidō. The city is laid out in a checkerboard pattern on the alluvial fan of the river Toyohiragawa. It became the administrative center of Hokkaidō after the establishment of a colonial office (KAITAKUSHI) in 1869. Since World War II, its commercial and industrial significance has increased. Major industries include food processing, printing, machinery repair and maintenance, and construction. The Toyoha mines in the western section produce lead and zinc. Sapporo is also known for its beer. It was host to the Winter Olympic Games in 1972 (see SAPPORO WINTER OLYMPIC GAMES). Attractions include the forests of Maruyama and Moiwayama, the campus of Hokkaidō University, Hokkaidō University Botanical Gardens, Nakajima Park, Maruyama Zoological Gardens, and JŌZANKEI HOT SPRING. Area: 1,118 sq km (432 sq mi); pop: 1,671,742.

Sapporo Breweries, Ltd
サッポロビール［株］

(Sapporo Bīru). One of Japan's leading breweries, commanding a large share of the domestic market for draft beer. The company was founded in 1876, and Sapporo is the oldest brand of beer in Japan. Sapporo beer is exported to Hong Kong, Singapore, Australia, the United States, France, Germany, and other countries. The company also produces wines, spirits, and soft drinks. Sales for the fiscal year ending December 1990 totaled ¥492.6 billion (US $3.7 billion), and capitalization stood at ¥41.2 billion (US $308.5 million) in the same year. Headquarters are in Tōkyō.

Sapporo Winter Olympic Games
札幌冬季オリンピック大会

(Sapporo Tōki Orimpikku Taikai). Held in Sapporo, Hokkaidō, 3–13 February 1972. The 11th Winter Olympic Games and the first to take place in Asia. The competitors totaled 1,128 athletes from 35 countries. KASAYA YUKIO took first place in the 70-meter ski-jump event, becoming the first Japanese to receive a gold medal in a Winter Olympics. The silver and bronze medals in the event were also won by Japanese.

sararīman
サラリーマン

Loanword derived from the English "salaried man." The term was coined in the Taishō period (1912–26) to distinguish the emerging class of white-collar workers, who received a regular salary, from blue-collar workers, usually paid an hourly wage. Today, sararīman is often used in reference to middle-class, white-collar workers such as managers, salesmen, salaried professionals, and office workers employed by private companies or government agencies. The sararīman usually works for the same company or organization until he reaches retirement age, although midcareer company changes have become increasingly common. Status is strongly influenced by the employee's academic background, and advancement is seen mainly in terms of a gradual upward movement within the company. The model sararīman is expected to be intensely loyal to his employer, putting company considerations before those of family and personal life, working many hours of overtime, and taking only the minimum number of holidays each year. See also EMPLOYMENT SYSTEM, MODERN; LABOR. ▶1316–1317

sarasa
更紗

(calico or batik). Cotton calico, or sarasa, was first imported from India to Japan by Spanish, Portuguese, and Dutch merchants in the late 16th and early 17th centuries. In the late Edo period (1600–1868), local sarasa began to be produced. At first domestic sarasa imitated Indian and Indonesian cottons in motif and color, but eventually a Japanese-style sarasa, called wasarasa (or wazarasa), appeared. Japanese sarasa may be hand-painted, stenciled, or block printed; composite methods are sometimes used. Patterns are often exotic, with designs generally filling the whole surface of the fabric. There are several different kinds of Japanese sarasa, their names reflecting their place of origin: Amakusa sarasa (Amakusa islands in Kumamoto Prefecture), Nabeshima sarasa (former name of Saga Prefecture), Kyō sarasa (Kyōto Prefecture), and Edo sarasa (Tōkyō). SILK sarasa was first produced after World War II. Today sarasa silk KIMONO are valued for their high artistic quality.

Sarashina nikki
更級日記

(Sarashina Diary; tr As I Crossed a Bridge of Dreams, 1971). Confessional memoirs in prose and poetry written shortly after 1059 by a woman of the Heian period (794–1185). The Sarashina nikki was originally anonymous and untitled. Poems from it have been included in other collections with authorship indicated, making it possible to deduce that the author was a lady known by the name of SUGAWARA NO TAKASUE NO MUSUME (Daughter of Sugawara no Takasue). Although other works—the HAMAMATSU CHŪNAGON MONOGATARI and the YORU NO NEZAME—are also believed to be hers, the Sarashina nikki is the only work that can be attributed to her with a degree of certainty.

Unlike other diaries by court ladies of the Heian period, which were usually kept for shorter periods of time (e.g., one year), the Sarashina nikki covers almost the entire life span of the author, starting at age 12 and ending in her early fifties (much of it written long after the fact). Most details about her life are known only through the Sarashina nikki. She spent most of her childhood in a province near what is now Tōkyō, where her father served as vice-governor. In 1020 she went with her family to the capital (now Kyōto), where she remained except for pilgrimages. Around age 31 she became a lady-in-waiting to an imperial princess. She soon left to marry a provincial governor and had three children. The last poem of the Sara-

shina nikki strongly suggests that after her husband's death she spent her last days in a nunnery.

Rather than a diary with daily entries, the Sarashina nikki is a later record of the main emotional events and poetic correspondences in the author's life. Happy events like marriage and childbirth are ignored in favor of more tragic events, such as the deaths of her nurse, the daughters of Fujiwara no Yukinari (972–1028), her cat, her sister, and her husband—the last in 1058.

The Sarashina nikki seems to develop around a central theme—the author's passion for romantic tales. It belongs to a category of literature to which the TOWAZUGATARI also belongs—a confession. The Sarashina nikki includes elements of diary, tale (monogatari), and travel literature. Of its beautiful passages in prose and poetry, the most celebrated is an account of a three-month journey from what is now Chiba Prefecture to the capital, which includes tales and poems about places and human encounters. Also of interest, especially to the literary historian, is the fact that the Sarashina nikki mentions the Genji monogatari (TALE OF GENJI) at a time (1021) when it may have been still unfinished.

sardines
鰯

(iwashi). In Japanese, iwashi is the general term for several species of small fish of the order Clupeiformes, class Osteichthyes, but refers particularly to the maiwashi (Sardinops melanosticta) of the family Clupeidae. Others are the round herring, urume iwashi (Etrumeus micropus), also of the family Clupeidae, and the anchovy, katakuchi iwashi (Engraulis japonica), of the family Engraulidae.

Maiwashi attain 20 centimeters (8 in) and resemble the Pacific sardine (Sardinops caerulea) of North America. The annual haul exceeds 1 million metric tons (1.1 million short tons) in some years in Japan, but falls below 10,000 metric tons (11,000 short tons) in other years. Sardines are broiled with salt or preserved by salting and drying and then broiled or deep fried. Most, however, are used for extracting oil, for processing, and as fish feed.

Continued on page 1318 ➡

Sapporo Winter Olympic Games The 1972 Winter Olympics, the first held in Asia, focused world attention on this northern city. **1** Before the Games officially opened in Sapporo, the Olympic Torch was brought to Japan from Greece, and a special ceremony was held in Tōkyō's National Stadium. **2** At the opening ceremony, young skaters holding balloons performed as the Olympic Flame was lit. **3** Kasaya Yukio, the gold medalist in the 70-meter ski jump. **4** The women's figure skating medalists greet the crowd.

San'yūtei Enshō VI This master rakugo storyteller's extensive repertory included anecdotes from the worlds of both the theater and the pleasure quarters.

Japan's Corporate Warriors: A Dying Breed

*The role of the traditional Japanese "salaryman,"
whose life revolves around his company,
is being challenged by a new generation of
male and female professionals.*

In early 1990, a 40-year-old civil servant in the Kagoshima Labor Standards Inspection Office became aware of a new social phenomenon. *Karōshi*, meaning "death from overwork," had become a hot topic in the national media. Men and women in their prime were being struck down by heart disease and other illnesses commonly associated with the elderly. In one case, a female bank clerk in her early twenties died after putting in months of strenuous overtime. Her parents demanded compensation for her death from her employer. In another case, a trading company executive in his early forties died of exhaustion following six months of nonstop business trips, client entertainment, and weekend work. Similar cases were cropping up almost every week, and each received extensive coverage in the press.

The Labor Standards Office became concerned over these incidents and began investigating. The civil servant in the Kagoshima division, who was a specialist in industrial injury cases, began researching the potential effects of this phenomenon on the government insurance program. Mountains of documents accumulated on his desk. He worked frantically, often late into the night. He took files home on weekends and gave up his holidays in order to master the ever-growing mass of data. Colleagues reported that he worked as if he were engaged in battle.

The ironic conclusion to his struggle came suddenly. One spring morning, he suffered a massive heart attack and was rushed to the hospital, where he later died. The Labor Standards Office had another case of *karōshi* on its hands.

This phenomenon, though often sensationalized by the media, is highly revealing of the Japanese attitude toward work, duty, and social identity. The behavioral pattern that culminates in *karōshi* is all too familiar, and Japan's "salarymen," or white-collar salaried workers, have probably been dying of stress-induced illnesses for several decades. The fact that *karōshi* has now been recognized and elevated to the status of a legal and social problem, however, indicates that the Japanese work ethic itself is being critically examined. As evidence of this trend, 1990 marked the largest drop in the number of working hours in manufacturing industries for 20 years. In the culture of the Japanese salaryman, something is definitely stirring.

Corporate culture, as it evolved from the end of World War II to Japan's emergence as an economic superpower, was based on a simple trade-off. In return for job security, steadily increasing wages, and excellent benefits, Japanese salarymen pledged total loyalty to a company, to a "marriage" that would last from university graduation to the end of their careers. This often meant complete identification of the individual's interests with the organization in which he worked.

It should be noted that the model of the Confucianist company—with its lifetime employment, seniority system, subsidized accommodations, and other benefits—generally only reflects the experience of Japanese salarymen employed by large companies. Employees in such companies make up less than one-fifth of the total work force. In small and medium-sized firms, wages are lower and benefits are scaled down.

Salarymen head for their offices
as another workday begins.

Of course, "time spent at work" is not necessarily the same as "time spent working." Despite their reputation for high productivity and fierce competitiveness, most large Japanese companies have an extremely relaxed atmosphere. The contrast with the extraordinary efficiency of the factory floor could not be more pronounced.

Desks are cluttered with documents, comic books, namecards, ashtrays, back scratchers, and calculators. People give each other shoulder massages and practice their golf swings with rolled-up newspapers. Middle-aged ladies selling yogurt drinks push their trolleys from desk to desk as if in a street market. However, all the jumble, casualness, and apparently wasted time helps to foster *ningen kankei* (human relations)—in Japanese eyes, the very foundation of a healthy company.

Kaisha is the Japanese word for "company." Interestingly, if the two characters that make up the word are reversed, they read *shakai*, which means "society." The company is the salaryman's society, providing him with a network of relationships that gives meaning to his existence. Consequently, the standard answer to the question "What do you do?" is "I work for X company." Whether as a lathe operator, a software programmer, or an accountant is a detail that need not be mentioned. Since job rotation is standard within Japanese companies, the employee usually has little attachment to a particular job. What matters above all else is the company's prestige, which is synonymous with the employee's. Indeed, people outside the company will sometimes refer to him by his company's name—for example, a man working for Toyota may be called Toyota san, meaning "Mr. Toyota."

Office Routine in Large Companies

By Western standards, Japanese salarymen put in exceptionally long hours at the office. A walk through the business districts of Tōkyō in the late evening will reveal office lights blazing in the headquarters of many companies and government offices. Although the minimum paid vacation is 10 days per year, most employees feel reluctant to take their full allowance and content themselves with a few days in midsummer and at New Year's. In a bid to cut working hours, the personnel departments of some organizations have had to resort to incentive schemes to persuade people to take more time off.

Despite recent reductions in the overall number of hours worked, Ministry of Labor statistics indicate that the Japanese working year is the equivalent of one month longer than the British working year and two months longer than that of the French. Since much overtime goes unreported, and average figures include those of non-career-track female employees, it is likely that official data significantly understate the time spent at work by the ordinary salaryman.

The Salaryman's Lifestyle

Traditionally, salarymen spend 30 or more years with the same set of colleagues. Young bachelors, especially those hailing from distant areas, often live in company dormitories, with fellow workers occupying tiny rooms above, below, and on either side of them. They eat breakfast and dinner together in the dormitory cafeteria, perform ablutions together in the communal bath, and even spend weekends together at the company sports center.

They may well date and then marry one of the OLs (office ladies) who make their tea, clean their ashtrays, and photocopy their documents. If a salaryman has trouble finding a suitable mate, he can sometimes look to his department head to find a prospective marriage partner for him. Once married, the employee may move into the company's married quarters, where he is again surrounded by colleagues and their families. Thereafter, he is likely to spend many evenings drinking in hostess clubs and playing Mah-Jongg with his coworkers. He will take skiing and fishing trips with them, leaving his wife behind to take care of the children. Altogether, the average salaryman will spend a greater proportion of his life with his colleagues than with anyone else—including his wife, children, and

Behind the scenes at a large Japanese company.

"Family service": a pair of young fathers relax with their children at the Tōkyō Dome.

parents. Home, for the Japanese employee, is the basic support system that allows the mechanics of life to be carried out with maximum efficiency. Naturally, the family unit has to be kept in good running order, but that can safely be left to the wife, who is the "home manager."

Katei sābisu, or "family service," is the revealing phrase that Japanese men use to describe activities like shopping with their families on Sunday afternoons, taking the kids to an amusement park, or visiting relatives. As a result of the clear separation of roles, Japanese wives have much greater control over household affairs than their counterparts in other industrialized countries. Major decisions about matters such as household finances and the children's education are left to the wife. And if an exhausted husband does decide to spend more time at home with his family, his intrusion into the traditionally female realm will not necessarily be welcomed.

In some companies, family members are expected to support, even participate in, the QC (quality control) movements that help to boost efficiency. Matsushita Electric boasts a Stakhanovite worker who, in the course of his career, has submitted 20,000 suggestions for productivity improvements. He claims that the most satisfying times in his life are when he and his wife are preparing new proposals together.

It is not uncommon for the family unit to be temporarily broken up to serve corporate needs. Some major companies dispatch their most promising young executives—almost always men in their late twenties—to study at US and European business schools for a couple of years. If married, they are discouraged from taking their wives with them. Every year, tens of thousands of midlevel executives suffer a milder version of the same fate. When the husband is transferred to a branch office, many families choose not to move because of the difficulties of placing children in good schools. Instead, the husband lives on his own in a small apartment near his new place of work, often for several years, and makes visits home once a month or so.

Membership in the corporate group is reinforced by symbols and rituals. At some leading companies, the day's work is preceded by compulsory calisthenics and the singing of the company song. In most factories, managers wear the same overalls as production line workers, and in nearly all offices and banks OLs are attired in uniforms. Lapel badges bearing the company crest are considered *de rigueur*. Homogeneity of appearance, as of mind-set, is highly valued.

| Changes for the Future | The work culture prevalent in large, respected companies has acted as a paradigm for Japanese society as a whole. That paradigm is gradually becoming outmoded is more the result of its success than its failure. The Japanese economy has grown richer and more service-oriented, and labor has become a scarce and valuable resource. Large companies have evolved into complex, dynamic enterprises with global ambitions. Information technology has begun to erode the traditional pyramid of paper shufflers, just as automated manufacturing removed whole job categories from the factory floor. Battalions of loyal, flexible generalists who could be shifted from section to section were appropriate to an industrial structure based on mass production and mass marketing. In a value-added, "software-driven" economy, companies have an entirely different set of personnel needs, particularly in creative areas and fields requiring specialized knowledge.

Inevitably, the old absolutes are being challenged. The introduction of payment for merit—as opposed to payment for seniority—and fast-track promotion have weakened the sense of solidarity with fellow workers that was once an article of faith. Mergers and acquisitions have grown more common as companies seek to buy their way into new markets. Workers are being treated as assets, like equipment and machinery, instead of as family members. The recession of the mid-1980s saw a wave of layoffs and closures of heavy industry plants, for example, proving that the "marriage" contract between worker and employer could sometimes end in abrupt divorce.

Attitudes among workers have been changing, too. Headhunting, formerly a taboo activity, has developed into a minor growth industry, with more and more Japanese employees willing to change companies. The trigger was the arrival in the mid-1980s of dozens of Western financial institutions with large bankrolls and immediate requirements for whole teams of well-qualified managers and traders. Even for those who choose to remain where they are, the headhunter's telephone call has become something to brag about to friends.

Employment magazines have become one of the most profitable segments of the publishing industry, selling more than a million copies a week. The title of one of the most successful of these magazines, *Torabāyu* (from the French *travail*, meaning "work"), has become slang among its young female readership for changing companies.

The move of female workers out of OL positions into positions of responsibility also threatens the traditional Mah-Jongg and *mizuwari* (whiskey-and-water) male camaraderie that lies at the heart of large-scale corporate culture. The real agent of change was not the passing of the Equal Employment Opportunity Law for Men and Women in 1985 or a raising of political consciousness among Japanese women. It was the most powerful force of all—economics. In an era of labor shortages, Japan simply cannot afford to have legions of intelligent, capable women graduates confined to making tea, photocopying, and cleaning ashtrays. Large companies have been slower to respond, but in small companies women are already making their mark.

The labor market, like any other market, contributes to the efficient allocation of resources within an economy. During the period following World War II, a time of great uncertainty and wrenching economic change, the interests of both workers and companies were generally well served.

Now, however, just as corporate behavior is changing, so are the attitudes and expectations of the new generation of male and female employees. While no less diligent than their elders, they place increasing value on time spent on hobbies and with their families and friends outside the company. They have little respect for less competent but senior colleagues. They are more interested in developing specialized skills than in endlessly cultivating human relations in *karaoke* bars and Mah-Jongg clubs. They are prepared to bargain for higher pay and, if necessary, to move on to new challenges.

Where does this leave the *samurai* salaryman—the loyal retainer on whose sacrifices so much has been built? Probably wondering, when his work gives him the time to think, whether it is still worth the effort. In television dramas, comic books, and conversations among younger colleagues, he is becoming an old-fashioned, slightly ridiculous figure. He has endured much in the service of his company over the years, but mockery may be the final straw.

Peter Tasker

saru mawashi
A trained monkey performs in the city of Hikari, Yamaguchi Prefecture, where a society has been founded for the preservation of this traditional form of street entertainment.

Sasaki Nobutsuna
A *tanka* poet, Sasaki is also well known for his studies of and commentaries on traditional Japanese poetry.

The fish has long been in demand as a source of protein and as fertilizer. It was once believed that the head of a sardine attached to the front door in early spring served to ward off evil spirits.

Saris, John セーリス, J.

(1580?–1643). Captain of the first English voyage to Japan in 1613. Saris, who had been chief factor of the trading post maintained at Bantam in Java by the British East India Company (founded in 1600), was sent to Japan with instructions to establish a trading factory. With the help of William ADAMS, the English pilot of a Dutch ship who had become TOKUGAWA IEYASU's adviser on foreign affairs, Saris obtained audiences with the retired Ieyasu in Sumpu and with the shōgun TOKUGAWA HIDETADA in Edo (now Tōkyō). He was promised extensive trading privileges for the English; Saris chose Hirado in Kyūshū as the site of the English factory. After Saris departed for England in December 1613, Richard COCKS was left in charge at Hirado. Their trading venture proved unsuccessful, and the Hirado factory was abandoned in 1624. Saris's journal was edited by Ernest M. SATOW as *The Voyage of Captain John Saris to Japan, 1613* (1900).

Sarobetsu Plain サロベツ原野

(Sarobetsu Gen'ya). Located in northern Hokkaidō. Consists of the floodplains of the rivers Teshiogawa and Sarobetsugawa and bordering the Sea of Japan. With its cold climate and vast peat bogs, it consists of largely undeveloped pastureland. A part of the Rishiri-Rebun-Sarobetsu National Park, it is renowned for its wildflowers. Area: approximately 150 sq km (60 sq mi).

Saroma, Lake サロマ湖

(Saromako). Lagoon on the coast of the Sea of Okhotsk, northeastern Hokkaidō. It is the largest lake in Hokkaidō and the third largest in Japan. Scallop, oyster, and seaweed culture flourish here. Area: 152 sq km (59 sq mi); circumference: 90 km (55.9 mi); depth: 20 m (66 ft).

sarugaku 猿楽

Also called *sangaku* (Ch: *sanyue* or *san-yüeh*). Genre of performing art in ancient Japan that developed into a dramatic form known as the precursor of the classical NŌ drama. Also an old name for Nō.

Sangaku (or *sarugaku*), the Chinese repertory of variety arts (including acrobatics, juggling, conjuring, and pantomime), had reached Japan by the 8th century. At court, temples, and shrines, *sarugaku* intermingled with other traditions and gradually changed in character. It absorbed new elements such as the dances of another type of performing art known as DENGAKU. In the 11th century, dramatic sketches of a comic nature had become most important, while acrobatics and other elements dropped out of the rep-

ertory. By the late 12th century, the term *sarugaku* had come to encompass humorous dialogues based on word play (*tōben*), improvised comical party dances (*rambu*), short plays involving several actors, and musical arrangements based on the courtesan tradition. During the 13th century there was a general development toward standardization of words, gestures, musical arrangement, and program combinations, as well as the adoption of the guild (*za*) system to which all present-day Nō schools can be traced. This tradition formed the basis on which outstanding *sarugaku* players of the 14th century created Nō and the comic genre called KYŌGEN.

Sarugawa 沙流川

River in southern Hokkaidō, originating in the northern Hidaka Mountains and emptying into the Pacific Ocean. The town of Biratori, a center of Ainu culture, is located in the river basin. Length: 104 km (65 mi); area of drainage basin: 1,350 sq km (521 sq mi).

Sarukani kassen 猿蟹合戦

(The Battle between the Monkey and the Crab). Folktale. A sly monkey trades his persimmon seed for a crab's rice ball. The crab plants the seed, which grows into a large tree. The monkey climbs the tree and takes the ripe fruit for himself but throws green fruit at the crab and kills it. The crab is avenged by its children, aided by such other characters as wasps, chestnuts, and a walking mortar.

saru mawashi 猿回し

The training of monkeys to perform in shows staged for profit by the trainer; also, the word used to refer to such trainers. The practice of *saru mawashi* began during the Kamakura period (1185–1333). Because of a Chinese belief that horses who saw performing monkeys would be blessed with good health, during the Edo period (1600–1868) monkey trainers in Japan traveled to the stables of *samurai* and held shows for the horses. Later, monkey shows came to be regarded as generally auspicious and gave traveling performances at New Year's. This form of entertainment can be seen today in Hikari, Yamaguchi Prefecture, where it is maintained by a small society for that purpose.

Sarumino 猿蓑

(tr *The Monkey's Straw Raincoat*, 1981). The fifth of seven collections of *haikai* (see HAIKAI SHICHIBUSHŪ) composed by Matsuo BASHŌ and poets of his school; compiled by MUKAI KYORAI and NOZAWA BONCHŌ in 1691. Parts 1 through 4 are compilations of *hokku*, the antecedent of the modern-day HAIKU. The *hokku* are grouped under the rubrics of the seasons in the manner of the IMPERIAL ANTHOLOGIES. In contrast to those in the imperial anthologies, however, the seasons fall in the unorthodox order of winter (94 poems), summer (94 poems), autumn (76 poems), and spring (118 poems). Part 5 contains four *kasen*, or 36-stanza *haikai* linked verses, that begin with *hokku* whose season words (KIGO) trace the same irregular seasonal order. Part 6, the final section, contains a piece in the prose genre known as HAIBUN, *Genjūan ki* (Record of Genjū Cottage), and *hokku* composed by visitors to Genjūan. There is a preface by Enomoto Kikaku (1661–1707) in Japanese and a postface by the priest Naitō Jōsō (1662–1704) in Chinese. Many of the *hokku* illustrate the astringent aesthetic of SABI, but a spare humor, characteristic of *hai-*

kai, often tempers the somber tone: in one of Bashō's *hokku*, the source of the work's title, a monkey huddled against the first drizzling rain of autumn seems to wish for a straw rain cape.

Sarusawa Pond 猿沢池

(Sarusawa no Ike). Artificial pond in the eastern part of the city of Nara, Nara Prefecture, central Honshū. Situated within Nara Park. The image of the five-story pagoda of the temple Kōfukuji reflected in the pond's water makes it a tourist attraction. Width: 100 m (328 ft); length: 70 m (230 ft); circumference: 360 m (1,180 ft).

sasa → bamboo

Sasagawanagare 笹川流れ

Coastal area on the Sea of Japan, Niigata Prefecture, northern Honshū. It is noted for its oddly shaped rocks and cliffs. Length: 10 km (6 mi).

Sasago Pass 笹子峠

(Sasago Tōge). Located on the eastern fringe of the Kōfu Basin, central Yamanashi Prefecture, central Honshū. Formerly a pass of the highway Kōshū Kaidō, it lost its importance first with the completion of the Sasago Tunnel of the Japanese National Railways' Chūō Main Line in 1903, and further with the completion of the New Sasago Tunnel Route No. 20 in 1958. Altitude: 1,096 m (3,596 ft).

Sasakawa Peace Foundation 笹川平和財団

(Sasakawa Heiwa Zaidan). A foundation established in 1986 by Sasakawa Ryōichi (b 1899), a wealthy Japanese industrialist who is a key figure in Japan's motorboat-racing industry. The foundation provides funding for international studies, surveys, and symposia in the economic and political fields; financial support for the Japan Exchange and Teaching Program (JET) and for programs directed at graduate students studying in Japan; and financial support for various activities in Southeast Asian countries, including scholarships for students in the Philippines. Most of the foundation's funding comes from motorboat-racing revenues. In 1989 total assets were ¥22.2 billion (US $160.9 million). Headquarters are in Tōkyō.

Sasaki Kōzō 佐々木更三

(1900–1985). Politician and leader of the JAPAN SOCIALIST PARTY. A graduate of Nihon University, he was active in the agricultural labor union movement before World War II. Following the war he joined the Japan Socialist Party, becoming a major ideologist of its left wing, and was elected to the House of Representatives in 1948. He served as party chairman between 1965 and 1967.

Sasaki Nobutsuna 佐佐木信綱

(1872–1963). TANKA poet and scholar. Born in Mie Prefecture. Graduated from Tōkyō University. He founded the poetry society Chikuhakukai in 1898 and edited the society's magazine KOKORO NO HANA (1898–). He was the author of 12 volumes of *tanka*, including *Omoigusa* (1903) and *Yama to mizu to* (1952). His poems are known for their freshness of expression and richness of feeling. As a scholar, he is known for his research on traditional Japanese poetry, including *Wakashi no kenkyū* (1915), a study of the history of WAKA, and *Kōhon man'yōshū* (1924–25), a commentary on the 8th-century anthology MAN'YŌSHŪ. He was awarded the Order of Culture in 1937.

Sasaki Ryōsaku 佐々木良作

(1915–). Politician. Born in Hyōgo Prefecture; graduate of Kyōto University. He was elected to the House of Councillors in 1947 after working as a labor leader. He was elected to the House of Representatives in 1955, and in 1960 he left the Japan Socialist Party to help form the DEMOCRATIC SOCIALIST PARTY. He was appointed party secretary-general and became its vice-chairman in 1975. Following KASUGA IKKŌ's retirement in 1977, Sasaki succeeded to the post of chairman but resigned in 1985.

Sasaki Sōichi 佐々木惣一

(1878–1965). Legal scholar. Born in Tottori Prefecture, he became a lecturer at Kyōto University after his graduation there in 1903 and studied administrative law in Germany and France from 1909 to 1912. He became a professor at the university in 1913, but in 1933 he resigned in protest against an infringement of academic freedom, the dismissal of his colleague TAKIKAWA YUKITOKI (see KYŌTO UNIVERSITY INCIDENT); he then became president of Ritsumeikan University. Immediately after World War II, Sasaki and KONOE FUMIMARO were assigned by the lord keeper of the privy seal (naidaijin) to suggest possible revisions of the Meiji Constitution of 1889. His interpretations of constitutional and administrative law were characterized by meticulous logic and thorough objectivity. Sasaki was awarded the Order of Culture in 1952.

Sasaki Tadashi 佐々木直

(1907–88). Businessman and governor of BANK OF JAPAN (1969–74). After graduating from Tōkyō University in 1930, he entered the Bank of Japan, where he worked continuously until his retirement in 1974. He showed considerable boldness during his tenure as governor in carrying out several elevations of the yen's exchange rate and the currency's eventual shift to the floating rate system. After retirement he became chairman of the JAPAN ASSOCIATION OF CORPORATE EXECUTIVES (1975–85) and was active as a leader in business circles.

Sasaki Takaoki 佐々木隆興

(1878–1966). Medical scientist, noted for cancer research. Born in Tōkyō. Graduate of Tōkyō University. After serving as professor of internal medicine at Kyōto University, he became director of the Kyōundō Hospital. He received the Order of Culture in 1940.

Sasaki Takatsuna 佐々木高綱

(?–1214). Warrior of the Kamakura period (1185–1333); related to the Minamoto family. Most of his family was destroyed in the HEIJI DISTURBANCE of 1160. In 1180 Sasaki joined MINAMOTO NO YORITOMO against the TAIRA FAMILY. He helped in the destruction of the Taira and was made military governor (SHUGO) of Nagato Province (now part of Yamaguchi Prefecture).

Sasaki Takauji 佐々木高氏

(1306–73). General of the early Muromachi period (1333–1568); better known as Sasaki Dōyo. Born in Ōmi Province (now Shiga Prefecture). Sasaki helped ASHIKAGA TAKAUJI overturn the KEMMU RESTORATION (1333–36) and establish the Muromachi shogunate. He helped compile the 1336 KEMMU SHIKIMOKU, the shogunate's administrative code. He was a military governor (SHUGO) of six provinces and chief officer of the Administrative Board

(MANDOKORO). Sasaki was a noted *waka* and *renga* poet. He figures in the 14th-century war tale TAIHEIKI as the quintessential military aristocrat.

Sasaki Takayuki 佐々木高行

(1830–1910). Politician. Born in the Tosa domain (now Kōchi Prefecture). With fellow activists SAKAMOTO RYŌMA and GOTŌ SHŌJIRŌ, Sasaki participated in the imperial restoration movement in Tosa. Sasaki joined the ministry of justice after the Meiji Restoration (1868) and traveled to Europe with the IWAKURA MISSION in 1871. He later served on the Privy Council and as tutor to the crown prince (later Emperor TAISHŌ).

Sasaki Toyoju 佐々城豊寿

(1853–1901). Feminist and social activist. Born in the Sendai domain (now Miyagi Prefecture), the daughter of a Confucian scholar; original name Hoshi Toyoshi. She attended the Eigakujuku (the predecessor of the Ferris Girls' School) in Yokohama. With YAJIMA KAJIKO and others, in 1886 she helped found the KYŌFŪKAI (Japan Woman's Christian Temperance Union). In 1889 she also organized the Fujin Hakuhyō Kurabu (Women's Ballot Club) to study political questions.

Sasamegoto ささめごと

(Murmured Conversations). Muromachi-period (1333–1568) poetic treatise on RENGA (linked verse) written by the poet-priest SHINKEI in 1463–64. A profound expression of the principles of *renga* as a serious art equal to WAKA, the treatise integrates religious ideas into a poetic theory. *Sasamegoto* attaches primary importance to the nature and spirit (*kokoro*) of the poet, over and above the diction or technique of the verse (*kotoba*). Consequently, it sees the poet's training as akin to Buddhist *shugyō* (see ASCETICISM), the ascetic discipline for attaining enlightenment through liberation from worldly illusions and cultivation of the sense of mutability. Such an enlightened spirit manifests itself in a verse having a "chill and meager" (*hie-yase*) or "withered" quality (see SABI). The ideal *renga* poet, when linking his own verse to the preceding one, strives by mystic contemplation to enter the inner world of the preceding verse in order to re-create it in a different form. *Sasamegoto* had a profound influence on such poets as SŌGI and, indirectly, BASHŌ.

Sasameyuki 細雪

(tr *The Makioka Sisters*, 1957). Novel by TANIZAKI JUN'ICHIRŌ (1886–1965); published 1943–48. Set in Semba, a commercial district of Ōsaka, the story centers on the lives of four sisters of the Makioka family—Tsuruko, Sachiko, Yukiko, and Taeko. In telling of the family's search for a husband for Yukiko, the main thread of the plot, Tanizaki vividly depicts the annual observances and daily customs in the life of the bourgeoisie of Japan's Kansai (Kyōto-Ōsaka) area during the late 1930s. The emphasis on the seasons, the portrayal of the lives of women, and the episodic nature of the narrative all suggest Tanizaki's indebtedness to the TALE OF GENJI, which Tanizaki translated into modern Japanese between 1939 and 1941. When *Sasameyuki* was first serialized in CHŪŌ KŌRON, its publication was halted under pressure from the military authorities: the quiet scenes of domestic life, far removed from the urgencies of war, were thought to be out of keeping with the times.

Despite such obstacles Tanizaki persevered in his work, chronicling the demise of the Makioka household. The novel gives voice to the affection Tanizaki came to feel for the Kansai culture, a sentiment he had pursued in earlier works such as *Tade kuu mushi* (1928–29; tr *Some Prefer Nettles*, 1955).

sasara A folk musician helps celebrate the harvest festival in the village of Taira, Toyama Prefecture, with a sasara made of flat pieces of wood threaded onto a string.

sasara 筬

Folk music instrument; the name is onomatopoeic. The two most common types are: (1) those in which a bamboo whisk is scraped along a serrated length of wood or bamboo; (2) those in which small, flat pieces of wood are threaded onto a string and shaken. Both types are frequently used in DENGAKU performances.

Sasayama 篠山[町]

Town in eastern Hyōgo Prefecture, western Honshū. A former castle town, Sasayama was a military base from the Meiji period (1868–1912) to the end of World War II. Principal products are chestnuts and *matsutake* (a kind of mushroom). Pop: 21,841.

Sasaki Sōichi A legal scholar whose interpretations of constitutional and administrative law demonstrated rigorous logic and objectivity.

Sasazawa Saho 笹沢左保

(1930–). Novelist. Real name Sasazawa Masaru. Born in Kanagawa Prefecture. Sasazawa received the Detective Story Writers Club Prize for *Hitokui* (1960, Cannibalism). His other works include *Roppongi shinjū* (1962, Love Suicide in Roppongi) and a popular series of period novels, *Kogarashi Monjirō* (1971–).

Sasebo 佐世保[市]

City in northern Nagasaki Prefecture, Kyūshū. It has been a naval base since 1886 and suffered great damage during World War II. It was rebuilt and modernized after it was taken over by the US Navy and the Japanese Maritime Self Defense Force during the Korean War. Its principal industry is shipbuilding. Pop: 244,677.

Sasebo Heavy Industries Co, Ltd 佐世保重工業[株]

(Sasebo Jūkōgyō). Shipbuilder, ship repairer, and manufacturer of machinery and steel structures. Incorporated in 1946 as a successor to the former naval arsenal located in the city of Sasebo. Commonly known for its production of supertankers, the company recently has begun to remodel idle vessels into special-purpose ships, such as restaurant ships, cruisers, and car-carrying vessels. Sales for the fiscal year ending March 1991 totaled ¥57.5 billion (US $419.1 million). Capitalization stood at ¥8.4 billion (US $61.2 million) in the same year. Headquarters are in Tōkyō.

sashiko 刺子

Garments made of one or more layers of INDIGO-dyed hemp or cotton fabric and

Sata Ineko An active participant in the pre-World War II proletarian literature movement, Sata later became estranged from leftist politics and wrote novels concerned with the impact of historical events on ordinary people.

quilted in various patterns for the purpose of mending, reinforcement, warmth, or decoration. Also, a style of weaving in imitation of this stitching. Originally, simple running stitches were made in straight lines to reinforce areas of work garments, cloths, and rags that were apt to wear. Later, as the decorative element became increasingly important, the stitches became more elaborate, each region of Japan developing distinct designs. *Sashiko* stitching runs in all directions, attaching two layers of fabric so that the front and reverse sides show the same patterns. Although since the Meiji period (1868–1912) mass-produced fabrics have become more accessible and the need to recycle fabrics has virtually disappeared, the decorative use of *sashiko* has survived under the influence of the *mingei* (FOLK CRAFTS) movement led by YANAGI MUNEYOSHI. See also EMBROIDERY.

sashimi　　　　　　　　　　刺身

Also called *tsukuri*. Fresh seafood fillets cut into bite-sized pieces and eaten raw with soy sauce and *wasabi* (Japanese horseradish). Almost any fish can be used for *sashimi*, but most common are red-meat fish such as tuna and bonito; white-meat fish such as seabream, flounder, horse mackerel, and sea bass; and freshwater fish such as carp. In addition shrimp, squid, abalone, and ark shell are often used.

Sashimi is served on a bed of finely shredded *daikon* (Japanese radish), with *wasabi* as a condiment, and garnished with one or more of the following: SHISO (beefsteak plant) leaves or buds, edible chrysanthemum flowers, freshly grated ginger, or lemon slices. Soy sauce is served separately in a small saucer. To eat *sashimi* one dips it into soy sauce in which *wasabi* has been dissolved or places a small amount of *wasabi* on it and then dips it into the soy sauce.

sashimi Slices of raw fish are here presented in a miniature boat. The arrangement includes sea bream, sea urchins, squid, and yellowtail.

sata　　　　　　　　　　沙汰

Word used chiefly in premodern times with a wide range of meanings (judgment, proceedings, report, incident) and important during the Kamakura (1185–1333) through the Edo (1600–1868) periods as a legal and administrative term referring to trials, decisions, and other governmental actions. The original meaning of *sata* was the sifting of gold, rice, or other valuable matter from sand; it was extended to the distinguishing of good from evil, right from wrong. In the 13th to 16th centuries *sata* referred chiefly to official decisions and proceedings. More extended meanings such as "report" and "rumor" came in the Edo period.

Sata Ineko　　　　　　　　佐多稲子

(1904–). Novelist and leftist social critic. Born in Nagasaki. After an unsuccessful marriage in Tōkyō (1924), she attempted suicide in 1925 and was taken home to Hyōgo Prefecture. In 1926 she returned to Tōkyō and met the writers and leftist social critics producing the literary magazine *Roba* (1926–28, Donkey), among them NAKANO SHIGEHARU, who encouraged her to write. She married a member of this group, KUBOKAWA TSURUJIRŌ. Sata became an active participant in the PROLETARIAN LITERATURE MOVEMENT following the success of her first short story, "Kyarameru kōba kara" (1928, From the Caramel Factory), and joined the outlawed JAPAN COMMUNIST PARTY in 1932.

While caring for her two children, she suffered poverty and political oppression. Kubokawa and Nakano were arrested in 1932, and she was imprisoned for two months in 1935. She wrote about these experiences in her novel *Kurenai* (1936, Scarlet). Her estrangement from the leftist movement (see TENKŌ) around this time led to her divorce in 1945.

She wrote candidly on the theme of wartime collaboration and her disillusionment with the Communist Party in such works as *Sozō* (1966, Plastic Sculpture). Later works dealt mainly with the complex impact of historical events on essentially apolitical people. Her other works include *Suashi no musume* (1940, Barefoot Girl), *Watakushi no Tōkyō chizu* (1946–48, My Tōkyō Map), *Kikai no naka no seishun* (1954, Youth among Machines), *Onna no yado* (1963, Women's Lodgings), *Omoki nagare ni* (1968–69, On the Heavy Tide), and "Toki ni tatsu" (1975, tr "Standing Still in Time," 1977).

Satake family　　　　　　佐竹氏

(Satakeshi). A warrior branch of the Seiwa line of the MINAMOTO FAMILY, named for the village of Satake in Hitachi Province (now Ibaraki Prefecture), where its founder, Minamoto no Yoshimitsu (1045–1127), established himself. Originally powerful enough to oppose MINAMOTO NO YORITOMO, the Satake joined Yoritomo's rebellion against the Taira in 1180 and became a major power in northern Kantō. After the fall of the KAMAKURA SHOGUNATE in 1333, the Satake supported the ASHIKAGA FAMILY. During the Sengoku period (1467–1568), under Satake Yoshishige, the family extended its rule to most of Hitachi and Shimotsuke provinces (the latter now Tochigi Prefecture). Supporters of TOYOTOMI HIDEYOSHI, who confirmed their landholdings of 545,800 *koku* (see KOKUDAKA), the family moved its base to Mito Castle. After the Battle of SEKIGAHARA in 1600, the Satake were shifted by

TOKUGAWA IEYASU to a smaller fief in the Akita domain (now Akita Prefecture). After the Meiji Restoration in 1868 Satake Yoshitaka was made a marquis for services during the BOSHIN CIVIL WAR.

Satake Shozan　　　　　　佐竹曙山

(1748–85). *Daimyō* of the Akita domain (now Akita Prefecture) and founder of the AKITA SCHOOL of Western-style painting. Also called Satake Yoshiatsu. Born in Edo (now Tōkyō), Shozan became daimyō of Akita in 1758. In 1773 he invited HIRAGA GENNAI to Akita to give advice on local copper production. While there, Gennai introduced his theories of Western art to Shozan and Shozan's retainer ODANO NAOTAKE. In 1778, with the assistance of Naotake, Shozan composed three essays entitled, respectively, "Gahō kōryo" (Art of Painting), "Gato rikai" (Understanding Painting and Composition), and "Tanseibu" (Red and Blue, a technical discussion of pigments). These essays constituted the first theoretical works on Western-style painting written in Japan.

Sata mirensho　　　　　沙汰未練書

(Book for Those Unversed in Lawsuits). Manual of legal terminology and litigation procedures of the Kamakura shogunate (1192–1333). Although its authorship is unclear, the manual is thought to have been completed around 1323. It consists of an explanation of legal terms and clerical procedures for initiating lawsuits, an explanation of the rank system of court nobles in Kyōto, and examples of documentary forms for lawsuits.

Satamisaki　　　　　　　　佐多岬

Cape on southern Ōsumi Peninsula, Kagoshima Prefecture; southernmost point of Kyūshū; part of Kirishima-Yaku National Park. Known for its rocky coastline, reefs, and subtropical plants.

Satchō Dōmei→Satsuma-Chōshū Alliance

satellites→space technology

Satō Aiko　　　　　　　　佐藤愛子

(1923–). Novelist. Born in Ōsaka Prefecture; graduated from Kōnan Higher Girls' School. Her father was the novelist SATŌ KŌROKU and her brother was the poet SATŌ HACHIRŌ. She received the Naoki Prize for her story of a woman shouldering the burden of her husband's bankruptcy, *Tatakai sunde hi ga kurete* (1969, The Battle Is Over, Day Is Done). Satō's style is light and humorous, though touched with an element of pathos. Her other works include a biographical novel of her father, *Hana wa kurenai* (1967, The Flowers Are Crimson), and *Nagi no kōkei* (1987–88, A Calm Scene).

Satō Chūryō　　　　　　　佐藤忠良

(1912–). Sculptor. Born in Miyagi Prefecture. A graduate of Tōkyō Bijutsu Gakkō (now Tōkyō University of Fine Arts and Music), Satō founded the sculpture group Shin Seisaku Kyōkai (New Works Society). Characterized by a humanistic realism, his works have received numerous awards, including the 1959 Takamura Kōtarō Prize. In 1956 he became the first Japanese artist to have a one-man show at the Rodin Museum in Paris.

satodairi 里内裏

(literally, "rustic" imperial palace). Provisional imperial residence outside the imperial palace complex in Kyōto. During the Heian period (794–1185) emperors frequently moved to temporary quarters when fires damaged or destroyed the palace or when inauspicious events occurred. They usually took up residence in the mansions of maternal relatives. The first *satodairi* was designated after a fire in 976 when Emperor En'yū (959–991; r 969–984) moved to the Horikawa mansion of imperial regent (*kampaku*) FUJIWARA NO KANEMICHI for nearly a year. Beginning in the reign (1073–87) of Emperor SHIRAKAWA, the main palace was reserved for ceremonial purposes, and some 30 different places served as provisional palaces thereafter.

Satō Eisaku 佐藤栄作

(1901–75). Prime minister from 9 November 1964 to 6 July 1972. Recipient of the Nobel Peace Prize in 1974, he normalized Japan's relations with South Korea (1965) and achieved the reversion of Okinawa from the United States to Japanese administration (1972) during his ministry.

Satō was born in Yamaguchi Prefecture, the younger brother of postwar premier KISHI NOBUSUKE. Upon graduation from Tōkyō University in 1924, Satō joined the Ministry of Railways. In the 1930s he traveled in the United States and in Japanese-occupied China. At the end of World War II, he was appointed director of the Ōsaka District Railway Bureau, and in 1947 he became vice-minister of transportation.

In 1948 Satō was named director of the Cabinet Secretariat. He won a seat in the House of Representatives as a member of the Democratic Liberal Party (Minshu Jiyūtō) in 1949. In 1953 he was chosen to be secretary-general of the LIBERAL PARTY. In 1954 he was accused of accepting bribes from a shipbuilders association (see SHIPBUILDING SCANDAL OF 1954). He was indicted but released in 1956 in a general amnesty. He reemerged as finance minister in 1958. In 1964 he succeeded IKEDA HAYATO as president of the LIBERAL DEMOCRATIC PARTY (Jiyū Minshutō). A consummate politician, he continued the policy of high economic growth, signed the nuclear nonproliferation treaty (1970), and maintained good US relations. His political fortunes waned after the so-called NIXON SHOCKS.

satogo 里子

A child reared by foster parents (*satooya*). This practice has taken special forms in Japanese history. From shortly before the Edo period (1600–1868) into the 19th century some aristocratic families in Kyōto and merchant families in Ōsaka, Kyōto, and Edo (now Tōkyō) sent their children to live as *satogo* for several years with peasant families in the surrounding countryside. It was thought that this arrangement would help the children grow up strong and healthy. Some scholars believe that it is related to the practice whereby natural parents would temporarily leave their offspring, born perhaps in an inauspicious year (YAKUDOSHI), with others to thwart evil influences.

In other ranks of society an illegitimate, orphaned, or poor child was sent to live with another family as its *satogo.* Since 1948 *satogo* have been cared for under a foster family program established in accord with the Child Welfare Law (Jidō Fukushi Hō).

Satō Hachirō サトウ・ハチロー

(1903–73). Poet and songwriter. Son of author SATŌ KŌROKU. Born in Tōkyō. In 1926 he published his first collection of poems, *Tsumeiro no ame* (Fingernail-Colored Rain), about life among the lower classes in the SHITAMACHI area of Tōkyō. He composed a number of well-known songs, including the immensely popular postwar hit "Ringo no uta" (The Apple Song), and was a televison and radio personality.

Satō Haruo 佐藤春夫

(1892–1964). Poet and novelist. Born in Shingū, Wakayama Prefecture. Satō devoted his school years to writing traditional WAKA poetry and modern verse. Upon graduation from school in 1910, he entered Keiō University to study literature under NAGAI KAFŪ.

Satō's early poems are recognizable by their statements of protest. In works such as *Gusha no shi* (1911, Death of a Fool), about a young socialist implicated in the alleged plot to assassinate Emperor MEIJI (see HIGH TREASON INCIDENT OF 1910), he voiced his strong concern for social and political justice. After he left Keiō, his poetry took on a more personal note, reflecting his concerns about resolving emotional problems born out of romantic entanglements and justifying the choice of a way of life. His first collection, *Junjō shishū* (1921, Poems of Innocence), contains the best examples of his lyrical poems from this period.

Satō's most acclaimed works in fiction are *Den'en no yūutsu* (1919, Pastoral Melancholy) and its companion novel, *Tokai no yūutsu* (1922, Urban Melancholy). The former is in the style of an expanded prose poem and traces the troubled mind of its poet through the recurring symbol of the ailing rose; the latter portrays the hero's progress in the city following his return from the country.

Satō experimented with the stream-of-consciousness technique as early as 1914 with the short story "Arukinagara" (While Walking) and was one of the first Japanese writers to introduce Freudian psychoanalysis in fiction, with the highly acclaimed mystery *Kōseiki* (1929, A Chronicle of Rebirth). His love of fantasy and cosmopolitan characters and settings is most clearly witnessed in "Supeinken no ie" (1917; tr "The House of a Spanish Dog," 1961). In *Kono mittsu no mono* (1925–26, These Three), a serialized novel, Satō attempted to weave into fiction the story of the love triangle that involved himself, his friend TANIZAKI JUN'ICHIRŌ, and the latter's first wife. In 1948 Haruo was elected a member of the Japan Art Academy, and in 1960 he received the Order of Culture. *Akiko mandara* (1954, Akiko Mandala), an artistic rendering of the life of YOSANO AKIKO, Japan's foremost woman poet of the early 1900s, won Satō the Yomiuri Literary Prize in 1954.

Satō Issai 佐藤一斎

(1772–1859). Confucian scholar of the late Edo period (1600–1868). Born the son of a high-ranking retainer of the Iwamura domain (now part of Gifu Prefecture), Satō studied in Ōsaka and Kyōto before going to Edo (now Tōkyō) in 1793 to study with HAYASHI JUSSAI. In 1805 he was appointed principal teacher of the SHŌHEIKŌ, the shogunal school for Confucian studies, of which Jussai was the head. Following Jussai's death in 1841, Satō was made professor at the

Shōheikō. His students included the prominent scholars Ōhashi Totsuan (1816–62), SAKUMA SHŌZAN, and WATANABE KAZAN. As an official shogunate scholar Satō was obliged to teach the Zhu Xi (Chu Hsi) school of Neo-Confucianism (see SHUSHIGAKU), although his personal leanings were toward the Wang Yangming school (YŌMEIGAKU). His best-known work is the collection of essays entitled *Genshi shiroku.*

Satō Kōgyō Co, Ltd 佐藤工業[株]

(Satō Kōgyō). Company engaged in civil engineering, construction, and real estate. Incorporated in 1931. It is a leader in tunneling shield projects. It has affiliates in Singapore, Malaysia, and the United States and plans to expand its operations further in Southeast Asia and the United States. Sales for the fiscal year ending September 1991 totaled ¥502.9 billion (US $3.7 billion), and the company was capitalized at ¥19.4 billion (US $141.4 million). Headquarters are in Tōkyō.

Satō Kōroku 佐藤紅緑

(1874–1949). Novelist. Born in Aomori Prefecture. A middle-school dropout, he was a storyteller before turning to juvenile fiction, for which he is best known. He also participated in the modern HAIKU movement led by MASAOKA SHIKI. He was the father of the poet SATŌ HACHIRŌ and the writer SATŌ AIKO. His principal works include the play *Kyōenroku* (1906, Records of Heroism) and the novel *Aa gyokuhai ni hana ukete* (1927–28, Into a Jeweled Cup a Blossom Falls).

Satomi Ton 里見弴

(1888–1983). Novelist. Real name Yamauchi Hideo. Born into the Arishima family in Kanagawa Prefecture, he was legally adopted by his mother's family, Yamauchi. After withdrawing from Tōkyō University, he joined the literary coterie known as the SHIRAKABA SCHOOL in 1910 with his brothers ARISHIMA TAKEO and Arishima Ikuma (1882–1974). From the 1920s he remained independent of any literary school or political ideology. He is known for his consummate craftsmanship and refinement of expression in both narrative and dialogue. In 1959 he received the Order of Culture. His principal novels include *Tajō busshin* (1922–23, The Compassion of the Buddha) and *Gokuraku tombo* (1961, A Carefree Fellow).

Satomura Jōha 里村紹巴

(1525–1602). Also known as Satomura Shōha. Poet of RENGA (linked verse); foremost *renga* master of the late 16th century. He changed his surname from Matsumura to Satomura when his teacher, Satomura Shōkyū, died in 1552. At the age of 12, Jōha became a novice at the Kōfukuji monastery in Nara; he began his study of linked verse soon afterward. In 1545 he took the name Jōha and accompanied the *renga* master Shūkei (1470–1544) to Kyōto. On Shūkei's death, Jōha became a disciple of Shōkyū. Jōha was the author of several influential handbooks and critical treatises on linked verse. His most important work is *Renga shihō shō* (1585, Treasures of Linked Verse), in which he denigrates the contemporary emphasis upon the techniques of linking stanza to stanza and urges the consideration of a *renga* poem as an integral literary structure.

Satō Eisaku The 1974 Nobel Peace Prize recipient was Japan's longest continuously serving prime minister (1964–72).

Satō Haruo This poet and novelist also published essays and translations of Chinese poetry.

Satomi Ton This novelist is known for his refinement of expression in both narrative and dialogue.

Satō Naokata 佐藤直方

(1650–1719). Neo-Confucian scholar of the early Edo period (1600–1868). Born in Fukuyama (in what is now Hiroshima Prefecture). He studied with YAMAZAKI ANSAI in Kyōto and, together with ASAMI KEISAI and Miyake Shōsai (1662–1741), was regarded as one of Ansai's three outstanding disciples. Naokata and Keisai were expelled, however, for opposing Ansai's attempts to reconcile Shintō with Neo-Confucianism (SHUSHI-GAKU). Naokata is remembered for criticizing the deeds of the masterless *samurai* who avenged the death of their lord in the FORTY-SEVEN RŌNIN INCIDENT.

Satō Naotake 佐藤尚武

(1882–1971). Diplomat and politician. Born in Ōsaka; graduate of Tōkyō Kōtō Shōgyō Gakkō (now Hitotsubashi University). Satō entered the Ministry of Foreign Affairs in 1905. In 1937 he became foreign minister in the HAYASHI SENJŪRŌ cabinet. In 1942 Satō was named ambassador to the Soviet Union. As Japan's war situation rapidly deteriorated, Satō, under instructions from Foreign Minister TŌGŌ SHIGENORI, tried in vain to have the Soviets act as an intermediary with the Allies, and he personally urged the Japanese government to accept the terms of surrender as articulated in the POTSDAM DECLARATION. Satō was elected to the House of Councillors in the first postwar election (1947). He served as president of the House from 1949 to 1953 and withdrew from politics in 1965.

Satō Nempuku 佐藤念腹

(1898–1979). HAIKU poet. Born Satō Kenjirō in Niigata Prefecture, he settled in a Japanese agricultural colony at Aliança, Brazil, and worked as a farmer. Associated with the magazine HOTOTOGISU, Satō taught haiku in Brazil and worked to enrich the cultural life of Brazil's Japanese immigrants.

Satō-Nixon Communiqué 佐藤・ニクソン共同声明

(Satō-Nikuson Kyōdō Seimei). Joint communiqué issued on 21 November 1969 by Prime Minister SATŌ EISAKU of Japan and President Richard Nixon of the United States, following three days of talks in Washington. The communiqué stated that they had agreed to speed up consultations "with a view to accomplishing the reversion in 1972" of OKINAWA to the administrative control of Japan after its administration by the United States since World War II.

In the 1969 communiqué Japan recognized the security of South Korea as "essential" and that of Taiwan as "a most important factor" for its own security; also embodied in the communiqué were understandings that the United States–Japan Security Treaty (see UNITED STATES–JAPAN SECURITY TREATIES) would be applied "without modification" to Okinawa and that the United States would withdraw its nuclear weapons stored on Okinawa. The reversion treaty was signed on 17 June 1971 and administrative control was turned over to Japan on 15 May 1972. The Satō-Nixon agreement on Okinawa settled the last of the major issues between Japan and the United States arising from World War II.

Satō Nobuhiro 佐藤信淵

(1769–1850). Agronomist of the late Edo period (1600–1868). Born in Dewa Province (now Akita Prefecture). As a child he traveled with his father and was deeply moved by the desperate conditions of peasants suffering from the TEMMEI FAMINE. After his father's death he went to Edo (now Tōkyō) to study with the Rangaku (see WESTERN LEARNING) scholar Udagawa Genzui (1755–97). After a brief service with the Tsuyama domain (now part of Okayama Prefecture), he traveled, acquiring practical knowledge about agriculture. He became interested in Shintō and entered the school of the KOKUGAKU (National Learning) scholar HIRATA ATSUTANE. He also became friends with TAKANO CHŌEI and WATANABE KAZAN and narrowly escaped punishment in the shogunate arrest of Rangaku scholars (BANSHA NO GOKU). His fame gradually spread, and he was invited by several *daimyō* to advise them on agriculture, the economy, and maritime defense. At MIZUNO TADAKUNI's request he wrote *Fukkohō gaigen*, in which he proposed unifying Japan under a single ruler and placing all land, production, commerce, and transportation under direct government control.

satori 悟り

(awakening; enlightenment). The heart of the Buddhist faith, the concept of *satori* (Ch: *wu*) achieved prominence particularly in the ZEN tradition. Because all people are considered to be already Buddhas and because enlightenment must be total, the radical Zen tradition has insisted on "sudden, not gradual, enlightenment." By mere recognition of one's a priori enlightenment, one awakens suddenly to one's innate Buddhahood. The experience has been compared to that of a "sudden falling out of the bottom of a wooden bathtub." Although self-validating, the *satori* experience traditionally requires the seal of approval from one's master.

Satō Satarō 佐藤佐太郎

(1909–87). TANKA poet. Born in Miyagi Prefecture. In 1926 he joined the *tanka* poets' society associated with the magazine ARARAGI, and in 1940 he published *Hodō*, his first collection of *tanka*. His fifth collection, *Kichō* (1952), won the Yomiuri Literary Prize. His works are not particularly innovative or exciting, but they are well wrought and poetically intense. Satō was a principal editor of the collected works of his mentor, SAITŌ MOKICHI. He has published studies of Saitō Mokichi as well as numerous critiques of *tanka*.

Satō Tatsuo 佐藤達夫

(1904–74). Government official. Born in Fukuoka Prefecture. After graduating from Tōkyō University in 1928, Satō joined the Home Ministry and later moved to the Legislative Bureau (Hōseikyoku). As chief of the bureau's Second Department after World War II, he helped prepare the draft of the 1947 constitution. His book *Nihonkoku kempō seiritsu shi* (2 vols, 1962, 1964; History of the Creation of the Japanese Constitution) is an instructive account of the Japanese negotiations with OCCUPATION authorities over the postwar political structure of Japan. As president of the NATIONAL PERSONNEL AUTHORITY from 1962 until his death, Satō was instrumental in improving the salaries of civil servants. He distinguished himself also as a poet, essayist, and botanist.

Satow, Ernest Mason サトー、E. M.

(1843–1929). English diplomat, linguist, and scholar. Active on the British diplomatic staff in Japan from 1862 to 1882; minister plenipotentiary to Japan (1895–1900) and China (1900–1906). Born in London, Satow graduated from London University. He arrived in Yokohama as an interpreter in 1862, after the ANSEI COMMERCIAL TREATIES had opened Japan to Western trade. He was an eyewitness to the sequence of events culminating in the Meiji Restoration of 1868 and became secretary to the embassy shortly afterward. He was sympathetic to the leaders of the new regime as they charted Japan's transition from a feudal to a modern state.

Satow left Japan in 1883 for a succession of other diplomatic postings but returned in 1895 after being knighted and appointed minister plenipotentiary. His return coincided with Japan's emergence as a major factor in Far Eastern politics with its victory over China in the SINO-JAPANESE WAR OF 1894–1895. After his tour in Japan, he was sent to China, where he is credited with negotiating the accord that ended the BOXER REBELLION. He retired from diplomatic service in 1907. Among his numerous writings, Satow is best remembered for his memoirs, entitled *A Diplomat in Japan* (1921).

Satsuei Sensō → Kagoshima Bombardment

Satsuki → calendar, dates, and time

satsuki → azaleas

Satsuma-Chōshū Alliance 薩長同盟

(Satchō Dōmei; also known as the Satchō Rengō). A military coalition formed in 1866 against the Tokugawa shogunate by the powerful Satsuma (now Kagoshima Prefecture) and Chōshū (now Yamaguchi Prefecture) domains. In the early 1860s Satsuma tended to take a moderate position toward the failing Tokugawa shogunate, while Chōshū acted as the center of the movement to overthrow the shogunate. By 1865, however, Satsuma leaders, particularly SAIGŌ TAKAMORI and ŌKUBO TOSHIMICHI, had come to agree with Chōshū that the shogunate must be removed by force. In March 1866 SAKAMOTO RYŌMA brought together Saigō and Ōkubo of Satsuma and KIDO TAKAYOSHI of Chōshū and persuaded them to form a secret military pact between their two domains. The alliance was a major factor in the failure of the second of the CHŌSHŪ EXPEDITIONS in 1866 and in the shogunate's fall in 1867–68. The two domains dominated the new imperial government (see HAMBATSU). See also MEIJI RESTORATION.

Satsuma domain 薩摩藩

(Satsuma *han*). Also known as Kagoshima domain. Edo-period (1600–1868) domain that extended over Satsuma and Ōsumi provinces and part of Hyūga Province; all of present-day Kagoshima Prefecture and part of Miyazaki Prefecture. The domain was granted in 1602 to Shimazu Iehisa (1578–1638; see SHIMAZU FAMILY), who, having sided with TOKUGAWA IEYASU following the Battle of SEKIGAHARA, received the status of TOZAMA (outside vassal). Profitable trade with the Ryūkyū Islands and successful economic policies made Satsuma a wealthy and influential domain. It played an important role in the MOVEMENT FOR UNION OF COURT AND SHOGUNATE and the MEIJI RESTORATION of 1868, producing such leaders as SAIGŌ TAKAMORI and ŌKUBO TOSHIMICHI. OMOTEDAKA (estimated annual production of rice): 729,000 KOKU (1 *koku* = 180 liters or 5 US bushels).

Satsuma Peninsula   薩摩半島

(Satsuma Hantō). Located in western Kagoshima Prefecture, southern Kyūshū; part of Kirishima-Yaku National Park. Occupying the western half of the prefecture, it is composed of volcanic hills and plateaus. The principal agricultural products are sweet potatoes, tea, tobacco, and dairy products. Makurazaki, Yamagawa, and Kushikino are bases for deep-sea fishing.

Satsuma Province   薩摩国

(Satsuma no Kuni). One of the 11 provinces of the Saikaidō (Western Sea Circuit) in Kyūshū; established under the KOKUGUN SYSTEM in 646, it comprised what is now the western half of Kagoshima Prefecture. From the mid-Heian period (794–1185) many landed estates (SHŌEN) in Satsuma were owned by the Fujiwara regent families (see GOSEKKE) and by temples and shrines of the capital region. From the 12th through the 16th century the SHIMAZU FAMILY acted as military governors (SHUGO) of Satsuma and neighboring provinces, but their defeat by TOYOTOMI HIDEYOSHI in 1587 resulted in a great diminution of their domain. Because of its geographical position Satsuma served as the point of entry for foreign goods. It was at what is now the city of Kagoshima that Francis XAVIER landed in 1549. The Shimazu remained powerful and eventually played a leading role in the MEIJI RESTORATION of 1868. With the establishment of the prefectural system in 1871 Satsuma was combined with Ōsumi Province to form KAGOSHIMA PREFECTURE.

Satsuma Rebellion.   西南戦争

(Seinan Sensō). The last major armed uprising against the new Meiji government and its reforms. Carried out by former *samurai* of the Satsuma domain (now Kagoshima Prefecture) under the leadership of SAIGŌ TAKAMORI, the rebellion lasted from 29 January to 24 September 1877. Its suppression proved the effectiveness of the government's new conscript army in modern warfare.

The reform program of the government had caused the disestablishment of the samurai class, the abolition of their social privileges, a drastic reduction of their income, and the destruction of their traditional way of life. When their hero, Saigō Takamori, was politically discredited and resigned from the government in October 1873 as a result of a debate over whether to wage war on Korea (see SEIKANRON), a number of former Satsuma samurai left their posts in the army and police force en masse to return to Kagoshima with Saigō.

Seizure of arms and ammunition from a naval yard and army munitions depot by some of Saigō's followers was the spark that touched off open rebellion. Presented with this *fait accompli*, Saigō saw no choice but to come out of semiretirement to lead a hastily organized and poorly equipped rebel army of about 40,000 men.

After a battle between the rebels and the local garrison at Kumamoto lasting about 50 days, the arrival of government reinforcements turned the tide and forced Saigō's retreat. For the next few months the remnants of the Satsuma army fought their way through the mountains of southern Kyūshū, arriving in Kagoshima with about 400

troops. The rebellion came to an end with a last charge by Saigō and his men, followed by Saigō's suicide.

Satsuma ware   薩摩焼

(*satsuma-yaki*). Ceramic ware for the TEA CEREMONY and general use made at kiln sites in Kagoshima Prefecture (formerly the Satsuma domain) in southern Kyūshū. Production includes Naeshirogawa ware (Naeshirogawa, 1604–present), Tateno ware (Kagoshima, 1601–1871), Ryūmonji ware (Kajiki, 1598–present), Nishimochida ware (Kajiki, 1663–1763) and Hirasa ware (Sendai, 1768–ca 1915). Several of the earliest kilns were founded by potters from Korea.

So-called black Satsuma, with dull, somber black or warm, reddish-brown ash glazes, was made at the Naeshirogawa and Ryūmonji kilns from their start, but true black Satsuma with a lustrous black glaze was rare before the Meiji period (1868–1912), when black glazes using manganese were introduced. White wares were first made in 1602. Other Satsuma ware products include sharkskin ware, Hirasa tortoiseshell ware, three-color ware, scorpion ware, and brocade ware. Brocade ware has been exported to the West in vast quantities.

Satsumon culture   擦文文化

(Satsumon *bunka*). An iron-tool-using culture that flourished in Hokkaidō and the northern Tōhoku region between the 8th and 12th centuries (some scholars assign its farthest limit to a later period). Satsumon culture developed from the influence of KOFUN culture (ca 300–710) on the so-called Continuing Jōmon culture (vestiges of the earlier JŌMON CULTURE that survived in the far north). It is distinguished by the following traits: the exterior of Satsumon pottery was finished by wood-scraping (hence the term *satsumon*, or "scraped design"), as was HAJI WARE; modified versions of Kofun-period mounded tombs were built for some burials; spindle whorls were used in making cloth; iron swords and other iron implements such as axes and spades were in use; and interior hearths were constructed against one wall of the square PIT HOUSES.

Satsunan Islands   薩南諸島

(Satsunan Shotō). Group of islands extending from southern Kagoshima Prefecture, Kyūshū, to Okinawa. They form the northern half of the RYŪKYŪ ISLANDS and are administratively a part of Kagoshima Prefecture. The group includes the TOKARA ISLANDS and AMAMI ISLANDS. The principal activities are the cultivation of sugarcane, bananas, and pineapples.

Satte   幸手[市]

City in northeastern Saitama Prefecture, central Honshū. During the Edo period (1600–1868), Satte prospered as a post-station town. Textile, machinery, and food-processing factories are located here. The boundaries of the city encompass a rice-producing area, but in recent years large tracts have been developed as housing for commuters to Tōkyō. Pop: 54,342.

Saudi Arabia and Japan
サウジアラビアと日本

(Sauji Arabia *to* Nihon). Japanese contacts with Arabia and the Middle East developed in the wake of the Russo-Japanese War of 1904–05. The exchange of official envoys began in 1938. Relations between the two

countries, interrupted by World War II, were resumed in 1956, following ratification by Saudi Arabia of the San Francisco Peace Treaty in 1954. Talks were initiated on the granting of oil concessions and led in 1960 to the development of oil fields in the neutral zone between Saudi Arabia and Kuwait by the Japanese-owned ARABIAN OIL CO, LTD. In 1971 King Faisal became the first Arab head of state to visit Japan. Economic relations were set on a firm footing in 1975 with the signing of an economic and technological cooperation agreement. Saudi Arabia has been one of the largest suppliers of oil to Japan in the postwar period. In 1990 Japan's exports to Saudi Arabia, chiefly automobiles and machinery, totaled US $3.3 billion and its imports $10.5 billion, of which $10.1 billion was petroleum.

Sawachi Hisae   澤地久枝

(1930–). Nonfiction writer. Born in Tōkyō; graduated from Waseda University. Sawachi received the Kikuchi Kan Prize for *Umi yo nemure* (1984–85, Sleep, Sea), which examines the deaths that resulted from combat between the United States and Japan during World War II. Her other works include *Tsumatachi no niniroku jiken* (1972, The February 26th Incident from the Perspective of the Wives) and *Hi wa waga kyōchū ni ari* (1978, A Fire in Our Hearts), which centers on the soldiers involved in the Takehashi Insurrection of 1878.

Sawada Kyōichi   沢田教一

(1936–70). Photographer. Born in Aomori Prefecture, Sawada took a job in the photography department of UPI's Tōkyō bureau in 1961. In 1966 he was transferred to the Saigon bureau to take photographs of the Vietnam War. "Escape to Safety," his photograph of two women and three children crossing a swift-running river in the midst of

Satsuma Rebellion
This 1877 woodblock print depicts rebel forces from Satsuma clashing with the garrison at Kumamoto in the opening battle of the last serious attempt to overthrow the Meiji government.

Sawada Kyōichi
"Escape to Safety," Sawada's 1966 Pulitzer Prize–winning photograph of Vietnamese civilians fleeing an attack on their village.

Sawada Miki The Elizabeth Saunders Home for racially mixed orphans in Japan was founded by this social worker in 1948.

Sawada Shōjirō The actor and founder of the Shinkokugeki theater troupe in a 1929 photograph.

sazanka
1 A cultivated variety of *sazanka* (sasanqua). Flowers appear from October to December. Oil pressed from the seeds has been used for cooking and hair grooming.
2 The wild variety.

flames and gunfire in the heart of Vietnam, received a Pulitzer Prize in 1966. Sawada died at the Cambodian battlefront in 1970. *Doromamire no shi* (1971, Muddy Death) is a collection of his photographs.

Sawada Miki   沢田美喜

(1901–80). Social worker and founder and director of the ELIZABETH SAUNDERS HOME for racially mixed orphans in Japan after World War II. Born in Tōkyō, she was a granddaughter of IWASAKI YATARŌ, founder of the MITSUBISHI industrial empire. In 1922 she married Sawada Renzō (1888–1970), a diplomat and administrator in the Japanese Foreign Ministry. Disturbed by widespread hostility toward orphans born of Japanese women and Occupation soldiers, she founded a home for them in 1948 and named it after Elizabeth Saunders, an impoverished British national and longtime resident of Japan who contributed $170, her life savings, toward its establishment. Sawada continued as director until her death.

Sawada Seikō   沢田政広

(1894–1988). Sculptor. Real name Sawada Torakichi. Born in Shizuoka Prefecture. A graduate of Tōkyō Bijutsu Gakkō (now Tōkyō University of Fine Arts and Music), he studied under the sculptor Yamamoto Zuiun (1867–1941). Sawada won the Japan Art Academy Award (Geijutsuin Shō) in 1952 for his sculpture *Sange* (Three Flowers). He received the Order of Culture in 1979.

Sawada Shōjirō   沢田正二郎

(1892–1929). Actor; founder of the SHINKO-KUGEKI (New National Theater) troupe. Born in Ōtsu, Shiga Prefecture, Sawada graduated from Waseda University, where he became one of TSUBOUCHI SHŌYŌ's first acting students and took minor roles in the professor's Bungei Kyōkai SHINGEKI (new theater) performances. Upon the dissolution of the Bungei Kyōkai, Sawada joined MATSUI SUMAKO's Geijutsuza troupe in 1913, but he left within a year.

In 1917 Sawada established the Shinkokugeki troupe. He steered Shinkokugeki into melodramatic period plays with spectacular action. In the early 1920s the troupe made film versions of several of its swordfighting plays that strongly influenced the early development of the *jidaigeki* (period drama) motion picture. Although specializing in costume drama, Sawada mixed his stage repertoire with plays in contemporary domestic settings as well as with a few adaptations of modern European works.

Sawada had a commanding stage presence that he used to create the definitive characterization of the nihilistic sword fighter, which became the model for heroes in many period films and plays. With the Shinkokugeki, Sawada sought to fill the wide gap between *shingeki* and traditional KABUKI.

Sawamura Sōjūrō   沢村宗十郎

One of the most prestigious names among the KABUKI acting families. Sōjūrō I (1685–1756) was an actor of extraordinary versatility who excelled in both *jidai-mono* (historical plays) and *sewa-mono* (domestic plays). Sōjūrō II (1713–70) was recognized for his portrayal of villains taken from an earlier period of Japanese history. His son, Sōjūrō III (1753–1801), was a gifted actor particularly noted for his portrayal of romantic leads. Sōjūrō V (1802–53) specialized in gen-

tle, romantic roles and performed brilliantly as an ONNAGATA (female impersonator).

In recent times, Sōjūrō VII (1875–1949) was regarded as the last great kabuki actor who retained the distinctive acting style of the *wagotoshi* (performers of male romantic leads) associated with the Edo tradition. Sōjūrō VIII (1908–75), the son of Sōjūrō VII, specialized in *onnagata* roles. His son, Sawamura Tosshō V (b 1933), who became Sōjūrō IX in 1976, is also an *onnagata*.

Sawa Nobuyoshi   沢宣嘉

(1836–73). Court noble who advocated loyalty to the emperor and expulsion of foreigners (see SONNŌ JŌI). In 1858 he denounced the ANSEI COMMERCIAL TREATIES and, with other courtiers, persuaded the emperor to withhold his sanction from the treaties. After the MEIJI RESTORATION of 1868 Sawa held several posts in the new national government.

Sawara   佐原[市]

City in northeastern Chiba Prefecture, central Honshū. Located on the river TONEGAWA. Developed as a port in the Edo period (1600–1868), it was known for its rice, soy sauce, and vegetables. It is being rapidly industrialized with the development of the Kashima Coastal Industrial Region and the opening of the NEW TŌKYŌ INTERNATIONAL AIRPORT. Historic attractions include KATORI SHRINE and the home of the cartographer-geographer INŌ TADATAKA. Pop: 49,546.

Sawayanagi Masatarō   沢柳政太郎

(1865–1927). Educator. Born in Nagano Prefecture. Graduate of Tōkyō University. Sawayanagi served as vice-minister of education, first president of Tōhoku University, and president of Kyōto University. He devoted his energies to applying new educational theories, founding in 1917 Seijō Elementary School, one of the early experimental schools of its day, and later adding a middle school and high school. Sawayanagi was one of the leaders of progressive education in Japan (see SHIN KYŌIKU UNDŌ).

Sayama   狭山[市]

City in southern Saitama Prefecture, central Honshū. The site of the Imperial Japanese Army's Air Force Academy, which was taken over by the US Army after World War II; returned to Japan in 1963, it is now a base for the Japanese Air Self Defense Force. Sayama has a number of industrial complexes and is a commuter suburb of Tōkyō. Local products are tea, burdock, and carrots. Pop: 157,309.

Sayama, Lake   狭山湖

(Sayamako). Also called Yamaguchi Reservoir. Artificial reservoir in southern Saitama Prefecture, central Honshū. Constructed in 1934, it is fed by water from the Hamura Dam on the river Tamagawa and is one of the main sources of water for Tōkyō. It is a popular recreational area, with the UNESCO Village situated next to the lake. Area: 1.9 sq km (0.7 sq mi); circumference: 23 km (14 mi); storage capacity: 19.5 million cu m (688.5 million cu ft).

Sayo no Nakayama   小夜ノ中山

Mountain pass located east of the city of Kakegawa, Shizuoka Prefecture, central Honshū. Formerly a pass of the old highway Tōkaidō. National Route No. 1 runs through a tunnel under the pass. Altitude: 200 m (656 ft).

sazanka   山茶花

(sasanqua). *Camellia sasanqua*. Evergreen tree of the tea family (Theaceae) native to mountainous areas of western Honshū, Shikoku, and Kyūshū; also cultivated as an ornamental and for hedges. It reaches about 7–10 meters (23–33 ft) in height and has many branches. Its alternate leaves are elliptical, with finely serrated edges. Toward the end of autumn it bears five-petaled flowers. In the wild form the flowers are white, while in the cultivated varieties they may be red, pink, or parti-colored. Double-flowered varieties have also been developed. Unlike the camellia, the *sazanka*'s flower petals do not form a cylinder but are attached to each other at the base.

Like the other Japanese CAMELLIAS, this tree was not cultivated as an ornamental until the Edo period (1600–1868). *Sazanka* is now exported extensively to Western countries. Its wood is widely used for the handles of farming and carpentry tools.

SCAP   連合国最高司令官

(Supreme Commander for the Allied Powers; J: Rengōkoku Saikō Shireikan). A term used to refer both to the chief executive of the Allied OCCUPATION of Japan and, especially as an acronym, to his General Headquarters (GHQ) in Tōkyō. GHQ-SCAP was part of the combined US Headquarters that carried out both Allied responsibilities for the Occupation of Japan as GHQ-SCAP and US military responsibilities throughout the Far East as General Headquarters, Far East Command (GHQ-FEC; see FAR EAST COMMAND). General Douglas MACARTHUR and his successor, General Matthew B. RIDGWAY, both served as supreme commander for the Allied powers and as commander in chief, US Far East Command.

The supreme commander served as the sole executive authority for the Allied powers in Japan and was subject to the policymaking authority of the FAR EASTERN COMMISSION in Washington. GHQ-SCAP consisted of the basic military staff sections and, by August 1947, of 17 additional nonmilitary sections, such as the Government Section, the Economic and Scientific Section, the Diplomatic Section, the International Prosecution Section, and the Public Health and Welfare Section. The Occupation authorities did not institute direct military government. Each SCAP section was responsible for direct contact with the Japanese government on matters within its jurisdiction. United States military government teams were set up throughout Japan under the control of the US Eighth Army, based in Yokohama, to oversee the implementation of SCAP orders and to maintain contact with local Japanese officials. The BRITISH COMMONWEALTH OCCUPATION FORCE in 1947 occupied the Chūgoku region (the western end of Honshū) and the island of Shikoku under the operational control of the commanding general of the US Eighth Army, initially General Robert L. EICHELBERGER, and later, General Walton Walker.

GHQ-FEC exercised unified command over all US forces in the Far East and included among its missions support of the Occupation forces in Japan. A number of its staff sections, such as G-1, G-2, G-3, and G-4, performed functions for GHQ-SCAP as well.

scarecrows → kakashi

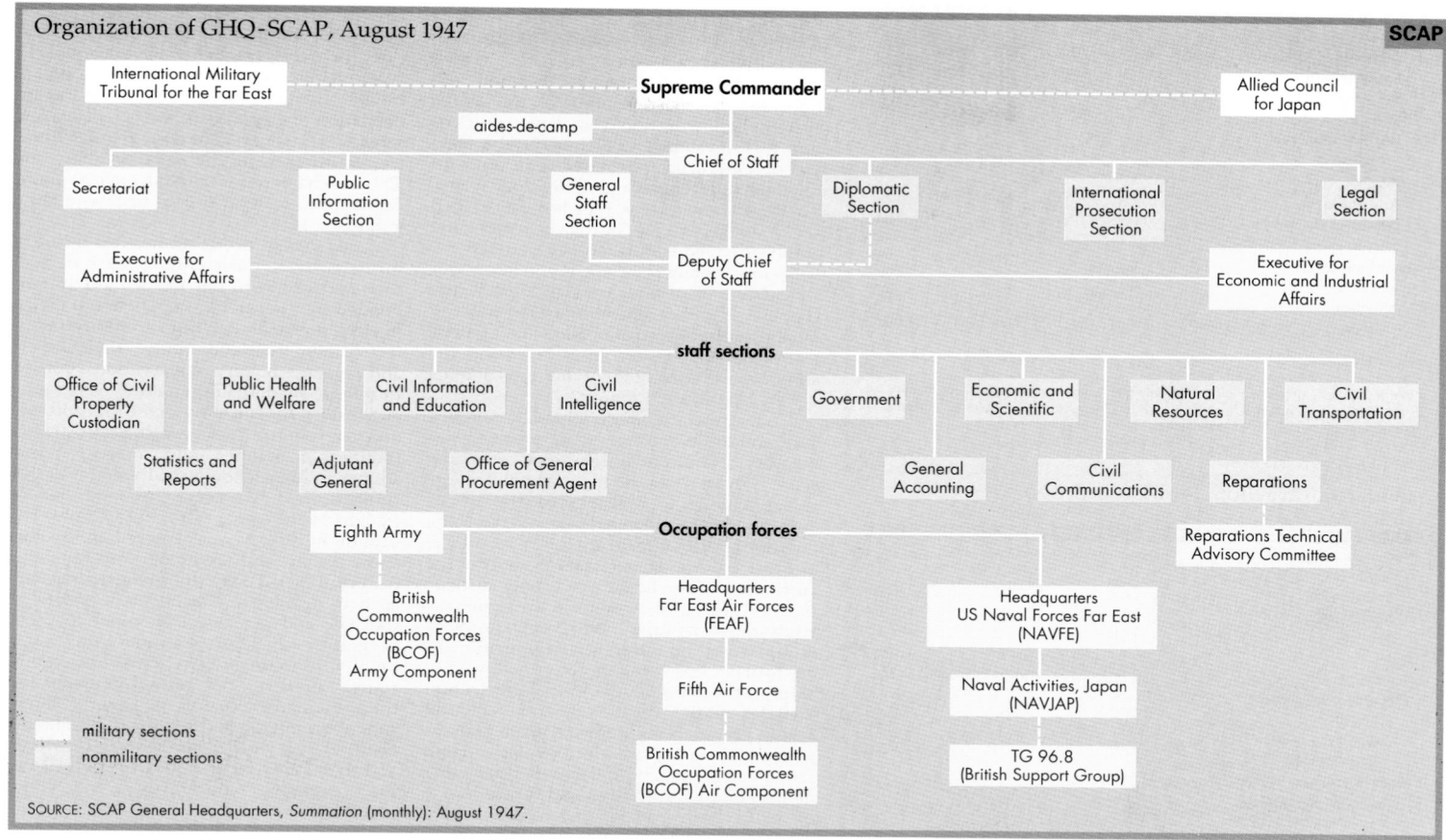

Organization of GHQ-SCAP, August 1947

SCAP

military sections
nonmilitary sections

SOURCE: SCAP General Headquarters, *Summation* (monthly): August 1947.

school administration 学校運営

(*gakkō un'ei*). Administration in the elementary, middle, and high schools in Japan is the responsibility of the principal (*kōchō*) and vice principal (*kyōtō*), supported by heads of departments and other teaching and nonteaching staff members. The school administration is organized into such groups as the faculty council, composed of the principals and faculty, various committees of teachers, and office personnel.

The principal has overall responsibility for school management and administration. Principals of public schools are selected by the prefectural superintendent of schools through examinations and are appointed by the prefectural board of education. As an aide to the principal, the vice principal acts on the principal's behalf and has the right of proxy. Selection is made through examination and appointment by the prefectural superintendent of schools. Selection of department heads is made by either the principal or the area superintendent of schools. See also SCHOOL SYSTEM.

school allergy 登校拒否

(*tōkō kyohi*). Condition, increasingly prevalent among Japanese schoolchildren, in which the child is unable to attend school for emotional reasons. As the time for school approaches, the child develops headaches, fever, or nausea and becomes unable to leave home. It has been suggested that school allergy develops in response to the intensification of such problems as BULLYING among students, competitive school entrance examinations, and the administrative rigidity of the school atmosphere. According to a Ministry of Education survey, the number of middle-school pupils who had missed

30 or more days of school for emotional reasons in 1974 was 7,310. In 1991 the number had increased to 54,112. The corresponding numbers for elementary-school pupils were 2,651 in 1974 and 12,637 in 1991.

school architecture 学校建築

(*gakkō kenchiku*). In Japan school construction first began on a large scale with the establishment of the modern education system in 1872. In the beginning most school buildings were designed and constructed in a Western or pseudo-Western style using traditional Japanese materials and building techniques. After 1900 school construction was standardized.

A number of reinforced concrete buildings were built about 1920, and, after the great Tōkyō Earthquake of 1923 demonstrated their resistance to fire and their durability, reinforced concrete rapidly came to be used in the construction of new schools, particularly in big cities. In the 1950s, several so-called new-style schools were constructed employing a battery or cluster arrangement of classrooms, as opposed to the earlier one-sided corridor system. A second group of new-style schools built in the 1960s utilized higher ceilings, floor-level variation, and rich colors. Around 1970 a third group of new-style schools began to be built that employed the open-classroom plan common in the United States. A number of public schools built in recent years have integrated unique elements of the architectural traditions of their regions into the overall designs of the buildings.

school course guidelines 学習指導要領

(*gakushū shidō yōryō*). Basic outlines stating the scope of each subject taught in Japanese

schools and the objectives and contents of teaching in each grade. First drawn up by the Ministry of Education in 1947, in reaction to prewar methods of standardized, textbook-centered education, they sought to relate knowledge to a student's life experiences. Yet the 1958 guidelines, revised extensively in reaction to postwar trends, became a mechanism for the standardization of curricula with the force of law.

The 1989 revisions, to be introduced in 1992, are the most extensive yet. In addition to stressing computer and foreign language literacy for a new age of information and internationalization, they also require primary, middle, and high school students to salute the flag and sing the national anthem at matriculation ceremonies and graduation. "Life environment studies" replace "social studies" and "science" in the early years; high school students are given civics and a combined course in geography and history rather than a single course in social studies. See also SCHOOL CURRICULUM.

school curriculum 教育課程

(*kyōiku katei*). The modern Japanese educational system was established in the early Meiji period (1868–1912) with the assistance of such American advisers as David MURRAY and Marion SCOTT. In 1886 the government set up the first regular curriculum. Under Japan's system of COMPULSORY EDUCATION (initially four years of elementary school), the required subjects were SHŪSHIN (courses instilling patriotism), arithmetic, reading and writing, composition, penmanship, and physical education. Drawing and singing were sometimes included.

In 1890 the government issued the IMPE-

Standard Curriculum for Elementary Schools

Subjects	Year 1	2	3	4	5	6
	(school hours per year)					
Japanese language	306	315	280	280	210	210
Social studies	—	—	105	105	105	105
Arithmetic	136	175	175	175	175	175
Science	—	—	105	105	105	105
Life environmental studies	102	105	—	—	—	—
Music	68	70	70	70	70	70
Arts and crafts	68	70	70	70	70	70
Physical education	102	105	105	105	105	105
Homemaking	—	—	—	—	70	70
Moral education[1]	34	35	35	35	35	35
Extracurricular activities[2]	34	35	35	70	70	70
Total	850	910	980	1,015	1,015	1,015

[1]Private elementary schools may substitute religious education for a portion of the school hours required for moral education.
[2]"Extracurricular" activities include not only after-school activities but also activities scheduled into the normal school day, such as class assemblies, field trips, library-use training, and traffic safety training.
NOTE: The average school hour is a class period of 45 minutes.
SOURCE: Ministry of Education.

Standard Curriculum for Middle Schools

Required subjects	Year 1	2	3
	(school hours per year)		
Japanese language	175	140	140
Social studies	140	140	70–105
Mathematics	105	140	140
Science	105	105	105–140
Music	70	35–70	35
Fine arts	70	35–70	35
Health and physical education	105	105	105–140
Industrial arts or homemaking	70	70	70–105
Elective subjects			
Foreign language[1] or other special subject	105–140	105–210	140–280
Other subject[2]	—	—	35
Moral education	35	35	35
Extracurricular activities[3]	35–70	35–70	35–70
Total	1,050	1,050	1,050

[1]Nearly all middle school students study English.
[2]Students are required to take one of the following subjects: music, fine arts, health and physical education, industrial arts, or homemaking.
[3]"Extracurricular" activities include not only after-school activities but also activities scheduled into the normal school day.
NOTE: Where ranges are indicated, individual schools are allowed to offer classes whose total hours fall within these limits. Yearly total hours of instruction must add up to 1,050. The average school hour is a class period of 50 minutes.
SOURCE: Ministry of Education.

RIAL RESCRIPT ON EDUCATION. This document, based on traditional Confucian tenets, articulated the guiding principles of education in Japan; it remained in effect until the end of World War II. After the Sino-Japanese War of 1894–95, the government consolidated the school system and introduced more up-to-date subject matter into the curriculum. After 1907 compulsory education was increased to six years and the courses taught were *shūshin*, Japanese, arithmetic, physical education, Japanese history, geography, science, drawing, singing, and, for girls, sewing. This curriculum continued basically unchanged until 1941, when elementary schools were reorganized as KOKUMIN GAKKŌ (national people's schools), and the curriculum was drastically revised to meet the objective of "training loyal subjects of the emperor." Such courses as *shūshin* and history were infused with a strong militaristic and nationalistic tone, and almost every aspect of schooling stressed absolute loyalty to the emperor.

After Japan's defeat in 1945, OCCUPATION authorities suspended the teaching of *shūshin*, Japanese history, and geography and forbade the formal reading of the Imperial

Rescript on Education. In 1946 a team of American education specialists (see UNITED STATES EDUCATION MISSIONS TO JAPAN) visited Japan and made a number of recommendations for the reorganization of the school system. Following this visit a new curriculum was developed, and the school system was decentralized and revised to accord with regional differences and individual needs. The EDUCATIONAL REFORMS OF 1947 established social studies as a part of the curriculum and emphasized educating students to be responsible members of society. The SCHOOL EDUCATION LAW OF 1947 provided for the basic framework and organization of the postwar Japanese school system, while SCHOOL COURSE GUIDELINES, first issued in 1947, stated the aim of each subject taught and the contents of teaching in each grade.

Under the contemporary system, compulsory education consists of six years of elementary school and three years of middle school; three years of high school are optional. Owing to revisions of the school course guidelines, schools now have some measure of discretion in organizing curricula, but national standards dictate the bulk of the curriculum. The elementary school curriculum is uniform: all students in the same year study the same topics; no special classes or groups based on different attainment levels are formed; and students are not allowed to skip grades. The middle school curriculum includes basic vocational and technical classes geared to the students' needs and aptitudes, some on an elective basis. High schools stress matching electives to each student's abilities, aptitudes, and future course of study. Both primary and middle school curricula include one hour of MORAL EDUCATION per week, and additional guidance is provided in all educational activities. Religious education is not included in the public school curriculum. Extracurricular activities receive strong emphasis. Curriculum standards are reviewed by the Curriculum Council (Kyōiku Katei Shingikai) of the Ministry of Education and are usually revised every 10 years, most recently in 1989.

The Structure of Education ── Elementary schools teach Japanese language, social studies, arithmetic, science, music, arts and crafts, physical education, and homemaking. The 1989 course guidelines mandate life environmental studies, rather than social studies and science, to teach first- and second-graders about society and nature through activities and experiences geared to their immediate environment. In middle school, Japanese language, social studies, mathematics, science, and industrial arts and homemaking (one course for boys and girls) are required subjects; music, art, and health and physical education are partly required and partly elective. Foreign language is an elective, but nearly all middle school students study English; a few schools offer other languages (generally French or German). In high school, Japanese language, geography and history, civics, mathematics, science, health and physical education, the arts, and home economics (for boys and girls) are common required courses. Foreign language, usually English, is an elective taken by the majority of students; far fewer students take French or German, although more high schools than middle schools offer these languages. Specialized vocational courses are available, and extracurricular activities are required in all grades. The contents of the principal courses are as follows:

Japanese language. Reading and writing is

stressed. By the time students complete their elementary and middle school education, they are expected to have learned the 1,945 characters known as the JŌYŌ KANJI. In middle and high schools the reading and appreciation of CLASSICAL JAPANESE (*kobun*) and KAMBUN (classical Chinese) are included. Composition using the KANA syllabary and Chinese characters is taught from first grade; calligraphy, using a brush, begins in third grade.

Social studies. Social studies was included in the postwar curriculum to teach democracy and pacifism, but the subject is now divided into geography, history, and civics. In elementary school, third- to sixth-graders learn about their community, their nation, and Japanese history in a combined course. In middle school children study geography and history concurrently in the first and second years; in the third year they study civics (politics, economics, and society). Social studies in high school was divided into two subjects in 1989: geography and history (taught as one course) and civics. Prewar education in history was centered on the emperor system, and mythology was taught as historical fact. Today the student is encouraged to develop independent judgment of the past and present. The initial focus of geography education is on one's own community (as in the life environmental studies course for first- and second-graders) and then gradually expands to cover a larger sphere. In middle and high school students begin with a view of the world as a whole and then study Japan and their own city in the geography and history and civics courses.

Mathematics. Elementary school programs cover four areas: numbers and calculation, quantity and measurement, geometry, and quantity relationships. In middle school numbers and formulas, functions, geometry, and qualitative relationships including probability and statistics are taught. High schools offer general math, algebra, geometry, basic analysis, differentiation and integration, and probability and statistics.

Science. To learn about the world around them, third- to sixth-graders study living things and their environment, matter and energy, the earth and the universe. In middle school, science comprises physics, chemistry, biology, and earth science. High school students must take two of the following: comprehensive science, basic science, physics, chemistry, biology, or earth science.

Music and art. Singing, instrumental music, composition, and appreciation of both Western and traditional Japanese music are taught. Elementary school students learn to play the harmonica in the lower grades and later the recorder. Elementary and middle school students are taught to appreciate and express themselves through drawing, sculpture, design, and handicrafts. High-schoolers choose two from among music, art (painting, drawing, sculpture, graphic design), calligraphy, and crafts.

Health and physical education. In physical education students may take gymnastics, track and field, swimming, various kinds of ball games, *kendō*, *sumō*, *jūdō*, and dancing. There are swimming pools in 78.1 percent of the public elementary schools and 67.6 percent of the public middle schools, and swimming is required from the fourth grade on. In health classes, students study the functions and development of the body and mind, the prevention of accidents and illness, and, at the middle school level, the effects of smoking, alcohol, and recreational drug use on health.

Home economics. Students acquire basic knowledge and skills relating to food, clothing, shelter, child care, and welfare for the aged. Both boys and girls must take home economics from the fifth grade through high school; the middle and high school courses are coeducational. Classes in industrial arts and homemaking teach middle school students the rudiments of cooking and sewing, the child-parent relationship, consumer life, and computer use. From the preparation of simple egg dishes in elementary school, or practical skills such as sewing on buttons, students progress during the high school years to more complex tasks such as making their own skirts and shirts, or cooking full meals.

Foreign language. English is taught in middle and high school, and German and French are offered in some middle and high schools. See ENGLISH LANGUAGE TRAINING.

Extracurricular activities. Additional student activities include class assemblies, club activities, ceremonies, athletic meets (UNDŌKAI), school plays and concerts (GAKUGEIKAI), excursions (SHŪGAKU RYOKŌ) and field trips (ENSOKU), and educational guidance relating to student life, such as traffic safety guidance and training in the use of the school library. See also EDUCATION, HISTORY OF.

School Education Law of 1947　学校教育法

(Gakkō Kyōiku Hō). The basic law providing for the framework and organization of the Japanese school system, passed in 1947 together with the Fundamental Law of Education (see EDUCATION, FUNDAMENTAL LAW OF), which outlines the ultimate objectives of education. Before World War II, different types of schools (i.e., kindergartens, elementary and special schools, etc) were governed by separate ordinances called SCHOOL ORDERS. The present law applies to the entire school system; it sets forth rules and guidelines on the organization, purpose, curriculum, and duration of study for schools at each level.

school libraries　学校図書館

(gakkō toshokan). From the early Meiji period (1868–1912), when compulsory education was instituted in Japan, until the end of World War II, schools generally ignored written materials other than those textbooks adopted for use by the Ministry of Education. With the exception of some private schools, school and classroom libraries generally had small collections.

After World War II, textbooks came to be regarded as merely one aspect of the entire educational process. The use of other kinds of educational materials, both printed and audiovisual, was stressed. In 1948 the Ministry of Education put out a *School Library Handbook* as a guide to establishing and managing school libraries. In 1950 the Japan School Library Association was founded to promote and conduct studies on school libraries. The association was able to push through the School Library Law (Gakkō Toshokan Hō) in 1953, which led to funding for public school libraries.

School libraries have become a fixed part of the Japanese educational system, with nearly 100 percent of primary, middle, and high schools maintaining libraries. Problems remain, however. In 1989, throughout Japan,

only 0.25 percent of elementary schools, 0.85 percent of junior high schools, and 7.7 percent of senior high schools employed trained and qualified librarians. The remaining school libraries are managed by teachers with no library training or qualifications.

school lunch program　学校給食

(gakkō kyūshoku). Program of providing lunches in elementary and middle schools, special education schools, and evening high schools. During the post–World War II food shortage the Allied Occupation started a nationwide school lunch program. With the School Lunch Law of 1954 the practice was established on a permanent basis. The school lunch menu was based on bread until 1976, when a rice-based menu was introduced. By 1989 rice-based school lunches were being served two or three times a week. That year 98.0 percent of elementary schools and 85.4 percent of middle schools had lunch programs.

school orders　学校令

(gakkōrei). A general term for government education ordinances issued from 1886, when the Education Order of 1879 was repealed, until the enactment of the SCHOOL EDUCATION LAW OF 1947. In 1886 the first minister of education, MORI ARINORI, issued the following ordinances: the Imperial University Order, the Normal School Order, the Middle School Order, and the Elementary School Order (supplemented 1890, 1900). Other orders followed in rapid succession: the Higher School Order (1894), the Teacher Education Order (1897), and in 1899 the second Middle School Order, the Girls' Higher School Order, and the Vocational School Order.

After World War I, the University Order and second Higher School Order were passed to augment the higher education system. These were followed by the Blind, Deaf, and Dumb Schools Order (1923), Kindergarten Order (1926), and the Youth Order (1935; see SEINEN GAKKŌ). After World War II, a single composite law called the School Education Law (Gakkō Kyōiku Hō) of 1947 superseded the school orders.

school principals　校長

(kōchō). The principal of a Japanese elementary, middle, or high school is in charge of school management and administration and is ultimately responsible for all institutional functions (educational and otherwise) as well as the supervision of faculty and staff. As the chief representative of the school, the principal devotes most of his time to external affairs and entrusts daily operations to the vice principal (kyōtō). To become a public school principal, a teacher must first pass a competitive examination given to prospective vice principals; a test given to those serving as vice principals determines who may take a position as principal. No educational requirements beyond those to be met by faculty are required of principals. Most school principals in Japan are male. The percentage of female principals of high schools in 1989 was 2.4; of middle schools, 0.6; and of elementary schools, 3.2.

schools for Japanese children abroad　海外子女教育

(kaigai shijo kyōiku). School facilities provided for the children of Japanese nationals residing temporarily in foreign countries. In 1989 there were over 47,118 Japanese children of school age (6–15 years) living

school lunch program
1 An elementary school classroom at lunchtime. Most schoolchildren in Japan eat at their desks, rather than in a central cafeteria.
2 A notable feature of the lunch program is the assignment of students as servers. Intended to help students develop a sense of responsibility, serving assignments are rotated within each class.

abroad, 43 percent of them in North America and 23 percent in Asia. The increasing number of such children (nearly a fourfold increase over a period of 20 years) has led to the establishment of a number of special educational facilities to address their needs.

Postwar overseas education for Japanese children began in the late 1950s and early 1960s when schools were established in a number of cities throughout the world, developing out of informal Japanese-language classes that had been set up by concerned parents. At present these schools are of two main types: part-time "supplementary schools" (hoshūkō), which meet afternoons and/or weekends and concentrate on language and mathematical skills, and full-time Japanese schools (nihonjin gakkō), which replicate the curriculum of schools in Japan. As of 1989 there were 136 part-time and 84 full-time Japanese schools overseas.

The Ministry of Education now sends teachers and free textbooks to both types of overseas schools, and in the 1980s there was a significant effort by various Japanese private educational institutions to establish branch schools in foreign countries, many of which are beginning to attract applicants directly from Japan. See also EDUCATION FOR CHILDREN OF RETURNEES.

schools for the blind　盲学校

(mōgakkō). Schools for the blind in Japan provide regular education courses from kindergarten through high school and also offer special vocational training in such fields as massage, acupuncture, MOXA TREATMENT, physical therapy, and piano tuning. The first school for the blind in Japan was the Kyōto Institute for the Blind and Deaf, established in 1878. Education for the blind became compulsory under the SCHOOL EDUCATION LAW OF 1947. As of 1989 there were 6,000 students enrolled nationwide in 67 public and 3 private schools for the blind. See also SPECIAL EDUCATION.

schools for the deaf　聾学校

(rōgakkō). Schools for the deaf in Japan provide regular education courses from kindergarten through high school and also offer special training in techniques to cope with hearing disabilities. The first such school in Japan was the Kyōto School for the Blind and Deaf, established in 1878. Education for the hearing impaired became compulsory under the SCHOOL EDUCATION LAW OF 1947. As of 1989 there were 8,319 students nationwide enrolled in 106 public and 2 private schools for the deaf. See also SPECIAL EDUCATION.

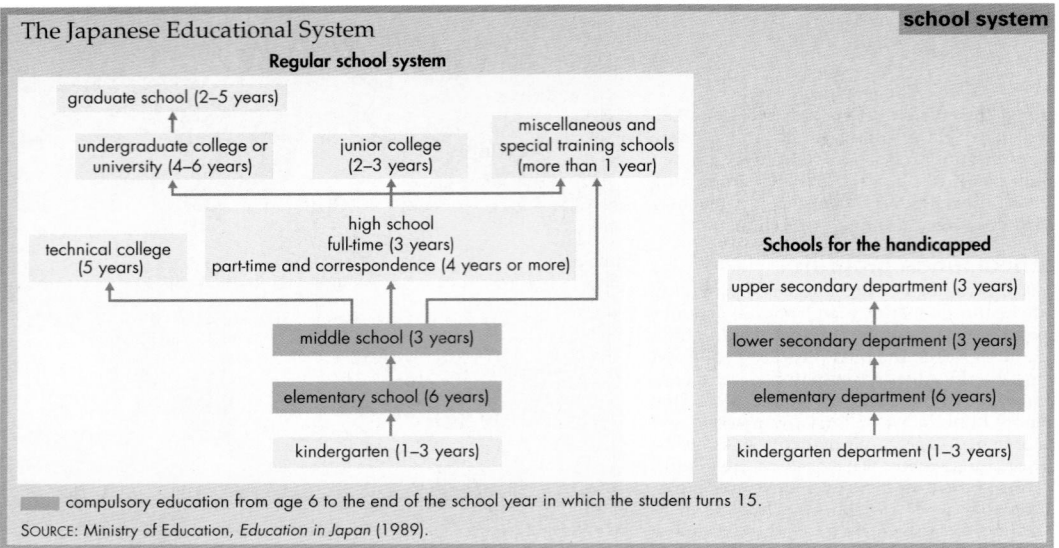

The Japanese Educational System

Regular school system

- graduate school (2–5 years)
- undergraduate college or university (4–6 years)
- junior college (2–3 years)
- miscellaneous and special training schools (more than 1 year)
- technical college (5 years)
- high school: full-time (3 years); part-time and correspondence (4 years or more)
- middle school (3 years)
- elementary school (6 years)
- kindergarten (1–3 years)

Schools for the handicapped

- upper secondary department (3 years)
- lower secondary department (3 years)
- elementary department (6 years)
- kindergarten department (1–3 years)

compulsory education from age 6 to the end of the school year in which the student turns 15.

SOURCE: Ministry of Education, *Education in Japan* (1989).

schools for the handicapped
養護学校

(*yōgo gakkō*). In Japan, schools for the handicapped are of three types: those that address the needs of physically handicapped students, those offering programs for mentally retarded students, and those providing physical rehabilitation for students recuperating from illness or injury. Besides providing courses of study equivalent to those offered at kindergartens, elementary schools, middle schools, and high schools, *yōgo gakkō* inculcate knowledge and skills to help students cope with their handicaps. Although the SCHOOL EDUCATION LAW OF 1947 mandated that local governments construct such facilities, sufficient funding was not allocated until 1979. As of 1989, there were 760 schools (703 of them public) for the handicapped serving 80,680 students.

school system
教育制度

(*kyōiku seido*). The first modern school system in Japan was established by the EDUCATION ORDER OF 1872 (Gakusei). Curricula for pre–World War II schools were established by the government, and textbooks for elementary and middle schools were either compiled or authorized by the government. Employees of public schools were considered government officials, and even private schools were required to conduct their educational activities according to government guidelines. The Japanese school system has undergone substantial change since World War II. The EDUCATIONAL REFORMS OF 1947, carried out under the direction of the American Occupation, decentralized control of education, authorized autonomous private schools, and encouraged the development of COMMUNITY EDUCATION. Textbooks for elementary, middle, and high schools are now compiled under the sponsorship of private publishing houses; however, authorization by the Ministry of Education is still required (see also SCHOOL TEXTBOOKS).

The nucleus of the school system is the system of six-year ELEMENTARY SCHOOLS, three-year MIDDLE SCHOOLS, three-year HIGH SCHOOLS, and four-year universities. In addition there are kindergartens (see PRESCHOOL EDUCATION), five-year TECHNICAL COLLEGES for graduates of middle school, and schools for the handicapped (see SPECIAL EDUCATION). Universities include undergraduate colleges, junior colleges, and graduate schools (see UNIVERSITIES AND COLLEGES). Aside from these regular schools there are MISCELLANEOUS

SCHOOLS (*kakushu gakkō* and *senshū gakkō*). Education is compulsory through middle school, and over 95 percent of elementary and middle schools are public; PRIVATE SCHOOLS play a larger role at the secondary and university level (24 percent of Japan's high schools and 73 percent of its universities are private institutions).

In 1971 the CENTRAL COUNCIL FOR EDUCATION (Chūō Kyōiku Shingikai) submitted a report to the Ministry of Education that cited the need for major reform of the school system. The PROVISIONAL COUNCIL ON EDUCATIONAL REFORM, established in 1984, proposed the introduction of a system without grades, under which graduation would be based solely on the accumulation of a set number of course credits. The first such institution, a high school, opened in 1991. Rapid changes in industry and technology and increased leisure time and income have increased the demand for continuing education, resulting in the expansion of university extension programs and graduate programs. In 1988 the Graduate University for Advanced Studies was established by the Japanese government. It is the first educational institution in Japan to be given over entirely to postgraduate study. The education of overseas Japanese has also become increasingly important as Japanese business has expanded abroad. See EDUCATION FOR CHILDREN OF RETURNEES.

school system administration and finance
教育行財政

(*kyōiku gyōzaisei*). The basic policy for educational administration in postwar Japan was established by the Fundamental Law of Education (see EDUCATION, FUNDAMENTAL LAW OF) in 1947: "Education shall not be subject to improper control, but it shall be directly responsible to the whole people" (art. 10). Postwar educational administration can be contrasted with the prewar system in the following ways: First, educational regulations are now established under the law, while in the prewar period, with few exceptions, they were issued as imperial ordinances. Second, in principle, administration is now comparatively decentralized. Boards of education serve as the primary administrative bodies on the local level. Third, the primary role for the central administration is now the provision of professional guidance and advice, rather than authoritarian control.

National Administration——As the central organ of education administration, the MINISTRY OF EDUCATION comes under the supervision of the cabinet and handles all administrative affairs concerning education,

science, and culture at the national level. Its jurisdiction also includes establishment and administration of national schools, approval of the establishment of public and private universities, authorization of SCHOOL TEXTBOOKS, and approval of appointments of prefectural superintendents and superintendents in cities with populations over 1 million. The minister of education is appointed by the prime minister. He has the authority to propose laws and ordinances concerning education, issue Ministry of Education orders, and issue SCHOOL COURSE GUIDELINES. He also develops educational policy after hearing the opinions of professional scholars through various advisory organs, including the CENTRAL COUNCIL FOR EDUCATION.

Local Administration——The board of education is the local educational administrative body. There are boards of education at the prefectural and municipal levels. Board members are appointed by the head of the prefectural or municipal assembly. Nonprofessionals in educational administration are preferred as committee members. The board of education appoints an administrative superintendent as executive agent and establishes board-of-education regulations. The board of education has authority over the establishment and administration of public schools, curriculum management, the appointment of personnel, and the planning of study and training projects for teachers. The head of the local government retains supervisory authority over public universities, private schools, the acquisition and disposition of educational property, and educational budgets. The Ministry of Education plays a leadership role with respect to prefectural and municipal assemblies, and prefectural boards of education give direction to municipal boards of education.

Educational Finance——Both national and local educational financing come under the general fiscal system. Therefore, the authority over national educational finance is centered in the minister of education's power to prepare draft budgets for annual expenditures. In 1988, 8.0 percent of the general account of the national budget was appropriated for expenses for education and culture and the promotion of science and technology. The itemized breakdown of the 1988 education budget was as follows: 47.9 percent for government subsidy of expenditures for compulsory education, 22.9 percent for expenditures for national schools, 5.3 percent for capital expenditures for public educational facilities, 4.9 percent for financial assistance to private colleges and universities, and the remaining 19.0 percent for such other expenses as LIFELONG LEARNING programs and the promotion of science and technology education. The distribution of national treasury funds for local education is done through a system of aid and subsidies under the jurisdiction of the Ministry of Education and through a system of revenue sharing under the jurisdiction of the Ministry of Home Affairs.

The planning and implementation of local education-related budgets come under the jurisdiction of the head of the prefectural or municipal government. The opinion of the board of education must be taken into account in the preparation of the budget. Half of the expense is borne by prefectures, and the other half by the national government. The total amount spent by the national government, prefectural assemblies, and municipal assemblies for education in 1988 was ¥19.5 trillion (US $152.2 billion). Public fi-

nancial expenditures for education constituted about 6.5 percent of the national income. See also EDUCATIONAL EXPENSES.

school textbooks 教科書

(*kyōkasho*). In Japan all schools are obliged to use government-approved textbooks as their main teaching materials. Textbooks are compiled by private publishers, who are given a certain amount of freedom in the style of presentation and choice of illustrations, but are also required to conform to government-issued SCHOOL COURSE GUIDELINES. Authorization is given only after evaluation of the texts by Ministry of Education specialists and appointed examiners and a final review by the Textbook Authorization and Research Council, an advisory organ of the ministry.

A system of free distribution of textbooks for compulsory education was established in 1963. The textbooks used in each school district are chosen by the local board of education from among those authorized by the central government; in the case of private schools the responsibility lies with the school principal. The law requires that once adopted, a textbook must be used for three consecutive years.

The purpose of the official authorization of textbooks, a system that has been in effect in Japan since 1886, is the standardization of education and the maintenance of objectivity and neutrality on political and religious issues. Despite these goals, the textbook approval process has engendered considerable controversy and has led to at least one famous court case, a suit brought against the government by historian Ienaga Saburō (b 1913) in 1965, charging that the authorization process was both illegal and unconstitutional (see IENAGA TEXTBOOK REVIEW CASE; TEXTBOOK ISSUE).

school violence 校内暴力

(*kōnai bōryoku*). Violent acts committed by students, either against other students or against teachers, became a serious problem in Japanese schools—chiefly middle and high schools—during the 1980s. In 1984 the police handled 1,683 incidents of school violence, of which 742 were directed against teachers. By 1987 reported incidents of violence in the schools had decreased to 482.

After 1987 school violence increased again, with 1,588 incidents occurring in 1989. Of these, 70 percent were at the middle school level, and 47 percent of those involved were third-year students. Among middle school students involved in such incidents, 1 in 10 was suspended from or otherwise disciplined by the school, while 1 in 3 was placed in police custody or otherwise dealt with outside the school's jurisdiction. In contrast, most high school students were punished within the school system. In recent

years violence by teachers, in the form of excessive corporal punishment for infringement of school regulations, has also become a controversial issue.

Science and Technology Agency 科学技術庁

(Kagaku Gijutsu Chō). Agency of the national government responsible for the formulation, coordination, and implementation of many programs and research in science and technology. Established in 1956, it is attached to the Prime Minister's Office and is headed by a cabinet-level director-general. It plays a major role in formulating government policies toward science and technology, budgets funds for some government-associated programs and research, assists in formulating budgets of other government offices in science and technology, and coordinates joint research and development programs. The agency supervises the ATOMIC ENERGY RESEARCH INSTITUTE, JAPAN, the NATIONAL AEROSPACE LABORATORY, the NATIONAL SPACE DEVELOPMENT AGENCY OF JAPAN, and the Japan Information Center for Science and Technology. Its Atomic Energy Bureau forms and implements policies and programs for the peaceful uses of atomic energy, and its Nuclear Safety Bureau regulates and enforces nuclear safety standards.

Science and Technology, Council for 科学技術会議

(Kagaku Gijutsu Kaigi). Organ established within the Prime Minister's Office in 1959. It advises the prime minister concerning basic and comprehensive policies to be adopted on matters of science and technology. The prime minister serves as council chairman. The council is made up of 10 members: the minister of finance, the minister of education, the director-general of the Economic Planning Agency, the director-general of the Science and Technology Agency, the president of the Science Council of Japan, and 5 other members appointed by the prime minister for three-year terms.

Science Council of Japan 日本学術会議

(JSC; J: Nihon Gakujutsu Kaigi). Organization that represents Japanese scientists both domestically and abroad. Established in 1949. It is a deliberative body created to improve and develop the level of scientific research and to communicate its findings to the governmental and industrial spheres as well as to the public.

Although the Science Council is a government agency, it operates autonomously. The JSC represents Japan in such international organizations as the International Council of Scientific Unions and takes a central role in international scientific exchange. The JSC is composed of 210 representatives, with 30 in each of its seven departments. The tenure of

office is three years. Council members are elected based on recommendations made by individual scientific research groups.

science fiction SF

(*esuefu*; SF). Before World War II, science fiction was regarded in Japan as a variant form of detective fiction and was read mainly by young boys. However, since World War II it has established its popularity among adult readers as well. As early as the Edo period (1600–1868), the Japanese public enjoyed free-spirited, fantastic adventure stories. The year 1774 marked the publication of *Wasobei ikoku monogatari*, a Japanese novel similar to *Gulliver's Travels.*

With the opening of Japan to the West after the Meiji Restoration (1868), new information concerning the social systems of the United States and Europe and scientific technology started pouring into Japan. In 1878 Jules Verne's *Around the World in Eighty Days* was translated into Japanese; it was followed by translations of the works of H. G. Wells. In the 1930s, works by Unno Jūza (1897–1949), Kigi Takatarō (1897–1969), and OGURI MUSHITARŌ appeared, influenced by the progenitors of the American science-fiction boom such as Hugo Gernsback and Edmond Hamilton. In the 1940s, translations of such Western authors as Villiers L'Isle-Adam, Selma Lagerlöf, Karel Čapek, Aldous Huxley, Guillaume Apollinaire, Comte de Lautréamont, and Franz Kafka were popular in Japan. They influenced ABE KŌBŌ, the foremost author in the first period of science-fiction writing in Japan after World War II.

TEZUKA OSAMU started doing outstanding work in science-fiction comics for children during the late 1940s, and science-fiction films like *Godzilla* were hits in the mid-1950s. During the 1960s Japanese science fiction found its place as light reading material second in popularity only to mystery fiction. In 1960 the Japanese *SF magajin* (published in association with the American magazine *Fantasy & Science Fiction*) started publication, introducing British and American science-fiction writers to Japan. Another science-fiction magazine, *Kisō tengai*, started up in 1975.

Leading contemporary science-fiction writers in Japan include HOSHI SHIN'ICHI, known for the extreme brevity and wit of his many short stories; KOMATSU SAKYŌ, who utilizes scientific knowledge and injects social criticism into his tales about the future; TSUTSUI YASUTAKA, popular for his satire and experimentation; and Mitsuse Ryū (b 1928), who writes tales about outer space. Other science-fiction writers include Hammura Ryō (b 1933), Mayumura Taku (b 1934), Toyoda Aritsune (b 1938), Hirai Kazumasa

school textbooks
1 An array of the textbooks used by first-year middle school students in Chiyoda Ward, Tōkyō. Throughout Japan, the local boards of education choose from a collection of government-approved textbooks those to be used in their public elementary and middle schools.
2 Pages from an English-language textbook for first-year middle school students.

(b 1938), Ishikawa Takashi (b 1930), and Kōsai Tadashi (b 1938). Women science-fiction writers include Nakajima Azusa (b 1953), Yamao Yūko (b 1955), and Arai Motoko (b 1960).

Japanese science fiction has changed dramatically since the late 1970s. Televised animation and science-fiction series swept action-oriented space adventures and prehistoric fantasy fiction into the mainstream of science-fiction writing. Although more serious science fiction has not entirely disappeared, the younger generation of readers and writers seems to be enjoying science fiction as youth-oriented, fast-paced adventure. Representative science-fiction authors of this new era include Yamada Masaki (b 1950), Hori Akira (b 1944), Kambe Musashi (b 1948), Takachiho Haruka (b 1951), Yumemakura Baku (b 1951), and Ōhara Mariko (b 1959).

Science Museum 科学技術館

(Kagaku Gijutsukan). Museum in Chiyoda Ward, Tōkyō. Established by the Japan Science Foundation in 1964 to educate the general public regarding new developments in science and technology. Covering such fields as robotics, electronics, and space exploration, the exhibits are designed to encourage visitor participation through the use of models, experimental equipment, and simulations.

Science University of Tōkyō
東京理科大学

(Tōkyō Rika Daigaku). A coeducational private university located in Shinjuku Ward, Tōkyō. Originally established as the Tōkyō School of Science in 1881, it attained university status in 1949. The university has faculties of science, science and technology, engineering, industrial science and technology, and pharmaceutical science. Enrollment in 1988 was 17,619.

scientific thought, premodern
前近代の科学思想

(*zenkindai no kagaku shisō*). The introduction from Korea of bronze, iron, and irrigated farming precipitated the transformation of ancient Japanese society from migratory tribal life to settled agrarian communities, beginning in the 3rd century BC. As the country was unified during the Kofun period (ca AD 300–710), there was a gradual accumulation of practical knowledge of weather, farming, fishing, and simple architecture (with rudimentary skills in numerical calculation and measurement), along with development of a limited materia medica and a typical folkloric sense of closeness to nature, related to early SHINTŌ beliefs.

Following the TAIKA REFORM of 645, an effort was begun to reshape both Japanese society and state according to the model of Tang (T'ang) dynasty (618–907) China. Diplomatic envoys and students returning to Japan helped introduce Chinese administrative organization, Buddhism, crafts, and such early sciences as astrology, calendrical astronomy, mathematics, and medicine, all of which had undergone over a millennium of development in China. The active pursuit of Chinese knowledge continued to the end of the 9th century, but since teachers and students alike first had to master Chinese writing and calculation methods, the Japanese were, even after two centuries, far behind their Chinese mentors.

In both China and Japan, there was no

study of astronomy independent of its astrological and calendrical uses. Production of the civil calendar was among the principal tasks of the Chinese emperor, making astronomy, like other sciences, an official function of government. Reinforced by Chinese practice, official sponsorship of scientific inquiry, established during the Taika Reform, remained a prominent feature of Japanese scholarship.

The Chinese believed that their emperor conducted the affairs of state under the Mandate of Heaven and was charged with keeping the political world in accord with the order of nature, which was to be discerned through observation of regular natural (especially celestial) phenomena. The Japanese, with a supposedly unbroken imperial line, had less interest in the "mandate" notion. It was not eternal truths gleaned from the regularities of mathematical astronomy but the irregularities of unforeseeable omens that attracted more attention from Japanese astrologers.

Although premodern Eastern and Western knowledge of nature often overlapped, there were enormous differences in style and methods. The conviction that eternal patterns underlay the flux of nature was central in the West, but Chinese science considered ultimate reality too subtle to be fully measured or comprehended by empirical investigation. The Japanese paid even less attention to the general, while showing a keen interest in the particular and evanescent. Medical theory in both China and Japan viewed man as a microcosm of the natural order. Health was maintained, or restored, by bringing bodily functions into harmony with cosmic phases, mainly through drug therapies or auxiliary methods such as massage, acupuncture, and incantations. The physical organs were of little interest because the human body was understood as a complex of systems defined in terms of vitality or energy.

Between the 10th and 15th centuries, Japanese attraction to the irregular and particular became even more pronounced as the country lost interest in further adoption from China and virtually ended travel abroad. The calendrical system adopted from China in 862 remained in use until it was revised by SHIBUKAWA SHUNKAI in 1684, by which time there was a disparity of two days with the tropical year. Official sponsorship was neglected: each of the scientific disciplines was made the hereditary province of a noble family that did little more than preserve its inherited knowledge. Mathematical ability declined drastically, reviving only with the growth of a large merchant class, while the popularity of divination and other superstitious practices rose.

Western influence reached Japan by the mid-16th century through European traders and Catholic missionaries, briefly stimulating interest in technical subjects such as navigation and gunnery. But when a new period of NATIONAL SECLUSION (1639–1854) was imposed by the Tokugawa shogunate, residual European influences could not sustain a revival of scientific effort in Japan. Stimulus came, rather, from renewed contact with China following the reopening of trade relations in the 15th century. During the 16th century, Buddhist priest-practitioners, Japan's most learned class, devoted themselves to medical study, teaching, and practice to catch up with the more advanced Chinese.

From the early 17th century books were

printed in virtually every scholarly field in an intellectual renaissance embracing the entire spectrum of Chinese learning and science. OGYŪ SORAI, the influential Edo-period (1600–1868) Confucian philosopher, believed that the heavens were imbued with vital force, which could not be explained solely by physical cosmology. This moralistic, anthropocentric, and often anthropomorphic view of nature was common among Confucian thinkers throughout East Asia.

Perhaps due to its alliance with Confucian thought, MEDICINE also had a strong vitalistic bias. Until modern times, the Japanese did not locate thought processes in the head. As knowledge was not viewed as localized and stored, there was no reason to investigate the physiological basis of cognition. Similarly, it was believed that health was related to the balance of energy (KI), which resembled the Stoic pneuma of the West and was ultimately responsible for all vital functions.

Not until the 18th century did some Japanese find fault with the utility of Chinese medicine. YAMAWAKI TŌYŌ, who probably had access to a Western anatomical chart and performed his own dissections, criticized the traditional Chinese charts for inaccuracy. Those loyal to traditional physiology claimed nothing could be learned from a cadaver since it was no more than a container emptied of its vital energy. But as dissections were increasingly performed, functional analysis lost its importance and physical organs were studied for their own sake.

In the late 18th century, SUGITA GEMPAKU and others studied anatomy because it seemed the most tangible and readily comprehensible part of Western medicine. It soon became clear, however, that to understand Western medicine fully it was also necessary to study physics, biology, and chemistry. By the late 19th century, scholarship in science was firmly linked with a mastery of Western scientific theory, and the long-standing Japanese orientation toward the extraordinary gave way to scientific practice dedicated to observation and classification of the general. Since the introduction of scientific thought from the West, scientific disciplines have exhibited a high degree of institutionalization within university, industry, and military organizations. These institutional settings continue to influence the course of scientific thought in Japan.

Scott, Marion McCarrell
スコット, M. M.

(1843–1922). US educator who contributed to the establishment of a modern educational system in Meiji-period (1868–1912) Japan, working as a textbook editor and adviser on teaching methods. Scott came to Japan in 1871 and taught at the Daigaku Nankō (now Tōkyō University). From 1872 to 1874 he worked at Tōkyō Normal School (Tōkyō Shihan Gakkō; later Tōkyō University of Education; now TSUKUBA UNIVERSITY). At the latter he introduced American methods of elementary education into the training of elementary-school teachers. He left Japan in 1881.

screen and wall painting 障屏画

(*shōheiga*). Paintings executed on screens or walls of traditional Japanese-style buildings; one of the major formats in the history of Japanese painting. The term *shōheiga* embraces paintings executed on sliding screens (*fusuma-e*), on walls (*hekiga*), and on folding screens (*byōbu-e*). *Fusuma-e* are painted on screens (*fusuma*) constructed of paper or

screen and wall painting

Artworks on folding and standing screens, doors, and walls represent some of Japan's most important painting.

Six sliding-door panels from a group of 16 titled *Birds and Flowers* by Kanō Eitoku. 1566. Ink on paper. Panels range from 176 × 74 cm to 176 × 143 cm. Jukōin, Kyōto. National Treasure.

silk stretched over a light wooden frame, which open and shut by sliding in grooves in a stationary outer frame. *Hekiga* refers to all forms of wall painting, though in its broadest sense it can also include paintings on pillars or ceilings. The earliest wall paintings in Japan date to the protohistoric Kofun period (ca 300–710; see ORNAMENTED TOMBS). The artist often painted first on silk or paper, which was then pasted on a wall. *Byōbu-e* are painted on freestanding, portable folding screens (*byōbu*) that range in size from about 1.0 to 1.8 meters (3.3 to 5.9 ft) high and 1.0 to 5.5 meters (3.3 to 18.0 ft) wide and have two, three, four, six, or eight panels. Most commonly, however, folding screens have been arranged in pairs, each screen having six panels and measuring approximately 1.5 meters (4.9 ft) high by 3.7 meters (12.1 ft) wide.

Early folding screens were rather awkward and heavy. Panels were linked together at the corners with silk or leather cords. The holes for these cords were reinforced by wooden washers shaped like Japanese coins, in what was known as *zenigata* ("coin-shaped") construction. The panels were usually edged with silk brocade that separated the panels compositionally. Beginning in the 14th century layers of strong paper were stretched over light wooden frames. These panels were then linked with overlapping and interlocking strips of paper pasted between panels. When the screen was unfolded, a single, unbroken surface with no intrusive borders resulted. With few modifications, this method of construction is still used.

In addition to the standard folding and sliding screens, there are also freestanding, single-panel screens called *tsuitate*. These screens, constructed entirely of wood, are supported on low wooden feet.

Early Shōheiga——The majority of wall and screen paintings can be traced to Chinese prototypes that were introduced to Japan beginning in the late 6th and the 7th centuries (see ASUKA CULTURE; HAKUHŌ CULTURE). Buddhist religious themes were a dominant motif. In Japan screen painting was well established by the Nara period (710–794). Important wall paintings of the period at the temple HŌRYŪJI were almost entirely destroyed in a fire in 1949; however, they may be studied through photographs and repro-

Two sliding-door panels from a group of five on the theme of blossoming cherry trees by Hasegawa Kyūzō. 1593. Colors and gold leaf on paper. Each panel 172 × 139 cm. Chishakuin, Kyōto. National Treasure.

A two-panel folding screen entitled *Bamboo and Plum Tree* by Kōrin. Early 18th century. Ink and gold leaf on paper. 66 × 183 cm. Tōkyō National Museum.

ductions. In the Heian period (794–1185) native Japanese subject matter began to develop. Though wall painting continued to be devoted almost exclusively to Buddhist subjects, screen painting—that is, *fusuma-e* and *byōbu-e*—was more commonly used as decoration in the homes of aristocrats and at court, generally with secular subjects. In the later part of this period these secular subjects were often designated as YAMATO-E (Japanese-style painting), as distinguished from *kara-e* (Chinese-style painting). Al-

most no examples of screen painting have survived from the Heian period; there are no *fusuma-e* extant, and only one example of *byōbu-e* survives. Illustrated handscrolls (EMAKIMONO), however, give a clear picture of screen painting during the Heian and Kamakura (1185–1333) periods. Interior scenes in these works often include detailed depictions of screens in which both the subject and the style of the painting can be seen.

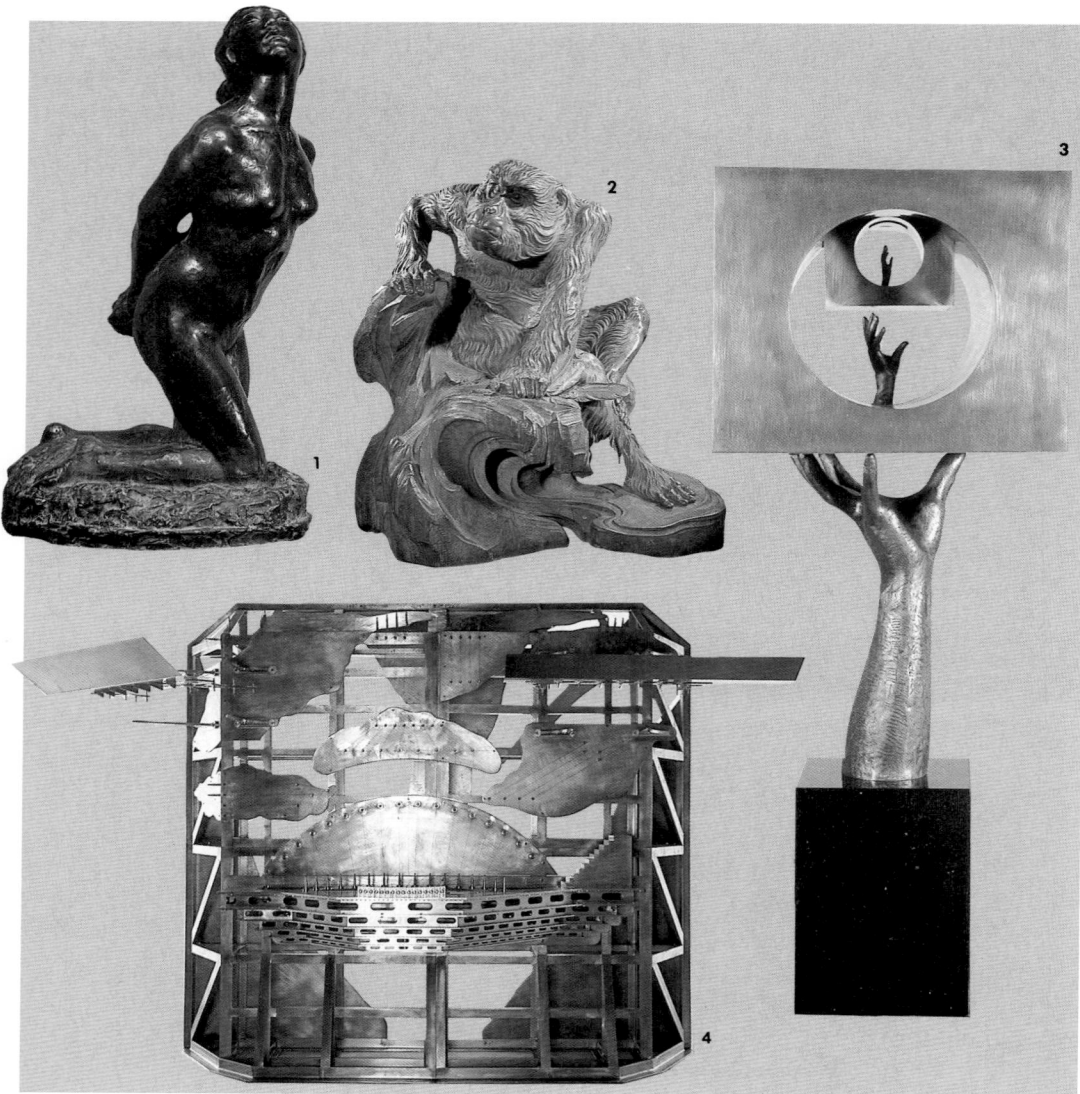

modern sculpture
1 *Woman*, the last work of Ogiwara Morie, who studied painting in New York and Paris at the turn of the century. 1910. Bronze. Height 99 cm. National Museum of Modern Art, Tōkyō.
2 *The Aging Monkey* won international acclaim for Takamura Kōun. 1893. Wood. Height 106 cm. Tōkyō National Museum.
3 *A Box Returning to the Sky, No. 5*, by Horiuchi Masakazu. Bronze. 86 × 30 × 30 cm. Tōkyō Metropolitan Art Museum.
4 *TC5908* by Shinoda Morio. 1991. Aluminum, stainless steel, and brass. 275 × 395 × 162 cm. Private collection.

Medieval Shōheiga—The tradition of Buddhist paintings for walls and secular *yamato-e* painting for screens continued into the Kamakura period. However, in the mid-Kamakura period, under the influence of renewed contacts with China, monochrome ink painting inspired by paintings of the Song (Sung) dynasty (960–1279) began gradually to supplant *yamato-e* for screens.

In the Muromachi period (1333–1568), Buddhist painting declined, and with it wall painting. The most important subject for secular screens was still landscape, though Chinese literary themes and paintings of flowers and birds were also popular. Landscape paintings of the 15th century often represented the four seasons. The paintings were subdued and detailed, with few bright colors. An early example of *shōheiga* in this period is JŌSETSU's *Catching a Catfish with a Gourd*, which, though now mounted on a hanging scroll, originally decorated a single-panel *tsuitate*.

The Azuchi-Momoyama period (1568–1600) is referred to as the golden age of screen painting. During this time screens with backgrounds sprinkled with gold dust or covered with wafer-thin gold leaf became prominent. This is largely attributable to the rise of wealthy and powerful military warlords and to the fact that gilt screens served to brighten gloomy castle interiors. These screens, the precursors of which had been known in the Muromachi period, were often brightly colored and the compositions boldly simplified, with stronger and more immediate appeal than naturalistic Muromachi-period treatments.

Edo-Period Shōheiga—For the most part, painters of the Edo period (1600–1868) continued the tradition of *shōheiga* developed by the Azuchi-Momoyama–period artists. The KANŌ SCHOOL, which had dominated Azuchi-Moyomama–period screen painting, continued to be extremely influential. In the same conservative vein, the TOSA SCHOOL continued the *yamato-e* tradition. Many anonymous paintings illustrating scenes from everyday life were produced in shops by *machi eshi* (town painters) for the growing class of wealthy merchants. The most creative and innovative of the Edo-period schools were the RIMPA, BUNJINGA, and Nagasaki schools (see NAGASAKI SCHOOL). However, it was chiefly the artists of the Rimpa school, such as Tawaraya SŌTATSU and KŌRIN, whose simple yet elegant compositions brought screen painting to new heights of accomplishment. After the 18th century, screen paintings of genre subjects favored by the UKIYO-E school were executed in large numbers to satisfy the demand from wealthy townsmen. However, most of the major schools of Edo-period painting were in decline, and *shōheiga* declined with them.

scrolls → emakimono

sculpture, modern　　近代彫刻

(*kindai chōkoku*). The notion of sculpture (*chōkoku*) as an independent genre of the plastic arts did not emerge in Japan until the Meiji period (1868–1912), when an imported European ideology of art began to affect traditional aesthetics. Before the Meiji period, sculpture was referred to as *horimono* (carved and engraved objects) and was either religious (see BUDDHIST SCULPTURE) or decorative (see NETSUKE).

In 1876 the Meiji government opened the Kōbu Bijutsu Gakkō (Technical Fine Arts School) and invited the Italian bronze sculptor Vincenzo RAGUSA to head its department of Western-style sculpture. Ragusa taught academic realism and introduced current European techniques in modeling in clay preparatory to bronze casting. Prominent among Ragusa's students was Ōkuma Ujihiro (1856–1934), who produced the portrait *Ōmura Masujirō* (1893), a pioneering work in Japanese Western-style bronze sculpture.

The Kōbu Bijutsu Gakkō was closed in 1882, and Western-style sculpture entered a temporary period of decline. This was due in part to a resurgence of interest in conservative Japanese-style sculpture; also, many Western-style sculptors were abroad. In 1887 the Tōkyō Chōkōkai (Tōkyō Sculptors Association) was formed to encourage traditionalist currents in sculpture. Among its members was TAKAMURA KŌUN, a member of an old Edo family of *busshi* (Buddhist sculptors), and Ishikawa Kōmei (1852–1913) and TAKEUCHI KYŪICHI, both from established families of ivory carvers.

In 1889, following the ideas of promoting traditional art held by OKAKURA KAKUZŌ and Ernest FENOLLOSA, the Tōkyō Bijutsu Gakkō (now Tōkyō University of Fine Arts and Music) was opened, but it did not offer any courses in Western-style sculpture, concentrating instead on training in traditional wood carving. Both Takamura and Takeuchi taught there, emphasizing small-scale works with a strong decorative content.

Renewed interest in Western-style sculpture gained momentum as artists returned from study abroad. With the institution in 1907 of the government-sponsored BUNTEN painting and sculpture competition, Western-style sculptors gained official recognition with the added advantage of a public arena for their works. They exhibited alongside their more conservative Japanese-style counterparts and were judged by representatives from both camps.

A small group of artists inclined to newer trends in European sculpture, which had developed away from academicism toward the romantic realism epitomized by Auguste Rodin (1840–1917). Most influential of this group was OGIWARA MORIE, who sought to express through sculpture the inner rhythms of living form. His *Onna* (Woman) of 1910 exemplifies his style.

By the early years of the Taishō period (1912–26), Rodin's works had been widely publicized in the literary journal *Shirakaba*. Takamura Kōun's eldest son, TAKAMURA KŌTARŌ, a Western-style sculptor who equaled Ogiwara in influence and also was recognized as an outstanding poet, translated Rodin's views on art as *Rodan no kotoba* (1915–20). This book became a pillar of the aesthetics of modern Japanese sculpture.

Rodin's romantic realism displaced neoclassicism in Japan, and most Western-style sculptors were attracted to it as an avenue of greater individual expression. While Western ideals and Rodin's stylistic influence were dominant, they were not all-encompassing. A number of sculptors continued to work in wood in the more conservative vein of Takamura Kōun, among them HIRAGUSHI DENCHŪ. By the end of the Taishō period, conceptually and stylistically Japanese sculpture consisted of two streams, European and traditional. Although occasionally these merged into a successful hybrid, as in the works of Hiragushi, the general trend was parallel development.

In the Shōwa period (1926–89) two general trends became apparent. First, as an outgrowth of the Taishō-period concern with the art and philosophy of Rodin, modern sculptors explored the possibilities of individual expression to an increasingly pronounced degree. Second, Japanese sculpture evolved an international as opposed to a derivative or provincial character. During the 1920s and 1930s sculptors who had studied in Europe returned to Japan and laid the groundwork for new formal and conceptual directions. For example, Shimizu Takashi (1897–1981), Kinouchi Yoshi (1892–1977), and Yasuda Ryūmon (1891–1965), all of whom had worked under Émile-Antoine Bourdelle (1861–1929) at his studio in Paris, introduced a monumental, almost architectural style much influenced by archaic Greek sculpture. Yamamoto Toyoichi (1899–1987) studied under Aristide Maillol (1861–1944), whose energetically depicted figures of women are based on classical Greek and Roman sculpture, and he brought this distinctive style to Japan. Other sculptors active in introducing new trends during this period included SATŌ CHŪRYŌ, whose work reflects the influence of contemporary Italian sculpture; Funakoshi Yasutake (b 1912), skilled in the working of marble; and Yodoi Toshio (b 1911), who was much influenced by Alberto Giacometti (1901–66).

After World War II, Japanese sculptors began to participate actively in the international art world. Formal and conceptual trends current in Europe and the United States soon surfaced in Japan as well. Outdoor sculpture was taken up with enthusiasm during the 1950s and 1960s, and the first generation of Japanese abstract sculptors also became active, among them HORIUCHI MASAKAZU, Mukai Ryōkichi (b 1918), and Tatehata Kakuzō (b 1919).

Contemporary sculptors have attempted to relate sculpture to urban space, introduced technology to their art, and actively developed new methods and materials. Among the more innovative experimental sculptors are Miyawaki Aiko (b 1929) and Shinoda Morio (b 1931). On the other hand, TOMINAGA NAOKI's realistic, powerful male figures and ENTSUBA KATSUZŌ's poetic wood sculptures maintain the traditional idiom.

sea bream 鯛

(tai). In Japanese, tai is used both as a general name for saltwater fish of the family Sparidae, order Perciformes, class Osteichthyes, and specifically for the madai (Pagrus major), a popular species in Japan. Of the approximately 120 species of Sparidae known worldwide, 11 are found in Japan; these resemble the sea bream of the United Kingdom and the porgy of the United States. The madai is native to Japan and its vicinity; it grows to over 80 centimeters (32 in). Over 200 species of fish that are not of the family Sparidae, but that have slightly flattened bodies, are given names suffixed with -tai, indicating the popularity of the tai itself. It is eaten raw, broiled with salt, or in soups.

Bones of the madai and other tai have

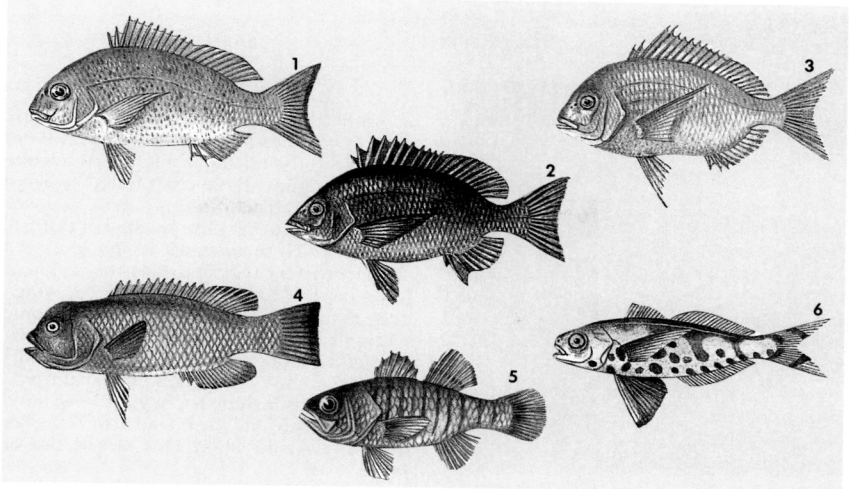

been found in archaeological sites from the Jōmon period (ca 10,000 BC–ca 300 BC). Poems praising the taste of tai are found in the 8th-century anthology, the Man'yōshū. However, it was only with the development of the fishing industry in the early modern period that the common people came to eat tai. The tai is regarded as a celebratory fish and is often served at ceremonious occasions such as weddings.

sea cucumbers 海鼠

(namako). Members of the class Holothuroidea, phylum Echinodermata. Species are numerous. The manamako (Stichopus japonicus), distributed in shallow seas, spawns in April through June (July through August in Hokkaidō) and estivates when the water temperature rises. It is eaten raw, dipped in vinegar and soy sauce; the salt-pickled internal organs (konowata) are relished as a side dish for sake. The kinko (Cucumaria frondosa japonica), found in northern Japan, and baika namako (Thelenota ananas), found in southern Japan including Okinawa, are used in Chinese cooking. The sea cucumber appears in Japanese folklore and in haiku.

seals 印章

(inshō; also called hanko; in). Official or private seals or stamps engraved with the name of the office, institution, or individual to which each belongs. The impressions of these seals are used to endorse documents of all kinds. On most occasions that would call for a signature in the West, Japanese custom requires the impression of a person's seal, called inshō or hanko. No legal document is valid, no contract is binding, without the required seals affixed to it. Seals are also indispensable in many day-to-day activities.

Seals were formally introduced to Japan in 701 when, in imitation of Chinese practice, the TAIHŌ CODE established the first system regulating their manufacture and use. Four types were authorized: the imperial seal; the seal of the Dajōkan (Grand Council of State); seals of various government departments and bureaus; and seals for each province

Some of the great religious establishments also possessed seals.

Government seals were seldom used after the FUJIWARA FAMILY created the regency and took effective control of the government in the 10th century (see REGENCY GOVERNMENT). The powerless imperial court continued to use seals.

With the rise of Zen Buddhism in the 12th and 13th centuries, use of seals by individuals—particularly Chinese monks visiting Japan or Japanese monks returning from study in China—spread for the first time. Following the ŌNIN WAR (1467–77), powerful independent daimyō began to set their personal seals to documents issued within their domains. During the reign of the third Tokugawa shōgun, Iemitsu (1623–51), personal seals were adopted by the general populace.

In 1871, after the MEIJI RESTORATION, the government revived and expanded the 8th-century Taihō system of government seals. Use of the imperial seal was discontinued after World War II, but seals are still used by all central and local government agencies. Also in 1871 a nationwide system for the registration and certification of private seals was established that remains in effect today.

Individuals must register their jitsuin ("true seals") with the head of their local government unit. Only jitsuin may be used on legal documents. For this reason everyone possesses other seals for daily use. When jitsuin are used they are normally affixed below one's signature, and a certificate from the local government must be furnished as proof that the seal used is in fact the legally registered jitsuin.

Sea of Japan 日本海

(Nihonkai). One of the three marginal seas around Japan (see EAST CHINA SEA; OKHOTSK, SEA OF). It is situated between the Asian continent and the Japanese archipelago and is connected to adjacent seas by the straits of Mamiya, Sōya, Tsugaru, Kammon, and Tsushima. It is the smallest of the three marginal seas (1,008,000 sq km; 389,000 sq mi) and the

sea bream The term tai is commonly used to refer to the madai (**1**) and broadly to other fish of the family Sparidae, such as the kurodai (**2**) and the chidai (**3**). It also occurs in the names of more or less related fish, such as the kobudai (**4**) of the family Labridae, the tenjikudai (**5**) of the family Apogonidae, and the eboshidai (**6**) of the family Nomeidae.

seaweed
1 Makombu, a staple seaweed used in making stock, grows to lengths of 2 to 6 meters.
2 Hijiki is another staple seaweed, often used in simmered dishes. It grows to 1 meter in length.
3 Hondawara, a branched seaweed that grows to 2 meters, is used as a New Year's decoration.
4 Tengusa is used to make the vegetable gelatin kanten (agar-agar).
5 Aosa, which grows in shallow waters, has very tough leaves that are used only for feeding livestock.
6 Aonori grows along much of the Japanese coastline. When dried it releases a distinctive fragrance and rich flavor.
7 Wakame has been part of the Japanese diet for centuries.

seaweed cultivation
Nets stretched between poles for the older and still most widely used method of *nori* cultivation, in which seaweed spores are spread on the netting and the resulting crop of seaweed is exposed for drying at low tide.

deepest (maximum depth: 3,712 m; 12,178 ft; average depth: 1,350 m; 4,430 ft). The Sea of Japan provides good fishing grounds and is an important factor in the heavy winter snowfalls on parts of Honshū.

sea urchins   海胆

(*uni*). Members of the class Echinoidea, phylum Echinodermata. Species commonly found in Japan include the dark purple *murasaki uni* (*Anthocidaris crassispina*), the red *aka uni* (*Pseudocentrotus depressus*), and the grayish green *bafun uni* (*Hemicentrotus pulcherrimus*), all of which live on coastal reefs washed by warm currents. The *kita murasaki uni* (*Strongylocentrotus nudus*) and *ezo bafun uni* (*S. intermedius*) are distributed on the coasts of northern Japan. These two species are gathered for food. Other Japanese species include the *gangaze* (needle-spined sea urchin; *Diadema setosum*) in southern Japan and the *futozao uni* (slate-pencil sea urchin; *Heterocentrotus mamillatus*) in Okinawa. Part of the Japanese diet since prehistoric days, the sea urchin is used today mainly in SUSHI and other fancy cuisine, commanding high prices.

seaweed   海藻

(*kaisō*). Stretching from north to south and surrounded by both cold and warm currents, Japan is favored with a rich variety (almost 1,200 kinds) of seaweed. The cold-water region around Hokkaidō to the north is especially rich in KOMBU (genus *Laminaria*), which grows to a length of 10 meters (33 ft). WAKAME (genus *Undaria*), HIJIKI (genus *Hizikia*), *hondawara* (genus *Sargassum*), *arame* (genus *Eisenia*), and *kajime* (genus *Ecklonia*) are found in warmer water from Honshū to Kyūshū. Red algae, such as *amanori* (genus *Porphyra*), *tsunomata* (genus *Chondrus*), and *tengusa* (genus *Gelidium*), are also found in quantity. In waters south of Kyūshū there are *kasanori* (genus *Acetabularia*), *iwazuta* (genus *Caulerpa*), *kirinsai* (genus *Eucheuma*), and *makuri* (genus *Digenea*).

The Japanese more than any other people make use of seaweed in their diet. Certain kinds are used in the manufacture of starch, alginic acid, and insecticides. *Kanten*, or vegetable gelatin, is obtained from *tengusa*. — *See illustrations, previous page.*

seaweed cultivation   海藻養殖

(*kaisō yōshoku*). The major seaweeds cultivated in Japan are NORI (laver; *Porphyra*), *hitoegusa* (*Monostroma*), *wakame* (*Undaria pinnatifida*), and *kombu* (kelp; *Laminaria japonica*). Of these the most important is *nori*. The history of Japanese *nori* cultivation goes back about 300 years. However, recent advances in technology for such procedures

as artificial seeding, low-temperature storage of *nori* nets, and floating cultivation, along with the raising of highly productive cultured strains, have contributed to large production gains.

In addition to the older method of cultivation, in which the *nori* net is spread over a supporting fence and exposed for drying at low tide, the floating-fence method, which does not allow the *nori* to dry, has become widespread. This has resulted in the utilization of offshore areas in addition to traditional shoreline cultivation. The main production areas include Ise Bay, Mikawa Bay, the Ariake Sea, and the Inland Sea. There are only a few cultivation sites on the Sea of Japan coast.

Sebald, William Joseph

シーボルト, W. J.

(1901–80). US diplomat. He headed the Diplomatic Section of SCAP (headquarters for the Allied OCCUPATION of Japan) from 1947 to 1952 and, as General Douglas MACARTHUR's deputy and US member, served as chairman of the ALLIED COUNCIL FOR JAPAN from 1947 to 1951. Born 5 November 1901 in Baltimore, Maryland, he graduated from the US Naval Academy in 1922 and served as a naval language officer in Japan. Sebald earned a degree at the University of Maryland Law School in 1933 and then practiced law in Japan. After naval service in World War II, he entered the Foreign Service, went to Japan in 1946, and later became US political adviser to General MacArthur, with the rank of ambassador. He thereafter served as ambassador to Burma (1952–54), deputy-assistant secretary of state (1954–57), and ambassador to Australia (1957–61). His works include *With MacArthur in Japan* (1965) and several studies of Japanese laws and legal procedures.

SECOM Co, Ltd   セコム[株]

(Sekomu). Security service company. Incorporated in 1962. It provides comprehensive security services, including research and development, manufacture, installation, maintenance, computerized monitoring, guard service, armored car service, training, and consulting. It has expanded from fire and burglary prevention to energy conservation and overall building management. International operations include subsidiaries and affiliates in the United States, the Republic of Korea, Taiwan, and Thailand. Sales for the fiscal year ending March 1991 totaled ¥133.5 billion (US $973.0 million), and the company was capitalized at ¥32.7 billion (US $238.3 million). Headquarters are in Tōkyō.

secondary education   中等教育

(*chūtō kyōiku*). "Secondary education" refers to the three years of compulsory education at MIDDLE SCHOOLS (see also ELEMENTARY EDUCATION) and to the three optional years offered at HIGH SCHOOLS. Pre–World War II secondary education consisted of old-system middle schools, vocational schools, separate HIGHER SCHOOLS for boys, and KŌTŌ JOGAKKŌ for girls. Though widely available, it discriminated against those from less prestigious social and economic backgrounds. After the war the current school system based on the American model was established to standardize education. The goals of teaching, the content, and the number of hours of instruction are prescribed by the state (see SCHOOL CURRICULUM). As of 1989 some 94.5 percent of middle school graduates went on to high school, where they had a choice of either academic or vocational course work.

High school study is also available part time (see TEIJISEI KŌTŌ GAKKŌ) or on a correspondence basis for working students.

Second Provisional Commission for Administrative Reform

第二次臨時行政調査会

(Dainiji Rinji Gyōsei Chōsakai; abbreviated as Dainiji Rinchō). A Japanese government advisory commission formed in March 1981 to investigate and make recommendations concerning the government's administrative structure in order for the nation to adapt to a period of lower economic growth. The chairman of the commission was DOKŌ TOSHIO, former chairman of the Federation of Economic Organizations (KEIDANREN). The commission was composed of nine members drawn from the financial community, former government officials, labor, the press, and the academic community. They were supported by numerous specialists and advisers.

The commission's Final Report, submitted in March 1983, recommmended "restoration of fiscal balance without increased taxation," but had little to say about specific reforms. It stressed reorganization and rationalization of departments and bureaus, the relationship between administrative reform and fiscal balance, reorganization of the regional branch offices of the central government, reorganization and rationalization of subsidies, and the partition and PRIVATIZATION of the nation's three largest public corporations (the *sankōsha*). It was criticized by some for advocating reductions in administrative organizations and curtailment of administrative services. Prime Minister NAKASONE YASUHIRO promised to pay close attention to the commission's reports. On 1 July 1984 he combined the Administrative Management Agency with parts of the Prime Minister's Office to form the MANAGEMENT AND COORDINATION AGENCY. As for the three public corporations, the privatization of the Japan Tobacco and Salt Public Corporation and the Nippon Telegraph and Telephone Public Corporation was put into effect in April 1985, and the breakup and privatization of the Japanese National Railways was put into effect in April 1987.

Second United Front   第二次国共合作

(Dainiji Kokkyō Gassaku). The name for the cooperation between the Chinese Guomindang (Kuomintang) Party and the Chinese Communist Party in the late 1930s that suspended civil war in a common cause against Japanese aggression. This term is distinguished from an earlier, abortive united front (1924–27).

After Japan's takeover of Manchuria in 1931 (see MANCHURIAN INCIDENT), the Communist Party called for a united front against Japan in the AUGUST FIRST DECLARATION of 1935. The Guomindang under CHIANG KAISHEK, however, continued to follow a policy of appeasement toward Japan and of suppression toward the communists. Disagreement with Chiang's Japan policy sparked armed revolts from forces nominally under Guomindang control, in Fujian (Fukien) and in North China, where the XI'AN (SIAN) INCIDENT of December 1936 finally compelled Chiang to accept the principle of a united front. The final agreement between the Guomindang and the Communist Party was not concluded until 22 September 1937, two months after the outbreak of the SINO-JAPANESE WAR OF 1937–1945. After Japan's surrender in 1945, the civil war resumed, ending with the communist victory in 1949.

Sect Shintō　　　　　　　　教派神道

(Kyōha Shintō; also called Shintō Jūsampa). Originally the 13 independent Shintō sects recognized by the Japanese government between 1876 and 1908. They were for the most part founded in the 18th and 19th centuries by charismatic teachers. Each generally had its own scriptures, composed or revealed by its founder. In contrast to shrines officially recognized as "public," these sects were not permitted to maintain shrines or to copy the shrine architectural styles for their places of worship.

The 13 traditional Shintō sects may be classified in 5 groups: (1) Pure Shintō (three sects), which emphasize Shintō themes found in the KOJIKI (712, Records of Ancient Matters) or in RESTORATION SHINTŌ; (2) Confucian (two sects), which stress Confucian ethical principles; (3) Purification (two sects), which encourage the practice of MISOGI (purification rite) and asceticism; (4) Mountain (three sects), which are organized around the traditional worship of sacred mountains; and (5) Faith Healing (three sects), which seek to effect cures through Shintō rituals. When government controls over religion were removed after 1945, the number of sect Shintō groups proliferated. By 1989 there were 80 sects, plus another 48 sects that described themselves as belonging to the "New Sect Shintō" (Shin Kyōha Shintō). See also SECT SHINTŌ, ASSOCIATION OF; SHRINE SHINTŌ.

Sect Shintō, Association of
　　　　　　　　　　　　　　教派神道連合会

(Kyōha Shintō Rengōkai). One of the five constituent groups that make up the membership of the Nihon Shūkyō Remmei (JAPAN RELIGIOUS LEAGUE); established in 1946. The Kyōha Shintō Rengōkai is a liaison organization that represents and speaks on behalf of SECT SHINTŌ. It is supported by 11 Shintō sects. Of the 13 Shintō sects officially recognized before 1945, the Shinshūkyō, Shintō Taiseiha, and TENRIKYŌ are not currently members. The ŌMOTO is the only Shintō sect not recognized before 1945 to have membership in the association.

Securities Exchange Law
　　　　　　　　　　　　　　証券取引法

(Shōken Torihiki Hō). Law enacted in 1948, and revised in 1988, for the purpose of protecting investors by ensuring that securities are issued and traded fairly. Modeled after the US Securities Act of 1933 and Securities Exchange Act of 1934, the law regulates both the market in which securities are issued and the market in which they are traded. Under this law, securities are defined narrowly. The only domestic securities covered are stocks, convertible bonds, and unsecured bonds, and there are no provisions to cover such transactions as investment contracts. Foreign government bonds are subject to the law's disclosure requirements.

The Securities Exchange Law provides that issuers of securities must register with the MINISTRY OF FINANCE before making any public offering. Sales of securities must be accompanied by a prospectus. An obligation to file annual financial disclosure statements is imposed on all issuers of listed securities, certain over-the-counter securities, and publicly offered securities. These types of securities are also subject to regulations on tender offers made outside an exchange. Brokers and securities exchanges must be licensed by the government.

When this law was enacted, the Securities Exchange Commission was placed in charge of its execution. This commission was abolished in 1952, however, and replaced by the Securities Bureau of the Ministry of Finance. A person who makes an untrue statement or otherwise commits an unlawful act in connection with the issuance or trading of protected securities is criminally as well as civilly liable. The 1988 revision further provided criminal sanctions against insider trading. The procedures to be followed when a company issues stock or bonds are regulated by the COMMERCIAL CODE and other laws that fall under the jurisdiction of the minister of justice.

Securities Exchange Law, article 65　　　　　　　証券取引法65条

(Shōken Torihiki Hō Rokujūgojō). Legislation prohibiting financial institutions, such as commercial banks, from engaging in securities-related transactions (the dealing and underwriting of bonds and securities). In Japan such transactions are restricted to securities firms (although both types of institutions can deal in government bonds). Japan's legislation was based on similar restrictions in the United States. In contrast, most European countries practice universal banking, in which commercial banks are free to deal in securities. In 1991 the Ministry of Finance announced plans to allow banks and securities firms to set up subsidiaries to enter each other's businesses.

Security Council　　　　　安全保障会議

(Anzen Hoshō Kaigi). Cabinet body in charge of matters related to national defense. Established in 1956 as the National Defense Council (Kokubō Kaigi), it assumed its present name in 1986. Its members are the prime minister (chairman), the ministers of foreign affairs and finance, the directors-general of the Defense and Economic Planning agencies, and others appointed by the prime minister. The prime minister is obliged to consult the council on all matters relating to defense, including decisions on emergency military action.

Sefuri Mountains　　　　　背振山地

(Sefuri Sanchi). Also called Seburi Mountains. Mountain range in Saga and Fukuoka prefectures, northern Kyūshū, running east to west along the northern edge of the Saga Plain. The highest peak is Sefurisan (1,055 m; 3,460 ft).

Segawa Jokō　　　　　　瀬川如皐

Name of a succession of important playwrights in the KABUKI theater. Jokō I (1739–94), an onnagata (female impersonator) in the Ōsaka kabuki theater, later became a leading playwright for the Edo (now Tōkyō) stage. Jokō II (1757–1833), a pupil of Jokō I, was regarded as second only to the great Tsuruya Namboku IV (see TSURUYA NAMBOKU) in ability. Others included Jokō III (1806–81), Jokō IV (1857–1938), and Jokō V (1888–1957).

segregation of Japanese schoolchildren in the United States
　　　　　　　　　　　　日本人学童隔離

(nihonjin gakudō kakuri). Refers to a regulation passed by the San Francisco Board of Education on 11 October 1906 requiring children of Japanese descent to attend special segregated schools. By 1900 there were about 24,000 Japanese immigrants on the US mainland. Most of them lived on the West

Coast and made up 1 percent of the population of California. After Japan's success in the Russo-Japanese War of 1904–05, Californians became increasingly exclusionist and xenophobic, and a strong anti-Japanese movement emerged. When the San Francisco Board of Education ordered schoolchildren of Japanese descent to attend an Oriental public school, the Japanese government registered an official protest. To ease tensions, President Theodore Roosevelt persuaded the board to rescind the order and later persuaded the Japanese government not to issue passports to laborers who intended to go to the US mainland. See GENTLEMEN'S AGREEMENT.

seibo　　　　　　　　　　歳暮

Custom of giving year-end gifts and the gifts themselves; presented as an expression of appreciation for favors received in the past year. The Chinese characters for seibo mean "year end." The custom is said to have arisen from the practice of sharing with others offerings initially made to ancestors. Those in a socially superior position, such as a marriage mediator (nakōdo), are typical recipients of seibo, as well as of midyear CHŪGEN gifts. Gifts are presented by those in inferior positions and are usually considered to be from family to family or from business to business. There is some discontent with the custom of seibo, probably because it is obligatory, but of all calendrically determined gift-giving occasions, seibo is by far the most important. Traditionally, seibo were personally delivered, but today people often will have stores deliver or send the gifts through the mail. See also GIFT GIVING.

Seibu Department Stores, Ltd
　　　　　　　　　　　　［株］西武百貨店

(Seibu Hyakkaten). Department store chain comprising 33 stores. The Seibu Department Stores group consists of 49 affiliated companies in such fields as fashion import and wholesaling, product licensing, and interior design. The group employs over 20,000 persons. A unique feature of Seibu's operations are its "concept stores," separate stores that specialize in such areas as audiovisual equipment, books, music, and home needs. Seibu Department Stores, Ltd, is one of the retailing companies of the Saison group. Sales for the fiscal year ending February 1991 totaled ¥985.0 billion (US $7.5 billion), and capitalization stood at ¥3.6 billion (US $27.6 million). Headquarters are in Tōkyō.

Seibu Railway Co, Ltd　　西武鉄道［株］

(Seibu Tetsudō). Private railway company based in the northwestern part of the Tōkyō metropolitan area and engaged in transportation, tourism, real estate, and leisure enterprises. The predecessor of Seibu Railway was the Musashino Tetsudō, a railway company incorporated in 1912, which started operations in 1915 on a 43.8-kilometer (27.2-mi) route between Ikebukuro and Hannō using steam locomotives. It gradually developed by electrifying its lines, laying double tracks, extending its routes, and absorbing other railway firms. It took its current name in 1946. In 1991 the company had 2 trunk lines and 11 branch lines totaling 178.4 kilometers (110.8 mi) in length and transported approximately 3.6 million passengers daily. Total sales for the fiscal year ending March 1991 were ¥203.6 billion (US $1.5 billion), of

Edward George Seidensticker This scholar is known for his many superlative translations of both classical and modern Japanese literature.

which railway operations accounted for 36 percent; tourism, 42 percent; and real estate, 22 percent. The company was capitalized at ¥21.7 billion (US $158.2 million) in the same year. Headquarters are in Tokorozawa, Saitama Prefecture.

Seichō no Ie 生長の家

(House of Growth). Contemporary religious sect founded in 1930 by TANIGUCHI MASAHARU, when he first began publishing *Seichō no ie*, a journal of spiritual guidance. In 1934 Taniguchi began disseminating his teachings throughout Japan. He emphasized man's filial relationship with the divine through each individual's effort to realize "the truth of life." One who returns to this truth, he maintained, will be free of misfortunes. He claimed that the doctrines of Shintō, Buddhism, Christianity, and all other true religions are truly one. In addition to propagation in Japan, Seichō no Ie has heavily emphasized overseas proselytizing. In 1989 there were reportedly 821,998 adherents and 126 missionary centers in Japan; overseas there were 1,257,907 adherents and 133 missionary centers.

Seidan 政談

(Discourses on Government). Four-volume work by the Confucian scholar OGYŪ SORAI; originally written as a memorial to the eighth shōgun, TOKUGAWA YOSHIMUNE; presumably completed between 1725 and 1727. Sorai discusses the Tokugawa shogunate's political and economic problems and recommends, among other things, advancement based on merit and the relocation of *samurai* to the countryside to alleviate their financial hardship.

Seidensticker, Edward George

サイデンステッカー, E. G.

(1921–). US scholar and translator of Japanese literature. Professor emeritus of Japanese at Columbia University. Born in Castle Rock, Colorado, he graduated from the University of Colorado and studied Japanese literature at Harvard University and Tōkyō University. Seidensticker is known for his perceptive, subtle translations of many works of Japanese literature, both classical and modern. He completed a full-length translation of the TALE OF GENJI (*Genji monogatari*) in 1976. Among his many other translations are TANIZAKI JUN'ICHIRŌ's *Sasameyuki* (1943–48; tr *The Makioka Sisters*, 1957) and KAWABATA YASUNARI's *Yukiguni* (1935–48; tr *Snow Country*, 1956) and *Sembazuru* (1949–51; tr *Thousand Cranes*, 1959). It is widely recognized that Kawabata's receipt of the Nobel Prize for literature (1968) owed much to Seidensticker's translations. His scholarly studies include *Kafū the Scribbler* (1965), *Low City, High City* (1983), and *Tōkyō Rising* (1990).

seidō 西堂

(literally, "western hall"). Status title of monks in ZEN monasteries. Originally the western hall of a monastery or the monks who lived there, *seidō* gradually came to designate a monk who upon retiring from the abbacy of one monastery took up residence in the western hall of another. In the Muromachi period (1333–1568) *seidō* came to designate a monk who had served as abbot in any monastery of *jissatsu* or *shozan* rank in the official ranking system for Zen monasteries (see GOZAN).

seii tai shōgun →shōgun

Seijin no Hi →holidays, national

seiji shōsetsu 政治小説

("political novel"). Term referring specifically to novels written mainly during the 1880s in connection with the FREEDOM AND PEOPLE'S RIGHTS MOVEMENT (Jiyū Minken Undō). From the late 1870s, journalists belonging to the democratic movement tried writing fiction to get across to uneducated people the basic ideas of "freedom" and "people's rights." A number of them, such as Komuro Angaidō (1852–85), Miyazaki Muryū (1853–89), and Sakazaki Shiran (1853–1913), who had originally been political activists, became rather popular authors; their subject matter ranged from the Restoration movement at the end of the Edo period (1600–1868) to the French Revolution and the Russian nihilists.

More sophisticated politically oriented fiction was written by YANO RYŪKEI, who in 1883–84 published his *Keikoku bidan* (A Noble Tale of Statesmanship). This book was directed at the educated reader and made fiction seem socially acceptable. SUEHIRO TETCHŌ, in his *Setchūbai* (1886, Plum Blossoms in the Snow), sought to combine a political message with elements of the novel of manners. TŌKAI SANSHI published *Kajin no kigū* (1885–97, Chance Meetings with Beautiful Women), an imaginative romance about the battles for freedom in contemporary Asia, Africa, and Europe.

In general, the *seiji shōsetsu* mirrored the basic weakness of the people's rights movement it had served: an inability to reconcile ambitious concepts of state and nation with the actual subtleties of human thought and feeling. However, by showing that fiction, in addition to entertaining, could disseminate new ideas capable of influencing the emerging middle class, the *seiji shōsetsu* took a significant step toward establishing the novel at the center of modern literature.

Seijō University 成城大学

(Seijō Daigaku). A coeducational private university in Setagaya Ward, Tōkyō. The university, which was established in 1950, traces its origins to the Seijō Shōgakkō (Seijō Elementary School), an experimental school that was founded in 1917 by SAWAYANAGI MASATARŌ. It maintains faculties of economics, arts and literature, and law. Enrollment in 1989 was 4,200.

Seikadō Bunko 静嘉堂文庫

(Seikadō Library). A major repository of East Asian culture containing nearly 200,000 volumes and some 5,000 art objects. Located in Setagaya Ward, Tōkyō, this private collection was founded in 1892 by Iwasaki Yanosuke (1851–1908), a son of the founder of the MITSUBISHI financial combine, and his son IWASAKI KOYATA.

Concerned about the Westernization of East Asian culture and the reported loss of its cultural heritage to foreign collectors, Yanosuke sought to preserve East Asian cultural objects in Japan. In 1924 the collection was moved to its present site. MOROHASHI TETSUJI was its director from 1921 to 1955. The collection survived World War II unscathed and is now administered by a private foundation.

Seikanron 征韓論

The debate (*ron*) over whether Japan should send a punitive expedition to Korea (*seikan*),

an issue that divided the Japanese government in 1873. The new Meiji government sought to reorganize relations with Korea. Korea, however, had long been a Confucian dependent state of China and regarded the Japanese overture as an attempt by Japan to arrogate China's rank in the Confucian hierarchy. Accordingly, the Koreans responded negatively and, the Japanese thought, insultingly. Negotiations at Pusan proved fruitless, and the idea of "punishing" Korea arose in Japan. However, many key members of the Meiji government were absent from Japan on the IWAKURA MISSION (1871–73), and it had been agreed that no large projects would be undertaken until their return.

Meanwhile, the caretaker government at home, which included SAIGŌ TAKAMORI, ITAGAKI TAISUKE, and Foreign Minister SOEJIMA TANEOMI, decided to pursue the Korean issue independently. In August Saigō obtained approval from the Grand Council of State (Dajōkan) to go as an ambassador to Korea and provoke war if a settlement could not be reached, but the president of the council, SANJŌ SANETOMI, brought back to the council the imperial "decision" that the young emperor wished to defer the matter until "after the return of Iwakura."

IWAKURA TOMOMI returned in September, determined to counter Saigō's plans. He had ŌKUBO TOSHIMICHI, who had accompanied him on the mission to the West, appointed to the Grand Council of State, and it was Ōkubo who took the lead in the argument against Saigō and his supporters. The debate was so intense that Sanjō suffered a breakdown, and Iwakura assumed the council presidency. He announced that he would not permit the emperor to approve the appointment of Saigō to Korea and forced the resignations of all the prowar councillors.

Saigō left Tōkyō in a fury and returned to his home base in Satsuma (now Kagoshima Prefecture). As prowar and other *samurai* dissidents gathered there, he gradually emerged as the leader of the antigovernment movement that was to culminate in the SATSUMA REBELLION of 1877. The rebellion was crushed by the government's new conscript army, which was being developed by YAMAGATA ARITOMO, and Saigō committed suicide. A year later Ōkubo was assassinated in Tōkyō by followers of Saigō. But Iwakura, his protégé ITŌ HIROBUMI, and others of the "antiwar" faction of 1873 continued to guide the destinies of the Meiji state and to chart its course toward modernization.

Seikan Tunnel 青函トンネル

(Seikan Tonneru). Railway tunnel under the Tsugaru Strait, connecting the Oshima Peninsula on the island of Hokkaidō with the Tsugaru Peninsula, Aomori Prefecture, on the island of Honshū. Under construction since 1964 by the Japan Railway Construction Public Corporation, the tunnel was completed in March 1985. The longest undersea tunnel in the world, it has a total length of 53.9 kilometers (33.5 mi), 23.3 kilometers (14.5 mi) of which is undersea. Its deepest point is 140 meters (459 ft) below sea level. The tunnel was opened to railway traffic in March 1988.

Seikatsu Tsuzurikata Undō

生活綴方運動

(literally, "Life Composition Movement"). An educational movement for free, realistic self-expression in writing, conducted in primary schools during the early part of the Shōwa period (1926–89). In the second decade of the 20th century, ASHIDA ENOSUKE, a primary school teacher, began to promote a new method of teaching composition that emphasized free expression by the students rather than ideological indoctrination as had been the practice. In 1918 the writer SUZUKI MIEKICHI, through his children's literary magazine AKAI TORI (Red Bird), began to advocate the principle "Ari no mama ni kaku" (To write about things as they are), encouraging free expression.

The Seikatsu Tsuzurikata Undō developed from these beginnings. The 1929 publication of *Tsuzurikata seikatsu*, edited by the popular educator Sasaoka Tadayoshi (1897–1937), helped to spread the movement. With the beginning of World War II in 1941, however, the movement was suppressed by state authorities who considered it leftist.

Seikei University 成蹊大学

(Seikei Daigaku). A coeducational private university in the city of Musashino, Tōkyō Prefecture. It traces its origins to the Seikeien, a private academy opened in 1906. It became a university in 1949 and currently maintains faculties of economics, engineering, humanities, and law. Enrollment in 1989 was 6,560.

Seike Kiyoshi 清家清

(1918–). Architect. Born in Kyōto. Graduate of the Tōkyō School of Fine Arts (now Tōkyō University of Fine Arts and Music) and the Tōkyō Institute of Technology. Among Seike's major works is the Hakone Prince Hotel Lakeside Lodge (1985), which typifies his style: modern functionalist design imbued with traditional Japanese atmosphere. Seike taught at both the schools he graduated from and became president of the Architectural Institute of Japan in 1981.

Seiken igen 靖献遺言

(Last Words of Loyalists). A two-volume work on loyalty and duty written in 1687 by the Confucian scholar ASAMI KEISAI (1652–1712). Each of the work's eight chapters contains a short biography and pertinent sayings and writings of one of eight exemplars of loyalty from Chinese history—for example, Qu Yuan (Ch'ü Yüan), Tao Qian (T'ao Ch'ien), and Zhu Geliang (Chu Ko-liang). *Seiken igen* had a great influence on antishogunate thinkers and activists of the late Edo period (1600–1868).

Seikō Corporation [株]服部セイコー

(Hattori Seikō). Major worldwide supplier of quality watches and clocks. It also markets a broad range of electronic and consumer products, among which are eyeglass lenses and frames, jewelry and accessories, computers, liquid-crystal-display (LCD) color televisions, tuners, and other consumer products.

In 1881 Hattori Kintarō (1860–1934) established K. Hattori & Co, Ltd, in Tōkyō; the company's name was changed to Seikō Corporation in 1990. In 1969 it introduced the world's first quartz watch under the Seikō brand name, revolutionizing the timepiece industry. With Seikō Corporation functioning as the marketing headquarters, all watches are manufactured on automated production lines in the factories of SEIKŌ INSTRUMENTS, INC, and SEIKŌ EPSON CORPORATION; clocks are manufactured at Seikōsha Co, Ltd.

In the fiscal year ending March 1991, annual sales were ¥305.7 billion (US $2.2 billion), with sales of watches accounting for 60 percent; clocks, 15 percent; and jewelry and other goods, 25 percent. The export ratio was 37 percent and capitalization stood at ¥10.0 billion (US $72.9 million) in the same year. Headquarters are in Tōkyō.

Seikō Epson Corporation セイコーエプソン[株]

(Seikō Epuson). Producer of computers and related office equipment. It is the largest manufacturing unit in the Seikō group. Since its founding in 1942, the company has developed precision "mechatronics" technology, which it applied to the development of quartz watches. It has 35 overseas sales and manufacturing affiliates in 21 countries. Sales for the fiscal year ending March 1990 totaled ¥470.0 billion (US $3.1 billion), and capitalization stood at ¥12.5 billion (US $81.7 million). Headquarters are in the city of Suwa, Nagano Prefecture.

Seikō Instruments, Inc セイコー電子工業[株]

(Seikō Denshi Kōgyō). Manufacturer of watches and industrial machines and tools. Incorporated in 1937 as a manufacturer of Seikō brand watches. For the fiscal year ending March 1990, sales totaled ¥160.3 billion (US $1.1 billion), of which watch sales accounted for 41 percent, and capitalization stood at ¥1.0 billion (US $6.5 million). Headquarters are in Tōkyō.

Seikōkai 聖公会

(Anglican-Episcopal Church). The foundations of this church in Japan were laid by missionaries from the Protestant Episcopal Church in the United States, the Church Missionary Society of England, and the Society for the Propagation of the Gospel of England. These three groups united in 1887 to form the Nihon Seikōkai; the Missionary Society of the Church of England in Canada joined in 1888. In 1989 the church consisted of 11 dioceses with 277 churches and claimed 57,478 members. It runs RIKKYŌ UNIVERSITY in Tōkyō and ST. ANDREW'S UNIVERSITY in Ōsaka, as well as hospitals and other institutions.

Seikyōsha 政教社

(Society for Political Education). Cultural and political association established in 1888 that opposed government acceptance of the Unequal Treaties (see UNEQUAL TREATIES, REVISION OF) imposed by Western powers. Members included SUGIURA SHIGETAKE, MIYAKE SETSUREI, SHIGA SHIGETAKA, and NAITŌ KONAN. In its magazine, NIHONJIN, the group advocated a pluralistic world culture in which Japan would play an active role. After 1923 the association espoused a militaristic PAN-ASIANISM. It was dissolved in February 1945.

Seikyō yōroku 聖教要録

(Essentials of the Sacred Teachings). Work by YAMAGA SOKŌ, Confucian scholar and founder of the Yamaga school of military science; published in 1665. Sokō criticizes the contending schools of Confucianism, particularly the officially supported Zhu Xi (Chu Hsi) school of Neo-Confucianism (SHUSHIGAKU), as too theoretical and impractical; he then explains his own position, which called for a return to the original Confucian teachings (see KOGAKU). This work angered the Tokugawa shogunate, and Sokō was banished temporarily from Edo (now Tōkyō).

Seimi kaisō 舎密開宗

A Japanese translation, published 1837–49, of the Dutch version of the British Chemist William Henry's (1775–1836) *An Epitome of Experimental Chemistry* (1801). Translated by UDAGAWA YŌAN, *Seimi kaisō* consists of 18 main volumes and 18 supplementary volumes. The work greatly influenced the development of chemistry in Japan, and some of Udagawa's terminology is still in use today.

Seimikyoku 舎密局

Two government institutes established in Ōsaka and Kyōto during the early Meiji period (1868–1912) as educational and research facilities in the natural sciences. The word *seimi* is a phonetic rendering of *chemie,* the Dutch word for chemistry. The Ōsaka Seimikyoku, established in 1868, was considered the most advanced facility for Western scientific learning in the Kyōto-Ōsaka-Kōbe area. It later developed into the Third Higher School. The Kyōto Seimikyoku was founded in 1870 with the WESTERN LEARNING scholar Akashi Hiroakira (1839–1910) as director. The German scholar Gottfried WAGENER also lectured there. It closed in 1884. The bureaus contributed to scientific and technological education and to the development of industry.

Seinan Sensō → Satsuma Rebellion

seinendan → youth clubs

seinen gakkō 青年学校

(youth schools). Secondary education facilities for working boys and girls that were operated between 1935 and the educational reforms of 1947. Classes were conducted at night for young people who did not attend either middle or high school. In 1939 attendance was required of all boys from 12 to 19 who were not enrolled in another educational facility. All students were taught Japanese history and "moral education" (SHŪSHIN); in addition, boys were given military training and girls were taught home economics. By 1945 there were 15,000 youth schools with a total enrollment of 2.6 million students.

Seinō Transportation Co, Ltd 西濃運輸[株]

(Seinō Un'yu). Company specializing in overland cargo transport. Incorporated in 1946. The company is engaged in general cargo haulage, trucking, air carrier service, warehousing, transportation, marine carrier service, and general vehicle maintenance and repair. In 1983 Seinō began door-to-door service between Japan and the United States. The company has European tie-ups for air-

Sei Shōnagon A 17th-century portrait of the poet and diarist, whose brilliantly written observations are important documents for understanding aristocratic life in the Heian period.

cargo and small-package services. Sales for the fiscal year ending April 1991 totaled ¥230.6 billion (US $1.7 billion), and capitalization stood at ¥30.7 billion (US $223.6 million) in the same year. Headquarters are in the city of Ōgaki, Gifu Prefecture.

seirei → cabinet order

Seiryōki 清良記
Chronicle of the life of Doi Kiyoyoshi (Doi Seiryō; 1546–1629), lord of Ōmori Castle in Iyo Province (now Ehime Prefecture); ascribed to Doi Mizunari (d 1654). It is thought to have been completed in the Kan'ei (1624–43) era. Belonging to the genre known as GUNKI MONOGATARI (military tales), the work focuses on Kiyoyoshi's military exploits. One section, which contains information on the agricultural technology of the time, is considered the earliest Japanese treatise on the subject.

seishō 政商
(literally, "political merchants"). Merchants and financiers who made use of their close connections with the early Meiji government to found commercial empires. They included the MITSUI and SUMITOMO families, IWASAKI YATARŌ (who founded MITSUBISHI), YASUDA ZENJIRŌ, ASANO SŌICHIRŌ, SHIBUSAWA EIICHI, and GODAI TOMOATSU. They received government patronage, either through grants of monopolies, direct subsidies, easy financial terms, or purchase of government enterprises at nominal prices. From the late Meiji period (1868–1912) on, Mitsui and Mitsubishi were particularly skillful in forming alliances with political parties. Mitsui contributed regularly to the political party RIKKEN SEIYŪKAI, and Mitsubishi gave financial backing to a rival party, the RIKKEN MINSEITŌ.

Sei Shōnagon 清少納言
(fl late 10th century). One of the best known of the brilliant women writers of the Heian period (794–1185); author of MAKURA NO SŌSHI (996–1012; tr *The Pillow Book of Sei Shōnagon*, 1967). Two superlative prose works distinguish Japanese literature of the period around the year 1000. One is the *Genji monogatari* (TALE OF GENJI), the best-known early court novel; the other is *Makura no sōshi*, a slender volume of short eyewitness narratives, casual essays, impressions, reflections, lists, and imagined scenes. *Makura no sōshi* established a genre known as ZUI-HITSU, a term meaning "to follow the brush," implying a total absence of premeditated direction.

Sei Shōnagon, the only name by which she is now known, is merely the nickname given her during her service at the imperial court in the 990s. She was a Kiyohara, and Sei is the Sino-Japanese reading of the first character used in writing this family name. Shōnagon means "lesser counselor," a typical court lady's cognomen. Her father was

Motosuke (908–990), a noted scholar and poet of some repute. As one of the Five Gentlemen of the Pear Chamber (Nashitsubo no Gonin), he helped compile the second imperial WAKA (classical poetry) anthology, the *Gosen wakashū*, in 951.

As with most women writers of the period, it is only the middle part of Sei Shōnagon's life about which much is known. She was a rival to her contemporary MURASAKI SHIKIBU, the author of the *Tale of Genji*, who disparages Sei Shōnagon in her diary of 1008–10. Sei Shōnagon emerges with startling brilliance in her own writings, but she does not deal with her childhood, and her late years are recorded more in legend than in fact. Speculation centers on 966 as the year of Sei Shōnagon's birth. At some time in the early 990s she became a lady-in-waiting at the court of Sadako (976–1001; see FUJIWARA NO TEISHI), the consort of the young emperor ICHIJŌ (r 986–1011). She presumably remained in service until Sadako's death, and although her subsequent fate is obscure, she may have stayed on to care for Sadako's daughter Shūshi (997–1049) or may even have entered service with Sadako's cousin Akiko. Tradition has it that she ended her days old and impoverished.

Makura no sōshi is valued not only as a literary masterpiece, but as a work of considerable historical significance as well. The impressions of the world about her that Sei Shōnagon recorded in it result in a detailed account of events and customs at the Heian court. More important, it provided a vehicle for the revelation of a brilliant author's vivacious personality and style. Sei Shōnagon was opinionated and abrasive, but at the same time she was possessed of a rare sensitivity to the colors of the passing scene and of a talent for rendering her impressions with sharp economy. In addition to *Makura no sōshi* she left a small collection of her poems, the *Sei Shōnagon shū*.

Seitaisho 政体書
Also known as the "Constitution of 1868" or the "Organic Act." The first "constitution" of the Meiji government; issued on 11 June 1868. Under the Seitaisho all authority was vested in the DAJŌKAN (Grand Council of State), within which were seven administrative departments. It also provided for a bicameral deliberative assembly (Giseikan), but this was virtually ignored from the outset and eventually abandoned. The Dajōkan, however, remained the central executive organ of government until the cabinet system was adopted in 1885.

Seitōsha 青鞜社
(Bluestocking Society). An organization, lasting from 1911 to 1916, that marked the beginning of the Japanese feminist movement. The first women's group to arouse nationwide interest, the Seitōsha started by publishing the literary magazine *Seitō* ("Bluestocking") in September 1911. The idea of a magazine by and for women only, as well as its name, was inspired by literary critic IKUTA CHŌKŌ, who proposed the plan to his pupil HIRATSUKA RAICHŌ. Raichō founded the group and its magazine with Yasumochi Yoshiko and others. As many as several hundred women joined the Seitōsha and took part in its activities. The Seitōsha gained its reputation as an association of "new women," who since the turn of the century had begun penetrating the world of men by becoming teachers, nurses, artists, officials, and office workers and who were

becoming more and more aware of their own rights as women in society.

In November 1914 Raichō, faced with family and financial hardships, thought of giving up publication of the *Seitō* altogether. However, ITŌ NOE decided to continue it on her own. She took over editorship of the *Seitō* in January 1915 and dealt with issues such as prostitution, abortion, and chastity. Itō discontinued publication of the magazine in February 1916 and the Seitōsha disbanded.

Seiyō jijō 西洋事情
(Conditions in the West). Work in three volumes by FUKUZAWA YUKICHI, the preeminent scholar of the MEIJI ENLIGHTENMENT movement, based on the knowledge he acquired on three trips abroad (1860–67). Volume 1 (1867) discusses numerous Western institutions: schools, newspapers, libraries, government bonds, orphanages, museums, steamships, telegraphs—in short, those aspects of modern Western life that Fukuzawa hoped Japan would emulate. Volume 2 (1868) contains translations of excerpts on governments and economics from a popular British series, *Chambers' Educational Course*. Volume 3 (1870) presents general material by British jurist Sir William Blackstone (1723–80) on human rights and by American educator Francis Wayland (1796–1865) on taxes and then supplies data on Russia and France. Throughout, Fukuzawa sought to explain Western political systems, particularly the concepts of liberty and rights. The book had a powerful influence on the Japanese public of the time. FUKUOKA TAKACHIKA, a drafter of the CHARTER OATH and of the SEITAISHO, the Meiji government's protoconstitution, later wrote that in formulating ideas for a new political structure, he and his colleagues had relied almost exclusively on the *Seiyō jijō*.

Seiyū Foods Co, Ltd [株]西友フーズ
(Seiyū Fūzu). Food-processing company. Incorporated in 1953. It supplies foodstuffs to companies of the Saison group such as SEIYŪ, LTD. In 1988 it had 225 outlets in Seiyū stores and SEIBU DEPARTMENT STORES, LTD. Sales for the fiscal year ending February 1990 totaled ¥153.2 billion (US $1.1 billion), and capitalization stood at ¥909.0 million (US $6.2 million) in the same year. Headquarters are in Tōkyō.

Seiyū Hontō 政友本党
(True Seiyū Party). Conservative political party formed in January 1924 by TOKONAMI TAKEJIRŌ and other RIKKEN SEIYŪKAI members unhappy with the TAKAHASHI KOREKIYO faction's dominance of the Seiyūkai. They left that party to support the KIYOURA KEIGO cabinet. Closely allied with the bureaucratic elite, the Seiyū Hontō advocated national harmony and opposed expansion of the electoral franchise. It was initially the largest party in the Diet, with 149 seats. However, in the 1924 election it won only 109 seats. In 1926 it retained only 87 seats, for 22 members returned to the Seiyūkai when TANAKA GIICHI replaced Takahashi as the Seiyūkai's president. In June 1927 it joined the relatively progressive KENSEIKAI to form the RIKKEN MINSEITŌ. See also POLITICAL PARTIES.

Seiyūkai → Rikken Seiyūkai

Seiyū, Ltd [株]西友
(Seiyū). Chain store and supermarket operator. A member of the Seibu Saison group, it

was originally established as Seibu Stores in 1956 and took its present name in 1983. The firm is developing a range of new activities, including reservation booking and sales of theater, movie, and other tickets. Seiyū is building on-line computer systems to link its stores with other Seibu Saison group companies. It has business tie-ups in South Korea, Indonesia, and Thailand and representative offices in Seoul, Beijing, Hong Kong, Bangkok, Los Angeles, Chicago, Seattle, and Taipei. Sales for the fiscal year ending February 1991 totaled ¥1.0 trillion (US $7.7 billion), and capitalization was ¥10.0 billion (US $76.6 million). Headquarters are in Tōkyō.

seizōbutsu sekinin → product
liability

seizonken　　　　　　　　生存権
(literally, "right to live"). The responsibility of the state, established in article 25 of the CONSTITUTION OF JAPAN, to protect citizens from poverty and destitution and to develop policies to guarantee the welfare of the people. Article 25 provides: "All people shall have the right to maintain the minimum standards of wholesome and cultured living." Furthermore: "In all spheres of life, the State shall use its endeavors for the promotion and extension of social welfare and security, and of public health."

The *seizonken* of article 25 is considered to be a "program provision" that directs government policy but does not carry the right to claim relief by lawsuit when the laws and resources of the state do not provide these minimum standards.

Specific legislation enacted under the principles of *seizonken* includes the LIVELIHOOD PROTECTION LAW (Seikatsu Hogo Hō), the CHILD WELFARE LAW (Jidō Fukushi Hō), the Social Welfare Activities Law (Shakai Fukushi Jigyō Hō; see SOCIAL WELFARE), and the National Pension Law (Kokumin Nenkin Hō; see PENSIONS).

Seji kembunroku　　　　　世事見聞録
(Record of Personal Observations of Society; also called *Seji kemmonroku*). A 7-volume collection of essays completed in about 1816 by an unidentified writer using the pen name Buyō Inshi. The author addresses a wide variety of subjects, ranging from class and occupational groups to crop production, *kabuki* plays, and contemporary mores. The work is an important source of information on social conditions at a time when the merchant class was in the ascendant.

Sejima Ryūzō　　　　　　　瀬島竜三
(1911–). Businessman and chairman (1978–81) of C. Itoh & Co, Ltd (now ITŌCHŪ CORPO-

RATION). Born in Toyama Prefecture. After graduating from the Army War College in 1938, he served as a staff officer of the Imperial General Headquarters (DAIHON'EI) and of the GUANDONG (KWANTUNG) ARMY. After World War II, he was detained in Siberia for 11 years. Sejima returned to Japan in 1956 and joined C. Itoh & Co in 1958, transforming it from a trading company specializing in textiles into one of Japan's leading general trading companies. He was vice chairman (1987–90) of the Provisional Council for the Promotion of Administrative Reform.

Sekai　　　　　　　　　　世界
(World). A general monthly magazine (*sōgō zasshi*) published since 1946 by IWANAMI SHOTEN, PUBLISHERS. A forum for intellectuals and their views on current national and international political and social topics. It is characterized by strong ideological tendencies and by contributions from both foreign and Japanese scholars. Many of its articles, serial novels, and short fiction stories have stirred controversy and sensation.

Sekai fujin　　　　　　　　世界婦人
(Women of the World). First socialist women's journal in Japan; published from January 1907 to August 1909 (39 issues) by FUKUDA HIDEKO, aided by Kanagawa Matsuko. It espoused socialism and women's independence and carried articles on political issues in Japan and women's movements abroad. Its contributors included such major leftists as KŌTOKU SHŪSUI, SAKAI TOSHIHIKO, and especially ISHIKAWA SANSHIRŌ.

Sekai Kyūsei Kyō　　　　世界救世教
(The Religion for the Salvation of the World). Also called Sekai Meshiya Kyō. One of Japan's NEW RELIGIONS, founded in 1935 by OKADA MOKICHI (1882–1955). Its central teachings are that the world is rapidly approaching the day of final judgment, after which a paradise will be built on earth; that people must purify themselves to participate in the creation of the earthly paradise; and that Okada was a messiah sent by God to lead men in the building of paradise. He rejected medicines, fertilizers, and agricultural chemicals as sources of poison and evil. Followers are drawn to the faith-healing powers of *jōrei* (purification of the spirit).

The group grew rapidly after World War II. Okada proselytized actively and claimed to have received divine revelation. His elaborate cosmology and system of beliefs were strongly influenced by the ŌMOTO religion and Christianity. He emphasized the uplifting value of art, and the group's HAKONE MUSEUM OF ART and MOA MUSEUM OF ART contain some great art treasures. Its membership was about one million in 1990.

Seken munesan'yō　　　　世間胸算用
(tr *Worldly Mental Calculations*, 1976). The last of Ihara SAIKAKU's (1642–93) "books of the floating world" (see UKIYO-ZŌSHI) to be published, in 1692, during his lifetime. Subtitled "The Last Day of the Year is Worth a Thousand Pieces of Gold," the work depicts the stratagems debtors use to pay their bills or fend off their creditors on the last day of the year, when accounts were traditionally settled. *Seken munesan'yo*, which includes 20 stories, focuses on the townsmen (see CHŌNIN), highlighting those from the lower and middle classes. Neither sentimental nor gloomy, this tragicomic portrait of the less affluent characters living in the money-centered "floating world" takes a humorous approach to the harsh realities they face. The work is written in a blend of literary and vernacular Japanese, the latter generally reserved for dialogue. A lengthy introduction, often didactic in nature, precedes most of the vignettes. Saikaku's genius as a storyteller has given the work its enduring appeal and its reputation, among some critics, as the apex of its author's prolific career.

Seki　　　　　　　　　　関[市]
City in southern Gifu Prefecture, central Honshū. Seki has been known for its swordsmiths since the 12th century. The city produces about 90 percent of all the safety razor blades in Japan, as well as fine-quality scissors and knives. Pop: 68,386.

Seki　　　　　　　　　　関[町]
Town in northern Mie Prefecture, central Honshū. Suzuka no Seki, an important barrier station (SEKISHO), was established here in the 7th century. During the Edo period (1600–1868) it prospered as a post-station town on the highway Tōkaidō. Industries include forestry and the cultivation of rice and tea. Pop: 7,413.

Sekigahara　　　　　　　関ケ原[町]
Town in southwestern Gifu Prefecture, central Honshū. Fuwa no Seki, one of three important barrier stations (SEKISHO), was situated here in the 7th century. In the Battle of Sekigahara (1600) TOKUGAWA IEYASU won control of all Japan. Sekigahara retained its strategic importance as a post-station town for the next 300 years and is still a transportation center. Pop: 9,544.

Sekigahara, Battle of　　関ケ原の戦い
(Sekigahara no Tatakai). The decisive battle in the rise of TOKUGAWA IEYASU to the shogunate. It took place in 1600 at Sekigahara in Mino Province (now Gifu Prefecture). After

Sekine Shōji *Boy*. 1917. Oil on canvas. 45 × 37 cm. Private collection.

sekisho This barrier station in the town of Arai in Shizuoka Prefecture was one of the most important on the Tōkaidō and is the only such station still standing. The building is an 1855 reconstruction.

sekihan This mixture of glutinous rice and *azuki* beans is often served on shrine festival days, birthdays, and other auspicious occasions.

the death of TOYOTOMI HIDEYOSHI in 1598 the principal *daimyō* of Japan soon fell to quarreling, and during the summer of 1600 two armies mobilized for war. One, composed mostly of warriors from western Japan, was led by ISHIDA MITSUNARI. The other, made up primarily of eastern warriors, was led by Ieyasu.

The two armies met in a narrow valley just west of the village of Sekigahara. Ieyasu's forces were composed of units led by his fourth son, MATSUDAIRA TADAYOSHI, major vassals such as Honda Tadakatsu (1548–1610) and II NAOMASA, and about 15 *daimyō*, including YAMANOUCHI KAZUTOYO, IKEDA TERUMASA, KURODA NAGAMASA, and TŌDŌ TAKATORA. Ishida was supported by forces of the MŌRI FAMILY, SHIMAZU FAMILY, and Ukita family in addition to troops commanded by KONISHI YUKINAGA, ANKOKUJI EKEI, KOBAYAKAWA HIDEAKI, and Wakizaka Yasuharu (1554–1626).

The two armies deployed their troops during the night of 20 October and fighting began the following morning, with more than 100,000 men committed to the battle. In the afternoon the forces of Kobayakawa, Wakizaka, and three other *daimyō* defected to Ieyasu's eastern army. Their subsequent surprise assault led to the utter rout of the western army. The victory tipped the balance of power in favor of Ieyasu, who was able to solidify his hold in the realm.

Sekigunha → Red Army faction

sekihan 赤飯

(literally, "red rice"). Parboiled rice dish served on festive occasions in Japan. *Sekihan* is prepared by steaming glutinous rice (*mochigome*) together with AZUKI beans and is eaten sprinkled lightly with toasted black sesame seeds and salt.

Seki Hironao 瀬木博尚

(1852–1939). Founder of the advertising agency HAKUHŌDŌ, INC. Born in Toyama Prefecture. On the advice of a friend who had seen such operations in the United States, Seki started an advertising agency in 1895. He first inserted advertisements in newspapers that specialized in education and gradually extended his business to include advertisements in all kinds of publications. Hakuhōdō is now the second largest advertising agency in Japan, after DENTSŪ, INC. Seki donated his collection of Meiji-period (1868–1912) periodicals to Tōkyō University.

Sekine Hiroshi 関根弘

(1920–). Poet and critic. Born in Tōkyō. Sekine began publishing his poetry while employed as a factory worker and a trade paper journalist. Written from the viewpoint of the common people, his works employ allegory and scathing irony to criticize the hypocrisy of modern society. His works include a poetry collection, *E no shukudai* (1953, Art Assignment), and a collection of essays on poetics, *Ōkami ga kita* (1955, The Wolf Has Come).

Sekine Shōji 関根正二

(1899–1919). Western-style painter. Born in Fukushima Prefecture. At the encouragement of the Japanese-style (NIHONGA) painter ITŌ SHINSUI, he took up *nihonga* painting, but soon switched to working in the Western style. In 1918 he won the Chogyū Prize at the Nikaten (Exhibition of the Nikakai). In the few years before his death at the age of 20, he developed a unique style marked by a lyrical illusionism.

Sekirankai 赤瀾会

(Red Wave Society). Women's socialist group founded in April 1921 with some 40 members, including YAMAKAWA KIKUE, ITŌ NOE, Kutsumi Fusako (1890–1980), and Sakai (later Kondō) Magara (1903–83). An auxiliary of the NIHON SHAKAI SHUGI DŌMEI (Japan Socialist League), it was composed largely of female relatives of active male leftists. The group worked specifically for equal wages, mothers' welfare, and the abolition of prostitution. Facing suppression, in March 1922 the group was reorganized (without its anarchist faction) as the Yōkakai (Eighth Day Association), taking its name from 8 March, the date of International Women's Day. The Yōkakai disbanded in 1923.

sekirei → wagtails

sekisen 関銭

(literally, "barrier money"). Tolls, originally collected in the form of rice as stipends for guards at barrier stations (SEKISHO) or for upkeep of temples. Tolls began in the Heian period (794–1185), when many barrier stations came into the hands of the local aristocracy and owners of private estates (SHŌEN). In the Muromachi period (1333–1568) the imperial court, the shogunate, aristocrats, and *shōen* proprietors came to depend on *sekisen*, now paid in coins, as a major source of income. For example, along the 50 kilometers (31 mi) of the river Yodogawa between Kyōto and Ōsaka, there were more than 600 toll gates. The collection of tolls discouraged travel and disrupted the circulation of goods, resulting in higher prices. To encourage development of a national economy, ODA NOBUNAGA and TOYOTOMI HIDEYOSHI abolished

barrier stations and tolls in the late 16th century. They were revived in the Edo period (1600–1868).

sekisho 関所

(barrier stations). Government installations at strategic points along traffic routes, where travelers were stopped for inspection. The system of barrier stations was established under the TAIKA REFORM of 645. The barrier stations at Suzuka (Suzuka no Seki) in Ise Province (now part of Mie Prefecture), Fuwa (Fuwa no Seki) in Mino Province (now part of Gifu Prefecture), and Arachi (Arachi no Seki) in Echizen Province (now part of Fukui Prefecture)—the so-called Sankan, or Three Barriers—were considered particularly important. The Sankan fell into disuse in the mid-Heian period (794–1185), and proprietary lords (*ryōshu*) set up and maintained within their estates (SHŌEN) private barrier stations that levied tolls (SEKISEN) in one form or another. These *sekisho* were abolished in the late 16th century by the national unifiers ODA NOBUNAGA and TOYOTOMI HIDEYOSHI. *Sekisho* were revived under the TOKUGAWA SHOGUNATE (1603–1867), more than 50 being established at Hakone, Imagire, Kobotoke, Usui, and other points on the main roads (GOKAIDŌ) leading to the shogunal capital at Edo (now Tōkyō). Especially stringent inspections were made for "incoming weapons and outgoing women" (*irideppō deonna*), i.e., contraband weapons and distaff members of *daimyō* families required to reside in Edo (see SANKIN KŌTAI). *Sekisho* were abolished by the Meiji government on 2 March 1869.

Sekisui Chemical Co, Ltd
積水化学工業[株]

(Sekisui Kagaku Kōgyō). Chemical company that ranks first in Japan in the production and processing of synthetic resins and prefabricated homes. Sekisui Chemical was incorporated in 1947 by seven former employees of the Nippon Chisso Fertilizer Co. In 1949 it constructed a new plant in Ōsaka and started to manufacture a wide variety of industrial components and consumer goods made of vinyl-related resins. In the late 1950s the company created a nationwide network of 50 production subsidiaries (such as Sekisui Resin and Sekisui Kaseihin Industries) and sales firms to form the Sekisui group. In 1960 it established SEKISUI HOUSE, LTD, and in 1971 started mass production of prefabricated homes called Haim. Sales for the fiscal year ending March 1991 totaled ¥617.1 billion (US $4.5 billion), of which housing accounted for 49 percent; pipe and related products, 16 percent; industrial materials, 10 percent; building materials, 10 percent; household products, 7 percent; and chemicals, 8 percent. The company was capitalized at ¥92.7 billion (US $675.7 million) in the same year. Headquarters are in Ōsaka.

Sekisui House, Ltd 積水ハウス[株]

(Sekisui Hausu). Builder of houses, condominiums, dormitories, offices, and other buildings; a leading member of the Sekisui group. Incorporated in 1960 as a subsidiary of SEKISUI CHEMICAL CO, LTD. The company has a number of plants and subsidiary companies, including subsidiaries in Germany and the Netherlands. Sales for the fiscal year ending January 1991 totaled ¥1.0 trillion (US $7.7 billion), with housing construction accounting for 76 percent and real estate for 24 percent; capitalization stood at ¥134.4 billion (US $1.0 billion). Headquarters are in Ōsaka.

Seki Takakazu 関孝和

(1640?–1708). Mathematician; considered the greatest figure in premodern Japanese mathematics. Believed to have been self-educated, he developed a method for approximating the roots of a higher-order algebraic equation quite similar to the well-known "Newton's method," and it is now generally recognized that Seki's formulation of the theory of determinants preceded that of the German mathematician Gottfried Leibnitz (1646–1716), previously considered the originator of this theory. His algebraic techniques were later expanded upon by his pupil TAKEBE KATAHIRO.

sekkan seiji → regency government

sekke shōgun 摂家将軍

(shōguns from the regents' house). Refers to Fujiwara (or Kujō) Yoritsune (1218–56) and Fujiwara (or Kujō) Yoritsugu (1239–56), the fourth and fifth shōguns of the KAMAKURA SHOGUNATE. After the second Kamakura shōgun, MINAMOTO NO YORIIE, and the third, MINAMOTO NO SANETOMO, were assassinated in 1204 and 1219, respectively, their maternal relatives, the HŌJŌ FAMILY, took control of the shogunate but lacked sufficient status to assume the title of shōgun. They arranged with the court to appoint a scion of the KUJŌ FAMILY, one of the five Fujiwara regents' houses (GOSEKKE), as nominal shōgun to legitimate their control. Yoritsune, distantly related to the first shōgun MINAMOTO NO YORITOMO, was made shōgun in 1226 and was succeeded by his son Yoritsugu in 1244. In 1252, however, the shogunal regent (shikken) HŌJŌ TOKIYORI sent Yoritsugu back to Kyōto, and the imperial prince MUNETAKA was installed in his place.

sekku 節句

(seasonal festival). A term that originally applied to offerings (ku) of food made on certain days traditionally recognized as marking changes in the seasons (sechi), it came to refer to the actual days. Sekku are also referred to as monobi or mombi, that is, the days on which people dress in formal kimono bearing the family crest (mon).

In the Edo period (1600–1868) the Tokugawa shogunate prescribed the following days as sekku: 7 January (Jinjitsu no Sekku), commonly referred to as Nanakusa no Sekku (Seven Herb Festival); 3 March (Jōshi no Sekku; see DOLL FESTIVAL), commonly known as Momo no Sekku (Peach Festival); 5 May (Tango no Sekku; see CHILDREN'S DAY), commonly called Shōbu no Sekku (Iris Festival); 7 July (TANABATA FESTIVAL); and 9 September (Chōyō no Sekku), commonly known as Kiku no Sekku (CHRYSANTHEMUM FESTIVAL). These have been informally observed by families up to the present and customarily involve special foods.

Self Corporation 大西衣料[株]

(Ōnishi Iryō). Cash-and-carry wholesaler of apparel, personal and household accessories, bedding, toiletries, and home appliances. Incorporated in 1944. It has seven overseas offices. For the fiscal year ending August 1990, sales totaled ¥134.2 billion (US $910.3 million) and capitalization stood at ¥909.0 million (US $6.1 million). Headquarters are in Ōsaka.

Self Defense Forces 自衛隊

(SDF; J: Jieitai). Armed forces responsible for the ground, sea, and air defense of Japan. The term "Self Defense" is used in the official title because the 1947 CONSTITUTION OF JAPAN prohibits the nation from possessing military forces (see RENUNCIATION OF WAR), but, according to the government, does not prohibit the nation from maintaining the ability to defend itself.

Historical Development——After World War II, Japan's army, navy, and air force were dismantled, but, with the outbreak of the Korean War in 1950, General Douglas MACARTHUR, commander of the Allied OCCUPATION of Japan, ordered the establishment of a NATIONAL POLICE RESERVE of 75,000 men to fill the gap created by the dispatch of Occupation forces to Korea. From its inception, this force was recognized as possessing greater firepower and mobility than the regular police force. In 1952 its name was changed to NATIONAL SAFETY FORCES and, together with the Maritime Guard, it was administered by the newly established National Safety Agency.

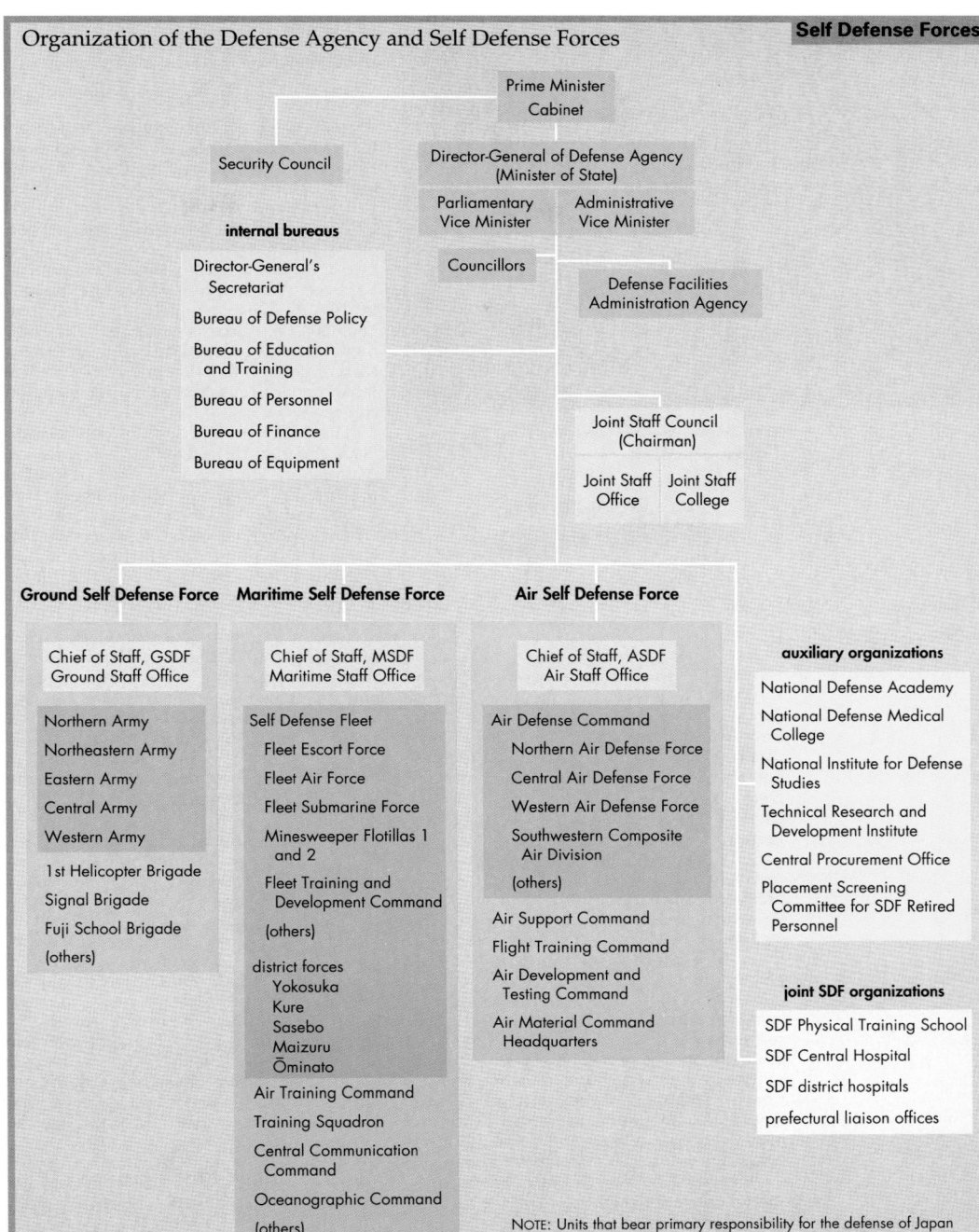

Organization of the Defense Agency and Self Defense Forces

NOTE: Units that bear primary responsibility for the defense of Japan are highlighted in dark green. Those shown in light green are examples of support units.
SOURCE: Defense Agency, *Defense of Japan* (annual): 1990.

International Military Strength in the Late 1980s

Country	Ground forces	Naval forces		Air forces
	(thousands of personnel)	(number of vessels)	(displacement in thousands of tons)	(number of combat aircraft)
United States	767	1,350	6,428	5,120
Soviet Union	1,900	2,990	7,666	9,490
China	2,300	2,060	1,000	6,050
United Kingdom	156	420	977	660
West Germany	341	290	246	690
France	293	340	492	670
Japan	156	170	303	430

NOTE: The figure for Japan's combat aircraft includes both ASDF combat aircraft and MSDF fixed-wing combat aircraft. Combat aircraft statistics for all other countries include aircraft belonging to air, naval, and marine forces.
SOURCE: Defense Agency, *Bōei hakusho* (annual): 1990.

1341

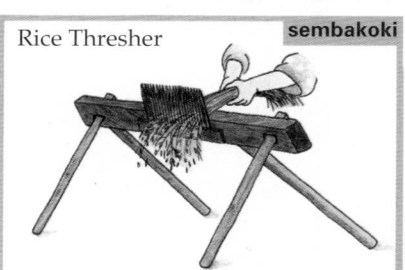

Rice Thresher **sembakoki**

With the passage of the Self Defense Forces Law in 1954, the Safety Agency became the DEFENSE AGENCY, and the existing forces were reorganized as the Self Defense Forces, with three services: the Ground Self Defense Force (GSDF; J: Rikujō Jieitai), the Maritime Self Defense Force (MSDF; J: Kaijō Jieitai), and the Air Self Defense Force (ASDF; J: Kōkū Jieitai).

Organization and Command—Supreme command rests with the prime minister, who represents the cabinet. The director-general of the Defense Agency, a member of the cabinet, receives his orders from the prime minister and is assisted by civilian and military personnel and by the JOINT STAFF COUNCIL. The chiefs of staff of the three forces carry out within their commands the orders of the director-general and supervise the activities of their respective branches. In wartime, the chairman of the Joint Staff Council would assume command, but in peacetime his powers are limited to the formulation and coordination of overall defense planning.

Personnel—Self Defense Forces personnel enlist between the ages of 18 and 25 for voluntary two- or three-year terms. In 1970 the SDF formed a reserve corps of volunteers on inactive status, and in 1974 it began recruiting women. Officers are selected from among graduates of the NATIONAL DEFENSE ACADEMY, graduates of regular universities who have passed a qualifying examination, and noncommissioned officers who score high on the qualifying examination. Each service has its own officer candidate school, but there is also a NATIONAL INSTITUTE FOR DEFENSE STUDIES for higher study by selected officers.

Defense Budget—Defense appropriations totaled approximately ¥4.2 trillion (US $29.0 billion) in 1990, or 0.997 percent of the estimated gross national product (GNP; see ONE-PERCENT DEFENSE CEILING). Since its inception the SDF's share of the GNP has decreased, though real appropriations have continued to climb. In 1990 the breakdown of expenditures by organization was GSDF, 35.5 percent; MSDF, 23.5 percent; ASDF, 27.0 percent; Defense Facilities Administration Agency, 10.5 percent; and others, 3.5 percent. Of the overall defense budget, 40.1

percent went for personnel expenses and 59.9 percent for non-personnel-related expenses (equipment, training, bases, research and development, etc).

Units and Their Deployment—The GSDF is divided into 12 infantry divisions and 1 armored division, which are grouped into 5 regional armies. The greatest emphasis has been placed on the defense of Hokkaidō. In 1990 GSDF personnel numbered about 150,000. The force is equipped with 1,200 medium tanks of Japanese design and manufacture and 400 helicopters produced in Japan under license from their US manufacturer.

The MSDF comprises the Self Defense Fleet and five district units. It regards antisubmarine warfare as its most important mission. In 1990 personnel numbered about 43,000 and the MSDF deployed 60 destroyers and destroyer escorts, 14 nonnuclear submarines, and about 160 antisubmarine anticraft and helicopters produced in Japan under license from their US manufacturers.

The men and equipment of the ASDF are divided into four air zones. Operational emphasis is placed on the swift identification of aircraft encroaching on Japanese airspace and on quick response to a possible consolidated air attack. In 1990 personnel numbered some 45,000, and the ASDF possessed some 330 fighter planes, chiefly F-15s and F-4s produced in Japan under license from their US manufacturers, as well as Patriot and Nike surface-to-air missiles, which were also produced under license.

The Constitution and the SDF—Since its inception the SDF has faced the charge that its existence is a violation of article 9 of the constitution. To this, the government has responded that although the constitution forbids war as a means of resolving international disputes, it does not negate the right of self-defense (see SELF-DEFENSE, NATIONAL RIGHT OF). Although criticism continues, the SDF has won general acceptance from the Japanese public, and the voices calling for abolition are fewer. However, with the end of the cold war, there has been a growing call for arms and personnel reductions. See also NATIONAL DEFENSE.

Self Defense Forces group enshrinement case　自衛官合祀訴訟

(Jieikan *gōshi soshō*). Legal case brought against the Japanese government in which the Christian widow of a member of the SELF DEFENSE FORCES (SDF) who had died in the line of duty sought nullification of his enshrinement with other deceased SDF members at the Shintō Gokoku Shrine in Yamaguchi Prefecture, and the award of a solatium, on the grounds that her constitutional right to freedom of religion had been violated. In its judgment, handed down on 1 June 1988, the Supreme Court rejected the widow's claim, stating that the request for enshrinement had been the independent action of the Committee of Friends of the Forces (Taiyūkai) and that, as her legal interests had not been violated, she must tolerate the committee's "right to enshrine." Critics contend that the decision reflects a weakening of the constitutionally stipulated separation of religion and state (art. 20, para. 3).

self-defense, national right of　自衛権

(*jieiken*). The concept of international law used to justify the creation of Japan's SELF DEFENSE FORCES (SDF), in apparent violation

of article 9 of the CONSTITUTION OF JAPAN, which prohibits the establishment of land, sea, or air forces or other war potential. Article 51 of the Charter of the United Nations recognizes "the inherent right of individual or collective self-defense" for all its members. The peace treaty between Japan and the Allied nations signed in San Francisco in September 1951 states that the Allied powers recognize that Japan "as a sovereign nation possesses the inherent right of individual or collective self-defense" as referred to in article 51, even though they had earlier adopted the policy of complete disarmament and demilitarization of Japan.

The Japanese government, with some public support, has taken the view that the right of self-defense, because it is "inherent," justifies the creation of the SDF. In addition, it is argued that because article 9 does not prohibit military forces for purposes of defense, these forces are therefore not unconstitutional. Those who oppose the SDF argue that the maintenance of armed forces—even for the purposes of self-defense—violates the letter and the spirit of the constitution. See also RENUNCIATION OF WAR; CONSTITUTION, DISPUTE OVER REVISION OF.

self-help　自力救済

(*jiriki kyūsai*). The preservation of one's rights by one's own means without resort to official resources. Japanese law, unlike that of England and the United States, does not recognize the principle of self-help. One example of self-help would be the use of force by a property owner to expel a person who was occupying the former's property without authorization. In Japan, as in other countries whose legal systems are based on the European continental model in which authority is concentrated in the state, the basic premise is that to preserve one's rights one must first obtain a judgment from a court and then a compulsory execution of that judgment by the proper authorities. Even an unauthorized possessor has a possessory right. Therefore, if the owner should by force seize the thing possessed, the possessor may obtain its return, and the owner would have no recourse but to institute a separate action. Academic theory recognizes an exception in cases involving robbery or other emergency situations in which the disadvantage would be very great if force were not used in asserting one's rights. However, there are not many actual court decisions in Japan based on the principle of self-help.

Semba　船場

Commercial district in the city of Ōsaka. The name (literally meaning "boat place") derives from its use as a landing point for cargo brought in on a system of canals built by TOYOTOMI HIDEYOSHI (1537–98) to serve the city that rapidly grew up around his headquarters at ŌSAKA CASTLE. The district is laid out on a grid, with streets (-*dōri*) running east to west and avenues (*suji*) north to south. Textile wholesalers are found on Hommachi-Dōri and Dobuike Suji, pharmaceutical wholesalers on Doshōmachi-Dōri, securities firms on Kitahama-Dōri, and numerous high-rise office buildings on Midō Suji.

sembakoki　千歯扱

("thousand-tooth thresher"). A threshing implement used by farmers in less developed areas as late as the 1940s. It had about 20 flat, pointed iron tines (1.5 cm by 40.0 cm [0.6

in by 16.0 in]) attached to a crossbar frame. Rice stalks drawn through the tines were stripped of their ripe grains. Attributed to an Ōsaka carpenter, it came into general use around 1700. It was also called *gokedaoshi* ("widow-killer") because it replaced threshing by poor widows using primitive tools.

sembazuru 千羽鶴

A string of folded paper cranes (see ORIGAMI). Like turtles, cranes have long been considered auspicious in Japan as a symbol of longevity. Because of the belief that the diligence required to fold each one of a large number of paper cranes will be rewarded, a string of them is often offered at a shrine or temple along with a prayer. *Sembazuru* may also be given to a person suffering from illness as a prayer for their recovery and an expression of the giver's sympathy.

sembei 煎餅

(rice crackers). Crackers usually made from a dough of rice flour and water, though wheat flour or dried MOCHI (glutinous rice cakes) may also be used. To make *sembei*, the dough is shaped in a mold, dried in an oven, grilled over a low fire, and then basted with soy sauce, wrapped in *nori* (a type of dried seaweed), or sprinkled with sugar. The types of *sembei* common today originated in the Edo period (1600–1868).

Semboku New Town 泉北ニュータウン

(Semboku Nyū Taun). Planned residential community in south-central Ōsaka Prefecture, central Honshū. Construction began in 1961 as part of a plan to develop the urban areas of the prefecture; the town contains both public and private housing. Area: 15.2 sq km (5.9 sq mi). Projected pop: 152,000.

Sembon Matsubara 千本松原

Pine grove in the city of Numazu, Shizuoka Prefecture, central Honshū. Located west of the mouth of the river Kanōgawa, it constitutes part of a great belt of wooded area that protects against wind and tidal waves. There are memorial plaques here for WAKAYAMA BOKUSUI and INOUE YASUSHI, men of letters. The area also offers good swimming resorts.

semburi 千振

Swertia japonica. Biennial herb of the gentian family (Gentianaceae) that grows wild in sunny fields and hills throughout Japan. The dark purple stem is 25–30 centimeters (10–12 in) high with opposite, paired, purplish green, thin leaves along the branches. In autumn many white flowers with purple stripes bloom in clusters.

Semburi has been used as a stomach medicine from ancient times. The entire plant is collected when in blossom, then dried in the shade and boiled down. It has a bitter taste that supposedly survives a thousand immersions in boiling water; hence the name *semburi* (from *sen*, one thousand, and *furi*, decoctions). Two similar species not usable as medicine are *murasaki semburi* (*S. pseudochinensis*) and *inusemburi* (*S. diluta* var. *tosaensis*).

sembutsu → Buddha tiles

Semenov, Grigorii Mikhailovich セミョーノフ, G. M.

(1890–1946). Cossack leader and Japanese protégé in Siberia and Manchuria from 1918 until 1945. Born in the Trans-Baikal region of eastern Siberia, he joined the Russian army in 1908. He took advantage of chaotic conditions attending the Russian Civil War and Allied Intervention (see SIBERIAN INTERVENTION) to become a virtually independent warlord. Styling himself a White (anti-Bolshevik) leader, Semenov won Japanese patronage. After the anti-Bolshevik cause foundered in 1920, he wielded (under Japanese guidance) influence among Russian and Cossack communities throughout Manchuria and China for the next 20 years. Captured in Dalny (J: Dairen; Ch: Dalian or Talien) by Soviet paratroopers on 22 August 1945, he was hanged for counterrevolutionary activities on 30 August 1946.

semi → cicadas

semiconductor industry 半導体産業

(*handōtai sangyō*). Industry that produces integrated circuits (ICs) and discrete semiconductors such as transistors and diodes. Japan's semiconductor industry got its start through the acquisition of US technology. In the early 1950s, Kōbe Kōgyō imported transistor technology from RCA, and Tōkyō Tsūshin Kōgyō (now Sony Corporation) imported similar technology from Western Electric Co. The technology gap between Japan and the United States was closed in the late 1970s. Japan was able to surpass the United States in the area of very large scale integration (VLSI) technology through combined government and private-sector VLSI research and development projects from 1976 to 1979.

Early in its development the Japanese semiconductor industry was supported by the growth in production of discrete semiconductors. However, integrated circuits came to dominate the semiconductor industry from 1975 onward; in 1984 the IC industry approached the ¥2.0 trillion (US $8.4 billion) level. Among integrated circuits, semiconductor ICs are particularly important, and among semiconductor ICs, digital ICs have shown remarkable growth. Japan's IC production is centered on digital-type metal-oxide semiconductor (MOS) ICs.

In contrast to the US semiconductor industry, which achieved its development primarily in industrial machinery, the semiconductor industry in Japan has centered on consumer products. There are also differences in the industry's structure in the two countries. While venture-business specialty firms, many of which started out as small entrepreneurial manufacturers, are the heart of the US semiconductor industry, the industry in Japan is based in major corporate manufacturers for which semiconductors are only one of many business areas, such as NEC CORPORATION; HITACHI, LTD; TŌSHIBA CORPORATION; and FUJITSŪ, LTD. Only such giant manufacturing firms have access to the vast funds needed for the continual research, development, and production of the kind of multiapplication VLSI super-capacity memory chips on which they have chosen to focus. Many such chips are used in the multitude of consumer goods that these same firms also produce. Since they have the financial resources to weather any short-term deficits or drops in demand, they are able to maintain continuous production and investment schedules. Japanese semiconductor production reached US $35.1 billion in 1991. With the successful development by the Japanese industry in 1990 of the 64-megabit dynamic random access memory (DRAM) chip, the IC marketplace has now entered the age of ultra-large integration (ULSI).

Semimaru 蝉丸

Legendary blind lute player and poet, the subject of several premodern works of poetry, fiction, and drama. His name first appeared in the imperial WAKA anthology GOSEN WAKASHŪ (ca 955–966), where authorship of a single poem is attributed to Semimaru. Throughout history Semimaru has been associated with Ōsaka (now Ōsakayama), a slope east of the center of modern Kyōto, which is mentioned in the above poem.

The most important prose work concerning Semimaru is a story in the KONJAKU MONOGATARI (12th century). The Semimaru legend reaches its peak of pathos with the NŌ play *Semimaru*, generally ascribed to the major Nō playwright ZEAMI Motokiyo (1363–1443). The last major work concerning Semimaru is the puppet drama *Semimaru*, an early work of the great playwright CHIKAMATSU MONZAEMON (1653–1724).

semmin 賤民

("lowborn" or outcasts). Generally hereditary groups classified below free commoners (RYŌMIN) in ancient Japan. Under the 7th-century RITSURYŌ SYSTEM, there were five levels in this lowest class of society. The *gosen* ("five *semmin*") were, in descending order: the *ryōko*, guards of the imperial tombs; the *kanko*, government menials; the *kenin*, servants of aristocratic families; the *kunuhi* (or *kannuhi*), slaves of government officials; and the *shinuhi*, slaves of aristocratic families. The *kunuhi* and *shinuhi* could actually be bought and sold and were not allowed to establish families. In the Nara period (710–794), 10 percent of the population was *semmin*, but in the early 10th century the *semmin* system was abolished.

semmon gakkō 専門学校

(professional school). A type of higher-education institution in the pre–World War II education system, established by the Professional School Order of 1903. Graduation from middle school or girls' higher school was required for entrance, and the course of study was three years or more. Some professional schools were affiliated with universities and some were independent. Most of them were private institutions. Many taught medicine, law, economics, and commerce;

sembei These rice crackers are a popular Japanese snack food and are enjoyed in many varieties.
1 At some traditional *sembei* shops, like this one in Tōkyō's Asakusa district, the crackers are still carefully hand roasted.
2 These seed-shaped crackers are flavored with red pepper and soy sauce.
3 Seaweed-wrapped *sembei* seasoned with soy sauce.
4 The basic *sembei* is a simple rice-flour cracker that is brushed with soy sauce.

semburi This biennial herb, which grows wild throughout Japan, has long been used as a stomach medicine.

Sendai

1 Downtown Sendai seen from Sendai Castle. The city was completely rebuilt after being destroyed in World War II.

2 Famous for its elaborate celebration of the Tanabata Festival in early August, Sendai draws crowds of visitors from throughout Japan.

those that taught agriculture, technology, and business were called *jitsugyō semmon gakkō* (technical colleges).

The professional schools worked to produce a pool of trained personnel rather than an intellectual elite. In the prewar period, the majority of students of higher learning were in the professional schools; all institutions of higher education for women were professional schools. After World War II, the professional school system was abolished, and most of the schools became four-year universities.

semmyō 宣命

(literally, "to proclaim a decree"). Ancient imperial decrees composed in Japanese. Before the Nara period (710–794) all imperial proclamations (*mikotonori*) were written in Japanese, and only in the 8th century, when the Chinese-influenced RITSURYŌ SYSTEM of government was consolidated, were most decrees and statements of the emperor written in KAMBUN (classical Chinese). Imperial edicts in *kambun* were called *shō* (or *shōsho*) and *choku* (or *chokushi*). The term *semmyō* for edicts in Japanese has been used since the Heian period (794–1185).

Semmyō were drawn up in the Ministry of Central Imperial Affairs (Nakatsukasashō) and read aloud on the emperor's behalf by a special herald (*semmyōshi*). In tone, *semmyō* are similar to ancient Japanese ritual prayers (NORITO). The texts of the *semmyō* followed a fixed formula (*semmyōtai*) prescribed in chapter 21 of the TAIHŌ CODE (702). *Semmyō* were written in Chinese characters but were intended to be read in Japanese with assistance of a special writing system, known as *semmyōgaki*. It can be considered a forerunner of the mixed Sino-Japanese writing system (*wakan konkōbun*) of medieval and modern Japanese. See also DIPLOMATICS.

sempai-kōhai 先輩・後輩

(senior-junior). An informal relationship ubiquitous in Japanese organizations, schools, and associations, in which older, experienced members offer friendship, assistance, and advice to inexperienced members,

who reciprocate with gratitude, respect, and, often, personal loyalty.

The *sempai-kōhai* tie is determined by the date of entrance into a particular organization. The *sempai*, perhaps a graduate of the same school or a senior in the work group, acts as a friend and patron, disciplining and teaching the neophyte appropriate conduct. *Sempai-kōhai* ties permeate Japanese society. HABATSU, BATSU, and other personal networks function to some extent in *sempai-kōhai* terms, and *sempai-kōhai* alliances often smooth the way toward a quick, satisfactory resolution of a problem. Successful careers have often been promoted by these long-term relationships, though they can also have negative aspects, as when the *sempai* exploits his *kōhai*.

Senaga Kamejirō 瀬長亀次郎

(1907–). Politician and Okinawan social activist. Vice-chairman of the JAPAN COMMUNIST PARTY (JCP). Born in Okinawa, Senaga became interested in Marxism-Leninism while a student. Under US military rule after World War II, Senaga was active as a leader and later chairman of the Okinawa People's Party (Okinawa Jimmintō). In 1956 he was elected mayor of the city of Naha but was removed from office by the US military government. In 1970 he was elected to the lower house of the Diet as a candidate of the Okinawa People's Party; in 1973 his party merged with the JCP. Senaga was elected to the House of Representatives seven times. He retired from political life in 1990.

Senchakushū 選択集

(abbreviation of *Senchaku hongan nembutsu shū*; The Selection of the Nembutsu of the Original Vow). Also known as *Senjakushū*. A treatise by HŌNEN (1133–1212), founder of the JŌDO SECT, detailing the principles of his Pure Land Buddhist faith; written in 1198. In it Hōnen explains the scriptural bases of his doctrine and responds to hypothetical questions and criticisms. He identifies the threefold scripture of the "Pure Land school" and its major patriarchs. He claims on the basis of these teachings that ultimate liberation comes either through strenuous efforts of saintly beings or through trust in the Buddha AMIDA's vows of salvation, and that only the latter is feasible because of the decadence of the age. And he maintains that invoking NEMBUTSU guarantees rebirth in the Pure Land because it is Amida's promise or original vow (*hongan*) to save all who call on him. The *Senchakushū* set down the doctrinal basis for an independent Pure Land Buddhist movement. It gave to what had been an amorphous piety and marginal monastic cult a firm grounding in the continental Buddhist tradition and a clear set of doctrines consistent with the Mahāyāna ideal of universal salvation. It brought Pure Land Buddhism to the forefront of Japanese religious life.

Sendai 仙台[市]

Capital of Miyagi Prefecture, northern Honshū. It is the largest city in northeastern Japan and the political, economic, and cultural center of the region. The town developed around Sendai Castle (also called Aoba Castle), built by DATE MASAMUNE in 1601. There are petrochemical, foodstuffs, and printing plants. The city is the site of Tōhoku University. The former site of the castle, the Ōsaki Hachiman Shrine, and the Tanabata Festival, held in August, draw visitors. Pop: 918,398.

Sendai 川内[市]

City in northwestern Kagoshima Prefecture, Kyūshū. During the Nara period (710–794) it was the seat of a provincial capital (*kokufu*) and temple (KOKUBUNJI). Industries include paper, of which it is the leading manufacturer in the prefecture, ceramics, and foodstuffs. Rice is its principal agricultural product. Pop: 71,735.

Sendai Bay 仙台湾

(Sendai Wan). Inlet of the Pacific Ocean, on the southeastern coast of Miyagi Prefecture, northern Honshū. Extends from the Oshika Peninsula to Unoozaki, a cape in northeastern Fukushima Prefecture. It serves as an ocean port area for the Sendai Industrial Zone.

Sendai domain 仙台藩

(Sendai han). Edo-period (1600–1868) domain situated in central MUTSU PROVINCE; all of present-day Miyagi Prefecture and part of Iwate Prefecture. It was founded in 1603 by DATE MASAMUNE, who, as a former vassal of TOYOTOMI HIDEYOSHI, was granted the status of TOZAMA (outside vassal) by TOKUGAWA IEYASU. In 1868 the domain led an anti-imperial alliance, ŌUETSU REPPAN DŌMEI, that was defeated by the superior forces of Emperor MEIJI in the BOSHIN CIVIL WAR, resulting in a major reduction in domainal lands. OMOTEDAKA (estimated annual production of rice): 620,000 KOKU (1 *koku* = 180 liters or 5 US bushels).

Sendaigawa 川内川

River in northern Kagoshima Prefecture, Kyūshū, flowing west to enter the East China Sea at the city of Sendai. It is the second largest river in Kyūshū. The Tsuruta Dam, located on the middle reaches, is used for flood prevention and electric power generation. The water is used for irrigation. Length: 137 km (85 mi); area of drainage basin: 1,600 sq km (620 sq mi).

Sendai Plain 仙台平野

(Sendai Heiya). Located in central Miyagi Prefecture, northern Honshū. Bordering the Pacific Ocean, the northern part consists of the floodplain of the river Kitakamigawa, and the southern part consists of the floodplain of the rivers Natorigawa and Abukumagawa. High-quality rice is cultivated. The major cities are Sendai and Ishinomaki. Area: approximately 1,000 sq km (400 sq mi).

Senda Koreya 千田是也

(1904–). Producer and actor. Real name Itō Kunio. Born in Tōkyō. As a student Senda participated in the establishment of the Tsukiji Shōgekijō (Tsukiji Little Theater) in 1924. He left that group in 1926 to become involved in the proletarian theater movement, and from 1927 to 1931 he studied in Germany. With Aoyama Sugisaku (1889–1956) and others, Senda helped form the troupe known as the GEKIDAN HAIYŪZA in 1944. With his numerous productions of works by Bertolt Brecht, Senda played a key role in the development of the SHINGEKI ("new theater") movement in postwar Japan.

sendan → chinaberry

Sengai Gibon 仙厓義梵

(1750–1837). ZEN painter and calligrapher whose works are animated by a warm, satiric, and often self-mocking humor. Born in Mino (now Gifu Prefecture), Sengai became a Rinzai-sect monk at the age of 11. (Gibon was his Buddhist priest name.) After 50 years as a monk, he retired in 1811 from the position of 123rd abbot of Shōfukuji in Hakata (now the city of Fukuoka), the oldest Zen temple in Japan. Sengai devoted his final 26 years to teaching, painting, and calligraphy. His works treat a wide variety of themes, from traditional Buddhist figures such as Daruma (Skt: Bodhidharma) and Kannon (Skt: Avalokiteśvara) to landscapes, flowers, plants, and animals. Sengai frequently added inscriptions to his works in free, unassuming calligraphy, often containing puns and jokes. One of his most famous works is *Circle, Triangle, and Square.* The Idemitsu Art Gallery in Tōkyō owns the largest collection of his works.

Sengaku   仙覚

(1203–?). Scholar and monk of the TENDAI SECT of Buddhism in the early Kamakura period (1185–1333). Born in Hitachi Province (now Ibaraki Prefecture). His research laid the foundation for future studies of the MAN'YŌSHŪ. His main work was *Man'yōshū chūshaku* (1269), also known as *Sengakushō.*

Senge Motomaro   千家元麿

(1888–1948). Poet. Born in Tōkyō. His poetry, known for its optimistic and humanistic tone, reflects the philosophy of the SHIRAKABA SCHOOL. He wrote prolifically, in some years publishing 30 to 40 poems each month. As he said, his poems were often too "artless." But from such artlessness came his best poems: those that describe daily occurrences without forced emotionalism. Notable among his books are *Jibun wa mita* (1918, I Saw), whose opening poem, "Kuruma no oto" (The Noise of the Carts), is frequently anthologized, and *Mukashi no ie* (1929, House of Long Ago), a long narrative poem that describes his aristocratic upbringing.

Sengen Shrine   浅間大社

(Sengen Taisha; officially Fujisan Hongū Sengen Taisha). Shintō shrine in the city of Fujinomiya, Shizuoka Prefecture, dedicated to the goddess Konohana no Sakuyahime no Mikoto and two other deities. The Sengen Taisha is the central shrine of a cult that venerates the volcano Mt. Fuji (Fujisan) as a sacred mountain (see MOUNTAINS, WORSHIP OF). Based primarily in the prefectures in the vicinity of Mt. Fuji, the cult has more than 1,300 shrines, most of which bear the name Sengen (or Asama) Jinja. Belief in the mountain as a benefactor gradually spread throughout much of eastern Japan after the 17th century, as a result of proselytizing by itinerant priests (OSHI). One of these *oshi*, Hasegawa Kakugyō (1541–1646), established regional Fuji associations (Fujikō; see KŌ) designed to promote pilgrimages to the mountain. The major annual festival is held on 3–5 November; YABUSAME (archery on horseback) is held 4–6 May.

Sengoku daimyō   戦国大名

Powerful local lords who, during the Sengoku or Warring States period (1467–1568), displaced the military governors (SHUGO DAImyō) appointed by the Muromachi shogunate (1338–1573). Sengoku daimyō had their origins as important vassals of *shugo daimyō*, as local proprietors, as masterless *samurai*, or as *shugo daimyō* themselves. By the 1540s they had gained considerable independent control of the lands they held. As they grew, they recruited as their housemen provincial

warrior-landowners (KOKUJIN) and through them increased their military capacities and their control over the peasantry.

In their efforts to establish their domains as independent political and economic entities, they built castles, laid down house laws, made cadastral surveys, developed new rice lands, built irrigation systems, and erected post stations along major highways. However, unlike the daimyō of the Edo period (1600–1868), the Sengoku daimyō were obliged to leave their more powerful retainers in possession of private fiefs and thus were unable to set up a fully centralized power structure. As they increased in strength they began to fight among themselves for regional hegemony, but were in turn subjugated by the unifiers ODA NOBUNAGA and TOYOTOMI HIDEYOSHI in the 1570s and 1580s, preparing the way for the emergence of the Edo-period *kinsei daimyō* under the centralized authority of the Tokugawa shogunate. See DAIMYŌ.

Sengokuhara   仙石原

Highland north of the lake ASHINOKO, near the town of Hakone, southwestern Kanagawa Prefecture, central Honshū. It was formed from an old volcanic crater of HAKONEYAMA. Until recently a wild and desolate area, it now has golf courses and ice-skating rinks as well as a few modern hotels. Elevation: 650–700 m (2,100–2,300 ft).

Sengoku period   戦国時代

(1467–1568; Sengoku *jidai*). Also known as the Warring States period. The years from the beginning of the ŌNIN WAR (1467–77) until ODA NOBUNAGA entered Kyōto in 1568. The Sengoku period is also dated by some historians from the early 1490s, when Hosokawa Masamoto (1466–1507), the KANREI or shogunal deputy, took over the power of the MUROMACHI SHOGUNATE, and when HŌJŌ SŌUN conquered Izu Province (now part of Shizuoka Prefecture) and began to control the Kantō region.

The term GEKOKUJŌ (the overturning of those on top by those below) characterizes this period. Local *shugodai* (deputy military governors) and KOKUJIN (local military proprietors) established military and political control over provinces formerly ruled by SHUGO (military governors). SENGOKU DAIMYŌ waged constant war to defend or enlarge their domains until Nobunaga asserted hegemony.

The Sengoku period saw remarkable economic growth. The Sengoku daimyō enriched their domains and built up their armies. Increase in trade resulted in formation of commercial cities, such as Sakai, Hyōgo (now Kōbe), Kuwana, and Hakata. Kyōto became the nation's industrial and commercial center. Merchants managed the affairs of these cities and towns and attained a degree of political autonomy. CASTLE TOWNS developed and served as political and commercial centers.

The Sengoku period also spawned a nationwide diffusion of culture. ZEN priests taught Confucianism, classical Chinese poetry (*kanshi*), and INK PAINTING and were also influential in the publication of books. RENGA and *haikai* (see HAIKU) poetry and the Japanese classics were taught. Traditional arts, the TEA CEREMONY, NŌ, and music flourished. Books aimed at the general public, such as OTOGI-ZŌSHI collections of moralistic stories) and the KANGINSHŪ (a collection of popular songs), were published, as was the SETSUYŌSHŪ, a dictionary for everyday use.

After Christianity was introduced by Francis XAVIER in 1549, missionaries exposed Japan to European, or *namban* ("southern barbarian"), culture.

Sen Hime   千姫

(1597–1666). Daughter of the shōgun TOKUGAWA HIDETADA (r 1605–23) and wife of TOYOTOMI HIDEYORI, son of TOYOTOMI HIDEYOSHI; her mother, Tatsu Hime, and Hideyori's mother, YODOGIMI, were sisters. Sen Hime was wedded to Hideyori on 4 September 1603; the union between the two children was evidently a political design by the Tokugawa to paper over growing differences between the two families. The conflict was resolved in favor of the Tokugawa in the Ōsaka campaigns of 1614–15 (see ŌSAKA CASTLE, SIEGES OF); as Ōsaka Castle was about to fall on 3 June 1615, Sen Hime was sent to her father to plead for her husband's life, but failed, and Hideyori committed suicide. The next year Sen Hime was remarried to Honda Heihachirō Tadatoki, son of the *daimyō* of Kuwana (later of Himeji), and after his death in 1626 lived in Edo (now Tōkyō).

seniority system   年功序列

(*nenkō joretsu*). System of employment in Japan in which an employee's rank, salary, and qualifications within a firm are based on the length of service in the company. In this system, wage increases and promotions are tightly regulated by one's school background, sex, and type of work.

Workers, upon hire, are expected to stay with the company until their retirement. Starting wages are determined by educational background, age, sex, and type of job, while wage increases are primarily governed by age and length of service; retirement pay is based on length of employment, position, and wage level at the time of retirement. Seniority is also an important factor in promotions.

The seniority system enables employees to benefit from stability of employment: the longer they work at a single company, even at comparatively low wages, the greater their overall remuneration. It is a mixed blessing to employers. They can benefit from strong worker loyalty and stability and the resultant ease with which they can formulate personnel plans. They suffer, however, from the necessity of carrying along surplus workers, difficulty in assigning employees to appropriate tasks, and growing inflexibility within their organizations.

In the 1970s, with the steady increase in numbers of employees in higher age brackets, the pyramidal personnel structure started to crumble as Japanese corporations began to suffer from skyrocketing labor costs. A growing number of corporations started reviewing the seniority system in the late 1970s, and some even stopped giving pay raises to workers in their forties or older. Particularly since the 1980s, faced with a severe shortage of young workers, rapid obsolescence of technology, and internationalized activities, Japanese corporations have been forced to place more emphasis on their employees' talents and abilities. Japan's seniority system has thus been placed at an important crossroads. See also EMPLOYMENT SYSTEM, MODERN; WAGE SYSTEM.

Seni Pramot   セーニー

(1905–   ). Thai politician, lawyer, and poet. Also known as M. R. Seni Pramoj. While

Senda Koreya This producer and actor played a key role in Japan's post–World War II *shingeki* ("new theater") movement.

Senjōgahara Seen here in autumn, this highland was formerly a great bog; except for areas along the banks of the river Yukawa, it has now become dry grassland.

serving as Thai ambassador to the United States in 1942, he was informed by Prime Minister PHIBUL SONGKHRAM that Thailand had declared war against the United States. Instead of formally transmitting this message, Seni asked the US government for support in organizing military units for the anti-Japanese FREE THAI MOVEMENT. Seni's units provided intelligence services for the United States until the end of the war. Appointed prime minister in September 1945, he retired from office in January 1946, shortly after concluding peace treaties with Great Britain and China. See THAILAND AND JAPAN.

senji 宣旨

Form of imperial edict used during the Heian period (794–1185); developed after the establishment of the KURŌDO-DOKORO (Bureau of Archivists or Chamberlains' Office) in 810. It was less complicated than the *shō* (or *shōsho*) and *choku* (or *chokusho*), earlier forms of imperial edict. An imperial handmaid (*naishi*) conveyed the orders of the sovereign to an official in the Kurōdodokoro, who relayed them to the ranking noble on duty at the court that day. The noble then had it drafted and issued either through the secretary (*geki*) or the Controlling Board (Benkan). Edicts issued through the Benkan were termed *kansenji*.

Senjinkun 戦陣訓

(Instructions for the Battlefield). Military code issued to soldiers on 8 January 1941 in the name of TŌJŌ HIDEKI, then army minister. It was an addition to the IMPERIAL RESCRIPT TO SOLDIERS AND SAILORS (1882) and several other exhortative codes. The code was a series of injunctions concerning the Japanese empire, the imperial armed forces, military regulations, esprit de corps, combat readiness, faith in ultimate victory, veneration of Shintō deities, filial piety, sense of responsibility, attitudes toward life and death, and so on. The concept of Japan's unique national

sennimbari In this 1937 photograph, a woman adds one stitch of red thread to a "thousand-stitch" sash, a protective amulet given to soldiers leaving for the war in China.

polity (KOKUTAI) was stressed. The code enjoined absolute obedience to orders and forbade retreat or surrender. All soldiers on active duty were given copies of the Senjinkun. Toward the end of World War II, copies of the Senjinkun were distributed among the civilian population, including schoolchildren, to prepare them for the expected Allied invasion.

Senjōgahara 戦場ケ原

Highland. In the mountain Nantaisan's western foothills, northwestern Tochigi Prefecture, central Honshū; part of Nikkō National Park. Popular with campers, hikers, and trout fishers, it is known for its alpine flora and autumn foliage. Average elevation: 1,400 m (4,600 ft); area: approximately 10 sq km (4 sq mi).

Senjōgatake 仙丈ケ岳

Also known as Senjōdake. Mountain on the border between Nagano and Yamanashi prefectures, central Honshū; in the northern part of the Akaishi Mountains. Near the summit are three cirques. Height: 3,033 m (9,951 ft).

Senjōsan 船上山

Hill on the northern slope of DAISEN, western Tottori Prefecture, western Honshū. Surrounded on the east, north, and west by 30–50 m (100–165 ft) vertical cliffs. It is known for its historical sites associated with the KEMMU RESTORATION, during which Emperor GO-DAIGO was restored to the throne (1333). Height: 616 m (2,021 ft).

Senjuji 専修寺

Head temple of the Takada branch of the JŌDO SHIN SECT of Buddhism, located in the city of Tsu, Mie Prefecture. It was probably built by Shimbutsu (1209–58), disciple of SHINRAN, Jōdo Shin founder, but tradition attributes its establishment to the latter, whose handwritten manuscripts are among the temple's treasures. Originally in the Takada district of Shimotsuke Province (now Tochigi Prefecture), Senjuji was moved to Tsu in 1465 by the 10th abbot, Shin'e (1434–1512). In 1477 it became a *chokuganji*, a temple commissioned to offer prayers for the well-being and prosperity of the imperial family and the empire. In 1574 Senjuji gained the status of *monzekidera*, a temple whose chief abbot is of the imperial family or aristocracy. In 1989 the Takada branch claimed about 267,000 followers.

Senju Woolen Mill 千住製絨所

(Senju Seijūsho). Japan's first woolen mill; one of a number of model factories established by the Meiji government. Set up in the Senju district of Tōkyō, it was built by German technicians with machinery imported from Germany and began operation in 1879. It remained the major producer of woolen textiles until after the turn of the century. See GOVERNMENT-OPERATED FACTORIES, MEIJI PERIOD.

Senkaku Islands 尖閣諸島

(Senkaku Shotō). Group of uninhabited islands 160 km (100 mi) north of the YAEYAMA ISLANDS, western Okinawa Prefecture, including Uotsurishima, Kōbisho, Kita Koshima, Minami Koshima, and Sekibisho. The surrounding seas are rich fishing grounds for bonito. Taiwan and the People's Republic of China have claimed the islands, although the United States returned them to Japan with the reversion of Okinawa in 1972.

Senki 戦旗

(Battle Flag). Major leftist literary journal published from May 1928 to December 1931; until September 1930 it was the organ of the Zen Nihon Musansha Geijutsu Remmei (All-Japan Federation of Proletarian Arts), better known by the acronym NAPF (J: Nappu; from the Esperanto, Nippona Artista Proleta Federacio). *Senki* was opposed by the leftist journal BUNGEI SENSEN, the organ of another faction of the PROLETARIAN LITERATURE MOVEMENT. *Senki* was managed and edited principally by TSUBOI SHIGEJI and Yamada Seizaburō (1896–1987). Contributors included KURAHARA KOREHITO, NAKANO SHIGEHARU, KOBAYASHI TAKIJI, TOKUNAGA SUNAO, and SATA INEKO. Not only did its circulation exceed 20,000 by 1930, but NAPF's distribution system—which formed *Senki* study groups at factories, farms, and schools—had given it an even larger audience.

senkyo kanshō 選挙干渉

("election interference"). Government obstruction of the election campaigns of opposition candidates. Three instances are particularly well known. In February 1892 Home Minister SHINAGAWA YAJIRŌ used every possible measure against the opposition parties. There was even bloodshed in some areas; the official report listed 25 dead and 388 wounded. The antigovernment parties emerged with a majority of 163 seats.

In the March 1915 campaign Home Minister ŌURA KANETAKE flagrantly bought votes for candidates of the RIKKEN DŌSHIKAI and other progovernment parties. He also brought considerable pressure to bear on prefectural governors to assure government victories in their districts. As a result, the Dōshikai won.

In the election of February 1928, the first held after the passage of the Universal Manhood Suffrage Law, interference was led by Home Minister SUZUKI KISABURŌ. The government party (Seiyūkai) was returned with a majority of one seat, but Suzuki was severely criticized and soon forced to resign.

Sennan 泉南[市]

City in southwestern Ōsaka Prefecture, central Honshū, on Ōsaka Bay. Long known for its Izumi cotton, it is still a textile center. Principal agricultural products are rice and onions. Pop: 60,065.

sennimbari 千人針

("thousand-stitch" cloths). A strip of white cloth embellished by 1,000 women with 1,000 stitches (French knots) sewn with red thread. Red was traditionally an auspicious color. Worn as sashes, these *sennimbari* were given to soldiers to ward off bullets and ensure a safe return. The custom originated during the SINO-JAPANESE WAR OF 1894–1895.

sennin 仙人

(immortal one; Ch: *xianren* or *hsien-jen*). Persons manifesting the ideals of religious Taoism, who were imagined to have attained supernatural powers, especially immortality, by means of ascetic exercises practiced in remote mountain regions. *Sennin* were similar to the Hindu ṛṣi (holy man), Vedic seers who lived in mountain forests, possessed psychic powers, and were able to levitate. In China, *xianren* were believed to preserve a youthful appearance indefinitely by drinking elixirs containing such ingredients as powdered cinnamon, mica, deer antlers, and cinnabar.

They allegedly could levitate, ride clouds, and make the winds blow. The concept of the *xianren* was introduced to Japan along with Taoism in the second half of the 7th century. The term was adopted by Buddhists and occasionally used as a designation for the Buddha, because of his mastery over life and death, but more often for religious figures of great accomplishment who belonged to heterodox faiths.

Sen no Rikyū 千利休

(1522–1591). Tea master of the Azuchi-Momoyama period (1568–1600); founder of the Sen school of TEA CEREMONY. His grandfather, Tanaka Sen'ami, is said to have been one of the DŌBŌSHŪ (special retainers to the Muromachi shogunate who practiced the tea ceremony and other arts) in the service of the shōgun ASHIKAGA YOSHIMASA. Rikyū's father, Yohei, moved to Sakai in Izumi Province (now part of Ōsaka Prefecture); tradition has it that Yohei took the character *sen* of his father's name as his family name. The family apparently became wholesale fish dealers and eventually joined the ranks of the EGŌ-SHŪ, a group of wealthy merchants who formed a virtually autonomous city government.

Rikyū was born in Sakai and first studied the tea ceremony under Kitamuki Dōchin (1504–62) of the Nōami school and later under Takeno Jōō (1502–55) of the school founded by Murata Shukō (or Jukō, 1422–1502). He also studied Zen under the master Shōrei Shūkin at the temple DAITOKUJI in Kyōto. From 1570 to 1573, with IMAI SŌKYŪ and TSUDA SŌGYŪ, Rikyū served as *sadō* (tea-ceremony officiant) for the military hegemon ODA NOBUNAGA. He went on to perform the same duties for the national unifier TOYOTOMI HIDEYOSHI, from whom he received extensive landholdings. In 1585 Sen no Rikyū officiated at the sumptuous tea ceremony that Hideyoshi held for Emperor Ōgimachi (1517–93; r 1557–86) in the Imperial Palace. With Tsuda Sōgyū, he also officiated at Hideyoshi's magnificent outdoor tea ceremony held at the KITANO SHRINE in 1587.

In 1591 Rikyū suddenly fell afoul of Hideyoshi and was forced to commit suicide. Several reasons have been suggested for this: that he had placed a life-sized statue of himself in the Kimmōkaku, a structural addition to the main gate of the Daitokuji that he and his family donated, that he had refused to give his daughter to Hideyoshi, or that he had demanded exorbitant prices for his tea utensils. He died on 21 April 1591 (Tenshō 19.2.28).

Sen no Rikyū imposed his unerring taste on the tea ceremony, introducing implements such as flower holders fashioned from bamboo, rough black teabowls known as RAKU WARE, and the *Amida no kama,* a type of iron kettle. He preferred to use simple objects close at hand and to emphasize the ordinary, everyday aspect of the tea ceremony. In one of his poems he reminds his disciples that "the tea ceremony is nothing more than boiling water, steeping tea, and drinking it." He was also responsible for reducing the size of the teahouse (CHASHITSU). The trend that had begun in the Muromachi period (1333–1568), when the so-called *shoin*-style teahouse was simplified to produce a rustic effect (see SHOIN-ZUKURI). Sen no Rikyū reduced the size to only two TATAMI mats, or even one and a half, in his pursuit of the ideal of *yoriai,* the special communion among participants in the tea ceremony.

Sen'oku Hakkokan 泉屋博古館

Large collection of Chinese bronze vessels, Chinese and Japanese mirrors, and a few Chinese bronze Buddhist figures brought together by Sumitomo Kichizaemon VII (1864–1926) before his death in 1926. Located in Kyōto, it is housed in a building erected in 1970. The quality and variety of the more than 500 pieces make this one of the world's great oriental bronze collections.

Senri New Town 千里ニュータウン

(Senri Nyū Taun). Planned residential community located in north-central Ōsaka Prefecture, central Honshū. The prefectural government began construction of the town in 1961. The Expo '70 Commemoration Park and two universities are nearby; the town also serves as a subcenter of the prefecture. Area: 11.6 sq km (4.5 sq mi). Projected pop: 150,000.

senryō 千両

Sarcandra glabra. An evergreen shrub of the family Chloranthaceae that grows wild in warm regions of central Honshū, Shikoku, and Kyūshū. The stem is 50–80 centimeters (19.7–31.5 in) high. Leaves are opposite, oblong, serrated, and glossy dark green in color. In June a compound spike forms at the tip of the branch and produces numerous small greenish yellow flowers. The fruit is a globular drupe that turns red when ripe. In warmer regions the *senryō* is planted as a garden shrub. The *senryō* (literally, "much money") is thought to bring wealth.

senryōbako 千両箱

("thousand-*ryō* box"). Edo-period (1600–1868) cash box made of wood reinforced with external iron fittings. One box would hold about 1,000 *ryō* in KOBAN coins, a considerable sum in those days. A 2,000-*ryō* box appeared in the late Edo period.

senryū 川柳

A type of humorous verse, originating in the Edo period (1600–1868), which is composed in three lines of 5, 7, and 5 syllables each. *Senryū* derived from the practice of *maekuzuke* (see ZAPPAI), in which customarily a given couplet (the *maeku,* or "leading stanza") of 7-7 syllables was capped by a comic 7-5-7 tercet (the *tsukeku,* or "capping stanza"). *Tsukeku* were widely popularized through anthologies of anonymous verses selected and published by KARAI SENRYŪ and came to be appreciated independently of their *maeku,* eventually becoming known as *senryū.*

Beginning with *Mutamagawa* (1750–76), there appeared, without accompanying *maeku,* a number of collections of *tsukeku* that had been judged superior in competitions in which the citizens of Edo (now Tōkyō) had entered their verses. *Yanagidaru* (1765), an anthology in this tradition, contained *tsukeku* that had been solicited and selected by Karai Senryū, according to critical and procedural standards that evoked immense enthusiasm. Subsequently there appeared 22 further collections of *senryū* selected by him, and after his death an additional 144 collections by other compilers—all entitled *Yanagidaru.* The early editions displayed a marked preference for a style similar to that of contemporary *zappai* poetry, but Senryū's treatment of *tsukeku* as independent entities and his willingness to accept superior verses that were unrelated to the assigned *maeku* went a step beyond *Mutamagawa.*

The popularity of the *Yanagidaru* series

led to an increased emphasis on the independence of the *tsukeku,* and in his last years Senryū abandoned entirely the use of *maeku* in competitions. However, the use of *kudai* (set topics) as compositional guides contributed to a shift from the light, witty, and realistic sketches of everyday life that had predominated in the early collections to indulgence in bawdy, often obscene humor and extravagant wordplay. Nevertheless *senryū* survives to this day as a form of satirical poetic amusement and is composed, as in the past, primarily by amateurs.

senshū gakkō 専修学校

(special training schools). Vocationally oriented schools enrolling a minimum of 40 students and offering programs at least one year in length (over 800 hours for full-time students, or 450 hours for part-time students). Established in 1976 as an alternative to university or junior college study, *senshū gakkō* offer high school equivalency courses for middle school graduates and college-level courses for high school graduates. The latter, known as special programs (*semmon katei*), usually consist of two-year courses in engineering, business, medicine, hygiene, or foreign languages. There are also general programs open to all applicants. In 1989 there were some 740,000 students enrolled in 3,254 *senshū gakkō.* See also MISCELLANEOUS SCHOOLS.

Senshū University 専修大学

(Senshū Daigaku). A coeducational private university located in Chiyoda Ward, Tōkyō. Founded in 1880 as Senshū Gakkō, a two-year night school, it became Senshū University in 1922. The university maintains facul-

sentai butsu The "thousand Buddhas" (actually 1,001) at Sanjūsangendō in Kyōto were carved by Tankei and others during the 12th and 13th centuries.

ties of economics, law, business administration, commerce, and literature. Enrollment in 1989 was 21,053.

Sensōji　　　　　　　　　　浅草寺

Also called Asakusa Kannon. Buddhist temple in the Asakusa section of Taitō Ward, Tōkyō. Sensōji originally belonged to the Tendai sect, but in 1950 it became the head temple of the Shōkannon sect. According to tradition, the statue of the bodhisattva Kannon enshrined at Sensōji was found in the river Sumidagawa in 628 by two fishermen, the brothers Hinokuma Hamanari and Hinokuma Takenari. The village head Haji no Nakatomo recognized the statue's divinity and remade his own house into a temple dedicated to it. After numerous fires, the temple was rebuilt during the Kamakura period (1185–1333) and became the center of worship for Kannon's many ardent devotees, who included shōguns and *samurai*. Sensōji is the site of many events throughout the year, with July's HŌZUKI ICHI, a traditional fair, one of the most popular. It is also a popular destination for HATSUMŌDE (New Year's temple visits). The arcade known as Nakamise, which extends from the temple's front gate, Kaminarimon, to its main hall, is lined with shops specializing in Japanese confections and goods. The ASAKUSA SHRINE, well known as the site of the Sanja Festival, is located on the grounds of Sensōji. See also ASAKUSA.

Sen Sōshitsu　　　　　　　千宗室

(1923–). Fifteenth head of URA SENKE, a 400-year-old school of the TEA CEREMONY. Born in Kyōto. After his graduation from Dōshisha University, Sen Sōshitsu took Buddhist vows and underwent Zen training at the temple Daitokuji. He succeeded to the position of school head in 1964. Believing that "with a bowl of tea, peace can truly spread," he traveled throughout the world as an envoy of the tea ceremony and interna-

tional friendship. He is also a professor of history at the University of Hawaii.

Sensuijima　　　　　　　　仙酔島

Small island in the central Inland Sea, about 300 m (985 ft) east of Tomonoura, southeastern Hiroshima Prefecture. Sea-eroded caves, good beaches, and demonstrations of traditional net fishing for sea bream attract tourists. Area: 0.9 sq km (0.3 sq mi).

sentai butsu　　　　　　　　千体仏

(literally, "thousand Buddhas"). Groups of 1,000 small images of the Buddha. The idea of making sets of 1,000 images of AMIDA or 1,000 images of KANNON began in India, spread to China, and eventually came to Japan, where it became very popular by the Heian period (794–1185). It was popularly believed that the multiplication of images enhanced the power of the Buddha. These icons were carved or cast and sometimes painted. Two notable Japanese examples of *sentai butsu* are the copperplate relief sculpture (see OSHIDASHIBUTSU) inside the Tamamushi Shrine of the temple HŌRYŪJI in Nara and the larger-scale images in the SANJŪSANGENDŌ in Kyōto.

sentō → bath

Sentsūzan　　　　　　　　船通山

Mountain on the border between Tottori and Shimane prefectures, western Honshū. It is the setting for legends mentioned in the 8th-century record KOJIKI. It has an excellent mountain-climbing trail. Sentsūzan is part of Hiba-Dōgo-Taishaku Quasi-National Park. Height: 1,142 m (3,747 ft).

Senuma Shigeki　　　　　瀬沼茂樹

(1904–88). Critic. Real name Suzuki Tadanao. Born in Tōkyō; graduated from Tōkyō Shōka Daigaku (now Hitotsubashi University). Senuma began publishing essays, poetry, and fiction while still a student. He is known for his careful scholarship and broad perspective on modern literature. His principal works include *Gendai bungaku* (1933, Contemporary Literature), a collection of essays that provides a detailed historical analysis of the modernist literature of the early Shōwa period (1926–1989); *Kindai Nihon bungaku no naritachi* (1951, Origins of Modern Japanese Literature), a systematic study of the nature and structure of modern Japanese literature focusing on the central themes of family and self; and *Nihon bundanshi* (1977–78, A History of the Japanese Literary Community).

sen'yū　　　　　　　　　　占有

(possession). Legal term referring to a person's intentional holding of property for his or her own purposes. The CIVIL CODE classifies the right of possession, the substance of which is occupancy, as one kind of *bukken*, or RIGHTS IN REM (Civil Code, art. 180).

If a possessor's right of possession is in danger of being interfered with, the Civil Code recognizes the right of the holder of the possessory rights to demand the removal of the disturbance. This is known as the right to sue for possession (*sen'yū soken*). The owner of the property has no legal recourse against the party in possession other than the right to sue.

A person who, with the intent of owning a certain piece of property, possesses that property for a period of 20 years, or a period of 10 years in good faith and without negligence, can acquire ownership of that prop-

erty (acquisition by prescription). A person who purchases movable property from a possessor who he or she believes has ownership of the property can acquire ownership immediately even though the person in possession is not actually the owner of the property. This is called immediate acquisition (*sokuji shutoku*). A possessor in good faith can acquire the fruits of the possessed property. Also, that person can demand from the owner reimbursement for expenditures made for the benefit of the possessed property. If the possessor destroys or damages the possessed property, he or she is liable to the owner for compensation for damages.

Senzai wakashū　　　　　千載和歌集

(Collection of a Thousand Years; usually abbreviated to *Senzaishū*). Seventh of the IMPERIAL ANTHOLOGIES (*chokusenshū*) of classical Japanese poetry (WAKA). It was ordered in 1183 by former Emperor GO-SHIRAKAWA (r 1155–58) and was completed in 1187 or 1188, with a few later additions. Compiled by FUJIWARA NO TOSHINARI (Shunzei; 1114–1204), who also wrote the Japanese preface, it consists of 20 books containing 1,288 poems. Compiled during the struggles of the Taira and Minamoto clans for military and political supremacy (see TAIRA-MINAMOTO WAR), the final text officially presented to the former emperor, probably in 1188, consisted of 20 manuscript scrolls in Shunzei's own hand.

There are 385 individuals represented in the anthology. Shunzei strikes a balance between older and newer poets, men and women, and poetic conservatives and innovators. By numbers of poems included, the most prominent poets are MINAMOTO NO TOSHIYORI, 52 poems; Shunzei, 36 poems (most of them added by Go-Shirakawa's command); FUJIWARA NO MOTOTOSHI, 26 poems; former emperor SUTOKU, 23 poems; priest SHUN'E (Toshiyori's son and heir), 22 poems; and Lady IZUMI SHIKIBU, 21 poems. A neoclassicist, Shunzei advocated a return to the standards of decorum, elegance, dignity, and refinement embodied in the KOKINSHŪ (ca 905, Collection of Ancient and Modern Times).

Seoul, Treaty of　　　　　漢城条約

(J: Kanjō Jōyaku). Agreement between Japan and Korea signed on 9 January 1885. The treaty restored diplomatic relations disrupted by the KAPSIN POLITICAL COUP of 1884. Korea agreed to apologize to Japan and pay a ¥110,000 indemnity for harm done to Japanese citizens and their property, to provide a new site and buildings for Japan's legation, and to provide facilities and maintenance for Japan's legation guard. This paved the way for the TIANJIN (TIENTSIN) CONVENTION between China and Japan. See also KOREA AND JAPAN.

Seppuku　　　　　　　　　切腹

(foreign release title: *Harakiri*). A 1962 film directed by KOBAYASHI MASAKI and starring NAKADAI TATSUYA and MIKUNI RENTARŌ. The film dramatizes the cruelty of the warrior code of ethics (BUSHIDŌ). A young masterless *samurai* (RŌNIN) with a destitute and starving family to support visits the Edo (now Tōkyō) headquarters of a prosperous warrior household. He asks permission to commit HARAKIRI (more formally known as *seppuku*) in the garden of the mansion, obviously hoping to be taken in and employed or sent away with a sum of money. Domainal officers call the young man's bluff, forcing him to commit *harakiri* with the only sword he now carries, one of bamboo. He had previously pawned his blade, the symbol of his class standing.

A few months later another, somewhat older, man arrives at the same household and makes the same request. He, too, is ordered to make good his threat. He reveals that he is the young man's father-in-law and succeeds in slaying many of a large band of swordsmen set upon him by those responsible for his son-in-law's death, before also disemboweling himself. This film is an implicit criticism of the rigid rules by which contemporary Japanese society seemingly operates.

seppuku (ritual suicide)→harakiri

sericulture　　　　　　　養蚕

(yōsan). The raising of silkworms for the production of raw silk. Japan's climate is suitable for raising both the mulberry (J: kuwa) and the silkworm (kaiko), which feeds on mulberry leaves, and sericulture has been practiced there since ancient times. Silkworms were traditionally reared in family dwellings, but today they are reared in specially built silkworm houses. The development of the automatic leaf feeder and other such technology has greatly lessened the work involved. Harvested about four times a year from May through October; cocoons are either reeled by agricultural cooperative associations (which also weave the fabric) or sold to manufacturers of silk fabrics through factors.

Sericulture probably came to Japan from China via the Korean peninsula. The earliest mention of sericulture in Japan is found in a 3rd-century Chinese history, the WEI ZHI (Wei chih). According to the 8th-century chronicle NIHON SHOKI, the government encouraged sericulture and collected silk as taxes as early as the 5th century. By the 1900s Japan came to lead the world in silk production. Export was mostly to the United States until World War II. In 1929 more than 2.2 million households engaged in sericulture, and in 1930 total production of cocoons peaked at 399,000 metric tons (438,900 short tons). In 1990, however, some 52,060 households produced a total of only 24,925 metric tons (27,418 short tons). Japan was fourth in the world in terms of total cocoon production in 1990 after the People's Republic of China, India, and the Soviet Union; however, domestic demand for silk fabrics has grown in recent years, and Japan must import silk from China and Korea. See also SILK.

Serizawa Keisuke　　　芹沢銈介

(1895–1984). Textile designer; illustrator; painter. Born in the city of Shizuoka. He adapted an Okinawan method of stencil dyeing called bingata-zome ("red-pattern dyeing"; see OKINAWAN TEXTILES) and infused it with a modern sense of design and bold color. In 1956 the Japanese government designated him one of its LIVING NATIONAL TREASURES for preserving this indigenous craft and developing it into a recognized art.

Serizawa Kōjirō　　　芹沢光治良

(1897–1993). Novelist. Born in Shizuoka Prefecture. A graduate of Tōkyō University, he studied economics at the University of Paris (1925–29). His recuperation from tuberculosis in a Swiss sanatorium became the basis of his short story "Burujoa" (1930). This was followed by the novels Asu o oute (1931) and Isu o sagasu (1932), which depicted the internal turmoil of Japanese intellectuals in the midst of the PROLETARIAN LIT-

sericulture

▶ Silkworms eat rapaciously before making their cocoons and are traditionally fed large amounts of fresh mulberry leaves every day; recently, however, concentrated mulberry food has been developed, and this is used in the early stages.

▲ Cocoons are sorted for quality.

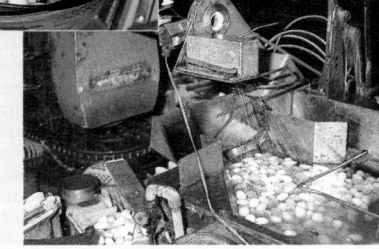

▲ Cocoons are soaked in hot water to make reeling easier. This photograph shows the traditional hand-reeling process.

▼ Shown here is the reeling process done by machine.

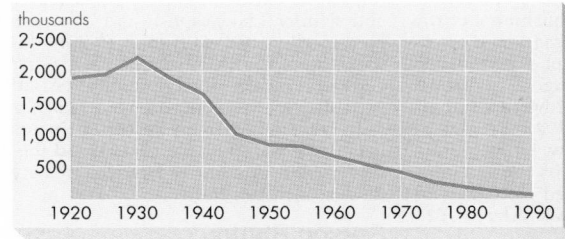

▼ Silk yarn of uneven thickness, spun manually from floss silk as shown here, is used to make the traditional fabric tsumugi (silk pongee).

Japanese Households Raising Silkworms

thousands
2,500
2,000
1,500
1,000
500
1920 1930 1940 1950 1960 1970 1980 1990

SOURCE: Ministry of Agriculture, Forestry, and Fisheries.

ERATURE MOVEMENT. After World War II, he wrote about Japan's wartime experiences. Serizawa's works are colored by a deep religious outlook and show a close relationship to the logical structure of the European novel. Many of his works have been translated into French, including Pari ni shisu (1942; tr J'irai mourir à Paris, 1954) and Pari fujin (1955; tr Madame Aida, 1958). He was chairman of the Japan P.E.N. Club from 1965 to 1974 and received an award from the French Academy in 1957. Other works include Ningen no ummei (1962–68) and Hitotsu no sekai (1952–53; tr One World, 1954).

service industries　　サービス産業

(sābisu sangyō). Service industries (also referred to as the tertiary sector) in Japan include wholesale and retail sales, finance and insurance, real estate, transport, communications, and utilities. The number of service-related enterprises in Japan totaled 5.2 million in 1986: this figure was led by wholesale and retail firms and food service establishments. Service industries employed 34.3 million people, or about 60 percent of the nation's work force.

The service sector can be divided into industries that provide services to businesses and those that cater to individuals. Business-oriented services include leasing and renting, information-related services such as advertising and data processing, and legal and accounting services. Service businesses catering to individuals include barbershops and beauty salons, laundry and dry-cleaning services, and convenience stores. In recent years travel agencies, rental shops, and health clubs have also enjoyed dramatic growth.

The growth of service industries is a natural economic phenomenon associated with the development of a country's economy. Service industries in Japan will continue to grow, given the growing Japanese acceptance of the five-day workweek and the increased demand for leisure activities. In addition, the increase in the number of working women has given rise to many new industries, such as those providing housework, catering, and child care services. Many service businesses, such as beauty salons and language schools, have begun to accommodate the changing schedules of customers by staying open late or opening very early in the morning.

Serizawa Kōjirō The works of this novelist, whose career as a writer was given impetus by a number of years spent in Europe, are colored by a deep religious outlook.

Sesshū Tōyō
Amanohashidate, a landscape scroll depicting the famous scenic spot on the Sea of Japan coast. Ca 1501. Ink and colors on paper. 89 × 169 cm. Kyōto National Museum. National Treasure.

Setouchi Harumi
After becoming a Buddhist nun in 1973, this novelist began publishing her fiction under the name Setouchi Jakuchō.

sesame → goma

sesshō 摂政

Imperial regent for a minor emperor as opposed to KAMPAKU, regent for an adult emperor. A *sesshō* was originally a member of the imperial family appointed when the emperor was a child or a woman. Prince SHŌTOKU, for example, acted as *sesshō* (593–622) for the empress SUIKO. The first person outside the imperial family to be appointed was FUJIWARA NO YOSHIFUSA, in 866, after having placed his own grandson, the child emperor Seiwa (850–881; r 858–876), on the throne. For the next two centuries, Yoshifusa's descendants held exclusive control over both the office of *sesshō* and of *kampaku*, the latter created in 887 (see REGENCY GOVERNMENT). With the establishment of the INSEI system of rule by retired emperors in the 11th century, the office of *sesshō* lost its political significance, although it remained an important post until the Meiji Restoration (1868). The 1889 and 1947 versions of the IMPERIAL HOUSEHOLD LAW both contain provisions for appointment of a *sesshō*. Emperor SHŌWA (Hirohito) acted as regent for his ailing father Emperor TAISHŌ from 1921 to 1926. See also EMPEROR.

Sesshū Tōyō 雪舟等楊

(1420–1506). Ink painter active during the second half of the 15th century. Born in Bitchū Province (now part of Okayama Prefecture), he went to Kyōto in his early years, becoming a monk at the temple SHŌKOKUJI. There he acted as attendant to the priest Shunrin Shūtō (fl 1430–65) and studied painting with the monk-painter SHŪBUN. Sesshū moved to the Unkokuan studio in Yamaguchi (in what is now Yamaguchi Prefecture) in 1464.

Setsubun Playfully carrying out this traditional ceremony, two children throw beans to chase away the demon, impersonated by a third child wearing a mask.

In 1467 Sesshū traveled to China with a trade mission dispatched by the ŌUCHI FAMILY. While in China Sesshū did a wall painting in the building of the Board of Rites in Beijing (Peking) and made many village sketches, some of which survive today through later copies. In 1469 he returned to Japan. By 1476 he had opened a studio in Bungo Province (now part of Ōita Prefecture), which he named the Tenkai Togarō.

Sesshū is best known for his landscapes. His works are characterized by dynamic brushwork and structured composition, a clear departure from the lyrical mode associated with Shūbun. Sesshū's best-known work is *Haboku sansuizu* (1495, Haboku Landscape). Also noteworthy are his sketch of *Amanohashidate* (ca 1501), a pair of hanging scrolls entitled *Shūtō sansuizu* (Autumn and Winter Landscapes), and a horizontal handscroll entitled *Sansui chōkan* (1486, Landscape). Sesshū also painted portraits and other figure subjects, and his versatility extended to the genre of BIRD-AND-FLOWER PAINTING. He had many disciples (including Josui SŌEN and SHŪGETSU TŌKAN), and the UNKOKU SCHOOL of painters later claimed stylistic descent from him.

Sesson Shūkei 雪村周継

(1504?–89?). Ink painter whose career spanned a half-century following the deaths of the luminaries SESSHŪ TŌYŌ, SHŌKEI, and SŌAMI. Sesson was born in Hitachi Province (now Ibaraki Prefecture), remote from the major centers of Japanese INK PAINTING. In the 1550s he worked in close association with the ZEN Buddhist temple Sōunji in Odawara. Sesson's known corpus of over 60 paintings, few of which are dated, includes a rich variety of subjects and formats. His figure and animal subjects, especially Taoist immortals and dragons among clouds, have a turbulent vivacity, and even landscape forms in his later paintings seem mutable and vital. His treatise on painting, *Setsumon teishi* (1542), sets forth the theories embodied in his later work: the importance of observing nature and of copying master paintings to achieve a simplification of nature. He gave considerable attention to the use of ink, especially the suggestive use of light and dark tonalities.

Sesson Yūbai 雪村友梅

(1290–1346). ZEN monk of the RINZAI SECT and poet; with KOKAN SHIREN, one of the two great figures in early GOZAN LITERATURE (Chinese learning in medieval Japanese Zen monasteries). Born in Echigo Province (now Niigata Prefecture); disciple of ISSAN ICHINEI. In 1307

he went to China, where, because of a worsening in diplomatic relations between China and Japan, he was jailed in 1310 and subsequently sent West into exile. Released after more than ten years, Sesson was refused permission to return home until 1329. His poems are collected in the anthology *Mingashū*.

Setagawa 瀬田川

River in Shiga Prefecture, central Honshū. It originates in Lake Biwa and flows into Kyōto Prefecture, where its name becomes UJIGAWA. It is thus the upper part of a longer river with three names, the lower reaches being called YODOGAWA, which empties into Ōsaka Bay. Tourist attractions include the Karahashi bridge at Seta and the temple ISHIYAMADERA. Length: 15 km (9 mi).

Setagaya Ward 世田谷区

(Setagaya Ku). One of the 23 wards of Tōkyō. On the Musashino Plateau. Bordered on the southwest by the river Tamagawa, this residential area is Tōkyō's largest ward with an area of 58.8 sq km (22.7 sq mi). After the Tōkyō Earthquake of 1923 private railway companies began various land development projects here. Among the numerous recreational facilities are the Komazawa Olympic Park and Baji Kōen, an equestrian park. Pop: 789,051.

Setchūgakuha 折衷学派

A school of Confucianism during the mid-Edo period (1600–1868); it was a composite of theories of the three major schools of Confucianism, SHUSHIGAKU, KOGAKU, and YŌMEIGAKU. Advocates of the Setchūgakuha in the late 18th century included the scholar HOSOI HEISHŪ.

Seto 瀬戸〔市〕

City in northern Aichi Prefecture, central Honshū, 18 km (11 mi) northeast of NAGOYA. Its ceramics industry (the Japanese word for ceramic ware is *setomono*), dating from the 13th century, is the largest in the country. Pop: 126,340.

Seto Naikai → Inland Sea

Setō Shōji 瀬藤象二

(1891–1977). Electrical engineer. Born in Wakayama Prefecture, he graduated from Tōkyō University in 1915. After studying abroad, he became a professor at Tōkyō University and began his work on anodized aluminum at its Institute of Physical and Chemical Research. He was active in Japan's independent electron microscope development project during World War II and for this work received the Order of Culture in 1973.

Setouchi Harumi 瀬戸内晴美

(1922–). Novelist. Born in Tokushima Prefecture. Graduate of Tōkyō Christian Women's University. Setouchi's biographical novel of the feminist author TAMURA TOSHIKO was awarded the first Tamura Toshiko Prize in 1960. In addition to biographical novels of feminists she has also published semiautobiographical novels. In 1973 she became a Buddhist nun but continued to publish fiction under the name Setouchi Jakuchō. Setouchi's principal works include *Natsu no owari* (1962, The End of the Summer), a novel, and *Kanoko ryōran* (serialized 1962–64; published in book form 1971), a biographical novel of the contemporary woman writer OKAMOTO KANOKO.

Setouchi region 瀬戸内地方

(Setouchi *chihō*). General term for an area that includes the southern part of the CHŪGOKU REGION facing the INLAND SEA, the northern part of the SHIKOKU REGION, and the islands in the Inland Sea. It has placid seas and a mild climate even in the winter. Long an important travel route to and from the Asian continent, Setouchi developed into one of Japan's more culturally advanced districts. Cities and industries grew rapidly after World War II.

Seto ware 瀬戸焼

(*seto-yaki*). Important glazed ceramic ware in Japan from the 12th century to the present. The remains of kilns are scattered around the present-day city of Seto, near Nagoya in Aichi Prefecture. The oldest wares, dating from the 12th century, were glazed with ash; the technology originated in China but appears to have spread to Seto from the SANAGE kilns east of Nagoya.

Seto ware of the Kamakura (1185–1333) and Muromachi (1333–1568) periods is customarily referred to as *koseto* or "old Seto." The 14th century was the most prosperous for the Seto kilns. Decorative techniques included stamped, carved, applied, and combed patterns. A finer, more even ash glaze of light green color was used. Production of iron-glazed wares began during this century at Seto, but it was not until the 15th century that the Seto potters achieved a beautiful, dark, iron-brown glaze. Most Seto products during the 15th and early 16th centuries were for household use. Fine TEA CEREMONY utensils were also made in large numbers. The ash-glazed wares of this period have a deep green color.

During the Muromachi period the major production center for ceramic ware was Mino (now Gifu Prefecture; see MINO WARE). However, early in the Edo period (1600–1868) the ascendancy of the Seto area was restored. In the late Edo period Seto was renowned for its porcelains. After the Meiji Restoration (1868), Western ceramic techniques were introduced and the predominance of Seto ware was such that *setomono* ("Seto things") became a generic term for ceramic ware.

Setsubun 節分

Traditional ceremony to dispel demons, now observed on 3 or 4 February. The practice of scattering beans (*mamemaki*) to drive away demons is one of a number of magical rites performed to ward off evil (see MAYOKE).

The term *setsubun* originally referred to the eve of the first day of any of the 24 divisions of the solar year known as *setsu*. Later it came to be applied more specifically to the last day of the *setsu* called *daikan* ("great cold"), which corresponded to the eve of Risshun ("the first day of spring"), the New Year's Day of the ancient solar calendar and the traditional beginning of spring (see CALENDAR, DATES, AND TIME).

On Setsubun, beans (usually soybeans) are scattered inside and outside the house or building to the common chant of *oni wa soto, fuku wa uchi* ("Out with demons! In with good luck!"). It is customary for family members to eat the same number of beans as their age.

setsuwa bungaku 説話文学

("tale" or "anecdotal literature"). Originally coined by scholars as a term equivalent to the Western folk or fairy tale, as distinct from *densetsu* (legend) or *shinwa* (myth), the word *setsuwa* now has a very general meaning. Legends, myths, fairy tales, episodes in Chinese history, war tales, and anecdotes about ordinary life are all included in *setsuwa*, collections compiled between 800 and 1300.

Many collections deal exclusively with Buddhism and are written in Chinese. The earliest is NIHON RYŌIKI. Later collections in Japanese include one possibly compiled by SAIGYŌ (*Senjūshō*), one attributed to KAMO NO CHŌMEI (*Hosshinshū*, about the awakening of faith), and two by Mujū Ichien (see SHASEKISHŪ).

Secular collections, found from the 12th century on, vary in subject matter: *Kyōkunshō* has tales about music; *Kara monogatari*, tales about China. Some collections record anecdotes about famous figures such as ŌE NO MASAFUSA (*Gōdanshō*) or Fujiwara no Tadazane (1078–1162; *Chūgaishō, Fukego*). Noteworthy collections of the mid-13th century include JIKKUNSHŌ and KOKON CHOMONJŪ.

The *setsuwa* collection of greatest importance to Japanese literature is the vast *Konjaku monogatari shū* (also known as the KONJAKU MONOGATARI; compiled about 1120). It influenced the works of such 20th-century writers as AKUTAGAWA RYŪNOSUKE, who first brought its quality to the attention of the modern reading public.

Setsuyōshū 節用集

Mid-15th-century Japanese-language dictionary. Also known as *Setchōshū*. Editor unknown. Essentially a lexicon of the spoken language of the Muromachi period (1333–1568), it also contains some material of a more encyclopedic nature. The words are entered in *kana* (the Japanese phonetic syllabary) together with their corresponding Chinese characters. Words are grouped by first syllable in *iroha* order (the old order of the *kana* syllabary; see IROHA POEM) and within these groups by subject. The dictionary, which was convenient and easy to use, went through many revisions and enlargements, the last of which appeared in the late 19th century.

settai 接待

(entertaining; often used particularly to refer to entertaining of business clients). Despite less favorable tax treatment for entertainment expenses in recent years, one of the most common ways of showing gratitude to a company's best customers is still to provide entertainment. This typically consists of an invitation to a substantial meal at a high-quality Japanese or Western restaurant, followed by one or more visits to Japanese-style hostess bars. Because of the high cost of these evenings, the less favorable tax treatment of such expenses, and the trend among younger persons to spend more time with their families, there has been a tendency toward less conspicuous consumption.

All major Japanese cities have their entertainment districts containing expensive Japanese-style restaurants (*ryōtei*) and bars. The typical *ryōtei* is patterned after traditional Japanese houses, with liberal use of fine woods, *tatami* mats, and Japanese-style decorations, plus, of course, waitresses dressed in *kimono*. The typical evening on the town for a valued client usually begins with a meal of 10 or more courses (all rather small in volume) at one of these *ryōtei*, beginning at about seven in the evening and lasting between two and three hours. If the guest is to be particularly honored, the host

may call in a GEISHA or a group of geisha to play the *shamisen* and dance for the party.

The most common alternative to an evening of eating and drinking is an invitation to a round of golf. Since memberships in golf courses can run from nearly ten million yen for a new, relatively unknown, and distant course to several hundred million yen for some courses convenient to the Tōkyō area, golf is regarded as an appropriately prestigious activity with which to reward customers. See also EXPENSE ACCOUNTS; ENKAI.

▶▶1352–1353

settlement → jidan

Settsu 摂津[市]

City in central Ōsaka Prefecture. Formerly a rice-producing area, Settsu is now a suburb of Ōsaka, with many industrial plants, transport companies, and warehouses. Pop: 87,453.

Settsu Corporation セッツ [株]

(Settsu). Manufacturer of paperboard and corrugated packaging products. Incorporated in 1947. In 1986 the company changed its name from Settsu Paperboard Mfg Co, Ltd, to Settsu Corporation. In the United States, it owns Uarco, Inc, the third-largest business form producer, and Medasonics, Inc, a medical equipment producer. Sales for the fiscal year ending March 1991 were ¥69.0 billion (US $502.9 million). Capitalization stood at ¥40.0 billion (US $291.5 million) in the same year. Headquarters are in the city of Amagasaki, Hyōgo Prefecture.

Seven Deities of Good Fortune 七福神

(Shichifukujin). The seven gods who are said to bring wealth and long life. Widely wor-

Continued on page 1354 ►

Seven Deities of Good Fortune

1 A set of *kimekomi*-type dolls representing the Seven Deities of Good Fortune.
a Fukurokuju, a deity of long life (sometimes identified with Jurōjin), can be recognized by his large head.
b Jurōjin, a deity of long life, is accompanied by a deer.
c Benzaiten, a deity of water and music, plays the *biwa* (a kind of lute).
d Bishamonten, a deity of good fortune, is dressed in armor.
e Hotei, a deity of good fortune and happiness, is known for his large stomach.
f Daikokuten, a deity of wealth, stands on a bag of rice.
g Ebisu, a deity of wealth and fishing, carries a large fish.
2 The Seven Deities of Good Fortune aboard a treasure ship. Placing a picture such as this under one's pillow on the night of 1 or 2 January is said to ensure that the year's first dream will be a lucky one.

Mixing Business and Pleasure

In the corporate culture of Japan, socializing plays an important part in solidifying business relationships.

Japanese businesspeople are fond of characterizing the difference between themselves and their Western counterparts as "wet" and "dry." To them, dry signifies a strictly businesslike association that is not concerned with developing long-term personal ties, while wet represents the more intimate approach to business favored in Japan.

Japanese managers tend not to make decisions based solely on sales presentations, no matter how persuasive, nor are they necessarily swayed by lower prices. Instead, they prefer to build close relationships with clients so that they will be able to sense any change in behavior that might affect the provision of goods and services. Business socializing (*settai*) is one way in which managers and clients can get to know each other and begin to build trusting relationships.

Cultivating the Client

Rather than using company expense accounts to woo new clients, the general practice in Japan is for a supplier to invite an important established client out for an evening of entertainment. This is done with great attention to business protocol. A section head (*kachō*) or department head (*buchō*) of the supplier company extends the invitation, by telephone or in person, to his counterpart in the client company. (Written invitations are sent only for large functions.)

The *buchō* or *kachō* of both firms attend the get-together, along with a few lower-ranking staff members. Care is taken to ensure that the corresponding associates of each guest are present. It would be inappropriate to invite a *buchō* from a client company to an outing attended only by junior staff from your own company. Likewise, the positions of those attending from the client company—assuming there are no schedule conflicts—can be indicative of how the client views the relationship. If major problems have occurred in the recent past, the client company may decline altogether, or make the host wish he had done so by voicing strident complaints during the course of the evening.

A typical evening out may begin with a leisurely dinner at a high-class Japanese restaurant serving *kaiseki ryōri* (Japanese haute cuisine). The meal, which usually consists of 10 or more courses, may total ¥40,000 (US $320) or more per person, depending on the restaurant and the menu selected. To avoid the social awkwardness of studying the menu, the courses are usually ordered in advance.

The meal begins with an exchange of pleasantries and a toast, often with beer. The host makes sure that the choice of beer does not clash with the corporate affiliation (*keiretsu*) of his guests. For example, employees from Mitsubishi Bank expect to be served Kirin beer, while those of Sumitomo Metal Industries expect Asahi beer. Over the next couple of hours, the conversation roams over a wide range of topics, from light subjects such as golf handicaps to weightier matters such as what the client did or did not like about the previous year's service. Some personal matters, like the marital status of the young people present, might also be brought up.

After dinner, the host may invite his guests for more drinks at one of the hostess bars or clubs in Tōkyō's fashionable Ginza or Akasaka districts. Budget permitting, he may have arranged in advance for limousines to take the party there and home afterward. The establishment chosen is sure to be one that the inviting company patronizes frequently, where the host is on friendly terms with the head hostess. The conversation at such places seldom touches on business, unless there is some pressing issue. Hostesses sitting with the guests help to lighten the mood. After an hour or so, if the guests are still sober enough, the host may take them to another bar nearby. Most likely this one will have a *karaoke* system, and everyone in the group will take turns singing. Each person is expected to sing at least one song or face a certain amount of ribbing. By 11 PM the revelers are usually ready to call it a night.

As the host bows farewell to his guests, he may review the cost of the evening and wonder if it was worth it. For six people, the total—including dinner, drinks at the hostess club and *karaoke* bar, complimentary gifts to take home, and chauffeur-driven limousine service—may have come to about ¥650,000 ($5,200). But if the client company places the order the host company hopes for, they may stand to make 10 times that or more.

A number of recent government measures have curbed the growth of business entertaining expenses, including a reduction in the amount that is tax-deductible. For companies capitalized at ¥50 million ($400,000) or more, no deduction is allowed, which means that all entertainment expenses must be paid out of taxable income. So unless the host in the previous example is

from a small company, his organization will have to absorb the full cost of the evening outing.

Social trends, such as the desire of young people to spend evenings with their families, are discouraging this type of entertaining. Likewise, as more women assume positions of responsibility, drinking in hostess bars is becoming less frequent. There is also increasing reluctance to use company expense accounts for purposes that many see as little more than conspicuous consumption.

Social Visits and Gift-Giving

Although everyday business with major clients is generally conducted at the level of assistant section head (*kakarichō*) or below, the section or department head pays a personal visit to key clients several times a year. In addition to extending his greetings (*aisatsu*), the purpose of these semiformal meetings is to feel the pulse of the relationship and obtain feedback on areas that may need improvement.

Paying calls on clients is also an expected courtesy at year-end and on the first or second working day of the new year. These seasonal visits are usually brief, and sometimes unannounced. If the client is out, the practice is to leave a name card with New Year's greetings.

Another important element of business socializing is gift-giving. Called *chūgen* in the summer (June–July) and *seibo* in the winter (December), gifts are sent to associates in the most important client companies. The value of the gift, which often consists of soft drinks, beer, or cookies, averages between ¥3,000 and ¥5,000 ($24–$40) but varies according to the position of the recipient. The gift may be considerably more for a valued customer in a powerful position. Gifts are also given when a business associate in a client company is promoted or retires.

Attending the weddings of close business associates and providing a suitable monetary gift is customary as well. Lower-level employees frequently send congratulatory telegrams on the marriage of peers.

Good Sports

Among businessmen in Japan, the most popular sport is golf, which provides a relaxed setting in which managers can discuss business. Since golf courses are crowded and reservations have to be made well in advance, minor annoyances such as rain, sleet, and fog do not usually deter golfers from playing their appointed rounds.

Golf is hardly a cheap pastime in Japan, where club membership fees range from several million yen to several hundred

million. The cost of a game is about ¥30,000 ($240) per head, which includes green fees, caddy costs, and a small present for each guest. Transportation is extra, and the cost of this varies according to the location of the course. The thoughtful host often provides a taxi or limousine to pick up his guests and take them home in the evening. The cost of this may exceed that of the game itself.

For nonmanagerial personnel, a common form of socializing is Mah-Jongg. Employees often invite clients, or are invited by them, for a game after work or sometimes on weekends. This game, however, is less popular among younger people.

Advice for Non-Japanese Managers

All personnel, especially those at the management level, will find that careful attention paid to the finer details of business socializing is useful, if not essential, in building strong relationships with Japanese clients. As a rule, major clients should be entertained at least once or twice a year. Golf outings of the same frequency are also important, provided, of course, both parties enjoy the game. Although entertaining in the evening is one of the more colorful aspects of business socializing, any kind of socializing serves the purpose of reinforcing business ties.

Taking clients to lunch is an appropriate way of getting together, but keep in mind that except for senior-level personnel, Japanese employees are not accustomed to spending two or three hours over the meal. So luncheon meetings tend to be rather brief by Western standards. Breakfast meetings, although common among foreign companies in Japan, are relatively rare among Japanese firms.

Paying visits to clients several times a year is highly recommended. Good occasions for such visits are the conclusion of a major contract and to introduce new staff members. Giving gifts at the semiannual summer and winter seasons—and when promotions take place—is also advisable, but the value of gifts should not exceed accepted practice.

Remember that while some aspects of business are formal in Japan, others, such as after-work get-togethers, can be very casual. Do not be surprised by an out-of-the-blue call inviting you for a drink in the evening. Although a prior engagement is an acceptable excuse for declining, the reason for such a call may be that some important issue has arisen, so always try to arrange an alternative time. Take business socializing seriously because it is an integral part of Japan's corporate culture.

C. Tait Ratcliffe

Illustrations by Odagiri Akira

Shakkyō Toward the end of this Nō play the character known as the lion attendant, played here by Kanze Yoshiyuki III, arrives to dance among peonies that have fallen from the sky.

shiped from the 15th to 17th century, the group usually consists of EBISU, DAIKOKUTEN, Bishamonten (Skt: Vaiśravaṇa), Benzaiten (Skt: Sarasvatī), Fukurokuju (sometimes identified as Jurōjin), Hotei, and Kichijōten (Skt: Śrīmahādevī) or Shōjō. The grouping includes gods and sages of Indian, Chinese, and Japanese origin. Specifically, Ebisu, Daikokuten, Bishamonten, and Kichijōten are considered gods of fortune; Ebisu is also venerated as the fishing deity; and Daikokuten in folk religion is identified with the mythic figure ŌKUNINUSHI NO MIKOTO. Benzaiten is the deity of water and music, and Fukurokuju the deity of long life. Hotei (Ch: Budai or Putai) is thought to be an eccentric Zen priest who was believed to be an incarnation of the bodhisattva Maitreya. Still popular is the custom of placing a picture of the seven gods, aboard a treasure ship, under one's pillow on the night of 1 January to guarantee that the first dream of the year will be a lucky one.

Seven-Eleven Japan Co, Ltd

[株]セブン-イレブン・ジャパン

(Sebun-Irebun Japan). Operator of convenience stores. Incorporated in 1973. Its parent company, ITŌ-YŌKADŌ CO, LTD, purchased the rights to franchise Seven-Eleven convenience stores in Japan from the owner of Seven-Eleven in the United States, Southland Corporation. When debt problems forced Southland to file for bankruptcy in 1990, Itō-Yōkadō agreed to buy 70 percent of the company. Seven-Eleven Japan is known for its computerized point-of-sale inventory-control system, which enables store managers to track sales and place orders. Sales for the fiscal year ending February 1991 totaled ¥932.0 billion (US $7.1 billion), and the company was capitalized at ¥17.2 billion (US $131.8 million) in the same year. Headquarters are in Tōkyō.

Seven Samurai 七人の侍

(Shichinin no samurai). A 1954 film directed by KUROSAWA AKIRA that has been called Kurosawa's best picture and one of the finest Japanese films ever made. It is an epic—well over three hours long in the uncut version—about a farm village menaced by bandits during the 15th-century period of civil wars. The village elders ask an unemployed samurai, Kambei (played by SHIMURA TAKASHI), to help them. He gathers six other warriors, and these seven samurai (one of whom is played by MIFUNE TOSHIRŌ) undertake to protect the village and defeat the bandits. This they eventually do although four of them are killed in battle. Peace restored, the remaining three gaze at the farmers, now busily planting their spring rice, and the leader, Kambei, says the famous closing lines of the film: "And again we lose. They, the farmers, they are the real winners." A heroic film, it affirms action in a good cause and yet at the same time questions it.

Seventeen-Article Constitution 十七条憲法

(Jūshichijō no Kempō). Principles of government said to have been promulgated by Prince SHŌTOKU in 604. Although the word kempō has traditionally been translated as "constitution," in this instance it has neither the connotation nor the binding power of the modern sense of the term. The Seventeen-Article Constitution is a set of moral injunctions based on Confucian and Buddhist doctrines to exhort government officials to work in harmony for the good of the central government. To this end the divine origin of the emperor's authority and the role of officials as the emperor's loyal servants are strongly emphasized. This "constitution" strongly influenced later codes, most notably the KEMMU SHIKIMOKU of 1336 and the 17-Article Code of the late 15th century (see ASAKURA TOSHIKAGE, 17-ARTICLE CODE OF).

sexagenary cycle →jikkan jūnishi

sex education 性教育

(seikyōiku). Sex education is not taught as an independent subject in Japanese public schools. Although there is now little debate over the necessity of providing guidance about sex to students, this is done in the context of other classroom studies; private counseling is also provided to students experiencing difficulties with sexual matters. Before the late 1960s, sex education had been limited to education in sexual morality and the prevention of venereal disease for teenage boys and girls. Education now includes lessons in sexual growth and the physical and psychological characteristics of boys and girls, as well as discussion of the social and personal facets of sex and love. While not yet taught in a systematized fashion, sex education is incorporated in the national curriculum guidelines in the following subject areas: health and physical education, science, social studies, and home economics. Guidance is also provided in homerooms, in student activity clubs, and by student counselors.

sex in Japanese folk culture 性と日本人

(sei to nihonjin). In traditional Japanese society, particularly among farming and fishing folk, sex was not considered something to be hidden, whether the relations were within or outside the family. In plays and dances at village festivals, the depiction of sexual activities and symbols was common; furthermore, men and women were permitted to engage in promiscuous sex on festival days. Such aspects of commoner life are rarely discussed in written sources; however, the great number of ethnographical studies by folklorists and cultural anthropologists during the last century attests to the accuracy of these occurrences (see EMBREE, JOHN FEE). Many of Japan's folk songs have erotic verses, although these verses are rarely heard in public performances today. Also, especially in the snowy areas of northern Japan, there are erotic tales and legends known as enshōtan.

The deification and worship of sexually explicit objects is widespread in Japan (see KONSEI) and takes many forms. Among the many festivals dealing with sex, a typical example is a pair of festivals held jointly on 15 March in Aichi Prefecture: the Henoko Matsuri (Penis Festival) at Tagata Shrine in the city of Komaki and the Ososo Matsuri (Vagina Festival) at Ōagata Shrine in the city of Inuyama. These festivals traditionally took place just before the onset of rice cultivation or at thanksgiving rites just after harvest.

seyakuin 施薬院

(medical dispensaries). Charitable institutions to provide medical care for the poor. Prince SHŌTOKU is said to have built one at the temple SHITENNŌJI in Ōsaka, but the first confirmed foundation was at the temple KŌFUKUJI

in 723. It was operated in conjunction with the HIDEN'IN, a refuge for the destitute and orphaned in the same compound. Similar facilities were built in Kyōto during the Heian period (794–1185) under the patronage of the FUJIWARA FAMILY. Later, such institutions survived at a few temples. The seyakuin in Kyōto was revived under TOYOTOMI HIDEYOSHI, and during the Edo period (1600–1868) the Yōjōsho, the shogunate hospital in Edo (now Tōkyō), and similar institutions were referred to as seyakuin.

shabushabu しゃぶしゃぶ

One-pot dish cooked at the table. Paper-thin slices of marbled beef are cooked by dipping them into a pot of simmering kombu (kelp) broth for a few seconds with chopsticks. To Japanese ears shabushabu is the sound made when one swishes meat in the broth. The morsels of meat are eaten with either a sesame-flavored sauce (tare) or a citron-flavored sauce (ponzu). Other ingredients, such as tōfu, Chinese cabbage, chrysanthemum leaves (shungiku), scallions, and mushrooms, are simmered in the stock.

shaga →irises

Shakai Minshu Rengō →United Social Democratic Party

Shakai Minshutō 社会民主党

(Socialist Democratic Party). Japan's first socialist party, formed on 18 May 1901 by ABE ISOO, KATAYAMA SEN, KŌTOKU SHŪSUI, KINOSHITA NAOE, and other members of the Shakai Shugi Kyōkai (see SHAKAI SHUGI KENKYŪKAI). The government proscribed the party two days later, when it announced its goals in several newspapers. See also POLITICAL PARTIES.

Shakai Minshutō 社会民衆党

(Socialist People's Party). A proletarian political party formed in December 1926 by the right wing of the RŌDŌ NŌMINTŌ (Labor-Farmer Party). The first chairman was ABE ISOO and the secretary-general KATAYAMA TETSU. It advocated anticommunist socialism and parliamentarianism and drew support from the SŌDŌMEI (Japan Federation of Labor) and the Nippon Kaiin Kumiai (Japan Seamen's Union). At the time of the MANCHURIAN INCIDENT of 1931, the party announced its policy of supporting Japanese expansionism abroad. It was split by internal dissension in April 1932 and in July of that year merged with the Zenkoku Rōnō Taishūtō (National Labor-Farmer Masses Party) to form the SHAKAI TAISHŪTŌ (Socialist Masses Party).

Shakai Shugi Kenkyūkai 社会主義研究会

(Society for the Study of Socialism). The first Japanese socialist study group; founded in October 1898; members included KATAYAMA SEN, KŌTOKU SHŪSUI, and ABE ISOO. In January 1900 it was reorganized as the Shakai Shugi Kyōkai, some of whose members in 1901 formed Japan's first socialist party, the SHAKAI MINSHUTŌ. See also POLITICAL PARTIES.

Shakai Taishūtō 社会大衆党

(Socialist Masses Party). Moderate-leftist political party formed in July 1932 through a merger of the Zenkoku Rōnō Taishūtō (National Labor-Farmer Masses Party) and the SHAKAI MINSHUTŌ, with ABE ISOO as chairman. Attempting to occupy a middle position in the polarized political world of the 1930s, the party was inevitably riven with contradictions. It favored economic relief for the impoverished countryside but criticized the rising military budget. Abroad, it supported Japanese aggression in Manchuria but opposed Japan's withdrawal from the League of Nations; it advocated international cooperation, but in 1937 declared the invasion of China a "holy war." The only "leftist" party legally allowed to operate in the 1930s, it espoused the nationalistic and militaristic policies of ASŌ HISASHI, the leader of its dominant faction. It purged members caught up in the repression of liberals and leftists known as the POPULAR FRONT INCIDENT. Thereafter the dispute between the party's main faction and its leftist faction became more serious. In July 1940 the party was dissolved. See also POLITICAL PARTIES.

Shakaitō   車会党

(literally, "Rickshaw Party," a play on its homophone "Shakaitō," meaning "Socialist Party"). A political association of rickshawmen established in October 1882 in Tōkyō by JIYŪTŌ (Liberal Party) politician OKUMIYA TAKEYUKI and the rickshawman "boss" Miura Kamekichi to oppose horse-drawn streetcars (see HORSECARS). The party was dissolved in December 1882.

Shakkintō → Kommintō

Shakkyō   石橋

(The Stone Bridge). NŌ play. Author unknown. It is classified as a gobamme-mono ("part-five play"). The monk Jakushō (d 1034; the waki or subordinate character) has traveled to China and reached the slopes of the mountain Shōryōsen (Seiryōzan; Ch: Qingliangshan or Ch'ing-liang-shan). About to cross a narrow stone bridge spanning a chasm, he is stopped by a woodcutter (the maejite or main character at the beginning of a play) who tells him that the bridge leads to a pure land inaccessible to common travelers. Soon red and white peonies begin to fall from the sky, and the lion attendant (the nochijite or main character at the end of a play) of the bodhisattva Monju (Skt: Mañjuśrī) arrives to dance among the flowers. This play is often performed as hannō ("half Nō"), in which the first half of the play is omitted and only the latter half is staged.

Shakotan Peninsula   積丹半島

(Shakotan Hantō). Located in western Hokkaidō; part of Niseko Shakotan-Otaru Coast Quasi-National Park. It juts into the Sea of Japan and has a hilly terrain with little level land. Stretches of sea cliffs extend along the coast. The fishing ports of Yoichi, Iwanai, and Furubira, which once flourished as bases for herring fishing, are found here.

Shaku Chōkū → Orikuchi Shinobu

shakuhachi   尺八

Vertical bamboo flute with a notched mouthpiece and five finger holes. It takes its name from the standard length of the instrument in traditional measuring units, 1 shaku, 8 (hachi) sun, or 54.5 centimeters (21.46 in). The shakuhachi is made from madake bamboo (Phyllostachys bambusoides). The bamboo is severed near the root, which becomes the bell of the instrument. Four finger holes are placed equidistant on the front face, with an upper thumb hole on the rear face, and the inner bore is lacquered.

Imported from China with other imperial court instruments, the shakuhachi first appeared in Japan in the late 7th century. This

early shakuhachi, with six finger holes in the Chinese manner, was a regular member of the Japanese court orchestra (GAGAKU) until the end of the 9th century. Occasional historical references to the shakuhachi continue to appear throughout the Kamakura (1185–1333) and Muromachi (1333–1568) periods, but when and how the six-hole form gave way to the five-hole instrument is unclear.

In the early 16th century, the shakuhachi began its association with the wandering beggars called komosō ("straw-mat priests"). In the 17th century, the players became known as komusō ("priests of nothingness"). The komusō comprised a sect of Zen Buddhism called the Fuke sect, the theoretical basis of which was the playing of shakuhachi as a spiritual discipline. They claimed legitimacy by tracing their origins to the 9th-century Chinese priest Fuke (Ch: Puhua or P'u-hua). The Fuke sect was granted official recognition by the government in the 17th century, and licensed komusō were given the exclusive right to play the shakuhachi. The Zen practice of playing the shakuhachi was maintained throughout the Edo period and even after the abolition of the Fuke sect by the new Meiji government in 1871. Many performers encouraged the development of the shakuhachi as a secular instrument, while others strove to revitalize the Zen tradition with its unique repertoire of spiritually oriented solo pieces (honkyoku). Of the various schools that developed, the Myōan, Kinko, and Tozan schools are the best known. The Myōan represents the original Zen ideals of the Fuke sect; the Kinko descends from the 18th century but developed in later years with stylistic influence from koto and shamisen music; and the Tozan, founded in 1896, signals a new departure under the influence of Western music. See also MUSIC, TRADITIONAL.

shakunage → rhododendrons

Shaku nihongi   釈日本紀

The oldest extant commentary on the chronicle NIHON SHOKI (or Nihongi; 720); compiled by Shintō priest Urabe Kanekata (late 13th–early 14th centuries). Kanekata collected court records of Heian period (794–1185) discussions of the Nihon shoki and published them in the 28 volumes of the Shaku nihongi. The work is valued for its inclusion of materials that have not survived elsewhere, including the Kōnin shiki (810–824, Private Records of the Kōnin Era) and fragments of the FUDOKI.

Shaku Sōen   釈宗演

(1859–1919). Monk of the RINZAI SECT of Zen Buddhism. Born in Takahama, Wakasa Province (now part of Fukui Prefecture). Studied at the temples MYŌSHINJI in Kyōto and ENGAKUJI in Kamakura; graduate of Keiō University in 1887. He traveled extensively in Ceylon (now Sri Lanka) and India. In 1892 he became the abbot general of Engakuji and its dependent abbeys. In 1905–06 he lectured in the United States and held the first Zen meditation (zazen) session there, a seed cultivated by his disciple D. T. SUZUKI. Sōen died at Engakuji. His writings are collected in Shaku Sōen zenshū (10 vols).

shakuyaku → peonies

shakyō   写経

Devotional copying of Buddhist scriptures (sutras), often regarded as a religious service

Shakotan Peninsula Before modern navigation, the rugged coastline of this Hokkaidō peninsula made fishing treacherous.

or as spiritual training. In Japan, the earliest mention of this practice is in the NIHON SHOKI (720, Chronicle of Japan), which says that the imperial court ordered a version of the DAIZŌKYŌ copied at the temple Kawaradera in 673. The court, aristocratic families, and temples built scriptoria (shakyōsho; literally, "sutra-copying offices") in the Nara period (710–794), when shakyō was performed for the well-being of deceased ancestors.

Sutras were most commonly copied using a brush and Chinese ink on a variety of media from paper to tiles and wooden tablets. Among them were lavishly decorated manuscripts called SŌSHOKUKYŌ, one of the most famous of which is the Heike nōkyō (1164), an illustrated sutra executed in gold and silver ink on dyed paper. Sutra copying as a means of disseminating the Buddhist scriptures declined from the late Heian period (794–1185) onward with the introduction of woodblock-printing technology from Song (Sung) dynasty China. It continued to be practiced, however, as a form of spiritual training and supplication and is still common in contemporary Japan. One of the most frequently copied texts is the HEART SUTRA.

shamanism   シャーマニズム

(shāmanizumu). The shaman is a particular kind of religious specialist, of whom the prototype is found in Siberia. Characteristically, shamans receive their "call" in a visitation by a supernatural spirit during which their souls are dispatched to the underworld to undergo terrifying initiatory experiences. After ascetic training, they emerge gifted with powers of healing, prophesy, and exorcism, enabling them to act for the community as medicine man, oracular mouthpiece, and sometimes guide to the afterlife.

In Japan, where shamanism displays influences from both northern Asia and the South Pacific, early chronicles show shamanic practices in the YAMATO COURT of the 6th and 7th century. Because of sinicizing reforms in the mid-7th century, however, these were abandoned by the central government and relegated to the level of folk religion. Present-day practitioners are principally of two types: (1) the MIKO, or medium, usually a woman, whose trance enables a spiritual being (kami) to speak through her and (2) the YAMABUSHI, an ascetic whose powers include healing, exorcism, out-of-body travel, and summoning kami into the body of the medium.

Mediums and ascetics used to be employed in tandem at village rituals seeking an oracle (takusen matsuri) to pronounce upon the village's future. Though such rituals are almost extinct, the ascetic's services as a

shakuhachi This type of bamboo flute is central to Japanese traditional music and has also been employed by contemporary composers and jazz musicians.

shamisen Musician Takahashi Chikuzan plays the *tsugaru-jamisen*, which has especially thick strings and fingerboard and is plucked with a heavier plectrum than is the standard *shamisen*.

healer and exorcist are still in wide demand. Ascetic training includes fasting, bathing in icy water, and reciting a sacred text; for *yamabushi*, it also requires a retreat to a holy mountain.

The Tōhoku (northern Honshū) region's *itako* are examples of mediums who still operate alone rather than in conjunction with ascetics. Blind from birth, these women are apprenticed to a teacher and undergo rigorous training culminating in an initiatory marriage to a god (*kamizukeshiki*), thereby allowing them to act as professional mouthpieces for the spirits. However, *itako* rarely experience the call and internal initiation characteristic of true shamans.

Modern examples of the shaman in Japan occur among founders of NEW RELIGIONS. Most successful new sects were inspired by a man or woman exhibiting shamanistic traits, such as NAKAYAMA MIKI, founder of Tenrikyō. See also DEGUCHI NAO; KITAMURA SAYO.

shamisen   三味線

Three-stringed plucked lute. Originally associated with the urban world of the pleasure quarters and theaters of the Edo period (1600–1868), it later became a concert instrument as well. It is called *samisen* in the Kyōto-Ōsaka area and *sangen* when used in classical chamber music. It developed from an instrument apparently imported from the Ryūkyū Islands in the mid-16th century and may be of mainland Chinese origin. Both the Okinawan (*sanshin* or *jamisen*) and the Chinese (*sanxian* or *san-hsien*) forms are still used, but they differ greatly from the instrument used in Japan.

Shamisen come in many different sizes, varying from 1.1 to 1.4 meters (3.6 to 4.6 ft) in length, and are generally distinguished by the thickness of their unfretted fingerboard. The wooden parts of *shamisen* are made of red sandalwood, mulberry, or quince, and the heads that cover the front and back of the body are cat or dog skin. Pegs and plectrums are ivory, wood, or plastic. Strings are twisted silk or nylon. *Shamisen* notation indicates intervals rather than specific pitches. Three basic tunings are *honchōshi* (a fourth and a fifth), *niagari* (a fifth and a fourth), and *sansagari* (two fourths). See also MUSICAL INSTRUMENTS.

Shandong (Shantung) Expeditions   山東出兵

(Santō Shuppei). A series of three Japanese military interventions in Shandong Province, China, ordered by the TANAKA GIICHI cabinet in 1927–28 in attempt to block the Northern Expedition mounted by CHIANG KAI-SHEK in order to unify China under the rule of the Nationalist Government.

The first of the Japanese expeditions to Shandong took place between May and September of 1927. Some 4,000 Japanese troops were sent to the Qingdao (Tsingtao) and Jinan (Tsinan) areas on the pretext of protecting Japanese residents from the advancing Nationalist forces. The troops were withdrawn when Chiang temporarily suspended his northward advance. When the Northern Expedition was resumed in 1928, Japan intervened once again. This second Shandong Expedition resulted in a clash between Japanese and Nationalist forces at Jinan (known as the Jinan Incident) in May 1928, with significant military and civilian casualties on the Chinese side. This military confrontation occasioned the third dispatch of Japanese forces, in even greater numbers, and their stationing throughout Shandong Province and other parts of northern China. Japanese troops were finally withdrawn in March 1929 after the signing of an agreement resolving the Jinan Incident, but the net result of the three Shandong Expeditions was primarily an intensification of the anti-Japanese movement in China.

Shandong (Shantung) Question   山東問題

(Santō Mondai). Controversy over Japanese control of China's Shandong Province that took place from the Paris Peace Conference of 1919 to the WASHINGTON CONFERENCE of 1921–22.

Shandong, a peninsula jutting into the Yellow Sea south of Manchuria, early attracted the attention of foreign powers. Seeking a foothold for Asian naval and economic expansion, Germany seized the principal port of Qingdao (Tsingtao) in 1896 and also obtained a concession to build a railway linking the city with the provincial capital of Jinan (Tsinan).

When war broke out in Europe in August 1914, Japan, which was allied with Great Britain, declared war on Germany and invaded Qingdao in September 1914. Japan demanded that China recognize the transfer of German rights in Shandong to Japan as one of the TWENTY-ONE DEMANDS. The Chinese viewed any Japanese-German agreement on the future of the region as invalid. Shandong became a symbol of China's nationalistic resistance to Japanese imperialism, and the Shandong Question was born.

The Chinese appealed to the United States to intercede, but the United States only issued a declaration that it would not recognize any agreement concerning China that violated the OPEN DOOR POLICY. Undeterred, the Japanese entered into secret agreements with Britain, France, and Russia in which these nations pledged to support Japanese claims for Shandong.

During the Paris Peace Conference, Japanese determination to hold onto its gains led Chinese delegates to refuse to sign the peace treaty. In China, university students, merchants, and intellectuals began a boycott of Japanese goods which developed into the MAY FOURTH MOVEMENT of 1919. Finally, as part of an arrangement worked out during the Washington Conference, all Japanese forces were evacuated from the area and China indemnified Japan for the cost of improving and maintaining the railway.

Shanghai Incident   上海事変

(Shanhai Jiken). Military confrontation between Chinese and Japanese troops in Shanghai from 28 January to 5 May 1932. It marked the first clash between the two nations in China proper following the MANCHURIAN INCIDENT of 18 September 1931. While Japan's Guandong (Kwantung) Army held virtually complete control of Manchuria, the cabinet of WAKATSUKI REIJIRŌ was replaced by a cabinet under INUKAI TSUYOSHI, who was more inclined to accept the military faits accomplis in Manchuria. China retaliated with a boycott of Japanese goods.

In Shanghai on 18 January 1932 Japanese Buddhist monks were attacked by a Chinese mob. The incident, which had actually been fomented by a few Japanese officers, generated tension between the city's Japanese and Chinese populations. On 28 January Chinese army forces skirmished with Japanese marines. Skirmishes escalated to extensive fighting between armies of both countries until the Chinese withdrew on 3 March. The two countries signed a truce agreement on 5 May that provided for a demilitarized zone around Shanghai's international settlement, an end to the boycott, and the evacuation of Japanese forces from that area.

It is not clear why the Japanese provoked such an incident, which cost Japan dearly in the long run. By involving the international community of Shanghai in its war against China, it turned the Manchurian Incident into an international crisis. The British government sought cooperation from the United States to check further Japanese expansion. Although little came of this cooperation, Japan's disregard for foreign rights and interests only undermined whatever good will it could still expect from other nations. How to prevent Japan from threatening the security and stability of East Asia would become the principal Asian issue for China and the Western powers. Ten days after the signing of the Shanghai truce agreement, Prime Minister Inukai and members of his government were assassinated by right-wing ultra-nationalists (see MAY 15TH INCIDENT), an act that put an end to party politics in prewar Japan and increased the importance of the military.

Shanghai International Settlement   上海共同租界

(Shanhai Kyōdō Sokai). Formed in 1863 by the merger of the British and US settlements north of the old walled city of Shanghai, the Shanghai International Settlement was a product of the treaty port system whereby foreign merchants, under the principle of extraterritoriality, governed areas leased in perpetuity. After the signing of the Treaty of SHIMONOSEKI (1895), Shanghai became the most important manufacturing, commercial, and financial center in China. The settlement also provided a sanctuary for Chinese dissidents. At the same time, since it was ruled by foreigners through the Shanghai Municipal Council, it became the target for radical and nationalistic movements as a symbol of foreign exploitation.

In the 1920s an increase in union organizing and strikes in Shanghai culminated in the 1925 MAY 30TH INCIDENT. Patriotic sentiment emerged again in 1936 with the growth of the NATIONAL SALVATION ASSOCIATION in response to Japan's aggression in North China.

Sharaku   写楽

(fl 1794–95). Also known as Tōshūsai Sharaku. UKIYO-E artist who specialized in portraits of KABUKI actors. A relatively obscure artist in his own day, Sharaku was first discovered in the Meiji period (1868–1912) by Westerners. Over the years various hypotheses have been put forward concerning

Sharaku

The enigmatic *ukiyo-e* artist Sharaku's entire known body of work was created in a nine-month period in 1794–95. Little known in his own day, his works have been highly valued by later collectors.

▲ Portrait of *kabuki* actors Segawa Tomisaburō II and Nakamura Manse in female roles. 1794. Tōkyō National Museum.

▲ Portrait of the *sumō* wrestler Dai-dōzan. 1794. Woodblock print. MOA Museum of Art, Shizuoka Prefecture.

▶ Portrait of the kabuki actor Segawa Tomisaburō II playing a female role. 1794. Woodblock print. Tōkyō National Museum.

◀ Portrait of the kabuki actor Arashi Ryūzō in a male role. 1794. Tōkyō National Museum.

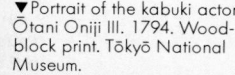

▼ Portrait of the kabuki actor Ōtani Oniji III. 1794. Woodblock print. Tōkyō National Museum.

Sharaku's true identity and the course of his career. His known oeuvre consists of 145 color woodblock prints, a group of 8 block copies of drawings for an illustrated book, and a group of 10 drawings of wrestlers, only 1 of which survives. The woodblock prints were all published in Edo (now Tōkyō) by Tsutaya Jūzaburō (1750–97).

Prints—Sharaku's earliest and most important work is a series of 28 large half-length portraits of 30 kabuki actors printed with dark mica backgrounds that reflect a metallic sheen like a mirror. The actors are portrayed in roles they acted in plays at the three major Edo kabuki theaters in the fifth month of 1794.

The second group of Sharaku prints is a series of seven large sheets with full-length portraits of pairs of actors in plays performed in the summer of 1794. Most of these prints have a light mica background, often with a glossy pinkish cast. It seems likely that an eighth print, the portrait of the theater director Miyako Dennai, was published at the same time since it has the same background.

Sharaku also designed 30 panel prints depicting full-length portraits of actors in the summer plays, against plain gray or yellow backgrounds. Many of these panels were designed in groups forming larger compositions of two or more figures.

Sharaku produced 60 portraits of actors in plays performed in late 1794, including 47 panel prints, 11 large heads in medium format with yellow backgrounds, and 2 prints in medium format designed as a memorial for a deceased actor. In addition, he designed 4 portraits of wrestlers. Sharaku's last prints were 10 full-length panel portraits of actors in plays performed in the first month of 1795, 2 portraits of wrestlers, 2 pictures of warriors, and a picture of Ebisu, one of the Seven Deities of Good Fortune.

Drawings—Eight block copies for an unpublished book of actors' portraits may have been drawn by Sharaku or by a professional draftsman from Sharaku's designs at the end of 1794. Sharaku's last recorded works seem to have been a series of 10 drawings, apparently for an unpublished series of full-length woodblock portraits of pairs of *sumō* wrestlers. The one extant drawing of the series may well be the only surviving work direct from the artist's hand.

Influence—Sharaku's influence on his contemporaries has been exaggerated. They may have found license in Sharaku's work for their own exaggerations in pose and expression, but these artists were not much affected by his vision or style of portraiture. Sharaku's greatest influence was not on contemporary artists, but on collectors and writers of his own and later periods who have been deeply moved by the power and dignity of his work.

sharebon   洒落本

(literally, "witty book"). A genre of Edo-period (1600–1868) popular fiction (GESAKU) that flowered in the 1770s and 1780s. It is concerned exclusively with life in the pleasure quarters, mainly in the capital city, Edo (now Tōkyō). The prototypes in the 1750s were mock-learned guidebooks to the pleasure quarters. The pattern of most subsequent *sharebon* was fixed about 1770 by the pseudonymous author of *Yūshi hōgen* (Playboy's Dialect). Notable writers in the genre were ŌTA NAMPO; Hōraisanjin Kikyō; Tanishi Kingyo; and SANTŌ KYŌDEN, also an important UKIYO-E artist.

The central protagonist of standard *share-bon* is the TSŪ or *tōrimono*, the sophisticated man-about-town, well-informed about the pleasure quarters and fashions. Through stock characters and colloquial dialogue, the author enumerates the minute details of the quarter's customs. This demonstration of mastery of arcane detail that only the insider could know was called *ugachi* ("piercing").

An obsession with *ugachi* in the 1780s led to *sharebon* in which the more sordid side of life in the quarters was meticulously recorded. Morishima Chūryō (also known as Manzōtei; 1756?—1810?), a disciple of HIRAGA GENNAI (1728–80), tried to restore to *sharebon* its original gaiety. His *Inaka shibai* (1787, Village Theater) ignored the pleasure quarters altogether, depicting rustic scenes instead. He pioneered the way for the KOK-KEIBON writers who emerged as the literary heirs of the comic aspects of *sharebon*. A shift in emphasis, to stories of "true love," led to an entirely new genre, the NINJŌBON.

Sharp Corporation   シャープ[株]

(Shāpu). Comprehensive electronics manufacturer, producing liquid crystal displays (LCDs), televisions, audio equipment, videocassette recorders (VCRs), home appliances, office automation and communications equipment, computers, semiconductors, integrated circuits, solar cells, and other electronic products. The company began operations in metal processing in Tōkyō in 1912. Three years later, founder Hayakawa Tokuji (1893–1980) invented the Ever Sharp mechanical pencil, from which the Sharp Corporation name is derived. Hayakawa succeeded in mass-producing the Sharp Dyne AC vacuum-tube radio set in 1929 and television sets in 1953. In 1964 Sharp introduced the world's first all-transistor-diode electronic desktop calculator, followed by pioneering developments in integrated circuit technology. Sharp developed the world's first long-life laser in 1981. More recently, it introduced the super-semiconductive magnetic sensor. Sharp's research and development network consists of 12 labora-

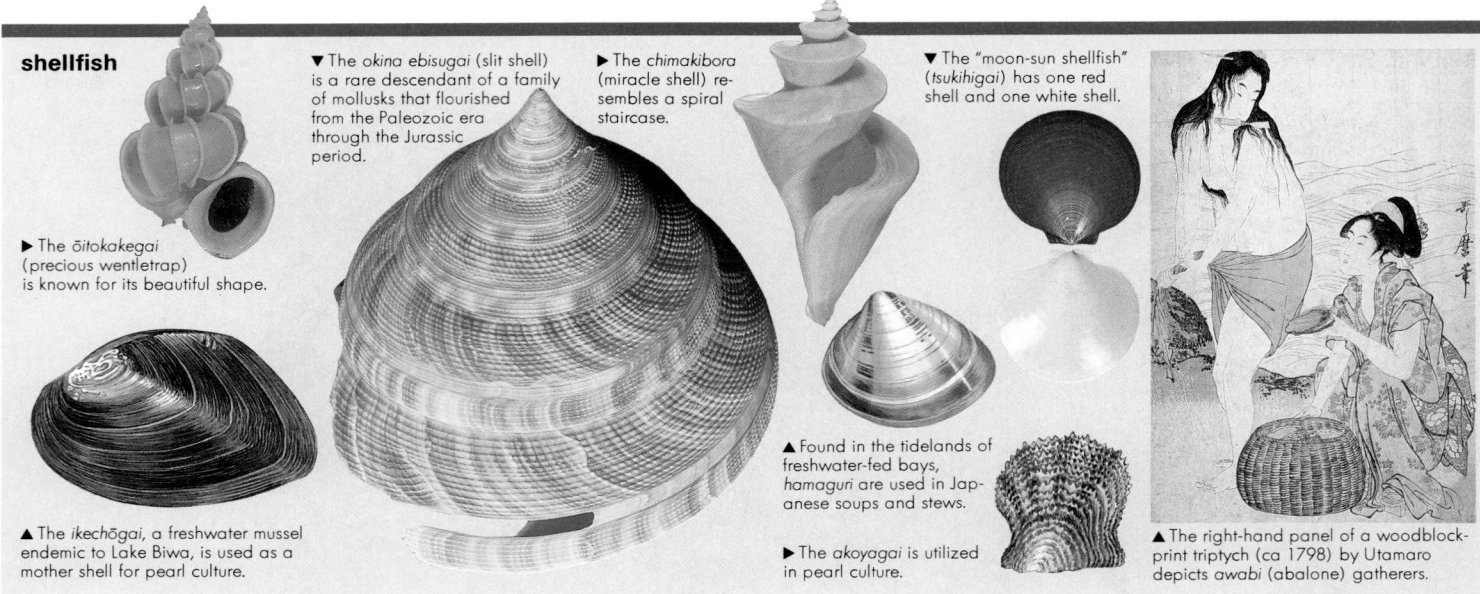

shellfish

▶ The *ōitokakegai* (precious wentletrap) is known for its beautiful shape.

▼ The *okina ebisugai* (slit shell) is a rare descendant of a family of mollusks that flourished from the Paleozoic era through the Jurassic period.

▶ The *chimakibora* (miracle shell) resembles a spiral staircase.

▼ The "moon-sun shellfish" (*tsukihigai*) has one red shell and one white shell.

▲ The *ikechōgai*, a freshwater mussel endemic to Lake Biwa, is used as a mother shell for pearl culture.

▲ Found in the tidelands of freshwater-fed bays, *hamaguri* are used in Japanese soups and stews.

▶ The *akoyagai* is utilized in pearl culture.

▲ The right-hand panel of a woodblock-print triptych (ca 1798) by Utamaro depicts awabi (abalone) gatherers.

tories employing more than 6,000 researchers. Overseas, Sharp maintains sales subsidiaries in 13 countries, representative offices in 9 countries, and manufacturing bases in 27 countries. Its products now reach consumers in 135 countries worldwide. Sales for the fiscal year ending March 1991 totaled ¥1.2 trillion (US $8.7 billion). Capitalization stood at ¥171.2 billion (US $1.2 billion) in the same year. Headquarters are in Ōsaka.

Shasekishū 沙石集

(Collection of Sand and Pebbles). Collection of 134 didactic tales composed by the Buddhist monk Mujū Ichien (1227–1312) between 1279 and 1283. Like similar collections of legends and anecdotes (see SETSUWA BUNGAKU), the *Shasekishū* reveals a lack of sustained narrative and character development. However, it records the practical and earthy aspects of ordinary life in the Kamakura period (1185–1333), and it is a valuable document on the popular Buddhism of its time. It is sometimes classified as a vernacular tract or *kana hōgo*. The work left its impression on the SASAMEGOTO, a theoretical work on RENGA (linked verse) by SHINKEI. The KYŌGEN farce *Busu* also owes its inspiration to the *Shasekishū*.

The author, Mujū Ichien, was born in Kamakura. He took the tonsure in 1243. Standard biographies identify Mujū as a ZEN monk of the RINZAI SECT by virtue of his having become, in 1261, a disciple of ENNI (1202–80), founder of the temple Tōfukuji; but the bias of Mujū's writings is toward the eclecticism of the TENDAI SECT, encompassing Shintō, Shingon, Zen, and Pure Land doctrines. In 1262, with the support of HŌJŌ TOKIYORI (1227–63), Mujū rebuilt a rural temple in what is now the city of Nagoya, renaming it Chōboji. Mujū's other works include a second collection of Buddhist *setsuwa*, the *Zōtanshū* (Collection of Casual Digressions), completed in 1305; *Shōzaishū* (Collection of Sacred Assets), a doctrinal work composed in 1299; and *Tsuma kagami* (Mirror for Women), a Buddhist tract thought to have been written in 1300.

shasō 社倉

Granaries established by village organizations and domainal governments during the Edo period (1600–1868) as a precaution against famines. In contrast to central government charitable granaries (*gisō*), *shasō* received voluntary contributions according to each participant's income and status. Based on systems in China and Korea, the idea was introduced into Japan by YAMAZAKI ANSAI. The first *shasō* was established in 1655 by HOSHINA MASAYUKI; most were abolished after the Meiji Restoration (1868).

Shaw, Glenn William ショー, G. W.

(1886–1961). American educator, writer, translator, and government official, active in Japan from 1916 to 1940 and from 1949 to 1957. Born in Los Angeles; graduate of Colorado College. Prior to World War II he lived in Ōsaka, where he taught and worked as a radio broadcaster and newspaper columnist while translating a number of works by important modern Japanese writers into English. From 1940 to 1949 he served in a civilian capacity with the US Navy, first as director of the Navy Language School in Boulder, Colorado, where he organized Japanese-language instruction, and then as dean of the Navy Intelligence School in Washington, DC. He returned to Japan in 1949 as a State Department historian, and served with the American Embassy in Tōkyō as a cultural officer from 1952 until his retirement in 1957. His published works include *Ōsaka Sketches* (1929), *Japanese Scrap-Book* (1932), and *Living in Japan* (1936), as well as translations of novels and short stories by Japanese writers such as KURATA HYAKUZŌ, FUTABATEI SHIMEI, KIKUCHI KAN, and AKUTAGAWA RYŪNOSUKE.

Shayō 斜陽

(tr *The Setting Sun*, 1956). Novel by DAZAI OSAMU (1909–48); published 1947. Set amid the ruins of post–World War II Japan, *Shayō* describes the relationships between Kazuko, a divorced woman approaching 30; her mother; her brother, Naoji; and a novelist, Uehara Jirō. Bankrupt in the economic chaos of the time, Kazuko and her mother, an elderly and dying member of the aristocracy, are forced to surrender their home in Tōkyō for less opulent surroundings in Izu. Naoji, recently released from the army, where he became addicted to drugs, suddenly appears, compounding the difficulties of life. In the company of Uehara, Naoji leads a life of dissipation and alcoholism, placing Kazuko under extreme emotional and financial duress. Their mother dies and Naoji, who believes he has inherited her aristocratic nature, commits suicide. Kazuko, pregnant from an affair with Uehara, remains to carry on: her role, so she believes, is to forge a new moral order. *Shayō*, which sets Kazuko's desire for a moral revolution against the destruction that surrounds her, presents an apt portrait of Japan in its immediate postwar years.

shellfish 貝

(*kai*). Invertebrate animals with univalve or bivalve shells that belong to the phylum Mollusca. For crustaceans, see SHRIMPS, PRAWNS, AND LOBSTERS; CRABS; HORSESHOE CRAB.

About 6,000 species of marine shellfish are found in Japan. On the Pacific coast are warm-water shellfish, such as the *takaragai* (cowrie; genus *Cypraea*) and *imogai* (cone shell; genus *Conus*); they decrease in number toward the north. Cold-water shellfish, such as the *ezobai* (whelk; genus *Buccinum*) and *ezobora* (neptune whelk; genus *Neptunea*), decrease toward the south until the molluscan fauna show major changes at the Bōsō Peninsula. A similar distribution is seen on the Sea of Japan coast, but there is no distinct boundary between these two elements. In the Inland Sea and large bays, there are shellfish different from those mentioned above. They are the remains of species distributed in Japan when it was still connected with the continent.

About 90 species of freshwater shellfish are found in Japan, many of which are similar to those of the Asian continent. In particular Lake Biwa, which formed during the Miocene epoch of the Tertiary period, abounds in endemic species, such as the *ikechōgai* (*Hyriopsis schlegelii*), *setashijimi* (*Corbicula sandai*), and *nagatanishi* (*Heterogen longispira*).

Scientifically, the most interesting Japanese species is the *okina ebisugai* (slit shell; *Mikadotrochus beyrichi*) belonging to the family Pleurotomariidae, which flourished from the Paleozoic era; of 12 remaining species in this family, 6, including the *okina ebisugai*, are found in Japan. The *ōitokakegai* (precious wentletrap; *Epitonium scalare*) and *chimakibora* (miracle shell; *Thatcheria mirabilis*) are notable for their beautiful shapes.

Among the snails, the important edible mollusks are ABALONES (*awabi*), *sazae* (spiny turban shell; *Turbo cornutus*), *bai* (ivory shell; *Babylonia japonica*), *ezobai* (*Buccinum middendorfi*), and *ezobora* (*Neptunea polycostata*). Among the important bivalves are the *asari* (Japanese littleneck; *Ruditapes philippinarum*), *hamaguri* (*Meretrix lusoria*), *bakagai* (*Mactra chinensis*), *ubagai* (*Spisula sybillae*), *magaki* (Japanese oyster; *Crassostrea gigas*), and *hotategai* (Ezo giant scallop; *Patinopecten yessoensis*). The *akoyagai* (*Pinctada fucata martensii*) and the *ikechōgai*, a freshwater mussel living in Lake Biwa, are used as mother shells for pearl culture.

Shell mounds attest the importance shellfish had in the life of the ancient Japanese. Edward Sylvester MORSE first took notice of Japanese shell mounds during his visit to Japan to study brachiopod shellfish in 1877. The research initiated by Morse on the ŌMORI SHELL MOUNDS, which he had noticed from a train window, was the beginning of Japanese archaeology.

In addition to the use of shells in fashioning various implements and in inlay, nobles of the court in Kyōto during the Heian period (794–1185) played a game called KAI-AWASE, or shell matching. The *kai oke* (shell pot) used to hold the shells for this game came to be a part of the bridal trousseau in the Edo period (1600–1868).

shell mounds 貝塚

(*kaizuka*). Heaps of shells or kitchen middens left by shellfish eaters, dating from the Jōmon (ca 10,000 BC–ca 300 BC) and, to a lesser extent, Yayoi (ca 300 BC–ca AD 300) and Kofun (ca 300–710) periods. Besides shells these mounds contain animal, fish, and bird bones; small quantities of floral remains, such as nuts and gourds; discarded cultural materials, especially pottery; and human burials, and thus serve as valuable repositories of archaeological information. About 3,000 shell mounds are known from Hokkaidō (see MOYORO SHELL MOUND) to Okinawa Prefecture (see IHA SHELL MOUND; OGIDŌ SHELL MOUND). Most are found along the eastern coast of Japan where warm water and natural sandy inlets and beaches provided good conditions for shellfish breeding; nearly half of the known total are concentrated in the Kantō region.

Shell mounds of the Initial and Early Jōmon periods (ca 7500 BC–ca 3500 BC) are only of modest dimensions, but in Middle and especially Late Jōmon times (ca 3500 BC–ca 1000 BC) they increased greatly in size (see KASORI SHELL MOUNDS). Dependence on shellfish decreased after the beginning of wet-rice agriculture in the Early Yayoi period (ca 300 BC–ca 100 BC); however, sporadic disposal of shells in midden form continued in peripheral areas until modern times.

Shell mounds are used to reconstruct the prehistoric environment. Since specific shell species survive only within certain temperature ranges, their presence in the shell mounds indicates that those conditions prevailed in the area when the shells were collected. Shell rings indicate that about 65 percent of the collecting was done in the spring. Thus prehistoric coastal environments, fluctuations in water temperature, and changes from marine to freshwater shells can be recognized. Moreover, the geographical distribution of shell mounds when matched with their contents can be used to identify prehistoric shorelines. Skeletal remains of the Jōmon people seldom survive in Japan's acidic soil, but those that were buried in the shell mounds have been preserved by the calcium content of the shells. Several thousand skeletons have been recovered. See also MUKŌGAOKA SHELL MOUND; ŌMORI SHELL MOUNDS.

Shen Nanpin (Shen Nan-p'in) 沈南蘋

(fl mid-18th century; J: Chin Nampin, or Shin Nampin). Chinese practitioner of BIRD-AND-FLOWER PAINTING. Real name Shen Quan (Shen Ch'üan; J: Chin Sen, or Shin Sen). Born in Zhejiang (Chekiang) Province. In 1731 he traveled to Japan where he remained for approximately two years. Despite the brevity of his visit, his influence was considerable and brought about the flourishing of colorful and realistic painting of birds and flowers (*kachōga*) in Japan. Among his disciples who formed the Nampin school within the so-called NAGASAKI SCHOOL of painting was KUMASHIRO YŪHI.

Shen Weijing (Shen Wei-ching) 沈惟敬

(?–1597; J: Shin Ikei). Envoy of the Ming dynasty (1368–1644) of China who was sent to Korea and Japan at the time of TOYOTOMI HIDEYOSHI's first invasion of Korea in 1592 (see INVASIONS OF KOREA IN 1592 AND 1597), when the Ming came to the aid of the Koreans. Shen was sent to meet with the Japanese general KONISHI YUKINAGA, who was encamped at Seoul, but no truce could be reached since China insisted that Japan admit vassalage to the Ming. In 1596 Shen was dispatched to Japan to negotiate directly with Hideyoshi. Because the mission ended in failure Shen was put to death on his return to China. Hideyoshi launched a second invasion in 1597.

shiatsu 指圧

(literally, "finger pressure"; often referred to as acupressure). Curative and preventive therapy consisting of pressing specific points and areas of the body with the fingers, palms, elbows, knees, or feet. The *shiatsu* therapist is expected to have empathy with the patient's state of body and mind and to awaken and stimulate the natural healing powers of the patient. The practitioner stimulates specific points (called *tsubo* or *keiketsu*) in the body and thereby regulates the flow of energy or life force (*ki*) in the meridians (*keiraku*) throughout the body. According to the philosophy of traditional Chinese and Japanese medicine, this meridian system is a fundamental, life-sustaining mechanism present in some form even in the most primitive life forms, and *shiatsu* aims at stimulating the innate healing powers of the patient by restoring the harmony of the organism that has been disturbed by disease. It has proven to be effective in healing many diseases, especially functional diseases, stress-induced diseases, and kinetic disorders.

Shiba family 斯波氏

(Shibashi). One of the three warrior families that monopolized the post of KANREI (shogunal deputy) during the Muromachi period (1333–1568), with the HATAKEYAMA FAMILY and the HOSOKAWA FAMILY. A branch of the ASHIKAGA FAMILY, the Shiba were based in Mutsu, in northern Honshū, but also inherited the governorship of Owari (now part of Aichi Prefecture). Shiba Takatsune (1305–67) sided with ASHIKAGA TAKAUJI against Emperor GO-DAIGO in 1335 and was appointed military governor (SHUGO) of Echizen and Wakasa (now Fukui Prefecture) after Takauji established his shogunate. Takatsune's son Yoshimasa (1350–1410) greatly extended the family's power as *kanrei*. His son Yoshishige (1371–1418) and grandson Yoshiatsu also served as *kanrei*. In the mid-1400s the Shiba family fell into a bitter succession dispute; this and similar disputes in other warrior families was one cause of the ŌNIN WAR (1467–77). After the war Shiba lands were taken over by the IMAGAWA FAMILY and the ASAKURA FAMILY, and the family stronghold was destroyed by ODA NOBUNAGA in 1561. The CHIKUBASHŌ, a set of moral rules for samurai, was written by Shiba Yoshimasa.

Shibaki Yoshiko 芝木好子

(1914–91). Novelist and short-story writer. Real name Ōshima Yoshiko. Born in Tōkyō. Shibaki graduated from Tōkyō Prefectural First Girls' Higher School. She won the Akutagawa Prize for her short story "Seika no ichi" in 1941. The three novels *Yuba* (1960), *Sumidagawa* (1961), and *Marunouchi Hachigōkan* (1962) form an autobiographical trilogy. Many of Shibaki's works, including her short story "Susaki paradaisu" (1954), describe the lives and traditional arts and crafts of the people of Tōkyō's SHITAMACHI district. *Seiji kinuta* (1972) is a collection of her short stories. In 1982 Shibaki received the Japan Art Academy Prize, and she became a member of the academy in 1983. In 1989 she published *Sumidagawa boshoku*, a love story.

Shiba Kōkan 司馬江漢

(1747?–1818). Artist, innovator, and pioneer in the Westernization of Japan who achieved revolutionary advances in Western-style oil painting and created the first copperplate etchings in the country. Kōkan was born in Edo (now Tōkyō). He studied geography, etched copperplate maps of the world, and wrote texts to accompany them. He also turned his attention to astronomy and introduced the theories of Copernicus to a society imbued with an antithetical, Confucian world order. He regarded himself as the chief prophet of Western culture in Japan.

Kōkan's early training was in the KANŌ SCHOOL style of painting, but at the age of 15 he became the student of Sō Shiseki (1712–86), a master of Chinese-style BIRD-AND-FLOWER PAINTING. At age 23 he turned to making woodblock prints. He created his first Western-style oil paintings around 1780 and in 1783 made his first copperplate etching on the basis of techniques learned from a Dutch encyclopedia. In 1788 Kōkan embarked on a historic journey to Nagasaki, traveling on foot from Edo and keeping a diary, which he later published. He was a prolific writer. In old age Kōkan became a disciple of ZEN Buddhism and retired to a monastery. — See *photo, next page.*

Shibano Ritsuzan 柴野栗山

(1736–1807). Confucian scholar of the Edo period (1600–1868); he is thought to have formulated MATSUDAIRA SADANOBU's 1790 edict, the "Ban on Heterodoxy" (Kansei Igaku no Kin), making knowledge of Zhu Xi (Chu Hsi) Confucianism (SHUSHIGAKU) as taught by the Hayashi family a prerequisite for entering the shogunate administration (see also KANSEI REFORMS). Shibano was born in Sanuki Province (now Kagawa Prefecture) and after studying at SHŌHEIKŌ, the shogunal academy for Confucian studies, was tutor in the Tokushima domain (now Tokushima Prefecture). In 1788 he was named official Confucian scholar to the shogunate and was appointed to the staff at Shōheikō.

Shibaraku 暫

(One Moment). KABUKI play; one of the celebrated kabuki numbers known as the KABUKI JŪHACHIBAN. A *jidai-mono* (historical play) by Ichikawa Danjūrō I (1660–1704), it was first performed in 1697. A ruthless courtier is about to execute the members of a clan whose lands he has expropriated. As the lord's minions prepare to carry out his com-

Shiba Kōkan Detail from *View of Ryōgokubashi.* 1787. Copperplate and colors on paper. 26 × 38 cm. Kōbe City Museum.

Shiba Ryōtarō
A historical novelist known for his entertainments that reinterpret periods of history.

mands, a voice calls from offstage, "One moment!" A superhuman figure, dressed in a costume and wig calculated to make him five-times human size, makes his way down the *hanamichi* (a ramp connecting the stage to the rear of the theater). He frees the captives, excoriates the villain for his oppression of the weak, and proceeds to dispatch him with an eight-foot sword.

Shiba Ryōtarō   司馬遼太郎

(1923–   ). Novelist. Born in Ōsaka. Graduate of Ōsaka Gaigo Gakkō (now Ōsaka University of Foreign Studies), where he studied Mongolian. Working as a newspaper reporter, he started writing popular historical novels and received the Naoki Prize for *Fukurō no shiro* (1959). His works, which are primarily entertainments, depict the lives and behavior of people in turbulent times of history, such as the Meiji Restoration, and provide a new interpretation of those times. Principal works include *Ryōma ga yuku* (1962–66), *Yo ni sumu hibi* (1969–70), *Saka no ue no kumo* (1969–72), and *Na no hana no oki* (1982).

Shibata   新発田［市］

City in northern Niigata Prefecture, central Honshū. It was a castle town from the 15th century through the Edo period (1600–1868). Local products include *sake* (rice wine) and pears. There is an emerging plastics and machine industry. Pop: 78,170.

Shibata   柴田［町］

Town located at the confluence of the rivers Abukumagawa and Shiraishigawa in southern Miyagi Prefecture, northern Honshū. Shibata is a growing residential suburb of the city of Sendai. Pop: 37,315.

Shibata Katsuie   柴田勝家

(1522?–83). Principal captain of the hegemon ODA NOBUNAGA. He distinguished himself in Nobunaga's major campaigns from 1569 to the destruction of the *daimyō* ASAI NAGAMASA and ASAKURA YOSHIKAGE in 1573 and against armed confederations (IKKŌ IKKI) of the Buddhist JŌDO SHIN SECT, 1570–75. He governed Echizen Province (now part of Fukui Prefec

ture) from 1575 under a set of "regulations" (*okite*) and the supervision of three inspectors (*metsuke*) imposed by Nobunaga. His policies in Echizen, namely the separation of the peasant from the *samurai* status (*heinō bunri*), a SWORD HUNT, a land survey (KENCHI), and a prototypal religious inquisition, illustrate important features of Nobunaga's approach to provincial governance, later followed by TOYOTOMI HIDEYOSHI and TOKUGAWA IEYASU. The conquest of the Ikkō sect in Kaga and Noto (now Ishikawa Prefecture) in 1580 was Shibata's last major accomplishment. During the struggle for the succession after Nobunaga's death in 1582, Shibata was defeated by Hideyoshi in the Battle of SHIZUGATAKE on 11 June 1583 and committed suicide.

Shibata Keita   柴田桂太

(1877–1949). Plant physiologist and biochemist. Born in Tōkyō. His father, Shibata Shōkei (1849–1910), was a famous pharmacologist. A graduate of Tōkyō University, Keita later taught there. He studied in Germany under the plant physiologist Wilhelm Pfeffer (1845–1920). In addition to his research on the distribution of flavonoid compounds in the plant world, he also carried out successful research in such fields as respiration and metabolism. He also trained many outstanding scientists.

Shibata Kyūō   柴田鳩翁

(1783–1839). Propagator and scholar of SHINGAKU, a commoner-oriented school of ethics of the Edo period (1600–1868). In his twenties he became a professional teller of heroic tales (KŌDAN). He began study of Shingaku under Satta Tokuken (1778–1836) in his late thirties, traveling and lecturing despite the loss of his sight at age 44. His *Kyūō dōwa* (1835), a collection of moral tales, is considered a masterpiece among Shingaku writings.

Shibata Renzaburō   柴田錬三郎

(1917–78). Novelist. Born in Okayama Prefecture. Graduate of Keiō University. Shibata received the Naoki Prize in 1951 for his short story "Iesu no sue." He wrote a period novel, *Nemuri Kyōshirō burai hikae* (serialized 1956–58 in the weekly magazine *Shū*

kan shinchō), in which he created a new hero, Nemuri Kyōshirō, a tough and unemotional swordsman. The novel was very successful, and he wrote many sequels. Together with GOMI YASUSUKE's similar novels, it created the so-called *kengō* (strong swordsman) fiction boom in the late 1950s. Other works by Shibata include *Akai kagebōshi* (1960, Red Shadow).

Shibata Shō   柴田翔

(1935–   ). Novelist. Born in Tōkyō. A graduate of and later teacher of German literature at Tōkyō University. After winning the Japan Goethe Society Award in 1961, he traveled to Germany. In 1964 his *Saredo warera ga hibi* won the Akutagawa Prize and triggered a "Shibata Shō boom" among young Japanese, who were attracted by his sentimental, introverted, nostalgic style and basic positivism. From 1970 to 1972 he participated in the publication of the coterie magazine *Ningen to shite* with TAKAHASHI KAZUMI, ODA MAKOTO, KAIKŌ KEN, and MATSUGI NOBUHIKO.

Shiba Tatto   司馬達等

(6th century; Ch: Sima Dadeng or Ssu-ma Ta-teng). Early promoter of BUDDHISM in Japan. According to an account in the 12th-century history *Fusō ryakki*, Shiba Tatto was Chinese and immigrated to Japan in 522. He soon established a hermitage containing a Buddhist image at Sakatahara in Takechi no Kōri (now the Asuka region in Nara Prefecture). His actual date of arrival, however, is more likely to have been 582. The chronicle NIHON SHOKI (720) says that in 584 SOGA NO UMAKO asked Shiba Tatto to help search for people already practicing Buddhism in Japan. His son Kuratsukuri no Tasuna produced Buddhist images for Japan's oldest large temple, the Sakatadera. Tasuna's son KURATSUKURI NO TORI created the bronze image of the Buddha at the temple ASUKADERA in 606 and the bronze Shaka triad of the temple HŌRYŪJI in 623.

Shibata Yūji   柴田雄次

(1882–1980). Chemist. Born in Tōkyō. Graduate of Tōkyō University. In 1910 he went to Europe to study inorganic chemistry, returning to Japan in 1913 and becoming a professor at Tōkyō University in 1919. Shibata pioneered Japanese research in many areas of chemistry. He founded the field of spectrochemical research in Japan, importing and using Japan's first spectral analyzer to investigate the absorption spectrum of metallic complex salts. Shibata then applied the results of his research to the chemical analysis of natural substances. In conjunction with KIMURA KENJIRŌ, he also initiated the geochemical investigation of Japan's volcanoes.

Shibata Zeshin   柴田是真

(1807–91). Outstanding lacquer artist, noted for the originality and elegance of his designs. In his youth Zeshin studied lacquer for eight years with Koma Kansai II (1767–1835). He went on to acquire training as a painter in the naturalistic style of the Shijō school (see MARUYAMA-SHIJŌ SCHOOL), working with Suzuki Nanrei (1775–1844) and Okamoto Toyohiko (1773–1845) in Kyōto. His subject matter is generally restricted to pleasant and uncontroversial bird-and-flower or genre themes. From the 1870s Zeshin added the unusual technique of lacquer painting (*urushi-e*) to his repertoire. These works won numerous prizes at international expositions in Europe and America. Be tween 1886 and 1889 Zeshin assisted in the lacquer decoration of the Imperial Palace in Tōkyō.

Shiberia Shuppei → Siberian Intervention

Shibetsu 士別[市]

City in north-central Hokkaidō, on the river Teshiogawa. It was developed from 1899 by colonist militia (TONDENHEI). Agriculture, food processing, sugar refining, and lumber are the principal industries. Pop: 25,754.

shibori → tie-dyeing

Shibue Chūsai 渋江抽斎

(1805–58). Physician and philologist. Although he served as physician to the Tsugaru family of the Hirosaki domain (now part of Aomori Prefecture), Chūsai was born and spent most of his life in Edo (now Tōkyō). In 1844 he was appointed professor at the shogunate school of Chinese medicine, the Seijukan, where he remained until his death. As a scholar of Confucianism, Chūsai was a figure in the Kōshōgaku (Textual Criticism) school. He continued the tradition of philological studies begun by his teachers Ichino Meian (1765–1826) and Kariya Ekisai (1775–1835) and, with his friend Mori Kien (1807–85), wrote a comprehensive bibliography of classical Chinese texts, *Keiseki hōko shi.* He was a leading member of the staff responsible for publishing *Ishimpō,* the rediscovered medical book from the Heian period (794–1185). He also wrote commentaries on the classics of Chinese medicine and was the subject of a biography by MORI ŌGAI.

Shibugaki 渋柿

(Sour Persimmons). Collection of Kamakura-period (1185–1333) writings; compiler and date unknown. It contains four items: (1) an account of the life of MYŌE; (2) a letter from MONGAKU to the shōgun MINAMOTO NO YORIIE, advising him on principles of governance; (3) a letter, dated 13 February 1192, in which MINAMOTO NO YORITOMO sends condolences to Sasaki Sadatsuna (1142–1205), who had lost a son; and (4) advice from HŌJŌ YASUTOKI to his son Tokiuji (1203–30).

Shibu Hot Spring 渋温泉

(Shibu Onsen). Located in the town of Yamanouchi, northeastern Nagano Prefecture, central Honshū. A weak saline spring; water temperature 50°–98°C (122°–208°F). Opened in 1305, it is still famous for its curative properties.

shibui 渋い

An adjective designating a subtle, unobtrusive, and deeply moving beauty, cherished by artists and connoisseurs since the Muromachi period (1333–1568). The term is applied to color, design, taste, and voice as well as to human behavior in general. Originating in medieval aesthetic sensibility, it is related to and sometimes overlaps such concepts as WABI, SABI, and *iki* (see IKI AND SUI). Its noun form is *shibusa* or *shibumi.*

The use of *shibui* became widespread when urban commoners of the Edo period (1600–1868) asserted their preference for a quietly appealing ambience. The subdued voice of a master singer, the disciplined performance of a seasoned actor, or the simple pattern designed by an expert ceramic artist had a beauty of understatement and as such was praised as *shibui.* Colorful beauty was

for the unsophisticated, but *shibui* was for connoisseurs who were not to be misled by the dazzling surface.

The penchant for *shibui* still survives in Japan, forming part of the basic aesthetic taste and manifesting itself in architecture, interior design, ceramic art, and other arts. The term is even applied to baseball: a player is said to be *shibui* when he makes no spectacular plays on the field but contributes to the team in an unobtrusive way.

Shibukawa 渋川[市]

City in central Gumma Prefecture, central Honshū. Near the confluence of the rivers TONEGAWA and Agatsumagawa, it developed as a market and post-station town on the Mikuni Kaidō highway. It has chemical, lumber, electrical-appliance, and cement-block industries. Shibukawa is a gateway to the volcano HARUNASAN, Lake Haruna, and the Ikaho Hot Spring. Pop: 49,062.

Shibukawa Shunkai 渋川春海

(1639–1715). Astronomer and scholar of calendrical science. Also known as Shibukawa Harumi and Yasui Santetsu, the latter being also the name of his father. He began astronomical and calendrical studies at an early age and, after making observations over a period of years, discovered that the Xuanming (Hsüan-ming) calendar (J: Semmyōreki), a calendar of Chinese origin in use in Japan for more than 800 years, was two days behind the solar year. Shunkai succeeded in having his own calendar, the Jōkyōreki, which was based on a calendar of the Yuan (Yüan) dynasty (1279–1368), officially adopted by the Tokugawa shogunate in 1684; he entered the Bureau of Astronomy the same year. (This calendar was used until 1754.) See also CALENDAR, DATES, AND TIME.

Shibusawa Eiichi 渋沢栄一

(1840–1931). Entrepreneur and business leader; played a central role in the establishment of modern industry in Japan. Born in what is now Saitama Prefecture, Shibusawa came from a farming family that also engaged in sericulture and the production of indigo. In 1864 he was enlisted as a retainer of the Hitotsubashi family, a branch family of the Tokugawa, and three years later became aide-de-camp to the shōgun's younger brother TOKUGAWA AKITAKE, who led the Japanese delegation to the Paris International Exhibition. On his trip to Europe Shibusawa was deeply impressed with the modern technology and economic systems of the Western nations.

Returning to Japan in the wake of the Meiji Restoration of 1868, Shibusawa gained appointment to the Ministry of Finance. As a protégé of ŌKUMA SHIGENOBU and INOUE KAORU, he played a key role in the establishment of the government-operated TOMIOKA SILK-REELING MILL in 1872 and in the introduction of a modern banking system the same year. He resigned from the Ministry of Finance in 1873, having secured for himself the presidencies of Dai-Ichi Bank (now DAI-ICHI KANGYŌ BANK, LTD) and ŌJI PAPER CO, LTD, both of which he had persuaded MITSUI and other merchant houses to establish in the form of modern corporations. He and his bank were consulted and emulated when other private and national banks mushroomed during the years 1877–80.

In 1882 Shibusawa organized the ŌSAKA SPINNING MILL, and throughout the 1880s and 1890s he was involved in the organization of dozens of other enterprises in areas such as

textiles, insurance, shipping, rail transport, manufacturing, and the like. He was instrumental in the establishment of the Tōkyō Shōhō Kaigisho, Japan's first Chamber of Commerce, serving as its president from 1878 to 1905, and was active in the creation and management of a number of other business organizations. Shibusawa was also a philanthropist who founded schools, homes for the aged, and other social welfare projects. In the latter part of his career he was active in efforts to improve international relations, organizing and heading a committee on Japanese-American relations as well as a goodwill mission to the United States.

Shibusawa Eiichi The establishment in 1872 of a modern Japanese banking system was among the many achievements of this entrepreneur and advocate of Western business practices.

Shibusawa Keizō 渋沢敬三

(1896–1963). Businessman. Grandson of the entrepreneur SHIBUSAWA EIICHI. Born in Tōkyō, he graduated from Tōkyō University. He went into banking and became the president of the Bank of Japan in 1944. Shibusawa served as minister of finance in the SHIDEHARA KIJŪRŌ cabinet (1945–46). He later was active as a business leader, becoming president of KOKUSAI DENSHIN DENWA CO, LTD, and chairman of NIPPON CULTURAL BROADCASTING, INC. Shibusawa was deeply interested in Japanese folk culture; in 1921 he established in his home the Attic Museum, which later became the Nihon Jōmin Bunka Kenkyūjo (Japanese Folk Culture Research Institute), and supported the research of young ethnology students. As president of the Japanese Society of Ethnology (Nihon Minzokugaku Kyōkai) and the Anthropological Society of Japan (Nihon Jinruigaku Kai), he worked to bring together the various disciplines related to Japanese folk studies.

Shibusawa Tatsuhiko 澁澤龍彦

(1928–87). Critic; novelist; scholar of French literature. Real name Shibusawa Tatsuo. Born in Tōkyō; graduate of Tōkyō University. *Akutoku no sakae* (1959–60), Shibusawa's abridged translation of the Marquis de Sade's *L'Histoire de Juliette; ou, Les Prosperités du vice,* was the subject of an important obscenity decision by the Japanese Supreme Court (see DE SADE CASE). Shibusawa has produced many translations and critical studies in the fields of French literature, medieval demonology, and art. Other works include *Erotishizumu* (1967, Eroticism) and the fantasy tale *Takaoka Shinnō kōkai ki* (1987, The Ocean Voyages of Imperial Prince Takaoka).

Shibushi Bay 志布志湾

(Shibushi Wan). Formerly called Ariake Bay (Ariake Wan; not to be confused with Ariake Sea). Inlet of the Pacific Ocean on the northeastern coast of the Ōsumi Peninsula, Kagoshima and Miyazaki prefectures, Kyūshū. Extends from the cape TOIMISAKI to the cape Hizaki. There has been much debate over plans for the industrial development of the area, which is a good fishing ground.

Shibuya Tengai 渋谷天外

(1906–83). Comic actor and playwright. Born in Kyōto. Real name Shibutani Kazuo. He formed the Shōchiku Kateigeki theater in 1928. Reacting against earlier comedy in the all-male KABUKI tradition, he cast Naniwa Chieko and other actresses in plays of his own writing. In 1948 he created the Shōchiku Shinkigeki (Shōchiku New Comedy). The nonsensical humor of his plays was well received by the youth of the post–World

Shibusawa Tatsuhiko This novelist and scholar translated many French literary works; his version of a work by de Sade was the focus of a famous obscenity trial.

Shichigosan In observance of this festival, a traditionally attired seven-year-old girl and five-year-old boy visit Kanda Shrine in Tōkyō in order to pray for health and safety.

shichishitō The seven-pronged iron sword belonging to Isonokami Shrine, with a 61-character gold inlay inscription recording its manufacture in AD 369. Length 75 cm.

War II generation. A great comic star, he also appeared in movies.

Shibuya Ward 渋谷区

(Shibuya Ku). One of the 23 wards of Tōkyō. On the Musashino Plateau. Although Shibuya is primarily a residential area, the district near Shibuya Station has become one of the major commercial and amusement centers of Tōkyō. With its many department stores, movie houses, and restaurants, this district is particularly popular among Japanese young people. Located in Shibuya are the Meiji Shrine, the Yoyogi National Stadium, and the NHK Broadcasting Center. Pop: 205,625.

shichi 質

A kind of material collateral for loans. The usage and definition of this term have varied throughout history. In ancient times, it referred to pawning, in which the possession of the object offered as collateral is transferred to the creditor, and to mortgaging, in which the possession of the object is not transferred to the creditor.

Under the RITSURYŌ SYSTEM of government, enacted in the late 7th century, in the event of nonfulfillment of a debt, the security object was to be sold off to settle the account. When the security was in the form of real estate, the rights of possession belonged to the creditor. It was common at this time for nobles and priests to take crops or land from farmers as collateral for loans.

In the Kamakura (1185–1333) and Muromachi (1333–1568) periods, *shichi* continued to refer to pawned security and mortgaged security, but the terms *irejichi* (pawned security) and *kenjichi* (mortgaged security) came to be used to differentiate the two. Hostages (HITOJICHI) were also given as collateral.

In the Edo period (1600–1868) the word *shichi* was in its broad sense still used to include nonpossessory (mortgaged) security but in practice was more commonly used to mean possessory (pawned) security, and it is in this sense that the term is used today. *Shichibōkō* (collateral labor), in which human beings were used as security, was also practiced.

---

shichigenkin This 8th-century *shichigenkin*, shown from the front (above) and back (below), is preserved in the Shōsōin collection in Nara.

In the early Meiji period (1868–1912) the use of human beings as collateral was prohibited. However, the term *shichiire* (pawnage) remained in use until the enactment in 1898 of Japan's first modern civil code, in which pledge rights (*shichi-ken*) were classified as one category of RIGHTS IN REM.

shichibukin tsumitate 七分金積立

(literally, "seven-tenths of the cash reserves"). Emergency reserve fund established in 1791 by MATSUDAIRA SADANOBU as a part of the KANSEI REFORMS. After analyzing the municipal expenditures of Edo (now Tōkyō) for the years 1785–89, Sadanobu reduced the city's annual expenses by 10 percent, of which one-tenth was allocated for unbudgeted outlays and two-tenths was refunded to the taxpayers of Edo. The remaining seven-tenths, called *shichibukin tsumitate*, was annually deposited at the Edo Office for Town Affairs (Edo Machikaisho) for emergencies. Approximately half was spent on rice, kept in storehouses (SHASŌ). The cash reserve was lent to the poor at low interest. During the TEMPŌ FAMINE (1833–36) these reserves fed the people of Edo. After the MEIJI RESTORATION (1868) the accumulated *shichibukin tsumitate*, amounting to 1.43 million *ryō*, was used for public buildings and social welfare under supervision of SHIBUSAWA EIICHI.

Shichifukujin → Seven Deities of Good Fortune

shichigenkin 七弦琴

Also known as *kin* (Ch: *qin* or *ch'in*). A seven-stringed musical instrument of the zither type, made of hollowed wood; now approximately 110 centimeters (43 in) long and 20 centimeters (8 in) wide.

Broadly speaking, it is a kind of KOTO (the same written character is used for *kin* and *koto*), though, unlike the more common and slightly larger *koto*, the *kin* does not utilize movable bridges for each string. Instead, the strings are stopped by the fingers of the left hand and plucked in various ways by the fingers of the right hand.

For 2,000 years in China, the *shichigenkin* has been considered the instrument of the sage, poet, and scholar. It was first imported into Japan during the Nara period (710–794) and remained popular among literati until the end of the Edo period (1600–1868). But its popularity did not outlive the taste for Chinese culture in Japan and declined during the Meiji period (1868–1912).

Shichigosan 七五三

("Seven-Five-Three" Festival). The custom, observed on 15 November, of taking five-year-old boys and seven- or three-year-old girls to the local Shintō shrine to pray for their safe and healthy future. It was originally connected with the belief that children of certain ages were especially prone to bad luck and hence in need of divine protection. A newborn infant was thought of as unformed flesh that gradually took shape as an adult only after a series of ritual observances; at the age of seven the child was finally recognized as a social entity. In many parts of Japan, the child is received as a member of the shrine parish (*ujiko*) at seven. Recently, parents have tended to take their children to large and prestigious shrines, rather than to the local one. After the visit many people buy *chitose-ame* ("thousand-year candy"), sold at the shrine, to distribute to relatives and neighbors.

Shichihakase Jiken 七博士事件

(Seven Professors Incident). Incident in June 1903 surrounding a written statement by seven professors (most of them members of the law faculty of Tōkyō University) before the outbreak of the RUSSO-JAPANESE WAR (1904–05). TOMII MASAAKI, Tomizu Hirondo (1861–1935), and five other professors urged Prime Minister KATSURA TARŌ to declare war immediately. Their statement, published in the newspaper *Tōkyō nichinichi shimbun*, influenced public opinion in favor of the war. After the war the government dismissed Tomizu from his post at Tōkyō University, but he was reinstated after faculty protests, and the minister of education, Kubota Yuzuru (1847–1936), was compelled to resign.

Shichikyō Ochi 七卿落

The flight of seven court nobles from Kyōto to the Chōshū domain (now Yamaguchi Prefecture) in 1863. These nobles, of whom SANJŌ SANETOMI was the most famous, supported the Chōshū-led antiforeign, antishogunate activists. When the extremists were driven out of Kyōto in the COUP D'ETAT OF 30 SEPTEMBER 1863, the nobles followed them to the Chōshū port of Mitajiri. In 1864 Chōshū requested the pardon of the seven nobles. Denial of this contributed to tensions that culminated in an unsuccessful countercoup by Chōshū that same year (see HAMAGURI GOMON INCIDENT). The nobles remained in exile until the MEIJI RESTORATION (1868).

Shichinin no samurai → Seven Samurai

Shichirigahama 七里ケ浜

Coastal area southwest of the city of Kamakura, Kanagawa Prefecture, central Honshū. Located on Sagami Bay, it is famous as a vacation and health resort and for its views of Mt. Fuji (FUJISAN) and ENOSHIMA. Land development and housing projects have increased rapidly in recent years. Length: 4 km (2.5 mi).

shichishitō 七支刀

(seven-pronged sword). Ancient iron sword located in the ISONOKAMI SHRINE in the city of Tenri, Nara Prefecture. The total length of the sword is 75 centimeters (29.55 in). Each side of the blade has three branchlike prongs which, added to the tip of the sword, make a total of seven prongs. Gold inlay inscriptions are carved on both sides of the blade. The inscriptions read "I made this seven-pronged sword during the fourth year of Taiwa (AD 369), tempering it over and over. He who possesses this sword will drive away calamity. This sword is fit to be possessed by someone with the rank of king and will probably be passed down from generation to generation through eternity." Because the *shichishitō* is believed to correspond to the seven-pronged sword mentioned in the 8th-century chronicle *Nihon shoki* as having been given to the Japanese emperor by the early Korean kingdom of Paekche, it constitutes important evidence of the relationship between Japan and the Korean peninsula during ancient times.

shichiya 七夜

("seventh night"). A celebration on the seventh day after the birth of a child. Still widely observed in Japan, it traditionally includes inviting relatives and giving the child

---

a name, which is written on paper and posted. The impurity (*imi*) resulting from childbirth is usually deemed to end after 21 days, with each 7-day period marking a stage. It is considered safe to take the infant out of the house on this day, and in some places it is presented to whatever Shintō gods may be enshrined in the house.

Shidehara Kijūrō　幣原喜重郎

(1872–1951). Minister of foreign affairs two times (1924–27 and 1929–31) and prime minister once (1945–46). The so-called Shidehara diplomacy of the 1920s was distinguished by its advocacy of international cooperation among the imperialist nations and a "conciliatory" attitude toward China.

Born in Ōsaka, he attended Tōkyō University, graduating in law in 1895. After passing the foreign service examination in 1896, he served in Korea, Tōkyō, the United States, and Europe. In 1915 he returned home to become vice-minister for foreign affairs and retained this position under five different ministers until 1919, when he was named ambassador to the United States. He was one of Japan's delegates to the WASHINGTON CONFERENCE in 1921–22. His negotiations led to the return of Shandong (Shantung) Province to China (see SHANDONG [SHANTUNG] QUESTION).

First Term as Foreign Minister (1924–1927)—In 1924 he accepted the post of minister of foreign affairs in the KATŌ TAKAAKI cabinet. An admirer of Great Britain and the United States, Shidehara hoped to retain friendly ties with the West, and in his initial Diet speech as foreign minister, he pledged a policy of international cooperation in accordance with the Covenant of the League of Nations and the recently signed treaties in Washington.

Regarding China, Shidehara is associated with policies of nonintervention in the republican revolution and expansion of Japan's economic influence on the continent. At the Beijing (Peking) Customs Conference in October 1925 Japan surprised other delegates by announcing approval of the Chinese demand for tariff autonomy. Although no agreement was reached, Shidehara always pointed to the customs conference as an instance of Japan's conciliatory China policy. One of the last affairs of the first Shidehara period, the celebrated NANJING (NANKING) INCIDENT of March 1927, tested as never before the durability of conciliation. Shidehara refused to allow Japan to participate in an ultimatum that foreign officials prepared to send to Chiang Kai-shek after Chinese Nationalist troops had entered Nanjing and attacked foreign consulates and settlements. Criticism in Japan of Shidehara's noninterventionist policy was largely responsible for the collapse of the WAKATSUKI REIJIRŌ cabinet in April 1927.

Second Term as Foreign Minister (1929–1931)—In Shidehara's second term as foreign minister, the hands-off policy was renewed. China was seemingly united under the Nanjing government of Chiang Kai-shek, but the TANAKA GIICHI administration, whose policy concerning China urged "positive" action, had intervened several times in the previous two years. Now, moreover, there were other preoccupations, such as the LONDON NAVAL CONFERENCES. Approval of the London treaty by Shidehara and the Ministry of Foreign Affairs in April 1930 precipitated a major political crisis in Japan, where Shidehara's policy of compromise with the West was harshly criticized. When in 1930

Prime Minister HAMAGUCHI OSACHI was seriously wounded by an assassin, Shidehara assumed the post of interim premier until March 1931 and represented the government's views in the Diet.

Shidehara's final crisis was the MANCHURIAN INCIDENT in September 1931. He and the cabinet were powerless to stop the occupation of Manchuria by the Japanese GUANDONG (KWANTUNG) ARMY. This brought to an end the cabinet and Shidehara's career as foreign minister. Though a member of the House of Peers, from 1931 to 1945 Shidehara was in semiretirement. For this reason, and because of his pro-American reputation, Shidehara was selected, at 73, as the second postwar prime minister in 1945. As prime minister he tried to preserve the emperor system. He suggested that he was the author of the famous article 9 of the 1947 constitution, which outlawed war (see RENUNCIATION OF WAR). General Douglas MACARTHUR also stated that the idea was Shidehara's, but his role remains subject to controversy. Shidehara was later elected twice to the House of Representatives and became speaker of the house in 1949. His memoirs, *Gaikō gojūnen* (Fifty Years of Diplomacy), appeared in 1951.

shiden　私田・賜田

1. (private fields). Rice lands assigned by the government for private use under the RITSURYŌ SYSTEM initiated in the late 7th century. Under this system all land belonged to the central government, to be distributed as it chose. The produce of "public fields" (KŌDEN) went to the government. Remaining lands (*shiden*) included KUBUNDEN fields distributed by the government to cultivators under the HANDEN SHŪJU SYSTEM and fields awarded to individuals on the basis of court rank or government service (*iden* and *shikiden*, respectively). Holders received only the right of usufruct. Tenure was either for life (*kubunden* and *iden*), or for the duration of official appointment (*shikiden*). From the mid-8th century, *shiden* referred to lands recognized as the permanent private property of their original developers (see KONDEN EISEI SHIZAI HŌ).

2. (bestowed fields). Rice lands granted by the emperor during the Nara (710–794) and Heian (794–1185) periods in recognition of extraordinary service to the state.

Shidō Bunan　至道無難

(1603–76). Also known as Shidō Munan. ZEN monk of the RINZAI SECT. Around 1654 (or 1649?) he became a disciple of Gudō Tōshoku (1579–1661), the celebrated Zen master and sometime abbot of the temple MYŌSHINJI in Kyōto. He eventually became a monk in Edo (now Tōkyō). Bunan gained renown as a great spiritual master; until his death he resided in a hermitage at Koishikawa, Edo. His disciple Dōkyō Etan (1642–1721) handed down his discipline to HAKUIN, a Rinzai-sect Zen master. These three were largely responsible for the immense popularization of Zen during the Edo period (1600–1868). Bunan's instruction is collected in his *Kana hōgo* (first published in 1671).

shidō yōroku → cumulative guidance record

Shie Incident　紫衣事件

(Shie Jiken; literally, "Purple Robe Incident"). Intervention in 1627 by the Tokugawa shogunate (1603–1867) in a tradi-

tional prerogative of the imperial court: the conferral of *shie*, purple robes that symbolized the highest order of priesthood. The court had been receiving a considerable portion of its income in return for granting this honor. In 1613, to demonstrate its power, the Tokugawa shogunate stated that imperial conferral of *shie* required shogunal approval. When Emperor GO-MIZUNOO (r 1611–29) bestowed *shie* on priests of the temples Daitokuji and Myōshinji in 1627, the shogunate pronounced the *shie* invalid and confiscated them. Emperor Go-Mizunoo abdicated in protest in 1629, and others who objected, including the priest TAKUAN SŌHŌ, were exiled.

shigajiku　詩画軸

Hanging scrolls (KAKEMONO) containing paintings accompanied by poetry or prose. In most cases, the painting and writing are done by different people, and the text may even be written by more than one person. Most of the paintings are landscapes in the INK PAINTING genre. The concept of uniting poetry and painting originated in China and was developed independently in Japan during the middle part of the Muromachi period (1333–1568), principally by Zen priests at GOZAN temples. The oldest surviving example of a Japanese *shigajiku* is *Saimon shingetsu zu*, which dates to 1405.

Shiga Kiyoshi　志賀潔

(1870–1957). Bacteriologist. Original surname Satō. Born in what is now Miyagi Prefecture. He graduated from the Faculty of Medicine of Tōkyō University in 1896. Working at the Institute for Infectious Diseases under KITASATO SHIBASABURŌ, Shiga discovered the bacillus causing dysentery (*Shigella dysenteriae*) in 1897. After study in Germany with Paul Ehrlich, he returned to Japan and helped establish the Kitazato Institute. He was appointed professor at Keiō Gijuku (now Keiō University) in 1920 and was later president (1929–31) of Keijō University in Seoul, Korea. He was awarded the Order of Culture in 1944.

Shiga Kōgen　志賀高原

Highland in northeastern Nagano Prefecture, central Honshū. Surrounded by towering mountains, it is noted for its numerous lakes and ponds, dense white birch forests, and alpine flora. With its many excellent ski slopes and hot spring resorts, including Kumanoyu and Hoppo, it is a popular year-round resort area and a major attraction of Jōshin'etsu Kōgen National Park. Elevation: 1,300–2,000 m (4,300–6,600 ft); approximately 400 sq km (155 sq mi).

Shiga Naoya　志賀直哉

(1883–1971). Novelist; short-story writer. Born in Miyagi Prefecture; attended Gakushūin (the Peers' School) and Tōkyō University. Shiga has widely been considered by critics the perfecter of the *watakushi shōsetsu*, or the "personal novel" (see I-NOVEL). Although several of the short stories that established his reputation—"Kamisori" (1910; tr "The Razor," 1979), "Seibei to hyōtan" (1913; tr "Seibei and Gourds," 1979), "Manazuru" (1920; tr "Manazuru," 1979)—are clearly not autobiographical, such ventures into longer fiction as *Ōtsu Junkichi* (1912), *Wakai* (1917, Reconciliation), and AN'YA KŌRO (1921–37; tr *A Dark Night's Pass-*

Shidehara Kijūrō
During his two terms as foreign minister (1924–27 and 1929–31), this career diplomat advocated cooperation with the Western powers and a conciliatory policy toward China. In 1945 he became Japan's second postwar prime minister.

Shiga Kiyoshi The bacillus that causes dysentery was discovered by this bacteriologist in 1897.

Shiga Naoya Figuring prominently in the standard intellectual and social histories of modern Japan, this writer is widely regarded as the perfecter of the "personal novel," or I-novel.

ing, 1976) are certainly rooted in the events of his own life.

What seems most intense in Shiga's life and most germane to his works as a whole can be partially reconstructed from some of his confessional early stories. His fictional alter ego as a child and young man is characterized by obsessive involvement in emotional tangles with family and a few friends, and by remarkably satisfying, if transitory, retreats into nature and art.

An'ya kōro recapitulates the central themes of Shiga's earlier works. The "long night" of the title stands for the protracted passage of the still-adolescent hero (though he is roughly 30 at the outset) through a sequence of disturbing and often "regressive" experiences into a hard-won truce with destructive forces within himself. Themes such as the re-emergence of childhood passions, lyrical descriptions of nature, the imminence of death, and the combination of private moralism and noninstitutional religious faith bring to mind the earlier works "Haha no shi to atarashii haha" (1912, Mother's Death and a New Mother), *Wakai,* "Takibi" (1920; tr "Night Fires," 1979), and others.

Shiga suffered the fate of many authors of personal fiction in his apparent failure to find something new to say once he had reached the final telling of his own experience, which he did in *An'ya kōro.* The last 35 years of his life were spent in the enjoyment of a reputedly happy domestic life and in an often half-hearted performance of the role allotted him by various journalists and literary entrepreneurs, that of *bungaku no kamisama,* or patron saint of literature. Largely on account of his youthful association with the SHIRAKABA SCHOOL and his brief infatuation with the Christian movement of UCHIMURA KANZŌ, Shiga has figured prominently in the standard intellectual and social histories of modern Japan.

Shiga Prefecture 滋賀県

(Shiga Ken). Located in central Honshū and bordered by Kyōto, Mie, Gifu, and Fukui prefectures. The prefecture takes the form of a basin surrounded by mountains on all sides. Lake BIWA, in central Shiga, is the largest lake in Japan. The climate is moderate, with heavy snowfall in the northern half.

Known as Ōmi Province after the TAIKA REFORM of 645, the area was important from early on. The city of ŌTSU served briefly as the imperial capital in the 7th century (see ŌTSU NO MIYA). Various warlords gained dominance through the feudal period, and its proximity to the capital of Kyōto made it the site of several major battles. In the late 16th century the national unifier ODA NOBUNAGA established his base at AZUCHI CASTLE, near the eastern shore of Lake Biwa. Under the Tokugawa shogunate the area was divided

among the Ii family of HIKONE and several lesser domains. The merchants of Ōmi were noted for their entrepreneurial skills during the Edo period (1600–1868). The present name and boundaries were established in 1881.

Agriculture is still a major occupation, with rice as the main crop. Lake Biwa provides an abundant supply of freshwater fish. Major industries, centered in the southern portion on the fringe of the Kyōto-Ōsaka metropolitan area, include textiles, electrical products, transportation equipment, and chemicals.

The main tourist attraction is the Lake Biwa area, which has been made into a quasinational park. It includes the temple EN-RYAKUJI on Mt. Hiei (HIEIZAN), the HIE SHRINE (Hie Taisha), and the temples ISHIYAMADERA and MIIDERA in Ōtsu. The city of Hikone on the lake's eastern shore retains the atmosphere of an old castle town. The Suzuka Mountains have been designated as a quasinational park. Area: 4,016 sq km (1,550 sq mi); pop: 1,222,411; capital: Ōtsu. Other major cities include Hikone, NAGAHAMA, KUSATSU, and ŌMI HACHIMAN.

Shigaraki 信楽[町]

Town in southern Shiga Prefecture, central Honshū, on the river Daidogawa. With plentiful supplies of good-quality clay and feldspar, it has long been known for its SHIGARAKI WARE. Shigaraki was the site of SHIGARAKI NO MIYA, an imperial palace built by the emperor Shōmu (r 724–749). Pop: 14,215.

Shigaraki no Miya 紫香楽宮

(Shigaraki Palace). Also known as Kōka no Miya. One of the imperial residences in the Nara period (710–794); located in what is now the town of Shigaraki in the Kōka district of Shiga Prefecture. In 741, following the Rebellion of Fujiwara no Hirotsugu (see FUJIWARA NO HIROTSUGU, REBELLION OF) Emperor SHŌMU moved his capital from HEIJŌKYŌ (Nara) to KUNI NO MIYA (in the present Sōraku district of Kyōto Prefecture). In the following year he built a separate residence at Shigaraki with the aim of eventually moving the capital there. He changed his plans, however, and moved instead to NANIWAKYŌ. In February 745 Shōmu suddenly moved the capital to Shigaraki; but the inaccessibility of the place and the prevalence of earthquakes and forest fires persuaded him to return to Heijōkyō barely four months later. The only archaeological remains in the Shigaraki area are those of a later temple.

Shigaraki ware 信楽焼

(*shigaraki-yaki*). Stonewares produced by several villages in the Shigaraki valley in southern Shiga Prefecture. The ceramic tradition in Shigaraki is said to have begun in the Kamakura period (1185–1333), when pottery was produced there for purely local domestic use. The larger vessels were coil built; smaller items were thrown on the wheel from the 16th century on. Intentionally glazed wares appeared in the 16th century, although streaks of natural ash glaze are frequently found on the shoulders of larger vessels.

From the beginning of the 16th century, Shigaraki ware was used for the TEA CEREMONY. Since the late 19th century, Shigaraki has shifted to the production of various wares, including molded planters, braziers, and miscellaneous garden furniture, along with large ceramic *tanuki* (raccoon dogs) holding *sake* jugs. The body fabric of tradi-

tional wares is generally reddish brown and coarse grained; Shigaraki pottery can be identified by the white specks and grains of feldspar and quartz that melt during firing and protrude from the surface.

Shigarami sōshi しがらみ草紙

(The Weir). Literary journal edited by MORI ŌGAI. A total of 59 issues appeared between October 1889 and August 1894. The magazine featured a broad range of critical essays on literature, art, and drama and also published translations of Western literature, such as the initial portion of *Sokkyō shijin* (1892–94), Ōgai's version of Hans Christian Andersen's *Improvisatoren.* Influential in introducing the style and sensibility of European romanticism to Japan, *Shigarami sōshi* was succeeded in 1896–1902 by the journal *Mezamashi-gusa,* also edited by Ōgai.

Shiga Shigetaka 志賀重昂

(1863–1927). Geographer and proponent of enlightened nationalism at a time when Westernization was rampant. Also known as Shiga Jūkō. Born in the Mikawa domain (now part of Aichi Prefecture); educated at Sapporo Agricultural College (now Hokkaidō University). On a trip through the South Pacific in 1886, Shiga was struck by what he thought were the principles of social Darwinism at work in Western colonialism. On his return to Japan he published *Nan'yō jiji* (1887, Conditions in the South Seas), in which he stressed both the strength and the vulnerability of Japan as an island country and the importance of strengthening the country through commerce and industry. The following year, with MIYAKE SETSUREI, he founded the SEIKYŌSHA (Society for Political Education). In its journal *Nihonjin* (The Japanese), he expounded his notion of *kokusui hozon* (preservation of the national essence) in the face of indiscriminate modernization. Shiga was a member of the lower house of the Diet from 1902 to 1904. His *Nihon fūkeiron* (1894, The Landscape of Japan) and *Sekai sansui zusetsu* (1911, Illustrated Geography of the World) and his lectures at Waseda University helped popularize geographical studies.

Shiga Yoshio 志賀義雄

(1901–89). Politician. Born in Fukuoka Prefecture. While still a student at Tōkyō University he joined the leftist study group SHIN-JINKAI and became a member of the Japan Communist Party (JCP). Upon graduating in 1926, together with TOKUDA KYŪICHI and others he reestablished the JCP, which had been dissolved the year before. Following the mass arrest of communists in 1928 (see MARCH 15TH INCIDENT) he was imprisoned for 18 years. Shiga steadfastly refused to recant (see TENKŌ). Upon his release after World War II, he helped form the postwar JCP and became editor in chief of the party organ, AKAHATA (Red Flag). He was elected to the Diet in 1946 but was debarred from office in the so-called RED PURGE by American Occupation authorities in 1950. He resumed public activity in 1955 and was elected to the Central Committee of the JCP. In 1964 Shiga was expelled from the party for supporting ratification of the 1963 Nuclear Test Ban Treaty.

Shigemitsu Mamoru 重光葵

(1887–1957). Career diplomat who served as foreign minister during and after World War II. Born in Ōita Prefecture, he graduated from Tōkyō University in 1911 and entered the Ministry of Foreign Affairs the same year. He served in Europe and was a member of Japan's delegation at the Paris Peace Conference in 1919. In 1928 he was appointed consul general in Shanghai. He was made minister to China in August 1931.

In 1933 Shigemitsu was named vice-minister of foreign affairs, a post he retained until 1936. He was associated with the so-called Asia faction, which urged an aggressive foreign policy toward China. He was appointed ambassador to the USSR in 1936 and to Britain in 1938. Upon his return to Japan in 1941 he cautioned against war with the United States. As foreign minister from 1943 to 1945, Shigemitsu became a leading member of the group seeking peace. He tried unsuccessfully to institute a policy that would return China to the Chinese. As foreign minister he also represented the Japanese government at the official surrender ceremony on the USS *Missouri* on 2 September 1945.

In 1946 Shigemitsu was indicted as a war criminal by the International Military Tribunal for the Far East (see WAR CRIMES TRIALS). He was sentenced to seven years but released in 1950. Shigemitsu promptly returned to politics. He joined the Nihon Kaishintō (Japan Reform Party) in 1952 and became its president. In 1954 the Kaishintō merged with the Nihon Jiyūtō (Japan Liberal Party) to form the NIHON MINSHUTŌ (Japan Democratic Party), and Shigemitsu became vice-president. When the party came to power in 1954, Shigemitsu became foreign minister and deputy premier, positions he retained until 1956. His *Gaikō kaisō roku* (Reflections on Diplomacy) was published in 1953.

Shigemitsu Takeo　　重光武雄

(1922–). Businessman and head of the Lotte group of companies. Korean name Shin Kyuk-Ho. Born in Urusan, Korea, he emigrated to Japan in 1930 and graduated from Waseda University in 1946. In 1948 Shigemitsu established LOTTE CO, LTD, and, as its president, led the company to success in the chewing gum business. As of 1990 he was the head of 14 companies in Japan and 27 in Korea, in fields such as confectioneries, real estate, electronics, fast foods, petrochemicals, and leisure. He also is owner of two professional baseball teams: the Lotte Orions in Japan and the Lotte Giants in Korea.

Shigeno Yasutsugu　　重野安繹

(1827–1910). Historian. Born in the Satsuma domain (now Kagoshima Prefecture), he studied at the Shōheikō, the shogunate academy in Edo (now Tōkyō). After the Meiji Restoration (1868) he supervised the compilation of historical records at the Office of Historiography (Shūshikyoku). Shigeno was appointed professor of history at Tōkyō University in 1888. Adamantly opposed to the moralistic use of history, he was forced to resign in 1893 after attacks by Shintō nationalists.

shigi kempō　　私擬憲法

(private draft constitutions). Various constitutional drafts prepared by government officials, political groups, or private individuals before the promulgation of the CONSTITUTION OF THE EMPIRE OF JAPAN in 1889. A forerunner of such drafts was composed in 1867 by NISHI AMANE. His proposal was a last-ditch effort to preserve the shogunate's political authority. A *shigi kempō* that followed the Prussian model was written in 1872 by AOKI SHŪZŌ.

In 1878 the GENRŌIN, the government's legislative body, presented a draft constitution (Nihon Kokken An), rejected by government, that would have limited the power of the emperor. While the government continued to prepare a constitution to be granted by the emperor, forces outside the government, particularly the FREEDOM AND PEOPLE'S RIGHTS MOVEMENT, campaigned on behalf of a constitution drawn up by the people themselves. Between 1873 and 1887, more than 40 drafts were composed. The most radical was by UEKI EMORI, a leader of the people's rights movement. His 1881 draft (Nihonkoku Kokken An) placed sovereignty in the hands of the people and provided for civil rights, including the right to resist an oppressive government. Most took the British or American constitutions as models. After the POLITICAL CRISIS OF 1881, the government firmly decided to follow the Prussian model for the constitution that was ultimately granted in 1889.

Shigisan　　信貴山

Hill in the southern Ikoma Mountains, northwestern Nara Prefecture, central Honshū. On the slopes is Shigisanji, a temple of the Kōyasan Shingon sect of Buddhism. The temple possesses the SHIGISAN ENGI EMAKI, a famous set of picture scrolls. Height: 437 m (1,434 ft).

Shigisan engi emaki　　信貴山縁起絵巻

(The Legends of Mt. Shigi). A set of three narrative handscrolls, dated circa 1156–80, preserved at Chōgo Sonshiji, Mt. Shigi (Shigisan), Nara Prefecture, a mountain monastery restored in the late 9th century by the monk Myōren (see SHIGISANJI). The *Shigisan* scrolls illustrate three miracles attributed to Myōren, who lived most of his adult life in retreat at Mt. Shigi.

Scroll I, popularly titled *The Flying Granary*, tells of Myōren's rice bowl, which flew daily to be filled at a rich landlord's estate; after having been locked inside the granary, the bowl carried storehouse and contents to the sequestered monk. Scroll II, *The Exorcism of the Engi Emperor*, narrates the miraculous cure of the emperor Daigo (r 897–930) through Myōren's prayers. Scroll III, *The Story of the Nun*, tells of Myōren's elder sister's search for her brother and their reunion after her prayers to the Great Buddha at the temple Tōdaiji, Nara.

The *Shigisan engi emaki* is the earliest surviving example of the continuous narrative method of illustration. Executed in flexible ink lines and light color washes on paper, each scroll unfolds the plot in an unbroken sequence of events. The leading characters are repeatedly shown before changing architectural and landscape backdrops. See also EMAKIMONO.

Shigisanji　　信貴山寺

SHINGON SECT temple located on the eastern slope of the mountain Shigisan in the town of Heguri, Nara Prefecture; properly called Chōgo Sonshiji. Its founder is said to be Prince SHŌTOKU (574–622), but it was made famous by the priest Myōren, who, during the Kampyō era (889–898), donated the statue of Vaiśravaṇa (J: Bishamonten), the temple's chief deity. During the Sengoku period (1467–1568) a local military ruler, Matsunaga Hisahide (1510–77), built a castle on Shigisan and made temple repairs. After Hisahide revolted against ODA NOBUNAGA, the entire complex was laid to waste (1577) by Nobunaga's troops. The temple was reconstructed by TOYOTOMI HIDEYORI in 1602. Among the possessions of the temple are three 12th-century picture scrolls, the SHIGISAN ENGI EMAKI.

Shihōshō　　司法省

(Ministry of Justice). Government ministry charged with the administration of the judicial system in the pre–World War II period. Established on 24 August 1871. According to the CONSTITUTION OF THE EMPIRE OF JAPAN (1889) the courts were to function as an independent judiciary, but the Shihōshō, with its wide-ranging authority over judicial matters, retained control of the appointment of judges. In 1947 the ministry was abolished; thereafter administration of the courts and appointment of their personnel were transferred to the SUPREME COURT. A new MINISTRY OF JUSTICE (Hōmushō), with different functions and authority than the prewar version, was created in 1952.

Shiiba　　椎葉[村]

Village in northwestern Miyazaki Prefecture, Kyūshū. Located in a remote, sparsely inhabited mountainous area, Shiiba relies on lumbering and farming. In 1960, Japan's first arched dam was built here on the river Mimikawa. Shiiba is also known as the refuge of the warriors of the Taira family who were defeated in the TAIRA-MINAMOTO WAR in the 12th century. Pop: 4,611.

Shiina Makoto　　椎名誠

(1944–). Essayist and novelist. Born in Tōkyō; attended Tōkyō College of Photography (now Tōkyō Institute of Polytechnics). Shiina's writing is characterized by a deft and witty conversational style. In addition to the essay collection *Saraba Kokubunji*

Shigisan engi emaki
Detail of *The Flying Granary* (Scroll I), a depiction of the legend of the monk Myōren's rice bowl, which flew daily to be filled at a rich landlord's estate. Ca 1156–80. Ink and colors on paper. 32 × 872 cm. Chōgo Sonshiji, Nara. National Treasure.

1365
Shiina Makoto

shiitake The *shiitake* mushroom, eaten in both fresh and dried form, is cultivated by planting mycelia on lengths of oak. Harvesting takes place in the spring and autumn.

Shoten no obaba (1979, Farewell to the Lady Who Owned the Kokubunji Bookstore), Shiina has written a book about his relationship with his son Gaku called *Gaku monogatari* (1985–86, Tales of Gaku).

Shiina Rinzō   椎名麟三

(1911–73). Novelist. Real name Ōtsubo Noboru. Born in Sosa village (in the city of Himeji, Hyōgo Prefecture). Three days after his birth his mother, Misu, attempted suicide; consequently she and her son were sent by the police to join her husband, who was working in Ōsaka. Misu returned to Sosa with her children in 1920, and Shiina attended the local primary school. He entered the Himeji Middle School in 1924, but in his third year the family experienced an acute economic crisis when his father stopped sending money from Ōsaka. Shiina went to his father to ask for money, was refused, and became a vagrant in the streets of Ōsaka.

He got a job as a railroad conductor, helped organize a new labor union, and later became head of a Communist Party cell of railroad employees. Arrested during a mass roundup of communists in August 1931, he was imprisoned until April 1933, during which time he turned away from the Communist Party. He returned after his release to Himeji, then moved to Tōkyō.

Shiina's literary debut came with the publication in 1947 of his novella *Shin'ya no shuen* (tr *Midnight Banquet*, 1970). Its protagonist, a starving ex-communist and street peddler, seeks to endure in the face of life's meaninglessness and the certainty of death, rejecting all ideology. Shiina maintained a prolific output of fiction, drama, translations, and essays on literature and Christian existentialism. In December 1950 he converted to Christianity and was baptized. His fictional works after 1950, which express a Christian existentialist vision and comic sense of the absurd, include *Jiyū no kanata de* (1953–54, This Side of Freedom), *Utsukushii onna* (1955, A Beautiful Woman), and *Eien naru joshō* (1958, Eternal Prologue).

Shiina Takeo   椎名武雄

(1929–). Businessman and president of IBM JAPAN, LTD (1975–). Born in Gifu Prefecture. After graduating from Keiō University in 1951, he studied at Bucknell University in Pennsylvania. Upon graduating from that university in 1953, he joined IBM Japan, Ltd, becoming its president in 1975. In 1989 Shiina became a vice-president of IBM Corporation in the United States. He serves as executive director of NIKKEIREN (Japan Federation of Employers' Associations; 1980–) and as trustee of the JAPAN ASSOCIATION OF CORPORATE EXECUTIVES (1983–).

Shiina Rinzō Growing up in extreme poverty, this prolific writer was influenced first by communism, then by existentialism and Christianity.

shiitake   椎茸

Lentinus edodes. A mushroom of the family Tricholomataceae that grows wild throughout Japan and is also widely cultivated. The pileus (cap) is 5–10 centimeters (2.0–3.9 in) in diameter, with a light to dark brown upper surface and whitish lower surface. Its flesh is thick and white. The *shiitake* is generally found growing on rotting trunks or stumps of deciduous oaks. It has been cultivated since the Edo period (1600–1868). The *shiitake* is an important ingredient in many Japanese dishes, including TEMPURA. Dried *shiitake* have a strong fragrance and are used in soup stock and as an ingredient in *sushi*.

Shijōnawate   四条畷[市]

City in northeastern Ōsaka Prefecture; 13 km (8 mi) northeast of Ōsaka, of which it is a suburb. A former farming area, one of its attractions is the Shijōnawate Shrine, associated with Kusunoki Masatsura (d 1348), a military hero of the period of the Northern and Southern Courts (1337–92). Pop: 50,035.

Shijō school → Maruyama-Shijō school

Shijūhattai Butsu   四十八体仏

("The 48 Buddhas"). Collection of small 7th- and 8th-century gilt bronze Buddhist images, averaging 30 centimeters (11.8 in) in height. Actually 59 in number, they were presented to the imperial household in 1878 by the temple HŌRYŪJI in Nara and are preserved in the Tōkyō National Museum. Some of the images are inscribed with the dates 651 and 666. In the Edo period (1600–1868) the collection became associated with the so-called 48 vows of the Buddha Amida (*shijūhachigan;* see AMIDA), and it began to be popularly known as "The 48 Buddhas." See also HŌRYŪJI, TREASURES OF.

shijuku   私塾

(private school). Educational facility of the Edo period (1600–1868) that used the teacher's own home as the classroom and based the curriculum on the particular learning of the teacher. Standards were higher than those at the TERAKOYA (village schools). Pupils came from all parts of the country and from most social classes.

Representative *shijuku* were the Tōju Shoin of NAKAE TŌJU, the Kōyō Sekiyō Sonsha (also called Renjuku) of KAN SAZAN, the KOGIDŌ of ITŌ JINSAI, and the Kangien of HIROSE TANSŌ, which were all under the direction of Confucian scholars. National Learning (KOKUGAKU) was represented in such schools as the Suzunoya of MOTOORI NORINAGA and the Ibukinoya of his disciple HIRATA ATSUTANE. The Tekijuku of OGATA KŌAN emphasized WESTERN LEARNING.

Shikanoshima   志賀島

Island at the mouth of Hakata Bay, Fukuoka Prefecture, northern Kyūshū. There are gardens and rice fields on the western slopes of the island; fruits and vegetables are also cultivated. The scene of fighting during the MONGOL INVASIONS OF JAPAN, the island is also known as the site where a historic gold seal (see KAN NO WA NO NA NO KOKUŌ NO IN) was discovered. It is part of the Genkai Quasi-National Park. Area: 5.8 sq km (2.2 sq mi).

shikashū   私家集

Personal poetry collections, as distinguished from the IMPERIAL ANTHOLOGIES (*chokusen wakashū* or *chokusenshū*), in the WAKA tradition of Japanese classical poetry. There are several hundred extant collections compiled from the late 9th to the early 19th century, the earliest being *Kudai waka* (894), which contains poems by Ōe no Chisato. *Shikashū* may consist of fewer than 50 poems, or of more than 1,000. Some are arranged according to the formal categories of the imperial anthologies; others are arranged in chronological order with long prose headnotes (see KOTOBAGAKI) and may be read as a species of diary. The traditional term for *shikashū* is *ie no shū* (house collections), and early examples often exhibit a strong sense of family pride. *Shikashū* constituted the basic material for the first imperial anthology, the KOKINSHŪ (ca 905). There is also a significant link between *shikashū* and the birth of *uta monogatari* (tales about poems; see MONOGATARI BUNGAKU). Renowned examples of *shikashū* are *Sanjūrokuninshū* (ca 1112), a compilation of the collections of 36 poets (see SANJŪROKKASEN), MINAMOTO NO TOSHIYORI's *Samboku kikashū* (ca 1127), and SAIGYŌ's *Sankashū*.

Shikatsu   師勝[町]

Town in northwestern Aichi Prefecture, central Honshū. An agricultural area producing cabbage, spinach, and other vegetables, Shikatsu is now being transformed into a commuter suburb of Nagoya. Pop: 39,610.

Shikatsube Magao   鹿都部真顔

(1753–1829). Also known as Koikawa Sukimachi. KYŌKA poet and KIBYŌSHI writer. Born in Edo (now Tōkyō). He studied with KOIKAWA HARUMACHI and Yomo no Akara (also known as ŌTA NAMPO). Poems by him are included in Nampo's anthology *Manzai kyōkashū*.

Shika wakashū   詞花和歌集

(Collection of Verbal Flowers). Usually shortened to *Shikashū*. Sixth of the IMPERIAL ANTHOLOGIES (*chokusenshū*) of classical Japanese poetry (WAKA); ordered in 1144 by former emperor Sutoku (1119–64; r 1123–42). Compiled by FUJIWARA NO AKISUKE, head of the most prominent family of court poets of the day, the first draft was probably completed in 1151; the second, official draft was accepted in 1152 or 1153 and consisted of 10 books and 409 poems. The shortest of the imperial anthologies, it falls into two halves, the first dominated by nature poems arranged by season, and the second by poems on love and miscellaneous topics. Between the two halves are a book each of celebration and of parting. The poems are by 189 individuals, generally represented by a single poem each. Major poets by number of entries include SONE NO YOSHITADA, 17 poems; Lady IZUMI SHIKIBU, 16; ŌE NO MASAFUSA, 14; and MINAMOTO NO TOSHIYORI, 11.

Shiki   志木[市]

City in southern Saitama Prefecture, central Honshū. It prospered in the Edo period (1600–1868) as a river port and is now primarily a commuter suburb of Tōkyō. Pop: 63,491.

Shiki   四季

(The Four Seasons). Poetry coterie magazine, published in four series. The first series, edited by HORI TATSUO, was published in May and July of 1933. The best known and most influential was the second series, coedited by Hori, MIYOSHI TATSUJI, and MARUYAMA KAORU and published monthly by Shikisha from

October 1934 to June 1944. An important forum for the lyric poetry of the 1930s, this series of *Shiki* published work by leading poets such as HAGIWARA SAKUTARŌ, NAKAHARA CHŪYA, MUROO SAISEI, and ITŌ SHIZUŌ, as well as cultural criticism by KUWABARA TAKEO, YASUDA YOJŪRŌ, and others. A third and fourth series were published in the postwar period.

Shikibō, Ltd　敷島紡績[株]

(Shikishima Bōseki). Manufacturer and marketer of cotton yarn, synthetic fibers and textiles, secondary textile products, and interior decorating materials. Incorporated in 1892. For the fiscal year ending March 1991, sales totaled ¥69.3 billion (US $505.1 million) and capitalization stood at ¥10.3 billion (US $75.1 million). Headquarters are in Ōsaka.

Shikidō ōkagami　色道大鏡

(The Great Mirror of the Erotic Way). Study of prostitution in Japan by Hatakeyama Kizan (d 1704). Published in 1678, it is a scholarly and encyclopedic work that describes the history, customs, and day-to-day operations of the pleasure districts of the early Edo period (1600–1868). It also functioned as a book of etiquette and detailed guide to the manners, language, arts, and practices of the licensed quarters (*yūkaku*), which were a focal point for the burgeoning popular culture of the period. The novelist Ihara SAIKAKU was well acquainted with the *Shikidō ōkagami*, and he may have used Kizan as the prototype for the profligate hero of his KŌSHOKU ICHIDAI OTOKO (1682; tr *The Life of an Amorous Man*, 1964).

Little is known of Kizan's life. He was born in Kyōto in 1626 or 1628 and studied under the *haiku* poet MATSUNAGA TEITOKU. He is also known as Fujimoto Kizan.

shikikin→rental deposit

shikimi　樒

Illicium religiosum or *I. anisatum.* Evergreen tree of the family Illiciaceae that grows wild in the warm areas of Kyūshū, Shikoku, and central and western Honshū. It is also cultivated in cemeteries and Buddhist temple grounds as an offering flower. It reaches 3–5 meters (10–16 ft) in height. The leaves are alternate, oblong, 6–8 centimeters (2.5–3.0 in) long, and fragrant. Around April the plant opens light yellow flowers, each with a total of 12 petals and sepals of nearly the same shape and color. The star-shaped fruits (follicles) split open when ripe in autumn and scatter yellow seeds. Although the seeds are poisonous, the fresh branches of the *shikimi* are used as offerings on household Buddhist altars (*butsudan*), and incense powder is made from the leaves.

shikimoku　式目

1. Compilations of regulations for the behavior of *samurai* retainers or "housemen" (GOKENIN) issued by warrior governments or warlords from the 13th through the 16th centuries. Examples include GOSEIBAI SHIKIMOKU (1232), KEMMU SHIKIMOKU (1336), and YOSHIHARU SHIKIMOKU (1567). See also BUKEHŌ; BUNKOKUHŌ.

2. In literature, rules for composing RENGA and *haikai* (see HAIKU) verse.

shikinaisha　式内社

(*shikinai* shrines). Also called *shikisha* or *kansha.* The Shintō shrines listed in the "register of deities" (*jimmyōchō*) in books 9 and 10 of the ENGI SHIKI (Procedures of the Engi Era) of 927. It listed a total of 2,861 shrines throughout Japan, enshrining 3,132 deities (*kami*). These were divided into major shrines (*taisha*) and minor shrines (*shōsha*), which were classified into those directly supported by offerings from the Jingikan (Office of Shintō Worship) of the central government and those supported by provincial governments. Shrines not in this system were called *shikige* or *shikigai*. See also SHRINES.

Shiki no Miko　志貴皇子

(?–716; Prince Shiki). Imperial prince and poet of the early literary period (late 7th–early 8th centuries). Although his extant works consist of a mere six 31-syllable *tanka* ("short poems") in the MAN'YŌSHŪ, the first great anthology of Japanese vernacular poetry, he is nonetheless regarded as one of the finest poets of the age. Since the emperors TENJI (626–672) and TEMMU (d 686) each had a son known as Prince Shiki, his exact identity is uncertain, but the Prince Shiki who is represented in the *Man'yōshū* is believed to be the son of Emperor Tenji.

shikishi and tanzaku　色紙と短冊

(*shikishi to tanzaku*). Types of paper, of a set size and either plain white or decorated with gold or silver leaf, that are used especially for writing WAKA or HAIKU poetry or for painting. *Shikishi* are nearly square; *tanzaku*, long and rectangular.

Shikishi originated in the late Heian (794–1185) and Kamakura (1185–1333) periods, a time when court nobles amused themselves by composing *waka* and then affixing the sheets of paper on which they had written the poems to decorative screens and sliding doors. The *shikishi* of today come in a standard size of 27.3 by 24.2 cm (10.8 by 9.5 in) and are still used when composing poetry. *Shikishi* are also used by famous actors and other celebrities when handing out autographs.

Tanzaku of various sizes came to be used for writing *waka* during the Kamakura period, and during the Muromachi period (1333–1568) the size of the *tanzaku* used was an indication of the writer's social status. Since the Meiji period (1868–1912) the size of *tanzaku* has been standardized at 36.4 by 6.1 cm (14.3 by 2.4 in).

Shikishi, Princess　式子内親王

(?–1201; Shikishi Naishinnō). Also known as Shokushi Naishinnō (Princess Shokushi). Poet; Shintō high priestess. Daughter of Emperor GO-SHIRAKAWA. Visits to her by the famous poets Fujiwara no Shunzei (FUJIWARA NO TOSHINARI) and his son Fujiwara no Teika (FUJIWARA NO SADAIE) indicate her interest in poetry. Shunzei included nine of her poems in the seventh imperial anthology, SENZAI WAKASHŪ, which he completed in 1188. Shunzei also wrote the treatise KORAI FŪTEI SHŌ (Notes on Poetic Style through the Ages) at her request. Forty-nine of her poems, more than any other woman, appear in the imperial anthology SHIN KOKINSHŪ (1205).

Shikitei Samba　式亭三馬

(1776–1822). Early-19th-century GESAKU fiction writer. Real name Kikuchi Taisuke. Born in Edo (now Tōkyō). One of the earliest Japanese writers to earn a living from fiction, Samba is best known for his KOKKEIBON ("funny books"), principally UKIYOBURO (1809–13, The Bathhouse of the Floating World), but was author as well of best-selling stories in the GŌKAN ("bound volume") format—lavishly illustrated fiction popular from the early 19th century onward—and many works in other genres of fiction. Samba's first published works were KIBYŌSHI ("yellow cover"), a variety of illustrated fiction. His first real success came in 1799 with a *kibyōshi* entitled *Kyan taiheiki mukō hachimaki*, which treated satirically a battle that had recently taken place between two neighborhood fire brigades in Edo.

In 1806 Samba published a 10-volume *kibyōshi*-style story entitled *Ikazuchi Tarō gōaku monogatari*, regarded as the first example of a book published in the *gōkan* format. The 10 volumes of this work were bound in 2 larger volumes of 5 each, instead of each separately. The new format encouraged the development of longer, more complicated stories and soon displaced the *kibyōshi* as the dominant form of illustrated fiction. Samba went on to write over 70 *gōkan*, many of them extremely popular. Samba also wrote several SHAREBON, late-18th-century *gesaku* fiction that deals exclusively with the pleasure quarters. *Tatsumi fugen* (1798) and its sequels are examples of a trend toward the greater, almost novelistic complexity of later NINJŌBON romances.

The works for which Samba, who considered himself a disciple of HIRAGA GENNAI, is best remembered are his *kokkeibon*, which were influenced by RAKUGO and other humorous storytelling forms. His *Ukiyoburo* and its sequel *Ukiyodoko* (1813–14, The Barbershop of the Floating World) have enjoyed enduring popularity. Collections of vignettes from a bathhouse and a barbershop, the stories consist of conversations of ordinary middle-class people who reveal their personalities, quirks, and obsessions.

shikken　執権

(shogunal regent). An office of the KAMAKURA SHOGUNATE (1192–1333), first assumed in 1203 by HŌJŌ TOKIMASA after the death of MINAMOTO NO YORITOMO, his son-in-law and the founder of the shogunate. As regent for MINAMOTO NO SANETOMO and as head of the MANDOKORO (Administrative Board), Tokimasa became de facto ruler in 1203. His son and successor, HŌJŌ YOSHITOKI, increased this power; in 1213 Yoshitoki became simultaneously head of the SAMURAI-DOKORO (Board of Retainers). Thereafter the office was held by successive members of the HŌJŌ FAMILY. The post of assistant regent (RENSHO, or cosigner) was established by HŌJŌ YASUTOKI in 1225, and the creation of the HYŌJŌSHŪ (Council of State) in 1226 allowed for further collegial sharing of power. After the MONGOL INVASIONS OF JAPAN in 1274 and 1281, political power shifted to the TOKUSŌ, the patrimonial head of the Hōjō family.

Shikoku Electric Power Co, Inc　四国電力[株]

(Shikoku Denryoku). Supplier of electric power to the island of Shikoku. Incorporated in 1951. The company maintains a close relationship with various foreign companies in order to secure energy sources and financing in international markets. In the fiscal year ending March 1991, the company sold 20 billion kilowatt-hours, worth ¥435.4 billion (US $3.2 billion), and was capitalized at ¥145.6 billion (US $1.1 billion). Headquarters are in the city of Takamatsu, Kagawa Prefecture.

shikimi A *shikimi* branch, with flowers and buds. Because of the plant's association with Buddhist funeral rites, it is not usually planted in private gardens.

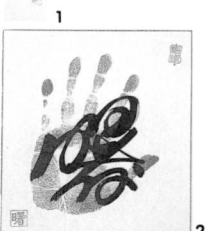

shikishi and tanzaku
1 A delicate polychrome bird-and-flower painting decorates this *tanzaku*.
2 *Shikishi* are commonly used by celebrities for autographs, as seen in this handprint and signature of *sumō* wrestler Akebono.

Shikotsu-Tōya National Park Four volcanic islands lie within Lake Tōya. The small island Kannonjima (Bodhisattva Island) is the site of a temple dedicated to Kannon, the bodhisattva of infinite compassion.

Shikoku Karst　　　四国カルスト

(Shikoku Karusuto). Japan's highest limestone plateau. It overlaps Ehime and Kōchi prefectures, Shikoku. It is noted for its karst topography, with numerous dolines and limestone caves. Elevation: 900–1,400 m (3,000–4,600 ft); area: 7.4 sq km (2.9 sq mi).

Shikoku Mountains　　　四国山地

(Shikoku Sanchi). Series of mountain ranges extending east to west about 250 km (155 mi) from the Kii Channel to the Bungo Channel, central Shikoku. The highest peak is ISHIZUCHISAN (1,982 m; 6,503 ft). The mountains are noted for their rugged and wild terrain. There is heavy precipitation, and large areas are covered with forests. Lumbering and the cultivation of *mitsumata* and *kōzo* trees for making *washi* (Japanese paper) are carried on. Tourist attractions include the Shikoku Karst Prefectural Natural Park and gorges, such as ŌBOKE and IYADANI.

Shikoku region　　　四国地方

(Shikoku *chihō*). Region consisting of Shikoku, the smallest of Japan's four main islands, and numerous surrounding islands. Shikoku lies to the south of western Honshū, across the INLAND SEA and across the Bungo Channel from northeastern Kyūshū. It consists of Kagawa, Tokushima, Ehime, and Kōchi prefectures. Shikoku's high mountains and steep slopes severely limit agriculture, habitation, and communication. The climate is subtropical with short, mild winters and long, hot summers. On the Pacific Ocean side of the island there is heavy rainfall in summer, and typhoons are frequent.

Much of the island is a thinly populated agricultural region, with few natural resources and little large-scale industry. Two recently completed chains of bridges linking Shikoku with Honshū (a third was still under construction in 1990) are expected to bring in many new industries. Extensive land reclamation in Kagawa and Tokushima prefectures should provide more room for this industrial expansion. TAKAMATSU and MATSUYAMA are the largest cities. Area: 18,808 sq km (7,262 sq mi); pop: 4,195,069.

Shikotan　　　色丹

Island approximately 75 km (47 mi) northeast of the Nemuro Peninsula, eastern Hokkaidō. The island is hilly, averaging 300 m (985 ft) in elevation. It is surrounded by sea cliffs. Shakotan, in the northeast, is an excellent natural port. The principal activity is fishing; marine products include cod, crab, and kelp. The island was occupied by the Soviet Union in 1945, and in early 1992 it was still under occupation by the Russian Federation (see TERRITORY OF JAPAN). Area: 255 sq km (98 sq mi).

Shikotsu, Lake　　　支笏湖

(Shikotsuko). Caldera lake in the city of Chitose, southwestern Hokkaidō. Japan's northernmost ice-free lake and second deepest lake after Lake Tazawa in Akita Prefecture. Located within Shikotsu-Tōya National Park, it attracts numerous anglers between June and August. Area: 77 sq km (30 sq mi); circumference: 42 km (26 mi); depth: 360 m (1,181 ft); altitude: 248 m (814 ft).

Shikotsu-Tōya National Park　　　支笏洞爺国立公園

(Shikotsu-Tōya Kokuritsu Kōen). Situated in southwest Hokkaidō, 10 km (6.2 mi) southwest of the city of SAPPORO. The chief features of this mountainous region are active volcanoes, numerous hot-spring resorts, and three large caldera lakes. In the east lies Lake SHIKOTSU, ringed by high cliffs and active volcanoes such as Eniwadake and TARUMAEZAN. To the southwest lies Lake TŌYA, on whose southern shore are two active volcanoes: USUZAN, noted for its frequent eruptions, and SHŌWA SHINZAN, formed in 1944. North of Lake Tōya is the volcano YŌTEIZAN. At the southern edge of the park is Lake KUTTARA, with Noboribetsu Hot Spring nearby. JŌZANKEI HOT SPRING is in the north of the park, near Shiraito Falls. Typical trees of the area are the Yeddo spruce (*ezomatsu*), Sakhalin fir (*todomatsu*), silver birch, and Japanese oak (*nara*). Area: 983.3 sq km (380 sq mi).

Shikunshi　　　四君子

(The Four Gentlemen; Ch: Si Junzi or Ssu Chün-tzu). Chinese painting subject. The combination of blossoming plum, orchid, chrysanthemum, and bamboo as a painting subject alludes to the purity and nobility of the Confucian gentleman. In China, each of these four plants has a long literary history of association with virtue, and one by one became scholar-painter subjects during the Song (Sung; 960–1279) and Yuan (Yüan; 1279–1368) dynasties. Their union as The Four Gentlemen was established by the early 15th century. In Japan, Shikunshi was a favored subject of literati painting (BUNJINGA).

Shimabara　　　島原[市]

City in Nagasaki Prefecture, Kyūshū. During the Edo period (1600–1868) Shimabara was a castle town of the Matsudaira family and the site of the SHIMABARA UPRISING (1637–38), a rebellion by Christians and peasants. Principal products are mandarin oranges, tobacco, and tea. Rainbow-trout hatcheries are located here. Among its tourist attractions are the remains of Shimabara Castle, old warrior houses, and the Shimabara Hot Spring. Pop: 44,828.

Shimabara Peninsula　　　島原半島

(Shimabara Hantō). Located in Nagasaki Prefecture, western Kyūshū, separating the Ariake Sea from Tachibana Bay. As the center of Christianity when it was first introduced to Japan in the 16th century, it has many historical sites associated with this era. Site of Unzendake and other peaks in Unzen-Amakusa National Park. The Shimabara and Unzen hot springs are located here.

Shimabara Uprising　　　島原の乱

(Shimabara no Ran). Peasant uprising (IKKI) that broke out on 11 December 1637 in the overtaxed Shimabara domain (now part of Nagasaki Prefecture) of the *daimyō* Matsukura Katsuie (d 1638) and immediately spread to the Amakusa Islands (now part of Kumamoto Prefecture). Both areas had been Christianized before the Tokugawa shogunate (1603–1867) began its general persecution of the faith in February 1614. The shogunate viewed the rebellion as Christian-inspired, a critical factor in its final decision to cut off all contact with Catholic lands (see NATIONAL SECLUSION).

However, it was not orthodox Christianity but millenarian hopes for deliverance from chronic poverty, recurrent famine, extortionate taxation, and religious persecution that motivated the rebellion. The discontented peasants were joined by large numbers of masterless *samurai* (*rōnin*), former vassals of the *daimyō* KONISHI YUKINAGA, who had been defeated and executed by the Tokugawa in 1600. The rebellion was led by Amakusa Shirō (also known as Masuda Shirō Tokisada; 1622?–38), a charismatic youth whose father had been a Konishi vassal.

The rebels were put under siege at Hara Castle on the Shimabara Peninsula by a huge army mobilized by the shogunate. When it fell on 12 April 1638, Amakusa Shirō and 37,000 of his followers, women and children included, are said to have perished in the slaughter.

Shimada　　　島田[市]

City in central Shizuoka Prefecture, central Honshū. In the Edo period (1600–1868) it was a crossing point for the river Ōigawa and a prosperous post-station town on the highway TŌKAIDŌ. Now a distribution center for lumber, it also produces pulp, foodstuffs, and machinery. Tea and mandarin oranges are cultivated on the Makinohara Plateau. Pop: 73,810.

Shimada Junko　　　島田順子

(1941–). Fashion designer. Born in Chiba Prefecture. Shimada, who graduated from the Sugino College of Dressmaking in Tōkyō, is based in Paris. In 1981 she launched her "49AV Junko Shimada" label. Her designs feature simple, basic lines.

Shimada Masahiko　　　島田雅彦

(1961–). Novelist. Born in Tōkyō. Graduated from Tōkyō University of Foreign Studies. Shimada writes sharply parodic novels about the social consciousness of contemporary youth. He received the Noma Literary Prize for New Talent for *Muyū ōkoku no tame no ongaku* (1984, Music for the Kingdom of Sleepwalking) and is also the author of *Yasashii sayoku no tame no kiyūkyoku* (1983, Divertimento for Gentle Leftists).

Shimada Saburō　　　島田三郎

(1852–1923). Politician and journalist. Born in Edo (now Tōkyō), he studied at Daigaku Nankō, the predecessor of Tōkyō University. In 1873 he became a reporter for the newspaper *Yokohama mainichi shimbun* and a champion of the FREEDOM AND PEOPLE'S RIGHTS MOVEMENT. In 1875 Shimada entered government service but resigned at the time of the POLITICAL CRISIS OF 1881. He joined in the founding of the RIKKEN KAISHINTŌ (Constitutional Reform Party) and at the same time resumed his journalistic career with the *Yokohama mainichi*, of which he became manager. He was elected to 14 successive terms in the Diet, beginning with the first election in 1890, and was known as a gifted orator. He was outspoken in his condemnation of political corruption, particularly in connection with the SIEMENS INCIDENT and the ASHIO COPPER MINE INCIDENT.

Shimadzu Corporation

[株]島津製作所

(Shimazu Seisakusho). Manufacturer of precision measuring, medical, aviation, and industrial instruments. Incorporated in 1917. It has 7 overseas offices, 4 foreign subsidiaries, and more than 100 overseas sales agencies. Annual sales totaled ¥163.4 billion (US $1.2 billion) in the fiscal year ending March 1991, and the company was capitalized at ¥16.7 billion (US $121.7 million). Headquarters are in Kyōto.

Shima Hot Spring

四万温泉

(Shima Onsen). Located in the northern part of the town of Nakanojō, northwestern Gumma Prefecture, central Honshū. A voluminous, weak saline hot spring; water temperature 70°C (158°F). Located within Jōshin'etsu Kōgen National Park, this spa is situated along the river Shimagawa and is a summer and health resort.

Shimai Sōshitsu

島井宗室

(1539?–1615). Merchant and tea connoisseur of the Azuchi-Momoyama (1568–1600) and early Edo (1600–1868) periods. The Shimai family were *sake* brewers and pawnbrokers in the port city of Hakata (now Fukuoka; see HAKATA MERCHANTS). Sōshitsu engaged in trade with Tsushima and Korea. He had by the 1570s established ties with counterparts in SAKAI, Japan's other major trading city, and with powerful *daimyō* such as ŌTOMO SŌRIN; by 1583 he had come to the notice of TOYOTOMI HIDEYOSHI. Upon Hideyoshi's conquest of Kyūshū in 1587, Sōshitsu together with KAMIYA SŌTAN was assigned responsibilities in the reconstruction of war-torn Hakata. Sōshitsu participated in the negotiations that preceded Hideyoshi's invasions of Korea, traveling to that country in 1589 and 1592 as the associate of Sō Yoshitomo (1568–1615), daimyō of Tsushima, and KONISHI YUKINAGA. Sōshitsu assisted Kobayakawa Takakage (1533–97), KOBAYAKAWA HIDEAKI, ISHIDA MITSUNARI, and KURODA NAGAMASA in their successive administration of the Hakata area but is said to have refused elevation to *samurai* status.

Shimaji Mokurai

島地黙雷

(1838–1911). Buddhist priest and reformer of the JŌDO SHIN SECT; ardent spokesman for Buddhists in Japan and advocate of freedom of religion in the Meiji period (1868–1912). Born in Suō Province (now part of Yamaguchi Prefecture). After taking his priestly vows he went to the temple Nishi Hoganji in Kyōto, where he was active in the sect reform movement. Impressed by the separation of religion and state he observed while traveling in Europe, Shimaji submitted a number of written petitions to the government calling for the dissolution of the Daikyōin (Office of Religion, established in 1872), through which the Meiji government attempted to spread SHINTŌ as the national creed. His efforts were instrumental in securing abolition of this office in 1875 and promoting a government religious policy more tolerant toward Buddhism. Despite his espousal of religious freedom, Shimaji was critical of Christianity. He was a reporter for the *Shimbun zasshi*, a weekly news magazine, and editor of *Nihonjin*, a national magazine. He also helped found a school for women and the Japanese Red Cross.

Shimaki Akahiko

島木赤彦

(1876–1926). TANKA poet. Real name Kubota Toshihiko. Born in Nagano Prefecture. Graduate of Nagano Normal School (now part of Shinshū University). An elementary-school teacher, he started composing *tanka*, inspired by the *tanka* reformer MASAOKA SHIKI. In 1908 he became a contributor to ARARAGI, a *tanka* magazine, and in 1914 he became its editor. He combined a crisp style, reminiscent of the school of Japanese naturalism, with a moralizing tone, which he advocated as a principal element in *tanka*. His major collections are *Taikyoshū* (1924) and *Shiinshū* (1926).

Shimaki Kensaku

島木健作

(1903–45). Novelist. Real name Asakura Kikuo. Born in Hokkaidō. Inspired by the proletarian movement of the 1920s, he left Tōhoku University in 1926 and participated in labor and farmers' union movements. He joined the Communist Party and was arrested in the mass arrests of 1928 (see MARCH 15TH INCIDENT). He developed tuberculosis in prison and was released in 1932 after promising to forsake communism. After his forced withdrawal from political activities, he began to write while living in Tōkyō with his mother and older brother. His novels evoke his painful struggles of conscience in abandoning his political commitments. His principal works are *Saiken* (1935, Reconstruction), *Seikatsu no tankyū* (1937–38, The Quest for Life), and "Akagaeru" (1946, Red Frog).

Shimamura Hōgetsu

島村抱月

(1871–1918). Literary critic, novelist, and playwright. Real name Shimamura Takitarō. Born in Shimane Prefecture. Graduate of Tōkyō Semmon Gakkō (now Waseda University), where he was a student of TSUBOUCHI SHŌYŌ. After studying in Europe, he returned to Japan in 1905 and became a professor at Waseda. He emerged as an important critic through his studies of works written by authors of the naturalist school. A founding member, together with Shōyō, of the Bungei Kyōkai (Association of Literary Arts; 1906–13), he participated in the modern theater movement, introducing a number of modern European plays. Hōgetsu founded an independent theater group, the Geijutsuza, with Matsui Sumako (1886–1919), a star actress and his lover. Hōgetsu's major contribution as a dramatist was the popularization of modern-day Western issues such as greater freedom for women. His name is best remembered in association with Sumako, who played Katusha in his dramatization of Tolstoy's *Resurrection*. His principal works include *Ran'unshū* (1906), a collection of stories, and *Kindai bungei no kenkyū* (1909), literary essays.

Shimanaka Incident

嶋中事件

(Shimanaka Jiken). The planned murder in 1960 of Shimanaka Hōji (b 1923), president of the publishing firm CHŪŌ KŌRON SHA, INC. After the short story "Fūryū mutan" (An Elegant Fantasy) by FUKAZAWA SHICHIRŌ appeared in the December 1960 issue of the magazine CHŪŌ KŌRON, rightist groups and the Imperial Household Agency filed protests with the magazine, citing as blasphemous the scene in which the imperial family are executed. A young right-wing terrorist broke into Shimanaka's house; failing to find Shimanaka, he stabbed the maid to death and seriously wounded Shimanaka's wife.

The magazine published a statement apologizing for having offended the dignity of the imperial house.

Shimanaka Yūsaku

嶋中雄作

(1887–1949). Editor, publisher, and president of CHŪŌ KŌRON SHA, INC. Born in Nara Prefecture. After graduating from Waseda University, Shimanaka entered Chūō Kōron Sha, the publisher of CHŪŌ KŌRON, a leading journal for intellectuals. He worked as an editor under TAKITA CHOIN. In 1916 he brought out FUJIN KŌRON, a magazine for educated women. Shimanaka became president of the company in 1928 and started publishing books in 1929. Some of his most successful publishing ventures were translations of Western works. Due to military repression, in 1944 he dissolved his company. It resumed publication in 1945.

Shimane Peninsula

島根半島

(Shimane Hantō). Located in northeastern Shimane Prefecture, western Honshū. Composed chiefly of mountains, it runs parallel with the Chūgoku Mountains and is separated from them by Lake Shinji and Lake Nakaumi. The heavily indented northern coast forms part of the Daisen-Oki National Park. Tourist attractions include the Miho Shrine, Izumo Shrine, and Hinomisaki Shrine. Length: east to west about 65 km (40 mi); greatest width: 20 km (12 mi).

Shimane Prefecture

島根県

(Shimane Ken). Located in western Honshū and bounded on the north by the Sea of Japan, on the east by Tottori Prefecture, on the south by Hiroshima Prefecture, and on the west by Yamaguchi Prefecture. The terrain is largely mountainous, with the main level areas situated near the coast in the northeast. The small Oki Islands, located north of the city of MATSUE in the Sea of Japan, are administratively a part of the prefecture. The climate is relatively mild, with many overcast days.

Formerly the area was divided into the provinces of Izumo, Iwami, and Oki. The Izumo region is mentioned in the mythic cycles of the KOJIKI (712), Japan's first chronicle, and the IZUMO SHRINE remains one of the most important centers of the Shintō religion. The area came under the control of a succession of warrior families from the late Heian period (794–1185) to the Edo period (1600–1868) and was incorporated into the modern prefectural system in 1881.

Agriculture, especially rice production, remains the main occupation. Fishing is also important. Industry is limited to textiles, farming tools, and woodworking, as well as to molybdenum mining. Attractions include the city of Matsue with its castle, Izumo Shrine, and the Oki Islands. The mountain SAMBESAN and Shimane Peninsula are part of the DAISEN-OKI NATIONAL PARK. Area: 6,629 sq km (2,559 sq mi); pop: 781,021; capital: Matsue. Other major cities include HAMADA, IZUMO, and MASUDA.

Shimantogawa

四万十川

River in southwestern Kōchi Prefecture, Shikoku, originating in the western Shikoku Mountains and flowing through the Nakamura Plain into Tosa Bay. It is the second largest river in Shikoku. The river basin is mountainous. The volume of water is abundant, but the river's hydroelectric potential is

Shimamura Hōgetsu
This critic and playwright was a major force in introducing modern European drama and its social concerns to a Japanese audience.

Shimane Prefecture
Location and Prefectural Crest

undeveloped. Length: 196 km (122 mi); area of drainage basin: 2,270 sq km (876 sq mi).

Shimao Toshio   島尾敏雄

(1917–86). Author. Born in Yokohama. Shimao was drafted immediately after graduating from Kyūshū University and in the final days of World War II was the commander of a naval suicide-mission unit. He began publishing soon after the war, writing about war and love in an abstract, often surrealistic style. Several of his works, among them *Shima no hate* (1948, Island's End) and *Shuppatsu wa tsui ni otozurezu* (1962, Orders for Departure Never Came), are based on his wartime experiences. Perhaps his best-known work is *Shi no toge* (1960; tr *The Sting of Death*, 1985), an account of his reaction to his wife's mental illness.

Shima Peninsula   志摩半島

(Shima Hantō). Located in eastern Mie Prefecture, central Honshū. With Atsumi Peninsula it encloses Ise Bay. The southern part has heavily indented coasts with an abrasion platform called Sakishima. Pearl culture flourishes in Ago and Matoya bays; women divers fish for shellfish off the eastern and southern coast. The peninsula has numerous tourist attractions, particularly near the cities of Toba and Sakishima. The entire peninsula is designated as Ise-Shima National Park.

Shimazaki Tōson   島崎藤村

(1872–1943). Poet; novelist; most famous Japanese proponent of NATURALISM. Born in Magome in Nagano Prefecture. Real name Shimazaki Haruki. Tōson entered Meiji Gakuin, a college with Protestant Christian affiliations, and graduated in 1891. He became

one of the coterie that began the noted literary journal BUNGAKUKAI (1893–98, World of Literature). In 1896 he left Tōkyō for Sendai to teach; while there he published his first collection of verse, *Wakanashū* (1897, Collection of Young Herbs), which immediately established him as a leading "new style" poet.

The publication in 1906 of his first novel, HAKAI (tr *The Broken Commandment*, 1974), began Tōson's distinguished career as a novelist. The novel is considered a landmark of modern Japanese realism. The hero, a schoolteacher who keeps his outcaste origin as a member of the minority BURAKUMIN group a secret until near the end of the novel, is drawn with great insight and force and remains to this day one of the memorable characters in modern Japanese fiction. His next novel, *Haru* (1908, Spring), is weakly plotted and much less explicit in language than *Hakai*. It is a lyrical and often too sentimental autobiographical account of Tōson's youthful days with the *Bungakukai* group.

Ie (1910–11; tr *The Family*, 1976), however, is often considered to be the "classic" Japanese naturalistic novel. Understated in tone, carefully maintaining objectivity, it is a slow-moving and detailed account of the decline of two provincial families to which the protagonist is closely related. The gestures and silences of the characters, as well as the surroundings, subtly convey meaning. *Shinsei* (1918–19, New Life), a more explicitly emotional work, describes the author's seduction of one of his nieces, her pregnancy, and his ignominious flight from confrontation with his relations by exiling himself to France for a while. It caused a sensation when it was published and was attacked by some critics and fellow writers for its alleged hypocrisy in the author's presentation of himself and his motives. YOAKE MAE (1929–35; tr *Before the Dawn*, 1987), the most ambitious Tōson novel in scope, is a historical novel in which the author tries both to describe the era of the Meiji Restoration of 1868 from the point of view of a provincial loyalist—his own father—and to describe the tragedy of this man, who dies in bitter disillusionment. Very uneven, it is often marred by the author's description of the mundane and his penchant for extreme understatement.

All in all, however, Tōson's reputation as a novelist will survive; for, at least in *Hakai* and *Ie*, he wrote two masterpieces in their respective genres.

Shimazono Junjirō   島薗順次郎

(1877–1937). Scientist and specialist in internal medicine. Born in Wakayama Prefecture; graduate of the Faculty of Medicine of Tōkyō University. By analyzing meals served in factories and school dormitories where beriberi was prevalent, Shimazono proved that a shortage of vitamin B_1 was the cause of the disease. Shimazono taught at both Kyōto and Tōkyō universities. He received the Japan Academy Prize in 1926 for his study on vitamin B_1 deficiency, carried out in cooperation with OGATA TOMOSABURŌ.

Shimazu family   島津氏

(Shimazushi). Provincial leaders and later *daimyō* in southern Kyūshū from the 12th century to 1868. In 1197 Shimazu Tadahisa (1179–1227), a vassal of MINAMOTO NO YORITOMO, was appointed military governor (*shugo*) of Ōsumi and Satsuma provinces (now Kagoshima Prefecture) and later also Hyūga Province (now Miyazaki Prefecture). Under Shimazu Yoshihisa (1533–1611) the family came to control most of Kyūshū. When Yoshihisa was defeated by TOYOTOMI HIDEYOSHI in 1587 the Shimazu holdings were reduced to the original three provinces. Yoshihisa's brother SHIMAZU YOSHIHIRO fought on the losing side at Sekigahara in 1600 (see SEKIGAHARA, BATTLE OF), and the family barely escaped confiscation of their lands by the victor, TOKUGAWA IEYASU. Nonetheless, under the Tokugawa shogunate (1603–1867) the heads of the Shimazu served as *daimyō* of the TOZAMA ("outside vassal") domain of Satsuma. Yoshihiro's son Iehisa (1578–1638) conquered Okinawa in 1609. In the 19th century SHIMAZU NARIAKIRA strengthened the financial and military position of his domain during the TEMPŌ REFORMS, and SHIMAZU HISAMITSU was prominent in the MOVEMENT FOR UNION OF COURT AND SHOGUNATE and the MEIJI RESTORATION (1868). See also SATSUMA PROVINCE.

Shimazu Genzō   島津源蔵

(1869–1951). Inventor and industrialist. Born in Kyōto. He took over the family company, Shimazu Seisakusho, Ltd, after his father's death in 1894 and developed the small firm into a large enterprise (see SHIMADZU CORPORATION). Among his accomplishments was the introduction of mass-production techniques in the manufacture of lead-acid storage batteries. In 1896 he was successful in taking the first X-ray photographs in Japan, and in 1928 he developed the Shimazu-type induction generator. In 1930 he was formally recognized by the government as one of Japan's 10 leading inventors.

Shimazu Hisamitsu   島津久光

(1817–87). De facto ruler of the Satsuma domain (now Kagoshima Prefecture) in the years immediately preceding the MEIJI RESTORATION of 1868. The fifth son of the Shimazu Narioki (1791–1895), *daimyō* of Satsuma. When his elder half brother SHIMAZU NARIAKIRA died in 1858, Hisamitsu's son Tadayoshi (1840–97) succeeded. In 1860 Hisamitsu sought to bring Satsuma into national politics by promoting the MOVEMENT FOR UNION OF COURT AND SHOGUNATE. In 1862 he led a force of over 1,000 men to Kyōto, where he ordered activist Satsuma *samurai* to return to their domain, urged the court to control radical elements, and sent troops to suppress Satsuma samurai holding out at an inn outside Kyōto (see TERADAYA INCIDENT). Hisamitsu and his troops then went to

Shimao Toshio
A number of this author's works are based on his experiences in World War II, when he served as commander of a naval *kamikaze* squad.

Shimazaki Tōson
Tōson began his career as a romantic poet, but went on to establish himself as the major Japanese proponent of naturalism with a series of novels ranked by some as masterpieces of modern literature.

Edo (now Tōkyō), where he had TOKUGAWA YOSHINOBU appointed as shogunal regent (*kōkenshoku*). On his way back to Kyōto, members of his retinue killed one of a group of Englishmen they thought had failed to show him proper respect (see RICHARDSON AFFAIR). Finding Kyōto held by extremists from Chōshū (now Yamaguchi Prefecture), Hisamitsu withdrew to Satsuma. He returned to Kyōto following the COUP D'ETAT OF 30 SEPTEMBER 1863. Hisamitsu later served briefly in the Meiji government but, largely ignored for his extreme conservatism, resigned in 1875 and returned to Satsuma.

Shimazu Nariakira 島津斉彬

(1809–58). *Daimyō* of the Satsuma domain (now Kagoshima Prefecture); his Westernization program enabled Satsuma to assume a principal role in the MEIJI RESTORATION of 1868. In 1851 he succeeded his father as daimyō with the support of ŌKUBO TOSHIMICHI, SAIGŌ TAKAMORI, and others. Nariakira initiated modernizing reforms, building a refinery for the manufacture of munitions; a reverberatory furnace (HANSHARO) to make heavy artillery and machinery; the Shūseikan, a Western-style factory that produced gunpowder, glass, ceramics, and chemicals and carried out experiments in photography and telegraphy; and several naval vessels. Convinced that a sweeping reform of the Tokugawa shogunate (1603–1867) was necessary, in 1853 he urged the shogunate to employ men of talent regardless of rank and to pursue a policy of Westernization. He also called for a national league of powerful domains to supplant the autocratic rule of the Tokugawa family; to that end he supported TOKUGAWA YOSHINOBU in the 1858 shogunal succession dispute but was unsuccessful.

Shimazu Yasujirō 島津保次郎

(1897–1945). Film director. Born in Tōkyō. He joined the film production company SHŌCHIKU CO, LTD, in 1920 and directed his first film in 1923. A true craftsman who worked in all the film genres dealing with contemporary life, Shimazu helped to develop and define "the Shōchiku style." By 1931 he had directed 100 silent features. With the advent of "talking pictures," Shimazu directed two films that are still considered minor classics of the *shōshimin geki* genre (dramas of lower-middle-class life): *Tonari no Yae-chan* (1934, Our Neighbor, Miss Yae) and *Ani to sono imōto* (1939, A Brother and His Younger Sister). He is also remembered for *Okoto to Sasuke* (1935, Okoto and Sasuke). Among those who trained under Shimazu as assistant directors at Shōchiku were GOSHO HEINOSUKE, TOYODA SHIRŌ, YOSHIMURA KŌZABURŌ, and KINOSHITA KEISUKE.

Shimazu Yoshihiro 島津義弘

(1535–1619). *Daimyō* of the Azuchi-Momoyama period (1568–1600). Yoshihiro's father, Takahisa (1514–71), had consolidated the SHIMAZU FAMILY's control over Satsuma and Ōsumi (now Kagoshima Prefecture). In 1587 TOYOTOMI HIDEYOSHI defeated the Shimazu, but from 1592 Yoshihiro served Hideyoshi in several campaigns. Yoshihiro fought against TOKUGAWA IEYASU at the Battle of SEKIGAHARA in 1600, but later reached an accommodation with his opponent. His breakthrough to safety through the enemy's camp as the battle was lost is famous.

Shimbunshi Hō → Press Law of 1909

Shimbunshi Jōrei → Press Ordinance of 1875

shimbun shōsetsu 新聞小説

Novels serialized in newspapers, generally in 100 to 300 installments, each consisting of several hundred words accompanied by an illustration. The number and readership of newspapers in Japan grew rapidly after 1871, when the first modern daily, the *Yokohama mainichi shimbun*, appeared. There were two categories of early modern newspapers: *ōshimbun*, which emphasized political issues, and *koshimbun*, which centered on crimes, missing persons, advice, and entertaining reading. Most editors and writers for the *koshimbun* were authors of the traditional popular literary genre known as GESAKU. It was from their articles, which tended to be anecdotal, didactic, or humorous, rather than straightforward news, that newspaper serials first developed. The first serialized story was *Iwata Yasohachi no hanashi* (1875) by Maeda Kōsetsu (1841–1916), which appeared in the newspaper *Hiragana eiri shimbun*. Because of the popularity of stories such as this, the *ōshimbun* also began to publish serialized political novels as well as translations of foreign novels. The distinction between *ōshimbun* and *koshimbun* gradually began to disappear.

The years from 1907, when NATSUME SŌSEKI became literary editor of the *Asahi shimbun*, to 1918 were the golden age of newspaper fiction, and most of the classics of modern literature written at that time were first published as newspaper serials. In the years following World War I, the quality of newspaper fiction declined, and the popular novel known as the *taishū shōsetsu* came to be the mainstay of newspaper serials. After World War II, notable newspaper serials appeared in rapid succession. With the spread of television starting in the early 1950s and the growth of new weekly magazines, newspaper fiction began to lose much of its audience. Even so, the form remains popular today.

shimbutsu bunri → Shintō and Buddhism, separation of

shimbutsu shūgō → syncretism

Shime 志免[町]

Town on the eastern border of the city of Fukuoka in northern Fukuoka Prefecture, Kyūshū. Once a coal-mining town, Shime is now a growing commuter suburb of Fukuoka. Pop: 34,626.

shimenawa 注連縄

A cord or rope made by twisting together strands of rice straw. *Shimenawa* are used to mark a place considered sacred and set it off from the realm of the profane; they are traditionally believed to have the power to ward off evil and sickness. At Shintō shrines, *shimenawa* are hung in front of the main worship hall (*haiden*), before the altar, and across the TORII (entrance gate). They may also be hung around old trees that are revered as *shintai* (abodes of the divine) or unusually large rocks upon which deities have been thought to sit. They are also hung from Shintō altars in homes or, most commonly at New Year's, over doorways or the front bumpers of automobiles.

Shimizu 清水[市]

City in central Shizuoka Prefecture, central Honshū, on Suruga Bay. It developed as a post-station town on the highway TŌKAIDŌ during the Edo period (1600–1868). The port is a base for deep-sea fishing. Principal industries are shipbuilding and canned-goods production; main agricultural products are mandarin oranges, strawberries, and tea. Many tourists visit the scenic hills of NIHONDAIRA as well as MIHO NO MATSUBARA, a famed pine grove. Pop: 241,523.

Shimizu 清水[町]

Town on the river Kanogawa in the northern part of the Izu Peninsula, eastern Shizuoka Prefecture, central Honshū. A local spring produces a large volume of water that is used in industry and agriculture and to supply drinking water to the city of Numazu. There are textile and paper factories in Shimizu, and it is a commuter suburb of Numazu and Mishima. Pop: 27,755.

Shimizu Corporation 清水建設[株]

(Shimizu Kensetsu). One of Japan's leading construction firms, Shimizu traces its history back to 1804. It is now active in the construc-

shimenawa A display of these sacred ropes at the worship hall of the Izumo Shrine, Shimane Prefecture, one of the most important Shintō shrines in Japan. This immense *shimenawa* is 4 meters in circumference and weighs 1,500 kg.

Shimomura Kanzan
Byakko (The White Fox). One of a pair of folding screens. 1914. Colors on paper. 186 × 207 cm. Tōkyō National Museum.

Shimmura Izuru
This philologist was the chief editor of the 1955 edition of *Kōjien*, the most widely used dictionary of the Japanese language.

tion of high-rise buildings, atomic power facilities, and local development projects. It has 30 subsidiaries overseas and 44 overseas offices. Sales for the fiscal year ending March 1991 totaled ¥1.9 trillion (US $13.8 billion), of which construction accounted for 81 percent; civil engineering, 15 percent; and real estate and engineering, 4 percent. Overseas construction projects accounted for 5 percent of this total. The company was capitalized at ¥74.2 billion (US $540.8 million) in the same year. Headquarters are in Tōkyō.

Shimizu Hamaomi　　　清水浜臣

(1776–1824). Also known as Sazanaminoya. KOKUGAKU (National Learning) scholar and WAKA poet of the late Edo period (1600–1868). Born in Edo (now Tōkyō). A practicing physician, his works include the *waka* collection *Sazanaminoyashū*, published in 1829 by his son Mitsufusa, and *Gorin ruiyō*, a glossary of Heian-period (794–1185) poetry.

Shimizu Hiroshi　　　清水宏

(1903–69). Film director. Born in Shizuoka Prefecture. He joined SHŌCHIKU CO, LTD, in 1920, making his directorial debut in 1924. His films are characterized by depictions of nature and of the cheerful, spontaneous behavior of children. His major works include *Kaze no naka no kodomo* (1937, Children in the Wind) and *Kodomo no shiki* (1939, Children of the Four Seasons).

Shimizu Muneharu　　　清水宗治

(1537–82). Vassal of the MŌRI FAMILY who is famous for the dramatic circumstances of his suicide. Muneharu held Takamatsu Castle in Bitchū (now part of the city of Okayama), which was besieged in 1582 by TOYOTOMI HIDEYOSHI on behalf of ODA NOBUNAGA. By di-

verting the waters of the river Ashimorigawa, Hideyoshi flooded the castle and prevented the Mōri from relieving it; moreover, Hideyoshi expected strong reinforcements, including Nobunaga himself. Hence, the Mōri were prepared to sign an armistice under the conditions that called for the surrender of the castle and Muneharu's suicide. In return, the garrison would be spared. When word reached Hideyoshi that Nobunaga had been assassinated by AKECHI MITSUHIDE (see HONNŌJI INCIDENT), the news was successfully kept from the Mōri, and Muneharu committed suicide. With the armistice concluded, Hideyoshi rushed to Kyōto to eliminate Mitsuhide, thus beginning his career as national unifier.

Shimizu Shikin　　　清水紫琴

(1868–1933). Novelist and essayist. Born Shimizu Toyoko in Okayama Prefecture; raised in Kyōto. She joined in early campaigns for women's rights with FUKUDA HIDEKO, then taught at Meiji Jogakkō (Meiji Girls' School) in Tōkyō. She was a contributor to the pioneering women's magazine JOGAKU ZASSHI. Her stories and essays centered on contemporary women's problems. In 1892 she married the agricultural chemist Kozai Yoshinao (1864–1934), a professor at and later president of Tōkyō University. Shimuzu's works include "Koware yubiwa" (1897, The Broken Ring).

Shimmei Masamichi　　　新明正道

(1898–1984). Sociologist. Born in Taiwan. A graduate of Tōkyō University, he taught at Tōhoku University. Shimmei developed a theoretical system integrating what he called general sociology, historical sociology, and practical sociology. He also contributed to the advancement of Japanese sociology through his critical introductions to Japan of US sociology and his studies of the develop-

ment of various social theories. His works include *Shakai honshitsu ron* (1942, On the Nature of Society).

Shimmi Masaoki　　　新見正興

(1822–69). Official of the Tokugawa shogunate. Appointed as commissioner of foreign affairs (GAIKOKU BUGYŌ) in 1859. The following year he was chosen as a leader of the delegation to Washington, DC, to exchange ratifications of the United States–Japan Treaty of Amity and Commerce (see UNITED STATES, MISSION OF 1860 TO).

Shimminato　　　新湊[市]

City in northern Toyama Prefecture, central Honshū, at the mouth of the river Shōgawa. The opening of the port Toyama Shinkō in 1968 has led to industrialization. Fishing is also important. Pop: 39,434.

Shimmura Izuru　　　新村出

(1876–1967). Philologist. Born in Yamaguchi Prefecture, Shimmura graduated from Tōkyō University. After studying in Europe he taught at Kyōto University and in 1956 was awarded the Order of Culture. Continuing in the tradition of UEDA KAZUTOSHI, he introduced Western linguistic methods to Japan and devoted himself to the establishment of the scientific study of language and of the Japanese language in particular. He is also known for his research on the introduction into Japan of NAMBAN or Western culture by Europeans in the 16th and 17th centuries. He was the editor of *Jien* (1935) and its revised and expanded version, *Kōjien* (1955), which is still the most famous and widely used one-volume dictionary of the Japanese language. His complete works were published in 15 volumes in 1971–73.

Shimobe　　　下部[町]

Town in southwestern Yamanashi Prefecture, central Honshū. It is primarily known for its hot springs, which were patronized by the 16th-century warlord TAKEDA SHINGEN. A Takeda Shingen festival is held every May at Kumano Shrine here. Pop: 6,638.

Shimoda　　　下田[市]

City in eastern Shizuoka Prefecture, central Honshū, on the Izu Peninsula. In the Edo period (1600–1868) Shimoda was a prosperous port of call for ships transporting goods between Edo (now Tōkyō) and Ōsaka. At the conclusion of the KANAGAWA TREATY with the United States in 1854 it became an open port. In 1856 the first American consulate general was opened with Townsend HARRIS as its head. Shimoda is a fishing port, and it has a marine-food-processing industry as well as abalone and sea bream farming. Attractions include the temples Ryōsenji and Gyokusenji, Shimoda Hot Spring, and the Black Ship Festival. Pop: 30,081.

Shimoda Takesō　　　下田武三

(1907–). Also known as Shimoda Takezō. Career foreign ministry officer and Supreme Court justice (1971–77). Born in Tōkyō. After graduating from Tōkyō University, Shimoda joined the Ministry of Foreign Affairs. He held such important posts as ambassador to the Soviet Union (1963–64), administrative vice-minister (1965–66), and ambassador to the United States (1967–70). Among the major negotiations that he conducted were the conclusion of the United States–Japan Security Treaty of 1951, its replacement by a new treaty in 1960, and the "automatic extension" of the latter in 1970 (see UNITED STATES–JAPAN SECURITY TREATIES).

After he retired from the foreign service, he was appointed to the Supreme Court in 1971.

Shimodate 下館[市]

City in western Ibaraki Prefecture, central Honshū. At one time known for textiles used in making *tabi* (cotton socks worn with *kimono*), Shimodate now has electrical-appliance and confectionery plants. Pop: 66,028.

Shimoda Utako 下田歌子

(1854–1936). Educator. Original name Hirao Seki. Born in the Iwamura domain (now Gifu Prefecture), she began seven years of service at the imperial court in 1872. She was given the name Utako by the empress in recognition of her poetic talents. From 1881 to 1885 she ran a private school for women and girls of the elite called the Shimoda Gakkō (or Tōyō Jojuku). In 1885 she helped establish an official school for female relatives of the peerage (called Kazoku Jogakkō; from 1906, Gakushūin Jogakubu).

In 1898 Utako and other women from the elite formed the Teikoku Fujin Kyōkai (Imperial Women's Society), which published the magazine *Nihon fujin* (Japanese Women). In 1899 she founded two schools, the Jissen Jogakkō (now Jissen Joshi Gakuen) and the Joshi Kōgei Gakkō (Women's Crafts School). She helped form the patriotic women's society AIKOKU FUJINKAI in 1901 and later served as its president from 1920 to 1931.

Shimokita Peninsula 下北半島

(Shimokita Hantō). Located in northeastern Aomori Prefecture, northern Honshū, projecting north into the Tsugaru Strait and embracing Mutsu Bay to the southwest. This desolate mountain region includes OSOREZAN, a volcanic group, and several hot springs. ŌMAZAKI, a cape at the northern tip of the peninsula, is the northernmost point of Honshū. Fishing, forestry, and sightseeing are the main industries; Mutsu is the major city.

Shimokōbe Chōryū 下河辺長流

(1624–86). WAKA poet and classical scholar of the early Edo period (1600–1868). Also known as Shimokōbe Nagaru. Born in Yamato Province (now Nara Prefecture). He is known for research on the poetic anthology MAN'YŌSHŪ (ca 759), culminating in the *Man'yōshū kanken* (ca 1661). Influenced by KINOSHITA CHŌSHŌSHI, he compiled the anthology *Rin'yō ruijinshū* (1670). KEICHŪ compiled the *Bankashū* (1686), a posthumous anthology of Chōryū's poetry.

Shimomoto Kenkichi 下元健吉

(1897–1957). A leader of the Japanese immigrant community in Brazil. Born in Kōchi Prefecture, Shimomoto emigrated to Brazil at the age of 16. He helped establish the Cotia Cooperative Society, one of Brazil's first agricultural cooperative societies and, as its managing director, continued to guide immigrant farmers until his death.

Shimomura Kanzan 下村観山

(1873–1930). Eclectic Japanese-style painter. Born in Wakayama Prefecture to a family of NŌ artists. Kanzan studied with KANŌ HŌGAI and HASHIMOTO GAHŌ. He attended the Tōkyō Bijutsu Gakkō (now Tōkyō University of Fine Arts and Music), where he became a faculty member in 1894. When OKAKURA KAKUZŌ resigned its directorship in 1898 to found the JAPAN FINE ARTS ACADEMY (Nihon Bijutsuin), Kanzan joined him. He also resumed a post at the Tōkyō Bijutsu Gakkō from 1901 to 1908 and spent from 1903 to 1905 studying in England. In 1914 he helped form the reorganized Japan Fine Arts Academy and in 1917 was appointed an artist for the imperial household. He was both a judge and exhibitor at the BUNTEN and Inten exhibitions. A student of early Buddhist painting and TOSA SCHOOL narrative scrolls, Kanzan was also influenced by the KANŌ SCHOOL and RIMPA painters, blending these elements with a dash of Western realism to evolve a distinctive style for traditional subjects. See also NIHONGA.

Shimonaka Yasaburō 下中弥三郎

(1878–1961). Founder of the publishing house Heibonsha (see HEIBONSHA, LTD, PUBLISHERS); educator and political activist. Born in Hyōgo Prefecture. Largely self-educated, he began his career as a teacher. In 1914 he founded Heibonsha, which published popular fiction and works on the fine arts in the 1920s and a multivolume dictionary and encyclopedia in the 1930s. A social reformer, he founded Japan's first teachers' union, the Keimeikai, in 1919. In the 1930s Shimonaka gradually adopted a more nationalistic stance, founding several rightist organizations, and after World War II he was purged by OCCUPATION authorities. Returning to Heibonsha in 1951, he published several encyclopedias, establishing Heibonsha as one of Japan's foremost publishers of reference works.

Shimonita 下仁田[町]

Town in southwestern Gumma Prefecture, central Honshū. It is known for its Welsh onions and *konnyaku* (a common ingredient in Japanese cooking). Pop: 13,683.

Shimonoseki 下関[市]

City in southwestern Yamaguchi Prefecture, western Honshū. It was the seat of the provincial capital (*kokufu*) of Nagato Province in the ancient past. The Battle of DANNOURA, in which the Taira were destroyed by the Minamoto, was fought in the sea near here in 1185. The city was bombarded by foreign battleships during the closing days of the Tokugawa shogunate (see SHIMONOSEKI BOMBARDMENT). Today it is one of the biggest deep-sea fishing bases in the country. Shimonoseki is served by several railway lines and is connected to Kyūshū by two undersea rail tunnels and a highway tunnel (the Kammon Tunnels) and the 1,068-m (3,503-ft) Kammon Bridge (a highway bridge). Tourist attractions include the Sumiyoshi Shrine, Akama Shrine, Hinoyama Park, and Shimonoseki Aquarium. Pop: 262,635.

Shimonoseki Bombardment 四国艦隊下関砲撃事件

(Shikoku Kantai Shimonoseki Hōgeki Jiken; also known as Bakan Sensō). Naval expedition of September 1864 against the Chōshū domain (now Yamaguchi Prefecture) by the joint forces of Britain, France, the Netherlands, and the United States in retaliation for Chōshū's attacks on Western ships passing through the Shimonoseki Strait.

The ANSEI COMMERCIAL TREATIES signed in 1858 by the Tokugawa shogunate opened Japan to trade with Western nations. Antiforeign, antishogunate activists persuaded the imperial court to issue an edict setting 25 June 1863 as the date for "expelling the barbarians" (see SONNŌ JŌI). On that day Chōshū fired on a US ship and, in the next month, attacked other Western ships.

In retaliation, 17 Western ships bombarded the Shimonoseki emplacements between 5 and 8 September 1864, and a landing party seized and destroyed Chōshū's weapons and fortifications. A truce was reached on 14 September that exacted from the shogunate an immense indemnity. This incident helped discredit Chōshū's antishogunate, anti-Western faction. Moreover, the shogunate's inability to pay the indemnity was used by the new British minister, Sir Harry PARKES, to secure further trade concessions in return for deferral of payment.

Shimonoseki, Treaty of 下関条約

(Shimonoseki Jōyaku). Treaty concluding the SINO-JAPANESE WAR OF 1894–1895; signed at Shimonoseki, Yamaguchi Prefecture, on 17 April 1895. The terms that ITŌ HIROBUMI presented to his Chinese counterpart LI HONG-ZHANG (Li Hung-chang) demanded that China recognize Korea as an independent country; cede the Liaodong (Liaotung) Peninsula, Taiwan, and the Pescadores Islands; pay an indemnity of 200 million taels over seven years; and sign a commercial treaty similar to those the Chinese government had concluded with the Western powers. A few days after the treaty was signed, Germany, France, and Russia forced Japan to give up the Liaodong Peninsula (see TRIPARTITE INTERVENTION) but concurred with Japan's demand that China increase the indemnity by 30 million taels as compensation. There is little doubt that the treaty marked the beginning of Japanese imperialistic expansion at China's expense.

Shimōsa Plateau 下総台地

(Shimōsa Daichi). Group of diluvial uplands in northern Chiba Prefecture, central Honshū. Developed as farmland in the premodern period, in recent years large-scale housing developments have been built here. New Tōkyō International Airport is located in the nearby city of Narita. Elevation: 10–150 m (33–492 ft).

Shimose Masachika 下瀬雅允

(1859–1911). Developer of Shimose gunpowder, the powerful explosive that gave the Japanese Imperial Navy an important edge against the Russian fleets during the RUSSO-JAPANESE WAR of 1904–05. Born in what is now Hiroshima Prefecture, he graduated from Tōkyō University's College of Engineering in 1884. He became a navy technician in 1887 and a year later developed his superior gunpowder, using picric acid as its main ingredient. He was one of Japan's earliest doctors of engineering.

Shimo Suwa 下諏訪[町]

Town in central Nagano Prefecture, central Honshū, on Lake Suwa. In the Edo period (1600–1868) it developed as one of the POST-STATION TOWNS. From the Meiji period (1868–1912) silk reeling flourished, but this has been replaced since World War II by the precision-instrument, knitting, and *miso* (bean paste) industries. A hot spring, Suwa Shrine, Lake Suwa, and the Kirigamine highland are the town's major attractions. Pop: 25,519.

shimotsuke 下野

Spiraea japonica. Deciduous shrub of the rose family (Rosaceae) that grows wild in mountainous regions throughout Japan,

Shimoda Utako This turn-of-the-century educator founded a number of schools for women and advocated improved women's education in Japan.

shimotsuke The beautiful flowers and many varieties of this deciduous shrub of the rose family make it a popular garden plant.

Shimoyama Incident Investigators stand at the site where the dismembered body of Shimoyama Sadanori, president of the Japanese National Railways, was discovered on 6 July 1949.

Korea, and China; also cultivated as an ornamental. The stems grow in bundles and reach about 1 meter (3 ft) high. The serrated leaves are alternate and oblong to broadly lance-shaped. Around June clusters of small pink aromatic flowers with five petals develop. Similar species found in Japan include *iwashimotsuke* (*S. nipponica*) with white flowers; *maruba shimotsuke* (*S. betulifolia*) with round leaves and white flowers; *yukiyanagi* (*S. thunbergii*) with numerous small, almost stalkless white flowers; and *kodemari* (*S. cantoniensis*) with ball-like clusters of white flowers.

Shimotsuki → calendar, dates, and time

Shimotsuma 下妻[市]
City in western Ibaraki Prefecture, central Honshū, on the river Kinugawa. Shimotsuma developed as a castle town and river port. Its mainstay has been agriculture, and industry is being developed. Pop: 33,731.

Shimoyama Incident 下山事件
(Shimoyama Jiken). A controversial criminal incident of the Allied OCCUPATION period. On 6 July 1949 the dismembered body of Shimoyama Sadanori (1900–1949), then president of the Japanese National Railways (JNR), was found alongside some railroad tracks in Adachi Ward in northern Tōkyō. He had been run over by a train.

Shimoyama had been under orders from the government and the Occupation authorities to fire some 97,000 national railway employees during July, and two days previously had approved dismissal notices for 37,000 workers. Occupation officials and the government of Prime Minister YOSHIDA SHIGERU intended to use the firings to break the hold of the Communist Party over the National Railway Workers' Union (NRWU).

The dispute over whether Shimoyama's death was murder or suicide has continued without resolution. The significance of the incident lies in the belief of the press and public during 1949 that Shimoyama, a high-ranking public official, had been murdered by communist railroad workers. Together with the MATSUKAWA INCIDENT and the MITAKA INCIDENT, both of which occurred during 1949, the Shimoyama case was a factor in turning public opinion against the Communist Party and in favor of the policies of economic recovery and alliance with the United States advocated by the Liberal Party (Jiyūtō).

Shimozawa Kan 子母沢寛
(1892–1968). Novelist. Real name Umetani Matsutarō. Born in Hokkaidō. Graduate of Meiji University. He worked as a newspaper reporter in Tōkyō and wrote popular historical novels about the late Edo period (1600–1868). His principal novels include *Shinsen-*

shimpa This modern theatrical movement is rooted in the *kabuki* tradition. Pictured is the actress Mizutani Yoshie as Otsuta in a 1988 production of one of the best-known *shimpa* works, Izumi Kyōka's *Onna keizu* (1907, The Genealogy of Women).

gumi shimatsuki (1928), *Kunisada Chūji* (1932–33), and *Oyakodaka* (1955–56).

shimpa 新派
The first modern Japanese theatrical movement and tradition. *Shimpa* means "new school," in opposition to KABUKI, the old school of actors. *Shimpa* is distinct from SHINGEKI (new theater), which closely resembles the modern Western theater.

Shimpa began in 1888 as a political form of drama. Early adherents included Sudō Sadanori (1867–1907), KAWAKAMI OTOJIRŌ, and II YŌHŌ. It later turned to melodrama, as well as to plays based on Japanese history. *Shimpa* troupes came to use actresses, ending the ban of two and a half centuries on mixed casts of men and women. *Shimpa* dominated the Japanese theater during the first decade of the 20th century. This "Golden Age of *Shimpa*" set the essential *shimpa* form: women's roles shared by ON-NAGATA (female impersonators) and a few actresses; a realistic acting style that stressed virtuoso performance; contemporary stories; and melodramatic plots.

Shimpa underwent major reform after the success of Seto Eiichi's (1892–1934) *Futasujimichi* (Two Paths) in 1931. The primary focus shifted from melodrama to slice-of-life stories set in the world of the GEISHA and other feminine subcultures. The principal creator of the new repertoire was KAWAGUCHI MATSUTARŌ with his *Fūryū Fukagawa uta* (1935, Song of the Elegant Fukagawa), *Meiji ichidai onna* (1935, Life of a Meiji Era Woman), and *Tsuruhachi Tsurujirō* (1934, Tsuruhachi and Tsurujirō). Yagi Ryūichirō (1906–65), TANIZAKI JUN'I-CHIRŌ, IZUMI KYŌKA, and other major novelist-playwrights also wrote finely crafted vehicles for female impersonators KITAMURA ROKURŌ and HANAYAGI SHŌTARŌ and for *shimpa* actresses, principally MIZUTANI YAEKO. With the deaths of its irreplaceable female impersonator stars, *shimpa* productions are now dominated by strong actresses. *Shimpa* continues to face shrinking audiences but remains dedicated more to preservation than to change.

shimpan 親藩
(related houses, or collateral *daimyō*). The Tokugawa shogunate (1603–1867) designated the 20-or-so lineages that were descended by birth or adoption from TOKUGAWA IEYASU and were of daimyō status (and hence held domains, or HAN) as *shimpan*—literally, "related (*shin*) domains (*han*)." These lineages mostly derived from Ieyasu through the GOSANKE daimyō of the Mito (now part of Ibaraki Prefecture), Owari (now part of Aichi Prefecture), and Kii domains (now Wakayama Prefecture) and through Ieyasu's descendants living in Echizen Province (now part of Fukui Prefecture). See also TOKUGAWA FAMILY; GOSANKYŌ.

Shimpeitai Incident 神兵隊事件
(Shimpeitai Jiken; literally, "Divine Soldiers" Incident). Conspiracy by rightist civilians and military officers to establish by force a nationalist-military regime; uncovered in July 1933. Suzuki Zen'ichi (b 1903) of the ultranationalist Dai Nippon Seisantō (Great Japan Production Party), members of the Aikoku Kinrōtō (Patriotic Labor Party), and Commander Yamaguchi Saburō of the navy (brother of the ultranationalist INOUE NISSHŌ) planned to organize several thousand "divine soldiers" (*shimpei*), drop bombs on the prime minister's residence and the Diet

building, take over the headquarters of the liberal parties and the Metropolitan Police, attack a bank and an industrialists' club, and assassinate prominent politicians. An advance party assembled at the Meiji Shrine on 10 July. Their arrest led to the discovery of the plot. The conspirators, tried in late 1937, were given mild sentences for reduced charges, not conspiracy, and were all released in March 1941.

Shimpotō 進歩党
(Progressive Party). Political party established in March 1896 through a merger of the RIKKEN KAISHINTŌ, the Rikken Kakushintō, and several minor Diet parties; it sought to counterbalance the temporary alliance between ITŌ HIROBUMI and the rival party JIYŪ-TŌ. Shimpotō leader ŌKUMA SHIGENOBU joined the second MATSUKATA MASAYOSHI cabinet in September 1896; after a disagreement, he resigned in November 1897. In June 1898 the Shimpotō allied itself with the Jiyūtō to create the KENSEITŌ. See also POLITICAL PARTIES.

Shimura Takashi 志村喬
(1905–82). Film actor. Real name Shimazaki Shōji. Born in Hyōgo Prefecture. He began making films at age 30, appearing in a succession of KUROSAWA AKIRA pictures in which he was acclaimed for his unaffected performances. These films included Kurosawa's first film, *Sugata Sanshirō* (1943; shown abroad as *Sanshirō Sugata*), *Waga seishun ni kui nashi* (1946, No Regrets for Our Youth), *Yoidore tenshi* (1948, Drunken Angel), *Norainu* (1949, Stray Dog), RASHŌMON (1950), IKIRU (1952), *Shichinin no samurai* (1954, SEVEN SAMURAI), *Kumonosujō* (1957, Throne of Blood), *Kakushi toride no san'aku-nin* (1958, The Hidden Fortress), *Yōjimbō* (1961), and *Tsubaki Sanjūrō* (1962, Sanjūrō).

Shinagawa Fuel Co, Ltd 品川燃料[株]
(Shinagawa Nenryō). Integrated fuel dealer affiliated with ITŌCHŪ CORPORATION. Incorporated in 1934. The company is now diversifying into real estate and other new businesses. Sales for the fiscal year ending March 1991 totaled ¥117.0 billion (US $852.8 million), and capitalization stood at ¥8.4 billion (US $61.2 million) in the same year. Headquarters are in Tōkyō.

Shinagawa Refractories Co, Ltd 品川白煉瓦[株]
(Shinagawa Shirorenga). Ceramic company engaged in the production of refractories and in engineering projects. It traces its origins back to 1875; the present company was incorporated in 1903. After World War II, it expanded its operations to match the rapid development of Japan's steel industry. It is now active in exporting plants and technologies for the manufacture of refractories. Sales for the fiscal year ending March 1991 totaled ¥63.7 billion (US $464.3 million), and the company was capitalized at ¥3.3 billion (US $24.1 million) in the same year. Headquarters are in Tōkyō.

Shinagawa Ward 品川区
(Shinagawa Ku). One of the 23 wards of Tōkyō. During the Edo period (1600–1868) Shinagawa was a post-station town on the highway TŌKAIDŌ. After the Meiji Restoration (1868) it underwent rapid industrialization. Today eastern Shinagawa, built on alluvial and reclaimed land along Tōkyō Bay, is an industrial area with numerous electronics and machine factories and is part of the

Keihin Industrial Zone. Western Shinagawa Ward is a residential district. The ward is a vital transportation center. Pop: 344,611.

Shinagawa Yajirō 品川弥二郎

(1843–1900). Politician. Born in the Chōshū domain (now Yamaguchi Prefecture). With KIDO TAKAYOSHI, he was instrumental in bringing about the SATSUMA-CHŌSHŪ ALLIANCE that preceded the MEIJI RESTORATION in 1868. In 1870 he was sent to England and Germany to study local government and agricultural policy. He returned six years later and in 1882 was appointed vice-minister (*tayū*) of agriculture and commerce. He set up the Kyōdo Un'yu Kaisha, a transportation company. In 1891 Shinagawa became home minister but incurred criticism for interference in the Diet election of 1892 and was forced to resign (see SENKYO KANSHŌ). With SAIGŌ TSUGUMICHI, he founded the KOKUMIN KYŌKAI.

Shinanogawa 信濃川

River in Nagano and Niigata prefectures, central Honshū; originating in the mountain Kobushigatake in the Kantō Mountains and flowing through the Saku, Ueda, Nagano, Iiyama, and Tōkamachi basins and across the Niigata Plain to enter the Sea of Japan at the city of Niigata. It is the longest river in Japan and has approximately 280 tributaries. Called CHIKUMAGAWA in Nagano Prefecture, it joins with its largest tributary, Saigawa, at Kawanakajima in the Nagano Basin. The lower reaches were the site of frequent floods before the digging, completed in 1922, of the Shin Shinanogawa (New Shinanogawa), which carries most of the river's volume to the sea from a point some 9 km (6 mi) upstream of the river's mouth. The water is utilized for irrigation, electric power, industry, and drinking. Length: 367 km (228 mi); area of drainage basin: 11,900 sq km (4,595 sq mi).

Shin Caterpillar Mitsubishi, Ltd 新キャタピラー三菱[株]

(Shin Kyatapirā Mitsubishi). Manufacturer, distributor, and seller of construction machinery. Incorporated in 1963 as a joint venture between Caterpillar, Inc, of the United States and MITSUBISHI HEAVY INDUSTRIES, LTD. For the fiscal year ending March 1990, sales totaled ¥242.0 billion (US $1.6 billion) and capitalization stood at ¥23.1 billion (US $150.9 million). Headquarters are in Tōkyō.

Shinchō 新潮

(New Currents). Major literary monthly published since 1904 by SHINCHŌSHA, LTD. It was launched by Satō Giryō (1878–1951), founder of the magazine *Shinsei* (July 1896–August 1903). *Shinchō* rapidly became Japan's premier literary magazine, helping to establish Shinchōsha as a major publishing house. In content it tended toward aestheticism; when proletarian literature was enjoying its great popularity in the late 1920s and early 1930s, *Shinchō* emphasized works by the more aesthetically minded SHINKANKAKU SCHOOL (School of New Sensibilities) and later the SHINKŌ GEIJUTSU HA ("New Art school") writers. Contributors of original works included such well-known writers as ARISHIMA TAKEO, AKUTAGAWA RYŪNOSUKE, KIKUCHI KAN, ITŌ SEI, and MISHIMA YUKIO. Among more recent contributors are ŌE KENZABURŌ, INOUE MITSUHARU, YASUOKA SHŌTARŌ, and KURAHASHI YUMIKO.

Shinchō Kō ki 信長公記

(Chronicle of Nobunaga). Also known as *Nobunaga Kō ki*. An account of the career of

the hegemon ODA NOBUNAGA by Ōta Gyūichi (1527–after 1610). The work, completed around 1600, consists of an introduction and 15 parts. The introduction is a summary of Nobunaga's career up to the eve of his emergence into national prominence in 1568. Part 1 treats his embrace of the cause of ASHIKAGA YOSHIAKI and his entry into Kyōto to install Yoshiaki as shōgun in late 1568; each of the subsequent 14 parts gives a detailed chronological account of the events of a single year, concluding with 1582 and Nobunaga's assassination in the HONNŌJI INCIDENT. Although uncritical and sometimes inaccurate, the work is remarkable for its comprehensiveness. The *Shinchō Kō ki* is an important source for a study of Nobunaga's policies and campaigns and for broader studies of the Azuchi-Momoyama period (1568–1600).

Shinchōsha, Ltd [株]新潮社

(Shinchōsha). Publishing company. It is active in all fields of publishing, particularly of Japanese literary works and foreign literature in Japanese translation. In 1896 Satō Giryō (1878–1951) founded Shinchōsha's forerunner, which published the magazine *Shinsei*. In 1904 he brought out the monthly magazine *Shinchō* and at the same time changed the company name to Shinchōsha. In 1956 it launched *Shūkan shinchō*, the first weekly magazine to be brought out by a major Japanese publishing house. In 1981 the company launched the magazine *Fōkasu* (Focus), which started a boom of weekly photojournalistic magazines.

shinden 神田

(literally, "Shintō fields"). Also called *mitoshiro* or *mitoshiroda*. Tax-exempt land owned by Shintō shrines under the RITSURYŌ SYSTEM of government (instituted in the 7th century), which abolished private ownership of land. However, shrines, temples, and certain noble families were allowed to retain some holdings. By the mid-Heian period (794–1185) *shinden*, like other private holdings, had increased greatly in size through commendation and reclamation and had developed into private estates (SHŌEN).

shinden kaihatsu 新田開発

(development of new fields). Also called *shinkai*. The opening of new lands to cultivation and the conversion of dry fields to paddy during the Edo period (1600–1868), which was one of the most active periods of land reclamation in Japanese history. New farmland producing an estimated 1.3 million *koku* (1 *koku* = about 180 liters or 5 US bushels; see KOKUDAKA) of rice was brought under cultivation during this time. Most of this growth occurred before the 18th century, but another major increase in reclaimed land came in the first half of the 19th century.

There were three major categories of reclamation. *Shinden* (called *konden* before the Edo period) referred to reclamation of new land for use as paddy. Reclamation of land for dry-field crops such as wheat, barley, cotton, and tobacco was called *hatakebiraki*. Dry fields converted to paddy were called *hatakenaoshi shinkai*. The Tokugawa shogunate and the *daimyō* encouraged land reclamation in order to increase the base for their major source of revenue, the annual land tax (NENGU). In order to stimulate reclamation, various kinds of tax relief, for legally specified lengths of time, were granted to cultivators of reclaimed land.

shinden-zukuri 寝殿造

One of the two major styles of traditional Japanese domestic architecture, the other being SHOIN-ZUKURI. Used mainly in the palatial mansions of the aristocracy and also in private residences of high-ranking warriors and Buddhist clerics, *shinden-zukuri* was perfected in the Heian period (794–1185) and continued to influence Japanese residential architecture until the mid-15th century. The name is derived from its central feature, the *shinden* (master quarters or main hall).

The *shinden* style was patterned after ornate Chinese architectural models, especially Buddhist temple architecture, and achieved its distinctively Japanese expression around the 10th century. No authentic examples of the *shinden*-style residence are extant.

Sites for the *shinden* conformed naturally to the grid pattern layout of the capital, HEIANKYŌ (now Kyōto). The standard size lot as prescribed by law measured one *chō* square—approximately 120 meters (394 ft) to a side—and was enclosed by small streets. Larger residences were built on lots that were two or four times this size.

The typical *shinden* mansion was originally arranged in a right-left pattern of symmetry. This may have derived in part from its Chinese models, but a more direct influence was probably the Shishinden, or main hall of the Imperial Palace, which was itself symmetrical in ground-plan design. The *shinden*, or main hall, of such a mansion was constructed in the center of the lot; it faced south and was slightly more wide than deep. The sloping roof was semigabled and covered with cypress bark. There was an extension of the roof on the south side that covered the steps up to the *shinden* from an elaborate landscaped garden that usually included a pond with an island and bridges. To the east, west, and north there were attached pavilions and annexes (*tai no ya*). It later became the practice, as with the Tōsanjō Palace constructed in 1043, to employ an asymmetrical design that excluded either the east or the west *tai no ya*. Each pavilion was connected to the *shinden* or to another pavilion by various types of passageways, such as the walled *watadono* and the open-sided *sukiwatadono*. Water was diverted from one of the streams that coursed north to south through Heiankyō and drawn into the compound between the *shinden* and a *tai no ya* to supply the man-made pond in the south garden. Used as a place for holding ceremonies, the south garden was laid out over a broad area of level ground. A *tsuridono*, or open pavilion for musical entertainment, which was connected to the main building through a series of passageways, was erected on piles over the pond.

The main hall was composed of an inner area (*moya*), usually two bays by three or five bays (one bay is the distance between two pillars), surrounded on all four sides by another series of pillars that marked off an area known as *hisashi*. The building could be extended on one or more sides by adding rows of pillars to form an area called *magobisashi*. Beneath the eaves was a veranda (*en*). There were doors at both sides, and the area encompassed by the outer pillars of the *hisashi* or *magobisashi* was enclosed by latticed wall panels (*shitomido*) that swung open upward. Except for a small room called a *nurigome* used for sleeping or

shinden-zukuri

The exposed rafters and wide floorboards of the throne room of the Imperial Palace in Kyōto (originally designed during the Heian period) typify this domestic architectural style.

Shinden-zukuri Architecture

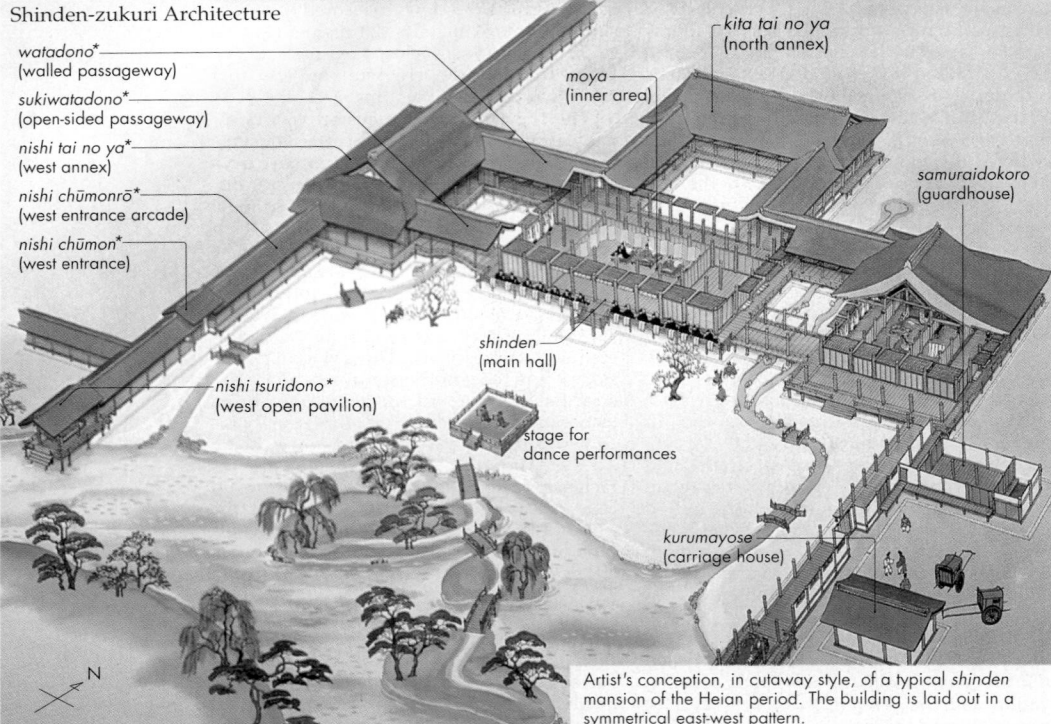

watadono* (walled passageway)

sukiwatadono* (open-sided passageway)

nishi tai no ya* (west annex)

nishi chūmonrō* (west entrance arcade)

nishi chūmon* (west entrance)

nishi tsuridono* (west open pavilion)

kita tai no ya (north annex)

moya (inner area)

samuraidokoro (guardhouse)

shinden (main hall)

stage for dance performances

kurumayose (carriage house)

Artist's conception, in cutaway style, of a typical *shinden* mansion of the Heian period. The building is laid out in a symmetrical east-west pattern.
SOURCE: Ōbayashi Corporation.

*Parallel structures exist on the east side of the complex.

storage, there were few partitions within. The floor was boarded, and rush mats and cushions were placed here and there for sleeping or sitting. Privacy was obtained by the use of folding screens and curtain stands, and by bamboo screens that were suspended from the transoms of the hinged wall panels.

Shindō Kaneto 新藤兼人

(1912–). Scenarist and film director. Born in Hiroshima Prefecture. Shindō began his movie career in 1934 as an assistant art director. He has also written screenplays for such directors as MIZOGUCHI KENJI, KINOSHITA KEISUKE, ICHIKAWA KON, and YOSHIMURA KŌZABURŌ.

In 1950, with Yoshimura, Shindō formed an independent production company, Kindai Eiga Kyōkai, and made his first film, *Aisai monogatari* (1951, The Story of a Beloved Wife). In the 1950s Shindō also made several so-called *rumpen-mono*, which showed the oppressed lives of the "lumpen proletariat." These include *Shukuzu* (1953, Epitome) and *Dobu* (1954, Gutter). In 1952 Shindō directed *Gembaku no ko* (1952, Children of the Atom Bomb).

Shindō's best-known film is a much-acclaimed semidocumentary, HADAKA NO SHIMA (1960, Naked Island; shown abroad as *The Island*). Without dialogue, the film portrays the lives of an impoverished rural couple and their children on a barren island in the Inland Sea. During the mid-1960s Shindō shifted from social observation and began to emphasize the role of erotic feelings, as in *Onibaba* (1963, Hags) and *Yabu no naka no kuroneko* (1968, Black Cat in the Bushes; shown abroad as *Kuroneko*). Shindō's work includes such thrillers as *Kagerō* (1969, Heat Wave Island) and an adaptation of NATSUME SŌSEKI's novel *Kokoro* (1973, The Heart).

Shin-Etsu Chemical Co, Ltd
信越化学工業[株]

(Shin-Etsu Kagaku Kōgyō). Manufacturer of an array of synthetic resins and electronic materials. Incorporated in 1926. The company is known for its technology for the production of silicone resins, polyvinyl chloride, and silicon wafers. Shin-Etsu has an international network of subsidiaries, affiliates, liaison offices, and licensees. Sales for the fiscal year ending March 1991 totaled ¥283.6 billion (US $2.1 billion), and capitalization was ¥35.6 billion (US $259.4 million). Headquarters are in Tōkyō.

Shin Fujin Kyōkai 新婦人協会

(New Woman's Association). Japan's first national women's rights group (1920–22); led by HIRATSUKA RAICHŌ, ICHIKAWA FUSAE, and OKU MUMEO. The group advocated equal opportunity for both sexes and protection of mothers' and children's interests. It published a magazine, *Josei dōmei* (Women's League). The group's major achievement was persuading the Diet in 1922 to delete the provisions of the Public Order and Police Law that prohibited women from joining political associations.

Shingaku 心学

(literally, "Heart Learning"). The teachings of ISHIDA BAIGAN and his school. The term Shingaku (Ch: Xinxue or Hsin-hsüeh) was originally used to refer to a school of Chinese philosophy developed by Lu Xiangshan (Lu Hsiang-shan; 1139–92) and Wang Yangming (1472–1529; see YŌMEIGAKU). Japanese Confucian scholars of the early Edo period (1600–1868), such as NAKAE TŌJU, also called their scholarly activities Shingaku. It was not, however, until the emergence of the Sekimon Shingaku movement, founded by Ishida Baigan, that the term became popular.

Ishida Baigan's teachings were based primarily on the Zhu Xi (Chu Hsi) school of Confucianism (see SHUSHIGAKU) but contained elements of Shintō and Buddhism as well. The first task of learning, according to Baigan, was the subjective investigation of human nature through personal experience and reflection. He insisted that the merchant—who ranked lowest in the traditional division of society (see SHI-NŌ-KŌ-SHŌ)—should be equal to the *samurai*, farmer, or craftsman when it came to moral practices. He proposed the establishment of a merchant ethic, emphasizing the importance of the merchant's role in society (see CHŌ-NINDŌ). Baigan's followers later expanded Shingaku into a broad philosophy of life envisioning the integration of all classes in a harmonious world.

Shingei → Geiami

Shingeki 新劇

(New Drama). Theater magazine published since April 1954 by Hakusuisha. Founded as a successor to an earlier coterie organ of a drama group headed by KISHIDA KUNIO, *Shingeki* has stayed abreast of and influenced current developments in modern theater by recruiting young playwrights to help write and staff the journal. Among its members, TANAKA CHIKAO, KINOSHITA JUNJI, MISHIMA YUKIO, and FUKUDA TSUNEARI have played central roles. It has published several special collections of original one-act plays, as well as criticism and essays on modern European theater. Among contemporary dramatists whose work has been published and discussed in its pages are BETSUYAKU MINORU, KARA JŪRŌ, TSUKA KŌHEI, SUZUKI TADASHI, and NODA HIDEKI.

shingeki 新劇

(literally, "new theater"). Form of theater roughly comparable to 20th-century Western theater. Unlike traditional Japanese theater such as KABUKI and NŌ, where dancing and a musical form of declamation play an important part, shingeki uses a conversational form of dialogue and psychological realism.

The leaders of the new theater movement, which began at the turn of the 20th century, developed shingeki out of a desire to create a drama responsive to the rapid changes in the economy, politics, and psychology of Japanese life. The movement can be said to have begun in earnest with the introduction of translations of Henrik Ibsen's plays in Japan. The most influential Ibsen enthusiast was OSANAI KAORU (1881–1928), who in 1909 formed his own company, the Jiyū Gekijō (Free Theater). Osanai's company produced both Western and new Japanese plays until 1919.

Another important figure in the movement, TSUBOUCHI SHŌYŌ (1859–1935), realized the necessity for training actors and actresses capable of performing this new kind of drama, since the training of kabuki actors was inadequate for modern drama. Additionally, in kabuki the female roles were played by female impersonators, so Tsubouchi decided to train amateurs, both male and female. His group, the Bungei Kyōkai (Literary Society), was formed in 1906.

The next impetus for the development of the new theater movement came in 1924, after the great Tōkyō Earthquake of 1923 had destroyed most theaters. Osanai constructed a small theater equipped with the most modern stage machinery available. Osanai's Tsukiji Shōgekijō (Tsukiji Little Theater) became the training ground for modern theater and presented a wide variety of modern plays (mostly European). Through the work and influence of Osanai, theatrical companies, rather than individual dramatists, became the focal point of the modern theater movement. Osanai's company also brought politics into the theater, introducing a Marxist influence that was already becoming widespread in many other areas of Japanese artistic and intellectual life.

With the death of Osanai in 1928, the new theater movement seemed to be moving far to the Left. Beginning in the early 1930s, however, the government began to restrain the activities of the politically active companies, closing theaters and imprisoning important theatrical figures. The pre–World War II political theater produced some playwrights of considerable merit, notably KUBO SAKAE (1901–58). KINOSHITA JUNJI (b 1914), the leading playwright of the postwar period and an admirer of Kubo, shows in his own work the same degree of political commitment.

Others in prewar years sought a new theater more closely allied to literary and aesthetic ideals. Chief among these was the playwright KISHIDA KUNIO (1890–1954), who encouraged younger playwrights such as MORIMOTO KAORU (1912–46), KATŌ MICHIO, (1918–53), and TANAKA CHIKAO (b 1905). Kishida also helped foster the development of several theater companies, notably the BUN-GAKUZA, which began its productions in 1938. Another influential troupe was the Haiyūza, founded in 1944 by SENDA KOREYA (b 1904).

Post–World War II——In the early postwar years, a new flowering of acting, directing, and writing talent brought the new theater to a gratifying level of accomplishment. Two acting companies, GEKIDAN MINGEI (founded in 1950 by members of an earlier shingeki troupe with a different name) and GEKIDAN SHIKI (founded in 1953) were at the forefront of these developments, and such theater troupes have continued to provide the focus for actors and dramatists alike. The theater troupes have also undertaken to expand their work to the provincial cities outside Tōkyō. Through touring productions, the new theater has come to attract a wide national audience, although it remains more a white-collar and intellectual group than the audience of "worker-spectators" sought by the more active leftist groups. Because of the rising prestige and ever greater performing skill of these theater companies, a number of prominent contemporary novelists have written for the stage, such as ABE KŌBŌ (1924–93), MISHIMA YUKIO (1925–70), YAMAZAKI MASAKAZU (b 1934), YASHIRO SEIICHI (b 1927), and BETSUYAKU MINORU (b 1937). See also DRAMA, MODERN; SHŌGEKIJŌ UNDŌ.

Shingen Kahō 信玄家法

Collective name for two codes established in the mid-16th century by the TAKEDA FAMILY, daimyō of Kai (Kōshū) Province (now Yamanashi Prefecture). The first is the Kōshū Hatto no Shidai (Legal Articles of Kōshū), a domainal legal code (BUNKOKUHŌ) of 57 articles enacted by TAKEDA SHINGEN in 1547 and 1554. It shows the influence of the IMAGAWA KANA MOKUROKU. The second is the Takeda Nobushige Kakun (Household Precepts of Takeda Nobushige), a collection of household precepts (KAKUN) or house regulations (kahō) in 99 articles drawn up by Shingen's brother in 1558. The two codes were combined under the title Shingen Kahō by an unknown editor of the Edo period (1600–1868).

shingikai → ministerial deliberative council

shingon → mantra

Shingon sect 真言宗

(Shingonshū). Major Buddhist sect. A branch of Mahāyāna Buddhism, founded by KŪKAI in the early 9th century. It is also referred to as the Shingon-darani (Skt: mantra-dhāraṇī) sect, the Tōmitsu sect, and generally as Mikkyō (ESOTERIC BUDDHISM). The basic doctrines and practices were established by Kūkai, who synthesized Indo-Chinese esoteric Buddhism on the basis of Mādhyamika, Yogācāra, and Huayan (Huayen; J: Kegon) thought. Among the major sects of Japanese Buddhism, the Shingon sect maintains the closest affinity with Hinduism and with the Lamaist Buddhism of Tibet and the Himalayan countries.

In contradistinction to the common belief that the Buddhist teachings are derived from the historical Buddha Śākyamuni, Shingon takes the stand that its basic sutras, the Mahāvairocana-sūtra (J: Dainichikyō) and the Vajraśekhara-sūtra (Kongōchō-gyō), were expounded by the Buddha Mahāvairocana (J: DAINICHI), who is the Dharmakāya (Body of Dharma), the Ultimate Reality. Śākyamuni is interpreted as one of many manifestations of Mahāvairocana. According to Kūkai's Transmission of Dharma (Fuhōden), Vajrasattva received the teachings directly from Mahāvairocana and sealed the sutras in an iron stupa in South India; 800 years after

Śākyamuni's demise, Nāgārjuna (J: Ryūju or Ryūmyō; ca 150–ca 250) opened the iron stupa and revealed the sutras to the world.

The first missionary of Indian esoteric Buddhism, Śubhakarasiṃha (J: Zemmui; 637–735), traveled to Tang (T'ang; 618–907) China, arriving in the capital of Chang'an (Ch'ang-an) in 716. Śubhakarasiṃha translated the Mahāvairocana-sūtra from Sanskrit into Chinese with the help of Yixing (I-hsing; J: Ichigyō; 683–727). The second esoteric Buddhist master, Vajrabodhi (J: Kongōchi; 671–741), arrived in Canton in 720 and undertook the translation of the Vajraśekhara-sūtra. Amoghavajra (J: Fukū; 705–774) became the chosen disciple of Vajrabodhi. The successor of Amoghavajra was the first native Chinese master of esoteric Buddhism, Huiguo (Hui-kuo; J: Keika; 746–805), under whom Kūkai studied.

Kūkai interpreted the Buddha as the Dharmakāya Mahāvairocana who revealed the Mahāvairocana and Vajraśekhara sutras. Kūkai's identification of Mahāvairocana with the Dharmakāya, or Ultimate Reality, was a great leap in Buddhist speculation, for hitherto Dharmakāya had been regarded as totally transcendent. All phenomena point to Ultimate Reality, Mahāvairocana, and at the same time are expressions of that Reality. To attain enlightenment means to realize the "glorious mind, the most secret and sacred" (J: himitsu shōgon shin). Kūkai taught that man is intrinsically capable—through the grace (kaji; Skt: adhiṣṭhāna) of Mahāvairocana and through his own practice of yoga-samādhi—of participating here and now in the Real, of becoming Mahāvairocana (J: sokushin jōbutsu).

In Attaining Enlightenment in This Very Existence (Sokushin jōbutsu gi), Kūkai explains his conception of Mahāvairocana as the Body of Six Great Elements, consisting of the three constituents: the Six Great Elements, the Four Mandalas, and the Three Mysteries. These three correspond respectively to the essence (J: tai), the attributes (sō), and the functions (yū) of the Dharmakāya Mahāvairocana. The Six Great Elements are earth, water, fire, wind, space, and consciousness. These Six Great Elements create all Buddhas, all sentient beings, and all material worlds.

Of the Four Mandalas, Kūkai explains that the mahā-maṇḍala is the great (mahā) circle; that is, the universe, or Mahāvairocana seen in his physical extension. The samaya-maṇḍala is the same circle seen from the viewpoint of the omnipresence of Mahāvairocana's "intention" (samaya). The dharma-maṇḍala is the same circle viewed as the sphere where the revelation of the truth (dharma) takes place. Finally, the karma-maṇḍala is the same circle seen from the viewpoint of his action (karma). The Three Mysteries are the suprarational activities of the body, speech, and mind of Mahāvairocana.

Shingon meditation, the integration of the microcosmic activities of individual exis-

Lake Shinji The island of Yomegashima as seen from the eastern shore of this lake, famous for its beautiful scenery at sunset.

tence into the macrocosmic activities of Mahāvairocana, is done through symbolic acts of the body (the pose of sitting in meditation and the use of hand gestures, *mudrā* [J: INZŌ]), of speech (the recitation of mantras, the symbols of the essence of speech of Mahāvairocana), and of mind (practices involving thinking, feeling, imagining, visualizing, listening, and ceasing the activities of the mind). Among methods are meditation on the Diamond Realm (KONGŌKAI) and Womb Realm (TAIZŌKAI) mandalas and on the moon (symbol of the enlightened mind), each of which is a manifestation of Mahāvairocana.

The Sanskrit title Mahāvairocana (J: Dainichi) means "Great Sun." Similarly, the great sun goddess AMATERASU ŌMIKAMI is the central figure in the Shintō pantheon. With the development of RYŌBU SHINTŌ in the medieval period, Amaterasu came to be widely recognized as an avatar of Dainichi. Esoteric Buddhism, embracing many native Indian Hindu deities, provided, in part, the ground for the fusion of Buddhism and Shintō. Shingon Buddhism was also instrumental in forming SHUGENDŌ. Today, the headquarters of Shugendō (Tōzan branch) is a Shingon temple, DAIGOJI in Kyōto.

There are two major divisions in the Shingon sect: Old (*kogi*) and New Shingon (*shingi*). KAKUBAN (1095–1143), an ardent follower of Kūkai's teachings, established on Mt. Kōya (Kōyasan) an institute for the transmission of dharma (the Dai Dembōin), which came into conflict with the mountain's time-honored headquarters, Kongōbuji. The New Shingon division was founded by Raiyu (1226–1304), a descendant in Kakuban's line who, after a fierce theological controversy, left Mt. Kōya and established, about 25 kilometers (15.5 mi) northwest of Mt. Kōya, the temple Negoroji, the headquarters of the New Shingon. After Negoroji's destruction in 1585, two new centers were created by the followers of Kakuban: one at the temple HASEDERA, also called Chōkokuji (Buzan branch); another at CHISHAKUIN (Chizan branch). The Old Shingon sect includes the following subsects: the TŌJI, Daigo, DAIKAKUJI, Omuro (see NINNAJI), Sennyūji, Yamashina, and ZENTSŪJI. In 1989 the Shingon sect consisted of 45 subsects, 12,394 temples, and approximately 16 million followers.

Shingū　　　　　新宮[市]

City in southeastern Wakayama Prefecture, central Honshū. It originally developed as a shrine town around the Kumano Hayatama Shrine (see KUMANO SANZAN SHRINES). Today lumber and paper industries flourish. It is the gateway to the Yoshino-Kumano National Park and to the scenic gorge DOROKYŌ. Pop: 35,925.

Shinji, Lake　　　　宍道湖

(Shinjiko). In northeastern Shimane Prefecture, western Honshū. Part of the Shinji Trough between the Chūgoku Mountains and the Shimane Peninsula. The river Hiigawa flows into the lake, while the Ōhashigawa flows out of it into the Nakaumi lagoon. Lake Shinji is connected with the Sea of Japan by the man-made river Sadagawa. Catches include pond smelt, icefish, *shijimi* or corbicula (a small shellfish), eels, perch, prawns, and carp. The city of Matsue is located on its eastern shore. Area: 79.7 sq km (30.8 sq mi); circumference: 45 km (28 mi); depth: 6 m (20 ft).

Shinjinkai　　　　新人会

(New Man Society). Political organization founded on 7 December 1918 by a group of students of the Faculty of Law at Tōkyō University. Espousing political democracy and social reform, the Shinjinkai became the largest and most influential group in a flourishing left-wing student movement in Japan.

At first, the Shinjinkai sought to proselytize for democracy and reform through a wide variety of activities, including the publication of a magazine as well as agitation and organization of the growing labor movement. Later, in efforts to mobilize the "student masses," the Shinjinkai came to have a preponderant influence in the university newspaper (*Teikoku daigaku shimbun*), the student government (Gakuyūkai), the debating club, and the university-affiliated settlement project in the slums of east Tōkyō. Shinjinkai members were also prominent in the leadership of the Gakuren (Gakusei Shakai Kagaku Rengōkai; Student Federation of Social Science). By this time, the early Shinjinkai emphasis on "liberal democracy" had shifted in the direction of orthodox Marxism-Leninism. Although only a minority of the membership of the Shinjinkai ever joined the underground JAPAN COMMUNIST PARTY, most considered themselves Marxists and devoted much time to the reading and discussion of Marxist literature.

Shinjinkai members were among those arrested in the government's mass roundup of suspected communists on 15 March 1928 (see MARCH 15TH INCIDENT), and official university pressure forced the dissolution of the Shinjinkai as a legal association on 17 April. The Shinjinkai survived as an underground group until its formal dissolution on 23 November 1929.

At its peak in the late 1920s the Shinjinkai had about 40 members in each graduating class of Tōkyō University. Many went on to prominent careers in politics, academic life, and literature. See also STUDENT MOVEMENT.

Shinjō　　　　新庄[市]

City in northern Yamagata Prefecture, northern Honshū. It developed as a castle town of the Tozawa family during the Edo period (1600–1868). The principal agricultural product is rice. Furniture and electronics products are manufactured here. Visitors are drawn to the Shinjō Hot Spring and the boat rides down the river Mogamigawa. Pop: 43,125.

Shinjō Basin　　　　新庄盆地

(Shinjō Bonchi). In northern Yamagata Prefecture, central Honshū. Flanked by the Ōu, Dewa, and Asahi mountains, it consists of alluvial fans covered with volcanic ash and the floodplain of the river Mogamigawa. It is a rich rice-producing area. Thick Japanese cedar forests grow in the hilly northern part. The major city is Shinjō. Area: approximately 200 sq km (77 sq mi).

shinjū　　　　心中

(plural suicide). Suicide involving a small number of closely related persons. Collective orientation and group cohesion are two of the hallmarks of Japanese society and are reflected in the prevalence of plural suicides. *Shinjū* may be subdivided into *jōshi* (love suicide) and *ikka shinjū* (family suicide). *Jōshi* typically involves two lovers, either heterosexual or homosexual. Stifling customs and rigid social codes in the Edo period (1600–1868) resulted in numerous love suicides, providing a rich source for novels and plays by writers such as CHIKAMATSU MONZAEMON. Though Japanese society has changed immensely since that time, *jōshi* remains a common form of suicide even in contemporary Japan.

Ikka shinjū involves at least two family members and may appear in a number of configurations; in the most typical, a mother takes the lives of her children and then her own. Various social factors lead some Japanese parents to feel that it is more "humane" to take their children along in suicide rather than to leave them behind.

Plural suicide can be further classified according to whether the suicide is committed by mutual consent (*gōi shinjū*) or not (*muri shinjū*).

Shinjuku Gyoen National Garden　　　　新宿御苑

(Shinjuku Gyoen). Park and landscape garden in Shinjuku and Shibuya wards, Tōkyō. Famous for cherry blossoms in April and chrysanthemums in November. Designed in 1906 in the manner of a European park, it occupies the site of the Naitō *daimyō*'s mansion, which had been turned over to the imperial household in 1872. It became a public park in 1949. Area: 58.5 hectares (144.5 acres).

Shinjuku Ward　　　　新宿区

(Shinjuku Ku). One of the 23 wards of Tōkyō. During the Edo period (1600–1868), Shinjuku was a post-station town on the Kōshū Kaidō (Kōshū Highway). It developed rapidly beginning in the 1920s, and today is one of the major business and entertainment centers of Tōkyō (see URBAN SUBCENTERS). Department stores, restaurants, bars, theaters, and shops surround Shinjuku Station, an important transportation center. Redevelopment of the area around the west exit of Shinjuku Station began in the 1960s, and there are now 18 high-rise office buildings located there, including the new Tōkyō Metropolitan Government headquarters. Eastern and central Shinjuku Ward are principally commercial and residential. In northern Shinjuku Ward, on the river Kandagawa, are numerous dyeing and printing plants. Points of interest include the Shinjuku Gyoen National Garden, the Outer Gardens of the Meiji Shrine, and the National Sports Stadium. Pop: 296,790.

Shinkankaku school　　　　新感覚派

(Shinkankaku Ha). Modernist literary group of the mid-1920s. Its name is often translated as Neo-Impressionist school, but School of New Sensibilities would be closer to its actual meaning. Among the 18 young writers who were members were YOKOMITSU RIICHI, KAWABATA YASUNARI, KATAOKA TEPPEI, NAKA-

GAWA YOICHI, KON TŌKŌ, KISHIDA KUNIO, Ishihama Kinsaku (1899–1968), Sasaki Mosaku (1894–1966), and Jūichiya Gisaburō (1897–1937). These writers published the coterie magazine *Bungei jidai* (Literary Age) from October 1924 to May 1927; however, many of the works most often cited as examples of the Shinkankaku style were actually printed in other periodicals. The word *shinkankaku* (new sensibilities) was applied to the group by the critic Chiba Kameo (1878–1935) in a sympathetic review of the first issue of their magazine, and they quickly adopted it as their name.

The Shinkankaku writers, who saw it as their mission to provide an art-centered alternative to the drab confessional fiction of Japanese NATURALISM on the one hand and the politically oriented writings of the Japanese PROLETARIAN LITERATURE MOVEMENT on the other, were strongly attracted to such post–World War I European artistic movements as futurism, cubism, expressionism, and dadaism. Yokomitsu Riichi developed the writing style that is most closely associated with the Shinkankaku movement, a highly polished style marked by careful attention to rhythm and imagery, by conscious use of symbolism, and by ways of looking at and describing things that were startling to the Japanese readers of his day. As a group of writers, the Shinkankaku school had ceased to exist by 1928.

Shinkansen   新幹線

(New Trunk Line). A high-speed passenger railroad system operated by companies of the JR group. Often called the "bullet train" because of its shape and speed. The Shinkansen provides first-class, or "Green Car," service as well as reserved and unreserved ordinary-car service. There are no sleeping facilities and few dining facilities on Shinkansen trains, since most runs can be made in a few hours.

The first line to be completed was called the Tōkaidō Shinkansen, because it was a new trunk line on the route of the TŌKAIDŌ between Tōkyō and Ōsaka. The San'yō line has since been constructed from Ōsaka west to Hakata in Kyūshū. The combined route, with a total length of 1,069 kilometers (664 mi), is known as the Tōkaidō-San'yō Shinkansen. The train has a maximum speed of 270 kilometers per hour (168 mph), and the minimum trip time between Tōkyō and Hakata is 5 hours 51 minutes. A Shinkansen train departs Tōkyō for Ōsaka or some point

further west about every seven minutes throughout most daytime schedules, lasting from approximately 6 AM to 12 PM. In 1991, 278 trains were scheduled on the route per day, each with a uniform 16 cars. Between the inauguration of service on the line in 1964 and early 1991, the Tōkaidō San'yō Shinkansen had carried 3 billion passengers.

The Tōhoku Shinkansen and Jōetsu Shinkansen commenced service in 1982. The former connects Tōkyō and Morioka in northern Japan, with a route length of 535.3 kilometers (332.6 mi) and a minimum trip time of 2 hours 36 minutes. On average 115 trains are scheduled daily and passengers number over 30 million per year. The latter connects Tōkyō and Niigata on the coast of the Sea of Japan, with a route length of 333.9 kilometers (207.5 mi) and a minimum trip time of 1 hour 40 minutes. On average 85 trains are scheduled daily and passengers number 20 million per year. From the inauguration of service to 1991, the two lines carried over 400 million passengers.

Development of the System—The railroad that serves the 500-kilometer (311-mi) corridor between Tōkyō and Ōsaka has always been considered the main artery of Japan. Located on the Pacific coast of central Honshū, this zone is the industrial and socioeconomic nucleus of the country; almost half the population and two-thirds of the nation's industry are concentrated there, on only 16 percent of the total land area.

In the 1950s innovations on the conventional Tōkaidō rail line, which served this district, were given priority over other lines in an effort to meet steadily increasing demand. Nevertheless, by 1961 the double-track line reached its transport capacity with 26,000 route kilometers (16,150 mi) of traffic per day. Because of the significance of the line, it became imperative to increase the capacity. The eventual solution was to construct a high-speed railroad on a separate double track—the Shinkansen. Initial plans estimated a construction cost of ¥194.8 billion (US $541.0 million), a construction period of five years, and a three-hour travel time between Tōkyō and Ōsaka. Ground was broken for the project in April 1959, with a proposed completion date of mid-1964, in time for the fall opening of the Tōkyō Olympics. The total construction cost was ¥380.0 billion (US $1.1 billion), double the original estimate. Construction was completed in July 1964 and service was begun on 1 October 1964, 10 days before the opening

of the Olympics, with initial daily service of 60 trains with 12 cars each. Expedited production of equipment enabled an increase in service to 110 trains per day in November 1965.

The Shinkansen reduced the minimum trip time between Tōkyō and Ōsaka from 6 hours and 30 minutes to 2 hours and 30 minutes. A business trip between the two cities was no longer an overnight journey, a fact that considerably altered business activities. The Shinkansen was enthusiastically welcomed by the public because of its high speed, short trip time, good ride comfort, and superb on-time operation. Many trains were operating at full capacity within months, and the numbers of trains and cars in each train have increased steadily since the service was introduced. In the 1960s and 1970s the image of the Shinkansen speeding past a snow-capped Mt. Fuji was seen as a symbol of modern Japan.

The line's popularity and the rapid growth in traffic volume brought about a need for the westward extension of the Shinkansen system. The San'yō Shinkansen opened for service with a 160.9 kilometer (100-mi) stretch between Ōsaka and Okayama in March 1972. The project had taken five years to complete at a cost of ¥224.0 billion (US $739.0 million). The line was extended to Hakata in Kyūshū through the Kammon undersea tunnel in March 1975. The construction for this stretch of 392.8 kilometers (244 mi) also took five years, and the cost was ¥729.0 billion (US $2.4 billion).

In 1971 the construction of two new lines was begun from Ōmiya in Saitama Prefecture north to Niigata and northeast to Morioka. These lines were completed in 1982 and extended from Ōmiya to Tōkyō in 1991. Additional routes are under construction, and others are being planned.

Technical Aspects—The Shinkansen track is a conventional ballasted track on either embankments or viaducts between Tōkyō and Ōsaka. This track structure, however, requires a great deal of time and labor to maintain the track geometry. Consequently, concrete slab track, which is maintenance free and contributes to the quality of the ride, was adopted for further line extensions. The Shinkansen has a DC series traction motor installed on each single-wheel axle, allowing dynamic brakes to be applied

Shinjuku Ward The area surrounding Shinjuku Station has become one of the most important administrative and commercial subcenters of the metropolis of Tōkyō.

1 Japan's largest concentration of skyscrapers—including the new Tōkyō Metropolitan Government Offices (the two structures in the center and right foreground), completed in 1991—lies to the west of Shinjuku Station.

2 To the east of the station is a busy shopping and entertainment district; pictured is one of the entrances to Kabukichō, center of Shinjuku's frenetic nightlife.

Shinkansen
A view from the engineer's seat. State-of-the-art equipment monitors the train's performance.

With Mt. Fuji as a backdrop, a train on the Tōkaidō Shinkansen speeds toward Tōkyō.

to all axles at once, and uses electric multiple-unit trains fed by AC 25 kilowatts. This system was selected over locomotive-hauled coaches for a number of reasons: the even distribution of axle load results in less strain on track structure; the turnaround operation is simple; and a failure of one or two units does not interrupt the operation of the entire train. The car body is streamlined and the cars are air-conditioned and airtight. Windows cannot be opened, but the train is well ventilated throughout. Automatic Train Control (ATC) is used to prevent collisions by maintaining a safety distance between trains and to prevent excess speeds by applying brakes automatically. All trains are continuously monitored and controlled from large display boards, control panels, and computer-aided traffic control systems located in two central control rooms in Tōkyō. The computer system is also capable of a certain degree of conflict resolution, as when, for example, trains are running late and require rescheduling. Electric power supply to the trains is also monitored and controlled from the same rooms by electric power dispatchers. In case of accidents or other problems, the dispatchers act promptly to secure alternative power to restore the failure.

Since it was inaugurated in 1964, the Shinkansen has had a remarkable record of high-speed operation, safety, volume of transport, and punctuality. The success of the Shinkansen revolutionized thinking about high-speed trains. It has been described as the "savior of the declining railroad industry" since its example has stimulated many other countries to take on the new construction or the modernization of railroads as national projects, among which are the French TGV, the Italian Direttissima, the English HST, the German InterCity service, and the Northeast Corridor Rail Improvement Project in the United States.

Shinkawa 新川[町]

Town on the northwestern border of the city of Nagoya in northwestern Aichi Prefecture, central Honshū. Located within the Chūkyō Industrial Zone, Shinkawa has many machinery, pharmaceutical, and food-processing factories. Pop: 18,708.

Shinkawa Kazue 新川和江

(1929–). Poet. Born in Ibaraki Prefecture. Graduate of Yūki Higher Girls' School. Shinkawa studied with SAIJŌ YASO. With masterful rhetoric and evenly flowing rhythm, Shinkawa draws on everyday occurrences to depict the various guises of human love and longing for freedom. Her principal collections of poetry are *Hitotsu no natsu takusan no natsu* (1963) and *Rōma no aki; sono ta* (1965). In 1983–84, she chaired the Japan Modern Poets' Society, the first woman to hold that position.

Shinkei 心敬

(1406–75). Poet of WAKA and RENGA (linked verse) and Buddhist priest. Shinkei embarked upon the priestly life at a very young age, taking the name Shin'e, which at around the age of 50 he changed to Shinkei. He became resident priest of the temple Jūjūshin In in the Kiyomizu district of Kyōto and attained the rank of acting archbishop (*gon daisōzu*). Shinkei was a poetic disciple of the *waka* poet-priest SHŌTETSU from around 1430 until Shōtetsu's death in 1459. He also studied linked verse and in his forties and fifties became widely known as a poet of both genres. In 1467, when Kyōto became the battlefield of the destructive ŌNIN WAR, Shinkei left the area and traveled. From 1471 he settled in a hermitage in the mountains of Sagami Province (now Kanagawa Prefecture). Among the disciples of his later years was the young Kensai (1452–1510), a prominent *renga* poet of his generation. Shinkei's critical writings include SASAMEGOTO (1463–64, Murmured Conversations), *Hitorigoto* (1468, Talking to Myself), and *Oi no kurigoto* (1471, An Old Man's Repetitious Talk), which contend that *waka* and linked verse are products of the same artistic sensibility and that devotion to poetry is of equal value to religious devotion.

Shinkiron 慎機論

(literally, "On Prudence in Acting"). Treatise by the WESTERN LEARNING scholar WATANABE KAZAN, written in 1838. In 1825 the Tokugawa shogunate (1603–1867), in accordance with the NATIONAL SECLUSION policy, called on coastal domains to repel any foreign vessel that might enter Japanese waters. When in 1837 the American ship *Morrison* was driven off by artillery (see MORRISON INCIDENT), Kazan was moved to criticism of shogunate policy. In *Shinkiron* he wrote about world conditions and predicted that Japan's isolation would make it "prey to ravenous wolves." Although Kazan's work remained in manuscript form, he was arrested and imprisoned during the BANSHA NO GOKU suppression of Western Learning scholars. His prison sentence was commuted to domiciliary confinement for life, but Kazan committed suicide lest he cause embarrassment to the *daimyō* of his domain.

Shinkō Geijutsu Ha 新興芸術派

("New Art school"). A loose coalition of writers in the late 1920s sharing a common interest in art for its own sake and a dislike for Marxist notions of art. They formed a kind of club that competed with the PROLETARIAN LITERATURE MOVEMENT, which then dominated the literary scene. Its two principal spokesmen were Ryūtanji Yū (1901–92) and Kuno Toyohiko (1896–1971). Other early participants included Nakamura Murao (1886–1949) and KAMURA ISOTA. Nakamura functioned as the group's unofficial sponsor, working behind the scenes as editor of the literary magazine *Shinchō* (New Currents), whose parent company, Shinchō-sha, published anthologies of the group's short stories and individual novels. Such later well-known writers as KAWABATA YASUNARI, FUNAHASHI SEIICHI, KOBAYASHI HIDEO, IBUSE MASUJI, ABE TOMOJI, and others were also associated with the group early in their careers.

During 1931 and 1932 the Shinkō Geijutsu Ha split into several smaller factions and finally disappeared. Its rapid demise was due in part to its increasing tendency toward commercialization and journalism and in part to the growing enforcement of militarist controls after 1931. Although literary critics characterize the literature of the Shinkō Geijutsu Ha as *ero guro nansensu bungaku*, or literature of the erotic, grotesque, and nonsensical, it did contribute indirectly to the flowering of postwar literature in the late 1940s and early 1950s.

Shin kokinshū 新古今集

(New Collection from Ancient and Modern Times; full title *Shin kokin wakashū;* often cited by court poets as *Shin kokin*). The eighth—and with the KOKINSHŪ, one of the two greatest—of the 21 IMPERIAL ANTHOLOGIES (*chokusenshū*) of classical Japanese poetry (WAKA). The *Shin kokinshū*, with its dominant feeling of melancholy (*sabi*), is one of the most studied and written about of Japan's classical literary works. It profoundly influenced later literature, from linked verse (RENGA) to the NŌ drama, and contemporary poets have come to appreciate its tone, technique, and unique beauty.

Ordered in 1201 by retired emperor GO-TOBA (r 1183–98), the *Shin kokinshū* was nominally completed in 1205 but underwent numerous later revisions. It was compiled by Fujiwara no Teika (FUJIWARA NO SADAIE), Fujiwara no Ariie (1155–1216), FUJIWARA NO IETAKA, the priest JAKUREN, Minamoto no Michitomo (1171–1237), and ASUKAI MASATSUNE, with a Japanese preface by FUJIWARA NO YO-SHITSUNE and a Chinese preface by Fujiwara no Chikatsune (dates unknown). The work has 20 books; there are 1,981 poems in the common text (based on the pre-1210 ver-

A train enters a tunnel near the city of Hashima, Gifu Prefecture.

A Tōkaidō Shinkansen train.

Passenger-Kilometers Traveled on the Shinkansen Lines

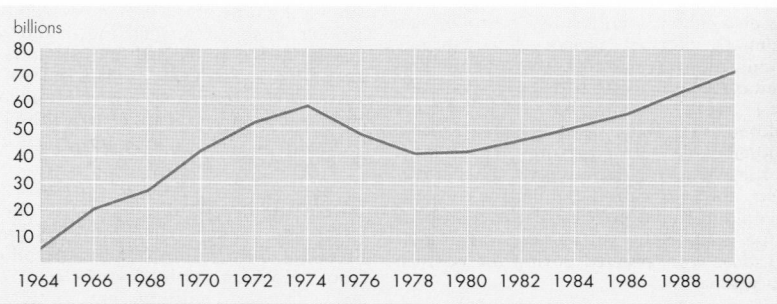

billions

SOURCE: Ministry of Transport.

The Shinkansen Railroad System

Line	Termini	Route length (km)	Travel time of fastest train	Maximum speed (km/h)
Tōkaidō	Tōkyō–Ōsaka	515.4	2 hrs 30 min	270
San'yō	Ōsaka–Hakata	553.7	2 hrs 50 min	230
Tōhoku	Tōkyō–Morioka	535.3	2 hrs 36 min	240
Jōetsu	Tōkyō–Niigata	333.9	1 hr 40 min	275

in operation
under construction
scheduled for construction
in planning stages

NOTE: Information as of March 1992.
SOURCE: Ministry of Transport.

sion, but including 3 poems previously deleted).

The *Shin kokinshū* was a personal project of Go-Toba, who exercised editorial control, calling for extensive revisions (*kiritsugi*) of earlier drafts and retaining veto power over the grouping of poems in books and their ordering into sequences. The "Age of the *Shin kokinshū*"—the generation of Go-Toba and such younger poets as Teika, Ietaka, Ariie, and Jakuren, together with the preceding generation of Fujiwara no Shunzei (FUJIWARA NO TOSHINARI) and the priest SAIGYŌ—was a brilliant poetic age. The poets represented in the *Shin kokinshū* are among the foremost talents of this and the previous age. The most prominent contemporary poets in terms of the number of poems selected are Priest Saigyō, 94; Archbishop JIEN, 92; Fujiwara no Yoshitsune, 79; Fujiwara no Shunzei, 72; Princess SHIKISHI, 49; Fujiwara no Teika, 46; Fujiwara no Ietaka, 43; Jakuren, 35; ex-Emperor Go-Toba, 33; and FUJIWARA NO TOSHINARI NO MUSUME (Shunzei's daughter), 29. Poets of earlier periods include KI NO TSURAYUKI, 34; Lady IZUMI SHIKIBU, 25; KAKINOMOTO NO HITOMARO, 23, of which several are false attributions; MINAMOTO NO TSUNENOBU, 19; and SUGAWARA NO MICHIZANE and SONE NO YOSHITADA, 16 each.

Like the *Kokinshū*, the *Shin kokinshū* consists of 20 books: Books 1–6, *The Seasons* (1

Shinoda Masahiro
1 Shinoda. A notable feature of this film director's work is his innovative use of traditional dramatic forms.
2 Nakamura Kichiemon (right) and Iwashita Shima (Shinoda's wife) in a scene from the film *Shinjū ten no Amijima* (1969, Double Suicide), inspired by a *bunraku* puppet play.

and 2, *Spring;* 3, *Summer;* 4 and 5, *Autumn;* 6, *Winter*); Book 7, *Felicitations;* Book 8, *Laments;* Book 9, *Partings;* Book 10, *Travel;* Books 11–15, *Love;* Books 16–18, *Miscellaneous;* Book 19, *Shintō Poems;* Book 20, *Buddhist Poems.* Great care was taken, as was also the case with the *Kokinshū,* in the ordering and integration of the poems in terms of association and progression; that is, poems were linked one to the next to portray the advance of the seasons or the development of a love affair. Within these larger progressions were embedded subprogressions: a series of poems might move from first light to dawn to twilight and then night.

The most distinctive feature of the poetry written in the age of the *Shin kokinshū* is its tonal depth—a depth achieved in part by frequent allusion to older poetry (HON-KADORI) and in part by employing natural images as symbols of tone and feeling.

Shinkokugeki 新国劇

(New National Theater). Modern drama troupe founded in 1917 by actor-manager SAWADA SHŌJIRŌ. Sawada sought to create with the Shinkokugeki troupe a popular, indigenous, contemporary theatrical form. Sawada's small group of actors and actresses found success with swashbuckling period plays dominated by athletic, realistic action. Yukitomo Rifū (1879–1959), the troupe's first important playwright, created the initial core of the Shinkokugeki repertoire with works about famous swordsmen, *Kunisada Chūji* (1919) and *Tsukigata Hampeita* (1919).

During the early 1920s the troupe's appearances in silent film versions of several of its hit plays became an important base on which the *jidaigeki* (period drama) film tradition of Japan was built. Shinkokugeki became the dominant theatrical troupe of the 1920s as Sawada produced SHIMPA standards and plays out of the SHINGEKI tradition, such as Shakespeare's *Coriolanus.*

Following the sudden death of Sawada in 1929, the troupe lost momentum for several years. Although it continued to emphasize its hallmark sword-action plays, Shinkokugeki in the mid-1930s also developed a strong line of local-color, slice-of-life plays in modern settings. After World War II, Shinkokugeki increased its production of plays about contemporary low life. The troupe eventually revived its sword-fighting spectaculars and returned to a balanced mixed repertoire. During the 1950s, Shinkokugeki became active in film, radio, and eventually television. However, because of increasing financial difficulties, the troupe disbanded in 1987 after more than six decades of uninterrupted activity.

Shinkokushi 新国史

(New National History). Court history compiled in the mid-10th century by Fujiwara no Saneyori (900–970), Ōe no Asatsuna (886–957), or both, by command of Emperor Murakami (r 946–967). It continues the *Nihon sandai jitsuroku* (901; see RIKKOKUSHI). Now lost, it probably recorded the reigns of emperors UDA (r 887–897), DAIGO (r 897–930), and Suzaku (r 930–946).

shinkō shūkyō → new religions

Shin Kyōiku Undō 新教育運動

(New Education Movement). Early-20th-century educational movement emphasizing the individuality and initiative of children. The principles and methods espoused were those of the European and American progressive education movement of the late 19th and early 20th centuries.

The need for such a movement in Japan was suggested by TANIMOTO TOMERI, who studied (1900–1903) new educational theories in Europe and the United States. These ideas were first put into practice in Japan in the early Taishō period (1912–26) by OIKAWA HEIJI, who adopted group education methods based on the German *Gruppenunterricht* at the elementary school attached to Akashi Women's Normal School. Such private schools as SAWAYANAGI MASATARŌ's Seijō Elementary School, HANI MOTOKO's Jiyū Gakuen, Akai Yonekichi's (1887–1974) Myōjō Gakuen, and OBARA KUNIYOSHI's Tamagawa Gakuen made "new education" a basic tenet of their teaching philosophy. The movement, however, suffered under the conservative educational policies of the militarists in the 1930s. Many of the movement's central ideas were revived during the postwar educational reform.

Shinkyō Kyōdōtai 心境共同体

(literally, "State of Mind Community"). Small cooperative community in Kasama, Haibara Chō, Nara Prefecture. It operates the Shinkyō Nōsan, a factory producing *fusuma* (sliding doors), as well as the Shinkyō Sōen (established 1966), a facility for the mentally retarded. The group was started by Ozaki Masutarō (b 1900), a proselytizer for the religious group TENRIKYŌ who underwent a religious crisis and was ostracized (see MURAHACHIBU) by Kasama villagers for smashing Shintō altars. The community, composed of 20 families, seeks a way of life in which its members may live in harmony and equality. A memoir by Sugihara Yoshie (b 1907) of the founding of the community has been translated as *Sensei and His People: The Building of a Japanese Commune* (1969).

Shin Meiwa Industry Co, Ltd 新明和工業[株]

(Shin Meiwa Kōgyō). Manufacturer of special-duty motor vehicles, industrial machinery, and aircraft. Incorporated in 1949. The company manufactures hydroplanes for Japan's DEFENSE AGENCY and has division-of-labor arrangements with McDonnell Douglas Corporation and Boeing Co for production of passenger planes. In 1990 the company's production comprised 47 percent special-duty vehicles, 40 percent industrial machinery, and 13 percent aircraft. The company's sales for the fiscal year ending March 1991 amounted to ¥122.8 billion (US $895.0 million); capitalization stood at ¥13.6 billion (US $99.1 million). Headquarters are in the city of Nishinomiya, Hyōgo Prefecture.

Shin Nampin → Shen Nanpin (Shen Nan-p'in)

Shin Nan'yō 新南陽[市]

City in southern Yamaguchi Prefecture, western Honshū. The city consists of two noncontiguous districts separated by the city of Tokuyama. The district located to the north of Tokuyama is mainly rural, producing rice and tea. The southern district is industrialized and is the site of a petrochemical complex. Pop: 32,988.

Shin Nihon bungaku 新日本文学

(New Japanese Literature). Literary magazine founded immediately after World War II by the Shin Nihon Bungaku Kai (New Japanese Literature Society), an organization of veterans of the prewar PROLETARIAN LITERATURE MOVEMENT. The society was founded in December 1945, and a preliminary issue, including articles by members MIYAMOTO YURIKO, TOKUNAGA SUNAO, and NAKANO SHIGEHARU, appeared the next month; regular publication started in March 1946. FUJIMORI SEIKICHI, Akita Ujaku (1883–1962), Eguchi Kan (1887–1975), KURAHARA KOREHITO, KUBO-KAWA TSURUJIRŌ, and TSUBOI SHIGEJI were also among the nine original members, and later arrivals included ODAGIRI HIDEO and NOMA HIROSHI. It has published original works by SATA INEKO, KAIKŌ KEN, FUJIEDA SHIZUO, and KUROI SENJI. Despite recurring factionalism and a succession of disputes with the Japan Communist Party, *Shin Nihon bungaku* has survived to the present.

Shinoda Hajime 篠田一士

(1927–89). Literary critic; scholar of English literature. Born in Gifu Prefecture; graduated from Tōkyō University. In his *Dentō to bungaku* (1964, Tradition and Literature), Shinoda examines the literature of MORI ŌGAI, SHIMAZAKI TŌSON, and YOKOMITSU RIICHI from the dual perspectives of tradition and the avant-garde. His other works include *Nihon no kindai shōsetsu* (1973, The Modern Japanese Novel) and *Nihon no gendai shōsetsu* (1980, The Contemporary Japanese Novel). Shinoda has also written extensively on the subject of modern poetry, including *Shiteki gengo* (1968, Poetic Language).

Shinoda Masahiro 篠田正浩

(1931–). Film director. Born in Gifu Prefecture; studied at Waseda University. He joined the film production company SHŌCHIKU CO, LTD, in 1953. In 1960 management gave Shinoda, ŌSHIMA NAGISA, and Yoshida Yoshishige (b 1933) their first directing jobs, creating a "Shōchiku Nouvelle Vague" in hopes of duplicating the French New Wave's success in reaching the youth market. Early Shinoda films like *Kawaita hana* (1964, Pale Flower) were acclaimed for depicting the nihilistic sensibility of postwar Japanese youth. For the independent production company Hyōgensha, which he founded in 1967, Shinoda directed *Akane gumo* (1967, Clouds at Sunset) and *Shinjū Ten no Amijima* (1969, Love Suicide at Amijima; Double Suicide), his most acclaimed film. In the latter, based on a play written for the BUNRAKU (classic puppet) theater, he juxtaposed the puppeteers and other devices of the bunraku stage with living actors, a bold approach that unleashed the sensuality of the classic original. The voluptuous imagery of traditional theater is also captured on screen in *Buraikan* (1970, The Scandalous Adventures of Buraikan) and *Yari no Gonza* (1986, Gonza the Spearman). Among his other films are *Setouchi shōnen yakyūdan* (1984, MacArthur's Children) and *Maihime* (1989, The Dancer).

Shinoda Tōkō   篠田桃紅

(1913–). Avant-garde calligrapher. Real name Shinoda Masuko. Born in Manchuria. She was almost entirely self-taught in traditional calligraphy, and later turned to avant-garde forms. After World War II, her work gained attention overseas in one-woman exhibitions held in New York, Paris, and Brussels. Her calligraphy separates writing from its semantic function, allowing it to operate as a medium of purely formal expression. She has brought calligraphy as close as possible to the boundary that separates it from painting.

Shinohara Miyohei   篠原三代平

(1919–). Economist and specialist in economic theory and the Japanese economy. Born in Toyama Prefecture. He graduated from Hitotsubashi University in 1942 and later became a professor there (1962–70) and at Seikei University (1973–85). Studying under NAKAYAMA ICHIRŌ, he devoted himself to the analysis of the dual structure of the Japanese economy. He also developed some highly controversial hypotheses, including that of medium-term business cycles.

shi-nō-kō-shō   士農工商

(warrior-farmer-artisan-merchant). The four classes into which the Japanese people were divided during the Edo period (1600–1868); a system of occupational class distinction that originated in China. This system was officially established in the mid-17th century. Besides the four main categories, there existed small outcaste groups, HININ and *eta* (see BURAKUMIN). For all practical purposes, however, Japanese society was divided into *samurai* (warriors) and non-*samurai*. Artisans and merchants were often collectively called "townsmen" (CHŌNIN). The four-class system was abolished a year after the Meiji Restoration of 1868. At that time, of a population of 30,090,000, the samurai class constituted 6.4 percent, the lower three classes 90.62 percent, outcastes 1.73 percent, and others (court nobles, monks, and nuns) 1.25 percent. The Meiji government established three new categories: *kazoku* (nobility; see PEERAGE); *shizoku* (former samurai); and *heimin* (commoners). The Meiji system was abolished at the end of World War II.

Shino ware→Mino ware

Shinran   親鸞

(1173–1263). Founder of the JŌDO SHIN SECT OF PURE LAND BUDDHISM, a sect based on the principle of birth into the Pure Land (attainment of enlightenment) through faith (*shinjin*) alone. Shinran entered the monastic life at about age eight and served as a *dōsō* (menial monk) at the temple ENRYAKUJI on Mt. Hiei (Hieizan) outside Kyōto until 1201, when he became a disciple of HŌNEN, the founder of the JŌDO SECT. While associated with Hōnen he was permitted to copy the master's major work, the *Senchaku hongan nembutsu shū* (SENCHAKUSHŪ; The Selection of the Nembutsu of the Original Vow), and his portrait.

As Hōnen's NEMBUTSU group became popular and influential, however, criticism and opposition by the monks of Mt. Hiei and the temple Kōfukuji in Nara, as well as alleged indiscretions by his disciples, led to government abolition of the community, the exile of major followers, and the execution of two members. Hōnen was banished to Shikoku, while Shinran was exiled to Echigo Province (now Niigata Prefecture).

Shinran's life during the four-year period of exile is obscure, though it is known that he married and began to raise a large family. Shinran was the first Buddhist priest to be publicly married; thereafter the practice became fairly common. He did not return to Kyōto after his pardon at the end of 1211, for his master died at the beginning of the following year. Instead, he migrated with his family to the Kantō region, where he gathered a body of followers, of whom 74 are known. A major development in this phase of his life was the compilation of his monumental work, KYŌGYŌSHINSHŌ. Interspersed with interpretive comments, it is an anthology drawing from sutras and commentaries in order to make clear the true teaching (*kyō*), living (*gyō*), faith (*shin*), and realizing (*shō*) of the Pure Land school. Shinran made faith, conferred upon the individual by the Buddha Amida, the sole precondition for attainment of birth into the Pure Land. Its themes were popularized in WASAN (poems or hymns in Japanese).

From his return to Kyōto around 1235 until about 1260 Shinran devoted himself to literary efforts. He counseled his disciples through a variety of writings, especially correspondence. Shinran communicated his insights in such works as *Jinen hōni shō* (Treatise on the Ultimate Truth of Things). He died in 1263 in Kyōto. His ashes were interred in the Ōtani area, west of Higashiyama in Kyōto; the site became a devotional center and later the location of the temple HONGANJI.

The central thesis of Shinran's teaching developed from his deep awareness of the inadequacy of individual, self-motivated efforts to achieve enlightenment in the face of profound and persistent egoism and the ineradicability of passion. He came to the conclusion that the possibility of birth in the Pure Land and attainment of enlightenment arise solely from the working and fulfillment of the 48 vows of Amida, and particularly the 18th vow as expounded in the *Muryōju kyō* (Skt: [Larger] *Sukhāvatī-vyūha-sūtra;* one of the three canonical sutras of Pure Land Buddhism) in which Amida declares his intention to lead all sentient beings who recite his name (*nembutsu*) to enlightenment and birth in the Pure Land.

Shinritsu Kōryō   新律綱領

The first national code of criminal law in modern Japan; promulgated in 1870 by the DAJŌKAN (Grand Council of State). Consisting of 192 statutes, it was based on the criminal codes of the Ming (1368–1644) and Qing (Ch'ing; 1644–1912) dynasties of China. Together with its amendment and supplement, the KAITEI RITSUREI (1873), it remained in force until 1882.

Shinron   新論

(New Discourse). Two-volume work completed in 1825 by AIZAWA SEISHISAI, a scholar of the MITO SCHOOL of historical studies. Writing in response to the increase in foreign ships frequenting Japanese waters in defiance of the NATIONAL SECLUSION policy, the au-

Shinran A 13th-century portrait of Shinran, founder of the Jōdo Shin sect of Pure Land Buddhism.

thor discussed world conditions and his belief in Japan's innate superiority as manifested by its unique national polity (*kokutai*). He argued that Western nations were subverting people with Christianity and attempting to conquer the world through trade and military power. To counter this, Seishisai stated that the Japanese should carry out political reforms, build up their military, and under imperial leadership properly venerate the Shintō gods and act as one. *Shinron* provided an ideological framework for the SONNŌ JŌI (Revere the Emperor, Expel the Barbarians) movement that would culminate in the Meiji Restoration of 1868.

Shinryō Corporation

新菱冷熱工業[株]

(Shinryō Reinetsu Kōgyō). Comprehensive engineering company engaged in air-conditioning and ventilation work. Incorporated in 1956. It has overseas engineering and construction projects completed or in progress in over 40 countries. For the fiscal year ending September 1990, sales totaled ¥145.2 billion (US $1.0 billion) and capitalization stood at ¥2.4 billion (US $17.3 million). Headquarters are in Tōkyō.

shin sangyō toshi→new industrial cities

Shin seinen   新青年

Monthly magazine of popular fiction and entertainment. Published by HAKUBUNKAN from 1920 to 1948 and then successively by three other publishers before it ceased publication in 1950. In its early years, *Shin seinen* introduced the Western detective story to its readers. After the magazine ran EDOGAWA RAMPO's debut detective story, "Nisen dōka" (1923, Two-Sen Copper Coin), it went on to feature similar stories by authors such as YOKOMIZO SEISHI, YUMENO KYŪSAKU, and OGURI MUSHITARŌ, and mysteries became its focal point. In 1927, under the editorship of Yokomizo, the magazine began to include humorous stories and comics.

Shinsengumi   新撰組

Small group of *rōnin* (masterless *samurai*) swordsmen commissioned by the Tokugawa shogunate in 1863 as a special police unit to counter antishogunate activities in Kyōto. Called at first the Rōshigumi, the group was organized in Edo (now Tōkyō) in 1863 and sent to Kyōto to guard the shōgun, who was visiting that city. However, Kiyokawa Hachirō (1830–63) and his faction were recalled to Edo for expressing proimperial sentiments. Some 20 remaining members reorganized and took the name Shinsengumi, and KONDŌ ISAMI and Hijikata Toshizō (1835–69) emerged as the new leaders. The Shinsengumi acted under orders from KYŌTO SHUGO-SHOKU, the commissioner newly appointed to keep peace in Kyotō. The group was involved in the massacre at the Ikedaya inn in 1864 (IKEDAYA INCIDENT) and in the defense of the Imperial Palace in the HAMAGURI GOMON INCIDENT. After the Meiji Restoration (1868) the Shinsengumi remained loyal to the shōgun, fighting against imperial forces in the BOSHIN CIVIL WAR.

Shinsen jikyō 新撰字鏡

A Chinese-Japanese character dictionary compiled by the Buddhist monk Shōjū (dates unknown) in the late 9th or early 10th century. It contains more than 20,000 Chinese characters (KANJI) arranged by radical with the Japanese approximation of the Chinese pronunciation (see ON READINGS). It also includes the Japanese pronunciation (see KUN READINGS) of some 3,000 words (single characters or character compounds), being the oldest existing Japanese dictionary to provide such information. The *Shinsen jikyō* is an important resource work for the study of ancient documents and of Chinese characters and for research into the phonology and vocabulary of ancient Japanese. See also DICTIONARIES.

Shinsen shōjiroku 新撰姓氏録

(Newly Compiled Record of Surnames). A genealogy of noble families of the early Heian period (794–1185). Begun at the order of Emperor KAMMU (r 781–806) in 799, it was completed in the reign of Emperor SAGA (r 809–823) and presented to the throne in 815. The work, in 30 sections, lists 1,177 (originally 1,182) families (UJI) living in the capital and the five surrounding provinces. They are grouped in categories including *kōbetsu* (offshoots of the imperial line, descended from Amaterasu Ōmikami), *shimbetsu* (those claiming descent from other deities), and *shoban* (those of foreign origin).

Shinsen tsukubashū 新撰菟玖波集

Second important anthology of RENGA (linked verse) following the pioneering TSUKUBASHŪ (1356–57); it marked the high point of *renga*'s development in the Muromachi period (1333–1568). Compiled in 1495 by SŌGI and INAWASHIRO KENSAI, it was designated an "honorary imperial anthology" (*jun chokusenshū*). It includes some 2,053 verses composed roughly between 1429 and 1495 by some 255 poets. One-fourth of the verses are by SHINKEI and others of the so-called Renga Shichiken (Seven Sages of Renga), the poet-monks who dominated the art from the mid-15th century on. This, coupled with the deliberate omission of *haikai no renga* (comic *renga;* a precursor of HAIKU), which was becoming increasingly popular at the time, indicates Sōgi's desire to make the anthology representative of the orthodox *renga* style.

Shinshichō 新思潮

(New Currents of Thought). Literary magazine whose publication extended through 20 series, with lapses, from 1907 to 1987. Series 1 *Shinshichō* (October 1907–March 1908) was founded by OSANAI KAORU. Its aim was

the introduction of modern drama and new literary trends from abroad. It also introduced original essays, stories, and poems by writers such as MASAMUNE HAKUCHŌ, OGURI FŪYŌ, KAMBARA ARIAKE, and IWANO HŌMEI. *Shinshichō* was a precursor of the SHINGEKI ("new theater") movement and was opposed to Japanese NATURALISM.

Series 2 *Shinshichō* (September 1910–March 1911) was also edited by Osanai. Most of its collaborators were Tōkyō University literature students. Series 3 *Shinshichō* (February–September 1914) was the product of a group including KUME MASAO, AKUTAGAWA RYŪNOSUKE, and YAMAMOTO YŪZŌ, all Tōkyō University graduates, who were joined by KIKUCHI KAN. Series 4 (February 1916–March 1917) comprised mostly members of the series 3 group. Series 5 through 20, published intermittently between 1918 and 1987, continued *Shinshichō* as a college coterie magazine and included the work of such writers as KAWABATA YASUNARI, KON TŌKŌ, ŌYA SŌICHI, DAN KAZUO, YOSHIYUKI JUNNOSUKE, and ARIYOSHI SAWAKO.

Shinshiro 新城［市］

City in eastern Aichi Prefecture, central Honshū, on the river Toyogawa. It prospered in the Edo period (1600–1868) as a river port and market town. It has many lumber mills and rubber plants. Pop: 35,633.

shinsho → paperback books

Shinshōji 新勝寺

Major temple of the Chizan branch (see CHISHAKUIN) of the SHINGON SECT of Buddhism, located in the city of Narita, Chiba Prefecture. Popularly known as Naritasan or Narita Fudō, Shinshōji was built to house an image of the ferocious Buddhist divinity Fudō Myōō (Skt: Acalanātha; see MYŌŌ). The image, reputedly carved by KŪKAI, founder of the Shingon sect, had been brought from the temple JINGOJI in the Takao district of Kyōto to Narita in the hope that it could help crush the rebellion of TAIRA NO MASAKADO. Shinshōji was built shortly after Masakado's defeat and death in 940. Popular since the Edo period (1600–1868), the temple attracts pilgrims year-round. It has become the center of Fudō worship.

Shinshōsetsu 新小説

(New Fiction). Literary magazine of the late Meiji and Taishō periods (roughly 1889 to 1926), which sought to present new forms of the novel. Founded by AEBA KŌSON, Sudō Nansui (1857–1920), and Morita Shiken (1861–97), the original *Shinshōsetsu* appeared briefly from January 1889 to June 1890. In addition to original works of fiction, it carried plays, translations, and essays. The second series of *Shinshōsetsu* was published from July 1896 to November 1926. It was created to compete with the literary magazine BUNGEI KURABU. The editorship of *Shinshōsetsu* passed through several hands, including KŌDA ROHAN, ISHIBASHI NINGETSU, SUZUKI MIEKICHI, AKUTAGAWA RYŪNOSUKE, and KIKUCHI KAN. Writers whose works appeared in *Shinshōsetsu* include HIROTSU RYŪRŌ, IZUMI KYŌKA, SHIMAZAKI TŌSON, NATSUME SŌSEKI, TAYAMA KATAI, IWANO HŌMEI, and NAGAI KAFŪ.

Shinshū University 信州大学

(Shinshū Daigaku). A coeducational national university located in the city of Matsumoto, Nagano Prefecture. Founded in 1949, the university has faculties of arts, education, economics, science, medicine, engi-

neering, agriculture, and textile science and technology. The university has five campuses and a television system for transmission of lectures from one area to another. Enrollment in 1989 was 8,471.

Shinsui Kyōyo Rei 薪水供与令

(Order for the Provision of Fuel and Water). Decree issued in 1842 by the Tokugawa shogunate ordering that foreign ships be provided with food, water, and other necessities, on condition that they leave Japan immediately. In the face of mounting pressure from Western powers to open its ports to trade, the shogunate recognized that it could no longer enforce its earlier order to repel foreign ships (GAIKOKUSEN UCHIHARAI REI). It thus issued the Shinsui Kyōyo Rei as a compromise, hoping to retain the more essential features of its NATIONAL SECLUSION policy.

shintai 神体

(literally, "body of the divine"). A sacred object in Shintō, regarded as the "support" of the divine, evidencing its presence. Also called *mitama no mikata, mitamashiro, mishōtai.* Natural objects used as *shintai* include trees or branches, stones, bodies of water, and mountains; man-made objects include mirrors, swords, polished comma-shaped stones (*tama*), bells, clothes, dishes, and later, under the influence of Buddhism, statues or paintings. At the time of religious ceremonies, it is believed that a divinity that is called upon descends and locates itself in the object in question, which then becomes a focus for ritual activity. Regarded as sacred, this object generally is kept concealed in a box retained in th main sanctuary of a Shintō shrine. When it is paraded, it is installed by the priests in a portable shrine (*mikoshi*), which is also closed. See also IMPERIAL REGALIA, MISHŌTAI.

Shin Taisei Undō → New Order Movement

shintaishi 新体詩

(new-style poetry). The term *shintaishi* refers chiefly to verse of the Meiji period (1868–1912) written in literary Japanese and in a flexible number of lines but employing the traditional seven-five or five-seven meter of classical WAKA poetry. It marked an attempt to create a new mode of poetic expression suitable to the times, and to a significant degree developed under the influence of Western poetry. In the first anthology of poems in this genre, the *Shintaishi shō* (1882, Collection of New-Style Poetry), 15 of the 19 poems included were translations from French and English. Among prominent practitioners of the genre were YAMADA BIMYŌ, MORI ŌGAI, SHIMAZAKI TŌSON, KAMBARA ARIAKE, and YOSANO TEKKAN, publisher of the magazine MYŌJŌ. By 1910 verse written in free meter and colloquial Japanese had gained ascendancy over *shintaishi.*

Shintō 神道

Japan's indigenous religion. The word Shintō is written with two Chinese characters; the first, *shin,* is also used to write the native Japanese word *kami* ("divinity" or "numinous entity"), and the second, *tō,* is used to write the native word *michi* ("way"). The term first appears in the historical chronicle NIHON SHOKI (720), where it refers to religious observance, the divinities, and shrines, but not until the late 12th century was it used to denote a body of religious doctrines. The worship of *kami* slowly emerged at the dawn of Japanese history, crystallized as an imperial religious system during the Nara (710–794) and Heian (794–1185) periods, and subsequently was in constant interaction with Buddhism and Confucianism, which were introduced from the Asian continent. This interaction gave birth to various syncretic cults that combined the worship of *kami* with the imported religions. In the Muromachi (1333–1568) and Edo (1600–1868) periods, however, there was a revival of Shintō as the "Ancient Way," and an attempt was made to pare away all foreign influences. This expurgated system became the state religion of Japan during the Meiji period (1868–1912), but in 1945 Shintō was disestablished and again became one among other forms of worship.

Shintō can be regarded as a two-sided phenomenon. On the one hand it is a loosely structured set of practices, creeds, and attitudes rooted in local communities, and on the other it is a strictly defined and organized religion at the level of the imperial line and the state. These two basic aspects, which are not entirely separate, reflect fundamental features of the Japanese national character as it is expressed in sociopolitical structures and psychological attitudes.

Origins and Formative Period—Archaeological evidence of the Jōmon period (ca 10,000 BC–ca 300 BC) has yielded scant information concerning religious practices. However, artifacts of the Yayoi period (ca 300 BC–ca AD 300), during which important population movements occurred and contacts with the continent intensified, show that religious life was becoming complex. Wetland agriculture necessitated stable communities, and agricultural rites that later played an important role in Shintō were developed. Metal implements, such as weapons and mirrors, were deposited in burial sites as emblems of political legitimacy. Cups and jars for food offerings have been found, a significant matter in the light of later practice, in which the primary form of worship consists in offering food. Oracular bones show the increasing importance of divination.

The Kofun period (ca 300–710) was marked by influences from the continent and by the emergence of Japan as a nation. The 100 or so Japanese "kingdoms" mentioned in the late-3rd-century Chinese chronicle WEI ZHI (*Wei chih*) were gradually unified as relationships of clientage and allegiance were formed around the leaders of the powerful Yamato clan, from which developed the imperial line. Not only the Yamato kings, but also the chiefs of major clans (UJI)—each worshiping its own tutelary divinity (UJIGAMI)—were buried in stone chambers covered by earthen mounds (KOFUN) and accompanied by swords, curved gemstones (*magatama*), and mirrors, suggestive of the myth of the three IMPERIAL REGALIA. It was during this period that the ISE SHRINE and IZUMO SHRINE, the most important shrines of the imperial tradition of Shintō, were established. The introduction of Confucianism contributed to the formalization of the Shintō moral precepts TSUMI (hindrance of the life force) and KEGARE (ritual impurity).

On the one hand religious activity was grounded in each community and was concerned with agriculture and seasonal acts of worship, while on the other hand it was central to the ritual and political life of the leading clans. Imperial legitimacy, based on mythical, ritual, and religious coherence, was established through the compilation of the histories KOJIKI (712) and *Nihon shoki*. In the chapters of these works that recount mythology, the structure of the pantheon is connected to the structure of early society: the relationship of major clans to the imperial family is stated to be the result of relationships established between their respective ancestors. The centrality of religious practices to the RITSURYŌ SYSTEM of government, created after the Taika Reform (645) and under which all the lands and people of Japan belonged to the emperor, is reflected in the fact that the Office of Shintō Worship (Jingikan) was in form, if not in practice, preeminent over the Grand Council of State (DAJŌKAN). The Jingikan, presided over by the Nakatomi, Imbe, and Urabe clans, administered a system of shrines (some 3,000 in the early 10th century) at which prayers were offered for the benefit of the state. The Shintō rituals surrounding the imperial family and its satellite clans were codified at the end of the 9th century in the Jōgan Gishiki and in the early 10th century in the ENGI SHIKI. Imperial Shintō thus achieved the status of a coherent religion, with a system of myths, rituals, sacerdotal lineages, and shrines.

The official recognition of Buddhism by Empress SUIKO (r 593–628) in 594 and its acceptance by the upper strata of society not only contributed to the systematization of the traditions that came to be known as Shintō, but also initiated a process of SYNCRETISM that was formalized in the medieval period (mid-12th–16th centuries). At the beginning of the 8th century, Buddhist temples were already being built on or next to the grounds of Shintō shrines and were called *jingūji* (literally, "shrine-temples"). Buddhist monks considered the Shintō divinities (*kami*) to be in need of salvation and read and lectured on the Buddhist sutras in front of Shintō shrines. In 741, members of the emperor's court offered up a set of Lotus Sutra scrolls to the USA HACHIMAN SHRINE, and in 745 the shrine sent funds for the completion of the state-sponsored temple TŌDAIJI. This service, among others, resulted in the granting of the Buddhist title "bodhisattva" to the *kami* Hachiman in 783.

Crucial developments in the interaction between Shintō and Buddhism occurred during the Heian period, following the introduction from China of the Tiantai (T'ien-t'ai; J: Tendai) sect by SAICHŌ (767–822) and esoteric Shingon teachings by KŪKAI (774–835), founder of the Shingon sect (see ESOTERIC BUDDHISM). The Tendai sect was permeated by Shingon doctrines after Saichō died, and the two sects established a close relationship with Shintō, resulting in the development of syncretic ritual and philosophical systems in the medieval period. The facility with which esoteric Buddhism adapted itself to Shintō worship can be explained in part by the fact that it incorporated numerous syncretic practices that had developed in India and that its fundamental teaching was that all things in the phenomenal world are emanations of the Buddha Mahāvairocana (J: DAINICHI).

The Medieval Period: Syncretism—Of several pivotal theories of amalgamation introduced by Buddhism, the HONJI SUIJAKU ("original prototype and local manifestation") theory played a key role in the evolution of Shintō-Buddhist relationships. At its core lies the notion that Shintō divinities are manifestations of Buddhas and bodhisattvas. Hence worship of a *kami* was worship of a Buddha in its *kami* form. Associations between Shintō divinities and Buddhas, such as that which obtained between AMATERASU ŌMIKAMI, chief divinity of the Ise Shrine, and Dainichi, were established at the level of particular shrines and temples, and each devised its own system of rituals and practices surrounding its syncretic pantheon. Legends explaining the origin of these associations and descriptions of ritual systems were recorded in *engi-mono*, a type of picture scroll (EMAKIMONO). While these were for proselytization among the masses, there was also developed between the 13th and 19th centuries a vast body of mythicohistorical and philosophical treatises composed by scholarly monks and priests. Its major categories are treatises based on schools of Buddhism, especially the Tendai and Shingon sects; treatises based on shrine traditions; and treatises written by Shintō priests. Examples of the first category are works dealing with Sannō Shintō and SANNŌ ICHIJITSU SHINTŌ, which arose from the Tendai sect, and RYŌBU SHINTŌ, which arose from the Shingon sect. The second category includes works of cults that originated at major shrines, such as the KUMANO SANZAN SHRINES, IWASHIMIZU HACHIMAN SHRINE, and KASUGA SHRINE. The third category is represented by works of the imperial tradition of Shintō, such as Watarai Shintō at the Ise Shrine and Yuiitsu Shintō at the Yoshida Shrine, that evince a reaction to Buddhist influence.

Sannō Shintō developed from the relationship between the guardian divinity Sannō of the Hie Shrine on the eastern slope of Mt. Hiei near Kyōto and Buddhist deities of the temple ENRYAKUJI on the summit of Mt. Hiei. Sannō and Amaterasu Ōmikami came to be considered local manifestations of, respectively, Shaka (Skt: Śākyamuni) and Dainichi. However, the Tendai monk Tenkai (1536–1643), founder of the teaching known as Sannō Ichijitsu Shintō, later held that all Buddhas and Shintō divinities were in fact manifestations of Amaterasu, and in 1617 TOKUGAWA IEYASU (1543–1616), the unifier of Japan and founder of the Tokugawa shogunate, was buried according to its rituals.

Ryōbu Shintō also attempted a combination of Buddhism with the great tradition of Shintō at Ise. *Ryōbu* denotes the dual Shingon mandalas (RYŌBU MANDARA), which are graphic representations of the universe seen in its twofold aspect of noumenon/phenomenon. The *Tenchi reiki ki* (Notes on the Numinous Energy of Heaven and Earth), composed during the latter half of the Kamakura period (1185–1333), is the fundamental treatise on the subject. Its main point resides in the connection of the two mandalas with the Outer Shrine (Gekū) and Inner Shrine (Naikū) of Ise. As is usual with syncretic phenomena in Japan, numerous associations of a philosophical, ritual, phonetic, graphic, and numerologic nature were proposed in order to indicate the essential identity of Shintō and Buddhism. Ryōbu Shintō declined as the imperial Shintō tradition reacted against Buddhist influence, first with its own brand of syncretism, and then with an outright rejection of Buddhism.

Watarai Shintō was developed by a series of scholarly priests of the sacerdotal lineage charged with the administration of the Outer Shrine of Ise. By the end of the 13th century they had composed texts, the *Shintō gobusho* (Five Books of Shintō), which they attributed to distant imperial and divine figures. Regarded as revealed scripture, they deal with mythology, history, ritual, purification, and ethics and contain symbolic explanations of rituals, myths, and architectural details. Although Buddhism is mentioned, it remains in the background. The summa of medieval Shintō scholarship, however, was the *Ruijū jingi hongen* (1320), a compendium of Shintō knowledge assembled by Watarai Ieyuki (1256–1351). An important characteristic of Watarai Shintō is its emphasis on a primordial divinity that preceded the birth of the cosmos and was responsible for it.

The appearance of Yuiitsu Shintō ("Only Shintō") or Yoshida Shintō marked the eclipse of the *honji suijaku* doctrine and heralded a national decline of Buddhist-centered Shintō. Though it was based on the scholarship of several generations of the Yoshida family (formerly Urabe), it was essentially the creation of Yoshida Kanetomo (1435–1511). The school regarded Shintō as the origin of all phenomena—Confucianism, Taoism, and Buddhism included. In the major scripture of the school, the *Yuiitsu Shintō myōbō yōshū*, Kanetomo established a distinction between exoteric and esoteric Shintō; the exoteric teachings are based on the *Kojiki* and the *Nihon shoki*, while the esoteric teachings are based on scriptures that he claimed had been revealed by various divinities in mythical times.

By the beginning of the 15th century, Kanetomo had established himself as the foremost figure in Shintō. However, though he considered Buddhism to be a mere manifestation of Shintō, it is clear that esoteric Buddhism pervaded his thinking, his symbolism, and his rituals. In 1598, when TOYOTOMI HIDEYOSHI died, the Yoshida school was charged with the funeral rites and the deification of the warrior at the Toyokuni Shrine. Although the school supervised the initiation and nomination of Shintō priests in much of the country during the Edo period, the Meiji Restoration in 1868 marked the end of its influence.

The Edo Period——There developed in the Edo period a shift of Shintō away from Buddhism and a rapprochement with Neo-Confucianism. At the same time scholars of the KOKUGAKU (National Learning) movement attempted, through rigorous philological study of old texts, to gain new insights into the culture and religious beliefs of ancient Japan as they had existed before the introduction of Confucianism and Buddhism.

HAYASHI RAZAN (1583–1657), who became the Confucian adviser to four shōguns, founded the first school that harmonized Shintō and Neo-Confucianism. Among other works, he composed the *Honchō jinja kō* (Reflections on the Shrines of This Nation) and the *Shintō denju* (Shintō Transmission), in which he emphasized the union between Shintō and the Imperial Way, the immanence of the absolute as *kami* within the human heart, ethical behavior as the mark of the divine, and the correct conduct of government as the manifestation of divine virtue.

Suika Shintō was a school founded by YAMAZAKI ANSAI (1619–82), a Zen monk who became a Neo-Confucianist and a passionate proponent of Shintō. Ansai compared Neo-Confucianism with the main philosophical and ethical aspects of Shintō and found many similarities, though he never advocated a syncretism of the two. It is in this

light that he proposed Neo-Confucian interpretations of mythology, which led him to state that the Heavenly Way and the Human Way were identical in foundation and nature.

There also appeared in the early Edo period thinkers who, though outside the major schools of Shintō, proposed interpretations that resulted in a popular revival of a form of Shintō that had no Buddhist overtones. KUMAZAWA BANZAN (1619–91), ISHIDA BAIGAN (1685–1744), and the popular street-corner preacher Masuho Nokoguchi (1656–1742) belonged to this category and were precursors of Kamo no Norikiyo (1798–1861), Inoue Masakane (1790–1849), and others who were responsible for the appearance of SECT SHINTŌ.

Important contributors to the movement known as Restoration Shintō (Fukko Shintō) were KEICHŪ (1640–1701), KAMO NO MABUCHI (1697–1769), MOTOORI NORINAGA (1730–1801), and HIRATA ATSUTANE (1776–1843). These scholars proposed a return to the sources of Japanese identity through close study of the language of ancient literary and historical texts. Norinaga devoted 34 years to his *Kojiki den* (1798), an annotated study of the *Kojiki* that is an encyclopedic source of knowledge about ancient Japan. The ardent nationalist Hirata Atsutane, who proposed a return to imperial rule and to Shintō as the sole Way, popularized his views among the masses, thus helping to lay the groundwork for the introduction of STATE SHINTŌ following the Meiji Restoration, a development in which his adopted son Kanetane (1799–1880) played a major role.

The Meiji Period and After——The 19th century was a crucial turning point in Shintō history: on the one hand a number of religious movements emerged to form Sect Shintō, and on the other the expurgated imperial tradition of Shintō became the state religion, giving to the Meiji Restoration of 1868 the superficial appearance of a return to the Age of the Gods. The system of national shrines was reinstated, as well as the classical Office of Shintō Worship. Shrines were supported by the government, and Shintō, whose doctrines were taught in schools, took on an increasingly nationalistic coloration. Buddhism came under attack after the government decreed the separation of Shintō and Buddhism, but quickly reacted with its own brand of scholarship. After Japan's defeat in World War II, State Shintō was disestablished and replaced by SHRINE SHINTŌ, which represents the bulk of Shintō shrines at the regional and local levels. See also FOLK SHINTŌ.

The religious picture of Japan today is complex. Statistics fail to suggest the numerous layers of interaction that have emerged, disappeared, and reemerged through history; syncretic tendencies and a general nonchalance concerning religious phenomena make it impossible for the uninitiated to come up with a clear image. There is no doubt that the identification of imperial Shintō with nationalism has hurt the tradition considerably, even though in many ways the essence of Shintō has been preserved only at the local shrines, which have had little to do with the imperial tradition. Industrialization and fundamental social changes are now confronting Shintō with what may be its greatest challenge.

Shintō Worship and Ritual——Shintō practice is circumscribed within the context of sacred space and sacred time. The oldest known form of sacred space is a rectangular

area covered with pebbles, surrounded by stones, and marked off by a rope linking four corner pillars; in the middle of this area is a stone (*iwasaka* or *iwakura*), a pillar, or a tree (*himorogi*). This ritually purified place where divinities were invoked (*kanjo*) was located in the midst of a sacred grove. The typical shrine (*jinja*) is located near the source of a river at the foot of a mountain. Surrounded by a fence (*tamagaki*), its entrance is marked by a wooden gate (*torii*) of simple style, on which a rope (*shimenawa*) has been fixed.

The etymology of the term *kami*, which is often rendered as "deity" or "god" but is translated here as "divinity," is unclear. The Shintō pantheon, which is structured only at the level of the imperial tradition, consists of the *yaoyorozu no kami* (literally, "800 myriads of divinities"). Therefore, the presence of the *kami* is overwhelming and pervades all aspects of life. Natural phenomena—wind, sun, moon, water, mountains, trees—are *kami*. Specialized *kami* overlook and patronize human activities and even dwell in man-made objects. Certain *kami* are divinized ancestors or great figures of the past (see SUGAWARA NO MICHIZANE), and until 1945 the emperor was regarded as divine.

Each *kami* is endowed with an efficient force called *tama*, which is the object of religious activity and may be seen as violent (*aramitama*) or peaceful (*nigimitama*). *Tama*, the force that supports all life, dwells in human beings as *tamashii* and departs at the time of death. The *tama* of a *kami* is called upon at the outset of a ceremony to listen to the praise of the community and to its wishes. It is then offered food, praised again, and sent back. During ceremonies the *tama* of a divinity is thought to invest itself in the sacred tree or stone described above, or, more commonly, in a stone, root, branch, sword, mirror, or other object that is kept out of sight in a shrine. As the *tama* is inexhaustible, it may be invoked at many different locations.

Sacred time is that of the myths of the origin of the gods and of the land, as well as the time during which these origins are commemorated. Rituals and ceremonies are performed at each shrine by priests or by a rotating group of community members, on a cyclical and yearly basis (see FESTIVALS). Each word uttered, each gesture and movement, and each ceremony is prescribed in ritual codes that are today set for all shrines in the *Saishi kitei*, published by the National Organization of Shrines (Jinja Honchō).

Food offerings are the core of each ceremony and festival (*matsuri*); products from the sea, rivers, plains, and mountains are prepared in the shrine's kitchen (*shinsendokoro*) on a special fire (*kiribi*). Food is either cooked (*jukusen*) or raw (*seisen* or *marumono*), or comes from live animals (*ikenie*) such as birds or fish. In offering, a distinction is made between food that is intended to be ingested by the divinities (*kyōō shinsen*) and food that is to be viewed by them (*kyōkan shinsen*). Modes of offering include placing on a table, hanging, scattering on the ground, putting into the earth, or releasing into water. Each major shrine has its own style of offering and of preparation. At the level of the imperial tradition, much of the enthronement ceremony of the emperor consists essentially of food preparation and partaking (see DAIJŌSAI).

The other central aspect of Shintō ritual is purification. Grounded in mythology, it takes two forms: MISOGI, purification from contact with sullying elements (*kegare*) such as disease or death, and HARAE, the restoration of proper relationships after wrongdoing, through the offering of compensation. *Misogi* is held to have originated in the myth of the deity Izanagi no Mikoto, who, having followed his consort Izanami no Mikoto to the Land of Darkness (Yomi no Kuni; the netherworld) and seen her in a state of decomposition, returns to the world and cleanses himself in a stream (see IZANAGI AND IZANAMI). As he does so, the purification of his left eye results in the birth of the solar divinity Amaterasu Ōmikami, the purification of his right eye results in the appearance of the lunar divinity Tsukuyomi no Mikoto, and the purification of his nose causes the appearance of the storm divinity SUSANOO NO MIKOTO.

The second form of purification, *harae*, is held to derive from the myth of Susanoo no Mikoto, who, after rampaging through the palace of his sister Amaterasu, is compelled to make recompense by offering up a great quantity of goods and having his beard cut and nails pulled off (see MYTHOLOGY). Ritual implements, such as the folded paper strips (*shide*) that are affixed to ropes, gates, and sacred trees, and offerings of hemp, ramie, salt, and rice derive from the tradition of *harae* and serve the function of *misogi*; hence the origin of the general term *misogi harae* for purificatory practices. The emphasis on purity in Shintō worship is also manifested in the custom of undergoing a period of interdiction (*imi* or *kessai*) of as long as 30 days, which requires avoidance of contact with death, disease, menstruating women, and disfigured persons and abstention from sexual activity and the eating of meat, as well as adherence to conventions in food preparation, clothing, and bathing.

Shintō and the Arts——Japanese scholarship has not established a category of Shintō literature, perhaps because the distinction between "Japanese" and "Shintō" is often obscure. It is, nevertheless, possible to distinguish two subcategories of literature: poetry and Shintō-Buddhist literature. Poetry is intimately related to Shintō; poems are offered to the divinities and the divinities themselves speak "poetically," both in form and substance. There is evidence that poems were seen in religious circles as potent magical formulas, whose function was to pacify the heart. The second subcategory, Shintō-Buddhist literature, includes all examples of SETSUWA BUNGAKU (didactic and popular literary works dealing with extraordinary events) that involve Shintō, such as the UJI SHŪI MONOGATARI, the KOKON CHOMONJŪ, the SHASEKISHŪ, the *Shintōshū*, and the *Fusō ryakki*, as well as works presenting the myths and legends of the origins of shrine temples (*jisha engi*). Theater was linked to shrines as well, both in origin and content. The NŌ dramatist ZEAMI (1363–1443) was connected with the Kasuga Shrine, and Izumo no OKUNI (fl 1600), who developed the earliest form of KABUKI, was connected with the Izumo Shrine. It is generally agreed that theater began in the dances (KAGURA) and songs offered to Shintō divinities.

Important objects of Shintō art are the artifacts found in archaeological sites, such as polished gemstones (*tama, magatama*), mirrors, swords, earthenware statuettes (*dogū*), and other ritual implements. It has been suggested that wooden sculptures representing anthropomorphic divinities owed their appearance to the introduction of Buddhism, or, perhaps, to Chinese influence in general. In any case, a number of statues that have been preserved are of extreme beauty, characterized by august simplicity (those in the Matsunoo Shrine and Kumano Hayatama Shrine), or by stern but refined elegance (Tamayori Hime of the Yoshino Mikumari Shrine). A type of painting used in syncretic ritual is the shrine mandala. Depicting shrine-temple complexes, such mandalas served as maps for mental pilgrimages and as objects of meditation. Famous examples are the Fuji mandala of the Fuji Hongū Sengen Shrine, the Kasuga Jōdo mandala of the Nōman'in, and the Kumano Nachi mandala of the Tōkei Shrine. Because anthropomorphic images are generally alien to Shintō practice, shrines did not support schools of painting as the *ritsuryō* government and later schools of Buddhism did, and, outside of syncretic iconography, one cannot find what could be called Shintō painting. See also SHINTŌ ART.

Shintō and Buddhism, separation of 神仏分離

(*shimbutsu bunri*). The Meiji government (1868–1912) policy of separating Shintō and Buddhism in order to reinforce the Shintō-based divine status of the emperor. Some members of the new government who had been influenced by KOKUGAKU (National Learning), especially the school of HIRATA ATSUTANE, hoped to establish a Shintō-oriented government modeled on the rule of the legendary emperor JIMMU. Through the so-called Dual Shintō (RYŌBU SHINTŌ) system, Buddhist priests had gained administrative control of a large proportion of Shintō shrines. According to a March 1868 decree, these Buddhist priests were now ordered to relinquish their positions, and all Buddhist images were to be removed from Shintō shrines. This decree set in motion a nationwide anti-Buddhist outburst (see HAIBUTSU KISHAKU).

Shintō architecture 神社建築

(*jinja kenchiku*). The architecture of the buildings located within the precincts of Shintō shrines. The precinct not only designates where a deity or deities (KAMI) are enshrined but serves as a place where people can worship and can stage ceremonies and festivals for the *kami*. Consequently, there are buildings for the *kami* and buildings for worshipers. Because some Shintō shrines are dedicated to historic personages, Shintō architecture has influenced mausoleum design, especially since the Kamakura period (1185–1333).

Origin of Shintō Architecture——Shintō is basically a pantheistic religion that believes in the *kami*'s existence in practically every natural object or phenomenon. Often particularly beautiful mountains or deep forest areas were venerated as sacred sites (*kannabi*). Active volcanoes were also considered sacred. The *kami* were thought to dwell in ponds, waterfalls, the confluence of rivers, giant trees, and large or strangely shaped rocks. A rocky crag or precipice might be considered a *kami*'s seat and called *iwakura*. The temporary shelters for the *kami* during a festival (*otabisho*) were also sacred.

Thus, a natural object that was itself a *kami* or a place indicating a *kami*'s existence was marked off as sacred, and a place for worship was created. The demarcation of the sacred area is accomplished simply by placing a straw rope (SHIMENAWA) around the site. More elaborate fences can be used, such as a horizontally stacked wooden plank fence (*mizugaki*), which totally blocks the view into the enclosure, or the *aragaki*, which allows the worshiper to see between the vertically arranged planks in the fence. The TORII probably began as a gate in the fence surrounding the sacred area and marked the farthest point in the compound that the ordinary worshiper could enter. The Ōmiwa Shrine in Nara Prefecture and the Kanasana Shrine in Saitama Prefecture illustrate Shintō shrine types in which there is a sacred precinct but no shrine buildings within it.

Shrine Complexes and Buildings——Shrine buildings are situated to suit the environment and do not follow a uniform arrangement. From the precinct gate a path or roadway will lead to the main shrine building, *honden*, and often stone lanterns will mark the route. To maintain the purity of the shrine precinct, water basins are provided for worshipers to wash their hands and mouths. Often shrines are located in relation to Buddhist temples.

There are two main sources of architectural style for the *honden*. One is the temporary building type constructed for special occasions to house the *kami*. This building style probably dates to the early agrarian period in Japan, about 300 BC. Examples of this type of structure can be seen in the Suki and Yuki halls, which are constructed as part of the ceremonies for the formal enthronement of an emperor (see DAIJŌSAI). The main shrine building of the SUMIYOSHI SHRINE in Ōsaka resembles the temporary building type and is said to preserve the appearance of ancient religious buildings.

The second source of architectural style for the *honden* is domestic architectural forms, both storehouses (*kura*; see STOREHOUSES, TRADITIONAL) and dwellings. This so-called *shimmei* style is said to derive its simple two-bay by three-bay rectangular shape (one bay is the distance between two pillars) from the granaries and treasure storehouses of prehistoric Japan. The ISE SHRINE most clearly exemplifies this style. The inner shrine, Naikū, is consecrated to AMATERASU ŌMIKAMI, the sun goddess and traditional ancestress of the imperial family. The Naikū buildings are raised above the ground and are entered by steps on the longer side. Freestanding columns support the ridge of the roof at each gabled end and are decorated with *chigi*, the ornamental members that cross above the roofing. Ten *katsuogi* (short logs) lie horizontally across the ridge, and a railed veranda encircles the building. The outer shrine, Gekū, at Ise is dedicated to the grain goddess, Toyouke no Ōkami, and is similar to the Naikū.

The shrine at Izumo in Shimane Prefecture, like that of Ise, dates from "the age of myths," and its buildings reflect the residential style of the Kofun period (ca 300–710). When the deity ŌKUNINUSHI NO MIKOTO, who ruled this area, built his own palace, he is said to have copied the design of the Imperial Palace of the Yamato area. The main building of IZUMO SHRINE (Izumo Taisha) was modeled on his palace. The Izumo Taisha style of Shintō architecture reveals construction features suggestive of residential architecture, with columns set directly into the ground and floors raised high. The main shrine building at Izumo is two bays square with a central pillar and a gabled *kirizuma* roof. The veranda that encircles the building is reached

A view from the veranda of the main hall of the Inner Shrine within the Ise Shrine complex; at right is the west treasury. The buildings of the Inner Shrine are built in the *shimmei* style of Shintō architecture.

by stairs off center on the gable end, and the doors to the shrine are on the right side.

After the introduction of Buddhism, the nature of Shintō worship changed, and shrine architecture evolved as well. Shrine buildings adopted elements from BUDDHIST ARCHITECTURE, and many shrines were painted with Chinese red (cinnabar) on the columns and white over the walls. Metal and sculpted-wood ornaments were added, often using the same decorative motifs as Buddhist temples. The most important shrines increased the number of buildings within their precincts, and the *honden* itself was expanded to provide a roofed area for the worshipers. These changes occurred during the Nara (710–794) and Heian (794–1185) periods, and four distinct building forms developed for the *honden*. These styles are the *nagare* style (*nagare-zukuri*), the Kasuga style (*kasuga-zukuri*), the Hachiman style (*hachiman-zukuri*), and the Hie style (*hie-zukuri*).

Among existing main shrine buildings, the *nagare* style is most common, with the Kasuga style a close second. The *nagare* is typified by the KAMO SHRINES in Kyōto. They are distinguished by their small size in comparison to the more ancient shrines and by their construction atop a raised earthen base. A second characteristic is that a roof, or canopy, is extended to cover the stairs and area in front of the shrine. In the *nagare* style the whole roof on one side sweeps forward and down, and thus worship is conducted on the narrower side of these two-bay by three-bay structures. In the Kasuga style, named

for the four small shrines that stand in a row at the KASUGA SHRINE in Nara, a pent roof has been added to the gable end of the one-bay square to cover the stairway leading to the shrine doors. In the Hachiman style, seen in the IWASHIMIZU HACHIMAN SHRINE and various other shrines dedicated to the war god HACHIMAN, a separate building for the worshipers has been added immediately in front of the main shrine building so that the roofs touch along the eaves. The Hie style found primarily at the HIE SHRINE (Hie Taisha) outside Kyōto has a pent roof added to the front and two sides of the main shrine and approximates the design of the worship hall (*kondō*) of the Buddhist temple.

In the Heian period the *ishinoma* style (later called the *gongen* style) separated the shrine from the worship hall with an intervening space. The area between these two parallel buildings was paved with stone and covered with a gable roof set perpendicular to the two parallel ridges. This style can be most clearly seen in the KITANO SHRINE.

Periodic Reconstruction—Even the oldest existing main shrine buildings date only as early as the 11th to 12th century. This is a result of fire and natural disaster as well as of the tradition of regular reconstruction. Shrine buildings were often rebuilt to purify the site and to renew the materials, a practice followed by most of the larger shrines until the Edo period (1600–1868) and still followed by the Ise Shrine.

Shintō art　　　　　　　神道美術

(Shintō *bijutsu*). SHINTŌ, the native religion of Japan, is associated with a wide variety of

art forms, including ritual objects, architecture, sculpture, and painting, in a tradition that dates from the 5th century. Whether in theme or usage, all forms of Shintō art radiate around the KAMI, the focal point of Shintō worship; loosely rendered in English as "deity," *kami* denotes any object or being possessed of a numinous quality.

The introduction of Buddhism to Japan in the 6th century provided both the impetus and the artistic resources for the creation of Shintō statues and paintings and made significant technical contributions in the field of architecture. The influence of aristocratic values on Shintō art is also considerable, stemming from the fact that the nobility traced its privileged status to descent from *kami* and that shrine priests were generally of the aristocratic class. Elements of court culture are apparent in the architecture of certain shrines, in the representation of *kami* as courtiers, and in the paraphernalia used in shrines.

Definition—The phrase Shintō *bijutsu* can be used to denote any art form pertaining to *kami*, so many scholars prefer the term *shūgō bijutsu* or *suijaku bijutsu*. *Shūgō bijutsu*, which designates imagery produced through the merging of Buddhism and Shintō, is applied primarily to painting and statuary. *Suijaku bijutsu* refers more specifically to paintings and statues in which *kami* are presented as traces or avatars (*suijaku*) of the Buddhist deities who are their true forms (*honji*). Art became one of the principal tools for the dissemination of this concept, called the HONJI SUIJAKU theory; from the 12th through the 19th century, imagery

Styles of Shrine Honden

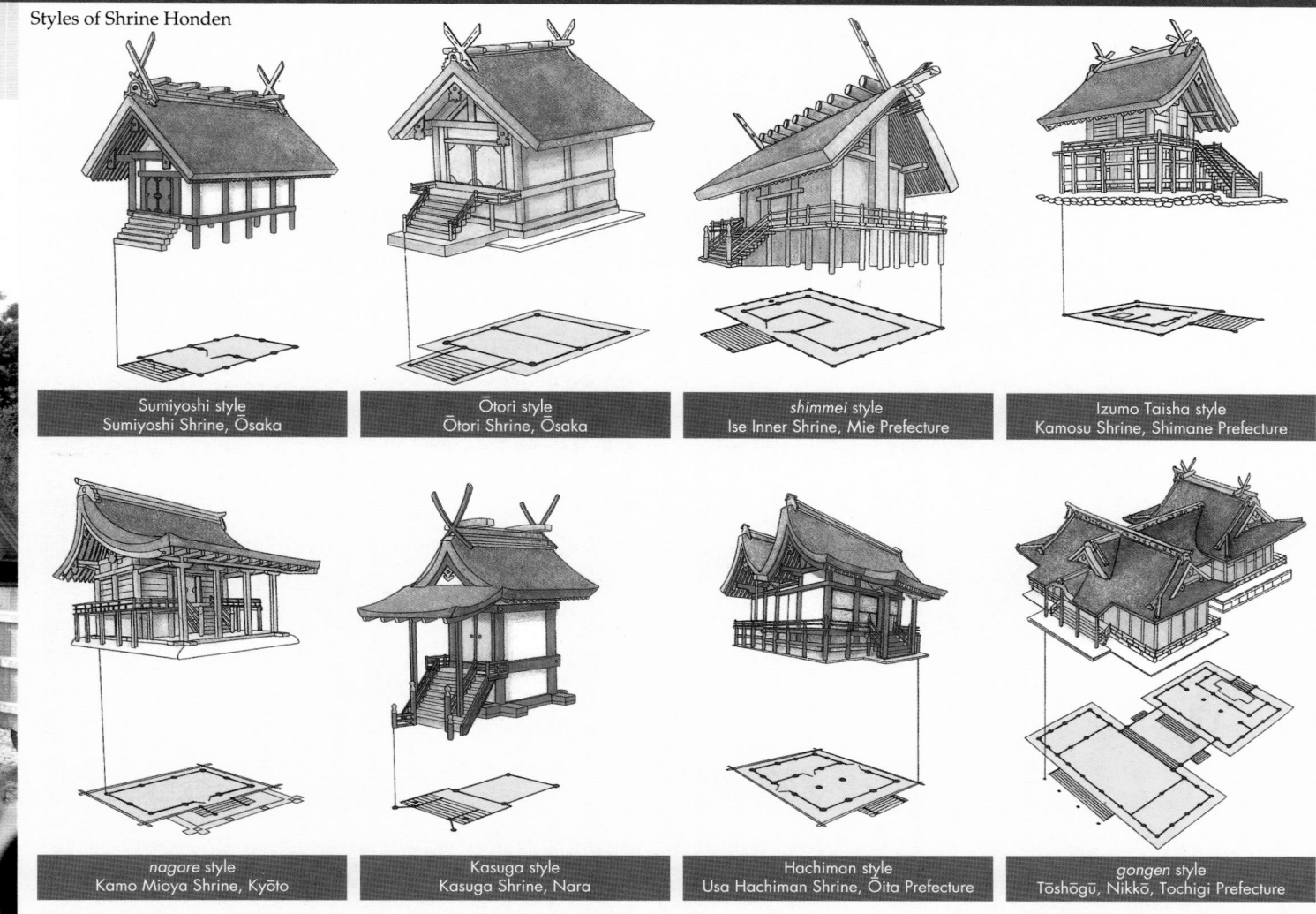

Sumiyoshi style
Sumiyoshi Shrine, Ōsaka

Ōtori style
Ōtori Shrine, Ōsaka

shimmei style
Ise Inner Shrine, Mie Prefecture

Izumo Taisha style
Kamosu Shrine, Shimane Prefecture

nagare style
Kamo Mioya Shrine, Kyōto

Kasuga style
Kasuga Shrine, Nara

Hachiman style
Usa Hachiman Shrine, Ōita Prefecture

gongen style
Tōshōgū, Nikkō, Tochigi Prefecture

graphically illustrating the relationship between specific Buddhist divinities and Shintō *kami* became a predominant mode of Shintō art. See also SYNCRETISM.

Imperial Regalia—Mirrors, swords, and comma-shaped *magatama* jewels constitute the most ancient known forms of Shintō art. Initially they were attributes of power or personal ornaments. Their special esteem within the Shintō tradition stems in part from the combination of religious and political leadership embodied in the rulers of early Japan who possessed them. Today, possession of the mirror, sword, and jewels, which are regarded as IMPERIAL REGALIA, is solely the prerogative of the emperor.

As the special emblem of AMATERASU ŌMIKAMI, supreme goddess of the Shintō pantheon and ancestress of the imperial family, the mirror is the most highly revered of the three. The mirror that, according to Japanese mythology, was given by this goddess to the founder of the imperial family is today the divine emblem housed in ISE SHRINE. In other shrines also, ancient mirrors, swords, and jewels may function as *shintai*, or the material embodiment of the *kami*.

Numerous variations of the basic circular mirror with a reflecting surface on one side and a design on the other exist. One is the bell mirror, characterized by the knoblike bells attached to the mirror's circumference. Another, which developed in the late part of the Heian period (794–1185), is the MISHŌTAI (or *kakebotoke*), embellished with either incised or raised representations of one or more Buddhist or Shintō deities and often

used as the material embodiment of the divine spirit.

Architecture—The Shintō shrine, with its distinctive TORII gate, is the residence of the *kami* and the place where ceremonies and prayers are performed. The first shrines were either natural sites selected for their unusual configuration or strategic location or spots designated as sacred for the duration of a ceremony. The temporary nature of many sanctuaries underlies the practice of *sengū*, or periodic reconstruction, once common to many shrines but today almost exclusive to Ise. Individuals do not worship within the structure (*honden* or *shōden*) housing the deity. The special worship hall (*haiden*) is thought to have made a rather late appearance on the shrine compound.

In the Nara period (710–794) the influence of continental building techniques introduced to Japan through Buddhism became increasingly apparent in the preference for complex bracketing systems, curved, often multiple roofs, and vermilion-painted structures. The gabled KASUGA SHRINE in Nara is the forerunner of sanctuaries of this type. Subsequently another style, the so-called flowing or *nagare-zukuri* style, became one of the most widespread in shrine construction. From the Heian period (794–1185) onward, the distinction between Buddhist and Shintō architecture became increasingly blurred, and numerous styles developed. See SHINTŌ ARCHITECTURE.

Sculpture—Shintō sculpture comprises portrayals of *kami* in various guises, human or animal guardian figures, and, occasionally, images of personages who participate

in ceremonies held on shrine precincts. Wooden statuary has long held a special place among Shintō arts because of the deep reverence within the Shintō tradition for certain kinds of trees and indeed for all natural phenomena.

Shintō statuary falls into two categories: images closely modeled after those current in Buddhist circles (in some cases renowned Buddhist sculptors were commissioned to make these) and images of deities dressed in court garb, reflecting the influence of aristocratic tastes and values. Stylistically, the development of the latter mode of statuary diverges considerably from contemporary Buddhist works, and the identity of the artists is often unknown.

Painting—Shintō painting is unsurpassed in thematic range. It comprises portrayals of *kami*, individually or in groups, with or without their Buddhist *honji;* maplike representations of shrines and their activities; votive plaques; and many variations thereof. It is likely that most types of painting emerged in the late Heian period as court culture reached a peak and the *honji suijaku* theory attained widespread acceptance.

Many forms of Shintō painting are designated as MANDALA, a term of Sanskrit origin that initially referred to a sacred circle, cosmic diagram, or arrangement of divinities showing their interrelationship and respective places in the universe. In Japan, however, the word mandala came to be applied to various forms of religious painting, including those with Shintō affiliations. Among

Shintō art

▶ A shrine mandala depicting the sacred Nachi waterfall comes close to being a pure landscape painting. 13th century. Colors on silk. 159 × 58 cm. Nezu Art Museum, Tōkyō. National Treasure.

◀ This Muromachi-period Shintō painting illustrates a scene from the legend of the founding of the Kasuga Shrine. Colors on silk. 140 × 41 cm. Nara National Museum.

▼ A famous example of a Shintō mandala, the *Mt. Fuji Pilgrimage Mandala* illustrates a procession of devotees climbing the mountain. Attributed to Kanō Motonobu. Late Muromachi period. Colors on silk. 180 × 118 cm. Sengen Shrine, Shizuoka Prefecture.

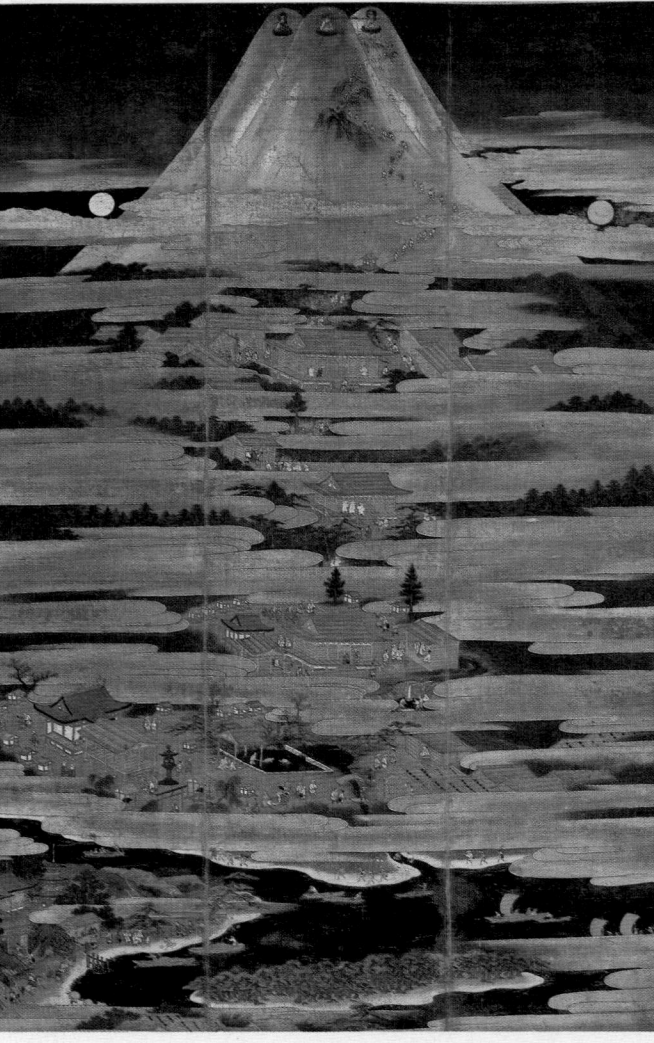

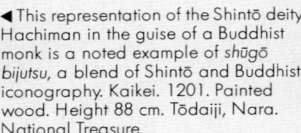

◀ This representation of the Shintō deity Hachiman in the guise of a Buddhist monk is a noted example of *shūgō bijutsu*, a blend of Shintō and Buddhist iconography. Kaikei. 1201. Painted wood. Height 88 cm. Tōdaiji, Nara. National Treasure.

Shintō mandalas are works of an iconographic nature illustrating the relationship between Buddhist and Shintō divinities (*honji suijaku* mandala), or those in which the *honji* or *suijaku* alone (*honji* or *suijaku* mandala) are depicted. In some cases, a shrine and its surroundings become the subject of a painting, as in the Kasuga mandala. Closely related to these so-called shrine mandalas are the festival and pilgrimage mandalas in which the human activity at a shrine replaces the sanctuary as the composition's focus. This tendency developed in the late Muromachi (1333–1568) and subsequent periods. See SUIJAKUGA.

Many paintings in the long EMAKIMONO, or illustrated handscroll, format may also be included among Shintō arts. Most numerous are those illustrating the origins of a shrine and miracles performed by its deities, such as the 13th-century *Kitano Tenjin engi.*

The EMA is basically a form of votive art. *Ema* initially designated a representation of a horse. Painted on a wooden plaque, it was dedicated to a shrine for the fulfillment of a prayer, but in time even the object of that prayer—a child, success in battle—came to be depicted.

Applied Arts—As in most religious systems, ritual implements and other accessories were made for use within the Shintō tradition. Peculiar to Shintō is the *mikoshi*, or sacred palanquin, used to carry, hidden from public view, the emblem of the *kami* during festivals or other ceremonies. Elegant garments, fans, and other personal items prevalent among the aristocracy were also commonly presented to shrines for the use of the *kami.*

Shintō family altars 神棚

(*kamidana*; literally, "god shelf"). Altar placed in the home for traditional worship of Shintō deities (KAMI). Typically, it is placed on a shelf built above a door lintel of the room in which visitors are received. It is customary to place talismans of gods such as those of the ISE SHRINE or the local tutelary deity (CHINJU NO KAMI) on the altar. The location of the altar may differ, however, according to the god or gods being worshipped: EBISU and DAIKOKUTEN, two of the SEVEN DEITIES OF GOOD FORTUNE, are usually lodged above a kitchen lintel; the fire and kitchen god KŌJIN has his own altar next to the oven. A temporary altar may be built to receive the TOSHIGAMI, gods who visit at NEW YEAR, or the returning ancestral spirits during the BON FESTIVAL. Offerings placed on the *kamidana* include *sake* (rice wine), food, and candles. The number of households that have *kamidana* is declining.

Shintō gobusho → Gobusho

Shintō Hisashi 真藤恒

(1910–). Businessman and president (1985–88) of NIPPON TELEGRAPH AND TELEPHONE CORPORATION (NTT). Born in Fukuoka Prefecture. After graduating from Kyūshū University in 1934, Shintō entered the shipbuilding firm Harima Zōsenjo. He eventually became president of ISHIKAWAJIMA-HARIMA HEAVY INDUSTRIES CO, LTD (1972–79). He became the first president of the privatized NTT in 1985. He was forced to resign his post in 1988 because of his involvement in the RECRUIT SCANDAL. He was convicted in October 1990 of accepting bribes.

Shin Tōhō 新東宝

(Shin Tōhō). Company engaged in film production, distribution, and exhibition. It was established in 1947 by several of the employees and actors of the TŌHŌ CO, LTD, in the unrest leading up to the TŌHŌ STRIKE of 1948. Successful for a brief time, it produced some excellent pictures, including NARUSE MIKIO's *Okāsan* (1952, Mother). It went bankrupt in 1961 after many of its staff returned to the reorganized Tōhō Co.

Shintō rites 神道祭祀

(Shintō *saishi*). SHINTŌ could well be termed a religion of ceremony. As a religion without official founders, Shintō has no tales of the conversions or revelations of early personalities, no official dogma, and no sacred texts (it does have several classics of myth, ritual, and history). Thus, Shintō is a popular religion based not on doctrine but on elaborate ceremonial rites.

Various governments in Japanese history have attempted to codify Shintō rites. There were sections on Shintō rites in the Ritsuryō Code (see RITSURYŌ SYSTEM) and other statutes for warriors to observe in feudal times, including the Jōei Shikimoku (see GOSEIBAI SHIKIMOKU) in the Kamakura period (1185–1333) and the Statutes concerning Shintō Priests and Deacons issued in the Edo period (1600–1868). The Meiji government passed laws concerning Shintō and Shintō rites, as did the OCCUPATION forces following World War II. More particularly, the *Ryō no gige* (835), a commentary on the YŌRŌ CODE, has a section entitled "Rules on Shintō," which states that "all gods in the heavens and on the earth shall be revered according to the traditional rituals." The ENGI SHIKI (927, Procedures of the Engi Era) includes a section on ceremonies at the Grand Shrine of Ise (ISE SHRINE) decreeing that ritual offerings follow precedent.

In the period before World War II, Shintō was divided into STATE SHINTŌ, SHRINE SHINTŌ, and SECT SHINTŌ, with rites classified as imperial house rites, rites conducted at the Grand Shrine of Ise, rites at other shrines, rites at sect shrines, and other ceremonies. The main rites in these categories were based upon laws dating from the Meiji period (1868–1912). However, at the end of World War II, many rites were either revised or completely revoked upon the abolition of the government offices concerning Shintō shrines and practices.

Buildings and Facilities—Before Shintō deities began to be viewed as personal gods or ancestral spirits, they were worshiped at sites called *saijō*, holy ground that was the prototype of the *jinja*, or shrine. The spirits of gods were thought to be attracted to natural objects such as a grove of evergreens (*himorogi*), a forested mountain (*kannabi*), or ground surrounded by boulders (*iwasaka*). The designation of gods by name is a comparatively recent phenomenon (see MOUNTAINS, WORSHIP OF). As Japanese culture developed, rites began to be performed in special shrine buildings. These facilities include the *shinden* (sanctuary), *noritoya* (prayer hall), *heiden* (hall of offering), *haiden* (hall of worship), *shinsenjo* (culinary hall), *sanrōjo* (hostel for abstinence), *shamusho* (shrine affairs office), *chōzuya* (washing place), *haraijo* (place of exorcism), *rōmon* (entrance gate), *emaden* (votive picture repository), *kaguraden* (KAGURA dance platform), *hōmotsuden* (treasure repository), *torii* (ceremonial arch), and *mizugaki* (shrine

fence). See also SHRINES; SHINTŌ ARCHITECTURE.

Body of Worshipers—The worshipers were drawn from ancient settlements in Japan, often located near marshy areas at the bases of hillsides. They formed an *ujiko chiiki* (parish) surrounded by a natural border of mountains, hills, or rivers, with the shrine in the center. Older families that were leaders in the village performed rites on a rotating basis and chose from among themselves officers (*tōnin*) to be in charge of the services held by shrine guilds (MIYAZA). Since the fate of the village and the success of the crops were thought to depend on these Shintō services, the ritual officers were obliged to observe strict abstinence. This group of ritual officers in a sense belonged to "the territory of the gods." From this special group of people were chosen the *negi* and *hafuri*, the basis of the Shintō ministry (see KANNUSHI), and these offices were usually transmitted from generation to generation through family succession. The shrine ministry, particularly at larger shrines, grew more diversified as society became more complex, with varied names for different ministerial duties (see also PRIESTHOOD).

Ritual Prayers—Shintō ritual prayers (NORITO) constitute the high point of the union between god and man in a Shintō ceremony. In this spoken ceremony, the officiant makes clear to the venerated god the meaning and purpose of the given ritual. The *norito* follows either the proclamation style of a deity addressing the faithful or the reporting style of the faithful speaking to a deity.

Accessories and Offerings—Shintō festivals center on the wait for the visitation of a god and entreaties and supplications preliminary to that arrival. Pillars, banners, and streamers are symbols (*yorishiro*) employed to implore the gods to descend. Persons performing these actions belong to "the territory of the gods," and preparations for the festivals were traditionally performed by the devoted faithful (see also SACRIFICE). Since offerings had to be acceptable to the gods, proper ritual objects such as sacred jewels, furniture, clothes, and food offerings were chosen according to various rites before the standardization of Shintō ritual. These accessories and offerings tell much about the background of the modern ceremonies. Rituals may be classified according to their purpose: (1) supplication, (2) thanksgiving, (3) memorials, (4) incantations, (5) divination, and (6) exorcism and purification; the motive behind a particular ceremony is often a combination of two or more of these.

Festivals—Shintō FESTIVALS (*matsuri*) are a means of reactualizing the sacred presence through reenactment of the ancestral rituals and thereby affirming the relationshp between deity and devotee. One early reference to Shintō festivals appears in the 8th-century *Yamashiro no Kuni fudoki* (Gazetteer of the Province of Yamashiro [now Kyōto Prefecture]), which mentions the festival days kept at the Inari shrines on HATSUUMA (the first horse day of the second month according to the sexagenary cycle; see JIKKAN JŪNISHI). A reenactment of the original rite held when the god was first enshrined, this festival is thus an annual event bringing back the god and his glory.

Shintō rites center on AGRICULTURAL RITES; these include the Toshigoi no Matsuri (a festival for good crops, observed in the second month of the year according to the lunar calendar), KANNAMESAI (blessing of new rice at

Shintō family altars
At the center of this elaborate *kamidana* is a miniature Shintō shrine, before which hangs a sacred rope (*shimenawa*). Also visible are sprays of the sacred *sakaki* tree, which serve to attract the gods, and white paper decorated with auspicious designs. Ishikawa Prefecture.

Ise Shrine), Ainame no Matsuri (rice offering formerly made to 71 enshrined gods), and NIINAMESAI (offering of new rice made by the emperor). Festivals praying for peace and happiness in daily life include the Hanashizume no Matsuri (a festival for protection against pestilence, observed in the spring) and the Michiae no Matsuri (a festival to ward off evil spirits, observed in June and December).

Purification Rites—Shintō rites also emphasize fasting and abstinence (*imi*); it was believed that such practices prepared people for their approach to the gods. *Imi* includes both spiritual and physical mortification, involving the spirit, body, words, and actions and necessitating an abandonment of everyday life during the period of abstinence. Abstinence is divided into *sansai* (also called *araimi*) or preliminary purification rites and *chisai* (also called *maimi*) or main purification rites. The *chisai* rites are performed on the day of the festival itself, and the *sansai* are performed on the days immediately preceding and following the festival.

For purification rites (*saikai*), Shintō officiants changed their clothes, performed *misogi* (purification ablution), cooked vegetarian meals on special purified fires, and remained in the purification hall in order to devote themselves completely to the services. Similarly, in the past the families performing shrine duties, including the head priest and his successor, his son, were not permitted to carry barrels of fertilizer, handle dead things, or the like. On festival days, they hung a rope (SHIMENAWA) around their residence and set up a bamboo fence to prevent the entry of unclean persons and objects. See also MISOGI; KEGARE.

Religious Banquets—Banquets were the central focus of the ancient rites. In the practice known as NAORAI, the offerings are taken from the altar following a ceremony and eaten at the *ainame* ceremony, in which the participants receive the favor and blessing of the gods by partaking of this food with them. *Naorai* refers to the dishes served at the *gesai*, or release from the period of abstinence, as well as to the ritual banquet held at the end of Shintō ceremonies. Regulations ordain that *sansai* take place both before and after the *chisai*. Thus the *gesai* may in a certain sense be considered a part of the purification rites. *Gesai*, however, is also the final stage in a Shintō ceremony and marks a return to everyday life from a unity with the gods.

At the climax of Shintō services, *kagura* (ritual dances) or similar religious performances are staged as an act of praise to the divine virtues. Similarly, at the funerals for ancient emperors, propitiatory offerings of rice wine and food were served by the *asobibe* (clan for funeral services) on seven successive days and nights, accompanied by dances employing drums, flutes, and banners. See also SACRED, THE.

Shintō Shrines, Association of
神社本庁

(Jinja Honchō). Umbrella association of Shintō shrines established on 3 February 1946 with the ISE SHRINE as the principal shrine. The Jinja Honchō does not regulate the doctrines of its member shrines but promotes SHRINE SHINTŌ and supervises the prefectural associations of Shintō shrines. In 1989 it comprised the majority of Shintō shrines (79,152 shrines) and had registered 18,799 certified priests and 1,564 certified priestesses.

Shinwa Kaiun Kaisha, Ltd
新和海運[株]

(Shinwa Kaiun). Steamship operator primarily engaged in the transporting of raw materials and finished products for the NIPPON STEEL CORPORATION. Incorporated in 1950. It is also engaged in the tanker and bulk carrier businesses. It has subsidiaries in Melbourne, Jakarta, London, and New York. Annual revenue at the end of March 1991 was ¥75.2 billion (US $548.1 million), and the company was capitalized at ¥8.1 billion (US $59.0 million) in the same year. Headquarters are in Tōkyō.

Shin Yakushiji
新薬師寺

Temple of the Kegon Buddhist sect; located in the city of Nara. It is said to have been founded in 747 by Empress KŌMYŌ for the recovery of her husband, Emperor SHŌMU, from an eye infection. Dedicated to the healing Buddha Yakushi Nyorai, the temple was called Shin, or "New," Yakushiji to distinguish it from the Yakushiji built earlier in another section of the capital. Only the main hall survives from the early 8th century. The main image of the temple is a 2-meter (6.6-ft) Yakushi Nyorai, dating from the early Heian period (794–1185); enshrined on a circular altar, it is surrounded by images of the Twelve Divine Generals.

Shin'yei Kaisha
神栄[株]

(Shin'ei). Firm engaged in the production and trading of silk yarn. Incorporated in 1887. After World War II, it began the production of secondary textile goods and electronic parts. It has played a significant role in Japanese trade with China in recent years. The firm has a subsidiary in New York. Sales for the fiscal year ending March 1991 totaled ¥62.7 billion (US $457.0 million), and the company was capitalized at ¥2.0 billion (US $14.6 million). Headquarters are in Kōbe.

Shinzō inu tsukubashū
新増犬筑波集

Two-volume collection of *haikai* (see HAIKU) verse and criticism by MATSUNAGA TEITOKU; published 1643. Entitled *Aburakasu* and *Yodogawa*, the volumes were written as a commentary on the INU TSUKUBASHŪ (ca 1540) and as a handbook for novices of the verse form. Its rules evolved to form the core of the first true handbook of the Teimon school, *Haikai gosan* (1651).

Shiobara
塩原[町]

Town in northern Tochigi Prefecture, central Honshū. It is known primarily for its complex of 11 hot springs. The area is noted for its scenic gorges; it is also a popular summer and winter resort, with good skiing on nearby mountains. Pop: 9,825.

Shioda Hiroshige
塩田広重

(1873–1965). Surgeon. Born in Kyōto Prefecture. Graduate of Tōkyō University. Shioda is known for his achievements in the pathogenesis and treatment of actinomycosis (1911) and in other areas of visceral surgery. He was a professor at Tōkyō University, president of Nihon Ika Daigaku (Nihon Medical School), and a member of the Japan Academy from 1949.

Shiogama
塩竈[市]

City in central Miyagi Prefecture, northern Honshū, on Matsushima Bay. In the Edo period (1600–1868) it developed as a fishing port and as a shrine town around the Shiogama Shrine. Principal industries are fishing and seafood processing. A large number of people are drawn to the Shiogama port festival each August. Pop: 62,025.

Shiogama Shrine
塩竈神社

(Shiogama Jinja). Shintō shrine in the city of Shiogama, Miyagi Prefecture; dedicated to Shiotsuchinooji no Kami (a deity associated with the sea) and two other deities. The precise origins of the shrine are not known, but it is mentioned in the early-10th-century ENGI SHIKI. It was thought to offer particular protection to seafarers, saltmakers, and pregnant women. The annual festival, held on 10 July, includes a spectacular exhibition of YABUSAME (archery on horseback).

shiohigari
潮干狩

(literally, "gathering at low tide"). Pleasure excursions to gather seashells, shellfish, and the like on tidewater beaches; they have been popular since the Edo period (1600–1868). April is the best time for such outings because the variation in tides is greatest. From very early times excursions called *iso asobi* ("beach play") marked the beginning of farm work in the spring. Modern shell-gathering picnics in April and the custom of serving clam soup at the DOLL FESTIVAL in March are thought to be derived from this ancient practice. These excursions have declined recently because of seashore reclamation projects and pollution.

Shioiri Matsusaburō
塩入松三郎

(1889–1962). Agrochemist. Born in Nagano Prefecture; graduate of Tōkyō University. Shioiri worked successively as a technician at the Agricultural Experiment Station of the Ministry of Agriculture and Forestry, as a professor at Tōkyō University, and as president of the Prefectural College of Agriculture and Forestry, Shiga Prefecture. His many research achievements included the analysis of soil colloids; his most outstanding study was on the chemical structure of rice paddy soil layers, completed during World War II. He also developed techniques for fertilizing fields in every layer and for revitalization of deteriorated paddy fields, both of which help to increase rice yields during periods of food shortages. He is the author of *Dojōgaku kenkyū* (1952).

Shiojiri
塩尻[市]

City in central Nagano Prefecture, central Honshū. In the Edo period (1600–1868) it prospered as a post-station town. Grapes (used by the local wineries) and vegetables are grown. There is an electrical and precision-instruments industry. The HIRAIDE SITE, an ancient settlement dating from the Middle Jōmon period (ca 3500 BC–ca 2000 BC), is located here. Pop: 57,331.

Shiojiri Pass
塩尻峠

(Shiojiri Tōge). Pass on the border of the cities of Shiojiri and Okaya in Nagano Prefecture, central Honshū. It links the Matsumoto and Suwa basins, and is traversed by National Route No. 20. The pass offers a panoramic view of the Japanese Alps and Lake SUWA. Elevation: 999 m (3,278 ft).

shioki
仕置

(criminal punishments). The general term for criminal punishments and their imposition during the Edo period (1600–1868). *Shioki* varied somewhat between shogunal and *daimyō* domains, but they generally followed the KUJIKATA OSADAMEGAKI (also called the Hyakkajō or Hundred Articles), a criminal code enacted by the Tokugawa shogunate (1603–1867) in 1742. The punishments were in six categories: (1) *seimeikei* (capital punishments); (2) *shintaikei* (corporal punishments), imposed only on commoners; (3) *jiyūkei* (loss of liberty), which often meant exile (ENTŌ, earlier called RUKEI) or house arrest (HEIMON) for a *samurai* and priests but imprisonment (*jurō*) or placement in manacles (*tejō*) for a commoner; (4) *zaisankei* (loss of property), often imposed in addition to exile; (5) *mibunkei* (loss of status), which included KAIEKI (demotion of a samurai to commoner status) and the reduction of a commoner to HININ, or pariah, status; and (6) *eiyokei* (loss of honor), which entailed forms of official reprimand. The *shioki* punishments of the Hyakkajō code were abolished with the enactment of the Provisional Penal Code (Kari Keiritsu) in 1868.

Shiomidake
塩見岳

Mountain on the border of Nagano and Shizuoka prefectures, central Honshū, in the central part of the Akaishi Mountains. It is composed of Paleozoic sandstone strata. Height: 3,047 m (9,997 ft).

Shionogi & Co, Ltd
塩野義製薬[株]

(Shionogi Seiyaku). Pharmaceutical company engaged in the manufacture, distribution, export, and import of pharmaceuticals, industrial and agricultural chemicals, veterinary drugs, diagnostics, and clinical testing services. Established in 1878, it assumed its present name in 1943. The company has overseas subsidiaries in Germany, the United States, and Taiwan, and technical alliances with several international pharmaceutical companies. Total sales for the fiscal year ending March 1991 were ¥215.8 billion (US $1.6 billion), and capitalization was ¥21.3 billion (US $155.2 million). Headquarters are in Ōsaka.

Shionomisaki
潮岬

Cape on southern Kii Peninsula, southern Wakayama Prefecture; projecting south into the Pacific Ocean, it is the southernmost point of Honshū (lat. 33°26′ N). A fishing port, Kushimoto, and an island, Ōshima, 2 km (1.2 mi) off the coast, are popular resorts. It is part of Yoshino-Kumano National Park.

Shiozawa
塩沢[町]

Town in southern Niigata Prefecture, central Honshū. It developed as a post-station town and is known for its fine silk fabrics such as *tsumugi* and *omeshi*. Pop: 20,872.

Shiozawa Masasada　塩沢昌貞

(1870–1945). Economist. Born in Ibaraki Prefecture. He initially studied Chinese literature but later entered Tōkyō Semmon Gakkō (now Waseda University) and studied English. After studying in the United States and Germany from 1896 to 1902, he was appointed professor at Waseda University and later became its president. An influential member of the Nihon Shakai Seisaku Gakkai (Japanese Association for the Study of Social Policy), he was particularly active in the field of labor relations.

shipbuilding industry　造船業

(*zōsengyō*). The modern Japanese shipbuilding industry had its beginning in the late Edo period (1600–1868). After the Meiji Restoration of 1868 the government targeted it as a priority industry, and between 1897 and 1913 shipbuilding and shipping received about three-quarters of all government subsidies to industry. After the Russo-Japanese War of 1904–05, the Japanese navy became a major source of demand for ships. The total tonnage of ships launched increased from 65,000 gross tons in 1913 to 612,000 gross tons in 1919, and Japan became an exporter of ships to England, France, and the United States. During World War II the industry was under government control and supplied ships to the Japanese navy and merchant fleet.

After World War II, Japan and its shipbuilding industry had to make a new start. While in the prewar period Japanese shipbuilding had catered mainly to domestic demand, after the war its main targets became export markets. A revolution in Japanese shipbuilding took place, based on new techniques of electric welding, automatic cutting of steel plates, and the clock-building system, and the industry grew rapidly through the postwar period. Widespread technological borrowing coupled with highly skilled labor helped Japan become competitive in the world shipbuilding market. Government assistance also played a significant role through a system of long-term, low-interest loans to shipping companies for the purchase of ships. In 1956 Japan became the world's major supplier of tankers, surpassing the million-ton mark in total ship production, and by the late 1950s Japan had become a world leader in ship production.

After the oil crisis in 1973 a glut of tankers caused cancellation of orders and a substantial change in the composition of Japanese ship production: cargo ships increased from 18 percent of total production in 1973 to 93 percent in 1975. Demand decreased steadily through the mid-1980s, and measures were taken to reduce industry capacity and employment. However, in the late 1980s such factors as increased demand for sea transport of raw materials led to increased ship orders for Japan and the Republic of Korea (South Korea), Japan's main competitor in shipbuilding. In 1988 Japan received orders for ships totaling over 5.6 million gross tons, an increase of over one-half million gross tons from 1983.

The five largest Japanese shipbuilding companies in 1989 were MITSUBISHI HEAVY INDUSTRIES, LTD; KAWASAKI HEAVY INDUSTRIES, LTD; ISHIKAWAJIMA-HARIMA HEAVY INDUSTRIES CO, LTD; HITACHI ZŌSEN CORPORATION; and Shin-Kurushima Dock Co, Ltd. In an effort to remain competitive with the shipbuilding industries of South Korea and other countries, some Japanese shipbuilding companies are researching superconductivity propulsion systems and various technologically advanced building techniques. Japanese shipbuilding companies are also involved in the production of industrial machinery. These "on-land activities" enable companies to reduce risk through diversification and to withstand fluctuations in demand for any single product.

Shipbuilding Scandal of 1954　造船疑獄

(Zōsen Gigoku). Also known as the Zōsen Oshoku (Shipbuilding Kickback) case. In January 1954 it was discovered that shipbuilding companies were paying bribes to high government officials in return for government contracts and subsidies. Among the 71 suspects arrested were the heads of Hitachi Shipbuilding and Engineering Co, Ltd, and Ishikawajima-Harima Heavy Industries Co, Ltd. Several politicians, including SATŌ EISAKU and IKEDA HAYATO, were indicted. Under pressure from Prime Minister YOSHIDA SHIGERU, the minister of justice refused to approve prosecution of Satō, who was secretary-general of the Liberal Party. A number of businessmen and government officials were eventually convicted of bribery and misuse of public funds, and Satō himself was eventually indicted for violation of the Political Fund Control Law but was released in a general amnesty before completion of his trial. This incident contributed to the fall of the fifth Yoshida cabinet.

Ship Research Institute　船舶技術研究所

(Sempaku Gijutsu Kenkyūjo). Ministry of Transportation–affiliated institute that conducts research on new shipbuilding technologies. Located in the city of Mitaka, Tōkyō Prefecture, the institute was founded in 1963 to research and develop energy-saving technologies, nuclear-powered propulsion, pollution-reducing technologies, and automation systems for the shipping industry.

ships, traditional　和船

(*wasen*). Water transportation has been of great importance in Japanese history. That ships existed in Japan from ancient times is known from the discovery of primitive canoes at various archaeological sites and from numerous references to boats and ships found in ancient historical records. The occurrence of gaffs and fishhooks made of bone or horn in SHELL MOUNDS dating from the Jōmon period (ca 10,000 BC–ca 300 BC) shows that the early inhabitants of the Japanese archipelago had ties to the sea and fishing. Jōmon-period sites have yielded specimens of dugout canoes, presumably made by burning and scraping with stone implements. Early Chinese accounts such as the *Han shu* (1st century AD) and the *Hou Han shu* (4th or 5th century) record that various communities of Japanese (Ch: Wo; J: WA) sent tribute to China as early as the 1st century BC. From this it may be assumed that sea transportation between Japan and China existed even in the Yayoi period (ca 300 BC–ca AD 300). What sorts of boats were used, however, can only be conjectured from such scanty evidence as outlines found scratched on rock faces.

Japanese historical records, such as the KOJIKI (712, Records of Ancient Matters) and NIHON SHOKI (720, Chronicle of Japan) and the 8th-century regional gazetteers called FUDOKI, contain descriptions of many kinds of early boats: *ama no iwakusubune* (a dugout made from camphor wood, relics of which have been found at Yayoi-period diggings), *ashibune* (a type of raft made of papyrus reed), *morotabune* (a dugout rowed with oars by a large crew), *manashikatama obune* (a kind of coracle made of closely woven bamboo), and other types. Attempts are being made to clarify the designs of these boats through etymological study of their names and archaeological investigation. According to the *Nihon shoki* and the *Kojiki*, a boat named the *Karanu* was built during the reign of Emperor ŌJIN (late 4th–early 5th centuries). No details are recorded except that it measured 30 meters (98 ft) in length. In the 8th-century gazeteer *Hitachi fudoki* there is a record of a large boat said to have measured 45 meters (148 ft) long and 3 meters (10 ft) wide.

The most common boat of the time was the canoe or dugout made by hollowing out a single log. Compound-hulled craft were built by joining together two or more dugouts. Further technical development made it possible to build semicomposite boats—dugouts with vertically attached planking on each side for protection against waves—and finally composite craft.

The *Nihon shoki* reports that shipbuilding techniques were imported from the kingdom of SILLA on the Korean peninsula during Ōjin's reign. A clay image of a ship (*funagata haniwa*; see HANIWA) found at the SAITOBARU TOMB CLUSTER in Miyazaki Prefecture is said to date from the 5th or 6th century. It has tholepins in the gunwales for oars and is considered a copy of the largest boats commonly in use at the time. Similar model boats dating from the same period have also been discovered in Korea.

In 600 the Japanese began sending missions to China on a systematic basis, and by 838 some 20 missions had been sent to Sui (589–618) and Tang (T'ang; 618–907) dynasty China (see SUI AND TANG [T'ANG] CHINA, EMBASSIES TO). Japanese shipbuilding techniques improved considerably during this period, but precise data regarding the type of craft used by the envoys have not survived. We can only guess at the scale and structure of these ships from the number of crew members and passengers said to have been on board and from early paintings.

Ships used by the embassies sent to Sui China (*kenzuishi*) were apparently of the semicomposite type, but by the time of the second dispatch of envoys to Tang China (*kentōshi*) in 653 shipbuilding technology

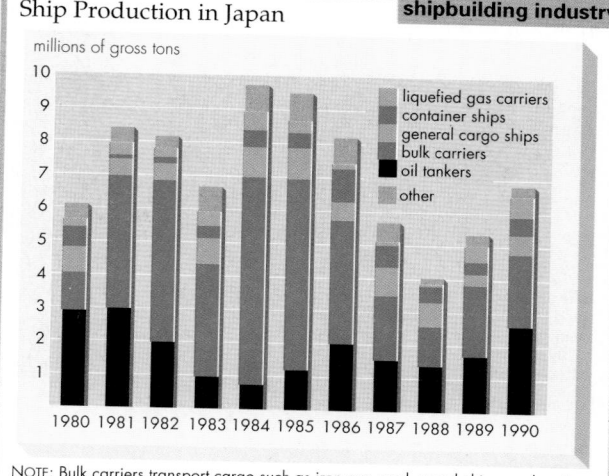

Ship Production in Japan　shipbuilding industry

millions of gross tons

liquefied gas carriers
container ships
general cargo ships
bulk carriers
oil tankers
other

1980 1981 1982 1983 1984 1985 1986 1987 1988 1989 1990

NOTE: Bulk carriers transport cargo such as iron ore, coal, wood chips, and grain. "Other" includes fishing and passenger boats, ferries, etc.
SOURCE: The Shipbuilders' Association of Japan, *Saikin no zōsen jijō* (annual): 1991.

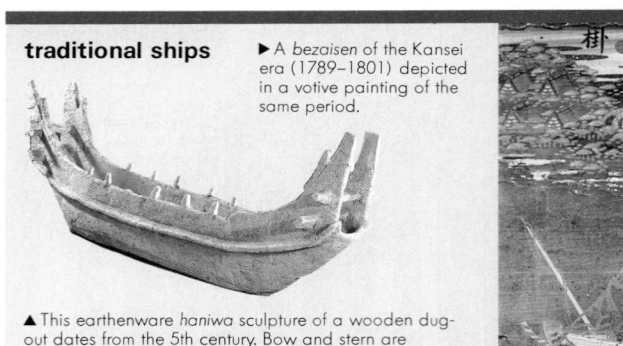

traditional ships

▶ A bezaisen of the Kansei era (1789–1801) depicted in a votive painting of the same period.

▲ This earthenware *haniwa* sculpture of a wooden dugout dates from the 5th century. Bow and stern are identical, and the boat has pin-type oarlocks. It was excavated from the Saitobaru tomb cluster in Miyazaki Prefecture. Length 101 cm. Tōkyō National Museum.

The Structure of a Bezaisen

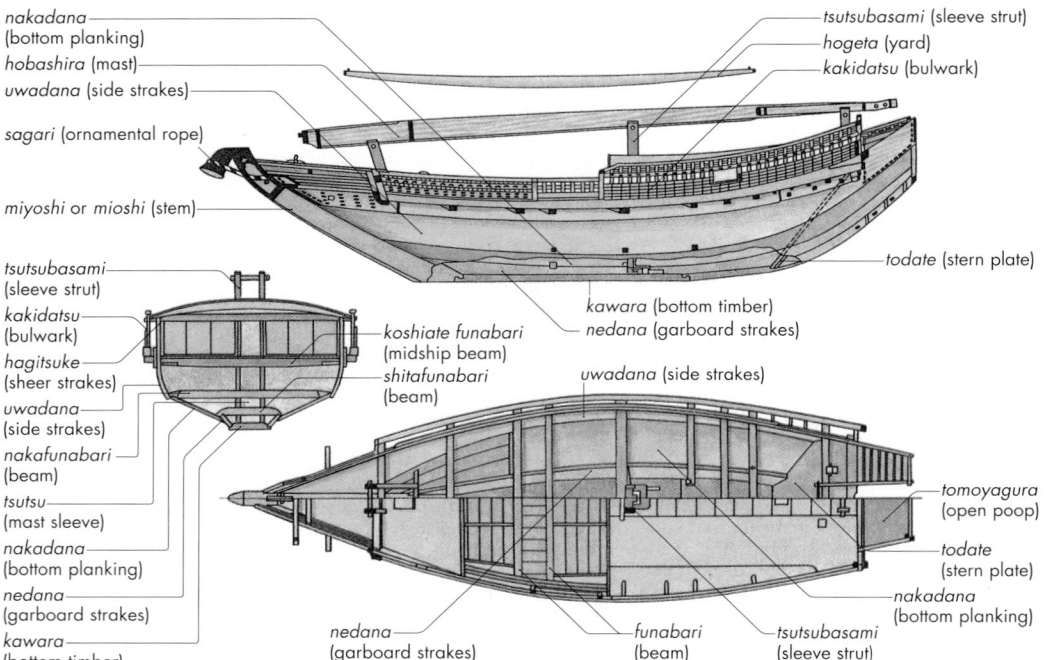

nakadana (bottom planking)
hobashira (mast)
uwadana (side strakes)
sagari (ornamental rope)
miyoshi or *mioshi* (stem)
tsutsubasami (sleeve strut)
kakidatsu (bulwark)
hagitsuke (sheer strakes)
uwadana (side strakes)
nakafunabari (beam)
tsutsu (mast sleeve)
nakadana (bottom planking)
nedana (garboard strakes)
kawara (bottom timber)

tsutsubasami (sleeve strut)
hogeta (yard)
kakidatsu (bulwark)
todate (stern plate)
kawara (bottom timber)
nedana (garboard strakes)
koshiate funabari (midship beam)
shitafunabari (beam)

uwadana (side strakes)
tomoyagura (open poop)
todate (stern plate)
nakadana (bottom planking)
nedana (garboard strakes)
funabari (beam)
tsutsubasami (sleeve strut)

had developed to such a degree that in Aki Province (now part of Hiroshima Prefecture) it was possible to build seaworthy craft like the *kudarasen* ("Korean-type ship"), with room for about 120 people. It is thought that these were single-masted junks, the largest of which may have had a capacity of 1,500 *koku* (147 gross tons) and accommodated around 150 passengers. A European sailing ship of this tonnage was usually about 30 meters (98 ft) long, but in view of its shallow draft and flat-bottomed hull the *kentōshi* ship must have been around 40 meters (131 ft) and could have sailed only with a tail wind. There are some reports of ships of this type breaking in two because of these characteristics.

The sending of embassies from Japan to China was halted after 838, and the only further development in shipbuilding between the 9th and 12th centuries was in the size of ships. During the Kamakura period (1185–1333) a number of merchant ships carried on limited trade with Southern Song (Sung) dynasty (1127–1368) China. The official exchange of envoys between Japan and China resumed under the government of the shōgun ASHIKAGA YOSHIMITSU and continued intermittently from about 1401 to 1547, during which time 17 embassies were sent to Ming dynasty (1368–1644) China (see TALLY TRADE). These envoys were called *kemminshi*, and the ships they used were called *kem-*

minsen. Each *kemminsen* carried 150–200 people. Contemporary records describe their capacities as 1,000–2,500 *koku* (98–245 gross tons). They appear in picture scrolls as vessels with a cabin on the deck and two masts fitted with simple square sails made of matting.

Foreign trade was conducted from 1592 under government license, and merchants in Nagasaki, Sakai, and Kyōto carried on a lively overseas trade. TOYOTOMI HIDEYOSHI, who wished to keep the NAMBAN TRADE with Europeans in Southeast Asia under his control, took measures against pirates (see WAKŌ) and illegal traders by issuing to selected merchants official licenses with vermilion seals that verified the protected status of their ships, which were referred to as *shuinsen* ("vermilion seal ships"; see VERMILION SEAL SHIP TRADE). Spanish and Portuguese influences are apparent in the introduction of the quadrant and the astrolabe, and in the adaptation to the *shuinsen* of features of the structure and rigging of the galleon. Although its two lugsails were similar to those of the Chinese junk, its stern, rudder, and auxiliary sails were of European design. The largest of the *shuinsen* had an estimated gross tonnage of 750 tons.

In the first decade of the 17th century, two English-style ships of about 80 and 120 gross tons were built under the direction of the Englishman William ADAMS. A galliot-type ship in the 500-gross-ton class, 35 meters (115 ft) long and 11 meters (36 ft) wide, was built in

1612–13 under the direction of the Spaniard Sebastian VISCAINO. Although Japanese shipwrights were apparently eager to master Western shipbuilding techniques, further development in ship design was suspended due to the policy of NATIONAL SECLUSION imposed by the Tokugawa shogunate (1603–1867) in 1639.

In the early decades of the period of seclusion, the shogunate strictly prohibited the construction of ships with capacities exceeding 500 *koku* (49 gross tons). However, as the major urban centers were situated near the sea, ships were by far the most efficient means of transport, and the restriction was soon lifted to encourage the development of a coastal shipping industry. In 1673 the shogunate itself established a system whereby commercial ships were hired to transport its rice.

One of the largest types of ship of the 17th century was the *hokkokubune* (also known as *kitamaesen*), some examples of which had a capacity of 1,000 *koku* (98 gross tons) or more, and which, in addition to their traditional square sail, were fitted to be rowed. The *hokkokubune*, which plied the waters of the Sea of Japan, was rivaled in the second half of the 17th century and largely displaced in the 18th century by the *bezaisen*, which sailed south from ports on the Sea of Japan, traversed the Inland Sea to Ōsaka, and then sailed on to Edo (now Tōkyō), or sailed north to the Tsugaru Strait between Hokkaidō and Honshū and then south to Edo. Although the *bezaisen* had no keel, ribbing, or stanchions, it was an extremely sturdy vessel: a bottom timber that served in place of a keel was joined to the first of four stages of broad and stout planking that were strengthened by four tiers of beams. As its chief purpose was to transport the maximum amount of cargo, the beam of a *bezaisen* was often half the length of its bottom timber. Early ships of this design had a capacity of only 30 gross tons, but by the second half of the 17th century the standard size of *bezaisen* was 1,000 *koku* (98 gross tons), with a crew of about 15, and they came to be referred to as *sengokubune* (1,000-*koku* ships). In the late 17th century passage from Ōsaka to Edo required about 30 days, but by the late 18th century technical innovations cut this figure in half; moreover, with a fair wind Edo could be reached in 4 days. See also KAISEN.

After the Meiji Restoration of 1868, the government established a SHIPBUILDING INDUSTRY based on Western technology. Nevertheless, the predominance of the *bezaisen* in domestic marine transportation continued. In 1887, in order to hasten the proliferation of Western-style ships, the government prohibited the construction of *bezaisen* of over 500 *koku*; however, shipwrights replied by introducing design features of Western vessels to produce a hybrid type of ship called *ainokobune*, which was widely used into the Taishō period (1912–26).

shirabyōshi　　　　　　白拍子

Type of song and dance performance, characterized by a strongly marked rhythm, that became popular in the 12th century; also, the female performers of this type of dance. *Shirabyōshi* performers invariably dressed in white, male attire. Their costume also included fans, court caps, and swords. Drums and small cymbals were the accompanying musical instruments. The performers sang songs and a kind of ballad called *imayō* as they danced. *Shirabyōshi* performances are

1394
shirabyōshi

recorded as part of court and temple festivities in the 12th and 13th centuries, but they declined in popularity thereafter. Famous semilegendary *shirabyōshi* performers are Giō, Hotake Gozen (fl ca 1170), and SHIZUKA GOZEN, who formed liaisons with members of the nobility and the warrior class. See also DANCE, TRADITIONAL.

Shiragi →Silla

Shirahama   白浜[町]
Town in southwestern Wakayama Prefecture, central Honshū, on the Pacific Ocean. It is known for its hot springs and for Senjōjiki and Sandanheki, rocky cliffs jutting out into the sea. Pop: 19,243.

Shirahama   白浜[町]
Town in Chiba Prefecture, central Honshū. It is the center of the Minami Bōsō Quasi-National Park, with attractions such as the AMA (women divers), flower farms, and the Nojimazaki lighthouse, built by François VERNY in 1869. Pop: 6,634.

Shirahone Hot Spring   白骨温泉
(Shirahone Onsen). Located on the northern slope of Norikuradake at an altitude of 1,400 m (4,593 ft), western Nagano Prefecture, central Honshū. A hydrogen sulfide spring; water temperature 50°C (122°F). It features limestone caves and ball-shaped limestones that have been designated as natural monuments.

Shirai Kyōji   白井喬二
(1889–1980). Novelist. Real name Inoue Yoshimichi. Born in Kanagawa Prefecture; graduate of Nihon University. His major work is the period novel *Fuji ni tatsu kage* (1924–27) whose hero, Kumaki Kōtarō, is often contrasted with Tsukue Ryūnosuke, the nihilistic hero in NAKAZATO KAIZAN's novel *Daibosatsu Tōge* (1913–41). These two novels, of which several film versions have been made, are representative works of modern POPULAR FICTION. As editor in chief of the magazine *Taishū bungaku*, Shirai was a leading critic in the field of popular literature. Other novels include *Shimpen goetsuzōshi* (1922–24), *Shinsengumi* (1924–25), and *Bangaku no isshō* (1932).

Shirai Seiichi   白井晟一
(1905–83). Architect. Born in Kyōto. Graduate of Kyōto Technical School. His early buildings, such as the Kankisō House (1937), show obvious European influences, but his postwar designs are characterized by distinctive sculptural forms and closed, introspective spaces. His notable buildings include Akinomiya Town Hall (1949), Matsuida Town Hall (1955), the main temple building of Zenshōji in Asakusa (1958), the Shinwa Bank main office in Sasebo (1968) and its computer center, the Kaishōkan (1975), and the Shōtō Museum of Art (1981).

Shiraishi Kazuko   白石かずこ
(1931–). Poet and essayist. Born in Vancouver. Graduate of Waseda University. Shiraishi first gained attention as the author of *Tamago no furu machi* (1951, The Street That Rains Eggs), a poetry collection that revealed her indebtedness to surrealist and modernist influences. After a 10-year hiatus, she again drew public attention with her jazz-inspired verses, establishing herself as a poet of sexual liberation. She won the H-Shi Prize in 1970 for the collection *Sei naru inja no kisetsu* (Season of the Saintly Prostitutes).

Shiraito Falls   白糸ノ滝
(Shiraito no Taki). Located on the upper reaches of the river Shibakawa, in the city of Fujinomiya, eastern Shizuoka Prefecture, central Honshū. It is said to resemble countless white threads dangling over a cliff, hence the name Shiraito no Taki (literally, "White Thread Falls"). Located at the foot of Mt. Fuji (FUJISAN) on its western side and a part of Fuji-Hakone-Izu National Park, it has been designated a natural monument. Height: 26 m (85 ft); width: 130 m (427 ft).

Shirakaba   白樺
(White Birch). Monthly journal of literature and the arts. One hundred sixty issues were published between April 1910 and August 1923. A forum for the writings of the SHIRAKABA SCHOOL, the magazine featured works by MUSHANOKŌJI SANEATSU, SHIGA NAOYA, SATOMI TON, YANAGI MUNEYOSHI, ARISHIMA TAKEO, and others. It also played a major role in the introduction of modern Western art to a Japanese audience, publishing critical essays on and reproductions of the work of artists such as Cézanne, van Gogh, and Rodin. The humanist aestheticism of *Shirakaba* was one of the more powerful and emblematic currents of Taishō-period (1912–26) culture, and the demise of the magazine in the wake of the TŌKYŌ EARTHQUAKE OF 1923 is often seen as symbolic of the transition to the more turbulent and politically oriented art and literature of the early Shōwa period (1926–89).

Shirakaba, Lake   白樺湖
(Shirakabako). Artificial lake in central Nagano Prefecture, central Honshū. Located on the western slope of the mountain Tateshinayama, the lake was completed for irrigational purposes in 1946. Area: 0.4 sq km (0.2 sq mi); circumference: 6 km (4 mi); depth: 10 m (33 ft); altitude: 1,400 m (4,593 ft).

Shirakaba school   白樺派
(Shirakabaha; "White Birch school"). School of writers—most prominent among them MUSHANOKŌJI SANEATSU, SHIGA NAOYA, and the three brothers ARISHIMA TAKEO, Arishima Ikuma (1882–1974), and SATOMI TON—that took its name from *Shirakaba*, a monthly journal of literature and art appreciation, published between 1910 and 1923, to which they were regular contributors.

Shirakaba was a direct outgrowth of several little literary clubs and their magazines at the Peers' School (see GAKUSHŪIN UNIVERSITY), which all of its founding editors and contributors had attended. Although the members of the school did not have the common literary program or consistency in

style and theme that the designation "school" would imply, the magazine is remembered for its role in introducing and interpreting the works of European impressionist and postimpressionist painters, its connection with the development of the influential "international" style of ceramics (see LEACH, BERNARD HOWELL), and its advocacy of such writers as Romain Rolland and Anatole France. Among the early contributors to the magazine were YANAGI MUNEYOSHI and KISHIDA RYŪSEI. During the 1920s and 1930s there was some reaction among younger and more egalitarian writers against the *Shirakaba* group's supposed elitism and egotism. After World War II, the nonfiction of such surviving members as Mushanokōji and Shiga was widely interpreted as the last gasp of a quintessentially Taishō-period (1912–26) blend of old-fashioned libertarianism, self-involved idealism, and a fundamental cultural conservatism. The image created by the *Shirakaba* journal and its contributors was a shifting one, but without doubt it affected subsequent writers, some of whom may have drawn on the supposed ideology of the group, while others clearly reacted consciously against it.

Shirakami Mountains   白神山地
(Shirakami Sanchi). Mountain range on the border of Aomori and Akita prefectures, northern Honshū. Covered with virgin forests of beech trees, it is the object of an active preservation campaign. The highest peak is Mukai Shirakamidake (1,250 m; 4,101 ft).

Shirakawa   白河[市]
City in southern Fukushima Prefecture, northern Honshū. In ancient times Shirakawa was a barrier station (SEKISHO) for travelers entering northeastern Japan (see

Shiretoko National Park
1 An autumn view of one of the lakes that make up the Shiretoko Five Lakes.
2 Fed by a hot spring that flows from a sulfur vein, Kamuiwakka Falls is popular among bathers.

shiran Unlike most orchids, this popular ornamental variety can be grown in ordinary soil. The perennial herb is also found in the wild.

Shirase Nobu This explorer led Japan's first successful Antarctic research expedition in 1912.

SHIRAKAWA NO SEKI). During the Edo period (1600–1868) it developed as a castle town of the Matsudaira family. Principal industries are electrical appliances, construction materials, and clothing. Attractions include the remains of Komine Castle and the site of the barrier station. Pop: 45,646.

Shirakawa   白川[村]

Village in northwestern Gifu Prefecture, central Honshū, on the river Shōgawa. It is said to have been founded by surviving members of the TAIRA FAMILY, defeated by the Minamoto in the late 12th century. It is known for its large farmhouses in the *gasshō-zukuri* style (see MINKA). The MIBORO DAM, to the south of the village, is the largest rock-fill dam in East Asia. Pop: 1,892.

Shirakawa   白川

River in central Kumamoto Prefecture, Kyūshū; originating from a caldera on the volcano Asosan and flowing west into Shimabara Bay. The city of Kumamoto is located on the lower reaches. Electric power plants are located on the upper and middle reaches of the river. Length: 74 km (46 mi); area of drainage basin: 480 sq km (185 sq mi).

Shirakawa, Emperor   白河天皇

(1053–1129; Shirakawa Tennō). The 72nd sovereign (*tennō*) in the traditional count (which includes several legendary emperors); reigned 1073–87; son of Emperor GO-SANJŌ and Fujiwara no Moshi. Shirakawa continued to dominate court politics for 43 years after his own retirement in 1087. Credited with establishing the system of "cloister government" (INSEI), Shirakawa united the imperial house, neutralized the Fujiwara REGENCY GOVERNMENT, and restored great political and economic power to the ruling dynasty during the reigns of his successors, emperors Horikawa (1079–1107; r 1087–1107), TOBA, and SUTOKU. He achieved much of this by aligning himself with the newly emergent class of wealthy provincial tax managers (ZURYŌ) and with such warrior leagues as the TAIRA FAMILY and the MINAMOTO FAMILY.

Shirakawa no Seki   白河関

(Barrier of Shirakawa). One of the three ancient fortified barriers in northeastern Honshū (the others being NAKOSO NO SEKI and Nezu no Seki). Located in what is now the city of Shirakawa, Fukushima Prefecture, it served from the 8th to 10th centuries to prevent southward incursions by the aboriginal EZO people (regarded as barbarians by the Japanese) and to restrict travel to and from the north. Shirakawa no Seki acquired many historical and literary associations. It appears in classical *waka* poetry as a conventionalized setting (UTA MAKURA), evoking the desolation of remote frontiers. Excavations in

1959–63 showed the barrier to have been an earthwork surrounded by a moat and surmounted by a palisade.

shiran   紫蘭

Bletilla striata. Perennial herb of the orchid family (Orchidaceae) that grows wild in bogs and on rocks from central Japan westward; also widely cultivated as an ornamental. Five or six oblong, furrowed leaves 30 centimeters (12 in) long grow alternately at the bottom of the stem. In late spring the plant produces six or seven attractive, reddish purple flowers about 3 centimeters (1.2 in) across. Cultivated varieties include the *shirobana shiran*, with very light red flowers, and the *fukurin shiran*, with white-margined leaves. The *shiran* is popular as a cut flower, and its bulb is used for medicinal purposes and as the source of a low-quality adhesive.

Shiranesan   白根山

Also called Nikkō Shirane. Active volcano on the border between Gumma and Tochigi prefectures, central Honshū. Eruptions have been recorded from the Edo period (1600–1868) up to 1889. Erosion has created dammed lakes. Shiranesan is part of Nikkō National Park. Height: 2,578 m (8,458 ft).

Shiranesan   白根山

Also called Kusatsu Shirane. Active volcano in the Nasu Volcanic Zone, on the border between Gumma and Nagano prefectures, central Honshū. Yugama, one of three craters, is noted for the dense vapor clouds ascending from it. Shiranesan is part of JŌSHIN'ETSU KŌGEN NATIONAL PARK. Height: 2,160 m (7,086 ft).

Shirane Sanzan   白根三山

Also called Shiranesan and Kai Shirane. General name for a three-mountain group in the northern part of the AKAISHI MOUNTAINS, consisting of KITADAKE (3,192 m; 10,472 ft), Ainotake (3,189 m; 10,462 ft), and Nōtoridake (3,026 m; 9,928 ft). The mountains are composed of Paleozoic strata and have ice-scoured regions.

Shiranui Sea → Yatsushiro Sea

Shiraoi   白老[町]

Town in southern Hokkaidō on the Pacific Ocean. Shiraoi has been the site of lumber, paper, and pulp mills since 1960. There is an AINU settlement on the shore of Shiraoi's Lake Poroto. The town is part of the SHIKOTSU-TŌYA NATIONAL PARK. Pop: 23,229.

Shirase Nobu   白瀬矗

(1861–1946). Explorer of the Antarctic. Born in what is now Akita Prefecture. Inspired by Robert Falcon Scott's expedition to the South Pole, Shirase embarked with 26 men aboard the 204-ton *Kainan maru* in 1910. In his second try he succeeded in landing on the Antarctic continent from the Ross Sea in

January 1912 and reached the point of 80°05' south latitude and 156°37' west longitude, which he named Yamato Yukihara (The Yamato Snow Field).

shirasu   白州

(literally, "white sandbar"). Courtyards, spread with white gravel, in commissioners' offices of the Edo period (1600–1868). Usually attached to the offices of the commissioners of temples and shrines (JISHA BUGYŌ), city affairs (MACHI BUGYŌ), and finance (KANJŌ BUGYŌ), as well as the offices of regional intendants (DAIKAN), such courtyards were used for adjudicating both civil and criminal cases. Peasants, townsmen, and other members of the lower classes were made to sit on the white gravel during their trials, while priests, *samurai*, and other upper-class defendants sat on stairs leading from the gravel to the commissioner's desk.

Shiratori Incident   白鳥事件

(Shiratori Jiken). Controversial incident in which Shiratori Kazuo, an officer of the Sapporo Police Department, on the island of Hokkaidō, was shot and killed on 21 January 1952. The police apprehended and prosecuted Murakami Kuniharu and Murate Hiromitsu, both members of the Japan Communist Party, on a charge of conspiracy to murder. Although nine other suspects (including one alleged to have been the killer) escaped arrest and fled to China, in May 1959 the Sapporo District Court found the two men guilty and sentenced Murakami to life imprisonment and Murate to 3 years in prison. On appeal the higher court reduced Murakami's sentence to 20 years, and in 1963 the Supreme Court upheld the decision. By the end of 1980 seven of the nine escaped suspects had returned but had not been indicted due to lack of evidence.

Shiratori Kurakichi   白鳥庫吉

(1865–1942). Scholar of Asian history. Born in what is now Chiba Prefecture; graduate of Tōkyō University. After a period of study in Europe, he was appointed in 1904 to the chair of the department of Oriental history at Tōkyō University. He wrote on Korea, Manchuria, Mongolia, and Central Asia. Shiratori was also instrumental in founding in 1908 the Research Bureau of the SOUTH MANCHURIA RAILWAY to carry out studies of the area and in building up the collection of the TŌYŌ BUNKO library.

shirauo → whitebait

Shiretoko National Park
知床国立公園

(Shiretoko Kokuritsu Kōen). Situated in northeastern Hokkaidō, on the Shiretoko Peninsula. This virgin mountain region consists of forests, caldera lakes, waterfalls over sea cliffs, and volcanoes. The highest volcano is RAUSUDAKE (1,661 m; 5,449 ft) in the south; on its slopes is Rausu Hot Spring, a popular tourist resort. The forests in the region consist mainly of Yeddo spruce (*ezomatsu*) and Sakhalin fir (*todomatsu*). Among the numerous species of wildlife that inhabit the region are the brown bear (*higuma*), a fox called the *kita kitsune* (*Vulpes vulpes schrencki*), and the white-tailed sea eagle (*ojirowashi*). Area: 386.3 sq km (149 sq mi).

Shiretoko Peninsula   知床半島

(Shiretoko Hantō). Located in eastern Hokkaidō, bounded on the northwest by the Sea of Okhotsk and on the southeast by the Nemuro Strait. One of the wildest and most

remote regions of Japan, the peninsula is covered by dense coniferous forest and a massive volcanic range. It is famous for a long coastline, which includes overhanging precipices that are 30–100 m (98–328 ft) high and rocks eroded by the sea. Fishing is the principal industry. Most of the peninsula has been designated as Shiretoko National Park.

Shiribetsugawa　尻別川

River in southwestern Hokkaidō near Lake Shikotsu and flowing west by Yōteizan, a volcanic mountain, to Kutchan where it changes to a southwesterly course before emptying into the Sea of Japan. Several electric power plants are located on the upper reaches. Length: 126 km (78 mi); area of drainage basin: 1,640 sq km (633 sq mi).

Shiroishi　白石[市]

City in southern Miyagi Prefecture, northern Honshū. In the Edo period (1600–1868) it developed as a castle town and post-station town on the highway Ōshū Kaidō. Traditional products are handmade Japanese paper (WASHI) and wooden dolls (KOKESHI); there are also flour mills and noodle factories. Pop: 42,030.

Shirone　白根[市]

City in central Niigata Prefecture, central Honshū. Situated between the rivers Shinanogawa and Nakanokuchigawa, it is a major rice-producing region. Pears and grapes are also cultivated. Traditional products are sickles and Buddhist altars. Pop: 35,801.

Shiroumadake　白馬岳

Mountain on the border of Nagano and Toyama prefectures, central Honshū, in the northern part of the Hida Mountains. Together with Shakushidake and Yarigatake, it is one of the three mountains of Shirouma and is made up mostly of Paleozoic strata. Shiroumadake has excellent ski slopes and is popular with climbers. It is part of Chūbu Sangaku National Park. Height: 2,932 m (9,619 ft).

Shiroyama　城山

Small hill in the northern part of the city of Kagoshima, Kagoshima Prefecture, Kyūshū. A battlefield during the SATSUMA REBELLION (1877). The rebellion's leader, SAIGŌ TAKAMORI, committed suicide at this historical site. The observation platform on the hill provides a view of SAKURAJIMA and Kagoshima Bay. Height: 108 m (354 ft).

Shiroyama Saburō　城山三郎

(1927–). Novelist. Real name Sugiura Eiichi. Born in Aichi Prefecture; graduate of Tōkyō Shōka Daigaku (now Hitotsubashi University). He is known for his novels of the business and financial world. The 1958 Naoki Prize was awarded to his *Sōkaiya Kinjō* (1958), in which he revealed the behind-the-scenes workings of stockholders' meetings. His novels examine the life and fate of the average person struggling to survive in a complex, capitalist society. He is also known as a biographer of modern business leaders. Principal works are *Shōsetsu Nihon ginkō* (1963), a novel about the banking industry, and *Rakujitsu moyu* (1974; tr *War Criminal: The Life and Death of Hirota Kōki*, 1977), a biographical novel.

shiruko　汁粉

Sweet soup consisting of a simmered mixture of red *azuki* beans, sugar, and water, to which a grilled piece of MOCHI (rice cake) is added. The *azuki* beans may be strained to make a smoother *shiruko*. When the beans are left whole, the dish is called *inaka-jiruko* or *zenzai*. *Shiruko* has been eaten in Japan since the late Edo period (1600–1868), when it achieved mass popularity.

shiryō　私領

(privately owned lands). (1) From the 10th century onward, lands held by private persons. (2) In the Kamakura (1185–1333) and Muromachi (1333–1568) periods, lands obtained through reclamation or private acquisition. (3) In the Edo period (1600–1868), lands owned by the *daimyō* or the shōgun's direct vassals (HATAMOTO and GOKENIN).

Shisakajima　四阪島

Group of islands in the central Inland Sea, approximately 18 km (11 mi) northeast of the city of Niihama, Ehime Prefecture, Shikoku; part of Ehime Prefecture. The group consists of Minoshima, Ienoshima, Kajishima, Nezumishima, and Myōjinshima. These islands were uninhabited until 1895. Area: 1.3 sq km (0.5 sq mi).

Shiseidō Co, Ltd　[株]資生堂

(Shiseidō). Company engaged in the manufacture and sale of cosmetics, pharmaceuticals, and toiletries. Incorporated in 1927. Its products are sold abroad under the brand names Shiseido Facials, Bio-Performance, and Shiseido Makeup. Shiseidō is known for its high level of research and development. The company markets its products in Japan through a nationwide network of 25,000 stores under 15 sales companies. Overseas its products are sold in 7,700 stores in more than 20 nations, and production facilities have been established in the United States, France, New Zealand, Taiwan, South Korea, and China. In 1986 the company acquired Carita SA in France, followed by the acquisition of the US corporation Zotos International in 1988. In the fiscal year ending March 1991 sales totaled ¥352.3 billion (US $2.6 billion), and the company was capitalized at ¥26.4 billion (US $192.4 million). Headquarters are in Tōkyō.

shisekibo → dolmen burials

Shishi Bunroku　獅子文六

(1893–1969). Novelist and theatrical director. Real name Iwata Toyoo. Born in Kanagawa Prefecture; attended Keiō University. In 1937, with KISHIDA KUNIO and others, he organized the BUNGAKUZA theatrical company and helped to introduce modern French drama to Japan. He wrote *Etchan* (1936–37), a popular novel rich in humor and irony; *Jiyū gakkō* (1950), a novel portraying the customs and manners of the immediate postwar period; *Musume to watashi*

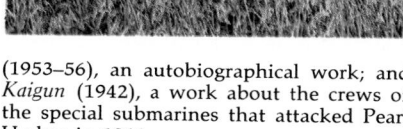

(1953–56), an autobiographical work; and *Kaigun* (1942), a work about the crews of the special submarines that attacked Pearl Harbor in 1941.

Shishigatani Conspiracy → Shunkan

shishi-mai　獅子舞

Dance (often referred to in English as the lion dance) performed in the guise of a *shishi*, an imaginary beast, supposedly a lion or, in some areas, a deer. Usually, performers wear a headdress in the shape of a *shishi*. The type of *shishi-mai* in which two or more dancers form one lion belongs to the KAGURA (sacred dance) category. This type spread throughout Japan during the medieval period (mid-12th–16th centuries) as a form of exorcism. In the DENGAKU type of *shishi-mai*, the costume is worn by only one dancer. This form, found throughout eastern Japan, is derived from the deer dance (SHISHI ODORI) and influenced by NEMBUTSU ODORI. A large group of classical dance pieces derive from this tradition and form a category called *shishi-mono*, for example, the NAGAUTA (song) "Echigo-jishi." See also DANCE, TRADITIONAL; KADOZUKE; KAKUBEI-JISHI.

shishi odori　鹿踊

(deer dance). Also called *taiko odori*. Group dance of northeastern Japan (primarily Iwate and Miyagi prefectures) performed by 8 to 12 or, in some areas, 3 male dancers. They wear masks resembling deer and beat two-headed drums attached to their waists. It was traditionally danced door-to-door during late summer or autumn to avert evil.

Shisho Gokyō → Four Books and Five Classics

shiso　紫蘇

(beefsteak plant). *Perilla frutescens* var. *crispa*. Annual culinary herb that has been cultivated in Japan since the Nara period (710–794). The leaf of the type of *shiso* known as *aojiso* (green *shiso*) is prepared as

shishi odori An October performance of the deer dance at a local shrine in Esashi, Iwate Prefecture. A slim pole decorated with white paper extends from the back of each dancer as an invocation to the deities.

Shishi Bunroku A popular novelist and theatrical director, Shishi helped introduce modern French drama into Japan.

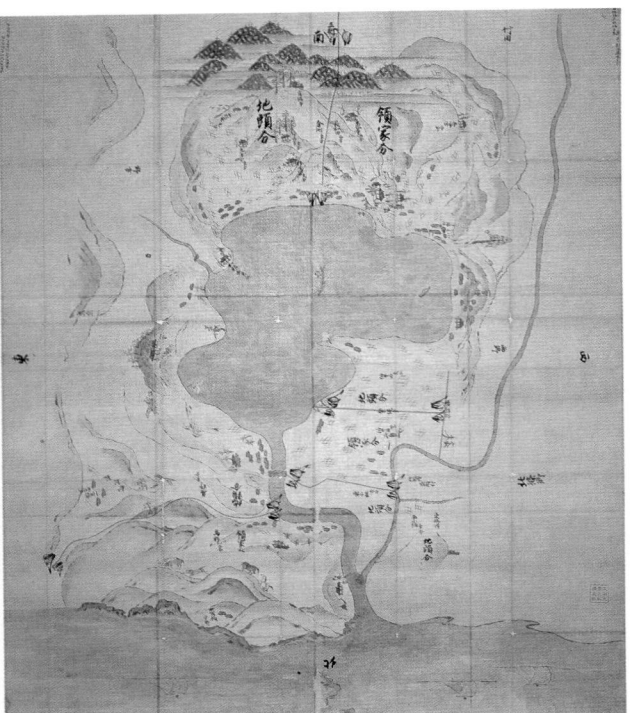

shitaji chūbun This mid-13th-century map depicts divisions of land accomplished under the *shitaji chūbun* system. The red lines mark the boundaries of landed estates. Other straight lines are caused by folds in the map.

TEMPURA and is also used in *shisomaki* (meat, fish, or MISO rolled in a *shiso* leaf and broiled or deep-fried), as a flavoring for the thin noodles known as SŌMEN, and as a garnish for SASHIMI (sliced raw fish). The *akajiso* (red *shiso*) leaf is used in pickling *ume* (Japanese plum; see UMEBOSHI) or vegetables to give them a red color. Flower stalks of both green and red *shiso*, when in the bud, are also used to garnish *sashimi*.

Shisō 思想

(Thought). Journal of philosophy issued by IWANAMI SHOTEN, PUBLISHERS, beginning in 1921. Devoted to important philosophical problems, the journal's early contributors included KUKI SHŪZŌ, WATSUJI TETSURŌ, and NISHIDA KITARŌ. It has recently been publishing articles with wider audience appeal.

Shisō no kagaku 思想の科学

(The Science of Thought). An intellectual movement and its journal of the same name founded in 1946 by young intellectuals who felt they had not opposed World War II vigorously enough. They were the physicists Taketani Mitsuo (b 1911) and Watanabe Satoshi (b 1910), the economist Tsuru Shigeto (b 1912), the political scientist MARUYAMA MASAO (b 1914), the sociologist Tsurumi Kazuko (b 1918), the philosopher Tsurumi Shunsuke (b 1922), and the intellectual historian Takeda Kiyoko (b 1917).

The movement's aims were to carry out intellectual activity based on logic and experience and to selectively introduce Anglo-American philosophy and thought to a Japan hitherto enamored of German idealistic metaphysics. In 1949 the movement's members formed the Shisō no Kagaku Kenkyūkai

Shitakiri suzume An honest old man, the hero of this folktale, bids farewell to a family of sparrows who have treated him kindly, as depicted in this scene from a 1950 children's book.

(Science of Thought Research Group). By 1954 total membership reached over 200; there were 243 members in 1990. In addition to liberal scholars, researchers, and journalists, the group also includes educators, government workers, and laborers, embodying the movement's emphasis on "populist scholarship" as opposed to "government-university scholarship." Its publications include *Tetsugaku, ronri yōgo jiten* (1959, Dictionary of Terms in Philosophy and Logic), *Tenkō* (3 vols, 1959–62, Conversion; see TENKŌ), *Nihon senryō* (1972, The Occupation of Japan), and *Nihon senryōgun* (1978, The Occupation Army in Japan). The journal *Shisō no kagaku* continues to be published as a monthly review of culture, society, and politics.

shitaji chūbun 下地中分

(literally, "halving of land"). Division of a private landed estate (SHŌEN) between its original proprietor (RYŌSHU) and its shogunate-appointed land steward (JITŌ), practiced mainly from the mid-13th to the mid-14th century. Disputes became inevitable when the *jitō* took over many of the *ryōshu*'s rights of tax collection and law enforcement. Various compromises, such as WAYO, were made, but when the concept of shared power proved unworkable, it was simplest to divide the estates. In most cases of *shitaji chūbun*, the land itself (*shitaji*) was divided; in other cases, the fruits of the land (*jōbun*) were divided between the two. Divisions could be decided through "mutual understanding" (called *wayo-chūbun*), but more often one of the two parties involved—usually the *ryōshu*—would petition the shogunate to settle the dispute. Actual territorial possession further strengthened the position of the *jitō* and speeded the disintegration of the *shōen* system.

Shitakiri suzume 舌切雀

(The Tongue-Cut Sparrow). Folktale. A sparrow owned by an honest old man eats some rice paste prepared by a greedy old woman (in some versions the man's wife). Enraged, the woman cuts out the tongue of the sparrow and drives it away. The grieving old man goes in search of his sparrow and is well treated by the sparrow's family. On leaving them, he is offered a choice of two boxes; he takes the lighter one, which turns out to be full of treasure. The greedy woman then pays a visit to the sparrows and demands the heavier box, from which emerge goblins and serpents; the woman dies of shock. The archetype of this story is found in the 13th-century collection of tales UJI SHŪI MONOGATARI.

shitamachi 下町

Term used to refer to the traditional commercial districts of older Japanese cities, and particularly to the eastern wards of Tōkyō (formerly Edo), i.e., to Chūō, Taitō, and Sumida wards. Although the term is often translated as "downtown," the *shitamachi* should not be confused with modern central business districts. Properly speaking, it refers to the merchant (*shōnin*) and craftsman (SHOKUNIN) quarters usually found in low-lying areas of feudal CASTLE TOWNS (*jōka machi*), and by extension to present-day neighborhoods with strong ties to the traditions of preindustrial urban merchant life. Contemporary survival of those traditions is associated with the so-called old middle classes—small-scale merchants and artisans—often clustered in older commercial

neighborhoods. The *shitamachi* is often contrasted with the YAMANOTE (literally, "the foothills"), the districts and the traditions associated historically with *samurai* and now with the white-collar new middle class. Thus the *shitamachi* is a distinctive segment of urban society, distinguishable in terms of geography, historical background, social and cultural traditions, social identity, and economic subsistence.

The *shitamachi* was largely the product of rigid segregation imposed on the mercantile and manufacturing classes (the CHŌNIN or townspeople) by the feudal elite just prior to and early in the Edo period (1600–1868). With the increasing economic prosperity of the *chōnin* in the middle and late Edo period, *shitamachi* blossomed, developing a sophisticated urbanity centering on the amusements of the great cities' pleasure quarters: Edo's Yoshiwara and Asakusa, Kyōto's Shimabara and Gion, Ōsaka's Shimmachi and Dōtombori. The *chōnin* subculture created the arts of the KABUKI theater, RAKUGO storytelling, the BUNRAKU puppet theater with its SHAMISEN music, and the UKIYO-E print, which so often portrayed the world of the GEISHA quarters.

Throughout the *chōnin* districts particular styles of dress, speech, spending, and consumption were developed, as well as social norms of relative informality, contrasting sharply with the severe standards of samurai society. There arose distinctive *chōnin* temperaments or personalities, such as the *edokko* ("children of Edo"), free-spending and studiously nonchalant in their adherence to the aesthetic canons of *iki* ("chic"; see IKI AND SUI) and TSŪ ("connoisseurship").

Since the Meiji restoration, however, with the homogenization of social and cultural patterns, the distinctiveness of the *shitamachi* and the *chōnin* tradition has lessened. However, some areas still retain their *shitamachi* aura and newer areas have assumed *shitamachi* characteristics, keeping alive traditional cultural elements. The present-day *shitamachi* is inhabited by members of the old middle class: shopkeepers, artisans, wholesalers, and industrial subcontractors. They retain traditional social relationships and neighborhood associations, but their way of life is gradually disappearing.

Shitennōji 四天王寺

A Buddhist temple compound located in the Tennōji Ward of Ōsaka. The head temple of the Wa sect since the end of World War II, Shitennōji retains close connections with the TENDAI SECT, with which it had been affiliated since 1010. The temple is said to have been founded in 593 by Prince SHŌTOKU, who, in gratitude for a victory over his anti-Buddhist foes, had vowed to honor the Shitennō (Four Heavenly Kings; see TEMBU). Gutted in an air raid in World War II, the site was excavated during 1950–57, revealing the foundations to be intact. The temple, originally of wood, was reconstructed with every detail in reinforced concrete. It is the oldest temple compound in Japan that preserves the original Asuka-period (593–710) design. According to a traditional plan widely used in China and Korea, the buildings are arranged along a north-south axis. The temple's most prominent building is the five-story pagoda, behind which is the image hall (*kondō*) that houses a large altar-platform (*shumidan*) symbolic of Mt. Sumeru (J: Shumisen), the cosmological center of the Buddhist universe.

Shitetsu Sōren　　私鉄総連

(abbreviation of Nihon Shitetsu Rōdō Kumiai Sōrengō Kai; General Federation of Private Railway Workers' Unions of Japan). Formed in 1947 as the single national union organization for private railway workers, Shitetsu Sōren had about 160,000 members in 1990. It was one of the most influential members of the now-defunct union organization SŌHYŌ. In November 1987 it joined the newly established union organization RENGŌ. Shitetsu Sōren continues to play an important role in labor negotiations.

shitōkan　　四等官

(the four ranks; also called *shibukan*). Collective term for the four highest ranks of bureaucrats under the RITSURYŌ SYSTEM of government during the Nara (710–794) and Heian (794–1185) periods. The hierarchy was modeled after the practice of the Sui (589–618) and Tang (T'ang; 618–907) dynasties of China. The four ranks were *kami* (bureau chief) and *suke* (assistant bureau chief), who were jointly responsible for administration; *jō* (supervisors), who oversaw the clerical work; and *sakan* (clerks), who compiled records and drafted documents.

Shi to shiron　　詩と詩論

(Poetry and Poetics). Quarterly poetry journal published by Kōseikaku Shoten. A total of 20 issues appeared between September 1928 and June 1933 (for the last six the magazine's title was changed to *Bungaku* [Literature]). *Shi to shiron* was known as a forum for the freshest and most avant-garde poetry of its time. Principal poets published in its pages included Haruyama Yukio (b 1902), KITAGAWA FUYUHIKO, ANZAI FUYUE, NISHIWAKI JUNZABURŌ, and MIYOSHI TATSUJI.

Shiwaku Islands　　塩飽諸島

(Shiwaku Shotō). Group of 28 islands in the Inland Sea sandwiched between Okayama Prefecture, western Honshū, and Kagawa Prefecture, Shikoku; part of Kagawa Prefecture. Also called the Shiaku Islands. The Shiwaku Islands constitute the western half of the Bisan Archipelago. Located along an important water transportation route, the islands have prospered since ancient times. The principal industry is stone quarrying.

Shiwasu → calendar, dates, and time

Shizen shin'eidō　　自然真営道

Principal work of ANDŌ SHŌEKI (1703?–62). On the one hand, it is a book of social criticism purporting to demonstrate, through clarification of the laws of nature, that people suffer in existing society because their lives run counter to the laws of nature. At the same time it is a medical book claiming to show the way to attain a sound mind and body. The book existed in a manuscript version in 93 volumes (101 chapters) and in a printed edition in 3 volumes (3 chapters). The latter was published in Edo (now Tōkyō) and Kyōto in 1753. Some of the manuscript volumes are thought to date from the years after 1755. The manuscript volumes were discovered by KANŌ KŌKICHI in about 1899, but the bulk of them were lost in the Tōkyō Earthquake of 1923. Only 15 volumes survive.

shizen shugi → naturalism

shizoku　　士族

Term designating people of *samurai* descent. In 1869, the year after the MEIJI RESTORATION, the traditional class distinctions of *shi* (samurai), *nō* (farmer), *kō* (artisan), and *shō* (merchant) were replaced by three broad categories: *kazoku* (former court nobles and *daimyō*; see PEERAGE), *shizoku* (those of samurai descent), and HEIMIN (commoners). The imperial family (*kōzoku*) formed a fourth class. However, by 1882 the legal rights of *shizoku* had been abolished, by 1914 the use of the term *shizoku* in household registers (*koseki*) ended, and in 1947 the very title and all other distinctions were abolished.

The *shizoku* were a large class, making up 5 percent of the population. (According to the January 1873 census, there were 408,823 *shizoku* families, or 1,892,449 persons, in a population of 34.3 million.) Moreover, their hereditary stipends were an intolerable fiscal burden to the government, consuming 25–33 percent of the annual budget. The government phased out *shizoku* political, social, and economic privileges on a gradual but sustained basis in the 1870s. The most serious blow to the *shizoku* was the loss of their monopoly over military and civil office. The CONSCRIPTION ORDINANCE OF 1873 established the principle that military service would henceforth be a duty of all classes. The Meiji government also phased out special *shizoku* social privileges and symbols of rank or else made them available to all citizens. Commoners were allowed to wear the *haori* jacket and the *hakama* split-skirt, once exclusive to the samurai. The right of samurai to cut down commoners for "disrespect" was abolished (see KIRISUTE GOMEN). Class lines dissolved further with permission for marriages between *shizoku* and commoners, with the requirement that commoners take surnames similar to the *shizoku* and with permission for *shizoku* to enter farming or business. The Sword Ban Order of 1876 (HAITŌREI) completed the process by denying *shizoku* their most cherished badge of rank.

Finally, between 1873 and 1876, the *shizoku* lost their economic base. Voluntary, then compulsory conversion of their hereditary stipends into cash settlements and government bonds brought ruin to many (see CHITSUROKU SHOBUN). At the same time, SHIZOKU JUSAN, the economic rehabilitation of the former samurai class, was initiated through land reclamation or settlement, the establishment of national banks capitalized with *shizoku* bonds, and government loans of industrial capital to *shizoku*. *Shizoku* entered banking through policies that led to their holding 75 percent of the stock in more than 100 banks set up under the National Banking Ordinance of 1872, but with indifferent results. By 1889 the *shizoku jusan* program was suspended.

Shizoku Dissidence —— Bitterness over loss of status and pensions or because of economic ruin expressed itself in assassinations, riots, and civil war; in some cases it assumed more enduring form as part of the movement to establish representative government. "Righteous assassins," who had once cut down shogunate officials, now eliminated Meiji leaders such as ŌMURA MASUJIRŌ and ŌKUBO TOSHIMICHI. The assassinations of Ōmura in 1869 and Ōkubo in 1878 bracketed a series of riots and rebellions. Chief among these were the HAGI REBELLION of October 1876, the SAGA REBELLION of February 1874, the JIMPŪREN REBELLION in October 1876, and

the SATSUMA REBELLION of 1877. *Shizoku* also expressed their discontent more constructively through the FREEDOM AND PEOPLE'S RIGHTS MOVEMENT, developing a political consciousness that nurtured the modern democratic tradition in Japan. *Shizoku* dissidence, however, should not obscure the fact that *shizoku* elites dominated the emerging society as bureaucrats, military officers, teachers, and even as entrepreneurs.

shizoku jusan　　士族授産

(employment for former *samurai*). An economic policy of the early Meiji period (1868–1912) designed to provide a livelihood for former samurai (SHIZOKU) who had been stripped of their hereditary stipends. As a result of the abolition of domains and the establishment of prefectures (1871; see PREFECTURAL SYSTEM, ESTABLISHMENT OF) and the adoption of a universal conscription system (see CONSCRIPTION ORDINANCE OF 1873), most former samurai were without income. In 1873 the government gave money and bonds to samurai who voluntarily surrendered their stipends. In 1876 all former samurai were ordered to exchange their stipends for government bonds (see CHITSUROKU SHOBUN). To provide employment, the government established a colonist-militia system (TONDENHEI), sending former samurai to settle in Hokkaidō. It also sold them public land cheaply, lent them capital to form new businesses, and encouraged them to develop wasteland. Few samurai were equipped with the skills needed for modern commerce and many were forced to sell their government bonds, although former *daimyō* tended to invest theirs profitably.

Shizugatake, Battle of　　賤ケ岳の戦い

(Shizugatake no Tatakai). A major military encounter fought on 11 June 1583 between the forces of the national unifier TOYOTOMI HIDEYOSHI and SHIBATA KATSUIE, the powerful *daimyō* of Echizen (now part of Fukui Prefecture) and Kaga (now part of Ishikawa Prefecture), in northern Ōmi Province (now the town of Kinomoto, Shiga Prefecture) near the mountain Shizugatake. Shibata's defeat ended the first stage of the succession struggle that had broken out among ODA NOBUNAGA'S (1534–82) generals after his assassination the previous year. Shibata committed suicide three days after the battle, his ally Oda Nobutaka (1558–83), son of Nobunaga, a week later. Takigawa Kazumasu (1525–86), another ally, capitulated and was pardoned. Hideyoshi's victory immensely strengthened his position, so that in 1584 he was able to confront successfully his remaining opponents in the succession struggle in the KOMAKI NAGAKUTE CAMPAIGN.

Shizuka Gozen　　静御前

(fl late 12th century). SHIRABYŌSHI dancer; mistress of MINAMOTO NO YOSHITSUNE. When

Shitennōji The western gate of the temple (center) is believed to face toward the eastern entrance to the Pure Land of Amida Buddha and is known as the Gokurakumon (Gate to Paradise). The temple's five-story pagoda is visible in the background.

shō A musician in concert (top) playing the *shō* (above), a type of mouth organ used for court music.

MINAMOTO NO YORITOMO turned against his younger brother Yoshitsune after the latter's brilliant victories in the TAIRA-MINAMOTO WAR (1180–85), Shizuka accompanied Yoshitsune in his flight. Unable to keep up, Shizuka was abandoned in the Yoshino region, south of Nara, where she was seized by monks loyal to Yoritomo. Taken to Kamakura for questioning, she was forced to dance for Yoritomo at the TSURUGAOKA HACHIMAN SHRINE, after which he allowed her to return to Kyōto. Numerous works of medieval fiction give accounts of Shizuka's life, the most complete being that in the GIKEIKI, a 15th-century compilation of legends about Yoshitsune; however, the mention of her performance at the Tsurugaoka Hachiman Shrine in the historical text AZUMA KAGAMI is evidence that she actually lived.

Shizuki Tadao　志筑忠雄

(1760–1806). Translator and scholar of the Dutch language. Born in Nagasaki, Shizuki was adopted into a family who had served as hereditary translators (*tsūji*) to Dutch traders. He contributed to the study of astronomy in Japan by translating numerous works on astronomy from Dutch into Japanese. *Rekishō shinsho* (1798–1802), a translation from the Dutch version of John Keill's commentaries on Newton's *Principia*, was the first book in Japanese on modern physics and astronomy. In it Shizuki introduced much information acquired from his own studies of astronomy, including a theory concerning nebulas.

Shizunai　静内[町]

Town in the Hidaka region on the Pacific coast of southern Hokkaidō. The town contains the ruins of a fortress associated with the late-17th-century AINU chieftain Shakushain. The local economy is based on commerce, agriculture, and lumbering; government-operated pasturelands are also located here. Pop: 24,184.

Shizuoka　静岡[市]

Capital of Shizuoka Prefecture, central Honshū, on Suruga Bay. It was the site of Sumpu Castle, built by TOKUGAWA IEYASU in 1589. It also prospered in the Edo period (1600–1868) as one of the post-station towns on the highway TŌKAIDŌ and as a distribution center of regional products. Traditional goods such as lacquer ware, sewing boxes, and *geta* (wooden clogs), as well as electrical appliances, textile goods, paper, and plastic mod-

els are made here. Principal agricultural products are tea, mandarin oranges, strawberries, and Japanese horseradish. Of interest are the TORO SITE, the Sengen Shrine, the ruins of Sumpu Castle, the Kunōzan-Tōshōgū Shrine, and the garden of the temple Togetsuhō-Saiokuji. Pop: 472,196.

Shizuoka Bank, Ltd　[株]静岡銀行

(Shizuoka Ginkō). Regional bank (*chihō ginkō*) with its principal base of operations in Shizuoka Prefecture. Incorporated in 1943. The bank has about 200 branches covering the area between Tōkyō and Ōsaka. It has representative offices in Los Angeles and Hong Kong and a subsidiary in Hong Kong. For the fiscal year ending March 1991 total deposits amounted to ¥6.5 trillion (US $47.4 billion), total assets stood at ¥7.7 trillion (US $56.1 billion), and capitalization was ¥89.2 billion (US $650.1 million). Headquarters are in Shizuoka.

Shizuoka Municipal Toro Site Museum　静岡市立登呂博物館

(Shizuoka Shiritsu Toro Hakubutsukan). Located in the city of Shizuoka, Shizuoka Prefecture, on the grounds of the Late-Yayoi-period (ca 100–ca 300) TORO SITE, now a historical park. Architecturally resembling a Yayoi-period (ca 300 BC–ca AD 300) raised storehouse, the museum, built in 1972, houses artifacts excavated from the site.

Shizuoka Plain　静岡平野

(Shizuoka Heiya). Located in central Shizuoka Prefecture, central Honshū. Bordering Suruga Bay, it consists principally of the alluvial fans of the river Abekawa. A spectacular view of Mt. Fuji (FUJISAN) can be obtained from the top of the hill called Udosan. The major city is Shizuoka, and the scenic area of MIHO NO MATSUBARA is a tourist attraction. Area: approximately 110 sq km (40 sq mi).

Shizuoka Prefecture　静岡県

(Shizuoka Ken). Located on the Pacific coast of central Honshū and bordered by Yamanashi and Nagano prefectures to the north, Kanagawa Prefecture to the east, the Pacific Ocean to the south, and Aichi Prefecture to the west. The terrain is principally mountainous, and the eastern half of the prefecture includes part of Mt. Fuji (FUJISAN) and the rugged IZU PENINSULA. Rivers such as the FUJIKAWA, ABEKAWA, ŌIGAWA, and TENRYŪGAWA run between the mountains, creating deep gorges. The climate is humid and mild, especially in the southern part of the Izu Peninsula.

Under the 7th-century system of provinces (KOKUGUN SYSTEM) the area was designated as the three provinces of Suruga, Tōtōmi, and Izu. The region gave rise to several important warrior families, such as the HŌJŌ FAMILY and TOKUGAWA FAMILY. The prefecture was created in its present form in 1876, with minor alterations in 1878.

Shizuoka is especially noted for its green tea and mandarin oranges. Fishery and forestry are also important, and eel cultivation is carried out in Lake HAMANA. The manufacture of textiles, musical instruments, looms, foodstuff, and paper dates from the late 19th century. Since World War II, the metal, machinery, motorcycle, automobile, shipbuilding, and oil-refining industries have become important.

Proximity to the Tōkyō area and attractions such as FUJI-HAKONE-IZU NATIONAL PARK, SOUTHERN ALPS NATIONAL PARK, and numerous

hot-spring resorts make Shizuoka a popular tourist area. Area: 7,773 sq km (3,001 sq mi); pop: 3,670,840; capital: SHIZUOKA. Other major cities include HAMAMATSU, NUMAZU, SHIMIZU, and FUJI.

Shizuoka University　静岡大学

(Shizuoka Daigaku). A coeducational national university located in the city of Shizuoka, Shizuoka Prefecture. Founded in 1949, the university maintains faculties of humanities and social sciences, education, science, engineering, and agriculture. Enrollment in 1989 was 7,448.

shō　笙

The mouth organ of Japanese court music. The *shō* consists of a lacquered wooden cup-shaped body, into which 17 narrow bamboo pipes of varying length are inserted vertically to form a circular cluster. Two of the pipes are mute; the remainder are fitted with small metal tongues vibrating freely through a small slot and made to speak by closing a finger hole on the pipe. The instrument plays single notes and chords identified in the notation by the names of the pipes, and the player can maintain a continuous sound by sucking and blowing alternately. The *shō* is related to the Chinese *sheng* and to other East Asian mouth organs. See also GAGAKU.

Shōbara　庄原[市]

City in northeastern Hiroshima Prefecture, western Honshū. It developed as an iron-mining center of the Chūgoku Mountains and later flourished as a market town. Principal activities are rice cultivation, cattle raising, dairy farming, and *sake* production. Pop: 22,677.

Shōbō genzō　正法眼蔵

(Treasury of the True Dharma Eye). The magnum opus of DŌGEN, founder of the SŌTŌ SECT of Japanese ZEN Buddhism. It is a collection of his sermons and commentaries on selected KŌAN, composed over a period of 22 years (1231–53). The 95-chapter corpus is written in Japanese, unlike other Japanese Buddhist works of the day, which were customarily written in Chinese. Throughout the work Dōgen expounds matters of monastic life and examines Buddhist concepts and symbols at the limit of their semantic possibilities. Today the work is considered a Buddhist classic and one of the most important Japanese philosophical texts.

shōbu　菖蒲

(sweet flag). *Acorus calamus* var. *asiaticus*. Often wrongly translated as "iris." Evergreen perennial herb of the arum family (Araceae) growing wild in colonies along the edges of ponds, marshes, and streams throughout Japan. The thick white rhizomes grow laterally and have numerous small fibrous roots. The sword-shaped leaves are about 80 centimeters (32 in) long. In early summer a leaflike stalk bears a fingerlike light yellowish green inflorescence (spadix) crowded with minute light yellowish green flowers. In ancient times this herb was known as *ayame* (see IRISES).

The *shōbu* is known for the pleasant smell of its rhizome and leaves. The leaves were traditionally used to decorate the eaves of houses and added to bathwater during celebrations of Boys' Day (now CHILDREN'S DAY) in May. A similar species called *sekishō* (*A. gramineus*) grows wild along mountain streams and is also cultivated in gardens.

shōchikubai 松竹梅

(pine, bamboo, plum). The pine and bamboo, which stay green throughout the winter, and the plum, the first tree to flower in spring, have been collectively regarded as a symbol of hope and good fortune in Japan since the Nara period (710–794), when this notion was imported from China. Since that time, the three have been planted together, combined in flower arrangements, employed as a design motif, and used in decorations for New Year's and other auspicious occasions. Pine, bamboo, and plum are often used to name different meal combinations in Japanese restaurants; "pine" corresponding to deluxe, "bamboo" to special, and "plum" to regular.

Shōchiku Co, Ltd 松竹[株]

(Shōchiku). A major producer and distributor of movies. Also produces and promotes stage shows and television programs and does business in prerecorded videotapes. Established in 1902 as a *kabuki* production company, the company began producing movies in 1920 through the establishment of a subsidiary, the Shōchiku Kinema Co. The company consolidated and assumed its present name in 1937. Sales for the fiscal year ending February 1991 totaled ¥48.6 billion (US $372.5 million), and capitalization stood at ¥3.0 billion (US $23.0 million). Headquarters are in Tōkyō.

shōchū 焼酎

Japanese distilled liquor made from grain. *Shōchū* is classified into two types, A (*kō*) and B (*otsu*); the latter, distilled by the pot-still method, is less severely taxed and is the standard type. A-type *shōchū* uses molasses as its main ingredient, while B-type uses chiefly rice, sweet potatoes, barley, rye, buckwheat, corn, or raw sugar. Both use malted rice for fermentation. The alcohol content varies from 40 to 90 proof, depending on the type and where it is produced; it averages 50 proof. *Shōchū* is generally drunk mixed with hot or cold water, or with any of a variety of flavorings.

Shōchū is assumed to have been introduced from the Ryūkyū Islands (present-day Okinawa). The *shōchū* of that area is called *awamori* (millet brandy) and first appeared in the Ryūkyūs in the 15th century. The first written mention of *shōchū* in Japan was in the 16th century. At present, *shōchū* is used only as an alcoholic drink, but until the end of the Edo period (1600–1868) it had an important medical use as a disinfectant.

Shōchū Conspiracy 正中の変

(Shōchū no Hen). An unsuccessful plot to overthrow the KAMAKURA SHOGUNATE; led by Emperor GO-DAIGO in 1324 (Shōchū 1). Since the time of Emperor FUSHIMI (r 1287–98) members of the Jimyōin and Daikakuji lines of the imperial family had succeeded to the throne in alternation. In 1321 the retired Emperor Go-Fushimi (r 1298–1301) of the Jimyōin line sought to replace Go-Daigo's son (of the Daikakuji line) with his own son as heir apparent and succeeded in enlisting the support of the shogunate. Go-Daigo conspired with the courtiers Hino Suketomo (1290–1332) and Hino Toshimoto (d 1332) to raise an army against the shogunate. The plot was discovered by the Rokuhara *tandai*, the shogunal deputy stationed in Kyōto. Go-Daigo denied all knowledge of the plot and managed to survive the incident. Go-Daigo failed to wrest power from the shogunate again in the GENKŌ INCIDENT of 1331, but in 1333 he finally achieved his aims. See KEMMU RESTORATION.

Shōda Heigorō 荘田平五郎

(1847–1922). Businessman and leader of the MITSUBISHI *zaibatsu* (financial and industrial combine). Born in what is now Ōita Prefecture; graduate of Keiō Gijuku (now Keiō University). Shōda first taught at Keiō Gijuku, but later joined Mitsubishi & Co through FUKUZAWA YUKICHI's introduction. He engineered the company's participation in capitalizing the Tokio Marine & Fire Insurance Co, Ltd. In 1886 Shōda became general manager of Mitsubishi & Co. He masterminded the company's real estate acquisitions in Tōkyō's MARUNOUCHI area, the construction of office buildings, and the expansion and modernization of what is now MITSUBISHI HEAVY INDUSTRIES, LTD.

Shōda Hidesaburō 正田英三郎

(1903–). Businessman. Born in Gumma Prefecture, the third son of Shōda Teiichirō (1870–1961), founder of NISSHIN FLOUR MILLING CO, LTD. Graduated from Tōkyō Commercial University (now Hitotsubashi University). After first working for MITSUBISHI CORPORATION, Shōda joined Nisshin Flour Milling in 1929 and became its president in 1945. He added many new production lines, including formula feeds, foodstuffs, and chemicals. Shōda is the father of Empress MICHIKO.

Shōda Kenjirō 正田建次郎

(1902–77). Mathematician who led the development of abstract algebra in Japan. Uncle of Empress MICHIKO. Born in Gumma Prefecture, he graduated from Tōkyō University in 1925. After studying in Germany he became a professor at Ōsaka University in 1933, later becoming its president. He also served as president of Musashi University. He received the Order of Culture in 1969.

Shōdan chiyō 樵談治要

(A Woodcutter's Chats on the Essentials of Government). An essay on government and social conditions composed in 1480 by the high-ranking courtier and scholar ICHIJŌ KANEYOSHI for the young shōgun Ashikaga Yoshihisa (1465–89; r 1474–89). The work contains interesting observations on affairs in the aftermath of the ŌNIN WAR.

shodō → calligraphy

Shōdoshima 小豆島

Island in the eastern Inland Sea, between southeastern Okayama Prefecture, southwestern Honshū, and northeastern Kagawa Prefecture, Shikoku. Administratively part of Kagawa Prefecture. It is the second largest island in the Inland Sea after AWAJISHIMA. Agricultural products include olives and chrysanthemums. It is known for its high-quality soy sauce, *sōmen* (noodles), and building stone. Part of Inland Sea National Park, the island is a tourist area. One attraction is the gorge Kankakei. Religious sanctuaries on the island attract a large number of pilgrims. Area: 152.5 sq km (59 sq mi).

shōen 荘園

(landed estate). One of the most important institutions for organizing the economic life of medieval Japan. The first landed estates appeared in the 8th century, and the last of them did not disappear until the 16th century during the turbulent Sengoku (Warring States) period (1467–1568). The mature estate, emerging in the mid-11th century,

proved to be an extremely successful way of securing a balance between the demands of the ruling class for income and the demands of the populace for a stable livelihood. Not only did the *shōen* serve as the primary means through which the ruling class tapped the wealth of the countryside, but it also provided the residence, the workplace, and the source of sustenance for peasants and estate managers alike. Before the development of regional market economies in the 13th century, the workshops and craftsmen on the estate produced the hoes, plows, and other equipment needed by the farmers. Moreover, the estates frequently manufactured special products such as roof tiles, reed mats, and pottery to supply their proprietors in the capital. As one of the primary production units in medieval Japanese society, the *shōen* held a central place in the economic and social history of Japan.

The Early Shōen—In 743 the government promulgated a law (KONDEN EISEI SHIZAI HŌ) that granted tenure in perpetuity over reclaimed lands, thus removing them from the land allotment system (HANDEN SHŪJU SYSTEM) under the RITSURYŌ SYSTEM of government. The *shōen* that emerged from this legal basis were quite simple in both physical and administrative structure. Based on these lands granted by the imperial government for reclamation, the *shōen* had parcels in close proximity to each other. (The government supported land reclamation to encourage the development of new paddy fields. Although estates were also acquired by purchase of existing rice land, the development of new fields provided the richest source.) Clusters of cultivated fields might be separated by unreclaimed tracts since the order of reclamation was often dependent upon the availability of irrigation and other geographical factors. Administratively, the proprietor, court noble, or religious institution that had supplied the capital for the reclamation project controlled the early *shōen* directly. Agents appointed by the central proprietor resided on the estate and oversaw the day-to-day administration of the land and its cultivators. They were responsible for recruitment of cultivators and the collection of rents and dues.

Early estates gained tax immunities in a variety of ways. One way was by borrowing or extending the exemptions of lands already acquired under different circumstances. Thus temples and shrines often gained tax immunity for newly acquired estates by having them classified as temple or shrine land (*jiden* or SHINDEN). A more secure way was to submit a petition to the central government. When the petition was approved, the estate holder received a charter that specified the location and area of the estate and the extent of its tax immunity. A proprietor who established an estate without a clear charter from the central government, or who extended its territories beyond those listed in a charter, faced a constant struggle to maintain its tax-exempt existence.

The Mature Shōen—From the 10th century, as the central government's interest in the provinces declined, landed estates grew in size, number, and complexity. Court nobles and religious institutions enlarged their holdings through purchase, further reclamation, and the outright annexation of public fields (KŌDEN). Frequently, provincial governors or district officials extended immunities to these new holdings through the

shōbu The lateral rhizome, leaves, and yellowish green inflorescence (spadix) of the sweet flag. It was traditionally believed that the plant could ward off plagues and demons.

issuance of tax exemption certificates. The most widespread method used by local magnates to expand their *shōen* was commendation (*kishin;* the placing of land under a more powerful person's protection). This practice led to the formation of the conglomerate or commendation-type estate, which flourished in the 12th and 13th centuries and formed the basis of the *shōen* system.

The organization of a typical conglomerate estate can be viewed as a pyramid with the cultivators (*shōmin*) at the base. Next came the resident managers (SHŌKAN or *shōke*). Above the resident managers were the central proprietors or *ryōke.* At the peak of the hierarchy was the guarantor or *honke* (see HONKE AND RYŌKE).

Although central proprietors occasionally used commendation, it was most often local magnates—local proprietors who held positions of influence in their areas—who took this means of protecting their interest in the land. Using the power and prestige of their offices to extend their holdings, the local magnates held their land as "private lands" (*ryō*) and were recognized as proprietors (RYŌSHU). A *ryōshu* possessed all fiscal and administrative power over his land. However, because of the constant threat of interference by provincial governors, the *ryōshu* sought protection by borrowing prestige from court nobles or religious institutions. To do this he commended his rights of ownership to a powerful individual or institution in the capital in return for political influence in seeking protection. Commendation added a new dimension to tenurial relationships and a new complexity to the estate hierarchy.

The *ryōshu,* the key figure in the practice of commendation, generally took the initiative in turning his property over to a central proprietor or *ryōke.* In doing so, the *ryōshu* gave up little in terms of income since it was customary for the *ryōshu* to take the title of manager (*shōkan*) under the terms of commendation. The *ryōshu* exchanged the title of proprietor for more secure immunity. The *ryōke* was to act as legal protector for the estate, using his influence to maintain tax immunities and to intervene with government authorities as the necessity arose. In return, the *ryōke* received a specified share of income from the estate. If additional influence was needed, the *ryōke* could secure an even more influential nobleman or religious institution to act as guarantor or *honke.* The *ryōke* commended a portion of his share from the estate to the *honke.*

Although the basic posture of estate hierarchy took the form of the cultivator-manager-proprietor-guarantor pyramid, there was room for great flexibility and variation within that form. It was possible for changes to take place at one level with little effect on the other levels. For example, a change in *honke* or *ryōke* would scarcely be noticed in the day-to-day operations of the estate. Conversely, the central proprietors cared little who did the actual work on the estate as long as the income flowed to their storehouses in the capital. The estate system was based not on direct proprietary control of the land but rather on income from the land. Total income, the goods and services provided by the cultivators, was conceived of as subject to allotment or sharing, according to the relationships between the levels in the estate tenure hierarchy. These shares were defined for each estate in terms of *shiki,*

which specified the share or amount of revenue due each rank in the hierarchy. Since *shiki* were alienable and divisible, it was possible for income from the estate to be widely distributed. Moreover, shares could change hands without disturbing the functioning of the estate. Most important, *shiki* holders could receive income from more than one estate, and they could hold shares of different hierarchical ranks on different estates.

From the mid-11th century, as they accumulated numerous *shiki* in different *shōen,* central proprietors began to create conglomerates of estate holdings. Court nobles, the imperial family, and religious institutions grouped *shōen,* often from widely scattered provinces, together into portfolios and assigned the portfolios to family chapels, temples, or the like, which assumed the position of *ryōke* or *honke.* The imperial government made periodic attempts to limit the expansion of the *shōen.* The most effective effort came during the era of the retired emperors (1087–1192; see INSEI), a time of particularly rapid *shōen* expansion. Edicts issued by the retired emperors were administered by the Shōen Records Office (KIROKU SHŌEN KENKEIJO), which confiscated the lands of proprietors with improper charters and reduced the immunities of others. This was not, however, an attempt to abolish *shōen* altogether. In fact imperial *shōen* increased noticeably from the time of the retired emperors.

At the cultivator level, some tenures had become secure enough to be regarded as private rights in the land, and the cultivators' names were attached to the plots. By the late 11th century name land (*myōden*) functioned as the basic unit of landholding in both *shōen* and public land. The holder (*myōshu*) became the person responsible for dues and labor services and had, in fact, become a small-scale proprietor who exercised managerial rights over his land in the *shōen.*

As the estate system matured in the 12th century, the feature that distinguished such holdings from publicly administered land (*kokugaryō*) became the possession of complete immunity from taxation and from entry by government officials. Winning and protecting such immunities became one of the main incentives for local proprietors to commend their lands to a higher authority. As land holdings expanded or as local officials became more assertive, the government frequently challenged the validity of the immunities. Thus, the *ryōke* often had to intervene at court on behalf of the *shōen.* A *shōen*'s immunity was not complete, therefore, until it was free from entry by all government officials (see FUYU AND FUNYŪ). Once this was accomplished, estate administrators gained full power of jurisdiction over both the land and the cultivators, making them the true successors to provincial government officials in the lands that composed their estates.

Kamakura-Period Shōen ── The establishment of the Kamakura shogunate (1192–1333) and creation by MINAMOTO NO YORITOMO of the offices of SHUGO (military governor) and JITŌ (military estate steward) introduced a new layer of tenurial rights into the *shōen* hierarchy. Appointment of *jitō* by the shogunate marked the beginning of a long process that resulted in the diminution of the rights of the central proprietor and the growth of the warriors' authority over the land, its revenues, and its inhabitants. By the 13th century some *jitō* had acquired full

proprietary rights to *shōen* lands, mostly in the Kantō region, where the influence of the Minamoto and their followers was strongest. This process evolved later where the imperial court and central religious institutions had strong ties to the land.

The office of *jitō* initially fit into the *shōen* hierarchy at the manager or *shōkan* level; the *jitō*'s function was to keep the peace and to assure delivery of dues and services to the central proprietors. Initially, the shogunate allowed the *jitō* a one-eleventh share for his services. As time went on, however, the *jitō,* using his military power, extended his fiscal and administrative authority over the *shōen,* often taking control out of the hands of the manager appointed by the central proprietors. This led to numerous disputes between *jitō* and central proprietors, particularly over income from the land. As the shogunate's judicial court increasingly favored the *jitō,* the central proprietors turned to direct negotiations with the *jitō,* which often resulted in a physical division of the holdings—commonly on a 50-50 basis (see SHITAJI CHŪBUN).

By the Kamakura period (1185–1333) it is also possible to make a more accurate appraisal of how the estate system provided a wide distribution of its income among the many holders who had interests in the estate. For officials of the estate there was a small amount of demesne from which they received a direct yield. Rent and service payments from the *myōden,* assessed on a volume-per-area basis, provided the major portion distributed to the many *shiki* holders. The *ryōke* and high-level managers took between 25 and 35 percent. Lesser officials on the estate claimed between 7 and 10 percent of the yield. This left 55 to 68 percent in the hands of the *myōshu* and the other cultivators. The tenant-cultivators, however, also had to pay rent to the *myōshu* and were, in addition, liable for payments in local products and for labor service. The demands of the *ryōke* and the *myōshu* combined often came close to 60 percent of the total yield. For the proprietors, the products and services rendered in addition to the payment in grain commonly proved to be the most valuable part of their holding.

During the Muromachi shogunate (1338–1573), as power increasingly moved into the hands of local military leaders, a gradual but perceptible decay crept into the *shōen* system. Because the central government had lost much of its authority, it could no longer enforce its demands for income from the *shōen,* and the *shōen* system weakened as an effective means to share the wealth of the land. After the ŌNIN WAR (1467–77), both the shogunate and *shugo* were greatly weakened, and control of the land and its inhabitants fell increasingly to local military leaders (SENGOKU DAIMYŌ). As political decentralization grew, many *shōen* simply disappeared, with new physical and political boundaries springing up to coincide more closely with the local military lord's scope of power.

shōga → ginger

Shōgakukan, Inc ［株］小学館
(Shōgakukan). One of Japan's major publishing houses; established in 1922 by Ōga Takeo (1897–1938). The company at first limited production to juvenile and educational publications and became known for its publication of magazines aimed at specific primary-school grade levels. With the post-

war rise in the birthrate and the subsequent changes in educational programs, the company expanded into a general publishing house. It continues to publish magazines as well as a variety of books, including art and reference works.

Shōgatsu → New Year

Shōgawa
庄川

River in Gifu and Toyama prefectures, central Honshū; originating in Eboshidake, a peak in the highland Hida Kōchi, and flowing north into Toyama Bay. The villages of SHIRAKAWA and GOKAYAMA, noted for their *gasshō-zukuri*-style farmhouses with steeply pitched roofs (see MINKA), are along the river. The water is utilized for electric power and for irrigating the Tonami Plain. Length: 133 km (83 mi); area of drainage basin: 1,180 sq km (455 sq mi).

shōgekijō undō
小劇場運動

(literally, "little-theater movement"). Also known as *angura geki* (underground theater). The Japanese version of the underground theater movement that started in the 1960s in locations such as New York's Off Broadway. The movement based itself in small theaters seating around 100; performances were also staged in tents or open-air settings. The best-known troupes of young theater professionals active between the mid-1960s and the mid-1970s were the Jōkyō Gekijō (Situation Theater, now known as Karagumi), run by KARA JŪRŌ; the Waseda Shōgekijō (Waseda [University] Little Theater, now known as SCOT), run by SUZUKI TADASHI and BETSUYAKU MINORU; the Tenjō Sajiki (Galley Theater), run by TERAYAMA SHŪJI; the Gendaijin Gekijō (Theater of Contemporary Man), run by NINAGAWA YUKIO and others; and the Tenkei Gekijō (Theater of Change), run by Ōta Shōgo (b 1939). The *shōgekijō undō* troupes burst onto the theater scene as an aggressive reaction against the limitations of established theater. They experimented with the structure of plays, the emotive aspect of acting, and the use of theatrical space and soon overtook SHINGEKI ("new theater") to become the new center of contemporary theater in Japan. Rather than concentrate on Western plays in translation, as had been the case with *shingeki*, these troupes breathed new life into contemporary Japanese drama. Directors such as Suzuki Tadashi and Ninagawa Yukio built international reputations through their participation in the *shōgekijō undō*. Although the movement as such peaked in the early 1970s, such figures as TSUKA KŌHEI, Yamazaki Tetsu (b 1946), Kitamura Sō (b 1952), Takeuchi Jūichirō (b 1947), and NODA HIDEKI continue its tradition.

shōgi
将棋

A board game involving two players and 40 pieces; commonly referred to in the West as "Japanese chess." The object of the game is to checkmate the opponent's king. There are many similarities to chess in the way the pieces move, but what is different is that a captured piece can be used again as one's own piece. There are an estimated 20 million *shōgi* players in Japan. The present-day JAPAN SHŌGI FEDERATION (Nihon Shōgi Remmei) was founded in 1947.

The prototype of *shōgi* is believed to have originated in India. From there it made its way to Europe via Persia, becoming what is known today as Western chess. It also moved east, to China, where it became known as *xiangqi* (*hsiang-ch'i;* Japanese pronunciation *shōgi*). *Shōgi* may have been introduced to Japan in the Nara period (710–794) by Japanese envoys who were sent to Tang (T'ang) dynasty (618–907) China. In the Heian period (794–1185) several forms of *shōgi* were popular among the nobility, but by the Muromachi period (1333–1568) the rules of the game had been modified, and the game had become very much like present-day *shōgi*.

In 1607 the Tokugawa shogunate established an office for *shōgi* and GO, under the jurisdiction of the commissioner of shrines and temples; a monk named Hon'imbō Sansa (1558–1623) was made its head. Later the office was turned over to Ōhashi Sōkei (1555–1634), who was installed as its first lifetime *meijin* ("master"). The *meijin* rank was inherited within a *shōgi* "family"; a *meijin* remained one for life, with no alteration of status despite any change in his actual ability. The lifetime *meijin* system was abolished in 1935, and annual contests for the title of *meijin* were begun. Kimura Yoshio (1905–86) was the first to win the title; he has since been followed by six others: Tsukada Masao (1914–78), Ōyama Yasuharu (1923–92), Masuda Kōzō (1918–91), Katō Hifumi (b 1940), Tanigawa Kōji (b 1962), and Nakahara Makoto (b 1947), titleholder as of 1991. Championship matches, usually sponsored by newspaper companies, are held regularly, and game moves in such matches are featured daily in newspaper columns.

The Game—The *shōgi* board is a square wooden block with a grid of 81 squares. Each player uses 20 flat wooden pieces of an elongated, irregular pentagon shape. Each piece is placed on the grid with its apex pointing toward the opponent. The pieces are distinguished by characters written on each side. Captured pieces are placed to the player's right and returned ("dropped") to the board at the discretion of the player who captured the piece, for his or her own use.

The *ōshō* (king; *ō* for short) and *gyokushō* (jewel; *gyoku* for short) are in essence the same piece, i.e., a king. Making one king a "jewel" (by adding one stroke to the character for "king") avoided having two kings on the same board, a custom that supposedly originated on the request of an emperor in ancient times. The better player has the king and the other player has the jewel. The *ōshō* or *gyokushō* can move one square in any direction, like a king in chess.

The other pieces are the *hisha* (abbreviated, only in writing, as *hi*), which moves like a rook in chess; the *kakugyō* (*kaku* for short), which corresponds to the chess bishop; the *kinshō* (*kin* for short), or "gold," which can move one square in any direction except diagonally backward; the *ginshō* (*gin* for short), or "silver," which moves one square in any direction except sideways or straight backward; the *keima* (*kei* for short), which is similar to the knight in chess except that it may jump only to one of two squares two ranks ahead and one file to the left or right; the *kyōsha* (*kyō* for short), or "lance," which moves any number of squares straight forward only; and the *fuhyō* (*fu* for short), which corresponds the chess pawn except that it captures forward, not diagonally. The forward, sideways, backward, or diagonal movement of each piece is therefore restricted in *shōgi*, in ways similar to (but not exactly corresponding to) the various moves permitted to the pieces in chess.

The pieces can take enemy pieces that are

shōgi Two amateur players test their skill at a *shōgi* club. Captured pieces are placed on the small board to each player's right.

in range of their movements. The two aspects of *shōgi* that distinguish it from chess are *utsu*, the use of captured pieces, and *naru*, the promotion of one's own pieces. All the pieces except the *ō* or *gyoku* and *kin* can be promoted after penetrating enemy territory. The piece is turned over to show its new name. The *hisha* becomes a *ryūō* (*ryū* for short), which has the combined powers of a rook and a king. The *kaku* becomes a *ryūma* (*uma* for short), which has the combined powers of a bishop and a king. The *ginshō* becomes the *narigin*, which has the same powers as the *kin*. The *kei*, *kyō*, and *fu* can all be promoted to the powers of a *kin*. Their names after promotion are, respectively, *narikei*, *narikyō*, and *tokin*. To promote or not is a matter of choice. A promoted piece returns to its original status when captured.

To begin play, the board is placed between two players and the pieces are lined up as in the diagram. Players alternate, moving one piece at a time. There are three important restrictions: one cannot drop a *fu* on a file in which there is already a friendly *fu*, one cannot drop a piece where there is no room for its next move, and one cannot checkmate the enemy *gyoku* by dropping a *fu*. It is permissible to checkmate using a *fu* on the board. One forfeits immediately upon violation of any of the above three rules. In the case of a stalemate, the game must be played over. When both players' kings enter enemy territory and neither player can check the other, victory is determined by the number of pieces left.　☎ 1404–1405

Shōgitai
彰義隊

A military unit formed in Edo (now Tōkyō) by former retainers of the Tokugawa shogunate (1603–1867) to resist the Imperial Restoration (ŌSEI FUKKO) of January 1868. Organized in March 1868, its headquarters were established at Kan'eiji, a temple in the Ueno district. The group, some 2,000 strong, acted as police for the city, which was in confusion because of the impending attack by imperial forces, and as self-appointed protectors of the deposed shōgun, TOKUGAWA YOSHINOBU. Even after the city had been formally surrendered to imperial forces in May, the Shōgitai resisted but were finally defeated in the Battle of Ueno on 4 July 1868. Survivors escaped to northern Japan, and several participated in the Battle of GORYŌKAKU (1869). See also BOSHIN CIVIL WAR.

Shōgoin
聖護院

Head temple of the Honzan Shugenshū sect, located in Sakyō Ward, Kyōto. Originally named Jōkōin, it was built by Tendai monk ENCHIN and reestablished in 1090 as Shōgoin by Zōyo (1032–1116), a monk from the tem-

Continued on page 1406 ➡

Japan's Game of Kings: A Shōgi Primer

The game of *shōgi* is derived from the same ancient prototype that gave birth to Western chess. In both games the object is checkmate—overwhelming the enemy king with an attack from which it cannot escape. Shōgi, however, has two features that set it apart from chess in ways that radically alter the nature of the contest: *utsu*, a rule that permits players to use the pieces they capture as their own, and *naru*, a rule that allows most pieces to be promoted and become more powerful. These features greatly influence strategy, making it difficult but also highly rewarding to master this complex game.

Glyndon Townhill

How to Play

The Board—In shōgi, two players face each other across a board marked with a grid that divides it into 81 squares: nine horizontal rows (ranks) and nine vertical columns (files). In the conventional notation used by Western shōgi players to record their games, "White" occupies the top three ranks at the beginning of the game and "Black" the bottom three; files are numbered 1 to 9 from right to left and ranks are assigned letters "a" to "i" from top to bottom. Thus, any square on the board can be located by specifying its file number and rank letter.

The Pieces—Each player begins the game with 20 pieces. These two sets of pieces are virtually identical, the two sides are differentiated not by color but by being oriented in opposite directions. For the sake of convenience, however, one side is designated White and the other Black, as in chess. Shōgi diagrams represent the board viewed from the black side, which plays first. Chess terminology has also been adopted by Western players to designate certain shōgi pieces since, for the most part, these pieces function the same way their chess counterparts do. Each of the pieces used in shōgi is listed below under its English name, along with its notational symbol and an explanation of its moves. For the Japanese names, see the accompanying article.

The king (**K**) can move one square in any direction, but not onto a square where it would be threatened by an enemy piece. A king under attack is said to be "in check," just as in chess.

The gold general (**G**), also called the gold, can move one square in any direction except diagonally backward.

The silver general (**S**), also called the silver, can move one square diagonally in any direction or one square straight forward.

The knight (**N**) can move to either of two squares—two ranks forward and one file to the left or right—jumping over any piece that occupies an intervening square.

The lance (**L**) can move any number of squares straight forward, provided its path is not obstructed by another piece.

The pawn (**P**) can move one square straight forward.

Diagram 1 shows the moves of the six pieces discussed so far.

The rook (**R**) can move any number of squares along a rank or file, as demonstrated in diagram 2, provided its path is not obstructed by another piece.

The bishop (**B**) can move any number of squares diagonally, as demonstrated in diagram 3, provided its path is not obstructed by another piece.

Diagram 4 shows the setup of the pieces at the start of the game.

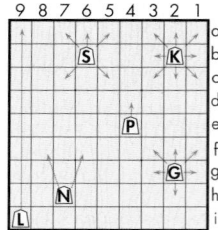

Diagram 1

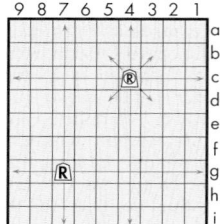

Diagram 2

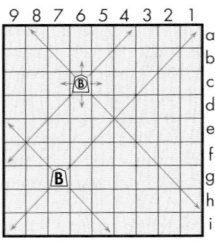

Diagram 3

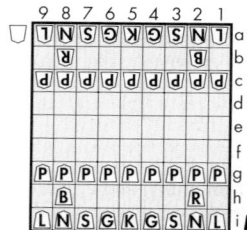

Diagram 4
In shōgi diagrams Black and White are indicated by the black and white symbols shown here outside the corners of the board.

In the figure below, the various faces of the pieces used in shōgi are shown in both their Japanese (top row) and Western (bottom row) versions. The reverse side of each promotable piece—the side displayed upon promotion—is shown below the piece's original face. The king and the gold are not promotable.

Promotion—When any piece other than a king or gold general reaches the promotion zone—the three ranks occupied by the opposing pieces at the beginning of the game—it becomes eligible for promotion. A piece may be promoted upon the completion of a move that begins, ends, or both begins and ends within the promotion zone. Promoted pieces have new powers of movement: rooks and bishops add to their own moves the moves of a king upon promotion, while silver generals, knights, lances, and pawns lose their old moves upon promotion and gain those of a gold general. To indicate its new status a promoted piece is turned over to reveal a new face (see the figure at left below). As a rule, promotions are optional, but if a pawn or lance reaches the last rank in the promotion zone or if a knight reaches either of the last two ranks—positions from which, unless promoted, these pieces cannot move—promotion is compulsory. Eligibility for promotion does not carry over to any subsequent moves; once declined, a promotion must be earned again. Promotions are irreversible, but if a promoted piece is captured, it reverts to its original status.

Captures and Drops—Players can capture enemy pieces—but not the enemy king—by moving their own pieces onto squares occupied by the opponent. Pieces that have been captured, now referred to as being "in hand," are removed from the board to an area just off the right-hand corner nearest the player who captured them, in full view of the opponent. Instead of moving a piece on the board, a player with pieces in hand may elect to use a turn by returning one of them to the board. Known in English as "dropping" a piece, such a move is subject to the following restrictions:
1. Pieces can be dropped only onto unoccupied squares.
2. Pawns and lances cannot be dropped onto the last rank in the promotion zone, nor can knights be dropped onto either of the last two ranks. This rule, like the compulsory promotion rule, precludes the possibility of permanently immobilizing any of these pieces.
3. A pawn cannot be dropped onto a file on which an unpromoted friendly pawn is already situated.
4. A player cannot, in a single move, drop a pawn and thereby achieve checkmate.

Draws—There are two circumstances under which a game can end in a draw. The first involves the repetition of moves: if the same position occurs four times in a game, the result is a draw. Here, po-

KING (1)	ROOK (1)	BISHOP (1)	GOLD (2)	SILVER (2)	KNIGHT (2)	LANCE (2)	PAWN (9)
玉将	飛車 / 龍王	角行 / 馬竜	金将	銀将 / 金	桂馬 / 金	香車 / 金	歩兵 / と
K ✳	R ✛ / R ✛	B ✕ / B ✳	G ✛	S ✲ / S ✛	N ⅄ / N ✛	L ↑ / L ✛	P ⌂ / P ✛

Numbers in parentheses indicate how many of each piece a player has at the start of the game.

sition includes not only the placement of the pieces on the board but also the pieces in hand and the side whose turn it is. Repeated checking moves that force the opponent to repeat moves are not allowed; by causing a position to recur four times, the checking player forfeits the game. The second type of draw can result when a game reaches the point where there is no prospect of a checkmate by either side. Then the point values of the pieces on the board and those in hand on each side are added up, with rooks and bishops worth 5 points each and all other pieces except the kings, which are ignored, worth 1 point each. If both players have 24 points or more, the game ends in a draw. A player who ends up with less than 24 points, however, loses.

Castling——Castling means defending one's king by positioning it on one side of the board, usually the side farthest from its own rook, and surrounding it with up to three generals. There are many ways to castle. The choice of which to use in a given game is primarily determined by the opening strategy that has been adopted. Some standard castling configurations are explained below.

Diagram 5: Black, having selected the opening style known as Ranging Rook, has moved her rook to the left and then positioned her king in what is called a High Mino castle, defended by one silver and two gold generals. The key point is the combination of the silver on 3h and the gold on 4i. White, who answered with a Static Rook opening, has secured his king in the castle called *anaguma*, or bear-in-the-hole. Both castles are effective against attacks from the side.

Diagram 5

Diagram 6

Diagram 6: Here both players have selected the same castling setup, known as *yagura*—the tower. This variation works particularly well against frontal attacks. The configuration seen here may be described as a double *yagura*.

Classic Game: Learning from the Masters

The best way to appreciate the effectiveness of various moves and strategies is to consider them in the context of an actual game. To this end many shōgi contests, particularly those between highly regarded players, are recorded by means of a shorthand notation system. In the Western version of this system, which closely resembles chess notation, the piece being moved or dropped is identified by a one-letter symbol (see the list of pieces on the facing page), and its new position is identified by file number and rank letter. If two or more pieces of the same type could be moved to the square thus designated, the relevant piece is identified both by a letter and by its square of origin. A move is indicated by a dash when the square moved to is vacant and by an × when it results in a capture. An asterisk indicates a drop. To show that a piece has been promoted, + is appended to its symbol; = indicates that a promotion has been declined.

What follows is the record of a game played in April 1990, the first of a best-of-seven championship match. Nakahara Makoto, the challenger at the time, plays Black; White is played by Tanigawa Kōji, then shōgi's reigning *meijin*, or champion.

Diagram 7

1	P—2f	P—8d	2	P—2e	P—8e
3	G—7h	G—3b	4	P—2d	P×2d

As a result of this double Static Rook opening, each rook will operate primarily on its own file. Note that Black defended with his gold before exchanging pawns.

5	R×2d	P*2c	6	R—2f	S—7b
7	P—1f	P—1d	8	S—3h	P—9d
9	P—9f	P—3d	10	P—7f	K—4b

It is always important to move the king off its original square. Black's king will take a somewhat more aggressive position.

| 11 | K—5h | P—8f | 12 | P×8f | R×8f |
| 13 | P*8g | R—8d | 14 | P—3f | P*8f |

Black has advanced a pawn to develop his right-hand knight. White initiates another pawn exchange so as to threaten the pawn on 7f.

| 15 | P×8f | R×8f | 16 | P—3e | R—8b |

White threatens to drop a pawn on 8f and then promote it on 8g.

| 17 | N—7g | P—9e | 18 | R—5f | P—6d |
| 19 | P×3d | P×9f | 20 | P*8g | R—9b |

The position on the board at this point is shown in diagram 7.

| 21 | P*9h | R—9e | 22 | R—3f | R—2e |

Black's next move demonstrates the usefulness of the gold as a defensive weapon. He

could drop a pawn on 2f or 2g to prevent a promotion on 2h, but it is important to keep a pawn in hand.

| 23 | G—3i | P*3e | 24 | R—5f | R—2d |
| 25 | P—7e | R×3d | 26 | R—8f | P*8c |

White has captured Black's forward pawn, but he has also been forced to drop a pawn to counter Black's rook.

| 27 | S—6h | K—4a | 28 | P—9g | P×9g+ |
| 29 | L×9g | P*9e | 30 | P—7d | P×7d |

The pawn sacrifice does not pay off for Black. Instead, it paves the way for an unexpected counterattack.

| 31 | P*9c | P—3f | 32 | L×9e | P*9g |
| 33 | B×9g | R—3e | 34 | R—9f | P—7e |

Black will now move his lance off the White rook's rank so as to be able to defend 7f with his own rook.

35	L—9d	P—7f	36	R×7f	R—9e
37	B×6d	P*7c	38	P*7d	R×9d
39	N—6e	S—4b	40	N×5c=	S×5c
41	B×5c+	R—9i+	42	G—7i	L*5b

White's lance has driven the promoted bishop off and now aims at Black's king. But the promoted Black bishop will provide a strong defense.

43	+B—8f	P×7d	44	R×3f	N*7e
45	P*7f	P*3e	46	R—2f	N—7c
47	P×7e	N—6e	48	G—4h	B—7g+
49	S×7g	N×7g+	50	+B×7g	+R×7i
51	+B—6h	+R—8i	52	S*7h	G*5i
53	+B×5i	+R×7h	54	N*5i	S*6h
55	B*6d	S—6c	56	B×9a+	L×5g+
57	G×5g	S*4h	58	G*6i	S×6h=
59	G×6h	S×5i+	60	K×5i	B*7g

Black sacrifices the bishop to draw White's gold away from the defense.

| 61 | G×7g | +R×3h | 62 | P*5h | S*4h |
| 63 | K—6h | N*6e | | | |

Seeing that White cannot yet checkmate him, Black will attempt a checkmate of his own.

			64	L*3d	S×5g=
65	K—7i	N—3c	66	N*5c	K—5b
67	L×3c+	+R—4i	68	K—8h	N×7g+
69	K×7g	+R—7i	70	N*7h	+R—6h
71	K—8f	G×3c	72	B*4a	Resigns

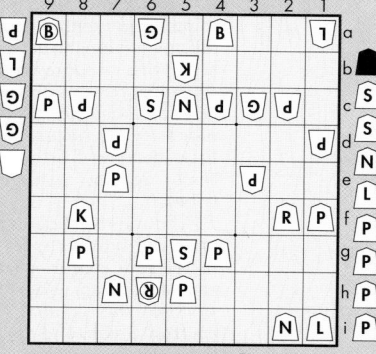

Diagram 8

The position at the end of the game is shown in diagram 8. If White took the knight, Black would have a checkmate with N*4e. If White moved his king, Black would respond with B×6c+, threatening checkmate while defending his own king. Recognizing that his position is hopeless, White resigns.

Shōheikō Lectures at this Edo-period academy for shogunal retainers and Confucian scholars were grounded in the Shushigaku school of Confucian teachings. Late-Edo-period painting.

ple Onjōji (MIIDERA). Since the late 12th century Shōgoin has been a *monzekidera* (i.e., its chief abbot is of the imperial family or aristocracy). Shōgoin's abbot exercised jurisdiction over the temples of the Jimon branch (i.e., the Miidera line) of the Tendai sect (ENRYAKUJI headed the Sammon branch), as well as over the three KUMANO SANZAN SHRINES. In 1613 Shōgoin was designated head temple for the Tendai line of SHUGENDŌ, a Buddhist-Shintō syncretic mountain cult. In 1946 Shōgoin separated from the Tendai sect and became the head temple of the independent religious organization Honzan Shugenshū, which in 1989 claimed about 76,300 followers.

shōgun 将軍

An abbreviation of *seii tai shōgun*, which is customarily translated as "barbarian-subduing generalissimo." Shōguns were in theory military dictators whose regimes dominated the Japanese polity for most of Japanese history between 1192 and 1867 (see WARRIOR GOVERNMENT). Their regimes were known as *bakufu* or "tent governments," a term commonly translated as shogunate. There were three shogunates, the first (1192–1333) situated in Kamakura, the second (1338–1573) in the Muromachi district of Kyōto, and the third (1603–1867) in Edo (now Tōkyō).

During the Nara period (710–794), the imperial government ordered several expeditions against tribal groups known as the EZO, who occupied northeastern Honshū. The most famous of the commanding generals, SAKANOUE NO TAMURAMARO, was designated *seii tai shōgun*, one of several ancient titles bestowed on officials leading expeditions against insurgents or indigenous tribes.

Though the shogunal title fell into disuse once the borders were quiet, it was resurrected four centuries later during the TAIRA-MINAMOTO WAR, when the brilliant warrior MINAMOTO NO YOSHINAKA drove the Taira leaders from Kyōto and appropriated for himself the title *seii tai shōgun*. After Yoshinaka's death and the subsequent triumph of his cousin MINAMOTO NO YORITOMO in the civil wars, the emperor designated Yoritomo as shōgun in 1192, giving him standing authority to undertake military action against anyone challenging his regime. Yoritomo's control over his own domains and vassals was thus legitimized, and he was given the right to appoint supervisory officials (JITŌ and SHUGO) over much of the country, creating

the power base which sustained the KAMAKURA SHOGUNATE (1192–1333).

Yoritomo's sons proved unable to dominate their powerful vassals, the HŌJŌ FAMILY. The Hōjō seized power and, after the Minamoto line died out, selected malleable Kyōto aristocrats to receive the title of shōgun and become the figureheads of the shogunate they now controlled as regents. The Hōjō established the principle that the shogunal title be held only by a man who nominally headed a shogunate, a ruling military regime sanctioned by the emperor.

ASHIKAGA TAKAUJI, a military leader who helped destroy the Hōjō regime, overcame other rivals to establish the MUROMACHI SHOGUNATE (1338–1573) and claim the title of *seii tai shōgun*. For the next 30 years he and his son were constantly at war with rivals. From the 1370s, however, ASHIKAGA YOSHIMITSU and his successors were able to govern by maintaining an alliance with a few powerful regional warlords (SHUGO DAIMYŌ). During the century after the ONIN WAR (1467–77), the shogunal position weakened as regional warriors (SENGOKU DAIMYŌ) gained control of more and more of the country. In 1573 the Ashikaga shogunate ceased to exist, its last shōgun driven from Kyōto by ODA NOBUNAGA, the man who had earlier installed him. Nobunaga and, later, TOYOTOMI HIDEYOSHI never sought the title of shōgun. Both apparently accepted the tradition that the title, if not its power, was reserved for men of Minamoto descent, which neither could claim.

Years of civil war among regional warlords culminated in 1600 with a major battle at SEKIGAHARA. The triumphant TOKUGAWA IEYASU, tracing a tenuous link to Minamoto ancestors, accepted the title of shōgun from the court. During the next century and a half, his descendants, the shōguns of the TOKUGAWA SHOGUNATE (1603–1867), were able to retain power by manipulating regional *daimyō* and their own vassals. However, the elaborate institutional structure, detailed regulations, and balancing mechanisms that held these groups in check also gradually deprived later shōguns of political flexibility, eventually creating a nearly powerless figurehead. The opening of Japan to Western influence during the 19th century culminated in overturning the country's political institutions and forcing the resignation of the last shōgun, TOKUGAWA YOSHINOBU, in 1867 (see MEIJI RESTORATION).

shogunate 幕府

(*bakufu*; literally, "tent government"). Any of the three military governments ruling

Japan during most of the period from 1192 to 1867, as opposed to the civil government under the emperor at Kyōto. The word *bakufu* was originally used to refer to the Headquarters of the Inner Palace Guards (Konoefu), to the residence of their commander, or to the commander himself (*konoe no taishō*). Thus when MINAMOTO NO YORITOMO was appointed commander of the inner palace guards of the right (*ukonoe no taishō*) in 1190, his residence was called the *bakufu*. After he was named SHŌGUN in 1192 the term was applied both to Yoritomo and to the headquarters of his military government. Modern scholars have used the term *bakufu* or shogunate to designate the type of power structure presided over by a shōgun, specifically the KAMAKURA SHOGUNATE (1192–1333), the MUROMACHI SHOGUNATE (1338–1573), and the TOKUGAWA SHOGUNATE (1603–1867).

shogunate missions to the West 幕府遣外使節

(*bakufu kengai shisetsu*). Official missions sent to Western nations by the Tokugawa shogunate shortly before its collapse at the time of the MEIJI RESTORATION of 1868. There were six major missions, dispatched for somewhat different purposes. The missions in 1860, 1862, 1864, and 1866 were sent to negotiate problems connected with the ANSEI COMMERCIAL TREATIES of 1858, while the missions of 1865 and 1867 were primarily charged with obtaining technological knowledge.

Beyond their specific purposes, these missions were significant in that they opened up unexpected perspectives for the delegates and the students who accompanied them; they began to question the wisdom of the traditional social and political order and to look to the West for a new model. Many of them—such as FUKUZAWA YUKICHI, whose SEIYŌ JIJŌ (1867–70, Conditions in the West) was based on his observations as a member of the 1862 mission—went on to play leading roles in the Meiji-period (1868–1912) movement for "civilization and enlightenment." See also IWAKURA MISSION; MEIJI ENLIGHTENMENT.

Shōhaku 肖柏

(1443–1527). Poet of WAKA (classical poetry) and RENGA (linked verse). Also known as Botange (Peony Blossom). He had been initiated by the poet SŌGI into the "secret mysteries" of the TALE OF GENJI and ISE MONOGATARI by 1474 or 1475 and the KOKINSHŪ by 1481. In 1488 Shōhaku participated with Sōgi and SŌCHŌ in composing perhaps the most famous *renga* of 100 links, MINASE SANGIN HYAKUIN (Three Poets at Minase). In 1491 the same three poets composed another poem of 100 links, *Yuyama sangin* (Three Poets at Yuyama). In 1495 Shōhaku collaborated with Sōgi and other poets in compiling the *renga* anthology SHINSEN TSUKUBASHŪ (Tsukuba Collection, Newly Selected). A collection of his poetry is entitled *Shummusō* (1515, Book of a Spring Night's Dream).

shōheiga → screen and wall painting

Shōheikō 昌平黌

An official academy (KANGAKU) of the Tokugawa shogunate during the Edo period (1600–1868). Also called Yushima Seidō or Shōheizaka Gakumonjo. In 1630 HAYASHI RAZAN, under the patronage of the third shōgun, TOKUGAWA IEMITSU, built a school and library in the Ueno district of Edo (now Tōkyō). In 1691 the school was moved to Yu-

shima in the Kanda district of Edo. As a result of the KANSEI REFORMS (1787–93), the school was reorganized and an official shogunal academy (*gakumonsho*) was established alongside it. This was named Shōheizaka Gakumonsho, though it was commonly referred to as Shōheikō. It served as a school for HATAMOTO and GOKENIN (shogunal retainers) and for Confucian scholars. The Zhu Xi (Chu Hsi) school of Confucian teachings (SHUSHIGAKU) was taught as the official doctrine. After the Meiji Restoration of 1868, the school was taken over by the Meiji government but was discontinued in 1870.

Shōhō →Commercial Code

shoin-zukuri   書院造

Style of Japanese residential architecture. *Shoin* means "library" or "study" and was originally the name given to the abbot's quarters at a Zen temple; the style came to be widely used both in temple living quarters and guest halls and in the mansions of the military elite during the Azuchi-Momoyama (1568–1600) and Edo (1600–1868) periods. Developing out of the classic *shinden* style (see SHINDEN-ZUKURI) in the course of the Kamakura (1185–1333) and Muromachi (1333–1568) periods, *shoin-zukuri* still serves as the prototype for today's traditional-style Japanese house.

The earliest extant structure incorporating a room that is clearly in the *shoin* style is the Tōgudō at the temple GINKAKUJI in Kyōto, built by the shōgun ASHIKAGA YOSHIMASA about 1486. The design of mature *shoin-zukuri* structures, such as the Kōjōin Guest Hall (1601) of the temple Onjōji (MIIDERA), incorporates sliding louvered doors (*mairado*) with one latticed paper sliding screen (SHŌJI) behind each pair; floors completely covered with woven rush mats (TATAMI); and subdivision of the rooms into a number of fixed spaces by square posts, walls, and sliding screens (*fusuma*). All of these features were innovations that were not used in *shinden* structures. The main room of the Kōjōin Guest Hall includes four other characteristic *shoin* elements. These are the TOKONOMA (decorative alcove) located on the room's far wall, staggered shelving (*chigaidana*) flanking it, a built-in desk (also called a *shoin*), and decorative doors (*chōdaigamae*) on the wall opposite the veranda. In many *shoin* buildings these four interior elements are located on a *jōdan*, a floor area raised one step above the surrounding space and fronted with a decorative molding (*kamachi*). The *shoin* style reached its peak in the early Edo period, and the most magnificent *shoin* still extant is the Ninomaru Palace of NIJŌ CASTLE in Kyōto, dating from the beginning of the 17th century.

shoji   障子

Sliding screen, used since the Heian period (794–1185) to set off a room from a hallway or another room. The present *fusuma*, a wooden sliding door frame with cloth or paper applied on both sides, was initially called *fusuma shōji*, but now the term *shōji* refers only to screens comprising a wooden frame on one side of which translucent paper (*shōjigami*) is applied. Since *shōji* admit light, they are also used for window fixtures and ornamentation. With the contemporary trend toward Western-style interiors, *shōji* are becoming less common as fittings in modern buildings.

Shōji Kaoru   庄司薫

(1937–). Novelist. Real name Fukuda Shōji. Born in Tōkyō; graduate of Tōkyō University. His short story "Sōshitsu" (1958, Loss) received the Chūō Kōron New Writer's Prize. He abandoned writing until 1969, when *Akazukin-chan ki o tsukete* (Look Out, Little Red Riding Hood!) won the Akutagawa Prize and became a best seller. A first-person narrative of the actions and emotions of an upper-middle-class youth born in the postwar baby boom, this book and its three sequels, known as the "Kaoru-chan series" from the name of their main character, established Shōji as a spokesman for young people in the 1970s.

Shōji, Lake →Fuji Five Lakes

shōjin ryōri   精進料理

Type of vegetarian cooking introduced into Japan together with Buddhism in the 6th century. *Shōjin* is a Buddhist term that refers to asceticism in pursuit of enlightenment, and *ryōri* means "cooking." In the 13th century, with the advent of the Zen sect of Buddhism, the custom of eating *shōjin ryōri* spread. Foods derived from soybeans—including TŌFU—and vegetable oils—including sesame, walnut, and rapeseed—were popularized in Japan as a result of their use in *shōjin ryōri*.

Shōjōkōji → Yugyōji

Shōkadō Shōjō   松花堂昭乗

(1584–1639). Monk, painter, and one of the great calligraphers of his age. Born in Yamato Province (now Nara Prefecture). While a young man, he became a monk at the Hachiman Shrine at Otokoyama, southwest of Kyōto. Upon the death of his master, Takimoto Jitsujō, in 1627, Shōkadō became head of the shrine, which combined Shintō with Shingon Buddhism. He became known as an accomplished WAKA poet and painter and as an expert on the tea ceremony. He was most famous for his calligraphy, being counted as one of the Kan'ei no Sampitsu (Three Brushes of the Kan'ei Era), along with HON'AMI KŌETSU and KONOE NOBUTADA. Shōkadō's brushwork is generally restrained in

comparison with that of Kōetsu, but more elegant than that of Nobutada. His line ranges from thick to thin, and his characters are rounded with occasional angularities.

Shōkai shingo   捷解新語

(Kor: Ch'ŏphaesinŏ). Korean reference work on the Japanese language; first published in 10 volumes in 1676 but completed about 40 years earlier. Its author was Kang U-sŏng (J: Kō Gūsei; b 1581), who as a young boy was captured by the Japanese during the invasion of Korea in 1592 and taken back to Japan. Kang's work reflects the Japanese colloquial language of the late 16th and early 17th centuries. Japanese sentences and phrases are written in the *hiragana* phonetic syllabary with their pronunciation indicated in the Korean alphabet, *han'gul*. Each sentence or phrase is followed by a Korean translation.

Revised editions of this work were in use in Korea until the end of the 19th century. Extant today are the original edition, the 1781 revision, *Jūkan kaishū shōkai shingo* (Kor: Chunggan kaesu ch'ŏphaesinŏ), and a 1796 version, *Shōkai shingo bunshaku* (Ch'ŏphaesinŏ munsŏk). These three versions are valuable materials for linguistic research, for, taken together, they reflect changes in the Japanese and Korean spoken languages during the 16th to 18th centuries.

shōji These sliding screens are a characteristic feature of traditional Japanese architecture, as seen here at the Gepparō pavilion of the Katsura Detached Palace in Kyōto.

shōkan 荘官

(*shōen* managers). General term for functionaries responsible for management, assignment of duties, tax collection, and providing protection for landed estates (SHŌEN). Their specific titles differed according to period, region, and individual estate; some of the most common were *azukari-dokoro* (proprietary deputy), *geshi* or *gesu* (steward), or *kumon* (clerk). There were originally two types: those the estate proprietors dispatched from the capital and those chosen from local notables. From the middle Heian period (794–1185) local proprietors began to commend their lands in name to powerful families or religious institutions in the capital, retaining or receiving some sort of *shōkan* title. With the appointment of military land stewards (JITŌ) by the KAMAKURA SHOGUNATE after 1185, conflict arose between these new officials and the previously appointed *shōkan*. By the 13th century most managerial and proprietary rights to the *shōen* had passed to the *jitō*.

Shōkei 祥啓

(fl mid-15th to early 16th century). Also known as Kenkō Shōkei. ZEN monk and painter. Shōkei developed a distinctive style of landscape and figure painting that established a flourishing regional school of INK PAINTING in the Kantō area and influenced many followers. His official title at the Kenchōji, a Zen Buddhist temple in Kamakura, was that of record keeper (*shoki*), hence his popular name, Kei Shoki. Later accounts relate that Shōkei initially studied painting with the Kenchōji monk-painter Chūan Shinkō (fl mid-15th century).

His surviving works include excellent copies of Chinese paintings of the Southern Song (Sung; 1127–1279) and Yuan (Yüan; 1279–1368) dynasties, which in turn served as model paintings for Shōkei's many followers. Shōkei's landscapes, painted after his first period of study with GEIAMI in Kyōto from 1478 to 1480, strongly reflect the latter's distinctive style, itself evolved from Geiami's study of the work of the Southern Song academy painter Xia Gui (Hsia Kuei; fl ca 1195–1224). Shōkei's late landscapes following his second visit to Kyōto in 1493 reflect the influence of Japanese master-painters of the mid-15th century, especially the

circle of SHŪBUN, the leading monk-painter of Shōkokuji, the Kyōto Zen temple.

Shō Ki 鍾馗

(Ch: Zhong Gui or Chung Kuei). Chinese mythic being who dispels demons. The pictorial subject of "the demon queller" originated in the Chinese legend that the scholar-recluse Zhong Gui cured the ailing Tang (T'ang) emperor Xuan-zong (Hsüan-tsung; r 847–859) by driving away his devils in a dream. Zhong Gui is portrayed wearing a Chinese robe, high boots, and a black scholar's hat. He strikes a threatening pose with bulging eyes, abundant beard, and sword in hand. In Japan Shō Ki first appeared in the 12th-century JIGOKU-ZŌSHI (Scrolls of Hells). He is associated with the Boys' Festival in May (see CHILDREN'S DAY), when his image is displayed to overpower evil and pestilence.

shokkan seido → foodstuff control system

Shokkō Giyūkai 職工義友会

(Workers' Fraternal Society). The first modern Japanese labor organization, formed in April 1897. The group's founders included TAKANO FUSATARŌ and Jō Tsunetarō (1863–1906). In July 1897 it changed its name to Rōdō Kumiai Kiseikai (Society for Formation of Labor Unions) to reflect its commitment to union organizing and soon became active nationwide. The group disbanded in the face of increasing government pressure in 1901.

Shokkō jijō 職工事情

(Conditions of Factory Workers). Five-volume report on labor conditions in the textile, iron, cement, glass, match, tobacco, and other industries published by the Ministry of Agriculture and Commerce in 1903. The investigative project was undertaken as preparation for legislation that eventually emerged as the FACTORY LAW OF 1911. The report contains information on housing, health care, welfare facilities, work hours, wages, and general morale within each industry. Like YOKOYAMA GENNOSUKE's *Nihon no kasō shakai* (1899, Japan's Lower Classes), it is considered a classic study in the history of labor relations.

Shōkō Chūkin Bank 商工組合中央金庫

(Shōkō Kumiai Chūō Kinko). Government-affiliated financial institution; one of the world's largest financial institutions serving small businesses. Incorporated in 1936. It has 96 branches throughout Japan, a branch in New York, and a representative office in London. As of March 1991 total assets stood at ¥14.5 trillion (US $105.7 billion). In the same year the bank was capitalized at ¥267.5 billion (US $1.9 billion), of which the government's investment totaled ¥196.1 billion (US $1.4 billion). Headquarters are in Tōkyō.

Shōkōkan 彰考館

Office where the DAI NIHON SHI (History of Great Japan) was compiled. Begun in 1657 by TOKUGAWA MITSUKUNI, *daimyō* of the Mito domain (now part of Ibaraki Prefecture), at his mansion in the Komagome district of Edo (now Tōkyō), the massive history project continued until 1906. The office was named Shōkōkan in 1672, when it was moved to Mitsukuni's mansion in the Koishikawa district of Edo. It was later moved permanently to the city of Mito and in 1907 was con-

verted into a library that houses many historically and culturally valuable works. Although the building was partially burned during World War II, the library continues to serve a large community of scholars.

Shōkokuji 相国寺

Head temple of the Shōkokuji branch of the RINZAI SECT of Zen Buddhism, located in Kami-Gyō Ward, Kyōto. Shōkokuji was founded in 1383 under the sponsorship of shōgun ASHIKAGA YOSHIMITSU. It is said that Yoshimitsu and Zen monk GIDŌ SHŪSHIN participated in the temple's construction, which was regarded as a national enterprise. Appointed first abbot, Shun'oku Myōha (1311–88) insisted that his late master MUSŌ SOSEKI be designated honorary first abbot. In 1386 Shōkokuji was designated second in rank among the GOZAN Zen temples in Kyōto. Between 1394 and 1788 Shōkokuji suffered extensive damage from six major fires; the temple was restored each time. Shōkokuji now consists of 15 subtemples (*tatchū*). Its main hall (*hondō*), rebuilt by the warrior general TOYOTOMI HIDEYORI in 1605, is of great architectural significance, representing the *karayō* or Chinese style of building used in Japanese Zen temples from the 12th century onward.

shokudō 食堂

General term for eating place or dining hall. Popular, inexpensive restaurants for serving the kinds of noodles called *soba* and *udon* (called *sobaya* in the Kantō region and *udon'ya* in the Kansai region) were first established in the late 17th century. Shops, chiefly teahouses (*chamise*) serving light meals, were built along the highways in the Edo period (1600–1868). From the Meiji period (1868–1912) these became luncheonettes (*ichizen meshiya*). In the Taishō (1912–26) and Shōwa (1926–89) periods, inexpensive *shokudō* for the common people increased dramatically, including quick-lunch rooms and dining rooms in department stores. Unlike other more expensive restaurants, *shokudō* display realistic wax or plastic models of the food on their menus in their front windows. Some *shokudō* will deliver food and drinks, a service called *demae*.

Shokugenshō 職原抄

(Origins of Office). A two-volume book on government offices compiled by KITABATAKE CHIKAFUSA for the Southern Court's child emperor Go-Murakami (r 1339–68) during the dynastic schism between the NORTHERN AND SOUTHERN COURTS (1337–92). It traces the development of government offices, both statutory and extrastatutory, since the establishment of the RITSURYŌ SYSTEM of government in the 7th century and explains their functions.

Shokuhō seiken 織豊政権

(Shokuhō regime). The regime of national unification founded by ODA NOBUNAGA (1534–82) and developed by his successor TOYOTOMI HIDEYOSHI (1537–98) during the Azuchi-Momoyama period (1568–1600). Shokuhō is an acronym formed from alternate pronunciations of the initial characters of the names Oda and Toyotomi. The regime marked the transition from the medieval period to the early modern age. See AZUCHI-MOMOYAMA PERIOD.

shokunin 職人

(artisans). General term for makers of traditional handicrafts. Around the 8th century the construction, metalwork, and weaving needs of the state were handled by offices called *shiki*. From the 9th to the 12th century, throughout the country, groups of skilled workmen were attached to estates (SHŌEN) under the control of court nobles and powerful temples. The Edo period (1600–1868) was the golden age of handcraft production. Following the Meiji Restoration in 1868, mechanized factory production became widespread, with the result that many handcraftsmen became factory laborers.

In the past, master craftsmen were organized into a type of guild. The usual procedure was to become apprenticed to a master at age 12 or 13, learn the skill until about age 20, and spend a year working for, or sometimes with, one's master in gratitude and as repayment (called *orei bōkō*) before becoming an independent, full-fledged *shokunin* (see also APPRENTICE SYSTEM). Today there are virtually no guilds, and competition is open. The Japanese government has begun to designate and protect both traditional handicrafts and those who possess traditional technical skills, but the lack of young people who might succeed these *shokunin* threatens the survival of traditional crafts. See also LIVING NATIONAL TREASURES.

Shokuryō Mēdē   食糧メーデー

(Food May Day). Popular name for Shokuryō Kiki Toppa Jimmin Taikai (People's Meeting to Overcome the Food Crisis). Also known as Kome Yokose Mēdē ("Give Us Rice" May Day). A demonstration in front of the Imperial Palace in Tōkyō on 19 May 1946; 300,000 people demonstrated against the food shortages that had plagued Japan since the end of World War II. Occurring in the midst of a serious political crisis, it was considered by OCCUPATION authorities to be a threat to the democratic government and to law and order. The following day General Douglas MACARTHUR issued a warning against future demonstrations.

When communist demonstrators carried a placard reading "I, the Emperor, have eaten my fill; but you subjects can starve to death," one person was arrested and charged with LESE MAJESTY (*fukeizai*); however, Occupation authorities declared that the emperor was not entitled to special protection, and the charge was changed to simple libel. The person arrested was sentenced to prison for eight months but was pardoned and released three days later.

Shokusanjin → Ōta Nampo

Shokusan Jūtaku Sōgo Co, Ltd
殖産住宅相互[株]

(Shokusan Jūtaku Sōgo). Construction company specializing in building houses, stores, and apartment houses. Incorporated in 1950. It has grown rapidly, owing in large part to its method of taking payment for its construction work in monthly installments. Sales for the fiscal year ending March 1991 totaled ¥206.3 billion (US $1.5 billion), of which construction accounted for 63 percent; real estate, 22 percent; sales of goods, 14 percent; and other sources, 1 percent. Capitalization stood at ¥7.2 billion (US $52.5 million) in the same year. Headquarters are in Tōkyō.

shokusan kōgyō   殖産興業

("Increase Production and Promote Industry"). Government policy of the early Meiji period (1868–1912) intended to encourage industries to realize the ideal of a "rich country and strong military" (FUKOKU KYŌHEI). The Ministry of Public Works (Kōbushō) was established in 1870, and the Home Ministry (Naimushō) in 1873, to organize industrialization. The two ministries were responsible for introducing modern technology from abroad, constructing railways, and supervising government enterprises. They also founded model factories for cotton-spinning and silk-reeling (see GOVERNMENT-OPERATED FACTORIES, MEIJI PERIOD) and emphasized the modernization of marine transport, agriculture, and other areas. The policy produced positive results, but many government-operated enterprises encountered financial difficulties, and the government sold them off to private entrepreneurs (see KAN'EI JIGYŌ HARAISAGE).

Shōmei Incident   鐘銘事件

(Shōmei Jiken; "Incident of the Bell Inscription"). The immediate cause of the outbreak of hostilities between TOKUGAWA IEYASU and TOYOTOMI HIDEYORI. In 1614 Hideyori finished rebuilding the Hōkōji, a temple in Kyōto. The bell for the rededication (still on view in Kyōto) contained an inscription in which the two characters composing the name Ieyasu were split by a third. When some advisers interpreted this as an imprecation to overthrow the Tokugawa, Ieyasu seized this excuse to demand Hideyori's submission. His demand rejected, Ieyasu mounted the campaign that destroyed the Toyotomi (see ŌSAKA CASTLE, SIEGES OF).

Shōmonki   将門記

(Record of Masakado). Also known as *Masakadoki*. Considered the prototype of GUNKI MONOGATARI, or war tales. It was written by an unknown author after TAIRA NO MASAKADO's death in the mid-10th century. Written in the heavily Japanized form of Chinese known as HENTAI KAMBUN, the tale follows the life of Masakado through the Jōhei and Tengyō rebellions. The only extant manuscripts are the version dated 1099, found in the temple Shimpukuji in Nagoya, and that in the Katakura Takeo collection in Tōkyō (formerly in the Yang Shoujing [Yang Shou-ching] library).

shōmono   抄物

General term for Muromachi-period (1333–1568) commentaries on the classic texts of Buddhism, Confucianism, Chinese medicine, earlier Japanese literature, and so forth, by masters in these various fields. These commentaries typically consist of notes made by the masters themselves or of notes taken down by their disciples from lectures. While some *shōmono* are written in classical Chinese, most are in an easily understandable form of the colloquial Japanese of the period. They include not only interpretations of the wording of the classical Chinese (KAMBUN) or classical Japanese of the texts but also explanations of the thoughts they embody. The term *shōmono* is also used to refer to similar materials of the early Edo period (1600–1868); however, *shōmono* are usually distinguished from the GOROKU (recorded oral teachings of Zen masters) of the Kamakura period (1185–1333) and the commentaries of Edo-period Confucian scholars. The *shōmono* that are written in Japanese contain many examples of contemporary colloquial expressions and are thus valuable materials for the study of the Japanese language of the Muromachi period.

Shōmu, Emperor   聖武天皇

(701–756; Shōmu Tennō). The 45th sovereign (*tennō*) in the traditional count (which includes several legendary emperors); reigned 724–749. He was the eldest son of Emperor MOMMU. His mother, Kyūshi, was a daughter of FUJIWARA NO FUHITO, and his consort, Empress KŌMYŌ, was also a daughter of Fuhito. During Shōmu's reign, the government was dominated first by the imperial prince Nagaya no Ō (684–729), later by the FUJIWARA FAMILY, and finally by a clique comprising TACHIBANA NO MOROE, KIBI NO MAKIBI, and the priest GEMBŌ. Political strife was a constant problem (see NAGAYA NO Ō, REBELLION OF; FUJIWARA NO HIROTSUGU, REBELLION OF). During the period 741–745 the capital was moved from HEIJŌKYŌ (Nara) to three other locations (KUNI NO MIYA, NANIWA-KYŌ, and SHIGARAKI NO MIYA) only to return to Nara in 745.

In 741 Shōmu ordered the establishment of state-maintained temples (KOKUBUNJI) in each province. With the priests RŌBEN and GYŌGI, he sponsored the building of the temple TŌDAIJI and the casting of its image of the Buddha (see DAIBUTSU). Shōmu's reign was marked by a flourishing of the arts under strong Chinese influence; the Tempyō era (729–749) is known as one of the most brilliant in the history of Japanese culture (see TEMPYŌ CULTURE). In 749 Shōmu abdicated in favor of his daughter Empress KŌKEN and took holy orders.

shōmyō   声明

(Buddhist liturgical chant). Choral chanting of prayers and texts extolling the virtues of the Buddha; performed by priests as a part of religious ceremonies and services (see MUSIC, RELIGIOUS). *Shōmyō* is said to have reached Japan in the mid-6th century with the introduction of Buddhism. Written records indicate that *shōmyō* was performed at the dedication ceremony for the Great Buddha image at the temple TŌDAIJI in 752. During the Heian period (794–1185) monks such as ENNIN and KŪKAI traveled to China, where they learned differing forms of *shōmyō* that were passed down through generations of their followers. Over time these settled into two distinct styles, named for two of the major Buddhist sects: Tendai *shōmyō* and Shingon *shōmyō*.

Shōmyō is still practiced in contemporary Japan. The chanters are priests and the music remains a component of Buddhist ceremonial, linked to specific ritual forms and procedures. It may be performed while

Shōsōin This 8th-century repository at the temple Tōdaiji incorporates the architectural style known as *azekura* (log house); the structure utilizes no vertical supporting pillars, relying instead on the overlapped triangular wall logs for roof support.

seated, standing, or walking; the melody is usually chanted in unison but may also be chanted alternately by a head priest and a chorus. Percussion instruments such as gongs (*nyō*) or cymbals (*hachi*) may accompany the chants, but melodic instruments are rarely used. *Shōmyō* has had a major impact on the development of many forms of traditional Japanese music. It has also begun to attract increasing attention on purely aesthetic grounds, and concerts combining *shōmyō* with *bugaku* (court dances) and even with modern dance performances have been staged in recent years.

Shōnai Plain 庄内平野

(Shōnai Heiya). Located in northwestern Yamagata Prefecture, northern Honshū. Consists of the floodplains of the lower part of the river Mogamigawa and other rivers, as well as deltas. Bordering the Sea of Japan, its coastline is characterized by high sand dunes. High-quality rice is produced. The plain's major cities are Sakata and Tsuruoka. Length: 50 km (30 mi); width: 5–15 km (3–9 mi).

Shōnan 湘南

Coastal area of Sagami Bay in southern Kanagawa Prefecture, central Honshū. Because of its warm climate and beautiful scenery, the area has been popular for sightseeing and as a health resort since the Meiji period (1868–1912). The city of KAMAKURA and the island of ENOSHIMA are the two main tourist attractions. It is increasingly becoming a residential and industrial area.

Shōnen 少年

(Boy). A 1969 film directed by ŌSHIMA NAGISA. Written by Tamura Tsutomu (b 1933). A mother and father use their 10-year-old son to stage fake traffic accidents in order to collect accident insurance or extort money from drivers. This nuclear family, a metaphor for the Japanese nation, survives only through deceit, violence, and repression. They make their living illicitly as they travel the length of the Japanese archipelago to the northern shores of Hokkaidō. The boy, who prefers his own fantasies to his parents' world, sees that his only way out will be rescue by creatures from outer space. The estranged visual style of *Boy* is dominated by unbalanced compositions that make full use of the edges of the wide screen and by a seemingly random mixture of monochrome and color photography.

Shōnen kurabu The cover of the first issue of *Boys' Club*, a popular boys' magazine published from 1914 to 1962.

Shōnen kurabu 少年倶楽部

(Boys' Club). One of the most popular boys' magazines in Japan in the first half of the 20th century. Published by KŌDANSHA, LTD, beginning in November 1914, the magazine completely changed the image of boys' magazines that had developed during the Meiji period (1868–1912) with its easy-to-read, interesting style and polished illustra-

tions. Outstanding features of the magazine included the cartoon about a dog named "Norakuro" (Blackie) in the early years of the Shōwa period (1926–89) and novels such as YOSHIKAWA EIJI's *Shinshū temma kyō* (Seven Riders for Justice), SATŌ KŌROKU's *Aa gyokuhai ni hana ukete* (Ah! A Blossom in My Cup), and EDOGAWA RAMPO's *Kaijin nijūmensō* (The Man of 20 Faces). Circulation reached 750,000 in 1936. *Shōnen kurabu* was discontinued in December 1962.

Shōni family 少弐氏

(Shōnishi). Warrior family in northern Kyūshū from the 12th to the mid-16th centuries; they claimed descent from FUJIWARA NO HIDESATO. The family founder, Mutō Sukeyori (fl 1189–after 1227), was appointed by MINAMOTO NO YORITOMO as junior-assistant governor (*shōni*) of DAZAIFU, the government headquarters in Kyūshū. The position was hereditary, and his descendants adopted the title as their name. Shōni Sadatsune (1272–1336) and Shōni Yorihisa (1293–1371) allied themselves with ASHIKAGA TAKAUJI in the 1330s, and subsequently the Shōni fought supporters of the Southern Court (see NORTHERN AND SOUTHERN COURTS), notably the KIKUCHI FAMILY. During the 14th and 15th centuries the Shōni, deeply involved in military rivalries in Kyūshū, gradually lost lands and power to neighboring *daimyō*, especially the ŌUCHI FAMILY. In 1559 the Shōni were destroyed by their vassals the RYŪZŌJI FAMILY.

shōnin 上人

A title of respect given Buddhist monks for their wisdom, virtue, or good works. Its first known usage is in the appellation Ichi no Shōnin (Saint of the Marketplace) for the 10th-century monk KŪYA. The term *shōnin* originally designated monks devoted to seclusion or itinerant HIJIRI (ascetics with charismatic powers) proselytizers, but later it came to be applied more honorifically, especially in the Pure Land and Nichiren Buddhist traditions. It was institutionalized as one of the honorary titles conferred upon Buddhist monks by the imperial court.

Shōno Junzō 庄野潤三

(1921–). Novelist. Born in Ōsaka; graduate of Kyūshū University. In 1954 he won the Akutagawa Prize for his short story "Pūrusaido shōkei," (tr "Near the Swimming Pool, 1958), which describes the psychological crisis of a middle-class housewife whose life is unexpectedly disrupted when her husband is fired from his job. Many of his subsequent novels in traditional autobiographical style deal with similar domestic situations. His novel *Yūbe no kumo* (1964–65) won the Yomiuri Literary Prize, and *E-awase* received the Noma Prize in 1971. Other works include *Seibutsu* (1960) and *Ukitōdai* (1961).

Shōriki Matsutarō 正力松太郎

(1885–1969). Businessman and politician. Born in Toyama Prefecture, he was a graduate of Tōkyō University. Shōriki began a career in the Tōkyō Metropolitan Police Department but resigned in 1924 after taking responsibility for the TORANOMON INCIDENT. He then became president of YOMIURI SHIMBUN, developing it into Japan's most widely circulated newspaper. He inaugurated professional baseball in Japan in 1934 (see BASEBALL, PROFESSIONAL). After World War II, Shōriki was purged by Occupation authorities, but the purge was lifted in 1951, and in 1952 he founded the NIPPON TELEVISION NET-

WORK CORPORATION (NTV), becoming its president. He also served as director of the Science and Technology Agency and chairman of the Atomic Energy Commission.

Shōrui Awaremi no Rei 生類憐みの令

(Edicts on Compassion for Living Things). A series of edicts issued by the shōgun TOKUGAWA TSUNAYOSHI (1646–1709) prohibiting cruelty to animals. The first, issued in 1685, prohibited hawking, strictly limited hunting to authorized persons, and forbade the processing of certain horsehide products. From 1687 onward the edicts became more and more extreme. The trapping and killing of all birds and animals were forbidden, and a government post, commissioner for living things (*shōrui bugyō*), was established to enforce the edicts. In 1695 Tsunayoshi had large kennels erected in Nakano, Yotsuya, and Ōkubo in Edo (now Tōkyō), which were supported by levies imposed on the Edo populace, who dubbed Tsunayoshi "the dog *shōgun*" (*inu kubō*). It is said that by the end of its first year of operation the kennel in Nakano housed some 100,000 dogs.

The accepted explanation for these edicts is that Tsunayoshi took the death of his son and his inability to sire another as evidence that he was not governing properly. A Buddhist monk explained the problem to Tsunayoshi, in Buddhist terms, as a consequence of Tsunayoshi's having taken the lives of many sentient beings in a prior incarnation. He was advised that he might nullify his bad karma by showing compassion for living things, in particular for dogs, because Tsunayoshi had been born in the year of the dog (see JIKKAN JŪNISHI). His nephew and successor, TOKUGAWA IENOBU, rescinded the edicts soon after taking office in 1709.

Shōsenkyō 昇仙峡

Gorge on the river Arakawa, north central Yamanashi Prefecture, central Honshū. Consisting of towering granite cliffs and numerous strangely shaped rocks, it is located within Chichibu-Tama National Park. Length: 4 km (2.5 mi).

Shōsetsu gendai 小説現代

(Contemporary Stories). Monthly popular fiction magazine. Published since February 1963 by KŌDANSHA, LTD. With its emphasis on CHŪKAN SHŌSETSU ("middlebrow fiction"), which strove to bridge the gap between "pure" and "popular" literature, *Shōsetsu gendai* appealed to a new class of readers when it first appeared. Fiction by former television scriptwriters NOSAKA AKIYUKI and INOUE HISASHI, as well as a series of period novels by SASAZAWA SAHO, were indicative of this innovative editorial policy.

Shōsetsu shinchō 小説新潮

Monthly literary magazine, published since September 1947 by SHINCHŌSHA, LTD. One of the new popular-literature magazines of the post–World War II period, *Shōsetsu shinchō* made a significant contribution to the development of the genre known as CHŪKAN SHŌSETSU ("middlebrow fiction"). The magazine's contributors have included such writers as FUNAHASHI SEIICHI, ISHIZAKA YŌJIRŌ, OZAKI SHIRŌ, SAKAGUCHI ANGO, UCHIDA HYAKKEN, GENJI KEITA, and INOUE HISASHI.

Shōshikai 尚歯会

Study group formed around 1836 by scholars and intellectuals interested in Western knowledge and its practical application to Japan. Also known as Bansha, an abbreviation of Bangaku Shachū, or "Companions of Barbarian Studies." Its members included noted scholars of Rangaku (Dutch Learning, the study of Western science and culture through Dutch; see WESTERN LEARNING) such as WATANABE KAZAN, TAKANO CHŌEI, and KOSEKI SAN'EI. The group became the target of a governmental crackdown on progressive intellectuals that culminated in the BANSHA NO GOKU incident in 1839. (See also MORRISON INCIDENT.) The term *shōshikai* (literally, "honor-the-aged society") is otherwise a generic term used for informal groups that elderly people organized to share mutual interests.

Shōshō Hakkei
瀟湘八景

(Eight Views of the Xiao and Xiang [Hsiao and Hsiang] Rivers). Painting subject. The term refers to paintings evocative of the humid lake and river scenery near Lake Dongting (Tung-t'ing) in China. Originating with the painter Song Di (Sung Ti; ca 1015–80), by the 13th century the "Eight Views" became a standard theme in Chinese painting. The original eight titles were: *Geese Descending on Sandbanks, Returning Sails from a Distant Shore, Mountain Village in Clearing Rain, Evening Snow over the River, Autumn Moon over Lake Dongting, Night Rain over Xiao and Xiang, Evening Bell from a Misty Temple,* and *Sunset Glow over a Fishing Village.* The Ashikaga shōguns from ASHIKAGA YOSHIMITSU (1358–1408) onward acquired some remarkable examples of this genre that provided the core models for works in a similar mode by Japanese painters from the 15th to the 17th century. "Eight Views" paintings on folding screens and sliding doors, often bearing theme poems in Chinese by leading GOZAN monks, flourished in the school of INK PAINTING started by SHŪBUN. While mid-15th century works appear to have been modeled mainly on Southern Song (Sung) Dynasty (1127–1279) academic styles, the abbreviated style of Yujian (Yü-chien) gained favor in the SOGA SCHOOL and with the followers of SESSHŪ TŌYŌ. In the hands of SŌAMI a landscape style in the manner of Muqi (Mu-ch'i; J: MOKKEI) was perfected; it exerted a profound influence on the KANŌ SCHOOL.

shōshū reijō
召集令状

Draft notification slips first issued at the time of the IMO MUTINY in 1882; the last one was issued at the end of World War II. *Shōshū reijō* were issued by the commanders of the regimental districts into which Japan was divided. Printed on red paper, these notifications were commonly called *akagami* (red papers).

Shōsōin
正倉院

The wooden storehouse at the temple TŌDAIJI in Nara. It originally housed several thousand precious ornamental and fine art objects from the 8th century. In the 8th century the term *shōsō* described the imperial warehouses where rice and other items collected as tax were stored, and the term *in* referred to a fenced enclosure. The Shōsōin, now under the jurisdiction of the Imperial Household Agency, is a raised rectangular building made of Japanese cypress (*hinoki*); it is divided into 3 sections and sits above the ground on 40 thick piles, each 2.4 meters (7.9 ft) in height. The north and south sections were built in the *azekura* style with triangular cross-section logs stacked horizontally, giving a smooth surface to the interior and a corrugated effect to the facade. The middle section joins the north and

south sections with thick planks layered horizontally, and the whole building is covered by a *yosemune* hipped tile roof. All 3 sections were in place by 761.

Treasures of the Shōsōin—The treasures of the Shōsōin are from two main sources: the core collection donated by the empress KŌMYŌ to Tōdaiji following the death of her husband, the emperor SHŌMU, in 756; and the articles transferred to the Shōsōin from the storehouse of the Kensakuin, a subtemple of Tōdaiji, in the mid-Heian period (794–1185). Many of the articles donated by the empress were lost, and the treasures from the Kensakuin make up the bulk of the collection. The Shōsōin treasures include calligraphy samples, official documents, stationery, furniture and utensils, ornaments, Buddhist altar fittings, musical instruments, dance costumes, weapons and armor, objects used in annual observances, and perfumes and medicines. Art and handicraft works represented in the collection range from paintings and sculpture to lacquer ware, ceramics, glassware, and textiles. Although the majority of the treasures were made in Japan, many reflect foreign sources in their design motifs, materials, and production methods. Tang (T'ang) China is the most direct influence; but works in the collection bear traces of cultures as distant as India, Sassanid Persia, and Greece.

Preservation of the Treasures—In general the treasures in the Shōsōin have been remarkably well preserved. One important reason for this is that the repository was built off the ground on pillars. The treasures were also placed in wooden chests, which helped ward off damage from humidity. Imperial permission had to be obtained to open the doors of the repository, and the treasures were not allowed to be handled without sufficient reason. During the Edo period (1600–1868), when the treasures began showing signs of decay, repairs were initiated. Since 1883 the repository house has been opened for airing once a year in the fall. In 1963 the treasures were transferred to two new ferroconcrete buildings, one completed in 1953 and one in 1962. A check of the items is conducted every fall, and an exhibition of selected treasures is held, principally at the NARA NATIONAL MUSEUM for two weeks during this period.
☎ *1412–1413*

shotai
書体

(script style; specifically, the style in which Chinese characters or KANJI are written). The three basic styles of Chinese calligraphy, in use in China and Japan since ancient times, are known in Japanese as *santai* (the three styles). They are, in the Japanese pronunciations of their Chinese names: *kaisho,* the standard angular, noncursive style; *gyōsho,*

the semicursive style; and *sōsho,* the fluid cursive or "grass" style. *Kaisho* developed during the Later Han dynasty (AD 25–220) out of earlier styles, and *gyōsho* and *sōsho* had both developed on the basis of *kaisho* by the 5th and 6th centuries. A larger classification known as *gotai* (the five styles) consists of the above three plus two archaic styles: the *tensho* or seal script, dating from the Qin (Ch'in) dynasty (221 BC–206 BC); and the *reisho* or clerical script, dating from the Former Han dynasty (206 BC–AD 8).

Kaisho is the style of character in widest use today. *Gyōsho* and *sōsho* are used for informal occasions or for calligraphy. *Tensho* and *reisho* are used decoratively, but many of their forms are not readily recognizable to the public. The most common styles of characters used in printing in Japan, all *kaisho,* are based on the printed styles of various Chinese dynasties. The *sōchōtai* 宋朝体 (Song or Sung dynasty [960–1279] style) and *seichōtai* 清朝体 (Qin dynasty style) are used for formal invitations and calling cards, while the *minchōtai* 明朝体 (Ming dynasty [1368–1644] style) is the style used in most books, newspapers, and magazines. There is also a so-called *kyōkashotai* 教科書体 or textbook style.

Shōtetsu
正徹

(1381–1459). Classical (WAKA) poet and critic; Buddhist priest. Shōtetsu stands out in his time as one of the two foremost opponents of the dominant conservative Nijō poetic school. At about the age of 16 Shōtetsu became an acolyte at Kōfukuji, a temple in Nara, and around 1417 became a secretary at Tōfukuji, a temple in Kyōto.

In his poetics Shōtetsu was somewhat at variance even with the Reizei school of poetry. He called for a return to the ideals and practice of Fujiwara no Teika (FUJIWARA NO SADAIE), whom he idolized, writing in his important poetic record known as *Shōtetsu monogatari* (ca 1450, Tales of Shōtetsu) that anyone who presumed to criticize Teika should be punished in the life to come. In addition to *Shōtetsu monogatari,* Shōtetsu left a collection of his own poems, *Sōkonshū* (1473, Collection of the Roots of Plants), containing more than 11,000 poems. His distinctive style is both convoluted and elliptical and makes him one of the most difficult of the classical poets.

Shōtoku Nagasaki Shinrei
正徳長崎新令

Also called Shōtoku Shinrei; officially the Kaihaku Goshi Shinrei (New Regulations on

Continued on page 1414➤

Basic Character Styles

Script					Print			
kaisho (noncursive style)	gyōsho (semicursive style)	sōsho (cursive style)	tensho (seal script style)	reisho (clerical script style)	sōchōtai (Song dynasty style)	seichōtai (Qin dynasty style)	minchōtai (Ming dynasty style)	kyōkashotai (textbook style)

Read from top to bottom, these Chinese characters form the phrase *onko chishin* (to learn from the past; literally, "respect the old, know the new") from *The Analects* (Ch: *Lun yu*), a collection of sayings by Confucius and his disciples.

Treasure House of Ancient Japan

The **Shōsōin** is built of Japanese cypress and rests on 40 thick pillars, each 2.4 meters high. Interlocking triangular logs were used to construct two of the building's three sections.

Gigaku mask. This paulownia-wood mask was used in *gigaku*, a kind of dance drama. The character it represents was known as Konron, the Japanese name for the seafaring Malay people of Champa, now southern Vietnam. Height 39 cm.

The Shōsōin stands in a pinewood glade behind the temple Tōdaiji in Nara. From the mid-8th century until 1963, when the last of its contents were moved to modern facilities, the huge log structure was the repository of treasures submitted to the temple. The nucleus of the collection was composed of some 110 items offered to the Buddha Vairocana at Tōdaiji in the middle of the 8th century by Empress Kōmyō following the death of her husband, Emperor Shōmu. The vast majority of the treasures, however, were probably moved to the Shōsōin in the middle of the Heian period (794–1185) from the storehouse of a Tōdaiji subtemple.

Most of the 8,000 objects in the collection were fashioned in Japan during the 8th century, but few display what today are considered distinctive aspects of the Japanese aesthetic. Many of the treasures feature motifs and techniques that found their way to Japan from Central Asia via the Silk Road, while the touch of exoticism that distinguishes the collection as a whole derives from the expertise of immigrant Chinese and Korean artisans who took up residence in Nara or who were dispatched to the provinces. In this way the treasures of the Shōsōin document the spread of cultural influences from West to East.

Each of the 19 artifacts shown on these pages was selected for some quality that evokes a distant culture along the Silk Road. The backdrop is provided by the *Kokka chimpō chō* (Record of Treasures of the Nation), a partial list of the offerings bestowed on Tōdaiji by Empress Kōmyō, which was compiled in 756.

Ink painting of a bodhisattva. This bodhisattva, seated on a cloud, is rendered in the Tang Chinese style, typified by bold, fluid lines and the figure's rounded features and narrow waist. Ink on hemp cloth. 138 × 133 cm.

Folding screen. Two of six panels, each employing the Persian motif of a beautiful woman posed under a tree. The women pictured here are dressed in the Tang style. 136 × 56 cm each.

Red-sandalwood five-stringed biwa. The unusual five-stringed variety of the lute-like *biwa* originated in India. This one has an inlaid mother-of-pearl soundboard depicting a musician astride a camel. Length 108 cm.

Cushion slip. Silk twill with a symmetrical pattern of trees and leashed lions, a motif that originated in the ancient Near East and spread throughout Asia. 99 × 53 cm.

Red-sandalwood go board. Fashioned as a low table (height 13 cm), this board has side panels decorated with various inlaid ivory motifs that originated on the Silk Road. Top 49 × 49 cm.

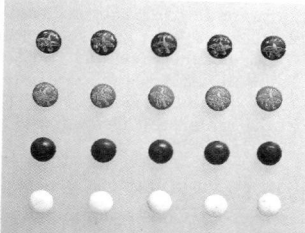

Two sets of go stones. The figure of a bird is carved on each of the black- and red-dyed ivory pieces shown above. The white stones below are quartz; the black stones, serpentine.

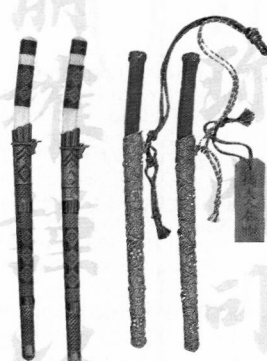

Two sets of knives. The birchwood scabbards (length 15 cm) at left are mounted with insect wings of iridescent silver. The knives at right, presented to the temple by Lady Tachibana, have handles made of rhinoceros horn.

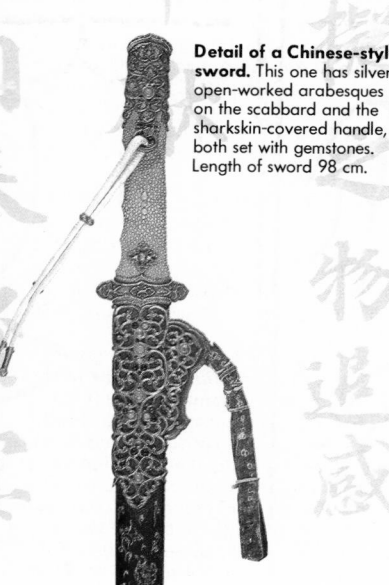

Detail of a Chinese-style sword. This one has silver, open-worked arabesques on the scabbard and the sharkskin-covered handle, both set with gemstones. Length of sword 98 cm.

Maple wood four-stringed biwa. The leather plectrum guard is decorated with a painting of four musicians performing on the back of a white elephant. Length 97 cm.

Cloisonné back of a silver mirror. The interstices at the outer edge of the stylized flower pattern are filled with gold. Diameter 19 cm.

Cut-glass bowl. This bowl is made of an alkaline lime glass. Similar bowls have been excavated in Iran and from the tomb of the early-6th-century Japanese emperor Ankan. Diameter 12 cm; height 9 cm.

Bowl with three-color glaze. Contrasting light and dark glazes were used on this bowl in imitation of the three-color ceramics of Tang China. The predominance of green, however, is typically Japanese. Diameter 27 cm; height 16 cm.

Silver censer. This item was placed under robes in order to scent them with incense. The decorative motif of fantastic lions developed along the Silk Road. Diameter 18 cm; height 19 cm.

Aromatic aloewood. Used for incense, it was brought to Japan from India. Pieces cut from this block were presented to the 15th-century shōgun Ashikaga Yoshimasa, the 16th-century hegemon Oda Nobunaga, and Emperor Meiji. Weight 11.6 kg.

Ewer. Its shape derives from a Persian model. The lacquered surface is decorated with silver-foil appliqués depicting animals and flowers. Height 41 cm.

Storage cabinet. Used to hold religious objects. Black persimmon wood from Southeast Asia. Height 52 cm.

Prince Shōtoku Of the many representations of the great Asuka-period statesman, this painting from the early Nara period (710–794) is the oldest known; it is also acknowledged as the earliest surviving example of Japanese portraiture.

Ships and Trade). Regulations issued by the Tokugawa shogunate (1603–1867) in 1715 to limit trade with China and the Netherlands, the only countries allowed to trade with Japan under the NATIONAL SECLUSION policy (see NAGASAKI TRADE). They were drafted by ARAI HAKUSEKI to curtail outflow of gold and silver, to restrict export of copper (then Japan's largest export item), and to reduce smuggling by issuing certificates called *shimpai*. The regulations specified the number of ships (2 for the Dutch and 30 for the Chinese) and limited the value of trade to 3,000 *kan* or 11.3 metric tons of silver for the Dutch and 6,000 *kan* or 22.5 metric tons for the Chinese annually. These regulations remained in effect until the 1830s.

Shōtoku no Chi　　　正徳の治

Reforms under the sixth and seventh Tokugawa shōguns, TOKUGAWA IENOBU and Tokugawa Ietsugu (1709–16; r 1713–16); named for the era name (NENGŌ) Shōtoku (1711–16). Ienobu's adviser, ARAI HAKUSEKI, and his chamberlain (*sobayōnin*), MANABE AKIFUSA, were key figures in these reforms, which were intended to implement a conservative fiscal policy and to enhance the authority of the shōgun by transforming him into a Confucian monarch. They included discontinuation of currency debasement, stricter regulation of the NAGASAKI TRADE, change in the protocol for the reception of embassies from Korea (CHŌSEN TSŪSHINSHI), adoption of monarchical ritual, and betrothal of the child shōgun Ietsugu to an imperial princess. The fiscal aspect was continued under the eighth shōgun, TOKUGAWA YOSHIMUNE, but the ideological and ritual dimensions were abandoned.

Shōtoku, Prince　　　聖徳太子

(574–622; Shōtoku Taishi). Statesman of the Asuka period (593–710); second son of Emperor Yōmei (r 585–587). As regent for the empress SUIKO (r 593–628), Prince Shōtoku instituted the KAN'I JŪNIKAI ("twelve cap

ranks") and the SEVENTEEN-ARTICLE CONSTITUTION to strengthen imperial authority. He compiled histories with SOGA NO UMAKO and initiated diplomatic relations with the Sui dynasty (589–618) in China. He was first known as Umayado no Miko. The title Shōtoku Taishi (Prince of Sagely Virtue), by which he is generally known, is first mentioned in a temple inscription of the 8th century.

Following the death of Emperor Yōmei in 587, a power struggle broke out between Soga no Umako and MONONOBE NO MORIYA (see SOGA FAMILY). Shōtoku sided with Umako, who succeeded in having Sushun (r 587–592) installed as emperor. Sushun was murdered in 592. Umako's niece and widow of the deceased emperor Bidatsu (r 572–585) was selected as the next ruler, Empress Suiko; in 593 Suiko appointed Shōtoku as regent, delegating all powers to him.

With the institution of a system of 12 cap ranks for courtiers in 604, Shōtoku replaced KABANE ranks based on UJI lineage groups (see UJI-KABANE SYSTEM). The same year Shōtoku promulgated the Seventeen-Article Constitution, or "splendid law," stressing the importance of the emperor. In 594 Shōtoku issued an imperial edict calling for the promotion of Buddhism. He gave direct imperial support to the building of the temples ASUKADERA (Hōkōji), SHITENNŌJI, and HŌRYŪJI and is credited with written commentaries on sutras (see SANGYŌ GISHO; LOTUS SUTRA). In 620, together with Umako, Shōtoku also compiled the historical chronologies TENNŌKI AND KOKKI.

After the conquest of the Japanese enclave of KAYA by the adjacent Korean kingdom of SILLA in 562, successive emperors made repeated efforts to regain a foothold on the Korean peninsula. Shōtoku planned an expeditionary force against Silla in 602, although it was never sent. In 600 Shōtoku dispatched an envoy to China. A second embassy was sent in 607, when ONO NO IMOKO was dispatched. Imoko set off again the following year, accompanied by a large delegation of scholar-monks and students. Some of these scholars later contributed directly and indirectly to the TAIKA REFORM of 645. See SUI AND TANG (T'ANG) CHINA, EMBASSIES TO.

Shōtoku died at IKARUGA NO MIYA. Some documents relating to him are preserved in the collection JŌGŪ SHŌTOKU HŌŌTEI SETSU.

Shoup mission　　　シャウプ使節団

(Shaupu Shisetsudan). Group of seven American tax specialists, headed by Professor Carl S. Shoup of Columbia University, which arrived in occupied Japan for its initial visit on 10 May 1949. The mission's purpose was to study and recommend revisions for Japan's system of taxes. These tax reforms were to complement the balanced budget and other stabilization measures implemented under the DODGE LINE and to aid in Japan's economic rehabilitation.

The mission proposed that the central government rely on personal and corporate income taxes for the bulk of its revenue. In order to reduce the highly centralized power of the national government, the mission recommended that the revenue base of local governments be strengthened, the authority of local tax administrators be increased, and the tax jurisdictions for the respective levels of government be specified. In order to facilitate capital accumulation, the mission recommended that corporations be allowed to revalue their assets with only a 6 percent tax on the revaluation profits.

After considerable debate the Diet passed the Shoup mission's recommendations in 1950. Although many of the measures were subsequently modified or repealed, the Japanese system has essentially remained in the pattern established by the Shoup mission. See also ECONOMIC HISTORY.

Shōwa Aluminum Corporation　　　昭和アルミニウム[株]

(Shōwa Aruminiumu). Diversified manufacturer of aluminum products. Incorporated in 1935, the company produces sheets and coils, extruded products, foils, and fabricated products, which have applications ranging from automobile parts and electronic components to household goods. Sales for the fiscal year ending November 1990 totaled ¥171.3 billion (US $1.3 billion). Capitalization stood at ¥18.8 billion (US $137.0 million) in the same year. Headquarters are in Ōsaka and Tōkyō.

Shōwa Denkō KK　　　昭和電工[株]

(Shōwa Denkō). Chemical company. Incorporated in 1939 through the merger of Nippon Electric Industries and Shōwa Fertilizer Co. Its chief operations are manufacturing petrochemical products and smelting aluminum. In 1966 Shōwa Denkō constructed a petrochemical plant in Ōita Prefecture, where it produces ethylene, polyethylene, polypropylene, acetaldehyde, and vinyl acetate. Its subsidiary firm SHŌWA ALUMINUM CORPORATION manufactures aluminum products. Smelting companies have been established in New Zealand, Venezuela, and Indonesia. Sales for the fiscal year ending December 1990 totaled ¥569.7 billion (US $4.3 billion), of which petrochemical products accounted for 48 percent and other products 52 percent. The firm was capitalized at ¥105.4 billion (US $789.2 million) in the same year. Headquarters are in Tōkyō.

Shōwa Denkō Scandal　　　昭電事件

(Shōden Jiken). A major political scandal of 1948 involving SHŌWA DENKŌ KK, Japan's largest fertilizer producer, and many political leaders and government officials. The scandal was revealed in April 1948, when opposition party members accused government officials of accepting bribes from Shōwa Denkō in return for special consideration in arranging a low-interest loan from the RECONSTRUCTION FINANCE BANK. Members of ASHIDA HITOSHI's cabinet were implicated, and in October the cabinet was forced to step down. It was not until 1962 that final judgments were handed down by the Tōkyō High Court: 2 of the 64 indicted were found guilty, the rest having been acquitted earlier.

Shōwa Depression　　　昭和恐慌

(Shōwa Kyōkō). Great Japanese financial depression of the 1930s; so called from the Shōwa period (1926–89). One of a series of world financial crises triggered by that in the United States in 1929, it lasted from 1930 until 1935.

In November 1929 the Japanese government declared its intention to return to the gold standard, and in January 1930 it lifted its gold embargo. However, only two months later, as prices in the consumer and stock markets began to plummet and foreign trade declined, there was a huge gold outflow. The double blow of the world economic crisis and the adverse effects of the return to the gold standard thrust the Japanese economy into an unprecedented depression. Between 1929

▲Symbolic of Japan's economic growth in the 1980s, newly manufactured automobiles await shipping at the port of Yokosuka in Kanagawa Prefecture.

▼The funeral ceremony for Emperor Shōwa (Hirohito), held in Tōkyō on 24 February 1989, drew dignitaries from around the world.

◀At this 1943 rally in support of the war effort, the huge poster displayed on the Nichigeki Theater in Tōkyō was part of a campaign that featured the war slogan *uchiteshi yaman* (Attack to the End).

Hagiwara Sakutarō, the group extolled the beauty of traditional Japanese culture and called for the revival of a spirit of dedication and self-sacrifice.

Despite the temper of the times, some of the masterpieces of Shōwa literature appeared during this period, such as Kawabata's YUKIGUNI (1935–37, revised 1948; tr *Snow Country*, 1956) and NAGAI KAFŪ'S BOKUTŌ KIDAN (1937; tr *A Strange Tale from East of the River*, 1958). But as World War II intensified, an increasing number of works were banned, including TANIZAKI JUN'ICHIRŌ's monumental SASAMEYUKI (1943–48; tr *The Makioka Sisters*, 1957), and literature was made an instrument of the state as popular authors were drafted to write laudatory reports from the front (see WAR LITERATURE). KANEKO MITSUHARU, the only major antiwar poet, continued to write but did not dare attempt to publish.

After the war ended, Tanizaki published *Sasameyuki* and Kawabata produced his elegy to prewar Japanese culture, *Yama no oto* (1949–52; tr *The Sound of the Mountain*, 1970). Left-wing writers reemerged, and there appeared a group of writers known as the Buraiha ("Outsiders' school") that included DAZAI OSAMU, who examined a widespread postwar feeling of personal loss in such works as SHAYŌ (1947; tr *The Setting Sun*, 1956). Another group, the so-called first generation of postwar writers, which included NOMA HIROSHI, ŌOKA SHŌHEI, HANIYA YUTAKA, and SHIINA RINZŌ, viewed the war from a political and philosophical point of view. Postwar poetry, some of the best of which was published in the journals ARECHI (Waste Land) and REKITEI (Historical Course), was marked by a return to a distinctly personal world view. A major achievement of the early postwar theater was KINOSHITA JUNJI's *Yūzuru* (1949; tr *Twilight Crane*, 1956), which combined a folk theme with an experimental use of dialect.

Following the appearance in 1949 of his highly praised first novel, KAMEN NO KOKUHAKU (tr *Confessions of a Mask*, 1958), MISHIMA YUKIO went on to publish a series of carefully wrought works, most of which have been translated into English. ABE KŌBŌ's SUNA NO ONNA (1962; tr *The Woman in the Dunes*, 1964), like much of his literature,

depicts the alienation of the city-dweller. Both authors wrote popular plays for the theater and Abe in particular contributed to the formation of the underground (*angura*) theater movement that arose in the late 1960s.

A number of novelists, such as YASUOKA SHŌTARŌ and KOJIMA NOBUO, whose first works appeared in the 1950s, examined the collapse of the traditional family system. Other writers turned to historical or folk themes. In CHIMMOKU (1966; tr *Silence*, 1969) ENDŌ SHŪSAKU depicted the persecution and suffering of Christians and apostates in Edo-period (1600–1868) Japan, and ENCHI FUMIKO described in ONNAZAKA (1949–57; *The Waiting Years*, 1971) a Meiji-period woman, who, though she submits to extreme sexual oppression, is not dominated by it. INOUE YASUSHI set many of his historical novels, such as TEMPYŌ NO IRAKA (1957; tr *The Roof Tile of Tempyo*, 1975), in China. In MAN'EN GANNEN NO FUTTOBŌRU (1967; tr *The Silent Cry*, 1974), ŌE KENZABURŌ combined personal experience with an engaged social conscience.

CHŪKAN SHŌSETSU, or "middlebrow" fiction, was stimulated by the growth of the mass media, and the MYSTERY STORIES of MATSUMOTO SEICHŌ and the SCIENCE FICTION novels of KOMATSU SAKYŌ became enormous best sellers, a number of which were made into films. There has also been a notable increase since the 1960s in the number of women writers of the first rank, among them ARIYOSHI SAWAKO, KŌNO TAEKO, and SONO AYAKO, and in the early 1980s a succession of young women won the prestigious AKUTAGAWA PRIZE. Among the most popular writers of fiction in the early 1990s were TSUSHIMA YŪKO, MURAKAMI RYŪ, NAKAGAMI KENJI, and MURAKAMI HARUKI. See also FICTION, MODERN; POETRY, MODERN; DRAMA, MODERN.

Shōwa Memorial Park　昭和記念公園

(Shōwa Kinen Kōen). National park on the border between the cities of Tachikawa and Akishima in Tōkyō Prefecture; former site of a US Air Force base. Construction was begun in 1978 to commemorate the 50th year of the reign of Emperor Shōwa (Hirohito), which had been celebrated three years earlier, and one part of the park was opened to the public in 1983. As of 1990 more than half of the pro-

jected 180 hectares (445 acres) had been developed. A pond for boating, a swimming pool, and cycling courses are provided for public use.

Shōwa period　昭和時代

(1926–89; Shōwa *jidai*). The reign of Emperor SHŌWA (Hirohito), from 25 December 1926 to 7 January 1989, was the longest imperial reign in Japanese history, and one of the most tumultous and controversial. In the course of this 62-year period Japan traversed a complex and often contradictory course that led it from parliamentary democracy and peaceful international cooperation into militarism and global war, and then from defeat and occupation by foreign troops to recovery and a level of prosperity that has astonished the Japanese themselves as much as the rest of the world.

Parliamentarianism and International Cooperation—When Emperor Shōwa ascended the throne, Japan appeared to be moving toward convergence with the Western democracies. Universal manhood suffrage had been instituted in 1925 (see UNIVERSAL MANHOOD SUFFRAGE MOVEMENT), and the GENRŌ or elder statesmen, the oligarchic group that had been the moving force behind Japan's establishment as a modern state, were gradually withdrawing from the scene. In their place, POLITICAL PARTIES vied for power within Japan's fractious yet vital parliamentary system, and progress was being made in passing legislation to address some of Japan's more acute problems in the areas of tenant farming, labor, and health. Internationally, Japan had committed itself at the WASHINGTON CONFERENCE (1921–22) to a policy of naval arms limitation and cooperation with the United States, Great Britain, and other nations in the effort to preserve peace through international diplomacy. During most of the 1920s the Japanese economy grew at a respectable 3.2 percent a year, and there were signs of the development of a mass consumer culture increasingly integrated in a global system of trade.

Grave problems, however, were concealed in the background of these generally positive developments. Economic growth seemed to primarily benefit the burgeoning financial conglomerates (ZAIBATSU) and the urban areas of the country; smaller businesses and the rural population were largely left behind to face increasingly difficult times. Then, in the FINANCIAL CRISIS OF 1927 and the SHŌWA DEPRESSION touched off by the New York stock market crash of 1929, even the leading sectors of the Japanese economy were thrown into confusion, shaking public confidence in the government. The deflationary policies and the various military and bureaucratic budget cuts attempted by Prime Minister HAMAGUCHI OSACHI did little to restore faith in the political system or in party rule. Fearful of a growing Marxist movement, government officials used the PEACE PRESERVATION LAW OF 1925, which had been passed in conjunction with universal manhood suffrage, to suppress dissent in the name of eradicating communism.

Militarism and Authoritarianism— During the course of the 1930s a squabbling, constantly shifting antidemocratic coalition of ultranationalist ideologues, disgruntled army officers, "reform" bureaucrats, and ambitious politicians gradually pushed Japan away from the parliamentarianism and internationalism of the 1920s toward militarism, authoritarianism, and a "go-it-alone" policy in Asia. The Hamaguchi cabinet's efforts to continue a policy of international arms control at the London Naval Conference of 1930 (see LONDON NAVAL CONFERENCES) were met with deep displeasure by an increasingly restive military, and Hamaguchi himself was shot by a right-wing assailant, ushering in an era of political assassinations and coup attempts. The situation worsened in September 1931 when insubordinate army officers staged the MANCHURIAN INCIDENT, initiating a course of military expansionism in continental Asia that led to increasing friction with the Western powers, the creation of the puppet state of MANCHUKUO in 1932, and Japan's withdrawal from the League of Nations in 1933 (see LEAGUE OF NATIONS AND JAPAN).

This was followed in 1936 by a shocking full-fledged military revolt in Tōkyō (see FEBRUARY 26TH INCIDENT) that shook the very foundations of civilian government in Japan. The revolt was suppressed, but as the government tried to deal with these and other acts of lawlessness and insubordination, power increasingly slipped from the hands of party politicians into those of men who, it was hoped, might better be able to control the militarists. Foremost among these new leaders was Prince KONOE FUMIMARO, who served as prime minister from June 1937 to January 1939, and again from July 1940 to October 1941.

Konoe was an ambiguous figure. Though he no doubt desired an end to conflict and chaos, he was weak and indecisive, and was enough of a nationalist that he did little to thwart those calling for a "SHŌWA RESTORATION," the slogan of the reactionary right. Moreover, in 1937 he permitted the MARCO POLO BRIDGE INCIDENT to escalate into a full-scale war between China and Japan (see SINO-JAPANESE WAR OF 1937–1945), a bitter and protracted conflict that, despite military victories, only deepened Japan's problems. During his second term of office, Konoe committed Japan to the fateful TRIPARTITE PACT (1940) with Italy and Germany. This decision to join the Axis alliance, as well as the neutrality pact signed with the Soviet Union

in April 1941, reflected Foreign Minister MATSUOKA YŌSUKE's conviction that a firm stand and new allies would persuade the United States and Great Britain to give Japan a free hand in Asia and the Pacific—especially given their preoccupation with the stunning German victories in the early phases of World War II in Europe.

War in the Pacific— Far from discouraging the United States, however, Japan's actions merely served to increase tensions. As early as 1931, the United States had said that it would not recognize further Japanese conquests in Asia (see NONRECOGNITION POLICY). When Japanese forces occupied northern French Indochina in September 1940, the United States stopped iron and steel exports to Japan. Undeterred, the Japanese moved into southern Indochina in July 1941, and the United States responded by organizing an international embargo on oil exports to Japan. This had a more serious impact, and, faced with dwindling oil reserves and confusion over how to resolve the dilemma, the Konoe cabinet resigned in October 1941, to be succeeded by a government formed by General TŌJŌ HIDEKI. After attempts at negotiation between Japan and the United States foundered over the issue of whether or not Japan should be permitted to maintain its military presence in China, Japan struck at Pearl Harbor on 7 December 1941 and quickly occupied a vast area of Southeast Asia and the Pacific that it designated as the GREATER EAST ASIA COPROSPERITY SPHERE.

Initially, the war went well for the Japanese, as they overran British Malaya and Singapore, took Hong Kong and Burma, and defeated the US forces in the Philippines. However, by the time of the Battle of MIDWAY (June 1942) and the bloody campaign for GUADALCANAL (August 1942–February 1943), it was clear that Japan did not have the forces necessary to control such far-flung territories, nor the material and logistic resources to sustain its war effort. US submarine warfare cut off the Japanese home islands from the resources of Southeast Asia, and the island-hopping campaign across the Pacific brought US long-range bombers within striking range of Japan's urban and industrial heartland.

By 1945 Japan's situation was desperate. Japan turned to the USSR in the hope of finding an intermediary that could help in negotiating some sort of compromise peace, but this hope was shattered by the firmly worded call for "unconditional surrender" enunciated by the United States, Great Britain, and China in the POTSDAM DECLARATION of July 1945. As Japan hesitated, atomic bombs were dropped on Hiroshima (August 6) and Nagasaki (August 9), and the Soviet Union declared war on Japan (August 8). Still unable to decide whether to fight on or to accept the Potsdam Declaration, the deadlocked cabinet of Prime Minister SUZUKI KANTARŌ, in an unprecedented move, appealed to Emperor Shōwa for guidance. The emperor responded that Japan would have to "bear the unbearable" and accept its defeat. On 15 August 1945, WORLD WAR II came to an end.

Occupation— As a result of its defeat, Japan was subjected to the Allied OCCUPATION, which lasted from August 1945 to April 1952. During this period the Japanese government was subject to the authority of the supreme commander for the Allied powers (SCAP), a term that referred both to the commander himself (General Douglas MACARTHUR until 1951 and then General Matthew

B. RIDGWAY) and to the supporting bureaucracy of several thousand officials, most of them Americans. During the early years of the Occupation, these officials pushed through a sweeping series of reforms that included a new constitution (see CONSTITUTION OF JAPAN), the LAND REFORMS OF 1946, a revamping of the educational system, curtailment of the economic activities of the zaibatsu (see ZAIBATSU DISSOLUTION), and major changes in the legal codes to support equality of the sexes and lessen the authority of Japan's traditional patriarchal family system. Underlying these and other Occupation actions, including the WAR CRIMES TRIALS, was an American belief that a small clique of military and civilian leaders had led the great majority of Japan's overly compliant but basically innocent citizenry into an immoral war. Democratic reforms, it was hoped, would create a more peaceful and stable Japan.

The many sudden changes instituted under the Occupation shocked Japan's conservatives. Particularly galling were the constitution's reduction of the emperor to purely symbolic status, the renunciation of a military establishment contained in article 9, the decentralization of the police and educational system, and the banning from public life of thousands of prewar political and business leaders (see OCCUPATION PURGE). At the same time, Japanese leftists and progressives were disappointed that even more fundamental structural reforms had not been carried out, and in the later years of the Occupation they were dismayed by what they saw as a "reverse course" in Occupation policy, reflecting cold war tensions. In this later period the scheduled GENERAL STRIKE OF 1947 was banned, strikes by government employees were outlawed, a RED PURGE of suspected communists was initiated, the police and school system were recentralized, and, after the outbreak of the Korean War in 1950, the NATIONAL POLICE RESERVE (which later evolved into the present SELF DEFENSE FORCES) was created. Women, although they had received the right to vote and made important legal and social gains, also found that they did not achieve the degree of equality their most vigorous representatives desired.

The Occupation officially ended in April 1952 with the implementation of the SAN FRANCISCO PEACE TREATY, which Japan had signed with 48 noncommunist nations in September 1951. At the same time, Japan concluded a security treaty with the United States that permitted US military bases to remain on Japanese soil in return for an American commitment to protect Japan from foreign aggression (see UNITED STATES–JAPAN SECURITY TREATIES).

Toward Prosperity— Japan's economy was still in the arduous process of recovery from the war, but US aid, a stable ¥360-to-$1 exchange rate, a rush of special military procurements (TOKUJU) to support the US and United Nations forces in the Korean War (1950–53), and hard work by Japanese business and labor combined to push the average annual growth of Japan's gross national product (GNP) to 8.6 percent in 1951–55, and over 9.1 percent in 1955–60.

The political scene was more turbulent. Attempts by the ruling LIBERAL DEMOCRATIC PARTY (LDP; established in 1955 by a merger of two existing conservative parties) to alter or roll back a number of the Occupation reforms, including article 9 of the constitution, were met with fierce protests by the JAPAN SOCIALIST PARTY (JSP) and the JAPAN COMMUNIST

Upheaval and Transformation: The Shōwa Period

The 62-year reign of Emperor Shōwa (Hirohito), from 25 December 1926 to 7 January 1989, was the longest and perhaps the most turbulent in all of Japanese history. Its opening decades were scarred by economic hardship, domestic unrest, and the horrors of war. But Japan's defeat in 1945 marked a turning point, ushering in a new era of reform, recovery, and rapid growth that established Japan as an economic superpower in less than a single generation. The photographs that follow are an impressionistic record of this tumultuous time and its impact on the lives of the Japanese people.

1930 In the depths of the worldwide depression, striking Japanese workers protest pay and personnel cutbacks.

1931 Despite hard times, some of Japan's young people can afford to follow Western fashions. They are dubbed *mobo* ("modern boys") and *moga* ("modern girls").

1940 Even children's clothing reflects the nation's involvement in a bitter war in China and its mobilization for wider conflict.

1944 With Japan losing the war, an urgent labor shortage leads to the recruiting of unmarried women between the ages of 14 and 25 to work in ordnance factories.

1945 Most of Japan's major cities are devastated by Allied air raids. This is the city of Gifu in Gifu Prefecture, central Honshū.

1945 Japan surrenders on 15 August. Food shortages are acute. Here children beg chocolate bars from US soldiers.

1947 A father returns from service overseas and offers a military salute to his family. Demilitarization of Japanese society is a principal goal of Occupation reforms.

1956 The economy recovers sufficiently to meet basic needs. Householders dream of owning a washing machine, a refrigerator, and a television.

1965 Riding the crest of rapid economic growth, Japanese develop a taste for mass consumption, leisure activities, and Western popular culture.

1975 A generation after the war, the traditional extended family is being replaced by the nuclear family.

1988 A strong yen makes foreign travel accessible to all. During a holiday period, the international airport at Narita is as packed with people as a rush-hour commuter train.

Shōwa Shinzan The action of the volcano Usuzan in 1943 caused low-lying fields to rise and create, in just a few months, the lava dome Shōwa Shinzan.
1 The fields before the eruption, with the volcano Usuzan in the background.
2 The same location after the appearance of Shōwa Shinzan.
3 Another view of Shōwa Shinzan.

PARTY (JCP). Tension reached a fever pitch in June 1960, when Prime Minister KISHI NOBU-SUKE rammed a revised United States–Japan Security Treaty through the Diet in the hope of resolving the controversy over the US bases in Japan before President Dwight D. Eisenhower arrived for a scheduled official visit. After massive rioting, the revised treaty went into effect, but the turmoil forced Eisenhower to cancel his visit and Kishi to resign. The new prime minister, IKEDA HAYATO (1960–64), and his successor, SATŌ EISAKU (1964–72), now concentrated on an "income-doubling" policy of high economic growth, and some of the ideological tensions associated with the immediate post-Occupation period began to subside.

Rapid economic growth provided the dominant theme of the last 20 years of Emperor Shōwa's reign. During this time annual growth in GNP rose from the 8–9 percent that characterized the 1950s to 9.7 percent between 1960 and 1965, and 13.1 percent between 1965 and 1970, declining to roughly 7 percent throughout the 1970s. By the early 1970s Japan was the world's largest producer of ships, radios, and televisions, the second largest manufacturer of cars and rubber products, and the third largest producer of cement and iron. By the 1980s, Japan had become the leading manufacturer of cars in the world, and the dominant producer of such high-technology electronic products as videocassette recorders, computer chips,

video games, televisions, and audio equipment. Despite pressures from abroad for voluntary restraints on exports, and despite vigorous efforts to correct the imbalance in the yen-dollar exchange rate, Japanese goods remained attractive to consumers in the United States and other countries, and Japan's favorable trade balances, especially with the United States, remained large. Japanese purchases of US bonds, securities, and property also worried some Americans, while many others competed to draw Japanese investment to their regions.

There were many reasons for Japan's high rate of growth during this period. First, Japan's demographic growth from a population of 72 million in 1945 to more than 120 million in 1989 made it the seventh most populous nation in the world. Roughly 60 percent of this population, which was characterized by both a stable birth rate (since 1956) and a relatively small number of elderly people, was able and willing to work. Second, Japan's low military expenditures (usually below 1 percent of GNP), relatively low investment in social services, and generally high rate of savings contributed to heavy capital investment in the latest technology and innovative plants and equipment. Aided by the comparatively easy international access to technology and markets that characterized the 1960s, given generous support by conservative governments, and guided by the policy planning of agencies such as the MINISTRY OF INTERNATIONAL TRADE AND INDUSTRY (MITI), the Japanese business community made use of a well-educated and hard-working labor force to turn out a stream of highly successful products. Although this led to unfavorable stereotypes of government-business collusion—as represented by the phrase JAPAN INCORPORATED—it was clear that the Japanese way of doing business and the unprecedented level of prosperity it was generating were rooted in a much more complex and diverse set of economic and social factors.

Japanese Society at the End of the Shōwa Period—By the 1980s, Japan's rapid industrialization had brought more than 80 percent of the Japanese population into urban areas, and there was a shift from the traditional extended-family ideal to the more modern nuclear family. The divorce rate rose slightly but remained one-fifth that of the United States, both because opportunities for women were improving and because there was strong social pressure to make marriage work. Few families professed to be very religious, yet the established Buddhist and Shintō sects prospered, while the so-called NEW RELIGIONS such as SŌKA GAKKAI, TENRIKYŌ, and PL KYŌDAN kept the adherents they had won during their explosive growth in the 1960s. Marxism in Japan, on the other hand, lost much of its vitality, as it was doing in the rest of the world. Criminal gangs (known as YAKUZA) provided lurid copy for the media, and yet the level of crime and the proliferation of illegal drugs remained surprisingly low in comparison to other advanced industrial nations. Some progress was also made in dealing with the problem of prejudice toward BURAKUMIN, KOREANS IN JAPAN, and other minority groups, and the status of women also slowly improved.

Nonetheless, difficult problems remained. Early in the 1970s, for example, various outbreaks of POLLUTION-RELATED DISEASES demonstrated to a shocked nation some of the environmental costs of high growth. The OIL CRISIS OF 1973 and a series of unilateral actions

by US president Richard M. Nixon (see NIXON SHOCKS) during the 1970s also reinforced a sense of the Japanese economy's vulnerability to external events and pressures, a sense that many Japanese continue to hold today, amid the mounting chorus of foreign protests against Japan's massive trade surpluses. By the end of the 1980s, a steep rise in land prices had created a rapidly widening gap between owners and nonowners, young people were worrying about whether they could ever afford to purchase a home, and income distribution in Japan was becoming increasingly unequal. Meanwhile, government efforts to control budget deficits led to a tightening of expenditures, to the PRIVATIZATION of various government-run corporations such as the national railways, and, in 1988, to the imposition of an unpopular 3 percent CONSUMPTION TAX, intended in part to help finance improved social services for Japan's rapidly aging population.

A series of political scandals beginning in the 1970s has also provoked continuing criticism of the nature of party politics in Japan. Prime Minister TANAKA KAKUEI (1972–74) was initially praised for his energetic approach to national issues, but was soon forced to resign after he was implicated in the LOCKHEED SCANDAL. Resentment flared up once again after the 1988 passage of the consumption tax, not only because the tax itself was an irritant, but also because its passage coincided with the disclosure that the Recruit Company had involved a host of leading politicians in illegal stock deals (see RECRUIT SCANDAL). The ruling LDP managed to stay in power throughout this period, largely because the opposition (including the JSP, JCP, and KŌMEITŌ) were too weak and divided among themselves to form an effective coalition, but also because the LDP itself has been relatively skillful in polishing its periodically tarnished image and in adapting its political program to meet new popular demands.

The Shōwa period thus drew to a close on a rather ambiguous note. Pessimists could look at various of the problems outlined above and offer a negative assessment of the state of Japanese society and politics as the nation moved into the last decade of the 20th century; optimists, pointing to the remarkable story of Japan's recovery from war and defeat and its subsequent economic "miracle," could argue that it contained lessons for the rest of the world in management techniques, fiscal restraint, macroeconomic policy, and simple hard work. Whether given to optimism or pessimism, the Japanese themselves felt a sense of uncertainty at the end of the longest period of their modern history, and saw it as a time to begin a renewed questioning of their country's present state and of its future role within the world community.

☞ 1419

"Shōwa Restoration" 昭和維新

(Shōwa Ishin). Slogan used by right-wing extremists of the 1920s and 1930s who hoped for a sweeping national reform on the order of the MEIJI RESTORATION of 1868, Shōwa being the reign name of Emperor Hirohito, who succeeded to the throne in 1926. To radical young military officers and nationalists such as TACHIBANA KŌZABURŌ, INOUE NISSHŌ, GONDŌ SEIKYŌ, and KITA IKKI, the term "Shōwa Restoration" meant social reform, reconstruction of the machinery of government, and a thorough reorganization of the national economic structure. Its ideology underlay a series of abortive coups d'état by radical rightists in the 1930s.

Shōwa Sangyō Co, Ltd

昭和産業[株]

(Shōwa Sangyō). A food-processing company that produces flour, edible oils, dextrose, high fructose corn syrup, animal feeds, noodles, and *tempura* flour. It also stores grain and leases buildings. Incorporated in 1936. The company has been concentrating its efforts on the production of processed foods. Sales for the fiscal year ending March 1991 totaled ¥154.2 billion (US $1.1 billion), and capitalization stood at ¥12.7 billion (US $92.6 million). Headquarters are in Tōkyō.

Shōwa Shell Sekiyu KK

昭和シェル石油[株]

(Shōwa Sheru Sekiyu). Leading oil refiner and distributor. Affiliated with the Royal Dutch Shell group. The company was incorporated on 1 January 1985 through the amalgamation of Shōwa Oil Co (established in 1942) and Shell Sekiyu KK (started around 1876 by the Samuel & Samuel Co, forerunner of the Shell group). The company operates five oil refineries across Japan with a combined capacity of approximately 500,000 barrels per day. Domestic sales derive from 7,100 service stations supplying gasoline, kerosene, and automotive lubricants. International sales include aviation fuel as well as lubricants for oceangoing vessels. The company imports crude oil, petroleum products, and liquefied petroleum gas on vessels owned and chartered by Shōwa Shell Sempaku KK, a related firm. Sales for the fiscal year ending December 1990 totaled ¥1.7 trillion (US $12.4 billion), of which naphtha accounted for 37 percent; kerosene and gasoline, 24 percent; fuel oil, 16 percent; and lubricants and other products, 23 percent. The company was capitalized at ¥13.7 billion (US $102.6 million) in the same year. Headquarters are in Tōkyō.

Shōwa Shinzan

昭和新山

Volcanic hill, a parasitic volcano of USUZAN, south of Lake Tōya, southwestern Hokkaidō. When Usuzan erupted smoke and volcanic ash in 1943, the land adjacent to Lake Tōya rose and lava domes, including Shōwa Shinzan, were created. Shōwa Shinzan's volcanic activities ended in 1945, although it still emits steam and sulfuric fumes. It has been designated as a natural monument and is part of Shikotsu-Tōya National Park. Height: 402 m (1,319 ft).

shōya

庄屋

(village headman). Village official in the Edo period (1600–1868). The term *shōya* was used primarily in the Kansai region, *nanushi* in the Kantō region, and *kimoiri* in the Hokuriku and Tōhoku regions of northern Japan.

The village headman stood at the second level of peasant officialdom, ranking below officials variously called *ōjōya*, *warimoto*, or *tomura*, who presided over groups of villages known as *gō*, *kumi*, or *tomuragumi*. The village headman acted as the principal intermediary between the villagers and higher authorities. He was responsible for allotting and collecting village taxes, for maintaining village order, and often for introducing new agricultural techniques. The position, hereditary in many villages, allowed the headman's family to acquire broad social and economic privileges.

The headman was assisted by several *kumigashira* (household group leaders, also

known as OSABYAKUSHŌ or *toshiyori*) and *hyakushōdai* (peasant representatives). The three offices were known collectively as *murakata san'yaku* or *jikata san'yaku*. See also MURA YAKUNIN.

shōyō jurin bunka

照葉樹林文化

(laurilignosa culture). Term coined by the ethnobotanist Nakao Sasuke (b 1916) to refer to an assembly of material and nonmaterial cultural traits that appear to have spread among a broad range of ethnically distinct peoples along a belt of broadleaf evergreen forests extending from the southern foothills of the Himalayas through China south of the Yangzi (Yangtze) River and the highlands of Vietnam, Laos, Thailand, and Burma (Myanmar) to southwestern Japan. Such forests of laurels (Lauraceae) and evergreen oaks—which flourish in the warm temperate zones, where the January mean temperature is above freezing—had spread throughout most of southwestern Japan by about 5000 BC. It is proposed that the *shōyō jurin* (laurilignosa, or laurel and evergreen oak forest) culture had its origins in the area extending from Annam to the Yunnan (Yün-nan) Plateau and had become well established in Japan before the introduction of intensified wet-rice cultivation in the Yayoi period (ca 300 BC–ca AD 300).

Features of the culture included leaching of evergreen oak acorns, horse chestnuts, bracken rhizomes, and kudzu roots to prepare them as foodstuffs; processing tea for drinking; weaving silk from the cocoon of the silkworm; gathering lacquer-tree sap for the production of LACQUER WARE; and the slash-and-burn cultivation of millet, buckwheat, soybeans, *azuki* beans, taro, and dryland rice. The practice of using the fungal fermenting agent *kōji* to produce rice wine and soybean paste was also common to the region and persists today. Nonmaterial cultural elements that are still observed in parts of the region include the use of rice cakes as religious offerings and the belief that ancestral spirits dwell in the mountains (see YAMA NO KAMI). There are also numerous correspondences among myths and legends, such as the marriage of brother and sister divinities (see IZANAGI AND IZANAMI) and the creation of agricultural crops from the corpse of a goddess.

shōyu→soy sauce

Shōyūki

小右記

Also known as *Yafuki*. Diary of the minister of the right Fujiwara no Sanesuke (957–1046), also known as Ononomiya Sanesuke because he founded the Ononomiya school of rites. The diary covers the years 978–1032 and is a source of information on court ceremony and politics when the regents FUJIWARA NO MICHINAGA and FUJIWARA NO YORIMICHI dominated Kyōto. It provides details and

comments about Michinaga, with whom the author was not on cordial terms. The original number of chapters (*kan*) is unknown. Extant manuscripts preserve from 5 to 32 *kan*.

shōzei

正税

Tax rice collected by the government and stored in provincial granaries (*shōsō*) under the Chinese-style RITSURYŌ SYSTEM of administration begun in the late 7th century. Of the three major forms of tax levied by the government (see SO, YŌ, AND CHŌ), the *shōzei* or rice weighed the most, so it was more practical to store it locally than to transport it to the capital. The locally stored tax rice was managed by the provincial governors (KOKUSHI), who used it to make loans (SUIKO) to local farmers. From the mid-8th century, the term *shōzei* began to be used more narrowly to mean interest from such loans. The *kokushi* sent annual reports (*shōzeichō*) to the Grand Council of State (DAJŌKAN) on their *shōzei* income and expenses; 23 of these reports, dated 730–739, are preserved in the SHŌSŌIN repository at Nara.

shrikes

百舌

(*mozu*). In Japanese, *mozu* is the common name for any member of the numerous species of predatory songbirds of the family Laniidae, genus *Lanius*, that breed throughout Japan. It also refers specifically to the bull-headed shrike (*Lanius bucephalus*). Distinguished by its sharply hooked beak and longish tail, the shrike averages 20 centimeters (8 in) in length. The male has an orange head, black eye lines, a grayish streaked back and pale orange underbelly, and black wings and tail. The female has an overall brown plumage. Shrikes hunt insects, lizards, and other small animals and often impale their prey on sharp branches or thorns. Other species include the *akamozu* (Japanese red-tailed shrike; *L. cristatus*), the *chigomozu* (thick-billed shrike; *L. tigrinus*), the *ōmozu* (great gray shrike; *L. excubitor*), and the *ōkaramozu* (Chinese gray shrike; *L. sphenocercus*).

When first mentioned in Japanese literature in the 8th century, the *mozu* was depicted as a spring bird. Centuries later, among *haiku* poets, the shrike became associated with autumn.

shrimps, prawns, and lobsters

海老

(*ebi*). Crustaceans of the order Decapoda, suborders Natantia and Palinura, are collectively called *ebi* in Japanese. They are found in freshwater, brackish, and saltwater environments, near the shore as well as deep in the sea. Major Japanese species include the *kurumaebi* (*Penaeus japonicus*), the *sakuraebi* (*Sergestes lucens*), the *tenagaebi* (*Macrobrachium nipponense*), the Ise *ebi* (Japanese

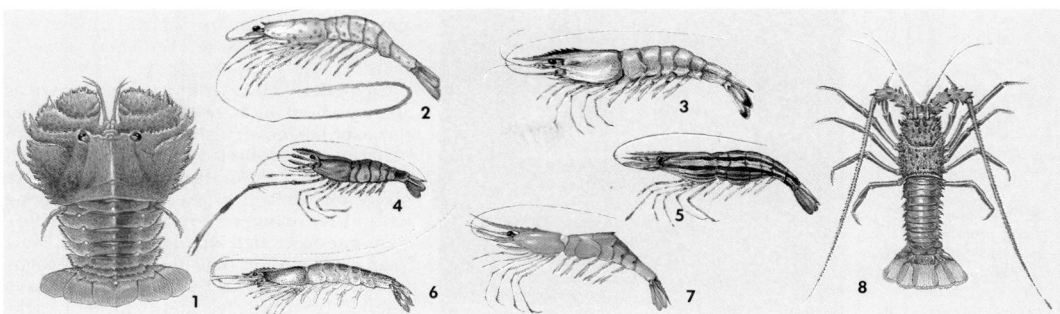

shrimps, prawns, and lobsters

1 The *uchiwa ebi* ("fan shrimp") is named for its fanlike shape.
2 The *sakuraebi* spends the daylight hours in deep waters but rises toward the surface at night.
3 The Taishō *ebi*, first commercially harvested in the Taishō period, is a favorite in *tempura*.
4 The *tenagaebi* has very long claws.
5 The *hokkai ebi* has distinctive stripes.
6 The shell of the *shibaebi* is relatively thin, and this variety is often cooked as *tempura*.
7 Also known as *amaebi*, the *hokkoku akaebi* is often eaten raw.
8 The 350-mm-long Ise *ebi* is a spiny lobster prized for its flavor.

shrines

▶ The main sanctuary of the Mitake Shrine, Akita Prefecture, a small rural shrine established in 1290.

▼ A tree-lined path leads from the gate (*torii*) to the main buildings of the Kirishima Shrine, believed to date from the mid-6th century. Kagoshima Prefecture.

Plan of a Medium-Size Shrine

kaguraden (hall of sacred dance and music)

temizuya (pavilion for ritual washing of hands and mouth)

haiden (hall of worship or oratory)

honden (main sanctuary)

komainu (lionlike guardian figures)

torii (shrine gateway)

This woodblock print of the Kasuga Shrine in Tōkyō is taken from the *Edo meisho zue*, a 19th-century illustrated guidebook.

spiny lobster; *Panulirus japonicus*), and the *semiebi* (locust lobster; *Scyllarides squamosus*).

In modern Japan shrimp is best known as an ingredient in TEMPURA, SUSHI, and other forms of Japanese cuisine. In the premodern period deep red, boiled spiny lobsters called *okazari ebi* ("decoration lobsters") were placed on round rice cakes, and these, along with bitter oranges, fern, and KOMBU (kelp), were put on a small wooden stand as a New Year's decoration. The traditional conception of *ebi* as auspicious creatures may have resulted from the idea that their bent backs symbolized old age and thus long life, or that the periodic shedding of their shells signified renewal. *Ebi* appear in WAKA and HAIKU poetry, as well as in woodblock prints. In cooking, the *kurumaebi* and *shibaebi* (*Metapenaeus joyneri*) are the most highly prized species.

shrines   神社

(*jinja*). A Shintō shrine is an enclosed area containing a wooden sanctuary and several auxiliary buildings where SHINTŌ RITES are performed and prayers offered. The shrine is the focal point of organized Shintō religious practice, including annual festivals and KAGURA (sacred dance and music). In urban areas it provides a sense of community to those living within its parish. In rural areas it tends to create a feeling of kinship among villagers by stressing the common tie that all have to the shrine deity.

A typical medium-size shrine might be laid out as follows: Toward the rear of the shrine precinct, which is often rectangular and surrounded by a fence marking it off as a sanctified area, stands the *honden* (main sanctuary), which houses the SHINTAI, a sacred object in which the spirit of the deity (KAMI) is believed to reside. Usually more than one deity is enshrined. Directly in front of the *honden* is the *haiden* (hall of worship or oratory), where the priests conduct their rituals and individuals make their offerings. Worshipers announce their presence to the deity or deities enshrined in the *honden* by clapping their hands and tugging on a heavy bell rope hanging from the eaves of the *haiden*. A wooden box stands in front of the *haiden* to receive money offerings. The interior of the *haiden* may be entered by laymen only on special ritual occasions, and the *honden* only by priests on rare occasions.

At the entrance to a shrine stands a TORII, the characteristic shrine gateway of two erect pillars pierced at the top by two crossbeams. A path, over which may arch additional *torii*, leads directly to the *haiden*. Away from the path but close to the *haiden* stands a *temizuya*, a pavilion where worshipers purify themselves by a ritual washing of hands and mouth. A pair of highly stylized stone lions called KOMAINU (Korean dogs) stand guard in front of the gate or *haiden* of the shrine. A medium-size shrine may also include a storehouse for ritual objects such as portable shrines (MIKOSHI), a hall for preparing food offerings, a miniature shrine to protect the precincts, and an office where amulets are sold.

There are many variations in the layout, structure, and relation of shrines. Some shrines have a single sanctuary, with the front half used as the *haiden* and rear as the *honden*. In some shrines the *haiden* and *honden* are located miles apart, typically with the *haiden* easily accessible in the village and the *honden* on an outlying peak away from possible human defilement. A shrine dedi-

cated to a mountain, hot spring, or waterfall deity often may have only a *haiden*, since the natural phenomenon itself takes the place of a *honden* (see ŌMIWA SHRINE). There are even cases of a shrine having a *honden* but lacking a *haiden*. Some shrines are a compound of equally important or hierarchically related shrines, and others preside over subordinate shrines located throughout the country. See also SHINTŌ ARCHITECTURE.

Shrine Shintō   神社神道

(Jinja Shintō). The term Shrine Shintō came into use in the Meiji period (1868–1912) and was used in contrast to SECT SHINTŌ to refer to that aspect of Shintō that was associated with all public shrines, of which there were 109,712 by the end of World War II. Sect Shintō was the designation applied to the 13 Shintō sects recognized by the government as independent religious organizations. Because the Home Ministry granted official status to shrines in 1870, appointed their priesthood, determined their liturgy, and generally used the shrines for the dissemination of the official ideology, Shrine Shintō was sometimes held to be synonymous with STATE SHINTŌ. After a period of disarray in the wake of the OCCUPATION order in 1945 to separate religion and state and the consequent withdrawal of state support for shrines, most shrines were organized into an incorporated body, Jinja Honchō (see SHINTŌ SHRINES, ASSOCIATION OF), which is made up of about 90 percent (79,165 shrines in 1989) of all shrines in Japan. Shrine Shintō at present refers to the religious observances performed at these shrines.

Shūbun   周文

(?–ca 1460). Also known as Tenshō Shūbun. Monk-painter of the ZEN temple SHŌKOKUJI in Kyōto; the harbinger of the style of ink landscape painting (*suibokuga*) that arose in Kyōto during the 15th century. Shūbun is considered the founder of the Japanese-Chinese style (*karayō*) of painting, followed by his pupil SESSHŪ TŌYŌ.

The earliest reference to Shūbun is as a Zen monk sent with a diplomatic mission to Korea by the Muromachi shogunate in 1423 to secure a printed edition of the Korean *Tripitaka*. Other sources record that he was the *tsukansu* (secretary-general) of Shōkokuji. Shūbun learned painting from JOSETSU, a monk also affiliated with Shōkokuji.

The Shūbun style is distinctive in its handling of space. Although individual motifs—rocks, trees, hills, and huts—are inspired by Chinese landscapes of the 12th through the 14th centuries, the space that surrounds them permeates every corner of the composition in a manner surpassing that of their Chinese models and rendering the landscape images other-worldly. See also INK PAINTING.

Shūbun no Hi → holidays, national

shūdan shūshoku → group hiring

Shūeisha Publishing Co, Ltd

[株]集英社

(Shūeisha). Established in 1926 as a subsidiary of SHŌGAKUKAN, INC, it initially published recreational magazines for school-age children. It became independent in 1949 and thereafter gained a reputation as one of Japan's leading magazine publishers. Since 1953 the company has also published literature and books on the fine arts. Its numerous magazines include *Myōjō* (Stars), *More*, and the Japanese edition of *Playboy*.

Shufuren

主婦連

(Japan Housewives Association). Abbreviation of Shufu Rengōkai. Consumer organization devoted to the improvement of family life through consumer education and public action, founded in 1948 by OKU MUMEO, a member of the House of Councillors. Oku believed that in order to improve the quality of life, housewives should organize and exert direct influence on government decisions. By the late 1970s Shufuren was a nationwide organization, composed mainly of middle-class married women, with a membership of around 1 million. The organization has maintained a leading role in Japan's CONSUMER MOVEMENT. In addition to political action, Shufuren engages in commodity safety research, presents lecture series, and, to a limited degree, operates consumer cooperatives. Its activities have focused on consumer protection, inflation, and environmental issues. As of 1992, Shufuren had 391 local affiliates.

Shūgaishō

拾芥抄

(literally, "Collection of Dust"). Encyclopedic work in three volumes that classifies information into 99 categories. It was compiled in the middle Kamakura period (1185–1333) and expanded later. Several versions exist. Authorship is unknown, but it has been ascribed to such court officials as Tōin Sanehiro (b 1409) and Tōin Kinkata (1291–1360). It is a valuable source of information on court life of the period.

Shugakuin Detached Palace

修学院離宮

(Shugakuin Rikyū). Detached imperial palace begun by the abdicated emperor Go-Mizunoo (1596–1680; r 1611–29) in the mid-17th century. Located in the foothills of Mt. Hiei (HIEIZAN) in the northeast part of Kyōto, the estate was originally planned as an imperial family retreat having three garden areas stepped down the hillside, separated and surrounded by rice fields, and connected by paths. Several small pavilions were completed by Go-Mizunoo in 1659, establishing the upper and lower gardens. After his death in 1680, his daughter Akenomiya built and occupied a nunnery, the Rinkyūji, which became the middle garden. The architecture of several pavilions exemplifies the *sukiya* style (see SUKIYA-ZUKURI) popular in the Edo period (1600–1868), and the gardens are famed for their ponds, paths, and so-called bor-rowed scenery (*shakkei;* see GARDENS). The buildings at Shugakuin are modest in size but highly refined in craftsmanship. The main structures are of wood post-and-beam construction, with plaster walls or movable panels (*fusuma*), mat flooring (*tatami*), and cypress bark or clay tile roofs.

shūgakuritsu

就学率

(enrollment rate for compulsory education). The percentage of children between the ages of 6 and 14 (excluding those entitled to exemptions or postponements for health or other reasons) actually enrolled in Japan's compulsory primary and middle schools. When the EDUCATION ORDER OF 1872 went into effect, the *shūgakuritsu* surged, passing the 90 percent mark by the early 1910s. Behind this surge was the government's faith in a policy of rapidly introducing compulsory education to aid Japan in achieving modernization. Today the *shūgakuritsu* has reached 99.99 percent. More important, 99.5 percent of those who enroll actually graduate.

shūgaku ryokō

修学旅行

(school excursion). A traditional class excursion, led by teachers, which normally lasts several days and is perhaps the most memorable of the school events (GAKKŌ GYŌJI) for students of Japanese elementary and secondary schools. In order to gain exposure to experiences and places beyond the confines of their region or ordinary school life, students may visit historic cities (such as Tōkyō, Kyōto, Nara, Nikkō, or Hiroshima), culturally significant buildings, or other cultural treasures, or they may make excursions to areas renowned for their natural beauty. Recently trips to foreign countries such as China and Korea have also become frequent. The trips are expressly intended to acquaint students with the dynamics of group living. These trips are usually taken during the student's last year at a school.

Shugei Shuchiin

綜芸種智院

Private educational institute established for the sons of commoners in the early Heian period (794–1185). It was founded in 828 by the Shingon monk KŪKAI. The school offered education to people regardless of their class background, in contrast to the DAIGAKURYŌ and the *kokugaku* (provincial academies), which trained candidates for the bureaucracy. The school gave instruction on Buddhist and Confucian teachings, emphasizing both moral discipline and intellectual development. After Kūkai's death in 835, the school was closed.

Shugendō

修験道

A religious order that prescribes ascetic practices in mountains to attain holy or magic powers beneficial to the community. The order combines elements of ancient pre-Buddhist worship of certain mountains as holy ground (*sangaku shinkō;* see MOUNTAINS, WORSHIP OF) with esoteric Buddhism. Its members are known as YAMABUSHI.

Shugendō emerged as a coherent religious group in the late 12th century. Its predecessors were the HIJIRI, solitary Buddhist hermits who practiced ascetic disciplines in the depths of certain mountains and recited holy texts, such as the LOTUS SUTRA (*Hokekyō*). In the Heian period (794–1185) these solitary ascetics became organized into groups, with a prescribed body of ascetic exercises performed at stated seasons under the leadership of officers known as *sendatsu.* The order has no historical founder, though its members ascribe its origin to EN NO GYŌJA, a semilegendary sorcerer.

Shugendō was not until recently considered a separate religious sect, its members being affiliated with either the TENDAI SECT or the SHINGON SECT of Buddhism. The principal ritual exercises of the Shugendō are known as *nyūbu* or *mineiri,* "entering the mountain." These comprise an ascent of a particular holy mountain at each of the four seasons. The climb represents a passage from a profane to a sacred state. Austere exercises

Shugakuin Detached Palace In a famous example of the use of "borrowed scenery" (*shakkei*), the distant hills provide a backdrop to the pond in the palace's upper garden.

Shugendō Participants in this religious order's ritual exercises en route to the holy mountain Gassan, one of the three Dewa Sanzan peaks.

are enacted to endow the disciple with various magic powers and bring about his transformation into a Buddha. The principal holy mountains where these exercises are performed are ŌMINESAN (see also KIMPUSENJI), Katsuragisan (in Nara Prefecture, see KONGŌSAN), the mountains around Kumano (see KUMANO SANZAN SHRINES), DAISEN, Dewa Sanzan (see DEWA SANZAN SHRINES), and Ushiroyama (in Okayama Prefecture).

Shūgetsu Tōkan 秋月等観

(ca 1427–ca 1510). Priest-painter of the Muromachi period (1333–1568); direct pupil of the artist SESSHŪ TŌYŌ. Born to a *samurai* family serving the Shimazu *daimyō* of the Satsuma domain (now Kagoshima Prefecture), his original name was Taki Kantō (or Takagi Gonnokami). He entered the priesthood in 1462. In the mid-1460s he went to Yamaguchi to study painting with Sesshū at his Unkokuan studio, becoming one of the great master's closest disciples. About 1494–95 he took a trip to China and probably followed the route Sesshū had taken on his 1467–69 trip.

Shūgetsu painted abbreviated landscapes in splashes of ink wash (see HABOKU) as well as detailed scenes constructed on the basis of strong outlines and linear texturing of forms. He created portraits in precise classical silhouettes filled in with heavy color (see YAMATO-E) as well as figure subjects painted with the viscous ink contours of the Muromachi INK PAINTING tradition. He also designed bird-and-flower compositions.

shūgi 祝儀

Rite of celebration on happy occasions; gift given at such an occasion; tip or gratuity. These celebrations are usually public occasions for announcing the attainment of a new stage in life or a new state of affairs and usually require formal or traditional clothing and some kind of special food. The most important events requiring *shūgi* are births and marriages. In contrast, rites performed during inauspicious occasions, such as funerals and memorial services, are called *bushūgi*.

By extension, *shūgi* also refers to gifts given to the individuals in whose honor the rite is performed. Such gifts on formal occasions are wrapped in special white paper with an ornamental string (MIZUHIKI) and a special symbolic element (NOSHI) signifying happiness, but on lesser occasions money may be placed in store-bought envelopes with these symbols printed in red (*shūgibukuro*).

Shūgi may also refer to tips given to a *geisha*, to the maid in a Japanese-style inn, and to other service personnel. In this sense, *shūgi* is synonymous with terms such as *hana* (tip given to geisha), KOKOROZUKE, and *chippu* (from "tip").

shugo 守護

(provincial constables; later, military governors). *Shugo* and JITŌ (estate stewards) represent the two major governing networks of the KAMAKURA SHOGUNATE (1192–1333). *Shugo* were assigned from among the regime's favored vassals and exercised limited authority over Kamakura's vassals (GOKENIN) and criminal jurisdiction over certain types of offenders. Little is known about the origins of the office or the range of its jurisdiction. *Shugo* may have first been irregularly appointed during the years of the TAIRA-

MINAMOTO WAR (1180–85) and authorized on a national basis late in 1185.

The shogunate assigned *shugo* to identify and register warriors who deserved recognition as *gokenin*. The *shugo*'s only formal authority over them was in organizing and leading an occasional palace guard duty (*ōban'yaku*) in Kyōto. The *shugo* was also given jurisdiction over punishment for murder and rebellion, although murder cases were sometimes handled directly by Kamakura. This dated from the 1190s, though these responsibilities (called DAIBON SANKAJŌ, "three regulations for great crimes") were not formalized until 1232 in the GOSEIBAI SHIKIMOKU. For the remainder of the Kamakura period (1185–1333), this definition served as the basis for the *shugo*'s public authority.

Shugo took up residence in their assigned provinces only rarely, being content to operate through regular deputies (*shugodai*). The number of deputies was restricted to one per province, and many extant instructions from the shogunate are addressed to the *shugodai*. Not until the specter of the MONGOL INVASIONS OF JAPAN loomed in the 1270s did Kamakura order any of its *shugo* to take up local residence.

The shogunate limited the power of the office of *shugo*. *Shugo* titles were not intended to be hereditary and did not include the right to income-producing lands. *Shugo* were prohibited from confirming the private land rights of *gokenin*, save for pro forma validations of Kamakura's own confirmations (ANDO). No *shugo* was permitted to distribute new perquisites.

The shogunate's leading house, the HŌJŌ FAMILY, came to possess a disproportionate share of *shugo* titles by the late 1280s, but the family was totally destroyed in the 1330s. Only four or five Kamakura *shugo* retained the post under the MUROMACHI SHOGUNATE (1338–1573). The new wave of *shugo* were drawn from two sources: kinsmen of the ASHIKAGA FAMILY and locally entrenched *jitō*. See also SHUGO DAIMYŌ.

shugo daimyō 守護大名

Term used by modern historians to refer to provincial military lords of the early and middle Muromachi period (1333–1568) as distinguished from the SHUGO (military governors) of the Kamakura period (1185–1333) and SENGOKU DAIMYŌ of the Sengoku period (1467–1568). Appointed as *shugo* by the MUROMACHI SHOGUNATE, they gradually attained the status of semiautonomous lords (DAIMYŌ) ruling over one or more provinces. The acquisition of landholdings by *shugo* was accelerated when many court-based aristocratic estate (SHŌEN) proprietors, attempting to stem gradual encroachment upon their incomes, ceded their lands to the *shugo* in exchange for a fixed annual compensation (*shugo uke*). In this way *shugo daimyō* eventually gained control over 30 to 40 percent of the country's rice land. Among these daimyō were the HOSOKAWA FAMILY, HATAKEYAMA FAMILY, SHIBA FAMILY, IMAGAWA FAMILY, ŌUCHI FAMILY, TAKEDA FAMILY, ŌTOMO FAMILY, and the YAMANA FAMILY. Under the Muromachi shogunate the *shugo daimyō* of central Japan were obliged to reside in Kyōto. Increasingly, governance of the provinces was delegated to deputies (*shugodai*). By the end of the 15th century most *shugo daimyō* had either been defeated in conflicts among themselves (see ŌNIN WAR) or overthrown by provincial proprietors (KOKUJIN) and *shugodai*. These victors over

the *shugo daimyō* subsequently established themselves as Sengoku daimyō.

Shugō Incident 殊号事件

(Shugō Jiken; also called Title Incident). A controversy over the official title by which the Tokugawa shōgun should be addressed in diplomatic documents from Korea. Despite much opposition, in 1711 the shogunal adviser ARAI HAKUSEKI temporarily succeeded in replacing the customary term Nihonkoku *taikun* ("great ruler of Japan") with the grander term Nihon *kokuō denka* ("his highness the king of Japan"), which placed the shōgun on an equal level with the king of Korea diplomatically. Soon after Hakuseki's removal from influence, the original title was restored. The English word *tycoon* is derived from *taikun*.

Shūhōdō→Akiyoshidō

Shūhō Myōchō→Sōhō Myōchō

shuinjō 朱印状

(vermilion-seal certificate). A diplomatic form originating in the Sengoku period (1467–1568); the earliest extant *shuinjō* is dated 1512. With the *kokuinjō* (black-seal certificate), the *shuinjō* belongs to a category called *imbanjō*, i.e., documents authenticated by the impression of a seal (*imban*; see SEALS) rather than the subscription of a monogram or cypher (KAŌ), the customary medieval practice. ODA NOBUNAGA used *shuinjō* for various purposes, ranging from the confirmation of land rights (ANDO), the mobilization of vassals, and the grant of "off-limits" privileges (*kinzei*), to correspondence with other daimyō. *Shuinjō* were also issued by the other two national unifers, TOYOTOMI HIDEYOSHI and TOKUGAWA IEYASU; their use as licenses for overseas voyages originated the term *shuinsen* (see VERMILION SEAL SHIP TRADE). See also DIPLOMATICS.

shuinsen bōeki→vermilion seal ship trade

Shūi wakashū 拾遺和歌集

(Collection of Gleanings). Usually shortened to *Shūishū* or *Shūi*. Third imperial anthology (*chokusenshū*) of classical Japanese poetry (WAKA). It consists of 20 books containing 1,351 poems. With the first imperial anthology, the KOKINSHŪ (ca 905, Collection from Ancient and Modern Times), and the second, the GOSEN WAKASHŪ (after 951, Later Collection of Japanese Poetry), the *Shūishū* is counted as one of the *sandaishū*, or "anthologies of three eras," the group revered over the centuries as the orthodox canon of classical poetry and the accepted source of elegant, decorous diction and expression. As the title suggests, the purpose of the anthology was to gather together worthy poems of earlier times that had for one reason or another missed inclusion in the first two imperial collections. Its compilation was ordered by former emperor KAZAN and was carried out perhaps by FUJIWARA NO KINTŌ, who is thought to have prepared a draft under the title *Shūishō* (Draft of the *Shūishū*), which came to be regarded by many as superior to the *Shūishū*. Kazan himself has also been suggested as compiler. Probably completed between 1005 and 1007. The arrangement of the 20 books follows the general principles established by the *Kokinshū*, with differences in detail. Some 196 poets are represented. In terms of numbers of poems selected, the most important include KI NO TSURAYUKI, with 113 poems; KAKINOMO-

TO NO HITOMARO, 104; ŌNAKATOMI NO YO-SHINOBU, 59; Kiyohara no Motosuke (908–990), 46; Taira no Kanemori (d 990), 38; ŌSHIKŌCHI NO MITSUNE, 34; MINAMOTO NO SHI-TAGAU, 27; and Lady ISE, 25.

Shūkai Jōrei　　　　　　　集会条例

(Public Assembly Ordinance). Ordinance restricting political assembly; issued in April 1880. Together with the PRESS ORDINANCE OF 1875, it was aimed at controlling the FREEDOM AND PEOPLE'S RIGHTS MOVEMENT. It required registration with, and prior approval from, local police authorities for all political organizations and meetings and provided for surveillance by uniformed police, who were empowered to break up meetings. It also prohibited outdoor meetings, contact between different political associations, and political activity by servicemen, police, teachers, and students. More restrictions were added in 1882. After further revision in 1890, the ordinance was replaced by the even more repressive PUBLIC ORDER AND POLICE LAW OF 1900.

shukuba machi → post-station towns

Shumarinai, Lake　　　　　朱鞠内湖

(Shumarinaiko). Also known as Lake Uryū. Artificial lake in northwestern Hokkaidō. Composed of two lakes, it was created in 1943 by damming the upper reaches of the Uryūgawa, a tributary of the Ishikarigawa, to construct a hydroelectric power station. Area: 23.7 sq km (9.1 sq mi); depth: 31 m (102 ft).

Shumbun no Hi → holidays, national

shūmeigiku → anemone, Japanese

shūmon aratame　　　　　　宗門改

(religious inquisition). Institution of the Edo period (1600–1868) designed to eradicate Christianity throughout Japan. Under it, persons discovered to be Christian were forced to apostatize; the recalcitrant were subjected to psychological and physical tortures until they recanted, and those who refused to abandon their faith were executed. By the mid-17th century, the last priests had been captured, some 3,000 Japanese martyred, the majority of the religion's adherents driven into apostasy, and Christianity in Japan reduced to a few underground groups of believers, the KAKURE KIRISHITAN (Hidden Christians), among whom Catholicism was gradually transmuted into a syncretic folk creed. The inquisition next developed into an elaborate mechanism of surveillance over the country's entire population. All persons were required to show that they were not Christian by affiliating themselves with approved Buddhist temples under the "temple guarantee" (TERAUKE) system. "Religious inquiry census registers" (shūmon aratame nimbetsu chō), compiled by the temples, attested to their parishioners' religious purity.

The Appointment of Inquisitors — In 1640 the shogunate instituted the office of the shūmon aratame yaku (inquisitor) as the central organ for the supervision of its anti-Christian measures. On 11 January 1665 the daimyō were ordered to follow the shogunate's example and to appoint inquisitors charged with a yearly scrutiny of Christians; the analogous offices of shūmon bugyō and the like appeared in the tables of organization of domains from Yonezawa through Okayama to Kagoshima.

There was little left to do for the inquisitors after the 1660s, although shūmon aratame yaku continued to be appointed by the shogunate until 1792. But the routine set in motion for the purposes of the inquisition had developed an inertia and an identity of its own that made the shūmon aratame process continue in existence past the end of the Edo period. That routine took the form of the previously mentioned compilation of shūmon aratame nimbetsu chō. These were prepared on the basis of periodic surveys that classified individuals according to their religious affiliations. The process utilized the "five-household neighborhood groups" (GONINGUMI), through which collective responsibility was enforced among the populace, and gave rise to the "temple guarantee system" (terauke seido), through which the Buddhist church was made into an instrument of the Tokugawa regime.

The Survival of Christianity — For all its thoroughness, the shūmon aratame did not succeed in totally extirpating Christianity in Japan. The hermetic religion of the Kakure Kirishitan survived the inquisition's best efforts. Four times between 1790 and 1865, groups of Hidden Christians were discovered near Nagasaki. (These incidents are known as the Urakami kuzure; see PERSECUTIONS AT URAKAMI). The persecution that followed the last and most spectacular of these discoveries carried over from the Tokugawa regime into the first years of the "modern" Meiji government, which punished 3,384 of these survivors of the Edo period's inquisition with exile to various provinces of Japan. Not until 1873 was the prohibition of Christianity ended. See also CHRISTIANITY; ANTI-CHRISTIAN EDICTS.

Shun'e　　　　　　　　　　俊恵

(1113–ca 1190?). One of the major poets and critics of the 12th century; the son of the famous poet MINAMOTO NO TOSHIYORI and the teacher of FUJIWARA NO TOSHINARI (Shunzei), one of Japan's greatest poets. In about 1130 he became a priest at the temple Tōdaiji in Nara. He named his dwelling the Karin'en (Garden of the Forest of Poetry) and held monthly poetry parties there, creating a type of literary circle. Although no treatise of his own is extant, his views have been preserved in the Mumyōshō (Nameless Notes) of his pupil KAMO NO CHŌMEI and in the Eigyokushū (Collection of Bright Jewels), a poetic treatise spuriously attributed to Chōmei. His ideal in poetry was profundity through simplicity and direct description, and he did much to foster the style of YŪGEN (mystery and depth). His own poetry is preserved in his collection, the Rin'yōshū (Collection of Forest Leaves), which he compiled in 1178, and he has 84 poems included in imperial anthologies from the SHIKA WAKASHŪ onward.

shunga　　　　　　　　　　春画

(literally, "spring pictures"). The Japanese term for erotic paintings, prints, and illustrations. As opposed to the native term makura-e ("pillow pictures"), shunga was originally an elegant, Chinese-derived expression. Today it is somewhat in disrepute in Japan, the term higa ("secret pictures") being considered more refined. In their heyday shunga were considered a perfectly normal subject for the Japanese artist—no more improper or degrading than the painting of a nude or a classical love scene would have seemed to a contemporary Western artist.

Early Shunga — Fragmentary evidence indicates that the earliest Japanese shunga were a diversion of Buddhist artists and artisans, graffiti sketched for relaxation in the midst of more serious endeavors. Illustrated sex manuals are known from the Nara period (710–794). The official TAIHŌ CODE of the year 701 even specified that physicians were required to study such illustrated texts, osokuzu no e ("posture-pictures"), as they were termed. And in 1288 the Eisei hiyō shō (Secret Essentials of Hygiene), a Japanese sex manual that summarized earlier Chinese texts, was even presented to the throne. With the development of the EMAKIMONO, the lateral handscroll, shunga became an established art form in Japan.

Shunga in Ukiyo-e — During the Edo period (1600–1868) erotic art came into its own as an object of appreciation by the urban populace in general, no longer merely a pleasure of the wealthier samurai and of the priesthood or aristocracy. A critical element in the popularization of the shunga art form was the expansion of woodblock printing—formerly limited to a few monastic presses—to the secular world. As with printing in general, the early-17th-century examples of shunga were yet very "limited" editions, produced in Kyōto by and for a restricted group of affluent connoisseurs. The first major development of printed shunga appeared not in the old imperial capital but in the new samurai administrative center of Edo (now Tōkyō). The year 1660 marks the first extant, dated shunga publication in Edo, and this may be taken as the general starting point of fully developed shunga in its printed form. The first Edo UKIYO-E artist of shunga was MORONOBU's anonymous mentor, the KAMBUN MASTER. Other ukiyo-e artists noted for their shunga are Moronobu, SUGIMURA JIHEI, TORII KIYONOBU I, OKUMURA MASANOBU, NISHIKAWA SUKENOBU, and Tsukioka Settei (1710–86).

The Tokugawa shogunal government was more afraid of sedition than of erotica, and actual cases of censorship were infrequent, despite the sumptuary government edicts of 1722 and thereafter. However, the mere existence of such laws meant that shunga publication became more surreptitious and the number of prints and books fewer. The great revival of ukiyo-e in all categories came with the "golden age" of the mid-1760s. Known for their shunga of this era are Suzuki HARUNOBU, ISODA KORYŪSAI, IPPITSUSAI BUNCHŌ, KITAO SHIGEMASA, KATSUKAWA SHUNSHŌ, TORII KIYONAGA, and Kitagawa UTAMARO. Utamaro is probably the best known abroad of any of the Asian masters of the erotic.

Later Shunga — From the "golden age" of Utamaro, decadent elements gradually came to predominate, and the innocent sexual curiosity of the earlier years was increasingly replaced by a manifestly lubricious, near-pornographic interest. Later shunga work includes that of Katsushika HOKUSAI, KEISAI EISEN, UTAGAWA KUNISADA, and UTAGAWA KUNIYOSHI.

The shunga print followed the destiny of the figure print in general, reaching a peak in the late 18th century, then declining gradually. By the mid-19th century, it was a rare artist or publisher who could design or issue a print approaching the level of the earlier masters and publishers. In modern Japan—what with strong government censorship and prosecution—shunga have played only a minor role, in the hidden shadows of art.

Shunkan　　　　　　　　　俊寛

(1142?–79). Buddhist priest of the Shingon sect and administrative director of Hosshōji, a temple in the Shirakawa area of Kyōto. In

Shuri Castle remains
1 Restored sections of the Okinawan castle city include stone arches, which in the 15th century were still unknown in mainland Japan.
2 The influence of Chinese architecture can be seen in the ornate roof of the castle, shown here as it appeared in about 1933.

cies cultivated in Japan include Shina *shunran*, or Chinese *shunran* (*C. forrestii*), and *surugaran* (*C. ensifolium*); both are native to China.

Shunshoku umegoyomi
春色梅児誉美

(Spring Love: A Plum Blossom Almanac). A four-volume work of popular fiction written by TAMENAGA SHUNSUI (b 1789); published 1832–33. It became the prototype of the NINJŌBON—an Edo-period (1600–1868) genre of literature emphasizing romance. Although *Shunshoku umegoyomi* resembles the SHAREBON and other genres of comic fiction, it was the first to portray romantic love in a positive light, rather than as a snare to be avoided. In contrast to the wealthy, witty, and suave hero of the classic *sharebon*, its protagonist is the handsome but weak-willed Tanjirō, adopted heir to a YOSHIWARA brothel, who, having been cheated out of his inheritance, is left bedridden and miserable. However, his very weaknesses endear him to the courtesans, who vie with each other for his affection. Shunsui's gift for dialogue allowed him to present his characters through their own words and to impart a vivid realism that set his work apart from earlier popular fiction. His unique blend of social and psychological realism and sentimentality also paved the way for the development of realistic fiction in the Meiji period (1868–1912).

shuntō
春闘

(spring wage offensive). Unified campaign mounted by Japanese LABOR UNIONS every year in April to demand wage increases. Wage bargaining negotiations take place in the spring because April is both the beginning of the fiscal year in Japan and the time when most companies do their annual hiring of new graduates. At this time each year since 1955, a number of industrywide federations of unions have coordinated demands for increases in wage levels and have joined together to negotiate settlements with management. These negotiations have become the basic pattern of wage bargaining, involving all the major industries. Each year a particular industry is chosen to negotiate a wage settlement, the outcome of which sets the pattern for subsequent settlements made by other industries that year.

Shuppan Hō → Publication Law of 1893

Shuppan Jōrei → Publication Ordinance of 1869

Shuri Castle remains
首里城跡

(Shurijō *ato*). Early-15th-century castle site located at the highest point of the Shuri hills on the outskirts of the city of Naha, Okinawa Prefecture. The exact date of the castle's construction and its original size are not clear, but it is known to have been built on the grounds of an earlier castle by Shō Hashi (see CHŪZAN'Ō), founder of the first Shō dynasty, soon after his unification of the three Okinawan kingdoms in 1429. The castle was enlarged in the reigns of Shō Shin (r 1477–1526) and Shō Sei (r 1527–56) of the second Shō dynasty. Architecturally, the Shuri castle was a late representative of the Okinawan GUSUKU (castle) style. The castle was destroyed during World War II, but archaeological excavations have recently been undertaken.

shuriken
手裏剣

Knifelike weapon for throwing; used in one of the traditional MARTIAL ARTS of the Edo period (1600–1868), although known since the 11th century. *Shuriken* were made of steel in a number of different shapes. Some were shaped like small four-pointed stars, crosses, or swastikas and were thrown with a spin. Others were nail-shaped or needle-shaped. The former were sized to fit the hand for throwing, and the latter ranged up to 21 centimeters (8 in) in length. The Yagyū, Tsugawa, Shirai, and Negishi were well-known schools of *shuriken* throwing.

Shushigaku
朱子学

(Zhu Xi or Chu Hsi school). General name in Japan for the Neo-Confucianism that developed in Song (Sung) dynasty (960–1279) China. This, the most fully developed philosophical system of premodern China, was established by Zhu Xi (1130–1200), also known as Zhuzi or Chu-tzu (J: Shushi; hence Shushigaku, *gaku* meaning school). Whereas the already established interpretive studies of the Han (202 BC–AD 220) and Tang (T'ang; 618–907) dynasties were concerned with practical ethics (i.e., proper forms of conduct, especially in terms of social and familial relationships) and based this concern on the ethically oriented "Five Classics" of Confucianism, the Zhu Xi school was, in addition, concerned with abstract metaphysical principles. It developed an interpretation of nature and society based on the more philosophically oriented "Four Books" of the Confucian tradition (see FOUR BOOKS AND FIVE CLASSICS) and, influenced by Buddhist and Taoist ideas, formed a philosophy integrating the metaphysical and the physical.

Basic Teachings of the Zhu Xi School of Confucianism—The basic concept in Zhu Xi Confucianism is the *li-qi* (*li-ch'i*) dualism. *Li* (J: *ri*) is the principle that is basic to the existence of all things as well as to natural law and social norms. Because *li* does not assume any shape, function, or motion, it cannot result in phenomena by itself; only in conjunction with *qi* (*ch'i*; J: *ki*) does it take on a concrete existence in the form of animate or inanimate beings. *Qi* is a kind of gaseous matter and by self-induced motion can become *yin* and *yang* and the five elements (wood, fire, earth, metal, and water) that determine the shape and quality of all things. Yet, the basis for the functioning of *qi* is found in *li*. When *li* and *qi* combine, *qi* is condensed and beings are produced; when they separate, beings cease to exist.

After Zhu Xi's death, a division occurred in the Zhu Xi school: one side inclined toward regarding *li* as substance, the basis of existence of all things; the other side inclined toward regarding *li* as natural law and social norm. The former side became fixed as the national teaching in China. In Japan, however, this division into two schools was not particularly significant at the time.

The Zhu Xi School in Japan: Shushigaku—Zhu Xi's writings were introduced to Japan in the early Kamakura period (1185–1333); but it was later, in the Muromachi period (1333–1568), that they were particularly studied by Zen monks of the GOZAN temples. At the end of that period their influence appeared in the laws of *daimyō* domains (*kahō*). However, it was in the Edo period (1600–1868) that Zhu Xi's teachings, as Shushigaku, became rooted in the social fabric of Japan and became the official teaching of the Tokugawa shogunate.

1177 he joined the retired emperor GO-SHIRAKAWA in a plot (known as the Shishigatani Conspiracy) against TAIRA NO KIYOMORI, then the dominant power in the capital. Kiyomori arrested the conspirators and banished Shunkan to the island of Kikaigashima (believed to be what is now Iōjima, Kagoshima Prefecture). The following year an amnesty was declared, but Shunkan's name was not included, and he remained there until his death. His grief and rage at the moment he realized he would not be recalled from exile provide the dramatic climax of several Nō, *bunraku*, and *kabuki* plays, the most famous of which is *Heike nyogo no shima* (1719) by CHIKAMATSU MONZAEMON.

shunran
春蘭

Cymbidium georingii. An evergreen perennial herb of the orchid family (Orchidaceae) that grows wild on wooded mountains and hills throughout Japan and is also cultivated. The dark green leaves (20–50 cm [8–20 in]) are broad, linear, and drooping. In early spring a pale yellow flower (3–5 cm [1–2 in] wide), sometimes with reddish purple lines, opens on a stalk rising from the roots. The Japanese decorate bowls of soup with *shunran* flowers and drink boiled water with the salted flower floating on it.

All the plants known as *ran* (orchid) that are cultivated in Japan and China belong to the genus *Cymbidium* and are referred to as *tōyōran* (oriental orchids), in distinction to *yōran* (Western orchids). Other *tōyōran* spe-

Shushigaku is central to an understanding of the development of ideas in the Edo period. KOGAKU (Ancient Learning), a development within Japanese Confucianism and essentially a reaction against Shushigaku, advocated a return to the works of the ancient sages of China. Both KOKUGAKU (National Learning), which idealized Japan's earliest age and its ancient social mores and sentiments, and the so-called KOKUTAI ("national polity") theory, which found in the emperor system the special national characteristic of Japan, were influenced significantly by the development of Shushigaku. Shushigaku also influenced the acceptance of modern European science, which entered Japan via the Dutch in the late Edo period. See WESTERN LEARNING.

Confucianism and Buddhism, which had arrived in Japan by the 6th century, were regarded as more or less noncontradictory until the 16th century. Beginning with FUJIWARA SEIKA (1561–1619), however, Buddhism and Confucianism became clearly distinguished. Seika found in Confucianism a system of practical ethics by which to live in society and consequently abandoned the other-worldly teachings of Buddhism. The recognition of this contradistinction was also the rediscovery of the attractiveness of the moral rigor of Shushigaku, and it was thus that the interest of the warrior class in Shushigaku was heightened. In 1607 the shogunate employed HAYASHI RAZAN (the first important Japanese thinker to be exclusively identified with Shushigaku) as the shogunal Confucianist, giving him funds and land to build a private school and a Confucian temple in Edo (now Tōkyō). Razan drafted the BUKE SHOHATTO, the basic legal codes for the daimyō. During the KANSEI REFORMS of the 1780s and 1790s, Shushigaku was recognized as the orthodox teaching of the shogunate, which it remained until the MEIJI RESTORATION of 1868.

Until the mid-17th century, Edo-period Shushigaku was influenced by the Zen Buddhism of the Gozan or Five Monasteries and was accommodating toward a li-qi monism, as seen in Fujiwara Seika and Hayashi Razan. However, what is most characteristic of Shushigaku in Japan is its development of a position regarding li as law. YAMAGA SOKŌ, ITŌ JINSAI, OGYŪ SORAI, and DAZAI SHUNDAI—generally referred to as Kogaku scholars—developed a position regarding li as the law of qi and even arrived at a denial of the authority of Zhu Xi's interpretations of the classics.

The second most characteristic element of Edo-period Shushigaku is its emphasis on loyalty (Ch: zhong or chung; J: chū) over filial piety (Ch: xiao or hsiao; J: kō). Loyalty became directed at the state or domain rather than at the lord as an individual. Among Confucianists of the MITO SCHOOL, loyalty to the emperor came to be emphasized, developing into emperor-reverence by the end of the shogunate.

The third characteristic is the union of Shintō and Confucianism. A theory of Shintō incorporating elements of Zhu Xi's teaching (see SUIKA SHINTŌ) developed hand in hand with the growing call for reverence for the emperor.

The final important characteristic of Edo-period Shushigaku is its advancement of philological research. The inclination to verify history, institutions, and phenomena resulted in a proliferation of major studies in history, philosophy, and the natural sciences. See also CONFUCIANISM.

shūshin 修身

("moral" training). Name of a course devoted to "moral" training that was instituted by the Education Order of 1872. It was taught in primary and middle schools before Japan's defeat in World War II.

The term shūshin is taken from the Analects of Confucius and means to "establish or conduct oneself." The value system of shūshin was basically Confucian, with elements of modern civic morality and nationalism. The basic ideology underlying it was made clear in 1890 in the IMPERIAL RESCRIPT ON EDUCATION. Textbooks for moral training were made by the government, which used edifying stories and examples from everyday life. They gradually acquired a more nationalistic and militaristic tenor. Shūshin as a school subject was eliminated from the curriculum at the end of the war, but there has been a search for a new way to inculcate moral principles since then. See also MORAL EDUCATION.

shūshin koyō → employment system, modern

Shu Shunsui 朱舜水

(1600–1682; Ch: Zhu Shunshui or Chu Shun-shui). Expatriate Chinese scholar. Loyal to the Ming dynasty (1368–1644), he fled the rule of the succeeding Qing (Ch'ing) dynasty (1644–1912) and settled in Nagasaki in 1659. In 1665 he was invited by TOKUGAWA MITSUKUNI, daimyō of the Mito domain (now part of Ibaraki Prefecture), to live in Edo (now Tōkyō) under his patronage. There he cultivated the friendship of KINOSHITA JUN'AN, YAMAGA SOKŌ, and other Confucian scholars; lectured on various subjects, including Confucian etiquette, gardening, and agriculture; and greatly influenced the MITO SCHOOL of historical studies.

Shutoken → Tōkyō Metropolitan Area

Shuzenji 修善寺[町]

Town in eastern Shizuoka Prefecture, central Honshū. Situated on the river Kanogawa, it developed as a hot-spring resort in the Edo period (1600–1868). Of interest is the temple Shuzenji, associated with MINAMOTO NO YORIIE of the Kamakura shogunate (1192–1333) and made famous by OKAMOTO KIDŌ's play Shuzenji monogatari (1911). Pop: 17,490.

Sian Incident → Xi'an (Sian) Incident

Siberia, Japanese prisoners of war in シベリア抑留者

(Shiberia yokuryūsha). Soldiers and civilians captured by the Red Army and held for varying terms in prisons or labor camps throughout Soviet Asia between 1939 and 1959. Prisoners taken during the NOMONHAN INCIDENT along the Outer Mongolian–Manchurian frontier in 1939 spent several years at Karaganda in the Kazakh Soviet Socialist Republic (Kazakh SSR; now Kazakhstan). Of the nearly 2 million Japanese captured by the Red Army during August 1945, several hundred thousand soldiers and a few civilian officials were transported to labor camps across the Soviet Union. Most of these prisoners were repatriated between 1947 and 1950. In 1950 the Japanese Foreign Ministry claimed that 370,000 of its nationals remained unaccounted for and were presumably in Soviet custody. In 1953 the Japanese and Soviet Red Cross organizations began talks on the repatriation problem, resulting

in a boatload of 811 prisoners of war being returned. During the next six years, aided by the SOVIET-JAPANESE JOINT DECLARATION of 19 October 1956, some 4,500 were repatriated. The vast majority of those unaccounted for probably died at the end of the war or during the first few months of captivity.

Siberian Intervention シベリア出兵

(Shiberia Shuppei). Expedition of Japanese troops to Siberia from 1918 to 1922; part of a larger effort by Allied forces to intervene in the Bolshevik Revolution. The closing years of World War I witnessed the overthrow of the tsarist regime and the conclusion of a separate peace treaty between the newly established Soviet government and Germany in March 1918. The railway towns of Siberia and the Russian Far East passed into Soviet hands, but some 600,000 tons of Allied munitions had accumulated at Vladivostok, and about 50,000 Czechoslovak troops, many of whom had deserted from the Austrian armies to join the tsarist forces, were making their way westward across Siberia from Vladivostok along the Trans-Siberian Railway in an attempt to reach the Allied front in Europe. With the cooperation of the United States, the Allies decided to send troops to Vladivostok to protect their supplies and support the Czechoslovak troops. In July 1918 President Woodrow Wilson of the United States suggested that Japan contribute 7,000 troops to an international contingent of 25,000. After heated debate over whether to join the Allied plan or act alone, the TERAUCHI MASATAKE cabinet replied that it would send 12,000 troops.

Once the expedition was launched, the army took control, and by November 1918 more than 70,000 Japanese were entrenched in the Maritime Province and northern Manchuria. The Allies withdrew from Siberia in June 1920 after Admiral Aleksandr Vasilievich Kolchak, the counterrevolutionary leader they supported, had been captured and executed by the Bolsheviks. The Japanese remained, and a local military conflict continued between the Japanese-backed Priamur government in Vladivostok and the FAR EASTERN REPUBLIC established by the Soviets. Criticized domestically for the campaign's economic and human cost and pressured by the United States and Britain, Japan finally withdrew in October 1922. See also SOVIET UNION AND JAPAN; NIKOLAEVSK INCIDENT.

sickles → kama

Siddham 悉曇

(Shittan). Also known as Siddhamātrkā. A script used to write the form of Sanskrit used in the Buddhist world. Deriving from a script that in turn developed out of Brāhmī, Siddham was introduced to Japan via China in the Nara period (710–794). The traditional order of listing vowels and consonants in

shuriken At top, a multiple exposure photograph showing a straight, nail-shaped shuriken being thrown by a practitioner of the Negishi school of shuriken throwing. Above, three examples of shuriken, designed to be thrown with a spin.

shunran The 5-cm-long fruit (left) of this cold-resistant member of the orchid family stands upright on the stem. Shunran is cultivated both as a potted plant and in gardens.

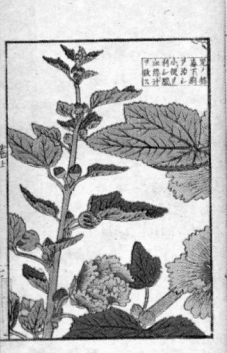

Siddham influenced the order of syllables in the traditional Japanese syllable chart (see GOJŪON ZU). Some premodern Japanese treatises on Siddham describe the sounds of the Japanese language of their time and are thus valuable materials for the historical study of Japanese phonology.

Sidotti, Giovanni Battista

シドッチ, G. B.

(1668–1714). The last Roman Catholic missionary to penetrate Japan while the policy of NATIONAL SECLUSION was in effect (1639–1854). This Sicilian priest arrived from the Philippines on Yakushima, an island off Kyūshū, in 1708. He was captured immediately and transported first to Nagasaki, then to Edo (now Tōkyō). In late 1709 and early 1710 he was questioned four times by ARAI HAKUSEKI, principal policy adviser to the shōgun TOKUGAWA IENOBU. Hakuseki, a great Confucian scholar who welcomed the opportunity to learn from Sidotti about the West, concluded that Christian missionary activity was not external aggression but noted that the spread of Christianity inevitably led to internal subversion. Although he recommended that Sidotti be repatriated, the priest was imprisoned in the KIRISHITAN YASHIKI, the seat of the anti-Christian inquisition. When Sidotti converted two of his caretakers to Christianity, he was confined in a hole in the ground, where he died on 28 November 1714. Hakuseki's interrogations of Sidotti resulted in Hakuseki's famous treatise *Seiyō kibun* (Tidings of the West), drafted in 1715.

Siebold, Philipp Franz von

シーボルト, P. F.

(1796–1866). Pioneer of Japanese studies in Europe. Born in Würzburg, Bavaria, he studied medicine at the university there and took his degree in 1820. Two years later he entered Dutch government service as an army doctor and was dispatched to the Netherlands East Indies. In 1823 he was appointed physician at the tiny Dutch settlement on DEJIMA, Nagasaki. In 1824 he established a boarding school called the Narutakijuku at Narutaki, then on the outskirts of the city of Nagasaki. Upon his disciples—who included ITŌ GEMBOKU and TAKANO CHŌEI—he conferred "doctor's" degrees in exchange for "dissertations" that dealt with a wide variety of subjects and were later used by him in his compendium, *Nippon, Archiv zur Beschreibung von Japan* (1832–51, Nippon, An Archive for the Description of Japan). He befriended the shogunate astronomer TAKAHASHI KAGEYASU, as well as MOGAMI TOKUNAI. In exchange for Dutch books, Takahashi provided Siebold

with maps of Japan, an act forbidden by shogunal policy. Eventually, enemies of Takahashi denounced him as a traitor and intercepted his correspondence with Siebold. Siebold was expelled from Japan at the end of December 1829; many of his Japanese friends were arrested, and Takahashi died in prison. Via Batavia he returned to the Netherlands, where he settled at Leiden in July 1830. During the next two decades he prepared his Japanese materials for publication.

His collection of Japanese ethnographic material was bought by the Dutch government in 1837 and became the foundation of the present National Museum of Ethnology (Leiden). His botanical and zoological collections are preserved at the Botanical Garden, the National Herbarium, and the National Museum of Natural History, all at Leiden.

Siemens Incident

シーメンス事件

(Shīmensu Jiken). The Siemens Incident of January 1914 was one of several spectacular political scandals between 1905 and 1915. A common theme in the popular disturbances that accompanied these scandals was clique (HAMBATSU) domination of the navy and army by men from the former domains of Satsuma (now Kagoshima Prefecture) and Chōshū (now Yamaguchi Prefecture). The Siemens Incident involved collusion between the navy and the German firm of Siemens.

The Siemens company had provided a 15-percent kickback to Japanese naval authorities in order to retain a monopoly over naval contracts. At the same time the navy had also contracted with the British firm of Vickers with a more favorable 25-percent commission. Hearing of this, the headquarters of Siemens demanded clarification through its Tōkyō office. A Tōkyō employee of Siemens (K. Richter) stole incriminating documents, sold them to a reporter for Reuters News Service, and returned to Germany. The *London Telegram* reported on 21 January 1914 that Richter had been sentenced to two years' imprisonment in Germany for his theft. The article also noted that some of the documents exposed corrupt contractual agreements with the Japanese navy.

Japanese newspapers immediately reported the details of the scandal. In the lower house, members of the Rikken Dōshikai party denounced the navy and the cabinet of YAMAMOTO GONNOHYŌE, who was backed by the Rikken Seiyūkai and who was the acknowledged head of the navy. Mass demonstrations followed in early February, culminating in violent confrontations with the police in Hibiya Park on the 10th and 14th. Naval officers in charge of procurement and shipbuilding were dismissed. Challenged even by the House of Peers, Prime Minister

Yamamoto resigned on 24 March, bringing down the entire cabinet with him.

signboards

看板

(kamban). *Kamban* became popular with the rapid development of commerce and industry in the 17th century. NOREN, cloth or rope curtains with the shop crest, apparently developed first. By the Edo period (1600–1868) signboards had become so gaudy that in 1682 the Tokugawa shogunate decreed that they must be wooden boards inscribed in india ink or made of copper. At night *andon* (a paper-covered lamp stand) and *chōchin* (a paper-covered lantern; see LANTERNS) bearing the store name were displayed. Some stores hung out their wares or representations of them, while other more established shops showed only their crest. Theatrical signboards were designed according to strict regulations regarding form and size. In Kyōto, where streets were narrow, rooftop signs were favored; in Edo (now Tōkyō) hanging signs were more common. With the Westernization of buildings in the late 19th century, painted and electric signboards became popular.

silk

絹

(kinu). Traditional Japanese textile. The fibers may be treated to produce either raw or glossed silk. Types of raw silk fabrics produced in Japan include *habutae* (a fine, smooth silk), *chirimen* (crinkly silk crepe), *kurēpu de shin* (crepe de chine), and *kiginu* (raw silk). Japanese glossed silk fabrics include NISHIJIN-ORI, *omeshi* (a kind of *chirimen*), *hakata-ori* (silk made in Fukuoka Prefecture), and TSUMUGI (pongee).

At the same time that silkworms and silk cloth were introduced into Japan from China around AD 200, Chinese and Korean weavers and sericulture experts settled in Japan and began producing fine silk *aya* (figured twill) and NISHIKI (brocade). From the Kamakura period (1185–1333) textile production fell into decline but revived in the 16th century, mainly in Hakata (now Fukuoka), Sakai (in Ōsaka Prefecture), and the Nishijin district of Kyōto, and soon new Chinese weaves were being produced (see KARA-ORI; KINRAN AND GINRAN).

Under the Tokugawa shogunate (1603–1867) restrictions on importation stimulated the domestic industry, and Ashikaga and Kiryū, near Edo (now Tōkyō), emerged as silk-weaving centers rivaling Nishijin. The end of the NATIONAL SECLUSION policy in the mid-19th century brought another expansion in the Japanese silk industry. From 1859 exportation of silk products became the mainstay of foreign trade.

The silk industry achieved its highest production in 1934: 45,243 metric tons (49,858 short tons). In 1990 Japan produced approximately 6,000 metric tons (6,600 short tons), or .8 percent of the world's silk. But since Japan consumes 17 percent of the total world production, it must rely on imports to meet domestic demand. See also SERICULTURE; TEXTILES.

Silk Road

シルクロード

(Shiruku Rōdo). General term for the overland trade routes by which Chinese silk was transported to Europe through Central and West Asia in premodern times. Broadly, the term refers to all the ancient land and sea routes between East Asia and Europe. As the main artery for commercial, cultural, and religious exchanges between East and West for nearly two millennia, the Silk Road played a

▲ A profusion of billboards dominate this early-20th-century street scene in Minatogawa, the theater district of Kōbe.

▲ Electric signs advertise shops, restaurants, and bars stacked high in buildings in Shinjuku, a Tōkyō business and entertainment district.

▶ An old and well-known merchant house in Kyōto announces its business with roof tiles reading "spice dealer."

▲ This Meiji-period sign for an Ōsaka pharmacy advertises medicinal candy.

▲ An old wooden signboard declares that this Nara shop sells narazuke, a type of Japanese pickle.

signboards

◀ Traditional signboards in the town of Narai in Nagano Prefecture hang above a store selling lacquer ware.

▼ Like many traditional establishments in Kyōto, the Tawaraya Inn uses a distinctive curtain (noren) as a kind of signboard.

▼ In Ōsaka's Dōtombori entertainment district, the signboard for a chain of crab restaurants features a huge crab whose legs wave back and forth.

vital role in the evolution of Chinese and Japanese culture in the Nara (710–794) and Heian (794–1185) periods.

The Silk Road from China to the Mediterranean had many branches. Most of them began in Chang'an (Ch'ang-an; now Xi'an or Sian), capital of the Former Han dynasty (206 BC–AD 8), or later in Luoyang (Loyang), capital of the Later Han dynasty (AD 25–220), and passed westward through Lanzhou (Lanchow) and Suzhou (Suchow) to Dunhuang (Tunhuang), the westernmost outpost of China proper.

From Dunhuang the most common route followed the southern foothills of the Tianshan (T'ien-shan) range along the northern rim of the Tarim Basin to Kashi (Kaxgar or Kashgar), in what is now western Xinjiang (Sinkiang) Province. It then crossed the Pamirs and passed through Fergana, Tashkent, Samarkand, and Bukhara to Merv. After crossing the Iranian plateau it divided into a northern branch, passing through Turkey to end at Antioch, and a southern branch, which passed through Baghdad and Palmyra to Damascus and Tyre on the eastern shore of the Mediterranean. From Kashi an alternative, more southerly route crossed the Pamirs to the headwaters of the Oxus (now Amu Darya) River and on into Bactria, passing through Balkh to meet the northerly route at Merv.

Another branch of the Silk Road, after leaving Dunhuang, followed the northern foothills of the Kunlun range (the southern rim of the Tarim Basin) through Ruoqiang (Qarkilik or Charklik) to Hotan (Khotan) in southwestern Xinjiang and then crossed the Pamirs and descended through the Hindu Kush into Afghanistan, passing through Bagram (near what is now Kabul) and Kandahār and thence to the northwest through Balkh to Merv.

A third route went further south into Afghanistan and passed through Ghazni, Kandahār, and Zaranj before turning northward to connect with the above routes at Merv.

Yet a fourth route, independent of the others, went from Dunhuang to Turpan (Turfan) and then struck out northward, along the foothills of the Altai range, and passed north of the Tianshan over the Eurasian steppe in what is now Kazakhstan, crossing the upper reaches of the Ob, Irtysh, Ishim, and Tobol rivers, as well as the Ural Mountains and the Volga River, to arrive at Tana at the mouth of the river Don.

Through this continuum of high mountains, deserts, and grassy plains traveled large caravans of traders from Central and West Asia, India, Armenia, Greece, Italy, and other countries along the routes. Braving climatic extremes and brigands' attacks, they dealt in goods and currencies at the numerous markets along the way. The bulk of their China trade, however, was conducted with Chinese merchants, who were legally barred from leaving their country by land.

The Silk Road and Japan——From the Nara period into the early Heian period, Japan sent embassies to the Asian continent (see SUI AND TANG [T'ANG] CHINA, EMBASSIES TO). Along with the resulting import of Chinese culture into Japan came somewhat sinicized elements of Central and West Asian cultures. Imported cultural artifacts from these areas, many of which survive in the SHŌSŌIN repository in Nara, received lavish attention from Japanese emperors and their courts and helped to stimulate advances in Japanese arts and crafts.

Cultural imports included the masked musical drama known as GIGAKU, which was derived from the drama of the Chinese Sui (589–618) and Tang (618–907) dynasties called Xiliang ji (Hsi-liang chi; J: Seiryōgi), itself an amalgam of folk music from the Dunhuang area in China and the music of Kuqa (Kucha) in Central Asia. It was introduced to Japan in 612 and has been regularly performed ever since. The masks of the various characters in gigaku represent Chinese, Indian, and Central Asian facial types.

Among the musical instruments stored at

Buddhism's Journey to the East

The ancient trade routes linking Europe to China served as a conduit for more than commerce. The network of roads that are known collectively as the Silk Road passed through areas of Central Asia in which Buddhism, spreading northward from India, had established itself as the dominant religion. Buddhism was then carried eastward via these trade routes over the Tarim Basin to Dunhuang, the westernmost outpost of China, and on across China to Korea and eventually to Japan. Along the way the motifs of Indian Buddhist art and architecture were filtered through the intervening cultures of Central Asia, China, and Korea in ways that produced a whole range of variations on the basic themes.

Below are photographs of icons (①–⑦) and structures (⑧–⑫) arranged to reflect Buddhism's journey from west to east. The precise rendering of facial features and drapery folds in sculpture ① attests to Greco-Roman influence resulting from the commercial and diplomatic ties between the Kushan dynasty and Rome. Sculpture ② is an Indian work that dates from the Gupta dynasty and shares many traits with sculpture ③, created at Tumxuk in the Tarim Basin. In both works, the Gupta preference for essential form reduces the robe to a thin layer that clings to the voluptuous outlines of the body. Stylistic resemblances to Chinese cave sculpture ④ can be seen in Japanese sculpture ⑥. Folds of drapery spill over the bases of both sculptures, and the treatment of the body is more abstract than in the Gupta-dynasty prototypes. Parallel similarities can be seen between Chinese sculpture ⑤ and Japanese sculpture ⑦. Photographs ⑧ to ⑫ show the transformation undergone by the rounded Indian Buddhist stupa as it traveled east to become the highly stylized Japanese pagoda.

Hayashi Ryōichi

① Seated Buddha. Gandhara (northwestern Pakistan). Kushan dynasty. 3rd century. Schist.

② Seated Buddha. Sarnath (Uttar Pradesh state, northern India). Gupta dynasty. 5th century. Sandstone.

③ Seated Buddha. Tumxuk (Uygur Autonomous Region of Xinjiang, western China). 5th century. Wood.

④ Seated Buddha. Longmen Binyang Cave (Henan Province, China). Northern Wei dynasty. 6th century. Stone.

⑤ Buddha (Mahāvairocana). Longmen Fengxiansi Cave (Henan Province, China). Tang dynasty. 675. Stone.

⑥ Shaka (Śākyamuni) Triad. The temple Hōryūji, near Nara, Japan. Nara period. 623. Gilt bronze.

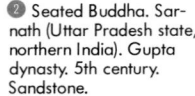
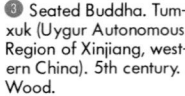
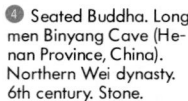
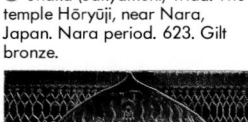

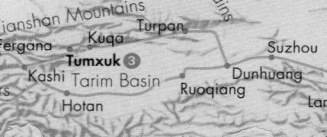

⑦ Buddha Amida (Amitābha) by Jōchō. The temple Byōdōin at Uji, near Kyōto, Japan. Late Heian period. 1053. Gilt wood.

Overland Trade Routes between Asia and Europe in Ancient Times

⑧ Great Stupa. Sanchi (Madhya Pradesh state, central India). 2nd century BC. Brick and stone. The first stupas were built as repositories for the earthly remains of Buddha and his disciples. The stupa shown is the best-preserved of three at this site.

⑨ Miniature stupa with relief scenes of Buddha's life. Gandhara (northwestern Pakistan). Kushan dynasty. 3rd century. Schist.

⑩ Pagoda Dayanta. The temple Ciensi at Chang'an (Xi'an, Shaanxi Province, China). Tang dynasty. 7th century. Brick.

⑪ West pagoda. The temple Kamŭnsa (Kyŏngju, North Kyŏngsang Province, South Korea). Silla dynasty. 8th century. Stone.

⑫ Pagoda. The temple Hōryūji, near Nara, Japan. Nara period. 711. Wood. This is Japan's oldest remaining wooden pagoda.

the Shōsōin, the *kugo* (a kind of harp) and the BIWA (a lutelike instrument) display characteristics similar to instruments from Central and West Asia. Among the Shōsōin's collection of *biwa*, there is a four-stringed instrument as well as the sole surviving five-stringed example. The origin of these two *biwa* is unclear, but scholars have proposed a Persian, West Asian, or Indian origin for the five-stringed instrument because its mother-of-pearl inlay depicts a man playing a *biwa* astride a camel. The Shōsōin's *genkan* (a type of *biwa*) is also the sole surviving example in the world. Since this instrument appears in wall paintings at Kyzyl, near Kuqa, the Shōsōin example may have come from that region. Among the game pieces of West Asian origin are a board (*kyoku*), pieces (*koma*), two dice (*sai*), and a cylinder for shaking the dice, all employed in the dice game SUGOROKU, which entered China from the West in the 5th century and may have originated in India or West or Central Asia.

Chairs, pitchers, and 8- or 12-lobed drinking cups are among the many pieces of furniture and utensils manifesting Central and West Asian influence. Some fabrics and other artifacts of the Shōsōin have Chinese versions of flowing patterns that originated in Central and West Asia, Persia, India, and the Eastern Roman Empire. Two famous examples, the *Hekiji shuryō mon nishiki* (Hunting Scene with Blue Background Brocade) and the *Shitennō mon nishiki* (Four Devas Brocade; stored at Hōryūji) are either Chinese products of the early Tang or slightly later Japanese copies. The hunting-scene brocade and lion-taming scenes on fabric and on a silver urn show evidence of Persian influence, as do dyed fabrics with bird and animal designs. Many of the Shōsōin treasures contain motifs and designs that came to Japan via Tang China, often Chinese versions of patterns from West and Central Asia. The Japanese of the Nara period were thus unconsciously assimilating a considerable amount of Central and West Asian culture. ☎ *1430*

silkworms 蚕

(*kaiko*). The larvae of the silkworm moth (*Bombyx mori*) of the family Bombycidae, whose cocoon is collected and turned into silk. There are more than 3,000 varieties, divided into Japanese, Chinese, European, and tropical groups. The native Japanese silkworm is sturdy, and it reproduces in great numbers; its principal food is mulberry leaves. The cocoon is peanut-shaped and colored white, yellow, or pale green. The breeding cycle of the silkworm moth is either six months or a year. The silkworm was used in a series of experiments by TOYAMA KAMETARŌ in 1906 to establish the validity of Mendel's law of heredity in the insect world. See also SERICULTURE.

Silla 新羅

(J: Shiragi). One of the Three Kingdoms of ancient Korea (see KOREAN THREE KINGDOMS PERIOD). Founded in 57 BC, Silla initially controlled the southeastern third of the Korean peninsula with its capital at Kyŏngju, 64 kilometers (40 mi) north of modern Pusan. When Silla embarked on its unification of the peninsula with Tang (T'ang) Chinese military support in 660, the kingdom of PAEKCHE requested aid from Japan; the Japanese expeditionary force was defeated, however, at the naval battle of HAKUSUKINOE (663). Silla then conquered KOGURYŎ in 668 and

ruled Korea until overthrown by the KORYŎ dynasty in 935.

sin → tsumi

Sin'ganhoe 新幹会

(J: Shinkankai). National coalition of Korean patriotic groups formed in 1927 with the goal of undermining Japanese rule from within Korea. Its founder was Yi Sang-jae (J: Ri Shōzai; 1850–1927). Although he opposed violence and political radicalism, his death shortly after the coalition's birth enabled radical elements, both left and right wing, to take control of the organization. The Sin'ganhoe turned violent, backing and coordinating the KWANGJU STUDENT RESISTANCE MOVEMENT of 1929–30. Korean communist involvement in the coalition and its violent tactics led to the arrest of many leaders, splintering the coalition and resulting in its membership voting for disbandment in 1931.

Singapore and Japan

シンガポールと日本

(Shingapōru *to* Nihon). As a trading center and port, Singapore has been of great importance to Japan throughout the modern era. Consular relations were established in 1889, and, by the end of the century, a number of large trading and shipping companies and banks had established offices in Singapore. These companies had been preceded by KARAYUKI SAN, women who were sold into prostitution and sent abroad, who first arrived in Singapore in the early Meiji period (1868–1912). By 1919 Japan was an important trading partner for the British crown colony and more than 3,000 Japanese were living there.

Japanese expansion into China in the 1920s and 1930s touched off anti-Japanese boycott movements by Chinese residents of Singapore. When Japanese forces attacked Malaya in December 1941, British colonial authorities released imprisoned Chinese communists and helped them organize a voluntary force to fight the Japanese. Prewar and wartime anti-Japanese activities led to massacres of Chinese by the Japanese following the 1942 fall of Singapore, which was renamed Shōnan. The Japanese military administration also coerced Singaporean Chinese to contribute 50 million Singapore dollars as reparations for their past activities against Japan.

Japan's postwar relations with Singapore were marred in 1962 when the "BLOOD DEBT" INCIDENT renewed the Singaporeans' determination that Japan atone for past military atrocities. The controversy was settled amicably in 1966, aided by Prime Minister Lee Kuan Yew's conciliatory attitude and the Japanese government's willingness to pay reparations. Following the settlement, Japanese capital was used to help finance government-sponsored industrial projects in Singapore and to set up joint ventures with local Chinese partners.

Located at the entrance of the Strait of Malacca connecting the Indian Ocean and the South China Sea, Singapore is extremely important to Japan's economy and security. In 1977 the Japanese government signed a treaty with Singapore, Malaysia, and Indonesia regulating navigation of the Strait of Malacca, through which passes 80 percent of the oil Japan imports from the Middle East. In 1989 Japanese investments in Singapore's manufacturing sector reached US $678 million, while investments in nonmanufac-

ing businesses reached US $1.2 billion. Since 1987 Japan has been Singapore's second largest trading partner, behind the United States. In 1990, 8.7 percent of Singapore's exports went to Japan, and Japan was the largest source of Singapore's imports, with 20.2 percent of the total. Singapore's trade deficit with Japan, US $7.1 billion in 1990, continues to be a problem in the trade between the two nations.

As it has already achieved considerable economic development, Singapore now receives a much smaller share of Japan's official development assistance (ODA) than it has in the past. In 1990 it received US $14.3 million in grants and funds for technical cooperation projects. Japan has also contributed to educational programs in Singapore. The Japanese government assisted the National University of Singapore in establishing a department of Japanese studies, which opened in 1981. In addition, hundreds of Singaporeans have studied at Japanese universities under the scholarship program set up by the Ministry of Education.

About 10,000 Japanese live in Singapore, many of them working for the approximately 600 Japanese companies that have operations there. Singapore is also one of the most popular spots for Japanese tourists, with more than 800,000 visiting in 1989.

Singh, Mohan シン, M.

(1909–). First commander of the anti-British INDIAN NATIONAL ARMY (INA) during World War II. Born in Punjab, he graduated from the Indian Military Academy in 1934. Captured in Malaya by the Japanese in 1941, Mohan Singh was persuaded to accompany Japanese advance troops during the attack on Singapore. In March 1942 he went to Tōkyō as a member of a mission composed of Indians from the parts of Southeast Asia then under Japanese control to learn Japanese intentions regarding the setting up of the INA and the achievement of Indian independence. Mohan Singh was allowed to raise the first INA division in late 1942, but as Japanese authorities stalled on the issue of further expansion of the organization, he began to lose confidence in the Japanese government's support of Indian independence. When one of his closest associates was arrested by the Japanese military police in December 1942 on charges of being a secret British agent, Mohan Singh issued secret instructions to disband the INA if he himself were arrested or assassinated. A week later he was arrested, and the INA dissolved itself. When Subhas Chandra BOSE, the Indian nationalist leader, set about raising the Second INA in 1943, he hoped to use Mohan Singh's good offices, but the meeting between the two was unsuccessful. Confined by the Japanese until the end of the war, Mohan Singh later participated in Indian politics.

Sino-French War 清仏戦争

(Shin-Futsu Sensō). War fought between China and France from 1883 to 1885 for domination of Vietnam, traditionally a tributary state of China. Vietnam became a protectorate of France in June 1885, in accordance with the Tianjin (Tientsin) Convention. In Japan, the French victory was seen as the start of Western imperialism in East Asia and led to a shift in emphasis from popular rights (*minkenron*) to national rights (*kokkenron*) by the leaders of the FREEDOM AND PEOPLE'S RIGHTS MOVEMENT.

1 Units of the Japanese army disembark at Inch'ōn in Korea in June 1894, preparing for war with
China. Japan would declare war on August 1.
2 The Japanese attack on Port Arthur in November 1894.

Sino-Japanese War of 1894–1895

Japanese Troop Movements during the Sino-Japanese War of 1894–1895

- China
- Niuzhuang 5 March 1895
- Tianzhuangtai 9 March 1895
- Fengtian Province
- Yingkou
- Yalu River 17 September 1894
- Liaodong Peninsula
- P'yŏngyang 16 September 1894
- Wŏnsan
- Dalian
- landing 24 October 1894
- Port Arthur (Lüshun) 21 November 1894
- Inch'ŏn 12 June 1894
- Korea
- Seoul
- Sea of Japan
- P'ungdo 25 July 1894
- Weihaiwei 12 February 1895
- Sŏnghwan 29 July 1894
- Asan
- Pusan
- Yellow Sea
- Shimonoseki
- Japan
- → Japanese troop movements
- ceded to Japan under the Treaty of Shimonoseki, 17 April 1895, returned to China, 8 November 1895

Sino-Japanese Amity Treaty of 1871 　日清修好条規

(Nisshin Shūkō Jōki). First modern treaty between Japan and China; signed in Tianjin (Tientsin) on 13 September 1871 by special envoy Date Munenari (1818–92) and LI HONGZHANG (Li Hung-chang). Tōkyō initiated the treaty, which emphasized the regularization of commercial relations between the two countries. Mutual rights of extraterritoriality were established, and a most-favored-nation clause was deliberately omitted. The treaty was abrogated with the outbreak of the SINO-JAPANESE WAR OF 1894–1895. See also CHINA AND JAPAN.

Sino-Japanese War of 1894–1895 　日清戦争

(Nisshin Sensō). A war between China and Japan formally declared on 1 August 1894 and concluded with the Treaty of SHIMONOSEKI on 17 April 1895. Japan quickly and utterly defeated the superior forces of China and emerged as the dominant power in East Asia. In Japanese history it marked the point when the armed forces gained a controlling influence in official decision making, foreign policy came to emphasize territorial expansion and power politics, China became an object of Japanese exploitation, and industrialization began in earnest. The war is a landmark in modern Asian international relations.

Almost from the establishment of the Meiji government in 1868, the Japanese had pressed for a bold interventionist policy in Korea (see SEIKANRON). China became directly involved in 1882, when it sent a fleet with 3,000 troops to Korea to deal with an anti-Japanese riot in Seoul. Two years later, when a Korean faction led by KIM OK-KYUN staged a coup d'état with overt Japanese assistance, Queen MIN called in 1,500 Chinese troops (see KAPSIN POLITICAL COUP). From this time on, and especially after the signing of the TIANJIN (TIENTSIN) CONVENTION in 1885, it became impossible for Japan to interfere in Korean politics without incurring Chinese retaliation.

In the spring of 1893 a domestic uprising in Korea soon turned into the large-scale TONGHAK REBELLION, threatening the Korean dynasty. The ruler again appealed to China for aid and received a force of 2,800 soldiers. The Japanese also quickly dispatched troops. Although the Tonghaks were easily suppressed, Tōkyō's leaders were determined to seize this opportunity for war. After a series of encounters, all resulting in Japanese victories, Japan formally declared war on 1 August. Quick victories over Chinese land forces at P'yŏngyang (16 September) and Chinese warships in the YALU RIVER naval battle (17 September), followed by the seizure of PORT ARTHUR (21 November) and the final destruction of the Chinese fleet at Weihaiwei (12 February 1895), whetted the appetite of a resource-poor nation for territorial acquisitions.

The Chinese negotiator, LI HONGZHANG (Li Hung-chang), arrived in Shimonoseki in February 1895. The Japanese delegation, headed by ITŌ HIROBUMI and MUTSU MUNEMITSU, demanded the independence of Korea; the cession of the southern part of Fengtian (now Liaoning) Province (in Manchuria), Taiwan, and the Pescadores; the payment of 300 million taels (more than ¥500 million) as a war indemnity; and the conclusion of a new commercial treaty allowing Japan to navigate the Yangzi (Yangtze) River and to operate manufacturing establishments in the treaty ports, as well as the opening of four additional ports. Li eventually yielded when the Japanese reduced the indemnity to 200 million taels and confined territorial claims in Manchuria to the Liaodong (Liaotung) Peninsula.

When the Treaty of SHIMONOSEKI was signed on 17 April, Japan became the first Asian imperialist power. Japan's "Manchurian empire," however, was soon aborted by the so-called TRIPARTITE INTERVENTION. Russia, France, and Germany "advised" Japan to give up the Liaodong Peninsula. The Japanese government had no choice but to return the peninsula to China in exchange for an additional indemnity of 30 million taels. This humiliating retreat only stiffened the Japanese resolve to persevere in the game of imperialist politics.

A significant by-product of the war was Japan's industrial revolution. The requirements of the enlarged armed forces and the newly opened markets of Korea and China provided an impetus for the growth of the textile, iron and steel, shipbuilding, and other industries.

The Sino-Japanese War also defined the framework in which Japan would deal with its external and internal problems for the next half-century. It marked modern Japan's active entry into international power politics and set the stage for internal economic, social, and cultural developments. A sense of national unity had been achieved, but this unity also called forth a rising tide of industrial disputes, labor movements, selfish pursuits, and extremist ideologies. The resulting tension would characterize the history of Japan over the next half-century.

Sino-Japanese War of 1937–1945 　日中戦争

(Nitchū Sensō). War between Japan and China, from 7 July 1937 to 15 August 1945. Fought on the Chinese mainland by forces of the Japanese Imperial Army against CHIANG KAI-SHEK's Nationalist army and MAO ZEDONG's (Mao Tse-tung) communist army centered in Yan'an (Yenan). The war claimed untold numbers of civilian lives and, by conservative estimate, 1,871,000 military lives (571,000 Japanese; 1,300,000 Chinese) and destroyed vast amounts of land and property.

Outbreak of Hostilities—The first incident of the war occurred at a bridge called Lugouqiao (Lukouchiao) about 19 kilometers (12 mi) southwest of Beijing (Peking; called Beiping or Peiping from 1928–1949), known by Westerners as the Marco Polo Bridge (see MARCO POLO BRIDGE INCIDENT). On the night of 7 July 1937, Japanese troops, part of a brigade permitted in the area under terms of the Boxer Protocol of 1901 (see BOXER REBELLION), were conducting routine field exercises in the darkness when some blank shots were fired from a Japanese machine-gun position. These were answered by a round of live shots fired toward the Japanese position—perhaps from Chinese troops. When the Japanese detachment commander called roll, a soldier was missing from the ranks. The Japanese officer demanded the right to search the nearby town of Wanping. The Chinese refused, and the Japanese responded by forcibly trying to breach the town's defenses.

After a month of skirmishing in the Beijing-Tianjin (Tientsin) area and a series of futile attempts to arrive at a local settlement in the north, the confrontation spread to

Shanghai in August and then veered out of control. What had been called the North China Incident (J: Hokushi Jihen) grew in violence and scope to become the China Incident (J: Shina Jihen).

Military Operations—While Chinese armies withdrew after only a token defense of Beijing and Tianjin in the north, Chiang Kai-shek ordered a determined defense of the lower Yangzi (Yangtze) River area, beginning with Shanghai. From August to November 1937, the city suffered first aerial and naval bombardment and then hand-to-hand combat as approximately 200,000 Japanese troops gradually forced a 500,000-man Chinese army into retreat in savage street fighting.

The Chinese resistance in Shanghai collapsed in November after a task force of about 30,000 Japanese troops landed unopposed at Hangzhou (Hangchow) Bay, about 48 kilometers (30 mi) south of Shanghai. The Japanese troops outflanked Shanghai and joined other units to begin a race westward to the Nationalist capital of Nanjing (Nanking). The capital fell after only a few days of fighting on 13 December 1937. Soldiers under the command of General Matsui Iwane (1878–1948; hanged as a war criminal after the WAR CRIMES TRIALS in Tōkyō) engaged in an orgy of looting, arson, torture, rape, and murder that lasted for three weeks. The casualty toll of the NANJING (NANKING) MASSACRE will never be known with certainty, but estimates range upward from 42,000 killed.

The Nationalists retreated farther inland to a new capital at Hankou (Hankow), about 970 kilometers (600 mi) upriver on the Yangzi. In the north, Mao Zedong's partisans used guerrilla warfare that effectively tied down large numbers of Japanese soldiers; occasionally they defeated the Japanese in pitched battles. The first significant Chinese victory in the war came in September 1937 when communist general Lin Biao's (Lin Piao; 1908–71) 115th Division entrapped and decimated a Japanese division at Pingxingguan (P'ing-hsing-kuan) in northern Shanxi (Shansi). The Chinese also employed "scorched earth" tactics in 1938—the incineration of the city of Changsha and the intentional breaching of the dikes of the Yellow River near Zhengzhou (Chengchow)—but this delayed Japanese motorized columns for no more than six to eight weeks.

Japan's battlefield strategy was centered on the seizure of "points" (cities) and "lines" (railways). In the spring of 1938 attention was fixed on the crossroads city of Xuzhou (Süchow), at the junction of the north-south Jinpu (Tsinpu) and east-west Longhai (Lunghai) railways. In April 1938 Chinese forces under the personal command of Deputy Chief of Staff General Bai Chongxi (Pai Ch'ung-hsi; 1893–1966) defeated two Japanese divisions at Tai'er Zhuang (Taierh Chuang) in Jiangsu (Kiangsu), about 65 kilometers (40 mi) northeast of Xuzhou. Chiang failed to exploit his success at Tai'er Zhuang, pulled back, and allowed the Japanese to replenish their forces. Consequently, on 15 May 1938, Japanese armies encircled Xuzhou and four days later captured the city.

Continued Chinese resistance forced the Japanese to turn their attention to Hankou. As the campaign for Hankou got under way, Major General ISHIWARA KANJI, one of the few Japanese to challenge the official view that the war was nearly over, cautioned military colleagues against becoming hopelessly mired in China. His outspokenness led to his

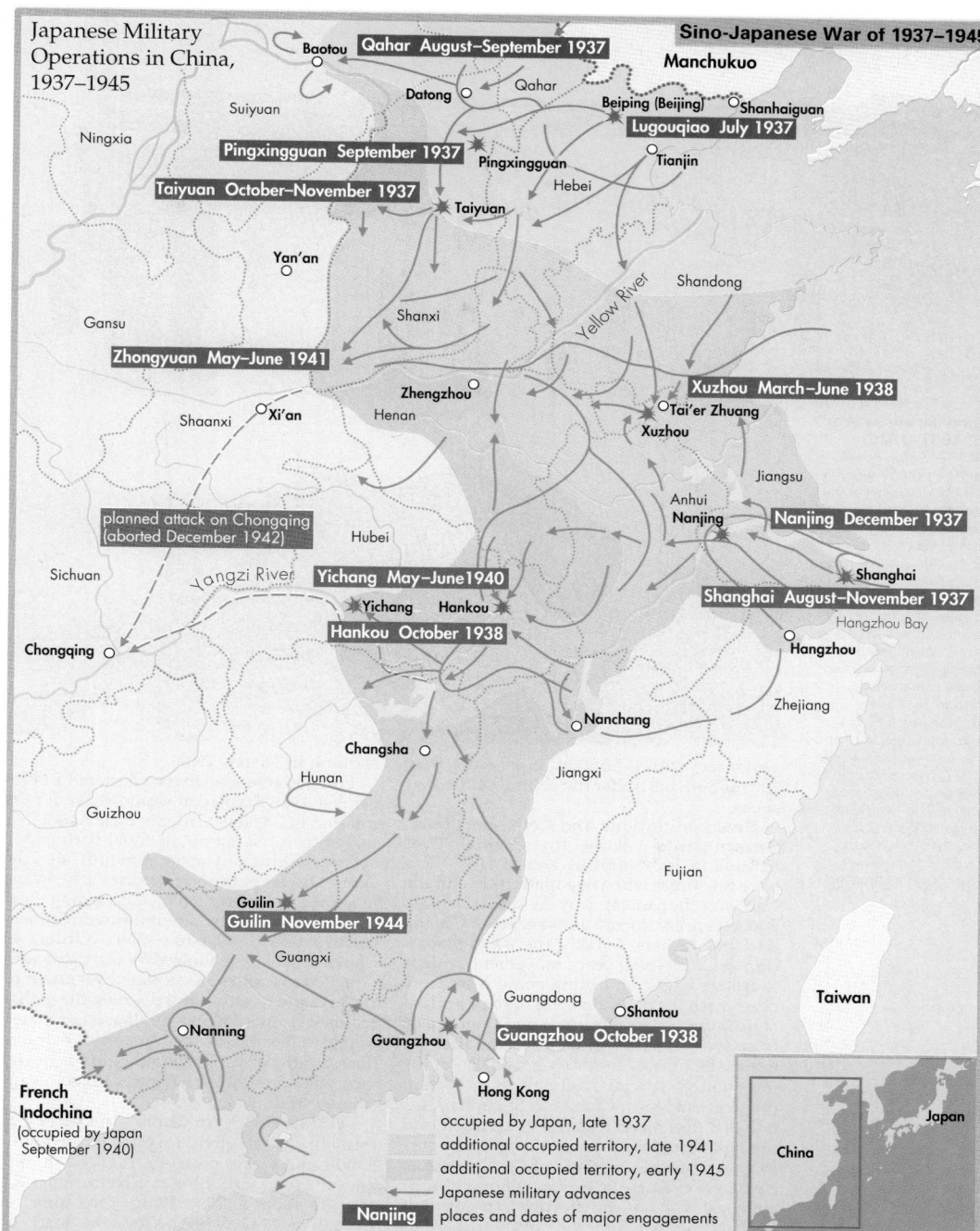

assignment to garrison duty in Kyōto and eventual demotion. The four-and-a-half-month pincer campaign to capture Hankou came to a climax when five Japanese columns poured into that city on 25 October. The Nationalist government had already vacated the city. Government, industry, schools, hospitals—the working capacity of Free China—were relocated westward beyond the Yangzi gorges to Chongqing (Chungking) in one of the great mass migrations of human history. Meanwhile, the great southern city of Guangzhou (Canton), the last remaining seaport through which China could hope to import war matériel, fell to Japan on 21 October. From that time on, the war fronts gradually stabilized. Chongqing was subjected to devastating air raids, but there were only a few large-scale land operations after October 1938.

The expansion of the China Incident into WORLD WAR II (or the Greater East Asia War, as it was officially designated) on 8 December 1941 brought the United States into the Asian war. US air power, provided through General Claire Chennault (1890–1958), helped to preserve Chongqing and other Chinese cities from Japanese attack. US general Joseph W. Stilwell was designated as chief of staff to Chiang Kai-shek and assigned the task of defending Burma. The Chinese and British armies and American advisers there, however, were overrun by Japan in the spring of 1942. Stilwell felt that Chiang was reluctant to commit his army to battle with the Japanese in Burma and in China because he was using so many forces to blockade communist guerrilla armies in the north. His criticism of the Nationalist army's lethargic resistance to Japan was confirmed in May 1944 when Japan launched a highly successful six-month campaign on the Chinese mainland. Known as OPERATION NUMBER ONE, this offensive overran the US base at Guilin (Kweilin) and was advancing in the direction of Chongqing before Chinese lines finally held in late 1944. Almost 500,000 Chinese soldiers were lost, and eight

Sino-Japanese War of 1937–1945

1 The Marco Polo Bridge near Beijing, in 1937. A skirmish in the vicinity of this bridge marked the beginning of the war.

2 Continuing Japanese assaults forced the Chinese to relocate their capital to Chongqing in Sichuan Province. Japanese navy medium bombers, shown here, strike at the new capital.

3 Nanjing, China's capital, fell to the Japanese on 13 December 1937, two days before this photograph was taken. The Japanese army embarked on nearly a month-long campaign of killing, rape, and destruction.

provinces, with a population of more than 100 million, fell under the control of the Japanese.

Peace Initiatives and Collaborationist Governments—From the beginning of fighting in 1937 until its end in 1945 there were few times when negotiations to end the war were not under way in some fashion. Some were conducted with agents of Chiang Kai-shek; others, notably the WANG JINGWEI (Wang Ching-wei) peace movement, sought to isolate China and bring about a separate peace with his rivals. In spite of their mutual anticommunist posture Japan did not see fit to soften the peace terms it offered the Nationalist Chinese, continuing to insist on the retention of special economic and military privileges in North China and Shanghai. Nationalist diplomats rejected these terms and the Japanese turned to recruiting collaborators from outside the ranks of the Nationalist Party. For example, after parts of Inner Mongolia as well as the northern portion of Shanxi Province and the southern part of Qahar (Chahar) Province were overrun by the Japanese GUANDONG (KWANTUNG) ARMY, these areas were amalgamated in November 1937 into a federation known as Mengjiang (Meng-chiang; J: Mōkyō; Mongolian Borderlands). The Japanese recruited Mongolian tribal leaders to administer the federation, with guidance from the Guandong Army.

One month after the appearance of Mengjiang, agents of Japan's North China Area Army sponsored the creation of the PROVISIONAL GOVERNMENT OF THE REPUBLIC OF CHINA in Beijing. This puppet regime, which survived until March 1940, had jurisdiction over all or parts of the five provinces of North China. Japanese advisers called upon the Provisional Government to charter "national policy companies" (kokusaku kaisha) under rules that allowed Japan to increase its grip on virtually all industries related to resource development. Similar arrangements were made between the Japanese Central China Area Army and its REFORM GOVERNMENT OF THE REPUBLIC OF CHINA, launched in

Nanjing in March 1938.

Premier KONOE FUMIMARO declared in November 1938 that Japan would strive for the creation of a "New Order in East Asia" (TŌA SHINCHITSUJO) based on an equal partnership between China and Japan. A month later, the deputy leader of the Nationalist Party, Wang Jingwei, defected from Chongqing and began to explore the possibilities of Chinese participation in Japan's New Order. In March 1940 Japan allowed Wang to inaugurate the REORGANIZED NATIONAL GOVERNMENT OF THE REPUBLIC OF CHINA and dissolve the earlier regional regimes. However, Japan continued to regard North China as an area of extraordinary military and economic privilege and refused to present Wang with a timetable for troop withdrawal.

A "New Policy for China" and Anticommunism—Battlefield reverses in the South Pacific and severe pressure from communist guerrilla forces in China caused the Japanese army to adopt a "New Policy for China" in December 1942. This policy (the work of SHIGEMITSU MAMORU, ambassador to the Reorganized Government) allowed Wang a more independent government. In 1943 Japan returned the SHANGHAI INTERNATIONAL SETTLEMENT to Chinese administration. Japan encouraged the Wang regime to maintain armed forces—known to the Nationalists as weijun (wei-chün; puppet armies). Defections from the Nationalist army swelled the size of these forces so that they numbered perhaps as many as 900,000 by the final year of the war.

As the war drew to an end, the fear of communism impelled the Nationalist army, the weijun, and the Japanese Imperial Army to put aside their differences in order to check growing communist strength. The Japanese faced the difficult task of transferring power in major cities to the Nationalists when, in many cases, communist forces had sufficient strength to contest the Nationalists. Shanghai, Nanjing, and other great Yangzi and coastal cities were eventually turned over to Chiang's forces by puppet and Japanese troops and denied to Mao's armies. In the North China countryside,

communist attempts to take over the Shandong-Hebei region were hampered because Nationalist commanders received Japanese and weijun reinforcements in the immediate postsurrender period. On 23 November, well over three months after the Japanese surrender, the commanding general of US forces in China, Albert C. Wedemeyer (1897–1989), reported to his chief of staff that the disarming of Japanese forces by the Chinese was not proceeding rapidly because the Japanese were being employed to protect communication lines and installations against the communists.

On 2 September 1945 a Chinese representative was aboard the battleship *Missouri* in Tōkyō Bay to witness the Japanese signing of the instrument of surrender. On 29 April 1952 Japan signed a peace treaty with the Republic of China. Finally, in October 1978, the formal end to the war came with the exchange of instruments of ratification of the CHINA-JAPAN PEACE AND FRIENDSHIP TREATY in ceremonies held in Tōkyō.

sister cities　　　　　姉妹都市

(*shimai toshi*). As of 1990 there were 730 Japanese cities, towns, wards, and villages linked with foreign sister counterparts. The first Japanese sister-city combination was arranged by the United Nations and linked Nagasaki with St. Paul, Minnesota, in 1955. Thereafter, many Japanese cities became linked with other cities all over the world. The Kokusai Shinzen Toshi Remmei (International Federation for the Promotion of Sister Cities), founded in 1962, promotes these activities.

skating　　　　　スケート

(*sukēto*). Ice skating was introduced into Japan in 1877 by Americans in Sapporo. Between 1908 and 1915 Lake SUWA in Nagano Prefecture became a favorite locale for recreational and competitive skating. Japanese have participated in the Winter Olympics in skating events since 1932 and in ice hockey since 1936. The National Skating Union of Japan and the Japan Ice Hockey Federation comprise approximately 10,000 skaters, with over 900 hockey teams. Recreational skating has become more popular with widespread construction of skating rinks in the cities.

skiing　　　　　スキー

(*sukī*). Skiing was introduced into Japan in 1911 under the direction of Major Theodor von LERCH, an Austrian military attaché serving in Japan. Under his supervision, soldiers of the Imperial Army practiced skiing in Takada, Niigata Prefecture. In the same year the first ski club was founded. The Japanese made their Olympic debut at the second Winter Olympics in 1928, and at the 1956 Winter Olympics IGAYA CHIHARU won a silver medal in the men's slalom event. The 11th Winter Olympics were held in Sapporo, Hokkaidō, in 1972 (see SAPPORO WINTER OLYMPIC GAMES).

Interest in skiing has continued to grow in recent decades. Approximately 93,000 skiers are currently registered with the Ski Association of Japan.

Skylark Co, Ltd [株]すかいらーく

(Sukairāku). Suburban restaurant chain operator. Incorporated in 1948. Skylark operates 633 outlets, including family restaurants, casual dining restaurants, coffee shops, fast-food outlets, traditional Japanese and Chinese restaurants, and restaurants featuring French cuisine. It operates a gourmet hamburger chain on the West Coast of the United States. Sales for the fiscal year 1990 totaled ¥126.0 billion (US $918.4 million). The company was capitalized at ¥11.6 billion (US $84.5 million) in the same year. Headquarters are in Tōkyō.

small and medium enterprises 中小企業

(chūshō kigyō). Small and medium enterprises in Japan are defined by a law passed in 1972 as those having no more than 300 employees or ¥100.0 million (US $729,927) in paid-in capital; small-scale wholesalers, however, are defined as those with no more than 100 employees or ¥30.0 million (US $218,978) in capital, while for small-scale retailers the limits are 50 employees or ¥10.0 million (US $72,992) in capital.

The most important characteristics of small and medium enterprises in Japan are these: (1) very small (fewer than four employees) or family-owned businesses are the most numerous; (2) small and medium enterprises are widely distributed in almost all sectors of the economy, with most found in manufacturing, wholesaling, retailing, and services; (3) about two-thirds of the enterprises are subcontractors of large companies (shitauke kigyō) and thus subject to a degree of influence from large firms; and (4) local industries (jiba sangyō), or businesses that are identified with a particular region or regional product, play an important role in the economic structure.

The Japanese government's system for assisting small and medium enterprises is one of the most extensive of its kind in the world. Financial assistance is offered by three government-affiliated institutions: the SMALL BUSINESS FINANCE CORPORATION, the PEOPLE'S FINANCE CORPORATION, and the SHŌKO CHŪKIN BANK.

Before the expansion of the Japanese economy in the 1960s, a widely held assumption was that small and medium enterprises hindered economic development. This view was buttressed by the low productivity, unfavorable wages, and inferior product quality that plagued small and medium enterprises before the high economic growth period. From the mid-1960s on, however, small and medium enterprises grew rapidly in number and increased production. Their growth was mainly due to rapid growth of demand and the expansion of the consumer market, in which small and medium businesses dominated; the composite effect of capital investment for modernization of equipment; and government assistance in strengthening small-business management.

The sudden slowdown in growth following the oil crisis of 1973, coupled with export difficulties and increased competition due to the sharp appreciation of the yen (in 1977 and again in 1985), was expected to hit smaller enterprises harder then the larger firms. While many of the less-efficient firms did fail, most smaller firms adapted to these changes in the economic structure and survived. As the position of small and medium enterprises improved, the focus of government assistance shifted from direct financial assistance, tax breaks, and the supply of credit to more indirect aid, such as guidance in improving marketing techniques and the promotion of cooperative efforts among small and medium firms. In 1989 small and medium enterprises totaled 6,571,942, or 99.2 percent of all firms in Japan. This figure includes 873,615 manufacturers, 3,045,133 wholesalers and retailers, 1,519,093 companies in service industries, and 1,134,101 in other industries. It excludes agricultural, forestry, and fishery establishments.

small and medium enterprises, laws concerning 中小企業関係法

(chūshō kigyō kankei hō). Body of legislation, centered on the Small and Medium Enterprises Basic Law (Chūshō Kigyō Kihon Hō, 1963), that forms the basis of Japanese government policy toward the large number of smaller enterprises that operate in the economy. Official policy, as stated in the basic law, is to rely chiefly on the independent efforts of the small and medium enterprises, with government assistance where appropriate, especially in the area of promoting cooperative efforts. Many laws have been passed to implement this policy. Various laws also promote the modernization and improvement of enterprises, the restructuring of the traditional crafts and textile industries, capital loans, credit, business guidance, financial security and prevention of bankruptcy, employee welfare, and labor relations.

Small Business Finance Corporation 中小企業金融公庫

(Chūshō Kigyō Kin'yū Kōko). Government-funded financial institution. Established in 1953 to provide small and medium-sized businesses with low-interest operating funds and equipment funds for modernization and reorganization. The corporation had success in the 1970s helping small businesses to improve their pollution control systems, upgrade safety and sanitary setups, and computerize and modernize operations. As of the end of March 1991, the corporation had outstanding loans totaling ¥7.4 trillion (US $53.9 billion), of which equipment investment funds accounted for 52 percent. The government is the sole provider of the corporation's capital; capitalization stood at ¥87.7 billion (US $639.2 million) in the same year. Headquarters are in Tōkyō.

SMC Corporation エスエムシー[株]

(Esu Emu Shī). Pneumatic compressor manufacturer. It began operations in 1959 as Shōketsu Kinzoku Kōgyō (Sintered Metal Corporation) of Tōkyō and has become one of the world's largest makers of pneumatic compressors. Overseas expansion of the SMC group began in earnest in 1967 with capital participation in an Australian company. Today SMC has locally incorporated subsidiaries in 13 countries in North America, Europe, Asia, and Oceania. For the fiscal year ending March 1991, the company had annual sales of ¥102.9 billion (US $750.0 million), and capitalization was ¥21.1 billion (US $153.8 million). Headquarters are in Tōkyō.

smiths 鍛冶屋

(kajiya). In Japan this profession was passed down through family lines from early times. Kajiya belonged to the kanuchibe, one of many hereditary service groups that specialized in a craft (see BE); many of these smiths were naturalized immigrants (KIKAJIN) who introduced ironworking techniques from the Asian mainland. After the TAIKA REFORM (645) they came under the authority of the Bureau of Smiths (Kaji no Tsukasa) and lived in the capital area of Nara. They later scattered throughout the country to work on landed estates (SHŌEN). With the rise to power of the warrior class, professional swordsmiths appeared; there was further specialization when firearms were introduced by the Portuguese in 1543 (see FIREARMS, INTRODUCTION OF). During the Edo period (1600–1868) the increased demand for metal agricultural tools and household goods led to regional specialization. There were also smiths who went from village to village at harvesttime to repair farm tools.

SMON disease スモン病

(subacute myelo-opticoneuropathy; J: sumombyō). A disease of the nervous system associated with a disorder of the optical nerve and due primarily to the toxic effects of the drug chinoform (lodochlorhydroxyquin), used for treatment and prevention of amoebic dysentery. The disease frequently commences with abdominal pain and diarrhea and is characterized in its advanced stages by damage to the central and peripheral nervous systems resulting in severe sensory and motor impairment. Cases of SMON disease began appearing in Japan in 1955, and the number increased rapidly in the late 1960s, involving a total of about 11,700 patients, with 500 deaths. New outbreaks effectively stopped when the sale of chinoform was banned in 1970.

The etiology of SMON disease became a highly controversial issue. In October 1969 newspapers reported that public health experts believed it to be an infectious disease. Some sufferers subsequently committed suicide. In March 1972 a special investigation commission appointed by the Ministry of Health and Welfare rejected the virus theory and concluded that chinoform had caused the vast majority of SMON cases. Some authorities attribute the relatively high incidence in Japan to an interaction between chinoform and environmental factors.

snakes 蛇

(hebi). In Japanese, hebi is the general name for reptiles of the suborder Serpentes, order Squamata. Five families are found in Japan: Typhlopidae, Colubridae, Elapidae (Okinawa Prefecture), Hydrophiidae, and Viperidae. The most common species are the shimahebi (Elaphe quadrivirgata); aodaishō (E. climacophora); and yamakagashi (Rhabdophis tigrinus) of the family Colubridae, which are distributed widely in paddy fields, dry fields, grasslands, and woods. The mamushi (Agkistrodon halys), the only poisonous

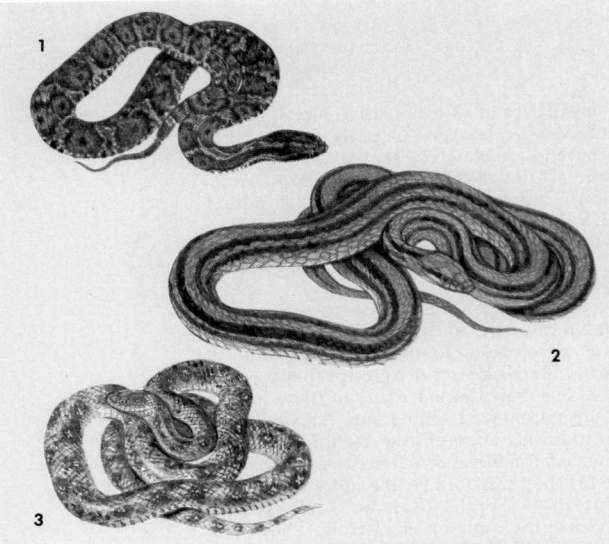

snakes
1 The pit viper known as *mamushi* is 40 to 60 cm in length. It is well known as Japan's most common poisonous snake.
2 The common *shimahebi* is found throughout Japan north of Okinawa. This snake, which reaches 1 to 1.5 meters, eats small birds, frogs, and mice.
3 The *yamakagashi* lives near water throughout Japan south of Hokkaidō and feeds largely on frogs and fish.
4 The *aodaishō*, which reaches 2 meters, lives throughout Japan. It is an excellent climber and often eats birds' eggs.

snake widely distributed throughout Japan, is commonly seen in paddy fields and other damp areas, and hikers and outdoor workers are often bitten by it. The *habu* (*Trimeresurus flavoviridis*), which inhabits the Amami Islands and Okinawa, is more aggressive and fatally poisonous. The Erabu *umihebi* (*Laticauda semifasciata*) sea snake is found southward from southern Kyūshū.

In ancient times snakes were venerated as beings possessed of an eternal life because of their ability to shed their skins. The snake was also regarded as a deity of paddy fields and mountains as well as of houses.

Snow Brand Food Co, Ltd
雪印食品[株]

(Yukijirushi Shokuhin). Meat-packer. Its main products are processed meat, fresh and frozen meat, preserved food, and institutional foods. Affiliated with SNOW BRAND MILK PRODUCTS CO, LTD, it was incorporated in 1950. The company specializes in the processing of meat products for commercial use and the development of prepared foods for restaurants. The firm has a tie-up for sales of Gatorade in Japan. Products are imported from the United States, Australia, France, Canada, Brazil, and Taiwan for sale in Japan. Sales for the fiscal year ending March 1991 totaled ¥126.8 billion (US $924.2 million), and capitalization was ¥2.1 billion (US $15.3 million). Headquarters are in Tōkyō.

Snow Brand Milk Products Co, Ltd
雪印乳業[株]

(Yukijirushi Nyūgyō). Manufacturer and seller of food products. Founded in 1925 as the Hokkaidō Dairy Cooperative, it assumed its present name in 1950. As Japan's largest dairy product company in annual sales, it produces and sells a variety of products, including milk, butter, cheese, powdered baby formula, soft drinks, frozen foods, and wine. Some of its products are well known abroad, and its powdered baby formula is widely used in Thailand, Malaysia, and the Middle and Near East. It has offices in Hamburg, New York, Melbourne, Bangkok, and Taipei. Sales for the fiscal year ending March 1991 totaled ¥515.0 billion (US $3.8 billion). Capitalization stood at ¥27.8 billion (US $202.6 million) in the same year. Headquarters are in Tōkyō.

Snow Festival
雪祭

(Yuki Matsuri). 1. A festival of prayer for a good harvest, held on 14–15 January at the Izu Shrine in the town of Anan, Nagano Prefecture. Snow, thought to bring about a bumper crop for the coming year, is offered before the gods.
   2. A tourist-oriented festival held in Sapporo, Hokkaidō, in early February, featuring a contest of snow and ice sculptures. Similar festivals are held elsewhere in northern Japan.

snow viewing
雪見

(*yukimi*). Custom of gathering to partake of food and *sake* (rice wine) while viewing a snow-covered landscape. Records of such events appear in chronicles of the Nara period (710–794). In the Heian period (794–1185), aristocrats held gatherings or accompanied imperial excursions to view the snow. By the Edo period (1600–1868), the custom had spread to the common people.

Snyder, Gary
スナイダー, G.

(1930–   ). American poet. Born in San Francisco, he spent his childhood in the Pacific Northwest. Graduating in 1951 from Reed College, he enrolled in 1953 as a graduate student in the Department of Oriental Languages of the University of California at Berkeley to study Chinese and Japanese. He wrote poetry and participated in the Beat movement on the West Coast. In 1956 Snyder left for Japan, where he spent most of the following decade studying ZEN with Oda Sessō of the temple DAITOKUJI in Kyōto. He was much influenced by BASHŌ's *haiku* and MIYAZAWA KENJI's life and work as a Buddhist, poet, and agricultural worker in the mountains. His works include four collections of poems: *The Back Country* (1968), *Turtle Island* (1974), which won a Pulitzer Prize in 1975, *Myths and Texts* (1978), and *Axe Handles* (1983).

sō
惣

Also called *sōchū*, *sōshō*, or *sōmura*. Self-governing bodies, generally corresponding to a village unit, that existed in rural areas from the 14th through 16th centuries. As the estate (SHŌEN) system eroded, local groups began to manage village affairs independently. On occasion they even resisted attempts at outside control in uprisings called TSUCHI IKKI. Each *sō* took care of irrigation, communal lands (IRIAI), law and order, and defense. Its decisions were reached at group meetings called YORIAI and were administered by the headmen (OTONA) and elders (TOSHIYORI). Especially after the ŌNIN WAR (1467–77), *sō* often linked together into groups including whole districts (*gunchūsō*). From the mid-1500s on, many rural leaders became warrior retainers and placed their *sō*

under the control of *daimyō* (see GŌSON SYSTEM).

Sōami
相阿弥

(ca 1455–1525). Also known as Shinsō. Painter and connoisseur-curator (DŌBŌSHŪ) of the Ashikaga shōguns' collection; the son of GEIAMI, whose duties he assumed after his father's death in 1485. He contributed to the historical *Kundaikan sō chōki* (1511) art records by adding notations taken from Xia Wenyan's (Hsia Wen-yen) paintings, together with his own opinions on works he had seen. The true measure of his genius may be found in his development of a landscape style based on very close study of works attributed to Muqi (Mu-ch'i; J: MOKKEI). In this way he produced Japan's first truly "Southern school" landscape style (see BUNJINGA). Sōami's paintings in the Daisen'in, a subtemple of Daitokuji in Kyōto, show that he developed this style in a manner reminiscent of YAMATO-E traditions. See also AMI SCHOOL; INK PAINTING.

soba
蕎麦

Type of noodle principally made from buckwheat flour, with wheat flour, yam, or egg white serving as a thickener. Water is added and the dough is kneaded and ripened, then rolled out and cut into strips. *Soba* is thought to have come to Japan from China by way of Korea, and references to it are found in works dating from the Nara period (710–794).
   Boiled *soba* is frequently served cold, topped with pieces of the dried seaweed known as *nori*, on a slatted bamboo drainer inside a lacquer box, accompanied by a small bowl of cold dipping sauce (*tsuyu*) consisting of soy sauce, *mirin* (sweetened *sake*), sugar, and stock (*dashi*) made with bonito flakes (see KATSUOBUSHI). Finely sliced green onions and *wasabi* (Japanese horseradish) are used as condiments. In this form it is called *zaru soba*. *Kake soba* is *soba* that is put in a bowl immediately after boiling and to which is added a hot broth similar to *tsuyu*, but less concentrated. If *tempura* is added to *kake soba*, it is called *tempura soba;* if raw egg, *tsukimi soba;* if *aburaage* (deep-fried *tōfu*), *kitsune soba*. TOSHIKOSHI SOBA is a traditional New Year's Eve dish.

sobayōnin
側用人

(grand chamberlain). Aide of the Tokugawa shōgun who relayed messages between the shōgun and the RŌJŪ, the shōgun's senior councillors (see TOKUGAWA SHOGUNATE). The influence of the *sobayōnin* position, which was established in 1681, increased after 1684 when the assassination of *tairō* (great elder) HOTTA MASATOSHI in his office prompted the shōgun to move his own quarters farther away from the administrative offices. YANAGISAWA YOSHIYASU and TANUMA OKITSUGU were *sobayōnin* who used the position to enhance their own power.

Sobosan
祖母山

Mountain on the border of Ōita and Miyazaki prefectures, Kyūshū. The highest peak of the KYŪSHŪ MOUNTAINS. Primeval forests of beech trees grow on the upper part, while fir and hemlock-spruce are found at lower levels. Height: 1,757 m (5,764 ft).

soccer
サッカー

(*sakkā*). Soccer was first introduced to Japan in 1873 by visiting British instructors at the Japanese Naval Academy and soon won popularity among Japanese students. In

soba

Made primarily of buckwheat flour, this type of noodle is eaten in a variety of ways, both cold and hot. The preparation of handmade *zaru soba* (a cold *soba* dish) is illustrated here.

▲ Buckwheat and wheat flours, in a ratio of about 8:2, are mixed with a small amount of water to make the dough.

▼ After kneading, the dough is allowed to rest for 30 minutes.

▲ The dough is then liberally sprinkled with flour to prevent sticking and rolled out to a thickness of 1–2 mm.

▲ A special knife is used to cut the dough into noodles of the desired width.

◄ The noodles are boiled briefly and then immediately rinsed with cold water.

▶ The cooled noodles are served in a bamboo basket (*zaru*), along with grated radish, green onion, and dipping sauce.

1921 a national soccer association (the Dai Nippon Shūkyū Kyōkai) was established and began sponsoring national championship matches. Elementary school competitions were initiated the following year, and soccer became a sport with a broad nationwide following among all age groups. Today the Football Association of Japan (Nihon Sakkā Kyōkai) is the governing body for the sport at the amateur level. The Japan Professional Football League (Nihon Puro Sakkā Rīgu), comprising 10 teams, was scheduled to be launched in May 1993.

Sōchō 宗長

(1448–1532). Master of linked verse (RENGA), author, critic, and Zen Buddhist priest. Born in the province of Suruga (now part of Shizuoka Prefecture). In his early years he was called Sōkan, first taking the name Sōchō in his late thirties. He took Buddhist orders at 17 and became a disciple, first, of the Rinzai Zen master IKKYŪ and then, from 1466, of the poet SŌGI.

Sōchō's *renga* verses are included in MINASE SANGIN HYAKUIN (1488, One Hundred Links by Three Poets at Minase) and *Yuyama sangin* (1491, Three Poets at Yuyama). Other works include poetry collected in *Kabekusa* (1512, Grasses on the Wall) and the diary *Sōgi shūenki* (1502, Record of Sōgi's Last Days), as well as travel accounts and *haikai* (informal or comic linked verse; see HAIKU).

Social Democratic Party of Japan (SDPJ)→ Japan Socialist Party

Socialist Democratic Party→ Shakai Minshutō

Socialist Masses Party→ Shakai Taishūtō

Socialist People's Party→ Shakai Minshutō

social overhead capital 社会資本

(*shakai shihon*). Capital invested in the social infrastructure, primarily by government. Social overhead capital is broadly divided into two categories: capital for public amenities such as sewage systems, waterworks, schools, and parks, and capital for industry-related facilities such as ports, docks, airports, and expressways. In addition to public investments and the fixed capital of public corporations, social overhead capital includes private-company investments in facilities such as railroads and communications networks that are used by the public, although this private investment is difficult to measure statistically. In 1990 total fixed capital investment by the government and public corporations was ¥25 trillion (US $181 billion), 6.7 percent of the gross national product. There has been large-scale growth in public investment in recent years. Compared to fiscal 1980, in fiscal 1990 investment in urban parks had increased 107.5 percent; sewers, 66.2 percent; and airports, 225.3 percent. Still, with only 40 per-

cent of all households connected to sewage systems and only 2.5 square meters (26.9 sq ft) of urban park land per resident, Japan lags considerably behind most other industrialized countries in social infrastructure. Public investment in such lifestyle-related areas is likely to be a major social issue for some time. See also PUBLIC WORKS.

Social Policy Council 国民生活審議会

(Kokumin Seikatsu Shingikai). Advisory organization that reports to the prime minister and other cabinet ministers concerned with economic affairs. Established in 1961 under the aegis of the ECONOMIC PLANNING AGENCY, it investigates and advises on basic policies and plans related to economic stability and progress. There are two divisions in the council: the division of general policies advises on medium-range general policy issues, while the division of consumer policy advises on long-range consumer policies and issues.

social security legislation 社会保障法

(*shakai hoshō hō*). Legislation establishing social insurance and public assistance programs to guarantee minimum standards of living for all citizens. Social security legislation in Japan authorizes the following: public assistance for the impoverished and those with low incomes; social insurance programs, particularly for workers; social welfare programs for children, senior citizens, and the mentally and physically disabled; and programs for public hygiene or medical care.

The CONSTITUTION OF JAPAN guarantees the people's right to live (SEIZONKEN) and clearly establishes the responsibility of the state to promote and improve welfare, social security, and public health. The LIVELIHOOD PROTECTION LAW was enacted in 1946. The Workmen's Compensation Insurance Law and the Unemployment Insurance Law were enacted in 1947. The CHILD WELFARE LAW was enacted in 1947, the PHYSICALLY HANDICAPPED WELFARE LAW in 1949, and the Social Welfare Services Law in 1951. The National Health Insurance Law was completely revised in 1958, and additional legislation was enacted—the Mentally Retarded Welfare Law in 1960, the OLD-AGE WELFARE LAW in 1963, and a series of laws between 1964 and 1971 to provide for the welfare of mothers, children, and the mentally and physically disabled. The social security system's quantitative expansion and qualitative improvement have been accomplished, but this has greatly increased the expenses borne by the nation, and ensuring the continued financing of these programs has become a major concern. See also MEDICAL AND HEALTH INSURANCE; NATIONAL HEALTH INSURANCE; PENSIONS.

social security programs→ social welfare

social welfare 社会福祉

(*shakai fukushi*). Social welfare in Japan is designed to guarantee a minimum standard of living and to protect citizens from certain

types of social and economic risk. Japan's social welfare system consists of four major components: public assistance, social insurance, social welfare services, and public health maintenance. In 1991 social welfare–related expenses accounted for 17.4 percent of the national budget.

Development of Social Welfare— Modern social welfare in Japan began in the early Meiji period (1868–1912), when a system of disability and retirement allowances for military personnel and public officials was instituted. Aid for the general work force did not come until some years later. The Poor Relief Regulation of 1874, a government reaction to popular unrest, provided limited support to workers, but it was not until the passage of the Health Insurance Law of 1922 (implemented in 1927) that Japan had its first true social welfare legislation for workers. In 1938 the NATIONAL HEALTH INSURANCE system was established to cover those excluded by the 1922 law. Though these steps were important in the development of social welfare in Japan, they were largely conciliatory gestures by the government to appease labor during a period of social unrest caused by rapid industrialization and modernization.

Post–World War II Reforms—After World War II, the Allied OCCUPATION established new legal and philosophical bases for social welfare in Japan and extensively reformed the administration of the existing welfare system. The philosophy of this time is set forth in the CONSTITUTION OF JAPAN, which states that "All people shall have the right to maintain the minimum standards of wholesome and cultured living" (see SEIZONKEN), and is further codified in the LIVELIHOOD PROTECTION LAW of 1946. Although the initial social welfare programs established were small-scale, the postwar legal reforms clearly established the responsibility of the government to promote and improve social welfare. Through subsequent legislation, mainly in the 1950s and 1960s, and through a series of reforms in the 1980s, Japan has established a comprehensive welfare system that is comparable in most respects to systems in other advanced countries. See also SOCIAL SECURITY LEGISLATION.

Categories of Social Welfare—Programs designed to assure a minimum level of security to those who are unable to generate subsistence-level income are classed as PUBLIC ASSISTANCE. In recent years the number of people receiving public assistance has decreased steadily, with only 0.8 percent of the population receiving such assistance in 1990. The national government provides 75 percent of public assistance benefits; local governments provide the remainder.

Social insurance, the second component of Japan's system of social welfare, covers four main areas: health and medical insurance, public pensions, unemployment insurance, and workers' compensation. All citizens are entitled to coverage under one of Japan's basic health insurance programs, depending on employment status or place of residence. The main program, based on the Health Insurance Law of 1922, automatically covers all employees in firms with more than five workers. The National Health Insurance program covers many of the remaining noninsured, including the self-employed, the elderly, and foreign residents. Seamen, public officials, and schoolteachers are covered by separate insurance programs. Health insurance is financed by contributions from employers and employees, as well as by subsidies from the national treasury. See also MEDICAL AND HEALTH INSURANCE.

Since 1961 all Japanese of working age have been legally required to be covered by one of the public pension programs, all of which provide old-age, disability, and survivor benefits. In 1986 public pensions were organized into a two-tiered system. At one level, the NATIONAL PENSION provides mandatory basic pensions for all citizens. Aside from this basic pension, a second level of support that includes the EMPLOYEES' PENSION INSURANCE program and MUTUAL AID ASSOCIATION PENSIONS provides additional coverage and benefits for private- and public-sector employees. See also PENSIONS.

Legislation protecting workers against unemployment began when the government passed the EMPLOYMENT SECURITY LAW OF 1947, which set up a network of government-operated employment offices. In the same year the Unemployment Insurance Law was passed, providing for benefits for those unemployed persons actively seeking employment. Programs are funded jointly by employees and employers.

Current WORKERS' COMPENSATION programs, based on the Factory Law of 1911 and two postwar laws, the Labor Standards Law and the Workers' Compensation Law, assign liability to employers to provide compensation for workers in the event of injury or death resulting from work-related accidents.

Social welfare services, the third main component of the Japanese welfare system, are of three major types: services for the handicapped, services for the aged, and services for children, which include aid to fatherless families. Government programs for the handicapped include pensions, institutional care, rehabilitation programs, SPECIAL EDUCATION, and cash subsidies. Emphasis is given to services for the handicapped outside of institutional settings, including medical counseling and "home helper" programs. Programs for vocational guidance and employment opportunities are offered by the Ministry of Labor. See also WELFARE FOR THE HANDICAPPED; PHYSICALLY HANDICAPPED WELFARE LAW.

Japan's rapidly AGING POPULATION has made welfare services for the elderly a pressing social problem. The OLD-AGE WELFARE LAW of 1963 introduced NURSING HOMES, free annual health examinations, a system of home helpers, and local welfare centers for the aged. In 1973 the government introduced free medical care for all persons 70 years or older. However, the 1983 LAW CONCERNING HEALTH AND MEDICAL SERVICES FOR THE AGED reintroduced the requirement that certain healthcare fees be paid by the individual. See also WELFARE FOR THE AGED.

Welfare services are also offered to needy families with children. The CHILD WELFARE LAW of 1947 established the government's responsibility to protect children in need. The 1964 Law for the Welfare of Mothers, Children, and Widows provides financial assistance and such services as vocational counseling and homes for fatherless families. See also CHILD WELFARE.

PUBLIC HEALTH maintenance, the fourth component of the social welfare system, includes public sanitation and the prevention and treatment of infectious diseases, including POLLUTION-RELATED DISEASES. Rapid economic growth has brought about considerable progress in all aspects of public health in Japan. See also ENVIRONMENTAL QUALITY.

Administration—Most social welfare–related activities are administered by the MINISTRY OF HEALTH AND WELFARE, although the ministries of labor and education also fulfill important social welfare functions. Within the Ministry of Health and Welfare, separate bureaus for social affairs, children and families, pensions, public health, environmental sanitation, and medical affairs are responsible for overall supervision and planning. The Social Insurance Agency administers the key public pension programs. However, implementation of most programs is left to local governments: independent bureaus for health and welfare services operate at prefectural, city, town, and village government levels. In addition, welfare offices at the city and district level administer public assistance and engage in other welfare activities. At the private level, SOCIAL WELFARE COUNCILS coordinate local welfare activities under contract with local governments. Volunteer WELFARE COMMISSIONERS designated by the welfare minister carry out much of the casework investigation, counseling, and referral services. In 1989 the Ministry of Health and Welfare initiated licensing tests for social workers and case workers who provide counseling, guidance, and home service to bedridden elderly or handicapped patients.

social welfare councils
社会福祉協議会

(*shakai fukushi kyōgikai*). Private local councils organized with the goal of enhancing the social welfare of area residents. These local councils are connected with prefectural social welfare councils and, on a higher level, with the National Council of Social Welfare (Zenkoku Shakai Fukushi Kyōgikai), established in 1951. In recent years social welfare councils, which are subsidized by the national treasury, have served as focal points for community social welfare activists, fostering citizen volunteers and senior citizens' clubs and developing and implementing home services for the elderly, such as delivery of meals.

society
社会

(*shakai*). Japan today is one of the most industrially advanced societies in the world, highly urbanized and reliant on advanced technology and communications. Once the most culturally isolated of countries, Japan is now thoroughly integrated into the international system. At the same time, traditional patterns of social relations and social ethics remain a significant part of the contemporary picture. Elements of tradition—best exemplified by the traditional household, village society, and Confucian morality—have mixed with modernization to produce a nation that shares a great deal with the rest of the modern world while at the same time retaining its own particular character.

Legacies of the Past—The traditional household (IE) was the fundamental form of social organization among the farmers, warriors, and merchants of the premodern period. Every individual understood his or her place in life first as a member of an immediate household, which was part of an ancestral line with inheritance by the eldest male. The practice of ANCESTOR WORSHIP was in fact the worship of the household itself and its morality. The household was a highly interdependent group in which all members shared resources, a common identity, and responsibility for the enterprise upon which the household depended. The internal organization of the household was based on a status hierarchy and a clear division of labor. Age seniority and male superiority were the two basic principles establishing rank. The group was, however, built upon the spirit of cooperative unity, and all adult members were often given a voice in decision making. The formal autocracy was thus typically balanced by an informal democracy of joint discussion and consensus. See FAMILY; IE; KINSHIP.

The *ie* was also the basis for the organization of the traditional business enterprise. As enterprises grew, households expanded by adding outsiders to the business "family" through such practices as fictive kinship (see ADOPTION). Apprentices worked their way up to positions of responsibility, all the while being cared for in the style of a household servant-member. Several of the great commercial households of the premodern era, including the MITSUI and the SUMITOMO, survived and evolved into the most powerful ZAIBATSU, or financial and industrial combines, of the modern era. Agricultural villages, the economic backbone of premodern society, were characterized by considerable autonomy of internal affairs but strict subordination to higher authority in such matters as taxation. Many common economic interests—from irrigation to joint ownership of forests and communal labor activities—fostered strong tendencies toward village solidarity, as did the common worship of local deities (UJIGAMI). Between villages, competition and hostility were strong, resulting in an "in-group" psychology for each village.

The internal structure of villages was characterized by a leadership hierarchy based on age, wealth, kinship, and length of household residence. Decision making, however, involved most or all households and followed a process aimed at consensus.

Within this general framework, there was much variation, and in some cases the ideals of cooperation and mutuality were far from realized. Any conflicts were, nevertheless, confined within the limits of a social framework that strongly discouraged schism, so interdependent were households. Compromise and accommodation to group norms were notable characteristics of village life.

The traditional household and village thus shared common characteristics of social solidarity based on common practical interests. Each had a particular religious focus, each was corporate in significant ways, and each combined the notion of participation in decision making with that of a status hierarchy and formal authority.

The morality of CONFUCIANISM was first spread as an official ideology during the EDO PERIOD (1600–1868) rather than being an outgrowth of everyday relationships. Nevertheless, it reinforced inherited practice in households and villages, and it, too, helped to shape the natural evolution of modern institutions. At the heart of this morality was the notion of society as an ordering of different but interdependent roles and statuses. In Japan during the Edo period this took the form of an officially instituted fourfold class system at the top of which were the *samurai*, and beneath them, in declining order of precedence, farmers, artisans, and merchants (see SHI-NŌ-KŌ-SHŌ). If each class carried out its prescribed duties, the whole system would work and all would prosper. The virtuous individual was one who observed the duties and behavior proper to his or her social place. The family served as a model of this, with each generation and each sex having a distinct place. Morality centered on relationships, particularly the parent-child relationship, rather than on individual conscience or abstract principles. Hierarchy was considered the natural product of age and experience. Relationships were seen as reciprocal, with nurturance and guidance from above being returned with obedience and loyalty from below. Confucianism permitted the extension of the analogy of ideal family relationships to almost any social situation. Familism, PATERNALISM, and LOYALTY became three dominant values of society in general. The EMPEROR was later to be seen as the father of the family comprising all Japanese (KAZOKU KOKKA), and contractual relationships such as that between employer and employee could be understood in the Confucian perspective as analogous to the parent-child bond.

Social Changes in Modern Times—Since the end of its policy of NATIONAL SECLUSION in 1854, Japan has experienced enormous change and modern development accompanied by an extremely high rate of economic expansion. Within less than 100 years the country experienced two great political upheavals, one following the MEIJI RESTORATION of 1868 and the other in the years immediately after World War II. Each of these dramatically altered the traditional social landscape.

In the first of these upheavals, the institutions of the Edo period were replaced with a modern state dedicated to building an industrial nation. The samurai who overthrew the Tokugawa government in the name of the emperor began—as soon as they had consolidated power in a central government dominated by themselves—to create a wholly new society based on modern institutions that they observed to be successful in the West. By the turn of the century, modern industries, public education, private stock companies, mass transportation, banks, national taxation, a conscripted military, and a host of other social and economic institutions replaced the less integrated, Confucian-inspired feudal order and its fourfold class system.

Much of the creative effort and cultivation of the new institutions came from the government. Private banks were largely founded with government bonds, and experiments in building heavy industry were initiated by the government and later sold to private entrepreneurs at low prices. The process of generating a strong, modern society centered on cooperation between the government and private businesses. Prominent among the new institutions were *zaibatsu* composed of many companies owned by a central holding company. The gap between small and large enterprises widened progressively. However, the larger companies developed complex subcontracting networks utilizing the lower wage costs of smaller firms, while their own employees developed into a managerial class and a skilled labor elite. A dual structure emerged in the economy, in which thousands of small manufacturers paying low wages existed alongside internationally competitive industrial giants.

The second upheaval occurred during the OCCUPATION following Japan's defeat in World War II. The US Occupation officials, who indirectly ruled Japan for nearly seven years, intended to root out the social causes of prewar ultranationalism and to create a new democratic Japan. There were wide-reaching reforms affecting the military, land ownership, education, and labor. The *zaibatsu* were broken up and the ownership of their companies more widely distributed. There was a significant reduction in the gap between rich and poor. Women were given legal equality with men. Individuals, not households, became the legal units of society.

Japanese Society Today—Japanese social structure today, however, is not simply a reflection of the Occupation blueprint. Increased URBANIZATION, modernization, and economic growth have led to still further changes in the pattern of life. At the same time, any examination of present Japanese society in detail reveals the democratic ideals of contemporary public culture existing in uneasy truce with more traditional values.

Fishing and agriculture, once pillars of Japanese society, now play relatively minor roles in the overall economy. Both, however, cater to complex national markets that are affected by government price supports and protectionist import policies. Farmers have learned to be businessmen and to play interest-group politics. Prosperity has brought consumerism to the villages, and there is no significant difference today between the standard of living of villagers and city dwellers. Rapid social change has also reduced the significance of many older social ties. The importance of patrilineal kinship between main and branch households and that of lateral relationships among in-laws and neighbors has been weakened in economic terms, but in other respects patrilineal kinship remains important. Some hamlets remain more hierarchical and tightly structured than others, but in general local interests are being superseded by more distant ones as the necessity for local cooperation diminishes. Greater equality of income has meant less hierarchical authority. The most persistent ideal is that of hamlet solidarity, as for centuries all households have had to face crises together. Block voting in politics is one expression of this sentiment.

Marriage and Family—In the family, relationships between husbands and wives show a strong tendency to role separation, with the man away from home for long hours and the woman taking exclusive responsibility for home and children. The overall stability of the family is a notable quality of Japanese society, and the DIVORCE rate remains quite low by Western standards (see MARRIAGE). The notion of the household as a single intergenerational entity retains significance only in the case of family businesses and farms, and in general, modern employment and urban living have severed all but personal ties with parents once the children are grown. Due to the shift from agriculture to wage employment, the inheritance of land is no longer significant to most Japanese, and primogeniture is quite limited. Today, the most significant contribution of parents to their children's future is to assist them in education. Saving to pay for college and to buy a family house are the two major financial goals of most parents.

Education—Japan has an elaborate and advanced educational system, one that produces the highly educated population that forms the basis for other general characteristics of Japanese society today. MASS COMMUNICATIONS are highly developed, with the rate of newspaper readership per capita among the highest in the world. Japanese society, despite being crowded, busy, and rapidly changing, is remarkably orderly and stable. Lives are lived with a degree of care and circumspection that some observers find prejudicial to the growth of individualism and others consider worthy of international emulation.

At school, children are thoroughly drilled by teachers trained to place great emphasis on students' cooperative behavior, group discipline, and mutual empathy. Teaching in schools is somewhat formalized. Large classes of about 40 students, nationally standardized textbooks, a lecture approach, rote learning of large quantities of detail, little independent work by students, regular tests, and a somewhat longer school year than in Western countries are all features of the Japanese system.

Commonly cited faults of the system are that it provides too little opportunity for self-expression and too little time for nonacademic pursuits; it also encourages excessive parental pressure. In order to gain some advantage at examination time, more than half the middle school students in Tōkyō commute to JUKU or CRAM SCHOOLS after their regular classes several days a week or take extra lessons from private tutors.

While group solidarity and the high degree of national integration have never failed to win the admiration (and, sometimes, the jealous criticism) of foreign observers, the fact remains that Japan is a highly competitive society. Just as individuals (indeed whole families) compete intensely to get ahead in education, so do interest groups, businesses, localities, and religious groups. An ideal of social harmony is accompanied by a national character in which competitive inclinations and loyalties to competing groups provide great dynamism. Japan is not divided by deep religious, ethnic, or racial schisms, but economic and political conflict

Soejima Taneomi This politician was a leading member of a group within the early Meiji government that argued unsuccessfully for an invasion of Korea in 1873.

it knows well.

Differences of individual position and income based largely on education and employment are sources of a minutely graded status hierarchy of great concern to many Japanese. The favored career paths are within powerful, prestigious institutions—the bureaucracy, the largest companies, and the top universities. Since those who enter desirable companies protect their advantage by staying until retirement, opportunities for upward social mobility are largely limited to the period of education. In the widest sense, Japanese employment is composed of a "core" group, consisting of workers enjoying permanent status in medium-sized and large private companies or governmental organizations, and a "marginal" group, including temporary or part-time employees and employees of enterprises too small to afford job guarantees. It is the "core" group who enjoy the benefits of Japanese "lifetime employment." The degree of identification between the worker and his organization implied in this arrangement would signify an alarming degree of dependence to most Westerners, but to Japanese the security provided is highly valued. The hardworking "company man" is a high ideal in Japan, one reminiscent of the loyal samurai of Japanese history and legend. See EMPLOYMENT SYSTEM, MODERN.

Class Consciousness—Despite an acute awareness of status, class consciousness is relatively weak. Horizontal social affiliations based on occupation or class lines appear here and there, but the great majority of people share what they believe to be middle-class incomes, ambitions, attitudes, and lifestyles. Class-based organizations such as labor unions prove on close examination to be less rooted in class interests than their charters would imply. In the case of unions, "vertical" ties to the company turn out to be more important than "horizontal" ties to class. (Japanese unions are constructed on an enterprise basis rather than along occupational or industrywide lines.) Self-interest is aligned with company fortunes, undermining the idea that the interests of employer and employee are antagonistic.

Minorities—In Japan MINORITY GROUPS first became a major focus of political and public policy discussion in the 1960s. The largest minority group consists of about 3 million Japanese known as the BURAKUMIN, a euphemism for descendants of people who occupied outcaste villages in a pattern of discrimination that was formalized and legalized in the Edo period. The government has spent large amounts of money to stop illegal discrimination against the *burakumin.* It has also made efforts to improve facilities in *burakumin* areas; however, considerable economic and social discrimination against the *burakumin* persists in Japan. Koreans compose the next largest minority group. Totaling about 690,000 as of 1990, KOREANS IN JAPAN do not enjoy Japanese citizenship or many of the civil rights that go with it. Other minorities—the AINU and the Chinese—are very small in number. They too suffer discrimination, particularly in marriage and employment. All of the minority groups combined make up less than 4 percent of the population.

Social Problems—When asked about their society, Japanese typically list its problems: expensive and insufficient housing; overpriced food; want of leisure; burdensome educational competition; inadequate SOCIAL WELFARE, especially for the aged; deteriorating ENVIRONMENTAL QUALITY; intolerable urban congestion; lack of discipline and ambition among the young; corruption in politics; and excessive materialism. All of these complaints underline the fact that economic success is accompanied by social problems that seem very great to Japanese. The problems reflect a set of governmental priorities that have placed economic growth first, and there is now much pressure and a growing consensus for a new set of priorities that places the quality of life ahead of growth for its own sake. Slower economic growth may give Japan latitude to focus on improvements in the quality of life, but it also will mean economic insecurity and require people to make completely new adjustments. The Japanese social system is particularly finely tuned, however, and the constraints on major changes are great indeed.

Among the most pressing problems in the last quarter of the century is the rapidly increasing proportion of older people in the population. This means higher average wages, greater welfare costs, and painful problems of readjustment for the old. The multitude of inconveniences and costs that stem from the overconcentration of population in a few urban centers is another fundamental challenge to be met.

Interpretations of Japanese Society—Scholars differ in their understanding and interpretations of contemporary Japanese society, some emphasizing the influence of tradition and others seeing the same forces shaping modern Japan as have shaped other industrialized societies. One well-known psychological approach focuses on the relative strength of dependency relationships (AMAE) among the Japanese and points out that Japanese are not raised to seek social independence as are Europeans and Americans. Another approach emphasizes the solidarity and hierarchical structure of small groups and sees Japan as essentially a VERTICAL SOCIETY. A Marxist approach sees the remnants of feudalism, as it survives in traditional social relations, as inhibiting the rise of class consciousness among the Japanese. A "liberal" interpretation sees Japan as having achieved a relatively stable and healthy society without revolution by imposing a modern institutional superstructure on a base that remains essentially Japanese. Some scholars emphasize Japan's peculiar geographic and economic situation as an overpopulated island nation with few natural resources, where social cooperation has always been important for survival. Each of these perspectives offers useful insights, but a reliable understanding of modern Japan is likely to be gained only if they are taken in combination.

Sōda Kiichirō   左右田喜一郎

(1881–1927). Economic theorist. Born in Yokohama. After graduation from Tōkyō Higher Commercial School (now Hitotsubashi University) in 1904, he studied philosophy in Germany under Heinrich Rickert. After returning to Japan, Sōda was appointed lecturer at his alma mater and established an original economic philosophy known as "Sōda philosophy," which was concerned with the methodological basis of economics. Also president of the Sōda Bank, he was an influential and powerful businessman. He was a member of the House of Peers (1925). His works on economics include *Keizai tetsugaku no shōmondai* (1917, Problems of Economic Philosophy).

Sodegaura   袖ケ浦[市]

City on Tōkyō Bay in western Chiba Prefecture, central Honshū. In the past, *nori* (a type of seaweed) and littleneck clams were harvested here. Oil refineries and petrochemical plants have been built on reclaimed coastal land, and the city has become part of the KEIYŌ INDUSTRIAL REGION. Pop: 52,818.

Sōdōmei   総同盟

(abbreviation of Nihon Rōdō Sōdōmei; Japan Federation of Labor). Labor federation originally organized in 1912 as the YŪAIKAI (Friendship Association); reorganized in 1919 as the Dai Nihon Rōdō Sōdōmei Yūaikai. It took the name Nihon Rōdō Sōdōmei in 1921. Although the federation was influenced initially by radical theories of trade unionism, Sōdōmei came to represent the right wing of the Japanese labor movement by the late 1920s. Sōdōmei merged with centrist workers' unions in 1936, split in 1939, and was dissolved by the government in 1940. In 1946 the federation was reorganized as Nihon Rōdō Kumiai Sōdōmei (Japan Federation of Labor Unions) by its previous leaders, including MATSUOKA KOMAKICHI. The remaining members formally dissolved the organization in 1964 when Dōmei (Japanese Confederation of Labor) was formed by right-wing unions.

Soejima Taneomi   副島種臣

(1828–1905). Politician-statesman of the Meiji period (1868–1912). Born in the Saga domain (now Saga Prefecture), he became a leader of the antishogunate movement in Saga. After the Meiji Restoration (1868), Soejima became a junior councillor (*san'yo*). With FUKUOKA TAKACHIKA, he drew up the "Constitution of 1868" (SEITAISHO), the first official statement on the structure and functions of the new government. While key government leaders toured Europe (see IWAKURA MISSION), Soejima served as foreign minister, and in 1873 he led an ambassadorial mission to Beijing (Peking). His real purpose in Beijing was to lay the diplomatic groundwork for a program of Japanese expansion in both Korea and Taiwan. In opposition to the government policy that rejected his own proposal to invade Korea (see SEIKANRON), he resigned from the government in October 1873. He then joined in forming the AIKOKU KŌTŌ political association.

Sōen   宗淵

(fl 1495–99). Priest-painter in the Muromachi-period (1333–1568) INK PAINTING tradition who studied with SESSHŪ TŌYŌ in Yamaguchi and returned with the new style to his home temple in Kamakura. Also known as Josui Sōen. Born in Sagami Province (now Kanagawa Prefecture), Sōen attained the high rank of *zōsu* (sutra keeper) in Kamakura's important Zen temple ENGAKUJI before going to Yamaguchi to become one of Sesshū's closest disciples.

A relatively large number of Sōen's paintings survive, attesting to a breadth of subject matter characteristic of a Sesshū follower who was painting to meet the requirements of a Zen temple. His artistic foundation in Sesshū's style is undeniable in the brawny drapery contours and substantial forms of his figure paintings; his landscapes also bear ample evidence of the Sesshū techniques. However, Sōen's personal style is softer than that of his master and is distinguished by his smooth handling of moist ink to create atmospheric effects.

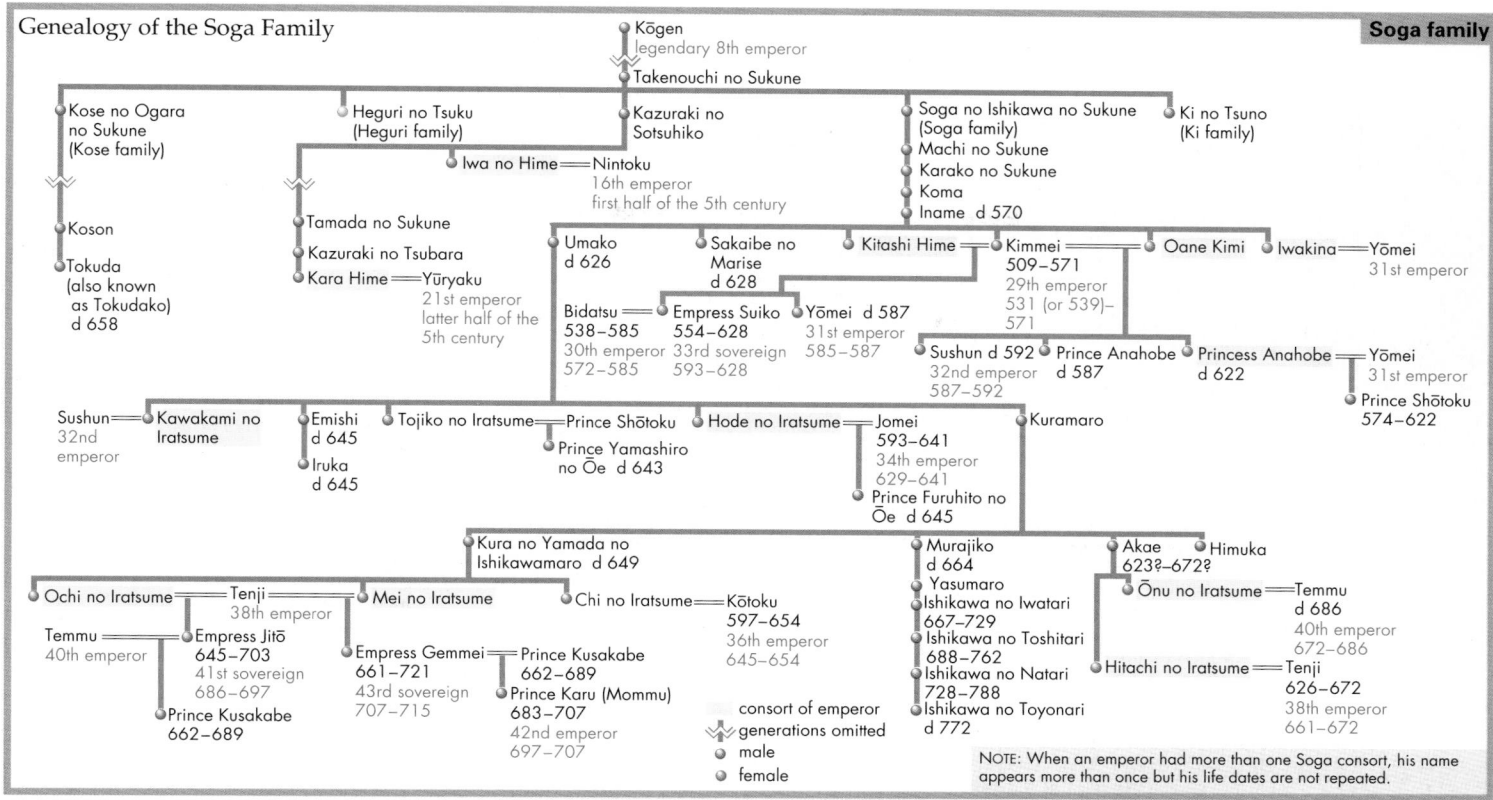

Genealogy of the Soga Family — Soga family

NOTE: When an emperor had more than one Soga consort, his name appears more than once but his life dates are not repeated.

Sō family
宗氏

(Sōshi). *Daimyō* family of the island of Tsushima (now part of Nagasaki Prefecture). Because the island is situated between northern Kyūshū and Korea, the family was constantly involved in the interactions between Korea and Japan. The Sō became military governors (*shugo*) of Tsushima under the Kamakura shogunate (1192–1333) and were nearly destroyed when the island was overrun in the first of the MONGOL INVASIONS OF JAPAN (1274). In 1419 they repulsed a Korean force sent in retaliation against Japanese pirates (see ŌEI INVASION) and in 1443 concluded a treaty with Korea to regularize the foreign trade on which Tsushima thrived. In 1592 and 1597 they contributed troops to TOYOTOMI HIDEYOSHI's Korean expeditions (see INVASIONS OF KOREA IN 1592 AND 1597). After Hideyoshi's death in 1598 Sō Yoshitomo (1568–1615) led the peace negotiations and in 1605 established diplomatic relations with Korea on behalf of the Tokugawa shogunate (1603–1867). As a reward the Sō domain was enlarged. The Sō continued to serve as intermediaries between Japan and Korea throughout the Edo period (1600–1868).

soft drinks
清涼飲料水

(*seiryō inryōsui*). With the opening of Japan to foreign influences after the Meiji Restoration (1868), carbonated drinks with names derived from English, such as *saidā* (from cider) and *ramune* (from lemonade), became popular, as did lactic-acid beverages. At present beverages flavored with cola and various fruits are also sold. The long-favored Calpis (a trade name), made with milk, sweetener, artificial color, and lactic-acid bacteria, has been displaced in popularity by cola drinks.

software industry
ソフトウエア産業

(*sofutouea sangyō*). Industry concerned with the production, distribution, and sale of the programs needed for computer operation. It is one part of the information services industry.

Software was established as an independent industry in 1969 after IBM set forth its "unbundling" policy, separating software and hardware prices. The Japanese industry developed with great rapidity in the late 1970s and 1980s due to the pace of computerization of all aspects of manufacturing and the diffusion of information technology. Whereas the Japanese computer hardware market is led by between 10 and 20 manufacturers, the software industry—the product of which is largely of an intellectual nature, and in which there is little need for substantial initial capital investment—developed in a more fragmented fashion, as a multitude of software producers sprang up to cater to the specific and variegated needs of a wide spectrum of users. Since about 1982 two distinct software markets have developed: general-application software package development and sales, and customized software offered on a contract or per diem basis. As of 1990 customized software accounted for some 90 percent of the market, while generalized software packages and applications accounted for only 10 percent.

According to statistics from the MINISTRY OF INTERNATIONAL TRADE AND INDUSTRY (MITI), in 1989 software was being produced by 5,587 general computer-related companies and more than 3,148 specialized software houses. Sales of Japan's software industry in 1986 amounted to ¥875.5 billion (US $5.2 billion); three years later sales had risen to ¥4.4 trillion (US $31.9 billion). The 1989 sales showed a 32.6 percent increase over 1988 and indicated remarkable growth at 6.6 times the software sales of 1980.

Soga brothers → Soga monogatari

Soga family
蘇我氏

(Sogashi). A family (UJI) of the Yamato region (now Nara Prefecture) whose leading members in the 6th and 7th centuries came to exercise political influence rivaling that of the imperial house. Accounts in the chronicles NIHON SHOKI (720) and KOGO SHŪI (807) link the Soga to financial administration, foreign relations, and the promotion of Buddhism and other aspects of continental culture. Soga no Iname (d 570), the first of four generations of Soga who consecutively held the post of *ōomi* (chief minister) at the YAMATO COURT, showed interest in Korean affairs and was one of the first converts to Buddhism, recently introduced from PAEKCHE. Two of his daughters were married to Emperor KIMMEI (r 531 or 539 to 571) and three of his grandchildren reigned in succession as Emperor Yōmei (r 585–587), Emperor Sushun (r 587–592), and Empress SUIKO (r 593–628).

SOGA NO UMAKO (d 626), Iname's son, built the temple ASUKADERA as the Soga family temple and helped Prince SHŌTOKU compile two histories, TENNŌKI AND KOKKI. He and his supporters in 587 waged a victorious battle against the anti-Buddhist MONONOBE FAMILY and Nakatomi family.

Umako's son Emishi (d 645) and grandson SOGA NO IRUKA (d 645) increasingly abused their authority. In 641 they requisitioned other people's private groups of laborers (*kakibe*) to build for themselves grandiose twin mausoleums; Iruka made an armed attack on the residence of Shōtoku's surviving son, Prince YAMASHIRO NO ŌE. In a coup d'état in 645 Iruka was killed by Prince Naka no Ōe, the future emperor TENJI; Emishi committed suicide the next day. Soga no Akae (623?–672?), a grandson of Umako, survived to serve as *ōomi* during the TAIKA REFORM.

Soga monogatari
曽我物語

(Tale of the Soga Brothers). Medieval prose tale of revenge in which Kudō Suketsune, angry at being deprived of his inheritance by his uncle Itō Sukechika, has Sukechika's son murdered. Eighteen years later, in 1193, the dead man's two sons exact revenge by killing Suketsune at a hunt near Mt. Fuji (Fujisan). The elder Soga brother (the surname is that of their stepfather), Jūrō Sukenari, is killed in the melee, but the younger, Gorō Tokimune, is captured and brought before MINAMOTO NO YORITOMO, who, impressed by his filial piety, would have pardoned him had not Suketsune's son demanded his execution.

This historical incident is treated in several Nō plays and ballad dramas (KŌWAKAMAI). The form of the Soga prose tale most widely current in the 15th and 16th centuries contained many dramatic and romantic elements ideally suited for later adaptation to the popular theater (see KABUKI). However, many of these elements are absent from the earliest known form of the story, that written in a Japanized form of Chinese (kambun) perhaps between 1300 and 1350.

Soga no Iruka 蘇我入鹿

(?–645). Court official of the 7th century; son of Soga no Emishi (d 645) and grandson of SOGA NO UMAKO. He worked with his father to preserve the SOGA FAMILY's control of the imperial throne. The death of the Soga-created Empress SUIKO in 628 led to a succession dispute between Prince Tamura, supported by the Soga, and Prince YAMASHIRO NO ŌE, son of Prince SHŌTOKU. Prince Tamura prevailed and ascended the throne as Emperor Jomei (593–641; r 629–641). On Jomei's death the Soga intervened again to install his widow, Empress Kōgyoku (later Empress SAIMEI), on the throne. Yamashiro no Ōe, still a threat to Soga ambitions, was forced by Iruka to commit suicide in 643. In 645 Prince Naka no Ōe (later Emperor TENJI) conspired with Nakatomi no Kamatari (later FUJIWARA NO KAMATARI) and succeeded in assassinating Iruka. Emishi committed suicide, and Empress Kōgyoku was deposed. These events marked the end of Soga tyranny and paved the way for the TAIKA REFORM.

Soga no taimen 曽我の対面

(The Soga Confrontation). KABUKI play of the jidai-mono (historical play) category. The generic title for a set piece that was a fixture of the New Year's program of Edo (now Tōkyō) kabuki from the early 18th century to the late 19th century, it was rewritten under a different title each year to give a new twist to the familiar story (from the SOGA MONOGATARI) of the initial confrontation between the Soga brothers Jūrō and Gorō and their enemy Kudō Suketsune. The earliest known version, Tsuwamono kongen Soga, was presented by Ichikawa Danjūrō I (see ICHIKAWA DANJŪRŌ) in 1697; the variant most frequently presented today bears the title Kotobuki Soga no taimen. However, it is not the plot but the festive beauty of the tableau that makes this play noteworthy, for at the climax, the entire range of lead actors strikes a set pose (mie).

Soga no Umako 蘇我馬子

(?–626). Political figure of the YAMATO COURT (ca 4th century–ca mid-7th century). Son of Soga no Iname (d 570), Umako sought to establish the SOGA FAMILY's dominance through kinship ties with the imperial house and patronage of Buddhism. In an imperial succession dispute of 587, he destroyed the anti-Buddhist MONONOBE FAMILY and installed his nephew on the throne as Emperor Sushun (r 587–592). When Sushun resisted his high-handed conduct of government, Umako had him assassinated in 592 and set up a niece as Empress SUIKO. Umako collaborated with the regent and heir apparent Prince SHŌTOKU in strengthening the central government. Some scholars believe that he is buried in the ISHIBUTAI TOMB in the village of ASUKA in Nara Prefecture.

Soganoya Gorō 曽我廼家五郎

(1877–1948). Comic actor, playwright, and director known as the father of modern Japanese comedy. Born Wada Hisakazu in Sakai, the port city near Ōsaka, he spent 10 years touring the provinces in second-rate KABUKI troupes until he met Ōmatsu Fukumatsu (1869–1925). They borrowed the names of the Soga brothers (see SOGA MONOGATARI) to become Soganoya Gorō and Soganoya Jūrō. In 1904 they organized the Soganoya Ichiza (Soganoya Troupe) to create a contemporary comic form.

Gorō played low-life, carefree churls in a bombastic manner to contrast with Jūrō's restrained interpretations of pessimistic semi-intelligentsia. Gorō also originated the definitive caricature of the nasty, crafty old woman. The two separated around 1915. Using the pen name Ikkai Gyojin, Gorō wrote more than 1,000 short comedies.

Soga school 曽我派

(Sogaha). School of painters active from the 15th century into the 18th century who specialized in INK PAINTING. The early Soga artists centered their activity around the Kyōto temple DAITOKUJI. Traditional art histories cite Soga Dasoku as the primary figure in the school's development. Existing Soga-school paintings reflect a manner evolved from the style of the great Shōkokuji priest-painter SHŪBUN, but they also contain Korean elements, giving some credence to the claim that the founder of the line was Yi Chuman (J: Ri Shūbun), a Korean artist who came to Japan in 1424. Soga-school paintings include the important panels in the Daitokuji subtemple Shinjuan, as well as numerous scrolls treating a wide range of subject matter: portraits of the Zen master IKKYŪ Sōjun, bird-and-flower paintings, and ink landscapes in both a neatly drafted manner and an abbreviated HABOKU ("break ink") style.

When ODA NOBUNAGA destroyed the Asakura family, patrons of the Soga school, in 1573, the artists dispersed, and Soga Chokuan founded another school. Although Nichokuan, his son, wrote a Soga-school lineage in 1656 claiming that his father, Chokuan, was heir to Soga Shōshō, there was probably no strong connection between the early Soga painters and the later school founded by Chokuan. Nichokuan, active during the early 17th century, preserved his father's style and used his father's seal, which has resulted in frequent confusion of their works. A series of painters continued to work in the Soga style, culminating in the work of the 18th-century master SOGA SHŌHAKU.

Soga Shōhaku 曽我蕭白

(1730–81). Painter whose works exemplify the spirit of experimentation and diverse, innovative modes of expression that are characteristic of 18th-century painting in Japan. Shōhaku's birthplace and family background are unclear, but he may have been a member of a merchant family from Kyōto and his family name may have been Miura. As a young man he studied painting under Takada Keiho (1674–1755).

Shōhaku felt a strong artistic affinity with the 15th-century SOGA SCHOOL of painters that had been founded by Soga Dasoku, but he stood apart, both in temperament and creative predilection, from any of the institutionalized schools of painting of his time. Chinese legend and folklore provided the subjects for most of his figurative works. A

similar inventory of traditional pictorial components is evident in his landscapes, which show the influence of the suibokuga (INK PAINTING) of the Muromachi period (1333–1568), which was dependent on Chinese traditions as well as, more directly, the 17th-century KANŌ SCHOOL and UNKOKU SCHOOL.

A good deal of Shōhaku's time seems to have been spent on the road, working independently as an itinerant painter. Although Shōhaku experimented with colors occasionally, his most representative works are in monochrome ink. Shōhaku's works are characterized by incisive brushwork and a spontaneous style, as can be seen in a pair of folding screens in the Museum of Fine Arts, Boston. They depict the Four Sages of Mt. Shang, a theme drawn from Chinese legend.

Sōgetsu school 草月流

(Sōgetsuryū). A school of ikebana (FLOWER ARRANGEMENT) founded in 1927 by Teshigahara Sōfū (1900–1979), one of the leaders of the movement that transformed this traditional pursuit into an avant-garde, highly expressive art form. In 1979 he was succeeded by his daughter, Teshigahara Kasumi (1932–80), who became the second head of the school. Following her death, her brother, TESHIGAHARA HIROSHI, an accomplished filmmaker, became the third head. In Sōgetsu ikebana the student acquires a base of fundamental understanding systematically by actively imitating a number of different forms. Called the kakeihō approach, it quickly renders ikebana accessible even to students with no prior experience. The school is headquartered at the Sōgetsu Kaikan in the Minato Ward, Tōkyō, and has 44 chapters in Japan and 50 branches and 26 study groups overseas.

Sōgi 宗祇

(1421–1502). The leading RENGA (linked verse) poet of the late 15th century. He was revered as the epitome of the traveler-poet and served as the chief compiler of the second honorary imperial renga anthology, the SHINSEN TSUKUBASHŪ (1495). Born in either Kii Province (now Wakayama Prefecture) or Ōmi Province (now Shiga Prefecture), he was of humble origin. He moved to Kyōto and entered the Buddhist priesthood at Shōkokuji, a Zen temple of the RINZAI SECT. He studied renga under TAKAYAMA SŌZEI, Senjun (ca 1411–76), and SHINKEI. Sōgi's patron was ICHIJŌ KANEYOSHI, a scholar and court official.

Sōgi traveled much between 1466 and 1474. During this period he wrote Chōrokubumi (1466) and Azuma mondō (1470), critical works on renga composition, and a travel diary, Shirakawa kikō (1468). In 1471 he received the KOKIN DENJU—the transmission of a secret body of knowledge concerning the KOKINSHŪ—from TŌ NO TSUNEYORI. This qualified Sōgi as an official authority on court literature. In 1473 he built a hermitage in Kyōto. Wasuregusa, the first of three personal renga anthologies, was completed in 1474; two years later he compiled the Chikurinshō, an anthology of verses by the seven most famous renga poets of the mid-15th century; in 1479 he analyzed verses by these same poets in Oi no susabi. In 1480 he visited Suō Province (now part of Yamaguchi Prefecture) and Kyūshū, where he recorded Tsukushi no michi no ki, a travel diary later admired by the great poet BASHŌ.

In the spring of 1488 Sōgi was appointed by the shogunate to administer the Kitano

Soganoya Gorō This comic actor and playwright was especially inspired by Molière and by traditional improvised comic skits (niwaka).

Shrine *renga* sessions, the highest official honor accorded a *renga* poet. Sōgi and his disciples, SHŌHAKU and SŌCHŌ, gathered at Minase (between Ōsaka and Kyōto) and composed the 100-verse MINASE SANGIN HYAKUIN. Three years later the same poets produced *Yuyama sangin*. In 1495.Sōgi was commissioned for the *Shinsen tsukubashū*, succeeding the *renga* masters NIJŌ YOSHIMOTO and GUSAI, who compiled the original TSUKUBASHŪ (1356). He considered this his greatest honor.

Sogō Co, Ltd
[株]そごう

(Sogō). One of Japan's largest department store chains, with branches in Ōsaka, Kōbe, and Tōkyō. Its history can be traced back to an Ōsaka clothing store that opened in 1830. It has 17 domestic subsidiary stores and overseas subsidiaries in areas such as Hong Kong and Singapore. Sales for the fiscal year ending February 1991 totaled ¥313.4 billion (US $2.3 billion), of which clothing accounted for 41 percent; accessories, 10 percent; sundry goods, 18 percent; foodstuffs, 18 percent; household goods, 10 percent; restaurants, 2 percent; and others, 1 percent. In the same year Sogō was capitalized at ¥14.4 billion (US $105.0 million). Headquarters are in Ōsaka.

sōgo kaisha → mutual company

sōgo shōsha → general trading
companies

sōhei → warrior-monks

Sōhō Myōchō
宗峰妙超

(1282–1337). Also known as Shūhō Myōchō. Monk of the RINZAI SECT of ZEN Buddhism. Born in Harima Province (now part of Hyōgo Prefecture), he first studied TENDAI SECT teachings but later traveled to Kyōto, where he practiced Zen under the noted master Kōhō Kennichi (1241–1316) and subsequently under RANKEI DŌRYŪ's disciple Nampo Shōmyō (or NAMPO JŌMYŌ). In 1315 he established a temple in Murasakino. With his great virtue, he attracted many followers, who also built temples on the same site. It eventually developed into the complex known as DAITOKUJI. Emperor Hanazono (r 1308–18) bestowed on him the title Daitō Kokushi ("National Teacher of the Great Lamp"), by which he has been remembered.

Sōhyō
総評

(abbreviation of Nihon Rōdō Kumiai Sō Hyōgikai; General Council of Trade Unions of Japan). Japan's largest nationwide federation of LABOR UNIONS before disbanding in 1989. Sōhyō was formed in 1950 through a merger of Sambetsu Minshuka Dōmei, which had seceded from SAMBETSU KAIGI (Congress of Industrial Labor Unions of Japan), and the left and centrist factions of Nihon Rōdō Sōdōmei (General Federation of Japan Trade Unions). Although Sōhyō originally took an anticommunist position, it soon took a leftist stand in opposing the Korean War and formed a close relationship with the left wing of the JAPAN SOCIALIST PARTY. Sōhyō maintained its leading position even after the secession of its right-wing faction in 1953 and organized a nationwide spring wage offensive (SHUNTŌ) every year from 1955.

While Sōhyō included almost all unionized government employees in Japan, it did not extend its power comparably in the private sector. In 1989, the year it dissolved,

Sōhyō consisted of 49 trade unions with a membership of 3,977,000. After Sōhyō's disbanding, many of its former member unions joined RENGŌ (Japanese Trade Union Confederation).

Sōja
総社[市]

City in southern Okayama Prefecture, western Honshū. It developed as a shrine town around the Sōja Shrine and as the seat of the provincial capital (*kokufu*) of Bitchū Province. Formerly a farming area, Sōja now has spinning, foodstuff, machinery, and metal plants. Mounded tombs (KOFUN), the Kibi Historical Prefectural Park, and the remains of the ancient state-established provincial temple (*kokubunji*) are of interest. Pop: 52,724.

Sōjiji
総持寺

One of the two major centers, along with EIHEIJI, of the SŌTŌ SECT of ZEN Buddhism in Japan. Founded in 1321 by KEIZAN JŌKIN (1268–1325) in Noto Province (now part of Ishikawa Prefecture), the center was moved in 1911 to its present location in Tsurumi Ward in the city of Yokohama. (A branch temple sits on the original site.) In 1321 Keizan Jōkin converted Morookaji, a RITSU SECT temple, into the original Sōjiji, a Sōtō Zen monastery and training center for monks from all over Japan. In 1322 Emperor GODAIGO officially recognized Sōjiji as a Sōtō monastery. As one of the largest and most active Buddhist institutions in the eastern part of Japan, Sōjiji serves Zen followers in the Tōkyō and Yokohama areas.

sōjutsu
槍術

The ancient martial art of attack and defense with a spear. One of the seven primary military arts. The spear that is used in *sōjutsu* is called the *yari*. It commonly has a double-edged blade or head ranging in size from 30 to 75 centimeters (12–29 in). The shaft length varies depending on the size of the spearhead.

Various methods of spear handling were developed by experts using different kinds of *yari*, and many different schools of *sōjutsu* developed. During the Sengoku period (1467–1568), infantry divisions armed with long spears, called *yaribusuma* ("screen of spears"), often played a decisive role in battle. During the peace of the Edo period (1600–1868), the *yari* became a symbol of *samurai* status and was borne by the retainers of high-ranking warriors. After the Meiji Restoration (1868), *sōjutsu* fell into decline, and today only a few schools preserve its traditions. See also MARTIAL ARTS.

Sōka
草加[市]

City in southeastern Saitama Prefecture, central Honshū. In the Edo period (1600–1868) it developed as a post-station town on the highway Ōshū Kaidō. The leather, textile, and machine industries are active. A well-known local product is *sembei* (rice crackers). Today the city is a dormitory suburb of Tōkyō. Pop: 206,132.

Sōka Gakkai
創価学会

The largest of Japan's NEW RELIGIONS; founded in 1930 by MAKIGUCHI TSUNESABURŌ. It is an independent lay organization of the Buddhist sect Nichiren Shōshū; its chief temple is TAISEKIJI. The organization was originally called the Sōka Kyōiku Gakkai (Value-Creating Educational Society) and was composed mainly of schoolteachers interested in Makiguchi's educational theories. Makigu-

chi converted to Nichiren Shōshū in 1928 and, when his plan to reform Japan's society through its educational system received little attention, became convinced that his educational ideals could be realized best through NICHIREN's teachings. He founded his organization in 1930 with this aim in mind.

The Sōka Kyōiku Gakkai grew slowly during the 1930s. In 1943 Makiguchi, his chief disciple, TODA JŌSEI, and 19 others were jailed by the government, having been charged with violating the 1941 revision of the PEACE PRESERVATION LAW OF 1925 by advising their followers not to venerate Shintō, then the state religion, and by opposing the government's war policy. Makiguchi died in prison. Toda began to reconstruct and expand the organization following his release in 1945; the name was changed to Sōka Gakkai to reflect its emphasis on religious rather than educational aims. Toda, having assumed the presidency in 1951, was succeeded in 1960 by his close associate IKEDA DAISAKU (b 1928). Under his leadership the Sōka Gakkai grew rapidly.

The Sōka Gakkai assumes as a central idea that the Buddha nature is inherent in each human being, who can manifest it through religious practices. The essence of its teachings can be summarized as faith, practice, and study. Faith is the chanting of NAMU MYŌHŌ RENGE KYŌ ("Devotion to the Lotus Sutra") and the reciting of parts of the Lotus Sutra. Practice signifies the incorporation of Buddhist activities into one's daily life, the most important being the communication of the doctrines of Nichiren Shōshū to other people (*shakubuku*). Study refers to that of Nichiren's teachings. In 1989 it claimed a membership in Japan of 7.95 million families; sister organizations overseas in 115 countries had some 1.26 million members.

The Sōka Gakkai carries out a broad range of educational, cultural, and social programs. It has launched a campaign for world peace and developed its own educational system at Sōka University, founded in Tōkyō in 1971. The organization publishes numerous books and periodicals; its daily newspaper, *Seikyō shimbun*, claimed a circulation of about 5.5 million in 1989. It also founded a political party, the KŌMEITŌ, in 1964 but separated the party from itself in 1970.

sōkaiya
総会屋

Certain individuals or groups of individuals (often called "professional stockholders") who sell their services as "protection" for companies, ostensibly to prevent disruption at annual shareholders' meetings. They attend shareholders' meetings because they generally own a small amount of the com-

Sōma Kokkō A patron of the arts and proprietor of Nakamuraya, a Tōkyō bakery-restaurant that became a favorite haunt of early-20th-century artists and writers.

sōmen A very fine wheat-flour noodle, *sōmen* is often eaten in summer with a cold dipping sauce to which ginger and aromatic herbs such as chives (left) may be added.

pany's stock and can threaten disruption themselves if their monetary requests are not met. Changes in Japan's Commercial Code in recent years, intended to bring the *sōkaiya* under control, seem to have had little effect. Instead, more and more leading companies have resorted to holding their annual shareholders' meetings on the same day to make it impossible for the *sōkaiya* to turn out in force for a large number of company meetings. Despite this strategy, it has proved impossible to remove fully the influence of these elements because of their skill at intimidation, and the *sōkaiya* remain an embarrassment and problem for Japan in this era of supposedly rational, global capital markets.

sokushin jōbutsu 即身成仏

("Buddhahood in this very body"). A central tenet of the SHINGON SECT of Buddhism, which holds that perfect enlightenment can be attained in one's present lifetime and is as much a bodily as a spiritual process. The doctrine was explicated by KŪKAI (774–835), who, in his *Sokushin jōbutsu gi* (817–818; tr *Attaining Enlightenment in This Very Existence*, 1972), traced its origins to the treatise known in Japanese as *Bodaishin ron* (Treatise on the Bodhicitta "Mind of Enlightenment"), attributed to the Indian sage Nāgārjuna.

The concept of *sokushin jōbutsu* derives from the radically immanentalist view that the potentiality for Buddhahood exists latently in all creatures and needs not so much to be developed as simply evoked. This is related to the immanentalist HONGAKU (primordial enlightenment), in contrast to the developmental *shigaku* (incipient enlightenment) viewpoint. Broadly construed, *sokushin jōbutsu* suggests an organic, pantheistic view of the universe and became important for Japanese Buddhism not only as an explicit doctrine but also as an interpretive tendency.

sōkyoku 箏曲

Music for KOTO. The *koto* was used in the 11th century to accompany court songs from the SAIBARA and *imayō* repertoires; as a solo instrument from at least the Kamakura period (1185–1333); and to accompany Buddhist chant from at least the late 16th century. However, the term *sōkyoku* (sometimes *zokusō*) generally refers to the solo repertoire developed from the late 16th century, when Kenjun (1534–1623), a Buddhist monk, composed a group of song suites (*koto kumiuta*) inspired by Japanese court music and by the technique and music of the Chinese *qin* (*ch'in*; a seven-string zither). This music was known as Tsukushi *sō* or Tsukushi *gaku*. Certain pieces were based closely on court music, while others included more purely instrumental music. These last pieces inspired a series of instrumental solos (*danmono*), which are usually credited to the blind SHAMISEN master Yatsuhashi Kengyō (1614–85), a pupil of one of Kenjun's disciples. Today there are very few players in the Tsukushiryū and Yatsuhashiryū schools, but their influence on later *koto* music has been of fundamental importance.

The repertoire was extended under the influence of *shamisen* music, especially JIUTA, a genre that comprised both *kumiuta* and concert arrangements of theater pieces, particularly *nagauta* and *hauta*. *Shamisen* pieces were rearranged for *koto* or as *sankyoku* trios.

In the late Edo period (1600–1868) a new movement was led in Edo (now Tōkyō) by Yamada Kengyō (1757–1817), the blind son of a Nō actor, whose 36 *koto* compositions include some elaborate program music. Since his day there have been two main schools of *sōkyoku*, Ikutaryū (centered in Kyōto) and Yamadaryū (in Tōkyō).

During the Meiji period (1868–1912) the *koto* world was in some disarray. The 20th century, however, brought a strong revival led by MIYAGI MICHIO (1894–1956) and NAKANOSHIMA KIN'ICHI (1904–84).

solatium 慰謝料

(*isharyō*). In Japanese law, compensation for pain and suffering. Compensation for damages arising out of torts (CIVIL CODE, art. 709) can be divided into compensation for economic loss and compensation for pain and suffering. Solatium is usually paid in cases of injury to person or reputation, but even in the case of invasion of property rights, it is provided that compensation must be paid for nonfinancial damages (Civil Code, art. 710). However, in the case of invasion of property rights, solatium is limited to intentional damage and to damage to property of great sentimental value. Solatium may be included not only in compensation for damages arising from torts but also in compensation for damages arising out of the nonperformance of obligatory duties (Civil Code, arts. 415–416). In practice, however, such consolation payments are usually limited to special cases (such as personal injury, defamation, or injury to property of great sentimental value). In the past, solatium was paid to the wife in divorce cases, but this has now been almost completely absorbed into the distribution of property system (Civil Code, art. 768).

Personal injuries caused by traffic accidents, pollution, and pharmaceutical products are prime examples of cases in which payment of solatium is required. At trial, it is the judge who decides whether solatium is to be paid and, if so, the amount to be awarded (in Japan there is no jury system).

Sōma 相馬[市]

City in northeastern Fukushima Prefecture, northern Honshū, on the Pacific Ocean. Sōma developed as a castle town of the Sōma family. It is now a distribution center for rice. Port facilities and industries are developing along Sōma Bay. A tourist attraction is the Sōma Nomaoi (literally, "wild horse chase") Festival held in July. Pop: 39,134.

Sōma family 相馬氏

(Sōmashi). Provincial leaders and later *daimyō* of the northern part of what is now the northeastern corner of Fukushima Prefecture (originally part of Mutsu Province) from the 12th century through the Edo period (1600–1868). In 1189 Sōma Morotsune (1139–1205) was awarded the Namekata district of Mutsu Province for helping MINAMOTO NO YORITOMO subjugate the northern region. Sōma Yoshitane (1548–1635) allied himself with TOYOTOMI HIDEYOSHI; his domain was confiscated after the Battle of SEKIGAHARA (1600). In 1604 the family was again granted its traditional lands and settled in Nakamura (now the city of Sōma, Fukushima Prefecture).

Sōma Kokkō 相馬黒光

(1876–1955). Businesswoman and patron of the arts. Original name Hoshi Ryō. Born in Sendai, niece of the feminist SASAKI TOYOJU.

She attended the Ferris Girls' School in Yokohama and graduated from the Meiji Girls' School (Meiji Jogakkō) in 1895. In 1897 she married Sōma Aizō (1870–1954), and in 1901 they opened the Nakamuraya, a bakery and restaurant still flourishing in the Shinjuku district of Tōkyō. The store became famous for its Western pastries and curried rice. The Sōmas encouraged the artists and writers who gathered there, such as sculptor OGIWARA MORIE and SHIMAMURA HŌGETSU's drama group. They also befriended the exiled Indian independence-movement leader Rash Behari BOSE and the blind Russian poet Vasilii EROSHENKO.

Sōma ware 相馬焼

(*sōma-yaki*). Ceramics produced in two centers in Fukushima Prefecture, one in Nakamura in the city of Sōma, the other at Ōbori in the town of Namie. The Nakamura kiln was set up around 1630 and initially produced wares in the Ninsei style (see NONOMURA NINSEI). Sometimes called *komayaki*, this stoneware (because of the *koma* or horse motif) is easily identified by the underglaze painted design of a leaping horse that appears on almost all vessels. The kiln, constructed in the late 1640s, is one of the oldest kilns still in continuous use in Japan. The second kiln, at Ōbori, is thought to have been established in the 1680s. This kiln produces a wide range of wares with a variety of glazes and decorations.

sōmen 素麺

Type of very thin noodle. *Sōmen* is made from a dough consisting of wheat flour and salted water that is kneaded and cut into thick strips. These are coated with cottonseed oil, pulled out into long strings, and ripened overnight. The strings are then attached to two poles, pulled out to the appropriate fineness, and dried in the sun. *Sōmen* is usually considered a food for summer, when it is boiled, rinsed in a colander, and served in a bowl containing cold water or ice. It is accompanied by a cold dipping sauce (*tsuyu*) consisting of soy sauce, MIRIN (sweetened *sake*), sugar, and stock (*dashi*) made from bonito flakes (see KATSUOBUSHI).

Sōmin 僧旻

(?–653). Buddhist priest and scholar of the YAMATO COURT; also known as Bin, Sōbin, or Min. In 608 he accompanied a mission to the Sui dynasty of China (see SUI AND TANG [T'ANG] CHINA, EMBASSIES TO) headed by ONO NO IMOKO, remaining until 632. With TAKAMUKO NO KUROMARO he was appointed state scholar (*kunihakase*) in 645 and assisted Prince Naka no Ōe (later Emperor TENJI) in drawing up the provisions of the TAIKA REFORM.

Sompi bummyaku 尊卑分脈

(Lineages of the Noble and the Humble). Comprehensive collection of genealogical tables begun in the late 14th century by the court noble Tōin Kinsada (1340–99) and continued by his adopted son Tōin Mitsusue (dates unknown) and Mitsusue's son Sanehiro (1409–57). The work originally planned comprised three parts: (1) a genealogy of the imperial family; (2) genealogies of leading families such as the FUJIWARA, TAIRA, and MINAMOTO; and (3) lines of transmission of the largely hereditary learned traditions recognized by the court, such as law and mathematics. The work was elaborated upon and distorted by the later editors, notably Kanroji Chikanaga (1424–1500), SANJŌNISHI SANETAKA, and Nakamikado Noritane (1442–

1525). The imperial genealogy appeared as the independent work *Honchō kōin jōun roku* (A Record of Imperial Descent and Succession in This Realm) compiled in 1416 by Tōin Mitsusue.

Sone no Yoshitada 曽禰好忠

(fl ca 985). Also called Sotan. Classical (WAKA) poet and eccentric innovator. Reputed to be an odd, carelessly dressed character, Yoshitada's poetic eccentricities were mostly confined to the use of startling colloquialisms, crude images, and "low," "vulgar" metaphors. His experiments with unusual diction, in which he persisted despite the indignation of his contemporaries, were unique in the age. It is said that Yoshitada's innovations were inspired in part by the coarse, homely imagery of early Japanese poetry as preserved in the first great anthology, the MAN'YŌSHŪ (ca 759), and in part by the example of Chinese poetry, and particularly the colloquial verse of the very popular Bo Juyi (Po Chü-i; 772–846). He also composed in a more quiet, reflective mode of natural description, foreshadowing the descriptive poetry of retirement in nature practiced in the 11th century by MINAMOTO NO TSUNENOBU and his son MINAMOTO NO TOSHIYORI and preeminently by FUJIWARA NO TOSHINARI (Fujiwara no Shunzei) and FUJIWARA NO SADAIE (Fujiwara no Teika) in the 12th and 13th centuries. Nine of his poems were chosen for the third imperial anthology, the SHŪI WAKASHŪ (ca 1005, Collection of Gleanings), while 89 more were included in various imperial anthologies from the *Go shūishū* (1086, Later Collection of Gleanings) on. His personal collection, *Sotanshū*, contains 586 poems.

Sonezaki shinjū 曽根崎心中

(tr *The Love Suicides at Sonezaki*, 1961). KABUKI play of the *sewa-mono* (domestic play) category by CHIKAMATSU MONZAEMON. Originally written as a puppet play; first performed in 1703. Based on an actual incident that was the talk of Ōsaka, this play recounts the tragic love story and death pact of the shop clerk Tokubei and the courtesan Ohatsu, who are driven to suicide by a friend's betrayal. After a secret reunion and a pathos-filled *michiyuki* (journey) to Sonezaki Wood, Tokubei stabs Ohatsu and then slashes his own throat as a temple bell tolls. The passage recited by the chanter to accompany the *michiyuki* scene is regarded as one of the lyrical masterpieces of the Japanese traditional theater.

Song Hŭi-gyŏng 宋稀璟

(1376–1446; J: Sō Kikei). Korean government official; pen name Nosongdang (J: Rōshōdō). Song came to Japan in 1420 as an envoy to reciprocate a visit by a Japanese delegation sent by shōgun Ashikaga Yoshimochi (r 1395–1423). His record of the trip, *Nosongdang Ilbon haengnok* (J: *Rōshōdō Nihon kōroku*), provides valuable information on Japanese society.

Song Jiaoren (Sung Chiao-jen) 宋教仁

(1882–1913; J: Sō Kyōjin). An anti-Manchu revolutionary, a follower of HUANG XING (Huang Hsing), and a founder of the Guomindang (Kuomintang; Nationalist Party). In 1904 Song Jiaoren fled to Japan, where he studied Western political thought and participated in the anti-Manchu movement among Chinese students in Tōkyō. He founded the journal that later became the organ of the revolutionary United League

(Tongmeng Hui or T'ung-meng Hui), led by SUN YAT-SEN. During this period Song became a close friend of Japanese socialist and nationalist KITA IKKI. In 1910 Song returned to China and worked to counter the growing authoritarianism of President YUAN SHIKAI (Yüan Shih-k'ai). On 20 March 1913 Song was fatally shot by followers of Yuan. His assassination marked the end of the initial optimism concerning democratic government in the new Republic of China.

Song Zheyuan (Sung Che-yüan) 宋哲元

(1885–1940; J: Sō Tetsugen). Military figure directly involved in Sino-Japanese confrontations in North China in the 1930s. Until 1930 Song was a subordinate of a warlord in northwest China and not directly loyal to CHIANG KAI-SHEK, leader of the Guomindang (Kuomintang; KMT; Nationalist Party). With the outbreak of the MANCHURIAN INCIDENT on 18 September 1931, Song (then a commander of the 29th Army) called for war against Japan. He resisted the invasion of the Japanese GUANDONG (KWANTUNG) ARMY in spring 1933 and fought on until the TANGGU (TANGKU) TRUCE of 31 May. In 1935 Song assumed the chairmanship of the JI-CHA (CHI-CH'A) AUTONOMOUS POLITICAL COUNCIL created by the Japanese military. In the face of anti-Japanese demonstrations (see DECEMBER NINTH MOVEMENT), he informed the Japanese that he would not be responsible for order in Beiping (Peiping; now Beijing [Peking]). After the MARCO POLO BRIDGE INCIDENT (7 July 1937) Song tried to negotiate a settlement with Japan. When Japanese troops moved toward Beiping, Song evacuated the city. Song's troops were defeated in the autumn, marking the end of what had been a major military force in North China.

Sonkeikaku Library 尊経閣文庫

(Sonkeikaku Bunko; more correctly, Maeda Ikutoku Kai Sonkeikaku Bunko). The MAEDA FAMILY library; located in Komaba, Meguro Ward, Tōkyō. Five generations, beginning with MAEDA TOSHIIE (1538?–99), founder of the family, collected the riches of Ming-dynasty (1368–1644) Chinese classics and printed scriptures, old manuscripts and household records, rare books and art works of the Heian (794–1185) and Kamakura (1185–1333) periods, and valued handicrafts from the Edo period (1600–1868), including publications. By the time of the fifth family head, MAEDA TSUNANORI (1643–1724), the library held some 80 priceless works recognized today as National Treasures and Important Cultural Properties by the Japanese government. A handwritten copy by FUJIWARA NO SADAIE of KI NO TSURAYUKI's TOSA NIKKI (Tosa Diary) is one of these treasures.

sonnō jōi 尊王攘夷

(literally, "Revere the Emperor, Expel the Barbarians"). The idea that Japan should be unified under the imperial rule (*sonnō*) and incursions by foreigners resolutely repelled (*jōi*). *Sonnō jōi* as a political doctrine developed during the late Edo period (1600–1868). As the guiding principle of the movement to overthrow the Tokugawa shogunate, it played a significant role in bringing about the MEIJI RESTORATION of 1868.

The sacrosanct character of the imperial institution and Japan's superiority over other nations were upheld by such 17th-century Confucian scholars as YAMAZAKI ANSAI and YAMAGA SOKŌ. In the 18th century this view was vigorously expounded by MOTOORI

NORINAGA and other scholars of the Japanese classics (see KOKUGAKU). As Russian and British ships intruded into Japanese waters at the end of the 18th century, the viability of the 150-year-old policy of NATIONAL SECLUSION was questioned. Scholars and intellectuals put forth theories and proposals to ensure Japan's independence and future development.

The concepts *sonnō* and *jōi*, originally distinct ideas traceable to ancient China, were first systematically combined by the scholar AIZAWA SEISHISAI of the Mito domain (now part of Ibaraki Prefecture) in his treatise SHINRON (1825). The *sonnō jōi* doctrine became a distinguishing mark of the MITO SCHOOL of historical studies. In *Kōdōkan ki* (1838), a manifesto drafted by FUJITA TŌKO and read publicly under the name of the Mito *daimyō*, TOKUGAWA NARIAKI, *sonnō* was used to describe the reverence paid to the imperial court by TOKUGAWA IEYASU, the founder of the shogunate, and *jōi* meant the proscription of Christianity.

Some historians have regarded *sonnō jōi* thought as originating in a conservative ideology aimed at maintenance of the shogunal ruling structure, but the fact that *sonnō jōi* had as its main object the preservation of national unity meant that, in the face of shogunal impotence, it led inevitably to an antishogunate position. The partial opening of Japan in the late 1850s under pressure from the Western powers exposed the weakness of the shogunate both within and without. Fervent advocates of *sonnō jōi*, like YOSHIDA SHŌIN and MAKI IZUMI, criticized the shogunal institution and called for its abolition. The expression came to represent a militant rallying cry for the movement to overthrow the shogunate and restore imperial rule. Therefore, *sonnō jōi* can be seen positively as an impetus in the formation of the modern Japanese nation.

Sono Ayako 曽野綾子

(1931–). Novelist. Real name Miura Chizuko; maiden name Machida. Born in Tōkyō. In 1953 she married the novelist MIURA SHUMON and the following year graduated from the University of the Sacred Heart in Tōkyō. She gained prominence with her story "Enrai no kyakutachi" (1954, Guests from Afar), about the US Occupation forces. Her principal works include *Tamayura* (1959, A Moment), *Rio Gurande* (1961, Rio Grande), *Ikenie no shima* (1969, Island of Sacrifice), and *Kami no yogoreta te* (1979, The Dirty Hands of the Gods).

Sonoda Takahiro 園田高弘

(1928–). Pianist. Born in Tōkyō. He studied under Leo Shirota (1885–1965) and Toyomasu Noboru (1912–75) at the Tōkyō Music School (now Tōkyō University of Fine Arts and Music), graduating in 1948. He studied in France and Germany in 1952–53 but was forced to return home due to illness. In 1954 he was discovered by Herbert von Karajan (1908–89) during the Austrian conductor's first visit to Japan. He made his debut recital in Paris in 1957, achieving international recognition in 1959 when he played with the Berlin Philharmonic Orchestra. He became a member of the Japan Art Academy in 1980.

Sony Corporation ソニー[株]

(Sonī). Japan's leading electronics manufacturer, producing mainly audio and visual

余時佛告諸大衆乃往古世過無量無邊不
妙法蓮華經妙莊嚴王本事品第二十七
可思議阿僧祇劫有佛名雲雷音宿王華智

sōshokukyō Detail from one of the 33 scrolls of the *Heike nōkyō*, an illustrated sutra donated by Taira no Kiyomori to the Itsukushima Shrine, Hiroshima Prefecture, in 1164. Colors on paper. 26 × 813 cm. National Treasure.

Sorge Incident Richard Sorge was arrested by Japanese authorities and executed for espionage in one of the most famous spy incidents of World War II.

electronic equipment. It was incorporated in 1946 by IBUKA MASARU and MORITA AKIO. In 1958 it changed its name from Tōkyō Tsūshin Kōgyō (Tōkyō Telecommunications Engineering Corporation) to its present one. The Sony trademark is now registered in 178 countries and territories around the world. Its exports are distributed overseas through locally managed subsidiaries. It has established production facilities in various countries, including the United States and the United Kingdom. Sony's stocks are listed on 18 major stock exchanges in 10 countries. It was the first Japanese company to offer shares on the US stock market. At the end of March 1991 its consolidated net sales were ¥1.9 trillion (US $13.8 billion), of which overseas sales accounted for 63 percent. Sales were distributed as follows: televisions, 17 percent; other video equipment, 38 percent; audio equipment, 26 percent; and other products, 19 percent. In that same year the company was capitalized at ¥297.3 billion (US $2.2 billion). Headquarters are in Tōkyō.

Sony Foundation of Science Education   ソニー教育振興財団

(Sonī Kyōiku Shinkō Zaidan). A foundation established in 1972 by the SONY CORPORATION to support research in and promotion of education, especially science education. It also supports a Japan-US high-school-teacher exchange program. In 1989 total assets were ¥2.2. billion (US $15.9 million). Headquarters are in Tōkyō.

Sophia University   上智大学

(Jōchi Daigaku). Located in Chiyoda Ward, Tōkyō. A private, Catholic, coeducational university based on the Jōchi Gakuen, it was founded by the German Hermann Hoffman in 1911; it was granted university status in 1928. It maintains an international division for foreign students and faculties of letters, economics, law, theology, foreign languages, and science and engineering. It is known principally for its foreign language studies. It has an affiliated two-year women's junior college. Enrollment was 10,322 in 1989.

Sorge Incident   ゾルゲ事件

(Zoruge Jiken). Espionage incident uncovered immediately before Japan's entry into World War II. On 18 October 1941 Tōkyō

police took into custody Dr Richard Sorge, a leading German newspaper correspondent; Branco Vukelic, a Yugoslav national who worked for a French news agency; and Max Klausen, a German businessman. Some days earlier the police had arrested MIYAGI YOTOKU, a Japanese artist, and OZAKI HOTSUMI, a political commentator and journalist. These five men were the principal figures in a spy ring organized and directed by Soviet military intelligence in Moscow. However, the brief press release by the Ministry of Justice in May 1942 stated that the five men, together with certain other persons, were charged with espionage "on behalf of the Communist International." By its reference to the Comintern rather than to Soviet military intelligence, the Ministry of Justice could take the view that the Soviet Union itself (then linked to Japan by a nonaggression pact) was not involved in the affair. Moreover, the accused, as members of a communist party, could be tried for violation of the 1941 revision of the PEACE PRESERVATION LAW OF 1925, which came within the ministry's jurisdiction, rather than for a breach of the National Defense Security Law, which would have to be dealt with by the military authorities.

At their trials in September 1943 Sorge and Ozaki were sentenced to death and Vukelic and Klausen to life imprisonment. Miyagi died in custody before being brought to trial, Sorge and Ozaki were hanged on 7 November 1944, and Vukelic died in prison in January 1945. Klausen survived to be released in October 1945, following the arrival of the Allied Occupation forces.

A great deal of top-secret economic, military, and political information (some of it from German sources) was sent to the Soviet Union by the Sorge ring. Possibly the two most dramatic items were an almost perfect order-of-battle chart of the Japanese army in June 1941 and an assurance that Japan would *not* attack the Soviet Union in 1941, following Germany's assault in the summer, but would move south, probably against British and Dutch possessions in Southeast Asia.

The major source of such information was Ozaki, who had been a member of the Shōwa Research Association (SHŌWA KENKYŪKAI) and who for several years had maintained close contact with more than one member of Prime Minister KONOE FUMIMARO's inner circle of consultants. Thus Konoe himself and certain of his friends faced questioning by prosecu-

tors of the Ministry of Justice. The arrest, trial, and execution of Ozaki sent out political shock waves whose ripples did not die down for many years.

It was in the fall of 1945 that fuller coverage of the Sorge Incident was given by the Japanese press. Ozaki emerged as a resistance leader and as a symbol of the opposition in high circles to Japan's entry into the war. In 1956 a society was founded in Tōkyō to keep alive the memory of Ozaki and his associates. After many years of denying that Sorge had been a Soviet-controlled agent, the Soviet Union in 1964 gave him the posthumous decoration of Hero of the Soviet Union.

Sōrifu → Prime Minister's Office

soroban → abacus

sōrōbun   候文

(epistolary style). Style of written Japanese used mainly for letters and certain types of documents. *Sōrōbun* developed in the late Heian period (794–1185) and the Kamakura period (1185–1333) from an earlier documentary style called HENTAI KAMBUN, which was itself a form of classical Chinese heavily modified by an admixture of Japanese words and grammatical constructions. The distinctive feature of *sōrōbun* is the frequent use of the polite auxiliary verb *sōrō* (originally meaning "to serve"), which eventually lost its independent semantic value and came to correspond in function to the auxillary verb *arimasu* "to be" or merely to the polite verbal suffix *-masu* of modern Japanese.

The grammatical structure of *sōrōbun* was based on that of CLASSICAL JAPANESE, but its orthography made extensive use of Chinese characters and Chinese word order and omitted Japanese particles and conjugational suffixes wherever possible, thus to a certain extent requiring the reader to perform a rather complex decoding operation to read a *sōrōbun* text as Japanese. Although *sōrōbun* originated as a style for personal letters, in the Edo period (1600–1868) it was also widely used in official letters, a practice that continued into the modern era. In fact, *sōrōbun* was the standard form for all formal correspondence until the end of World War II and was sometimes used even in commercial notices and advertisements. *Sōrōbun* and *mairase sōrōbun*, a variant used only by women, are now obsolete. Nevertheless, many epistolary conventions—particularly salutations and closing phrases—developed in *sōrōbun* are still used in letter writing.

sōryō system   惣領制

(*sōryōsei*). Internal organization of regional landholding families on the basis of divided inheritance under the absolute leadership of a main heir (*sōryō*), who was usually the eldest son. The practice first emerged in the late Heian period (794–1185) and continued through the Kamakura period (1185–1333). All sons and even daughters were originally entitled to a share of family property, but the *sōryō* came to be responsible for the distribution and overall administration of the fields (*myōden*) and cultivators controlled by his family (see MYŌSHU and RYŌSHU). The most powerful *sōryō* served as vassals (GOKENIN) under the Kamakura shogunate (1192–1333). Toward the close of the Kamakura period the shogunate directly confirmed collateral family members' rights of proprietorship (ANDO), thus making the system ineffective.

Sosei 素性

(fl ca 859–923). Classical (WAKA) poet and Buddhist priest. Lay name Yoshimine no Harutoshi; also called Yoshiyori no Ason. Son of the poet HENJŌ (Yoshimine no Munesada). One of the "Thirty-Six Poetic Geniuses" (SANJŪROKKASEN); 36 of his poems are included in the first imperial anthology of classical poetry (chokusenshū), the KOKINSHŪ. His personal collection, Soseishū, contains 65 poems.

sōsen 宋銭

(literally, "Song [Sung] coins"). Copper coins minted in China during the Song dynasty (960–1279). After the last minting of Japanese coins (KŌCHŌ JŪNISEN) in 958, coins imported from China and Korea were used in increasing numbers. Sōsen circulated widely in Japan as a result of trade in East Asia in the 13th century. With KŌBUSEN and EIRAKU-SEN—both coins of the Ming dynasty (1368–1644)—sōsen were the major currency until coins were once again minted in Japan by ODA NOBUNAGA and TOYOTOMI HIDEYOSHI. These coins stimulated the money economy because they were sometimes used in place of rice for paying taxes.

sōshoku kofun → ornamented tombs

sōshokukyō 装飾経

(ornamented sutra). Also called sōgonkyō. A decorated handscroll onto which a sutra is copied. Methods of decoration include dyeing the paper, copying the sutras in gold or silver distemper, and painting Buddhist images on the cover or frontispiece. During the latter part of the Heian period (794–1185), many elaborate sōshokukyō were produced by the aristocracy. A well-known example of a sōshokukyō is the Heike nōkyō (1164), which is housed at the Itsukushima Shrine in Hiroshima Prefecture.

Sosogi Coast 曽々木海岸

(Sosogi Kaigan). Coastal area on the northern Noto Peninsula, Ishikawa Prefecture, central Honshū. Noted for its oddly shaped rocks, rugged cliffs, and the Tarumi Falls, it is part of Noto Peninsula Quasi-National Park. Length: about 2.5 km (1.6 mi).

Sōtan → Oguri Sōtan

Sōtatsu 宗達

(?–1643?). Also known as Tawaraya Sōtatsu. Artist and founder of the RIMPA style of painting. Sōtatsu headed the workshop Tawaraya in Kyōto, which flourished between 1600 and 1640, and is said to have attempted a revival of the tradition of medieval painting. The repertoire of his workshop comprises paintings done in color and gold and silver on screens and sliding-wall panels, fans, writing paper, and album leaves, as well as paintings done in ink.

Sōtatsu may have been related by marriage to the great calligrapher HON'AMI KŌETSU and to Ogata Dōhaku (d 1604), great-grandfather of Sōtatsu's later follower KŌRIN. Sōtatsu had an enormous impact on later Japanese painting, especially in his use of color and ink, which allowed tonal modulation similar to that of watercolor technique. In the genre of flowers and grasses, Sōtatsu's school started a new tradition of representation based on detailed observation.

Some of the literary sources for Sōtatsu's illustrative works are the classical tales HEIJI MONOGATARI, HŌGEN MONOGATARI, ISE MONOGATARI, and the TALE OF GENJI. The greater part of Sōtatsu's figurative repertoire is taken from medieval picture scrolls (EMAKIMONO), which he used as his source book. Major works such as the Fūjin Raijin zu (Wind and Thunder Gods) screens (Kenninji, Kyōto) and the Bugakuzu (Bugaku Dancers) screens (Daigoji, Kyōto) also draw on mythology and classical dance for their themes.

In his ink paintings Sōtatsu chose mostly bird-and-flower and Zen Buddhist subjects. He created a new "boneless" technique by applying several wet layers of ink or paint on specially prepared paper, producing an accidental fusion of the pigments, a technique known as tarashikomi.

Sōtatsu's art reveals the difference between painting in the Chinese mode as represented by the KANŌ SCHOOL and the indigenous Japanese tradition of YAMATO-E painting. He combined yamato-e subject matter with the new preference for grandiose compositions and lavish materials, such as gold and silver, that had developed in the Azuchi-Momoyama period (1568–1600). In the late 19th and early 20th centuries, his tradition became one of the major roots of modern Japanese-style painting (NIHONGA).

sotetsu 蘇鉄

(Japanese sago palm). Cycas revoluta. Evergreen tree of the family Cycadaceae, commonly cultivated as an ornamental and found growing wild in southern Kyūshū and the Ryūkyū Islands. Its rough, dark, columnar stem grows to 1–4 meters (3–13 ft). The stem is crowned with stiff, glossy, dark green, frondlike leaves, 0.5–2.0 meters (1.6–6.6 ft) long, which uncoil like fern leaves. Around August the sotetsu produces male and female flowers on separate trees. In 1896 IKENO SEIICHIRŌ clarified the reproductive process of the sotetsu and its relationship to other gymnosperms. In the past starch taken from the stem was used as food in times of emergency, and the seeds were used for medicinal purposes.

Sotomo 蘇洞門

Coastal area on the Uchitomi Peninsula, city of Obama, Fukui Prefecture, central Honshū. Noted for its granite joints, oddly shaped rocks, caves, and cliffs created by the erosion of the sea, it is part of Wakasa Bay Quasi-National Park. Length: 2 km (1.2 mi).

Sōtō sect 曹洞宗

(Sōtōshū). One of the two major schools of ZEN Buddhism introduced to Japan from Song (Sung) China (960–1279) early in the Kamakura period (1185–1333). Sōtō Zen was established in Japan by DŌGEN, who returned from study in China in 1227. The RINZAI SECT of Zen had been introduced by EISAI in 1191. The Sōtō sect initially grew under the shadow of Rinzai, but Sōtō became one of the largest Japanese Buddhist sects after moving from Kyōto into the provinces.

Basic Teachings—Zen, together with other schools of Mahāyāna Buddhism, teaches that all people inherently possess the Buddha nature and that, by awakening to this Buddha nature, a person may achieve enlightenment. Zen places special emphasis on meditation as the means to enlightenment. Zen was the principal school of Buddhism in Song China; two branches, the Rinzai (Ch: Linji or Lin-chi) and Sōtō (Ch: Caodong or Ts'ao-tung), flourished. Dōgen was one of the few to study under a Sōtō sect master; his teacher was Zhangweng Rujing (Chang-weng Ju-ching; J: Chōō Nyojō;

Sōtatsu A pair of two-panel folding screens entitled *Wind and Thunder Gods*. Based on a mythological theme, this work typifies Sōtatsu's mature style. Early 17th century. Colors and gold leaf on paper. Each screen 157 × 173 cm. Kenninji, Kyōto. National Treasure.

sotetsu The system of reproduction of this evergreen tree is one of the simplest among all seed-bearing plants.
1 The male sotetsu plant and cone.
2 The female plant and cone.

Sōunkyō Hiking trails wind around and through the high cliffs of this scenic gorge, forming part of Daisetsuzan National Park.

1163–1228). Sōtō and Rinzai differed in that Sōtō placed a greater emphasis on a tranquil form of meditation sitting, characterized as *mokushō* Zen, or "silent illumination Zen," whereas Rinzai advocated the more active *kanna* Zen, or "*kōan*-introspection Zen," in which one meditated upon a brief Zen story (KŌAN) under the direction of a Zen master.

Early History——When Dōgen returned from China in 1227 he went first to the Rinzai temple, KENNINJI, in Kyōto, but was dissatisfied with the teachings practiced there. In 1230 he moved to Fukakusa, south of Kyōto (now in Kyōto), where in 1233 he began setting up the Song-style meditation temple later called Kōshō Hōrinji. His students were largely former members of a school known as Nihon Daruma Shū (Japan Bodhidharma sect), founded by Dainichi Nōnin (dates unknown). Its members left Kyōto in 1194 when the propagation of Zen by Eisai and Nōnin was forbidden, and several, including Ejō (1198–1280), Gikai (1219–1309), and Gien (d 1314) came to study under Dōgen. In 1243 Dōgen set out for the remote province of Echizen (now part of Fukui Prefecture) and eventually founded the monastery Daibutsuji, later renamed EIHEIJI. In 1253 he died, and Ejō took over Eiheiji; he in turn handed over the duties of running the temple to Gikai. An opposing faction, centering on Gien and Jiyuan (Chi-yüan; J: Jakuen; 1207–99), objected to Gikai's attempts to gain a local following by enlarging the temple and adding elements from esoteric Buddhism, which they saw as a violation of Dōgen's austere style. This quarrel is known as the *sandai sōron,* or "third-generation dispute." Gikai finally left Eiheiji for Kaga Province (now Ishikawa Prefecture), where he changed a former Tendai temple, Daijōji, into one of the Sōtō sect. Eiheiji eventually lost its local support and fell into disrepair.

Popularization——Sōtō gained popular appeal under KEIZAN JŌKIN, the fourth patriarch and Gikai's heir. He incorporated elements from mountain religious activities, Hakusan Tendai beliefs in KANNON, and various local Shintō guardian deities, and he absorbed ascetic practices of the SHUGENDŌ mountain monks. A conscious effort was made to offer solace to the people, and great emphasis was placed on public works and services. Assemblies such as the *gōkoe,* gatherings of monks from throughout the country, and *jukaie,* gatherings for conferring the precepts, flourished. Since the general public was allowed to attend, these meetings gained great popularity and furnished the public with a general knowledge of Zen.

Edo-Period Revitalization——By the Edo period (1600–1868) the Sōtō sect had spread throughout the country, but both it and Rinzai Zen had virtually abandoned any serious Zen study and practice. In 1612 the Tokugawa shogunate established *hatto* (regulations) for the Sōtō sect. In 1615 an order establishing both Eiheiji and SŌJIJI as *honzan* (main temples), where people might enter the priesthood, was issued. Despite the rigid governmental controls and the emergence of Neo-Confucian and other teachings, the Edo period saw a revitalization of Buddhist teaching. Gesshū Sōko (1618–96) was one of the leaders of a movement known as *shūtō fukko,* or restoration of the lineage, which sought to clarify the line of teaching passed from master to disciple in the Sōtō sect. Gesshū was also a leader in the renewed interest in Dōgen's major work, the SHŌBŌ GENZŌ (1231–53, Treasury of the True Dharma Eye). A succession of Sōtō sect scholars studied Dōgen's work, bringing about a reassessment of his position as the founder of Sōtō Zen and the first publication of *Shōbō genzō* between 1796 and 1811.

During the Genroku era (1688–1704) a school, the Sendanrin, was established in Edo (now Tōkyō), to instruct Sōtō monks. Chinese studies and poetry were also taught. It was the forerunner of present-day Komazawa University. The Sōtō sect had about 14,700 temples and nearly 7 million adherents as of 1989.

Sōunji Dono Nijūikkajō
早雲寺殿廿一箇条
(The Twenty-One Articles of Lord Sōunji). A set of household precepts (KAKUN) attributed without direct evidence to HŌJŌ SŌUN (1432–1519), a Sengoku-period (1467–1568) adventurer who rose to lordship over Izu and Sagami provinces (now comprised in Shizuoka and Kanagawa prefectures) and founded the Later Hōjō Family (see HŌJŌ FAMILY). Unlike other documents of the same category, these articles were addressed principally not to the author's family and descendants but to the vassals of his house, providing them with basic rules of conduct. The *samurai* are told to believe in the Buddhas and the gods; to practice reading and writing no less than riding; and to be prudent, straightforward, and truthful.

Sōunkyō
層雲峡
Gorge near the upper reaches of the river Ishikarigawa, central Hokkaidō. Its sheer cliffs reach a height of more than 160 m (525 ft) on both sides of the gorge, presenting a grand spectacle of columnar joints and waterfalls. Sōunkyō Hot Spring is located here. Length: approximately 24 km (15 mi).

South Africa and Japan
南アフリカと日本
(Minami Afurika *to* Nihon). The first Japanese consulate on the continent of Africa was established in 1918 in Cape Town, South Africa, and was followed in 1937 by the opening of a Japanese legation in Pretoria. Amicable relations between the two countries continued until 1941.

A Japanese consulate general was opened in Pretoria when the SAN FRANCISCO PEACE TREATY went into effect in 1952, and a consulate general of South Africa was established in Tōkyō in 1962. Relations remained at the consular level, however, due to the international outcry, led by the nations of Africa, against the South African domestic policy of apartheid. In 1969 Japan prohibited direct investment in South Africa, and in 1974 it restricted sporting, cultural, and educational exchange programs with that country.

In 1985, following United Nations resolutions against South Africa, the United States and European countries instituted sanctions against South Africa, and that country's total import-export trade shrank. In the same year Japan also prohibited the export to South Africa of certain items of computer equipment that could be used by the military and the police to further apartheid policies, and in 1986 Japan banned the import of South African iron and steel. Nevertheless, Japan's trade with South Africa in 1987 expressed in dollars expanded by some 20 percent over the previous year, owing to the appreciation of the yen. African nations responded by condemning Japan for, in effect, supporting apartheid.

In 1990 Japan was South Africa's fifth largest trade partner; Japanese exports, chiefly automobiles and machinery, totaled US $1.5 billion, and imports, largely rare metals such as chromium and manganese, $1.8 billion. Nelson Mandela, vice-president of the African National Congress, visited Japan in 1990; his organization had opened an office in Tōkyō two years earlier. It is anticipated that, with the repeal of apartheid laws in 1991 and the lifting of the international community's sanctions against South Africa, Japan will review its economic policies in regard to that country, a course of action indicated by the decision of the TOYOTA MOTOR CORPORATION and the NISSAN MOTOR CO, LTD, in June 1991 to lift the policies of voluntary restraints on automobile exports to South Africa that they had introduced in 1988.

South China Sea, Battle of
マレー沖海戦
(Marē Oki Kaisen; literally, "Battle off the Malay Coast"). Naval engagement between Japan and Great Britain at the beginning of World War II. On 10 December 1941 the British Far Eastern Fleet, consisting of the battleship *Prince of Wales,* the battle cruiser *Repulse,* and four destroyers, and commanded by Adm. Sir Thomas Phillips, went into action to prevent Japanese forces from landing on the Malay Peninsula. Both the *Prince of Wales* and *Repulse* were sunk by Japanese naval airplanes. The battle, together with the attack on Pearl Harbor, proved conclusively the importance of air power in naval operations.

Southeast Asia and Japan

東南アジアと日本

(Tōnan Ajia to Nihon). Relations between Japan and Southeast Asia first flourished in the late 16th century. Until 1635 the Tokugawa shogunate (1603–1867) promoted VERMILION SEAL SHIP TRADE with the region, and Japanese settlements (NIHOMMA-CHI) were established in commercial centers such as Manila in the Philippines and Ayuthaya in Siam (now Thailand). However, trade came to an abrupt end with the enforcement of the NATIONAL SECLUSION policy, and it was not until the mid-19th century that relations were resumed.

Meiji Period—A large majority of Japanese who went to Southeast Asia in the early Meiji period (1868–1912) were prostitutes (see KARAYUKI SAN). They plied their trade throughout Southeast Asia, especially on the Malay Peninsula; of the Japanese living in Southeast Asia at the time, it is estimated that 80 to 90 percent were women engaged in prostitution and related occupations.

Toward the turn of the century, private Japanese shipping companies opened sea routes between Japan and major ports in the region, and the Foreign Ministry established consulates in Manila (1888), Singapore (1889), and Batavia (1909), as well as a legation in Bangkok (1897). Communities of Japanese merchants arose in all regions of Southeast Asia: in the Dutch East Indies, Japanese sundries stores, called toko jepang, did a thriving business; in Davao in the Philippines, a Manila hemp industry was developed; and on the Malay Peninsula, rubber plantations were established. At the same time, large trading firms and banks opened networks of branches in the area.

Japanese Expansion—Several important developments in relations with the region arose after the outbreak of World War I. The Japanese occupied a number of Pacific Islands that had been German protectorates (among them the Marshall, Palau, Caroline, and Mariana islands) and its mandate was confirmed by the VERSAILLES Peace Treaty of 1919. The Japanese considered the Pacific Islands an important part of Southeast Asia, and possession of the islands represented a strong tie to the region. During the period 1914–20, trade volume with Southeast Asia, particularly in cotton textiles, increased dramatically as Japan moved to meet the demand that the European nations, due to the war, were no longer able to supply. At the same time Japanese capital investment in the region, particularly by large corporations in rubber and coconut plantations, also increased. The expansion of trade relations was accompanied by an increase in shipping routes between Japan and Southeast Asia and a corresponding increase in migration from Japan. In contrast to the prewar era, Japanese expansion into the area during the postwar period derived from economic planning by both the Japanese government and private business.

Expansion to the South and World War II—The SOUTHERN EXPANSION DOCTRINE, which had been advocated by some in Japan since the late 19th century, was adopted as national policy in 1936. It held that the whole of Southeast Asia was destined to come within Japan's sphere of influence and that the Pacific Ocean would become a "Japanese lake." Implementation of the doctrine was decided upon by July 1940 and incorporated in the proposal for the GREATER EAST ASIA CO-PROSPERITY SPHERE.

In September of the same year, Japan occupied northern French Indochina. In November, the Pacific Islands Bureau (Nan'yōkyoku) was established within the Foreign Ministry. After the outbreak of the Pacific War in December 1941, Japan took, in quick succession, New Guinea and the Solomon Islands, the Philippines, Singapore, the Dutch East Indies, and Burma, before being turned back by US forces at the Battle of Midway in June 1942. On 1 November 1942, the Greater East Asia Ministry (Dai Tōa Shō) was formed to coordinate relations between Japan and the various nations and territories of the Coprosperity Sphere, and a year later the Greater East Asia Conference was held in Tōkyō. This was the only meeting of the leaders of the major nations of the Coprosperity Sphere held during the sphere's existence. During the war era, by far the larger portion of Japan's diplomatic efforts were directed not toward China, but toward Southeast Asia. With defeat in 1945, all but a few Japanese nationals, military and civilian, were repatriated. See also WORLD WAR II; COLONIAL POLICY.

Post–World War II Relations—The first issue of postwar relations was the payment of war reparations to the countries of Southeast Asia. On the basis of the SAN FRANCISCO PEACE TREATY, the Philippines and Vietnam demanded reparations and started negotiations with Japan. Although Burma did not attend the San Francisco peace conference, and Indonesia signed the peace treaty but did not ratify it, both countries demanded reparations from Japan. Cambodia and Laos renounced their claims to indemnity. Japan signed reparations agreements with Burma, the Philippines, Indonesia, and Vietnam between 1954 and 1959. The reparations negotiations played a major role in the establishment of formal relations between Japan and these countries. See REPARATIONS FOR SOUTHEAST ASIA.

The Japanese economy benefited much from the long-term payment of reparations in services and products, principally capital goods. The automobile and electrical machinery industries were stimulated by contracts for capital goods, while stockpiles of ceramic wares, rayon, canned fish, and galvanized sheet iron were set as reparations payments, aiding the revitalization of depressed industries. Of greater significance was the fact that the reparations payments primed the pump for the advance of trading firms and other enterprises into the markets of Southeast Asia. The Japanese construction industry, which before the war had had little involvement overseas, established itself in the area. Reparations in the form of trucks, buses, bicycles, sewing machines, household electric appliances, and pumps created markets for the later sale of goods. Reparations also contributed to capital formation in the recipient countries.

The Resurgence of Japanese Influence in Southeast Asia—The postwar advance into Southeast Asia by Japan has been remarkable, considering the legacy of resentment that accrued from its wartime activities. Japan's entrance into the area was in part eased by the United States, which, during and after the Korean War, wielded considerable influence in Southeast Asia. Another factor was the desire on the part of the nations of the region for assistance in economic development. As the only industrialized country in Asia at the time, Japan quite naturally assumed that role. In April 1954 Japan joined the United Nations Economic Commission for Asia and the Far East (ECAFE), and in October of the same year Japan became a signatory of the Colombo Plan for the development of South and Southeast Asia, paving the way for expanded Japanese involvement in the area.

From the mid-1960s economic ties between Japan and Southeast Asia became increasingly close. The governments of Thailand and Indonesia enacted legislation to facilitate the introduction of foreign capital and began to implement policies aimed at industrialization. Japan's aggressive entry into the markets of Southeast Asia, however, aroused increasing resentment, culminating in violent anti-Japanese demonstrations, particularly in Bangkok and Jakarta in January 1974, when Prime Minister Tanaka Kakuei visited the member countries of the Association of Southeast Asian Nations (ASEAN). In addition to latent antagonism attributable to the human suffering and loss of civic pride inflicted by Japan during the war, it was charged that the economic advance of Japan was obstructing development of the region's economies and the welfare of its peoples, as well as having an adverse effect on political systems of the region.

Relations with the ASEAN Nations—ASEAN was founded in August 1967 by Thailand, Indonesia, Malaysia, the Philippines, and Singapore and joined in 1984 by Brunei. Although initially the cooperation of ASEAN nations was limited to nonpolitical areas, following the resumption of diplomatic relations between the United States and China and the end of the Vietnam War, ASEAN moved toward a stronger emphasis on political and mutual security issues. This change is apparent in its declaration at Kuala Lumpur in November 1971 concerning the creation of a neutral zone in Southeast Asia and in the Declaration of Concord and the Treaty of Amity and Cooperation, both of which issued from the first ASEAN summit meeting held in Bali in February 1976. Japan has consistently supported ASEAN in the belief that the growing unity and influence of the organization would contribute to stability in Southeast Asia. Although in the first half of the 1970s relations were occasionally strained, the second half of the decade saw marked improvement, in part as a result of Prime Minister Fukuda Takeo's speech in Manila in 1977, in which he expressed Japan's desire to cooperate with ASEAN. Regular meetings have been held once or twice a year since 1977, when the first ASEAN-Japan forum was held in Jakarta.

In the 1970s and 1980s the ASEAN economies experienced remarkable growth and industrial development, and trade relations with Japan grew increasingly close. In 1967, when the organization was founded, Japan exported goods valued at US $1.1 billion to ASEAN nations and imported $0.8 billion worth of goods; in 1989, exports stood at $26.0 billion and imports at $25.8 billion. In 1988, ASEAN's shares in Japan's import and export markets were 9.4 percent and 12.2 percent, respectively, while Japan's shares of ASEAN imports and exports were 24.6 percent and 19.4 percent. The percentage of total imports by Japan from ASEAN countries accounted for by manufactured goods, such as machinery and textiles, rose from 8.4 percent in 1985 to 24.2 percent in 1989. Japan's direct investments in the area in 1988 reached a record high of $1.4 billion.

Southern Alps National Park Winter shadows fall on one of the snowy, windswept peaks of the Southern Alps. These rugged mountains are accessible only to experienced mountain climbers.

Relations with the Nations of Indochina——Until the defeat of South Vietnam in 1975, Japan supported the Vietnam policy of the United States. Although Japan recognized unified Vietnam in 1976, relations have been restricted due to the invasion of Cambodia by Vietnam in 1978, and improvement of relations depends largely on resolution of that problem. Japan has, nevertheless, increased contact on the governmental level. In 1990, Japan joined with Thailand to organize the Tōkyō Meeting on Cambodia in order to assist in the resolution of the crucial political issue of the region, namely how to bring peace and stability to Cambodia by first securing a cessation of hostilities between the Phnom Penh government and the three opposition groups fighting to oust it. Relations with Laos, which were limited in the period following the establishment of a socialist regime in 1975, have improved in recent years; the visit to Japan in 1989 of Prime Minister Kaysone Phomvihane was his first to an economically advanced noncommunist nation. Relations with Myanmar (until 1988, Burma), one of the chief recipients of Japanese overseas development aid, were temporarily severed in the wake of the coup d'état of September 1988. However, the Japanese government recognized the new regime in February 1989 and economic assistance has been resumed. See also BURMA AND JAPAN; CAMBODIA AND JAPAN; INDONESIA AND JAPAN; LAOS AND JAPAN; MALAYSIA AND JAPAN; PHILIPPINES AND JAPAN; SINGAPORE AND JAPAN; THAILAND AND JAPAN; VIETNAM AND JAPAN.

Southern Alps → Akaishi Mountains

Southern Alps National Park
南アルプス国立公園

(Minami Arupusu Kokuritsu Kōen). Situated in central Honshū, in Shizuoka, Nagano, and Yamanashi prefectures. The park extends 55 km (34 mi) north to south and has a maximum width of 18 km (11 mi). It is set in an entirely mountainous region, and its chief features are towering peaks, gorges, waterfalls, and granite cliffs. The Southern Alps, also called the AKAISHI MOUNTAINS, include KOMAGATAKE; SENJŌGATAKE; HŌŌZAN; KITADAKE, the second highest mountain in Japan after Mt. Fuji (FUJISAN); and AKAISHIDAKE. Three rivers, the TENRYŪGAWA, ŌIGAWA, and FUJIKAWA, flow southward into the Pacific. The park is noted for forests of Japanese beech (*buna*), Japanese stone pine

(*haimatsu*), and hemlock spruce (Amerika *tsuga*). The Japanese antelope (KAMOSHIKA) and such birds as the ptarmigan (*raichō*) inhabit it. Area: 358 sq km (138 sq mi).

southern expansion doctrine
南進論

(*nanshinron*). A doctrine that regarded Southeast Asia and the Pacific Islands as Japan's sphere of interest and considered that the potential value of expansion there was greater than anywhere else. It was used until World War II to justify Japan's territorial and political expansion into the area. The term was used in contrast to the "northern expansion doctrine" (*hokushinron*) advocating Japanese expansion into Korea and Manchuria. A related phrase was "guard the north and advance to the south" (*hokushu nanshin*). Advocating the strengthening of the Imperial Navy, the expansion of Japan's shipbuilding capacity, the extension of sea routes, the promotion of trade, and free immigration, the southern expansion doctrine concerned the area referred to as Nan'yō ("the southern seas" or the southwest Pacific), an area including those Pacific Islands lying north of the equator. Although Southeast Asia was considered part of Nan'yō, in its original sense the primary focus of the doctrine was on the Pacific Islands.

Possibly originating in the Edo period (1600–1868), the doctrine occupied an increasingly important place in Japanese diplomacy between the Meiji (1868–1912) and the Shōwa (1926–89) periods. The outbreak of WORLD WAR I in 1914 presented an opportunity for its application, when Japan occupied the Pacific Islands that had been held by Germany (the Caroline, Palau, Marshall, and Mariana islands). In 1919 these islands came under the mandate of Japan.

In 1936 the doctrine was incorporated for the first time in national policy in a statement issued by a conference of five ministers. During this time, the concept of the GREATER EAST ASIA COPROSPERITY SPHERE also emerged. Shortly after the formation of the second KONOE FUMIMARO cabinet on 22 July 1940, Japan launched its southern expansion on a broad front. In September 1940 Japan occupied northern French Indochina; it occupied the rest of Indochina and took New Guinea and the Solomons in 1941 and the Philippines, Singapore, the Dutch East Indies, and Burma in early 1942. The southern expansion doctrine was brought to an end only by Japan's defeat in World War II. See also PANASIANISM; COLONIALISM.

South Manchuria Railway
南満州鉄道

(SMR; J: Minami Manshū Tetsudō; abbreviated as Mantetsu). Often referred to as South Manchurian Railway. Semiofficial Japanese company founded in 1906 and engaged from 1907 to 1945 in the management of railways, the administration of railway zones, and the economic development of Manchuria. Control of railways was crucial for establishing Japanese control over Manchuria, a potential base for further penetration in East Asia.

Founding of the Company——The Treaty of PORTSMOUTH, ending the Russo-Japanese War of 1904–05, provided for the transfer to Japan of Russia's rights and leases on the Liaodong (Liaotung) Peninsula and the railway between Changchun and PORT ARTHUR. In 1896 Russia had obtained from China the right to build the CHINESE

EASTERN RAILWAY across Manchuria to its port of Vladivostok. In 1898 Russia obtained a 25-year leasehold to the southern Liaodong Peninsula, also acquiring the right to extend this line south to Port Arthur and Dalian (Ta-lien; J: Dairen). Construction of this portion (later the SMR) was completed in 1902.

Initially, Japanese government leaders were divided on how the railway should be operated: Prime Minister KATSURA TARŌ favored a proposal by E. H. Harriman of the United States for joint international operation of the SMR, while chief of the general staff KODAMA GENTARŌ and the governor of Taiwan, GOTŌ SHIMPEI, advocated the "Japan alone" policy. The issue was resolved in favor of the latter when the SMR was founded and Gotō became its first president in November 1906. The company took over management of the railroad in April 1907.

From the beginning, the company was dominated by the Japanese government and its military policies. The Japanese government was the major supplier of capital and the major authority on personnel and financial matters. The administration of the GUANDONG (KWANTUNG) TERRITORY (as the leased area was now called) controlled the company's railway guards and police.

The SMR's Administrative and Economic Empire, 1907–1937——The SMR exercised special jurisdictional and administrative power in its railway zone, which included not only the land along the railway but also many cities and settlements. The Chinese government was excluded from exercising its sovereign power within the zone, whose population rose from 30,000 in 1908 to 545,000 in the mid-1930s. In 1937, however, Japan formally relinquished its special powers to the puppet state of MANCHUKUO.

Between 1907 and 1931 the SMR dominated and monopolized the economic life of Manchuria through the management of harbors, water transportation, railways, warehousing, coal mines, electric power, real estate, ironworks, industrial plants, natural resources, the labor market, and monetary facilities. The giant Anshan steelworks, the Fushun coal mine, and other mines operated by the railway contributed tremendously to the economic development of Manchuria. Moreover, the SMR invested in and gained control over a growing number of business and industrial companies. The Chinese were not the beneficiaries of this development, carried out under Japanese control for Japanese interests.

Conflict with China——The SMR's ever-increasing control of Manchuria and the encroachment into Chinese territory led to a conflict with China that threatened the Japanese hegemony. In 1931 the Guandong Army used a bombing incident engineered by some of its officers as a pretext to occupy almost all of Manchuria (see MANCHURIAN INCIDENT). This use of force indicated the military's shift from its previous policy of indirect colonial rule through the SMR to one of direct control. After the creation of Manchukuo in 1932, the management of the entire nationalized railway system in Manchuria was placed under SMR control.

The SMR after 1937——In 1937, the Guandong Army asked the Nissan (Nihon Sangyō Kabushiki Kaisha) interests under AIKAWA YOSHISUKE to organize the Manchuria Heavy Industry Co to manage the region's heavy industries. All of the SMR's heavy industries, technicians, and facilities were transferred to the new corporation, and the railway's function narrowed to the transportation of goods and people, especially military personnel in Manchuria; these efforts reached a peak in 1942, when the SMR transported over 80 million tons of freight. However, due to military requisitioning and the construction of strategic railways, profits began to decline. With the Japanese surrender in 1945, the SMR was placed under the control of the Chinese Changchun Railway, a joint Chinese-Soviet operation.

Soviet-Japanese Basic Convention   日ソ基本条約

(Nisso Kihon Jōyaku). Signed at Beijing (Peking) between Lev Mikhailovich KARAKHAN and YOSHIZAWA KENKICHI on 20 January 1925, the convention constituted Japanese recognition of the new Soviet regime. It provided for the withdrawal of Japanese troops from northern Sakhalin (J: Karafuto) and restored diplomatic relations between the two countries. In exchange, the Soviets agreed that the Treaty of PORTSMOUTH (1905) ending the RUSSO-JAPANESE WAR would remain in full force and that the other treaties, conventions, and agreements signed between Japan and tsarist Russia would be reexamined.

The Basic Convention furthermore provided for the revision of the Fishery Convention of 1907, the conclusion of a treaty of commerce and navigation, and the granting of concessions to Japanese individuals and companies for the exploitation of natural resources in the USSR. It also guaranteed reciprocal freedom of movement and protection for each country's nationals in the other's territories. See also SOVIET UNION AND JAPAN.

Soviet-Japanese development of Siberia   日ソシベリア開発

(Nisso Shiberia kaihatsu). Japanese interest in Siberian resources dates from the late 18th century and centered on oil and coal until 1944. Following World War II, a resumption of diplomatic relations, and the steady growth of bilateral trade, an ongoing series of joint projects was undertaken in 1968 to develop the region extending from the Ural Mountains to the Pacific, with Japan providing capital, technology, and equipment in exchange for raw materials—principally lumber, coal, copper, iron ore, oil, and natural gas. Major projects included the joint development of timber resources along the Amur River and the joint construction of a container port at Wrangel Bay, near Nakhodka.

The oil crises of the 1970s led to drastic retrenchment in Japan's industrial structure and a loss of interest in developing resources in Siberia, where lack of transportation is a major drawback. Due to Soviet political liberalization in the mid-1980s, however, the vast resources of Siberia and the Soviet Far East once again became attractive to Japanese business. At the sessions of the Soviet-Japanese Joint Economic Committee held in 1991, both sides agreed on the exploitation of timber resources in the Far East, which would involve the exchange of $1.4 billion worth of timber for Japanese machinery over a five-year period. The construction of paper and pulp mills in Sakhalin and the development of oil and natural gas off the coast of the island were also discussed.

Soviet-Japanese Joint Declaration   日ソ共同宣言

(Nisso Kyōdō Sengen). Joint declaration issued on 19 October 1956 by the governments of Japan and the Soviet Union, ending the state of war that had existed between them since 9 August 1945 and reestablishing diplomatic relations. Both sides agreed to terminate the state of war, restore diplomatic and consular relations, adhere to the United Nations Charter with respect to the right of self-defense and noninterference in one another's internal affairs, mutually waive claims arising out of World War II, activate an existing fisheries and marine safety treaty, and continue negotiations for commercial agreements and a peace treaty. The Soviet Union pledged to support Japan's entry into the United Nations, to repatriate all remaining Japanese prisoners of war, and to hand over Shikotan and the Habomai Islands after the signing of a peace treaty. The Soviet-Japanese impasse over Japan's claims to KUNASHIRI and ETOROFU in the southern Kurils, however, still prevented the two countries from concluding a peace treaty (see NORTHERN TERRITORIES ISSUE). See also SOVIET UNION AND JAPAN.

Soviet-Japanese Neutrality Pact   日ソ中立条約

(Nisso Chūritsu Jōyaku). A pact signed on 13 April 1941 in Moscow by Foreign Minister MATSUOKA YŌSUKE and Ambassador TATEKAWA YOSHITSUGU on behalf of Japan and Foreign Minister Viacheslav M. Molotov on behalf of the Soviet Union. The pact obliged each party to remain neutral should the other go to war against another country. The outbreak of the war between Germany, France, and England in September 1939 had convinced the Soviet Union of the need to come to an agreement with Japan. The Japanese, in turn, with military operations bogged down in China and Japan-US relations deteriorating rapidly, hoped for an agreement with the USSR that would improve Japan's international position. The pact remained precariously in effect through most of World War II. On 5 April 1945 Molotov denounced the pact in accordance with the promise made by Joseph Stalin at Yalta in February 1945 to enter the war against Japan after the surrender of Germany. The Soviet Union declared war on Japan on 8 August 1945.

Soviet Union and Japan   ソ連と日本

(Soren to Nihon). Japan's relations with the Soviet Union were deeply affected not only by the foreign policies and ideology of the Soviet state but also, in the pre–World War II period, by the competing colonial ambitions of the two countries in northern Asia. After 1945 Soviet-Japanese relations became locked in the confrontation between the Communist bloc and the West, and tension was heightened by the issue of former Japanese territories occupied by the Soviet Union at the close of the war. In the late 1980s it appeared that an improvement in relations between the two nations might be at hand, but the dissolution of the Soviet Union in 1991 took place before it could actually be achieved.

The Siberian Intervention—Following the defeat of Russia in the RUSSO-JAPANESE WAR of 1904–05, cooperative relations had been established on the basis of the four RUSSO-JAPANESE AGREEMENTS OF 1907–1916. However, the Bolshevik Revolution of 1917, civil war, and Japanese intervention brought an end to the Russo-Japanese Alliance of 1916 and created feelings of distrust between Japan and the newly founded Soviet Union that lingered for years. Japan's dispatch of an expeditionary force to Siberia in 1918 constituted part of similar forces sent to Russia

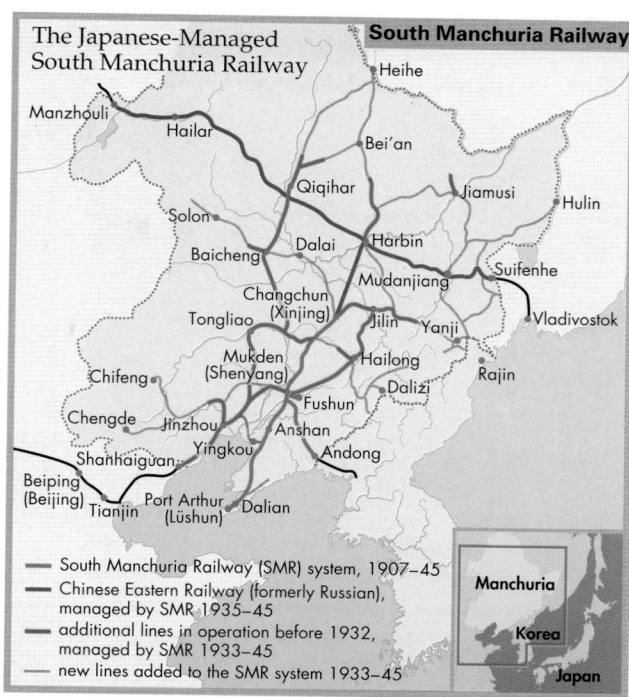

The Japanese-Managed South Manchuria Railway | South Manchuria Railway

— South Manchuria Railway (SMR) system, 1907–45
— Chinese Eastern Railway (formerly Russian), managed by SMR 1935–45
— additional lines in operation before 1932, managed by SMR 1933–45
— new lines added to the SMR system 1933–45

by Great Britain, the United States, and France. Japan's motives were complex and only half articulated. Safeguarding military stores in Vladivostok and "rescuing" the beleaguered Czech legion were given as official reasons. Hostility to Bolshevism, determination to recoup lost investments, and perceptions of an opportunity to settle "the northern problem" by territorial acquisitions or to create a buffer state figured as important but unpublicized incentives among various Japanese civilian and military leaders.

The SIBERIAN INTERVENTION turned out to work against Japan's interests. Patronage of various "White" leaders left the Japanese in bad repute when the Bolsheviks eventually achieved the upper hand in the civil war. Japan's occupation of northern Sakhalin (1920) in retaliation for a massacre of Japanese nationals further embittered relations (see NIKOLAEVSK INCIDENT). Japan withdrew from Siberia in 1922, only after the other Allies had withdrawn.

Japanese Recognition of the USSR—Despite the ideological cleavage between the Soviet Union and Japan, the desire for a rapprochement persisted, particularly since geographic relationships and economic needs remained basically the same. Negotiations began in 1923, first "privately" between GOTŌ SHIMPEI and Soviet diplomat Adolf Abramovich IOFFE. By the SOVIET-JAPANESE BASIC CONVENTION signed in January 1925, Japan recognized the Soviet Union at a price: the continuation of Japanese fishing rights in Russian waters and the granting to Japanese subjects, companies, and associations of new concessions for the exploitation of minerals, forests, and other natural resources in all the territories of the USSR.

In the late 1920s Japanese bureaucrats and businessmen worked for the development of mutual understanding and the strengthening of cultural ties between the two countries. The complementary character of the Soviet and Japanese economies might well have led to increased collaboration had it not been for the revival of militarism in Japan.

When the Japanese field army in the Guandong (Kwantung) Territory overran Manchuria in 1931 (see MANCHURIAN INCIDENT), the Chinese Eastern Railway became a source of friction between the USSR and

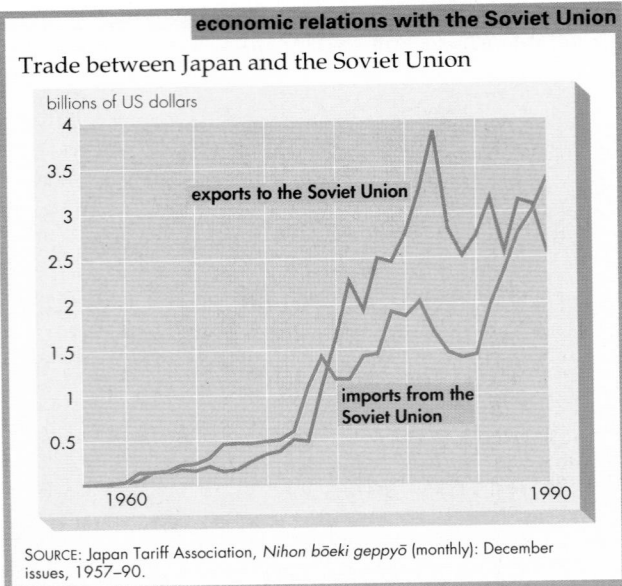

economic relations with the Soviet Union

Trade between Japan and the Soviet Union

billions of US dollars

exports to the Soviet Union

imports from the Soviet Union

SOURCE: Japan Tariff Association, *Nihon bōeki geppyō* (monthly): December issues, 1957–90.

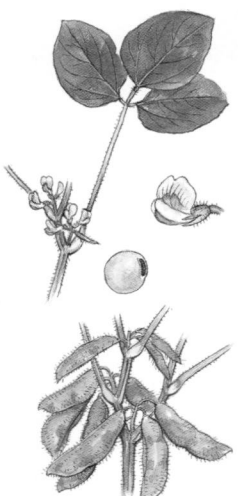

soybeans The high-protein bean is used to produce such basic Japanese foods and flavoring agents as *tōfu*, *miso*, and soy sauce. *From top:* the stem with compound leaf; the flower; the mature bean; pods.

Japan. Since its retention by the Soviet Union increased the likelihood of a conflict with Japan, for which the USSR was not ready, and as the Japanese could be expected to run the railroad efficiently, in 1935 the Soviet government sold the railway to the newly created Japanese puppet state of MANCHUKUO at a fraction of its cost.

Uneasy Neutrality—Relations between the Soviet Union and Japan underwent a reversal in 1936 when Japan joined Nazi Germany in the ANTI-COMINTERN PACT and in 1937 invaded China proper. The USSR immediately extended military aid to China. The mounting tension between the Soviet Union and Japan precipitated a number of incidents along the often poorly marked borders between the USSR and Korea (under Japanese rule since 1910), the USSR and Manchukuo, and Soviet-backed Outer Mongolia and Manchukuo. Major clashes occurred at Zhanggufeng (Chang-ku-feng) near Lake Khasan in the summer of 1938 (see ZHANGGUFENG [CHANG-KU-FENG] INCIDENT), and a year later at Nomonhan, at the border between Outer Mongolia and Manchukuo (see NOMONHAN INCIDENT). Paradoxically, the Japanese defeat at Nomonhan had a salutary effect on Soviet-Japanese relations, impressing upon Japan's leaders the realization that diplomatic measures might be less costly and more effective in resolving issues.

The outbreak of war among Germany, France, and Great Britain in September 1939 convinced the Soviet Union of the need to come to an agreement with Japan. On 13 April 1941, the SOVIET-JAPANESE NEUTRALITY PACT was signed in Moscow. The neutrality pact between the USSR and Japan remained in effect precariously through most of World War II, for it shielded them both from a dreaded two-front war.

Toward the end of the war, unaware of the promise Joseph Stalin had made to Prime Minister Winston Churchill and President Franklin Delano Roosevelt at Yalta in February 1945 to enter the Pacific War within 90 days after the surrender of Germany, Japan tried to obtain Russian mediation in bringing hostilities to a close. But the decision for war with Japan had already been cast, and Tōkyō's reluctance to accept the unconditional surrender demanded by the Allies gave Moscow the pretext for declining the role of mediator. On 9 August the Red Army launched a massive offensive against the Japanese forces in Manchuria; operations

in the Kuril Islands, southern Sakhalin, and Korea followed. On 14 August, Japan surrendered.

Relations during the Occupation—The United States barred the USSR from an effective role in the OCCUPATION of Japan; Russian membership in the FAR EASTERN COMMISSION in Washington and the ALLIED COUNCIL FOR JAPAN in Tōkyō had little effect on the policies of the Allied supreme commander, General Douglas MACARTHUR. As relations between the Soviet Union and the United States continued to deteriorate and communism swept across China, the United States began to view Japan as a bulwark against communist expansion in Asia. Even after the Occupation of Japan formally ended in 1952, American forces remained in the country under a bilateral security treaty to defend Japan. The Soviet Union viewed the American bases as a threat to its own security, and it linked the return of SHIKOTAN and the HABOMAI ISLANDS, which it had occupied during the war, to the evacuation of all foreign troops from Japan. See NORTHERN TERRITORIES ISSUE.

Normalization of Relations—The need to settle a long-standing fisheries problem, and the desire to hasten the repatriation of prisoners of war who had been retained by the Soviet Union, induced Japan to "normalize" relations with the USSR. A joint declaration in 1956 effectively ended the state of war that had existed since World War II. The territorial issue was left open until the conclusion of a peace treaty sometime in the future. The inability of either side to give in on the territorial question remained a lasting irritant, but the breakup of the Sino-Soviet alliance, fear of a Sino-American rapprochement, and the threat of American curtailment of Japanese imports increased interest on both sides in closer Soviet-Japanese relations.

The striking increase in Soviet-Japanese trade that took place in the 1960s was further stimulated by the five-year trade and payments agreements signed in 1971 and by a series of joint conferences held by the Soviet-Japanese and Japanese-Soviet Commissions for Business Cooperation. The mounting participation of Japanese industry and finances in Siberian development also boosted commercial relations. Soviet-Japanese collaboration in the construction of a new port in Wrangel Bay, near Nakhodka, also facilitated trade.

Relations in the 1970s and 1980s—After Japan normalized relations with China in 1972, Prime Minister TANAKA KAKUEI turned to improving relations with the Soviet Union. In 1973 he visited Moscow and issued a joint declaration with Soviet Communist Party chairman Leonid I. Brezhnev, in which both countries recognized the existence of unsettled issues and called for continuing negotiations to conclude a peace treaty.

However, in the context of worsening overall East-West relations, Soviet-Japanese relations deteriorated beginning in the mid-1970s. In 1976, when a defecting Soviet military pilot landed his MiG-25 fighter in Hokkaidō, Japan caused a diplomatic backlash by allowing the United States to inspect the plane before returning it to the Soviet Union. The conclusion of the CHINA-JAPAN PEACE AND FRIENDSHIP TREATY in 1978, which included an "antihegemony" clause clearly directed against the Soviet Union, further hardened Moscow's attitudes toward Japan. The Soviet invasion of Afghanistan in 1979 deliv-

ered another blow to already tense relations, and Japan joined the West in imposing economic sanctions on the Soviet Union and boycotting the 1980 Olympic Games held in Moscow. Signs that the Soviet Union was building up its military capabilities in the Far East contributed to increasing tension. The shooting down of a Korean civilian airliner by a Soviet warplane further outraged many in Japan. Political developments affected economic relations as well: Japan's trade with the Soviet Union decreased from US \$5.6 billion in 1982 to US \$3.9 billion in 1984, and a number of projects to develop Siberian resources were postponed or canceled.

Mikhail Gorbachev's rise to power in 1985 was a turning point in the Soviet-Japanese relationship. Departing from Moscow's conventional focus on US-Soviet relations, Gorbachev placed greater emphasis on relations with Western Europe and Japan. When Soviet foreign minister Eduard Shevardnadze visited Japan in 1986, the two nations agreed to resume ministerial consultations, after a two-year break. In 1987 Japanese foreign minister Abe Shintarō (1924–91) visited Moscow and signed an agreement to promote cultural exchange.

The overall improvement in East-West relations contributed to the improvement of Japan's relations with the Soviet Union, and economic relations expanded accordingly. Trade volume in 1988, amounting to US \$5.9 billion, finally surpassed the level reached in 1982. In addition, a number of joint ventures were established in the Soviet Union: in 1990, 27 Japanese companies operated there.

In April 1991 President Gorbachev paid an official visit to Japan, the first such visit by a chairman of the Soviet Communist Party. In the joint communiqué Gorbachev signed with the Japanese prime minister KAIFU TOSHIKI, both sides agreed to accelerate work to conclude a peace treaty. However, in August of that year the Soviet government was irrevocably destabilized by a coup attempt, and Soviet-Japanese relations came to an end in December with the breakup of the Soviet Union into 15 independent states. Japan recognized the three Baltic states in September 1991, and all but Georgia among the remaining 12 states in December. It was anticipated that it would fall to the Russian Federation to negotiate with Japan the issues of a peace treaty and reversion of the Northern Territories. See also SOVIET UNION, ECONOMIC RELATIONS WITH; RUSSIA AND JAPAN.

Soviet Union, economic relations with
日ソ経済関係

(Nisso *keizai kankei*). The Soviet Union and Japan were unable, because of political obstacles such as the NORTHERN TERRITORIES ISSUE, to establish close economic relations in the post–World War II era. While their economies were complementary—in the sense that the Soviet Union was rich in natural resources while Japan is a source of manufactured goods, technology, and capital—potential mutual benefits from trade went largely unrealized.

Historical Background—Japan and the Soviet Union normalized diplomatic relations with the Soviet-Japan Joint Declaration of October 1956, ending the formal state of war that had existed since World War II. This led to the establishment of a framework for commercial relations through the conclusion of a treaty of commerce in December 1957. From 1957 through the early 1980s Soviet-Japanese trade volumes showed a consistent annual increase of 9 percent and reached US $5.6 billion in 1982. Trade then began to deteriorate, however, reflecting the stagnation of the Soviet economy as a result of increasing military budgets in the late 1970s and the rigidities inherent in the Soviet economic system. It also reflected worsening political relations between the two nations, as well as the growing East-West tensions of the early 1980s.

The coming to power of Mikhail Gorbachev in March 1985 and his subsequent efforts to reform and modernize the Soviet economic system created a degree of optimism that bilateral economic relations could be improved. Gorbachev also tried to ease strained relations with Western nations in general and made efforts to tap the economic vitality of the noncommunist economies. In this context, the Soviet Union made new overtures to Japan for the joint development of Siberian resources. In an address in Vladivostok in July 1986, Gorbachev also expressed his desire to strengthen and improve Soviet relations with the nations of the Asia-Pacific region.

Extent and Importance of Recent Trade Relations—Between 1980 and 1988 the dollar value of bilateral trade increased by an average of 3.0 percent per year (Japanese exports increased annually by 1.5%, while imports from the Soviet Union increased by 5.1%). Total trade between Japan and the Soviet Union in 1988 was valued at US $5.9 billion. This represented only 1.3 percent of Japan's total worldwide trade in that year and 2.4 percent of the Soviet Union's total trade. In 1988 Japan ranked third among Western nations trading with the Soviet Union, behind West Germany and Finland. Japan ran a consistent trade surplus with the Soviet Union in the 1980s. From a surplus of US $1 billion, the margin decreased to US $210 million in 1987 and then rose slightly in 1988 to US $360 million.

While Japan's trade with the Soviet Union was small in terms of absolute volume, it was important in certain sectors. For example, steel accounted for 40 percent of Japanese exports to the Soviet Union, making it a major market for Japanese steel producers. Also, the Soviet Union was second in importance only to the United States as an export market for Japan's construction and mining machinery industries. The Soviet Union was, for Japan, an important source of nonferrous metals such as palladium, platinum, and nickel, as well as resources such as oil, coal, and lumber. In the overall trade pattern, Japan exported manufactured goods to the Soviet Union while importing natural resources.

The Siberian Far East Development Project, initiated in the 1970s, was an example of this trade pattern. Japan exported machinery to the Soviet Union to aid in developing Siberian resources and imported a portion of those resources, which included lumber, wood chips, coal, and natural gas. Japan's interest in this project stemmed largely from its desire to increase its access to Soviet energy resources following the oil crises of 1973 and 1979. Afterward many Japanese industries economized on energy consumption, reducing the need to participate further in the large-scale development of Siberian resources.

In the late 1980s the Soviet Union further attempted to encourage Japanese companies to enter into Soviet-led joint ventures by proposing these ventures as a centerpiece of Soviet-Japanese economic cooperation. In particular, the Soviet Union was interested in joint ventures in high-technology sectors. The response by major Japanese companies, however, was marked by caution. By the end of 1988 only seven joint ventures were registered, and no major Japanese firms were involved. New joint ventures were primarily small-scale operations in industries such as fisheries, processed marine products, and catering.

Developments in the Early 1990s—Following the dissolution of the Soviet Union in December 1991, some Western nations moved aggressively to provide aid to the former Soviet republics. Japan announced that support already promised to help the Soviet Union meet its economic crisis, including the underwriting of trade insurance and loans for food purchases, would be provided to the former Soviet republics; however, Japan was slow to make major new aid commitments with the Northern Territories issue still unsettled. The Japanese representative to a January 1992 Washington conference on aid to Russia and the other republics took the position that the discussions should be limited to short-term humanitarian aid.

Many Japanese businesses are interested in developing closer economic ties with the republics, particularly with Russia, which now administers the island of Sakhalin as well as resource-rich Siberia. As of late 1992, however, little concrete progress had been achieved.

Sōyamisaki 宗谷岬

Cape in the city of Wakkanai, northern Hokkaidō. Forms the northernmost tip of Japan at latitude 45°31′ north. An extension of the Sōya Plateau, its cliffs jut out into the Sōya Strait. Until World War II, Sōyamisaki was a major base for transportation to Sakhalin (J: Karafuto).

Sōya Strait 宗谷海峡

(Sōya Kaikyō). Between the cape Sōyamisaki, the northernmost tip of Hokkaidō, and Sakhalin (J: Karafuto) in the Russian Federation, connecting the Sea of Japan with the Sea of Okhotsk. Narrowest point: 43 km (27 mi); average depth: 50 m (165 ft); deepest point: 74 m (243 ft).

soybeans 大豆

(daizu). Glycine max, annual herb of the family Leguminosae, now cultivated throughout the world. Said to have first been cultivated in an area ranging from North China to Siberia in ancient times, soybeans were introduced to Japan in the early Yayoi period (ca 300 BC–ca AD 300) and have continued to be one of Japan's main food crops.

Soybeans are rich in protein and fat and traditionally have been an important source of these nutrients for the Japanese people. Soybeans are used to make MISO (a paste made from cooked soybeans mashed and fermented with malted rice), SOY SAUCE (shōyu), TŌFU (bean curd), soybean oil, and NATTŌ (fermented beans), as well as to grow bean sprouts.

To supplement domestic soybean production, large quantities were imported from Manchuria before World War II, and from the United States after the war. Japanese consumption in 1989 was 4,748,000 metric tons (5,223,000 short tons), while domestic production in 1990 was about 220,400 metric tons (242,400 short tons). Besides this, about

100,000 metric tons (110,000 short tons) of soybeans are produced in Japan each year for green soybeans (edamame), which are boiled in the pod and shelled.

soy milk →tōnyū

so, yō, and chō 租庸調

(soyōchō). Basic taxes under the RITSURYŌ SYSTEM established in the 7th century. Following the TAIKA REFORM (645), taxation was modified to conform with the land allotment system whereby all rice land became public domain and was assigned to the peasantry (see HANDEN SHŪJU SYSTEM).

So, the rice tax, was imposed on KUBUNDEN, plots distributed to every person over six years of age. Most of the tax was used for local expenses. A part was lent as seed rice (see SUIKO). Yō, also known as chikarashiro, was a local product tax paid in lieu of corvée labor (see YŌEKI) and was usually paid in the form of a certain length of cloth. Chō, also called mitsugi, were handicrafts or local products paid to the imperial court. Those rendering military service were exempt from chō, yō, and zōyō (corvée labor). The proceeds of the yō and chō taxes went to pay the stipends (FUKO) of nobles and officials. The so, yō, and chō were an enormous burden on the peasants, who tried to evade these taxes. From the 10th century, with the breakdown of central authority, these taxes were gradually diverted by the proprietors of private estates (SHŌEN).

soy sauce 醤油

(shōyu). Basic flavoring agent used in Japanese cuisine; made by fermenting water, salt, and a yeast of soybean and wheat—a process that may take over a year. Its prototype, a pasty substance called hishio, made by adding fish to salt, is known to have been made in the Yayoi period (ca 300 BC–ca AD 300). Shōyu as it is known today was first made in Japan in the Muromachi period (1333–1568).

Shōyu is distinguished according to the

Sōyamisaki
A geographic marker indicates Japan's northernmost point, located at latitude 45°31′ north.

soy sauce A number of varieties of this basic seasoning are produced, almost all by fermenting a mixture of steamed soybeans, water, salt, and a yeast made from soybeans and wheat.
1 Soy sauce fermentation tubs. The fermentation process may last more than a year for some types of soy sauce.
2 Koikuchi shōyu is the most widely used soy sauce. It is hearty and flavorful, with a full-bodied fragrance.
3 Light-flavored soy sauce, or usukuchi shōyu, has a high salt content and is usually fermented for less than a year. It is typically used when regular soy sauce would impart an undesirable color to a dish.

The H-II Rocket

space technology

payload fairing
payload attachment fitting
on-board equipment
second-stage liquid hydrogen tank
second-stage liquid oxygen tank
interstage section
second-stage engine
first-stage liquid oxygen tank

center body section
first-stage liquid hydrogen tank
first-stage engine section

first-stage main engine
solid rocket booster

The centerpiece of the Japanese space program of the 1990s, the H-II rocket is capable of launching satellites of up to two metric tons.

ingredients used in its preparation and the length of fermentation. *Koikuchi shōyu*, widely used, is fermented for a longer time and is thick; *usukuchi shōyu* is fermented for a shorter period. The addition of MIRIN (sweet *sake*) gives the latter a delicate color, flavor, and aroma, making it suitable for seasoning vegetables, white-fleshed fish, and clear soups. Both types are now produced mainly in Chiba and Hyōgo prefectures. There are also local variations: the sweeter *tamari*, made in central Honshū; the pale yellow *shottsuru* of Akita Prefecture, made with fish; and the white *shiroshōyu* of the Nagoya area. Since aroma is most important, it is advisable to add *shōyu* just before a dish is ready to be served. Also, once the container is opened, the flavor and color of *shōyu* begin to deteriorate, so it should be used quickly.

sozei seido → taxes

SOZŌ 塑像

Modeled statues of naturally dried, unbaked clay. *Sozō* sculpture flourished in the Nara period (710–794), when it was used in the production of large-scale, realistically conceived Buddhist images. Straw was wrapped around a wooden armature over which clay, fortified with fiber and glue, was applied in layers of increasingly fine detail. Sometimes thin layers of clay were applied to a wooden image. After drying, colors were added. *Sozō* reached Japan in the 7th century; the earliest extant example is considered to be the image of the bodhisattva MIROKU in the Nara temple Taimadera. The best-known *sozō* are the figures of the bodhisattvas Nikkō and Gakkō in the *hokkedō* of the temple TŌDAIJI at Nara.

space technology 宇宙開発

(*uchū kaihatsu*). Space technology is relatively new to Japan; although there were attempts at developing military rockets near the end of World War II, the foundations laid by this work were lost with Japan's defeat.

Japan's space technology development is currently coordinated by two organizations: the INSTITUTE OF SPACE AND ASTRONAUTICAL SCIENCE (ISAS; established 1981) and the NATIONAL SPACE DEVELOPMENT AGENCY OF JAPAN (NASDA; established 1969). ISAS is primarily involved in the development of scientific satellites and a series of solid-propellant rockets used to launch them. NASDA concentrates on the development and launching of applications satellites (communications, broadcasting, and weather satellites). While in the past NASDA has made extensive use of technology imported from the United States, in recent years it has relied increasingly on domestic technology.

Rockets—Japan's postwar rocket research began in 1954, as interest in the peaceful use of rockets grew throughout the world and plans to use them for an extensive survey of the upper atmosphere were developed for the International Geophysical Year (IGY) of 1957–58. Early research was carried out by Tōkyō University's Institute of Industrial Science, which developed the first small-scale sounding rockets for upper atmospheric research, the Kappa series. Japan was able to participate in the IGY in 1958 with the two-stage Kappa model 6 rocket, which weighed 260 kilograms (572 lb) and climbed to 60 kilometers (37.3 mi). This was followed by the Lambda rocket series, which had as one of its main aims the raising of the altitude range and payload of Japanese rockets. By 1964 a Lambda rocket had reached 1,000 kilometers (621 mi), and in 1970 a four-stage Lambda L-4S rocket launched Japan's first successful experimental satellite, *Ōsumi*, in 1970, making Japan the fourth country to achieve satellite launch capability, following the Soviet Union, the United States, and France.

The sounding rockets advanced work in X-ray astronomy, including the study of cosmic X rays and solar X-ray flares, and knowledge about the nature of ionospheric plasma. They were followed by the Mu rocket series of the 1970s and 1980s, which was developed to launch satellites specifically for scientific research. These programs were coordinated by the Institute of Space and Aeronautical Science at Tōkyō University (established 1964) until it was reorganized in 1981 as the Institute of Space and Astronautical Science

(ISAS), a research facility independent of Tōkyō University and intended to coordinate the scientific satellite research programs of various cooperating universities. The rocket currently used to launch scientific satellites, the solid-propellant Mu-3S II, is 28 meters (91.9 ft) long and is capable of putting 770 kilograms (1,697.9 lb) into orbit.

In 1975 a new rocket, the N1, was completed and thereafter used to launch applications satellites. The N series rockets consisted of a US Delta rocket for the first and third stages, and the Japanese-developed LE-3 rocket for the second stage. They were launched by the National Space Development Agency of Japan (NASDA) from its new launch site at the Tanegashima Space Center on the island of Tanegashima in Kagoshima Prefecture. In the late 1970s, the need to launch heavier applications satellites made it necessary to commission US launch systems until a series of larger Japanese vehicles became available. This was the H series, the first of which (H-I) was completed in 1986. The H-I, a three-stage rocket, 40 meters (131.2 ft) in length and weighing 140 metric tons (154 short tons), was capable of placing a 550-kilogram (1,212.8-lb) satellite into geostationary orbit. The two-stage liquid-propellant H-II rocket, intended to place a 2-metric-ton (2.2-short-ton) satellite into geostationary orbit, was under development for use in the 1990s. Based entirely on domestic technology, H-II is 49 meters (160.8 ft) long, weighs 260 metric tons (286 short tons), and was scheduled for its first test launch in 1993. It was also being considered as a launch vehicle for a Japanese-developed manned reusable spaceplane, now at the design stage.

Scientific Satellites—Japan's space-science satellite program, administered by ISAS, began with the launch of the first full-scale Japanese scientific satellite, *Shinsei*, in 1971 to carry out ionospheric studies and measure cosmic rays and solar waves. Since the failure of the fourth satellite in 1976, the program has had an unbroken string of successes. In all, Japan has launched 13 satellites for atmospheric and magnetospheric studies, 3 X-ray astronomy satellites, 1 solar observation satellite, and two missions to Halley's comet; the launch vehicles for these scientific satellites have been Mu series rockets. Despite its late start, Japan's flexible small-satellite program is highly rated, particularly in view of the worldwide downward trend in scientific funding.

Applications Satellites—The development of applications satellites and their launch vehicles, the N and H series rockets, has been conducted by NASDA. Applications satellites have been used in the areas of communications, broadcasting, meteorology, and observation of the Earth. Whereas communications satellites transmit signals to large centralized ground stations, broadcast satellites transmit directly to antennae in individual homes.

The first Japanese applications satellite, an 83-kilogram (182.6-lb) experimental technology satellite named *Kiku*, was launched in September 1975 by an N1 rocket. The first geostationary weather satellite, the 350-kilogram (770-lb) *Himawari*, was launched in 1977. The first experimental communications satellite, *Sakura* (1977), and the first experimental broadcasting satellite, *Yuri* (1978), were both largely US-built owing to the lack of suitable Japanese launchers for such heavy satellites. The failure of the following two experimental broadcasting satellites, *Ayame* and *Ayame 2*, in 1979 and 1980, led to an extensive reorganization of Japan's space technology development effort.

In 1983 Japan successfully launched its first two working communications satellites, *Sakura 2a* and *2b*, which provided communications links to outlying islands and contingency channels in case of natural disasters. Two broadcasting satellites, *Yuri 2a* and *2b*, identical to the earlier *Yuri* in weight and shape, were launched by Japanese N-rockets in 1984 and 1986 into geostationary orbits. After overcoming an initial malfunction in their microwave transmitters, these satellites have not only fulfilled their original function of covering areas where normal TV reception is difficult, but have also been used by NHK (the Japan Broadcasting Corporation) to begin a 24-hour satellite broadcasting service that has drawn considerable attention and supplanted the satellites' original purpose, indicating one likely future direction that the utilization of space will take. They have also earned praise for their role in the first practical broadcasts of HIGH-DEFINITION TELEVISION.

Meanwhile, a growing demand for channel capacity and more types of service led to the launching of the communications satellites *Sakura 3a* and *3b* in 1987 and 1988. These provided a capacity equivalent to 6,000 telephone circuits. The satellite *Kiku 5* was launched in 1987 to conduct developmental tests for future high-technology communications. A further experimental communications satellite, *ETS-VI*, was scheduled for launch in 1993.

Although NASDA has over the years subcontracted a considerable amount of the actual construction of satellites to private companies such as MITSUBISHI ELECTRIC CORPORATION, TŌSHIBA CORPORATION, and NEC CORPORATION, the first fully commercial Japanese satellite, owned by the Japanese Satellite Communications Company, went into orbit only in March 1989. The *JC/SAT-1*, which provides 32 channels, was built by Hughes Co and launched by the European Space Agency using an Ariane IV rocket. A second commercial satellite, *JC/SAT-2*, was launched in 1990 by a US Titan rocket.

Space Development Policy—The Japanese space research program is proceeding in line with the Fundamental Policy of Space Development, formulated in 1978 by the Space Activities Commission (which was established in 1968 under the chairmanship of the minister for science and technology). The policy outlines the following basic directives:

First, technical development that will allow Japan to participate in joint international projects on an equal basis with other countries will be pursued. Also, technology that can be provided to other countries for global-scale activities such as weather observation and scientific research will be developed.

Second, a manned space program will be pursued, including the development of a Japanese manned space vehicle.

Third, while space research in Japan has primarily been a national undertaking since its inception, the participation of the private sector will be encouraged and an appropriate balance found between public and private investments.

Based on these fundamental policies,

space development was proceeding through satellite, rocket, spaceplane, and other projects. The government's space technology budget for 1991 allocated ¥128.3 billion (US $935.2 million) to NASDA, ¥20.8 billion (US $151.8 million) to ISAS, and ¥20.5 billion (US $149.4 million) to other groups. The money was earmarked for these projects: development of launch vehicles; projects related to global environmental problems such as the Advanced Earth Observation Satellite (ADEOS); satellites for scientific purposes and for the development of new technologies; and utilization of the space environment through the development of manned space stations.

Spain and Japan   スペインと日本

(Supein *to* Nihon). Spain was among the first European nations to open relations with Japan. The dispatch of a mission to the governor of the Philippines by TOYOTOMI HIDEYOSHI in 1592 led to the opening of diplomatic relations, conducted through Spain's colonies in the Philippines and Mexico. Spanish Franciscan monks came to Japan the following year as Philippine envoys and also began missionary activities. See CHRISTIANITY.

From the Spanish the Japanese acquired knowledge concerning Europe and the New World. However, these contacts intensified Japanese suspicions that Spanish missions were a precursor of eventual territorial aggression. Hideyoshi confiscated the Spanish galleon *San Felipe* in 1596 and began prosecution of Catholic missionaries in Japan (see SAN FELIPE INCIDENT). The anti-Spanish campaign of the Dutch and the English further damaged Spain's reputation, and diplomatic relations were severed by the Japanese in 1624.

Following the Meiji Restoration of 1868, formal relations between the two countries were resumed. After World War II, diplomatic relations were broken for a while and then reestablished. Today, commercial relations between Spain and Japan are growing stronger, and technology exchanges are being pursued. The economic relationship with Japan is expected to grow especially rapidly now that Spain has become a member of the European Community (EC). In 1990 Spain's exports to Japan totaled US $792.5 million, while imports from Japan were US $2.1 billion. Japanese direct investment in Spain has also increased, with investments in 1990 of US $320.0 million. On a cumulative basis, Japan's investments in Spain as of March 1990 totaled US $1.9 billion. See also MEXICO AND JAPAN; PHILIPPINES AND JAPAN; NAMBAN TRADE.

sparrows   雀

(*suzume*). In Japanese, *suzume* is the common name for small, brownish, streaked songbirds of the genus *Passer*, family Ploceidae. They average approximately 14 centimeters (6 in) and live close to human habitation. The most typical species found in Japan are the Japanese tree sparrow (*Passer montanus saturatus*) and the *nyūnai suzume* or russet sparrow (*P. rutilans rutilans*). The common house sparrow (*P. domesticus*) is not found in Japan.

The *suzume* is first mentioned in Japanese literature in the ancient chronicle KOJIKI (712). The 11th-century court lady SEI SHŌNAGON categorized the *suzume* among things that are lovable in MAKURA NO SŌSHI (The Pillow Book), and the sparrow occupies an especially high place in the fauna of court

sparrows Japanese tree sparrows feeding in a rice field. Sparrows and other small grain-eating birds can do considerable damage to rice crops.

literature. The *suzume* has also been a favorite bird of Japanese poets such as the *haiku* poet Kobayashi ISSA and appears in folktales such as SHITAKIRI SUZUME.

special adoption system   特別養子制度

(*tokubetsu yōshi seido*). A new category of legal adoption created by the 1987 revision to adoption regulations in Japan's civil law. The special adoption system provides an emphasis on the welfare of the adopted child and the stability of the new parent-child relationship not found in prior adoption regulations. Under this system a child of up to 6 years of age can be adopted by a married couple in which one member is at least 25 years of age. Family court approval and a minimum six-month trial period are also required. The adoptee becomes the legitimate child of the adoptive parents with the same relationship to the adoptive parents and their relatives as their natural child would have. All legal relationships between the adopted child and his or her natural parents and relatives are severed. In principle, the dissolution of special adoption is prohibited.

Prior to the creation of special adoption, only "general" adoption was possible. Under general adoption the adoptee is entered in the family register (*koseki*) of the adoptive parents; however, he or she also maintains a legal relationship with the natural parents and under certain circumstances the adoption can be dissolved. The most common purpose of general adoption is to provide a successor for the household (*ie*), and the adoptee is often an adult. General adoption is still the most common type of adoption in Japan. See also ADOPTION; PARENT AND CHILD, LEGAL DEFINITION OF.

special education   特殊教育

(*tokushu kyōiku*). Special education, in the wording of the SCHOOL EDUCATION LAW OF 1947, is directed at the blind and nearly blind, the deaf and nearly deaf, the mentally retarded, and those with speech impairments, emotional disorders, and multiple disorders. Special education facilities are of three types: SCHOOLS FOR THE BLIND, SCHOOLS FOR THE DEAF, and SCHOOLS FOR THE HANDICAPPED. In addition, there are special education classes for the mildly handicapped within the regular elementary and middle school systems. Compulsory education was

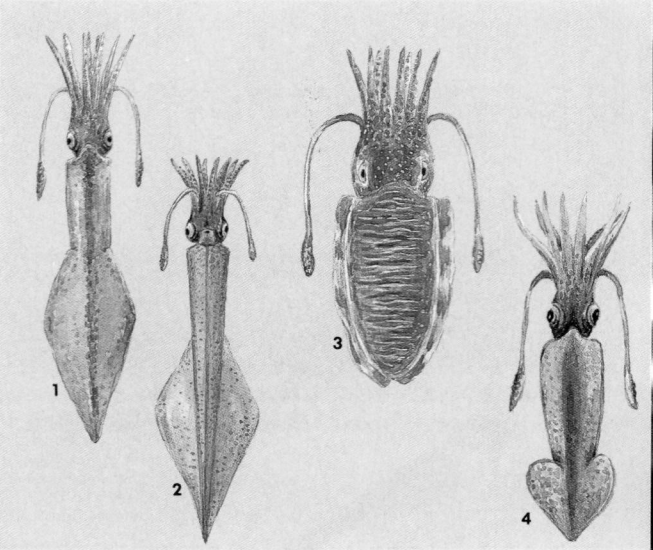

squid and cuttlefish
1 The *kensaki ika* is often caught off southern Japan and is commonly used for dried squid (*surume*), a popular snack.
2 A number of varieties of squid are imported into Japan under the name *yariika*; this squid is often eaten raw.
3 A cuttlefish, the small *kōika* is located off southern Japan. It feeds near the bottom in shallow coastal waters, hiding in the sand to avoid predators.
4 The *surumeika* is the most commonly eaten squid variety in Japan, both dried and raw.
5 The *aoriika* is found off Japan from mid-Honshū southward. Said to be the most delicious of all squid, it is usually eaten raw as *sashimi*.

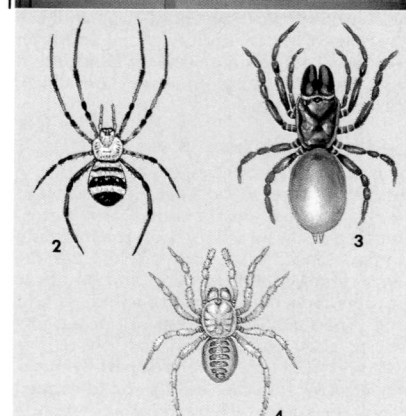

spiders
1 In a scene from the Nō play *Tsuchigumo* (Earth Spider), the victim (right) cowers as the monstrous spider spins its beautiful web, represented by thin strands of white paper.
2 Recognizable by the black and gold bands on its abdomen, the *koganegumo* reaches 3 cm in length and is found throughout Japan, except Hokkaidō.
3 The *jigumo* reaches 2 cm in length; it is found throughout Japan.
4 The 1.5-cm-long *kimuragumo* is found in Kyūshū and on Japan's Nansei Islands. It is known for the vestiges of primitive segments that are visible on its abdomen.

extended to include schools for the blind and deaf from 1948, and to include schools for the handicapped in 1979. As of 1989, there were 70 schools for the blind, 108 schools for the deaf, and 760 schools for the handicapped. The number of children within the compulsory education age bracket (ages 6–15) who were enrolled at these schools was 95,008. In addition, there were 81,053 children enrolled in special education classes within the regular elementary and middle schools.

Special Higher Police   特別高等警察

(Tokubetsu Kōtō Keisatsu; often abbreviated as Tokkō). A police organization created in 1911 to investigate and control the activities of political groups and to prevent the spread of ideologies regarded by the government as a threat to public order. Also known as the "peace police" (*chian keisatsu*) or the "thought police" (*shisō keisatsu*), the Tokkō achieved great notoriety as the eyes and ears of the powerful HOME MINISTRY until the end of World War II.

The HIGH TREASON INCIDENT OF 1910 appears to have been the direct stimulus for the creation of the Tokkō. The Russian Revolution, the RICE RIOTS OF 1918, the upsurge of strikes and agrarian disputes after World War I, agitation for universal suffrage, and the huge SAMIL INDEPENDENCE MOVEMENT in Korea in 1919 prompted the expansion of the organization and its role by the HARA TAKASHI cabinet (1918–21) and later governments.

The Special Higher Police achieved greatest power in the period after the passage of the PEACE PRESERVATION LAW OF 1925. Using this broad law, and cooperating with the Ministry of Justice, the Tokkō launched a sustained campaign to destroy the JAPAN COMMUNIST PARTY in a wave of mass arrests and prosecutions (see MARCH 15TH INCIDENT). Meanwhile, it expanded into a nationwide system with units stationed in every Japanese prefecture and major city and even began to send agents overseas. This growth had implications for socialists, liberals, Christians, and radical rightists within indigenous religious sects as well: they, too, became targets for ideological suppression in the deteriorating international and domestic political climate of the 1930s. By 1945 arrests of those involved in violations of the Peace Preservation Law totaled nearly 70,000. The activities of the Special Higher Police continued until the organization was abolished by OCCUPATION authorities in October 1945.

special tax measures   租税特別措置

(*sozei tokubetsu sochi*). Measures, adopted mainly under the Special Tax Measures Law (Sozei Tokubetsu Sochi Hō) of 1957, in which certain tax bases are assessed at reduced rates or exempted from taxation in order to achieve specific economic policy objectives. The first such measures were instituted shortly after World War II to spur the rebuilding of lost capital stock. Postwar Japanese economic policy aimed at achieving economic recovery as quickly as possible without causing inflation, and special tax measures were initiated to achieve this objective through the favorable treatment of savings and the promotion of investment. Special tax measures instituted to promote land sales have caused controversy. Another controversial tax measure levies a low tax rate upon payments to physicians for medical services under social insurance programs. Corporation tax measures include special depreciation allowances and exemptions for special reserves.

spiders   蜘蛛

(*kumo*). In Japanese, *kumo* is the common name for arthropods of the order Araneae.

Japanese spiders belong to three suborders, and about 1,000 species have been identified; some of the most common of these are the *kimuragumo* (*Heptathela kimurai*), the *jigumo* (*Atypus karschi*), the *onigumo* (*Araneus ventricosus*), the *koganegumo* (*Argiope amoena*), and the *ashidakagumo* (*Heteropoda venatoria*).

Japanese folklore frequently casts the spider in the role of the villain or the pursued, probably because of the association of spiders with a legendary race of cave dwellers known as *tsuchigumo* (literally, "earth spiders"), who are said to have lived in parts of Japan until the 7th or 8th century.

sports   スポーツ

(*supōtsu*). Sports and sports-related activities are extremely popular in Japan. Most secondary schools and universities provide facilities for team sports, and many large companies encourage and support sports activities for their employees. In addition, professional spectator sports draw large crowds. Japanese teams and individual athletes participate in numerous international competitions.

Modern Western-style sports, including BASEBALL, GYMNASTICS, TENNIS, and WINTER SPORTS, were first introduced during the Meiji period (1868–1912) by foreign teachers (see FOREIGN EMPLOYEES OF THE MEIJI PERIOD) and by Japanese students returning from abroad. In the days preceding World War II, however, Western sports were discouraged in the schools, and traditional martial arts received official support. After World War II, following the first NATIONAL SPORTS FESTIVAL in 1946, the JAPAN AMATEUR SPORTS ASSOCIATION (JASA), originally formed in 1911 to direct athlete training for Olympic Games, was reorganized to form the governing body for all amateur sports.

The most popular leisure sports in Japan are baseball, tennis, SWIMMING, SKIING, GOLF, and fishing. The most popular spectator sports are baseball, SUMŌ wrestling, and VOLLEYBALL.

Professional sports in Japan include baseball, *sumō*, boxing, tennis, and golf, baseball and *sumō* being the most popular. Professional baseball drew more than 20 million spectators in 1989. Around 780 professional *sumō* wrestlers in Japan draw about 800,000 spectators to the six annual tournaments. In 1989 there were more than 120 professional golf tournaments. Since 1912 Japan has participated in such international events as the ASIAN GAMES and the Olympic Games, hosting both the 1964 TŌKYŌ OLYMPIC GAMES and the 1972 SAPPORO WINTER OLYMPIC GAMES.

spring wage offensive→shuntō

squid and cuttlefish   烏賊

(*ika*). In Japanese, *ika* is the general name for cephalopods of the order Decapoda. About 120 species live in waters off Japan and many are important in fishery. The thick-shelled *kōika* (*Sepia esculenta*), a species of cuttlefish, is eaten raw or cooked. The thin-shelled *surumeika* (*Todarodes pacificus*), *yari-ika* (*Loligo bleekeri*), and *kensaki ika* (*L. edulis*), which migrate in groups, are eaten raw or dried (*surume*). The luminous *hotaruika* (fire squid; *Watasenia scintillans*) is caught when the female migrates to the shallow water of Toyama Bay to spawn in early summer. The area has been designated a natural monument for its beautiful luminescence.

Raw squid has become a popular food in modern Japan since the development of refrigeration, but squid was eaten in dried form (*surume*) in ancient times. As *surume* was traditionally used as an offering to Shintō deities, the Japanese still use it for presents on auspicious occasions.

Sri Lanka and Japan スリランカと日本

(Suriranka *to* Nihon). Before World War II, Japan had good commercial relations with Sri Lanka, then a British colony known as Ceylon. During the war, however, the Japanese navy attacked British bases in Colombo and Trincomalee. In 1951 Ceylon, by then independent, took part in the San Francisco Peace Conference and concluded a peace treaty with Japan. At this time it decided to forgo its right to seek war reparations from Japan. This act of goodwill by the Sri Lankan people became the basis of friendly relations between the two countries. Since the adoption of a liberal economic policy by the Sri Lankan government in 1977, economic relations have been growing. In 1990 Japan imported US $134.1 million in goods from Sri Lanka and exported US $314.9 million in goods to the country. Japan's main imports were pearls and gemstones, prawns, and tea, while its exports consisted mainly of vehicles and machinery. Japan's direct investments in Sri Lanka have also been growing. From 1977 to 1988, 57 Japanese investments were approved by the Sri Lankan government. Japan's official development assistance (ODA) to Sri Lanka more than tripled between 1984 and 1988, to US $199.8 million. This made Sri Lanka the eighth largest recipient of Japanese ODA funds. By 1990, however, ODA funds had gradually decreased to US $176.1 million. The ethnic conflict between the Sinhalese and the Tamils casts a shadow over future relations with Japan.

standard-form contract 普通取引約款

(*futsū torihiki yakkan*). Prepared contract containing standard terms and conditions pertaining to specified transactions. Such contracts are used to execute a large number of transactions promptly and with uniform conditions. They are often used in banking, carriage, warehousing, insurance, and maritime transactions. A CUSTOMARY LAW (*kanshūhō*) has developed to the effect that transactions of a certain type are generally undertaken pursuant to standard terms and conditions. See also CONTRACTS.

standard Japanese → kyōtsūgo

standard of living 生活水準

(*seikatsu suijun*). Measure of the average economic well-being of the citizens of a society. Since the late 1950s there has been a dramatic rise in average household income in Japan, and the standard of living has reached a level comparable to that of other advanced countries. There has also been a shift in consumption patterns, with discretionary purchases exceeding expenditures on basic necessities.

Japan ranked 16th in a 1980 survey of per capita NATIONAL INCOME in OECD countries, but by 1990 Japanese income of US $19,242 was in 4th or 5th place (depending on the method of calculation used). The large increase in Japan's per capita income compared to other countries since 1985 can be largely attributed to the increase in the value of the yen. In 1991 the gross average monthly income of the household of a male office worker (SARARĪ-

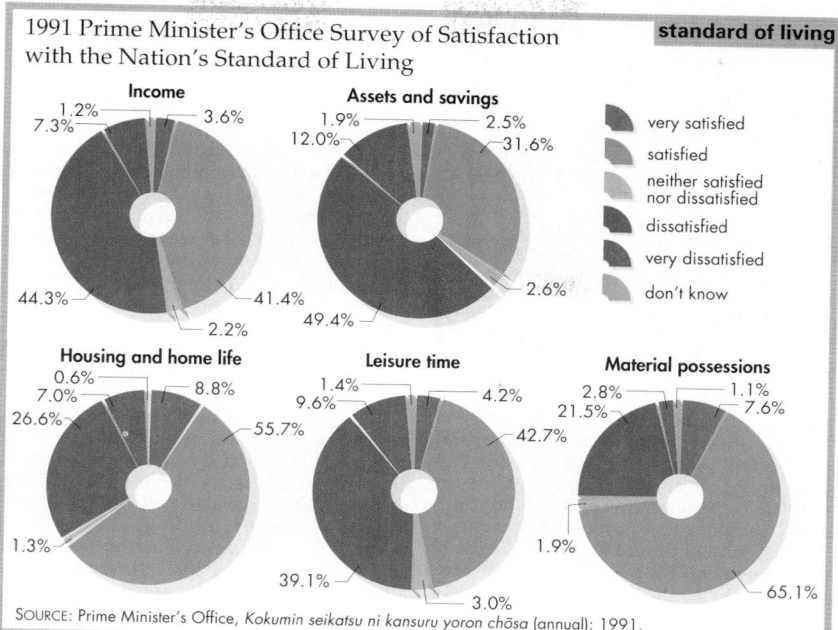

1991 Prime Minister's Office Survey of Satisfaction with the Nation's Standard of Living

standard of living

Income: 3.6%, 1.2%, 7.3%, 44.3%, 41.4%, 2.2%

Assets and savings: 2.5%, 31.6%, 1.9%, 12.0%, 49.4%, 2.6%

Legend: very satisfied, satisfied, neither satisfied nor dissatisfied, dissatisfied, very dissatisfied, don't know

Housing and home life: 0.6%, 8.8%, 7.0%, 26.6%, 55.7%, 1.3%

Leisure time: 1.4%, 4.2%, 9.6%, 42.7%, 39.1%, 3.0%

Material possessions: 2.8%, 1.1%, 21.5%, 7.6%, 1.9%, 65.1%

SOURCE: Prime Minister's Office, *Kokumin seikatsu ni kansuru yoron chōsa* (annual): 1991.

MAN) was ¥548,769 (US $4,074), of which disposable income accounted for ¥463,862 (US $3,443).

Changes in consumption patterns are illustrated by the decline in food expenditures, as measured by the Engel coefficient, from 36.2 percent of income in 1965 to 30.0 percent in 1975 and to 24.0 percent in 1991. During the 1975–91 period expenditures on transportation and communication rose from 6.6 to 10.0 percent of all expenditures, cultural pursuits and entertainment from 8.5 to 9.5 percent, and education from 2.7 to 5.0 percent. In 1991 nearly 100 percent of all households had a color television, refrigerator, and washing machine; 63.8 percent, a videocassette recorder; 69.8 percent, an air conditioner; 78.6 percent, an automobile. See CONSUMPTION AND SAVING BEHAVIOR.

While the consumption level of the average Japanese household has increased considerably over the past 20 years, the same cannot be said for the quality of life, given the continued restricted size of residential units, long commuting distances for workers, and high prices of all types of products. Land prices have increased to the point where it is virtually impossible for an average urban office worker to afford a single-family dwelling. At an average price of ¥59.0 million (US $438,000), even a MANSHON-type apartment with only 68 square meters (732 sq ft) of floor space costs the equivalent of 7.1 years' disposable income. Most urban families must endure living in cramped conditions or move far from the center of the city.

According to 1990 ECONOMIC PLANNING AGENCY statistics, the price of food in Tōkyō was 1.4 times that of New York; clothing and footwear, 1.5 times; fuel, lighting, and water, 2.0 times. As for specific products, beef prices were 3.3 times higher than those in New York; milk, 1.8 times; gasoline, 3.4 times.

Despite this high cost of living, however, most people declare themselves satisfied with their lifestyles. In the 1991 results of the annual opinion survey on the nation's standard of living published by the Prime Minister's Office, 67.1 percent of the respondents were satisfied with their own standard of living, compared to 32.1 percent who were dissatisfied. Since 1976 the proportion of those declaring themselves satisfied has never fallen below 60 percent. Surveys of class consciousness show that 89.9 percent of the Japanese people consider themselves members of the middle class and 54.4 percent see

themselves as in "the middle of the middle class." An increase in middle class consciousness took place during the growth period of the 1960s when there was a rapid increase in the average person's economic status.

With the widespread ownership of automobiles and many other consumer durables, as well as new problems with overeating and garbage disposal brought on by overconsumption, it is clear that life in Japan has reached a high level of economic and material well-being. Some people, however, are beginning to question the value of a constant drive for economic gains that, even when achieved, do little to increase their enjoyment of life.

Stanley Electric Co, Ltd スタンレー電気[株]

(Sutanrē Denki). Manufacturer of electrical equipment for automobiles. Incorporated in 1933. It has six overseas subsidiaries. Sales for the fiscal year ending March 1991 totaled ¥180.9 billion (US $1.3 billion), of which automotive electrical equipment accounted for 60 percent; semiconductors, 26 percent; light bulbs, 10 percent; and other products, 4 percent. The company was capitalized at ¥20.5 billion (US $149.4 million) in the same year. Headquarters are in Tōkyō.

Star Micronics Co, Ltd スター精密[株]

(Sutā Seimitsu). Manufacturer of electronic printers, automatic lathes, and wristwatch components. Incorporated in 1950, the company assumed its current name in 1965. It has overseas sales subsidiaries in the United States, the United Kingdom, Germany, France, and Hong Kong and manufacturing subsidiaries in the United Kingdom, Korea, and China. Sales for the fiscal year ending February 1991 totaled ¥62.7 billion (US $480.3 million), and capitalization stood at ¥12.6 billion (US $96.6 million). Headquarters are in the city of Shizuoka, Shizuoka Prefecture.

State Shintō 国家神道

(Kokka Shintō). Term used chiefly after 1945 for those Shintō ideas, rituals, and institutions that were fostered by the government to create belief in the divinity of the emperor and the uniqueness of Japan's "national polity" (KOKUTAI). State Shintō began in

stick dance
A performance of this folk dance at the November Kofun Festival in the city of Saito, Miyazaki Prefecture. Accompanied by drum and gong, the dance is dedicated to local ancestors enshrined in the nearby Saitobaru tomb.

1868, when the Meiji government proclaimed as its goal *saisei itchi*, "the unity of religious ritual and government administration," established the Shintō Worship Bureau (Jingi Jimukyoku), and called for the complete separation of Shintō and Buddhism (see SHINTŌ AND BUDDHISM, SEPARATION OF). An Office of Shintō Worship (Jingikan) was created. In 1872 its Office of Propaganda (Senkyōshi) became the Agency for Spiritual Guidance (Kyōdōshoku), to which all Shintō priests were appointed.

The formal structure of State Shintō was created in 1871 with decrees declaring that shrines were places for the observance of "national rites" (*kokka no saishi*), that is, they were government institutions; that priests were to be appointed by the government; that all citizens must register with their local shrines; and that shrines would be assigned an official rank and supported by the state. The constitution of 1889 reaffirmed State Shintō by declaring the emperor "sacred and inviolable," and in 1932 the Ministry of Education declared that shrines were nonreligious institutions whose primary purpose was to foster patriotism and loyalty.

State Shintō ended abruptly in 1945 when General Douglas MACARTHUR ordered the Japanese government to dissociate itself from all shrine affairs. This principle of separation of church and state was incorporated into the 1947 constitution, and today all shrines are private religious organizations. See also SHRINE SHINTŌ.

Statistical Mathematics, Institute of   統計数理研究所

(Tōkei Sūri Kenkyūjo). Institute administered by the Ministry of Education. Located in Tōkyō. It was established in 1944 for the purpose of studying statistical concepts and developing statistical methods and techniques. Its publications include the *Annals of the Institute of Statistical Mathematics*, which appears thrice yearly.

statute of limitations→prescriptive period

statutes→hōritsu

steel industry→iron and steel industry

Stein, Lorenz von   シュタイン, L.

(1815–90). German scholar whose conservative views on government influenced the framers of the CONSTITUTION OF THE EMPIRE OF JAPAN. In 1882 ITŌ HIROBUMI, a leader of the Meiji government, headed a mission to Europe to study constitutional systems. The members of the delegation, which included ITŌ MIYOJI and AOKI SHŪZŌ, went first to Berlin, where they were instructed privately by the jurist Rudolf von GNEIST. They went on to Vienna to listen to Stein, who was lecturing

at the university there. Like Gneist, Stein was opposed to universal suffrage and party government. He held that the state should be above society, that its aim was to bring about social reform, and that the latter should be implemented by a "social monarchy." Stein's ideas, as well as Gneist's, had a strong influence on the final drafting of the 1889 constitution.

stick dance   棒踊

(*bō odori*). Any of several mainly ceremonial folk dances involving the clashing of sword-length sticks or poles. These are usually vigorous dances performed by groups of young men. In Kyūshū and Shikoku, stick dances are often conducted at festivals honoring the UJIGAMI (local tutelary deity) or at the BON FESTIVAL and harvest festival; in the Kantō (eastern Honshū) region the stick dance serves as a preliminary for the lion dance (SHISHI-MAI). In some areas the sticks are replaced by scythes or long swords. The Okinawan stick dance is clearly martial, but in most regions the clashing of sticks is thought simply to have the power to exorcise evil spirits.

stilts   竹馬

(*takeuma*; literally, "bamboo horse"). Japanese stilts are made of bamboo poles with wooden footstands attached. The present form of stilts, in use since the 17th century, is a variation of a kind of footgear used in the performance of DENGAKU. The word *takeuma* is also used to refer to a hobbyhorse made of one bamboo pole.

Stimson Doctrine→nonrecognition policy

Stimson, Henry Lewis   スチムソン, H. L.

(1867–1950). US lawyer and statesman; secretary of war (1911–13; 1940–45), secretary of state (1929–33), and governor-general of the Philippines (1928–29). His name is identified with the so-called NONRECOGNITION POLICY applied to Japan as a result of its military takeover of Manchuria in 1931 (see MANCHURIAN INCIDENT). A Republican, Stimson served in the cabinets of both Herbert Hoover and Franklin D. Roosevelt. He was chief delegate at the London Naval Conference of 1930 (see LONDON NAVAL CONFERENCES).

During World War II, Stimson made the decision to evacuate Japanese, alien and citizen alike, from the West Coast of the United States into relocation camps (see JAPANESE AMERICANS, WARTIME RELOCATION OF). He was head of the War Department during the development of the atomic bomb and helped determine the list of target cities where the bomb might be dropped. He eliminated Kyōto as a possible target. Stimson worked closely with Under-Secretary of State Joseph C. GREW in making it possible for Japan to accept the surrender terms of the POTSDAM DECLARATION without renouncing its imperial institution.

stock exchanges   証券取引所

(*shōken torihikijo*). Japan has stock exchanges in eight major cities, with the TŌKYŌ STOCK EXCHANGE (TSE) being by far the largest and the Ōsaka Securities Exchange the second largest. The remaining exchanges are located in Nagoya, Kyōto, Hiroshima, Fukuoka, Niigata, and Sapporo. The Tōkyō Stock Exchange is now one of the world's largest in terms of the value of listed issues.

The development of Japan's stock exchanges began in the late 1870s when provisions were made for the trading of government bonds issued to members of the former *samurai* class (see KINROKU KŌSAI). Although trading was suspended during World War II, it was resumed in 1949, after the formulation of a SECURITIES EXCHANGE LAW patterned on similar legislation in the United States. Stock exchanges have expanded along with Japan's economy and have grown especially rapidly in value of transactions since the mid-1980s.

Portfolio investment by foreign investors in Japanese securities is fully deregulated. In addition, a growing number of foreign companies have listed their shares on the foreign section of the TSE. See also CAPITAL MARKETS.

stockholders' general meeting   株主総会

(*kabunushi sōkai*). Essential organ of joint-stock companies (*kabushiki kaisha*) that determines fundamental corporate matters by resolution of the stockholders. Stockholders' general meetings can be annual meetings (*teiji sōkai*), which must be convened at least once in each fiscal year, or extraordinary meetings (*rinji sōkai*), which may be convened as necessary.

Under the COMMERCIAL CODE, stockholders' general meetings are to decide on such matters as election and replacement of corporate directors (see BOARD OF DIRECTORS), comptrollers, and liquidators; approval of financial records; stock dividends; ex post facto incorporation (German: *Nachgründung*); remuneration of directors and comptrollers; amendment of the articles of incorporation; reduction of stated capital; dissolution of the corporation; continuation of the corporation; mergers and consolidations; and transfers of all or substantially all assets of the corporation.

stock market   証券市場

(*shōken shijō*). The market in which securities exchanges are established for the purpose of trading negotiable securities. The eight securities exchanges in Japan are in Tōkyō, Ōsaka, Nagoya, Kyōto, Hiroshima, Fukuoka, Niigata, and Sapporo.

The negotiable securities that can be traded in the Japanese stock market are defined in article 2, section 1, of the Securities Exchange Law. The main securities traded are government bonds, municipal bonds, and public corporation bonds, as well as unsecured securities, including unsecured debenture bonds, stocks, warrants, and securities investment trusts.

Issue Market and Trading Market— Functionally, the stock market can be divided into the issue or primary market, for direct acquisition by the investor of newly issued securities, and the trading or secondary market, for trading of issued securities between securities companies and investors. The 1990 issue markets for the main Japanese securities included bonds and debentures, ¥38.0 trillion (US $262.4 billion); stocks, ¥3.8 trillion (US $26.2 billion); convertible bonds, ¥3.6 trillion (US $24.9 billion); and fund-raising in foreign markets, ¥5.7 trillion (US $39.3 billion). The 1990 securities trading market comprised ¥231.8 trillion (US $1.6 trillion) in stock transactions including all the Japanese exchanges, ¥3,400 trillion (US $23.9 trillion) in public and corporate bond transactions, and ¥1,600 trillion (US $11.1 trillion) in bond futures transactions.

Stock Market Changes and Trends—
Recent changes and trends in the stock market include (1) interest rate liberalization, resulting in the creation of deregulated interest rate products such as investment trusts utilizing public and corporate bonds; (2) a significant increase in capital movement both inside and outside Japan, including investment in foreign securities and the issuing of foreign bonds by Japanese companies, as a result of the liberalization of capital transactions by the 1980 revision to the Foreign Exchange Control Law; (3) deregulation, allowing movement by banks into the securities business and by securities companies into the banking business; (4) relaxation of the standards for issuing corporate bonds and the rules on collateral; (5) membership of foreign securities companies in the Tōkyō Stock Exchange; and (6) the lifting of the prohibition on the issuing of domestic commercial paper in 1987.

The progress in recent years of the securitization of finance can be seen in the shift of capital funding from loans to negotiable securities and in the issuing of asset-backed securities by financial and other institutions. Securitization already has gained general acceptance in the European market, as shown by the issuing of floating rate notes (FRN), and in the United States, as shown by the issuing of housing mortgage securities. This trend is expected to continue in Japan as well.

stone tools 石器

(*sekki*). The origin of stone tools in Japan probably dates back 100,000 years to the early paleolithic period (see PALEOLITHIC CULTURE). This age was characterized by the use of rough or chipped stone implements, in contrast to the polished stone tools common in the subsequent neolithic period. Sites remaining from the early paleolithic period are extremely rare. Stone tools that have been excavated include chopping implements, prototype hand axes, and elliptical stone tools. In the late paleolithic period, various types of backed-blade stone tools were developed.

Japan's neolithic period included the Jōmon (ca 10,000 BC–ca 300 BC) and part of the Yayoi (ca 300 BC–ca AD 300) periods. During the period stone tools were used not only for labor but also for religious ceremonies and festivals and for personal adornment. Work tools were mostly arrowheads, axes, and adzes, including polished stone tools and chipped stone implements. Chipped stone axes and adzes were formed mainly from slate and shale. Polished stone axes and adzes were made of serpentine, sandstone, diorite, and other stones. Other stone tools include arrowheads, spearheads, and sinkers for fishing nets, as well as some tools whose uses are unknown. Since rice cultivation began during the Yayoi period there are numerous stone tools related to rice cultivation. Among these were chipped and polished harvesting knives and the stone sickle.

Arrowheads were used chiefly for hunting during the Jōmon period, then as battle weapons in the Yayoi period along with stone spearheads. Both chipped and polished arrowheads exist, the latter said to have been patterned after bronze arrowheads. The spread of bronze tools from the end of the Early Yayoi period (ca 300 BC–ca 100 BC) led to their use as models for stone tools (see BRONZE WEAPONS). Like the polished stone arrowhead, polished stone swords and stone halberds indicate the close contact between Japan and the Korean peninsula. The use of

all stone tools disappeared in the Late Yayoi period (ca 100–ca 300).

storehouses, traditional 倉・蔵

(*kura*). Storehouses have been used in Japan for rice and other grains since ancient times. The log-cabin style granary reconstructed on the basis of excavations at the ruins of a Yayoi-period (ca 300 BC–ca AD 300) farm village in Shizuoka Prefecture was probably used for seed rice (see TORO SITE). The central role played by *kura* in prehistoric village life is reflected in the fact that the architectural style of the ISE SHRINE is clearly that of a storehouse.

In the process of extending its rule over Japan, the YAMATO COURT set up between the 4th and 7th centuries a number of granaries at outposts for storing harvests. In the Nara period (710–794) the court nobility constructed *kura* to house their treasures and archives, and major Buddhist temples kept their sutras in storage buildings known as *kyōzō*. Many of the storehouses of the period had raised floors, which helped to reduce humidity within, and walls were built with logs, often triangular in section (see SHŌSŌIN), or thick boards. In the Kamakura period (1185–1333) there appeared storehouses (*dozō*) with earthen walls, reducing the risk of fire. Earthen warehouses (DOSŌ) were built by moneylenders in Kyōto during the Muromachi period (1333–1568), and the word *dosō* became the standard term for a pawnshop.

During the first century of the Edo period (1600–1868) sumptuary regulations limited the construction of *dozō*, but in the Kyōho era (1716–36), following a series of major conflagrations in Edo (now Tōkyō), the erection of fire-resistant structures was encouraged and urban merchants built storehouses with tile roofs and earthen walls 20 to 30 centimeters (8 to 12 in) thick. In addition to commercial items they were used for the storage of household goods and clothing. The Tokugawa government built warehouses (*okura*) in Ōsaka, the Asakusa district of Edo, and at other sites around the country to house rice that it bought or received from lands under its direct control (see TENRYŌ). In farm villages cooperatively administered warehouses were built for the storage of tax rice and rice set aside to tide villagers over in the event of a poor crop.

Straight, Willard Dickerman ストレート, W. D.

(1880–1918). US diplomat, financier, and journalist. Born in New York State. Graduating from Cornell University, Straight went to China to work for the Imperial Maritime Customs Service. He then went to Korea as correspondent for the Reuters News Agency. After a stay in Mukden (now Shenyang) as the US consul general, he worked at the State Department in Washington. In 1909 he returned to Asia to consider developing railways in Manchuria and northern China, but met opposition from Russia and Japan. In 1912, shortly after the Chinese Revolution, Straight returned to the United States and worked for J. P. Morgan and Co as its Far Eastern expert. Interested in public affairs, he and his wife financed the magazine *New Republic*.

Strategic Bombing Survey, United States アメリカ戦略爆撃調査

(Amerika Senryaku Bakugeki Chōsa). Study of the effectiveness of Allied bombing of Japan and Germany during World War II;

made at the request of US President Harry S. Truman and carried out under the auspices of the US Department of the Army. The survey pertaining to Japan was initiated in August 1945. In 1946–47, 108 reports were drawn up that dealt with the effect of bombing on the Japanese government, the military, the livelihood of the people, and the economy; the events leading to the war; the stages of the war's development; the effects of the atomic bombs dropped on Hiroshima and Nagasaki; and US miscalculations in evaluating the Japanese war effort.

traditional storehouses This refurbished Yamaguchi Prefecture storehouse, which dates from the 1750s, has thick plaster walls and small, easily closed windows designed to protect against fire.

straw raincoats 蓑

(*mino*). Type of rainwear woven from the stalks or leaves of straw, sedge, or other plants; used in Japan since ancient times, though seen only rarely today. The main varieties of straw raincoats were the *koshimino*, which covers the waist and hips; the *katamino*, which is worn over the shoulders and covers the entire back; the *dōmino*, which extends from the shoulders down to the mid-calf; the *marumino*, which protects the body from the shoulders down; the *seimino*, which covers only the shoulders and top of the back; and the *minobōshi*, which covers the head and upper torso.

straw ware 藁細工

(*warazaiku*). Rice straw or, less frequently, barley or wheat straw have traditionally been employed in Japan to make both utilitarian and sacred objects. The religious significance of straw is best demonstrated by the *shimenawa*, sacred straw ropes used in Shintō shrines to set apart a holy space or to suspend offerings to the deities. Adorned with purificatory paper strips (GOHEI), such ropes are also used to decorate gateways during the observance of the New Year's festivities.

Straw has also played a significant role in

traditional Japanese architecture. Straw or pampas grass is employed in the large thatched roofs or *kayabuki* of Japanese peasant houses (see MINKA), splendid examples of which may be found in the village of Shirakawa in Gifu Prefecture. The straw mats or TATAMI in Japanese houses are made in large part of thickly wadded straw matting (*toko*) covered with rushes. In ancient times, prior to the development of *tatami*, wooden floors were typical, and straw cushions (*enza*), wadded sitting mats (*okidatami*), and sleeping mats (*shikidatami*) were used. Simple straw mats called *mushiro* are still in use today.

Straw and grass were also once widely used, especially in rural areas, for all kinds of utensils, such as baskets, boxes, and bags. Of particular interest are the boxes made with straw mosaic decorations. Straw was also used for traditional STRAW RAINCOATS (*mino*) and rain hats (*amigasa;* see HEADGEAR) as well as for sandals, both light ZŌRI and sturdier WARAJI. In northern Japan straw boots (WARAGUTSU) and gloves were once common. Straw folk toys, especially straw horses, are still found in all parts of Japan. See also FOLK CRAFTS; MINGU.

street entertainment 大道芸

(*daidōgei*). Street entertainment in Japan had its beginnings in ancient court and religious functions. It reached the height of its popularity with the growth of cities during the Edo period (1600–1868) and came to rank with KABUKI and JŌRURI as an important form of popular entertainment. The street performer, however, was an itinerant and landless outcast.

Perhaps 300 different types of street entertainers were active during the Edo period. Among them were illusionists and candy and medicine peddlers, who entertained crowds with their lively monologues and dexterous gestures. There were performances of simple dramas, freak shows, exhibitions, peep shows, and trained-animal acts. Only a few types of traditional street entertainment have survived to the present. The *saru mawashi* (monkey show) is preserved in its original form in Hikari, Yamaguchi Prefecture, and MANZAI (witty dialogues), GOZE (troupes of blind women singers), *daikoku-mai* (dances performed by people wearing the costume of Daikoku, one of the SEVEN DEITIES OF GOOD FORTUNE), and *ningyō mawashi* (street puppeteers) can be seen in certain rural areas.

street stalls 露店商

(*rotenshō*). Stalls set up to sell miscellaneous articles for daily use, food, and so forth, usually on a busy street corner. The word *rotenshō* also applies to the keepers of such stalls, who are distinguished from STREET VENDORS, who travel throughout the country, and from shopkeepers, who have a fixed, permanent shop. Stalls that appear only at night are called *yomise;* these first appeared in the late Edo period (1600–1868) in Ōsaka. Some stalls open only on special days such as festival or feast days (ENNICHI) at shrines and temples, but many stalls, including night stalls, appear every day in a regular location. *Rotenshō* who attract their customers by some performance such as top-spinning, sword-drawing exhibitions, or hypnotism are called *yashi* or *tekiya*. At festivals, the head *yashi* used to have the authority to assign places for each stall. Presently, the officials of the Cooperative

Association of Street-Stall Keepers have that power.

street vendors 行商人

(*gyōshōnin*). Itinerant merchants and peddlers. In the Heian period (794–1185) peddlers went from Heiankyō (now the city of Kyōto) into the countryside, and vice versa, at regular intervals. In the Edo period (1600–1868), the Ōmi (now Shiga Prefecture) peddlers were so successful that they soon established large shops in Edo (now Tōkyō), Ōsaka, Kyōto, and other cities. In the late Edo period, medicine dealers from Toyama created a nationwide sales route and sales distribution system: a peddler would leave medicines in the customer's home and calculate the amount actually used the following year when he returned to receive payment and to replace the used products. Many peddlers could be distinguished by their cries. In recent years, however, most peddlers of wares such as baked sweet potatoes (YAKIIMO) use microphones or recordings. See also STREET STALLS.

strict liability 無過失責任

(*mukashitsu sekinin*). Liability to compensate for damages where there was no intent or neglect involved; distinguished from LIABILITY BASED ON NEGLIGENCE. With regard to TORTS, the Japanese CIVIL CODE takes liability based on negligence as a basic principle. However, the development of industry has resulted in a situation where many enterprises make large profits from types of business that create unavoidable dangers to society, and it is no longer considered adequate to base liability solely on the negligence principle. As a result, a number of theories recognizing liability without fault have been advocated.

The responsibility for compensation theory, for example, holds that a party receiving benefits from a profitable activity is liable for damages arising therefrom, while the hazard liability theory holds that a party creating a danger to society is liable for any resulting damages. In various rulings the courts have recognized both of these theories of liability.

However, it has been difficult to impose a fair share of the liability on all parties concerned, and it has proven necessary to provide solutions through legislation. Damage compensation systems had already been established for industrial accidents, but new systems were necessary to administer liabilities occurring outside the factory. Since the 1960s compensation systems have been established for damages arising from the operation of mines and nuclear power plants and from the harmful side-effects of pharmaceutical products. Protests against environmental pollution have resulted in the enactment of strict liability laws for the prevention of air and water pollution.

Strike, Clifford Stewart
ストライク, C. S.

(1902–79). US engineer and industrial expert. Born in Marion, Illinois, Strike graduated in 1924 with an engineering degree from the University of Illinois. As a consultant to the US Department of the Army he led two missions to Japan after World War II to study the reparations issue in the light of Japan's industrial needs and economic potential. The report, known as the Strike report and issued in February 1948, concluded that Japan would require much greater productive capacity than that prescribed by the existing US policy.

strikes and other forms of labor dispute 争議行為

(*sōgi kōi*). The Japanese use the English word "strike" (*sutoraiki* or *suto*) only to describe full-scale strike activity; a broad range of other labor tactics is encompassed by the term "dispute activities" (*sōgi kōi*). See also LABOR DISPUTES.

It is rare to encounter all-out strikes, which continue until the workers' demands are either met or abandoned. Most Japanese strikes are short ones of scheduled duration (*jigen suto*); an example is the "spring offensive" (SHUNTŌ), which lasts one or two days, before collective bargaining begins. Often only one group of workers engages in a so-called partial strike (*bubun suto*) or a designated workers' strike (*shimei suto*).

Dispute activities take place at enterprise facilities, and an attempt is often made to interfere with the employer's control over the facilities and the means of production. Examples are picketing, demonstrations, or the posting of leaflets. A partial rather than a complete work stoppage is often employed. For example, all workers will take a holiday on the same day, refuse to work overtime, or enforce safety rules in an extremely strict manner. These measures are often adopted by public employees, to whom the RIGHT TO STRIKE is denied. See also GRIEVANCE PROCEDURE; LABOR; LABOR DISPUTE RESOLUTION PROCEDURES; LABOR LAWS.

Structural Impediments Initiative talks 構造協議

(Kōzō Kyōgi). Series of high-level negotiations between the US and Japanese governments. The first phase of the talks included five rounds held between September 1989 and June 1990. The purposes of the talks are, first, to achieve mutual recognition of the domestic structural factors in each country that are responsible for the large US-Japan trade imbalance, and, second, to discuss measures to rectify these structural problems. The Japanese problems covered by the talks include the balance between savings and investment, price differentials between Japan and other countries, the distribution system, land use, business groupings (KEIRETSU), and restrictive business practices. The US problems include the balance between savings and investment, corporate investment activities, management practices, research and development, export promotion, and labor training and education.

A report was prepared in June 1990 at the fifth and final round of the first phase of talks. In this report Japan committed itself to invest ¥430 trillion (US $2.9 trillion) in public works projects between 1991 and 2000, improve application of the LARGE-SCALE RETAIL STORES LAW, strengthen ANTIMONOPOLY LAW provisions and their enforcement, reduce the time required for consideration of patent applications to 24 months within the next 5 years, and require disclosure of transactions between *keiretsu* companies. For its part, the United States committed itself to work to reduce its budget deficit, encourage increased savings and investment, and promote research and development. Follow-up meetings are planned twice a year to monitor progress in achieving the objectives. See also UNITED STATES, ECONOMIC RELATIONS WITH.

student movement 学生運動

(*gakusei undō*). A vocal and well-organized Marxist student movement has been a conspicuous feature of the Japanese political scene ever since the 1920s—with the obvious and important exception of the years leading up to and during World War II. At certain times, most dramatically in 1968–69, student radicalism has become the center of national attention.

Of course, not all student political activists in Japan are Marxists. Liberal and anarchist student organizations have long existed in Japan, and a wide range of traditionalist and patriotic student groups has flourished in opposition to the Marxist Left. But the Marxist mainstream has been by far the most conspicuous and influential and has come to monopolize the conventional understanding of the term "student movement" in Japan.

Origins of the Student Movement

The roots of student political activity in Japan may be found in late-Edo-period (1600–1868) patterns of *samurai* education, which while emphasizing the virtues of loyalty and obedience also tended to encourage a Confucian spirit of political activism and criticism. But it remained for the creation of the Japanese university system in the late 19th century to provide the framework of the modern student movement, and it is from this time that large-scale student political activity dates. In addition to strikes over issues of education and living conditions, students participated in national protest movements, first in the FREEDOM AND PEOPLE'S RIGHTS MOVEMENT of the 1880s and then on a far more conspicuous scale in the socialist movement of the early 1900s.

Various new student groups were founded in the first decade of the 20th century in support of political and social reform. The most important were the Rōgakkai (Study of Labor Society) at Tōkyō and Kyōto universities, the SHINJINKAI (New Man Society) at Tōkyō University, and the Minjin Dōmeikai (People's League) at Waseda University.

The Prewar Gakuren

The liberal-democratic spirit that initially dominated this vigorous new student movement gave way steadily to the growing influence of Marxism-Leninism as propagated by the Comintern. There were strong links between the students and the Communist Party movement in Japan, culminating in the founding of the first JAPAN COMMUNIST PARTY (JCP) in 1922.

The JCP was thus to some degree involved in the organization in November 1922 of Japan's first national left-wing student federation, the Gakusei Rengōkai (Student Federation), generally known as the Gakuren, which by September 1924 claimed a membership of 1,600 students on 53 campuses. In the fall of 1924 the official name was expanded to Gakusei Shakai Kagaku Rengōkai (Student Federation of Social Science), to which the prefix Zen Nihon (All-Japan) was added a year later.

Suppression and Decline

The first case of large-scale suppression of the student Left was a dramatic incident at Kyōto University in the winter of 1925–26, in which 38 Gakuren activists from several universities were arrested and convicted under the PEACE PRESERVATION LAW OF 1925 (see KYŌTO UNIVERSITY INCIDENT). Suppression of the campus Left escalated greatly after the 15 March 1928 mass arrests of communists, in which students were conspicuously involved (see MARCH 15TH INCIDENT). In response to these pressures and to directives from Moscow, the Gakuren was formally dissolved on 7 November 1929.

student movement
A police helicopter drops tear gas on Tōkyō University's Yasuda Hall in an attempt to disperse the radical student groups that held the building and blockaded much of the campus in January 1969.

Ironically, the police suppression of the student Left after 1928 coincided with, and itself stimulated, a tremendous wave of on-campus student rebellion that reached a peak in the winter of 1930–31. However, the dozens of student strikes and boycotts were limited almost exclusively to on-campus issues.

Following the MANCHURIAN INCIDENT of 1931, however, the wave of campus protest rapidly subsided under increased suppression and the mounting mood of nationalism. Nationalistic student groups rapidly multiplied after 1931, effectively ending the prewar student Left.

Postwar Reconstruction

The early postwar years were a period of reconstruction and reorganization by the student Left. Strong antiwar feelings among many students combined with the generally favorable attitude of US OCCUPATION (1945–52) authorities to create an environment hospitable to the student movement.

A league of student governments at major universities was founded in November 1946. In September 1948 this organization expanded into the ZENGAKUREN (an abbreviation for Zen Nihon Gakusei Jichikai Sōrengō; All-Japan Federation of Student Self-Governing Associations). The system of compulsory membership for all students in a *jichikai*, or self-governing association, enabled the Zengakuren to claim from the start a massive membership of 300,000 students on 145 campuses, although in fact only a tiny fraction of these were committed radicals.

The Early Zengakuren

The Zengakuren was founded chiefly by student members of the Japan Communist Party. From 1950, with the emergence of a strongly

anticommunist policy by the Occupation authorities, the Zengakuren, along with the JCP, was put on the defensive. The violent May Day demonstrations (see MAY DAY INCIDENT) of 1952 worked to discredit the student movement in the eyes of the general public.

The end of the Korean War in 1953 and the reconciliation of factions within the JCP in the mid-1950s led to a new phase of aggressive activity by the student Left. They supported the movement to ban the hydrogen bomb and opposed the US military presence in Japan (see UNITED STATES–JAPAN SECURITY TREATIES).

The Break with the JCP

In the late 1950s factions within the Zengakuren emerged in opposition to the Japan Communist Party. In 1958 a majority of the representatives broke completely with the JCP. The anti-JCP forces, known from the mid-1960s as the New Left, were already divided between the Revolutionary Communist League (Nihon Kakumeiteki Kyōsan Shugisha Dōmei or Kakkyōdō; founded November 1957) and the Communist League (Kyōsan Shugisha Dōmei; founded December 1958 and popularly known as the Bund).

Geba: Armed Confrontation

The early 1960s were years of organizational regrouping, and the Zengakuren split into several separate federations, each claiming the title of Zengakuren. The JCP-led group came to be known from 1964 as the MINSEI (an abbreviation of Minshu Seinen Dōmei; Democratic Youth League) Zengakuren and throughout the tumultuous late 1960s claimed control of some two-thirds of all

subways

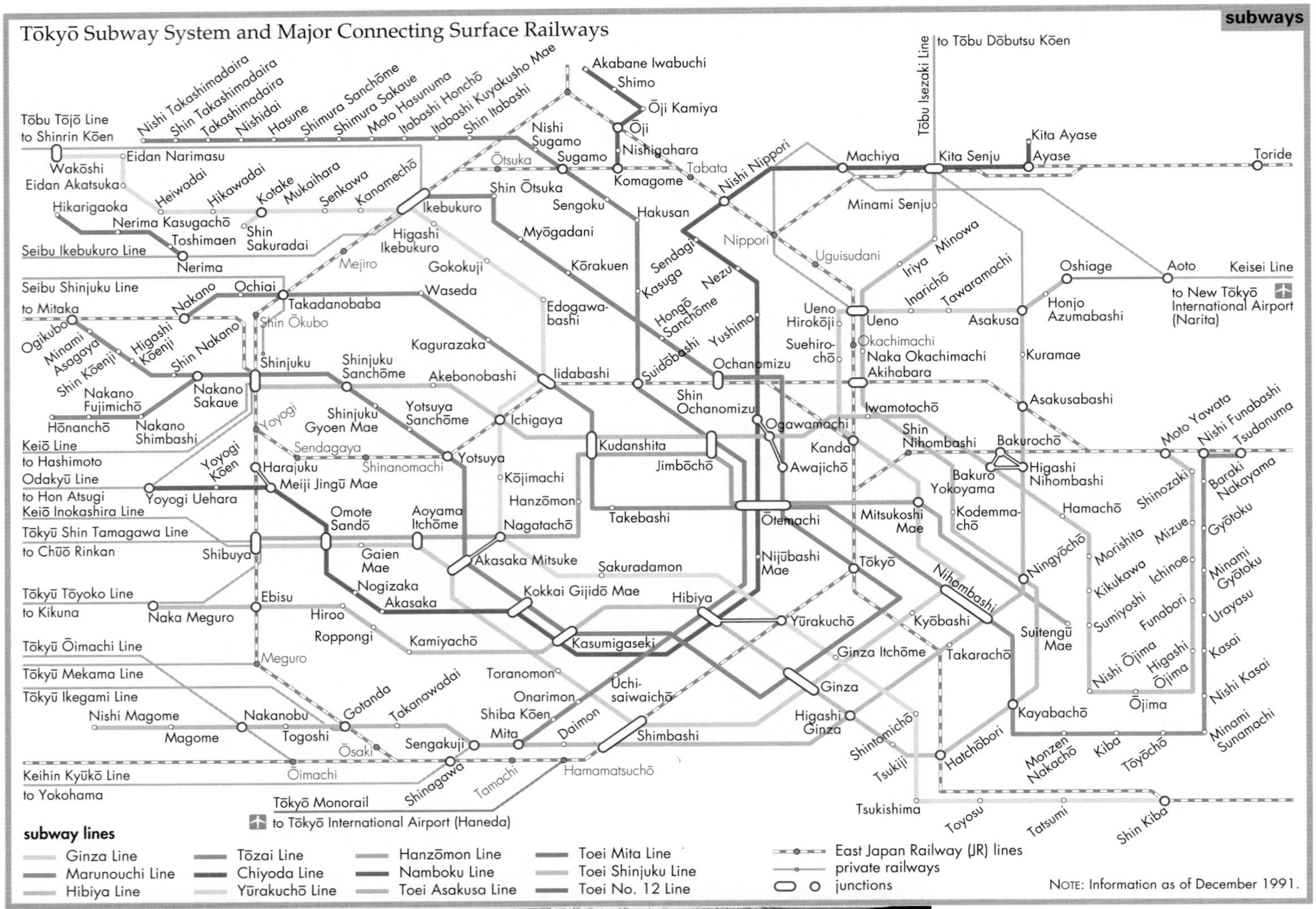
Tōkyō Subway System and Major Connecting Surface Railways
Tōbu Tōjō Line
to Shinrin Kōen
Wakōshi
Eidan Akatsuka
Hikarigaoka
Eidan Narimasu
Nerima Kasugachō
Toshimaen
Seibu Ikebukuro Line
Nerima
Nishi Takashimadaira
Shin Takashimadaira
Takashimadaira
Nishidai
Hasune
Shimura Sanchōme
Shimura Sakaue
Moto Hasunuma
Itabashi Honchō
Itabashi Kuyakusho Mae
Shin Itabashi
Heiwadai
Hikawadai
Kotake Mukaihara
Senkawa
Kanamechō
Shin Sakuradai
Ikebukuro
Higashi Ikebukuro
Mejiro
Akabane Iwabuchi
Shimo
Ōji Kamiya
Ōji
Nishigahara
Nishi Sugamo
Sugamo
Ōtsuka
Shin Ōtsuka
Komagome
Tabata
Sengoku
Hakusan
Myōgadani
Gokokuji
Kōrakuen
Nishi Nippori
Nippori
Machiya
Kita Senju
Tōbu Isezaki Line
to Tōbu Dōbutsu Kōen
Kita Ayase
Ayase
Toride
Minami Senju
Uguisudani
Iriya
Minowa
Inarichō
Tawaramachi
Oshiage
Aoto
Keisei Line
to New Tōkyō International Airport (Narita)
Honjo Azumabashi
Asakusa
Ueno
Ueno Hirokōji
Suehiro-chō
Okachimachi
Naka Okachimachi
Akihabara
Kuramae
Sendagi
Nezu
Kasuga
Hongō Sanchōme
Yushima
Suidōbashi
Ochanomizu
Shin Ochanomizu
Seibu Shinjuku Line
to Mitaka
Ochiai
Nakano
Takadanobaba
Waseda
Shin Ōkubo
Edogawa-bashi
Ogikubo
Minami Asagaya
Shin Kōenji
Higashi Kōenji
Shin Nakano
Nakano Sakaue
Nakano Fujimichō
Hōnanchō
Nakano Shimbashi
Shinjuku
Shinjuku Sanchōme
Kagurazaka
Akebonobashi
Iidabashi
Shinjuku Gyoen Mae
Yotsuya Sanchōme
Ichigaya
Iwamotochō
Asakusabashi
Keiō Line
to Hashimoto
Odakyū Line
to Hon Atsugi
Keiō Inokashira Line
Yoyogi
Sendagaya
Shinanomachi
Yotsuya
Kudanshita
Jimbōchō
Ogawamachi
Kanda
Awajichō
Shin Nihombashi
Bakurochō
Bakuro Yokoyama
Higashi Nihombashi
Moto Yawata
Nishi Funabashi
Tsudanuma
Yoyogi Kōen
Harajuku
Meiji Jingū Mae
Yoyogi Uehara
Kōjimachi
Hanzōmon
Omote Sandō
Aoyama Itchōme
Nagatachō
Takebashi
Ōtemachi
Mitsukoshi Mae
Kodemma-chō
Hamachō
Shinozaki
Baraki Nakayama
Tōkyū Shin Tamagawa Line
to Chūō Rinkan
Shibuya
Gaien Mae
Akasaka Mitsuke
Sakuradamon
Nijūbashi Mae
Tōkyō
Ningyōchō
Morishita
Mizue
Gyōtoku
Nogizaka
Akasaka
Kokkai Gijidō Mae
Hibiya
Nihombashi
Kikukawa
Ichinoe
Minami Gyōtoku
Tōkyū Tōyoko Line
to Kikuna
Naka Meguro
Ebisu
Hiroo
Roppongi
Kamiyachō
Kasumigaseki
Yūrakuchō
Kyōbashi
Suitengū Mae
Sumiyoshi
Funabori
Urayasu
Tōkyū Ōimachi Line
Meguro
Ginza Itchōme
Takarachō
Nishi Ōjima
Higashi Ōjima
Kasai
Tōkyū Mekama Line
Tōkyū Ikegami Line
Nishi Magome
Magome
Nakanobu
Togoshi
Gotanda
Takanawadai
Toranomon
Onarimon
Shiba Kōen
Uchi-saiwaichō
Ginza
Higashi Ginza
Ōjima
Nishi Kasai
Ōsaki
Sengakuji
Mita
Daimon
Shimbashi
Shintomichō
Kayabachō
Minami Sunamachi
Keihin Kyūkō Line
to Yokohama
Ōimachi
Shinagawa
Tamachi
Hamamatsuchō
Tsukiji
Hatchōbori
Monzen Nakachō
Kiba
Tōyōchō
Tōkyō Monorail
to Tōkyō International Airport (Haneda)
Tsukishima
Toyosu
Tatsumi
Shin Kiba
subway lines
Ginza Line
Marunouchi Line
Hibiya Line
Tōzai Line
Chiyoda Line
Yūrakuchō Line
Hanzōmon Line
Namboku Line
Toei Asakusa Line
Toei Mita Line
Toei Shinjuku Line
Toei No. 12 Line
East Japan Railway (JR) lines
private railways
junctions
NOTE: Information as of December 1991.

6119

subways
1 A subway train pulls into a station in central Tōkyō. Subways play a vital role in Japan's urban transportation networks.
2 Automated ticket machines line the entrance to one of Tōkyō's numerous subway stations.

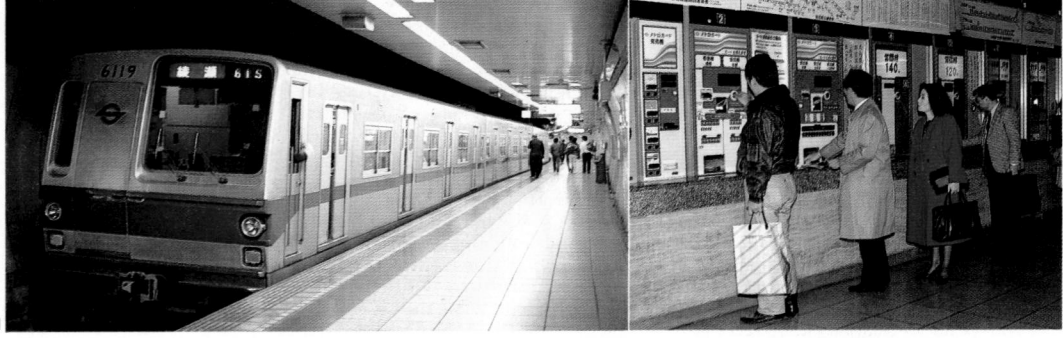

left-wing *jichikai.* The anti-JCP New Left forces were fragmented into several different factions, although an alliance known as the Sampa (Three-Faction) Zengakuren was in force from December 1966 to July 1968.

Student revolts against rising university costs and the decreasing quality of instruction in the middle and late 1960s were paralleled by an intensification of the broader political movement in opposition to the security treaty with the United States, particularly as a result of the war in Vietnam. The specific goal of this movement was the revocation of the Security Treaty ("Ampo") in mid-1970. It was this emerging "Ampo 70" campaign that gave birth in late 1967 to a dramatic new mode of left-wing student protest that came to be known as *geba.* The *geba* (short for *gebaruto;* from the German *Gewalt,* meaning force) was an armed confrontation with the riot police. The *geba* techniques became the standard mode of operation of the student Left.

The Crisis of 1968–1969—From mid-1968 into early 1969, these off-campus campaigns against the "Ampo" system were joined by a new wave of on-campus revolts. The turning point came in January 1969 with the mobilization of riot police to evict radical students who had blockaded much of the Tōkyō University campus. From this point, the student movement began to lose momentum both on and off campus, the victim of severe factional rivalry, mounting public opposition, and increasingly severe control measures by police and educational authorities.

In the early 1970s, the student Left turned increasingly against itself in the form of the *uchigeba* ("internal *geba*") in which rival factions fought with one another. It was also in the aftermath of the 1968–69 crisis that the Sekigunha (RED ARMY FACTION) emerged with a program of guerrilla terrorism. In Japan the Sekigunha activists carried out a series of bombings and robberies, finally collapsing under police pressure and internal violence in February 1971. An international wing of the same group, known as the Japanese Red Army (Nihon Sekigun), was responsible for a spectacular series of international terrorist attacks and hijackings throughout the 1970s. These acts caused many students to lose interest in political movements and the activities of student government, and the student movement continued to decline. In 1990 only some 40 percent of Japanese universities had student governments. See also UNIVERSITY UPHEAVALS OF 1968–1969.

student protests of 1968–1969

→university upheavals of 1968–1969

study abroad 留学

(*ryūgaku*). The first Japanese to study abroad were the groups of students who accompanied the series of Japanese embassies to Sui and Tang (T'ang) China from the 7th to the 9th century (see SUI AND TANG [T'ANG] CHINA, EMBASSIES TO). After the embassies were discontinued in the late 9th century, no government students were sent abroad until the Meiji period (1868–1912). In order to help Japan modernize, the Meiji government strongly encouraged overseas study in Europe and America, especially the study of Western science and technology and systems of government and law. In 1872 a government-financed Ministry of Education scholarship was established, and by 1945 over 3,200 students had studied overseas in this program.

Since World War II, major foreign study programs have included the Fulbright Exchange Program (see JAPAN–UNITED STATES EDUCATIONAL COMMISSION); the various international exchange and overseas study programs sponsored by the Japanese government or by the governments of other countries; and programs established by privately funded organizations such as the American Field Service (see AFS JAPAN ASSOCIATION, INC) and the ROTARY CLUB. In recent years study abroad has become very popular, especially among Japanese high school and college students. In 1988 there were nearly 85,000 Japanese studying in some 80 foreign countries (chiefly the United States and the various countries of Europe). The overwhelming majority of these students were privately funded; fewer than 600 were supported by domestic or foreign government scholarships. See also FOREIGN STUDENTS IN JAPAN.

Subarjo, Raden Akhmad

スバルジョ, R. A.

(1897–1978). Indonesian nationalist and minister of foreign affairs after World War II. From 1942 to 1945 he worked for the Japanese navy in Jakarta. Upon Japan's defeat in 1945 he supported the decision of SUKARNO and Mohammad HATTA to declare Indonesia's independence. In the 1950s he played an instrumental role in Indonesia's negotiations with Japan on war reparations. See also INDONESIA AND JAPAN.

Subaru

スバル

(The Pleiades). Literary magazine published from January 1909 to December 1913; a successor to MYŌJŌ. This monthly opposed Japanese NATURALISM, publishing poetry and prose works in a style often labeled as decadent or neoromantic. MORI ŌGAI intervened to reunite the defunct Myōjō's feuding poets in Subaru, whose members and contributors included ISHIKAWA TAKUBOKU, TAKAMURA KŌTARŌ, KINOSHITA MOKUTARŌ, YOSANO AKIKO, KITAHARA HAKUSHŪ, SATŌ HARUO, and YOSHII ISAMU. NAGAI KAFŪ and UEDA BIN introduced translations of European poetry, and Ōgai and TANIZAKI JUN'ICHIRŌ published prose works. The magazine was weighted in favor of poetry, putting out several special numbers of TANKA, but also devoted space to original critical essays, stories, and plays. Subaru is viewed as one of the most influential magazines of the period.

Subaru

すばる

(The Pleiades). Journal of literature and criticism. Published by SHŪEISHA PUBLISHING CO, LTD, since July 1970. It began as a quarterly, became a bimonthly in 1977, and a monthly in May 1979. At first Subaru was dominated by academic criticism, but it came to place increasing emphasis on original literary work, publishing such writers as ISHIKAWA JUN, INOUE MITSUHARU, and INOUE HISASHI. Since January 1986 it has broadened its coverage of areas other than literature, evolving into a general-interest magazine.

subsidiary companies

子会社

(kogaisha). Joint-stock or limited liability companies whose majority stocks or shares are owned by another company (oyagaisha, or parent company) as defined by the COMMERCIAL CODE, article 211 (2). The COMPTROLLER of the parent company is authorized to request a business report from and to inspect the subsidiary company (art. 274 [3]).

Subversive Activities Prevention Law

破壊活動防止法

(SAPL; J: Hakai Katsudō Bōshi Hō; abbreviated Habō Hō). Internal security law, enacted in 1952 in response to the violent MAY DAY INCIDENT of that year. The law permits the government to restrict the activities of or to dissolve organizations that are engaged in terrorist subversive activities. Fears that this would mean a reinstitution of the prewar thought-control system made possible by the PEACE PRESERVATION LAW OF 1925 aroused a vehement demonstration. Probably because of this strenuous opposition, but also because of restrictions written into the law and the government's apparent policy of using it only in unusual circumstances, the SAPL was invoked only about 10 times between 1952 and the late 1970s, and so far no organization has been ordered to dissolve by its invocation. The Public Security Investigation Agency (Kōan Chōsa Chō) was created to investigate possible violations of the SAPL.

subways

地下鉄

(chikatetsu). Japan's first underground rail service started operating in December 1927 over a 2.2-kilometer (1.4-mi) route between Ueno and Asakusa stations in Tōkyō under the management of the Tōkyō Underground Railway Co. The line later became part of the present Ginza Line, operated by the Teito Rapid Transit Authority. The rapid concentrations of population in large cities since World War II and the resulting transport congestion have led to successive subway-network-building programs in Tōkyō, Ōsaka, Nagoya, Kōbe, Sapporo, Yokohama, Kyōto, Fukuoka, and Sendai. In 1991 there were some 34 lines totaling 523.6 kilometers (325.3 mi) operating in nine cities. More than 8 million passengers a day travel on the 12 Tōkyō lines (230.3 km; 143.1 mi) and 3 million on the 7 Ōsaka subway lines (99.1 km; 61.5 mi). Many of the subway lines currently under construction are designed to connect directly with existing suburban surface rail networks, the intention being to ease congestion at terminus stations and to improve convenience for passengers. See also TRANSPORTATION.

Sūden

崇伝

(1569–1633). Also known as Ishin Sūden, Konchiin Sūden, and Honkō Kokushi. ZEN cleric of the RINZAI SECT; diplomatic and political adviser to the first three Tokugawa shōguns and a major figure in the early institutional development of the TOKUGAWA SHOGUNATE (1603–1867).

Born into the Isshiki family, important vassals of the MUROMACHI SHOGUNATE (1338–1573), in early childhood Sūden entered the temple NANZENJI in Kyōto, a major Rinzai center, and studied Zen under several masters, including Saishō Shōtai (1548–1607), diplomatic adviser to both TOYOTOMI HIDEYOSHI and TOKUGAWA IEYASU. Sūden became abbot of Nanzenji in 1605 but was called to Ieyasu's retirement capital at Sumpu (now the city of Shizuoka) in 1608 to succeed Shōtai as his diplomatic adviser. His duties quickly expanded to include domestic political affairs. In 1612 Sūden began to draft legislation for Ieyasu, particularly laws dealing with the control of the imperial court, the warrior houses, and various Buddhist sects (see BUKE SHOHATTO; KINCHŪ NARABI NI KUGE SHOHATTO). His diplomatic papers in the IKOKU NIKKI (Register of Foreign Affairs), and

his office log, Honkō Kokushi nikki (Diary of Honkō Kokushi), are important historical sources.

Sue

須恵［村］

Village in southern Kumamoto Prefecture, Kyūshū. Sue is known primarily in the West as the subject of a book, Suye Mura: A Japanese Village (1939), by John F. EMBREE. About 60 percent of the village is forest land. Rice is also cultivated. Pop: 1,594.

Suehiro Izutarō

末弘厳太郎

(1888–1951). Legal scholar. Born in Yamaguchi Prefecture. A 1912 graduate of Tōkyō University, Suehiro joined its faculty in 1914. His exposure during studies abroad (1918–20) to the case-study method at the University of Chicago and, in Switzerland, to the ideas of Eugen Ehrlich (1862–1922), founder of the discipline of the sociology of law, led him to take a positivist approach to civil law. He stressed the importance of judicial precedent and organized a study group, the Mimpō Hanrei Kenkyūkai, at Tōkyō University. He also became interested in the problems of farming villages and of labor and was the first scholar before World War II to lecture on labor law. Suehiro retired from the university in 1946 to become the first chairman of the CENTRAL LABOR RELATIONS COMMISSION and arbitrated numerous labor disputes. His writings include Nōson hōritsu mondai (1924, Legal Problems of Farming Villages) and Mimpō zakkichō (2 vols, 1940, 1949; Notes on Civil Law).

Suehiro Tetchō

末広鉄腸

(1849–96). Politician, journalist, and novelist. Real name Suehiro Shigeyasu. Born in what is now Ehime Prefecture. Suehiro joined the staff of the liberal newspaper Chōya shimbun and was jailed twice during the 1870s for his resistance to government oppression of freedom of speech. In 1881 he participated in founding the JIYŪTŌ (Liberal Party), Japan's first political party. He wrote political novels (SEIJI SHŌSETSU) such as Nijū-sannen miraiki (1886) and Setchūbai (1886). In 1890 he was elected to the lower house of the newly founded Diet as a member of the RIKKEN KAISHINTŌ.

Suekawa Hiroshi

末川博

(1892–1977). Legal scholar. Born in Yamaguchi Prefecture. He graduated from Kyōto University in 1917, joined its faculty in 1919, and taught there until 1933, when he resigned in the wake of the KYŌTO UNIVERSITY INCIDENT. In 1940 he became a professor at Ōsaka Municipal University and in 1945 president of Ritsumeikan University in Kyōto, where he remained until 1969. Suekawa made many significant contributions to the study of the CIVIL CODE. His book Kenri shingai ron (1929, Theory of Infringement of Rights) led to a basic change in the law of torts in Japan. Other works include Mimpō ni okeru tokushu mondai no kenkyū (1925, Study of Special Problems in the Civil Code), Kenri ran'yō no kenkyū (1949, The Abuse of Rights), Bukkenhō (1956, Real Rights), Keiyakuhō (1958, Contract Law), and Sen'yū to shoyū (1962, Possession and Ownership).

Suematsu Kenchō

末松謙澄

(1855–1920). Politician and scholar. Born in what is now Fukuoka Prefecture. In 1878 Suematsu went to England to work in the

Suekawa Hiroshi
A legal scholar who made important contributions to the study of the Civil Code and served for almost 25 years as president of Ritsumeikan University.

Japanese embassy and to study at Cambridge University. He won a seat in the first Diet elections of 1890 and went on to serve in various government posts, including communications minister and home minister. He also produced the partial first English translation of the TALE OF GENJI.

Suenaga Masao 末永雅雄

(1897–1991). Archaeologist. Born in Ōsaka Prefecture, in 1926 Suenaga studied archaeology and ancient history with HAMADA KŌSAKU at Kyōto University. He was the head of the Nara Prefectural Kashihara Archaeological Institute from 1938 to 1980, playing a leading role in excavation activities in the prefecture. He participated in over 200 excavations, including those of the 7th-century ISHIBUTAI TOMB and the Yayoi-period (ca 300 BC–ca AD 300) KARAKO SITE. Suenaga's publications include *Nihon jōdai no katchū* (1936, Armor of Ancient Japan) and *Nihon no kofun* (1961, Japanese Tomb Mounds). He received the Order of Culture in 1988.

Suetsugu Heizō 末次平蔵

(?–1630). Overseas trader. Born into a family of wealthy merchants of Hakata (now Fukuoka). His father moved to Nagasaki in 1571, when that port was opened to foreign trade, and amassed a great fortune. Heizō succeeded to his father's business and in 1619 was appointed local intendant (DAIKAN) of Nagasaki. After obtaining an official license to engage in the VERMILION SEAL SHIP TRADE, he dispatched ships to the Philippines and Siam (now Thailand). One of his captains, HAMADA YAHYŌE, fought with the Dutch factor in Taiwan and brought Taiwanese hostages back to Nagasaki. Because of this skirmish, on Heizō's advice the shogunate discontinued trade with the Dutch for some time. In 1676 Heizō's grandson was discovered to have been secretly trading with Cambodia, a violation of the NATIONAL SECLUSION policy. The Suetsugu family was severely punished, and their name and business were discontinued.

sue ware 須恵器

(*sueki*). A gray stoneware manufactured in Japan from the 5th through 10th centuries. This pottery was known as *iwaibe doki* or Chōsen *doki* (Korean pottery) until the 1950s when the word *sue*, derived from a reference to the vessels in the 8th-century anthology MAN'YŌSHŪ, was generally adopted. Originally a ceramic tradition of the southern part of the Korean peninsula, *sue* ware was one of several crafts brought to Japan by immigrant (KIKAJIN) craftsmen during the 5th and 6th centuries. Differing greatly from the native HAJI WARE—a porous, reddish earthenware—*sue* ware was fired stone-hard at temperatures exceeding

1,000°C (1,832°F); the atmospheric oxygen was then reduced to produce a gray color. *Sue* ware was generally unglazed, and, contrary to popular belief, it was mainly coil-made and beaten, smoothed, or carved into shape, rather than wheel-thrown.

Sue production, initially established in the hills of southern Ōsaka Prefecture, spread quickly throughout Japan. By the 6th century kilns existed in several localities along the Inland Sea, the Sea of Japan coast, and the eastern seaboard. In the early 7th century, *sue* began to be mass produced, replaced as an elite product by new imports such as three-color ware from China. Continued throughout the Heian period (794–1185) as a utilitarian ware, *sue* gave birth to a number of regional wares (e.g., YAMACHAWAN). See also CERAMICS.

Sueyoshi Magozaemon 末吉孫左衛門

(1570–1617). Wealthy merchant and overseas trader of the early Edo period (1600–1868); also known as Sueyoshi Yoshiyasu. At the behest of TOKUGAWA IEYASU, Sueyoshi and his father helped establish the Ginza, an office for minting silver coins, in 1601. During the Ōsaka campaigns of 1614–15 (see ŌSAKA CASTLE, SIEGES OF), he constructed the military headquarters for the Tokugawa and was appointed DAIKAN (intendant) of two districts in Kawachi Province (now part of Ōsaka Prefecture). He also received a SHUINJŌ (vermilion-seal certificate) and dispatched ships (known as *sueyoshibune*) annually to Luzon in the Philippines and Tonkin in Vietnam. His family remained involved in the VERMILION SEAL SHIP TRADE until the prohibition of voyages abroad in 1635 under the NATIONAL SECLUSION policy. Three famous *ema* (votive pictures) donated by the Sueyoshi family in gratitude for a safe voyage are preserved in the temple KIYOMIZUDERA in Kyōto.

Sugadaira 菅平

Highland in northeastern Nagano Prefecture, central Honshū, on the southwestern slopes of Azumayasan and Nekodake; part of Jōshin'etsu Kōgen National Park. The central part is a swamp created by lava flows. Vegetables are grown here, and livestock raising is carried out. In winter skiing is available; in summer it is a resort area. Elevation: 1,200–2,200 m (4,000–7,200 ft).

Sugae Masumi 菅江真澄

(1754–1829). KOKUGAKU (National Learning) scholar and writer; known for his descriptions of local folk customs. Real name Shirai Hideo. Born near Toyohashi (now in Aichi Prefecture). He began to write about his travels in 1783 and eventually completed over 70 accounts, consisting of dated journal entries, poems, and drawings, and generally concerning rural life. He traveled mainly in the central and northeastern regions of Japan's main island, Honshū, but he also visited briefly the northern island Hokkaidō. In 1811 Sugae was commissioned by Satake Yoshimasa (1775–1815), *daimyō* of the Akita domain, to write a geographical description of the six districts (*gun*) of Dewa Province (now Yamagata and Akita prefectures). His works, long circulated in manuscript form, were published under the title *Sugae Masumi yūranki* (5 vols, 1965–68).

Suganuma Teifū 菅沼貞風

(1865–89). Scholar of economic history. Born in Nagasaki Prefecture. Educated at a do-

mainal school, he entered the classics department of Tōkyō University in 1884 while also studying economics at the Senshū Gakkō (now Senshū University). In 1888 he became a professor at the Tōkyō Higher Commercial School (now Hitotsubashi University). Six months later he resigned his post. While investigating industrial and economic conditions in Southeast Asia, he died of cholera in Manila. His principal works include *Hirado bōeki shi* (1883), a survey of the history of trade in HIRADO, Japan's foreign trade center until the early 17th century.

Sugawara denju tenarai kagami 菅原伝授手習鑑

(The Secrets of Sugawara's Calligraphy). One of the most famous plays of the BUNRAKU and KABUKI repertories. A *jidaimono* (historical drama) written jointly by Takeda Izumo II (1691–1756), Namiki Senryū (1695–1751), and two other playwrights, this five-act play was first performed on the puppet stage in 1746. The story concerns the fate of the legendary statesman-scholar SUGAWARA NO MICHIZANE, who was banished to Kyūshū for life after being unjustly accused by a political adversary, Fujiwara no Tokihira (871–909), of plotting against the throne. Triplet brothers, whose father is indebted to Michizane, are forced to take sides against each other in the political turmoil that ensues. Unique to this play are the three parting scenes in which children are separated from a parent for the last time, the most famous of which occurs in act 4 and is popularly known as "Terakoya."

Sugawara no Michizane 菅原道真

(845–903). Leading court scholar, poet, and political figure of the Heian period (794–1185) who challenged the powerful FUJIWARA FAMILY. His father and grandfather were actively involved in Japan's enthusiastic adoption of Chinese culture during the 9th century. In 877 he was appointed professor of literature at court, an office he held for 10 years. In 886 he was named to a 4-year term as governor of Sanuki Province (now Kagawa Prefecture) in Shikoku. After his return to the capital, he was rapidly promoted to high court office by Emperor UDA, who sought to rule without interference by the Fujiwara family. In 899 Michizane was appointed minister of the right (*udaijin*). By this time, however, Uda had abdicated in favor of his young son Emperor DAIGO, who had closer ties with the Fujiwara. In 901 Fujiwara leaders falsely accused Michizane of plotting against the throne, and he was exiled to DAZAIFU, the government headquarters in Kyūshū. He died there in 903 after writing a series of famous poems bemoaning his fate and protesting his innocence.

Michizane's most important political contribution was his proposal, accepted in 894, that Japan cancel its last proposed official mission to Tang (T'ang) dynasty China because of unstable political conditions there. He is also considered early Japan's greatest master of poetry in Chinese. Michizane's poetry in Chinese survives in two anthologies that he compiled. He also helped write the *Nihon sandai jitsuroku*, last of Japan's six official histories (RIKKOKUSHI), and compiled a version of all six arranged topically rather than chronologically (the RUIJŪ KOKUSHI).

When after his death a number of misfortunes at court were ascribed to his angry spirit, Michizane was posthumously pardoned and promoted to the highest of court ranks in order to placate his ghost. Shrines dedicated to him were established in Kyōto (KITANO SHRINE) and Dazaifu (DAZAIFU SHRINE). Deified as Temman Tenjin, Michizane is venerated as the patron saint of scholarship. See TEMMANGŪ.

Sugawara no Takasue no Musume　菅原孝標女

(1008–?; Sugawara no Takasue's Daughter). Writer of the mid-Heian period (794–1185). Her real name unknown, she was a sixth-generation descendant of SUGAWARA NO MI-CHIZANE and niece of the author of KAGERŌ NIKKI (974; tr *The Gossamer Years*, 1964). She spent her childhood in the province of Kazusa (now Chiba Prefecture), where her father was stationed. She returned at the age of 12 to Kyōto and eventually entered service at the court. At about age 33 she married Tachibana no Toshimichi. Two years after her husband's death, when she was 51, she wrote the SARASHINA NIKKI (ca 1060, The Sarashina Diary; tr *As I Crossed a Bridge of Dreams*, 1971). She is also said to be the author of YORU NO NEZAME (ca mid-11th century, Nights of Fitful Waking) and HAMAMATSU CHŪNAGON MONOGATARI (11th century, Tale of the Hamamatsu Middle Counselor).

sugi　杉

(Japanese cedar). *Cryptomeria japonica*. Evergreen tree of the family Taxodiaceae, common throughout Japan. The largest Japanese conifer, it grows to 40 meters (130 ft). The crown has a distinctive conical shape; the short needles are aligned in spiral fashion on twigs. In early spring the yellowish male flowers and the green, ball-shaped female flowers are borne on the tips of twigs of the same tree (monoecious), and the fruit turns brown in October.

All *sugi* belong to a single species, but shape or color of needles and bark may vary according to region. Some *sugi* grow very large. For example, one particular tree, a cedar on the island of YAKUSHIMA popularly known as Jōmon Sugi, has a girth of 16 meters (50 ft) and is some 3,000 to 7,000 years old. *Sugi* wood is used for buildings, bridges, ships, and furniture. It has been traditionally prized as *sake* cask material because of its crisp scent. *Sugi* bark is used for incense.

Sugihara Sōsuke　杉原荘介

(1913–83). Archaeologist. Born in Tōkyō, Sugihara graduated from Meiji University, where he became a professor in 1953. He pioneered research into the culture of Japan's paleolithic period and also researched the culture of the Yayoi period (ca 300 BC–ca 300 AD), devoting himself to the analysis of primitive agriculture. In addition, he made significant contributions to typological and chronological studies of YAYOI POTTERY and HAJI WARE. Sugihara's publications include *Nihon seidōki no kenkyū* (1972, Research into Japanese Bronze Ware) and *Nihon sendoki jidai no kenkyū* (1974, Research into Japan's Preceramic Period).

Sugi Michisuke　杉道助

(1884–1964). Corporate executive and business leader. Born in Yamaguchi Prefecture, he was a graduate of Keiō Gijuku (now Keiō University). After working at Kuhara Kōgyōsho, a mining firm, Sugi shifted to the textile business in Ōsaka, becoming president of Yagi Shōten in 1938. He had close connections with the Ōsaka Chamber of Commerce and Industry from 1929 and acted as its chairman from 1946 through 1960. Sugi

made great contributions to the resurgence of the Kansai (Ōsaka-Kōbe area) business and industrial community and also promoted foreign trade by helping to establish the Japan External Trade Organization (JETRO) and serving as its chairman.

Sugimori Hisahide　杉森久英

(1912–). Novelist and critic. Born in Ishikawa Prefecture. Graduated from Tōkyō University. Sugimori received the Naoki Prize for his *Tensai to kyōjin no aida* (1960–61, Between Genius and Madman), an account of the life of writer Shimada Seijirō (1899–1930). He is known as a leading writer of biographical fiction. Sugimori's works include *Tokuda Kyūichi den* (1963–64, The Life of Tokuda Kyūichi), *Takuboku no kanashiki shōgai* (1965, The Tragic Life of Takuboku), and *Konoe Fumimaro* (1986). He also wrote *Noto* (1986, The Noto Peninsula), an autobiographical novel about his birthplace.

Sugimoto Eiichi　杉本栄一

(1901–52). Economist. Born in Tōkyō. After graduating from the Tōkyō University of Commerce (now Hitotsubashi University), Sugimoto studied in Germany at the universities of Berlin, Kiel, and Frankfurt. He became a professor at his alma mater upon his return to Japan. He was primarily interested in econometrics, then still in its infancy. His brilliant contributions to the field included a classic analysis of the principles of supply and demand in regard to rice. Sugimoto touched off a series of debates in postwar academic circles by maintaining that the analytical tools of modern economics could be utilized to perfect Marxist economic theory. Sugimoto also contributed to the development of the theory of dynamics. His works include *Riron keizaigaku no kihon mondai* (1939, Basic Problems of Theoretical Economics) and *Kindai keizaigaku shi* (1953, History of Modern Economics).

Sugimoto Sonoko　杉本苑子

(1925–). Novelist. Born in Tōkyō; graduate of Bunka Gakuin. Sugimoto studied under YOSHIKAWA EIJI. She won the Naoki Prize for *Koshū no kishi* (1962, The Shores of Lonely Contemplation), which tells the story of 51 retainers of the Satsuma domain (now Kagoshima Prefecture) who committed ritual suicide (*seppuku*) in 1765 because they could not complete a levee project ordered by the shogunate. She has written many historical novels, including *Takizawa Bakin* (1977) and *Edo sōgon* (1986). Sugimoto also writes excellent travel literature, one example of which is *Asukaji no tera* (1970, The Temples on the Asuka Road).

Sugimura Haruko　杉村春子

(1909–). Actress. Born in Hiroshima Prefecture. In 1927 Sugimura interned at the Tsukiji Shōgekijō (Tsukiji Little Theater). In 1937 she helped found the theater troupe BUNGAKUZA. From then on she was not only the leading actress of that group but also the outstanding SHINGEKI ("new theater") actress of her era. In the MORIMOTO KAORU play *Onna no isshō* (A Woman's Life), which was first produced near the end of World War II, she received particular acclaim for the leading role, which she had played 900 times by 1990. A very popular actress whose artistic horizons have not been limited to *shingeki*, Sugimura has worked with KABUKI and SHIMPA (new-style *kabuki*) actors. She has also appeared in numerous films by such directors as OZU YASUJIRŌ and KOBAYASHI MASAKI, among them TŌKYŌ MONOGATARI and KWAIDAN.

Sugimura Jihei　杉村治兵衛

(fl ca 1681–1703). Prominent early UKIYO-E print artist and illustrator. The most striking of Hishikawa MORONOBU's followers, Sugimura (who, unlike other traditional Japanese artists, preferred to use his surname on his works) illustrated at least 70 novels and picture books as well as several series of SHUNGA (erotica) prints. In *shunga* his flamboyant, decorative style often surpasses Moronobu in erotic effectiveness. His peak years also coincided with the rising popularity of large-sized prints, and his extant works include several of the early masterpieces in this format.

Sugimura Kōzō　杉村広蔵

(1895–1948). Economic theorist. Born in Hokkaidō. After graduating from Tōkyō Higher Commercial School (now Hitotsubashi University), he did graduate work there

sugi A forest of Japanese cedar (top) in the Kitayama district of Kyōto; the area has produced some of Japan's finest *sugi* wood for more than 1,000 years.

Sugimura Haruko This *shingeki* stage actress has also appeared in numerous films.

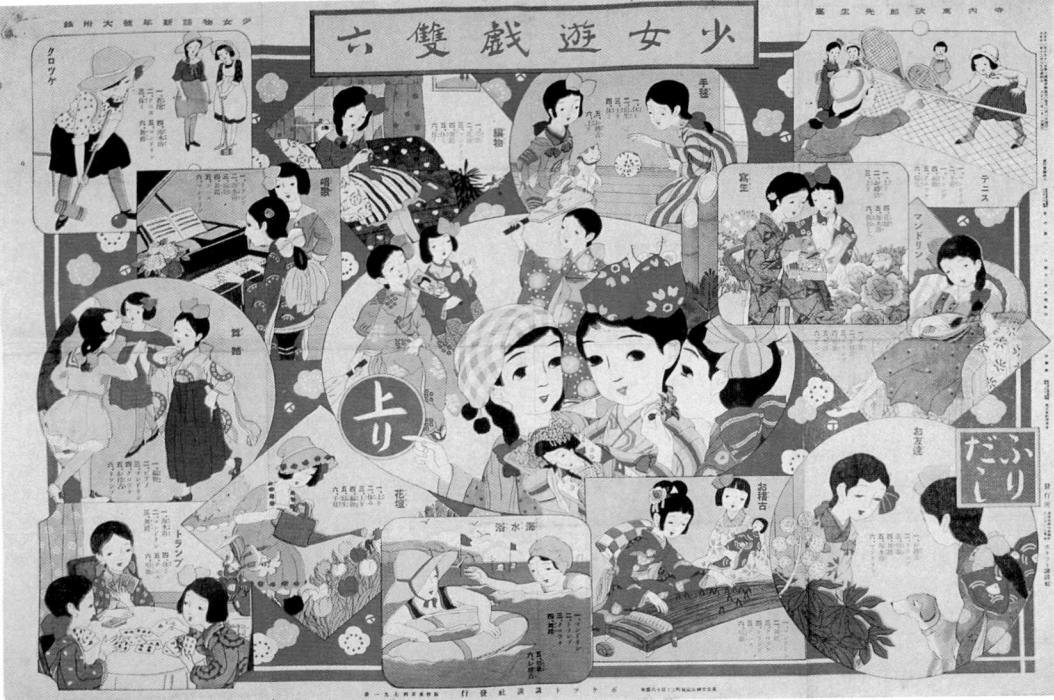

sugoroku A girls' "picture *sugoroku*" game sheet from the early 1920s. This version of the backgammon-like board game developed in the 1600s.

disciples, including ŌTSUKI GENTAKU, played leading roles in this movement.

Sugita Hisajo　　　杉田久女

(1890–1946). *Haiku* poet. Real name Sugita Hisako. Born in Kagoshima Prefecture; graduated from Ochanomizu Higher Girls' School. Sugita studied under TAKAHAMA KYO-SHI. In 1932 she joined the magazine HOTO-TOGISU. Her poetic style is strong and passionate, but her uncompromising individualism and eccentric behavior alienated her from her mentor, and she was expelled from the *Hototogisu* circle in 1936. Her works include *Sugita Hisajo kushū* (1952, The Haiku of Sugita Hisajo).

Sugiura Kōhei　　　杉浦康平

(1932–). Graphic designer. Born in Tōkyō, Sugiura graduated from Tōkyō University of Fine Arts and Music. He made his artistic debut with a record jacket he submitted to the sixth annual show of the Nihon Senden Bijutsukai (Japan Advertising Artists Club). His use of geometric patterns, innovative coloring, and novel typography had a strong impact upon Japanese design. Sugiura went on to apply his original graphic design skills to a wide variety of media, including books and magazines. In 1981 he became a design consultant to the government of Bhutan. His published works include *Moji no uchū* (1985, The Universe of Letters).

Sugiura Mimpei　　　杉浦明平

(1913–). Literary critic and novelist. Born in Aichi Prefecture. Graduate of Tōkyō University. After World War II, Sugiura returned to the farming village where he had been born and became involved in local politics, serving on the town council. His experience resulted in *Norisoda sōdō ki* (1953, A Record of the Norisoda Disturbance), an account of a local dispute that is considered a pioneering work in the genre of documentary literature. His other works include *Shōsetsu Watanabe Kazan* (1968–70, Watanabe Kazan: The Novel), a historical novel based on the life of the Edo-period (1600–1868) artist and scholar WATANABE KAZAN, and *Kōshō no shisō* (1966, The Philosophy of the Belly Laugh), a selection of his critical essays.

Sugiura Shigetake　　　杉浦重剛

(1855–1924). Educator and thinker of the Meiji (1868–1912) and Taishō (1912–26) periods. Also known as Sugiura Jūgō. Born into the family of a Confucian scholar of the Zeze domain in Ōmi Province (now Shiga Prefecture), Sugiura traveled to Tōkyō in 1870 to study at the Daigaku Nankō (a forerunner of Tōkyō University). He served as an administrator for Kokugakuin University, ran a private school called Shōkōjuku, and established the Tōkyō English Institute (later the Nippon Middle School). Sugiura joined journalist MIYAKE SETSUREI and others in publishing the periodical NIHONJIN (The Japanese) in 1888. Here one finds his peculiar viewpoint: an emphasis on human development rooted in a fusion of Western natural science and nationalist ideology. Sugiura lectured the then crown prince and princess (later Emperor SHŌWA [Hirohito] and Empress Nagako) as an imperial household official, a position he held from 1914 to 1921.

Sugiyama Hajime　　　杉山元

(1880–1945). General of the Imperial Japanese Army. Also known as Sugiyama Gen. Born in Fukuoka Prefecture, the son of a for-

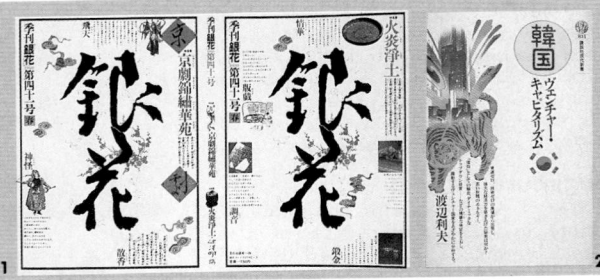

Sugiura Kōhei
This graphic designer created innovative jackets for a great number of books. **1** Sugiura also designed covers for a number of magazines. Pictured is the cover of the spring 1980 issue of *Ginka* (Silver Flower). **2** Sugiura is known as the designer of more than 1,000 covers for Kōdansha's *Gendai Shinsho* series of paperback books. Shown is his design for a 1986 book on venture capitalism in Korea.

under SŌDA KIICHIRŌ. After studying in Berlin from 1929 to 1932, he returned to his alma mater as a professor of philosophy and economic history. He resigned in 1935 when he failed to obtain committee approval for his doctoral thesis, which concerned the theory of value. He entered the business world and became a director of the Shanghai Chamber of Commerce and Industry and an auditor of Mitsubishi Shōji (now MITSUBISHI CORPORATION). Continuing the work of his mentor, Sōda Kiichirō, he was the first to give definition to economic philosophy in Japan. His works include *Keizai tetsugaku no kihon mondai* (1935, Basic Problems of Economic Philosophy).

Sugimura Sojinkan　　　杉村楚人冠

(1872–1945). Newspaper reporter and essayist. Real name Sugimura Kōtarō. Born in Wakayama Prefecture, Sugimura joined the predecessor of the ASAHI SHIMBUN in 1903. While in England as a foreign correspondent for the newspaper, Sugimura established a reputation for his informative coverage. After his return to Japan, he convinced the *Asahi shimbun* to adopt certain features of leading foreign newspapers, such as a research department and data-checking system. *Sojinkan zenshū*, an 18-volume collection of his articles and essays, was published in 1937–43.

Sugimura Takashi　　　杉村隆

(1936–). Oncobiochemist and doctor of medicine. Graduate of the Tōkyō University School of Medicine, where he has also served as a lecturer and professor. Sugimura is noted

for his studies on the relationship between mutagenicity and carcinogenesis, particularly in the field of stomach cancer, which has a high incidence in Japan. His work on the experimental induction of stomach cancer is an important contribution to oncological research. He became president of the National Cancer Center in 1974. Sugimura was awarded the Order of Culture in 1978.

Suginami Ward　　　杉並区

(Suginami Ku). One of the 23 wards of Tōkyō. On the Musashino Plateau. During the Edo period (1600–1868) it was a farming area. Beginning in the 1920s it became a residential and commercial area, with shopping centers developing around stations of the Chūō railway line. Pop: 529,485.

Sugino College of Dressmaking　　　ドレスメーカー学院

(Doresumēkā Gakuin). A private, coeducational fashion training school located in Shinagawa Ward, Tōkyō. Founded in 1926 by Sugino Yoshiko (1892–1978). In addition to its courses of study in sewing, design, and other aspects of general dressmaking, the institute offers dressmaking courses in English for the benefit of its students from overseas, who constituted about 50 of the 1,408 students enrolled in 1988.

Sugita Gempaku　　　杉田玄白

(1733–1817). Physician and scholar of WESTERN LEARNING. In 1769 he succeeded his father as personal physician to the *daimyō* of the Obama domain (now part of Fukui Prefecture). As he relates in his book RANGAKU KOTOHAJIME, in 1771 he was invited to witness the dissection of the body of a female criminal executed in Edo (now Tōkyō) and compared his observations with the *Ontleedkundige Tafelen* (1734, Anatomical Tables), a Dutch translation of the German work *Anatomische Tabellen* (1722) by Johann Adam Kulmus (1689–1745). He began the following day to translate it into Japanese, aided by MAENO RYŌTAKU, NAKAGAWA JUN'AN, KATSURAGAWA HOSHŪ, and others. Published in 1774, this translation, entitled *Kaitai shinsho* (New Book of Anatomy), aroused great interest in Western scientific knowledge and methods as the first Japanese translation of a European medical work. Many of Sugita's

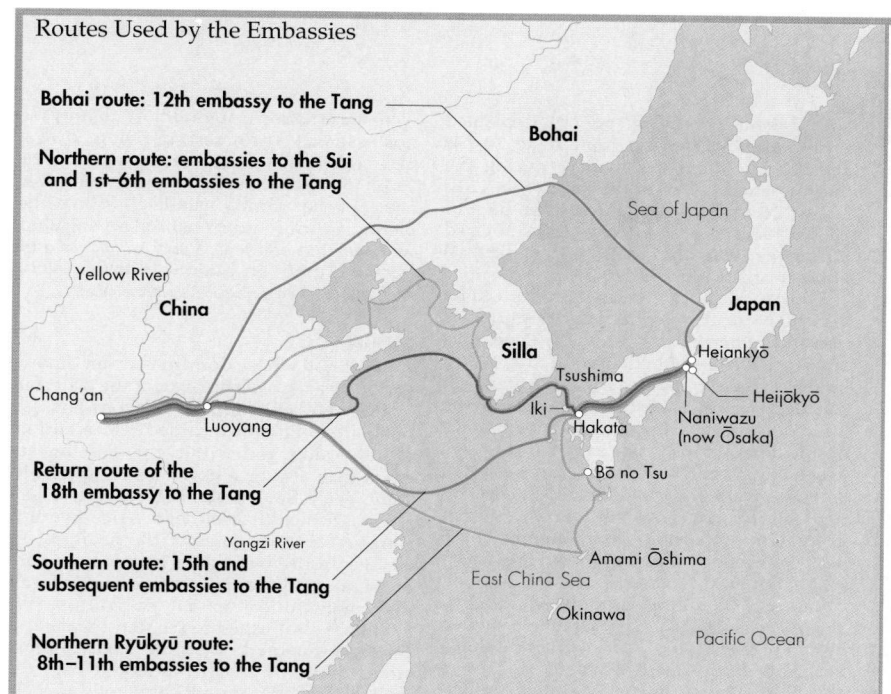

Routes Used by the Embassies

Bohai route: 12th embassy to the Tang

Northern route: embassies to the Sui and 1st–6th embassies to the Tang

Return route of the 18th embassy to the Tang

Southern route: 15th and subsequent embassies to the Tang

Northern Ryūkyū route: 8th–11th embassies to the Tang

Bohai · Sea of Japan · Japan · Yellow River · China · Silla · Tsushima · Heiankyō · Iki · Heijōkyō · Chang'an · Luoyang · Hakata · Naniwazu (now Ōsaka) · Bō no Tsu · Yangzi River · East China Sea · Amami Ōshima · Okinawa · Pacific Ocean

Mission number	Year of departure from Japan	Year of return to Japan	Comments
Sui dynasty			
1	?	?	Chinese sources note a Japanese envoy at the Sui court in 600; not mentioned in Japanese sources
2	607	608	Accompanied by Chinese envoy on return
3	608	609	Escorted Chinese envoy back to Japan
4	610	?	Mentioned only in Chinese sources; not accepted by some scholars
5	614	615	—
Tang dynasty			
1	630	632	Accompanied by Chinese envoy on return
2	653	654	Two ships sent with separate ambassadors; one ship lost
3	654	655	Departed before previous mission returned
4	659	661	One of two ships lost
5	665	667	Escorted Chinese envoy back to China
6	667	668	Escorted Chinese envoy, possibly only as far as Korea
7	669	?	—
8	702	704	One official did not return until 707, another not until 718 with the next mission
9	717	718	First time four ships sent; Kibi no Makibi and Abe no Nakamaro sent as students
10	733	734–736	Two of four ships lost; one returned late; Kibi no Makibi brought back
11	752	753–754	One ship drifted to Annam; Japanese ambassador eventually entered service of Chinese court; Chinese priest Ganjin brought to Japan
12	759	761	Unsuccessful attempt to bring previous Japanese ambassador back to Japan; accompanied by Chinese envoy on return
13	761	—	Two missions appointed to escort Chinese envoy back to China with military supplies requested by Chinese court when facing civil war; both missions abandoned because of bad weather
14	762	—	
15	777	778–779	One ship lost; accompanied by Chinese envoy on return
16	779	781	Escorted Chinese envoy back to China
17	804	805–806	Brought priests Saichō and Kūkai to China; two ships departed late after having been blown back to Japan; one ship lost; another brought Kūkai back to Japan
18	838	839–840	One ship lost; brought priest Ennin to China; returned on Korean ships
19	—	—	In 894, Sugawara no Michizane named ambassador to the Tang, but at his suggestion mission was abandoned

mer *samurai*, he graduated from the Army Academy in 1900. Sugiyama rose to become chief of the ARMY GENERAL STAFF OFFICE from 1940 until February 1944. In July 1945 he became commander of the First Theater Army to direct the defense of the Japanese mainland against the anticipated Allied invasion. On 12 September 1945, after finishing preparations for the final dissolution of Japan's military forces, he shot himself in his office; the same day, his wife, the daughter of an army general, killed herself.

Sugiyama Naojirō   杉山直治郎

(1878–1966). Professor of law and founder of comparative legal studies in Japan. Graduate of Tōkyō University. After studying in France, Switzerland, and Germany, he taught at Nagasaki University (then Nagasaki Kōtō Shōgyō Gakkō) from 1908 to 1913. In 1916 he was named the first Japanese professor to teach French law at Tōkyō University. After World War II, he was director of the Institute of Comparative Law at Chūō University. Sugiyama insisted that in adopting foreign systems Japan should first consider historical sources of each law. His principal publication is *Hōgen to kaishaku* (1957, Source and Interpretation in Law).

Sugiyama Sampū   杉山杉風

(1647–1732). HAIKU poet and prosperous fish wholesaler of the early Edo period (1600–1868). A faithful disciple of BASHŌ. Bashō's cottage in Fukagawa (now part of Tōkyō) had been a warehouse of Sampū's, named "Bashōan" after a plantain tree (*bashō*) in its yard; from this Bashō took his pen name. Sampū's main collection of haiku is *Sampū kushū* (1785).

Sugiyama Yasushi   杉山寧

(1909–). Japanese-style (NIHONGA) painter. Born in Tōkyō, Sugiyama graduated from Tōkyō Bijutsu Gakkō (now Tōkyō University of Fine Arts and Music) and studied under the *nihonga* painter MATSUOKA EIKYŪ. He won the highest award at the Teiten (Exhibition of the Imperial Fine Arts Academy) while still a student. From 1934 to 1938, along with YAMAMOTO KYŪJIN and others, Sugiyama participated in the association of painters known as Rusō Gasha. Sugiyama's

work is characterized by its precise composition and innovative use of color. He won the Japan Art Academy Award (Geijutsuin Shō) in 1957 and received the Order of Culture in 1974.

sugoroku   双六

A board game similar to backgammon that is played by two or more persons using dice. There are two main varieties of *sugoroku*. In *bansugoroku* ("board *sugoroku*"), believed to have been introduced from China in the 6th century, two people advance their pieces (15 each) across a wooden board according to the numbers on the dice. The player who succeeds in advancing all his or her pieces into enemy territory wins. *Esugoroku* ("picture *sugoroku*"), developed during the 17th century, is played on a large sheet of paper divided into sections with various colored illustrations. The first *esugoroku* games had religious themes and were called *Jōdo sugoroku* ("Pure Land *sugoroku*"); the goal was to reach heaven and avoid hell. Today picture *sugoroku* have illustrations of popular tourist spots or theater personalities. The game is mainly played by children at New Year's.

Sugup'a   守旧派

(J: Shukyūha; Conservative Faction). A late-19th-century Korean political clique that advocated maintenance of traditional ties with China. It backed the policy of *sadae* (J: *jidai*; literally, "serve the great") that symbolized Korea's ritual submission to imperial China and adherence to Confucian ideology. See KOREA AND JAPAN.

Sui and Tang (T'ang) China, embassies to   遣隋使と遣唐使

(*kenzuishi to kentōshi*). Japanese diplomatic embassies sent to China during the Sui (589–618) and the Tang (T'ang) (618–907) dynasties. Between 600 and 614, 4 or 5 missions were sent to the Sui, and from 630–894 at least 19 missions to the Tang were appointed; however, some of the latter did not actually make the trip, and others were not designated *kentōshi*. In addition to their diplomatic functions, these embassies fostered trade and cultural exchange with China.

Japan's first mission to the Sui in 600 was to gain Chinese support for Japanese acti-

vities in Korea. In 607 the regent Prince SHŌTOKU appointed the court official ONO NO IMOKO to lead a second embassy, which returned to Japan in 608 accompanied by a Sui envoy. Later missions included lay scholars and Buddhist monks sent to learn more about Chinese culture and institutions. Eight scholars and Buddhist monks accompanied the third mission (608), among them TAKAMUKO NO KUROMARO, MINABUCHI NO SHŌAN, and the monk SŌMIN; these men had great influence on Japanese culture and on the administrative innovations embodied in the TAIKA REFORM of 645.

The first embassy to the Tang in 630 was honored with a Chinese escort on its return, but relations were interrupted when in 663 a Japanese fleet was defeated by a joint Chinese-Korean force in the Battle of HAKUSUKINOE. After six Chinese missions to Japan and three Japanese missions to China the tension was eased. In the 8th century the Japanese resumed sending envoys to the Tang in a peaceful and increasingly grand manner. A few scholars and monks remained in China for long periods (see ABE NO NAKAMARO), and many, upon their return, made important contributions to Japan's in-

embassies to Sui and Tang China This detail from the 11th-century *Illustrated Biographical Tales of Prince Shōtoku*, a series of screen paintings, depicts a seaborne Japanese mission to the Sui dynasty court.

creasingly sinified culture (see KIBI NO MAKIBI; GEMBŌ; ENNIN; KŪKAI; SAICHŌ).

In 894 the scholar SUGAWARA NO MICHIZANE was named ambassador to the Tang. His proposal that the mission be canceled because of political instability in China was accepted, and regular diplomatic relations were not resumed until the 15th century.

suibokuga → ink painting

suicide 自殺

(*jisatsu*). Japan has one of the highest rates of suicide in Asia, but, contrary to popular belief, in worldwide comparisons it stands in the middle between the high-rate countries of Europe on the one hand and the low-rate countries of Asia, Africa, and Latin America on the other.

Japan's traditional culture, which has never condemned suicide, is known for a highly ritualized and institutionalized form of self-disembowelment (*seppuku* or HARA-KIRI) that has, however, virtually disappeared in modern Japan. Official statistics on suicide in Japan, first compiled in 1882, show that the suicide rate during the Meiji (1868–1912)

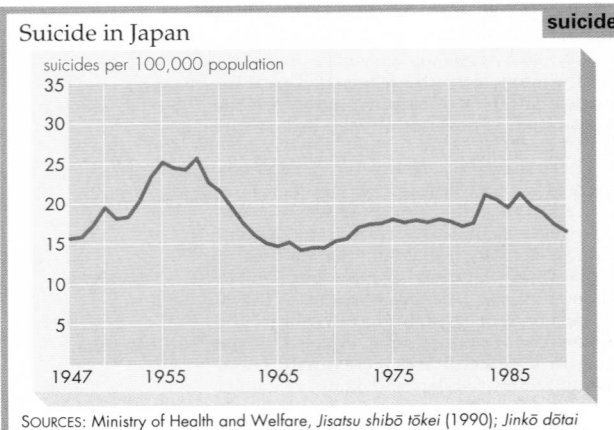

Suicide in Japan

suicides per 100,000 population

SOURCES: Ministry of Health and Welfare, *Jisatsu shibō tōkei* (1990); *Jinkō dōtai tōkei* (annual): 1990.

and Taishō (1912–26) periods remained fairly constant, ranging from 16 to 20 per 100,000 but fluctuated widely during the Shōwa period (1926–89), ranging from 12 to almost 26, and reaching an all-time high of 25.7 in 1958. The rate more or less stabilized during the 1980s at 17 to 21. In 1990 the total number of suicides was 20,088.

Until recently Japan was characterized by very high suicide rates in the elderly population and among youths below 25, a phenomenon known as bimodality. In the 1980s, however, there was a steady decline in youth suicide as well as a substantial increase in the middle-age group, bringing Japan's pattern of suicide closer to Europe's than it had been. Much higher rates of suicide are recorded among the elderly who live with their married children and grandchildren in a three-generation household than among those who live alone or separately from their married children.

Like their counterparts in the Middle East and the rest of East Asia, Japanese women have a higher ratio of suicide than do European and North American women. In Europe and North America, highly skilled professionals often register very high rates of suicide, but in Japan the highest rates are among less-skilled workers in agriculture, fishing, and mining. In Europe and North America, suicide is more common in densely populated areas, but in Japan much higher rates have been observed historically in sparsely populated, rural, impoverished areas. One feature of suicide in Japan is the large number of plural suicides (SHINJŪ) involving lovers or family members, either voluntarily or in the form of homicide-suicide. Though not a uniquely Japanese phenomenon, these types of plural suicide have a long history in Japan, and love suicide in particular has been a powerful theme in many plays and novels.

Suigō 水郷

Name given to a district extending from northern Chiba Prefecture to southern Ibaraki Prefecture in central Honshū. Situated on the swampy lower reaches of the river Tonegawa and the shores of the lake Kasumigaura, Suigō is famous for its irises.

suigun 水軍

General term for naval forces in Japan from ancient times to the 1850s. According to the chronicle NIHON SHOKI (720), ABE NO HIRAFU led naval expeditions between 658 and 660 to subdue the EZO tribes of northern Japan. His navy was defeated, however, in 663 at the Battle of HAKUSUKINOE in Korea. In the Heian period (794–1185) sea forces were maintained by local families along the Inland Sea and northern Kyūshū. They participated in the Taira-Minamoto War (1180–85) and played an important role in the Battle of DAN-NOURA. Naval forces were also mobilized against the MONGOL INVASIONS OF JAPAN in the late 13th century. Because of the policy of NATIONAL SECLUSION, *daimyō* during the Edo period (1600–1868) were prohibited from building large ships. When the Tokugawa shogunate began to modernize its military forces after the mid-1850s, the term *kaigun* (navy) was used.

suijakuga 垂迹画

Genre of Shintō paintings derived from Buddhist iconography, often showing Shintō deities (KAMI) portrayed with, or in the form of, their Buddhist avatars. These paintings were based on the belief that Shintō *kami*

were incarnations of Buddhist deities (see HONJI SUIJAKU). The oldest surviving *suijakuga* date from the Kamakura period (1185–1333). *Suijakuga* were anonymous and were often in the "shrine mandala" format, depicting a shrine and its natural setting along with related deities. Some *suijakuga* portrayed Shintō or Buddhist deities alone, without a shrine. See also SHINTŌ ART.

suijin 水神

Type of god whose domain is water; known variously as god of the river, of the waterfall, of the well, and so forth. Dragons and serpents are commonly regarded as incarnations of the water god, while the mischievous KAPPA may also be a degenerate form of the water deity. Since water is absolutely essential for rice cultivation, many rice-planting songs refer to the gods of the fields (TA NO KAMI) or of rice harvests as having been born of the sun and a female water deity. In farming communities, special fraternities (*suijinkō*) are established to see that the deity is properly honored. In some households a stone statue of a *suijin* is placed near the well. Festivals honoring water gods are held in June and December.

Suijinroku 吹塵録

Collection of the financial records of the Tokugawa shogunate (1603–1867); published in 1890. It was compiled at the behest of Finance Minister MATSUKATA MASAYOSHI by KATSU KAISHŪ and others. Besides containing data on the land system, rice yields, population, currency, and commerce, it is an important source of information on the Tokugawa regime's financial policies. A supplement, the *Suijin yoroku*, was published the same year.

Suika Shintō 垂加神道

An eclectic school of Shintō founded by YAMAZAKI ANSAI (1619–82). Ordained as a Buddhist monk, Yamazaki later returned to lay life to devote himself to the study of the Zhu Xi (Chu Hsi) school of Confucianism (see SHUSHIGAKU). In his fifties Yamazaki traveled, studying the doctrines of the major Shintō schools, and ultimately evolved a grand synthesis of Neo-Confucian metaphysical, cosmological, and ethical concepts with the doctrinal traditions of various Shintō schools.

The term *suika* (grace and protection), which in Yamazaki's view signified the essence of Shintō, is taken from a passage in the *Yamatohime no Mikoto seiki* (one of the five scriptures of WATARAI SHINTŌ), which states, "To receive divine grace (*sui*), prayer must be foremost in your mind; to enjoy the protection (*ka*) of the deities, uprightness must be the root of your conduct." From Neo-Confucianism Yamazaki borrowed the Chinese concepts of *jing* (ching; J: *kei*; reverence), which he held to be the basis of all human behavior, and *li* (J: *ri*), "the all-pervading and unifying principle," to establish the fundamental unity between the Shintō deities and man as well as between the emperor and his subjects. Yamazaki stressed the uniqueness and divinity of the imperial line. The ideas of Suika Shintō exerted a great influence on the Mito school of historical scholarship as well as on HIRATA ATSUTANE (1776–1843), a leading exponent of Restoration Shintō, and contributed to the movement that led to the divinization of the emperor and the overthrow of the shogunate.

suikazura → honeysuckle, Japanese

suiko 出挙

(loans). Government loans, often seed rice, made to peasants in Japan from the 7th through 12th centuries. Interest rates varied from 30 to 100 percent annually. The loans originated with the need to lend food and seed to peasants as relief in the spring and summer.

Many borrowers were forced to sell their lands to pay off their debts to private lenders. The heavy burden of interest caused many peasants to abandon their land and flee to other districts. Repeated government measures to deal with this problem by prohibiting private loans (*shisuiko*) or by offering compensatory tax reductions generally failed. Eventually the government itself began making loans to peasants, and by the 12th century the interest on such loans had in effect become a part of the tax burden.

Suiko, Empress 推古天皇

(554–628; Suiko Tennō). Reigning empress (*tennō*), the 33rd sovereign in the traditional count (which includes several legendary emperors); reigned 593–628. The third daughter of Emperor KIMMEI (r 531 or 539 to 571), her mother came from the SOGA FAMILY. She became empress (*kōgō*) to Emperor Bidatsu (r 572–585), her half brother. When Emperor Sushun (r 587–592; another half brother) was killed in a plot masterminded by her uncle SOGA NO UMAKO, Suiko ascended the throne. She ruled with the help of her nephew Prince SHŌTOKU.

Suiko's reign saw the establishment of the twelve cap ranks (KAN'I JŪNIKAI), the promulgation of the SEVENTEEN-ARTICLE CONSTITUTION, the beginning of diplomatic contact with the Sui dynasty of China (see SUI AND TANG [T'ANG] CHINA, EMBASSIES TO), the compilation of the national histories TENNŌKI AND KOKKI, the building of the HŌRYŪJI and other temples, and a general flowering of Buddhist arts.

suiren → water lily

suisen 水仙

(narcissus). *Narcissus tazetta* var. *chinensis.* A perennial plant of the family Amaryllidaceae. Native to North Africa and the Mediterranean coast, the narcissus was brought from China to Japan at the end of the Heian period (794–1185). It is cultivated as a garden plant and also grows wild in coastal regions. The bulb produces an erect stem of 20–40 centimeters (7.9–15.8 in), and four to six linear leaves grow from its base. The white or yellow fragrant flowers bloom from December to March and are extremely cold-resistant. There are about 30 principal species. The *suisen* is often used as a New Year's decoration.

Sui shu 隋書

(J: *Zuisho*). History of the Sui dynasty (589–618) of China, compiled in the mid-7th century. Its chapter "Records of the Eastern Barbarians" ("Dongyi zhuan" or "Tung-i chuan"; J: "Tōiden") contains a section on "the country of Wo" (J: Wakoku; see WA), or Japan, which is called in Japanese "Tōiden Wakoku no jō" or "Zuisho wakokuden." Much of the general information on Japan in this section is taken from such earlier Chinese histories as *Hou Han shu* (History of the Later Han Dynasty), *Wei lüe* (*Wei lüeh;* Summary of the Wei Dynasty), the WEI ZHI

(*Wei chih;* Records of the Wei Dynasty) section of *Sanguo zhi* (*San-kuo chih;* History of the Three Kingdoms), and *Song shu* (*Sung shu;* History of the [Liu-] Song Dynasty [420–479]). *Sui shu* contains valuable records of Sino-Japanese relations in the late 6th–early 7th centuries and objective descriptions of Japan absent from early Japanese chronicles.

Suita 吹田[市]

City in central Ōsaka Prefecture, central Honshū. A residential suburb of Ōsaka, Suita also has many industrial plants. Located in its northern section are Kansai University and SENRI NEW TOWN. East of Senri New Town is the Expo '70 Commemoration Park. Pop: 345,206.

Suita Incident 吹田事件

(Suita Jiken). A disturbance of 24–25 June 1952 by leftist groups in the city of Suita, near the American military base in Itami, Ōsaka Prefecture. On 24 June about 900 demonstrators gathered at the city of Toyonaka to protest the presence of American military bases and the continuation of the Korean War. After the rally, several hundred demonstrators went on to Suita Station, throwing stones and Molotov cocktails at police stations and patrol cars. Forty-two policemen and 12 demonstrators were injured. Of 102 tried, 46 were found guilty in 1968 under the Riot Law. The incident was ultimately regarded as a result of the decision by the mainstream faction of the JAPAN COMMUNIST PARTY to resort to violence.

Suiyuan Incident 綏遠事件

(J: Suien Jiken). Military excursion into Suiyuan Province, Inner Mongolia, in November 1936 by Inner Mongolian troops, accompanied by advisers from the Japanese GUANDONG (KWANTUNG) ARMY. Seeking to create a buffer zone between MANCHUKUO (the Japanese-controlled puppet state in Manchuria) and China, the Japanese government had earlier called for the neutralization of five provinces of North China, including Suiyuan. The Guandong Army had also fostered an anti-Chinese, Inner Mongolian separatist movement. Inner Mongolian troops based in Qahar (Chahar) Province attacked Chinese troops in eastern Suiyuan but were routed within a week. The Guandong Army sent fighter planes to support the Inner Mongolians, and the Nationalist Chinese sent reinforcements north. The Tōkyō government, embarrassed by the independent action taken by the field army, issued an official statement denying that Japanese troops had been involved in the fighting. The incident further stimulated the growth of Chinese nationalism and resistance.

Sujin, Emperor 崇神天皇

(Sujin Tennō). The legendary 10th sovereign (*tennō*) in the traditional count (which includes several other legendary emperors). In the chronicle NIHON SHOKI (720) he is said to have reigned 97 BC–30 BC, an implausibly early date. The KOJIKI (712) and *Nihon shoki* accounts of his reign have a decidedly legendary cast. Sujin reputedly sent the so-called generals of the four quarters (*shidō shōgun,* referring to four regions of Japan still known as San'yōdō, San'indō, Hokurikudō, and Tōkaidō) to extend imperial authority throughout the country. He is credited with having developed agriculture through the construction of ponds and irrigation canals and to have improved court

finances by levying taxes called *yuhazu no mitsugi* (edible birds and animals, provided by men) and *tanasue no mitsugi* (woven goods, provided by women). Sujin was known by the laudatory name Hatsukunishirasu Sumeramikoto, which in part suggests "being first" in ruling the country. The same name is traditionally ascribed to the putative first emperor, JIMMU, and some scholars have concluded that the chronicles' accounts of an Emperor Jimmu of doubtful historicity are projections of an Emperor Sujin who did exist.

Sukagawa 須賀川[市]

City in central Fukushima Prefecture, northern Honshū. Situated on the river ABUKUMAGAWA, Sukagawa developed as a market and post-station town on the highway Ōshū Kaidō during the Edo period (1600–1868). It has electrical and precision machinery plants. Pop: 60,695.

Sukarno スカルノ

(1901–70). Indonesian nationalist leader and statesman. Born in Surabaya, he became a prominent opponent of colonial rule in the Dutch East Indies even before his graduation from Bandung Technological Institute in 1925. From February 1934 to March 1942 he was exiled to the islands of Flores and Bengkulu. Forced to collaborate with Japanese occupation authorities during World War II, he held a series of leading positions in Japanese-sponsored bodies but remained committed to the goal of Indonesian independence. Two days after the Japanese surrender in 1945, he proclaimed Indonesia's independence, finally winning the formal transfer of sovereignty from the Dutch in 1949. He served as president of Indonesia until 1967, becoming a major spokesman for the nonaligned nations. Toward the end of his presidency he married Nemoto Naoko (b 1940), a Japanese woman whom he had met during a visit to Tōkyō. See also INDONESIA AND JAPAN.

Sukayu Hot Spring 酸ケ湯温泉

(Sukayu Onsen). Located in the Hakkōdasan Mountains in the southern part of the city of Aomori, central Aomori Prefecture, northern Honshū. This sulfur spring, located within Towada-Hachimantai National Park, has been designated a National Health Resort Hot Spring. Water temperature: 48°–60°C (118°–140°F).

sukegō 助郷

Labor service requisitioned by the Tokugawa shogunate (1603–1867) from peasants living near post stations. Villages supplying this corvée labor were also called *sukegō.* The shogunate had established *shukueki* or post stations along the main highways (GOKAIDŌ),

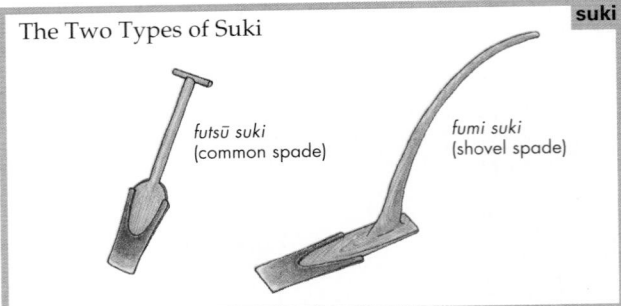

The Two Types of Suki

suki

futsū suki
(common spade)

fumi suki
(shovel spade)

holding post station officials responsible for providing labor, horses, and other supplies. With the increase in travel in the 17th century, especially under the SANKIN KŌTAI system, under which *daimyō* spent alternate years in Edo (now Tōkyō), it became necessary to requisition supplementary labor. At first temporary, in time the levying of *sukegō* became permanent. In some cases substitution of money payment for labor was accepted; the money was used to hire homeless drifters (KUMOSUKE) as porters. An enormous burden on peasants, especially during the harvest season, *sukegō* frequently caused them to rebel and was abolished soon after the MEIJI RESTORATION (1868).

Sukeroku yukari no Edo-zakura
助六由縁江戸桜

KABUKI play; one of the celebrated kabuki numbers known as the KABUKI JŪHACHIBAN. Popularly called *Sukeroku*, it is a *jidai-mono* (historical play) by Tsuuchi Han'emon (dates unknown) and was first performed in 1713. *Sukeroku* is named after the hero of the play, a chivalrous commoner who bests a vicious warrior for a courtesan's favors. In the process he recovers for his lord an heirloom sword stolen by the villain; it is revealed at the end of the play that he is actually a *samurai* disguised as a commoner to facilitate the search. The action takes place in the Yoshiwara pleasure quarters. Sukeroku makes his entrance when the villain, rebuffed by a courtesan, threatens to become violent. It is one of the great entrances in kabuki. Three-quarters of the way along the ramp, he stops, turns to the audience, and delivers a monologue introducing himself. In early kabuki, all the main actors did this, but this is the only example that has survived into modern times.

sukiyaki A young man reads while savoring *gyūnabe*, or "beef pot"—thought to be a precursor of *sukiyaki*—in this illustration from a 19th-century book.

suki
鋤

Traditional Japanese spade consisting of a hollowed-out blade or scoop attached to a handle. Historically, its use precedes that of the hoe (KUWA) in ancient Japan. Examples of spade-shaped *suki* dating back to the Yayoi period (ca 300 BC–ca AD 300) have been unearthed at the KARAKO SITE in Nara Prefecture. These consist of a blade extending more or less straight out from a wooden handle. Japanese spades are of two types: the "common spade" (*futsū suki*) and the "shovel spade" (*fumi suki*). The former consists of a blade attached to the handle at an angle of nearly 180 degrees and is used by holding it in front of the body and digging into the soil while walking backwards. The latter has a blade fixed to a long handle at more or less 150 degrees and is pushed into the ground with the foot. Both types are common in Japanese farming communities.

sukiyaki
鋤焼き

Thinly sliced beef, vegetables, *tōfu*, and other ingredients cooked at the table in a large skillet or iron pot in a broth of soy sauce, *mirin* (sweet *sake*), and sugar.

Although meat dishes such as *sukiyaki* are now popular among the Japanese, traditional Buddhist injunctions against the consumption of the flesh of four-legged animals effectively prevented the widespread eating of meat in Japan for much of its history. The word *sukiyaki* first appears in documents from the early 19th century as the name of a dish in which goose, duck, or venison was broiled on top of a spade (*suki*) and basted with *tamari* (a thick soy sauce). However, *sukiyaki* as it is known today was created during the Meiji period (1868–1912), after Western influence helped make the consumption of beef and other types of meat common among large segments of the Japanese population. "Western-style" restaurants began by serving a dish of thinly sliced beef with chopped scallions. Flavoring the meat with soy sauce, *mirin*, and sugar soon became popular.

Today, the most typical recipe for *sukiyaki*, among many regional and personal variations, calls for beef (usually a high-quality, well-marbled variety), spring onions (*negi*), a type of thin, gelatinous noodle known as *shirataki*, *tōfu*, chrysanthemum leaves (*shungiku*), and a type of mushroom (*shiitake*). After first browning the sliced beef, the soy-sauce-based broth and other ingredients are added, and the resulting stewlike mixture is brought to a boil. The cooked meat is dipped in beaten raw egg before eating. In the Kantō (Tōkyō area) version of *sukiyaki*, the meat and vegetables are cooked together, while in the Kansai (Kyōto–Ōsaka–Kōbe area) variety they are cooked separately. There are also such variations as *uosuki*, in which fish, rather than beef, is used, and *udonsuki*, in which *udon* noodles are added. ☎ 1472–1473

sukiya-zukuri
数寄屋造り

Style of residential architecture. *Suki* refers to the enjoyment of the elegantly performed TEA CEREMONY; *sukiya* denotes a building in which the tea ceremony was performed. *Sukiya-zukuri* is a style incorporating features characteristic of the *sukiya*.

The Azuchi-Momoyama period (1568–1600) saw the perfection of not only the *sukiya* as a distinctive style but also the SHOIN-ZUKURI as a contrasting style of residence of the warrior class. The *sukiya* comprised a

small space, simple and austere. The *shoin-zukuri* was meant for a large, magnificent reception area, the setting for the pomp and ceremony of the feudal system. In the fusion of the two styles, the delicate features of the *sukiya* were introduced into *shoin-zukuri*, and the result was *sukiya-zukuri*. During the Edo period (1600–1868) *sukiya-zukuri* became popular among the townspeople, and the majority of houses came to be built in this style.

Sukiya-zukuri was first used in the private areas of residences and in villas. An example of the former is the Kuro Shoin, a building at the temple NISHI HONGANJI in Kyōto. As *sukiya-zukuri* this is still relatively formal. An example of the latter is KATSURA DETACHED PALACE. In particular, the Koshoin, the Chūshoin, and the Shinshoin there can be considered representative works of *sukiya-zukuri*. The beauty of *sukiya-zukuri* comes from its delicate sensibility, its slender wood elements, the use of natural materials, and the elimination of ornament.

Sukumo
宿毛[市]

City in western Kōchi Prefecture, Shikoku. It developed in the Edo period (1600–1868) as a castle town. Agricultural products are rice, *igusa* (for *tatami* mats), and citrus fruits. Marine products are. sardines, yellowtail, cultured pearls, and coral. Pop: 25,828.

Sukumo Bay
宿毛湾

(Sukumo Wan). Inlet of the Pacific Ocean on the coast of southern Ehime and southwestern Kōchi prefectures, Shikoku. Between the Nishiumi and the Ōtsuki peninsulas. Site of the city of Sukumo. The principal activities here are pearl culture and the cultivation of oysters and yellowtail. The bay is part of the Ashizuri-Uwakai National Park.

Suku site
須玖遺跡

(Suku *iseki*). One of several archaeological sites of the Yayoi period (ca 300 BC–ca AD 300) located on some low hills projecting out into the Fukuoka Plain in the Suku section of the city of Kasuga, Fukuoka Prefecture. The site consists mainly of a cemetery where a burial jar, containing more than 30 Former Han dynasty (206 BC–AD 8) Chinese BRONZE MIRRORS, bronze daggers and spearheads, and glass *magatama* (see BEADS, ANCIENT), was discovered in 1899. Excavations in 1929 and 1962 unearthed more than 50 additional jar burials. This site is thought to be the burial place of the rulers of the ancient country of NAKOKU.

Suma
須磨

District in the western part of the city of KŌBE, Hyōgo Prefecture, western Honshū. Its scenic coastline facing ŌSAKA BAY has been famous since ancient times for its pine trees and white sandy beaches. Suma is mentioned in the 8th-century poetry anthology *Man'yōshū* and is the setting for a chapter in the *Genji monogatari* (Tale of Genji). It was a battlefield during the Taira-Minamoto War (1180–85) and a resort area in the early modern period.

Suma Aqualife Park
須磨海浜水族園

(Suma Kaihin Suizokuen). A municipal aquarium in the city of Kōbe, Hyōgo Prefecture; opened in 1957. The aquarium features a specially constructed tank with a capacity of 1,200 metric tons (1,320 short tons) that mechanically simulates the ocean's natural wave action. The tank is the first aquarium display tank of its kind in the world.

Sumatakyō 寸又峡

Gorge of the river Sumatagawa, a tributary of the Ōigawa, in northwestern Shizuoka Prefecture, central Honshū. Countless waterfalls drop from sheer cliffs, and the surrounding mountains are covered with virgin forest. Length: 20 km (12.4 mi).

Sumidagawa 隅田川

River in Tōkyō, central Honshū; the lower reaches of the ARAKAWA. It originates in the Kantō Mountains and flows through the eastern part of Tōkyō Prefecture into Tōkyō Bay. It flows north to south through Tōkyō's SHITAMACHI and is connected with a network of canals. Wholesale stores, warehouses, and industrial plants are located along the river. The lower reaches are called Asakusagawa or Ōkawa. Industrial pollution of the water has been decreased by strong measures to control effluents. Length: 23.5 km (14.6 mi).

Sumidagawa 隅田川

NŌ play by KANZE MOTOMASA. It is classified as a *yobamme-mono* ("part-four play"). A madwoman (the *shite* or main character) in search of her lost child travels the great distance from Kyōto to the banks of the Sumidagawa (a river flowing through the eastern part of what is now Tōkyō). The boatman (the *waki* or subordinate character) who ferries her across the river tells her that her beloved child is dead. She also learns from him that the people gathered before a burial mound on the opposite shore are chanting a Buddhist prayer on behalf of her child, who had been forsaken by slave dealers. The madwoman rushes into the group and, striking a gong, begins to chant the prayer herself. The ghost of her child emerges from behind the burial mound but recedes with the light of dawn; only the grass-covered mound remains.

Sumida Ward 墨田区

(Sumida Ku). One of the 23 wards of Tōkyō. On the east bank of the river Sumidagawa. A farming area until the end of the Edo period (1600–1868), the area developed into an industrial district with numerous plants manufacturing beer, timepieces, and cosmetics. The KOKUGIKAN, a *sumō* wrestling stadium, is also located here. Pop: 222,944.

sumi-e →ink painting

Sumii Sue 住井すゑ

(1902–). Novelist. Real name Inuta Sue. Born in Nara Prefecture. Together with her husband, Inuta Shigeru (1891–1957), she was a leader in the agrarian literary movement. Her moving epic novel *Hashi no nai kawa* (1961–73; tr *The River with No Bridge*, 1990), the story of a BURAKUMIN youth who comes of age in the midst of a prejudiced world and goes on to become a leader in the *burakumin* liberation movement, has long been a best seller in Japan. Sumii is also the author of *Yoake asaake* (1954, Dawn, Daybreak).

suminagashi 墨流し

("ink-flow"). Design technique used to produce marbled patterns in handmade paper, pottery, and hand-dyed textiles. With paper and textiles, swirling designs are created by adding drops of ink to a pan of oily water. The surface of the water is gently disturbed by blowing or touching it lightly with the tip of a brush; the ink, prevented by the oil from diffusing, forms delicate patterns following the natural surface movements of the water. The paper or cloth is then applied to the surface and the pattern is absorbed. In ceramics, an unfired leather-hard piece is coated with slip (liquid clay), followed by a few drops of slip in a contrasting color. The two are swirled together by moving the piece through several angles until the desired marbled effect is achieved. The piece is then fired. In the Edo period (1600–1868) indigo and crimson inks were added to the previous gray-black repertoire. *Suminagashi* paper is still being made in Imadate, Fukui Prefecture.

Suminokura Ryōi 角倉了以

(1554–1614). Wealthy merchant and overseas trader. Born in Kyōto as Yoshida Mitsuyoshi, of a family of physicians and moneylenders (DOSŌ). Suminokura was the name his family had adopted for business purposes. In the 1590s he obtained from TOYOTOMI HIDEYOSHI an official license (SHUINJŌ; see also VERMILION SEAL SHIP TRADE) to engage in overseas commerce, and he began sending trade ships to Annam and Tonkin (both now part of Vietnam). The ships, known as *suminokurasen*, brought in huge profits for Ryōi and his son Soan (1571–1632) before foreign trade was ended under the NATIONAL SECLUSION policy in 1635. Ryōi also devoted himself to opening the rivers Ōigawa, Fujikawa, Kamogawa, and Takasegawa to navigation.

sumire →violets

Sumishō Lease Co, Ltd
住商リース[株]

(Sumishō Rīsu). Comprehensive leasing company; a member of the Sumitomo group. Incorporated in 1968. The company has 21 domestic offices and overseas subsidiaries in Hong Kong, Singapore, and the United States. Sales for the fiscal year ending March 1991 totaled ¥266.2 billion (US $1.9 billion), and capitalization stood at ¥7.1 billion (US $51.7 million) in the same year. Headquarters are in Tōkyō and Ōsaka.

Sumitomo 住友

Merchant house founded in the early 17th century; major business combine (ZAIBATSU) of the pre–World War II era; enterprise grouping (KEIRETSU) of the postwar period. The House of Sumitomo was founded by Sumitomo Masatomo (1585–1652). The 1690 acquisition of the Besshi Copper Mine in Shikoku was of great importance to the Sumitomo House. Sumitomo became the official purveyor of copper to the Tokugawa shogunate and a major exporter of copper. Sumitomo also became the chartered agent (GOYŌ SHŌNIN) for the three senior branches of the Tokugawa family, managing their annual tax receipts.

During the Meiji period (1868–1912) Sumitomo branched out into copper rolling, steel manufacture, and other fields. In 1921 the firm was reorganized as Sumitomo, Ltd (Sumitomo Gōshi Kaisha), a limited partnership that served mainly as a holding company for the joint-stock subsidiaries. During the 1920s and 1930s Sumitomo expanded into machinery and electricity, becoming the third most important *zaibatsu*, with diverse business interests centered in a top holding company controlled by the House of Sumitomo.

Sumitomo was much more centralized than other prewar business combines. Unlike the families controlling other combines, the Sumitomo remained a single house with its wealth concentrated accordingly. The house rules of the Sumitomo prescribed primogeniture at its most extreme. In 1937 the head of the House of Sumitomo, the 16th in line from the founder, held over 90 percent of the shares.

Because of wartime expansion, the number of companies controlled by the Sumitomo holding company increased from 40 firms in 1941 to 135 firms in 1946. As a result of the ZAIBATSU DISSOLUTION directed by the Allied Occupation, the holding company was dissolved in February 1948.

In the 1950s the Sumitomo group was reconstituted in *keiretsu* form, and the role of the family was greatly diminished. A presidents' club, The White Waters Club (Hakusui Kai), now serves as a consultative forum for the grouping but has no power to direct overall business activities. The Sumitomo group today comprises some 80 firms, 21 of which are represented in the presidents' club. See also CORPORATE HISTORY.

Sumitomo Bakelite Co, Ltd
住友ベークライト[株]

(Sumitomo Bēkuraito). Firm engaged in the manufacture of plastics. Incorporated in

Continued on page 1474►

sukiya-zukuri The first room (*ichi no ma*) of the Kuro Shoin residential building, a part of the temple complex Nishi Honganji in Kyōto, is an example of the restrained elegance of this architectural style. Completed 1657. National Treasure.

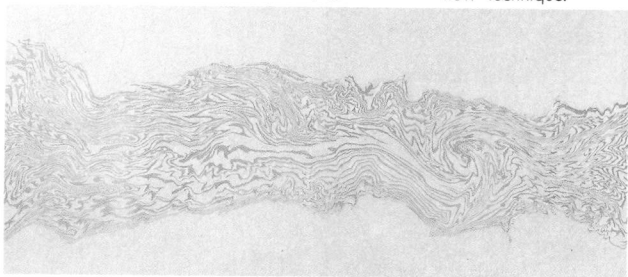

suminagashi Japanese paper decorated by use of the "ink-flow" technique.

Into the Pot: Sukiyaki and Shabushabu

Sukiyaki and *shabushabu* are two of the most popular varieties of a Japanese style of cooking known as *nabemono* ("one-pot dishes"). Sukiyaki, a savory, stew-like blend of beef and vegetables, is known by many outside Japan. Shabushabu is a lighter dish in which paper-thin slices of beef are cooked by being dipped in a pot of boiling stock. This style of cooking allows diners to cook what they like from among a variety of ingredients, while the communal dipping of chopsticks into one pot promotes an atmosphere of warmth and conviviality. It's easy—prepare the ingredients, set the pot on the table, and invite your family and friends to take part in communal dining, Japanese-style.

Yamada Katsumi

SUKIYAKI

Sukiyaki is usually cooked in a cast-iron pan on a portable gas ring, but an electric skillet will do as a substitute.

Ingredients (for 4 servings)

600 g (1¼ lbs) well-marbled beef, in bacon-thin slices
1 cake *tōfu*, drained and cut into 6 cubes
6 Welsh onions, sliced into 4-cm (1½-in) lengths (if unavailable, substitute leeks)
8 fresh *shiitake* mushrooms, stems removed and caps scored (see Helpful Hints)
2 bunches *shungiku* (chrysanthemum leaves), washed and trimmed
2 packets *shirataki* (gelatinous filaments made from a processed starch called *konnyaku*)
4 eggs
40 g (1⅓ oz) beef suet
1 cup soy sauce
1 cup *mirin* (sweet cooking *sake*)
2–3 Tbsp sugar

Preliminary Steps

1 Wash and prepare all vegetables; arrange on a platter. To prepare *shirataki*, boil for 1 to 2 minutes, drain, and cut into 10-cm (4-in) lengths.
2 Prepare the cooking sauce, or *warishita*, by heating soy sauce, *mirin*, and sugar in a pan until the sugar dissolves. Bring to a boil; simmer for a few seconds. Transfer to a spouted cup or bowl.
3 Set each diner's place with a dipping bowl containing 1 beaten raw egg.

Cooking Steps

1 Melt suet in pan over medium heat until bottom of pan is well greased.

2 Add *shirataki*, Welsh onions, and *shiitake*; fry lightly for 1 to 2 minutes.

3 Add beef, spreading the slices open to ensure even cooking. Add *tōfu*.

4 Pour in enough cooking sauce to just cover bottom of pan. (Ingredients should not swim in the sauce.) Cook on high heat for a few minutes.

5 Reduce heat and add *shungiku*; cook for 1 to 2 minutes. Sukiyaki should now be ready to eat.

6 Invite diners to serve themselves. To eat, dip cooked meat and vegetables lightly into beaten raw egg. There is no other garnish.

Helpful Hints

If presliced beef is unavailable, freeze a cut of well-marbled sirloin; slice it as it thaws.

To create a pleasing appearance and release the flavor of the *shiitake*, make notches across the caps as shown.

Other ingredients that may be used include (clockwise from top): rice cakes (*mochi*), *udon* noodles (on small plate), bok choy (*chingensai*), sliced potatoes, white mushrooms, bean sprouts.

SHABUSHABU

A brass Mongolian hot pot is the classic utensil for shabushabu, but you can use any flameproof casserole placed over a tabletop heating unit.

Ingredients (for 4 servings)

600 g (1¼ lbs) well-marbled beef, sliced paper-thin
1 bunch *enoki* mushrooms, stems trimmed
4–6 leaves Chinese cabbage
10-cm (4-in) square of *kombu* (giant kelp)
Bottled *goma-dare* (sesame dipping sauce)

Bottled *ponzu* (citrus–soy sauce dressing)
Bottled *rāyu* (cayenne-flavored sesame oil)
Chives, finely chopped
Salt and pepper
Prepare as for sukiyaki: 1 cake *tōfu*, 2 packets *shirataki*, 1 bunch *shungiku*, 6 Welsh onions, 8 *shiitake* mushrooms.

Preliminary Steps

1 For easier handling, arrange beef slices on a large platter as shown.
2 Prepare all other ingredients; arrange on another platter.
3 Set out dipping sauces in individual bowls.
4 Prepare stock. Fill ⅔ of hot pot or casserole with water. Wipe *kombu* with damp cloth; add to pot and turn on heat. Just before water starts to boil, remove *kombu*.

Cooking Steps

1 Each diner picks up a slice of beef with chopsticks and dips it into the boiling stock, swishing from side to side for only a few seconds. The beef is done when the center is pink.

2 Diners dip the cooked beef in the *goma-dare*. To give the sauce more flavor, finely chopped chives or *rāyu* may be added.

3 Use a ladle to periodically skim off the film that develops on the surface of the broth.

4 After diners have had a few servings of beef, add some of the *tōfu* pieces, *shirataki*, and vegetables to the broth, cooking for 1 or 2 minutes.

5 Diners dip these ingredients in the tangy *ponzu* sauce. Chives can be added to the sauce as desired.

6 Keep alternating between beef slices and other ingredients. When finished, ladle remaining broth into cups. For each serving, add a scant teaspoon of salt and a dash of pepper to make a delicious soup. Garnish with chives.

Other Suggestions

1 After finishing the beef and vegetables, skim off any remaining film and add *udon* noodles.

2 Put noodles into individual cups filled with shabushabu broth. Diners can add salt and pepper to taste and *zāsai* (Chinese pickles) if desired.

Experiment with a variety of condiments (clockwise from top right): *rāyu*, *ponzu*, minced garlic, chopped chives, grated *daikon* radish with red pepper, soy sauce with garlic, *goma-dare*.

1932. It supplies finished and semifinished products to the electronics, telecommunications, packaging, transportation, and medical industries. It has seven affiliated companies worldwide. It has a joint-venture operation in Japan with the Hooker Chemical Corporation. Annual sales in 1991 totaled ¥152.8 billion (US $1.1 billion), and capitalization stood at ¥23.6 billion (US $172.0 million). Headquarters are in Tōkyō.

Sumitomo Bank, Ltd　[株]住友銀行

(Sumitomo Ginkō). One of the largest city banks in Japan and a central member of the SUMITOMO group. SUMITOMO KICHIZAEMON VII established the bank in 1895, although its history can be traced back to a money-changing business founded by Izumiya Rihei in 1743. Until the end of World War II, it was the principal financial organ of the Sumitomo ZAIBATSU. It absorbed a great number of smaller local banks to become one of Japan's major banks. After the war, it concentrated its efforts on capturing the deposits of the general public. Sumitomo Bank was the first private bank in Japan to expand its business abroad, establishing branches in San Francisco and Hawaii in 1916. In 1925 it established the Sumitomo Bank of California, and in 1958 it set up a subsidiary in Brazil. It currently has a total of over 300 branches, including 19 overseas. In March 1991 total assets were ¥61.4 trillion (US $447.5 billion), total deposits stood at ¥43.6 trillion (US $317.8 billion), and capitalization was ¥502.1 billion (US $3.7 billion). Headquarters are in Ōsaka.

Sumitomo Cement Co, Ltd
住友セメント[株]

(Sumitomo Semento). Cement company affiliated with the SUMITOMO group. Incorporated in 1907 under the name of Iwaki Cement Co, Ltd, in Fukushima Prefecture. The Iwaki company joined the Sumitomo group in 1963. Sales for the fiscal year ending March 1991 totaled ¥147.3 billion (US $1.1 billion), and capitalization stood at ¥33.3 billion (US $242.7 million). Headquarters are in Tōkyō.

Sumitomo Chemical Co, Ltd
住友化学工業[株]

(Sumitomo Kagaku Kōgyō). Chemical company producing a wide range of petrochemical and fine chemical products; one of the mainstays of the SUMITOMO group. Its forerunner was the Sumitomo Fertilizer Manufacturing Co, incorporated in 1925. It entered the petrochemical field in the late 1950s and has diversified its operations into basic chemicals, fine chemicals, agricultural chemicals, pharmaceuticals, aluminum-related products, and other goods. Sumitomo Chemical has joint-venture production affiliates in the United States, Singapore, and Brazil. Sales for the fiscal year ending December 1990 totaled ¥716.8 billion (US $5.4 billion). The company was capitalized at ¥81.5 billion (US $610.3 million) in the same year. Headquarters are in Ōsaka and Tōkyō.

Sumitomo Construction Co, Ltd
住友建設[株]

(Sumitomo Kensetsu). Comprehensive construction company affiliated with the SUMITOMO group. Incorporated in 1950. It has undertaken construction projects in Iraq, Kenya, Indonesia, Singapore, Guam, the United States, and Thailand and is also en-gaged in the real estate business. The company receives many orders from government offices. Sales for the fiscal year ending March 1991 totaled ¥364.7 billion (US $2.7 billion), and the company was capitalized at ¥14.5 billion (US $105.7 million). Headquarters are in Tōkyō.

Sumitomo Corporation　住友商事[株]

(Sumitomo Shōji). One of Japan's largest GENERAL TRADING COMPANIES (sōgō shosha) and a leading member of the Sumitomo group. The company, incorporated in 1919, is a global trader and distributor of a diverse range of commodities, industrial goods, and consumer goods. Its trading operations center on metals (especially iron and steel), machinery, chemicals, and fuels. The company is noted for its extensive domestic distribution channels and has the largest real-estate portfolio of any general trading company. One of Japan's leading precious metals traders, Sumitomo Corporation is active as an investor in diverse businesses that complement its trading and distribution operations. It also engages in substantial offshore-trading activities.

For the fiscal year ending March 1991, gross trading volume was ¥19.2 trillion (US $140.0 billion). Of this, the domestic market, including imports, accounted for 61.1 percent; exports, 14.2 percent; and offshore business, 24.7 percent. The company was capitalized at ¥170.0 billion (US $1.2 billion) in the same year. Headquarters are in Tōkyō and Ōsaka.

Sumitomo Electric Industries, Ltd
住友電気工業[株]

(Sumitomo Denki Kōgyō). Manufacturer of electric wire and cable. Established in 1897, it is one of the major enterprises in the SUMITOMO group. The company has diversified into such product lines as special steel wires, sintered alloy products, disk brakes, rubber and plastic products for industrial use, traffic and vehicle control systems, electronics materials, and fiber-optic communication systems. It has 30 overseas subsidiaries in 13 countries, covering North and South America, Asia, and Europe. Sales for the fiscal year ending March 1991 totaled ¥781.8 billion (US $5.7 billion); capitalization was ¥65.3 billion (US $475.9 million) in the same year. Headquarters are in Ōsaka and Tōkyō.

Sumitomo Forestry Co, Ltd
住友林業[株]

(Sumitomo Ringyō). Forestry company engaged in a wide range of activities including sales of building materials, timber wholesaling, construction and sales of residential houses, and forest management. A member of the SUMITOMO group; incorporated in 1948. The company owns extensive forests, centering in the Shikoku region and including large stands of 300-year-old high-quality Japanese cypresses and cedar trees. Overseas offices are located in Seattle, Vancouver, Hong Kong, Singapore, Jakarta, Sandakan (Malaysia), and New Zealand. Sales for the fiscal year ending March 1991 totaled ¥532.2 billion (US $3.9 billion). Capitalization in the same year was ¥17.9 billion (US $130.5 million). Headquarters are in Tōkyō and Ōsaka.

Sumitomo Heavy Industries, Ltd
住友重機械工業[株]

(Sumitomo Jūkikai Kōgyō). Company engaged in the manufacture of industrial machinery and ships. Established in 1969 through the merger of the Sumitomo Machinery Industries Co and Uraga Heavy Industries Co. A member of the SUMITOMO group, it is the largest manufacturer of reduction gears in Japan and also produces steelmaking machinery, presses, and haulage machinery. Overseas it has nine affiliates, four offices, and four companies to which it provides technical assistance. The company is expanding its mass-production machinery department. Sales for the fiscal year ending March 1991 totaled ¥274.3 billion (US $2.0 billion), with capitalization standing at ¥30.9 billion (US $225.2 million) in the same year. Headquarters are in Tōkyō.

Sumitomo Kichizaemon
住友吉左衛門

Name adopted by successive heads of the SUMITOMO merchant family, 17th–20th centuries. The first Kichizaemon (real name Sumitomo Tomonobu; 1647–1706) was the third head of the family and fifth son of Sumitomo Tomomochi, the second head. In 1690 his son Tomoyoshi, or Kichizaemon II (1670–1719), discovered rich copper deposits at Besshi (in what is now Ehime Prefecture), which he exploited. He diversified into the money-changing, minting, and lumbering businesses, laying the foundation for SUMITOMO CORPORATION (see ZAIBATSU).

Sumitomo Life Insurance Co
住友生命保険[相]

(Sumitomo Seimei Hoken). One of the three largest life insurance companies in Japan and a member of the SUMITOMO group. Founded in 1907, it became a mutual company in 1947. The company operates 121 branch offices in Japan. Sumitomo Life owns 16 overseas subsidiaries and 7 overseas representative offices. It has business tie-ups in the international group life insurance business with 14 life insurance companies in 13 countries. Total assets for the fiscal year ending March 1991 reached ¥16.5 trillion (US $120.3 billion). The company received premiums totaling ¥3.2 trillion (US $23.3 billion) in the same year. Headquarters are in Ōsaka.

Sumitomo Light Metal Industries, Ltd
住友軽金属工業[株]

(Sumitomo Keikinzoku Kōgyō). Nonferrous metal company principally producing rolled aluminum products. It also manufactures rolled copper products. A member of the SUMITOMO group, the company traces its roots to the pre–World War II aluminum operations of the Sumitomo ZAIBATSU, centered on SUMITOMO METAL INDUSTRIES, LTD. When it became independent in 1959, it began producing rolled aluminum products, and it continued to expand the scale of its rolling operations. It has also moved into the fields of aluminum foil and substrates for magnetic disks. Sales for the fiscal year ending March 1991 totaled ¥229.6 billion (US $1.7 billion), and capitalization stood at ¥13.4 billion (US $97.7 million). Headquarters are in Tōkyō.

Sumitomo Marine & Fire Insurance Co, Ltd　住友海上火災保険[株]

(Sumitomo Kaijō Kasai Hoken). Nonlife insurance company belonging to the SUMITOMO group. Incorporated in 1944. The company has emphasized fire and automobile insurance. It is a pioneer in the marketing of long-term accident insurance to women. It also has an international sales network with 28 overseas representative offices worldwide, mainly in the United States, Canada, Asia, and Europe. Total assets for the fiscal year ending March 1991 reached ¥2.1 trillion (US $15.3 billion), and capitalization was ¥56.7 billion (US $413.3 million). Net income from premiums for the same year was ¥420.7 billion (US $3.1 billion). Headquarters are in Tōkyō.

Sumitomo Metal Industries, Ltd
住友金属工業[株]

(Sumitomo Kinzoku Kōgyō). Steel maker; member of the SUMITOMO group. With origins dating back to 1590, when a forerunner of the Sumitomo family started the refining of copper in Kyōto, the company has the longest history of any major Japanese enterprise. The company now has affiliates and offices in many countries, including the United States. For the fiscal year ending March 1991, sales totaled ¥1.2 trillion (US $8.7 billion), and capitalization stood at ¥204.3 billion (US $1.5 billion). Products comprised steel plates (43 percent of sales) and steel pipes (25 percent), plus wires, forgings, and other products. Exports accounted for 22 percent of sales. Headquarters are in Ōsaka.

Sumitomo Metal Mining Co, Ltd
住友金属鉱山[株]

(Sumitomo Kinzoku Kōzan). Producer of nonferrous metals. The company is engaged in mining, smelting, and processing of metals such as gold, copper, nickel, and zinc. It has also diversified into metal processing, engineering, and the manufacture of electronic parts. Incorporated in 1950, the company traces its history to 1590, when a forerunner of the Sumitomo family began a copper smelting and manufacturing business in Kyōto. In 1985 the company commenced operation of the Hishikari Gold Mine. It is also engaged in the development of fine chemicals and magnetic materials. Sales for the fiscal year ending March 1991 totaled ¥505.6 billion (US $3.7 billion). The company was capitalized at ¥65.3 billion (US $475.9 million) in the same year. Headquarters are in Tōkyō.

Sumitomo Pharmaceuticals Co, Ltd
住友製薬[株]

(Sumitomo Seiyaku). Manufacturer of pharmaceuticals, food additives, veterinary drugs, and medical equipment. Incorporated in 1984. A member of the SUMITOMO group. The company is known for its work in biotechnology and chemical synthesis. Sales for the fiscal year ending December 1990 totaled ¥180.4 billion (US $1.4 billion), and capitalization stood at ¥8.0 billion (US $59.9 million). Headquarters are in Ōsaka.

Sumitomo Realty & Development Co, Ltd
住友不動産[株]

(Sumitomo Fudōsan). Real estate company; member of the Sumitomo group. Incorporated in 1949. It specializes in development, leasing, and sale of commercial buildings, apartments, and houses. The company started overseas activities in 1963 when building development projects in Hong Kong and is expanding into Thailand, California, Hawaii, and New York. It is also building hotels in Sydney. Sales for the fiscal year ending March 1991 totaled ¥187.2 billion (US $1.4 billion), and capitalization was ¥86.7 billion (US $631.9 million). Headquarters are in Tōkyō.

Sumitomo Rubber Industries, Ltd
住友ゴム工業[株]

(Sumitomo Gomu Kōgyō). Company engaged in the manufacture and sale of auto-

mobile, motorcycle, and other types of tires; sporting goods such as golf and tennis balls; and allied goods such as flooring and marine materials. Incorporated in 1917. Its products are known abroad under the brand names Dunlop and Sumitomo. The company is a member of the SUMITOMO group. Its annual sales totaled ¥244.8 billion (US $1.8 billion) in December 1990; it was capitalized at ¥15.4 billion (US $115.3 million) in the same year. Headquarters are in Kōbe.

Sumitomo 3M, Ltd
住友スリーエム[株]

(Sumitomo Surīemu). Importer and manufacturer of 3M products. Incorporated in 1960 as a joint-venture company of 3M Co of the United States; Sumitomo Electric Industries, Ltd; and NEC Corporation. For the fiscal year ending October 1990, sales totaled ¥128.7 billion (US $992.1 million), and capitalization stood at ¥9.5 billion (US $73.2 million). Headquarters are in Tōkyō.

Sumitomo Trust & Banking Co, Ltd
住友信託銀行[株]

(Sumitomo Shintaku Ginkō). One of Japan's leading financial institutions. Incorporated in 1925 as a trust company for the SUMITOMO group, it added commercial banking to its business activities in 1948. It contributed to Japan's postwar economic recovery and expansion by supplying mainly long-term loans to such key industries as electric power, steel, chemicals, and shipbuilding. Sumitomo Trust maintains six overseas branches, eight representative offices, and eight wholly owned subsidiaries. As of March 1991 the volume of the bank's funds was ¥28.0 trillion (US $204.1 billion). The bank's total assets were ¥17.6 trillion (US $128.3 billion). The bank was capitalized at ¥181.4 billion (US $1.3 billion) in the same year. Headquarters are in Ōsaka.

Sumitomo Warehouse Co, Ltd
[株]住友倉庫

(Sumitomo Sōko). Company engaged in warehousing and harbor and land transportation. Incorporated in 1923. It has played a pioneering role in international freight forwarding and is actively engaged in intermodal transportation services. Sales for the fiscal year ending March 1991 totaled ¥60.2 billion (US $438.8 million), and the company was capitalized at ¥9.3 billion (US $67.8 million). Headquarters are in Ōsaka.

Sūmitsuin → Privy Council

Sumiyaki chōja
炭焼長者

(The Charcoal-Maker Millionaire). Folktale. Variations are known as *Asahi chōja* (The Rising-Sun Millionaire) or *Imohori chōja* (The Potato-Digger Millionaire). A poor and honest charcoal maker makes a fortune when his wife finds a gold mine. Stories about discovery of gold exist throughout Japan. This version may have been spread

by itinerant ironcasters, who made their own charcoal.

Sumiyoshi monogatari
住吉物語

Anonymous tale of the early Kamakura period (1185–1333) that resembles the Cinderella story. Believed to be a revision of a Heian-period (794–1185) work, now lost, of the same title. The councillor Saemon no Kami begets two daughters by one wife and another daughter, Himegimi, by a second wife, who dies when Himegimi is still a child. Shii no Shōshō, the son of a high minister, hears of Himegimi's beauty and asks for her hand in marriage. Himegimi's stepmother, who is concerned only for the fortunes of her own daughters, tricks him into marrying one of them instead. Learning that her stepmother is plotting to have her kidnapped, Himegimi runs away to Sumiyoshi (now part of Ōsaka) in the company of her wet-nurse's daughter, Jijū. Shii no Shōshō realizes he has been deceived, finds Himegimi, and takes her back to Kyōto, banishing his wife. The stepmother dies impoverished, while Himegimi and her husband thrive; he becomes regent to the emperor.

Sumiyoshi school
住吉派

(Sumiyoshiha). School of painting founded in 1662 by Sumiyoshi Jokei (original name Tosa Hiromichi; 1599–1670); an offshoot of the TOSA SCHOOL. The Sumiyoshi painters worked primarily for the shogunate in Edo (now Tōkyō), while the Tosa family served the imperial court in Kyōto. The Sumiyoshi artists worked in the Tosa style, revitalizing to some extent its depleted traditions, but they are remembered mainly for their services as art historians and connoisseurs to the Tokugawa shōguns. They traced their artistic lineage to a 13th-century painter known as Sumiyoshi Keion, whose identity is not clear.

Hiromichi, probably the younger brother of painter Tosa Mitsunori (1583–1638), changed his family name to Sumiyoshi at the order of the emperor Gosai (1637–85; r 1655–63), who appointed him the official painter of the Sumiyoshi Shrine in Ōsaka. He took the priestly name Jokei. He moved to Edo, where he set up the Sumiyoshi school and worked as *goyō eshi* (official painter). Jokei's son Gukei (original name Hirozumi; 1631–1705) followed a career very similar to his father's.

Father and son worked together on such projects as the *Tōshōgū engi* of 1665, a pictorial history of the shrine of TOKUGAWA IEYASU at Nikkō. Gukei became known as a painter of genre scenes, the most famous of which is the scroll *Rakuchū rakugai* (Scenes in and around Kyōto), now in the Tōkyō National Museum.

Sumiyoshi Shrine
住吉大社

(Sumiyoshi Taisha). Shintō shrine in Sumiyoshi Ward, Ōsaka, dedicated to four

Sumiyoshi Shrine
1 The gabled roof, distinctive ornaments, and cypress-bark roofing of the shrine buildings are typical of Sumiyoshi-style architecture.
2 The shrine's Otaue Festival, held annually in June, is centered on the ritual planting of a sacred rice crop.

deities. Three of the deities, born of the god Izanagi no Mikoto, are called collectively Suminoe no Ōkami. The fourth is Okinagatarashihime no Mikoto (i.e., the legendary empress Jingū deified) who according to legend founded this shrine. The shrine was believed to offer protection and prosperity for mariners, fishermen, *waka* poets, and merchants. The four buildings, each housing one deity, are in the so-called Sumiyoshi style of architecture (see SHINTŌ ARCHITECTURE), and are designated a National Treasure. The annual festival is held on 31 July.

Summers, James　　サマーズ, J.

(1828–91). British scholar and teacher of English literature. Born in Ritchfield, England. Summers traveled to China and studied its dialects. In 1848 he became a tutor at St. Paul's School in Hong Kong. He became professor of Chinese at King's College, London University, in 1852. There Summers studied Japanese, and when the IWAKURA MISSION visited England in 1872 he was invited to teach English in Japan. In 1873 he traveled to Japan to teach English literature and logic at Kaisei Gakkō (a predecessor of Tōkyō University). In 1882 he opened his own English school in Tōkyō. He was the first person in Japan to give lectures on Shakespeare and Milton.

sumō　　相撲

A 2,000-year-old form of wrestling that is considered by many to be the national sport of Japan. *Sumō* became a professional sport in the early Edo period (1600–1868), and although it is practiced today by clubs in high schools, colleges, and amateur associations, it has its greatest appeal as a professional spectator sport.

The object of this compelling sport is for a wrestler to force his opponent out of the center circle of the elevated cement-hard clay ring (DOHYŌ) or cause him to touch the surface of the *dohyō* with any part of his body other than the soles of his feet. The wrestlers may spend as much as the first four minutes in the ring in a ritual of stamping, squatting, puffing, glowering, and tossing salt in the air, but the actual conflict is only a matter of seconds. To decide who has stepped out or touched down first is often extremely difficult and requires the closest attention of a referee (GYŌJI), dressed in the court costume of a 14th-century nobleman, on the *dohyō* and judges (*shimpan*) sitting around the *dohyō* at floor level.

The Japan Sumō Association (Nihon Sumō Kyōkai), the governing body of professional *sumō*, officially lists 70 winning techniques consisting of assorted throws, trips, lifts, thrusts, shoves, and pulls. Of these, 48 are considered the "classic" techniques but the number in actual daily use is probably half that. Of primary concern in *sumō* are ring decorum and sportsmanship.

Unique to *sumō* is the use of a belly band or belt called a *mawashi*, which is folded, looped over the groin, wrapped tightly around the waist, and knotted in the rear. Most *sumō* matches center on the wrestlers' attempts to get a firm, two-handed grip on their opponent's *mawashi* while blocking him from getting a similar grip on theirs. With the right grip they then have the leverage to execute a throw, trip, or lift. During tournaments, but not in practice, a string apron (*sagari*) is also worn tucked into the front folds of the *mawashi*, whence it falls frequently in the heat of the match.

The Wrestlers——Traditionally *sumō* has drawn the majority of its recruits from rural communities. Most wrestlers start in their mid-teens and retire from this rigorous sport in their early thirties. Top-ranking wrestlers have an average height of 185 centimeters (6 ft) and an average weight of 148 kilograms (326 lb), with successful exceptions running from as light as 102 kilograms (225 lb) to as heavy as 239 kilograms (527 lb).

The wrestlers in professional *sumō* are organized into a pyramid. Progress from the ranks of beginners at the bottom to the grand champion's pinnacle at the top depends entirely on ability. The speed with which a wrestler rises or falls depends entirely on his win-loss record at the end of each tournament. Based on this, his ranking is calculated for the next tournament and then written with his name and those of other wrestlers in Chinese characters on a graded list called the *banzuke*. The only permanent rank is that of *yokozuna*, "grand champion," but a *yokozuna* who cannot maintain a certain level of championship performance is expected to retire.

Only wrestlers in the top two divisions, *jūryō* and *makuuchi*, receive regular salaries. They also enjoy the title *sekitori*, "top-ranking wrestler," and the right to have their long, oiled hair combed into the elegant *ōichōmage* (ginkgo-leaf knot) during tournaments.

The world of *sumō* is filled with ceremonies, all of which must be performed precisely. One such ceremony is the *yokozuna dohyōiri*, "the ring entrance of the grand champions." Another is the *dampatsushiki*, the "hair-cutting ceremony" performed at a senior wrestler's public retirement (*intaizumō*). The wrestler, dressed in his best formal *kimono*, his oiled hair combed into the handsome *ōichōmage* knot, sits in the middle of the *dohyō*. Beside him stands a chief referee in ceremonial tournament dress holding a pair of scissors (usually goldplated). One by one friends, relatives, fellow wrestlers, celebrities, and *kōenkai* (fan club) members climb into the ring to take a ritual snip at the back of the knot.

Annual Tournaments——Traditionally only two tournaments were held each year, but by 1958 this number had grown to six, where it stood in the early 1990s. The big six are held every other month in four different cities.

In 1949 the length of a tournament increased from the traditional 10 days to 15 days. A tournament day starts with the apprentices of *maezumō* (pre-*sumō*) fighting in the qualifying rounds, then the long march of the four lower divisions across the *dohyō* begins. The boy-men in these divisions— *jonokuchi*, *jonidan*, *sandamme*, and *makushita*—wrestle on 7 of the 15 days of the tournament. For them a winning record (*kachikoshi*) begins with 4 wins against 3 losses, which ensures promotion. Anything less is a losing record (*makekoshi*) and demotion. A *zenshō* record (all wins, no losses) of course boosts a wrestler way up the ladder, usually into a higher division.

Sekitori in the *jūryō* and *makuuchi* divisions wrestle once a day for 15 days. *Sekitori* must win 8 of their 15 bouts for a *kachikoshi* record. *Makekoshi* starts with 8 losses. The entire tournament is won by the *makuuchi* wrestler with the most wins.

The Stable System——The *sumō* stable system has as its purpose the training of young wrestlers into senior champions while inculcating them with the strict eti-

sumō

Depictions of *sumō* flourished as a genre of woodblock print during the late Edo period. This late-18th-century example is by Hokusai.

quette, discipline, and special values of *sumō*.

Physically, a stable (*heya*; literally, "room") is a self-contained unit complete with all living-training facilities. Every professional *sumō* wrestler belongs to one, making it his home throughout his ring career and often even into retirement. The only exceptions to the live-in rule are the married *sekitori*, who may live outside with their wives and commute to daily practice at the *heya*. As of June 1992 there were 44 active *heya*.

A stable is managed under the absolute control of a single boss (*oyakata*). All *oyakata* are former senior wrestlers and members of the Japan Sumō Association. The stable they run is usually the stable where they wrestled. *Oyakata* are generally married and live in special quarters with their wives, known by the title of *okamisan*, the only women to live in *heya*. *Okamisan* play an important behind-the-scenes role in the smooth operation of a stable, but their duties never include cooking or cleaning for the wrestlers. These and all other housekeeping chores outside the *oyakata*'s quarters are performed by apprentices and low-ranked wrestlers. *Heya* expenses are paid for by regular allowances from the Japan Sumō Association and gifts from the *heya* fan club.

Sumō Practice——*Keiko*, "practice," is a sacred word in *sumō*, and a brief description of the morning practice that takes place every day in every *heya* will give an idea of the *sumō* way of life.

The day begins at 4:00 or 5:00 AM for the youngest, lowest-ranked wrestlers, who ready the ring and begin their exercises. The higher a wrestler's rank, the longer he may sleep. *Makushita* are up at 6:30 and in the ring at 7:00. *Jūryō* wrestlers enter the ring around 8:00 and *makuuchi* shortly after.

The physical essentials for success in *sumō* are balance, agility, and flexibility, combined with a pair of powerful thighs and the lowest possible center of gravity. To achieve all this, wrestlers practice endlessly three traditional exercises, *shiko*, *teppō*, and *matawari*.

For *shiko* one stands with feet wide apart, draws in the breath, tips the body to the left, raises the right leg sideways as high as possible, and then stamps it down with a hissing exhalation. The action is repeated with the left foot, and so on. Beginners should practice *shiko* at least 500 times a day.

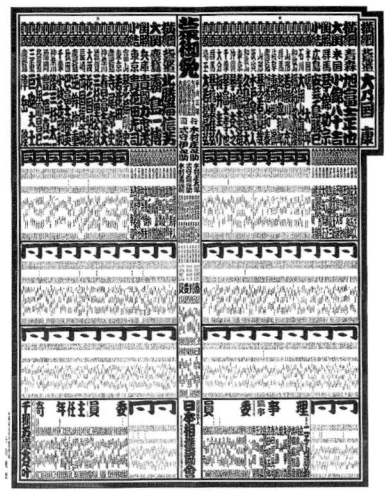

The *banzuke*, a graded list that announces the wrestlers' names, ranks, and birthplaces, is published before each tournament.

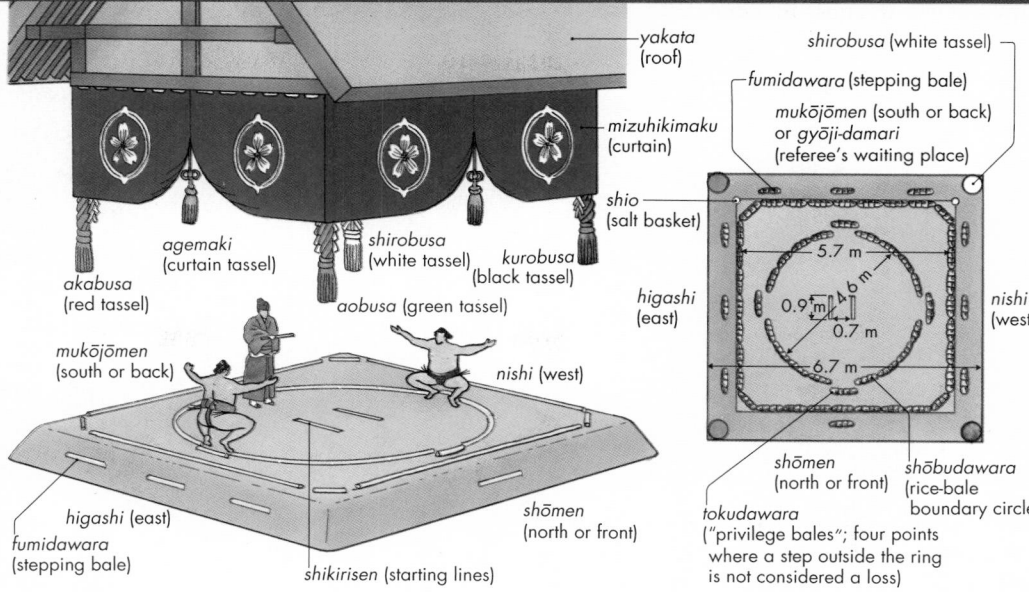

yakata (roof)

mizuhikimaku (curtain)

agemaki (curtain tassel)

akabusa (red tassel)

shirobusa (white tassel)

kurobusa (black tassel)

aobusa (green tassel)

mukōjōmen (south or back)

higashi (east)

nishi (west)

shōmen (north or front)

higashi (east)

fumidawara (stepping bale)

shikirisen (starting lines)

shirobusa (white tassel)

fumidawara (stepping bale)

mukōjōmen (south or back) or gyōji-damari (referee's waiting place)

shio (salt basket)

higashi (east)

nishi (west)

5.7 m

6 m

0.9 m

0.7 m

6.7 m

shōmen (north or front)

tokudawara ("privilege bales"; four points where a step outside the ring is not considered a loss)

shōbudawara (rice-bale boundary circle)

Sumō Dohyō

Matawari involves sitting in the dirt with legs spread as wide as possible, the closer to 180° the better. Next, one leans forward until the entire upper body from the navel to the cheekbone is pressed against the ring. A senior wrestler will help a struggler by standing on his back, an incredibly painful procedure.

Teppō is the *sumō* punching bag, a pillar of wood sunk in the earth that the wrestler slams his open hand against—right, left, right, left—to develop timing and coordination.

Wrestling techniques are learned by watching and in practice bouts (*mōshiai*), there being no formal, Western-style teaching of the various throws and lifts. Instead the wrestler learns from wrestling with a senior and then practicing with one of his peers. When the session is almost over, wrestling ends and *butsukari-geiko* (literally, "collision training") begins. This requires the younger wrestlers to charge a senior and drive him across the ring in one long slide, turn and drive him back, and repeat until the junior is exhausted. During this exercise the junior is occasionally thrown down so that he will learn how to hit the hard *dohyō* and roll without hurting himself. After *butsukari-geiko* comes *matawari*, and then all join in a final round of *shiko*.

At 11:00 AM the wrestlers head for the baths, seniors first, followed by the lower ranks. Next is brunch, the first and largest *sumō* meal of the day. This consists of *chankonabe*, a high-calorie stew made with a seaweed-base stock and containing chicken, pork, fish, *tōfu*, bean sprouts, cabbage, carrots, onions, and other vegetables. The senior wrestlers eat bowl upon bowl of this stew together with bowl upon bowl of rice washed down with quarts of beer; the younger wrestlers get what is left.

Except for the housekeeping chores of junior wrestlers, the official business of the day is over at the *heya* after lunch until the next morning's *keiko*. Whenever a wrestler leaves the *heya* he must be dressed neatly in a *kimono*; and his hair, if it is long enough, must be carefully oiled, combed, and tied in the *chommage* topknot of the 18th-century townsman.

The Japan Sumō Association—Every aspect of professional *sumō* is controlled by the Japan Sumō Association, composed of 105 retired wrestlers known as elders (*toshiyori*) and including representation from *sumō*'s "working ranks," i.e., active wres-

Ring-entrance ceremonies open each day of a tournament. *Makuuchi* (top division) wrestlers, with elaborately embroidered aprons covering their belly bands, file into the ring during the ceremony.

Chiyonofuji, a *yokozuna* (grand champion) from 1981 to 1991, performs the separate ring-entrance ritual that precedes the day's higher-division matches.

A ring steward calls out the names of the two wrestlers before a match.

Under the referee's supervision, the wrestlers take their places at the starting lines called *shikirisen*.

At some point within the four minutes allowed for "warming up," the wrestlers charge, angling for the best grip on their opponent.

The decisive moment: the wrestler on the right has stepped outside of the ring, losing the match.

Immediately following most matches, the winning wrestler is offered money in an envelope placed on the referee's fan.

After the day's last match, a lower-division wrestler performs a bow-twirling rite dating from the Heian period (794–1185).

yorikiri
(forcing out)

oshidashi
(pushing out)

tsukiotoshi
(dodging and forcing down)

uwatenage
(arm throw with an outside grip)

hatakikomi
(slapping down)

hikiotoshi
(pulling down)

okuridashi
(pushing out from behind)

sukuinage
("scooping" beltless throw)

shitatenage
(arm throw with an inside grip)

tsuridashi
(lifting out)

tsukidashi
(pushing out with alternating hand thrusts)

uwate dashinage
(throwing out with an outside grip)

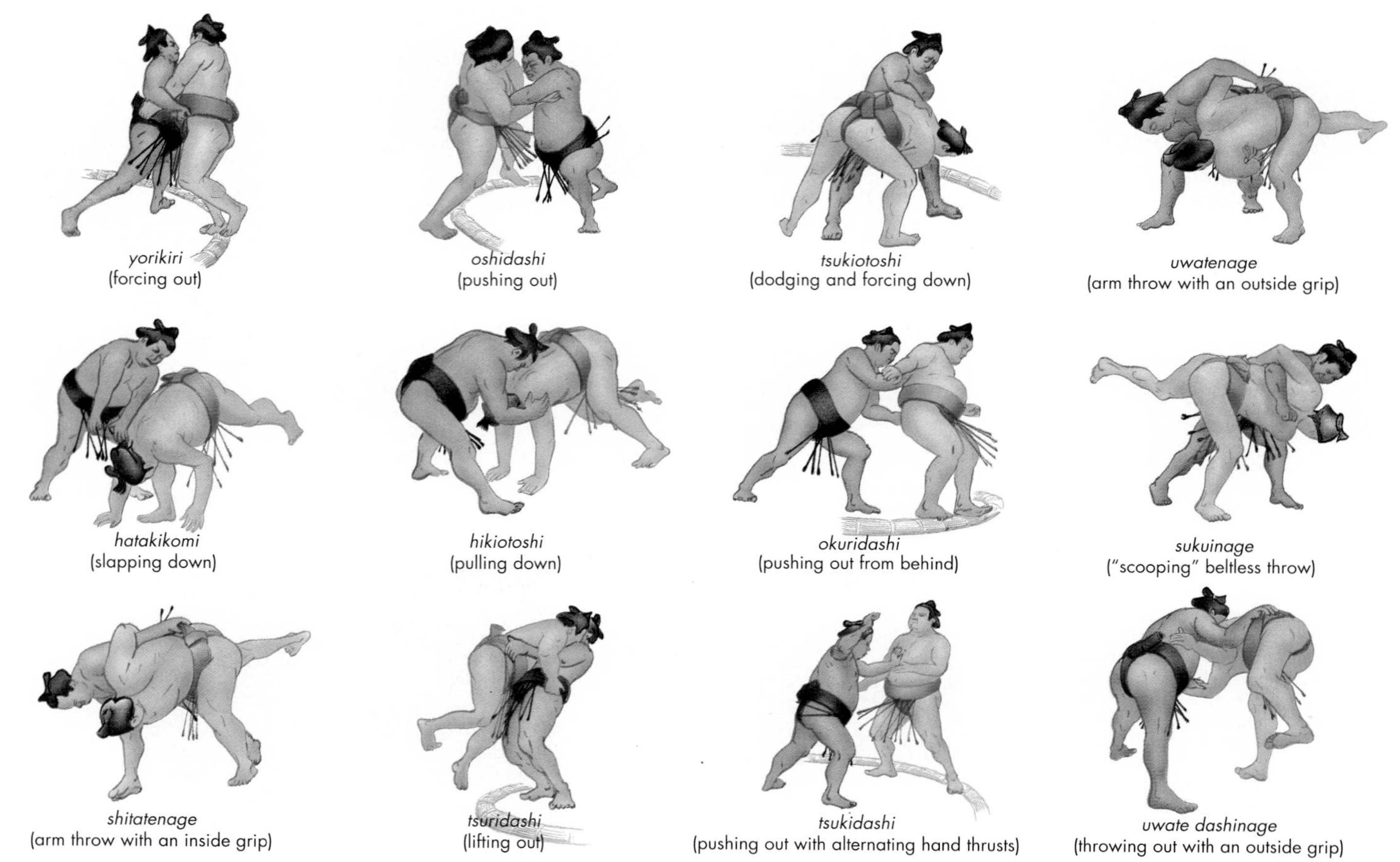

NOTE: The wrestler wearing the black loincloth is executing the winning technique.

---

tlers, referees, and ring stewards (*yobidashi*). The Japan Sumō Association is organized in several divisions such as Business, Judging, Off-Season Tours (Jungyō), Out-of-Tōkyō Tournaments (Chihō Basho), Training, and Guidance, supervised by an elected 10-man board of directors under the leadership of a president or managing director (*rijichō*). See also KOKUGIKAN.   ☛ 1480–1481

Sumō Museum   相撲博物館

(Sumō Hakubutsukan). Museum of memorabilia related to SUMŌ wrestling. Part of the KOKUGIKAN, the new *sumō* stadium in the Ryōgoku district of Sumida Ward, Tōkyō. Established in 1954 at the old Kokugikan in Taitō Ward, Tōkyō, the museum has been at its present location since the new stadium was built in 1985. It houses such items as woodblock prints depicting *sumō* wrestlers, belts (*mawashi*) and other *sumō* apparel, articles and books on *sumō*, and the records of active wrestlers of junior rank (*jūryō*) and above.

Sumoto   洲本〔市〕

City on the island of AWAJISHIMA in the INLAND SEA; administratively a part of Hyōgo Prefecture. A castle town during the Edo period (1600–1868), it is the political and economic center of the island. Principal industries are spinning and the manufacture of electrical appliances. It is part of the Inland Sea National Park. Pop: 43,817.

Sumpu   駿府

The *kokufu* (seat of provincial government) of "Sunshū" (that is, Suruga Province)

under the RITSURYŌ SYSTEM formed in the 7th and 8th centuries. The town's name euphonically combines the syllables "*sun*" and "*fu*" from these two terms. Sumpu was renamed Shizuoka in 1869 and has been the capital of Shizuoka Prefecture since 1871. From the 14th century it was the seat of the IMAGAWA FAMILY. TOKUGAWA IEYASU moved his headquarters to Sumpu in early 1587. In 1607, two years after he retired from the shogunate, Ieyasu established in Sumpu a governmental apparatus (the so-called Sumpu *seiken*) that had national responsibilities and overshadowed the shogunate itself, in effect creating a dyarchy, which Ieyasu dominated as retired shōgun (*ōgosho*). Ieyasu died in Sumpu on 1 June 1616. Sumpu Castle, built by Ieyasu in 1607–08, ranked with ŌSAKA CASTLE as one of the shogunate's most important fortifications outside Edo (now Tōkyō).

Sumpuki   駿府記

(Chronicle of Sumpu). Work, variously attributed to GOTŌ MITSUTSUGU and HAYASHI RAZAN, which examines TOKUGAWA IEYASU's relations with TOYOTOMI HIDEYORI (see ŌSAKA CASTLE, SIEGES OF) as well as Ieyasu's views on literature, religion, and the arts. It covers the period of Ieyasu's retirement in Sumpu (now the city of Shizuoka) from 1611 to 1616.

Sunagawa   砂川〔市〕

City in west-central Hokkaidō, on the river Ishikarigawa. Sunagawa was once a vital coal transportation center but has declined in recent times. Principal industries are chemical fertilizer, plywood, and concrete. Pop: 23,152.

Sunagawa case   砂川事件

(Sunagawa *jiken*). Criminal trial in which seven Japanese were indicted for trespassing on a US military base in 1957. They challenged the stationing of the US armed forces in Japan on the grounds that it violated article 9, the controversial RENUNCIATION OF WAR clause, of the CONSTITUTION OF JAPAN. The seven defendants were charged with violating a special law that set more severe penalties for such trespassing than the general law did with regard to other property. On 30 March 1959 the Tōkyō District Court reached a verdict of not guilty and acquitted all defendants. The court ruled that the stationing of US forces in Japan violated article 9 of the constitution. The court concluded that, since the stationing of the US forces in Japan was unconstitutional, the privileged treatment of the forces because of the special law was null and void under the due-process-of-law principle enunciated in article 31 of the constitution.

The public prosecutor, bypassing the High Court, appealed directly to the Supreme Court for review of the case. In its verdict of 16 December 1959, the Grand Bench of the Supreme Court quashed the first-instance decision and remanded the case to the Tōkyō District Court for retrial. The majority opinion held that although article 9 renounces war and prohibits the maintenance of war potential, it in no way denies Japan the right of self-defense that a sovereign nation inherently possesses. The Tōkyō District Court had to accept the legal validity of the special law under which the defendants had been indicted. Thus the lower court's role was restricted merely to determining the

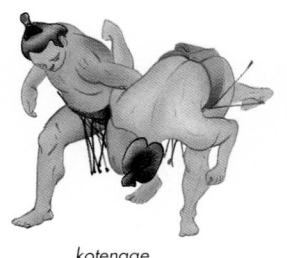

kotenage
(forearm throw)

kimedashi
(thrusting out by locking
the opponent's arms)

katasukashi
(pushing the opponent's shoulder
to force him down)

utchari
(leaning back and throwing the
opponent out at the edge of the ring)

sotogake
(outside leg trip)

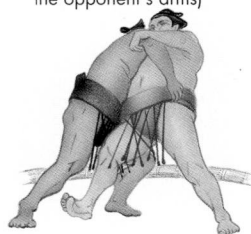

kirikaeshi
(outside knee trip)

shitatehineri
(inner-hand twist down using
the opponent's belt)

watashikomi
(grabbing the opponent's
calf and pushing him out)

abisetaoshi
(toppling the opponent inside the ring)

makiotoshi
(grappling the opponent's torso
and twisting him down)

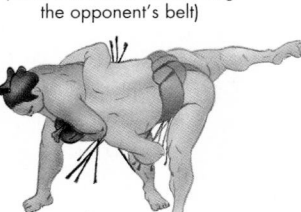

kubinage
(neck or head throw)

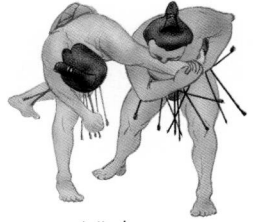

tottari
(arm-twist throw)

appropriate punishment. The trespassers were punished with a fine.

The legal and political significance of the Supreme Court's decision at home and abroad can hardly be overstated. For the first time Japan's highest tribunal had interpreted the problematic war-renunciation clause and made a ruling on JUDICIAL REVIEW of international treaties. With its reversal of the first-instance court decision, the Supreme Court had deprived those who were opposing Japan's alliance with the United States of their major legal weapon.

Suna no onna 砂の女
(tr *The Woman in the Dunes*, 1964). Novel by ABE KŌBŌ (1924–93); published 1962. The story focuses on the paradoxical fate of Niki Jumpei, an elementary school teacher and amateur insect collector. While searching for insect specimens in the dunes, Jumpei is himself entrapped in a sand pit and forced to replace the husband of the widow who lives there. He contributes to the survival of the small community of sand-dwellers by endlessly clearing away the accumulating sand. As his various attempts to escape end in failure he gradually undergoes a personal transformation, so that when escape becomes possible he is less interested in leaving than in discovering ways of coping with his new existence. Commenting on the absurdity and stifling conditions of urban life, Abe's allegorical tale is representative of postwar avant-garde Japanese literature. It was the basis of a widely acclaimed 1964 film directed by TESHIGAHARA HIROSHI.

sunao 素直
Used in the adjectival form *sunao na*, meaning "upright and compliant." Considered

one of the most desirable personality traits in Japanese boys and girls, *sunao na* is the opposite of *hinekureta* (warped, twisted). According to the psychologist Doi Takeo (b 1920), when a Japanese person's AMAE (dependency need) is not satisfied, he or she feels acute frustration and resorts to the kind of sulking described by the verb *suneru* (to pretend indifference to one's *amae*) or the verb *higamu* (to pretend not to need to depend, while envying others who are apparently favored). When this becomes a chronic attitude and is seen as an integral part of the personality, the person is described as a *hinekureta* person (distrustful, embittered, begrudging, and resentful). In contrast, a *sunao na* person, whose *amae* has been sufficiently gratified since childhood, has a basic trust in and acceptance of authority and acts on the assumption that he or she will be taken care of should special needs arise.

Sung Che-yüan →Song Zheyuan
(Sung Che-yüan)

Sung Chiao-jen →Song Jiaoren
(Sung Chiao-jen)

sun goddess →Amaterasu Ōmikami

Suntory Foundation サントリー文化財団
(Santorī Bunka Zaidan). A foundation established by SUNTORY, LTD, in 1979 to provide funding and prizes for various types of international and domestic research and other activities in the humanities and social sciences. It also sponsors international symposia and funds the translation and publication of books about Japan. In 1989 assets were ¥1.6

billion (US $11.6 million). Headquarters are in Ōsaka.

Suntory, Ltd サントリー[株]
(Santorī). The oldest and largest distiller of whiskey in Japan and a major producer of spirits, beer, wine, and soft drinks. Founded in 1899 by TORII SHINJIRŌ and later led by his son, SAJI KEIZŌ. Suntory, Ltd, is one of the world's top three whiskey producers, and its Old Suntory (sold in Japan as Suntory Old) is the world's best-selling whiskey. The company exports its products to more than 60 countries and has several overseas subsidiaries. It also owns a restaurant chain with a total of eight overseas branches. Suntory is involved in cultural activities as well, operating the Suntory Foundation (which promotes cultural exchange between Japan and foreign countries), the Suntory Museum of Art, and the Suntory Music Foundation. Sales for the fiscal year ending December 1990 totaled ¥796.4 billion (US $6.0 billion). In the same year the company was capitalized at ¥30.0 billion (US $224.6 million. Headquarters are in Ōsaka.

Suntory Museum of Art サントリー美術館
(Santorī Bijutsukan). Museum in Minato Ward, Tōkyō. Established in 1961 by the president of Suntory, Ltd, SAJI KEIZŌ. The 2,000-piece collection centers on items associated with everyday life in Japan, including lacquer ware, ceramics, glassware, and combs.

Sun Wen →Sun Yat-sen

The Everyday Life of a Sumō Wrestler

1

The origins of *sumō* wrestling date back 2,000 years, but this combination of sport and ritual has never been more popular than it is today.

All wrestlers must belong to a sumō stable (*heya*; literally, "room"), a combined practice and communal living facility managed by a former senior wrestler called an *oyakata*. Only married wrestlers are allowed to live off the premises. For a junior member, life in the stable means not only eating, sleeping, and practicing there but also cooking, cleaning, and being at the beck and call of his seniors.

The daily routine has a simple, overriding objective: to improve each wrestler's win-loss record in the next tournament. In a grueling training regimen that for junior members often starts before dawn, wrestlers must concentrate all their energy on a series of traditional exercises designed to improve agility and balance and to increase strength.

Next to practice, the second most important task for the sumō wrestler in his quest for victory is eating, and what he eats is a sort of potluck stew called *chankonabe*, which contains vegetables, meat, and fish.

The sumō wrestler's public appearances are not limited to the six 15-day tournaments held throughout the year. After most of these major tournaments he sets off on promotion tours to the far corners of Japan and sometimes abroad. While the tour's demonstration competitions, called *hanazumō* ("flower sumō"), lack the intensity of a real tournament, they provide a rare chance for fans in remote areas to get a close-up view of sumō.

2

3

1 — **Surrounded by fans and supporters,** Chiyonofuji, one of the greatest *yokozuna* (grand champions) of all time, prepares to drink from a giant *sake* cup following one of the 31 tournament victories he achieved before retiring in 1991.

2 — **Practice bouts** in which the wrestlers test themselves for 10 or even 20 consecutive matches are considered the most demanding and effective of the traditional sumō practice techniques.

3 — **Young wrestlers train** under the sharp eye of Fujishima Oyakata (left), head of the Fujishima Stable.

4 — **The popular Takahanada** (now called Takanohana), in 1992, at the age of 19, became the youngest wrestler ever to win a tournament.

5 — **Two young up-and-coming wrestlers** show the dedication to practice necessary for success in sumō.

6 — **Opportunities for fans** to meet the wrestlers are a special feature of the *hanazumō* competitions held during the sumō promotions that tour Japan.

7 — **Wrestlers demonstrate practice techniques** before fans at a temporary open-air arena during a promotion tour.

8 — **Kitanoumi Oyakata** (seated) calls out the weight of an aspirant for entrance to a stable. In principle, new wrestlers must weigh at least 75 kg (165 lb) and be at least 173 cm (5 ft 8 in) tall.

9 — **A great variety of ingredients** are used in *chankonabe*, which is traditionally served every day for lunch, the first and the main meal in the sumō stable.

10 — **A stable's higher-ranking wrestlers,** such as the pair pictured here, get their *chankonabe* first. Later, junior members will take their turn.

11 — **The number of foreign wrestlers** in sumō is growing. Here Hawaiian-born Akebono, the first foreign wrestler to be named *yokozuna*, poses with a young fan. It is said that a baby held by a sumō wrestler will grow up strong and healthy.

Supreme Court
1 The Supreme Court Building, Chiyoda Ward, Tōkyō.
2 The Supreme Court in a grand bench session, which requires the presence of at least 9 court justices. Most cases are examined not by the grand bench but by one of the three petty benches into which it is divided.

sun worship   太陽崇拝

(*taiyō sūhai*). Sun worship has been practiced in Japan since ancient times. According to Japanese mythology, the sun goddess, AMA-TERASU ŌMIKAMI, is the highest deity and a direct ancestor of the imperial family. A sun deity, *amateru kami*, is still worshiped in several Shintō shrines in the Kansai and Kyū-shū regions. Traces of sun worship are also seen in festivals held on the days of the solstice or equinox (HIGAN) and in the custom of welcoming the rising sun on the peak of a mountain, especially on New Year's Day.

Sun Yat-sen   孫逸仙

(1866–1925; Ch: Sun Yixian or Sun I-hsien; J: Son Issen). Also known as Sun Wen (J: Son Bun). Leading revolutionary against the Qing (Ch'ing) dynasty (1644–1912) and first provisional president of the Chinese republic. Known as the father of modern China. Born in Guangdong (Kwangtung) Province, he was educated in Honolulu, Guangzhou (Canton), and Hong Kong, where he graduated from medical school in 1892.

In 1894 Sun organized the Revive China Society (Ch: Xingzhong Hui or Hsing-chung Hui). After his first, unsuccessful uprising against the Qing in 1895, he went abroad to raise money for the revolutionary cause. In Japan in 1897 Sun began his close friendship with MIYAZAKI TŌTEN and through him made the acquaintance of TŌYAMA MITSURU, ŌKUMA SHIGENOBU, and INUKAI TSUYOSHI.

In 1905 Sun organized the revolutionary United League (Ch: Tongmeng Hui or T'ung-meng Hui), the forerunner of the Guomindang (Kuomintang; Nationalist Party), in Tōkyō. Under Qing pressure Sun was expelled from Japan in 1907. In the United States at the time of the successful Chinese Revolution of October 1911, Sun returned to China and accepted the post of provisional president of the Republic of China on 1 January 1912. One month later Sun resigned and was succeeded by YUAN SHIKAI (Yüan Shih-k'ai). When Yuan began a movement to end the republic and enthrone himself emperor, Sun launched the abortive Second Revolution of 1913. The campaign failed, and Sun fled to Japan seeking further monetary and political support. Influential Japanese such as MORI KAKU reportedly gave him considerable financial aid in return for promises of sizable territorial concessions for Japan. In 1914 Sun reorganized the Guomindang in Tōkyō with the aim of wresting power from Yuan. Sun returned to China in 1916, and for brief periods between 1916 and 1924 he was the leader of a separatist government. In 1923–24, under Soviet guidance, Sun again reorganized the Guomindang, this time on the model of the Soviet Communist Party. In 1924 he elaborated in public lectures his three famous principles of nationalism, democracy, and people's livelihood. During a visit to Beijing (Peking) to confer with political leaders he fell ill and died on 12 March 1925.

Suō Province   周防国

(Suō no Kuni; also called Bōshū). One of the eight provinces of the San'yōdō ("South of the Mountains Circuit") in southern Honshū; established under the KOKUGUN SYSTEM in 646, it is now the southeastern part of YAMAGUCHI PREFECTURE. In the 8th through 10th centuries copper from the region was used to mint Japan's earliest coins, the KŌCHŌ JŪNISEN. During the Heian period (794–1185) large landed estates (SHŌEN) were established in Suō by temples and shrines of the Kyōto-Nara area. In the Kamakura period (1185–1333) the entire province was designated revenue land for the temple TŌDAIJI in Nara; it was administered first by the FUJIWARA FAMILY and the HŌJŌ FAMILY and later by the ŌUCHI FAMILY and the MŌRI FAMILY. Under the Ōuchi the castle town of Yamaguchi became a major cultural center. Products included rice, salt, paper, and wax. With the establishment of the prefectural system in 1871, Suō was combined with Nagato to form Yamaguchi Prefecture.

Suō Sea   周防灘

(Suō Nada). Westernmost part of the Inland Sea, extending from the southern coast of Yamaguchi Prefecture, western Honshū, to the northern coast of Ōita Prefecture, Kyūshū. It is bounded by the Kammon Strait to the west and the Iyo Sea to the east. Globefish and *nori* (a kind of seaweed) are cultivated here.

Superconductivity Research Laboratory   超電導工学研究所

(Chōdendō Kōgaku Kenkyūjo). Laboratory established in 1988 in Kōtō Ward, Tōkyō. The laboratory is affiliated with the International Superconductivity Technology Center, a private foundation that conducts research there. Researchers from about 100 firms use the laboratory in the development of high-performance superconducting materials. The laboratory is financed by national subsidies and dues from supporting member companies. A branch laboratory in Nagoya, Aichi Prefecture, studies critical current density.

support   扶養

(*fuyō*). Under the CIVIL CODE of 1898, which was influenced by the traditional Japanese family system, the head of the household was responsible for the support of the family. Today, however, support is construed primarily as economic assistance determined by the relationships of rights and obligations between individuals. Book IV, chapter 6 of the present Civil Code makes support obligatory only in relationships between lineal relatives and among siblings. Under extenuating circumstances, the FAMILY COURT may impose the obligation of support upon a relative within the third degree of relationship by blood. The obligation to provide support arises when two conditions exist: first, a person with a right to receive support must need it, and second, the party obliged to provide support must be capable of providing it while maintaining his own livelihood. This second, limiting condition does not apply, however, to a parent's responsibility to support a minor child or to one spouse's responsibility to support the other, since a distinction is made between these and other familial relationships. See also CIVIL PROCEDURE, CODE OF.

Supreme Commander for the Allied Powers → SCAP

Supreme Court   最高裁判所

(Saikō Saibansho). Highest tribunal in Japan. The 1947 CONSTITUTION OF JAPAN states: "(1) The whole judicial power is vested in a Supreme Court and in such inferior courts as are established by law. (2) No extraordinary tribunal shall be established, nor shall any organ or agency of the Executive be given final judicial power" (art. 76). The Supreme Court is literally the highest organ of judicial power in civil and criminal cases, as well as in administrative law cases or any other forms of legal litigation. Furthermore, article 81 of the constitution makes the Supreme Court "the court of last resort with power to determine the constitutionality of any law, order, regulation or official act." This reflects the obvious influence of the US system of judicial review.

The Supreme Court consists of a chief justice and 14 associate justices. The chief justice is formally appointed by the emperor in accordance with the designation by the cabinet. Other justices are appointed by the cabinet, and their appointments are reviewed by voters in the first general election of members of the House of Representatives after each appointment. The justices' retirement age is 70. The Supreme Court is divided into three petty benches, and each bench is able to decide most cases. The grand bench, consisting of the full membership of the court, examines cases referred by one of the petty benches.

Su, Prince   粛親王

(1863–1922; J: Shuku Shinnō). Prince Su was the hereditary title of Su Shanqi (Su Shan-ch'i), a member of the Manchu imperial family whom the Japanese supported to foster independence in Manchuria and Inner Mongolia. After the overthrow of the Manchu dynasty in 1911 the Japanese military concluded that China's new president, YUAN SHI-KAI (Yüan Shih-k'ai), was not favorable to their interests in China and began to work

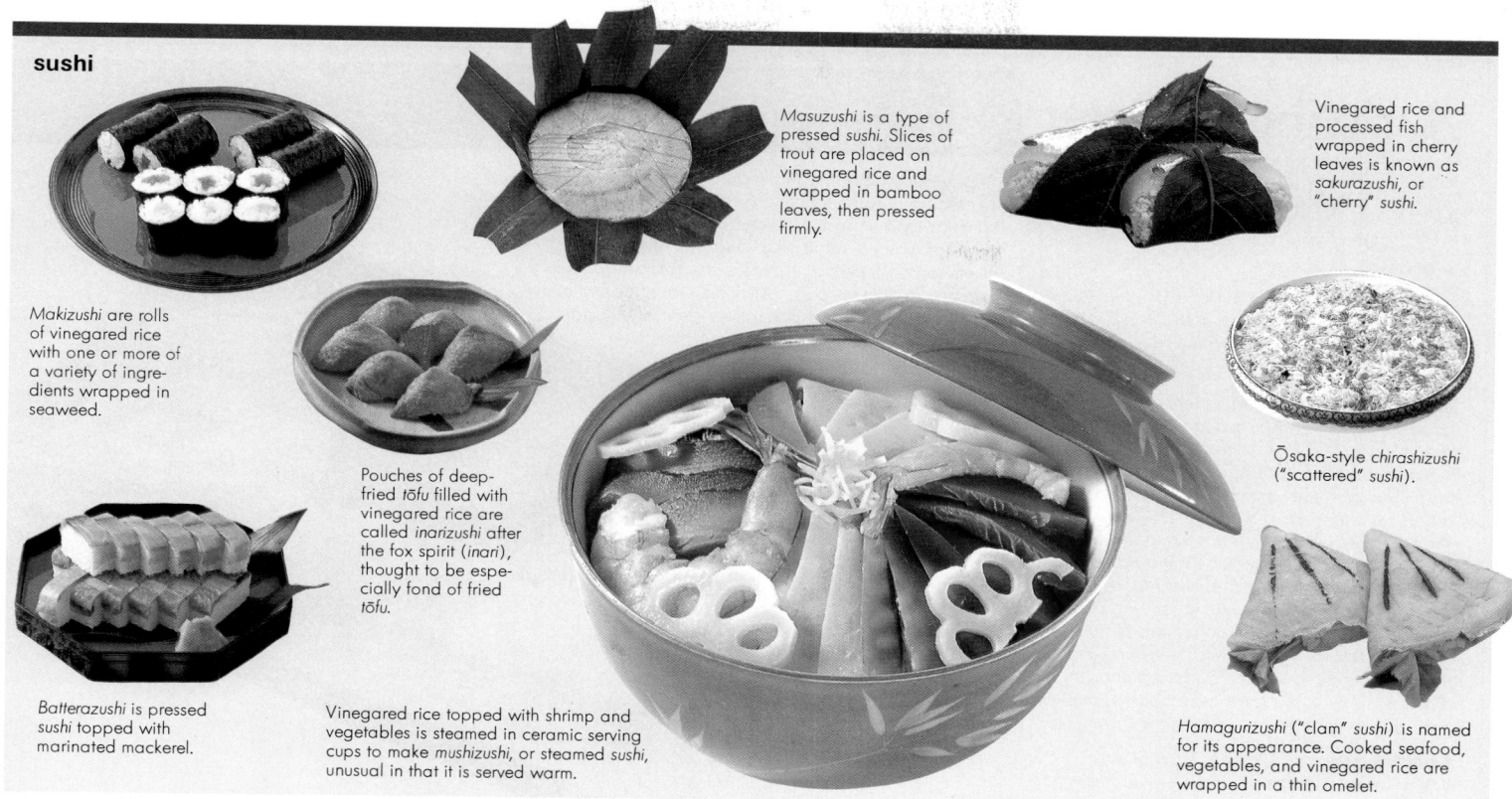

Makizushi are rolls of vinegared rice with one or more of a variety of ingredients wrapped in seaweed.

Masuzushi is a type of pressed sushi. Slices of trout are placed on vinegared rice and wrapped in bamboo leaves, then pressed firmly.

Vinegared rice and processed fish wrapped in cherry leaves is known as sakurazushi, or "cherry" sushi.

Pouches of deep-fried tōfu filled with vinegared rice are called inarizushi after the fox spirit (inari), thought to be especially fond of fried tōfu.

Ōsaka-style chirashizushi ("scattered" sushi).

Batterazushi is pressed sushi topped with marinated mackerel.

Vinegared rice topped with shrimp and vegetables is steamed in ceramic serving cups to make mushizushi, or steamed sushi, unusual in that it is served warm.

Hamagurizushi ("clam" sushi) is named for its appearance. Cooked seafood, vegetables, and vinegared rice are wrapped in a thin omelet.

toward a separate Manchu state in Manchuria. When Yuan proclaimed himself emperor at the end of 1915, Japan gave aid to both SUN YAT-SEN and to Prince Su's separatist movement, which collapsed in 1916. Prince Su retired to Japanese-controlled PORT ARTHUR. See also MANCHURIAN-MONGOLIAN INDEPENDENCE MOVEMENT.

suretyship 保証

(hoshō). Legal duty (hoshō saimu or the suretyship obligatory duty) of a third party (hoshōnin or the surety) to perform the principal obligatory duty to the obligee when the principal obligor fails to perform the principal obligatory duty. It also refers to a contract (hoshō keiyaku or suretyship contract) giving rise to such a duty. Suretyships are most commonly given by relatives or friends, but suretyship by public or cooperative surety organizations is becoming frequent. The suretyship obligatory duty is secondary to the principal obligatory duty.

surimono 摺り物

(literally, "printed thing"). Specifically, surimono refers to a luxurious kind of woodblock print on unsized paper, made to special order and used for greetings, announcements, etc, notably as New Year's gifts. Surimono vary in size. Most surimono include one or more poems, usually KYŌKA. Surimono are distinguished from other woodblock prints in several ways: they are invariably made in short editions, as few as one of a kind; in addition to the usual woodblock printing, much embossing (blind printing) is used to give texture and depth to the impressions; and, frequently, the prints are enhanced with gold, silver, and copper onlays.

Surimono emerged from the calendar prints that came into vogue in the 1770s. Although many exceptional surimono were made by various UKIYO-E artists before and after the early 19th century surge of surimono art, the form reached its peak between 1795 and 1835 with the work of two outstanding surimono artists, Gakutei (1786?–1868) and TOTOYA HOKKEI (1780–1850), although excellent surimono by such

artists as HOKUSAI (1760–1849) and KUBO SHUMMAN (1757–1820) survive. As the production of surimono tapered off, elegant stationery was made, incorporating fine surimono art with space for adding a poem or special message.

Surrender, Instrument of 降伏文書

(Kōfuku Bunsho). The formal document whereby Japan surrendered to the Allied powers. Signed on 2 September 1945 aboard the USS Missouri by Foreign Minister SHIGEMITSU MAMORU and Chief-of-Staff General UMEZU YOSHIJIRŌ, it was accepted by General Douglas MACARTHUR, supreme commander for the Allied powers (SCAP). Japan agreed to the immediate cessation of all hostilities, formal acceptance of the terms of the POTSDAM DECLARATION, and the placement of all administrative powers of the Japanese government under SCAP, establishing the basic conditions for the OCCUPATION of Japan. On the same day the emperor issued a proclamation stating that he had ordered the government to sign the instrument and commanding his subjects to adhere to its provisions.

Suruga Bay 駿河湾

(Suruga Wan). Inlet of the Pacific Ocean, on the southern coast of Shizuoka Prefecture, central Honshū. Extends from OMAEZAKI, a cape in the west, to IRŌZAKI, a cape on the southern tip of the Izu Peninsula in the east. The warm Kuroshio Current makes this area a fertile fishing ground, now threatened by pollution resulting from industrialization. Much of the eastern coast of the bay along the Izu Peninsula is included in the Fuji-Hakone-Izu National Park.

Suruga Province 駿河国

(Suruga no Kuni). Established in 680, its territory roughly corresponded to the eastern half of present-day Shizuoka Prefecture, excluding Izu Peninsula. Situated along the highway TŌKAIDŌ, the province was the site of a battle fought at Fujigawa in 1180 during the Taira-Minamoto War and two battles in 1335 that led to the turmoil of the era of Northern and Southern Courts (1337–92). In

the Muromachi period (1333–1568) the IMAGAWA FAMILY became military governors (SHUGO) of Suruga but were destroyed in 1560 by ODA NOBUNAGA in the Battle of OKEHAZAMA. TOKUGAWA IEYASU assumed control of the region in 1582, and during the Edo period (1600–1868) the castle at Sumpu (now part of the city of Shizuoka) was occupied by shogunal appointees (see JŌDAI), who administered Tokugawa lands (TENRYŌ). Three small domains were governed by hereditary vassals (FUDAI) of the Tokugawa family.

Susaki 須崎[市]

City in central Kōchi Prefecture, Shikoku. It has a good natural harbor on Tosa Bay. Principal occupations are fish (yellowtail) farming and raising rice, vegetables, and citrus fruits. Cement plants make use of abundant limestone deposits. Pop: 30,295.

Susanoo no Mikoto 素戔嗚尊

A complex and composite deity in Japanese mythology. Susanoo no Mikoto figures variously as god of the storm, the underworld, agriculture, the waters, and disease. In the Yamato myth cycle he is the son of Izanagi (see IZANAGI AND IZANAMI) and the capricious younger brother of the sun goddess AMATERASU ŌMIKAMI. When Susanoo's offensive behavior drives Amaterasu into a cave, he is banished from the High Celestial Plain (TAKAMAGAHARA) and descends to Izumo in western Japan. The Izumo myth cycle portrays Susanoo as its hero and ancestral deity. In his most famous exploit, Susanoo intoxicates and slays the YAMATA NO OROCHI, a great, eight-headed, eight-tailed serpent, thereby rescuing a maiden and acquiring the sword later known as Kusanagi, one of the IMPERIAL REGALIA. Susanoo subsequently came to be associated with the tutelary deity Gozu Tennō and as such is worshiped at the YASAKA SHRINE in Kyōto. See also MYTHOLOGY.

sushi 鮨

Vinegared rice topped or combined with such items as raw fish, shellfish, or cooked

Continued on page 1486 ►

A Sushi Sampler

Sushi in its finest form is far from being a simple dish—the nimble white-smocked chefs working briskly behind the sushi counter have usually undergone many years of rigorous training. But with imagination and a little patience, you can make sushi at home, using fresh, locally available seafood and other delicacies.

Ōmae Kinjirō

Toppings and Fillings——Here are a few hints for selecting sushi topping and filling ingredients, known collectively as *tane*.

For raw seafood, freshness is the key. Look for freshly caught saltwater fish and shellfish, preferably in their peak seasons. (Freshwater fish should not be eaten raw.) Someone who works at a fish market can advise you on the best catches of the day as well as skin and fillet the fish for you. Fish roe is also delicious as *tane*.

But if fresh seafood is unavailable, try using prepared fish such as canned tuna, smoked salmon, and marinated seafoods or other ingredients such as sliced roast beef or pork, smoked ham, sliced cheese, avocado, asparagus, etc.

Condiments——All the varieties of sushi mentioned here are eaten dipped in soy sauce. Aside from soy sauce, the main condiments for sushi are *wasabi* and vinegared ginger. Nose-tingling *wasabi*, or Japanese horseradish, is used to season raw seafood *tane*, while slices of vinegared ginger (*amazu shōga*), popularly known as *gari*, are eaten between servings of sushi to cleanse the palate.

Sushi Rice

To make proper sushi rice, or *shari*, you will need short-grain, polished white rice and rice vinegar. Sushi rice should always be eaten the same day it is prepared.

Cooking the Rice——Wash 3½ cups of rice until water rinses clear. Drain rice in a colander and let stand for 1 hour. Place rice in a pot with a close-fitting lid; add 4 cups water. Cover and bring to a boil over medium heat. Raise to high heat and boil for 2 minutes. Reduce to medium heat; boil for another 5 minutes. Reduce to low heat and cook until all water has been absorbed. Remove from heat; allow to steam 10–15 minutes. Makes about 6½ cups cooked rice.

Seasoning the Rice——Make vinegar dressing by heating 5⅓ Tbsp rice vinegar, 5 Tbsp sugar, and 4 tsp salt in a pan over low heat until sugar dissolves. Spread out cooked rice in a shallow wooden bowl and pour dressing evenly over rice. With a wooden spatula, mix vinegar evenly into rice using swift, horizontal slicing motions. Fan rice until it cools to room temperature.

Nigirizushi (Hand-Molded Sushi)

Nigirizushi—hand-molded fingers of rice topped with a colorful assortment of *tane*—is probably the most familiar type of sushi outside Japan. For about 6–8 servings, you will need 1 kg (roughly 2 lb) skinned fish fillets for the topping, 4 cups sushi rice, and 6 Tbsp *wasabi*. To keep rice from sticking, wet hands with a mixture of water and a small amount of vinegar.

Nigirizushi with traditional ingredients. Front row (left to right): squid, ark shell (*akagai*), conger eel (*anago*). Middle row: shrimp, salmon roe, gizzard shad (*kohada*). Back row: tuna, sea bass, vinegared ginger. (Shrimp and eel have been precooked.)

Molding the nigirizushi:

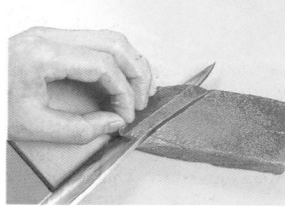

1 Using a long, slender knife, insert blade at a 75° angle to left edge of fillet and cut into 5-mm (¼-in) slices.

2 With right hand, take a small handful of sushi rice and shape into a firm ball.

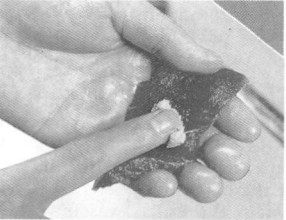

3 Place a slice of fish across fingers of left hand. With right index finger, dab a small amount of *wasabi* onto fish.

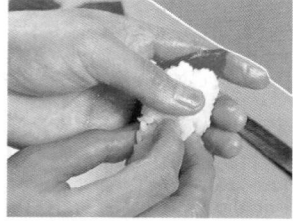

4 Put rice on top of fish and press down rice with left thumb. Press down again with right index and middle fingers.

5 Turn over so fish is on top. Press in sides with right thumb and middle finger, then press down top with index and middle fingers. Rice should form a firm, oblong shape.

Gunkammaki (Seaweed-Wrapped Nigirizushi)

For *gunkammaki*, seaweed (*nori*) is used to hold in salmon roe, sea urchin roe, and other toppings that normally will not stay in place atop the rice. Follow the steps above to make fingers of rice, omitting the topping. Cut sheets of toasted seaweed into 6 strips each. (For more information on seaweed, refer to the section on *makizushi*.)

1 Place finger of rice on a flat surface and dab a small amount of *wasabi* on top. Wrap a strip of seaweed around rice.

2 Hold ends of the seaweed together with a mashed grain of cooked rice. Fill with topping.

Makizushi (Rolled Sushi)

Makizushi refers to all types of sushi rolled in seaweed (*nori*). The *makizushi* here have been rolled in a traditional bamboo mat called a *makisu*, but a flexible place mat or dry kitchen towel can be used as a substitute. Seaweed is sold packaged in standard-sized sheets. Before using, toast each sheet by passing one side over an open flame.

An assortment of *makizushi*. Left to right: *futomaki* with assorted vegetables; *uramaki* with avocado, crab, and cucumber (known as "California roll"); *kappa-maki*, or *hosomaki* with cucumber; *kampyōmaki*, or *hosomaki* with gourd.

Utensils and ingredients for making *makizushi*. Clockwise from top: seaweed, *makisu* (rolling mat), *wasabi*, grater for *wasabi*, grated *wasabi*.

For hosomaki (thin roll):

1 With shiny side facing down, lay a half sheet of seaweed along bottom edge of *makisu*. Take a handful of sushi rice.

2 Spread an even layer of sushi rice, about 1 cm (⅜ in) thick, across the seaweed, leaving the top 1½ cm (⅝ in) of seaweed uncovered.

3 Form a groove across the middle of rice with fingers; spread *wasabi* along groove.

4 Lay filling on top of *wasabi*. For *kappamaki* (pictured), use a strip of cucumber about 1 cm (⅜ in) thick.

5 Lift up the bottom edge of *makisu* with thumbs while holding in the filling with other fingers. Roll it over once to bring together bottom and top edges of rice; press.

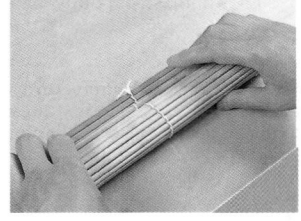

6 Finish rolling to the other edge of *makisu*. Grip rolled *makisu* with both hands and press firmly to mold. Slice roll into 4 rounds.

Futomaki (Thick Roll)——Make *futomaki* when you wish to roll several ingredients together. Spread sushi rice across a whole sheet of seaweed, leaving the top 2 cm (¾ in) of seaweed uncovered. Arrange ingredients horizontally along rice; roll as for *hosomaki*. Ingredients for *futomaki* on platter above: shrimp, conger eel, ground white fish (*oboro*), *shiitake* mushrooms, lotus root, cooked egg, gourd (*kampyō*), *shiso* (beefsteak plant), trefoil (*mitsuba*), and cucumber.

Uramaki (Reverse Roll)——Spread sushi rice on top of a half sheet of seaweed; set aside. Lay a damp towel on top of *makisu* and sprinkle it with toasted sesame seeds or crab roe. Carefully lay rice and seaweed on top of towel, with rice side facing down. Place ingredients along center of seaweed, and roll. To make a "California roll," use a combination of avocado, crab, and cucumber.

Temakizushi (Hand-Rolled Sushi)

Fun to make and easy to prepare, *temakizushi*, or hand-rolled sushi, is the ideal course for a buffet-style party. Just set the sushi rice, *tane*, seaweed, and condiments out on the table and invite your guests to roll the sushi of their choice.

On large platter (clockwise from top): avocado, tuna, salmon roe, shrimp, omelet strips, salmon, *daikon* radish sprouts, ark shell (*akagai*) mantles, cucumber, shrimp, conger eel, squid. (The cone-shaped *temakizushi* pictured here have been rolled in half sheets of seaweed.)

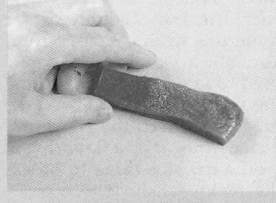

1 Slice larger ingredients into palm-sized strips. Cut seaweed into quarter sheets.

2 Place a heaping tablespoon of sushi rice in middle of seaweed. (For easier handling, have sushi rice shaped into small balls, as shown.)

3 Flatten rice with chopsticks and dab a small amount of *wasabi* in the center.

4 Lay filling on top of rice and bring together the right and left corners of seaweed.

susuki
1 A field of wild *susuki* in the village of Soni, Nara Prefecture. Some varieties are cultivated domestically.
2 This reedlike perennial herb is known in Japan as one of the traditional seven flowers of autumn.

Susukida Kyūkin This writer of symbolist verse later worked as a newspaper editor and became known for his finely crafted essays.

egg. Served in restaurants and sold at supermarkets and take-out shops, *sushi* can also be prepared at home. It is enjoyed in many regional varieties all over Japan and is one of a handful of Japanese foods, along with TEMPURA, that have become popular internationally.

Sushi cuisine originated in ancient China as a method of preserving fish. After packing the fish in rice and salt, the mixture was left to ferment for anywhere from two months to one year. After fermentation the rice was discarded and the pickled fish was eaten. This method probably came to Japan with the introduction of wet rice culture sometime in the Yayoi period (ca 300 BC–ca AD 300); a variant of the ancient process is used today in making certain regional varieties of *sushi*. Variations on the fermentation process reduced the waiting time and introduced vinegar as a flavoring agent, and after a time the rice came to be eaten along with the pickled fish. It was not until the early 19th century, however, in Edo (now Tōkyō), that the pickling process was dropped and fresh raw fish was served on freshly cooked vinegared rice. The *sushi* of this period was sold from stalls as a snack food; the stalls were the precursors of today's *sushi* restaurants.

Today *sushi* can be divided into four broad categories:

Nigirizushi (hand-pressed *sushi*) is the *sushi* developed in Edo in the 1800s. It is also known as *edomaezushi*. It consists of a bite-sized portion of vinegared rice topped with a small slice of raw fish or shellfish (cooked shellfish is also used) and seasoned with a dab of *wasabi* (Japanese horseradish) between the rice and the topping. Some of the most popular fish used in *nigirizushi* are tuna (*maguro*), sea bream (*tai*), swordfish (*makajiki*), bonito (*katsuo*) and sea bass (*suzuki*). Also used are shrimp (*ebi*), salmon roe (*ikura*), octopus (*tako*), squid (*ika*), eel (*anago*), abalone (*awabi*), and cockle (*torigai*). *Nigirizushi* is dipped lightly in soy sauce before eating.

For *makizushi* (rolled *sushi*), vinegared rice is spread over a sheet of lightly toasted seaweed (*nori*) and various types of seafood and/or vegetables are arranged along the center; a thin bamboo mat placed beneath the seaweed beforehand is used to roll the *makizushi* into a cylinder, which is sliced crosswise into bite-sized pieces. Some of the most popular types of *makizushi* are *tekkamaki* (tuna roll), *kappamaki* (cucumber roll), *kampyōmaki* (gourd roll), and *futomaki* (a thick roll of omelet, gourd, bits of vegetables, and other ingredients). For *temakizushi* the seaweed and other ingredients are loosely rolled by hand (without the bamboo mat) into a conelike shape that is not cut into pieces. The various types of *makizushi* may also be dipped in soy sauce for eating.

The category of *chirashizushi* ("scattered" *sushi*) is divided into two regional varieties. In the Tōkyō variety cooked and uncooked seafood, vegetables, and sliced omelet are arranged over a bowl of vinegared rice. Soy sauce is served on the side for dipping. In the Ōsaka version cooked seafood and vegetables are chopped and mixed into the rice, a sweetened sauce is poured over the mixture, and the whole is topped with thin strips of omelet.

Oshizushi (pressed *sushi*) is a specialty of the Kansai (Kyōto-Ōsaka-Kōbe) area made by pressing marinated seafood and rice in a small, boxlike wooden mold. It is sliced into bite-sized pieces and eaten dipped in soy sauce. *Batterazushi* is *oshizushi* topped with mackerel. In making *sugatazushi* (figure *sushi*), a whole fish (head intact) is cleaned, deboned, and stuffed with vinegared rice so as to reproduce the original shape of the fish. *Inarizushi* consists of a pocket of deep-fried bean curd (*aburaage*) filled with vinegared rice mixed with roasted poppy or sesame seeds. ☎ 1484–1485

Susono 裾野〔市〕

City in eastern Shizuoka Prefecture, central Honshū. Industries include automobile parts, aluminum, and electrical-cable plants. Fuji Safari Park and Nippon Land are among its many tourist attractions. Pop: 49,039.

susuki 薄

(eulalia). *Miscanthus sinensis.* Sometimes referred to as Japanese pampas grass. One of the traditional seven flowers of autumn (*aki no nanakusa*), this reedlike perennial herb of the family Gramineae grows wild on hills and in fields, often in large masses, throughout Japan and the rest of East Asia. Its narrow stem with alternate leaves grows to a height of 1.0–1.5 meters (3.3–5.0 ft). From late summer through autumn several flower spikes develop at the top of the stem; from their resemblance to animal tails, these spikes have given *susuki* the nickname *obana* ("tail flower"). Dried *susuki* stems have been used to make roofs, sacks, sandals, ropes, and curtains, and young leaves have been used as fodder.

Several varieties of *susuki* grow wild in Japan. The *itosusuki* has very slim leaves and a larger spike and is often planted in gardens. The *shimasusuki* has white-spotted leaves and is also planted in gardens and used in *ikebana* (FLOWER ARRANGEMENT).

Susukida Kyūkin 薄田泣菫

(1877–1945). Poet and essayist. Real name Susukida Junsuke. Born in Okayama Prefecture. In 1899 his first poetry collection, *Botekishū*, was published, followed in 1901 by his second collection, *Yuku haru*. Known as one of Japan's early symbolist poets, he first wrote in a romantic style and later turned to symbolist expression. After 1910, as chief literary editor of the newspaper *Ōsaka mainichi shimbun*, he became known as an essayist. Other works include *Hakuyō-kyū* (1906), a collection of poems, and *Sōmoku chūgyo* (1929), a collection of essays.

sutego 捨子

(abandoned children; also, the abandoning of children). The term *sutego* refers both to actual abandonment of unwanted children and to ritual abandonment for purposes of exorcism, a custom that was once fairly widely practiced in Japan. Ritual abandonment was practiced when an infant was weak and sickly or it was born in an unlucky year according to Chinese and Japanese zodiacal traditions (see JIKKAN JŪNISHI). The parents left the infant at a crossroad or on the bank of a river, and a previously chosen "finder parent" (*hiroioya*) then took the child and returned it to its real parents. Those selected for the task were usually parents who had raised strong and healthy children, powerful and respected members of the community, Shintō priests, or Buddhist monks.

Sutoku, Emperor 崇徳天皇

(1119–64; Sutoku Tennō). The 75th sovereign (*tennō*) in the traditional count (which includes several legendary emperors); reigned 1123–42. Son of Emperor TOBA and Taiken Mon'in, he was enthroned as a small child while his great-grandfather, the former emperor SHIRAKAWA, and later his father ruled in his stead from retirement (see INSEI). In 1142 Toba forced Sutoku to relinquish the throne to a young half brother, who became Emperor Konoe (1139–55; r 1142–55). Sutoku tried to secure the succession for his own son after Konoe's death but another half brother was enthroned as Emperor GO-SHIRAKAWA. After Toba's death in 1156, Sutoku conspired to depose Go-Shirakawa (see HŌGEN DISTURBANCE). He failed and was exiled to Sanuki Province (now Kagawa Prefecture), where he died.

sutra mounds 経塚

(*kyōzuka*). Small earthen mounds beneath which Buddhist sutras were buried. The practice of burying sutras was especially popular late in the Heian period (794–1185) when people believed that the world had entered the last, degenerate period of history (*mappō*; see ESCHATOLOGY) and that it was necessary to preserve sutra texts. Later, texts were buried for other purposes, such as ensuring one's rebirth into paradise, worldly gain, or the repose of the souls of the dead. The practice continued through the Edo period (1600–1868). Copies of the sutras were placed in stone or metal containers inscribed with the depositor's intentions or wishes. These containers, together with other articles such as BRONZE MIRRORS and knife talismans, were then placed in stone-lined pits 1 to 4 meters (3.3 to 13.1 ft) in diameter and about 1 meter (3.3 ft) deep. Earth was mounded over the pit, and a stone stupa or GORINTŌ was usually erected on the spot.

Suwa 　　　　　　　　　　　諏訪[市]

City in central Nagano Prefecture, central Honshū, on Lake Suwa. In the Edo period (1600–1868) it developed as a castle town. The traditional silk-reeling industry was replaced after World War II by precision-instrument, *miso* (bean paste), and wood-working industries. Local attractions are Lake Suwa, the Kami Suwa Hot Spring, the Kirigamine highland, and Suwa Shrine. Pop: 52,464.

Suwa Basin 　　　　　　　諏訪盆地

(Suwa Bonchi). A graben basin in central Nagano Prefecture, central Honshū. It spreads around Lake Suwa, forming a delta and fans, and is basically a rice-producing area. The basin is also noted for the production of raw silk and precision instruments. The major cities are Suwa and Okaya. Area: 714 sq km (276 sq mi).

Suwa, Lake 　　　　　　　　諏訪湖

(Suwako). In Suwa Basin, central Nagano Prefecture, central Honshū. The lake boasts abundant fishing with catches including carp, crucian carp, and pond smelt. It is popular for ice-skating in winter. Numerous hot springs are located on the eastern bank and also within the lake. Area: 14.1 sq km (5.4 sq mi); circumference: 18 km (11 mi); depth: 7.6 m (24.9 ft); altitude: 759 m (2,490 ft).

Suwa Shrine 　　　　　　　諏訪大社

(Suwa Taisha). Shintō shrine in Nagano Prefecture combining two shrines, the Kami Sha (Upper Shrine) and the Shimo Sha (Lower Shrine). The Kami Sha consists of the two compounds Moto Miya, in the city of Suwa, and Mae Miya, in the city of Chino. Shimo Sha's two compounds, Haru Miya and Aki Miya, are both located in the town of Shimo Suwa. The gods enshrined in Suwa Shrine are Takeminakata no Kami, Yasakatome no Kami, and Yaekotoshironushi no Kami. The Moto Miya has no main hall (*honden*), and the surrounding forest is venerated as the sacred abode of the god. In ancient times the gods enshrined were revered as hunting deities and later as farming deities and as the preeminent gods of war. Of the numerous religious ceremonies performed at the shrine, the most famous one is the Ombashira Matsuri, held every sixth year in early May. The annual festival of the Kami Sha is on 15 April and that of the Shimo Sha on 1 August.

Suzaka 　　　　　　　　　　須坂[市]

City in northeastern Nagano Prefecture, central Honshū. It prospered as a silk-reeling town from the Meiji period (1868–1912), but since World War II, it has become the center of an electronics industry. Apples and grapes are grown. Prefectural agricultural experimental stations are located here. It is the gateway to the Jōshin'etsu Kōgen National Park. Pop: 53,662.

Suzu 　　　　　　　　　　　　珠洲[市]

City in northeastern Ishikawa Prefecture, central Honshū, on the tip of the Noto Peninsula. It is known for its portable cooking stoves (*konro*) and its beautiful coastline. It is a part of Noto Peninsula Quasi-National Park. Pop: 23,471.

suzu 　　　　　　　　　　　　　鈴

(bell). Small enclosed bell with a tiny pellet for a clapper, much like a jingle bell or sleigh bell; also, a small bell with a dangling clapper. The word *kane* is used for larger bells. *Suzu* came to be made of metal after the introduction of Chinese culture in about the 5th century. Funerary goods of the Kofun period (ca 300–710) indicate that *suzu* were used to decorate hats, BRONZE MIRRORS, and horse trappings (see HORSE TRAPPINGS, ANCIENT). A string of *suzu* is traditionally used in KAGURA dances for the repose of departed souls.

Suzuka 　　　　　　　　　　鈴鹿[市]

City in northern Mie Prefecture, central Honshū; known as Suzuka no Seki. A barrier station (SEKISHO) from the 8th to the 12th centuries, it developed as a castle town and post-station town during the Edo period (1600–1868). Synthetic fiber and transport machinery industries are active. The technique for patterned paper made in the Shiroko district has been designated an Important Intangible Cultural Property. The Suzuka Circuit is known for its automobile races. Pop: 174,105.

Suzuka Mountains 　　　　　鈴鹿山脈

(Suzuka Sammyaku). Mountain range forming the border between Mie and Shiga prefectures, central Honshū. It consists of numerous mountains in the 1,000 m (3,300 ft) range, including Gozaishoyama (1,212 m; 3,976 ft). During the Nara period (710–794) two check stations were established in the mountains, forming a boundary between the Kantō and Kansai regions.

Suzuka Pass 　　　　　　　　鈴鹿峠

(Suzuka Tōge). Located in the Suzuka Mountains, on the border of Mie and Shiga prefectures, central Honshū. Important pass connecting the Kinai (Kyōto-Nara-Ōsaka) region with eastern Japan in ancient days. The post-station towns of Sakashita and Tsuchiyama flourished in the Edo period (1600–1868). The Mie side of the pass is steep, and National Route No. 1, which runs over the pass, sometimes becomes impassable due to heavy winter snowfall. The pass is mentioned in the famous song "Suzuka magouta" (Song of the Suzuka Packhorse Man). Altitude: 378 m (1,240 ft).

Suzuken Co, Ltd 　　　　[株]スズケン

(Suzuken). Comprehensive supplier of medical equipment and pharmaceuticals to the medical community. Incorporated in 1946. The company offers a wide range of products, including high-technology scanners and laser equipment. For the fiscal year ending March 1990, sales totaled ¥382.9 billion (US $2.5 billion) and capitalization stood at ¥1.5 billion (US $9.8 million). Headquarters are in Nagoya.

Suzuki Akira 　　　　　　　鈴木朖

(1764–1837). Confucian scholar and Japanese grammarian of the Edo period (1600–1868). Born in the Owari domain (now part of Aichi Prefecture). Suzuki was a student of

MOTOORI NORINAGA and was instrumental in synthesizing the grammatical work on the Chinese language of Confucians such as OGYŪ SORAI (1666–1728) and Minagawa Kien (1734–1807) with the work on Japanese of Norinaga and FUJITANI NARIAKIRA (1738–79). His ideas influenced MOTOORI HARUNIWA and TŌJŌ GIMON.

Suzuki's most noted contribution to Japanese grammar was his theory of word classes, similar to the parts of speech in traditional European grammar. His major classes were *tai no kotoba* (substance words), corresponding to nouns; *arikata no kotoba* (state words), corresponding to adjectives; *shiwaza no kotoba* (action words), corresponding to verbs; and *tenioha* (particles), corresponding to nonderived adverbs, prepositions, conjunctions, and interjections. He made a distinction between the first three classes, which express concepts used by the mind to organize experience, and the fourth class, which expresses the mind's activity directly. This distinction was later developed further by the modern grammarian TOKIEDA MOTOKI.

Suzuki's best-known works on Japanese grammar are *Gengyo shishu ron*, first printed in 1824, and *Katsugo danzoku fu*, published posthumously. He also wrote a treatise on the origin of language, *Gago onjō kō*, first printed in 1816. See also JAPANESE LANGUAGE STUDIES, HISTORY OF.

Suzuki Bokushi→Hokuetsu seppu

Suzuki Bunji 　　　　　　　鈴木文治

(1885–1946). Labor leader. Born in Miyagi Prefecture. He became a Christian while a student at Tōkyō University and, under the influence of YOSHINO SAKUZŌ and ABE ISOO, became interested in social problems. In 1912

Suwa Shrine This shrine actually consists of two separate shrines, the Kami Sha (Upper Shrine) and the Shimo Sha (Lower Shrine). **1** During the Suwa Shrine's Ombashira Festival, 16 tall fir trees are felled and then slid down steep hillsides to be used to replace the *ombashira*, or four sacred posts, at each of the four compounds of the shrine. **2** The Aki Miya compound, pictured here, and the Haru Miya compound make up the Shimo Sha.

Daisetz Teitarō Suzuki A Buddhist philosopher and translator whose English-language works played a key role in popularizing Zen Buddhism worldwide.

Suzuki Miekichi This novelist and children's story writer founded the landmark children's magazine *Akai tori* (Red Bird) in 1918.

Suzuki Mosaburō A founder of several pre–World War II proletarian parties, Suzuki became chairman of the Japan Socialist Party in 1951.

he founded the YŪAIKAI, a society to promote the welfare of workers, which gradually developed into the first major labor organization in Japan, with 30,000 members by 1919. Suzuki advocated moderation, attempted to reconcile labor and management, and opposed communism. He was elected four times as a Japanese representative to the International Labor Organization (ILO) and served as vice-chairman of the general assembly at the 14th ILO conference in 1930. In the 1928 national election, the first with universal manhood suffrage, Suzuki was elected to the House of Representatives, serving a total of three terms. Among his works is *Nihon no rōdō mondai* (1919, Labor Problems of Japan).

Suzuki, Daisetz Teitarō 鈴木大拙

(1870–1966). Philosopher. Known in Japan as Suzuki Daisetsu. Through his numerous books in both Japanese and English, he was instrumental in engendering the worldwide popularity of ZEN Buddhism. Born in Kanazawa, Ishikawa Prefecture, he entered Tōkyō University and concurrently undertook Zen training at the temple Engakuji in Kamakura under its abbot, SHAKU SŌEN. In 1897 he moved to La Salle, Illinois, to assist the Open Court Publishing Co with the English translation of Oriental philosophical and religious works.

Upon his return to Japan in 1909, Suzuki was appointed lecturer and later professor of English at the Peers' School (now Gakushūin University). In 1911 he married Beatrice Lane, who was his close collaborator until her death in 1939. In 1921 he became professor of Buddhist philosophy at Ōtani University, Kyōto, and over the next several years published many works. His three-volume *Essays in Zen Buddhism* (1927–34) comprised virtually the first Western-language discourses on Zen. In 1938 appeared another major work, *Zen Buddhism and Its Influence on Japanese Culture*. In 1949 he was elected to the Japan Academy and received the Order of Culture. From then on he spent much time lecturing on Zen outside Japan, most notably as visiting professor at Columbia University. Suzuki's collected works in Japanese number 32 volumes and in English, about 30.

Suzuki Eiji 鈴木永二

(1913–). Business leader. Born in Aichi Prefecture. Graduated from the Tōkyō Higher Commercial School (now Hitotsubashi University). In 1937 he joined Nippon Kasei Co, Ltd (now MITSUBISHI KASEI CORPORATION). He became president of Mitsubishi Kasei in 1974 and chairman in 1982. Between 1987 and 1991 he served as chairman of NIKKEIREN (Japan Federation of Employers' Associations). While at Nikkeiren he greatly expanded the chairman's role by representing business interests in political and national economic affairs as well as in labor matters. In 1990 he was appointed chairman of the Third Provisional Commission for Administrative Reform.

Suzuki Eitarō 鈴木栄太郎

(1894–1966). Sociologist. Born in Nagasaki Prefecture. A graduate of Tōkyō University, he later held professorships at Hokkaidō and Tōyō universities. Suzuki is held in high regard for having devised a system of rural and urban sociology, as well as an original theory of local sociology. After World War II,

Suzuki did research on urban sociology and criticized urban studies for tending to focus on slums and crime. He then turned to the structural pattern produced by the lives of the average population of a city. Maintaining that the city serves as a medium for social intercourse, he theorized that the size of a city is determined by the size of the integrative organization and class composition. His publications include *Nihon nōson shakaigaku genri* (1940, Principles of Japanese Rural Sociology) and *Toshi shakaigaku genri* (1957, Principles of Urban Sociology).

Suzuki Harunobu → Harunobu

Suzuki Kantarō 鈴木貫太郎

(1867–1948). Admiral and prime minister of Japan's last wartime cabinet. Born in Ōsaka; graduate of the Naval Academy and the Naval War College. Promoted to admiral in 1923, he was named chief of the Naval General Staff two years later. Late in World War II, in April 1945, Suzuki became prime minister. With the landing of American forces in Okinawa and Russian notification that it would not extend the Soviet-Japanese Neutrality Pact (see SOVIET UNION AND JAPAN), Japan's military situation had become desperate. Although Suzuki publicly maintained an unyielding posture, he secretly asked the Soviet Union to mediate for peace, but his overtures were rebuffed. In early August, Hiroshima and Nagasaki were destroyed by atomic bombs; on the 8th the Soviet Union declared war. A series of imperial conferences (GOZEN KAIGI) was held, and on the 14th the Suzuki cabinet decided to accept the terms of the POTSDAM DECLARATION. The following day the cabinet resigned.

Suzuki Kiitsu 鈴木基一

(1796–1858). Painter of the RIMPA style and a favorite disciple of SAKAI HŌITSU. Real name Suzuki Motonaga. The son of a dyer, Kiitsu was born in Ōmi Province (now Shiga Prefecture) and moved to Edo (now Tōkyō). He married the elder sister of a fellow student of Hōitsu, Suzuki Reitan (1782–1817). When Reitan died Kiitsu became head of the Suzuki family. Kiitsu specialized in paintings of figures as well as birds and flowers. He was also known as an accomplished HAIKU poet and a master of the various polite classical arts (*geinō*) practiced by members of the nobility.

Suzuki Kisaburō 鈴木喜三郎

(1867–1940). Conservative bureaucrat and a leader of the RIKKEN SEIYŪKAI political party. Born in Kawasaki, Musashi Province (now part of Kanagawa Prefecture), and graduated from the law faculty of Tōkyō University in 1891, Suzuki entered the Ministry of Justice. As prosecutor for the Great Court of Cassation (1912), prosecutor-general (1921), and minister of justice (1924), Suzuki worked to suppress heterodox social movements and was influential in securing passage of the PEACE PRESERVATION LAW OF 1925. Joining the Rikken Seiyūkai in 1925, Suzuki was awarded the post of home minister in 1927. Under Suzuki the Home Ministry arranged the mass arrests of Communist Party members in 1928 (see MARCH 15TH INCIDENT). However, his interference in the elections of 1928 (see SENKYO KANSHŌ) forced him to resign in May.

With the assassination of Prime Minister INUKAI TSUYOSHI in May 1932, Suzuki became president of the Seiyūkai and a candidate to succeed Inukai as prime minister. The elder

statesman (*genrō*) SAIONJI KIMMOCHI could not tolerate Suzuki's antiliberalism, so Suzuki was passed over. He resigned as president of the Seiyūkai in 1937.

Suzuki Masatsugu 鈴木雅次

(1889–1987). Civil engineer. Authority on harbor construction and systems concepts applied to the design of large-scale industrial areas. Born in Nagano Prefecture, he graduated from Kyūshū University in 1914 and entered the Department of Public Works of the Home Ministry, serving until 1945. He later became a professor at Nihon University. His publications include *Kōwan kōgaku* (1933, Harbor Engineering). He received the Order of Culture in 1968.

Suzuki Masaya 鈴木馬佐也

(1861–1922). Businessman and leader of the SUMITOMO *zaibatsu* (financial and industrial combine) in the early 20th century. Born in Miyazaki Prefecture, Suzuki graduated from Tōkyō University in 1887. He joined Sumitomo in 1896 after serving in the Home Ministry and the Agriculture and Commerce Ministry. As manager of Sumitomo's Besshi Copper Mine he promoted construction of the Shisakajima smelting works. He became executive director of Sumitomo's main office in 1904. He promoted the diversification and modernization of Sumitomo-affiliated businesses by turning Sumitomo Sōhonten (the combine's private holding company) into Sumitomo Gōshi Kaisha (a limited partnership).

Suzuki method スズキ・メソッド

(Suzuki *mesoddo*). Method of early musical talent development. The Suzuki method was established and developed by the violin teacher SUZUKI SHIN'ICHI. The principle of the method is simple: all talent is "equal," and any child can develop his or her talent provided that adequate training is given. Using this method, young children begin lessons on an instrument, usually a violin, to learn a fixed repertoire of pieces (predominantly, the music of 18th- and 19th-century composers) by ear and by rote. Musicality and technique are emphasized and aided by recordings; score reading is not introduced until the student has acquired a basic technique. Although this method is well known for teaching violin, it is also used to teach piano, flute, and cello. Suzuki started a music school in the city of Matsumoto in Nagano Prefecture. Today there are over 100 affiliated schools in Japan, and the method is well known all over the world.

Suzuki Miekichi 鈴木三重吉

(1882–1936). Novelist and writer of children's stories. Born in Hiroshima Prefecture; graduate of Tōkyō University. While still a student, he associated with NATSUME SŌSEKI and his disciples and wrote his first lyrical short stories, "Chidori" (1906) and "Yamabiko" (1907). In July 1918 he founded *Akai tori* (Red Bird), a magazine that was a landmark in the history of CHILDREN'S LITERATURE in Japan, enlisting such prominent authors as AKUTAGAWA RYŪNOSUKE and KITAHARA HAKUSHŪ as contributors. Other works include *Kosui no onna* (1916), a collection of children's stories, and *Kotori no su* (1910), an autobiographical novel.

Suzuki Mosaburō 鈴木茂三郎

(1893–1970). Politician and socialist leader. Born in Aichi Prefecture, Suzuki graduated from Waseda University in 1915. He worked for the newspaper *Hōchi shimbun* and, while covering the SIBERIAN INTERVENTION and the RICE RIOTS OF 1918, became interested in socialism. He joined the *Tōkyō nichinichi shimbun* (now the *Mainichi shimbun*) in 1922. Suzuki helped found the Proletarian Masses Party (Musan Taishūtō, 1928), the Japan Masses Party (Nihon Taishūtō, 1928–30), and the Japan Proletarian Party (NIHON MUSANTŌ, 1937). In December 1937 he was arrested in the POPULAR FRONT INCIDENT. After World War II, he helped form the JAPAN SOCIALIST PARTY, serving as secretary-general from 1948 and as chairman in 1951. He was elected to the first of nine terms in the Diet in 1946. When his party split in 1951, Suzuki became chairman of the Left Faction (Saha); when it was reunited in 1955 he was reelected chairman. In 1960 he withdrew from all formal posts.

Suzuki Motor Corporation
スズキ[株]

(Suzuki). Company manufacturing minicars, motorcycles, and outboard motors that is affiliated with General Motors Corporation and Isuzu Motors, Ltd. It is the largest producer of minicars and the third largest manufacturer of motorcycles in Japan. The company's predecessor was the Suzukishiki Loom Co, incorporated in 1920. With the decline of the textile industry, it switched to the manufacture of motor vehicles. It took on its current name in 1954. Suzuki has automobile assembly plants in Canada, India, Indonesia, and Spain. Sales for the fiscal year ending March 1991 totaled ¥1.0 trillion (US $7.3 billion), with an export ratio of 48 percent. The company was capitalized at ¥49.1 billion (US $357.9 million) in the same year. Headquarters are in Hamana District, Shizuoka Prefecture.

Suzuki Seijun
鈴木清順

(1923–). Film director. Born in Tōkyō, in 1948 joined SHŌCHIKU CO, LTD, as an assistant director. He moved to NIKKATSU CORPORATION in the same capacity in 1954 and made his directorial debut in 1956. Refusing to manipulate emotions, he strives for interesting images, creating his own unique kind of cinematic beauty with a fresh sense of color and finely studied technique. Among his most important films are *Kenka erejī* (1966, Elegy for a Quarrel) and *Chigoineruwaizen* (1980, Zigeunerweisen).

Suzuki Shigetane
鈴木重胤

(1812–63). Classical scholar of the late Edo period (1600–1868). Born on the island of Awaji (now part of Hyōgo Prefecture). In 1832 Suzuki took up the study of National Learning (KOKUGAKU). He journeyed to visit Kokugaku scholar HIRATA ATSUTANE; Hirata had died, but Suzuki considered himself his disciple. In 1848 he completed *Engi shiki norito kōgi* (Discourse on Shintō Rituals in the Engi Legal Code), and about 1853 he began his *Nihon shoki den*, a commentary on the 8th-century chronicle NIHON SHOKI that was never completed. Suzuki was murdered in 1863 for motives that remain unclear.

Suzuki Shin'ichi
鈴木鎮一

(1898–). Creator of the world-famous SUZUKI METHOD. Born in Aichi Prefecture. Son of a noted violin maker, he studied violin in Japan with Andō Kō (1878–1963). Later he studied violin in Germany. In 1946 he started the Talent Education Movement with the motto "Anyone's talent can be developed through education." His method spread

---

worldwide. About 25,000 people are studying his method in Japan and about 400,000 worldwide.

Suzuki Shōsan
鈴木正三

(1579–1655). Zen teacher and moralist. Born in Mikawa (now part of Aichi Prefecture). He fought at the Battle of SEKIGAHARA (1600) and at the sieges of Ōsaka Castle, then in 1621 became a monk. Shōsan acknowledged no master and therefore was outside both Sōtō and Rinzai Zen, although he supported Sōtō. Intensely combative and loyal, he aspired to conquer all fear of death and to have the shōgun proclaim true Buddhism—his own simple and strenuous teaching—as the moral guide for Japan. He succeeded in the first aim but failed in the second. Shōsan taught that each man's work was deeply worthwhile and itself a path to enlightenment. He also urged recitation of the NEMBUTSU, a practice not commonly associated with the Zen tradition. Shōsan's writings include *Ninin bikuni* (1664, Two Nuns), a KANA-ZŌSHI tale; and *Bammin tokuyō* (1661, Right Action for All), a moral essay.

Suzuki Shōten
鈴木商店

A trading firm active during the Meiji (1868–1912) and Taishō (1912–26) periods; founded by Suzuki Iwajirō around 1877. Initially dealing in sugar and camphor, the firm grew rapidly. After the SINO-JAPANESE WAR OF 1894–1895, in which Japan acquired the island of Taiwan, the company obtained the right to sell 65 percent of Taiwan's camphor. When World War I broke out, the firm expanded its holdings in ships, agricultural products, and iron ore. It soon rivaled MITSUI and MITSUBISHI. After World War I, the firm was weakened by disclosures of improprieties with the Bank of Taiwan (TAIWAN GINKŌ), and it finally collapsed in the FINANCIAL CRISIS OF 1927. KŌBE STEEL, LTD, TEIJIN, LTD (a textile firm), and Harima Shipbuilding, which is now a part of ISHIKAWAJIMA–HARIMA HEAVY INDUSTRIES CO, LTD, emerged from the subsequent reorganization.

Suzuki Tadashi
鈴木忠志

(1939–). Stage producer and head of the theater group Suzuki Company of Toga (SCOT). Born in Shizuoka Prefecture. Graduated from Waseda University. In 1966 Suzuki established the Waseda Shōgekijō (Waseda Little Theater) with a former classmate, the playwright BETSUYAKU MINORU, and others; in 1984 the group adopted the name SCOT. Suzuki's innovative productions, which include *The Trojan Women* (1974), contributed to his emergence as one of the leaders of Japan's SHŌGEKIJŌ UNDŌ (little theater movement). Suzuki developed an original style of footwork in acting that came to be called the Suzuki method. In 1976 Suzuki shifted most of his activities from Tōkyō to the village of Toga in Toyama Prefecture. Since 1982 an international drama festival called the Toga Festival has been held there each summer.

Suzuki Takeo
鈴木竹雄

(1905–). Scholar of commercial law. Born in Kanagawa Prefecture, Suzuki graduated from Tōkyō University in 1928. He was a professor there from 1940 to 1966 and from 1966 until 1976 was a professor at Sophia University. Suzuki is a member of the Japan Academy and Chairman of the Commercial Law Division of the Ministry of Justice Legislative Council. In the post–World War II era he was the leading contributor to amend-

---

ments of and new legislation dealing with the Commercial Code—in particular, those sections covering corporate law. His writings on corporate and negotiable instruments law display a flexibility derived from close observation of actual practice and have strongly influenced both academics and legal practitioners. His publications include *Tegata, kogitte hō* (1957, Bills and Notes Law and Checks Law) and *Shimpan: Kaisha hō* (1974, Company Law: New Edition). He was awarded the Order of Culture in 1989.

Suzuki Torao
鈴木虎雄

(1878–1963). Scholar of Chinese literature and writer of both Chinese and Japanese poetry. Born in Niigata Prefecture. Graduated from Tōkyō University. As a professor at Kyōto University, he made a substantial contribution to the study of Chinese poetry with *Shina shironshi* (1927, A History of Chinese Poetics). He also translated the complete works of the poet Du Fu (Tu Fu; 712–770) into Japanese and wrote many critical works and commentaries on Chinese poetry. He was awarded the Order of Culture in 1961.

Suzuki Umetarō
鈴木梅太郎

(1874–1943). Agricultural chemist and one of the pioneers of biochemistry in Japan. Born in Shizuoka Prefecture, he graduated from Tōkyō University in 1896. In 1901 he went to Germany to do research on proteins under Emil Fischer. In 1907 he became a professor at Tōkyō University. In 1910 Suzuki succeeded in extracting the substance later known as vitamin B_1. At the INSTITUTE OF PHYSICAL AND CHEMICAL RESEARCH, he conducted research on the chemistry of nutrition and successfully compounded synthetic rice wine (*sake*). Suzuki received the Japan Academy Prize in 1924 for research on secondary nutrients, and the Order of Culture in 1943.

Suzuki Zenkō
鈴木善幸

(1911–). Politician and prime minister (1980–82). Born in Iwate Prefecture. Suzuki graduated from the Agriculture and Forestry Ministry's Fisheries Institute (now Tōkyō University of Fisheries). In 1947 he was elected to the House of Representatives as a candidate of the Japan Socialist Party. He joined the Minshu Jiyūtō (now LIBERAL DEMOCRATIC PARTY or LDP) in 1949 and was elected to the House of Representatives. Elected thereafter 16 times, he was minister of posts and telecommunications in the first IKEDA HAYATO cabinet (1960), chief cabinet secretary in the third Ikeda cabinet (1964), and welfare minister in the first SATŌ EISAKU cabinet (1965–66). Suzuki also served as chairman of the Executive Board of the LDP. In 1980, upon the sudden death of Prime Minister ŌHIRA MASAYOSHI, Suzuki was appointed his successor. Two years later he resigned and was succeeded by NAKASONE YASUHIRO. He retired from political life in 1990. Suzuki was known more for his skill in mediating differences than for strong leadership.

suzuri
硯

(inkstone). A CALLIGRAPHY implement. Used in conjunction with a solid inkstick to make liquid ink. *Suzuri* are usually made of stone, but may be ceramic or tile. Commonly flat and rectangular in shape with a raised lip along the side, they are indented at one end to form a shallow receptacle. To make liquid

Suzuki Shin'ichi
The originator of the internationally known Suzuki method of violin study as photographed in 1985.

Suzuki Umetarō
A pioneer of biochemistry in Japan, Suzuki succeeded in 1910 in isolating the chemical compound that came to be known as vitamin B_1.

swimming
Considered a martial art in premodern Japan, swimming was part of the training of every *samurai*. Here a modern-day "samurai" demonstrates a stroke from one of the 12 surviving schools of traditional swimming.

ink the calligrapher drips water onto the *suzuri* while slowly rubbing the tip of the inkstick over the moistened area until the desired amount and consistency of ink has been produced. The ink collects in the receptacle end of the *suzuri*, which then serves as an inkwell.

swallows   燕

(*tsubame*). Birds of the family Hirundinidae; the name *tsubame* may be used to refer to all species in this family or specifically to the barn swallow (*Hirundo rustica*). About 17 centimeters (7 in) long, this bird has a deeply forked tail, black back, reddish brown throat, and white belly. It migrates to Japan from Southeast Asia in the spring, appearing in settled areas throughout the country, and builds nests of grass and mud under the eaves of buildings. In autumn it moves to reedy marshes along seacoasts. The species is also very common in Eurasia and North America. Other swallow species found in Japan include the *koshiaka tsubame* (Japanese striated swallow; *H. daurica*), the *iwatsubame* (house martin; *Delichon urbica*), the *ryūkyū tsubame* (Pacific swallow; *H. tahitica*), and the *shōdō tsubame* (sand martin; *Riparia riparia*).

Because barn swallows have the unusual habit of building their nests in people's houses and because pairs of swallows may return to the same house spring after spring, they came to be revered by the Japanese people as birds of good fortune.

swearwords   罵りの言葉

(*nonoshiri no kotoba*). There are no Japanese swearwords with as strong religious or sexual connotations as those commonly employed in other languages. Perhaps the major exception is *chikushō* ("beast"), an insult with religious overtones because of the Buddhist belief that one could be consigned to the realm of beasts in a future existence as a result of actions in this life. Another Japanese swearword is *kuso* (excrement, filth), but this lacks the taboo connotations of the English "shit" and is much milder in effect. There are many even milder expressions of disdain, roughly equivalent to "fool" or "idiot," like *baka*, *bakayarō*, *ahō*, and *manuke*.

Sweden and Japan スウェーデンと日本

(*Suēden to Nihon*). Relations between Sweden and Japan were initiated in 1868 with the signing of a treaty of amity and commerce. Crown Prince (now Emperor) AKIHITO visited Sweden in 1953 and in April 1980 King Carl XVI Gustaf visited Japan. The king also attended the funeral of Emperor

SHŌWA in 1989 and the enthronement of Emperor Akihito in 1990.

Japan and Sweden have held annual trade talks since 1975. In April 1988 a joint corporation was set up in Japan by Swedish and Japanese businesspeople to promote the import of Swedish products. Although the balance of trade between the two nations has risen overwhelmingly in favor of Japan, Sweden's deficit shrank substantially in 1990, when Japan's exports decreased 10 percent from the previous year to US $2.0 billion, and its imports rose 19 percent to $1.3 billion.

swimming   水泳

(*suiei*). Traditional Japanese-style swimming developed chiefly during Japan's medieval period (mid-12th–16th centuries) as one of the MARTIAL ARTS (*bujutsu*) practiced by the *samurai*, or warrior class. Techniques were developed for swimming while carrying weapons, for moving underwater, and for swimming silently. During the Edo period (1600–1868) various *daimyō* domains developed their own schools of swimming. These swimming methods, which are still practiced today and are known collectively as Nihon *eihō*, contributed to the modern popularity of swimming as a sport. Western-style swimming was introduced to Japan during the Taishō period (1912–26). In 1928 TSURUTA YOSHIYUKI became the first Japanese swimmer to win an Olympic event. Japanese swimmers remained active on the international scene until World War II, after which they were less prominent. Swimming has remained popular as a sport, however, and swimming clubs have proliferated throughout Japan. Suzuki Daichi (b 1967) won a gold medal for backstroke in the 1988 Seoul Olympics.

Switzerland and Japan スイスと日本

(*Suisu to Nihon*). Diplomatic relations between Japan and Switzerland began with the conclusion of a treaty of amity and commerce in 1864. Legations were established in 1916 and elevated to the status of embassy in 1955. During World War II Switzerland, as a nonbelligerent country, represented Japanese interests vis-à-vis the Allied powers. Japan's acceptance of the POTSDAM DECLARATION was communicated to the Allies through this channel.

In 1989 President René Felber attended the funeral of Emperor Shōwa, and in 1990 Foreign Minister Nakayama Tarō visited Bern. In recent years a number of Japanese economic missions have visited Switzerland and in 1989 the country drew 472,000 Japanese tourists. In 1990 Japan's exports to Switzerland, chiefly automobiles and electronics and optical equipment, totaled US $2.9 billion and its imports, mainly precious metals, machinery, timepieces, and chemicals, totaled US $4.1 billion. As of 1989, 93 Japanese corporations, including banks and securities firms, had opened offices in Switzerland.

sword guards →tsuba

sword hunt   刀狩

(*katanagari*). Name given to programs of weapons confiscation carried out by military authorities especially in the 16th century. The best known of these was ordered in 1588 by TOYOTOMI HIDEYOSHI. There had been sword hunts from early times, and Hideyoshi and other 16th-century *daimyō* had al-

Swordsmith Sumitani Seihō, who is designated a Living National Treasure by the Japanese government, heats the raw steel for a sword in his forge in the city of Mattō, Ishikawa Prefecture.

During the early stages of forging, a power hammer is now used in place of assistants wielding sledge hammers.

Using a small hammer, Sumitani pounds the blade into its final shape.

An assistant does the initial rough polishing of the sword.

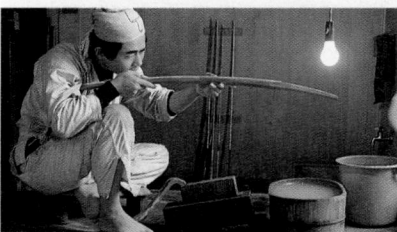

The sword is repeatedly inspected during the rough-polishing process.

ready carried out confiscations directed toward specific areas or against specific groups, such as the armed monks of certain temples. The 1588 order was distinguished by the fact that it applied to the entire nation. The sword hunt was a means of reducing the level of violence in the countryside to the benefit of higher military authority and of disarming the farming class to make the status of *samurai* and the authority of the daimyō secure. By the start of the Edo period (1600–1868) the pacification of the countryside was complete. The wearing of two swords had become the samurai's badge of status, denoting the monopoly of arms bearing by the warrior aristocracy.

swords   日本刀

(*nihontō*). The origins of the Japanese sword go back to the 8th century and the earliest development of steel in Japan. Japanese

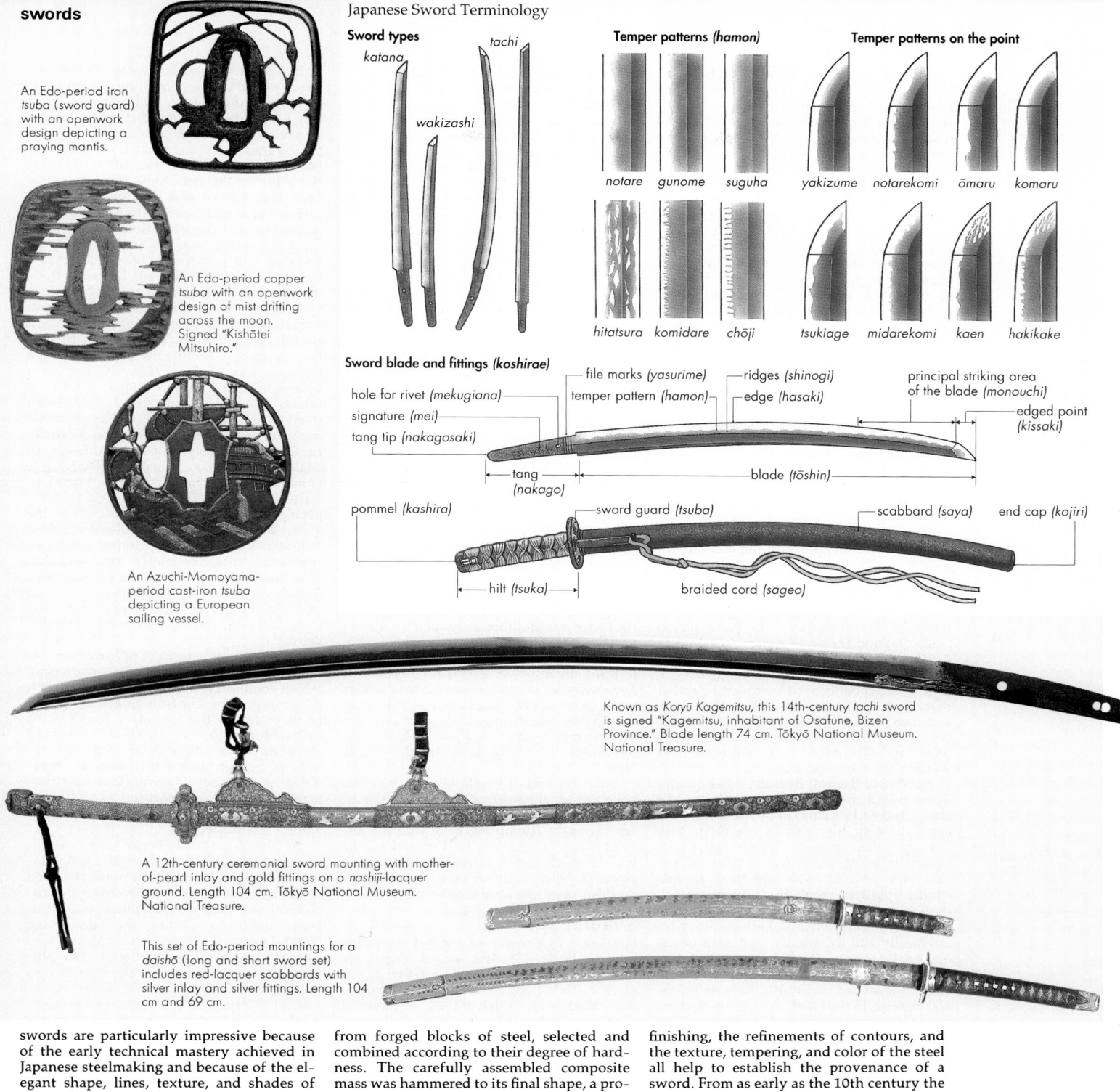

An Edo-period iron *tsuba* (sword guard) with an openwork design depicting a praying mantis.

An Edo-period copper *tsuba* with an openwork design of mist drifting across the moon. Signed "Kishōtei Mitsuhiro."

An Azuchi-Momoyama-period cast-iron *tsuba* depicting a European sailing vessel.

Japanese Sword Terminology

Sword types

katana tachi wakizashi

Temper patterns (hamon)

notare gunome suguha

hitatsura komidare chōji

Temper patterns on the point

yakizume notarekomi ōmaru komaru

tsukiage midarekomi kaen hakikake

Sword blade and fittings (koshirae)

hole for rivet (mekugiana)
signature (mei)
tang tip (nakagosaki)
file marks (yasurime)
temper pattern (hamon)
ridges (shinogi)
edge (hasaki)
principal striking area of the blade (monouchi)
edged point (kissaki)
tang (nakago)
blade (tōshin)

pommel (kashira)
sword guard (tsuba)
scabbard (saya)
end cap (kojiri)
hilt (tsuka)
braided cord (sageo)

Known as *Koryū Kagemitsu*, this 14th-century *tachi* sword is signed "Kagemitsu, inhabitant of Osafune, Bizen Province." Blade length 74 cm. Tōkyō National Museum. National Treasure.

A 12th-century ceremonial sword mounting with mother-of-pearl inlay and gold fittings on a *nashiji*-lacquer ground. Length 104 cm. Tōkyō National Museum. National Treasure.

This set of Edo-period mountings for a *daishō* (long and short sword set) includes red-lacquer scabbards with silver inlay and silver fittings. Length 104 cm and 69 cm.

swords are particularly impressive because of the early technical mastery achieved in Japanese steelmaking and because of the elegant shape, lines, texture, and shades of color of the steel fabric. For more than 12 centuries the sword has had a spiritual significance for the Japanese; along with the mirror and jewels, it is one of the three IMPERIAL REGALIA.

From as early as the 8th century, the Japanese sword was fabricated from steel of controlled carbon content rather than iron. From the first the sword was made with varying degrees of hardness appropriate to the different parts of the blade. Even the earliest examples are characterized by a very densely forged, repeatedly folded, cross-welded, laminar structure with as many as 10,000 strata of steel of alternating higher and lower carbon content hammered to exceptional toughness. In later years swords were made from forged blocks of steel, selected and combined according to their degree of hardness. The carefully assembled composite mass was hammered to its final shape, a process of hardening that provided nearly the hardness of file steel at the edge with resultant unsurpassed sharpness.

Swordsmiths—The Japanese swordsmith was traditionally held in high regard. The earliest swordsmiths were often *yamabushi*, members of the SHUGENDŌ sect, who with their apprentices lived an austere and religiously dedicated life. The approximately 200 schools of Japanese swordsmith-artists were scattered throughout Japan, each with its own history and its own identifiable and surprisingly consistent blade characteristics that can be traced down through the centuries.

The file marks (*yasurime*) on the tang (*nakago*) of the blade, the shape and style of finishing, the refinements of contours, and the texture, tempering, and color of the steel all help to establish the provenance of a sword. From as early as the 10th century the signature of the smith was often chiseled on the tang. In the case of individual schools the inscription often included not only the name of the smith, but the province, the town, and the date when the blade was tempered.

Forging—Iron-working technology was introduced to Japan from about the 3rd to the 5th century AD, and, as early as the 8th to 10th century, sword blades of high-quality steel were being made in Japan. After the steel was forged, the "skin steel" (*kawagane*) was some 10 to 20 times hammered into plates, which were then hardened, broken into coin-sized pieces, stacked, and welded.

This hardened steel was later welded onto the surface of the less brittle inner steel (*shingane*). This repeated folding and welding gave the Japanese blade one of its unique qualities—a texture (*jihada*) like that of the grain of wood.

Tempering and Polishing—The *hamon*, or temper pattern of the blade, is one of the most noticeable and beautiful features of the sword and also an important means of identifying its origin. By the early Kamakura period (1185–1333), this *hamon* was made to exhibit many shapes and forms. Generally a specific type of temper or group of types was employed by an individual school or smith. The final polishing and sharpening were done by a sword polisher, who set the sword to a series of stones of increasing fineness that were lubricated with water. When completed, the final curving outlines of the sword exhibit extraordinary symmetry. A cross section of the edge shows that the two sides meeting at the edge form a slim Gothic arch, a stable structure that strengthens the edge.

Jōkotō (Ancient Sword) Period—*Jōkotō*, or ancient swords, have come down to us almost exclusively from the ancient burial mounds of the Kofun period (ca 300–710) and are badly rusted. Swords preserved in the 8th-century SHŌSŌIN imperial art repository in Nara have been kept in nearly perfect condition for centuries. These ancient blades were nearly always straight, with a very small and sharply angled slanted point (*bōshi*). Swords of the Nara period (710–794) and the early Heian period (794–1185) were similar to those found in the mounds. Being rather short and lightweight, they were probably used for thrusting rather than slashing. From approximately the 9th and 10th centuries, blades were made longer with a slightly curved shape and with ridge lines on both sides, a far more efficient weapon for mounted warriors.

Kotō (Old Sword) Period—The quality of the sword greatly improved in the middle Heian and early Kamakura periods, or from approximately the 10th to the early 13th century, when its use markedly increased, especially by mounted warriors. In the period from 1040 to 1400, schools of swordsmiths appeared in all the principal provinces of Japan. The swords of the Kamakura period (*tachi*) are of the highest quality, both artistically and technically, and most of the National Treasure (Kokuhō) blades derive from this period. With improvements in armor the sword necessarily became longer and heavier. In the late Kamakura period the sword became very long—in many instances as long as 1 to 1.5 meters (3–5 ft)—and was used exclusively by mounted warriors. Many of these were later shortened for use in hand-to-hand combat.

In the Muromachi period (1333–1568), as a result of prolonged strife and feudal combat, the production of swords increased in number but quality declined. Swords became somewhat heavier and less curved, wider and considerably shorter, so that they could cut through the heavier armor then coming into use. This new blade was called *katana* and was upward of 60 centimeters (2 ft) in length. It was soon accompanied by a somewhat shorter blade, *wakizashi*. The *katana* and *wakizashi* were worn thrust through the sash, edge up and parallel to or crossing each other in the sash. These swords were called *daishō*, "long and short."

Shintō (New Sword) Period—During the Azuchi-Momoyama (1568–1600) and Edo (1600–1868) periods individual swordsmiths founded new schools, and an interest developed in the largely lost skills of the Kamakura period. They attempted to copy the swords of the past but were restricted by the requirements of hand-to-hand combat. Many swords had extraordinarily brilliant tempering patterns, a substantial structure of well-hammered and well-tempered steel, and beautiful chiseled engravings (*horimono*) and grooves. Sword guards (TSUBA) and other fittings (KOSHIRAE) for the *samurai*'s long and short swords and for daggers became highly ornate.

The years from 1800 to the close of the Edo period are known in sword history as the Shinshintō (New, New Sword) period. It was a brief renaissance marked by a final effort to revive the beauty and quality of the ancient sword.

Modern Period—In 1868 the emperor Meiji promulgated regulations forbidding the making or wearing of swords but permitted a small number of smiths to continue their work in order to keep the art alive. A further quickening of interest occurred during the Russo-Japanese War of 1904–05 and before and during World War II. For the most part these later military swords are not genuine art swords (*nihontō*) but are made from machine-made steel.

After World War II, the Allied Occupation forces ordered all swords destroyed, but the order was modified to exclude swords of artistic, religious, or spiritual significance belonging to museums, shrines, or private collections. Even so an enormous number of good swords were destroyed. Many others were taken out of the country as souvenirs during the immediate postwar period when it became mandatory that all swords be registered with the police, as is still the case in Japan.

Since the end of World War II, there has been a gradual renewal of interest in the art of the ancient sword, and a number of smiths are currently attempting to restore the ancient skills. The Agency for Cultural Affairs has designated two swordsmiths and two sword polishers as LIVING NATIONAL TREASURES. See also ARMS AND ARMOR; IRON AND STEEL.

Syahrir, Sutan シャフリル, S.

(1909–66). Indonesian nationalist and prime minister (1945–47). Also spelled Sjahrir. He helped to establish a national education movement in the Dutch East Indies in 1931, but he was exiled by the Dutch in 1934. He returned to the East Indies in 1942, but refused to cooperate with the Japanese. He served as prime minister during the struggle for independence, but was forced to resign because of his conciliatory diplomatic policies.

syncretism 習合

(*shūgō*). A conscious or unconscious admixture of two or more different traditions or ideas—cultural, philosophical, or religious. In modern Japanese usage, *shūgō* signifies "mixing" or "blending" and is sometimes used to mean "eclecticism." With the introduction of Buddhism and Confucianism between the 4th and 6th centuries and again with the influx of Western culture after the Meiji Restoration of 1868, syncretism in Japan has been constantly increasing in scope and depth, and it continues to be in evidence in all aspects of Japanese culture to this day. See also WAKON KANSAI; WAKON YŌSAI.

In religious syncretism we see the assimilation of the native cult, Shintō, with Buddhism, Confucianism, and religious Taoism. Shintō-Buddhist syncretism, known as *shimbutsu shūgō* or *shimbutsu konkō*, spread among the masses and had a lasting and important impact on Japanese culture. Despite the order of the new Meiji government in 1868 that Shintō and Buddhism be completely separated (see SHINTŌ AND BUDDHISM, SEPARATION OF), by this time Shintō-Buddhist syncretism had been so thoroughly integrated into Japanese religious life that it has never been eradicated. Japanese Buddhists devised a particular form of religious syncretism commonly known as HONJI SUIJAKU, which refers to a manifestation of a Buddha or bodhisattva (*honji*) in the temporary form of a Shintō deity (*suijaku*). The Shingon sect of Buddhism constructed a system of Dual Shintō (RYŌBU SHINTŌ) in which the deities of the Inner Shrine (Naikū) and Outer Shrine (Gekū) of the ISE SHRINE (Amaterasu Ōmikami and Toyouke no Ōkami) are respectively identified with Mahāvairocana (the Great Sun Buddha; J: Dainichi Nyorai) in the Matrix World (J: Taizōkai) and the Diamond World (J: Kongōkai) of the two mandalas known as the RYŌBU MANDARA. In the Sole Reality Shintō (Ichijitsu Shintō or SANNŌ ICHIJITSU SHINTŌ) of the TENDAI SECT, the native deities of Mt. Hiei (HIEIZAN) were first made protectors of Buddhism and of the temple erected on that mountain (ENRYAKUJI) and later identified with various Buddhas and bodhisattvas.

Another unique form of religious syncretism is SHUGENDŌ (mountain asceticism), which emphasizes the attainment of magico-religious powers. The founding of Shugendō is attributed to the legendary figure EN NO GYŌJA. Shugendō is a syncretistic mixture of elements of the native belief in the sacredness of certain mountains, esoteric Buddhism, and religious Taoism. Traveling Shugendō ascetics (YAMABUSHI) contributed greatly to the spread of religious syncretism among the masses.

As Shintō gradually began to develop its own systematized metaphysical, cosmological, and ethical doctrines around the 13th century, it borrowed heavily from Confucianism and Neo-Confucianism as well as from Buddhism. During the Edo period (1600–1868), when Neo-Confucianism (SHUSHIGAKU) was made the orthodox state philosophy, many scholars attempted to create a syncretism of Shintō and Neo-Confucianism. The 18th- and 19th-century KOKUGAKU thinkers also covertly syncretized elements of foreign thought into their own overtly nativistic philosophy.

Thus, the Japanese mind has endeavored through syncretism to maintain and enrich the "indigenous" Japanese culture, which itself is syncretistic and defies efforts at precise characterization. It is this ambiguity that has led the Japanese mind to produce a complex and essentially multilayered syncretistic culture, with the indigenous culture as its substratum. Syncretism can be found in practically all phases of Japanese culture, but it has never formed a coherent system. Its most conspicuous form (and the form that has been the object of most research) is religious syncretism, which has affected all segments of the Japanese society. The ramifications of popularized syncretism in Japanese literature, fine arts, and folklore have yet to be extensively studied and analyzed. See also SETCHŪGAKUHA.

T

Tabaruzaka 田原坂

Hill in the town of Ueki, northern Kumamoto Prefecture, Kyūshū; formerly an important transportation center and the site of an engagement between rebel and imperial troops during the SATSUMA REBELLION in 1877. A monument and museum commemorating the battle are located in the town. Height: 50–100 m (165–330 ft).

Tabei Junko 田部井淳子

(1939–). Alpinist; first woman to climb Mt. Everest. Born in Fukushima Prefecture. Graduate of Shōwa Women's University. In 1970 she reached the summit of Annapurna III in the Himalayas. Despite injuries received in an avalanche, she reached the summit of Mt. Everest on 16 May 1975. In 1981 she made a successful ascent of Xixabangma (Shisha Pangma; also known as Gosainthan) in the Himalayas, and in 1991 she climbed Vinson Massif, the highest mountain in Antarctica.

tabi 足袋

A kind of sock worn with traditional Japanese clothing. Originally *tabi* were made of deer or monkey skin (*kawa tabi*) and had no separation between the toes, but as thonged ZŌRI sandals became popular in the Kamakura period (1185–1333), *tabi* were divided between the big toe and the other toes to accommodate the thong. Originally *tabi* fastened at the ankle with a string, later buttons, and finally metal clasps called *kohaze*. Because of the scarcity of skins, after the 17th century silk and cotton were used. White *tabi* were worn with formal *kimono*, while solid dark colors were for ordinary occasions. Today *tabi* come in cotton, satin, and stretch nylon.

Tablada, José Juan タブラダ, J. J.

(1871–1945). Noted Mexican poet, essayist, and journalist. Though written in Spanish, many of his poems were modeled on the form of Japanese HAIKU. These innovative poems are said to have significantly influenced Latin American literature. For several months in 1900 Tablada worked in Japan as a correspondent for the literary journal *Revista Moderna.* In 1911 he spent a short time in Paris. Interest in Asian culture (and particularly in Japanese haiku) was very high there, and Tablada's literary career blossomed. When he returned to Mexico, he published poetry, a number of essays on Japanese art and artists, and a book on the *ukiyo-e* artist HIROSHIGE.

table tennis 卓球

(*takkyū*). Table tennis, now enjoyed by millions of Japanese, was introduced into Japan around 1900. In 1921 the Japan Imperial Table Tennis Association was founded, and in 1934 the All-Japan Table Tennis Championships began. A softer nonstandard ball unique to Japan was used exclusively at first, but in 1934 the standard ball also began to be used. International matches began to be played at about the same time. Since both the softer ball and the standard ball are still in use, national table tennis matches are separated into two classes. Japan has participated in the World Table Tennis Championships since 1952 and has achieved excellent records.

tableware 食器

(*shokki*). Almost contemporaneous with the perfection of what is now considered "tradi-

tabi Japanese-style socks, known as *tabi*, are worn with *kimono* and are usually made of white or colored cotton.

tional" Japanese cuisine, the development of Japanese tableware culminated during the Edo period (1600–1868) in nearly the same form that it has today. The use of *hashi* (CHOPSTICKS) as eating utensils was a shaping force in that development. Unlike metal knives and forks, *hashi* are usually made of softer materials such as wood or lacquered wood, so dishes could be made of similar materials as well as ceramics. Also, because *hashi* can be maneuvered in smaller areas, dishes could be made in a variety of shapes and sizes. The *wan* (bowl) was developed so that, in the case of soup for example, one could alternately drink the broth and use *hashi* to pick up the solid ingredients. Since *hashi* cannot readily be used for slicing, food is usually cut into small pieces beforehand and served in individual dishes. The amount of tableware needed for a Japanese meal, therefore, is much greater than that for a Western meal.

Characteristic of Japanese cuisine is the emphasis placed on seasonal awareness, and tableware plays an important role in conveying this sense. There are fixed designs and patterns that distinguish seasonal tableware, and the way in which chefs select and combine tableware from various regions, made of diverse materials, is a measure of their skill.

Traditional forms of Japanese cuisine include KAISEKI RYŌRI, HONZEN RYŌRI, and *chakaiseki ryōri* (see TEA CEREMONY). The fundamental rule governing the menu for all of these is formulated as "one soup and three side dishes." For example, a meal of *kaiseki ryōri* (the typical cuisine for banquets and gatherings) corresponding to a Western dinner would consist of the following: *shirumono* (soups), SASHIMI (raw fish), *yakimono* (grilled foods), and *nimono* (simmered foods). At the conclusion of the meal, rice and PICKLES are served. The kind of tableware necessary for such a meal includes individual place settings of *hashi*, lacquer soup bowls (*shiruwan*), plates for *sashimi* as well as tiny dipping bowls for soy sauce, plates for *yakimono*, bowls for *nimono*, rice bowls (CHAWAN), and small dishes for pickles. Also, if SAKE is served, SAKAZUKI (*sake* cups) and TOKURI (*sake* decanters) might be added. Depending on the menu, the number of side dishes for *kaiseki ryōri* can be increased to 5, 7, or as many as 11. As a rule, tableware for *chakaiseki ryōri* is made of lacquered wood, but in actual practice ceramic dishes are often mixed in with the lacquer ones. Noodles (such as UDON and SOBA), *sushi*, and foods for formal ceremonies all have their own specialized tableware.

With increasing availability of Western food, Western tableware has come to play a prominent role in Japan. Recently tableware that can be used for both Japanese and Western foods has become prevalent. However, almost every home is supplied with *chawan*, soup bowls, and *hashi*, since these are the basic eating utensils for Japanese food. Most tableware come in sets of five, but generally all members of a family have their own individual *chawan* and *hashi* for daily use.

taboo 忌

(*imi*). Ritual avoidance of things, persons, places, times, actions, or words believed to be inauspicious or, in contrast, sacred. The concept of taboo is closely allied to the notion of ritual impurity (KEGARE): anything impure must be avoided so as not to offend or defile the sacred; at the same time, the sacred itself must occasionally be avoided to insure that no offense to its sanctity occurs. Examples of the former category are the traditional taboos surrounding birth, menstruation, and death. Inauspicious words (*imikotoba*; see TABOO EXPRESSIONS) or numbers (*imikazu*) that are homonyms of tabooed phenomena may also be taboo: hence the avoidance of the number four (*shi*), which is a homonym of the word for death (*shi*). In the Heian period (794–1185), directional taboos (KATATAGAE) were observed so as to avoid transgressing the direction believed to be occupied by certain deities.

taboo expressions 忌詞

(*imikotoba*). Words or expressions considered to bring or be associated with bad luck; also, the euphemisms and alternative expressions used in their place. For example, in Shintō ceremonies Buddhist terms such as *hotoke* (Buddha) and *sō* (Buddhist monk) are generally avoided (Buddhism being associated with funerals), as are words like *shi* (death) and *chi* (blood). There are expressions to be avoided after nightfall; instead of saying *shio* for salt (near-homophone of *shi*, death), one says *nami no hana* (flowers of the waves). In speeches at wedding parties, words like *kaeru* and *modoru* (to go back home) are carefully avoided. Among *imikotoba* used by fishermen are *nagamono* (long object) for snake (*hebi*) and *eteko* ("honorable monkey") for monkey (*saru*, homophone of the verb "to depart"), while hunters and charcoal makers refer to the bear (*kuma*) as *yamaoyaji* (old man of the mountains), and so forth. Some *imikotoba* have become part of the secular argot used exclusively by particular groups (such as craftspeople, entertainers, and gangsters) to reinforce in-group solidarity and exclusivity.

Tabuchi Setsuya 田淵節也

(1923–). Businessman and chairman (1985–91) of NOMURA SECURITIES CO, LTD. Born in Okayama Prefecture. Upon graduation from Kyōto University in 1947, he joined Nomura Securities Co, becoming its president in 1978. In 1980 he launched the medium-term government bond (*chūki kokusai*) fund, which became an extremely popular financial instrument. In 1984 the company became the largest financial firm in the world, and by 1985 it had taken in more than ¥25 trillion (US $104.8 billion) in client deposits. Tabuchi promoted internationalization of the securities business and acquired a seat on the New York Stock Exchange in 1981. He served as vice-chairman of the JAPAN ASSOCIATION OF CORPORATE EXECUTIVES from 1985 to 1991.

Tachibana Akemi 橘曙覧

(1812–68). Pen name Shinobunoya. WAKA poet. Born in Echizen (now part of Fukui Prefecture). He was an admirer of the classical style based upon the MAN'YŌSHŪ and advocated by KAMO NO MABUCHI. With Tanaka Ōhide (1777–1847), he was a student of the KOKUGAKU (National Learning) scholar MOTOORI NORINAGA. At the age of 35 he turned to a life of austere and impoverished seclusion. He supported the SONNŌ JŌI (Revere the Emperor, Expel the Barbarians) movement. His chief works include a collection of poetry, *Shinobunoya kashū* (1878), and a volume of essays, *Irori-gatari* (date unknown).

Tachibana family 橘氏

(Tachibanashi). Ancient noble family (UJI), particularly prominent during the Nara period (710–794). In 708 Agata no Inukai no Michiyo, the wife of Prince Minu, a descendant of Emperor Bidatsu (538–585), was granted the name Tachibana no Sukune (see AGATA NO INUKAI NO TACHIBANA NO MICHIYO). Her son Prince Katsuragi changed his name to TACHIBANA NO MOROE and later received the honorific cognomen of *ason* (see YAKUSA NO KABANE), indicating his status as a kinsman of the imperial house. Moroe's son Naramaro (721?–757) unsuccessfully challenged the power of FUJIWARA NO NAKAMARO in a failed rebellion. Tachibana no Kachiko (786–850), popularly known as Empress DANRIN, became principal consort (*kōgō*) to Emperor SAGA and the mother of Emperor Nimmyō (r 833–850). After TACHIBANA NO HAYANARI's involvement in the JŌWA CONSPIRACY (842) and the downfall of imperial favorite Tachibana no Hiromi (837–890) in the AKŌ INCIDENT OF 887, the family's influence declined. By the late Heian period (794–1185) people bearing names of the central nobility had become common in the provinces, and the Tachibana became one of the "Four Great Surnames" together with the Fujiwara, Taira, and Minamoto families.

Tachibana Kōzaburō 橘孝三郎

(1893–1974). A farm educator, rural utopian, and agrarian nationalist who helped to plan an unsuccessful coup d'état to rescue Japan from excesses that he attributed to capitalism, bureaucracy, and the urban way of life. Born in Mito, Ibaraki Prefecture, Tachibana studied European literature at the First Higher School in Tōkyō. He founded a "fraternal village," Kyōdai Mura, in 1915. This utopian community became the basis for a cooperative he founded in 1929 and a school known as the AIKYŌJUKU (Academy for the Love of One's Community) in 1931.

On 15 May 1932, 24 of Tachibana's students and an equal number of young military officers attacked power stations, civilian leaders, and the Tōkyō police headquarters. Prime Minister INUKAI TSUYOSHI was assassinated in the incident (see MAY 15TH INCIDENT). Convicted at a sensational trial, Tachibana spent six years in prison and turned to a quiet life of scholarship after World War II.

Tachibana believed the essence of Japanese life was "mutual love and cooperation," qualities he found mainly in rural society. Like all agrarian nationalists, he vilified absentee landlords but thought the chasm between city and village was the crucial social division in Japan, not the gap between tenants and landlords. See also NŌHON SHUGI.

Tachibana Moribe 橘守部

(1781–1849). KOKUGAKU (National Learning) scholar and WAKA poet of the late Edo period (1600–1868). Born in Ise (now part of Mie Prefecture). In *Itsu no kotowaki* (1846), an annotated study of the songs contained in the 8th-century chronicles KOJIKI and NIHON SHOKI, he opposed the views of Kokugaku scholar MOTOORI NORINAGA.

Tachibana no Hayanari 橘逸勢

(?–842). Court official of the early Heian period (794–1185), who accompanied a mission to China in 804 that included the Buddhist monks KŪKAI and SAICHŌ. In 842 he was charged with leading the JŌWA CONSPIRACY and died on his way into exile. He was a distinguished calligrapher and, with Kūkai and Emperor SAGA, was ranked one of the so-called Sampitsu (Three Brushes) of his time. See also CALLIGRAPHY.

Tachibana no Kachiko → Danrin, Empress

Tachibana no Moroe 橘諸兄

(684–757). Court official of the Nara period (710–794); son of the imperial prince Minu and the court lady AGATA NO INUKAI NO TACHIBANA NO MICHIYO, who later became the wife of FUJIWARA NO FUHITO and the mother of Empress KŌMYŌ, consort of Emperor SHŌMU. In 737 Moroe was appointed great counselor (*dainagon*) and dominated court affairs with the priest GEMBŌ and the scholar-official KIBI NO MAKIBI. He suppressed the Rebellion of Fujiwara no Hirotsugu (740; see FUJIWARA NO HIROTSUGU, REBELLION OF). In 749 Moroe was elevated to the senior first rank (*shōichii*; see COURT RANKS) with full administrative control of the state, but his power was soon eclipsed by FUJIWARA NO NAKAMARO. Moroe, accused of plotting a coup d'état in 755, was forced to withdraw from public life. He was responsible for the construction of two imperial palaces between 740 and 745—the KUNI NO MIYA and the SHIGARAKI NO MIYA. Several of his poems are preserved in the 8th-century anthology *Man'yōshū*.

Tachibana Shiraki 橘樸

(1881–1945). Sinologist. Born in Ōita Prefecture, Tachibana studied at the Fifth Higher School in the city of Kumamoto. He became interested in Chinese agriculture, economics, and folk beliefs and traveled widely, collecting material for the newspaper for which he worked. He later worked for the SOUTH MANCHURIA RAILWAY and became editor in chief of the magazine *Manshū hyōron* (Manchurian Review) in 1931. In the course of his studies he came to view Confucianism as the guiding principle of the Chinese social revolution and to criticize Japan's imperialistic policies on the Asian mainland. He also influenced many Japanese intellectuals through his published works on Chinese culture, history, and philosophical thought such as *Shina shisō kenkyū* (1936, Studies on Chinese Philosophy). His collected works in three volumes were published posthumously as *Tachibana Shiraki chosakushū* (1966).

Tachibana Shūta 橘周太

(1865–1904). Army officer. Born in Hizen Province (now Nagasaki and Saga prefectures). He graduated from the Army Academy in 1887. He was killed during the RUSSO-JAPANESE WAR of 1904–05. Together with the naval officer HIROSE TAKEO, he was honored as a *gunshin* ("war god") until the end of World War II.

Tachibana Takashi 立花隆

(1940–). Journalist. Born in Nagasaki Prefecture; graduated from Tōkyō University. Publication of Tachibana's *Tanaka Kakuei kenkyū*, an examination of the political and financial dealings of then prime minister TANAKA KAKUEI, serialized in the magazine BUNGEI SHUNJŪ in 1974, was a factor in Tanaka's resignation. Tachibana writes about a variety of social and political issues. He received the Mainichi Book Award for *Nōshi* (1986, Brain Death). Tachibana's other works include *Nihon Kyōsantō no kenkyū* (1978, A Study of the Japan Communist Party).

Tachihara Masaaki 立原正秋

(1926–80). Novelist. Born in Korea to Korean parents; later acquired Japanese citizenship. Studied at Waseda University. His works are noted for their intricate construction, sensitive depiction of human psychology, and evocation of loneliness. He was awarded the Naoki Prize for his novel *Shiroi keshi* (1965, White Poppy). Other novels include *Tsurugigasaki* (1965) and *Kinuta* (1973, The Fulling Block).

Tachihara Michizō 立原道造

(1914–39). Poet. Born in Tōkyō; graduate of Tōkyō University. He became a contributor to the poetry magazine SHIKI, founded in 1933 by HORI TATSUO. He left two collections of lyric poems, mostly in a sonnetlike form, *Wasuregusa ni yosu* (1937, Flowers of Forgetfulness) and *Akatsuki to yūbe no shi* (1937, Sonnets of Dawn and Dusk).

Tachikawa 立川[市]

City in central Tōkyō Prefecture. An army airfield was constructed here during the Taishō period (1912–26), and during World War II it was a center for aircraft production. After the war it became a United States Air Force base; the site was returned to Japan in 1977 and has been turned into a park, the Shōwa Kinen Kōen. Formerly a regional railroad center, the city has now developed into a residential and commercial area as well. Industrial products include automobiles and machinery. Pop: 152,824.

Tachikawa Bunko 立川文庫

(Tachikawa Library). Series of books—mostly period pieces read by boys and girls—published by the Ōsaka firm Tachikawa (more properly pronounced Tatsukawa) Bummeidō between 1911 and the mid-1920s. In Japan, there is a tradition of oral storytelling called KŌDAN, whose stories were often highly dramatized retellings of historical events. The Tachikawa Bunko consisted of *kōdan* stories that were adapted by the *kōdan* storyteller Tamada Gyokushūsai (dates unknown) for juvenile readers and published as paperback books. Almost 200 such books were published in a period of 15 years. The movie director MAKINO SHŌZŌ completed a series of *samurai* adventure movies based on the Tachikawa books.

tachimono 断物

(literally, "that which is cut off"). Certain types of food that an individual voluntarily abstains from eating for a set period of time as an ascetic practice in preparation for the observance of an important festival or to fulfill a personal or religious vow (see GANKAKE).

There are examples of whole villages avoiding *tachimono* on special occasions.

Tada Fumio 多田文男

(1900–1978). Geographer. Born in Tōkyō; graduated from Tōkyō University in 1924. Professor at Tōkyō, Komazawa, and Hōsei universities. President of the ASSOCIATION OF JAPANESE GEOGRAPHERS and vice-president of the International Geographical Union. Tada was an expert on both physical and applied geography. His works include *Shizen kankyō no hembō* (1964, Changes in the Natural Environment).

Tadamigawa 只見川

River in western Fukushima Prefecture, northern Honshū; originating in the lake Ozenuma, which straddles the border of Fukushima and Gumma prefectures, it flows into the Agagawa in the Aizu Basin. The Agagawa flows into Niigata Prefecture, where it is known as the Aganogawa and eventually empties into the Sea of Japan. Large electric power plants are located along the Tadamigawa. Its great volume of water is due to melting snow. Length: 137 km (85 mi); area of drainage basin: 2,260 sq km (873 sq mi).

tadokoro 田荘

Private rice lands and granaries owned by local chieftains (*gōzoku*) before the TAIKA REFORM (645). The term is used in distinction to *miyake*, rice lands owned by the ruling family in Yamato. *Tadokoro*, like the imperial estates, are thought to have been worked by serfs or service groups (BE) belonging to the landowners.

Taehan Empire 大韓帝国

(Kor: Taehan Cheguk; J: Daikan Teikoku). Replaced Chosŏn (J: Chōsen) as the official name of Korea in October 1897 and was used until Japan's annexation of Korea in 1910. *Tae* means great, while *han* was the name of ancient Korean tribes living in southern Korea prior to the KOREAN THREE KINGDOMS PERIOD. The name was intended to symbolize Korea's independence from all foreign powers. See KOREA AND JAPAN.

Taewŏn'gun 大院君

(1820–98; J: Taiinkun). Father of the Korean king KOJONG (r 1864–1907); personal name Yi Ha-ŭng; enfeoffment title Hŭngsŏn'gun. *Taewŏn'gun* (J: *taiinkun;* grand prince) is a royal title reserved for a monarch's father who has not occupied the throne. After his son's succession to the throne in 1864, the Taewŏn'gun became the dominant figure at court. He implemented an exclusionist foreign policy that resulted in a number of confrontations with foreign powers, including the Japanese SEIKANRON affair of 1873. He retired from the palace in late 1873. Returned to power briefly after the IMO MUTINY of 1882, the Taewŏn'gun was abducted by Chinese forces and taken to Tianjin (Tientsin), where he was held until 1885. The Japanese reinstalled him in the summer of 1894, but he sided with the rebels of the TONGHAK REBELLION and was again removed from power. A longtime rival of his son's consort, Queen MIN, he remained a rallying point for Confucian conservatives and anti-Japanese sentiment until his death.

Tagajō 多賀城[市]

City in central Miyagi Prefecture, northern Honshū. In the 8th century Tagajō was the

site of a military outpost for subduing the Ezo tribesmen. It is now a satellite city of Sendai. Industries include the manufacture of electrical and electronic machinery. Pop: 58,456.

Tagajō 多賀城

(Taga Castle). Eighth-century civil and military headquarters established in northern Honshū primarily to carry out the war against the aboriginal EZO people. Originally called Taga no Ki (Taga Stockade), it was later known as Tagajō. Situated on a hill south of the modern city of Shiogama in Miyagi Prefecture, Tagajō consisted of several buildings in a walled central area. Tagajō was eventually abandoned after the Ezo were crushed in 802, but the site of the castle's guardian temple—with the base stones for a pagoda, a main hall, a lecture hall, and other buildings—is well preserved today.

Tagawa 田川[市]

City in central Fukuoka Prefecture, Kyūshū. Part of the CHIKUHŌ COALFIELD, it was once the center of a thriving coal-mining industry. The closing down of all the mines has led to a drastic drop in the population. Pop: 57,700.

Tagawa Suihō 田河水泡

(1899–1989). Cartoonist. Real name Takamizawa Chūtarō. Born in Tōkyō. Graduate of the Art College of Japan (Nihon Bijutsu Gakkō). His children's comic strip *Norakuro* (Blackie the Stray) recounted the adventures of a dog who joins the army and finds himself promoted in spite of his repeated bumbling. It appeared in the magazine *Shōnen kurabu* (Boys' Club) for 10 years beginning in 1931 and was very popular with children.

tageta 田下駄

A type of footwear formerly worn in paddy fields. They are based on the same principle as the snowshoe and consist of sandals resting on large wooden frames that distribute the weight and enable the wearer to walk in muddy fields. *Tageta* are also used for trampling seedbeds before transplanting. *Tageta* have been traced back to the Yayoi period (ca 300 BC–ca AD 300).

Tagokura Dam 田子倉ダム

(Tagokura Damu). Located on the upper reaches of the river TADAMIGAWA, southwestern Fukushima Prefecture, northern Honshū. Completed in 1959, the dam created Lake Tagokura. The dam is utilized for electric power generation with a maximum output of 380,000 kilowatts. Height: 145 m (476 ft); length of embankment: 462 m (1,516 ft); storage capacity: 370 million cu m (13 billion cu ft).

Tagawa Suihō
1 Tagawa's *Norakuro*, a popular comic strip of the 1930s about a bumbling stray dog that joins the Imperial Army, was compiled into 10 hardcover books. **2** *Norakuro* in battle dress. Though the series appeared to support the Japanese military, the Imperial Army frowned on *Norakuro* as bad for its image.

Tachihara Michizō
This poet produced two collections of lyric poems before his death at age 25.

Taguchi Ukichi This historian and laissez-faire economist was also a politician and the president of a railway company.

Tagonoura　田子ノ浦

Coastal area near the mouth of the river Fujikawa, Shizuoka Prefecture, central Honshū. Celebrated in ancient poems, the coast offers a beautiful view of Mt. Fuji (FUJISAN). The important Tagonoura Port is in the city of Fuji. There are large pulp, chemical, and starch manufacturing plants on the coast.

Tagore, Rabindranath　タゴール, R.

(1861–1941). Indian poet and philosopher; recipient of the 1913 Nobel Prize in literature. Born in Calcutta; son of Debendranath Tagore, the Bengali philosopher and religious reformer. Tagore wrote plays, novels, and literary criticism, composed music, and painted, but it is for his Bengalese poems that he is best remembered. He worked for the independence movement in India. OKAKURA KAKUZŌ met Tagore in India in 1902; Okakura's works, *The Ideals of the East* (1903), *The Awakening of Japan* (1904), and *The Book of Tea* (1906), all bear witness to Tagore's influence. Tagore visited Japan on three occasions.

Taguchi Ukichi　田口卯吉

(1855–1905). Economist and cultural historian. Born in Edo (now Tōkyō). He studied economics and English in the Translation Bureau of the Ministry of Finance. In 1879 Taguchi founded the *Tōkyō keizai zasshi* (*Tōkyō Journal of Economics*), through which he helped to introduce the theories of the British "liberal" economists. He criticized protectionist theories and government economic policies from the standpoint of laissez-faire economics. He was the author of *Nihon kaika shōshi* (1877–82, A Short History of the Enlightenment of Japan), a systematic study of Japan's political, economic, religious, and literary history. He also edited the KOKUSHI TAIKEI and the modern edition of the GUNSHO RUIJŪ, two major compilations on Japanese history and culture. He was active in politics and business, serving first in the Tōkyō prefectural and municipal assemblies and, from 1894 on, in the lower house of the Diet and as president of the Ryōmō Railway Co.

Tahara　田原[町]

Town in the central part of the Atsumi Peninsula in southeastern Aichi Prefecture, central Honshū. Tahara has cement and food-processing factories and a Toyota factory built on reclaimed land in what was formerly Tahara Bay. Pop: 34,450.

Tahata Eitai Baibai Kinshi Rei
田畑永代売買禁止令

Also known as Dempata Eitai Baibai Kinshi Rei. Ordinance issued by the Tokugawa shogunate (1603–1867) in 1643 forbidding the sale and purchase of farming land. Issued to check the accumulation of land by rich peasants, it was also intended to prevent pauperization of peasants, their flight from rural areas, and the deterioration of farmland. Similar ordinances were issued in individual domains. Decrees reinforcing the ordinance were issued, but since peasants were allowed to put up their land as security against loans (*shichiire*) in order to pay their taxes (NENGU), land did change hands. By the 18th century the law had become almost meaningless. The Confucian scholar OGYŪ SORAI contended that because the land belonged to the peasant, it was therefore at his

disposal. The magistrate ŌOKA TADASUKE argued that the law might as well be abolished, since people gave up their land only as a last resort, and it was at his suggestion that punishments were mitigated. The ordinance was revoked in 1872, four years after the Meiji Restoration (1868).

tai→sea bream

taian→rokuyō

Tai Chi-t'ao→Dai Jitao (Tai Chi-t'ao)

Taiga→Ike no Taiga

Taigyaku Jiken→High Treason Incident of 1910

Taihei Housing Co, Ltd　太平住宅[株]

(Taihei Jūtaku). Construction company. Incorporated in 1950. Taihei Jūtaku markets its made-to-order construction services through a nationwide business network. For the fiscal year ending November 1990, sales totaled ¥120.2 billion (US $931.2 million) and capitalization stood at ¥500.0 million (US $3.9 million). Headquarters are in Tōkyō.

Taiheiki　太平記

GUNKI MONOGATARI (war tale) of unknown authorship recounting the conflict between the NORTHERN AND SOUTHERN COURTS over the period 1318–67. In 40 volumes, the work, whose title translates as "Chronicle of the Great Peace" (reflecting, no doubt, the author's desire for more stable times), was probably completed about 1370–71. In contrast to the lyricism of the HEIKE MONOGATARI and its Buddhist-oriented emphasis on the transience of life, this account emphasizes the natural order of cause and effect and seems Confucian in outlook. The *Taiheiki* (tr *Taiheiki*, 1959; vols 1-12 only) depicts a period of turmoil and shifting loyalties in which the low displace the high (GEKOKUJŌ). It was initially recited by storyteller-priests known as *taiheiki-yomi*, without musical accompaniment. The narrative, written in *wakan konkōbun*, mixed Chinese-Japanese style, is embellished with tales from the Chinese classics and Buddhist mythology. The first section covers Emperor GO-DAIGO's plot to overthrow the HŌJŌ FAMILY and the establishment of the KEMMU RESTORATION (Kemmu no Chūkō). The second section covers the rebellion of ASHIKAGA TAKAUJI, and the third covers the gradual emergence of the Northern Court and the establishment of the MUROMACHI SHOGUNATE.

Taiheiyō Kouhatsu, Inc
太平洋興発[株]

(Taiheiyō Kōhatsu). Company dealing in real estate, oil, construction materials, and coal. Incorporated in 1920 as Taiheiyō Coal Mining Co. The company belongs to the Mitsui group and is ranked second in the wholesale coal business. Sales for the fiscal year ending March 1991 totaled ¥80.0 billion (US $583.1 million), of which real estate accounted for 24 percent; trading, 13 percent; and coal, 63 percent. The company was capitalized at ¥3.1 billion (US $22.6 million) in the same year. Headquarters are in Tōkyō.

Taihō　大鵬

(1940–　). SUMŌ wrestler; 48th grand *sumō* champion (*yokozuna*). Real name Naya Kōki. Born in Sakhalin. Taihō entered the Nishonoseki stable and made his debut as a *sumō* wrestler in 1956, achieving top-divi-

sion (*makuuchi*) status by 1960 and championship (*ōzeki*) status in 1961. In the same year he became *yokozuna*. He maintained his *yokozuna* status in 58 tournaments over a nine-and-a-half-year period. Taihō won a total of 32 tournament victories, establishing a record that, as of late 1990, remained unbroken. Combining a low center of gravity with great pliancy of movement, his outstanding technique places him in the *sumō* pantheon alongside such masters as FUTABAYAMA. He retired in 1971 and was allowed to establish his own stable.

Taihō Code　大宝律令

(Taihō Ritsuryō). Early-8th-century legal code of 6 volumes of penal law (*ritsu*) and 11 volumes of administrative law (*ryō*). It is believed to have been a revision of the ASUKA KIYOMIHARA CODE (689), which had been modeled on the legal code of the Tang (T'ang) dynasty (618–907) of China. Compiled by an imperially appointed commission that included Prince Osakabe (d 705), FUJIWARA NO FUHITO, and Awata no Mahito (d 719), the Taihō Code was completed in 701 and became effective in 702 (Taihō 2). It was the first code to be formally promulgated. The original text has not survived; a 9th-century commentary, the RYŌ NO SHŪGE, indicates that it was similar to the YŌRŌ CODE, which superseded it in 757. See also RITSURYŌ SYSTEM.

Taiiku no Hi→holidays, national

Taiji Whale Museum
太地町立くじら博物館

(Taiji Chōritsu Kujira Hakubutsukan). Museum of the history of Japanese whaling. Established in 1969 in the town of Taiji, Wakayama Prefecture, the traditional birthplace of whaling in Japan. The exhibits include specimens of whale skeletons and traditional whaling equipment. The museum also stages dolphin and whale shows.

Taika Nijūikkajō Yōkyū→Twenty-One Demands

Taika no Kaishin→Taika Reform

Taika Reform　大化の改新

(Taika no Kaishin). In its strictest sense, the political and economic reforms carried out in the name of Emperor KŌTOKU from 645 to 649. After eliminating the SOGA FAMILY in a coup d'état in the sixth month of 645 (Taika 1), Nakatomi no Kamatari (later FUJIWARA NO KAMATARI) and Prince Naka no Ōe (later Emperor TENJI) strove to break the power of the UJI (chieftain families) and place the imperial house in control of Japan. In 646 they issued an edict announcing plans to establish a new system of regional administration, compile household registers, allocate land to peasants, and collect taxes from all male adults. The reformers aimed for a Chinese-style centralized state (see RITSURYŌ SYSTEM). Development of this state was furthered by the ASUKA KIYOMIHARA CODE in 689 and by compilation of the Kōinnen-Jaku population register in 690. In its broadest sense the term Taika Reform refers to political changes throughout the second half of the 7th century.

　Immediate Reform Efforts—One of the first steps of Japan's new leaders in 645 was to dispatch officials called *kokushi* or *kuni no mikotomochi* to all Yamato-controlled areas in eastern Japan and to the six districts (*mutsu no agata*) under direct court control in Yamato Province (now Nara Prefecture). The officials sent east consisted of eight groups with jurisdiction over local chieftains (*kuni no miyatsuko*). By dispatching them, the court hoped to strengthen its hold on the militarily important Kantō area. Often in the past, local chieftains, particularly those in eastern Japan, had been hostile to Yamato interests. The officials were to survey the land, count the population, guarantee communal rights to forests, prevent the exaction of excess taxes by local rulers or the exercise of vigilante justice, report all false claims to KABANE titles such as *kuni no miyatsuko*, and collect and store all weapons.

The NIHON SHOKI (720) reports other reform efforts in 645. Complaint boxes were installed throughout the country. Rules governing interclass marriage and divorce were established. Laws for state support of Buddhist temples and the nomination of monks to posts of authority in their monasteries were promulgated. Kōtoku's court moved to Naniwa (see NANIWAKYŌ) on the Inland Sea to facilitate communication with the continent.

The Reform Edict—In 646 Emperor Kōtoku and Prince Naka no Ōe proclaimed the Taika Reform edict. The edict had four articles: It abolished imperial and local-magnate service communities (*koshiro*, *kakibe*; see BE) and lands (*miyake*, TADOKORO), setting up a system of government stipends instead. It made arrangements for a permanent imperial capital and a new system of local government. It ordered the compilation of population and tax registers and the state allocation of land (HANDEN SHŪJU SYSTEM) and described land measurements (see JŌRI SYSTEM) and village government. It substituted a produce tax, levied both on paddy land and households, for the prior labor tax (see SO, YŌ, AND CHŌ). Thus the goal of the reform edict was government control of land and populace (*kōchi komin*). In addition to this edict, the Hakusōrei of 646, a sumptuary law, limited the size of burial mounds (KOFUN) and the number of workers employed in building them—a reform probably aimed at the *kabane* rank system.

Emergence of the Ritsuryō State— Setbacks in Japan's position in Korea (see HAKUSUKINOE, BATTLE OF) led to further attempts to strengthen centralized government. In 664 Naka no Ōe (who became emperor in 661 but was not formally enthroned as Emperor Tenji until 668) had his brother Prince Ōama proclaim the Kasshi Reform, which established a 26-step rank system for government offices and ordered the selection of *uji* representatives (*uji no kami*). In 667 Tenji moved his capital to ŌTSU NO MIYA. The following year Japan's first statutes, the ŌMI CODE, were proclaimed. In 670 Tenji carried out the first nationwide census of population, the KŌGONEN-JAKU. In this register people were granted surnames and their statuses were fixed.

A period of instability followed Tenji's death in 672 (see JINSHIN DISTURBANCE), but Prince Ōama ascended the throne as Emperor TEMMU that same year. His empress, JITŌ, succeeded him. The Asuka Kiyomihara Code of 689 became the direct ancestor of the TAIHŌ CODE and YŌRŌ CODE of the 8th century. In 690 the Kōinnen-Jaku was compiled as a preliminary to the first nationwide allocation of state land. This *handen shūju* system was the basis of the *ritsuryō* state.

Although there is no question that the Taika reforms took place, recent scholarship has cast doubt upon the version of the reform edict of 646 that appears in the *Nihon shoki*. Most scholars agree that it was altered by

the compilers of the *Nihon shoki*, one of whom was FUJIWARA NO FUHITO, Kamatari's son. Some scholars contend that the reforms were the result of late-7th-century events and that the roles of Emperor Kōtoku and Prince Naka no Ōe were exaggerated.

Taika Shakkandan   対華借款団

(International Banking Consortium for China). A group of European, American, and Japanese banks that sought to coordinate their loan policies toward China in the first decades of the 20th century. Organized in 1909, it originally consisted exclusively of European banks, but US and Japanese banks soon became participants as well. The idea was to pool the banks' resources in cooperative efforts to develop the Chinese economy and stabilize the country's monetary affairs.

In 1911, when revolution broke out in China, the banks found it difficult to work together. The consortium was reactivated in 1919–20, but continued instability in China discouraged banking efforts. When the consortium was dissolved in 1946 it had failed to extend a single joint loan to China.

The consortium's goals conflicted with Japan's unilateral policies in East Asia, but the organization provided a framework for Japanese economic activities in China and symbolically reinforced Japan's status as a great power. The consortium is significant as a precursor of more recent multinational endeavors by capitalist industrial nations to undertake joint projects in the developing areas of the world.

Taiki   台記

Diary of the Heian-period (794–1185) court official Fujiwara no Yorinaga (1120–56); also known as *Ukaiki* and by other names. The diary covers 1136 (when Yorinaga was appointed inner minister, or *naidaijin*) to 1155, but entries are sporadic, and many years are missing. Yorinaga was a scholar, and his career was advanced by the patronage of retired Emperor TOBA. As the result of political rivalry with his elder brother, the regent Tadamichi (1097–1164), Yorinaga lost his influence and his patron's favor. He joined with Minamoto no Tameyoshi (1096–1156) and Taira no Tadamasa (d 1156) in an unsuccessful coup d'état, the HŌGEN DISTURBANCE of 1156, and died of his wounds. His diary is an important source for the cultural life and political developments of the late Heian period, when retired emperors controlled the government (see INSEI).

taiko   太鼓

Any of various kinds of large drum. (1) Three types of *taiko*, known collectively as *gakudaiko*, are used in court music: *dadaiko*, an enormous laced drum; *tsuridaiko*, a nailed drum, the most commonly used type; and *ninaidaiko*, a laced drum on a carrying pole, played in processions. (2) The large *shimedaiko* of the NŌ drama, a barrel-shaped laced drum, is also used in KABUKI and popular KAGURA music. (3) The *ōdaiko*, a large barrel-shaped, nailed drum, is used in festival music and also to announce kabuki performances. (4) The *hirazuridaiko*, a thin barrel-shaped drum suspended on a stand, is used in kabuki and in popular Sino-Japanese music. Since the 1970s *taiko* performance groups such as Kodō and Ōedo Sukeroku Taiko have popularized Japanese drumming in Japan and abroad.

taikō   太閤

Honorific title applied in the Heian period (794–1185) to the grand minister of state

taiko Pictured is the largest of these traditional drums, the double-sided *ōdaiko*, which is used in festival music. The physical energy and excitement of *taiko* performances have made them popular with audiences abroad.

(*dajō daijin*) or the regent of the realm (SES-SHŌ) and later used to refer to an imperial regent (KAMPAKU; see REGENCY GOVERNMENT) who had passed on his office to his son. TOYOTOMI HIDEYOSHI was called *taikō* after the office of *kampaku* was transferred to his adopted son TOYOTOMI HIDETSUGU in 1592.

Taikō kenchi →kenchi

Taikyō Sempu   大教宣布

(Proclamation of the Great Doctrine). The government policy immediately after the Meiji Restoration (1868) to promote SHINTŌ as the national religion to help foster national unity. Because a renewed interest in Shintō had been part of the movement to restore direct rule to the emperor in the early 19th century, some of the leaders in the new government sought to revive the ancient Japanese ideal of "unity of religion and government" (*saisei itchi*). In 1869 the Office of Shintō Worship (Jingikan) was established, ranked above the Grand Council of State (DAJŌKAN) in the administrative hierarchy. In 1870 the government issued the Proclamation of the Great Doctrine, which declared the "way of the gods" to be the guiding principle of the state. The government also ordered (1871) compulsory registration at local Shintō shrines. These efforts to promote Shintō were severely criticized, especially by Buddhists, and more restrained policies were adopted. See also STATE SHINTŌ.

Taimadera   当麻寺

Temple of the SHINGON SECT and JŌDO SECT of Buddhism; located in the village of Taima in Nara Prefecture. According to temple tradition, in 612 Prince Maroko, the son of Emperor Yōmei (d 587), built the monastery Mampōzōin in Kawachi Province (now part of Ōsaka Prefecture); in 682 the monastery was moved to its present site and called Zenrinji. Its name was later changed to Taimadera. It houses the *Taima mandara* of 763, one of the oldest surviving mandalas in the world.

The central image in the main hall (*kondō*), rebuilt in 1184, is of the Buddha Maitreya. The structure also houses a set of the Four Heavenly Kings (see TEMBU) from the Nara period (710–794). In front of the *kondō* are the three-storied East and West pagodas, both from the 8th century. The Taimadera lecture hall (*kōdō*), burned in 1180 and rebuilt in 1303, houses a 4.9-meter (16-ft) wooden image of the Buddha Amida from the 10th or 11th century.

Tainoura   鯛ノ浦

Coastal area in the town of Amatsu Kominato, southern Chiba Prefecture, central Honshū. It is famous for sea-bream

Genealogy of the Taira Family

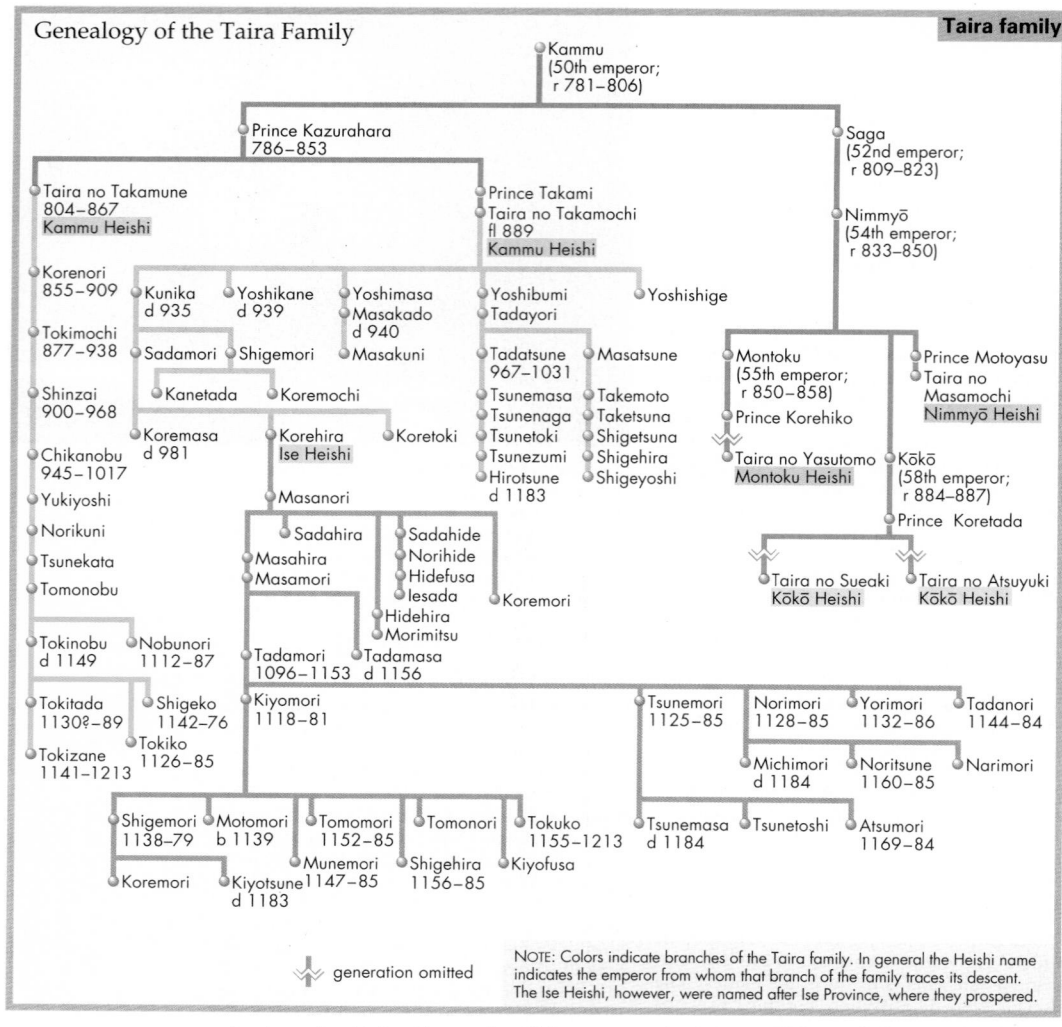

NOTE: Colors indicate branches of the Taira family. In general the Heishi name indicates the emperor from whom that branch of the family traces its descent. The Ise Heishi, however, were named after Ise Province, where they prospered.

〰️ generation omitted

viewing; a boat takes the tourist off the coast, where bait is thrown into the sea, and sea bream (*tai*) leap out of the water at the sound made by slapping the side of the boat. Tainoura is the birthplace of the monk NICHIREN, founder of the Nichiren sect of Buddhism.

Taira family 平氏

(Heishi). One of the four great families, including also the MINAMOTO FAMILY, FUJIWARA FAMILY, and TACHIBANA FAMILY, that dominated court politics during the Heian period (794–1185). The Taira family, like the Minamoto and Tachibana, was an offshoot of the imperial family. In the Heian period, offspring of sovereigns were periodically cut off from the imperial line and given surnames. This practice, held over from pre-Heian times, helped to limit succession disputes within large imperial families. In 814 Emperor SAGA created the surname Minamoto for several of his children, and in 825 Emperor KAMMU's grandson Takamune (804–867) was awarded the surname Taira. Thereafter all members cut off from the imperial line were surnamed Minamoto or Taira. The Taira family is better known through alternate pronunciations of its Chinese characters (Taira [*hei*] and family [*shi*] or [*ke*] = Heishi or Heike).

Several Taira branches were established, but the branch destined to flourish traced its origin to Prince Takamochi, Kammu's great-grandson. His descendants held provincial posts in eastern Japan. A number of families that would play major roles in the late-12th-century TAIRA-MINAMOTO WAR trace their beginnings to Takamochi's sons Yoshishige and Yoshibumi: the Ōba family, MIURA FAMILY, Kajiwara family, and HATAKEYAMA FAMILY among them. Together, these provincial warriors came to be known as the "Eight Bands of Taira from the East" (Bandō Hachi Heishi). However, two major rebellions involving Taira leaders would diminish Taira influence: the defeats of TAIRA NO MASAKADO in 940 and TAIRA NO TADATSUNE in 1031.

Another branch of the Kammu Heishi moved to Ise Province (now part of Mie Prefecture) under Taira no Korehira. His great-grandson Masamori became a client of the retired sovereign SHIRAKAWA. Masamori's son TAIRA NO TADAMORI also served Shirakawa as well as the next retired emperor, TOBA. The high point of Taira influence came in the late Heian period under Tadamori's son TAIRA NO KIYOMORI, victor in the HŌGEN DISTURBANCE of 1156 and HEIJI DISTURBANCE of 1160, who rose to the position of grand minister of state. In 1180 MINAMOTO NO YORITOMO rebelled against and crushed the Taira and established warrior government in Japan (see KAMAKURA SHOGUNATE). Kiyomori and all the major Taira leaders died or were killed during the Taira-Minamoto War, and the house never again achieved prominence. The story of the Taira is recounted in *The Tale of the Heike* (HEIKE MONOGATARI).

Taira Incident 平事件

(Taira Jiken). The seizure of a police station in Taira, Fukushima Prefecture, on 30 June 1949 by several hundred people, mostly local members of the JAPAN COMMUNIST PARTY (JCP) and labor unions. Demonstrators occupied the police station for about eight hours, protesting police removal of a JCP billboard. More than 150 demonstrators were indicted on rioting charges (*sōjōzai*, article 106 of the Criminal Code). This was the first time under the postwar constitution that article 106—often used by the prewar government to suppress the freedoms of the press and assembly—had been invoked. In 1955 most of the demonstrators were acquitted by the local court, but a higher court reversed the lower court's ruling and found the defendants guilty of rioting. In 1960 the Supreme Court dismissed their appeal.

Taira-Minamoto War 源平の争乱

(Gempei no Sōran; literally, "Gempei Disturbance"). Conflict from 1180 to 1185 between two warrior leagues, one under the TAIRA FAMILY (Heishi or Heike), and the other under the MINAMOTO FAMILY (Genji).

By the late 12th century the Seiwa Genji branch of the Minamoto family had established a warrior hegemony in eastern Japan, after the victories of Minamoto no Yoriyoshi (988 or 994–1075) and his son MINAMOTO NO YOSHIIE. However, in the HŌGEN DISTURBANCE (1156), much of the main line was killed or executed by the Taira, and in 1160, after the HEIJI DISTURBANCE, the Seiwa Genji leader MINAMOTO NO YOSHITOMO was killed. His three surviving sons—MINAMOTO NO YORITOMO, Minamoto no Noriyori (d 1193), and MINAMOTO NO YOSHITSUNE—were exiled. The other major military lineage of the period, the Ise branch of the Taira family, was based in central Japan under Taira no Masamori and his son TAIRA NO TADAMORI. The Taira entered the service of retired emperors SHIRAKAWA and TOBA (see INSEI) and succeeded in infiltrating the ranks of the court nobility. TAIRA NO KIYOMORI became grand minister of state (*dajō daijin*). His infant grandson was enthroned as Emperor ANTOKU in 1180. The Taira by this time had become so powerful that even elements within the court began to turn against them.

Retired emperor GO-SHIRAKAWA's second son, Prince Mochihito (1151–80), frustrated at having twice been passed over for the succession, and MINAMOTO NO YORIMASA, the sole remaining Minamoto at court, rebelled and lost their lives in a battle near the river Ujigawa. Kiyomori also burned the temples TŌDAIJI and KŌFUKUJI, which had tried to support the uprising.

While in exile Yoritomo developed a close relationship with his captor HŌJŌ TOKIMASA, who became his father-in-law, and was able to gather a small army of men. Marching eastward into Sagami (now Kanagawa Prefecture), Yoritomo confronted a major Taira force at the Battle of Ishibashiyama. He was defeated but escaped. Over the course of several months he gathered 200,000 warriors and established headquarters in Kamakura, later riding off to Suruga (now part of Shizuoka Prefecture) to meet a large Taira army. In the Battle of FUJIGAWA Yoritomo won his first major victory.

From late 1180 to 1183 warfare virtually ceased, and Yoritomo devoted himself to consolidation of the eastern territories under his control. In 1183 Yoritomo's cousin MINAMOTO NO YOSHINAKA, a rough provincial *samurai* from Shinano Province (now Nagano Prefecture) in north-central Japan, met and routed Taira troops, chasing them back to Kyōto. The Taira fled westward with Emperor Antoku when Yoshinaka entered the city later that month.

Yoshinaka and Yoritomo's uncle Yukiie (d 1186), now in control of the capital, were unacceptable to the court since their men created havoc throughout the city. Estrangement and growing suspicion between Yoshinaka and Yoritomo reached the point where Yoshinaka declared him a rebel. Yoritomo then sent his brothers Noriyori and Yoshitsune to Kyōto, where they defeated Yoshinaka in late February 1184. The Minamoto commanders then pursued the Taira to the west, winning a major victory at Ichinotani in early March.

Yoshitsune, appointed sole commander of the Minamoto by Yoritomo, launched a successful attack against the fortress of Yashima in March 1185 and sent the Taira fleeing farther west with their young emperor. The Minamoto and Taira fleets met on 25 April 1185 at Dannoura, off the southern tip of Honshū, in the final battle of the war (see DANNOURA, BATTLE OF). The major Taira figures were killed or committed suicide, Emperor Antoku was drowned, and it is believed that even the sacred jewels and sword of the IMPERIAL REGALIA sank beneath the waves.

Yoritomo's relationship with Yoshitsune deteriorated, and he had his brother branded a rebel by the court. Yoshitsune sought refuge with the ŌSHŪ FUJIWARA FAMILY in northeastern Japan but was eventually forced by his hosts to commit suicide; Yoritomo nevertheless reduced the Ōshū Fujiwara capital at HIRAIZUMI and brought the north under his control.

By the end of the decade Yoritomo was master of most of Japan and had established the KAMAKURA SHOGUNATE (overthrown in 1333). Thus, the Taira-Minamoto War ushered in an era of WARRIOR GOVERNMENT rule, which would last in one form or another until the Meiji Restoration of 1868.

Taira no Atsumori 平敦盛

(1169–84). Son of Taira no Tsunemori (1124–85) and nephew of the powerful TAIRA NO KIYOMORI. Atsumori is famous only for the poignant literary accounts of his death at the age of 16 in the Battle of Ichinotani during the TAIRA-MINAMOTO WAR. The Minamoto warrior KUMAGAI NAOZANE caught Atsumori but, moved by the youth's beauty and resemblance to his own son, he wished to spare him. Several other Minamoto warriors appeared, and Kumagai, seeing that they would kill Atsumori, killed the boy himself. This probably apocryphal story became a favorite subject of literature and drama, including the NŌ play ATSUMORI and the play Ichinotani futaba gunki in the BUNRAKU and KABUKI repertories.

Taira no Kiyomori 平清盛

(1118–81). Prominent political figure of the late Heian period (794–1185). Of warrior origin, he rose to dominate the court and saw his grandson become emperor. He is the central figure in Japan's greatest war chronicle, HEIKE MONOGATARI. His grandfather Masamori and his father, TAIRA NO TADAMORI, were military commanders in the service of retired emperors SHIRAKAWA and TOBA (see INSEI). Although official genealogies record Kiyomori as Tadamori's son, the Heike monogatari asserts that he was in fact the son of Shirakawa.

A skillful politician, Kiyomori benefited from his participation in two major factional struggles. In the HŌGEN DISTURBANCE of 1156 Kiyomori and MINAMOTO NO YOSHITOMO defended Emperor GO-SHIRAKAWA against an attempted coup. Yoshitomo, displeased with his rewards, attempted unsuccessfully to eliminate both Kiyomori and the retired Go-

Shirakawa in the HEIJI DISTURBANCE of 1160, which was crushed by Kiyomori. Kiyomori held military control of the capital and dominated the court for 20 years. In 1160 he became an imperial adviser (sangi) and the first member of a warrior house to sit in the Grand Council of State (Dajōkan). In 1167 he was made grand minister of state (dajō daijin). When Kiyomori tried to enthrone a Taira prince, opposition to him grew, and finally even his patron Go-Shirakawa turned against him.

In 1177 a plot against him by several of Go-Shirakawa's associates was suppressed. In 1180 Prince Mochihito (1150–80), a son of Go-Shirakawa, with MINAMOTO NO YORIMASA (1104–80), enlisted the aid of warrior monks of the temple Onjōji, or MIIDERA, at what is now the city of Ōtsu, and called for the Minamoto and other loyal warriors to rise against the Taira. This revolt, too, was quickly put down. To guard against further conspiracies, Kiyomori transferred the court, together with the reigning and retired emperors, to FUKUHARAKYŌ (now part of Kōbe) in his own domain, but public protests forced him to return the government to Kyōto after six months. Late in 1180 Kiyomori placed his grandson Emperor ANTOKU on the throne.

After Kiyomori's death in 1181 the Taira clung briefly to power, but their decline was rapid. MINAMOTO NO YORITOMO, a son of Yoshitomo, had begun a revolt against them in 1180. In 1183 Minamoto forces drove the Taira from Kyōto, in 1184 dislodged them from their base of power in western Honshū, and in the spring of 1185 destroyed them in the Battle of DANNOURA. See TAIRA FAMILY; TAIRA-MINAMOTO WAR.

Taira no Masakado 平将門

(?–940). Warrior of the Heian period (794–1185) who led the first major rebellion by the rising warrior class against the central government; a grandson of Taira no Takamochi (fl 889), the princely founder of the TAIRA FAMILY. According to the military chronicle SHŌMONKI (also known as Masakadoki; ca 940), an intrafamily quarrel over a woman in 931 developed into a military struggle (935–936) for predominance and control over land. From 938 the conflict widened into a struggle for preeminence in the entire Kantō region. It turned into a rebellion against the state when, early in 940, Masakado attacked and occupied government quarters and installed his own governors. He even assumed the title "New Emperor," making the Kantō into an autonomous state, but was killed by forces under FUJIWARA NO HIDESATO on 25 March 940 (Tengyō 3.2.14). This rebellion and a contemporaneous revolt in Shikoku led by FUJIWARA NO SUMITOMO are collectively known as the rebellions of the Jōhei (931–938) and Tengyō (938–947) eras.

Taira no Munemori 平宗盛

(1147–85). Warrior of the late Heian period (794–1185); third son of TAIRA NO KIYOMORI. Munemori succeeded as the family head at his father's death (1181) and assumed leadership of Taira forces in the TAIRA-MINAMOTO WAR (1180–85). In 1183 he was forced to abandon Kyōto under pressure from MINAMOTO NO YOSHINAKA, and the Taira fled to the western provinces with their kinsman, the child emperor ANTOKU. Munemori was a commander in the Battle of Ichinotani (1184), in which MINAMOTO NO YOSHITSUNE defeated the Taira. When Yoshitsune crushed the Taira in the naval battle at DANNOURA

(1185), Munemori cast himself into the sea but was captured and later killed.

Taira no Shigehira 平重衡

(1156–85). Warrior; fifth son of TAIRA NO KIYOMORI. In 1180 Shigehira defeated at Uji (near Kyōto) the forces led by MINAMOTO NO YORIMASA in support of the imperial prince Mochihito (1151–80), whose rising against Taira authority marked the outbreak of the TAIRA-MINAMOTO WAR. Late in the same year Shigehira led a punitive expedition against the warrior-monks of the temple Onjōji, or MIIDERA (in what is now the city of Ōtsu), for their support of Mochihito. Two weeks later Shigehira's forces burned the great Buddha hall (daibutsuden) of the temple TŌDAIJI and razed the nearby temple KŌFUKUJI. In 1182 Shigehira commanded Taira forces in the eastern provinces, and in 1184 he was captured in the Battle of Ichinotani. After the Taira defeat in the Battle of DANNOURA in 1185, Shigehira was beheaded by the monks of Nara for his sacrileges.

Taira no Shigemori 平重盛

(1138–79). Eldest son of TAIRA NO KIYOMORI and reputedly a moderating influence on his father in the series of civil disturbances leading up to the TAIRA-MINAMOTO WAR (1180–85). The courtier and diarist KUJŌ KANEZANE, however, blamed Shigemori for initiating a serious confrontation between the Taira family and the court in 1170. Shigemori fought alongside his father in the HŌGEN DISTURBANCE of 1156 and the HEIJI DISTURBANCE of 1160. Shigemori was rapidly promoted at court and in 1177 became inner minister (naidaijin), an unusual honor for a scion of a warrior family. In the same year, Kiyomori discovered the so-called Shishigatani Conspiracy against him, led by the priest SHUNKAN; only Shigemori's intercession prevented his father from incarcerating the retired emperor GO-SHIRAKAWA as a conspirator. After his death he became known for combining the best qualities of the warrior and the aristocrat.

Taira no Tadamori 平忠盛

(1096–1153). Warrior and leader of the TAIRA FAMILY; father of TAIRA NO KIYOMORI; later married to IKE NO ZENNI. He consolidated the economic and military strength of his family and established it as an important force in imperial court politics through his faithful service to retired emperors SHIRAKAWA and TOBA. In 1129 and 1135 Tadamori led expeditions to suppress piracy on the Inland Sea. He and his warriors were also charged by the imperial court with the task of policing the unruly WARRIOR-MONKS of the ENRYAKUJI monastic complex northeast of Kyōto, and of temples in Nara. Tadamori's successful supervision of building projects for Toba gained him permission to attend the emperor at court, a privilege unprecedented for a warrior and resented by courtiers. Only three years after Tadamori's death, the political and military alliances in which he had participated were ruptured by armed conflict in the HŌGEN DISTURBANCE of 1156.

Taira no Tadanori   平忠度

(1144–84). Warrior and poet of the late Heian period (794–1185); youngest brother of TAIRA NO KIYOMORI. Tadanori studied poetry under FUJIWARA NO TOSHINARI. In the TAIRA-MINAMOTO WAR, he was a commander of Taira armies. He was killed in the Battle of Ichinotani in 1184. Poems attributed to Tadanori are included in the imperial anthologies SENZAI WAKASHŪ and GYOKUYŌ WAKASHŪ, but are listed as anonymous, supposedly because the compilers did not wish to offend the court by naming a member of the defeated Taira family as author.

Taira no Tadatsune, Rebellion of   平忠常の乱

(Taira no Tadatsune no Ran). Rebellion of 1028 in which Taira no Tadatsune (967–1031), a magnate and former vice-governor of Kazusa Province (now part of Chiba Prefecture), killed the governor of neighboring Awa Province (now also part of Chiba Prefecture), seized control of the entire region, and defied the central government. Taira no Naokata (dates unknown) led court forces against Tadatsune in 1028 but was defeated. Finally, in 1031, Minamoto no Yorinobu (968–1048) forced Tadatsune to surrender without a fight. Tadatsune soon died of illness. From this time the MINAMOTO FAMILY began to consolidate its power in the Kantō region of eastern Japan; the descendants of Tadatsune's sons, who became retainers (kenin) of Yorinobu, flourished there as the Chiba family.

Taira no Tomomori   平知盛

(1152–85). Fourth son of TAIRA NO KIYOMORI; warrior in the TAIRA-MINAMOTO WAR (1180–85). In 1180 Tomomori and his younger brother TAIRA NO SHIGEHIRA defeated the forces of the imperial prince Mochihito (1151–80) and MINAMOTO NO YORIMASA. With his elder brother TAIRA NO MUNEMORI, in 1181 he defeated Minamoto no Yukiie (d 1186). Tomomori was in command when the Taira abandoned Kyōto in 1183 and fled to the western provinces with the child emperor ANTOKU. He also led Taira forces in the Battle of Ichinotani in 1184 and at the final destruction of the Taira in the naval battle at DAN-NOURA in 1185. There Tomomori, seeing that the battle was lost, leaped into the sea and drowned. In the Nō and kabuki plays entitled Funa Benkei (Benkei and the Boat), Tomomori's ghost rises from the waves to obstruct the passage of MINAMOTO NO YOSHITSUNE across the Inland Sea; only the prayers of Yoshitsune's retainer BENKEI can subdue the vengeful Taira spirits.

Taira no Yoritsuna   平頼綱

(?–1293). A vassal and house official of the HŌJŌ FAMILY, late in the Kamakura period (1185–1333). When Hōjō Sadatoki (1271–1311) succeeded as shogunal regent (shikken) in 1284, Yoritsuna became a house steward (naikanrei or uchikanrei). He soon came into conflict with Adachi Yasumori (1231–85), Sadatoki's father-in-law, and in the so-called Shimotsuki Incident of 1285, he destroyed the Adachi. Yoritsuna's power over-shadowed even Sadatoki's, but when he schemed to have his second son named regent, his eldest son betrayed him to Sadatoki, who destroyed Yoritsuna's family.

tairiku rōnin   大陸浪人

(rōnin or wanderers on the continent; an allusion to the RŌNIN or masterless samurai of the Edo period). An expression referring to Japanese civilians active on the Asian mainland in the late 19th century and early 20th century. They supported Asian revolutionaries and promoted Japan's imperialist aims in China, Korea, and Manchuria. These activists often served as agents of Japanese military officers, politicians, and businessmen for whom they gathered intelligence and engaged in covert political activities. Many of them were affiliated with such ultranationalist organizations as the GEN'YŌSHA and the AMUR RIVER SOCIETY. Some, like MIYAZAKI TŌTEN, were idealistic pan-Asianists who worked for the Chinese revolution and the Philippine independence movement in the early 1900s. Others were mere adventurers.

tairō   大老

(great elder). Nominally the highest-ranking position below that of shōgun in the TOKUGAWA SHOGUNATE (1603–1867). The post was in fact rarely occupied. During the 17th century several shōguns promoted distinguished advisers such as SAKAI TADAKIYO to the office. From the 18th century until 1867 only FUDAI daimyō of the Ii family of Hikone held the title, and then only as an infrequent political sinecure, until 1858 when II NAOSUKE took decisive control of the shogunate as tairō and pursued repressive policies that led to his assassination.

Tairo Dōshikai   対露同志会

(Anti-Russia Society). Political organization formed in August 1903, on the eve of the RUSSO-JAPANESE WAR, by KONOE ATSUMARO and others. It advocated a strong foreign policy toward Russia, which was pressing China to declare Manchuria a Russian protectorate. Successor to Konoe's 1901 Kokumin Dōmeikai (Nationalist Alliance), the organization sought a declaration of war on Russia.

Taisei Corporation   大成建設[株]

(Taisei Kensetsu). One of the largest general contracting companies in Japan. It is engaged in public works, design and construction, plant engineering, housing, and real estate. Founded in 1873, it became independent and took on its current name in 1946 following the post–World War II ZAIBATSU DISSOLUTION program. Its numerous subsidiary firms include Taisei Road Construction Co, Taisei Prefab Construction Co, and Yūraku Real Estate Co. Taisei is expanding its business into the area of hotel management. Taisei is also very active in international markets. In Southeast Asia, the Near and Middle East, and South America, Taisei's projects include hospitals, power-generating plants, commercial buildings, and dams. Net sales in the fiscal year ending March 1991 totaled ¥1.5 trillion (US $10.9 billion). It was capitalized at ¥94.1 billion (US $685.9 million) in the same year. Headquarters are in Tōkyō.

Taisei Hōkan   大政奉還

(Return of Political Rule to the Emperor). A statement issued by the last shōgun, TOKUGAWA YOSHINOBU, on 9 November 1867—two months before the MEIJI RESTORATION—surrendering to the emperor the shōgun's de facto right to rule the country. By midsummer 1867, anti-Tokugawa forces led by the Satsuma (now Kagoshima Prefecture) and Chōshū (now Yamaguchi Prefecture) domains had decided to restore imperial rule. However, more moderate samurai of the Tosa domain (now Kōchi Prefecture) tried to avoid war with a compromise plan (the KŌGI SEITAI RON), by which the shōgun would voluntarily relinquish political authority, act as head of a council of daimyō, and retain his domainal holdings. YAMANOUCHI TOYOSHIGE, the daimyō of Tosa, persuaded Yoshinobu to relinquish political authority. Yoshinobu issued a formal statement, the Taisei Hōkan, thus ending the Tokugawa shogunate, which had ruled Japan since 1603. But on 3 January 1868 Satsuma and Chōshū forces, dissatisfied with this, surrounded the Imperial Palace in Kyōto and proclaimed an "imperial restoration" (ŌSEI FUKKO), which precipitated a civil war in which the Tokugawa forces were defeated (see BOSHIN CIVIL WAR).

Taisei Yokusankai →Imperial Rule Assistance Association

Taisekiji   大石寺

Head temple of the Buddhist sect Nichiren Shōshū, located in the city of Fujinomiya, Shizuoka Prefecture. It was built in 1290 by Nikkō (1246–1333), a prominent disciple of NICHIREN. It became a center for the Fuji Tradition (Fuji Monryū), a subschool based on Nikkō's interpretation of Nichiren's teachings. In 1900 Taisekiji announced the formation of its own independent religious organization under the name of Nichirenshū Fujiha (the Fuji branch of the Nichiren sect). In 1912 the latter name was changed to Nichiren Shōshū (True Nichiren sect), around which later arose the SŌKA GAKKAI. Taisekiji continues to be a center of Sōka Gakkai pilgrimage.

Taisetsuzan →Daisetsuzan

Taisha   大社[町]

Town in northern Shimane Prefecture, western Honshū, on the Shimane Peninsula. Taisha developed around the IZUMO SHRINE (Izumo Taisha) and is still economically dependent on it. Pop: 17,284.

Taishakukyō   帝釈峡

Gorge on the river Taishakugawa (a tributary of the TAKAHASHIGAWA), eastern Hiroshima Prefecture, western Honshū. Taishakukyō is dotted by numerous fantastically shaped rocks, deep pools, and caves. It is the location of the artificial Lake Shinryū and a National Vacation Village. Length: 20 km (12 mi).

Taishakusan   帝釈山

Also called Taishakuzan. Mountain in northern Tochigi Prefecture on the border with Fukushima Prefecture, northern Honshū; the highest peak in the Taishaku Mountains. Natural forests of hemlock-spruce, Japanese black pine (Pinus thumbergii), and oak cover the slopes. Height: 2,060 m (6,758 ft).

Taishō Democracy   大正デモクラシー

(Taishō Demokurashī). A term coined by Japanese historians after World War II to refer to the democratic ideals, practices, and movements of early-20th-century Japan; generally used to refer to political currents between the end of the Russo-Japanese War in 1905 and the end of party government in 1932, a time spanning the Taishō period (1912–26). The term is commonly used to refer to government institutions and political parties as well as to ideas and movements in cultural and intellectual circles, in education, and in popular media.

One major feature of Taishō Democracy was increased power for the popularly elected House of Representatives (Shūgiin) of the IMPERIAL DIET. This political ideal was expressed in terms of party government, whose cabinets would be based on the strength of political parties in the House of Representatives. Such cabinets would have predominant influence over nonelected organs and forces of government: the GENRŌ (elder statesmen), the HOUSE OF PEERS (Kizokuin), the PRIVY COUNCIL (Sūmitsuin), the military, and the career bureaucracy. Another important aspect of Taishō Democracy was increased popular involvement in politics, primarily through expansion of male suffrage and more widespread freedom of political expression. Emphasis on the broader ideals of social democracy included the recognition of labor and tenant-farmer unions and of greater equality for women.

Strengthening Elected Bodies——Institutionally, Taishō Democracy was marked by the growing prominence of political parties (such as the RIKKEN SEIYŪKAI), whose strength lay in their control of seats in the House of Representatives. After 1910 there was growing acceptance of party government, either as an ideal or as a practical necessity. The House electorate, while never more than one-quarter of the adult male population before 1925, was still over 1.5 million as early as 1908, making these parties the only political force responsible in any direct sense to a substantial popular base. In 1918 HARA TAKASHI's formation of a cabinet composed of Seiyūkai members except for the army, navy, and foreign ministers was hailed as the advent of true party government. For many, party government meant reducing the independent power of unelected bodies and their ability to interfere in the work of cabinets. The *genrō* continued to claim an informal but potent voice as the emperor's chief advisers. They also continued to select the prime ministers, but, with the exception of a two-year period, from 1918 until 1932 the premiership was held by the leader of a major party. The party politicians, notably Hara, also took steps to make top bureaucrats responsive to party leadership and to end the virtual monopoly by the career bureaucracy of positions below the ministerial level.

While Taishō Democracy generally supported imperial rather than popular sovereignty, its theorists were forthright about the desirability of limiting the emperor's powers. They argued that the emperor did not make policy decisions in Japan and that the selection of prime ministers by the *genrō* limited the emperor's sovereignty just as much as selection by the popularly elected House. Professor MINOBE TATSUKICHI of Tōkyō University asserted that under the constitution the emperor was an organ of the state, and Minobe sought to preclude mystical and irrational invocation of the emperor in politics. Likewise, Prime Minister Hara Takashi advocated bringing the military under cabinet control, rather than having it act independently under the control of the emperor.

Expansion of Popular Involvement—— The most direct form of public political involvement, the mass demonstration, became markedly more prominent under Taishō Democracy. In fact, the choice of 1905 as the beginning of Taishō Democracy may be based primarily on the outbreak—particu-

larly in the so-called Hibiya riots (see HIBIYA INCENDIARY INCIDENT)—of popular indignation over the peace settlement following the Russo-Japanese War. Mass demonstrations that sometimes turned into riots became frequent. In early 1913 the riots sparked by *genrō* interference with the Saionji Kimmochi government led to the resignation of the successor cabinet two months after its formation (see TAISHŌ POLITICAL CRISIS). Wider in scope though less political and specific in their objectives, the RICE RIOTS OF 1918 were further evidence of a growing tendency to mass expression and involvement in public issues. Mass rallies of the UNIVERSAL MANHOOD SUFFRAGE MOVEMENT were held in 1919 and 1920. Public enthusiasm waned somewhat thereafter, but the movement, and the enactment of the universal suffrage law in 1925, have been seen by some as the central feature of Taishō Democracy. Another major feature was the refusal to identify individual interests with state interests. Businessmen participated in antitax movements, suggesting a decline in the earlier unquestioning acceptance of the sacrifices required for the state's military preparedness. Scholars emphasized academic freedom and intellectual cultivation for its own sake. People came to think of themselves as members of particular classes or interest groups.

Limits of Taishō Democracy——The trend away from personal identification with the state sometimes took the form of withdrawal from public affairs. Political competition was materially inhibited by restrictions on freedom of expression, including the PEACE PRESERVATION LAW OF 1925 (Chian Iji Hō). While the objective of creating party cabinets was attained at least before 1932, party cabinet control over other government organs was only partially realized. Moreover, by the time party cabinets were achieved, there was also considerable popular disillusionment with the parties as bearers of democracy. In evaluating Taishō Democracy, one can focus on its "failure" to survive into the 1930s and early 1940s or see it as providing the indigenous roots essential for the "success" of democracy after 1945.

Taishō, Emperor　　　大正天皇

(1879–1926; Taishō Tennō). The 123rd sovereign (*tennō*) in the traditional count (which includes several legendary emperors); so called posthumously from the name of the era, Taishō (1912–26), during which he reigned. The third son of Emperor MEIJI. His personal name was Yoshihito. In a nontraditional upbringing, he was educated publicly at the Peers' School (now Gakushūin University), where he studied Western subjects as well as Japanese and Chinese classics.

Emperor Taishō did not play an active role in the political process, largely because of his

ill health. Soon after his birth he contracted what appeared to be meningitis. His health remained poor and of constant concern to court and government leaders. Although Yoshihito was deemed competent to ascend the throne in 1912, by 1919 he had become unable to perform basic state ceremonies, and he spent longer periods at imperial villas away from the palace in Tōkyō. Finally, in 1921, Crown Prince Hirohito was made regent (*sesshō*) for his father. Emperor Taishō died on 25 December 1926 and was succeeded by Hirohito (Emperor SHŌWA).

Taishō literature　　　大正時代の文学

(Taishō *jidai no bungaku*). The first significant development in Taishō-period (1912–26) literature was the emergence of the SHIRAKABA SCHOOL. Critical of the earlier trends of NATURALISM and aestheticism, members of the group were united by their upper-class backgrounds, and also by their basic humanism. MUSHANOKŌJI SANEATSU, the group's leader, expressed his free-spirited ideas in straightforward prose in the novel *Yūjō* (1920; tr *Friendship*, 1958). Other writers in the group included SHIGA NAOYA, who depicted a male character groping toward self definition in AN'YA KŌRO (1921–37; tr *A Dark Night's Passing*, 1976), and ARISHIMA TAKEO, who depicted the clash of ideals and instincts, social pressures, and individual inspirations in ARU ONNA (1919; tr *A Certain Woman*, 1978).

Other prominent writers of the period were affiliated with the literary magazines SHINSHICHŌ, MITA BUNGAKU, and *Kiseki.* AKUTAGAWA RYŪNOSUKE was the foremost writer for the first: he examined the contradictions of human nature with biting irony in such works as "Rashōmon" (1915; tr "Rashomon," 1930) and "Haguruma" (1927; tr "Cogwheels," 1965). Other writers for *Shinshichō* included KIKUCHI KAN and YAMAMOTO YŪZŌ, who mostly contributed plays—the former, for example, *Chichi kaeru* (1917; tr *The Father Returns*, 1925), and the latter, *Eijigoroshi* (1920; tr *A Case of Child Murder*, 1930). Members of the *Mita bungaku* group included KUBOTA MANTARŌ and SATŌ HARUO, who published collections of poetry as well as the novel *Den'en no yūutsu* (1919, Pastoral Melancholy). While the writers for *Mita bungaku* inclined toward social criticism in a nevertheless highly polished style, the writers for *Kiseki* were marked by a sense of malaise and morbid hopelessness. They included HIROTSU KAZUO, who wrote about mental instability in "Shinkeibyō jidai" (1917, The Neurotic Age), and KASAI ZENZŌ, whose *Kanashiki chichi* (1912, Sad Father) is an obvious exercise in self-criticism.

The emergence of the so-called I-NOVEL in the mid-Taishō period marked an important

Emperor Taishō

1 The Taishō emperor, whose personal name was Yoshihito, ascended the throne in 1912, but lifelong health problems forced the appointment of his son Hirohito as regent in 1921.

2 The future empress Teimei on the day of her marriage to Crown Prince Yoshihito in May 1900.

3 Yoshihito, while still crown prince, shown here with his son Hirohito in 1904.

literary trend. I-novels continued anti-idealistic inclinations inherited from naturalism, and a tendency toward self-revelation on the part of the author from the Shirakaba school. Their material was taken from everyday life, obvious fabrication was eschewed, and little concern was shown for society at large. While Kasai, UNO KŌJI, and others stressed their protagonists' increasing alienation from reality, Shiga, TAKII KŌSAKU, and others depicted protagonists struggling through emotional crises toward acceptance and inner peace.

Important works from writers who had emerged during the Meiji period (1868–1912) included NATSUME SŌSEKI's *Michikusa* (1915; tr *Grass on the Wayside*, 1969) and *Meian* (1916; tr *Light and Darkness*, 1971), MORI ŌGAI's *Shibue Chūsai* (1916), SHIMAZAKI TŌSON's *Shinsei* (1918–19, New Life), and TANIZAKI JUN'ICHIRŌ's *Chijin no ai* (1924–25, A Fool's Love; tr *Naomi*, 1985).

The socialist movement that arose in the early Taishō period produced such writers as FUJIMORI SEIKICHI and Akita Ujaku (1883–1962). The leftist journal TANE MAKU HITO began publication in 1921, marking the beginning of the PROLETARIAN LITERATURE MOVEMENT.

The leading poet of the Taishō period was MIKI ROFŪ, who wrote symbolist poetry in classical Japanese. Poets who sustained the modern poetry of the Meiji period included KITAHARA HAKUSHŪ, HAGIWARA SAKUTARŌ, Satō Haruo, and HORIGUCHI DAIGAKU. Hagiwara's *Tsuki ni hoeru* (1917; tr *Howling at the Moon*, 1978) used the rhythms of the colloquial language to convey a morbid sensibility and exerted a profound influence on Taishō poetry. MIYAZAWA KENJI, a poet and author of children's literature from northern Japan, was an important literary figure of the period. TAKAMURA KŌTARŌ, a sculptor as well as a poet, was noted for his sincere realism and humanism.

In the field of TANKA poetry, the journal ARARAGI fostered such poets as ITŌ SACHIO and SAITŌ MOKICHI, who was central in reviving *tanka* as a major genre of Japanese literature. The traditional HAIKU form was promoted by TAKAHAMA KYOSHI, who published in the journal HOTOTOGISU. See also FICTION, MODERN.

Taishō period　　　大正時代

(1912–26; Taishō *jidai*). The reign of Emperor TAISHŌ, which one Japanese historian has characterized as "an era of great possibilities." Some historians, employing the term TAISHŌ DEMOCRACY, associate the period with the emergence of political and social trends that ultimately made possible the post-1945 democratization of Japan. Looking at a different set of trends, others have found it equally plausible to see in the Taishō period the roots of the radical nationalism, expansionism, and antiliberalism that later marked the 1930s and early 1940s.

The ambiguity of the Taishō period may be especially pronounced because historians have trouble discovering a defining event, such as the MEIJI RESTORATION (1868) or World War II, that provides an obvious interpretive perspective. For that reason it makes more sense to abandon the entirely arbitrary boundaries set by the accession and death of a monarch and to think instead of "World War I Japan" and "Japan in the 1920s," a distinction that not only situates Japan in the context of world history but also suggests a chronological break that many Japanese sensed at the time.

The Impact of World War I——The outbreak of WORLD WAR I had a profound social and economic impact on Japan. The withdrawal of European business interests from Asian markets after the war began provided a boost to the industrial sector. The rupture of trade with Germany stimulated the chemical, dye, and drug industries; military orders prompted the expansion of the iron, steel, and machine-tool industries; the output of cotton-spinning and textile factories grew to meet Asian demand no longer satisfied by British mills; the shipping industry expanded precipitously to handle expanded trade; and the hydroelectric power industry grew in response to the demand of industrial growth.

The wartime boom brought with it a quick and easy prosperity. Between 1912 and 1919 the national income more than tripled in nominal terms, from ¥4.2 billion to ¥13.3 billion. Astute investors and speculators made quick fortunes, and the newly wealthy (called *narikin*) indulged in ostentatious consumption. The wages of factory workers rose sharply, and farm households enjoyed good times as the demand for rice and other food products rose and the expanding industrial sector provided jobs for their offspring.

The boom had other social effects as well. The factory labor force nearly doubled in size, and the proportion of male workers in heavy industry rose significantly. Male workers, many with families to support, were more likely to express labor militance than the young, unmarried female textile workers who had dominated the factory labor force before the war. Not surprisingly, the number of labor disputes increased. In 1914 there were only 50 recorded labor disputes, but by 1918 there were 417. Workers demanded not only better compensation but recognition of their place in Japanese society as well.

If any single event symbolized the wartime changes, it was the nationwide disturbance known as the RICE RIOTS OF 1918. Demonstrations against an exorbitant rise in rice prices began in Toyama Prefecture in late July and spread to most major cities and towns, and many villages as well, during August and September. Crowds milled through the streets, attacking and looting the shops of rice brokers, moneylenders, and other merchants. Nationwide, between 1 million and 2 million people may have participated in the rioting.

To many observers the rice riots marked the beginning of a "popular awakening" that would lead Japan along the path of "democracy." And when the war ended in the victory of the Western democracies over the central European monarchies, many journalists, intellectuals, and politicians concluded that the future held the promise for "emancipation" of the masses the world over.

The Postwar Years: The Seeds of Democracy——When the war came to an end, so did the economic boom. Although the economy continued to grow, it did so at a much slower rate. The collapse of overseas markets brought about a recession in 1920. Prices fell, exports dropped, and stock prices tumbled. Many firms found themselves saddled with debt and unable to raise new capital. Workers faced wage cuts and discharges, and the import of colonial rice brought about a sudden end to wartime prosperity in the countryside.

Against this background there emerged new and vocal movements for democratic reform. Intellectuals such as YOSHINO SAKUZŌ argued that even though sovereignty was formally vested in the emperor it was possible to have Japanese-style democracy—what Yoshino called *mimpon shugi* (literally, "people-as-the-foundation-ism"). In 1919 and 1920 intellectuals, students, and workers took to the streets to demonstrate for universal manhood suffrage (see UNIVERSAL MANHOOD SUFFRAGE MOVEMENT). They saw the extension of voting rights as a way to break the hold of the "privileged classes" on politics. Although the opposition parties in the Diet favored an end to tax qualifications for voting, the party cabinet of HARA TAKASHI defeated a universal suffrage bill introduced into the 1920 Diet.

Frustrated by this failure, urban intellectuals and popular movements took a radical turn in the early 1920s. Attracted by the apparent success of the new "socialist experiment" in the Soviet Union, they shifted their focus from political reform to demands for major structural changes in the capitalist socioeconomic system. The labor movement, dominated by the Japan Federation of Labor (SŌDŌMEI), organized in 1921, came under the influence of leaders committed to anarchosyndicalism, democratic socialism, or Marxism. Student associations became radicalized as well. Worker and student activists took to the countryside to organize tenant unions and rent strikes against landlord oppression. To confirm the worst fears of the conservative political establishment, the JAPAN COMMUNIST PARTY was organized in 1922.

This inescapable evidence of popular and intellectual discontent prompted Diet politicians and concerned bureaucrats to devise ways of accommodating the demands for greater social and political democracy. The Diet passed moderate reform legislation such as a labor exchange bill, a tenancy dispute arbitration law, and a minimum wage law. Most dramatically, in 1925 it passed a universal manhood suffrage law that gave the vote to adult males over 25. To attract the newly enfranchised electorate, a number of small "proletarian parties" such as the Labor-Farmer Party (RŌDŌ NŌMINTŌ) and the Japan Labor-Farmer Party (NIHON RŌNŌTŌ) were organized in 1926. The activists in these parties were drawn from the ranks of the student and labor union movements.

The Seeds of Reaction——The call for democratization and reform was centered mainly in large cities. Most of the votes cast for the proletarian parties in the 1928 election were cast in urban constituencies. The cities fostered intellectual ferment. The educated urban middle classes and even some workers avidly read the latest translations of Western books and provided the audience for new experiments in literature, art, and music. New kinds of mass media—large-circulation newspapers, general monthlies such as *Chūō kōron* and *Kaizō*, and inexpensive paperback books—propagated cultural fads and the latest ideas from the West.

But the trend toward democracy, reform, and change rested on a narrow base. The vast majority of the population still lived in rural communities where traditional folkways and values remained strong. The primary school system, with its emphasis on inculcating patriotic ideas and loyalty to the emperor, reinforced conservative tendencies in the countryside. Newfangled middle-class reform ideas, whether about labor unions or love marriages, were deeply threatening to

Taishō period

▶ Women joined the work force in ever-greater numbers during World War I. This 1925 photograph shows a female conductor collecting streetcar fares.

▼ In response to continued domination of the political scene by elder statesmen, reformist parties met in December 1912 to discuss how to "protect constitutional government." The movement eventually brought down the Katsura Cabinet in 1913 and led to the formation of Japan's first party-dominated cabinet in 1918.

▼ A policeman manipulates a traffic signal at a busy intersection in Ginza in the mid-1920s.

rural villagers. A profound cultural gap separated city and country.

The postwar years also saw the emergence of a new right wing. Alarmed by the growth of popular unrest, the increase in labor disputes, the spread of alien ideas, and leftist militance, right-wing activists organized to counter what they regarded as a deplorable weakening of the traditional social order. Fearing that the country was on the brink of social revolution, they called for a renewal of patriotism, devotion to the emperor, respect for parents and elders, and other traditional values.

While the right wing did not use the tactics of popular protest or street demonstrations, its ideas appealed to a broad spectrum of Japanese society. In rural communities and provincial towns organizations such as the Reservists Associations and Youth Associations provided forums for patriotic activities. In the universities conservative students organized themselves to counter the influence of student radicals. And organizations such as the KOKUHONSHA (National Foundations Society), founded in 1924 by Minister of Justice HIRANUMA KIICHIRŌ, included in their numbers high-ranking bureaucrats, military and naval officers, and university professors.

If the passage of the universal suffrage bill in 1925 marked the emergence of democratic trends, the PEACE PRESERVATION LAW OF 1925, passed by the same Diet, marked countervailing conservative and right-wing tendencies. Intended to control the spread of "dangerous thoughts," the latter law made it illegal to criticize either the KOKUTAI (the "national polity" or state structure of Japan as embodied in the imperial institution) or the system of private property. In 1925 and 1926 the law was invoked to crack down on stu-

dent radicalism in the universities, and in March 1928 it was used to carry out a national roundup of communists and other "subversive elements" shortly after the first election was held under the new manhood suffrage law. In the late 1920s the forces of the SPECIAL HIGHER POLICE, a secret political police organization (also known as the "thought police"), were expanded, and in the 1930s they were the principal instrument for controlling not only radicalism but all kinds of political dissent.

The Legacy of the Taishō Period——The historical legacy of the Taishō period is an ambiguous one. If the 1920s saw the emergence of a nascent democratic movement, they also saw the revival of an older traditionalism and conservatism. Since historians are more often drawn to examine new trends or new developments than old ones, it is easy to understand why many of them were attracted to the concept of "Taishō Democracy." But it is clear that one as readily can find "Taishō Conservatism" or "Taishō Authoritarianism." When severe economic crisis struck in the late 1920s, particularly in the countryside, it was these older and more persistent tendencies that overwhelmed the movement for democratization.

Taishō Pharmaceutical Co, Ltd
大正製薬[株]

(Taishō Seiyaku). Pharmaceutical manufacturer specializing in over-the-counter drugs. Incorporated in 1928. The company has developed its own direct-sales system. A joint research contract has been concluded with the Institute of Medical Materials of the Chinese Academy. Overseas joint ventures have been set up with Sanofi SA of France and Knoll AG of Germany. Sales for the fiscal year ending March 1991 totaled ¥173.3 bil-

lion (US $1.3 billion), and the company was capitalized at ¥23.6 billion (US $172.0 million). Headquarters are in Tōkyō.

Taishō Political Crisis   大正政変

(Taishō Seihen). Political crisis of the Taishō period (1912–26) in which the third cabinet of KATSURA TARŌ was overthrown in 1913 by the first MOVEMENT TO PROTECT CONSTITUTIONAL GOVERNMENT, a popular protest movement organized by opposition parties, businessmen, and journalists. In December 1912 the second cabinet of SAIONJI KIMMOCHI fell with the army's refusal to replace former Army Minister UEHARA YŪSAKU. General Katsura was named to form the next cabinet. He was unpopular, however, with the public. When the navy threatened to withhold its minister if its demand for new battleships was not met, Katsura had an imperial edict issued ordering the navy to furnish a minister. Critics saw this as proof of Katsura's authoritarian nature. The first Movement to Protect Constitutional Government now took the form of a popular front against Katsura and quickly won support throughout the country. Katsura countered by forming his own party, the RIKKEN DŌSHIKAI, and by suspending the Diet three times. On 10 February 1913 thousands of angry demonstrators surrounded the Diet building, set fire to police stations, and raided several progovernment newspaper companies. Katsura resigned the following day. The Taishō Political Crisis was the first instance in modern Japanese history in which a popular movement brought down a cabinet.

Taishō Seihen→Taishō Political Crisis

Taishō University　大正大学

(Taishō Daigaku). A coeducational private university located in Toshima Ward, Tōkyō. Founded in 1926 by four major sects of Japanese Buddhism. The university has faculties of letters and Buddhism and also operates the Institute for the Comprehensive Study of Buddhism. Enrollment in 1989 was 2,930.

Taiso Yoshitoshi　大蘇芳年

(1839–92). The major UKIYO-E artist of the early Meiji period (1868–1912). Born in Edo (now Tōkyō). Although his real name was Yoshioka Kinzaburō, he was adopted by the ukiyo-e artist Tsukioka Sessai (dates unknown) and so became known as Tsukioka Yoshitoshi (alternate pronunciation, Tsukioka Hōnen). As a youth he studied with UTAGAWA KUNIYOSHI, and by the age of 15 he was producing his first ukiyo-e prints. He soon became famous for shockingly realistic prints based on sketches made from life. After 1868 he worked in Tōkyō as a newspaper illustrator, pioneering in the adaptation of print designs for journalism. He died insane at the age of 53.

Taitō Co, Ltd　台糖[株]

(Taitō). Major sugar manufacturer, affiliated with MITSUI & CO, LTD. Its forerunner, the Taiwan Seitō Co, was founded in 1900. It was reorganized as the Taitō Co in 1946 and later became Japan's leading maker of penicillin. In 1955 the pharmaceuticals division was transferred to Pfizer Pharmaceuticals, Inc (formerly a joint venture with Pfizer, Inc, USA, called Pfizer Taitō Co, Ltd). Sales in the fiscal year ending March 1991 totaled ¥37.0 billion (US $269.7 million). In the same year the company was capitalized at ¥3.1 billion (US $22.6 million). Its headquarters are in Tōkyō.

Taitō Ward　台東区

(Taitō Ku). One of the 23 wards of Tōkyō. On the west bank of the river Sumidagawa. With an area of 10 sq km (3.9 sq mi), Taitō Ward is the smallest of the wards. It has numerous small and medium-sized factories. Taitō Ward contains the UENO and ASAKUSA districts and is noted for its traditional Japanese urban atmosphere (see SHITAMACHI). Pop: 162,969.

Taiwan　台湾

(Taiwan). The island of Taiwan (Formosa) is situated 1,060 kilometers (660 mi) southwest of Japan and 130 kilometers (80 mi) east of China's Fujian (Fukien) Province. The first Japanese contacts with Taiwan may have been the bands of Japanese pirate-traders (WAKŌ) who stopped at the island early in the 16th century. By the late 1500s Japanese merchants had begun to use Taiwan as a way station for trade with China. In 1593 TOYOTOMI HIDEYOSHI issued licenses to Japanese merchants that authorized them to open offices on the island. Later, the shōgun TOKUGAWA IEYASU systematically developed the VERMILION SEAL SHIP TRADE, which had been initiated under Hideyoshi. Both men made unsuccessful attempts to gain military control of Taiwan.

Early formal Japanese contact with Taiwan ended during the 1630s under the NATIONAL SECLUSION policies of the Tokugawa shogunate (1603–1867). However, the flow of Taiwanese imported goods (chiefly sugar and deerskins) to Japan continued through the trading activities of the Dutch, who were driven out of Taiwan by the Zheng (Cheng) family in 1661. The Zheng continued overseas trade with Japan, but, by the time Taiwan came under the rule of China during the Qing (Ch'ing) dynasty (1644–1912) in 1683, the island had lost its position as an important intermediary port for trade with Japan and other Asian countries.

Japanese political interest in Taiwan resumed upon the lifting of the policy of National Seclusion in the 1850s, and after the Meiji Restoration in 1868 Japan's Taiwan policy reflected the Meiji government's expansionist ambitions (see TAIWAN EXPEDITION OF 1874). Japan eventually gained control of Taiwan at the close of the SINO-JAPANESE WAR OF 1894–1895 as part of China's terms of surrender, and Taiwan remained a colony of Japan for the next 51 years.

Under the Japanese colonial system, modeled closely after Western colonial empires in Asia and elsewhere, Taiwan was administered by a Japanese governor-general, and the island's economy was subordinated to the needs of Japan. The Japanese exerted tight control over Taiwanese internal affairs and gave preferential treatment to the resident Japanese population, who were the chief beneficiaries of the modern technology and industry that was introduced during colonial rule. The Taiwanese resisted the Japanese military takeover in 1895. Thereafter, colonial police and the military occasionally took action against restive local elements including native tribal peoples. Nevertheless, relative peace and stability, as well as economic growth, were brought about in Taiwan after the fourth governor-general, KODAMA GENTARŌ, and his chief of civil administration, GOTŌ SHIMPEI, assumed office in 1898. Kodama and Gotō introduced an effective police system and public health program, and reinstated the traditional Chinese system of mutual household surveillance. They also stimulated agricultural and commercial development by introducing a modern-type infrastructure to the island.

Kodama also implemented new fiscal policies and, by the time he left office in 1906, Taiwan was no longer dependent on subsidies from the Japanese government. Subsequently, Japan used Taiwan to satisfy growing Japanese demand for agricultural products and raw materials. The colony became a major supplier of rice and sugar to Japan. During the 1920s colonial authorities promoted modern light industry in Taiwan, securing investment capital from sources within the colony as well as from business concerns in Japan, including the ZAIBATSU. During this time educated Taiwanese continued to call for autonomy for their homeland, but the colonial government dissolved the home-rule movement in the 1930s.

During the SINO-JAPANESE WAR OF 1937–1945 and World War II, Japan used Taiwan as a staging area for assaults on southern China, the Philippines, and Southeast Asia. Taiwan was also assessed heavy wartime contributions, and young Taiwanese men were mobilized for military and labor duties. Not until 1944, however, did the island begin to experience directly the effects of war; around that time Allied submarines interrupted shipping between Taiwan and Japan and heavy American air strikes commenced. By then severe shortages and inflation had already disrupted the economy. Finally, on 25 October 1945, Governor-General Andō Rikichi (1884–1946) relinquished control of Taiwan and Penghu (P'eng-hu; the Pescadores) to the Republic of China, in accordance with the CAIRO DECLARATION of 1943 and the POTSDAM DECLARATION of 1945.

In the bilateral peace treaty concluded with the Republic of China—by then based in Taiwan—on 28 April 1952, Japan formally renounced "all right, title, and claim" to its former colony. After the 1971 United Nations resolution ousting Taiwan as the representative of China and US president Richard M. Nixon's trip to China in 1972 (see NIXON SHOCKS), Japan extended diplomatic recognition to the People's Republic of China in September and acknowledged Taiwan and Penghu as inalienable territory of the mainland communist government. Within two months, however, Japan and the Republic of China in Taiwan had established mutual exchange agencies to protect the commercial ties that had been forged between them since 1952. Under this arrangement trade between Japan and Taiwan has grown steadily, as has Japanese investment in Taiwan. However, as of the early 1990s the Republic of China's large trade deficit with Japan remained a serious problem.

Taiwan Expedition of 1874　台湾出兵

(Taiwan Shuppei; also known as Seitai no Eki). A punitive expedition by Japanese military forces using as a pretext the murder of 54 shipwrecked Ryūkyū islanders by Taiwanese aborigines in December 1871. In May 1874 the Japanese government sent more than 3,000 men led by SAIGŌ TSUGUMICHI to southwestern Taiwan. The ulterior aims of the expedition were to force Chinese acknowledgment of Japanese claims of sovereignty over the RYŪKYŪ ISLANDS, and gain a foothold in Taiwan. After meeting fierce resistance from the Taiwanese, Japanese forces withdrew, but China agreed to pay an indemnity of 500,000 taels and thus tacitly acknowledged Japanese suzerainty over the Ryūkyū Islands. The expedition mollified those in the new Meiji government pressing for a more assertive foreign policy.

Taiwan Ginkō　台湾銀行

(Bank of Taiwan). Semiofficial colonial bank established by the Japanese government in 1899 to serve as the central bank for Taiwan, a Japanese colony from 1895 to 1945; to promote the resource exploitation and economic development of that island; and to facilitate the expansion of trade between Taiwan and South China and the South Sea Islands. During World War I, the bank moved aggressively into Japan proper and by the 1920s was lending more to businesses in Japan than to those in Taiwan. Disclosure of its reckless lending to the Suzuki conglomerate, in particular, helped to bring on the FINANCIAL CRISIS OF 1927. During World War II, it helped to finance the administration of the Japanese-occupied areas of South China and Southeast Asia. Following the war the bank was ordered dissolved by the OCCUPATION authorities, its liquidation being completed by 1957.

Taiyō　太陽

(The Sun). One of Japan's first general-interest magazines; published by HAKUBUNKAN, a leading Tōkyō publishing house, from 1895 to 1928. The magazine was launched in January 1895, along with Shōnen sekai and BUNGEI KURABU, in a move by Hakubunkan to consolidate its magazine division. Taiyō came out monthly (bimonthly 1896–99). It published articles on a wide variety of practical and intellectual topics and was among the leading periodicals of the 1900–1920 era. Its literary columns attracted particular attention because of the critical articles of literature editor TAKAYAMA CHOGYŪ. With the rise of TAISHŌ DEMOCRACY and changing social trends after World War I, it was overshadowed by CHŪŌ KŌRON and KAIZŌ and ceased publication in February 1928. Two other magazines with the same name were later published by CHIKUMA SHOBŌ PUBLISHING CO, LTD (October 1957–February 1958), and HEIBONSHA, LTD, PUBLISHERS (July 1963 to the present).

Taiyō Fishery Co, Ltd 大洋漁業[株]

(Taiyō Gyogyō). One of the world's leading fishery and seafood companies. Incorporated in 1943. It has expanded its line of business to include processed foods (such as canned foods, fish, ham and sausages, frozen foods, and sugar), cold storage, and shipping. The company has a total of 61 domestic subsidiaries, 28 joint enterprises overseas, and 11 representative offices overseas. It also owns a professional baseball team, the Taiyō Whales. Sales for the fiscal year ending January 1991 totaled ¥542.2 billion (US $4.0 billion), and the company was capitalized at ¥15.0 billion (US $112.0 million). Headquarters are in Tōkyō.

Taiyō Mutual Life Insurance Co
太陽生命保険[相]

(Taiyō Seimei Hoken). Life insurance company. Incorporated in 1893. Taiyō is Japan's leading short-term insurance company. Total assets at the end of March 1990 reached ¥4.4 trillion (US $28.7 billion), and the company received total premiums of ¥1.2 trillion (US $7.8 billion). Headquarters are in Tōkyō.

Taizōkai 胎蔵界

(Skt: Garbhadhātu; Matrix or Womb Realm). A realm symbolizing one of two aspects of the Dharmakāya Buddha Mahāvairocana (J: DAINICHI), the central Buddha in ESOTERIC BUDDHISM. The Taizōkai refers to Mahāvairocana's aspect of dynamic enlightenment, an all-embracing principle underlying and nurturing all phenomena (hence the use of the word "womb"). The *Taizō mandara* (Skt: *Garbha-maṇḍala*), or *Taizōkai mandara* (Mandala of the Garbhadhātu), is the pictorial representation of this realm, and the sacred text *Dainichikyō* (*Mahāvairocana-sūtra*) expounds the mandala. The Taizōkai and the KONGŌKAI (Diamond or Thunderbolt Realm), the other aspect of Mahāvairocana, are often paired and known as Kontai Ryōbu. Together these realms formulate the two central tenets of SHINGON SECT esoteric Buddhism. See also RYŌBU MANDARA; MANDALA.

Tajima Naoto 田島直人

(1912–90). Track and field athlete; specialist in the triple and long jump. Born in Ōsaka Prefecture; graduate of Kyōto University. Professor of physical education at Chūkyō University from 1966. Tajima won a gold medal in the triple jump in the 1936 Berlin Olympic Games, setting a world record of 16 meters (52.5 ft), and also won a bronze medal in the long jump. Tajima was a member of the Japanese Olympic Committee from 1961 to 1964 and from 1969 to 1985.

Tajimi 多治見[市]

City in southeastern Gifu Prefecture, central Honshū. Tajimi has been known since ancient times for its MINO WARE. With the opening of a rail line in 1900, Tajimi's ceramic industry developed further. Today it manufactures tile and tableware. Pop: 94,036.

taka → hawks and eagles

Takabatake Motoyuki 高畠素之

(1886–1928). Social theorist. Born in Gumma Prefecture; attended Dōshisha University. Influenced by the thought of KŌTOKU SHŪSUI, he started a socialist newspaper in his hometown. While briefly imprisoned in 1908 for an article he had published, he began reading an English translation of Marx's *Das Kapital*. In 1911 he joined SAKAI TOSHIHIKO's socialist organization, the BAIBUNSHA, and became a frequent contributor to its journal, *Shin shakai*, introducing the ideas of European socialist thinkers such as Karl Kautsky (1854–1938) to Japan. By 1919 he had begun to fall out with his leftist colleagues and move in the direction of national socialism, but it was in this year that he began his main work—the first complete Japanese translation of *Das Kapital*, published 1920–24 as *Shihonron*.

Takachiho 高千穂[町]

Town in northwestern Miyazaki Prefecture, Kyūshū. The principal activity is stock raising; agricultural products include rice, vegetables, and tobacco. Tourist attractions include the scenic gorge TAKACHIHOKYŌ and the *yokagura*, a sacred Shintō dance performed at the Amanoiwato shrine, where it is claimed the sun goddess AMATERASU ŌMIKAMI once hid herself (see MYTHOLOGY). Pop: 18,093.

Takachihokyō 高千穂峡

Gorge on the upper reaches of the river GOKASEGAWA, northern Miyazaki Prefecture, Kyūshū. Famous for its rocky formations and foliage. The area is associated with the mythic beginnings of Japan, as recounted in the *Kojiki* (712) and the *Nihon shoki* (720). Length: 5 km (3 mi).

Takachihonomine 高千穂峰

Craterless stratovolcano, on the southern edge of the Kirishima Volcanic Group, on the border between Miyazaki and Kagoshima prefectures, Kyūshū. Legend has it that the grandson of AMATERASU ŌMIKAMI, the sun goddess, descended from heaven to the summit of this mountain. It is part of Kirishima-Yaku National Park. Height: 1,574 m (5,164 ft).

Takada → Jōetsu

Takada Hiroatsu 高田博厚

(1900–1987). Western-style sculptor and art critic. Born in Ishikawa Prefecture. He learned Italian at the Tōkyō University of Foreign Languages and later studied sculpture with TAKAMURA KŌTARŌ. Strongly influenced by the SHIRAKABA SCHOOL, a movement of young writers and artists, in 1927 he helped found a short-lived artists' commune on the outskirts of Tōkyō. In 1931 he left for Paris, where he associated with leading French artists. He returned to Japan in 1957. In addition to his original writings and numerous translations, he is noted for his portrait sculptures.

Takada Kenzō 高田賢三

(1939–). Fashion designer. Born in Hyōgo Prefecture; graduate of Bunka Fashion College. Kenzō's "big silhouette" designs attracted world-wide attention, and his work

Takachihokyō The waterfall Manai no Taki is one of the famous features of this gorge, which was cut through a volcanic plateau by the river Gokasegawa.

is regarded as an indicator of fashion trends for the young throughout the world. He combines the spirit of Paris with Japanese sensibilities. He is esteemed highly in Japan as a pioneer who opened the way for world appreciation of Japanese designers.

Takada Plain 高田平野

(Takada Heiya). Also called the Jōetsu Plain. Alluvial plain of the river Sekigawa in southwestern Niigata Prefecture, central Honshū. It was developed into a rice production area early in the Edo period (1600–1868). Snowfall is heavy. In recent years major industries have been attracted to the plain; natural gas and oil fields have been developed. Area: 280 sq km (108 sq mi).

Takada Sanae 高田早苗

(1860–1938). Educator and politician. Born in Edo (now Tōkyō). Upon graduation from Tōkyō University in 1882, he helped ŌKUMA SHIGENOBU found Tōkyō Semmon Gakkō (now WASEDA UNIVERSITY). In 1890 and on five later occasions he was elected to the House of Representatives from Saitama Prefecture. In 1915 he was appointed to the House of Peers. In addition, he held such eminent posts as director-general of the Ministry of Foreign Affairs and of the Ministry of Education and later served as education minister in the second Ōkuma cabinet (1914–16). His greatest achievement, however, lay in the sphere of private university management, particularly at Waseda. He was appointed its provost (*gakuchō*) in 1907 and became its third chancellor (*sōchō*) in 1923.

takagari → falconry

Takagi Kenkan 高木兼寛

(1849–1920). Naval surgeon and medical educator. Also known as Takagi Kanehiro. Born in what is now Miyazaki Prefecture. Takagi studied under Ishigami Ryōsaku (1821–75) and William WILLIS and graduated from St. Thomas's Hospital Medical School in London. In 1880 he became director of the Tōkyō Naval Hospital. The following year he founded the Seiikai School (now the JIKEI UNIVERSITY SCHOOL OF MEDICINE), as well as

Takada Kenzō This designer has been one of the pioneers in the introduction of Japanese fashion to a worldwide audience.

Takagi Teiji A leading modern Japanese mathematician, Takagi made a significant contribution to algebraic number theory.

Takahama Kyoshi A *haiku* poet and novelist who promoted new writing as editor of the magazine *Hototogisu*.

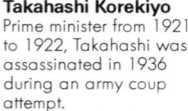

Takahashi Korekiyo Prime minister from 1921 to 1922, Takahashi was assassinated in 1936 during an army coup attempt.

Japan's first nursing school. Takagi became medical inspector general of the navy in 1885. As a member of the Beriberi Investigation Committee, Takagi proved that beriberi was mainly related to a dietary imbalance resulting from a diet of polished rice.

Takagi Teiji   高木貞治

(1875–1960). Mathematician. The leading figure in modern Japanese mathematics, Takagi is known for his far-reaching contributions in algebraic number theory. Born in Gifu Prefecture, he graduated from Tōkyō University in 1897. From 1898 to 1901 he studied at the universities of Berlin and Göttingen. In 1904 Takagi became professor at Tōkyō University, where he taught until his retirement in 1936. He made his most significant contribution to the advance of modern mathematics in 1920 with the introduction of the Takagi class-field theory, which generalized and gave structure to Hilbert's concept of a class field and became the framework for the study of algebraic number theory. In 1932 he was elected to the selection committee for the prestigious Fields Prize, and he received the Order of Culture in 1940. His publications include *Kaiseki gairon* (1938, Introduction to Analysis) and *Daisūteki seisūron* (1948, Algebraic Number Theory).

Takahagi   高萩[市]

City in northeastern Ibaraki Prefecture, central Honshū, on the Pacific Ocean. The ABUKUMA MOUNTAINS occupy about 70 percent of the city's area. Formerly a coal-mining center, it now has pulp and lumber mills. Pop: 35,320.

Takahama   高浜[市]

City in central Aichi Prefecture, central Honshū; on Chita Bay. Long known for its tiles, it has diversified into machinery and other industries. Poultry farming is also active. Pop: 33,478.

Takahama Kyoshi   高浜虚子

(1874–1959). HAIKU poet and novelist. Real name Takahama Kiyoshi. Born in Matsuyama, Ehime Prefecture. He is noted for his leading role in the haiku world during the first half of this century and for his achievements as editor of the magazine HOTOTOGISU, where he introduced the work of other writers and new types of poetic prose.

Ignoring the advice of his mentor MASAOKA SHIKI, Kyoshi left school in 1894 and went with his friend KAWAHIGASHI HEKIGOTŌ to live in Tōkyō, where he studied Edo-period (1600–1868) literature. In 1895 he entered Tōkyō Semmon Gakkō (now Waseda University) but soon abandoned his studies and took a job with the magazine *Nihonjin* (The Japanese) as haiku editor and critic. While there he produced poems notable for their experimentation with lines containing irregular numbers of syllables and for carrying on the general tradition of the haiku poet BUSON but with an increased emphasis on human affairs.

Kyoshi married in 1897, the year that Masaoka Shiki established the magazine *Hototogisu*. He took over the magazine when it fell into difficulty and contributed verses; *shaseibun* ("sketch pieces"); short, poetic pieces; and prose, including short stories. A collection of his stories, *Keitō* (1908, Cockscomb), had a preface by NATSUME SŌSEKI that described the stories as "leisurely

tales," thus giving rise to the appellation "Leisure School" (Yoyū Ha).

In 1908 Kyoshi began serialization of his first full-length novel, *Haikaishi* (The Haiku Master). In 1909 a second volume of short stories, *Bonjin* (An Ordinary Person), appeared. Trips to Korea in 1911 inspired another novel, *Chōsen* (Korea), but from 1912 on, Kyoshi showed a renewed interest in haiku. In *Susumubeki haiku no michi* (1915–17, The Path Haiku Ought to Take), he stressed objective observation as the basis of the haiku. He continued to write short stories and the novel *Kaki futatsu* (1915; tr *The Two Persimmons*, 1951), while as editor of *Hototogisu* he helped to launch the careers of many other poets and novelists. Kyoshi took an interest in NŌ theater, writing some new plays himself. Visits abroad inspired him to write several travel pieces and helped to widen the scope of his verse. His major postwar work was the novel *Niji* (1947, Rainbow). He was awarded the Order of Culture in 1954.

Takahashi   高梁[市]

City in western Okayama Prefecture, western Honshū. A regional commercial and agricultural center. Products include tobacco, lumber, Christmas decorations, and straw hats. Bitchū Matsuyama Castle is on the summit of the mountain Gagyūzan. Pop: 26,003.

Takahashigawa   高梁川

River in western Okayama Prefecture, western Honshū; originating in the mountains on the border of Tottori Prefecture and flowing south into the Inland Sea at the city of Kurashiki. The middle reaches flow through the plateau Kibi Kōgen, and there are stalactite grottoes where the river has carved through limestone. The lower reaches form the agricultural belt of the Okayama Plain, and the Mizushima Industrial Area is located at its mouth. The water is used for drinking, irrigation, industry, and electric power. Length: 111 km (69 mi); area of drainage basin: 2,670 sq km (1,030 sq mi).

Takahashi Hideo   高橋英夫

(1930–). Critic. Born in Tōkyō; graduated from Tōkyō University. Takahashi first became known in 1968 for his *Orikuchigaku no hassō josetsu* (Introduction to the Thought of Orikuchi Shinobu) and has continued to write criticism from a mythological and ethnological perspective. His principal works include *Hihyō no seishin* (1970, The Spirit of Criticism), *Yakuwari to shite no kami* (1975, God as a Role), and *Shiga Naoya: Kindai to shinwa* (1981, Shiga Naoya: Myth and the Modern Age).

Takahashi Kageyasu   高橋景保

(1785–1829). Geographer and scholar of WESTERN LEARNING who produced some of the earliest scientifically surveyed maps of the Japanese archipelago. Born in Ōsaka. Succeeding his father, TAKAHASHI YOSHITOKI, as shogunal astronomer in 1804, he published maps of Japan based upon the surveys of INŌ TADATAKA and two northern explorers, MAMIYA RINZŌ and MOGAMI TOKUNAI. In 1811 he established a translation office for foreign books and personally translated part of Engelbert KAEMPFER's history of Japan. Bavarian naturalist Philipp Franz von SIEBOLD visited Edo (now Tōkyō) in 1826; when Japanese maps were discovered among Siebold's effects in 1828, shogunal authorities arrested Takahashi and some of his disciples (giving

maps to foreigners was prohibited). Takahashi died in prison, and his corpse was formally "executed."

Takahashi Kazumi   高橋和巳

(1931–71). Scholar of Chinese literature and novelist. Born in Ōsaka; graduate of Kyōto University. His novel *Hi no utsuwa* (1962) depicts the fall of a university dean from prominence and power as a result of his self-centered love affairs. During the nationwide student uprisings of the late 1960s, Takahashi conscientiously supported the radical students, with whom he was very popular. Principal works include the novels *Yūutsu naru tōha* (1965, A Melancholy Faction) and *Jashūmon* (1965–66, Heretical Faith) and the essay "Waga kaitai" (1969, Self-Dissection).

Takahashi Kenji   高橋健自

(1871–1929). Archaeologist. Born in Miyagi Prefecture, he graduated from Tōkyō Higher Normal School (later Tōkyō University of Education), where he studied under MIYAKE YONEKICHI. Takahashi began archaeological research in Nara Prefecture while employed as a middle-school teacher. In 1904 he joined the staff of the Tōkyō Imperial Household Museum (now Tōkyō National Museum). Among his publications are *Dōhoko dōken no kenkyū* (1925), on bronze weapons; *Kagami to ken to tama* (1911), on bronze mirrors, swords, and beads; *Nihon fukushokushi ron* (1927), on ancient clothing; and *Kofun to jōdai bunka* (1922), on ancient culture.

Takahashi Kiichirō   高橋揆一郎

(1928–). Novelist. Real name Takahashi Yoshio. Born in Hokkaidō. Attended Sapporo Normal School. Takahashi achieved recognition as a writer in 1973 with the publication of *Popura to gunshin* (The Poplar Tree and the God of War), the story of a youth who is intimidated by the corporal punishment he suffers at the hands of a militaristic teacher. He received the Akutagawa Prize for *Nobuyo* (1978), about a widowed schoolteacher's love affair with one of her former male students.

Takahashi Korekiyo   高橋是清

(1854–1936). Politician and financial expert. Prime minister (1921–22); president of the RIKKEN SEIYŪKAI political party (1921–25); and intermittently finance minister in six cabinets between 1913 and 1936. His major accomplishments were to bring under control the FINANCIAL CRISIS OF 1927 and to help the economy recover rapidly from the SHŌWA DEPRESSION.

Born in Edo (now Tōkyō), Takahashi served as a low-ranking bureaucrat in various government ministries and eventually became an employee of the BANK OF JAPAN in 1892. He became vice-president of the bank in 1898. For his services in obtaining foreign loans during and immediately after the Russo-Japanese War of 1904–05, he was appointed to the House of Peers in 1905. He continued his rise in the banking world, becoming president of the Yokohama Specie Bank in 1906 and of the Bank of Japan in 1911.

In 1921 he took over leadership of the government and of the Seiyūkai. His term as prime minister lasted less than seven months, mainly because of his inability to control factions within his own party. When one faction of the Seiyūkai deserted to support a nonparty cabinet (see "TRANSCENDENTAL" CABINETS), Takahashi joined the second MOVEMENT TO PROTECT CONSTITUTIONAL GOVERN-

MENT, becoming minister of agriculture and commerce in KATŌ TAKAAKI's coalition cabinet in 1924. Resigning the Seiyūkai presidency in 1925, he served as finance minister in the cabinets of TANAKA GIICHI (1927–29), INUKAI TSUYOSHI (1931–32), SAITŌ MAKOTO (1932–34), and OKADA KEISUKE (1934–36). Despite his successes in combating the economic depression of the late 1920s and early 1930s, he was assassinated in the FEBRUARY 26TH INCIDENT by army critics of his policies limiting armaments expansion.

Takahashi Michitsuna 高橋三千綱

(1948–). Novelist. Born in Ōsaka Prefecture; attended Waseda University. In 1974 he received the Gunzō Prize for New Talent for *Taikutsu shinogi* (Fending Off Boredom). In 1978 Takahashi received the Akutagawa Prize for *Kugatsu no sora* (September Sky). He writes refreshing, bright novels of adolescence. Takahashi's other works include *Mayonaka no bokusā* (1982, Midnight Boxer).

Takahashi Mutsuo 高橋睦郎

(1937–). Poet. Born in Fukuoka Prefecture; graduate of Fukuoka University of Education. The poetry of his teens was collected in his first published work, *Mino, atashi no oushi* (1959, Mino, My Bull). His second collection of poems was *Bara no ki: Nise no koibitotachi* (1964, The Rose-Tree: Imitation Lovers). A prolific writer, he has also published the autobiographical work *Jūni no enkei* (1970, Twelve Perspectives); short stories, including "Sei sankakukei" (1972, The Holy Triangle); a full-length novel, *Zen no henreki* (1974, Zen's Pilgrimage), in which a young provincial journeys through Tōkyō's erotic underground, seen as a transmutation of the various realms of the Buddhist cosmos; and travel essays. Running through his works is a dual preoccupation with homosexual eroticism, as in "Homeuta" (1971, Ode), and religion. Takahashi's religious interests extend from Roman Catholicism to Eastern Orthodoxy and Mahāyāna Buddhism.

Takahashi no Mushimaro 高橋虫麻呂

(fl ca 730). Poet and court official. Practically nothing is known of his life apart from references in the MAN'YŌSHŪ (ca 759), the first great anthology of Japanese vernacular poetry. He is believed to have compiled Book 9 of the *Man'yōshū* and may also have collected the local dialect songs and poems gathered in Book 14 under the rubric Azuma *uta* (Poems of the Eastland). Noted for his verse adaptations of legends, he is accepted as the author of 34 poems in the anthology and has been posited as the author of two others.

Takahashi Oden 高橋お伝

(1851–79). Murderess; the most notorious *dokufu* (wicked woman) of the modern era. Accused of several sex-related murders, Oden was the first woman to be executed by beheading after the Edo period (1600–1868). Born in what is now Gumma Prefecture, she was known from girlhood for her beauty and promiscuity. Her life of crime began after her husband contracted leprosy. When the disease proved incurable, Oden allegedly poisoned her husband and embarked on a career of prostitution, larceny, and homicide. Arrested in 1876 for slitting the throat of a used-clothing merchant at an inn in Asakusa, she was convicted and ultimately executed. It was the most sensational crime story of the day, and lurid accounts of Oden's escapades filled the newspapers. The popular author KANAGAKI ROBUN wrote a spicy novel based on her life, *Takahashi Oden yasha monogatari* (1879, Tale of Takahashi Oden, the She-Devil), which Kawatake MOKUAMI adapted as a *kabuki* play.

Takahashi Osamu 高橋治

(1929–). Novelist. Born in Chiba Prefecture; graduated from Tōkyō University. Takahashi received the Naoki Prize for *Hiden* (1984, Secret Tradition), the story of an old fisherman. His other works include *Hahei* (1973–77, 4 vols, Dispatch of Troops), a nonfiction work about the SIBERIAN INTERVENTION; *Kenrantaru kage-e* (1982, Dazzling Shadow Picture), a portrait of the filmmaker OZU YASUJIRŌ; and *Jihaku no kōzu* (1984, Draft for a Confession).

Takahashi Satomi 高橋里美

(1886–1964). Philosopher. Born in Yamagata Prefecture. After graduating from Tōkyō University in 1910, he studied in Germany and France (1924–27) and then became a professor at Tōhoku University. Early in his life, he was influenced by the Marburg school of Neo-Kantianism and NISHIDA KITARŌ's philosophy of "Absolute Nothingness," but he later became critical of Nishida and TANABE HAJIME (whose position is related to Nishida's) and came to expound his own philosophy of the "comprehensive dialectical whole" (*hō benshōhōteki zentaisei*). His writings are collected in the *Takahashi Satomi zenshū* (7 vols, 1973).

Takahashi Seiichirō 高橋誠一郎

(1884–1982). Economist. Born in Niigata Prefecture. After graduating from Keiō University in 1908, Takahashi studied in England and came to be known as an international authority on mercantilism. He was a professor at Keiō University from 1914 to 1944 and was minister of education in 1947, during the promulgation of the 6-3-3-4 education system. Takahashi served as director of the Tōkyō National Museum (1949–51) and as committee chairman of the Council for the Protection of Cultural Properties (1950–56). He was also widely known as a collector and scholar of UKIYO-E. He received the Order of Culture in 1979.

Takahashi Shinji 高橋信次

(1912–85). Radiotherapist and doctor of medicine. Born in Fukushima Prefecture. Graduate of Tōhoku University School of Medicine. Takahashi is noted for his development of rotary, multicolor, and magnification X-ray radiography, which enables three-dimensional imaging of the body and studies of pathological anatomy. He also made significant contributions in the field of radiological diagnosis and served as president of the Aichi Cancer Center. Takahashi was awarded the Order of Culture in 1984.

Takahashi Shinkichi 高橋新吉

(1901–87). Poet. Born in Ehime Prefecture. As a young man, he was inspired by the dadaist manifestos of Romanian poet Tristan Tzara (1896–1963), which were carried in a Tōkyō newspaper. Takahashi's dadaist poetry collection *Dadaisuto Shinkichi no shi* (1923) created an immediate sensation. It combined the dadaist opposition to all convention and tradition with a Buddhist sense of nihilism, often achieving in his poems an effect reminiscent of the Zen KŌAN. Other collections include *Gion matsuri* (1926) and *Kūdō* (1981).

Takahashi Takako 高橋たか子

(1932–). Novelist. Born in Kyōto Prefecture; graduated from Kyōto University. Her husband is the writer TAKAHASHI KAZUMI. Her works depict the struggles of people to grasp the essence of existence. The influence of Christianity, to which the author converted in 1975, can be seen in the lonely souls in her works who wander in search of unconditional love. Takahashi's principal works include *Yūwakusha* (1976, The Seducer), *Yosōiseyo, waga tamashii yo* (1982, Adorn Yourself, My Soul), and *Ikari no ko* (1985, Child of Anger).

Takahashi Yoshitoki 高橋至時

(1764–1804). Astronomer of the mid-Edo period (1600–1868). With his son TAKAHASHI KAGEYASU, he advanced the study of astronomy and the calendar in Japan. Born in Ōsaka. In 1795 he was made official astronomer to the Tokugawa shogunate and, with Hazama Shigetomi (1756–1816), devised the Kansei Calendar, which was officially adopted in 1798. Takahashi translated and published *Rarande rekisho kanken*, a Dutch version of a work by French astronomer Joseph Lalande (1732–1807).

Takahashi Yuichi 高橋由一

(1828–94). Western-style painter who is best known for his realistic still lifes. Born in Edo (now Tōkyō), he studied the KANŌ SCHOOL style of painting until his interest in Western art was aroused by Western lithographs. In 1862 he entered the shogunal Institute for the Investigation of Western Books (see BANSHO SHIRABESHO), where he studied under KAWAKAMI TŌGAI. In 1866 he furthered his study of Western art under the direction of the English illustrator Charles WIRGMAN in Yokohama. In 1870 Takahashi became professor at Daigaku Nankō, the predecessor of Tōkyō University. In 1873 he left to found his own art school, Tenkai Gakusha. In 1880 he began publication of Japan's first art magazine, *Gayū sekichin*.

Takahata Seiichi 高畑誠一

(1887–1978). Businessman. Born in Ehime Prefecture. After graduation from Kōbe Kōtō Shōgyō Gakkō (now Kōbe University), Takahata joined the firm SUZUKI SHŌTEN in 1909. Handpicked in 1913 by its head manager KANEKO NAOKICHI to act as London branch manager, he helped build the firm into a leading trading company during the course of World War I, through third-country trade (trade not involving Japan). After the company's failure in 1927, Takahata established the general trading firm Nisshō & Co (now NISSHŌ IWAI CORPORATION) in 1928. He served as the company's chairman from 1945 through 1963.

Takahira Kogorō 高平小五郎

(1854–1926). Diplomat. Born in what is now Iwate Prefecture, he attended the Kaisei Gakkō, a precursor of Tōkyō University. In 1876 Takahira joined the Ministry of Foreign Affairs. He served as minister to Italy and Austria before becoming vice–foreign minister in 1899. As minister to the United States from 1900, he helped negotiate the Treaty of PORTSMOUTH (1905) concluding the Russo-Japanese War; as ambassador, he signed the 1908 TAKAHIRA-ROOT AGREEMENT, which sanctioned the status quo in the Pacific and pro-

Takahashi Seiichirō
An international authority on mercantilism, this economist was appointed minister of education in 1947.

Takahashi Yuichi
Salmon. Ca 1877. Oil on paper. 140 × 47 cm. Tōkyō University of Fine Arts and Music.

Takamatsuzuka tomb
The paintings on the walls of this tomb, which is dated to about 700, are National Treasures.
1 A detail from paintings on the west wall shows a group of four women, thought to represent mourners, dressed in Korean-style jackets and skirts.
2 A painting of the "Azure Dragon of the east" appears in the center of the east wall.

vided for equal Japanese-US commercial opportunities in China.

Takahira-Root Agreement
高平・ルート協定

(Takahira-Rūto Kyōtei). An agreement between Japan and the United States regarding their respective roles in China and the Pacific Ocean area following the RUSSO-JAPANESE WAR of 1904–05. Negotiated by Secretary of State Elihu Root and Ambassador TAKAHIRA KOGORŌ, it was signed on 30 November 1908. The agreement consisted of an official recognition of the status quo; provisions included affirmation of the independence and territorial integrity of China, maintenance of free and equal commercial opportunities, Japanese recognition of American interests in Hawaii and the Philippines, and American recognition of Japan's position in Manchuria. See also KATSURA-TAFT AGREEMENT; OPEN DOOR POLICY.

Takai Kitō
高井几董

(1741–89). HAIKU poet. Born in Kyōto. A faithful disciple of BUSON, he compiled and edited the texts of his master's school and devoted himself to the haiku revival movement of the late 18th century. Noted for their delicacy and subtlety, his verses are mainly collected in *Seikashū* (1789).

Takaishi
高石［市］

City in southwestern Ōsaka Prefecture, central Honshū, on Ōsaka Bay; 20 km (12 mi) southwest of Ōsaka. It was once an exclusive suburb of Ōsaka, but since the 1960s it has undergone rapid industrialization. An older textile industry produces blankets and cotton fabrics. Pop: 65,086.

Takai Yūichi
高井有一

(1932–). Novelist. Real name Taguchi Tetsurō. Born in Tōkyō. Graduate of Waseda University. In 1965 he received the Akutagawa Prize for *Kita no kawa* (North River), which told the story of his mother's suicide during World War II. Other works include

Takakura Ken The gangster film genre enjoyed huge popularity in the 1960s, largely as a result of this actor's energetic performances.

Shinjitsu no gakkō (1980, The School of Truth), about the educational movement SEIKATSU TSUZURIKATA UNDŌ, and *Chiri no miyako ni* (1988, In the Capital of Dust), which depicts the life of SAITŌ RYOKUU.

Takakura Ken
高倉健

(1931–). Real name Oda Toshimasa. Screen actor known for his tough-guy roles in numerous YAKUZA (gangster) films. Born in Fukuoka Prefecture. After graduating from Meiji University, he joined the motion picture company TŌEI CO, LTD in 1955. His first role was in *Denkō karate uchi* in 1956. After playing the lead in *Jinsei gekijō: Hishakaku* in 1963, Takakura became the undisputed archetypical hero of *yakuza* movies for his performance in an 18-segment *yakuza* movie series collectively titled *Abashiri bangaichi* (1965–72). This and another series, *Shōwa zankyō den* (1965–72), made him one of Japan's most popular box-office stars. He left Tōei in 1976 to become a free-lance actor in such films as *Hakkōdasan* (1977) and *Shiawase no kiiroi hankachi* (1977). Takakura has also appeared in several American films, including *Black Rain* (1989).

Takakura Tokutarō
高倉徳太郎

(1885–1934). Protestant theologian. Born in Kyōto Prefecture, he graduated from Tōkyō Union Theological Seminary, where he also became a professor after serving as a pastor in various areas. Influenced by the English Congregationalist minister Peter Taylor Forsyth (1848–1921), he embarked on a reform movement and stimulated the church in Japan to a new theological awareness. In opposition to rationalistic or naturalistic Christianity, as well as a Catholic-type pietism and mysticism, his Gospel-oriented Christianity emphasized original sin and the grace of atonement, laying the foundation for evangelicalism prior to the influence of the theology of Karl Barth (1886–1968).

Takakusu Junjirō
高楠順次郎

(1866–1945). Scholar of Indian philosophy and Buddhism. His pen name was Takakusu Setchō. Born in Hiroshima Prefecture, he graduated from Ryūkoku University. In 1890 he went to England and studied Indian religion and philosophy and Sanskrit under the German philologist and orientalist Max Müller (1823–1900) at Oxford. Returning to Japan in 1897, he lectured on Sanskrit literature at Tōkyō University. Assembling a group of scholars of Buddhism, he poured all his energies and personal resources into publishing a series of translations of Buddhist literature and original Indian documents, among which was *Taishō shinshū daizōkyō* (1924–34, 100 vols, The Taishō Tripitaka). He was a professor at Tōkyō University from 1899 to 1927. He was awarded the Order of Culture in 1944.

Takamagahara
高天が原

(literally, "High Celestial Plain"). Also called Takamanohara. Standard term for the abode of the heavenly divinities (*tenjin* or *amatsukami*) in Japanese MYTHOLOGY. It is generally considered that the High Celestial Plain is opposed to the "Land of Roots" (Nenokuni), to which some dead persons go; between these two realms the human world, the "Central Land of Reeds" (Ashihara no Nakatsukuni), is located. This term therefore symbolizes a vertical view of the universe and suggests its association with shamanistic tradition.

Takamatsu
高松［市］

Capital of Kagawa Prefecture, Shikoku, on the Inland Sea. Takamatsu developed as a castle town after Ikoma Chikamasa (1526–1603) constructed a castle in 1588. It later came under the rule of the Matsudaira family. The opening in 1910 of a ferryboat service between Honshū and Takamatsu led to its emergence as a transportation center. A series of bridges, completed in 1988, have largely superseded the ferry. The city's main industries are machinery and foodstuffs. Traditional products are LACQUER WARE, tissue paper, and *udon* (noodles). Attractions include the remains of Takamatsu Castle; RITSURIN PARK; and YASHIMA, the site of a battle in the TAIRA-MINAMOTO WAR. Pop: 329,684.

Takamatsu, Prince
高松宮宣仁親王

(1905–87; Takamatsu no Miya Nobuhito Shinnō). Third son of Emperor TAISHŌ and younger brother of Emperor SHŌWA (Hirohito). Named Teru no Miya Nobuhito, in 1913 he succeeded to the headship of the Takamatsu family, a princely house established in 1625 by a son of Emperor Go-Yōzei (1571–1617; r 1586–1611). He graduated from the Naval Academy and the Naval Staff College and married a daughter of Tokugawa Yoshihisa (1884–1922), a son of the last Tokugawa shōgun. Attached to the military command during World War II, the prince was involved in a conspiracy to overthrow the cabinet of TŌJŌ HIDEKI.

Takamatsuzuka tomb
高松塚古墳

(Takamatsuzuka *kofun*). A small tomb mound with plastered and painted walls located in the southern hills of ASUKA, Nara Prefecture. Dated to around AD 700, it is the sole Japanese example of the so-called international artistic style then current in East Asia. The tomb was excavated in 1972. Although illustrated and identified in documents of the Edo period (1600–1868) as the mausoleum of Emperor Mommu (683–707; r 697–707), the Takamatsuzuka was taken off the list of imperial tombs when a large mound to the south was later identified with Mommu. The excavation yielded skeletal remains of a male in his forties (Mommu had been cremated), fragments of a lacquered coffin, and a small variety of grave artifacts. The east and west walls each bear two groups of four human figures, men at the south end and women at the north, divided by representations of the Azure Dragon of the east and the White Tiger of the west, the sun and moon respectively above them. The "Black Warrior" (the snake and tortoise) appears on the north wall. Overhead are 72 red dots, some still showing a little gold; a few are grouped in recognizable constellations. The women wear jackets and pleated skirts as seen in Sui dynasty (589–618) China but more familiar in Korea, and the men wear long robes and trousers best known in China. All the objects in the paintings—satchels, round fans, and priests' staffs—with the exception of a folding stool, have their counterparts in China.

Takami Jun   高見順

(1907–65). Novelist and poet. Real name Takama Yoshio. Born in Fukui Prefecture; graduate of Tōkyō University. He participated in left-wing politics, but after being arrested in the early 1930s he renounced Marxism. He wrote about the anguish of this ideological "conversion" (see TENKŌ) in *Kokyū wasureubeki* (1935–36, Should Auld Acquaintance Be Forgot). His autobiographical novels are characterized by ironic self-pity over his decadence and intellectual confusion following his "conversion" in the 1930s. In 1962 he helped found the Nihon Kindai Bungakukan (MUSEUM OF MODERN JAPANESE LITERATURE). In 1964 his poetry collection *Shi no fuchi yori* (From the Abyss of Death) received the Noma Prize. Other works include the novels *Ikanaru hoshi no moto ni* (1939–40, Beneath What Star) and *Iya na kanji* (1960–63, A Disagreeable Feeling) and a nine-volume diary, *Takami Jun nikki* (1964–66), which provides a detailed account of his experiences during World War II and the immediate postwar era.

Takamine Hideko   高峰秀子

(1924–). Film actress. Real name Matsuyama Hideko. Born in the city of Hakodate, Hokkaidō. She joined what is now SHŌCHIKU CO, LTD, at the age of five, earned a name for herself as a child actress, and then became an adult dramatic star. She appeared in Japan's first color picture, *Karumen kokyō ni kaeru* (1951, Carmen Comes Home). She scored a critical triumph as the wife in the film *Na mo naku mazushiku utsukushiku* (1961, Nameless, Poor, Beautiful), written and directed by her husband, MATSUYAMA ZENZŌ. Her other films include NARUSE MIKIO'S UKIGUMO (1955, Floating Clouds) and KINOSHITA KEISUKE'S NIJŪSHI NO HITOMI (1954, Twenty-Four Eyes). Retired from acting since 1979, she now devotes herself to writing.

Takamine Hideo   高嶺秀夫

(1854–1910). Educator of the Meiji period (1868–1912); born in the Aizu domain (now part of Fukushima Prefecture); graduate of Keiō University. In 1875 Takamine went to the United States, where he studied teacher training in Oswego, New York, at a state college that was a center for the theories of Swiss educator Johann Heinrich Pestalozzi (1746–1827), who stressed the need for student participation. After returning to Japan in 1878, he took a teaching post at Tōkyō Normal School (later Tōkyō University of Education; now TSUKUBA UNIVERSITY). He be-

came president of this school and, subsequently, of Tōkyō Women's Higher Normal School (now Ochanomizu Women's University) and Tōkyō Bijutsu Gakkō (now Tōkyō University of Fine Arts and Music).

Takamine Jōkichi   高峰譲吉

(1854–1922). Applied chemist. Born in what is now Toyama Prefecture. After graduating in 1879 from the applied chemistry course of the Kōbu Daigakkō (a predecessor of Tōkyō University), Takamine went to England and studied there until 1883. Returning to Japan, he worked for the Agriculture and Commerce Ministry. In 1890 he went to the United States, where he produced a powerful digestive, Taka-Diastase. He also succeeded in isolating adrenaline in crystalline form from bovine adrenal glands. In 1917 he founded a chemical laboratory in Clifton, New Jersey. In 1912 Takamine was awarded the Imperial Academy Prize for his work on adrenaline.

Takamine Mieko   高峰三枝子

(1918–90). Actress. Real name Suzuki Mieko. Born in Tōkyō. In 1936 she joined the Shōchiku Kinema Co (now SHŌCHIKU CO, LTD). Recognized for her graceful beauty, she played the leading role in *Shu to midori* (1937, Crimson and Green), directed by SHIMAZU YASUJIRŌ. She also became well known as a singer with her recording of "Kohan no yado" (Lakeside Cottage). Her other films incude *Danryū* (1939, A Warm Current), directed by YOSHIMURA KŌZABURŌ, and *Tsuma* (1953, Wife), directed by NARUSE MIKIO.

Takami Senseki   鷹見泉石

(1785–1858). Official of the Koga domain (now part of Ibaraki Prefecture) and scholar of WESTERN LEARNING, which he began to study under the guidance of ŌTSUKI GENTAKU. Appointed chief retainer (*karō*) to the *daimyō* Doi Toshitsura (1789–1848), he went to Ōsaka with Doi, who had been named keeper (*jōdai*) of Ōsaka Castle. Takami was instrumental in capturing ŌSHIO HEIHACHIRŌ, the leader of an 1837 rebellion. He accompanied Doi to Edo (now Tōkyō) when Doi became a shogunal senior councillor (*rōjū*). There Takami associated with official interpreters and scholars of Western Learning such as MITSUKURI GEMPO and WATANABE KAZAN. He was particularly interested in maps and built up a collection of atlases. After Commodore PERRY's visits in 1853 and 1854 Takami urged the shogunate to open the country to trade, invite foreign advisers, and send study missions abroad.

Takamiyama   高見山

(1944–). SUMŌ wrestler. Born in Hawaii. Real name Jesse Kuhaulua; Japanese name Watanabe Daigorō. Takamiyama entered the Takasago stable in 1964 and rose to the highest division of sumō wrestlers (*makuuchi*) in 1968. His victory in the 1972 Nagoya Tournament was the first ever for a non-Japanese. An extremely popular wrestler, Takamiyama set a number of sumō records. In 1980 he applied for and was granted Japanese citizenship, which qualified him for membership in the Japan Sumō Association, the organization that regulates professional sumō. He retired in 1984, having attained the rank of *sekiwake* (champion second-class), to become one of the *toshiyori*, or elders—the respected retired wrestlers who maintain the traditions of sumō. Taking the

toshiyori name Azumazeki he set up his own stable and began training a new generation of wrestlers, including a grand champion (*yokozuna*) from Hawaii, Akebono.

Takamuko no Kuromaro   高向玄理

(?–654). Scholar and adviser on government at the YAMATO COURT. Descended from an immigrant Korean (KIKAJIN) family that had come to Japan in about 400. In 608 Takamuko was sent to study in China (see SUI AND TANG [T'ANG] CHINA, EMBASSIES TO) with a group led by ONO NO IMOKO. He remained there for 32 years. With the TAIKA REFORM of 645, he was named a state scholar (*kuni hakase*) with the priest Min (see SŌMIN), who had been a fellow student in China; they were charged with establishing the central administrative organs of the new Japanese government. In 654 Takamuko was sent as an envoy to the Tang (T'ang) dynasty of China, where he died.

Takamura Kōtarō   高村光太郎

(1883–1956). Sculptor and poet. Born in Tōkyō. Eldest son of the sculptor TAKAMURA KŌUN. Takamura Kōtarō was raised to succeed his father as head of a sculpture studio. He was sent to the Tōkyō Bijutsu Gakkō (now Tōkyō School of Fine Arts and Music) and went abroad in 1906 to study in the United States, England, and France. Kōtarō returned to Japan three years later. Increasingly estranged from his family, he began spending his days with the decadent writers and artists of the Pan Society (PAN NO KAI).

Kōtarō, who in youth had composed HAIKU and TANKA, found his creative energies influenced by such Pan Society poets as KINOSHITA MOKUTARŌ and KITAHARA HAKUSHŪ. Suggestive of this influence are Kōtarō's poems "Mona Lisa" and "Loneliness," composed soon after his return to Japan. The simplicity that emerges in the later poetry can already be noticed in the defiant "Journey," the title poem of *Dōtei* (1914), his first collection of verse. Almost all of his poems of note are in free verse.

Kōtarō claimed that he was rescued from a decadent existence by Naganuma Chieko (d 1938), who became his wife. The love poems Chieko inspired in Kōtarō were composed over the years from 1912 to 1952. These 40-odd poems, compiled in *Chieko shō* (1941; tr *Chieko's Sky*, 1978), are remarkable during a period when marital love was seldom evoked in Japanese poetry. For some years before her death Chieko was schizophrenic, and her alienation from Kōtarō and the world became the subject of a number of his poems. World War II followed Chieko's

Takamura Kōtarō
Strongly influenced by Rodin, this sculptor was also an accomplished free-verse poet whose treatment of marital love is a landmark in the history of modern Japanese poetry.

Takami Jun A recurring theme in this poet and novelist's autobiographical works is the intellectual confusion that followed his "conversion" from Marxism in the 1930s.

Takamine Hideko The actress in the 1961 film *Na mo naku mazushiku utsukushiku* (Nameless, Poor, Beautiful), about a deaf-mute couple who communicate eloquently in sign language.

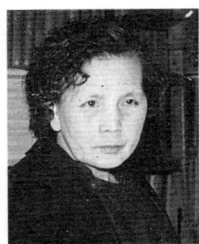

Takamure Itsue
Among the works of this historian and feminist are pioneering studies of the development of Japanese marriage patterns.

Takano Iwasaburō
Appointed director of the Ōhara Institute for Social Research in 1920, this statistician conducted the first domestic budget survey of Japanese working families.

death, and Kōtarō emerged as a writer committed to the war effort, serving as head of the Poet's Division of the Japanese Literature Patriotic Association (Nihon Bungaku Hōkokukai). After Japan's defeat, he led a hermitlike existence in a rural cabin in Iwate Prefecture for seven years. A striking work entitled "Reverence" serves indirectly as an apologia for the poet's wartime conduct.

Although Kōtarō is considered chiefly a poet rather than a sculptor, he thought of himself primarily as a sculptor. His major sculptures include the monumental nudes on the shore of Lake Towada, a bronze hand in the Tōkyō Museum of Modern Art, and small wood carvings of insects and fish.

Takamura Kōun   高村光雲

(1852–1934). Sculptor. Born Nakajima Mitsuzō in Edo (now Tōkyō), apprenticed in 1863 to the traditional-style Buddhist sculptor Takamura Tōun (dates unknown), and later adopted into the Takamura family. On the recommendation of OKAKURA KAKUZŌ, he was appointed professor of Tōkyō Bijutsu Gakkō (now Tōkyō University of Fine Arts and Music) in 1889. His most distinguished pupil was HIRAGUSHI DENCHŪ. Kōun worked in wood, ivory, and bronze in an exceptionally realistic style that reflected Western influence. His statue of KUSUNOKI MASASHIGE, the 14th-century warrior noted for his devotion to the imperial house, stands in front of the Imperial Palace in Tōkyō, and his statue of SAIGŌ TAKAMORI stands in Ueno Park, Tōkyō. *Rōen* (1893, The Aged Monkey), an early sculpture in wood exhibited at the Chicago World's Fair in 1893, won international acclaim. His eldest son, TAKAMURA KŌTARŌ, was a well-known poet and sculptor.

Takamure Itsue   高群逸枝

(1894–1964). Historian and feminist, known for her pioneering research in women's history. Born in Kumamoto Prefecture. In 1919 she married Hashimoto Kenzō (1897–1976), who later helped with her studies of social issues and women's history. In 1926 she published *Ren'ai sōsei* (The Genesis of Love), in which she advocated "a new feminism." This work can be said to be a source of the radical feminist theory exhibited in the women's liberation movement of the early 1970s, the so-called second stage of feminism. In 1930 she joined with several other feminists, including HIRATSUKA RAICHŌ, in forming the Musan Fujin Geijutsu Remmei (Proletarian Women's Art League), a group sympathetic to anarchism. Her direct involvement with activism, however, was brief, and today she is best known for her many historical studies. Her major works include *Bokeisei no kenkyū* (1938), a study of matrilineal practices in ancient Japan, and her monumental history of Japanese women, *Josei no rekishi* (4 vols, 1954–58).

Takanabe   高鍋[町]

Town on the Hyūga Sea in central Miyazaki Prefecture, Kyūshū. A castle town during the Edo period (1600–1868), Takanabe is now a center for commerce, livestock raising, and vegetable cultivation. There are many *kofun* (tomb mounds) in the area. Pop: 22,970.

Takano Chōei   高野長英

(1804–50). Scholar of Rangaku, or Dutch Learning (see WESTERN LEARNING). Born in Mizusawa, Mutsu Province (now the city of Mizusawa in Iwate Prefecture). He studied

medicine at the Narutakijuku, the school operated by Philipp Franz von SIEBOLD, and in 1826 was awarded the degree of "Doktor."

In 1830 Takano began medical practice in Edo (now Tōkyō), while lecturing and working on his book *Seisetsu igen sūyō* (1832, Outline of Principles of Western Medicine). He formed, with WATANABE KAZAN, KOSEKI SAN'EI, and others, the SHŌSHIKAI, an informal study group. After the MORRISON INCIDENT Takano wrote *Bojutsu yume monogatari* (1838, Tale of a Dream), criticizing the government's NATIONAL SECLUSION policies. In 1839 he was arrested in the shogunate's roundup of Rangaku scholars known as the BANSHA NO GOKU. Sentenced to life imprisonment, he escaped in 1844. In 1850 he was captured by shogunal officials and committed suicide. His autobiography, *Tori no naku ne* (The Song of a Bird), is included in his collected works.

Takano Fusatarō   高野房太郎

(1869–1904). Pioneer in the Japanese labor movement. Born in what is now Nagasaki Prefecture. He went to the United States in 1886 and worked as a laborer in the San Francisco area, returning to Japan in 1896. With KATAYAMA SEN and other labor leaders, in 1897 he formed the SHOKKŌ GIYŪKAI (Workers' Fraternal Society), Japan's first significant labor organization. With the government's enactment of the oppressive PUBLIC ORDER AND POLICE LAW OF 1900 (Chian Keisatsu Hō), the embryonic labor movement suffered an immediate setback. Discouraged, Takano left Japan for China, where he died.

Takano Iwasaburō   高野岩三郎

(1871–1949). Statistician. He was the first in Japan to apply social statistics to labor problems. Born in Nagasaki Prefecture. After graduating from Tōkyō University in 1895, he studied statistics in Germany under George von Mayer. After returning to Japan he was appointed professor at the law and economics schools of Tōkyō University, giving the first lectures in Japan on statistics. He later became director of the ŌHARA INSTITUTE FOR SOCIAL RESEARCH and conducted the first family budget survey of working people. He served as chairman of NHK (Japan Broadcasting Corporation) from 1946 to 1949. Labor leader TAKANO FUSATARŌ was his elder brother.

Takano Minoru   高野実

(1901–74). Labor union leader. First secretary-general of SŌHYŌ (General Council of Trade Unions of Japan). Born in Tōkyō. Takano joined the labor movement while a student at Waseda University, becoming a member of the JAPAN COMMUNIST PARTY in 1922. After World War II, he helped reorganize SŌDŌMEI (Japanese Federation of Labor) and was appointed its secretary-general in 1948. When Sōhyō was established in 1950, he became its first secretary-general (1950–55). Takano was known for his support of the so-called three principles of peace (*heiwa sangensoku*): a comprehensive peace treaty, neutrality in the cold war, and opposition to military bases in Japan.

Takano Sujū   高野素十

(1893–1976). HAIKU poet and physician. Real name Takano Yoshimi. Born in Ibaraki Prefecture; graduate of Tōkyō University, where he specialized in medicine. Although a long-time professor of medical jurisprudence, he is best remembered for his haiku poems. He studied with the poet TAKAHAMA KYOSHI and contributed regularly to the liter-

ary magazine HOTOTOGISU. From 1915 to 1925 Sujū was one of the "Four S's," the members of the Hototogisu haiku school that also included MIZUHARA SHŪŌSHI, YAMAGUCHI SEISHI, and AWANO SEIHO. His collections of haiku include *Hatsugarasu* (1947) and *Seppen* (1952). His poems are noted for pure descriptions that are simple, yet buoyant.

Takaoka   高岡[市]

City in northwestern Toyama Prefecture, central Honshū. In the Nara period (710–794) Takaoka developed as the seat of a provincial capital (*kokufu*) and provincial temple (*kokubunji*). It was briefly a castle town after a castle was built in 1609 by Maeda Toshinaga (1562–1614). It is now a major commercial and industrial center, with traditional products such as copper ware and lacquer ware and emerging pharmaceutical, pulp, and metal-goods industries. Pop: 175,466.

Takaosan   高尾山

Mountain in the city of Hachiōji, southwest of Tōkyō Prefecture, central Honshū, on the southeastern edge of the Kantō Mountains. It has been an object of worship since ancient times. Because of its proximity to Tōkyō, it is a crowded recreational spot throughout the year. A cable car runs to the summit, where there is the Buddhist temple Yakuōin and an observation platform. It is part of Meiji no Mori Takao Quasi-National Park. Height: 600 m (1,968 ft).

Takarabe Takeshi   財部彪

(1867–1949). Navy minister (1923–27 and 1929–30) and delegate to the London naval arms limitation conference of 1930; a central figure in the controversy over the London naval treaty. Born in Hyūga Province (now Miyazaki Prefecture). After graduating from the Naval Academy and the Naval Staff College, he served in the Sino-Japanese War (1894–95). Takarabe then held posts that prepared him for service in the naval section of Imperial Headquarters during the Russo-Japanese War of 1904–05. In 1909 Takarabe was promoted to rear admiral and became vice-minister of the navy; he was promoted to full admiral in 1919. In 1923 he became navy minister and was beset with problems rooted in the conflict between Japan's commitment to arms limitations and the navy's desire to secure more ships, aircraft, and submarines.

In 1929 Takarabe was appointed as a delegate to the first of the LONDON NAVAL CONFERENCES. The conference ended with a compromise on arms limitations that angered the chief of the Naval General Staff, Admiral KATŌ HIROHARU, who protested that the cabinet had not taken his views into proper consideration (see TŌSUIKEN). Determined to overcome opposition, Takarabe replaced his vice-minister and the vice-chief of the Naval General Staff. Prime Minister HAMAGUCHI OSACHI was able to help neutralize dissent among navy members of the Supreme War Council, and the treaty was approved. Exhausted by the struggle, Takarabe resigned the day after ratification of the treaty.

Takarai Kikaku   宝井其角

(1661–1707). Also known as Enomoto Kikaku. HAIKU poet of the early Edo period (1600–1868). Born in Edo (now Tōkyō). Considered a leading disciple of BASHŌ, Kikaku founded the Edoza school of haiku, which diverged from Bashō's style in its urbane spirit and its emphasis on novelty, wit, and rhetorical flourish. Kikaku edited *Mina-*

shiguri (1683), the first collection of haiku by Bashō and his disciples. The most complete collection of his own haiku is *Gogenshū* (1747).

takara kuji → lotteries, public

Takara Shuzō Co, Ltd   宝酒造[株]

(Takara Shuzō). A distiller of such alcoholic beverages as SAKE, it is the largest domestic producer of *mirin* (a sweetened cooking wine) and *shōchū* (a distilled drink made from rice or sweet potatoes). Incorporated in 1825. Since the 1970s it has been developing new fermented products, including pharmaceuticals. Sales for the fiscal year ending March 1991 totaled ¥140.5 billion (US $1.0 billion), and the company was capitalized at ¥10.6 billion (US $77.3 million). Headquarters are in Kyōto.

Takarazuka   宝塚[市]

City in southeastern Hyōgo Prefecture, western Honshū. Known for its hot springs since the 8th century, it is now a residential satellite of ŌSAKA and KŌBE. Tree and plant nurseries, as well as several zoological and botanical gardens, are located here. The city is known for its all-female revue troupe (the TAKARAZUKA KAGEKIDAN). Pop: 201,862.

Takarazuka Kagekidan   宝塚歌劇団

(literally, "Takarazuka Opera Company"). All-female troupes specializing in musical extravaganzas; organized by the entertainment tycoon and politician KOBAYASHI ICHIZŌ in 1913 as the principal attraction for his Takarazuka resort area near Ōsaka. Within a few years several Takarazuka troupes were touring Japan's major cities and theaters were constructed for them in Takarazuka (1924) and Tōkyō (1934); even today these troupes remain a unique fixture of Japanese popular culture.

Takarazuka is a manifestation of the Japanese fascination with the androgynous performer. The major stars are "beauties in men's clothing" who perform the male roles. A Takarazuka program is usually a potpourri arranged to show off the versatility of its performers in a pastiche of musical styles ranging from European operatic aria, chanson, and the latest international pop tunes through Japanese classic NAGAUTA and folk songs. Spectacular production numbers and star turns are the rule in these gaudy performances. Landmark Takarazuka shows during the last half century have included *Mon Pari* (1927, Mon Paris), *Kaze to tomo ni sarinu* (1952, Gone with the Wind), and *Berusaiyu no bara* (1974, The Rose of Versailles).

Takasago   高砂[市]

City in southern Hyōgo Prefecture, western Honshū, on the INLAND SEA. The city developed as a port and rice-shipping center during the Edo period (1600–1868). It has textile, machinery, concrete, firebrick, pharmaceutical, and paper factories. Pop: 93,273.

Takasago   高砂

NŌ play by ZEAMI. It is classified as a *shobamme-mono* ("part-one play"). A Shintō priest (the *waki* or subordinate character) travels to Takasago, a pine-forested beach in Harima Province where he meets an aged couple (the *maejite* or main character at the beginning of a play, and the *tsure* or "companion" character) sweeping the forest floor. They tell him that two aged pine trees, one there at Takasago and the other at Sumiyoshi (in Settsu Province), are husband and

wife; although they are separated by a great distance, their hearts are one. The couple then reveal that they are the spirits of the two trees and disappear. In the second half of the play, the god Sumiyoshi no Kami (the *nochijite* or main character at the end of a play) performs a *kamimai* ("god dance").

Takasago Thermal Engineering Co, Ltd   高砂熱学工業[株]

(Takasago Netsugaku Kōgyō). Firm specializing in the design and installation of air-conditioning equipment. Incorporated in 1923. Since the early 1980s it has expanded its operations in the field of industrial air-conditioning to include the installation of "clean rooms" for semiconductor production. Sales for the fiscal year ending March 1991 totaled ¥212.5 billion (US $1.5 billion), and the company was capitalized at ¥12.0 billion (US $87.5 million). Headquarters are in Tōkyō.

Takasaki   高崎[市]

City in southern Gumma Prefecture, central Honshū. During the Edo period (1600–1868) it flourished as a castle town and post-station town. Traditional products include silk, dyes, and flour. Machinery, chemicals, and metal goods are also manufactured. A huge statue of the bodhisattva KANNON and an annual DARUMA fair in January, at which *daruma* dolls are sold, attract visitors. Pop: 236,461.

Takasakiyama   高崎山

Volcano near Beppu Bay, Ōita Prefecture, Kyūshū. It is part of Inland Sea National Park and a habitat for more than 2,000 wild monkeys. Height: 628 m (2,060 ft).

Takasegawa   高瀬川

Canal in the eastern part of the city of Kyōto, central Honshū. It flows north to south from the road known as Nijō-Dōri parallel to the river KAMOGAWA before joining the BIWAKO CANAL at Fushimi. Built in the Edo period (1600–1868) by SUMINOKURA RYŌI, it was a vital link in a system of waterways for transporting passengers and goods between Kyōto and Ōsaka. Length: 10 km (6 mi).

Takashima Coal Mine   高島炭鉱

(Takashima Tankō). One of the largest and most important mines in Japan; discovered in the early 18th century on the small island of

Takashima, south of Nagasaki. First controlled by Saga domain and then by the government, it was later sold to GOTŌ SHŌJIRŌ (see KAN'EI JIGYŌ HARAISAGE), who in turn sold it to MITSUBISHI in 1881. The mine was closed in November 1986.

Takashima Shūhan   高島秋帆

(1798–1866). Gunnery expert and pioneering authority in Western military science. Born in Nagasaki, Takashima became interested in Western arms through contact with Dutch traders. In 1814 he was placed in charge of the fortification at DEJIMA. He imported Western firearms and tried to reproduce them; the TOKUGAWA SHOGUNATE (1603–1867) ordered him to give an artillery demonstration in 1841 but disapproved of Takashima's dissemination of his specialized knowledge. In 1842 he was jailed, and from 1846 to 1853 he was banished and placed under protective custody. But in 1855 he was appointed head instructor of the newly established shogunal military training center and thereafter was invited by many *daimyō* to instruct their men in his teachings, known as Takashimaryū.

Takashimaya Co, Ltd   [株]高島屋

(Takashimaya). Major department store company. Incorporated in 1919. The company has 10 department stores in Ōsaka, Tōkyō, Kyōto, Sakai, Wakayama, and other cities. It leads the Takashimaya group, with six other companies and an additional 8 stores in Japan. In 1991 the group had 4 overseas stores in London, Paris, Sydney, and New York and 14 overseas offices. Sales in the fiscal year ending February 1991 totaled ¥767.7 billion (US $5.6 billion); sales for the entire Takashimaya group amounted to ¥1.3 trillion (US $9.5 billion). In the same year the company was capitalized at ¥16.9 billion (US $123.2 million). Headquarters are in Ōsaka.

Takashima Zen'ya   高島善哉

(1904–90). Economist. Born in Gifu Prefecture. He graduated from Hitotsubashi University in 1927 and became a professor there in 1941, retiring in 1966. Beginning before World War II, he devoted himself to Marxism, analyzing Adam Smith and Friedrich List from a Marxist viewpoint. After World

Takarazuka Kagekidan A scene from the finale of the 1986 *Revue Symphonique* at the Takarazuka Daigekijō, Takarazuka. To enter the all-female company, known for its exacting standards, performers must study for two years at the Takarazuka Music School.

Takayama A street lined with traditional buildings in this highland city. Several buildings have been restored and converted into museums and galleries.

Takasugi Shinsaku A retainer of the Chōshū domain who played a central role in the movement to overthrow the Tokugawa shogunate.

Takayama Chogyū This literary critic and novelist profoundly influenced literature and culture at the turn of the century with his brand of romantic individualism.

War II, he promoted a social science–based humanist movement. His followers have been grouped under the name of the Takashima school.

Takasugi Shinsaku　　　　高杉晋作

(1839–67). A retainer of the Chōshū domain (now Yamaguchi Prefecture) and a central figure in the movement to overthrow the Tokugawa shogunate (1603–1867). Born in the castle town of Hagi. From 1857 he studied at the Shōka Sonjuku, the school run by the proimperialist YOSHIDA SHŌIN. In 1862 he traveled to Shanghai, where he witnessed the Taiping (T'ai-p'ing) Rebellion and the foreign presence in China. He became convinced that Japan must strengthen itself to avoid a similar semicolonial status and came to see the overthrow of the shogunate as a necessary means to this end.

On 25 June 1863 (Bunkyū 3.5.10) Chōshū fired on foreign ships in the Shimonoseki Strait. Takasugi organized a militia called the KIHEITAI to defend the domain, but in 1864 Western forces demolished Chōshū's coastal fortifications (see SHIMONOSEKI BOMBARDMENT). Weakened by the attack, Chōshū was defeated by a punitive expedition sent by the shogunate (see CHŌSHŪ EXPEDITIONS) in retaliation for prior attempts by Chōshū to capture Kyōto. From late 1864 to the beginning of 1865 Takasugi led Kiheitai units in a coup against the conservative clique in Chōshū and joined KIDO TAKAYOSHI in taking over leadership of the domain. In 1866 he led domainal forces in repelling a second shogunal punitive expedition. Chōshū's victory discredited the shogunate and opened the way for united action against it. Takasugi died of tuberculosis on the eve of the Meiji Restoration.

Takataya Kahei　　　　高田屋嘉兵衛

(1769–1827). A wealthy trader of the early 19th century who opened new trade routes to EZO (now Hokkaidō and the Kuril Islands). Born in Awaji Province (now part of Hyōgo Prefecture). In 1795 Kahei founded his own shipping business, specializing in transporting commodities such as clothing, tobacco, and salt to northeastern Japan. In 1799 the shogunate decided to survey Etorofu, the largest of the Kuril Islands. Hoping to win sole trading rights for Ezo products, Kahei volunteered as an aide to KONDŌ JŪZŌ, a shogunate official who explored Ezo. Kahei built up a thriving business between Ezo and the home islands. In 1812 Kahei and four members of his crew were seized by a Russian ship in retaliation for Japan's detention of the Russian naval officer Vasilii Mikhailovich GOLOVNIN a year earlier. Kahei was taken to Kamchatka but persuaded his captors to free him and returned to Japan in 1813. He

then worked successfully to have Golovnin released.

Takata Yasuma　　　　高田保馬

(1883–1972). Sociologist and economist who contributed significantly to the development of sociological theory in Japan before World War II. Born in Saga Prefecture. After graduating from Kyōto University, he taught at Kyūshū and Ōsaka universities. He strove to establish sociology as a separate and independent scientific discipline in Japan, criticizing the then dominant school of sociology, which, heavily influenced by Herbert Spencer and Auguste Comte, sought to incorporate the principles of political science and other social sciences. Influenced by the theories of Georg Simmel and Robert MacIver, he adopted a psychological approach. Takata was also critical of Marxist theory; he felt that the cause of all social change lay in population growth and called his approach the third or sociological view of history in contrast to materialistic and idealistic interpretations. Representative writings are *Shakaigaku genri* (1919, Principles of Sociology) and *Shakaigaku gairon* (1922, Outline of Sociology).

Takatō　　　　高遠[町]

Town in south-central Nagano Prefecture, central Honshū. During the Edo period (1600–1868) it developed as a castle town. The cherry blossoms at the site of Takatō Castle attract visitors. Pop: 8,074.

Takatori ware　　　　高取焼

(*takatori-yaki*). Ceramics made at kiln sites in or near present-day Nōgata and Fukuoka, Fukuoka Prefecture, Kyūshū. Produced from 1601 to almost the end of the Edo period (1600–1868). The kilns were started by Korean potters and operated under the auspices of the Kuroda *daimyō* family. The kilns produced thickly and freely potted everyday and tea-ceremony wares with emphasis on the former, employing sea-slug glazes or thick, opaque white-straw or wood-ash glazes. In the mid-17th century, under the guidance of the famous tea master KOBORI ENSHŪ, they began producing sophisticated, elegant, thin-walled pieces with what was to become a characteristic lustrous, dark toffee-brown glaze. Beginning in the 18th century, two kilns were operated near Fukuoka Castle, one making tea wares for *daimyō* use and the other making everyday wares for general consumption. In 1860 the Sarayama kilns were reopened for the mass production of high-quality porcelains, but production has not been continuous. Among the modern ceramists who specialize in Takatori ware, the best known is the 11th-generation woman potter Takatori Seizan (1907–83).

Takatsuki　　　　高槻[市]

City in northeastern Ōsaka Prefecture, central Honshū. During the Sengoku period (1467–1568) Takatsuki developed as a post-station town on the highway Saigoku Kaidō. It then became a castle town of the 16th-century Christian *daimyō* TAKAYAMA UKON. It is now a residential and industrial suburb of Ōsaka. Principal products are electric appliances, machinery, chemicals, and foodstuffs. Tumuli (KOFUN) and other prehistoric remains are located here. Pop: 359,867.

Takayama　　　　高山[市]

City in northern Gifu Prefecture, central Honshū. Takayama developed from 1586 as

a castle town of the Kanamori family. It came under the direct jurisdiction of the Tokugawa shogunate in 1692. Its chief industry is lumbering. *Shunkei-nuri*, a type of LACQUER WARE, has long been famous. Its beautiful setting and old houses, several of which have been converted into folk-art museums, draw visitors. The Takayama Festival in April and the Hachiman Festival in October are added attractions. Pop: 65,243.

Takayama Basin　　　　高山盆地

(Takayama Bonchi). In northern Gifu Prefecture, central Honshū. Situated along the river Miyagawa and the upper reaches of the Jinzūgawa. Because of its high altitude, the basin has severe winters. Rice is cultivated along the Miyagawa. The major city is Takayama. Area: approximately 30 sq km (12 sq mi).

Takayama Chogyū　　　　高山樗牛

(1871–1902). Literary critic and novelist. Real name Saitō Rinjirō. Born in Yamagata Prefecture; graduate of Tōkyō University. After gaining recognition for his historical romance *Takiguchi Nyūdō* (1894), he wrote critical essays for the magazines TEIKOKU BUNGAKU and TAIYŌ. He advocated Japanese nationalism (Nihon *shugi*) but later embraced the philosophy of Nietzsche and the 13th-century Buddhist leader NICHIREN. His brand of romantic individualism greatly influenced literature and culture during the 1890s and early 1900s.

Takayama Hikokurō　　　　高山彦九郎

(1747–93). Emperor worshiper famed for the extremity of his infatuation with the nobility and the imperial line. Born in Kōzuke Province (now Gumma Prefecture); son of a rural *samurai* (GŌSHI). Takayama made several trips to Kyōto to visit the graves and residences of court nobles and royal personages and to advocate the legitimacy of the emperor's authority. The Tokugawa shogunate (1603–1867) exerted pressure in an attempt to stop his activities, even destroying the home of a noble who had housed him. Takayama then left for Kyūshū, hoping to inspire more imperial loyalists, but, still hounded by shogunate authorities, finally committed suicide. Takayama's bizarre acts of homage earned him inclusion among the Three Eccentrics (Sankijin) of the Kansei era (1789–1801), with GAMŌ KUMPEI and HAYASHI SHIHEI.

Takayama Sōzei　　　　高山宗砌

(?–1455). Poet of RENGA (linked verse), critic, and Buddhist priest. Studied with SHŌTETSU and ASAYAMA BONTŌ. In 1448 he was appointed grand master (*sōshō*) of the Renga Center at the Kitano Shrine in Kyōto. Ranked by SŌGI as one of the "Seven Sages of Renga" (Renga Shichiken), he collaborated with ICHIJŌ KANEYOSHI on *Renga shinshiki kon'an*, an elaboration of the rules of *renga*. He also wrote *Shoshin kyūei shū* (Principles of Composition for Aspiring Poets), a collection of his teacher Bontō's pronouncements; *Hana no magaki* (1452, Blossoms by the Sacred Fence), an exposition of various kinds of *renga* linkings and styles; and *Kokon rendan shū* (late 1440s, Discussions of Renga, Ancient and Modern).

Takayama Tatsuo　　　　高山辰雄

(1912–). Japanese-style (NIHONGA) painter. Though he was briefly influenced by Gauguin, Takayama is known mainly for color compositions dispensing with lines, in which he depicts nature as part of an imaginary landscape. Born in Ōita Prefecture, he graduated from the Tōkyō Bijutsu Gakkō (now Tōkyō University of Fine Arts and Music). He was a student of MATSUOKA EIKYŪ. In 1946 his painting *Yokushitsu* (Bath) won a special Nitten (Japan Art Exhibition) prize. In 1972 he became a member of the Japan Art Academy, and in 1975–77 he was chairman of the board of directors of Nitten. He received the Order of Culture in 1982.

Takayama Ukon 高山右近

(1552?–1615). The best known of the CHRISTIAN DAIMYŌ. Ukon was baptized in 1564. He first made a name for himself by killing his lord Wada (or Wata) Korenaga in 1573. In 1578 Ukon betrayed his new lord, Araki Murashige (d 1586), in favor of ODA NOBUNAGA to prevent a threatened persecution of Christianity; thereafter he ordered the Christianization of the people of Takatsuki (southwest of Kyōto). Ukon played a key role in the Battle of YAMAZAKI (1582), helping TOYOTOMI HIDEYOSHI to win the succession to Nobunaga's hegemony. In 1585 Ukon was transferred from Takatsuki to Akashi in Harima Province (now part of Hyōgo Prefecture); here he again endeavored to convert the entire populace. When Hideyoshi issued his ANTI-CHRISTIAN EDICTS in 1587, he dispossessed Ukon. Eventually Ukon attained high status in the Maeda house but was dispossessed again when the Tokugawa shogunate undertook a general persecution of Christianity in 1614. Banished from Japan, Ukon died in Manila on 5 February 1615.

Takayanagi Kenjirō 高柳健次郎

(1899–1990). Electrical engineer. The father of Japanese television. He engineered the first television transmission in Japan in 1926 and in 1933 developed an iconoscope (the main component in a television camera), only months behind the work of Vladimir K. Zworykin (1889–1982) of the United States. Born in Shizuoka Prefecture, Takayanagi studied at a technical school in Tōkyō. He became professor at Hamamatsu Kōtō Kōgyō Gakkō (Hamamatsu Higher Technical College) in 1930, and in 1937 he joined the Japan Broadcasting Corporation (NHK), moving to VICTOR CO OF JAPAN, LTD, in 1947. He was awarded the Order of Culture in 1981.

Takayanagi Kenzō 高柳賢三

(1887–1967). Scholar of Anglo-American law. Born in Saitama Prefecture, he graduated from Tōkyō University in 1912 and, apart from a period of study in the United States and Europe (1915–20), taught in its law faculty until his retirement in 1948. Takayanagi was particularly interested in Anglo-American legal history and comparative law. In 1946, as a member of what was then the House of Peers, he was appointed to a committee to discuss the draft of the new postwar CONSTITUTION OF JAPAN. When the question of revising the 1947 constitution arose in the 1950s, Takayanagi was named chairman of the COMMISSION ON THE CONSTITUTION (1957–65) and, because of his impartiality, became one of the most respected defenders of the new constitution.

take → bamboo

Takebe Ayatari 建部綾足

(1719–74). HAIKU and WAKA poet, author of YOMIHON, and artist. Real name Kitamura Hisamura. Born in Edo (now Tōkyō), he was the maternal grandson of DAIDŌJI YŪZAN, the famous theoretician of BUSHIDŌ (the *samurai* code). At the age of 20 he ran away when his love affair with his elder brother's wife was discovered. He went first to Kyōto and then to Edo, where he studied haiku and became established as a poet and master, writing under the name Ryōtai. He advocated that haiku should be returned to older forms and attempted to revive a verse form known as *katauta*. In his 30s he went to Nagasaki, where he studied the literati style of painting known as NANGA and painted under the name Kan'yōsai. In his later years Takebe wrote novels that are chiefly noteworthy as early examples of *yomihon*. His best-known novels are *Nishiyama monogatari* (1768) and *Honchō suikoden* (1773).

Takebe Katahiro 建部賢弘

(1664–1739). Mathematician. Coauthor of *Taisei sankyō* (1710), a 20-volume compilation of achievements in Japanese mathematics. Born in Edo (now Tōkyō), he entered the school of SEKI TAKAKAZU at age 13. His published works on algebra, actually commentaries and notes on algebraic techniques developed by Seki, helped spread knowledge of higher mathematics in Japan.

Takechi no Kurohito 高市黒人

(fl ca 690–710). Court official and poet. Very little is known about him apart from notes accompanying his poems. His 18 known *tanka* poems are in the MAN'YŌSHŪ (ca 759). It is believed that like KAKINOMOTO NO HITOMARO and YAMABE NO AKAHITO he was an official of low rank who served as one of the "poets laureate" who accompanied sovereigns on excursions, composing auspicious and laudatory poetry on demand. That all of Kurohito's surviving poems are on travel is not surprising, but that he is so celebrated for such a relatively meager number of surviving poems is due to his skill at "objective description" of nature—a mode of which he is considered one of the pioneers of his age and which is highly prized by modern critics and enthusiasts.

Takechi Zuizan 武市瑞山

(1829–65). Master swordsman and proimperial activist from the Tosa domain (now Kōchi Prefecture). Also known as Takechi Hampeita. The son of a rural *samurai* (GŌSHI), Zuizan early established himself as a master of swordsmanship. In 1861 he went to Edo (now Tōkyō), where he met SONNŌ JŌI (Revere the Emperor, Expel the Barbarians) activists from the domains of Satsuma (now Kagoshima Prefecture) and Chōshū (now Yamaguchi Prefecture). Influenced by their ideas, he returned to Tosa and organized a loyalist group called the Tosa Kinnōtō (Tosa Loyalist Party), whose members included SAKAMOTO RYŌMA and NAKAOKA SHINTARŌ. In 1862 his group murdered YOSHIDA TŌYŌ, an influential domainal adviser who supported the MOVEMENT FOR UNION OF COURT AND SHOGUNATE. The group was temporarily able to control domainal politics, but, after the expulsion of *sonnō jōi* extremists from Kyōto in the summer of 1863, Tosa once again reverted to a position favoring reconciliation between the court and the shogunate. Zuizan and other loyalist leaders were arrested and ordered to commit suicide in the summer of 1865.

Takeda Chemical Industries, Ltd 武田薬品工業[株]

(Takeda Yakuhin Kōgyō). Manufacturer of pharmaceuticals and other chemical products. Established in 1925. Its products include fine chemicals and various chemical products such as food additives, industrial and agricultural chemicals, and animal health products. Active in overseas markets, the company exports many varieties of fine chemicals, such as vitamins and raw materials for local processing. Processing plants have been established in the United States and Southeast Asia, and development and sales centers have been set up in the United States, Germany, France, Italy, and several locations in Southeast Asia. Recently, research and development centers have been established in the United States and Germany. Sales for the fiscal year ending March 1991 totaled ¥550.9 billion (US $4.0 billion). In the same year the company was capitalized at ¥47.9 billion (US $349.1 million). Headquarters are in Ōsaka.

Takeda family 武田氏

(Takedashi). Prominent military house of the Kamakura (1185–1333), the Muromachi (1333–1568), and the Azuchi-Momoyama (1568–1600) periods. It took its name from Takeda in Kai Province (now the city of Nirasaki, Yamanashi Prefecture). Takeda Nobuyoshi (d 1186) fought for MINAMOTO NO YORITOMO in the TAIRA-MINAMOTO WAR (1180–85); his son Nobumitsu (d 1248) served the Kamakura shogunate during the JŌKYŪ DISTURBANCE of 1221, eventually being appointed SHUGO (military governor) of Aki Province (now part of Hiroshima Prefecture). In the Eikyō Disturbance (1438) the Takeda helped the shogunate destroy the rebellious governor-general Ashikaga Mochiuji (1398–1439). The family's position in Kai was consolidated by Takeda Nobutora (1494–1574), who established the Takeda as a SENGOKU DAIMYŌ house. TAKEDA SHINGEN displaced his father Nobutora in 1541, but the Takeda house of Kai fell in 1582 when ODA NOBUNAGA destroyed Shingen's son TAKEDA KATSUYORI.

Although the Takeda of Kai are the best known, other branches of the family are as noteworthy. At least 10 Takeda were *shugo* of Aki Province under the MUROMACHI SHOGUNATE from 1336 to 1520. An offshoot of this lineage were military governors of Wakasa Province (now part of Fukui Prefecture) from 1440. The Takeda of Wakasa were known for their cultural pursuits; heads of this house compiled a set of rules of chivalrous bearing, especially of mounted archery (YABUSAME), developing a "Takeda school" of military etiquette (*kyūba kojitsu*). By the late 16th century, Wakasa also fell under Nobunaga's sway; in 1582, when Nobunaga was killed in the HONNŌJI INCIDENT, Takeda Motoaki (1552–82) adhered to the assassin, AKECHI MITSUHIDE, but was captured and committed suicide, as had his relative Takeda Katsuyori of Kai. Thus the two major branches of the Takeda family were destroyed within four months and one week of each other.

Takeda Izumo 竹田出雲

The name of a succession of managers of the Takemotoza, a puppet theater in Ōsaka established in 1684 by TAKEMOTO GIDAYŪ I. According to tradition, Takeda Izumo I (also

Takayanagi Kenjirō
This electrical engineer achieved the first television transmission in Japan in 1926.

Takeda Shingen
A 16th-century portrait of this prominent *daimyō* of the Sengoku and Azuchi-Momoyama periods in his later years.

Takeda Taijun A writer influenced by both his Buddhist upbringing and his love of Chinese literature.

Takehara Han Shown here in 1983 at the National Theater in Tōkyō, Takehara performs *Matsugasane*, an example of *jiuta-mai*, the style of dance for which she is renowned.

known as Geki, Koizumo I, and Senzenken; d 1747) assumed control of the Takemotoza in 1705 and founded the well-known line. He was a business manager as well as a writer and director of JŌRURI puppet plays and staged *Kokusen'ya kassen* (1715; tr *The Battles of Coxinga*, 1951), a masterpiece by CHIKAMATSU MONZAEMON. Like his father, Takeda Izumo II (also known as Oyakata Izumo; 1691–1756) was a gifted dramatist and director. He is best known for his collaborative efforts with NAMIKI SŌSUKE, Miyoshi Shōraku (1696?–1772?), and others. His collaborations include YOSHITSUNE SEMBONZAKURA (1747, The Thousand Cherry Blossoms of Yoshitsune) and KANADEHON CHŪSHINGURA (1748; tr *Chūshingura: The Treasury of Loyal Retainers*, 1971). Eventually Takeda's son Izumo III relinquished title to the theater, thus ending the Takeda Izumo succession.

Takeda Katsuyori　　　　武田勝頼

(1546–82). *Daimyō* of the Azuchi-Momoyama period (1568–1600); also known as Takeda Shirō. At the death of his father, TAKEDA SHINGEN, in 1573, Takeda rule extended over a vast but unconsolidated domain that Katsuyori, neither an effective nor a popular administrator, could not preserve against ODA NOBUNAGA and TOKUGAWA IEYASU. When he invaded Ieyasu's home province of Mikawa (now part of Aichi Prefecture), he was routed by Nobunaga and Ieyasu in the Battle of NAGASHINO. His ally Hōjō Ujimasa (1538–90), daimyō of Odawara, transferred his support to Nobunaga and Ieyasu. Early in 1582 some of Katsuyori's most important vassals, such as Anayama Nobukimi (d 1582), went over to Nobunaga, who launched a massive invasion of the Takeda territories. Katsuyori fled but was hunted down and committed suicide.

Takeda Kōunsai　　　　武田耕雲斎

(1803–65). *Samurai* activist of the Mito domain (now part of Ibaraki Prefecture) and leader of the 1864 antiforeign MITO CIVIL WAR. As a high-ranking official, Takeda supported TOKUGAWA NARIAKI's domainal reforms and shared his SONNŌ JŌI (Revere the Emperor, Expel the Barbarians) ideology. In response to the growing sentiment against the Tokugawa shogunate (1603–1867) for having opened the country, hundreds of antiforeign activists gathered at Mt. Tsukuba in 1864 to press for expulsion of foreigners from Japan. Takeda attempted to pacify the activists but in the end decided to lead them in a march to Kyōto to present their demands to the shōgun, who was then in attendance at the imperial court. The shogunate ordered the domains en route to suppress the revolt, and the insurgents were defeated after three months of fighting. Takeda es-

caped but was captured and executed soon after.

Takeda Rintarō　　　　武田麟太郎

(1904–46). Novelist. Born in Ōsaka Prefecture; studied at Tōkyō University. Influenced by the SHINKANKAKU SCHOOL of writers, he also participated in the labor movement. As a writer of the PROLETARIAN LITERATURE MOVEMENT he published an antiwar short story, "Bōryoku" (1929), but he later adopted a more conventional style, borrowing 17th-century novelist Ihara SAIKAKU's techniques to depict urban society in such novels as *Nihon sammon opera* (1932) and *Ginza hatchō* (1934). His works are commonly referred to as *shiseimono* (urban life stories), although behind the description of urban life there is sharp criticism of social injustice. Other works include the short story "Ichi no tori" (1935) and the unfinished novel *Ihara Saikaku* (1936–37).

Takeda Shingen　　　　武田信玄

(1521–73). *Daimyō* of the Sengoku (1467–1568) and Azuchi-Momoyama (1568–1600) periods. He was named Harunobu at his coming of age in 1536; Shingen is a Buddhist name that he used from about 1559. Shingen succeeded to the position of *shugo* (military governor) in Kai Province (now Yamanashi Prefecture) in 1541 by expelling his father, Nobutora (1494–1574), and usurping the family headship. In 1542 Shingen invaded Shinano Province (now Nagano Prefecture). In 1559 the shōgun Ashikaga Yoshiteru (1536–65) appointed him *shugo* of Shinano, in effect legalizing the conquest.

Shingen and UESUGI KENSHIN, daimyō of Echigo Province (now part of Niigata Prefecture), were involved in a famous rivalry after 1553. Particularly celebrated is the series of battles they fought at KAWANAKAJIMA. From 1554 onward, Shingen fought steadily to gain power in a series of treacherous, shifting alliances with daimyō such as IMAGAWA YOSHIMOTO, ODA NOBUNAGA, TOKUGAWA IEYASU, and the HŌJŌ FAMILY. In 1572 Shingen mounted an offensive toward the west. Shingen's early successes, particularly his victory over the combined forces of Ieyasu and Nobunaga at Mikatagahara on 6 January 1573, enticed the shōgun ASHIKAGA YOSHIAKI into an open break with Nobunaga, a move that led to the downfall of the MUROMACHI SHOGUNATE. A mortal disease forced Shingen to break off the campaign, and he died on 13 May. Nine years after Shingen's death, Nobunaga eliminated his heirs and partitioned his domains.

Takeda Taijun　　　　武田泰淳

(1912–76). Writer. Born in Tōkyō; son of a JŌDO SECT Buddhist priest. He entered Tōkyō University to study Chinese literature but withdrew. In 1932 he was ordained a Buddhist priest. With other sinologists he founded the magazine *Chūgoku bungaku geppō* (later renamed *Chūgoku bungaku*). Takeda was drafted into the army and served in China from 1937 to 1939. In 1943 he published *Shiba Sen*, a critical biography of the Chinese historiographer Sima Qian (Ssu-ma Ch'ien).

Takeda was a prolific writer whose narrative style was much influenced by Chinese literature. He wrote 9 full-length novels, 9 novellas, 126 short stories, and 3 plays, as well as 33 books of essays. *Shiba Sen*, his most noted work, was reissued as *Shiba Sen: Shiki no sekai* in 1952. Some of his other

works are *Mamushi no sue* (1947; tr *This Outcast Generation*, 1967), set in Shanghai at the time of Japan's defeat; *Igyō no mono* (1950; tr *The Misshapen Ones*, 1957); *Mori to mizuumi no matsuri* (1955–58, The Festival of Woods and Lakes); and *Fuji* (1969–71, Mt. Fuji Sanatorium).

Takefu　　　　武生[市]

City in central Fukui Prefecture, central Honshū. It has been known for its cutlery since the Kamakura period (1185–1333). Silk and linen textiles, handmade Japanese paper (*washi*), furniture, chemical products, and electrical machinery are also produced. Pop: 70,187.

Takefuji Corporation　　　　[株]武富士

(Takefuji). Consumer finance company. Incorporated in 1968. It is known for quick and simple procedures for obtaining secured and unsecured loans. The company's funding sources include foreign financial institutions. Loans outstanding in November 1990 exceeded ¥494.2 billion (US $3.8 billion), and revenue was ¥132.3 billion (US $1.0 billion). Capitalization stood at ¥10.5 billion (US $81.3 million) in the same year. Headquarters are in Tōkyō.

Takegoshi Yosaburō　　　　竹越与三郎

(1865–1950). Historian and politician. Also known as Takekoshi Yosaburō. Born in what is now Saitama Prefecture, Takegoshi attended Keiō Gijuku (now Keiō University). As a writer for the liberal *Jiji shimpō* and several other newspapers, he came to the attention of the oligarch SAIONJI KIMMOCHI, who chose Takegoshi as editor in chief of his magazine, *Sekai no Nihon* (Japan in the World). On Saionji's recommendation Takegoshi then worked for the Ministry of Education. He was elected to the Diet in 1902 as a member of the political party RIKKEN SEIYŪKAI and reelected four times. Takegoshi was appointed to the House of Peers in 1923 and to the Privy Council in 1940. He established his reputation as a historian with *Shin nihonshi* (1891–92, A New History of Japan), but his principal work is *Nihon keizai shi* (1920, Economic History of Japan).

Takehara　　　　竹原[市]

City in southern Hiroshima Prefecture, western Honshū, on the Inland Sea. A private estate (SHŌEN) of the Shimo-Gamo Shrine in Kyōto during the Heian period (794–1185), Takehara flourished as a salt-making town during the Edo period (1600–1868). Its principal industries are metallurgy, food processing, *sake*, and ceramics. Pop: 34,771.

Takehara Han　　　　武原はん

(1903–). Performer of the Japanese-style dance and a specialist in the style known as *jiuta-mai*. Real name Takehara Yukiko. Born in Tokushima Prefecture. Takehara began studying the *jiuta-mai* in Ōsaka in 1914 under Yamamura Chiyo and made her debut in the piece called *Bōshibari* in 1918. In 1930 she moved to Tōkyō and mastered the KABUKI dance, studying under FUJIMA KANJŪRŌ VI and Nishikawa Koisaburō (1909–83). With a graceful figure and a remarkable talent, she is known for the refined style of her dancing. She is particularly celebrated for her dancing in such pieces as *Yuki* and *Aoi no Ue*. She became a member of the Japan Art Academy in 1985. She published *Nochi no yuki*, a book of essays, in 1978.

Takehashi Insurrection 竹橋騒動

(Takehashi Sōdō). Uprising in 1878 by soldiers of the elite Konoe Artillery, First Battalion, stationed near the Takehashi bridge in Tōkyō. Angered by a reduction of wages and meager rewards following the SATSUMA REBELLION (1877), over 260 soldiers led by Mizoe Unosuke and Nagashima Takeshirō rose up on the night of 23 August 1878. Killing the battalion commander and another officer, they occupied the barracks and fired shots into the residence of the finance minister. They planned to proceed to the nearby Imperial Palace, but were thwarted by soldiers sent out from the Tōkyō garrison. At the military trial held on 15 October, Mizoe and 52 others were sentenced to death and 118 others were banished from Tōkyō. The incident prompted the government to reinforce army discipline.

Takehisa Yumeji 竹久夢二

(1884–1934). Painter, illustrator, and poet. Real name Takehisa Shigejirō. Born in Okayama Prefecture. After he left a vocational school in Tōkyō, he became associated with socialist periodicals, such as the HEIMIN SHIMBUN, to which he contributed sketches and caricatures. He later joined the newspaper YOMIURI SHIMBUN, where he became established as an illustrator and prose writer. In 1909 he published his first collection of prints, *Haru no maki*, which created a sensation. Said to be a composite image of the women in his life, a certain type of feminine beauty, slightly consumptive with large eyes and a sad expression, became the basic theme of his work. In addition to oil and watercolor paintings, Japanese-style paintings (NIHONGA), and prints, Yumeji designed book and magazine covers. His work is said to epitomize the lyricism of the Taishō period (1912–26).

Takeiri Yoshikatsu 竹入義勝

(1926–). Politician. Born in Nagano Prefecture, he attended the Army Academy. In 1953 he joined the religious organization SŌKA GAKKAI and later became a missionary. In 1961 he became a central committee member of the Kōmei Political Federation (Kōmei Seiji Remmei), the political arm of the Sōka Gakkai. Following the formal establishment of the KŌMEITŌ party in 1964, Takeiri served in several central posts, becoming the party's leader in 1967. He was elected to the House of Representatives that year, and under his leadership the Kōmeitō made significant advances on the political front. He resigned as party leader of the Kōmeitō in 1986.

Takekurabe たけくらべ

(tr "Growing Up," 1956). Short story by HIGUCHI ICHIYŌ (1872–96); published 1895–96. One of the finest of the Meiji period (1868–1912), the story depicts a group of children growing up just outside the YOSHIWARA, the former licensed prostitution quarter in Tōkyō. In her depiction of the Yoshiwara, Higuchi combines an irony reminiscent of SAIKAKU (1642–93) with deep sympathy for the children who are about to enter that world. As summer turns to autumn and the childhood games of the characters give way to adolescent preoccupations, the main character, Midori, faces the sad realization that her passage to womanhood signifies the beginning of a life of prostitution. The circumscribed destiny of the Meiji-period woman, as illustrated by Midori's fate, is a recurrent theme in Higuchi's work.

Takemi Tarō 武見太郎

(1904–83). Physician. Born in Kyōto Prefecture. Graduate of Keiō University. He served as president of the JAPAN MEDICAL ASSOCIATION from 1957 to 1982. In this post Takemi was a strong leader who campaigned aggressively for doctors' interests. He sought to secure a prominent role for the Japan Medical Association in the formation of government medical policies and fought for the removal of certain government-enforced regulations and standards that placed restrictions on the nature of medical examinations. By using the tactic of threatened refusals of service by doctors in private practice in 1961 and again in 1971, he succeeded in securing the abolition of the restrictions and also of regional differences in consulting fees.

Takemitsu Tōru 武満徹

(1930–). Composer. Born in Tōkyō. He first heard the music of the French modernists in 1946 with the resurgence of Western musical styles in Japan following World War II. This influence, coupled with his private studies with Kiyose Yasuji (1900–1981) and additional influences from Hayasaka Fumio (1914–55) and Matsudaira Yoritsune (b 1907), continues to have a profound impact on his composition style.

Takemitsu developed his individual, eclectic style as one of the founding members of Jikken Kōbō (The Experimental Workshop), a group of artists who worked together throughout the 1950s to set the standards for the major developments in contemporary Japanese music. In 1967 he composed *November Steps 1*, a monumental work for BIWA, SHAKUHACHI, and symphony orchestra, which was dedicated to and commissioned by the New York Philharmonic in celebration of its 125th anniversary.

Since his debut in 1950 with the piano composition *Futatsu no rento* (Lento in Due Movimenti) and *Gengaku no tame no rekuiemu* (1957, Requiem for Strings), Takemitsu has gained a considerable reputation as a major figure in international contemporary music. He has been the director of Music Today, a festival of contemporary music held annually in Tōkyō since its founding in 1973; the author of several books; and a composer of film scores, such as *Suna no onna*, KWAIDAN, and *Kuroi ame* (1989, Black Rain). Other compositions include *Coral Island* (1962) and *Arc* (1963–66).

Takemoto Gidayū I 竹本義太夫1世

(1651–1714). Chanter (*tayū*) in the JŌRURI form of narrative chanting that is associated with the BUNRAKU professional puppet theater. Originator of the GIDAYŪ-BUSHI style of chanting. Born in Ōsaka. Among his early performing names was Kiyomizu Gorobei.

In 1684 he established the Takemotoza puppet theater in Ōsaka and, through stylistic and repertorial innovation, soon brought to *jōruri* an unprecedented popularity. Although Gidayū's voice alone ranked him as the preeminent figure in contemporary *jōruri*, it was his collaboration with the playwright CHIKAMATSU MONZAEMON (1653–1724) that had the most profound effect on *jōruri*

as an art. The collaborators gave to *jōruri* a new dramatic appeal by touching upon popular themes familiar to the audiences. The *gidayū-bushi* style of chanting continues to predominate in the modern puppet theater.

Takenaka Corporation ［株］竹中工務店

(Takenaka Kōmuten). A design, engineering, and construction company that traces its history to 1610. The company places greater emphasis on special construction orders than on contracts obtained by bidding. One of the company's main characteristics is that it adopts an integrated system, from the planning and designing to the completion of construction projects. It is active overseas, with six subsidiaries and affiliates in the United States, seven in Europe, and seven in Asia. It also has an office in Singapore. Sales totaled ¥1.4 trillion (US $9.7 billion) in 1990, and the company was capitalized at ¥50.0 billion (US $345.3 million). Headquarters are in Ōsaka.

Takenishi Hiroko 竹西寛子

(1929–). Critic and novelist. Born in Hiroshima Prefecture; graduated from Waseda University. Takenishi first became known for *Ōkan no ki* (1964, Departures and Returns), in which she alternates between criticism of classical and modern literature. She has also published many novels that are based on her experience as a survivor of the atomic bomb dropped on Hiroshima. Takenishi's principal works include *Shikishi Naishinnō, Eifuku Mon'in* (1972, Princess Shikishi, Eifuku Mon'in), the short-story collection *Tsuru* (1975, Cranes), *Kangensai* (1978, Music Festival), and *Yamakawa Tomiko: "Myōjō" no kajin* (1985, Yamakawa Tomiko: Poet of *Myōjō*).

Takenouchi no Sukune 武内宿禰

Legendary figure who supposedly served several early Japanese emperors, most of whom were themselves legendary. According to the KOJIKI (712) and the NIHON SHOKI (720), Takenouchi was the great-grandson of the legendary emperor Kōgen and served under the legendary emperors Keikō, Seimu, and Chūai, as well as the emperors ŌJIN (late 4th to early 5th century) and NINTOKU (early 5th century). He is said to have recommended to the emperor that he send troops to northeastern Honshū to subjugate the inhabitants, to have played an active role in Empress JINGŪ's expedition to Korea, and to have expanded the territories of the Yamato court. The five families of Kose, Soga, Heguri, Ki, and Katsuragi all claimed to be descendants of Takenouchi no Sukune, but this too is doubtful.

Takenouchi Shikibu 竹内式部

(1712–67). Japanese classical scholar; early proponent of imperial loyalty and of curbing shogunate arrogance toward the emperor. Born in Echigo Province (now Niigata Prefecture). In 1759 Takenouchi was banished from Kyōto (see HŌREKI INCIDENT). In the wake of the MEIWA INCIDENT, he was sen-

Takeuchi Seihō *Tabby Cat.* 1924. Colors on silk. 83 × 102 cm. Yamatane Museum of Art, Tōkyō.

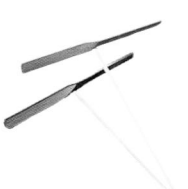

taketombo Because of their simple design, these "bamboo dragonflies" are often made in primary school arts and crafts classes.

Takikawa Yukitoki Dismissed from the Kyōto University faculty in 1933 for his liberal views, this law professor was reinstated after the war and became the university's president in 1953.

tenced to exile on Hachijōjima but died before reaching the island.

Takenouchi Tsuna   竹内綱

(1840–1922). Politician and entrepreneur. Born in Tosa Province (now Kōchi Prefecture). After the establishment of the Meiji government in 1868, he was appointed to the Ministry of Finance. For a time he operated the TAKASHIMA COAL MINE on an island off Kyūshū but was imprisoned briefly for attempting to incite an antigovernment insurrection in Tosa in response to SAIGŌ TAKAMORI's Satsuma Rebellion (1877). He joined the JIYŪTŌ, Japan's first political party, upon its formation in 1881 and was elected to the Diet for three terms beginning in 1890. Takenouchi was involved in enterprises in Korea, including the Seoul-Pusan Railway. The postwar prime minister YOSHIDA SHIGERU was his fifth son.

Takenouchi Yasunori   竹内保徳

(1806–?). Official of the Tokugawa shogunate and leader of a shogunal mission to Europe in 1862–63. Born in Edo (now Tōkyō). In 1861 he was appointed commissioner of finance (*kanjō bugyō*) and commissioner of foreign affairs (*gaikoku bugyō*). In 1862 he headed a mission to Europe to negotiate delaying until 1868 the opening of Japan's ports to foreign trade as provided by the ANSEI COMMERCIAL TREATIES. See also SHOGUNATE MISSIONS TO THE WEST.

Takeo   武雄[市]

City in western Saga Prefecture, Kyūshū. Takeo has long been known for its hot springs. Traditional products include the pottery wares known as *kuromuta-yaki* and *tatarō-yaki.* Rice is cultivated in the lowlands, and mandarin oranges, tea, and persimmons are grown in the hills. Pop: 34,490.

Takeshima   竹島

Uninhabited island in the Sea of Japan that has become the focus of a territorial dispute between Japan and the Republic of Korea (ROK). Located just south of the 38th parallel and approximately equidistant from Honshū and the Korean peninsula, the island is called Takeshima by the Japanese and Tokto by the Koreans. It is also known as the Liancourt Rocks, after the French ship *Liancourt.* Small (0.23 sq km; 0.09 sq mi) and barren, the island is little more than a cluster of reefs. Japan occupied the island for strategic reasons during the Russo-Japanese War (1904–05), and it was incorporated into Shimane Prefecture in 1905. Since the end of World War II, the ROK has claimed rights to the island and has had control over it.

Attempts to resolve the dispute have been unsuccessful. See also TERRITORY OF JAPAN; KOREA-JAPAN TREATY OF 1965, SUPPLEMENTARY AGREEMENTS.

Takeshita Noboru   竹下登

(1924–). Politician; prime minister from 1987 to 1989. Born in Shimane Prefecture, Takeshita graduated from Waseda University. He was first elected to the House of Representatives in 1958 as a LIBERAL DEMOCRATIC PARTY candidate from Shimane Prefecture. After holding a succession of cabinet posts and important positions in his party, Takeshita became Japan's 74th prime minister in November 1987. One of his most important acts as prime minister was the introduction of the CONSUMPTION TAX in December 1988. Throughout his career Takeshita has shown himself to be a successful behind-the-scenes negotiator, both in his own party and in the Diet at large. It was expected that he would remain prime minister for a considerable length of time, but the unpopularity of the consumption tax and considerable criticism of his involvement in the RECRUIT SCANDAL forced his resignation in June 1989.

Taketa   竹田[市]

City in southwestern Ōita Prefecture, Kyūshū. Taketa developed as a castle town in the 12th century. Principal products are rice, tobacco, and *shiitake* mushrooms. It was the childhood home of the composer TAKI RENTARŌ. TANOMURA CHIKUDEN, the Edo-period (1600–1868) painter, was born here. Of interest also are the remains of a secret Christian chapel (see KAKURE KIRISHITAN) and a cluster of mounded tombs (KOFUN). Pop: 20,164.

Taketani Mitsuo   武谷三男

(1911–). Theoretical physicist. Born in Fukuoka Prefecture. Graduate of Kyōto University. Taketani was a professor at Rikkyō University from 1952 to 1969. He has been active in theoretical research on subatomic particles. Taketani has strongly advocated the peaceful uses of atomic energy, and in 1952 he proposed three principles for atomic energy research: peaceful development, public control, and openness. In 1955 these principles were incorporated into Japan's Basic Law concerning Atomic Energy (Genshiryoku Kihon Hō).

taketombo   竹蜻蛉

("bamboo dragonfly"). A children's toy made of bamboo carved into the shape of a propeller with a shaft attached at the center. It is set in motion by rubbing the shaft between the palms of the hands and then releasing it upward in the air to fly. Some say the toy was invented by HIRAGA GENNAI (1728–80). Today *taketombo* are often made of plastic.

Taketomijima   竹富島

Island 4 km (2.5 mi) southwest of the island of Ishigakijima, southwestern Okinawa Prefecture; one of the YAEYAMA ISLANDS. It is a level island surrounded by coral reefs, with beaches covered with *hoshisuna* ("star sand"), the remains of tiny sea animals. The principal activity is sugarcane cultivation. Area: 5.5 sq km (2.1 sq mi).

Taketori monogatari   竹取物語

(tr *The Tale of the Bamboo Cutter,* 1956). Early-Heian-period (794–1185) prose work, probably written between 850 and 950, about a supernatural being found by a bam-

boo cutter and brought up as his daughter under the name Kaguyahime, "The Shining Princess." He becomes rich and urges her to marry one of five noble suitors, to each of whom she sets a fantastic quest; all either fail or resort in vain to trickery. She also refuses the suit of the emperor. Eventually she explains that she is from the Palace of the Moon, whose messengers are coming to take her back. She dons a robe of feathers that obliterates her memories of the world and departs. She leaves behind a letter and an elixir of life for the emperor, but loath to prolong life without her, he has both items burned on the mountaintop nearest heaven (Mt. Fuji). In the *Genji monogatari* (TALE OF GENJI) *Taketori monogatari* is referred to as "the archetype and parent of all romance." See also FOLKTALES.

Taketoyo   武豊[町]

Town in the central part of the Chita Peninsula in western Aichi Prefecture, central Honshū. Facilities are being built on reclaimed land here as part of a project for developing a coastal industrial zone and the port of Kinuura. Pop: 38,105.

Takeuchi Kyūichi   竹内久一

(1857–1916). Japanese-style sculptor. Born in the Asakusa district of Edo (now Tōkyō). In 1880 Takeuchi decided to devote himself to the study and revival of traditional techniques of Japanese painted wood sculpture. When the Tōkyō Bijutsu Gakkō (now Tōkyō University of Fine Arts and Music) opened in 1889, he became an instructor in the sculpture department. On the advice of OKAKURA KAKUZŌ, de facto director of the school, he made several reproductions of Nara-period (710–794) sculptural masterpieces. Takeuchi is considered one of the three leading sculptors of the early Meiji period (1868–1912), along with TAKAMURA KŌUN and Ishikawa Kōmei (1852–1913).

Takeuchi Seihō   竹内栖鳳

(1864–1942). Japanese-style painter. Real name Takeuchi Tsunekichi. Born in Kyōto. With his fluent and refined style, grounded in a meticulous realism, Takeuchi became a master among the artists of Kyōto and a pioneer of modern NIHONGA (Japanese-style painting). In his youth he studied under KŌNO BAIREI of the MARUYAMA-SHIJŌ SCHOOL. In 1882 two of his paintings won awards at the Naikoku Kaiga Kyōshinkai (Domestic Painting Competition), one of the first modern painting competitions to be held in Japan. On a tour of Europe in 1900–1901 Takeuchi absorbed the influence of Turner, Corot, and other artists, adding Western techniques to his repertoire and new elements to his depictions of light and air. He was a BUNTEN exhibition judge from its inauguration in 1907. In 1909 he became a professor at Kyōto Municipal College of Painting (now Kyōto City University of Arts); in 1913 he was appointed artist to the imperial household (*teishitsu gigeiin*); and in 1919 he became a member of the Imperial Fine Arts Academy (Teikoku Bijutsuin). He received the Order of Culture in 1937.

takeuma → stilts

Takezaki Suenaga   竹崎季長

(1246–?). A warrior of Higo Province (now Kumamoto Prefecture) who distinguished himself in the defense of the northern Kyūshū coast during the MONGOL INVASIONS OF JAPAN of 1274 and 1281. His military exploits are immortalized in a pair of polychrome painted scrolls, dated 1293, entitled *Mōko shūrai ekotoba* (Scrolls of the Mongol Invasion) or *Takezaki Suenaga ekotoba*. Tentatively attributed to Tosa Nagataka, the scrolls are preserved in the Tōkyō National Museum.

takiginō　薪能

NŌ drama performed outside by the light of a bonfire. It originated in the practice of burning sacred firewood (*takigi*) during the *shunie* ceremony at the east and west *kondō* buildings of the temple KŌFUKUJI in Nara Prefecture. In the Muromachi period (1333–1568) *takiginō* performances, often lasting several days, were given at Kōfukuji and the KASUGA SHRINE. Today *takiginō* is still performed at those places every 11 and 12 May. Similar performances are given in many places throughout Japan during the summer months.

takiguchi no bushi　滝口の武士

(literally, "warriors of the mouth of the waterfall"). A unit of armed guards in the imperial palace. Established during the reign (887–897) of Emperor UDA, they were attached to the KURŌDO-DOKORO (Chamberlain's Office or Bureau of Archivists) and named for their station at the waterfall in the garden of the Seiryōden, the emperor's living quarters. The unit originally comprised 10 warriors, later expanded to 20, and at one time 30. Selected for skill in archery, they served as imperial messengers and accompanied the emperor on outings. During the reign of Emperor Horikawa (1079–1107; r 1087–1107), some of the *takiguchi no bushi* were seconded to the service of the retired emperor SHIRAKAWA and became known as HOKUMEN NO BUSHI.

Takii Kōsaku　滝井孝作

(1894–1984). Novelist and HAIKU poet. Haiku pen name Sessai. Born in Gifu Prefecture. He became a disciple of the haiku poet KAWAHIGASHI HEKIGOTŌ, who is known for his nontraditional "new trend" haiku, and later became acquainted with the writers AKUTAGAWA RYŪNOSUKE and SHIGA NAOYA. He established his reputation as a novelist with *Mugen hōyō* (1921–24), an autobiographical account of his love for a prostitute, who died soon after their marriage. Like those of Shiga Naoya, his lifelong mentor, his works depict interpersonal family relationships. However, most of his later works are plotless essays that reflect the haiku tradition. Other works include the haiku collection *Sessai kushū* (1931) and the short stories "Kekkon made" (1927) and "Yokuboke" (1934). In 1960 he became a member of the Japan Art Academy (Nihon Geijutsuin).

Takikawa　滝川[市]

City in central Hokkaidō, at the confluence of the rivers Ishikarigawa and Sorachigawa. Takikawa was developed from 1889 by colonist militia (TONDENHEI). It is an agricultural distribution center; principal products are rice, apples, and onions. Pop: 49,591.

Takikawa Incident → Kyōto University Incident

Takikawa Yukitoki　滝川幸辰

(1891–1962). Law professor and central figure in the Takikawa Incident of 1933 (see KYŌTO UNIVERSITY INCIDENT), in which university autonomy and academic freedom were seriously undermined by the government.

Also known as Takigawa Kōshin. Born in Okayama Prefecture, Takikawa graduated from Kyōto University. He became a professor there in 1924. Attacked in 1932 by right-wing groups for his liberal views, he was forced out of his job in 1933 by Education Minister HATOYAMA ICHIRŌ. After World War II, Takikawa was reinstated at Kyōto University (1946) and became its president in 1953. Notable among his works is *Hanzairon josetsu* (1937, Introduction to Criminology).

Taki Mototaka　多紀元孝

(1695–1766). Edo-period (1600–1868) physician and founder of a long line of physicians to the TOKUGAWA FAMILY. Born in Edo (now Tōkyō). A descendant of TAMBA YASUYORI, a court physician of the 10th century, Taki taught medicine at his own school and later served as the administrator of the shogunate medical bureau; he was regarded as the highest medical authority of the time.

Taki Rentarō　滝廉太郎

(1879–1903). Composer; pianist. Born in Tōkyō. He attended school in Ōita, Kyūshū, before entering in 1894 the music school founded in Tōkyō by IZAWA SHŪJI (1851–1917) that later became part of Tōkyō University's of Fine Arts and Music. There he studied Western music, one of his teachers being Kōda Nobu (1870–1946), whose sister Andō Kō (1878–1963) had studied violin in Germany with Joseph Joachim (1831–1907). Taki was also influenced by Raphael von Koeber (1848–1923), who came to Japan in 1893 and taught him piano and composition. Taki entered the music academy in Leipzig, Germany, in 1901 but became ill and returned to Japan in 1902. His work included the first serious Western-style songs by a Japanese composer, notably "Hana" (1900) and "Kōjō no tsuki" (1901).

Takisada & Co, Ltd　滝定[株]

(Takisada). Textile trading company. Incorporated in 1940. It sells only to wholesalers, including apparel makers. Exports are shipped worldwide and mainly consist of cotton, synthetic fiber, and woolen goods. Imports comprise fabrics, garments, and accessories from Europe, Korea, Taiwan, and China. Sales for the fiscal year ending January 1991 totaled ¥226.9 billion (US $1.7 billion), and capitalization was ¥2.1 billion (US $15.7 million). Headquarters are in Nagoya.

Takita Choin　滝田樗陰

(1882–1925). Editor of the monthly magazine CHŪŌ KŌRON. Real name Takita Tetsutarō. Born in Akita Prefecture. While still a student at Tōkyō University, Takita joined the staff of CHŪŌ KŌRON SHA, INC, the publisher of a then relatively obscure monthly. Soon after his promotion to editor in chief in 1912, *Chūō kōron* became one of Japan's leading general-interest magazines. He encouraged such writers as TOKUTOMI SOHŌ, NATSUME SŌSEKI, TAYAMA KATAI, TOKUDA SHŪSEI, SHIMAZAKI TŌSON, and YOSHINO SAKUZŌ.

Takita Minoru　滝田実

(1912–). Born in Toyama Prefecture. President of Dōmei (Japanese Confederation of Labor) from 1968 through 1972. After serving as president of the Nisshin Spinning Co labor union and Zensen (Japan Federation of Textile Industry Workers' Unions), Takita became president of Zenrō (Congress of Trade Unions of Japan) when it was formed in 1954 as a splinter group of SŌHYŌ (General Council of Trade Unions of Japan). Zenrō

was expanded in 1964 to become Dōmei. As a leader of the anticommunist trade union movement, Takita forged Dōmei into a labor presence larger than Sōhyō in Japanese private industry.

Takizawa Bakin → Bakin

Takizawa Katsumi　滝沢克己

(1909–84). Philosopher and systematic theologian. Born in Tochigi Prefecture, he graduated from Kyūshū University, where he also became a professor (1950–71). Under the influence of the philosopher NISHIDA KITARŌ, Takizawa interpreted the meaning behind the name "Jesus Christ" as the ontological foundation for human existence, and "Jesus Christ" as the materialization of the universal concept of "Emmanuel," or "God with us." He posited the ubiquitous nature of Emmanuel by separating it from its Christian context. This interpretation of the name of Jesus Christ and of revelation (the realization of "Emmanuel") as a part of human history that is independent of Christian doctrine opened the way for interreligious dialogue.

Takizawa Osamu　滝沢修

(1906–). SHINGEKI ("new theater") actor. Born in Tōkyō. In 1925 Takizawa became a member of the Tsukiji Shōgekijō (Tsukiji Little Theater), a group known for its introduction of modern European plays to Japan. In 1947 he formed the Minshū Geijutsu Gekijō (People's Art Theatre; precursor of the GEKIDAN MINGEI) with UNO JŪKICHI and became one of the group's principal actors. Takizawa's acting style, with its emphasis on the accurate portrayal of real-life situations, is said to epitomize the *shingeki* acting tradition. His best-known roles have been in a theatrical adaptation of SHIMAZAKI TŌSON's novel *Yoake mae* (1929–35; tr *Before the Dawn*, 1987) and in *Death of a Salesman* (1954).

tako → kites

takoyaki　蛸焼き

Snack consisting of octopus (*tako*), chopped scallions, and pickled ginger cooked in wheat-flour batter. It is often sold at outdoor stalls. To make *takoyaki*, batter is poured into hemispheric cavities in a special griddle and the other ingredients added. A pick is used to turn the hemispheres so that the uncooked batter falls to the bottom of the cavity. The resulting spheres are topped with a Japanese version of Worcestershire sauce and sprinkled with green *nori* (a type of dried seaweed).

takiginō Outdoor performances of Nō drama by bonfire light were revived in the 1950s and continue to be popular. Here, a scene from the "madwoman play" *Yamamba* is performed at the temple Kōfukuji in Nara.

Taki Rentarō This musician was the first Japanese composer to write Western-style art songs.

takoyaki Made from bits of octopus and other ingredients cooked in batter, *takoyaki* is sprinkled with green dried seaweed and sometimes, as here, with dried bonito flakes (*katsuobushi*).

takuan-zuke This popular variety of pickled radish is named after the Zen priest Takuan Sōhō, who is reputed to have originated it in the 17th century.

Taku 多久[市]

City in central Saga Prefecture, Kyūshū. Under the rule of the Taku family (vassals of the Kamakura shogunate) from the 12th century, it later came under the Ryūzōji, and subsequently the Nabeshima family. It became a center of Confucian studies in the Edo period (1600–1868). It later flourished as a coal-mining town, but all the mines have now been closed and new industries are being encouraged. The southern section is noted for its loquats and mandarin oranges. Pop: 25,162.

Takuan Sōhō 沢庵宗彭

(1573–1645). Zen monk, calligrapher, and painter. Born in Izushi (in what is now Hyōgo Prefecture). He was given the name Sōhō in 1594 at Daitokuji, the leading Rinzai Zen temple in Kyōto. After serving in other temples, he returned to Daitokuji to become abbot at age 35. In 1629 he was banished for three years to Kaminoyama (in what is now Yamagata Prefecture) over a disagreement with the shogunate about temple succession. He founded the temple Tōkaiji in 1638 at the behest of shōgun TOKUGAWA IEMITSU. Takuan's bold and free brushwork is exhibited in both his calligraphy and painting, achieving a maximum of expression with a minimum of lines. He is also known as a poet and tea master. See also ZENGA.

takuan-zuke 沢庵漬け

One of the most common PICKLES of Japan. It is made by placing dried *daikon* (Japanese white radish) in a barrel of salt and rice bran for three to seven months, a process which gives it a distinctive flavor and yellow hue. *Takuan-zuke*, which keeps extremely well, is eaten in thin slices. Although it was once the custom for each household to prepare its own *takuan-zuke*, today it is usually bought ready-made. Legend attributes the origins of this variety of pickle to the Zen priest TAKUAN SŌHŌ (1573–1645).

Takubo Hideo 田久保英夫

(1928–). Novelist. Born in Tōkyō; graduated from Keiō University. His parents' traditional Japanese-style restaurant and his upbringing in the old SHITAMACHI section of Tōkyō are important elements in Takubo's literature. He first became known for *Kaikin* (1961, Removal of the Ban), an account of his boyhood, and received the Akutagawa Prize for *Fukai kawa* (1969, Deep River), the story of a student who takes care of horses on a US military base in Japan. Takubo's other works include *Kami no wa* (1976, Coil of Hair), *Kaizu* (1985, Nautical Chart), and the short story collection *Tsujibi* (1986, Roadside Fire).

Takuma Eiga 宅磨栄賀

(fl late 14th century). Buddhist painter (*ebusshi*) of the TAKUMA SCHOOL. The inscription on his painting of the poet KAKINOMOTO NO HITOMARO in the Tokiwayama Collection, Kamakura, may be dated 1395, thus providing one point of reference for his activity as a painter toward the end of the 14th century. His other surviving paintings include a set of 16 hanging scrolls in the Fujita Art Museum, Ōsaka, depicting the 16 arhats, or RAKAN; a painting of the Buddhist deity Fudō in the Seikadō Collection, Tōkyō, and three hanging scrolls of Shaka (the Buddha Śākyamuni) and the bodhisattvas Monju

(Mañjuśrī) and Fugen (Samantabhadra) in the Chōmyōji, a Kyōto temple, as well as a painting of Fugen in the Freer Gallery of Art, Washington, DC.

Eiga's paintings show a remarkable diversity of style. His paintings of Buddhist subjects range from fully colored icons based on traditional Japanese and Chinese iconographic and stylistic models to paintings executed entirely in ink, which reflect the 14th-century trend toward assimilation of ideas from Chinese paintings of the day.

Takuma school 宅磨派

(Takumaha). School of EBUSSHI (artists specializing in Buddhist painting) that flourished from the mid-12th to the late 14th century. Its founder was claimed to be TAKUMA TAMETŌ (fl mid-12th century). However, its association with the temples KŌZANJI and JINGOJI, in northwest Kyōto, did not occur until during the lifetime of the founder's oldest son, TAKUMA SHŌGA. After Shōga, there followed such noted artists as Takuma Tamehisa (fl ca 1184–85), Takuma Shunga (fl 1201–32), Takuma Ryōga (fl 1202–17), and others. Within a generation after the death of TAKUMA EIGA (fl late 14th century), the school ceased to exist. The school has been considered a pioneer of a new realism in painting, characterized by vigorous brushwork inspired by Chinese works of the Song (Sung) dynasty (960–1279).

Takuma Shōga 宅磨勝賀

(fl late 12th century). Buddhist painter. Son of TAKUMA TAMETŌ. Surviving paintings attributed to Shōga indicate his important role in incorporating stylistic and iconographic elements from Song (Sung) dynasty (960–1279) Chinese painting. Paintings attributed to Takuma Shōga include the *Jūniten byōbu* (1191, Screen Paintings of 12 Devas) in the collection of the Kyōto temple TŌJI; the *Ryōkai mandara* in the same temple collection; and the *Jūniten* in the JINGOJI, a temple northwest of Kyōto. All these works show the delicate color harmonies associated with Song Chinese paintings.

Takuma Tamenari 宅磨為成

(fl mid-11th century). Buddhist painter known only through a later account recorded in the Kamakura-period (1185–1333) collection of anecdotes, *Kokon chomonjū*. According to this account, Tamenari painted the door panels of the BYŌDŌIN. The extant paintings of the Hōōdō (Phoenix Hall) of the Byōdōin were executed in 1053. Tamenari's participation in the project, however, as well as his relationship to later TAKUMA SCHOOL artists such as TAKUMA TAMETŌ and TAKUMA SHŌGA, both active in the second half of the 12th century, is unverified.

Takuma Tametō 宅磨為遠

(fl mid-12th century). Buddhist painter. Tametō is the earliest painter whose name has been associated with the TAKUMA SCHOOL, which was especially active in Buddhist painting of the 12th to the 14th century, and he has been claimed as its founder. As a Buddhist priest he took the ecclesiastical name Shōchi and attained the rank of *hōin*. He is recorded to have executed paintings for the interior of the Kakuōin, a subtemple of the temple KONGŌBUJI at Kōyasan in Wakayama Prefecture. The extant work attributed to Tametō comes from the *Kontai butsuga chō*, an album of iconographic drawings in ink

and light colors. His son, TAKUMA SHŌGA, also specialized in painting Buddhist subjects.

Takushoku University 拓殖大学

(Takushoku Daigaku). A coeducational private university located in Bunkyō Ward, Tōkyō. Founded in 1900 as the Taiwan Kyōkai Gakkō, it was granted university status in 1922. In addition to operating a cooperative venture with Vancouver Community College (the Takudai Canadian School), the university has schools in China, Taiwan, Spain, and Mexico. Takushoku University maintains faculties of commerce, political science and economics, foreign languages, and engineering. Many students from Southeast Asia study Japanese at Takushoku's Language Research Institute. Enrollment in 1989 was 8,717.

Tale of Genji 源氏物語

(*Genji monogatari*). By general repute the supreme masterpiece of Japanese prose literature. Written in the early 11th century, it has been called the first great novel in world literature. More than 1,000 pages in translation, or some three-quarters of a million words, it has an essentially simple plot, describing the life and loves of an erstwhile prince known, from his family name, as "the shining Genji"; after his death, the work describes the less successful loves of a youth, Kaoru, who passes as Genji's son, but is in fact the grandson of his best friend.

The earliest surviving texts from the late Heian period (794–1185) are fragmentary, and it is only from the medieval period (mid-12th–16th centuries) that complete texts can be put together. The absence of a holograph manuscript and of detailed information about the author, a court lady known as MURASAKI SHIKIBU, means that no final answers can be given to questions concerning the circumstances of composition. From evidence in the work known as the *Murasaki Shikibu nikki* (Murasaki Shikibu Diary), it seems undeniable that at least part of the work is by Murasaki Shikibu. From the SARASHINA NIKKI, the diary or memoirs of another court lady, it seems equally certain that a prose work, approximately the length of the present *Genji*, had been completed and widely circulated by about 1025.

Early Stages of the Story—The action covers almost three-quarters of a century. Genji is born in the first chapter and is 52 by the Oriental count in "The Wizard," the last chapter in which he is still living. (Chapter titles and names of characters in this article derive from Edward Seidensticker's translation: *The Tale of Genji*, 1976.) Kaoru, the youth who passes as his son, is 5 in "The Wizard" and 28 in the last of the 54 chapters that make up the present *Genji*.

Genji is born the son of the reigning emperor by his best-loved wife, a lady of undistinguished lineage. She dies before Genji is old enough to remember her. He is his father's favorite son, but the possibility of his succeeding to the throne is early dismissed, and he is given commoner status and the family name Genji or Minamoto, commonly bestowed by emperors upon sons not granted royal status.

After the death of Genji's mother, the emperor transfers his affections to a princess, Fujitsubo, who is brought to court because she closely resembles the dead lady. Genji is strongly attracted to her as a substitute for the mother he never knew. He has a brief affair with her, and the son who is the result later succeeds to the throne and is known after his abdication as the Reizei emperor.

Marriages and Love Affairs—The search for affinities with his dead mother also attracts Genji to the great love of his life. Known as Murasaki—and it is quite possible that the name by which the author has traditionally been known derives from this designation—she is a niece of Fujitsubo, whom she closely resembles. Her marriage to Genji and his love for her form the principal strand of the plot.

Genji has already made a political marriage to Aoi, a lady somewhat older than he and the daughter of the Minister of the Left. She is also the sister of Tō no Chūjō, Genji's best friend. Aoi dies after the birth of a son, Yūgiri, who is to rise to great eminence and figure prominently in the later plot. Genji is persuaded that the jealous spirit of the Rokujō lady, with whom he has had an affair, is responsiible for the death. A belief that disturbed spirits wander forth and do great mischief was prevalent in the Heian period.

The youthful Genji has a variety of love affairs, with, among others, the lady of the evening faces, a former mistress of his best friend, Tō no Chūjō; the comic safflower lady, an impoverished princess to whom Genji remains steadfast (steadfastness is among his more conspicuous traits) despite her uncomeliness; and Oborozukiyo, a daughter of the Minister of the Right, the most powerful political rival of Genji's father-in-law and Tō no Chūjō's father, the Minister of the Left.

The abdication of Genji's father is announced in the ninth chapter, and Aoi dies. The Minister of the Right and another of his daughters, the Kokiden lady, who is the mother of the new emperor and greatly dislikes Genji, come into political ascendancy with the abdication, and the Oborozukiyo affair gives them the occasion they need for driving Genji into exile.

A Secure Future—The exile is the one major setback of his career, which after a few years recovers brilliantly. Ill and determined to abdicate, the Suzaku emperor, who is Genji's brother and Kokiden's son, summons him back from exile, and with the accession of Genji's son, the Reizei emperor, who is thought to be Genji's brother, his future prospects are secure. Genji's prospects are further brightened by the fact that a liaison with a lady of Akashi, one of his places of exile, gives him a much-needed daughter. He does as the FUJIWARA FAMILY did through much of the Heian period: he marries the girl to the crown prince and thus gains control of future emperors.

There are deaths in the early chapters, bringing sorrow into Genji's life: of Aoi, of the Rokujō lady, of Fujitsubo, and of Genji's father. His career is triumphantly successful, however. By age 40 he is the most powerful statesman in the land, and he has been accorded the honors and emoluments of a retired emperor.

Genji moves into a magnificent new mansion at Rokujō and discovers and brings into his house Tamakazura, Tō no Chūjō's lost daughter by the lady of the evening faces. Yūgiri courts his cousin Kumoinokari. The courtship is initially thwarted by the girl's father, Tō no Chūjō, but presently brought to a happy conclusion. Genji makes Tamakazura unhappy by his obvious designs upon her, but in the end she makes a prudent, if loveless, marriage to a man with a bright political future.

Genji's Death—Genji's career reaches a brilliant climax, but as he prepares to go into retirement tragedy enters his private life. Murasaki becomes seriously ill and indeed is briefly taken for dead. Although she makes a partial recovery, she eventually dies, never having fully regained her strength. At the behest of his brother, the Suzaku emperor, now abdicated, Genji marries the emperor's favorite daughter. She is seduced by Kashiwagi, the oldest son of Tō no Chūjō, and the result of the liaison is Kaoru. Though in no way responsible for what has happened, except through a certain carelessness, the princess is so consumed with guilt that she becomes a nun.

Kashiwagi languishes and dies, the Third Princess, Genji's young wife, is seen in her nunnery; and in alternation with these somber episodes Yūgiri is followed in his earnest, somewhat ludicrous, and finally successful pursuit of Kashiwagi's widow, a sister of the Third Princess. Genji goes through the first year of his bereavement, and his death is suddenly announced.

The Later Stages—The 2 chapters that follow Genji's death introduce the characters who are to dominate the last 10 chapters. These include an "Eighth Prince," a brother of Genji and the Suzaku emperor who, at the end of a life of disappointment, is living in the village of Uji and pursuing religious devotions. Kaoru visits him and becomes interested in his two daughters, especially the older one. She turns him away in terror and starves herself to death after her father dies. Kaoru has meanwhile acted as intermediary for his good friend Prince Niou, Genji's grandson and the son of the reigning emperor, in his courtship of the younger princess. Niou marries her, and Kaoru is left with bitter regrets that he brought the two together. He has learned, from an old lady attending the two Uji princesses, the secret of his birth, which intensifies his unhappiness and sense of ineffectuality.

Another daughter of the Eighth Prince is introduced after the removal of the second princess to the city. Traditionally known as Ukifune, she is an unrecognized daughter, the result of a brief liaison after the death of the prince's wife. Kaoru is interested in her and thinks of making her a concubine, but she has the misfortune of also attracting the interest of Niou and of returning it. Paralyzed at the prospect of choosing between two gentlemen so much higher in rank than herself, she attempts to drown herself. However, she is rescued and taken to a nunnery in the hills east of Kyōto, where she becomes a nun. The story ends on an uncertain note, as she refuses to see her brother, Kaoru's emissary, and as Kaoru becomes suspicious that Niou has spirited her away and hidden her.

Social and Religious Pessimism—A deep pessimism pervades the latter part of the work. The great day was that of Genji, and it is over. Kaoru and Niou are lesser men, the author seems to say. There is an element of social criticism in the pessimism. Genji comes from the royal family and not from the Fujiwara clan, which dominated affairs of state in Murasaki's day. His successes would have been unthinkable now, and Murasaki is implicitly expressing her dissatisfaction. The pessimism has a religious as well as a social grounding. The Buddhist notion of the ephemeral was among those that the Japanese found most congenial. It is everywhere in the *Genji*. Certain forms of Buddhism went to the extreme of applying the principle of evanescence to Buddhism itself. The day would come when the Good Law would wither away. The final decline (*mappō*; see ESCHATOLOGY) was to begin in the mid-Heian period, it was thought, and Murasaki's grand story of decline can be read as a parable, a symbolic recounting of this ultimate decline. The falling away of society as Ukifune is left alone with her fate becomes the withering away of the Buddhist law itself.

The *Genji* can be read as another sort of Buddhist parable. The principle of karma, or retribution, is also a notion to which the Japanese were strongly attracted. Early in the story Genji has an affair with one of his father's wives, and toward the end of his career he is similarly cuckolded. He is aware of this last happening and wonders if his father was also aware and remained silent. He is convinced that his youthful misdeeds have come back to make him unhappy. There can be little doubt that Murasaki meant her story to be read as an instance of the inexorable workings of karma.

Characterizations—It is above all the characterization that supports the claim of the *Genji* to be the oldest of novels. The total number of characters runs into the hundreds. Although there is not a great deal of explicit inquiry into emotions and states of mind, the characters are skillfully delineated and kept distinct from each other with remarkable consistency. It has been averred that the *Genji* takes the form of theme and variations, with the theme announced in the second chapter in a discussion of the states

Tale of Genji Detail from one of the 12th-century *Genji* scrolls (*Genji monogatari emaki*) illustrating the 49th chapter, "Yadorigi." The reigning emperor (facing the viewer) has decided that Genji's putative son Kaoru would be a suitable match for his own daughter and deliberately loses at go in order to offer Kaoru a spray of chrysanthemum, symbolizing the daughter he is willing to give. At left, ladies-in-waiting watch the match.

and varieties of femininity, and the several varieties of courtly love introduced in subsequent chapters. For so long a work, the plot is essentially simple, and the hold upon the reader's attention depends chiefly on characterization. There are no extremes of good and evil, except perhaps in the early, more romantic chapters. The illusion of life is achieved for the most part without exaggeration or caricature.

Popularity and Influence—Initially read to and by a small circle of court ladies, the *Genji* seems to have gained an immediate popularity that has not flagged in the years since.

A confusing proliferation of medieval texts—and it is from the medieval period that the earliest complete texts survive—makes the establishment of a definitive text impossible. In the early medieval period the preferred text was the "Kawachi Book." Since the late medieval period the "Blue Book" (Aobyōshi) has been preferred. The latter derives ultimately from the work of FUJIWARA NO SADAIE (Fujiwara no Teika), the great poet and scholar of the late Heian and early Kamakura (1185–1333) periods. There are numerous medieval texts that seem to fit into neither line.

The *Genji monogatari* has been an enormous influence on later literature and other art forms and on popular lore as well. It is one of the principal sources for the NŌ drama, and it has been adapted for the KABUKI stage, the cinema, and television. Of several renditions in modern Japanese, more than one has become a best seller. The remoteness of the language from modern Japanese means that few people except specialists read the entire *Genji* in the original, but every high-school student gets a smattering. The *Genji* has been a continuing source of inspiration for artists. The 12th-century *Genji* scrolls, traditionally known as the Takayoshi scrolls, are the earliest and most famous of many graphic representations. See also GENJI MONOGATARI EMAKI.

Tale of the Heike →Heike monogatari

tally trade   勘合貿易

(*kangō bōeki*). Trade carried on between Japan and the Ming dynasty (1368–1644) of China from the early 15th to the mid-16th century. Although the Ming government prohibited Chinese merchant ships from trading in foreign countries, they permitted ships of "tributary" countries to trade by issuing *kangō* (Ch: *kanhe* or *k'an-ho*), or tallies. In 1401 retired shōgun ASHIKAGA YOSHIMITSU sent an envoy to China and complied with its request to prohibit the activities of the WAKŌ (Japanese pirates). Diplomatic relations were opened in 1402, the Ashikaga shōgun thereafter signing all diplomatic correspondence as the "King of Japan." In 1404 an envoy arrived bearing tallies and a register for the shōgun. Thenceforth all official ships going to China carried sequentially numbered tallies. Between 1404 and 1547 a total of 87 tally ships made 17 voyages in fleets of as many as 9 ships. In principle, the tally trade represented tribute on the part of the "king of Japan" to the Ming emperor, and the ships flew banners that read "tribute-bearing ship of Japan." The goods that the Japanese received in return were "gifts" from the emperor to his loyal subject the "king." The actual operation of the tally trade, however, was carried out by *daimyō* and Buddhist temples, sometimes joined by Hakata (see FUKUOKA) and SAKAI merchants. The Japanese sent horses, swords, sulfur, gold screens, copper, fans, and gold lacquer ware to be exchanged for silver or copper coins, raw silk, and silk textiles. As the Ashikaga declined, the HOSOKAWA FAMILY and ŌUCHI FAMILY competed for the right to send tally ships. In 1523 the Ōuchi gained a monopoly. With the collapse of the Ōuchi in 1551, the tally trade ceased to exist.

Tama   多摩[市]

City in southern Tōkyō Prefecture on the river Tamagawa. Formerly a farming village, Tama is now a residential area with large housing complexes. One development, TAMA NEW TOWN, has a projected future population of 400,000. Pop: 144,489.

tama   霊

Also called *mitama*. Name applied in the Shintō tradition to a metaphysical substance of being. Different from *mono* and *mi*—spiritual entities inseparable from material being—*tama* functions through the medium of material substance but is independent from that substance. Disease or misfortune occurs when the function of *tama* declines, and death when this *tama*-spirit escapes from the body. Historically, four separate aspects or functions of *tama* have been recognized: the harmonious and harmonizing *nigimitama*, the active and valiant *aramitama*, the gracious and beneficent *sakimitama*, and the wondrous and wonderworking *kushimitama*. Shintō deities have proliferated in accordance with the degree and function of *tama*. Thus there is separate enshrinement and worship of the *aramitama* of the sun goddess and imperial ancestress, AMATERASU ŌMIKAMI, at the Aramatsuri no Miya, a subshrine of the ISE SHRINE, and the *sakimitama* and *kushimitama* of the god ŌKUNINUSHI NO MIKOTO at the ŌMIWA SHRINE. *Tama* whose functions are maleficent are regarded as vengeful spirits (*onryō* or GORYŌ) that must be placated through rites of pacification.

Tamagawa   多摩川

River in Tōkyō Prefecture, central Honshū, originating in Yamanashi Prefecture in the Chichibu Mountains and flowing east through the western part of Tōkyō Prefecture into Tōkyō Bay. The lower reaches separate Tōkyō from Kanagawa Prefecture. The upper reaches beyond the city of Ōme, a scenic area known as OKU TAMA, are part of Chichibu-Tama National Park. Tōkyō International Airport (Haneda) is located on the northern bank of the river's mouth. Lake Oku Tama, created by a dam in the upper reaches of the river, is a major source of drinking water for Tōkyō. Length: 126 km (78 mi); area of drainage basin: 1,240 sq km (480 sq mi).

Tamagawa Aqueduct   玉川上水

(Tamagawa Jōsui). Canal in Tōkyō Prefecture, central Honshū. Completed in 1654, it was created by diverting water from the river Tamagawa across the Musashino Plateau and into the city of Edo (now Tōkyō); its terminus was in the Yotsuya district. It was one of the three main aqueducts supplying water to the city during the Edo period (1600–1868). It also provided irrigation for the Musashino region, accelerating the creation of new rice fields there. It remained in use until 1965.

Tamagawa University   玉川大学

(Tamagawa Daigaku). Private, coeducational university located in the city of Machida, Tōkyō Prefecture. Founded in 1929 by the progressive educator OBARA KUNIYOSHI as Tamagawa Gakuen, it adopted its present name in 1947. It has departments of letters, agriculture, and engineering. It has affiliated kindergartens, elementary, junior high, and high schools, and a two-year women's junior college. Enrollment was 6,587 in 1989.

Tama Hills   多摩丘陵

(Tama Kyūryō). Group of hills in southern Tōkyō and Kanagawa prefectures, central Honshū. Portions have been incorporated into parks serving as major recreation areas for Tōkyō residents. In the l960s numerous large housing projects were built here.

Tama, Lake   多摩湖

(Tamako). Also called Murayama Reservoir. Artificial reservoir in north-central Tōkyō, central Honshū. It was constructed in 1927 and is one of the main sources of water for Tōkyō. Located in the densely wooded region of the Sayama Hills, the lake is noted for its clear water and is a popular recreation area. Area: 1.4 sq km (0.5 sq mi); storage capacity: 14.8 million cu m (523 million cu ft).

Tamana   玉名[市]

City in northwestern Kumamoto Prefecture, Kyūshū. Situated at the mouth of the river Kikuchigawa, Tamana has been an active port since the 14th century. Principal industries are printing, foodstuffs, and rubber. *Nori* (a kind of seaweed) and shellfish are cultivated; grapes and mandarin oranges are grown. Tamana Hot Spring attracts visitors. Pop: 45,284.

Tama New Town   多摩ニュータウン

(Tama Nyū Taun). Planned residential community in western Tōkyō Prefecture. The development is sited on land from four cities in the area: Hachiōji, Machida, Tama, and Inagi. Construction began in 1967 and has been chiefly sponsored by the Tōkyō metropolitan government and the national government's Housing and Urban Development Corporation; the first residents began occupancy in 1971. Large-scale commercial, cultural, and business facilities have also been constructed here. Area: 30.2 sq km (11.7 sq mi). Projected pop: 313,000.

Tamano   玉野[市]

City in southern Okayama Prefecture, western Honshū, on the Inland Sea. Tamano was a fishing port and salt producer until the Meiji period (1868–1912). From the early 1900s it was known for the port of Uno—which provided connections to the island of Shikoku—and shipbuilding. With the opening of the Honshū/Shikoku bridge route and the decline in shipbuilding, it is being developed as a resort area. Copper smelting and the manufacturing of school uniforms are also important. Pop: 73,238.

Tamatsukuri Hot Spring   玉造温泉

(Tamatsukuri Onsen). Located in the town of Tamayu, southwest of the city of Matsue, northeastern Shimane Prefecture, western Honshū. This sulfate spring is one of the best-known hot-spring spas in the San'in region. Water temperature 50°–70°C (122°–158°F).

Tama Zoological Park 多摩動物公園

(Tama Dōbutsu Kōen). Metropolitan zoological park in the city of Hino, Tōkyō Prefecture. Opened in 1958 as Japan's first open-range zoo, it is situated in the natural environment of the TAMA HILLS and is surrounded by a moat. The park initially contained chiefly Asian animals, but in 1962 African animals were also introduced. In 1964 a system of bus tours was initiated so that the park's lions could be observed. One objective of the park is to breed colonies of animals, and it has made contributions to the study of the propagation of giraffes. The Koala Pavilion houses a number of small Australian animals, and in the Insect Pavilion there are 138 species of insects, including butterflies. As of 1991, the 52.3-hectare (129.2-acre) park accommodated 1,368 animals of 183 species.

Tamba Mountains 丹波山地

(Tamba Sanchi). Mountain range running from north-central Kyōto Prefecture to eastern Hyōgo Prefecture, central Honshū. Aside from the monadnocks of Mikunidake (959 m; 3,146 ft) and ATAGOYAMA (924 m; 3,031 ft), most of the range is 600–700 m (2,000–2,300 ft) in height. The rivers Yuragawa and Ōigawa have carved the mountains to create basin lands. Special products are *matsutake* (a kind of mushroom) and chestnuts.

Tamba ware 丹波焼

(*tamba-yaki*). Ceramics produced in the southwestern part of Tamba Province (now the town of Konda, Hyōgo Prefecture). Production appears to have begun early in the Kamakura period (1185–1333). The kilns originally produced wares for local farmers, including storage jars. Except for some incised designs and inscriptions, surface decoration grew out of the firing process: falling wood ash formed an accidental greenish glaze on the shoulders of pots, and flame flashing resulted in variegated reddish hues elsewhere.

Expanding inventories emphasized such items as TEA CEREMONY wares, *sake* bottles, rice bowls, small *hibachi* (braziers), and mortars. Reddish brown, black, or amber glazes were used, and simple designs predominated. Demand for Tamba pottery declined rapidly after the Meiji Restoration (1868) but was revived during the FOLK CRAFTS (*mingei*) movement of the early 1960s. Today approximately 55 ceramic workshops produce folk craft ceramics.

Tamba Yasuyori 丹波康頼

(912–995). Heian-period (794–1185) physician and author of the *Ishimpō* (984), the oldest extant medical treatise in Japan. Born in Tamba Province (now parts of Kyōto and Hyōgo prefectures) of a naturalized Chinese family, he served as a high-ranking court physician. Consisting of 30 fascicles, the *Ishimpō* is a compilation of Chinese medical books of the Sui (589–618) and Tang (T'ang; 618–907) dynasties, many of which would otherwise have been lost.

Tamenaga Shunsui 為永春水

(1789–1843). Late-Edo-period (1600–1868) GESAKU fiction writer. He brought to maturity the genre of fiction known as NINJŌBON. Shunsui's real name was Echizen'ya Chōjirō, and he was originally the proprietor of a commercial lending library (*kashihon'ya*) in Edo (now Tōkyō). Tradition pictures him as an itinerant book lender walking the streets of Edo with his nose always in a book. He became a student of the KŌDAN storyteller Itō Enshin (1761–1840) and appeared irregularly on the YOSE stage as a raconteur under the name Tamenaga Shōsuke. Shunsui became a student of SHIKITEI SAMBA and formed an association with RYŪTEI TANEHIKO.

In 1819, using the pen name Nansenshō Somabito with the permission of that earlier writer's heirs, Shunsui published the first three volumes of a work entitled *Akegarasu nochi no masayume*, on which he had collaborated with Ryūtei Rijō (d 1841). (Two more volumes appeared in 1824.) Rijō, an associate of Shikitei Samba, may have been Shunsui's elder brother. This work, closely akin to GŌKAN ("bound volumes," a form of popular illustrated fiction) and YOMIHON ("reading books," a genre of *gesaku* fiction), is regarded as Shunsui's first important *ninjōbon*.

The 1820s saw Shunsui's gradual emergence as a popular writer, although a great number of his works (all published under the name Somabito) were either plagiarisms or written to his outlines by assistants. Shunsui announced in 1829 that he would hereafter call himself Tamenaga Shunsui. His reputation for using collaborators and for plagiarism survived this change of names, however. Shunsui's best works, chief among them his masterly SHUNSHOKU UMEGOYOMI (1832–33, Spring Love: A Plum Blossom Almanac), were entirely his own.

Published in four volumes in 1832 and 1833, *Shunshoku umegoyomi* met with great success. Like all *ninjōbon*, *Umegoyomi* shows much influence from the SHAREBON—as well as elements derived from *gōkan* and *yomihon* sources, the earlier UKIYO-ZŌSHI tradition, and the KABUKI stage—but is distinguished by its blend of social and psychological realism and sentimental romance. *Umegoyomi* caused a sensation because Shunsui's honest, sympathetic portrayal of romantic love was a novelty in the fiction of his day. Shunsui wrote two dozen or more similar works, chief among them *Shunshoku tatsumi no sono* (1833–35), but none equaled *Umegoyomi*.

He ran afoul of the moral conservatism of the TEMPŌ REFORMS initiated by MIZUNO TADAKUNI. He was arrested and charged with harming public morals. Shunsui spent several months in manacles, his publisher and illustrator were fined heavily, and the blocks from which his books were printed were confiscated and destroyed. Broken in health and spirit, he died soon after. The *ninjōbon* never regained the eminence to which Shunsui raised it, but *Umegoyomi* and the best of Shunsui's other works maintained their popularity and would have a considerable influence on modern Japanese fiction.

Tamiya Hiroshi 田宮博

(1903–84). Plant physiologist. Born in Ōsaka. Graduate and professor of Tōkyō University. With his former teacher, SHIBATA KEITA, he carried out research on the activities of enzymes, especially respiratory enzymes, in living creatures and joined in the worldwide debate concerning these matters. In connection with his research in photosynthesis, he devised a method for the synchronized culture of CHLORELLA, making its mass cultivation possible. He was awarded the Order of Culture in 1977.

Tamiya Torahiko 田宮虎彦

(1911–88). Novelist. Born in Tōkyō; graduate of Tōkyō University. After World War II, he gained recognition for his historical novel *Kiri no naka* (1947). He wrote other historical novels, including *Rakujō* (1949), and he developed an autobiographical form of fiction exemplified by *Ashizurimisaki* (1949). Tragic historical figures or contemporary people in adverse situations are the main characters in his works. He later wrote novels of unhappy marriages and other family situations. *Ehon* (1951) is a collection of his short stories.

Tamon'in nikki 多聞院日記

(Tamon'in Diary). A journal of 46 volumes (*kan*) kept by successive heads of the Tamon'in chapel of the temple KŌFUKUJI in Nara between 1478 and 1618. The oldest extant copy dates from the early 18th century. The scope of the work is broad, and it is a rich source of information for political, social, economic, and cultural history.

Tampopo タンポポ

A film comedy released in 1986, written and directed by ITAMI JŪZŌ, starring Yamazaki Tsutomu (b 1936) and Miyamoto Nobuko (b 1945). Humorously described as the first "noodle western," the film concerns a truck driver who happens one night into a noodle shop that has seen better days. Taken with the female proprietor, he stays with her long enough to coach her through a rigorous training program that results in the reinstatement of her shop as the best in the neighborhood. Then, true to the Western-movie format, he drives off into the sunset. The main plot is interspersed with short humorous vignettes illustrating how the Japanese see food. A hit in Japan, the film was also quite popular with European and American audiences.

Tamura Ransui 田村藍水

(1718–76). Specialist in *honzōgaku* (traditional pharmacognosy), known for his cultivation of ginseng (Chōsen *ninjin*). Also known as Tamura Gen'yū. Born in Edo (now Tōkyō). He was a student of ABE SHŌō. During and after the rule of the shogun TOKUGAWA YOSHIMUNE (r 1716–45), he is said to have worked as an adviser to help carry out the government's plan of encouraging domestic production of certain products, including ginseng. The first national trade fair was held in Edo (now Tōkyō) in 1757 mainly through his efforts. One of his students was HIRAGA GENNAI. He wrote *Chōsen ninjin kōsakuki* (The Cultivation of Ginseng) in 1764.

Tamura Ryūichi 田村隆一

(1923–). Poet. Born in Tōkyō; graduated from Meiji University. In 1947 Tamura organized the second series of the poetry magazine ARECHI (1947–48) and became an important figure in postwar poetry. Tamura's poetry expresses the sense of crisis experienced by modern civilization in the wake of two world wars, employing paradox, innovative metaphors, and sharp, fresh images. His poetry collections include *Yonsen no hi to yoru* (1956, Four Thousand Days and Nights), *Kotoba no nai sekai* (1962, World Without Words), and *Shinnen no tegami* (1973, New Year's Letter).

Tamura Taijirō 田村泰次郎

(1911–83). Novelist. Born in Mie Prefecture; graduate of Waseda University. Shortly after World War II, he created a sensation with his novel *Nikutai no mon* (1947, Gate of Flesh), which describes the world of prostitutes. Other works include the novels *Shumpuden*

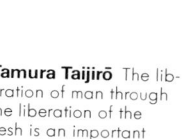

Tamura Ryūichi This poet's work is known for its innovative metaphors and sharp, fresh images.

Tamura Taijirō The liberation of man through the liberation of the flesh is an important theme in this novelist's works.

Tanabata Festival
After this festival ends, the decorated bamboo branches are placed in rice paddies in the hope of a bountiful harvest. Toyokawa, Aichi Prefecture.

Tamura Toshiko This novelist's early, best-selling works were thought to reflect the new women's consciousness of the early 20th century.

Tanakadate Aikitsu
A geophysicist considered the father of Japanese seismology and geophysics.

(1947, Tales of Prostitutes) and *Jiraigen* (1964, Minefield).

Tamura Toshiko 田村俊子

(1884–1945). Novelist. Real name Satō Toshi. Born in Tōkyō; studied briefly at Nihon Joshi Daigaku (Japan Women's University). She began writing as a disciple of KŌDA ROHAN. Her novel *Akirame* (1911, Resignation) won first place in the *Ōsaka asahi shimbun* newspaper fiction contest, and she became a best-selling writer. In 1918 she left her first husband, Tamura Shōgyo (dates unknown), to follow Suzuki Etsu (1886–1933) to Vancouver, British Columbia. They married, and she lived there until after Suzuki's death. She returned to Japan in 1936 and had a difficult affair with the leftist KUBOKAWA TSURUJIRŌ. In 1942 she went to Shanghai, where she edited a women's literary magazine before her death there. Her works include *Miira no kuchibeni* (1913, Lip Rouge on a Mummy), *Onna sakusha* (1913, Woman Writer), and *Yamamichi* (1938, Mountain Road). The posthumous royalties from her works were used to establish a literary prize for women in her name. Its first winner in 1960 was SETOUCHI HARUMI for the biography *Tamura Toshiko*.

Tamura Tsutomu 田村孟

(1933–). Screenwriter. Born in Gumma Prefecture; graduated from Tōkyō University. In 1955 Tamura began to work as an assistant director for the film production company SHŌCHIKU CO, LTD. He became a screenwriter in 1960, working chiefly with the director ŌSHIMA NAGISA. His screenplays characteristically explore the tension between individuals and the social groups—from the family to the nation—to which they belong. His major scripts include *Nihon shunka kō* (1967, A Treatise on the Japanese Bawdy Song) and *Kōshikei* (1968, Death by Hanging) for Ōshima; *Seishun no satsujinsha* (1976, Youth to Kill) for the director Hasegawa Kazuhiko (b 1946); and *Setouchi shōnen yakyūdan* (1984, MacArthur's Children) for SHINODA MASAHIRO.

Tanabata Festival 七夕

(Tanabata). One of Japan's traditional five festivals, or *gosekku* (see SEKKU), currently observed on 7 July, or, in some locales, 7 August. Its celebration originated in a Chinese folk legend concerning two stars—the Weaver Star (Vega) and the Cowherd Star (Altair)—who were said to be lovers who could meet only once a year on the seventh night of the seventh lunar month. When introduced to Japan, it merged with native legends concerning a celestial weaving maiden (Tanabatatsume) believed to fashion clothing for the gods. Termed Tanabata (a shortened form of Tanabatatsume), this festival became one of the annual events (NENCHŪ

GYŌJI; see also FESTIVALS) observed by the imperial court. Since Tanabata fell close to the time of the BON FESTIVAL for the souls of the dead, its celebration became associated with some of the practices involved in welcoming and seeing off the spirits of one's departed ancestors.

Although the modern celebration of Tanabata varies according to locale, a common feature of this festival is the display of bamboo branches decorated with long narrow strips of colored paper and other small ornaments and talismans. The paper strips are inscribed with wishes and romantic aspirations. The cities of Sendai and Hiratsuka are particularly known for their elaborate celebrations of the Tanabata Festival. Both cities observe Tanabata on 7 August, which is closer to the traditional festival date.

Tanabe 田辺[市]

City in southern Wakayama Prefecture, central Honshū, on Tanabe Bay. Tanabe developed as a port town, military base, and transportation center. Principal industries today are lumber and fishing. Scenic attractions include the gorge Kizetsukyō and the Kikyōiwa, an unusual rock formation. Pop: 69,859.

Tanabe Hajime 田辺元

(1885–1962). Philosopher. Born in Tōkyō, he graduated from the philosophy department of Tōkyō University, and from 1922 he studied phenomenology in Europe, chiefly under the direction of Edmund Husserl (1859–1938). He became professor at Kyōto University in 1927. Tanabe first worked on a philosophical theory of science, influenced by the Neo-Kantian school. He later took a critical stance on German idealism, Marxism, and the philosophical views of NISHIDA KITARŌ and developed his own philosophical system based on the "logic of species" theory (*shu no ronri*). However, his *Zangedō to shite no tetsugaku* (1946, Philosophy as the Way of Atonement) criticized his own previous methods. He moved to a position stressing the TARIKI (salvation through the power of the "other") tenets found in the Jōdo Shin sect of Buddhism. His works are collected in *Tanabe Hajime zenshū* (15 vols, 1963–64). He received the Order of Culture in 1950.

Tanabe Makoto 田辺誠

(1922–). Politician; chairman of the Social Democratic Party of Japan (SDPJ; the former JAPAN SOCIALIST PARTY). Born in Gumma Prefecture. He worked at the prefectural post office from 1941. After World War II Tanabe was a labor activist and won election to the Gumma Prefectural Assembly in 1955. In 1960 he was elected to the national HOUSE OF REPRESENTATIVES. A Christian and a specialist in welfare issues, he is viewed as a moderate within the SDPJ. He is a veteran of the kind of negotiations with other political parties that are necessary to facilitate the smooth operation of parliamentary business. Tanabe served as secretary-general of the Japan Socialist Party at the urging of Chairman ISHIBASHI MASASHI from 1983 to 1986 and succeeded DOI TAKAKO as chairman of the SDPJ in July 1991.

Tanabe Seiko 田辺聖子

(1928–). Novelist. Born in Ōsaka; graduate of Ōsaka Shōin Women's College. Most of Tanabe's stories, set in the Ōsaka area, use Ōsaka dialect. Her novel *Senchimentaru jānī* (1964, Sentimental Journey) won the Akutagawa Prize. She has also written scripts for

television and radio dramas, as well as a novel about the poet YOSANO AKIKO, titled *Chisuji no kurokami* (1972), and *Hanagoromo nuguya matsuwaru* (1987) about the poet SUGITA HISAJO.

Tanabe Seiyaku Co, Ltd 田辺製薬[株]

(Tanabe Seiyaku). Company engaged in the manufacture and sale of pharmaceuticals. It traces its roots back to 1678. While Tanabe is ranked fifth in sales, its export sales ratio is first in the industry. It has wholly owned subsidiaries in the United States, Belgium, and Brazil and joint ventures in Taiwan, Indonesia, France, and Switzerland. In the fiscal year ending March 1991, sales totaled ¥200.2 billion (US $1.5 billion), and the company was capitalized at ¥33.8 billion (US $246.4 million). Headquarters are in Ōsaka.

Tanabe Taichi 田辺太一

(1831–1915). Diplomat who served both the Tokugawa shogunate (1603–1867) and the Meiji government (1868–1912). Also known as Tanabe Yasukazu. The son of a Confucian scholar, Tanabe attended the Shōheikō, the shogunate's Confucian academy. He accompanied several Tokugawa and Meiji diplomatic missions abroad, including the IWAKURA MISSION (1871–73), and was later appointed to the GENRŌIN (Chamber of Elders).

Tanaka Chikao 田中千禾夫

(1905–). Playwright and director. Born in Nagasaki Prefecture; graduate of Keiō University. He studied acting before writing the one-act play *Ofukuro* (1933). Influenced by French existentialism and interested in Catholicism after World War II, he explored such themes as female sexuality and the concept of original sin. In 1934 he married the playwright and novelist TANAKA SUMIE. In 1954 his play *Kyōiku* won the Yomiuri Literary Prize. Other plays include *Kumo no hatate* (1947), *Maria no kubi* (1959), and *Jikan to iu kisha* (1972). Since 1981 he has been a member of the Japan Art Academy.

Tanakadate Aikitsu 田中館愛橘

(1856–1952). Geophysicist. Father of Japanese seismology and geophysics. Born in Iwate Prefecture, he graduated in 1882 from Tōkyō University, where he studied with Thomas C. MENDENHALL. Following study in England and Germany, he became a professor at Tōkyō University. He was a prime mover behind the establishment of what is now the MIZUSAWA ASTROGEODYNAMICS OBSERVATORY, and he received the Order of Culture in 1944. He also had a lifelong interest in the movement to replace the traditional Japanese writing system with roman letters, having devised a system of his own.

Tanaka Fujimaro 田中不二麻呂

(1845–1909). Politician of the Meiji period (1868–1912); promoted progressive educational administrative policies during the 1870s. Tanaka was born in Owari Province (now part of Aichi Prefecture). As a member of the IWAKURA MISSION, which toured the United States and Europe from 1871 to 1873, he carefully observed Western educational systems. After his return home he was appointed vice-minister of education in 1874. He made a second inspection of the US school system from 1876 to 1877, then set out to reform the Japanese school-administration system. He revised the EDUCATION ORDER OF 1872, which he criticized for making the educational system too highly centralized and uniform, and thus paved the way for the enactment of the EDUCATION ORDER OF 1879, which was based on the more decentralized US system. The criticism of the new order as inviting confusion and decadence in education resulted in Tanaka's leaving the Ministry of Education and becoming minister of justice in 1880. He subsequently served in diplomatic and cabinet-level posts.

Tanaka Fuyuji   田中冬二

(1894–1980). Poet. Real name Tanaka Kichinosuke. Born in Fukushima Prefecture; graduate of Rikkyō Middle School in Tōkyō. He contributed poems to SHIKI, the magazine started by the poet HORI TATSUO. Tanaka's poems are reminiscent of HAIKU—being short, concise, and unadorned in style—and reflect the life and landscape of the various Japanese cities he lived in as an employee of the Yasuda Bank. His poems have been translated into English, French, and other languages. Principal collections are *Umi no mieru ishidan* (1930) and *Banshun no hi ni* (1961).

Tanaka Giichi   田中義一

(1864–1929). General, prime minister (1927–29), foreign minister, and president of the RIKKEN SEIYŪKAI political party. Born in the Chōshū domain (now Yamaguchi Prefecture), he attended the Army Academy and the Army War College. During the RUSSO-JAPANESE WAR (1904–05) he served as an aide to KODAMA GENTARŌ, chief of staff of the Manchurian army. In 1906 he drafted a defense plan, which became basic policy. In 1911, now a major general, he became director of the Military Affairs Bureau of the Army Ministry.

In 1923 Tanaka, now a full general, became army minister. When the Seiyūkai invited him to be party president in 1925, he accepted. Tanaka became prime minister in 1927. He served concurrently as foreign minister and minister of colonization. In the MARCH 15TH INCIDENT of 1928 and the APRIL 16TH INCIDENT of 1929, the Tanaka cabinet ordered arrests of members of the Communist Party and other leftist parties.

In foreign policy Tanaka favored maintaining Japan's position in China and expanding Japanese interests in Manchuria (see TŌHŌ KAIGI; TANAKA MEMORANDUM). On three occasions from 1927 to 1928 the Tanaka cabinet sent troops to Shandong (Shangtung). After ZHANG ZUOLIN (Chang Tso-lin) was assassinated by Japanese military officers in Manchuria in 1928, criticism of the Tanaka cabinet increased, especially from the emperor. The cabinet resigned in July 1929.

Tanaka Hidemitsu   田中英光

(1913–49). Novelist. Born in Tōkyō; graduate of Waseda University. Influenced by his brother, a newspaper reporter, he became a communist sympathizer but was subsequently disenchanted by the corrupt leadership of the Communist Party. He participated in the founding of a literary coterie and started writing for its magazine. After graduation he met his lifelong mentor, the novelist DAZAI OSAMU. During the early 1940s he wrote two novels based upon his experience as a rower at the 1932 Los Angeles Olympics: *Orimposu no kajitsu* (1940) and *Tantei sōshu* (1944). After World War II, he joined the Communist Party but again became disenchanted and was eventually expelled. His later years were colored by drugs, alcoholism, and decadence. He committed suicide in 1949 at the grave of Dazai Osamu.

Tanaka Hisashige   田中久重

(1799–1881). Inventor. Also known as Karakuri Giemon. Born in Kurume (now in Fukuoka Prefecture). Even as a child he was known for his cleverness with mechanical devices (*karakuri*). Among his numerous and varied inventions were a pump for extinguishing fires and a "perpetual" clock. In 1854 he entered the service of the Saga domain (now part of Saga Prefecture) and made contributions to the manufacture of cannons and rifles as well as boilers for ships. He was the founder of Tanaka Manufacturing Works, a forerunner of the Tōshiba group.

Tanaka Jirō   田中二郎

(1906–82). Scholar of administrative law. Born in Hyōgo Prefecture. A graduate of Tōkyō University and a professor there from 1941 to 1964, Tanaka served as a Supreme Court justice from 1964 to 1973. He also contributed to the drafts of numerous laws as a member of various committees and deliberative bodies, such as the Chihō Zaimu Kaikei Seido Chōsakai (Board for Investigation of Local Financial Systems). A leading figure among legal scholars, Tanaka published articles during both the pre– and post–World War II eras based on the notion of a liberal state founded upon the rule of law. In *Gyōseihō sōron* (1957), he presents the results of his study of administrative law.

Tanaka Kakuei   田中角栄

(1918–). Politician; prime minister from 1972 to 1974. Born in Niigata Prefecture. As a young man he formed his own construction firm, which prospered during World War II, enabling him after the war to make substantial contributions to the Nihon Shimpotō (Japan Progressive Party), easing his entry into politics. Elected to the House of Representatives in 1947 as a candidate of the MINSHUTŌ (Democratic Party), the following year he joined the newly formed Minshu Jiyūtō (Democratic Liberal Party), a forerunner of the Liberal Democratic Party (LDP; formed in 1955). He served as minister of postal services and communications in the first KISHI NOBUSUKE cabinet and as minister of finance in the second and third IKEDA HAYATO and first SATŌ EISAKU cabinets. He was twice secretary-general of the LDP before becoming party president and prime minister in 1972. Tanaka advocated the "remodeling" of the Japanese islands—that is, a geographical redistribution of Japanese industry (see NIHON RETTŌ KAIZŌ RON)—a program that served only to spin an inflationary rise in land prices. He resigned from the government in December 1974 and was arrested in 1976 in connection with the LOCKHEED SCANDAL. Though Tanaka was sentenced to four years' imprisonment at the first hearing in 1983, he pleaded innocent to all charges and is still in the process of appealing to the higher courts. In 1985 he suffered a stroke and was hospitalized. He retired from politics in 1990.

Tanaka Kikinzoku Kōgyō KK
田中貴金属工業[株]

(Tanaka Kikinzoku Kōgyō). Manufacturer of precious-metal products for use in the electronics and communications industries. Also sells precious-metal ingots. Incorporated in 1918. The company is an authorized melter and assayer on the London Gold Market. Sales for the fiscal year ending March 1990 totaled ¥307.4 billion (US $2.0 billion), and capitalization stood at ¥250.0 million (US $1.6 million). Headquarters are in Tōkyō.

Tanaka Kinuyo   田中絹代

(1909–77). Film actress and director. Born in Yamaguchi Prefecture. She is better known for her work as an actress in a career that began in 1924 and spanned over 50 years. Her best-known films and greatest critical acclaim came from her long association with director MIZOGUCHI KENJI, for whom she worked in *Saikaku ichidai onna* (1952, The Life of Oharu) and UGETSU MONOGATARI (1953, Ugetsu).

Tanaka directed six films in all, beginning with *Koibumi* (1953, Love Letter). She continued to act through the 1970s and was awarded the prize for best actress at the 1975 Berlin International Film Festival for her performance in KUMAI KEI's *Sandakan hachiban shōkan: Bōkyō* (1974; shown abroad as *Sandakan No. 8; Brothel No. 8*).

Tanaka Kōtarō   田中耕太郎

(1890–1974). Legal scholar and second chief justice of the postwar Supreme Court. Born in Kagoshima Prefecture, he graduated from Tōkyō University in 1915. In 1917 he joined the faculty of Tōkyō University, where he taught jurisprudence and commercial law. He was minister of education (1946) in the first YOSHIDA SHIGERU cabinet and a member of the House of Councillors (1947–50). As chief justice of the Supreme Court (1950–60) Tanaka took part in rulings on the TEIGIN INCIDENT and the SUNAGAWA CASE. Politically a conservative, he was a devout Roman Catholic who believed that the antiwar, democratic 1947 constitution embodied what medieval scholastics termed natural law. He served on the International Court of Justice from 1960 to 1970. His writings include *Sekaihō no riron* (3 vols, 1932–34, Theory of World Law) and *Kyōiku kihonhō no riron* (1961, The Theory of the Basic Education Law).

Tanaka Kyūgu   田中丘隅

(1663?–1729). Civil administrator of the Edo period (1600–1868). Born in what is now Tōkyō Prefecture, he was adopted into the family of a village official in the post-station town of Kawasaki (now in Kanagawa Prefecture). He studied under Confucian scholars Narushima Kinkō (1689–1760) and OGYŪ SORAI. In 1721 he published *Minkan seiyō*, a 3-volume treatise on taxation, flood control, and other aspects of civil administration. In 1723 he was commissioned by the shōgun TOKUGAWA YOSHIMUNE to supervise river control and irrigation on the rivers Arakawa and Tamagawa. Later he completed the dikes of the river Sakawagawa. For his services he was made an intendant (DAIKAN), or administrator, over Tokugawa land valued at 30,000 KOKU, a great honor for a commoner.

Tanaka Memorandum
田中メモランダム

(Tanaka Memorandamu). A memorandum, dated 25 July 1927, supposedly presented to Emperor SHŌWA (Hirohito) by Prime Minister TANAKA GIICHI following the Far Eastern Conference (TŌHŌ KAIGI); it contained a detailed plan for the conquest of Manchuria and Mongolia. Its text was published in 1929 in the Nanjing (Nanking) Chinese-language monthly review *Shishi yuebao* (Shih-shih

Tanaka Giichi This general served as prime minister from 1927 to 1929, pursuing an aggressive policy toward China before he was forced to resign as a result of the assassination of the Chinese warlord Zhang Zuolin.

Tanaka Kinuyo During a career lasting more than half a century, this popular actress worked with most of Japan's leading directors and also directed six films of her own.

Tanaka Kōtarō A legal scholar and second chief justice of the postwar Supreme Court, Tanaka also served on the International Court of Justice.

Tanaka Shōzō
Although few listened at the time, this pioneer environmentalist and reformer expounded the need for man to respect the natural environment.

Taneda Santōka
Ordained a Buddhist priest in 1925, Taneda spent the rest of his life as a wandering mendicant, composing the *haiku* poetry for which he is remembered.

yüeh-pao) and in 1931 in the Shanghai English-language *China Critic.* The latter version became the basis for anti-Japanese pamphlets circulated in China (by the Comintern) and in the United States, while the former was translated into Japanese, reportedly by the Japan Communist Party. The Japanese government officially denied the authenticity of the memorandum. Nevertheless, it had considerable international impact, and as Japanese armies occupied Manchuria in 1931 and later advanced into China, the memorandum gained credibility among the Western powers. The issue of the supposed memorandum, for which no corroborative archival material has ever been found, was taken up inconclusively at the International Military Tribunal for the Far East following World War II.

Tanaka Michitarō　田中美知太郎

(1902–85). Philosopher. Born in Niigata Prefecture. Tanaka graduated from Kyōto University, where he taught from 1950 to 1965. Founder of the Classical Society of Japan (Nihon Seiyō Koten Gakkai), he did translations and philological-historical research in classical Greek philosophy centered on Plato. His activities extended to the philosophy of life, cultural criticism, and commentary on politics. His works include *Rogosu to idea* (1947) and *Zen to hitsuzen to no aida ni* (1952). In 1978 he received the Order of Culture.

Tanaka Mitsuaki　田中光顕

(1843–1939). Government official of the Meiji period (1868–1912). Born in the Tosa domain (now Kōchi Prefecture). After the Meiji Restoration of 1868, he served the new government in various posts, including positions as head of the Audit Bureau, chief of the Tōkyō Metropolitan Police, and principal of the Peers' School. In 1898 Tanaka became imperial household minister. As a confidant of Emperor Meiji he exercised great authority in the palace.

Tanaka Ōdō　田中王堂

(1867–1932). Popular essayist for CHŪŌ KŌRON and other journals during the late Meiji period (1868–1912) and the Taishō period (1912–26); an unusual Japanese thinker who supported individualism, liberalism, and democracy. Real name Tanaka Kiichi. Tanaka was born in the village of Nakatome (now part of the city of Tokorozawa) in Saitama Prefecture and attended missionary schools in Tōkyō and Kyōto. He studied in the United States at the College of the Bible (now Lexington Theological Seminary) and the University of Chicago, where he studied with the four men who formed the Chicago school of pragmatism: James H. Tufts, George Herbert Mead, James R. Angell, and John Dewey, whose ideas are reflected in Tanaka's later writings.

As a Japanese writer Tanaka addressed different issues from those that preoccupied his American teachers. Rising to prominence in the journalistic boom that followed the RUSSO-JAPANESE WAR (1904–05), he attacked government censorship and paternalism, repressive education, and the patriarchal family system. He also articulated the social function and responsibilities of the essayist (*hyōronka*) in forming public opinion and public policy. During the 1910s, in harmony with the rising TAISHŌ DEMOCRACY movement, he attempted to reinterpret the MEIJI

RESTORATION as a commitment to cosmopolitanism and representative government; to develop a conception of national and cultural autonomy that would advance democracy and respect for the autonomy of other nations; and to promote democratic reforms—such as universal suffrage—that would ensure a more representative relationship between government and people.

During the 1920s Tanaka fell out of step with new trends in Japanese intellectual life, Marxism and Neo-Kantian culturalism, and in doing so lost his prestige as an essayist and his reading audience. Nevertheless, his influence remained strong among a small group of his former students at Waseda University, where he taught philosophy. Tanaka's leading publications were the critical biographical studies *Ninomiya Sontoku* (1911) and *Fukuzawa Yukichi* (1915) and essay anthologies such as *Shosai yori gaitō ni* (1911, From the Study to the Streets) and *Tettei kojin shugi* (1918, Radical Individualism).

Tanaka Shōsuke　田中勝助

(fl early 17th century; Western name, Don Francisco de Velasco). Kyōto merchant thought to have been the first Japanese to cross the Pacific. In 1610, leading about 20 Japanese, he accompanied Don Rodrigo VIVERO Y VELASCO, who had been shipwrecked in Japan the previous year, to New Spain (Mexico). Bearing a personal message and gifts from the shōgun TOKUGAWA IEYASU, Tanaka hoped to establish Japanese trade with Mexico. Unsuccessful, he returned to Japan in 1611 with Sebastian VISCAINO, the Spanish envoy sent to thank the shogunate formally for its hospitality to Don Rodrigo.

Tanaka Shōzō　田中正造

(1841–1913). Pioneer environmentalist and reformer who campaigned on behalf of the peasants against political oppression and industrial pollution. Born in what is now Tochigi Prefecture. He became a leader of the FREEDOM AND PEOPLE'S RIGHTS MOVEMENT in Tochigi and a moving spirit in launching its first liberal newspaper, the *Tochigi shimbun.*

Industry versus Agriculture—After the Meiji Constitution was promulgated in 1889, Tanaka was elected to the first Diet in 1890. He soon became involved in fighting the pollution of the Kantō Plain by the copper mine at Ashio, in the mountains northeast of Tōkyō (see ASHIO COPPER MINE INCIDENT). Large quantities of rock bearing waste copper were dumped into the river Watarasegawa, contaminating the stream as it flowed across the farmlands below, poisoning crops, and affecting the livelihood of thousands of households.

Tanaka called on the government to order the mine's closure, but the government took little notice. Tanaka refused to withdraw his demand, insisting on two principles: first, that agriculture is the basis of a nation's life and must take priority over industry, and second, that in no circumstances must a people be sacrificed to the demands of "industrial progress." In 1897 the government imposed pollution-control regulations on the mine, but these measures proved ineffective. In 1901 Tanaka resigned from the Diet in disgust at its indifference to his appeals. Two months later, in a final attempt to rouse the nation's conscience, he tried to thrust a petition into the emperor's state carriage when the latter was on his way back from opening the Diet. Tanaka was arrested but soon released.

Fight for a Village—Though this incident ended his career on the national stage, Tanaka persisted in his fight on behalf of the peasants. In 1903 a scheme for the containment of the floodwaters of the Watarasegawa was drawn up by the government, but it required the creation of a reservoir that would result in the destruction of the village community of Yanaka. Tanaka went to live in Yanaka and led the villagers in their resistance to this scheme, but they were unsuccessful in preventing the demolition of the village in 1907.

During the years in Yanaka his outlook underwent a remarkable change. He came to see himself as a fellow worker with the peasants, from whom he had as much to learn about simplicity and quiet endurance as he had to give by way of encouragement and wider vision. With a few of the peasants, Tanaka stayed on in Yanaka in makeshift huts. The last great effort of his life was to expound the need for man to respect the natural environment if he was to survive.

Tanaka's long career of protest was rooted in traditional values whose relevance was scarcely perceived during his lifetime. Today, however, he is seen as the prophet of an age when the ideal harmony between man and nature, as well as between man and man, will win permanent acceptance.

Tanaka Sumie　田中澄江

(1908–). Playwright and novelist. Maiden name Tsujimura Sumie. Born in Tōkyō; graduate of Tōkyō Women's Higher Normal School (now Ochanomizu Women's University). In 1934 she married playwright TANAKA CHIKAO. Her plays, which examine women's psychology, include *Tsuzumi no onna* (1958, The Woman with the Drum), a retelling of an Edo-period (1600–1868) tragedy; *Garashia Hosokawa fujin* (1959), based upon the life of the 16th-century Christian woman HOSOKAWA GRACIA; and *Genshi, josei wa taiyō de atta* (1971, In the Beginning, Woman Was the Sun), recounting the struggles of the feminist HIRATSUKA RAICHŌ. Some of her short stories are collected in *Kakitsubata gunraku* (1973, A Clump of Irises).

Tanaka Yoshio　田中芳男

(1838–1916). Natural history scholar, known for developing the variety of loquat called the Tanaka *biwa.* Born in Iida in present-day Nagano Prefecture, he was a student of ITŌ KEISUKE. He worked for the government after the Meiji Restoration (1868), establishing museums and writing textbooks for children. The Tanaka *biwa* is an improved version of a superior type of Japanese loquat he obtained in Nagasaki. He wrote *Yūyō shokubutsu zusetsu* (1891), a botanical encyclopedia in seven volumes containing illustrations and descriptions of Japanese flora that are of practical use.

Tanaka Yutaka　田中豊

(1888–1964). Civil engineer and authority on bridge engineering and design in Japan. Born in Nagano Prefecture, he graduated from Tōkyō University and served as a professor there. After the TŌKYŌ EARTHQUAKE OF 1923, he directed the design and construction of numerous bridges in the Tōkyō area.

Tanashi　田無[市]

City in central Tōkyō Prefecture. It is principally a residential area, although many industrial plants have been constructed in recent years. There are several public-housing complexes. Pop: 75,144.

tandai 探題

(shogunal deputies). Officials appointed in strategic areas by the Kamakura (1192–1333) and Muromachi (1338–1573) shogunates to oversee political, military, and judicial affairs. Among those appointed by the Kamakura shogunate were the ROKUHARA TANDAI in Kyōto and the Chinzei *tandai* in Kyūshū. The Muromachi shogunate set up the Ōshū *tandai* and the Ushū *tandai* in northwestern Honshū and the Kyūshū *tandai* in Kyūshū.

The term *tandai* originally referred to high-ranking priests who examined novices on the Buddhist scriptures. In the world of WAKA it was used to refer to the extemporaneous composition of a poem on a theme drawn by lot at literary gatherings.

Taneda Santōka 種田山頭火

(1882–1940). HAIKU poet. Born in Yamaguchi Prefecture; studied at Waseda University. From 1904 to 1925 he worked at various jobs in Kumamoto and Tōkyō. In 1925, having divorced his wife, he became a Buddhist monk of the Sōtō sect, but in 1926 he left the temple and became a mendicant priest. For most of the remainder of his life he was on the road, begging, visiting his friends, composing haiku, and writing travel diaries. In 1936 he went as far as Sendai in northeastern Japan on a trip reminiscent of the haiku poet BASHŌ's famous journey north in 1689.

He is remembered for his anthology containing 701 free-verse haiku, *Sōmokutō* (1940, Monument of Grass and Trees), which he edited from over 9,000 poems composed between 1925 and 1940, and *Gochū nikki*, a five-volume diary that was published posthumously. His best haiku are simple and reflect his love of drink and travel and his appreciation of nature.

Tanegashima 種子島

Island approximately 40 km (25 mi) south of the Ōsumi Peninsula, Kagoshima Prefecture, southern Kyūshū; part of Kagoshima Prefecture. Nishinoomote is the island's only city. Subtropical plants flourish on the coasts. The chief agricultural activities are the cultivation of sweet potatoes and sugarcane and stock raising. The first musket was introduced to Japan by a Portuguese whose ship was stranded on Tanegashima in 1543. A space center for launching rockets and satellites is located on the cape Takezaki. Area: 446 sq km (172 sq mi).

Tanegashima Tokitaka 種子島時尭

(1528–79). Lord of Tanegashima, an island south of Kyūshū where the first Portuguese traders arrived in 1543. He obtained the harquebus, a portable Western shoulder gun; firearms modeled after it became known as *tanegashima*. By 1549 Tokitaka received inquiries about these guns from the MUROMACHI SHOGUNATE; by the 1570s, various *daimyō* and warlike monastic institutions had organized units of musketeers (*teppō ashigaru*) and revolutionized Japanese military tactics. See also FIREARMS, INTRODUCTION OF.

Tane maku hito 種蒔く人

(The Sowers). Small but influential leftist literary monthly that was published from February 1921 to August 1923 and marked the beginning of the PROLETARIAN LITERATURE MOVEMENT. The first three issues were printed in Tsuchizaki in northern Akita Prefecture, of which five of the magazine's six original members, including founder Komaki Ōmi (1894–1978) and Kaneko Yōbun (1894–

Tange Kenzō For the 1964 Tōkyō Olympic Games the architect designed two dynamically paired structures known as the Yoyogi National Stadium, a noted example of steel suspension roofing.

1985), were natives. After six months it shifted to Tōkyō. New members were added, including leftist critics HIRABAYASHI HATSUNOSUKE and AONO SUEKICHI and journalist HASEGAWA NYOZEKAN. The journal was antiwar, supported the Russian Revolution, and called for the liberation of all oppressed peoples. It moved steadily leftward until the TŌKYŌ EARTHQUAKE OF 1923, and the increasing clampdown on all leftist activities forced its closure. As a parting shot it published a final special issue in January 1924 detailing atrocities committed against leftists by the police and military in the aftermath of the earthquake.

Tange Kenzō 丹下健三

(1913–). Internationally recognized architect and city planner. Born in Imabari, Ehime Prefecture; graduated from Tōkyō University. Tange is known for boldly shaped buildings and urban complexes showing that functionalism does not demand a rigidly geometric style and for his conscious blending of modern expression with traditional Japanese aesthetics. He has brought a number of technological innovations to architecture, notably the "shell structure."

Tange established himself as a major architect early in his career with an impressive series of public buildings, including the Shizuoka Assembly Hall (1953), the Hiroshima Peace Memorial Hall and Memorial Museum (1955), the Tōkyō Metropolitan Government Offices (1957), and the Kagawa Prefectural Government Offices (1958). Examples of his extremely dramatic work in the 1960s include the Yoyogi National Stadium designed for the Tōkyō Olympic Games (1964), the Yamanashi Press and Broadcasting Center (1966), and the theme pavilion for Expo '70 in Ōsaka. Later work included the Hanae Mori Building (1978), the Turkish embassy in Tōkyō (1979), and the massive new TŌKYŌ METROPOLITAN GOVERNMENT OFFICES (1991). Tange's experiments in urban planning produced his ambitious Tōkyō Plan of 1960. He also helped in the reconstruction of the city of Skopje, Yugoslavia (1965), after its destruction by earthquake.

Tanggu (Tangku) Truce 塘沽停戦協定

(Tankū Teisen Kyōtei). An armistice between the Japanese GUANDONG (KWANTUNG) ARMY and Chinese officials; concluded on 31 May 1933 at Tanggu, a coastal city near Tianjin (Tientsin). The truce designated the Great Wall as the boundary between Chinese and Japanese forces in Hebei (Hopeh) Province and established a demilitarized zone north and east of the Tianjin-Beiping

(Peiping; now Beijing or Peking) area up to the Great Wall. In March 1933 the Guandong Army annexed Rehe (Jehol) Province and moved south into Hebei but withdrew as far as the Great Wall after the truce was negotiated. Within two years the Guandong Army again exerted pressure southward, and the movement of Chinese troops into the demilitarized zone in response to the MARCO POLO BRIDGE INCIDENT of 7 July 1937 provided one pretext for the SINO-JAPANESE WAR OF 1937–1945.

Tango 丹後[町]

Town in northern Kyōto Prefecture, central Honshū. Main industries are agriculture and fishing, although with a decline in the catch, there has been a major effort to introduce fish farming. Textiles, most notably Tango *chirimen* (silk crepe), are also an important local product. The beautiful peninsular coastline attracts many sightseers. Pop: 8,042.

Tango Mountains 丹後山地

(Tango Sanchi). Mountain range forming the border between Kyōto and Hyōgo prefectures, west central Honshū. ŌEYAMA (833 m; 2,733 ft) is the highest peak. Composed primarily of granite, it is located between the rivers Maruyamagawa and Yuragawa and is known for its Tango beef cattle.

Tango Peninsula 丹後半島

(Tango Hantō). Peninsula on the western side of Wakasa Bay in northwestern Kyōto Prefecture, central Honshū. Coastal fishing and production of textiles, particularly a type of silk crepe called Tango *chirimen*, are the principal industries here. The scenic pine-covered sandbar AMANOHASHIDATE is located in the southeastern part of the peninsula.

Tani Bunchō 谷文晁

(1763–1840). Painter who introduced BUNJINGA (literati painting) to Edo (now Tōkyō); author of and contributor to many illustrated books. Born Tani Masayasu of a *samurai* family in Edo, the son of the poet Tani Rokkoku (1729–1809). Bunchō first studied the KANŌ SCHOOL style under Katō Bunrei (1706–82), then worked with the Chinese academic-style painter Kitayama Kangan (1767–1801), whose repertoire included Western-influenced subjects. Bunchō also received instruction in the *bunjinga* tradition and BIRD-AND-FLOWER PAINTING. He also studied other styles of Japanese painting, including those of the TOSA SCHOOL, UKIYO-E, and the MARUYAMA-SHIJŌ SCHOOL. His career was

Taniguchi Yoshirō This architect, whose Imperial Theater (1966) in Tōkyō is pictured here, is known for buildings that incorporate traditional motifs into modern design.

sponsored by MATSUDAIRA SADANOBU, regent to the shōgun TOKUGAWA IENARI. His reputation as a leading artist of the Edo period (1600–1868) brought him a great number of pupils, including WATANABE KAZAN, TANOMURA CHIKUDEN, and TSUBAKI CHINZAN.

In the late 18th century Bunchō achieved a synthesis of the Northern and Southern schools of Chinese landscape painting (see NANGA), distinct from the lyricism of his earlier landscapes. His 19th-century style is characterized by the use of heavy, wet inks in more spontaneously constructed compositions.

Tanigawadake 谷川岳
Mountain on the border between Gumma and Niigata prefectures, central Honshū. The Niigata side has gentle slopes but the Gumma side forms a precipitous wall of rocks. Because of the easy access by public transportation from the Tōkyō area it attracts many climbers, but its precipices and changeable weather have claimed many lives. It is part of Jōshin'etsu Kōgen National Park. Height: 1,963 m (6,440 ft).

Tanigawa Kotosuga 谷川士清
(1709–76). Classical scholar of the mid-Edo period (1600–1868). Born in Ise (now Mie

Tanizaki Jun'ichirō The author in his study. In his writing, Tanizaki explored the fear, fascination, and potential for spirituality that beautiful women held for him.

Prefecture) to a family of physicians, he went to Kyōto to study medicine and Shintō. He studied KOKUGAKU (National Learning), the Shintō-oriented school of classical learning, and corresponded with MOTOORI NORINAGA. He wrote *Nihon shoki tsūshō* (1748, Commentary on the *Nihon shoki*) and also compiled a dictionary of the Japanese language, WAKUN NO SHIORI (A Guide to Japanese).

Taniguchi Masaharu 谷口雅春
(1893–1985). Religious leader and founder of SEICHŌ NO IE. Born in Hyōgo Prefecture. From 1917 to 1922 he was an adherent of ŌMOTO. In 1929, claiming to have received revelations, he began writing profusely on the subject of religion. His organization began in 1930 with the first publication of his magazine *Seichō no ie.* In 1934 he began popularizing his doctrines through writings and lectures. After World War II, he continued his activities as leader of Seichō no Ie.

Taniguchi Yoshirō 谷口吉郎
(1904–79). Architect. Born in the city of Kanazawa, Ishikawa Prefecture. Taniguchi graduated from Tōkyō University and went on to a teaching career at the Tōkyō Institute of Technology. His noted works include the Keiō University Hiyoshi Dormitory (1938), Tōson Memorial Hall (1948), Shiga House (1955), Hotel Ōkura (1962), the Tōkyō National Museum of Modern Art (1969), and the Yoshikawa Eiji Memorial Hall (1977). As head of the MEIJI MURA, an open-air museum in Inuyama near the city of Nagoya, he played a key role in the preservation of Meiji-period (1868–1912) architecture. He was awarded the Order of Culture in 1973.

Tani Jichū 谷時中
(1598–1649). Confucian scholar of the early Edo period (1600–1868); associated with NANGAKUHA, a branch of Zhu Xi (Chu Hsi) Confucianism (see SHUSHIGAKU) in the Tosa domain (now Kōchi Prefecture). As a youth Jichū entered a local Buddhist temple. He later studied Confucianism with Minamimura Baiken (dates unknown), founder of the Nangakuha, and abandoned Buddhist orders in order to teach. Jichū's disciples included NONAKA KENZAN and YAMAZAKI ANSAI.

Tani Kanjō 谷干城
(1837–1911). General and politician. Also known as Tani Tateki. Born in the Tosa domain (now Kōchi Prefecture). He joined the new Meiji government after the MEIJI RESTORATION of 1868 and occupied various important army posts, distinguishing himself as the commander of the defense of Kumamoto Castle during the SATSUMA REBELLION of 1877. Tani also served as head of the Army Academy. After he retired from active duty in 1881, he and another military man, Torio Koyata (1847–1905), founded the Chūseitō, a conservative political group. In 1885 he joined the first ITŌ HIROBUMI cabinet as minister of agriculture and commerce but resigned in objection to what he considered the insufficiently forceful demands of Foreign Minister INOUE KAORU for revision of the socalled Unequal Treaties with Western nations. See UNEQUAL TREATIES, REVISION OF.

Tanikawa Shuntarō 谷川俊太郎
(1931–). Poet. Born in Tōkyō; son of the philosopher Tanikawa Tetsuzō (1895–1989). He made his debut with *Nijūoku kōnen no kodoku* (1952), a collection of poems on the theme of man's universal insignificance and

isolation. Beginning in 1953, Tanikawa contributed to the poetry journal *Kai,* which was published by a circle of poets that included ŌOKA MAKOTO and which did much to foster a new spirit in postwar lyric poetry. Since then he has explored various poetic forms in an attempt to bring new life to the sonority and rhythms of the Japanese language. Among his volumes of poetry are *Rokujūni no sonetto* (1953), *Rakushu kyūjūkyū* (1964), and *Kotoba-asobi uta* (1972).

Tanimoto Tomeri 谷本富
(1867–1946). Educator. Born in the Takamatsu domain (now part of Kagawa Prefecture), he studied at Tōkyō University. At first an advocate of the educational theories of German educator Johann F. Herbart (1776–1841), he later supported education for the benefit of the state. Then, during the liberal Taishō period (1912–26), he became a leader of the progressive education movement (SHIN KYŌIKU UNDŌ) in Japan.

Tanizaki Jun'ichirō 谷崎潤一郎
(1886–1965). Author. Tanizaki made his literary debut in 1910 as an adherent of the romantic movement in Japanese literature, which had emerged in opposition to Japanese naturalism, then at the height of its influence. In his later writings he went on to explore his own sexual conflicts and sought to discover how man could wrest spiritual salvation from the baser struggles of the flesh. The Great Tōkyō Earthquake of 1923 marked an important turning point in Tanizaki's career. At that time, he moved from the cosmopolitan atmosphere of Tōkyō to the more traditional Kansai (Kyōto-Ōsaka-Kōbe) area. Inspired by this intimate and intense contact with a pure form of Japanese culture, he forced his imagination to new heights of richness and vigor.

During World War II, Tanizaki delved into his own creative powers, turning toward wholly fabricated tales, seeking to discover the essential truths of literature through imaginary works, not in current events. In his masterful storytelling and loving appreciation of traditional Japanese concepts of beauty, he carried on the classical literary tradition of the Heian period (794–1185). In work after work, he describes the humiliations, the pitifully small victories, and the persistent desires that drive his male characters to ignominy because of their yearning for women.

Tanizaki was born in the Nihombashi district of Tōkyō, which, in the first half of the Meiji period (1868–1912), represented a unique mix of the old traditions of the Edo period (1600–1868) and the new influences of the West. He possessed an urbanite's sophistication in his frankly sensual approach to life and required more than the bare, inelegant "true-to-life" aesthetic of the naturalists. In his short story "Shisei" (1910; tr "The Tattooer," 1963) a tattoo artist inscribes a gigantic spider, symbolic of evil, upon the flesh of a beautiful young woman. Suddenly her beauty seems to take on a compelling, demonic power; masochism is seen to be an inescapable component of erotic yearnings. This theme is repeated in most of Tanizaki's other early short stories, including "Kirin" (1910), "Shōnen" (1910), "Hōkan" (1911), and "Akuma" (1912). His Taishō-period (1912–26) works "Shindō" (1916) and "Oni no men" (1916) reflect autobiographical tendencies.

Both Tanizaki's first marriage in 1915 and the so-called Odawara episode—a triangular relationship involving Tanizaki, his wife Chiyoko, and the writer SATŌ HARUO—had great psychological effects upon him. In several works, including the play *Aisureba koso* (1921, If Indeed One Loves) and the novel *Kami to hito no aida* (1924, Between Men and the Gods), Tanizaki seems to believe that complete happiness can be achieved only out of the anguish and guilt that result from the struggle of two men for the love of one woman. In *Chijin no ai* (1924–25, A Fool's Love) Tanizaki succeeded in setting this theme against the background of the rapid modernization of Taishō society.

Two transitional works followed. The novel *Manji* (1928–30) shows the new influence of the Kansai area as Tanizaki, inspired by the feminine charms of the Kansai dialect, wrote about lesbianism. *Tade kuu mushi* (1928–29; tr *Some Prefer Nettles*, 1955) shows how the superficial effects of Tōkyō culture were effaced by stronger, more traditional strains. Tanizaki's return to classical literature and the traditional storytelling techniques that had developed since the Heian period began with *Yoshinokuzu* (1931, The Arrowroot of Yoshino), a fine study of maternal love.

During his second marriage, to Furukawa Tomiko, Tanizaki became involved with a married woman, Morita Matsuko. The effects of his relationship with Matsuko, who eventually became his third (and last) wife, figured in many of his later works. "Mōmoku monogatari" (1931; tr "A Blind Man's Tale," 1963), "Ashikari" (1932; tr "Ashikari," 1936), *Shunkinshō* (1933; tr *A Portrait of Shunkin*, 1965), and "Kikigakishō" (1935) were Tanizaki's chief works during this period. These are the stories of men who find their ultimate happiness in absolute devotion to women who are either haughty or pure and unapproachable. The male protagonists all cower in fear before these women, and, although they experience countless humiliations, the men do not seem to be crushed spiritually. Instead their subjugation seems to help them transcend their own sorry state, elevating them to an undefiled, almost religious realm of existence.

In 1939 Tanizaki took up the formidable task of rendering the entire *Genji monogatari* (TALE OF GENJI) into modern Japanese. The novel SASAMEYUKI (tr *The Makioka Sisters*, 1957), which he started writing in 1942, was probably prompted by the affinity he felt with the splendid but sorrowing court ladies in the *Genji monogatari.* For the background material of *Sasameyuki*, Tanizaki turned to his own family and that of Matsuko. His novel is an elegy to a bygone era, an exaltation of "beauty in ruin," as depicted in the decline of the once proud and prosperous family. The serialization of *Sasameyuki* began in 1943 but was halted during World War II. Tanizaki completed the novel in 1948.

Shōshō Shigemoto no haha (1949–50; partial tr "The Mother of Captain Shigemoto," 1956) represents another aspect in Tanizaki's treatment of the femme fatale. It is a brilliant culmination of other works that deal with the theme of love between mother and son. The concluding scene, in which mother and son are reunited, is one of the most beautiful in modern Japanese literature. At the same time, he introduced another theme—the problem of sexuality in old age—that was further developed in *Kagi* (1956; tr *The Key*, 1961), a lurid psychological study that chronicles the sexual struggle of an aging professor and his wife. In an

attempt to stimulate his flagging appetite for sex, the protagonist arranges for his wife to commit adultery. By falling in love with her paramour she achieves dominance over her husband, who suffers intense sexual frustration and collapses with a stroke. In his next work, "Yume no ukihashi" (1959; tr "The Bridge of Dreams," 1963), Tanizaki returns to the themes of the sublimated sexual attraction of son for mother and the search for redemption through sexuality. Nevertheless, it was only with one of his last novels, *Fūten rōjin nikki* (1961–62; tr *Diary of a Mad Old Man*, 1965), that Tanizaki combined the themes of the femme fatale and the mother figure to bring his protagonist toward a resolution that allows him a final, troubled salvation.

tanka 短歌

(literally, "short poem"). A 31-syllable poem consisting of five lines in the pattern 5–7–5–7–7; the dominant form in classical Japanese poetry (WAKA) from the 7th century to the present. In the oldest anthology of native poetry, the 8th-century MAN'YŌSHŪ, the term *tanka* is used to distinguish the short 31-syllable poem from the "long poem" (CHŌKA or *nagauta*), a form consisting of an indefinite number of pairs of 5- and 7-syllable lines, with an extra line of 7 syllables at the end. Following the virtual disappearance of the *chōka* and other less important genres by the end of the 8th century, the *tanka* became essentially the only form of sophisticated Japanese vernacular poetry and retained its dominance for 1,200 years. For this reason, *tanka* came to be synonymous with *waka* ("Japanese poetry" as distinguished from *kanshi*, "Chinese verse"). Since about 1900, *tanka* has replaced *waka* as the preferred generic term for poetry in the 31-syllable form. Poets of the 31-syllable form active prior to the Meiji period (1868–1912) are, in this encyclopedia, called "*waka* poets," whereas those active since then are called "*tanka* poets."

Tankai 湛海

(1629–1716). Buddhist monk and sculptor of the early Edo period (1600–1868). Also called Hōzan Tankai. At age 17 he became a priest of the SHINGON SECT and left his home in Ise Province (now part of Mie Prefecture) to practice austerities at various mountain temples. He lived for several years in a cave on the mountain IKOMAYAMA near Nara before founding the temple Hōzanji in Nara in 1678. He is best known for his statues of Fudō Myōō (Skt: Acalanātha), which are preserved in the temples Hōzanji, HŌRYŪJI, and TŌSHŌDAIJI. See also MYŌŌ.

Tankei 湛慶

(1173–1256). Sculptor of Buddhist images in the Kamakura period (1185–1333). A member of the KEI SCHOOL of sculpture, he was the eldest son and principal pupil of UNKEI; his grandfather was the sculptor KŌKEI. One of the most distinguished sculptors of the period, Tankei assisted in the restoration of the temples Tōdaiji and Kōfukuji and received the honorary Buddhist titles *hokkyō* (1194), *hōgen* (1208), and *hōin* (1213). Among his best-known works are the Senju Kannon (Skt: Sahasrabhujā; 1254) in the temple Rengeōin in Kyōto and the figures of Bishamonten (Skt: Vaiśravaṇa) and two attendants in the temple Sekkeiji in Kōchi Prefecture. They are noted for their understated and refined realism.

Tannishō 歎異抄

(Lamenting the Deviations). Religious treatise of the 13th century compiled from the basic ideas of SHINRAN, founder of the JŌDO SHIN SECT of Buddhism, by his disciple Yuien. The text purports to make explicit the true teachings of PURE LAND BUDDHISM in order to settle doctrinal disputes that had arisen among Shinran's followers; hence the title. Its sayings and insights concern AMIDA's Primal Vow as well as the legalistic interpretations of faith and other related issues. Before its popularization by the philosopher KIYOZAWA MANSHI (1863–1903), the *Tannishō* was largely unknown even to followers of the Jōdo Shin sect. Today it is one of the most widely read of Japanese Buddhist classics.

Tanno Setsu 丹野セツ

(1902–87). Labor activist and social reformer. Born in Fukushima Prefecture. In 1921 she went to Tōkyō, where she joined the socialist women's group SEKIRANKAI and was involved in the 1923 KAMEIDO INCIDENT. In 1924 she married fellow labor activist WATANABE MASANOSUKE. The next year they helped form the leftist labor group Hyōgikai (Council of Japanese Labor Unions), a radical offshoot of SŌDŌMEI. Tanno joined the outlawed JAPAN COMMUNIST PARTY in 1926 and became the first head of its women's section. She was arrested in the MARCH 15TH INCIDENT of 1928, and later that year her husband committed suicide while fleeing from police in Taiwan. She was imprisoned from 1932 to 1938 for anderground activities. After World War II, she turned her attention to health-care reforms and hospital administration.

ta no kami 田の神

(god of the paddies). Shintō god who protects rice plants and brings about abundant rice crops. Also known as *sakugami* and *tsukurigami*. Festivals to this god are often observed in conjunction with the various stages of rice cultivation. These include the major festivals "welcoming of the god of the fields" (*kamimukae*) just prior to spring planting; "the festival of the water gates" (*minakuchi matsuri*), held on the day when seed rice is sown in the rice plant nurseries; the festival of the first rice planting (*saori*); the festival held on the final day of planting seedlings in the paddies (*sanaburi*); and many harvest festivals. It is believed that the god of the paddies does not dwell in the human world but descends at times of festivals (*kyoraishin*). Old legends tell that the god of the mountain (YAMA NO KAMI) comes down to the villages in the spring in the form of the god of the paddies to protect the growth of the rice and returns to his perma-

tanuki The *tanuki*, which often plays an amusing role in Japanese folklore, resembles the North American raccoon in appearance.

taranoki
1 Young shoots of the Japanese angelica tree are collected or cultivated as early spring vegetables.
2 Clusters of *taranoki* flowers bloom in August. Each flower has five petals and bears a round black fruit.

nent abode after the fall harvest, once again becoming the god of the mountain.

Tanomura Chikuden　田能村竹田

(1777–1835). Painter in the Chinese manner ranked in Japan among the leading *nanga* (see BUNJINGA) artists. Born in the small castle town of Taketa in Bungo Province (now Ōita Prefecture) in Kyūshū. He served briefly in his inherited role as domain physician and later was appointed to a commission that was to write a gazetteer of the domain for the shogunate. Although he maintained his home in Taketa, Chikuden continually traveled to various parts of Japan, visiting such artists and scholars as RAI SAN'YŌ (1781–1832), AOKI MOKUBEI (1767–1833), URAGAMI GYOKUDŌ (1745–1820), and OKADA BEISANJIN (1744–1820). On one of these extended journeys he became ill and died in a small village near Ōsaka.

Chikuden developed his own style based on his studies of Chinese painting of the Ming (1368–1644) and Qing (Ch'ing; 1644–1912) dynasties. His paintings, with their compositions carefully built with layers of delicate color and fine brushwork, possess a close relationship to the literati painting of China.

Tanomura Chokunyū　田能村直入

(1814–1907). Literati painter. Born in Bungo Province (now Ōita Prefecture) in Kyūshū. At age eight he began studying literati painting (BUNJINGA) with TANOMURA CHIKUDEN, who adopted him two years later. He was active in Kyūshū painting circles until 1868, when he established himself in Kyōto. The Kyōto Prefectural Painting School (Kyōto Fu Gagakkō), Japan's first painting school, opened in 1880, largely through his efforts. Tanomura served as a juror for the Domestic Expositions (Naikoku Kangyō Hakurankai) from their inception in 1877 and was instrumental in founding the Japan Literati Painting Association (Nihon Nanga Kyōkai) in 1897. See also NIHONGA.

tansen and tammai　段銭と段米

(*tansen to tammai;* acreage coin and acreage rice). Land tax levied on peasant cultivators by the imperial court, shogunate, military governors, and sometimes temples and shrines to cover the cost of special projects or important ceremonies during the Kamakura (1185–1333) and Muromachi (1333–1568) periods. It was levied in addition to the annual land tax (NENGU). The terms *tansen* and *tammai* derive from the practice of levying a certain amount of rice (*mai*) or an equivalent amount of money (*sen*) per *tan* (1 *tan* = about 0.10 hectare or 0.25 acre) of land. It could be levied on a national or provincial basis and was collected by commissioners (*tansen bugyō*) dispatched from a central office in Kyōto. Military governors (SHUGO) were at first allowed to levy *tansen* only to cover personal expenses, but

by the 15th century they were able to exact it without restriction. In the 16th century such *daimyō* as the HŌJŌ FAMILY of Odawara (now part of Kanagawa Prefecture) levied it regularly. See also MUNABETSUSEN.

Tan Taigi　炭太祇

(1709–71). HAIKU poet; one of the forerunners of the late 18th-century haiku revival. Born in Edo (now Tōkyō). His early training was in the Edoza school of haiku established by TAKARAI KIKAKU. In 1751 he moved to Kyōto and became a priest in the temple Daitokuji. He later established himself in the Shimabara pleasure quarter in the capacity of haiku master and mingled with its courtesans and their wealthy merchant clients. It was here that he met the haiku poet BUSON, whose close friendship stimulated his finest haiku, written in his final years. His principal haiku anthology is the *Taigi kusen* (1772).

tanuki　狸

(raccoon dog). *Nyctereutes procyonoides.* Often referred to in English as badger. Mammal of the family Canidae, native to East Asia but also introduced to northern Europe. It resembles the North American raccoon, but it lacks the ring pattern on the tail. Its head and body measure about 60 centimeters (24 in) and the tail about 16 centimeters (6 in). It inhabits Hokkaidō, Honshū, Shikoku, and Kyūshū and frequents suburban gardens. It eats snails and fruits, nests in caves or tree hollows, and bears a litter of four or five in spring.

The *tanuki* has long been compared with the fox in Japan as a crafty animal possessing supernatural powers, but unlike the latter it is considered to be amusing rather than fearsome. Since ancient times the Japanese have caught the *tanuki* for its meat and used its fur for brushes. It appears in many folk songs and tales, the most famous of which is probably the fairy tale BUMBUKU CHAGAMA, in which a *tanuki*, freed from a trap, repays his liberator's kindness.

Tanuma Okitsugu　田沼意次

(1719–88). Official of the Tokugawa shogunate (1603–1867) who gained prominence as a favorite of the 9th and 10th shōguns, TOKUGAWA IESHIGE and Tokugawa Ieharu (1737–86; r 1760–86), and who attained the status of *daimyō* from very humble origins. Tanuma entered shogunate service in 1734 as a page (KOSHŌ) to the shōgun's heir, Ieshige. On his father's death he inherited an annual stipend of 600 *koku* (see KOKUDAKA). When Ieshige became shōgun in 1745, Tanuma remained in his service. He was named chamberlain (*sobashū*) in 1751 and acquired the status of daimyō in 1758, having received lands assessed at 10,000 *koku;* eventually he was to receive a total of 57,000 *koku*. In 1760, a year before his death, Ieshige relinquished his position as shōgun to his son Ieharu, whose trust Tanuma also enjoyed. The subsequent period (1767–86), during which Tanuma exerted his greatest influence on shogunate policy, is commonly referred to as the Tanuma period. In 1767 he was appointed grand chamberlain (SOBAYŌNIN), and in 1772 he was named a senior councillor (RŌJŪ) concurrently with his post of grand chamberlain.

Ieharu died in 1786 and was succeeded by TOKUGAWA IENARI, then a minor. Being dependent on the support of the shōgun, Tanuma's position was precarious, and the accession of a minor permitted the Tokugawa senior collateral houses (GOSANKE) to intervene in

shogunate affairs. Tanuma was stripped of his offices and reduced in rank and income. His memory was vilified by his successor as chief shogunal adviser, MATSUDAIRA SADANOBU, and by contemporary popular opinion. Tanuma was accused of gaining an unhealthy hold over the shōgun Ieharu, under whom the shogunate was seen to have condoned corruption and luxurious living while neglecting the moral foundations of *samurai* government, and of plunging the country into economic dislocation and social unrest. Recent scholarship, however, has suggested that Tanuma's role was part of a growing effort of the finance commissioner's office (KANJŌ BUGYŌ) to improve the shogunate's economic position within the country and to secure greater centralization of shogunal authority. As this policy was generally opposed by the daimyō it was necessary to circumvent the senior councillors, who were among the most powerful of daimyō. Tanuma supplied the mechanism that enabled this, and therefore the daimyō, who wished to protect their local autonomy, attacked him.

The policies for which Tanuma was criticized were directed toward expanding the commercial economy of the shogunal domains (TENRYŌ), a portion of which had been mandated to daimyō, and thereby increasing the tax income of the shogunate. Some policies were quite traditional, such as the attempt to increase farmland through reclamation of swamp areas like IMBANUMA. Others were more innovative, such as the licensing of commercial agents and monopoly associations (KABUNAKAMA) to extend shogunate control over important commodities, and the expansion of foreign trade. In an effort to increase circulating currency and to create a unified currency system that could be controlled by the shogunate, Tanuma ordered the minting of silver coins as an auxiliary to gold. Tanuma's personal weaknesses, his lowly origin, and his openness to corruption were factors that complicated but did not create the bad repute of the policy with which he became associated.

Tan'yū　→Kanō Tan'yū

Tanzawasan　丹沢山

Also called Tanzawayama. Mountain in northwestern Kanagawa Prefecture, central Honshū; a prominent peak in the Tanzawa Mountains and Tanzawa-Ōyama Quasi-National Park. It attracts many climbers and hikers. Height: 1,567 m (5,141 ft).

Taoka Reiun　田岡嶺雲

(1870–1912). Literary critic and journalist. Real name Taoka Sayoji. Born in the Tosa domain (now Kōchi Prefecture), he graduated from Tōkyō University, where he studied the Chinese classics. At the university he became known for his iconoclastic views, especially his opposition to the KEN'YŪSHA, then a dominant literary coterie. In 1895 he started a magazine, *Seinembun* (Literature for Youth), through which he advocated a new literature based on social criticism. He also worked for the *Yorozu chōhō* and other newspapers and traveled to China, where he associated with Chinese revolutionaries. Taoka became increasingly outspoken in his opposition to the government's commitment to capitalism, and many of his books were censored. His writings are collected in *Taoka Reiun zenshū* (3 vols as of 1991; 1969–).

Tappizaki　竜飛崎

Cape on the northern Tsugaru Peninsula, northwestern Aomori Prefecture, northern Honshū. Separated from the cape Shirakamimisaki on Hokkaidō, 19 kilometers (12 mi) away, by the Tsugaru Strait. The closest point on Honshū to Hokkaidō, it is the southern exit for the Seikan (Aomori-Hakodate) Tunnel, a railway tunnel linking the islands, which was completed in 1988. It is famous for its caves and grottos in cliffs along the shore and for fantastically shaped rocks.

Taradake　多良岳

Group of volcanoes in the Aso Volcanic Zone, Saga and Nagasaki prefectures, Kyūshū. The main peaks are Kyōgadake (1,076 m; 3,530 ft) and Taradake (983 m; 3,225 ft). Deep valleys extend radially from the peak to the foot of each mountain. Large tracts of azaleas and rhododendrons cover the slopes. The volcanoes are part of Taradake Prefectural Natural Park.

taranoki　楤の木

(Japanese angelica tree). *Aralia elata.* Deciduous shrub of the ginseng family (Araliaceae) that grows wild in uncultivated fields and on hills throughout Japan. It grows to a height of about 4 meters (13 ft) and has spiny branches. The large leaves are bipinnate compound; clusters of small white five-petaled flowers bloom in August. The young shoots of the *taranoki* are greatly appreciated for their taste and fragrance.

tarashikomi　たらし込み

A technique used in NIHONGA (Japanese-style painting). *Tarashikomi* refers to the application of an additional layer of ink or paint onto the first layer before it is completely dry. This causes the ink or paint to blur, resulting in uneven patches of light and dark. SŌTATSU (d 1643?) is believed to have been the first painter to consciously employ *tarashikomi.* Thereafter it was practiced by his school, the Rimpa, and influenced other artistic movements as well. Sōtatsu's *Fūjin Raijin zu byōbu* (early 17th century) is a well-known example of *tarashikomi.*

tariffs　関税

(*kanzei*). Tariffs in Japan, as in most nations, have been used to protect domestic industries from foreign competition. For an extended period following World War II, import controls were a major component of Japan's trade policies. In order to join international organizations such as the General Agreement on Tariffs and Trade (GATT), however, Japan was required to remove or lower tariffs on a great number of products. Tariff reductions continued through the 1960s and 1970s, largely as the result of multilateral discussions sponsored by GATT. See TRADE LIBERALIZATION.

Also in the late 1960s, Japan agreed to extend preferential duties to developing countries. Although this system exposed Japan's small businesses and farmers to increased competition, Japan cooperated with other developed nations and instituted the preferential tariff system. This system has not worked satisfactorily, however, and Japan has had to respond to complaints from developing countries.

The seventh round of mulitlateral trade negotiations under GATT was held from 1973 to 1979. Launched by GATT in Tōkyō, the entire series of negotiations is referred to

as the Tōkyō Round. The actual negotiations were mainly held in Geneva with the participation of 99 nations. Among a wide range of subjects discussed, it was decided that tariffs were to be lowered evenly over an eight-year period beginning in January 1980. Japan lowered its tariffs by 50 percent on 2,600 categories of mining and manufacturing products worth US $24.7 billion in imports. The final average tariff rate resulting from this eight-year series of reductions was targeted at a little over 4 percent for the United States, slightly less than 5 percent for the European Community, and a little under 3 percent for Japan, the lowest of all.

In the 1970s and 1980s, Japan continued to remove or reduce tariffs, usually as the result of international pressure. In 1984 Japan's trade surplus reached an unprecedented US $37 billion. Critics abroad asserted that Japan's closed market was the cause of this huge surplus, and there were increasing demands for the further opening of the Japanese market. The Japanese government responded to this criticism by introducing the Action Program for Improving Market Access, in which a top-priority item was the lowering or abolition of tariffs. Accordingly in 1986 there was a 20 percent across-the-board tariff reduction on 1,853 items, and in the same year a three-nation pact was signed between Japan, the United States, and Canada to abolish tariffs on computers, computer peripherals, and computer parts. In addition to the reductions of tariffs on mining, manufacturing, and wood products from developing countries that were introduced in line with the Action Program, tariffs on leather, aluminium, cigarettes, alcohol, and chocolate were also reduced or removed between 1986 and 1988.

In 1988, as a measure intended to balance the effects of the liberalization of the Japanese agricultural market, tariffs were raised on beef and processed cheese. In that year, however, Japan's average tariff rate of 3.4 percent, while not yet under the 3 percent envisaged in the Tōkyō Round, was still the lowest of all of the members of the Organization for Economic Cooperation and Development (OECD), standing in comparison with the average tariff rate of the European Community (3.9 percent), the United States (3.8 percent), Canada (3.5 percent), and Australia (7.9 percent).

tariki　他力

(literally, "another's power"). In Buddhism, *tariki* refers to the power of the Buddhas and bodhisattvas to save others as well as to the process of approaching enlightenment through the power of Buddhas and bodhisattvas. In the JŌDO SECT, *tariki* refers to the power of the vow made by the Buddha AMIDA to save all who invoke his name. People who place their trust in the power of this vow are born into paradise (*gokuraku*), achieve *satori* (enlightenment), and become Buddhas. The JŌDO SHIN SECT teaches that any person who relies on the power of Amida is assured rebirth in paradise, and the practice of NEMBUTSU (reciting the name of the Buddha) is interpreted as an expression of thanks. The opposing term *jiriki* (literally, "one's own power") refers to enlightenment through one's own resources and efforts, but not without Buddha's assistance.

taru　樽

General term for barrellike traditional lidded wooden containers used for storing and transporting liquids such as rice wine (*sake*),

cooking oil, and soy sauce or nonliquids such as bean paste (*miso*) and pickles (*tsukemono*). *Taru* were traditionally constructed of Japanese cedar or willow staves bound with bamboo-strip hoops. Some were lacquered or encased in rice-straw coverings. For convenience in storage, they were wider at the top than at the bottom and had no bulging sides.

Tarui Tōkichi　樽井藤吉

(1850–1922). Politician and founder of the TŌYŌ SHAKAITŌ (Oriental Socialist Party). Born in what is now Nara Prefecture, he studied Confucianism and KOKUGAKU (National Learning) in Edo (now Tōkyō). He joined the FREEDOM AND PEOPLE'S RIGHTS MOVEMENT, and in May 1882 he helped organize the Oriental Socialist Party. The party's objectives were morality, social equality, and the happiness of the masses. It attracted peasants who thought that Tarui's "socialism" would end tenancy and establish a system of equal distribution of wealth. Within a month of its formation the government ordered the party to dissolve, but Tarui continued to hold meetings until his arrest in 1883; he was sentenced to one month in jail. Thereafter he was implicated in the ŌSAKA INCIDENT and other schemes by radical members of the People's Rights Movement to increase Japanese influence in Asia. In 1892 he was elected to the lower house of the Diet as a representative from Nara Prefecture.

taru kaisen → kaisen

Tarumaezan　樽前山

Also called Tarumaesan. A triple volcano southeast of Lake Shikotsu, southwestern Hokkaidō, formed on the crater rim of the Lake Shikotsu caldera. Height: 1,041 m (3,415 ft).

1　**2**

tatami
1 The rooms of this Japanese-style interior have floors of *tatami* matting and are separated by *fusuma* sliding doors.
2 A *tatami* maker sews a cloth border along the edge of a mat. Such artisans are becoming rarer in metropolitan areas.

Tarumizu   垂水[市]

City in southern Kagoshima Prefecture, Kyūshū, on the Ōsumi Peninsula. During the Edo period (1600–1868) Tarumizu was a castle town. Principal agricultural products are vegetables, mandarin oranges, and loquats; livestock are also raised. Marine catches include sardines and yellowtail. The Kaigata Hot Spring is here. Pop: 22,264.

Tasaka Tomotaka   田坂具隆

(1902–74). Film director. Born in Hiroshima Prefecture. He joined the NIKKATSU CORPORATION in 1924 and became a director in 1926. His films are noted for close attention to details of period and locale. Tasaka made masterpieces in two different genres in 1938. GONIN NO SEKKŌHEI (Five Scouts) virtually created the Japanese war-film genre. That same year he adapted *Robō no ishi* (A Pebble by the Wayside), a novel by YAMAMOTO YŪZŌ. It is considered one of the finest films about the Meiji period (1868–1912). Tasaka suffered serious radiation poisoning from the bombing of Hiroshima in 1945 and was hospitalized until 1949. His postwar work included *Jochūkko* (1955, The Maid's Kid), *Hi no ataru sakamichi* (1958, Street in the Sun) and *Gobanchō Yūgirirō* (1963, Yūgiri Brothel of Gobanchō, Kyōto).

tashidaka   足高

(literally, "added amount"). Temporary supplementary stipend paid by the Tokugawa shogunate (1603–1867) to officials who had been promoted to posts above their hereditary rank in order to make up any income gap between their hereditary stipends and those normally granted to holders of those posts. Initiated in 1723 as part of the KYŌHŌ REFORMS by the eighth shōgun, TOKUGAWA YOSHIMUNE,

tasuki Participants in the famous Nebuta Festival, their sleeves bound up with *tasuki*, make their way through the streets of Aomori, Aomori Prefecture.

the *tashidaka* helped the shogunate recruit new talent from the lower ranks.

Tashiro Sanki   田代三喜

(1465–1537). Muromachi-period (1333–1568) physician. One of the founders of *goseihō*, a school of traditional Chinese medicine in Japan. A native of Musashi Province (now Tōkyō Prefecture, Saitama Prefecture, and part of Kanagawa Prefecture). Tashiro studied for 12 years in China, mastering the knowledge of the Jin-Yuan (Chin-Yüan) school of medicine assembled during the Jin (1125–1234) and Yuan (1279–1368) dynasties. Upon his return to Japan he taught MANASE DŌSAN. Tashiro enjoyed the patronage of the KOGA KUBŌ, a branch of the powerful Ashikaga family in eastern Japan.

Tashiro Shigeki   田代茂樹

(1890–1981). Businessman. Born in Fukuoka Prefecture. After graduating from Meiji Semmon Gakkō (now Kyūshū Institute of Technology), Tashiro joined Mitsui & Co in 1913. He moved to Tōyō Rayon (now TŌRAY INDUSTRIES, INC), a subsidiary, in 1936 and became president in 1945. Purged by the Allied Occupation authorities after World War II but soon reinstated, Tashiro became the company chairman and started full-scale production of nylon by introducing Du Pont's technological innovations in 1951.

tasuki   襷

Cloth band or cord used by workers and warriors dressed in traditional Japanese garb to tie up the wide sleeves of their KIMONO, giving the arms and hands unimpeded movement. The *tasuki* is usually tied together at the ends and twisted to form loops through which the arms are passed, the band or cord thus forming an "X" across the back between the shoulders. The donning of a *tasuki* along with a HACHIMAKI (headband) traditionally indicated the wearer's preparation for a ceremonial occasion or strenuous task. The earliest *tasuki*, found on clay HANIWA figures of the Kofun period (ca 300–710), probably had a mostly decorative function. But in ancient times *tasuki* were clearly worn by both men and women as part of formal attire during festivals or rice-planting rituals, as well as for practical purposes. It has almost disappeared in the 20th century with the predominance of Western clothing, but its ceremonial function can still be observed in the dress of festival partici-

pants or when candidates campaigning for election drape a single *tasuki* sash diagonally across the chest from shoulder to waist with their name inscribed in large characters.

tatami   畳

Mat used as a flooring material in traditional Japanese-style rooms. The noun *tatami* is derived from the verb *tatamu*, meaning "to fold" or "pile"; this derivation is taken by some to be evidence that the earliest floor mats were thin and could be either folded up when not in use or used piled in layers.

In the Heian period (794–1185) *tatami* were used as isolated pieces. They came in various thicknesses, with the colors of the cloth borders (*herinuno*) signifying the householder's social rank. By the Muromachi period (1333–1568), the floors of some residences were covered completely with *tatami*.

Since the Muromachi period *tatami* have been made of a thick base (*toko*) of straw covered with a soft surface (*omote*) of woven rush (*igusa*). The size of *tatami* was gradually standardized within each region of Japan, and today *tatami* continue to be used as a unit of measure (pronounced *jō*) for Japanese and sometimes even for Western-style rooms. For example, a room with floor space for six mats is called a *rokujōma* ("six-mat room"). A *tatami* generally measures 1.91 by 0.95 meters (6.3 by 3.1 ft) in the Kyōto area, 1.82 by 0.91 meters (6.0 by 3.0 ft) in the Nagoya area, and 1.76 by 0.88 meters (5.8 by 2.9 ft) in the Tōkyō area. The thickness is on the average 6 centimeters (2.4 in). A half-size mat is called a *hanjō*, and a mat of three-quarter size, which is used in tea-ceremony rooms, is called a *daime-datami*.

tatara-buki   踏鞴吹き

The traditional Japanese iron- or steel-making process. Blasts of air are blown from bellows into a clay furnace called *tatara*, raising the temperature inside to melt iron sand into iron or steel. Primitive forms of *tatara-buki* (*buki*, from *fuki*, means air blowing) were used before the Nara period (710–794), and variations of the process were widely used until the end of the 19th century.

Iron is usually refined from ore, but in Japan iron ore is scarce. Iron sand, however, is found in abundance, and *tatara-buki* was developed to make use of this resource. The idea of using hand bellows in iron making was brought from China via Korea. Use of the bellows was developed into *tatara-buki* in Izumo Province (now Shimane Prefecture). Hand bellows were used at first, then simple foot bellows, and finally a kind of seesaw foot bellows that was operated by several men at once.

Detailed manuals on *tatara-buki* practices, such as the classic eight-volume *Tetsuzan hitsuyō kiji* (1784, Essential Articles on Iron Mines), were published during the Edo period (1600–1868). In 1858 the first Western-style blast furnace was built in Japan, and in the 1920s *tatara-buki* was abandoned for all practical purposes.

tateana jūkyo → pit houses

Tatebayashi   館林[市]

City in southeastern Gumma Prefecture, central Honshū. Tatebayashi developed as a castle town from the late 16th century. The city was formerly known for its silk (Yūki *tsumugi*). Principal industries include the manufacture of electrical machinery, metal goods, and chemicals. It also has flour, soy-sauce, and silk-yarn factories. Of note are the temple Morinji, familiar to many through the tale (*Bumbuku chagama*) about a "badger" (TANUKI), and the azaleas in Tsutsujigaoka Park. Pop: 76,221.

Tatebayashi Kagei   立林何帠

(fl mid-18th century). Artist of the RIMPA style; specialized in pines, plum blossoms, and flowering grasses. Real name Shirai Rittoku. Born in Kaga (now Ishikawa Prefecture), he lived in Edo (now Tōkyō) and painted in the style of KŌRIN with some influence from the KANŌ SCHOOL. Kagei is also said to have once studied with Kōrin's younger brother, KENZAN. His paintings often bear seal impressions similar to the ones used by Kōrin, to whom his works have sometimes been mistakenly attributed.

Tatekawa Yoshitsugu   建川美次

(1880–1945). Army general. Born in Niigata Prefecture; graduate of the Army Academy and the Army Staff College. He distinguished himself during the RUSSO-JAPANESE WAR (1904–05). As a member of the General Staff Office in Tōkyō, he associated with the right-wing SAKURAKAI and is noted for his participation in the MARCH INCIDENT of 1931, an unsuccessful attempt to establish a military government, and for his involvement in the MANCHURIAN INCIDENT that same year in which he declined to dissuade Japanese GUANDONG (KWANTUNG) ARMY officers from taking over Manchuria, a military action he was sent to restrain.

tatemae and honne   建前と本音

(*tatemae to honne*). Pair of words used to describe a situation in which a person's stated reason (*tatemae*) differs from his real intention or motive (*honne*). It is analogous to the expressions *omote* and *ura* (front and back), which describe public character or behavior as opposed to private interactions. Traditional Japanese social norms have greatly emphasized harmonious interpersonal relations and group solidarity. Self-assertion has been strongly discouraged, and the individual often finds that he must sacrifice personal needs and emotions so as to avoid confrontation in the group. Social norms are considered indispensable, and Japanese people are taught early to follow their personal aims but not to defy *tatemae* openly. The result is that in certain social situations it becomes difficult to discern the person's real intentions. A host may offer hospitality to conform with the formalities of etiquette, yet hope that the guest will interpret the excessive cordiality as a sign to leave. The word *tatemae* alone can also refer to the etiquette of the TEA CEREMONY or the ceremony for erecting the framework of a house or building (see KENCHIKU GIREI). See also HAJI; GIRI AND NINJŌ.

Tatematsu Wahei   立松和平

(1947–). Novelist. Real name Yokomatsu Kazuo. Born in Tochigi Prefecture; graduated from Waseda University. Tatematsu received the Noma Literary Prize for New Talent for *Enrai* (1980, Distant Thunder), which depicts a suburban farming village that is gradually being urbanized. Tatematsu's other works include *Kanki no ichi* (1981, Market of Joy) and *Shunrai* (1983, Spring Thunder), a sequel to *Enrai*.

tateshakai━▶vertical society

Tateshina Kōgen   蓼科高原

Highland in the foothills of Tateshinayama, central Nagano Prefecture, central Honshū. Covered mainly with dense birch and larch forests, it has several lakes, numerous hot spring resorts, and camping grounds. Elevation: 1,200–1,500 m (3,900–4,900 ft).

Tatewaki Sadayo   帯刀貞代

(1904–90). Labor activist. Born in Shimane Prefecture. A graduate of Matsue Higher School of Domestic Science. In 1925 she married Orimoto Akira (1900–1954), a member of Tōkyō University's SHINJINKAI political club who was later active in the NIHON RŌNŌTŌ (Japan Labor-Farmer Party). In 1927 she worked with Iwauchi Tomie (1898–1986) to found the leftist Zenkoku Fujin Dōmei (All-Japan Women's League, a predecessor of the Musan Fujin Dōmei or Proletarian Women's League founded in 1929). She was imprisoned for her activities from 1932 to 1934 and again in 1944.

Tateyama   館山[市]

City in southern Chiba Prefecture, central Honshū, on the BŌSŌ PENINSULA. Rice, vegetables, flowers, and fruit are grown here. It is known for its fine beaches. Pop: 54,575.

Tateyama   立山

A group of three mountains (Oyama, Ōnanjiyama, and Fujinooritate) in eastern Toyama Prefecture, central Honshū, in the northern part of the Hida Mountains. The mountainous area contains numerous snowy ravines, lava plateaus, a crater called Jigokudani (Hell's Valley), and abundant alpine flora. Yamasaki cirque is a natural monument. The Tateyama group is considered one of Japan's three holy mountains together with FUJISAN and HAKUSAN. More than a million tourists and climbers have visited Tateyama annually since the 1971 opening of the Tateyama-Kurobe Alpine Route (a combination of train, bus, and ropeway) connecting Toyama and Nagano prefectures. The highest peak is Ōnanjiyama (3,015 m; 9,892 ft).

Tateyama Toshibumi   竪山利文

(1923–). Trade union leader. Born in Kagoshima Prefecture; attended Kyūshū University. He is the first and current chairman of RENGŌ (Japanese Trade Union Confederation). As leader of Tōshiba Rōren (the Tōshiba employees' union), he led the anticommunist wing of the trade union movement. He has been chairman of DENKI RŌREN (All-Japan Federation of Electrical Machine Workers' Unions) and CHŪRITSU RŌREN (Federation of Independent Unions) and played a leading role in the formation of Rengō.

Tatsuno   竜野[市]

City in southwestern Hyōgo Prefecture, western Honshū. Tatsuno developed as a castle town during the late 17th century. It has long been known for its soy sauce and *sōmen* noodles. The city is the birthplace of the poet MIKI ROFŪ and the philosopher MIKI KIYOSHI. Pop: 40,843.

Tatsuno Kingo   辰野金吾

(1854–1919). Pioneer modern architect. Born in what is now Saga Prefecture. In 1879 he was among the first graduates of the building-engineering department of Kōbu College, a predecessor of Tōkyō University, where he was a student of Josiah CONDER. Upon graduating he went to England and trained under the Gothic revival architect

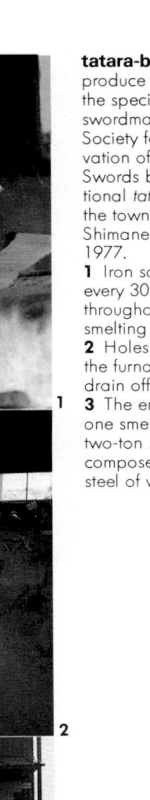

William Burges. Returning to Japan in 1883, Tatsuno became professor and then dean of the school of engineering at Tōkyō University. He served as head of the Architectural Institute of Japan and was the most influential Japanese architect of his day. Among his many buildings are the BANK OF JAPAN BUILDING (1896) and the Tōkyō Station Building (1914). ━ *See photo, next page.*

Tatsutagawa   竜田川

River in Nara Prefecture, central Honshū, flowing south through the lowlands east of the Ikoma Mountains. It is a tributary of the YAMATOGAWA. Tatsutagawa refers to the lower reaches; the upper reaches are called Ikomagawa and the middle reaches Herugigawa. The area is famous for its maple trees and its autumn foliage. Length: 13.2 km (8.2 mi).

Tateyama Even the unathletic can ascend mountains via the Tateyama-Kurobe Alpine Route, a combination of train, bus, and ropeway. The Murodōdaira stop pictured here is located at an elevation of 2,450 meters on one of the area's volcanic plateaus.

tattoos Mentioned in the 8th-century *Nihon shoki* (Chronicle of Japan), tattoos have a long history in Japan. The two men pictured here are tattooed with maple leaf (left) and chrysanthemum (right) motifs.

Tatsuta Shrine 竜田大社

(Tatsuta Taisha). Shintō shrine in Ikoma District, Nara Prefecture; dedicated to the deities Amenomihashira no Mikoto and Kuninomihashira no Mikoto. According to tradition, it was built by the legendary emperor Sujin. The shrine has long been associated with good harvests and a supposed power over destructive winds, and it is often paired with the HIROSE SHRINE, which is believed to have the power of avoiding water-related disasters. In addition to the annual festival on 4 April, a well-known ceremony for warding off typhoons (Fūchinsai) is held on the first Sunday of July.

tattoos 入墨

(*irezumi*). Also called *horimono*. Western experts agree that in Japan the ancient and worldwide practice of tattooing reached its highest level of artistic expression with bold, colorful, integrated pictorial designs based on traditional themes that were skillfully "engraved" over large areas of the body. This singular preeminence in decorative design appeared suddenly and developed rapidly in urban areas during the mid-19th century.

In ancient Japan, as in other primitive societies, tattoos were probably associated with ritual and indicated status. Over the centuries, tattooing as a punishment followed a curious pattern of falling in and out of favor. Its final official use was ordered in 1720 by the eighth Tokugawa shōgun, TOKUGAWA YOSHIMUNE. Markings varied by region and were applied to the arm as well as to the face, with designs allowing for additions for repeated offenses. In the Genroku era (1688–1704) it became a minor vogue

among prostitutes of the gay quarters in Edo (now Tōkyō) and Ōsaka to have the name of a favored client tattooed on the upper arm or inner thigh. A more discreet affirmation could be made with a series of small dots numbering a lover's age or with a shared pattern on fingers and hands that was completed when the lovers' hands met. Called *kishō-bori* ("pledge marks"), these love tattoos appear in woodblock prints illustrating the risqué literature of the period.

The Edo Explosion——In the 1820s and 1830s there developed a significant demand among townsmen for tattoos that covered the entire back, most of the front, and often the upper arms and legs as well. To meet this demand, a distinct trade group emerged. Its members were called *horishi* (tattooists). They possessed the techniques, tools, and skills to execute masterpieces on a grand scale with secondary design elements artfully integrated into a harmonious whole. Members of this select guild included street barbers and the artisans who carved the woodblocks used to make UKIYO-E prints. Their customers were initially from the so-called naked trades (porters, palanquin bearers, etc). Laborers, volunteer firemen, and *geisha* also employed tattooists; *samurai*, it seems, seldom succumbed to the temptation. It was the printmaker UTAGAWA KUNIYO-SHI, with his bold colors and dramatic designs, who established the canons of the tattooists' art.

Meiji Suppression——As foreigners entered Japan after the Meiji Restoration, government officials became sensitive to the possibility of odious comparisons between Eastern "backwardness" and Western "enlightenment." Tattooing was banned as barbaric. The practice nonetheless continued, even being favored occasionally by foreigners, including King George V of England and Tsar Nicholas II of Russia, both said to have been tattoed in Yokohama as young men.

The State of the Art Today——Tattooing is still done in Japan today. Taken from religion and popular mythology, pictures are chosen to help the bearer gain strength, health, wealth, wisdom, and various magical powers. They include Buddhist deities, folk heroes, auspicious animals, flowers, and assorted angels and rogues. A fine, large-scale tattoo takes several months to complete and costs several thousand dollars. The people with the time, money, and greatest need for group identification are usually gangsters (see YAKUZA), although customers may come from any profession or social class.

Taue-zōshi 田植草紙

Late-16th-century book of transplanting songs sung each year at the time of trans-

planting rice seedlings from nursery beds into the main fields. The work is done by women, who sing responsively with the director of the day's labor to the accompaniment of drums, flutes, and cymbals. There are many similar collections from a later period, but this one is generally regarded as the finest and most representative. It is preserved at Tōkyō University in the form of two tracings.

The collection is divided into 16 sets to be sung at specific times during the working day. Secular and religious songs were integrated into a whole series sung at the time of this crucial agricultural, social, and religious event, in order to bring it to a successful conclusion. Some songs were originally extemporaneous; others were reworkings of contemporary popular songs.

Taut, Bruno タウト, B.

(1880–1938). German expressionist architect who was influential in generating increased interest in traditional Japanese architecture. Born in Königsberg (now Kaliningrad). In 1933 Taut moved to Japan to escape Nazism. In Japan he extolled the functionalism and rationalism of what he called "emperor art," as represented by the ISE SHRINE and KATSURA DETACHED PALACE, and condemned the decorative style of temples and the TŌSHŌGŪ, which he labeled "shōgun art." His writings on architecture include *Nippon* (1934).

tawara 俵

Large straw sacks of standardized size used for the storage or transport of rice, potatoes, charcoal, and so forth. Since rice taxes were delivered in *tawara* in ancient Japan, their size was presumably standardized quite early, at least regionally, and this led to the use of *hyō* (another reading of the Chinese character for *tawara*) as a unit for measuring rice. The circular straw cap at either end of the *tawara* (called *sandawara*) is used as a ritual object in some regions.

Tawara Kuniichi 俵国一

(1872–1958). Metallurgist known for his metallographic study of steel. Born in Shimane Prefecture, Tawara graduated from Tōkyō University in 1897 and immediately became an assistant professor. He went to Germany in 1899 to study metallurgy and upon his return became a full professor at Tōkyō University. He is also known for his analytical studies of traditional methods of refining iron sand and of making Japanese swords. He received the Order of Culture in 1946.

Tawaramoto 田原本[町]

Town in northwestern Nara Prefecture, central Honshū. During the Edo period (1600–1868), Tawaramoto flourished as a castle and market town, with goods being transported

on the nearby river Teragawa. Watermelons and vegetables are grown, and it is a distribution center for agricultural products. Pop: 31,533.

Tawara Sunao 田原淳

(1873–1952). Pathologist and medical scientist. With Ludwig Aschoff, discoverer of the Aschoff-Tawara node (the atrioventricular node). Born in Ōita Prefecture; graduate of Tōkyō University. Tawara studied in Germany from 1903 to 1906, and at Aschoff's laboratory at the University of Marburg the two described the atrioventricular node, which is associated with the heartbeat mechanism in mammals. Tawara taught at Kyūshū University. He received the Imperial Prize of the Japan Academy in 1914.

Tawarayama Hot Spring 俵山温泉

(Tawarayama Onsen). Located in the city of Nagato, western Yamaguchi Prefecture, western Honshū. A simple alkaline spring; water temperature around 40°C (104°F). This spa has been designated as a National Health Resort Hot Spring.

Tawaraya Sōtatsu →Sōtatsu

Tawara Yoshizumi 田原良純

(1856–1935). Pharmacologist. Born in Hizen Province (now Saga Prefecture and part of Nagasaki Prefecture). Graduate of Daigaku Nankō (now part of Tōkyō University). Tawara succeeded in extracting tetrodotoxin, a poisonous compound of medicinal value found in *fugu* (GLOBEFISHES). As head of the Tōkyō Institute of Hygienic Sciences of the Home Ministry for many years, he contributed greatly to the development of the domestic pharmaceutical industry.

tax accountants 税理士

(*zeirishi*). Qualified tax and accounting professionals licensed under the Tax Accountant Law (Zeirishi Hō). Tax accountants are approved separately from CERTIFIED PUBLIC ACCOUNTANTS. In response to client requests, tax accountants provide tax agent, financial statement preparation, and other financial services. Tax accountants must pass a national examination that covers tax law and accounting theories and practices.

tax accounting 税務会計

(*zeimu kaikei*). In Japan, tax accounting (the calculation of taxable income for profit-making personal business ventures and corporations) is done in accordance with the Income Tax Law and Corporation Tax Law. Tax accounting takes as its basis the results of business accounting, computed in accordance with the Commercial Code and the Securities Exchange Law. Whereas business accounting seeks to assess the company's operating results, financial condition, and profit available for dividends, the purpose of tax accounting is to calculate the tax obligation based on principles of fairness and ability to pay. Because of their different objectives there is considerable variation in concepts and methods of calculation between the two types of accounting, and net income from business accounting must be adjusted under the tax law to produce taxable income. See also ACCOUNTING FOR BUSINESS ENTERPRISES; TAXES; TAX LAW.

Tax Commission 税制調査会

(Zeisei Chōsakai). Institution attached to the Prime Minister's Office as an advisory organ on matters of tax reform. Created in 1962, the commission is composed of academics,

industrialists, labor union leaders, and others. Since tax problems are of a highly political nature, however, the actual initiation of tax reform proposals and the final decision making on key tax issues are performed by the Tax Research Council of the ruling Liberal Democratic Party.

taxes 租税制度

(*sozei seido*). The present Japanese tax system is largely a result of reform measures passed in the 1950s on the recommendation at the SHOUP MISSION, an American advisory group that visited Japan in 1949. Although many of the Shoup reform measures were later repealed, the mission's basic recommendations had a lasting impact on Japanese tax policy and administration. Since that time a dominant characteristic of the Japanese tax system has been its heavy reliance on direct taxes (mainly taxes on personal and corporate income) relative to indirect taxes (sales and excise taxes). In the 1980s well over 70 percent of tax revenues in Japan came from direct taxes. This percentage is comparable to the percentage of direct tax revenue generated in the United States but is high compared to the percentages of other industrialized nations.

In 1986 the Japanese government undertook a major tax reform effort, with the objective of a fundamental revision of the Shoup tax system. One of the goals of this reform was to reduce the excessive reliance on direct taxes by increasing the importance of indirect taxes. As a result, the government imposed a 3-percent CONSUMPTION TAX and a decrease in income and corporate tax rates. However, since the consumption tax rate is low, and many small and medium-sized companies are exempt from the tax, it provides less than 10 percent of all national tax revenues. As a result, the system continues to depend primarily on direct taxes. See also TAXES, NATIONAL AND LOCAL.

Direct taxes in Japan consist of taxes on individual income, corporate income, and inheritance. One notable difference between the Japanese tax system and that of other advanced nations is that in Japan there tends to be less of a disparity between the percentage of revenues derived from corporate taxes and the percentage of revenues derived from individual taxes. For example, in 1991, according to Ministry of Finance figures, 39.5 percent of total tax revenues came from individual income taxes, compared to 29.5 percent from corporate taxes. One explanation for the high level of corporate tax revenues in Japan is that most small businesses are incorporated, providing a large pool of corporate taxpayers.

Tax rates on individual income in Japan were previously divided into 15 progressive brackets. However, a second tax reform in 1989 simplified this system. Today individual income is taxed in 5 brackets of 10, 20, 30, 40, and 50 percent.

taxes, national and local 国税と地方税

(*kokuzei to chihōzei*). There are currently three types of national taxes in Japan: personal income tax, corporate tax, and CONSUMPTION TAX. Local taxes consist of both prefectural and municipal taxes. The prefectural taxes include the enterprise tax imposed on the profits of individuals and corporations and a resident tax imposed on individual and corporate residents. Municipal taxes are a similar resident tax and a fixed asset tax on the owners of land,

Revenue Estimates, 1991 taxes

Direct taxes	Amount (in billions of yen)	percent
Income tax	25,738	39.5
Corporate tax	19,267	29.5
Inheritance tax	2,046	3.1
Special provisional corporate surtax[1]	436	0.7
Subtotal	47,487	72.8

Indirect taxes	Amount (in billions of yen)	percent
Consumption tax	4,944	7.6
Stamp revenue	2,148	3.3
Gasoline and fuel taxes	2,075	3.2
Liquor tax	2,000	3.1
Stock exchange and securites taxes	1,068	1.7
Tobacco tax	987	1.5
Customs duty	850	1.3
Motor vehicle and other tonnage taxes	649	1.0
Other[2]	3,015	4.6
Subtotal	17,736	27.3
Total	65,223 ($484 billion)	—

[1] A special assessment in 1991 to pay for Japan's contribution to the Persian Gulf War effort.
[2] Taxes appropriated for special accounts.
NOTE: US dollar value is calculated at the average April 1991 exchange rate of $1.00=¥134.71. Percentages do not add up to 100 due to rounding.
SOURCE: Ministry of Finance, *Zaisei kin'yū tōkei geppō* (monthly): April 1991.

houses, and depreciable assets.

The 1989 tax reform that introduced the national consumption tax was viewed as a fundamental revision of the postwar tax system, which had been based on the SHOUP MISSION tax recommendations of 1949. With the introduction of the consumption tax, the commodity tax previously levied on automobiles, consumer electronics, etc, was abolished. A portion of the consumption tax revenue is made available to local governments in the form of a transfer tax. See TAXES.

tax law 税法

(*zeihō*). The modern Japanese tax system is based on the SHOUP MISSION recommendations passed by the Diet in 1950. Rather than a general tax code, Japan has a series of separate statutes, cabinet orders, and ministerial orders that govern particular taxes and cover certain common problems. The most significant tax by far is the national income tax, producing some 75.4 percent of the ¥51 trillion (US $391 billion) in total national tax revenue received for fiscal year 1989. This tax can be classified into two categories. The first is the individual income tax defined in the Income Tax Law (Shotokuzei Hō) and its supporting enforcement orders and regulations. This tax produced 35.6 percent of fiscal 1989 national tax revenue. The second category of national income tax is the corporate income tax imposed on all legal entities (known as *hōjin* or juristic persons). This tax is defined in the Corporation Tax Law (Hōjinzei Hō) and its supporting enforcement orders and regulations; it provided some 36 percent of fiscal 1989 national income tax revenue.

Historically the major emphasis of the Japanese tax system has been on direct rather than indirect taxation. One of the main objectives of the tax reform undertaken in 1988 was to reduce the overdependence on direct taxes like the income tax. Six tax reform bills were enacted in December 1988 that, among other things, reduced individual and corporate income tax rates and introduced a new major indirect tax, the national CONSUMPTION TAX. The consumption tax provided 7.1 percent of national tax revenue in 1989. Also important is the Special Tax Measures Law

Lake Tazawa This caldera lake in northern Honshū forms a backdrop for the gilt-bronze statue called *Tatsuko zō*, representing a figure from a local legend.

(Sozei Tokubetsu Sochi Hō; see SPECIAL TAX MEASURES), which includes special incentive measures affecting other taxes.

Income taxation in Japan is based on self-assessment rather than government assessment. Therefore, all corporate and other legal entity taxpayers must file a final corporate tax return with the tax office having jurisdiction over their head office within two months of the end of their business year. However, most individual taxpayers need not file a tax return provided that they have received only remuneration income and all or almost all of that income is from one employer. Their employer calculates their tax amount, which is withheld at source, and makes a year-end adjustment, either collecting additional tax or refunding tax to the taxpayer. Individual taxpayers who have significant renumeration income from two or more sources or who have other types of income are required to file a final income tax return by 15 March of the year following the calendar year for which they are being taxed.

The national Japanese domestic tax system is administered by the NATIONAL TAX ADMINISTRATION, a semi-independent agency of the MINISTRY OF FINANCE. This body oversees 12 regional taxation bureaus and 517 local tax offices throughout the country. Tax policy and international tax negotiations, such as tax treaties, are handled by an internal bureau of the Ministry of Finance called the Tax Bureau. Customs matters come under the Customs and Tariff Bureau of the Ministry of Finance.

For local tax matters, a general framework is established by the Local Tax Law, which is overseen by the Local Tax Bureau of the Ministry of Home Affairs. As the type of local taxes that can be imposed and their rates are regulated by the national government, the local tax burden tends not to vary substantially between districts. See also TAXES, NATIONAL AND LOCAL.

A formal procedure exists for settling tax disputes with the government. Protests must first be filed with the chief of the tax office or the director of the regional taxation bureau responsible for the determination being questioned. If this proves unsatisfactory, the taxpayer may claim review by the tax court called the NATIONAL TAX TRIBUNAL. A ruling by the tax court may then be appealed to the regular judicial courts. See also TAXES.

tax office → National Tax Administration

tax system, international   国際税制

(*kokusai zeisei*). Japanese laws regulating international taxation basically follow international customs. Nonresident individuals or corporations that have branches, factories, shops, or other fixed places of business ("permanent establishments") in Japan must file tax returns in the same way as residents with respect to any Japanese sources of income including investment income (interest, dividends, and royalties) and remuneration

to which 15 to 20 percent withholding taxation is applied. Nonresidents without any permanent establishment are subject to taxation on income from sales of real estate and subject to separate withholding taxation on investment income and remuneration.

Residents of Japan (individuals and corporations) are subject to worldwide income taxation. However, foreign tax paid on foreign sources of income can be credited against Japanese income tax liabilities. This foreign tax credit system is provided for in the Japanese domestic tax laws.

Japan has also concluded tax treaties with 36 countries (as of 1990). They provide for the maximum withholding tax rates on investment income paid to residents of another country, principles of business income taxation, obligation of double taxation relief, and exchange of information between authorities.

Tayama Katai   田山花袋

(1872–1930). Real name Tayama Rokuya. A prominent writer of the Japanese naturalist school. He is the author of more than 400 short stories and full-length novels, as well as poetry and works of criticism and travel. Born in Tatebayashi, Gumma Prefecture. Katai's schooling was irregular, but even so he decided to pursue a literary career through self-study. He was associated with both OZAKI KŌYŌ's conservative KEN'YŪSHA group and the young writers KUNIKIDA DOPPO and Miyazaki Koshoshi (1864–1922), with whom he produced a collection of "new style" poetry entitled *Jojōshi* (1897, Lyric Poetry).

In 1902 the publication of "Jūemon no saigo" (The Death of Jūemon), an account of the life of a beastlike man, lifted Katai from obscurity. In 1904 he published the essay "Rokotsu naru byōsha" (Straightforward Description) in the magazine *Taiyō*, in which he set forth his ideas on a revolutionary writing style that would eschew all adornment. His story "Futon" (1907, The Quilt) did much to establish the personal, confessional mode as a hallmark of the fledgling naturalist movement (see I-NOVEL). Katai's experience as a correspondent in the Russo-Japanese War (1904–05) enabled him to write one of his most powerful naturalist stories, "Ippeisotsu" (1908; tr "A Soldier," 1956). INAKA KYŌSHI (1909, Country Teacher) is often considered his best work.

Tayasu Munetake   田安宗武

(1715–71). WAKA poet and KOKUGAKU (National Learning) scholar of the 18th century. Born in Edo (now Tōkyō); second son of the shōgun TOKUGAWA YOSHIMUNE. A student of the poet and Kokugaku scholar KAMO NO MABUCHI, he wrote over 300 *waka* in the MAN'YŌSHŪ style. His main collection is *Amorigoto* (after 1771).

Tazaki Hirosuke   田崎広助

(1898–1984). Western-style painter. Real name Tazaki Hiroji. Born in Fukuoka Prefecture. Studied at Kansai Art Academy (Kansai Bijutsuin). His work was first shown at the Nikaten (Exhibition of the Nika Society) in 1927. Subdued colors and strongly modeled forms characterize his work, which skillfully portrays the natural scenery of Japan. He received the Order of Culture in 1975.

Tazaki Sōun   田崎草雲

(1815–98). Painter and book illustrator. Born in Edo (now Tōkyō) to a *samurai* family serving the *daimyō* of the Ashikaga domain (now part of Tochigi Prefecture). He studied

under several minor painters in the BUNJINGA (literati painting) style as well as with the literati master TANI BUNCHŌ. In 1882, and again in 1884, Sōun won silver medals at the first and second Domestic Competitive Painting Exhibitions (Naikoku Kaiga Kyō-shinkai). He was a member of the conservative Japan Art Association (Nihon Bijutsu Kyōkai) and in 1890 he was one of the first four painters to be named artists for the imperial household (*teishitsu gigeiin*). See also NIHONGA.

Tazawa, Lake   田沢湖

(Tazawako). Caldera lake in eastern Akita Prefecture, northern Honshū. Deepest lake in Japan. Located in the Ōu Mountains, it is said to have been created when the Tazawa volcano caved in. Area: 25.5 sq km (9.8 sq mi); circumference: 21 km (13 mi); depth: 423 m (1,388 ft); altitude: 249 m (817 ft).

Tazoe Tetsuji   田添鉄二

(1875–1908). Socialist. Born in Kumamoto Prefecture. Tazoe was converted to Christianity while a student at a missionary school in Kumamoto. While studying at the University of Chicago (1898–1900), he became interested in socialism. He went to Tōkyō to work on a book, *Keizai shinkaron* (1904, Economic Evolutionism), in which he tried to apply the theories of social Darwinism to economics. He joined the Shakai Shugi Kyōkai, a socialist study group and successor to the SHAKAI SHUGI KENKYŪKAI, and helped found the JAPAN SOCIALIST PARTY in 1906. At the annual convention of the party in 1907 Tazoe opposed KŌTOKU SHŪSUI, who advocated radical tactics to advance the socialist movement; Tazoe advocated working through the Diet but was outvoted. Several days later the government banned the party.

TDK Corporation   ティーディーケイ[株]

(Tī Dī Kei; formerly called Tōkyō Denki Kagaku Kōgyō). Japan's largest producer of magnetic tapes, ferrite cores, and magnetic products. Incorporated in 1935 to produce ferrite, the firm expanded by developing high-performance magnetic materials and their applications. TDK's overseas manufacturing companies are located in the United States, Mexico, Brazil, Germany, South Korea, Taiwan, and Hong Kong. Sales for the fiscal year ending March 1991 totaled ¥414.0 billion (US $3.0 billion), and the overseas sales ratio was 38 percent. In the same year the company was capitalized at ¥24.7 billion (US $180.0 million). Headquarters are in Tōkyō.

tea   茶

(*cha*). Green tea is one of the most popular beverages in Japan. It is the only kind of tea produced in Japan and it is drunk plain, without milk or sugar. In 1989 Japan produced 89,000 metric tons (98,780 short tons) of green tea and imported 2,245 metric tons (2,470 short tons) of green tea and 10,261 metric tons (11,287 short tons) of black tea. Tea is grown in the warmer southern regions of Japan. Half of all tea produced in Japan comes from Shizuoka Prefecture, but production has recently increased in Kyūshū.

Types—The various types of tea produced today in Japan differ according to cultivation practices and methods used in leaf processing. *Sencha*, which constitutes 80 percent of all Japanese processed leaf teas, is made by sterilizing the leaves with steam to stop fermentation (oxidation); this prevents the leaves from changing color. The treated

Tayama Katai This prolific writer's concern for strict realism made him a pioneer in modern Japanese fiction.

tea ceremony 茶の湯

(chanoyu) literally, "tea's hot water"; also called chadō or sadō, the Way of tea). A highly structured method of preparing powdered green tea in the company of guests. The tea ceremony incorporates the preparation and service of food as well as the study and utilization of architecture, gardening, ceramics, calligraphy, history, and religion. It is the culmination of a union of artistic creativity, sensitivity to nature, religious thought, and social interchange.

History of Tea in Japan—According to tradition, Bodhidharma, who left India and introduced Zen (Ch: Chan or Ch'an) Buddhism to China in 520, encouraged the custom of tea drinking for alertness during meditation in Buddhist temples during the Tang (T'ang) dynasty (618–907), a ritual was performed using tea in brick form. This was ground to a powder, mixed in a kettle with hot water, and ladled into ceramic bowls.

Buddhism was brought to Japan sometime in the first half of the 6th century. During the Nara period (710–794), the influence of Chinese culture included the introduction of tea in conjunction with Buddhist meditation. Early in the Kamakura period (1185–1333), the Japanese priest Eisai (1141–1215) returned from Buddhist studies in China, bringing the tea ritual practiced in Chinese Buddhist temples during the Song (Sung) dynasty (960–1279). In this ritual, powdered green tea (matcha) is whisked in individual conical bowls called temmoku ("heaven eye"), after the Chinese mountain where they were used in Buddhist temples. The bowl is supported on a lacquered stand called yotsugashira ("four heads"), powdered green tea (matcha) is whisked in individual conical bowls called temmoku ("heaven eye"), after the Chinese mountain where they were used in Buddhist temples. The bowl is supported on a lacquered stand called yotsugashira ("four heads"), bringing the tea ritual practiced in (idō). Eisai also brought tea seeds from the wild tea that was to become the source of much of the tea grown in Japan today. Although wild tea grew in Japan, it was considered inferior, and the tea from Eisai's seeds became known as "true tea" (honcha).

In the early 13th century, the priest Eizon (1201–90) traveled around Japan preaching and extolling the curative powers of tea. His mission made tea drinking a widespread custom. The monk Ikkyū (1394–1481), one of the greatest figures in Zen Buddhism, believed that the tea ceremony produced greater enlightenment than did hours of meditation. One of Ikkyū's disciples was the monk Murata Shukō (Jukō; 1422–1502), who became tea master and curator of Chinese art to the shōgun Ashikaga Yoshimasa (1436–90). When making tea, Shukō displayed a hanging scroll of Buddhist calligraphy that he had received from Ikkyū. Shukō urged the aristocracy to avoid ostentation and observe Buddhist principles when drinking tea. At the shōgun's villa, later known as the Temple of the Silver Pavilion (Ginkakuji), is the Tōgudō, a small shrine dedicated to Amida, the Buddha of Compassion; within is a room called Dōjinsai, the first four-and-a-half-mat room designed for serving tea.

In Sakai, south of Ōsaka, there was a group of wealthy merchants called the nayashū ("warehouse school"), which espoused a modest manner of tea drinking. Out of this tradition came Takeno Jōō (1502–55), who taught the use of the daisu (the stand for the tea utensils), as it had been handed down from Shukō, as well as a sensitive connoisseurship and the aesthetic sensibility known as wabi, the contrast of refinement and rusticity. His influence was widely felt but was most important in his instruction of his student SEN NO RIKYŪ (1522–91).

Rikyū transformed the tea ceremony, perfected the use of the daisu, and substituted common Japanese objects for the rare and expensive Chinese tea utensils used previously. Tea was no longer made in one room and served to guests in another, but rather made in their midst, in emulation of Shukō's method. Many people began to practice the tea ceremony following the precepts and example of Rikyū.

Rikyū's successor, FURUTA ORIBE (1544–1615), introduced a decorative style that some considered superficial. Oribe's pupil KOBORI ENSHŪ (1579–1647) continued the grand style and was teacher to the Tokugawa shōguns, moving freely among the nobility, while also designing gardens and teahouses.

There were many masters of tea, with heirs and followers who eventually gathered into schools that served either the aristocracy or the commoners. Rikyū's way was passed to his grandson Sōtan (1578–1658), who was renowned for his humility and sensitivity. In turn, each of Sōtan's sons headed his own school: URA SENKE, OMOTE SENKE, and MUSHANOKŌJI SENKE. Ura Senke, representative of

Continued on page 1538→

TEAC Corporation テアック[株]

(Tīakku). Manufacturer of information processing and audio equipment. Incorporated in 1953. It is the largest manufacturer of floppy disk drives for the world. Sales for the fiscal year ending March 1991 totaled ¥116.4 billion (US $587.6 million). The company was capitalized at ¥7.7 billion (US $56.1 million) in the same year. Headquarters are in Tōkyō.

tea 茶

History—The use of tea is said to have originated in China. During the Nara period (710–794) numerous Japanese Buddhist monks visited China and supposedly brought tea seeds back to Japan. The most widely accepted theory fixes the beginning of Japan's tea industry in 1191, when the monk Eisai brought tea seeds from China on temple lands. He then encouraged the cultivation of tea in other areas of Japan by extolling the benefits of tea drinking.

For some 500 years after tea was introduced to Japan it was used in its powdered form (matcha) only. It was not until the mid-16th century that the processing method for sencha was invented. The tea ceremony was perfected by SEN NO RIKYŪ in the late 16th century, and prior to the Edo period (1600–1868) the consumption of tea was limited to the ruling class. The special cultivation methods for gyokuro were developed in the 19th century. Only after the beginning of the 20th century, with the introduction of mass production techniques, did tea achieve widespread popularity among the general populace.

Gyokuro is the top grade of leaf tea in Japan. It is made from the choicest, most tender leaves of tea bushes protected by bamboo blinds during cultivation. It is processed in the same manner as sencha.

Matcha is a powdered form of green tea used mainly in the TEA CEREMONY. Like gyokuro it is made from the choicest tea leaves, which are steamed, dried, and then ground into a powder rather than crushed into pieces. Matcha is not brewed by steeping; hot water is added to the powder and then rapidly beaten with a bamboo whisk. The tea is cloudy and dark green and has a pleasing, astringent flavor.

Bancha is low-grade coarse tea. It is essentially the same as sencha but is made from older, brittle leaves. Bancha has a yellowish brown tint and a slightly astringent taste. Hōjicha, which is made from sencha and bancha, is dark reddish brown and has a strong, robust, roasted flavor.

Sencha, brewed with hot (not boiling) water, has a mildly astringent yet agreeable flavor. Gyokuro is the top grade of leaf tea in Japan. It is made from the choicest, most tender leaves are rolled to liberate juices and enzymes sealed within and then dried with warm air, producing tiny, dark green, needle-shaped pieces ready for packaging.

tea

Green tea is an everyday drink for most Japanese. Tea leaves are placed in a pot and steeped briefly in boiled water that has been allowed to cool slightly.

Tea cultivation in Kanaya, Shizuoka Prefecture. Picking commences in May, the earliest leaves are considered the most delicious.

Bancha is made from those leaves remaining after the more tender ones are picked for sencha.

In genmaicha roasted genmai (brown rice) is mixed with bancha.

The most common green tea is called sencha (pictured), of which the highest grade is composed of deep green leaves.

Hōjicha, roasted bancha. The roasting gives the tea a smoky flavor.

The Way of Tea

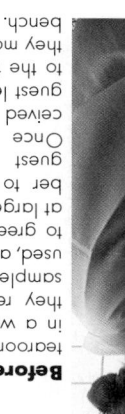

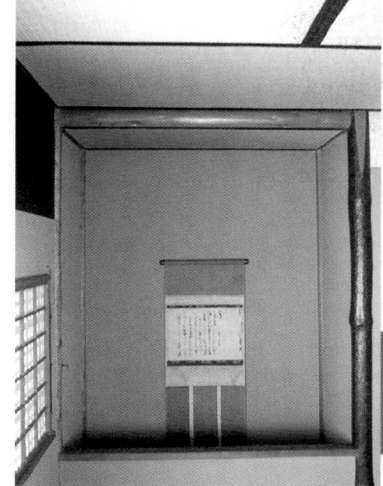

Every human encounter is a singular occasion. This is the truth that the tea ceremony consciously underscores. The uniqueness of the seasonal moment, the setting, and the time of day at which a host convenes a particular group of guests must be savored, for it will never recur. In planning a *chaji*, or tea ceremony, a host selects a theme and spends days pondering the arrangements. Who should be invited on this occasion? What combination of bowls and utensils would be best? Which scroll hanging on the wall, which flowers in which vase will suggest most vividly the time of year? What flavors and ingredients unique to the season should be included in the meal that is served before the tea is drunk? Guests, well aware of their host's devotion to such nuances, approach the small world of the tearoom with a reverent readiness to play their part in enacting and appreciating the ritual drama of tea.

Before entering the tearoom, the guests gather in a waiting room where they remove their coats, sample the hot water to be used, and wait for the host to greet them. The group at large selects one member to act as the main guest in the ceremony. Once the host has received them, the main guest leads the group into the tea garden, where they may rest briefly on a bench.

Pure, clear water fills the stone basin called the *tsukubai*. Guests take up a ladle and lightly rinse their hands and mouths. This ritual is meant to cleanse them of mundane concerns. The order followed by guests as they make their way through the garden and purify themselves at the *tsukubai* is maintained throughout the *chaji*, with the principal guest taking the lead.

Crawling into the teahouse through the *nijiriguchi*, a sliding door only 90 centimeters tall, obliges guests to bow their heads and crouch. The *nijiriguchi* serves to underscore the fact that worldly status or social position means nothing within these walls, where all participants are treated alike.

Once inside, each guest admires the scroll displayed in an alcove called the *tokonoma*. The host reveals the theme of the occasion through his or her choice of scroll. Guests also inspect the brazier and kettle before seating themselves in spots determined by their positions in the order established earlier. When the host enters, the principal guest leads the others in greeting him or her. The host then presents them each with a tray bearing a light meal—the *kaiseki*—designed to stave off hunger during the course of the ritual. Sake is also served. After the meal, guests consume a sweet offered by the host, the sweet is meant to offset the slightly bitter taste of the *koicha*, or thick tea, that will next be served. While the host begins the initial preparations, the guests retire to the garden or the waiting room to relax.

Bowls of thin tea are prepared and served to each guest by the host. These tea bowls tend to have a slightly more light-hearted or festive look. The word for the tea container used here is usuchaki. Guests admire the container and scoop before departing, and the chaji is over.

Dry sweets are passed around as usucha is pre-pared. Each guest places a sweet on his or her kaishi, a paper napkin for the purpose, and passes the remaining sweets to the next guest. The flavor and form of such sweets often reflect the season.

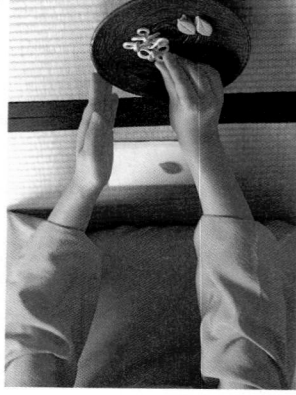

Koicha (thick tea), made by adding a very small amount of hot water to the powdered tea, is prepared by the host in a single bowl from which all guests drink. After savoring it, each wipes the rim of the bowl before passing it to the next guest. Inquiries concerning the tea and its poetic name are exchanged at this time. Guests then inspect the tea container, its wrapper, and the tea scoop.

Rebuilding the fire in the brazier, the host now prepares thin tea. Usucha calls for more hot water to be added to the powdered tea, which is whipped into a fine froth with a chasen, or tea whisk.

Flowers displayed in the tokonoma greet guests as they make their goiri, or second entry, into the tearoom. The flow-ers, which have replaced the scroll dis-played earlier, should consist of one or two varieties that are slightly ahead of season. As before, guests take turns admiring the tokonoma display and the utensils before seating themselves in the prescribed arrangement.

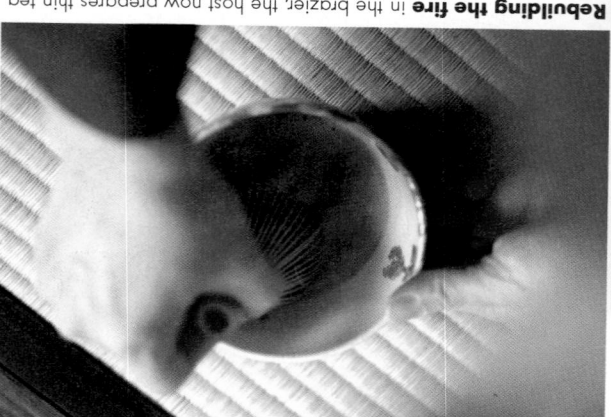

the commoners' tea, and Omote Senke of the aristocrats' tea, are the leading schools in Japan today.

Practice of the Tea Ceremony—The manner of preparing powdered green tea may be influenced by many styles and techniques, depending on the practices of the various schools. The following procedure is adapted from the Ura Senke way of preparation. A full tea presentation with a meal is called a *chaji*, while the actual making of the tea is called *temae*. A simple gathering for tea may be called a *chakai*. The selection of utensils (*dōgu*) and the service of tea is determined by time of year, season, and time of day or night, as well as special occasions such as welcoming someone, bidding farewell, a memorial, a wedding, flower viewing, and so on.

The tea is prepared in a specially designated and designed room, the *chashitsu*. It is devoid of decoration with the exceptions of a hanging scroll (*kakemono*) and flowers in a vase (*hanaire*). The scroll, inspired by Buddhist thought, provides the appropriate spiritual atmosphere for serving tea. The Buddhist writing, usually by a recognized master, is called *bokuseki* ("ink traces"). Flowers for tea (*chabana*) are simple, seasonal, and seemingly "unarranged," unlike those in *ikebana*. See FLOWER ARRANGEMENT.

The following are some of the highlights of a *chaji*. The guests, ideally four, assemble in a *machiai* (waiting room) and are served *sayu* ("white" hot water) by the host's assistant, the *hantō*, in order to sample the water used in making tea. The guests enter the *roji* ("dew ground"), a water-sprinkled garden path devoid of flowers, in which the guests rid themselves of the "dust," or of the world. They take seats at the *koshikake machiai* (waiting bench), anticipating the approach of the host, who is called *teishu* (house master).

The host replenishes the water in the stone basin set in a low arrangement of stones called *tsukubai* (literally, "to crouch"). The host purifies his hands and mouth and proceeds through the *chūmon* (middle gate) to welcome the guests with a silent bow. This gate separates the mundane world from the spiritual world of tea. The guests purify their hands and mouths and enter the tearoom by crawling through the small door, or *nijiriguchi*, which the last

guest latches. Individually they look at the scroll in the *tokonoma* (alcove), the kettle, and the hearth and take their seats.

Prior to the guests' entry, the kettle of water (*kama*) is placed in the room on a portable hearth (*furo*) with a charcoal fire. In winter a *ro*, a hearth set into the floor, replaces the *furo* to provide warmth. The host greets the guests. A charcoal fire to heat the water is built in the presence of the guests; this presentation (*sumi-demae*) is performed after the meal in the *furo* season and before the meal in the *ro* season. Incense, held in a *kōgo* (incense container), is put into the fire; sandalwood (*byakudan*) is used in the *furo*, and kneaded incense (*nerikō*) in the *ro*.

The Tea Meal—The host serves the tea meal, which is called *kaiseki* or *chakaiseki* (the name derives from that of a warmed stone that Buddhist monks placed in the front fold of their garments to ward off hunger pangs). The foods are fresh, seasonal, and carefully prepared without decoration. Each guest is served a tray set with three bowls: *gohan* (cooked white rice) and miso-*shiru* (soup flavored with fermented bean paste), served in covered lacquered bowls, and *mukōzuke* ("opposite place"), plain or vinegared raw fish or vinegared vegetables served in a ceramic dish and placed on the far side of the tray. New *hashi* (chopsticks) of cedar are used.

Sake is served in an iron pitcher (*kannabe*) and drunk from lacquered wooden saucers called *hikihai*. *Nimono* (foods simmered in broth) are served in separate, covered lacquered bowls. *Yakimono* (grilled foods) are served in individual portions on ceramic plates. All the serving chopsticks are of freshly cut green bamboo. Additional rice and soup are offered. The host may join the guests. The palate is cleared with a simple light broth, *kosuimono*, served in covered lacquered cups, which is used to rinse the chopsticks. This rinsing, or *hashiarai*, names the course.

Hassun is the name of the next course, which is inspired by Shintō reverence for nature. *Hassun* (8 *sun*; about 24.1 cm or 9.5 in) is also the length of the plain wood tray that is used to serve morsels of *uminomono* (seafood) and *yamanomono* (mountain food), representing the abundance of sea and land. During this course the host, who has been serving the guests, eats and is served *sake* by each guest; the role of server is consid-

ered a higher position. *Kōnomono* ("fragrant things"), pickled vegetables, are served in a small ceramic bowl, and browned rice, representing the last of the rice, is served in salted water in a lacquered pitcher (*yutō*). Guests clean their own utensils with soft paper (*kaishi*) that they have brought. The meal concludes with *omogashi*, the principal sweet. In order to make preparations for serving the tea, the host then asks the guests to leave the room.

Preparing and Serving Tea—Alone, the host removes the scroll and replaces it with flowers, sweeps the room, and sets out utensils for preparing *koicha* (thick tea), which is the focal point of the gathering. The *mizusashi*, a jar filled with fresh water, is displayed; the water represents the *yin* to complement the fire in the hearth, which is *yang*. The *chaire*, a small ceramic jar containing the powdered tea, covered by a fine silk bag (*shifuku*), is set in front of the water jar. An appropriate *tana*, or stand, on which to display the tea utensils is chosen for the occasion. A gong (*dora*) is struck to summon the guests during the day; at night a small bell (*kanshō*) is rung. The guests once again purify their hands and mouth at the *tsukubai* and reenter, look at the flowers and displayed utensils, and latch the door.

The host enters with the *chawan* (tea-bowl), which holds the *chakin* (tea cloth), a bleached white linen cloth used to dry the bowl; *chasen* (tea whisk); and *chashaku* (tea scoop), a slender bamboo scoop used to dispense the tea powder. The *chashaku* often bears a poetic name. These are set next to the tea jar, which represents the sun (symbolic of *yang*); the bowl represents the moon (symbolic of *yin*). The host brings in the *kensui*, a waste-water bowl; the *hishaku*, a bamboo water ladle; and the *futaoki*, a rest for the kettle lid made of green bamboo, and closes the *sadōguchi* (tea way entrance). The host uses a *fukusa*, a silk cloth representing the host's spirit, to purify the tea container and scoop, examining, folding, and handling the *fukusa* to deepen the host's concentration and meditation. Hot water is ladled into the bowl to warm it; the whisk is examined and rinsed. The emptied bowl is dried with the linen cloth. Three scoops of tea in increasing amounts are put into the bowl; then the tea jar is emptied into the bowl, sufficient to form a thin paste when kneaded with the whisk. A little

tea ceremony

Pictured here are various tea utensils used in the preparation and service of the tea ceremony.

▲ The container for the powdered tea varies according to the type of tea and the season. The ceramic tea container at left is for *koicha*, thick tea. The tea container is covered by a fine silk bag (right) called a *shifuku*.

▲ Water utensils arranged in the way the host would bring them into the tearoom. A bamboo *hishaku*, or ladle, rests on a metal rinse-water container (*kensui*). Inside is a bamboo *futaoki*, a rest for the kettle lid.

▲ Kettles in which the water is heated vary widely in shape.

▲ Utensils used in building the charcoal fire. The basket (far left) contains a feather duster to sweep the brazier, metal fire tongs, metal rings to lift the kettle, a hot pad, and several pieces of charcoal. The ash container (left) holds ash made from wisteria vines.

▲ From left to right are a teabowl, a linen cloth for wiping the bowl, a bamboo tea scoop, and a tea whisk. This teabowl is an example of *akaraku*, red Raku ware.

▲ A fan is used by guests (unopened) to accompany certain gestures. The *fukusa* (upper right) is used by the host to wipe utensils. For thick tea the host hands to guests on a cloth called a *kobukusa* (lower right).

▲ There are a variety of stands for the display of tea utensils; this paulownia stand holds a *natsume*, a container for thin tea (top shelf), and a *mizusashi*, a water container (bottom shelf).

more water is added to bring it to a drinkable consistency. The bowl is offered to the guests.

The first guest takes the bowl, drinks, and passes it to the others. The preferred wares for the teabowl are RAKU WARE, HAGI WARE, and KARATSU WARE, although many others may be used—Shino, Seto, and Oribe, for example. The bowl is returned and rinsed. The whisk is rinsed, the chashaku wiped, and the kettle replenished. The tea jar is cleaned and, with the tea scoop, is offered to the guests to examine more closely. The utensils are taken from the room. During the presentation, the utensils and related subjects are discussed.

The fire may be rebuilt in anticipation of serving usucha (thin tea), which helps to rinse the palate and to prepare the guests psychologically for their return to the mundane world. Smoking articles—a hiire (fire receptacle), a ceramic cup with a lighted piece of charcoal set in a bed of ash; a haifuki (ash blow), a length of green bamboo containing water to extinguish the ash; and a kiseru (pipe)—are offered on a tabakobon (tobacco tray). Since one rarely smokes in the tearoom, the tray is presented as a sign for relaxation. Zabuton (cushions) and tea-bun (hand warmers) may be offered. Higashi (dry sweets) are served on a wooden tray to complement the bitterness of the thin tea. Thin tea is prepared in a way similar to that of thick tea, except that less tea powder, of a lesser quality, is used, and it is dispensed from a natsume, a date-shaped lacquered wooden container; the bowl has a more casual or decorative character; and the guests are served individually prepared bowls of frothy, light tea. At the conclusion, the guests thank the host and leave; the host watches their departure from the open door of the tearoom.

The Japanese tea ceremony, a social act founded on reverence for all life and all things, is enacted in an idealized environment to create a perfect life. Its quiet atmosphere of harmony and respect for people and objects, with attention to cleanliness and order, strives to bring peace to body and spirit.

◐ 1536–1537

teachers 教師

(kyōshi). There have been three major developments in the system of teacher training in Japan since the Meiji Restoration in 1868: the first was the establishment of normal schools in accordance with the EDUCATION ORDER OF 1872; the second was the issuance of the Normal School Order (1886) by MORI ARINORI; the third was the abolition of a new system and the establishment of schools in accordance with educational reforms after World War II.

Teacher training. In 1872 the Ministry of Education established the Tōkyō Normal School (later Tōkyō University of Education, now TSUKUBA UNIVERSITY) to train elementary school teachers. In 1874 the Tōkyō Women's Normal School (now OCHANOMIZU WOMEN'S UNIVERSITY) was founded for the training of women teachers; it became a center for women's education and for the training of kindergarten teachers. Normal schools, especially the Tōkyō Normal School under the guidance of Marion SCOTT, introduced the organization of classes according to grade level, uniform instruction, and modern textbooks. After 1886, however, not all teachers were educated at normal schools; applicants who passed the certification exams and university graduates could also obtain a teaching certificate.

After World War II, a drastic reform of the teacher-training system was instituted. The United States Education Mission to Japan of 1946 advised that the curriculum for teacher training should comprise three areas—general education, course-related professional education, and professional education. It also related to teaching; that normal schools should be reorganized into four-year teachers' colleges; and that teacher-training programs could be administered by regular universities.

Today, the training of teachers for primary schools and special schools (SCHOOLS FOR THE BLIND, SCHOOLS FOR THE DEAF, and SCHOOLS FOR THE HANDICAPPED) is carried out primarily in education departments of universities and at national teachers' colleges; for middle and high schools, it is carried out primarily in regular universities. The training of kindergarten teachers is done in private junior colleges or training institutes designated by the Ministry of Education.

Teacher qualification. In 1949 the Educational Personnel Certification Law (Kyōiku Shokuin Menkyo Hō) was enacted and (except for university instructors) it became necessary to obtain a teaching certificate in order to become a teacher. At present, certificates are divided into first and second classes depending on the teacher's level of education and the grade taught. In addition, temporary certificates are sometimes granted. Through such means as in-service training, teachers can be promoted from temporary to second-class certification or from second-class to first class.

In-service training. In-service training today is carried out in three general ways: study and training individually, in school, or with various organizations; in-service training in such organizations as education centers run by the Ministry of Education; and in-service training at universities. In order to ensure the opportunity for in-service training, teachers' colleges offer in-service training, teachers' colleges offer dence courses for those who want higher certification. Middle-rank administrators are often selected from among graduates of these institutions.

Appointment, dismissal, and remuneration. Teachers at national schools (such as schools affiliated with national universities) are appointed or dismissed by the minister of education; teachers at public elementary and middle schools, by the prefectural board of education; and teachers at public high schools, by prefectural or city boards of education. Teachers' salaries are regulated according to a standardized scale. Starting salaries are determined by educational background, type of certification, and experience. In order to prevent stagnation of personnel it is customary to transfer teachers from one school to another within the same prefecture periodically.

Teaching responsibility. Teachers are completely responsible for guidance, club activities, student councils, and homeroom activities. In addition to these tasks and those related to PTA activity, teachers also bear responsibility for certain student activities outside the school. Working conditions are in general quite demanding.

Teachers' unions. The first teachers' union, the Keimeikai, was organized in 1919 by SHIMONAKA YASABURŌ. The union NIKKYŌSO, founded in 1947, has consistently regarded the educational policies of the Ministry of Education as reactionary and opposed them. Among more conservative teachers' organizations are the Nihon Kyōshokuin Remmei (Japan Federation of Teachers), the Nihon Shin Kyōshokuin Kumiai Rengō (New Japanese Federation of Teachers Union), and several other national organizations.

Composition of teaching personnel. In 1989, 49.5 percent of elementary-school teachers, 35.7 percent of middle-school teachers, and 20.1 percent of high-school teachers were women. Almost all kindergarten teachers were women. According to a 1986 survey, the age of 55 percent of elementary- and middle-school teachers was 38 or younger.

Problems affecting the teaching profession. A major problem has been the adjustment of new teachers to school environments. Consequently, in 1989 the Training Program for Newly Appointed Teachers (Shoninsha Kenshū Seido) was initiated. Under this program teachers are for the first year hired provisionally and are obligated to undergo on-the-job training under the guidance of a veteran teacher in methods of instruction and the handling of students. Another problem of increasing concern is juvenile delinquency, requiring teachers to offer guidance to students with personal problems.

teaching methods 教育方法

(kyōiku hōhō). In the Edo period (1600–1868) there were two main teaching methods, represented by the temple schools (TERAKOYA), where both teaching materials and instruction were individualized, and domain schools (HANKŌ), where emphasis was placed on the rote memorization of Chinese and Japanese classics. After the Meiji Restoration (1868), efforts were directed at forming a national system of education. The Meiji government hired the American Marion McCarrell SCOTT in 1871 to teach at the government-operated normal school in Tōkyō, and it was Scott who introduced American teaching methods to Japan.

Government control over curriculum was increased in 1886, after which nationalistic teaching methods became prevalent. With the spread of democratic ideas, the New Education Movement (SHIN KYŌIKU UNDŌ) emerged in opposition to the uniformity of Meiji-period (1868–1912) education. Numerous Western educational theories, broadly referred to as the Progressive Education Movement, were introduced. Most of these efforts, however, were conducted at elementary schools attached to normal schools or at private schools operated by such progressive educators as SAWAYANAGI MASATARŌ and HANI MOTOKO (see also SEIKATSU TSUZURI KATA UNDŌ). The public schools were not greatly affected by these new movements, which were suppressed during the militaristic early Shōwa period (1926–89).

Since the end of World War II, increased emphasis has been placed on the interests of the student and the individual's stages of development. Nonetheless, schools continue to focus on the transmission of formal knowledge, a system reinforced by ENTRANCE EXAMINATIONS and multiple-choice testing.

Teatoro テアトロ

Important theater journal originally established in 1934 and presently in its fourth revival. Teatoro is the Esperanto word for theater. From its inception Teatoro has focused

on the introduction and development of Western dramatic theories and techniques, frequently serializing translations of foreign dramatic criticism and plays. Series one of the journal appeared from May 1934 to August 1940 and was active in the promotion of leftist theater. Revived after World War II, series two of *Teatoro* was published from October 1946 to July 1956 under editors Hijikata Yoshi (1898–1959) and MURAYAMA TOMOYOSHI. Series three, revived by Akutagawa Hiroshi (1920–81), KINOSHITA JUNJI, SENDA KOREYA, and others, appeared from September 1956 to May 1964. It continued to be devoted to SHINGEKI ("new drama") and functioned as an organ of the progressive theater movement. Series four began publishing in June 1964 and continues to the present.

technical colleges
高等専門学校

(*Kōtō semmon gakkō*). Five-year institutions for professional and technical education, started in 1962. Graduation from middle school is a prerequisite for entrance. There are two types of technical colleges: industrial and merchant marine. Among the main courses are machinery, electricity, industrial chemistry, public works, and metalworking. There were 52,930 students enrolled in 62 technical colleges in 1990. To meet the demand for further technical education, two national universities opened in 1976: the Technological University of Nagaoka and Toyohashi University of Technology.

technology, modern
現代科学技術

(*gendai kagaku gijutsu*). Japan, which began to industrialize much later than most nations of the West, invested considerable time and capital in laying the industrial, economic, and educational foundations for technologies that were already in use abroad. From the beginning of the Meiji period (1868–1912) the Japanese government promoted the development of industry and technology as part of its plan to create a wealthy and strong nation. Victories in the SINO-JAPANESE WAR of 1894–1895 and the RUSSO-JAPANESE WAR and economic prosperity during WORLD WAR I spurred the development of industry and technology. The INSTITUTE OF PHYSICAL AND CHEMICAL RESEARCH was organized in 1917 under the joint sponsorship of government and industry for the purpose of developing and applying creative technology. Of particular significance was the rapid development of Japan's heavy and chemical industries in the 1930s as part of a general mobilization of industry and technology by the military, and significant advances were made in shipbuilding, optics, and aircraft technologies.

Although most of Japan's technology has been imported, the following are early examples of Japanese technological innovation: a power loom designed in 1897 by TOYODA SAKICHI; the seasoning Ajinomoto (L-monosodium glutamate; MSG) developed in 1908 by IKEDA KIKUNAE; the high-performance alloy KS Magnetic Steel, developed in 1917 by HONDA KŌTARŌ; a nitrogen-fixation process developed in 1920 by the National Chemical Laboratory for Industry; and the Yagi antenna, the most commonly used television and radio antenna configuration, developed in 1926 by YAGI HIDETSUGU.

Following World War II, industry, under the supervision of the Japanese government, again turned to Western technology, which it adapted to domestic needs and standards. The SCIENCE AND TECHNOLOGY AGENCY was established in 1956 to coordinate technological development, and the MINISTRY OF INTERNATIONAL TRADE AND INDUSTRY (MITI) provided guidance to prevent excessive competition and the consequent payment of unreasonably high licensing fees and royalties for imported technologies. While assisting the introduction of foreign technology, the ministry was also able to foster the development of domestic industries.

Although dependence on foreign technology remains a characteristic of native industry, the implementation of this technology has not been merely imitative. The Japanese have endeavored not only to improve imported technology but to adapt it to serve new purposes. For example, while all the fundamental technology for television, including video recording, is based on foreign patents, Japanese engineers succeeded in developing video recording for home use. Major Japanese enterprises are intensely competitive and constantly endeavor to be the first to introduce advanced technology from abroad. Technologies introduced by large enterprises are then swiftly adopted by the smaller manufacturers that serve them as subcontractors.

By the early 1990s Japan had overtaken the United States in the technological level of certain production processes, such as the manufacture of automobiles, television sets, and semiconductors. Japan had also introduced advanced technology in such areas as the prevention of pollution and environmental science. According to a survey made in 1985 by MITI, Japanese technologies for high-tensile steel, videocassette recorders, and plants for the solar generation of electric power were unexcelled by any similar foreign technologies. By 1990 fine ceramics, semiconductor memories, and spectrum analyzers had achieved a similar high level of technological excellence. Areas in which Japanese technology still lagged behind that of the West included those of airplane engines and microprocessors, as well as data base technology.

The technological revolution in postwar Japan has been effected largely through liberal investments made by private industries for the development of innovative applications of foreign technologies. Whereas in the United States 47 percent of funds for research and development was supplied in 1989 by the government, in Japan only 18 percent (1988) was provided by the government, the remainder coming from private investors. The emphasis placed by Japanese enterprises on developing improved applications of existing technology, rather than expending funds for the development of new technology whose commercial application may be impractical, has resulted in the relatively swift transformation of imported technologies into innovative industrial products, which, if commercially successful, provide a generous return on investment. However, it is anticipated that in the future the portion of total research funds directed to basic research, which at present is very small, will steadily increase. See also RESEARCH AND DEVELOPMENT.

technopolis
テクノポリス

(*tekunoporisu*). An English word coined in Japan to refer to a number of planned cities (urban concentrations of high technology) that were being proposed by the Ministry of International Trade and Industry (MITI) in the mid-1980s for realization some 10 years in the future. The proposal was first made in "The Vision of MITI Policies in the 1980s," a publication issued by MITI's Industrial Structure Council in March 1980. In April 1983 it became a definite government policy with passage of the so-called Technopolis Law (more properly, Law for Accelerating Regional Development based upon High-Technology Industrial Complexes). The proposed technopolises would be organic combinations of an industrial sector, an academic sector, and a residential sector, all featuring the most advanced technology. More specifically, they would be located near existing mother cities with populations of 150,000 or more. The technopolises would be designed to attract high-technology industry in such fields as semiconductors and computers, as well as related universities and research institutions. These areas would eventually develop into cities of 40,000 to 50,000 people. In 1984, 14 areas, including the Hamamatsu area of Shizuoka Prefecture, were designated for the development of such technological cities, and by February 1989 the number had been increased to 26.

Tedorigawa
手取川

River in southern Ishikawa Prefecture, central Honshū, originating in Hakusan, the highest peak in the Hakusan National Park, and flowing north into the Sea of Japan. The water is utilized for irrigation and electric power. Length: 73 km (45 mi).

Teganuma
手賀沼

Lake in the northwestern part of Chiba Prefecture, central Honshū. Located within Imba-Teganuma Prefectural Natural Park. This narrow lake was originally an inlet that later was sealed off by deposits of the river Tonegawa. Large-scale land reclamation was completed in 1968. Famous for duck hunting, it is also a popular fishing spot with catches including carp and eels. Area before land reclamation: 10 sq km (4 sq mi); present area: 3.7 sq km (1.4 sq mi); circumference: 25 km (15.5 mi); depth: 2.9 m (9.5 ft); altitude: 2 m (6.6 ft).

tegata → commercial paper

Teigin Incident
帝銀事件

(*Teigin Jiken*). Mass murder and robbery at a branch of the Teikoku Ginkō (Imperial Bank, abbreviated Teigin) in Tōkyō on 26 January 1948. A man posing as a public health official announced an outbreak of dysentery in the neighborhood and induced the bank's employees to drink an "antidote" containing cyanide. Twelve people died and about ¥160,000 (US $445) was stolen. Seven months later the police arrested Hirasawa Sadamichi (1892–1987), an artist. On the strength of a confession, which he later repudiated, Hirasawa was convicted and sentenced to death in each of two lengthy trials; the sentence was upheld by the Supreme Court in 1955. His execution delayed by protracted appeals, Hirasawa died after 38 years in prison, still maintaining his innocence.

Teijin Incident
帝人事件

(*Teijin Jiken*). Scandal of the 1930s involving the sale of shares in TEIJIN, LTD, a rayon manufacturer. Charges of official collusion and corruption caused the fall of the SAITŌ MAKOTO cabinet in 1934.

In June 1933 the Banchōkai (a group of young financiers including SHŌRIKI MATSUTARŌ and KOBAYASHI ATARU) purchased from

the Bank of Taiwan 100,000 shares of Teijin stock at ¥125 per share. When by the year's end the value of Teijin stock had risen to nearly ¥200 per share, the Banchōkai was widely suspected of having manipulated the stock market. Right-wing officials in the Ministry of Justice, hoping to damage the Saitō cabinet, claimed that cabinet ministers, high officials of the Ministry of Finance, and directors of the Bank of Taiwan had conspired to allow the Banchōkai to buy the Teijin shares at an artificially low price in return for Teijin shares and cash. In April and May 1934 the government arrested the vice-minister of finance, the president of Teijin, and a director of the Bank of Taiwan. Learning that certain cabinet ministers would soon be arrested as well, Saitō dissolved his cabinet on 3 July. Eventually 16 men were charged with corruption. In December 1937 the court declared the stock transaction regular and the defendants blameless, but the public was left with an impression of corruption in both the bureaucracy and financial circles.

Teijin, Ltd 帝人[株]

(Teijin). Textile company manufacturing synthetic fibers, plastics, films, and pharmaceuticals. Incorporated in 1918 as the Teikoku Jinzō Kenshi Co under the leadership of KANEKO NAOKICHI. In 1957 the company acquired polyester fiber technology from the United Kingdom to consolidate its position as Japan's leading manufacturer of polyester fibers. It has numerous overseas subsidiaries and 17 joint-venture companies with offices in New York, São Paulo, Düsseldorf, London, Singapore, Hong Kong, and Athens. Sales for the fiscal year ending March 1991 totaled ¥325.7 billion (US $2.4 billion), with 51 percent derived from polyester fibers, 22 percent from chemicals, 9 percent from nylon, 12 percent from pharmaceuticals, and 6 percent from other sources; the export ratio was 16 percent. The company was capitalized at ¥70.2 billion (US $511.7 million) in the same year. Headquarters are in Ōsaka and Tōkyō.

teijisei kōtō gakkō 定時制高等学校

(part-time high school programs). A type of high school program established in 1948 that offers a four-year part-time curriculum as an alternative to the three-year regular program. The part-time program admits working students unable to pass the regular high school entrance examination, and high school dropouts. Classes are scheduled to meet the needs of students with regular employment. Enrollment peaked in 1955 with 540,000 students and has been on the decline since then due to increased enrollment in regular high schools. In 1989 there were 152,253 students enrolled in part-time programs, a figure representing only 3 percent of the total high school enrollment in Japan.

Teiki 帝紀

(Record of the Emperors). A record of imperial succession, probably written down in the 6th century. Now lost, it may have been a primary source for Japan's oldest extant histories, the KOJIKI (712) and NIHON SHOKI (720), and for the genealogical chapters of JŌGŪ SHŌTOKU HŌTEI SETSU, a biography of Prince SHŌTOKU. See also TENNŌKI AND KOKKI.

Teikin ōrai 庭訓往来※

(Household-Precept Letter Writer). One of the best-known examples of the genre called ŌRAIMONO (collections of models for letter writing). Believed to have been written by GEN'E (1279-1350), a Buddhist priest of the TENDAI SECT, the model letters deal with social affairs of the higher samurai class. This book brought about the standardization of correspondence forms and was used as a writing textbook for about 400 years, to the end of the Edo period (1600-1868).

Teikoku bungaku 帝国文学

(Imperial Literature). Literary magazine. There were 296 issues published between January 1895 and January 1920. Teikoku bungaku was the product of the Teikoku Bungakkai, a group of professors, students, and graduates of the Faculty of Literature at Tōkyō Imperial University (now Tōkyō University). The magazine combined scholarly research in the humanities with literary works. Contributors included TAKAYAMA CHOGYŪ, UEDA BIN, WATSUJI TETSURŌ, and MORI ŌGAI.

Teikoku Nōkai 帝国農会

(Imperial Agricultural Association). Central organization for agricultural associations (nōkai) that had been formed separately from about 1880 onward. Established in 1910, it provided guidance to individual associations, made recommendations to the government, conducted research, and facilitated the sale of farm products. In 1943 it was absorbed by the Chūō Nōgyōkai (Central Agricultural Association).

Teikoku Oil Co, Ltd 帝国石油[株]

(Teikoku Sekiyu). The largest domestic oil and gas producer in Japan. Incorporated in 1941. It has been engaged in the exploration and development of oil fields along the coast of the Sea of Japan as well as on continental shelf areas. In Niigata Prefecture it has discovered large amounts of natural gas, which now constitutes its main line of business. The company is also active in the exploration of overseas oil fields through its subsidiaries. Zaire Petroleum Co commenced production of crude oil in 1976; the current daily production rate is 20,000 barrels. Egyptian Petroleum Development Co has produced crude oil at a daily production rate of 4,500 barrels since 1980. Other subsidiaries are active in explorations in Indonesia, Gabon, and China. Annual sales for December 1990 totaled ¥29.4 billion (US $220.1 million), of which natural gas accounted for 70 percent and oil products 25 percent. The company was capitalized at ¥13.3 billion (US $99.6 million) in the same year. Headquarters are in Tōkyō.

Teikōkutō 帝国党

(Imperial Party). Progovernment political party. Founded in July 1899 by former members of the KOKUMIN KYŌKAI, the Teikōkutō provided support in the House of Representatives for programs favored by the ruling oligarchy and bureaucracy. In December 1905 it joined other groups to form the Daidō Kurabu. See also MEIJI POLITICAL PARTIES.

teinensei 定年制

(age limit system). System of employment that designates ages for compulsory retirement. Promulgated from about the time of World War I, the age limit system now plays an important role in Japan's system of promotion through seniority.

The most common compulsory retirement age is 60. Many small and medium-sized enterprises, however, have either higher compulsory retirement ages or have no compulsory retirement regulations at all. Although no compulsory retirement regulations are set for public servants, they usually leave office when they reach the age of 60. At retirement, workers are paid allowances calculated from their basic monthly wages multiplied by the number of their years of service.

Retirees at age 60 face a variety of serious postretirement problems. Finding new jobs is extremely difficult, except for those workers in administrative posts who are assured of other jobs in affiliated companies. In many cases, workers must accept lower wages in exchange for extensions of compulsory retirement age. On their part, corporations are faced with the problem of sharply growing labor costs. See also RETIREMENT; EMPLOYMENT SYSTEM, MODERN.

Teisan KK テイサン[株]

(Teisan). Company producing oxygen, nitrogen, and other industrial gases. Incorporated in 1930. Among its other products are low temperature equipment, deep-sea diving equipment, and rapid freezing systems for food. It has an overseas subsidiary in South Korea. Annual sales for the fiscal year ending December 1990 totaled ¥54.1 billion (US $405.1 million), and the company was capitalized at ¥6.2 billion (US $46.2 million). In the same year the L'Air Liquide group of France held 64.4 percent of its capital stock and also provided technical assistance. Headquarters are in Tōkyō.

Teito Rapid Transit Authority 帝都高速度交通営団

(Teito Kōsokudo Kōtsu Eidan). A public enterprise incorporated in 1941 with capital furnished by the Tōkyō Metropolitan Government and Japanese National Railways to construct and operate subway lines in Tōkyō and adjacent areas. In 1991 the authority operated a total of eight lines—the Ginza, Marunouchi, Hibiya, Tōzai, Chiyoda, Yūrakuchō, Hanzōmon, and Namboku lines, with a total length of 162.2 kilometers (101 mi). In the fiscal year 1990 these lines (excluding the Namboku line, which began operating in 1991) carried an average of 5.9 million passengers daily. Although the authority is a public enterprise, it differs from other public corporations in that its capital includes no national government funds, and it is treated legally as a private railway company. The authority was capitalized at ¥58.1 billion (US $423.5 million) in March 1991. Headquarters are in Tōkyō.

Teizanbori 貞山堀

Canal in central Miyagi Prefecture, northern Honshū. This landlocked canal runs parallel to the coast of Sendai Bay from the city of Shiogama to near the mouth of the river Abukumagawa. Said to have been constructed in the early 17th century for transporting rice, it is no longer in use. Length: 36 km (22 mi).

Tejima Seiichi 手島精一

(1849-1918). Educator who worked for the establishment of modern technical education in Japan. Born in the Numazu domain (now part of Shizuoka Prefecture). From 1870 to 1874 he studied educational practices throughout the United States and England. After returning to Japan, he served as dean of students of the Tōkyō Kaisei Gakkō (a predecessor of Tōkyō University) and cura-

tor of the Tōkyō Kyōiku Hakubutsukan (now National Science Museum). He later became president of Tōkyō Kōgyō Gakkō (now Tōkyō Institute of Technology) and experimented with practical training in technical education.

Tekijuku 適塾 →→ Ogata Kōan

Tekken Construction Co, Ltd 鉄建建設[株]

(Tekken Kensetsu). General contractor. Incorporated in 1944. Tekken's projects include the SEIKAN TUNNEL, linking Honshū and Hokkaidō, and the bridge Kojima Ōhashi, part of the HONSHŪ-SHIKOKU BRIDGES. It has an overseas office in Singapore and subsidiary companies in the United States. For the fiscal year ending March 1991, the company had sales of ¥218.0 billion (US $1.6 billion) and capitalization stood at ¥17.9 billion (US $130.5 million). Headquarters are in Tōkyō.

tekkō 手っ甲

Coverings made of leather or cloth for the back of the hand and wrist to protect them from injury, cold, and sunburn; traditionally used by peddlers, travelers, and outdoor laborers. Today they are worn only by some farmers. The section covering the back of the hand is cut in a triangle or semicircle, and the part going over the wrist is square or cylindrical.

Tekkō Rōren 鉄鋼労連

(abbreviation of Nihon Tekkō Sangyō Rōdō Kumiai Rengōkai; Japan Federation of Steel Workers' Unions). Federation formed in 1951 by the unions of the five dominant steel-producing firms and related companies. The federation is a powerful force in the trade-union movement and frequently sets the pace for wage-level increases in the nationwide spring wage offensives (SHUNTŌ). In 1966 it became the nucleus of the new IMF-JC (International Metalworkers' Federation–Japan Council; see KINZOKU RŌKYŌ) and has since followed a policy of cooperation with employers, promoting the need for moderation by Japanese trade unions. Tekkō Rōren was affiliated with SŌHYŌ before joining RENGŌ in November 1987. In 1989 the federation had 201,400 members.

telecommunications laws 電気通信法

(denki tsūshin hō). Japanese telecommunications laws comprise both detailed technical regulations and laws governing the social uses of telecommunications. All present telecommunications laws were enacted after World War II with the objective of permitting the wide use of telecommunications by citizens. These laws govern both public and private use of all forms of telecommunications, including wire, cable, and broadcast media.

Basic laws include the Radio Law (Dempa Hō, 1950), which provides for fair and efficient use of radio waves; the Broadcasting Law (Hōsō Hō, 1950), which established the principle that broadcasts must conform to the public welfare; the Cable Television Broadcasting Law (Yūsen Terebijon Hōsō Hō, 1972); and the Telecommunications Business Law (Denki Tsūshin Jigyō Hō, 1984), which was promulgated to rationalize and stimulate the telecommunications industry. See also TELECOMMUNICATIONS SYSTEMS.

telecommunications systems 通信制度

(tsūshin seido). Telegraph and telephone services were established in Japan in the late 19th century. Relying initially on the advanced technology and equipment of Europe and the United States, Japan soon raised the level of its own technology and the size of its telecommunications networks. Telecommunications facilities deteriorated seriously during World War II, but their reconstruction was rapid after the war. The Nippon Telegraph and Telephone Public Corporation (now the NIPPON TELEGRAPH AND TELEPHONE CORPORATION, NTT) carried out a series of five-year plans, the first one starting in 1953, completing a nationwide automatic telephone dialing system in 1978 and eliminating its backlog of telephone orders in 1977. By 1991 there were over 55 million domestic telephone circuits, or about 45 for every 100 people. International telecommunications, under the aegis of KOKUSAI DENSHIN DENWA CO, LTD (KDD), also increased. Since its inauguration in 1952 NTT has actively promoted technological development in all fields of telecommunications, from telephone sets to switching equipment and transmission systems. Efforts are being made toward the development and introduction of nontelephone services in pursuit of the digitalization of telecommunications networks, as part of a plan to create a single integrated services digital network (ISDN). With the liberalization of the telecommunications market in 1985, a number of new companies began to offer a vast array of services ranging from international telecommunications to mobile telephone facilities. See also TELECOMMUNICATIONS SYSTEMS INDUSTRY.

telecommunications systems

Overseas Communications to and from Japan

Media	1980	1982	1984	1986	1988	1990
Telephone calls* (in millions)	23.4	38.1	68.9	134.6	255.5	388.9
Telex transmissions* (in millions)	38.0	45.7	52.1	43.8	27.1	17.5
Leased circuits (in millions)	812	842	961	1,149	1,461	1,632
Television transmissions†	2,559	3,593	3,312	5,546	10,599	16,355
Telegrams* (in millions)	3.3	2.6	1.9	1.2	0.8	0.6
Postal items (in millions)	229.2	235.1	239.3	242.5	275.7	308.5

*Includes relayed transmissions.
†International transmission of television signals using facilities provided by Kokusai Denshin Denwa Co, Ltd (KDD).
SOURCE: Ministry of Posts and Telecommunications, Tsūshin hakusho (annual), 1991.

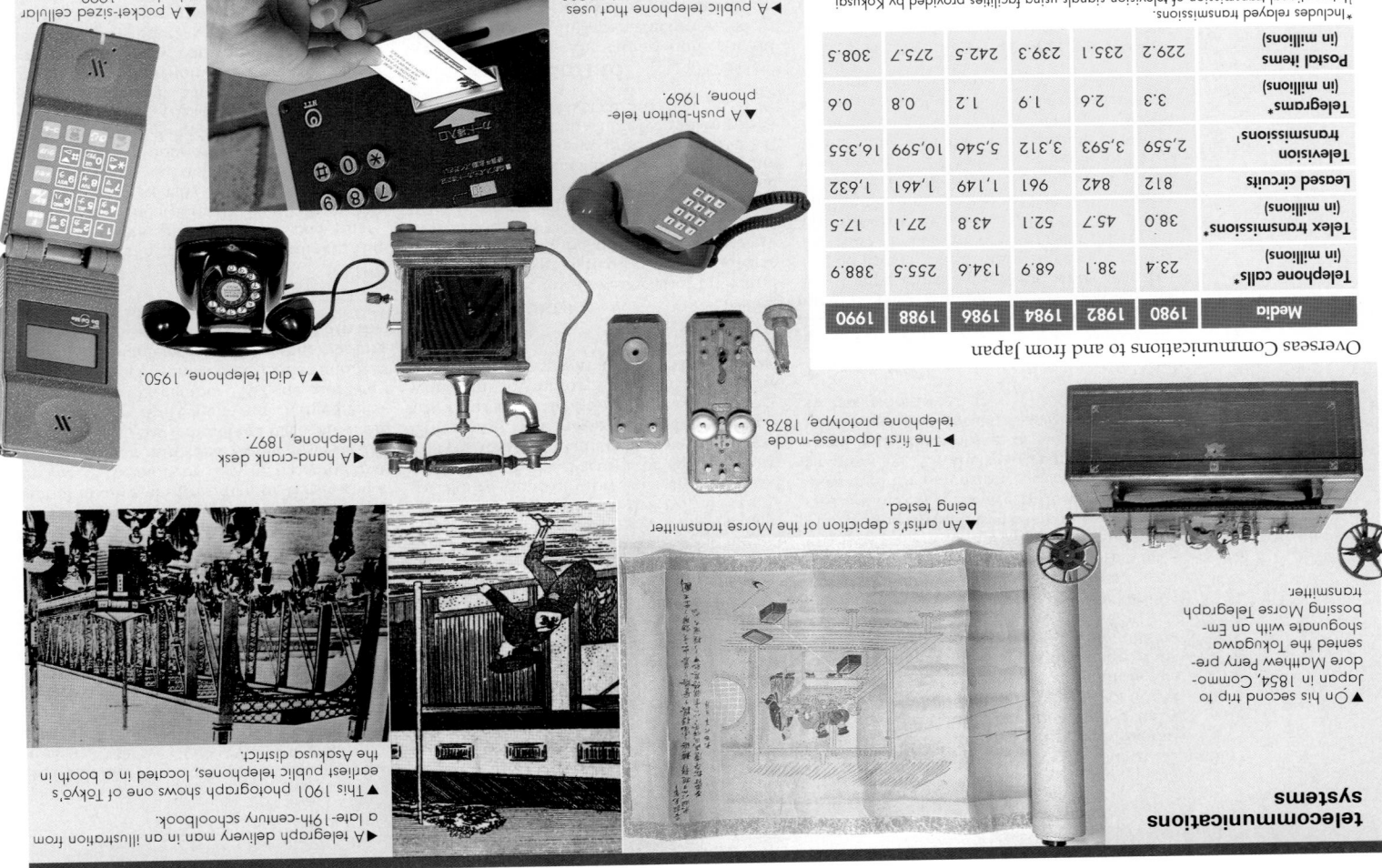

▶On his second trip to Japan in 1854, Commodore Matthew Perry presented the Tokugawa shogunate with an Embossing Morse telegraph transmitter.

▲An artist's depiction of the Morse transmitter being tested.

◀The first Japanese-made telephone prototype, 1878.

▲A hand-crank desk telephone, 1897.

▲A dial telephone, 1950.

▲A telegraph delivery man in an illustration from a late-19th-century schoolbook.

▲This 1901 photograph shows one of Tōkyō's earliest public telephones, located in a booth in the Asakusa district.

▶A push-button telephone, 1969.

▶A public telephone that uses prepaid telephone cards, 1982.

▲A pocket-sized cellular telephone, 1992.

History—Japan's age of modern telecommunications began in 1854 when Commodore Matthew Perry, who had come to Japan seeking to conclude a treaty of friendship and trade, presented the Tokugawa shogunate (1603–1867) with a Morse telegraph apparatus. After the MEIJI RESTORATION of 1868, government leaders quickly decided to make the establishment of telegraph service one of their top policy objectives. Two years later a telegraph service between Tōkyō and Yokohama was provided to the general public. The telegraph service was expanded rapidly and a nationwide network was completed by 1878.

The telephone was introduced into Japan in 1877, only one year after its invention in the United States. In 1890 the first general public telephone service was inaugurated in both Tōkyō and Yokohama. It was some years before the public recognized the importance of the telephone, but the demand for telephone service grew with the modernization of the economy. The TŌKYŌ EARTHQUAKE of 1923 caused extensive damage to telephone and telegraph facilities in both Tōkyō and Yokohama. In reconstructing these facilities, the government introduced automatic switching equipment. Until the end of WORLD WAR II, domestic telephone and telegraph services were operated entirely by the government, whereas both private enterprise and government were involved in international communications. The private International Telephone Co, Ltd, maintained international radiotelegraph facilities, and the International Telephone and Telegraph Co, Ltd, and Nippon Radio and Telegraph Co, Ltd, were involved in the construction and maintenance of international telephone equipment. The two companies were merged into the International Telecommunications Co, Ltd, in 1938 in an attempt to improve the overall effectiveness of both organizations.

In 1948 General Douglas MACARTHUR, commander of the Allied OCCUPATION forces, ordered the Japanese government to separate the telephone and telegraph service from the postal service in order to promote efficiency. As a result, the Communications Ministry was abolished in 1949, and in its place two separate ministries were established, the Ministry of Telecommunications and the Ministry of Postal Service (Yūseishō). With the end of the Occupation in 1952 a further reorganization took place. The Ministry of Telecommunications was abolished, and the newly created Nippon Telegraph and Telephone Public Corporation was given exclusive authority to provide domestic telecommunications services. The following year saw the establishment of KDD, with a monopoly over international services. Both of these corporations were placed under the supervision of the Yūseishō (now known in English as the MINISTRY OF POSTS AND TELECOMMUNICATIONS).

Telex service began in Japan in 1956. The number of telex subscriber lines increased from 188 at the time of inauguration to more than 73,000 over the next 20 years. With the diversification of data communications terminal equipment and the diffusion of facsimile systems, however, the number of telex subscriber lines has decreased greatly. In 1985, as a response to the growing sophistication and diversity of telecommunications services, NTT was privatized and the telecommunications market was liberalized. A number of new companies were allowed to offer their services, thus ending the monopoly on telecommunications services held by NTT and KDD throughout the postwar period. As of 1991 there were three new domestic telecommunications companies and two more companies offering international services.

The Revolution in Telecommunications Technology—Since its inception, NTT has actively promoted technological development in all fields of telecommunications, from telephone sets to switching equipment and transmission systems. NTT possesses state-of-the-art technologies in all these fields. Moreover, NTT has become one of the world leaders in the development of such new transmission systems as advanced microwave and coaxial cable systems. During the 1980s there was a remarkable growth in the use of computer networks, data base services, facsimile machines, and other related communications technologies in the Japanese workplace. In order to respond to the increased demand for data transmission, NTT early on began to plan for the digitalization of communications networks, the shift to a fiber optics system, and the introduction of satellite communications. By 1990 Japan's largest data communications company, NTT Data Communications, began offering the INFORMATION NETWORK SYSTEM (INS), an integrated services digital network that provides voice, picture, and data transmissions, in cities with a population of over 100,000. The size of the fiber optics network had grown to 41,800 kilometers (26,000 mi) by 1991. In addition, following the liberalization of the telecommunications market, a number of private companies began offering paging services, cellular telephones, and other mobile communications services.

telephones → telecommunications systems

television

(terebi hōsō). Including public, commercial, and satellite stations, 111 television stations were broadcasting throughout Japan in 1990. More than 99 percent of Japanese households have at least one television set, and many have one or more sets. The average length of time the Japanese spend watching television is three hours a day.

Television broadcasting was begun in Japan in 1953 by Nippon Hōsō Kyōkai (NHK), the national public broadcasting system. Black-and-white televisions spread rapidly at the time of the 1959 wedding of the present emperor and empress. Color televisions sold similarly well at the time of the Tōkyō Olympics in 1964 and replaced black-and-white sets by the mid-1970s.

In the early days of television in Japan, the television set held an honored place in the home and was a focal point of family gatherings. However, with the diversification of lifestyles and the number of sets per household increasing to two or more, television viewing has increasingly become an individual activity. In response, programs have increasingly been tailored to the interests and tastes of specific viewer age groups.

Especially in the 1980s, the number of after-midnight viewers sharply increased. In 1987 NHK commenced 24-hour satellite broadcasting, which was soon followed by all-night programming on regular commercial television stations. After midnight, information-oriented programs for young people, movies, and all-night debate shows are broadcast. Around 1985 prime-time programming, which had until then been devoted to entertainment programs, began to feature long news programs and documentaries, with considerable success. Outside production companies have increased their share to over one-half of commercially broadcast programs. Television has also become a major advertising medium, accounting for ¥1.6 trillion (US $11.1 billion), or about 30 percent of total advertising expenses.

NHK broadcasts throughout Japan and private stations broadcast on a local basis. Private stations in different parts of the country, however, generally belong to one of the nationwide networks centered on key stations headquartered in Tōkyō, so programs seen in Tōkyō can be seen elsewhere. The number of original programs produced by local stations is very small, but creating locally centered programming has become increasingly important for local stations.

In the second half of the 1980s, television reached an important turning point: videocassette recorders came into wide use in Japanese homes, direct satellite broadcasting began, and CABLE TELEVISION broadcasting services using communication satellites have created a multichannel television age. The development of HIGH-DEFINITION TELEVISION (HDTV), providing much clearer visual images by increasing the number of scanning lines and using larger screens, is expected to greatly increase the pleasures and potentials of television broadcasting.

▶ 1544–1545

television drama

(terebi dorama). Regular television broadcasting in Japan commenced in 1953 and live dramas were an important element in programming from the beginning. The first drama series was Kōfuku e no kifuku (The Rocky Road to Happiness), broadcast on NHK (Japan Broadcasting Corporation) in 1953–54, Toshiba nichiyō gekijō (Toshiba Sunday Theater), featuring family dramas, first appeared in 1956 on TBS (Tōkyō Broadcasting System, Inc) and is still on the air, making it Japan's longest-running television show. The earliest detective series was Daiyaru hyakutōban (Dial 110), broadcast by NTV (Nippon Television Network Corporation) beginning in 1957. Watashi wa kai ni naritai (A Clam is What I Want to Be), aired on TBS in 1958, was the first program to use a combination of live and videotaped material and demonstrated that television drama was capable of original artistic expression, both in terms of substance and in

Continued on page 1546 →

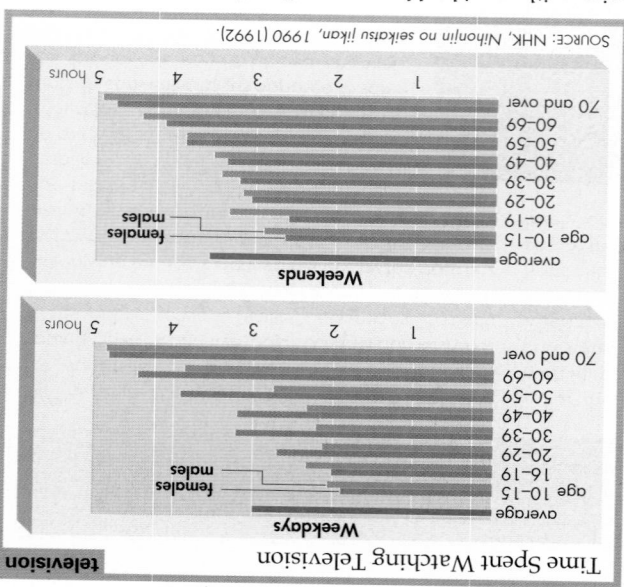

television

Time Spent Watching Television

Weekdays / Weekends

average, age 10–15, 16–19, 20–29, 30–39, 40–49, 50–59, 60–69, 70 and over — females, males — 1 2 3 4 5 hours

SOURCE: NHK, Nihonjin no seikatsu jikan, 1990 [1992].

There are two types of television broadcasting in Japan today: a single national public broad-casting network and five major commercial networks. The public network, NHK (Nippon Hōsō Kyōkai; Japan Broadcasting Corporation), operates a nationwide service. Financed neither by the state nor by private enterprise, it receives 98 percent of its op-erating revenues from reception fees paid by televi-sion-set owners. (Most people pay the fees, despite being under no legal obligation to do so.) NHK does not air commercials and is therefore relatively free of ratings pres-sures. Its conventional (as opposed to satel-lite) broadcasts consist of two channels, "General Television" and "Educational Television," and are transmitted from 6 AM until midnight.

Commercial broadcasting is dominated by five major national networks: Nippon Television Network Corporation (NTV); Tōkyō Broadcasting System, Inc (TBS); Fuji Telecasting Co, Ltd; Asahi National Broad-casting Co, Ltd; and Television • Tōkyō Channel 12, Ltd. All of these depend on advertising sponsorship and are thus con-stantly engaged in cutthroat competition for audience ratings.

Most of the commercial networks' pro-grams for national consumption are produced at the key stations of the "big five" in Tōkyō or at secondary stations in Ōsaka. The five also control smaller local commercial stations, which produce a limited number of their own programs. All the major Tōkyō-based networks operate on a 24-hour basis, and each is affiliated with one of Japan's five leading national daily newspapers.

Programming

Although the types of programs broadcast by NHK General Televi-sion and by the commercial networks are very similar—consisting mostly of news, cultural presenta-tions, entertainment, and sporting events—NHK is dis-tinct in that it has certain public obligations and tends to be seen as a custodian of public values. Its live relay broadcasts from the Diet (Japan's parliamen-tary body) and feature coverage at election times of the political positions and personal histories of all declared candidates are examples of the kind of broadcasting unique to NHK.

NHK Educational Television differs from other channels in that it is mainly oriented to serving the needs of viewers who wish to study specific subjects. For example, many Japanese feel that, as a conse-quence of their nation's insular location and history, they lack conversational ability in foreign languages. So for the large numbers of people seeking to learn a foreign language or improve their speaking skills, NHK broadcasts language lessons in English, French, Chinese, German, Italian, Spanish, Korean, and Rus-sian. Other educational programs include those intended for use in school classrooms; programs for children, such as Sesame Street; programs giving in-struction in various hobbies; and programs devoted to the arts and culture; and programs examining social issues. Ratings for these shows remain at a modest but steady level.

The Public and Private Faces of Japanese Television

Japan's huge public broadcasting network, NHK, and five major commercial networks offer televi-sion viewers a diverse selection of programming.

For the commercial networks, prime time means quizzes, comedies, talk shows, dramas, and variety programs. One of the first things to strike people when they flip through Japanese television channels is the high-speed banter maintained by program hosts and studio guests. The main role of the host is to ensure that the guests are able to express themselves freely and to create a smooth, easygoing atmo-sphere. Japanese-speaking foreigners often appear as guest panelists on quiz, game, and talk shows and many are treated as celebrities simply because they are able to keep up with the pace of the speedy repartee of the Japanese participants.

Many Japanese quiz shows are based on bizarre happenings in foreign countries, a theme which was first introduced by Naruhodo za wārudo (It's the World!; Fuji) in 1981. The shows present unusual foreign customs and lifestyles about which the panel-ists are quizzed. Panel members are generally select-ed from a wide range of media personalities, pop stars, comedians, cartoonists, actors, university pro-fessors, and foreigners.

Another feature of Japanese game and talk shows is the obvious amateurism of the guests. Even on talk shows dealing with politics and current affairs, which might seem to require a certain level of expertise, one sees amateurs—former sports stars, actors, and televi-sion comedians—in the role of host or commentator. Interestingly, the practice of using amateurs in this way was introduced by NHK, when it successfully used an amateur as a program hostess on Yume de aimashō (1961–66, Let's Meet in Dreamland). Since that time viewers have enjoyed the fresh approach of nonprofessionals—their interesting angles on topics, their way of thinking, their movements and behavior, and even their slips and fumbles. The use of amateurs removes much of the distance between the viewer and the people on screen. The viewer is able to feel a kinship with media stars even though the latter move in a different circle.

Commercial network talk shows are not limited to prime-time viewing. The major channels also broad-cast talk shows in the morning and early afternoon. The "wide shows," as they are known, mostly feature scandals and events in the lives of media personalities and are aimed at housewives.

A number of late-night talk shows are directed at young urban singles living on their own. Programs like Puresuté! (1988–92, Pre-Stage; Asahi) offer a hard-and-soft mixture of trendy topics that studio guests discuss into the small hours. Viewers can inter-act by telephone and facsimile. All-night television in general, and talk shows in particular, ease many city-dwellers' feelings of loneliness.

A popular prime-time genre is the drama, both historical and contemporary. "The just are rewarded and evildoers are punished"—this is the theme of most Japa-nese period pieces. The heroes of these dramas are usually high-ranking samurai who hide their rank and live among the common people. Through superior knowl-edge and guile, not to mention swords-manship, they outwit and chastise hard-nosed criminals, corrupt merchants, and malevolent officials. Although viewers know in advance how things will turn out, they enjoy watching the heroes in action. Each of the major commercial networks has had success with a long-running period drama of this type. Among the most popular have been Happpyakuya chō yume nikki (1989–92, Tales of Ward 808; NTV), Mito Kōmon (1969–, Counsellor Mito; TBS), and Tōyama no Kin san (1970–, Kin of Tōyama; Asahi).

NHK produces its own period dramas, which are shown every Sunday evening over the course of a year. The NHK dramas are aimed at the kind of view-er who is drawn to historical sagas as much for in-struction as amusement. These dramas focus on his-torical figures, usually military, who helped forge new epochs. Although factually based, the events and personalities in the dramas are often given a modern interpretation. Examples of NHK dramas include Tai-heiki (1991, Chronicle of the Great Peace), about the 14th-century feudal lord Ashikaga Takauji; and Nobunaga, King of Zipangu (1992), about Oda Nobunaga, who began the process of reunifying Japan in the 16th century.

When it was common for Japanese households to have only one television set, families used to watch programs together in the living room. Most of the "modern" dramas of 20 or 30 years ago were set in family situations and were known by the term hōmu dorama (family dramas). Indeed, the phrase "just like a family drama" came to be used to describe a con-tented urban middle-class family. Today, however, the family is no longer center stage; the focus has shifted to the lives and romantic adventures of young, single men and women who live in the big city. Neverthe-less, as was evident in the highly popular 1991 drama, Tōkyō rabu sutōrī (Tōkyō Love Story; Fuji), a peculiarly Japanese element continues to pulse through the latest programs—a view of human rela-tionships in which communication takes place without recourse to words. Tacit agreement or the belief that one should simply bear something without making a fuss are attitudes that can sometimes lead to great confusion. While the unraveling of the misunder-standing provides the very stuff of the drama, the conclusion is invariably harmonious. Modern dramas

not only depict the life situations of young people today, they also influence to a considerable extent young people's attitudes, language, and fashion.

Travelogues, another popular genre, are shown every day on at least one of the main channels. In days when foreign travel was regarded as a luxury, television travelogues gave viewers enticing glimpses of the unknown world beyond the shores of their island country. The prosperity of the high-growth years, which began in the 1960s, created a foreign travel boom. Today, when overseas travel is common, television travelogues have turned their attention back home to rediscover aspects of rural Japan. Shows that incorporate local culinary traditions have proved especially popular.

While the commercial networks' travelogues invariably feature some television personality as tour guide and are lighthearted and upbeat, NHK travelogues are somewhat more sedate, but also more diverse. Some are highly detailed portrayals of small regions in Japan, such as *Chiisana tabi* (1983– , A Little Trip), a long-running series that covers the Kantō and Kōshin'etsu regions of eastern Japan. Others are made abroad and cover vast areas over long periods of time, such as *Shiruku rōdo* (1980–86, The Silk Road) and *Dai Kōga* (1986–87, The Yellow River). The rich content of these programs exemplifies the type of quality programming in which NHK, a public broadcasting institution, is properly engaged.

Popular documentaries on the commercial networks try to tap into viewers' curiosity. Topics range from what it's like inside women's prisons to how *rāmen* noodles are made. Successful documentary series have included *Tsuiseki* (1988– , The Chase; NTV), *Suteki ni dokyumento* (1987–92, A Nifty Documentary; Asahi), and *Soko ga shiritai* (1982– , That's What I Want to Know!; TBS).

NHK examines serious subjects, such as current affairs issues, in its documentaries. For example, the *NHK supesharu* (1989– , NHK Special) series has included *Hōkai suru sorengun* (1992, The Collapse of the Soviet Military), on the coup d'état that took place in the former Soviet Union in August 1991. The documentary was based on unpublished documents of the former Soviet Army. In the *Puraimu 10* (1991– , Prime 10) series, one of the programs showed footage of fetal diagnosis. Both NHK series present the latest information on a variety of topics of public interest.

Nyūsu sutēshon (1985– , News Station; Asahi) was the first long-format (75-minute) news program in a prime-time slot on commercial network television. Although NHK General Television had been running long-format (40-minute) news programs since 1974, the understanding in commercial television had been that only entertainment shows could guarantee good ratings. The main reason for the success of *Nyūsu sutēshon* is the personality of its main presenter, Kume Hiroshi.

Unlike NHK's newscasters, who are professional journalists, Kume had been a popular presenter on TBS entertainment shows. On *Nyūsu sutēshon*, Kume sometimes makes provocative personal comments and asides. Viewers appreciate his witty exchanges with the other commentators and guests. NHK newscasters, ever mindful of their company's public status,

keep any personal comments to the barest minimum. While they can always be relied on to give an accurate and balanced account of the news, NHK news programs are relatively bland. When major news stories break, many viewers like to compare the heavier approach taken by NHK's evening bulletin *Nyūsu 21* (1990– , News 21) with the lighter treatment of the same subject on *Nyūsu sutēshon*.

Animated cartoon programs comprise another genre often shown in prime time. With its humorous portrayal of daily life in a three-generation household, *Sazae san* (1969– , Fuji) is a popular animated version of the classic, nationally known *manga* (comics) by Hasegawa Machiko.

Also set in the context of a three-generation family, *Chibimaruko chan* (1990–92, Fuji) centered on a precocious nine-year-old girl, who often made telling criticisms of adults and her classmates. Chibimaruko chan represented a new breed of child character not seen before in Japanese animated cartoons. Like today's more-knowing children, she could see through the deceits of the adult world.

Another television cartoon program worth noting is *Manga Nihon mukashi-banashi* (1975– , Folktales of Japan; TBS), which is still on the air after more than 15 years.

Satellite Broadcasting

By 1992 households in Japan were able to receive satellite transmissions on three broadcast satellite (BS) channels and six communications satellite (CS) channels.

NHK's BS-1 broadcasts a 24-hour service of news using extracts from a variety of foreign news telecasts: the BBC and ITN from Great Britain; Antenne 2 from France; ZDF from Germany; the All-Russian Television and Radio Company; ABC, CNN, and PBS from the United States; CCTV from the People's Republic of China; KBS from South Korea; and Channel 9 from Thailand. Simultaneous translation into Japanese is available for these newscasts, and certain stories are shown in real time. NHK's BS-2 offers a variety of general programming.

The third BS channel, WOWOW, is commercial and features mostly movies and foreign sports events. In 1992 the six commercial CS channels began broadcasting. Each channel offers a specific type of programming. Viewers can tune in to see foreign movies, Japanese movies and theater, CNN news, rock music, popular music, and sports. To receive these broadcasts, it is necessary to pay entry and reception fees to the individual stations.

The existence of NHK as a public institution has allowed the commercial networks considerable leeway in which to develop their own identity and types of programming. Not so long ago, each of the major networks was seen before to specialize in a particular area; TBS was known for its dramas, for example, and Fuji for its entertainment. In today's more fiercely competitive environment, in which ratings play such an important part, these categories are breaking down. With their journalism, documentaries, dramas, and entertainment shows, commercial networks are able to take more liberties and be more adventurous than is possible for NHK. Nevertheless, in recent years, NHK has been trying to lighten up its image a bit by using media personalities that were once seen only on commercial channels. Indeed, NHK has gone so far in this direction that these days there is often little discernible difference between some NHK programs and programs on commercial networks.

Fujitake Akira

terms of exploring the technical potential of the new medium. This program exerted a strong influence on the development of subsequent television dramas in Japan, and the genre firmly established itself as a staple of television broadcasting, generating such variant forms as the family drama, the literary drama, and historical, suspense, and socially oriented dramas.

Renzoku terebi shōsetsu (The Television Novel Series), a fifteen-minute-long daytime program broadcast Monday through Saturday on NHK since 1961, has enjoyed 30 years of steady popularity, consistently drawing nearly 30 percent of the viewing audience with its dramatizations of the lives of women and achieving a smash hit in the 1983–84 season with Oshin, a tale of the trials and tribulations of a poor farm girl and her eventual success as a supermarket entrepreneur. TBS's historical drama Mito Kōmon has maintained a similarly loyal following since 1969 with its tales of good triumphing over evil in Edo-period (1600–1868) Japan. As the television drama genre has matured and diversified, it has attracted many talented dramatists, including YAMADA TAICHI, HASHIDA SUGAKO, HAYASAKA AKIRA, MUKŌDA KUNIKO, KURAMOTO SŌ, and James Miki (b 1935).

In their early days, television dramas were usually one hour in length, but recently longer pieces have become common. They are usually broadcast during three time slots: at 8 AM, at 1 PM, and between 7 PM and 12 AM. Almost all are videotaped rather than live or shot on motion picture film.

Some commentators have indicated that the ever-increasing homogenization of program content, the popularity of nonfiction programs, and the impact of other forms of home entertainment other than network programming (such as videocassettes) may well be signs that viewers are beginning to tire of television drama. Despite these predictions, production has continued unabated—in a given week in Tōkyō in the late 1980s, for example, 50 television dramas with a total length of 60 hours were broadcast—and the future of the genre does not seem radically threatened.

Television Tōkyō Channel 12, Ltd
[株]テレビ東京

(Terebi Tōkyō). A Tōkyō-based commercial television station established in 1964. It began as a station devoted to special programs on science and technology backed by the Japan Science Foundation (Nihon Kagaku Gijutsu Shinkō Zaidan). Broadcast operations were initially limited to the immediate Tōkyō area. It later became a general programming station, with significant additions of financial programs and shows imported from the United States. As of 1992 the channel had acquired five network affiliates and reached the Ōsaka, Aichi, and Hokkaidō areas.

temari
手まり

(literally, "handball"). A small ball fashioned from cloth wound about with brightly colored thread. It is used in playing a kind of handball, a variant of KEMARI (kickball), which had been introduced from China around the 7th century. Originally used in a tossing game such as otedama (see BEANBAG), from the 17th century on it was bounced against the hard surface of the floor. Rubber balls (gomu mari) appeared in the 1880s. Ball-bouncing games are usually played to the accompaniment of rhythmic songs known as temari uta.

tembimbo
天秤棒

(carrying poles). Wooden poles formerly used to transport heavy loads, particularly liquids in pots or barrels, or salable goods. Loads of equal weight are suspended from the ends of a pole that is borne over one shoulder or across both shoulders and steadied with the hands. The poles normally measure 1.8 meters (5.9 ft) in length.

temari This traditional cloth handball is wound about with cotton thread in an intricate chrysanthemum pattern.

tembimbo An 18th-century ukiyo-e print by Harunobu showing a vendor using tembimbo (carrying poles) to bear a water-based drink.

Tembo
展望

(Outlook). Monthly journal of literature and criticism published by CHIKUMA SHOBŌ PUBLISHING CO, LTD. It ran for 69 issues between January 1946 and September 1951 before suspending publication. USUI YOSHIMI was editor in chief, assisted by KARAKI JUNZŌ and NAKAMURA MITSUO. The magazine was known for its broadly informed, in-depth treatment of literary and philosophical issues. Usu's own column, "Tembo," set the tone with its incisive social and cultural criticism. NAKANO SHIGEHARU, DAZAI OSAMU, ŌOKA SHŌHEI, and SHIINA RINZŌ were major contributors. A second version of Tembō, under different editorship, was published for 167 issues between October 1964 and August 1978.

tembu
天部

(heavenly beings; Skt: deva). The fourth-ranking category in Japanese Buddhist iconography, after NYORAI (Buddha), bosatsu (BODHISATTVA), and myōō (Kings of light or wisdom). The category of tembu comprises miscellaneous deities adopted from the Hindu pantheon into the Buddhist tradition. The best known types of deva images are as follows: (1) Bonten (Skt: Brahmā) and Taishakuten (Skt: Indra), examples of which are found in the temples of TŌDAIJI, TŌSHŌDAIJI and TŌJI. (2) Niō or Kongōrikishi (Skt: Vajrapāṇi), for example those at Tōdaiji. (3) the Shitennō or Four Heavenly Kings, i.e. Jikokuten (Skt: Dhṛtarāṣṭra), Zōchōten (Skt: Virūḍhaka), Kōmokuten (Skt: Virūpākṣa), and Tamonten or Bishamonten (Skt: Vaiśravaṇa), for example, those at Tōdaiji. (4) the popular feminine deities Kisshōten or Kichijōten (Skt: Śrīmahādevī), Benzaiten or Benten (Skt: Sarasvatī), and KISHIBOJIN (Skt: Hārītī); and (5) Daikokuten (Skt: Mahākāla, i.e., Śiva), sometimes identified with the native Japanese deity ŌKUNINUSHI NO MIKOTO. Many of these deities have become objects of local cults, especially since the introduction of esoteric BUDDHISM in the 9th century.

Temiya Cave
手宮洞窟

(Temiya Dōkutsu). A cave in Temiya Park, city of Otaru, Hokkaidō, noted for its unusual prehistoric markings, discovered in 1866. In 1989 it was learned from the study of surrounding soil strata that the Temiya Cave markings are of the period AD 200–400. Whether the markings are phonograms or other symbols remains uncertain, as does their relationship to the abstract pictographs in the nearby Fugoppe Cave (dated AD 500–1000).

Temmangū
天満宮

Also known as tenmangū. General term for shrines dedicated to SUGAWARA NO MICHIZANE (845–903), a scholar-statesman who was exiled on false charges to Dazaifu in Kyūshū, where he died unpardoned. Kyōto, the capital, suffered repeated storms and earthquakes after his death. These were interpreted as acts perpetrated by the vengeful ghost (see GORYŌ) of Michizane, and he soon came to be associated with Tenjin, a god of heaven. By the end of the Heian period (794–1185) Michizane had come to be honored as the god of literature. Several centuries later he was also regarded as the god of calligraphy. Temmangū are found throughout the country. The head shrines are KITANO SHRINE in the city of Kyōto and DAZAIFU SHRINE in Fukuoka Prefecture.

Temmei Famine
天明の飢饉

(Temmei no Kikin). A severe famine that affected nearly all of Japan during the Temmei era (1781–89). Several hundred thousand people died as a result of the famine, one of the worst in the Edo period (1600–1868). Unseasonable weather caused crop failures, and the difficulties were compounded by the eruption of the volcano Asamayama and by poor administration. Rice prices soared as speculators, often with the connivance of officials, hoarded the meager harvest. The Tokugawa shogunate attempted to meet the crisis by distributing relief food and money and setting up shelters. Riots (HYAKUSHŌ IKKI; UCHIKOWASHI) broke out in unprecedented scale and numbers. The famine was one of several factors that led to the fall of TANUMA OKITSUGU from control of the shogunate government. See also KYŌHO FAMINE; TEMPŌ FAMINE.

Temmon Hokke Rebellion
天文法華の乱

(Temmon Hokke no Ran). A disturbance in August 1536 (Temmon 5.7; the name of the era can also be pronounced Temmon, hence the name of the disturbance) by adherents of the NICHIREN SECT (also known as the Hokke or Lotus sect), who held sway in Kyōto from 1532 to 1536 (the so-called Hokke Ikki). By the late 15th century about half the populace of Kyōto were followers of the Nichiren sect, which itself was becoming an armed power, with its Kyōto temples fortified against attacks by rival sects. The people of Kyōto, organized by townsmen (MACHISHŪ) for self-defense and other political activities, acted as the chief support of the military power of the

Temmu, Emperor 天武天皇

(?–686). Temmu Tennō. The 40th sovereign (*tennō*) in the traditional count (which includes several legendary emperors); reigned 672–686. He was also known as Prince Ōama. His father was the 34th sovereign, Emperor Jomei (593–641; r 629–641). His mother, Jomei's consort (*kōgō*) ruled twice—first as Empress Kōgyoku, then as Empress Saimei. Temmu's consort, a daughter of his elder brother Emperor Tenji, later reigned as Empress Jitō. Temmu emerged into political affairs after Japan's defeat in the Battle of Hakusukinoe in 663. Following the enthronement of Tenji's son Ōtomo as Emperor Kōbun in 672, Temmu successfully rebelled (see JINSHIN DISTURBANCE). He established his capital at ASUKA KIYOMIHARA NO MIYA. His formal enthronement was the following year (673).

Temmu furthered Tenji's administrative reforms by establishing an efficient central bureaucracy. The system of ranks for imperial princes and other members of the court nobility was revised (see COURT RANKS), and the various important families were classified according to lineage and social status (see YAKUSA NO KABANE). In 681 Temmu ordered compilation of the ASUKA KIYOMIHARA code, and he commissioned a national history. The laws formed the basis of the TAIHŌ CODE (701) and the historiographical project, which produced the Kojiki (712) and NIHON SHOKI (720).

temples 寺院

(*jiin*). The word temple (*tera* or *jiin*) refers to a Buddhist establishment in which Buddhist images are enshrined, priests or nuns usually reside, and ceremonies and religious practices take place. Today there exist over 77,000 temples of various sects in Japan.

The first temple in Japan is said to be the Mukaharadera, founded in 552, when Soga no Iname (d 570), leader of a faction favoring the introduction of BUDDHISM to Japan, converted his residence at Mukahara into a temple (see SOGA FAMILY). In 587 SOGA NO UMAKO, Iname's son, defeated the anti-Buddhist Mononobe family in battle. He then built ASUKADERA, the first full-fledged temple complex in Japan, in 596. Prince SHŌTOKU is said to have built the so-called Seven Great Temples of Nara, including SHITENNŌJI, HŌRYŪJI, and DAIANJI. During the reign of Emperor Temmu (r 672–686) Buddhist chapels were set up in each provincial capital and staffed with monks called *kokushi* (national teachers).

In the year 742, Emperor Shōmu, after the practice of Tang (T'ang) China, ordered the construction of a kokubunji (provincial temple) and kokubunniji (provincial nunnery) in each province. TŌDAIJI was built in the capital, HeijōkyŌ (now the city of Nara), as the head *kokubunji*. By the Nara period (710–794), there were some 360 temples in Japan.

During the Heian period (794–1185), the TENDAI SECT and SHINGON SECT, which eventually replaced NARA BUDDHISM as the central force in Japanese Buddhism, were established. The Tendai temples ENRYAKUJI and MIIDERA and the Shingon temples KONGŌBUJI and KyŌŌ Gokokuji (also known as TŌJI) gained adherents from among the imperial family and the nobility. In the late Heian period, the belief that one could be reborn in the Amida's Pure Land became widespread (see PURE LAND BUDDHISM). The nobility constructed many Buddhist halls enshrining Amida, including the Hōōdō at the temple BYŌDŌIN.

In the late 12th century, the Kamakura shogunate extended its patronage to the Zen RINZAI SECT. Later, following the practice of Song (Sung) China, KENCHŌJI, ENGAKUJI, and other Zen temples were organized into the GOZAN system. During this period, older sects, such as Tendai and Shingon, established *monzeki* (temples headed by members of the imperial family) and *inge* (subtemples of *monzeki* in which monks of noble origins monopolized the highest offices).

The Muromachi period (1333–1568) saw the rapid spread among the common people of various Pure Land, Zen, and Nichiren sects. In particular, the JŌDO SHIN SECT, with its head temple, the HONGANJI, developed by systematically organizing adherents who gathered at its branch temples and preaching centers (*dōjō*).

The Tokugawa shogunate (1603–1867) moved to establish control over the various Buddhist sects. It issued a series of regulations and structures and decreed that all Japanese register with a local temple (see TERAUKE; SHŪMON ARATAME).

After the Meiji Restoration in 1868, the new government, intent on establishing Shintō as the national religion, ordered the separation of Buddhism from Shintō (see SHINTŌ AND BUDDHISM, SEPARATION OF; STATE SHINTŌ). Concurrently, an often violent anti-Buddhist movement erupted (see HAIBUTSU KISHAKU). The temple registration system was abolished. In 1871 many temple lands were confiscated by the government. Until the end of World War II, Buddhism was subordinated to State Shintō and placed under stringent state control. The building of new temples was strictly regulated, and religious activities of temples declined. Under the 1947 constitution, FREEDOM OF RELIGION FAITH was guaranteed. Buddhist temples tried to attract new followers, but most experienced financial difficulties and competition with the more modern NEW RELIGIONS for funds and members.

Tempo Famine 天保の飢饉

(Tempo no Kikin). Nationwide famine between 1833 and 1836 (Tempo 4–7), years when rice crops were exceptionally poor. Scarcity sent rice prices higher, and destitute peasants flocked to the cities. Many died of starvation and disease, particularly in northeastern Japan. The Tokugawa shogunate and the various domains tried to meet the crisis by distributing rice, setting up shelters, regulating prices, prohibiting hoarding, and restricting *sake* production. Domainal assistance measures were largely ineffective. It was to seek relief that ŌSHIO HEIHACHIRŌ rebelled in Ōsaka, and peasant uprisings broke out in many other areas as well. See also KyŌHŌ FAMINE; TEMMEI FAMINE; TEMPO REFORMS.

Tempo Reforms 天保の改革

(Tempo no Kaikaku). Reforms undertaken during the Tempo era (1831–45). The term refers to reforms initiated by the TOKUGAWA SHOGUNATE (1603–1867) under the leadership of MIZUNO TADAKUNI during the years 1841–43 (Tempo 12–14); it also embraces reforms undertaken by DAIMYŌ of various domains.

temporary workers 臨時労働者

(*rinji rōdōsha*). The most stable employment in Japan is provided by the lifetime employment system, in which companies recruit regular workers upon graduation from schools and universities. To guarantee these regular workers continuous employment even when business is slow, companies hire only the number of regular workers that they are able to maintain under all economic conditions. In good times, however, the companies' demand for labor is greater than the fixed number of regular workers can supply, so they supplement their staffs by hiring temporary workers. The lifetime employment system established itself in the 1930s, and the accompanying system of hiring temporary workers was widely taken up.

At first, there was strong demand for skilled workers as temporary staff, and the conditions of their employment were frequently superior to those of the regular employees. Gradually, however, as companies were able to train enough of their own skilled staff, they increasingly moved in the direction of hiring mostly unskilled temporary workers at low wage rates.

In the postwar period of high economic growth, most temporary workers were seasonal migrant (*dekasegi*) laborers from rural areas, but gradually, with the increase in the number of housewives taking on part-time work to supplement the family income, along with the number of students and teenagers doing part-time jobs, the categories of temporary employment became more varied. After the oil crisis of 1973, companies were particularly eager to achieve flexibility in their employment policies, and temporary workers were hired in a more systematic fashion until they accounted for over half the total number of new employees. Most were paid by the hour at the lowest wage rates. Labor mobility was very high, and contracts, as a result, were kept very simple. In 1985 the Labor Services Temporary Assignment Bill became law. This was passed in response to the growing number of employment agencies that were specializing in supplying companies with cheap temporary labor to do such jobs as office cleaning. In addition to such unskilled workers, however, skilled workers such as computer operators and office staff were also becoming available, and companies began to hire people with special skills from the agencies whenever they had a need for them. In order to secure the services of such skilled staff, contract employee systems were devised under which companies began to offer fixed-period contracts directly to individuals instead of going through agencies.

During the 1830s Japan experienced widespread crop failures (see TEMPŌ FAMINE). Foreign ships appeared offshore in unprecedented numbers, and the MORRISON INCIDENT of 1837 and Western imperialist activity in China suggested the imminence of a major foreign crisis. Mizuno Tadakuni, chief among senior councillors (RŌJŪ), and others were alarmed, and the death of retired shōgun TOKUGAWA IENARI in 1841 enabled them to initiate vigorous reforms. That summer Tadakuni had the new shōgun, Tokugawa Ieyoshi (1793–1853), announce his intention to restore the spirit of the KYŌHŌ REFORMS and the KANSEI REFORMS of the previous century.

To increase food production, Tadakuni forbade peasants to divert their energies from agriculture and later ordered those living in Edo (now Tōkyō) to return to their home villages (see HITOGAESHI). To improve the morals and morale of samurai and the general public, he ousted men from office, punished others for corruption, and ordered daimyō and lesser samurai to practice frugality and self-discipline. He reissued sumptuary regulations and outlawed gambling and unregulated prostitution. He ordered merchants to reduce prices and prohibited production of luxury items. Merchant monopoly associations (KABUNAKAMA) were abolished. To meet shogunate fiscal needs, Tadakuni instructed merchants to make monetary contributions and tried to increase the effectiveness of tax collection. He also initiated a program to bring under direct shogunate control all accessible arable lands in fiefs surrounding Edo and Ōsaka (see AGECHIREI).

To strengthen military capabilities, Tadakuni ordered samurai to practice military arts, instructed EGAWA TARŌZAEMON to cast firearms, authorized TAKASHIMA SHŪHAN to train soldiers in their use, and opened a new artillery training area. To avoid a foreign crisis, Tadakuni had the shogunate modify its policy of forbidding foreign ships to approach the coastline (see GAIKOKUSEN UCHIHARAI REI). Then, to pacify domestic critics, he took steps to strengthen coastal defenses and control unauthorized foreign trade. By early 1843 Tadakuni was facing stiff criticism, and his order transferring fief holders away from Edo and Ōsaka was the last straw; the order was retracted and Tadakuni resigned.

The Tempō Reforms were not limited to the shogunate, because the issues they addressed, most notably the problem of governmental debt, were shared by most domains. In some domains, reformers tried to strengthen control of certain businesses to increase domainal revenue (see HAN'EI SEMBAI). In others, reformers attacked monopolies, but this policy seems to have invariably failed. Prior to the institution of reforms by the shogunate, reforms were undertaken in the domains of Mito (now a part of Ibaraki Prefecture), Saga (now Saga Prefecture) and Satsuma (now Kagoshima Prefecture) in Kyūshū, Tadakuni's domain of Hamamatsu (now a part of Shizuoka Prefecture), and Chōshū (now Yamaguchi Prefecture). However, neither on the shogunal nor the domainal level were the Tempō reforms completely successful. Some historians see them as marking the emergence of new "absolutist" forces that eventually led to the MEIJI RESTORATION in 1868.

Tempyō no iraka 天平の甍

(tr The Roof Tile of Tempyō, 1975). Historical novel by INOUE YASUSHI (1907–91); published 1957. The work depicts the lives of five Japanese priests who go to Tang (T'ang) dynasty (618–907) China as part of an effort to invite the famous priest GANJIN to Japan. Although all five are portrayed as being at the mercy of their fate, each persists singlemindedly on his chosen path. Yōei dies in China, never seeing his lifelong efforts to bring Ganjin to Japan bear fruit. Kaiyū becomes a mendicant priest and runs away. Although homesick for Japan, Genrō settles in China with his Chinese wife and two children. After spending over 10 years copying the sutras and dreaming of taking them back to Japan, Gyōkō drowns en route, and the sutras share his fate. Only Fushō, who inherited Yōei's mission to bring Ganjin to Japan, realizes his ultimate goal. While focusing on these characters, the novel accurately depicts the great historical events of the times and the drama of ancient Japan's assimilation of the culture of China.

ten → heaven

tenant farmer disputes 小作争議

(kosaku sōgi). Between 1917 and 1941 there occurred 72,696 tenant disputes with landlords, usually at the subadministrative village or hamlet (buraku) level. The most common tenant demands were rent reductions to compensate for harvest losses caused by natural disasters (especially in the 1920s) and continued tenancy when landlords attempted to change tenants or cultivate the land themselves (especially in the 1930s). Over 90 percent of the disputes ended in compromise, frequently mediated through the government's tenancy conciliation system established in 1924. The rest were mostly resolved in the tenant's favor. The spread of rural poverty was the major cause of tenant farmer unrest.

Tenchi, Emperor → Tenji, Emperor

Tenchūgumi Rebellion 天誅組の乱

(Tenchūgumi no Ran). An uprising in 1863 by the Tenchūgumi (Heavenly Retribution Band), antishogunate, proimperial loyalists in Yamato Province (now Nara Prefecture). Like the IKUNO DISTURBANCE, it is considered important today because some participants were peasants. The SONNŌ JŌI (Revere the Emperor, Expel the Barbarians) movement peaked in 1863, when imperial loyalists from Chōshū (now Yamaguchi Prefecture) dominated Kyōto. Planning to have the emperor personally lead an army against the foreigners, activists from several domains first organized an imperial visit to Yamato shrines to pray for success. The visit was announced on 25 September. The next day some 75 Tenchūgumi activists set out for Yamato to raise an imperial army, destroy shogunate authority in the region, and welcome the emperor. Yoshimura Toratarō (1837–63), a village headman (shōya) from the Tosa domain (now Kōchi Prefecture) acted as principal commander, while the young court noble NAKAYAMA TADAMITSU was the nominal leader. On 29 September the group killed the shogunal intendant (DAIKAN) at Gojō and his deputies. Local peasants joined the cause, attracted by promises of tax relief. However, in the coun-

Tempyō culture 天平文化

(Tempyō bunka). The culture of the Tempyō era (729–749), a subperiod of the Nara period (710–794), it roughly coincides with the reign (724–749) of the emperor SHŌMU. In this period the Chinese-inspired RITSURYŌ system of government was further developed, and through missions to China (see SUI AND TANG [T'ANG] CHINA, EMBASSIES TO) Japan received direct influence from the cosmopolitan culture of Tang China.

Under the patronage of the devout Shōmu, Buddhism was adopted as the national religion, and provincial temples (KOKUBUNJI) were built throughout Japan, with TŌDAIJI in Nara as the head temple. Many outstanding temple buildings (the Octagonal Hall, or Yumedono, at HŌRYŪJI; the main hall at SHIN YAKUSHIJI), Buddhist statues (the Jū Dai Deshi, or Ten Great Disciples of the Buddha, at KŌFUKUJI), Buddhist paintings (the Kichijōten, or goddess of good fortune, at YAKUSHIJI), and other Buddhist works were produced. In addition to wood and gilt bronze, clay and dry lacquer (kanshitsu) were used in sculpture, making possible a wide range of expressive techniques. Several thousand articles from this period have been preserved at the SHŌSŌIN repository at Tōdaiji. See also BUDDHIST SCULPTURE; BUDDHIST PAINTING; BUDDHIST ART.

tempura 天麩羅

Fresh fish, shellfish, or vegetables dipped in a batter (koromo) of flour mixed with egg and water and then deep-fried. Tempura tastes best eaten right after frying, accompanied by a side dish of special tempura dipping sauce and grated radish. The sauce is a mixture of soy sauce, mirin (sweet sake), and dashi (stock).

The origins of tempura date to the mid-16th century, a time when many items of Portuguese and Spanish culture, including methods of frying game, were brought to Japan (the word tempura is generally thought to be a corruption of the Portuguese tempero or cooking). Cooking with oil had already been introduced in Japan from China as part of a vegetarian diet. The merging of these two elements, after adaptation to Japanese tastes and customs, resulted in tempura as it is known today. Open-air tempura stalls became popular in early-19th-century Edo (now Tōkyō), and many of these stalls developed into full-scale tempura restaurants.

A wide variety of foods can be used as ingredients for tempura. Low-fat fish such as smelt (kisu), a kind of whitebait (shirauo), conger eel (anago), cuttlefish (ika), shrimp, and such shellfish as scallops are commonly used. Vegetables used include lotus root, mushrooms, ginkgo nuts, beefsteak plant (shiso), and green peppers. Shrimp tempura is commonly served in a bowl atop a bed of rice in a dish known as TENDON, or atop noodles as tempura soba or tempura udon.

☞ 1550–1551

Tendai sect The interior of the Kompon Chūdō, one of the principal buildings of this Buddhist sect's head temple, Enryakuji.

Tendai sect 天台宗 (Tendaishū). Buddhist sect founded in Japan in 806 by SAICHŌ. The Japanese counterpart of the Chinese Tiantai (T'ien-t'ai) sect, Tendai was, together with the SHINGON SECT, a dominant sect of the Heian period (794–1185). Popular Buddhist movements of the Kamakura period (1185–1333) such as the JŌDO SECT (Pure Land sect) and NICHIREN SECT evolved from it, although Tendai itself was closely identified with the court nobility through much of its history.

Chinese Tiantai — The Tiantai sect in China was founded by Zhiyi (Chih-i; 538–597) and along with the Huayan (Hua-yen;) sect was considered one of the two great sects of Chinese Buddhism. Tiantai synthesizes the diverse teachings of the historical Buddha as found in the Hinayana and Mahāyāna scriptures, utilizing the message of the LOTUS SUTRA as its unifying framework. Tiantai philosophy is based on the fundamental Mahāyāna teaching of emptiness—that all things, being impermanent, are devoid of self-entity. According to the Tiantai formulation, lack of self-entity means that nothing exists of itself; everything partakes of Ultimate Reality, which is beyond conceptualization in terms of existence. However, Ultimate Reality is never abstract, for it is identical with the phenomenal world. Hence, "everything is real," and "the unenlightened state is identical with Buddhahood." Tiantai also emphasized the need for meditation and established a set of meditational practices.

Saichō and the Founding of Japanese Tendai — As a young man, Saichō had become dissatisfied with the worldliness of the Buddhism of his day (called NARA BUDDHISM) and in 785 secluded himself on Mt. Hiei (HIEIZAN), where he created a small monastic community by attracting disciples and lay patrons including the reigning emperor KAMMU. He went to China in 804 to receive accreditation from a Chinese Tiantai master, and while there also learned some rituals from a master of ESOTERIC BUDDHISM.

Upon returning to Japan in 805, Saichō received from Emperor Kammu official recognition of the Tendai sect on Mt. Hiei. Kammu, however, stipulated that esoteric Buddhism be part of the sect. The first challenge to the Tendai sect came from KŪKAI, the founder in Japan of the Shingon sect, who had acquired a mastery of esoteric Buddhism in China. Between 809 and 816 Saichō regarded Kūkai as a teacher and a colleague, but their friendship ended when Kūkai refused to return one of Saichō's disciples who had defected to him. In 818 Saichō asked the court for authority to ordain monks based on Mahāyāna precepts. However, due to the opposition of the Nara sects to which the ordination of all novice monks according to Hinayāna precepts was vouchsafed, permission was not granted until shortly after Saichō's death, when the court gave official recognition to the Tendai center on Mt. Hiei by naming it ENRYAKUJI.

Tendai after Saichō — Kūkai's center was on Mt. Kōya (KŌYASAN) in what is now Wakayama Prefecture. Kūkai had a deeper understanding of esoteric Buddhism than any Tendai monk and his influence at court waxed. In 835 the court formally recognized Kūkai's sect of esoteric Buddhism, and Shingon became Tendai's great rival.

Tendai's fortunes were revived by ENNIN, who reestablished the Tendai sect's position at court through his mastery of esoteric Buddhist rituals, attained during a nine-year stay in China. ENCHIN also enriched the Tendai sect through his study in China between 853 and 858. In the 10th century, a bitter rivalry developed between monks of Ennin's line and those of Enchin's line, and in 993 the latter moved out of Enryakuji and established themselves at Onjōji (see MIIDERA) at the foot of Mt. Hiei.

Two of the most significant developments in Tendai after the 9th century were the growth of HONGAKU, a philosophy that greatly influenced the sects that grew out of Tendai. The Tendai Pure Land movement culminated in the Kamakura period (1185–1333) with the establishment of independent Pure Land sects, such as the JŌDO SECT of HŌNEN and the JŌDO SHIN SECT of SHINRAN. The Nichiren sect was founded by a priest, NICHIREN, who had studied at Mt. Hiei and based his religious beliefs on the Lotus Sutra.

The influence of Tendai itself declined with the fortunes of the court aristocracy. ODA NOBUNAGA destroyed almost all of Enryakuji in 1571, signaling the end of Tendai's political influence and prominence, although the sect recovered somewhat during the Edo period (1600–1868). As of 1989, there were approximately 4,300 Tendai temples, 20,000 clergymen and religious personnel, and 3 million lay members affiliated with the sect.

Tendō 天童[市] City in central Yamagata Prefecture, northern Honshu. It developed as a castle town of the Tendai family during the 14th century and later as a market town. In 1830 it became the castle town of the Oda family. Tendō makes about 95 percent of all shōgi (Japanese chess) pieces in the country. Agricultural tools and furniture are also produced. Farm products include cherries, apples, and grapes. The Tendō Hot Spring is located here. Pop: 57,339.

tendon 天丼 One-dish meal consisting of a bowl of rice topped with TEMPURA, over which tempura sauce is poured. Tendon was originally made with shrimp tempura, but now fish or vegetable tempura as well as kakiage, a tempura made with a mixture of finely chopped ingredients, may be used.

tengu 天狗 Uncanny and ambivalent creature in Japanese folklore with long beak and wings, glittering eyes, and a man's body, arms, and legs. A variant form, sometimes credited with higher rank, has a long nose, white hair, and red face and carries a feather fan.

The tengu is principally seen as a keshin (AVATAR) of YAMA NO KAMI, the guardian of certain mountains with a particular affinity for huge trees. References to him in medieval literature reveal him as a subtle enemy of Buddhism, kidnapping Buddhist priests and tying them to the tops of trees, implanting thoughts of greed and pride in their minds, or feasting them on dung magically disguised as delicious food. He is also feared as an abductor of children and for his powers of illusion and demoniacal possession. Conversely the tengu is often represented as a benign protector and transmitter of supernatural skills. He is closely associated with the YAMABUSHI, being often depicted as wearing items of the yamabushi's distinctive costume. See also BAKEMONO.

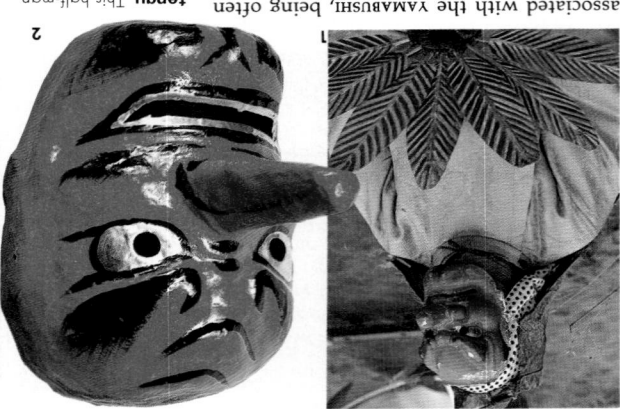

1 A villager costumed as a tengu for an autumn festival in Shizuoka Prefecture. 2 Tengu masks and carvings are popular as decorative talismans in rural areas and are often seen in shops and inns.

Tenguto no Ran → Mito Civil War

Tenji, Emperor (626–672; Tenji Tennō; also called Tenchi Tennō). The 38th sovereign (tennō) in the traditional count (which includes several legendary emperors); reigned 661 to 672, although his formal enthronement did not take place until 668. The son of Emperor Jomei (593–641; r 629–641); known before his ascension to the throne as Prince Naka no Ōe. His mother, Jomei's consort (kōgō), became Empress Kōgyoku (see SAIMEI, EMPRESS). The SOGA FAMILY was then at the peak of its power, virtually eclipsing the imperial house. Naka no Ōe plotted with FUJIWARA NO KAMATARI (then called Nakatomi no Kamatari) to overthrow the Soga. They carried out a coup in 645 and reorganized the government on the Chinese model (see TAIKA REFORM). Naka no Ōe became regent for his uncle Emperor Kōtoku, who had succeeded Kōgyoku at the time of the coup. After Kōtoku's death, Naka no Ōe's mother reascended the throne as Empress Saimei. She died in 661, but for seven years Naka no Ōe was unwilling to relinquish the regency—the real locus of power—and refused to be enthroned. In 667 he moved the capital to Ōtsu no miya and in 668 formally ascended the throne as Emperor Tenji. As emperor, he established a standardized system of household registration (KŌGONEN-JAKU) and drew up the Ōmi CODE of laws.

tenjōbito 殿上人 General term for court officials of the Heian period (794–1185) who enjoyed the privilege of imperial audience (shōden) in the Seiryōden, the emperor's living quarters. They included all officials of third rank or higher, those of fourth and fifth ranks who were specially favored, and sixth-rank chamberlains (or archivists; kurōdo; see KURŌDO-DOKORO). They were also known as kumonoue-bito ("people above the clouds"), although this could refer to any member of the court nobility. Those not allowed audience were jigenin ("people on the ground"; see jige). The number of tenjōbito was set at 30 but later increased to about 100. Restricting the privilege of audience was practiced also by retired emperors, retired imperial consorts, and crown princes.

tenjōgawa 天井川 (river with a raised bed). A river whose bed has become higher than the adjacent land. Most rivers in Japan have swiftly flowing currents and carry large quantities of silt and sand. As a result, tenjōgawa can occur naturally.

Continued on page 1552→

tendon This popular tempura and rice dish is one of a class of Japanese foods known as donburimono (one-bowl rice dishes).

D'ÉTAT OF 30 SEPTEMBER 1863 the extremist forces were expelled from Kyōto by moderates, and the shogunate dispatched troops to quell the Tenchūgumi rebellion.

Tempura Techniques

It is no wonder that tempura has won so many devotees outside Japan. The appeal is obvious: golden crisp on the outside, tender and succulent on the inside, tempura is a glorious way of savoring the freshest seafood and vegetables of the season. While every chef has his or her own carefully guarded secrets for tempura frying, most will agree that the key to success lies in properly mixing the batter and controlling the oil frying temperature. Care must also be taken in selecting the oil for frying. The rich, nutty flavor of tempura fried in sesame oil was at one time considered superior, but modern palates now seem to prefer the lighter, less heavily flavored tempura fried in vegetable oil. You can fry either, or a combination of both—but whichever you use, be sure that the oil is fresh.

Since tempura should be served and eaten right away, have everything prepared before you begin frying, so that no time is wasted between the frying pan and the table.

The steps for making tempura are: (1) Prepare dipping sauce and condiments. (2) Prepare items of food to be fried. (3) Heat oil. (4) Make batter. (5) Fry food and serve immediately with dipping sauce and condiments.

Kawabe Kōji

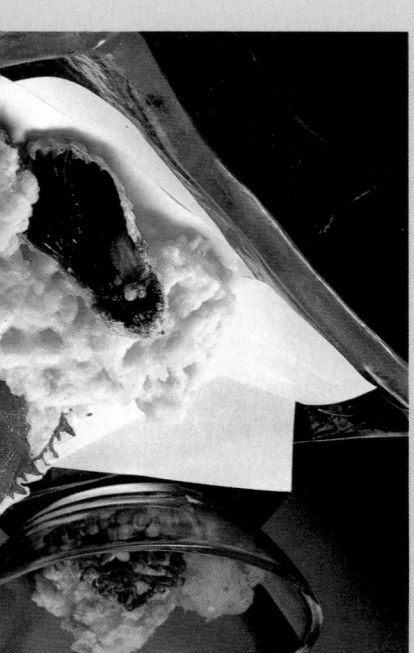

Tempura Batter

A crisp, lacy coating is the essential for good tempura. To achieve this, the batter must be thin and lumpy—not smooth and creamy. A smooth mixture will prevent excess moisture from escaping and allow air pockets to form between the batter and the food, resulting in a plasterlike coating that falls off easily. Only a few swift strokes with a pair of thick chopsticks are needed to mix the batter. Refrigerating the ingredients beforehand will also help to keep the batter from becoming sticky. Mix the ingredients *just before* you begin frying, and keep the batter chilled by putting the mixing bowl into a larger bowl filled with ice water.

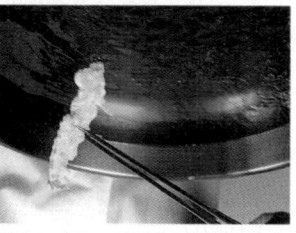

1 Ingredients for batter: chilled water; beaten egg, all-purpose flour. Prepare egg-water by mixing 1 part beaten egg with 3–4 parts water. (One egg makes enough batter for about 4 servings.)

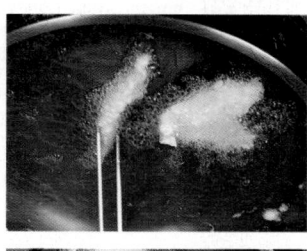

2 Just before frying, loosely combine equal parts of sifted flour and egg-water mixture, using swift, slicing strokes. Traces of dry flour should remain in batter.

Frying

It is essential to maintain the proper oil temperature throughout the frying process. Using a flat, thick-bottomed pan and frying in a large quantity of oil—enough to fill about ⅓ of the pan—will help to reduce temperature fluctuations. Adding ingredients will naturally bring down the temperature of the oil, so fry only a few pieces at a time.

Dredge seafood lightly in flour before dipping in batter. When frying, begin with the low-temperature foods and gradually move up to the high-temperature group. To keep oil clean, occasionally skim the surface of the oil for loose crumbs.

Testing the Oil: If using a cooking thermometer, keep checking the temperature and adjusting the heat as you fry. But if you can, try the traditional method of judging the correct oil temperature by sight.

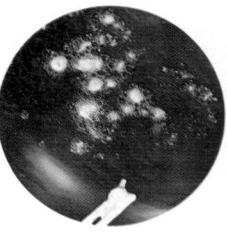

At 170°C (338°F): Drops of batter will fall to the bottom of the pan before quickly floating back up to the surface.

At 180°C (356°F): Drops of batter will spatter near the surface of the oil.

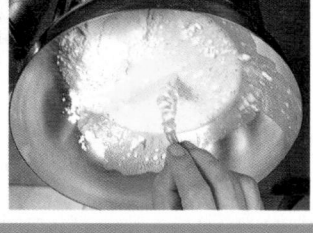

1 Dip item to be fried into the batter. Only a thin film is needed; allow excess batter to drip off.

2 Lower into middle of pan.

3 Deep-fry until crisp, turning only once for even frying. Tempura is done when the large bubbles of oil around the edges are reduced to a fine froth.

4 As you remove tempura from pan, briefly allow excess oil to drain off. Serve immediately on individual plates lined with absorbent paper.

Ingredients for Frying

A whole array of seafood and vegetables from conger eel to string beans will make for delicious tempura—the only rules are that the ingredients be fresh and in season. Chicken, beef, and pork are generally not used because of their heavier taste.

All ingredients can be divided roughly into low (170°C/338°F) and high (180°C/356°F) temperature groups.

Low-temperature ingredients: Foods that require more thorough cooking—vegetables such as potatoes, acorn squash, carrots; saltwater fish such as conger eel and flathead; most varieties of freshwater fish. Pictured (clockwise from top): flathead (*megochi*), conger eel (*anago*), sweet potato, carrot, Japanese eggplant (*nasu*), squash.

Kakiage-Style Tempura

A combination of ingredients can be fried together to make *kakiage*-style tempura. Try using 2 or 3 different types of ingredients that all require about the same frying time. The batter for *kakiage* should be slightly sticky; mix it a little more thoroughly than you would for regular tempura. The oil should be kept at about 170°C (338°F).

Some suggestions for *kakiage*-style tempura (pictured below): baby shrimp and green soybeans (*edamame*); corn and julienne carrots; baby scallops and trefoil (*mitsuba*).

Dipping Sauce

The delicately seasoned dipping sauce (*tentsuyu*) enhances the natural flavors of tempura. The secret to making the dipping sauce lies in the soup stock, known as *dashi*. The main ingredients for the stock are dried bonito flakes (*katsuobushi*) and giant kelp (*kombu*). Have the dipping sauce prepared before you begin frying so that the tempura can be eaten right away.

The ingredients for the dipping sauce are (clockwise from top): water, *mirin* (sweet cooking *sake*), soy sauce, salt, sugar, kelp, bonito flakes.

1 Put 1 liter (1 qt) of water in pan. Add 30 g (1 oz) of kelp and heat. Just before water comes to a boil, remove kelp.

2 When liquid begins to boil, sprinkle in 30 g (1 oz) of bonito flakes; remove from heat. When the flakes have settled to bottom of pan, filter remaining stock through a sieve.

3 Heat 500 ml (17 fl oz) of stock and 100 ml (3½ fl oz) each of *mirin* and soy sauce, 1 heaping Tbsp sugar, and 1 tsp salt. Bring to a boil, reduce heat, and simmer for 10 minutes.

Condiments

To enhance the natural flavors of tempura, try adding condiments like grated *daikon* radish and ginger to the dipping sauce. But piping-hot tempura can also be just as delicious with nothing but a sprinkle of salt or a squeeze of lemon.

Mix and match condiments of your choice (clockwise from top): grated *daikon* radish mixed with grated zest of citron (*yuzu*), dipping sauce, curry powder, powdered *sansho* spice, salt, lemon, fine powdered green tea (*matcha*).

Preparing Ingredients Cut larger ingredients into bite-size portions that are thin enough to allow heat to penetrate quickly. Pat ingredients dry before frying.

Squid: Remove skin and cut into bite-size squares. Cross-score surface.

Smelt and other small fish: Remove scales and entrails. Slice along back; open and flatten. Remove backbone.

Shrimp: Devein and shell; make 3 incisions along belly. Cut off tip of tail; use flat of knife to squeeze out moisture.

Shiitake mushrooms: Remove stem; make decorative notches along cap.

High-Temperature Ingredients: Foods that taste best with minimal cooking—fragrant vegetables and herbs, shellfish, white-fleshed fish, other seafood that can be eaten almost raw. Pictured (clockwise from top): smelt (*kisu*), squid, asparagus, celery, string beans, *shiitake* mushrooms, ginger shoots, baby scallops, shrimp.

1 For each serving, place a small handful of ingredients in a bowl.

2 Mix with just enough batter to hold ingredients together; transfer mixture to a ladle.

3 Carefully slide mixture into oil from side of pan.

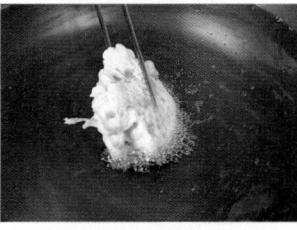

4 When bottom begins to harden, bring mixture to middle of pan and turn over.

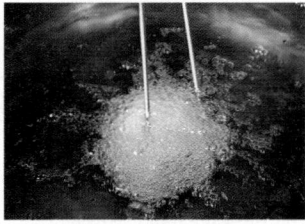

5 With a pair of chopsticks, gently hold down center of mixture in oil to allow heat to penetrate inside. Fry until golden.

rally where embankments have been built to prevent river flooding, since deposits build up along these embankments. The riverbeds become higher, the danger of flooding increases, and the embankments are made still higher. The Jōganjigawa, a river in Toyama Prefecture, and the Kusatsugawa, a river in Shiga Prefecture, are two examples of *tenjōgawa*.

tenkō   転向

(literally, "change of direction"). Term used figuratively to refer to an individual's formal rejection of an ideological commitment, usually under some pressure. Originally used to describe a recantation of affiliations with the JAPAN COMMUNIST PARTY (JCP) and belief in communist ideology; subsequently used for other ideological shifts. *Tenkō* is sometimes translated as "ideological conversion," but its emphasis is on the rejection of a previously held ideological belief rather than the acceptance of a new one.

The term was coined in 1933 by SANO MANABU and Nabeyama Sadachika (1901–79), two high officials of the JCP. They were arrested in 1929 for violating the PEACE PRESERVATION LAW OF 1925, tried with over 250 others in 1931–32, found guilty, and sentenced to life imprisonment. As Peace Preservation Law violators, they were considered "thought criminals" (*shisōhan*). Their crime had been to lead an organization (the JCP) that advocated overthrow of the KOKUTAI (the national polity that was thought to be unique to Japan) and the capitalist economic system.

On 10 June 1933, eight months after their sentencing, Sano and Nabeyama announced from prison that they had made a political "change of direction" and were breaking their ties with the Communist Party. They published a statement that listed their reasons for leaving the party and set forth their new beliefs, which acknowledged the special role of the emperor and their acceptance of the *kokutai*. The authorities publicized the statement and used it to pressure others. Within a month, 548 others had made similar recantations, and it soon became government policy to resolve thought crimes by inducing thought criminals to recant.

Various forms of coercion, both physical and psychological, were used to achieve *tenkō*. For minor offenders, a potent inducement was the promise of release from custody. There was some beating and torture, but such techniques were more often used to extract confessions and evidence than to obtain *tenkō* statements. The most powerful tactic was to instill a sense of guilt and obligation toward other family members, and toward the emperor and nation. In the initial wave of recanting following Sano and Nabeyama's joint *tenkō*, any expression of *tenkō*, written or oral, was accepted at face value. Later, as *tenkō* became a matter of policy, systematic procedures evolved. After 1936 a new THOUGHT CRIMINAL PROBATION LAW provided supervised probation and rehabilitation services for *tenkōsha* (persons who underwent *tenkō*) who were released from custody. The pervasiveness of *tenkō*, especially at early stages of the judicial process, is demonstrated by the fact that over 13,000 persons were handled under the new law during its first two years of operation, although fewer than 3,000 persons were ever convicted of thought crimes during the 20-year life of the Peace Preservation Law.

Tenkō played an important part in integrating even the most divisive elements in prewar Japanese society into the war effort. The phenomenon of ideological recantation is certainly not unique to Japan, but seldom has it been so formally elaborated, nor has it had such far-reaching implications for a nation.

tenkoku   篆刻

(seal carving). Carving of a name or sobriquet in a durable material, such as stone or wood, to fashion a seal. *Tenkoku* (Ch: *zhuanke* or *chuan-k'o*) refers to the carving of seals used in an unofficial capacity to imprint works of graphic art, and in particular to seals carved for their own use by *bunjin* (Ch: *wenren* or *wen-jen;* literati artists; see BUNJINGA). The term derives from *tensho* (Ch: *zhuanshu* or *chuan-shu;* archaic script), the calligraphic style in which seals are usually carved. Seal carving came to Japan from China in the Kamakura period (1185–1333) but did not flourish until the Edo period (1600–1868), when the practice spread among *bunjin*. Carving of seals and the study of old imprints continues today, and exhibitions are well attended by aficionados. See also RAKKAN.

Tenninkyō   天人峡

Gorge on the upper reaches of the river Chūbetsugawa (a tributary of the ISHIKARIGAWA), central Hokkaidō. Towering cliffs formed by columnar joints rise from the gorge, and many huge rocks dot the area. Site of Hagoromo Falls, the largest in Hokkaidō, and of Tenninkyō Hot Spring. Length: approximately 8 km (5 mi).

tennis   テニス

(*tenisu*). The American surgeon Dr George A. Lealand is credited with formally introducing tennis to Japan (1878). Because of the difficulty of obtaining standard balls, Japanese-style tennis using a softer ball was invented around 1890. Keiō University in Tōkyō began to use the standard ball in 1913, and since then both types of tennis have been played in Japan. Japanese players made their first appearance in international matches at the 1921 Davis Cup, and the Japan Lawn Tennis Association was founded the following year. As of 1988 there were an estimated 13 million amateur players in Japan, making tennis one of the nation's most popular sports.

tennō →emperor

Tennōki and Kokki   天皇記と国記

(*Tennōki to Kokki*; Record of the Emperors and Record of the Nation). Early written histories of Japan. No longer extant, they were probably organized around the genealogy of the imperial house. The chronicle *Nihon shoki* (720) states that they were compiled by Prince SHŌTOKU and SOGA NO UMAKO in 620 and destroyed by fire during the TAIKA REFORM of 645.

tennō kikan setsu   天皇機関説

The theory that the emperor is an organ of the state, the state being a legal person in which sovereignty is vested. It achieved considerable influence in academic and bureaucratic circles in the period 1920–35, when it enjoyed quasi-official sanction as the basis of a "liberal" interpretation of the 1889 CONSTITUTION OF THE EMPIRE OF JAPAN.

The phrase gained currency when it became identified with "liberal constitutional heresy," a principal target of right-wing criticism in the great academic and official purge of 1935–37. A dramatic episode was the Affair of the Emperor-as-Organ-of-the-State Theory. Gaining front-page coverage in 1935 and early 1936, it brought a previously obscure academic theory to public notice and culminated in the forced withdrawal from official and academic positions and honors of its most noted advocate, MINOBE TATSUKICHI, emeritus head of the law school of Tōkyō University and member of the House of Peers. The animus behind his critics' allegations of lese majesty was the realization that such theories could serve as the basis of an interpretation of the constitution that elevated the authority of the Diet at the expense of the military and the bureaucracy.

An important corollary of the idea of the state as a legal person was the notion that the monarch was but one organ of the state, albeit a centrally important one as the "bearer in his own person of the state's sovereignty." A vision of a tamed monarchy, operating in the context of political, legal, and economic liberalism, lay behind the promotion of the theory in Japan as part of a general theory of constitutional interpretation that reflected middle class and popular urban interests.

According to the official definition of "national polity" (KOKUTAI) and the plain language of the 1889 constitution and its attendant rescripts, the emperor was (as lineal descendant of a transcendent being) possessor in his own right of absolute authority. To those who affirmed this position the theory of the emperor as an organ of the state was blasphemous, and the liberal constitutional inferences drawn from it were seditious. Until the early 1930s Minobe's interpretation of the constitution was able to withstand criticism from conservative factions. However, the rise of militarism, carried out under the banner of "national polity clarification" (see KOKUTAI DEBATE), eventually made Minobe the first and most famous victim of a general academic and political purge.

tennō ningen sengen →emperor, renunciation of divinity by

Tennō Tanjōbi →holidays, national

Tennōzan   天王山

Hill in southern Kyōto Prefecture, central Honshū. The Yamazaki district at the foot of the hill was the site of a decisive battle where TOYOTOMI HIDEYOSHI defeated the forces of AKECHI MITSUHIDE, the murderer of ODA NOBUNAGA, in 1582 (see YAMAZAKI, BATTLE OF). Height: 270 m (886 ft).

Tenri   天理[市]

City in northern Nara Prefecture, central Honshū. Originally a market town near Isonokami Shrine, it is now known as the headquarters of TENRIKYŌ, a contemporary religious group. There are numerous buildings connected with Tenrikyō, including those of the TENRI CENTRAL LIBRARY and TENRI UNIVERSITY. Pop: 68,815.

Tenri Central Library   天理図書館

(Tenri Toshokan). Library in the city of Tenri in Nara Prefecture. It serves a multiple role in its support of the activities of the TENRIKYŌ sect of Shintō. Opened in 1926 with 26,000 volumes, the library has grown to become an important repository of Japanese and Western collections, with about 1.5 million items. The Tenri collection boasts over 80 titles designated as National Treasures or Important

Tenryūgawa The sheer cliffs of Tenryūkyō, a scenic gorge in the middle reaches of this river in central Honshū, tower over a boatload of sightseers.

Cultural Properties by the Ministry of Education.

Tenrikyō 天理教

(literally, "religion of divine wisdom"). One of Japan's largest contemporary religious groups. Founded by NAKAYAMA MIKI (1798–1887), a resident of Shōyashiki (now Mishima in the city of Tenri in Nara Prefecture), who claimed she had received a revelation from God. Miki wanted to deliver people from suffering and social evils and to bring about a perfect world. Because the movement seemed to conflict with established interests, Miki and her followers were persecuted. Miki wrote the main scriptures of Tenrikyō and taught her disciples the hand movements for the *kagura-zutome* (salvation dance service), the most important rite in Tenrikyō. She also determined the precise location of the *jiba* (a sacred spot in the main temple). In 1887, as her disciples performed the prohibited service around a symbolic monument (*kanrodai*) erected at the *jiba*, Miki allegedly passed into a purely spiritual state. The faithful believe that her soul remains in the sanctuary of the *jiba*. Miki's passage into this new state became the doctrinal core of Tenrikyō.

After Miki's death Tenrikyō was finally recognized by the government as a religious organization (see SECT SHINTŌ), but it was forced to adjust its religious activities to conform to nationalist government policies. Privately, the church struggled to keep Miki's teachings intact. After 1947 Tenrikyō entered a third phase of development, characterized by the *fukugen* (restoration of the original teachings) movement. By the late 1980s the sect had more than 16,000 churches around the world and operated TENRI UNIVERSITY, a museum, a hospital, a radio station, and TENRI CENTRAL LIBRARY.

Doctrine——God, as revealed through Miki, is called Tenri Ō no Mikoto (literally, "Lord of Divine Wisdom"). His attributes are explained symbolically as the *tohashira no kami* (10 deities), each representing a specific function of God in relation to human life. According to Tenrikyō, God the parent (*oyagami*) created human beings in order to delight in their life of joy and harmony. But because of man's selfishness, the condition of the world became contrary to his expectation, hence the need for a revelation, which took place through the three preordinations——soul, place, and time——historically represented by the soul of Miki, the *jiba* or holy place of the original creation, and the time of the revelation. These form the point where man can come into direct contact with God's *tasuke* (salvation). To participate in *tasuke*, one must purify one's heart and mind, reflecting therein the will of God through *makoto shinjitsu* (sincerity). The purification process involves removing the *yattsu no hokori* (eight dusts), which accumulate in the mind from selfish motivations and the improper use of human freedom; these are not evils as such but rather pollutions that can be cleansed from the mind. Only with a pure heart and mind can one recognize the world as a manifestation of God's work. To distinguish the true and eternal self from one's phenomenal existence, one must realize that one's body is *kashimono-karimono*, "something lent, something borrowed," from God.

Three actions are encouraged in order to attain salvation. Of these, receiving *osazuke* (holy grant) is considered most essential, after which a person can perform works for others as an agent of God. The practice of *hi no kishin* (daily service) is another way to achieve personal perfection. Finally, repeated pilgrimages to the *jiba* are urged for renewal of faith. Three scriptures constitute the basic canon of Tenrikyō: the *Mikagura uta* (Songs for the Sacred Dance) and the *Ofudesaki* (Tip of the Divine Writing Brush), written by Miki, and the *Osashizu* (Divine Directions), which were revealed to Iburi Izō (1823–1907).

Tenri University 天理大学

(Tenri Daigaku). A private, coeducational university located in the city of Tenri, Nara Prefecture. Its predecessor was Tenri Gaikokugo Gakkō (Tenri School of Foreign Languages), founded in 1925 by the religious organization TENRIKYŌ. Japan's first private coeducational institute of foreign languages, it was recognized as a college in 1944. It adopted its present name in 1948. It maintains faculties of letters, foreign languages, and physical education. The TENRI CENTRAL LIBRARY, the university library, is well known. Enrollment was 2,783 in 1989.

tenryō 天領

The personal domain of the Tokugawa shōguns, administered by the shogunate (*bakufu*) and others on its behalf during the Edo period (1600–1868). Although the term has been used loosely to denote all Tokugawa land, one-third of the land was awarded in fief to HATAMOTO ("bannermen"; senior shogunal vassals) and therefore was technically not *tenryō* but *hatamoto ryō*, land administered and taxed by individual *hatamoto*.

At the beginning of the 17th century TOKUGAWA IEYASU, the first Tokugawa shōgun, had direct control of land with an assessed productivity of 2.5 million *koku* (see KOKUDAKA). The tax from this land, roughly 40 percent of each crop, sustained most of his *samurai*, who held no fiefs, and also the Tokugawa shogunate (1603–1867). By the end of the 17th century that inheritance had doubled; where the *daimyō* domains (HAN) produced 18 million *koku*, and *hatamoto* fiefs another 2.5 million, the Tokugawa *tenryō*, at a little over 4 million, represented some 17 percent of Japan's agricultural production.

By 1804 more than 15 percent of *tenryō* had been assigned to neighboring daimyō for administration; known as mandated territory (*azukari-dokoro*), it tended to become part of the domain entrusted with it. Management of the remaining *tenryō* was in the hands of civil servants called intendants (DAIKAN or GUNDAI) under the general supervision of the commissioners of finance. Despite occasional purges, intendants seem to have controlled their areas as much in their own interests as in those of the Tokugawa. Rice production, which had reached its peak in 1744 (4.6 million *koku*), had declined to 4.2 million *koku* by 1840. Moreover, taxes paid into the Tokugawa coffers in the same years declined from 1.8 million *koku* to less than 1.4 million *koku*.

Tenryō Distribution, 1804 — tenryō

Region	Mandated territory	Intendant control	Total tenryō
		(in *koku*)	
Kantō[1]	—	1,022,000	1,022,000
Kinai[2]	115,000	572,000	687,000
Tōkaidō[3]	70,000	618,000	688,000
Hokkoku[4]	387,000	966,000	1,353,000
Chūgoku[5]	51,000	361,000	412,000
Saigoku[6]	40,000	136,000	176,000
Total	663,000	3,675,000	4,338,000

[1] A region encompassing the present Tōkyō, Chiba, Saitama, Kanagawa, Ibaraki, Tochigi, and Gumma prefectures.
[2] The Kyōto-Ōsaka-Nara region.
[3] The Pacific Ocean side of central Honshū.
[4] The Sea of Japan side of central Japan and all of northern Honshū.
[5] The Inland Sea side of Honshū and all of the Shikoku region.
[6] The Kyūshū region.
NOTE: One *koku* = approximately 180 liters or 5 US bushels.
SOURCE: Kitajima Masamoto, *Edo bakufu no kenryoku kōzō* (1964).

Tenryūji The blossoms of a *shidarezakura* (weeping cherry tree) frame this view of the abbot's quarters at this temple in Kyōto.

Tenryū 天竜[市]

City in western Shizuoka Prefecture, central Honshū, on the river TENRYŪGAWA. Its lumber industry draws on the forests nearby. Tea and *shiitake* (a Japanese mushroom) are cultivated. Attractions include the ruins of Futamata Castle. Pop: 24,519.

Tenryūgawa 天竜川

River in Nagano and Shizuoka prefectures, central Honshū, originating in Lake Suwa and flowing south into the Enshū Sea in western Shizuoka Prefecture. The Ina Basin, on the upper reaches, is a rich farming area, and the plain area on the lower reaches produces fruit and vegetables. In its middle reaches, past the city of Iida, the river forms rapids near TENRYŪKYŌ, a scenic gorge. With five dams, the Tenryūgawa is an important power source for central Japan. The city of Hamamatsu is located on the lowlands. Length: 213 km (132 mi); area of drainage basin: 5,090 sq km (1,965 sq mi).

Tenryūji 天竜寺

Head temple of the Tenryūji branch of the RINZAI SECT of Zen Buddhism; located in Ukyō Ward, Kyōto. ASHIKAGA TAKAUJI decided to establish Tenryūji in 1339 in memory of Emperor Go-Daigo (r 1318–39) and in honor of those fallen in the civil war that preceded the founding of the Muromachi shogunate (1338–1573). The temple was built 1340–44, and Zen master MUSŌ SOSEKI was named its first abbot. In 1386 the massive Tenryūji was ranked first among the major Zen temples (GOZAN) in Kyōto. During the HAMAGURI GOMON INCIDENT of 1864 the temple suffered its eighth major fire. Reconstruction was completed in 1900. Tenryūji became an independent branch of the Rinzai sect in 1876. See also TENRYŪJI-BUNE.

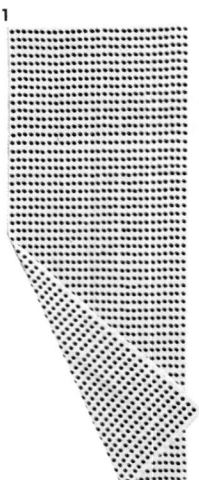

tenugui
1 This towel is decorated with a spotted pattern known as *mameshibori*.
2 A variety of Edo-period styles for wearing a *tenugui* as a head covering are shown on this facsimile of a broadside from that period.

Tenryūji-bune 天竜寺船

(Tenryūji temple ship). Japanese trading vessel that sailed to and from China on a government-approved voyage in the mid-14th century; the first Japanese ship authorized to sail to China after the MONGOL INVASIONS OF JAPAN. Its trip to Yuan (Yüan) dynasty (1279–1368) China was commissioned in 1341 by ASHIKAGA TADAYOSHI. The shogunate hoped to raise funds to build the temple TENRYŪJI to appease the spirit of GO-DAIGO, the emperor it had deposed. MUSŌ SOSEKI, founding father of the Tenryūji, was put in charge of the project. He secured the appointment of the Hakata trader Shihon as captain. Shihon guaranteed a profit of 5,000 *kan* (see MONEY, PREMODERN) in return for shogunate protection from pirates. The *Tenryūji-bune* appears to have left Japan in 1342 and returned the following year.

Tenryūkyō 天竜峡

Transverse valley in the city of Iida, Nagano Prefecture, central Honshū. Located where the river TENRYŪGAWA cuts its way through the Akaishi Mountains. Sheer cliffs tower on both sides, and the flow of the river is rapid. It is the terminus for boating trips on the Tenryūgawa.

Tenshō Ken'ō Shisetsu → mission

to Europe of 1582

tenugui 手拭い

Rectangular cotton gauze cloth used as a towel or headcovering. A *tenugui* is approximately 34 centimeters (13.5 in) wide; its length varies. *Tenugui* were originally made of undyed linen, but from the Edo period (1600–1868) cotton was used. Red or indigo dyeing, tie-dyeing, and other techniques for adorning them were gradually developed. The practice arose of printing *tenugui* with the crests of famous *kabuki* actors, and schools of traditional dance and music began designing their own. Often shops and business firms distribute *tenugui* at their openings, and most localities print souvenir *tenugui* for tourists. *Tenugui* are often used as headbands for absorbing perspiration (see HACHIMAKI). As head coverings, *tenugui* were draped and tied in styles that often indicated the wearer's status, or, in the theater, the character type being portrayed. Although they have all but been replaced by terry cloth as towels, *tenugui* are still used as head coverings, rags, souvenirs, and advertisements. See also HEADGEAR.

Terada Torahiko This physicist is best known for his literary essays.

Terada Torahiko 寺田寅彦

(1878–1935). Also known as Yoshimura Fuyuhiko. Physicist and essayist. Born in Tōkyō. He attended the Fifth Higher School in Kumamoto, where he was inspired by NATSUME SŌSEKI to write HAIKU. A graduate of Tōkyō University, he received a doctorate in 1908 and went to Europe in 1909 in order to further his study of geophysics and seismology. In 1916 he became a professor at Tōkyō University. Although a physicist by profession, his fame is based largely upon his skill as an essayist. Some of his literary essays can be found in the collections *Fuyuhiko-shū* and *Yabukōjishū*, both published in 1923. His complete works were collected in the *Terada Torahiko zenshū* (1950–51).

Terada Tōru 寺田透

(1915–). Literary critic and scholar of French literature. Born in Kanagawa Prefecture; graduate of Tōkyō University. Terada's first collection of critical essays, *Sakka shiron* (1949, Writers: A Personal View), dealt with MASAOKA SHIKI, MORI ŌGAI, and other Japanese writers. He also wrote on modern French literature, producing essays on such writers as Balzac, Valéry, and Camus. He fashioned these essays from his close, sensitive readings of literary works. His works include *Bungaku: Sono naimen to gaikai* (1959, Literature Inside and Out), *Baruzakku: Ningen kigeki no kenkyū* (1953, Balzac: A Study of The Human Comedy), and *Terada Tōru: Hyōron* (1969–75, Critical Essays).

Teradaya Incident 寺田屋事件

(Teradaya Jiken). Incident of 21 May 1862 at the Teradaya, an inn on the outskirts of Kyōto, in which antiforeign imperial loyalists were killed. In the spring of 1862 SHIMAZU HISAMITSU, the de facto leader of the Satsuma domain (now Kagoshima Prefecture), went to Kyōto with 1,000 Satsuma troops to suppress radical loyalists. ARIMA SHINSHICHI and other Satsuma activists in Kyōto mistakenly assumed that Hisamitsu had come to assist the court in expelling foreigners who had been permitted to live in Japan. They planned a general uprising against the Tokugawa shogunate but, receiving no encouragement from Hisamitsu, decided to assassinate shogunate officials. Hearing of this, Hisamitsu sent a party of nine *samurai* to the loyalists' lodgings to instruct them to abandon their plan. When Arima and his men refused, violence broke out, and seven conspirators, including Arima, were killed, considerably weakening the loyalist movement in Satsuma.

Terakado Seiken 寺門静軒

(1796–1868). Writer of the late Edo period (1600–1868). Born in Edo (now Tōkyō). He studied Confucianism and the Chinese classics and opened a school in Edo. In 1832 he began writing *Edo hanjō ki* (1832–36), a series of humorous and gently satiric essays describing various aspects of life in Edo. The first of several such works, it immediately became popular but was banned for its criticism of the Tokugawa shogunate. Terakado was forced to leave Edo during the TEMPŌ REFORMS.

terakoya 寺子屋

Generic term used today for the popular schools of the Edo period (1600–1868). *Terako* means "schoolchild," literally, "temple child," an etymology that presumably reflects an earlier state of affairs when priests provided such formal instruction as was available. *Terakoya* simply means a shop or house that takes in pupils for a living.

Such schools were mostly family affairs of a single teacher or married couple (in Edo [now Tōkyō], one-third were run by women) and 50 or 60 pupils. Some (often those run by *samurai*) catered primarily or exclusively to samurai children, some to commoners. In the villages, older retired men, usually of the rich farmer or headman class, often taught as a benevolent exercise of their community responsibilities. Parents' payments were generally made in the form of thank-you gifts.

The staple activity of these schools was writing practice. Some schools taught more gracious accomplishments such as *utai* (the dramatic poetry recited at weddings and festivals) and, to girls, sewing and flower arrangement. The basic form for the copybooks used by the *terakoya* was the ŌRAIMONO, a collection of model letters. The pattern for these was set by the TEIKIN ŌRAI, a famous text of the 14th century. More contemporary texts often concentrated on the vocabulary of specific occupations, intermixed with a wide range of worldly wisdom. *Terakoya* principally provided moral exhortation stressing obedience, neighborliness, and responsibility.

Terashima Munenori 寺島宗則

(1832–93). Diplomat. Born in the Satsuma domain (now Kagoshima Prefecture). In 1862 he went to Europe as a member of a mission from the Tokugawa shogunate (see SHOGUNATE MISSIONS TO THE WEST). He returned to Japan in 1863 and was involved in the hostilities between Britain and Satsuma that year (see KAGOSHIMA BOMBARDMENT). After the Meiji Restoration of 1868 Terashima became a junior councillor (*san'yo*) in the new government. In 1873 he was named foreign minister; in that capacity he negotiated the Treaty of ST. PETERSBURG (1875) with Russia and in 1878 planned the Yoshida-Evarts Convention, in which the United States recognized tariff autonomy for Japan (it was never put into effect because of British opposition). Terashima was also responsible for the negotiations concerning the MARIA LUZ INCIDENT involving a Peruvian ship carrying Chinese laborers that stopped in Japan. In 1891 he became vice-president of the Privy Council.

Terauchi Hisaichi 寺内寿一

(1879–1946). Field marshal and commanding general of the Imperial Japanese Army who served as commander in the South Pacific throughout World War II. Born in Yamaguchi Prefecture, the oldest son of General and Prime Minister TERAUCHI MASATAKE, he graduated from the Army Academy in 1899 and the Army War College in 1909. He served as army minister after the aborted coup d'état by army officers in the FEBRUARY 26TH INCIDENT of 1936 and further intensified the confrontation between the military and political parties by engaging in a heated debate in the Diet with Hamada Kunimatsu (1868–1939) of the RIKKEN SEIYŪKAI in 1937. Terauchi also served as commander of the army in North China immediately following the outbreak of the SINO-JAPANESE WAR OF 1937–1945 in July.

Terauchi Masatake 寺内正毅

(1852–1919). General and prime minister. Born in the Chōshū domain (now Yamaguchi Prefecture). As the first inspector general of military education (1898), he worked to systematize military training. Terauchi served as army minister during the Russo-Japanese War (1904–05) and remained in the post until 1910, when he was appointed the first governor-general of Korea, having directed its annexation by Japan. In 1916 he was named prime minister. The main foreign policy events of Terauchi's premiership were the so-called NISHIHARA LOANS to shore up the government of Duan Qirui (Tuan Ch'i-jui) in China; the LANSING-ISHII AGREEMENT, recognizing Japan's special interests in China; and Japanese participation in the SIBERIAN INTERVENTION by Allied forces during World War I. Terauchi was forced to step down with the outbreak of the nationwide RICE RIOTS OF 1918 that resulted from wartime inflation.

terauke
寺請

(temple guarantee). A method of social control used in the Edo period (1600–1868) by the Tokugawa shogunate (1603–1687) and the *daimyō* domains, ostensibly to search out adherents of the proscribed Christian faith but actually with the wider effect of the surveillance of the entire population. The system developed as part of the period's religious inquisition (SHŪMON ARATAME) from the 1630s, when the certificate of affiliation with a Buddhist temple came to be required as proof that a suspect was not a Christian; in 1665 the shogunate ordered a detailed scrutiny of the population, "listing the name of the temple that stood as guarantor of each person's religion."

At birth every person was enrolled as a parishioner of his family's temple and listed as such in the so-called religious inquiry registers (*shūmon aratame chō*), which were compiled by the temple and forwarded to the domainal lord. In addition the temple's attestation was required prior to marriage, travel, change of residence, or entry into service.

The *terauke* system was also directed against other proscribed religious groups, such as the uncompromising FUJU FUSE SECT of Nichiren Buddhism from 1669. The system collapsed along with the Tokugawa regime in the MEIJI RESTORATION (1868).

Terayama Shūji
寺山修司

(1935–83). Avant-garde playwright; also a critic, scriptwriter, novelist, filmmaker, essayist, and poet. Born in rural Aomori Prefecture. At age 19, Terayama won a major national prize for TANKA poetry and dropped out of Waseda University. After publication of a collection of his miscellaneous poems, *Den'en ni shisu* (1965, To Die in the Country), he began to write and produce plays. In 1967 he founded his personal troupe, the Tenjō Sajiki (Upper Balcony).

Among Terayama's chief plays are *Aomori Ken no semushi otoko* (1967, The Hunchback of Aomori) and *Nuhikun* (1978, Instructions to Servants). Terayama wrote feature film scripts as well as radio and television plays. He directed the films *Sho o suteyo machi e deyō* (1971, Throw Away the Books, Take to the Streets) and *Den'en ni shisu* (1974).

Most of Terayama's main characters are children in revolt. Performance for him was not a show to create illusion or to display talent but the "means to generate and experience chaos."

Terazaki Kōgyō
寺崎広業

(1866–1919). Japanese-style painter. Also called Terasaki Kōgyō. Born to an impoverished *samurai* family in what is now Akita Prefecture, he studied first with a KANO

SCHOOL painter, later with the MARUYAMA-SHIJŌ SCHOOL artist Hirafuku Suian (1844–90) and the painter Sugawara Hakuryū (1833–98). In 1891 he was active in the formation of the progressive Japan Youth Painting Society (after 1897 the Japanese-Style Painting Society, Nihonga Kai). Kōgyō taught at the Tōkyō Bijutsu Gakkō (now Tōkyō University of Fine Arts and Music) until 1898. He was a judge at the BUNTEN government-sponsored art exhibitions and was named an artist for the imperial household (*teishitsu gigeiin*). Kōgyō's best-known work is his set of four paintings, *Tani yondai* (1909, Valleys: Four Themes), from sketches done in Nagano Prefecture. See also NIHONGA.

teriyaki
照り焼き

A method of cooking fish or meat by broiling over an open flame and repeatedly basting with a sauce made of strong soy sauce and *sake* or *mirin* (sweet *sake*). The fish or meat is cooked until its surface is glazed and slightly burned. *Teriyaki* is a popular method of cooking fish with a high fat content or more delicate fish and shellfish. Beef, pork, chicken, and duck may also be prepared this way. The *teriyaki* method is also used for YAKITORI, or bite-sized pieces of chicken meat or giblets threaded on a skewer, and *unagi no kabayaki*, eel or conger split and grilled.

territorial waters
領海

(*ryōkai*). Japan's first official declaration concerning territorial waters came in 1870, when the Franco-Prussian War broke out in Europe and the Japanese government issued a proclamation of neutrality (Proclamation No. 546 of 1870) stipulating that "the contending parties are not permitted to engage in hostilities in Japanese harbors or inland waters, or within a distance of 3 nautical miles (1 nautical mile = 1.85 km or 1.15 mi) from land at any place, such being the distance to which a cannonball can be fired." Since then, Japan has continued to adhere to the 3-mile limit not only for its own territorial waters but also as a rule of international law that should be applied throughout the world.

The Law on Territorial Waters (Ryōkai Hō) enacted in 1977 provides for a limit of 12 nautical miles, except for the Sōya Strait, the Tsugaru Strait, the eastern channel of the Tsushima Strait, the western channel of the Tsushima Strait, and the Ōsumi Strait, for

which the 3-mile limit remains in effect pending the outcome of the Third United Nations Conference on the Law of the Sea (UNCLOS III). See also FISHERY AGREEMENTS.

territory of Japan
領土

(*ryōdo*). The territory of a state in international law comprises the land, the TERRITORIAL WATERS, and the territorial airspace to which the sovereignty of the state extends. The land territory of Japan in the mid-19th century consisted of four main islands—Honshū, Kyūshū, Shikoku, and Hokkaidō—and a number of small islands.

In the area bordering Russia there have been territorial disputes, especially concerning the Kuril Islands and Sakhalin. These have been the subject of several treaties, most notably the Sakhalin–Kuril Islands Exchange Treaty of 1875 (see ST. PETERSBURG, TREATY OF), the 1905 Treaty of Portsmouth (see PORTSMOUTH, TREATY OF), and the SAN FRANCISCO PEACE TREATY of 1951, by which Japan renounced claim to the Kuril Islands and Sakhalin. By the San Francisco Peace Treaty of 1951 Japan also renounced claim to Korea, which it had attached in 1910, and to Formosa (TAIWAN) and the Pescadores (Penghu), acquired from China by the Treaty of Shimonoseki in 1895 (see SHIMONOSEKI, TREATY OF).

Japan acquired the RYŪKYŪ ISLANDS when the lord of the Satsuma domain in Kyūshū forced the ruler of the Ryūkyūs to swear allegiance in 1609. The Ryūkyūs became Okinawa Prefecture in 1879 (see OKINAWA). The OGASAWARA ISLANDS (Bonin Islands), claimed by several states, were put formally under the administration of Japan in 1875. Other islands were included in the territory of Japan in the late 19th and early 20th centuries, including MINAMI TORISHIMA (Marcus Island), the Volcano Islands (Kazan Rettō; see IŌ ISLANDS), the SENKAKU ISLANDS, the Daitō Islands, and TAKESHIMA.

There is ongoing dispute over the Northern Territories, which comprise the islands of KUNASHIRI, ETOROFU, SHIKOTAN, and the HABOMAI ISLANDS, occupied by the Soviet Union at the end of World War II and, as of late 1992, still occupied by the Russian Federation; Takeshima (Tokto), occupied by the Republic of Korea; and the Senkaku Islands, claimed by the People's Republic of China and Taiwan.

Terayama Shūji This avant-garde playwright also wrote and directed several films.

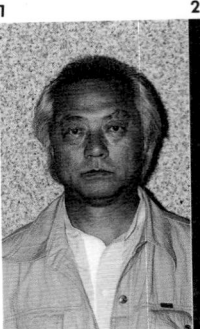

Teshigahara Hiroshi
1 The director. Teshigahara is also the head of the Sōgetsu school of *ikebana* (flower arrangement).
2 Kishida Kyōko (center) and Okada Eiji in a montage scene from the director's most famous film, *Suna no onna* (1964, Woman in the Dunes), an adaptation of the Abe Kōbō novel.

Terumo Corporation　テルモ［株］

(Terumo). Manufacturer and seller of pharmaceuticals, blood bags, single-use medical supplies, artificial organs, electronic medical instruments, home health-care products, and other medical devices. Incorporated in 1921. Terumo's products are supplied to over 120 countries through an overseas sales network. Production facilities are in Japan, the United States, Belgium, and Australia. For the fiscal year ending March 1991, sales reached ¥109.4 billion (US $797.4 million), and capitalization stood at ¥19.3 billion (US $140.7 million). Headquarters are in Tōkyō.

teruteru bōzu　照る照る坊主

Doll hung from the eaves in the hope that the result will be fair weather the following day. A *teruteru bōzu* is made by placing round padding in the center of a square of paper or cloth (usually white) and pushing it up to make a round head, which is secured at the "neck" with thread. If the wish for fair weather comes true, facial features are often drawn on the doll. This custom began during the Edo period (1600–1868). In some parts of Japan farmers color the heads of the dolls black and use them to pray for rain instead. Japanese children still make *teruteru bōzu* today, often on the night before a field trip or athletic event.

Teshigahara Hiroshi　勅使河原宏

(1927–). Film director; *ikebana* (FLOWER ARRANGEMENT) master. Born in Tōkyō, the son of the *ikebana* master Teshigahara Sōfū (1900–1979), founder of the SŌGETSU SCHOOL of flower arrangement. Teshigahara graduated from Tōkyō University of Fine Arts and Music. Particularly interested in the visual aspects of filmmaking, Teshigahara completed his first feature film, *Otoshiana* (Pitfall), scripted by the novelist ABE KŌBŌ in 1962. This began a collaboration that extended through the next decade of the director's career. *Suna no onna* (1964, Woman in the Dunes), his best-known film, as well as *Tanin no kao* (1966, The Face of Another) and *Moetsukita chizu* (1968, The Ruined Map), were both based on novels by Abe. These were followed by *Natsu no heitai* (1972, Summer Soldiers), written by John Nathan. After this film he turned his attention to ceramics and continued an earlier interest in experimental cinema. In 1980, following the deaths of his father and his sister, Teshigahara became the third head of the Sōgetsu school. In 1989 he made *Rikyū*, his first feature film in 17 years.

Teshikaga　弟子屈［町］

Town in eastern Hokkaidō. On the upper reaches of the river Kushirogawa. Principal farm products are potatoes and sugar beets. Dairy farming and forestry are also active. The greater part of the town is located in the Akan National Park. Attractions include the caldera lakes KUSSHARO and MASHŪ and hot springs. Pop: 10,630.

teruteru bōzu Quickly fashioned from a square of cloth or paper and a bit of stuffing, the dolls are hung from the eaves in supplication for sunny weather.

Teshima Toan　手島堵庵

(1718–86). Religious and moral teacher. Born in Kyōto. A disciple of ISHIDA BAIGAN, he laid the basic institutional foundations for the SHINGAKU movement, which became a major source of ethical guidance for the merchants and townsmen (CHŌNIN) of the Edo period (1600–1868). Toan, an eloquent speaker, drew large crowds to his lectures. In 1765 he moved his family to a larger residence, part of which served as a lecture hall. This hall, called the Gorakusha, became the prototype for others. By 1782 three additional halls had been set up by Toan's followers: the Shūseisha, the Jishūsha, and the Meirinsha. These three halls later came to be regarded as the organizational and spiritual core of the national Shingaku movement. Toan's most influential writings were the *Zadan zuihitsu* (1771), *Chishin bengi* (1773), and *Kaiyū taishi* (1773).

Teshiogawa　天塩川

River in northern Hokkaidō, originating in the Kitami Mountains, flowing north through the Nayoro Basin to enter the Sea of Japan near the town of Teshio. The lower reaches meander through the Sarobetsu Plain. Length: 256 km (159 mi); area of drainage basin: 5,590 sq km (2,158 sq mi).

Teshio Mountains　天塩山地

(Teshio Sanchi). Mountain range running north to south along the Sea of Japan coast, northwestern Hokkaidō. The highest peak is Pisshirizan (1,032 m; 3386 ft), noted for its dense primeval forests. Extensive lumbering is done throughout the range. There are coal mines in the Rumoi and Tempoku districts.

Teshio Plain　天塩平野

(Teshio Heiya). Extends along the lower reaches of the river Teshiogawa, northwestern Hokkaidō. Comprises Kamisarobetsu, Shimosarobetsu, and Ubushi plains. A low and swampy plain along the Sea of Japan, it is composed of peat bogs, pastureland, and wild, uncultivated land. Area: approximately 500 sq km (200 sq mi).

tesō → palmistry

Tessai → Tomioka Tessai

Tesshū Tokusai　鉄舟徳済

(?–1366). Early *suibokuga* (INK PAINTING) artist of the Muromachi period (1333–1568). A Zen monk, he was a disciple of MUSŌ SOSEKI, the founder of the Kyōto temple Tenryūji. After studying in China Tesshū went back to Kyōto as the primate (*shuso*) of Tenryūji; in 1347 he became the abbot of the temple Hodaji in Awa Province (now Tokushima Prefecture) and shortly thereafter of the temple Zuikōji in Harima Province (now part of Hyōgo Prefecture). In 1362 he was appointed abbot of Manjuji, one of the five major Zen monasteries in Kyōto (see GOZAN). He retired to Ryūkōin, a subtemple of Tenryūji, where he died in 1366.

Some paintings traditionally attributed to Tesshū were inspired by Zen allegorical themes such as monkeys, reeds, and geese, but it is his ink paintings of orchids, bamboos, and grapes—subjects favored by the literati and literati monk-painters—for which he is best known.

Tetsugen　鉄眼

(1630–82). Also known as Tetsugen Dōkō. Zen monk of the ŌBAKU SECT. Born in Higo

Province (now Kumamoto Prefecture). He became a disciple of the Chinese master Yinyuan (Yin-yüan; J: INGEN) and later of his student Muan (J: Mokuan; 1611–84). Learning that the Buddhist canon (*daizōkyō*) had not yet been printed in its entirety in Japan, he collected funds and labored for more than 10 years, completing the task in 1678. This printing is known as the Tetsugen or Ōbaku edition and even today is considered an important legacy. The printing blocks are still at the temple MAMPUKUJI. Tetsugen is remembered for his charitable works during the great famine that beset the Kyōto-Ōsaka area in 1682.

teuchi　手打

The custom of clapping hands to confirm a negotiation concluded between two parties; also known as *tejime*. It is believed to have been derived from the Shintō custom of clapping one's hands (*kashiwade*) in front of the shrine. It is customary to clap three times in unison. Even today, among merchants, it is not unusual to close special meetings and commemorative events with clapping of the hands.

Texas Instruments Japan, Ltd
日本テキサス・インスツルメンツ［株］

(Nippon Tekisasu Insutsurumentsu). Semiconductor component maker. Incorporated in 1968 as a wholly owned subsidiary of Texas Instruments, Inc, of the United States. It manufactures and sells semiconductors and components and has 4 factories and 12 offices in Japan. For the fiscal year ending December 1990, sales totaled ¥149.0 billion (US $1.1 billion) and capitalization was ¥5.0 billion (US $37.4 million). Headquarters are in Tōkyō.

textbook issue　教科書問題

(*kyōkasho mondai*). In the years since World War II, conservative and progressive forces in Japan have confronted each other repeatedly over the issue of governmental approval of textbooks. As part of the educational reforms that were instituted after the war, the previous system of government-compiled textbooks was abolished and replaced by a system in which all textbooks were produced by private textbook companies and then subjected to approval by the Ministry of Education, which often demanded revisions, before being adopted by elementary, middle, and high schools. Confrontations have been particularly marked in the fields of social studies (especially government, economics, and history) and the Japanese language. Controversial topics include war, the SELF DEFENSE FORCES, nuclear weapons, and nuclear power plants. The process of government approval has been a favorite target of opposition politicians. In 1982, China and South Korea officially protested textbook revisions they felt minimized Japanese aggression in World War II; the Japanese government made corrections. However, the system of government approval and the political content of public school education continue to be important issues. See also IENAGA TEXTBOOK REVIEW CASE.

Textbook Scandal of 1902–1903
教科書疑獄

(Kyōkasho Gigoku). The discovery in 1902–03 of nationwide bribery in the selection of elementary school textbooks. Textbooks were published by private companies, which submitted them for selection by prefectural committees after approval by the Ministry of

Education. Following widespread rumors of bribery to influence book selection, the Ministry of Justice initiated secret investigations in December 1902. As a result, by March 1903 more than 200 people had been arrested; 116 were found guilty. Minister of Education KIKUCHI DAIROKU resigned. The scandal convinced the government of the need to centralize the selection of textbooks in the Ministry of Education. In 1903 the first *kokutei kyōkasho* (national textbooks) were issued.

textile industry   繊維産業

(*sen'i sangyō*). The textile industry was the first modern industry established in Japan and the largest in the country prior to World War II. During the war, however, much of the industry's equipment was scrapped or destroyed. Production capacity at the end of the war was only 30 percent of the prewar level. Early in the postwar period measures were taken to rehabilitate the industry, since textile exports were an important source of foreign exchange. By 1956, production had exceeded its prewar peak, led by rapid growth in the chemical and synthetic fiber sectors.

However, the Southeast Asian nations, once major markets for Japanese textiles, gradually developed their own industries. The appreciation of the yen in the 1970s and rising energy costs further reduced Japan's export competitiveness. Since 1973, Japan's textile imports have exceeded exports. A bright spot for the industry is that Japan's per capita consumption of textiles is increasing (17.5 kg [38.6 lb] per person in 1988 compared with 11.9 kg [26.2 lb] in 1975). In response, the industry is shifting to higher value-added products to meet new demand for diverse and high-quality articles.

textiles   織物

(*orimono*). The arts of weaving, dyeing, and decorating fabrics were developed to a high level of skill and beauty in Japan from a relatively early period. Throughout premodern times the Japanese imported textiles and technical knowledge from the continent, especially from Korea and China, as well as from India and the Ryūkyū Islands, making adaptations to suit their own needs and tastes. As in other areas of East Asia, artisans worked primarily with bast fibers (see ASA) and SILK until the introduction of cotton from India via China and Korea in the 16th century. Since the Meiji Restoration (1868), European and American influences have been strong, and other fibers have come into common use, notably wool and, more recently, various man-made synthetic fibers. There has been a general preference for composite designs and colors derived from nature, scenery, and everyday life rather than abstract or mythological creations. The most innovative and important Japanese contributions have been in dyeing techniques.

Early Textiles——The inhabitants of Japan during the Jōmon period (ca 10,000 BC–ca 300 BC) pulled fibers from the inner bark of certain plants and twisted them by hand to form cords and later straw mats and other coarse textiles with such preweaving techniques as netting, plaiting, and twining. The earliest evidence of weaving consists of loom parts excavated from sites in Nara and Shizuoka prefectures dating from around 300 BC.

The people of the Yayoi period (ca 300 BC–ca AD 300) cultivated fiber-bearing plants.

They spun and dyed thread and wove it into cloth, which they pounded until smooth and pliant with wooden mallets. Sericulture was introduced from China in the early 3rd century AD, and textiles played an important role in subsequent official interchanges. In the first recorded tribute/gift exchange with China in AD 243, the priestess-ruler HIMIKO is reported to have sent well-woven *asa* (hemp; ramie) and rough silk to the Chinese court and received in return complex figured silks. Yamato rulers of the 4th and 5th centuries recruited Korean and Chinese weavers to improve textile production, giving them clan status and land. The names of some of these early artisans linger as technical terms in the 20th-century weaving vocabulary.

Asuka (593–710) and Nara (710–794) Periods——The Asuka period saw a wave of continental influence that reached its peak in the Nara period. Due in part to Chinese influence, textiles became an important part of material culture. At court, ranks were distinguished by differently colored garments. Cloth was a major form of tribute payment and could be substituted for corvée service. The TAIKA REFORM of 645 called for central supervision of textile production, and in 701 the Office of the Guild of Weavers was established to direct the textile craft, sending weavers to several outlying districts in 711 to teach patterned silk weaving. Common artisans as well as master craftsmen were welcomed from the continent.

Buddhism, introduced in the mid-6th century, was associated with many textiles intended for ritual use. Newly constructed temples employed continental masters and local apprentices to produce an array of artifacts for Buddhist ceremonies. These temples came to serve as repositories for great collections of textiles of both foreign and domestic manufacture.

The SHŌSŌIN repository in Nara contains over 100,000 textiles donated to or used in the temple TŌDAIJI in the 8th century; many date from the consecration of the image of the Great Buddha in 752 and include gifts brought by foreign dignitaries from as far away as India. The Shōsōin also contains imperial clothing and other palace textiles belonging to Emperor SHŌMU (r 724–749), workmen's uniforms, and provincial tribute cloth. The collection includes plain-weave monochrome silk and *asa*, *nishiki* (brocade), *aya* (figured twill), *ra* and *sha* (gauze), as well as woven materials dyed with SANKECHI (literally, "three press-dyes") techniques—and gives a good indication of the range, technical skill, and variety of textile arts as they were practiced in the greater Tang (T'ang) dynasty (618–907) cultural area.

Heian (794–1185) and Kamakura (1185–1333) Periods——The move of the capital to HEIANKYŌ (Kyōto) in 794 marked the beginning of a period of comparative isolation in Japan. The major categories of Nara weaves, *ra*, *aya*, and *nishiki*, all continued to be manufactured in simplified form, subdued monochromatic *aya* being preferred to the more ornate *nishiki*. Aristocratic households of the Heian period skillfully dyed silk tribute cloth many shades of solid colors and stitched them into *kimono*-like garments, which were worn in layers with the full range of colors visible only at the neck and at the deep sleeve openings and fanlike hems. The subtly gradated or contrasting colors of the layers were chosen with great care to echo the season and occasion and suggest the aesthetic sense of the wearer.

With the gradual impoverishment of the

court, the Office of the Guild of Weavers declined and, in the early 13th century, collapsed. It was replaced by guildlike groups of private weavers in the capital and in a few provincial areas.

The most interesting extant textiles from the turbulent Kamakura period were those used in the assembly of armor (see ARMS AND ARMOR). Armor was typically made of small metal or lacquered leather plates laced together by rows of silk braid (KUMIHIMO) executed in a carefully conceived variety of techniques and color combinations. Leather edges and breastplates were decorated with small patterns made by stamping a metal stencil into the softened deerskin and smoking the leather or rubbing color (often safflower crimson and INDIGO blue) through the stencil. This is the earliest definitive evidence of the use of stencils in Japan. Underarmor garments show motifs that appear to have been executed with a paste resist, which by the Muromachi period (1333–1568) was applied through stiffened paper stencils to create tiny all-over patterns (see KOMON).

Muromachi (1333–1568) and Azuchi-Momoyama (1568–1600) Periods——Beginning in the late Heian period, private trade ships had brought back small quantities of cloth from China. Trade increased after official relations were established with the Chinese Ming dynasty (1368–1644). In the 16th century significant numbers of textiles began to enter the country from Southeast Asia and India as European traders found their way to Japan. From China came new types of patterned silk weaving, damasks (*donsu*), simple and figured satins (*shusu* and *rinzu*), woven stripes (*kantō*), rich and heavy brocades woven of gold and silver threads (KINRAN AND GINRAN), embroidery (*shishū*), gold leaf imprint (*inkin*), new patterned gauzes (RO AND SHA; *monsha; kinsha*), and, at the very end of the period, light crinkly silk crepe (CHIRIMEN). From India came cotton calico (SARASA) and handsome stripes (*tōzan*).

These imported textiles were coveted by aristocrats, military lords, priests, and affluent merchants alike, enriching dealers in port towns and stimulating domestic attempts to imitate them. The finest were so valuable that they were used only in tiny bits (MEIBUTSUGIRE) as edgings of scrolls or for TEA CEREMONY appurtenances. Chinese fabrics and domestic imitations were also used in the NŌ drama as it developed into a symbol of the culture and wealth of its military patrons.

During the devastating ŌNIN WAR (1467–77), most of the weavers fled Kyōto, some to the port city of Sakai (near Ōsaka), others to Nara. Much of the capital was burned and the old weaving district was completely destroyed. It was this period that saw the full emergence of the *kosode*, the direct forerunner of the modern KIMONO, originally one of the inner robes of the women's court costume. Its simple but distinctive form fostered the development of free-style graphic designs that used the whole robe as a canvas. One of the first of these was TSUJIGAHANA ("flowers-at-the-crossing"), a garment characterized by stitch-resist graphic designs of native flora and fauna enhanced with delicate ink brushwork and, later, embroidery. The weavers returned to the capital in the latter part of the 15th century and settled in what had been the western camp (*nishijin*) during the Ōnin War, an area still

Continued on page 1560——

Japanese Textiles: A Patchwork Survey

Traditional Japanese attire at its best is distinguished by the quality of the material itself, rather than the tailoring or design. Japan's enduring fascination with *kimono* has thus inspired a deep appreciation for fabric and a great deal of interest in how it is produced. Many dyeing and weaving techniques were imported centuries ago from China, Korea, and Southeast Asia, and some of these evolved into sophisticated regional manufacturing traditions that are still being employed today.

 Notable for weaving method.

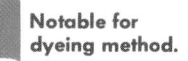 Notable for dyeing method.

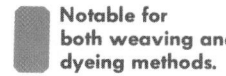 Notable for both weaving and dyeing methods.

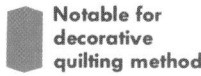 Notable for decorative quilting method.

The fabrics presented here are numbered according to place of origin, indicated on the map below.

This silk crepe furisode, a woman's kimono with long, flowing sleeves, was dyed by the Kyō yūzen method and dates from the Edo period (1600–1868).

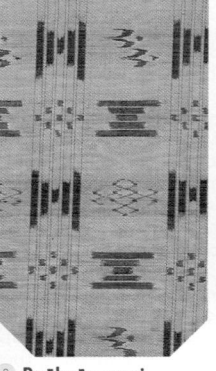

2 Ryūkyū-gasuri (Okinawa Prefecture). *Kasuri* woven in a variety of lively patterns.

3 Bingata (Okinawa Prefecture). Produced by a centuries-old paste-resist stencil technique, *bingata* is often decorated with designs taken from nature.

1 Miyako jōfu (Okinawa Prefecture). A type of *kasuri*, or ikat, made from hand-spun ramie that has been dyed with indigo. In the *kasuri* technique, selected portions of thread are tied before dyeing; when the thread is woven into fabric, the undyed sections produce calculated but hazy patterns.

14 Kaga yūzen (Ishikawa Prefecture). Although dyed in the same way as Kyō yūzen, Kaga designs are more intricate.

15 Kihachijō (Tōkyō Prefecture). Checked or striped silk in yellow, brown, and black is produced on Hachijōjima, one of the Izu Islands.

16 Edo komon (Tōkyō Prefecture). From a distance the fabric looks unfigured; up close, intricate patterns emerge in the tiny spots of resist.

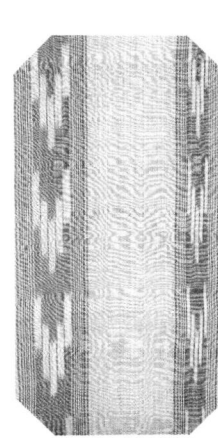

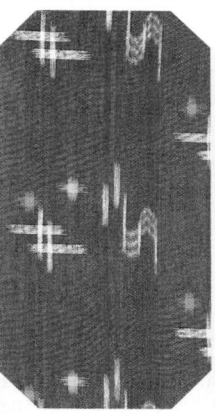

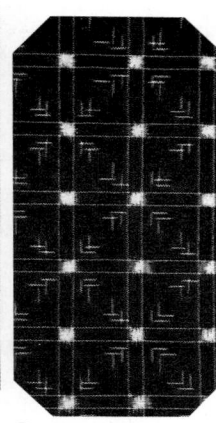

6 **Kurume-gasuri** (Fukuoka Prefecture). A cotton *kasuri* woven in complex geometric patterns.

5 **Ōshima tsumugi** (Kagoshima Prefecture). The island of Amami Ōshima is well known for *tsumugi* (pongee) colored with plant dyes and iron-rich mud.

7 **Hakata-ori** (Fukuoka Prefecture). Thick weft and fine warp threads create a dense and stiff silk used mostly for *obi*, or sashes.

8 **Awa shijira** (Tokushima Prefecture). This fabric's crepelike texture is achieved by varying the number of warp threads and by shrinking the material in hot water.

9 **Yumigahama-gasuri** (Tottori Prefecture). Made with cotton thread and decorated with folk patterns, this type of *kasuri* has traditionally been used for everyday household goods.

4 **Bashōfu** (Okinawa Prefecture). In the oldest-known Okinawan weaving technique, fibers of the *bashō* (a plant in the banana family) are spun into thread, then dyed and woven in *kasuri* or striped patterns to produce *bashōfu*, also known as abaca cloth.

12 **Kyō kanoko shibori** (Kyōto Prefecture). Hand-tied resist dots, used to make broad patterns on fine silk, are said to resemble the white spots of a fawn (*kanoko*).

13 **Kyō yūzen** (Kyōto Prefecture). Formal kimono become a canvas for hand-painted, ornate designs, which are paste-resist dyed.

11 **Nishijin-ori** (Kyōto Prefecture). One of the best-known Japanese textiles, brocaded with intricate and colorful patterns.

10 **Tango chirimen** (Kyōto Prefecture). This white silk crepe is primarily used in the Kyō *yūzen* method of dyeing.

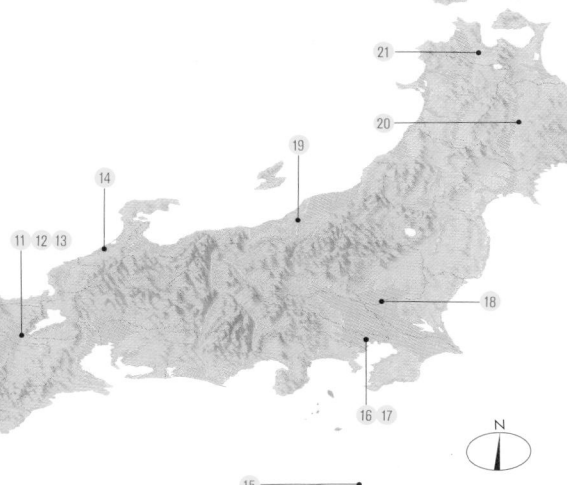

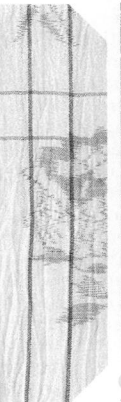

17 **Nagaita chūgata** (Tōkyō Prefecture). Cotton decorated by stenciling paste-resist designs on both sides and dyeing with indigo; used for *yukata*.

18 **Yūki tsumugi** (Ibaraki and Tochigi prefectures). A single bolt of this minutely patterned silk *kasuri* can take a year to produce.

19 **Ojiya chijimi** (Niigata Prefecture). A ramie crepe *kasuri* used for summer garments.

20 **Nambu kodai kata-zome** (Iwate Prefecture). Stencil-dyed fabric in traditional patterns from the Edo period.

21 **Tsugaru kogin** (Aomori Prefecture). In the far north, cotton thread is stitched into indigo-dyed hemp garments to serve as decorative quilting.

22 **Yūkara-ori** (Hokkaidō). Developed in the 1960s, this Hokkaidō weaving technique employs wool, rich plant dyes, and design motifs from nature.

Tezuka Osamu
1 The author in his trademark beret.
2 Representative works of Tezuka. *Top: Hi no tori* (1954–88, *Phoenix 2772*). Left to right: *Bampaiya* (1966–67, *Vampire*); *Tetsuwan Atomu* (1952–68, *Astro Boy*); *Burakkujakku* (1973–83, *Blackjack*).

known today as Nishijin (see NISHIJIN-ORI). By the end of the 16th century they were able to produce luxurious Ming-style gold and silver brocades, damasks and figured satins, silk crepes, and patterned gauzes, adapting continental techniques to suit the needs and tastes of their *kosode*-wearing patrons (see KARA-ORI).

Edo Period (1600–1868)——Although the Tokugawa shogunate (1603–1867) continued to sponsor the production of rich woven textiles for the Nō drama, strict sumptuary laws affected the production of textiles for use by urban merchants throughout much of the period. Forbidden to wear heavy brocades and damasks, 17th-century merchants and their wives turned to the dyers, who were soon producing textiles to rival the finest woven products in style, variety, skill, and even sheer expense. Silk *kosode* made of tiny-pointed tie-dye (*kanoko*) and YŪZEN, a composite painterly technique employing rice-paste resist, characterized the mid-Edo period. Recently domesticated cotton, as well as *asa* stripes, checks, stencil and paste resist (KATAZOME), and hazy-patterned ikat (KASURI) textiles were typical of the late 18th and 19th centuries. Many of the latter were woven and dyed in the countryside for sale in the cities. Color was also regulated, and a full range of browns and grays and deep indigo blue dominated the palette. Textiles from India and the Ryūkyū Islands (see OKINAWAN TEXTILES) were important influences.

Meiji-Period (1868–1912) and Modern Textiles——The Meiji Restoration of 1868 started Japan on a course of rapid industrialization. The TEXTILE INDUSTRY, already quite well organized, absorbed simple modernization easily, and the export of raw silk (to a Europe suffering from severe silkworm blight) soon comprised a significant portion of Japan's foreign trade. After World War II, during which the textile industry suffered considerably (equipment was scrapped for munitions and facilities damaged by air raids), emphasis was redirected toward chemical and synthetic fibers, which were exported in increasing amounts in the 1960s. The international competitiveness of Japanese industrially manufactured textiles declined thereafter, however, as cotton and synthetic textile enterprises in Southeast Asia arose to challenge Japanese manufacturers.

Interest in traditional textiles was maintained to a certain extent (see FOLK CRAFTS) by the 20th-century folk-craft movement associated with YANAGI MUNEYOSHI. Government legislation now protects individual textiles designated as National Treasures and supports the continuation of traditional techniques. Today, such internationally ac-

claimed fashion designers as MIYAKE ISSEI look to Japan's rich textile heritage to create contemporary fashion, and textile designers such as Arai Jun'ichi (b 1932) work closely with manufacturers to develop highly complex textile structures that challenge the potential of late-20th-century industrial equipment. ☎ *1558–1559*

Tezuka Osamu   手塚治虫

(1926–89). One of the leading comic-strip authors of post–World War II Japan. Born in Ōsaka Prefecture. A graduate of the Ōsaka University Medical School and holder of an MD, Tezuka made his debut as a newspaper comic-strip artist in 1946 while still a university student. Influenced by TAGAWA SUIHŌ and Walt Disney, he broke new ground in such fields as the comic-strip novel and comic-strip science fiction. An extremely prolific artist, Tezuka produced a wide range of comics for both adult and juvenile audiences. His best-known series include *Janguru taitei* (1950, Jungle Emperor; known in English as *Kimba, the White Lion*), *Ribon no kishi* (1953, Knight of the Ribbon; known in English as *Princess Knight*), and *Tetsuwan Atomu* (1952–68, Mighty Atom; known in English as *Astro Boy*). From 1954 to 1988 he produced a long-running series entitled *Hi no tori* (Firebird; known in English as *Phoenix 2772*), which dealt in comic-strip form with serious issues relating to human life; Tezuka described it as his lifework. In 1962 Tezuka began making animated versions of his own works for television and movies.

Thai-Japanese Alliance   日タイ同盟

(Nittai Dōmei). Military alliance between Thailand and Japan during World War II, established under a pact signed in Bangkok on 21 December 1941. Thailand and Japan agreed to respect each other's sovereignty, provide mutual aid against military attack from any third power, and refrain from making any separate peace with enemy countries. The pact is also said to have included a secret protocol whereby Japan agreed to help Thailand regain the four states of northern Malaya lost to Britain, and Thailand agreed to assist Japan in its war effort. Thailand did, in fact, declare war against the United States and Britain in January 1942. The alliance ended with Japan's defeat in 1945.

Thailand and Japan   タイと日本

(Tai *to* Nihon). Thailand and Japan have a natural affinity, sharing a heritage of a rice-based economy, Buddhist religion and culture, and a history of independence from colonial domination. Thailand was allied with Japan during World War II, and although postwar relations have at times been strained by controversies over war reparations and continuing Thai fears of Japanese economic domination, relations between the two countries have increased in scale and importance, especially since the 1970s.

Early Relations——Early in the 17th century, a settlement of Japanese merchant-adventurers led by YAMADA NAGAMASA was established in Ayutthaya, then the capital of Siam (Thailand). This NIHOMMACHI, or Japanese town, was burned down by the Siamese in 1630 shortly after the death of Yamada. During the period of Japan's NATIONAL SECLUSION (1639–1858), Siamese goods were brought into Japan by Chinese merchants.

Siam and Japan issued a declaration of friendship in 1887 and signed a trade and navigation treaty in 1898. At the turn of the century Siam invited Japanese advisers to

help modernize its legislation, medical science, railway technology, silkworm cultivation, and arts and crafts. Siam's name became Thailand in 1939, following a 1932 constitutional revolution.

Relations during World War II——Japan and Thailand signed a friendship treaty in June 1940, and Thailand regained border states from French Indochina through Japanese intervention in July 1941. Under the terms of the friendship treaty, immediately after the outbreak of World War II, the Thai government gave permission to Japanese troops to use Thai territory as a base for operations against British Malaya and Burma. Field Marshal PHIBUL SONGKHRAM, premier of Thailand at the time, concluded an alliance with Japan on 21 December 1941 and declared war on the United States and Great Britain in January 1942 (see THAI-JAPANESE ALLIANCE). At the same time, PRIDI PHANOMYONG, regent of the king of Thailand, directed the anti-Japanese FREE THAI MOVEMENT (FTM) with the aim of cooperating with similar movements in the United States and Britain.

In July 1943 Prime Minister TŌJŌ HIDEKI of Japan visited Thailand and reached an agreement with Phibul ceding territory under Japanese occupation in British Malaya and Burma to Thailand. In return for control over this territory, Phibul was expected to participate in the Greater East Asia Conference held in Tōkyō in November 1943, but he sent Prince Wan Waitayakorn instead and hoped to disassociate himself from the Japanese since defeat seemed inevitable. At the end of 1943 the FTM launched an underground movement against the Japanese army and sent secret information to the British air force for use in air raids on Thailand. In July 1944 Phibul resigned from the premiership and was succeeded by Kuang Aphaiong and a cabinet of FTM ministers.

When the Japanese army in French Indochina arrested Vichy French officials and imposed a military government, the FTM in Thailand began preparing a military coup against the Japanese army, a plan that did not materialize until 15 August 1945, the date of the Japanese surrender. On 16 August, Pridi renounced the 1942 declaration of war. Although the United States accepted this move, Britain did not and occupied Thailand in September to disarm both the Japanese and FTM armies.

The Postwar Period——Within two years of the end of the war, the civilian government in Thailand concluded peace treaties with Great Britain and China. It joined the United Nations in December 1946. In 1947, however, the military overthrew the civilian government and in 1948 Field Marshal Phibul was reinstated as premier. He adopted anticommunist and pro-American policies in the cold war period. Meanwhile, occupied Japan began to import Thai rice again early in 1948, and a Japanese government liaison office was set up in Bangkok in March 1951. After the signing of the SAN FRANCISCO PEACE TREATY in September of the same year, diplomatic relations were reestablished, and an embassy was opened in Bangkok in 1952.

Remaining unresolved between the two countries was the problem of the wartime special yen account debt that had been accumulated by the Japanese military in Thailand. In April 1955 Phibul, as prime minister, visited Japan and accepted partial payment of ¥5.4 billion (US $15.0 million). The remaining payment of ¥9.6 billion (US $26.7

million) was postponed until 1961. Phibul withdrew from politics after being overthrown in a coup in 1957 and was exiled in Japan from 1958 to 1964. In November 1961 Japanese prime minister IKEDA HAYATO visited Thailand and announced the payment of the balance of the special yen account debt. At the same time, Japan also began to provide development assistance to Thailand, including factory facilities, technicians, and machinery.

Trade between the two countries increased steadily in the 1960s. By the end of that decade annual imports from Japan reached US $470.0 million (36 percent of Thailand's total imports), while exports to Japan reached US $160.0 million (27 percent of total exports). The imbalance of trade led to a long series of governmental and civilian trade negotiations and conferences. As Japanese firms continued to expand their presence in Thailand, anti-Japanese sentiments deepened. In November 1972 the National Student Center of Thailand initiated a drive to boycott Japanese goods to protest the Japanese domination of the Thai economy. In order to moderate anti-Japanese feelings, Japanese prime minister TANAKA KAKUEI visited the Southeast Asian nations in January 1974. In Thailand, however, he was greeted with demonstrations against Japan's economic advances in Thailand. The years 1975 to 1979 marked a period of adjustment in Thai-Japanese relations, induced by the anti-Japanese movement, which was related, behind the scenes, to the antigovernment movement within Thailand.

In November 1981 Premier Prem Tinsulanonda visited Japan and indicated that Thailand would have no objection to a larger Japanese military role in Southeast Asia if this would contribute to regional peace and stability. Between 1980 and 1985 Thailand was the second largest recipient—next to Indonesia—of Japan's official development aid (ODA), a jump from seventh largest in the 1969–79 period. The bilateral trade imbalance remained a problem throughout the 1980s, however. In 1990 Japan's exports to Thailand totaled US $9.13 billion, while imports from Thailand amounted to US $4.15 billion.

thalidomide children サリドマイド児

(saridomaido ji). Children born between 1958 and 1963 with extreme deformities of the arms and legs (phocomelia) and other external and internal body parts, because their mothers had used sedatives or nausea-controlling drugs during pregnancy that contained the chemical thalidomide. West Germany, where thalidomide was developed, had the greatest number of victims, 2,000–3,000; Japan was second, with more than 1,000.

In January 1958, Dainippon Pharmaceutical Co, Ltd, began selling the drug, and within three years 14 other companies were marketing thalidomide under various names throughout Japan. By the end of 1961, most Western European nations had prohibited thalidomide use, following West Germany's lead. However, thalidomide was allowed in Japan through September 1962. According to one scientific estimate, this one-year delay led to the birth of nearly one-half of the thalidomide children in Japan. Only in the early 1970s, after testimony for a class-action case had concluded at the Tōkyō District Court, did the government and the company admit a cause-and-effect relationship between the drug and defects and accept responsibility and provide compensation for the tragedy.

theater, traditional 古典芸能

(koten geinō). The five major genres of Japanese traditional theater, all still in performance, are bugaku (see GAGAKU), NŌ, KYŌGEN, BUNRAKU, and KABUKI. Although different in content and style, they are linked by strong aesthetic relationships, derived from a confluence of sources both inside and outside Japan. The assumption of an integral relationship among dance, music, and lyrical narrative governed the evolution of performing arts throughout Asia. These three elements were held to be an extension of the poetic art in classical Sanskrit treatises on dance and drama, which strongly influenced traditional stage practices throughout Asia. The synthesis of the disparate elements of speech, music, and dance led to highly developed styles, of which the five Japanese genres represent supreme examples.

Among the five Japanese genres, bugaku stands apart as a ceremonial dance associated only with court ritual, in which the theatrical element is minimal and music predominates. Ceremonial dance was common in ancient Chinese ritual, and as far back as the Zhou (Chou) dynasty (1027 BC–256 BC) dance in China was divided into civil and military styles performed for propitiation. Bugaku incorporates aesthetic and structural principles current in the 8th century—admixtures of Central Asian, Indian, and Korean elements assimilated by China and adopted by Japan during a period of cultural borrowing. One can trace the symmetrical, rigidly patterned choreography, paired dancers, and compartmented dance forms of bugaku to its ancient Chinese sources. Although it has undergone transmutation into a wholly Japanese form, symbolic of Japan's movement away from external cultural influences and toward cultural independence, bugaku still embodies forms and principles long obsolete in continental Asia.

Nō, kyōgen, bunraku, and kabuki, by contrast, are indigenous forms representing successive periods of political and social change in Japan. The first two belong to an age when Chinese influences were still potent; the latter two come from a time when Japan was politically isolated. But all adhere to Asian dramatic principles emphasizing symbolism and allusive imagery, as opposed to the Aristotelian concept of mimesis, the imitation of reality, which dominates Western dramatic theory. Japanese theater, whatever the genre, strives to induce a mood, to create an immediate aesthetic experience drawing an instantaneous response from the spectator.

Nō drama, for example, seeks to reveal the ephemeral nature of reality through stage techniques stressing imagery, metaphor, and symbolism. Medieval Buddhist thought, which profoundly influenced Nō, rejected factual reality as illusory: in Buddhist theory it is only at the moment of perception that anything exists; thus, all existence is fleeting. Just as classical Sanskrit drama was governed by the theory of rasa, so is Nō based upon the aesthetic ideal of YŪGEN; both are untranslatable terms originally indicating an object lying too deep to be seen or comprehended, that refer to the aesthetic communication between performer and spectator. Both Nō and Sanskrit drama matured into highly refined, nonrealistic styles concerned with the affinity between performer and spectator.

Kyōgen, the comic interludes that are an integral part of Nō performance, poke fun at human frailties as did the traditional Asian storytellers, jesting at social pretensions, marital discord, quackery, and so forth. Through stylized vocal forms, pantomime, and spatial control, kyōgen preserves some of the formal elegance of Nō. In its artless humor and oral techniques there is also a great deal that is reminiscent of traditional Chinese stage clowning, for the Chinese comic actor is also descended from a long storytelling tradition. In both kyōgen and Chinese performance the comic action is physical and situational, playing off the discrepancies between what people would be and what they really are. In both, the comic actor becomes a catalyzing agent, relieving tension through the arrangement of his appearance between (or, in the case of the Chinese comic, within) the serious plays.

Bunraku, or puppet theater, is unique in being accepted in Japan as the equal of orthodox drama. Indeed, it is impossible to speak of bunraku without mentioning kabuki, since a sizable part of the latter's repertoire consists of plays originally written for puppet drama, which has also greatly influenced the style of kabuki acting. In turn, bunraku has taken much from the sophisticated technical presentation of kabuki and has incorporated some of its popular dance dramas into its own repertoire. Bunraku puppets bear a family resemblance to puppets once common in southern China, although they are more technically complex and are characterized by a degree of realism not found elsewhere in Asia. The artistry involved in the unique bunraku practice of using three puppeteers to manipulate a single character in coordination with a sung narrative and SHAMISEN music produces a theatrical experience of considerable emotional intensity.

Kabuki carries even further the deployment of speech, sound, movement, and space as equal contributory forces. Theatrical synthesis reaches a powerful degree of instantaneous communication by using visual and aural techniques cumulatively to assail the playgoer's senses and emotions. Stylization conditions every level of performance. Narrative musical forms are used constantly to convey mood, emphasize emotional tensions, and provide exposition.

There is much in the background and methods of kabuki that is reminiscent of the Beijing (Peking) theater, at least as the latter existed in the past. Like its Chinese counterpart, kabuki catered to habitués for whom virtuoso acting was the main attraction. In both, the female impersonator was, and in kabuki still is, central to the nature of the performance, the use of actresses at one time being proscribed in the interests of public decency. Although the ban on actresses was lifted after the Meiji Restoration of 1868, female impersonation continues as an accepted feature of kabuki.

Typical of Japanese and Chinese traditional theatrical music is the use of stereotyped modal patterns to create mood, tempo, and rhythm, dramatically complementing the progression of events on stage. One major difference between the Beijing and kabuki stages is that in the former the actors do their own singing to musical accompaniment, whereas in kabuki a narrative chorus seated on stage along with musicians pro-

Three Monkeys The image of the Three Monkeys is associated with a variety of folk and religious beliefs in Japan. Pictured is one of eight carved panels adorning the stable of the Tōshōgū Shrine in Tochigi Prefecture.

vides all vocal accompaniment. The actors stress dramatic climaxes with dance and pantomime.

Archetypal characterization is the basis for both Chinese and Japanese acting styles, and this has led to highly systematized vocal techniques, gestures, dance forms, and combat styles. Together with costume and makeup these are used to identify the specific character roles. Costumes stress theatrical function and spectacle rather than historical accuracy, making symbolic use of color, decoration, and motifs. The fantastic facial makeup (KUMADORI) used in kabuki to symbolize such qualities as good, evil, and power has its counterpart in Beijing stage makeup, but the elaborate wigs worn by actors are distinctively Japanese. Also, in contrast to the spareness of Chinese staging, kabuki uses complex stage settings and properties together with a runway (HANAMICHI) designed to carry the action into the auditorium and close to the audience. These settings, a powerful factor in developing the synthesis of theatric form, have inspired a method of acting unique to kabuki.

In kabuki, as in other Japanese theatrical forms, the aesthetics of performance combine to provoke a total sensory response from spectators, in contrast to the Western tradition with its emphasis on the literary and textual qualities of the dramatic work.

theatrical costumes 舞台衣装

(*butai ishō*). The theatrical costumes worn in the traditional performing arts of Japan reflect the periods of history in which the stage arts developed and the social classes that patronized the performances. In ancient *bugaku* (see GAGAKU) court dances one sees the flowing trousers and broad sleeves of Heian-period (794–1185) court apparel. In NŌ and KYŌGEN plays one sees 15th- and 16th-century robes and fabrics reflecting the development of complex weaving techniques. On the BUNRAKU and KABUKI stages, the ordinary cotton dress of the Edo-period (1600–1868) merchant class appears alongside silks with stenciled and painted designs. The types of costumes worn for stage performances have been prescribed for centuries; costumes have been preserved and collected, and some that are worn today date from the 18th and 19th centuries.

Bugaku Costumes——The oldest of Japan's stage arts still performed is the court dance, or *bugaku*. These slow dances use free-flowing, layered costumes. A broad-sleeved cloak of silk gauze called a *hō* is worn over several layers of silk KIMONO, wide trousers, and figured vest. The color of the *hō* indicates the style of the dance.

Nō and Kyōgen Costumes——Nō costumes have been recognized as works of art and are collected and displayed by museums. In the 14th century most of these garments were of plain silk, but in the 15th century

thistles Three varieties of Japanese thistle. *Moriazami* (top) blooms in the fall. *Fujiazami* (center), named for its abundance on Mt. Fuji, has flowers that reach 9 cm in diameter. *Noazami* (bottom) is a common perennial found in hills and alpine meadows.

brocade (KARA-ORI, ATSUITA, etc), satin, and complex weaves saw increased use on the Nō stage. Only in the 17th century did Nō costumes develop into stylized garments distinct from everyday wear. Today most of the Nō costumes produced are imitations of older ones.

Nō costumes are worn in layers. The stiffness of the fabric, aided by liberal padding around the body, gives the costumed figure a well-defined outline and larger-than-life appearance. MASKS, wigs, and headgear complete the sublimation of the actors' individuality. Each school of Nō has its wardrobe, and the finest costumes are reserved for the use of the school's greatest actors.

Costumes for the comic *kyōgen*, which are performed during the intervals of Nō plays, typify the clothing and manners of lower-class *samurai* and servants. The stencil dyes on the cotton *kataginu* (a type of vest) show imaginative use of common objects to create striking designs.

Bunraku Costumes——The puppet theater developed in the early 17th century and was patronized by the rising merchant class and low-ranking samurai. Costumes for the large wooden puppets were devised to suggest body contour and to allow three men to operate each puppet. Costume changes involved momentarily ducking out of sight and transferring the head to a new body. Patterns and colors of costumes suggested character traits such as wickedness or submissiveness as well as social status and role.

Kabuki Costumes——Kabuki also prospered in the Edo period. Stories based on historical episodes used reconstructions of samurai dress and armor, but romances among the merchant class featured costumes reflecting the everyday clothing of the merchant, wife, GEISHA, and dandy. New fashions and colors introduced by the actors were often adopted by the audience. Kabuki helped popularize the use of family CRESTS (*mon*) as decoration on the kimono. Emphasis on splashy effects gave rise to the art of onstage quick costume changes (*hikinuki*). By removing a few key threads, a costume is unsewn in seconds, and the actor appears in new array. See also CLOTHING; TEXTILES.

theocracy 神政

(*shinsei*). The ancient Japanese state was, at least in theory, a theocracy in that religious ceremonies (*matsuri*) and the act of governing (*matsurigoto*) were regarded as one, the emperor (*tennō*) being the central figure in both the government and the indigenous Japanese Shintō religion. The emperor was held to be "a god in the form of a man" (*arahitogami*), not just a representative of the gods, and his sovereign function as chief-of-state and high priest was to perform those ceremonies upon which the welfare of the nation was believed to rest. Although actual government power was almost always exercised by secular figures, this system re-

mained a basic principle until the 1947 constitution established the separation of religion and state and ensured freedom of religion.

thistles 薊

(*azami*). *Cirsium* spp. Perennial herbs of the family Compositae. The species most commonly found in Japan is the *noazami* (*Cirsium japonicum*), which is widely distributed throughout the country except in Hokkaidō. It reaches a height of 60–90 centimeters (2–3 ft). The spiny stem branches at the head and bears reddish purple, tubular flowers in May and June. Many varieties are found in Japan, with flowers ranging from white to pale red and dark purple. The *hanaazami*, also called *doitsuazami*, used in flower arrangements, is a variety of the *noazami*.

Other Japanese thistle species include the *noharaazami* (*C. tanakae*), which closely resembles the *noazami*; the *taiazami* (*C. fauriei*), with spiny leaves, which grows to over 1 meter (3.3 ft) in height; the *moriazami* (*C. dipsacolepis*), with thick, edible roots; the *hamaazami* (*C. maritimum*), found on beaches; and the largest of all, *fujiazami* (*C. purpuratum*).

this-worldliness 現世主義

(*gense shugi*). Generally speaking, Japanese religions emphasize not death and the afterlife but the procurement of blessings in the present life; thus they are often described as "this-worldly." There is a strong tendency among Japanese to see this world as continuous with the next, or other, world. As a result the solution to the problems of sin and suffering is sought in the present world, and acquisition of material benefits through the agency of gods and Buddhas in the other world holds an important role in religious activities. Consequently self-denial and rejection of the things of this world do not in general have the importance given them by other religions. This tendency is found not only in the indigenous SHINTŌ faith but in BUDDHISM (introduced in the 6th century) as well.

Thought Criminal Probation Law
思想犯保護観察法

(Shisōhan Hogo Kansatsu Hō). Law passed by the Diet on 18 May 1936 that provided for a probationary period *hogo kansatsu* (literally, "protective supervision") for so-called thought criminals (*shisōhan*) arrested under the PEACE PRESERVATION LAW OF 1925 (Chian Iji Hō), whether indicted or not. The law solidly established the category of "thought crime" (*shisō hanzai*) in the legal system. Its aim was to keep thought criminals under surveillance, reform their thinking, and help them find employment. A key concept in this law was TENKŌ (conversion), i.e., ideological recantation by radicals who had undergone self-criticism and accepted the ideology supported by the state.

Three Monkeys 三猿

(San'en or Sanzaru; also called Sambikizaru). Figures of three monkeys (*saru*) who clasp both hands over eyes, ears, or mouth, thus not seeing (*mizaru*), not hearing (*kikazaru*), or not speaking (*iwazaru*). Beginning in the late Muromachi period (1333–1568), it became customary to carve these figures on *kōshintō*, stone pillars used during the observances of KŌSHIN. According to the KIYŪ SHŌRAN, an early-19th-century reference work, the Three Monkeys may also be related to the Sannō belief complex, wherein

monkeys play the role of divine messengers. The Three Monkeys represent the Santai (Three Truths) advocated by the TENDAI SECT of Buddhism. The Tendai founder, SAICHŌ, is said to have carved a representation of this ideal in the form of monkeys.

thrushes 鶫

(*tsugumi*). Birds of the family Muscicapidae, subfamily Turdidae. The best-known in Japan is the *tsugumi* (dusky thrush; *Turdus naumanni*). It is about 24 centimeters (9 in) long, with a spotted breast, white feathers above the eye ("eyebrows"), and chestnut-colored wings. Breeding in Siberia, it migrates to Japan in the fall. It is a legally protected species.

Besides the *tsugumi*, other thrushes of this subfamily found in Japan are the resident birds *toratsugumi* (White's ground thrush; *T. dauma*), *akahara* (brown thrush; *T. chrysolaus*), and *akakokko* (Izu island thrush; *T. celaenops*). The *kurotsugumi* (gray thrush; *T. cardis*) and *mamijiro* (Siberian thrush; *T. sibiricus*) summer in Japan; the *shirohara* (pale thrush; *T. pallidus*) and *mamichajinai* (gray-headed thrush; *T. obscurus*) winter there.

Thunberg, Carl Peter ツンベリ, C. P.

(1743–1828). Swedish physician and botanist. After studying medicine and botany with Carolus Linnaeus (1707–78) at the University of Uppsala, he joined the Dutch East India Company as a ship's doctor. He arrived in 1775 at Nagasaki, the only Japanese port then open to foreign (Dutch and Chinese) trade under the Tokugawa shogunate's NATIONAL SECLUSION policy. During his year-long stay, Thunberg collected more than 800 specimens of flora and lectured to such scholars as KATSURAGAWA HOSHŪ and NAKAGAWA JUN'AN. He wrote several books on Japan, including the *Flora Japonica* (1784).

Tianjin (Tientsin) Convention 天津条約

(Tenshin Jōyaku). Agreement that resolved Sino-Japanese misunderstandings growing out of the Korean-led KAPSIN POLITICAL COUP of 1884; also known as the Li-Itō Convention. Chinese representative LI HONGZHANG (Li Hung-chang) and ITŌ HIROBUMI of Japan met at Tianjin, China, in April 1885. It was agreed that both nations would withdraw troops from Korea within four months of the treaty's conclusion; that King KOJONG would be advised to hire instructors from a third nation to train the Korean army, and that neither nation would send troops to Korea without prior written notice. The last provision proved to be no deterrent when the next serious confrontation in Korea escalated into the SINO-JAPANESE WAR OF 1894–1895. See also KOREA AND JAPAN.

tie-dyeing 絞り染め

(*shiborizome*; also called *shibori*). A method of resist dyeing in which the required design is securely tied or stitched onto the fabric before it is dyed. There is evidence that it was used as early as the Heian period (794–1185). By the mid-Muromachi period (1333–1568) tie-dyeing became a popular textile art form, and a technique called TSUJIGAHANA, which combined stitch-resist tie-dye and hand-drawn motifs, was developed. During the Edo period (1600–1868) an exotic type of *kanoko shibori* emerged, in which the wrinkles left after tie-dyeing were preserved. Also fashionable was *sō-*

kanoko, where the entire surface of a garment is tie-dyed into mini-resist dots on a uniform background color.

Tie-dye methods are traditionally used for KIMONO, *haori* (kimono jacket), and OBI (sash) fabrics as well as for accessories and *futon* (bed) and *zabuton* (cushion) covers. In modern tie-dye production, dot stencils with the desired design are used to mark the design onto the fabric. With different color zones indicated, the material is tied by hand or with a hook and shuttle device according to the stencil design. The fabric is then either hand painted with dye or vat-dyed before being steamed and untied. See SANKECHI.

Ting Ju-ch'ang → Ding Ruchang

(Ting Ju-ch'ang)

Titsingh, Izaak ティツィング, I.

(1744?–1812). Dutch trade commissioner in Nagasaki; diplomat. Born in Amsterdam. A medical doctor, he joined the Dutch East India Company and went in 1768 to its Asian headquarters at Batavia in Java. He was sent to Japan three times (1779–80, 1781–83, and 1784). He met Japanese scholars of WESTERN LEARNING and made two official visits to the shogunate in Edo (now Tōkyō). In 1784 Titsingh returned to Batavia and in 1809 to Holland. His *Mémoires et anecdotes sur la dynastie régnante des djogouns, souverains du Japon* (1820) and *Cérémonies usitées au Japon pour les mariages et les funérailles* (1819) are valuable sources for knowledge of late-18th-century Japan.

Tōa Corporation 東亜建設工業[株]

(Tōa Kensetsu Kōgyō). General construction contractor and pioneer of offshore engineering in Japan. Incorporated in 1920. It has nine overseas offices, mostly in Southeast Asia and the Middle East. For the fiscal year ending March 1991, sales totaled ¥201.7 billion (US $1.5 billion) and capitalization stood at 8.9 billion (US $64.9 million). Headquarters are in Tōkyō.

Tōa Dōbunkai 東亜同文会

(East Asia Common Culture Society). Organization founded in 1898 by pan-Asianist politician KONOE ATSUMARO to promote mutual understanding between Japan and China in the wake of the SINO-JAPANESE WAR OF 1894–1895. The society stressed a "common culture" because both nations used written characters (*kanji*) developed in ancient China. In 1900 the society opened a school, the Dōbun Shoin, in Nanjing (Nanking). In 1901 the school was moved to Shanghai and renamed the Tōa Dōbun Shoin; it recruited students from Japan to study Chinese language and culture. Accredited as a college in 1939, this institution also had a high school for Chinese students. The society sponsored a preparatory school in Tōkyō for Chinese students seeking higher education in Japan. The Tōa Dōbunkai published several journals, including *Shina* (China). Graduates of the college in Shanghai numbered nearly 5,000, and many promoted Japan's expansionist interests on the Asian continent. Both the college and the society were abol-

ished at the end of World War II. See also PAN-ASIANISM.

tie-dyeing Cloth decorated with a peony pattern using the *sōkanoko* technique, in which the entire fabric is tie-dyed.

Tōagōsei Chemical Industry Co, Ltd 東亜合成化学工業[株]

(Tōa Gōsei Kagaku Kōgyō). Company engaged in the manufacture and sale of caustic soda, chlorine products, fertilizer, synthetic resins, and other chemicals. Incorporated in 1942. It operates joint-venture companies with the Rohm & Haas Co of the United States and Ato Chimie SA of France. Total sales in 1990 were ¥116.0 billion (US $868.6 million), and the company was capitalized at ¥14.3 billion (US $107.1 million). Headquarters are in Tōkyō.

Tōa Remmei 東亜連盟

(East Asian League). An ultranationalist organization formed in October 1939 by pan-Asianist military man ISHIWARA KANJI and others to support Prime Minister KONOE FUMIMARO's "New Order in East Asia" (TŌA SHINCHITSUJO). The league had about 15,000 members and published the magazine *Tōa remmei*. It advocated pooling the economic resources of Japan, MANCHUKUO (Japan's puppet state in Manchuria), and China; the establishment of an integrated defense effort; and political autonomy for participating nations in order to oppose Western imperialism. A branch was established in Nanjing (Nanking), with WANG JINGWEI (Wang Ching-wei) as its head. In 1942 the organization dissolved. It was reorganized as the Tōa Remmei Dōshikai and concentrated on domestic problems such as agricultural reform, but it was disbanded by order of the OCCUPATION authorities after World War II.

Tōa Shinchitsujo 東亜新秩序

("New Order in East Asia"). Slogan proclaiming the objective of Japan's China policy. It was first used on 3 November 1938 in a statement by Prime Minister KONOE FUMIMARO announcing that the purpose of Japan's military presence in China was to help build a new order in East Asia based on political, economic, and cultural ties and cooperation among China, MANCHUKUO (the Japanese puppet state in Manchuria), and Japan.

On 16 January 1938 Konoe had declared (in what is known as the first Konoe statement) that Japan would no longer deal with the Nationalist Chinese government. The second Konoe statement, on 3 November 1938, proposed the creation of a "New Order" in East Asia. Konoe issued a third statement, reasserting Japan's intention to establish a New Order based on the principles of "mutual friendship, anticommunism,

▼An Edo-period (1600–1868) *tabako-bon* (tobacco tray) with smoking implements. *Clockwise from upper left*: charcoal for lighting the tobacco, a tobacco case, a container for ashes, and two pipes.

◀A cloth tobacco pouch and a carved pipe holder of the type that was worn on the sash of a man's *kimono* (Meiji period).

▼Three ornate pipes, the top one made of metal and bamboo and the other two of silver (Edo period).

◀This woodblock print showing the typical smoking "style" of an Edo-period townsman depicts the actor Matsumoto Kōshirō IV in a male *kabuki* role. Sharaku. Late Edo period.

and economic cooperation," in December 1938 when he saw indications that WANG JINGWEI (Wang Ching-wei; an important member of the Nationalist Chinese government) might be willing to work with Japan. The slogan, which was no more than a rationalization for the Japanese invasion of China, prefigured another phrase, Dai Tōa Kyōei Ken (GREATER EAST ASIA COPROSPERITY SPHERE), that was used later during World War II.

Tōa Washinkai   東亜和親会

(East Asia Friendship Society; Ch: Dongya Heqin Hui or Tung-ya Ho-ch'in Hui). Group formed in Tōkyō in 1907 by Chinese revolutionaries Zhang Ji (Chang Chi; 1882–1947) and Liu Shipei (Liu Shih-p'ei; 1884–1919) to oppose colonization of Asia by the West. In addition to Chinese participants, membership included Indians, Filipinos, and Japanese. The group's activities ceased in 1908.

Toba   鳥羽[市]

City in eastern Mie Prefecture, central Honshū; a landing point for pilgrims to ISE SHRINE during the Edo period (1600–1868). Still a transportation center, it also has an active fishing industry. The cultured-pearl industry was developed here. It is a base for tourists to Ise-Shima National Park. Pop: 27,320.

tobacco   煙草

(*tabako*). Tobacco is thought to have been introduced into Japan in the late 16th century, probably brought from the Philippines or Macao by Spanish or Portuguese merchants. Records show that tobacco was first cultivated in Nagasaki in 1605. Only four years later fights broke out in Kyōto between two gangs who used long, heavy, iron tobacco pipes as weapons; this resulted in an ordinance prohibiting the use of tobacco.

The Tokugawa shogunate (1603–1867) had a house rule against smoking and repeatedly issued ordinances against using tobacco, but these injunctions were rarely heeded. Wealthy merchants of Edo (now Tōkyō) became so fond of such extravagances as gold and silver tobacco pipes and cases that the shogunate issued statutes prohibiting excessively ornate smoking paraphernalia. The Japanese used a long, slender tobacco pipe (*kiseru*) with a small metal bowl big enough for only two or three puffs at a time.

During the Meiji period (1868–1912) the cigarette (also referred to as *tabako*) came into fashion in Japan. In 1875 the Japanese government began issuing licenses for tobacco dealers. In 1904, in order to raise revenue for the Russo-Japanese War (1904–05), the government made the sale of tobacco a government monopoly. While it is no longer government controlled, the production of tobacco remains a monopoly (see JAPAN TOBACCO, INC). Distribution has been deregulated. Although most Japanese cigarettes are made from domestically grown tobacco, some imported tobacco is added for improved taste and aroma. In 1990, approximately 37 percent of the adult population were smokers (61 percent of adult men and 14 percent of adult women). Total domestic and import sales stood at over 300 billion cigarettes, worth roughly ¥4.8 trillion (US $25.0 billion). See also NONSMOKERS' RIGHTS.

Toba, Emperor   鳥羽天皇

(1103–56; Toba Tennō). The 74th sovereign (*tennō*) in the traditional count (which includes several legendary emperors); reigned 1107–23. Eldest son of Emperor Horikawa (1079–1107; r 1087–1107). Toba's grandfather, retired emperor SHIRAKAWA, controlled the government from his cloistered quarters during Toba's reign; after Toba retired, he himself exercised power for 27 years during the reigns of his sons SUTOKU, Konoe (1139–55; r 1142–55), and GO-SHIRAKAWA (see INSEI). In 1142 he forced Sutoku to abdicate, replacing him with Konoe. When Konoe died, Toba, instead of enthroning Sutoku's son, installed another of Sutoku's younger brothers as Emperor Go-Shirakawa. The bitterness between Toba and Sutoku was a cause of the HŌGEN DISTURBANCE of 1156. Toba also acquired a vast number of landed estates (SHŌEN) and bequeathed them to his wife and Go-Shirakawa the year before his death. He was a devout Buddhist, making more than 22 pilgrimages to the Kumano Shrine and establishing the temple Saishōji in Kyōto.

Toba-Fushimi, Battle of
鳥羽伏見の戦い

(Toba-Fushimi no Tatakai). The first of the military conflicts that accompanied the Meiji Restoration (see BOSHIN CIVIL WAR); fought on 27 January 1868. Hoping to dislodge the forces of the Satsuma (now Kagoshima Prefecture) and Chōshū (now Yamaguchi Prefecture) domains, which had seized the Kyōto palace and proclaimed an "Impe-

rial Restoration" (ŌSEI FUKKO) on 3 January, Tokugawa shogunate troops set out for Kyōto on 25 January. On the 27th they were intercepted at Toba and Fushimi, south of Kyōto, and defeated by Satsuma-Chōshū forces.

tōbaku no mitchoku   討幕の密勅

(secret imperial orders to overthrow the shogunate). Imperial orders to depose the shōgun TOKUGAWA YOSHINOBU; believed to have been secretly transmitted in 1867 to the political leaders of the Satsuma (now Kagoshima Prefecture) and Chōshū (now Yamaguchi Prefecture) domains, the centers of the movement to overthrow the Tokugawa shogunate (1603–1867). By arrangement of ŌKUBO TOSHIMICHI of Satsuma and the influential court noble IWAKURA TOMOMI, a court official named Ōgimachi Sanjō Sanenaru (1820–1909) is said to have delivered a letter addressed to the *daimyō* of Satsuma to Ōkubo himself and a similar one addressed to the daimyō of Chōshū to Hirosawa Saneomi (1833–71). The orders were nullified the day they were issued, 9 November, when the shōgun "returned" his mandate to the emperor (see TAISEI HŌKAN). The supposed letters survive, but since they contain neither the emperor's handwriting nor the seals of any court officials, some scholars believe them to be forgeries.

Toba Sōjō   鳥羽僧正

(1053–1140). Painter and priest of the TENDAI SECT who held many official posts, including that of *sōjō* (high priest); his popular name combines this title with Toba, the place of his residence as *bettō* (intendant) of the Shōkongōin in Kyōto. The son of the courtier Minamoto no Takakuni (known as Uji Dainagon; 1004–77), his Buddhist name was Kakuyū. His career as a Buddhist official began with his appointment to the post of *bettō* of the temple Shitennōji in 1081. He subsequently held various other posts and in his late years resided at the Hōrin'in of the Onjōji (Miidera), becoming its *chōri* (head priest) in 1135. He is also sometimes referred to as Hōrin'in no Sōjō.

His name is recorded in various literary sources as a painter of Buddhist icons, including the *tobira-e* (door paintings) in NINNAJI in 1135. He was annotator of the *Hōrin'in zuzō*, a compendium of iconographic drawings produced at the temple where he resided. Toba Sōjō's name has long been associated with lively and even humorous paintings as well as with Buddhist iconography. Although he was formerly considered to have painted the SHIGISAN ENGI EMAKI and the CHŌJŪ GIGA, it is now known that the *Shigisan engi emaki* is not his work and that only the first two of the four scrolls of the *Chōjū giga* may be his. At present no known painting is acceptably documented as the work of Toba Sōjō.

Tobata 戸畑
Ward in the northern part of the city of Kita Kyūshū in northern Fukuoka Prefecture, Kyūshū. After the opening of the government-owned Yawata Steel Mill in 1901, Tobata developed as a harbor town. Today Nippon Steel Corporation plants occupy nearly half of Tobata's total area.

Tobe 砥部[町]
Town in central Ehime Prefecture, Shikoku. Its Tobe ware (mainly vases, china, utensils for the tea ceremony, and, more recently, porcelain insulators) dates from the early 17th century. Mandarin oranges are grown, and there is some dairy farming. Pop: 19,561.

tobera 海桐花
(tobira or Japanese pittosporum). *Pittosporum tobira.* Evergreen shrub of the family Pittosporaceae that grows wild in the coastal areas of central and western Honshū, Shikoku, and Kyūshū, as well as in China and southern Korea. It is also cultivated as an ornamental. The plant reaches a height of 2–3 meters (7–10 ft). The slightly glossy, oblong leaves are alternate and grow densely on the upper part of the branch. The fragrant flowers are dioecious and bloom about June, changing from white to yellow. Fruits are three-sectioned capsules with sticky red seeds. The name *tobera* or *tobira* (door) comes from the custom of inserting branches of this tree in house doorways on the day of SETSUBUN to keep demons out. Infusions of *tobera* leaves are a folk remedy for skin diseases.

Tobishima 飛島
Island in the Sea of Japan, 39 km (24 mi) northwest of the city of Sakata, northwestern Yamagata Prefecture, northern Honshū; part of Yamagata Prefecture. Fishing is the principal industry. The island is famous as a breeding ground for black-tailed gulls. Area: 2.5 sq km (0.9 sq mi).

Tobishima Corporation 飛島建設[株]
(Tobishima Kensetsu). Company engaged in public works, construction, and real estate operations. Incorporated in 1947. Its specialties are the construction of hydroelectric plants and railroad projects. It is active in the procurement of overseas contracts, particularly in Southeast Asia. Sales for the fiscal year ending March 1991 totaled ¥419.6 billion (US $3.1 billion), and the company was capitalized at ¥30.0 billion (US $218.7 million). Headquarters are in Tōkyō.

Tōbu Railway Co, Ltd 東武鉄道[株]
(Tōbu Tetsudō). Major railway company operating bus and rail services and real estate businesses. Incorporated in 1897, it is the leading company of the Tōbu group in Japan. Sales for the fiscal year ending March 1991 totaled ¥206.4 billion (US $1.5 billion), and capitalization stood at ¥64.2 billion (US $467.9 million) in the same year. Headquarters are in Tōkyō.

Tochigi 栃木[市]
City in southern Tochigi Prefecture, central Honshū. Tochigi developed as a post-station town on the highway to NIKKŌ. Since the beginning of the Meiji period (1868–1912) lime, *sake*-brewing, and *geta* (wooden clogs)

industries have flourished. There are also food-processing and machine industries. Pop: 86,216.

Tochigi Prefecture 栃木県
(Tochigi Ken). Located in central Honshū and bordered by Gumma, Fukushima, Ibaraki, and Saitama prefectures. The YAMIZO MOUNTAINS on the east and Taishaku and Ashio mountains on the west are separated by a central plain watered by the Nakagawa and several other rivers. The climate is distinguished by moist, hot summers and dry, cool winters.

Known after the TAIKA REFORM of 645 as Shimotsuke Province, the area came under the control of the ASHIKAGA FAMILY in the late Kamakura period (1185–1333). It was divided into numerous *daimyō* domains in the Edo period (1600–1868) and given its present name and boundaries in 1873.

Rice is the principal crop, and other grains and vegetables are produced in the central plains area. Forestry and woodworking industries are active. Copper mining was formerly a major industry, but since World War II, the machine, metal, and textile industries have become more prominent.

NIKKŌ NATIONAL PARK, which includes the TŌSHŌGŪ mausoleum built by the Tokugawa shogunate; Lake Chūzenji; Kegon Falls; the mountain known as Shiranesan; the river Kinugawa; and the Nasu Highland draw visitors from far and wide. The town of Mashiko in southeastern Tochigi is famed for its handmade pottery (see MASHIKO WARE). Area: 6,414 sq km (2,476 sq mi); pop: 1,935,168; capital: Utsunomiya. Other major cities include ASHIKAGA, TOCHIGI, SANO, KANUMA, and OYAMA.

tochinoki → horse chestnut, Japanese

Tochio 栃尾[市]
City in central Niigata Prefecture, central Honshū. Noted for its heavy snowfall. Tochio was traditionally known for its Tochio *tsumugi* (a silk cloth); since World War II, it has developed as a manufacturing center for synthetic fibers. Pop: 27,809.

Toda 戸田[市]
City in southeastern Saitama Prefecture, central Honshū; separated by the river Arakawa from Tōkyō. Toda developed as a river crossing point on the highway Nakasendō during the Edo period (1600–1868). Today it is a transportation center on National Route No. 17, as well as a residential area. Pop: 87,599.

Toda Construction Co, Ltd 戸田建設[株]
(Toda Kensetsu). Construction firm. Established in 1881. The company was a pioneer in the early stages of Western-style architecture in modern Japan. It has diversified into civil engineering, real estate development, and international operations. It has subsidiaries in the United States, Brazil, Malaysia, Thailand, and China and offices in the United Kingdom and Sri Lanka. Sales for the fiscal year ending March 1991 totaled ¥735.5 billion (US $5.4 billion), and the firm was capitalized at ¥22.6 billion (US 164.7 million) in the same year. Headquarters are in Tōkyō.

Tōdaiji 東大寺
Major monastery-temple belonging to the KEGON SECT of Buddhism. It was erected by order of the emperor SHŌMU (r 724–749) in Nara, the capital of Japan from 710 to 784, to

become the most important religious institution within the network of provincial monasteries and convents (KOKUBUNJI) throughout Japan. Immense in scale, Tōdaiji represented the culmination of Buddhist architecture under imperial sponsorship. The principal image of the temple, a colossal bronze statue popularly called the Nara Daibutsu (Great Buddha of Nara), completed in 752, was installed in its *daibutsuden* (great Buddha hall). The image embodied the Buddha Birushana (Skt: Vairocana), who was regarded by the Kegon sect as the cosmic, central Buddha. Over the centuries the icon was severely damaged several times and finally restored to its present form in 1692. Most of the extant Tōdaiji buildings are restorations of earlier structures.

The origin of Tōdaiji goes back to the Kinshōji, a temple that had existed in the eastern sector of the present Tōdaiji compound. Here, Rōben (689–773), a scholar-monk of the Kegon sect who was to become the first abbot of Tōdaiji, had been active in 733. Rōben is commemorated by a portrait-statue made around 1019 and kept in the *kaisandō* (founder's hall). The *kondō* (main hall) of Kinshōji probably is the extant inner sanctuary of the *hokkedō* (lotus hall), popularly known as the Sangatsudō (Third Month Hall), where the Lotus Sutra (*Hokekyō*) is chanted yearly during the third month (*sangatsu*). The main icon of the *hokkedō* is the Fukūkensaku Kannon, a splendid, dry-lacquer statue, made around 746. In 741 the Kinshōji became the provincial monastery-temple for Yamato Province (now Nara Prefecture). At that time the temple was renovated and renamed Konkōmyōji after the Sutra of the Golden Light (J: *Konkōmyō kyō*).

The temple was first referred to as Tōdaiji in 747, when construction of its major buildings was begun. An immense area extending over seven city blocks was allocated for the Tōdaiji compound. The eastern sector stretched into the Kasuga hills. The main entrance was through the *nandaimon* (great south gate), which was on an axis with the *daibutsuden*. Between the *nandaimon* and the *chūmon* (inner gate) that led to the precinct of the *daibutsuden* were two seven-storied pagodas, one to the east and the other to the west, each 100 meters (328.1 ft) high. On an axis to the north of the *daibutsuden*, flanked by a belfry and a sutra repository, was the *kōdō* (lecture hall), enclosed on three sides by monks' quarters that were connected to a refectory by a corridor. In 754 a hall for the ordination of monks, the *kaidan'in*, was established by GANJIN (Ch: Jianzhen or Chien-chen). It burned down three times; the present one dates from 1731. On its altar are placed images of the Shitennō (Four Heavenly Kings), which are outstanding examples of Tempyō-era (729–749) clay modeling. By 798 the vast compound of Tōdaiji and its buildings were completed. According to Tōdaiji records, 50,000 carpenters, 370,000 metal workers, and 2.18 million laborers worked on its construction and furnishings. The enormous expenses virtually brought the nation to the brink of bankruptcy.

Little remains of the 8th-century buildings of Tōdaiji except the Tegai Gate of the western wall and the inner sanctuary of the *hokkedō*. After the destruction of the *daibutsuden*, the towering pagodas, and most of the other buildings in 1180, the Tōdaiji was reconstructed under the direction of the

tobera An evergreen shrub whose leaves are used to treat skin diseases, the *tobera* blooms in early summer.

Tochigi Prefecture Location and Prefectural Crest

▲ An aerial view of the Tōdaiji central compound. The present *daibutsuden* (great Buddha hall), above center, was built in 1709 and is generally regarded as the largest wooden structure in the world. It is a National Treasure.

▲ The huge bronze statue known as the Nara Daibutsu (Great Buddha of Nara) viewed from above. A representation of the Buddha Birushana, the 15-meter-high statue, a National Treasure, has been severely damaged and restored several times since its creation in 752.

◄ The *daibutsuden* lighted by torches for a New Year's ceremony. The face of the Nara Daibutsu can be seen through the small window at the center of the photograph.

abbot Shunjōbō Chōgen (1121–1206), in a style Chōgen had observed in Southern Song (Sung; 1127–1279) China. This new architectural style, known as the "great Buddha style" (*daibutsuyō*) or the "Indian style" (*tenjikuyō*), is well preserved in the *nandaimon*, for which in 1203 the famed sculptors UNKEI and KAIKEI made the powerful guardian statues of the Niō (Benevolent Kings). After great damage in 1567, the rebuilding of Tōdaiji was sponsored by the Tokugawa shogunate in 1692. The *daibutsuden* visible today dates for the most part from 1709 and lacks the stylistic uniformity and refinement of its 8th-century predecessor. However, it remains to this day the most prominent edifice in Nara and is generally regarded as the largest wooden structure in the world. The SHŌSŌIN, a storehouse located on the grounds of Tōdaiji, houses several thousand precious ornamental and fine-art objects from the 8th century. Tōdaiji is also famous as the temple where OMIZUTORI, a central rite in the Buddhist religious calendar, is conducted each year in early spring.

Toda Jōsei 戸田城聖

(1900–1958). Religious leader and second president of the SŌKA GAKKAI, a lay organization of the Nichiren Shōshū sect of Buddhism. Born in Kaga, Ishikawa Prefec-

ture. In 1920 he became a teacher in a school whose principal was MAKIGUCHI TSUNESABURŌ, founder of the forerunner of the Sōka Gakkai in 1930. Toda became Makiguchi's close friend and chief disciple. During the 1930s Toda became increasingly involved in the Sōka Gakkai. In 1943 he, Makiguchi, and 19 other Sōka Gakkai officials were arrested for opposing the state religion, Shintō, and the government's war policies. Toda was released in 1945 and immediately began to rebuild the Sōka Gakkai into one of Japan's largest NEW RELIGIONS.

Toda Mosui 戸田茂睡

(1629–1706). WAKA poet and theoretician of the early Edo period (1600–1868). Real name Toda Yasumitsu. Born in Suruga Province (now part of Shizuoka Prefecture). Critical of the secretly transmitted poetics of the KOKIN DENJU, his work in Edo (now Tōkyō) paralleled that of KEICHŪ and SHIMOKŌBE CHŌRYŪ in Ōsaka. The main statement of his views is contained in *Nashimotoshū* (1698), a treatise on poetics. Also of note is his *Murasaki no hitomoto* (1682), whimsical descriptions of famous places in Edo, where he lived as an eccentric recluse.

Toda Teizō 戸田貞三

(1887–1955). Sociologist. Born in Hyōgo Prefecture. A graduate of and later professor at Tōkyō University. He introduced US

methods of sociological research to Japan. Toda was particularly interested in the Japanese family. Where previous scholars had specialized in abstract analyses of the family system, he used actual case studies and statistics from Japan's first population census (1920) to formulate his theories. He published his findings in *Kazoku kōsei* (1937, Family Structure). In 1923 he founded the Japan Sociological Society.

Todoroki Falls 轟ノ滝

(Todoroki no Taki). Located on the upper reaches of the river Kaifugawa, the town of Kainan, southern Tokushima Prefecture, Shikoku. Also called Todoroki Kujūku Taki (99 Falls of Todoroki) because there are dozens of falls within a distance of 5 kilometers (3 mi), with Todoroki Falls the main one. During Todoroki Shrine's autumn festival, a shrine (*mikoshi*) is carried into the basin of the falls. Height: 60 m (197 ft).

Tōdō Takatora 藤堂高虎

(1556–1630). Warrior and *daimyō* of the Azuchi-Momoyama (1568–1600) and early Edo (1600–1868) periods. Born in Ōmi Province (now Shiga Prefecture). Takatora entered the service of ASAI NAGAMASA, later became a vassal of Hashiba Hidenaga (1541–91), half brother of TOYOTOMI HIDEYOSHI, and fought in Hideyoshi's campaigns in Kyūshū and the INVASIONS OF KOREA IN 1592

AND 1597. With the deaths of Hidenaga and Hidenaga's son, Hidetoshi, Takatora took holy orders but resumed secular life to become castellan (*jōdai*) of Uwajima Castle in Shikoku. After Hideyoshi's death Takatora allied himself with TOKUGAWA IEYASU; in recognition of his services in the Battle of SEKIGAHARA (1600), he was awarded half of Iyo Province (now Ehime Prefecture).

Tōei Co, Ltd   東映[株]

(Tōei). A major producer and distributor of movies. Incorporated in 1949 as Tōkyō Eiga Haikyū to distribute movies produced by Tōyoko Eiga Haikyū and Ōizumi Eiga. The three merged in 1951 to form the present Tōei Co. The company grew through the mass production of popular historical dramas and enjoyed a golden era in its early years. Tōei also produced various *yakuza* (gangster) series, creating a boom and ushering in such stars as TAKAKURA KEN, YOROZUYA KINNOSUKE, Ōkawa Hashizō (1929–84), Tsuruta Kōji (1924–87), and Sugawara Bunta (b 1933). The company has produced films by such directors as UCHIDA TOMU, IMAI TADASHI, and FUKASAKU KINJI. Sales for the fiscal year ending March 1991 totaled ¥133.5 billion (US $973.0 million) and capitalization stood at ¥11.7 billion (US $85.3 million). Headquarters are in Tōkyō.

Tōei Movieland   東映太秦映画村

(Tōei Uzumasa Eigamura). A section of the TŌEI CO, LTD's, film studios in the Uzumasa section of Kyōto that consists of an open, working film set and a museum of the history of the Japanese film. Opened to the public in 1975. Visitors to the set can observe the filming of motion picture and television period dramas (JIDAIGEKI). Uzumasa is one of the centers of Japan's motion picture industry.

tōfu   豆腐

(bean curd). *Tōfu* was first made by the Chinese some 2,000 years ago and was introduced to Japan in the 7th century. It is high in protein, easily digestible, and inexpensive. *Tōfu* is made from soybeans that are soaked in water, mashed to a pastelike consistency, boiled, and then separated into pulp (*okara*, which is edible) and liquid (TŌNYŪ). For *momengoshi*, the type of *tōfu* most commonly used in Japan, the liquid is then poured into a settling tank lined with cloth and a coagulant is added. The cloth is used to drain the curds that form, giving *momengoshi* a coarse texture. For *kinugoshi*, a more delicate, smoother *tōfu*, the curds are not drained.

Tōfu cut into thin sheets and then deep-fried is called *aburaage*. *Namaage* are thicker cakes of *tōfu* prepared in the same way. *Gammodoki* is made by adding bits of carrot or sesame seeds to patties of *tōfu* and grated mountain yam and then deep-frying. *Kōyadōfu* is freeze-dried *tōfu*. Lightly toasted *tōfu* is called *yakidōfu*.

Tōfu is used in many different types of dishes, such as soups or *sukiyaki*, and may also be eaten alone. As *yudōfu* it is heated in a pot of hot water and dipped in a mixture of soy sauce, minced scallion, and spices. For *hiyayakko*, soy sauce is poured over chilled *tōfu* topped with minced scallion, shaved bonito flakes, and spices.

👁 *1568–1569*

Tōfukuji   東福寺

Head temple of the Tōfukuji branch of the RINZAI SECT of ZEN Buddhism; one of the five GOZAN temples. Located in Higashiyama

tōfu

High in protein, low in fat, and easily digested, this staple food has an unobtrusive taste suited to a wide variety of preparations.

Okara, the edible pulp by-product that remains after the boiled beans are strained, is used in vegetable dishes.

Yuba, a *tōfu* by-product, is made from the film that forms on the surface of heated soy milk.

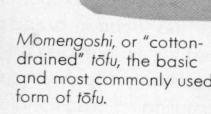

Momengoshi, or "cotton-drained" *tōfu*, the basic and most commonly used form of *tōfu*.

Gammodoki is deep-fried mashed *tōfu* that is mixed with sesame seeds and minced carrot and then fried.

Small neighborhood shops that make and sell *tōfu* on the premises like the one pictured here are less common than they once were; now most people buy mass-produced *tōfu* at supermarkets.

Aburaage, thin deep-fried slices of *tōfu*, are very light and are used in a variety of dishes.

Thick deep-fried cakes of *tōfu*, called *namaage* or *atsuage*, are popular in boiled dishes.

Ward, Kyōto. Founded by the priest ENNI in 1236, it was built upon the remains of Hosshōji, the main temple of the FUJIWARA FAMILY. The name Tōfukuji was derived from the names of the temples TŌDAIJI and KŌFUKUJI. Three major fires at Tōfukuji since 1319 have resulted in much reconstruction. There were at one time 53 *tatchū* (subsidiary temples) within the complex, but after the Meiji Restoration (1868) the number declined; today there are 25. The *sammon* (main gate), built sometime between 1394 and 1428, is the oldest of its kind in Japan and is now a National Treasure; inside are such works as MINCHŌ's paintings, Ashikaga Yoshimochi's (1387–1428) calligraphy, and images of the Buddha Śākyamuni and 16 RAKAN (Skt: *arhat*, "worthy ones"). Tōfukuji boasts numerous Important Cultural Properties: the *tōsu* (lavatory), the *yokushitsu* (bathhouse), the *aizendō* (a hall dedicated to Aizen Myōō [Skt: Rāgarāja]), and the bell tower. At Manjuji, a nearby subordinate temple, there is an image of AMIDA, claimed to be the work of Tendai monk GENSHIN in 1007. Tōfukuji preserves many artworks, documents, and manuscripts and has several magnificent gardens in the style of the Kamakura period (1185–1333).

Tōfutsu, Lake   濤沸湖

(Tōfutsuko). Lagoon on the coast of the Sea of Okhotsk, northeastern Hokkaidō. Located east of the city of Abashiri, it is famous for its white swans and wildflowers, which grow on the coastal sand dunes. Area: 9.3 sq km (3.6 sq mi); circumference: 31 km (19 mi); depth: 2.5 m (8.2 ft).

Togakushi Kōgen   戸隠高原

Highland between the mountains Iizunayama and Togakushiyama, northern Nagano Prefecture, central Honshū. Famous for its bird nesting area and alpine flora. Popular for camping and skiing. Part of Jōshin'etsu Kōgen National Park. Elevation: 1,200 m (3,940 ft).

Togakushiyama   戸隠山

Mountain in northern Nagano Prefecture, central Honshū. Composed of agglomerate, it has sharp cliffs. The mountain is a noted training place for mountain ascetics (see SHUGENDŌ), and women were once forbidden to climb it. The mountain is part of JŌSHIN'ETSU KŌGEN NATIONAL PARK. Height: 1,911 m (6,270 ft).

Tōgane   東金[市]

City in central Chiba Prefecture, central Honshū. During the Edo period (1600–1868) it was the distribution center for marine products from the KUJŪKURIHAMA coastal area and for farm products from the Kujūkurihama Plain. Chief activities are commerce and agriculture. Industrialization is proceeding with the construction of chemical and machinery plants. Pop: 45,179.

Togariishi site   尖石遺跡

(Togariishi *iseki*). Archaeological site of the Middle Jōmon period (ca 3500 BC–ca 2500 BC; also dated as ca 3500 BC–ca 2000 BC); located in Nagano Prefecture near the foot of the group of volcanoes known as Yatsugatake, at an altitude of 1,070 meters (3,510 ft);

Continued on page 1570→

Tōfukuji The temple's south garden is a 20th-century dry landscape garden designed in the Zen style of the Kamakura period by Shigemori Mirei, a modern expert on garden design.

1567
Togariishi site

A Tōfu Primer

Protein-rich yet low in fat and calories, *tofu* has earned a reputation in the West as an ideal food for the health-conscious. In Japan, however, this soybean-based product is appreciated for more than its nutritional value alone. Long prized for its light, delicate flavor and velvety consistency, tōfu is featured in numerous dishes in traditional Japanese cuisine.

The recipes presented here are a sampling of traditional tōfu favorites, along with two Western-style dishes inspired by the recent popularity of tōfu abroad. They specify either *momengoshi-dōfu* ("cotton" tōfu) or *kinugoshi-dōfu* ("silk" tōfu). Although the smooth, "silk"-like consistency of *kinugoshi-dōfu* is preferred in certain dishes, the more common *momengoshi-dōfu* can be used as a substitute.

To make the *dashi* stock required for some of these recipes, you may use commercially pre-pared instant *dashi* powder. For 1 cup *dashi*, dissolve $\frac{1}{4}$ tsp *dashi* powder in 1 cup simmering water. *Dashi* powder and most of the other ingredients mentioned here can be found at Asian specialty markets. All recipes are for four servings.

Kurihara Harumi

Yudōfu (Simmered Tōfu)

This simple, Zen-inspired dish is the perfect meal for cold winter nights.

As soon as the tōfu is ready, transfer it to a plate with a straining spoon.

Ingredients
2 cakes "silk" tōfu
10-cm (4-in) square of *kombu* (kelp)
Soy sauce
Bonito flakes
Shichimi tōgarashi ("seven-spice" cayenne pepper)

Preparation
1 Set an earthenware casserole $\frac{3}{4}$ full of cold water on top of a heating element at the table. Wipe *kombu* with a damp cloth and place in casserole.
2 Cut each block of tōfu into 6 equal pieces; carefully add tōfu to casserole with a straining spoon.
3 Bring liquid to a simmer; remove *kombu*. When water comes to a gentle boil, the tōfu is ready to serve.
4 Transfer to individual plates and top with soy sauce, bonito flakes, and *shichimi tōgarashi*.

Nikudōfu (Tōfu with Sliced Beef)

This hearty, stewlike dish is typical of Japanese home-style cooking.

When the broth has reduced as shown, the dish is ready.

Ingredients
1 cake "silk" tōfu
200 g (7 oz) beef, thinly sliced
1 large onion
1 Tbsp sugar
4 Tbsp soy sauce
2 Tbsp *mirin* (sweet cooking *sake*)
Shichimi tōgarashi ("seven-spice" cayenne pepper)

Preparation
1 Drain tōfu in colander; cut into 6 pieces. Cut beef into bite-size pieces.
2 Cut onion into wedges and place in medium-deep pot; add beef and tōfu.
3 Combine sugar, soy sauce, *mirin*, and 2 Tbsp water. Add to pot and bring to boil.
4 Reduce heat and cover; simmer over medium heat until ingredients are tender. Serve in individual bowls and season with *shichimi tōgarashi*.

Agedashi-dōfu (Fried Tōfu in Sauce)

A crispy coating is augmented by a light, salty-sweet sauce in this tōfu favorite.

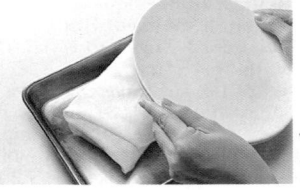

Weigh down tōfu with a plate or similar heavy object to drain.

Ingredients
2 cakes "cotton" tōfu
1 cup *dashi* stock
1 Tbsp *mirin*
1 Tbsp *sake*
$1\frac{1}{2}$ Tbsp soy sauce
Flour
Cooking oil
Grated *daikon* radish
Grated ginger
Chopped chives

Preparation
1 Wrap each tōfu cake in a kitchen towel and weigh down with a heavy plate to drain off excess moisture.
2 Bring to boil *dashi* stock, *mirin*, *sake*, and soy sauce. Turn off heat and set aside.
3 Halve each tōfu cake; coat lightly with flour.
4 Heat cooking oil to 170°C (338°F). Deep-fry tōfu until golden brown; remove and drain.
5 Transfer tōfu to bowls; top with grated *daikon*, ginger, and chives. Pour heated sauce over tōfu and serve.

Hiyayakko (Chilled Tōfu)

Enjoy the fresh, natural flavor of tōfu with this simple but delicious dish.

Ingredients

2 cakes "cotton" tōfu
Soy sauce
Chopped chives
Dried bonito flakes
Grated ginger

Sesame Sauce
2 Tbsp *dashi* stock
2 Tbsp ground sesame seeds
1 Tbsp soy sauce
1 Tbsp *mirin*

Chinese-Style Sauce
1 Tbsp spring onion, minced
1 Tbsp grated ginger
1 Tbsp grated garlic
3 Tbsp soy sauce
1 Tbsp *sake*
2 Tbsp vinegar
$\frac{1}{2}$ Tbsp sugar
1 tsp Chinese red-pepper paste
Sesame oil (to taste)

Preparation

1 Cut tōfu into 4-cm (1$\frac{1}{2}$-in) blocks and place in ice water.
2 Assemble the sesame and Chinese-style sauces.
3 Transfer chilled tōfu to 4 plates. Top with one of the two sauces or with plain soy sauce; add condiments to taste.

There are a number of ways to enjoy *hiya-yakko*. Try different combinations of condiments and sauces.

Shira-ae (Tōfu with Vegetables)

This Japanese-style "tōfu salad" features julienne vegetables and crushed tōfu.

Ingredients

1 cake "cotton" tōfu
30 g (1 oz) carrots, peeled
3 dried *shiitake* mushrooms
10 snow peas
$\frac{1}{2}$ cake *konnyaku*
1 Tbsp *dashi* stock
1 Tbsp soy sauce

1 Tbsp sugar
$\frac{1}{2}$ tsp salt

Sesame Dressing
3 Tbsp tahini
$\frac{1}{2}$ Tbsp soy sauce
$\frac{1}{2}$ Tbsp sugar
$\frac{1}{2}$ Pinch of salt

Preparation

1 Soak *shiitake* mushrooms in water for about 2 hours. Remove stems; slice caps into thin strips.
2 Wrap tōfu in kitchen towel and squeeze gently to remove excess moisture.
3 Boil *konnyaku* for 1 to 2 minutes. Slice *konnyaku* and carrots into julienne strips. String snow peas; parboil and cut into thin diagonal strips.
4 In pan, combine carrots, *konnyaku*, *shiitake*, *dashi*, soy sauce, sugar, and salt. Cook until sauce is almost gone, stirring constantly. Let cool.
5 Mix ingredients for sesame dressing in a bowl. Add tōfu and cooked ingredients; mix well. Garnish with sliced peas.

WESTERN-STYLE TŌFU DISHES

Avocado Tōfu Dip

The light, unobtrusive taste of tōfu makes it perfect for dips.

Ingredients

$\frac{1}{2}$ cake "silk" tōfu
1 avocado
2 Tbsp sour cream
1 Tbsp mayonnaise
2 Tbsp lemon juice
$\frac{1}{2}$ Tbsp bouillon
Salt and pepper (to taste)

Crush drained tōfu gently with the back of a spoon.

Preparation

1 Drain tōfu as for *agedashi-dōfu*; crush with the back of a spoon.
2 Cut avocado in half lengthwise; remove pit and scoop out flesh. Combine with crushed tōfu and the rest of the dip ingredients; mix well.
3 Serve dip with toasted bread, crackers, fresh vegetables, etc. Suggestions (on large platter, clockwise from top): french bread, roast pork slices, celery sticks, radishes, watercress, red cabbage leaves.

Tōfu Steak

This healthy soybean "steak" is low in calories and cholesterol.

Fry tōfu until both sides turn golden brown.

Ingredients

2 cakes "cotton" tōfu
1 Tbsp salad oil
1 Tbsp sesame oil
4 Tbsp soy sauce
2 Tbsp lemon juice
4 lemon wedges
4 leaves green *shiso* (beef-steak plant), cut into thin strips
Spring onion, minced
Bonito flakes
Roasted white sesame seeds

Preparation

1 Drain tōfu as for *agedashi-dōfu*. Slice each cake in half horizontally to create 2 thin "steaks." Mix soy sauce and lemon juice; set aside.
2 For each steak, heat $\frac{1}{2}$ Tbsp salad oil and $\frac{1}{2}$ Tbsp sesame oil in pan and fry tōfu until both sides turn golden brown. At edge of pan, pour in $\frac{1}{4}$ of the soy sauce–lemon mixture. Coat tōfu evenly with the sauce.
3 Transfer to individual plates and top with spring onion, bonito flakes, and sesame seeds. Garnish with lemon wedges.

Tōgō Heihachirō As chief of Japan's naval operations during the Russo-Japanese War, Admiral Tōgō led the Japanese fleet to victory in the Battle of Tsushima.

Tōhata Seiichi Beginning in 1946, this agricultural economist served as the director of several government agriculture research facilities.

named for the jagged rocks (*togariishi*) found in the area. The site was discovered in 1893; excavations in 1940–42 and in 1954 uncovered the remains of 33 PIT HOUSES and a large number of stone implements as well as beads (see BEADS, ANCIENT), JŌMON FIGURINES, and clay earplugs (see EAR ORNAMENTS, ANCIENT). Large Middle Jōmon settlement sites like Togariishi are abundant in the mountainous region around Yatsugatake (see IDOJIRI ARCHAEOLOGICAL HALL). Because of the size, number, and close proximity of these sites, it is believed that some cultivation sufficient to sustain a large community was practiced in addition to hunting and gathering. See also JŌMON CULTURE.

Togashi family   富樫氏

(Togashishi). Warlords of the Togashi district of Kaga Province (now part of Ishikawa Prefecture) during the early Kamakura period (1185–1333). Military governors (SHUGO) of Kaga from the early Muromachi period (1333–1568). In 1447 the Togashi split into two branches, with the head of each branch governing half of Kaga. The family was reunited some 30 years later under Togashi Masachika (1455?–88). He was killed in 1488 in an uprising of the Jōdo Shin sect (see IKKŌ IKKI), and the Togashi fell into obscurity. A member of the family served as a model for the character Togashi (an official in charge of guards at the barrier or checkpoint) in several literary works, including the military chronicle GIKEIKI.

Tōgatta Hot Spring   遠刈田温泉

(Tōgatta Onsen). Located on an eastern foothill of the Zaōzan Mountains, southwestern Miyagi Prefecture, northern Honshū. A radioactive spring; water temperature 60°–70°C (140°–158°F). This famous spa sits on the left bank of the river Matsukawa, a tributary of the Abukumagawa, and has been known since ancient days for its medicinal waters. Tōgatta *kokeshi* (wooden dolls) are a famous product of this area.

Togawa Masako   戸川昌子

(1933–   ). Mystery writer and chanson singer. Born in Tōkyō Prefecture. Togawa received the Edogawa Rampo Prize for her first mystery, *Ōinaru gen'ei* (1962; tr *The Master Key*, 1984). Her work is noted for its graceful style and sensual descriptions. Other mysteries are *Ryōjin nikki* (1963; tr *The Lady Killer*, 1985) and *Shinkirō no obi* (1967, The Illusory Sash).

Tōgō Heihachirō   東郷平八郎

(1848–1934). Fleet admiral in the IMPERIAL JAPANESE NAVY. Born in the Satsuma domain (now Kagoshima Prefecture). He served on the domainal warship *Kasuga* during the BOSHIN CIVIL WAR in 1868. He studied naval science in Great Britain from 1871 to 1878 and was commissioned a lieutenant, first class, upon his return to Japan. A captain at the time of the SINO-JAPANESE WAR OF 1894–1895, he was a commanding officer of the *Naniwa* when it sank a British merchant ship carrying Chinese soldiers off the Korean peninsula.

Following the war he served successively as head of the Naval War College, commander of Sasebo Naval Station, commander in chief of the standing fleet during the BOXER REBELLION in China (1900), and commander of the Maizuru Naval Station. Tōgō was appointed commander in chief of the Com-

bined Fleet in December 1903. Becoming an admiral in 1904, he led naval operations during the RUSSO-JAPANESE WAR, including Japan's stunning victory in the Battle of TSUSHIMA on 27–28 May 1905, which made him a national hero.

After the war he was named chief of the NAVAL GENERAL STAFF OFFICE and war councillor to the emperor. He was promoted to the rank of fleet admiral in 1913. From 1914 to 1924 he was in charge of the education of Prince Hirohito, the eventual emperor SHŌWA. Tōgō Shrine, located in Harajuku, Tōkyō, was founded in his memory.

Tōgō Shigenori   東郷茂徳

(1882–1950). Diplomat. Born in Kagoshima Prefecture. Having graduated from Tōkyō University, he joined the Ministry of Foreign Affairs and became ambassador to Germany in 1937 and ambassador to the Soviet Union in 1938. He played an important role in settling Japanese fishing and territorial disputes with the Soviet Union. He was opposed to the formation of the Axis alliance. Joining the TŌJŌ HIDEKI cabinet as minister of foreign affairs in 1941, he participated in the unsuccessful prewar negotiations with the United States. He resigned the following year in protest against the formation of the Greater East Asia Ministry. Favoring an early peace, Tōgō joined the SUZUKI KANTARŌ cabinet as minister of foreign affairs in 1945 and led the effort to negotiate Japan's surrender. He was sentenced to a 20-year prison term as a class A war criminal by the International Military Tribunal for the Far East in 1946 (see WAR CRIMES TRIALS).

Togura Kamiyamada Hot Spring
戸倉上山田温泉

(Togura Kamiyamada Onsen). Hot spring region extending across the towns of Togura and Kamiyamada, northern Nagano Prefecture, central Honshū, along both banks of the river CHIKUMAGAWA. A sulfur spring; water temperature 40°–57°C (104°–135°F).

tōgyū → bullfighting

Tōhaku → Hasegawa Tōhaku

Tōhata Seiichi   東畑精一

(1899–1983). Agricultural economist. Born in Mie Prefecture; graduate of and later professor at Tōkyō University. He studied under J. A. Schumpeter (1883–1950) in Germany and became a leading authority in his field. After World War II, he served as director of the National Research Institute of Agricultural Economics (under the Ministry of Agriculture and Forestry) and the Institute of Developing Economies. He was also president of the Agricultural Administration Council and of the Tax System Council. He wrote *Nihon nōgyō no tenkai katei* (1936, The Development of Japanese Agriculture) and translated Schumpeter's *History of Economic Analysis* (1955–62). He was awarded the Order of Culture in 1980.

Tōhō Co, Ltd   東宝[株]

(Tōhō). A major producer and distributor of movies. Also engaged in theatrical and television production, video software, and real estate leasing. Established in 1937 as the Tōhō Eiga Co through the merger of the Shashin Kagaku Kenkyūjo Co with the J. O. Film Studio and two other companies. In 1943 the company merged with the Tōkyō Takarazuka Gekijō to form the present Tōhō Co, Ltd. In 1943 the company produced

KUROSAWA AKIRA's first film, *Sugata Sanshirō*. MIFUNE TOSHIRŌ also made his debut at Tōhō. Although the company was hard hit by the TŌHŌ STRIKE of 1948 and the creation of the SHIN TŌHŌ company, it recovered through the adoption of a producer system and the production of big-budget films. Tōhō was especially known for its comedies. The company now leads the industry in the distribution of foreign films, which are imported by its subsidiary, Tōhō Tōwa Co. Sales for the fiscal year ending February 1991 totaled ¥85.1 billion (US $652.2 million), and capitalization stood at ¥9.9 billion (US $75.9 million) in the same year. Headquarters are in Tōkyō.

Tōhō Gakuen School of Music
桐朋学園大学

(Tōhō Gakuen Daigaku). A private, coeducational music college, located in Chōfu, Tōkyō Prefecture. It began as the Sansui Girls' High School in 1941 and became a junior college in 1955. In 1961 it was established as a four-year college. The faculty of music offers two majors: composition and performance. OZAWA SEIJI is one of the school's outstanding graduates. Enrollment was 926 in 1989.

Tōhō Gas Co, Ltd   東邦瓦斯[株]

(Tōhō Gasu). City gas utility, serving more than 1 million households in Aichi, Gifu, and Mie prefectures. Incorporated in 1922. Liquefied natural gas (LNG) accounted for 77 percent of the company's energy supplies in 1991. Tōhō Gas is promoting the use of LNG as a substitute for other fuels. It is also working on high-efficiency combustion technology and other city-gas-related projects. Most of the company's raw materials such as LNG, naphtha, and coke are imported. Sales for the fiscal year ending March 1991 totaled ¥160.8 billion (US $1.2 billion), and capitalization was ¥33.1 billion (US $241.3 million). Headquarters are in Nagoya.

Tōhōkai   東方会

(Far East Society). Rightist political group founded by NAKANO SEIGŌ in May 1936. Four years earlier, Nakano and ADACHI KENZŌ had formed the political organization KOKUMIN DŌMEI; disagreeing with Adachi over policy, Nakano left to form the Tōhōkai. Inspired by the writings of the ultranationalist ideologue KITA IKKI, the Tōhōkai called for national reform by parliamentary means. Absorbed by the IMPERIAL RULE ASSISTANCE ASSOCIATION in 1940, it broke away a year later and fared poorly in the 1942 wartime election. In October 1943 Nakano was arrested on charges of conspiring to overthrow the TŌJŌ HIDEKI cabinet. Nakano committed suicide, and the Tōhōkai ceased to exist.

Tōhō Kaigi   東方会議

(Far Eastern Conference). Name given to two policy conferences convened by Japanese prime ministers. The more important one was called by Prime Minister TANAKA GIICHI in the summer of 1927 to formulate a China policy in the aftermath of a dispatch of Japanese troops to northern China (see SHANDONG [SHANTUNG] EXPEDITIONS). Participants included personnel from the foreign ministry, general staff, and army and navy ministries, as well as Japanese colonial officials. The meeting endorsed a "positive" China policy that consisted of maintaining Japan's position in China by force if necessary and of expanding Japan's special interests in Manchuria by encouraging native separatist movements. In 1929, the Nationalist Chinese government made public the so-called TANAKA MEMORANDUM, a document containing detailed plans for the conquest of Manchuria and Mongolia that the Chinese alleged had been presented by Tanaka to the emperor. Doubts continue to exist regarding the authenticity of this memorandum, but at the time it provoked violent anti-Japanese sentiment in China.

The name Tōhō Kaigi is also given to a policy conference convened by Prime Minister HARA TAKASHI in May 1921 to discuss Japanese interests in Manchuria and Mongolia and the withdrawal of Japanese troops stationed in Shandong Province and Siberia since the end of World War I. Attended by ministerial, military, and colonial officials, the meeting resolved to protect Japanese interests in Manchuria, largely through support of the Manchurian warlord ZHANG ZUOLIN (Chang Tso-lin).

Tōhoku Electric Power Co, Inc 東北電力[株]

(Tōhoku Denryoku). Supplier of electric power to six prefectures in the Tōhoku area and to Niigata Prefecture. Incorporated in 1951. The company has 10.1 million kilowatt-hours of total power generation capacity: 2.3 million kilowatt-hours as hydroelectric power, 7.3 million kilowatt-hours as thermal power, and 0.5 million kilowatt-hours as nuclear power. The firm is pushing diversification of energy sources into nuclear power, liquefied natural gas, and coal. It opened an office in New York in 1988. Operating revenues for the fiscal year ending March 1991 totaled ¥1.1 trillion (US $8.0 billion), and capitalization was ¥249.1 billion (US $1.8 billion). Headquarters are in Sendai, Miyagi Prefecture.

Tōhoku Gakuin University 東北学院大学

(Tōhoku Gakuin Daigaku). A coeducational private university located in the city of Sendai, Miyagi Prefecture. Founded in 1886 as the Sendai Theological Seminary, it attained university status in 1949. The university is affiliated with the United Church of Christ in Japan and offers an education based on Christian principles. It has faculties of letters, economics, law, and engineering. Enrollment in 1989 was 12,413.

Tōhoku region 東北地方

(Tōhoku chihō). Also called Ōu region. Region encompassing the entire northern end of the island of Honshū and consisting of Aomori, Iwate, Akita, Yamagata, Miyagi, and Fukushima prefectures. The Tōhoku region is largely mountainous, and most towns and cities are concentrated along the Pacific and Sea of Japan coasts and in the centers of several basins. The climate is highly seasonal, with short summers and long winters.

In ancient times the area was inhabited by the aboriginal people known as EZO. Today it is primarily an agricultural area where rice, vegetables, and fruit are grown. Forestry and fishing are also important. There is some petroleum and natural-gas production, and the iron, steel, cement, chemical, pulp, and petroleum-refining industries have been developing since the 1960s. The principal city is SENDAI. Area: 66,912 sq km (25,835 sq mi); pop: 9,738,285.

Tōhoku University 東北大学

(Tōhoku Daigaku). A national, coeducational university located in the city of Sen-

dai, Miyagi Prefecture. Founded as Tōhoku Imperial University in 1907, it became Tōhoku University in 1949. It now maintains faculties of letters, education, law, economics, science, medicine, dentistry, pharmacology, engineering, and agriculture. It is known for its research institutes in iron, steel, and other metals; agricultural research; mineral dressing and metallurgy; tuberculosis and cancer; scientific measurements; high-speed mechanics; electrical communication; and non-aqueous chemical solutions. Enrollment was 11,102 in 1989.

Tōhō Mutual Life Insurance Co 東邦生命保険[相]

(Tōhō Seimei Hoken). Company providing life and other kinds of insurance, security services, and financial investment services to individuals and businesses. Incorporated in 1898. The company was a pioneer in private pension insurance. It operates offices in New York, London, and Beijing (Peking). Total assets for the fiscal year ending March 1990 totaled ¥4.1 trillion (US $26.7 billion), and premiums received totaled ¥1.2 trillion (US $7.8 billion). Headquarters are in Tōkyō.

Tōhō Pharmaceutical Co, Ltd 東邦薬品[株]

(Tōhō Yakuhin). Pharmaceutical wholesaler handling drugs, chemical reagents, and medical equipment. Incorporated in 1948. Sales for the fiscal year ending March 1990 totaled ¥141.0 billion (US $921.1 million), and capitalization stood at ¥3.3 billion (US $21.6 million). Headquarters are in Tōkyō.

Tōhō Rayon Co, Ltd 東邦レーヨン[株]

(Tōhō Rēyon). Fiber spinning company for acrylic and rayon fibers; it also spins acrylic, rayon, cotton, and other fibers into yarn and manufactures carbon fiber. Founded in 1934, it was incorporated under its present name in 1950. Sales for the fiscal year ending March 1991 totaled ¥77.9 billion (US $567.8 million). In the same year the company was capitalized at ¥9.1 billion (US $66.3 million). Headquarters are in Tōkyō.

Tōhō Strike 東宝争議

(Tōhō Sōgi). Celebrated labor dispute of the OCCUPATION period between the management and the employees' union of the motion picture company TŌHŌ CO, LTD. The dispute arose in April 1948, when the financially troubled company announced the dismissal of 270 union employees. The union launched a strike on 17 April and occupied the company's studio in Kinuta, Tōkyō, while the management countered by obtaining a court injunction forbidding union members to enter the studio grounds. On 19 August the injunction was implemented by some 1,800 armed policemen, with the support of Occupation forces armed with tanks and airplanes. The dispute ended on 19 October when the management agreed to sharply reduce the number of dismissals.

Tōhō Zinc Co, Ltd 東邦亜鉛[株]

(Tōhō Aen). Smelter of nonferrous metals, mostly zinc and lead. Incorporated in 1937, the company consistently has used imported ores as raw materials. It is expanding its nonsmelting sectors, including electronic components, chemicals, processed-metal products, and engineering. For the fiscal year ending March 1991, sales totaled ¥73.7 billion (US $537.2 million) and capitalization stood at ¥5.0 billion (US $36.4 million). Headquarters are in Tōkyō.

Toi 刀伊

Korean term for the Jürchen, a Tungusic people of Manchuria who were subjects of the Khitan Liao dynasty (907–1125) and the Korean state of KORYŎ during the 11th century but went on to found their own Jin (Chin) dynasty (1125–1234). In 1019 some 50 Toi ships sailed from Korea and attacked Tsushima, Iki, and northwestern Kyūshū. The attack was repulsed by officials at DAZAIFU, but many Japanese prisoners were carried off to Korea. Ultimately, some 270 Japanese rescued by Koryŏ were returned to Japan.

Toi Hot Spring 土肥温泉

(Toi Onsen). Hot spring located on the shores of Suruga Bay in the town of Toi, eastern Shizuoka Prefecture, central Honshū. It is a saline and sulfur spring with a water temperature of 50°–60°C (122°–140°F). During the summer the area attracts many beachgoers.

toimaru 問丸

Shipping agents of the Kamakura (1185–1333) and Muromachi (1333–1568) periods who lived in port towns and major trading centers. In the late Heian period (794–1185) these men (called *toi*) had been employed at a few ports as salaried shipping agents for the proprietors of landed estates (SHŌEN). By the Kamakura period they were becoming independent of *shōen* proprietors and were found in most of the major ports as middlemen who arranged for storage, handling, and shipping of tax rice and other commodities. They also provided lodging and transportation for estate owners and travelers. By the late Muromachi period many had become wholesale dealers called TOIYA. They gathered in trade centers, such as Kyōto and Nara, specializing in rice, *sake*, salt, fish, and oil, and came to play an important role in commerce during the Edo period (1600–1868).

Toimisaki 都井岬

Cape in southern Miyazaki Prefecture, Kyūshū; part of Nichinan Coast Quasi-National Park. Extending south into the Pacific Ocean, embracing Shibushi Bay, it is a mountainous region that ends abruptly in a series of cliffs along the coast. It is noted for a herd of wild horses and for the sago palms that grow near Misaki Shrine.

Toita Yasuji 戸板康二

(1915–93). Drama critic and novelist. Born in Tōkyō; graduated from Keiō University. Toita published *kabuki* criticism, such as *Waga kabuki* (1948, Our Kabuki), while he was working at a dramatic publishing company. After he resigned he published such works as *Kabuki e no shōtai* (1950, Invitation to Kabuki) and *Engeki gojūnen* (1950, Fifty

Tōji This Kyōto temple, founded in 796, is the head temple of the Tōji branch of the Shingon sect of Buddhism. The present main hall (pictured) dates from 1603.

Tōjō Hideki The army general and prime minister of Japan from 1941 to 1944 in a photo taken during the Tōkyō war crimes trials. Indicted as a class A war criminal, he was hanged on 23 December 1948.

Years of Theater). Toita received the Naoki Prize for one his mystery novels, *Danjūrō seppuku jiken* (1959, The Case of Danjūrō's Disembowelment). He is also known as an essayist. In 1977 he received the Japan Art Academy Award.

toiya   問屋

Also pronounced *ton'ya*. Type of middleman-merchant who played a key role in Edo-period (1600–1868) commerce. Called TOIMARU in the Kamakura (1185–1333) and Muromachi (1333–1568) periods. These merchants included the *niuke-doiya*, who sold goods on commission to the *nakagai* (distributor or retailer), and the *shiire-doiya*, who bought and sold on speculation. Some specialized in specific products, and others concentrated on goods from specific regions of the country. *Toiya* formed associations (KABUNAKAMA) that maintained a monopoly on commerce throughout the Edo period. After the MEIJI RESTORATION of 1868 the distinction between the *toiya* and the *nakagai* became blurred, and the modern wholesaler came into existence. See also NIJŪSHIKUMI-DOIYA; TOKUMI-DOIYA.

Tōji   東寺

A monastery-temple, officially called the Kyōō Gokokuji, located in Minami Ward, Kyōto. Founded in 796 by imperial order, Tōji is now the head temple of the Tōji branch of the SHINGON SECT of Buddhism. The original buildings of the temple were replaced with later reconstructions. Sponsored in 1599 by TOYOTOMI HIDEYORI and completed in 1603, the existing *kondō* (main hall) was one of the largest Buddhist buildings erected during this period. The five-storied pagoda, rebuilt in 1644 with support from shōgun TOKUGAWA IEMITSU, is the tallest in Japan and a Kyōto landmark.

After the capital was moved to Kyōto in 794, two temples were founded for the protection of the city: Tōji (East Temple) and the short-lived Saiji (West Temple). When the emperor SAGA appointed KŪKAI abbot of Tōji in 823, the temple was effectively transformed into a Shingon monastery. Kūkai enlarged Tōji by adding buildings to suit the needs of esoteric rituals and established it as Kyōto's main Shingon monastery, where the study and practice of esoteric Buddhism flourished.

tōji   杜氏

Also pronounced *toji*. Japanese SAKE (rice wine) brewer. Specifically, the occupational title for the head overseer of the crew that carries out *sake*-brewing operations. It is thought that the word *tōji* originally stood for the wife of the household (*toji*) whose job it was to make *sake* in ancient times. Because *sake* was brewed during approximately 100 days from December through March, the off-season for farming, *tōji* were also known as "100-day men" (*hyakunichi otoko*).

Tōjimbō   東尋坊

Scenic spot on the Sea of Japan, Fukui Prefecture, central Honshū. Pillarlike joints of pyrozene andesite thrust up about 25 m (80 ft) high from the sea, presenting a spectacular sight.

Tōjin Okichi   唐人お吉

(1841?–90; "Foreigner's Okichi"). Real name Saitō Kichi. Young girl sent to serve Townsend HARRIS, the first American consul in Japan, in response to his request for "female attendants." Born in Izu Province (now part of Shizuoka Prefecture). She entered Harris's service in May 1857 but was soon returned home because Harris complained that her skin was infected. Though she had been handsomely paid, the double stigma of having been sent to the American and then rejected made Okichi an object of ridicule; hence her nickname. She moved to Yokohama and later returned to Shimoda to work as a hairdresser. In 1882 she opened a small restaurant. Faced with bankruptcy eight years later, she drowned herself. Okichi's tragic life has been the subject of many works, including *Tōjin Okichi* (1928–31) by Jūichiya Gisaburō (1897–1937).

Tōji Treasure House   東寺宝物殿

(Tōji Hōmotsuden). Located at TŌJI, a SHINGON SECT temple in Kyōto. This treasure house, opened in 1965, holds many of the famous Buddhist statues, paintings, sutras, and other objects owned by the temple. The paintings include portraits of seven patriarchs of the Shingon sect. Of these, five are by Chinese artists and were brought back from China in 806 by KŪKAI, the founder of the Shingon sect in Japan. There is also a set of the Jūniten (12 Devas Who Protect Buddhism) painted by TAKUMA SHŌGA. The manuscripts include a letter in Kūkai's hand and his *Shōrai mokuroku* (Memorandum on the Presentation of the List of Newly Imported Sutras).

Tōjō Gimon   東条義門

(1786–1843). Japanese-language scholar of the Edo period (1600–1868). Born in Wakasa Province (now part of Fukui Prefecture), he later succeeded his father as the head of a Buddhist temple. Tōjō's research focused chiefly on Japanese conjugated words (verbs and adjectives), and he devised the names for conjugational forms still in use today. His writings include *Katsugo shinan* (2 vols, 1844, A Guide to Conjugation). See JAPANESE LANGUAGE STUDIES, HISTORY OF.

Tōjō Hideki   東条英機

(1884–1948). Army general and prime minister (1941–44). Born in Tōkyō, Tōjō graduated from the Army Academy and the Army Staff College. He was a military attaché in Switzerland and Germany from 1919 to 1922. Tōjō joined the Issekikai, a group formed by NAGATA TETSUZAN, and the so-called Control faction (TŌSEIHA), which called for technological innovation within the military. He was transferred to the headquarters of the GUANDONG (KWANTUNG) ARMY in Manchuria in 1935. While there, Tōjō built up a new power group, the so-called Manchuria faction.

In 1938 he returned to Tōkyō. As army vice-minister he continued to support the expansion of the war with China. In July 1940 he was appointed to the posts of army minister and chief of the Manchuria Bureau. He pushed for the conclusion of the TRIPARTITE PACT with Germany and Italy and supported the formation of the IMPERIAL RULE ASSISTANCE ASSOCIATION. Tōjō was named prime minister in 1941. The succession of victories after the attack on Pearl Harbor strengthened his position.

In February 1944 Tōjō became chief of the General Staff. With Japan's deteriorating fortunes in the war, he was removed from office in July 1944. After Japan's defeat, he attempted to kill himself. He was hanged as a war criminal on 23 December 1948 (see WAR CRIMES TRIALS). Loyal to the end, he did everything he could to exonerate Emperor SHŌWA (Hirohito) from any blame for his role in the war.

Tōjō Misao   東条操

(1884–1966). Linguist. Born in Tōkyō, he graduated from Tōkyō University and was a professor at Gakushūin University. He was the founder of dialectology in Japan, his most important work being the classification of Japanese dialects. Among his major publications are *Dai Nihon hōgen chizu: Kokugo no hōgen kukaku* (1927), a dialect atlas of Japan; and *Hōgen to hōgengaku* (1938), a study of dialects and dialectology.

Tokachidake   十勝岳

Active stratovolcano, in Chishima Volcanic Zone, central Hokkaidō. Two great eruptions occurred, in 1926 and 1962, causing loss of life and crop damage. The volcano erupted again in 1988. It is part of Daisetsuzan National Park. Height: 2,077 m (6,814 ft).

Tokachigawa   十勝川

River in central Hokkaidō, originating on Tokachidake, one of the major peaks that are part of Daisetsuzan National Park, and flowing southeast through Tokachi Plain to the Pacific Ocean. Riverbank terraces and swampland form much of the area along the middle and lower reaches. The water is utilized for irrigation, industry, and electric power. Length: 156 km (97 mi); area of drainage basin: 9,010 sq km (3,479 sq mi).

Tokachi Plain   十勝平野

(Tokachi Heiya). Located in southeastern Hokkaidō. Most of the plain consists of diluvial upland covered with volcanic ash, but there are also alluvial lowlands on the river Tokachigawa and a coastal plain along the Pacific Ocean. This plain is Japan's greatest producer of beans, sugar beets, potatoes, and wheat. Dairy farming also flourishes. The major city is Obihiro. Area: approximately 3,600 sq km (1,400 sq mi).

tokage   蜥蜴

Eumeces latiscutatus. The *tokage* is a small lizard native to Japan with a blackish brown body, fine yellow or green longitudinal stripes, and a blue-green tail. It reaches a length of 16–21 centimeters (6–8 in). Commonly found in flatlands and low mountains of Hokkaidō, Honshū, Shikoku, and Kyūshū, it is especially numerous in western Japan, often inhabiting gardens. It preys on earthworms and insects. Another common lizard, the *kana hebi* (*Takydromus tachydromoides*), resembles this species in shape and size but is brown all over.

Tōkai   東海[市]

City in Aichi Prefecture, central Honshū, on the Chita Peninsula, Ise Bay. Formerly known for its *nori* (seaweed), it now has many steel and heavy industrial complexes and is a commuter suburb of NAGOYA. Pop: 97,358.

Tōkai   東海[村]

Village in eastern Ibaraki Prefecture, central Honshū, on the Pacific Ocean. Since the construction of the ATOMIC ENERGY RESEARCH INSTITUTE, JAPAN, here in 1956, Tōkai has developed as the atomic power center of the country. Pop: 31,557.

Tōkai Bank, Ltd   [株]東海銀行

(Tōkai Ginkō). City bank that has its main center of business in the Nagoya area. Although Tōkai traces its roots back to the 1870s, it took its present form in 1941. It has an international network covering key financial and business centers in Europe, the United States, Asia, and Oceania. Tōkai Bank had 268 domestic branches and 50 overseas offices and affiliates as of March 1989. At the end of March 1991 its total assets amounted to ¥37.5 trillion (US $273.3 billion) on a nonconsolidated basis. It was capitalized at ¥310.4 billion (US $2.3 billion) in the same year. Headquarters are in Nagoya.

Tōkaidō   東海道

(literally, "Eastern Sea Road"). The highway that ran from Edo (now Tōkyō) to Kyōto, a route of approximately 488 kilometers (303 mi) generally following the Pacific coast; an extension continued to Ōsaka. During its heyday in the Edo period (1600–1868) there were 53 POST-STATION TOWNS along the Tōkaidō offering services for the convenience of travelers. These became famous in art and literature (especially the woodblock prints of HIROSHIGE) as the Fifty-Three Stations of the Tōkaidō (Tōkaidō Gojūsantsugi).

From the time that a central government first crystallized in the Yamato area (around present-day Nara; see YAMATO COURT), the Tōkaidō was the most important route to the east. In the late 12th century the headquarters of the shōgun MINAMOTO NO YORITOMO was established at Kamakura, and the Tōkaidō became the main artery between the imperial capital at Kyōto and the military capital at Kamakura. At the beginning of the Edo period the Tokugawa shogunate systematically directed a policy of road improvement with emphasis on the Five Highways (GOKAIDŌ) radiating from Edo, where the shogunate established its capital. The Tōkaidō was one of these. The roadbed averaged about 5.5 meters (18 ft) wide. It consisted of a deep layer of crushed gravel covered with sand, but on mountainous slopes subject to erosion it was paved with stone. Each *ri* (3.93 km; 2.44 mi) was marked by a mound (ICHIRIZUKA) planted with a nettle or pine tree, and stone guideposts pointed the way at crossroads. There was almost no wheeled traffic on the road; bulky cargo moved by sea. Packhorses were shod with straw and led by hostlers (BASHAKU). The standard vehicle on the Tōkaidō was the palanquin (KAGO). Most rivers were bridged, had ferries, or could be forded. Large rivers were sometimes rendered impassable by floods. At such times travelers might use the normally more difficult alternate road, the NAKASENDŌ (Central Mountain Road), also called the Kiso Kaidō (Kiso Road).

At governmental barriers (SEKISHO) travelers were inspected for proof of identity and travel permits. The strictest was HAKONE NO SEKI at Hakone Pass, considered the gateway to the Kantō Plain and Edo. There officials were on the watch for guns being smuggled into the city or women escaping from it; either could signal rebellion (wives and daughters of the *daimyō* who were away in the provinces were required to reside in Edo as hostages under the system of alternate attendance; see SANKIN KŌTAI). Most post stations were under direct shogunate control; the rest were managed by daimyō. Most stages maintained a force of 100 packhorses and 100 porters. When heavy official travel warranted it, each stage had authority to levy men and horses from a designated surrounding area (see SUKEGŌ).

Every stage had from about 50 to 200 inns, of varying quality. At the top were one or more HONJIN (officially appointed inns for daimyō), which had fine rooms and gardens. There were lesser inns (*waki honjin*, "side" or subsidiary *honjin*) for officials and *samurai*, inns for ordinary travelers, and flophouses for porters (see KUMOSUKE). Travelers of every status used the road. Of the country's approximately 250 daimyō, about 150 used the Tōkaidō to and from Edo on the journeys required by the system of alternate attendance at the shōgun's court (see DAIMYŌ PROCESSIONS). Swift couriers (HIKYAKU) carried official tidings, and associations of merchants set up courier services to link operations and carry private messages.

A modern highway now overlays part of the Tōkaidō and its route is now roughly paralleled by the tracks of the modern "bullet train" (SHINKANSEN); however, a few short stretches of the old road still exist.

Tōkaidō bunken ezu   東海道分間絵図

A series of woodblock prints by the artist Hishikawa MORONOBU (d 1694) depicting the 53 post stations of the TŌKAIDŌ, the highway linking Edo (now Tōkyō) and Kyōto, with descriptions of famous places along the way; published in 1690 as a set of five folding books. Considered the prototype of Japanese guidebooks, the set is a valuable source for local geography and history.

Tōkaidōchū hizakurige   東海道中膝栗毛

(tr *Shank's Mare*, 1960). Also known as *Dōchū hizakurige*. Comic novel (KOKKEIBON)

series by the popular and prolific GESAKU writer JIPPENSHA IKKU. The first volume, an instant success, appeared in 1802 and was followed by seven more volumes in as many years. In 1810 Ikku began a 12-volume sequel, *Zoku hizakurige*, completed in 1822. The same year, he added an introduction to the original *Tōkaidōchū hizakurige*. The series features Yajirobei and Kitahachi, a footloose pair of commoners from Edo (now Tōkyō) with a penchant for coarse humor and an eye for women, who spend any money that comes their way, never plan a day in advance, and persist in seeing life as one long series of pleasures. Affectionately known as Yaji and Kita, the two become involved in a myriad of comic intrigues on their journey along the road from Edo to Kyōto and Ōsaka. Sheltered from harm by their quick wit and endless banter, Yaji and Kita continue to charm readers today.

Tōkaidō megalopolis   東海道メガロポリス

(Tōkaidō *megaroporisu*). General term for the region along the Pacific coast of Honshū extending west from Tōkyō to Ōsaka and Kōbe. It is the political, economic, and cultural center of Japan with approximately 45 percent of its population and 60 percent of its industrial output in a stretch of land that accounts for only 17 percent of the nation's area. It encompasses Tōkyō, Yokohama, Kawasaki, Nagoya, Kyōto, Kōbe, and Ōsaka along with their numerous satellite cities and suburbs.

Tōkaidō Yotsuya kaidan   東海道四谷怪談

(The Ghost Story of Tōkaidō Yotsuya; tr *Les Spectres de Yotsuya*, 1979). KABUKI play by TSURUYA NAMBOKU. First performed in 1825. Often called *Yotsuya kaidan*, it is the most famous ghost play of the classical Japanese theater. The story is about a *rōnin* or masterless *samurai*, Tamiya Iemon, who is per-

Tōjimbō A section of the geological formation known as Tōjimbō. The jagged pillars of rock have been formed by the Sea of Japan through erosion.

tokage Found in all of Japan's four main islands, this small lizard likes dry ground and lives in small holes or embankments.

toki A Japanese crested ibis foraging in a rice paddy prior to 1981 when the few remaining individuals were brought into captivity. At present, the total extinction of the species seems likely.

Tokieda Motoki This linguist and Japanese grammarian's ideas are widely regarded as being the most influential in Japanese language studies after World War II.

suaded to abandon his wife, Oiwa, to achieve social status and wealth. The play shows Oiwa's disfigurement by poison, the sadistic treatment by her husband, and then her transformation into a revengeful ghost. The play is similar to *Kanadehon chūshingura*, the celebrated play about the revenge of the 47 *rōnin* (see FORTY-SEVEN RŌNIN INCIDENT), in that the characters are from the same camps of loyal and disloyal retainers; the two plays were originally performed over two days in alternating parts. However, whereas *Kanadehon chūshingura* depicts a revenge of honor and loyalty, *Tōkaidō Yotsuya kaidan* portrays those who have failed to be loyal and have, therefore, incurred the revenge of frightful ghosts. This play appears to criticize the role of the samurai that served the shogunal court, which fell in the Meiji Restoration (1868), only 43 years after the play's first performance.

Tōkai Industrial Region
東海工業地域

(Tōkai Kōgyō Chiiki). Industrial zone extending along the coast of the Pacific Ocean in Shizuoka Prefecture, central Honshū. Part of the PACIFIC COASTAL BELT, it connects with the KEIHIN INDUSTRIAL ZONE to the north and with the CHŪKYŌ INDUSTRIAL ZONE to the south. There are many rivers in the area, providing an abundance of water and hydroelectric power. Products include musical instruments, motorcycles, paper, processed foods, and textiles.

Tōkai Kōgyō Co, Ltd
東海興業[株]

(Tōkai Kōgyō). Construction firm; also engaged in civil engineering and real estate. Incorporated in 1946. The company's strength is in the construction of facilities for marine and food products, including cold-storage warehouses. Overseas projects include cold-storage facilities, fishing ports, hospitals, housing complexes, and educational facilities. Sales for the fiscal year ending October 1990 totaled ¥248.5 billion (US $1.9 billion) and capitalization stood at ¥6.9 billion (US $53.2 million). Headquarters are in Tōkyō.

Tōkai region
東海地方

(Tōkai *chihō*). The region of Honshū's Pacific coast that lies between the KANTŌ REGION and the KINKI REGION; it encompasses Shizuoka, Aichi, Gifu, and Mie prefectures. The region has a typical coastal climate, with mild temperatures and heavy rainfall; mandarin oranges, green tea, and vegetables are grown here. Since the Meiji period (1868–1912) the area has undergone heavy industrialization, and today the TŌKAIDŌ MEGALOPOLIS is an important part of the PACIFIC COASTAL BELT.

Tōkai Sanshi
東海散士

(1852–1922). Novelist and politician. Real name Shiba Shirō. Born in Kazusa Province (now part of Chiba Prefecture). He fought for the losing Tokugawa side in the BOSHIN CIVIL WAR. He worked his way through school, then went to the United States in 1879 to study. Back in Japan after six years, he wrote his epic-length political novel, or SEIJI SHŌSETSU, *Kajin no kigū* (1885–97, Chance Meetings with Beautiful Women). Despite its length and absence of real plot, the novel became a best seller and exerted great influence on the younger generation. He became involved in politics, serving several terms in the lower house of the Diet after 1892. Other works are *Tōyō no kajin* (1888, A Beauty of the Orient), a novel, and *Ejiputo kinsei shi* (1889, Modern History of Egypt).

Tōkai Shizen Hodō
東海自然歩道

Nature trail beginning in Takao Quasi-National Park in Tōkyō Prefecture and ending in Minoo Quasi-National Park in Ōsaka Prefecture, a total distance of 1,343 kilometers (834 mi). The trail, which was begun in 1969 and completed in 1974, passes through many points of natural beauty or historical interest, including the Tanzawa Mountains, ASAGIRI KŌGEN, HŌRAIJISAN, the SUZUKA MOUNTAINS, Mt. Hiei (HIEIZAN), and ARASHIYAMA.

Tōkai University
東海大学

(Tōkai Daigaku). A private, coeducational university whose central administrative offices are located in Shibuya Ward, Tōkyō. The School of Aeronautics in the city of Shimizu, Shizuoka Prefecture, and the School of Radio Science in Tōkyō, both founded by Matsumae Shigeyoshi (1901–91) in 1943 and 1944, respectively, were combined in 1945 to form Tōkai College of Science (Tōkai Kagaku Semmon Gakkō). In 1946 the school adopted its present name and acquired university status. The university has been expanding throughout Japan. It maintains faculties of letters, political science and economics, law, humanities and culture, science, physical education, engineering, medicine, and marine science and technology, as well as its Foreign Student Education Center. Enrollment was 30,912 in 1989.

Tōkamachi
十日町[市]

City in southern Niigata Prefecture, central Honshū. Tōkamachi has long been known for its fine silk. It is also known for its very heavy snowfall. The Torioi Festival in January and the Snow Festival in February are famous. Pop: 46,278.

Tōkan kikō
東関紀行

Travel diary of the Kamakura period (1185–1333); authorship unknown. It records a journey from Kyōto to Kamakura in the autumn of 1242. Imbued with Buddhist feelings, its sensitive observations of people and places during some two weeks on the road and a two-month residence in Kamakura are recorded in the elegant *wakan konkō* prose style (classical Japanese with a heavy admixture of classical Chinese). An important travel work of the period along with the KAIDŌKI, its prose style has influenced such later works as the HEIJI MONOGATARI. See also TRAVEL DIARIES.

Tokara Islands
吐噶喇列島

(Tokara Rettō). Group of islands extending from southern Kagoshima Prefecture, Kyūshū, to the island of AMAMI ŌSHIMA. Part of the SATSUNAN ISLANDS. Farming and fishing are the principal activities.

Tōka zuiyō
桃華薬葉

(Leaves from the Peach Blossom [Manse]). Ichijō family (see GOSEKKE) book written in 1480 by ICHIJŌ KANEYOSHI as a guide for his son Fuyuyoshi (also pronounced Fuyura; 1464–1514). *Tōka zuiyō* contains rules of deportment, descriptions of traditional family customs, records of inheritance, and an inventory of family estates and possessions.

Tōkeiji
東慶寺

Also known as Matsugaoka Gosho. Temple in the city of Kamakura, Kanagawa Prefecture, belonging to the Engakuji branch of the RINZAI SECT of ZEN Buddhism. Tōkeiji was founded in 1285 by the widow of HŌJŌ TOKIMUNE, regent of the Kamakura shogunate (1192–1333), to serve as a refuge for women escaping from unhappy marriages and thus was popularly known as Enkiridera, or Temple for Divorce (see KAKEKOMIDERA). After becoming almost defunct with the establishment of the Meiji government in 1868, Tōkeiji was reestablished as a monastery by Shaku Sōen (1859–1919), the famous abbot of ENGAKUJI. The temple's library, Matsugaoka Bunko, was built in memory of the Zen scholar D. T. SUZUKI.

Toki
土岐[市]

City in southeastern Gifu Prefecture, central Honshū, on the river Tokigawa. Toki is known primarily for its ceramics; many of its wares are exported. Pop: 64,946.

toki
朱鷺

(Japanese crested ibis). *Nipponia nippon.* A wading bird of the family Threskiornithidae. Mature birds are about 76 centimeters (30 in) in length. The *toki's* plumage is white except for the wings and tail, which are pink; its unfeathered forehead and legs are red. It nests in broadleaf trees 10 meters (33 ft) or more above the ground. Although the *toki* was once widely distributed in lakes and wetlands throughout Japan, extensive land development narrowed its environment and pollution by agricultural chemicals further reduced its numbers. In 1952 the *toki* was designated a protected species, but by 1981 wild *toki* were extinct, and in 1991 only two *toki* remained in captivity. The bird has become a symbol of the destruction of Japan's natural environment. Efforts are now being made to breed the *toki* with a closely related Chinese species.

Tokico, Ltd
トキコ[株]

(Tokiko). Automobile equipment manufacturer affiliated with HITACHI, LTD. Incorporated in 1949. The company is the industry's largest producer of shock absorbers and gasoline flowmeters. Robots used in industrial painting are among the company's fastest-growing products. The company sells suspension systems to US automakers, including the "Big Three" (Chrysler, Ford, and General Motors). Tokico's sales in 1990 were composed of automobile equipment, 68 percent; instrumentation equipment, 19 percent; and air compressors, 13 percent. In the fiscal year ending March 1991, sales totaled ¥108.7 billion (US $792.3 million) and capi-

tokonoma Decorative alcoves of this type, a key element of traditional Japanese architecture, typically include the raised flooring, hanging scroll, and flower arrangement visible here.

talization stood at ¥8.2 billion (US $59.8 million). Headquarters are in Kawasaki, Kanagawa Prefecture.

Tokieda Motoki 時枝誠記

(1900–1967). Linguist and Japanese grammarian. Born in Tōkyō; graduate of Tōkyō University in 1926. He served as professor of Japanese at Seoul University from 1927 until 1943, when he succeeded HASHIMOTO SHINKICHI as professor of Japanese at Tōkyō University.

Tokieda investigated the grammar of both classical and modern Japanese. He is noted for his *gengo katei setsu* (process theory of language), which he placed in opposition to European structural linguistics. His approach showed the strong influence of earlier studies of Japanese, particularly those of SUZUKI AKIRA. Tokieda's grammatical system is based on the distinction between *shi* (those words that express the mind's experience) and *ji* (those words that express the mind's activity); that is, between conceptualized and affective elements or perhaps between semantic and pragmatic elements. It thus follows the tradition of YAMADA YOSHIO and MATSUSHITA DAISABURŌ as against that of Hashimoto Shinkichi. Another key idea is the *irekogata kōzō* (nested box structure), which Tokieda adopted in contrast to the linear *bunsetsu* (phrase) structure used by Hashimoto. Tokieda's ideas have been much criticized, but his is probably the most influential approach to Japanese grammar of the post–World War II period. See also JAPANESE LANGUAGE STUDIES, HISTORY OF.

Toki family 土岐氏

(Tokishi). Powerful provincial leaders in Mino (now part of Gifu Prefecture) from the 12th to the mid-16th century. Claiming descent from MINAMOTO NO YORIMITSU, the Toki were prominent vassals (*gokenin*) of the Kamakura shogunate (1192–1333). For his support of ASHIKAGA TAKAUJI, Toki Yoriyasu (1318–87) was appointed military governor (SHUGO) of the family base in Mino as well as of Owari and Ise provinces (now Aichi and Mie prefectures, respectively). Toki power eroded during the ŌNIN WAR (1467–77), when the family was gradually displaced by the Saitō, who were deputy military governors (*shugodai*). In 1542 Toki Yorinari (1502–82) was defeated by SAITŌ DŌSAN, and the family lost its domain in Mino. The Toki later became direct vassals (*hatamoto*) of the Tokugawa shogunate (1603–1867).

Tokio Marine & Fire Insurance Co, Ltd 東京海上火災保険[株]

(Tōkyō Kaijō Kasai Hoken). Japan's largest property and casualty insurance company. Incorporated in 1879 by SHIBUSAWA EIICHI. It was the first such company founded in Japan and is a member of the MITSUBISHI group. It began overseas operations early, opening offices in Paris, London, and New York in 1880 under the name Tokio Marine. In 1944 the original Tokio Marine & Fire Insurance Co merged with the Mitsubishi Marine & Fire Insurance Co and the Meiji Fire & Marine Insurance Co to form the present company. Aside from its main office in Tōkyō, the company has a total of 43 major offices and 415 branches in Japan. It also has 39 offices in 26 countries overseas. The company's total assets of ¥4.6 trillion (US $33.5 billion) at the end of March 1991 ranked first among property and casualty insurance companies in the world. In the same year the company's

net income from premiums totaled ¥1.0 trillion (US $7.2 billion). The firm was capitalized at ¥99.8 billion (US $727.4 million) in 1991. Headquarters are in Tōkyō.

Tokitsugu Kyō ki 言継卿記

Thirty-seven-volume diary by Yamashina Tokitsugu (1507–79), a court noble responsible for imperial household finances, covering the years 1527–76. The diary is useful for its account of conditions in the capital and in the KINAI region, as well as for its references to literature, court rituals, and music.

tokiwazu-bushi 常磐津節

Type of music for KABUKI, accompanied by SHAMISEN and other instruments. A variety of *jōruri* narrative chanting. In 1730 Miyakoji Bungonojō (?–1740) and his follower Mojidayū (1709–81) brought from Kyōto to Edo (now Tōkyō) a new style of kabuki chant, which rapidly became popular there but was banned by the government in 1739, perhaps because of an intrigue by rival singers. Bungonojō returned to Kyōto, and the old Miyakoji style eventually disappeared. Under the name Tokiwazu, Mojidayū obtained permission to continue in Edo and, from 1747 onward, performed a series of new pieces, together with the *shamisen* player and composer Sasaki Ichizō I (d 1768). The main *shamisen* school of *tokiwazu-bushi* was founded by Kishizawa Shikisa I (1730–83), Ichizō I's successor.

As music, *tokiwazu-bushi* drew on the traditions of GIDAYŪ-BUSHI, which it adapted for the kabuki theater, particularly to accompany dance episodes. It has a more dignified character than KIYOMOTO-BUSHI: the singing is purer and less nasal, and the accompanying ensemble is less bright in sound. The present repertoire contains over 70 pieces of various types.

Toki Zemmaro 土岐善麿

(1885–1980). Pen name Toki Aika. TANKA poet and scholar of Japanese literature. Born in Tōkyō; graduate of Waseda University. His *tanka* were unusual in that they were written and printed in roman letters and in three lines (independent of their syllable count) instead of the traditional two. They were often compared with the *tanka* of his friend ISHIKAWA TAKUBOKU. An editorial staff member of the newspaper *Asahi shimbun*, Toki was also active in the postwar national language reform program. In 1947 he received the Japan Academy Award for *Tayasu Munetake* (1942–46), a study of the poet TAYASU MUNETAKE. Toki's principal poetry collection is *Nakiwarai* (1910).

Tokkō → Special Higher Police

Tokkōtai → Kamikaze Special Attack Force

Tōkō, Inc 東光[株]

(Tōkō). Manufacturer of coils and switches. Incorporated in 1955. The company developed the world's first intermediate-frequency transformer, supplying it to Japan's leading radio makers. Later the company extended its product line to include coils for television and stereo sets. Tōkō has 10 overseas subsidiaries in Germany, France, the United Kingdom, the United States, Brazil, Korea, Taiwan, and Malaysia. Sales for the fiscal year ending March 1991 totaled ¥48.2 billion (US $351.3 million), and capitalization stood at ¥16.2 billion (US $118.1 million). Headquarters are in Tōkyō.

tōkō kyohi → school allergy

Tokoname 常滑[市]

City in Aichi Prefecture, central Honshū. High-quality clay from nearby mountains is used for making TOKONAME WARE. There is a ceramics museum featuring both old and contemporary products. Fishing, manufacture of cotton cloth, and cultivation of *nori* (a kind of seaweed) are also carried out. Pop: 51,784.

Tokoname ware 常滑焼

(*tokoname-yaki*). A strong, heavy, reddish brown ware made from the early 12th century to the first half of the 16th century, with some production continuing to the present. The kilns are distributed throughout the Chita Peninsula, a narrow strip of land jutting into Mikawa Bay south of the present-day city of Nagoya, Aichi Prefecture.

The earliest datable (ca 1125) Tokoname piece is a jar with three lines incised horizontally around the body. Because the Chita Peninsula was a farming area, the kilns prospered by producing durable, functional products needed by the farmers in their daily lives, such as small unglazed bowls (YAMA-CHAWAN), large jars (some with wide mouths), grinding bowls, and water vases. Many of these jars were used for cinerary urns or sutra burials.

Tokonami Takejirō 床次竹二郎

(1867–1935). Politician. Born in Satsuma Province (now Kagoshima Prefecture). Tokonami entered government service after graduation from Tōkyō University. He was elected to the Diet in 1914 as a member of the RIKKEN SEIYŪKAI party. He became home minister in the HARA TAKASHI (1918) and TAKAHASHI KOREKIYO (1921) cabinets. He led a group of Seiyūkai members who supported the nonparty cabinet of KIYOURA KEIGO to form the SEIYŪ HONTŌ party (1924). The party merged with the KENSEIKAI to form the RIKKEN MINSEITŌ in 1927. Two years later Tokonami rejoined the Seiyūkai but was expelled when he joined the OKADA KEISUKE cabinet (1934) without party consent. He helped to found the nationalistic DAI NIPPON KOKUSUIKAI (Great Japan National Essence Society) in 1919.

tokonoma 床の間

A decorative alcove found in Japanese-style rooms and dwellings that adds an element of formality and grace to an otherwise unadorned interior. The main features of the *tokonoma* include a decorative corner post (*tokobashira*); floor frame (*tokogamachi*); TATAMI or wooden flooring, usually raised a few inches higher than the rest of the room; and the upper-frame beam (*otoshigake*). The back wall is hung with one to three hanging scrolls (see KAKEMONO), on the floor in front of which are placed a flower arrangement and often some object of art.

Tokoname ware A vessel discovered in Kanagawa Prefecture, incised with images of autumn grass, dragonflies, and other nature motifs. 12th century. Height 42 cm. Keiō University. National Treasure.

Tokuda Kyūichi
A founding member of the Japan Communist Party, Tokuda spent the years 1928–45 in prison for his political beliefs, emerging to lead the party in the years immediately following World War II.

Tokonoma originated in the Muromachi period (1333–1568) with the practice in upper-class homes of hanging a Buddhist picture scroll on the wall and placing a low table set with a flower vase and incense burner in front of it. The arrangement came to occupy a fixed place in houses—a feature of the style of architecture known as SHOIN-ZUKURI. Although in the Edo period (1600–1868) *tokonoma* were forbidden in the houses of commoners, less formal versions became widespread from the middle of the 18th century (see SUKIYA-ZUKURI). *Tokonoma* still held a central position in Japanese homes after World War II, but they have become less common with the modification of housing along American and European lines.

Tokorogawa   常呂川

River in northeastern Hokkaidō, originating in the Ishikari Mountains and flowing through Kitami Basin into the Sea of Okhotsk. Areas along the upper reaches are covered with forests. The middle and lower reaches form an agricultural district. Length: 120 km (75 mi); area of drainage basin: 1,930 sq km (745 sq mi).

Tokorozawa   所沢[市]

City in southern Saitama Prefecture, central Honshū, some 30 km (19 mi) from Tōkyō. Tokorozawa developed as a market town in the Edo period (1600–1868) and in the Meiji period (1868–1912) became a production center for textiles. Japan's first airport was built here by the Imperial Japanese Army. Local products include tea. Today it is a principal residential suburb of Tōkyō and an important shopping center. Attractions include Lake Sayama, Seibuen Yūenchi (an amusement park), and a professional baseball stadium. Pop: 303,040.

Tokoyo   常世

(the "eternal land"). An imaginary realm in Japanese MYTHOLOGY. Of uncertain location, Tokoyo is generally conceived as a world beyond the sea, an oceanic paradise vaguely connected with immortality and fertility. According to the KOJIKI (712, Record of Ancient Matters) and NIHON SHOKI (720, Chronicles of Japan), the dwarf deity Sukunahikona no Kami came mysteriously riding over the waves in a miniature boat fashioned from the pod of the *kagami* plant. Sukunahikona assisted the god ŌKUNINUSHI NO MIKOTO in creating and solidifying the land, whereupon he departed for Tokoyo. Human heroes may visit Tokoyo, but their return to the earthly realm is fraught with grief because of the time differential between this world and the eternal land. One legend tells of Urashima no Ko, who was transported to Tokoyo by a beautiful woman. After three years he returned to his native village, only to find that 300 years had elapsed. Another legend tells of Tajimamori, who was sent to Tokoyo by Emperor Suinin to retrieve the fruit of the "seasonless, ever-fragrant tree." Upon his return Tajimamori found the emperor had already died, and died of grief himself. The *Nihon shoki* version of this episode reveals the influence of the Chinese beliefs surrounding the realm of the Taoist immortals (*sennin*), with which the notion of Tokoyo later became amalgamated in the popular consciousness.

Tokuda Shūsei This naturalist writer's best works are known for their frank, autobiographical style and nuanced treatment of female characters.

Tokto→Takeshima

Tokuda Kyūichi   徳田球一

(1894–1953). Politician and JAPAN COMMUNIST PARTY (JCP) leader. Born in Okinawa, Tokuda graduated in 1920 from Nihon University. In the same year he joined the Shakai Shugi Dōmei, a socialist study group. He attended the Far Eastern People's Conference (January–February 1922) held under Comintern auspices in Moscow and helped form the JCP in 1922. Soon after running unsuccessfully for the Diet as a candidate of the RŌDŌ NŌMINTŌ (Labor-Farmer Party) in February 1928, he was arrested in the MARCH 15TH INCIDENT. Along with SHIGA YOSHIO and other JCP activists, he remained in prison until October 1945. Tokuda became secretary-general of the postwar JCP that year and was elected to the House of Representatives in 1946 for the first of three terms. With the RED PURGE by OCCUPATION authorities in 1950, Tokuda persuaded the party to resort to violent tactics, and he himself went underground. He died in Beijing (Peking).

Tokuda Shūsei   徳田秋声

(1871–1943). Author. Real name Tokuda Sueo. Born in the city of Kanazawa (in what is now Ishikawa Prefecture). Much of Shūsei's fiction is autobiographical; his name is usually associated with Japanese NATURALISM (*shizen shugi*). Unlike some Japanese naturalists, Shūsei was relatively unconcerned with the intellectual bases and philosophical implications of literary naturalism. The realistic style and frank autobiography of Japanese naturalism suited him perfectly. Philosophically, his work is marked more by a familiar Japanese fatalism than by Western determinism.

He began his writing career as one of the principal followers of the author OZAKI KŌYŌ; after Kōyō's death in 1903 he moved from the romantic style associated with Kōyō to the blend of realism and confession known as *shizen shugi*. This move is reflected in *Arajotai* (1908, The New Household), which treats the frustrations of a young working-class couple he had observed. Thereafter, however, Shūsei wrote mostly autobiographical fiction. *Kabi* (1911, Mold) is a classic example of the Japanese genre known as the I-NOVEL (*watakushi shōsetsu*). In *Tadare* (1913, Festering), Shūsei dealt with a favorite subject: a woman of the demimonde. When his wife died in 1926, Shūsei began a series of affairs with younger women that provided the inspiration for a long string of stories, including his best-known works, *Kasō jimbutsu* (1935–38, Masquerading Characters) and *Shukuzu* (1941, Miniature).

Tokugawa Akitake   徳川昭武

(1853–1910). *Daimyō* of the Mito domain (now part of Ibaraki Prefecture); son of TOKUGAWA NARIAKI. In 1867 he attended the Paris Exposition as shogunal representative. Returning to Japan, he joined the imperial side in the BOSHIN CIVIL WAR. Upon the establishment of the prefectural system by the new Meiji government, he was appointed governor of Mito Prefecture.

Tokugawa Art Museum   徳川美術館

(Tokugawa Bijutsukan). Located in the city of Nagoya, Aichi Prefecture. Established in 1935. The collection of well over 10,000 pieces includes armor, swords, tea ceremony objects, Nō costumes, and household objects owned by the Owari branch of the TOKUGAWA FAMILY. Exhibits reconstruct the lifestyle of domainal lords (DAIMYŌ). Eight National

Treasures are housed in the museum, including portions of the GENJI MONOGATARI EMAKI (the illustrated handscrolls of the *Tale of Genji*).

Tokugawa family   徳川氏

(Tokugawashi). One of the major warrior lineages in Japanese history, the Tokugawa dominated politics from 1600 to 1868. Their period of rule is known as the Tokugawa period or, more commonly, as the EDO PERIOD (1600–1868), after their seat of government at EDO (now Tōkyō). The family's fortunes were established by TOKUGAWA IEYASU, who founded the TOKUGAWA SHOGUNATE (1603–1867), which ruled Japan until the MEIJI RESTORATION of 1868.

Origins——During the 15th century, Ieyasu's ancestors were a local warrior family called the Matsudaira in the foothills of Mikawa Province (now part of Aichi Prefecture) east of Nagoya. The first identifiable Tokugawa ancestor, Matsudaira Chikauji, lived around 1400. About six generations later Matsudaira Kiyoyasu (1511–35) established control over most of Mikawa Province. After he was killed in 1535, he was succeeded by his young son Hirotada (1526–49).

Hirotada preserved his family's position only by commending himself to his powerful neighbor, the *daimyō* IMAGAWA YOSHIMOTO. Later he sent his four-year-old son Takechiyo to Yoshimoto as a hostage until 1560, when Yoshimoto died in battle. In the winter of 1567 Takechiyo changed his name to Tokugawa Ieyasu.

Ieyasu's rapid rise to national power culminated in his victory in the Battle of SEKIGAHARA in 1600. In 1603 the court formally designated him SHŌGUN, signifying that he ruled the land at the behest of the emperor.

The Tokugawa Kinship Group——In basic character the Tokugawa family was an ordinary Japanese familial unit or "house" (*ie* or *ke*) consisting of the main lineage (*honke*) and its collaterals (*bunke*). The main lineage was that of the shogunal succession. The collateral lines were the related or SHIMPAN daimyō. The greatest of the Tokugawa *shimpan* houses in time produced branches of their own, including the GOSANKE, or Three Successor Houses. The three domains of Mito (now part of Ibaraki Prefecture), Owari (now part of Aichi Prefecture), and Kii (now Wakayama Prefecture) were established as the domains of the younger sons of Ieyasu. They and their descendants kept the family name Tokugawa. Less prestigious branch lines established in the 18th century by the shōguns Yoshimune and Ieshige were known collectively as the GOSANKYŌ, or Three Lords. They also retained the name Tokugawa. The other *shimpan* used the name Matsudaira and were known collectively as *kamon* (related houses).

The Shogunal Line——There were 15 shōguns during the Edo period. Ieyasu held the shogunal title for only two years before transferring it to his son TOKUGAWA HIDETADA in 1605 to establish a precedent for shogunal succession. Ieyasu died in 1616. Hidetada retired in 1623 and until his death in 1632 supervised his son TOKUGAWA IEMITSU. Iemitsu's rule was distinguished by diplomatic shrewdness and the use of restrictive administrative procedures, notably SANKIN KŌTAI, the system of alternate attendance at Edo. Upon his death in 1651 he was succeeded by his eldest son, TOKUGAWA IETSUNA. Until his death in 1680 Ietsuna remained a passive ruler. He was succeeded by his

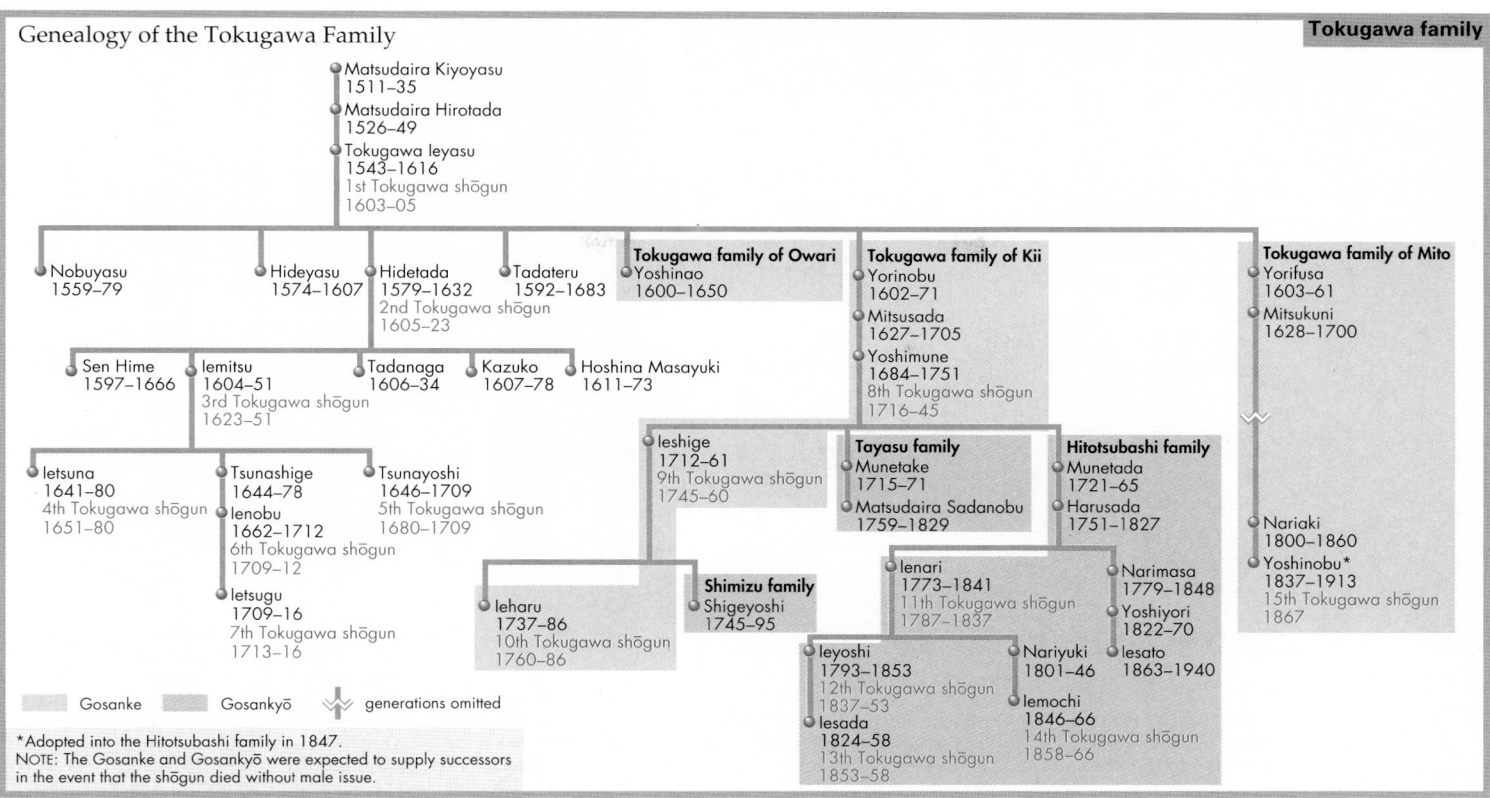

Genealogy of the Tokugawa Family

younger brother TOKUGAWA TSUNAYOSHI. Tsunayoshi was succeeded by his nephew TOKUGAWA IENOBU. He was succeeded by his son Ietsugu, who died in 1716 at the age of seven.

The forceful leadership of Ietsugu's successor, TOKUGAWA YOSHIMUNE of Kii, strengthened the shogunate's control over the daimyō through the KYŌHŌ REFORMS. In 1745 he retired and for six years supervised his eldest son, TOKUGAWA IESHIGE. Ieshige's son and successor was Ieharu (1737–86). Ieharu's heir was TOKUGAWA IENARI, a son of Ieharu's cousin Harusada (1751–1827). Ienari held office for 50 years, longer than any other shōgun, and supervised his son Ieyoshi (1793–1853) even after retirement. The KANSEI REFORMS took place during his tenure.

Toward the end of Ienari's long rule, accumulated difficulties and new national hardships (see TEMPŌ FAMINE) generated a ground swell of reformism, which resulted in the TEMPŌ REFORMS. Ieyoshi succeeded Ienari in 1837. Ieyoshi was shōgun when Commodore Matthew C. PERRY's fleet reached Japan in 1853. On Ieyoshi's death in July 1853, his sickly son Iesada succeeded but died five years later. Iesada was succeeded in turn by his young cousin TOKUGAWA IEMOCHI. By the time Iemochi died in 1866 and TOKUGAWA YOSHINOBU succeeded him, the regime was on the verge of collapse because of the movement to restore direct imperial rule.

In the settlement that followed the Meiji Restoration of 1868, the former shogunal family received a large domain in the area around Sumpu (now the city of Shizuoka). Three years later, when the daimyō domains were abolished by imperial decree (see PREFECTURAL SYSTEM, ESTABLISHMENT OF), the Tokugawa received a substantial financial settlement and various honors. The principal branches of the Tokugawa family survived, and a few of their members, such as TOKUGAWA IESATO, had distinguished careers in public service.

Tokugawa Hidetada   徳川秀忠

(1579–1632). Second shōgun of the Tokugawa shogunate (1603–1867); third son

of its founder, TOKUGAWA IEYASU. Hidetada served as a general in the campaign that led to the Battle of SEKIGAHARA (1600) and in the sieges of Ōsaka Castle (1614–15). Although he officially became shōgun when Ieyasu retired in 1605, father and son ruled jointly until Ieyasu's death in 1616, with Ieyasu and his staff at Sumpu (now the city of Shizuoka) retaining the preponderance of power, especially in foreign affairs. Hidetada followed this precedent by retiring in 1623 and installing his son TOKUGAWA IEMITSU as the third shōgun. The two ruled jointly until Hidetada's death in 1632. Hidetada's reign was a period of institutional consolidation in the new shogunate, which strengthened central control over the *daimyō*, the Tokugawa collaterals, and the imperial court; reorganized the executive organs of the shogunate; and regulated Christianity and foreign trade more closely.

Tokugawa Iemitsu   徳川家光

(1604–51). Third shōgun of the TOKUGAWA SHOGUNATE (1603–1867); ruled 1623–51. Second son of the second shōgun, TOKUGAWA HIDETADA; his mother was a younger sister of Lady YODOGIMI. His elder brother, Nagamaru, died in infancy. For a time it appeared that Iemitsu would be denied the succession in favor of his younger brother Tadanaga (1606–33), but thanks to the intercession of his wet nurse, KASUGA NO TSUBONE, he was confirmed as shōgun in 1623 when his father abdicated. After his father's death in 1632, in anticipation of further trouble, Iemitsu forced his brother to commit suicide. Drawing on the advice of such men as DOI TOSHIKATSU, ABE TADAAKI, and MATSUDAIRA NOBUTSUNA, Iemitsu carried out important administrative reforms to consolidate shogunal rule. He stiffened the discipline of the military houses by augmenting the BUKE SHOHATTO promulgated by his grandfather TOKUGAWA IEYASU, the founder of the shogunate. He tightened his control over the *daimyō* by compelling them to reside at the shogunal capital in alternate years (see SANKIN KŌTAI) and strengthened the internal organization of villages (see GŌSON SYSTEM) by enacting

such measures as the TAHATA EITAI BAIBAI KINSHI REI, which forbade the sale of rice land. He intensified the persecution of Christians and, after suppressing the SHIMABARA UPRISING (1637–38) in southern Kyūshū, enforced a strict NATIONAL SECLUSION policy that closed Japan to all but a handful of Chinese and Dutch merchants. The shogunate reached the height of its power during Iemitsu's rule and assumed the form that it was to retain until its collapse in the 1860s. Iemitsu was succeeded by his eldest son, TOKUGAWA IETSUNA.

Tokugawa Iemochi   徳川家茂

(1846–66). The 14th shōgun of the Tokugawa shogunate; reigned 1858–66. Born Tokugawa Yoshitomi, in the Wakayama domain (now Wakayama Prefecture and part of Mie Prefecture; see GOSANKE). When the question of choosing a successor to the shōgun Iesada (1824–58) arose in 1858, reform-minded forces led by MATSUDAIRA YOSHINAGA supported TOKUGAWA YOSHINOBU, while conservative forces led by II NAOSUKE supported Yoshitomi. Ii's forces won, and twelve-year-old Yoshitomi became shōgun and was renamed Iemochi. Following Ii's assassination in 1860 (see SAKURADAMONGAI INCIDENT), his successors put into action Ii's plan for a MOVEMENT FOR UNION OF COURT AND SHOGUNATE. To effect this reconciliation, in 1862 Iemochi married Princess KAZU, the sister of Emperor KŌMEI. In an attempt to check the antishogunate movement incited by the ANSEI COMMERCIAL TREATIES, Iemochi made three trips to the imperial court in Kyōto. On the last of these, taken in 1866 to command a punitive expedition against Chōshū (see CHŌSHŪ EXPEDITIONS), Iemochi fell ill and died. He was succeeded by Yoshinobu, who became the 15th and last Tokugawa shōgun.

Tokugawa Ienari   徳川家斉

(1773–1841). The 11th shōgun of the Tokugawa shogunate; ruled 1787–1837. Ienari was the son of Harusada (1751–1827), *daimyō* of the branch family of Hitotsubashi

Tokugawa Ieyasu
1 A posthumous portrait of Ieyasu deified as Tōshō Daigongen ("Great Incarnation Who Illuminates the East"), attributed to Kanō Tan'yū. Early Edo period (1600–1868).
2 Emblazoned with a rising sun motif, this suit of armor worn by Ieyasu is an example of the bold designs and magnificent workmanship characteristic of the Azuchi-Momoyama period (1568–1600).

(see GOSANKYŌ), and was designated heir to the childless shōgun Ieharu (1737–86; r 1760–86) in 1781; he became shōgun six years later at the age of 13. At first the KANSEI REFORMS of the senior councillor (*rōjū*) MATSUDAIRA SADANOBU dominated, but with Sadanobu's retirement from office in 1793, Ienari came into his own. His rule, which embraced the BUNKA AND BUNSEI ERAS (1804–30), was characterized by the absence of political movement. These years were blessed with a succession of good harvests, and the government supplemented its land-tax income through monetary manipulation. At the heart of the stability, however, was Ienari's vigorous program of nepotism and political bargaining. During the 1830s, crop failures gave rise to widespread distress (see TEMPŌ FAMINE) and declines in shogunate revenues. The shogunate resorted to massive recoinages that weakened the currency and fostered more inflation. Ienari's political success was obscured by the great stress and political crisis of his final years.

Tokugawa Ienobu　　徳川家宣
(1662–1712). The sixth shōgun (r 1709–12) of the TOKUGAWA SHOGUNATE; eldest son of the lord of the Kōfu domain (now part of Yamanashi Prefecture), Tokugawa Tsunashige (1644–78), who was a brother of the fourth and fifth shōguns, TOKUGAWA IETSUNA and TOKUGAWA TSUNAYOSHI. Ienobu succeeded his father as lord of Kōfu in 1678. He was adopted in 1704 as the heir to his childless uncle Tsunayoshi, whom he succeeded as shōgun on the latter's death in 1709. Ienobu's short rule was marked by a series of Confucian-inspired reforms (SHŌTOKU NO CHI) urged by his tutor and political adviser ARAI HAKUSEKI. Another prominent figure in his shogunate was his chamberlain (*sobayōnin*) MANABE AKIFUSA. On his death Ienobu was succeeded by his four-year-old son, Ietsugu (1709–16; r 1713–16), whose death ended the main line of the Tokugawa house.

Tokugawa Iesato　　徳川家達
(1863–1940). The first head of the Tokugawa family after the Tokugawa shogunate was overthrown in the MEIJI RESTORATION of 1868. In 1877 he went to England to study; he returned to Japan in 1882 and was given the title of prince. He became a member of the House of Peers at its inception in 1890 and

became its president in 1903, remaining in that position until his retirement in 1933. Following World War I, he was a delegate to the WASHINGTON CONFERENCE on naval disarmament. He also served as president of the Japan Red Cross and the Nichibei Kyōkai (Japan-America Society).

Tokugawa Ieshige　　徳川家重
(1712–61). The ninth shōgun (r 1745–60) of the TOKUGAWA SHOGUNATE; eldest son of the eighth shōgun, TOKUGAWA YOSHIMUNE. Ieshige suffered chronic ill health and had a severe speech defect. His succession to the office of shōgun at the age of 34 created a controversy among shogunate leaders because his younger brothers Munetake (1715–71) and Munetada (1721–65) were obviously better qualified. Nevertheless he was elevated by his aging father, who, during the first two years of Ieshige's rule, continued to direct state affairs as retired shōgun (ŌGOSHO). Uninterested in government, Ieshige left shogunate affairs in the hands of his chamberlain Ōoka Tadamitsu (1709–60). Ieshige retired in 1760 and assumed the position of *ōgosho* but died the following year. His eldest son, Ieharu (1737–86), succeeded him.

Tokugawa Ietsuna　　徳川家綱
(1641–80). The fourth shōgun (1651–80) of the TOKUGAWA SHOGUNATE; eldest son of the third shōgun, TOKUGAWA IEMITSU. He took office at age 10 and was assisted by members of his father's entourage, including HOSHINA MASAYUKI, MATSUDAIRA NOBUTSUNA, and SAKAI TADAKIYO. Ietsuna, who suffered from ill health, continued to rely on advisers, remaining a figurehead shōgun. He died without issue at the age of 39 and was succeeded by his younger brother TOKUGAWA TSUNAYOSHI.

The three decades under Ietsuna were a transitional period between the martial formative years of the shogunate and the peaceful middle years. The KEIAN INCIDENT, an unsuccessful coup d'état against the Tokugawa shogunate, took place at the very beginning of Ietsuna's rule. Under Ietsuna the custom of committing suicide after one's master's death (JUNSHI) was prohibited (1663), Confucian learning was encouraged, and the history *Honchō tsugan* (1670, Comprehensive Mirror of Our Nation's Dynasty) was compiled by HAYASHI RAZAN and his son.

Tokugawa Ieyasu　　徳川家康
(1543–1616). The warrior chieftain who, outwitting many of his major contemporaries and outliving and outprocreating the rest, survived Japan's late-16th-century wars of unification to set up the TOKUGAWA SHOGUNATE.

Background——Born Matsudaira Takechiyo in the small castle of Okazaki in Mikawa Province (now part of Aichi Prefecture), he was the first son of Matsudaira Hirotada (1526–49), a petty chieftain. His mother, known to posterity as Odai no Kata (1528–1602), was the daughter of a neighboring warrior leader, Mizuno Tadamasa of Kariya in Mikawa. Ieyasu spent his youth first as a captive of his father's enemies, the Oda family, and then as a hostage to his father's allies to the east, the Imagawa. During this time he took the personal names Motonobu and then Motoyasu.

Early Career——In 1561 Ieyasu, having recently gained his independence from the Imagawa and taken control of his father's domains, abandoned his alliance with the Imagawa, allying himself instead with ODA NOBUNAGA. This action secured his western flank, and by 1568 his eastward expansion had made him master of the provinces of Mikawa and Tōtōmi (now part of Shizuoka Prefecture). He had also changed his personal name to Ieyasu and had been permitted by imperial order to substitute for Matsudaira the more ancient family name of Tokugawa.

In 1570 at Anegawa near Lake Biwa, the Oda and Tokugawa forces combined to destroy the power of two local warrior houses, the Asai and Asakura, in a decisive battle (see ANEGAWA, BATTLE OF). From 1572 to 1582 Ieyasu gradually expanded his territorial grasp, fighting for much of the time against the TAKEDA FAMILY. In 1572 the redoubtable TAKEDA SHINGEN gave Ieyasu the worst defeat of his career in a battle at Mikatagahara. Shingen soon died, however, and was succeeded by his son Katsuyori (1546–82). Successive battles—at Nagashino in 1575 and Takatenjin in 1581—drove the Takeda back, leaving Ieyasu master of Mikawa, Tōtōmi, and Suruga (now part of the Shizuoka Prefecture).

In 1579 Ieyasu was obliged to put his wife (who was from an Imagawa vassal family) to death and force his firstborn son to commit suicide to reassure Nobunaga of his own loyalty. (Both were suspected by Nobunaga of having colluded with the Takeda.) Ieyasu reacted to the turmoil after Nobunaga's assassination in 1582 by making himself master of the Takeda heartland—the provinces of Kai and Shinano (now Yamanashi and Nagano prefectures)—which gave him an important position among the contending factions in central Japan.

His relations with Nobunaga's successor, TOYOTOMI HIDEYOSHI, began inauspiciously. In 1583 Ieyasu resisted several overtures from Hideyoshi, and in 1584 Hideyoshi attacked a Tokugawa fortress on Mt. Komaki (see KOMAKI NAGAKUTE CAMPAIGN). Both men then decided that a rough alliance was to be preferred to further fighting. Therefore, in 1584 Ieyasu sent a son to Hideyoshi for adoption, receiving in return two years later Hideyoshi's 43-year-old sister, specially divorced so that she might marry him. In 1590 the two men joined forces to attack the great Kantō chieftain, Hōjō Ujimasa (1538–90), in his castle at Odawara.

Move to Edo—By overthrowing the Hōjō at Odawara in 1590 (see ODAWARA CAMPAIGN), Hideyoshi won a degree of control in eastern Japan unrivaled since the Kamakura period (1185–1333). Ieyasu was required to surrender his five provinces, including Mikawa, his native province, and move to a new domain including the provinces of Musashi, Izu, Sagami, Kazusa, and Shimōsa, together with parts of Hitachi, Awa, Kōzuke, and Shimotsuke—effectively, the KANTŌ PLAIN and its surrounding hills. Although his unfamiliarity with the new domain was a strategic, administrative, and probably fiscal disadvantage, the domain was larger, more productive, and geographically more unified than his former holdings. As headquarters he chose Edo (now Tōkyō), a little fishing town on the edge of what is now Tōkyō Bay.

In 1592 Hideyoshi began his invasion of Korea, an enterprise that consumed the remainder of his life and the resources of those warrior-leaders forced to take part. Ieyasu, however, was able to preserve his resources by maintaining a comfortable distance from this campaign. Shortly before Hideyoshi died in 1598 he made his senior generals, Ieyasu among them, swear to serve his son, TOYOTOMI HIDEYORI, faithfully. Within two years Ieyasu had broken that promise, forming alliances with four powerful warrior families. In response ISHIDA MITSUNARI, one of Hideyoshi's vassals, armed with promises of support from several families, declared war against him in 1600. On 21 October 1600 Ieyasu led an army of 104,000 men into battle at Sekigahara (see SEKIGAHARA, BATTLE OF) and won an easy victory. As a result Tokugawa Ieyasu came to assume a great many of Hideyoshi's powers, establishing his control over the city of Kyōto (and hence over the emperor) and claiming authority over all Japanese DAIMYŌ.

Shōgun—After 1600 Ieyasu was the most powerful warrior leader in Japan. In 1603 he assumed the ancient title of *seii tai shōgun* ("barbarian-subduing generalissimo") with the assent of Emperor Go-Yōzei (1571–1617). Thenceforth he and his descendants were, like their predecessors of the Minamoto and Ashikaga families, held to be entitled to speak for the emperor on national affairs. It was expected that the SHŌGUN, as commander in chief of the entire *samurai* class, would be obeyed by all military overlords and their vassals.

In 1605 Ieyasu, then 63, resigned from office in favor of his third son, TOKUGAWA HIDETADA, and two years later retired to Sumpu (now the city of Shizuoka). Although retired, Ieyasu had by no means relinquished his authority, especially in foreign affairs.

Above all Ieyasu was concerned about Japan's internal strategic balance, as the Tokugawa were dependent upon other warriors who could withdraw their support at any time. Any discontent with the Tokugawa shogunate would inevitably gather around Hideyoshi's son, Toyotomi Hideyori. Thus, in the winter of 1614 and again in the following spring, Ieyasu launched two attacks on Ōsaka Castle, Hideyori's fortress, finally taking it and destroying its outer fortifications. Hideyori chose to commit suicide, while his seven-year-old son, Kunimatsu, was beheaded (see ŌSAKA CASTLE, SIEGES OF).

After the fall of Ōsaka Castle and the destruction of the Toyotomi house, Ieyasu's major accomplishment was having his advisers draw up in 1613–14 the two basic documents of early Tokugawa legislation. The BUKE SHOHATTO (Laws for Military Houses) and the KINCHŪ NARABI NI KUGE SHOHATTO (Laws Governing the Imperial Court and Nobility) were both issued in 1615. Ieyasu died on 1 June 1616. A year later his remains were removed to NIKKŌ, where by imperial decree he was canonized under the title of Tōshō Daigongen, a manifestation of the Buddha as healer. Luck was an important factor in Ieyasu's success. He outlived his great contemporaries, Oda Nobunaga and Toyotomi Hideyoshi, and was survived by five sons, four of whom were entrenched in powerful positions. Ultimately, the achievement of Tokugawa Ieyasu was that by the time of his death he had brought peace and an unprecedented degree of unity to Japan and had provided a succession stable enough to withstand his passing. Others of his contemporaries could perhaps have achieved as much, but none could have done more.

Tokugawa jikki 徳川実紀

(True Chronicle of the Tokugawa). Historical work compiled by the TOKUGAWA SHOGUNATE that records the political achievements of the first 10 shōguns, from TOKUGAWA IEYASU to Tokugawa Ieharu (1737–86; r 1760–86). Some 20 historians, under HAYASHI JUSSAI, were engaged in the project, begun in 1809 and completed in 1849. A sequel, *Zoku Tokugawa jikki*, intended to cover the rule of the 11th shōgun, TOKUGAWA IENARI, and his successors, was interrupted by the MEIJI RESTORATION of 1868 and never completed.

Tokugawa Kazuko 徳川和子

(1607–78). Also known as Tōfuku Mon'in. Daughter of the shōgun TOKUGAWA HIDETADA and consort of Emperor GO-MIZUNOO. Her marriage to the emperor in 1620 was part of the shogunate's strategy to bolster its legitimacy by strengthening ties with the imperial court. Kazuko bore the emperor two sons and five daughters, but both sons died young. Go-Mizunoo, upset over the SHIE INCIDENT and shogunate interference in court affairs, abdicated in favor of Kazuko's eldest daughter, Okiko, who became Empress Meishō (1623–96; r 1629–43). Kazuko continued to exert influence in the court as stepmother of the emperors Go-Kōmyō (r 1643–54), Gosai (r 1655–63), and Reigen (r 1663–87).

Tokugawa Keiki → Tokugawa Yoshinobu

Tokugawa kinrei kō 徳川禁令考

A 102-volume collection of the laws and regulations of the Edo period (1600–1868); compiled by the Ministry of Justice, 1878–95. It is divided into two sections, the first containing regulations for the imperial court, *daimyō*, shrines and temples, and transactions with foreign countries and the second containing penal codes and cases.

Tokugawa Mitsukuni 徳川光圀

(1628–1700). Popularly known as Mito Kōmon. The second *daimyō* (1661–90) of the Mito domain (now part of Ibaraki Prefecture); a grandson of TOKUGAWA IEYASU. Mitsukuni was the driving force behind the compilation of the DAI NIHON SHI (History of Great Japan), a comprehensive account of Japanese history from the country's origins to the 14th century, begun in 1657 and completed in 1906. He invited 130 Japanese and Chinese scholars to participate in this project at his domain's residences (see SHŌKŌKAN) in Edo (now Tōkyō); the most famous participants were Sassa Sōjun (1640–98),

KURIYAMA SEMPŌ, MIYAKE KANRAN, and ASAKA TAMPAKU. The chronicles of the first 100 emperors were completed in 1697. In 1698 the work was shifted to Mito, where it came to serve as the scholarly basis for the MITO SCHOOL of learning.

Mitsukuni was known as an effective and benevolent ruler who actively promoted business and trade. This image of Mitsukuni as the ideal feudal ruler was later reinforced by a mid-19th-century fictional account of his travels around the country and subsequent versions of the tale, most recently taking the form of a popular television series.

Tokugawa Musei This popular radio and television broadcaster began his career as a narrator for silent films.

Tokugawa Musei 徳川夢声

(1894–1971). Entertainer and writer. Real name Fukuhara Toshio. Born in Masuda, Shimane Prefecture. He began as a narrator (BENSHI) for silent movies and became chief narrator for the Shinjuku Musashinokan Theater in Tōkyō. He was popular, particularly among intellectuals, for his witty and eloquent style. After the introduction of talkies he became a comedian, helping to organize the troupe Warai no Ōkoku in 1933, and appeared in stage plays and films. He also charmed radio and television audiences with his gift for words.

Tokugawa Nariaki 徳川斉昭

(1800–60). *Daimyō* of the Mito domain (now part of Ibaraki Prefecture) and father of the 15th and last Tokugawa shōgun, TOKUGAWA YOSHINOBU. Nariaki became lord of the powerful senior collateral (GOSANKE) domain of Mito in 1829, and as daimyō he initiated administrative reforms, giving prominent posts to such capable men of the reform faction as FUJITA TŌKO and AIZAWA SEISHISAI. In 1841 he established a school named the Kōdōkan to foster WESTERN LEARNING and the SONNŌ JŌI (Revere the Emperor, Expel the Barbarians) cause. Nariaki's activities aroused the enmity of the shogunate, and in 1844 he was removed as daimyō and ordered into domiciliary confinement. He relinquished the leadership of the family to his eldest son, Yoshiatsu. The confinement order was lifted in 1849.

During the national turmoil following the visit of Matthew C. PERRY in 1853, Nariaki was invited by the senior councillor (*rōjū*) ABE MASAHIRO to serve the shogunate as an adviser on maritime defenses. In the succession dispute of 1857–58 following the death of the 13th shōgun, Iesada, Nariaki was at the center of the Hitotsubashi faction. The group backed his seventh son, Yoshinobu, who had been adopted as head of the Hitotsubashi house (see GOSANKYŌ). Nariaki was thus in opposition to II NAOSUKE, a strong backer of TOKUGAWA IEMOCHI. After Ii had become great elder (*tairō*) and installed Iemochi as the 14th shōgun in 1858, Nariaki again came into conflict with Ii over the HARRIS TREATY signed that year. He criticized Ii for signing it without imperial approval. The shogunate retaliated (see ANSEI PURGE) by condemning Nariaki to lifetime confinement in Mito, where he died.

Tokugawa period → Edo period

Tokugawa shogunate 徳川幕府

(1603–1867; Tokugawa *bakufu*). Last, and longest-lived, of Japan's three warrior governments, the first two being the KAMAKURA SHOGUNATE (1192–1333) and the MUROMACHI SHOGUNATE (1338–1573). It was founded in

Principal Officials of the Tokugawa Shogunate

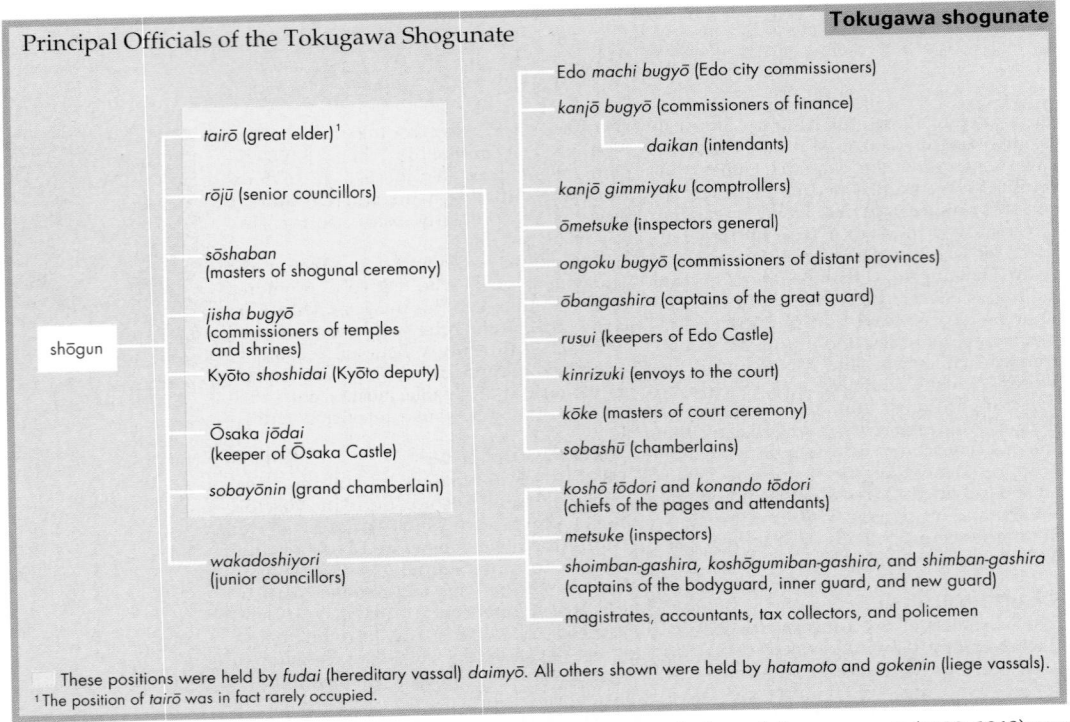

These positions were held by *fudai* (hereditary vassal) *daimyō*. All others shown were held by *hatamoto* and *gokenin* (liege vassals).
[1] The position of *tairō* was in fact rarely occupied.

1603 when TOKUGAWA IEYASU took the title *seii tai shōgun* ("barbarian-subduing generalissimo"; see SHŌGUN). His government, military in origin, carried the appropriately military designation of bakufu, or general headquarters, referred to in this encyclopedia as shogunate. Thereafter the office of shōgun, and with it nominal leadership of the shogunate, was invested in 15 successive heads of the TOKUGAWA FAMILY in a progression that came to an end with the resignation of TOKUGAWA YOSHINOBU, the last shōgun, late in 1867 (see MEIJI RESTORATION).

Responsibilities — The title of shōgun, granted to Ieyasu by the emperor in 1603, carried with it no guarantee of security. Won by force, it could be forfeited to anyone else strong enough to claim it. Nevertheless, those who assumed the title also assumed certain responsibilities. As chief of Japan's warriors, a shōgun was expected to keep the peace, controlling foreign trade and diplomacy while preserving law and order at home. To help with the first, the Tokugawa came to restrict all foreign contact under the Sakoku (NATIONAL SECLUSION) edicts of 1633–39. To assure the second, they claimed the right to limit regional independence and to levy contributions of men and money from potential rivals. Moreover, the Tokugawa shogunate tried to preserve social stability through a four-class system (SHI-NŌ-KŌ-SHŌ) in which everyone, whether *samurai*, farmer, artisan, or merchant, would know his place and keep it.

It was also expected that, like its predecessors, the Tokugawa shogunate would assume the functions of lawgiver and moral arbiter. In the former capacity, Tokugawa Ieyasu unified the currency, standardized weights and measures, and restricted the prerogatives of both the imperial court and the provincial overlords. His grandson, TOKUGAWA IEMITSU, established the HYŌJŌSHŪ (Judicial Council) in 1635 to settle complex legal disputes, while in 1742 TOKUGAWA YO-SHIMUNE, the eighth shōgun, introduced the most comprehensive legal code Japan had yet seen (see KUJIKATA OSADAMEGAKI). As moral arbiter, the shogunate issued a never-ending succession of minutely detailed instructions whose impact on the moral and political vo-

cabulary of the EDO PERIOD (1600–1868) was profound.

Powers — The Tokugawa victory at the Battle of SEKIGAHARA (1600), which had brought Ieyasu pledges of fealty from all surviving warrior leaders, established him as Japan's single most powerful military figure, a position enhanced in 1615 by the destruction of TOYOTOMI HIDEYORI (1593–1615), the most plausible of his rivals. Ieyasu quickly put his preeminence to good use. In 1615 he issued the 17-clause KINCHŪ NARABI NI KUGE SHOHATTO, an order to the imperial court removing it from political life and claiming veto power over its personnel. Just 10 days earlier, with the 13-clause BUKE SHOHATTO, the DAIMYŌ had been forbidden to harbor fugitives, to undertake new fortifications, or to contract marriages without official approval. This intrusion of the central government into entrenched regional prerogatives was to continue in 1635, when daimyō were also deprived of the right to impose tolls or build large ships.

Control of the provinces was crucial to Tokugawa authority and was affirmed symbolically at the accession of every new daimyō and every new shōgun, with an exchange of documents in which, in return for a pledge of fealty, the daimyō received certification of his right to the income of his domain (HAN). Beyond symbolism, however, and especially in the years 1600–1650, the Tokugawa government was active in the allocation and withdrawal of domains. During that half-century 172 new daimyō were created and 206 were given fief increases, all as a reward for notable service. On 281 occasions over the same period daimyō were transferred from one domain to another, with the quality of the new fief corresponding to the quality of service rendered, while 213 daimyō lost all or part of their domain in punishment for some offense, real or fictitious.

Control took other forms as well. Daimyō were subject to various forms of surveillance, overt and covert, while in 1635 the introduction of the SANKIN KŌTAI system obliged each of them to spend every alternate year in residence in Edo (now Tōkyō), the seat of the shogunate, where his activities could be subjected to regular scrutiny. Travel to and from Edo and the upkeep of official residences

there, together with shogunal demands for contributions to a series of ambitious building projects early in the 17th century, helped keep the daimyō poor and the shogunate, in consequence, more powerful.

Military Position — The Tokugawa vassals, divided into HATAMOTO ("bannermen"), GOKENIN ("housemen"), and their retainers, constituted the core of the shogunate's military machine. They resided permanently in Edo and for the most part possessed no domains. At any given time there were perhaps 60,000 of them, but only a small percentage could have been considered a standing army. Many were bureaucrats or household servants, others had only nominal employment of any kind, and all, as the peaceful period of Tokugawa rule continued, were more accustomed to drawing salaries than swords.

In any case, even such a figure as 60,000 is dwarfed beside the more than 200,000 other samurai who, through their daimyō employers, were Tokugawa vassals only at second hand: in the event of any conflict between daimyō and shogunate their support would go to the former. The shogunate, therefore, at no stage enjoyed absolute military supremacy. Its rule depended on the tacit support of two groups of daimyō—the SHIMPAN, cadet houses of the Tokugawa, and the FUDAI ("hereditary" vassals), who had been Tokugawa vassals before the Battle of Sekigahara and who had been raised to the rank of daimyō after 1600. It also required the neutrality of at least some of the TOZAMA ("outside lords"), who had attained eminence independently.

Financial Position — Like its military position, the Tokugawa shogunate's financial base fell short of total superiority. True, the shōgun's personal domain (TENRYŌ) included Japan's largest cities, as well as major gold and silver mines. Other sources of revenue were fees from the vestigial foreign trade at Nagasaki and from merchants receiving shogunal patents of monopoly. Nevertheless, the shogunate held no more than 25 percent of Japan's registered arable land. The rest was in the possession of the daimyō.

Administrative System — The Tokugawa shogunate functioned on two different levels: as a national government and as the government of the Tokugawa house. Consequently, apart from the shōgun and the TAIRŌ or great elder, who was occasionally appointed to advise him, the shogunate's administrative structure reflected this duality. National affairs, including foreign relations, defense, and daimyō control, were conducted by the RŌJŪ (senior councillors), usually five or six *fudai* daimyō who met in formal council to discuss important issues, each in turn taking charge of general administration for a month at a time. Beneath them were the KYŌTO SHOSHIDAI, or Kyōto deputy, who acted as ambassador to the imperial court, and the ŌSAKA JŌDAI, or keeper of Ōsaka Castle, charged with the security of western Japan. These offices were also held by *fudai* daimyō, as was the post of JISHA BUGYŌ, or commissioner of temples and shrines.

By contrast, the affairs of the Tokugawa household—that is, the management of Tokugawa land and vassals—were in the charge of the WAKADOSHIYORI, or junior councillors. These posts, and those subordinate to them, were filled by *hatamoto*, *gokenin*, and lesser samurai, themselves all direct vassals of the Tokugawa house.

Such, at least, was the shogunate's administrative system in theory. In practice it was

Tokugawa Yoshimune The eighth Tokugawa shōgun instituted a series of reforms and rejected the luxurious lifestyles of his predecessors.

not so neatly organized. Few shōguns, although ultimately accountable for the actions of their government, had anything like absolute authority. Those who did, such as TOKUGAWA TSUNAYOSHI (1646–1709) and TOKUGAWA IENARI (1773–1841), had to fight for it, making themselves generally disliked in the process. For the most part, however, the shōgun was overshadowed by others. The rotation of office among senior officials also failed in its objective, which was to prevent any single *rōjū* from taking control. Powerful individuals, such as TANUMA OKITSUGU, MATSUDAIRA SADANOBU, and MIZUNO TADAKUNI, emerged from time to time to dominate the council; without them, indeed, any decisive response to critical situations would have been impossible.

It could be claimed that by restricting high office to *fudai* daimyō the shogunate alienated both *shimpan* and *tozama*, but there is little evidence to support this. A more substantial criticism is invited by the restricted recruitment for official positions in the shogunate: the most responsible offices were limited either to certain daimyō or to *hatamoto* and *gokenin*, who represented only a tiny minority of the samurai class.

Achievement — Politically and financially the Tokugawa shogunate was at its strongest in the 17th century. Thereafter many of its forms of daimyō control fell into disuse, while at the same time its revenues began to decline. Attempts were undertaken to restore both authority and solvency, first with the KYŌHŌ REFORMS of the early 18th century, subsequently with the KANSEI REFORMS toward the end of that century, and finally with the TEMPŌ REFORMS of the mid-19th century. These, however, did not have lasting success. Accordingly, Japan was to confront the crisis of the 1850s and 1860s with no more than the remnants of a strong central government.

It is true that the two and a half centuries of Tokugawa rule were a time of unparalleled peace for Japan, but this peace came not from a strong and active shogunate but rather from a combination of foreign indifference and daimyō passivity and unwillingness to cooperate with each other. When these latter conditions came to an end in the mid-19th century, so too did the government that had relied on them. See also EDO PERIOD.

Tokugawa Tsunayoshi　徳川綱吉

(1646–1709). Fifth shōgun of the Tokugawa shogunate; ruled 1680–1709. The fourth son of TOKUGAWA IEMITSU, the third shōgun, Tsunayoshi served as *daimyō* of the Tatebayashi domain in Kōzuke Province (now part of Gumma Prefecture) before succeeding his elder brother TOKUGAWA IETSUNA as shōgun in 1680. In the early part of his rule Tsunayoshi had the assistance of the great elder (*tairō*) HOTTA MASATOSHI. After Masatoshi's death in 1684 the government deteriorated steadily as Tsunayoshi began to rely on his grand chamberlain (*sobayōnin*) YANAGISAWA YOSHIYASU, while he himself retired more and more from his duties. Tsunayoshi's rule largely coincided with the GENROKU ERA, characterized by lavish spending and spiraling prices resulting from misguided financial policies and legislation. He also drew criticism for his "Edicts on Compassion for Living Things" (SHŌRUI AWAREMI NO REI), which forbade the killing of birds and animals and were enforced with severe punishments. Tsunayoshi's particular concern with the welfare of dogs led him to be dubbed "the dog shōgun" (*inu kubō*).

Tokugawa Yoshimune　徳川吉宗

(1684–1751). Eighth shōgun of the Tokugawa shogunate and initiator of the KYŌHŌ REFORMS; ruled 1716–45. Born the third son of Tokugawa Mitsusada (1627–1705), head of the Kii branch of the Tokugawa family, Yoshimune was made *daimyō* of the minor domain of Sabae (now part of Fukui Prefecture) in 1697. In 1705, following the deaths of his two elder brothers, he became daimyō of the Kii domain (now Wakayama Prefecture). When the death in 1716 of the child shōgun Ietsugu (b 1709) brought the main line of the Tokugawa family to extinction, the 32-year-old Yoshimune was chosen as successor. The branch families founded by Yoshimune and his son TOKUGAWA IESHIGE supplied the remaining shōguns of the Edo period (1600–1868).

Benefiting from his previous practical experience as daimyō, Yoshimune developed various means to maximize his direct knowledge of shogunate affairs and administration. The most novel of these was the MEYASUBAKO, a box posted at one of the gates of Edo Castle from 1721 in which townspeople could deposit complaints and suggestions for the shōgun's personal consideration.

Yoshimune's active involvement with government enabled him to remain far less dependent than his predecessors on personal attendants appointed to high rank. Early in his rule Yoshimune was constrained by the presence of particular senior councillors, but after they retired or died, Yoshimune designated his own appointee "senior councillor responsible for financial affairs" (*kattegakari rōjū*), and rapidly developed a core of officials from the finance and judicial commission (KANJŌ BUGYŌ) under the direct jurisdiction of this senior councillor. It was this core of officials that was largely responsible for the series of reforms known from the name of the era as the Kyōhō Reforms.

The reforms, intended to restore the shogunate and the *samurai* class to financial solvency, bore Yoshimune's personal imprint. Calling for a general retrenchment, he led the way in rejecting the luxurious lifestyle of his predecessors for one of spartan frugality. He sought to counter the seductive lure of urban life and to improve samurai morale and physical fitness by sponsoring a revival of martial activities.

Tokugawa Yoshinobu　徳川慶喜

(1837–1913). The 15th and last shōgun of the Tokugawa shogunate, who ruled during most of 1867. Also known as Tokugawa Keiki. Born in Edo (now Tōkyō), he was head of the Hitotsubashi house, one of the three junior collateral houses (GOSANKYŌ) of the Tokugawa family.

In 1857 the shōgun Iesada (1824–58), who had no heir, became ill. Yoshinobu's candidacy for shōgun was supported by a number of powerful *daimyō*, but II NAOSUKE and others close to Iesada arranged the succession of TOKUGAWA IEMOCHI. In 1866 the shogunate sent a punitive expedition against the Chōshū domain (now Yamaguchi Prefecture) in an attempt to reassert Edo's control over the country (see CHŌSHŪ EXPEDITIONS). The war went badly for the shogunate and, when the shōgun Iemochi sickened and died, Yoshinobu succeeded him as head of the Tokugawa family. In 1867 he accepted the title of shōgun.

Following the defeat by Chōshū, Yoshinobu and other officials set energetically to work to reform the government. Proim-

perial leaders in Satsuma and Chōshū were alarmed by his reforms and in late 1867 carried out a coup d'état in Kyōto. They proclaimed an "imperial restoration" and ordered Yoshinobu to surrender his domains. Attempts to reverse the coup precipitated the BOSHIN CIVIL WAR, in which the shogunal armies were defeated. Thoroughly disheartened by the abrupt military collapse, Yoshinobu decided to capitulate. He soon retired to Sumpu (now the city of Shizuoka), where he lived quietly, receiving honors and titles from the new Meiji government and leaving politics to the victors. See MEIJI RESTORATION.

Tokugawa Yoshinobu The last of the Tokugawa shōguns, Yoshinobu attempted in 1867 to reform the shogunal government, but his efforts to prevent its collapse came too late.

tokuju　特需

(special procurements). Foreign procurements of goods and services that helped Japan's economy recover and expand after World War II. The first surge of such procurements occurred during the KOREAN WAR, when Japanese firms received a huge quantity of special orders for goods and services for the United Nations, primarily American, military forces in Korea and later for materials to be used in Korea's reconstruction. These special procurement expenditures raised domestic production, improved business profits, and contributed to Japan's economic independence. Later, orders for goods and services by the American military during the Vietnam War provided further stimulus for the Japanese economy.

Tokumi-doiya　十組問屋

(Ten Groups of Wholesalers; also pronounced Tokumi-don'ya). A merchant asso-

Tokushima Prefecture
Location and
Prefectural Crest

Tokutomi Roka A turn-of-the-century novelist whose work, often concerned with the repressive power of family authority, reflects a candor and outspokenness unusual for its time.

ciation of the EDO PERIOD (1600–1868) consisting of wholesale dealers in EDO (now Tōkyō) who bought commercial goods from a group of suppliers in Ōsaka known as the NIJŪSHIKUMI-DOIYA. The association originally had 10 (*tō*) groups (*kumi*) of wholesale dealers (TOIYA), each handling a different set of commodities. The organization was formed in 1694 to deal with disputes among shipowners, wholesalers, and merchants over damaged and lost cargo. With its Ōsaka counterpart, the association controlled the *higaki kaisen* (see KAISEN), cargo ships that specialized in transport between Ōsaka and Edo. In 1730 the *sake* wholesalers seceded and used another kind of ship, known as *taru kaisen*, leading to competition between the two shipping lines. The Tokumi-doiya gradually expanded to nearly 100 groups. It was temporarily abolished under the TEMPŌ REFORMS (1841–43), revived in 1851, and disbanded after the Meiji Restoration (1868).

Tokunaga Sunao 徳永直

(1899–1958). Novelist. Born in Kumamoto Prefecture. A member of a working-class family, he completed middle school while working for a living. Beginning in 1922 he was a typesetter in Tōkyō, where he participated in labor activities and the PROLETARIAN LITERATURE MOVEMENT. His novel *Taiyō no nai machi* (1929, Streets without Sun) was about the 1926 KYŌDŌ PRINTING COMPANY STRIKE, in which he had participated. After writing mainly autobiographical novels during the war years, he reemerged as a major left-wing author with such works as *Tsuma yo nemure* (1946–48, Sleep, My Wife) and *Shizuka naru yamayama* (1949–54, Quiet Mountains).

Tokunoshima 徳之島

Island 50 km (30 mi) southwest of the island of AMAMI ŌSHIMA of Kagoshima Prefecture, Kyūshū. One of the Amami Islands, it is surrounded by coral reefs. The climate is subtropical. Principal activities are cattle raising and the growing of sugarcane, bananas, and pineapples. The island also has a well-developed tourist industry; one well-known local event is fighting between black bulls. Area: 248 sq km (96 sq mi).

Tokuoka Shinsen 徳岡神泉

(1896–1972). Japanese-style (NIHONGA) painter. Real name Tokuoka Tokijirō. Born in Kyōto, he graduated from Kyōto Shiritsu Kaiga Semmon Gakkō (now Kyōto City University of Arts) and studied under the *nihonga* painter TAKEUCHI SEIHŌ. As a young man he underwent Zen training at a Buddhist temple. In 1926 he won the highest prize at the Teiten (Exhibition of the Imperial Fine Arts Academy). His paintings are pervaded with a sense of stillness and ineffable mystery. He was awarded the Order of Culture in 1966.

tokuri 徳利

Often pronounced *tokkuri*. Vessel from which *sake* is poured into small cups (SAKAZUKI). Usually ceramic, *tokuri* come in various sizes and shapes with the most common sizes holding 180 or 360 milliliters (6 or 12 fl oz). *Sake* is often warmed before drinking by placing a *tokuri* of *sake* in a pot of hot water over a low flame. Larger *tokuri*, holding 500–1800 milliliters (17–61 fl oz), were traditionally used to bring *sake* home from the *sake* merchant's shop.

tokusei 徳政

(literally, "virtuous acts of government"). Decrees issued by the government during the medieval period (mid-12th–16th centuries) to give relief—usually amnesty or remission of taxes or debts—to certain groups. They arose from the ancient Chinese Confucian belief that natural and human disasters occur when a ruler is not "virtuous." As early as the 8th century Japanese sovereigns granted *tokusei* to increase their apparent virtue and to cure an ailing member of the imperial house, end a famine or epidemic, or put down some threatening disturbance. *Tokusei* were also issued to ward off calamities at an important state event.

Under the Kamakura shogunate (1192–1333) a different kind of *tokusei* was proclaimed in 1297 by the military government to strengthen the economic position of its retainers; it was later rescinded. Toward the mid-Muromachi period (1333–1568) *tokusei* were proclaimed to quell peasant rebellions (*tokusei ikki*). The Ashikaga military government collected a percentage of every loan canceled by a *tokusei*. Thirteen *tokusei* were issued during the rule (1443–74) of ASHIKAGA YOSHIMASA alone. During the late Muromachi period many lords issued *tokusei* in times of economic stress. Employed by the hegemons ODA NOBUNAGA and TOYOTOMI HIDEYOSHI, this practice continued into the Edo period (1600–1868). By then the remissions were called KIENREI (debt cancellations).

Tokushima 徳島[市]

Capital of Tokushima Prefecture, Shikoku, on the river Yoshinogawa. The city developed as a castle town and prospered as a shipping port for indigo during the Edo period (1600–1868). Designated as one of the NEW INDUSTRIAL CITIES in 1964, Tokushima is the location of lumber, furniture, foodstuff, chemical, and textile industries. Attractions are the ruins of Tokushima Castle, Bizan Park, and the AWA DANCE festival held every August. Pop: 263,356.

Tokushima Plain 徳島平野

(Tokushima Heiya). Located in northern Tokushima Prefecture, Shikoku. Bordered by both the Pacific Ocean and the Kii Channel, and situated along the Median Tectonic Line, this floodplain of the river Yoshinogawa consists of extensive alluvial fans below the scarps, some river terraces, and the delta. Rice, mulberry trees, tobacco, and vegetables are grown. The major city is Tokushima. Length: 15 km (9 mi); width: 80 km (50 mi).

Tokushima Prefecture 徳島県

(Tokushima Ken). Located on eastern Shikoku and bordered by Kagawa Prefecture and the Inland Sea to the north, the Kii Channel and the Pacific Ocean to the east, Kōchi Prefecture to the south, and Kōchi and Ehime prefectures to the west. The terrain is predominantly mountainous, and the largest plains are found around the YOSHINOGAWA, Shikoku's longest river, and the river NAKAGAWA. The climate is generally mild.

Formerly known as Awa Province, the area was dominated successively by the Hosokawa, Chōsokabe, and Hachisuka families during the feudal period and was a center of salt, tobacco, and indigo production. The prefecture took its present boundaries and name in 1880.

It is a predominantly rural prefecture. Rice, fruits, and vegetables are grown mainly

in the north. Forestry and fishing are important in the south. Paper manufacturing and chemical production are gradually being added to traditional industries such as textiles, woodworking, and food processing.

Tourist attractions are the whirlpools off NARUTO, part of the INLAND SEA NATIONAL PARK, and the mountain TSURUGISAN. The Awa *odori* (Awa dance) festival in August attracts visitors to TOKUSHIMA, the capital of the prefecture. Area: 4,146 sq km (1,607 sq mi); pop: 831,598. Other major cities include Naruto and ANAN.

tokusō 得宗

Patrimonial head of the main branch of the HŌJŌ FAMILY, which monopolized the position of SHIKKEN (shogunal regent) during the Kamakura period (1185–1333). The term was originally the Buddhist name of HŌJŌ YOSHITOKI, who became the second *shikken* and consolidated the political power of his family. The positions came to be held separately in 1256 when HŌJŌ TOKIYORI took holy orders and relinquished the *shikken* post to his father's cousin Hōjō Nagatoki (1230–64), since his own son and heir, HŌJŌ TOKIMUNE, was only five years old. Tokiyori continued to control the shogunate, however. He operated outside the formal structures of the shogunate, holding secret meetings with retainers who had a personal allegiance to him. This practice was continued by Tokimune, and in time the *tokusō* came to dominate the *shikken*. The *tokusō*'s tenure as military governor (SHUGO) of more than a half-dozen provinces and his possession of lands (*tokusō ryō*) throughout Japan further increased his political power.

Tokutomi Roka 徳冨蘆花

(1868–1927). Novelist. Real name Tokutomi Kenjirō. Born in Higo Province (now Kumamoto Prefecture); studied at what is now Dōshisha University. Part of his fame is due to his resistance to the traditional authority of the family, a resistance that culminated in 1902 in a dramatic "parting message" addressed to the head of the family, his elder brother Iichirō (pen name TOKUTOMI SOHŌ). His novel HOTOTOGISU (1898–99; tr *Namiko*, 1904) reflects this impulse to question the harshness with which the supremacy of the family often bore on individuals. In 1900 Tokutomi published *Shizen to jinsei* (tr *Nature and Man*, 1948), a collection of 87 prose poems whose subject matter is nature. It was followed by *Omoide no ki* (1901; tr *Footprints in the Snow*, 1971), a classic of the period. In this novel of a young man's development in the 1880s and 1890s, inspired in part by *David Copperfield*, Tokutomi conveys the excitement of a period of dramatic change and the impact on Japanese youth of notions of political freedom, Christianity, and romantic love. But Tokutomi lacked the intellectual equipment to go beyond attractive popular fiction to a deeper probing of the problems of his time, and the rest of his work does not live up to its early promise.

His life, however, continued to evince a powerful if eccentric individuality. Some of its highlights include a visit to Tolstoy at his estate, Yasnaya Polyana; a stormy marriage, the vicissitudes of which he chronicled unashamedly in his writing; a "conversion" experience on the summit of Mt. Fuji (Fujisan); and a naive but courageous personal appeal (in English) for racial equality and disarmament addressed to the statesmen gathered at Versailles after World War I.

Continuing Japanese interest in Tokutomi's outspokenness and "sincerity" is demonstrated by the publication of a massively detailed, three-volume biography (*Roka Tokutomi Kenjirō*, 1972–74) by NAKANO YOSHIO.

Tokutomi Sohō 徳富蘇峰

(1863–1957). Journalist and historian. Real name Tokutomi Iichirō. Older brother of the author TOKUTOMI ROKA. Born in Minamata, Higo Province (now Kumamoto Prefecture). He was educated in Western subjects at the KUMAMOTO YŌGAKKŌ and the Dōshisha (now DŌSHISHA UNIVERSITY) in Kyōto. In 1887 Sohō founded a publishing house, the Min'yūsha (Society of the People's Friends), which from 1887 to 1898 put out KOKUMIN NO TOMO (The Nation's Friend). This review was Japan's first general magazine and the most influential of the 19th century. The Min'yūsha published two other journals, *Katei zasshi* (Home Journal, 1892–98) and an English-language version of *Kokumin no tomo* called *The Far East* (1896–98). It also published and edited, from 1890 to 1929, the *Kokumin shimbun* newspaper. Sohō wrote more than 350 works on such subjects as domestic and international affairs, history, biography, and literature. His 100-volume *Kinsei Nihon kokumin shi* (A History of Early Modern Japan) was written between 1918 and 1952.

Sohō's early conception of how Japan could become modern, "wealthy and strong," and equal to the great Western nations was called *heimin shugi* ("populism"). It represented the general notion of a free, open, and democratic political, economic, and social order. From the early 1890s Sohō's views changed, and he began to develop collectivist and statist-oriented principles for the nation. After 1895 he became a friend, confidant, and adviser to the Meiji oligarchy and was particularly close to KATSURA TARŌ. After World War II, because of his prominence as a nationalist, he was held under house arrest by the Allied OCCUPATION from December 1945 until August 1947. See OCCUPATION PURGE.

Tokuyama 徳山[市]

City in southeastern Yamaguchi Prefecture, western Honshū. Tokuyama flourished originally as a castle town. Industrialization began with the construction of giant soda and metal plants during the 1920s. A huge petrochemical industrial complex is located here. Pop: 110,900.

Tokuyama Soda Co, Ltd 徳山曹達[株]

(Tokuyama Sōda). Major manufacturer of caustic soda and cement. Also produces plastics and organic and inorganic chemicals. Other products include ion membranes, medical materials, and electronics-related ceramics. The company is attempting to diversify into the fields of electronics and biomedicine. Incorporated in 1918. Sales for the fiscal year ending March 1991 totaled ¥169.7 billion (US $1.2 billion). The company was capitalized at ¥19.3 billion (US $140.8 million) in the same year. Headquarters are in Tōkyō.

Tōkyō 東京

Capital of Japan. Located on the Kantō Plain, on the Pacific side of central Honshū. Bordered by the prefectures of Chiba on the east, Saitama on the north, Yamanashi on the west, and Kanagawa on the southwest, and by Tōkyō Bay on the southeast. Under its

administration are islands scattered in the western Pacific, among them the IZU ISLANDS and the OGASAWARA ISLANDS.

Tōkyō Prefecture comprises the 23 wards (*ku*) of urban Tōkyō, 27 cities (*shi*), 1 county (*gun*), and 4 island administrative units (*shichō*). The county and the island units contain 14 towns and villages (*chō, son*). Area: 2,168 sq km (837 sq mi); pop: 11,855,563.

The residents of Tōkyō live in a total of 4,028,600 dwellings, with an average floor space of 60 square meters (645 sq ft). The average household has 3.5 members.

Geography and Climate——Tōkyō was known by the name Edo (literally, "Rivergate") before the MEIJI RESTORATION (1868), and the principal rivers of the Kantō region—the EDOGAWA, ARAKAWA, and SUMIDAGAWA—still flow to the sea through eastern Tōkyō. Along the alluvial plains of the old river TAMAGAWA, volcanic ash emitted from the Fuji-Hakone Volcanic Range accumulated to form the MUSASHINO PLATEAU, where the western wards (commonly known as the YAMANOTE district) and outlying districts are located. Some areas in the eastern wards (the SHITAMACHI district) lie 2–3 meters (6.5–10 ft) below sea level; the highest point in Tōkyō Prefecture is Mt. Kumotori (Kumotoriyama) to the west (2,018 m; 6,619 ft).

The four seasons of the year are sharply delineated, and the climate is generally mild, with the highest average monthly temperature in August (26.7°C; 80.1°F) and the lowest in January (4.7°C; 40.5°F). The annual precipitation is 1,460 millimeters (57.5 in).

Fauna and Flora——Pollution and unchecked land development ravaged the animal and plant population in Tōkyō Prefecture during the 1960s, but, with stricter pollution controls, 370 out of the approximately 570 bird species found throughout Japan have been sighted within Tōkyō. Other wildlife found in the mountainous areas within the boundaries of Tōkyō Prefecture include the Japanese antelope, raccoon dog (*tanuki*), fox, flying squirrel, rabbit, and squirrel.

The official tree of Tōkyō is the ginkgo, which is utilized as a shade tree throughout the city. Other common trees in Tōkyō include the cherry, zelkova, Japanese oak, and *kunugi* (*Quercus acutissima*, a kind of oak).

History——Where Tōkyō now stands relics have been found dating from the Jōmon (ca 10,000 BC–ca 300 BC), the Yayoi (ca 300 BC–ca AD 300), and the Kofun (ca 300–710) periods. During the 7th century Japan was divided into some 50 provinces, and MUSASHI PROVINCE was established in what is today Tōkyō, Saitama, and eastern Kanagawa prefectures. Its administrative center was located in what is now the city of FUCHŪ, which served as the political center of the province for nearly 900 years. During the civil wars of the 15th century, the warrior ŌTA DŌKAN constructed the predecessor of EDO CASTLE at the present site of the Imperial Palace.

After nearly a century of warfare, TOYOTOMI HIDEYOSHI partially united the country and dispatched TOKUGAWA IEYASU to Kantō in 1590 as lord of Edo Castle. After Hideyoshi's death Ieyasu completed the unification of Japan and established the TOKUGAWA SHOGUNATE in Edo in 1603. He constructed a castle town there with a samurai residential district on the castle's western side. To the east marshland was reclaimed, and a commercial and industrial area taking advantage of river and canal transportation came into being. As the city flourished mer-

chants and artisans flocked to Edo; the population reached one million by 1720, making Edo the largest city in the world at that time.

In 1867 the Tokugawa shogunate came to an end, and, with the Meiji Restoration the following year, Edo, renamed Tōkyō ("eastern capital"), became the national capital. The imperial family took up residence at Edo Castle in 1869. In the following years Tōkyō grew steadily in importance as the political, commercial, and financial center of Japan. Almost completely destroyed in the TŌKYŌ EARTHQUAKE OF 1923, the city was largely rebuilt by 1930 and administratively enlarged in 1943 through the amalgamation of surrounding districts and suburbs to form Tōkyō To (Tōkyō Prefecture; officially, Tōkyō Metropolis).

Much of Tōkyō was destroyed during World War II by American bombing, especially in the spring of 1945. After Japan's defeat Tōkyō remained the seat of government, with the General Headquarters of the Supreme Commander for the Allied Powers (SCAP) located there until the end of the Occupation in 1952. During the period of economic recovery starting in the 1950s, large enterprises increasingly concentrated their managerial operations in Tōkyō. This resulted in an increase in population from 6.3 million in 1950 to 9.7 million in 1960.

The city undertook a feverish building program in preparation for the 1964 TŌKYŌ OLYMPIC GAMES, and by 1965 the population had reached 10.9 million, resulting in serious housing problems and skyrocketing land prices. A program of building urban subcenters has since been carried out to alleviate the concentration of company head offices in the central Tōkyō area, and the pollution problems that were severe in the late 1960s and early 1970s have now been alleviated to a degree; the waters of the river Sumidagawa in eastern Tōkyō are relatively clean once more. The four-lane intracity expressway system that was begun in the 1960s is still often severely congested, however, and a further period of rapidly spiraling land prices since the mid-1980s has put home ownership beyond the reach of most Tokyoites.

Local and Traditional Industry——Local industries were long centered in the three *shitamachi* wards of Taitō, Sumida, and Arakawa, but in recent years the surrounding wards, particularly Adachi and Katsushika, have witnessed the influx of plants and factories. Products include clothing, knitted goods, precious metals, toys, and leather goods. Among traditional industries, fabric making has been prominent. Cities within Tōkyō Prefecture such as HACHIŌJI, ŌME, and MUSASHI MURAYAMA have been noted for the production of fabrics since the Edo period (1600–1868), and the island of HACHIJŌJIMA is noted for its *kihachijō* dyed fabric. Many of the craftsmen making traditional products face the problems of weak consumer demand and the difficulty of financing successors.

Modern Industry and Finance——A consumer city in the Edo period, Tōkyō developed into a center of manufacturing and heavy industry from the Meiji period (1868–1912) until the end of World War II. After 1965, however, tertiary industries—commerce, finance, transportation, communication, wholesale and retail stores, and service industries—began to surpass secondary

Tokutomi Sohō This journalist and historian founded the influential magazine *Kokumin no tomo* (The Nation's Friend) in 1887.

Tōkyō
Location and Prefectural Crest

Continued on page 1594➤

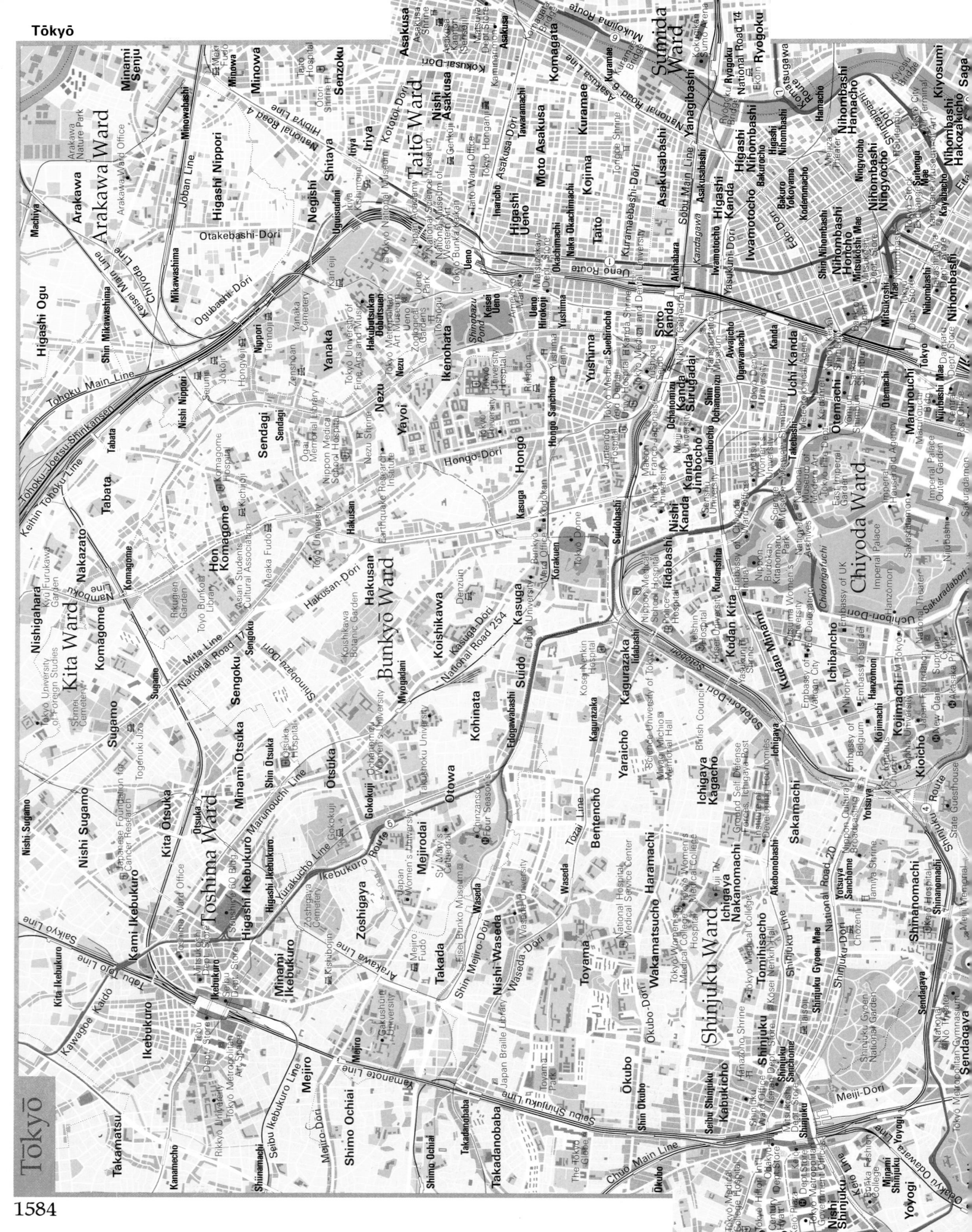

Tōkyō

1584

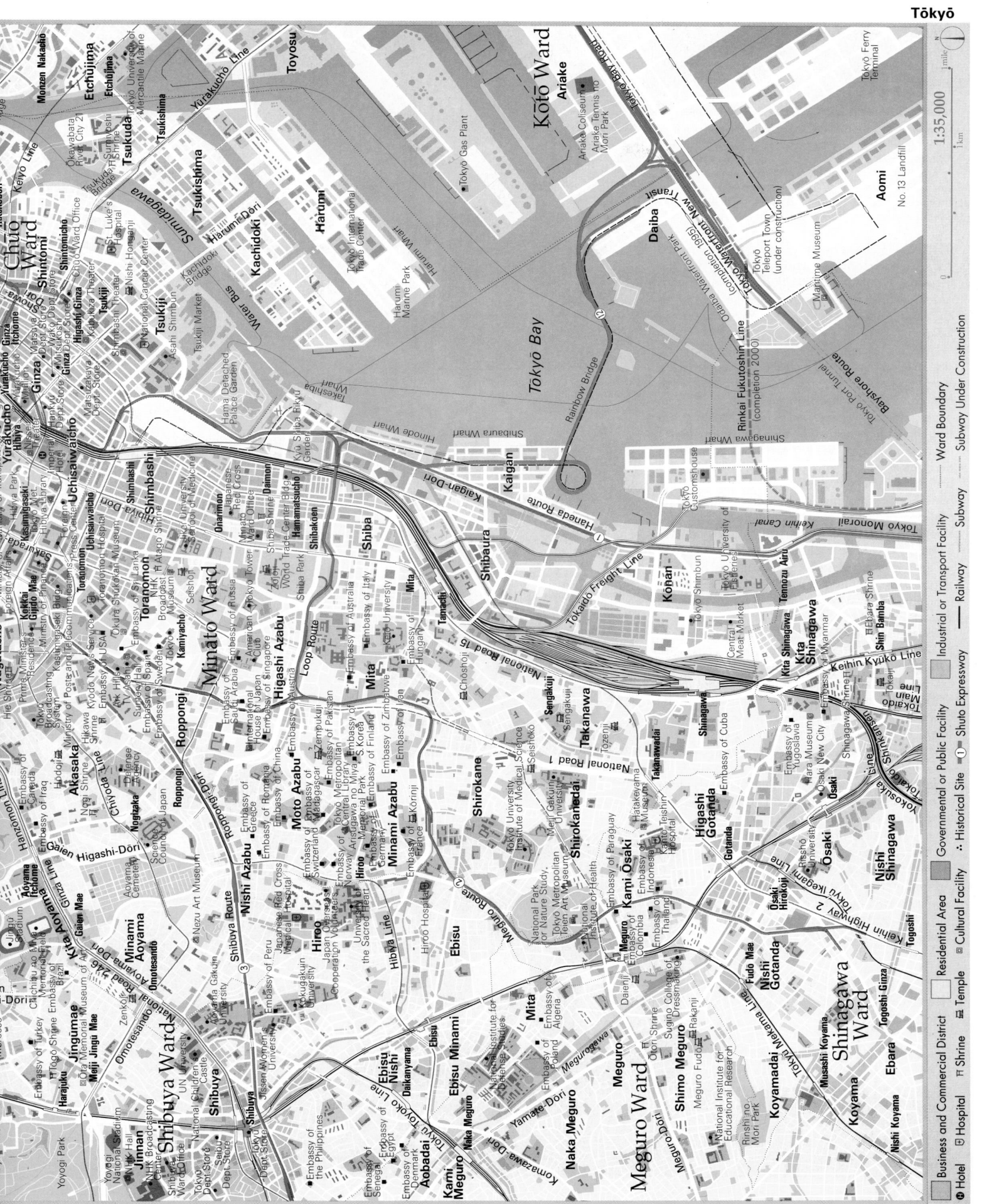

Letting Go of the Past

For millions of people, Tōkyō is a chaotic yet comfortable place to live—simultaneously maddening and endearing—and endlessly fascinating in its variety. For this section, a noted essayist and Tōkyō native has written a three-part *zuihitsu*, or impressionistic essay, that illuminates both the charms and shortcomings of his hometown—past, present, and future.

"From the balcony of our house where we used to hang out the wash, you could see the fireworks over the river Sumidagawa," I overheard one 29-year-old man say, recalling the days of his childhood. "Back then, this area was all two-story buildings."

Until fairly recently, Tōkyō was a ground-hugging city. The contours of the land shaped people's lives. Many downtown residents remember a time when they could see all the way to the Ginza district from one upper-story window and as far as Asakusa from another. Mt. Fuji could still be seen from the middle of town then, rising in the distance in the cool morning air. Place names such as Fujimizaka ("Fuji-View Hill") are still common in the metropolis, although the famed peak is no longer visible from these areas, crowded as they now are with high-rise buildings. Shiomizaka, a sloping street running by the US embassy, was once a bluff from which one could survey the broad expanse of Tōkyō Bay. The Sumidagawa ran its natural course, bearing lumber rafts from upriver down to the yards at Kiba, and children swam in its waters.

My grandparents came to Tōkyō from a village in the northern Kantō region at the end of the Meiji period (1868–1912). They opened a shoe store and prospered. The store was reduced to ashes in the firebombings of 1945, and my family fled to my grandmother's village and the safety of the countryside. The inflationary economy of the postwar era made it impossible to settle there, though, and before long the family was forced to return to Tōkyō to make a living. Many others found themselves in similar circumstances. Tōkyō put food on their tables, but their hearts remained in the country, amid nature. The ranks of potted plants that line the narrow back alleys of the city even now are mute testimony to this longing. The common vision of a native place, a country home to which one would someday return, made the Tōkyō of that time a city of the dispossessed, a city of wanderers.

The rusting pump of a disused well on one of Tōkyō's back streets.

The Hongōkan, built in 1905, is the city's oldest existing wooden apartment building.

A mail slot adorns the weathered wooden wall of an old residence.

The communal telephone on the ground floor of the Shinseikan, a vintage apartment block, hints at the structure's age.

In more traditional neighborhoods, New Year's is still an occasion for ritual celebrations of community spirit and friendship.

A rice shop preserves the look of a bygone Tōkyō—of an age when storefronts like this were the norm. Many of these shops have been replaced by convenience stores and fast-food outlets.

Back-street scenes like this one are rapidly falling victim to urban redevelopment.

Photographs by Ina Eiji

Living the Present

A crowd descending an escalator after a concert at the Tōkyō Metropolitan Art Space. The vertical growth of the metropolis has made elevators and escalators an inescapable part of daily life for many people.

Atriums such as this one in the headquarters of the NEC Corporation represent a new effort by architects to overcome the claustrophobic sensation imposed by such massive office blocks.

Tōkyō was once crisscrossed by a network of streetcars. Where the tracks ended, so did the city.

Now, however, only one streetcar line remains, the rest supplanted by a labyrinth of subways. Millions of people move beneath the city's streets. In just a quarter of a century, the relationship between the city and its inhabitants has been altered irrevocably. As people became increasingly cut off from the visual stimulation of the streets, the thread of memory connecting them to the natural world was strained. That thread has now snapped. In the meantime, however, Tōkyō residents have learned the intoxicating appeal of artificial space. The very artificiality of Tōkyō is a powerful stimulant.

I went to school clutching a strap in one of those old streetcars, watching the city streets flow past on the other side of the window. Now my daughter goes to school on the sightless subway, plugged into a Walkman, the soundscape of the music replacing the landscape of my day.

The horizontal expansion of the subways and Tōkyō's vertical thrust are simultaneous phenomena. The underground torrent of humanity bursts from the subway exits and spills into high-rise buildings. The recently completed metropolitan government offices in Shinjuku offer a symbol of the new Tōkyō; towering over the city, they will also be at the hub of a new subway system beneath it.

Many Tōkyō residents still return to their ancestral homes in the country for New Year's and the Bon Festival, but at the same time a counterflow from the countryside into the metropolis has begun. People head for the capital, check into the big hotels in the city's center, and explore the playground that is Tōkyō. A new tribe of "weekend Tokyoites" has come into being, invading the city to visit Disneyland, shop at the boutiques in Aoyama and Harajuku, and seek out the gourmet eateries now found all over town. Meanwhile, in the countryside, ancestral graves are left untended by a generation drunk on urban life.

The skyline west of Shinjuku Station, dominated by the twin towers of Tōkyō's new metropolitan government offices. Cranes rearing up high above the cityscape and the din of construction are part of everyday life in Tōkyō.

Photographs by Suzuki Yutaka

Imagining the Future

One evening I emerged from the subway at the last stop on one of the new lines. The streets were hushed. On the door of a shuttered sandwich shop was a notice saying the owner had moved away to live by the shores of a lake in a nearby prefecture. This district, with its roots in old Edo, seemed resigned to being swept away by the riptide of redevelopment.

Across the broad main street, a lonely patch of light—a terminal for the airport shuttle buses—shone in the distance. Overhead ran the elevated expressway that goes into the heart of town. Ascending a spiral staircase that resembled a human throat, I found myself atop a highway bridge. Downriver, a massive Hawaiian-blue arc of neon slashed across the water from bank to bank—another bridge, illuminated against the night sky. Behind it, countless other points of light leapt out of the surrounding darkness, no doubt emanating from the windows of the high-rise apartment buildings that now crowd the mouths of the rivers and estuaries that spill into Tōkyō Bay.

Looking over the railing, I could make out the dark outlines of a riverside park, a long narrow space extending from where I stood to the foot of a bridge that sprawled across the water like some prehistoric animal at rest. From a dimly lit pavilion in the park, laughter and the voices of teenagers rose up through the night air.

I still remember what the taxi driver said as he drove me through the deserted streets of Tōkyō's waterfront district.

"Not so long ago there were huge snakes in the weeds around here," he told me. "They must have come in on the ships bringing in lumber. But there was a big campaign mounted to exterminate them, and I guess it worked." The spot he was talking about is slated to become a telecommunications complex and international conference center. In such unlikely places, the future of the city stirs, soon to awaken.

Edagawa Kōichi

Contemporary architects are changing the face of the city in ways that shock some and delight others. This curious-looking object sits atop Super Dry Hall, a building in Tōkyō's Asakusa district that was named for a brand of beer.

The Tōkyō Budōkan complex, designed for martial arts competition and training, is another example of the wave of new construction that swept Tōkyō in the late 1980s and early 1990s.

Tōkyō Sea Life Park, an aquarium, is highly regarded for its design, which attempts to fuse the building with the surrounding seascape. As avant-garde architecture blurs the line between buildings and their environment, Tōkyō increasingly assumes the aspect of a single vast and borderless urban organism.

The Tōkyō Metropolitan Gymnasium's shape suggests a spacecraft poised for flight.

Photographs by Yokoyama Ryōichi

Tōkyō in Transition

While Kyōto embodies the spirit of old Japan,
Tōkyō resonates with the dynamism of modern life.

Tōkyō feels like the future, but the past is the adhesive that holds the city together as it races toward the 21st century. Like all great cities of the world, Tōkyō has a character all its own.

Despite its sprawling expanse, the city's overall scale remains small, much of the land still held in tiny parcels. This dichotomy of scale, combined with a mélange of cultural influences and an utter disregard for consistency in design and architecture accounts for jolting juxtapositions—Shintō shrines and Mc-Donald's restaurants, two-story wooden houses and high-tech apartment complexes.

The city changes at a dizzying pace, defying every attempt at control and planning. This internal, seemingly willful force of change defines Tōkyō. Complex and contradictory, the city confounds and challenges any attempt to make sense of it.

The People and the Lifestyle

Nearly 12 million people call Tōkyō home. Few were born there; most come from other parts of Japan, and increasing numbers now come from overseas. In the Edo period (1600–1868) a strict division of classes kept merchants and other commoners in the damp lowlands of the *shitamachi* district to the east, while the hilly areas in the west were reserved for the estates of the *samurai* elite. But at the end of the Edo period, the samurai returned to their homes in the provinces, and the wealthy merchants moved west to replace them. Nowadays, land prices and estate taxes are proving far more effective than Edo-period class divisions in determining residential patterns, although a surprising number of small two-story houses remain in neighborhoods throughout the city. Stubbornly resisting increasing offers for their properties, many Tokyoites remain admirably firm in their attachment to the land.

Neat, often tiny houses line winding back streets. Flower beds are lovingly tended, and early in the morning litter is swept clean in front of each home. Young children walk to school unescorted. Crime, though rising, is rare. Every neighborhood has its *kōban* (police box), and complaints are handled with a friendly, if not always satisfying, efficiency.

Tōkyō offers little to those seeking the old Japan, the Japan untouched and untainted by the West. The city only begrudgingly offers the quaint photo opportunities that confirm one's meeting with an exotic culture. *Kimono* have long been replaced as everyday attire by designer fashions, business suits, jeans, and sweatshirts emblazoned with nonsensical English phrases. Traditional corner groceries have given way to 7-Elevens, and Shintō shrines are not infrequently relocated to the roofs of office buildings. At times it seems that the worst of the West has invaded this city where *kabuki* and *ukiyo-e* once flourished, this former capital of the Tokugawa shōguns.

A City of Districts

Tōkyō has no real center. The city unfolds as a series of densely built villagelike districts, each centered around a subway or train station. The history of Tōkyō—political, economic, and cultural—can be traced in these districts. Many retain a flavor of their original character and purpose; others sprang up or evolved into commuter service centers.

The city's focus has moved from east to west, with the Imperial Palace remaining an awkward, if symbolic, central axis. This shift of focus became "official" in 1991 when the Tōkyō Metropolitan Government Offices moved from what had been the historical center of the inner city to the western edges in Shinjuku Ward. And yet, at the same time, there have been signs of a countertrend: ambitious plans abound for the redevelopment of the long-neglected waterfront and the city's still "developable" bay. As these plans are realized through the 1990s, it is tempting to imagine a Tōkyō centered around the *shitamachi* area again.

One can easily forget that Tōkyō is a waterfront city. It turned its back on what was once its lifeblood. The city used to be laced with rivers and canals, most of which were eventually filled in or covered by the roads and elevated freeways built in preparation for the 1964 Tōkyō Olympics. In parts of the city, however, the waterways remain. Crossing a bridge one may suddenly notice a small canal crowded with old wooden boats—the remains of a former fishing village.

A Boat Trip in Search of the Past

Travel by boat was common in the city during the Edo period, and it is still possible to go by boat from the waterfront up the Sumida River to Asakusa, one district that retains some traces of the city's past. It is not a scenic ride, though. Concrete warehouses and factories with rusting metal roofs line the shoreline and tell of the city's choice to side with the forces of commerce.

Spiritually and economically devastated by World War II, Tōkyō rebuilt itself from the ashes, finding strength in a populace that was willing to sacrifice many personal pleasures for the greater good. The city was reborn with a powerful will, a desire for peace and prosperity. The public has paid a stiff price for this achievement, but now that more attention is being placed on the quality of life, the river, perhaps more than any other resource in Tōkyō, holds the possibility for creating a more human city. Gradually, waterfront parks are being built, and public life is returning to its shores.

The boat that goes up the Sumida River leaves from a dock on the far side of the Hama Detached Palace Garden. The garden, with its ponds and wisteria, was once the site of a villa belonging to the Tokugawa family. In Asakusa, along the river's edge, the imposing Asahi Beer Azumabashi Hall looms as a harbinger of the district's future. The sleek, jewellike black box, which was designed by Phillipe Starck, is capped by a golden flame. It seems a fitting touch for Asakusa, a district where kitsch, culture, and religion have always clashed.

Sensōji, Asakusa's famous temple, was originally built in the 7th century but suffered greatly from the fires and earthquakes that plagued the city. Its main hall dates from a disappointingly recent 1958. The approach to the temple begins with the Kaminarimon (Thunder Gate) and proceeds along the Nakamise, an avenue lined with shops that leads to the temple. Many of these shops are filled with cheap souvenirs, but others still sell the products of true craftsmen who have been making boxwood combs, paper fans, and ceramic dolls for generations.

A fan-maker's shop in Yanaka.

Asakusa's Sanja Festival.

A sidewalk café along Omote Sandō.

Nearby is the Asakusa Shrine. This small Shintō shrine and its stone *torii* (archway) date from the Edo period and are officially designated Important Cultural Properties.

Not far from Asakusa is the Ueno district. Situated in the northeast, it housed the vast temple complex of Kan'eiji, which was built to protect the city of Edo from dangers that were traditionally thought to come from that direction. In one of the last battles between troops loyal to the Tokugawa shogunate and Meiji Restoration forces, most of the temple complex was destroyed. The city's first public park was later established on its grounds.

Ueno Park remains a valuable public resource, with a zoo, festival hall, and many museums. Most notable is the Tōkyō National Museum, which has splendid collections of art and archaeology. While it is a popular tourist destination, Ueno has also developed into a major shopping district for residents of the surrounding areas.

The old temple district continues to the north in Yanaka, one of the few areas in Tōkyō to survive both the city's destructive fires of the past and the more recent forces of development. Yanaka's still quiet, narrow streets are dotted with wooden houses, craft shops, temples, and shrines.

Much has been lost of the old Tōkyō, but the Japanese are unsentimental. For better or worse, many of the former bastions of traditional Japan are being redeveloped. Yet, as the old city fades, a new city is flowering that is just as Japanese as the one it is replacing. Contemporary art, design, and architecture are thriving. Exhibitions, concerts, and the performing arts, both local and foreign, are promoted and attended in staggering numbers. It is not difficult to imagine Tōkyō becoming a cultural as well as economic world capital in the not-too-distant future.

The Contemporary City

The Akasaka, Aoyama, Harajuku, and Shibuya districts of Tōkyō are showcases for contemporary Japanese design and architecture.

The Akasaka Prince Hotel, for example, was designed by internationally renowned architect Tange Kenzō, as was Akasaka's Sōgetsu Kaikan, headquarters of the Sōgetsu school of flower arrangement. This building also features a stunning plaza created by American sculptor Isamu Noguchi.

In Aoyama there is the Spiral Building by leading architect Maki Fumihiko as well as the Hanae Mori Building, another design by Tange. On the narrow street that leads from the Omote Sandō crossing toward the Nezu Art Museum one can find the main Tōkyō boutiques of top couturiers such as Miyake Issei, Kawakubo Rei, and Yamamoto Yōji. The La Collezione building by the Ōsaka-based architect Andō Tadao is located in this stretch, too.

On the other side of the Omote Sandō crossing, a

anything can be done in a department store—you can shop for food and fashion, finance a new car, plan a trip to Europe, or see an exhibition.

The Traditional City

The part of Tōkyō known as the Ginza is famous for having the highest rents per square meter in the entire country. Often called the Fifth Avenue of Japan, the Ginza is more elegant, perhaps more matronly, than Aoyama and Shibuya. Chic and expensive shops sell the most exclusive of Western and Japanese merchandise. Most of Tōkyō's contemporary art galleries are scattered among the back streets of this area, often tucked away on upper floors or in basements. Here one can also find galleries that specialize in locating multimillion-dollar postimpressionist paintings.

A step or two down the ladder of social respectability is the Shinjuku district. One of the main commuter terminals for the western suburbs, Shinjuku Station is among the largest stations in the world and, according to many visitors, is the hardest to find one's way in and out of. Perhaps more than any other district in Tōkyō, Shinjuku has the feel of the future as visualized in the film *Bladerunner*. The gentility of much of the rest of Tōkyō is not so apparent; the crowds are a bit less polite, the stores a bit downscale. Students from nearby universities haunt the local

overflow of people and its economic vitality. The waterfront warehouse districts, for example, are finding new tenants in discos, restaurants, and art galleries. The southwestern suburbs are spawning chic new shops and restaurants.

Tōkyō at Night

In the daytime, work seems an all-consuming passion, but in the evening, Tōkyō reveals a different face. The busy downtown streets take on a more leisurely air as the day begins to fade. Hurried businessmen become jolly; demure women become sophisticated. The city is transformed and almost seems beautiful.

A night out on the town for a prominent Tōkyō businessman often begins and ends in the Ginza. Here you can witness the Japanese "economic miracle" in progress. At around 11 PM, after the evening's festivities have come to an end, scores of tipsy movers and shakers are escorted to their limousines by kimono-clad bar hostesses.

The lower ranks of white-collar workers, without big expense accounts, gather in little drinking establishments beneath the tracks near Yūrakuchō Station. While crowded trains rumble overhead, streetside stalls and restaurants provide *yakitori* (grilled chicken on a skewer), beer or *sake*, and a relaxing break from the workday.

During the Meiji period (1868–1912), Akasaka

A secondhand bookstore in Kanda.

An amateur rock band at Yoyogi Park.

A pair of *sumō* wrestlers in Ryōgoku.

wide, tree-lined avenue leads to the center of the Harajuku district. This street and the surrounding area draw the most self-consciously fashionable young crowds of Japan. On Sundays a mass of teenagers swarms the section between Harajuku's landmark Laforet fashion building and the narrow shopping street called Takeshita-Dōri nearby. Few teens venture into the neighboring grounds of the Tōgō Shrine for its Sunday flea markets. Nor do they slip into the quiet serenity of the Ōta Memorial Museum of Art, an intimate Japanese-style building with an impressive collection of *ukiyo-e* prints.

On the other side of Harajuku Station is the Meiji Shrine, dedicated to Emperor Meiji and his empress. This shrine, with its graceful Shintō architecture, is surrounded by thick woods. In June, the shrine's iris garden is in glorious bloom. There is an odd fairy-tale quality about this shrine, perhaps because of its incongruous location.

In nearby Yoyogi Park teenagers gather each Sunday to perform and dance along to the latest pop music. Others imitate rock legends like Elvis Presley. Although the popularity of this weekly event has faded from its peak in the early 1980s, kids still show up in droves. This area has also become the Sunday morning meeting place for hundreds of transient foreign workers.

Near Harajuku is the Shibuya district, a major shopping area. With Tōkyō's scarcity of open space, shopping seems to be a favorite pastime. Just about

music shops, cheap bars, cafés, and movie houses. This is a district where the underworld wields a power that is hidden by day but unmistakable by night.

Tsukiji is the city's fish market. Almost every travel story on Tōkyō includes dramatic photographs of its morning auctions and the huge carcasses of steamy frozen fish lying across the docks. The mainstay of the Japanese diet is seen here in its freshest form. The outer market offers a quintessentially Japanese early-morning breakfast of *sushi*.

The Akihabara district is known for its many electronics discount stores. Merchandise spills out onto the streets—miniature vacuum cleaners in a range of pastel colors, complex self-timing rice cookers, "retro-1950s"-style TV sets. Huge discount stores dominate the main street; warrenlike arcades have booth after booth brimming with the parts and pieces of high technology.

Other districts have their specialties as well. Asakusabashi features doll shops, craft shops, and wholesalers for seasonal decorations. Kanda is characterized by booksellers and sporting goods shops. Nihombashi is both a shopping area and a financial center—the elegant Takashimaya and Mitsukoshi department stores are located there, as are the Bank of Japan and the Tōkyō Stock Exchange. Government offices can be found in Nagatachō and Kasumigaseki. Ryōgoku is the *sumō* district, Marunouchi the business district.

Many areas are changing in response to the city's

boasted one of the city's most fashionable *geisha* districts, catering to the new center of government nearby. The area continues to be known for its nighttime pleasures. Walking along the back streets, one finds the rickshaw still used to carry geisha to the discreet *ryōtei*, the often windowless, sand-colored stucco buildings that house the most exclusive and expensive of Japanese restaurants. An introduction is usually required for the privilege of spending an evening there complete with geisha entertainment—one that could easily run to several hundred dollars a head.

The Roppongi district reveals the international side of the city. The popularity of this area with foreigners adds to the distinctive flavor of its restaurants, bars, and nightclubs. The Japanese one sees here, mostly young and at least moderately well-off, seem in search of a future less constrained by tradition and the rules of Japanese society.

The future of Japan, of Tōkyō, is tested daily. New ideas are tried, old ones discarded or brought back into style. Tōkyō builds and rebuilds, becoming, to most observers, increasingly and disappointingly Westernized. But not even the most high-tech or avant-garde of its buildings goes up without a Shintō ceremony to placate the spirits of the place. The past lives on in the forms of the present. Behind the Western facade, Tōkyō is a city that could only be Japanese.

Judith Connor Greer

Tōkyō One of the many points of interest in Japan's largest city is the Nihombashi (literally, "Japan bridge"), from which all distances from Tōkyō to points throughout Japan are measured.
1 The Nihombashi in an early-19th-century woodblock print by Hiroshige. In the Edo period the Nihombashi served as the point of convergence for Japan's five main highways.
2 A horse-drawn streetcar crosses the Nihombashi in this early-Meiji-period photograph.
3 A contemporary view of the Nihombashi. A 1964 expressway runs directly above the modern bridge (1911).

← *Continued from page 1583*

industries. As of 1988 primary industries constituted only 0.2 percent of the total industries in Tōkyō; secondary industries 25.5 percent (compared to 50 percent in the 1960s); and tertiary industries, 74.3 percent. Tōkyō boasts a total of approximately 797,000 enterprises employing nearly 8 million workers. Most of these enterprises are small and medium-sized concerns. Forty-four percent of the nation's publishing and printing businesses are centered in Tōkyō with an annual turnover of US $34 billion. The total industrial output of Tōkyō Prefecture in 1988 was US $159 billion.

As new office buildings take over the central part of the city, small shops and permanent residents have been forced out to suburban areas, creating the so-called doughnut phenomenon. The pollution of the 1970s also forced large manufacturing plants (metals, textiles, foodstuffs, lumber) and related factories from the *shitamachi* lowlands to the outlying districts or to reclaimed land in TŌKYŌ BAY, and industrial plants formerly located on littoral districts have moved out of the city to adjacent prefectures. With the soaring urban and suburban land prices in recent years, more companies have been relocating their research and development centers and some of their head office departments to buildings equipped with the latest communications technology in outlying areas of Tōkyō. However, most large Japanese corporations, foreign companies, and the national press and mass media still have their head offices in Tōkyō; these are partic-

ularly concentrated in Chiyoda, Chūō, and Minato wards.

Another recent development has been the growth of the Shinjuku (see SHINJUKU WARD), Shibuya (see SHIBUYA WARD), and IKEBUKURO districts. Now known as satellite city centers or urban subcenters, they have become flourishing business and recreation districts, and large office buildings, including skyscrapers, have been constructed in these three districts over the last 20 years. The doughnut phenomenon, originally confined to the old city center, has spread to these satellite centers, and between 1985 and 1990 the population of the 23 urban wards of Tōkyō Prefecture fell by 190,000.

Tōkyō is also a major financial center. The TŌKYŌ STOCK EXCHANGE is one of the largest in the world in terms of aggregate market value and total sales, and deposits in Tōkyō banks constitute 34 percent of the nation's total deposits.

Transportation——Tōkyō is served by two airports: TŌKYŌ INTERNATIONAL AIRPORT (commonly called Haneda Airport), the main terminal for domestic flights in the southern end of the city, and NEW TŌKYŌ INTERNATIONAL AIRPORT (commonly called Narita Airport), located 66 kilometers (41 mi) east of Tōkyō.

The nation's main railway lines are concentrated in Tōkyō, with terminals at Tōkyō, Ueno, and Shinjuku stations. Trains for the west (Nagoya, Ōsaka, Kyōto) leave from Tōkyō Station (Tōkaidō and SHINKANSEN lines); trains for Tōhoku, Hokkaidō, and the Sea of Japan area originate from Ueno Station (Tōhoku, Takasaki, Jōban, and Jōetsu lines; the Tōhoku and Jōetsu Shinkansen lines originate from Tōkyō Station). From Shinjuku Station trains connect the city with the mountainous regions of central Japan (Chūō trunk line).

The principal commuter railway lines in Tōkyō are the Yamanote line, a loop around the heart of the city; the Keihin Tōhoku line, running through Tōkyō and Saitama and Kanagawa prefectures; the Chūō line, running through western Tōkyō; and the Sōbu line, connecting Tōkyō and Chiba. A network of private railway lines radiates outward from the principal stations on the Yamanote line, and 12 private and metropolitan subway lines (see SUBWAYS) have replaced the old network of streetcars in the heart of the city. Tōkyō is also well served by bus lines, and expressways connect the city to various regions.

Public Institutions and Services—— Government buildings are concentrated in the KASUMIGASEKI area in Chiyoda Ward. The DIET, the NATIONAL DIET LIBRARY, and the Supreme Court Building (see SUPREME COURT) are in neighboring Nagatachō. The Tōkyō metropolitan government, with offices in Shinjuku Ward, has jurisdiction over city services and in matters concerning corporations; ward, city, and town offices handle matters directly affecting their citizens.

Education——In recent years a number of colleges and universities have moved away from the crowded central city, but Tōkyō is still a major educational center, with 79 junior colleges and 106 universities as of 1989. The city is also the location of numerous academic societies, including the JAPAN ACADEMY, the SCIENCE COUNCIL OF JAPAN, and the JAPAN ART ACADEMY.

Cultural and Recreational Facilities—— *The arts.* Western culture was introduced into Japan through the gateways of Yokohama and Tōkyō after the Meiji Restoration, and Tōkyō today offers a variety of

modern arts as well as traditional arts such as KABUKI (drama), NAGAUTA (singing), *buyō* (see DANCE, TRADITIONAL), and RAKUGO (a form of comic storytelling). There are eight large-scale theaters in Tōkyō, including the Kabukiza and the NATIONAL THEATER. There are also numerous concert halls, MUSEUMS, and art galleries.

The media. Tōkyō is also a major information center. Eight general NEWSPAPERS are published in Tōkyō (including four in English), as well as three economic and industrial newspapers and seven sports newspapers; an average of more than 6,685,000 newspaper copies were printed each day in 1989. In addition, it is estimated that roughly 2,400 monthly and weekly magazines were being published in Tōkyō in the early 1990s.

A large proportion of television programming in Japan also orginates in Tōkyō, from the two noncommercial Japan Broadcasting Corporation (NHK) channels and the five commercial channels located there. There are also three satellite channels and numerous radio stations.

Parks and sports facilities. Although most parks are small by Western standards, a considerable number are scattered throughout Tōkyō. Major parks in central Tōkyō include the Imperial Palace grounds, HIBIYA PARK, UENO PARK, and the MEIJI SHRINE Outer Garden. There are also some 10 zoological and botanical gardens in the metropolitan area. Major national parks in Tōkyō Prefecture include CHICHIBU-TAMA NATIONAL PARK in the northwest, OGASAWARA NATIONAL PARK, and part of FUJI-HAKONE-IZU NATIONAL PARK.

Points of Interest——Situated in the center of Tōkyō and surrounded by a moat and high stone walls is the Imperial Palace, still retaining vestiges of its former glory as the residence of the Tokugawa family. To the east lies the GINZA, an area known for its fine shops, department stores, and numerous restaurants, bars, and cabarets.

North of the Ginza is NIHOMBASHI, the commercial hub of the city, from which all distances from Tōkyō to places throughout Japan are measured. Nearby are the districts of KANDA, renowned for its bookshops and universities, and AKIHABARA, famous for its discount stores selling all kinds of electrical appliances. Further to the north lie UENO and Ueno Park, a former shogunal estate that today houses the TŌKYŌ NATIONAL MUSEUM, the NATIONAL SCIENCE MUSEUM, the NATIONAL MUSEUM OF WESTERN ART, the UENO ZOOLOGICAL GARDENS, and the temple KAN'EIJI. To the east of Ueno is the oldest temple in Tōkyō, Asakusa Kannon (see SENSŌJI), in the heart of the *shitamachi* district, with its many shops still selling traditional handicrafts.

Another point of interest in the capital is the Diet Building in Nagatachō. Nearby ROPPONGI and AZABU, situated close to TŌKYŌ TOWER, house many foreign embassies. Neighboring AKASAKA is known for its luxurious nightlife. Near Shibuya Station lie Meiji Shrine, Yoyogi Park, the National Stadium, and HARAJUKU, a fashionable district popular with young people.

The area around Shinjuku Station—— which has the highest rate of passenger turnover in the country—is rapidly being developed, with restaurants and theaters in the Kabukichō area on the eastern side of the station and numerous skyscrapers on the western side, including the new TŌKYŌ METROPOLITAN GOVERNMENT OFFICES in the striking 48-story twin-tower building (243 m; 797 ft) designed by the world-famous architect

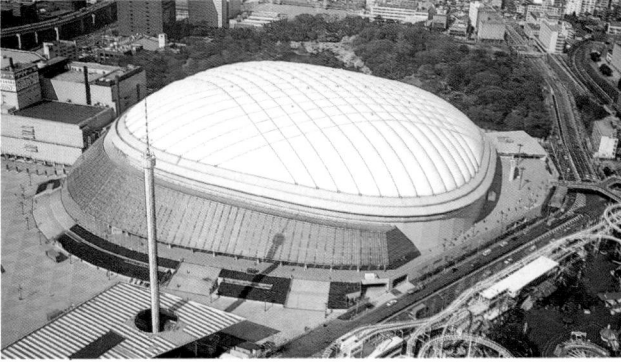

The Projected Tōkyō Bay Bridge and Tunnel

Tōkyō

Kawasaki

Chiba Prefecture

Tōkyō Bay

Kisarazu

SOURCE: Trans-Tōkyō Bay Highway Corporation.

TANGE KENZŌ. Another fast-growing commercial center is Ikebukuro, where the 60-story Sunshine City complex was completed in 1980.

A major project under way in the Tōkyō Bay area is the Tōkyō Frontier Project. This is a huge development on landfill sites that first had to be reclaimed from the sea, a process that was begun in the 1960s. New urban subcenters are planned for completion in the early 21st century on the Ariake and Daiba sites (448 hectares; 107 acres), which will include blocks of high-technology "INTELLIGENT" BUILDINGS, sports and leisure facilities, and international conference centers. Complementing this colossal undertaking is the equally ambitious TŌKYŌ BAY BRIDGE AND TUNNEL project, construction on which began in 1989 and is due for completion in 1996. Connecting the city of KAWASAKI in Kanagawa Prefecture with Kisarazu in Chiba Prefecture, this project will serve as a key link in the Tōkyō Bay ring road, which, it is hoped, will reduce traffic congestion in central Tōkyō. ― See map, pages 1584 and 1585.

☎ 1586–1591 ▮▶▶1592–1593

Tōkyō Bay
東京湾

(Tōkyō Wan). Inlet of the Pacific Ocean on the coast of Tōkyō, Kanagawa, and Chiba prefectures, central Honshū. Extends between the Miura and Bōsō peninsulas. Connected with the Pacific Ocean by the Uraga Channel. Fishing and aquiculture were active here until the beginning of the Shōwa period (1926–89) but ceased almost completely with the development of the Keihin Industrial Zone. A large number of industrial plants and port facilities are located on reclaimed land along the bay, and air and water pollution presents a serious problem. Some of Japan's largest ports are located on this important bay, including Tōkyō, Yokohama, Kawasaki, Yokosuka, and Chiba. The trade volume handled by the port of Yokohama is the largest in Japan.

Tōkyō Bay Bridge and Tunnel
東京湾横断道路

(Tōkyō Wan Ōdan Dōro). Official name Trans–Tōkyō Bay Highway. Bridge and tunnel system extending some 15 kilometers (9.3 mi) across Tōkyō Bay, connecting the city of Kawasaki in Kanagawa Prefecture with the city of Kisarazu in Chiba Prefecture. Construction began in May 1989 and completion is anticipated in March 1996. The roadbed will be a four-lane toll highway fully owned and operated by the JAPAN HIGHWAY PUBLIC CORPORATION; two tunnels, 14 meters (46 ft) in width, will extend for 10 kilometers (6.2 mi) from Kawasaki and join at a man-made island with a 4.4-kilometer (2.8-mi) bridge to Kisarazu. A crucial link in the construction of a ring road around Tōkyō Bay, the system is expected to be used by some 33,000 vehicles per day, thus significantly reducing the flow of traffic through central Tōkyō.

Tōkyō Broadcasting System, Inc (TBS)
[株]東京放送

(Tōkyō Hōsō). A Tōkyō-based commercial radio and television broadcasting company serving the Kantō (eastern Honshū) area. Established in 1951 as the first greater Tōkyō commercial radio station, it followed with television broadcasts in 1955. The company, which is presently allied with the large national newspaper MAINICHI SHIMBUN, operates with major funding from a group of banks and life insurance firms. It is affiliated nationally with 28 other commercial television stations (1992) comprising the Japan News Network (JNN). It is also a key affiliate of the Japan Radio Network (JRN).

Tōkyō City Hall→ Tōkyō
Metropolitan Government Offices

Tōkyō Collections
東京コレクション

(Tōkyō Korekushon). Biannual fashion shows sponsored by the Tōkyō Council of Fashion Designers and intended to give Tōkyō a place among the major international fashion capitals of Paris, London, Milan, and New York. The Tōkyō Collections, which attract journalists and buyers from around the world, were first held in November 1985. Thirty-two designers participated, with the collections centering on MIYAKE ISSEI, KAWAKUBO REI, MORI HANAE, YAMAMOTO KANSAI, and YAMAMOTO YŌJI. The fall/winter collections are held for 10 days starting the first week of April, and the spring/summer collections are held for 10 days beginning the first week of November. Forty designers participated in the November 1991 collections.

Tōkyō College of Pharmacy
東京薬科大学

(Tōkyō Yakka Daigaku). A coeducational private college located in the city of Hachiōji, Tōkyō Prefecture. Founded in 1880 as the Tōkyō Pharmacists' School, it became Tōkyō College of Pharmacy in 1949. The faculty of pharmacy is divided into a men's division and a women's division. Enrollment in 1989 was 2,006.

Tōkyō Denki University 東京電機大学

(Tōkyō Denki Daigaku). A coeducational private university in Chiyoda Ward, Tōkyō. The school originated as a nighttime vocational school, established in 1907, that offered courses in electrical engineering. It became a university in 1949 and currently maintains a faculty of engineering and a faculty of science and engineering. Enrollment in 1989 was 8,832.

Tōkyō Dental College 東京歯科大学

(Tōkyō Shika Daigaku). A coeducational private college located in the city of Chiba, Chiba Prefecture. Founded in 1946. It originated as the Takayama Shika Igakuin (Takayama Institute of Dentistry) established in 1890. Its one academic division is a faculty of dentistry. Enrollment in 1989 was 938.

Tōkyō Disneyland 東京ディズニーランド

(Tōkyō Dizunīrando). An amusement complex opened in April 1983 under license from the Walt Disney Company; located in the city of Urayasu, Chiba Prefecture. It is modeled closely on California's Disneyland, in terms of attractions, services, and operation. Tōkyō Disneyland is operated by the ORIEN-TAL LAND CO, LTD. About half of the total area of 82.6 hectares (204.1 acres) is occupied by five theme parks with 36 attractions: Adventureland, Westernland (Frontierland in the US Disneyland), Fantasyland, Tomorrowland, and World Bazaar (Main Street USA in the United States). The remainder is devoted to parking and service areas.

Tōkyō Dome 東京ドーム

(Tōkyō Dōmu). Japan's first indoor baseball stadium. Completed in 1988, it is situated in Bunkyō Ward, Tōkyō. The stadium contains Japan's first three-level grandstand, which seats 56,000 people. In addition to baseball games, such functions as concerts, exhibitions, and trade shows are held here. Tōkyō Dome is home to two professional baseball teams: the Central League's Yomiuri Giants and the Pacific League's Nippon Ham Fighters.

Tōkyō Dome Corporation
[株]東京ドーム

(Tōkyō Dōmu). Formerly Kōrakuen Co, Ltd. Company in the leisure industry. Incorporated in 1936. It built TŌKYŌ DOME, Japan's first air-supported dome stadium, in 1988. In partnership with Madison Square Garden Co, Inc, it promotes events in the Far East. Sales for the fiscal year ending January 1991 totaled ¥67.6 billion (US $492.7 million), of which Tōkyō Dome accounted for 32 percent; shops and restaurants, 27 percent; supermarkets, 18 percent; office building leasing, 9 percent; amusement parks, 6 percent; and other activities, 8 percent. The company was capitalized at ¥31.7 billion (US $231.0 million) in the same year. Headquarters are in Tōkyō.

Tōkyō Earthquake of 1923
関東大震災

(Kantō Daishinsai; literally, "Great Kantō Earthquake). Earthquake in Tōkyō and surrounding prefectures that struck at 11:58 AM on 1 September 1923. Damage was most ex-

Tōkyō Dome This indoor stadium is home to two professional baseball teams and also serves as a site for concerts, trade shows, and exhibitions.

1595
Tōkyō Earthquake of 1923

Tōkyō Earthquake of 1923
1 Postquake fires raged in the Hibiya district south of the Imperial Palace. Throughout Tōkyō, fires did more damage than the quake itself.
2 This brick tower, built in 1890 and long a symbol of the entertainment district of Asakusa, was broken off at the 8th of its 12 stories by the quake.
3 Thousands of people who had lost their homes sought shelter in makeshift houses constructed near the palace grounds.

tensive in the seven prefectures of Tōkyō, Kanagawa, Chiba, Ibaraki, Saitama, Yamanashi, and Shizuoka. The quake, which has since been assigned a magnitude of 7.9 on the scale used by the Meteorological Agency of Japan (see EARTHQUAKES), was followed by another severe tremor 24 hours later and by several hundred minor tremors. The intense fires that ensued—raging for almost two full days in Tōkyō—did more damage than the quakes themselves: in Tōkyō 63.2 percent of homes were destroyed (only 0.9 percent by the tremors and the rest by fire), and in Yokohama, which was closer to the epicenter, 72.5 percent were destroyed (9.8 percent by the tremors).

At the time the first quake occurred many people were preparing their noon meals over charcoal fires. The tremor scattered the coals, and fires, fanned by a steady breeze, spread rapidly and developed into firestorms. Intensely heated air rose to a high altitude, creating a partial vacuum that drew fresh air into the fires at ground level. The winds thus created were estimated at 70–80 kilometers (43–50 mi) per hour. Associated with the firestorms were cyclones that were especially deadly because they consisted primarily of superheated air from which most of the oxygen had been burned. One cyclone passed over the grounds of the Military Clothing Depot in Honjo, where many had sought refuge, and some 38,000 people died of suffocation. It is estimated that the total population of the affected areas was about 11,758,000 and that 3,248,205 people had their homes damaged or destroyed by the quakes or by fire. A total of 142,807 people were reported dead or missing and 103,733 injured.

The disaster destroyed city services and paralyzed administrative functions. Water mains and hydrants were ruptured and unavailable for firefighting; telephone and telegraph systems were knocked out, and even radio communication with the rest of the country was difficult, forcing the government to rely on military aircraft and carrier pigeons. The government itself was in disarray: Prime Minister KATŌ TOMOSABURŌ had died on 24 August, and on 2 September politicians hastily formed a new cabinet led by YAMAMOTO GONNOHYŌE. The disruption and anxiety caused by the disaster gave rise to hysteria and malicious rumors that Koreans were lighting fires and poisoning wells. Several thousand Koreans, many Chinese, and some Japanese were killed by organized neighborhood vigilante groups before order was restored.

The new cabinet had quickly declared martial law, and some 35,000 troops were dispatched into the disaster area. However, certain elements took advantage of the confusion to eliminate leftist radicals. Military police killed 10 labor union activists in the KAMEIDO INCIDENT of 4 September, and on 16 September anarchist ŌSUGI SAKAE, his wife, ITŌ NOE, and his six-year-old nephew also died at the hands of military police. These two incidents exemplify the breakdown of order in the devastated capital region even among those sworn to uphold it.

Tōkyō Electric Co, Ltd 東京電気[株]
(Tōkyō Denki). Company specializing in the manufacture and sale of electric and electronic equipment such as retail information systems, computer peripherals and software, home electrical appliances, and lighting fixtures. Incorporated in 1950. The company has overseas production facilities in the United States, Germany, and Singapore and 35 overseas sales offices. Sales for the fiscal year ending March 1991 totaled ¥190.4 billion (US $1.4 billion), with capitalization at ¥35.5 billion (US $258.7 million). Headquarters are in Tōkyō.

Tōkyō Electric Power Co, Inc
東京電力[株]
(Tōkyō Denryoku). Company supplying electricity to Tōkyō Prefecture and the eight surrounding prefectures of Tochigi, Gumma, Ibaraki, Saitama, Chiba, Kanagawa, Yamanashi, and Shizuoka (east of the river Fujikawa). The firm's forerunner was Tōkyō Electric Lighting, established in 1883. It took its present name in 1951. In March 1990 it had a capacity of 49.3 million kilowatts, of which 60 percent came from 29 thermoelectric plants, 27 percent from 3 nuclear power plants (in Fukushima and Niigata prefectures), and 13 percent from 156 hydroelectric plants. It imports approximately 9 million kiloliters (2.3 billion gal) of crude oil per year. It also imports liquefied natural gas (LNG) and nuclear fuel on long-term contracts. The company's annual sales totaled ¥4.4 trillion (US $32.1 billion) in the fiscal year ending March 1991, of which residential-use electric power accounted for 34 percent; other electric power, 63 percent; and other sales, 3 percent. It was capitalized at ¥670.4 billion (US $4.9 billion) in the same year. Headquarters are in Tōkyō. See also MATSUNAGA YASUZAEMON; KIKAWADA KAZUTAKA; HIRAIWA GAISHI.

Tōkyō Gakugei University
東京学芸大学
(Tōkyō Gakugei Daigaku). A coeducational national university in the city of Koganei, Tōkyō Prefecture. Founded in 1949 through the consolidation of four Tōkyō NORMAL SCHOOLS. The university's sole academic department is its faculty of education, which provides training for future kindergarten, elementary school, and junior high school teachers. Training for teachers of the handicapped and for teachers of specialized senior-high-school curriculum areas is also offered. Enrollment in 1989 was 5,119.

Tōkyō Gas Co, Ltd 東京瓦斯[株]
(Tōkyō Gasu). Company supplying city gas to approximately 7 million customers in the greater Tōkyō Metropolitan Area, including Tōkyō and Yokohama. It also sells various types of gas appliances and engages in gas facility contracting projects. Incorporated in 1885. In 1988 it became the first company in Japan to complete the process of conversion

to liquefied natural gas (LNG) caloric values, thereby guaranteeing the long-term safety and reliability of its supply systems. The company's development of the world's first compact heat-pump-type gas air conditioners, advanced district heating and air-conditioning systems, and advanced cogeneration systems is highly respected abroad. Annual revenue totaled ¥730.6 billion (US $5.3 billion) at the end of March 1991, and capitalization stood at ¥141.8 billion (US $982.5 million) in the same year. Headquarters are in Tōkyō.

Tōkyō Geographical Society　東京地学協会

(Tōkyō Chigaku Kyōkai). An academic society founded in 1879 for the purposes of introducing modern European scientific thought and furthering the spread of geographical research in Japan. In 1990 it had some 690 members who specialize in geography, geology, or geophysics. It promotes the exchange of ideas and information among specialists, sponsors lectures and research programs, and publishes a journal, *Chigaku zasshi* (Journal of Geography; first issued in 1889).

Tōkyō Institute of Technology　東京工業大学

(Tōkyō Kōgyō Daigaku). A national, coeducational college whose main campus is located in Meguro Ward, Tōkyō. Established in 1881 as the Tōkyō School of Technology (Tōkyō Shokkō Gakkō), it became a national college in 1929. It maintains faculties of science and engineering and research institutes in resources utilization, precision machinery and electronics, engineering materials, and nuclear reactor research. Enrollment was 4,652 in 1989.

Tōkyō International Airport　東京国際空港

(Tōkyō Kokusai Kūkō). Commonly referred to as Haneda Airport (Haneda Kūkō). Located on the shore of Tōkyō Bay in Ōta Ward, Tōkyō. The airport began operations in 1931 as Japan's first commercial airport. The US military requisitioned the facility following World War II; however, from 1952, when it was restored to Japanese control, until 1978, when the NEW TŌKYŌ INTERNATIONAL AIRPORT (Narita Airport) was opened, it was the chief gateway to Japan. Haneda Airport, which now serves largely domestic traffic, is operating at close to capacity, but a reclamation and construction project, due to be completed in 1995, will triple its size and add offshore runways that will permit an increase in air traffic from 157,000 takeoffs and landings annually to 230,000. The Tōkyō Monorail runs between Haneda Airport and Hamamatsuchō Station on the Yamanote Line.

Tōkyō International Film Festival　東京国際映画祭

(Tōkyō Kokusai Eigasai). Japan's first full-scale international film festival, held every other autumn since 1985. Festival events are concentrated in Shibuya Ward, Tōkyō. Since 1987 the festival has adopted a competitive format, with an international committee giving awards, including a Grand Prix. The Young Cinema division of the competition has attracted particular attention, for it awards budding directors substantial financial assistance to support their subsequent work.

Tōkyō Kyōiku Daigaku → Tsukuba University

Tōkyō Medical and Dental University　東京医科歯科大学

(Tōkyō Ika Shika Daigaku). A coeducational national university located in Bunkyō Ward, Tōkyō. Originally founded in 1928 as the Tōkyō School of Dentistry, Japan's only national dental education institution, it achieved university status in 1946. It has faculties of medicine and dentistry. Its research institutes include the Institute for Medical and Dental Engineering, the Institute of Stomatognathic Science, and the Medical Research Institute. Enrollment in 1989 was 882.

Tōkyō Medical College　東京医科大学

(Tōkyō Ika Daigaku). A coeducational private college located in Shinjuku Ward, Tōkyō. Founded in 1918 as the Tōkyō Medical School, it became Tōkyō Medical College in 1974. Its only academic department is the faculty of medicine. Enrollment in 1989 was 742.

Tōkyō Metropolitan Area　首都圏

(Shutoken). Also known as the National Capital Region. It consists of Tōkyō, Saitama, Chiba, Kanagawa, Ibaraki, Tochigi, Gumma, and Yamanashi prefectures, although for all practical purposes the Shutoken encompasses the area within a 150-km (93-mi) radius of central Tōkyō. It is the economic, political, and cultural center of the nation, with Japan's greatest concentration of population.

Tōkyō has expanded well beyond its administrative limits and has developed close economic relationships with its neighboring prefectures. Therefore the region has come to be viewed as a single entity in the formulation of urban plans for Tōkyō. The National Capital Region Development Law (Shutoken Seibi Hō) was implemented by the national government in 1956. Its aims were to stop the overconcentration of population and enterprise in central Tōkyō, to control the disorderly sprawl into the suburbs, and to define several outlying areas for urban development.

Tōkyō Metropolitan Art Museum　東京都美術館

(Tōkyō To Bijutsukan). Museum in Ueno Park, Tōkyō. From its establishment in 1926 until 1975, Tōkyō Metropolitan Art Museum served exclusively as a site for exhibitions of works by members of various art organizations and by private individuals. Since the erection of its new building in 1975, the museum has continued these exhibitions as well as mounting exhibitions of its own holdings and sponsoring lectures and workshops. It also maintains an art library. The museum holds some 3,000 items, consisting mostly of Japanese paintings, woodblock prints, and other works of art dating from the Meiji period (1868–1912) to the present.

Tōkyō Metropolitan Central Library　東京都立中央図書館

(Tōkyō Toritsu Chūō Toshokan). One of Japan's leading public libraries; located in Arisugawa no Miya Memorial Park, Minato Ward, Tōkyō. Opened in 1973. Among the library's features are a collection of Edo-period (1600–1868) materials such as colored woodblock prints and paintings; several im-

portant formerly private collections of rare books and manuscripts; materials concerning Tōkyō, including English-language guidebooks; and a periodical room with over 350 Japanese and foreign newspapers and magazines. In 1989 the library housed some 1.12 million volumes, approximately 80,000 of which were in foreign languages.

Tōkyō Metropolitan Government Offices　東京都庁舎

(Tōkyō Tochōsha). Building complex housing the government of Tōkyō Prefecture (officially Tōkyō Metropolis). Located in Shinjuku Ward, Tōkyō. Construction of the offices began in April 1988 and was completed in March 1991. The complex was designed by TANGE KENZŌ and consists of two office buildings, the Metropolitan Assembly Building, and a public courtyard. The 48-story Office Building Number One is 243 meters (797.2 ft) high, and the 34-story Office Building Number Two is 163 meters (534.8 ft) high. The Metropolitan Assembly Building is 41 meters (134.5 ft) high. The public courtyard is 5,000 square meters (53,800 sq ft) in area. The entire complex covers 42,940 square meters (462,034 sq ft) and has a total floor space of 381,000 square meters (4,099,560 sq ft). Some 13,000 metropolitan government employees work here, and the dramatic twin towers of the Number One building have already become a Tōkyō landmark.

Tōkyō Metropolitan Hibiya Library　東京都立日比谷図書館

(Tōkyō Toritsu Hibiya Toshokan). One of three prefectural libraries maintained by the Tōkyō metropolitan government. Since its establishment in 1908 it has remained at its present site in Hibiya Park in central Tōkyō, although it was destroyed by bombing in 1945. In 1949 service was restored. Many of its books and some of its previous functions have been transferred to a new facility, the TŌKYŌ METROPOLITAN CENTRAL LIBRARY, in Minato Ward.

Tōkyō Metropolitan Institute of Gerontology　東京都老人総合研究所

(Tōkyō To Rōjin Sōgō Kenkyūjo). The only research institute in Japan devoted to the ailments and problems of the aged. Located in Itabashi Ward, Tōkyō, the institute was established in 1972 as a center for research into the characteristics and problems associated with Japan's AGING POPULATION. Research is conducted into molecular, physiological, and pathological aspects of the aging process; human science and rehabilitation; sociology and sociomedical factors; and gerotechnology (technical support facilities for gerontological research). Projects include social support facilities for the aged and comprehensive studies of senile dementia.

Tōkyō Olympic Games

To many, the 18th Summer Olympic Games held in Tōkyō in October 1964 represented Japan's return to international society after the long period of reconstruction following World War II.

◄Cheered on by flag-waving crowds, one in a long series of relay runners carries the Olympic torch through a Tōkyō suburb.

▼Ethiopian Abebe Bikila became the first person to win consecutive Olympic marathons by taking the gold medal in Rome in 1960 and in Tōkyō in 1964.

▼Famous for the intensity of their practice sessions, the Japanese women's volleyball team provided some of the most dramatic moments of the games on their way to the gold medal.

▲ Opening ceremonies were held at the Kasumigaoka National Stadium.

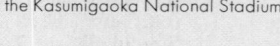

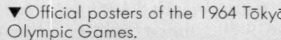

▼Official posters of the 1964 Tōkyō Olympic Games.

TOKYO ● 1964   TOKYO 1964   TOKYO ● 1964

Tōkyō National Museum The main building (pictured) of this museum of art and archaeology houses the most extensive collection of Japanese art in the world.

Tōkyō Metropolitan Police Department   警視庁

(MPD; J: Keishichō). The police force of Tōkyō Prefecture, with over 41,000 police officers. Established in 1874, it is commanded by a superintendent general who is appointed by the NATIONAL PUBLIC SAFETY COMMISSION with approval from the prime minister and the five-member Tōkyō Metropolitan Public Safety Commission (To Kōan Iinkai). With a population over 11.8 million, the 2,183.3-square-kilometer (842.9-sq-mi) area of Tōkyō Prefecture is divided into eight police districts, within which a total of 99 police stations (keisatsusho) and 1,250 police boxes (KŌBAN) are located.

Like the police in all prefectures, Tōkyō police officers are divided into administra-tive, personnel and training, traffic, guard, patrol, public security, criminal investiga-tion, and crime prevention specializations. Because Tōkyō is the political and economic hub of the nation, guard and public security duties are particularly crucial and are per-formed by the RIOT POLICE (Kidōtai) of the Metropolitan Police Department.

Tōkyō Metropolitan Teien Art Museum   東京都庭園美術館

(Tōkyō To Teien Bijutsukan). Located in Minato Ward, Tōkyō. Established in 1983. Originally built in 1933 as the mansion of Prince Asaka (1887–1981), who lived there with Princess Nobuko, the eighth daughter of Emperor MEIJI. The structure itself, its fur-nishings, and the surrounding gardens are the chief attractions of the museum. Planned chiefly by the French designer Henri Rapin (1873–1939), the building and many of its decorative features are in the Art Deco style of the 1920s and 1930s.

Tōkyō Metropolitan University   東京都立大学

(Tōkyō Toritsu Daigaku). A coeducational public university located in the city of Ha-chiōji, Tōkyō Prefecture. Founded in 1949, the university maintains faculties of social sciences and humanities, law, economics, science and technology, and a Center for Urban Studies. Enrollment in 1989 was 3,803.

Tōkyō monogatari   東京物語

(Tōkyō Story). A 1953 film directed by OZU YASUJIRŌ, starring RYŪ CHISHŪ and HARA SE-TSUKO. In the film, an elderly couple from the provinces come to Tōkyō to visit their chil-dren, a deceptively simple situation that gives Ozu the opportunity for an extended meditation on the sorrows of old age, the joy and disillusionments of parenthood, and the postwar breakdown of the traditional Japa-nese family. Centering on the parent-child relationship, a theme central to all his work, Tōkyō monogatari might be considered Ozu's most representative film in its use of the mundane and everyday to comment on deeper themes of human loneliness and the universal encounter with life and death.

Tōkyō National Museum   東京国立博物館

(Tōkyō Kokuritsu Hakubutsukan). Located in Ueno Park in Tōkyō. The collection origi-nated with a Ministry of Education exhibi-tion held in 1872 and was established at its present site in Ueno Park in 1881. The mu-seum has the finest and most extensive col-lection of Japanese art and archaeology in the world. Japanese art is housed in the main building (built in 1937); Japanese archaeol-ogy in a second building, called the Hyōkei-kan (built in 1908); and objects, largely of the Asuka period (593–710), presented by the authorities of the temple Hōryūji (see HŌRYŪJI, TREASURES OF) to the imperial house-hold in 1878 and now on loan to the museum, in a third building. The latest addition to the complex is the Tōyōkan (1968), which con-tains Chinese, Korean, and other Asian art.

The museum has notable collections of INK PAINTING, KAKEMONO (hanging scrolls), UKIYO-E prints, Western-style painting of the

Meiji period (1868–1912), Buddhist sculpture, pottery, porcelain, and lacquer ware. In 1968 the museum was placed under the jurisdiction of the Agency for Cultural Affairs. See also MUSEUMS.

Tōkyō National Research Institute of Cultural Properties
東京国立文化財研究所

(Tōkyō Kokuritsu Bunkazai Kenkyūjo). One of two national research institutes maintained by the Agency for Cultural Affairs under the Ministry of Education; located in Ueno Park, Tōkyō. Founded in 1930 as the Institute of Art Research with a bequest from the artist KURODA SEIKI, it became a government organization in 1952. The institute's research staff is divided among an archive and four other departments, with independent facilities for the study of the restoration and preservation of cultural objects. Library resources number about 54,000 volumes. See also NARA NATIONAL RESEARCH INSTITUTE OF CULTURAL PROPERTIES.

Tōkyō Ohka Kōgyō Co, Ltd
東京応化工業[株]

(Tōkyō Ōka Kōgyō). Manufacturer of photoresists, printing materials, processing equipment, fine chemicals, and specialty chemicals. Incorporated in 1940. The company is the leading manufacturer of photoresists for semiconductors, which is its main business. It established Ohka America, Inc, in California in 1987 and Ohka, Ltd, in the United Kingdom in 1988. In 1989 T.O.K. International, Inc, a wholly owned production subsidiary, was established in Oregon. Sales for the fiscal year ending March 1991 totaled ¥55.2 billion (US $402.3 million), and capitalization stood at ¥14.6 billion (US $106.4 million). Headquarters are in the city of Kawasaki, Kanagawa Prefecture.

Tōkyō Olympic Games
東京オリンピック

(Tōkyō Orimpikku). Held 10–24 October 1964. The 18th Summer Olympic Games and the first to be held in Asia. There were more than 5,500 participants from 94 nations. Twenty events were held, including newly added volleyball and *jūdō* competitions. Forty-seven world records and 111 Olympic records were set. The games were uniformly praised for their efficient operation, the fairness of the judges, and the splendor of the grounds.

Tōkyō ordinance decision
都条例事件

(To *jōrei jiken*). Supreme Court decision of 20 July 1960 affirming the constitutionality of a Tōkyō prefectural public safety ordinance (KŌAN JŌREI) regulating public demonstrations. The ordinance established a permit system under which sponsors of open-air assemblies were required to apply to the police, who had more or less discretionary power in dealing with applications. It was argued that the ordinance constituted an invalid prior restraint on the people's FREEDOM OF ASSEMBLY. The Supreme Court reversed a Tōkyō District Court decision of 13 October 1959, which had declared the ordinance invalid.

Tōkyō Philharmonic Orchestra
東京フィルハーモニー交響楽団

(Tōkyō Firuhāmonī Kōkyō Gakudan). Orchestra originating in 1911 as a small musical group formed in Nagoya. In 1938 it moved to Tōkyō and was renamed the Central Symphony Orchestra. The orchestra's first principal conductor was Manfred Gurlitt (1890–1972) of Germany. The group adopted its present name in 1952 and has become known for its annual premiere performances of new Japanese compositions.

Tōkyō Rope Mfg Co, Ltd
東京製綱[株]

(Tōkyō Seikō). Wire rope manufacturer. Incorporated in 1887; established in its present form in 1946. The firm produces various types of wire ropes, wires, and steel cords. The production of steel cords for auto tires is its main business. It is also engaged in the development of electromagnetic interference shielding materials. Sales for the fiscal year ending March 1991 totaled ¥77.3 billion (US $563.4 million), and capitalization was ¥10.0 billion (US $72.9 million). Headquarters are in Tōkyō.

Tōkyō Rose
東京ローズ

(Tōkyō Rōzu). Nickname given by US military men in the Pacific theater during World War II to a number of female announcers broadcasting entertainment and propaganda programs from Radio Tōkyō, the overseas bureau of the Japan Broadcasting Corporation (NHK). One such announcer was Iva Toguri D'Aquino (known in Japan as Toguri Ikuko), born in California in 1916 and a graduate of the University of California at Los Angeles, who was in Japan on a visit to relatives when the war broke out in 1941. In September 1945 D'Aquino was identified by two American newspapermen as the "one and only Tōkyō Rose." Arrested and imprisoned by US military authorities in October 1945, she was released in 1946. In 1948 the US Department of Justice, under heavy domestic political pressure, decided to prosecute her for treason. A San Francisco jury found her guilty in September 1949, and she was imprisoned for over six years. After revelation of false testimony at her trial, D'Aquino was pardoned by President Gerald Ford in January 1977.

Tōkyō Saiban→ war crimes trials

Tōkyō Sea Life Park
東京都葛西臨海水族園

(Tōkyō To Kasai Rinkai Suizokuen). Municipal aquarium located in the Kasai Coastal Park, in Edogawa Ward, Tōkyō, fronting Tōkyō Bay. Opened in 1989. The aquarium has the world's largest torus-shaped water tank, with a total diameter of 27 meters (89 ft) and an inner diameter of 19 meters (62 ft) allowing the aquatic life on display to be seen from both inside and outside the ring formed by the tank. Visitors also make use of the man-made beach and cycling paths in the park.

Tōkyō shimbun
東京新聞

A local daily newspaper serving readers of the Tōkyō area. The *Tōkyō shimbun* began publishing in 1942 as a result of the enforced wartime merger of two older established Tōkyō dailies, the MIYAKO SHIMBUN and the KOKUMIN SHIMBUN. Under government restrictions imposed on the use of paper during the last years of World War II, it dropped its morning edition in 1944 and became an evening paper. It continued to be Tōkyō's only evening newspaper for some years after the war, during which time it experienced considerable growth in readership. This was due in part to the serial publication of many popular novels (see SHIMBUN SHŌSETSU) beginning with volume 5 (earlier volumes appeared in the *Miyako shimbun*) of OZAKI SHIRŌ's *Jinsei gekijō* (7 vols, 1933–59). The morning edition was revived in 1956. In 1967 the *Tōkyō shimbun* was purchased by the publisher of the newspaper CHŪNICHI SHIMBUN. The *Tōkyō shimbun* is highly regarded for its comprehensive coverage of the arts and cultural events. In 1991 its morning edition had a circulation of 801,000 and its evening edition 525,000.

Tōkyō Station
東京駅

(Tōkyō Eki). Railroad station in Chiyoda Ward that serves as Tōkyō's central rail terminus. The station buildings consist of the Marunouchi Wing, completed in 1914, which is a historical landmark, and the modern Yaesu Wing, completed in 1968 and designed in the functional steel-and-glass block style of that period.

The Marunouchi Wing, designed by TATSUNO KINGO, was originally part of a much larger three-story structure that was severely damaged by bombing during World War II. Redesigned and rebuilt after the war, it preserves the neo-Renaissance style of the original, including the steel-reinforced red brick construction with white stone facing that was Tatsuno's trademark. Now two stories in height, its broad frontage is punctuated at either end by low octagonal towers. The building faces the IMPERIAL PALACE, and in the prewar period its central entrance was reserved for the use of the imperial family. Despite the postwar alterations, the Marunouchi Wing is still highly regarded as an example of the Western-inspired architecture of the Meiji (1868–1912) and Taishō (1912–26) periods.

Tōkyō Steel Mfg Co, Ltd
東京製鉄[株]

(Tōkyō Seitetsu). Manufacturer of steel bars, structural shapes, and H-shapes for construction use. Incorporated in 1934. In 1984

Tōkyō Stock Exchange The trading floor of the exchange in the Kabutochō district of central Tōkyō, Japan's Wall Street.

Tōkyō Tower The tallest structure in Tōkyō and a symbol of the city, the illuminated tower stands out against the night sky.

the company began to produce plates under the Universal Plate brand. Sales for the fiscal year ending March 1991 totaled ¥232.5 billion (US $1.7 billion), and capitalization stood at ¥24.7 billion (US $180.0 million). Headquarters are in Tōkyō.

Tōkyō Stock Exchange
東京証券取引所

(Tōkyō Shōken Torihikisho). The present Tōkyō Stock Exchange was established in April 1949 under the Securities and Exchange Law as a nonprofit, corporate-membership-based organization. It is located in Kabutochō, Chūō Ward. Membership is restricted to securities companies, and as of July 1991 there were 124 members, including 25 non-Japanese members. Stocks, bonds, and futures options based on securities are traded on the exchange. See STOCK EXCHANGES; STOCK MARKET.

Tōkyō Tanshi Co, Ltd
東京短資[株]

(Tōkyō Tanshi). Financial services company. Incorporated in 1909. The company's principal activities are the handling of short-term loans, short-term government bonds, and certificates of deposit. Revenue for the fiscal

year ending November 1990 totaled ¥513.1 billion (US $3.9 billion), and capitalization stood at ¥300 million (US $2.3 million). Headquarters are in Tōkyō.

Tōkyō Tatemono Co, Ltd
東京建物[株]

(Tōkyō Tatemono). Real estate developer, engaged in office building leasing and in the sale and brokerage of real estate. Incorporated in 1896. It is a member of the Fuyō group. It established its first overseas office in Los Angeles in 1989. Sales for the fiscal year ending December 1990 totaled ¥63.2 billion (US $473.2 million), and the company was capitalized at ¥45.6 billion (US $332.4 million) in the same year. Headquarters are in Tōkyō.

Tōkyō Tower
東京タワー

(Tōkyō Tawā). Tower built in 1958 in Minato Ward, Tōkyō, for the purpose of broadcasting throughout the Kantō region. It rises 333 meters (1,093 ft) and has two observation decks. In 1990 its antenna was broadcasting on eight television channels, from FM radio channels, and a number of channels that disseminate information of public importance, such as weather and fire reports.

Tōkyō Toyopet Motor Sales Co, Ltd
東京トヨペット[株]

(Tōkyō Toyopetto). Direct-sales company of TOYOTA MOTOR CORPORATION, selling all Toyota models both new and used. It also sells other domestic and foreign used cars in the Tōkyō district. Incorporated in 1953. Ranking first among 313 Toyota dealers nationwide, it sold 121,177 new cars in the Tōkyō district in 1990. Sales for the fiscal year ending March 1990 totaled ¥340.2 billion (US $2.5 billion), with ¥3.5 billion (US $25.5 million) in capital. Headquarters are in Tōkyō.

Tōkyō Union Theological Seminary
東京神学大学

(Tōkyō Shingaku Daigaku). A coeducational private university in the city of Mitaka, Tōkyō Prefecture. The school was founded in 1943 by the UNITED CHURCH OF CHRIST IN JAPAN through the merger of several Protestant seminaries. It achieved university status in 1949. It specializes in theological research and missionary training. Enrollment in 1989 was 160.

Tōkyō University
東京大学

(Tōkyō Daigaku). A national, coeducational university with campuses in Bunkyō and Meguro wards, Tōkyō. The first university established in Japan, it is one of the country's best-known and most prestigious schools. It was established in 1877 with the unification of Tōkyō Kaisei Gakkō (see BANSHO SHIRABE-SHO) and Tōkyō Igakkō. In 1886 the university was renamed Imperial University. Its name was changed to Tōkyō Imperial University with the establishment of Kyōto Imperial University in 1897. In 1947 the name was changed back to the original Tōkyō University, and in 1949 it was reorganized to incorporate the First Higher School and Tōkyō Higher School. The university has maintained a graduate school since 1886 and at present comprises 10 faculties: letters, education, law, economics, science, medicine, pharmacology, engineering, agriculture, and a college of general education. The university also houses the following research institutes: the Cosmic Ray Laboratory, the Institute for Nuclear Study, the Institute for Solid

State Physics, the Ocean Research Institute, the Institute of Medical Science, the Earthquake Research Institute, the Institute of Oriental Culture, the Institute of Social Science, the Institute of Journalism, the Institute of Industrial Science, the Historiographical Institute, and the Institute of Applied Microbiology. Enrollment in 1989 was 14,936.

Tōkyō University of Agriculture
東京農業大学

(Tōkyō Nōgyō Daigaku). A coeducational private university in Setagaya Ward, Tōkyō. Founded in 1925, the university traces its origins to the agriculture course established in 1891 at the Tokugawa Ikueikō, a private academy. The university's sole academic division is its faculty of agriculture. Enrollment in 1988 was 6,434.

Tōkyō University of Fine Arts and Music
東京芸術大学

(Tōkyō Geijutsu Daigaku). A coeducational national university in Taitō Ward, Tōkyō. It was formed in 1949 by uniting Japan's first official art academy, the Tōkyō School of Fine Arts (founded in 1887), with the Tōkyō School of Music (also founded in 1887). Its faculties of fine arts and music include departments of painting, sculpture, and Japanese music. It is the most prestigious school of its kind in Japan and has graduated many famous artists and musicians. Enrollment in 1989 was 1,995.

Tōkyō University of Fisheries
東京水産大学

(Tōkyō Suisan Daigaku). A coeducational national university located in Minato Ward, Tōkyō. Founded in 1888 as the Fisheries Institute, it was reorganized in 1949 to become Tōkyō University of Fisheries. The university maintains a faculty of fisheries with four departments: aquatic bioscience, fisheries resources management, food science and technology, and marine science and technology. Enrollment in 1989 was 1,307.

Tōkyō University of Foreign Studies
東京外国語大学

(Tōkyō Gaikokugo Daigaku). A national, coeducational university located in Kita Ward, Tōkyō. Established in 1897 as the Tōkyō School of Foreign Languages, it attained university status in 1949. It maintains a faculty of foreign languages, offering courses in 16 languages, as well as a Japanese language school for foreign students. Enrollment was 3,084 in 1989.

Tōkyō University of Mercantile Marine
東京商船大学

(Tōkyō Shōsen Daigaku). A coeducational national university located in Kōtō Ward, Tōkyō. It traces its origins to the Mitsubishi Nautical School, founded in 1875. In 1949 Tōkyō University of Mercantile Marine became a four-year college with a faculty of mercantile marine science. The college has traditionally served to train merchant marine officers for overseas service. Enrollment in 1988 was 737.

Tōkyō War Crimes Trial ⟶ war crimes trials

Tōkyō Women's Christian University
東京女子大学

(Tōkyō Joshi Daigaku). A private liberal arts university for women whose main campus is located in Suginami Ward, Tōkyō. It was founded in 1918 by the Presbyterian missionary August Karl REISCHAUER, Nagao Hampei (1865–1936), and their colleagues. In the following year NITOBE INAZŌ was elected its first president. He was succeeded in 1924 by Japan's first woman university president, YASUI TETSU. In 1948 the institution was recognized as a four-year university. It maintains faculties of arts and sciences and of culture and communication. Enrollment was 3,325 in 1989.

Tōkyō Women's Medical College
東京女子医科大学

(Tōkyō Joshi Ika Daigaku). A private women's college; the only women's medical school in Japan. Located in Shinjuku Ward, Tōkyō. Founded in 1900 by YOSHIOKA YAYOI, the school has existed under its current name since 1947. The school maintains a faculty of medicine, an Institute of Geriatrics, and an Institute of Rheumatology. Enrollment in 1989 was 624.

Tōkyū Agency, Inc
[株]東急エージェンシー

(Tōkyū Ējenshī). Advertising agency. Incorporated in 1961. A member of the Tōkyū group. In addition to being a full-service advertising agency, the company produces cultural and sports events. For the fiscal year ending March 1990, sales totaled ¥173.0 billion (US $1.1 billion) and capitalization stood at ¥3.6 billion (US $23.5 million). Headquarters are in Tōkyō.

Tōkyū Car Corporation
東急車輛製造[株]

(Tōkyū Sharyō Seizō). Manufacturer of rolling stock. Incorporated in 1948. A member of the Tōkyū group, the company comprises two major divisions: one manufacturing railway rolling stock for Japan Railways and other railway companies, and the other producing special-duty motor vehicles, including trailers and dump trucks. Sales for the fiscal year ending March 1991 totaled ¥89.0 billion (US $648.7 million), of which railway rolling stock accounted for 44 percent and special-duty vehicles 56 percent. The company was capitalized at ¥14.0 billion (US $102.0 million) in the same year. Headquarters are in Yokohama.

Tōkyū Construction Co, Ltd
東急建設[株]

(Tōkyū Kensetsu). General contractor. Incorporated in 1948. The company is a member of the Tōkyū group, one of the largest real estate developers in Japan. It engages in large-scale dam and tunnel projects, urban redevelopment, and the Tōkyū group's overseas projects. Sales totaled ¥521.0 billion (US $3.8 billion) in the fiscal year ending March 1991. Capitalization was ¥22.5 billion (US $164.0 million) in the same year. Headquarters are in Tōkyō.

Tōkyū Corporation
東京急行電鉄[株]

(Tōkyū Kyūkō Dentetsu). Company engaged in commuter transportation (railway and bus) throughout the southwest region of the Tōkyō metropolis. Tōkyū is also the largest real estate developer in Japan and the leader of a business group consisting of 334 companies. Incorporated in 1922 as a local railway company in southwest Tōkyō, it has diversified into real estate development, with projects throughout Japan and in Asia, Australia, the mainland United States, Hawaii, and the Pacific islands.

The Tōkyū group is engaged in four major areas: transportation, development, distribution and retailing, and recreation and lei-

sure. The major companies in the group are JAPAN AIR SYSTEM CO, LTD; TŌKYŪ LAND CORPORATION; TŌKYŪ HOTEL CHAIN CO, LTD (the largest in Japan); TŌKYŪ AGENCY, INC (the third largest); TŌKYŪ DEPARTMENT STORE CO, LTD; Tōkyū Hotels International; and TŌKYŪ CAR CORPORATION.

Gross sales of the Tōkyū group at the end of March 1990 were ¥3.8 trillion (US $27.7 billion). Total sales for Tōkyū Corporation in the fiscal year ending March 1991 were ¥277.7 billion (US $2.0 billion). It was capitalized at ¥107.1 billion (US $780.6 million) in the same year. Headquarters are in Tōkyō.

Tōkyū Department Store Co, Ltd
[株]東急百貨店

(Tōkyū Hyakkaten). Company chiefly engaged in the department store business. Incorporated in 1919. Tōkyū Department Store Co also operates restaurants and amusement centers, as well as engaging in the import-export business. A major member of the Tōkyū group's marketing branch, the company took its present name in 1958. In 1991 the company had six department stores in Japan and seven stores abroad. Sales for the fiscal year ending January 1991 totaled ¥393.2 billion (US $2.9 billion), and the company was capitalized at ¥37.6 billion (US $280.8 million) in the same year. Headquarters are in Tōkyō.

Tōkyū Hotel Chain Co, Ltd
[株]東急ホテルチェーン

(Tōkyū Hoteru Chēn). Urban hotel operator belonging to the Tōkyū group of companies. Incorporated in 1950. It operates 19 hotels (6,186 rooms altogether) in Japan's key cities. Sales for the fiscal year ending December 1990 totaled ¥60.0 billion (US $449.3 million). The company was capitalized at ¥12.5 billion (US $93.6 million) in the same year. Headquarters are in Tōkyō.

Tōkyū Land Corporation
東急不動産[株]

(Tōkyū Fudōsan). Company engaged in real estate, particularly development of housing projects. Incorporated in 1939. A member of the Tōkyū group, the company grew rapidly by developing land along the railway lines of the TŌKYŪ CORPORATION. It has a joint-venture company in Bandung, Indonesia. Sales totaled ¥230.9 billion (US $1.7 billion) in the fiscal year ending March 1991, and the company was capitalized at ¥31.5 billion (US $229.6 million). Headquarters are in Tōkyō.

Tomakomai
苫小牧[市]

City in southwestern Hokkaidō, on the Pacific Ocean. Tomakomai was settled by colonist militia (TONDENHEI) in the late 19th century. It is the leading producer of paper in Japan. Oil refineries and aluminum and lumber plants are also located here. Pop: 160,118.

Tomb period →Kofun period

Tōmen Corporation
[株]トーメン

(Tōmen). General trading company. Tōmen became independent from the cotton division of MITSUI & CO, LTD, in 1920 and now ranks seventh among the nine sōgō shōsha (general trading companies) in Japan. It has 23 branches and offices in Japan and 160 overseas branches, offices, and subsidiaries. By product, sales broke down in the year ending March 1991 as follows: metals and metal ores, 35 percent; machinery, 15 percent; chemicals and fuel, 24 percent; food, 9 percent; construction and lumber, 6 percent; and textiles, 11 percent. At the end of March

Tōkyō University
A view of Yasuda Hall on the Bunkyō Ward campus. The hall is the symbol of "Tōdai," as the university is popularly known.

1991, annual sales totaled ¥6.8 trillion (US $49.6 billion). The company was capitalized at ¥49.7 billion (US $362.2 million) in the same year. Headquarters are in Ōsaka.

tomeyama
留山

(literally, "mountain preserves"). Forest lands owned and regulated by the Tokugawa shogunate or by daimyō domains during the EDO PERIOD (1600–1868). Entry into and use of tomeyama for hunting and lumbering were controlled in order to maintain shogunal or domainal resources. Occasionally, areas in which disputes arose over IRIAI (commonage rights) were designated tomeyama and subject to the same regulations.

Tomii Masaaki
富井政章

(1858–1935). Legal scholar and codifier of the CIVIL CODE. Born in Kyōto. After graduating from the Tōkyō School of Foreign Languages in 1877, he studied law at the University of Lyons. Returning to Japan in 1883, he was appointed professor at Tōkyō University. He objected to the 1890 civil code for its exclusive reliance on the Napoleonic Code and suggested that elements from English and German civil law also be incorporated (see CIVIL CODE CONTROVERSY). In 1893 he was named, together with HOZUMI NOBUSHIGE and UME KENJIRŌ, to the commission to amend the code; the Civil Code, as finally enacted in July 1898, was almost entirely German in inspiration. In 1919 he was appointed to a committee to revise the parts relating to family law (Shinzoku Hō) and inheritance law (Sōzoku Hō). His principal work is Mimpō genron (3 vols, 1903–29, Principles of Civil Law). See also SHICHIHAKASE JIKEN.

tomikuji
富籤

(fortune lot). Type of lottery that flourished in cities during the Edo period (1600–1868). Derived from MUJIN (mutual-aid financial associations) that originated in the Muromachi period (1333–1568). It was also called tomi-tsuki (fortune stab), because the winning lot was selected by plunging a stick with a drill bit on its end into a large box and twisting it until a single wooden lot was pierced. Tomikuji were conducted to raise funds for the repair of temple or shrine buildings. Fraudulent practices were common, and in 1842 tomikuji were outlawed.

Tomimoto Kenkichi
富本憲吉

(1886–1963). Eminent modern potter. Specializing in porcelain, he also worked in earthenware and stoneware. He was also an influential teacher and a leading member of various organizations of artists and craftsmen. He was born in Ando, Nara Prefecture. He studied architectural design at the Tōkyō Bijutsu Gakkō (now Tōkyō University of Fine Arts and Music) in 1909 and went to England for further design study. From 1912 he studied ceramics under Kenzan VI.

Tomimoto's earliest pieces were low-fired

Tomioka Silk-Reeling Mill The Meiji government opened the Tomioka Mill with the help of French technology and know-how. Photograph ca 1872.

Tomioka Tessai *Two Divinities Dancing.* 1924. Hanging scroll. Colors on silk. 169 × 86 cm. Tōkyō National Museum.

Tomita Isao A composer and synthesizer player who has made major contributions to the establishment of electronic music as a performance medium.

RAKU WARE, a type he soon abandoned as too breakable, turning instead to stoneware. From 1926 to 1946 he made mainly porcelain: blue and white, overglaze enameled, and plain white. Later in life Tomimoto continued to produce porcelain but also made enamel-decorated earthenware. His complex, vigorous patterns of stylized blossoms in overglaze enamel, gold, and silver on white porcelain have never been surpassed. He was also a master of bold yet naturalistic plant motifs in underglaze cobalt blue. In 1955 the Japanese government designated him one of the first LIVING NATIONAL TREASURES. He received the Order of Culture in 1961.

Tominaga Nakamoto 富永仲基

(1715–46). Scholar of the Edo period (1600–1868) known for his critical views on Buddhism, Confucianism, and Shintō. Also known as Tominaga Kensai. Born in Ōsaka. In his work *Shutsujō kōgo* (also known as *Shutsujō gogo*; Buddha's Comments after His Meditation) of 1745, Tominaga noted that Buddhist teachings contained later accretions and did not represent original Buddhism. He maintained that many teachings claimed to be ancient were in fact newer. He later criticized Confucianism from the same perspective. His short critique *Okina no fumi* (1746, Writings of an Old Man) spelled out his views on Buddhism, Shintō, and Confucianism. Writing that both Buddhism and Confucianism had evolved under particular historical and geographical circumstances, he argued that it is both impossible and meaningless for the Japanese to adopt them; he found the ancient cult of Shintō, though native to Japan, equally impossible to practice. He concluded that those ethical and religious tenets that cannot be observed are invalid, that is to say, cannot be considered the true moral way (*makoto no michi*), and only those initial teachings that follow common sense and are easy to put into practice can be called true and valid. Tominaga called on his readers to concentrate on the work at hand, to be upright and circumspect in word and deed, to defer to their parents, and to be loyal to their lord.

Tominaga Naoki 富永直樹

(1913–). Sculptor. Real name Tominaga Yoshio. Born in Nagasaki Prefecture. A graduate of Tōkyō Bijutsu Gakkō (now Tōkyō University of Fine Arts and Music), he studied under KITAMURA SEIBŌ. In 1936, while still in school, he won a prize at the Bunten (Ministry of Education Fine Arts Exhibition). Powerful male figures sculpted with an assured realism are Tominaga's trademark. He received the Order of Culture in 1989.

Tomioka 富岡[市]

City in southwestern Gumma Prefecture, central Honshū, on the river Kaburagawa. The TOMIOKA SILK-REELING MILL, the country's first Western-style thread-reeling factory, was established here by the government in 1872. There are also electrical-appliance, automobile-parts, and rubber industries. Sericulture and poultry farming are active. Pop: 49,022.

Tomioka Silk-Reeling Mill 富岡製糸所

(Tomioka Seishisho). A model filature established in 1872 by the Meiji government in Tomioka, Gumma Prefecture (see GOVERNMENT-OPERATED FACTORIES, MEIJI PERIOD). The government hired a French engineer to supervise the construction and operations, imported machinery from France, and recruited workers primarily from the daughters of former *samurai* (SHIZOKU). The plant was sold to MITSUI in 1893 (see KAN'EI JIGYŌ HARAISAGE) then transferred to the Hara Gōmei Company in 1902. The Katakura Silk-Reeling and Spinning Company absorbed it in 1939. The mill ceased operations in February 1987.

Tomioka Taeko 富岡多恵子

(1935–). Poet and novelist. Born in Ōsaka. Graduate of Ōsaka Women's University. She received the H-Shi Prize for her first poetry collection, *Henrei* (1957, A Gift in Return). Tomioka's poems often express despair and are characterized by the frequent use of personal pronouns (unusual in Japanese) and a plainspoken narrative style. By 1971 she had turned to writing novels, such as *Shokubutsusai* (1973, Plant Festival), which examines the aimless lifestyle and resulting despondency of urban youth. In recent years Tomioka's writing has diversified to include collections of critical essays, plays, and translations.

Tomioka Tessai 富岡鉄斎

(1837–1924). Last major artist in the BUNJINGA (literati painting) tradition in Japan; one of the great modern masters of Japanese art. Real name Tomioka Yūsuke; later changed to Tomioka Hyakuren. Born in Kyōto, Tessai studied ancient Japanese classics under the KOKUGAKU scholar ŌKUNI TAKAMASA. At the age of about 20 he became a protégé of the Buddhist nun ŌTAGAKI RENGETSU.

During the Meiji period (1868–1912) Tessai championed old traditions against new Western styles and traveled throughout Japan, visiting famous and scenic places that became the subjects of many of his paintings. In 1882 Tessai settled in Kyōto, where he spent the rest of his life painting and reading the thousands of books he had collected. In 1907 he was commissioned to paint for the Meiji emperor. He was appointed as an artist to the imperial household (*teishitsu gigeiin*) in 1917 and named to the Imperial Fine Arts Academy (Teikoku Bijutsuin) in 1919. His most prolific and creative period was the decade of his eighties. His total life's output has been estimated at over 20,000 paintings.

Tessai's earliest paintings follow the *bunjinga* styles of the early 19th century. He also worked in virtually all the styles and traditions associated with Kyōto: the YAMATO-E style; the RIMPA style of SŌTATSU and KŌRIN; the semifolk art of ŌTSU-E; and the style (or form) of *haiga*, sketchy pictures done to accompany HAIKU poems.

Tessai's best works belong to the current within *bunjinga* that was based on the paintings of late-Ming-dynasty (1368–1644) artists of Suzhou (Soochow) in Jiangsu (Kiangsu) Province in China and introduced to Japan by SAKAKI HYAKUSEN. Tessai tended to use rich colors, to portray evocative scenes of people enjoying nature, to include lively figures in the landscapes, and to illustrate literary themes or episodes from history and legend. He often portrayed the bodhisattva KANNON and other Buddhist subjects, sometimes combining them with Taoist and Confucian figures to symbolize the unity of East-Asian religious and philosophical traditions.

Tessai's late works are powerful compositions, some in brilliant colors and some in ink monochrome or ink with light touches of color. He was also a master of calligraphy. The largest collection of his works is that of the Kiyoshikōjin Seichōji, a Buddhist temple near Takarazuka, Hyōgo Prefecture.

Tomita Isao 冨田勲

(1932–). Composer and synthesizer player. Born in Tōkyō. A graduate of Keiō University, he began composing while still a student. One of the first to recognize the potential of the synthesizer, he began to write electronic arrangements of well-known classical music. His album *Tsuki no hikari* (1974, released in the US as *Snowflakes are Dancing*), which included a version of Debussy's *Clair de Lune,* was nominated for a Grammy Award. Tomita has done similar arrangements of works such as Mussorgsky's *Pictures at an Exhibition*, Stravinsky's *The Firebird*, and Holst's *The Planets,* contributing greatly to the acceptance of the synthesizer and of electronic music as a performance medium.

Tomita Keisen 冨田渓仙

(1879–1936). Japanese-style (NIHONGA) painter. Real name Tomita Shigegorō. Born in Hakata (now the city of Fukuoka), he first studied painting at the local KANŌ SCHOOL atelier. In 1896 he moved to Kyōto and became a pupil of the MARUYAMA-SHIJŌ SCHOOL painter Tsuji Kakō (1870–1931). Fascinated with the life and art of SENGAI GIBON (1750–1837), he took up the practice of the Zen-related arts, but it was the paintings of his contemporary, TOMIOKA TESSAI, that excited his interest in literati painting (BUNJINGA). When Tomita

exhibited his masterpiece *Ubune* (1912, Cormorant Fishing), he attracted the attention of YOKOYAMA TAIKAN and soon after joined the reorganized Nihon Bijutsuin (JAPAN FINE ARTS ACADEMY).

Tomita Tsuneo   富田常雄

(1904–67). Novelist. Born in Tōkyō; graduate of Meiji University. He was essentially a writer of popular novels, most of them set in the early years of the Meiji period (1868–1912). He won the Naoki Prize for *Irezumi* (1947, Tattoo) and *Men* (1948, Mask). Tomita is best known for his earlier novel *Sugata Sanshirō* (1942), the story of a young man who dedicates his life to JŪDŌ; it was filmed in 1943 by KUROSAWA AKIRA. Other works include *Benkei* (1951–55) and *Yawara* (1964–65, Jūdō).

tomobiki→rokuyō

Tomoe   巴

NŌ play. Author unknown. Classified as a *nibamme-mono* ("part-two play"), it is based on a story from the HEIKE MONOGATARI and is the only *nibamme-mono* in which the *shite* (main character) is a woman. In a field near the banks of Lake Biwa, a traveling Buddhist priest (the *waki* or subordinate character) encounters a woman (the *maejite* or main character at the beginning of a play) who requests that he pray for the dead. As the priest recites a sutra, the apparition of a woman warrior (the *nochijite* or main character at the end of a play) appears before him. She identifies herself as TOMOE GOZEN, warlike mistress of the warrior MINAMOTO NO YOSHINAKA, and relates that she was not permitted to commit suicide with her lover at the time of his defeat. Wielding a halberd, she demonstrates her courage with a battle dance and then disappears.

Tomoe Gozen   巴御前

(fl late 12th century). Legendary female warrior; concubine of MINAMOTO NO YOSHINAKA, commander of Minamoto forces in the earlier phases of the TAIRA-MINAMOTO WAR (1180–85). According to the 13th-century military romance HEIKE MONOGATARI, Tomoe Gozen accompanied Yoshinaka when he fled Kyōto in 1184. When Yoshinaka was in danger of being captured, Tomoe was urged to leave him lest he be embarrassed by the enemy's discovery that a woman was with him; she refused to go until she had taken an enemy head to prove that her prowess was equal to that of any man. She escaped and is said to have remarried or lived as a nun. Her exploits are recounted in an early-16th-century Nō play, *Tomoe*.

Tomogashima Channel   友ケ島水道

(Tomogashima Suidō). Strait between the northwestern tip of Wakayama Prefecture, central Honshū, and the island of AWAJISHIMA; also called the Kitan Strait. An important sea route joining Ōsaka Bay and the Kii Channel. Width: 4 km (2.5 mi).

Tomonaga Sanjūrō   朝永三十郎

(1871–1951). Philosopher and historian of philosophy. Born in Nagasaki Prefecture, he graduated from Tōkyō University and then studied in Europe (1909–13). He became a professor at Kyōto University in 1913. Studying under Raphael Koeber (1848–1923) in Japan and Wilhelm Windelband (1848–1915) in Europe, he concentrated on Kantian and Neo-Kantian philosophy. In opposition to 19th-century pantheism and naturalism, he considered the "philosophy of reason" that began with Kant to be the core of philosophy because of its rigorousness, critical power, and personalism. He offered his own interpretation of the historical development from Descartes to Kant, based on his method of critical consideration of the facts. His major works include *Kinsei ni okeru "ga" no jikaku shi* (1916).

Tomonaga Shin'ichirō   朝永振一郎

(1906–79). Theoretical physicist and corecipient of the 1965 Nobel Prize in physics. Known for his pioneering contributions in fundamental physics, including a theory that reconciled the theory of quantum electrodynamics with the special theory of relativity. Born in Tōkyō, he graduated from Kyōto University in 1929. Returning to Japan after studying in Germany with Werner Heisenberg, he based his theory on insights by YUKAWA HIDEKI. He received the Order of Culture in 1952. His publications include the textbook *Ryōshi rikigaku* (1952–53; tr *Quantum Mechanics*, 1962).

tomo no miyatsuko   伴造

Leader of a hereditary service corporation (*tomo* or *be*) that furnished labor, goods, and services to the YAMATO COURT during the 5th and 6th centuries. Many held the honorary cognomen (KABANE) *miyatsuko*, indicating a lower status than the cognomen *atai* (see KUNI NO MIYATSUKO). Some of the more prominent were the Ōtomo and the Mononobe, who performed military services, and the Imbe and Nakatomi, who performed religious functions. After the TAIKA REFORM of 645 some were granted the more prestigious cognomen of *muraji*, thereby becoming court nobles. Others were made low-ranking officials (*tomobe*) under the RITSURYŌ SYSTEM. See also UJI-KABANE SYSTEM.

Tomo no Yoshio→Ōtemmon Conspiracy

Ton'a   頓阿

(1289–1372). Classical (WAKA) poet, critic, apologist of the conservative poetic school, and Buddhist priest of the TENDAI SECT. His lay name was Nikaidō Sadamune. He was a disciple of NIJŌ TAMEYO, head of the dominant conservative Nijō poetic house. He came to be known—with the priests Keiun, Jōben, and YOSHIDA KENKŌ—as one of the Four Guardian Kings of Classical Poetry (Waka Shitennō) of his age. In 1365 he was called

upon to complete the compilation of the 19th imperial anthology (*chokusenshū*) of classical poetry, the *Shin shūishū* (New Collection of Gleanings).

Some 45 of his poems are included in various imperial anthologies. His personal collection is *Sōanshū* (Collection of the Hermit's Cottage). He was also the author of *Seiashō* (Notes of a Frog at the Bottom of a Well), completed circa 1360–64, and *Gumon kenchū* (Wise Answers to Foolish Questions), completed in 1363. Among his students were the statesman and RENGA poet NIJŌ YOSHIMOTO and the shōgun ASHIKAGA TAKAUJI.

Tonami   砺波[市]

City in western Toyama Prefecture, central Honshū. Tonami developed as a market town during the Edo period (1600–1868). Principal products are rice and tulip bulbs. Pop: 37,070.

Tonami Plain   砺波平野

(Tonami Heiya). Located in western Toyama Prefecture, central Honshū. Bordering the Sea of Japan, it consists of alluvial fans of the river Shōgawa and graben valleys to the east and west. A rice-producing area, the plain is also noted for tulip bulbs. The major city is Tonami. Area: approximately 400 sq km (160 sq mi).

tonarigumi   隣組

(neighbor groups). Smallest unit of general mobilization during World War II. Units of 10 to 15 households had been established in large cities in 1938 for fire fighting and civil defense. On 11 September 1940, by order of the Home Ministry, these were officially organized into a nationwide network of neighborhood groups (*rimpohan*, commonly called *tonarigumi*). Participation was compulsory. Each unit was collectively responsible for such activities as allocating government bonds, civil defense, public health, fire fighting, and rationing consumer goods. Like the Edo-period (1600–1868) GONINGUMI

Tomita Keisen These four two-panel folding screens are titled *Man'yō Spring and Autumn*; they reflect Tomita's interest in identifying and painting the plants that are mentioned in the *Man'yōshū*, an 8th-century poetry collection. 1936. Detail. Colors on silk. Each screen 171 × 185 cm. National Museum of Modern Art, Kyōto.

Tomonaga Shin'ichirō A theoretical physicist who was corecipient of the 1965 Nobel Prize for physics.

Tonami Plain This fertile plain in western Toyama Prefecture is known for both its rice and its tulips.

Tonegawa Susumu
The 1987 Nobel laureate in physiology and medicine.

tonkatsu This fried pork cutlet dish is usually served with shredded cabbage.

system, it was an effective means of social control. It was abolished in 1947. See also CHŌNAIKAI; NATIONAL SPIRITUAL MOBILIZATION MOVEMENT.

Tonari no Totoro   となりのトトロ

(My Neighbor Totoro). A 1988 animated film written and directed by MIYAZAKI HAYAO. Set in a farming village in the 1950s, the film centers on two young sisters living with their father while their mother is hospitalized. In the woods nearby lives a strange ghostlike being, invisible to adults, named Totoro, who befriends the children. The lyricism of the film makes it Miyazaki's most memorable work and a major achievement in Japanese animation, and the character Totoro has been adopted as a symbol of the conservation movement in the areas surrounding the metropolis of Tōkyō.

Tondabayashi   富田林[市]

City in southeastern Ōsaka Prefecture, central Honshū; 22 km (14 mi) southeast of Ōsaka. Its principal industries are spinning and the manufacture of bamboo and glass products. Agricultural products include eggplants, cucumbers, mandarin oranges, and strawberries. At the center of the city is a JINAIMACHI, constructed in 1560 as a temple town of the JŌDO SHIN SECT temple Kōshōji. The headquarters of PL KYŌDAN, a religious organization, was built here in 1954. Pop: 110,447.

tondenhei   屯田兵

(colonist militia). A term applied to soldiers recruited to open up and defend new farmland in Hokkaidō. In 1869 the Meiji government established the Hokkaidō Colonization Office (KAITAKUSHI) in Sapporo. In 1873 the government adopted a plan suggested by KURODA KIYOTAKA in which former *samurai* in the northern prefectures (many of whom had been unemployed since the Meiji Restoration of 1868) were helped to establish themselves in Hokkaidō. When the Colonization Office was abolished in 1882 and authority over the *tondenhei* transferred to the Army Ministry, more than 2,400 people had been resettled. As Russia's interest in the Far East became more visible around 1890, Japan intensified efforts to increase its presence and strengthen its defenses in Hokkaidō by recruiting some 40,000 people, commoners as well as former samurai. With an increased civilian population and the establishment of an army division in the area, the *tondenhei* system was abandoned in 1904.

Tone Canals   利根導水路

(Tone Dōsuiro). General name for a system of small canals that transport water from the river TONEGAWA to Tōkyō, Saitama, and Gumma prefectures for agricultural, home, and industrial use. The canals include the Saitama Canal, the Musashi Canal, and the Asaka Canal. The YAGISAWA DAM on the upper reaches of the Tonegawa is one of the dams supplying these canals.

Tonegawa   利根川

River in the Kantō region, central Honshū, originating in the ECHIGO MOUNTAINS, entering the Kantō Plain at the city of Maebashi, and flowing southeast into the Pacific Ocean at the city of Chōshi, Chiba Prefecture. It is the second longest river in Japan; the area of its drainage basin is the largest. Until the Edo period (1600–1868), the Tonegawa followed the course of what is now the EDOGAWA and emptied into Tōkyō Bay, but early in the period its course was artificially changed in order to prevent floods in the city of Edo (now Tōkyō) and to secure water for irrigation. Numerous dams have been constructed to meet the increasing demands for drinking and industrial water in the Tōkyō area. The area where the river originates is part of Jōshin'etsu Kōgen National Park. Length: 322 km (200 mi); area of drainage basin: 16,840 sq km (6,502 sq mi).

Tonegawa Susumu   利根川進

(1939–   ). Immunologist. Born in Aichi Prefecture. Graduate of Kyōto University. After receiving a doctorate from the University of California at San Diego, Tonegawa became a researcher at the Basel Institute of Immunology in Switzerland in 1971. In 1981 he was appointed professor of biology and researcher at the Center for Cancer Research at the Massachusetts Institute of Technology. Tonegawa discovered the gene rearrangement mechanism by which a limited number of genes are able to produce a vast number of antibodies, each responding to a specific antigen. He was awarded the Order of Culture in 1984 and in 1987 was the first Japanese recipient of the Nobel Prize in physiology and medicine.

Tonegawa zushi   利根川図志

Gazetteer compiled by Akamatsu Sōtan (1806–62), a native of Fukawa, Shimōsa Province (now Ibaraki Prefecture), consisting of six fascicles and printed in 1855. The book covers historical and scenic sites as well as noteworthy temples and shrines along the river TONEGAWA from its middle reaches to the town of Chōshi, where the river flows into the Pacific.

In writing the book, Akamatsu drew on many written sources. A map of the entire river, as well as illustrations—many of them by leading artists—of such features as temples, shrines, festivals, castle ruins, local products, and vegetation are provided. A new edition was published in 1938.

Tōnen Corporation   東燃[株]

(Tōnen; formerly Tōa Nenryō Kōgyō). Refining company producing various petrochemical products. The company was incorporated in 1939 with capital provided by 10 oil companies. In 1949 it concluded an agreement with the Standard Vacuum Oil Co, Ltd (now the Esso Eastern Co and Mobil Petroleum Co), covering capital, technology, oil supply, and sale of oil products. Since 1949 the company has come to engage solely in refining. Its products are sold through Esso Sekiyu KK and Mobil Sekiyu KK, while its materials for petrochemical products are processed by Tōnen Sekiyu Kagaku. The company has advanced into a wide range of business areas through the creation of subsidiaries and joint ventures. In 1959 it established Tōnen Tanker, which is engaged in crude oil transport, and in 1972, with Nichimo Co, Ltd, it established a sales company, Kygnus Sekiyu Co, Ltd. The company is the principal member of the Tōnen group. Annual sales for the year ending December 1990 totaled ¥663.3 billion (US $4.3 billion), and capitalization was ¥32.3 billion (US $211.0 million). Corporate headquarters are in Tōkyō.

toneri   舎人

Attendants who served the sovereign and members of the imperial family before the development of the RITSURYŌ SYSTEM in the course of the 7th century. Recruited from the sons of local chieftains, *toneri* remained loyal to their masters in times of crisis. In the JINSHIN DISTURBANCE of 672, attendants of Prince Ōama (later Emperor TEMMU) played a significant role in gaining victory for their master. Later, under the TAIHŌ CODE (701), *toneri* became minor bureaucrats.

Toneri, Prince   舎人親王

(676–735; Toneri Shinnō). Court official of the Nara period (710–794). The third son of Emperor TEMMU; his mother was Princess Niitabe, a daughter of Emperor TENJI. After establishment of the RITSURYŌ SYSTEM of government, a struggle developed between the imperial family and the aristocratic faction that controlled the Grand Council of State (DAJŌKAN), the central organ of the government. As a leader of the imperial party, Prince Toneri became increasingly influential. In 718 he was given the rank of *ippon*, the highest granted to members of the imperial family, and in 719 he became an adviser to Crown Prince Obito, the future Emperor SHŌMU. With the death of FUJIWARA NO FUHITO in 720, Toneri became administrator (*chidajōkanji*) of the Dajōkan. Following the rebellion and forced suicide of Prince Nagaya no Ō in 729 (see NAGAYA NO Ō, REBELLION OF), he helped arrange the elevation of the imperial consort (see KŌMYŌ, EMPRESS) to the rank of nonreigning empress (*kōgō*). Toneri was the chief compiler of the NIHON SHOKI (720), Japan's first official history (see also RIKKOKUSHI).

Tonghak Rebellion   東学党の乱

(J: Tōgakutō no Ran). Korean peasant uprising that was the immediate cause of the SINO-JAPANESE WAR OF 1894–1895. Leaders of the Tonghak (J: Tōgaku; Eastern Learning) religious cult rallied peasants and marched on the capital in 1893 to petition King KOJONG for reforms. The religious movement, formed as a counter to Sŏhak (J: Seigaku; Western Learning, i.e., Catholicism) in the mid-19th century, had been suppressed by Kojong's father, the TAEWŎN'GUN, during the 1860s. The 1893 uprising developed into a massive rebellion in the spring of 1894. Kojong turned to China for military aid. Chinese forces arrived in June 1894. Japanese troops also landed in June and a month later attacked Chinese troops, igniting the Sino-Japanese War. When the Tonghak rose again after the fall harvest, the Japanese army suppressed them. The Tonghak Rebellion provided Japan with a pretext to further its aggressive designs against the Korean nation. See also KOREA AND JAPAN.

tonkatsu   豚カツ

(pork cutlet). Fried pork dish of Western origin. It is prepared by dredging a slice of pork loin or tenderloin lightly in flour, dipping it in beaten egg, breading, and deep-frying. *Tonkatsu* is customarily served with shredded cabbage and dressed with a Japanese version of Worcestershire sauce.

Tōno   遠野[市]

City in southeastern Iwate Prefecture, northern Honshū. It developed as a castle town of the Nambu domain and as a distribution center for regional products. The chief occupation is rice farming. Apples, tobacco, and hops are also grown. Dairy farming has replaced horse breeding. Tōno is the setting for TŌNO MONOGATARI, a collection of local legends by YANAGITA KUNIO. Pop: 28,946.

tops A colorful selection of the many types of Japanese tops; some tops make humming sounds and some do acrobatics on a string.

Tōnomine 多武峰

Hill in the city of Sakurai, Nara Prefecture, central Honshū. On the southern slopes is the Danzan Shrine, known for its ornate architecture and dedicated to FUJIWARA NO KAMATARI. Height: 619 m (2,031 ft).

Tōno monogatari 遠野物語

(The Legends of Tōno). Book by the folklorist YANAGITA KUNIO (1875–1962). Published in 1910, it is considered a modern Japanese literary and folklore classic. Set in the mountain village of Tōno in remote Iwate Prefecture, this volume represents Yanagita's most dramatic attempt to recreate in literary form the psychic landscape of the Japanese peasantry.

Tōno monogatari taps the most vigorous stream of Japanese oral narrative tradition, the legends (*densetsu*), which were more intimately bound up with daily village life and thought than the generally stereotyped FOLKTALES. The book is rich in the familiar Japanese imagery of festivals, animals, and mountain people. It offers a vision of a typical villager growing up in a world full of dangers from invisible forces and from malevolent creatures shuttling between the human and animal kingdoms.

Tonomura Shigeru 外村繁

(1902–61). Novelist. Born in Shiga Prefecture; graduate of Tōkyō University. He started a literary magazine with several classmates while at the university. He gained recognition with a trilogy composed of *Kusakada* (1935–38); *Ikada* (1954–56), winner of the Noma Prize; and *Hanaikada* (1957–58). These three works trace the saga of his family as well-established merchants since the mid-18th century. His later works are written in an autobiographical style. Other works include "Rakujitsu no kōkei" (1960), a short story, and *Miotsukushi* (1960, Channel Markers), a novel that won the Yomiuri Literary Prize.

Tonoshō 土庄[町]

Town in the western part of the island of SHŌDOSHIMA; part of Kagawa Prefecture, Shikoku. A base for ferryboats connecting Honshū and Shikoku, the town has numerous inns and shops catering to tourists. There are also spinning and stone-quarrying industries. Olive trees are cultivated on nearby hills. Pop: 20,191.

Tō no Tsuneyori 東常縁

(1401–84). Also known as Tōyashū. Classical (WAKA) poet and warrior. Tsuneyori was a key figure in the history of the esoteric ritual of "transmitting the secrets of the KOKINSHŪ" (KOKIN DENJU), especially to the poet SŌGI. His works include *Tōyashū kikigaki*, which records the teachings of Gyokō and SHŌTETSU, and *Tsuneyorishū*, a collection of his own poems.

ton'ya →toiya

tōnyū 豆乳

(soy milk). White, milklike liquid made from soybeans. *Tōnyū* is made by grinding soybeans that have been soaked in water, adding more water, and then heating. The resulting milk is strained through cloth. Soy milk also represents an intermediate stage in the manufacture of TŌFU. It is rich in protein and iron and has long been consumed in Japan as a health drink; however, production and sales increased markedly during the 1980s as a result of the growing public interest in health foods. It is available plain or in such flavors as orange and coffee.

tō on 唐音

(the Tang [T'ang] pronunciation). One of the several varieties of *on* readings of Chinese characters (KANJI) as used in Japan. *On* readings are Japanese approximations of the way the characters were pronounced in Chinese. For any one character there may be two or three possible *on* readings (reflecting the Chinese pronunciations of different periods and different regions). *Tō on* is a broad category that includes pronunciations introduced to Japan from southern areas of China over several centuries after the Tang dynasty (618–907). The *tō* (Tang) of the name refers to China as a whole rather than to the dynasty. These pronunciations are much closer to the pronunciation of modern Chinese than the earlier KAN ON (the Han pronunciation—i.e., pronunciations introduced during the Tang dynasty) or the still older GO ON (the Wu pronunciation). *Tō on* pronunciations are found mostly in Zen technical terms and in a few names of Chinese customs and artifacts from the Song (Sung; 960–1279), Yuan (Yüan; 1279–1368), and Ming (1368–1644) dynasties. See ON READINGS.

Topaz Relocation Center トパーズ収容所

(Topāzu Shūyōjo). Wartime relocation facility for Japanese Americans from California; located near Delta, Millard County, Utah. In operation from 11 September 1942 until 31 October 1945, it held a maximum of 8,130 inmates at any one time; a total of 11,212 persons were confined there. See also JAPANESE AMERICANS, WARTIME RELOCATION OF; WAR RELOCATION AUTHORITY.

topography →Japan

Toppan Moore Co, Ltd トッパン・ムーア[株]

(Toppan Mūa). Subsidiary company of TOPPAN PRINTING CO, LTD, specializing in business forms and office equipment. Incorporated in 1965. The company has joint ventures with Toppan Printing Co and Moore Incorporated, Ltd, in Canada. Sales for the fiscal year ending March 1990 totaled ¥130.4 billion (US $851.8 million). Capitalization was ¥7.5 billion (US $49.0 million) in the same year. Headquarters are in Tōkyō.

Toppan Printing Co, Ltd 凸版印刷[株]

(Toppan Insatsu). A comprehensive printing company. Toppan was incorporated in 1900 by technical experts originally with the Printing Bureau of the Ministry of Finance. It is the second largest printing company in Japan, after DAI NIPPON PRINTING CO, LTD. The company provides many services, including the printing of securities, publications, and commercial materials and the manufacture of packaging, interior decorating materials, and electronic precision components. Sales for the fiscal year ending March 1991 totaled ¥846.2 billion (US $6.2 billion), of which general printing accounted for 50 percent; packaging, 26 percent; publications printing, 20 percent; and securities printing, 4 percent. The company was capitalized at ¥90.1 billion (US $656.7 million) in the same year. Headquarters are in Tōkyō.

tops 独楽

(*koma*). For centuries the top has been a popular toy in Japan. Japanese tops, like their counterparts in other cultures, may be made of wood, bamboo, seashell, or metal, and come in a variety of shapes and sizes. They are spun either by hand or with a string. In the 8th century tops were introduced to Japan from China via Koma, one of the Japanese names for the Korean kingdom of Koguryō (hence the term *koma*). Originally tops were used for entertainment at court functions or as a means of diversion by the nobility. By the 17th century, however, the top had become a form of amusement for the common people and later developed as a children's toy. The shape of the Japanese top depends on the material used and where it is made. Many have holes cut or bored in them to produce a humming sound when spun. In Japan, the Hakata *koma* from the Hakata region of Kyūshū has been especially popular.

Topy Industries, Ltd トピー工業[株]

(Topī Kōgyō). Metal-processing company, whose products include presses and struc-

torii This *torii* at Tsushima Shrine, in Aichi Prefecture, is in the *myōjin* style, the type most commonly seen today.

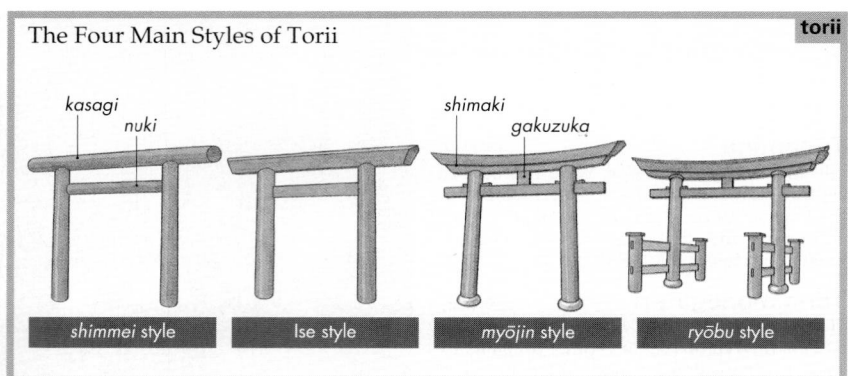

The Four Main Styles of Torii

kasagi
nuki
shimaki
gakuzuka

shimmei style · Ise style · *myōjin* style · *ryōbu* style

---

tural steel. Incorporated in 1934. It is a world leader in the production of wheels for cars, trucks, buses, and off-road vehicles and undercarriage components for construction and earth-moving machinery. It has a strong research and development program and is expanding overseas production facilities in the United States, the United Kingdom, and Taiwan. Annual sales for the fiscal year ending March 1991 were ¥180.3 billion (US $1.3 billion), and the company was capitalized at ¥14.6 billion (US $106.4 million). Headquarters are in Tōkyō.

toraijin → kikajin

Toranomon Incident   虎ノ門事件

(Toranomon Jiken). Assassination attempt on the life of the then prince regent Hirohito. On the morning of 27 December 1923, Namba Daisuke (1899–1924) attempted to assassinate Prince Regent Hirohito, who was on his way to open the new Diet session. The incident took place at the Toranomon intersection in Tōkyō. Namba's attempt was primarily motivated by leftist ideology and a strong desire to avenge the execution of KŌTOKU SHŪSUI, who had been implicated in the HIGH TREASON INCIDENT OF 1910. He was also angered by the brutal slaying of Koreans and Japanese socialists and anarchists in the aftermath of the TŌKYŌ EARTHQUAKE OF 1923. Justice officials carefully investigated Namba's motives—throughout he maintained it was a rational act—and announced to the public that he was insane (officials secretly held the view that Namba was rational); nevertheless, after a closed trial, he was sentenced to death on 13 November 1924 and executed two days later.

The new government of YAMAMOTO GONNOHYŌE took responsibility for the incident and resigned; other officials followed its example. The Toranomon Incident was cited by officials in the Justice and Home ministries as a compelling reason for the passage of the PEACE PRESERVATION LAW OF 1925.

Tora san   寅さん

Name of the main character in a long-running film series centering on the adventures of a carefree wanderer, always played by ATSUMI KIYOSHI. The series is popularly referred to by the name of this character; however, the formal series title is *Otoko wa tsurai yo* (It's Tough Being a Man). The first film in the series was released in 1969, and two new films have been released almost every year since; YAMADA YŌJI has written and directed all but two of them. Tora san, always well meaning but often misguided, travels from festival to fair as an itinerant hawker of trifling goods. The plots invariably involve

Tora san's kindhearted efforts to help out others and his love for a woman he can never attain. The series humorously shows how trying it can be to live up to society's expectations. In 1991 the 43rd film in the series was released.

Tōray Industries, Inc   東レ[株]

(Tōre). Largest manufacturer of synthetic fibers in Japan; also produces plastics, chemicals, and pharmaceuticals. Incorporated in 1926 as Tōyō Rayon Co, Ltd, to manufacture rayon, it was a subsidiary of MITSUI & CO, LTD. The company assumed its present name in 1970. In 1951 the company started nylon production with technology from E. I. DuPont de Nemours & Co of the United States. In 1964 it started producing Toraylon (an acrylic fiber) using its own technology. Since 1970 the company has diversified its operations into new business areas. Production of carbon fibers began in 1971, and in 1985 Tōray's natural interferon-B became the world's first interferon approved for commercial production. During the fiscal year ending March 1991, sales were ¥585.4 billion (US $4.3 billion), and the company was capitalized at ¥94.6 billion (US $689.5 million). Headquarters are in Tōkyō.

Toride   取手[市]

City in southern Ibaraki Prefecture, central Honshū, on the river Tonegawa. Now a commuter suburb of Tōkyō, Toride flourished from early times as a river port and a post-station town. Pop: 81,665.

torii   鳥居

A gatelike structure placed at key points in a SHINTŌ shrine precinct or path leading to the shrine and functioning both as a gate marking the sacred space and as a symbol of the shrine. Although *torii* were originally made of wood, since the Heian period (794–1185) many have been made of stone, and materials such as copper, porcelain, and concrete may also be employed. The basic structure of a *torii* is two columns, on top of which is placed a top rail (the *kasagi*); a little below the top rail is a second horizontal rail penetrating both columns (the *nuki*). There are four main styles of *torii* construction. The *shimmei*-style *torii* has a log for the top rail and a second rail that penetrates but does not protrude beyond the columns. The Ise-style *torii* uses a pentagonal top rail and a second rail that also does not protrude beyond the columns. The above-mentioned *torii* use straight members with no curves. Although there are variations, the style of *torii* most often seen today is the *myōjin* style. Its columns lean somewhat inward from the bases, the top rail curves gently upward toward the ends, and below the top rail there is a secondary top rail called a *shimaki*. Between this and the second rail (*nuki*)—at the center of both—is placed a vertical strut (*gakuzuka*), on which is hung a tablet (*gaku*) with the name of the shrine.

The next most common style after the *myōjin* is the *ryōbu* style. As its other name, *yotsuashi* (four-legged style), indicates, there are four posts located in the front and back of the columns, to which they are tied by penetrating horizontal ties. See also SHRINES.

Torii Kiyohiro   鳥居清広

(fl 1751–63). Torii-school printmaker. His date of birth is unrecorded; he is believed to have died young. Since the *Torii ga keifu* (a Torii family record) reports Kiyohiro's presence in the Torii atelier in 1763, it seems certain that he was at one time a pupil of TORII KIYOMASU II. However, he appears to have been most strongly influenced by TORII KIYOMITSU I, who was Kiyomasu's son and the third titular head of the Torii school. Kiyohiro's art reveals a dependence on that of Kiyomitsu and on that of his contemporary, ISHIKAWA TOYONOBU. His special genius was in the freshness of his compositions and the youthful character of his designs. He was also a master of *abuna-e* (risqué pictures) and illustrated several novelettes. He worked in either two-block or three-block color prints.

Torii Kiyomasu I   鳥居清倍1世

(fl 1697–1720s). Torii-school printmaker who specialized in Edo (now Tōkyō) KABUKI theatrical prints. No firm genealogical connection has ever been proven between TORII KIYONOBU I, the founder of the Torii school, and Kiyomasu I. According to one theory, these artists are one and the same person; according to other theories, Kiyomasu is a brother or son of Kiyonobu. It is possible that Kiyomasu and his namesake, TORII KIYOMASU II, originally represented a branch of the Torii family in Edo distinct from the Ōsaka-Kyōto branch headed by Kiyonobu and his father.

The earliest signed art by Kiyomasu I is a small group of single-sheet prints commemorating kabuki performances, dating from 1679 to 1704. His output was large and, along with hand-colored single sheets, he is known to have designed playbills and EMA (votive pictures). In addition, a number of unsigned illustrated books dating from 1697 to 1710 contain illustrations recently attributed to Kiyomasu I in collaboration with Kiyonobu I.

Torii Kiyomasu II   鳥居清倍2世

(1706–63). Torii-school printmaker specializing in Edo (now Tōkyō) KABUKI theatrical prints. Possibly the second titular head of the Torii school. Some critics believe that Kiyomasu II and TORII KIYONOBU II are the same person, but this theory does not conform with genealogical or artistic evidence. He began work in the mid-1720s designing picture books, one in collaboration with Kiyonobu II. His large output also included hand-colored prints of actors, and in later years, two-color block prints. His work is rather uneven, particularly in the hard lines of these later prints, but his earlier prints are very fine in a quiet, subdued way. His son TORII KIYOMITSU I became the third titular head of the school.

Torii Kiyomitsu I 鳥居清満1世

(1735–85). Torii-school painter and printmaker who specialized in Edo KABUKI actor prints. The third titular head of the Torii school. Born in Edo (now Tōkyō) at Naniwachō, he studied *ukiyo-e* under his father, TORII KIYOMASU II. Kiyomitsu produced actor pictures, kabuki placards, and kabuki posters for the Edo stage. He also designed a variety of illustrated books from the 1760s to the 1780s. Most of his single-sheet prints were done during the period 1740–65. Toward the end of this period he began to produce single sheets utilizing four or more colors printed from blocks, presaging the magnificent full-color prints of Suzuki HARUNOBU in 1765.

Torii Kiyonaga 鳥居清長

(1752–1815). Torii-school print designer and painter. Fourth titular head of the Torii school and last major Torii artist. His origin is uncertain. In the early Meiwa era (1764–72) he became a pupil of TORII KIYOMITSU I, the third head of the school.

The earliest extant works by Kiyonaga date from 1770. More than 1,000 works—color prints, picture-book illustrations, EMA (votive pictures), and paintings—by this gifted master survive and can be divided into three distinct periods. The first, ca 1770–80, is confined chiefly to actor prints of the KABUKI theater as well as illustrated books. In this formative period his style was influenced by his mentor Kiyomitsu and by the work of Suzuki HARUNOBU, KITAO SHIGEMASA, and ISODA KORYŪSAI. During his second period, 1781–85, he developed the "Kiyonaga beauty" in portraits of statuesque women, which exerted a strong influence on all artists toward the end of the 18th century. Around 1787 Kiyonaga is said to have given up illustrations of women, returning to the actor pictures that were the trademark of his school. Kiyonaga's art was part of a trend toward realism: the actor studies display an interest in portraiture, and his depictions of women employed Western perspective for backgrounds and landscape.

Torii Kiyonobu I 鳥居清信1世

(1664?–1729). *Ukiyo-e* painter and printmaker who specialized in illustrations for the Edo (now Tōkyō) KABUKI stage from 1697 to around 1727; considered the founder of the TORII SCHOOL. He was the son of Torii Kiyomoto (1645?–1702), a former actor who turned to sign painting for kabuki theaters. According to the *Torii ga keifu* (a Torii family record), he was born in Ōsaka in 1664, moved to Edo with his father in 1687, and settled at Naniwachō.

His earliest surviving woodblock works are two signed, illustrated books dated 1697. The prints and illustrated books dated from 1698 onward consist largely of scenes from plays and depictions of actors. His figures are round and full and drawn with a heavy curvilinear line, similar to that used in poster paintings. His signed masterpieces include two *orihon* (folding albums): *Fūryū yomo byōbu*, two volumes of illustrations of actors of the past and present, and *Keisei ehon*, a book of courtesan portraits, both published in 1700. Two copies of the *Fūryū yomo byōbu* survive, one at the Museum of Fine Arts, Boston, and the other at the Riccar Art Museum, Tōkyō. The only surviving copy

of *Keisei ehon* is owned by the Art Institute of Chicago. A number of artists were influenced by him, including OKUMURA MASANOBU and the KAIGETSUDŌ SCHOOL artists.

Torii Kiyonobu II 鳥居清信2世

(fl 1725–60?). Torii-school printmaker who specialized in Edo (now Tōkyō) KABUKI actor prints. According to one persistent theory, Kiyonobu II is the same artist as TORII KIYOMASU II. A more likely theory suggests that he was a son of TORII KIYONOBU I and adopted the name upon his father's retirement in 1727 or death in 1729. Kiyonobu II is known to have collaborated on a picture book with Kiyomasu II some time in the mid-1720s, proof that there were two independent artists. He produced a number of single-sheet prints of actors and theatrical scenes, hand-painted or printed from two blocks. One good surviving example of his work is a small, hand-colored print showing Ichikawa Danjūrō II as Soga no Jūrō Sukenari in a 1733 play.

Torii Pass 鳥居峠

(Torii Tōge). Located between the valley KISODANI and the Matsumoto Basin, western Nagano Prefecture, central Honshū. It was well traveled in ancient days as a pass on the highway NAKASENDŌ. Altitude: 1,197 m (3,927 ft).

Torii Ryūzō 鳥居竜蔵

(1870–1953). Archaeologist and anthropologist. Born in what is now Tokushima Prefecture. Interested in anthropology, archaeology, and history from an early age, Torii became a pupil of noted anthropologist TSUBOI SHŌGORŌ in 1892. Though Torii did not receive a formal college education, he went on to become head of the anthropology department at Tōkyō University. His studies covered a wide range of fields, including anthropology, folklore, and linguistics. Between 1895 and 1910, Torii led research expeditions to the Liaodong (Liaotung) Peninsula, the Yalu Basin, Taiwan, the Kuril Islands, Okinawa, Manchuria, Mongolia, Korea, and Sakhalin. During his later years he engaged in studies of the culture of the

Liao (907–1125) and Jin (Chin; 1125–1234) dynasties. From around 1917, he studied the cultures of the Jōmon (ca 10,000 BC–ca 300 BC) and Yayoi (ca 300 BC–ca AD 300) periods of Japan and wrote numerous treatises on these two periods. Torii lectured at Yanjing (Yenching) University in Beijing (Peking) from 1939 to 1951.

Torii school 鳥居派

(Toriiha). School of UKIYO-E print designers. The designing of theatrical billboards, programs, illustrated books, and prints for the Edo (now Tōkyō) KABUKI stage was a monopoly of the Torii school for most of the 18th century. Beginning in the late Genroku era (1688–1704) the Torii family of artists established a standard in the representation of kabuki subject matter that was to influence *ukiyo-e* for decades to come.

TORII KIYONOBU I has traditionally been regarded as the founder of the school and was its first titular head, but at least two artists using the Torii name preceded him. His father, Torii Kiyomoto (1645?–1702), a native of Ōsaka, began in 1692 to design *kamban-e* (theatrical posters) for the Ichimuraza kabuki theater. Another master, Torii Kiyotaka (dates unknown), was a teacher of Kiyonobu I and the "veteran artist" of the Torii school. He may have been part of an earlier branch of the Torii family in Edo. TORII KIYOMASU I may also have descended from this branch of the family.

Following the death of Kiyonobu I, a second artist of the school adopted the name Kiyonobu (see TORII KIYONOBU II), but he did not receive the school's titular mantle. TORII KIYOMASU II, Kiyonobu's son-in-law, is said to have received this honor. The school's third titular head was TORII KIYOMITSU I, the son of Kiyomasu II.

Three years after Kiyomitsu's death one of his best students, TORII KIYONAGA, officially became the fourth titular head of the school. The fifth head, Kiyomitsu's grandson Shōnosuke (1788–1868), assumed the name Kiyomitsu II. The Torii family of artists has continued to the present.

Torii Kiyonaga *July Evening,* from *The Twelve Months in the Gay Quarters of Shinagawa.* 1780s. Woodblock print. 38 × 51 cm. Honolulu Academy of Arts.

Torii Ryūzō A self-taught anthropologist, Torii was known for taking an interdisciplinary approach to research.

Torishima
1 Surrounded by steep cliffs, the island of Torishima is still an active volcano.
2 A pair of short-tailed albatross (*Diomedea albatrus*). Designated as a protected species, this albatross finds its home on Torishima.

Torii Shinjirō 鳥井信治郎

(1879–1962). Industrialist. Founder of SUNTORY, LTD. Born in Ōsaka. After a period of apprenticeship, Torii established Torii Shōten, the forerunner of Suntory, in 1899. Based on his success in producing Akadama port wine in 1907, Torii devoted his efforts to the domestic production of whiskey; he started marketing whiskey under the Suntory brand in 1929. After World War II, with the appearance of Torys, an inexpensive whiskey developed by the firm, Torii's position as leader of the Japanese whiskey industry became indisputable.

Torii Sosen 鳥居素川

tōrō nagashi On the final night of the Bon Festival, lanterns are floated toward the sea in the town of Kizukuri, Aomori Prefecture.

(1867–1928). Journalist. Real name Torii Teruo. Born in Kumamoto Prefecture. He studied at the Doitsu Kyōkai Gakkō in Tōkyō. In 1890 he joined NIHON, a newspaper noted for its nationalistic outlook, and be-

Torii Shinjirō

came known for his trenchant criticisms of government policy. In 1897 he changed to the newspaper *Ōsaka asahi shimbun*. His editorials were influential in promoting various democratic movements in the Taishō period (1912–26). In 1918 he was accused by the TERAUCHI MASATAKE cabinet of having violated the PRESS LAW OF 1909 and was forced to resign (see ŌSAKA ASAHI HIKKA INCIDENT). In 1919, along with other staff members who had left, he started the short-lived newspaper *Taishō nichinichi shimbun* and then withdrew from journalism.

Torii Yōzō 鳥居耀蔵

(1804?–74). City commissioner (MACHI BUGYŌ) of Edo (now Tōkyō), 1841–44. Architect of the BANSHA NO GOKU, the shogunate's crackdown on scholars of WESTERN LEARNING in 1839. Yōzō was appointed METSUKE (inspector) in 1837 and dealt harshly with an uprising in Ōsaka caused by a rice shortage (see TEMPŌ FAMINE; ŌSHIO HEIHACHIRŌ). Yōzō also played a major role in the TEMPŌ REFORMS before his fall from power in 1844.

Torii Yuki 鳥居ユキ

(1943–). Fashion designer. Real name Torii Yukiko. Born in Tōkyō. Torii graduated from Bunka Gakuin College. Her designs are often layered and make use of intricately patterned fabrics. In addition to Western-style clothes, she also designs *kimono* and handbags.

Torikaebaya monogatari とりかへばや物語

(A Tale of Changing Roles). Court narrative of the late Heian period (794–1185) whose extant texts are revisions from the early Kamakura period (1185–1333). Authorship

is unknown, but it is certain to have been the work of a lady familiar with court life. In *Torikaebaya monogatari* a court minister decides to allow his strident daughter to be initiated into court life with all the rank, role, and public responsibility of a man. Likewise, he permits his son to assume the role of lady companion in the service of the heir apparent (who is in this case a girl). Both children marry in their adopted social roles, which in the daughter's case creates inevitable difficulties. Conflicts are resolved when the children restore themselves to the social roles appropriate to their respective sexes; after a brief interlude in seclusion, each finds greater happiness in the life begun by the other. They end up switching lives, large families accrue to each, and all ends in conviviality.

tori no ichi 酉の市

(festival of the rooster). Festival held on the days of the rooster (*tori*; see JIKKAN JŪNISHI) in November at various Shintō shrines of the type called Ōtori shrines. The festival is also called *otorisama* and *tori no machi*. The first "day of the rooster" in the month (the day recurs in 12-day cycles) is called *ichi no tori*, the second *ni no tori*, and the third, if there is one that year, *san no tori*. It is thought that there will be many fires in a year that has a *san no tori*. The chief deity in Ōtori shrines was originally venerated by warriors as the god of success in war, but it later became the god of good luck in general (*tori* is a homophone for the verb "to fetch"). On the day of the festival, vendors line up on both sides of the street in front of the shrine, selling various charms such as *kumade* (rakes, to "rake in" fortune) decorated with imitation gold coins and the like.

Torishima 鳥島

Volcanic island approximately 280 km (175 mi) south of Hachijōjima of the IZU ISLANDS. Torishima is the southernmost of the Izu Islands. It was settled in 1886, but the population was killed in a volcanic eruption in 1902. A meteorological observatory was later established here, but renewed volcanic activity in 1965 forced the evacuation of the staff and the island became uninhabited. It is the home of an endangered species of albatross. Area: 4.5 sq km (1.7 sq mi).

tōrō → lanterns

tōrō nagashi 灯籠流し

(lantern floating). Customary practice that marks the end of the BON FESTIVAL, a Buddhist observance welcoming home the spirits of the dead. Today *tōrō nagashi* takes place on 15 or 16 August. Small paper lanterns containing lighted candles are floated on rivers or the sea to illuminate the way for the ancestral spirits as they depart.

Toro site 登呂遺跡

(Toro *iseki*). Archaeological site of the Late Yayoi period (ca 100–ca 300) located in the Toro district of the city of Shizuoka, Shizuoka Prefecture; discovered in 1943. Excavations in 1947–50 yielded the remains of 12 pit houses surrounded by wooden stakes, two storehouses, and more than 40 paddies. The dwellings had oval floor plans and central hearths. An excavation in 1965 revealed a primitive dam for irrigation. Recovered artifacts include YAYOI POTTERY and a variety of wooden household implements. Also found were a bronze bracelet, glass beads, baskets, nets, and fishhooks made of bone. These findings have enlarged our understanding of YAYOI CULTURE and in particular the life of Japan's earliest agricultural people. See also KARAKO SITE.

tortoiseshell ware　　　　鼈甲細工

(*bekkō-zaiku*). Handcrafted items made from the shells of tropical and subtropical tortoises. Japanese tortoiseshell was harvested in the seas off Nagasaki and Kagoshima prefectures and Okinawa in the past; today it is mostly imported.

Tortoiseshell, or *bekkō*, is often processed into uniform thickness and pieced together into the desired shape or design. The pieces are soaked in water for softening, layered, then shaped over wet wood and pressed between iron molds heated to between 100° and 150°C (212°–300°F). It can also be softened by heat before being molded into shape. These techniques are uniquely Japanese.

Tortoiseshell ware was very popular in Japan during the 17th and 18th centuries, especially for hair ornaments (see KANZASHI). Although demand is considerably reduced tortoiseshell continues to be used for eyeglass frames, necklaces, and earrings. In May 1991 the Ministry of International Trade and Industry announced its intention to prohibit the import of the shells of the hawksbill tortoise (*Eretmochelys imbricata*)—the source of tortoiseshell of the finest quality—after July 1993, which will effectively put an end to the *bekkō-zaiku* industry in Japan.

torts　　　　不法行為

(*fuhō kōi*). The body of private law defining the scope of a person's legal interests protected from unjustified interference by others and granting the injured person a right to compensation from the person responsible for the harm. Articles 709–724 of Japan's CIVIL CODE deal with torts and have remained unchanged since the code's promulgation in 1898. However, judicial interpretation of their content (especially of articles 709 and 710, which provide the basis of tort doctrine) has undergone considerable development because of the increase in environmental tort litigation.

There are three elements of tort liability in Japan today: substantial injury to a protected interest; proof of the defendant's intent or negligence; and legal causation. There has been a significant relaxation of the requirements for proof of negligence and of causation in recent environmental cases (see ENVIRONMENTAL LAW). Tort law protection has been extended to implied legal "interests" as well as explicit rights, to psychological and emotional harm, and to privacy and reputation.

Tosa　　　　土佐〔市〕

City in central Kōchi Prefecture, Shikoku. Takaoka, its central district, has long been known for its handmade Japanese paper (*washi*). Local products are rice, vegetables, *igusa* (rushes for *tatami* mats), bonito, and *katsuobushi* (dried bonito). Pop: 31,564.

Tosa Bay　　　　土佐湾

(Tosa Wan). Inlet of the Pacific Ocean, in southern Kōchi Prefecture, southern Shikoku. Extends from MUROTOZAKI, a cape in the east, to ASHIZURIMISAKI, a cape in the west. It is a major fishing area. Ports along the bay include Muroto, Kōchi, Susaki, and Shimizu.

Tosa dog　　　　土佐犬

(Tosa *inu*). The Japanese fighting dog, developed in Kōchi Prefecture (formerly Tosa

Province) after the Meiji period (1868–1912). The breed was formed through crossbreeding between the indigenous big-game-hunting dogs and imported large breeds. Throughout history DOGFIGHTING has been very popular in the Tosa area, and in order to increase body size and fighting ability, the "bloods" of larger foreign breeds (bulldog, mastiff, Great Dane, etc) were introduced. The Tosa dog is a very powerful, aggressive, mastifflike dog with a large stout body, pendulous ears, and a slender, stretched tail. The coat is short and brown with a more darkly colored muzzle. In dogfighting, dogs are divided into ranks, depending on ability and weight, much as *sumō* wrestlers are ranked.

Tosa domain　　　　土佐藩

(Tosa *han*). Also called Kōchi domain. Edo-period (1600–1868) domain that extended over all of Tosa Province; present-day Kōchi Prefecture. Granted in 1603 to YAMANOUCHI KAZUTOYO, who received the status of TOZAMA (outside vassal), the province had its administrative center in the castle town of Kōchi. In the late Edo period the domain supported the MOVEMENT FOR UNION OF COURT AND SHOGUNATE and later contributed to the return of power to the emperor (TAISEI HŌKAN). OMOTEDAKA (estimated annual production of rice): 240,000 KOKU (1 *koku* = 180 liters or 5 US bushels).

Tosaka Jun　　　　戸坂潤

(1900–1945). Educator and philosopher. Born in Tōkyō, he graduated from Kyōto University, where he studied philosophy. Early in his career he came under the influence of MIKI KIYOSHI, but he later turned from Miki's Neo-Kantianism to dialectical materialism, emphasizing the social responsibility of scholarship. In 1931 he joined the faculty of Hōsei University in Tōkyō but was dismissed in 1934 for allegedly harboring unsafe ideas. From 1932 to 1938 Tosaka was the guiding force behind the Association for the Study of Materialism (Yuibutsuron Kenkyūkai), which he founded to promote the scientific study of social phenomena. He was arrested in 1938 under the PEACE PRESERVATION LAW OF 1925 and died in prison. In his book *Kagakuron* (1935, On Science), he attempted to formulate a unitary philosophy that embraced the world of the natural and social sciences.

Tosa mizuki　　　　土佐水木

(winter, or flowering, hazel). *Corylopsis spicata.* A deciduous tree of the witch-hazel family (Hamamelidaceae) that grows wild in the limestone coast regions of Kōchi Prefecture (formerly Tosa Province) in Shikoku and elsewhere. It is also grown as an ornamental. Its height is about 2–3 meters (about 7–10 ft); leaves are alternate, broad, and

oval. Bell-shaped, creamy yellow, five-petaled flowers with red stamens bloom in drooping clusters in spring.

A similar plant is the Hyūga *mizuki* (*C. pauciflora*), a deciduous shrub that grows wild in mountainous regions of central Honshū and is also cultivated as an ornamental. It has thin branches and small leaves. Vivid yellow flowers grow in clusters of two or three. See also WITCH HAZEL.

Tosa nikki　　　　土佐日記

(tr *The Tosa Diary*, 1969). Also called *Tosa no nikki.* The first important work of NIKKI BUNGAKU (diary literature), written in 935 by KI NO TSURAYUKI. The diary describes the return to Kyōto, the national capital, by the governor of Tosa, Ki no Tsurayuki himself, as told by a woman in his entourage. Tsurayuki's use of a fictionalized female narrator distinguishes this diary from those of his male contemporaries. At the time, male aristocrats tended to confine themselves to rather banal, official diaries written in the hybrid form of Chinese known as HENTAI KAMBUN; only women were allowed to exploit the expressive potential of the "inferior" native idiom (see KANA). By choosing the point of view of a woman, Tsurayuki broadened the possible range of content in his diary. The female observer and narrator he created writes movingly of the sad departure of the governor, the grief she feels over her daughter's death, the dangers (pirates, storms) of the voyage by boat, and the joy of approaching the capital. Fifty-seven WAKA poems mark the high points of the journey. Tsurayuki's decision to write in Japanese influenced later writers, as did his use of a fictionalized narrator in a diary.

Tosa school　　　　土佐派

(Tosaha). School of painting that specialized in the native Japanese YAMATO-E style from the early 15th century to the late 19th century. Tosa-school painters worked primarily for the imperial court and specialized in courtly themes such as scenes from classical literature, especially the TALE OF GENJI. The Tosa style was characterized by a fine, delicate line, great attention to detail, lavish use of colors, and somewhat flat, decorative composition.

The Tosa family genealogy established in the Edo period (1600–1868) traces the lineage of the school to the 11th-century painter Fujiwara no Motomitsu. Reliable historical evidence of the use of the Tosa name by a painter begins in 1406, when a document refers to the painter Fujiwara no Yukihiro as Tosa Shōgen; Shōgen was one of his official titles, and Tosa referred to his position as governor of that province (now Kōchi Prefecture).

Tosa dog Bred from native and foreign stock, the Tosa dog is used for dogfighting and ranked in a system resembling that of *sumō* wrestling. The fighting dog pictured wears the symbols of a *yokozuna* (grand champion).

Tosa mizuki The nearly stalkless flowers of the deciduous Tosa *mizuki*, which grows wild in alkaline soils, bloom in drooping clusters before the leaves come out in spring.

Tōshōdaiji Statues of the Buddha Rushana (right) and the bodhisattva Kannon (left) are visible through the doors of this temple's main hall, which have been opened for the annual moon-viewing rites.

Yukihiro's father, Fujiwara no Yukimitsu, had held the position of *edokoro azukari* (superintendent of the imperial painting bureau), a post that became virtually hereditary in the Tosa family. The family's prestige reached its height under Tosa Mitsunobu (1434?–1525?), who is especially well known for his EMAKIMONO (illustrated handscrolls).

Mitsunobu's son Mitsushige (1496–1559) was less able than his father, and the family's status began to decline. In 1569 Mitsushige's heir, Mitsumoto (ca 1530–69), was killed in battle, and the leadership of the family and the position of *edokoro azukari* was inherited by the younger son or pupil Mitsuyoshi (1539–1613). Somewhat later Mitsuyoshi fled the capital and the post of *edokoro azukari* passed to the Kanō family (see KANŌ SCHOOL).

Mitsuyoshi's son Mitsunori (1583–1638) spent most of his life in Sakai, returning in his last years to paint fans for the imperial court. The revival of the Tosa school was brought about by Mitsunori's son Mitsuoki (1617–91), who was appointed *edokoro azukari* in 1654. He specialized in elegant paintings of flowers and birds, particularly quails, and was much influenced by his study of Chinese paintings of this type. Mitsuoki's descendants maintained their prominence at court throughout the Edo period, producing flower-and-bird paintings as well as paintings of traditional literary subjects. In their hands the Tosa style hardened into a highly formalized set of conventions featuring precise outlines filled in with strong, flat colors.

The Tosa school exerted a wide influence on other schools of painting, especially during the Edo period. Perhaps the most interesting of these connections was the influence of the Tosa style on book illustrations and hence on UKIYO-E. During the 16th and early 17th centuries crude versions of the Tosa style were used extensively for the brightly painted, illustrated editions of native literature known as Nara *ehon*. In the early 17th century, the *sagabon* printed editions of ISE MONOGATARI included woodcut illustrations in a Tosa-like style. Printed books usually were illustrated in this manner until the last quarter of the century, when artists such as Hishikawa MORONOBU (d 1694) transformed the style into true *ukiyo-e* woodblock prints.

Tosa Shimizu　土佐清水[市]

City in southern Kōchi Prefecture, Shikoku, on the Pacific Ocean. Most of the city is forested, but rice, tea, and vegetables are grown in the coastal areas. Its port is a base for deep-sea fishing. Attractions include ASHIZURIMISAKI, a cape in the ASHIZURI-UWAKAI NATIONAL PARK. Tosa Shimizu is the birthplace of NAKAHAMA MANJIRŌ, the first Japanese to go to the United States. Pop: 21,182.

Tōseiha　統制派

("Control" faction). Army officers united by their opposition to General ARAKI SADAO and his policies as army minister from 1931 to 1934. Consisting of the UGAKI KAZUSHIGE faction and other army groups blocked from promotions by Araki and his KŌDŌHA faction, the Tōseiha was a nonregional coalition that opposed Araki's reintroduction of regional politics into army appointment and policy decisions. Many army officers associated with the Tōseiha were very promising graduates of the Army War College. They strongly opposed Kōdōha policies that threatened to impede mechanization of the army and the integration of Manchuria into the Japanese economy. Lacking leadership, this coalition lasted only until TŌJŌ HIDEKI, MUTŌ AKIRA, and other members rose to power upon Araki's resignation in 1934. The term Tōseiha was actually a pejorative expression coined and used only by Kōdōha sympathizers.

Tō seikatsusha　党生活者

(Life in the Communist Party). Novella by KOBAYASHI TAKIJI (1903–33) published in 1933 and considered a monumental work of the PROLETARIAN LITERATURE MOVEMENT. *Tō seikatsusha*, set immediately following the MANCHURIAN INCIDENT, depicts the lives of underground communist party members active in a movement to resist temporary layoffs at a munitions factory. Based on the author's personal experiences, the work realistically portrays the hardships and activities of life within the party. When first published in CHŪŌ KŌRON, a large portion of the text had to be omitted and the title changed to *Tenkan jidai* (Time of Transition) to pass censorship restrictions of the time.

Tōshiba Ceramics Co, Ltd

東芝セラミックス[株]

(Tōshiba Seramikkusu). Manufacturer of semiconductor-related products and ceramics. Incorporated in 1928. The company is affiliated with TŌSHIBA CORPORATION. It has established overseas affiliates in the United States and the United Kingdom. Sales for the fiscal year ending March 1991 totaled ¥59.3 billion (US $432.2 million), and the company was capitalized at ¥17.9 billion (US $130.5 million). Headquarters are in Tōkyō.

Tōshiba Corporation　[株]東芝

(Tōshiba). Manufacturer of information and communication systems, electronic devices, heavy electrical apparatus, and consumer products. Its forerunner was Shibaura Engineering Works Co, Ltd, incorporated in 1904. After a 1939 merger with Tōkyō Electric Co, Ltd, it took its present name. It has long had close ties to General Electric Co of the United States and is affiliated with the Mitsui group. During the 1950s it grew as a result of the increasing demand for home electric appliances. It has also expanded into the fields of atomic power, energy-related equipment, semiconductors, office automation, and medical electronic equipment. Tōshiba's electricity generation technology is among the most sophisticated in the world, and the company sells facilities for hydroelectric, thermoelectric, geothermal, and atomic power generation worldwide. It has successfully marketed multipurpose process computers; automation systems for the steel, electric power, and chemical industries; and circulation systems for airports, harbors, and railways. It has a total of 61 overseas subsidiaries. Sales for the fiscal year ending March 1991 totaled ¥3.2 trillion (US $23.3 billion), and capitalization stood at ¥272.3 billion (US $2.0 billion). Headquarters are in Tōkyō, while the registered head office is in Kawasaki, Kanagawa Prefecture.

Tōshiba International Foundation

東芝国際交流財団

(Tōshiba Kokusai Kōryū Zaidan). A foundation established in 1989 by the TŌSHIBA CORPORATION to promote international cultural exchange and the understanding of Japan abroad. Activities include support for seminars, symposia, and research. Total assets in 1989 were ¥1.0 billion (US $7.2 million). Headquarters are in Tōkyō.

Tōshiba Machine Co, Ltd

東芝機械[株]

(Tōshiba Kikai). Integrated machine builder engaged in the production of precision machine tools, plastic-processing machinery, die-casting machines, printing presses, semiconductor manufacturing equipment, and industrial machinery. Incorporated in 1949. Affiliated with TŌSHIBA CORPORATION, Tōshiba Machine produces a wide range of equipment that provides ultrahigh precision and productivity—from computerized numerical control (CNC) units and factory automation equipment to massive machinery. It has

Tosa Shimizu

overseas subsidiaries and joint ventures in the United States, Canada, Singapore, Australia, Mexico, and Taiwan and liaison offices in Germany, the United Kingdom, Taiwan, and Hong Kong. Sales for the fiscal year ending March 1991 totaled ¥132.1 billion (US $962.1 million), and capitalization stood at ¥12.4 billion (US $90.4 million). Headquarters are in Tōkyō.

Tōshiba Medical Systems Corporation 東芝メディカル[株]

(Tōshiba Medikaru). Comprehensive marketer of medical equipment manufactured by TŌSHIBA CORPORATION. Incorporated in 1948. It also provides medical consultation for doctors. For the fiscal year ending March 1990, sales totaled ¥122.1 billion (US $797.6 million) and capitalization stood at ¥2.1 billion (US $13.7 million). Headquarters are in Tōkyō.

toshigami 年神

("god of the NEW YEAR," also called *wakato-shisama*, "lord of the New Year"). A type of deity invoked and welcomed at each household at the turn of the year. In archaic Japanese *toshi* means "rice" as well as "calendar year," and this observance was part of an annual cycle of AGRICULTURAL RITES.

On New Year's Day the *toshigami* pays an annual visit to bring blessings to each family, promising such benefits as a good crop to farmers, good business to merchants, and a big catch to fishermen. Traditional dishes are prepared on New Year's Eve and offered to the visiting deity on New Year's Day with *sake* (rice wine) and *mochi* (rice cakes), an indispensable part of this ritual throughout Japan. Images of the *toshigami* vary from those of an aged man and wife to that of a goddess, but most depict aged men and may represent the collective ancestral spirit of each family.

toshiiwai→ga no iwai

Tōshi kaden 藤氏家伝

(Biographies of the Fujiwara Family). Also known as *Kaden*. Three FUJIWARA FAMILY biographies, compiled around 760. In the first section FUJIWARA NO NAKAMARO recounts the life of his great-grandfather FUJIWARA NO KAMATARI. The second section, written by the priest Enkei, is an account of Kamatari's grandson Fujiwara no Muchimaro (680–737). A variant version includes a biography of Kamatari's son Jōe (643–665).

toshikoshi soba 年越しそば

("year-crossing noodles"). Type of *soba* (noodles made from buckwheat flour) cus-

tomarily eaten on New Year's Eve in Japan. These long, thin noodles are eaten in the hope that a family's fortunes will be similarly lengthened and extended during the New Year.

Toshima 利島

Volcanic island approximately 20 km (12 mi) south of the island of ŌSHIMA off the Izu Peninsula, central Honshū. Like Ōshima, Toshima is one of the Izu Islands and is under the administration of the Tōkyō prefectural government. Steep basalt cliffs descend to the coasts. The island's climate is warm, with strong winds and little precipitation. It is known for its camellias. Area: 4.2 sq km (1.6 sq mi).

Toshima Ward 豊島区

(Toshima Ku). One of the 23 wards of Tōkyō. During the Edo period (1600–1868) Toshima developed as a village on the highway Nakasendō. Since World War II, it has grown rapidly and is now a commercial and residential area centered on Ikebukuro Station. With numerous wholesale and retail stores, IKEBUKURO is one of Tōkyō's major shopping centers as well as a transportation hub. Pop: 261,870.

toshi no ichi→year-end fair

toshiyori 年寄

(elders). A generic term, *toshiyori* (literally, "grown old") came to refer to the acknowledged senior members of social groups and by extension to town and village officials. During the Muromachi period (1333–1568) the term was applied to some government officials, and during the Edo period (1600–1868) the title *toshiyori* (and such related terms as RŌJŪ, WAKADOSHIYORI, and KARŌ) was given to several political positions of great authority.

Tōshōdaiji 唐招提寺

Buddhist monastery founded in 759 in the western sector of the ancient capital of Nara by the Chinese monk Jianzhen (Chienchen), who is known to the Japanese as GANJIN. Tōshōdaiji became the head temple of the RITSU SECT, which was responsible for the ordination of the Buddhist clergy during the late 8th century. Tōshōdaiji has remained relatively untouched, so that the layout of its main buildings preserves the atmosphere of an 8th-century temple compound. The Tōshōdaiji *kondō* (main hall) is the only hall of its kind extant from the Nara period (710–794). The three main images housed within, the Buddha Rushana (Skt: Vairocana) flanked to the left by the Buddha Yakushi

(Skt: Bhaiṣajyaguru; the Buddha of Healing) and to the right by Senju Kannon (Thousand-Armed KANNON), are masterpieces of gilded lacquer sculpture made shortly after the temple was founded. The *kōdō* (lecture hall) was once an assembly hall (*chōshūden*) of the Imperial Palace in Nara, which was dismantled and rebuilt at Tōshōdaiji in 760. It remains the only extant specimen of Nara palace architecture.

The anniversary of Ganjin's death is celebrated yearly on 6 June in the *kōdō* and the *mieidō* (hall of the founder's image), where a statue of the monk is kept. Ganjin arrived in Nara in the spring of 754. At TŌDAIJI he administered the *bosatsukai* (precepts for Mahāyāna bodhisattvas) to some 400 persons (including members of the imperial family) and reordained 80 monks. There he also founded the *kaidan'in*, the hall containing the platform required by the Ritsu sect for proper ordination. After residing at Tōdaiji for five years, Ganjin was presented by the imperial family with a valuable plot of land, not far from YAKUSHIJI. There Ganjin built Tōshōdaiji, a monastery dedicated to the training of Ritsu monks. He moved there in 759. The widespread popularity of the esoteric Buddhism of the TENDAI SECT and SHINGON SECT led to a decline in the fortunes of the Tōshōdaiji during the Heian period (794–1185).

Tōshōgū 東照宮

Shintō shrine in the city of Nikkō, Tochigi Prefecture, dedicated primarily to the founder of the Tokugawa shogunate, TOKUGAWA IEYASU, and since 1873, to two other military figures, TOYOTOMI HIDEYOSHI and MINAMOTO NO YORITOMO. The shrine was established to house Ieyasu's remains. The extant highly ornate shrine buildings and gateways were erected in 1636. More than 100 Tōshōgū shrines have been built in other parts of Japan. The annual festivals, celebrated on 18 May and 17 October, feature a parade of parishioners dressed as warriors.

Tōshoku, Ltd [株]東食

(Tōshoku). Company selling agricultural and marine products, sugar, grain oil, and processed food. Tōshoku was incorporated as a result of the dissolution of the MITSUI *zaibatsu* (industrial and financial combine) in 1946. It has branches and subsidiaries in 18 cities around the world. It has increased its business in the fields of chemical products, machinery, and general merchandise. Sales for the fiscal year ending October 1990 totaled ¥722.6 billion (US $5.6 billion). Capi-

Tōshōgū The east corridor of the lavishly decorated Yōmeimon, the main gate of this ornate shrine. A National Treasure, Tōshōgū dates in its present form to 1636.

Tottori Sand Dunes
The dunes at sunset. The striated patterns are carved by gentle winds.

talization stood at ¥24.7 billion (US $190.4 million) in the same year. Headquarters are in Tōkyō.

Tōshūsai Sharaku →Sharaku

toso 屠蘇

Medicinal *sake* drunk at New Year's; formerly believed to prevent illness. The custom of drinking *toso* came to Japan from China and was practiced at court during the Heian period (794–1185). *Toso* is prepared by soaking in *sake* or MIRIN (sweet *sake*) a bag containing spices such as cinnamon bark and the seeds of the *sanshō* (Japanese peppertree) and roots of medicinal plants such as *bōfū* (*Siler divaricatum*) and OKERA.

Tōsoh Corporation 東ソー[株]

(Tōsō). Integrated chemical manufacturer. Incorporated in 1935 as Tōyō Sōda Manufacturing Co, Ltd, it assumed its current name in 1987. Tōsoh is a core member of the Industrial Bank of Japan group. It is engaged in the manufacture of basic chemicals, fine chemicals, polyvinyl chloride, polyolefin, synthetic rubber, metals, electronics, cement, and scientific and diagnostic instruments. The company is now diversifying into advanced materials, electronics, and biotechnology. It has overseas joint ventures and plants in the Netherlands, the United States, Canada, and Indonesia. Sales for the fiscal year ending March 1991 totaled ¥325.9 billion (US $2.4 billion), and capitalization stood at ¥40.6 billion (US $295.9 million). Headquarters are in Tōkyō.

Tostem Corporation トステム[株]

(Tōsutemu). Formerly known as Tōyō Sash Co, Ltd. Manufacturer of aluminum building materials, including house and building sashes. Incorporated in 1949. The company provides its building materials to 70 percent of Japanese construction projects involving buildings over 100 meters (328 feet) tall. In 1986 Tostem acquired Comalco Fabricators (Hong Kong), Ltd, and in 1988 it started op-

eration of a plant in Thailand. Sales for the fiscal year ending March 1991 totaled ¥462.5 billion (US $3.4 billion), and capitalization stood at ¥61.0 billion (US $444.6 million). Headquarters are in Tōkyō.

Tosu 鳥栖[市]

City in eastern Saga Prefecture, Kyūshū. A former post-station town, Tosu is still an important transportation center. Foodstuffs, flour, tobacco, bicycles, household medicines, and tires are produced here. Pop: 55,877.

tōsuiken 統帥権

(power of supreme command, i.e., of the military). The authority to command and use the armed forces. Article 11 of the 1889 CONSTITUTION OF THE EMPIRE OF JAPAN states that "the Emperor has the supreme command of the Army and Navy." It was maintained that the ARMY GENERAL STAFF OFFICE (established in 1878) and the NAVAL GENERAL STAFF OFFICE (separated from the former in 1893) were empowered to "assist" the emperor and that neither the cabinet nor the IMPERIAL DIET had the right to interfere. Referred to as the independence of the supreme command, this principle meant that the army and navy were independent of civilian government.

This independence was reinforced by the interpretation given to article 12 of the Constitution, which provided that "the Emperor determines the organization and peace standing [forces to be maintained in times of peace] of the Army and Navy." This position led to political conflict between the civil government headed by Prime Minister HAMAGUCHI OSACHI and the Naval General Staff Office over the ratification of the 1930 London Naval Limitations Treaty (see LONDON NAVAL CONFERENCES). The crisis signaled the increasing interference by the military in national politics that would come to characterize the following decade.

Totoki Baigai 十時梅厓

(1749–1804). BUNJINGA painter, poet, and calligrapher. Real name Totoki Shi. Born in Naniwa (now Ōsaka). In 1784 Baigai was invited to Nagashima in Ise (now Mie Prefecture) by the art-loving *daimyō* Masuyama Sessai (1754–1819) to serve as a resident Confucian scholar. In 1790, granted permission by his lord to visit Nagasaki, he overstayed his leave and lost his position. He subsequently retired to Ōsaka, where most of his dated paintings were done after 1792.

Baigai's themes were primarily landscapes and, secondarily, the "four gentlemen" (SHIKUNSHI: bamboo, plum, orchid, and chrysanthemum). Freedom of brushwork is characteristic of his style; he seems to have been more interested in spontaneity than in technical perfection.

Tōtō, Ltd 東陶機器[株]

(Tōtō Kiki). Manufacturing enterprise producing sanitary ceramic ware, metal fittings, bathtubs, washstands, toilet fixtures, and other sanitary equipment. Incorporated in 1917. The company grew rapidly after World War II to meet the great demand for sanitary ceramic ware caused by a housing boom and by Westernization of the Japanese lifestyle. The company later began producing bathtubs and washstands and became a comprehensive manufacturer of housing equipment. Sales for the fiscal year ending March 1991 totaled ¥394.6 billion (US $2.9 billion), and capitalization stood at ¥35.3 billion (US

$257.3 million). Headquarters are in Kita Kyūshū, Fukuoka Prefecture.

Totoya Hokkei 魚屋北渓

(1780–1850). UKIYO-E artist; a follower of *ukiyo-e* master Katsushika HOKUSAI. A native of Edo (now Tōkyō), his real name was Iwakubo Tatsuyuki. Originally a fishmonger (Totoya literally means "fish shop"), he studied painting under Kanō Yōsen'in (1735–1808). He later became a pupil of Hokusai and moved to the Akasaka district in Edo, where he became a professional artist, mastering Hokusai's style in both prints and *ukiyo-e* paintings. In prints he specialized in SURIMONO and illustrations of comic verse (KYŌKA).

Totsukawa 十津川[村]

Village in southern Nara Prefecture, central Honshū, on the river Totsukawa. Mentioned in medieval military chronicles such as the HŌGEN MONOGATARI and the TAIHEIKI, Totsukawa was the base of the Southern Court during the dynastic schism of the period of Northern and Southern Courts (1337–92). Following a flood in 1889 the village's population dwindled. Today there is a large lumber industry. Totsukawa Hot Spring draws tourists. Pop: 5,516.

Totsukawa 十津川

River in southern Nara Prefecture, central Honshū, flowing south through the Kii Mountains and joining the river Kitayamagawa to form the KUMANOGAWA. It has carved deep gorges along its course, and dams have been constructed for electric power. Length: 110 km (68 mi); area of drainage basin: 996 sq km (385 sq mi).

Tottori 鳥取[市]

Capital of Tottori Prefecture, western Honshū. It developed as a castle town of the Ikeda family from the 17th century. Seriously damaged by an earthquake in 1943 and fire in 1952, the city has been completely rebuilt, with active electrical-appliance, woodworking, food, and machinery industries. Tottori University is located here. Local attractions include TOTTORI SAND DUNES and Tottori Hot Spring. Pop: 142,467.

Tottori Plain 鳥取平野

(Tottori Heiya). Located in eastern Tottori Prefecture, western Honshū. This floodplain of the river Sendaigawa is a rice-producing area; pears are cultivated on the surrounding foothills and along the coastal sand dunes. Numerous tomb mounds (KOFUN) dot the plain. The major city is Tottori. Area: 80 sq km (30 sq mi).

Tottori Prefecture 鳥取県

(Tottori Ken). Located in western Honshū and bounded by the Sea of Japan on the north, Hyōgo Prefecture on the east, Okayama and Hiroshima prefectures on the south, and Shimane Prefecture on the west. Much of the terrain is mountainous, with the CHŪGOKU MOUNTAINS running across the southern part of the prefecture. Level areas are concentrated along rivers and near the Sea of Japan coast. The climate is temperate and relatively dry.

Archaeological remains from the Jōmon (ca 10,000 BC–ca 300 BC) and Yayoi (ca 300 BC–ca AD 300) periods have been found in this area. Formerly the area was composed of the provinces of Inaba and Hōki. It was ruled by various feudal lords until the Meiji Restoration of 1868. The present boundaries were

Tottori Prefecture
Location and Prefectural Crest

drawn up in 1881.

Because of its remoteness from major population and economic centers, Tottori has remained predominantly agricultural. Products include rice, livestock, fruits, vegetables, and tobacco. Its pears are especially prized. Other industries include fishing, forestry, and food processing. YONAGO and SAKAIMINATO have been designated NEW INDUSTRIAL CITIES in the Nakaumi Zone in line with the prefecture's plans to modernize its industries.

Attractions include the Sea of Japan coast, particularly the TOTTORI SAND DUNES in the SAN'IN COAST NATIONAL PARK; DAISEN, the training center for mountain ascetics in the DAISEN-OKI NATIONAL PARK; and hot spring resorts such as Misasa and Kaike. Area: 3,494 sq km (1,349 sq mi); pop: 615,722; capital: TOTTORI. Other major cities include KURAYOSHI and Yonago.

Tottori Sand Dunes   鳥取砂丘

(Tottori Sakyū). On the east coast of Tottori Prefecture, western Honshū. The dunes have been a notable feature of the area since ancient times, but their features are gradually changing today with the planting of trees and irrigation to turn them into arable land. Designated as a natural monument, the dunes are part of San'in Coast National Park. Length: 16 km (10 mi); width: 2 km (1.2 mi); highest point: 92 m (302 ft).

Towada   十和田[市]

City in southeastern Aomori Prefecture, northern Honshū. Towada was settled by a *samurai* from the Nambu domain in 1855. Principal products are rice and fruit; cattle and hogs are also raised. Pop: 60,911.

Towada-Hachimantai National Park   十和田八幡平国立公園

(Towada-Hachimantai Kokuritsu Kōen). Situated in northern Honshū, in Aomori, Akita, and Iwate prefectures. The park consists of two separate mountainous regions some 50 km (30 mi) apart. The northern Towada region has the volcanoes of HAKKŌDASAN in the north and Lake TOWADA in the south. From this large caldera lake, noted for its clarity and depth, the river OIRASEGAWA flows toward the Pacific Ocean through deep ravines and valleys. The southern Hachimantai region consists of an extensive plateau with numerous volcanoes, including HACHIMANTAI and Yakeyama in the north, KOMAGATAKE in the south, and IWATESAN in the east. The park is celebrated for numerous hot-spring resorts. The forests in both regions are noted for the Maries fir (Aomori *todomatsu*). Area: 854 sq km (330 sq mi).

Towada, Lake   十和田湖

(Towadako). Square-shaped double caldera lake. Between Aomori and Akita prefectures, northern Honshū, south of the Hakkōdasan volcano group. The river Oirasegawa flows out from the eastern side of the lake. Breeding of the *himemasu*, a type of salmon, has flourished since 1903. The lake is the principal attraction of Towada-Hachimantai National Park. Its water does not freeze in winter. This area is noted for its spring and autumn foliage. Area: 60 sq km (23 sq mi); circumference: 53 km (32.9 mi); depth: 327 m (1,072 ft); altitude: 400 m (1,312 ft).

Towazugatari   とはずがたり

(An Uninvited Confession; tr *The Confessions of Lady Nijō*, 1973). Autobiographical narrative of 36 years (1271–1306) in the life of Lady Nijō (also known as Go-Fukakusa In no Nijō), a high-ranking Kyōto aristocrat; completed ca 1307.

Little is known about the author except through her autobiography; even her name, Lady Nijō (Nijō Dono), is merely a court title. The first three books describe her gaining the affections of the retired emperor GO-FUKAKUSA, as well as the love of one of his close advisers, Saionji Sanekane (1249–1322), and of Go-Fukakusa's half brother, a Buddhist high priest. In 1283 Lady Nijō was expelled from Go-Fukakusa's palace because of his empress's jealousy and her own indiscretions. Book 4 opens in 1289 with Lady Nijō, now a Buddhist nun, setting out on a series of journeys that take her throughout Japan. She concludes Book 5 with an account of the services marking the third anniversary of Go-Fukakusa's death.

Towazugatari is the culminating work in the long court tradition of autobiographical writing (see NIKKI BUNGAKU). The work was completely forgotten by the 18th century, but a single manuscript survived to be discovered in 1940 by the literary scholar Yamagishi Tokuhei (1893–1987) in the Imperial Household Library in Tōkyō. The work's significance was not realized until annotated editions became available in the mid-1960s. What makes *Towazugatari* particularly important to students of Japanese culture is its description of life during a time of transition from an aristocratic culture to one dominated by the warrior class.

towns and villages, consolidation of   町村合併

(*chōson gappei*). Merger of two or more adjacent cities, towns, or villages. The purpose is to create administratively strong and effective local autonomous bodies. During the first consolidation (1889) 71,314 towns and villages were merged to create 39 cities and 15,820 towns and villages. Under the Towns and Villages Consolidation Promotion Law (Chōson Gappei Sokushin Hō) of 1953, the approximately 10,000 towns and villages in the country were reduced to 3,975 by 1956. By 1989 the number of towns and villages had been further reduced to 2,590.

Tōya, Lake   洞爺湖

(Tōyako). Caldera lake near Uchiura Bay, southwestern Hokkaidō. Located within Shikotsu-Tōya National Park. This round lake is one of the northernmost ice-free lakes in Japan. Nakajima, a volcanic cone, is located in the center of the lake. Tōyako Hot Spring and two volcanoes, SHŌWA SHINZAN and USUZAN, are nearby. Area: 69.4 sq km (26.8 sq mi); circumference: 52 km (32 mi); depth: 180 m (591 ft); altitude: 84 m (276 ft).

Toyama   富山[市]

Capital of Toyama Prefecture, central Honshū. Situated on the river Jinzūgawa, Toyama developed as a castle town of the Maeda family during the Edo period (1600–1868). It is now the center of the so-called Hokuriku Industrial Region, with aluminum-refining, shipbuilding, and machinery industries. Rice, pears, tea, and vegetables are grown here. Toyama University, the Museum of Modern Art Toyama, and a city science museum are located here. Pop: 321,254.

Toyama Bay   富山湾

(Toyama Wan). Inlet of the Sea of Japan in northern Toyama Prefecture, central Honshū. Known as the home of the firefly squid (*hotaruika*). Fishing is good in the western part of the bay. Commercial and industrial ports include Toyama and Shin Toyama. Forms part of the Noto Peninsula Quasi-National Park.

Toyama Kametarō   外山亀太郎

(1867–1918). Geneticist. Noted for his pioneering studies and experiments dealing with applied eugenics. Born in what is now Kanagawa Prefecture and a graduate of Tōkyō University, Toyama served as principal of a sericulture school and as a professor at Tōkyō University. While engaged in work to improve silkworm varieties, he discovered

Towada-Hachimantai National Park
1 Surrounded by spectacular foliage, Lake Towada is northern Japan's most popular spot for viewing autumn colors.
2 The peaks of Hakkōdasan form a volcano group.

Tōya maru Disaster
Following a typhoon, the passenger ferry *Tōya maru* capsized just off Hakodate, Hokkaidō, in September 1954 with a loss of 1,155 lives.

Toyama Prefecture
Location and Prefectural Crest

Tōyama Kinshirō　　　遠山金四郎

(1793–1855). City commissioner (MACHI BUGYŌ) of Edo (now Tōkyō); noted for his humanity and for his wise and impartial judgments; also known as Tōyama Kagemoto. In 1840 he became Kitamachi *bugyō*, or commissioner of the northern half of Edo. He soon fell afoul of TORII YŌZO, a strict reformist who served as commissioner of the southern half of Edo, and was demoted to the post of inspector general (ŌMETSUKE) in 1843. After Torii's downfall in 1844 Tōyama assumed his former foe's position. He retired seven years later and took Buddhist orders.

Toyama Masakazu　　　外山正一

(1848–1900). Educator and poet. Also known as Toyama Shōichi. Born in Edo (now Tōkyō). After studying at the BANSHO SHIRABESHO, he studied in England and at the University of Michigan. He became the first Japanese professor of philosophy and sociology at Tōkyō University. He was appointed president of the university in 1897 and served as education minister in 1898. Toyama was one of three editors of the *Shintaishi shō* (1882), a collection of modern-style Japanese and translated poetry.

Tōyama Mitsuru　　　頭山満

(1855–1944). Right-wing political leader, advocate of Japanese expansion on the Asian continent, and a founder of such ultranationalist groups as the GEN'YŌSHA. Born in the Fukuoka domain (now part of Fukuoka Prefecture). In 1879 he helped organize the Kōyōsha, a group supporting the FREEDOM AND PEOPLE'S RIGHTS MOVEMENT. In 1881 the Kōyōsha changed its name to Gen'yōsha and, headed by Tōyama's friend Hiraoka Kōtarō (1851–1906), began to promote the cause of Japanese expansion on the continent.

Just before the SINO-JAPANESE WAR OF 1894–1895 Tōyama helped organize the Ten'yūkyō, a paramilitary force whose activities in Korea were a prelude to those of the Japanese army (see KOREA AND JAPAN). He strongly favored establishment of Japanese control over Manchuria; in this connection he became a member of the anti-Russian TAIRO DŌSHIKAI when it was formed in 1903. He gave support to SUN YAT-SEN, and when the revolution of 1911 occurred, he went to China as an adviser to the new government.

Following the Chinese Revolution, Tōyama came to have great influence as a behind-the-scenes manipulator of Japan's Asian policy and domestic politics. Although Tōyama was in retirement during World War II, he maintained his standing as the grand old man of Japanese nationalism, reigning over right-wing groups such as the Gen'yōsha and the AMUR RIVER SOCIETY that he had helped bring into existence. See also RIGHT WING.

Toyama Plain　　　富山平野

(Toyama Heiya). Located in north-central Toyama Prefecture, central Honshū. Bordering the Sea of Japan, it consists of the piedmont alluvial fans of the rivers Kurobegawa, Jōganjigawa, and Jinzūgawa, all of which originate in the Hida Mountains. Rice is cultivated, and industries are being developed. The major cities are Toyama and Takaoka. Area: approximately 990 sq km (380 sq mi).

Toyama Prefecture　　　富山県

(Toyama Ken). Located in central Honshū and bounded by Toyama Bay and the Sea of Japan on the north, Niigata and Nagano prefectures on the east, Gifu Prefecture on the south, and Ishikawa Prefecture on the west. The central part of the prefecture is made up of plains surrounded by mountains to the east, south, and west and traversed by several rivers. The winters are marked by heavy snowfall and cloudy weather.

Known after the TAIKA REFORM of 645 as Etchū Province, the area came under the control of the MAEDA FAMILY in the Edo period (1600–1868). The present name of the prefecture dates from 1871, and its present boundaries from 1883.

Rice is the major agricultural crop. Tulip bulbs are exported. The availability of cheap hydroelectric power from Toyama's numerous rivers has spurred the development of the chemical, metal, machinery, lumber-processing, and textile industries. Fishing is also important.

Major attractions include the Kurobe Gorge-Tateyama district, part of CHŪBU SANGAKU NATIONAL PARK, and the seacoast around the city of HIMI, part of the Noto Peninsula Quasi-National Park. The Gokayama district in the southwestern part of the prefecture is noted for its farmhouses, which have steeply pitched roofs in the style known as *gasshō-zukuri* (see MINKA). The southwestern edge of the prefecture is a part of the HAKUSAN NATIONAL PARK. Area: 4,252 sq km (1,641 sq mi); pop: 1,120,161; capital: TOYAMA. Other major cities include TAKAOKA, Himi, UOZU, and SHIMMINATO.

Tōya maru Disaster　　　洞爺丸事故

(*Tōya maru* Jiko). The sinking on 26 September 1954 of the *Tōya maru*, a Japan National Railways passenger ferry, with a loss of 1,155 lives; one of the worst sea disasters in Japanese history. When a typhoon originating in Kyūshū hit northern Japan, five ships were sunk and many others damaged. The largest casualty was the *Tōya maru*, which capsized and sank after leaving the port of Hakodate on its run to Aomori. The incident brought into question navigation regulations and prompted improvements in hull structure.

Tōyo　　　東予[市]

City in eastern Ehime Prefecture, Shikoku, on the Hiuchi Sea. There are numerous textile mills and aluminum, machinery, and chemical plants. A ferry connects Tōyo with ŌSAKA. Pop: 33,749.

Toyoake　　　豊明[市]

City in central Aichi Prefecture, central Honshū. It has metal and machinery industries and is fast becoming a suburb of NAGOYA. It was the site of the Battle of OKEHAZAMA (1560). Pop: 62,160.

Tōyo Aluminium KK　　　東洋アルミニウム[株]

(Tōyo Aruminiumu). Manufacturer of aluminum foils and paste. Incorporated in 1931 jointly by Aluminium, Ltd, Canada, and Sumitomo. Originally engaged in the manufacturing of aluminum foil and sheet, it began production of aluminum powder in 1968 and high-purity aluminum nitride in 1987. It has joint manufacturing ventures in South Korea, France, and the United States. In 1990 sales totaled ¥45.8 billion (US $342.9 million), and the company was capitalized at ¥3.4 billion (US $25.5 million), of which 48.8 percent was invested by Alcan Aluminium, Ltd, of Canada. Headquarters are in Ōsaka.

Tōyōbō Co, Ltd　　　東洋紡績[株]

(Tōyō Bōseki). Leading comprehensive textile maker of both natural and synthetic fibers. Incorporated in 1914. In 1961 Tōyōbō developed and commercialized polyester fiber, and in 1966, after merging with Kureha Spinning Co, the firm started producing nylon. The company is expanding into non-textile products, including plastics, activated carbon fiber, reverse-osmosis membranes, enzyme-based diagnostic reagents, medical instruments, electronics materials, and pharmaceuticals. Sales for the fiscal year ending March 1991 totaled ¥338.5 billion (US $2.5 billion), of which synthetic fibers accounted for 39 percent; cotton-synthetic blends, 23 percent; wool, 4 percent; and plastic and other products, 44 percent. The company was capitalized at ¥43.3 billion (US $315.6 million) in the same year. Headquarters are in Ōsaka.

Tōyō Bunko　　　東洋文庫

(The Oriental Library). A world-famous research collection on Asian history and culture, the first of its kind privately established in modern Japan. In 1917 Iwasaki Hisaya (1865–1955), son of IWASAKI YATARŌ, founder of the Mitsubishi *zaibatsu*, began this library with the purchase of the Asiatic library of George Ernest Morrison (1862–1920), a long-term China correspondent for the *Times* of London. Known initially as the Morrison Bunko, it received its present name in 1924, when the Iwasaki family donated a building in Bunkyō Ward, Tōkyō. During World War II its books were moved for safety; upon their return to Tōkyō in 1948 the library was made part of the NATIONAL DIET LIBRARY.

Toyoda Automatic Loom Works, Ltd　　　[株]豊田自動織機製作所

(Toyoda Jidō Shokki Seisakusho). Manufacturer of textile machinery, forklifts, passenger and commercial vehicles, automobile engines, industrial rolling stock, compressors for automobile air conditioners, and casting machines. It is one of the world's leading producers of spinning and weaving machinery and of forklift trucks. Toyoda Automatic Loom Works was incorporated in 1926 to manufacture the shuttle-changing automatic looms invented by TOYODA SAKICHI. In 1933 an automobile division and a steelmaking division were added to begin production of automobiles. The automobile division became independent in 1937 as Toyota Motor Co, Ltd (see TOYOTA MOTOR CORPORATION), while the steel-making division became independent in 1940 as AICHI STEEL WORKS, LTD; these three companies are the primary companies of the Toyota group. The company's textile machinery division grew rapidly after World War II. In 1985 an electronics business division was organized to pursue emerging electronics technologies. Sales for the fiscal year ending March 1991 totaled ¥583.7 billion (US $4.3 billion). The company was capitalized at ¥30.9 billion (US $225.2 million) in the same year. Headquarters are in Kariya, Aichi Prefecture.

Toyoda Machine Works, Ltd
豊田工機[株]

(Toyoda Kōki). Manufacturer of machine tools and automotive parts and member of the Toyota group of companies. Incorporated in 1941. For the fiscal year ending March 1991, sales totaled ¥180.0 billion (US $1.3 billion) and capitalization stood at ¥20.7 billion (US $150.9 million). Headquarters are in Kariya, Aichi Prefecture.

Toyoda Sakichi
豊田佐吉

(1867–1930). Inventor and industrialist. Born in Shizuoka Prefecture. His early fascination with looms developed into a lifetime of research and innovation that produced the first Japanese-designed power loom in 1897 and an automatic power loom in 1924, at the time the most advanced weaving machinery in the world. His inventions revolutionized the Japanese textile industry and enabled Japan to assume virtual control of the international silk trade in the 1920s. The industrial research complex he developed became the base from which evolved many other industries, including TOYOTA MOTOR CORPORATION, the giant automobile manufacturer.

Toyoda Shirō
豊田四郎

(1906–77). Film director. Born in Kyōto. Toyoda began his career as a screenwriter for SHŌCHIKU CO, LTD, and eventually became an assistant director to SHIMAZU YASUJIRŌ. His first feature film as director was *Irodorareru kuchibiru* (1929, Painted Lips).

Toyoda was involved in the *jumbungaku* (pure literature) movement, a loosely organized group of directors who shared an interest in bringing works of serious literature to the screen, which flourished in the late 1930s. Toyoda's *Wakai hito* (1937, Young People) was based on a novel by ISHIZAKA YŌJIRŌ. The examples best known to American audiences are Toyoda's *Gan* (1953, The Wild Geese; shown abroad as *The Mistress*), an adaptation of a MORI ŌGAI novel, and *Yukiguni* (1957, Snow Country), from the novel by KAWABATA YASUNARI. Other notable films have been *Kojima no haru* (1940, Spring on Leper's Island), *Meoto zenzai* (1955, Marital Relations), *Neko to Shōzo to futari no onna* (1956, A Cat, Shōzo, and Two Women), and *Amai ase* (1964, Sweet Sweat).

Toyoda Shōichirō
豊田章一郎

(1925–). Businessman and president of TOYOTA MOTOR CORPORATION (1982–). Born in Shizuoka Prefecture. After graduating from Nagoya University in 1947, he worked with Nippondenso Co, Ltd, and other companies affiliated with Toyota, becoming a director of Toyota Motor Co, Ltd, in 1952 and president of Toyota Motor Sales Co in 1981. When Toyota Motor Corporation was estab-

lished in July 1982 through the merger of Toyota Motor Co and Toyota Motor Sales Co, he took office as president of the new company. Noted as an engineer as well as an executive, in 1980 he won the Deming Prize, the most renowned domestic prize for achievement in quality control. He was president of the Japan Automobile Manufacturers' Association (1986–90).

Toyogawa Canal
豊川用水

(Toyogawa Yōsui). Irrigation canal in southeastern Aichi Prefecture, central Honshū. Water sources are Lake Sakuma and the river Ōnyūgawa. The canal's eastern branch extends to the tip of the Atsumi Peninsula; the western branch extends to the city of Gamagōri. Completed in 1968, it irrigates approximately 20,000 hectares (49,400 acres) of farmland and provides water to the cities of Toyohashi and Toyokawa. Length of eastern canal: 76 km (47 mi); length of western canal: 37 km (23 mi).

Toyohashi
豊橋[市]

City in southeastern Aichi Prefecture, central Honshū, on the river Toyogawa. In the Edo period (1600–1868), it was known as Yoshida and flourished as a castle town and a post-station town. A silk-reeling center before World War II, it now produces textiles, lumber, machinery, and food. Water from the TOYOGAWA CANAL is used to irrigate vegetable fields. Eels are also raised. Urigō, a Yayoi-period (ca 300 BC–ca AD 300) archaeological site, is here. Pop: 337,982.

Tōyō Ink Mfg Co, Ltd
東洋インキ製造[株]

(Tōyō Inki Seizō). Company that manufactures and supplies printing inks, pigments, colorants, coatings, electronic materials, adhesives, and imaging systems and supplies. Incorporated in 1907. Tōyō is a partner in many joint-venture projects in North America, Asia, and Europe. Sales totaled ¥220.8 billion (US $1.6 billion) in the fiscal year ending March 1991, and the company was capitalized at ¥23.5 billion (US $171.3 million). Headquarters are in Tōkyō.

Tōyō Jiyūtō
東洋自由党

(Oriental Liberal Party). Populist political party formed in November 1892 by ŌI KENTARŌ and other defectors from the JIYŪTŌ (Liberal Party), with the support of TARUI TŌKICHI. It advocated constitutional representative government and government control of the economy. It also published Japan's first labor magazine, *Shin Tōyō* (New Orient). Internal dissension caused it to disband late in 1893. See also POLITICAL PARTIES.

tōyō kanji → jōyō kanji

Toyokawa
豊川[市]

City in eastern Aichi Prefecture, central Honshū. From the end of the Edo period (1600–1868) it developed around the temple Toyokawa Inari. Metal, machinery, and camera industries were set up after World War II. Pop: 111,730.

Tōyō keizai shimpō
東洋経済新報

(Eastern Economic Review). Economic journal founded in 1895 by journalist Machida Chūji (1863–1946) with financial support from SHIBUSAWA EIICHI and other influential businessmen. Editors after Machida included the economist Amano Tameyuki (1861–1938) and ISHIBASHI TANZAN. The general tenor of the magazine was liberal, demo-

cratic, and anti-imperialist; it was especially critical of Japan's expansionist policies on the Asian continent, making it unique for its time. Renamed *Shūkan tōyō keizai* (Weekly Eastern Economic Review) in 1961, it is still published.

Tōyō Kōhan Co, Ltd
東洋鋼鈑[株]

(Tōyō Kōhan). Company that manufactures and sells tin plates, tin-free steel, vinyl-coated steel, electro-galvanized steel, and cold-rolled steel sheet strips in coils. Incorporated in 1934. It has exported technology to West German, British, and Canadian mills. Sales for the fiscal year ending March 1991 totaled ¥124.0 billion (US $903.8 million). Capitalization was ¥5.0 billion (US $36.4 million) in the same year. Headquarters are in Tōkyō.

Toyokuni → Utagawa Toyokuni

Toyonaka
豊中[市]

City in northwestern Ōsaka Prefecture, central Honshū. It is a residential suburb of Ōsaka, with numerous small and medium-sized industrial plants. Toyonaka is the site of Ōsaka International Airport, Ōsaka University, and an open-air museum of Japanese farmhouses. SENRI NEW TOWN is located in the Senri Hills in the eastern part of the city. Pop: 409,837.

Toyooka
豊岡[市]

City in northern Hyōgo Prefecture, western Honshū. It flourished as a castle town of the Kyōgoku family during the Edo period (1600–1868). Local products include traditional wicker luggage (*yanagigōri*) and luggage made of vinyl and leather. Toyooka's coastal area is part of SAN'IN COAST NATIONAL PARK, the main attraction of which is the cave called GEMBUDŌ. Nakajima Shrine is a fine example of Muromachi-period (1333–1568) architecture. Pop: 47,244.

Toyosaka
豊栄[市]

City in northern Niigata Prefecture, central Honshū. Toyosaka developed as a market and weaving town. Today it is rapidly becoming a suburb of the nearby city of Niigata. It is known for the migratory birds that settle on the lagoon Fukushimagata. Pop: 45,962.

Tōyō Seikan Kaisha, Ltd
東洋製罐[株]

(Tōyō Seikan). Japan's largest manufacturer of canned food containers. Incorporated in 1941. After 1954 the company started modernization of its production methods through a technological tie-up with Continental Can Co of the United States. It started to manufacture soft drink cans and plastic containers in the 1970s. Tōyō Seikan Kaisha exports its technology to foreign countries. The company also owns TŌYŌ KŌHAN CO, LTD, a tin plate manufacturer. Sales for the fiscal year ending March 1991 totaled ¥523.7 bil-

Toyoda Sakichi This inventor's pioneering work on loom technology formed a base from which the Toyota Motor Corporation eventually evolved.

lion (US $3.8 billion), and the company was capitalized at ¥8.4 billion (US $61.2 million). Headquarters are in Tōkyō.

Tōyō Shakaitō   東洋社会党

(Oriental Socialist Party). Radical peasant political association organized by TARUI TŌKI-CHI and others on 25 May 1882. Calling for political morality and economic equality, and claiming the support of more than 3,000 peasants in Shimabara, Nagasaki Prefecture, it was quickly outlawed for being communistic or nihilistic and formally disbanded on 20 June.

Toyoshima Yoshio
This author's works include plays, short stories, children's stories, and translations of Western literature.

Toyoshima Yoshio   豊島与志雄

(1890–1955). Author. Born in Fukuoka Prefecture; graduate of Tōkyō University. A member of the Tōkyō University students' literary coterie magazine, SHINSHICHŌ (third series), he won recognition for his short story "Kosui to karera" (1914). Toyoshima wrote short stories, plays, and children's stories and translated Western literature, including Romain Rolland's *Jean Christophe* and, in collaboration with others, *The Thousand and One Nights*. His principal work is a collection of short stories, *Yamabuki no hana* (1954).

Toyoshina   豊科[町]

Town in central Nagano Prefecture, central Honshū. Toyoshina developed as a post-station town during the Edo period (1600–1868). Today it is the home of electronics and spinning industries. In addition to rice, *wasabi* (Japanese horseradish) is cultivated here. Pop: 25,265.

Tōyō Suisan Kaisha, Ltd   東洋水産[株]

(Tōyō Suisan). Japan's largest manufacturer of instant and frozen food. Incorporated in 1948. It has an overseas subsidiary in Los Angeles, Maruchan, Inc. Sales totaled ¥190.1 billion (US $1.4 billion) in the fiscal year ending March 1991, and the company was capitalized at ¥15.8 billion (US $115.2 million) in the same year. Headquarters are in Tōkyō.

Toyota   豊田[市]

City in central Aichi Prefecture, central Honshū, located on the river YAHAGIGAWA. It is the headquarters of the TOYOTA MOTOR CORPORATION; the first plant was built in 1937. Pop: 332,336.

Toyota Auto Body Co, Ltd   トヨタ車体[株]

(Toyota Shatai). Automobile body manufacturer affiliated with the TOYOTA MOTOR CORPORATION. Incorporated in 1945. It manufactures the bodies of Toyota Motor's small-sized passenger cars and is also developing special and multipurpose cars. Toyota Auto Body has grown with the development of the Toyota group. Sales for the fiscal year ending March 1991 totaled ¥487.1 billion (US $3.6 billion), practically all of which was accounted for by the Toyota group. The company was capitalized at ¥8.7 billion (US $63.4 million) in the same year. Headquarters are in the city of Kariya, Aichi Prefecture.

Toyota Foundation   トヨタ財団

(Toyota Zaidan). A foundation established in 1974 by the TOYOTA MOTOR CORPORATION. Its activities include support for research on society's responses to cultural diversity and technological change. The foundation also

supports efforts to preserve and maintain the cultural heritage of Southeast Asia. Its "Know Our Neighbors" program funds translations between Southeast Asian languages and Japanese as well as between different Southeast Asian languages. In 1989 total assets were ¥11.6 billion (US $84.0 million). Headquarters are in Tōkyō.

Toyotake Yamashiro no Shōjō   豊竹山城少掾

(1878–1967). Chanter (*tayū*) in the JŌRURI form of narrative chanting associated with the BUNRAKU puppet theater. Born in Tōkyō. Original name Kanasugi Yatarō. His theatrical career began as a child on the KABUKI stage. At the age of seven he commenced training in the GIDAYŪ-BUSHI style of chanting. In 1889 he became a disciple of Takemoto Tsudayū II (1839–1912) of Ōsaka's Bunrakuza puppet theater, with which he was to remain affiliated throughout his career. In 1909 he succeeded to the professional name Toyotake Koutsubodayū. The majority of chanters today have been stylistically and technically affected by him. In 1947 he was granted the court title Yamashiro no Shōjō by Prince CHICHIBU in recognition of his importance to *jōruri*.

Tōyō Takushoku Kaisha   東洋拓殖会社

(Oriental Development Company). A Japanese government-supported company formed in 1908, soon after the establishment of Korea as a Japanese protectorate (see KOREAN-JAPANESE CONVENTION OF 1905), to develop agriculture in Korea. One-third of its capital and extensive landholdings were provided by the Korean government. The main office was in Seoul. Besides agricultural management and irrigation projects, the company helped Japanese immigrants settle in Korea. Although ostensibly under joint Korean-Japanese management, it was in fact run by the Japanese, especially after their annexation of Korea in 1910. Through its control of numerous enterprises ranging from mining to rails and electricity, it became a major economic force and the largest landholder in Korea. In 1917 it moved its main office to Tōkyō and expanded to Manchuria, North China, and the South Pacific. It was dissolved by OCCUPATION authorities immediately after World War II.

Toyota Motor Corporation   トヨタ自動車[株]

(Toyota Jidōsha). Manufacturer of automobiles, industrial vehicles, parts and components, and prefabricated housing units. It is Japan's largest automaker and was the third largest in the world in 1988. The company began in 1933 as the Automobile Department of the Toyoda Automatic Loom Works, Ltd, and became independent of the parent firm in 1937. The company's first prototype passenger car, the Model A1, was completed in May 1935. World War II left the company in economic ruin, but with the introduction of the Toyopet Crown in 1955, passenger car production began in earnest. In the following years, new models were added in rapid succession as motorization took hold in Japan. In September 1987 Toyota became the fourth automaker to surpass the 60 million mark for cumulative domestic production, following General Motors, Ford, and Chrysler of the United States.

Today Toyota operates 14 domestic plants and 29 plants in 21 countries overseas. In 1990 it had about 69,000 domestic em-

ployees, and total vehicle production surpassed 4.0 million units. Sales for the fiscal year ending June 1990 were ¥8.0 trillion (US $52.3 billion), with exports accounting for 35 percent. The company was capitalized at ¥255.7 billion (US $1.7 billion) in the same year. Headquarters are in the city of Toyota, Aichi Prefecture.

Toyota Tsūshō Corporation   豊田通商[株]

(Toyota Tsūshō). Comprehensive trading company and a core member of the Toyota group of TOYOTA MOTOR CORPORATION. Incorporated in 1948. Toyota Tsūshō has 53 overseas business offices and 11 overseas subsidiaries in 45 countries. The company has diversified into telecommunications and new materials and has equity interests in a number of overseas joint ventures. Sales for the fiscal year ending March 1991 totaled ¥2.2 trillion (US $16.0 billion), and capitalization stood at ¥24.9 billion (US $181.5 million). Headquarters are in Nagoya and Tōkyō.

Tōyō Tire & Rubber Co, Ltd   東洋ゴム工業[株]

(Tōyō Gomu Kōgyō). Rubber company manufacturing automobile tires, industrial and chemical products, and shoes. It is the fourth largest manufacturer of car tires in Japan, specializing in radial tires for trucks and buses and large-size special tires. It was incorporated in 1943 when TŌYŌBŌ CO, LTD, purchased several rubber companies and merged them. The company has sales companies in the United States, Australia, and Germany. Sales for the fiscal year ending March 1991 totaled ¥219.7 billion (US $1.6 billion), and capitalization stood at ¥20.9 billion (US $152.3 million). Headquarters are in Ōsaka.

Toyotomi Hidetsugu   豊臣秀次

(1568–95). Also known as Toyotomi Hidetsugi. Nephew and adopted son of TOYOTOMI HIDEYOSHI; participated in Hideyoshi's military campaigns between 1583 and 1591, when Hideyoshi unified Japan. On 1 February 1592, after the death of his natural son Tsurumatsu (1589–91), Hideyoshi retired as imperial regent (KAMPAKU) and, 10 days later, had this post transferred to Hidetsugu. Hideyoshi also transferred the Jurakudai, his "Palace of Assembled Pleasures" in Kyōto, to Hidetsugu.

Hidetsugu proved unequal to the task of holding this highest post in the aristocratic hierarchy while having to subordinate himself to the wishes of Hideyoshi as TAIKŌ (a title applying to the father of the *kampaku*). He seems to have interfered with certain of Hideyoshi's decisions, and when Hideyoshi's natural son Hiroi (TOYOTOMI HIDEYORI; 1593–1615) was born, Hidetsugu's position became perilous. In 1595 he was disgraced, exiled to the Shingon monastery on Mt. Kōya (Kōyasan), and ordered to commit suicide.

Toyotomi Hideyori   豊臣秀頼

(1593–1615). Son of the national unifier TOYOTOMI HIDEYOSHI and his concubine YODOGIMI. His father tried to ensure Hideyori's succession to his own supreme position. The disgrace and forced suicide in 1595 of Hideyoshi's adopted son, TOYOTOMI HIDETSUGU, may partly be attributed to that wish, as may Hideyoshi's institution of a council of "Five Great Elders" (Gotairō) that same year. The five were TOKUGAWA IEYASU, MAEDA TOSHIIE, Mōri Terumoto (1553–1625),

UESUGI KAGEKATSU, and UKITA HIDEIE. Ieyasu had his own ambitions, and after Ieyasu's victory in the Battle of SEKIGAHARA in 1600 and the founding of the Tokugawa shogunate in 1603, Hideyori was reduced to the position of one among many *daimyō*. He was increasingly isolated in his stronghold at Ōsaka, and in 1614 Ieyasu used the SHŌMEI INCIDENT to provoke armed conflict. The Tokugawa were victorious in the two Ōsaka Campaigns that followed (see ŌSAKA CASTLE, SIEGES OF). On 3 June 1615 Hideyori's wife (Ieyasu's granddaughter) SEN HIME was sent to intercede for her husband. Her plea was fruitless. The next day Hideyori and his mother Yodogimi committed suicide.

Toyotomi Hideyoshi 豊臣秀吉

(1537–98). Warlord of humble origins who in 1590 completed the work of national reunification begun by ODA NOBUNAGA. A brilliant strategist and shrewd politician, he usually showed a generosity toward his enemies untypical of his time. His social reforms, while having the fundamental aim of strengthening his hold on the country, nevertheless showed an awareness of the many socioeconomic problems of the age. Despite his grandiose plans for conquest abroad and the megalomania of the last few years of his life, he is one of the great figures in Japanese history.

At his birth Hideyoshi was called Hiyoshimaru, later changed to Tōkichirō, the family name being Kinoshita. In 1558, on entering Nobunaga's service, he was called Kochiku; in 1562 he changed this name to Hideyoshi and in 1573 changed the family name Kinoshita to Hashiba. In 1585 he was appointed imperial regent (*kampaku*); in 1587 he was appointed grand minister of state (*dajō daijin*) and was given the family name Toyotomi. Hideyoshi is popularly known as TAIKŌ, the honorary title for a retired *kampaku*.

Early Years—Hideyoshi was born in 1537 (some scholars say 1536) at Nakamura in Owari Province (now part of Aichi Prefecture), the son of Kinoshita Yaemon, a foot soldier (*ashigaru*) in the service of Oda Nobuhide (1510–51), father of Nobunaga. In 1558 Hideyoshi presented himself to Nobunaga, who quickly took a liking to him and nicknamed him Saru ("Monkey"). At the time, in the struggle for military hegemony, the army of IMAGAWA YOSHIMOTO, lord of the provinces of Mikawa (now part of Aichi Prefecture), Tōtōmi, and Suruga (the latter two both now part of Shizuoka Prefecture), was advancing on Kyōto. But in his path lay the lands of Nobunaga, who defeated him in the Battle of OKEHAZAMA in 1560. By mid-1573 Nobunaga was firmly established in central Honshū, having destroyed his brother-in-law ASAI NAGAMASA (one of whose daughters, YODOGIMI, was to become Hideyoshi's favorite concubine) and his erstwhile ally ASAKURA YOSHIKAGE. The Asai lands in Ōmi Province (now Shiga Prefecture) were given to Hideyoshi.

General under Oda Nobunaga (1574–1582)—In 1575 Nobunaga was defeated in a naval battle in the bay of Ōsaka by the combined forces of Mōri Terumoto (1553–1625) and the temple-fortress ISHIYAMA HONGANJI. Nobunaga retaliated by dispatching two armies, one led by Hideyoshi, in a pincer movement aimed at subduing the Mōri home base in western Honshū. Hideyoshi took the strategic castle of Himeyama (later Himeji, in Harima Province; now part of Hyōgo Prefecture) in 1577. In 1581 he took

the fortress of Tottori in Inaba Province (now part of Tottori Prefecture); a year later he took Takamatsu Castle in Bitchū Province (now part of Okayama Prefecture) by employing the novel tactic of flooding (*mizuzeme*; see SHIMIZU MUNEHARU).

Taking the Reins of Power (1582–1588)—After Nobunaga was treacherously assassinated at the temple Honnōji in Kyōto by AKECHI MITSUHIDE (see HONNŌJI INCIDENT), Hideyoshi defeated Mitsuhide in the Battle of YAMAZAKI on 2 July 1582. Hideyoshi at 45 was master of the provinces of Ōmi, Harima, Yamashiro, Tamba (the last two now part of Kyōto Prefecture), and Kawachi (now part of Ōsaka Prefecture). Then, by defeating Shibata Katsuie at SHIZUGATAKE, he annexed Echizen, Kaga, and Noto (now Fukui and part of Ishikawa prefectures), and Etchū (now Toyama Prefecture). In 1584, after the KOMAKI NAGAKUTE CAMPAIGN, he arrived at a settlement with TOKUGAWA IEYASU, who had supported Oda Nobukatsu (1558–1630), Nobunaga's son. He then subdued all of Kii Province (now Wakayama Prefecture) and destroyed the organization (IKKŌ IKKI) of the JŌDO SHIN SECT of Saiga in that province. He proceeded to conquer the CHŌSOKABE FAMILY of Shikoku. By the end of 1585 Hideyoshi, newly appointed *kampaku*, or imperial regent, could lay claim to all civil and military powers by delegation of the emperor. In 1587 Hideyoshi extended his power in Kyūshū, thwarting the ambitions of the SHIMAZU FAMILY.

On 23 July 1587 Hideyoshi issued an 11-point edict denouncing Christianity and prohibiting forced conversion. The following day he presented the Edict of Expulsion to the Jesuit missionaries (see ANTI-CHRISTIAN EDICTS). In 1588 all the *daimyō* pledged obedience to the emperor and his regent, Hideyoshi. In the same year Hideyoshi carried out his famous SWORD HUNT. This reduced the likelihood of armed rebellion and separated the peasantry from the warrior class.

The Kantō Campaign (1590–1591)—Hideyoshi's conquest of the northeast remained barred by the Later Hōjō family (see HŌJŌ FAMILY), who occupied the Kantō region. Hideyoshi was able to destroy the allies of the Hōjō and besiege Odawara Castle (see ODAWARA CAMPAIGN). Odawara capitulated on 12 August 1590 and the Kantō provinces were reorganized. In order to remove Ieyasu from central Japan, Hideyoshi gave him six Kantō provinces in exchange for his former holdings in Mikawa, Tōtōmi, and Suruga. In 1591 Hideyoshi crushed all resistance in the

far north of Honshū. The military reunification of Japan was now complete; all territory belonged to Hideyoshi or to his vassals, and a new feudal hierarchy had been established.

Invasions of Korea (1592, 1597)—Once master of Japan, Hideyoshi in 1592 launched his first expedition to conquer Korea, which ended in a draw. The second expedition, in 1597, was abandoned with Hideyoshi's death in 1598. See INVASIONS OF KOREA IN 1592 AND 1597.

Final Years—In his last years, especially after 1593, Hideyoshi seemed almost to have lost touch with the reality around him. Two years earlier his son Tsurumatsu had died, and Hideyoshi had nominated his nephew TOYOTOMI HIDETSUGU as his heir. After he had another son, TOYOTOMI HIDEYORI, he became convinced that Hidetsugu was plotting against him and ordered Hidetsugu to commit suicide. Anxious for the future of Hideyori, now his successor, he created a council of Five Great Elders (Gotairō) and made them swear allegiance to Hideyori. He also became increasingly fearful of Western interference in Japan's internal affairs, especially after the Spanish ship *San Felipe* was shipwrecked on the Japanese coast in 1596 (see SAN FELIPE INCIDENT). Further irritated by the continuous bickering between the Jesuits and the Franciscans, Hideyoshi sentenced 26 Christians to death—the TWENTY-SIX MARTYRS of Nagasaki. Hideyoshi fell ill in the summer of 1598 and died on 18 September 1598. His private letters show him to have been open and affectionate, genial, and impatient with formality. Unfortunately, his insatiable thirst for power cast a shadow of terror during the last years of his life.

Tōyō Trust & Banking Co, Ltd
東洋信託銀行[株]

(Tōyō Shintaku Ginkō). Japanese trust bank. Incorporated in 1959 through the merger of the trust businesses of the SANWA BANK, LTD, and the Kōbe Bank, Ltd (now part of SAKURA BANK, LTD), as well as the securities agency business of the NOMURA SECURITIES CO, LTD. Tōyō Trust specializes in registered securities transactions, investment consultation, securities investment trusts, and other securities-related businesses. The company has diversified into individual annuity trusts and real estate. The company had ¥17.6 trillion (US $128.3 billion) in available funds at the

Toyotomi Hideyoshi
1 The warlord Hideyoshi, shown in an early-Edo-period portrait. He is said to have been small in stature, wearing oversized clothes and a false mustache in order to look more impressive.
2 In this screen from the early Edo period, Hideyoshi is shown standing beneath an umbrella at the extravagant cherry-blossom-viewing party that he held in 1598, five months before his death.

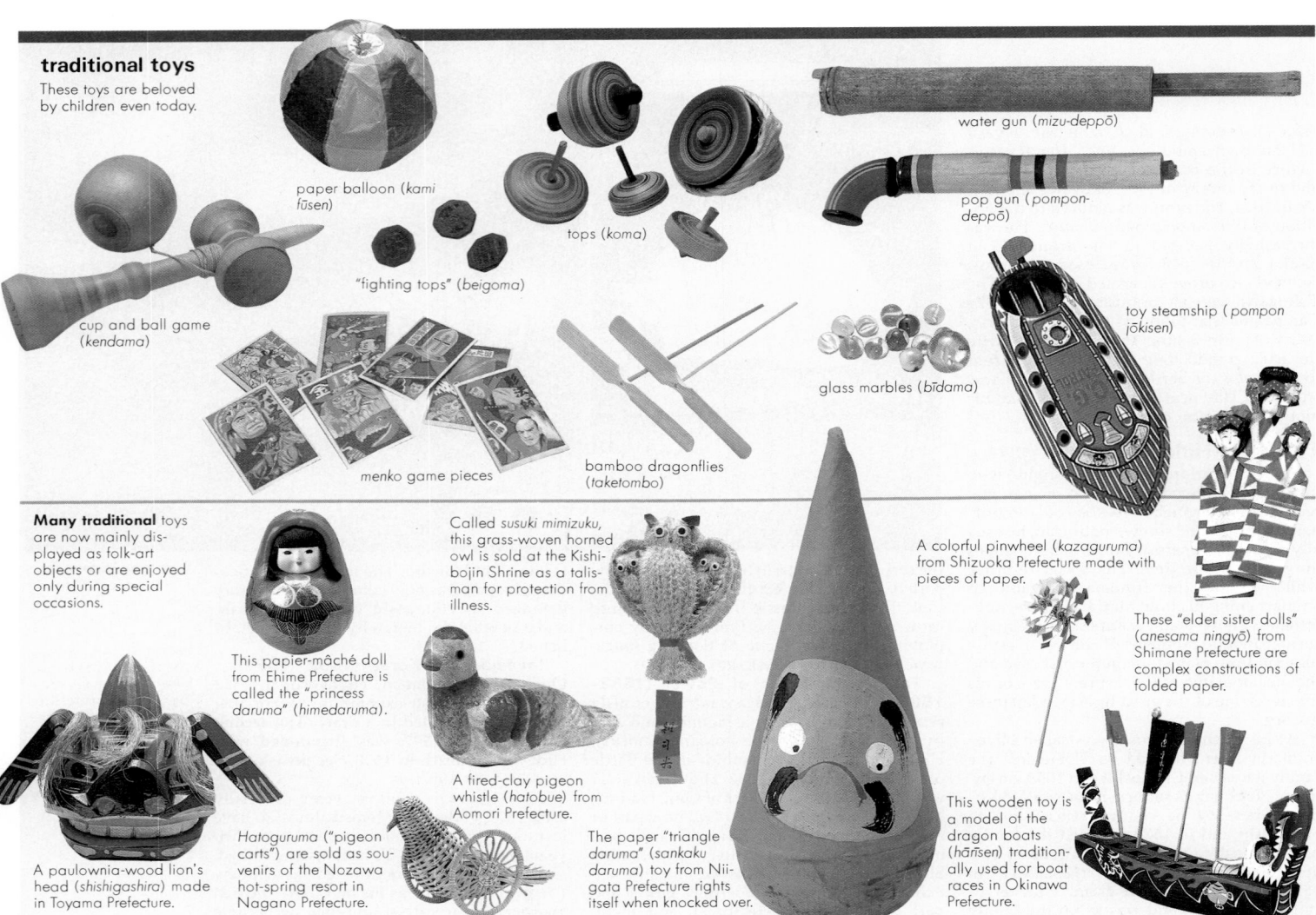

traditional toys
These toys are beloved by children even today.

paper balloon (*kami fūsen*)

cup and ball game (*kendama*)

"fighting tops" (*beigoma*)

tops (*koma*)

water gun (*mizu-deppō*)

pop gun (*pompon-deppō*)

toy steamship (*pompon jōkisen*)

glass marbles (*bīdama*)

menko game pieces

bamboo dragonflies (*taketombo*)

Many traditional toys are now mainly displayed as folk-art objects or are enjoyed only during special occasions.

This papier-mâché doll from Ehime Prefecture is called the "princess *daruma*" (*himedaruma*).

Called *susuki mimizuku*, this grass-woven horned owl is sold at the Kishibojin Shrine as a talisman for protection from illness.

A colorful pinwheel (*kazaguruma*) from Shizuoka Prefecture made with pieces of paper.

These "elder sister dolls" (*anesama ningyō*) from Shimane Prefecture are complex constructions of folded paper.

A paulownia-wood lion's head (*shishigashira*) made in Toyama Prefecture.

Hatoguruma ("pigeon carts") are sold as souvenirs of the Nozawa hot-spring resort in Nagano Prefecture.

A fired-clay pigeon whistle (*hatobue*) from Aomori Prefecture.

The paper "triangle *daruma*" (*sankaku daruma*) toy from Niigata Prefecture rights itself when knocked over.

This wooden toy is a model of the dragon boats (*harīsen*) traditionally used for boat races in Okinawa Prefecture.

---

end of March 1991. It was capitalized at ¥115.0 billion (US $838.2 million) in the same year. Headquarters are in Tōkyō.

Tōyō University   東洋大学
(Tōyō Daigaku). A coeducational private university located in Bunkyō Ward, Tōkyō. Founded in 1928. It originated as the Tetsugakukan (Academy of Philosophy) established by the Buddhist thinker INOUE ENRYŌ in 1887. It maintains faculties of literature, economics, business administration, law, sociology, and engineering. Enrollment in 1989 was 19,907.

toys, traditional   伝統玩具
(*dentō gangu*). The earliest documentary evidence for the existence of toys in Japan dates from the Heian period (794–1185), but there can be little doubt that their origin goes back even further. The greatest age for all kinds of toys was the Edo period (1600–1868). Until then toys had been made largely for members of the court and the aristocracy. The production of traditional toys continues today, but competition from cheap, machine-made toys of plastic, celluloid, metal, and wood is threatening to destroy the traditional toy industry, though such toys are collected by FOLK CRAFTS enthusiasts.

There are almost 1,000 different types of folk toys. These can be roughly divided into three main groups: simple playthings intended for children, more artistic toys that may be enjoyed by children but are also appreciated for their artistry by adults, and charms and dolls connected with local legends and traditions. Typical of the first category are clay and paper dolls, balls (TEMARI), and TOPS. Outstanding in the second group are the often large and magnificently decorated KITES. Other fine objects are the battledores and shuttlecocks still widely used (especially on New Year's Day) for a game known as HANETSUKI. The battledore, or HAGOITA, is usually decorated with a silk collage of actors or beautiful women on one side and floral designs on the other. But most characteristic are the toys belonging to the third category, which were originally religious in character. For example, in Tōkyō newborn infants are traditionally presented with toy dogs, believed to be protective charms. These are called INU HARIKO (or, in the Kyōto-Ōsaka area, Azuma *inu*) and are sold at local Shintō shrines. Other popular toys of this type are the horses often connected with sacred places, DARUMA dolls, KOKESHI (wooden dolls), and beckoning cat figures (MANEKINEKO). See also DOLLS; GAMES.

☎ *1620–1621*

tozama   外様
(literally, "outside" vassals). A term by which SAMURAI lords, such as the Hōjō regents of the Kamakura period (1185–1333) and the Ashikaga shōguns of the Muromachi period (1333–1568), distinguished samurai lineages that were not subordinate to their own family through kinship or hereditary service from their hereditary vassals (FUDAI). The TOKUGAWA SHOGUNATE (1603–1867) identified as *tozama daimyō* those lords who had acquired their daimyō status under ODA NOBUNAGA or TOYOTOMI HIDEYOSHI and who had sworn fealty to the Tokugawa family before or after the Battle of SEKIGAHARA (1600). Daimyō lineages descended from the dynastic founder, TOKUGAWA IEYASU, were called SHIMPAN, and hereditary vassal daimyō whose allegiance antedated Sekigahara were designated *fudai*. *Tozama* generally held higher rank and larger domains than *fudai*, but were less secure in their status. The relatively precarious position of the *tozama* is reflected in the changing numbers of daimyō due to dispossession (KAIEKI). Whereas in 1602 there were 117 *tozama* as opposed to 78 *fudai* and *shimpan*, by 1795 there were only 98 *tozama* as opposed to 168 *fudai* and *shimpan* lords.

track and field events   陸上競技
(*rikujō kyōgi*). Track and field events were introduced to Japan in the 1870s from England and the United States and developed as a student sport; the first school meet was held in 1874 at the Tsukiji Naval Academy in Tōkyō. Participation on the international level began with the 1912 Stockholm Olympic Games. In the 1924 Paris Olympics ODA MIKIO placed sixth in the triple jump, and Japan entered its "golden age," winning this event in the next three Olympic Games. Japanese athletes also did well in other Olympic events and international meets during these years. Since World War II, Japanese athletes have been less prominent except in MARATHONS.

trade balance   貿易収支
(*bōeki shūshi*). The difference over a period of time between the value of a country's exports and imports of merchandise. The trade balance is one of the most frequently

used indicators of a country's BALANCE OF PAYMENTS.

Japan experienced a continuing deficit trade balance after World War II since many of its production facilities had been destroyed or depleted during the war. It also suffered from a chronic shortage of foreign currency. After about 1964, however, Japan's trade balance began to show a surplus. Earlier equipment investments, particularly in the heavy-industry field, contributed to the improvement. Another factor was lower commodity price increases in Japan than in the United States and Europe, which strengthened the international competitiveness of Japanese products. In 1974 Japan's trade surplus fell sharply due to a rise in the value of the yen (a result of the changeover to a floating exchange rate system in August 1971) and steep increases in oil prices. However, Japan's trade surplus again expanded as a result of rapid progress in the development of Japan's industrial structure and the favorable effect of energy conservation measures.

In the 1980s such factors as macroeconomic structural disparities between Japan and the United States, Japan's high savings rate, and excess consumption in the United States and other Western countries contributed to further increases in the Japanese trade surplus, which in 1984 reached US $44.0 billion, a dramatic increase over the previous year's figure of US $9.5 billion. Up to the mid-1980s the relative weakness of the yen against the dollar tended to accelerate the growth of the trade surplus. Despite the reversal of the relative strengths of the dollar and the yen following the PLAZA ACCORD of 1985, Japan's yearly trade surplus continued to climb and in 1988 reached US $95.0 billion, of which US $47.6 billion was with the United States alone. Japan's one-sided trade balance with the United States is a major cause of continuing friction between the two countries. The series of STRUCTURAL IMPEDIMENTS INITIATIVE TALKS, which began in 1989, are an attempt to remove the underlying causes of this friction. See also FOREIGN TRADE.

trade friction 貿易摩擦

(bōeki masatsu). Trade friction has been a recurring issue in Japan's relationships with other nations since the mid-1950s. At various times trade disputes have erupted between Japan and the United States and also between Japan and the European Community (EC), the Association of Southeast Asian Nations (ASEAN), and Australia. Until the early 1980s, friction primarily involved efforts to control rising Japanese exports and to prevent alleged dumping of Japanese products. During most of the 1980s Japan's trade disputes with the United States typically involved attempts to gain greater access to the Japanese market. In contrast, in the 1980s trade disputes between Japan and Europe continued to focus on the issues of limiting Japanese imports and preventing alleged dumping in European markets. The STRUCTURAL IMPEDIMENTS INITIATIVE TALKS, which began in 1989, marked a new phase by addressing so-called nontariff obstacles to trade between the United States and Japan.

The history of Japan's trade friction is both lengthy and broad in scope. For example, until about 1981 Japan placed voluntary limits on exports to the United States through agreements in the following areas: cotton goods (1957), steel (1969), wool and synthetic fibers (1972), color televisions (1977), and automobiles (1981). (See VOLUNTARY EXPORT RESTRICTIONS.) Japan also agreed to restrain its steel exports to Europe in 1972. To counter dumping, the United States instituted a formula to trigger penalties on steel imported at unfairly low prices (1978); a similar settlement in machine tools was reached at about the same time.

Through the late 1970s and the 1980s, as a result of the US objective of improving access to the Japanese market, the following accommodations were reached: increases in Japanese import quotas in beef and oranges (1978), revision of Japanese import standards and certification procedures (1981), the Japanese government's Action Program to Improve Market Access (1985), the Japan–United States Semiconductor Agreement (1986, 1991), and the Market-Oriented Sector Selective agreement (see MOSS TALKS) covering Japanese markets for telecommunications equipment, electronics, pharmaceuticals, medical equipment, forest products, and transportation equipment (1987). Similarly, the "Super 301" clause of the US Omnibus Trade and Competitiveness Act (1988) was applied to improve access to Japan's supercomputer, satellite, and wood product markets (1988). In contrast with the market-opening approach adopted by the United States, from the early 1980s Japan has had a number of disputes with the EC countries and Australia concerning Japanese exports of videocassette recorders. Disputes with EC countries also occurred regarding exports of Japanese semiconductors (1986).

Under the Structural Impediments Initiative agreement of 1990, Japan and the United States established a wide-ranging basis on which each country will address structural issues affecting bilateral trade. Specifically, Japan has agreed to investigate price differentials existing betwen Japan and other countries, Japanese distribution and business group practices (see KEIRETSU), and other issues. For its part, the United States has agreed to address its fiscal deficit, the link between savings and investment, corporate capital spending and research-and-development practices, education, and other matters. While the General Agreement on Tariffs and Trade (GATT) provides a forum for Japanese participation in multilateral negotiations on trade among some 96 participating countries, disagreement among the nations of the European Community, the United States, and Japan over agricultural trade has stalled talks since the start of the so-called URUGUAY ROUND of 1986. In particular, since the mid-1980s the United States has been strongly urging Japan to liberalize its rice market, and the Japanese government has agreed to discuss the issue within the context of the Uruguay Round negotiations. However, there is considerable domestic opposition to liberalization, as was seen in September 1988, when all parties in both houses of the Diet were united in resolving to reject it. Some within the ruling Liberal Democratic Party are nevertheless prepared to accept partial liberalization.

The series of negotiated settlements covering Japan's trade friction has in turn spawned a number of significant economic developments. For example, Japan has responded to restrictions on exports by moving production of some products such as color televisions and automobiles to the United States. Japanese companies also increased the number of automobiles manufactured in Europe, notably the United Kingdom (see JAPANESE BUSINESSES OVERSEAS). In

1991 US automobile manufacturers filed dumping charges concerning exports of Japanese minivans. Measures have remained in place to limit Japanese exports to the European Community, while discussion prior to 1992 EC market integration focused on such matters as how to evaluate the local content of Japanese automobiles manufactured in Europe. See also FOREIGN TRADE; UNITED STATES, ECONOMIC RELATIONS WITH; EUROPEAN COMMUNITY, ECONOMIC RELATIONS WITH.

trade liberalization 貿易自由化

(bōeki jiyūka). Immediately after World War II, Japan was allowed to maintain a number of economic controls, including import restrictions. As a condition for joining international organizations such as the General Agreement on Tariffs and Trade (GATT) and the International Monetary Fund (IMF), however, Japan was required to liberalize substantially its trade policies. In 1955 the percentage of liberalized products was only 15 percent, but this figure rose to 90 percent by 1963. International trade was liberalized further in the 1960s as the result of multilateral tariff negotiations sponsored by GATT. In 1967 Japan instituted the across-the-board tariff reductions agreed to during the talks known as the Kennedy Round and removed tariffs from 2,147 items. Discussions in the mid-1970s known as the Tōkyō Round removed more tariffs and created rules for other trade issues.

In the 1980s Japan adopted other measures to open its domestic market to imports. In the Action Program for Improving Market Access announced in July 1985, tariffs were reduced on or removed from 1,853 items. Since 1986, tariffs have been lowered for such major products as leather and shoes, cigarettes, alcohol, chocolate, beef, and oranges. Japan's tariff rates are the lowest among the advanced industrialized countries. As of 1992, Japan still protected 12 agricultural products through import quotas, but international pressures were moving Japan closer to removing restrictions even in politically sensitive areas such as rice. See also TARIFFS; RESIDUAL IMPORT RESTRICTIONS.

Trademark Law 商標法

(Shōhyō Hō). The Trademark Law of 1959 sets forth a registration system under which trademarks having distinctive character are registered for designated goods or services. Registration confers on the registrant an exclusive right to use the registered trademark for the designated goods or services for 10 years. Registration is renewable for another 10 years if the registered trademark is in continuous use. "Trademarks" (shōhyō) are defined to include both marks (hyōshō)—i.e., "characters, letters, figures or signs, or any combination of these and colors"—to be used for goods (shōhin), and marks to be used for services (ekimu; art. 2[1]). Service marks have been made registrable by the 1991 revision of the Trademark Law.

trade name 商号

(shōgō). In Japanese law, a name used for an article or a service by a trader or company in the conduct of its business. A trader is not necessarily required to choose a trade name, but a company must select and register a specific trade name. The COMMERCIAL CODE provides rules applicable to trade names.

trade secrets → know-how

From Tin Toys to Game Boys

◀ **This pop-up book** depicts the chief events of a traditional Japanese story.

1868–1912 Meiji Period

A young girl plays with her toys in this illustration by Kawakami Shirō for *Dōyō gashū*, a 1937 picture book of children's songs and nursery rhymes.

▶ **When water** is poured down the back of this painted tin figure of a legendary *samurai* hero, a waterwheel is set in motion and the drumsticks begin to beat.

▲ **Metal toys** such as this station building and train set appeared in the late Meiji period.

▼ **A windup tin model** of a horse-drawn omnibus, a common form of urban transport in Meiji Japan.

◀ **Lithographs of famous places** were magnified when inserted in this viewer made of paulownia wood.

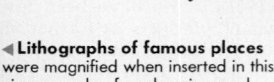

For centuries, Japanese children played with traditional toys made of paper, wood, and clay. Then came the toy revolution—the import in the Meiji period of Western playthings made of tin, rubber, and celluloid. While toys on traditional themes continued to be produced, Japanese craftsmen soon mastered the construction of rubber-band-powered, windup, and flywheel-driven mechanical toys, many modeled on novelties of the era such as railway trains.

In the Taishō period, propeller-driven airplanes and other complex products based on German models were available at the upper end of the toy market. The popular end was represented by such items as horses on springs and dolls in Western dress.

Older Japanese may still fondly recall the jack-in-the-boxes and tin toys sold by street vendors during the 1920s and 1930s. With the outbreak of the Sino-Japanese War in 1937, however, the making of metal toys was banned. During World War II, Japan's production was limited mostly to war toys made of wood, paper, and bamboo.

After the war ended, very little time passed before former toy makers were turning tin cans into toy jeeps and other such products. The 1960s and 1970s were the age of plastic models, electric toys, and, later, remote controls. More recently, Japanese toys have entered the age of electronics that is typified by portable computer games such as Nintendō's Game Boy.

▶ **This toy figure** of General Nogi Maresuke, who was glorified for committing ritual suicide following the death of Emperor Meiji, is made of celluloid. The wheeled platform is tin.

▲ **Aluminum zeppelins** appeared in the early 1920s. The zeppelin was suspended on a thread, and its propeller made it fly in a circle.

◀ **A hit product** of 1914. The pony bounds along when the spring is pushed down and released.

◀ **This stuffed doll** in Western clothes is made with a variety of fabrics, including rayon. Its features are painted.

1912–1926 Taishō Period

1926–1945 Early Shōwa Period

◀**Dressed like** a fashionable girl of the period, this doll is made of plaster and painted with opaque watercolors.

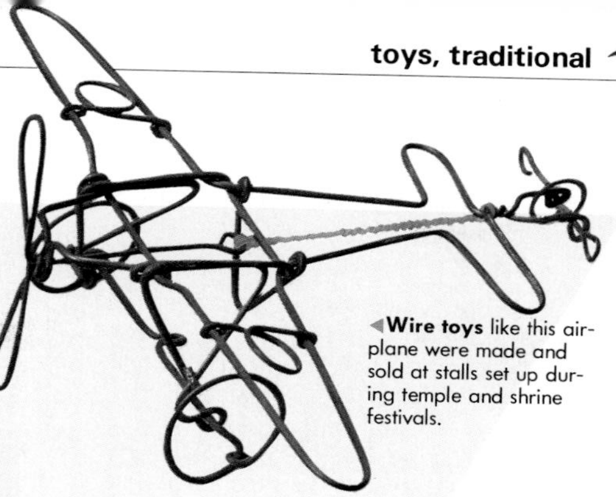

◀**Wire toys** like this airplane were made and sold at stalls set up during temple and shrine festivals.

▼**Changes of clothes,** bedding, and a trunk accompany a clay doll. As war approached, rayon came into use in place of silk.

▲**Painted tin goldfish** were floated in the bathtub. Similar toys are still made today.

▼**The use of tin** in toys for the domestic market was prohibited in 1938. During World War II, paper trumpets and bamboo antiaircraft guns, tanks, and pistols appeared.

▲**Jack-in-the-box toys** first appeared in the Meiji period and then returned to popularity in the late 1920s. The cat-in-the-box was a particular favorite.

1945–1989 Late Shōwa Period

▶**This windup airplane** does somersaults. Imprinted with the words "Made in Occupied Japan," it was exported to the United States.

▲**Plastic model airplanes** went on sale in Japan in 1958, and in the 1960s were hugely popular.

▼**Video games** were first sold in the late 1970s. Since the appearance of the Game & Watch, a pocket video game, in 1981, "electronics" has been the watchword of toy manufacturers.

▲**A toy jeep** was the desire of every child in the early postwar period of scarcity. This jeep was produced in 1947.

▶**The robot Tetsujin 28,** a comic book and TV cartoon character who gained a large following, was also a hit as a remote-control toy.

◀**The first Rika chan doll,** a dress-up doll whose tastes in fashion have evolved with the times, appeared in 1967.

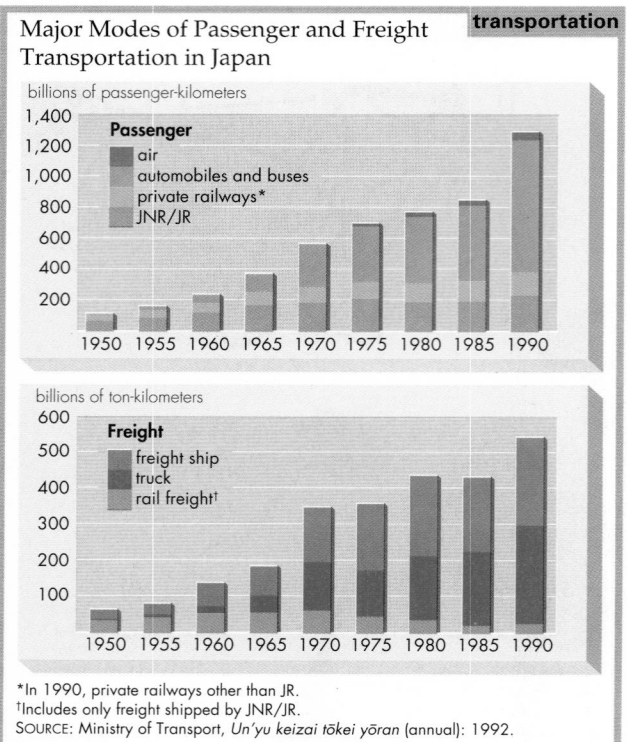

Major Modes of Passenger and Freight Transportation in Japan

billions of passenger-kilometers

Passenger
- air
- automobiles and buses
- private railways*
- JNR/JR

1,400 1,200 1,000 800 600 400 200

1950 1955 1960 1965 1970 1975 1980 1985 1990

billions of ton-kilometers

Freight
- freight ship
- truck
- rail freight†

600 500 400 300 200 100

1950 1955 1960 1965 1970 1975 1980 1985 1990

*In 1990, private railways other than JR.
†Includes only freight shipped by JNR/JR.
SOURCE: Ministry of Transport, *Un'yu keizai tōkei yōran* (annual): 1992.

---

trade unions → labor unions

"transcendental" cabinets

超然内閣

(*chōzen naikaku*). Cabinets intended to be above the partisan interests of political parties. The term was first used by Prime Minister KURODA KIYOTAKA on 12 February 1889. It reflected the profound distrust on the part of government leaders toward the political parties, which in turn assailed the idea of a nonparty cabinet as a pretext for government dominance by cliques (see HAMBATSU). The concept of "transcendental" cabinets was revived in the 1920s and 1930s.

translation rights

翻訳権

(*hon'yakuken*). The right to translate a book, article, or other original piece of writing into another language. Under the Japanese COPYRIGHT LAW (Chosakuken Hō) of 1970, the author of a work has the exclusive right to reproduce the work (art. 21) as well as the exclusive right to translate it into another language or dramatize, cinematize, or otherwise adapt it (art. 27). Translation rights can be assigned or licensed. When a copyright is assigned without specifically mentioning the translation rights, it is presumed that the original holder of copyright retains translation rights (art. 61[2]).

When a work is translated, the translation is a derivative work that is protected as an independent work of authorship. The translator's copyright protection for the translation lasts from the moment of its creation until 50 years after his or her death (art. 51).

transportation

交通

(*kōtsū*). Japan has a highly developed domestic and international transportation network. The system as it now exists was developed in the century following the Meiji Restoration of 1868, but even earlier the transportation system was relatively sophisticated for a preindustrial society.

Premodern Transportation—During the early periods of Japanese history, and especially during the official contacts of the 7th to 9th centuries, goods and people traveled extensively in ships (see SHIPS, TRADITIONAL) between Japan and the Asian mainland (see SUI AND TANG [T'ANG] CHINA, EMBASSIES TO). Within Japan, the establishment of a rice tax system and legal system in the late 7th century was accompanied by the construction of the first major roads. The Inland Sea was a major transportation route between settlements in Japan from early times, and by the 16th century the Japanese had also become major traders in the China Sea region.

After the establishment of the Tokugawa shogunate (1603–1867), international transportation activity was halted by the NATIONAL SECLUSION policy, which was in force from 1639 to 1854. Domestic transportation, on the other hand, grew and improved greatly during the peace, stability, and economic growth of the Edo period (1600–1868). Coastal shipping routes were extended to support the expanding commodity trade, and the road network was also improved.

Meiji Period (1868–1912) to World War II—Following the Meiji Restoration of 1868, Japan absorbed Western technology at a rapid pace. The first steam-powered train ran between Tōkyō and Yokohama in 1872, the first automobile was imported in 1899, the first automobile was produced domestically in 1907, and the first airplane in 1911. Western sailing and steam vessels quickly replaced most Japanese sailing ships, as the government took an active role in subsidizing shipbuilding of oceangoing vessels. From the 1880s onward the rail network expanded rapidly and in 1906 major portions of it were nationalized. In 1927 the first subway in Tōkyō began operation. Bus service began in 1919 and trucking companies in 1915, with rapid expansion taking place after the TŌKYŌ EARTHQUAKE OF 1923. During the 1930s taxis developed into an important means of urban transportation.

By the 1940s the mainstay of the domestic passenger transportation system was the railroads, while domestic freight transportation was conducted primarily through coastal shipping and the railroads. Trucks were used largely to deliver freight from railroad stations.

Postwar Transportation Network—At the conclusion of World War II, the transportation system was in ruins. The damaged rail network was burdened with meeting the major part of passenger and freight transportation needs: in 1950 the railroads provided 90 percent of total domestic passenger-kilometers, and 52 percent of domestic freight ton-kilometers.

The postwar era was characterized by an explosive growth in the number of automobiles, trucks, and airlines. By 1990 the rail share of total domestic passenger transportation had fallen to 30 percent, with automobiles increasing from less than 1 percent in 1950 to 57 percent in 1990. Buses also compete with the railroads to some extent, but they mainly provide feeder service to train stations or operate in rural areas where there is no rail service. SUBWAYS are an important means of urban transportation, with a total length of 523.6 kilometers (325.3 mi) in 1991. In addition to the vast network in Tōkyō, there are also subway systems in Fukuoka, Kōbe, Kyōto, Nagoya, Ōsaka, Sapporo, Sendai, and Yokohama.

Scheduled domestic airlines have grown rapidly but still occupy a small share (4 percent in 1990) of total passenger transportation. International air travel has also grown at a tremendous pace: the number of passengers carried by scheduled Japanese airlines was only 112,000 in 1955 but reached 10.5 million in 1990.

For freight transportation, the rail share of total domestic ton-kilometers fell to 5 percent by 1990, while trucks expanded from 8 percent in 1950 to 50 percent in 1990, and coastal shipping went from 39 percent to 45 percent.

Coordination and control of the transportation system has been a problem because different modes of transportation are governed by separate laws and represented by different bureaus within the MINISTRY OF TRANSPORT. In addition, certain transportation-related activities are under the jurisdiction of other ministries. Highway investment, for example, is under MINISTRY OF CONSTRUCTION control.

Railroads. The network of railways consists of the JR group and a number of private railways. The JR group is made up of six passenger railway companies, a freight railway company, and several other affiliated companies, all of which were created when long-term financial difficulties led to the privatization of the JAPANESE NATIONAL RAILWAYS (JNR) in 1987. In 1990 the rail system comprised 26,895 operation-kilometers (16,710 mi), of which JR companies operated 20,175 or 75 percent of the total. JR passenger service includes intercity trunk lines, urban feeder service, and a large number of rural lines. It also operates Japan's fastest passenger trains on the three SHINKANSEN lines. In 1950 the JNR alone generated 59 percent of all domestic passenger-kilometers, but this figure had fallen to 18 percent for the JR in 1990. The JR group's JAPAN FREIGHT RAILWAY CO provides almost all of the rail freight service in Japan. However, given the short distances involved in domestic transportation, railroads can no longer effectively compete with trucks for most freight business.

In addition to the JR group companies, there are 16 large railway companies and 58 smaller railways. Unlike the JR, whose predecessor, the JNR, was restricted from operating nonrail businesses, the other large railway companies have evolved into conglomerates of related activities, operating sports stadiums, baseball teams, department stores, amusement parks, and real estate. More of their profits often come from businesses operated along their railway lines than from the lines themselves.

Motor vehicles. Private automobiles have been one of the fastest growing segments of domestic passenger transportation because of three factors that were especially important during the 1960s. These were the rapid growth of income to a point where families could afford automobiles, the development of a domestic AUTOMOTIVE INDUSTRY geared to the specific needs of the domestic market (small-sized vehicles with right-hand drive), and the improvement of roads. The number of registered motor vehicles increased from only about 1.5 million in 1960 to over 43 million in 1990. Paving on national highways was extended from 29 percent in 1960 to 98 percent in 1991. Japan also completed its first limited-access expressway in 1965 and by 1991 had developed a total of 4,869 kilometers (3,025 mi) of EXPRESSWAYS. Even as late as 1960, 20 percent of all automobiles were business vehicles (taxis and company vehicles), but by 1990 private automobiles were 97 percent of total registrations. Despite the popularity of automobile ownership, problems such as urban traffic congestion, lack of parking, and the high cost of fuel continue to restrict the actual day-to-day use of private vehicles in Japan.

Freight motor carriers have also benefited from the improvement of highways during the postwar period. As roads have improved, trucks have increased in size. Whereas most commercial trucks did not exceed a 5-ton capacity in the mid-1950s, 18-ton trucks are now common and the number of trailer trucks is also increasing.

During the 1980s the parcel delivery service business grew rapidly. Small parcels such as gifts and catalog purchases are delivered on the day of or following their dispatch.

Highway safety continues to be a major problem. Although major safety campaigns led to a steady decline in traffic deaths between 1970 and 1980, since then the trend has reversed, and in 1988 highway fatalities exceeded 10,000.

Marine transportation. Seaborne freight is the primary means of transporting Japan's huge volume of raw-materials imports and finished-goods exports. Total tonnage handled by Japanese ports grew at an annual rate of 15 percent from 1980 to 1990. More than half of the tonnage handled in ports during this period was domestic coastal shipping freight. The most important of Japan's 121 international ports are the Tōkyō Bay area (Tōkyō, Yokohama, Kawasaki, and Chiba), Nagoya, the Ōsaka Bay area (Ōsaka and Kōbe), Kita Kyūshū, and Wakayama Shimotsu (a major oil port).

Supporting the rise in shipping volumes in the postwar era, the Japanese government invested considerable money in improved harbor facilities, including container-handling equipment. The government also provided financial assistance such as low-interest loans to the shipping industry for ship purchase and maintenance.

Since the OIL CRISIS OF 1973 an oversupply of ships worldwide has hurt the shipping industry as a whole. Japanese shipping companies have lost international competitiveness because of rising wages and the continuing high value of the yen since 1985. In 1990 only 6.9 percent of export tonnage and 28.6 percent of import tonnage was moved on Japanese vessels. Japanese-owned vessels under flags of convenience (registered in foreign countries) have been increasing to gain the advantage of lower-cost labor. By 1990 the total gross tons of vessels flying the Japanese flag had fallen about 42 percent from its peak of 35 million tons in 1982. The industry has responded to the difficult business environment by trying to increase efficiency through mergers and large-scale reductions in capacity. The overall 7.1 percent increase in operating income for Japan's top five shipping companies in 1990 indicates that industry recovery may finally have begun.

Along with the increases in maritime freight through the mid-1970s, Japan's SHIP-BUILDING INDUSTRY expanded to a point where Japan became the world's largest shipbuilder. Japan pioneered the construction of supertankers, which were instrumental in supplying Japan's energy needs at substantially reduced transportation costs. However, the oil crisis and ensuing severe recession brought depression to the shipbuilding industry. Since then the government has taken measures to reduce capacity and employment in the industry.

Air transportation. After World War II, passenger airlines were prohibited by SCAP (the supreme commander for the Allied

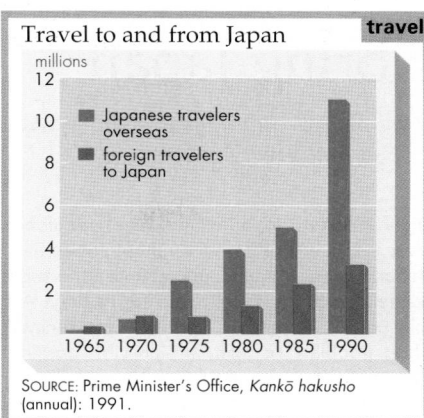

Travel to and from Japan

millions (0–12)

- Japanese travelers overseas
- foreign travelers to Japan

1965 1970 1975 1980 1985 1990

SOURCE: Prime Minister's Office, *Kankō hakusho* (annual): 1991.

powers) until 1951. At that time the Ministry of Transport was given control over licensing airline routes and fares. At the recommendation of the ministry's Civil Aviation Agency, JAPAN AIRLINES CO, LTD (JAL), was established in 1953 as an international airline (including domestic trunk lines) with 50 percent government capital participation. At the same time approval was also given to two private regional firms, which later merged to become ALL NIPPON AIRWAYS CO, LTD (ANA). JAL became a private company in 1987.

As of January 1991 there were 5 scheduled international airlines in Japan, including JAL and ANA, as well as 6 scheduled domestic airlines and 49 unscheduled air service companies. To handle the increased air traffic, AIRPORTS have also expanded. In the spring of 1978, the NEW TŌKYŌ INTERNATIONAL AIRPORT (Narita) replaced TŌKYŌ INTERNATIONAL AIRPORT (Haneda) as the main international airport for Tōkyō. KANSAI INTERNATIONAL AIRPORT is expected to open in 1994 in Ōsaka.

Transportation Museum 交通博物館

(Kōtsū Hakubutsukan). Museum in Chiyoda Ward, Tōkyō. Opened in 1921, the museum maintains a permanent collection and display of land, sea, and air vehicles, both originals and models, many equipped for actual operation.

travel 旅

(*tabi*). The archetype of Japanese travel is the pilgrimage (*junrei;* see PILGRIMAGES), popular since the Heian period (794–1185) among the aristocracy, who visited such holy places as ISE SHRINE, KUMANO SANZAN SHRINES, HASEDERA, and SHITENNŌJI. During the Edo period (1600–1868), a time of peace and prosperity, pilgrimages were made by all classes of people. Lodging houses and souvenir shops flourished, and several set circuits became established, among them the 88 Temples of Shikoku and the 33 Holy Places of the Western Provinces. More arduous journeys were made to holy mountains such as KŌYASAN (Mt. Kōya) and FUJISAN (Mt. Fuji). The requirement by the Tokugawa shogunate (1603–1867) that its vassals reside in Edo (now Tōkyō) in alternate years (see SANKIN KŌTAI) resulted in the systemization of highways (KAIDŌ) and the establishment of facilities for travelers. Although travel by ordinary citizens was closely regulated by the shogunal and domainal governments, journeys to shrines and temples were permitted, hence for commoners pilgrimages often became something of a jaunt.

In the Meiji period (1868–1912) a network of rail lines was constructed, making travel much less of an ordeal than it had once been. Nevertheless, though all were free to travel, few but the wealthy did so for pleasure. A tourist industry directed toward a mass market did not develop until the late 1950s,

when group tours—sponsored by companies for their employees—to hot springs such as Atami in Shizuoka Prefecture became popular.

In the 1980s a rising standard of living and the wide introduction of the five-day workweek contributed to an increase in tourism, and in 1990 the average annual per capita expenditure for domestic travel was ¥67,000 (US $463). The busiest times for travel in Japan are GOLDEN WEEK, a seven-day period (29 April through 5 May) that includes four national holidays, and a period of about a week centered on 15 August (see BON FESTIVAL). Although group tours are still common, Japanese today usually travel in the company of friends and family, often staying at resorts that provide sports and recreation facilities. Lodgings run the gamut from Western-style hotels and Japanese INNS to YOUTH HOSTELS and guesthouses (see MINSHUKU; PENSHON). The growing strength of the yen has led to a phenomenal increase in overseas travel. Between 1986 and 1990 the number of Japanese traveling abroad each year increased from 5.5 million to 11.0 million.
⏵⏵*1624–1625*

travel diaries 紀行文学

(*kikō bungaku*). The term *kikō* (travel diaries), more formally called *kikō bungaku* (travel diary literature), applies to a body of literature comprising generally short prose accounts of journeys, often anonymous and often containing many poems. The theme of travel has a long tradition in Japanese literature, with its roots in the *kiryoka* (travel poems) of the 8th-century anthology MAN'YŌSHŪ. Approximately 70 travel diaries written between the Heian period (794–1185) and 1600 are extant, and many more were produced during the Edo (1600–1868) and Meiji (1868–1912) periods.

The earliest Japanese literary work of note that could be called a true travel diary is the *Tosa nikki* (935, Tosa Diary) of KI NO TSURAYUKI. However, this is usually classified by Japanese literary historians as an example of the related genre of NIKKI BUNGAKU (diary literature), rather than as a *kikō* proper. The SARASHINA NIKKI (ca 1059) also begins with an extended passage describing the author's

Continued on page 1626 ➤

travel Ukiyo-e prints featuring travel scenes became popular during the Edo period as more people began to undertake journeys. Pictured are two prints from Hiroshige's series, *Fifty-Three Stations of the Tōkaidō Road.*
1 In the *Kanaya* print, a group crosses the river Ōigawa.
2 The *Hara* print depicts travelers walking near Mt. Fuji.

Exploring Japan

*There is no better way to capture the true nature of a country than to travel in it,
and Japan—the subject of so much mythmaking—has a lot to reveal.*

The greatest pleasure of traveling in Japan is discovering the subtle ways in which people and regions distinguish themselves in a culture where, as an old saying goes, "the nail that sticks up gets hammered down." After the Meiji Restoration in 1868, Japan cultivated the idea of seamless homogeneity, of a great, extended national family united in purpose. But before that, people from different areas had trouble understanding one another, so divergent were the local dialects. Each region had its own characteristic cuisine, customs, and architectural style. Today these variations are appreciated, particularly now that they are threatened with uniformity through standardized education, television, fast food, and prefab housing.

A few years ago a railway travel campaign exhorted people to "Discover Exotic Japan"—a back-to-the-roots directive aimed at the Japanese themselves. Traveling in Japan heightens one's senses and enhances one's powers of discernment, so that what once seemed an imposing monolith suddenly comes alive with color and contrast.

Tōhoku

If there is one area that serves as the "old country" for the collective Japanese consciousness, it is Tōhoku, the northern part of Japan's main island. Tōhoku people, with their earthy accents and customs, are affectionately regarded as country cousins by their compatriots, although they are now fast overtaking the rest of the nation.

Two of my favorite places in Tōhoku are the former castle towns of Morioka and Hirosaki, both proudly traditional but forward-looking, too. In Morioka, I enjoy visiting the eccentric Hashimoto Museum of Art and then sampling the regional cuisine at the Nambu Robata restaurant.

In Hirosaki, one can wander among shops that sell lacquer ware, baskets, textiles, kites, and toys made by traditional artisans. At night, a *shamisen* master plays Tōhoku ballads at the Yamauta restaurant.

Tōhoku also offers many opportunities for that quintessential old-country experience, the rustic hot spring. Tsurunoyu Onsen, two hours west of Morioka, and Aoni Onsen, near Hirosaki, are both wonderful spas deep in the mountains. While soaking in the communal open-air baths, you may find yourself sharing hot *sake* flavored with *mamushi*, a venomous snake, which is said to enhance virility.

Central Japan

Another area with a high nostalgia quotient is Chūbu, the mountainous zone lying between Tōkyō and Kyōto. Travelers of a bygone era made the journey between the cities by one of two major routes, the famed coastal Tōkaidō route and the inland Nakasendō route. Today most of the Tōkaidō has been covered over with expressways and Shinkansen "bullet train" tracks. But stretches of the Nakasendō remain almost unchanged.

In the former post-station town of Tsumago, you can hike along parts of the Nakasendō, reliving scenes immortalized in the woodblock prints of the famous Edo-period *ukiyo*-e artist Hiroshige. Then you can spend the night at one of the old roadside inns, where the bathtubs are still made of fragrant cypress wood. Tsumago remains well preserved because it was left out of the economic mainstream. Ironically, the town's survival now hinges on its ability

A hardworking woman from a rural village in Kanagawa Prefecture.

to attract the yen of tradition-hungry tourists. This is the case with many places throughout Japan, particularly in the remoter corners.

In Chūbu, tourism also supports bucolic areas such as Shirakawa, a village famed for its huge A-frame farmhouses (many of which take guests), and the Noto Peninsula, which has numerous hot springs and beautiful stretches of coastline. Without tourism, magnificent old buildings would not be preserved, nor would people be able to make a living. Yet hordes of visitors detract from the beauty of these places.

One of the prime examples is the highland city of Takayama. In spring and fall, its elegant streets, lined with Edo-period merchant houses, are nearly impassable. It is still worth visiting, but, for a less harried experience, go in the winter and stay at a place like the Nagase Ryokan or the more economical Ryokan Gōdo.

History and commerce seem to coexist comfortably in the vibrant city of Kanazawa, former capital of one of the wealthiest feudal domains of the Edo period. Kanazawa style is rich and sophisticated, influenced by that of Kyōto, yet bolder and more colorful. You can spend days exploring the superb mansions, the famed garden Kenrokuen, the old *samurai* mansions, pleasure quarters, temple districts, and artisans' workshops. If you have enough money for a splurge, stay at the Asadaya. This exquisite modern inn will give you a wonderful taste of Kanazawa-style refinement and cuisine. The Kotobukiya, a charming restaurant housed in a 120-year-old mansion, serves vegetarian meals, which are gorgeously presented on antique porcelain and lacquer ware.

The Chūbu region is home to two major pilgrimage centers, Ise and Nagano. The famed Ise Shrine, dedicated to the ancestral gods of the imperial family, is one of the most important Shintō shrines in Japan. During feudal times, the nation would occasionally be swept up in pilgrimage fervor, and throngs of people would descend on the town. The Asakichi Ryokan is a former pilgrims' inn that still takes guests.

At the temple Zenkōji in Nagano, pilgrims remain big business. Every year hundreds of thousands of them visit Zenkōji to touch the "key to paradise" located in a dark tunnel under the main hall. The roads leading to the temple are lined with subtemples, most of which offer lodging to guests.

Kansai

Once you've crossed Chūbu, you will arrive in Kyōto. After an appropriate sojourn in this glorious city—which reigned as capital of Japan for more than a thousand years—you would do well to continue onward to Nara, the 8th-century capital. There, every edifice, from the Kasuga Shrine to the Great Buddha Hall of Tōdaiji, and every image, from the compassionate guardian kings at the *kaidan'in* (ordination hall) of Tōdaiji to the impassive visage of the great Buddha, bear testimony to an era of opulence and spiritual expansion that was unique in Japanese history.

Although Nara was never to see such glory again, its legacy continues. An interesting souvenir of the city is a stick of *sumi*, the handmade ink used for calligraphy. You can watch it being made at Genrindō.

If you get hungry, try *kakinoha-zushi*, pickled mackerel slices and vinegared rice wrapped in a persimmon leaf, a regional delicacy. My favorite place to stay in Nara is Edosan, a lovely inn set in Nara Park that is so authentic it has yet to install modern plumbing!

From Nara, continue south to Asuka, Yoshino, and the sacred mountain Kōyasan. Asuka, the political and cultural center of Japan in the 6th and 7th centuries, is now a rural area strewn with burial mounds and mysterious carved stone figures. At Yoshino, the traditional stronghold of the *yamabushi* mountain priests, temples and inns line the top of a narrow ridge. The slopes of Yoshino are renowned for their cherry blossoms. Kōyasan is the mountaintop headquarters of the Shingon sect of Buddhism. More than 100 beautiful temples and monasteries stand in the shade of a cathedral-like cryptomeria forest, and an enormous cemetery contains tombs dedicated to famous personages, from emperors and shōguns to captains of industry. Elegant accommodations and superb Buddhist vegetarian food are provided by the temples, and guests can observe the services.

West of this region lies Ōsaka, the great metropolitan alternative to Tōkyō. Ōsaka is considerably older than Tōkyō and has played an important role as an international port since the dawn of Japanese history. The once grimy cityscape is transforming its image with some bold new architecture. In the arts, Ōsaka is known as the guardian of the grand tradition of *bunraku* puppet theater.

Western Honshū and Shikoku

The coast stretching west from Ōsaka offers a hit parade of attractions (all accessible by Shinkansen): Himeji Castle, the picturesque (but tourist-infested) old town of Kurashiki, and Itsukushima (also called Miyajima), a sacred island renowned for the exquisite Itsukushima Shrine. This coast is heavily industrialized but offers access to less developed regions. From the two main coastal cities, Okayama and Hiroshima, one can take a ferry to Shikoku, the smallest of Japan's four main islands. A rail link from Okayama, completed in 1988, may accelerate change on this sleepy island. In the meantime, the traveler can enjoy the calmer pace of life there.

The south coast of Shikoku has a noticeably different feel. The climate is almost subtropical, and palm trees line city streets. I have especially fond memories of Kiya Ryokan, a family-run inn in the old castle town of Uwajima. Another memorable evening was spent at Sotodomari, a tiny fishing village in the remote southwest corner of the island. As is the case in many such villages all over Japan, its people can no longer eke out a living by fishing. Most of the families have converted their homes into inns, or *minshuku*, in the hope that travelers will be attracted to the beautiful setting and unusual stone-terraced architecture of the village.

The north coast of western Honshū, facing the Sea of Japan, also possesses a distinctive character. To the Japanese this San'in coast conjures up images of dark, storm-swept shores. Traveling along the coast is time-consuming, so you should reward yourself with a stay at Yakumo Honjin, an inn originally built to accommodate the local lord during his pilgrimages to the Izumo Shrine. The magnificent building provides an apt setting for the inn's culinary specialty: wild duck breast broiled upon an abalone shell.

From Izumo, a train ride of three and a half hours west will bring you to Hagi, a seaside town celebrated for its pottery and splendid samurai mansions. A night at the Tomoe Ryokan will make you feel as if you've traveled back in time.

Kyūshū

Kyūshū, the westernmost of Japan's main islands, has historically been the gateway between Japan and the outside world. Japan's 16th-century invasions of Korea were launched from Kyūshū, and the island's many pottery villages are a legacy of that era. Korean-style tea ware was greatly prized by Japan's *daimyō*, who kidnapped hundreds of Korean potters and set them to work in Japan. At Arita, where Japanese porcelain was first made, one can see the successors of the Korean potters applying delicate decorations by hand. Rustic Korean-style ware is made in the scenic mountain villages of Onta and Koishiwara, and the villages reverberate with the thud of traditional water-powered clay mills.

No place embodies the ambiguities of Japan's interaction with the outside world better than

An Imari-ware potter at the wheel. Saga Prefecture, Kyūshū.

Nagasaki. The Tokugawa shogunate permitted a few Dutch and Chinese traders to operate in Nagasaki but closed off the rest of Japan and carried out inquisitions against suspected Japanese Christians.

Nagasaki retains a vaguely exotic air from its past, despite the atomic destruction it suffered at the end of World War II. The city is known for its Chinese-style temples, late-19th-century Western dwellings, *champon* noodles, and the famed Okunchi Festival in October, which features "Dutch" minstrels and Chinese dragon dances.

The drive across central Kyūshū, which is dominated by the volcano Asosan, is one of the most spectacular in Japan. The volcanic slopes are covered with grass, creating a rolling, open landscape. Among the mountains are numerous hot springs.

Local youngsters at play in the rice fields of Hiroshima Prefecture.

Perhaps the most fashionable is Yufuin, a rather self-consciously rustic spa town at the foot of the volcano Yufudake. The place to stay is the elegant Tamanoyu Inn. For those on a tighter budget, Sansō Yamashige, a thatched bungalow set in a garden, is a delightful alternative, but it has only two guest rooms.

Hokkaidō and Okinawa

Hokkaidō and the islands of Okinawa Prefecture, which are at the northern and southern ends of Japan, respectively, offer the greatest contrasts to the mainstream culture. Hokkaidō, Japan's version of the American Midwest, if not the Wild West, has been settled by the Japanese only since the late 19th century. Because Hokkaidō is largely populated by people who emigrated from other parts of Japan, it seems to have a less confining feel. The open landscape contributes to this sensation.

Hokkaidō does not have much in the way of historical relics, but its beautiful volcanic highlands and rugged coastline offer wonderful hiking. The annual Snow Festival in Sapporo, which is held every February, attracts visitors from around the world.

Okinawa, a subtropical archipelago south of Kyūshū, is politically the newest part of Japan (the islands were returned to Japan by the United States in 1972), but it is in some ways the oldest culturally. A number of linguists contend that the dialect spoken here is an archaic form of Japanese.

For centuries the Okinawans carried out sea trade throughout Asia and developed a unique culture that is a beguiling mixture of Japanese, Chinese, and Malay. This heritage can be experienced today in Okinawa's colorful festivals, haunting music, refined cuisine, and superb crafts.

For Americans and older Japanese, Okinawa is associated indelibly with the bloodiest fighting in the Pacific during World War II. For younger Japanese, the coral-fringed isles are a budget Hawaii. These stereotypes mask one of Asia's best-kept secrets: a unique land of diverse wonders, from the ghosts of Shuri Castle to the cane-swept tranquillity of outer isles such as Iriomotejima and Kumejima.

For all the diversity one finds in Japan, its people remain strongly unified by language, culture, history, and geography. Most non-Japanese are, and will forever be, *gaijin* (outsiders). But for travelers this presents an extraordinary opportunity. It is not uncommon for foreigners to be treated as confidants by innkeepers, restaurant operators, shop owners, and many others who, because of pressure to preserve social harmony, cannot reveal their true feelings to family or friends. Being on the outside can endow one with a fascinating perspective on the inner life of a nation.

June Kinoshita

TRISTAN A portion of the 3-km-ring accelerator. Electrons and positrons run through the tubes at nearly the speed of light.

journey, but it was not until the Kamakura period (1185–1333) that travel diaries flourished as a distinct genre.

In the late 12th century an increase in travel along the highway TŌKAIDŌ to Kyōto led to the proliferation of *kikō*, such as the IZAYOI NIKKI, KAIDŌKI, and TŌKAN KIKŌ. In the Muromachi period (1333–1568) many linked-verse (RENGA) poets, most notably SŌGI and SŌCHŌ, wrote diaries of their travels in the provinces. Matsuo BASHŌ, the peripatetic 17th-century *haiku* poet, wrote a number of *kikō* interspersed with verses describing his experiences. Certainly the most renowned travel diary of the period was his OKU NO HOSOMICHI, in which the journey becomes a metaphor for the passage of life itself.

A characteristic feature of *kikō* is the inclusion of poems dealing with places along the way around which a poetic tradition has evolved (see UTA MAKURA). The travel diary influenced other genres into which passages describing journeys (*michiyuki*) were introduced. There are examples in war tales such as the HEIKE MONOGATARI and the TAIHEIKI, and the *michiyuki* or travel section became a standard element in the NŌ drama and in BUNRAKU (the puppet theater).

Among the travel diaries of the Edo period are some by accomplished poets. KARASUMARU MITSUHIRO, who studied poetry under HOSOKAWA YŪSAI, wrote *Nikkōsan kikō* as a poetic account of the transfer of TOKUGAWA IEYASU's bones from Mikawa Province (now part of Aichi Prefecture) to the mausoleum at NIKKŌ. Among poetic *kikō* written by women of this period are the *Tōkai kikō* (1681) and *Kika nikki* (1689), by Inoue Tsūjo (1660–1738), and the *Kōshi michi no ki* (1720), by Takejo (dates unknown). Poetic *kikō* were often written by well-known scholars such as HAYASHI RAZAN, KAMO NO MABUCHI, and MOTOORI NORINAGA. MUKAI KYORAI's *Ise kikō* (1686) and HATTORI RANSETSU's *Sōyūkō* describe a journey coinciding with the seventh anniversary of Bashō's death. Tachibana Nankei (1753–1805; *Tōyūki* and *Seiyūki*) and SUGAE MASUMI (*Masumi yūranki*) are among the most noteworthy travel diarists of the Edo period.

Meiji-period *kikō* include those by TAYAMA KATAI, Ōmachi Keigetsu (1869–1925), and Chizuka Reisui (1868–1942). Contemporary *kikō* tend to resemble the genre known as ZUIHITSU, or the personal essay.

treaties 条約

(*jōyaku*). In Japan treaties are concluded by the cabinet, which, however, must obtain the prior or subsequent approval of the Diet. The attestation of the emperor is necessary as proof that the correct procedures were followed in concluding the treaty. A treaty is given the force of law upon its promulgation, which is effected by the emperor with the advice and consent of the cabinet. Promulgation makes the treaty and its provisions public and is accomplished through publication in the OFFICIAL GAZETTE (*Kampō*).

Article 98, paragraph 2, of the constitution declares that "treaties concluded by Japan and established laws of nations shall be faithfully observed." This is interpreted as meaning that treaties become part of Japanese domestic law. It is generally recognized that treaties take precedence over other laws, but opinion is divided as to whether treaties take precedence over the constitution.

Treaty of Peace with Japan→

San Francisco Peace Treaty

Tripartite Intervention 三国干渉

(Sangoku Kanshō). Diplomatic pressure brought to bear by Russia, France, and Germany that forced Japan to relinquish the Liaodong (Liaotung) Peninsula in southern Manchuria, the greatest prize it had won in the SINO-JAPANESE WAR OF 1894–1895. Even before the signing of the Treaty of SHIMONOSEKI between China and Japan on 17 April 1895, several European powers were particularly worried about the territorial disposition of China. If the Manchu dynasty (1644–1912) collapsed, international rivalries in China would intensify and the country would be thrown into political chaos. On 23 April 1895 the governments of France, Germany, and Russia "advised" Japan to restore the Liaodong Peninsula to China in return for an increased indemnity payment. Known as the Tripartite Intervention, this action caused a sensation in Japan. The Japanese realized at once that resistance was out of the question. They sought British and American intercession in vain. The only course left was to accept the "advice" in order to save the rest of the treaty. On 5 May the ITŌ HIROBUMI government notified the three powers that the Liaodong Peninsula would be restored to China, in return for the latter's payment of an indemnity of 30 million taels (about ¥450 million). All Japanese forces were withdrawn from the peninsula by December. In 1898 Russia demanded and obtained from China a 25-year lease of Port Arthur (Ch: Lüshun) and Dalian (Ta-lien; J: Dairen) at the southern tip of the peninsula (both now part of Lüda or Lü-ta). This precipitated a crisis between Japan and Russia that resulted in the RUSSO-JAPANESE WAR of 1904–05.

Tripartite Pact 日独伊三国同盟

(Nichidokui Sangoku Dōmei). Military pact signed by Japan, Germany, and Italy in Berlin on 27 September 1940; culmination of an increasingly strong relationship among the three countries from 1935 on as it became apparent that their aggressive military policies were drawing them closer together. In November 1936 the ANTI-COMINTERN PACT was signed by Japan and Germany. They were joined by Italy in November 1937. Japan allied itself with the fascist countries, ostensibly in the anti-Soviet, anticommunist cause, but also to advance its imperialist designs on the Asian continent.

In July 1938 the KONOE FUMIMARO cabinet, hoping to break the stalemate of the SINO-JAPANESE WAR of 1937–1945, decided to strengthen the Japanese-German-Italian alliance. Japan wanted this alliance to develop into a military pact against the Soviet Union and was therefore completely surprised by the conclusion of the German-Soviet nonaggression pact in August 1939. This development postponed the diplomatic initiatives Japan had been contemplating.

With the success of Germany's blitzkrieg tactics in Europe, the question of a pact with Germany and Italy was once again brought up. Before forming a new cabinet in 1940, Konoe had already decided to bolster the Axis alliance in order to establish what he called the "New Order in East Asia" (TŌA SHINCHITSUJO). Foreign minister MATSUOKA YŌSUKE was in charge of initiating negotiations for the three-nation pact. The pact, which was to last ten years, concerned the mutual recognition by the signatories of a new order in Europe and Greater East Asia. Each country committed itself to full-scale political, economic, and military aid if a signatory nation was attacked by a nation not presently involved in the European war or the Sino-Japanese conflict. Each country also maintained autonomy in its political relations with the Soviet Union. The Tripartite Pact was essentially an agreement on the redivision of the world by the three signatory countries and a military alliance against the United States. However, it served only to strengthen the anti-Axis alliance of the United States, Great Britain, Holland, and, after June 1941, the Soviet Union. The Tripartite Pact was shattered by Italy's surrender in September 1943 and Germany's collapse in May 1945.

TRISTAN トリスタン

(Transposable Ring Intersecting Storage Accelerator in Nippon; J: Torisutan). An electron-positron accelerator constructed by the National Laboratory for High Energy Physics (KEK) in the city of Tsukuba, Ibaraki Prefecture. Construction of the accelerator began in 1981 and was completed in 1986. Full-time collision experiments began in 1987. In the experiments, electrons and positrons are accelerated to 30 billion electron volts and rotated in opposite directions in a ring about 3 kilometers (9,843 ft) in circumference and 1 kilometer (3,281 ft) in diameter. The colliding positrons and electrons run close to the speed of light and collide at four intersections. Upon collision various new elementary particles are produced. Scientists examine the properties of these particles to learn more about the basic nature of matter.

TRON トロン

(The Realtime Operating System Nucleus; J: Toron). A Japanese computer architecture system, first proposed by Sakamura Ken (b 1951) of Tōkyō University in the early 1980s, which enables the user to operate Japanese machines of different manufacture by utilizing a uniform set of basic procedures. The need for such a system, which incorporates advanced Japanese language and complex image processing, was soon realized in industrial circles in the early 1980s; about 100 Japanese electrical and electronic equipment makers endorsed the proposed system in 1986, forming the TRON Association to investigate ways of developing basic TRON software in accordance with uniform domestic specifications. Development of the basic operating system was undertaken by MATSUSHITA ELECTRIC INDUSTRIAL CO, LTD, and that of the TRON central processing unit by MITSUBISHI ELECTRIC CORPORATION and HITACHI, LTD. The benefits of TRON are expected to include industrial applications with interchangeable programs and data, standardized peripheral equipment, and more efficient computer instruction. In 1988 the TRON Association was incorporated to form the central organization to coordinate the project, and in 1990 Matsushita marketed the first personal computer designed to TRON specifications. See also PERSONAL COMPUTERS.

Truman, Harry S. トルーマン, H. S.

(1884–1972). The 33rd president of the United States (1945–53). Born in Missouri. Truman entered the US Senate in 1934, was elected vice-president in 1944, and assumed the presidency in 1945 on the death of Franklin D. Roosevelt. He met with Winston Churchill and Joseph Stalin at the Potsdam Conference (see POTSDAM DECLARATION) in July 1945 to discuss surrender terms for Japan and plans for reorganizing the postwar world. While at the conference, he received word of the successful US testing of the ATOMIC BOMB and authorized its use against Japan. When the communist North Korean armies invaded South Korea in 1950, Truman sent US troops to Korea under the aegis of the United Nations. He recalled General Douglas MACARTHUR in 1951, when MacArthur insisted on carrying the war into Mainland China against presidential orders. This demonstration of the American concept of the preeminence of civil over military authority left a deep impression on the Japanese.

trust 信託

(shintaku). A system in which one person places property (such as money, securities, or immovable property) under the control and management of another. In Japanese law, the person requesting such management is referred to as the settlor (itakusha), and the person administering the assets is referred to as the trustee (jutakusha). The distinguishing characteristic of a trust is that certain specified property is transferred by contract or will from the settlor to the trustee to be managed by the trustee. However, Japanese law does not distinguish between legal interests and equitable interests, and trusts are not common among the general populace. Charitable trusts are recognized in addition to regular private trusts. In Japan the Trust Law (Shintaku Hō) of 1922 constitutes the legal basis of trusts.

Ts'ai O→Cai E (Ts'ai O)

Ts'ao Ju-lin→Cao Rulin (Ts'ao Ju-lin)

Tsingtao→Qingdao (Tsingtao)

Tsou T'ao-fen→Zou Taofen (Tsou T'ao-fen)

Tsu 津[市]

Capital of Mie Prefecture, central Honshū. Situated on Ise Bay, it was formerly called ANOTSU and known as a prosperous port town. During the Edo period (1600–1868) it developed as a post-station town on the road leading to ISE SHRINE and as a castle town of the Tōdō family. Tsu is a center of textile, electrical machinery, and shipbuilding industries. Agriculture, fishing, and commerce also flourish. Mie University is located here. The remains of Tsu Castle and the temple Senshūji draw visitors. Pop: 157,177.

tsū 通

An aesthetic ideal of the Edo period (1600–1868). A tsū was a man who was well informed about something, usually the YOSHIWARA licensed pleasure quarters. He was able to enjoy himself by putting to use his copious knowledge and experience, while always retaining the freedom assured by his status as a bystander. Those who were merely superficial imitations of tsū were

called hankatsū, while those who had no understanding whatsoever of the tsū concept were referred to as yabo. All three types were portrayed in KIBYŌSHI and SHAREBON, two genres of Edo-period popular fiction. After the Edo period, the term tsū was no longer restricted to familiarity with the pleasure quarters and assumed a broader meaning, akin to savoir faire.

tsuba 鐔

Japanese sword guard; the disk or plate that separates the blade from the handle of the sword. A typical tsuba is approximately 8 centimeters (3 in) wide and has a center hole (nakagoana) for the tang of the sword. Most commonly made of steel, but frequently of other metals or alloys, it ensures that the hand does not slip up onto the blade and affords some protection from an opponent's blade. The weight of the guard also brings the sword's center of gravity closer to the handle, adding "balance" and force to a blow and reducing fatigue to the wrist. Since the sword was the most important possession of the samurai warrior, tsuba and other metal fittings were considered appropriate objects for exquisite craftsmanship and beauty.

Tsuba were made in various shapes; the majority were round or oval but also common were squares, lozenges, and a shape known as mokkō, a circle with elliptic indentations around the edge giving the disk a lobed shape. Many fanciful shapes and irregular forms were also employed, the most important and common being the aoitsuba, a rounded square with a heart-shaped perforation at each corner, used especially on more formal sword mounts.

The surface finish of tsuba and other metal sword fittings (kodōgu) were intrinsic to the object's artistic value. A type of finishing done with special chisels to produce an effect like that of rough stone, termed ishime, was popular, as was nanako, a surface with tiny, raised dots. Often a steel surface was decorated with the marks of the hammer (tsuchime). Polished surfaces were used, particularly as a background for inlays (zōgan). Various types of engraving were also employed. In the case of older steel guards, the design was often an openwork silhouette (sukashibori) of a shrub or tree or sometimes of a geometric object, a family crest, animals, birds, or other objects drawn from nature.

The various ways in which the rim of a sword guard is finished indicate not only the period in which it was made but also the particular school where it was crafted. The rims were occasionally provided with a decorative cover (fukurin) of silver, bronze, or gold for preservation of the edge of the guard.

The earliest extant sword guards date from the Nara period (710–794). Distinctive tsuba were created during the Kamakura (1185–1333) and Muromachi (1333–1568) periods, but in caliber of construction, conception, and exposition, tsuba and other metal sword fittings reached a peak from the 17th century to the end of the 19th century. This art finally became extinct with the regulations of the new Meiji government in the 1870s, when it was forbidden either to make or to wear swords. Although metalworkers continued for some time to make small art objects in metal, the art of making tsuba and other sword fittings was substantially lost. See also SWORDS; KOSHIRAE.

tsubaki→camellias

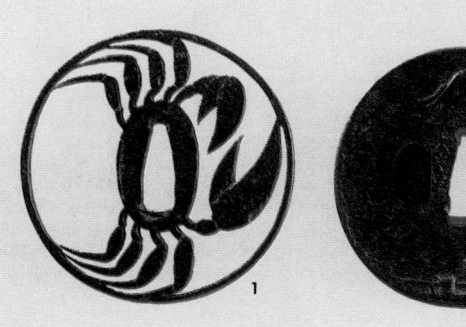

tsuba

1 A late-16th-century iron tsuba with an openwork depiction of a crab. Diameter 9 cm. Tōkyō National Museum.
2 An iron tsuba by Kaneie, a pioneer in the carving of pictorial decorations on sword guards. This landscape depicts a fisherman standing on a small boat. Late 16th–early 17th century. Diameter 9 cm. Tōkyō National Museum. National Treasure.

Tsubaki Chinzan 椿椿山

(1801–54). Painter in the BUNJINGA tradition. Real name Tsubaki Hitsu. Chinzan was a samurai official in the service of the shogunate in Edo (now Tōkyō), where he was born. He studied painting under Kaneko Kinryō (d 1817) and briefly under TANI BUNCHŌ, but his principal teacher was WATANABE KAZAN. Chinzan is especially noted for his BIRD-AND-FLOWER PAINTING (kachōga) and for his use of color. In his portraits he shows a strong debt to Kazan and to the West, especially in matters of brush tone and shading.

Tsubaki Hot Spring 椿温泉

(Tsubaki Onsen). Located in the southern part of the town of Shirahama, southwestern Wakayama Prefecture, central Honshū. A hydrogen sulfide spring; water temperature 34°–40°C (93°–104°F). Facing the Kumano Sea, this ancient spa is located in a coastal area that is popular with swimmers and anglers.

Tsubakimoto Chain Co [株]椿本チエイン

(Tsubakimoto Chein). Manufacturer of chains and conveyors; also produces power transmissions and material-handling systems. Incorporated in 1941. The company forms the core of the Tsubakimoto group. It has subsidiaries in the United States, Canada, the Netherlands, Australia, Singapore, Korea, and Taiwan. Sales for the fiscal year ending March 1991 totaled ¥107.7 billion (US $785.0 million), and capitalization stood at ¥16.8 billion (US $122.4 million). Headquarters are in Ōsaka.

Tsubakurodake 燕岳

Mountain in the central Hida Mountains, western Nagano Prefecture, central Honshū. Pure white rock towers of weathered granite stand near the summit. The hiking trail from this mountain to YARIGATAKE is one of the most popular in the JAPANESE ALPS. Height: 2,763 m (9,065 ft).

Tsubame 燕[市]

City in central Niigata Prefecture, central Honshū. Situated on the river Shinanogawa, Tsubame developed as a river port. During the Edo period (1600–1868) it became known for its files, kiseru (traditional smoking pipes), and copper ware. It is the country's leading manufacturer of tableware for export. Pop: 43,891.

Tsuboi Kumezō 坪井九馬三

(1858–1936). Historian. Born in Ōsaka. Tsuboi studied political economy and chemistry at Tōkyō University and, after teaching there briefly, went to Germany and Austria to study history. His book Shigaku kenkyū hō (1903, Methods of Historical Research) introduced German techniques of historical analysis to Japan.

Tsuchida Bakusen
One of a pair of four-panel folding screens titled *Women of Ōhara* by this artist who combined Western and traditional Japanese painting techniques. 1915. Colors on silk. Yamatane Museum of Art, Tōkyō.

Tsubouchi Shōyō This critic, novelist, and playwright was a major influence on the development of Japanese literature and was the first translator of the complete works of Shakespeare.

Tsuboi Sakae   壺井栄

(1900–1967). Novelist and children's story writer. Maiden name Iwai. Born on the island of Shōdoshima, Kagawa Prefecture. After marrying the anarchist poet TSUBOI SHIGEJI in 1925, she became active in the PROLETARIAN LITERATURE MOVEMENT. Her works, mostly set on Shōdoshima, are rich in local color and express her deep concern for social justice. Her novel *Nijūshi no hitomi* (1952; tr *Twenty-Four Eyes*, 1957), a sentimental story about the enduring friendship between a teacher and her 12 students, was filmed in 1954 by director KINOSHITA KEISUKE. Her other works include the children's story "Kaki no ki no aru ie" (1949; tr "Under the Persimmon Tree," 1965) and the novel *Uchikake* (1955, A Robe), about four generations of a village family.

Tsuboi Shigeji   壺井繁治

(1898–1975). Poet. Born in Kagawa Prefecture; studied at Waseda University. Tsuboi published his work in the anarchist poetry magazine *Aka to kuro* (1923–24), which he helped to found. He became active in the PROLETARIAN LITERATURE MOVEMENT, and in 1945 he helped to found the Shin Nihon Bungaku Kai, a Marxist literary group. He married the novelist TSUBOI SAKAE. His works include *Atama no naka no heishi* (1956), a collection of poems, and *Teikō no seishin* (1949), a collection of critical essays.

Tsuboi Shōgorō   坪井正五郎

(1863–1913). Anthropologist and archaeologist; born in Edo (now Tōkyō). In 1884, as an undergraduate in zoology at Tōkyō University, he excavated the MUKŌGAOKA SHELL MOUND with Arisaka Shōzō and discovered the first YAYOI POTTERY. In the same year, he also founded the Anthropological Association (now the Anthropological Society of Nippon). After completing graduate school in anthropology at Tōkyō University, he spent three years (1889–92) studying in Brit-

ain and France. Upon his return, he established the first courses in anthropology at Tōkyō University in 1893.

Tsuboi is known for his theories on the origin of the Japanese (i.e., that the Koropokkur, a people who appear in AINU legends, were the earliest occupants of Japan) and on the nature of KŌGOISHI sites—theories that are now defunct. He published numerous site reports on excavations of YOKOANA (tunnel tombs) and SHELL MOUNDS.

Tsubota Jōji   坪田譲治

(1890–1982). Novelist and writer of children's literature. Born in Okayama Prefecture; graduate of Waseda University. He first gained recognition with a collection of children's stories, *Shōta no uma* (1926, Shōta's Horse). His later trilogy of children's stories includes *Obake no sekai* (1935, World of Ghosts), *Kaze no naka no kodomo* (1936, Children in the Wind), and *Kodomo no shiki* (1938, Children's Four Seasons), the winner of the Shinchōsha Literary Prize. His stories portray the pure and innocent world of childhood, often set against the uglier aspects of reality. In 1955 he received the Japan Art Academy (Nihon Geijutsuin) Award and from 1964 was a member of the academy.

Tsubouchi Memorial Theater Museum of Waseda University
早稲田大学坪内博士記念演劇博物館

(Waseda Daigaku Tsubouchi Hakase Kinen Engeki Hakubutsukan). A privately operated museum opened in 1928. Built to commemorate the completion by TSUBOUCHI SHŌYŌ of a 40-volume translation of Shakespeare's collected works, the building is patterned after the 16th-century Fortune Theater used by Shakespeare in London. It is located on the campus of Waseda University in Tōkyō's Shinjuku Ward, where Shōyō taught for many years. A resource for theater studies, the museum contains costumes, small props, programs, and other items connected to the literature and performance of NŌ, KYŌGEN, BUNRAKU, and other theatrical forms.

Tsubouchi Shōyō   坪内逍遥

(1859–1935). Critic, playwright, translator, and novelist. A major figure in the modernization of Japanese literature, Shōyō ranks at the forefront of modern Japanese literary history. Born Tsubouchi Yūzō in the village of Ōta (now Mino Kamo) near Nagoya, he moved to Tōkyō in 1876. He graduated from Tōkyō University in 1883 and became a professor at what is now Waseda University.

Shōyō, who had read Western authors in college, began translating his favorites. His crowning achievement as a translator was

the complete translation of Shakespeare's works (1884–1928). Shōyō's contributions in criticism and fiction were influenced by his early translations. He wanted Japan to emulate the West's respect for fiction and drama. In his criticism he urged realism, objectivity, characterization, unity, and seriousness of tone. *Shōsetsu shinzui* (1885–86, The Essence of the Novel) contained Shōyō's most effective criticism. Shōyō felt that Japanese literature could be elevated by imbuing it with contemporary settings, modern manners and customs, objective description, philosophical depth, and psychological realism. To demonstrate his ideas, Shōyō produced nine fictional works between 1885 and 1890. Although none fully realized his goals, the best of these works, such as *Tōsei shosei katagi* (1885–86, The Character of Today's Students), would change the nation's literary course.

Shōyō turned to dramatic criticism after 1888. He again championed realism, asserting that the means of creating a new drama lay in combining selected elements of Western and traditional drama and music and then transmuting these into a sophisticated dramatic form. Between 1894 and 1920 he wrote dozens of plays to illustrate his concepts. With the exception of his masterpiece, "Shinkyoku Urashima" (1904), a drama based on the Urashima Tarō folktale, Shōyō failed to follow his own requirements or to surmount the models he wished to displace. Even so, these efforts pointed theater and drama in new directions.

Tsuboya ware   壺屋焼

(*tsuboya-yaki*). Ceramics produced in Tsuboya, in what is now the city of Naha, Okinawa Prefecture. Made from local clays with painted or incised floral, animal, or geometric patterns. Glazes are red and green and are lightly applied. For slip decoration a yellowish clay that fires a deep white is used.

There are two main categories of Tsuboya ware. *Arayaki* consists mostly of large vessels for *sake* or *miso* storage and is fired either unglazed or with manganese glaze. *Jōyaki*, which is more common, is a feldspathic glazed ware consisting mostly of smaller items such as tableware. Tsuboya-ware products include burial urns with sculpting. The history of Okinawan ceramics goes back about 500 years. In the 14th and 15th centuries, with the beginning of trade with China and the South Sea Islands, many foreign ceramics, the so-called *namban-yaki*, were imported, and their techniques were adopted locally. In 1682 the monarchical government moved all the kilns to Tsuboya. Today there are 12 functioning kilns in Tsuboya.

Tsuburaya Eiji   円谷英二

(1901–70). Real name Tsuburaya Eiichi. Special effects technician; known for his work on such monster pictures as *Gojira* (1954, GODZILLA) and numerous war films. Born in Fukushima Prefecture. Typical of his work were his special effects for *Hawai-Marē oki kaisen* 1942, The War at Sea from Hawaii to Malaya), a film directed by YAMAMOTO KAJIRŌ in which Tsuburaya recreated the attack on Pearl Harbor by the use of impressive miniature sets. He created the special effects in a number of other war pictures including *Taiheiyō no washi* (1953, Eagles of the Pacific).

Beginning with *Gojira* in 1954, Tsuburaya also created various prehistoric creatures, which wreaked havoc on modern so-

Tsubouchi Memorial Theater Museum of Waseda University
Built in honor of Tsubouchi Shōyō, scholar and translator of Shakespeare's collected works, this museum is modeled after the 16th-century Fortune Theater in London.

ciety in a series of science fiction and monster pictures. In 1963 he organized his own Tsuburaya Special Productions and began producing television programs such as *Urutoraman* (1966, Ultraman).

Tsuchida Bakusen　土田麦僊

(1887–1936). Japanese-style (NIHONGA) painter whose works combined Western and traditional Japanese painting techniques. Real name Tsuchida Kinji. Born on the island of Sado in Niigata Prefecture. He studied first with TAKEUCHI SEIHŌ and later at the Kyōto Kaiga Semmon Gakkō (now Kyōto City University of Arts). In 1918, with MURAKAMI KAGAKU, he founded the Kokuga Sōsaku Kyōkai (National Creative Painting Association); the works Bakusen exhibited with this group reveal a bold combination of Japanese and Western styles, which influenced the modernization of Japanese-style painting. In 1934 he was appointed to the Teikoku Bijutsuin (Imperial Fine Arts Academy).

Tsuchii Bansui→Doi Bansui

tsuchi ikki　土一揆

Also known as *do ikki.* Peasant uprisings of the Muromachi period (1333–1568), particularly during the 15th century. Most of them took place in the prosperous provinces adjacent to Kyōto, where the early development of village self-rule (see SŌ) contributed to solidarity and political consciousness among the peasantry. The term *tsuchi ikki* embraces a wide spectrum of uprisings, ranging from petition and protest to violent rebellion against authority. In the 14th century the most common demands involved reduction of tax burdens (NENGU) and corvée (BUYAKU) or removal of unpopular estate officials. In the 15th century debt cancellation (TOKUSEI) by the shogunate became the principal goal. These uprisings were no more than a temporary solution, because they disrupted a credit relationship that the peasants could not do without.

While *tsuchi ikki* were in general motivated by local economic concerns, they sometimes involved large numbers of peasants and considerable geographic areas. The largest uprisings occurred in times of turmoil within the shogunate, underlining their political significance. By the late 15th century the *tsuchi ikki* had begun to lose their impetus, largely because the *dogō* (affluent peasantry), who had provided the leadership for the *tsuchi ikki*, tended to become minor proprietors and to come to terms with the emerging KOKUJIN (local military leaders). See also IKKI; HYAKUSHŌ IKKI.

Tsuchimikado, Emperor　土御門天皇

(1195–1231; Tsuchimikado Tennō). The 83rd sovereign (*tennō*) in the traditional count (which includes several legendary emperors); reigned 1198–1210. The eldest son of Emperor GO-TOBA. While Tsuchimikado was on the throne, his father retained control of court politics as retired emperor (see INSEI). In 1210 he was forced to abdicate in favor of his younger brother, JUNTOKU. Although he was held blameless after the JŌKYŪ DISTURBANCE (1221), when both Go-Toba and Juntoku were exiled for attempting to overthrow the shogunal regent HŌJŌ YOSHITOKI, Tsuchimikado also chose exile.

Tsuchiura　土浦[市]

City in southern Ibaraki Prefecture, central Honshū, on Lake Kasumigaura. During the Edo period (1600–1868) Tsuchiura flourished as a castle town and post-station town. It has developed into a commuter suburb of Tōkyō. Vegetables and fruit are grown. Pop: 127,471.

Tsuchiya Bummei　土屋文明

(1890–1990). TANKA poet. Born in Gumma Prefecture. Graduate of Tōkyō University. Tsuchiya studied poetry with ITŌ SACHIO and in 1925 published his first collection, *Fuyukusa.* In 1930 he succeeded SAITŌ MOKICHI as editor of the *tanka* magazine ARARAGI. As a poet he upheld the traditions of realist *tanka.* Among his published works are *Ōkanshū* (1930) and *Sankokushū* (1935), two volumes of *tanka* verse, and the *Man'yōshū shichū* (1949–56), a 20-volume commentary on the MAN'YŌSHŪ, the oldest extant anthology of classical Japanese poetry. In 1986 he received the Order of Culture.

Tsuchiya Takao　土屋喬雄

(1896–1988). Economist. Born in Tōkyō. He graduated from Tōkyō University in 1921 and became a professor there in 1939. As a Marxist economic historian of the RŌNŌHA faction, he engaged in a historical debate with HATTORI SHISŌ of the rival KŌZAHA regarding the timing of Japan's entry into the manufacturing phase of economic development. He is known for his efforts to assemble and systematize important historical source materials on the early development of Japanese capitalism. Major works include *Nihon shihon shugi no keieishi teki kenkyū* (1954, A Managerial History of Japanese Capitalism).

Tsuchiyu Hot Spring　土湯温泉

(Tsuchiyu Onsen). Located in the city of Fukushima, Fukushima Prefecture, northeastern Honshū. A simple thermal spring; maximum water temperature 75°C (167°F). Part of BANDAI-ASAHI NATIONAL PARK. Tsuchiyu is known for its manufacture of KOKESHI, a type of wooden doll.

Tsuda College　津田塾大学

(Tsuda Juku Daigaku). A private women's college located in the city of Kodaira, Tōkyō Prefecture. Its origin lies in the Joshi Eigaku Juku (English School for Women) founded in 1900 by TSUDA UMEKO in Kōjimachi (now a part of Chiyoda Ward), Tōkyō. The school was moved to its present site in 1931 and renamed Tsuda Eigakujuku (Tsuda English School) in 1933. In 1948 the school adopted its present name. There is a faculty of liberal arts. Enrollment was 2,544 in 1989. See also WOMEN'S EDUCATION.

Tsuda Hisashi　津田久

(1904–). Businessman and president of SUMITOMO CORPORATION (1957–70). Born in Mie Prefecture. After graduating from Tōkyō University in 1928, Tsuda joined Sumitomo Gōshi Kaisha. When the Sumitomo interests were broken up by order of the Allied Occupation in 1946, Tsuda became executive director of Nihon Kensetsu Sangyō, Ltd, which carried on the general trading activities of the group. In 1952 the company changed its name to Sumitomo Shōji (English name Sumitomo Corporation from 1978), which Tsuda built into one of the largest trading companies in Japan during his tenure as president.

Tsuda Kyōsuke　津田恭介

(1907–). Pharmacologist and organic chemist. Born in Taiwan. Graduate of Tōkyō University. In 1951 he became a professor at

Kyūshū University and in 1955 a professor at Tōkyō University. Credited with much original research in the determination of the chemical structure and the synthesis of natural substances, he is especially known for his identification of the chemical structure of tetrodotoxin, the deadly poison of the Japanese globefish (*fugu*). He received the Order of Culture in 1982.

Tsuda Mamichi　津田真道

(1829–1903). Legal scholar and government official. Born in the Tsuyama domain (now part of Okayama Prefecture). As a youth Tsuda studied WESTERN LEARNING under MITSUKURI GEMPO and military science under SAKUMA SHŌZAN. He became an instructor at the BANSHO SHIRABESHO (the Tokugawa shogunate's bureau of Western Learning), and in 1862 he was sent to Holland to study at the University of Leiden. On his return in 1865, he became an instructor at the Kaiseijo, a successor to the Bansho Shirabesho. Based on his lecture notes at Leiden, he wrote *Taisei kokuhō ron* (1868, On Western Law), the first Japanese book on the subject. After the Meiji Restoration of 1868, Tsuda helped with the codification of the SHINRITSU KŌRYŌ. He subsequently helped to draft the Army Penal Code and served in the Genrōin (Chamber of Elders) and in the Diet. As a member of the MEIROKUSHA, a society organized to introduce Western ideas and culture, he wrote some 29 articles for its magazine, *Meiroku zasshi.*

Tsuda Sen　津田仙

(1837–1908). Leading agricultural writer of the Meiji period (1868–1912). He studied Dutch and English and, with FUKUZAWA YUKICHI, accompanied the government mission to the United States in 1867. In 1874 he won public attention with his work *Nōgyō sanji,* a study of natural and artificial crop pollination based upon observations he had made in Austria. He founded the Gakunōsha, a society for the study of agriculture, and published the popular agricultural magazine *Nōgyō zasshi.* His daughter, TSUDA UMEKO, founded Joshi Eigaku Juku, now known as Tsuda College.

Tsuda Sōgyū　津田宗及

(?–1591). Wealthy merchant and tea connoisseur. The oldest son of Tsuda Sōtatsu (1504–66), merchant of the city of Sakai, Sōgyū served ODA NOBUNAGA and TOYOTOMI HIDEYOSHI as master of the tea ceremony (*sadō*). With SEN NO RIKYŪ, he was responsible for organizing Hideyoshi's famous outdoor tea ceremony at Kitano Shrine in 1587 and ranks as one of the three tea masters of his age.

Tsuda Sōkichi　津田左右吉

(1873–1961). Historian; authority on ancient Japanese and Chinese history and thought.

tsujigahana A robe worn by the warlord Toyotomi Hideyoshi, displaying this textile design method. Late 16th century. Kyōto National Museum.

Tsuda Umeko The founder of what is now Tsuda College in Tōkyō was one of the first Japanese women to study abroad.

Born in Gifu Prefecture, he graduated from Tōkyō Semmon Gakkō (now Waseda University). Tsuda made his greatest contribution to scholarship in Japan by demonstrating textually in *Kojiki oyobi Nihon shoki no shin kenkyū* (1919, A New Study of the *Kojiki* and the *Nihon shoki*) that the 8th-century chronicles KOJIKI and NIHON SHOKI are not objective descriptions of historical facts but fabrications made by court compilers to justify imperial rule. For his work he came under attack from rightists and was briefly sentenced to jail. Tsuda's *Bungaku ni arawaretaru waga kokumin shisō no kenkyū* (1916–21), Studies on the Thought of Our People as Expressed in Literature) discusses the life of the Japanese people as it was reflected in literary works from the time of the empress Suiko (r 593–628) to the end of the 19th century.

The complete works of Tsuda have been published in 33 volumes as *Tsuda Sōkichi zenshū* (1963–65). His works concerning Chinese culture include *Rongo to Kōshi no shisō* (1946, The *Analects* and Confucian Thought). Tsuda received the Order of Culture in 1949.

Tsuda Umeko 津田梅子

(1864–1929). Educator and founder of TSUDA COLLEGE. Born in Edo (now Tōkyō); second daughter of TSUDA SEN, a *samurai* who became an expert on Western agricultural techniques. One of the first Japanese women to study abroad, she (then only age six) was among the 58 students sent in 1871 with the IWAKURA MISSION to the United States. In 1882 she returned to Japan, where she first became a tutor in the household of oligarch ITŌ HIROBUMI and then taught at the Kazoku Jogakkō, a new school for daughters of the nobility. She returned to the United States from 1889 to 1892 to study biology and education at Bryn Mawr College in Pennsylvania. In 1900 she founded the Women's English School (Joshi Eigaku Juku; now Tsuda College) in Tōkyō. It was officially recognized as a professional school in 1904. In 1905 Tsuda served as the first president of the Japanese branch of the Young Women's Christian Association (YWCA).

Tsugaru Peninsula 津軽半島

(Tsugaru Hantō). Located in northwestern Aomori Prefecture, northern Honshū;

tsuge The hard yellowish wood of the Japanese box tree has long been favored for making combs.

bounded to the east by Mutsu Bay, to the north by the Tsugaru Strait, and to the west by the Sea of Japan. The Tsugaru Plain, which covers the western half of the peninsula, is a rich agricultural region. The eastern portion comprises the Tsugaru Mountains. TAPPIZAKI, a cape on the northernmost tip of the peninsula, is the site of the southern exit of the Seikan (Aomori-Hakodate) Tunnel, an undersea railway tunnel between Honshū and Hokkaidō. Area: 1,300 sq km (502 sq mi).

Tsugaru Plain 津軽平野

(Tsugaru Heiya). Located in western Aomori Prefecture, northern Honshū. Bordering the Sea of Japan, this floodplain of the river Iwakigawa, which empties into Lake Jūsan, has been formed by filling marshlands. Rice is grown, and the output of apples, cultivated on the foothills of Iwakisan and on the levees, ranks first in Japan. The major city is Hirosaki. Area: approximately 1,000 sq km (400 sq mi).

Tsugaru Strait 津軽海峡

(Tsugaru Kaikyō). Between southern Hokkaidō and northern Honshū, connecting the Sea of Japan and the Pacific Ocean. The SEIKAN TUNNEL, an undersea railway tunnel, between the cape Tappizaki, Aomori Prefecture, northern Honshū, and Yoshioka near the cape Shirakamimisaki in Hokkaidō was completed in 1988. Length: 130 km (80 mi); width: 20–50 km (12–30 mi); deepest point: 449 m (1,473 ft).

Tsuga Teishō 都賀庭鐘

(1718–94?). Author and physician of the Edo period (1600–1868). Born in Ōsaka. He wrote adaptations of Chinese vernacular fiction (mostly ghost stories) that are considered forerunners of the YOMIHON genre. He also published a collated edition of the Chinese dictionary *Kangxi zidian* (*K'ang-hsi tzu-tien*). His major works are *Hanabusa sōshi* (1749, Blooming Branch Stories) and *Shigeshige yawa* (1766, Oft-Told Tales).

tsuge 黄楊

(Japanese box). *Buxus microphylla* var. *japonica*. Also called *asamatsuge*. An evergreen tree of the box family (Buxaceae) that grows wild on hills in Kyūshū, Shikoku, and western and central Honshū and is also cultivated in various parts of Japan. Its straight trunk reaches a height of 1–3 meters (3–10 ft). The elliptical, leathery leaves are about 2 centimeters (0.7 in) long. In the spring small, pale yellow flowers bloom on the shorter branches.

Naturally hard, heavy, and yellow in color, *tsuge* wood is a favorite material for combs, engraving blocks, and seals. A variety of cultivated *tsuge*, *himetsuge* (*B. microphylla*), grows only 60 centimeters (2 ft) high, with foliage so thick that the entire tree resembles a large ball.

tsugumi → thrushes

tsuihō → banishment

tsujigahana 辻が花

("flowers-at-the-crossing"). Decorative textile design method mainly using tie-dyeing (*shiborizome*); popular from the mid-Muromachi period (1333–1568) to the early Edo period (1600–1868) for *kosode* (an early form of KIMONO). The fabric was most often a silk called *nerinukiji*, woven with raw silk thread as warp and glossed silk thread as weft, then dyed with vegetable dyes. The

three main dyeing techniques included stitching the design closely with a fine thread of *asa* (flax), winding the cloth onto a water-resistant core, and immersing in dye; tying up undyed white areas of the cloth in bunches and dyeing those parts different colors from the rest of the cloth; and leaving the base white and dyeing the parts to be colored. Dyed fabrics were sometimes embellished with brush-painted or embroidered figures. See also TEXTILES.

tsujigiri 辻斬

(literally, "cutting down at the crossroad"). Random, unprovoked killing by *samurai*. The victims were innocent passersby who were usually attacked at nighttime by samurai wishing to test their swords, improve their martial skills, or simply rob. Such killings occurred most frequently in the early years of the Edo period (1600–1868). The Tokugawa shogunate (1603–1867) strictly forbade *tsujigiri* and set up patrol groups (see JISHIMBAN AND TSUJIBAN) to prevent it. The KUJIKATA OSADAMEGAKI code prescribed public humiliation (*hikimawashi*) followed by beheading as punishment for this crime.

Tsuji Jun 辻潤

(1884–1944). Critic. Born in Tōkyō. In 1909 he began teaching English at a women's school in Tōkyō but resigned as a consequence of an affair with his student ITŌ NOE. When Itō left him for the anarchist ŌSUGI SAKAE, he turned to drink. Influenced by the nihilist thought of Max Stirner (1806–56), he translated Stirner's *Der Einziger und sein Eigentum* into Japanese (1921, *Yuiitsusha to sono shoyū*). He followed this with a collection of original essays, *Furō mango* (1922, A Wanderer's Maunderings). He edited *Dadaisuto Shinkichi no shi* (1923), a collection of poems by TAKAHASHI SHINKICHI, which, along with Tsuji's own critical essays contained in *Desupera* (1924, Despair), was instrumental in the introduction of dadaism to Japan. His later years were plagued by mental illness and frequent hospitalizations.

Tsuji Kunio 辻邦生

(1925–). Novelist and scholar of French literature. Born in Tōkyō. Graduate of Tōkyō University. He studied in France from 1957 to 1961. After his return to Japan, his novel *Kairō ni te* (1962–63, In the Corridor) was serialized in the magazine *Kindai bungaku*. He continued to write while teaching French at Rikkyō University in Tōkyō. Free of the somber realism of mainstream postwar literature, his style conveys an inner liberation of the spirit. Other novels include *Azuchi ōkan ki* (1968) and *Haikyōsha Yurianusu* (1969–72, Julian the Apostate).

Tsuji Masanobu 辻政信

(1902–61?). Army officer and politician. Born in Ishikawa Prefecture. He graduated from the Army Academy in 1924. He was a staff officer of the GUANDONG (KWANTUNG) ARMY at the time of the NOMONHAN INCIDENT. During World War II, he played a leading role in developing strategy as a staff officer at Imperial General Headquarters (DAIHON'EI). He was twice elected to the Diet in the 1950s. He disappeared while traveling in Laos during the civil war there in 1961; his death was officially announced in 1968.

Tsujimura Jusaburō 辻村ジュサブロー

(1933–). Artist, puppeteer, and producer of puppet shows. Born in China. Tsujimura got his start at a theater workshop specializ-

Tsukiji Market

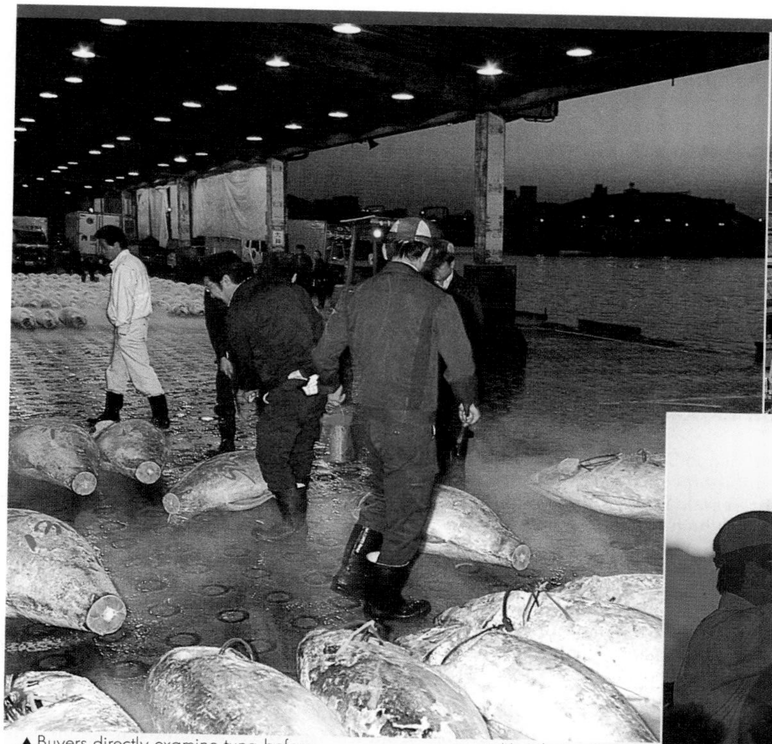

▲Buyers directly examine tuna before the early morning bidding starts.

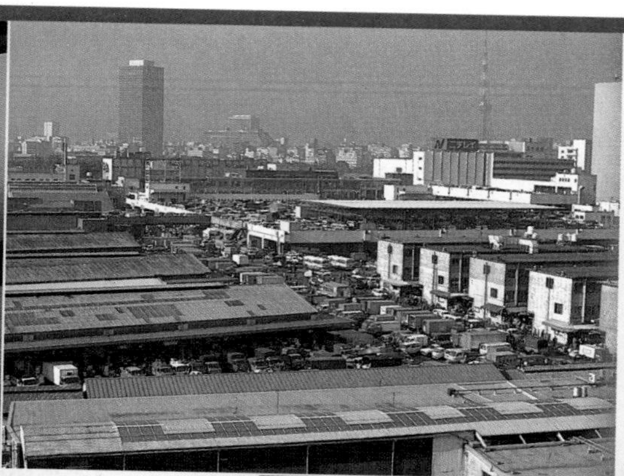

◀This huge Tōkyō wholesale market, particularly renowned as a fish market, has been in business since 1935.

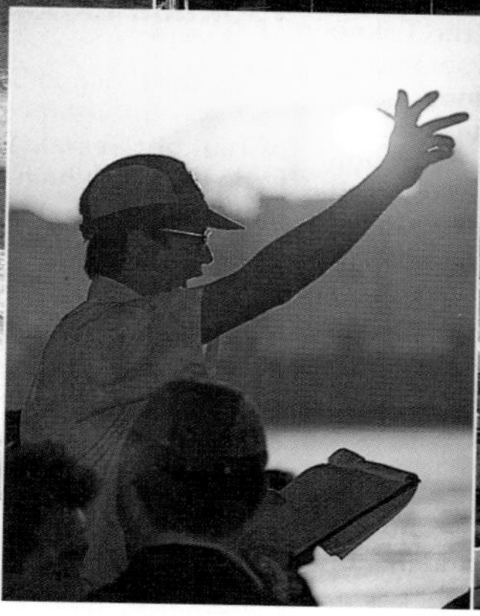

▶Hand signals at an auction.

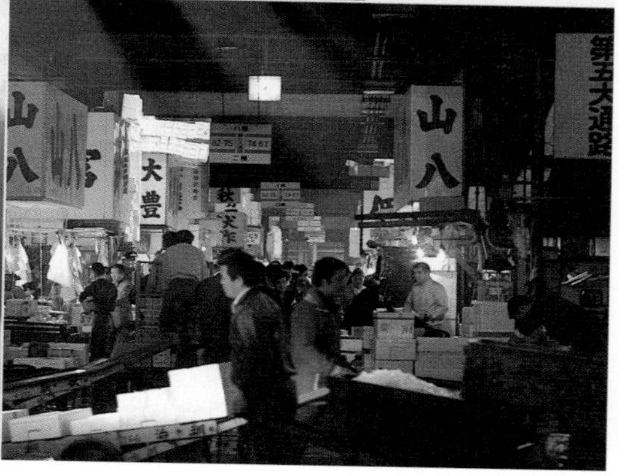

▼After being purchased in the primary auction, goods then pass through a series of middlemen (one such business is pictured here) before reaching retailers and restaurateurs.

ing in making small articles for use on the puppet stage. Around 1960 he decided to devote himself to the craft of puppetry. Over the years Tsujimura has introduced his audience to many different puppet characters, each with its own personality. In 1973 the public television network NHK aired puppet shows produced and performed by Tsujimura. Recently he has been active as an art director for stage and film.

tsujiura 辻占

Divining the future (*uranai*) by stationing oneself at a crossroads (*tsuji*) at dusk and listening to the chance words of passersby; these words were then regarded as oracular. The practice is related to the folk belief in MAREBITO, gods who were thought to appear from afar bestowing blessings. In ancient times this practice was termed *yūke*, or "evening divination." Eventually the rite of *tsujiura* became connected with the worship of DŌSOJIN, or roadside deities. By the Edo period (1600–1868), *tsujiura* had degenerated into the roadside hawking of rice crackers containing printed fortunes. See also DIVINATION.

Tsuji Zennosuke 辻善之助

(1877–1955). Historian. Born in Hyōgo Prefecture. He studied history at Tōkyō University and in 1902 joined the historiographical institute affiliated with the university. From 1911 onward he taught concurrently at the university, becoming a full professor in 1923. Tsuji was the author of numerous studies of Buddhism, including his 10-volume *Nihon bukkyō shi no kenkyū* (1944–55, Studies on the History of Buddhism in Japan). He received the Order of Culture in 1952.

Tsuka Kōhei つかこうへい

(1948–). Playwright and novelist. Real name Kanehara Mineo. Born in Fukuoka Prefecture. Tsuka attended Keiō University. He received the Kishida Drama Prize for *Atami satsujin jiken* (1973, The Atami Murder Case) and the Naoki Prize for *Kamata kōshinkyoku* (1981, Kamata March), a novel about movie stars and the people surrounding them.

Tsukamoto Kōichi 塚本幸一

(1920–). Businessman. Born in Shiga Prefecture. After graduating from Hachiman Commercial High School in Shiga Prefecture, he joined his father's wholesale textile business. Establishing the Wakō Shōji Company in 1946, he started the production and sale of women's underwear in 1949. He renamed the company WACOAL CORPORATION in 1957 and became its president. In 1987 he became chairman. During his career he has turned his company into the largest manufacturer of women's underwear in Japan.

Tsukamoto Kunio 塚本邦雄

(1922–). TANKA poet. Born in Shiga Prefecture. Graduate of Ōsaka University of Foreign Studies. He published two *tanka* poetry collections, *Sōshoku gakku* (1956) and *Nihonjin reika* (1958). His unconventional style—irregular line division, frequent use of uncommon Chinese characters and abstract terms—made him a leading avant-garde *tanka* poet in the late 1950s and 1960s. After 1970 he also wrote novels. His works include the poetry collections *Suisō monogatari* (1952) and *Saredo yūsei* (1975) and a collection of *tanka* criticism, *Yūgure no kaichō* (1971).

Tsukamoto Saburō 塚本三郎

(1927–). Politician. Born in Aichi Prefecture. Upon graduation from Chūō University in 1952, he was an unsuccessful candidate for the House of Representatives from Aichi Prefecture. On his fourth attempt, in 1958, he was elected as a candidate of the JAPAN SOCIALIST PARTY. When the DEMOCRATIC SOCIALIST PARTY was formed in 1960 as the result of a split within the Japan Socialist Party, Tsukamoto joined the new party, becoming its secretary-general in 1974. In April 1985 he succeeded SASAKI RYŌSAKU (b 1915) as chairman. He resigned that post in February 1989, acknowledging receipt of stock transfers from Recruit Co, Ltd. See RECRUIT SCANDAL.

Tsukamyōjin tomb 束明神古墳

(Tsukamyōjin *kofun*). A tomb mound of the mid to late 7th century in the Sada district of the town of Takatori, Nara Prefecture. The tomb mound is now round in shape but, judging from research conducted in 1984–85, it seems highly likely that it was originally octagonal. A corridor-type stone chamber constructed of 450 pieces of hewn stone was discovered in 1984. The funerary articles had been taken by grave robbers. It is known that there was originally a lacquered wooden coffin because of fragments of black lacquer, nails, and a gilt-bronze coffin ornament found on the floor of the chamber. A number of human teeth were also found. Experts estimated that the teeth were those of a person 20 to 30 years of age. This tomb had traditionally been thought to be that of Prince Kusakabe (662–689), the son of Emperor TEMMU (d 686). That tradition lost support in the 1860s when another tomb was suggested as that of Prince Kusakabe; however, the estimated age of the teeth found here provides some support for the traditional theory.

tsukemono ⟶ pickles

Tsukigase 月ヶ瀬[村]

Village in northwestern Nara Prefecture, central Honshū. Tsukigase is noted for its plum trees and the dye (*ubai*) made from the fruit. Lake Tsukigase, created by Takayama Dam, is located here. Pop: 2,084.

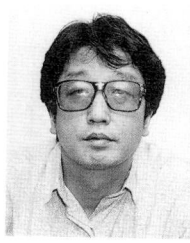

Tsuka Kōhei This writer has won awards both as a playwright and as a novelist.

Tsukiji Market 築地市場

(Tsukiji Shijō). One of the oldest of Tōkyō's 11 central wholesale markets; established in 1935. Located in the Tsukiji district of Chūō Ward. Although it also trades a large volume of produce, Tsukiji is particularly famous as a fish market, for it handles nearly 90 percent of the fish and marine products sold within the central wholesaling system. In 1988 average daily sales of fish at Tsukiji amounted to

2,735 metric tons (3,009 short tons), valued at ¥2.5 billion (US $19.3 million); daily produce sales were 1,674 metric tons (1,841 short tons), valued at ¥399 million (US $3.1 million).

tsukudani A gift assortment of this savory preserved food that includes small fish, shrimp, and mushrooms.

Tsukiji Uoichiba Co, Ltd
築地魚市場［株］

(Tsukiji Uoichiba). Marine products wholesaler dealing in fresh coastal fish, frozen pelagic fish, and dried and salted fish products. It also operates a freezing service and a cold-storage warehouse rental service. One of nine authorized wholesalers in the Tōkyō Central Wholesale Market. Incorporated in 1948 as a fresh and processed seafoods company in Tōkyō and as the main successor of Tōkyō Uoichiba Co, Ltd, in collaboration with other fish wholesalers and processors. It imports a large amount of frozen fish including tuna and shrimp from Africa and the Asia-Pacific region. Sales for the fiscal year ending March 1991 totaled ¥159.5 billion (US $1.2 billion), and capitalization was ¥2.0 billion (US $14.6 million). Headquarters are in Tōkyō.

tsukimono
憑物

Entities believed to "possess" a human being, causing a variety of bodily and mental torments. The term applies primarily to certain animals supposedly capable of becoming invisible and entering the human body through one of its orifices. Such animals are of two broad types: a four-legged creature usually described as a fox (*kitsune*) and a snake known as *tōbyō*. Instead of resembling their namesakes, the "fox" is described as resembling a small weasel, and the snake as short and fat like a fish.

Tsukimono can be divided into two categories: those that molest human beings by their own volition and those that are directed by another person, known as a *kitsunetsukai* or "fox employer." Such persons lure the creature into their power by feeding it, then use it as a servant or messenger to carry out their private grudges. The torments caused by *tsukimono* range from bodily aches and pains to apparent possession, in which the "fox" speaks through the victim's mouth. The approved method of cure is through the services of a Buddhist priest or ascetic. In addition to these animals, *tsukimono* also include dead ancestral spirits who possess a neglectful descendant, and KAMI enraged by profanation of their shrines.

Tsukuba
つくば［市］

City in southwestern Ibaraki Prefecture, central Honshū. Established in 1987 in order to provide the local governmental framework for the planned academic community called Tsukuba Academic New Town (Tsukuba Kenkyū Gakuen Toshi) that had been built in the area during the 1960s and 1970s following a plan approved by the cabinet in 1963. Tsukuba is the home of over 40 public and private technical and scientific research institutions, many of which were moved to the area from Tōkyō or its suburbs. The new institutions of higher education that were established in the area include Tsukuba University and the University of Library Information and Science. EXPO '85, an international exposition of science and technology, was held in the area in 1985. Pop: 143,396.

Tsukuba Botanical Garden
筑波実験植物園

(Tsukuba Jikken Shokubutsuen). Outdoor experimental botanical garden in the city of Tsukuba, Ibaraki Prefecture. Opened in 1983, it is affiliated with the National Science Museum. The 14-hectare (35-acre) garden contains 12 distinctive subdivisions that present the varied flora of central Japan. It also has indoor greenhouses that re-create tropical rain forest and savannah environments.

Tsukuba Expo Center
つくばエキスポセンター

(Tsukuba Ekisupo Sentā). Science and technology exhibition center located in the city of Tsukuba, Ibaraki Prefecture. The Tsukuba Expo Center, which opened in 1986, was established using exhibits and facilities from EXPO '85. In addition to exhibits introducing advanced technology in such fields as high-definition television (HDTV) and robotics, the center includes a planetarium and the Tomato Pavilion, where tomatoes, cucumbers, and melons are raised by a method known as moisture cultivation.

Tsukubasan
筑波山

Mountain in central Ibaraki Prefecture, central Honshū; main peak of the Tsukuba Mountains. The summit consists of two peaks, Nantaisan and Nyotaisan. It is mentioned in the MAN'YŌSHŪ (an 8th-century collection of poems) and is now a recreation site. Tsukuba Shrine and a meteorological observatory are located here. The scientific and academic city of TSUKUBA is at its foot. Tsukubasan is a part of Suigō Tsukuba Quasi-National Park. Height: 876 m (2,874 ft).

Tsukubashū
菟玖波集

RENGA (linked verse) anthology. Compiled in 1356–57 by NIJŌ YOSHIMOTO with the assistance of his teacher GUSAI. The title alludes to a passage in the 8th-century chronicle NIHON SHOKI in which the legendary hero Prince YAMATOTAKERU and an old man link verses to form what is said to be the first *renga*. Nearby Mount Tsukuba (Tsukubasan) was mentioned in the poem, and its name subsequently became almost synonymous with *renga*. The *Tsukubashū*'s 20 chapters contain over 2,000 individual verses (in the form of linked pairs, not entire *renga* sequences). These are arranged in categories based on the pattern of the IMPERIAL ANTHOLOGIES (*chokusen waka shū*). Over 400 poets are represented, from ancient times to the compilers and their contemporaries. *Tsukubashū* established *renga* as a respected literary form, and in 1357 it was designated the first imperially recognized anthology of *renga*.

Tsukuba University
筑波大学

(Tsukuba Daigaku). A national, coeducational university located in TSUKUBA in Ibaraki Prefecture. Founded in 1973, it absorbed Tōkyō University of Education (Tōkyō Kyōiku Daigaku) in 1978. The university is an attempt at reform within the Japanese university system, based upon a new system of cluster colleges. The first cluster comprises faculties of letters, law, economics, and general science; the second cluster, faculties of agriculture, biological sciences, and human sciences; and the third cluster, faculties of technological and information sciences and of socioeconomic planning. Three other clusters are devoted to medicine, physical education, and art and design. Enrollment was 8,608 in 1989.

tsukuda
佃

Rice land under the direct administration of the proprietor of an estate (SHŌEN). *Tsukuda* were cultivated by peasants and semiserfs (GENIN) as a form of corvée labor (BUYAKU). Until the 11th century *tsukuda* normally accounted for the largest and most fertile portion of an estate. From the 12th century *tsukuda* fell into the category of *myōden*, lands to which independent farmers (MYŌSHU) held hereditary rights of cultivation and obligation to pay rice taxes (NENGU). Estate managers (SHŌKAN) and later, during the Kamakura period (1185–1333), shogunate-appointed military land stewards (JITŌ) were assigned *tsukuda*. Thus began the process whereby estate proprietors, largely court nobles and religious institutions, lost control of their *shōen* in the 14th and 15th centuries.

tsukudani
佃煮

A preserved food made by simmering a broth of soy sauce, *sake*, and MIRIN (sweet *sake*) containing shrimp, diced tuna or bonito, clams, seaweed, or small fish until the liquid has been completely reduced. *Tsukudani* ("Tsukuda simmered") derives its name from the island Tsukudajima at the mouth of the river Sumidagawa (in Tōkyō Bay), where it was created during the Edo period (1600–1868).

Tsukumi
津久見［市］

City in southeastern Ōita Prefecture, Kyūshū. Rich deposits of lime have made it a center of the cement industry. Mandarin oranges are grown in the surrounding hills. Pop: 26,797.

Tsukushi Mountains
筑紫山地

(Tsukushi Sanchi). Also called Chikushi Mountains. A series of mountain ranges covering the greater part of Nagasaki, Saga, and Fukuoka prefectures, northern Kyūshū. The main range is the SEFURI MOUNTAINS to the west. The highest peak is Sefurisan (1,055 m; 3,461 ft). The Chikuhō and Saga coalfields are located here.

Tsukushi Plain
筑紫平野

(Tsukushi Heiya). Also known as Chikushi Plain. Located in Fukuoka and Saga prefectures, Kyūshū, and bordering the Ariake Sea. It consists of the floodplain and delta of the river Chikugogawa and has extensive alluvial fans. It is marshy land with numerous creeks. In this rich rice-producing area, dairy farming also flourishes. The major cities are Kurume and Saga. Area: approximately 1,200 sq km (460 sq mi).

Tsumago
妻籠

District in southwestern Nagano Prefecture, central Honshū. Part of the town of Nagiso, at the southern edge of the valley of KISODANI. In the Edo period (1600–1868), Tsumago was one of the POST-STATION TOWNS on the highway Nakasendō. It retains many of the features of the ancient post-station towns.

tsumi
罪

In modern Japanese the word *tsumi* is the equivalent of such English words as sin, offense, or crime. In ancient times it was a broad term applied to actions or conditions that cause the degeneration of or hinder the proper growth and development of the lifeforce; the concept of *tsumi* was closely related to the notion of KEGARE, or ritual impurity. The oldest extant enumeration of *tsumi* is the "Ōharae no Kotoba," found in the 10th century ENGI SHIKI. Examples include destroying ridges between rice paddies, polluting pure places with excrement, skin eruptions such as warts and tumors, actions such as incest and bestiality, and calamities caused by birds, insects, or lightning. The belief that *tsumi* may be brought on by powers outside the realm of individual responsibility underlies the importance of purification rites in Shintō ceremony. Hence, religious responsibility includes (1) maintaining one's purity and participating through worship in the gods' activities aimed at regenerating and creating this world, and (2) atoning for crimes or impurities. See also EVIL; HARAE.

Tsumoru koi yuki no seki no to 積恋雪関扉

(The Snowbound Barrier of Love). Popular title *Seki no to*. KABUKI dance piece (*shosagoto*) by Takarada Jurai (dates unknown), Tobaya Richō I (1738–94?), and Nishikawa Senzō II (d 1817); first performed in 1784. Accompanied by the type of music known as TOKIWAZU-BUSHI, it is based on legends associated with the Six Poetic Sages (ROK-KASEN). The play recounts the foiling of Kuronushi's plan to usurp control over the country by Munesada and his lover Komachi with the magical aid of the courtesan Sumizome, the spirit of a cherry tree in human form. At the play's climax near a snowbound barrier station in the mountains, Sumizome appears and engages Sekibei (an assumed name of Kuronushi) in banter about the pleasure quarters until she seduces him into revealing his identity; the two then engage in a fierce duel, and Kuronushi is vanquished.

tsumugi 紬

(pongee). Hand-woven fabric made from yarns of uneven thickness, manually spun from floss silk. Resembling cotton in texture, it has the luster unique to silk. Woven patterns of KASURI (ikat) and stripes are common. It is used mainly for traditional Japanese clothing. The best-known varieties are Ōshima *tsumugi*, Yūki *tsumugi*, Murayama-Ōshima *tsumugi*, and Oitama *tsumugi*. See also TEXTILES.

Tsumura Setsuko 津村節子

(1928–). Novelist. Real name Yoshimura Setsuko. Born in Fukui Prefecture; graduated from Gakushūin Women's Junior College. In 1965 Tsumura received the Akutagawa Prize for ''Gangu'' (Toy), which contains delicate descriptions of the psychology of women. Her other works include *Honoo no mai* (1975, Dance of the Flames), *Osozaki no ume* (1978, Late-Blooming Plum Tree), and *Shiroyuri no kishi* (1983, Bank of White Lilies).

tsunami 津波

Japanese term for a large sea wave originating from undersea earthquake or volcanic activity. Most *tsunami* originate from submarine earthquakes. When the *tsunami* reach land, they can cause serious damage, particularly in countries such as Japan, where the waterfront is densely populated. The largest *tsunami* to strike Japan in the 20th century was the 1933 Sanriku Tsunami, which took 3,008 lives in the Tōhoku region. Second most serious was the Nankai Tsunami of 1944, which claimed 1,330 victims on the island of Shikoku. The Meteorological Agency monitors earthquakes and issues *tsunami* warnings when conditions warrant.

Tsunashima Ryōsen 綱島梁川

(1873–1907). Religious philosopher and literary critic. Real name Tsunashima Eiichirō. Born in Okayama Prefecture; graduate of Tōkyō Semmon Gakkō (now Waseda University). Ryōsen converted to Christianity in his youth. He wrote literary criticism, and during an illness he came under the influence of EBINA DANJŌ, then a pastor at a church in Kōbe. He subsequently published his first work on comparative religion, *Hiai no kōchō* (1902), and wrote about his own religious experiences in *Yo ga kenshin no jikken* (1905). His work is collected in 11 volumes in *Ryōsen zenshū* (1921–23).

Tsunetō Kyō 恒藤恭

(1888–1967). Legal scholar specializing in jurisprudence. Born in Shimane Prefecture. After graduation from Kyōto University in 1916, he became a professor first at Dōshisha and then at Kyōto University. Resigning in 1933 in connection with the KYŌTO UNIVERSITY INCIDENT, he became a professor (1940) and later president of Ōsaka Commercial College (now Ōsaka Municipal University). After World War II, with SUEKAWA HIROSHI, he was active in the movement for constitutional government as a central figure in the Kansai Constitutional Study Group. In 1949 he was named to the JAPAN ACADEMY. His writings include *Hihanteki hōritsu tetsugaku no kenkyū* (1921, Critical Studies in the Philosophy of Law), *Hōritsu no seimei* (1927, The Life of the Law), *Hō no honshitsu* (1968, The Essence of the Law), *Tetsugaku to hōgaku* (1969, Philosophy and Law), and *Hō to dōtoku* (1969, Law and Morality).

Tsunoda Ryūsaku 角田柳作

(1877–1964). Scholar of Japanese history. Born in Gumma Prefecture. After graduating in 1896 from Tōkyō Semmon Gakkō (now Waseda University), he taught English in Japan. From 1909 to 1917 he was principal of the Hawaii Chūgakkō in Honolulu. He went to Columbia University in 1917 to study under John Dewey and planned to establish in New York a library for the study of Japanese culture. He returned to Japan to solicit gifts for what became in 1931 the Japanese Collection of Columbia University. He taught at Columbia from 1928 until he retired in 1955. His publications included *Ihara Saikaku* (1897), the first study of that author. His chief works in English were *Japan in the Chinese Dynastic Histories* (1951) and *Sources of Japanese Tradition* (1958), compiled jointly with two former students, William Theodore de Bary and Donald KEENE.

Tsurezuregusa 徒然草

(ca 1330; tr *Essays in Idleness*, 1967). A miscellany in the ZUIHITSU (''random jottings'') genre; written by YOSHIDA KENKŌ (ca 1283–ca 1352). *Tsurezuregusa* is one of the best-loved and most-admired examples of classical Japanese prose, often ranked with SEI SHŌNAGON'S MAKURA NO SŌSHI as one of the masterpieces of the *zuihitsu* genre. Its 243 entries range in length from a single sentence to a few pages and take many forms: reminiscences, anecdotes (often of an admonitory nature), meditations, judgments, notes and queries on factual matters, dreamlike fragments of narrative, descriptions, and emotional exclamations. The order in which they are arranged, though seemingly random, involves associative principles like those used in the collections of tales known

as *setsuwa* (see SETSUWA BUNGAKU) and in poetry anthologies. The transience of worldly things (see MUJŌ), be it of the glories of past ages, the beauties of the seasons, youth and vigor, or of life itself, is a dominant theme. The imminence of death makes each moment a gift of incalculable worth, which Kenkō is determined not to scant. At the same time, he finds nature's mutability, its beginnings and endings rather than its consummations, of greatest appeal; he prizes what is past and perishable and manifests a love for what is old and worn, incomplete, or doomed to obsolescence. His attitude is less a wholehearted acceptance of impermanence than an emotional resignation to the inevitability of change and loss. The irresolution between his determination to appreciate every moment to the full and his awareness of desire and the realities of life makes the text much more complex and contradictory than a work that is somewhat similar in tone, the HŌJŌKI by KAMO NO CHŌMEI (1156?–1216). *Tsurezuregusa*, a hymn to changeability that simultaneously reveres the past, has not lost its literary or philosophical value even for modern readers.

tsurigane ninjin 釣鐘人参

Adenophora triphylla var. *japonica*. A perennial herb of the bellflower family (Campanulaceae) that grows wild in mountain areas throughout Japan. Its height is 60–90 centimeters (24–35 in). The leaves generally grow in whorls around the stem. Small, drooping flowers with five bluish violet petals bloom in autumn. The spring shoots have been known as a delicacy since ancient times.

Tsuru 都留［市］

City in southeastern Yamanashi Prefecture, central Honshū, on the river Katsuragawa. Tsuru has been known since the Edo period (1600–1868) for its silk textiles. Pop: 33,903.

tsuru → cranes

Tsuruga 敦賀［市］

City in central Fukui Prefecture, central Honshū, on WAKASA BAY. In the Edo period (1600–1868) it prospered as an intermediate port between the ports of the Sea of Japan and the Ōsaka area. Today it mainly imports Siberian lumber. Industries are synthetic textiles, lumber processing, chemicals, cement, and marine-food processing. Attractions are the Kehi Shrine, Shibata Garden, and Kehinomatsubara, a stretch of pines on Wakasa Bay. Pop: 68,041.

Tsuruga Bay 敦賀湾

(Tsuruga Wan). Part of eastern Wakasa Bay, southwestern Fukui Prefecture, central Honshū. The deep-water port of Tsuruga is located on this bay. Coastal fishing is carried out, and the bay area is dotted with swimming beaches. Part of the Wakasa Bay Quasi-National Park.

Tsurugaoka Hachiman Shrine 鶴岡八幡宮

(Tsurugaoka Hachimangū). Shintō shrine in Kamakura, Kanagawa Prefecture, dedicated to the spirits of the legendary emperor ŌJIN (who was deified as HACHIMAN), the legendary empress JINGŪ (Ōjin's mother), and Ōjin's spouse Himegami (also known as Hime Ōkami). It was originally established as an extension of the IWASHIMIZU HACHIMAN SHRINE in 1063 in nearby Yuigahama by

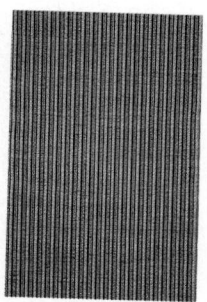

tsumugi Hand-woven silk fabric used chiefly for traditional Japanese clothing.

Tsunetō Kyō This legal scholar's wide-ranging research included international law, the history of political thought, and economic philosophy.

tsurigane ninjin This perennial herb grows in sunny meadows. The bell-shaped flowers open gradually on the stalk, beginning in late summer and ending in early fall.

Tsurugaoka Hachiman Shrine At the top of the stairs is the two-story gate and main shrine building, both reconstructed in 1828. The shrine is crowded with visitors at New Year's and during the annual shrine festival in September.

Minamoto no Yoriyoshi (988–1075) but was moved to its present site in 1180. Adopted as the tutelary shrine of the MINAMOTO FAMILY, the Tsurugaoka Shrine was richly supported by a succession of warrior families, including the Hōjō, Ashikaga, Toyotomi, and Tokugawa. Its annual festival is on 15 September.

Tsurugashima 鶴ヶ島[市]
City in central Saitama Prefecture, central Honshū; known for its production of tea and watermelons. Large-scale housing development and factory construction have increased the population in recent years. Pop: 63,064.

Tsurugidake 剱岳
Mountain in the northern Hida Mountains, eastern Toyama Prefecture, central Honshū; noted for its sharp cliffs and stony peaks. Along with HOTAKADAKE, it is one of the most popular rock-climbing areas in the JAPANESE ALPS. Part of Chūbu Sangaku National Park. Height: 2,998 m (9,836 ft).

Tsurugisan 剣山
Mountain in west-central Tokushima Prefecture, Shikoku; a major peak in the SHIKOKU MOUNTAINS and the second highest peak in Shikoku after ISHIZUCHISAN. It is composed chiefly of limestone and has been a holy mountain since ancient days. It is part of Tsurugisan Quasi-National Park, together with the gorges called IYADANI and ŌBOKE. Height: 1,955 m (6,414 ft).

Tsurumi Yūsuke 鶴見祐輔
(1885–1973). Social critic and writer. Born in Gumma Prefecture; graduated from Tōkyō University in 1910. Tsurumi worked for the Railway Ministry until 1924. Like his mentor NITOBE INAZŌ, Tsurumi was an exponent of liberalism and international cooperation. He assisted his father-in-law, GOTŌ SHIMPEI, with the Political Ethicization Movement (Seiji Rinrika Undō) of the mid-1920s and published the journal *Shin jiyū shugi* (The New Liberalism) from 1928 to 1935. He made extensive lecture tours in Japan and North America in the 1920s and 1930s. He helped organize the Japan committee of the INSTITUTE OF PACIFIC RELATIONS (IPR), and he founded the Taiheiyō Kyōkai (Institute of the Pacific). He was elected to the lower

house of the Diet five times. He served in the House of Councillors from 1953 to 1959 and as minister of welfare (1954–55) in the HATOYAMA ICHIRŌ cabinet.

Tsuru nyōbō 鶴女房
(The Crane Wife). Folktale about an honest man who rescues a crane that has been shot with an arrow by a hunter. The crane returns as a beautiful woman and becomes his wife. Out of her own plumage, she secretly weaves rich brocades that bring great wealth to her husband. When he breaks his promise not to watch her weaving and discovers her true nature, she leaves him in sorrow. The folktale combines the motif of an animal repaying human kindness with that of marriage between a human and an animal. Its numerous variants have other animals becoming the wife or the husband.

Tsuruoka 鶴岡[市]
City in northwestern Yamagata Prefecture, northern Honshū, on the Sea of Japan. The Shōnai Plain, on which the city is located, is a major producer of rice. Tsuruoka has electrical-machinery and automobile-parts industries. The Yunohama and Yudagawa hot springs are located here, as is the Chidō Museum, which houses historical materials and local folk art. Pop: 99,889.

Tsuru Shigeto 都留重人
(1912–). Economist and president of Hitotsubashi University (1972–75). Born in Tōkyō. He earned his doctorate at Harvard University in 1940 and entered the Ministry of Foreign Affairs in 1944. In 1947 he wrote the first Economic White Paper as vice-chairman of the General Coordinating Committee of the ECONOMIC STABILIZATION BOARD. From 1948 to 1975 he was a professor at Hitotsubashi University. He has helped to popularize knowledge of economics among the Japanese people and has addressed issues such as prices, pollution, and energy.

Tsuruta Yoshiyuki 鶴田義行
(1903–86). Swimmer. Born in Kagoshima Prefecture. In the 1928 Amsterdam Olympic Games he set a new Olympic record of 2:48.4 in the 200-meter breast stroke, becoming the first Japanese swimmer to win a gold medal. In the 1932 Los Angeles Olympic Games Tsuruta won the same event with a new Olympic record of 2:45.4.

Tsuruya Namboku 鶴屋南北
(1755–1829). KABUKI playwright of the late Edo period. The most noted dramatist of the Bunka-Bunsei eras (1804–30) and one of the most important writers of Japanese classic theatrical literature. He left more than 120 dramatic works. Namboku was born Ebiya Genzō in Edo (now Tōkyō). At about age 20 he apprenticed himself to a team of playwrights at one of the kabuki theaters. He married the daughter of a kabuki actor, Tsuruya Namboku III (dates unknown), and, after using many other pen names, eventually called himself Tsuruya Namboku IV. He was often called "Namboku the Great."

Namboku created a new type of Edo kabuki drama in the style known as *kizewa kyōgen*, a naturalistic form related to the *sewa kyōgen* of the Kamigata, or Ōsaka theaters. While the *sewa kyōgen* depict the world of the townsmen (CHŌNIN) and do not pretend to be critical of society, the *kizewa kyōgen* of Namboku describe a decaying society in which no social ethics remain effective. Namboku portrays characters who have fallen from social status and who are driven by an unquenchable thirst for money and power, or by lust. This thirst is the very one condemned by Buddhism as the core of all human suffering. Whether or not Namboku was a true Buddhist, his plays are permeated with popular Buddhist beliefs and refer, for example, to the texts of the NICHIREN SECT. His dramas also depict the decay of the warrior and clergy classes at the end of the Edo period. His major plays include *Tenjiku Tokubei ikokubanashi* (1804, Tokubei of India: Tales of Strange Lands), *Kokoro no nazo toketa iroito* (1810, Riddles of the Heart Unraveled in Colored Threads), *Sakurahime azuma bunshō* (1817; tr *The Scarlet Princess of Edo*, 1975), and TŌKAIDŌ YOTSUYA KAIDAN (1825; tr *Les Spectres de Yotsuya*, 1979), his most famous play dealing with ghosts and horror, a genre for which he was also noted.

Tsūsanshō → Ministry of International Trade and Industry

Tsushima 津島[市]
City in western Aichi Prefecture, central Honshū. Tsushima developed around the Tsushima Shrine. Its principal industry is woolen textiles. The shrine's River Festival attracts visitors each July. Pop: 59,343.

Tsushima 対馬
Island in the Tsushima Strait or Korea Strait, between Korea and northwestern Kyūshū; 50 km (30 mi) southeast of Korea. Part of Nagasaki Prefecture. It is divided into Kamishima (Upper Island) to the north and Shimoshima (Lower Island) to the south. The island is made up of an uplifted peneplain. Tsushima has long been a vital point of transportation between Japan and the Asian continent. Forestry is the chief industry, with 90 percent of the island covered with forests. Only 3 percent of the island is arable. Principal agricultural products are *shiitake* (a species of mushroom) and buckwheat. Marine products include squid and cultured pearls. The island is part of the Iki-Tsushima Quasi-National Park. Area: Kamishima, 413 sq km (159 sq mi); Shimoshima, 297 sq km (115 sq mi); pop: 46,064.

Tsushima, Battle of 日本海海戦
(known in Japan as Nihonkai Kaisen; literally, Battle of the Sea of Japan). Greatest naval engagement of the RUSSO-JAPANESE WAR

of 1904–05, in which Japan's combined fleet under Adm. TŌGŌ HEIHACHIRŌ annihilated most of Russia's Baltic squadron in the Tsushima Strait, 27–28 May 1905. In an attempt to restore Russian naval power in the Far East and to relieve Port Arthur (Ch: Lüshun, now part of Lüda), then under siege by the Japanese, 45 warships of the Baltic squadron under Vice Admiral Zinovii Rozhestvenskii embarked toward Vladivostok from the Gulf of Finland in October 1904. As this unwieldy squadron entered the Tsushima Strait between Japan and Korea on 27 May, it was intercepted by Tōgō's fast British-built battleships, cruisers, and scores of torpedo boats. By the next day, the Russians had lost 34 warships (including all of the squadron's battleships). Only three Russian vessels reached Vladivostok intact, others being scuttled at sea or interned in neutral ports. The battle confirmed Japan's naval supremacy in waters off northeast Asia. Until 1945, 27 May was celebrated as Navy Day (Kaigun Kinembi) in memory of the victory.

Tsushima Current   対馬海流

(Tsushima Kairyū). Warm ocean current that branches out of the KUROSHIO current south of Kyūshū and flows into the Sea of Japan by way of the Tsushima Strait. The current splits apart in the Sea of Japan but merges again near the Noto Peninsula. Most of the current eventually flows into the Pacific by way of the Tsugaru Strait. Being a warm current, it does not provide abundant fishing grounds.

Tsushima Incident   対馬事件

(Tsushima Jiken; also known as Tsushima Senryō Jiken or Roshia Gunkan Tsushima Senryō Jiken). Attempt by a Russian warship to obtain a base on the strategically located island of Tsushima in 1861. Under the pretext of stopping for repairs, in February 1861 the warship *Posadnik* anchored in the Osaki and Imozaki coves of Asō Bay on the island of Tsushima. Its crew built barracks on shore and its captain demanded a long-term land lease. The local villagers resisted the Russians, and the Tokugawa shogunate sent *gaikoku bugyō* (foreign affairs commissioner) OGURI TADAMASA to Tsushima. Finally, the British envoy Sir Rutherford ALCOCK sent two British warships, and the *Posadnik* departed after a stay of over six months.

Tsushima Strait   対馬海峡

(Tsushima Kaikyō). Between the islands of Tsushima and Iki, Nagasaki Prefecture, Kyūshū. In the broad sense it also includes the Korea Strait between Korea and Tsushima. The strait connects the Sea of Japan and the East China Sea. It is the site of the battle of TSUSHIMA, a famous naval engagement in the Russo-Japanese War. Narrowest point: 50 km (30 mi); deepest point: 130 m (427 ft).

Tsushima Yūko   津島佑子

(1947–   ). Novelist. Real name Tsushima Satoko. Born in Tōkyō; daughter of the novelist DAZAI OSAMU. Graduate of Shirayuri Women's College. Tsushima's writings explore fundamental relationships between men and women, or parents and children, that are unconstrained by morality or the contemporary social system. Her works include the novel *Chōji* (1978; tr *Child of Fortune*, 1983); the short-story collection *Hikari no ryōbun* (The Territory of Light), which won the 1979 Noma Literary Prize for New Talent; and *Yoru no hikari ni owarete* (1986, Pursued by Evening Light). A collection of her translated short stories, *The Shooting Gallery*, was published in Britain in 1986 and in the United States in 1988.

tsūshimbo → report cards

tsūshō kaisha   通商会社

(commercial companies). Companies formed in 1869 under the aegis of the Meiji government to foster foreign trade. The KAWASE KAISHA banking facilities and the *tsūshō kaisha* were the first Japanese enterprises organized as joint-stock companies (*kabushiki kaisha*). They were set up in eight key cities by MITSUI, ONO-GUMI, the KŌNOIKE FAMILY, and other wealthy merchant houses (see SEISHŌ) under the supervision of government commercial offices (*tsūshōshi*). The *tsūshō kaisha* promoted the establishment of subordinate trading companies. After abolition of the coordinating government offices in 1871, several *tsūshō kaisha* were converted into rice exchanges; the rest disbanded.

Tsutsui Junkei   筒井順慶

(1549–84). *Daimyō* of the Azuchi-Momoyama period (1568–1600). The Tsutsui family played a prominent role in the military organization (*kampu no shūto*) of KŌFUKUJI, the Buddhist monastery of the Hossō sect that had occupied the position of military governor (SHUGO) of Yamato Province (now Nara Prefecture) since the Kamakura period (1185–1333). The Tsutsui emerged in the Tembun era (1532–55) as a SENGOKU DAIMYŌ house. The warlord Matsunaga Hisahide (1510?–77) seized control of the province in 1559, and the young Junkei was displaced from Tsutsui Castle. When Hisahide turned against the hegemon ODA NOBUNAGA in 1577, Nobunaga destroyed him and installed Junkei in his place. Junkei was confirmed as Nobunaga's governor of Yamato, with his seat at Kōriyama Castle, in 1580. AKECHI MITSUHIDE, Nobunaga's vassal, called for Junkei's assistance after eliminating Nobunaga in the HONNŌJI INCIDENT of 1582, but Junkei adhered to TOYOTOMI HIDEYOSHI, who defeated Mitsuhide at the Battle of YAMAZAKI shortly afterward.

Tsutsui Yasutaka   筒井康隆

(1934–   ). Novelist. Born in Ōsaka; graduated from Dōshisha University. Tsutsui's tone ranges from parody to outright farce or black humor as he satirizes the modern world. He is especially well known for his science fiction. Tsutsui's principal works include *Afurika no bakudan* (1968; tr *The African Bomb*, 1986); *Kazoku hakkei* (1972; tr *Portraits of Eight Families*, 1989), which was nominated for the Naoki Prize; *Kyojintachi* (1981, False People); and *Yumenoki-Zaka bunkiten* (1987, Crossroads at Yumenoki-Zaka). His satire of Japanese academic life, *Bungakubu Tadano kyōju* (1989, Professor Tadano, Faculty of Letters), was a popular best seller.

tsutsuji → azaleas

Tsutsumi Chūnagon monogatari
堤中納言物語

(Tale of the Tsutsumi Middle Counselor). Collection of 10 narratives derived from incidents at the courts of the late Heian period (794–1185) through the early Kamakura period (1185–1333). The title refers to no one character named in the text but may be an attempt by the compilers to lend historical authenticity and novelistic intensity to a series of love affairs and court observances in which a highly attractive and amorous gentleman is always the initiator of strange and humorous events. "Tsutsumi Middle Counselor" was a sobriquet of the poet FUJIWARA NO KANESUKE (877–933), but there is no known connection between him and the *Tsutsumi Chūnagon monogatari*. The narrative style, consisting of elegant prose introductions to poem exchanges, is similar to that of the 10th-century ISE MONOGATARI (tr *Tales of Ise*, 1968). "Ausaka koenu gonchūnagon" (The Counselor Who Failed in Love), considered the oldest episode in the collection, may be reliably dated 1055, and its author is the otherwise unknown Lady Koshikibu. Authorship of the other episodes remains unknown. "Yoshinashigoto" (Things That Do Not Matter), which appears to be the most recent episode, may have been written as late as 1385. In most editions, the episodes are arranged in a seasonal sequence from spring to winter.

Tsutsumi Seiji   堤清二

(1927–   ). Businessman; chairman of the Saison group of companies (formerly known as Seibu Saison). Born in Tōkyō. After graduating from Tōkyō University in 1951, he worked as secretary to his father, TSUTSUMI YASUJIRŌ, speaker of the House of Representatives and founder of the Seibu conglomerate. In 1955 he assumed the positions of director and manager of SEIBU DEPARTMENT STORES, LTD. He became the head of the Seibu distribution group after his father's death in 1964, while his half brother, TSUTSUMI YOSHIAKI, assumed leadership of the SEIBU RAILWAY CO, LTD, and its related companies. In addition to founding the supermarket chain Seiyū, Ltd, he established, or formed by merger, FamilyMart Co, Ltd; Seibu Credit Co; Seibu Allstate Life Insurance Co; and the Continental Hotel chain. Under the pen name Tsujii Takashi he is also active as a poet and writer.

Tsutsumi ware   堤焼

(*tsutsumi-yaki*). Folk pottery of Tsutsumi, near Sendai, in Miyagi Prefecture, flourishing mainly in the early 19th century. Tsutsumi wares were made from granular, reddish brown clays. Most of the items produced were for household use, including mortars, bowls, and plates, but especially typical were the storage jars, varying in height from 10 centimeters (4 in) to a meter (3.3 ft). Traditional Tsutsumi pottery had a black or brown glaze, usually glossy, with a bluish or greenish white-flecked overglaze splashed on the rims or sides. Some pieces were glazed in the ordinary honey-colored (*ame*) translucent glaze.

After the BOSHIN CIVIL WAR (1868), the military conflict accompanying the MEIJI RESTORATION, the industry suffered greatly. Since the 20th century, production has switched mainly to the manufacture of tiles and drainage pipes, although some traditional works are still made.

Tsutsumi Yasujirō   堤康次郎

(1899–1964). Politician and entrepreneur. Born in Shiga Prefecture and a graduate of Waseda University, Tsutsumi was elected to the House of Representatives 13 times beginning in 1924 and acted as speaker in 1953 and 1954. Also active in the business world, he established a number of companies, including SEIBU RAILWAY CO, LTD, and created the Seibu group based on the railway, real estate, tourism, and bus transportation.

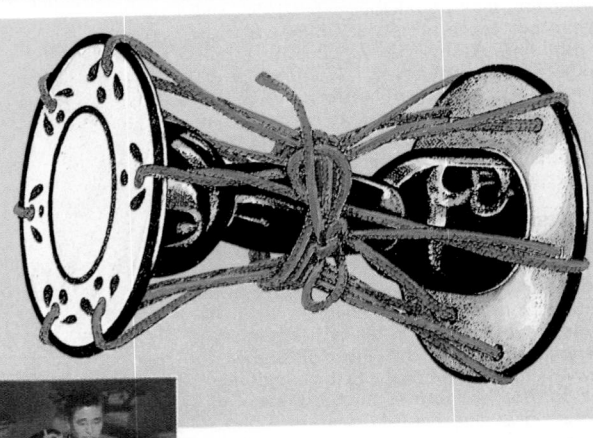

tsuzumi Above, an illustration of a *kotsuzumi* (small *tsuzumi*). In the photo, a musician plays a *kotsuzumi* during a Nō performance.

Tsutsumi Yoshiaki　堤義明

(1934–). Businessman and leader of the Seibu group of companies. Born in Tōkyō. After graduating from Waseda University, Tsutsumi entered Kokudo Keikaku Co, Ltd, in 1957. On the death of his father, TSUTSUMI YASUJIRŌ, in 1964, he took over the business and expanded the group's operations in such fields as transportation, real estate, tourism, and hotels. Its holdings now include SEIBU RAILWAY CO, LTD; Izuhakone Railway Co, Ltd; Kokudo Keikaku Co, Ltd; and PRINCE HOTELS, INC, as well as the Seibu Lions, a professional baseball team. Tsutsumi acted as president of the Japanese Olympic Committee in 1989–90. TSUTSUMI SEIJI, leader of the Seibu Saison group, is his half brother.

tsutsushimi　敬

(seriousness of mind; also pronounced *kei*; Ch: *jing* or *ching*). Philosophical concept elaborated by the Chinese Confucian philosopher Zhu Xi (Chu Hsi; 1130–1200; see SHUSHIGAKU) as in the phrase *cunxin chijing* (*ts'un-hsin ch'ih-ching*; J: *sonshin jikei*), "preserving one's mind/heart and maintaining seriousness." The notion of *chijing* differs from Zen's more direct method of attaining calmness of mind in that it involves objective knowledge. Among Japanese thinkers of the Edo period (1600–1868) there were essentially two views concerning *jing* or *tsutsushimi*. The school of YAMAZAKI ANSAI regarded it as the cardinal moral principle of Confucianism that regulated every aspect of daily conduct, while the school of ITŌ JINSAI insisted on liberation from moral rigorousness and regarded *jing* only as a moral method. In everyday parlance the Japanese word *tsutsushimi* has a range of other meanings, including "modesty," "discretion," and "self-restraint."

tsuwabuki　槖吾

tsuwabuki From October through December, this evergreen perennial herb grows a 60-cm flower stalk and bears yellow flowers in loose clusters. The leaf stalk is edible.

Ligularia tussilaginea or *Farfugium japonicum*. Also called *tsuwa*. An evergreen perennial herb of the chrysanthemum family (Compositae) that grows wild on the warm seacoasts of Kyūshū, Shikoku, and west of the Kantō region in Honshū. It is also widely planted as an ornamental. Long, edible leafstalks grow from underground stems; the thick leaves are roundish to kidney shaped. Loose clusters of composite yellow flowers bloom from fall to early winter. Cultivated varieties such as the *ōtsuwabuki* (*L.t.* var. *gigantea*) have large leaves. An infusion from the dried leaves or juice squeezed from raw leaves has been used as an antidote for poisonous fish.

Tsuwano　津和野[町]

Town in western Shimane Prefecture, western Honshū. *Samurai* residences from its days as a castle town remain. It is now a distribution center for lumber and Japanese paper (*washi*). Tourist attractions include the former residences of the men of letters MORI ŌGAI and NISHI AMANE. Pop: 7,072.

Tsuyama　津山[市]

City in northern Okayama Prefecture, western Honshū. Local products are textiles, handmade Japanese paper (*washi*), and paper goods. The cherry blossoms at the site of Tsuyama Castle, now a park, attract visitors. Pop: 89,400.

Tsuyama Basin　津山盆地

(Tsuyama Bonchi). In northern Okayama Prefecture, western Honshū. Situated between the Chūgoku Mountains and the highlands known as the Kibi Kōgen, it is drained by the river Yoshiigawa. The area's main products are rice, vegetables, and fruit. The major city is Tsuyama. Area: approximately 200 sq km (77 sq mi).

tsuyukusa　露草

(dayflower). *Commelina communis*. An annual herb of the family Commelinaceae that grows wild in forests or in moist soil along roadsides all over Japan. The stem is 20–50 centimeters (7.9–19.7 in) high and the alternate leaves are lanceolate and smooth. The flower has three petals: the larger two are blue and round and the smaller one is white and lanceolate. The *tsuyukusa* blooms during the day from summer to autumn. The blue sap of the flower has been used as a fabric dye since the early part of the 7th century. A variety of *tsuyukusa* known as the *ōbōshibana* is cultivated and used in the traditional YŪZEN textile-dyeing method.

tsuzumi　鼓

Traditional hourglass-shaped drum; it consists of two leather skins each sewn onto an iron ring larger in diameter than the drum body, then laced with cords onto the lacquered wooden drum. Several kinds of hourglass drums were introduced into Japan from the continent prior to the Nara period (710–794). The *ikko* and *san no tsuzumi* still used in the traditional court music of GAGAKU preserve in some measure their Nara-period shapes. Today, however, the word *tsuzumi* generally refers to the *ōtsuzumi* (big *tsuzumi*) and *kotsuzumi* (small *tsuzumi*) used in the NŌ and KABUKI drama. The *ōtsuzumi* is about 28 centimeters (11 in) long with horsehide heads; it is tightly laced and is held on the left thigh with the left hand. The heads are heated before each performance, contributing to the high, dry sound. The *kotsuzumi* is about 25 centimeters (10 in) long and has horsehide heads loosely laced. It is held on the right shoulder with the left hand; by squeezing the laces with the left hand, the player can alter the tone. In order to maintain the appropriate tension, the cords are readjusted before, and sometimes during, each performance.

tsuzura　葛

(clothes box). An old-fashioned piece of furniture used for storing clothes. It is made of woven vines, bamboo, or other flexible materials reinforced with tanned or lacquered paper. The *tsuzura* came into popular use during the Muromachi period (1333–1568). These boxes were originally made from vines of *tsuzurafuji*. The *tsuzura* is basically rectangular in shape and comes with a lid; some have refined lacquer work decorations (MAKI-E) or golden family CRESTS.

tsuzure-ori　綴れ織

(tapestry weave). Type of figured brocade and the technique for weaving it, brought to Japan from China circa 1400. Sometimes referred to as "fingernail weaving," since the weavers use their nails, filed to catch the threads, to execute the designs. This form of weaving has been used in making large decorative panels, temple hangings, and some religious clothing. Today it is used mainly for the type of sash known as Nagoya OBI and for special-occasion or family-crest gift covers called *fukusa*.

Tuan Ch'i-jui → Duan Qirui (Tuan Ch'i-jui)

Tule Lake Relocation Center　トゥーリーレイク収容所

(Tūrī Reiku Shūyōjo). Wartime relocation facility for Japanese Americans from California, Oregon, and Washington State; located near Newell, Modoc County, California. In operation from 27 May 1942 until 20 March 1946, it held a maximum of 18,789 inmates at any one time; 29,000 persons were confined there in all. Originally a "normal" camp, it became largely a concentration camp for those whom the government considered disloyal. There was more bloodshed and disorder at Tule Lake than at all the other centers combined. See also JAPANESE AMERICANS, WARTIME RELOCATION OF; WAR RELOCATION AUTHORITY.

tuna　鮪

(*maguro*). In Japanese, *maguro* is the common name for saltwater fish of the genus *Thunnus*, family Scombridae, order Perciformes, class Osteichthyes. Best known in Japan is the large and tasty *hommaguro* or *kuromaguro* (North Pacific bluefin tuna; *Thunnus thynnus orientalis*), which grows to 3 meters (10 ft), weighs over 300 kilograms (660 lbs), and is found, among other places, in the waters off the west coast of North America. Like other tuna species, its meat has a reddish color and is used for *sashimi* (sliced raw fish) and *sushi* (raw seafood over rice balls).

In ancient times tuna was known as *shibi* and appears in the *Kojiki* (completed in 712), Japan's oldest chronicle, and the 8th-century poetic anthology, the *Man'yōshū*. For a *sushi* menu *maguro* is indispensable; the fatty meat around the pectoral fins near the head, called *toro*, is particularly favored. In recent years much of the tuna consumed in Japan has come from foreign sources.

Turkey and Japan　トルコと日本

(Toruko *to* Nihon). Japan and Turkey underwent similar processes of radical modernization in the late 19th century, stem-

tsuzura A *tsuzura* figures prominently in the folktale "Shitakiri suzume" (The Tongue-Cut Sparrow), illustrated here in a 1960 children's book.

ming from the impact upon the two countries of the great powers of the West. In 1871, during the tour of the IWAKURA MISSION to the United States and Europe for the purpose of studying Western cultural institutions, IWAKURA TOMOMI dispatched a Foreign Ministry official to Constantinople to investigate the situation in Turkey. Both nations sought revision of the Unequal Treaties forced upon them by the Western powers and both considered Russia a threat to their security. The first diplomatic mission from Turkey arrived in Japan in 1890. On its return the vessel carrying the emissaries sank off the Kii Peninsula, but the survivors were rescued by Japanese and supplied with two cruisers for their homeward voyage. This incident and the victory of Japan in the RUSSO-JAPANESE WAR of 1904–05 promoted amity between the two nations, and in 1923 formal diplomatic relations were initiated, followed in 1930 by a treaty of commerce and navigation.

Turkey declared war on Japan in February 1945, some six months before the end of World War II. In 1951 it was a signatory of the San Francisco Peace Treaty and in 1952 diplomatic relations were resumed. Economic ties were expanded with the visit to Japan of Prime Minister Adnan Menderes in 1958. Since the early 1970s Japan has assisted numerous construction projects in Turkey, including dams and power stations. An agreement concerning the Second Bosporus Bridge (completed in 1988) was signed in 1985 during a visit to Japan by Prime Minister Turgut Ozar, and Japan loaned some $468 million (in 1988 US dollars) toward its construction. In 1990 Japan's exports to Turkey totaled US $992 million and its imports US $267 million.

turtles　　　　　　　　　　　亀

(*kame*). In Japanese, *kame* is the general name for reptiles of the order Chelonia. Four families are found in Japan: Cheloniidae and Dermochelyidae (marine); Testudinidae (terrestrial or freshwater); and Trionychidae (freshwater). Turtles of all four families are frequently found from Honshū southward, but around Hokkaidō only marine species are found. Among the marine turtles the *akaumigame* (loggerhead; *Caretta caretta*) is comparatively numerous on the Pacific coast of southwestern Japan. The *aoumigame* (green turtle; *Chelonia mydas*) is another common species. It lands on the OGASAWARA ISLANDS to lay eggs. The most common freshwater turtle is the *ishigame* (*Clemmys japonica*), which is often kept as a pet. The *suppon* (softshell; *Trionyx sinensis*) is raised for its meat.

As the proverb "a crane lives a thousand and a turtle ten thousand years" indicates, the turtle has traditionally been regarded as a symbol of longevity and bearer of good fortune. Turtles appear in many Japanese folktales, among which the story URASHIMA TARŌ is the most famous. Shells of the *taimai* (hawksbill; *Eretmochelys imbricata*) have been utilized for TORTOISESHELL WARE (*bekkōzaiku*) since ancient times.

Twenty-One Demands
　　　　　　　　　対華二十一ヵ条要求

(Taika Nijūikkajō Yōkyū). Set of 21 articles presented by the Japanese government in early 1915 to YUAN SHIKAI (Yüan Shih-k'ai), president of the new and weak Republic of China; the articles mainly specified the extension or introduction of Japanese territorial, political, and economic privileges in

China. Lengthy negotiations between the two governments reached their climax with a Japanese ultimatum in May 1915 for acceptance of a modified version of the original articles. The Chinese president capitulated, in an atmosphere of popular outrage at the Japanese demands and the high-handed manner in which they had been pressed.

Japanese Aspirations in China—With its successes in the SINO-JAPANESE WAR OF 1894–1895 and the RUSSO-JAPANESE WAR of 1904–05, Japan had joined the ranks of imperialist powers in China. In addition to acquiring Taiwan as a colony, it inherited part of the tsarist Russian position in northeast China, especially in South Manchuria (present-day Liaoning and Jilin [Kirin] provinces). The position included control of the SOUTH MANCHURIA RAILWAY and administration of the GUANDONG (KWANTUNG) TERRITORY on the Liaodong (Liaotung) Peninsula. After the 1911 Revolution, when China abandoned imperial for republican forms of government, leading Japanese became increasingly interested in expanding Japan's role in China.

The outbreak of general war in Europe in August 1914 was recognized by Japan as an unparalleled opportunity to advance its position in China. The Japanese government quickly declared entry into World War I on the Allied side, and a Japanese military expedition with token British participation attacked Germany's leased territory in China's Shandong (Shantung) Province (see JIAOZHOU [KIAOCHOW] CONCESSION). The Germans surrendered on 7 November 1914, and Japan acquired another foothold on Chinese soil.

Content of the Demands—The forceful foreign minister KATŌ TAKAAKI secured clearances from the GENRŌ (elder statesmen) and the emperor to proceed with a government agenda for Sino-Japanese negotiations and had a list of 21 demands delivered to President Yuan on 18 January 1915, with warnings of retaliation if Japanese desires were not served. The 21 articles were divided into five groups. The first pressed for confirmation of Japan's recent acquisitions in Shandong and an expanded railway network under Japanese control. It also demanded that no other country be granted territory in or off the coast of Shandong Province and that major cities in the province be opened to foreigners to live and engage in business, thus implying the establishment of a Japanese sphere of influence. In the second group the various railway and leasehold agreements that underlay Japan's dominance in South Manchuria were to be extended to the end of the 20th or into the 21st century. Retaining immunity from Chinese law, Japanese citizens would be allowed to rent or own land and buildings and establish businesses outside treaty ports and leaseholds in South Manchuria and eastern Inner Mongolia. This section also called for Japanese priority in the same regions in railway construction and loans, and in the appointment

of financial and administrative advisers to the government. The third group looked to Japanese participation as joint owners of the Hanyeping (Han-yeh-p'ing) Company, a mining and metallurgical complex in central China already heavily in debt to the Japanese. The fourth division barred China from making further cessions or leases of its coastal harbors or islands to any foreign country but Japan. The fifth group contained a miscellany of far-reaching demands, including appointment of advisers to the central government and Japanese participation in the administration of Chinese police departments, which would be a severe intrusion upon China's sovereignty. Japan conveyed to its ally Britain only the contents of the first four groups of articles.

The Chinese government's strategy was to procrastinate, hoping that the Western powers would react negatively to the Japanese demands. The popular response was an outpouring of patriotic sentiment and a widespread boycott of Japanese goods and shipping.

The Japanese Ultimatum—After China had rejected Japan's 26 April revised version of the original demands, the Japanese cabinet approved an ultimatum to the Chinese that, on the insistence of the *genrō*, deleted the main articles of the fifth group, which had gained a special notoriety, in part due to the Japanese attempt to veil it in secrecy. On 7 May the Chinese government was given two days to accept the reduced list of 13 articles. Yuan accepted; a series of treaties and notes between China and Japan were signed on 25 May 1915.

The revised version of the Twenty-One Demands gained little for Japan that it did not already have. However, the course of events leading to its acceptance had the effect of disenchanting Britain and the United States with Japan's China policy. To the people of China, the experience marked Japan as the most overbearing and dangerous of im-

turtles
1 The shell of the adult *akaumigame* (loggerhead) is 1–1.2 meters in length. This species' numbers are gradually decreasing.
2 Found in Japan's coastal waters, the adult *aoumigame* (green turtle) has a shell 1–1.2 meters in length.
3 The *suppon* (softshell), with a shell length of 25–35 cm, has a belligerent disposition, and its meat is customarily believed to impart vigor when eaten.
4 The *ishigame*, whose shell attains a length of 13–18 cm, is found in lakes and ponds from Honshū southward.

tsuyukusa The lower stems of this wild herb (also known as *aobana*, or "blue flower") trail along the ground, branching off in many directions.

The Muroto Typhoon destroyed or set adrift more than 2,000 boats in the waters off Ōsaka in September 1934. This photograph shows the devastation near the bridge Iwasakibashi in the port of Ōsaka.

Homes near the river Nigawa are half-submerged by flood waters after the Muroto Typhoon. Some 9,000 homes in Hyōgo Prefecture were damaged.

Major Typhoons in Japan and Resultant Damage

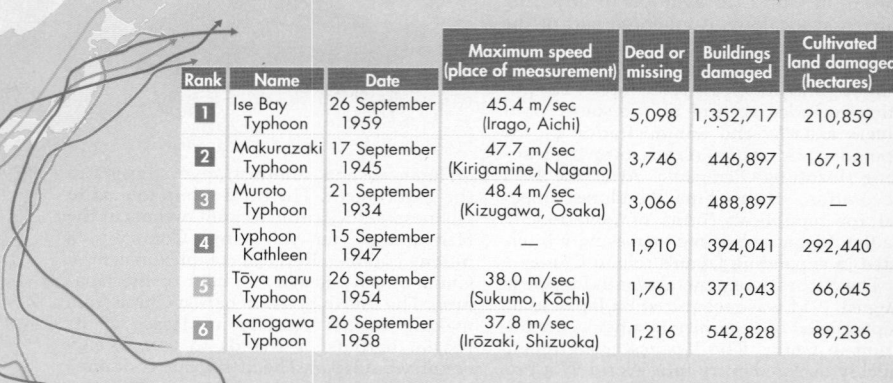

Rank	Name	Date	Maximum speed (place of measurement)	Dead or missing	Buildings damaged	Cultivated land damaged (hectares)
1	Ise Bay Typhoon	26 September 1959	45.4 m/sec (Irago, Aichi)	5,098	1,352,717	210,859
2	Makurazaki Typhoon	17 September 1945	47.7 m/sec (Kirigamine, Nagano)	3,746	446,897	167,131
3	Muroto Typhoon	21 September 1934	48.4 m/sec (Kizugawa, Ōsaka)	3,066	488,897	—
4	Typhoon Kathleen	15 September 1947	—	1,910	394,041	292,440
5	Tōya maru Typhoon	26 September 1954	38.0 m/sec (Sukumo, Kōchi)	1,761	371,043	66,645
6	Kanogawa Typhoon	26 September 1958	37.8 m/sec (Irōzaki, Shizuoka)	1,216	542,828	89,236

SOURCE: Meteorological Agency.

A 1990 photograph taken from the Japanese weather satellite *Himawari* shows the spiral-shaped cloud of Typhoon No. 19 heading northward.

perialist countries. See also WASHINGTON CONFERENCE.

Twenty-Six Martyrs　二十六聖人

(Nijūroku Seijin). The collective name given to the Japanese and foreign Christians crucified at Nagasaki on 5 February 1597 by order of TOYOTOMI HIDEYOSHI. Hideyoshi's motives for issuing this order are not clear, but they appear to have been connected with the seizure of the cargo of a Spanish ship that had run aground at Tosa (now Kōchi Prefecture) the previous December (see SAN FELIPE INCIDENT). The martyrs were 6 Franciscan missionaries (see FRANCISCANS), 3 JESUITS, and 17 laymen, including 3 young boys. This was the first time any Europeans had been put to death in Japan for professing CHRISTIANITY.

typhoons　台風

(*taifū*). Tropical storms occurring in the western Pacific. The Pacific equivalent of the hurricanes of the Western hemisphere, these tropical storms are prevalent in Japan during the late summer and early autumn.

Historic typhoons include those that thwarted the MONGOL INVASIONS OF JAPAN in 1274 and 1281. Typhoons during recent history that have been exceptionally destructive include the Muroto Typhoon of 1934 (over 3,000 people left dead or missing), the typhoon associated with the TŌYA MARU DISASTER of 1954 (over 1,000 dead or missing),

the Kanogawa Typhoon of 1958 (over 1,000 dead or missing), and the Ise Bay Typhoon of 1959 (over 5,000 dead or missing). Named for their place of entry into Japan or the area of heaviest damage, since 1953 typhoons have also carried serial numbers by year and order of formation. For example, the Ise Bay Typhoon is also called Typhoon No. 5915 (i.e., 59–15), as it was the 15th typhoon to form in 1959. Thanks to flood control works and improved warning systems, no typhoon since 1959 has left more than 1,000 people dead or missing.

Structure—Typhoons are small in comparison with storms outside the tropics. Their diameters are typically 500 kilometers (300 mi), though they sometimes reach 1,000 kilometers (600 mi). Pressure at the center of a typhoon can fall below 900 millibars. This extremely low pressure distinguishes tropical cyclones from storms in temperate zones, as does the presence of a calm area—the eye—20 to 50 kilometers (12–30 mi) in diameter in the storm center.

Development and Course—Most typhoons form in the Pacific Ocean east of the Philippines between latitudes 5°N and 25°N. Vast amounts of water vapor rise here, leaving behind a low-pressure area and an updraft for additional vapor. Hot vapor then condenses in the upper atmosphere and falls as rain. Soon after formation, the typhoon, pushed by easterly winds, travels to the west or west-northwest at 20 to 30 kilometers (12–18 mi) per hour. When it reaches the

North Pacific it hits a high-pressure zone moving southwest of Japan. In the summer months in particular, this high-pressure zone often extends far out to the west and thus deflects northwest-bound typhoons to the west toward the Philippines, the South China Sea, and the southern coast of China. When not deflected, the typhoon gradually moves north-northwest along the periphery of the high-pressure zone and eventually approaches the southern coast of Japan. The intensity of a typhoon varies over its course, but a medium-size typhoon exerts an average of 10^{25} ergs, an amount comparable to the energy released by 100 hydrogen bombs of the megaton range.

Observation and Forecasting—Accurate forecasting of a typhoon requires detailed observation of a wide area, including the typhoon and its surroundings. The Japanese METEOROLOGICAL AGENCY (Kishōchō) performs many of the essential observation and forecast services, collecting data on wind as well as atmospheric and high-altitude conditions. Information is collected from ships at sea, foreign meteorological agencies, and satellites, as well as from stations all over Japan. Although it is extremely difficult to plot the course of a typhoon, the agency provides charts displaying the projected position of the storm center 12, 24, and 48 hours in the future, and issues warnings and advisories to threatened areas. This information is also transmitted to meteorological facilities in Southeast Asia.

U

ubasoku 優婆塞

A Buddhist layman. (The term for Buddhist laywoman is *ubai*.) As a transliteration of the Sanskrit *upāsaka*, *ubasoku* is technically one who has taken the three refuges (in the Buddha, the DHARMA, and the *samgha*; i.e., the Buddha, the doctrine, and the priesthood) and keeps the five precepts (against killing, stealing, sexual misconduct, lying, and drinking intoxicants). In this orthodox sense, the term was used early in Japanese Buddhism to refer to those men who formed groups (*chishiki*) to erect temples or otherwise support Buddhism or to those in formal pursuit of monkhood.

Broadly, the term was applied to unordained holy men who, in the Nara (710–794) and early Heian (794–1185) periods, brought Buddhism to the common people. They defied government suppression and established a tradition for such ascetics and holy men as HIJIRI and SHUGENDŌ. Still a fundamental Buddhist term, *ubasoku* has not been used in the context of significant groups or movements since the Heian period.

Ube 宇部[市]

City in southwestern Yamaguchi Prefecture, western Honshū, on the Inland Sea. Ube grew rapidly as a mining town with the opening of coal mines in the Meiji period (1868–1912). The mines were closed in 1967. Steel, cement, fertilizer, and petrochemical plants are located on reclaimed land. Yamaguchi University's schools of medicine and engineering are here. Pop: 175,053.

Ube Industries, Ltd 宇部興産[株]

(Ube Kōsan). Comprehensive chemical company manufacturing petrochemical, chemical, cement, and machinery products. Incorporated in 1942. Sales for the fiscal year ending March 1991 totaled ¥467.8 billion (US $3.4 billion), and the company was capitalized at ¥41.8 billion (US $304.7 million). Headquarters are in the city of Ube, Yamaguchi Prefecture.

ubusunagami 産土神

The protective deity of one's birthplace. The term occurs as early as the 8th century. The category of *ubusunagami* has become confused with that of UJIGAMI, the local tutelary deity. In theory, the *ujigami* is the god of a consanguineous family or people, while the *ubusunagami* is the deity of a geographic territory. When all families of a village were related by blood, this distinction was irrelevant, but as unrelated families came to occupy the same village, a need was felt for a deity who could protect all the inhabitants. The newly adopted territorial deity was usually called *ubusunagami* or CHINJU NO KAMI and was responsible for a larger territory than the *ujigami*. Worshipers of a single *ubusunagami* came to be called its *ubuko;* the *ujigami*'s worshipers were termed *ujiko*.

UCC Ueshima Coffee Co, Ltd
ユーシーシー上島珈琲[株]

(Yū Shī Shī Ueshima Kōhī). Manufacturer of coffee, tea, cocoa, canned goods, and other foods. Incorporated in 1951. UCC is involved in all aspects of the coffee business, from cultivation of coffee beans to final sales. It maintains a subsidiary in Brazil. Sales for the fiscal year ending March 1990 totaled ¥197.1 billion (US $1.3 billion), and capitalization stood at ¥5.0 billion (US $32.7 million). Headquarters are in Kōbe and Tōkyō.

Uchida Ginzō 内田銀蔵

(1872–1919). Historian. Specialist in the history of the Edo period (1600–1868) and pioneer of the modern study of Japanese economic history (see HISTORIOGRAPHY). Born in Tōkyō, he graduated from Tōkyō University in 1896 and joined its faculty in 1899. After study in Europe he became a professor at Kyōto University. His works include *Kinsei no Nihon* (1919, Japan in the Edo Period).

Uchida Hyakken 内田百閒

(1889–1971). Novelist and essayist. Real name Uchida Eizō. Born in Okayama Prefecture; graduate of Tōkyō University. After a career spent teaching German, Uchida turned to professional writing. He is best known for his essays, which were written under the pen name Hyakkien. A disciple of NATSUME SŌSEKI, he worked as an editor and proofreader of Sōseki's complete works. Uchida's principal works include *Meido* (1922) and *Ahō ressha* (1952).

Uchida Hyakken This novelist and essayist turned to professional writing after a career as a German teacher.

Uchida Kōsai 内田康哉

(1865–1936). Diplomat and politician. Born in what is now Kumamoto Prefecture. A graduate of Tōkyō University, he entered the Ministry of Foreign Affairs and served as ambassador to Austria and the United States before being named foreign minister (1911–12). After a term as ambassador to Russia during the Bolshevik Revolution, he was again named foreign minister (1918–23). Appointed foreign minister a third time (1932–34), he called for the recognition of MANCHUKUO, the puppet state created by the GUANDONG (KWANTUNG) ARMY, and for Japan's withdrawal from the League of Nations following its censure of Japan's conduct in Manchuria (see LYTTON COMMISSION).

Uchida Mitsuko 内田光子

(1948–   ). Pianist. Born in Shizuoka Prefecture. At age 12 she accompanied her family to Vienna, where her father had been posted as a diplomat, and began her piano studies in earnest. She took first prize at the Beethoven Competition in Vienna in 1969 and placed second in the Chopin Competition in Warsaw in 1970. Best known as a gifted interpreter of Mozart, Uchida performed a complete cycle of Mozart piano concerti (with the English Chamber Orchestra under Jeffrey Tate) in Tōkyō in 1987 and a complete cycle of Mozart sonatas in New York in 1991.

Uchida Roan 内田魯庵

(1868–1929). Critic and novelist. Real name Uchida Mitsugu. Born in Tōkyō. He contributed to JOGAKU ZASSHI, Japan's first magazine for women. In 1889 he was profoundly moved by Dostoevsky's *Crime and Punishment*, which he later translated into Japanese. He advocated broadening the scope of popular literature by incorporating social dimensions and issues. His writings include essays on and translations of modern European literature and helped pave the way for the naturalist school of the early 20th century. His main works include the essay "Bungakusha to naru hō" (1894, How to Become a Man of Letters), the novel *Kure no nijūhachinichi* (1898, The Last Month of the Year), and his memoirs *Omoidasu hitobito* (1925, People I Remember).

Uchida Ryōhei 内田良平

(1874–1937). Ultranationalist leader. Born in Fukuoka Prefecture. As a youth he entered

Uchida Tomu
1 Yamamoto Kaichi (foreground), Kazami Akiko, and a child actor in a scene from this film director's early masterpiece of realism, *Tsuchi* (1939, Earth).
2 Uchida, who is known as a pioneer of realistic cinema.

the GEN'YŌSHA, a right-wing nationalist society, and soon became the leading disciple of its founder, TŌYAMA MITSURU. When the TONGHAK REBELLION broke out in Korea in 1894, Uchida went to help the rebels (see TAIRIKU RŌNIN). In 1901 he founded an ultranationalist organization, the AMUR RIVER SOCIETY, to press the government to adopt a strong policy toward Russia. In 1903 he joined the TAIRO DŌSHIKAI, a political association formed to advocate war with Russia. Following the Russo-Japanese War of 1904–05, Uchida called for the annexation of Korea (see KOREA, ANNEXATION OF). During the Taishō (1912–26) and early Shōwa (1926–89) periods, he turned his attention to attacking liberal currents at home. He was arrested in 1925 on suspicion of plotting to assassinate Prime Minister KATŌ TAKAAKI but was found innocent.

Uchida Tadao　　　　内田忠夫

(1923–86). Economist. Born in Mie Prefecture. After graduating from Tōkyō University in 1947, he went to study at the University of Chicago in 1951. In 1965 he became a professor at Tōkyō University. He was a leader in Japan in economic analysis using econometric models. The macroeconometric model he developed with Watanabe Tsunehiko was adopted by the government in its medium-term economic plan of 1960.

Uchida Tomu　　　　内田吐夢

(1898–1970). Film director. He was a pioneer of realistic cinema, exemplified by his film *Tsuchi* (1939, Earth), which used documentary realism to portray the lives of a fictional farming family that loses everything and then struggles to recover. Uchida started his career as a comic actor and production assistant. He later joined NIKKATSU CORPORATION as an assistant director making silent comedies. In the mid-1930s he became increasingly involved with movements toward greater realism in film and more cinematic adaptations of literature.

In 1945 Uchida went to Manchuria, and he remained there or in China until 1954. Upon his return to Japan he joined the TŌEI CO, LTD. There he specialized in remaking many classic period pieces, such as *Daibosatsu tōge* (1957–59, Daibosatsu Pass) and *Miyamoto Musashi* (1961–65, Musashi). His postwar masterpiece, *Kiga kaikyō* (1964, The Straits of Hunger), is, however, in a genre known as the "humanistic thriller" for its sympathetic examination of a criminal's motives.

Uchida Yōkō Co, Ltd　　　[株]内田洋行

(Uchida Yōkō). Trading and manufacturing company specializing in office equipment and machines. Incorporated in 1941. The company markets office computers under the PFU brand. Overseas offices are located in the United States, Germany, Italy, Taiwan, Hong Kong, Singapore, and Malaysia. Sales

for the fiscal year ending July 1990 totaled ¥157.8 billion (US $1.1 billion), and capitalization was ¥4.7 billion (US $31.5 million). Headquarters are in Tōkyō.

Uchida Yoshikazu　　　　内田祥三

(1885–1972). Architect and designer of earthquake-proof reinforced-concrete and steel-frame structures. Uchida graduated from Tōkyō University in 1907, became a professor there in 1921, and served as president of the university from 1943 to 1945. After the TŌKYŌ EARTHQUAKE OF 1923, he helped restore a large portion of the devastated Tōkyō University campus and participated in the design of the famous Yasuda Auditorium, which is considered one of his most important creations. Given the new set of architectural imperatives made evident by the earthquake, he also expanded his research to include fireproof architecture and participated in urban planning projects for the rebuilding of Tōkyō. He received the Order of Culture in 1972.

Uchigikishū　　　　打聞集

An anonymous collection of *setsuwa* (tales or anecdotes; see SETSUWA BUNGAKU) written near the end of the Heian period (794–1185). The bulk of the collection consists of 27 Buddhist tales from India, China, and Japan, 21 of which are also found in the KONJAKU MONOGATARI, with analogues in the UJI SHŪI MONOGATARI and the NIHON RYŌIKI as well. While it seems that each of these collections was developed independently, the *Uchigikishū* is extremely valuable for what it reveals of the tradition within which all of them were composed and transmitted, for its occasional unevenness of style suggests that it was still close in form to one of the sources of the *setsuwa* genre: the notes made by monks as an aid to memorizing their sermons. Its idiom, a blending of vernacular Japanese with literary Chinese, is rendered in a mixture of Chinese characters and Japanese phonetic script (*kana*) with a number of unusual orthographic features.

uchikowashi　　　　打毀

(literally, "smashing"). Urban riots of the Edo period (1600–1868). In protest against exorbitant rice prices, starving mobs destroyed the storehouses of rice merchants and pawnbrokers. (Similar riots by farmers are called HYAKUSHŌ IKKI.) *Uchikowashi* occurred sporadically during the 18th and 19th centuries in various cities. Early examples were riots in Nagasaki in 1713 and Edo (now Tōkyō) in 1733. A riot in Ōsaka led by ŌSHIO HEIHACHIRŌ in 1837 set off a series of urban disturbances in other parts of the country. The extensive riots of 1866 in Edo and Ōsaka helped to hasten the collapse of the TOKUGAWA SHOGUNATE. Modern instances of *uchikowashi* are known as *kome sōdō*; the RICE RIOTS OF 1918 are particularly famous.

Uchimura Kanzō　　　　内村鑑三

(1861–1930). Christian leader, essayist, and editor. Born in Edo (now Tōkyō), Uchimura showed an early ability in languages and began English lessons at age 11. By 1877 he gained admission to the Sapporo Agricultural College (now Hokkaidō University), where most lectures were in English. There he was converted to Christianity. He later went to study in the United States at Amherst College and Hartford Theological Seminary. He returned to Japan in 1888.

Uchimura taught in a number of schools, but in each case left after disagreement over

principles deriving from his Christian orientation. The most famous confrontation was with his colleagues at the First Higher School when they thought he failed to show sufficient respect to the signature of the emperor appended to a copy of the new IMPERIAL RESCRIPT ON EDUCATION. Realizing he could not continue as a teacher, Uchimura started to write. By 1897 he was senior editor of the popular newspaper YOROZU CHŌHŌ. He became an outspoken pacifist and resigned from the newspaper when the publisher endorsed the government's warlike policies on the eve of the Russo-Japanese War (1904–05).

Uchimura published 357 issues of his own monthly, *Seisho no kenkyū* (Biblical Studies), before his death. World War I convinced him of the need for renewed evangelical efforts, and for five years he addressed weekly audiences of 500 to 700 in downtown Tōkyō on the books of the Bible. His followers came to identify with Uchimura's attitude that the church is unnecessary and at times a hindrance to Christian faith. His word to describe his point of view, MUKYŌKAI, or Nonchurch Christianity, is still used to distinguish his tradition.

Whether directed to a Japanese or Western audience, Uchimura's writings reflect his struggle to serve the two J's (Jesus and Japan) simultaneously and to develop a Japanese, yet uncompromising, form of Christianity.

His works include *Kirisuto shinto no nagusame* (1893, Consolations of a Christian), *Japan and the Japanese* (1894), and *How I Became a Christian* (1895).

Uchimura Naoya　　　　内村直也

(1909–89). Playwright. Real name Sugawara Minoru. Born in Tōkyō; graduate of Keiō University. He studied drama with KISHIDA KUNIO and published plays in the late 1930s. His long-run serial radio drama, *Eriko to tomo ni* (Together with Eriko), was an enormous success after World War II. Uchimura also published studies of the dramatic arts and the mass media such as *Doramatorugī kenkyū* (1956, Dramaturgy Studies) and *Atarashii doramatorugī* (1962, New Dramaturgy).

Uchinada　　　　内灘[町]

Town in central Ishikawa Prefecture, central Honshū, on the Sea of Japan. The town was at the center of a controversy in 1953 when local residents opposed the construction of an artillery range by American military forces. Uchinada is now a commuter suburb of the city of Kanazawa. Pop: 24,688.

Uchinada Incident　　　　内灘事件

(Uchinada Jiken). Name given to a protest in 1952–53 against the location of an American military firing range in the village of Uchinada, Ishikawa Prefecture. The installation opened in March 1953 to train American personnel for the Korean War.

The first of many protests against American bases in Japan (see UNITED STATES MILITARY BASES, DISPUTES OVER), it rapidly expanded to become a national issue. The range was temporarily closed in May but reopened the following month. After negotiations the villagers accepted financial compensation. In 1957 the firing range was turned over to the Japanese government.

Uchinoura　　　　内之浦[町]

Town in southeastern Kagoshima Prefecture, Kyūshū; until recently an undeveloped agricultural region. Japan's first satellite was

launched in 1970 from the Kagoshima Space Center, which is located here. Pop: 5,744.

Uchiura Bay　内浦湾

(Uchiura Wan). Also known as Funka Bay. Inlet of the Pacific Ocean, on the eastern coast of the Oshima Peninsula, southwestern Hokkaidō. A circular bay with a diameter of approximately 50 km (30 mi). Principal activities are the catching of squid and the cultivation of scallops.

uchiwa → fans

Uda, Emperor　宇多天皇

(867–931; Uda Tennō). The 59th sovereign (tennō) in the traditional count (which includes several legendary emperors); reigned 887–897; abdicated in favor of his son Emperor DAIGO. Son of Emperor KŌKŌ (830–887; r 884–887), Uda was not closely related to the FUJIWARA FAMILY and was determined to curb its influence. Uda challenged the regent (KAMPAKU) Fujiwara no Mototsune (836–891) in the AKŌ INCIDENT OF 887. After Mototsune's death Uda refused to fill the regent's post, and tried to counteract Fujiwara power by promoting men of other families, most notably SUGAWARA NO MICHIZANE. Uda retired to the temple NINNAJI and became a priest, but remained influential throughout his son's reign. Fragments of his diary, UDA TENNŌ GYOKI, survive.

Udagawa Yōan　宇田川榕庵

(1798–1846). Scientist, physician, and scholar of WESTERN LEARNING. Born in Edo (now Tōkyō), he was adopted by Udagawa Shinsai (1769–1834), a doctor of Western medicine and translator of Dutch medical manuals. Interested in natural history, he studied Dutch under Baba Sajūrō (1787–1822), an interpreter with the Tokugawa shogunate. In 1826 Udagawa was put in charge of translation in the shogunate's department of astronomy and participated in the translation into Japanese of the Dutch version of a French encyclopedia (see KŌSEI SHIMPEN). Among his works were Shokugaku keigen (1833), a treatise on Western botanical science; and Seimi kaisō (1837–47), a translation of William Henry's (1775–1836) Elements of Experimental Chemistry.

Uda Tennō gyoki　宇多天皇御記

The diary of Emperor UDA (r 887–897); also known as Kampyō gyoki, after the Kampyō era (889–898). What remains today of the original 10-volume work was compiled in the late Edo period (1600–1868) by Nakatsu Hirochika from fragments quoted in other works. It describes court ceremony and the antagonism between Uda and the FUJIWARA FAMILY.

udon　饂飩

Type of wheat-flour noodle. The making of udon is thought to have been transmitted to Japan from China during the Nara period (710–794). Salt and water are added to flour to make a dough, which is kneaded, ripened, rolled out, and cut into strips. The noodles are then boiled and customarily served in a hot broth (tsuyu) consisting of soy sauce, MIRIN (sweet sake), sugar, and stock (dashi) made with flaked bonito (see KATSUOBUSHI). Any of a variety of ingredients, such as TEMPURA, raw egg, or aburaage (deep-fried bean curd), are often added. One notable variant of udon is the wide, flat noodle known as

kishimen, which originated in the city of Nagoya.

Udo Shrine　鵜戸神宮

(Udo Jingū). Shintō shrine in the city of Nichinan, Miyazaki Prefecture, Kyūshū, dedicated to Ugayafukiaezu no Mikoto and five other deities. The shrine is said to mark the birthplace of Ugayafukiaezu, the father of the legendary first emperor, Jimmu. According to tradition, the Udo shrine was erected in the time of the legendary emperor SUJIN. At the end of the 8th century the shrine became subordinate to a Buddhist temple, and, until the formal separation of Shintō and Buddhism in 1868, it served as a center for the syncretic school known as RYŌBU SHINTŌ. The annual festival is held on 1 February.

Ueda　上田[市]

City in eastern Nagano Prefecture, central Honshū, on the river Chikumagawa. In ancient times Ueda was the seat of the provincial capital (kokufu) of Shinano Province. It developed as a castle town from 1583. It was known until World War II for its sericulture. Present industries include textiles and electrical appliances. Rice, apples, and walnuts are cultivated. The remains of a provincial temple and Ueda Castle are of interest. Pop: 119,435.

Ueda Akinari　上田秋成

(1734–1809). Scholar, poet, and fiction writer, best known for his collection of nine tales of the supernatural, UGETSU MONOGATARI (1776; tr Tales of Moonlight and Rain, 1974). Born to a woman in Ōsaka's pleasure quarter, Akinari was adopted at the age of three by a former samurai named Ueda, who worked as an oil and paper merchant. His childhood was marked by a bout of smallpox and a seemingly miraculous recovery after a visit by his adoptive father to Kajima Inari Shrine; a slight deformity on his hands resulting from this illness led to his later use of the pen name Senshi Kijin ("Clipper-Handed Eccentric"). His scholarly inclinations were obvious from an early age; he attended a private academy, the KAITOKUDŌ, pursued classical studies, and took part in a HAIKU circle. In 1761, with the death of his adoptive father, he became responsible for the family business. In 1771, when his home and business were destroyed by fire, he turned to the study of medicine as a means of making a living, opening a practice in 1776 that lasted for 11 years. Even while engaged in medicine Akinari also supported himself by teaching, editing, and writing commentaries on classics he especially admired.

Best-Known Works—Akinari's two early works Shodō kikimimi sekenzaru (1766, The Worldly Monkey Who Knows All the Arts) and Seken tekake katagi (1767, Sketches of Worldly Mistresses) were written in the popular manner of the katagi-mono ("character sketches"), a subgenre of the UKIYO-ZŌSHI ("tales of the floating world"). Both were published by the Hachimonjiya ("Figure Eight Shop"; see HACHIMONJIYA-BON), the leading bookseller of popular fiction.

Akinari's Ugetsu monogatari ranks among the best-known works in the classical tradition. Classified as a YOMIHON ("reading book"), unlike the works mentioned above, it is set in times past. Employing a network of references and allusions to historical persons, places, and events, it also shows influence from Chinese classical and popular literary traditions—all of which combine to produce a work of great elegance and eerie beauty. The prominence of the theme of spirit possession in this work has been linked to Akinari's early brush with the Inari branch of Shintō theology, associated in the popular mind with fox spirits.

Poetry and Scholarship—Akinari wrote an essay on the grammatical particles in haiku in 1774; and he drew close to BUSON's circle of poets. After giving up his medical practice and moving to Kyōto in 1793, Akinari composed many WAKA; the waka poet OZAWA ROAN became his closest friend. Akinari left 2,454 verses and deserves to be counted among the best waka poets of his time.

Akinari also participated in the scholarly tradition known as KOKUGAKU (National Learning), although his stance was always an independent one. The most dramatic incident in his scholarly career was his dispute with the Kokugaku scholar MOTOORI NORINAGA, in which he took issue from a rationalist standpoint with the bases of Motoori's ethnocentric views.

Late Writings—Toward the end of his life Akinari returned to prose fiction, leaving a collection of 10 tales, Harusame monogatari (1808; tr Tales of the Spring Rain, 1975). A valuable revelation of Akinari's philosophical and moral outlook, it stands—together with Tandai shōshin roku (1808, Undaunted and Fainthearted Jottings), a collection of opinions and personal recollections—as a kind of last testament.

Ueda Bin　上田敏

(1874–1916). Poet, literary critic, and translator. Born in Tōkyō; graduate of Tōkyō University. Ueda became professor of English

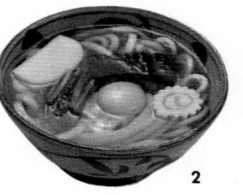

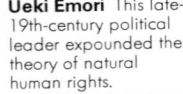

literature at Kyōto University. He published his own poems and translated European poetry into Japanese, including poems from the French of the Parnassians and symbolists. He is best known for *Kaichōon* (1905), a collection of poems that includes his translation of Baudelaire's "L'Albatros" and Verlaine's "Chanson d'automne," as well as poems from Robert Browning's *Pippa Passes*. This volume had a profound influence on the emerging symbolist poetry movement in Japan. Other works include *Uzumaki* (1910), a novel, and *Bokuyōshin* (1920), a collection of his own and translated poems.

Ueda Kazutoshi　上田万年

(1867–1937). Also known as Ueda Mannen. Scholar of the Japanese language and father of novelist ENCHI FUMIKO. Born in Tōkyō, he graduated from Tōkyō University, where he was especially influenced by his studies with Basil Hall CHAMBERLAIN. Ueda introduced Western linguistic research methods into the study of Japanese language, linguistics, and literature. While a professor at Tōkyō University and a member of the National Language Research Committee (Kokugo Chōsa Iinkai)—now the COUNCIL ON THE NATIONAL LANGUAGE (Kokugo Shingikai)—he trained researchers in Western linguistic research methods and contributed to national language policies. His works include *Kokugo no tame* (For a Japanese Language), written in two volumes between 1895 and 1903; a Chinese-character dictionary entitled *Daijiten* (1917); and, in collaboration with Matsui Kanji (1863–1945), a well-known Japanese language dictionary entitled DAI NIHON KOKUGO JITEN (1915–19).

Ueda Miyoji　上田三四二

(1923–89). TANKA poet, critic, and novelist. Born in Hyōgo Prefecture. Graduate of Kyōto University. Ueda's critical study of the poet SAITŌ MOKICHI, *Saitō Mokichi ron* (1961), received the Gunzō Prize for New Talent, and his *Shimaki Akahiko* (1986) was awarded the Noma Literary Prize. Other critical works include *Kono yo kono sei* (1984, This World, This Life), a study of the writings of monk-poets SAIGYŌ and RYŌKAN, whose semireclusive lives he emulated. His own poetry, as seen in the collections *Kiji* (1967, Pheasant) and *Wakui* (1975, Swirling

Well), is characterized by an introspective scrutiny of life.

Ueda Teijirō　上田貞次郎

(1879–1940). Scholar of business management. Born in Tōkyō, he graduated from Tōkyō Higher Commercial School (now Hitotsubashi University) in 1900 and soon after became a professor there. The school became a university in 1920, and Ueda was named university president in 1937. He also served as a representative director of the Dai Nihon Keiei Gakkai, a pre–World War II business-management academic society. Ueda's writings include *Kabushiki kaisha keizai ron* (1937, Economics of Joint Stock Corporations), *Shōkō keiei* (1930, Commercial and Industrial Management), and *Keiei keizaigaku sōron* (1937, Introduction to Business Economics).

Uehara Memorial Foundation
上原記念生命科学財団

(Uehara Kinen Seimei Kagaku Zaidan). A foundation established in 1985 by the TAISHŌ PHARMACEUTICAL CO, LTD, and the relatives of Uehara Shōkichi (1897–1983), Taishō's founder. The foundation's objective is the promotion of research in the life sciences. It provides funding for research and scholarships. In 1989 total assets were ¥3.9 billion (US $28.3 million). Headquarters are in Tōkyō.

Uehara Yūsaku　上原勇作

(1856–1933). Army general and field marshal who served as army minister, chief of the Army General Staff Office, and inspector general of military education. Born in Hyūga Province (now Miyazaki Prefecture), he graduated from the Army Academy in 1879 and studied in France (1881–85). Named army minister in April 1912, he resigned when his demand for an increase of two army divisions was rejected by the SAIONJI KIMMOCHI cabinet. The cabinet in turn was forced to step down when the army refused to nominate a replacement for Uehara.

Uejima Onitsura　上島鬼貫

(1661–1738). *Haikai* (see HAIKU) poet of the early Edo period (1600–1868). Real name Uejima Munechika. Born in Itami in Settsu Province (now Hyōgo Prefecture). He advocated the concept of *makoto* (sincerity) as the very essence of *haikai*, thus reasserting the emphasis on mental attitude—rather than technique—that has always been the predominant strain in classical Japanese poetics. At 16, he was a disciple of NISHIYAMA SŌIN. His *haikai* is distinguished by a complete absence of artifice and an almost conversational tone. His major works include the essay collection *Hitorigoto* (1718) and the *haikai* anthology *Taigo monogurui* (1690).

Ueki Emori　植木枝盛

(1857–92). Political leader and thinker associated with the FREEDOM AND PEOPLE'S RIGHTS MOVEMENT of the 1880s. The son of a *samurai* of the Tosa domain (now Kōchi Prefecture), he studied at the domainal school, Chidōkan, and briefly, in 1873, in Tōkyō. He came under the influence of ITAGAKI TAISUKE, helping him to organize the political groups RISSHISHA, AIKOKUSHA, Kokkai Kisei Dōmei (LEAGUE FOR ESTABLISHING A NATIONAL ASSEMBLY), and eventually the JIYŪTŌ, Japan's first political party. In 1879 he wrote a popular pamphlet, *Minken jiyū ron* (On People's Rights and Liberty), expounding the theory of naturally endowed human rights, the

people's right to political independence and freedom, and the necessity of constitutional government. In 1881 Ueki wrote a draft constitution in which he argued for popular sovereignty, a unicameral parliament, and the taxpayers' right to vote. He was editor of the newspaper *Jiyū shimbun*, the organ of the Jiyūtō. In the first national election (1890) he won a seat in the Diet. He died suddenly at the age of 35.

Uemura Kōgorō　植村甲午郎

(1894–1978). Businessman. Born in Tōkyō. After graduating from Tōkyō University, Uemura joined the Ministry of Agriculture and Commerce (now the Ministry of International Trade and Industry; MITI), becoming director of the Coal Control Board in 1941. He was purged by the Allied OCCUPATION after World War II but was later asked to become vice-president of KEIDANREN (Federation of Economic Organizations). Uemura attempted to abolish direct corporate contributions to political parties to avoid collusion between business and government. He became Keidanren's president in 1968, devoting himself to textile trade negotiations between Japan and the United States and to solving pollution problems.

Uemura Masahisa　植村正久

(1858–1925). Church leader, essayist, and translator. From the age of 13 he studied English and eventually became a Christian, going on to a mission school of theology in Yokohama and graduating in 1879. In 1880 he was ordained a minister of the Presbyterian Church.

While still a student, he had already started his career as an editor of numerous journals and in 1880 was one of the founders of the *Rikugō zasshi* (The Universe). Over the next decade he published *Shinri ippan* (On Truth); founded a church, the Fujimichō Kyōkai; served with other church leaders on numerous committees; and helped found MEIJI GAKUIN UNIVERSITY. In 1890 he launched his own literary journal, *Nihon hyōron*, and the Christian weekly *Fukuin shuhō*. He also lectured frequently on English literature. In 1904 he founded one of the schools that eventually became Tōkyō Union Theological Seminary.

Best known as a church leader, Uemura established the Presbyterian tradition in Japan with an emphasis on independence from missionary control. The main theme of Uemura's writings was the importance of the individual in society and the nurturing of Christians who could stand firm against social pressures. His translations of the Psalms, Song of Songs, Isaiah, and hymns became modern Japanese classics.

Uemura Naomi　植村直己

(1941–84). Mountaineer and adventurer. Born in Hyōgo Prefecture; graduate of Meiji University. He scaled the highest peaks on five continents (Everest, Kilimanjaro, Mont Blanc, Aconcagua, and McKinley) and, with the exception of Everest, he climbed alone. In 1978 he reached the North Pole by dogsled and was the first person to make an overland traverse of Greenland's interior. In February 1984 he failed to return to base camp after a solo winter ascent of Mt. McKinley; his body was never found. He was posthumously awarded the People's Honor Award in 1984.

Uemura Shōen　上村松園

(1875–1949). Painter; famous for her paintings of beautiful women. She was born

Ueno Zoological Gardens Huan Huan, an adult female panda (left), and Tong Tong, her female cub, are popular attractions at this zoo.

Uemura Tsune in Kyōto, the second daughter of a tea merchant. Shōen went to the Kyōto Prefectural Painting School, where she studied with Suzuki Shōnen (1849–1918), a Chinese-style landscape painter from whose name Shōen's own is derived. In 1894 she began studying under KŌNO BAIREI, later becoming a student of TAKEUCHI SEIHŌ, Bairei's most outstanding disciple.

She won her first award in the 1900 joint exhibition of the Japan Painting Association (Nihon Kaiga Kyōkai) and the JAPAN FINE ARTS ACADEMY (Nihon Bijutsuin). With the inauguration of the BUNTEN exhibitions in 1907, these exhibits became the main stage for her work. While historical and traditional subjects make up a large portion of her work, she is best known as a painter of women. In 1941 Shōen became a member of the Imperial Art Academy and in 1944 a court artist (teishitsu gigeiin). In 1948 she became the first woman to receive the Order of Culture.

Uemura Shōkō 上村松篁

(1902–). Japanese-style (NIHONGA) painter. Known for his elegant paintings of flowers and birds. Born Uemura Shintarō in Kyōto, the son of the painter UEMURA SHŌEN. Graduated from the Kyōto Municipal School of Fine Arts and Crafts (now the Kyōto City University of Arts). While still at the school Uemura became a student of NISHIYAMA SUISHŌ. In 1948 Uemura helped organize the group called Sōzō Bijutsu (Creative Arts). Afterward he belonged to the Shin Seisaku Kyōkai (New Creative Association) and helped found the Sōgakai (Creative Painting Association) in 1974. He taught at his alma mater from 1930, becoming a professor emeritus in 1968. He became a member of the Japan Art Academy in 1981 and received the Order of Culture in 1984. His works include Juka yūkin (1966, Birds under the Trees), which won the Japan Art Academy Prize in 1967.

Uemura Tamaki 植村環

(1890–1982). Christian activist. Born in Tōkyō, the daughter of the prominent Christian leader UEMURA MASAHISA. She attended Wellesley College in Massachusetts and later taught at Joshi Eigaku Juku (now Tsuda College). In 1921 she helped HANI MOTOKO establish the school Jiyū Gakuen. She then studied theology at the University of Edinburgh and returned to Japan to found and serve as minister for the Kashiwagi Church of the Nippon Kirisuto Kyōdan (Church of Christ in Japan, the influential union of Protestant sects founded in 1872). After World War II, she was a member of the COMMITTEE OF SEVEN TO APPEAL FOR WORLD PEACE.

Ueno 上野〔市〕

City in western Mie Prefecture, central Honshū. Ueno developed as a castle town of the Tōdō family in the beginning of the 17th century. A well-known local ceramic product is IGA WARE. The haiku poet BASHŌ was born here, and there are several sites associated with him, including his house. Ueno is where the school of martial arts known as Iga Ninjutsu (see NINJUTSU) originated. Pop: 60,242.

Ueno 上野

Commercial and recreational district in the western part of Taitō Ward, Tōkyō. Ueno has been a popular area for outings and excursions since the Edo period (1600–1868). Kan'eiji, a Buddhist temple established under the auspices of the Tokugawa family;

the Tōkyō National Museum; the National Museum of Western Art; and the Ueno Zoological Gardens are all located in UENO PARK. The southern part of Ueno is one of the busiest shopping areas in Tōkyō. High-speed trains of the Tōhoku and Jōetsu Shinkansen ("bullet train") lines stop at Ueno Station, one of Tōkyō's major transportation centers.

Ueno Basin 上野盆地

(Ueno Bonchi). In western Mie Prefecture, central Honshū. Also known as the Iga Basin. It is surrounded by fault scarps and consists of the floodplain of the upper reaches of the river Kizugawa. The area, a rice-producing region, is famous for sudden changes in temperature and thick fog. The major city is Ueno. Length: 30 km (19 mi); width: 15 km (9 mi).

Ueno Hikoma 上野彦馬

(1838–1904). One of Japan's first professional photographers. Born in Nagasaki Prefecture. His father, Ueno Toshinojō (1790–1851), was the first to import the daguerreotype camera into Japan. Hikoma studied chemistry at Seimi Kenkyūjo and then began a study of photography, going on to construct his own camera and make his own processing chemicals. In 1862 he opened Japan's first photography studio in Nagasaki. His photographs documenting the Satsuma Rebellion (1877) are invaluable historical reference materials.

Ueno Park 上野公園

(Ueno Kōen). In Taitō Ward, Tōkyō. The park, opened to the public in 1873, contains the Tōkyō National Museum, the Tōkyō Metropolitan Art Museum, the National Science Museum, the National Museum of Western Art, the Ueno Zoological Gardens, the Japan Art Academy, and the Tōkyō University of Fine Arts and Music. Shinobazu Pond, known for its waterfowl, and Kan'eiji, the Tokugawa family temple in the Edo period (1600–1868), are located in the park. The park is famous as a spot for cherry-blossom viewing (HANAMI). Area: 53.2 hectares (131 acres).

Ueno Riichi 上野理一

(1848–1919). Newspaperman; managing executive of the newspaper ASAHI SHIMBUN. Born in what is now Hyōgo Prefecture, he joined the Asahi shimbun in 1880, its second year. The following year he became one of its managers by providing one-third of the newspaper's capital; the other two-thirds were supplied by MURAYAMA RYŌHEI. After 1908, when the Asahi was incorporated, Murayama and Ueno served as president in alternate years. While Murayama was an expansionist, Ueno was said to be a steady, practical businessman.

Ueno Zoological Gardens 上野動物園

(Ueno Dōbutsuen). The first and most famous of Japan's ZOOLOGICAL GARDENS. Located in the Ueno district of Tōkyō. Founded in 1882 as part of the national museum at Ueno (now TŌKYŌ NATIONAL MUSEUM). After the Meiji Restoration of 1868 there was widespread recognition of the need for museums and zoos in Japan. TANAKA YOSHIO and others made a study tour of Europe and the United States, and the facilities at Ueno were the result. Since 1924 Ueno Zoo has been managed by the Tōkyō metropolitan government. Together with the affiliated TŌKYŌ SEA LIFE PARK

at Kasai, it houses 1,041 species. It serves both as a learning and a recreational facility.

Ueshiba Morihei 植芝盛平

(1883–1969). Founder of AIKIDŌ. Born in Wakayama Prefecture. Ueshiba began studying the Kitō and Yagyū schools of traditional jūjutsu (see JUDŌ) at the age of 18. In 1915 he became a student of the Daitō school under Takeda Sōkaku (1860–1943), which further intensified his interest in the MARTIAL ARTS. He became disillusioned, however, with the competitive character of these disciplines and their emphasis on winning. Having become a convert to the ŌMOTO sect of Shintō under the tutelage of its leader, DEGUCHI ONISABURŌ, he concentrated on the spiritual aspects of the martial arts. By 1922 he had developed a new set of techniques which he called aiki bujutsu; in 1942 he renamed it aikidō.

Uesugi family 上杉氏

(Uesugishi). 1. Territorial warlords (SHUGO DAIMYŌ) of the Muromachi period (1333–1568) who dominated the Kantō region for 100 years. The family founder, Uesugi Shigefusa (dates unknown), was descended from a cadet branch of the FUJIWARA FAMILY; his granddaughter became the mother of ASHIKAGA TAKAUJI, founder of the Muromachi shogunate. From the time of Uesugi Noriaki (1306–68) the Uesugi served as hereditary shogunal deputies for the Kantō (KANTŌ KANREI). In 1416–17 Uesugi Zenshū (d 1417) rebelled (see UESUGI ZENSHŪ, REBELLION OF). Toward the end of the Sengoku period (1467–1568) the family fell from power.

Uemura Naomi The adventurer and mountaineer is pictured here in May 1976, after completing a solo 12,000-kilometer, 313-day-long dogsled trip through the Arctic region.

Ueshiba Morihei Founder of the martial art aikidō.

1643
Uesugi family

1868) *daimyō* family. The last of the Uesugi Kantō deputies, Uesugi Norimasa (d 1579), fled to the north and took refuge with Nagao Kagetora (1530–78), on whom he bestowed his family name and official title. Under the name UESUGI KENSHIN, Kagetora became the most powerful daimyō in northern Japan. His adopted son UESUGI KAGEKATSU fought against TOKUGAWA IEYASU in the Battle of SEKIGAHARA (1600). The Uesugi endured as hereditary lords of Yonezawa in Dewa Province (now Yamagata and Akita prefectures) until the close of the Edo period.

Uesugi Harunori   上杉治憲

(1751–1822). Also known as Uesugi Yōzan. Tenth *daimyō* of the Yonezawa domain (now part of Yamagata Prefecture). His successful reforms earned him a reputation as one of the model lords (*meikun*) of the Edo period (1600–1868).

The second son of the daimyō of Akizuki (in what is now Miyazaki Prefecture), he was adopted into the Uesugi family and in 1767 became daimyō of Yonezawa, which was in severe financial straits. Harunori issued sumptuary edicts; ordered the development of new industries; encouraged land reclamation; established grain reserves; and opened a school, the Kōjōkan, employing HOSOI HEISHŪ as its head. Harunori also set an example, practicing frugality and reducing the number of his consorts. During the TEMMEI FAMINE of the 1780s it was said that Yonezawa did not suffer a single death from starvation. During the Kansei era (1789–1801) Harunori launched another series of reforms, closely aided by Nozokido Taika (1735–1804).

Uesugi Kagekatsu   上杉景勝

(1555–1623). *Daimyō* of the Azuchi-Momoyama (1568–1600) and early Edo (1600–1868) periods. Kagekatsu, the son of Nagao Masakage (d 1564), a provincial baron of Echigo (now Niigata Prefecture), was adopted by UESUGI KENSHIN, the great *daimyō* of that region. After Kenshin's death, he fought for the succession with another adopted son, Kagetora, driving him to suicide in 1579. Much of Kagekatsu's early lordship was spent in a struggle to check ODA NOBUNAGA; after Nobunaga's death he allied himself with TOYOTOMI HIDEYOSHI and in 1586 was confirmed by him in a vast domain of 550,000 *koku* (see KOKUDAKA) centered on Echigo. Kagekatsu participated in Hideyoshi's ODAWARA CAMPAIGN (1590) and invasion of Korea (1592) and was appointed to the position of great elder (*tairō*) in 1597; in 1598 he was transferred to a 1,200,000-*koku* domain at Wakamatsu in Mutsu Province (now the city of Aizu Wakamatsu, Fuku-

shima Prefecture), becoming Japan's fourth greatest daimyō. In the conflict that led to the Battle of SEKIGAHARA (1600), he ranged himself against TOKUGAWA IEYASU and after Ieyasu's victory was in 1601 transferred to a much diminished estate in Yonezawa.

Uesugi Kenshin   上杉謙信

(1530–78). *Daimyō* of the Sengoku (1467–1568) and Azuchi-Momoyama (1568–1600) periods. Kenshin was born into the Nagao family, who had since the 1340s served the Uesugi family as deputy governors (*shugodai*) of Echigo (now Niigata Prefecture). In 1507 Kenshin's father Nagao Tamekage (d 1537) rebelled against his overlords. He was succeeded by Kenshin's elder brother Harukage (d 1553), who proved unable to deal with recalcitrant provincial barons. Kenshin assumed the military leadership of his house in 1546. The brothers came into conflict, but peace was restored and Harukage adopted Kenshin as his son to give the appearance of orderly succession. On 28 January 1549 Kenshin was installed in the lordship and was at the time known as Nagao Kagetora.

In 1561 Uesugi Norimasa (d 1579), who had fled to Kagetora's protection, passed on to Kagetora the headship of the Uesugi family's Yamanouchi branch and the post of KANTŌ KANREI (shogunal deputy for the Kantō region). Kagetora assumed the name Uesugi Masatora. Kenshin is the name he bore as a Buddhist lay monk (*nyūdō*) from January 1571.

Kenshin's career was marked by conflict with ODA NOBUNAGA, with TAKEDA SHINGEN (with whom he fought a series of battles at KAWANAKAJIMA), and with the Later Hōjō (see HŌJŌ FAMILY). Kenshin died on 19 April 1578, in the middle of preparations for another campaign, ostensibly against the Hōjō in the Kantō. He was ultimately succeeded by his adopted son UESUGI KAGEKATSU.

Uesugi Norizane   上杉憲実

(1410–66). Military leader of the Muromachi period (1333–1568). Member of the warrior UESUGI FAMILY, whose members had held the powerful office of KANTŌ KANREI (shogunal deputy for the Kantō region) since 1363. Norizane was appointed to that post in 1419 to assist Ashikaga Mochiuji (1398–1439), the Kamakura KUBŌ (governor-general of the Kantō region). Mochiuji had on several occasions taken action independent of the Muromachi shogunate, and when ASHIKAGA YOSHINORI became shōgun in 1429, Mochiuji's antagonism toward the shogunate intensified. Norizane tried to mediate but incurred Mochiuji's distrust. Persecuted by him in 1438, Norizane left Kamakura. Mochiuji sent an army to pursue him, but it was intercepted by shogunal forces. Mochiuji was captured and eventually forced to commit suicide. (This incident is known as the Eikyō Rebellion.) Norizane soon took Buddhist orders and spent the rest of his life as an itinerant monk. While still in office, he was a patron of the ASHIKAGA GAKKŌ, a school founded by the Ashikaga family in the early Muromachi period.

Uesugi Shinkichi   上杉慎吉

(1878–1929). Scholar of constitutional law and nationalist leader. Born in Fukui Prefecture. On his graduation in 1903 from Tōkyō University, where he had studied under HOZUMI YATSUKA, Uesugi joined its faculty and in 1912 became a full professor. From 1906 to

1909 he studied in Germany. In 1912–13 he argued against MINOBE TATSUKICHI's theory that the emperor was simply an organ of the state (see TENNŌ KIKAN SETSU). He associated with the conservative YAMAGATA ARITOMO clique and formed right-wing student organizations such as the Shichiseisha (Seven Lives Society) at Tōkyō University. After Yamagata's death in 1922, Uesugi served as political adviser to the SEIYŪ HONTŌ (True Seiyū Party) and with TAKABATAKE MOTOYUKI formed the Keirin Gakumei (Statecraft Study Association). His works include *Teikoku kempō* (1922, The Imperial Constitution) and *Kempō tokuhon* (1928, A Reader on the Constitution).

Uesugi Yōzan →Uesugi Harunori

Uesugi Zenshū, Rebellion of   上杉禅秀の乱

(Uesugi Zenshū no Ran). Rebellion led by Uesugi Zenshū (or Uesugi Ujinori) in 1416–17 against Ashikaga Mochiuji (1398–1439), who was then governor-general of the Kantō region (Kamakura *kubō*; see KUBŌ). Zenshū served as shogunal deputy for the Kantō (KANTŌ KANREI), a post held for generations by members of the UESUGI FAMILY; but in 1415 he was forced from office by Mochiuji. Zenshū enlisted the aid of other malcontents and took up arms late in 1416. Their insurrection was suppressed by the shogunate early in 1417.

Uetsuka Shūhei   上塚周平

(1876–1936). A leader of the Japanese immigrant community in Brazil. Born in Kumamoto Prefecture, he studied law at Tōkyō University. In 1908 Uetsuka went to Brazil as the agent of a colonization firm that was sponsoring the first group of Japanese emigrants. In the early years of Japanese emigration to Brazil, Uetsuka made a great contribution by advocating independent farming and helping to found numerous Japanese agricultural settlements.

Ugaki Kazushige   宇垣一成

(1868–1956). General and army minister, highly influential in army circles in the 1920s and in political circles from the 1920s through World War II. Born in what is now Okayama Prefecture, he graduated from the Army Staff College in 1900. After World War I, he was principal of the college and commander of the Tenth Division. In 1923 he was appointed vice-minister of the Army Ministry. From 1924 onward he was army minister in several cabinets.

In 1931, although he refused to cooperate with them, Ugaki also failed to punish the insurgents responsible for the MARCH INCIDENT, an attempted coup d'état by young army officers and nationalistic civilians who had intended to make him prime minister. Having lost the support of his fellow officers, he left the military to become governor-general of Korea, where he strove to develop an industrial base for a Japanese invasion of China.

Ugaki was nominated to be prime minister in January 1937 but withdrew upon failing to complete a cabinet. In May 1938 he became foreign minister in the cabinet of KONOE FUMIMARO but resigned four months later. After the war he was purged and detained by Occupation authorities. Rehabilitated, in 1953 he was elected to the House of Councillors and was a member of the RYOKUFŪKAI.

Ugetsu monogatari　　雨月物語

(tr *Tales of Moonlight and Rain*, 1974). A collection of nine tales of the supernatural, written by scholar and poet UEDA AKINARI (1734–1809) and ranking among the best-known works of premodern fiction (see YOMIHON); published 1776. All nine tales are set in the past with references to historical persons, places, and events. Many are adaptations of Chinese ghost stories recast in ancient or medieval Japan and strung through with allusions to classical Japanese texts such as the TALE OF GENJI. Although each tale is complete in itself, the collection as a whole reveals an aesthetic unity, like the IMPERIAL ANTHOLOGIES of poetry or a sequence of RENGA (linked verse). Dreams and spirit possession play a prominent role in the collection; Akinari was drawing on NŌ drama, thus endowing his supernatural stories with a mysterious depth (see YŪGEN) and chilling beauty. In addition, Akinari imbues the collection with a special pathos as he explores the ties between friends, husband and wife, and parents and children. *Ugetsu monogatari* brought the supernatural tale in Japan to its highest artistic level.

Ugetsu monogatari　　雨月物語

(Tales of Moonlight and Rain). A 1953 film directed by MIZOGUCHI KENJI and starring KYŌ MACHIKO, TANAKA KINUYO, and MORI MASAYUKI. Released abroad as *Ugetsu*. KAWAGUCHI MATSUTARŌ and YODA YOSHIKATA wrote the screenplay, drawing on two stories from UEDA AKINARI's UGETSU MONOGATARI and a short story by Guy de Maupassant, "La Décoration." Set in 16th-century Japan, *Ugetsu monogatari* tells of two brothers-in-law, Genjūrō and Tōbei, who set out for Kyōto to take advantage of unsettled conditions in the war-torn capital. The confusion they hoped to profit by, however, visits disaster upon their families: Genjūrō, formerly a potter, returns to his now-ruined home to find the spirit of his wife, killed by soldiers; Tōbei, once a farmer, discovers his wife in a brothel. With excellent performances by the cast, cinematography by MIYAGAWA KAZUO, and music by HAYASAKA FUMIO, *Ugetsu monogatari* has a marvelous, otherworldly beauty. The movie won the Silver Lion at the 1953 Venice Film Festival.

uguisu → bush warbler

Ui Hakuju　　宇井伯寿

(1882–1963). Scholar of Indian philosophy and Buddhism. Born in Aichi Prefecture. After graduating from Tōkyō University in 1909 he studied in Europe from 1913 to 1917. Upon his return he commenced an extensive research career which laid the foundations for modern academic study of Indian philosophy and Buddhism in Japan. He taught at Tōhoku University and at Tōkyō University before being appointed president of Komazawa University. He received the Order of Culture in 1953. His major works include *Indo tetsugaku kenkyū* (1924–30, 6 vols, Research in Indian Philosophy).

Uji　　宇治[市]

City in southern Kyōto Prefecture, central Honshū, on the river Ujigawa. A residential suburb of Kyōto, Uji is known for its fine tea. There is a synthetic textiles industry. Of special interest are the temple BYŌDŌIN and MAMPUKUJI, a 17th-century Zen temple built by the Chinese monk INGEN. Pop: 177,010.

uji　　氏

Lineage groups before the Nara period (710–794). An *uji* was typically composed of the *uji no kami*, the head of the prime lineage, *uji-bito* (lineage members), and *kakibe* or BE, subordinate laborers. The *uji no kami* was given a hereditary title (KABANE). See also UJI-KABANE SYSTEM.

ujigami　　氏神

Originally, the tutelary deity of an UJI or "clan." Early Japanese society was composed of many *uji*, the members of which believed themselves to be descended from a common ancestor who looked after their interests (see ANCESTOR WORSHIP). This deified ancestor, *ujigami*, was worshiped at a shrine under the exclusive control of the *uji*. Occasionally the *ujigami* was not the direct ancestor of an *uji*, but rather a deity closely connected with it. The Minamoto (Genji), a famous warrior *uji*, adopted as its *ujigami* the deity HACHIMAN, who is associated with military prowess.

Only members of the *uji* were entitled to worship the *ujigami*. Services at the *uji* shrine were led by the nominal head of the *uji*. This privilege was carefully guarded. At the ISE SHRINE, prior to the 11th century, even the crown prince could not make an offering without specific approval of the emperor. The festival to honor the *ujigami*, called *ujigami matsuri*, was held normally twice a year.

The *uji* system declined in the 13th–16th centuries, and the term *ujigami* came to refer, as it still does today, to the local deity who protects all the inhabitants of a region. Supporters in the region of an *ujigami* are called UJIKO (*ko* meaning children, underlings), and shrines of *ujigami* thus differ from shrines that attract devotees (*sūkeisha*) from beyond local boundaries. The priesthood shifted to professional priests (see KANNUSHI) or to a household head chosen yearly (see MIYAZA). In some areas of rural Japan today, *ujigami* refers to a specific *yashikigami* ("household deity") enshrined at a small outdoor shrine (*hokora*) in the family plot.

Ujigawa　　宇治川

River in Kyōto Prefecture, central Honshū. The name is applied to the middle reaches of the YODOGAWA; that is, the part from the border of Shiga and Kyōto prefectures to where it joins the KIZUGAWA and KATSURAGAWA at the town of Ōyamazaki. Numerous gorges are located on the upper reaches, as well as the Ujigawa Rhine and Amagase Dam. Length: 30 km (19 mi).

uji-kabane system　　氏姓制度

(*uji-kabane seido*). Also known as the *shisei* system. Division of economic, military, and ritual functions among specially designated lineage groups, or *uji*, thought to have been predominant in the political organization of the YAMATO COURT from the late 5th to the early 7th century. *Uji* leaders primarily responsible for the performance of service to the Yamato king had hereditary titles, or *kabane*, indicative of their position in the king's retinue. Each *uji* chief, or *uji no kami*, typically presided over the worship of the *uji* deity or deities, called *ujigami*, while directing the labors of separately designated groups called *tomo* or BE in the service of the ruler. Most early *uji* had their own base territories in the Yamato area, but some were

able to establish branches widely throughout Japan.

The Structure of the Uji ── The corporate structure of the *uji* can be illustrated by the case of the *uji* known as the Imbe, whose leader was responsible for the conduct of certain major religious rituals. The chiefly line (or lines) resided in Yamato (now Nara Prefecture) and there presided over its own village of *uji* members. The organization included four or five widely scattered additional villages of several hundred persons apiece, each required to aid the chief in a specific way. The Imbe villages in Izumo, about 200 miles west of Yamato, and on the island of Shikoku provided ritualists and other helpers needed at the king's headquarters. The Imbe village in Kii (now Wakayama Prefecture), a forested area to the southeast of Yamato, was expected to supply lumber for palace construction, a function considered as ancillary to the conduct of religious ceremonies central to royal authority. Villages like this one, called *tomobe*, shared in the *uji*'s official obligations and were thus distinct from other villages subject to Imbe control called *kakibe*, which consisted of serfs regarded as a kind of property to be exploited by the chief and his kinsmen. Despite the probable status difference between the Yamato Imbe and the *tomobe*, and between the *tomobe* and the *kakibe*, all bore the name Imbe, although these various groups were of diverse ancestry. The Imbe chief's position was confined to a single line of descent, and his hereditary *kabane*, *obito* (ordinarily indicating a village headman), placed him among the king's retainers. The *uji* name Imbe, linked to the title *obito* by the genitive postposition *no*, made up the complete designation of the chief, Imbe no Obito.

The Kabane ── Despite some variations in structure, the defining characteristic of the *uji* was a quasi-proprietary hereditary power over subordinate persons or groups (*be*) to be impressed into the service of the Yamato king. In this sense the *uji* was a political institution of the emergent Yamato state rather than a pristine tribal organization. The *uji-kabane* system developed in the course of extensive interchange, including interchange of persons, between Yamato and the various states of Korea, notably PAEKCHE. The *kabane*, in particular, seems to be related to the Paekche "bone rank" system. It is noteworthy that the word *kabane* means "bone," and a number of *kabane* titles were of Korean linguistic origin. The application of *kabane* status, at first to those in the king's domestic service and later to the more submissive regional barons, produced a differentiated court structure able to marshal control over increasing supplies of economic and military resources and to survive the dynastic upheavals of the late 5th and early 6th centuries.

The *uji* system, besides assuring the Yamato monarch of needed services, reinforced his paramount authority in areas beyond Yamato itself. The Wani *uji*, whose base territory was in northern Yamato, had, by the late 6th century, acquired a great number of *kakibe*, called Wanibe, widely dispersed throughout western Honshū. These were in turn headed by hereditary subchiefs called Wanibe no Omi, *omi* being a *kabane*. These *omi* were almost certainly of regional origin, and their assimilation into the Wani *uji*, and hence the *uji-kabane* sys-

Uji shūi monogatari
Detail from an Edo-period (1600–1868) handscroll illustrating tales from this collection.

tem, shows how that system could promote the appropriation of local resources by the Yamato regime, even while the king was still little more than a mere primus inter pares vis-à-vis the regional chiefs.

Internal differentiation among *kabane*-holding nobles into two broad types, *omi* and *muraji*, seems to have taken place by the late 6th century, and possibly much earlier. This division seems to have resulted from the incorporation of regional lords, both beyond and within the Yamato area, into the retinue of *uji* chiefs who managed the king's *be*. Acceptance of a *kabane*, usually that of *omi*, amounted to a renunciation of parity with the royal nobles and thus sanctioned an appropriation of ultimate political authority by the kings over regional areas. The difference between this class of noble and the older service nobles such as the Imbe no Obito, who often took the title *muraji*, appeared in their relation to the monarch and his kin. Nobles of the *omi* type had few important roles in royal coronation ceremonies, which the *muraji* types dominated. Women from *omi* lineages often became royal consorts and the mothers of successors to the throne, but the *muraji* lines produced almost no such women.

The *uji-kabane* system thus served to expand the Yamato ruler's power widely through Japan while facilitating an integrated court structure of institutional permanency. With the appropriation of new *be*, the *uji* could divide into branches, while an interlocking network of marriage alliances provided linkages between higher and lower levels of the court hierarchy. This hierarchy consisted, by the late 6th century, of four major strata, known as *omi*, *muraji*, *tomo no miyatsuko* (leaders of *be*), and *kuni no miyatsuko* (regional chiefs), and there were below this level a number of other *kabane*-bearing lineages.

The interrelations among *uji* headship, *kabane* status, and position in the royal court are poorly understood, and there are a few references to trial by ordeal in ambiguous cases. Ancestry was the major qualification, and the keeping of long genealogies is well attested, the earliest example being an inscription from the late 5th century. A number of court functionaries of Korean origin used Korean titles such as *kishi* as *kabane* and presided over *be* of immigrant craftsmen. These often claimed descent from ancient Chinese rulers, but most others traced their ancestry to divine figures of the mythic past. Eventually, the various lineages were linked together by a complex theogony relating these origin legends to that of the kings. This development, however, coincided with the increasing bureaucratization of the Yamato court during the 6th and 7th

centuries, when an increasing number of *be* were performing clerical and administrative services for the rulers without subordination to particular *uji*. Finally, during the 7th century, the system of *uji* and *be* was gradually dismantled in favor of a more genuinely bureaucratic regime on the Chinese model, in which state functions were carried out by a corps of officials, each temporarily assigned to a specific post, and private authority over land and people was strictly limited.

The TAIKA REFORM of the mid-7th century emphasized the need for these changes to consolidate undivided power in the emperor. Concessions had to be made, however. In 664 *uji* were divided into three strata, "great *uji*," "small *uji*," and "*tomo no miyatsuko*," and officially recognized, as was control over *kakibe* by their chiefs. The remaining prerogatives of *uji* chiefs were soon thereafter preempted by privileges ancillary to rank and office, and a general system of family registration, begun in 670, made *kabane*, like *uji* names, automatically heritable by male descent. In 684 a graded series of eight *kabane* was promulgated (YAKUSA NO KABANE), and the higher four were distributed among the more prestigious lineages of the court. This attempt to reconcile *kabane* status with a hierarchy based on rank and office was supplemented by a legal rule making *uji* prestige a criterion for promotion in official rank, but the TAIHŌ CODE promulgated in 702 did away with this provision altogether. Corporate lineage groups continued to play an important role in the following centuries, but the *uji-kabane* system as such was permanently supplanted by newer institutions of officeholding and property.

ujiko 氏子

Parishioners of a community shrine enshrining the local Shintō deity (UJIGAMI); they are considered parishioners by the shrine authorities by virtue of their residence in the community under the *ujigami*'s protection. The *ujiko* system developed gradually throughout Japanese history, but by the Edo period (1600–1868) all families of a certain geographical area were considered the *ujiko* of the local shrine. The system was institutionalized by the Meiji (1868–1912) government as a means of keeping a census of the population, but this was abolished after World War II.

Ujina 宇品

District in the southern part of the city of Hiroshima, Hiroshima Prefecture, western Honshū, on Hiroshima Bay. Construction of the port of Ujina, now the port of Hiroshima, was completed in 1889, and it served as a base for the area's development. Ujina flourished as a transportation center for the army until World War II. Undamaged by the atomic bombing of Hiroshima, the district became a major commercial port after 1945 for Hiroshima and Inland Sea traffic.

Uji shūi monogatari 宇治拾遺物語

Anonymous collection of tales similar to KONJAKU MONOGATARI. Nearly half of the 197 stories in *Uji shūi* occur also in *Konjaku*, in some cases with virtually the same wording. Although the standard texts are divided into 15 books, these are not, as in *Konjaku*, classified into groups of stories, nor do the tales have *Konjaku*'s uniformity in their opening and closing formulae.

The standard view of *Uji shūi* is that it

was compiled in its present form, with perhaps some later interpolations, between 1180 and 1220 and that many of its tales are retellings of items from some text of the now lost *Uji dainagon monogatari*, "Tales of the Major Counselor from Uji," by Minamoto no Takakuni (1004–77), which is referred to in its preface.

Uji shūi's stories range from edifying accounts of miracles wrought by Kannon and of rebirth in Amida's paradise, to stories of the supernatural and stories of a folktale type, to humorous and even salty or grotesque incidents about the everyday life of people, high and low alike. Stylistically, the language of *Uji shūi* is less influenced by Chinese than that of *Konjaku*, and its tales less stereotyped, repetitious, and moralistic. Yet, like *Konjaku*, it gives a view of Heian-period (794–1185) life that does not appear in any other work of the time.

Uji-Yamada → Ise

ukai → cormorant fishing

ukebumi 請文

(literally, "request document"). Also known as *ukesho* or *sanjō*. Formal letter written during the ancient and medieval periods as an acknowledgement of a superior's orders, a pledge to carry them out, or a report on having fulfilled them. It later became a popular letter form or document of personal guarantee. See also DIPLOMATICS.

Ukigumo 浮雲

(Drifting Clouds; tr in *Japan's First Modern Novel: Ukigumo of Futabatei Shimei*, 1967). Novel by FUTABATEI SHIMEI (1864–1909), considered a landmark in Japanese literary history as the first successful attempt to write fiction in the spoken Japanese language (see GEMBUN ITCHI) and to create psychological realism; published 1887–89. The novel offers a picture of Meiji-period (1868–1912) life through the story of Utsumi Bunzō, a young and intellectual government employee who, true to the moral code of his *samurai* upbringing, refuses to curry favor with his superiors; as a result, Bunzō has already lost his job when the novel opens. Bunzō's aunt, Omasa, intent on pursuing wealth, quickly and callously cancels plans to have her daughter, Osei, a fickle and often peevish young woman, marry Bunzō. Omasa compares Bunzō to the sophisticated Noboru, another young government employee, who, as his name suggests, is an up-and-coming figure in the world. The contrast between Bunzō and Noboru grows more pronounced as the former sinks into gloomy introspection. Bunzō, Noboru, Omasa, and Osei are, to a certain extent, type characters, but they do embody contradictions; they are psychologically believable. It is this facet of *Ukigumo* in particular that earned it the epithet "Japan's first modern novel."

Ukigumo 浮雲

(Floating Clouds). A 1955 film directed by NARUSE MIKIO. MIZUKI YŌKO wrote the screen adaptation of the novel by HAYASHI FUMIKO. The film stars TAKAMINE HIDEKO as a typist who falls in love with an engineer played by MORI MASAYUKI while both are part of the Japanese occupation force in Indochina during World War II. Back in Japan after the war, the woman visits the man at his home and discovers that he is married. In spite of this, they continue their relationship. Naruse's best-known film, it is famous for the actors' performances.

Ukita Hideie   宇喜多秀家

(1572–1655). *Daimyō* of the Azuchi-Momoyama period (1568–1600). Hideie succeeded his father, Naoie (1529–81), in lordship of a large domain centered on Okayama in Bizen Province. Hideie was a favorite of TOYOTOMI HIDEYOSHI, who gave him his adopted daughter Gō Hime (1574–1634; the natural daughter of MAEDA TOSHIIE) in marriage. Hideie served in the conquest of Shikoku in 1585 and of Kyūshū in 1587, the ODAWARA CAMPAIGN in 1590, and the INVASIONS OF KOREA IN 1592 AND 1597. He became an imperial councillor (*sangi*) in 1587, provisional middle counselor (*gon chūnagon*) in 1594, and one of the "Five Great Elders" (Gotairō) of the Toyotomi regime in 1595. In the Battle of SEKIGAHARA (1600) Hideie opposed TOKUGAWA IEYASU; defeated, he lost his great domain and fled to Kyūshū, seeking the protection of the SHIMAZU FAMILY of Kagoshima. In 1603 the Shimazu delivered Hideie to the Tokugawa; in 1606 he was exiled to the Pacific Ocean island of Hachijōjima, where he lived until his death.

Ukita Kazutami   浮田和民

(1859–1946). Political scientist and educator. Born in the Higo domain (now Kumamoto Prefecture), he attended KUMAMOTO YŌGAKKŌ, Dōshisha (later Dōshisha University) in Kyōto, and Yale University. In 1897 he became a professor at Tōkyō Semmon Gakkō (now Waseda University). His social criticism from a liberal Christian viewpoint appeared in such magazines as *Taiyō* (Sun) and strongly influenced YOSHINO SAKUZŌ, the leading theorist of TAISHŌ DEMOCRACY.

ukiyaku   浮役

(literally, "floating tax"). A type of surtax, customarily collected in cash, that was levied during the Edo period (1600–1868); also known as *uki komononari*. Ukiyaku, which fall into the category of miscellaneous taxes known as KOMONONARI, could be levied at any time, on any item, and at any rate.

Ukiyoburo   浮世風呂

(1809–13, The Bathhouse of the Floating World). Work of GESAKU fiction, written by SHIKITEI SAMBA (1776–1822) and published in four books. One of the finest examples of the KOKKEIBON genre of humorous writing, it is also Samba's longest comic work. A plotless collection of vignettes set in a public bathhouse in Edo (now Tōkyō), it is loosely organized chronologically from dawn to dusk. The first and fourth book deal with the men's bath; the second and third with the women's. The vignettes consist almost entirely of conversations among the bathhouse patrons—primarily middle-class commoners—written with great fidelity to the dialects and speech habits of Edo. His characters are saved from stereotype by Samba's keen ear for dialogue and his ironic but essentially kindhearted vision of everyday human experience and behavior. In the preface, Samba states that *Ukiyoburo* was inspired by a humorous monologue (see RAKUGO) by the famous storyteller San'yūtei Karaku (dates unknown). The popularity of *Ukiyoburo* encouraged Samba to write a sequel, *Ukiyodoko* (1813–14, The Barbershop of the Floating World), which shifted the setting while retaining the flavor of his earlier work.

ukiyo-e   浮世絵

(literally, "pictures of the floating world"). A genre of art, chiefly in the medium of the woodblock print, that arose early in the Edo period (1600–1868) and built up a broad popular market among the middle classes. Subject matter tended to focus on the brothel districts and the KABUKI theaters, and formats ranged from single-sheet prints and greeting cards to albums and book illustrations. *Ukiyo-e* flourished throughout Japan, attaining their most characteristic form in the prints produced in Edo (now Tōkyō) from about 1680 to the 1850s.

Early Ukiyo-e—The distinctive milieu from which *ukiyo-e* would emerge was flourishing as early as the Kan'ei era (1624–44). Genre paintings (FŪZOKUGA) of the time depict pleasure seekers of every social class thronging the entertainment district beside the river Kamogawa in Kyōto. It was in such districts, in Kyōto, Ōsaka, and Edo, that there developed the freewheeling way of life of the *ukiyo*, or "floating world," and the genre of art, *ukiyo-e*, that glorified it.

Before the second half of the 17th century the history of *ukiyo-e* can be traced only through the study of paintings (*nikuhitsu ukiyo-e*). Although the first woodblock prints of consequence appeared around 1660, it was not until the early 18th century that *ukiyo-e* prints eclipsed paintings. Full-color print did not appear until about 1765, and until about 1745 all colors were added by brush to monochrome prints.

Sex manuals (SHUNGA; literally, "spring pictures") and courtesan critiques (*yūjo hyōbanki*) were among the earliest types of printed *ukiyo-e*. Shunga were either books or albums that depicted highly explicit love scenes, though rarely are couples completely naked. Few of the sex manuals from the 1660s and early 1670s have survived and none are signed; the earliest attributions are to Hishikawa MORONOBU and SUGIMURA JIHEI, who were active in the late 17th century, and thereafter *shunga* remained a genre at which most *ukiyo-e* artists tried their hand. The critiques of courtesans, essentially picture books with commentary, contained stylized portraits of the leading courtesans of the day, engaged in some casual activity such as reading or adjusting their hair. The interest of such scenes is chiefly in the poses and the draping of *kimono*. A similar type of picture was the *bijin-e* ("beautiful-woman picture"), in which courtesans of the highest rank (*tayū*) were depicted, often with their entourages. Pictures of courtesans remained popular throughout the history of *ukiyo-e*; the KAIGETSUDŌ SCHOOL (early 18th century) of *ukiyo-e* painters rarely turned to any other subject, and many of Kitagawa UTAMARO's most memorable prints were of these stylish beauties.

Woodblock Printing—Albums and books of the kinds described above seem to have antedated independent, single-sheet prints by perhaps as much as 20 years, though there is some question as to precisely when the first single prints appeared. Individual album sheets, found separately, have often been mistaken for (or passed on as) independent prints, and the same thing has been known to happen with book illustrations. A closer look at the craft of woodblock printing as it was actually practiced in the 17th century in Japan will explain how this might occur.

Prints and book pages were impressions taken by hand, without the use of a press, from carved wooden blocks (actually thin boards, usually of cherry wood). The surface of a block generally accommodated two book plates—printed sheets were folded and bound to form the front and back of a page—or one single-sheet plate. Pages of text, usually written in a flowing and highly cursive style of *hiragana* (see KANA), were carved and printed in the same way as illustrations. Movable type, though not unknown, was little used (see PRINTING, PREMODERN). The role of publishers was a central one: they gauged the market, determined subject matter, commissioned artists and writers, and then oversaw the work of engravers and printers. Artists merely supplied working drawings to a collaboration in which the publisher had the final say. So closely allied were the publication of prints and that of books that it was common for many publishers to be involved in both, leading to the appearance of works that combined their previously discrete stylistic features.

Edo Ukiyo-e—By the late 17th century, the center of *ukiyo-e* had shifted from Kamigata (the Kyōto-Ōsaka area) to Edo, where the single-sheet print, probably initially intended for mounting on scrolls (*kakemono-e*), seems to have become a specialty in the closing years of the Genroku era (1688–1704). Early *ukiyo-e* of Edo were primarily produced by publishers, called *jihon toiya*, of popular picture books and novelettes. In a growing market that reflected a remarkable increase in literacy, the works that enjoyed the greatest commercial success, such as the illustrated stories known as SHAREBON, took the YOSHIWARA pleasure quarters as their locale and the *tsūjin*—the sophisticated man-about-town—as their hero. Others, more satirical in character, drew from a wider range of experience (see KIBYŌSHI; KUSAZŌSHI).

It was the development of the single-sheet print, however, that marked a turning point in the history of *ukiyo-e*, the coming of age of which was closely joined to that of KABUKI. A major role in the development of kabuki was played by Ichikawa Danjūrō I (see ICHIKAWA DANJŪRŌ), who invented a bombastic style of acting known as *aragoto* that became immensely popular in Edo. Portrayals of actors (*yakusha-e*) in popular roles had already become standard subject matter of *ukiyo-e*, but it was the TORII SCHOOL that achieved the greatest success in rendering the pyrotechnics of an *aragoto* performance in graphic terms. TORII KIYONOBU I and TORII KIYOMASU I perfected a style that, with its vigorous use of line and robust forms, was particularly appropriate for theatrical subjects, and their school soon acquired a virtual monopoly over commissions in Edo for painted theatrical posters (*kamban*) and illustrated program notes (*ebanzuke*). The finest of the Torii school prints, recording a pose or entrance popularized by a particular actor, are in the large *kakemono-e* format, and provided a visual catalog of theatrical conventions that reinforced kabuki tradition. A separate theatrical print style arose in Ōsaka (see ŌSAKA SCHOOL).

Contemporary with the early Torii masters was the Kaigetsudō school, whose paintings of beautiful women (*bijin-e*) depicted tall, regal, somewhat haughty courtesans. Hugely popular in the first two decades of the 18th century, the school enjoyed a brief period of influence over the Torii school but had lasting impact only on *ukiyo-e* artists,

▶ Fireworks at Ryōgoku, a print from Hiroshige's series One Hundred Views of Edo, depicts the fireworks festival held on the river Sumidagawa. 1856–58. Ōban format (the largest ukiyo-e format). Tōkyō National Museum.

▼ The center panel of a triptych titled Seven Drunken Eccentrics by Utamaro. Ca 1800. Ōban format. Tōkyō National Museum.

▲ Okumura Masanobu's print depicting the interior of a theater is an example of both uki-e, prints using Western perspective, and urushi-e, prints using ink mixed with glue to give luster. Ca 1745. Ōban format. Tōkyō National Museum.

▶ Cover for an illustrated book by Utagawa Kunisada II. Ca 1860. Private collection.

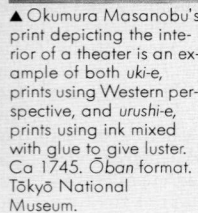

◀ Ichikawa Danjūrō I as Soga no Gorō, a print by Torii Kiyomasu I showing the famous kabuki actor in the role of a folk hero. Colors added by hand. 1697. Ōban format. Tōkyō National Museum.

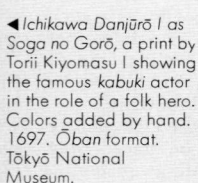

▶ Beauties in the East, Oshima and Onaka from Nakachō, from the series Beauties from the Four Directions by Kitao Shigemasa. 18th century. Ōban format. Tōkyō National Museum.

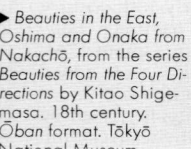

▲ Ōiso Station, from a series by Keisai Eisen. Ca 1842. Ōban format. Tōkyō National Museum.

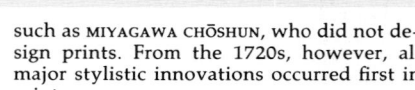

such as MIYAGAWA CHŌSHUN, who did not design prints. From the 1720s, however, all major stylistic innovations occurred first in prints.

Another major contemporary of the Torii masters was OKUMURA MASANOBU, some of whose earliest work is indistinguishable from that of the Torii. Masanobu, who was also a publisher, was associated with several major technical innovations, such as urushi-e (lacquer prints), so called because glue was mixed with the ink to give it luster, and uki-e (floating pictures), which employed Western perspective. At the height of their popularity in the 1740s, uki-e were chiefly interior scenes relying on architecture to control perspective. Later uki-e, especially those of UTAGAWA TOYOHARU, included landscapes. Another important ukiyo-e artist of the second quarter of the 18th century was NISHIKAWA SUKENOBU, a native of Kyōto, whose illustrated books presenting scenes from daily life or from classical poetry gained extraordinary popularity throughout the country. His work displayed a delicacy that set it apart from Edo ukiyo-e of the time and influenced the subsequent development of the genre.

Color Prints—In about 1745, a technique was conceived for registering successive blocks, each printing a different color on a single sheet. The resulting prints, called benizuri-e (pictures printed in red) because the most striking color was a red derived from the petals of the safflower (benibana), were produced only in two or three colors. It was not until 1764 that the first full-color prints appeared, a development that is closely associated with the sudden popularity of the work of Suzuki HARUNOBU. By 1766

almost every ukiyo-e artist was working in Harunobu's style. These new prints, called nishiki-e (brocade pictures) or edo-e (Edo pictures), represented the final stage of technical advancement in color printing achieved in the Edo period. Many of Harunobu's prints are imbued with a gentle nostalgia for the past, but others introduce the mocking, worldly spirit of mitate-e, parodies in contemporary dress of scenes from classical art or literature. Among other innovations that appeared at this time was a shift from the narrow hosoban print size, which continued to be used for yakusha-e, to the squarer chūban format.

The stylistic revolution brought about by the development of full-color printing soon affected the traditional genre of yakusha-e. From about 1770, in the work of the major innovators KATSUKAWA SHUNSHŌ and IPPITSUSAI BUNCHŌ, actors were for the first time presented as individuals with distinctive features, whereas previously they could be distinguished only by the crest (mon) on their kimono. Shunshō had particular influence as the teacher of KATSUKAWA SHUN'EI and Katsushika HOKUSAI, and the changes he set in motion laid the foundation for the work of Tōshūsai SHARAKU.

In the 1770s poets of KYŌKA, a type of comic verse, and artists began to collaborate in the production of some extraordinarily handsome books combining kyōka with ukiyo-e illustrations. The success of these works, particularly Utamaro's Ehon mushi erami (1788, Insect Book), helped give rise to SURIMONO. Popular in the 1790s, surimono, which combined kyōka or haikai (see HAIKU) and ukiyo-e, were prints that were produced on commission and issued in limited editions for use as announcements, invitations, or gifts. The printing was quite elegant,

making frequent use of burnished metallic pigments and of embossing, which gave texture and depth to the surface of prints. Some kyōka poets also wrote kibyōshi and sharebon stories, which were customarily illustrated by ukiyo-e artists.

The Golden Age of Ukiyo-e—The late 18th century was largely a period of consolidation rather than innovation; however, development of the more generous ōban format and the introduction of diptychs and triptychs led to more complex composition. Above all others TORII KIYONAGA is associated with this period. The ideal of feminine beauty that he perfected—tall, stately figures of unusual dignity and grace—dominated the 1780s. The composition of his prints, with its deliberate massing of volumes and studied balancing of horizontals and verticals, is among the most masterful in the tradition of ukiyo-e. Nevertheless, the work of some of his contemporaries, such as Katsukawa Shunchō, KUBO SHUMMAN, and Kitao Masanobu—the latter known also as a writer of sharebon, under the name SANTŌ KYŌDEN—though lacking Kiyonaga's assurance, often seems more daring. After 1790, ukiyo-e images acquired a new intensity and styles began to succeed one another with greater rapidity. Utamaro and Sharaku achieved a heightened closeness to their subjects by using the format of the ōkubi-e or bust portrait: Utamaro's women are extremely sensuous and the masculinity of Sharaku's female impersonators (ONNAGATA) infuses his portrayals. Utamaro was one of the first to isolate his figures against a brilliant mica background, and did so with a flair that other artists of the time, among them HOSODA EISHI and UTAGAWA TOYOKUNI, only rarely managed to equal.

After 1800, there appears to have been a

▲ *Zhang Shun*, from the series *108 Heroes of the Suikoden* by Utagawa Kuniyoshi. Ca 1830. *Ōban* format. Private collection.

► **Right:** *Ichikawa Danjūrō VI as Arakawa Tarō*, by Sharaku, an artist known for his theatrical prints. 1794–95. *Aiban* format (intermediate in size between the *chūban* and *ōban* formats). Tōkyō National Museum. **Far right:** *Kataoka Nizaemon VII as Fujiwara Shihei*, an *ōkubi-e* (close-up) portrait print by Utagawa Toyokuni. 1796. *Ōban* format.

► *Genre Scenes of the Twelve Months: Sixth Month*, an *ukiyo-e* painting by Katsukawa Shunshō. Ca 1783. 115 × 26 cm. Colors on silk. MOA Museum of Art, Shizuoka Prefecture.

▼ *Couple Reading a Letter*, a print by Harunobu. Ca 1765. *Chūban* ("medium size") format. Tōkyō National Museum.

▲ The left panel of Torii Kiyonaga's triptych *Sudden Evening Shower at Mimeguri Shrine*. 1786–87. *Ōban* format. Tōkyō National Museum.

► *Amida Falls on the Kiso Highway*, from Hokusai's series *The Waterfalls of Various Provinces*. Ca 1831. *Ōban* format. Tōkyō National Museum.

radical change in taste, accompanied by a faltering of inspiration in design and a deterioration in the quality of printing. Short figures with hunched shoulders and sharp features replaced the tall, elegant figures of the 1770s and 1780s, kimono patterns became coarser and more strident, and pictures of actors tended toward the exaggerated and grotesque. One reason for this was change in the print-buying public, which had grown larger and presumably less discriminating, resulting in prints that were produced hastily—many showing faulty registration of colors—and in great numbers.

Landscape—The emergence of the landscape print was a relatively late phenomenon in the history of *ukiyo-e.* Prior to Hokusai's *Fugaku sanjūrokkei* (1823, Thirty-Six Views of Mount Fuji), landscape as independent subject matter for *ukiyo-e* was largely unknown. Other artists soon followed Hokusai's lead, and landscape achieved a popularity that rivaled the established genres of portraiture. Active as an artist for some 60 years, Hokusai developed a style that was highly individual, combining Chinese and Western influences with elements drawn from the native KANŌ SCHOOL, the TOSA SCHOOL, and the RIMPA tradition. He was also a prolific draftsman who employed a variety of techniques to create the astounding array of images in his famous 13-volume *Hokusai manga* (1814–49, Hokusai's Sketches).

Hokusai's only true rival in landscape was Andō HIROSHIGE, whose great *Tōkaidō gojūsantsugi* (1833–34, The Fifty-Three Stations of the Tōkaidō Road) brought him fame and a host of imitators. Hiroshige displays in this and other works a greater concern than Hokusai with atmosphere, light, and weather. Drawing on the style of certain of the landscape paintings of the Southern Song (Sung) dynasty (1127–1279), his work was also influenced by the contemporaneous MARUYAMA-SHIJŌ SCHOOL and by Western realism. UTAGAWA KUNIYOSHI, who was also active at this time, stands out for his vivid imagination as well as his occasional use of Western perspective and chiaroscuro.

As an integral element of the Edo-period culture that it mirrored, *ukiyo-e* was unable to survive that society's demise in the wake of the radical Westernization that transformed Japan during the Meiji period (1868–1912). Nevertheless, a number of artists trained in the tradition, including TAISO YOSHITOSHI and KOBAYASHI KIYOCHIKA, continued to work into the late 19th century.

☎ *1650–1651*

ukiyo-zōshi　　　　　　浮世草子

(books of the floating world). Generic term for popular fiction written between the 1680s and 1770s in Kyōto and Ōsaka. SAIKAKU'S KŌSHOKU ICHIDAI OTOKO (1682, Life of an Amorous Man) is considered the first work in the genre. During Saikaku's time, all popular fiction was referred to as KANA-ZŌSHI. From about 1710 one finds mention of *ukiyo-zōshi* as a genre, used in reference to the amorous fiction earlier known as KŌSHOKU-BON. It was only in the Meiji period (1868–1912) that the Edo-period (1600–1868) literature describing the tribulations of this world was called *ukiyo-zōshi.* The *ukiyo-zōshi* generally fall into four categories: *kōshoku-mono,* or amorous pieces centered around the pleasure quarters, as in *Life of an Amorous Man; chōnin-mono,* dealing with the economic life of townsmen; *setsuwa-mono,* tales of the strange and curious; and *buke-mono,* dealing with *samurai* life.

Following Saikaku's death, the *ukiyo-*
zōshi tradition was carried on in Ōsaka by such writers as NISHIZAWA IPPŪ, MIYAKO NO NISHIKI, and HŌJŌ DANSUI. From around 1700 in Kyōto the writer EJIMA KISEKI and the bookseller Hachimonjiya Jishō (d 1745) produced numerous *ukiyo-zōshi,* known as HACHIMONJIYA-BON, that served to make the genre more popular and accessible. Kiseki developed a kind of *ukiyo-zōshi* known as the *katagi-mono,* or sketches of various types of townsmen, represented by such works as *Seken musuko katagi* (1715, Characters of Worldly Young Men). In 1766, after the deaths of both Kiseki and Jishō, the Hachimonjiya publishing house was sold, and *ukiyo-zōshi* ceased to be produced.

ultra-high-rise buildings
　　　　　　　　　　　超高層建築物

(*chōkōsō kenchikubutsu*). In Japan the term "ultra-high-rise" is used to classify buildings taller than 100 meters (328 ft). Frequent earthquakes and violent typhoons long deterred Japanese architects from erecting such buildings. However, post–World War II construction technology designed to withstand earthquakes, coupled with the easing of restrictions on building height in 1963 (see ARCHITECTURAL STANDARDS LAW), made possible their construction. The first ultra-high-rise was the Kasumigaseki Building, completed in 1968, with 36 stories and a height of 147 meters (482 ft). Plans for buildings over 60 meters (197 ft) must be approved by the Building Center of Japan (an auxiliary of the Ministry of Construction) to ensure their ability to withstand the effects of a major earthquake or typhoon. As of March 1991 there were 99 buildings over

Continued on page 1652➤

The Consummate Craftsmanship of Ukiyo-e

The art of the traditional woodblock print was a collaborative one, involving the combined efforts of the publisher, artist, wood-carver, and printer. As it was customary to include the names of both publisher and artist on the finished work, such master artists as Utamaro, Hokusai, and Hiroshige have achieved lasting fame. The essential contribution of the wood-carvers and printers, on the other hand, has not been as well recognized because they often labored anonymously. Yet without their special skills, the flowing lines and subtleties of color and texture that characterize *ukiyo*-e at its best could never have been fully realized. The delicate *kewari* technique used in expressing the line of the coiffure was left entirely to the skill of the wood-carver. Other techniques, such as vignette shading and *gauffrage* (blind printing or embossing), were largely made possible through the development of the printer's art. These fine details and the level of technical mastery they represent serve as the signatures of these generally unknown craftsmen and are a crucial source of the artistic richness of the mature ukiyo-e print.

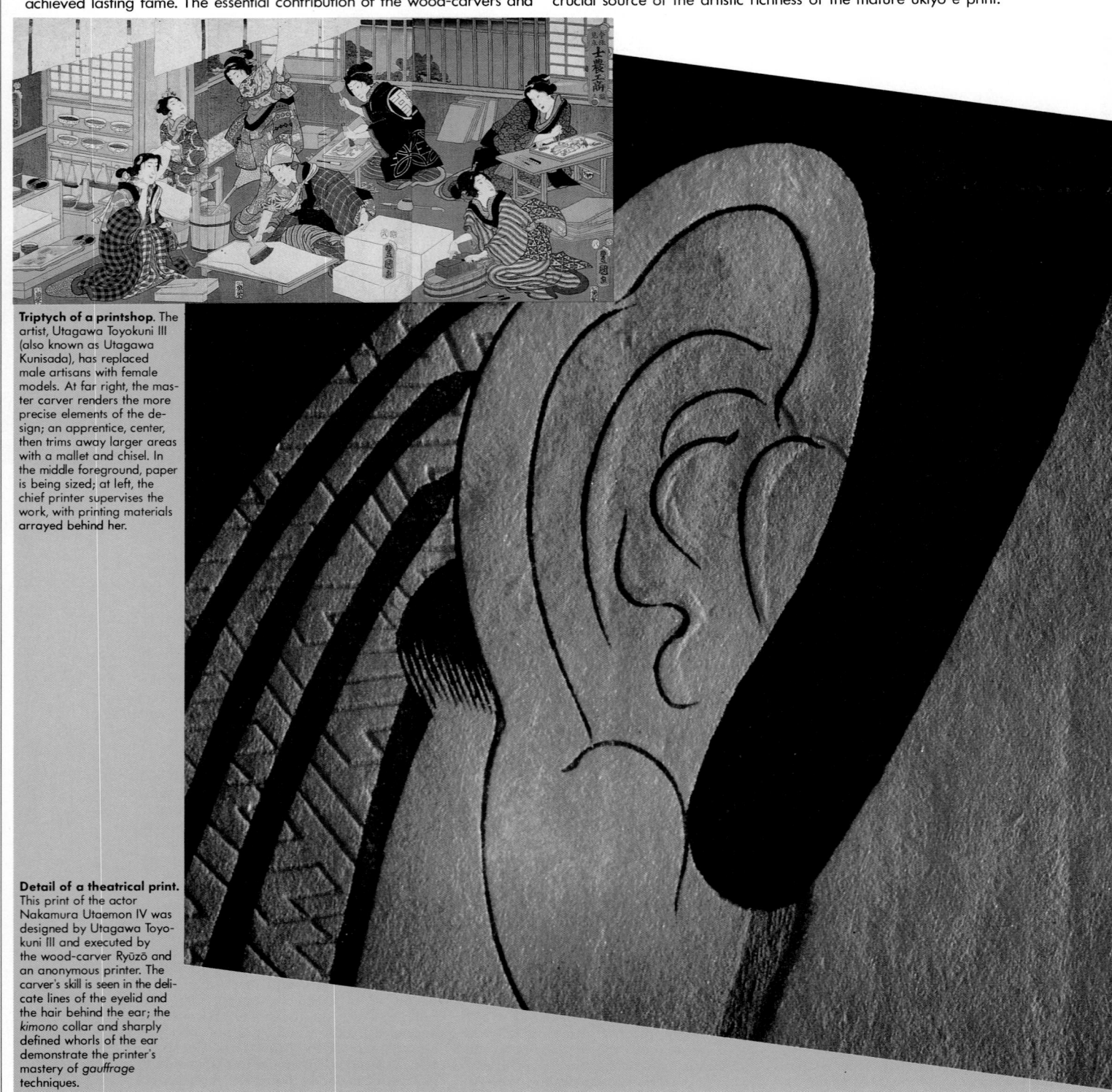

Triptych of a printshop. The artist, Utagawa Toyokuni III (also known as Utagawa Kunisada), has replaced male artisans with female models. At far right, the master carver renders the more precise elements of the design; an apprentice, center, then trims away larger areas with a mallet and chisel. In the middle foreground, paper is being sized; at left, the chief printer supervises the work, with printing materials arrayed behind her.

Detail of a theatrical print. This print of the actor Nakamura Utaemon IV was designed by Utagawa Toyokuni III and executed by the wood-carver Ryūzō and an anonymous printer. The carver's skill is seen in the delicate lines of the eyelid and the hair behind the ear; the *kimono* collar and sharply defined whorls of the ear demonstrate the printer's mastery of *gauffrage* techniques.

The wood-carver's tools. Cutting tools were of two main types: fine knives for detail work and various chisels and gouges for stripping away larger areas of the block. The mallet was used with larger chisels.

The printer's tools. An assortment of brushes for applying ink to the block, sticks for stirring pigment, and a finishing chisel. The disk-shaped pads (bottom), called *baren*, were used to press the paper onto the block; each pad had a core made of tightly plaited strands of bamboo wound in a spiral.

The Printing Process

Ukiyo-e printing utilized a sequence of carefully registered separate woodblocks. After the outline block was printed, smaller areas of color were set in (**1**). Larger color fields required additional blocks (**2**, **3**). The background was then filled in (**4**) and the hair and eyes enhanced with a final application of heavier black ink (**5**). Such special techniques as *gauffrage* were executed in the later print stages.

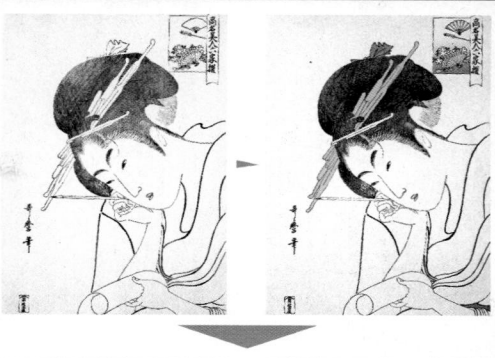

Reproduced, with omissions, by permission of the Adachi Woodblock Printing Research Center.

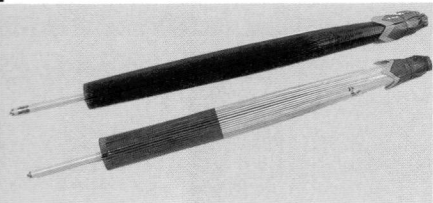

traditional umbrellas
1 An Aichi Prefecture craftsman works on a "snake-eye" umbrella.
2 Two closed *bangasa*-type umbrellas.

100 meters high in Japan, with 17 more under construction and 45 in the planning stages; the tallest building in Japan was the TŌKYŌ METROPOLITAN GOVERNMENT OFFICES, at 243 meters (797 ft). However, the Landmark Tower in Yokohama, scheduled for completion in 1993, will rise to a height of 296 meters (971 feet).

ultranationalism→nationalism

Umarete wa mita keredo

生れてはみたけれど

(Foreign release title: *I Was Born, but . . .*). A 1932 silent film directed by OZU YASUJIRŌ about two young boys learning to cope with the dictates of society. The two must adjust to a new neighborhood in Tōkyō, their new school, and new playmates, but they gradually win acceptance. Although they are eager to please their father, they cannot understand why he insists that they be nice to the company president's son, also a member of the neighborhood gang, but not nearly as smart or tough as they are. They cannot fathom the relationship between employer and employee but gradually come to understand and accept the adult code of behavior that demands greater honor for position than for ability, thereby marking their loss of innocence.

Umarete wa mita keredo is considered the first work of social criticism in Japanese cinema. One of its central themes is the tension between work and family life, a theme to which Ozu returned in many of his films. Yet the film is also a comedy with a prevailing sense of boyish mischief. Ozu later remade the film as *Ohayō* (1959, Good Morning).

umbrellas, traditional 傘

(*kasa*). Umbrellas in Japan are divided into *higasa* (sun umbrellas) and *amagasa* (rain umbrellas). Silk umbrellas were introduced to Japan during the mid-6th century from Korea and were used by aristocrats as sunshades. It was not until the Edo period (1600–1868) that common people started to use umbrellas. In the Genroku era (1688–1704) rain umbrellas made of oiled paper stretched over a bamboo rib frame became popular. These included the *janomegasa* ("snake-eye umbrellas"), which were black, red, or navy, with a white center ring; the *bangasa*, with wide ribs; and the *momijigasa*, with rattan handles. Paper parasols, such as the *ehigasa*, which were painted with pictures of birds and flowers, were also popular. Traditional paper umbrellas are expensive and have been largely replaced by Western-style rain umbrellas and cloth parasols. See also RAINGEAR, TRADITIONAL.

ume→plum, Japanese

umeboshi 梅干し

(pickled plums). *Umeboshi* have been a part of the Japanese diet since ancient times. They are made by salt-curing the fruit of the *ume* (see PLUM, JAPANESE) for about two weeks, then adding the salted leaves of the beefsteak plant (*shiso*) for red color. After three to four more weeks of marination the *umeboshi* are sun-dried for a few days and are then ready for eating. The typically salty-sour *umeboshi* is thought to aid digestion, stimulate the appetite, and combat fatigue. Because of their supposedly germicidal properties, *umeboshi* are frequently included with the rice in box lunches and are put in *onigiri* (rice balls; see NIGIRIMESHI) to prevent spoilage.

Umeda 梅田

Busy commercial and transportation district of Kita Ward in the city of Ōsaka, situated around the Japan Railways' Ōsaka Station and Hankyū and Hanshin Railways' Umeda Station. Once a small village, Umeda became the gateway to Ōsaka after what is now Ōsaka Station was opened in 1874. Today Umeda, also called Kita, or "north," is one of Ōsaka's two busiest districts, the other being Minami, or "south" (see NAMBA). A large transportation terminal, it has many high-rise buildings, department stores, underground shopping centers, and entertainment facilities.

Umeda Umpin 梅田雲浜

(1815–59). Imperial-loyalist *samurai* of the Edo period (1600–1868). Real name Umeda Genjirō. Born in the Obama domain (now part of Fukui Prefecture). He studied Confucianism in Edo (now Tōkyō) from 1829 to 1840. After traveling to Kyūshū, where he met YOKOI SHŌNAN, he became acquainted with YANAGAWA SEIGAN and Rai Mikisaburō (1825–59), the son of RAI SAN'YŌ, and joined the SONNŌ JŌI movement to restore imperial rule. In 1852 Umeda was stripped of samurai status for criticizing domainal policy and presuming to speak out on national defense. He then enlisted sympathizers for the proimperial movement in the Kyōto-Ōsaka area. He was arrested in the 1858 ANSEI PURGE and died in prison the following year.

Umehara Ryūzaburō 梅原竜三郎

(1888–1986). Western-style painter. Born in Kyōto, he studied painting under ASAI CHŪ at the Kansai Art School. From 1908 to 1913 he studied in Paris at the Académie Julian and then with Renoir. In Tōkyō he helped to found two artist groups—Nikakai in 1914 and Shun'yōkai in 1922—and joined the Western-art section of the group Kokuga Sōsaku Kyōkai in 1926. He returned to France in 1920–21, visited China in 1929 and Taiwan in 1933–35, and then lived in Beiping (Peiping; now Beijing or Peking) in 1939–43. From 1944 to 1952 he was a professor at the Tōkyō Bijutsu Gakkō (now Tōkyō University of Fine Arts and Music). A member of the JAPAN ART ACADEMY (Nihon Geijutsuin), in 1952 he received the Order of Culture. His paintings range from nudes and still lifes to Beijing street scenes and palaces. His use of color and sense of design made him one of the foremost Western-style artists of his time.

Umehara Sueji 梅原末治

(1893–1983). Archaeologist. Born in Ōsaka. After study in Europe (1925–29), he became a member of the Kyōto Institute of the Academy of Oriental Culture (now Kyōto University Research Institute for Humanistic Studies) and a lecturer at Kyōto University, attaining full professorship in 1939. Umehara's hypothesis concerning the distribution of BRONZE MIRRORS among Kofun-period (ca 300–710) rulers is important to the understanding of early political development. His publications include *Kodai hoppōkei bumbutsu no kenkyū* (1938, Studies on Ancient Northern-Style Civilization) and *Nihon kōkogaku ronkō* (1940, Thoughts on Japanese Archaeology).

Ume Kenjirō 梅謙次郎

(1860–1910). Scholar of civil and commercial law. Born in what is now Shimane Prefecture. He graduated from the law school attached to the Justice Ministry in 1884 and became a professor at Tōkyō University in the following year. He then studied at the University of Lyons and, after receiving a doctoral degree, studied for a year at the University of Berlin. In the so-called CIVIL CODE CONTROVERSY, he strongly urged the immediate enforcement of the civil code drawn up in 1890 by Gustave BOISSONADE DE FONTARABIE and others. When it was decided in 1892 to delay its enforcement, he appealed to Prime Minister ITŌ HIROBUMI to establish a committee to prepare a new draft. In 1893 he was appointed to the new body, together with HOZUMI NOBUSHIGE and TOMII MASAAKI; the CIVIL CODE was put into effect in 1898. Ume was also responsible, together with Tanabe Kaoru (1860–1936) and OKANO KEIJIRŌ, for the 1899 COMMERCIAL CODE. His principal work is *Mimpō yōgi* (5 vols, 1896–1900, Essentials of Civil Law).

umemodoki 梅擬

Ilex serrata var. *sieboldii*. Deciduous shrub of the family Aquifoliacae. Found wild in wet mountainous areas of Honshū, Shikoku, and Kyūshū, it is also cultivated as a decorative plant because of its attractive fruit. It grows to a height of 4–5 meters (13–16 ft). The serrated leaves are alternate, emerging either as ovals or as egg-shaped lanceolates. In June light purple flowers appear and bloom in a cluster, followed by round crimson berries that remain on leafless branches into early winter.

Variant species include the *kimino umemodoki*, with yellow fruit; the *shiro umemodoki*, with white fruit and flowers; and the *koshō umemodoki*, with relatively small leaves and berries. These varieties are grown mainly for use in BONSAI. Wild varieties include the *inu umemodoki* (*I. serrata* var. *argutidens*).

Umewaka Manzaburō I

梅若万三郎1世

(1868–1946). NŌ actor. Born in Tōkyō. *Shite* (principal player) of the KANZE SCHOOL of the Nō theater and the first son born to Umewaka Minoru I (1828–1909). Because Minoru I had already adopted an heir, Manzaburō did not inherit his father's position as head of the Kanze school; instead, he founded the separate Umewaka school with his two younger brothers in 1921. He returned to the Kanze school in 1933, leaving his brother Rokurō (1878–1959; later Umewaka Minoru II) to assume the headship of the Umewaka school. Regarded as the leading Nō actor of his day, Manzaburō gave 3,000 performances in the course of his career and set a record by appearing in all the plays that make up the modern Nō repertoire.

Umezaki Haruo　梅崎春生

(1915–65). Author. Born in Fukuoka Prefecture; graduate of Tōkyō University. He was drafted into the navy toward the end of World War II. His story "Sakurajima" (1946), based upon his war experiences, deals with the fear of death and a sense of the emptiness of human existence faced by a young intellectual soldier. He later turned to writing light satire, describing the lives of the common people in such stories as "Boroya no shunjū" (1954), which was awarded the Naoki Prize. His novels include the semiautobiographical *Kuruidako* (1963) and *Genka* (1965).

Umezawa Hamao　梅沢浜夫

(1914–86). Microbiologist. Born in Fukui Prefecture. Graduate of Tōkyō University. Umezawa is known as one of the world's foremost experts on the development of such antibiotics as sarcomycin, kanamycin, and bleomycin. He taught at Tōkyō University and served as director of its Institute of Microbial Chemistry. He received the Order of Culture in 1962.

Umezu Masakage nikki
梅津政景日記

The diary of Umezu Shume Masakage (1581–1633), a key administrator of the SATAKE FAMILY's Akita domain in Dewa Province (now Akita Prefecture); it covers the years 1612–33 and is an important source of information on domainal administration, particularly mining and fiscal policy.

Umezu Yoshijirō　梅津美治郎

(1882–1949). Army general and last chief of the ARMY GENERAL STAFF OFFICE. Born in Ōita Prefecture. A graduate of the Army Academy in 1903, he later served as commander of the Japanese forces in Tianjin (Tientsin) in North China, where in June 1935 he concluded the HE-UMEZU (HO-UMEZU) AGREEMENT, banishing the Guomindang (Kuomintang) and CHIANG KAI-SHEK's Nationalist Army from Hebei (Hopeh) and allowing the Japanese army to make advances into the province. In the early 1940s he commanded the Japanese GUANDONG (KWANTUNG) ARMY. Becoming chief of the Army General Staff Office in 1944, he served until the end of World War II. On 2 September 1945 he represented the Imperial High Command in signing the formal documents of surrender on board the USS *Missouri* (see SURRENDER, INSTRUMENT OF). Found guilty as a class A war criminal at the WAR CRIMES TRIALS, he died in prison.

Umi　海

(The Sea). Monthly literary journal published by CHŪŌ KŌRON SHA, INC, from July 1969 to May 1984. It sought to bring an international perspective to Japanese literature, placing an emphasis on the translation of foreign works and the introduction of new literary theories and trends from abroad. It also fostered important work by Japanese writers, such as TAKEDA TAIJUN's *Fuji* (1969–71, Mt. Fuji Sanatorium), and critical essays such as YOSHIMOTO TAKAAKI's series *Shomotsu no kaitaigaku* (1972–73, Textual Deconstruction).

umibōzu　海坊主

Also called *uminyūdō* or *umikozō*. In Japanese folklore, *umibōzu* is a ghost of the sea said to have a large round head. According to legend, if anyone speaks to this ghost, it will immediately capsize that person's boat. It is thought that people have mistaken large fish, large waves, and thunderheads for this ghost, but the origin of this belief is probably the superstition that the souls of people with no one to look after their graves, or who have suffered an untimely death, take refuge at sea.

Unazuki　宇奈月[町]

Town in eastern Toyama Prefecture, central Honshū, on the river Kurobegawa. Its hot springs, skiing facilities, and scenery, especially the Kurobe Gorge, attract many visitors. Pop: 7,261.

undōkai　運動会

Recreational athletic meets held in the spring or fall by schools (from preschool to college level), offices, and residential communities. At the typical school-sponsored *undōkai*, the entire student body is divided into two teams. The students compete in such events as relay races, tugs-of-war, three-legged races, and various ball-tossing games; they also take part in choreographed folk dances. The emphasis is on exercise and cooperation rather than serious competition. Teachers, parents, and local residents also attend and may participate in the activities.

Unebiyama → Yamato Sanzan

uneme　釆女

Female attendants in ancient times who served the ruler's daily needs. They were selected from among the sisters and daughters of local chieftains (KUNI NO MIYATSUKO) and presented as tribute to the sovereign at the YAMATO COURT (ca 4th century–ca mid-7th century). By the time of the TAIKA REFORM (645) the acquisition of *uneme* was firmly established as an imperial prerogative. These women held much lower status than the sisters and daughters of the pedigreed Yamato aristocracy, who might expect to enter the palace as junior consorts (or concubines, *nyōgo*) and eventually to become empresses (KŌGŌ or CHŪGŪ).

unemployment　失業

(*shitsugyō*). Japan's unemployment rates are low compared with those of Western countries. In the 1970s they remained below 2 percent and even in the 1980s did not exceed 3 percent. The main reason for this difference is the high growth rate of the Japanese economy, with its high demand for labor. Another significant factor has been the reluctance of Japanese employers, especially in larger companies, to dismiss workers in periods of economic downturn, due to the widespread custom of guaranteed lifetime employment. As a result, such companies are occasionally faced with the problem of excess employment; such surplus employees are in fact deemed to be internally unemployed. Companies have addressed this problem by cutting overtime, laying off TEMPORARY WORKERS, transferring workers to other departments, and suspending arrangements with subcontractors. Only as a last resort do they actually dismiss their full-time workers. Such an approach is considered to be conducive to maintaining good industrial relations. For their part, employ-

ees cooperate with management by working overtime when necessary and accepting transfers within the company even when business is good, in order to help prevent employee buildups that would lead to a surplus during economic slumps.

Types of Unemployed Workers— Those hit hardest by unemployment are temporary workers and those working for the subcontractors of big firms. The working conditions of such employees tend to be poor and their bargaining power weak, making it easier for their employers to cut labor costs by forcing dismissals when times are bad. In the years after World War II, there were many people from rural areas working away from home (*dekasegi rōdōsha*); when they became unemployed, they were simply reabsorbed into their farming communities. Today, in addition to large numbers of such migrant workers, there are also many temporary workers—housewives, for example, who return to their homes when dismissed from a job. This reabsorption process makes unemployment rates difficult to measure exactly.

Although the seniority wage system creates high average wages for elderly workers, the gap between customary retirement at age 55 and the age at which one becomes eligible for a pension (about age 60) causes workers to look for reemployment after their first retirement. A worker's previous skills and experience, however, may be of little use to other companies, and so there are high unemployment rates among the elderly. By contrast, demand for younger workers, who are quick to acquire skills and are paid a lower average wage, remains strong. Most unemployment among the young is accounted for by people who are changing jobs.

Depending on their age and their previous wage levels, unemployed people recognized to be looking for work receive unemployment benefits for a period of 90–300 days from the unemployment insurance system, which is supported by funds from the central government and employers' and workers' contributions. The highest postwar unemployment figure was recorded in 1987; the actual number was 1,730,000, just 2.8 percent of the total working population. See also PUBLIC EMPLOYMENT SECURITY OFFICES.

Unequal Treaties, revision of
条約改正

(*jōyaku kaisei*; literally, "treaty revision"). The term *jōyaku kaisei* refers to the extended diplomatic negotiations following the Meiji

Umehara Ryūzaburō Mt. Asama. Umehara was one of Japan's foremost Western-style artists in the first half of the 20th century. 1959. Mixed media on canvas. 67 × 83 cm. National Museum of Modern Art, Tōkyō.

umemodoki The crimson berries of this deciduous shrub reach about 5 mm in diameter and are favored by fruit-eating birds.

uniforms Uniformed Tōkyō schoolchildren on their way home from school.

Restoration of 1868 in which the Japanese government sought to revise and eventually replace the so-called Unequal Treaties concluded with the Western powers during the 1850s and 1860s.

Treaties and Problems—The foundations of the treaty system had been laid by the Tokugawa shogunate's (1603–1867) ANSEI COMMERCIAL TREATIES of 1858 with the United States, the Netherlands, Russia, Britain, and France. These agreements expanded upon earlier pacts that had opened several major ports to international trade. They also established a sliding scale of tariffs and acknowledged the right of foreigners to be tried in consular courts according to their own laws.

These treaties had provided for revision after 1 July 1872 but had been considerably modified before that date. Outbreaks of antiforeign violence had led to a series of tariff reductions that culminated in the Tariff Convention of 1866 (see KAIZEI YAKUSHO). The Western powers had taken advantage of the loosely worded treaties and most-favored-nation clauses to expand their privileges in other areas as well.

Initiatives and Negotiations—The new Meiji government accepted the treaties on 8 February 1868. Imperial officials at first hoped that revision might be easily obtained once domestic stability had been achieved, but difficulties became apparent by the time of the IWAKURA MISSION in 1871.

1875–1879. Foreign Minister TERASHIMA MUNENORI unsuccessfully offered the opening of more ports in return for tariff autonomy.

1880–1887. Terashima's successor INOUE KAORU sought to increase both tariff rates and Japan's jurisdiction over foreigners. His proposals led to joint preliminary talks in 1882 among representatives of the treaty states, and a compromise was reached in 1886. However, the French jurist and longtime government adviser Gustave Emile BOISSONADE DE FONTARABIE viewed the proposed agreement as a threat to Japan's jurisdiction, and it was also opposed by prominent traditionalists, such as General TANI KANJŌ. Objections sparked widespread opposition that proved a boon to the FREEDOM AND PEOPLE'S RIGHTS MOVEMENT (see SANDAI JIKEN KEMPAKU MOVEMENT). Negotiations were suspended, and Inoue resigned.

1888–1889. Under Foreign Minister ŌKUMA SHIGENOBU, negotiations were reopened in November 1888. Agreements were soon signed with Germany and the United States, and talks with England were under way when treaty revision once again ran afoul of public opinion. Negotiations were later broken off when Ōkuma was attacked and injured by a nationalist fanatic.

1890–1894. Discussions were renewed in February 1890, but little progress was made until MUTSU MUNEMITSU became foreign min-

ister in August 1892. By this time the government was again under considerable pressure from hardliners in the newly established Diet and from a public that, vulnerable to fears of racial and cultural extinction, seemed increasingly persuaded that the existing treaty port system was preferable to opening the country to mixed residence (NAICHI ZAKKYO). Turning public sentiment to its advantage, the government took a tougher negotiating stance. The ANGLO-JAPANESE COMMERCIAL TREATY OF 1894 (Aoki-Kimberley Treaty) that followed provided for the abolition of extraterritoriality in five years. By 1897 similar treaties had been signed with the other major treaty nations. Finally, in 1911, Japan successfully concluded a series of new treaties, which restored tariff autonomy.

UNESCO activities in Japan
ユネスコと日本

(Yunesuko *to* Nihon). Japan was admitted to the United Nations Educational, Scientific, and Cultural Organization (UNESCO) in 1951, signaling its return to the community of nations after World War II. UNESCO work in Japan is now handled by the Japanese National Commission for UNESCO. On the nongovernmental level, there is a National Federation of UNESCO Associations with more than 220 affiliates, which sponsors scientific, cultural, and educational activities. Since the US withdrawal from UNESCO in 1984, Japan has become the agency's largest contributor. The 1989 contribution of $25,657,811 constituted 10.71 percent of the total. See also UNITED NATIONS AND JAPAN.

unfair labor practices
不当労働行為

(*futō rōdō kōi*). Activities of an employer that infringe upon a worker's right to organize, bargain collectively, and engage in concerted action. These three FUNDAMENTAL LABOR RIGHTS are guaranteed by article 28 of the 1947 constitution. The prohibited practices are (1) dismissal or other adverse treatment of a worker in retaliation for the organization of a union, membership in a labor organization, or other legitimate union activity; (2) requirement that a worker sign, as a condition of employment, a promise to withdraw from or not to join a union; (3) refusal by an employer, without sufficient cause, to bargain collectively; (4) control of or interference in the formation or administration of a union; and (5) dismissal or other adverse treatment of a worker for requesting relief from unfair labor practices through a labor relations commission.

The Labor Union Law (Rōdō Kumiai Hō) initially contained penalties for employers who committed unfair labor practices, but a 1949 amendment to the law substituted the principle of returning a situation to its original condition, without the unfair practices. When an employer violates a relief order issued by one of the LABOR RELATIONS COMMISSIONS, a fine of up to ¥100,000, one year's imprisonment, or both may be assessed. See also LABOR LAWS.

Uni-Charm Corporation
ユニ・チャーム[株]

(Yuni Chāmu). Leading manufacturer of sanitary napkins and paper diapers. Incorporated in 1961. Pet food is another of its product lines. Uni-Charm has manufacturing plants in Taiwan and Thailand. It exports techniques for producing nonwoven fabric to Western countries. Sales for the fiscal year

ending March 1991 totaled ¥81.2 billion (US $591.8 million), and capitalization stood at ¥10.6 billion (US $77.3 million). Headquarters are in Tōkyō.

uniforms
制服

(*seifuku*). It was not customary in premodern Japan to wear uniforms to provide identification or to differentiate among occupations of groups in daily life. Only when Japan began to be influenced by the West in the late 19th century did uniforms come into wide use. About the time the Chinese-inspired RITSURYŌ SYSTEM of government was adopted in the 7th century, however, certain rules regulating clothing were laid down, and in one sense these clothes may be considered uniforms.

In 604 Prince SHŌTOKU, in imitation of China, devised a system of 12 court ranks (KAN'I JŪNIKAI) and designated the color of the headdress and clothing for each rank. The TAIHŌ CODE (701) and YŌRŌ CODE (718; effective 757) also meticulously prescribed for each rank the headwear, clothing, and accessories to be worn by male and female visitors to the imperial court. During the Heian period (794–1185), the Kamakura period (1185–1333), and the Edo period (1600–1868), various changes in style determined what was appropriate ceremonial dress for the aristocratic classes.

After the Meiji Restoration in 1868, uniforms were adopted for such occupations as the military, police, factory workers, and nurses. Today uniforms are usually worn by students from kindergarten through secondary school, but rarely in college. Many Japanese firms require certain women employees to wear uniforms to promote a sense of group identification. Although not limited to any particular industry, the practice is most noticeable in banks and department stores. See also CLOTHING.

Union of New Religious Organizations of Japan
新日本宗教団体連合会

(Shin Nihon Shūkyō Dantai Rengōkai, abbreviated Shinshūren). Association of 88 religious organizations as of 1989; with headquarters in Tōkyō and local branches. It was established in 1951 by 24 recently founded religious organizations (the so-called NEW RELIGIONS) to promote mutual communication and cooperation, especially in defense of religious freedom. It is a member of the Japan Religious League.

Union of Soviet Socialist Republics and Japan →Soviet Union and Japan

United Church of Christ in Japan
日本基督教団

(Nihon Kirisuto Kyōdan). Union of most Protestant Christian denominations and other groups, formed in 1941, partly to brace themselves against the mounting ideological and political pressures on Christians from the militarist government. The church absorbed more than 30 denominations and organizations, including the SALVATION ARMY, some of the Anglican-Episcopal churches, and the YMCA and YWCA. Although the Salvation Army, YMCA, and YWCA, along with many denominations, such as the Anglican-Episcopal, Lutheran, and some Baptist and Methodist denominations, withdrew from the union after the war, it remains the largest Protestant denomination in Japan. In 1946 the church stipulated a charter and in 1954 formulated its own creed. The church is governed by a general assembly and a standing executive committee. Nationwide, as of 1989, the church was divided into 16 districts with 1,437 churches, 139,720 members, and 2,550 Japanese and 203 foreign clergy.

United Kingdom and Japan

イギリスと日本

(Igirisu to Nihon). The arrival in Kyūshū of the shipwrecked English mariner William ADAMS in 1600 made Britain one of the first Western European nations to contact Japan. TOKUGAWA IEYASU valued Adams's skills and employed him as commercial agent, informant, pilot, shipbuilder, and interpreter. Ieyasu encouraged Adams to invite both the Dutch and the British to trade with Japan. With Adams's help, a Dutch trading post at Hirado in Kyūshū was set up in 1609. Adams then wrote to the English East India Company asking for trading ships to be sent to Japan. In fact, John SARIS had already departed from Britain with three trading ships; he arrived in 1613 and with Adams's aid obtained trading privileges with Japan. A British trading post was set up in Hirado, but it failed to prosper and was closed in 1623. Due to the shogunate's NATIONAL SECLUSION policy, further relations on the state level were held in abeyance until Japan was forced to reopen its doors to other countries in the 1850s.

In 1858 Great Britain, following the United States, the Netherlands, and Russia, signed a treaty of amity and commerce with Japan, thereby opening formal diplomatic and trade relations between the two nations (see ANSEI COMMERCIAL TREATIES). British consuls with extraterritorial jurisdiction were installed at various ports, and British merchants became quite numerous in the foreign settlements. Japanese who were hostile to trade with the United States and Europe responded to the foreign presence by assaulting foreigners or attacking their property. British nationals became frequent objects of attack, as in the RICHARDSON AFFAIR.

As the collapse of the Tokugawa shogunate (1603–1867) became imminent, the British minister Harry Smith PARKES advocated a position of strict neutrality toward the pro- and antishogunate forces. Britain continued to maintain a neutral stance during the BOSHIN CIVIL WAR, which erupted after the coup d'état of January 1868 in which the restoration of imperial rule was proclaimed. Parkes presented his diplomatic credentials to the emperor in May 1868, making Britain the first of the allied powers to recognize the new imperial government.

During the Meiji period (1868–1912) Britain served as a model for Japanese industrialization and the introduction of Western civilization. A number of Meiji leaders, among them ITŌ HIROBUMI and INOUE KAORU, studied in Britain in their youth. British foreign advisers and engineers, brought in to help implement the modernization of industry and institutions, made lasting contributions in such areas as the creation of a modern navy, the construction of railroads, and the establishment of a modern educational system (see FOREIGN EMPLOYEES OF THE MEIJI PERIOD).

Relations between the two nations remained cordial during the late 19th and early 20th centuries. In the first major success in its efforts to revise the "Unequal Treaties" imposed on it in 1858, Japan concluded the ANGLO-JAPANESE COMMERCIAL TREATY OF 1894, which ended British extraterritoriality and partially restored Japan's tariff autonomy (see UNEQUAL TREATIES, REVISION OF). Finding

that they also had common interests in containing Russian expansion in the Far East, Japan and Great Britain also concluded the ANGLO-JAPANESE ALLIANCE in 1902. The alliance worked to Japan's benefit during the RUSSO-JAPANESE WAR, but it was annulled when, at the 1921–22 WASHINGTON CONFERENCE, the FOUR-POWER TREATY, aimed at maintaining the status quo in the Pacific region, was concluded by Japan, Great Britain, the United States, and France.

Through the 1920s the foreign policy interests of the two nations remained bound together by a mutual desire to contain the Chinese nationalist movement, which had affected both nations' interests in China adversely. The Japanese move into Manchuria in 1931 and the outbreak of violence in Shanghai in 1932, however, spelled an end to any vestiges of the special relationship between Japan and Great Britain (see MANCHURIAN INCIDENT; SHANGHAI INCIDENT). Ongoing trade friction, centered on competition for third markets rather than Anglo-Japanese trade per se, further exacerbated tension between the two countries. Great Britain, in an effort to protect its markets, accepted proposals for imperial preference in trade with its colonies at the Ottawa Conference in 1932. Of necessity this "sterling bloc" had a detrimental effect on Japan's trade, even if Japan was not the sole target of this preferential trade policy.

The commercial disputes were dwarfed by the outbreak of the SINO-JAPANESE WAR OF 1937–1945. Relations were forced to the breaking point by Japan's signing of the TRIPARTITE PACT with Germany and Italy and the Japanese military's "southern advance" into Indochina. On 8 December 1941 Japan declared war against the United States and Great Britain. Shortly thereafter Japan attacked British possessions in Southeast Asia and China, occupying in rapid succession Hong Kong, Malaya, Singapore, and Burma (see WORLD WAR II).

After the Japanese surrender in 1945 the BRITISH COMMONWEALTH OCCUPATION FORCE took part in the Occupation of Japan. Relations between the two countries were restored with the ratification of the SAN FRANCISCO PEACE TREATY in 1952. In December 1960 an Anglo-Japanese cultural agreement and in November 1961 an Anglo-Japanese trade agreement were signed, and measures were taken to liberalize imports to Britain from Japan. Prime Minister IKEDA HAYATO visited Britain in November 1962 and signed a long-pending Anglo-Japanese commerce and navigation treaty. Britain also ended its invocation against Japan of article 35 of the General Agreement on Tariffs and Trade (GATT), which allows members to withhold most-favored-nation status from new members, thus creating the conditions for the first equal partnership between the two nations since the war.

The trade deficit has been a chronic problem in the Anglo-Japanese relationship. Since 1971 Japanese exports to Britain have exceeded Japanese imports from that country, and this has been the source of much British criticism of Japan. In September 1972 Prime Minister Edward Heath came to Japan to seek Japanese government cooperation in rectifying the trade imbalance, the first such visit by a British prime minister. A Japanese-government-dispatched economic mission to Europe headed by INAYAMA YOSHIHIRO, at that time chairman of the business federation Keidanren, visited Britain in October 1981. Britain appealed to the mission for the

wider opening of the Japanese market through such measures as the lowering of tariffs and greater imports of manufactured goods. While attending the London Summit of the major industrial powers in 1984, Prime Minister NAKASONE YASUHIRO held talks with Prime Minister Margaret Thatcher. They agreed to increase industrial cooperation in order to encourage Japanese investment and corporate expansion in Great Britain.

In 1990 figures the total amount of exports from Japan to Britain came to approximately US $10.8 billion, as opposed to total imports to Japan of $5.2 billion. Primary Japanese exports are electronic goods, transportation equipment, and general machinery. Imports to Japan include gold (for nonmonetary purposes), whiskeys and other alcoholic beverages, machinery, and chemicals.

The British have welcomed investment from Japan. In 1990 Japanese investment in Great Britain was $6.8 billion, which, at 48.0 percent of their total for Europe, is the largest share of Japanese investment in the European Community. As of 1990 there were 132 Japanese-owned companies in Britain, a major jump from a total of 32 companies in 1985. Great Britain now has a greater number of Japanese-owned companies than any other European nation except the Netherlands.

United Nations and Japan

国際連合と日本

(Kokusai Rengō to Nihon). The United Nations (UN) was established by charter on 24 October 1945. It is headquartered in New York City. Japan was admitted to the United Nations on 18 December 1956, and its foreign policy has since then included "the centrality of the United Nations" as one of its basic guidelines. Japan has established a UN bureau at the Ministry of Foreign Affairs and a permanent mission to the UN headquarters, as well as a permanent delegation to the United Nations' European sub-headquarters in Geneva, Switzerland. Since 1958 Japan has been elected to the UN Security Council as a nonpermanent (two-year-term) member six times and since 1960 has been a regular member of the Economic and Social Council. Tōkyō has been the base of the network of research facilities known as the UN University since the university's founding in 1974, and in 1991 there were 11 other UN organizations operating in Japan, including the United Nations Information Center, the United Nations Children's Fund (UNICEF) Office in Japan, the Japan branch office of the United Nations High Commissioner for Refugees (UNHCR), and the United Nations Development Program (UNDP) Tōkyō Liaison Office. The nongovernmental organizations registered with the United Nations in Japan include the Japan Red Cross Society, the United Nations Association of Japan, and the National Federation of UNESCO Associations in Japan. In 1992 Japan was the second largest payer of UN operating expenses, contributing over 12 percent of total expenses (the United States, which contributed 25 percent of operating expenses, was the largest).

Despite the increasing importance of Japan's role as a member of the United Nations, until 1992 it had not sent troops to participate in UN peacekeeping activities because of its renunciation of arms as embodied in article 9 of the Japanese constitution. Instead, Japan had supplied economic assistance and since 1988 was more active in

United Nations and Japan

UN Budget Assessments, 1992–1994

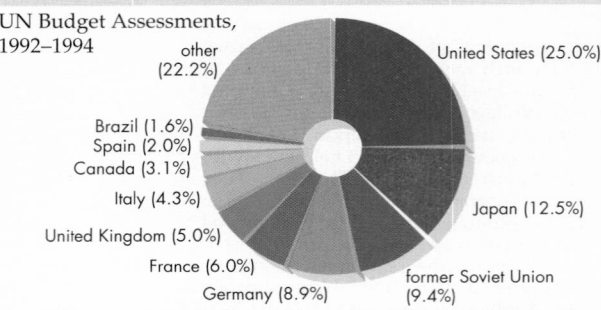

- United States (25.0%)
- Japan (12.5%)
- former Soviet Union (9.4%)
- Germany (8.9%)
- France (6.0%)
- United Kingdom (5.0%)
- Italy (4.3%)
- Canada (3.1%)
- Spain (2.0%)
- Brazil (1.6%)
- other (22.2%)

NOTE: The assessment rate for the Soviet Union will be allotted to the former soviet socialist republics (except Ukraine and Belarus, which have traditionally had separate seats in the United Nations).
SOURCE: United Nations.

Japan's Contribution to the UN Budget

Years	Japan's contribution	UN budget
	(millions of US dollars)	
1970–71	13.79	363.59
1972–73	19.68	446.95
1974–75	36.67	606.03
1976–77	52.75	783.93
1978–79	75.95	1,090.11
1980–81	103.78	1,339.15
1982–83	118.63	1,472.96
1984–85	134.97	1,611.55
1986–87	154.47	1,711.80
1988–89	163.51	1,786.75
1990–91	194.85	2,134.07

SOURCE: Ministry of Foreign Affairs, *Kokusai kikan sōron* (1991).

UN Staff Members, 1991

Country	Number of staff members (A)	Desired range of members	Desired mean number of members (B)	Achieved percent (A/B)
United States	385	327–442	385	100
Soviet Union	161	137–185	161	100
Germany	123	126–170	148	83
France	109	86–116	101	108
United Kingdom	88	68–93	81	109
Japan	88	152–206	179	49
Philippines	65	5–15	10	650
Canada	53	45–61	53	100
Italy	52	57–78	68	76
China	42	41–56	48	88

NOTE: A country's desired range of staff members is calculated on the basis of such factors as its contribution to the UN budget and its population.
SOURCE: United Nations.

Japan's Membership in Specialized Agencies of the United Nations

Organization	Year joined
FAO (Food and Agriculture Organization)	1951
IBRD (International Bank for Reconstruction and Development; World Bank)	1952
ICAO (International Civil Aviation Organization)	1953
IDA (International Development Association)	1960
IFAD (International Fund for Agricultural Development)	1977
IFC (International Finance Corporation)	1956
ILO (International Labor Organization)	1919/1951
IMF (International Monetary Fund)	1952
IMO (International Maritime Organization)	1958
ITU (International Telecommunication Union)	1879
UNESCO (UN Educational, Scientific, and Cultural Organization)	1951
UNIDO (UN Industrial Development Organization)	1967
UPU (Universal Postal Union)	1877
WHO (World Health Organization)	1951
WIPO (World Intellectual Property Organization)	1975
WMO (World Meteorological Organization)	1953

NOTE: Japan withdrew from the ILO in 1938 and rejoined in 1951.
SOURCES: Ministry of Foreign Affairs, *Kokusai kikan sōran* (1991); *Nihon gaikōshi jiten* (1979).

---

dispatching civilians to participate in UN observation teams operating in such problem areas as the Afghanistan-Pakistan border, the Iran-Iraq border, and Namibia. Japan's contribution of economic rather than military aid met with criticism from observers in the United States and other countries during the Persian Gulf War of 1990–91. In 1990 and again in 1991 the ruling Liberal Democratic Party proposed legislation in the Diet that would enable Self Defense Forces troops to participate in UN peacekeeping activities. But China and South Korea expressed concern, and the Japan Socialist Party argued that the legislation was unconstitutional. Nevertheless, in 1992 AKASHI YASUSHI, head of the UN Transitional Authority in Cambodia, and others again urged the Japanese government to provide more assistance there. In June 1992 the Diet passed the Law on Cooperation in United Nations Peacekeeping Operations, and, after a formal request from the United Nations, Japanese troops were sent to Cambodia in October of that year.

United Social Democratic Party
社会民主連合

(Shakai Minshu Rengō). Political party established in March 1978 by the merger of two groups led by people who had broken with the JAPAN SOCIALIST PARTY: (1) the Shakai Shimin Rengō (Socialist Citizens' League), which had been created by EDA SABURŌ in May 1977 and taken over by his son, EDA SATSUKI, after his death; and (2) a group led by DEN HIDEO and Hata Yutaka (b 1925), both of whom had broken with the Japan Socialist Party in September 1977. The party calls for the establishment of a free socialist democratic society.

United States and Japan
アメリカ合衆国と日本

(Amerika Gasshūkoku *to* Nihon). The United States has played a unique and important role in the history of modern Japan. The American people and their ideas, institutions, and tastes have exerted tremendous influence upon the Japanese people. The latter have likewise shaped the course of American history, most dramatically by threatening the national security of the United States in war but also through immigration and economic transactions. At various times during the 140-year history of direct encounter, the relationship between the two countries has been characterized by exclusiveness, separation, suspicion, and antagonism on one hand and by shared aspirations, interchanges, understanding, and compatibility on the other. The story forms an important part of the modern history of international and cross-cultural relations.

The First One Hundred Years (1853–1952)—The first century of US-Japanese relations, from the expedition undertaken by Commodore Matthew PERRY's fleet to the end of the American OCCUPATION of Japan following World War II, saw the two countries experimenting with different approaches to each other, sometimes successfully but at other times with disastrous consequences.

When they first came into contact in the 1850s, the two societies contrasted sharply. The Perry expedition brought about fundamental changes in Japan that, coupled with the transformation of American society that followed soon thereafter, ushered in several decades of harmonious, if still distant, relations between the two peoples. In the 1870s each was emerging as a "modern state," characterized by a unified national government, centralized armed forces, and progress toward industrialization and urbanization. In this process, the United States had hardly anything to learn from Japan, but the latter turned to America as well as to European nations for guidance. Individual Americans played important roles as government advisers and as teachers in the newly established universities and schools throughout Japan. Young Japanese men and women acquired their first knowledge of Western history, geography, mathematics, sciences, and religion from foreign teachers and visitors, among whom Americans were numerous, especially Protestant missionaries and secondary-school teachers (see FOREIGN EMPLOYEES OF THE MEIJI PERIOD). Likewise, young Japanese went abroad to study, and at this time more went to the United States than elsewhere.

But the development of a modernized Japan that devoted a higher portion of its resources (sometimes as much as 20 percent of its national income) to armament than did other countries was fated to complicate transpacific affairs. The United States, too, augmented its power and extended it westward toward the end of the century so as to emerge as an important factor in Asian-Pacific affairs. The SINO-JAPANESE WAR OF 1894–1895 was followed by the Spanish-American War of 1898, so that by the end of the decade both Japan and the United States had emerged as "great powers." Henceforth Japan and the United States would deal with each other not simply through trade or educational endeavors, but also with respect to naval strategies, colonies, and balances of power. Coincidentally, Japanese migration eastward also began at this time, first to the Hawaiian islands (see JAPANESE AMERICANS IN HAWAII) and then, after their annexation to the United States in 1898, to the West Coast as well. The number of Japanese there increased from about 20,000 in 1900 to more than 125,000 by 1907. The Japanese saw these settlers as forerunners of a still larger wave of emigrants to the United States, while Americans feared an unrestricted influx of Japanese workers.

The upshot of all these developments was to reverse the hitherto harmonious pattern of US-Japanese relations and to usher in a period of tension, misgiving, and crisis. Each country developed a naval battle fleet of sufficient size to be a potential threat to the other. After the RUSSO-JAPANESE WAR (1904–05), which annihilated the Russian fleet, each navy began devising war plans with the other as a hypothetical enemy. Economically, Japan was still among the poorest of modern nations. The realization of its relative poverty drove the country to colonial expansion, its leaders believing that whatever additional expenses this involved would be more than matched by the acquisition of new lands, resources, and markets. Japanese colonial administrators were determined to dominate the economies in Korea,

The Japanese flag is raised to mark Japan's admission to the UN in December 1956.

Taiwan, and southern Manchuria, territories added to the empire after the wars with China and Russia. In this process, they came into conflict with American merchants, bankers, and officials who sought an OPEN DOOR POLICY and protested against any infringement upon their equal access to markets.

The most serious aspect of the American-Japanese estrangement at that time, however, may have been cultural, in that there existed a heightened sense of mutual suspicion and misunderstanding. In part this was related to the immigration dispute. Americans often argued that the influx of immigrants from across the Pacific would debase the Western civilization that defined America (see "YELLOW PERIL"). The Japanese, because they believed themselves to be more "modern" or "Westernized" than other Asians, resented being labeled "oriental" or "yellow." Some Japanese, however, began talking of "Asia for Asians," which entailed developing a new identity for Asia distinct from Western civilization. The idea was vague but strong enough to impress on Americans the belief that the Japanese held firm to their cultural roots despite the veneer of Westernization.

It is clear that, during the first decades of the 20th century, the military, economic, and cultural dimensions of US-Japanese relations were creating a situation that boded ill for stability in Asia and the Pacific. Writers on both sides of the Pacific began publishing imaginary accounts of a US-Japanese war. The road to WORLD WAR II in the Pacific was not a direct one, however. During the 1920s both countries produced leadership—in the form of civilian bureaucrats, businessmen, and intellectuals—that was determined to put an end to the mutual antagonism and to redefine the bilateral relationship. These leaders supported naval disarmament agreements and at the same time did all they could to strengthen economic ties between the two countries. These ties were reinforced by social and cultural connections. To be sure, the 1924 immigration law (see UNITED STATES IMMIGRATION ACTS OF 1924, 1952, AND 1965), the so-called Oriental Exclusion Act, confirmed the US rejection of Japanese immigration and was a serious blow to the Japanese, but strong voices were heard within the United States condemning such an insensitive act, and the two governments began a quiet effort to have the law, if not repealed, then at least modified. In the meantime, serious efforts were undertaken by scholars, journalists, and artists on both sides to try to understand one another better, and Americans donated millions of dollars of relief goods

when Japan was hit by the TŌKYŌ EARTHQUAKE OF 1923.

The decade of the 1920s is also significant because the Japanese who grew up in those years and were affected by the Americanizing tendencies of the nation's life would emerge as influential leaders after World War II. Party politicians, businessmen, academic figures, journalists, bureaucrats, and others who had experienced the 1920s would reemerge after 1945 and be instrumental in redefining national life. Although their American counterparts did not share the same sense of the overriding importance of US-Japanese relations, they too would come to recall the 1920s fondly.

Unfortunately, the 1920s and the post-1945 years were separated by a 15-year period (1931–45) of renewed hostility culminating in World War II. It began with Japanese aggression in China and elsewhere. Despite apologetics and revisionist scholarship, the fact remains that the Japanese nation committed acts of unprovoked aggression and caused death and suffering to millions of Asians, Europeans, and Americans. The United States emerged as the major obstacle in the way of Japanese expansion in Asia.

The Japanese navy, chafing under the restrictions placed on it by various disarmament agreements (see LONDON NAVAL CONFERENCES), began calling for parity with the United States, and, when the latter rejected the demand, scrapped the agreements. After 1937 neither the United States nor Japan was bound by them, and both began rearming, each again considering the other a potential enemy. The Japanese army was determined to establish its control over Manchuria and, subsequently, most of China (see SINO-JAPANESE WAR OF 1937–1945). By 1940 the Japanese army came to view the United States as the major obstacle in the way of its victory in China. The United States started assisting China's war efforts from around 1938, and during 1940–41 the United States augmented its military forces in Hawaii and the Philippines.

The confrontation between the two countries became part of the global conflict when Japan signed the TRIPARTITE PACT with Germany and Italy in 1940 and a neutrality pact with the Soviet Union in 1941. The United States tied itself to Britain to prevent the latter's destruction, and it worked with the Chinese government and the Dutch East Indies to safeguard the status quo in the Asia-Pacific region (the ABCD alliance). When, in June 1941, Germany attacked the Soviet Union, Japan's dream of an Axis-Soviet partnership evaporated, while the United States, eager to prevent a Russian collapse, stepped up its pressure on Japan by freezing Japanese assets in the United States and imposing a de facto embargo on petroleum exports to Japan. Given this situation, the Japanese military, judging that time was running out, decided to strike at the ABCD.

Japanese civilians were also interested in establishing a sphere of self-sufficiency in East and Southeast Asia that would enable the nation to free itself from the vagaries of international economic conditions. There was a sense of urgency about this because of the world depression, which was driving nations to forsake economic internationalism for high tariffs, quotas, exchange control, devaluation, and imperial preferences. Japan followed suit, its leaders believing that the nation must ensure for itself stable sources of food, raw materials, and industrial goods and enough space to resettle farmers and others

hard hit by the economic crisis. The United States would not accept such a development and continued to insist on Japan's observance of the open door and other principles of economic multilateralism.

Japanese intellectuals became attracted to extremist alternatives such as fascism and communism. PAN-ASIANISM was eventually adopted as official doctrine, and, unlike its earlier manifestation, this time it had the widespread support of intellectual leaders, who embraced the vision of a new Asian cultural order pitting itself against what was believed to be a decaying Western civilization. Americans responded to the Japanese challenge ideologically by defining the US-Japanese relationship as a conflict of irreconcilable ideas.

Accommodation became increasingly difficult in the late 1930s and the early 1940s because the bilateral relationship merged into a global struggle between two hostile camps, the Axis and the democracies (and their not-so-democratic allies such as China and the Soviet Union). Even so, an American-Japanese war might have been averted if Tōkyō had been willing to reverse course, accept the open door in principle, and reduce Japanese military presence in China. But to do so would have taken a new leadership in Tōkyō, and it would seem that no one, not even the emperor, knew who the new leaders might be who could achieve such a feat. It would take four years of strenuous and disastrous fighting in the Pacific and on the Asian continent before such a leadership would emerge and, prodded by American Occupation authorities, undertake necessary reforms so as to restore national politics and policies to what they had been when the bilateral relationship had been more compatible.

The Last Forty Years (1952–1990s)

Japan's defeat and the destruction of its military power meant that new arrangements for the maintenance of order and security in the Asia-Pacific region had to be worked out, and the United States took the lead in defining them. This effort entailed a partial replacement of Japanese power with American power, with US naval bases established in the western Pacific, its land forces stationed on the Asian continent, and airfields built in the Philippines, Japan, and elsewhere. The United States, in effect, became the dominant power in the Pacific and part of Asia and from now on would seek to preserve the postwar status quo. Because the Soviet Union and then China would come to be seen as challenging this status quo, the United States would enter into various agreements and alliances with Asian and Pacific nations in order to contain the Soviet Union, China, and their allies, such as North Korea and North Vietnam.

Japan was but a passive participant in the drama, first because it had no say in the matter while it was occupied by Allied (mostly United States) forces, and then, after the SAN FRANCISCO PEACE TREATY of 1951, because it exchanged an end to the Occupation for a security treaty with the United States that gave the latter the right to continue to station bases and troops in Japan. The postwar Japanese leadership on the whole welcomed the arrangement, determined as it was not to repeat the disasters of the 1930s and the 1940s. After regaining independence in 1952, Japan resumed modest armament programs, devoting a small fraction of its national income to defense. Fundamentally, however, Japan

Trade between Japan and the United States

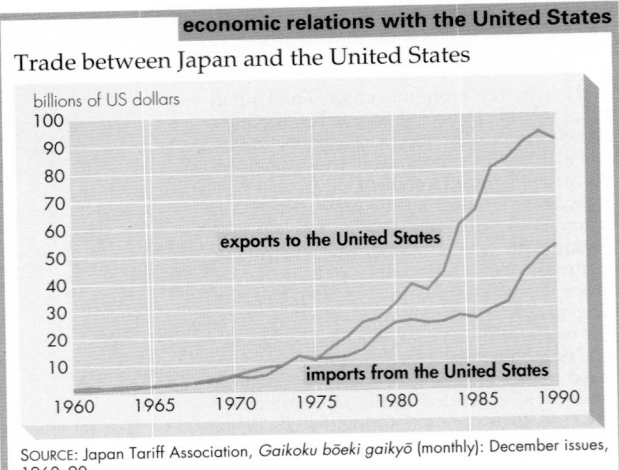

billions of US dollars

exports to the United States

imports from the United States

SOURCE: Japan Tariff Association, *Gaikoku bōeki gaikyō* (monthly): December issues, 1960–90.

continued to look to the United States for protection; the revised security treaties of 1960 and 1970 (see UNITED STATES–JAPAN SECURITY TREATIES) specifically mentioned America's obligation to defend Japanese security, in return for which Japan would continue to provide bases and facilities for American military personnel.

The American alliance enabled Japan to focus on economic recovery and growth. Although during the initial phase of the Occupation the United States supported a policy of exacting huge amounts of reparation payments from Japan, soon Washington changed its stance and came to view Japanese economic rehabilitation and development as an important means of preventing the spread of Soviet- or Chinese-supported radicalism. Reindustrialization and export trade were encouraged, and already by the mid-1950s Japan had regained its prewar level of economic performance. The United States further assisted Japan's recovery through nearly half a billion dollars' worth of purchases of Japanese goods during the KOREAN WAR (1950–54) and through its support of Japan's entry into GATT (General Agreement on Trade and Tariffs). Above all, by sponsoring the establishment and maintenance of a liberal international economic order, the United States, as the postwar "hegemon," made it possible for Japan to reenter the world economic arena.

The tempo of Japanese economic growth accelerated during the 1960s, again aided by American procurement orders during the Vietnam War and by Washington's high-growth policy, which aimed at expanding consumer spending as well as world trade. Japan's successful "income-doubling" policy was possible because the United States welcomed it and even acquiesced to Tōkyō's policy of "separation of politics and economics," under which Japan expanded its trade with China while refraining from dealing officially with the government in Beijing (Peking). It would be fair to say that Japan's almost single-minded devotion to economic growth was a major achievement of postwar US-Japanese relations.

Japan's postwar democratization was induced by the American Occupation authorities, but it is important to note that even after the end of the Occupation many features of the liberal reforms remained. This occurred because the prewar liberal, internationalist leadership regained positions of influence after the war and because the postwar generations self-consciously partook of American culture, including education, scholarship, and ways of life. More than 3,000 Japanese went to the United States to study in the 1950s; most of them became political, business, and scholarly leaders of Japan. Likewise, much as in the Meiji period (1868–1912), thousands of American missionaries, educators, and travelers went to Japan, helping Japan to regain self-respect and self-identity after its people had been shattered by the war. Already in the early 1960s, Edwin O. REISCHAUER, the American ambassador in Tōkyō, was referring to US-Japanese relations as a "partnership." Although it was not exactly a partnership of equals, there was widespread agreement that the two peoples had indeed come to share a great deal in common: their commitment to regional security, to economic internationalism, and to democracy.

Since 1970 US-Japanese relations have retained much of this pattern of mutuality, but the story has become vastly more complex because of changes in the two countries and in the world arena. American military superiority over Japan has remained, as has the presumption of American protection of Japanese security. But the US-Japanese alliance has undergone subtle changes reflective of the rapid shifts in Asian (and global) international affairs. To the extent that the years since 1970 or thereabout have been marked by a great-power détente, a solid military alliance has seemed less urgent. In 1972 both the United States and Japan established diplomatic relations with the People's Republic of China, a sure indication that geopolitical realities were changing. The US-Japanese alliance would now be linked to the two countries' developing ties to China. Although they would continue to view the Soviet Union as the primary object of the alliance, the US-Soviet détente would come to force rethinking as well.

Even more serious has been the economic aspect of the American-Japanese relationship in the last 20 years. The 1970s saw tremendous instability in world financial and economic conditions, exemplified by such landmarks as the collapse of the Bretton Woods system, petroleum shortages, and double-digit inflation. By then Japan had emerged as a major economic power; its gross national product (GNP) had approached the level of the more advanced European countries, and its share in world trade had approached 10 percent. But its dependence on the United States, if anything, deepened now that all the industrial economies were afflicted with severe problems. To control its inflation, obtain needed petroleum and other resources, and maintain a stable value for its currency, Japan had to rely on the United States to continue to open its doors to Japanese goods, to sell Japan what it needed, and to take the lead in the world economy to restore some semblance of order. The United States in fact did all of these things, which, coupled with Japan's aggressive efforts at industrial rationalization, helped Japan enter the 1980s with an even higher degree of competitiveness than earlier. The United States, on the other hand, began to suffer huge trade deficits.

The 1980s, in fact, witnessed sharply contrasting economic performances on the part of Japan and the United States. The former went on to accumulate trade surpluses, thanks to a considerable degree to the continued openness of the American market; for instance, between 1981 and 1986 Japanese exports to the United States increased from $38 billion to $82 billion, whereas its imports from the United States amounted to $22 billion and $27 billion, respectively. It was this sort of record that led to the first serious trade friction between the two countries. Earlier, American manufacturers of cotton textiles and cameras had complained of the influx of cheap Japanese goods, but their overall impact on the US economy had been limited. Now, however, it was Japanese automobiles, electronics, semiconductors, and other products of high technology that threatened to challenge the long-sustained American supremacy. Negotiations began for voluntary quotas and other agreements to keep Japanese imports under some control. Even so, the government in Washington strenuously opposed measures to adopt a policy of managed trade that would run counter to the principle of free enterprise. At the same time, the United States began strongly insisting that Japan also honor the free trade principle.

Huge trade deficits, coupled with accumulating governmental debts (due to increased armament spending and to the lowering of taxes), invited foreign loans and investment in the United States and in 1987 turned it into a net debtor nation for the first time since World War I. Japan accounted for about 20 percent of America's foreign debt, a startling development considering that only a decade or two earlier the picture had been the reverse. In a sense, Japanese loans, combined with funds from Britain, the Netherlands, and elsewhere, financed federal and local programs in the United States. In time, Japanese capital would make itself conspicuous in the private sector as well. At first taking the form of direct investment—the establishment of auto-manufacturing plants was the most graphic example—it soon extended into other areas, including the purchasing of real estate, golf courses, banks, and other businesses in the United States. Added to the visibility of Japanese-made automobiles, stereo systems, personal computers, and other items, the appearance of Japanese-owned companies and buildings created misgivings, even negative feelings, among the American people. They were appalled to recognize that Japan, at least at the current rate of exchange, was surpassing the United States in per capita income, that Japanese real estate prices were so high that the total value of land in Japan was greater than that of the United States, and that the Japanese were using their abundant funds not to improve the quality of life at home but to buy up businesses abroad.

This was a new phenomenon. In the past Japan had presented a security threat to the United States, and Japanese immigrants had been criticized for depriving American workers of jobs because the Japanese were willing to work for low wages. Now, however, it was the fear of Japanese economic power that created uneasiness. It was difficult to devise effective countermeasures as long as the United States kept its doors open to Japanese loans and investment, but to shut the doors would militate against the country's policy on free enterprise. Should the United States still abide by its traditional values but make an exception in the case of Japan, treating it as a kind of menace and applying to it a particular set of policies? Should it be assumed that the interests of the two countries were not complementary, as had long been thought, but in fact contradictory?

Evidently, US-Japanese relations are at a crossroads. The history of the bilateral relationship has undergone many shifts and turns, and undoubtedly there will be many more. It would seem that one thread that runs through the relationship's history is the theme of intertwined destinies. This has sometimes created tension, friction, and conflict, but at other times it has brought about economic interdependence and cultural interpenetration, conducive to shared consciousness and common concerns. If the two peoples can somehow reinforce this latter tradition and minimize the former, they will be contributing not only to their own stable relationship but also to a more congenial world community.

United States armed forces in Japan 在日米軍

(*zainichi beigun*). American military forces stationed in Japan under the provisions of the UNITED STATES–JAPAN SECURITY TREATIES. Article 5 of the treaty of 1960 states: "Each party recognizes that an armed attack against either party in the territories under the administration of Japan would be dangerous to its own peace and safety." This provision is the basis of the United States' obligation to render military assistance for Japan's defense and Japan's obligation to provide the Americans with the necessary land facilities for bases and services.

As a result of the 1957 Kishi-Eisenhower joint declaration, the US Army withdrew its combat divisions from Japan, leaving only supply and maintenance corps. The Fifth Air Force, which is responsible for the air defense of Japan and South Korea, is stationed at Yokota. The Seventh Fleet maintains two supply and repair bases at Yokosuka and Sasebo. Army headquarters in Zama, navy headquarters in Yokosuka. The commander of the US armed forces in Japan represents the three branches of the military and coordinates their activities. In 1952, when the first security treaty was put into effect, 260,000 American military personnel were in Japan, not counting Okinawa. In 1988 there were 49,800 US servicemen in Japan, including Okinawa. The breakdown was as follows: 2,100 army, 7,900 navy, 22,800 marines, 16,400 air force, and 600 others. The American military has jurisdiction over incidents, accidents, and crimes involving on-duty servicemen, and Japan has jurisdiction over those involving off-duty servicemen.

At the insistence of the Japanese, US forces have gradually reduced the number of bases in Japan. The United States has asked that Japan take responsibility for part of the expense of maintaining Japanese employees on American bases, and Japan has increased its share of the financial burden. See also UNITED STATES MILITARY BASES, DISPUTES OVER.

United States, economic relations with 日米経済関係

(*nichibei keizai kankei*). The economic relationship between Japan and the United States continues to increase in complexity and importance. In 1990 Japan was the second largest buyer, after Canada, of US products (12 percent) and the largest source of US imports (18 percent). The same year the United States was the largest buyer of Japanese products (31 percent) and the largest source of Japanese imports (22 percent).

According to MINISTRY OF FINANCE statistics, US direct investment in Japan was US $664 million in the fiscal year ending March 1990. In contrast, Japanese direct investment in the United States that year was US $26.1 billion.

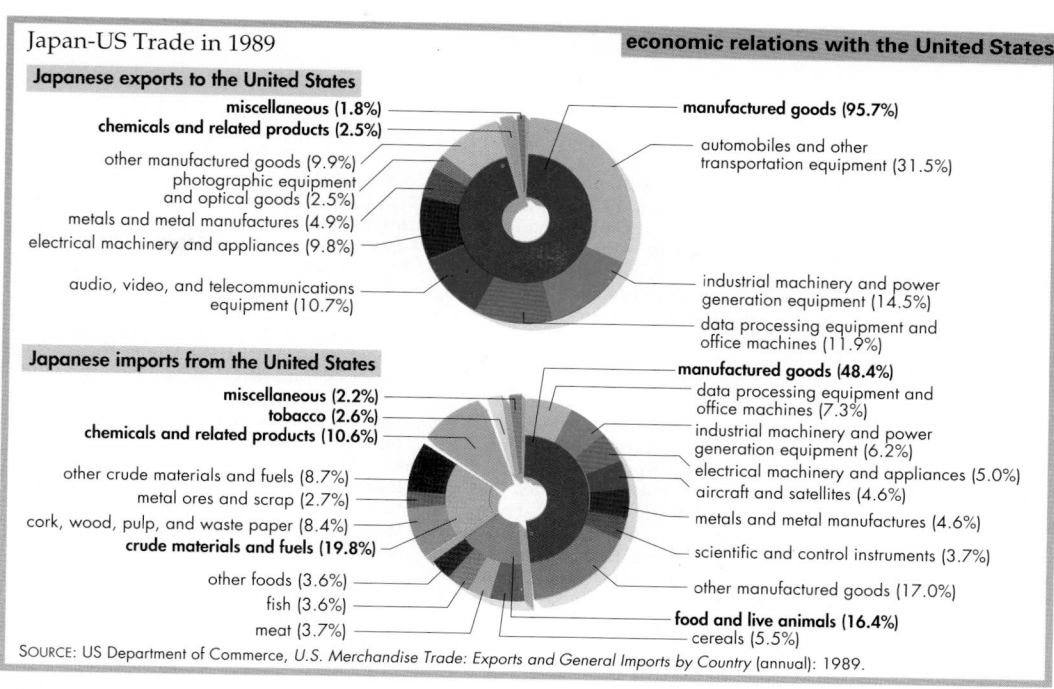

Japan-US Trade in 1989

Japanese exports to the United States

- miscellaneous (1.8%)
- chemicals and related products (2.5%)
- other manufactured goods (9.9%)
- photographic equipment and optical goods (2.5%)
- metals and metal manufactures (4.9%)
- electrical machinery and appliances (9.8%)
- audio, video, and telecommunications equipment (10.7%)
- manufactured goods (95.7%)
- automobiles and other transportation equipment (31.5%)
- industrial machinery and power generation equipment (14.5%)
- data processing equipment and office machines (11.9%)

Japanese imports from the United States

- miscellaneous (2.2%)
- tobacco (2.6%)
- chemicals and related products (10.6%)
- other crude materials and fuels (8.7%)
- metal ores and scrap (2.7%)
- cork, wood, pulp, and waste paper (8.4%)
- crude materials and fuels (19.8%)
- other foods (3.6%)
- fish (3.6%)
- meat (3.7%)
- manufactured goods (48.4%)
- data processing equipment and office machines (7.3%)
- industrial machinery and power generation equipment (6.2%)
- electrical machinery and appliances (5.0%)
- aircraft and satellites (4.6%)
- metals and metal manufactures (4.6%)
- scientific and control instruments (3.7%)
- other manufactured goods (17.0%)
- food and live animals (16.4%)
- cereals (5.5%)

SOURCE: US Department of Commerce, *U.S. Merchandise Trade: Exports and General Imports by Country* (annual): 1989.

The Japan-US trade balance favored the United States until 1964, but since then the United States has generally run a trade deficit with Japan. The deficit increased rapidly from 1981 to 1987, when it peaked at US $52.1 billion; it began declining in 1988 and fell to US $38.0 billion in 1990. Causes for the decline include Japan's expanding domestic demand and the increase in the value of the yen that followed the PLAZA ACCORD in 1985.

Japan and the United States have a highly interdependent economic relationship that is fundamentally cordial, but not without tension. Trade disputes are driven by increasing levels of international economic activity, greater parity in economic power, and the chronic Japan-US trade imbalance. Trade in high-technology goods has been a particularly contentious issue in recent years.

Trade negotiations have begun to move beyond product-specific talks to discussions of structural impediments in the Japanese market. In the past these impediments were considered a domestic issue in Japan, but a deepening sense of crisis in the Japan-US economic relationship has brought them into the international negotiating arena.

Issues through the 1970s—The first postwar trade dispute between the United States and Japan occurred in the mid-1950s over textile trade. In this period textiles were Japan's largest-volume export item. Trade tensions rose as the United States began to import large quantities of inexpensive Japanese textiles, and the US textile industry launched an import restriction campaign in 1955. The Japan–United States Cotton Agreement was concluded in 1957, with Japan agreeing to VOLUNTARY EXPORT RESTRICTIONS on cotton goods. This trade agreement was expanded to include wool and synthetic fibers in January 1972.

Steel was the next major trade issue. In 1967 some US congressmen began to call for compulsory import quotas on foreign steel. This was a factor leading to a three-year agreement negotiated through the US Department of State that was signed in 1969 and that set up a system of voluntary restrictions on Japan and the steel-exporting countries of Europe. The agreement was extended through 1974 and then allowed to lapse, partially as a result of a suit by the Consumers Union of the United States, which charged that the agreement violated antitrust law.

Steel reemerged as a trade issue in 1976 after a sudden increase in the volume of Japanese steel exports to the United States. A dumping suit was filed against Japanese steel producers in September 1977. The Japanese producers were willing to accept voluntary export restrictions, but the US government preferred the introduction of a price trigger mechanism. Under the mechanism instituted in 1978, dumping investigations were initiated automatically if steel prices fell below standards based on the production costs of the world's most efficient producers. Japan's steel exports to the United States declined as a result of this agreement, with peak volume at 7.4 million metric tons (8.2 million short tons) in 1976.

A dumping suit against Japanese color television manufacturers was filed in 1968, followed by various additional suits between 1970 and 1977. These ranged from requests for countervailing duties to charges that restraints violated US antitrust law. President Jimmy Carter concluded an orderly marketing agreement with the Japanese government in May 1977 that guaranteed a three-year period of voluntary export restrictions on the part of Japanese manufacturers.

Partly as a result of the protracted negotiations over color televisions, Japanese producers began to recognize the need to relocate a portion of their manufacturing activities to the United States. Eight color television manufacturers established US production facilities between 1972 and 1980. As a result Japanese exports of color televisions to the United States dropped dramatically, and the orderly marketing agreement was allowed to expire in June 1980.

Agricultural products were part of the General Agreement on Tariffs and Trade (GATT) agenda at the Tōkyō Round of trade talks held between 1973 and 1979. The United States requested full liberalization of Japan's beef and orange markets. Intense bilateral negotiations on this point began in September 1977 and resulted in the Ushiba-Strauss agreement to expand Japan's import quotas in these categories. This agreement was concluded in January 1978, even though the United States continued to press for full liberalization. Another compromise agreement, resulting in a further expansion of import quotas, was reached in December 1978.

1659

Issues after 1980 — Japan's share of the US auto market rose from 9.3 percent in 1976 to 21.3 percent in 1980, when sales totaled 1.8 million vehicles. In response the United Automobile, Aerospace and Agricultural Implement Workers of America (UAW) and Ford Motor Co filed a suit with the US International Trade Commission (ITC) seeking import relief. In this same period the US Congress introduced a resolution recommending a market-share agreement with Japan. A three-year voluntary export restriction agreement was concluded in May 1981 and has been continuously renewed. These restrictions have been set at 2.3 million vehicles per year since April 1985.

Since 1981 the United States has requested a simplification of Japan's import inspection procedures and improvements in its standards and certification system. Japan's first concessions in this area came in May 1982 when the Diet approved the amendment of 17 codes governing the standards and certification system.

In the 1980s US pressure to open Japan's financial services markets to participation by foreign firms increased. Considerable progress has been made in this area, and in overall financial market deregulation, since a Ministry of Finance policy report on financial liberalization and yen internationalization was issued in May 1984. Several US securities firms now have brokerage operations in Tōkyō.

In July 1985 the Japanese government adopted a package of market-opening measures called the Action Program. However, trade friction continued to worsen even as the Nakasone administration attempted to fulfill its commitment to structural reform in line with the proposals set out in the MAEKAWA REPORT of April 1986.

The Japan–United States Semiconductor Agreement was concluded in September 1986. The agreement was designed to monitor prices, guard against dumping in the US market, and raise the market share in Japan of foreign-made semiconductors. The United States was dissatisfied with Japan's performance under this agreement and introduced sanctions against Japan in March 1987, but most of these sanctions were discontinued the same year.

In response to complaints brought by the United States charging Japan with GATT infractions in 12 of 22 agricultural and marine product categories, in February 1988 GATT authorities determined that Japan was in violation in 10 product categories. The Japanese government pledged to liberalize 8 of these completely by April 1990, but withheld liberalization in the 2 categories of starch and milk products. An agreement was signed in 1988 that led to the end of beef and orange import quotas in April 1991, although tariffs were then raised to protect domestic producers during a transition period.

Rice is another area of ongoing trade disputes between Japan and the United States. The US Rice Millers Association filed suits against Japan in 1986 and 1988, claiming damage to US rice producers as a result of the closed Japanese rice market. Through negotiations the US trade representative (USTR) agreed to drop the suit on the condition that rice be added to the GATT agenda at the URUGUAY ROUND. Japan agreed, taking the position that the rice issue should be taken up in a multilateral forum.

The MOSS (Market-Oriented Sector-Selective) talks began in January 1985 (see MOSS TALKS). The first round ran one year and covered the sectors of telecommunications, electronics, pharmaceuticals, medical equipment, and forest products. Transportation equipment was added to the MOSS agenda in 1986, resulting in a second round that concluded in 1987.

The Omnibus Trade and Competitiveness Act was approved by both houses of the US Congress in April 1988. Under the so-called Super 301 provision of this law, the United States targeted supercomputers, satellites, and wood products as sectors where negotiations were needed to open the Japanese market. The law requires the United States to impose unilateral penalties if the negotiations fail. Japan opposes further talks on these sectors on grounds that the unilateral sanctions provided under Super 301 are nonnegotiable.

Structural impediments in the Japanese market do not fall within the Super 301 framework. They have been discussed separately at the STRUCTURAL IMPEDIMENTS INITIATIVE TALKS, which began in September 1989. These talks target structural problems in both the Japanese and US economies. A report was prepared in June 1990 at the fifth and final round of the first phase of the talks. This report included measures to be taken by Japan such as expansion of public investment, improvements in application of the LARGE-SCALE RETAIL STORES LAW, and strengthening of ANTIMONOPOLY LAW provisions and their enforcement. The report also specified actions for the United States to take, such as increasing efforts to reduce its budget deficit.

United States education missions to Japan アメリカ教育使節団

(Amerika kyōiku shisetsudan). Missions that visited Japan in March 1946 and August 1950, at the invitation of the OCCUPATION authorities, to evaluate the Japanese educational system. Their reports contributed to postwar educational reform (see EDUCATIONAL REFORMS OF 1947). The first mission was composed of 27 educational specialists headed by G. D. Stoddard. It relied largely on data prepared by the CIVIL INFORMATION AND EDUCATION SECTION OF SCAP, but through the cooperation of a Japanese group that later became the EDUCATION REFORM COUNCIL, it was also able to inspect the schools at firsthand. The mission recommended greater flexibility in the educational system, greater emphasis on learning through experience, the establishment of local school administrations, the adoption of a 6-3-3 system on the American model, coeducation, and greater access to higher education. The second mission, headed by W. E. Givens, studied the implementation of the reforms recommended four years earlier.

United States Immigration Acts of 1924, 1952, and 1965 アメリカ合衆国移民法

(Amerika Gasshūkoku Iminhō). Prior to 1924, immigration from Japan to the United States was governed largely by the GENTLEMEN'S AGREEMENT of 1907–08. The Immigration Act of 1924 denied admission as permanent immigrants to all "aliens ineligible to citizenship," a concept derived from the naturalization act of 1870, thus depriving Japan of a quota for immigration. This provision of the law was based upon race, not nationality.

The so-called McCarran-Walter Act of 1952 retained a modified form of the national origins quota system established in 1924 but amended the nationality act so that neither race nor ethnicity was a bar to becoming a US citizen. Children of Japanese immigrants who were born in the United States or its territories, the *nisei*, were and remained citizens. However, the same 1952 act provided for several categories of persons who were to be treated as "nonquota" entrants. These categories included wives of US citizens, mainly Occupation brides, and certain close relatives of US citizens. From 1952 to 1960, when only 800 quota spaces were allocated to Japan, some 40,000 Japanese actually migrated to the United States. The 1965 immigration act scrapped completely the national origins quota system while limiting total annual immigration to about 400,000 per year. See also JAPANESE AMERICANS.

United States–Japan Administrative Agreement 日米行政協定

(Nichibei Gyōsei Kyōtei). Formally entitled the Administrative Agreement under Article 3 of the Security Treaty between the United States and Japan, the agreement concerned the status of the US armed forces stationed in Japan under the treaty. The agreement was signed on 28 February 1952 and became effective together with the security treaty on 28 April 1952. In the agreement Japan agreed to grant the United States the use of facilities and land necessary to carry out the treaty. The agreement also specified the rights, powers, and authority of the United States in its military facilities; conditions for the entry into Japan of vessels, aircraft, members of the armed forces, and civilians attached to the military and their dependents; exemption from customs duties and taxes; extent of criminal and civil jurisdictions; and other matters.

The agreement became the subject of public controversy in Japan. Critics believed that it conferred excessive freedom of action on the US armed forces and made it possible for the United States to involve Japan in a conflict that Japan did not support. They also cited the fact that the agreement had not been submitted to the Japanese Diet for approval and that the jurisdictional privileges accorded the United States were broader in scope than those contained in similar US agreements with NATO countries.

A number of these problems were resolved in the years following the signing of the agreement. In a protocol signed on 29 September 1953 the scope of jurisdiction was revised to conform to NATO standards. A new document, known as the Status of Forces Agreement (Nichibei Chii Kyōtei), became effective with a new security treaty on 23 June 1960 after being approved by the Diet. The new arangements more clearly specified the requirement of prior consultation before the activation of US forces based in Japan. See also UNITED STATES ARMED FORCES IN JAPAN; UNITED STATES–JAPAN SECURITY TREATIES; UNITED STATES MILITARY BASES, DISPUTES OVER.

United States–Japan Commercial Treaty of 1858→Harris Treaty

United States–Japan Mutual Defense Assistance Agreement 日米相互防衛援助協定

(Nichibei Sōgo Bōei Enjo Kyōtei). Often called the MSA or Mutual Security Agreement. Signed on 8 March 1954 in Tōkyō, the agreement was intended to reinforce the United States–Japan Security Treaty of 1951 (see UNITED STATES–JAPAN SECURITY TREATIES) and to provide a legal basis for the United States to furnish Japan with military equipment and technology. It stated that the United States would make available military equipment and services to help Japan assume increasing responsibility for its own defense. Pursuant to the agreement, the United States established a military assistance advisory group in Japan. Under a related agreement, the United States granted to Japan $10 million from the sale of agricultural commodities to be used to develop Japan's defense industry and economic capacities. See also IKEDA-ROBERTSON TALKS.

United States–Japan security treaties 日米安全保障条約

(*nichibei anzen hoshō jōyaku*; abbreviated *ampo jōyaku*). A term encompassing both the United States–Japan Security Treaty (Nichibei Anzen Hoshō Jōyaku; abbreviated Ampo Jōyaku), which was signed at San Francisco on 8 September 1951 and implemented on 28 April 1952, and the successor Treaty of Mutual Cooperation and Security between the United States and Japan (Nichibei Sōgo Kyōryoku oyobi Anzen Hoshō Jōyaku; also abbreviated Ampo Jōyaku), which was signed at Washington on 19 January 1960 and has been in effect since 23 June 1960.

The Treaty of 1952—This treaty is inseparable from the SAN FRANCISCO PEACE TREATY and was the offspring of the cold war between the United States and the Soviet Union. In the first period of the postwar Allied OCCUPATION, General Douglas MACARTHUR, as supreme commander for the Allied powers (SCAP), thoroughly carried out the complete disarmament of Japan required by the Potsdam Declaration. In 1947 MacArthur announced that the objectives of the Occupation had been essentially achieved and that it was time to prepare a treaty of peace with Japan.

With the deterioration of relations between the two superpowers, US concern focused increasingly on the question of how to assure Japan's post-Occupation security from direct or indirect attack. Rearmament was unpopular within Japan, and its constitutionality—even for self-defense—had not yet been determined by the Supreme Court. A guarantee by the Allied nations of the security of a neutral Japan appeared too risky as long as mistrust prevailed between the United States and the Soviet Union. The remaining option was the retention of US forces in Japan after it regained sovereignty. Continuation of the US military presence in Japan was, however, certain to be unacceptable to the communist nations. In Japan the idea of "inviolable neutrality" guaranteed by the victor nations was favored by the people and, initially, by the government. The JAPAN SOCIALIST PARTY established four principles of peace, namely, settlements with all former enemies, neutrality, no military treaties with any country or military bases in Japan of another country, and no rearmament.

The outbreak of the KOREAN WAR in 1950 influenced US as well as Japanese thinking about a peace treaty. Negotiations between John Foster DULLES, President Harry Truman's personal representative, and Prime Minister YOSHIDA SHIGERU led to a basic agreement on the retention of US forces on bases in Japan under terms to be stipulated in a separate bilateral security treaty that would come into effect at the same time as the peace treaty. This solution became more palatable to the majority of the Japanese people, who decided, after the events in Korea, that the idea of neutrality had been unrealistic.

The security treaty was an extremely short framework of general principles, while the most difficult details were spelled out in the accompanying UNITED STATES–JAPAN ADMINISTRATIVE AGREEMENT. The treaty's preamble states that maintenance of US armed forces in and about Japan is legally justified by Japan's right to enter into collective security arrangements and the principle of the United Nations charter that all nations possess an inherent right of individual and collective self-defense. The main part of the treaty consists of five articles. Article 1 sets forth the agreement to station US forces in and about Japan to contribute to the maintenance of international peace and security and to the security of Japan against armed attack. Article 2 prohibits Japan from granting any bases or other military privileges to any third power without prior US consent. Article 3 delegates the implementation of the treaty pertaining to the stationing of US forces to administrative agreements. Article 4 makes the expiration of the treaty dependent upon agreement by both countries that other provisions for the maintenance of Japan's security have come into force. Article 5 stipulates that the treaty will come into force when instruments of ratification have been exchanged at Washington.

Ratification by the Japanese Diet took place on 19 November 1951. In the United States the president signed the security and peace treaties on 15 April 1952 after Senate ratification. The exchange of ratifications took place on 28 April 1952, the date both pacts took effect.

The Treaty of 1960—In the fall of 1958 the Japanese government under the premiership of KISHI NOBUSUKE proposed a liberalization of the security treaty. By this time Japan had achieved a considerable economic recovery, strengthened its military power through the establishment of the SELF DEFENSE FORCES, and been admitted to the United Nations. The United States, recognizing the need to render the treaty more equal and reciprocal, concluded with Japan a new Treaty of Cooperation and Security, which was signed in Washington on 19 January 1960 and implemented on 23 June 1960. An improved Status of Forces Agreement replaced the Administrative Agreement.

The 1960 treaty emphasizes peaceful intentions even more than the 1952 treaty and adds economic cooperation as an objective. The treaty omits the most objectionable features of its predecessor, such as interference in case of domestic riots and the ban on granting military rights to third nations. It explicitly commits the United States to "act to meet the common danger" in case of an armed attack in Japanese territories (art. 5), or in other words to defend Japan. Furthermore, by exchange of notes on the day the treaty was signed, the United States agreed, in consideration of Japanese sensitivity to atomic weapons, to prior consultation in case of "major changes in the deployment into Japan of US armed forces, major changes in their equipment and the use of facilities and areas in Japan as bases for combat operations to be undertaken other than those conducted under article 5 of the said treaty." However, as of 1990 the provision has never been exercised.

The United States–Japan Joint Committee, the consulting instrument for the Administrative Agreement, was continued under the Status of Forces Agreement. A higher-level Security Consultative Committee for the treaty replaced a similar one established in 1957. Finally, the expiration of the treaty is no longer dependent upon mutual agreement. Beginning 10 years after the implementation of the treaty, either party may give notice to the other of its intention to terminate it, and expiration will become effective a year later.

The date of assembling the House to consider the treaty was chosen in expectation of President Dwight Eisenhower's visit to Tōkyō, scheduled for 19 June 1960. Since ratification by the Diet would automatically become effective after 30 days, Prime Minister Kishi was eager to obtain it on 20 May at any price. There was continuous wrangling in various Diet committees, but Kishi finally rammed the approval through in a plenary session shortly after midnight on 20 May. The opposition parties, unaware that the majority party was voting for the treaty, had not been provided an opportunity for counterarguments.

This surprise move provoked a wild uproar, and now the target was not only the treaty, but also the premier. The streets of Tōkyō were suddenly filled with mass demonstrations by hundreds of thousands of ordinary citizens. The radical ZENGAKUREN (a federation of student associations) organized the most extensive and vociferous protests. The situation seemed chaotic, and the government had to cancel Eisenhower's visit, since his security could not be guaranteed. Kishi flew to Washington, where the exchange of the instruments of ratification took place. Upon his return, in the face of continuing criticism, Kishi announced his resignation.

After the treaty came into force and Kishi was replaced as prime minister by IKEDA HAYATO, the storm of protest dissipated surprisingly quickly, and the United States–Japan alliance grew more stable. After the escalation of US involvement in the Vietnam War, however, opposition to the treaty became linked with the antiwar movement and the effort to win the return of OKINAWA. Between 1965 and 1970, numerous large demonstrations were held against the treaty; these activities escalated in 1969 in anticipation of Japan's right to end the treaty in 1970. The SATŌ-NIXON COMMUNIQUÉ, issued in 1969, defused the protests by announcing the agreement to return Okinawa to Japan. The communiqué also reaffirmed US-Japanese ties in the region by announcing Japan's recognition that the security of Taiwan and South Korea is closely linked to its own security. The US military presence was later substantially reduced and made less conspicuous. This relieved tensions, and the end of the Vietnam War further defused the security treaty as a controversial political issue, both within Japan and between Japan and the United States. See also PEACE MOVEMENT; UNITED STATES MILITARY BASES, DISPUTES OVER.

United States–Japan Status of Forces Agreement → United States–Japan Administrative Agreement

United States–Japan Treaty of Amity, 1854 → Kanagawa Treaty

mission of 1860 to the United States
This Japanese diplomatic mission was sent to Washington, DC, to ratify the Harris Treaty. **1** The delegation received a grand reception in New York City. In this newspaper photo, members of the mission parade down Broadway in horse-drawn carriages. **2** The storm-tossed *Kanrin maru*, which accompanied the American ship that carried the mission, is depicted in this painting by Suzufuji Yūjirō, a member of the mission.

United States military bases, disputes over 基地問題

(*kichi mondai*). In Japan as of 1990 there were 105 US military bases occupying a total of 324.7 square kilometers (125.4 sq mi). The largest concentration of bases and personnel was in Okinawa Prefecture. The most important US military bases included the air bases at Yokota, Atsugi, Iwakuni, Kadena, and Futemma; the naval bases at Yokosuka and Sasebo; the maneuver area at Fuji; and the communications bases at Sobe, Misawa, Tokachibuto, and Iōjima.

After 1945 most of the existing Japanese military bases were taken over by the OCCUPATION authorities, that is, the US military, which also established new bases that were used during the Korean War (1950–53). Since rents for use of the bases and subsidies to surrounding areas were minimal, the discontent of the residents was great.

Even after the signing of the San Francisco Peace Treaty in 1951, under the terms of the UNITED STATES–JAPAN SECURITY TREATIES the US military continued to maintain bases in Japan. The few that were returned were taken over by the NATIONAL POLICE RESERVE, newly formed in 1950. (The National Police Reserve was reorganized as the NATIONAL SAFETY FORCES in 1952 and as the SELF DEFENSE FORCES in 1954.)

Popular opposition and resentment against the low rents for bases, accidents involving injury to Japanese citizens and property for which the United States paid no compensation, the noise caused by US aircraft, and the presence of nuclear weapons were strongest in Okinawa, which remained under military occupation until 1972 and where US bases were used during US involvement in the Vietnam War (1965–73). In ratifying the return of Okinawa from the United States, the Japanese House of Representatives in 1972 passed a resolution extending the Three Nonnuclear Principles (not to manufacture, possess, or allow the introduction of nuclear weapons; see HIKAKU SANGENSOKU) to Okinawa, along with a demand for reduction of the number of US bases there. The United States accordingly

removed Mace B missiles and B-52 bombers before reversion took place in May 1972, although accusations persisted that hidden nuclear weapons remained. In the 1980s, however, the United States reaffirmed the importance of its military bases in Okinawa, and today they are the keystone of its strategic forces in the Far East. See also UNITED STATES ARMED FORCES IN JAPAN.

United States, mission of 1860 to 万延遣米使節

(Man'en Kembei Shisetsu). The 81-man shogunate mission sent to Washington, DC, to ratify the United States–Japan Treaty of Amity and Commerce of 1858 (HARRIS TREATY). The group of shogunate officials and domain representatives, led by SHIMMI MASAOKI, MURAGAKI NORIMASA, and OGURI TADAMASA, left Japan in January 1860 aboard the American warship *Powhatan.* The KANRIN MARU, a Dutch-built ship with a Japanese crew captained by KATSU KAISHŪ, accompanied the *Powhatan* to San Francisco. The young FUKUZAWA YUKICHI was also on board as one of the mission's interpreters.

In Washington the mission met with President James Buchanan and exchanged documents on 17 May. Of particular interest to the Japanese was the upcoming presidential election that was to result in victory for Abraham Lincoln; they were greatly impressed by the ballot system. The mission left the United States in August 1860. The travel logs and diaries of the members of the mission have been collected in the seven-volume *Man'en gannen kembei shisetsu shiryō shūsei* (1962–63).

Unitika, Ltd ユニチカ[株]

(Yunichika). Comprehensive textile company engaged in the manufacture of cotton and woolen yarn and synthetic fibers. It traces its origins to a cotton-spinning company founded in 1889. It took its present form in 1969. The company has joint ventures in Brazil, Thailand, Indonesia, and Hong Kong. Sales for the fiscal year ending March 1991 totaled ¥294.1 billion (US $2.1 billion), of which 27 percent came from polyester, 16 percent from nylon, 9 percent from cotton yarn, 2 percent from secondary products, and 46 percent from other products. It was capitalized at ¥23.8 billion (US $173.5 million) in the same year. Headquarters are in Tōkyō and Ōsaka.

Universal Manhood Suffrage Movement 普通選挙運動

(Futsū Senkyo Undō). Movement to extend the vote to all adult Japanese males in elections for the House of Representatives in the pre–World War II IMPERIAL DIET. In reality the principal aim was to eliminate the tax-payment qualification for voting, thus enfranchising a large majority of adult males. The movement did not aim primarily at lowering the voting age (set at 25 from 1889 to 1946) or at enfranchising women. See WOMEN'S SUFFRAGE.

The first election law (1889) limited voting for the House of Representatives to adult males who annually paid direct national taxes of ¥15 or more. This legislation enfranchised about 450,000, roughly 1 percent of the total population. A movement for universal suffrage took shape in the 1890s and continued until the 1925 revision of the election law removed all tax qualifications for the vote, increasing the electorate from approximately 3 million to 12 million people, or 20 percent of the population.

Beginnings, 1897–1911—A sustained campaign for universal manhood suffrage dates from 1897 with the appearance of the League to Petition for Universal Suffrage (FUTSŪ SENKYO KISEI DŌMEIKAI, later called simply Futsū Senkyo Dōmeikai or Universal Suffrage League). Although the league sought public understanding through discussion groups and periodicals, it did not attempt to develop mass popular support. A Diet member associated with the movement presented the first, unsuccessful, universal-suffrage bill in 1902. Bills were again presented unsuccessfully in 1903, 1908, 1909, and 1910. The movement reached a premature climax in March 1911 when a bill for universal suffrage passed the House of Representatives. It was summarily rejected in the House of Peers.

Eclipse and Revival, 1911–1919—The movement then went into eclipse until late 1918, largely because of active government hostility. Government surveillance of radical groups had broadened to include the universal suffrage movement following the so-called HIGH TREASON INCIDENT OF 1910. In 1919 universal suffrage emerged as a major topic in journals of opinion and political discussion. Labor and student organizations began to stage well-publicized demonstrations for universal suffrage in major cities. Within political parties agitation for it appeared in late 1918. In December 1919 the major opposition party, KENSEIKAI, as well as the smaller RIKKEN KOKUMINTŌ, endorsed universal suffrage; the government party, RIKKEN SEIYŪKAI, took a firm negative stand.

Arguments for Universal Suffrage—Some proponents argued that universal suffrage was essential if Japan were to keep up with the world trend toward democracy; others reasoned that it would make bribing voters prohibitively expensive. Still others asserted that it would enable Japan to take a stronger stand in international politics. Many politicians saw universal suffrage specifically as a way to widen enfranchisement of the urban population, whereas by this time simply lowering the tax qualification would enfranchise only payers of the land tax, i.e., the rural population. Another argument for universal suffrage focused on the need to provide a safety valve for mass discontent. However, internal party pressure rather than these arguments persuaded the leadership of the Kenseikai to adopt universal suffrage as party policy.

Apathy and Success, 1920–1925—Popular demonstrations for universal suffrage declined in scope and intensity after mid-1920, when the Seiyūkai government won an overwhelming election victory on an explicitly anti-universal-suffrage stand. However, in 1924 a Kenseikai alliance with part of the Seiyūkai scored an electoral victory against the nonparty government of KIYOURA KEIGO (see MOVEMENT TO PROTECT CONSTITUTIONAL GOVERNMENT). KATŌ TAKAAKI, head of the Kenseikai, became premier. The Seiyūkai accepted Kenseikai policy on universal suffrage as a price of the coalition, and a government bill was passed by the Diet in 1925. The first national elections under universal manhood suffrage were held on 20 February 1928. See also TAISHŌ DEMOCRACY.

universities and colleges 大学

(*daigaku*). The first modern universities in Japan were established by the national government, beginning with TŌKYŌ UNIVERSITY in 1877 and continued with universities in

Kyōto in 1897, Tōhoku (northern Honshū) in 1907, and Kyūshū in 1910 (see IMPERIAL UNIVERSITIES). Private colleges—classified as "professional schools" (SEMMON GAKKŌ)—were also established, but private university status was not authorized until 1918. By 1935 there were 45 universities in Japan. The university system was thoroughly reformed after World War II, and the number and quality of Japan's institutions of higher learning has risen dramatically.

History of the University System

When a modern educational system was established in Japan after the Meiji Restoration of 1868, the university systems of Europe and the United States were used as models. Tōkyō University, the first comprehensive university, was founded in 1877 to train leaders needed for the modernization of the country. The university had four departments (jurisprudence, liberal arts, natural science, and medicine). The faculty was initially composed of Europeans and Americans, who taught in their own languages. In 1886 the government issued the Imperial University Order (Teikoku Daigaku Rei), reorganizing Tōkyō University as Imperial University (later renamed Tōkyō Imperial University after the establishment of other imperial universities). It also created five higher middle schools (later HIGHER SCHOOLS) in various parts of the country as preparatory schools for Imperial University.

By the late 1890s, Imperial University was employing Japanese instructors to teach classes in Japanese. A second imperial university was established in Kyōto in 1897. In addition, there were the institutions of higher learning called *semmon gakkō*. These received official authorization in the Professional School Order (Semmon Gakkō Rei) of 1903, and the number of such institutions increased. Higher education thus came to have a multilevel structure, composed of two types of institutions, universities and *semmon gakkō*. As the quality of the facilities of the *semmon gakkō* rose, pressure was exerted to raise their status to that of the universities. In 1918 the Ministry of Education promulgated the University Order (Daigaku Rei), which recognized public and private universities in addition to the imperial universities. Influential private *semmon gakkō*, often comprising several schools, thus became universities, while some of the government *semmon gakkō* with only a single school became colleges.

After World War II, the Allied Occupation attempted a radical reform of the education system as an important element of the effort to democratize Japan. The reform aimed at the unification of institutions of higher learning (universities, higher schools, *semmon gakkō*, and normal schools) into four-year colleges and universities. See EDUCATIONAL REFORMS OF 1947.

The greatest change was seen in the national institutions of higher learning. The seven imperial universities became national universities and, toward the goal of one national university per prefecture, various national institutions of higher learning within any one prefecture were combined into one university. Private universities remaining from the old system continued to operate as universities. While most private *semmon gakkō* were elevated to university status, some lacked the facilities and staff to qualify as universities, and they were thus temporarily accredited as two-year JUNIOR COLLEGES; permanent accreditation of junior colleges was extended in 1964. Public *semmon*

gakkō and most of the public universities were reorganized as four-year universities, and some of them became national universities. As a result, by 1949 a total of 173 new universities had been created: 68 national, 13 public, and 92 private universities.

Present Status—The power to accredit institutions was invested in the University Chartering Council (Daigaku Setchi Shingikai), which was composed of university authorities. It became very easy to establish private universities, and many were created. However, there were great differences among the universities in quality of education and research, resulting in a hierarchy of four-year universities, with certain of the national universities and a few long-established private universities at the top.

Most Japanese private institutions do not have large endowments. Government assistance to private universities began in 1970, but the amount they receive is small compared to support for the national universities, creating a significant difference between the tuition fees for private universities and those for the national universities. In 1990 the average yearly tuition for national universities was ¥339,600 (US $2,345), whereas the tuition for private universities was ¥615,000 (US $4,250).

The differences in quality among schools has led to intense competition in ENTRANCE EXAMINATIONS among those trying to enter higher-ranked universities. The university entrance examination issue is now a major social problem. Compared to the rigors of the entrance examinations, advancement after entrance is easy, and three-fourths of the students graduate after the prescribed four-year period. The vast majority of university students (81.0 percent in 1990) are employed as soon as they graduate, with 6.8 percent going on to attend GRADUATE SCHOOLS.

university autonomy　　　大学の自治

(*daigaku no jichi*). A university's independence in administering its own affairs, without which ACADEMIC FREEDOM cannot be guaranteed, since a university's distinctive function is to conduct research and disseminate knowledge. The Tōkyō Metropolitan Police Ordinance of 1950 required that police obtain prior university approval for intelligence and public security activities on university campuses. The principle of university autonomy was further supported by the Educational Public Employees Special Law and the Basic Law concerning the Execution of Duties by Police Officials. But in the case of an emergency affecting the public welfare, the police may enter a university campus without prior university approval. Thus a precarious balance exists between the university's need for self-government and society's need for the maintenance of peace and order. See POPORO PLAYERS CASE.

University Entrance Examination Center Tests　　大学入試センターテスト

(*Daigaku Nyūshi Sentā Tesuto*). A series of tests administered since 1990 to applicants to public and private colleges and universities. In 1979 national and other public universities in Japan introduced standardized tests in seven subjects called the Joint First-Stage Achievement Tests. The tests were to be administered by the National Center for University Entrance Examinations and used by national and other public institutions as an initial criterion for screening prospective students. Subsequently the Provisional

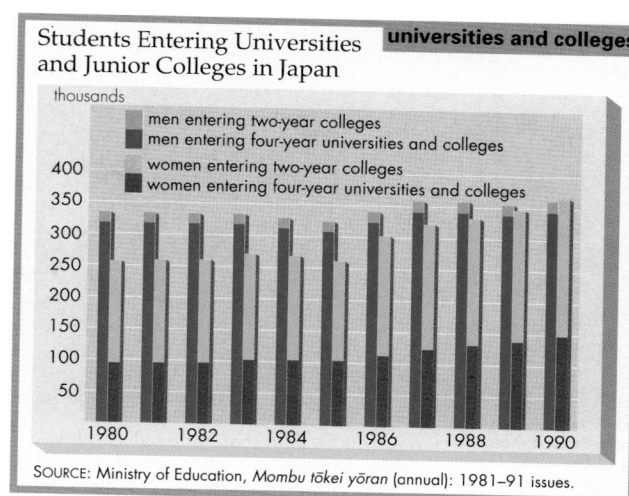

Students Entering Universities and Junior Colleges in Japan

thousands

Legend:
- men entering two-year colleges
- men entering four-year universities and colleges
- women entering two-year colleges
- women entering four-year universities and colleges

SOURCE: Ministry of Education, *Mombu tōkei yōran* (annual): 1981–91 issues.

Council on Educational Reform proposed that private colleges and universities be included within the scope of these entrance examinations, and in 1990 the University Entrance Examination Tests were instituted. Not only were private institutions included, but the number of fields in which the students were tested could be reduced to one at the discretion of the participating institutions. In 1991, 6 percent of all private institutions of higher education participated in the tests.

University of Electro-Communications　　　電気通信大学

(*Denki Tsūshin Daigaku*). A coeducational national university in the city of Chōfu, Tōkyō Prefecture. It was founded in 1918 as the Technical Institute for Wireless Communications and became a four-year university in 1949. The university's only academic department is its faculty of electro-communications. Enrollment in 1988 was 3,342.

University of the Air　　　放送大学

(*Hōsō Daigaku*). College administered by the Broadcast College Special Corporation, which broadcasts university-level courses on radio and television. Established in 1983; enrollment of students began in 1985. Seventy percent of its funding comes from the national budget, but it does not enjoy full national-university status. Qualification for admission requires that a person be a high-school graduate. However, special consideration is given to qualified non–high school graduates if they are at least 18 years old. Two credits are acquired by listening to fifteen 45-minute lectures and completing schooling provided by eight local study centers. Upon successful completion of all courses in the program the student is awarded a Bachelor of Arts degree. The University of the Air has three departments: domestic science, business–social science, and humanities–natural science. Approximately half of the students are over 40 years old. The administration office is located in the city of Chiba. Enrollment in 1989 was 22,504.

University of the Sacred Heart　　聖心女子大学

(*Seishin Joshi Daigaku*). A private women's university located in Shibuya Ward, Tōkyō. Founded in 1915 as the Seishin Joshi Gakuin Kōtō Semmon Gakkō, it became a university in 1948 and received its present name. Under the auspices of a Roman Catholic women's order, the Society of the Sacred Heart, the university offers an education that is based on Christian teachings. The school maintains

university upheavals of 1968–1969 In a rooftop meeting held in early January 1969, students at the strife-torn liberal arts campus of Tōkyō University, some equipped with staves and helmets, debated their course of action.

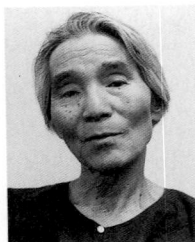

Uno Jūkichi This actor and stage director led the Gekidan Mingei and other theater groups.

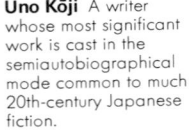

Uno Kōji A writer whose most significant work is cast in the semiautobiographical mode common to much 20th-century Japanese fiction.

only one faculty, that of liberal arts. It is actively engaged in international exchange with approximately 200 sister schools in 38 countries. Enrollment in 1988 was 1,909.

university upheavals of 1968–1969 　大学紛争

(*daigaku funsō*). The academic year 1968–69 witnessed a near total paralysis of Japan's university system as a majority of the nation's 377 universities were beset with student strikes, boycotts, and violent protests. The disturbances represented student discontent with the Japanese system of higher education, the most common points of dispute being increased tuition fees, jurisdiction over student dormitories and meeting halls, charges of corruption among university officials, and demands for greater student participation in university governance, for revocation of disciplinary measures, and for reform of educational programs. The upheavals were also linked with student opposition to what was viewed as Japanese and American imperialism, as manifested in the Vietnam War. In this sense, the 1968–69 upheavals were part of an international wave of student protest.

The first two major disturbances, in April 1968 at Nihon University and in June at Tōkyō University, sparked a contagion of often violent protests and demonstrations that had affected 110 schools by the end of the year. A massive assault by riot police on 18–19 January 1969 against student radicals at Tōkyō University stemmed, but did not stop, the wave of student protest. Strikes and demonstrations continued throughout the spring, resulting in a total for 1969 of 152 universities on strike, 10,000 student arrests, and 873 riot police mobilizations.

By late spring, however, the movement was beset by exhaustion, and public sentiment had turned increasingly against the students. The University Law that came into effect in August 1969 provided for sanctions against universities that failed within a certain time to resolve campus disputes. The law generated much debate over university reform but brought about very limited changes.

unjō 　運上

A fee collected from individuals such as urban tradesmen and craftsmen, hunters, and fishermen, during the Edo period (1600–1868). From the 12th to the 16th century *unjō* referred to the shipment of goods to Kyōto as tax payments. Belonging to a category of miscellaneous taxes (KOMONONARI), it was generally paid in cash. Since the tax base and rate varied from year to year, *unjō* was considered one of the "floating taxes" (UKIYAKU). In contrast to the other major levy collected from businesses at this time— MYŌGAKIN ("offertory money"), which in

theory was a voluntary cash donation—*unjō* was generally a fixed obligation.

unjust enrichment 　不当利得

(*futō ritoku*). Legal term referring to benefits that have been obtained without just legal cause. It also refers to the system by which the person who receives the benefit returns it (unjust enrichment) to the injured party (CIVIL CODE, art. 703–704).

Unkei 　運慶

(?–1223). Sculptor of Buddhist images in the early Kamakura period (1185–1333). Son of KŌKEI, colleague of KAIKEI, and father of TANKEI, all of the KEI SCHOOL of sculpture. He was based at the temple Kōfukuji in Nara; his masculine and dynamic style appealed to the warriors of the Kamakura period. Among his extant works are the Dainichi Nyorai (Skt: Mahāvairocana) at Enjōji in Nara as well as an Amida Triad, a Fudō Myōō (Skt: Acala), and a Bishamonten (Skt: Vaiśravaṇa) at Jōrakuji in Yokosuka, Kanagawa Prefecture. Considered the greatest master of the Kei school, Unkei revitalized the art of sculpture with his realistic and dynamic renditions of Buddhist figures.

Unkoku school 　雲谷派

(Unkokuha). Line of painters who traced their ancestry to SESSHŪ TŌYŌ (1420–1506). Founded by UNKOKU TŌGAN (1547–1618), who appropriated the name of Sesshū's painting studio, Unkokuan, in order to establish this artistic descent. Tōgan, a native of western Japan and a retainer to the MŌRI FAMILY of the Chōshū domain (now Yamaguchi Prefecture), studied KANŌ SCHOOL painting methods in Kyōto but then left to follow the brush manner and themes of Sesshū, whose paintings survived in the western provinces. Unkoku Tōeki (1591–1644), a son of Tōgan, studied and collaborated with his father on a number of projects both around Kyōto and in the Yamaguchi region. The school lasted into the 19th century. Combining the colorful Kanō-school painting canons with Unkoku ink-painting techniques, it forged a distinct approach to traditional painting themes.

Unkoku Tōgan 　雲谷等顔

(1547–1618). Ink painter and founder of the UNKOKU SCHOOL. Born into a *samurai* family from Hizen Province (now parts of Nagasaki and Saga prefectures) in Kyūshū; his real name was Hara Jihei Naoharu. After the death of his father, he entered the service of the MŌRI FAMILY in western Honshū. According to various records he studied painting in Kyōto at the KANŌ SCHOOL atelier. He left Kyōto to work for his patron, Mōri Terumoto (1553–1625), who resided at Hiroshima Castle.

Mōri Terumoto owned a landscape handscroll (*Landscape of the Four Seasons*; Mōri Collection), dated 1486, by the renowned ink painter SESSHŪ TŌYŌ. According to an inscription appended to the handscroll by Tōgan in 1592, this painting was entrusted to Tōgan so that he might revive Sesshū's painting style. Around this time Tōgan began using the professional name Unkoku, a reference to Sesshū's studio-retreat known as the Unkokuan (Cloud Valley Retreat). Tōgan even established his own studio at the same site. Perhaps his most famous work is represented by the two sets of *fusuma-e* (sliding-door paintings) entitled *West Lake* and *Seven Sages*, executed for the Ōbaiin, a subtemple of Daitokuji in Kyōto.

unlimited partnership company 　合名会社

(*gōmei kaisha*). Type of company incorporated under the COMMERCIAL CODE that is composed entirely of unlimited liability partners. Partners have a duty to contribute a specified amount of capital to the company and jointly and severally bear direct and unlimited liability to its creditors. Contributions are generally in the form of cash or other property, but contributions of services and credit are also allowed. Because they are exposed to substantial liability, partners have the right to administer the affairs of the company and to represent it but are not allowed to engage in business activities that compete with it. The *gōmei kaisha* is the least common type of corporation in Japan. See also PARTNERSHIP.

Uno Chiyo 　宇野千代

(1897–). Author. Born in Yamaguchi Prefecture. Her short story "Shifun no kao" (1921, A Face with Makeup) won a prize in a newspaper fiction contest. In the 1920s she associated with many literary celebrities while living with the novelist OZAKI SHIRŌ and later with the painter Tōgō Seiji (1897–1978), upon whom she based her novel *Irozange* (1933–35; tr *Confessions of Love*, 1989). Her second marriage (1937–64) was to the novelist KITAHARA TAKEO, with whom she published the magazine *Sutairu* (Style). Her works, often drawn from her own life, feature delicately sensual descriptions of women's psychology. Among her best-known works are *Ohan* (1947–57; tr *Ohan*, 1961), the autobiographical *Aru hitori no onna no hanashi* (1972, One Woman's Story), and the short story "Kōfuku" (1924; tr "Happiness," 1982).

unohana → utsugi

Uno Jūkichi 　宇野重吉

(1914–88). Actor and stage director. Born in Fukui Prefecture. After working with the Tōkyō Sayoku Gekijō (Left-Wing Theater of Tōkyō), Uno helped found the Shinkyō Gekidan (New Cooperative Theater Group) in 1934. In 1947 he formed the theater group Minshū Geijutsu Gekijō (People's Art Theatre; precursor of the GEKIDAN MINGEI) with TAKIZAWA OSAMU. He was the leader of the Gekidan Mingei from 1954 and also acted in many productions. He directed such plays as KOYAMA YŪSHI's *Taisamboku no ki no shita de* (1963, Under the Evergreen Magnolia Tree) and a Japanese version of *The Cherry Orchard* (1974). In September of 1986 he began a tour of Japan with his newly launched Uno Jūkichi Ichiza (Uno Jūkichi Theater Troupe), giving a total of 206 performances.

Uno Kōji 　宇野浩二

(1891–1961). Short-story writer, novelist, and essayist. Real name Uno Kakujirō. Born in the city of Fukuoka. Uno attended Waseda University but left before graduating. He first wrote using techniques of Japanese NATURALISM (*shizen shugi*). Uno's friend and fellow writer HIROTSU KAZUO helped him publish his best early short story, "Kura no naka" (1919, In the Storeroom). In the 1920s he was a regular contributor to such mainstream magazines as CHŪŌ KŌRON. By the late 1920s Uno, ill and also upset by the suicide of his friend AKUTAGAWA RYŪNOSUKE, gave up writing and spent some time in a mental institution but resumed writing with the short story "Kareki no aru fūkei" (1933, Landscape with Dead Tree). From the 1930s on, his stories were serious and mostly autobiographical. During the war years Uno published critical studies such as *Bungaku no sanjūnen* (1940, Thirty Years of Literature). The best of his postwar works is the novella *Omoigawa* (1948, Love Stream), which received the Yomiuri Literary Prize for 1951.

Uno Kōzō 宇野弘蔵

(1897–1977). Marxist economist and originator of theories that greatly influenced the Japanese academic world after World War II. Born in Okayama Prefecture and a graduate of Tōkyō University, Uno joined the ŌHARA INSTITUTE FOR SOCIAL RESEARCH, then went to Germany for further study. Upon his return to Japan he joined the faculty of Tōhoku University. Indicted for leftist beliefs in 1938, Uno was eventually acquitted but left the university. After World War II, he joined the faculty of the Social Science Research Institute of Tōkyō University and later became a professor at Hōsei University. Uno's economic theory sought to separate economics from ideological debates on social class and establish the field as a purely objective science. He worked out a bold revision of ideas in Marx's *Das Kapital* and formulated a unique theory regarding financial crises that emphasized capital surplus. His main works are collected in *Uno Kōzō chosakushū* (1973–74).

Uno Sōsuke 宇野宗佑

(1922–   ). Politician; prime minister June–August 1989. Born in Shiga Prefecture, Uno attended Kōbe University. He was first elected to the House of Representatives in 1960 as a LIBERAL DEMOCRATIC PARTY candidate from Shiga Prefecture. After serving in a variety of ministerial posts he became Japan's 75th prime minister in June 1989, replacing TAKESHITA NOBORU. His resignation in August was prompted by the defeat of the Liberal Democratic Party in the House of Councillors in July, the unpopularity of the CONSUMPTION TAX instituted by his predecessor, and public discontent over irregularities in his personal conduct.

Untei 芸亭

(Pavilion of Fragrant Herbs). Library of the 8th century. It was among the most famous *kuge bunko*—private libraries assembled by court nobles, including the Kōbaidono of SUGAWARA NO MICHIZANE and the Gōke Bunko of ŌE NO MASAFUSA. It is famous as the first library in Japan to be opened to public use. The Untei was built by ISONOKAMI NO YAKATSUGU, probably in the decade 770–780, and stood at a corner of his residence in Heijō-kyō (now Nara), which he had converted into a temple. The library was probably named for the aromatic herbs used to prevent destruction of paper and cloth by insect larvae. The Untei continued to flourish as a center of learning after Yakatsugu's death (781) before falling into disuse.

U Nu → Nu, U

Uny Co, Ltd ユニー[株]

(Yunī). Retail chain incorporated in 1950. It handles all types of merchandise, including clothing, food, household appliances, and leisure items. Uny has a total of 118 stores, mainly in central Japan. In addition to supermarkets and superstores, Uny has 32 subsidiaries and 11 affiliated companies; their activities include the operation of specialty stores, convenience stores, drugstores, and cable television stations, as well as computer-related, real estate, and insurance businesses. Uny opened its first store abroad in Hong Kong in 1987. Sales for the fiscal year ending February 1991 totaled ¥524.8 billion (US $4.0 billion), and the company was capitalized at ¥10.1 billion (US $77.4 million). Headquarters are in Nagoya.

Un'yushō → Ministry of Transport

Unzen-Amakusa National Park 雲仙天草国立公園

(Unzen-Amakusa Kokuritsu Kōen). Situated in western Kyūshū, in Nagasaki, Kumamoto, and Kagoshima prefectures. The park features volcanoes, islands, sheer cliffs, and hot-spring resorts. UNZENDAKE, a group of active volcanoes, lies in the center of the SHIMABARA PENINSULA. Unzen Hot Spring is on its slopes; in early summer and fall the mountain is covered with colorful wild Kirishima azaleas (*miyamakirishima*) and maples; in winter rime-covered trees are a particular attraction. South of the volcano in the YATSUSHIRO SEA are the AMAKUSA ISLANDS, whose coastal regions are included in the park. These islands are characterized by hills, white-sand beaches, and sea cliffs. In 1966 the Five Amakusa Bridges were completed, linking the larger islands to one another and to Kyūshū at MISUMI in the north. There are many historical sites related to the KAKURE KIRISHITAN (hidden Christians) in the Unzen and Amakusa areas. Area: 255 sq km (98 sq mi).

Unzendake 雲仙岳

Group of composite volcanoes, Shimabara Peninsula, Nagasaki Prefecture, Kyūshū. It is known for its tracts of *miyamakirishima* (a kind of azalea) and its hot springs. It is the main feature of Unzen-Amakusa National Park. There was an eruption at Fugendake (1,359 m; 4,459 ft), the group's highest peak, in May 1991.

Unzen Hot Spring 雲仙温泉

(Unzen Onsen). Located in the middle of the SHIMABARA PENINSULA, southern Nagasaki Prefecture, Kyūshū. A sulfur spring; water temperature 50°–97°C (122°–207°F). Its history goes back to the Nara period (710–794), and historical sites associated with the KAKURE KIRISHITAN of the Edo period (1600–1868) can be found nearby.

U Ottama → Ottama, U

Uozu 魚津[市]

City in northeastern Toyama Prefecture, central Honshū, on Toyama Bay. It first developed as a castle town and then as a fishing port from the Edo period (1600–1868). Besides fishing, it has carbide, textiles, and machinery industries. Pop: 49,514.

Uraga 浦賀

District in the city of YOKOSUKA, on the Miura Peninsula, Kanagawa Prefecture, central Honshū. In the Edo period (1600–1868) a commissioner's office here inspected vessels entering and leaving Tōkyō Bay. Commodore PERRY anchored off Uraga when he came to Japan in 1853. The district is the site of the Kannonzaki lighthouse and one of the largest shipbuilding industries in Japan.

Uraga bugyō 浦賀奉行

(commissioner of Uraga). One of the *ongoku bugyō* (commissioners for distant provinces) under the Tokugawa shogunate (1603–1867). The Uraga *bugyō*, whose office was established in 1720 to guard the sea approach to Edo (now Tōkyō), presided over the port of Uraga (now part of the city of Yokosuka). His duties included the administration of the city and the inspection and taxation of all ships entering Edo Bay.

Uraga Channel 浦賀水道

(Uraga Suidō). Between the Miura Peninsula, Kanagawa Prefecture, and the Bōsō Peninsula, Chiba Prefecture, connecting Tōkyō Bay with the Pacific Ocean. All commercial traffic to the Tōkyō-Yokohama area passes through the Uraga Channel. Commodore Perry passed through it with his "black ships" (KUROFUNE) in 1853. The coasts along this channel are popular for fishing and swimming. Width: 10 km (6 mi).

Uragami family 浦上氏

(Uragamishi). Powerful landholders who took their name from the Uragami estate in

Unzen-Amakusa National Park This park in western Kyūshū includes volcanoes, islands, cliffs, and hot-spring resorts.
1 Ash trails down Fugendake, the highest peak in the group of composite volcanoes known as Unzendake. In May 1991 eruptions of volcanic rubble and ash devastated nearby communities and left more than 40 people dead or missing.
2 Morning mist over Yōkaku Bay, on the southwestern side of the island of Amakusa Shimoshima. The floats in the foreground are used in the culturing of pearl oysters.

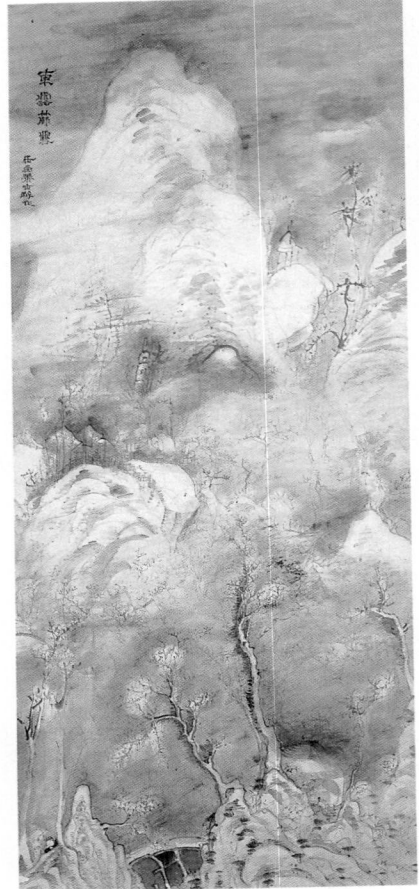

Uragami Gyokudō
Snow Sifted through Frozen Clouds. Ca 1820. Hanging scroll. Ink on paper. 134 × 56 cm. Kawabata Yasunari Kinen Kai, Kanagawa Prefecture. National Treasure.

Urashima Tarō A 1950 children's book illustration for this famous folktale depicts Tarō being borne home by the turtle whose life he saved.

Harima Province (now part of Hyōgo Prefecture); descendants of the scholar-official Ki no Haseo (845 or 851–912). During the Muromachi period (1333–1568) they rose in service to the AKAMATSU FAMILY, military governors (*shugo*) of Harima. Following the ŌNIN WAR (1467–77) Akamatsu Masanori (1455–96) was made head of the Board of Retainers (SAMURAI-DOKORO) in Kyōto, and Uragami Norimune (1429–1502) became his deputy. In 1521 Horimune's grandson Muramune (d 1531) assassinated Akamatsu Yoshimura (Masanori's son) and became lord of Harima, Bizen (now part of Okayama Prefecture), and Mimasaka (now part of Okayama Prefecture). In 1577 the Uragami were overthrown and destroyed by their vassal Ukita Naoie (1529–81).

Uragami Gyokudō   浦上玉堂

(1745–1820). BUNJINGA (literati painting) artist; better known in his day as a musician and poet. Born into a *samurai* family in Bizen Province (now part of Okayama Prefecture). He studied Confucianism, and during his stay in Edo (now Tōkyō) as personal attendant to his domainal lord, he learned to play the Chinese zither (Ch: *qin* or *ch'in*; J: SHICHI-GENKIN), compose poetry, and paint. His art name, Gyokudō Kinshi ("Jade Hall Zither Master"), was taken from the name of a Ming-dynasty (1368–1644) zither that he owned. After the death of his lord in 1768, Gyokudō devoted himself to scholarship and the arts. In his music Gyokudō revived SAIBARA, the ancient folk songs of Japan that had been incorporated into formal court music, by setting *saibara* poems to revised melodies with zither accompaniment.

In 1794, two years after the death of his wife, he gave up his hereditary position and became a wanderer with his two sons, URAGAMI SHUNKIN and Shūkin. During these years he began to paint seriously. In 1811 he settled down in Kyōto with Shunkin; during his final decade he painted most of his masterworks. Working in paper and monochrome ink, he developed a technique of overlaying gray and black ink, wet and dry brushwork; he often relied exclusively upon complex rhythmic patterns of horizontal dashes, rounded lines, short jabbing strokes, and vertical dots. His compositions are usually dominated by tall central mountains rising over a screen of trees in the foreground; frequently a tiny figure of a sage appears, sometimes carrying a zither.

Uragami Shunkin   浦上春琴

(1779–1846). BUNJINGA (literati painting) artist; the eldest son of URAGAMI GYOKUDŌ. Shunkin was born in Bizen Province (now part of Okayama Prefecture), where his father served as a *samurai* official. When Shunkin was 15, Gyokudō began a life of travel with his two sons, who became well-versed in music, poetry, calligraphy, and painting under their father's tutelage.

After almost two decades of travel, Shunkin married and settled down in Kyōto in 1811; he was joined by his father. Influenced by the literati circle of RAI SAN'YŌ, Shunkin developed a conservative painting style based on orthodox Chinese traditions, though his work extended beyond the conventional literati repertoire to bird-and-flower and figure paintings. The majority of his paintings, however, were landscapes. Shunkin's work featured short, overlapping brush strokes with darker ink overlaying grayer tones, clusters of dots to suggest vegetation, and pale color washes to soften the rocks and mountain forms.

Urakawa   浦河[町]

Town in south-central Hokkaidō on the Pacific Ocean. Settlers came here from Hiroshima and Hyōgo prefectures in 1880. A commercial center of the Hidaka region, it is known for its cattle and racehorses. Seafood processing is an important local industry. Pop: 17,862.

Uranouchi Bay   浦ノ内湾

(Uranouchi Wan). Inlet of western Tosa Bay on the coast of south-central Kōchi Prefecture, Shikoku. The chief activities are pearl culture and yellowtail cultivation. Popular for swimming and gathering shellfish, the bay has been designated a prefectural natural park.

Ura Senke   裏千家

A leading school of the TEA CEREMONY. Founded by Sen no Sōshitsu (1622–97) when he took over as master of the Konnichian tea hut in what is now Kami-Gyō Ward, Kyōto. Sen no Sōshitsu was the fourth son of Sen no Sōtan (1578–1658) and the great-grandson of the Azuchi-Momoyama period (1568–1600) tea master SEN NO RIKYŪ. The 15th-generation head of the school, SEN SŌSHITSU (b 1923), is noted for his work in fostering overseas cultural exchange through the tea ceremony, and Ura Senke operates a special program for foreign students. Ura Senke has about 150 chapters in Japan and about 70 abroad. Teachers are stationed in major cities throughout the world. See also OMOTE SENKE.

Urashima Tarō   浦島太郎

Folktale. A man named Urashima Tarō rescues a turtle that is being ill-treated by children. The turtle changes into a young woman, who invites Tarō to the sea-god's palace (*ryūgū*), where he spends three happy years with her. Finally returning to his village, he finds himself a stranger. At a loss, he opens a box that she has given him but has forbidden him to open. Instantly he becomes a hoary old man; it has been 300 years since he left. Folktales of the same motif are found throughout Japan. The earliest extant version, in which the man is referred to as Shima no Ko, appears in the *Tango fudoki itsubun* (Local Records of Tango Province; see FUDOKI).

Urasoe   浦添[市]

City on the island of Okinawa, Okinawa Prefecture. During the 12th–14th centuries Urasoe was the center of the Ryūkyū kingdom (see OKINAWA). It was a major battleground during World War II. Automobile dealers and foreign trading concerns are located here. The Urasoe Castle site contains the graves of several Ryūkyū kings. Pop: 89,994.

Urawa   浦和[市]

Capital of Saitama Prefecture, central Honshū. A post-station town in the Edo period (1600–1868), Urawa is now a satellite city of Tōkyō. It has large housing complexes and foodstuff, machinery, and metal industries. The primroses (*sakurasō*) at Tajimagahara draw visitors in May. Pop: 418,271.

urayaku   浦役

1. Tax levied on coastal villages during the Edo period (1600–1868); also called *kakoyaku*. Originating as a labor-service obligation (BUYAKU), it entailed rescuing vessels in distress, transporting government goods by sea, and expediting the obligatory travels of *daimyō* to the shogunal capital at Edo (now Tōkyō) under SANKIN KŌTAI. *Urayaku* was subsequently commuted to a currency or rice payment and classified as a miscellaneous tax (KOMONONARI).

2. A government official who supervised various marine activities in port towns and fishing villages during the Edo period. Also called *hamayaku* or *hamagakari*.

Urayasu   浦安[市]

City in northwestern Chiba Prefecture, central Honshū. In the Edo period (1600–1868) it was a thriving fishing village. Since land reclamation the city has become industrialized. TŌKYŌ DISNEYLAND was opened here in 1983. Pop: 115,675.

urbanization   都市化

(*toshika*). The development of an urban population in Japan can be traced back to the Nara (710–794) and Heian (794–1185) periods, when the first permanent capitals of HEIJŌKYŌ (now Nara) and HEIANKYŌ (now Kyōto) were established. By the Heian period Kyōto had a population of at least 100,000. Soon other urban centers were built, primarily for political and military purposes, although some, such as Naniwa (now Ōsaka) also developed to serve the needs of travelers. By the 13th century, KAMAKURA, seat of the Kamakura shogunate (1192–1333), had a population of over

10,000. As the central authority of the military government declined in the 15th and 16th centuries, towns increasingly evolved around castles built by regional warlords (DAIMYŌ) to defend their petty fiefdoms. During the Edo period (1600–1868) these CASTLE TOWNS continued to grow in size and stability. The castle town of Edo (now Tōkyō) had a population of over 1 million by the mid-18th century and is considered to have been the largest city in the world at that time.

Modern growth in urban population can be linked to changes that occurred in Japan's INDUSTRIAL STRUCTURE beginning in the late Meiji period (1868–1912). The shift in economic activity from agriculture, mining, forestry, and fishing to manufacturing encouraged large sectors of the work force to leave rural areas, towns, and villages for the industrial activity of urban centers. During the Meiji period the percentage of the population living in cities of 50,000 or more grew from less than 8 percent to more than 16 percent. The pace of urbanization accelerated during the period of high economic growth (1953–73). In 1950, 38 percent of the population lived in cities; by 1970 this figure had risen to 72 percent. This shift away from a rural-based population is further illustrated by the fact that as many as 25 of the so-called rural prefectures lost population in the first decade of high economic growth.

The pace of urbanization began to slow in the 1960s, with migration into the greater Tōkyō area reaching its peak in 1962. Statistics indicate that a similar peak in growth was also experienced in the 1960s by major urban centers like the Kyōto-Ōsaka-Kōbe area and Nagoya. By 1990 the population of the TŌKYŌ METROPOLITAN AREA (Tōkyō and the surrounding seven prefectures) had reached 39 million, a concentration of 32 percent of the nation's total population in a region equivalent to only 10 percent of the total land area. See also POPULATION REDISTRIBUTION.

Urban Planning Law 都市計画法

(Toshi Keikaku Hō). A law promulgating necessary measures regarding the substantive and procedural limitations of city planning to facilitate the sound and orderly development of cities. Enacted in 1968, the law was passed as a substitute for the old Urban Planning Law of 1919. There are seven main provisions to the law. First, city planning, as specified by this law, means that plans relating to land use, maintenance of city facilities, and urban development projects are to facilitate stable and orderly growth of cities. Second, it applies only to city planning areas designated by prefectural governors. Third, the law divides urban areas into urbanization promotion areas and urbanization control areas to promote planned growth. Fourth, in order to undertake development activity it is necessary to receive development approval from the prefectural governor in advance. Fifth, city planning includes city structures (such as streets, railways, parks, and plazas) as well as urban development projects (such as land regulation projects or residential development projects). Sixth, decision-making authority for city planning is delegated to the city, town, and village mayors, the prefectural governors, and the minister of construction. Seventh, the law establishes an approval system for city-planning projects.

urban subcenters 副都心

(fukutoshin). Secondary commercial and business centers that developed along with the expansion of large cities. These subcenters are usually located around major railway terminals and consist of department stores, specialty stores, markets, amusement and cultural facilities, restaurants, banks, and high-rise office and apartment buildings. Shinjuku, Shibuya, and Ikebukuro are major subcenters of Tōkyō; Ōsaka's include Umeda, Namba, and Tennōji.

Ureshino 嬉野[町]

Town in southwestern Saga Prefecture, Kyūshū. Ureshino has long been known as a hot-spring resort and producer of tea. A national hospital is located here. Pop: 20,356.

Urikohime 瓜子姫

(The Melon Princess). Folktale, somewhat resembling MOMOTARŌ. An old childless couple find a melon drifting downstream. Upon slicing it, they find a baby girl. She grows into a beautiful maiden and is betrothed to a prince, but a devil (AMANOJAKU), disguised as the princess, attempts to take her place at the wedding. A bird discloses the ruse, and the princess is properly married.

Uruguay Round ウルグアイ・ラウンド

(Uruguai Raundo). Multilateral international trade negotiations announced at the General Agreement on Trade and Tariffs (GATT) ministerial conference held in Uruguay in September 1986. Aiming to reach agreement by the end of 1992, the negotiations were centered on the reduction and removal of measures protecting the agricultural industry. There was a confrontation between food-exporting countries, such as the United States, Canada, and Australia, which were pushing for trade liberalization, and food-importing nations, such as Japan and some European countries, which were seeking to slow liberalization in order to protect their own food production capacities. The United States was specifically pressuring Japan to open its rice market, but the ruling Liberal Democratic Party as well as the opposition parties were opposed to rice imports. The Uruguay Round also included negotiations on service trade and intellectual property rights.

urushi-e 漆絵

(lacquer pictures). Technique employing lacquer as a painting medium on a paper or lacquer surface. The term is used to denote painted designs executed in a compound of lacquer and color pigments. Sabi, a grinding powder, is sometimes added in order to give more body to the compound and thereby to impart a greater clarity to the brushstrokes. Owing to the chemical properties of lacquer, the range of colors has, until recently, been restricted to red, black, brown, green, and yellow. Though there are pots decorated with lacquer that date from around 4,000–3,000 BC, the oldest extant example of pictorial urushi-e is the mid-7th-century Tamamushi Shrine in the Nara temple HŌRYŪJI, with figural and landscape subjects executed in colored lacquer. SHIBATA ZESHIN, a noted 19th-century lacquer artist and painter, is the most famous exponent of urushi-e on paper in the modern period.

Usa 宇佐[市]

City in northern Ōita Prefecture, Kyūshū. Usa developed as a shrine town around the USA HACHIMAN SHRINE. Farm products include rice, vegetables, and mandarin oranges. Industrial products include machinery, textiles, and processed marine foods. Pop: 50,829.

Usa Hachiman Shrine The main shrine building, a National Treasure, is distinguished by its "double roof," a key feature of Hachiman-style shrine architecture.

Usa Hachiman Shrine 宇佐八幡宮

(Usa Hachimangū). Also known as Usa Jingū. A Shintō shrine in the city of Usa, Ōita Prefecture, Kyūshū, dedicated to the legendary emperor ŌJIN; his mother, the legendary empress JINGŪ; and his deified wife, Hime Ōkami. The shrine first appears in historical records in the Yōrō era (717–724), when the deity HACHIMAN (the spirit of the deified emperor Ōjin) is said to have assisted the imperial forces in their campaign against the HAYATO rebels in Kyūshū. Hime Ōkami was enshrined soon after the establishment of the shrine. Hachiman has been thought of as a Japanese incarnation of a Buddhist divinity and was popularly called Hachiman Daibosatsu (Great Bodhisattva Hachiman). In 823 Empress Jingū was enshrined, and in 859 a branch of the Usa Shrine was built in Kyōto (see IWASHIMIZU HACHIMAN SHRINE). As a guardian deity of warriors and a protector of the land, Hachiman has a large following. The Usa Hachimangū is regarded as the central shrine for some 25,000 Hachiman shrines scattered throughout Japan. The annual festival is held on 18 March, and the Shinkōsai festival, with its famous procession of mikoshi (portable shrines), is held from 31 July to 2 August. See also HONJI SUIJAKU.

Usami Tadanobu 宇佐美忠信

(1925–). Labor leader. Born in Tōkyō. While working with Fuji Spinning Co, Ltd, he was influenced by the ideas of MATSUOKA KOMAKICHI. He succeeded TAKITA MINORU as president of ZENSEN DŌMEI (Japan Federation of Textile Industry Workers' Unions) in 1971 and then went on to become president of Zen Nihon Rōdō Sōdōmei (Dōmei; Japanese Confederation of Labor). Active in the formation of RENGŌ (Japanese Trade Union Confederation), Usami was its first vice-chairman.

Ushiba Nobuhiko 牛場信彦

(1909–84). Career foreign ministry officer. Born in Hyōgo Prefecture. After graduating from Tōkyō University, Ushiba joined the Ministry of Foreign Affairs. He held such posts as administrative vice-minister (1967–70) and ambassador to the United States (1970–73). Known as a tough negotiator, he took part in major diplomatic negotiations for Japan during the post–World War II period, including those for normalization of relations with Korea (see KOREA-JAPAN TREATY OF 1965) and the reversion of OKINAWA. After he retired from the foreign service he was given responsibility for coordinating Japan's trade policy vis-à-vis the United States and the European Economic Community.

Ushibuka 牛深[市]

City in Kumamoto Prefecture, Kyūshū. Located on Shimoshima, one of the AMAKUSA

usu
1 A grinding mortar (*suriusu*) used for milling grain. The lower section is fixed, while the handle turns the upper section around a vertical shaft.
2 A pounding mortar (*tsukiusu*) is used in the traditional way of preparing rice cakes (*mochi*), a staple of festive and solemn occasions.

ISLANDS. The city is a fishing port, with an abundant catch of sardines, horse mackerel, and sea bream. There is a major seafood-processing industry. Beds for cultivating pearls are also maintained. Pop: 21,443.

Ushijima Noriyuki 牛島憲之

(1900–). Western-style painter. Known for his poetic landscapes combining soft colors and simple compositions. Born in Kumamoto Prefecture. Graduated from the Tōkyō Bijutsu Gakkō (now Tōkyō University of Fine Arts and Music). His painting *Shibai* (Stage Play) was selected for the Teiten (Exhibition of the Imperial Fine Arts Academy) in 1927. In 1942 he joined the group called the Sōgenkai but resigned in 1949 to help found the Ryūkikai group. He taught at the Tōkyō University of Fine Arts and Music (1954–68). He became a member of the Japan Art Academy in 1981 and received the Order of Culture in 1983.

Ushiku 牛久[市]

City in southern Ibaraki Prefecture, central Honshū; established in 1986. Within easy commuting distance of Tōkyō, it has experienced rapid population growth in recent years. Pop: 60,693.

ushin 有心

(literally, "having heart, feeling"). Aesthetic term used from about the Kamakura period (1185–1333), particularly to distinguish serious, elegant WAKA or linked verse (see RENGA) from the light or comic forms thereof (see KYŌKA), for which the term MUSHIN ("lacking heart or depth of feeling") was used. Formerly referring to discretion or discernment, the word gradually came to mean having refined taste and aesthetic sensitivity. In Buddhism *ushin* takes on a radically different meaning, referring to worldly attachment as opposed to *mushin*, which means detachment or emptiness (enlightenment).

ushi no koku mairi 丑の刻参り

Also called *ushi no toki mairi*. The act of going to a shrine at approximately 2 AM to place the curse of death on an enemy. *Ushi*

no koku refers to an hour in the traditional sexagenary cycle (see JIKKAN JŪNISHI); *mairi* means a visit to a shrine. To place this curse, the petitioner nails a straw doll resembling the object of his or her enmity to a shrine gate (*torii*) or a tree on the shrine grounds and offers a prayer. This is repeated for seven consecutive days, after which it is believed that the accursed person will die after experiencing pain in the same part of the body where the straw doll was nailed. Today this practice is extremely rare.

Ushio, Inc ウシオ電機[株]

(Ushio Denki). Company specializing in the manufacture and sale of industrial lighting equipment. Incorporated in 1964. It produces various types of lighting apparatus and pioneered in the manufacture of special-purpose lamps, including halogen and xenon lamps. It also produces lamps for office automation and semiconductor manufacturing equipment and new products such as solar simulators. It has overseas offices, subsidiaries, and plants in the United States, the Netherlands, Singapore, Hong Kong, and Taiwan. Sales for the fiscal year ending March 1991 totaled ¥32.2 billion (US $246.8 million), and capitalization stood at ¥18.9 billion (US $144.8 million). Headquarters are in Tōkyō.

Ushio Jirō 牛尾治朗

(1931–). Businessman and chairman of USHIO, INC (1979–). Born in Hyōgo Prefecture. After graduating from Tōkyō University in 1953, he attended graduate school at the University of California (1956–57). After returning to Japan, he joined his family business, Ushio Industry, splitting off from it in 1964 to establish his own firm Ushio, Inc, and becoming its president. He was quick to enter high technology fields, such as electronics, information equipment, new materials, and space, and rapidly expanded the Ushio business.

USSR and Japan →Soviet Union and Japan

usu 臼

A mortar used in the threshing, refining, and milling of grain and in pounding cooked, glutinous rice (*mochi*). The *usu* was probably introduced to Japan along with rice cultivation early in the Yayoi period (ca 300 BC–ca AD 300); several bronze bells (DŌTAKU) from this period depict people using *usu*. Made of stone, wood, or clay, *usu* vary according to their function and shape. A variety of folk customs and rituals have developed around the use of the mortar and pestle (*kine*). As the *usu* is traditionally likened to the female and the *kine* to the male, they have played a role in many rituals related to occasions such as marriage and childbirth.

Usui Pass 碓氷峠

(Usui Tōge). Located on the border of Gumma and Nagano prefectures, central Honshū. Extends from Yokokawa station to the resort town of Karuizawa and has been known since ancient days as one of the most tortuous routes on the highway Nakasendō. A railway and a national highway both feature numerous steep slopes and hairpin turns. Altitude: 956 m (3,136 ft).

Usui Yoshimi 臼井吉見

(1905–87). Critic. Born in Nagano Prefecture; graduate of Tōkyō University. As editor in chief of the magazine TENBŌ after World War

II, Usui introduced such literary figures as SHIINA RINZŌ and Gomikawa Jumpei (b 1916). His major critical essays have been collected in the 12-volume series *Sengo* (1965–66, After the War). He also wrote a novel, *Azumino* (1964–74).

Usuki 臼杵[市]

City in southeastern Ōita Prefecture, Kyūshū. Usuki developed as the castle town of the Christian *daimyō* ŌTOMO SŌRIN, who built a castle in 1563. Traditional products are soy sauce and *miso* (bean paste). Whiskey distilleries and shipyards are also located here. A cluster of some 75 stone Buddhas carved into the mountainside has been designated a national historic monument. Pop: 37,871.

Usuzan 有珠山

Active double volcano in the Nasu Volcanic Zone, northeast of Uchiura Bay, western Hokkaidō. It erupted in 1663, 1822, 1910, 1943, and 1977. Meiji Shinzan and SHŌWA SHINZAN, new volcanoes, are on Usuzan's slopes. Height: 737 m (2,418 ft).

uta-awase 歌合

(poetry match). Literary competition in which poems composed on assigned themes by members of two opposing teams were paired and judged for superiority. Poetry matches emerged in the late 9th century, reached their greatest popularity in the 12th and early 13th centuries, and declined thereafter, though they continued to be held through the early 20th century.

The origins of poetry matches seem related to other ritualized contests that involved the matching of various objects. By the late 9th century the matching of poems had become a separate form of entertainment, complete with its own elaborate ceremonial. The oldest recorded poetry match was the Zai Mimbukyō no Ie no Uta-awase, held between 885 and 887. The Teijiin no Uta-awase in 913 was one of many poetry matches sponsored by Emperor Uda (r 887–897) and is the earliest competition for which there exist detailed records of the proceedings and judgments. By the 12th and 13th centuries poetry matches had become the most important formal social occasion for the composition of poetry, and decisions by judges such as FUJIWARA NO TOSHINARI were instrumental in shaping poetic standards.

The oral nature of the poetry match dictated a certain style of poetry. Since the poem was heard and not read, it was important to use familiar words and place names, avoid complicated puns, and structure the poem for easy comprehension. The matches, providing a formal occasion for the composition of poetry, produced vast quantities of poems, many of which were included in the imperially commissioned anthologies, and the judgments became the backbone of poetic criticism.

uta-e 歌絵

(literally, "poem-painting"). A decorative art form in which pictorialized letters of the Japanese syllabary (KANA) are employed along with natural imagery to allude to a poem. Such paintings, which often offered only a few cleverly disguised clues to the complete poem, achieved their most sophisticated development during the late Heian period (794–1185). The meanings of these cryptic picture-puzzles were often forgotten even in the Heian period, however, and today there are only a handful of *uta-e* whose hidden poems can be read with confidence. See also ASHIDE.

utagaki　歌垣

Also known as *kagai*. A type of ancient spring and autumn festival of the Nara period (710–794) or before in which men and women gathered on mountaintops or at the seashore to sing, dance, eat, and exchange poems. Poems said to be from those festivals are included in the MAN'YŌSHŪ and other ancient works.

Utagawa Kunimasa　歌川国政

(1773–1810). UKIYO-E artist. Born in Aizu in Iwashiro Province (now part of Fukushima Prefecture), Kunimasa went to Edo (now Tōkyō) where he worked as a craftsman in a dye shop. There his talent was recognized by the *ukiyo-e* master UTAGAWA TOYOKUNI, whose favorite pupil he became. Kunimasa specialized in portraits of KABUKI actors (*yakusha-e*). His best work, however, is in the *ōkubi-e* format, portraits focusing on the head and shoulders. He also designed full-length actor portraits and *bijinga*, pictures of beautiful women.

Utagawa Kunisada　歌川国貞

(1786–1865). UKIYO-E woodblock print designer and book illustrator, specializing in figures of women and portraits of KABUKI actors. Born Sumida Shōzō in the Honjo district of Edo (now Tōkyō). In his teens Shōzō entered the studio of the print designer UTAGAWA TOYOKUNI, from whom he received the name Kunisada. He made his public debut with two illustrated books and a portrait of the Ōsaka kabuki actor Nakamura Utaemon III in 1808. From this date until his death, Kunisada produced more than 20,000 single-sheet prints and many illustrations in a wide variety of styles. His early prints of women were more graceful than those of his contemporaries and did much to establish the new pictorial type of female beauty that was popular in the mid-19th century. Kunisada's late work is bold and brilliantly colorful, although its excellence often lies more in the realms of splendor, competence, and craft than in warmth or feeling.

During his career Kunisada used many secondary names. In 1844 the artist, who did not recognize Toyokuni's adopted son Toyokuni II as heir, began signing his prints as Ichiyōsai Toyokuni II. He is now usually referred to as Toyokuni III.

Kunisada II (1823–80)—A pupil of Kunisada, in 1846 he married his master's eldest daughter and was allowed to use the name Kunisada II. Around 1870, after his master's death, he changed his name to Toyokuni III; he is now usually referred to as Toyokuni IV.

Utagawa Kuniyoshi　歌川国芳

(1798–1861). Leading color-print designer, book illustrator, and UKIYO-E painter. Personal name Igusa Yoshisaburō, later Magosaburō. Born in Edo (now Tōkyō), the son of Yanagiya Kichiemon. In 1811 he was apprenticed to UTAGAWA TOYOKUNI, and in 1814 he was given the professional name Kuniyoshi and published his first illustrated book, *Gobuji chūshingura*. His first recorded actor prints appeared in 1815.

In 1827 Kuniyoshi made his name with the *Suikoden* series, a set of 108 large and forceful figures of Chinese warrior bandits featured in a translation by BAKIN from the Chinese novel *Shuihuzhuan* (*Shui-hu-chuan;*

The Water Margin). These gained immediate and immense popularity, being unlike anything that had happened before; they were even imitated by UTAGAWA KUNISADA.

From the early 1830s, in addition to theatrical prints and heroic subjects bearing his signature, there are SURIMONO (a type of luxurious print made on unsized paper) and landscapes. The latter were probably prompted by HIROSHIGE'S success in the field but are quite different, showing strong originality and some striking features derived from European prints. The years 1835 to 1850 were Kuniyoshi's greatest period. Heroic triptychs and series of historical biographies poured from his brush, many of them of startling originality. He also produced charming prints of women and of cats, for which he had a passion, as well as comic subjects, fan prints, and *surimono*. Vigor and versatility are the outstanding characteristics of Kuniyoshi's work. He illustrated about 300 books. See also UTAGAWA SCHOOL.

Utagawa school　歌川派

(Utagawaha). An important school of late-18th- to late-19th-century UKIYO-E artists who specialized in landscapes, portraits of KABUKI actors, and historical subjects. The founder of the school, UTAGAWA TOYOHARU, achieved popular success in the 1770s as a designer of landscapes and interiors for prints using Western perspective techniques.

Toyoharu taught UTAGAWA TOYOHIRO and UTAGAWA TOYOKUNI and allowed them to take the family name Utagawa. Toyohiro is remembered as the designer of a number of prints of women and a few landscapes. Toyokuni, however, invented a style of actor portraiture that was continued through the end of the 19th century by an unbroken string of artists whose names begin with the last two syllables of Toyokuni's name, UTAGAWA KUNIMASA and UTAGAWA KUNISADA being the best known. Another pupil of Toyokuni, UTAGAWA KUNIYOSHI, devised a style of his own suited to the heroic, legendary, and comic subjects in which he and his pupils, among them TAISO YOSHITOSHI, specialized. More than half the designs, and far more than half the surviving Japanese woodblock prints, are works of the Utagawa school.

Utagawa Toyoharu　歌川豊春

(1735–1814). UKIYO-E artist and founder of the UTAGAWA SCHOOL. Studied painting in Kyōto with the KANŌ SCHOOL artist Tsuruzawa Tangei (1688–1789). In the early 1760s he moved to Edo (now Tōkyō) and took up *ukiyo-e* printmaking. His prints and paintings after 1770 are numerous and include a series of landscape views of Edo using Western perspective (*uki-e*) that made him famous. It is said that Toyoharu adopted the Utagawa name from the district in Edo where he had his residence. His two most famous disciples are UTAGAWA TOYOHIRO and UTAGAWA TOYOKUNI.

Utagawa Toyohiro　歌川豊広

(1773?–ca 1830). UKIYO-E artist. Also known as Ichiryūsai; real name Okajima Tōjirō. Born in Edo (now Tōkyō), he was the disciple of UTAGAWA TOYOHARU and teacher of Andō HIROSHIGE. At Toyoharu's atelier he encountered UTAGAWA TOYOKUNI, a senior disciple, with whom he sustained a long and intense rivalry marked by occasional collaborative print publications. Toyohiro is known mainly for portraits of beautiful women (*bijinga*) and as an illustrator of novelettes

(KUSAZŌSHI), but it was his landscape series, such as *Edo hakkei* (Eight Views of Edo) and *Ōmi hakkei* (Eight Views of Ōmi), that made a deep impression on Hiroshige, his most illustrious disciple.

Utagawa Toyokuni　歌川豊国

(1769–1825). UKIYO-E print designer, book illustrator, and painter; inventor in the 1790s of a powerful and original style of actor portraiture that became the model for succeeding generations of *ukiyo-e* theater artists. Real name Kurahashi Kumakichi.

Toyokuni was born in Mishimachō in the Shiba district of Edo (now Tōkyō), the son of a sculptor of wooden dolls. He entered the studio of the *ukiyo-e* landscape print designer UTAGAWA TOYOHARU, from whom he received his artistic family name, Utagawa, and the first two syllables of his working name. His first signed works were published in 1786.

In 1794 Toyokuni designed his first portraits of KABUKI actors, which were entirely unconventional and became an enormous success. The kabuki theater inspired Toyokuni with its tension and drama, and he increasingly exaggerated expressions, gestures, and poses, often showing pairs of actors in dramatic involvement.

Nearly all artists of the 1790s to 1830s whose names begin with the word *kuni* were pupils of Toyokuni. His first and perhaps most brilliant pupil was UTAGAWA KUNIMASA; his most prolific and influential pupil was UTAGAWA KUNISADA; UTAGAWA KUNIYOSHI is noted for his prints and illustrations on historical themes.

Others with the Toyokuni Name—
Toyokuni II (1802–35?). Entered the studio of Toyokuni around 1820 and signed his early work Ichiryūsai Toyoshige. In 1825, on Toyokuni's death, he inherited his name. No work by Toyokuni II is known after the mid-1830s, and he is thought to have died before Kunisada assumed the name (Toyokuni III) in 1844.

Toyokuni IV (1823–80). Also known as Kunimasa II and Kunisada II, in his later years he designed *meiji-e*, genre prints with subject matter related to the MEIJI ENLIGHTENMENT.

utai　謡

A term denoting the sung portion of NŌ. (The term *yōkyoku* is used when referring to it in a literary context.) A given play may contain *utai* portions for the *shite* (leading character), the *waki* (subordinate character), or the *tsure* (companions or attendants of the *shite*), as well as for the *jiutai* (chorus). *Utai* portions may have melodies (*fushi*) written for them (with dotted notations), while other passages (called *kotoba* or prose) are chanted according to a set formula. As for rhythm, the two basic distinctions are between passages sung on the beat (*hyōshi-ai*) and those sung on the interval (*hyōshi-awazu*). Melodic styles are of two types: *tsuyogin* ("strong style," used in masculine, warlike scenes) and *yowagin* ("soft style," used in lyric scenes). The *utaibon* ("utai book" or libretto) contains the text of all *utai* passages with musical and stylistic notations. Recitals of *utai* by nonactors are also popular.

Utakai Hajime →Imperial New Year's Poetry Reading

uta makura 歌枕

Place names appearing in classical Japanese poetry in connection with traditional associations and wordplays. The term *uta makura* originally referred to compendiums of poetic lore that served as handbooks for aspiring poets. Works such as the *Nōin uta makura* by the poet-priest NŌIN (b 988) contained commentary on poetic diction and explanations of MAKURA KOTOBA (conventional epithets, or "pillow words") as well as lists of place names and their poetic associations. At the close of the Heian period (794–1185), *uta makura* referred exclusively to catalogs of place names and soon only to the toponyms themselves. Although not charged with set associations in the earliest poetry, by the late 9th century place names had come to be linked with certain standard images and feelings. Poets could enrich their poems by drawing on these conventional associations while demonstrating their originality by introducing subtle changes. The influence of *uta makura* is strong in the prose work TALE OF GENJI (early 11th century) and in NŌ plays.

Utamaro 歌麿

(1753–1806). Full name Kitagawa Utamaro. One of the most creative and influential artists in the history of UKIYO-E. Utamaro is famed for his superbly conceived paintings and woodblock-print depictions of beautiful women from the shops, teahouses, and plea-sure quarters of Edo (now Tōkyō). He received his initial artistic training during his adolescence under the supervision of Toriyama Sekien (1712–88).

Utamaro's artistic career evolved in a gradual, tentative manner, and his distinctive creative talents did not become really apparent until he reached his mid-thirties. The earliest group of his designs, beginning in the mid-1770s, consists of commonplace illustrations for cheap popular books, such as the librettos and guides to the theater produced for patrons of the KABUKI stage or the vernacular farces or novelettes known as KIBYŌSHI. Under the name Toyoaki he also began to design a few undistinguished single-sheet depictions of actors in the manner of KATSUKAWA SHUNSHŌ. About 1782 he took the name Utamaro. By the end of the decade he was not only producing multi-sheet compositions of figures superbly composed in interior and landscape scenes, but he was also designing some of the most beautiful illustrated books in the history of *ukiyo-e*, works such as *Ehon mushi erami* (1788, Insect Book), *Kyōgetsubō* (1789, Moon-Mad Monk), *Ginsekai* (1790, Silver World), and in the same or following year *Shiohi no tsuto* (Gifts of Ebb Tide) and *Momo chidori kyōka awase* (Bird Book).

Utamaro's creative efforts during the Kansei era (1789–1801), when he produced his most distinctive and memorable designs, were devoted mainly to exploring the compositional potentialities of single-sheet prints, most often in the standard *ōban* (38 by 25 cm; 15 by 10 in) size, vertically disposed. The figural subjects that appear in Utamaro's single-sheet prints of the 1790s range from full-figure to half-torso and close-up depictions. These prints of lovely courtesans and teahouse girls represent the final and most complete realization of this quintessential subject in the history of *ukiyo-e*. They are, in fact, among the most accomplished and eloquent expressions of feminine beauty in Japanese art. A salient aspect of Utamaro's conceptual preoccupation with women is his perennial interest in showing them in their most characteristic surroundings and revealing circumstances. Thus a significant number of his full-figure prints show the popular beauties and demi-mondaines situated either in their shops or in the great houses of pleasure in the YO-SHIWARA district. Utamaro's artistic evolution is marked by a persistent interest in scrutinizing these women from ever greater proximity, as shown by his taste for half-torso and *ōkubi-e* (bust-depiction) prints. Many of his representations of women are idealized stereotypes, but his prints of celebrated beauties such as Naniwaya Okita and Takashimaya Ohisa, with their attention to subtle differences of physiognomy, qualify as portraiture.

Utamaro produced designs for many publishers, but his closest relationship was with Tsutaya Jūzaburō (1750–97), who produced a significant number of his masterpieces. It was Utamaro's good fortune to come under his guidance in the late 1770s and benefit from his discerning patronage until Tsutaya's death. Utamaro is thought to have resided with Tsutaya during these years. Association with Tsutaya guaranteed an artist that the prints made from his designs would not only be faithful to the original but also be executed in the most meticulous and discerning fashion, for the wood engravers and printers who labored in Tsutaya's shop were unquestionably among the finest artisans of the day.

During the 1790s Utamaro was the most widely emulated artist in *ukiyo-e.* However, a decline in the originality and creative vitality of his works set in at the end of this period. In 1804 Utamaro was imprisoned for depicting the great historical figure TOYOTOMI HIDEYOSHI (1537–98) in a manner that the authorities considered disrespectful. Although his incarceration was relatively brief, his failing creative energies seem to have suffered further as a result, and he died two years later.

Utashinai   歌志内[市]

City in central Hokkaidō. Once a flourishing coal mining town, operations are greatly reduced today. It now has emerging textile and leather industries. Pop: 8,279.

Utility-Model Law   実用新案法

(Jitsuyō Shin'an Hō). The Utility-Model Law of 1959 sets forth a registration system in order to protect "devices" (*kōan*) that are "creations of technical ideas utilizing natural laws" (art. 2[1]). The first Utility-Model Law was enacted in 1905, modeled after the German law Gesetz betreffend den Schutz von Gebrauchsmuster of 1891. It was originally designed to protect and encourage small inventors. To obtain utility-model registration, a device must meet the requirements of novelty, utility, and inventive step or nonobviousness. While patentable inventions must be highly advanced, technical ideas do not have to meet such a high standard to be qualified for utility-model registration. Theoretically this difference must be reflected in the examination of the inventive step, but it is the general practice of the Patent Office to apply the same standard of inventive step for both patent and utility-model registrations. Registration establishes a utility-model right for 10 years from the date of publication of the application, but it cannot be longer than 15 years from the date of filing.

Uto   宇土[市]

City in Kumamoto Prefecture, Kyūshū. During the Edo period (1600–1868) Uto was a castle town of the HOSOKAWA FAMILY. It produces rice and vegetables; *nori* (a kind of seaweed) is cultivated offshore. There is also an active chemical industry. Japan's oldest extant water system, the Todoroki Aqueduct, is located here. Pop: 33,390.

utokusen   有徳銭

(literally, "virtue money"). A medieval form of taxation; special impost levied on wealthy persons (*utokunin*). Tributes exacted from *utokunin,* most notably pawnbrokers (DOSŌ) and *sake* brewers (SAKAYA), formed a substantial source of income for the Muromachi shogunate (1338–1573).

Utou   善知鳥

NŌ play. Author unknown. It is classified as a *yobamme-mono* ("part-four play"). An itinerant Buddhist priest (the *waki* or subordinate character) encounters an old man (the *maejite* or main character at the beginning of a play) on a mountain. Handing the priest a sleeve from his robe, the old man (actually the ghost of a hunter) asks that his wife and child be told of his death. Later, the priest and the old man's family hold a memorial service with the sleeve as a remembrance. During the ceremony, the ghost of the hunter (the *nochijite* or main character at the end of a play) appears and enacts the killing of birds with a club, after which he bewails his fate: having killed many birds in this fashion, he is now in hell and at the mercy of birds that torture him. He begs the priest to save him and fades away.

Utsubo monogatari   宇津保物語

(Tale of the Hollow Tree). Also known as *Utsuho monogatari.* Late-10th-century work of prose fiction in 14 chapters (divided into 20 fascicles, *kan*) of unknown authorship and date; believed to be the world's oldest extant novel. The story deals with the lives of a nobleman, Kiyowara no Toshikage, and three succeeding generations of his family. Setting out for China on an official mission, Toshikage is shipwrecked on the shores of a strange land, has fantastic adventures, and is taught to play the zither, or KOTO. Eventually he returns to Japan, bringing with him marvelous seven-stringed zithers (SHICHIGENKIN) and the musical knowledge he has gained during his journey. The focus then shifts to his descendants. His only daughter has a son, the filial Nakatada, who becomes one of the many suitors of the beautiful Atemiya. The tale describes the arduous efforts of Atemiya's suitors to win her hand, their disappointment when she marries the crown prince, and the power struggle that determines the successor to the throne.

The value of music, or the arts in general, seems to be the principal theme of the *Utsubo monogatari.* It appears in the first volume, runs through the greater part of the work as a contrastive motif, and dominates again at the end of the story. The chapters in between deal with love and political power, centering around the fair Atemiya with her numerous suitors (volumes 2–12) and the investiture of a new crown prince (volumes 13–18).

A 13th-century tradition attributes the work to the lexicographer and poet Minamoto no Shitagō (also known as MINAMOTO NO SHITAGAU). Allusions to *Utsubo* in the 11th-century *Genji monogatari* (TALE OF GENJI), SEI SHŌNAGON's *Makura no sōshi,* and FUJIWARA NO KINTŌ's *Kintōshū* indicate that it was probably completed in the late 10th century. See also MONOGATARI BUNGAKU.

utsugi   空木

Deutzia crenata. Also known as *unohana.* A deciduous shrub of the saxifrage family (Saxifragaceae) that grows wild in mountainous regions throughout Japan and is also planted near homes for hedges. It reaches a height of about 2 meters (6.6 ft) and has a hollow stem with shredded bark and numerous branches. The alternate leaves are ovate to broadly lance-shaped. The *utsugi* blooms from May to June, bearing clusters of five-petaled white flowers. A double-flowered variety is known as *yaeutsugi.* About 18 species of the genus *Deutzia* grow wild in Japan, including *himeutsugi* (*D. gracilis*), whose smaller flowers bloom earlier than those of the *utsugi,* and the pink-flowered variety, *akebono utsugi,* which is also raised as an ornamental. In ancient times the quality of the year's harvest was said to have been forecast by how abundantly the *utsugi* bloomed, perhaps because its white blossoms were likened to grains of rice. The tough wood has been used for pegs, toothpicks, and inlay work.

Utsukushigahara   美ヶ原

Lava plateau, east of the city of Matsumoto, central Nagano Prefecture, central Honshū. The plateau provides a spectacular view of the surrounding area, including the Northern Alps (HIDA MOUNTAINS). There is excellent hiking and good skiing. Part of Yatsugatake-Chūshin Kōgen Quasi-National Park. Average elevation: 2,000 m (6,600 ft); area: approximately 5 sq km (2 sq mi).

Utsunomiya   宇都宮[市]

Capital of Tochigi Prefecture, central Honshū. The city developed as the base of the Utsunomiya family, military governors (*shugo*) of the area in the Kamakura (1185–1333) and Muromachi (1333–1568) periods. During the Edo period (1600–1868) it was a castle town and post-station town. Principal manufactures are aircraft, tractors, and television sets. Attractions include the FUTARAYAMA SHRINE and the Ōya Stone Buddhas, carved into a mountainside. Pop: 426,795.

Uwai Kakuken nikki   上井覚兼日記

The diary of Uwai Kakuken (or Uwai Satokane; 1545–89), vassal of the powerful SHIMAZU FAMILY of Kyūshū; extant are fragments from the years 1574–76 and 1582–86. The diary covers the Shimazu campaigns of conquest and regional power alignments in Kyūshū and gives occasional glimpses into national politics. Kakuken's reflections on requirements to be an accomplished *samurai,* drafted in 1581, form a supplement.

Uwajima   宇和島[市]

City in southwestern Ehime Prefecture, Shikoku, on the Bungo Channel. An Edo-period (1600–1868) castle town, it is now a distribution center for marine products and lumber. Industries include shipbuilding and food processing. Mandarin oranges are grown. Local attractions are the bullfighting and summer festival at the Warei Shrine and Uwajima Castle. Pop: 68,034.

Uwa Sea   宇和海

(Uwa Kai). Inlet of the Pacific Ocean off the southwestern coast of Ehime Prefecture, Shikoku. Bounded by the Satamisaki Peninsula on the north, the Bungo Channel on the west, and the Pacific Ocean on the south, it has a heavily indented coastline. These waters offer good fishing for sardines and yellowtail. Pearl culture and yellowtail cultivation are also carried out here. Depth: 60–100 m (200–325 ft).

uyoku → right wing

Uzawa Hirofumi   宇沢弘文

(1928–). Economist. Born in Tottori Prefecture. A specialist in modern economics, he graduated from Tōkyō University in 1951. After serving as a professor at Stanford University and the University of Chicago, he became a professor at Tōkyō University in 1969. An acknowledged leader among modern economists in Japan, his research aims at a theoretical reconstruction of Keynesian economics.

Uzuki → calendar, dates, and time

utsugi Long a favorite of Japanese poets, the *utsugi* yields white trumpet-shaped flowers in May and June.

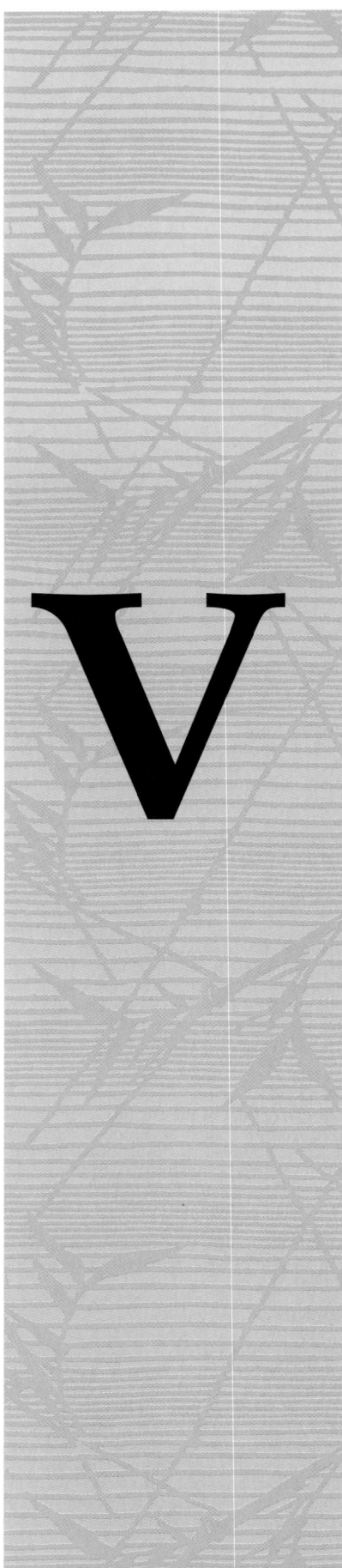

Valignano, Alessandro

バリニャーノ, A.

(1539–1606). Italian Jesuit (see JESUITS). Born in Chieti in 1539; studied law at Padua University; entered the Society of Jesus in 1566. Appointed visitor of the Jesuit missions in Asia (except the Philippines) in 1573, Valignano made three visitations of the Jesuit mission in Japan—1579–82, 1590–92, and 1598–1603—during which he met with several CHRISTIAN DAIMYŌ and national leaders. An outstanding administrator, he reorganized the Jesuit mission and founded a novitiate at Usuki (in what is now Ōita Prefecture) and two boys' schools at Funai and Azuchi (in what are now Ōita and Shiga prefectures, respectively). He promoted Japanese-language studies among the missionaries and urged adaptation to Japanese customs. Valignano died in Macao.

Vaughn, Miles Walter

ボーン, M. W.

(1891–1949). US reporter and correspondent for United Press International. Appointed correspondent for the Far East in 1924. His coverage of the LIUTIAOGOU (LIU-T'IAO-KOU) INCIDENT in 1931 received wide public attention. He died in a boating accident on 30 January 1949. The Vaughn Prize, the most prestigious prize given to Japanese reporters in international news, was established in 1950 by his Japanese friends. It is now known as the Vaughn-Ueda Prize in memory of Ueda Sekizō (1886–1949) of DENTSŪ, INC, who died in the same accident with Vaughn.

VCRs → videocassette recorders

vegetables, green

葉菜類

(*yōsairui*). Among the many leafy vegetables used by the Japanese, cabbage, Chinese cabbage, and spinach are especially popular. Cabbage (*kyabetsu*) was introduced from the West in the Meiji period (1868–1912) and has been cultivated widely since then. It is eaten in the same manner as in Europe and America and is popular as a salad ingredient. Chinese cabbage (*hakusai*) was introduced from China in the Meiji period and its popularity spread rapidly starting in the Taishō period (1912–26). Used mainly for pickling, especially with salt, it is also cooked in various dishes. Spinach (*hōrensō*) has been cultivated since its introduction from China in the 17th century. It is often eaten boiled and flavored with soy sauce. Other leafy vegetables include varieties belonging to the genus *Brassica*, which are used mainly for pickling, although they are also cooked, as well as varieties of mustard with largish leaves. These have a hot flavor and are used for pickling.

vegetables, Western

西洋野菜

(*seiyō yasai*). Vegetables introduced from Europe and the United States in the early part of the Meiji period (1868–1912) are known as Western vegetables in distinction to those traditionally cultivated in Japan. Of these, cabbage, onions, potatoes, and tomatoes have been assimilated so thoroughly into the Japanese diet that they are no longer distinguished as such. Among those still referred to as "Western vegetables," lettuce, cauliflower, celery, asparagus, and parsley have become especially popular.

vendetta → katakiuchi

Verbeck, Guido Herman Fridolin

フルベッキ, G. H. F.

(1830–98). Dutch-born American missionary. As one of the most important FOREIGN EMPLOYEES OF THE MEIJI PERIOD, he contributed to key government decisions in the years immediately following the Meiji Restoration of 1868. Verbeck was sent to Nagasaki in 1859 by the Dutch Reformed Church. In addition to his proselytizing activities he taught English, social sciences, and Western technology; his students included ITŌ HIROBUMI, ŌKUBO TOSHIMICHI, ŌKUMA SHIGENOBU, SOEJIMA TANEOMI, and others who were later prominent in the Meiji government. Recommended by Ōkuma, in 1869 Verbeck went to Tōkyō, where he became a trusted adviser to the new government. His recommendations contributed greatly to the establishment of the prefectural system (1871; see PREFECTURAL SYSTEM, ESTABLISHMENT OF), the sending of the IWAKURA MISSION to the West (1871), the EDUCATION ORDER OF 1872, and the CONSCRIPTION ORDINANCE OF 1873.

vermilion-seal certificate → shuinjō

vermilion seal ship trade

朱印船貿易

(*shuinsen bōeki*). Licensed foreign trade, initiated in the 1590s by TOYOTOMI HIDEYOSHI, in which ships carried licenses *(jō)* issued over the shōgun's vermilion seal *(shuin)*. Since Chinese law kept Japanese out of China after 1547, Japanese merchants and seafarers sought trade in the Philippines and Southeast Asia. Hideyoshi and TOKUGAWA IEYASU tried to bring this trade under their control, as part of their drive for national unification, to help limit the activities of Japanese pirate-traders (WAKŌ), and to ensure the safety of Japanese shipping on the high seas, by issuing special licenses for foreign trade.

Of over 350 licenses issued by the Tokugawa shōguns, most went to Japanese merchants, but some were issued to *daimyō* (37), to other *samurai* (10), and even to Chinese (43) and European (38) merchants. The 6 most common of the 19 recorded destinations are shown in the table.

Over 200 of the *shuinsen* voyages were to ports in Siam or the Indo-Chinese Peninsula, where Japanese merchants had established resident trading communities (see NIHOMMACHI). The principal Japanese exports in the *shuinsen* trade were copper, silver,

The Japanese merchant ship *Sueyoshi*, depicted here in a votive painting from 1633, was one of the ships licensed to trade in Southeast Asia under the vermilion seal of the Tokugawa shogunate.

Japanese Licensed Trade in Southeast Asia in the Early 17th Century

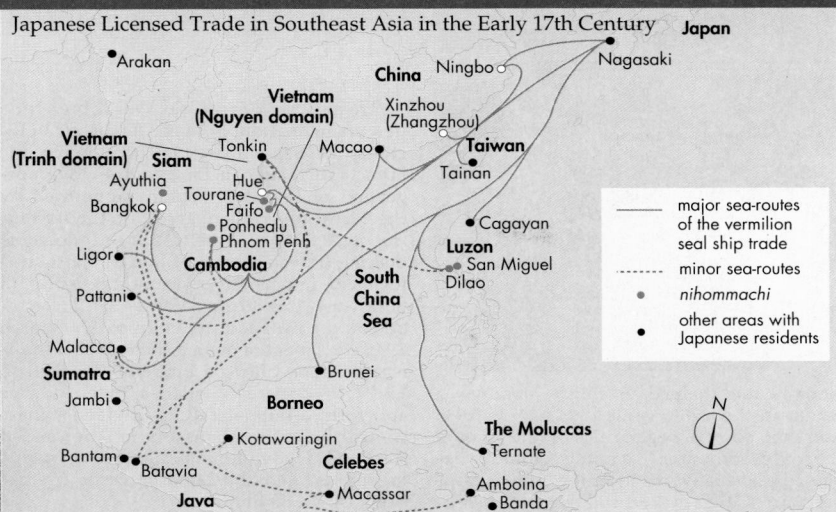

———	major sea-routes of the vermilion seal ship trade
- - -	minor sea-routes
•	*nihommachi*
●	other areas with Japanese residents

iron, Japanese craft items, and sulfur. The main imports were raw silk thread and silk cloth—by far the most important—as well as spices and medicines. In 1635 all foreign voyaging by Japanese was prohibited except for specially licensed voyages to the Ryūkyūs and Korea. See NATIONAL SECLUSION.

Verny, François Léonce

ベルニー, F. L.

(1837–1908). French engineer. Hired by the Tokugawa shogunate (1603–1867) in 1865 at the urging of the French minister Léon ROCHES, Verny supervised the construction of Japan's first lighthouse and a major government shipyard. Working first for the shogunate and later for the new Meiji government, Verny opened a pioneer foundry in Yokohama, expanded a small shipyard in Nagasaki, and constructed a new shipyard at Yokosuka. By 1870 Verny had built lighthouses at Kannonzaki, Nojimazaki, Jōgashima, and Shinagawa. The Yokosuka installation was officially opened by Emperor Meiji in January 1872. Before his return to France in 1876, Verny and his French co-workers taught a variety of Western architectural and industrial techniques to the Japanese. Verny's Shinagawa light, an Important Cultural Property, is now at MEIJI MURA in Aichi Prefecture. See also YOKOSUKA SHIPYARDS; NAGASAKI SHIPYARDS.

Versailles, Treaty of

ベルサイユ条約

(Berusaiyu Jōyaku). Treaty signed on 28 June 1919 at the conclusion of the Paris Peace Conference following World War I. The Japanese delegation, led by SAIONJI KIMMOCHI, sought to gain international recognition of its claims to former German privileges and property in the Shandong (Shantung) Peninsula of China and the Pacific Islands north of the equator. Japan acquired the Mariana, Caroline, and Marshall islands with little opposition but won US President Woodrow Wilson's assent to its Shandong claims only when it threatened not to sign the treaty and promised to return Shandong eventually to full Chinese sovereignty. Wilson yielded because the League of Nations Covenant was a part of the Treaty of Versailles, and he believed that Japanese participation in the league was essential. Japan also sought unsuccessfully to insert an affirmation of the principle of racial equality into the League of Nations Covenant. See SHANDONG (SHANTUNG) QUESTION.

vertical society

縦社会

(tateshakai). Popularized by anthropologist Nakane Chie (b 1926) in her best seller *Tateshakai no ningen kankei* (1967, Human Rela-

tions in a Vertical Society; tr *Japanese Society*, 1970), the term is commonly used to distinguish Japan from presumably more egalitarian societies. Nakane argued persuasively that the essential building blocks of Japanese society are didactic relationships based on a presumption of hierarchical difference. Age, power, sex, rank, role, and experience are the outstanding qualities differentiating superiors and subordinates in most societies, but in Japan such hierarchical differences do not inhibit the development of close personal ties.

Typical of such ties are those between employer or supervisor and subordinate, teacher and student, parent and child, and husband and wife. While some are clearly limited to particular institutions such as the family, others can be found at all levels and in all areas of Japanese life. For example, subsidiaries are known as "child" companies, and political bosses can be honored by their subordinates with the title "teacher."

Egalitarian ties do exist, and the implication that Japanese society is inherently and inevitably hierarchical can be misleading. Yet, since hierarchical personal relations are often central to work, religious, and other community affiliations, they tend to dominate the character of key Japanese social relationships. See also SEMPAI-KŌHAI; OYABUN-KOBUN; FAMILY.

vice-ministers

次官

(jikan). Government officials appointed to each ministry and agency that has a cabinet minister as its head official. Administrative vice-ministers (jimu jikan) are the highest career officials in the government bureaucracy and thus exercise great power. In contrast, the parliamentary vice-ministers (seimu jikan) are political appointees, usually members of the Diet.

Victor Co of Japan, Ltd

日本ビクター[株]

(Nippon Bikutā). Manufacturer of electronic audio and video products. Incorporated as a wholly owned subsidiary of Victor Talking Machine Co, USA (RCA), in 1927, it assumed its present name in 1945. It is a member of the Matsushita group. Its products include videocassette recorders, stereo equipment, color television sets, audio tapes and videotapes, compact discs, phonograph records, and computers and peripherals. The company has 23 sales subsidiaries and 13 production bases abroad. Its overseas brand is JVC. Sales for the fiscal year ending March 1991 totaled ¥638.7 billion (US $4.7 billion), and capitalization stood at ¥34.1 billion (US $248.5 million). Headquarters are in Tōkyō.

Main Destinations of the Voyages

Destination	Number of voyages
Central Vietnam (Nguyen domain)	87
Siam (Thailand)	56
Luzon (northern Philippines)	56
Cambodia	44
North Vietnam (Trinh domain)	37
Taiwan	36

SOURCE: Adapted by Robert Innes from Iwao Seiichi, *Nan'yō nihommachi no kenkyū* (1966).

videocassette recorders

ビデオテープ・レコーダー

(VCRs; J: *bideotēpu rekōdā*). Although video recording technology was developed in the United States in the 1950s, Japanese companies first recognized the potential popularity of a home video recording device that was small and affordable. The first VCR designated for home use was put on the market in 1975 by the SONY CORPORATION. In 1976 Sony's Betamax recording technology was joined (and soon after virtually eclipsed) by the VHS recording format developed by the VICTOR CO OF JAPAN, LTD (JVC). The two systems both use 13-millimeter (0.5-in) tape but are incompatible. Other Japanese companies soon began VCR production, and Japan is now the acknowledged leader in video recording technology development and marketing. In 1990 Japan produced some 31.6 million VCRs, or approximately 80 percent of world VCR production. Japanese companies have also brought onto the market "camcorders," or portable video camera/recorders, some of which use 8-millimeter (0.3-in) tape; VCRs for use with the HIGH-DEFINITION TELEVISION system; and digital VCRs, which process images digitally.

video games

ビデオゲーム

(bideo gēmu). Also called *terebi gēmu* (television games) in Japan. The earliest video games, such as "Pong" by the American company Atari, Inc, were manufactured in the United States in the early 1970s and imported to Japan. The first Japanese company to manufacture video games was Taitō Corp, which put "Elepong" on sale in 1973. In 1978 Taitō introduced its "Space Invaders" game, which was a big hit in Japan and also successful in the United States. The "Pacman" game, released by Namco Co, Ltd, in 1980, also became popular interna-

video games Children crowd around a home video game display at a department store. The Japanese company Nintendō is one of the world's largest manufacturers of such games.

tionally and helped establish Japan as a leader in the video game industry. In 1983 NINTENDŌ CO, LTD, began sales of its Famikon ("Family Computer"), a home computer designed especially for running video game software. Other makers followed with similar products, but Nintendō's popular "Super Mario Brothers" video game software, introduced in 1985, greatly expanded the company's market share and made it a leader in the home video game industry. In June 1991 Nintendō's family computer sales totaled 16.6 million units in Japan, 28.8 million units in the United States, and 5.4 million units in other foreign markets.

Vietnam and Japan ベトナムと日本

(Betonamu to Nihon). The first Japanese to be mentioned in historical records as having been in Vietnam was ABE NO NAKAMARO, who adopted a Chinese name (Chao Heng or Ch'ao Heng) and served there in the 760s as Chinese governor-general (Ch: *duhu* or *tuhu*; J: *togo*). It was not until the 16th and early 17th centuries, however, that trade between Japan and Vietnam developed and Japanese traders formed NIHOMMACHI (Japanese quarters) in Hoi An and Da Nang. Relations were severed in the 17th century with the adoption of the NATIONAL SECLUSION policy by the Tokugawa shogunate (1603–1867). See also NAMBAN TRADE.

Reestablishment of Contact—When Japan entered the Meiji period (1868–1912), most of Southeast Asia was being colonized, and the French conquered Vietnam during the Sino-French War (1884–85). Some Vietnamese nationalists came to Japan to seek support for their anticolonial struggle, but Japanese leaders were more concerned with maintaining good relations with the French colonists, and in 1907 the Japanese and French governments signed a treaty in which each promised to respect the other's sphere of influence in East Asia. This obliged the Tōkyō government to suppress the Vietnamese nationalists in Japan and to expel PHAN BOI CHAU and CUONG DE from Japan in 1909.

The outbreak of World War II brought a new era in relations between Japan and Indochina. In September 1940, following the French surrender in Europe, the governor-general of French Indochina appointed by the Vichy government agreed to the stationing of 30,000 Japanese troops in Indochina, making Indochina one of Japan's most strategically important bases of operation in Southeast Asia during World War II (see INDOCHINA, JAPANESE OCCUPATION OF). In March 1945 the Japanese ousted the French administration and allowed Emperor Bao Dai (b 1913) to declare Vietnam's independence and form a puppet cabinet under Japanese control. Once the Japanese occupation ended the Bao Dai government failed to win popular support and abdicated power to the nationalist Viet Minh.

Postwar Relations—In 1951 Japan signed a peace treaty at San Francisco with the French-backed Saigon government in the south but did not recognize the revolutionary Hanoi government led by Ho Chi Minh in the north. In 1959 Japan concluded a war reparations agreement with the Saigon government. From the mid-1960s the Japanese economy benefited from US military activity in Vietnam, and the Japanese government officially supported American policy; nevertheless antiwar movements flourished among Japanese citizens and Vietnamese students in Japan (see PEACE FOR VIETNAM COMMITTEE).

After the US-China rapprochement in 1971–72 and the conclusion of the Paris peace accord in early 1973, the Japanese government took a serious interest in the normalization of diplomatic relations with Hanoi. The Tōkyō and Hanoi governments signed an agreement in September 1973, but embassies were not actually opened until the end of the Vietnam War. After the fall of Saigon in April 1975, Tōkyō attempted to develop better relations with postwar Vietnam, and in October 1975 signed an economic aid agreement.

At that time Japan anticipated a rapid expansion of economic relations with Vietnam, which needed Japanese cooperation for its postwar recovery and future development. However, Japan joined China and the ASEAN countries in opposing the Vietnamese occupation of Cambodia in January 1979. Japan suspended its promised economic aid, and overall relations with Vietnam deteriorated.

In the meantime the outflow of Vietnamese boat people became a matter of international concern. Japan was finally obliged to remove its barriers against REFUGEES and in 1981 ratified the 1951 international Convention relating to the Status of Refugees. Japan, however, has been criticized for not accepting greater numbers of Indochinese refugees.

The Japanese business community has in recent years become increasingly interested in Vietnam, especially since the latter began in 1988 to actively encourage foreign investment. The future prospects for improved relations between Japan and Vietnam, however, depend on the resolution of the Cambodian conflict.

Vining, Elizabeth Gray
バイニング, E. G.

(1902–). American teacher who served as private tutor to Crown Prince Akihito (now Emperor AKIHITO) from 1946 to 1950. A native of Philadelphia, Vining was known as an author of children's literature. She was se-

lected to be private tutor to the crown prince and went to Japan in 1946. As she taught English to the then 12-year-old crown prince, she stressed the necessity of his possessing a broad vision of society and the world and developing an outstanding personal character. She also lectured at Gakushūin University and Tsuda College. After returning to the United States in 1950, she wrote a book about her experiences, *Windows for the Crown Prince* (1952).

violets 菫

(*sumire*). *Viola* spp. Perennial herbs of the family Violaceae. Of the approximately 400 species of violet that grow wild in temperate zones throughout the world, over 50 are found in Japan. The Japanese species generally fall into two categories: those whose petioles (leaf stems) and peduncles (flower stalks) grow directly from the rhizome, and those whose leaves and flowers grow from a main stem.

The name *sumire* is applied broadly to all Japanese violets but is also used to refer to the common stemless species *V. mandshurica* (7–11 cm [3–4 in] high) with lance-shaped leaves and deep purple blossoms. Similar species include the *shirosumire* (*V. patrinii*), which grows in cold areas and has white flowers; the *kosumire* (*V. japonica*), smaller than the *sumire*, with pale purple flowers; and the *fumotosumire* (*V. pumilio*), with purple-striped petals. Members of the stemmed group include the *tachitsubo sumire* (*V. grypoceras*), with purple-striped petals; the *nioi tachitsubo sumire* (*V. obtusa*), with fragrant, wine-colored flowers; and the *tsubosumire* (*V. verecunda*), often seen in fields and home gardens, with white blossoms.

Viscaino, Sebastian ビスカイノ, S.

(1551?–1615). Spanish envoy to Japan. In 1610 he was sent to Japan, ostensibly to thank the Tokugawa shogunate (1603–1867) for its generosity to Rodrigo VIVERO Y VELASCO, a former governor of the Philippines who had been shipwrecked in Japan in 1609 and returned home in 1610. Viscaino's ship reached Uraga in 1611. He met with the retired shōgun TOKUGAWA IEYASU in Sumpu (now the city of Shizuoka) and his son TOKUGAWA HIDETADA in Edo (now Tōkyō) before returning to Mexico in 1613 with a mission led by HASEKURA TSUNENAGA.

Vivero y Velasco, Rodrigo
ビベロ・イ・ベラスコ, R.

(d 1636). Colonial officer from New Spain (Mexico) who spent 10 months in Japan in 1609–10. A member of a noble family, Vivero was interim governor of the Philippines in 1608. In Manila he was contacted by William ADAMS, the English pilot and shogunal adviser, with the aim of establishing direct trade between the Tokugawa shogunate and New Spain, a project favored by TOKUGAWA IEYASU. At the end of September 1609, while returning to Mexico, Vivero was shipwrecked near Iwada in Kazusa Province (now Chiba Prefecture). Before leaving Japan on 1 August 1610 in the company of a group of Japanese merchants, Vivero negotiated with Tokugawa authorities in an attempt to establish relations between Japan and Spain.

Although never put into effect, a treaty was drafted that proposed extraterritorial privileges for a Spanish shipyard and naval base in the Kantō region in exchange for transpacific trade and Mexican silver-mining technology. Vivero's version of the draft also

violets
1 Highly adaptable, the *sumire* is found in low or slightly hilly areas, in sunny meadows, and, less frequently, in deciduous and pine forests.
2 The *tachitsubo sumire* grows wild throughout Japan in a wide variety of habitats. The striped flowers appear in April and May.

1

2

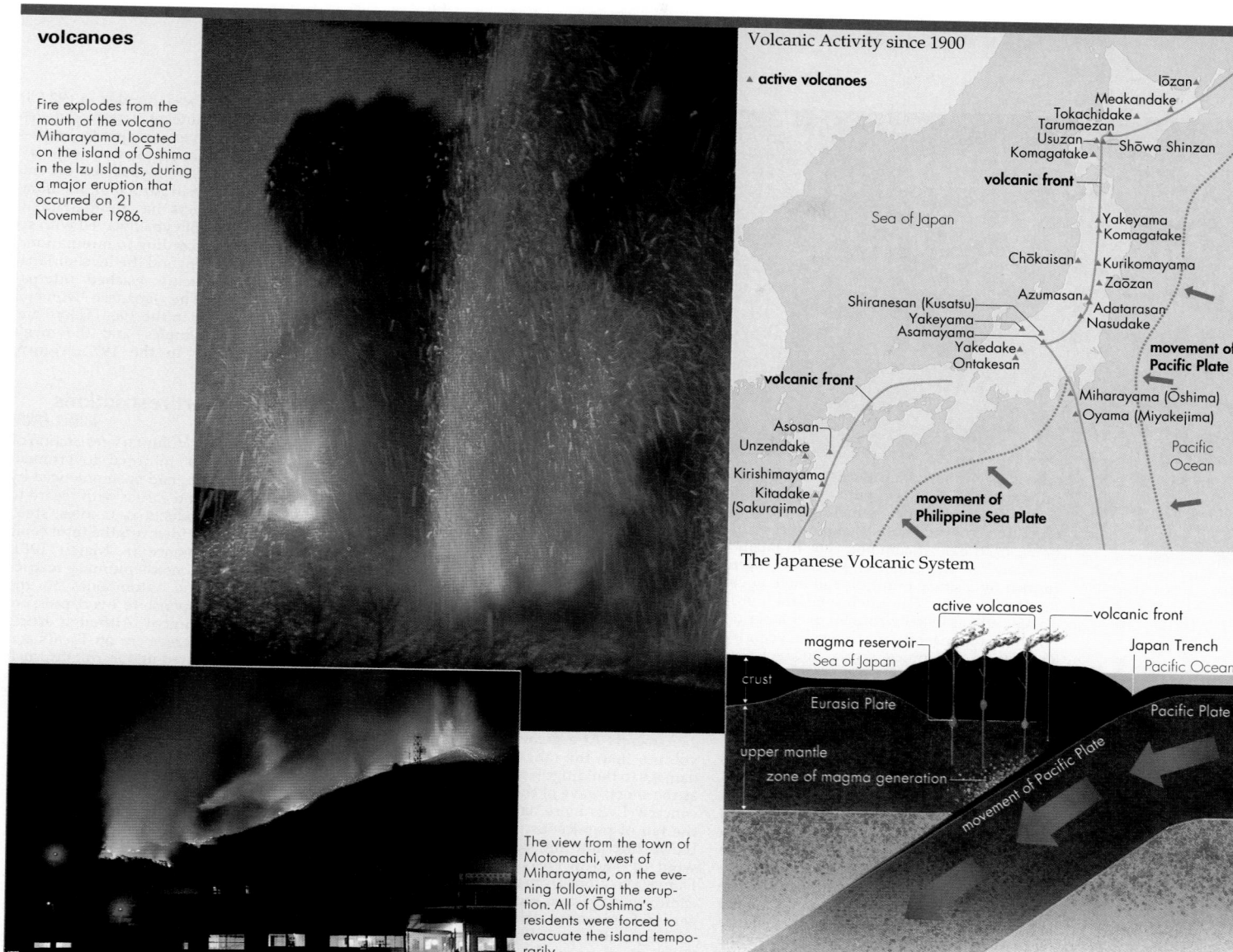

Fire explodes from the mouth of the volcano Miharayama, located on the island of Ōshima in the Izu Islands, during a major eruption that occurred on 21 November 1986.

Volcanic Activity since 1900

▲ active volcanoes

Iōzan
Meakandake
Tokachidake
Tarumaezan
Usuzan — Shōwa Shinzan
Komagatake ▲

volcanic front

Sea of Japan

Yakeyama
Komagatake

Chōkaisan ▲   Kurikomayama
                   ▲ Zaōzan
Azumasan ▲
Shiranesan (Kusatsu)   Adatarasan
Yakeyama   Nasudake
Asamayama
         Yakedake
         Ontakesan

volcanic front

movement of
Pacific Plate

Miharayama (Ōshima)
Oyama (Miyakejima)

Asosan
Unzendake

Kirishimayama
Kitadake
(Sakurajima)

movement of
Philippine Sea Plate

Pacific
Ocean

The Japanese Volcanic System

active volcanoes — volcanic front

magma reservoir
Sea of Japan   Japan Trench
crust   Pacific Ocean

Eurasia Plate   Pacific Plate

upper mantle
zone of magma generation

movement of Pacific Plate

The view from the town of Motomachi, west of Miharayama, on the evening following the eruption. All of Ōshima's residents were forced to evacuate the island temporarily.

called for the mapping of the Japanese coast; freedom for Christian missionary activities; and the expulsion of the Dutch, who had already won trading privileges.

Vocational Ability Development and Promotion Law

職業能力開発促進法

(Shokugyō Nōryoku Kaihatsu Sokushin Hō). Law that provides for a trade skill testing and vocational training system to give individual workers access to skills necessary for employment or promotion. Its ultimate purpose lies in the development of a skilled work force and the stabilization of employment. Its forerunner was the Vocational Training Law (Shokugyō Kunren Hō) enacted in 1958, which was revised in 1969 and replaced by the present law in 1985.

vocational education   職業教育

(shokugyō kyōiku). In Japan, vocational education is offered in high schools, technical colleges, vocational schools, public vocational training centers, and private industry. High schools offer vocational courses in business, nursing, industrial arts, agriculture, and fisheries. A total of 1,397,210 high school students were enrolled in vocational courses in 1990. Japan's 62 TECHNICAL COLLEGES offer rigorous five-year programs in such areas as electrical engineering, biotechnology, mechanical engineering, architec-

ture, and computers. In 1990, 52,930 students were enrolled in technical colleges. Numerous private vocational schools help students meet industry needs in computer programming, communications, fashion design, and other high-demand fields. Government-sponsored vocational training centers train unskilled young people in such areas as dressmaking, automobile maintenance, carpentry, and electronics. Companies also offer on-the-job training programs to employees in highly technical or supervisory positions (see CORPORATE EDUCATION AND TRAINING PROGRAMS).

volcanoes   火山

(kazan). The many active volcanoes in Japan form a part of the so-called circum-Pacific volcanic zone, which surrounds the Pacific Ocean. Volcanic eruptions have significantly influenced the life of the Japanese people since earliest times, frequently causing heavy loss of life. On the other hand, volcanoes have also produced beautiful natural views and features, provided fertile soil, and supplied a source of useful ore deposits.

Distribution of Volcanoes—The volcanoes formed during the Quaternary period are located in a line that generally runs parallel to the Japanese archipelago. The eastern edge of volcano distribution in Hokkaidō and northern Honshū forms a line running almost parallel to the central mountain range

that forms the backbone of the archipelago; to the west of this edge line, called the volcanic front, volcanoes are distributed as far as the Sea of Japan. It is notable that there are no volcanoes at all east of this edge line and that they are most densely distributed along the line itself and in the area immediately to its west. This distribution pattern is common to the entire circum-Pacific volcanic zone. The volcanic front turns abruptly southward in the northwest corner of the Kantō region of Honshū near Mt. Asama (ASAMAYAMA) and, by way of the YATSUGATAKE volcano group, FUJI-HAKONE-IZU NATIONAL PARK, and the eastern side of the Izu Peninsula, goes through the Izu Islands to the volcanic islands of the Marianas. In southwestern Japan the distribution is not so dense, but a volcanic front runs across western Honshū, extends southward to central Kyūshū, and is connected to the volcanoes of Taiwan by way of the Ryūkyū Islands.

Structure and Activity of Japanese Volcanoes—Many Japanese volcanoes have a conical shape similar to that of Mt. Fuji (FUJISAN), which has become a symbol of Japan. These volcanoes, called stratovolcanoes, were formed by the alternate accumulation of lava flows and of volcanic blocks and bombs emitted from the summit crater. One characteristic of this type of vol-

volleyball Intramural volleyball leagues are popular in Japan. Here, two women's teams, with nine players to a side, do battle at a local gymnasium.

cano is its profile, which consists of a beautiful exponential curve with wide, gentle skirts. Stratovolcanoes, which grow by the repetition of moderately explosive eruptions, are the most common type in Japan.

Many of the smallest volcanoes were formed by a single eruption and have never resumed activity. One such type, the pyroclastic cone, is usually formed over a period ranging from several days to several years by an effusion of pumice, scoria, and volcanic ash, which are piled into a cone-shaped volcano with a crater at its summit. Another type is the lava dome, in which highly viscous lava is gradually pushed up as a huge mass from the crater onto the ground, forming an umbrella hill. In many cases there is no explosive eruption but a violent steam explosion may occur when highly heated lava comes in contact with the underground water. Most pyroclastic cones and lava domes are no more than 200 meters (650 ft) in height, and they often occur in groups.

Two rarer kinds of eruption activity are known for their destructive power. One is a large steam explosion, which is a characteristic feature of the stratovolcano toward the end of its life. In the 1888 eruption of Mt. Bandai (BANDAISAN), a series of violent explosions lasting several minutes each was followed by a huge landslide. This type of eruption is not caused directly by magma, but by the high pressure of the steam heated by the magma. The other type of destructive eruption is caused by the effusion of an enormous amount of magma onto the ground within a brief period. Since the magmas characteristically found in the Japanese archipelago have a high viscosity, they cannot effuse rapidly in the form of large-scale lava flows. However, these magmas contain large quantities of gaseous components (mostly water vapor) that, under certain conditions during volcanic eruptions, separate themselves from the magma in the form of foam, much like the foam of beer that rises when a bottle is opened. The foamy magma splits into pieces and is violently ejected as a mixture of rocks, pumice, volcanic ash, and gas known as a pyroclastic flow. The eruption of KOMAGATAKE in Hokkaidō in 1929 is a small-scale example of this phenomenon.

Japanese Myths and Volcanoes—
Very few records of ancient volcanic activity have survived, but some people believe that several of these events are personified as figures in the Izumo myths. The violent Japanese volcanoes seem to have been regarded as objects of fear or worship. From the period of the YAMATO COURT (ca 4th century–ca mid-

7th century) on, volcano deities were given a high status in the Shintō pantheon. Special envoys were frequently appointed by the imperial court, apparently to pacify these volcano deities.

The History and Present Status of Volcanology—
With the introduction of Western scholarship in the 19th century came foreign geologists and geophysicists to study the volcanoes of the archipelago. Japan's scholars then undertook the research, and systematic geological surveys of the main volcanoes in Japan were made by Kotō Bunjirō (1856–1935). Detailed seismological studies of volcanic eruptions were made by ŌMORI FUSAKICHI and others. Later scientists postulated a relation between microearthquakes and volcanic eruptions. This was a beginning of efforts to predict eruptions.

Disasters Due to Eruptions and Their Prevention—
The degree of immediate threat to human life posed by volcanic activity depends upon the size of the eruption and the density of the population in a given area. In a vulcanian eruption, which is the most common type of eruption in Japan, it is only rarely that volcanic rocks and bombs are ejected from the crater over a horizontal distance of several kilometers. It has become possible to foretell explosive eruptions, and when warning signals occur, entry into the danger area around the crater is prohibited. These responsibilities are carried out as part of the wide-ranging meteorological observation and forecast system of the METEOROLOGICAL AGENCY. At a greater distance from the volcano than the range of volcanic bombs, damage to buildings from other factors, such as the shock wave of the eruption, is a major concern. Even more dangerous, however, is the fall of pumiceous rocks that have been blown high into the sky and drift with the wind to land in areas far from the crater. Damage to crops from accumulation of volcanic ash is a serious economic hardship, and several famines are attributed to destruction of rice paddies by volcanic eruptions. Landslides, though rare, have also caused large-scale destruction and death.

Microearthquakes and any change in the earth's crust (such as a tilt, rise, or subsidence) are observed regularly and continuously at 19 active volcanoes throughout Japan, including Asamayama, MIHARAYAMA, ASOSAN, and the UNZENDAKE group. At these volcanoes instruments such as seismometers, tiltmeters, extensometers, and laser beams are used to make precise measurements of any changes. The data recorded is transmitted by telemeter to the survey base, where it is entered into computers. The Global Positioning System (GPS), which uses artificial satellites, is also utilized to monitor conditions. Thus, it is unlikely that a major eruption could occur without some forewarning. However, means of preventing disasters stemming from volcanic eruptions remain inadequate, as volcanic eruptions are natural phenomena involving the release of huge amounts of energy.

In May 1991 there was an eruption at Fugendake, the highest peak of Unzendake, which last erupted in 1792. During the 1991 eruption pyroclastic flows claimed 41 lives.

volleyball　　　　　　　　バレーボール
(*barēbōru*). Volleyball was introduced to Japan in 1913 by F. H. Brown, an American YMCA worker. National volleyball championships began in 1921; the Japan Imperial Volleyball Association (later Japan Vol-

leyball Association) was founded in 1927. In 1925 the team of nine players was developed, and this number—unique to Japan—was soon adopted throughout the country. Since World War II, volleyball has become increasingly popular; in particular, the number of women players has risen dramatically. In the 1950s volleyball played with six players per team (according to international rules) was introduced, and the level of Japanese volleyball quickly reached international standards. The Japanese women's team won first place in the 1964 Tōkyō and 1976 Montreal Olympics, and the men's team came in first in the 1972 Munich Olympics.

voluntary export restrictions　　輸出自主規制
(*yushutsu jishu kisei*). Voluntary restriction of exports by means of informal government pressure on exporters had been practiced by Japan in the 1970s and earlier with regard to exports of such products as textiles, steel, and television sets. However, the term came into special prominence in March 1981, when Japan implemented voluntary restrictions on exports of automobiles to the United States in response to overt pressure from the US government. Although article 11 of the General Agreement on Tariffs and Trade (GATT) prohibited import quotas, such voluntary restrictions of exports fell into a gray area where legality could not be judged by the stated provisions of GATT. Voluntary export restrictions have been politically important in helping Japan reduce trade friction with the United States and the European Community. In recent years Japanese manufacturers have been expanding overseas sales despite voluntary export restrictions by building production facilities in the United States and other countries.

volunteer management of affairs　　事務管理
(*jimu kanri*). Legal term referring to the administration of the affairs of another in the absence of a legal or contractual duty to do so. Although such management of affairs is undertaken in good faith for the sake of another, and the right to claim a fee for such work is not usually recognized, the CIVIL CODE contains several provisions recognizing the right of the person undertaking such a task to, for example, claim reimbursement for expenses incurred (Civil Code, art. 702).

Vories, William Merrel　　ボーリズ, W. M.
(1880–1964). Christian educator and businessman. Known in Japan as Hitotsuyanagi Mereru. Born in Kansas, USA, Vories went to Japan in 1905 as a Christian missionary. After working as an English teacher at Ōmi Hachiman in Shiga Prefecture, he started an architectural office in 1908 and founded Ōmi Sales in 1920. This firm became Ōmi Kyōdaisha (Ōmi Brotherhood, Ltd) in 1934; it marketed and later also produced Mentholatum ointment. (Ōmi Kyōdaisha remains a unique self-supporting missionary enterprise.) In 1918 he established the Ōmi Mission, devoting himself to missionary work and education. In 1917 he married educator Hitotsuyanagi Makiko (1884–1969) and in 1941 became a Japanese citizen. In 1958 he was designated the first honorary citizen of the city of Ōmi Hachiman.

VTRs→videocassette recorders

W

Wa 倭

The Japanese pronunciation of a Chinese character used originally in China and Korea to designate Japan and the Japanese (Ch: Wo). The earliest extant references to Wa are brief geographical notations in the *Shanhai jing* (*Shan-hai ching;* Classic of Mountains and Waterways), date uncertain, and the *Han shu* (History of the Former Han Dynasty), a work of the 1st century. The first account of any length appears in the Eastern Barbarian section of the WEI ZHI (*Wei chih;* ca 297). After the late 7th century, Chinese records reflect the adoption by the YAMATO COURT of Nihon (or Nippon) as the official name of Japan; however, Wa persisted as an epithet in some Chinese texts. The etymology of Wa is uncertain, but it eventually took on disparaging connotations, as in its use in the word WAKŌ, referring to the Japanese pirates who raided the coasts of China and Korea during the 13th to 17th centuries. The Japanese themselves from early times used this Chinese character interchangeably with another, also pronounced *wa* in Japanese (but *he* or *ho* in Chinese), as a prefix in a number of words designating things as Japanese rather than Chinese or Western (e.g., WAKA; WAKON KANSAI); however, the latter character, which has more positive connotations (harmony and peace), was preferred and is now established.

wabi 侘

An aesthetic and moral principle advocating the enjoyment of a quiet, leisurely life free from worldly concerns. Originating in the medieval eremitic tradition, it emphasizes a simple, austere type of beauty and a serene, transcendental frame of mind. It is a central concept in the aesthetics of the TEA CEREMONY and is also manifest in some works of WAKA, RENGA, and HAIKU. Its implications partly coincide with those of SABI and FŪRYŪ.

The word *wabi* was derived from the verb *wabu* (to languish) and the adjective *wabishi* (lonely, comfortless), which initially denoted the pain of a person who fell into adverse circumstances. But ascetic literati of the Kamakura (1185–1333) and Muromachi (1333–1568) periods developed it into a more positive concept by making poverty and loneliness synonymous with liberation from material and emotional worries and by turning the absence of apparent beauty into a new and higher beauty. These new connotations of *wabi* were cultivated especially by masters of the tea ceremony, such as SEN NO RIKYŪ, who sought to elevate their art by associating it with the spirit of Zen and stressed the importance of seeking richness in poverty and beauty in simplicity. The following poem by FUJIWARA NO SADAIE (1162–1241) has been cited as suggesting the essence of *wabi:*

> As I look afar
> I see neither cherry blossoms
> Nor tinted leaves:
> Only a modest hut on the coast
> In the dusk of autumn nightfall.

Wacoal Corporation [株]ワコール

(Wakōru). Company engaged in the manufacture and sale of high-quality women's lingerie and clothing. The company was founded by TSUKAMOTO KŌICHI in 1946 and incorporated in 1949 as Wakō Shōji, a retailer of women's accessories. Its sales of women's underwear rank first in the industry. In 1970 the company established joint ventures in South Korea, Taiwan, and Thailand. In 1979 it initiated production operations in China. Sales for the fiscal year ending May 1991 totaled ¥119.5 billion (US $871.0 million). The company was capitalized at ¥13.3 billion (US $96.9 million) in the same year. Headquarters are in Kyōto.

Wada 和田[町]

Town in southern Chiba Prefecture, central Honshū. Its mild climate makes it ideal for horticulture, mainly flowers and vegetables. There is also dairy farming and fishing. Pop: 6,243.

Wadachi Kiyoo 和達清夫

(1902–). Geophysicist. Authority on deep-focus earthquakes (earthquakes with deep points of origin). Born in Aichi Prefecture. Graduate of Tōkyō University. Wadachi survived the TŌKYŌ EARTHQUAKE OF 1923 and resolved to make the study of earthquakes his career. Upon graduation he joined the Central Meteorological Observatory to specialize in the measurement and investigation of earthquakes. He became the director of the observatory in 1947, and after it became the Meteorological Agency in 1956 he continued as its chief until 1963. He served as head of the National Research Institute for Earth Science and Disaster Prevention from 1963 to 1966, as president of Saitama University from 1966 to 1972, and as director of the Japan Academy from 1974 to 1980. He received the Order of Culture in 1985.

Wada Eisaku 和田英作

(1874–1959). Western-style painter. Born in Kagoshima Prefecture. He studied painting in Tōkyō with HARADA NAOJIRŌ, Soyama Yukihiko (1859–92), and later KURODA SEIKI. Graduate of the Tōkyō Bijutsu Gakkō (now the Tōkyō University of Fine Arts and Music), where he began teaching in 1896. From 1898 through 1903 he lived in France. He served as director of the Tōkyō Bijutsu Gakkō from 1932 to 1935. In 1943 he received the Order of Culture.

Wada Emi ワダエミ

(1937–). Costume designer. Real name Wada Emiko. Born in Kyōto Prefecture; graduated from Kyōto City University of Arts. Wada designs costumes for plays, musicals, television commercials, and films. She received an Academy Award in 1986 for the costumes she created for KUROSAWA AKIRA's *Ran.*

Wada Pass 和田峠

(Wada Tōge). Located in central Nagano Prefecture, central Honshū, west of the highland Tateshina Kōgen. It was an important route on the highway Nakasendō in premodern times. Stone Age relics have been excavated near the pass. Altitude: 1,531 m (5,023 ft).

Wada Tsunashirō 和田維四郎

(1856–1920). Geologist and mineralogist. Born in Fukui Prefecture. A graduate of Kaisei Gakkō (now Tōkyō University), Fukui became the first director of the Japanese government's Geological Survey Office in 1882 and professor at Tōkyō University in 1885. In 1891 he resigned his university position to become head of the Bureau of Mines and contributed to the establishment of laws regulating the operation of mines. Wada's research is gathered in *Nihon kōbutsu shi* (1904, Studies on Japanese Minerals).

Wadachi Kiyoo This geophysicist resolved to study earthquakes after experiencing the Tōkyō Earthquake of 1923.

Monthly Wages by Employee Age and Company Size, 1989

thousands of yen

- over 1,000 employees
- 10–99 employees
- 100–999 employees

400, 300, 200, 100

up to 17 / 18–19 / 20–24 / 25–29 / 30–34 / 35–39 / 40–44 / 45–49 / 50–54 / 55–59 / 60–64 / 65 and over

SOURCE: Ministry of Labor, *Chingin kōzō kihon tōkei chōsa* (annual): 1990.

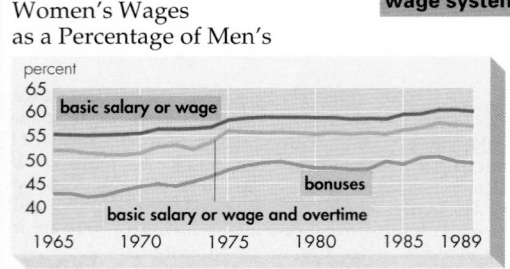

Women's Wages as a Percentage of Men's

percent
65, 60, 55, 50, 45, 40

- basic salary or wage
- bonuses
- basic salary or wage and overtime

1965, 1970, 1975, 1980, 1985, 1989

NOTE: Basic salary or wage includes such supplementary payments as transportation, housing, and family allowances.
SOURCE: Ministry of Labor, *Rōdō hakusho* (annual): 1991.

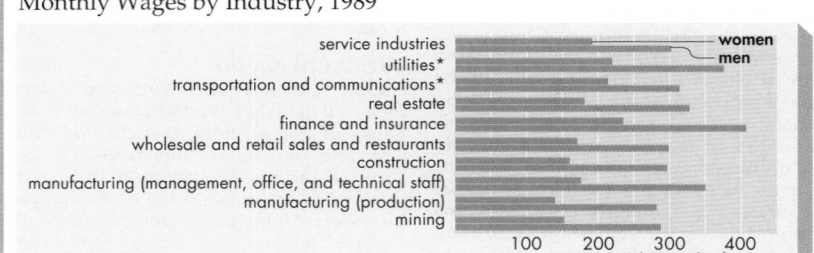

Monthly Wages by Industry, 1989

- service industries
- utilities*
- transportation and communications*
- real estate
- finance and insurance
- wholesale and retail sales and restaurants
- construction
- manufacturing (management, office, and technical staff)
- manufacturing (production)
- mining

women / men

100, 200, 300, 400
thousands of yen

*Includes public-sector as well as private-sector employees.
NOTE: Monthly wages listed here include basic salary, supplementary payments, and overtime pay.
SOURCE: Ministry of Labor, *Rōdō tōkei yōran* (annual): 1991.

Wada Yoshimori　和田義盛

(1147–1213). Military leader of the early Kamakura period (1185–1333); grandson of Miura Yoshiaki (1092–1180). Yoshimori took the surname Wada from his village on the Miura Peninsula in what is now Kanagawa Prefecture. He joined MINAMOTO NO YORITOMO in 1180 in rebellion against the TAIRA FAMILY (see TAIRA-MINAMOTO WAR) and was rewarded with the post of administrator (*bettō*) of the Board of Retainers (SAMURAI-DOKORO). Yoshimori served in campaigns that destroyed the Taira and led to the founding of the KAMAKURA SHOGUNATE. In 1203 he was ordered by the second shōgun, MINAMOTO NO YORIIE, to kill Yoriie's politically powerful maternal grandfather, HŌJŌ TOKIMASA. Yoshimori instead joined Tokimasa, and together they succeeded in replacing Yoriie with his younger brother MINAMOTO NO SANETOMO. In 1213 Tokimasa's son HŌJŌ YOSHITOKI provoked Yoshimori to revolt, and he was soon defeated and killed in a battle at Yuigahama in Kamakura.

Wadō kaihō　和同開珎

Currency of the Wadō era (708–715); also called Wadō *kaichin*. Japan's oldest coin; 1 of 12 types known as KŌCHŌ JŪNISEN (12 coinages of the imperial court), minted during the Nara (710–794) and Heian (794–1185) periods. The court established a minting office (the Chūsenshi) in 708 and began production of this coin in silver and from 709 in copper. Wadō *kaihō* were round with square holes in the center and with the four Chinese characters *wa*, *dō*, *kai*, and *hō* (the last sometimes read *chin*) arranged in clockwise fashion on the obverse. A mold used in minting the coins has been uncovered in the remains of the Nara-period capital HEIJŌKYŌ. Archaeological evidence suggests that the coins, though not in wide use, were minted and circulated in all regions under control of the imperial court.

waegwan　倭館

(J: *wakan*; Japanese residence). Walled compounds reserved for Japanese engaging in trade and diplomacy in Korea, from the early 15th century until shortly after the Meiji Restoration of 1868. From the early 1400s official contacts between Japan and the YI DYNASTY (1392–1910) of Korea were increasingly channeled through the SŌ FAMILY of Tsushima to the Korean ports of Pusanp'o (now Pusan) and Naeip'o (now Chep'o), where the first *waegwan* was located.

Korea allowed the Japanese only a strictly regulated trade within the 50-acre walled compound of the *waegwan*. The 1609 treaty that followed the Japanese INVASIONS OF KOREA IN 1592 AND 1597 barred Japanese from visiting the Korean capital of Seoul. After the Meiji Restoration of 1868 control of the *waegwan* was transferred in 1872 from the Sō family to the newly formed Ministry of Foreign Affairs. But Korea refused to recognize the new government or loosen the old trade limitations; this caused some Japanese to call for an invasion of Korea (see SEIKANRON) and led to Japanese "gunboat diplomacy" that resulted in the Western-style commercial Treaty of KANGHWA in 1876. The former *waegwan* became Japan's first consulate in Korea. See also KOREA AND JAPAN.

Wagahai wa neko de aru　吾輩は猫である

(tr *I Am a Cat*, 1961). NATSUME SŌSEKI's (1867–1916) first full-length novel; published 1905–06. In the work, a cat that speaks with a pompous air observes a variety of Meiji-period (1868–1912) character types, intellectuals in particular, who come to the house of its master, Kushami (literally "Sneeze"), a middle-school English teacher. Kangetsu, a doctoral student engrossed in his preposterous research experiments; Dokusen, a nihilistic philosopher; and Kaneda (literally, "Goldfield"), the parvenu of the neighborhood, are among the targets of Sōseki's criticism, which often expresses misgivings over Meiji Japan's rapid move toward Westernization and modernization. The influence of Swift's *Gulliver's Travels* is evident in the satirical and episodic style of the work, and perhaps even in the choice of an animal as narrator. *Wagahai wa neko de aru* typifies the author's early work, which had a comic and sometimes frivolous side.

wagashi →confections, traditional

Wagatsuma Sakae　我妻栄

(1897–1973). Legal scholar. Born in Yamagata Prefecture. After graduating from Tōkyō University in 1920, he studied civil law under HATOYAMA HIDEO. He was appointed to the faculty of his alma mater in 1922 and remained there until his retirement in 1957. As a member of numerous government commissions he participated in the drafting of the post–World War II CIVIL CODE, especially its section on family law, and other legislation. He received the Order of Culture in 1964. Wagatsuma's works include *Mimpō kōgi* (7 vols, 1932–62, Lectures on the Civil Code), widely regarded as the standard work on the code, and *Kindaihō ni okeru saiken no yūetsuteki chii* (1953, The Primacy of the Law of Obligations in Modern Law), a study that showed his interest in the question of the relation between capitalism and private law.

wage levels　賃金水準

(*chingin suijun*). Before World War II, Japanese wage levels were the lowest among the industrialized nations. The main reasons for this were the suppression of trade union activity and the abundance of workers recruited from farming families in which living standards were very low. Wages fell to bare subsistence levels in the immediate postwar period, but the removal of restrictions on labor union activities and the passage of land reform legislation, coupled with general economic recovery, led to gradual increases in wage levels. By about 1955 wages had recovered to prewar levels, and during the 1960s the labor unions capitalized on constant labor shortages and achieved large wage increases through the SHUNTŌ (spring wage offensive). Economic problems precipitated by the oil crisis of 1973, however, caused the rate of increases in wage levels to drop sharply. The resulting pattern of low wage increases persisted into the 1980s despite the recovery of the Japanese economy.

From an international perspective Japanese wages appeared to increase rapidly in the 1970s and 1980s. This was mainly the result of the strong rise in the value of the yen and represented very little in terms of increased purchasing power for the average Japanese. In 1988 the yen reached ¥120 to the US dollar, twice its average 1984 value and three times its 1971 value.

Although detailed statistical comparisons are difficult, as of 1990 it appeared that hourly wages in the manufacturing sector in Japan were comparable to those in the United States and had exceeded those of most European nations, with the notable exception of West Germany.

A comparison of wages based on actual purchasing power, however, gives very different results. Because of the high price of daily necessities and land, the real wages of the Japanese worker remain considerably lower than those in most industrialized Western countries.

Wagener, Gottfried　ワグネル, G.

(1831–92). German technical consultant and teacher who contributed to Japan's developing arts and industries, especially textiles and ceramics, in the Meiji period (1868–1912). Also known as Gottfried Wagner. Born in Hannover, Wagener graduated from Georgia Augusta University in Göttingen and went to Nagasaki in 1868 to help build a factory. In 1870 he aided local au-

Wagatsuma Sakae
This legal scholar trained many students and helped draft the post–World War II Civil Code.

thorities in improving the kilns for ARITA WARE. He went to Tōkyō to enter government service as a teacher in 1871. Over the years he taught physics, applied chemistry, and related courses at Daigaku Nankō and Tōkyō Kaisei Gakkō (predecessors of Tōkyō University), became a teacher at the Kyōto SEIMIKYOKU in 1878, and from 1884 was head of the pottery and glass department of the Tōkyō Shokkō Gakkō (now Tōkyō Institute of Technology). In his writings he urged the adoption of Western techniques to strengthen rather than replace traditional crafts—a suggestion that eventually became government policy. He helped establish a museum for Japanese art (now the TŌKYŌ NATIONAL MUSEUM).

wage system　　　　　　　　賃金制度

(*chingin seido*). The Japanese wage system basically operates on the principle of seniority. This principle, combined with other employment practices such as enterprise unionism and lifetime employment, has been credited with assuring workers' acceptance of technological innovation, job rotation, and in-house training, all key advantages enjoyed by large Japanese firms.

Under the seniority system, wages are determined in accordance with an employee's length of service and status within the company. No matter how the employee performs in a given job, length of service will count for more than individual ability when it comes to securing promotion and better pay. Workers in this system thus have strong incentives to remain in the same firm rather than seek to jump to another firm. Remuneration based on merit has grown in popularity among large firms, but the system of seniority-based wages remains largely intact.

Modern seniority wage and lifetime employment practices, which may be traced to the early 1920s, came about chiefly as Japanese industry responded to a shortage of skilled labor. The practices were popularized throughout the economy after World War II, as both management and the labor unions gradually came to recognize their advantages. Large firms (those with 1,000 employees or more) are now characterized by the use of a permanent labor force, which constituted 67.6 percent of their male workers in 1990. Only these permanent employees are members of the enterprise union and enjoy the benefits of the seniority wage and lifetime employment systems.

Another characteristic of the wage system in large firms is that the base wage tends to be a relatively small percentage of an employee's total remuneration. The total income of permanent workers in large firms consists of four components: the base wage, statutory allowances (overtime, paid vacations, etc), nonstatutory allowances, and seasonal bonuses. Of these other payments the bonus system is of particular importance: the average annual bonus in 1990 (paid in two installments) amounted to about one-third of annual base wages, and it is not uncommon for the bonus to equal the annual base wages. The company bonus system has served to increase the flexibility of the wage system.

Although the Japanese wage system has contributed to Japan's economic growth, two fundamental problems remain. First, the seniority wage system and lifetime employment guarantee have not become as well established in smaller firms as in larger enterprises, in part because job mobility is much higher in the former. This is one reason

for the significant wage differentials between small and large firms in Japan. Other factors contributing to these wage differentials include the wide gap in company welfare allowances, bonuses, and retirement and other allowances. Workers' total incomes will thus differ greatly depending upon the size of the firm where they are employed. Taking the average wage of regular workers in large firms as 100, in 1990 the wage index was 80.4 for workers in medium-sized companies (those with 100 to 999 employees), and 72.4 for workers in small companies (those with 10 to 99 employees).

Second, the system tends to discriminate against older workers and female employees. In Japan new employees' salaries are relatively low but tend to increase at an accelerating rate as their career with the company lengthens. By the time employees reach the age of 50 to 54, they are likely to be earning 2.34 times their salaries at age 20 to 24, a much wider differential than in the West. If employees continue to work after retirement, however, their wages often fall below the level they received when they entered the company. And although it is illegal to pay men and women different rates for the same job, the shorter average career of women employees puts them at a distinct disadvantage in the context of the seniority-based wage system.

wagtails　　　　　　　　鶺鴒

(*sekirei*). Birds of the family Motacillidae, with a long tail and a slender body about 20 centimeters (8 in) in length. Living near bodies of water, they forage on the ground, wagging their tails up and down. Five species are found in Japan: the *kisekirei* (gray wagtail; *Motacilla cinerea*), the *hakusekirei* (white wagtail; *M. alba*), and the *seguro sekirei* (Japanese wagtail; *M. grandis*) breed north of the island of Kyūshū; the *tsumenaga sekirei* (yellow wagtail; *M. flava*) breeds only in northern Hokkaidō; and the Iwami *sekirei* (forest wagtail; *Dendronanthus indicus*), which alone wags its tail sideways, breeds only in Kyūshū and western Honshū. The black-backed, white-bellied *seguro sekirei* is peculiar to Japan.

A passage in the *Nihon shoki* (720) relates how the male and female deities Izanagi no Mikoto and Izanami no Mikoto watched and then emulated a pair of mating wagtails, after which Izanami gave birth to the islands of Japan. For this reason a pair of wagtails is sometimes used as a decorative motif at weddings.

Wainai Sadayuki　　　　　和井内貞行

(1858–1922). Fish breeder. Known for his success at breeding trout (*masu*) in Lake TOWADA (northern Honshū), where it had been said that fish could not live. Born in Mutsu Province (now Akita Prefecture). Wainai introduced two varieties of carp into Lake Towada in 1884 without success. In 1902 he stocked the lake with *himemasu* (a kind of native trout similar to the kokanee salmon of Alaska) from Hokkaidō's Lake Shikotsu. By 1905 the fish were breeding and, later introduced throughout Japan, came to be known as Wainai *masu* (Wainai trout).

Wajima　　　　　　　　輪島［市］

City in northern Ishikawa Prefecture, central Honshū. Principal industries are fishing and the manufacture of *wajima-nuri* lacquer ware. Attractions include the Sosogi Coast and the female divers (*ama*) on the nearby island of HEGURAJIMA. Pop: 30,164.

Wajima A morning market is one of the attractions of this city on the Sea of Japan coast.

Wajima lacquer ware　　　　輪島塗

(*wajima-nuri*). A durable ware produced in the city of Wajima, Ishikawa Prefecture, through an elaborate process of layering and decoration. Early in the Edo period (1600–1868), clay containing oxidized iron and manganese was discovered in the area. This was fired and ground to a powder to produce *jinoko*, which was mixed with lacquer and layered on wood to provide an impervious foundation for the lacquer finish. Through a process known as MAKI-E, pictures or designs were painted with lacquer, and gold or silver dust or pigment powder was sprinkled over the lacquer while it was still damp. In the mid-Edo period the *chinkin* method of incising lines in patterns and inlaying them with strips of gold leaf was introduced from China. *Wajima-nuri* remains today an important Japanese lacquer ware.

Waji shōran shō　　　　　和字正濫鈔

(Notes on the Rectification of Japanese Writing). A comprehensive study of KANA (the Japanese phonetic syllabary) orthography written by KEICHŪ, a scholar of National Learning (KOKUGAKU), in the Edo period (1600–1868). It was published in five volumes in 1695. After carrying out research in old classical texts, Keichū corrected the Teika *kanazukai*, a long-practiced system of traditional *kana* usage attributed to FUJIWARA NO SADAIE (also known as Fujiwara no Teika). Arranging entries according to the old Japanese *iroha* syllabary order, he gave the corrected *kana* for problem words and cited the sources on which these were based.

wajū　　　　　　　　　輪中

(literally, "within a circle"). Type of community, surrounded by embankments for protection from flooding (the embankments containing both the community and its fields); found in the delta formed by the lower courses of the rivers Kisogawa, Nagaragawa, and Ibigawa. The area extends from the city of Ōgaki, Gifu Prefecture, in the north to the mouths of the three rivers in Aichi and Mie prefectures in the south. The

wagtails The gray wagtail is one of three species commonly seen along rivers and streams.

building of *wajū* in this area has a long history, the first dating as early as 1319. Some 80 *wajū* still exist.

waka 和歌

("Japanese poetry"). A genre of verse of various prosodic types that began to take form in the hands of the court aristocracy in the mid-6th century. By the late 8th century the term was used synonymously with TANKA ("short poem"), a type of verse that consists of five lines in 31 syllables in the pattern 5-7-5-7-7 and that is still composed today. EARLY JAPANESE SONG, from which *waka* arose, and the derivative genres RENGA ("linked verse") and *haikai* (see HAIKU) are distinguished from *waka*, as is modern free verse (see POETRY, MODERN). The sinicized term *waka*, in use by the Heian period (794–1185), replaced the previous term Yamato *no uta* (poetry of the land of Yamato), but both imply the distinction of native verse from *kanshi*, or verse composed in Chinese by Chinese or Japanese poets (see POETRY AND PROSE IN CHINESE).

A salient feature of *waka* verse is its tendency toward lyricism. Although this emphasis may be seen as a result of the brief 31-syllable form, many Japanese consider it a manifestation of a native disposition toward the logic of the heart as opposed to the logic of the mind. Moreover, much of the *waka* composed through the Kamakura period (1185–1333) was occasional. The exchange or capping of verses was an indispensable part of festive gatherings of courtiers and of communications between lovers. Another prominent aspect of *waka* is its restrictions and taboos concerning subject matter and vocabulary. In part this is a result of the religious origin of Japanese song, but of equal significance is the fact that *waka* developed in an aristocratic society that abhorred the common and the grotesque. A consequence was that *waka* came to be governed by convention down to the smallest details of imagery and phrasing, while invention was restricted to subtle readjustment of conventional elements.

Prosody and Rhetorical Devices—The primary sources of our knowledge of early Japanese poetry are the annals KOJIKI (712, Record of Ancient Matters) and NIHON SHOKI (720, Chronicles of Japan) and the late-8th-century anthology of poetry MAN'YŌSHŪ (Collection of Ten Thousand Leaves or Collection for Ten Thousand Generations), most of the more than 4,000 poems in which were culled from earlier anthologies that are no longer extant. The oldest poems display little prosodic regularity, although there was a tendency to alternate longer and shorter lines. In the 7th century, however, possibly arising from the influence of the five-character and seven-character lines of Chinese verse, the number of syllables per line became standardized at five and seven. From the mid-7th century the *tanka* form appears to have been paramount, but until the middle of the 8th century it was rivaled by the CHŌKA ("long poem"), consisting of an indefinite number of pairs of five- and seven-syllable lines with an extra seven-syllable line at the end. The longest *chōka*, by KAKINOMOTO NO HITOMARO, is one in 149 lines. Other forms were the KATAUTA ("half poem"), of 3 lines of five, seven, and five syllables, to which another poet replied to form a set; the *sedōka* ("head-repeated poem"), of 6 lines in the syllable pattern 5-7-7-5-7-7; and the *bussokuseki no uta*, also

of 6 lines but in the syllable pattern 5-7-5-7-7-7, the chief examples of which are inscribed on an ancient stela erected beside a stone (BUSSOKUSEKI) on which the Buddha's footprints are incised.

Alliteration, consonance, and assonance are found in the earliest Japanese verses and were used by poets of all periods to provide sonority and rhetorical complexity. Until the mid-8th century the dominant cadence of *waka* was 5-7, but thereafter the 7-5 cadence gained the ascendancy. It also became common for the cadence to be broken, usually at the end of the third line, by a caesura. In the following 12th-century poem by the priest JAKUREN, the third line terminates with a conclusive verb inflection and is followed by a noun phrase:

Sabishisa wa
Sono iro to shi mo
Nakarikeri
Maki tatsu yama no
Aki no yūgure

To be alone—
It is of a color that
Cannot be named:
This mountain where cedars rise
Into the autumn dusk.

Among prominent rhetorical devices of the *waka* tradition is the MAKURA KOTOBA ("pillow word"), a stylized epithet, normally of five syllables, used to modify certain fixed words in the fashion of Homeric epithets. JOKOTOBA (preface) is a freely composed modifying phrase of indeterminate length that often appears to be semantically unrelated to the ensuing line or lines of a poem but that supplies metaphorical amplification or tonal resonance. UTA MAKURA ("poem pillow") is the name of a place renowned for its beauty or for a mood that convention holds it evokes, and is often chosen because of the possibilities it offers for wordplay. KAKEKOTOBA ("pivot word") is a word or part of a word whose sense is rendered differently in conjunction with what precedes and what follows; both senses, however, contribute to the meaning of the poem, as in the lines *Ko no me mo haru no / Yuki fureba* (And the buds on the trees swell [*haru*] / But as a spring [*haru*] snow has fallen). ENGO ("associated word") is a word or words whose meaning or homophonous sound associates with another word basic to the sense of a poem. An instance of this would be the appearance of the verb *kiyu* "vanish" in a poem together with *yuki* "snow," but only when *yuki* is not the grammatical subject of *kiyu*.

Imagery and Subject Matter—Classical *waka* employed a high proportion of images drawn from nature, personification of which led increasingly to allegory. However, unlike Western allegory, with its personified conceptual abstractions, allegory in *waka* tended to be concrete and personal (e.g., a poem about an orange tree that awaits the arrival of the cuckoo in early summer might also represent a lady awaiting her dilatory lover). The conventions of *waka* militated against the innovative use of natural images—the stock of which, in the case of insects, included the cicada and the cricket, but not the butterfly, the bee, or the firefly—and a consequence of this narrowing of content was that a new poem inevitably alluded to earlier poems in the tradition.

Waka poets concentrated on a handful of subjects, primarily human affairs (celebration, separation, grief, and especially love)

and nature (natural beauty and the changing aspects of the seasons), avoiding war, physical suffering, death, and all that was ugly or low. The themes of beauty and sadness, infused by an awareness of the overarching effects of time, increasingly dominated *waka*. With the growing influence of a Buddhist world view holding all life to be ephemeral (see MUJŌ) and all human attachment to be an impediment to enlightenment, nature poetry came typically to express a lyric melancholy (see MONO NO AWARE; SABI), while poetry of love expressed a poignant consciousness of the impermanence of personal ties.

Historical Development—Following the *Man'yōshū*, the next major collection of *waka* was the KOKINSHŪ (905, Collection from Ancient and Modern Times), the first of 21 IMPERIAL ANTHOLOGIES. These anthologies varied considerably in size and quality, but each was considered the most important literary enterprise of its day. Among the chief sources from which poems were drawn for inclusion in the imperial anthologies were the *shikashū*, collections of poetry written and compiled by individual poets. Other important repositories of classical *waka*—and of critical judgments—are the records of poetry matches (UTA-AWASE).

Waka of the *Kokinshū* was much influenced by the mannered elegance and precious conceits of Chinese poetry of the late Six Dynasties period (222–589), in particular the monumental *Wen xuan* (*Wen hsüan*; J: *Monzen*). Nevertheless, the *Kokinshū* also displays in its verse, as well as in the vernacular preface written by one of its compilers, KI NO TSURAYUKI, a strong consciousness of a native poetics. Tsurayuki distinguishes between the essence or "heart" (*kokoro*) of a poem and the construct of language (*kotoba*) by means of which it is embodied. The ideal toward which the poet strives, Tsurayuki declares, is a harmony of *kokoro* and *kotoba*, of individual feeling and sincerity with rhetorical elegance and purity of diction.

By the 12th century, wit and elegant posturing had given way to a quest for depth and resonance. The prevailing sadness of poetry of the time was strongly influenced by the Buddhist doctrine of *mappō* (see ESCHATOLOGY), under which the era was viewed as the beginning of a last age of worldly degeneration. The greatest of the innovating poets of the 12th and early 13th centuries were Fujiwara no Shunzei (FUJIWARA NO TOSHINARI) and his son Fujiwara no Teika (FUJIWARA NO SADAIE). Shunzei adapted the Tendai-sect Buddhist meditative practice *shikan* ("concentration and insight") to the composition of *waka*—an art he felt to be as sure a means to enlightenment as Buddhism itself—and sought to express the essential nature (*hon'i*) of the human experience through concentration on and identification with the subjects of his verse. His dictum "old words, new treatment" called for the creation of innovative stylistic effects, such as YŪGEN (mystery and depth), through reverential application of the classical language of *waka*. Both he and Teika used the allusive device HONKADORI, the introduction of a phrase from a renowned older poem, in order to bestow a resonating montage effect upon their poetry.

The eighth imperial anthology, SHIN KOKINSHŪ (1205, New Collection from Ancient and Modern Times), one of whose editors was Teika, brought to fulfillment the organizational concepts, already apparent in the *Kokinshū*, of association and progression. Adjacent poems were linked by such devices as similarity of image or common allusion to an older poem, while all of the poems of the major divisions of the anthology, such as those devoted to individual seasons or to love, were ordered on the basis of the appearance of seasonal phenomena or the progress of a love affair. The principles of association and progression were among the influences that contributed to the development of the genre of linked verse (renga).

The last imperial anthology, Shin shoku kokinshū (New Collection from Ancient and Modern Times, Continued) was completed in 1439. Following the Shin kokinshū, imperial anthologies displayed an increasingly sterile style, marked by a slavish veneration of the conventions of the Heian period, and by the Edo period (1600–1868) the center of waka composition had passed from the court to society at large. These new practitioners felt freer to select from the entire range of Japanese tradition those styles and ideals that they wished to emulate, and some, such as TODA MOSUI and KADA NO ARIMARO, even called upon poets to liberate themselves from the restraints of the past and open new ground. In the late Edo period a number of innovative poets appeared, among them TACHIBANA AKEMI, HIRAGA MOTOYOSHI, and the priest RYŌKAN, whose influence persisted into modern times.

Early in the Meiji period (1868–1912), the influential poet-critics YOSANO TEKKAN and MASAOKA SHIKI called for a break with the past and, following their practice, the custom arose of referring to the art of 31-syllable poetry as tanka, rather than waka. In 1899, with other young tanka poets, Tekkan founded the Shinshisha (New Poetry Society), which in 1900 initiated the publication of the literary magazine MYŌJŌ (Bright Star). One of the leading contributors was YOSANO AKIKO, whose passionate lyricism brought a new vigor to the genre. Around Shiki, who urged the application of a painterly descriptive style (shasei) to the composition of tanka, there gathered such poets as ITŌ SACHIO and NAGATSUKA TAKASHI. Other notable modern tanka innovators were ISHIKAWA TAKUBOKU and SAITŌ MOKICHI.

Tanka continues in the post–World War II period to be a widely practiced form of verse; nevertheless, though today hundreds of societies and millions of practitioners carry on the tradition, the best Japanese poets have increasingly chosen to work in the genre of free verse. Moreover, the importance of convention in waka has led to the preservation of classical grammar in tanka composition, thus vitiating the immediacy of its effect on the majority of Japanese. A notable exception, however, is the vastly popular tanka of Tawara Machi (b 1962), who has preserved the subtlety of feeling and expressive grace of classical waka while employing colloquial diction.

wakadoshiyori   若年寄

Junior councillors or "young elders"; also known as shōrō or sansei. They stood second only to senior councillors (RŌJŪ) in the TOKUGAWA SHOGUNATE (1603–1867) and supervised direct vassals of the shōgun (HATAMOTO and GOKENIN), using the reports of inspectors (METSUKE). The wakadoshiyori also provided supervision of artisans, physicians, routine construction work, and most of the shōgun's guard units (BANKATA). In the event of war wakadoshiyori were to lead the hatamoto into battle. The office was established in 1633 by MATSUDAIRA NOBUTSUNA.

The number of wakadoshiyori varied from three to five, each (like the rōjū) serving for a month at a time on a rotating basis. They were chosen from the FUDAI daimyō.

wakai   和解

(compromise). Agreement between plaintiff and defendant to terminate a lawsuit. When an agreement is reached between parties in the course of civil litigation, the particulars of the agreement are presented to the court. In the event that the court records the particulars in a protocol, such a settlement protocol has the same effect as a final judgment (Code of Civil Procedure, art. 203).

A large percentage of lawsuits are disposed of by compromise. Generally speaking, negotiations can occur during three stages of a proceeding. The first opportunity for compromise is when the issues have been framed and documentary evidence has been produced, immediately before trial. The second opportunity is after the main witnesses on important issues have been examined. The last opportunity is after the conclusion of the presentation of evidence. Many judges take the initiative in suggesting figures and recommending payment in accordance with the extent of the evidence.

Wakakusayama   若草山

Also called Mikasayama. Hill in the eastern part of the city of Nara, Nara Prefecture, central Honshū; composed of andesite. On the summit is a mounded tomb (KOFUN) called Uguisuzuka. The hill is covered with turf and is known for the turf burning that is conducted there every January. It is part of Nara Park. Height: 342 m (1,122 ft).

Wakamatsu   若松

Harbor industrial zone located in the city of Kita Kyūshū, Fukuoka Prefecture, northeastern Kyūshū. Wakamatsu was a coal shipping port from the early part of the Meiji period (1868–1912) until about 1955. In recent years, large steel and machinery factories have been built on reclaimed land in the northern part of Wakamatsu, which constitutes part of the KITA KYŪSHŪ INDUSTRIAL ZONE.

Wakamatsu Kōji   若松孝二

(1936–). Film director. Born in Miyagi Prefecture. After working as an assistant director on films made for television, Wakamatsu began to direct low-budget pornographic films in 1963. Although this genre is generally ignored by critics, Wakamatsu's work attracted notice for its artistic quality. Among his major productions are Kabe no naka no himegoto (1965, Secrets within Walls) and Taiji ga mitsuryō suru toki (1966, When the Fetus Goes Poaching).

Wakamatsu Shizuko   若松賤子

(1864–96). Translator and author. Original name Matsukawa Kashi. Born in Wakamatsu in the Aizu domain (now part of Fukushima Prefecture). A graduate of the Ferris Girls' School in Yokohama in 1882, she later taught English there. In 1889 she married IWAMOTO YOSHIHARU, editor in chief of the influential women's magazine JOGAKU ZASSHI. Her original works reflect Christian influence. Wakamatsu is best known for her translation of F. E. Burnett's Little Lord Fauntleroy (1886; tr Shōkōshi, 1890–92).

wakame   若布

(lobe-leaf seaweed). Undaria pinnatifida. Eaten in Japan since ancient times, wakame

grows naturally in many areas, from the west coast of Hokkaidō to Kyūshū. Most commercial wakame, however, is cultivated. Dried wakame is softened in water, chopped, and used as an ingredient in MISO SOUP or served with a vinegar dressing.

wakamizu   若水

The first water drawn from a well or spring on New Year's morning. During the Heian period (794–1185) it was customary for members of the imperial court to take the first water drawn on the morning of the first day of spring and offer it to the emperor; later the practice shifted to New Year's Day. Because of the belief that wakamizu has the power to repel illness and attract good fortune, it is used in a variety of ways to pray for the year's happiness: to rinse out the mouth, purify the body, make ZŌNI (a kind of soup eaten at New Year's), and make the ink used in the first calligraphy of the year (KAKIZOME).

wakamono-gumi   若者組

A traditional male youth group found in rural communities. The wakamono-gumi played a central role in village society, directing festivals and rituals, performing communal village work, acting as night watchmen and firemen, and participating in rescue work in emergencies. Members also received training in work skills and engaged in social activities with the musume-gumi (girls' organization). Most boys entered the wakamono-gumi at around 15 years of age, but in some cases only the firstborn son of a family or one boy from a family became a member. It was usual to leave the group after marriage. Since membership in the wakamono-gumi meant that the youth was fully recognized as an adult by the villagers, strict initiation ceremonies were often performed. Members commonly lived together in communal lodgings called wakamono yado. From the late 19th century to the early 20th century, the role of the wakamono-gumi was largely taken over by the YOUTH CLUBS (seinendan).

Wakanoura   和歌浦

Coastal area in the city of Wakayama, Wakayama Prefecture, central Honshū. It forms the easternmost point of the Inland Sea National Park and is noted for the beauty of its beaches and surrounding scenery, which draw tourists. It is mentioned in the 8th-century poetry anthology Man'yōshū.

Wakan rōeishū   和漢朗詠集

(Collection of Chinese and Japanese Poems for Singing). Anthology of favorite Chinese couplets and Japanese tanka (31-syllable WAKA) for singing to fixed melodies, which were not included in the text. Compiled by FUJIWARA NO KINTŌ around 1013, it contains 588 couplets in Chinese by some 30 Chinese and 50 Japanese poets, including the very important and influential Tang (T'ang) dynasty poet Bo Juyi (Po Chü-i; 772–846) and Chinese poets Yuan Shen (Yüan Shen; 779–831) and Xu Hun (Hsü Hun; fl ca 850); Japanese poets of Chinese verse include Sugawara no Fumitoki (899–981), SUGAWARA NO MICHIZANE, Ōe no Asatsuna (886–957), MINAMOTO NO SHITAGAU, and Ki no Haseo (845–912). The 216 Japanese tanka in the collection are by 80 poets, including KI NO TSURAYUKI, ŌSHIKŌCHI NO MITSUNE, and KAKINO-

Wakasugi Hiroshi
Internationally known, Wakasugi is Japan's most accomplished operatic conductor.

Wakatsuki Reijirō
This adherent of party politics was prime minister in the years 1926–27 and 1931.

Wakayama Prefecture
Location and Prefectural Crest

MOTO NO HITOMARO. The work is divided into two books, poems on the four seasons occupying the first book and "miscellaneous" poems the second. Within these divisions, the poems are subclassified by common topics, Chinese couplets frequently alternating with Japanese *tanka* on the same subject.

Wakan sansai zue 和漢三才図会

(Japanese-Chinese Illustrated Assemblage of the Three Components of the Universe). Illustrated encyclopedia edited by Terashima Ryōan (dates unknown), an Ōsaka physician; completed in 1712. Closely patterned on the 1607 Chinese work *Sancai tuhui* (*San-ts'ai t'u-hui;* J: *Sansai zue*), the encyclopedia includes chapters covering astronomy, geography, plants, animals, clothing, implements, and other topics. The entries are written in Chinese prose (*kambun*).

Wakao Ayako 若尾文子

(1933–). Film actress. Born in Tōkyō. As a high-school student she joined HASEGAWA KAZUO and his Shin'engiza troupe and later moved to the Daiei Motion Picture Company. Appearing in Shima Kōji's (1901–86) *Jūdai no seiten* (1953, Teenager's Sex Manual) and *Chatarē fujin wa Nihon ni mo ita* (1953, Japan's Own Lady Chatterley), as well as Hisamatsu Seiji's (1912–90) *Jūdai no yūwaku* (1954, Temptation of Teenagers), she became a sex symbol. She also appeared in MIZOGUCHI KENJI's *Gion-bayashi* (1953, Gion Festival Music) and *Akasen chitai* (1956, Street of Shame) and in such films as MASUMURA YASUZŌ's *Tsuma wa kokuhaku suru* (1961, The Wife Confesses), *Manji* (1964), *Otto ga mita* (1964, The Husband Saw), *Seisaku no tsuma* (1965, The Wife of Seisaku), and *Nureta futari* (1968, Evil Duo). She has also acted on stage, on television, and in the Shōchiku film series *Otoko wa tsurai yo* (It's Tough Being a Man; see TORA SAN).

Wakasa Bay 若狭湾

(Wakasa Wan). Inlet of the Sea of Japan on the northern coast of central Honshū, extending between Echizemmisaki, a cape in Fukui Prefecture, in the east and Kyōgamisaki, a cape on the Tango Peninsula, Kyōto Prefecture, in the west. It has a heavily indented coastline with numerous small bays and peninsulas. A good fishing ground, the bay also has many fine beaches. Sections of the bay's shoreline form the Wakasa Bay Quasi-National Park.

Wakasugi Hiroshi 若杉弘

(1935–). Conductor. Born in Tōkyō, he graduated from Tōkyō University of Fine Arts and Music. He studied under SAITŌ HIDEO. As a student he began working as rehearsal pianist and associate conductor for the FUJIWARA OPERA and NIKIKAI. In 1963 he joined the NHK SYMPHONY ORCHESTRA as an associate. From 1977 on he became regular conductor of the Cologne Radio Symphony Orchestra. In 1981 he became music director of the German Opera of the Rhine. In 1986 he became music director of the Tōkyō Metropolitan Symphony Orchestra, and in 1990 he was appointed director of the Dresden State Opera. He specializes in conducting operas and the works of Mahler.

Wakatsuki Reijirō 若槻礼次郎

(1866–1949). Politician and prime minister (1926–27; 1931). Born in the Matsue domain (now Shimane Prefecture). Graduated from Tōkyō University. In 1912 he became finance minister and joined the RIKKEN DŌSHIKAI. In 1914 he joined the KENSEIKAI, successor to the Rikken Dōshikai. Named home minister in 1924, he worked for the passage of the universal manhood suffrage bill (see UNIVERSAL MANHOOD SUFFRAGE MOVEMENT) and the PEACE PRESERVATION LAW OF 1925.

When KATŌ TAKAAKI died in office in 1926, Wakatsuki took over as prime minister until 1927. As Japan's chief delegate to the 1930 London Naval Conference, he pressed for ratification of the proposed disarmament treaty. After Prime Minister HAMAGUCHI OSACHI was shot by a right-wing extremist in 1930, Wakatsuki assumed the presidency of the RIKKEN MINSEITŌ, successor to the Kenseikai, and then served once more as prime minister (1931). When the MANCHURIAN INCIDENT occurred in 1931, he worked hard to contain the hostilities but failed. He resigned in late 1931 and retired to the role of JŪSHIN (senior statesman). He opposed waging war against the United States.

Wakayama 和歌山〔市〕

Capital of Wakayama Prefecture, central Honshū, located at the mouth of the river Kinokawa. Its development began in 1585 with the construction of a castle by TOYOTOMI HIDEYOSHI. It later came under the rule of a branch of the Tokugawa family. Steel and chemical industries are active, along with traditional furniture making. Of interest are the temple Kimiidera, the Wakanoura coast, the Kada coast, and the island of Tomogashima in the Inland Sea. Pop: 396,553.

Wakayama Bokusui 若山牧水

(1885–1928). TANKA poet. Real name Wakayama Shigeru. Born in Miyazaki Prefecture; graduate of Waseda University. He began composing *tanka* under the influence of the noted Meiji-period (1868–1912) poet ONOE SAISHŪ. In 1910 he published a collection of poems, *Betsuri*. A wanderer and a lover of *sake*, he supported himself by writing numerous travel essays as well as poems. His style is generally that of the naturalist school of the early 20th century. His poems express the loneliness and sorrows of a traveler who seeks comfort in drink; they are known for their mellifluous quality. His principal works are *Umi no koe* (1908), a collection of poems, and *Minakami kikō* (1924), a collection of travel essays.

Wakayama domain → Kii domain

Wakayama Plain 和歌山平野

(Wakayama Heiya). Located in northwestern Wakayama Prefecture, central Honshū. Bounded by the Izumi Mountains to the north and the Kii Mountains to the south and situated along the Median Tectonic Line, this plain bordering the Kii Channel consists of the floodplain of the river Kinokawa. A rice-producing area, it has numerous mandarin orange orchards on the surrounding foothills. The major city is Wakayama. Area: approximately 100 sq km (40 sq mi).

Wakayama Prefecture 和歌山県

(Wakayama Ken). Located on the southwestern side of the Kii Peninsula in central Honshū, and bounded by Ōsaka Prefecture on the north, Nara and Mie prefectures on the east, the Kumano Sea and the Pacific Ocean on the south, and the Kii Channel on the west. With the exception of the plain around the capital, WAKAYAMA, the prefecture is almost entirely occupied by mountains. It is cut off from the main transportation routes by its mountainous terrain and remote location. The climate is generally warm, although some of the inland mountain regions are comparatively cool.

Known after the TAIKA REFORM of 645 as Kii Province, the Wakayama area has long been noted for its Shintō and Buddhist holy places. The Kumano district in the south came to have a special importance in the Shintō religion (see KUMANO SANZAN SHRINES), while the monastery complex on Mt. Kōya (KŌYASAN) is still a major center of Japanese Buddhism (see KONGŌBUJI). In the Edo period (1600–1868) the area was the domain of a Tokugawa branch family. The present prefectural boundaries were established in 1871.

Apart from mandarin oranges, agricultural production has been declining. Fishing and forestry continue to be important. Industry is largely concentrated in the area around Wakayama, where it forms a continuation of the Hanshin Industrial Zone. Major products include steel and electrical equipment. Papermaking and spinning plants dot the southern coast.

The Yoshino-Kumano and Inland Sea national parks span parts of the prefecture. The sandy beaches at Shirahama and rugged coves at Katsuura attract numerous vacationers from the Kyōto-Ōsaka-Kōbe area. NACHI FALLS is one of Japan's largest waterfalls. Area: 4,723 sq km (1,824 sq mi); pop: 1,074,325; capital: Wakayama. Other major cities include TANABE, KAINAN, and SHINGŪ.

Wake no Kiyomaro 和気清麻呂

(733–799). Court official of the late 8th century; principal adviser to Emperor KAMMU. Born Iwanasu no Wake no Kimi, the son of a powerful chieftain in the Fujino district of Bizen Province (now part of Okayama Prefecture), he is thought to have entered service at the imperial palace as a military guard. In 764 he distinguished himself in the suppression of the rebellion of FUJIWARA NO NAKAMARO. He was granted the honorific cognomen (*kabane;* see YAKUSA NO KABANE) *mahito* and was subsequently known as Fujino no Mahito. In 769 he sought to thwart the imperial ambitions of the priest DŌKYŌ, favorite of Empress Shōtoku (Empress KŌKEN). Wake no Kiyomaro was exiled to Ōsumi Province (now part of Kagoshima Prefecture) but was later recalled to the capital and granted the hereditary title *ason*. In 784 he was appointed to numerous offices by Emperor Kammu. He was responsible for improving the channel of the river Yamatogawa and for moving the capital, first to NAGAOKAKYŌ in 784 and then to HEIANKYŌ (Kyōto) in 794. In accordance with his last wishes, a school called the Kōbun'in was established for the education of males of the Wake family.

Wakimura Yoshitarō 脇村義太郎

(1900–). Economist. Born in Wakayama Prefecture. After graduating from Tōkyō University in 1924, he joined the faculty as an associate professor. He went to study in Europe and the United States in 1935. After his return to Japan, Wakimura was forced to leave his university post in 1938 because of his involvement in the POPULAR FRONT INCIDENT. After World War II, he returned to Tōkyō University, where he remained until his retirement in 1961. A RŌNŌHA Marxist, Wakimura is an expert on the international economy and on petroleum problems.

wakiōkan 脇往還

(side roads). Also called *wakikaidō.* Secondary routes in the Edo period (1600–1868) that connected with the five main highways (GOKAIDŌ). These roads included the Chūgokuji (from Ōsaka to Kokura in what is now Fukuoka Prefecture), the Mitoji (from the outskirts of Edo [now Tōkyō] to Mito in what is now Ibaraki Prefecture), the Sayaji (from Miya in what is now Aichi Prefecture to Kuwana in what is now Mie Prefecture by way of Saya in what is now Aichi Prefecture), and the Minoji (from Nagoya to Ōgaki in what is now Gifu Prefecture). Also included in the category of *wakiōkan* were two special routes reserved for official use: the Nikkō Onari Kaidō and the Reiheishi Kaidō, both leading to the shogunal mausoleum at Nikkō.

Wakkanai 稚内[市]

City in northern Hokkaidō, on the Sōya Strait. An ice-free port, Wakkanai flourished as a departure point for the island of Sakhalin until the end of World War II. It presently maintains ferry service to the islands of Rishiri and Rebun. It is a major fishing center, with abundant catches of crab, herring, cod, flatfish, and salmon. Major industries are marine-food processing, lumbering, and dairy farming. Pop: 48,232.

Wakō 和光[市]

City in southeastern Saitama Prefecture, central Honshū. Once an agricultural area, it now has machine and automobile plants as well as many housing complexes. Pop: 56,890.

wakō 倭寇

Japanese pronunciation of a Chinese and Korean term for Japanese pirates who pillaged the coasts of East Asia from the 13th into the 17th century. Initially the pirate bands were composed of Japanese, but at times they included Koreans, Chinese, Portuguese, and Southeast Asians. The character for *wa* (Ch: *wo*) was an ancient Chinese appellation for Japan, while the character for *kō* (Ch: *kou* or *k'ou*) means brigand or bandit. The term first appears on the KWANGGAET'O MONUMENT, a Korean stela erected in 414.

Wakō and Korea——From 1223 to 1265 raids originated on the islands of TSUSHIMA or IKI and the northern coast of Kyūshū and were directed against the southern coast of Korea. Raiding stopped for about a century but resumed in 1350 and reached a peak in the late 1370s and early 1380s. Both coasts of

Korea were ravaged, and rice, cloth, captives, and coins were seized. The loss of coins was so great that Korea returned to a barter economy. The Koreans sent diplomatic missions, the first in 1366, to protest to the MUROMACHI SHOGUNATE (1338–1573), but negotiating directly with the feudal lords who controlled western Japan was found to be more effective. In 1380 Korean warships armed with cannons destroyed a *wakō* fleet of 300–500 ships at the mouth of the Kŭm River. By 1385 the Koreans had begun eliminating Japanese pirate bases on offshore islands. In 1389 a Korean punitive expedition against Tsushima burned 300 Japanese ships.

The Korean court conducted diplomatic relations through the lords of Tsushima (see SŌ FAMILY) and held them responsible for the good behavior of the Japanese. Raids decreased, and Korea's YI DYNASTY government responded to incursions in 1419 by executing 737 Japanese traders and launching a punitive expedition against Tsushima (see ŌEI INVASION). After another century-long hiatus *wakō* again pillaged the southern coast of Korea in 1544, 1555, and 1589 but directed their main effort toward China.

Wakō and China——In 1358 *wakō* raided China's Shandong (Shantung) Peninsula and other coastal provinces. In 1363 they met defeat in an engagement on the Shandong Peninsula. Even after the founding of the Ming dynasty (1368–1644) the raids continued unabated and pushed south to Fujian (Fukien) Province. The Chinese built forts from Shandong to Fujian and forbade coastal trade and foreign voyages. The retired shōgun ASHIKAGA YOSHIMITSU joined the Ming in the licensed TALLY TRADE, during which the shogunate, the ŌUCHI FAMILY, the HOSOKAWA FAMILY, and others restrained the *wakō* based in their domains. With the assassination of ŌUCHI YOSHITAKA, who had controlled the Shimonoseki Strait, and the fragmentation of Japan into warring factions, the *wakō* once more sailed abroad in great numbers. Between 1552 and 1559 they raided from Jiangsu (Kiangsu) to Guangzhou (Canton). In many cases these "Japanese pirates" were predominantly Chinese. After TOYOTOMI HIDEYOSHI conquered Kyūshū in 1587, *wakō* activity was drastically reduced.

wakon kansai 和魂漢才

(Japanese spirit, Chinese knowledge). The ideal of using knowledge gained from China in accordance with Japan's native cultural traditions. The phrase was traditionally attributed to the 9th-century scholar SUGA-

WARA NO MICHIZANE but was surely coined much later. In the Meiji period (1868–1912) it was modified to WAKON YŌSAI (Japanese spirit, Western knowledge) and was advocated as a guiding principle for the adoption of Western culture.

wakon yōsai 和魂洋才

(Japanese spirit, Western knowledge). The ideal of adopting and applying Western learning and knowledge in conformity with native Japanese cultural traditions. The phrase was a modification of an earlier, similar sounding slogan, WAKON KANSAI (Japanese spirit, Chinese knowledge), said traditionally to have been coined in the 9th century to call attention to the importance of the native cultural heritage and the unique spirit inherent in Japanese civilization. In like fashion the phrase *wakon yōsai,* based on this same notion, gained currency in the Meiji period (1868–1912) as Western knowledge and technology began to be adopted on a large scale in Japan. It also echoed the expression "oriental ethics (spirit), Western technique (science and technology)" of the *samurai* thinker SAKUMA SHŌZAN (1811–64). The term *wakon yōsai* exemplifies the process by which traditional Japanese culture and Western technology were woven together in modern Japanese civilization.

Wakō Securities Co, Ltd
和光証券[株]

(Wakō Shōken). Medium-sized comprehensive securities company. Incorporated in 1947. Wakō maintains a close relationship with the INDUSTRIAL BANK OF JAPAN, LTD. Wakō's revenues derive largely from stock commissions, and it also distributes investment trusts. The company operates the Wakō Research Institute of Economics. Wakō has over 70 offices in Japan and 9 overseas offices. Sales for the fiscal year ending March 1991 totaled ¥107.2 billion (US $740.3 million), and capitalization stood at ¥41.9 billion (US $289.3 million). Headquarters are in Tōkyō.

Wakayama Bokusui Many of this *tanka* poet's verses express the loneliness of a traveler who seeks comfort in drink.

Wako Shungorō 輪湖俊午郎

(1890–1965). A leader of the Japanese immigrant community in Brazil. Born in Nagano Prefecture. After working as a newspaper reporter, Wako emigrated to Brazil in 1913 and helped establish Japanese agricultural settlements. Later Wako devoted himself to the education of Japanese farmers' children,

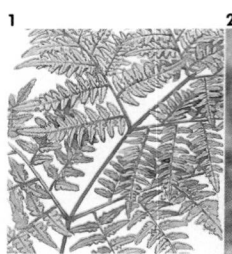

warabi
1 The mature pinnate frond of this perennial fern can grow to more than 1 meter in length. **2** The new shoots of wild bracken ferns have been savored as a springtime food for centuries. The plant is also cultivated.

helping to build a student center and the Harmonia dormitory in São Paulo.

Wakun no shiori 和訓栞

Japanese-language dictionary compiled by TANIGAWA KOTOSUGA in the late 18th century. A representative Edo-period (1600–1868) dictionary, the *Wakun no shiori* consists of 93 fascicles in 82 volumes, which are subdivided into three parts. The first and second parts were published during the period 1777 to 1862, after Tanigawa's death. The last part was not published until 1887. The *Wakun no shiori* contains an extensive selection of word entries drawn from ancient, classical, and colloquial vocabularies (including local dialects). Words are arranged in the order of the standard "50-sound" chart (GOJŪON ZU) of the KANA syllabary. It is considered the prototype of the modern Japanese-language dictionary and is a valuable research tool for Japanese vocabulary studies. The *Zōho gorin wakun no shiori*, a revised and enlarged three-volume edition without the final section, was published in 1898.

Wakura Hot Spring 和倉温泉

(Wakura Onsen). Located in the city of Nanao, Ishikawa Prefecture, central Honshū. The largest hot spring on the NOTO PENINSULA and a center for tourism in the area. A common salt spring; maximum water temperature 95°C (203°F).

Waley, Arthur David ウェーリー, A.D.

(1889–1966). Translator. Major figure in the introduction of classical Chinese and Japanese literature to Western readers. Born in England to a Jewish family originally named Schloss (the name was changed during World War I to avoid harassment as suspected enemy aliens). He attended Rugby School (1903–06) and King's College, Cambridge (1907–10). Essentially self-educated in Chinese and Japanese, he began his translation activities while employed as an assistant at the British Museum. He never accepted a regular university appointment, and he refused to visit Asia.

Waley's translations from the Japanese include *Japanese Poetry: The Uta* (1919), *The Nō Plays of Japan* (1921), and *The Pillow Book of Sei Shōnagon* (1928), as well as his masterwork, *The Tale of Genji*, which he produced

waraji The weaving of these straw sandals was an important evening task in farm households.

1684

Wakun no shiori

between 1925 and 1933. His translations have been criticized by later scholars, principally because of the freedom with which he treated some of his texts, but he was proud of the appeal of his work to the common reader and believed that an expressive English style was an essential aspect of fidelity to the original.

Waley's Chinese translations included *A Hundred and Seventy Chinese Poems* (1918), *The Book of Songs* (1937), and *The Analects of Confucius* (1938). Waley also wrote on Chinese and Japanese art, philosophy, and religion.

wall painting →screen and wall painting

Wamyō ruiju shō 倭名類聚抄

Also known as *Wamyōshō* or *Shitagau ga wamyō*. Chinese-Japanese dictionary compiled by MINAMOTO NO SHITAGAU around 934. There are both 10- and 20-volume editions extant, but the historical relationship between the two is unclear. Encyclopedic in nature, the work assembles the names of many objects and classifies them according to traditional categories (the *ruiju* of the title means "classified by categories"), e.g., heaven and earth, human relations, etc. Definitions in Chinese provide meanings, pronunciations, and literary sources, some no longer extant. Entries also record the Japanese pronunciation (*wamyō*) of the term in *man'yōgana* (Chinese characters used phonetically). It is a valuable research tool for bibliographers and cultural historians of the Heian period (794–1185) as well as for linguists.

Wamyōshō →Wamyō ruiju shō

Wang Jingwei (Wang Ching-wei) 汪精衛

(1883–1944; J: Ō Seiei). Also known as Wang Zhaoming or Wang Chao-ming (J: Ō Chōmei). Chinese Guomindang (Kuomintang; Nationalist Party) politician who collaborated with Japan as head of its puppet government in Nanjing (Nanking) during the SINO-JAPANESE WAR OF 1937–1945. While a student at Japan's Hōsei University, Wang became an enthusiastic disciple of SUN YAT-SEN. In the political struggles after Sun's death in 1925, Wang was alternately in and out of the Chinese Guomindang government, which came to be increasingly dominated by his rival, CHIANG KAI-SHEK.

Wang's determination to reach an accommodation with Japan led him in March 1940 to become the head of the newly created, Japanese-sponsored REORGANIZED NATIONAL GOVERNMENT OF THE REPUBLIC OF CHINA. Although vilified by many for treason, Wang argued that negotiating with Japan was necessary. He died in Japan in 1944. See also CHINA AND JAPAN.

Wang Kemin (Wang K'o-min) 王克敏

(1873–1945; J: Ō Kokubin). Leader of the Japanese-sponsored government in North China during World War II. After passing the provincial-level civil service examination, Wang was sent to Japan in 1900 to supervise Chinese students there. He served as a councillor to the Chinese legation in Tōkyō from 1902 until his return in 1907 to China, where he was active in banking and finance. In the 1930s Wang was a prominent pro-Japanese politician. After the SINO-JAPANESE WAR

OF 1937–1945 broke out, Wang headed the collaborationist PROVISIONAL GOVERNMENT OF THE REPUBLIC OF CHINA. When that regime was superseded by the puppet government in Nanjing (Nanking) under WANG JINGWEI (Wang Ching-wei) in 1940, Wang Kemin played a role in the North China Political Council, which he headed from 1943 to 1945. Arrested at the end of the war, he died in prison.

Wang Tao (Wang T'ao) 王韜

(1828–97?; J: Ō Tō). Founder of modern journalism in China, scholar, and early advocate of reform. Wang worked in Hong Kong as an editor and translator with English missionaries before pursuing a career in journalism. One of his books, *Pu-Fa zhanji* (*P'u-Fa chanchi*; The Franco-Prussian War), was widely read in Japan. In 1879 a group of Japanese scholars, including NAKAMURA MASANAO, invited Wang to Japan. Wang's *Fusang youji* (*Fu-sang yu-chi*; A Record of Travels in Japan), one of the earliest Chinese accounts of Meiji-period (1868–1912) Japan, resulted from this visit. In his book Wang expressed admiration for Japan's study of the West and its selective use of Western institutions. Wang later became distrustful of Japan's foreign policy, and he criticized Japan's seizure of the Ryūkyū Islands, using the DAI NIHON SHI (History of Great Japan) to support his argument that the islands belonged to China.

Wang Yangming school → Yōmeigaku

Wang Zhaoming (Wang Chao-ming) →Wang Jingwei (Wang Ching-wei)

Wang Zhengting (Wang Cheng-t'ing) 王正廷

(1882–1961; J: Ō Seitei). Also known as C.T. Wang. Chinese diplomat and minister of foreign affairs. The son of a Methodist minister, Wang studied in Japan from 1905 to 1907 and then in the United States, where he graduated from Yale University in 1910. In 1917 he joined SUN YAT-SEN's government in Guangzhou (Canton) and represented it at the 1919 Paris Peace Conference. In 1921 he was a member of the Chinese delegation to the WASHINGTON CONFERENCE. He joined the Nationalist government of CHIANG KAI-SHEK in July 1928 as foreign minister. Popular opinion blamed him for the Chinese government's lack of resistance to the Japanese occupation of Manchuria (see MANCHURIAN INCIDENT) and forced his resignation on 30 September 1931. Wang served as China's ambassador to the United States from 1936 to 1938.

Wani 王仁

(fl ca AD 400?). Also called Wani Kishi. Immigrant (KIKAJIN) who came to Japan from the Korean state of PAEKCHE in about AD 400 and became a scholar and administrator at the YAMATO COURT. According to the KOJIKI (712) and NIHON SHOKI (720), Wani was sent by the Paekche king to tutor a son of Emperor ŌJIN. He is said to have brought with him the *Analects* of Confucius and the "Thousand-Character Classic." The 9th-century historical work *Kogo shūi* states that in the reign of the legendary emperor Richū, Wani and Achi no Omi, ancestor of most of the immigrant AYA FAMILY, shared administrative responsibility for the Inner Treasury (Uchikura). The Kawachi no Fumi clan (which traced its ancestry to Wani) settled principally in what is now Ōsaka Prefecture. They built Sairinji, in what is now the city of Habikino, Ōsaka Prefecture, as their family temple. Perhaps Wani's best-known descendant was the itinerant priest and social activist GYŌGI (668–749).

Wa no Goō →Five Kings of Wa

warabe uta →children's songs

Warabi
蕨[市]

City in southeastern Saitama Prefecture, central Honshū. Warabi is chiefly a residential area, although textile and electrical-appliance industries are located here, as well. Pop: 73,620.

warabi
蕨

(bracken fern). *Pteridium aquilinum* var. *latiusculum.* A perennial fern of the family Denstaediaceae found on mountains and plains all over Japan. The rhizome extends deep into the ground where it ramifies. The frond is triangularly ovate, leathery, glossy, and covered with soft hair on the lower surface. The pinnate frond grows as long as 1 meter (3.3 ft) or more. The margin of the leaflet curls inside to form the indusia. The edible sprouts are collected in early spring and subjected to a process that removes their harsh taste. They may be served boiled, or they may be preserved by drying or salting. The starch extracted from the rhizome is used as an ingredient in *warabimochi* (*warabi* cakes) and *warabinori* (*warabi* glue).

warabidemon →fern frond design

waragutsu
藁沓

(straw shoes or straw boots). Also known as *yukigutsu* ("snow shoes"). Traditional footgear still used in the rural snowbound regions of northern Honshū. They range from straw sandals (*waraji*) with toe covers or straw slippers to low and high styles of boots.

waraji
草鞋

Traditional rough straw sandal, with a thong passing between the big and second toes; tied onto the foot with straw straps that pass through a series of loops on the sides of the sole. Not to be confused with the finer straw sandal, *zōri,* which is held onto the foot by the thong alone. Materials used include straw, flax (ASA) fibers, and wisteria or grape fibers, interwoven with cloth strips. *Waraji* were used throughout Japan and were worn when taking long journeys on foot.

Warashibe chōja
藁稭長者

(The Straw Millionaire). Folktale. A poor man prays to the bodhisattva Kannon (Skt: Avalokiteśvara) for good fortune and is told that the first thing he touches outside the temple shall be his. At the temple gate he stumbles on a stone and grabs a straw. He trades this straw for an orange and then trades each new acquisition for something more valuable (cloth, a horse, a field) so that he finally becomes wealthy. The story has been associated with the statue of Kannon at the temple HASEDERA.

war crimes trials
戦争犯罪に関する裁判

(*sensō hanzai ni kansuru saiban*). Series of military tribunals during and after World War II in which Japanese and German military and civilian leaders were tried by the victorious Allies for alleged war crimes. The trials of Japanese leaders culminated in the International Military Tribunal for the Far East (Kyokutō Kokusai Gunji Saiban; also known as the Tōkyō Trial or Tōkyō Saiban), held in Tōkyō from 1946 to 1948, which formed a Pacific counterpart to the trials of Nazi leaders at Nuremberg in 1945–46.

The term "war crimes" denotes activity in wartime that contravenes recognized standards of military conduct. Theoretically, it should include illegal activity by all participants and should exclude activity not clearly considered illegal. In the aftermath of the war in the Pacific, however, neither condition was applied. The various wartime and postwar trials and tribunals in the Far East considered only Japanese acts, not acts committed by the Allies. As regards the second condition, the bulk of the prosecution at the Tōkyō Trial rested on charges not clearly considered illegal. For example, the principal charge at Tōkyō was that of "aggression"; yet as recently as 1944, three Allied nations (France, Great Britain, and the United States) had agreed that aggressive war was not a crime. On both scores, then, the war crimes prosecutions relating to the Pacific War are open to the charge, first made by some of the defendants, that they were victors' justice—revenge dressed up in the trappings of legality.

The "Minor" Trials—The Allies tried some 6,000 Japanese in several thousand "minor" trials during and after the war. Of the accused, 920 were sentenced to death and executed. (The records of these trials are fragmentary and scattered, and the statistics are therefore inexact.) These trials primarily considered alleged atrocities committed in battle, during military occupation, or against prisoners of war.

The most famous of the "minor" trials is that of General YAMASHITA TOMOYUKI in 1946. Commander of most Japanese forces in the Philippines at the time of the Allied reconquest, Yamashita was tried before a military commission of five US generals. The charge against him was that he "unlawfully disregarded and failed to discharge his duty as commander to control the operations of the members of his command, permitting them to commit brutal atrocities and other high crimes." Found guilty as charged, he was sentenced to hang. That sentence was upheld on appeal by General Douglas MACARTHUR; both the Philippine Supreme Court and the US Supreme Court (5–2) refused to review the verdict.

The Tōkyō Trial—The International Military Tribunal for the Far East, known more often as the Tōkyō Trial, convened on 3 May 1946. It involved charges against 28 political and military leaders of the prewar and wartime Japanese governments, foremost among whom was TŌJŌ HIDEKI, prime minister during most of the war and general

The Tōkyō Trial

Defendant	Count and verdict										Sentence	Parole
	1	27	29	31	32	33	35	36	54	55		
Araki Sadao (1877–1966)	G	G	A	A	A	A	A	A	A	A	Life	1955‡
Doihara Kenji (1883–1948)	G	G	G	G	G	A	G	G	G	O	Death	
Hashimoto Kingorō (1890–1957)	G	G	A	A	A	—	—	A	A	A	Life	1955
Hata Shunroku (1879–1962)	G	G	G	G	G	—	A	A	A	G	Life	1954‡
Hiranuma Kiichirō (1867–1952)	G	G	G	G	G	A	A	G	A	A	Life*	
Hirota Kōki (1878–1948)	G	G	A	A	A	A	A	—	A	G	Death	
Hoshino Naoki (1892–1978)	G	G	G	G	G	A	—	A	A	A	Life	1955‡
Itagaki Seishirō (1885–1948)	G	G	G	G	G	A	G	G	G	O	Death	
Kaya Okinori (1889–1977)	G	G	G	G	G	—	—	A	A	A	Life	1955‡
Kido Kōichi (1889–1977)	G	G	G	G	G	A	—	A	A	A	Life	1955‡
Kimura Heitarō (1888–1948)	G	G	G	G	G	—	—	G	G	G	Death	
Koiso Kuniaki (1880–1950)	G	G	G	G	G	—	—	A	A	A	Life*	
Matsui Iwane (1878–1948)	A	A	A	A	A	—	A	A	A	G	Death	
Matsuoka Yōsuke (1880–1946)	Died during the trial											
Minami Jirō (1874–1955)	G	A	A	A	A	—	—	A	A	A	Life	1954
Mutō Akira (1892–1948)	G	G	G	G	G	A	—	A	G	G	Death	
Nagano Osami (1880–1947)	Died during the trial											
Oka Takazumi (1890–1973)	G	G	G	G	G	—	—	A	A	A	Life	1954‡
Ōkawa Shūmei (1886–1957)	Declared unfit for trial											
Ōshima Hiroshi (1886–1975)	G	A	A	A	A	—	—	A	A	A	Life	1955‡
Satō Kenryō (1895–1975)	G	G	G	G	G	—	—	A	A	A	Life	1956‡
Shigemitsu Mamoru (1887–1957)	A	G	G	G	G	A	—	A	A		7 years	1950
Shimada Shigetarō (1883–1976)	G	G	G	G	G	—	—	A	A	A	Life	1955‡
Shiratori Toshio (1887–1949)	G	A	A	A	A	—	—	—	—		Life*	
Suzuki Teiichi (1888–1989)	G	G	G	G	G	—	A	A	A	A	Life	1955‡
Tōgō Shigenori (1882–1950)	G	G	G	G	G	—	—	A	A	A	20 years†	
Tōjō Hideki (1884–1948)	G	G	G	G	G	G	—	A	A	O	Death	
Umezu Yoshijirō (1882–1949)	G	G	G	G	G	—	—	A	A	A	Life*	

Count 1: overall conspiracy; Count 27: waging war against China; Count 29: waging war against the United States; Count 31: waging war against the British Commonwealth; Count 32: waging war against the Netherlands; Count 33: waging war against France; Count 35: waging war against the Soviet Union (Lake Khassan); Count 36: waging war against the Soviet Union (Nomonhan); Count 54: ordering, authorizing, or permitting atrocities; Count 55: disregard of duty to secure observance of and prevent breaches of laws of war. The other 45 counts were dismissed or not dealt with in the majority judgment.
G: guilty; A: acquitted; O: charged but no finding made.
*Died in prison. †Died in US military hospital. ‡Released unconditionally by the Japanese Foreign Ministry on 7 April 1958.
SOURCE: Adapted from Richard H. Minear, *Victors' Justice: The Tokyo War Crimes Trial* (1971).

war crimes trials
Tōjō Hideki listens as his death sentence is read in the final verdicts handed down on 12 November 1948 during the military tribunal known as the Tōkyō Trial.

in the imperial army. Of the 28, 14 were generals, 3 were admirals, and 5 were career diplomats. On the bench were 11 justices, 1 each from the victorious nations and 1 each from the Philippines and India, which had not been independent at the time of the Pacific War. There were no judges from neutral nations. Only one judge (Radhabinod Pal [1886–1967] of India) had a background in international law. The Soviet judge understood neither of the official languages of the trial (English and Japanese). The Philippine judge was a survivor of the BATAAN "death march." The trial lasted two and one-half years, and the justices announced verdicts and sentences in November 1948.

The charges against the defendants in Tōkyō fell into three major categories: conspiracy to commit aggression, aggression, and conventional war crimes. Although the crime of conspiracy did not exist in international law until 1945, the majority of the justices convicted all but two defendants of conspiracy. Two of those so convicted were found guilty only on this charge; they were both sentenced to life imprisonment. Although the charge of having committed aggression rested upon a similarly fragile legal foundation, all but two of the Tōkyō justices held that aggression was or should be a crime in international law, and the majority convicted all but three of the defendants on at least one charge of committing it.

The charge of conventional war crimes consisted of two counts: that some defendants "ordered, authorized, and permitted" conventional war crimes (count 54); and that they "deliberately and recklessly disregarded their legal duty to take adequate steps to secure the observance and prevent breaches" of the laws and customs of war (count 55). On count 54, borrowed from Nuremberg, five defendants were found guilty, and all five were condemned to death. Count 55 was new to international law at Tōkyō, although it had figured earlier in the trial of General Yamashita. On this count, seven defendants were found guilty; of these, four were condemned to death, two were sentenced to life imprisonment, and one received the lightest sentence of all: seven years. One defendant was found guilty only on count 55; he was condemned to death.

The final judgment was a majority one, supported by 8 of 11 judges. Five judges prepared separate opinions. The most thorough dissenter was Radhabinod Pal of India, who found all the defendants innocent on all counts.

The defendants appealed the verdicts, first to General MacArthur and then to the US Supreme Court. After hearing preliminary arguments, the court voted six to one (with one abstention and one opinion reserved) that it lacked jurisdiction. Their appeals exhausted, the defendants condemned to death were hanged on 23 December 1948. Shortly after the trial the OCCUPATION authorities released the remaining class A suspects who had spent the years 1945–48 in prison without indictment.

From the vantage point of the 1980s and 1990s, some American historians have maintained that the postwar trials of Japanese war criminals can be explained but not justified. They point out that brutality was not confined to the Japanese side and that the Allies executed about 10 times as many Japanese as Germans on conventional war crimes charges. For these critics, the principal legacy

of the Tōkyō Trial seemed to lie in the realm of propaganda and popular images: it was an assertion that the Japanese cause was wrong and illegal, that the Allied cause was right and legal.

warigo 破り子

A type of traditional lunch box, made of thin sheets of *hinoki* (Japanese cypress). The oval, triangular, oblong, or fan-shaped box was usually discarded after use. The word *warigo* was also used to refer to MAGEMONO (woodstrip-craft containers) in general, or *kōri*, a type of suitcase made of woven strips of bamboo or willow bark.

war literature 戦争文学

(*sensō bungaku*). Unlike the classical GUNKI MONOGATARI (war tales), writing produced in modern Japan as a direct result of the Sino-Japanese, Russo-Japanese, and two world wars tends to focus on the experiences of individuals, rather than descriptions of battle or heroic deeds. The character types of modern Japanese war novels are usually conscripts who recognize the impossibility of controlling their own fate, making modern war literature highly introspective.

In the SINO-JAPANESE WAR OF 1894–1895, KUNIKIDA DOPPO submitted *Aitei tsūshin* (Letters to My Beloved Brother) to the newspaper *Kokumin shimbun* between 1894 and 1895, during his assignment as a war correspondent on board a warship. The work contains vivid descriptions of battle and is characterized by a strong nationalistic feeling in support of the war.

The RUSSO-JAPANESE WAR of 1904–05 engendered an outpouring of nationalistic war literature. Many journals were established for the sole purpose of publishing writings on war. One of the most popular and moving accounts was *Nikudan* (1906; tr *Human Bullets*, 1907) by Sakurai Tadayoshi (1879–1965), a young officer who fought in the war himself; in this work, soldiers' deaths are treated sympathetically and humanistically, but their sacrifice is also glorified as proof of the men's devotion to the nation.

TAYAMA KATAI presented the public with a different picture of war—its brutality and senselessness as far as the individual is concerned. His "Ippeisotsu" (1908; tr "One Soldier," 1956) deals with the agony and meaningless death of a nameless private for whom the glory of nationalism has no relevance. The same antiwar spirit can be seen in YOSANO AKIKO's poem "Kimi shinitamō koto nakare" (1904, Pray Thee, Do Not Die), whose publication led to accusations that she was anti-Japanese. That such writing was published, sometimes in establishment newspapers, shows that a certain freedom of expression was enjoyed by writers and intellectuals at this time, in sharp contrast with the situation that existed during WORLD WAR II.

The growing militarism of Japan, which culminated in the Sino-Japanese War of 1937–45 and World War II, fundamentally changed the situation of writers. They were deprived of freedom of expression (see FREEDOM OF SPEECH, REGULATION OF), and imprisonment and torture were used to silence or change the views of those who were critical. They were also subject to the draft and privileged only if they collaborated in the war effort. By 1941, even those writers who had been critical of the war in China were affected by the notion of the "sacred war," and in 1942 the NIHON BUNGAKU HŌKOKUKAI (Patriotic Association for Japanese Literature) was established to mobilize writers in support of

the war effort. The communists and socialists who had initially stood against the war (with such notable exceptions as KUROSHIMA DENJI and MIYAMOTO YURIKO) changed their views under censorship and police repression (see TENKŌ). Writers were used as reporters and served as information officers for the army and navy.

Among full-length novels, the best works of this period include ISHIKAWA TATSUZŌ's *Ikite iru heitai* (1937, Living Soldiers) and HINO ASHIHEI's trilogy *Mugi to heitai* (1938; tr *Barley and Soldiers*, 1939), *Tsuchi to heitai* (1938; tr *Mud and Soldiers*, 1939), and *Hana to heitai* (1938–39; tr *Flowers and Soldiers*, 1939). Ishikawa's novel describes the atrocities against the Chinese committed by the Japanese army attacking Nanjing (Nanking). Although it raises no questions about the war itself, the book was banned following publication, and Ishikawa and his publisher were convicted for violation of the PRESS LAW OF 1909. Hino's novels celebrate the nationalistic spirit but effectively present the sadness and strength of ordinary citizens and soldiers in a situation beyond their control.

Post–World War II literature began with writers' evaluation of their war experiences and their responsibility as intellectuals. Freed from censorship, the most significant war literature was written in the decade after the end of the war. UMEZAKI HARUO's "Sakurajima" (1946), ŌOKA SHŌHEI's *Nobi* (1952; tr *Fires on the Plain*, 1957), NOMA HIROSHI's *Shinkū chitai* (1952; tr *Zone of Emptiness*, 1956), and Gomikawa Jumpei's (b 1916) *Ningen no jōken* (1956–58, The Human Condition) are representative of the many literary treatments of the meaning of the war and of lives placed in extreme predicaments.

Among accounts of the war published retrospectively, *Kike wadatsumi no koe* (1949, Listen to the Voice of the Sea God), a collection of notes and diaries by student conscripts, some of whom had participated in KAMIKAZE suicide attacks toward the end of the war, is the single most moving document of human tragedy. IBUSE MASUJI's *KUROI AME* (1965–66; tr *Black Rain*, 1969), Ōta Yōko's (1903–63) "Hanningen" (1954, Half Human), and HAYASHI KYŌKO's "Matsuri no ba" (1975, Festival Site) all deal with either the Hiroshima or Nagasaki atomic bomb experience.

Many writers born in the 1930s also take the war as the starting point for their writing. Most of ŌE KENZABURŌ's works, including "Shiiku" (1958; tr "The Catch," 1959), present the war as the core of his generation's childhood experience. Postwar poetry by members of the modernist group ARECHI (Waste Land) also placed the war experience at the core of their disillusionment and alienation.

The KOREAN WAR and the Vietnam War have also figured in modern Japanese literature. HOTTA YOSHIE's *Hiroba no kodoku* (1951, Alone in the Marketplace) depicts the painful ambivalence of Japanese intellectuals toward the conflict in Korea. ODA MAKOTO's *Betonamu kara tōku hanarete* (1980–89, Far from Vietnam) and KAIKŌ KEN's *Kagayakeru yami* (1968; tr *Into a Black Sun*, 1980) are also of note. See also FICTION, MODERN.

Warner, Langdon ウォーナー, L.

(1881–1955). Teacher, author, and oriental art expert; curator of the oriental collection at Harvard's Fogg Museum. Graduating from Harvard in 1903, Warner was chosen by the university in 1906 to train for museum work in Asian art. He was apprenticed for several years under OKAKURA KAKUZŌ in Japan.

In 1912 Warner was selected as director of the American School of Archaeology in Beijing (Peking). After brief service with the State Department during World War I he became director of the Pennsylvania Museum of Art. Later he led two expeditions to China for the Fogg Museum.

During World War II Warner served with the Roberts Commission, which was charged with the protection and salvage of artistic and historic monuments in war areas. In March 1946 he went to Japan as a consultant to the Monuments, Fine Arts, and Archives Section of the Allied OCCUPATION headquarters. He was hailed in Japan as the man who had "saved" the cities of Nara and Kyōto from aerial bombing, a role he consistently denied. In fact Nara had never been a target and Kyōto had been stricken from the list of target cities with no prompting from Warner.

War Relocation Authority
戦時転住局

(WRA; J: Senji Tenjū Kyoku). Agency created in March 1942 by the US government to construct and administer the relocation centers needed to receive the more than 110,000 Japanese Americans whom the US Army was about to incarcerate in temporary assembly centers on the Pacific coast. In addition, the WRA was to relocate as many Japanese Americans as possible, particularly the *nisei* (second generation), who were citizens, out of the camps and into civilian life east of the Sierra Nevada Mountains. In these tasks the WRA was largely successful; by the end of the war, in August 1945, only 44,000 Japanese Americans remained behind barbed wire. The civilian agency established relocation centers at TULE LAKE and MANZANAR, California; MINIDOKA, Idaho; TOPAZ, Utah; POSTON and GILA RIVER, Arizona; HEART MOUNTAIN, Wyoming; AMACHE, Colorado; and ROHWER and JEROME, Arkansas.

A 1944 Supreme Court decision ruled that the WRA had exceeded its authority in detaining "conceded loyal" citizens against their will. The WRA was dissolved in June 1946. See also JAPANESE AMERICANS, WARTIME RELOCATION OF.

Warring States period—→Sengoku period

warrior government
武家政治

(*buke seiji*). Form of government in Japan for nearly 700 years, from the founding of the KAMAKURA SHOGUNATE in 1192 until the Meiji Restoration of 1868. The period can be divided into four phases: the Kamakura shogunate (1192–1333), the MUROMACHI SHOGUNATE (1338–1573), the rule (1568–98) of ODA NOBUNAGA and TOYOTOMI HIDEYOSHI, and the TOKUGAWA SHOGUNATE (1603–1867).

The shogunates were essentially nationwide warrior regimes organized on feudal principles of vassalage (see FEUDALISM) and headed as a rule by a warrior with the title SHŌGUN. By contrast, the regimes of Oda Nobunaga and Toyotomi Hideyoshi were short, and neither held the title of shōgun.

The warrior class (*buke, bushi,* or *samurai*) arose within the framework of the imperial state based on the RITSURYŌ SYSTEM. From the early Heian period (794–1185) the absence of any foreign threat or serious internal discontent led to the abandonment of conscript armies. However, the lawlessness on the frontiers of Heian society, especially in eastern Japan, encouraged the development of a permanent arms-bearing class.

Bands of warriors (BUSHIDAN) began to coalesce by the mid-Heian period. Local warriors came to function hereditarily as middle- and lower-level provincial officials and as administrative and police officers in estates (SHŌEN) owned by absentee court landlords. They carved out substantial holdings for themselves yet were subject to court authority. The greatest military leaders were members of the MINAMOTO FAMILY and the TAIRA FAMILY.

Early Development——The TAIRA-MINAMOTO WAR of 1180–85 resulted in the establishment of Japan's first warrior government. Establishing his headquarters at Kamakura in Sagami Province (now Kanagawa Prefecture), MINAMOTO NO YORITOMO set up three offices (see SAMURAI-DOKORO; KUMONJO; MONCHŪJO) to govern his expanding network of vassals and lands seized from vanquished enemies. Later Yoritomo received court sanction for his de facto control of eastern Japan, and in 1192 he was granted the title of shōgun.

The Kamakura period saw authority divided between the court and the shogunate. The court delegated some authority to the shogunate, and people increasingly turned to Kamakura for solutions to their problems. The crisis provoked by the MONGOL INVASIONS OF JAPAN of the 1270s and 1280s further strengthened warrior dominance.

This is not to say that the shogunate controlled the entire warrior class, let alone all of Japan. It relied on the SŌRYŌ SYSTEM, in which the family head apportioned land to family members. Vassalage and kinship ties were closely intertwined. Large numbers of warriors never even became direct vassals (GOKENIN) of the shogunate. After three brief generations of Minamoto control, shogunate leadership fell to 16 successive HŌJŌ FAMILY regents (SHIKKEN).

Disgruntled vassals, feeling insufficiently rewarded for their service, grew impatient with shogunate leadership. When Emperor GO-DAIGO attempted to unseat the Kamakura regime, many warriors, including Kamakura vassals, supported him. Go-Daigo's KEMMU RESTORATION proved anachronistic, however. ASHIKAGA TAKAUJI, having betrayed his Hōjō overlord, destroyed the shogunate in 1333 and turned on Go-Daigo, driving him south into the mountains. He enthroned his own puppet emperor in Kyōto (the Northern Court) to legitimize the establishment of his own shogunate in 1338. This regime is known as the Ashikaga shogunate, or as the Muromachi shogunate from the name of its Kyōto location. Takauji and his successors not only reduced Go-Daigo's Southern Court, but rendered the Northern Court powerless as well. However, the Ashikaga could not, as Yoritomo had done, reduce a large segment of warrior society to personal vassalage. The Muromachi shogunate represented a delicate balance of power between the shogunal house and the SHUGO DAIMYŌ, whose loyalty was necessary to ensure Ashikaga hegemony.

A factional dispute arose over shogunal succession in the mid-15th century, and from 1467 to 1477 Kyōto was engulfed in the ŌNIN WAR, which destroyed much of the city and spilled over into the provinces. For a century known as the Warring States (Sengoku) period, warfare swept Japan as vassal turned against lord (see GEKOKUJŌ). Although the Muromachi shogunate structure remained intact, the shōgun was virtually powerless.

By 1568 one baron, Oda Nobunaga, had subjugated most of his rivals, and in 1573 he deposed the last Ashikaga shōgun. Although

he created a regime more extensive than that of either Yoritomo or Takauji, Nobunaga did not establish a shogunate. By this time tradition seems to have dictated that only Minamoto descendants could claim the title of shōgun, and, without Minamoto genealogy, Nobunaga apparently felt unable to do so. When Nobunaga was killed by one of his generals, Toyotomi Hideyoshi avenged him and seized power, but for reasons similar to Nobunaga's he did not organize a shogunate. His actual control of Japan, nonetheless, was more complete, and he even launched massive INVASIONS OF KOREA IN 1592 AND 1597 in an effort to conquer China.

Nobunaga and Hideyoshi united the country out of feudal chaos and, by eliminating the last vestiges of the estate system, established the principle of legal ownership of land by farmers. Farmer and samurai were clearly distinguished and the latter became concentrated in CASTLE TOWNS. Foreign trade was encouraged, guilds were abolished (see RAKUICHI and RAKUZA), and Japan reached a high level of socioeconomic and cultural development.

Tokugawa Shogunate——Upon Hideyoshi's death a power struggle ensued. In the Battle of SEKIGAHARA in 1600 TOKUGAWA IEYASU defeated a coalition of generals and emerged as Hideyoshi's undisputed heir. In 1603 he organized a regime in the new city of Edo (now Tōkyō), known as the Tokugawa shogunate. He became shōgun, and the position was passed on through his descendants in 15 shogunal reigns until TOKUGAWA YOSHINOBU's resignation in 1867.

The Japanese refer to the balance of power between the shogunate at Edo and the various DAIMYŌ domains as "centralized feudalism" (see BAKUHAN SYSTEM). Daimyō were allowed great autonomy within their own domains, and feudal ties of vassalage still bound together daimyō and samurai retainers. The central shogunate administration, staffed mainly by FUDAI (vassals of the Tokugawa), was far more complex and pervasive than either the Kamakura or the Muromachi shogunate. The shōgun could reassign daimyō at will, and instituted a system of alternate attendance at the shogunal court (see SANKIN KŌTAI) that kept daimyō economically dependent. Ieyasu's successors proscribed CHRISTIANITY and severed communication with much of the rest of the world (see NATIONAL SECLUSION). Numerous legal codes regulated the lives of the citizenry (see BUKEHŌ).

During the 250 years of Tokugawa rule, warfare was virtually unknown. As a result, the samurai were converted into bureaucrats, and society changed tremendously. The toppling of the Tokugawa shogunate in 1867–68 paved the way for a dramatic period of industrialization along Western lines.

Thus for 700 years warrior regimes controlled Japan. The imperial system was not rejected; rather, warrior government was an institutional graft onto the body of imperial rule. Less concerned with precedents than with solutions, the institutions, laws, and ideals of warrior governments were pragmatic, rational, and firmly rooted in the contemporary society.

warrior house law—→bukehō

warrior-monks
僧兵

(*sōhei*). Armed monks attached to great Buddhist institutions from early times. Although forbidden to bear arms by secular

Waseda University
The tower of the Ōkuma Auditorium, built in 1927, is a campus landmark. It stands on the site of the residence of the university's founder, Ōkuma Shigenobu.

law and by religion, monks and menials from temples and monasteries participated in civil disturbances as early as the 8th century. As religious institutions became proprietors of estates (SHŌEN) by the late 10th century, they frequently mobilized warrior-monks in land disputes. By the 11th century, young soldiers from these estates shaved their heads in imitation of monks and were also called *sōhei*. The *sōhei* at times threatened the court and the shogunate with their military might. The warrior-monks of ENRYAKUJI, KŌFUKUJI, and MIIDERA were especially feared. Their power was broken by ODA NOBUNAGA (see ENRYAKUJI, BURNING OF) and TOYOTOMI HIDEYOSHI and by prohibitions of the early Edo period (1600–1868). See also GŌSO.

war songs → gunka

wasan   和讃

Buddhist poems or hymns composed in Japanese praising Buddhist doctrine and sutras, Buddhas, bodhisattvas, and founders of sects. Verses or *gāthā* appear in Buddhist sutras and texts from earliest times, and the *wasan* were modeled on chanted hymns from China and other hymns already existing in Japan. In *wasan* four lines of alternating seven- and five-syllable length form a stanza; a complete *wasan* may consist of up to 20 or 30 stanzas. From the early Heian period (794–1185), *wasan* were used to propagate PURE LAND BUDDHISM among the people. Prominent Buddhists of the Pure Land, Tendai, Yūzū Nembutsu, and Ji sects, such as ENNIN (794–864), KŪYA (903–972), GENSHIN (942–1017), RYŌNIN (1073–1132), and IPPEN (1239–89), relied on *wasan* to teach their doctrines.

SHINRAN (1173–1263), founder of the JŌDO SHIN SECT, was the most prolific and influential *wasan* composer. RENNYO (1415–99), the eighth patriarch, compiled a worship-service text, the *Sanjō wasan*, from three of Shinran's works: the *Jōdo wasan*, about the three Pure Land sutras; the *Kōsō wasan*, on the doctrines of the seven patriarchs; and the *Shōzōmatsu wasan*, about the three stages in Buddhist ESCHATOLOGY. Shinran's lyrical style had great appeal for ordinary people; his teachings could be recalled easily, thus merging faith with life's daily routine.

wasan   和算

(traditional Japanese mathematics). System of mathematics developed in Japan before the Meiji Restoration (1868), chiefly during the Edo period (1600–1868). The term is used in contrast to *yōsan*, mathematics introduced from Europe. Formal mathematics was first introduced to Japan from China sometime between the 7th and 8th centuries but most of this knowledge was later lost. Mathematical knowledge was imported anew from China in the 16th century in the form of

simple arithmetic, such as calculation on the ABACUS.

The oldest extant treatise on mathematics by a Japanese is Mōri Shigeyoshi's (dates unknown) *Warizansho* (1622, Writings on Division). *Jinkōki* (1627), by his disciple YOSHIDA MITSUYOSHI, greatly contributed to the spread of computation for practical purposes, and this title was long used as a generic term for arithmetic textbooks. SEKI TAKAKAZU, later revered as the "god of *wasan*," developed a workable system of algebraic notation, a theory of determinants, and a formula for calculating the circumference of a circle, and generally laid the foundation of *wasan*. His disciple TAKEBE KATAHIRO developed theories of series expansion and convergence speed. Although most *wasan* scholars of the 17th and 18th centuries were of the *samurai* class, the first half of the 19th century saw an increase in the number of mathematicians and the appearance of many amateurs from the merchant class. There was, however, little real progress in mathematical theory.

In the early Meiji period (1868–1912), *wasan* scholars helped set up the mathematics curriculum within the new school system. When Japan's oldest academic society, the Tōkyō Sūgaku Kaisha (forerunner of the present Mathematical Society of Japan, or Nihon Sūgakkai), was founded in 1877, more than half its members were scholars trained in *wasan*. By the end of the century, however, *wasan* had given way to Western-style mathematics. Nevertheless, many achievements of *wasan* scholars are interesting from the perspective of modern mathematics, and incorporating their spirit into present-day mathematical education has a relevance that goes beyond mere antiquarian curiosity.

Waseda bungaku   早稲田文学

(Waseda Literature). Literary journal of Waseda University (known until 1902 as Tōkyō Semmon Gakkō). *Waseda bungaku* was the first specialized literary magazine of its kind and was modeled on Western literary magazines. It has been issued in eight series, the first two being the most influential. Founded and edited by TSUBOUCHI SHŌYŌ, the first series appeared between October 1891 and October 1898, first semimonthly and later monthly. Among its contributors were SHIMAMURA HŌGETSU, TAKAYAMA CHOGYŪ, MORI ŌGAI, MASAOKA SHIKI, and KOSUGI TENGAI.

The second series was published from January 1906 to December 1927. Under the editorship of Shimamura Hōgetsu it became a major vehicle of the so-called Japanese NATURALISM. Contributors during this period included MASAMUNE HAKUCHŌ and TAYAMA KATAI. The third series was published from June 1934 to February 1949. Series four, five, and six appeared at intermittent intervals over a 10-year span from 1949 to 1959. Series seven comprised 72 issues published from 1969 to 1975. Series eight began publication in June 1976 and was still in existence in the early 1990s.

Waseda University   早稲田大学

(Waseda Daigaku). A private, coeducational university; main campus located in Shinjuku Ward, Tōkyō. Established in 1882 by ŌKUMA SHIGENOBU as the Tōkyō Semmon Gakkō, it was renamed Waseda University in 1902. It has faculties of political science and economics, law, letters, education, commerce, science and engineering, and human sciences as

well as a night curriculum in the social sciences and in literature. It also maintains an international division, where 102 foreign students studied in 1989. There were also 368 foreign undergraduates, 498 foreign graduate students, and 83 foreign students attending the Center for Japanese Language. The school also has affiliated high schools. The TSUBOUCHI MEMORIAL THEATER MUSEUM OF WASEDA UNIVERSITY is the only museum of theater in Japan. Enrollment was 43,341 in 1989.

washi   和紙

The collective term for Japanese hand-molded paper made principally from *kōzo* (paper mulberry; *Broussonetia kazinoki*), *gampi* (*Wikstroemia sikokiana*), or *mitsumata* (*Edgeworthia papyrifera*). Other bark fibers such as *asa* (hemp; *Cannabis sativa*) have been used at various times. Today wood pulp is frequently added to the stocks of the cheaper range of papers.

Invention and Transmission — The invention of paper in China dates from ancient times. A traditional date, supported by little factual evidence, has been accepted for the introduction of papermaking into Japan. The 8th-century NIHON SHOKI (Chronicle of Japan) states that the monk Donchō (Kor: Tamjing) arrived from Korea in 610 and that he knew the art of making pigments, ink, and paper. Actual introduction of paper may have been earlier.

Nara Period (710–794) — The centralization of political authority, the establishment of the imperial court at Nara with its attendant bureaucracy, and the dramatic expansion of the Buddhist priesthood created a new and heavy demand for paper. The finest examples of paper of this age are to be found in the SHŌSŌIN, the 8th-century imperial repository of the temple Tōdaiji in Nara. Here the oldest examples of Japanese paper have been collected: census registers from the provinces of Mino (now part of Gifu Prefecture), Chikuzen (now part of Fukuoka Prefecture), and Buzen (now parts of Ōita and Fukuoka prefectures). They clearly date from 702. Altogether the Shōsōin archive cites some 233 different types of paper.

Heian Period (794–1185) — The Heian period was the "golden age" of quality and variety in papermaking. The flowering of courtly culture created a wider demand for both official papers and luxuriously decorated sheets on which to keep diaries, write poems, and so forth. Demand was so great that the central government established its own mill, the Kamiyain (also called Kan'yain), which was set up during the period 806–809 on the banks of the river Kamiyagawa (also pronounced Kan'yagawa) in Kyōto. Collectively the papers of the mill were called *kan'yagami*. Tinted papers called *kan'ya no shikishi* were also produced. Toward the end of the period the mill found it increasingly difficult to acquire raw materials and was forced to make paper from recycled waste. This was known as *shukushi*. It was tinted gray because it was difficult to remove the ink; thus it was called *usuzumigami* ("pale ink paper") or *suiunshi* ("water cloud paper"), depending upon its tone. During this period *michinokugami* (Michinoku paper) came into vogue. This was the forerunner of *danshi* (fine crepe paper) and was made from *mayumi* (spindle tree; *Euonymus sieboldianus*). It was white, plump, and smooth, not creped like modern *danshi* made of *kōzo*. Other paper types from this period include papers with cloud patterns, marbled paper, and those decorated with silver or gold leaf.

Kamakura, Muromachi, and Azuchi-Momoyama Periods (1185–1600)—The rise of the warrior class, the change to a feudal form of government, and the decline in the economic and political fortunes of the imperial court reduced the demand for fancy paper but stimulated increased production of good-quality utility paper. *Sugiharashi*, a white, soft, and pliable paper, was less formal and somewhat cheaper than *danshi* and soon found favor among the warrior class. *Hōsho*, a white *danshi*-type paper, also became popular as formal stationery. *Torinoko* (eggshell) was a stout paper, having a tone and texture resembling the shell of an egg, and is the most famous of the *gampi* papers. It was much favored by calligraphers, and many of the finest manuscripts of the age were written on it. The development of printing, markets, and the freer architectural use of paper for screen and partition coverings added a new dimension to paper consumption.

Edo Period (1600–1868)—At the beginning of the politically stable Edo period, the pursuit of learning, which had suffered greatly during the Sengoku period (1467–1568), was revived. The Tokugawa shogunate established an official publishing house in Suruga (now part of Shizuoka Prefecture), and this in turn stimulated the opening of provincial printing centers. For the first time both books and paper became freely available for all.

The Tokugawa shogunate influenced *daimyō* feudal lords to establish papermaking centers in their own domains so they could have a personal source of supply. Many centers produced more than was locally needed, and surplus paper found its way into the markets of Edo (now Tōkyō), Ōsaka, and Kyōto.

Meiji Period (1868–1912) to the Present—Western papermaking technology was introduced into Japan in the 1870s, and since the early 20th century expense and limited production have made it difficult for artisan papermakers to compete with industrial paper manufacturers. In 1928, 28,532 families were recorded as engaged in papermaking; by 1973 the number had dropped to 851. Today, there is an increasing demand for fine-quality handmade paper, whatever the cost.

Techniques of Papermaking—The bark fibers of three shrubs (*kōzo*, *gampi*, and *mitsumata*) make up the papermaker's basic raw materials. All occur naturally in most parts of Japan. *Kōzo* and *mitsumata* shrubs are cultivated, but *gampi* bark is always gathered from the wild plant. Before bark is turned into paper it must be cropped, stripped, bleached, boiled in lye to remove the nonfibrous materials, washed, graded, and finally pulped. Techniques vary slightly for each of the raw materials.

Molding Paper—There are two methods of molding employed in Japan: *tamezuki*, introduced into Japan from China, is essentially the same method as that used in the West, and *nagashizuki*, the most commonly used method, is peculiar to Japan and probably evolved during the 8th century. In the case of *nagashizuki*, the stock or pulp water mix contains a mucilage obtained from one of several plants. *Tororo* (*Abelmoschus manihot*) or *noriutsugi* (*Hydrangea paniculata*) are those most commonly used. The inclusion of mucilage produces an emulsion in which fibers are suspended and do not knot, and

the slow-draining thickened liquid permits greater control in the determination of paper thickness. It also acts as a buffer between sheets when these are couched, no interleaving felts being used as in the case of *tamezuki*. The main differences between the two methods are that in *tamezuki* all excess liquid is allowed to drain through the mold, while in *nagashizuki* most of it is cast out. Each sheet or waterleaf requires several dips into the vat of stock. In the case of *tamezuki* the "face" or "right side" of the sheet is produced first, while in *nagashizuki* it is produced by the final dip. After some 400 to 600 sheets (one "block") have been molded, the sheets are pressed to remove excess water and are separated and brushed onto fine-grained wooden boards to dry. Finally the sheets are gathered, cut to size, packed, and marketed. Handcrafted paper is made in most parts of Japan, but the major centers are TŌYO and KAWANOE in Ehime Prefecture; Imadate and OBAMA in Fukui Prefecture; YAME in Fukuoka Prefecture; Adachi in Fukushima Prefecture; MINO and Kawai in Gifu Prefecture; Ino and TOSA in Kōchi Prefecture; AYABE in Kyōto Prefecture; IIYAMA in Nagano Prefecture; Yoshino in Nara Prefecture; OGAWA in Saitama Prefecture; Misumi and Yakumo in Shimane Prefecture; Saji and Aoya in Tottori Prefecture; and Nakatomi in Yamanashi Prefecture.　☎ 1690

Washington Conference

ワシントン会議

(Washinton Kaigi). An international meeting held from November 1921 to February 1922 in Washington DC to limit naval armaments and resolve outstanding East Asian international political problems. The conference produced treaties that ended the ANGLO-JAPANESE ALLIANCE of 1902, limited naval construction, and reaffirmed the principles of Chinese political and territorial integrity.

On 11 July 1921 President Warren G. Harding invited Japan, Great Britain, France, and Italy to send delegates to Washington to discuss naval and East Asian problems. American, British, and Japanese negotiators fashioned a replacement for the Anglo-Japanese Alliance called the FOUR-POWER TREATY, by which these nations and France pledged to respect the status quo in the Pacific and to confer if it were threatened. Naval forces were limited by a 10:10:6 capital-ship strength ratio between the American, British, and Japanese navies, respectively (despite Japan's original desire to establish a 10:10:7 strength ratio). The parties also agreed to respect the status quo of western Pacific fortifications.

Chinese and Japanese delegates met separately to resolve differences over the SHANDONG (SHANTUNG) QUESTION and misunderstandings generated by the TWENTY-ONE DEMANDS of 1915 and the LANSING-ISHII AGREEMENT of 1917. Japan and the United States joined seven other powers in two treaties. One provided for joint regulation of Chinese tariffs, and the other reaffirmed principles of Chinese political and territorial integrity and of equality of economic opportunity in China. The conference concluded on 6 February 1922 with the signing of the five-power naval agreement (WASHINGTON NAVAL TREATY OF 1922) and the China treaty (see NINE-POWER TREATY). (The Four-Power Treaty had been signed on 13 December 1921.) These accords profoundly influenced Japanese diplomacy and domestic politics for a decade. They laid the basis for the "coopera-

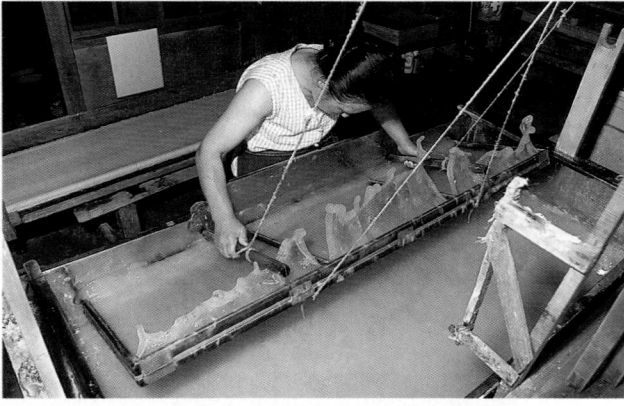

washi A key step in the *nagashizuki* method of making Japanese handmade paper is the casting out of excess water by shaking the paper mold, as illustrated here.

tive diplomacy" subsequently practiced by Japanese ambassador SHIDEHARA KIJŪRŌ. The naval treaties gave Japan maritime predominance in the western Pacific and made possible significant reductions first in navy, then in army, expenditures. Finally, the Washington Conference solidified the alliance between politicians and admirals. Their cooperation in constraining army political power at home and activism abroad was an essential feature of TAISHŌ DEMOCRACY.

Washington Naval Treaty of 1922

ワシントン海軍軍縮条約

(Washinton Kaigun Gunshuku Jōyaku). An agreement concluded on 6 February 1922 by Japan, France, Great Britain, Italy, and the United States to limit the size, armament, and deployment of capital ships of war.

On 11 July 1921 President Warren G. Harding invited Japan, Great Britain, France, and Italy to the WASHINGTON CONFERENCE to discuss naval limitation and East Asian international political problems. The resulting Five-Power Treaty on capital-ship limitation, signed in 1922, was to remain in effect for 15 years. The treaty specified the ships to be scrapped, and limited all capital ships (built and under construction) in size and armament in order to maintain a 10:10:6 strength ratio between the navies of the United States, Great Britain, and Japan, respectively. Article 19 required maintenance of the status quo of specified fortifications in the western Pacific. Japan ratified the treaty on 5 August 1922; it became effective 17 August 1923. Subsequent meetings for revision were held at Geneva in 1927 and at London in 1930 and 1935–36 (see LONDON NAVAL CONFERENCES).

The Washington Naval Treaty sparked debates within the Imperial Japanese Navy that led to a major political controversy in 1930 and to Japan's decision in 1934 to abrogate the agreement. Nonetheless, the treaty has come to be regarded as the first example of strategic arms limitation by international agreement.

Washūzan

鷲羽山

Hill in the southern part of the city of Kurashiki, Okayama Prefecture, western Honshū. Weathered granite rocks protruding from Washūzan form grotesque figures. Its summit commands a view of the Inland Sea. At its foot is Ōhama swimming beach. It is part of Inland Sea National Park. Height: 133 m (436 ft).

watakushi shōsetsu → I-novel

Watanabe Jōtarō

渡辺錠太郎

(1874–1936). Army general. Born in Aichi Prefecture. He graduated from the Army Academy in 1896 and became a general in

Japanese Paper: Art and Utility

Hand-molded Japanese paper (*washi*) is prized for its combination of strength and delicacy. Both qualities are contributed by the most important of the various plant materials customarily used in making washi—the bark fibers of the paper mulberry (*kōzo*). Washi's superior porosity and texture have long appealed to calligraphers. At the same time, the paper's translucence and durability have made it a popular feature in traditional designs for such utilitarian articles as *shōji* and *fusuma* screens, umbrellas, raincoats, and lampshades. Most of the paper intended for use in Japanese homes today is mass-produced; handmade washi represents only a tiny share of the output of the Japanese paper industry. To the extent that finely crafted washi is still made and used, however, it is valued more highly than ever.

An artisan making Japanese paper as depicted in the 1798 work *Kamisuki chōhōki* (Treasury of Papermaking).

The natural origins of washi made from paper mulberry are palpable.

Shōji screens were in use by the late 12th century and had become widespread by the 13th century, window glass being still unknown.

This 20th-century hand-crafted volume on camellias is printed on washi and bound in the traditional *fukurotoji* style.

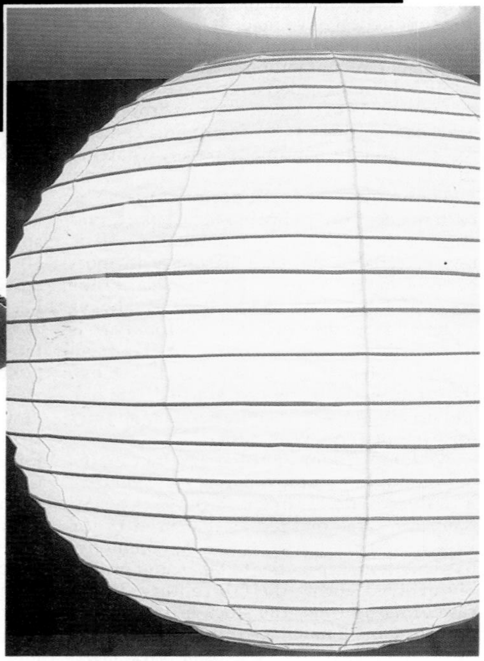

A washi lamp designed by Isamu Noguchi emits a soft, warm glow, much like that provided by premodern *chōchin* and *andon* lamps that employed washi.

1931. Watanabe was named inspector general of military education when a leader of the κōdōha faction, mazaki jinzaburō, was dismissed in 1935. Regarded as a leader of the rival tōseiha faction, Watanabe was assassinated by Kōdōha officers in the february 26th incident of 1936.

Watanabe Kazan   渡辺崋山

(1793–1841). Scholar of western learning and painter. Real name Watanabe Sadayasu. Pupil of tani bunchō. Most famous for landscapes in the bunjinga (literati painting) style and for realistic portraits, he also did bird-and-flower paintings and figure and nature studies.

Kazan served in Edo (now Tōkyō) as a high-ranking official of the Tawara domain (now part of Aichi Prefecture). In his early thirties he became fascinated with Western Learning and, with other *rangakusha* (scholars of "Dutch Learning") in Edo, formed the study group shōshikai. After criticizing the shogunate's national seclusion policy in the treatise shinkiron and advocating closer relations with the West, Kazan was arrested in 1839 on a false charge of conspiracy (see bansha no goku). His death sentence was commuted to life imprisonment, which he was later allowed to serve in his home domain. On 11 October 1841, worried lest he cause trouble to his *daimyō*, he committed suicide.

An eclectic painter, Kazan's combination of Western and Japanese methods makes his painting distinctive. Kazan made his greatest innovations in portrait painting, in which the fluid line and shading he employed gave a sense of anatomical structure and solidity new in Japanese portraiture.

Watanabe Masanosuke   渡辺政之輔

(1899–1928). Labor movement activist and communist leader of the Taishō period (1912–26). Born in Chiba Prefecture, he received an elementary-school education. While working at a celluloid factory in Tōkyō, Watanabe came into contact with members of the shinjinkai and with their help formed a union in the factory. In 1922 he joined the newly formed japan communist party and in 1923 was arrested for his activities. After his release from jail in 1924, he returned to labor-union activities and married tanno setsu, another labor activist. Active for a while in the left-wing faction of the sōdōmei (Japan Federation of Labor), he was expelled for being too radical. In 1926 he joined the Central Committee of the Japan Communist Party. He went to Moscow in 1927 for a Comintern meeting and helped to draft the comintern 1927 thesis on Japan. He escaped arrest in the march 15th incident of 1928. In the autumn of the same year he committed suicide while trying to escape police in Jilong (Keelung), Taiwan.

Watanabe Nangaku   渡辺南岳

(1767–1813). Painter of the maruyama-shijō school. Real name Watanabe Iwao. Born in Kyōto; studied under maruyama ōkyo and possibly under one of Ōkyo's disciples, Komai Ki (1747–97). Nangaku's subjects included figures, flowers, and animals. He was especially esteemed for his pictures of beautiful women (*bijinga*), his drawings of carp, and his impromptu sketches.

Watanabe Sadao   渡辺貞夫

(1933–). Jazz alto saxophonist. Born in Tochigi Prefecture. In the early 1950s he played in the Cozy Quartet with akiyoshi toshiko.

While studying at the Berklee College of Music in Boston from 1962 to 1965, he became interested in the bossa nova, African music, and fusion music. He carried these new musical forms back to Japan, where, now nicknamed "Nabe Sada," he exerted great influence upon younger musicians. His performances, characterized by a strong jazz spirit allied with a fluid expressive power, have won him critical acclaim in both Japan and the United States.

Watanabe Shikō   渡辺始興

(1683–1755). Painter of the rimpa school. Real name Watanabe Motome. Born and lived in Kyōto. A retainer of the court noble konoe iehiro, he began his artistic career by studying the painting style of the kanō school. He is said by some to have studied under kōrin and is counted, along with tatebayashi kagei, as one of Kōrin's most important followers. He is noted for his paintings of mountain landscapes and trees and flowers.

Watanabe Tetsuzō   渡辺銕蔵

(1885–1980). Businessman and politician. Born in Ōsaka; graduated from Tōkyō University, where he later taught. He was elected to the House of Representatives in 1936. After the outbreak of the Sino-Japanese War of 1937–45, Watanabe became active in the movement against militarism. From 1947 he served as president of the Tōhō film company and worked to settle the tōhō strike. After leaving Tōhō in 1950, Watanabe became active in the anticommunist and pro-rearmament movements.

Watarai Shintō   度会神道

Also called Ise Shintō, Gekū Shintō. An important school of Shintō founded by the Watarai family, hereditary priests of the Outer Shrine (Gekū) of ise shrine, which honors the food deity Toyouke no Ōkami. The Outer Shrine was originally moved to Ise so that its deity could serve amaterasu ōmikami, the imperial ancestress and sun goddess enshrined in the Inner Shrine (Naikū).

The inequality between the two Ise shrines diminished under the influence of ryōbu shintō, which held that the Inner and Outer Shrines were two aspects of a single reality. Resentful of the inferior position of the Outer Shrine, Watarai Yukitada (1236–1305) proclaimed the equality and interdependence of the two shrines. By the 13th century Watarai Shintō had produced the sacred corpus *Shintō gobusho* (Five Books of Shintō), which were attributed to semilegendary figures in order to provide authority for the school's views.

Some Watarai scholars developed a complex theology suggesting the ultimate superiority of Toyouke over all other deities, including Amaterasu. Watarai scholars also rejected the widely held view that Shintō deities were Japanese manifestations of Buddhist divinities (honji suijaku). With its emphases on the supremacy of the Ise Shrine over all other shrines, the divine origin of the imperial family, and the superiority of Shintō over Buddhism, Watarai Shintō strongly influenced other Shintō schools, such as the Yoshida and Suika, and contributed to the development of nationalist thinking.

Watarasegawa   渡良瀬川

River in central Honshū, originating in the mountains of western Tochigi Prefecture,

Watanabe Kazan Detail from *Portrait of Takami Senseki.* 1837. Hanging scroll. Colors on silk. 115 × 57 cm. Tōkyō National Museum. National Treasure.

flowing through the eastern part of Gumma Prefecture, and joining the tonegawa in northeastern Saitama Prefecture. A multipurpose dam has been constructed on the upper reaches. Water pollution by the Ashio Copper Mine, in operation until 1973, had been a problem since the Meiji period (1868–1912; see ashio copper mine incident). The water is utilized for irrigation and electric power as well as for drinking. Length: 108 km (67 mi); area of drainage basin: 2,612 sq km (1,008 sq mi).

watches → clocks and watches

water lily   睡蓮

(*suiren*). Of the more than 50 known species of the water lily family (Nymphaeaceae) in the world, the only one native to Japan is *Nymphae tetragona* var. *angusta,* a freshwater perennial found in ponds and marshes. Its long leafstalk grows up to the water surface from a rhizome in the marsh bed. Leafstalks bear thick, oval leaves with slits from their bordered edges to the center. A white flower about 5 centimeters (2 in) wide rises above the water in summer. Since Japanese water

water lily This variety of water lily, shown here at the Meiji Shrine, Tōkyō, was introduced from the West. The flowers bloom only for a few days in summer, opening at sunrise and closing at sunset.

waterwheels Though widely used in Japan through the Edo period, waterwheels, such as this one in Nagano Prefecture, are a comparatively rare sight today, even in rural areas.

Watsuji Tetsurō This philosopher sought to formulate a distinctly Japanese alternative to modern Western thought, with its emphasis on the individual.

lilies normally open their blossoms at about 2:00 PM, the hour of the sheep in the traditional Japanese calendar (see JIKKAN JŪNISHI), they are also called *hitsujigusa* (sheep plant).

Most of the species known as *suiren* in Japan today are actually of Western origin. They have relatively large leaves and bloom in a variety of colors. See also LOTUS.

Water Resources Development Public Corporation 水資源開発公団

(Mizushigen Kaihatsu Kōdan). Corporation established by the Japanese government in 1962 to meet the increased demand for water. Until 1962, flood control projects, waterworks, industrial waterworks, and agricultural waterworks were each under the supervision of a separate government ministry. Since that year, however, the corporation has been given the job of constructing dams, dikes, multipurpose irrigation channels, and other facilities in accordance with the Basic Plan for the Development of Water Resources. The corporation has centered its development efforts on the six major river systems: the Tonegawa, Arakawa, Yodogawa, Kisogawa, Yoshinogawa, and Chikugogawa.

Waters, Thomas James
ウォートルス, T. J.

(1830–?). English architect and engineer who, arriving in Japan at the beginning of the Meiji period (1868–1912), produced some of the nation's earliest foreign-designed buildings. His main accomplishments were to promote the local production and extensive use of brick for construction; to build one of the first modern foundries, the Ōsaka Mint; and to execute the new government's first urban plan by reconstructing the Ginza area in Tōkyō after a disastrous fire in 1872. Less visible but equally innovative was his introduction of modern waterpipes and sewage systems.

waterwheels 水車

(*suisha*). The first mention of a waterwheel in Japan is found in the chronicle NIHON SHOKI (720), which states that DONCHŌ, who came to Japan from the Korean kingdom of

weasels Weasels live in forested areas but also near farms and villages, where their raids on domestic fowl have made them pests.

KOGURYŌ in 610, made Japan's first millstone, which hulled rice by water power. Government records of 829 state that "orders were given to all the provinces that waterwheels be built." These wheels were used to lift water for irrigation and were run by human or animal power. This kind of waterwheel was developed in agricultural areas throughout the medieval period (mid-12th–16th centuries), and by the Edo period (1600–1868) it had become widespread, as had the water-driven mill wheel that was employed in producing textiles, oil, flour, and polished rice.

Watsuji Tetsurō 和辻哲郎

(1889–1960). Philosopher and cultural historian noted for his systematic studies of ethics and his inquiry into the particular philosophical components of Japanese culture. Born in Hyōgo Prefecture, Watsuji graduated from Tōkyō University. A prolific writer, he dealt with Western thinkers in his earliest works. He then underwent what he called an intellectual "about-face," which he described in *Gūzō saikō* (1918, Resurrecting Idols) as a renewed "appreciation for Buddhism and the Buddhist art of the Asuka and Nara periods." From this point on, Watsuji concentrated primarily on the intellectual roots of Japanese culture. Between 1920 and 1923 he wrote essays on DŌGEN, which revived interest in this neglected 13th-century Zen master. From 1925 until 1934 Watsuji taught ethics at Kyōto University, a position that gave him the context for his major project, *Rinrigaku*, a systematic treatise on ethics. From 1934 to 1949 he taught at Tōkyō University.

As a thinker, Watsuji strove to articulate a particularly Japanese alternative to modern Western thought, which he saw as overemphasizing man's existence as an individual. He held, for instance, that Japanese intellectual traditions contained the basis for a more sound and balanced ethics defining man as both an individual and a part of society. He cited certain classical aesthetic forms of Japan, such as the TEA CEREMONY, as expressive of this interdependence of the individual and society. Watsuji received the Order of Culture in 1955.

wax-resist dyeing 臈纈

(*rōkechi; rōketsu*). A textile dyeing process. The earliest known examples of Japanese wax-resist dyeing are four folding screens in the 8th-century SHŌSŌIN repository in Nara. These screens were done by a technique called *rōkechi* (see SANKECHI), which came to Japan from India via China during the Tang (T'ang; 618–907) dynasty. During the Heian period (794–1185), however, Japan isolated itself from foreign cultures, and the Japanese began to favor clothing without printed patterns; consequently, Tang-style *rōkechi* died out.

In the Taishō period (1912–26), a batik method of dyeing called *rōketsu* (written with the same characters as *rōkechi*) came into use, and it has been very popular ever since. In the *rōketsu* process, wax-resist and dye are applied to the fabric with a brush. The fabric generally goes through several repetitions of the waxing-dyeing process, then the wax is removed chemically and the dye is fixed into the fabric by steaming before a final washing.

Modern *rōketsu* motifs range from traditional flowers and birds to abstract designs. *Rōketsu* is common in Japanese daily life in such diverse items as KIMONO, folding

screens, framed pictures, NOREN curtains, and pillow covers.

wayo 和与

(literally, "peaceful giving"). A term originally used to mean the free and voluntary transfer of property and rights to either relatives or nonrelatives (in the latter case, it was called *tanin wayo*). It came to mean a peaceful out-of-court settlement between two disputants. *Wayo* (or, more correctly, *wayo chūbun*) settlements concerning division of revenue between SHŌEN (estate) proprietors (HONKE AND RYŌKE) and shogunate-appointed land stewards (JITŌ) became increasingly common from the mid-13th century. In order to be legally binding, *wayo* settlements had to be reviewed by the shogunate, which issued a document of confirmation (*gechijō*). These agreements reflected the KAMAKURA SHOGUNATE's (1192–1333) gradual retreat from control over its appointees. See also SHITAJI CHŪBUN.

weasels 鼬

(*itachi*). The principal species of weasel in Japan is the *itachi* (*Mustela sibirica*) of the family Mustelidae. Widely distributed in East Asia, it is native to all parts of Japan except Okinawa and Hokkaidō, where it has lately been introduced for the extermination of rodents. The body of a large male measures about 35 centimeters (14 in) and its tail 17 centimeters (7 in). Females are less than half this size. The body is brown with a darker head. The *itachi*'s habitat is near water in mountainous areas. It feeds on mice, frogs, and crayfish. The fur is of good quality and is exported under the name "Japanese mink." Related species of the same genus inhabiting Japan are the *iizuna* (least weasel; *M. nivalis*) and *okojo* (stoat; *M. erminea*).

Webb, Sir William Flood ウェッブ, W. F.

(1887–1972). Australian jurist and president of the International Military Tribunal for the Far East from 1946 to 1948. Born in Brisbane, Queensland, he had a distinguished legal career during which he occupied the positions of chief justice of Queensland (1940–46) and justice of the High Court of Australia (1946–58). While serving on the tribunal he proposed that no capital punishment be imposed on any of the accused because they had only been obeying orders, whereas the emperor had escaped trial. His belief in the emperors's complicity brought him into serious disagreement with the chief prosecutor, the American Joseph B. KEENAN, as well as some of his fellow judges. Nevertheless, when by majority decisions the tribunal pronounced death sentences on seven of the accused, Sir William did not press his dissent. See also WAR CRIMES TRIALS.

weddings 結婚式

(*kekkonshiki*). Weddings, perhaps the most important of the Japanese rites of passage, are one of the four major ceremonial occasions referred to as *kankon sōsai* (coming-of-age, marriage, funerals, ancestor worship). For a marriage to be official, a new family register (*koseki;* see HOUSEHOLD REGISTERS) must be compiled for the couple at the local administrative office. However, social and public recognition of a marriage in Japan is still often sought through the holding of extravagant weddings with elaborate formal costumes and large receptions.

Traditional Weddings—The "traditional" wedding of today was established as

weddings

Although modern weddings are popular, young couples today are also reviving older customs.

A bride and groom pose with their immediate families and the *nakōdo* (go-between) for a commemorative photograph following a traditional ceremony. The bride wears the white *tsunokakushi* head covering to hide her "horns of jealousy."

The wedding ceremony over, a bride and groom emerge from an old-fashioned farmhouse that is rented to couples who wish to hold a traditional ceremony.

After the wedding ceremony, a couple travels by boat to the hall where a reception will be held.

Reenactments of the tradition of escorting the bride to her new household have become a tourist attraction in the post-station town of Tsumago, Nagano Prefecture.

a pattern during the Meiji period (1868–1912). Although the marriage procedure varied a great deal with locality, most weddings included the customs described here. The day of the wedding was chosen carefully to avoid inauspicious days as determined by Chinese and Japanese astrological traditions (see ROKUYŌ). Traditional wedding rituals began the day before the wedding, when the bride prayed at the family shrine or temple or had a parting banquet with neighbors and parents. The wedding-day rituals primarily took place at the household of the groom, or at the household of the bride if the groom was adopted into her family in the kind of marriage called MUKOIRIKON. In cases where the bride entered the groom's household, she dressed in white as she took formal leave of her parents. The white was symbolic of the death of her natal ties to them. At the household of the groom she appeared wearing a colorful *furisode*-style KIMONO and a cotton or silk head covering called *tsunokakushi* (literally, "horn-hiding"), which was supposed to suppress and hide the feminine "horns of jealousy." The groom wore a kimono with family CRESTS and the loose trousers called HAKAMA.

Once at the home, various rites were performed, the most important being the couple pledge. This ritual exchange of *sake*, called

sansan kudo (three-three-nine times), was originally practiced in high-ranking households and is now standard in weddings throughout Japan. It consists of three formal sips of *sake* by the bride and groom from a set of three cups graduated from small to large size. Following the pledge, the introduction of the two households through a formal exchange of *sake* is held. A reception (*hirōen*) is held afterward.

Three or five days after the ceremony, the wife (and sometimes her husband) returned to her family home (a custom called *satogaeri*), bringing gifts for relatives and friends. The parents of the bride and groom might also visit each other, thus sealing the union and ending the marriage procedure.

Modern Weddings—Traditional weddings were basically secular rites decided upon by local customs and personal preference. Weddings today are still determined by these considerations but are more likely to include a religious ceremony, even when the couple has no particular belief or religious affiliation. Shintō weddings, which became popular after the Shintō marriage ceremony held for the crown prince in 1900, are more common than Buddhist or Christian weddings, although Christian ceremonies have become increasingly fashionable. The trend has shifted from weddings at home to wed-

dings in shrines, temples, and (since World War II) hotels, restaurants, churches, or special wedding halls, which are often furnished with special wedding chambers of Shintō or Christian design. Although the custom of *satogaeri* might still be observed by some, most Japanese try to take a honeymoon of at least a week. The couple may make their ritual trip after settling into their new home. Although large-scale, expensive weddings directed and financed by the parents are still common, there are also an increasing number of weddings that more closely reflect the personal wishes of the couple. See also MIAI; NAKŌDO.   ☎ 1694–1695

weekly magazines   週刊誌

(*shūkanshi*). The first widely read weekly magazines in Japan, the *Shūkan asahi* (published by the Asahi Shimbun Newspaper Co) and the *Sandei mainichi* (published by the Mainichi Shimbun Newspaper Co), were both launched in 1922. The subject matter of these early weeklies varied, ranging from such topics as current events, society, and the economy to women's interests and serialized novels. Their circulations were over 300,000 each, a large figure for the

Continued on page 1696 ➤

A Contemporary Wedding

The wedding rite of choice for most Japanese couples in the decades since World War II has been a version of the traditional Shintō marriage ceremony. The ritual is highly formalized, and attendance is strictly limited. Receptions are more open-ended affairs that allow couples and their families to display their social status to friends, coworkers, and relatives.

Western-style wedding rites are also popular. Whatever their beliefs, growing numbers of couples now choose to be married in churches or in the Christian-style chapels put up by many hotels and wedding halls.

The Ceremony

The Shintō wedding ceremony is conducted in the sanctuary of a shrine. Many shrines maintain reception halls on their grounds so that they can handle every phase of the marriage celebration; conversely, most hotels and independent wedding halls maintain shrines on their premises.

A Shintō priest, assisted by young women called *miko*, directs the ceremony, which takes between 20 and 30 minutes. Only close relatives and the go-between (*nakōdo*) and his or her spouse attend. After the participants take their appointed places, the priest waves a branch of the sacred *sakaki* tree, purifying those present and announcing the marriage to the gods. The bride and groom then drink *sake* together in a ritual known as *sansan kudo* (three-three-nine-times) and formally pledge to uphold the marriage bond. Often at this point a Western-style exchange of wedding bands takes place. The couple next offer *sakaki* branches at the Shintō altar, and those present sip *sake*, sealing the relationship between the two families, whose members are then formally introduced. The priest's closing statement ends the ceremony. Everyone retires to another room to have photographs taken.

The wedding photograph

The bride and groom appear after family members have been seated according to the traditional plan. Here the go-between escorts the groom while his wife leads the bride. The couple's seats (right foreground) face the altar (not shown). The go-between and his wife sit behind them.

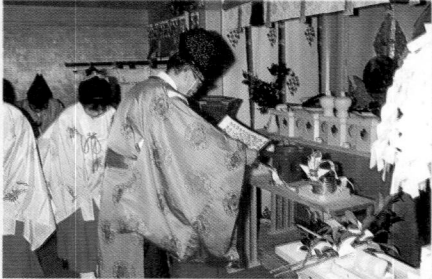
The priest announces the marriage to the gods after ceremonially purifying those present. He uses ritual language unintelligible to most participants.

The couple sips sake from a set of three cups, moving from the smallest to the largest.

Next the bride and groom make their pledge before the gods. The groom reads a prepared text. The bride simply speaks her own name.

The Reception

With the reception, the couple announce their union to friends and coworkers as well as to their families. Spending a total of ¥5 million (about US $40,000 in 1992) on a wedding is not unusual. The reception, lasting two to three hours, consumes the bulk of this expenditure.

Over the years receptions have become ever more elaborate, and ostentation has begun to meet with criticism. In an affluent age when one- or two-child families are the norm, however, many parents are willing to bear the entire financial burden for a magnificent wedding, and costs steadily escalate. It is taken for granted that the proceedings will be run by a professional master of ceremonies and videotaped, that the bride will appear in several different ensembles, and that the couple will light a central candle display and then candles at the guests' tables.

The average wedding reception is attended by 50 to 100 guests, who are treated to dinner and sent home with bags of presents. In turn, guests must present the couple with an envelope containing a set amount of money. The 1992 rate was ¥30,000 (about US $240) for guests unrelated to bride or groom; relatives must present a higher sum.

Receptions vary with the couple's tastes and budget, but a typical one will include speech making, cake cutting, and singing. Here are scenes from one such reception.

The once-in-a-lifetime experience. An "outdo the neighbors" mentality has made receptions increasingly extravagant.

The bride and groom appear. The go-between, seated beside the groom, greets the audience first.

The candle service is a recent addition to the ceremony.

Bride and groom are greeted by their guest of honor (usually a workplace superior) and toasted.

After the speeches and songs are over, the bride and groom each offer flowers to the other's parents.

The cutting of the cake. The dinner that follows features various speeches by selected guests, as well as singing.

The couple's parents thank the guests to end the reception. On their way out, guests greet the newlyweds.

Bride and groom reappear in wedding gown and morning coat.

The exchange of wedding bands is now as central to most ceremonies as the *sake* ritual, but it is a recent addition.

Traditional Weights and Measures as Standardized in 1891

Japanese units		Approximate metric equivalents	Approximate US equivalents
Length[1]			
bu		3.03 mm	0.119 in
sun	10 bu	3.03 cm	1.193 in
shaku	10 sun	30.30 cm	11.930 in
ken	6 shaku	1.818 m	5.965 ft
chō	60 ken	109.09 m	119.30 yd
ri	36 chō	3.927 km	2.440 mi
hiro	6 shaku	1.818 m	0.994 fathom
kairi		1.852 km	1 nautical mi
Area			
tsubo (or bu)	1 sq ken	3.306 sq m	35.58 sq ft
se	30 tsubo	99.175 sq m	118.61 sq yd
tan	10 se	0.099 ha (991.75 sq m)	0.245 a (1,186.11 sq yd)
chō (or chōbu)	10 tan	0.992 ha	2.451 a
Weight			
bu		0.375 gm	5.787 gr*
momme	10 bu	3.750 gm	57.870 gr* (0.132 oz)*
kin	160 momme	600.00 gm	1.323 lb*
kan (or kamme)	1,000 momme	3.75 kg	8.27 lb*
Capacity			
shaku		18.039 ml	0.033 pt (dry) or 0.610 fl oz
gō	10 shaku	180.39 ml	0.328 pt (dry) or 6.100 fl oz
shō	10 gō	1.8039 l	1.638 qt (dry) or 1.906 qt (liquid)
to	10 shō	18.039 l	2.048 pk or 4.766 gal
koku	10 to	180.39 l	5.119 bu or 47.655 gal

[1]Less frequently used measures of length include the rin (0.1 bu) and the jō (10 shaku). When used for cloth measure the bu, sun, and shaku were 25 percent longer than indicated here.
*Avoirdupois.
NOTE: The table shows values for the units as standardized in terms of the metric system in 1891. Actual values in the premodern period differed from time to time and place to place. Japan officially converted to the metric system in 1959.

time. After the MANCHURIAN INCIDENT of 1931, Japanese weekly magazines took on a distinctly nationalistic character, functioning in large part as dispensers of militaristic propaganda. This tendency became even more pronounced just before World War II, when the government began to use the allocation of paper as a way to influence the editorial content of all print media.

After the war, such weekly magazines as *Shūkan yomiuri*, *Shūkan Tōkyō*, and *Shūkan sankei*, all published by newspaper companies, made their appearance. Book publishers also issued weekly magazines, the most important of which was *Shūkan shinchō* (published by SHINCHŌSHA, LTD). These and other postwar weeklies achieved popularity by avoiding the restrained and factual reporting of the general-interest monthly magazines (*sōgō zasshi*), focusing instead on the "human side" of daily affairs.

Since the early 1970s weekly magazine readership in Japan has expanded greatly, and the magazines have become more specialized, often catering to very specific audiences and age groups. The 1980s saw the appearance of a special brand of tabloid-style weekly photo magazines, typified by the wildly popular *Focus* (published by Shinchōsha, Ltd) and *Friday* (published by KŌDANSHA, LTD), which specialize in exposing (or fueling) scandals in the entertainment and political worlds. A number of weekly newsmagazines, such as *Aera* and the Japanese-language edition of *Newsweek*, also began publication during this period. As of 1990 total circulation for weekly magazines in Japan was 1.8 billion.

weights and measures 単位と量

(*tan'i to ryō*). Two completely standardized systems of weights and spatial measures have been used in Japan since the Meiji period (1868–1912). One of these is the metric system, which has long been in use among scientists and for official purposes and which in 1959 was decreed to be the only system allowed for other common uses. The metric units seem to have moved a long way toward complete public acceptance, and the day is probably not far distant when they will have entirely replaced the units of the other modern system.

The other system may be referred to as native or Japanese. The names of the units in it are mostly of Chinese origin, but their values are not the same as those of the corresponding Chinese units. The native system has been standardized (i.e., defined in terms of the metric system) only since 1891. It contains units of the following kinds: weight, length, or distance; cloth measure; area; and volume or capacity.

When one comes to deal with units of measurement in use before the Meiji period, the situation becomes more complex. The intrinsic difficulty stems from three causes. First, at any given time there was not necessarily a standard definition throughout Japan of the value of any particular unit of measurement. For instance, whereas the official definition of the *ken* (the length of the standard architectural module) makes it 1.82 meters (5.97 ft), a common Kansai-region (Kyōto-Ōsaka-Kōbe area) use of the same unit takes it to be 1.97 meters (6.46 ft). Second, within the same area, the values of specific units did not necessarily remain constant over long periods of time. The standard span (distance between vertical supports) of the Kamakura-period (1185–1333) buildings in the city of Kyōto does not correspond to that used in the same city in the Edo period (1600–1868). Third, even with respect to different units of the same kind (e.g., units of weight, or of linear or volume measure) the ratios that existed at one time or place did not necessarily exist at another. The *kin*, a unit of weight equivalent to 0.60 kilograms (1.32 lb), now contains 160 *momme* (1 *momme* = 3.75 grams or 0.13 oz), but before standardization the same unit varied with the objects being weighed. It might be 160, 180, or 220 *momme*, the value of the *momme* being more or less constant.

Japanese specialists have done considerable work in tracing the history of each unit of measure. Fujita Motoharu's (1879–1958) *Shakudo sōkō* (1929) is a good historical study of linear measures in Japan, and most general and historical encyclopedias have entries describing and defining the principal premodern units of measurement.

Wei zhi (Wei chih) 魏志

(J: *Gishi*; The Wei Chronicle). History of the Chinese Wei dynasty (220–265). Its section dealing with the "Wa people" (Ch: *woren* or *wo-jen*; J: *wajin*; i.e., the Japanese) documents information on Japan in the 2nd and 3rd centuries. "Gishi wajinden," the name commonly used in Japan for this section, refers to the subsection on the Wa people in the "Dongyi zhuan" (Tung-i chuan; literally, "Eastern Barbarian Accounts"; J: "Tōiden") section of the *Wei zhi*. The *Wei zhi*, one of the post-Han *Chronicles of the Three Kingdoms* (*Sanguo zhi* or *San-kuo chih*) was compiled in the late 3rd century by Chen Shou (Ch'en Shou, 233–297), an official of the Western Jin (Chin) dynasty (265–317).

The "Wajinden" is about 2,000 Chinese characters in length and can be divided into 8 sections. The first section refers to the location of the "countries" of the Wa people and to changes in the number of countries maintaining a tributary relationship with China. The second is a brief description of the Wa countries. The third deals with Wa customs and products; politics and social ranking are discussed in the fourth. The fifth relates the life led by HIMIKO, the female ruler of YAMATAI, to which almost all the other Wa countries are said to have given allegiance. The sixth describes the existence of countries of "Wa ethnic stock" (J: *washu*) to the east of Yamatai, as well as countries across the sea to the south. The seventh describes relations between Wei China and Yamatai (239–247); the eighth is a concise account of Himiko's death and subsequent developments.

It was once thought that the "Wajinden" was based on a Chinese historical work known as the *Wei lue* (Wei lüeh; J: *Giryaku*). However, a more recent theory holds that it was probably based on the nonextant *Wei shu*, edited by Wang Shen (d 266).

welfare commissioners 民生委員

(*minsei iin*). Public servants who work on a voluntary basis to improve the lives of local residents. Based on the Welfare Commissioners Law (Minsei Iin Hō), which became effective in 1948, welfare commissioners are appointed to a term of three years of service in an assigned locality by the minister of health and welfare. Welfare commissioners observe the living conditions of residents who may need assistance and, working in cooperation with welfare offices, provide help to those who need it. In 1988 there were approximately 180,000 welfare commissioners in Japan.

welfare for the aged 老人福祉

(*rōjin fukushi*). The rapid aging of the Japanese population has made the provision of welfare services for the elderly one of the most pressing problems facing Japan. In 1990, 12 percent of the population was over 65, and by 1996 this number is expected to increase to 14 percent. See AGING POPULATION.

The OLD-AGE WELFARE LAW of 1963 guarantees a "wholesome and peaceful life" to the elderly. The law provides for free or low-cost placement in NURSING HOMES, free annual health examinations, and a system of home helpers and local welfare centers for the aged. As a symbolic indication of the importance of the elderly in Japanese society, the law also established 15 September as Respect for the Aged Day (Keirō no Hi), a national holiday. In 1973 the government began to pay all medical expenses not covered by health insurance for persons 70 years old or older. However, the LAW CONCERNING HEALTH AND MEDICAL SERVICES FOR THE AGED of 1982 reintroduced the requirement that a portion of health care fees be paid by the individual.

Welfare centers for the aged, another provision of the Old-Age Welfare Law, promote the formation of senior citizens' clubs, which numbered 129,600 in 1988, and sponsor a variety of activities that encourage social involvement on the part of the elderly. For those senior citizens who wish to continue working after retirement, the government sponsors organizations that assist them in finding jobs.

While many Japanese senior citizens remain active well into old age, in recent years the number of senior citizens who are bedridden or otherwise unable to care for themselves has increased. There are various kinds of nursing homes available for those in need of full-time care, and such short-term services as home helpers, day care, and temporary institutional stays are also available for those with less pressing care needs. In many cases Japanese families look after their elderly members, with a married son often living with his parents to care for them in their old age. However, the number of elderly being cared for by their children is decreasing and is expected to continue to do so, prompting growing demands on the government to expand the existing systems of care for the elderly or provide alternative systems.

welfare for the handicapped
障害者福祉

(*shōgaisha fukushi*). Welfare services for the handicapped, an integral component of Japan's system of SOCIAL WELFARE, include financial assistance, counseling, and rehabilitation services. In Japan welfare for the handicapped was not systematized until after World War II. Before that the only programs available were individual private social programs for retarded children and physically handicapped children. Today welfare for the handicapped is provided for in the PHYSICALLY HANDICAPPED WELFARE LAW, the Mentally Retarded Welfare Law (1960, Seishin Hakujakusha Fukushi Hō), and the Law concerning Basic Policies for the Emotionally and Physically Handicapped (1970, Shinshin Shōgaisha Taisaku Kihon Hō). Handicapped children under 18 are provided for in the CHILD WELFARE LAW. The basic disability component of the NATIONAL PENSION plan guarantees an income to the handicapped: in 1990 the severely handicapped received ¥70,967 (US $490) monthly and the moderately handicapped received ¥56,775 (US $392).

Special counseling centers for the rehabilitation of the physically or mentally handicapped, along with welfare offices, provide services to 2.3 million handicapped persons. Among the services provided are rehabilitation programs to enable the handicapped to function in society; residential facilities for those who require constant care but are unable to receive it at home; and home helpers, who travel to the homes of the handicapped and assist them with a variety of daily activities. In addition, programs to promote special employment opportunities are offered by the Ministry of Labor. By law, 1.6 percent of those employed by private industry and 1.9 to 2.0 percent of those employed by the government must be handicapped; as of yet, however, these goals have not been realized. See also SPECIAL EDUCATION.

Welsh onion
葱

(*negi*). *Allium fistulosum.* A biennial plant of the family Liliaceae that has long been an important winter vegetable in Japan. It was introduced to Japan from China before the 10th century. It is similar to the leek but smaller; its leaf base does not form an enlarged bulb, and its leaves and leaf sheaths are edible. In the eastern part of Japan, varieties that seldom grow in bunches are planted, and the stalks are covered high with earth to promote blanching. In western Japan, varieties that tend to bunch are grown and left relatively exposed for greater utilization of the green leaves. Welsh onion is used mainly in fish and meat dishes and is indispensable in SUKIYAKI.

Western Learning
洋学

(Yōgaku). Broadly speaking, the study of Western subjects by Japanese during the Edo period (1600–1868). For most of the period, however, it was called Dutch Learning (Rangaku), because the Japanese received Western culture only through the Dutch. The term Yōgaku came into common use only in the late Edo period, when Japanese interest in a wider range of Western knowledge led them to learn Western languages other than Dutch. The main subjects studied were medicine and other physical sciences, foreign languages, art, and, late in the period, military science and world affairs.

Origins of Western Learning—In the 16th and early 17th centuries, English, Dutch, Portuguese, and Spanish merchants and missionaries brought to Japan objects of Western material culture, such as clocks and firearms, as well as Western technical skills, such as navigation and surgery. But due to the Tokugawa shogunate's (1603–1867) policy of NATIONAL SECLUSION, by 1639 the Dutch were the only Westerners permitted to enter Japan—a limitation that continued for about two centuries. During the first century of seclusion, it was principally the official interpreters of the Dutch language at Nagasaki who became versed in Western culture. Although the Japanese authorities severely restricted personal contacts with the Dutch, the Japanese thirst for knowledge of the West persisted—sometimes even among the authorities themselves. In 1650 the physician of the East India Company on DEJIMA, Caspar Schambergen, accompanied the chief of the Dutch settlement on his annual mission to Edo (now Tōkyō). Requested by the shōgun to stay on in the capital for a few more months, he instructed the shogunal physicians in Dutch medicine.

The Nagasaki astronomer NISHIKAWA JOKEN and the Confucian scholar ARAI HAKUSEKI were pioneers in the development of Western Learning; another important figure was the shōgun TOKUGAWA YOSHIMUNE (r 1716–45). Hoping to correct the traditional Japanese calendar and thus improve agriculture, in 1720 he ended restrictions on the importation of Chinese books on Western subjects—except those specifically on Christianity, which remained banned. In 1740 Yoshimune ordered AOKI KON'YŌ and NORO GENJŌ to begin studying the Dutch language; both later wrote books on Western subjects. Japanese studies of the West advanced greatly between 1750 and 1790 due to research and publications by the scholar-officials MAENO RYŌTAKU, SUGITA GEMPAKU, and ŌTSUKI GENTAKU.

Medicine—Medicine was the most studied and appreciated branch of Western Learning. Medical knowledge was introduced by Western physicians employed by the Dutch East India Company (such as Engelbert KAEMPFER of Germany and Carl Peter THUNBERG of Sweden) and by Western

medical books. The completion in 1774 of KAITAI SHINSHO (New Book of Anatomy), a translated Western medical text, by Sugita and his colleagues was an epoch-making event because it symbolized Japanese recognition of the superiority of Western over traditional East Asian medical methods; it also stimulated further work in translation and lexicography. The most important Western teacher of medicine was Philipp Franz von SIEBOLD, but other foreign physicians introduced smallpox vaccination and the stethoscope. In 1861 J. L. C. POMPE VAN MEERDERVOORT opened a hospital, the Nagasaki Yōjōsho, where he treated 930 patients in the first year and issued medical certificates to Japanese doctors, some of whom became mainstays of medical science in the Meiji period (1868–1912).

Other Physical Sciences—The Portuguese introduced Ptolemaic astronomy before the seclusion policy began, but their efforts had no lasting influence. Later, the Nagasaki interpreter SHIZUKI TADAO publicized Copernican theories. Information provided by the Dutch allowed the shogunate to improve Japan's lunar calendar, a measure that was crucial to agriculture.

Surveying and mapmaking benefited from the geographical knowledge provided first by the Portuguese and later by the Dutch, which influenced Japanese explorers and cartographers such as HONDA TOSHIAKI, MAMIYA RINZŌ, MOGAMI TOKUNAI, and INŌ TADATAKA. Fields closely related to medicine, such as botany, physics, and chemistry, were also studied.

Language Studies—Knowledge of Dutch was largely transmitted orally until the 1774 publication of the *Kaitai shinsho*, which was followed by many books on the Dutch language. In 1788, Ōtsuki Gentaku published RANGAKU KAITEI (A Ladder to Dutch Learning), an introductory text for students of Dutch. INAMURA SAMPAKU compiled the first Dutch-Japanese dictionary, HARUMA WAGE (1796). In 1815–16 the manuscript for a second dictionary was completed by a group of shogunate interpreters under the supervision of Hendrik DOEFF, chief of the Dutch settlement in Nagasaki.

The Arts—Before the period of National Seclusion several Japanese artists had experimented with Western-style painting, but its influence soon faded (see NAMBAN ART). The versatile scholar and writer HIRAGA GENNAI made the first Japanese oil paintings, but he is known mainly as a teacher of this style (see AKITA SCHOOL). One of Gennai's disciples, SHIBA KŌKAN, studied Dutch under Maeno Ryōtaku and Ōtsuki Gentaku and became the greatest Western-style painter of the Edo period. Finally, the art of the NAGASAKI SCHOOL was influenced by Western subject matter and materials (see WESTERN-STYLE PICTURES, EARLY).

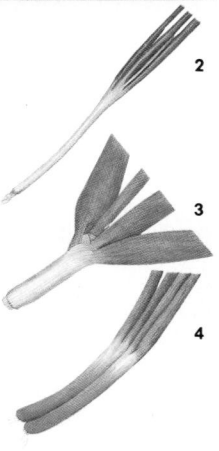

Welsh onion
1 White flowers appear on the tips of the onion stalks in spring.
2 The Hakushū is the most common variety and is used in *sukiyaki* and other one-pot dishes.
3 The Shimonita variety of Welsh onion, a specialty of Gumma Prefecture, is a favorite in one-pot dishes.
4 Grown in Ibaraki Prefecture, the reddish *akanegi* is frequently added to winter dishes to provide color.

The End of Seclusion—Near the end of the 18th century, some Japanese scholars started to warn of a foreign threat, first from Russia and later from Britain, France, and the United States. For example, in 1791 HAYASHI SHIHEI wrote *Kaikoku heidan* (Military Problems for a Maritime Nation), which advocated strengthening coastal defenses and building a strong navy. In time, shogunate leaders recognized the need to acquire much more systematic knowledge of the outside world, and in 1811 they appointed officials to translate foreign books. In 1855 the shogunate established the Yōgakusho (Institute for Western Learning) at Edo, where shogunate officials studied Western science and technology as well as European languages. The institute's name was changed to BANSHO SHIRABESHO (Institute for the Investigation of Barbarian Books) in 1856; it was one of the forerunners of TōKYō UNIVERSITY.

Military science became the most important field of Western Learning in the 19th century due to the impending foreign threat. TAKASHIMA SHūHAN, for example, avidly studied Western ballistics and gunnery techniques, becoming a pioneer of modern Japanese military technology. In 1855 the shogunate established the Naval Institute (KAIGUN DENSHūJO) at Nagasaki with instruction by Dutch navy officers. The shogunate and powerful *daimyō* vied with one another to buy or build Western-style ships and guns as Japan approached the civil war that led to the Meiji Restoration of 1868.

Japan's rise as a great power in the second half of the 19th century owed much to a rapid, systematic, and sustained assimilation of advanced Western knowledge. Although the information and skills gained by Edo-period Yōgaku students were quickly superseded by a new flood of Western knowledge in the Meiji period, the earlier forms of Western Learning created one undeniable legacy for Japan's modern development: unlike China, Japan had a tradition of acquiring Western knowledge in order to build national wealth and strength.

Western-style painting → yōga

Western-style pictures, early

洋風画

(*yōfūga*). Japanese art inspired by the styles of Europe, from the largely Portuguese-influenced NAMBAN ART ("southern barbarian" art) of the late 16th and early 17th centuries to the Dutch-influenced *kōmōga* ("red-hair" pictures) of the 17th to 19th centuries.

In 1590 the JESUIT MISSION PRESS was set up in Kyūshū, and the fathers there taught the art of engraving to Japanese converts. While Japanese Christians were adopting Western techniques for the purpose of imitating European religious paintings and engravings, traditional artists were incorporating Western nonreligious subject matter into their art.

With enforcement of NATIONAL SECLUSION in the 17th century, the chief inspiration for Western-style art became pictures introduced by the Dutch at the port of DEJIMA in Nagasaki. Pictures of foreigners became known as *kōmōga* ("red-hair" pictures), based on the belief that the Dutch all had red locks. A school of Western-style painting flourished in Nagasaki (see NAGASAKI SCHOOL) at this time. By the 18th century UKIYO-E prints depicting foreigners had become exceedingly popular.

Western art continued to influence Japanese arts and crafts (including LACQUER WARE and CERAMICS) throughout the Edo period (1600–1868) in spite of Japan's official seclusion policy. Through the influence of the Western-style artist, biologist, and author HIRAGA GENNAI, Akita in northern Japan became a center of Western art (see AKITA SCHOOL). However, the chief pioneer and popularizer of Western-style art in Japan was SHIBA KōKAN, the originator of copperplate etching in Japan and one of the first to develop the art of oil painting. See also YōGA.

West Japan Railway Co

西日本旅客鉄道[株]

(Nishi Nihon Ryokaku Tetsudō). Passenger railway company established in 1987 after the privatization of the former JAPANESE NATIONAL RAILWAYS. Now part of the JR group, it operates the San'yō SHINKANSEN from Shin Ōsaka to Hakata as well as 50 conventional lines, including 13 main routes in and around the Kansai metropolitan area. It also manages the JR group's New York and Paris offices in partnership with other members. Sales for the fiscal year ending March 1990 totaled ¥834.3 billion (US $5.5 billion), and capitalization stood at ¥100.0 billion (US $653.3 million). Corporate headquarters are in Ōsaka.

Weston, Walter

ウェストン, W.

(1861–1940). English missionary and alpinist; the "father of Japanese mountaineering." He came to Japan in 1888 as a missionary of the Church of England. During three periods of residency in Japan he climbed various peaks, including Mt. Fuji (Fujisan). He wrote *Mountaineering and Exploration in the Japanese Alps* (1896). A Weston Festival is held in his honor at KAMIKōCHI annually in June.

whales

鯨

(*kujira*). In Japanese, *kujira* is the general name for mammals of the order Cetacea. Whales of the suborder Mysticeti (baleen, or toothless, whales) are often seen in Japanese waters when Arctic summer populations migrate south for breeding in winter. The following species are the most common: the *semi kujira* (right whale; *Eubalaena glacialis*), the *zatō kujira* (humpback whale; *Megaptera novaeangliae*), and the *nagasu kujira* (fin whale; *Balaenoptera physalus*). The *makkō kujira* (sperm whale; *Physeter catodon*), one of the toothed whales (suborder Odontoceti), also frequents Japanese waters seasonally. In addition, among the dolphin family, the *mairuka* (common dolphin; *Delphinus delphis*), the *suji iruka* (blue-white dolphin; *Stenella caeruleoalba*), and the *kama iruka* (Pacific white side dolphin; *Lagenorhynchus obliquidens*) are common.

Among fishermen the whale has been regarded as a manifestation of EBISU (one of the Seven Deities of Good Fortune) and harbinger of a bounteous catch of fish. Once an important source of protein, it is now a rarity on Japanese tables. See also WHALING.

whaling

捕鯨

(*hogei*). The term *hogei* legally refers to the hunting of whales with a harpoon gun fired from a power-driven catcher boat. Until recently it included factory-ship whaling, land-based whaling, and small-scale whaling, all of which were designated as fishery operations and regulated in Japan by the Ministry of Agriculture, Forestry, and Fisheries. It is thus distinguished from dolphin hunting, which is subject to licensing by the prefectural government concerned.

History—The early Japanese caught whales that had run aground or wandered into bays, but by the beginning of the 17th century Japanese whaling had become an organized industry. In the early days of the industry, whales were hunted by hand harpooning. After a unique net whaling method was developed in 1675, whaling spread to a number of places along the coasts of western Japan and reached the height of its prosperity from 1810 to 1850. However, Japanese whalers were confined to nearby coastal waters by the NATIONAL SECLUSION policy of the Tokugawa shogunate (1603–1867). From about 1820, whalers from the United States and other Western countries began to appear in Japanese waters. The numerous Western whalers soon caused a rapid decline in the number of right whales, the main Japanese catch, causing the traditional Japanese whaling industry to languish. From the 1860s to the 1880s Japanese whalers tried US-style open-sea whaling methods but without much success.

At the turn of the century the appearance in the Sea of Japan of Russian whalers, who employed modern whaling methods, prompted Japanese whalers to modernize their equipment. In 1897 they adopted modern whaling techniques from Norway. From about 1906 onward, coastal whaling gathered momentum, and soon the Japanese extended their reach from Taiwan in the south to the Kuril Islands in the north. Beginning in the 1930s, they employed small catcher boats and specialized in the hunting of smaller species in which larger whalers were not interested.

In 1934 Japan sent a whaling fleet to Antarctic waters for the first time; this event marked the beginning of Japanese factory-ship whaling. In the ensuing years Japan rapidly increased the size of its whaling fleet. However, World War II dealt a near-fatal blow to the Japanese whaling industry. At war's end, coastal whaling was revived immediately in response to the food crisis. In 1946 factory-ship whaling was begun again in the waters surrounding the Bonin (J: Ogasawara) Islands, and another fleet was sent to Antarctic waters. In 1952 factory-ship whaling was resumed in the North Pacific as well. By the end of the first half of the 1960s, seven factory-ship whaling fleets were operating in the Antarctic and three in the North Pacific and their catch surpassed the prewar peak.

However, beginning in the late 1960s,

whaling regulations were stiffened by the International Whaling Commission (IWC), established pursuant to the International Convention for the Regulation of Whaling in 1948, and Japan's whaling industry came under increasing pressure to reduce its operations.

Whale Products—Primary products of the whale include whale meat, baleen whale oil, sperm whale oil, and meat extract. These are in turn processed into secondary and tertiary products. In Western countries, the primary objective of whaling was the production of whale oil. Whale meat was not usually used as food; instead, it was processed into meal, other forms of feed, or fertilizers. By contrast, whale meat constituted a significant (though proportionately small) source of protein in the Japanese diet during the decade following World War II, when animal protein was scarce. The whaling industry in Japan was thus supported in the past by the markets for both whale meat and oil.

Whaling Regulations—The introduction of modern whaling methods and the resulting growth of Japan's coastal whaling industry brought the question of conserving whale resources to the fore. To deal with the situation and to foster cooperation among the whaling companies, the government promulgated a Ministry of Agriculture and Commerce ordinance on "Whaling Control Regulations" in 1909 and followed it with several revisions. Regulations for the control of factory-ship whaling were promulgated in 1931 and amended in 1934, 1938, and 1949. While still under the Allied Occupation, Japan became in 1951 a signatory of the 1946 International Convention for the Regulation of Whaling. Since the late 1960s sentiment supporting the protection of whales has run high in the world, and the Japanese government has intensified the regulation of the domestic whaling industry.

Abandonment of Whaling—By the 1980s Japan was finally driven to a gradual abandonment of commercial whaling. In 1982 the International Whaling Commission, for the sake of preservation of natural resources, declared a moratorium on factory-ship whaling effective October 1985 and on coastal whaling effective April 1986. Four whaling nations—Japan, Norway, Peru, and the USSR—responded to this decision by filing statements of dissent. However, under pressure from the US government, Japan retracted its objection in 1986 and by 1988 discontinued commercial whaling entirely. Research whaling—the taking of whales for scientific purposes such as estimation of biological parameters required for stock man-

agement and elucidation of the roles of whales in the Antarctic ecosystem—has been carried out in the Antarctic Ocean since December 1987. Some 330 minke whales were taken in the 1990–91 season. See also WHALES.

wheat and barley   小麦と大麦

(*komugi to ōmugi*). Both grains were introduced to Japan from China in the 3rd or 4th century AD. They were cultivated as winter crops in dry fields and as second crops in paddy fields after the rice harvest. However, since Japan's climate is not particularly suitable for growing wheat and barley, productivity is low. Japanese wheat is mainly winter wheat and unfit for bread. Its main use is for noodles; it is also used in making soy sauce and *fu* (wheat-gluten). Production in 1990 was 951,500 metric tons (1,046,700 short tons). Two types of barley are grown: husked and naked. Both are polished, pressed or ground, mixed with rice, and boiled. Since the end of World War II, the new habit of eating bread has increased the demand for wheat, and the growth of livestock breeding has increased the demand for barley for feed. However, the import of large quantities of barley from the United States has resulted in a drastic decrease in production in Japan since 1962. Total 1990 production was 323,300 metric tons (355,600 short tons).

whitebait   白魚

(*shirauo*). *Salangichthys microdon;* a brackish-water fish of the family Salangidae, order Salmoniformes, class Osteichthyes. It swims upstream in the spawning season and grows to 10 cm (4 in) during its one-year life span. Distribution ranges from Lake Abashiri in Hokkaidō to Okayama Prefecture on the Pacific coast of Japan and from Sakhalin and Vladivostok to the west coast of Kyūshū along the coast of the Sea of Japan. The body of the *shirauo* is colorless, and it is often confused with the *shirouo* (*Leucopsarion petersi*) of the family Gobiidae. Both species are eaten.

For the common people of Edo (now Tōkyō) the arrival of the *shirauo* was a harbinger of spring; they were caught from the river Sumidagawa. It was customary to present the first catch of *shirauo* to the shōgun's family. Many works mentioning *shirauo* are found among the *haiku* poems of the Edo period (1600–1868). The frail beauty of the fish is captured in a haiku poem by Matsuo BASHŌ: "Frail fish, *shirauo* / You will splinter into nothingness / if you run into a rock."

white-collar workers →sararīman

White Paper on the Economy   経済白書

(*Keizai hakusho*). Annual report on current trends of the Japanese economy published each August since 1947 by the ECONOMIC PLANNING AGENCY. Each report has a title giving the primary policy problems of that year. In 1961, when the economy began its strong growth, the report was entitled "Problems of the Growth Economy"; in 1974, the year after the 1973 oil crisis, it was "Beyond the Growth Economy"; and in 1989, "The Dawning of the Heisei Era and the New Economic Trends." As a fundamental guide to present economic conditions and policies, the White Paper on the Economy is by far the most widely read of the "white papers" issued by the government.

White Paper on the National Life
国民生活白書

(*Kokumin seikatsu hakusho*). Annual report on national life published each December since 1956 by the ECONOMIC PLANNING AGENCY. In addition to analyzing household income, consumption, savings, and standards of living in detail, the report may also take up social welfare, income distribution, family structure, education, housing, and other important issues in the life of the people. Recent reports have dealt with reasons for the high prices in Japan relative to other countries and possible countermeasures, the effects of skyrocketing land prices and mounting financial assets on the Japanese economy as a whole, and proposals to increase leisure time for individuals.

white papers   白書

(*hakusho*). Reports released periodically by government ministries and agencies to inform the public of facts concerning the areas under their jurisdiction. The first white paper in Japan was the *Keizai jissō hōkokusho* (Report on Actual Economic Conditions) published in 1947. It explained in clear and simple terms the state of Japan's economy and the problems the nation faced immediately after World War II. The report was highly praised, and a *Keizai hakusho* (WHITE PAPER ON THE ECONOMY) has since been issued annually. Today almost all government ministries issue white papers. Although

whitebait The *shirauo* is a translucent fish used in a variety of dishes, including *sushi* and soup.

Major Annual White Papers

Subject	Title	Ministry or agency	Year first published
Agriculture	*Nōgyō hakusho*	Ministry of Agriculture, Forestry, and Fisheries	1961
Atomic energy	*Genshiryoku hakusho*	Atomic Energy Commission	1956
Civil servants	*Kōmuin hakusho*	National Personnel Authority	1978
Communications	*Tsūshin hakusho*	Ministry of Posts and Telecommunications	1974
Construction	*Kensetsu hakusho*	Ministry of Construction	1949
Crime	*Hanzai hakusho*	Ministry of Justice	1960
Defense	*Bōei hakusho*	Defense Agency	1970
Disaster prevention	*Bōsai hakusho*	National Land Agency	1963
Economic cooperation	*Keizai kyōryoku hakusho*	Ministry of International Trade and Industry (MITI)	1958
Economy	*Keizai hakusho*	Economic Planning Agency	1947
Economy, world	*Sekai keizai hakusho*	Economic Planning Agency	1959
Education	*Kyōiku hakusho*	Ministry of Education	1959
Enterprises, small and medium	*Chūshō kigyō hakusho*	Ministry of International Trade and Industry	1964
Environment	*Kankyō hakusho*	Environment Agency	1972
Environmental pollution disputes	*Kōgai funsō shori hakusho*	Environmental Disputes Coordination Commission	1973
Fire prevention	*Shōbō hakusho*	Fire Defense Agency	1960
Fishery	*Gyogyō hakusho*	Fisheries Agency	1964
Foreign policy	*Gaikō seisho*	Ministry of Foreign Affairs	1957
Forestry	*Ringyō hakusho*	Forestry Agency	1965
Health and welfare	*Kōsei hakusho*	Ministry of Health and Welfare	1956
International trade	*Tsūshō hakusho*	Ministry of International Trade and Industry	1949
Labor	*Rōdō hakusho*	Ministry of Labor	1950
Land use	*Tochi hakusho*	National Land Agency	1990
Living conditions	*Kokumin seikatsu hakusho*	Economic Planning Agency	1956
Local government finance	*Chihō zaisei hakusho*	Ministry of Home Affairs	1953
Maritime safety	*Kaijō hoan hakusho*	Maritime Safety Agency	1956
Monopoly	*Dokusen kinshi hakusho*	Fair Trade Commission	1948
Nuclear safety	*Genshiryoku anzen hakusho*	Nuclear Safety Commission	1981
Police	*Keisatsu hakusho*	National Police Agency	1973
Science and technology	*Kagaku gijutsu hakusho*	Science and Technology Agency	1958
Tourism	*Kankō hakusho*	Prime Minister's Office	1964
Transport	*Un'yu hakusho*	Ministry of Transport	1964
Transportation safety	*Kōtsū anzen hakusho*	Management and Coordination Agency	1964
Youth	*Seishōnen hakusho*	Management and Coordination Agency	1956

NOTE: Titles in bold are also issued in English translation.

they formerly released them without prior consultation, it has been the practice since 1963 to coordinate positions and predictions with other ministries before publication, so that white papers today may be regarded as expressing the official policy of the government as a whole.

White Russians 白系露人

(*hakkei rojin*). Originally, supporters of the tsarist regime who fought the Bolsheviks during the Russian Civil War (1918–20); subsequently, a term applied loosely to stateless Russian émigrés of any number of political persuasions. Of the more than 1 million Russians who abandoned their homeland in the wake of the October Revolution of 1917, approximately 250,000 entered China via Siberia and Mongolia. About 100,000 settled in Manchuria, principally in Harbin, while most of the remainder gravitated to Shanghai, Tianjin (Tientsin), and Qingdao (Tsingtao). A few joined older Russian communities in Tōkyō, Kōbe, and Hakodate. Today, ethnic Russians have all but disappeared from China, but a few thousand live in Japan and carry Japanese citizenship.

Whitman, Charles Otis
ホイットマン, C. O.
(1842–1910). US biologist who pioneered zoological studies in Japan. Born in Maine. Recommended by biologist Edward Sylvester MORSE, he came to Japan as Morse's successor at Tōkyō University. He taught zoology there from 1879 to 1881. Influenced by his training in Germany, he introduced German-style biological research methods to Japan, including the use of the microscope.

Whitney, Courtney ホイットニー, C.
(1897–1969). US lawyer, major general, and close adviser to General Douglas MACARTHUR. Head of the Government Section of SCAP (headquarters of the Allied OCCUPATION of Japan) from 1945 to 1951, he was a dominant figure in the constitutional and legal reform of Japan and in the purge of wartime leaders. He entered the army in 1917 and joined the newly created Air Service in 1920. He received a law degree from National University in Washington in 1923, then in 1927 resigned from the Army Air Corps and went to the Philippines, where he practiced law until 1939. Returning to active service in 1940, he was assigned to General MacArthur's staff in 1943. When the general was relieved of command in 1951, Whitney left military service. He wrote *MacArthur, His Rendezvous with History* (1956).

Wild Bird Society of Japan
日本野鳥の会
(Nihon Yachō no Kai). A private conservation organization founded in 1934, headquartered in Shibuya Ward, Tōkyō, and dedicated to the protection of wild birds and their habitats. The society's main activities are the creation and management of sanctuaries and wild bird parks, the monitoring of wild bird populations and habitats, sponsorship of bird watching trips, and support for conservation activities. As of 1990 there were ten sanctuaries around the country, each of which employed full-time rangers to educate visitors on the protection of the environment while conducting tours of the parks. As of 1990, the Wild Bird Society of Japan had 28,300 members in 72 chapters. See also BIRD WATCHING; BIRD SANCTUARIES.

wild boar 猪
(*inoshishi*). The Japanese wild boar (*Sus scrofa leucomystax*) is one of the subspecies of the Eurasian wild boar. Inhabiting Amami Ōshima, Kyūshū, Shikoku, and Honshū, it is most common in southern Japan. Head and body measure about 1.4 meters (5 ft); it weighs approximately 100 kilograms (220 lb). Body colors vary from black to yellowish. Along with deer, *inoshishi* have the highest commercial value of any game in Japan.

The *inoshishi* rivals the bear as the most ferocious of Japan's wild animals. Its fierce, direct charge has become a common meta-

wildcats Wildcats in Japan are on the brink of extinction.
1 The body shape of the Iriomote cat is thought to be similar to that of prehistoric cats.
2 Although the Tsushima cat is roughly the same size as the common house cat, its legs are relatively long.

2

1

White Russians

phor for strong action that ignores consequences. Warriors who only attacked and never retreated were once known as *inoshishi musha* (a wild boar *samurai*). The domestication and commercial raising of *inoshishi* for their meat first became a widespread practice in the Meiji period (1868–1912). The meat of the *inoshishi* is still a highly prized delicacy.

wildcats 山猫

(*yamaneko*). In Japanese, *yamaneko* is the common name of the medium- to small-sized wildcats of the family Felidae. Two rare species are found in Japan: the Tsushima *yamaneko* (*Prionailurus bengalensis manchurica;* head and body about 45 cm or 18 in long, tail about 20 cm or 8 in long) of the island of Tsushima, Nagasaki Prefecture; and the Iriomote *yamaneko* (*Mayailurus iriomotensis;* head and body about 50 cm or 20 in long, tail about 23 cm or 9 in long) of the island of Iriomotejima, Okinawa Prefecture. The former, a subspecies of the leopard cat distributed extensively in Southeast Asia, has an amber body and reddish brown, vertical stripes on the head. The latter, endemic to Iriomotejima and declared a new species in 1967, has a grayish brown body. In 1990 its population was estimated at around 80. Both species have been given protected status, but the deforestation of both islands and the small size of the cats' habitats may lead to their eventual extinction.

wild ducks 鴨

(*kamo*). The general name for small and medium-sized birds of the family Anatidae. Of the 36 species recorded in Japan, 24 are also found in Europe and 20 in North America. Among species not found in Europe and America are the *karugamo* (spotbill duck; *Anas poecilorhyncha*), which breeds throughout Japan; the *tomoegamo* (Baikal teal; *A. formosa*), a winter visitor; the *yoshigamo* (falcated teal; *A. falcata*), which breeds in Hokkaidō; the *ryūkyūgamo* (Indian whistling duck; *Dendrocygna javanica*), which breeds in the southern Ryūkyūs; the *akahajiro* (Baer's pochard; *Aythya baeri*), a rare visitor to Japan; and the *oshidori* (mandarin duck; *Aix galericulata*). The *kammuri tsukushigamo* (crested shelduck; *Tadorna cristata*) is now extinct; only three preserved specimens remain.

The *kamo* became particularly important in the lives of the common people starting in the Edo period (1600–1868) when it was welcomed as a culinary delicacy. Before that, duck hunting was a sport of the court elite.

wild roses 野茨

(*noibara*). *Rosa* spp. Wild roses are found throughout Japan in fields and coastal areas. The best-known species is the *noibara* (*Rosa multiflora*), which produces numerous heavily thorned branches and reaches a height of 2 meters (7 ft). The alternate and pinnately compound leaves are composed of seven to nine elliptical leaflets. In early summer attractive small white or pale red flowers appear in clusters. The lustrous berrylike red fruit is used in traditional Chinese medicine as a laxative and diuretic. Other species of wild rose found in Japan include the *teriha noibara* (*R. wichuraiana*), which trails along the ground; the vinelike *yamaibara* (*R. sambucina*); and the *fujiibara* (*R. fujisanensis*), with white blossoms, found in the Fuji-Hakone area.

Williams, Samuel Wells
ウィリアムズ, S. W.

(1812–84). American missionary and sinologist. A missionary in China from 1833, he sailed to Japan in 1837 aboard the American ship *Morrison* in its unsuccessful attempt to repatriate Japanese castaways, who taught him their language (see MORRISON INCIDENT). In 1853–54 Williams returned to Japan as official interpreter for Commodore Matthew PERRY in his trade negotiations with the Tokugawa shogunate. Around 1875 he translated the complete texts of Genesis and the Gospel of Matthew into Japanese, but his manuscripts were destroyed in a fire before they could be published. In 1876 Williams returned to the United States from China and the following year became professor of Chinese language and literature at Yale University.

Willis, William
ウィリス, W.

(1837–94). British physician who joined the British mission to Japan in 1861. He treated the British nationals attacked by *samurai* in the RICHARDSON AFFAIR and those injured in the KAGOSHIMA BOMBARDMENT. He was later appointed professor and clinical chief of the Igakkō (later Tōkyō University's faculty of medicine). In 1870 Willis resigned to become head of the hospital and medical school in Kagoshima that later became the medical department of Kagoshima University. With the outbreak of the SATSUMA REBELLION in 1877, Willis withdrew to Tōkyō until his return to England in 1881.

Willoughby, Charles Augustus
ウィロビー, C. A.

(1892–1972). US Army major general and longtime intelligence chief for General Douglas MACARTHUR. Born in Germany, Willoughby came to the United States as a young man, graduated from Gettysburg College in 1914, and was commissioned as an army officer. He served with MacArthur from 1941 to 1951. During the OCCUPATION period in Japan he was known for his disagreement with liberal policies advocated by other advisers to MacArthur, especially regarding the economic reform of Japan and the purge of wartime officials. His books include *Shanghai Conspiracy: The Sorge Spy Ring* (1952) and *MacArthur, 1941–1951* (1954).

willows 柳

(*yanagi*). *Salix* spp. Deciduous trees of the family Salicaceae. Various species grow throughout Japan and are widely appreciated for their graceful form. The name *yanagi* is used to refer to willows in general and, more specifically, to the weeping willow (*S. babylonica*). Also known as *shidareyanagi* or *itoyanagi*, this tree originated in China. It reaches a height of about 5–10 meters (15–35 ft).

The *unryū yanagi* (*S. matsudana* var. *tortuosa*) also originated in China. Its bent branches and twisted trunk are often used in flower arrangements. The *kinuyanagi* (*S. kinuyanagi*) is cultivated in southern Honshū, Kyūshū, and Shikoku; the undersides of its leaves are silvery. The *nekoyanagi* (*S. gracilistyla*) is cultivated for the fuzzy catkins that appear on its branches in early spring. The *furisode yanagi* (*S. leucopithecia* Kimura) is noted for its luxuriant autumn foliage. The *kuroyanagi* (*S. melanostachys*) has inflorescences covered with blackish bracts, which are used in flower arrangements. Branches of the *koriyanagi* (*S.*

koriyanagi) are used in making woven trunks and baskets. Willow wood is soft and pliable and is used for drafting boards, cutting boards, clogs (GETA), and matchsticks.

wills 遺言

(*yuigon; igon*). The legal expression or declaration, made in accordance with requirements of the CIVIL CODE, of a person's wishes as to the disposition of his or her property, to take effect after death. In Japanese law, wills can determine the disposition of property or status (such as household headship) or the execution of the will. With respect to property, a will can specify a bequest, an act of endowment, a trust, a disinheritance or revocation of disinheritance, the designation of a share of inheritance and its consignment to a trusteeship, the designation of special beneficiaries, the method and person in charge of dividing the estate, a prohibition against division of the estate, responsibility for bonding the heirs, or the method of reducing bequests. It can also specify the presiding officer for ancestral rites. A will can acknowledge or designate someone as guardian or guardian supervisor. It may also designate an executor or may delegate authority to make such a designation.

Anyone 15 years of age or older who has the mental capacity to make a rational judgment can independently make a valid will. Bequests specified within a will can modify the share of the estate that would otherwise pass to the decedent's successors by law. See also INHERITANCE LAW.

wind-bells 風鈴

(*fūrin*). Small bells of metal, glass, bamboo, or pottery that are hung under the eaves and tinkle when moved by a breeze. To the Japanese these *fūrin* have been a standard feature of summer since the Muromachi period (1333–1568). To catch the breeze, a feather or a small rectangular piece of poem paper (*tanzaku*) is attached to the clapper.

winter solstice 冬至

(*tōji*). The winter solstice, the day of the year on which the northern hemisphere experiences the shortest period of daylight, is one of the 24 Points (Nijūshi Sekki; see CALENDAR, DATES, AND TIME) relating to weather or agricultural phenomena in the old Japa-

willows The willow, or *yanagi*, with its slender, graceful shape, is often mentioned in Japanese literature as a metaphor for feminine beauty. The *yanagi* is also considered an auspicious tree, as it is hardy and early blooming. In the photograph *yanagi* line a path in an Ōsaka park.

wild roses The *noibara* (pictured) is the best-known species of wild rose in Japan. It produces small (2-cm) white or pale red flowers in early summer, and its berrylike red fruit ripens through autumn.

wind-bells A cast-iron wind-bell hangs next to a reed screen; together they evoke summertime in Japan. Wind-bells are said to have been originally imported from China.

Japanese wisteria Ornamental wisteria is usually supported on trellises, as here at the Kameido Shrine in Tōkyō. Fragrant clusters of blossoms begin to appear around April, with the trailing tips coming into flower last.

witch hazel The tree produces blossoms (right) in the spring and capsules containing black seeds (left) in the autumn.

nese solar calendar. In Japan it is customary to eat pumpkin and KONNYAKU (a paste made from the devil's tongue plant) on this day for health reasons. In addition, *yuzu* (citron) is placed in the bathwater for purification.

winter sports   ウィンタースポーツ

(*uintā supōtsu*). Winter sports in Japan consisted largely of children's sledding, snowshoeing, and snow games until the 20th century, when Western sports such as SKIING, ice skating (see SKATING), ice hockey, bobsledding, and the biathlon were introduced and became popular among adults. Japan's main winter sports areas are found in Hokkaidō, along the coast of the Sea of Japan, and in the central highlands of Honshū. See also SAPPORO WINTER OLYMPIC GAMES; SKATING; SKIING.

Wirgman, Charles   ワーグマン, C.

(1832–91). English painter, draftsman, and cartoonist. Brother of the painter Theodore Blake Wirgman, he arrived in Japan as a correspondent for the *Illustrated London News.* Landing in Yokohama in 1861, he remained there until his death. Wirgman exercised his humor in Japan's first magazine, *Japan Punch,* which he published almost monthly between 1862 and the spring of 1887. It was an amusing, often satirical, block-printed periodical illustrated with his sketches. He taught techniques of European painting to many eager Japanese artists of the Meiji period (1868–1912), including the painter and print designer KOBAYASHI KIYOCHIKA and the cartoonist Nozaki Bunzō (dates unknown). In the 1860s he traveled throughout the Japanese countryside with the English diplomat Ernest SATOW, who recorded the delight with which Wirgman's impromptu sketches were received by local maidens and shopkeepers. Little of his original work seems to have survived.

wisteria, Japanese   藤

(*fuji*). *Wisteria floribunda.* Also known as *nodafuji.* A deciduous climbing shrub of the family Leguminosae that grows wild in mountainous areas of Japan and is commonly planted in gardens. The extremely long stem coils around other objects in a clockwise direction. The alternate, compound leaves consist of 13–19 egg-shaped leaflets. Around April the plant produces fragrant, purple, butterfly-shaped flowers in large hanging clusters 30–90 centimeters (1–3 ft) long.

Many varieties have been cultivated as ornamentals, including the *kushakufuji,* whose flower clusters reach 2 meters (6.6 ft) long; the white-flowered *shirobanafuji;* the double-flowered *yaefuji;* and the pale red-flowered *akebonofuji.* A similar species called the *yamafuji* (*W. brachybotrys*) is found in southwestern Japan. Its stem coils counterclockwise and its flower clusters are shorter, but the flowers are larger. A white-flowered, cultivated type of *yamafuji* called *shirafuji* is particularly popular.

witch hazel   満作

(*mansaku*). *Hamamelis japonica.* Deciduous tree of the family Hamamelidaceae that grows wild in mountain areas of Japan and is also cultivated. It reaches a height of about 4–6 meters (13–20 ft). The oval leaves are alternate. In early spring the plant produces clusters of yellow flowers before the leaves come out. The flower has four sepals and four straplike petals that twist across each other when the flower opens. Varieties found in Japan include the *nishiki mansaku,* with purplish red flowers; the *akabana mansaku* and *atetsu mansaku,* with reddish flowers; and the *maruba mansaku,* with round leaves and red or purplish yellow flowers.

withholding tax   源泉徴収

(*gensen chōshū*). The deduction of a certain amount of income tax from those with earned income or other fixed income. The Japanese withholding tax rate ranges from 10 to 50 percent, depending on the amount of income. Payments are withheld by the national treasury. Withholding tax is imposed on interest and dividend income, earned income, severance pay, remuneration and fees such as those for lecturing or for entertainment and travel, and nonresident income.

witnesses   証人

(*shōnin*). Persons who appear before a judicial, quasi-judicial, or other investigating body to testify about what they personally experienced. As provided for in the Code of Civil Procedure and the Code of Criminal Procedure, witnesses are used in civil and criminal trials. Parties to civil actions and criminal defendants are not called as witnesses in their own cases. In civil cases examination of witnesses is made only on motion by one of the parties, but in criminal cases the court may examine a witness on its own motion. A duly summoned witness who does not appear is punishable and can be taken to the court under arrest. A witness is normally required to take an oath. A witness can refuse to give testimony that can lead to a criminal prosecution against him or against certain persons having a close relationship with him. Members of certain groups (such as physicians, dentists, pharmacists, lawyers, notaries, and clergymen) can refuse to testify about facts known through their professional activities.

Witte, Sergei Yulievich   ウィッテ, S. Y.

(1849–1915). Russian diplomat who, as finance minister, worked for the establishment of the Trans-Siberian Railway. The TRIPARTITE INTERVENTION, which forced Japan to return the Liaodong (Liaotung) Peninsula to China following the Sino-Japanese War of 1894–95, owed much to Witte's diplomatic skills. At the peace conference concluding the RUSSO-JAPANESE WAR of 1904–05, he was successful in inducing the Japanese to give up their demands for indemnity (see PORTSMOUTH, TREATY OF). Witte served as prime minister of Russia from 1905 to 1906.

wolf, Japanese   日本狼

(Nihon *ōkami*). *Canis lupus hodophilax,* Temminck. A now-extinct subspecies of the common wolf. Usually the term "Japanese wolf" does not include the very large Hokkaidō or Yezo wolf, which belonged to a different subspecies ranging in the Hokkaidō region. The Japanese wolf was confined to Honshū, Shikoku, and Kyūshū. Throughout history, the Japanese wolf has often been confused with the feral dog and vice versa, being called *yamainu* (mountain dog).

Intact stuffed or skeletal specimens of the Japanese wolf are rare, but a considerable number of osteological materials have been studied. The general conformation of the Japanese wolf is distinguished from that of the continental common wolf by a smaller body size and shorter legs. The average length of the body including the head is 104 centimeters (40 in) and the tail approximately 30 centimeters (12 in). The coat is generally gray, with some darker or brownish shades. The skull is rather broad and short.

The behavior of the Japanese wolf seems to have differed little from that of the continental common wolf; however, it adapted in ways better suited to the mountainous and heavily forested Japanese environment. It is thought that a considerable number of Japanese wolves existed on the major islands until quite recently and that they were eliminated either by an epidemic of canine distemper or by destruction of their habitats in the late 19th century. The last authentic specimen of the Japanese wolf was acquired in Nara Prefecture in 1904 or 1905 and sent to the British Museum. The Hokkaidō wolf disappeared around 1889 as a result of deliberate extermination.

The *ōkami* was worshiped as a god who could protect people from misfortune, disease, the dangers of traveling, and damage to crops by wild animals. Such worship of the wolf was once widely distributed in rural areas in Japan. Even now shrines sacred to the wolf and related folk rituals are found sporadically in remote regions. The skull of the wolf (or often, in fact, a dog's skull) was used as a charm for the security of the family and was thought to be useful in chasing the demons of mental disease, especially "fox possession" (see FOXES). At the same time, the wolf has also been feared and loathed, as seen in legends that describe wolves gathering in packs, scavenging graves, or attacking solitary travelers.

women in Japan, history of   女性史

(*joseishi*). Japanese history provides striking examples of how changes in the status of women can be linked with other broad socioeconomic trends. A woman-centered marriage pattern in ancient times contributed to considerable religious and political influence for women, but from the 6th century onward the growing acceptance of Confucian and Buddhist precepts that maintained women's inferiority reflected and reinforced a shift toward patriarchal family structure. However, upper-class women were often highly literate, and they retained such rights as property inheritance until these were eroded by the transition to a war-oriented feudal economy beginning in the 12th century. The harsh and sometimes precarious life of the provincial warrior class demanded courage and endurance from women as well as men, but the centuries of relative peace during the Edo period (1600–1868) seem to have led to a consolidation of the patriarchal family structure and women's dependent status within it. Only since the Meiji period (1868–1912), and especially since World War II, have increasing educational and employment opportunities, as well as improvements in legal status, allowed women some intellectual and financial autonomy once again.

The Early Period—Modern studies of Japanese women's history, pioneered by TAKAMURE ITSUE, show how Japanese marriages originally centered on women. Until at least the 11th century, it was customary at all social levels for a husband to join the family of his wife (see MUKOIRIKON) or to live separately and visit his wife on certain nights (*kayoi kekkon*). A daughter of a property-holding family was entitled to the family house and a share of income rights when an inheritance was divided. Such woman-centered families remained customary among peasants for some centuries after the upper classes, beginning with the warriors in the late Heian period (794–1185), adopted the practice of sending a bride to join her husband's family (see YOMEIRIKON), with more attention paid to economic or other advantages for both families than to the preferences of the couple. See also MARRIAGE.

Besides their central role in families, Japanese women have traditionally had an unusually prominent role in dealing with the supernatural. Japan's native religion, SHINTŌ, retains a principal female deity, AMATERASU ŌMIKAMI, who may have evolved from the concept of a shamaness mediating between humanity and supernatural beings (see SHAMANISM). Today women serve as Shintō shrine maidens (MIKO) and occasionally as priests (*negi* or KANNUSHI). Women's major role in Shintō and shamanism was apparently linked with ruling power in early Japan, as evidenced by such semilegendary figures as the priestess-queen HIMIKO and the empress JINGŪ. In the 7th and 8th centuries several women even reigned as "emperor" (*tennō*). See SUIKO, EMPRESS; SAIMEI, EMPRESS; JITŌ, EMPRESS; KŌKEN, EMPRESS.

There is much debate over the reasons for the shift to a patriarchal family pattern, but certain concepts found in the imported CONFUCIANISM and BUDDHISM could readily be used to justify such change. Under the new Confucian-style laws of the TAIKA REFORM in the mid-7th century, women were barred from becoming government officials, and a woman's share of government-distributed land (KUBUNDEN) was set at two-thirds of that for a man. Some sects of Buddhism taught that women were sinful temptresses who must be reborn as men before they could attain enlightenment. Yet many women of the elite actively promoted the spread of Bud-

Japanese wolf This subspecies of wolf, which died out in the late 19th century, was smaller than the continental common wolf. Illustration from Philipp Franz von Siebold's *Fauna Japonica* (1833–50).

dhism, and it became common for women of high-ranking families to take vows as Buddhist nuns in later life. See also NYONIN KINZEI.

Also emerging around the 6th century were two customs that would affect many women's lives throughout the rest of Japan's premodern history: one was the practice of sending hostages to cement alliances (see UNEME) and the other was the related practice, continued into modern times, of using marriages to establish ties between families (see KEIBATSU). Even before the capital was established at Nara in 710, the FUJIWARA FAMILY came to control the court largely through the practice of marrying Fujiwara women to emperors whenever possible.

While women's political authority was on the decline, however, women were making contributions in the cultural sphere that were to have a lasting impact on Japanese aesthetics. Centered on the imperial court, often portraying its affairs as well as their own, were the great women writers of the Heian period: ONO NO KOMACHI, SEI SHŌNAGON, MURASAKI SHIKIBU, IZUMI SHIKIBU, and the authors of the poetic diaries KAGERŌ NIKKI and SARASHINA NIKKI.

The Medieval Period—The ever-present danger of warfare from the 12th through the 16th century made it most practical for one person (the oldest or ablest son) to inherit family property, to consolidate and defend lands against outsiders. For many warrior families, the struggle to better their positions often led to "strategic marriages" or the outright surrender of female relatives as hostages. Women's loss of property rights made them dependent on their male relatives. Such altered family patterns, war, and the development of cities led to the growth of PROSTITUTION.

The unsettled conditions also encouraged the spread of new types of popular Buddhism (the JŌDO SECT and JŌDO SHIN SECT) with their promise of salvation for all believers, including women, in paradise after death. Itinerant singing nuns (*ura bikuni*) helped spread nationwide an oral tradition of both religious and secular tales. Other women entertainers and dancers, originally connected with Shintō shrines, were known as *arukimiko;* at the beginning of the 17th century, this tradition produced the woman performer OKUNI, who is credited with the founding of KABUKI theater.

Edo Period—The 18th-century Confucian-style moralistic work ONNA DAIGAKU, influential throughout the late Edo period, stressed that a woman should obey her parents until her marriage, then her husband and his family, and, in her old age, her sons; be humble, frugal, and hardworking; and remember that she could be divorced for disobedience, barrenness, jealousy, ill health, or garrulousness. DIVORCE was legally granted to a wife only if her husband abandoned her or committed a serious crime or in rare cases if she fled to one of the two official "divorce temples" (KAKEKOMIDERA). Women's adultery was punishable by death, but wealthy men

could maintain concubines outside or inside their homes. However, the status of such secondary wives or mistresses (*mekake*), which had been comparatively high in preceding eras, declined to that of near-servants.

Women's lives may not have been as harsh as the *Onna daigaku* and official laws indicate. Women took pride in controlling the management of their homes, as they do today. Older wives or mothers of the official household head were accorded considerable respect and freedom. A woman also had more social leverage if her husband had been "adopted" into her family, in a pattern resembling the former woman-centered marriages (see ADOPTION). Many young girls from the lower classes became servants for a few years in the homes of elite families, then married and introduced the customs of such homes into their own, thereby continuing the role of woman as a channel for contact between different areas and social levels. In many rural areas, girls in their midteens entered "girls' groups" (*musume-gumi*), which often allowed them to live separately from their parents and to have some part in the choice of their marriage partners (see also WAKAMONO-GUMI). Women's literacy in the Edo period has been estimated at around 15 percent, a relatively high figure for a premodern society.

At the higher levels of society, strategic marriages were still the rule. The keeping of female hostages was institutionalized in the practice of forcing *daimyō* lords to leave their wives in Edo (now Tōkyō) whenever they returned to their domains (see SANKIN KŌTAI). Certain families vied to send their daughters to the shōgun's harem (ŌOKU), since his favorites were supposedly able to promote the careers of their male relatives.

The Tokugawa shogunate (1603–1867), as did previous shogunates, licensed and supervised brothel districts (*yūkaku*), the best known of which was YOSHIWARA in Edo. Prostitutes' lives were restricted and often tragic; most had been indentured because of poverty. Yet certain high-ranking courtesans (*tayū* or OIRAN) became famous for their wit, artistic skill, character, and beauty. There also emerged a group of women dancers and musicians, more or less separate from the courtesans, called GEISHA. During the period, folk songs were spread and developed by wandering blind women musicians (GOZE).

Women and Modernization—Following the Meiji Restoration of 1868, the introduction of universal primary education in 1873 meant that increasing numbers of girls were educated at least through the primary grades, and in 1899 the Higher Girls' School Order stipulated that there should be at least one higher school for girls in each prefecture.

Continued on page 1706—

history of women in Japan A 1946 photograph of some of the 39 women who were elected to the House of Representatives after women were granted the right to vote and to run for office in 1945.

A Woman's Place

As the dawn of a new century approaches,
Japanese women are trying to balance traditional and contemporary roles.

In Japan today, there are several competing schools of thought about the role of women in modern society. Neotraditionalists maintain that women's lives should be organized around their role as wives and mothers. Any other roles women may play, in business, the community, etc, are considered secondary.

Proponents of a multirole ideology, or "New Women" as we call them, accept the primacy of the wife-mother role but believe that women should also be able to play other roles simultaneously and on an equal basis with men. Any individual pursuits, however, must fall within the limits imposed by home duties.

Radical Egalitarians, in contrast, reject the notion that any roles other than the biological role of childbearer should be assigned to women on the basis of sex. They contend that women should be able to enter all arenas of life with the same freedom accorded their male counterparts.

Although these three views exist in any advanced industrial nation, the degree to which each is a viable option for women depends on the laws, customs, and expectations of a given society. In Japan, the traditional view of a woman's role has evolved since World War II, which is why we refer to the postwar view as "Neotraditional." The core of this philosophy, however, has retained its essential staying power.

While some women in the United States may hesitate to identify themselves as housewives anymore, those following the Neotraditional role in Japan continue to win social approval. This is partly because women's employment opportunities, though improving, are constrained by custom and culture. As the educational level of women rises, however, the multirole ideology is gaining support, and in urban centers such as Tōkyō it is increasingly the dominant ideology. Finally, the Radical Egalitarian view, which represents a perspective that is identified as feminist in most societies, has its advocates but is still far from being embraced by the majority of women in Japan.

Pre- and Postwar Views

Before World War II, the Japanese upper classes viewed a woman's primary function as being wife and mother. Supporting this was the assumption that males and females were essentially different; that males were superior in most areas and therefore entitled to rights not shared by women. Men worked to provide for their families, while their wives stayed home and managed the household. In their youth, Japanese women prepared for this clearly defined role by studying cooking, sewing, flower arrangement, and the tea ceremony. On the farms and in the shops, mines, and factories of prewar Japan, married

women might work long and grueling hours, but they did so at their husbands' bidding. The orderly chain of authority dictated that women answered to men, and men to society.

Historically, women could escape the traditional role by joining the demimonde (*mizu shōbai*)—the underclass of *geisha*, entertainers, and prostitutes—or by leading the solitary life of a Buddhist nun, scholar, writer, or the like. These options generally meant living outside the security of a permanent marriage arrangement. Although urbanization and industrialization expanded women's opportunities, alternatives to the traditional role remained difficult to realize.

The laws upheld social convention. The Civil Code, promulgated in 1898 to establish greater control in Japanese society, set severe limits on women's rights. Under the code, women were forbidden to head households or own property and had limited recourse to divorce. Adultery constituted legal grounds for divorce only if committed by the wife. In cases involving disputes over the custody of children, the wishes of the husband prevailed. Similarly, if a man fathered children with women other than his wife, he was legally entitled to adopt them into his own family to bear his family name. Women thus became legal dependents of male household heads.

The Western tradition of chivalry never developed among the Japanese upper classes to soften the lines of status difference between men and women. Women deferred to men of equal or higher status by using honorific language, bowing more deeply, and walking behind their husbands in public. In the extended family arrangements common before the war, a new bride rose first in the morning, ate after all other family members, and went to bed last at night. She gained stature when she bore a son and acquired even more power in the family when her mother-in-law stepped aside or died, or when she became a mother-in-law herself.

After Japan's surrender in 1945, numerous measures giving new rights to women were introduced during the Allied Occupation. The 1947 constitution explicitly forbade discrimination on the basis of sex, and a complete overhaul of the Civil Code guaranteed women free choice of a spouse, equal recourse to divorce, and equal property rights.

The urbanization that accompanied Japan's postwar economic growth encouraged the demise of the extended family and the growth of the modern-day nuclear family. Democracy became the dominant ideology in public schools, made coeducational by the postwar reforms. Even though status differences are still recognized in the modern family, they are far less ritualized. Prosperity has made higher education available to women. Automation in the home has given Japanese women a higher standard of living and more free time to pursue outside interests.

The changes begun in the Occupation era, and reinforced by socioeconomic trends since then, have set in motion crosscurrents of thought on the subject of "a woman's place." How, then, do women in the 1990s respond to the tradition-based view of a female's role in society?

Neotraditionalists

Many typical Neotraditionalists of today work in corporations as OLs (office ladies), either with the hope of finding marriage partners or in order to make extra spending money before they marry. OLs do routine office work, answer telephones, serve tea several times a day, and create a pleasant office environment for the men, who do the serious work in the company. The work may be repetitious and boring, but it provides a chance to see a broader segment of society. Neotraditionalists tend to view their employment as a rite of passage between the comforts of the family home and school and the security of marriage.

As Japan leads the world into the information age, the large corporation is still at the top of the social pecking order. Women answer to their husbands, but men answer to their companies. Sasaki, a 50-year-old division chief (buchō) at a medium-sized corporation in Nagoya, explains his weekly interaction with his 45-year-old wife: "During the week, I say only three words to her at night. The first is meshi (food). She brings my dinner. Then I say furo (bath), and she draws my bath. Finally, I say futon, and she rolls out my bed and I go to sleep."

Sasaki's wife performs these chores to support her husband in his struggle to ascend the corporate ladder and provide for the family. The nature of corporate life in Japan—in which permanent employees are expected to devote most of their waking hours to the company—dictates, to some extent, the terms of their relationship. Salarymen are expected to work late and to go out with colleagues or entertain clients at bars, hostess clubs, and other popular night spots. Compared to Europe and the United States, Japan still has relatively few social settings in which husbands and wives can spend time together.

Although Neotraditionalists' views today echo those of prewar traditional women in many ways, there are a number of significant differences. Prewar public schools had a separate curriculum for girls to prepare them to become good wives and mothers. Today the study of all subjects is regarded as essential for both sexes; the public schools are coeducational, and the percentage of girls advancing to senior high school reached 96 percent in 1990.

More than 37 percent of women went on to college—either two-year or four-year schools—compared to 35 percent of men in 1990. For Neotraditionalists from the middle or upper classes, a college education is an extra credential for attracting a suitable marriage partner. However, in deference to men, who prefer to be better educated than the women they marry, Neotraditionalists often opt for two-year junior colleges over universities.

Although an arranged marriage (miai kekkon) was the accepted course in prewar Japan and is still an option today, the system serves mainly as a means of formal introduction, with both parties free to back out at will. Though able to choose their own mates, Neotraditionalists and the young men they marry tend to see married life as an end to carefree youth. Neotraditionalist women must take on the new responsibilities of managing the family budget and doing housework and, later on, looking after the education of their children and caring for elderly relatives. Marriage itself may require years of saving. In 1990 the average wedding package for the Kantō and Kansai regions, including the ceremony and honeymoon, cost about ¥5.7 million (US $39,000).

New Women

Today the multirole ideology is challenging the Neotraditional view. The working wife has gained wider acceptance with the increase in the number of working women: in 1990 there were 10.6 million working wives, compared with 14.8 million nonworking wives. However, almost 72 percent of women in their forties held full- or part-time jobs in 1990; and in a poll conducted by the Ministry of Health and Welfare in 1988, more than 64 percent of unemployed women with newborn children claimed they would like to work.

What New Women want in terms of work and marriage varies widely with the individual. Some try to balance the traditional obligations of the homemaker with a job or other activities and do not expect any help at home from their husbands. Others hope to find husbands who will be understanding and help with the housework. New Women are likely to expect greater mutuality and companionship in marriage than Neotraditionalists.

In the workplace, New Women are eschewing OL jobs for the management track. One New Woman interviewed in 1989 commented: "A lot of companies justify giving intelligent and capable women menial OL work by the fact that they don't want to waste time training women who will quit their jobs when they have children or marry. If these women were given more challenging work, they might stay longer."

In companies today, many New Women can be found in "katakana positions"—new jobs in Japan's internationalizing economy with English titles written in the phonetic script used for transliterating foreign words. A few examples of katakana positions are rikurūto konsarutanto ("recruit consultant" or headhunter), terehon māketā ("telephone marketer"), puroguramā ("programmer" or computer programmer), and shisutemu enjinia ("system engineer" or computer systems engineer).

New Women would like to be able to continue working after marriage. Many quit their jobs when they have children, however, because of husbands' attitudes, lack of adequate child care, social pressure, or limited work options. They generally hope to find interesting jobs when their children are well along in school, but traditional views of household responsibilities have been remarkably slow to change. According to a 1990 Ministry of Labor report, on an average weekday Japanese husbands spent only eight minutes a day on housework, compared to more than two and a half hours for working wives.

Radical Egalitarians

Representing a very small minority among Japanese women, Radical Egalitarians reject the concept of gender-determined roles entirely. Differing widely in educational background and socioeconomic class, they come to their views through a variety of routes. Some from wealthier families have had job experiences that contributed to significant changes in their attitudes toward life and the female role. Others were involved in feminist or political groups of the Left. Their views of equal roles are frequently reflected in their speech and behavior. Many prefer to speak directly, without honorifics, in what is commonly regarded as "men's language," and use slang that Neotraditionalists and New Women would consider unfeminine. They reject the concept of arranged marriage and even the terms of marriage itself.

The Radical Egalitarian ideology has won little support in Japan, compared to many other industrial societies. Numerous women's groups in Japan press for equality for women, but Japan has yet to experience a broad-based women's movement with commonly held goals and popular appeal. One stumbling block to more unified action has been the ambivalence that many women, including Radical Egalitarians, feel about striving for equality with men in the workplace of contemporary Japan. Looking at the exhausting routines of salarymen, "Who," they ask, "would want to lead the life of a Japanese man?"

The 1990s and Beyond

The young women of today and the future will tend to move back and forth among the views of the Neotraditionalists, New Women, and Radical Egalitarians at different stages of their lives. Social values, including those bearing on a woman's role and place, are in great flux. It is only natural for women to find themselves vacillating between views, unsure of what they want, undecided as to whether they are willing to undergo the substantial personal and psychological risks that come when human beings try to move in new directions. In present-day Japan, the central tension continues to be between the views of the Neotraditionalists and the New Women.

Many emerging forces challenge the Neotraditionalist view. The spread of the five-day workweek and increased affluence, for example, give young Japanese couples the leisure and resources to spend time together, leading to improved communication between them. However, societal expectations regarding motherhood, along with structural impediments in the workplace, make it unlikely that these changes will effectively alter the Japanese perception that homemaking and child care are primarily a woman's responsibility.

Demography is another force at work on the lives of men and women. In 1991 the average age at which Japanese women married was 25.9. Since family size in Japan is among the smallest in the world (with 1.5 offspring born to each woman), children are likely to be well along in school by the time their mothers reach their late thirties. With life expectancy for Japanese women at 81.8 years (75.9 years for men) in 1990, women face a long portion of their lives in which traditional demands upon them lessen, freeing them to pursue individual interests.

Changes in the structure of the labor force in Japan's aging society will probably benefit women. As the labor shortage intensifies, more firms are apt to offer training opportunities, managerial positions, and better compensation to Japanese women, thereby giving the New Women's route greater appeal. In 1990 women were greatly underrepresented in managerial jobs, and only one percent of working women had subordinates.

Finally, internationalization is another important catalyst for change. As Japanese companies continue to invest in the United States and Europe, more employees and their families will be posted overseas. In 1990 some 105,000 employees of Japanese companies and their family members were stationed in North America alone. The daughters of returnees, along with other young women who have studied or worked abroad, make up a new elite cultural class. Multilingual and eager for better work opportunities, they are the focus of media attention and have become another force for change.

Susan J. Pharr and Jeannie P.C. Lo

However, education for girls lagged behind that for boys, and government policy dictated that girls should be educated as homemakers, in keeping with the traditional ideal of women as "good wives and wise mothers" (*ryōsai kembo*). See WOMEN'S EDUCATION.

Women workers contributed to the success and speed of Japan's industrial revolution, particularly in the textile industry, which paid women little, housed them in dormitories, and required them to work long hours. As modernization proceeded, some women began to work in the new department stores, telephone exchanges, "milk bars," beer halls, and cabarets. A few began to advance into such fields as secretarial work and journalism, and growing numbers were employed as teachers. OGINO GINKO and YOSHIOKA YAYOI were pioneer women doctors. Although largely unacknowledged, women have contributed to the maintenance of Japan's rural productivity through unpaid family labor on farms and in small and medium-sized businesses and cottage industries. See WOMEN IN THE LABOR FORCE; WOMEN, RURAL.

Some women had participated in the struggles leading to the Meiji Restoration, and women such as KISHIDA TOSHIKO joined the FREEDOM AND PEOPLE'S RIGHTS MOVEMENT of the 1880s. Yet the 1898 Meiji CIVIL CODE granted women only limited rights to divorce or to own property, and a wife required her husband's consent in most legal actions. Other well-known women activists around the turn of the century included such diverse figures as the elite nationalist OKUMURA IOKO, the socialist FUKUDA HIDEKO, the anarchist KANNO SUGA, and a former prostitute who became a social commentator, YAMADA WAKA.

Labor strikes by women had begun as early as 1886, and in 1919 the women's section of the pioneer labor group YŪAIKAI sponsored a mass rally of textile workers to sanction a resolution to the International Labor Organization about the plight of women workers. In 1921 women socialists such as YAMAKAWA KIKUE formed the SEKIRANKAI (Red Wave Society) and made efforts to observe May Day and International Women's Day.

Around the same time, WOMEN'S MAGAZINES were beginning to publish articles and advertisements on contraceptives. Ishimoto Shizue was an active advocate of FAMILY PLANNING, and she continued such activities as a Diet member after World War II under her second-marriage name, KATŌ SHIZUE. In 1922 the government revealed its opposition to family planning when Margaret SANGER was nearly refused permission to visit Japan. In 1937, as the demand for new soldiers and workers was increased by war in China, the birth control movement was suppressed.

The earliest feminist group in Japan was the SEITŌSHA (Bluestocking Society), organized by HIRATSUKA RAICHŌ in 1911. Its endeavors were primarily intellectual and literary, but the focus of the group's journal, *Seitō*, gradually shifted to social concerns. Although disbanded in 1916, Seitōsha prepared the way for the 1920 founding of the SHIN FUJIN KYŌKAI (New Woman's Association), an organization dedicated to achieving political rights for women. Led by Raichō, OKU MUMEO, and ICHIKAWA FUSAE, it succeeded in achieving repeal of the law barring women from political meetings. Other feminists active around this time were KAMICHIKA ICHIKO, KUBUSHIRO OCHIMI, KAWASAKI NATSU, and YAMATAKA SHIGERI. Ichikawa Fusae, in-

spired by the feminist activities she had observed in the United States, organized the FUSEN KAKUTOKU DŌMEI (Women's Suffrage League) in 1924. It became the central organization of the nonsocialist feminist movement. This group's efforts to lobby for WOMEN'S SUFFRAGE at Diet sessions were weakened by a four-way split among the left-wing political parties, each of which had a women's section.

After 1930 many women's groups worked together for suffrage, led by the Fusen Kakutoku Dōmei. Under HAMAGUCHI OSACHI's cabinet in 1930, there was some shift in the climate of opinion concerning women, and the government even pushed a female civil rights bill through the lower house of the Diet. However, it encountered formidable opposition from city mayors, and even a weakened version failed to pass the House of Peers. By the early 1930s right-wing sentiment forced the women's movement, along with other protest movements, to modify its demands.

During World War II, women worked in government TONARIGUMI (neighborhood associations) and patriotic associations (see DAI NIPPON KOKUBŌ FUJINKAI; AIKOKU FUJINKAI; DAI NIPPON FUJINKAI). More significant was the mobilization of young women into the work force. However, it remained government policy during the entire war not to draft married women for labor service but to keep them at home producing more potential soldiers and citizens. Even at the height of the war effort, three-fourths of the workers in manufacturing and construction were male; it was not until the last phases of the war that married women were called upon.

Women in Contemporary Japan ——
Since the democratic system of the United States was the model for the US OCCUPATION, laws regarding women in Japan since the war have generally been similar to US laws. The constitution of 1947 forbade discrimination on the basis of gender in political, economic, or social relations and provided that "with regard to matters pertaining to . . . marriage and the family, laws shall be enacted from the standpoint of individual dignity and the essential equality of the sexes." The postwar reform of the Civil Code also supported the legal parity of husbands and wives, stating that both could divorce on the same grounds, for any serious reason that made continuation of the marriage difficult. Family courts intervene in matters such as child custody and property disputes (see FAMILY COURT). A woman can negotiate contracts without her spouse's consent. People can marry (and also divorce) on the consent of both parties without parental permission after legal age (18 for males; 16 for females).

In the prewar period the extended family played the decisive role in choosing marriage partners in a system of arranged marriages (*miai kekkon;* see MIAI). The number of "love matches" (*ren'ai kekkon*) has been increasing rapidly in the postwar period, and today many Japanese see the arranged marriage system as a method to introduce young people of carefully matched backgrounds who can then decide for themselves whether they will marry.

Traditionally, husbands and wives kept their worlds mostly separate from each other, and this is still generally the case, although there has been some movement toward greater communication and companionability. The husband centers his life on his work, spending much of his leisure time with his male coworkers in a social life that

does not include wives. The wife centers her life on home, children, and neighborhood. Within the home the wife's authority is great: she usually has full responsibility for managing the family budget and makes most of the decisions relating to her children. She generally does not ask for or expect help with home chores from her husband. This is true even when she works outside the home, as is increasingly the case.

In the prosperous 1960s the rate of marriage increased in Japan. But recently the average age at marriage has risen (in 1989 the average age of those marrying for the first time was 25.8 for women and 28.5 for men), and the number of women not marrying has grown because better educational and career opportunities have led to greater economic independence.

The 1947 constitution established the basis for women's equal educational opportunities (see EDUCATION, FUNDAMENTAL LAW OF; SCHOOL EDUCATION LAW OF 1947). New education laws opened the way for a public school system that has become largely coeducational and supportive of the democratization of family life. In 1955, 47 percent of girls and 56 percent of boys went beyond the nine years of compulsory education. By 1990, 96 percent of girls and 94 percent of boys advanced to secondary schools. In 1955, 15 percent of female and 21 percent of male high school graduates entered higher education; by 1990 those figures increased to 37 percent and 35 percent, respectively. These figures, however, do not mean that educational patterns for men and women are now the same. Although many women go on to higher education, a high percentage choose two-year JUNIOR COLLEGES rather than four-year institutions. In 1989 women made up 91 percent of the enrollment in junior colleges but only 26 percent of the enrollment in four-year institutions. But the number of women entering four-year institutions is growing annually, and, whereas in the past they studied mainly literature and home economics, more women are entering such fields as economics and engineering.

Postwar economic growth gave rise to labor shortages, which have brought women new opportunities for employment. Notably, married women and women in their forties and fifties have entered or reentered the work force. Yet women continue to do mainly nonprofessional and menial jobs, and their wages still average only about 60 percent of those for men. Also, a high percentage of women occupy part-time and temporary positions. The 1947 Labor Standards Law led to vast improvements in conditions for women workers (see LABOR LAWS; WOMEN WORKERS, PROTECTIVE LEGISLATION FOR), providing for a maternity leave and allowing mothers to nurse infants on the job. The 1991 Child Care Leave Law allows a mother or father with a child under one year old to take a leave of absence until the child's first birthday. The 1985 EQUAL EMPLOYMENT OPPORTUNITY LAW FOR MEN AND WOMEN stipulated that employers must make an effort to offer women equal opportunities for employment and promotion and that they are prohibited from dismissing women employees who require maternity leave. The law, however, lacks sanctions against employers who fail to comply. In three-generation households, many working mothers rely on relatives for child care, but, in urban areas where living space is tight and the nuclear-family structure is more common, many seek outside day care.

Men and Women in the Japanese Labor Force

Year	Population aged 15 and older (millions)		Labor force (millions)		Labor force participation rate		Percentage of the labor force occupied by women
	Male	Female	Male	Female	Male	Female	
1965	35.29	37.58	28.84	19.03	81.7	50.6	39.8
1970	38.25	40.60	31.29	20.24	81.8	49.9	39.3
1975	40.99	43.44	33.36	19.87	81.4	45.7	37.3
1980	43.41	45.91	34.65	21.85	79.8	47.6	38.7
1985	46.02	48.63	35.96	23.67	78.1	48.7	39.7
1990	49.11	51.78	37.91	25.93	77.2	50.1	40.6

NOTE: The labor force participation rate is the ratio of males or females in the labor force to the total population of males or females aged 15 or over.
SOURCE: Ministry of Labor, *Fujin rōdō no jitsujō* (annual): 1991.

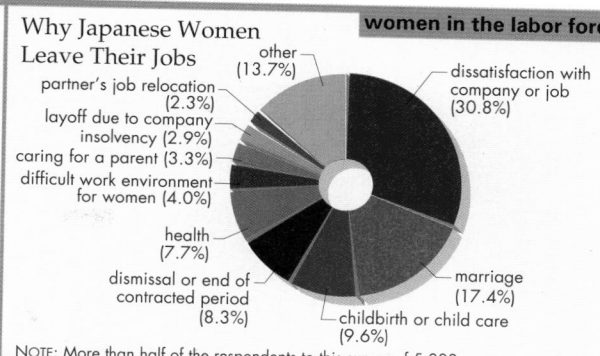

Why Japanese Women Leave Their Jobs

other (13.7%)
partner's job relocation (2.3%)
layoff due to company insolvency (2.9%)
caring for a parent (3.3%)
difficult work environment for women (4.0%)
health (7.7%)
dismissal or end of contracted period (8.3%)
childbirth or child care (9.6%)
marriage (17.4%)
dissatisfaction with company or job (30.8%)

NOTE: More than half of the respondents to this survey of 5,000 women were in their twenties.
SOURCE: Japan Institute of Women's Employment, *Joshi rōdōsha no rishoku ni kansuru jittai chōsa kekka hōkokusho* (1992).

Working Women by Age and Marital Status, 1990

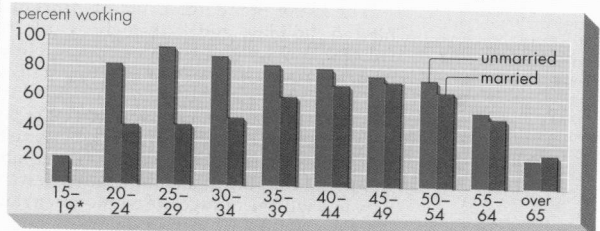

percent working
unmarried
married
15–19* 20–24 25–29 30–34 35–39 40–44 45–49 50–54 55–64 over 65

*Data for married women under 20 is not included because the number of women in this category is too small to be statistically significant.
SOURCE: Management and Coordination Agency, *Rōdōryoku chōsa* (annual): 1991.

Japanese women gained full political rights in 1945, when the Election Law was revised to permit them to vote and to run for political office. Today, although Japan is one of the few countries where women outvote men, women are underrepresented in the country's effective political life. Since the first postwar election brought 39 women into the Diet, women have held only between 20 and 25 Diet seats at a time (less than 3 percent of total membership). From the mid-1980s, however, this trend began to change, and in 1986 the appointment of the first woman leader of a major Japanese political party, the Japan Socialist Party (see DOI TAKAKO), marked the beginning of women's advance into the world of politics. In 1990, 46 women were members of the Diet, increasing women's membership to 6 percent. Even so, in national government, women are still being appointed to positions mainly in bureaus and commissions bearing directly on "women's concerns," and the number of women in civil-service managerial posts is quite low.

All major political parties have women's sections, and Japan has many women's groups that parallel such US organizations as the League of Women Voters and the Association of University Women (but not the National Organization of Women). There are approximately 25,000 regional women's organizations affiliated with the National Federation of Regional Women's Organizations (CHIFUREN). One of the most active women's groups is the Housewives Association (SHUFUREN). Women have also played a major role in the CONSUMER MOVEMENT, CITIZENS' MOVEMENTS, and the PEACE MOVEMENT. Since in legal terms, particularly in the specific constitutional guarantee of equality, Japanese women are far ahead of women in many other countries, including the United States, women activists now generally campaign not to change laws regarding women but to see them enforced.

▶1704–1705

women in the labor force 婦人労働

(*fujin rōdō*). Women were traditionally an important part of Japan's agrarian labor force, but the industrialization that followed the Meiji Restoration of 1868 initiated the flow of female workers into the textile industry, Japan's major source of foreign exchange. Most received very low wages; some even were indentured by their families in return for a lump-sum payment. Under an entrepreneurial attitude of laissez-faire, buttressed by growing nationalism, their working conditions deteriorated while their numbers increased.

The textile industry's poor working environment and overcrowded dormitories first received widespread attention with the 1903 publication of SHOKKŌ JIJŌ, a report by the Ministry of Agriculture and Commerce, and YOKOYAMA GENNOSUKE's *Nihon no kasō shakai* (1899, Japan's Lower Classes). A movement

for legislation to protect women and minors, begun in the 1890s but stalled during the Russo-Japanese War (1904–05), revived as part of a budding labor movement. The FACTORY LAW OF 1911, implemented in 1916, limited workdays for women to 12 hours, forbade night work between 10 PM and 4 AM, and required a minimum of 2 days off per month and 1 hour off for rest during the workday. The law applied, however, only to places employing 15 or more, thus excluding many women from its protection. See also JOKŌ AISHI.

Although concentrated in the textile industry, women outnumbered men in the total labor force until about 1930. The worldwide depression of the 1930s and Japan's growing militarism stimulated efforts to make the nation self-sufficient by expanding its heavy industry and armed forces. The chemical industry became a major employer of women; women also moved into other manufacturing jobs and skilled occupations as growing numbers of men joined the military.

After World War II, the labor movement gave priority to the needs of male household heads as primary breadwinners. But with many women left single and impoverished by the war, women's participation in the labor force remained necessarily high. Before World War II, most working Japanese women were young and single, but with rapid economic growth in the 1960s many companies began to offer part-time employment, and the number of married women employees rose considerably. Since 1955 the percentage of married women in the female labor force has almost tripled, rising to 64.9 percent in 1990, while the number of employed women under 19 has dropped because more women are continuing their education past senior high school.

Until about 1950, over 60 percent of working women were "family workers," mainly in agriculture. By 1990, family workers had declined to 16.7 percent. Nonetheless, the percentage of female family workers in Japan still is considerably higher than in other developed countries. Conversely, women's entry into "prestige professions" such as law and medicine has been slow, and fewer than 1 percent of female civil servants occupy managerial posts.

In 1990 clerical and related jobs accounted for the largest percentage of female employees (34.4 percent, excluding self-employed and family workers), followed by craft and production workers (20.6 percent), professional and technical workers (13.8 percent), sales workers (12.5 percent), service workers (10.7 percent), and other occupations (8.0 percent). The order of distribution has not changed for some time, although the number of women in each occupation has varied, increasing in professional and technical fields while decreasing in manual labor. The greatest gains for women in professional employment have been in public-school teaching

and social work.

The treatment of women in Japan's labor force resembles their treatment in other industrialized countries, with a negative correlation between their rate of participation and the income of the male household head. In both Japan and the West, female workers, more than half of whom are married, make up more than one-third of the total labor force and earn lower wages than men. Residual prejudice against women, however, has resulted in somewhat more discrimination against them in Japan than in the West. Tradition holds that women should devote themselves to the home after marriage, a view that causes the length of uninterrupted employment at the same firm to be rather short. Japanese court decisions have ruled against forcing women to retire upon marriage or upon having passed the "appropriate" age for marriage (commonly set at 30) but have been less clear on systems forcing women to retire at 50 (the normal retirement age for men is 55).

Japan's Labor Standards Law of 1947 stipulates equal pay for equal work, but this is rare in practice because of continuing tendencies to channel women into dead-end jobs, relabel their work, and favor men at promotion time. According to one survey, the average monthly wage paid female employees in 1990 was somewhat over 60 percent of that paid to male employees. The difference in Japan between men's and women's wages is still the greatest in the industrialized world, although it has narrowed slightly.

This disparity is due largely to the SENIORITY SYSTEM that presupposes "lifetime" employment of men, whereas the length of uninterrupted employment, average age, and educational level of women have tended to be considerably lower than those of men. Very few women attain positions of high responsibility in business, and few anywhere receive, as their male counterparts do, allowances for dependents and housing. Businesses still generally employ women only in low-level or temporary jobs because of the

woodenware Wooden vessels of the type known as *magemono*, or "bent things." These examples are from Kyōto. High-grade cypress or cedar is softened in hot water, bent into the desired shape, then secured with strips of cherry bark.

view that they are less able than men and should work only until marriage or childbirth.

The Labor Standards Law (art. 4[6]) prohibited holiday and late-night work by women and limited their overtime. However, the EQUAL EMPLOYMENT OPPORTUNITY LAW FOR MEN AND WOMEN of 1985 removed all restrictions for management and specialist positions except certain regulations applying to women workers in the period prior to and following childbirth. It is anticipated that the new law will encourage the employment and advancement of women on merit.

women, rural　　　　　　農村婦人

(*nōson fujin*). In the late 19th and early 20th centuries, Japan was still an agrarian society. However, by 1988 the agricultural population had fallen from 80 percent of the total in the early Meiji period (1868–1912) to 7 percent. The extremely rapid industrialization and urbanization that caused this population shift resulted in radical changes in the lives of rural women.

Under the Tokugawa shogunate (1603–1867), rural women faced heavy responsibilities. Besides engaging in agricultural production, women had to prepare clothing, food, and other necessities of life for their families. They spun thread, wove cloth, and sewed clothes. It was only in the mid-Meiji period, when raw cotton began to be imported and cheap clothing became available in rural areas, that women were released from these extra-agricultural duties. However, the social and economic problems caused by a suddenly emergent capitalism were particularly evident in rural areas. As a commodity economy rapidly developed, impoverished farmers who needed cash often sent their daughters to spinning mills and other factories in exchange for a small sum. When these young women became ill from the harsh labor conditions, they were simply returned without compensation to their villages. See JOKŌ AISHI.

Social scientists began to pay attention to the problems of working urban women only during the late 1920s and to the problems of rural women from about 1935. In *Nihon nōson fujin mondai* (1937, The Problems of Rural Women in Japan), MARUOKA HIDEKO lists some of the leading causes of the plight

of rural women: small family income and recurrent debts, the panic and shock of crop failures, heavy physical labor added to the traditional pressures of housework and family, and the scarcity of public welfare facilities. However, the role of women in farm communities has, in the postwar era, been given greater recognition, especially since the 1960s, and they have been liberated to some extent from their previous subordinate status. Mechanization and the adoption of scientific farming methods, as well as the wide use of electrical appliances such as refrigerators, washing machines, and vacuum cleaners, have lightened their work load.

A more recent concern has been the tendency of young women raised in farm communities to seek work in the major urban centers, and many young men, heirs to their family farms, have had great difficulty in finding marriage partners. Although in material respects the lives of rural women are no less comfortable than those of women in the city, farm communities remain the bastion of traditional thinking, and their women often lack full equality with their spouses. In a 1986 survey, about 60 percent of rural women were found to be incapable of handling basic household accounts, and only 11 percent participated in decisions concerning the family farm. To deal with such problems in an organized way, women's sections of agricultural cooperative associations have been established. The central organization is the National Council of Agricultural Cooperative Women's Associations. Young wives' groups have been especially active in improving the status and modernizing the lives of rural women. See also WOMEN IN JAPAN, HISTORY OF; WOMEN IN THE LABOR FORCE.

women's education　　　　女子教育

(*joshi kyōiku*). A concept and practice, weak in early Japanese history, that partially emerged in the Heian period (794–1185), gained strength from the 13th to 16th centuries, varied according to class during the Edo period (1600–1868), and was most highly developed during modern times (1868 to the present).

Early History—In ancient times, men and women seem to have been similarly "educated" for life. However, after several centuries of borrowing from China (where separate male and female spheres had long been differentiated), education of aristocratic women was increasingly restricted. Men studied Chinese (KAMBUN), the official language of court and politics, but women were supposed to read and write only Japanese. The essential calligraphic, musical, and poetic skills demanded of all aristocrats formed the backbone of education for both sexes.

Feudal Times—After 1185 the courtiers of the Heian period were replaced by a new ruling class of warriors, and between that date and 1600 Japan became a society increasingly dominated by males. Chinese Confucian ideas emphasizing the subordination of women gained ground among the *samurai* elite. This tendency reached a peak during the Edo period, when Confucianism became the state ideology. Samurai boys studied Chinese classics in domainal schools established by their lords, while their sisters stayed home learning to write simple characters from Confucian copybooks or memorizing the 19 injunctions for submissive behavior in the ONNA DAIGAKU (1716, The Great Learning for Women). Because substantial numbers of lower-class families wanted to

educate their children too, commoner schools (TERAKOYA) offered a curriculum of basic reading, writing, and arithmetic. There, schoolboys outnumbered schoolgirls four to one.

Modernizing Nation—After the Tokugawa shogunate was overthrown in 1867, the new government enthusiastically endorsed "modern" education for all classes and both sexes. The Education Order of 1872 made parents responsible for seeing that "boys and girls without distinction" attended primary school, and educational policy throughout the Meiji period (1868–1912) strove to narrow the gap between the school attendance of boys and that of girls. By 1910 primary school attendance of both sexes was approximately 98 percent. On the other hand, postprimary educational opportunities for women were soon drastically curtailed when in 1879 the government banned coeducation above the primary school level.

Because public education concentrated on males, private schooling for girls and women (a field in which Christian missionaries were active) played an enormously important role. It answered the heavy demand for female secondary schooling with institutions fashioned after government models: in 1899 all but 8 of the 28 girls' high schools (KŌTŌ JOGAKKŌ) were privately operated. At the same time, private educators founded postsecondary institutions for women that offered first-rate academic studies previously available only to men; among these was Joshi Eigaku Juku (now TSUDA COLLEGE).

Post–World War II—Under the Occupation government after World War II, a system of equal educational opportunity for the sexes was established in Japan. Many women's colleges (*tanka daigaku*) were elevated to the status of universities (*daigaku*), and institutions of higher learning opened their doors to women on an equal basis with men. However, a strong tendency remained on the part of parents, the Ministry of Education, and school administrators and teachers to favor unequal education based on traditional, stereotyped sex roles.

The number of women who pursue higher education in Japan has increased every year since World War II. In fact, in 1989 the percentage of females entering universities and junior colleges (36.8%) exceeded that of males (35.8%) for the first time. However, an overwhelming majority of female graduates opted to attend junior colleges, with only 26.4 percent of the total choosing to enroll in four-year institutions. Furthermore, three out of four female junior-college graduates and three out of five female university graduates majored in fields traditionally considered to be "female-oriented": the humanities, home economics, and education.

In recent years, as the women's liberation movement in Japan has become active, women's studies have begun to be available, particularly at women's colleges. In addition, much research is under way analyzing textbooks to uncover instances of sexism and sex-role stereotyping.

women's magazines　　　　女性誌

(*joseishi*). According to the 1990 *Shuppan nenkan* (Publishers' Yearbook), there were over 69 magazines for women in Japan with a total of over 300 million copies printed that year.

During the middle and latter part of the Meiji period (1868–1912), an array of new magazines appealing to specific audiences appeared. In 1884 the first women's maga-

women's suffrage Women were enfranchised under a law promulgated on 17 December 1945. Here two women cast ballots for the first time in the initial post–World War II general elections for the House of Representatives, held on 10 April 1946.

zine, *Jogaku shinshi*, was published. It was succeeded the next year by JOGAKU ZASSHI. Advocating a Christian and enlightened outlook, *Jogaku zasshi* sought to introduce Western ideas of family life. Toward the end of the Meiji period several magazines edited by women, notably SEKAI FUJIN by FUKUDA HIDEKO and *Seitō* by HIRATSUKA RAI-CHŌ, attracted public attention.

The years from the end of the Meiji period to the 1950s saw the consolidation of women's magazines as commercial enterprises. Magazines that appeared in the late Meiji, such as *Fujin gahō*, FUJIN NO TOMO, and *Fujokai*, rose in circulation. New magazines included FUJIN KŌRON (1916), *Shufu no tomo* (1917), and *Fujin kurabu* (1920–88). Although *Fujin kōron* purported to be a serious journal of opinion, most of the magazines of this period were eminently practical.

Beginning with *Shūkan josei* in 1957, there was a proliferation of weekly magazines for younger women: *Shūkan myōjō* (1958), *Josei jishin* (1958), *Josei sebun* (1963), and *Yangu redī* (1963, Young Lady). This no doubt reflected Japan's economic recovery in general, and, more specifically, technical improvements in mass production and marketing. It also reflected other changes: women were better educated, and the continuing increase in the number of nuclear families, with fewer children and more household appliances, meant more free time. The marriages and divorces of popular entertainers, fiction, comics, advice on romantic love, fashion, and similar topics formed the substance of these magazines. The circulations of some of these magazines have reached 1 million.

A new direction was opened up in the 1970s by magazines with exotic names such as *An-an*, *Non-no*, *More*, *Kurowassan* (Croissant), and *With*. *An-an* was clearly an imitation of the French magazine *Elle*, and *More*, of the American magazine *Cosmopolitan*. There was a marked trend toward internationalization, which was further evidenced by the publication of Japanese editions of *Cosmopolitan*, *Elle*, and the French magazine *Marie Claire*.

These new magazines used a large format and glossy displays of color photographs, full-page advertisements, and articles. Meant to be "looked at" rather than read, these magazines shifted from the traditional subjects of marriage, child care, and housekeeping to fashion, travel, and other leisure-time pursuits. A new emphasis on women as individuals rather than as wives and mothers was perhaps a result of the women's liberation movement.

This trend intensified in the 1980s, during which time a total of 39 women's magazines began publication (compared to 13 in the 1970s). Many of these magazines were targeted at single working women. A notable success was *Hanako*, an urban lifestyle and leisure magazine for young women in the Tōkyō area. *Hanako*'s popular "how-to guide" style inspired a wave of similar regionally based city lifestyle magazines.

women's suffrage   婦人参政権

(*fujin sanseiken*). A women's suffrage movement had existed in Japan long before the law granting women this right took effect in December 1945. Sweeping social changes after the Meiji Restoration of 1868 created new opportunities for women and led ultimately to their demand for political and other social rights. However, government leaders overlooked the early demands for women's rights made by a small number of male and female participants in the FREEDOM AND PEOPLE'S RIGHTS MOVEMENT.

Encouraged by widespread discussion of the "woman problem" (*fujin mondai*), in early 1920 women organized the SHIN FUJIN KYŌKAI (New Woman's Association). Of the numerous women's suffrage groups formed in the following years, the FUSEN KAKUTOKU DŌMEI (Women's Suffrage League) was the most influential. The women's suffrage movement ended with the dissolution of the Fusen Kakutoku Dōmei in October 1940, in the militarist suppression of all progressive movements in Japan.

During the Allied OCCUPATION a bill extending rights to women on the national level was promulgated on 17 December 1945. Women who had reached the age of 20 were allowed to vote for members of the House of Representatives and those 25 or over could become candidates in national elections. For the first postwar election in April 1946 there were 79 female candidates, of whom 39 were elected. Women's awareness of politics and social concerns has continued to grow since the war. Women who had reached the age of 20 were given full voting rights by the Public Office Election Law (see ELECTIONS).

women workers, protective legislation for   婦人労働者の保護

(*fujin rōdōsha no hogo*). Protection for women workers is provided by the Labor Standards Law (Rōdō Kijun Hō); this legislation was drafted in 1947 in accordance with the International Labor Conventions to set minimum standards for women's working conditions and extensively revised in 1985 when the EQUAL EMPLOYMENT OPPORTUNITY LAW FOR MEN AND WOMEN (Danjo Koyō Kikai Kintō Hō) was enacted. Chapter 1, article 4 establishes that men and women must receive equal pay for equal work. Chapter 6-2 makes various provisions for the protection of women. For example, the rights of pregnant women—and women who may in the future have children—to perform labor that is dangerous or endangers health are restricted; women who perform industrial labor may work only 6 overtime hours per week and a total of 150 hours overtime hours per year; with many exceptions, such as women who are administrators or who possess special skills, women are also prohibited from working between 10:00 PM and 5:00 AM; women are entitled to childbirth leave beginning six weeks before birth and extending to eight weeks after birth; pregnant women have the right to request work entailing less physical effort; new mothers are entitled to a minimum of two daily nursing periods of 30 minutes each. Women also have the right to take paid leave during their menstrual periods. See also LABOR LAWS; EQUALITY OF THE SEXES UNDER THE LAW; WOMEN IN THE LABOR FORCE.

woodblock prints → ukiyo-e; modern prints

woodenware   木工品

(*mokkōhin*). Wood has traditionally been an important building material in Japan. The grain, as well as the color of the wood, is considered an important aesthetic element. The oldest known wooden articles in Japan were made with stone tools during the second millennium BC. Around 200 BC iron tools and lathes were used to make wooden farm implements. By around 100 BC household utensils were made, and there was a sophisticated knowledge of lumbering, sawing, processing, cutting, lathing, and drilling. The many 4th- and 5th-century tools that have been unearthed indicate a high standard of workmanship. Woodcraft techniques reached a high point in the Nara period (710–794).

In the Heian period (794–1185), as LACQUER WARE and MAKI-E became popular, the role of woodcraft makers diminished to supplying unfinished material. However, in the 16th century the art was revived when tea masters began to adopt woodenware for their ceremonies. With the flourishing of the merchant class in the Edo period (1600–1868), demand for woodenware increased and production centers sprang up in various parts of the country. Common types of woodenware in use today are MAGEMONO containers, cabinets, and lathed bowls. See also FOLK CRAFTS.

woodpeckers   啄木鳥

(*kitsutsuki*). Birds of the family Picidae, noted for their sharply pointed bills with which they chip tree trunks for insects. Eleven species are found in Japan. Most of these are also found in Europe, but four are unique to Asia or Japan: the large red, white, and black *kitataki* (white-bellied black woodpecker; *Dryocopus javensis*), formerly found on the island of Tsushima and now believed to be extinct; the greenish yellow *aogera* (Japanese green woodpecker; *Picus awokera*), found from Honshū southward; the dark red *noguchigera* (Pryer's woodpecker; *Sapheopipo noguchii*), found on Okinawa; and the white-and-brown striped *kogera* (Japanese pygmy woodpecker; *Dendrocopos kizuki*).

word games   言葉遊び

(*kotoba asobi*). With its relatively simple phonetic structure and abundance of homophones, the Japanese language lends itself well to puns and other word games. The KAKEKOTOBA (pivot words) in WAKA poetry and the intricate system of capping verses through puns and word association in RENGA (linked verse) and *haikai* (see HAIKU) are evidence of the importance of word games in the Japanese literary tradition. Although there is much less emphasis on the use of puns and wordplay in modern literature, word games are still enjoyed by both adults and children. Apart from puns, the most popular forms are *nazo nazo* (RIDDLES), capping of verses, one-liners, tongue twisters, and palindromes (*kaibun*).

Shiritori (capping) was a favorite pastime of Heian-period (794–1185) courtiers. As one person read a *waka* poem of 31 syllables, the next person would take the last word or syllable from it and start a new verse. In this way, a chain of verses was created. Today it

Japanese-language word processors

The market for dedicated word processors is extremely large in Japan.

This 1992 desktop model by Sharp features a flat-screen liquid crystal display.

The first Japanese-language word processor, put on the market in 1978 by Tōshiba.

Keyboards like this are designed for the easy entry of Japanese text using *kana* script.

Word processors continue to shrink in size and weight; this 1991 pocket model was produced by Fujitsū.

Typical of Japanese laptop word processors, this 1991 Panasonic model has a thermal printer built into the back of the unit.

is exclusively a children's game in which single words are linked according to the last syllable. Tongue twisters (*hayakuchi*) also have long been popular; they now figure chiefly in the play of children. From early times palindromic poetry was composed by Chinese and Japanese poets as a diversion from more serious writing. Today palindromes are less intricate and usually are made up of single words and expressions.

word processors, Japanese-language
日本語ワープロ

(*nihongo wāpuro*). Before the advent of the electronic word processor, typing in Japanese (which makes use of Chinese ideographic characters, or *kanji;* two sets of phonetic characters, or *kana;* and, occasionally, the Roman alphabet) was a laborious process that could only be accomplished on large, printing-press-like Japanese typewriters. The development of microelectronics enabled Japanese engineers to devise a word-processing system whereby words and phrases are keyboarded phonetically, using either the Roman alphabet or one of the *kana* scripts, and then converted into the desired characters. The first Japanese-language word processor was put on the market in 1978 by the TŌSHIBA CORPORATION at a price of ¥6.3 million (US $29,937), but by the early 1990s a number of portable machines were priced as low as ¥50,000 (US $360). In 1990 more than 2.5 million Japanese-language word processors were sold, and nearly a dozen firms had developed a wide variety of models for home and office use.

work away from family
単身赴任

(*tanshin funin;* literally, "proceeding to a new post alone"). In the 1970s and 1980s increasing numbers of Japanese business and government employees who were transferred to distant cities within Japan or abroad left their families behind indefinitely and proceeded to their new posts alone. Despite the hardships involved (there were increasing reports of husbands whose health was affected and of wives and children suffering psychological disorders), most Japanese employees accepted such transfers as a matter of course. Acceptance was com-

monly seen as a passport to advancement.
There were strong pressures on the families of the transferred employees to remain behind in their existing homes. The most important factor was Japan's extremely competitive high-school and college entrance-examination system. Another factor, for home-owning families, was reluctance to endanger their equity in an expensive housing market (see HOUSING PROBLEMS). According to Ministry of Labor estimates, in the mid-1980s as many as 134,000 employees a year from firms employing 1,000 or more people were accepting transfers that made it necessary to leave their families behind. Of these employees, 30 percent were men in their forties and 40 percent men in their fifties. Three out of four companies provided special expense allowances to help with the cost of maintaining separate households.

workers' compensation
労働者災害補償

(*rōdōsha saigai hoshō*). Compensation given to a worker or surviving family members in the event of injury or death resulting from on-the-job accidents. The incidence of work-related injuries is relatively low in Japan. In addition, the system of workers' compensation is fairly well developed. The system originated with the FACTORY LAW OF 1911, which prescribed compensation by employers in the case of accidents that were not due to serious fault on the part of the employee. With the enactment of the 1947 Labor Standards Law (Rōdō Kijun Hō; see LABOR LAWS) and Workers' Compensation Law (Rōdōsha Saigai Hoshō Hoken Hō), workers' accident compensation was set up under a unified system and freed from the dependence on charity that had characterized such aid in the prewar years. The system requires employers to provide medical and disability benefits and aid to surviving family members sufficient to maintain their standard of living prior to the accident. Recently death from overwork (*karōshi*) has been added as a category of work-related injury.

work hours
労働時間

(*rōdō jikan*). Japanese workers work longer hours than workers in any other advanced industrialized nation; an annual total of 2,189 hours for production workers in the

manufacturing sector was recorded in a 1988 survey (the average for Japanese industry as a whole was 2,088 hours), compared with 1,962 hours in the United States and 1,642 hours in West Germany. This difference is accounted for mainly by long hours of overtime work and by the fact that the number of days worked per year in Japan is greater than elsewhere: 248 days, compared with 226 days in the United States and 210 days in West Germany. The six-day workweek is still operative in 46.2 percent of Japanese companies with just 7.4 percent of companies and 29.5 percent of the nation's employees working a true five-day workweek. (Nearly 50% of companies and 70% of employees had some form of five-day workweek.) Very few small companies have changed over to five-day workweeks. The average number of paid vacation days is 15.4 a year, but on average only 7.9 of these are used.

Reducing the number of work hours is now a priority for government and industry: the aim is to reduce the total number of hours worked per year to 1,800 by 1992. Banks, financial institutions, and local authorities are leading the way toward the five-day workweek, which is slowly spreading throughout industry. Flextime systems are being introduced, as well as shift systems that vary hours depending upon the nature of the work. However, the move toward reducing work hours is hampered by the practice of relying on employees' willingness to work overtime in order to help their company adjust to fluctuations in business volume rather than taking on extra staff or resorting to dismissals. See also HOLIDAYS AND VACATIONS.

work regulations
就業規則

(*shūgyō kisoku*). Rules governing the terms and conditions of employment. Work regulations may be set unilaterally or collectively by trade unions and by employers. In Japan they are usually set by employers, who take into consideration the union's opinion and seek its consent. The Labor Standards Law (Rōdō Kijun Hō) of 1947 (see LABOR LAWS) provides that an employer with more than 10 regularly employed workers must establish work regulations and stipulate working conditions. He must ask the opinion of the unions or representatives of a majority of his employees. He must also submit his regulations to the LABOR STANDARDS INSPECTION OF-

FICES and post them for employee examination.

World Bank   国際復興開発銀行

(Kokusai Fukkō Kaihatsu Ginkō). The World Bank (or International Bank for Reconstruction and Development; IBRD) was established in 1944, along with the IMF. Its purpose is to assist in the reconstruction of postwar economies and to aid less-developed countries. Japan became a member of the World Bank in 1952 and between 1953 and 1966 obtained 31 development loans totaling US $863 million. The loans were used primarily for electric power, steel, and highway projects. Full repayment of these loans was completed in 1990.

After 1960, Japan became a supplier of funds to the World Bank and by 1970 was one of the bank's five largest contributors. Since 1984 Japan has supplied 6.7 percent of the bank's funds, second only to the 18.9 percent contributed by the United States. In addition to the direct support of the Japanese government, the World Bank also raises part of its funds in Japanese capital markets. It also encourages cofinancing of development projects, together with such Japanese institutions as the EXPORT-IMPORT BANK OF JAPAN, the OVERSEAS ECONOMIC COOPERATION FUND, and the private sector banks.

World Co, Ltd   [株]ワールド

(Wārudo). Apparel manufacturer. Incorporated in 1959. World Co has subsidiaries in four cities: Paris, Milan, Shanghai, and Taipei. For the fiscal year ending March 1990, sales totaled ¥153.2 billion (US $1.0 billion) and capitalization stood at ¥3.0 billion (US $19.6 million). Headquarters are in Kōbe.

World War I   第一次世界大戦

(Daiichiji Sekai Taisen). On 1 August 1914 Germany, a member of the Triple Alliance with Austria and Italy, declared war on Russia, a member of the Triple Entente with Britain and France. The day after Germany declared war against France on 3 August, Britain declared war against Germany. On the Shandong (Shantung) Peninsula in China the German concession at Qingdao (Tsingtao; see JIAOZHOU [KIAOCHOW] CONCESSION) and the British concession at Weihaiwei were both fortified. A conflict between British and German troops in Shandong might have easily involved the British base at Hong Kong and German bases in the Mariana, Caroline, and Marshall islands. The ANGLO-JAPANESE ALLIANCE, as revised in 1911, would have required Japanese participation on the British side.

Immediately after the declarations of war in Europe, Japan announced neutrality but promised to support Britain if requested to repel a German attack on Hong Kong or Weihaiwei. On 7 August 1914 Japan received a British request to destroy armed German merchant cruisers in Chinese waters. On 8 August Japan decided to enter the war on Britain's side and declared war on 23 August, one week after sending to Berlin an ultimatum that had gone unanswered.

Japan moved swiftly against German possessions in the Shandong Peninsula and the Pacific Islands. On 2 September Japanese troops arrived in Shandong. During October the Japanese eliminated German power from the Mariana, Caroline, and Marshall islands. By the end of 1914 German possessions in Shandong and the Pacific Islands north of the equator were under Japanese control.

Twenty-One Demands—Almost immediately after these victories, Japan presented the so-called TWENTY-ONE DEMANDS to China's President YUAN SHIKAI (Yüan Shih-k'ai). When Yuan leaked to the foreign press these demands for recognition of much greater Japanese influence and privileges in China, Britain and the United States issued protests to Japan. Agreeing to drop some of the demands, Japan forced Yuan to accept the remainder in treaties and agreements signed on 25 May 1915.

Political Relations with the Allies—Throughout 1915 and 1916 German efforts to make a separate peace with Japan and Russia proved unsuccessful. On 3 July 1916 Japan and Russia signed an agreement not to make a separate peace and to consult each other on what common action might be required if the territorial rights or interests of either party were menaced by a third power in Asia (see RUSSO-JAPANESE AGREEMENTS OF 1907–1916).

In 1917 Japan attempted to consolidate its recent gains in China and the Pacific by improving relations with Britain and the United States. In January Japan agreed to send destroyers to the Mediterranean in return for British recognition of Japan's right to German possessions in Shandong and the Pacific Islands north of the equator. When the United States entered the war on 6 April, Americans and Japanese found themselves as allies despite their competition for influence in China and naval rivalry in the Pacific. Under the LANSING-ISHII AGREEMENT of 2 November 1917 the United States recognized Japan's "special interests" in China, and both sides affirmed the independence and territorial integrity of China, the principle of the Open Door, and equal opportunity for commerce and industry in China. During 1918 Japan continued to extend its influence and privileges in China (see NISHIHARA LOANS). It also joined in the US intervention in Siberia following Russia's separate peace with Germany (see SIBERIAN INTERVENTION).

Military Expansion and Economic Growth—Japanese military and economic power grew rapidly during the war. By the end of 1918, Japanese troops held, in addition to former German territory in Shandong and the Pacific, additional parts of China proper, part of northern Manchuria, and part of eastern Siberia.

During the war Japan profited from the inability of former suppliers to meet continuing demand in Asian markets. Orders for munitions poured in from the Allies, and the value of Japanese exports rose about threefold between 1913 and 1918; their volume rose 50 percent. Japan's industrial boom and the influx of capital during the war led to rampant inflation, and the steep rise in prices for daily necessities easily outstripped the rise in wages for Japan's growing urban population, resulting in the RICE RIOTS OF 1918. But on the whole, the spectacular growth of the economy, industry, armed forces, and empire during World War I was a source of pride to many Japanese. See also VERSAILLES, TREATY OF.

World War II   第二次世界大戦

(Dainiji Sekai Taisen). World War II was a vast and complex conflict, involving a number of separate but interrelated wars. The roots of the Asian and Pacific phase of the war can be traced largely to Japan's militarist expansionism on the Asian continent in the 1930s, and especially its war with China beginning in 1937. Historians now recognize,

however, that this expansionism was more complicated and less premeditated than was once thought. More than a decade of both international tension and domestic instability exacerbated Japan's aggressiveness and lay behind its decision to risk war with the United States, Great Britain, and their allies in December 1941.

The Context of Japanese Expansionism—In the wake of the New York stock market crash of 1929, international trade collapsed and the world seemed to be on the verge of shattering into a competing set of autarkic economic blocs. Japan, heavily dependent on foreign trade, felt increasing pressure to take control of sources of vital raw materials and markets. The world economic crisis weakened liberal party government in Japan while spurring totalitarian forces. Right-wing groups proliferated, with the most radical bent on eliminating the emperor's moderate advisers. A series of political assassinations from 1930 to 1936 intimidated Japan's centrist, Western-oriented leadership, paralyzing civilian government and forcing it to submit increasingly to the demands of the military.

Self-appointed guardian of the Japanese spirit, embittered by years of lean military budgets, the IMPERIAL JAPANESE ARMY was itself dangerously volatile through the early 1930s. With the original leaders of the Meiji period (1868–1912) gone, insubordination, plotting, and violence thrived within its ranks. A radical fringe engineered the MANCHURIAN INCIDENT of 1931, commencing Japan's military adventurism in continental Asia. Not until the failed military coup of 1936 (see FEBRUARY 26TH INCIDENT) did the army finally restore internal discipline. By then it was the dominant force in the Japanese government, its only rival the IMPERIAL JAPANESE NAVY, which had its own goal of expansion into Southeast Asia and the Pacific Islands (see SOUTHERN EXPANSION DOCTRINE).

The Japan that emerged from this turmoil of the early and mid-1930s was bent on conflict. With both the army and navy regarding wider war as inevitable, Japan concentrated on developing heavy industry, building up its armed forces, and mobilizing the population. The role of the Diet and political parties diminished as government became increasingly authoritarian and totalitarian. National self-sufficiency and Asian hegemony (often phrased in the rhetoric of PAN-ASIANISM) became the country's guiding assumptions, reflected in its break with the international order represented by the League of Nations and the Washington Treaty system (see LEAGUE OF NATIONS AND JAPAN; WASHINGTON CONFERENCE). Yet Japan had no rational scheme for achieving its aims. Policy remained haphazard, ambiguous, and lacking focus, for Japan's quest for hegemony implied a scale of conflict altogether beyond the nation's means—involving the possibility of both war in Northeast Asia with the Soviet Union and war in Southeast Asia and the Pacific with the Western powers.

War in China and the Axis Alliance—The first outbreak of hostilities, however, came closer to hand, with the MARCO POLO BRIDGE INCIDENT of 1937 in North China. Once the shooting started, Japan expected a quick end to Chinese resistance. Instead, Chinese forces retreated but refused to surrender, resulting in a horrible quagmire that drained Japan's resources and severely strained relations with the United States and other West-

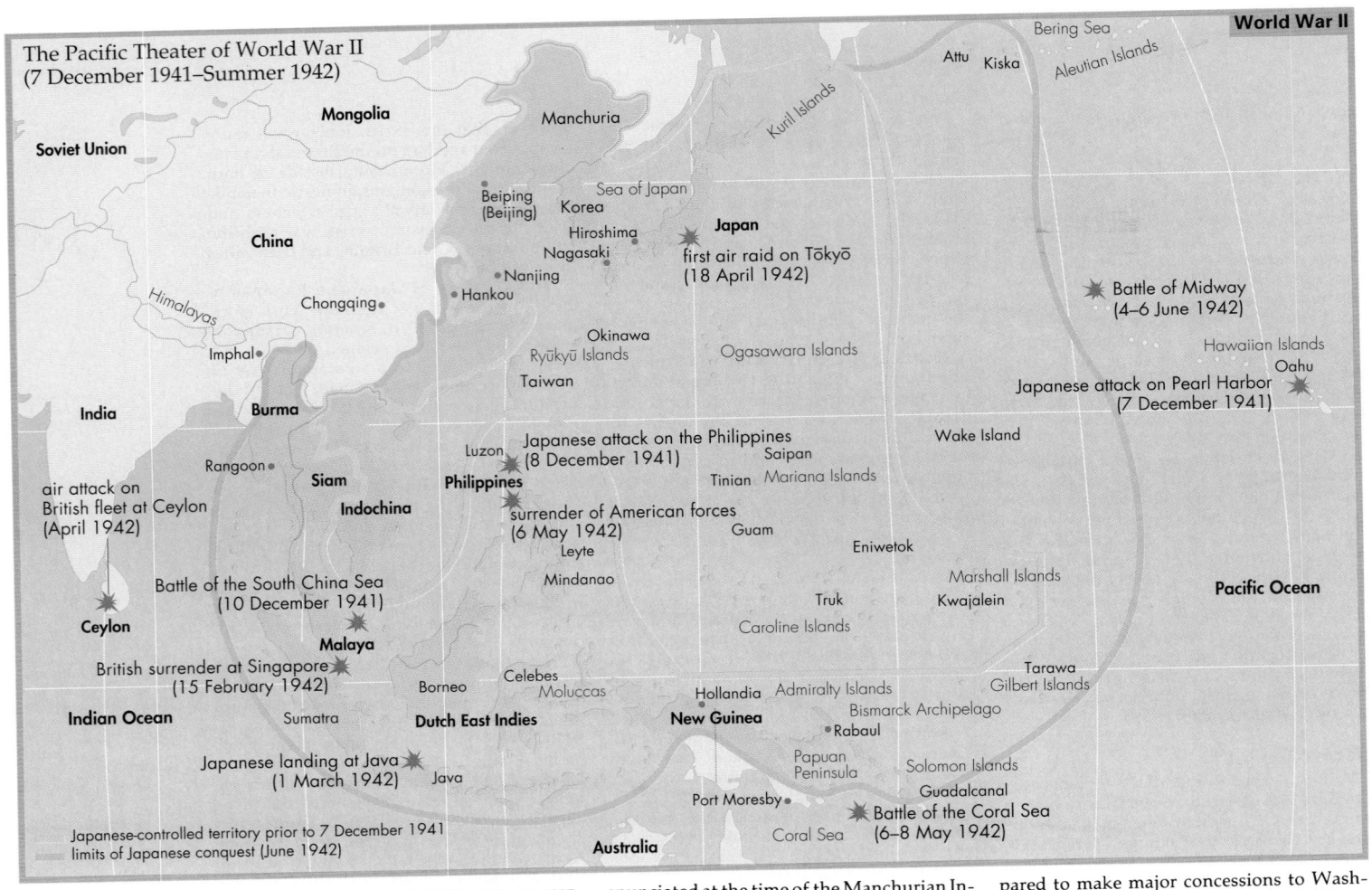

The Pacific Theater of World War II
(7 December 1941–Summer 1942)

Soviet Union
Mongolia
Manchuria
Kuril Islands
Bering Sea
Attu Kiska Aleutian Islands
Sea of Japan
Beiping (Beijing)
Korea
China
Hiroshima
Japan
Nagasaki
first air raid on Tōkyō (18 April 1942)
Nanjing
Hankou
Battle of Midway (4–6 June 1942)
Chongqing
Himalayas
Okinawa
Ryūkyū Islands
Ogasawara Islands
Hawaiian Islands
Imphal
Taiwan
Oahu
India
Japanese attack on Pearl Harbor (7 December 1941)
Burma
Japanese attack on the Philippines (8 December 1941)
Wake Island
Luzon
Saipan
Rangoon
Siam
Philippines
Tinian
Mariana Islands
air attack on British fleet at Ceylon (April 1942)
Indochina
surrender of American forces (6 May 1942)
Guam
Leyte
Eniwetok
Battle of the South China Sea (10 December 1941)
Mindanao
Marshall Islands
Truk
Kwajalein
Pacific Ocean
Ceylon
Caroline Islands
Malaya
British surrender at Singapore (15 February 1942)
Tarawa
Gilbert Islands
Borneo
Celebes
Moluccas
Hollandia
Admiralty Islands
Indian Ocean
Sumatra
Dutch East Indies
New Guinea
Bismarck Archipelago
Rabaul
Japanese landing at Java (1 March 1942)
Java
Papuan Peninsula
Solomon Islands
Guadalcanal
Port Moresby
Battle of the Coral Sea (6–8 May 1942)
Coral Sea
Japanese-controlled territory prior to 7 December 1941
limits of Japanese conquest (June 1942)
Australia
World War II

ern powers (see SINO-JAPANESE WAR OF 1937–1945). Meanwhile, Soviet forces dealt Japanese forces stationed in Manchuria resounding defeats in unpublicized encounters along the Mongolian border in 1939 (see NOMONHAN INCIDENT). Thus Japan was already deeply embroiled in conflict by the time war broke out in Europe in September 1939.

Cooperation among Germany, Italy, and Japan had begun with the ANTI-COMINTERN PACT of 1936, and the European war made closer ties look attractive. Germany's victories in the West in 1940 jeopardized the Asian colonial possessions of Great Britain, France, and the Netherlands, making them tempting prizes for the Japanese both for their natural resources and as bases for encircling and subduing China. Japan joined the Axis alliance by concluding the TRIPARTITE PACT in September 1940, but it turned out to be a fragile and largely ineffectual partnership. Despite common enemies, Japan and Germany possessed no common strategy. Japan refused to join Germany's attack on the USSR in 1941, instead entering a neutrality pact with Moscow.

A Growing Confrontation with the United States—For Tōkyō, the object of the Axis alliance had largely been to help neutralize the Soviet Union and to permit Japan to exploit unhindered the colonies of war-torn European powers. But it was also intended to paralyze the United States, self-styled protector of Chinese sovereignty and promulgator of discriminatory immigration policies bitterly resented by Japan. Throughout the 1930s, its navy below treaty limits and popular sentiment isolationist, the United States never risked open conflict with Japan, restricting itself to diplomatic protests, such as the NONRECOGNITION POLICY

enunciated at the time of the Manchurian Incident. Only at the very end of the decade did it turn to economic sanctions against Japan, until then a mutually profitable trade and investment partner.

Although President Franklin D. ROOSEVELT attempted to adopt a defensive strategy in the Pacific, German victories in Europe opened Southeast Asia to Japan's advance, which in turn prompted American countermeasures to protect Western interests there. Apprehensive, too, that Japan would join Hitler against the USSR if given any respite, American officals decided to deter further Japanese expansion. In July 1939, the United States gave notice abrogating the Japanese-American commercial treaty, thereby permitting the embargo of American exports to Japan. When Japan moved into northern Indochina the following year, Washington began embargoing exports, extending the list of restricted items month by month. In the summer of 1941, as Japan moved into southern Indochina, the United States mounted a coordinated international embargo that cut off all of Japan's foreign oil, dispatched heavy bombers and reinforcements to the Philippines, and extended Lend-Lease aid to China and the Soviet Union.

Japan's leaders knew they must do something, for the nation's capacity for war and defense would dwindle with its oil reserves. One alternative was to strike the United States soon, before its defenses were readied and its naval buildup, initiated in 1940, was completed. The other was to negotiate, in hopes that Japan might retain control of vital territory in North China and Manchuria, secure an honorable end to the war in China, and gain access to essential oil.

Through the summer and fall of 1941 Japan pursued both objectives. The government of Prime Minister TŌJŌ HIDEKI was pre-

pared to make major concessions to Washington, including Japan's withdrawal from Indochina and large parts of China (in return for American pressure on China to end the war), as well as assurances Japan would not come to Germany's aid, the Tripartite Pact notwithstanding. The Americans, however, would not accept any solution that impinged upon Chinese territorial integrity and sovereignty. Nor did they trust Japanese intentions, for intercepted cables indicated that Japan was preparing for attack. Japan's decision for war was a desperate gamble. Its leaders calculated that national security depended on maintaining dominance in East Asia, which in turn required access to the resources of Southeast Asia. This could be ensured only by force, which meant war with the Netherlands, the British Commonwealth, and almost inevitably the United States. Admiral YAMAMOTO ISOROKU, commander of the Combined Fleet, advised that a preemptive strike should be launched against Pearl Harbor to neutralize US naval forces before Japan struck southward. Japan's leaders realized that America's industrial capacity was vastly greater than theirs, but they hoped to buy some time in which to establish a far-flung perimeter of naval and air bases that would discourage American retaliation.

Japan Attacks—After months of negotiation US Secretary of State Cordell Hull concluded that further talk was useless, and on 26 November 1941 he presented the Japanese with a comprehensive restatement of the American position (see HULL NOTE). The Japanese leaders construed this as an ultimatum, though their military movements were already under way. At dawn on 7 December, Japanese bombers and torpedo planes dealt devastating blows to the American fleet at Pearl Harbor and to surrounding airfields

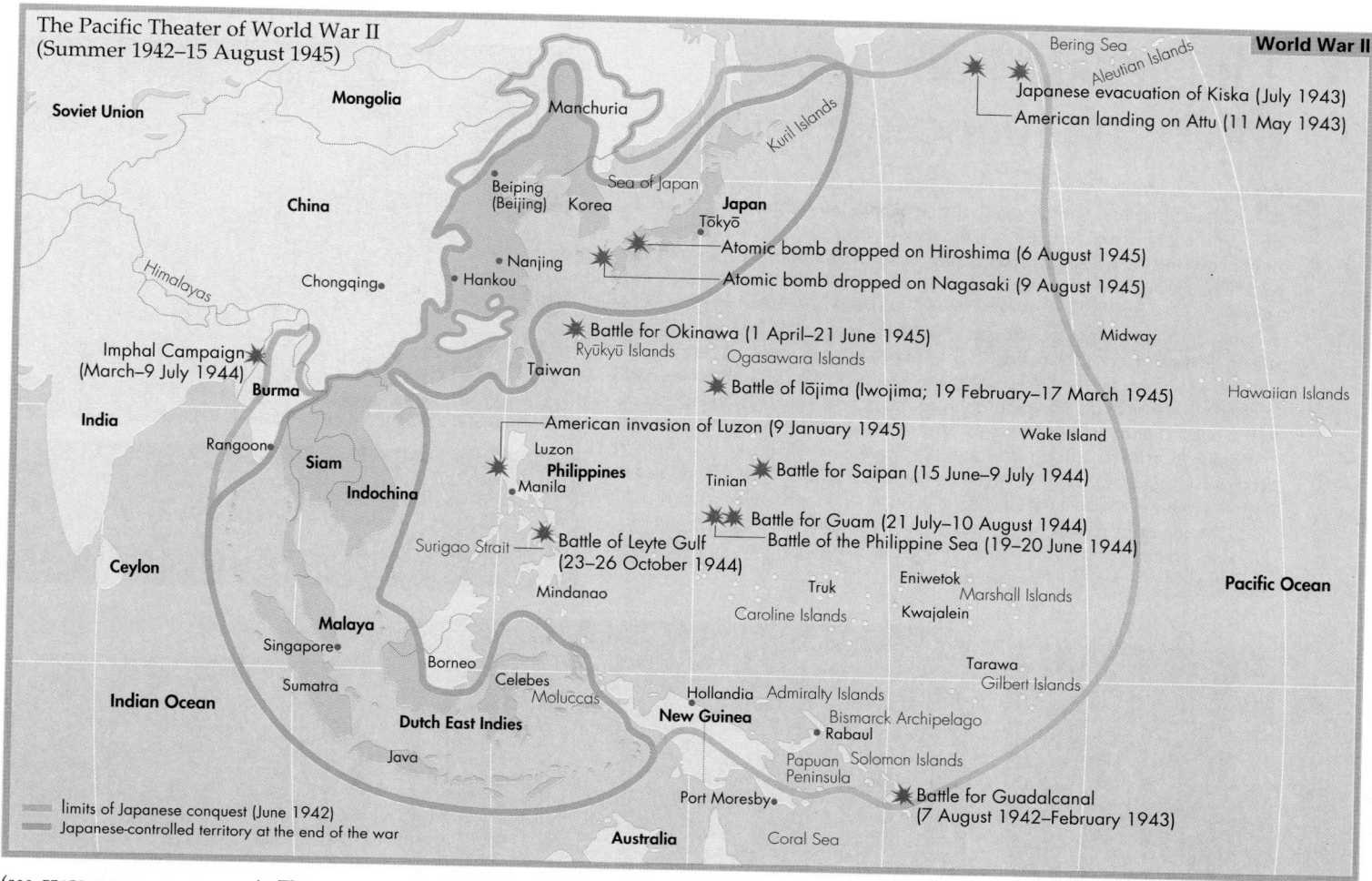

The Pacific Theater of World War II (Summer 1942–15 August 1945)

Soviet Union

Mongolia

Manchuria

Bering Sea

Aleutian Islands

World War II

Japanese evacuation of Kiska (July 1943)

American landing on Attu (11 May 1943)

Kuril Islands

China

Beiping (Beijing)

Korea

Sea of Japan

Japan

Tōkyō

Atomic bomb dropped on Hiroshima (6 August 1945)

Nanjing

Atomic bomb dropped on Nagasaki (9 August 1945)

Chongqing

Hankou

Himalayas

Battle for Okinawa (1 April–21 June 1945)

Ryūkyū Islands

Ogasawara Islands

Midway

Imphal Campaign (March–9 July 1944)

Taiwan

Battle of Iōjima (Iwojima; 19 February–17 March 1945)

Hawaiian Islands

Burma

India

American invasion of Luzon (9 January 1945)

Luzon

Wake Island

Rangoon

Siam

Philippines

Tinian

Battle for Saipan (15 June–9 July 1944)

Indochina

Manila

Battle for Guam (21 July–10 August 1944)

Battle of the Philippine Sea (19–20 June 1944)

Ceylon

Surigao Strait

Battle of Leyte Gulf (23–26 October 1944)

Mindanao

Truk

Eniwetok

Marshall Islands

Pacific Ocean

Caroline Islands

Kwajalein

Malaya

Singapore

Borneo

Tarawa

Gilbert Islands

Sumatra

Celebes

Moluccas

Hollandia

Admiralty Islands

Indian Ocean

Dutch East Indies

New Guinea

Bismarck Archipelago

Rabaul

Java

Papuan Peninsula

Solomon Islands

Port Moresby

Australia

Coral Sea

Battle for Guadalcanal (7 August 1942–February 1943)

limits of Japanese conquest (June 1942)

Japanese-controlled territory at the end of the war

(see PEARL HARBOR, ATTACK ON). The attack damaged or destroyed every battleship in the harbor, but success was not total, for it failed to find and destroy any of the US aircraft carriers stationed at Pearl Harbor or to cripple the base's repair and supply facilities. Worse, it angered the American people into abandoning the isolationism upon which Japan's leaders had counted.

The Philippines and Malaya lay in the path of Japan's advance on the Dutch East Indies, but both were overrun relatively early in 1942, allowing Japanese forces to leap from Borneo and Celebes to Sumatra and Java. The British stronghold at Singapore fell on 15 February 1942. By the time US resistance ceased in the Philippines, British forces in Burma were in full retreat, and Japan controlled the northern coast of New Guinea, the Bismarcks, the northern Solomons, the Gilberts, and Guam and Wake islands in the Central Pacific. These Japanese campaigns of December 1941 through early 1942 were some of the most stunning feats in military history. With the bulk of the Japanese army tied down in China and Manchuria, only 11 divisions were available for the southward advance. Through careful planning and coordination, Japan deployed these limited forces against successive targets, defeating its enemies piecemeal. Western prestige in Asia never recovered.

Japan designated its new realm the GREATER EAST ASIA COPROSPERITY SPHERE. The Tōjō government recognized that encouraging Asian nationalism in areas of marginal economic importance might foster cooperation and lessen the burden of rule. It was also of great propaganda value in strengthening the puppet Chinese government of WANG JINGWEI (Wang Ching-wei), belaboring the British in India, and dividing the colonial powers from the United States. The Copros-

perity Sphere, however, was a sham. For convenience Vichy France continued to govern Indochina; Japan itself expected to maintain colonial rule in the East Indies, Malaya, and strategic bases along its defense perimeter. The realities of the sphere were principally economic dislocation, inflation, military devastation, malnutrition, and political suppression.

The Tide Turns—Initial success encouraged Japan's leaders to attempt seizing Port Moresby in New Guinea as the first step in cutting communications between Australia and the United States. Alerted by "Magic," decoded top-secret Japanese messages, American naval forces met the Japanese in the Battle of the Coral Sea in May 1942. Although the Americans suffered greater losses, the Japanese met their first rebuff and were forced to withdraw.

Japanese forces were also stopped in the Central Pacific. To secure bases for defending the home islands from air attack and, more important, to challenge the US fleet to a decisive engagement while Japanese naval superiority lasted, Admiral Yamamoto moved against Midway Island in June 1942. Forewarned, the Pacific Fleet under Admiral Chester Nimitz destroyed four Japanese aircraft carriers, the heart of Japan's offensive naval power. After the Battle of MIDWAY, the Japanese navy was forced onto the defensive for the remainder of the war.

Yet by early 1943, despite another reversal at GUADALCANAL, Japan had no immediate reason to despair. China's CHIANG KAI-SHEK was still more interested in fighting his communist foes than in battling Japan, Britain was too weak to recapture Burma, and Japan's resource base in Southeast Asia remained intact. In Europe, however, Hitler had been defeated at Stalingrad, Allied offensives were gaining ground in North

Africa, and Italy would soon be coming under attack. America was also becoming steadily more powerful. Its carrier ranks began to swell, while American submarines tore away at Japan's merchant marine, straining the vital sea links of the Japanese empire.

Allied progress in the Pacific plodded along two fronts throughout 1943: the Southwest Pacific, with fighting in New Guinea and the Solomons; and the Central Pacific, with assaults on the Gilbert and Marshall islands. Air power became critically important. The Americans strove to gain air bases ever closer to Japan's vital communications links, leapfrogging Japanese strongpoints like Rabaul and Truk and isolating enemy troops before mounting amphibious invasions of suitable islands within combat radius of existing Allied bases. In April 1943 Admiral Yamamoto himself was shot down and killed by US planes operating out of the Solomons.

In June 1944, US amphibious forces landed on Saipan in the Marianas, a strategic island group in the Central Pacific that would put long-range B-29 bombers within striking distance of the home islands of Japan. Admiral Toyoda Soemu (1885–1957), Yamamoto's successor, saw this encounter as an opportunity for Japan to deal a knockout blow to the Allies. But American air strikes eliminated his land-based air support, freeing the US Navy to concentrate on Japanese carrier attacks. In the greatest naval air battle of the war, the Japanese Combined Fleet lost over 90 percent of its planes and was forced to withdraw.

The loss of the Marianas in July 1944 was a decisive defeat for Japan, leaving vulnera-

Continued on page 1716➝

The Pacific War through Japanese Eyes

For Japan, World War II in the Pacific consisted of three successive phases: glorious victories; humiliating setbacks; and hopeless resistance to the unbearable prospect of defeat. In late 1941, the nation attacked Western-held territories throughout the Pacific. Japan seemed invincible as its troops overran and captured Hong Kong, the Philippines, Singapore, oil-rich Indonesia, and other strategic targets in the South Pacific. By challenging the United States, Britain, and Holland on many fronts at once, Japan hoped to make them abandon their interests in the region. Achieving a decisive naval victory was central to the Japanese strategy, but defeat by US forces in the Battle of Midway in June 1942 transformed the Pacific conflict into a war of attrition that Japan could not win. Although its leaders clung to the belief that by inflicting heavy losses on the enemy they could negotiate a conditional surrender, Japan was steadily forced to withdraw from recently acquired territories. By 1944, when US forces took Saipan in July and crippled the Japanese navy in the Battle of Leyte Gulf in October, Japan could no longer command the sea or air. Unrestricted bombing of Japanese cities began. The military doggedly continued to resist enemy advances, but the war moved inexorably toward a total victory for the Allied forces.

The surprise attack on Pearl Harbor on 7 December 1941 was meant to cripple the US naval force based in Hawaii. Attacking from aircraft carriers, the Japanese sank or severely damaged 8 battleships and destroyed 188 planes. The *West Virginia*, shown here, was among those sunk.

Japan faced severe shortages of strategic materials by 1942. A dearth of metal led the government to commandeer temple bells and melt them down. This photograph, taken on 9 May 1942, shows bells gathered from temples in Ishikawa Prefecture.

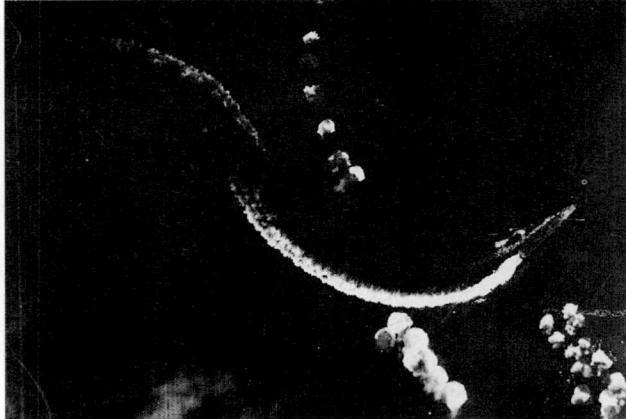

The Battle of Midway cost the Japanese navy much of its offensive strength. The Americans learned early of an attack on Midway Island by decoding a message. Surprising the Japanese fleet, they destroyed four carriers. Here the *Akagi*, caught as its planes prepared for takeoff, takes evasive action as bombs fall on 4 June 1942.

Forced to give up Guadalcanal after the American navy shut off their lines of supply to the island, the Japanese covertly evacuated a large number of their troops. Wounded and ill soldiers were left behind. US soldiers surround such a group on 10 February 1943.

American GIs raise the flag on Mt. Suribachi on 23 February 1945 as they battle for the island of Iōjima (Iwojima). The fierce attack against the entrenched Japanese force lasted a month and cost the lives of nearly 7,000 American and roughly 20,000 Japanese soldiers.

The most devastating attack in the firebombing campaign against Japanese cities took place on the night of 9–10 March 1945. American B-29 bombers reduced the heart of Tōkyō to ashes; at least 80,000 people were killed, and hundreds of thousands lost their homes.

Armored units like this one were needed in the Okinawa campaign that began on 1 April 1945. Sporadic resistance continued for nearly three months until the Japanese garrison was annihilated. Over 250,000 people died in the campaign, 12,520 of them American soldiers.

Japanese troops respond jubilantly on 16 February 1942 to the news that the British defenders of Singapore surrendered unconditionally the night before. Using bicycles to speed their advance through the Malay Peninsula, the Japanese army had captured Singapore in a mere two months.

Paratroopers in Malaya on 13 February 1942 prepare to launch an airborne assault against an oil refinery in Palembang, Sumatra. For the Japanese military, obtaining a stable supply of oil was a prime objective in the opening phase of the war.

On the Bataan Peninsula, the US forces under General Edward P. King, Jr, surrendered unconditionally on 9 April 1942. Marched 96 kilometers without adequate medical care, food, or water, thousands died. Above, one of King's officers is interrogated on 11 April.

The fight for Saipan (15 June to 9 July 1944) was Japan's last chance to prevent the United States from attaining an air base within striking distance of its cities. Unable to accept defeat, many Japanese on Saipan chose death over surrender. Some of the civilians who survived are shown here.

Evacuating all children between the ages of 8 and 12 to outlying areas became official government policy on 30 June 1944 as Japan's population centers faced the specter of aerial attack and invasion. Children without relatives in the country were housed in groups at temples and inns.

General Douglas MacArthur, who had fled Corregidor before the Japanese advance in 1942, landed at Leyte in the Philippines on 20 October 1944 with an American invasion force of 130,000 men.

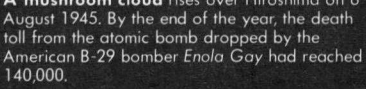

A mushroom cloud rises over Hiroshima on 6 August 1945. By the end of the year, the death toll from the atomic bomb dropped by the American B-29 bomber *Enola Gay* had reached 140,000.

The Japanese heard the imperial proclamation of unconditional surrender by radio on 15 August 1945. The prerecorded speech, broadcast nationwide, shocked the emperor's subjects, for his voice had never been heard in public. The listeners shown here are assembled near the Imperial Palace.

The formal surrender took place on 2 September 1945 aboard the US battleship *Missouri*, which was anchored in Tōkyō Bay. The Japanese and American representatives are shown at the signing of the surrender treaty.

Japanese society during World War II
Schoolchildren board a train at Ueno Station in Tōkyō on 4 August 1944 for evacuation to the countryside. Between February 1944 and November 1945 more than 10 million people sought refuge outside the cities.

ble the Philippines and the empire's inner line of communications. Prime Minister Tōjō resigned. Aware of the need to continue to appease the army, the senior statesmen settled on General KOISO KUNIAKI as his successor. Amid growing restiveness within the government, Japan's leaders and even Emperor SHŌWA (Hirohito) himself spoke of the need for a compromise peace. Japan's growing inclination for peace, however, was blunted by the Allied call for unconditional surrender. The Japanese government also erroneously believed that, in return for concessions, the Soviet Union would assist in negotiating an acceptable end to the war. Sustained by this illusion, Koiso's government determined to fight on.

After the Marianas victory it was even more clear to the Allies that the most direct route to the Japanese heartland lay through the Pacific. British progress in Burma was slow in 1944, and prospects on the China front dimmed as a Japanese counterattack overran US bases in southwest China and as Chiang Kai-shek became less cooperative. Moreover, B-29 bombers could now strike Japan more easily from Saipan than from the Asian mainland. As a result, General Douglas MACARTHUR's assault on the Philippines was accelerated and the Ogasawara and Ryūkyū islands began to look like the next stepping-stones for a final assault against the Japanese home islands.

The Last Assaults—The final phase of the Pacific War began in October 1944 in the Philippines. In the Battle of LEYTE GULF, Japan's southern naval force was virtually destroyed, while its northern force, restrained by caution and confusion, threw away the last Japanese hope for a dramatic sea victory. In January 1945 MacArthur invaded Luzon, recapturing Manila two months later. In February 1945 US marines landed on IŌJIMA (Iwojima), an island in the Ogasawara group halfway between Saipan and Japan proper.

Japan's leaders already realized they could neither win the war nor keep much, if any, of their new empire. They believed, however, that they might preserve national honor by giving ground only at costs so prohibitive that the enemy would settle for something short of unconditional surrender. Japan instituted a new defense for its remaining outlying islands: local commanders would concede the beaches to the enemy, retreat to hills honeycombed with underground emplacements and tunnels, and fight to the last man. Pinned down on the beaches and forced to advance foot by foot, the enemy would pay dearly. Iōjima, where American battle casualties ran as high as 60 to 75 percent, demonstrated the effectiveness of this strategy. A second tactic was the KAMIKAZE SPECIAL ATTACK FORCE, a corps of young pilots trained for suicide missions against enemy ships and used

for the first time in an organized fashion in the battle for Leyte.

The landings on Okinawa in the spring of 1945 heightened the crescendo of violence. In nearly three months of fighting, an American combat force of 172,000 suffered some 50,000 killed and wounded, with thousands more nonbattle casualties. Virtually the entire Japanese defending force of 110,000 perished, together with 150,000 Japanese civilians. *Kamikaze* and conventional air attacks destroyed 30 ships and craft and damaged another 368.

Allied plans called for an invasion of Kyūshū in November 1945, but the Japanese home islands were already being devastated from the air. In mid-March B-29 Superfortress bombers from Saipan and Tinian began massive incendiary raids on Japan's major cities. Perhaps as many as 100,000 died in the first firebombing of Tōkyō. By the end of May most of Yokohama, Nagoya, Ōsaka, and Kōbe had been incinerated, and at least 13 million Japanese were homeless.

The Path to Surrender—Loss of Okinawa led to the resignation of the ineffectual Koiso cabinet and selection of Admiral SUZUKI KANTARŌ as prime minister. Suzuki had the requisite military background and, more important, the emperor trusted his former grand chamberlain to seize any opportunity for peace. With Suzuki as prime minister, Admiral YONAI MITSUMASA as navy minister, and TŌGŌ SHIGENORI as foreign minister, peace advocates formed a significant force, yet they were still severely handicapped, for the army remained determined to fight. Rather than bow to the Anglo-American demand for unconditional surrender, Japan's leaders persisted in the delusion that the Soviet Union would help them negotiate better terms.

Aware of rising Japanese peace sentiment, a number of US officials feared that demanding unconditional surrender would prolong the war, especially if no assurances were given as to the future of the imperial system that the Japanese regarded as central to their way of life. President Harry S. TRUMAN preferred to await the test of an atomic device in July before deciding whether to offer any such assurances, which some American leaders felt might be construed as appeasement. In the end, what was offered was the POTSDAM DECLARATION, issued at the Allied summit held in late July 1945, which repeated the demand that Japan surrender unconditionally or face utter destruction. Nothing was said about the emperor.

The Suzuki cabinet, attempting to avoid the provocation of rejecting the declaration outright, chose to ignore it, which Washington took as contempt. Truman saw no reason to rescind authorization for use of the new atomic weapons. Like most other US officials, he found no moral difference between the ATOMIC BOMB and mass incendiary raids. On 6 August an American B-29 dropped the first atomic device on Hiroshima, obliterating the city and killing or injuring well over 100,000 people. Three days later the United States dropped a second atomic bomb that destroyed Nagasaki.

Shortly before the Nagasaki bomb fell, the Soviet Union declared war on Japan and attacked Manchuria. With the Japanese military adamant against surrender, Lord Keeper of the Privy Seal KIDO KŌICHI, the emperor's chief instrument in maneuvering for peace, turned in desperation to the throne for intervention. At an imperial conference on the night of 9 August, Emperor Shōwa sanc-

tioned acceptance of the Potsdam Declaration with Foreign Minister Tōgō's proviso that the lawful status of the throne be recognized by the victorious Allies. The cabinet complied.

The Allied reply stated that the emperor's authority to rule would be subject to the supreme commander for the Allied powers (SCAP) and that the ultimate form of government in Japan would be determined by the "freely expressed will of the Japanese people." Again, the service chiefs and war minister resisted, and again the emperor intervened. Young army officers attempted to prevent the broadcast of the imperial rescript announcing Japan's surrender, but their coup attempt was quelled and the rescript was transmitted as planned on 15 August. The war was over.

Japan had been continuously at war from 1937 to 1945, longer than any other nation involved in World War II except China. Three million Japanese died in those eight years, fewer deaths than the Soviet Union, Germany, or China suffered, but a high loss in relation to total population. Defeat deprived Japan not only of the fruits of conquest since 1931, but of all the territories, economic interests, and rights it had gained by war and diplomacy since the late 19th century. It also ushered in over six and a half years of OCCUPATION by Allied military forces, the next chapter in Japan's turbulent 20th-century history.   ☎ 1714–1715

World War II, Japanese society during   第二次世界大戦下の日本社会

(Dainiji Sekai Taisen *ka no* Nihon *shakai*). For the Japanese, WORLD WAR II was a total national effort affecting every citizen. The wartime period—which began with the outbreak of the SINO-JAPANESE WAR OF 1937–1945—brought enormous changes to civilian life, yet not even the shock of complete defeat in August 1945 upset the underlying stability of the Japanese social system.

Preparation for War—In October 1937 Prime Minister KONOE FUMIMARO began a three-year NATIONAL SPIRITUAL MOBILIZATION MOVEMENT to prepare the Japanese people for sacrifices. The state sponsored parades and public ceremonies to make citizens more conscious of the war in China. Symbolic economies were encouraged, such as simplified dress and hairstyle and the "rising-sun box lunch" (*hinomaru bentō*), a pickled red plum on a bed of white rice (reproducing the pattern of the national flag [Hinomaru]). Censorship, propaganda, and the state-controlled school system helped spread the spiritual mobilization to every village in the country.

During the first three years of the war, the government created a program to organize people into units to aid the national buildup. Households were obliged to form neighborhood associations (TONARIGUMI) for civil defense, street sweeping, fire fighting, sanitation, and public health—crucial local activities in a time of emergency.

Konoe's "New Order"—Having resigned as prime minister in early 1939, Konoe returned to power from July 1940 until mid-October 1941. He announced his NEW ORDER MOVEMENT in September 1940 to reorganize domestic society more tightly. At the political level parties were absorbed into the new IMPERIAL RULE ASSISTANCE ASSOCIATION, a huge amalgam of civilian organizations. At the local level the New Order Movement completed the drive to build neighborhood associations throughout the country. The

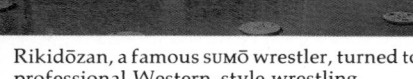

Imperial Rule Assistance Association soon proved to be clumsy and overcentralized in its organization, but it helped to muzzle the state's political opponents. So did the Cabinet Information Bureau, the main agency for media censorship and propaganda.

Full-Scale Mobilization——It was only after Japan plunged into war with the United States and Britain in December 1941 that the cabinet finally began a systematic program to put more people to work in farming and in arms plants. In 1944 the total civilian work force jumped to 33.5 million, including 1.8 million students who were now mobilized for full-time labor. Only 8 percent of male workers were recruited through the NATIONAL SERVICE DRAFT ORDINANCE; nearly all employees were on the job through inducement rather than coercion. The government never legally required married women to take jobs.

The economy of scarcity induced the government to begin food rationing in December 1940. Clothing was allocated by a ticket system. Because of victory gardens, the black market, and resourceful farmers, the food supply was reasonably adequate until the last year of the conflict. Then the American naval blockade, heavy aerial bombardments, and ruinously cold weather during the 1945 spring planting halved the amount of food available. After early 1944 formal school lessons were reduced to an hour or two per day so that older children could work full time. A majority of children were reared (at least temporarily) in fatherless homes because of conscription.

The Ravages of Wartime——During the last eight months of the war, more than 10 million Japanese fled the cities to escape American bombings, which eventually claimed a half-million civilian lives. Already the government had forcibly resettled 350,000 urban schoolchildren in village temples, shrines, and resort hotels.

In eight months US planes dropped 160,000 tons of explosives and incendiaries on 66 Japanese cities. The air raids destroyed nearly a quarter of all Japanese dwellings, in addition to 42 percent of urban industrial zones. The most severe of the fire bombings turned eastern Tōkyō into an inferno on 10 March 1945, killing 100,000 civilians. Only the agony caused by the bombing of Hiro-

shima on 6 August exceeded the disaster in Tōkyō.

War and Society——The simple need to fight for national survival accelerated many prewar changes caused by urbanization: crowding, the steady depopulation of the countryside in spite of temporary evacuation from the cities, the nuclearization of families, and the decline of patriarchy. The economy of scarcity forced women to take jobs in unprecedented numbers; their share of the work force remained permanently higher after the surrender.

The great manufacturing and trading companies substantially increased their wealth and oligopolistic powers during 1937–45. After the surrender they survived OCCUPATION efforts to trim their influence and now rank among the world's most powerful corporations.

Altogether, World War II claimed 3 million Japanese lives and destroyed $26 billion worth of national wealth. It obliterated the Japanese empire, reduced the influence of the military in Japanese society, trimmed the power of large landlords through forced rice-delivery schemes, and cleared the track for the dazzling economic expansion of the 1950s and 1960s. However, the war scarcely touched the underlying structures of Japanese society—particularly the family pattern of small groups. Core values such as teamwork, harmony, loyalty, and competence remained untouched. The greatest change was the permanent transformation of Japanese culture, leading to a revolutionary internationalization of Japanese fashion, taste, arts, and letters in the years after 1945.

wrestling　　　　　　　　　　レスリング

(*resuringu*). Amateur Western-style wrestling was introduced to Japan in 1931 with the founding of a wrestling club at Waseda University. The first national wrestling tournament was held in 1934. From the 1952 (Helsinki) to the 1988 (Seoul) Olympic Games there were 20 Japanese gold medalists in wrestling events. As of 1989, 8,000 wrestlers were registered with the Japan Amateur Wrestling Federation (established in 1932).

Professional Western-style wrestling was introduced to Japan from the United States in 1951. Its popularity increased when

Rikidōzan, a famous SUMŌ wrestler, turned to professional Western-style wrestling.

Wright, Frank Lloyd　　　ライト, F. L.

(1867–1959). American architect. Wright first visited Japan in 1905. He became a knowledgeable collector of woodblock prints and published a short appreciation of the genre in 1912. He designed the old Imperial Hotel in Tōkyō (see IMPERIAL HOTEL, LTD), which was completed in 1922. The facade and front lobby were disassembled and moved to the open-air museum MEIJI MURA in 1967 before the hotel was demolished. Some of Wright's other designs in Japan include the Odawara Hotel (1917), a Ginza movie theater (1918), the Yamamura House (1924), and the school Jiyū Gakuen (1921), the last of which was designed with his pupil Endō Arata (1889–1951).

Wu Peifu (Wu P'ei-fu)　　　呉佩孚

(1874–1939; J: Go Haifu). Important warlord in North China during the "warlord period" (1916–28) who was sought by the Japanese military in the 1930s to head a puppet government in China. Wu had first become known to the Japanese military in 1903. He was later decorated by the Japanese for reconnaissance missions made in Korea and Manchuria during the RUSSO-JAPANESE WAR (1904–05).

In 1935 the Japanese GUANDONG (KWANTUNG) ARMY stationed in Manchuria wanted to establish a separate, Japanese-controlled state in North China. Colonel DOIHARA KENJI tried to persuade Wu to head it, but he refused. When the Chinese communists and the Guomindang (Kuomintang; KMT; Nationalist Party) agreed to join together after the XI'AN (SIAN) INCIDENT (December 1936), Wu, who feared growing communist influence in China, looked more favorably on cooperation with Japan. He was again approached in 1938 to head a new government that would replace the PROVISIONAL GOVERNMENT OF THE REPUBLIC OF CHINA in Beiping (Peiping; now Beijing [Peking]) and the REFORM GOVERNMENT OF THE REPUBLIC OF CHINA in Nanjing (Nanking) but demanded more control of the proposed regime than the Japanese were willing to allow.

Frank Lloyd Wright
The well-known American architect had a long-standing interest in and association with Japan.
1 A ballroom in the original Imperial Hotel, which was designed by Wright.
2 The main entrance of the original hotel as relocated to the open-air museum Meiji Mura in Inuyama, Aichi Prefecture. It was moved here in 1967 before the hotel was demolished.

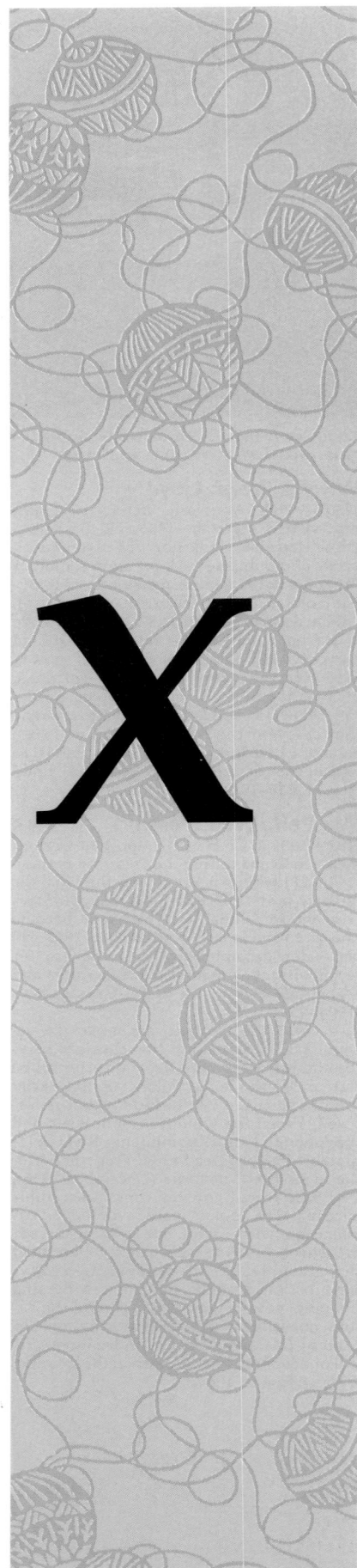

X

Xavier, Francis   ザビエル, F.

(1506–52). Anglicized form of the Spanish name Francisco de Javier. He introduced Christianity to Japan and set up the first Christian mission in the country. Born in northern (Basque) Spain in 1506, he studied at the University of Paris and was a founding member of the Society of Jesus (see JESUITS). Appointed apostolic delegate for Asia, he left Europe in 1541 and labored in India and Malacca. In 1547 he met in Malacca a Japanese fugitive named Anjirō, whose glowing account of his native country fired Xavier with enthusiasm to evangelize Japan. Xavier reached Kagoshima with two Jesuit companions on 15 August 1549, and with Anjirō as his less-than-adequate interpreter, he preached Christianity and compiled a simple catechism, with the result that about 100 people accepted baptism. A year after his arrival Xavier visited Hirado and Yamaguchi, but wishing to obtain permission to preach throughout Japan, he made his way to Kyōto in an unsuccessful bid to meet Emperor Go-Nara (r 1526–57). He left Japan for India at the end of 1551. His ultimate purpose was to evangelize the Chinese, but he died en route to China on 3 December 1552.

Xi'an (Sian) Incident   西安事件

(Seian Jiken). The arrest of CHIANG KAI-SHEK by one of his army commanders on 12 December 1936, resulting in a united Chinese resistance to Japanese aggression. Chiang believed that the domestic communist opposition had to be suppressed before China could actively resist Japanese encroachment. The largest contingent in the forces sent to eradicate the communists' base area in Yan'an (Yenan) in northwest China was the Manchurian army under ZHANG XUELIANG (Chang Hsüeh-liang). Having been driven from Manchuria by the Japanese in 1931, this army was sympathetic to communist proposals to end the civil war and unite against Japan.

On 3 December 1936 Chiang Kai-shek flew to Zhang's headquarters in Xi'an to urge more active fighting against the communists. Early on 12 December he was arrested by Zhang, who presented him with eight demands, including termination of the civil war. On 14 December Zhang and the communist armies announced the formation of a united anti-Japanese command. On 15 December a communist delegation led by ZHOU ENLAI (Chou En-lai) arrived in Xi'an, and Zhou helped to arrange a compromise settlement. Chiang apparently accepted Zhang's demands in principle while refusing to put his agreement on paper. On 25 December Chiang was released and flew back to Nanjing (Nanking) with Zhang, who had surrendered to him for punishment. The new policy of resistance led to the formation of the SECOND UNITED FRONT in 1937.

Xinmin Hui (Hsin-min Hui)   新民会

(Shimminkai; New People's Society). Organization launched by the Japanese army occupying North China in December 1937. It acted as the propaganda arm of the Japanese-sponsored PROVISIONAL GOVERNMENT OF THE REPUBLIC OF CHINA and sought to spread Japanese ideas to the Chinese through schools, libraries, newspapers, radio, cinema, and other media.

Y

Yabakei　耶馬渓

Gorge on the upper and middle reaches of the river YAMAKUNIGAWA, northwestern Ōita Prefecture, Kyūshū. Noted for strangely shaped rocks and peaks, narrow ravines, dense forests, and blue meandering streams. Part of Yaba-Hita-Hikosan Quasi-National Park. AONODŌMON, a tunnel through a large rock; the temple Rakanji; and hot springs are nearby.

Yabe Hisakatsu　矢部長克

(1878–1969). Geologist and paleontologist noted for his studies on the geological formation of the Japanese islands. He showed that the Japanese islands were separated from the Asian mainland during the Pleistocene epoch about 1 million years ago. Born in Tōkyō, he graduated from Tōkyō University and taught at Tōhoku University from 1911 to 1939. He received the Order of Culture in 1953.

yabukōji　薮柑子

Ardisia japonica. An evergreen shrub of the family Myrsinaceae that grows thickly on hills and in woods throughout Japan. It is often used as a ground cover in gardens. It propagates itself by means of a subterranean stem that produces a stalk (10–20 cm [4–8 in] high) tipped with whorls of alternate, glossy, oblong leaves. In the summer, inflorescences bear two to five small, white, hanging blossoms. *Yabukōji* is prized for its evergreen foliage and bright red berries and has customarily been used as a decoration at New Year's and wedding festivities. Many cultivated varieties have been developed, and it is cherished as a BONSAI plant. Its berries are used in traditional folk medicine as a detoxicant and diuretic. Similar species, such as *karatachibana* (*A. crispa*) and *manryō* (*A. crenata*), are also very popular.

yabusame　流鏑馬

(mounted archery). A warrior's form of prayer or religious exercise performed in shrine precincts by mounted archers who shoot at three stationary targets while riding at a full gallop. It is said that *yabusame* was first practiced by order of Emperor Kimmei (509–571; r 531 or 539 to 571) at the Usa Hachiman Shrine, Kyūshū, to pray for peace and abundant harvests. The first recorded instance is the *yabusame* performed in 1096 for retired emperor SHIRAKAWA.

There are four parts to a *yabusame* ceremony. First, the group leader, mounted on his horse, points a drawn bow and arrow at the sky and at the ground to symbolize eternal peace between heaven and earth. Next, all riders take turns shooting at three targets (60-cm [2 ft] square) having five rings of different colors. These targets are mounted about 63 meters (207 ft) apart in a straight line 2 meters (6.5 ft) from the track along which the horses gallop. Third, riders who hit all three targets are allowed to shoot at three clay bull's-eyes (about 9 cm [3.5 in] diameter). Finally, targets are presented to the leaders for inspection. In recent times *yabusame* has been performed annually at the TSURUGAOKA HACHIMAN SHRINE in Kamakura on 16 September and at MEIJI SHRINE in Tōkyō on 3 November.

Yabuta Teijirō　藪田貞治郎

(1888–1977). Chemist. Born in Shiga Prefecture; graduate of and professor at Tōkyō University. In 1938 he succeeded in isolating a crystalline substance, gibberellin, from cultured *Gibberella fujikuroi*, a rice blight fungus of the class Ascomycetes. This gibberellin, which accelerates the growth rate of young rice plants, was later proven to be a plant hormone. Yabuta also determined the chemical structure of kojic acid, which is a metabolic product of *Aspergillus oryzae*, the fermenting agent in malted rice. A member of the Japan Academy, Yabuta received the academy prize in 1943 and was awarded the Order of Culture in 1964.

Yachiyo　八千代[市]

City in northwestern Chiba Prefecture, central Honshū. Since World War II it has become a residential suburb of Tōkyō. Manufactures include machinery and metal products. Pop: 148,615.

Yaeyama Islands　八重山諸島

(Yaeyama Shotō). Group of islands southwest of the MIYAKO ISLANDS, southwestern Okinawa Prefecture. Part of Okinawa Prefecture. Forming the western half of the SAKISHIMA ISLANDS, the Yaeyama Islands include the two main islands of ISHIGAKIJIMA and IRIOMOTEJIMA, as well as TAKETOMIJIMA and YONAGUNIJIMA. Subtropical plants and mangroves flourish. The principal agricultural products are pineapples and sugarcane. The islands are noted for the production of traditional textiles (see OKINAWAN TEXTILES). Area: 584 sq km (225 sq mi).

Yagi Hidetsugu　八木秀次

(1886–1976). Electrical engineer. Noted for his pioneering research in shortwave and microwave signal propagation with Uda Shintarō (1896–1976), a junior colleague. Their efforts led to the development of the Yagi-Uda antenna, the basic antenna configuration used in the majority of today's outdoor television and radio antennas. Born in Ōsaka Prefecture, he graduated from Tōkyō University in 1909. In 1919 he became professor at Tōhoku University. He also served as president of Ōsaka University and Tōkyō Institute of Technology and received the Order of Culture in 1956.

Yagi Jūkichi　八木重吉

(1898–1927). Poet. Born in Tōkyō; graduate of Tōkyō Higher Normal School (later Tōkyō University of Education). In 1925 he published his first collection of poems, *Aki no hitomi.* He was a Nonchurch Christian (see MUKYŌKAI), and his verse is considered the best example of Christian poetry in Japan. He wrote poems in a simple, quiet style, independent of any particular poetry group. Yagi died of tuberculosis at age 29. His principal collections of poems are *Mazushiki shinto* (1928) and *Yagi Jūkichi shishū* (1942).

Yagisawa Dam　矢木沢ダム

(Yagisawa Damu). Dam located on the upper reaches of the river TONEGAWA in northern Gumma Prefecture, central Honshū. This arch dam, which created Lake Oku Tone,

yabusame After the Kamakura period, the emphasis in mounted archery shifted from its martial aspects to religious ritual. This performance of *yabusame* is at the Meiji Shrine in Tōkyō.

yabukōji The berries of this evergreen shrub appear in the fall, grow to about 5 mm in diameter, and turn bright red by midwinter.

Yagi Hidetsugu This electrical engineer was a developer of the configuration used today for most outdoor radio and TV antennas.

yakitori Skewers of vegetables like those shown are often served together with yakitori proper. From left, shiitake mushrooms, chicken, Welsh onions, chicken meatballs, chicken skin, shishitō (a type of green pepper), and chicken livers being grilled over a charcoal fire.

Yajima Kajiko Founder of the temperance society Kyōfūkai, Yajima was principal of the Christian girls' school Joshi Gakuin from 1889 to 1914.

yakiimo These baked sweet potatoes are sold as a snack by street vendors.

was completed in 1967 and is an important water source for Tōkyō. Height: 131 m (430 ft); storage capacity: 175.8 million cu m (6.2 billion cu ft).

yagō   屋号

(house name; also called *iena* or *kadona*). Identifying name, other than the family name, applied to a family residence or family line. In the former case *yagō* belonged to the house itself and was usually assumed by new inhabitants when the house changed hands, but in the latter case the name was retained by the family line even after the family moved. Although it is not known when the custom first developed, mention of *yagō* appears in Muromachi-period (1333–1568) chronicles. *Yagō* were often used in villages, where many people had the same family name, to distinguish lineages with higher status. Some *yagō* were derived from the locations of houses or from the relationship of main and junior lines (see HONKE AND BUNKE). Others were derived from family occupations, standing in the community, or the provinces from which families originated. During the Edo period (1600–1868) it became customary for KABUKI families to assume *yagō*. The renowned actor ICHIKAWA DANJŪRŌ, for example, was known as Naritaya. Today *yagō* frequently serve as names for Japanese businesses, especially retail stores.

Yagyū   柳生

District in the northeastern part of the city of Nara, Nara Prefecture, central Honshū. To alleviate Nara's water shortage, a reservoir has been built in Yagyū. The district is the home of the Yagyū family, which founded the Yagyū school of *kendō* (Japanese fencing).

Yagyū Munenori   柳生宗矩

(1571–1646). Master swordsman of the early Edo period (1600–1868). Born in Yagyūnoshō (now part of the city of Nara), he learned fencing from his father, Yagyū Muneyoshi (1527–1606), founder of the Yagyū or Shinkage school of swordsmanship. In the service of TOKUGAWA IEYASU, Munenori distinguished himself in the Battle of SEKIGAHARA (1600) and the sieges of Ōsaka Castle (1614 and 1615; see ŌSAKA CASTLE, SIEGES OF), winning the favor of the Tokugawa family. He was designated fencing instructor to the shōguns TOKUGAWA HIDETADA and TOKUGAWA IEMITSU. In 1632 he was appointed inspector general (ŌMETSUKE), charged with surveillance of *daimyō*. His descendants served as fencing instructors to the shogunal family throughout the Edo period.

Yahagigawa   矢作川

River in central Aichi Prefecture, central Honshū, originating in the mountain on the border of Nagano and Gifu prefectures, and flowing through Okazaki Plain to empty into Mikawa Bay at the city of Nishio. The

Yahagi Dam is located on the upper reaches. The water is utilized for irrigation, industry, and drinking. Length: 117 km (73 mi); area of drainage basin: 1,830 sq km (706 sq mi).

Yahata → Yawata

Yahikoyama   弥彦山

Also called Yahikosan. Mountain in central Niigata Prefecture, central Honshū, near the Sea of Japan coast. In its eastern foothills is Yahiko Shrine and a flourishing shrine town. The summit commands a panoramic view of the Sea of Japan, Sado Island, and the Niigata Plain. Height: 638 m (2,093 ft).

Yaita   矢板〔市〕

City in northern Tochigi Prefecture, central Honshū. Formerly a farming and lumbering city, it has become industrialized. Manufactures include electrical appliances, textiles, steel, and toys. Pop: 35,603.

Yaizu   焼津〔市〕

City in central Shizuoka Prefecture, central Honshū. Located on Suruga Bay, it has long been an important fishing port with a thriving seafood-processing industry. Yaizu Shrine is dedicated to the legendary hero, Prince YAMATOTAKERU. Pop: 112,186.

Yajima Kajiko   矢島楫子

(1833–1925). Educator and Christian activist. Born in Higo Province (now Kumamoto Prefecture). Studied at the Kyōin Denshūjo, a school for teachers. In 1878 she became a teacher at the Christian girls' school Shinsakae Jogakkō; in 1880 she became principal of the Sakurai Jogakkō. From 1889 to 1914 she served as head of the Joshi Gakuin (Women's Academy), which resulted from a merger of the two schools.

Baptized in 1879, in 1886 Kajiko founded the KYŌFŪKAI (Japan Woman's Christian Temperance Union). As its director for almost 35 years, she campaigned for women's rights, the abolition of licensed prostitution, and the temperance movement.

Yakai Incident   八海事件

(Yakai Jiken). One of Japan's most protracted and controversial court cases. It involved the legality of relying solely on the confession of one suspect and the possible use of police coercion. In 1951 an aged couple living in the Yakai district of the village of Ogō (now the town of Tabuse), Yamaguchi Prefecture, were robbed and murdered in their home. The police apprehended Yoshioka Akira, and as a result of his confession four other men were charged as his accomplices. Yoshioka was sentenced to life imprisonment, but the four others continued to appeal until, in October 1968, they were declared innocent by the Supreme Court. The case became the subject of IMAI TADASHI's film MAHIRU NO ANKOKU (1956, Darkness at Noon).

Yakedake   焼岳

Volcano on the border of Nagano and Gifu prefectures, central Honshū; the only active volcano in the Hida Mountains. An eruption in 1915 dammed the river Azusagawa, creating Taishō Pond. The volcano last erupted in 1963. It is part of Chūbu Sangaku National Park. Height: 2,455 m (8,054 ft).

yakiimo   焼き芋

Sweet potatoes (*satsumaimo*) that are baked in the skin and eaten as a snack. In autumn and winter vendors sell sweet potatoes cooked among heated stones from small trucks or hand-pulled carts. Passing from

neighborhood to neighborhood, the vendors call out *"ishi yakiimo"* (stone-baked potatoes) to draw customers.

yakitori   焼き鳥

Bite-sized pieces of chicken meat, giblets, or skin that are basted with a sweet soy-based sauce (*tare*) or sprinkled with salt and grilled on bamboo skewers over an open fire. Many small drinking establishments serve *yakitori* as their house specialty. It is also sold at street stalls.

yakko   奴

1. Before the Nara period (710–794) *yakko* referred to slaves, particularly male slaves. Under the RITSURYŌ SYSTEM, established in the 7th century, *yakko* became the lowest social stratum—public and private slaves (NUHI). The status of *nuhi* was officially abolished in the early 10th century, but in succeeding centuries the terms *yakko* and *nuhi* continued to refer to bond servants of wealthy families.

2. During the Edo period (1600–1868) servants attached to *daimyō* or *hatamoto* (direct shogunal vassal) houses were often called *yakko*. They formed bands (*kumi*) and were feared as rowdies. In imitation of these HATAMOTO YAKKO, the town rowdies without feudal affiliation referred to themselves as MACHI YAKKO.

3. In the Edo period *yakko* also referred to women forced into slavery as a form of punishment. Slavery was imposed on women who illegally bypassed barriers (SEKISHO) on the highways and on the wives and daughters of men condemned to exile or death.

yakubyōgami   疫病神

Also called *ekibyōgami, ekijin,* and *eyami no kami*. God believed to cause epidemics and plagues. Since the Heian period (794–1185) observances called *goryōe* were conducted to enshrine and pacify vengeful spirits (GORYŌ) believed responsible for plagues and other disasters. During the medieval period (mid-12th–16th centuries) the god of plagues was frequently personified, appearing as a white-haired old man in red robes or as an old woman with a monstrous visage. To keep this god away, protective talismans (GOFU) or dolls with frightening faces were placed at the entrance of houses. In some regions the *yakubyōgami* is placated by being invited at New Year's to lodge for a night in the household.

yakudoshi   厄年

(critical or unlucky years). According to Japanese folk belief, those ages when an individual is most likely to experience calamities or misfortunes. Although there are local and historical variations, according to the OMMYŌDŌ school of divination the ages 25 and 42 for men and 19 and 33 for women are deemed critical years. Of these, age 42 for men and 33 for women are considered especially critical. It is customary in these unlucky years to visit temples and shrines. The 61st and 70th years of life are also deemed *yakudoshi* for both men and women, but their observance is accompanied by celebration of longevity as well. See also SHICHIGO-SAN; KANREKI; KOKI; LIFE CYCLE.

Yakult Honsha Co, Ltd

〔株〕ヤクルト本社

(Yakuruto Honsha). Maker of Yakult, a well-known drink based on lactic acid milk; also manufactures other dairy products, foods, cosmetics, and pharmaceuticals. Incorporated in 1955, it is noted for its door-to-door sales system. It has overseas offices in Taiwan, Brazil, Hong Kong, Thailand, Korea, the Philippines, Singapore, and Mexico. Sales for the fiscal year ending March 1991 totaled ¥140.1 billion (US $1.0 billion). The company was capitalized at ¥30.6 billion (US $223.0 million) in the same year. Headquarters are in Tōkyō.

yakumi→herbs and spices

Yakumo mishō   八雲御抄

Treatise on Japanese classical (WAKA) poetry by Emperor JUNTOKU (1197–1242, r 1210–21). The work was completed during his exile to the island of Sado after the JŌKYŪ DISTURBANCE (1221). It is the first systematic study of *waka* history and techniques up to the end of the Heian period (794–1185). It discusses poetic style, rhetorical devices, subject matter, and vocabulary.

yakusa no kabane   八色の姓

A status system under which eight (*yakusa*) honorary cognomens (KABANE) were granted to certain families; instituted by the emperor TEMMU in 684 to strengthen imperial authority after the JINSHIN DISTURBANCE (672). The cognomens were *mahito, ason (asomi), sukune, imiki, michinoshi, omi, muraji,* and *inagi* (or *inaki*). *Mahito* and *ason* were granted to close relatives of the imperial family and *sukune* and *imiki* to members of other illustrious lineages; the other ranks were generally given to lesser officials. The cognomens were appended to the family names, as in Kibi no Ason Makibi. See UJI-KABANE SYSTEM.

Yakushidake   薬師岳

Mountain in the Hida Mountains, southeastern Toyama Prefecture, central Honshū. The summit, composed of quartz porphyry, forms a plateau. The mountain has been a center of worship since ancient days; on the summit is the temple Yakushidō. The mountain is rich in alpine flora. Height: 2,926 m (9,600 ft).

Yakushiji   薬師寺

One of the two head temples of the HOSSŌ SECT of Buddhism located in Nishinokyō, a western suburb of the city of Nara. Yakushiji was first built in the Asuka district on a site now located in the city of Kashihara in Nara Prefecture. When the capital was established at Nara, Yakushiji was rebuilt on its present site mostly during the 720s. The original Yakushiji in the Asuka district (now designated Moto Yakushiji) remained standing until the Heian period (794–1185). The Nara buildings perished but were rebuilt in later centuries. The temple was dedicated to the Buddha Yakushi (Skt: Bhaiṣajyaguru; the Buddha of healing).

The construction of Yakushiji derives from a vow of Emperor TEMMU in 680 to make an image of Yakushi to bring about the recovery of his ailing consort. She survived even though work did not actually begin until 687. After the death of the emperor in 686, his wife (who succeeded him as Empress JITŌ) carried out the work on the temple and the image. The latter was completed in 697.

The architects chose a plan that focused on the *kondō* (main hall). Although most early temple layouts in Japan emphasized a single, central pagoda, the architects opted for a Korean plan, which drew attention to the *kondō* by moving it into the center of the courtyard and flanking it with twin pagodas.

The West Pagoda was destroyed during the civil war of 1528–31 and was rebuilt in 1981. Other buildings were restored and rebuilt in styles ranging from those of the Kamakura period (1185–1333) to those of the Edo period (1600–1868). Only the East Pagoda, completed in Nara in 730, escaped the calamities that struck the temple over the years.

The Buddha Yakushi seated on a pedestal is installed inside the *kondō* on a white marble platform. He is flanked by standing figures of Nikkō (Skt: Sūryaprabha) and Gakkō (Skt: Candraprabha), the bodhisattvas of the sun and the moon respectively.

Southeast of the main compound is the Tōindō (East Hall), originally built in the early 720s. The present structure, dating from 1285, is in the native *wayō* style of architecture. Outstanding among the images it preserves is the stately Shō Kannon (Skt: Ārya Avalokiteśvara), the main deity worshiped at the Tōindō, now contained in a black tabernacle. The BUSSOKUSEKI, a stone monument carved in 753 that depicts the Buddha's footprints, is preserved at Yakushiji. Behind it stands a stele with 21 verses in praise of the footprints.

The monk Eishō had a shrine dedicated to HACHIMAN built between the years 889 and 897 on the grounds of the Yakushiji. The present shrine, dating from the Edo period, contains statues of Hachiman dressed as a Buddhist monk, the goddess Nakatsuhime, and Empress JINGŪ.

Yakushima   屋久島

Island 60 km (37 mi) south of the Ōsumi Peninsula, Kagoshima Prefecture, southern Kyūshū; part of Kagoshima Prefecture. It is a mountainous island; MIYANOURADAKE (1,935 m; 6,348 ft), in the central part of the island, is the highest peak in the Kyūshū region. Yakushima has the heaviest precipitation in Japan, with an annual rainfall of 4,000 mm (160 in) in the coastal regions and 10,000 mm (390 in) on the mountaintops. The climate is warm. Forestry is an important industry, and the Japanese cedar (*yakusugi*) grown here is especially valued. Agricultural products are sugarcane, sweet potatoes, and *ponkan* oranges (*Citrus reticulata*). The chief marine product is flying fish. One-third of the island forms the principal part of the Kirishima-Yaku National Park. Area: 500 sq km (193 sq mi).

yakuza   やくざ

(gangster, gambler, good-for-nothing). At present, *yakuza* almost always refers to those who participate in any form of organized crime, i.e., gangsters. In Japan gangster organizations have traditionally operated on the system of social or economic support known as OYABUN-KOBUN. Like their criminal counterparts around the world, Japanese gangsters attempt to dignify their cruel trade with elaborate codes of honor and behavior. In Japan these codes are a pastiche of the Neo-Confucian-based Tokugawa ethics (see GIRI AND NINJŌ; JINGI) and the *samurai* or warrior code (see BUSHIDŌ). The word *yakuza* is taken from a gambling game called "three-card" (*sammai karuta*), which became popular during the Tokugawa shogunate (1603–1867). *Yakuza* (literally, "8, 9, 3") is a losing hand in the game, which resembles blackjack or 21, in that the goal is to reach but not exceed 19. Gangsters adopted this apparently derogatory term with the bravado of the outsider who scorns conventional society and its ideas of success. Ac-

cording to a National Police Agency survey made in 1990, there are 88,259 members of 3,305 gangs in Japan. Of the 34,599 arrests involving organized crime in 1990, the major offenses involved stimulant drugs, infliction of bodily injury, blackmail, and gambling.
▶▶*1722–1723*

Yalta Conference   ヤルタ会談

(Yaruta Kaidan). Conference of the leaders of the Allied powers, held at Yalta in the Crimea on 4–11 February 1945, attended by Prime Minister Winston Churchill of the United Kingdom, President Franklin Roosevelt of the United States, and Premier Joseph Stalin of the Soviet Union. The major objective of the conference was to deal with the issues of the surrender and occupation of Germany and postwar European security. The summit was also important in determining Allied policy in the war against Japan, particularly plans for the Soviet entrance into the Pacific War after the defeat of Germany, and the political future of Japan's Asian empire after the war.

The United States promised the Soviet Union the Kurils and southern Sakhalin (and the adjacent islands), which were considered important by the Soviets for the security of the region north of Vladivostok. The United States and the Soviet Union also agreed to a Soviet lease of Port Arthur (Ch: Lüshun) and the internationalization of Dalian (Ta-lien; J:

Continued on page 1724▶

Yakushiji
1 The East Pagoda (right), West Pagoda (center), and main hall (left) of the temple Yakushiji, which was built on its present site in the 720s. Only the East Pagoda, a National Treasure, survives from the 8th century.
2 The temple's main image, of Yakushi Nyorai (the Buddha of healing), is shown here surrounded by paper flowers during the Shunie Hanaeshiki, an annual spring celebration. Early 8th century. National Treasure.

The *yakuza*, Japan's 250-year-old mafia, are quite unlike any organized crime groups in the West. Gang members sport business cards and operate offices with their gang insignia proudly displayed. Gang bosses hold press conferences and publish their own magazines. Gang members mark themselves for life with fantastic tattoos that stretch the length of their bodies from neck to calf. It is a politicized world as well—criminal gangs adhere to a right-wing agenda that calls on fellow Japanese to rearm the nation and worship the emperor.

Descended from medieval bands of gamblers and peddlers, the yakuza see themselves as latter-day *samurai*, the keepers of an ancient tradition of warriors and honorable outlaws. "The yakuza are trying to pursue the road of chivalry and patriotism," explained Inagawa Kakuji, the longtime boss of the Inagawa Kai, an 8,000-man criminal cartel spanning 24 of Japan's 47 prefectures. "That's our biggest difference with the Mafia in America; it's our sense of *giri* (obligation) and *ninjō* (chivalry)."

The 78-year-old Inagawa is regarded as the most esteemed "godfather" in all Japan, as peacemaker and power broker to gangs from Hokkaidō to Okinawa. Since founding the Inagawa Kai in 1945, he has built his organization into a sophisticated crime syndicate. But Inagawa is no longer the fighter he once was. In his later years, the aging patriarch has seen himself more as a reformer within the yakuza, hoping to change some of Japan's notorious gangland traditions.

Among them is *yubitsume*, the rite of finger-cutting, which is performed as punishment for an act against the group. With a swift, single stroke, a penitent gang member amputates the top of his little finger at the first joint, wraps the severed digit in cloth and solemnly presents it to the boss. Some repeat offenders have lost two finger segments or more. While viewed with high regard by the gangs, such practices have left a generation of disfigured yakuza. Up to half the members of some gangs have been affected.

After decreeing that *yubitsume* must stop within the Inagawa Kai, Inagawa was soon confronted with the problem of enforcing his new edict. Following a transgression of gang law, one of Inagawa's trusted lieutenants had ordered a lowly soldier in the organization to sever his finger as punishment. On hearing this, Inagawa was outraged. The godfather summoned his lieutenant and berated him before other gang members. The gangster, humiliated and ashamed, responded in the only way he knew how—he cut off his fingertip and presented it to Inagawa.

Inagawa points to the story with a certain pride, for it illustrates both the loyalty and adherence to tradition that permeate the Japanese underworld.

| **Yakuza, Inc** | On the Sunday closest to the fifth day of every month, an executive board of the Yamaguchi-Gumi, Japan's largest crime syndicate, meets at their headquarters in Kōbe, the port city where the gang began in 1915. The 12 bosses in attendance represent the 23,000 gangsters of the Yamaguchi organization. In some ways, their meetings are similar to those that take place every day at ordinary Japanese companies—there is talk of mergers, acquisitions, and investments. Later, the 12 men are joined by 92 "direct bosses" or their proxies, representing Yamaguchi gangs from across Japan.

Yamanouchi Yukio, an attorney for the syndicate, tried to put the Yamaguchi-Gumi in perspective for a Western reporter. "If you were to look at the Yamaguchi-Gumi as a company," he explained, "it would be one of the biggest in the nation, with more than 20,000 employees and branches all over the country. When their boss gives an order, it is obeyed."

Police estimate the syndicate's annual income to be well over ¥270 billion (US $2 billion). Its top 104 bosses reportedly pay a monthly membership fee of about ¥1 million ($8,000) each to cover the gang's basic operating costs. The Yamaguchi-Gumi has even published its own magazine, complete with poetry written by gang members, articles on legal advice and expanding one's territory, and announcements of weddings, funerals, and prison releases.

The Yamaguchi-Gumi is the largest of some 3,300 organized crime groups in Japan. The National Police Agency counts some 88,000 yakuza members in all, with a combined annual income of ¥1.4 trillion (about $10 billion). Independent observers believe these figures to be quite conservative, but the numbers are striking nonetheless. (By comparison, the US Department of Justice estimates there to be fewer than 20,000 members and associates of the Mafia in America.)

Yakuza membership is actually down from a peak in 1963, when police counted 184,000 members nationwide. Officials warn, however, that the size of the larger gangs has been increasing. Today, a handful of super-syndicates now dominate the under-

Yakuza: The Japanese Mafia

With Japan's ascent to the status of economic superpower, the yakuza, too, have grown rich and globally minded.

world, and they are the most effective in Japanese history. "Ultimately, the yakuza will become like the Mafia in the US," predicted godfather Inagawa. "In the future, there will be one national mob. The bigger firms, like my organization, will take over. You can see the move towards a more corporate structure."

Yakuza bosses like Inagawa boast a work force that other corporate chiefs could well envy. Bound together in a feudalistic system of *oyabun-kobun* (parent-child) relationships, gang leaders enjoy extraordinary levels of loyalty from their subordinates. According to one popular adage, "If the boss says a passing crow is white, you must agree."

The yakuza have proven to be as enterprising as they are loyal. Like organized crime outfits in the West, the gangs have thrived by offering Japanese society that which is forbidden—drugs, gambling, prostitution, and pornography. Also strong in the yakuza portfolio are loan sharking, debt collection, and "mediation" of disputes. And, like the mob in America, the yakuza control sizable chunks of construction and entertainment industries, including movie studios, nightclubs, and professional sports.

Yakuza front companies have made bids on subway and airport construction projects, have rigged baseball games and horse races, and have seized control of hospitals and amusement halls. They have invested in real estate, trucking, waste disposal, security services, and counterfeiting.

Recent scandals involving Japan's top securities firms, banks, and other corporations reveal substantial penetration by the yakuza into legitimate business. Yakuza front companies have reportedly gained access to more than ¥286 billion ($2.3 billion) in loans and loan guarantees and have used that money to invest in stocks, real estate, and various projects overseas. Given the high profile of the yakuza in Japan, it seems unlikely that their backers, including the Nikkō and Nomura securities companies, did not know with whom they were dealing.

The gangs have reached deeply into politics as well. For years they have acted as fund-raisers, canvassers, and hired muscle, typically for conservative members of Japan's ruling Liberal Democratic Party. They have been used to break up strikes, disrupt antipollution protests, and silence political dissenters. Some power brokers of Japanese politics, like Kodama Yoshio and, more recently, Kanemaru Shin, have relied on gangland support, thus extending the influence of the yakuza to the highest levels of government.

The emphasis on saving face in Japan can allow crimes of extortion to go largely unchecked. Most striking are the activities of *sōkaiya* ("professional stockholders"), a brazen class of corporate racketeers who try to control annual shareholders' meetings. "The stockholders' meeting is a solemn function," one *sōkaiya* told the newspaper *Yomiuri shimbun*. "We help it proceed smoothly and protect the interests of the innocent shareholders. We are the prop men of modern capitalism." So smoothly do the meetings proceed that some last only a few minutes.

The biggest money-maker for the gangs is drugs, especially methamphetamine. Known as "*shabu*," this powerful stimulant has long been the drug of choice in Japan. Since the mid-1970s, methamphetamine use has boomed, prompting one Tōkyō drug abuse expert to call Japan "the meth capital of the world."

While international attention has focused on the heroin traffic from southern Asia and the cocaine traffic from Latin America, a vast network of suppliers and smugglers has emerged in East Asia to provide Japan with methamphetamine. This illicit drug trade, originating primarily in Taiwan and South Korea, dumps billions of dollars worth of meth onto Japan's streets each year. Estimates of the number of Japanese users of the drug typically run at 500,000, putting it about even with the number of heroin users in the United States.

| **Patriotic Gangsters** | Despite their apparent similarities with organized crime groups in the West, the yakuza differ fundamentally in two respects. First, the Japanese mob has traditionally been tolerated to an extent that is unparalleled in most nations. Second, the gangs tend to be extraordinarily politicized.

The yakuza share in an unsavory tradition of ultranationalism in Japan. Bound by similar beliefs and practices, ultranationalist groups and yakuza gangs have grown so intertwined that it often becomes difficult to tell them apart. During the 1920s and 1930s, political yakuza played a key role in the rise of militarism and Japan's subsequent entry into World War II.

As in Europe, crime syndicates in Japan were devastated by the war, but postwar black markets paved the road to their recovery. With the increase in Cold War tensions, gangs received a boost from the American leaders of the Occupation forces, who found them useful in stopping the growth of the Communist Party and a militant labor movement.

The highly politicized nature of the underworld has led to several remarkable events in postwar Japan. As the Occupation drew to a close in 1952, Justice Minister Kimura Tokutarō attempted to recruit a 200,000-man force of yakuza to take on the Left. Kimura planned to bring this group, called the Aikoku Hankyō Battōtai, or Patriotic Anti-Communist Drawn Sword Regiment, under the direct auspices of the government—but the measure was vetoed by an alarmed Prime Minister Yoshida Shigeru.

A similar event occurred eight years later, amid heated demonstrations over the United States–Japan Security Treaty. As President Dwight D. Eisenhower prepared to visit Japan, Prime Minister Kishi Nobusuke's government, unsure that protests could be contained, turned to the underworld for help. The final plan called for deploying 28,000 yakuza and rightists, backed by government helicopters, cars and trucks, command posts, and first-aid units. The yakuza, though, never got the call. Fearing the worst, Japanese authorities decided to withdraw the invitation to Eisenhower.

Today, yakuza gangs still commonly belong to rightist organizations on the fringes of Japanese politics. Many are involved in paramilitary training. Others spend their time driving noisy sound trucks through Japanese cities, calling for a rearmed and more assertive military, reverence toward the emperor, and return of the islands north of Japan by the Russians. If Japan were to plunge into militarism once more, the role of the underworld could prove formidable yet again.

The Mob's Image

Despite the violent, exploitive nature of the yakuza, their subculture has become a popular subject for Japanese novels, plays, movies, magazines, and comic books. The yakuza have thrived on the image of the gangster as honorable outlaw, a tragic yet dedicated fellow who follows the criminal path because he has no other choice. The gangs envision themselves as preservers of noble traditions that have faded in modern Japan. Among yakuza leaders, considerable attention is paid to tracing these traditions—along with their gangs' imagined lineage—to legendary gangsters of centuries past, such as Banzuiin Chōbei and Jirochō of Shimizu.

Police have taken to calling the yakuza *bōryokudan* ("violence groups") in an attempt to dispel the romantic image of the mob. But relations between authorities and the gangs often resemble a *kabuki* play in which the characters follow carefully prescribed roles. Like other groups in Japan's group-centered society, the yakuza occupy a well-defined and accepted niche within their culture. As a result, few attempts have been made to strike seriously at the gangs.

Along with their provision of gambling, prostitution, and other services, the gangs are perhaps Japan's leading equal opportunity employer. Few other organizations will take in the juvenile delinquents, unemployed workers, and down-on-their-luck Japanese who fall through the cracks of the nation's highly structured society.

The Move Abroad

By the late 1960s, various economic forces were tugging at the yakuza to expand their activities overseas. Early experiences in South Korea had convinced many that their criminal talents were put to best use on an international scale. Some served as managers of huge yakuza-controlled corporations and watched with interest as their legitimate counterparts in business enjoyed repeated success in foreign markets.

The opportunity for expansion came with the explosion of Japanese tourism in the late 1960s and early 1970s. A strong yen and relaxed currency controls sent large numbers of Japanese vacationers abroad—including thousands of men on all-male sex tours to Southeast Asia. When controversy grew too heated over the sex tours, the yakuza and their local partners simply reversed the trade and imported thousands of Asian women to the brothels, bathhouses, and hostess bars of Japan.

The sex tours were an open invitation for the yakuza to cash in on the worst excesses of their countrymen overseas. Japanese gangsters soon began showing up in Taipei, Manila, and Bangkok, profiting from the seamier side of the tourist trade, smuggling guns and drugs back to Japan, and investing some of the proceeds from home into new ventures abroad.

By the early 1970s, police in Hawaii began to take note of suspicious Japanese visitors, many with full-body tattoos and missing fingertips. "It took a lot of learning to understand what was involved," recalled Michael Sterrett, a US attorney in Honolulu during the 1970s who brought the yakuza to the attention of other federal authorities. "Slowly, though, it began to dawn on us that we were dealing with a completely different kind of organized crime problem."

As American police learned to look for missing fingers and tattoos, yakuza were spotted coming into Los Angeles, San Francisco, New York, and other cities. Elsewhere, too, the Japanese underworld has made its presence felt. Authorities have found yakuza engaged in gunrunning in Italy and Brazil, extortion in Great Britain, and money laundering in Australia. The gangs have invested in the Southeast Asian heroin trade and are suspected of smuggling "ice," a crystal form of methamphetamine, into Hawaii. They have also met with South American cocaine bosses about opening up Japan as a major new market for that drug. Given the Japanese predilection for stimulant drugs, police worry that Tōkyō might become the world's next capital of cocaine use.

Taking on the Gangs

The growth of organized crime in Japan has paralleled that of the nation's legitimate economy. Thus, the underworld has at its disposal remarkable financial resources. Perhaps nowhere else today does one find sophisticated crime syndicates with access to huge amounts of capital, operating in a country that largely tolerates their activities.

In recent years, however, public acceptance of the yakuza has begun to erode. Spurred by growing disenchantment, the Diet, Japan's parliamentary body, passed a series of new laws in 1991 aimed at cracking down on the gangs. One measure, a money-laundering statute, allows authorities to confiscate assets linked to illegal drug money. Another, the Bōryokudan Countermeasures Law, is modeled loosely after US antiracketeering statutes. The new law allows police to officially designate yakuza groups as organized crime syndicates and prohibit them from engaging in a number of mob-tainted enterprises, such as "negotiating" accident settlements, evicting tenants, and offering protection.

True to form, the gangs have loudly and publicly protested the new laws, even taking to the streets with their wives in demonstrations. Yakuza leaders and their attorneys, joined in an unusual alliance with civil libertarians and leftists, call the antigang measures unconstitutional and claim they violate guarantees of freedom of association and choice of profession.

To cope with the new laws, some criminal groups have dropped the gang insignia from their business cards and offices and have adopted a lower profile. Smaller gangs have registered with the government as legitimate corporations, with the godfather listed as chairman. Others are using an old ploy of calling themselves right-wing political groups. One gang reportedly declared itself a religious sect.

What impact the new laws will have remains to be seen. Much depends on how aggressively the Japanese authorities enforce the measures. Given the extraordinary reach and longtime public acceptance of the yakuza, many observers remain skeptical that significant change is at hand. Indeed, Japan's organized crime groups appear to be stronger now than ever.

David E. Kaplan

Illustration by Tsurukai Shinsuke

yamabōshi The pale yellow flowers of the *yamabōshi*, a variety of dogwood, appear in June or July. Edible berries subsequently develop.

Dairen). Stalin accepted a proposal to operate the Manchurian railroads through a joint company with the Chinese. It was also agreed that the status quo in the Mongolian People's Republic would be maintained.

Yalu River, Naval Battle of　黄海海戦

(Kōkai Kaisen; literally, "Naval Battle of the Yellow Sea"). Naval battle of the SINO-JAPANESE WAR OF 1894–1895. On 17 September 1894, in the Yellow Sea off the mouth of the Yalu River, 12 warships of the Imperial Japanese Navy, under the command of Vice Admiral Itō Sukeyuki, engaged and defeated a Chinese fleet of 14 warships under Admiral Ding Ruchang (Ting Ju-ch'ang). After this battle Japan controlled the Yellow Sea.

Yamabe no Akahito　山部赤人

(fl 724–736). Poet and court official. One of the most important poets of the MAN'YŌSHŪ (ca 759, Collection for Ten Thousand Generations or Collection of Ten Thousand Leaves), which contains 37 *tanka* ("short poems"; see WAKA) and 13 *chōka* ("long poems") by him. He was one of the last of the "poets laureate"—semiprofessional poets and musicians who composed verse commemorating imperial births, deaths, and so forth and celebrating excursions of the sovereign. All of his surviving poems appear to have been written during the reign of Emperor SHŌMU (701–756; r 724–749). He evidently made several long journeys, composing poems on Mt. Fuji and other famous sites. He came to be known to later ages as the great nature poet of the *Man'yōshū*. KI NO TSURAYUKI singles out Akahito with KAKINO-

MOTO NO HITOMARO (fl ca 685–705) as the two great poets of the early literary period. In addition to Akahito's poems in the *Man'yōshū*, some 50 others by or attributed to him are found in various imperial anthologies.

yamabiraki　山開き

(literally, "mountain opening"). Ceremonies held annually at mountains on the first day of the climbing season. The ritual was traditionally conducted by mountain ascetics (YAMABUSHI) so that the general public could "enter" the sacred mountains. In the case of especially sacred mountains such as Mt. Fuji (FUJISAN) and Kiso Ontake (ONTAKESAN), the several pilgrim groups (KŌ) dedicated to each mountain would climb on its opening day. The term has in recent years been used simply to designate the beginning of the mountain climbing season. There is a similar rite for rivers (see KAWABIRAKI).

yamabōshi　山法師

Cornus kousa. A deciduous tree of the dogwood family (Cornaceae) that grows wild in hilly areas of Honshū, Shikoku, and Kyūshū. Its trunk reaches a height of 3–8 meters (10–26 ft). The oval leaves are alternate with wavy edges. In summer flower stalks produce clusters of flowers. Each cluster is composed of numerous florets surrounded by four large, white bracts that resemble petals. *Yamabōshi* flowers are popular as alcove decorations for the tea ceremony.

A flowering dogwood species similar to the *yamabōshi* called the Amerika *yamabōshi* (*C. florida;* also known as *hanamizuki*) is often planted in public parks and private gardens. It was first introduced to Japan from the United States in 1909, in gratitude for the cherry trees sent from Tōkyō to Washington, DC.

yamabuki　山吹

Kerria japonica. A deciduous shrub of the rose family (Rosaceae) found in mountainous areas throughout Japan and also widely cultivated in gardens. It has a delicate stem that can grow up to 2 meters (6.5 ft) high; alternate, ovate leaves with irregular serrations; and a single, five-petaled yellow blossom on each branch in the spring. Horticultural varieties include the double-flowered *yaeyamabuki* ("Japanese rose"; *K. japonica* f. *plena*), the most commonly cultivated variety; a six- to eight-petaled type called *kikuzaki yamabuki* (*K. japonica* f. *stellata*); and the *shirobana yamabuki* (*K. japonica* f. *albescens*), which has white blossoms with a yellow tint. Another commonly cultivated plant of the rose family called *shiroyamabuki* (*Rhodotypos scandens*) has white blossoms similar to those of the *yamabuki*, but its leaves are opposite and the blossoms have four petals.

yamabukisō　山吹草

Chelidonium japonicum. A perennial herb of the poppy family (Papaveraceae), akin to the celandine. It grows mainly under trees in mountainous sections of Honshū and is known as one of the most beautiful wild plants of spring. It grows to 30 centimeters (12 in). Pinnate, compound leaves with five to seven round or diamond-shaped serrated leaflets, grow from the base of the stem on long stalks. Four-petaled blossoms of a vivid color, similar to those of the YAMABUKI, appear during April or May.

yamabushi　山伏

(literally, "one who lies in the mountains"). The name given during the Heian period (794–1185) to ascetics, usually men, who practiced austerities in the mountains in order to attain holy or magic powers. It was later applied to the members of the SHUGENDŌ order.

The traditional costume of the *yamabushi* comprises 16 items that are of practical use during an ascetic sojourn in the mountains and that symbolically transform the disciple from a profane to a sacred state. The items include a small black cap (*tokin*), a tunic with baggy trousers (*suzukake*), a collar with six colored tufts (*yuigesa*), a Buddhist rosary (*nenju*), a conch-shell trumpet (*hora;* see HORAGAI), a staff with rings (*shakujō*), and a fur rug hanging down from the waist in the back (*hishiki*). Although the principal tasks of the *yamabushi* are healing and exorcism, they are also celebrated for such spectacular feats as fire-walking and climbing up ladders of swords. See also MIKO.

yamachawan　山茶碗

(literally, "mountain teabowl"). Simple unglazed stoneware food bowls produced in many parts of Japan during the mid-12th through the 13th centuries. Despite being wheel-thrown, *yamachawan* are generally rather misshapen. The clay used was seldom refined, and many examples show rather large pieces of quartz in the fabric body. In many respects these bowls may be considered the final representatives of the SUE WARE tradition. A feature that links them to that tradition is the foot rim, which, when present, was attached to the otherwise finished vessel and not "turned" or trimmed from the base of the bowl. *Yamachawan* are gray in tone and seldom exceed 17 centimeters (about 7 in) in diameter and 5 centimeters (2 in) in depth. See CERAMICS.

Yamada　山田[市]

City in central Fukuoka Prefecture, Kyūshū. The development of the CHIKUHŌ COALFIELD in the Meiji period (1868–1912) led to rapid growth, but now all the mines are closed. Efforts are being made to attract new industries. Pop: 13,266.

Yamada Bimyō　山田美妙

(1868–1910). Writer. Real name Yamada Taketarō. Born in Tōkyō; studied at Daigaku Yobimon (a preparatory school for what is now Tōkyō University), where he founded the literary magazine *Garakuta bunko* in 1885 with OZAKI KŌYŌ and others of the KEN'YŪSHA group. He established himself with *Natsukodachi* (1888), a collection of short stories of which the most famous is "Musashino." These were the first Japanese stories to be written exclusively in the spoken language (see GEMBUN ITCHI). Bimyō is remembered primarily for this contribution to the devel-

opment of modern Japanese literature. He was also an early advocate of the new-style poem (*shintaishi*), which was introduced in 1882. His works include the novels *Chōkai shōsetsu tengu* (1886–87) and *Kochō* (1889) and an essay on the new colloquial style, *Gembun itchi ron gairyaku* (1888).

Yamadadera remains　山田寺跡

(*Yamadadera ato*). The vestiges of the Buddhist temple Yamadadera located at Yamada, the city of Sakurai, Nara Prefecture. Construction of the temple is said to have taken place 641–676 at the behest of Kura no Yamada no Ishikawamaro (d 649), a member of the SOGA FAMILY. From the remaining stone and earthen foundations, it was long believed that the plan of the temple followed the SHITENNŌJI style—a rectangular compound with the pagoda and halls arranged in a straight line. Excavations in 1976 and 1978, however, revealed that the main hall and pagoda were surrounded by a corridor and formed a separate interior compound. Excavated artifacts include ROOF TILES and BUDDHA TILES. Portions of the eastern corridor were uncovered in excavations in 1982.

Yamada Fūtarō　山田風太郎

(1922–). Novelist. Real name Yamada Masaya. Born in Hyōgo Prefecture. Graduate of Tōkyō Medical College. Yamada's *Kōga nimpō chō* (1958–59) started the so-called *nimpō* (art of the *ninja;* see NINJUTSU) boom; subsequently the complete collection of his *ninja* stories, *Yamada Fūtarō nimpō zenshū* (15 vols, 1963–64), became a best seller. Yamada is also known as a writer of romantic period novels, including *Hakkenden* (1983).

Yamada Isuzu　山田五十鈴

(1917–). Real name Yamada Mitsu. Actress; born in Ōsaka. She appeared in ITAMI MANSAKU's masterpiece *Kokushi musō* (1932, Peerless Patriot); MIZOGUCHI KENJI's NANIWA EREJĪ (1936, Ōsaka Elegy) and *Gion no shimai* (1936, Sisters of the Gion); NARUSE MIKIO's *Tsuruhachi Tsurujirō* (1938, Tsuruhachi and Tsurujirō); KINUGASA TEINOSUKE's *Hebi Hime sama* (1940, Snake Princess); and MAKINO MASAHIRO's *Onnakeizu* (1942, Lineage of Women). After 1950 she also performed on stage, joining the GEKIDAN MINGEI from 1951 to 1952, and forming her own group, the Gendai Haiyū Kyōkai, in 1954. One of her greatest successes as a stage actress was in the play *Tanuki* (1974, Badger).

Yamada Kōsaku　山田耕筰

(1886–1965). Composer and conductor. Born in Tōkyō. After early musical studies at Tōkyō Music School (now Tōkyō University of Fine Arts and Music), he studied composition in Berlin with Max Bruch and K. L. Wolf from 1910 to 1913. In 1914, under the patronage of the entrepreneur IWASAKI KOYATA (1879–1945), he formed a symphony orchestra. He also became active in composition (particularly of songs) and in the spread of Dalcroze eurhythmics in Japan. In the period 1917–19 he was in the United States, where he had collections of his work published and conducted the New York Philharmonic at Carnegie Hall. In 1920 he formed the Japan Opera Association and gave the first Japanese performances of works by Wagner and Debussy. In the 1930s he made several visits to Europe and the Soviet Union. His more than 750 works include the opera *Ochitaru tennyo* (1912) and songs such as "Karatachi no hana" (1925) and "Akatombo" (1926).

He was awarded the Order of Culture in 1956.

Yamada Moritarō　山田盛太郎

(1897–1980). Marxist economist. Born in Aichi Prefecture. A graduate of Tōkyō University, Yamada became an assistant professor there but resigned in 1930 during a crackdown on communist sympathizers. He became a professor at Tōkyō University after World War II and taught there until his retirement in 1957. With NORO EITARŌ, Ōtsuka Kinnosuke, and HIRANO YOSHITARŌ, Yamada edited the massive *Nihon shihon shugi hattatsu shi kōza* (1932–33, Lectures on the History of the Development of Japanese Capitalism). *Nihon shihon shugi bunseki* (1934, Analysis of Japanese Capitalism), a collection of the articles he wrote for this series, became a theoretical mainstay of the KŌZAHA faction of Marxist economists. Among Yamada's major postwar works is *Nihon nōgyō seisanryoku kōzo* (1960), a study of agricultural productivity in Japan.

Yamada Nagamasa　山田長政

(?–1630). Adventurer; active in Siam (now Thailand). Born in Suruga Province (now part of Shizuoka Prefecture). About 1611 he traveled to Siam on a ship licensed by the shogunate to trade overseas (see VERMILION SEAL SHIP TRADE). He settled in the Siamese capital, Ayuthia (now Ayutthaya), and became the leader of its Japanese community (NIHOMMACHI), furthering diplomatic relations between Japan and Siam and engaging in trade. For having led a Japanese force in battle for King Songtham, he was awarded the prestigious official title *oya senaphimok*. When the king's death was followed by a succession dispute in 1628, Nagamasa led some 800 Japanese and 20,000 Siamese to secure the throne for the king's son. Soon afterward, however, he and 300 other Japanese were banished to Ligor, a remote southern region, by a rival in the royal family. There Nagamasa was wounded in a battle with invaders and died from poison administered by his Siamese servant. His son burned Ligor and escaped to Cambodia.

Yamada Saburō　山田三良

(1869–1965). Scholar of international law. Born in Nara Prefecture. An 1896 graduate of Tōkyō University, he was a professor there from 1901 until 1930. One of his best-known scholarly essays was a defense of article 2 of the CIVIL CODE, which granted foreigners equal rights under Japanese law. Yamada served as chairman of the Faculty of Law at Tōkyō University, as president of Keijō University (now Seoul National University) in Korea (then a Japanese colony), as president of the JAPAN ACADEMY, and as director in chief of the Japanese Association of International Law (Kokusai Hōgakukai). His publications include *Kokusai shihō* (2 vols, 1932–34, Private International Law).

Yamada Taichi　山田太一

(1934–). Television scriptwriter. Real name Ishizaka Taichi. Born in Tōkyō. Graduate of Waseda University. Yamada's works examine family problems, portraying the strains and conflicts experienced by each individual member. His principal works include *Otokotachi no tabiji* (1985, Men's Journey; televised in 1976), *Omoide-zukuri* (1987, Making Memories; televised in 1981), and the novel *Ijintachi to no natsu* (1988, Summer with Strangers). He received the Kikuchi Kan Prize in 1985.

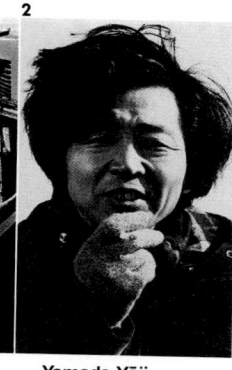

Yamada Yōji
1 Actors Atsumi Kiyoshi (left) and Mitsumoto Sachiko are shown here in a scene from this director's first "Tora san" episode (1969). **2** Yamada. His films combine artistic achievement with popular appeal.

Yamada Tomohiko　山田智彦

(1936–). Novelist. Born in Yokohama; graduate of Waseda University. Employed by a bank and also active as a writer. His works deal mainly with parent-child relationships or white-collar workers. Collections include *Chichi no shanikusai* (1971, Father's Carnival) and *Jikkenshitsu* (1972, The Laboratory).

Yamada Waka　山田わか

(1879–1957). Social commentator and reformer. Born in Kanagawa Prefecture; maiden name Asaba Waka. Seeking employment abroad to restore her family's fortunes, she was forced to work as a prostitute in Seattle, Washington, from around 1897 to 1903. She escaped to a Presbyterian-sponsored refuge in San Francisco, where she was baptized. She soon married Yamada Kakichi (1865–1934), and they returned to Tōkyō in 1906. He educated his wife and encouraged her to produce numerous translations and essays, which she began to publish in *Seitō* (Bluestocking), the magazine of the feminist group SEITŌSHA, in 1913. Yamada Waka became most widely known for her answers to letters from troubled women published in the newspaper *Tōkyō asahi shimbun* (now ASAHI SHIMBUN) beginning in 1931. She served as the first president of the Bosei Hogo Remmei (Motherhood Protection League) and established a refuge for mothers and children in Hatagaya, Tōkyō.

Yamada Yōji　山田洋次

(1931–). Film director. He graduated from Tōkyō University in 1954 and joined SHŌCHIKU CO, LTD, serving as an assistant director and screenwriter until his first directing opportunity in 1961. He began creating the popular TORA SAN series, known as *Otoko wa tsurai yo* (It's Tough Being a Man), in 1969. After that he turned out two Tora san episodes each year (as of April 1990, 42 Tora san films had been made) in addition to several other films, among them *Kazoku* (1970, Family; shown abroad as *Where Spring Comes Late*) and *Shiawase no kiiroi hankachi* (1977, Yellow Handkerchief of Happiness). Yamada's films, noted for both a high level of artistic achievement and popular, commercial appeal, promote the virtues of small-town or rural family life and depict the difficulties ordinary people face in coping with the expansion of technology and urbanization.

Yamada Yoshio　山田孝雄

(1873–1958). Philologist and grammarian. Born in Toyama Prefecture, Yamada in his early years taught at several junior high and high schools in various parts of Japan and participated in the work of the Kokugo Chōsa Iinkai (Commission to Investigate the National Language). He served on the faculty of Tōhoku University from 1924 through 1933.

Yamada Isuzu A well-known film actress in the 1930s and 1940s, Yamada also performed on the stage beginning in 1950.

Yamada Kōsaku This composer and conductor gave the Japanese premieres of works by Wagner and Debussy.

Yamagata Aritomo
A conservative military and political leader in the Meiji and Taishō periods, Yamagata engineered the building of a modern conscript army.

Yamada's most substantial contribution to Japanese language studies was a long series of grammatical works based on both Japanese and European traditional grammar. All of these books deal primarily with the Japanese literary language as it was generally used in the early part of the 20th century. Yamada's other works include studies of colloquial Japanese, studies of the historical development of Japanese grammar, and studies of the history of linguistics in Japan. He was awarded the Order of Culture in 1957.

Yamaga　　　　山鹿〔市〕

City in northern Kumamoto Prefecture, Kyūshū. Yamaga is known primarily for its hot springs. Rice, melons, and tobacco are grown. *Sake* breweries and silk-reeling and electrical-appliance plants are located here. The lantern festival of Ōmiya Shrine attracts visitors in August. Pop: 33,441.

Yamaga Sokō　　　　山鹿素行

(1622–85). Leading scholar of the Edo period (1600–1868), known for his contributions in Confucian studies, military science, and Japanese history. Born in Aizu (now part of Fukushima Prefecture). Educated in the school of the Confucian scholar HAYASHI RAZAN.

At age 30 Sokō became military instructor for the Akō domain, near modern Kōbe. In 1660 he opened his own school of classical and military studies in Edo (now Tōkyō), where he taught an original interpretation of Confucianism, rejecting the orthodoxy of the Zhu Xi (Chu Hsi) school (SHUSHIGAKU).

In 1665 Sokō published SEIKYŌ YŌROKU (Essentials of the Sacred Teachings), which openly questioned the validity of accepted interpretations of Confucian thought and attacked the ideological foundation of the Tokugawa shogunate. The book was banned by the authorities, and Sokō was exiled from Edo. He was later pardoned.

Sokō is credited with initiating the return to the original teachings of Confucius that came to be designated as KOGAKU (Ancient Learning). In military science he integrated the use of European firearms with traditional Chinese tactics. However, it was in his development of a *samurai* ethic (see BUSHIDŌ) and his patriotic view of Japanese history that Sokō's influence was greatest, for it was felt well into the 20th century. In 1656 he wrote the *Bukyō yōroku*, now considered one of the earliest works on *bushidō*. He argued that the function of the samurai in peacetime was to serve the nation as a living example of dedication to duty.

In his treatment of Japanese history, Sokō wrote primarily to enhance national pride and patriotism at a time when other scholars were completely engrossed in the study of China. His best-known historical work, the CHŪCHŌ JIJITSU (1669, True Facts of the Central Realm), ridiculed China-worshipers and demonstrated the many ways in which Japan excelled all other nations. Its emphasis on native Shintō beliefs and the divine nature of the unbroken imperial line stands in close relation to trends of thought prevalent from the 1870s to the 1940s.

Yamagata　　　　山形〔市〕

Capital of Yamagata Prefecture. During the Edo period (1600–1868) Yamagata prospered as a castle town, a post-station town at the junction of several highways, and a distribution center for *benibana* (safflower), wax,

and raw silk. Today principal products are rice, cherries, *sake*, canned fruits, foodstuffs, sewing machines, and cast-iron goods. Yamagata University is located here. The nearby mountain range ZAŌZAN, a popular ski area, the Hanagasa Festival in August, and the temple RISSHAKUJI are of interest. Pop: 249,487.

Yamagata Aritomo　　　　山県有朋

(1838–1922). Political leader of the Meiji (1868–1912) and Taishō (1912–26) periods. Architect of the modern Japanese army, he also played a major role in building the political institutions of Meiji Japan. He was born in Hagi, a castle town of Chōshū (now Yamaguchi Prefecture), into a family of low-ranking *samurai*. Early in his career, Yamagata devoted his energies to the radical, loyalist SONNŌ JŌI (Revere the Emperor, Expel the Barbarians) movement. He was leader of the semimodern militia of Chōshū, the KIHEI-TAI, in the MEIJI RESTORATION of 1868.

In 1870 he was appointed assistant vice-minister of military affairs following a year abroad to study European military systems, and in 1873 he assumed leadership of the Army Ministry, which had replaced the Ministry of Military Affairs the previous year. He is credited with the enactment of the CONSCRIPTION ORDINANCE OF 1873, the suppression in 1877 of the SATSUMA REBELLION led by SAIGŌ TAKAMORI, and the 1878 reorganization of the army along Prussian lines. Yamagata resigned as army minister in December 1878 and became the first chief of the General Staff. He issued a series of regulations culminating in the IMPERIAL RESCRIPT TO SOLDIERS AND SAILORS of 1882, emphasizing absolute loyalty to the emperor and enjoining soldiers to eschew politics. His initiation of a law (1900) that permitted only generals and admirals on active duty to serve as service ministers in the cabinet (see GUMBU DAIJIN GEN'EKI BUKAN SEI) set a pattern of military life free from outside interference.

In 1882 Yamagata became president of the Board of Legislation (Sanjiin), a post he held for 16 months, and then was home minister for over seven years. He reorganized the Home Ministry (Naimushō), reformed the police system, and was responsible for the enactment in 1888–90 of a new local government system. His response as home minister to the FREEDOM AND PEOPLE'S RIGHTS MOVEMENT was to devise laws restricting political party activities and controlling excessive agitation (see PEACE PRESERVATION LAW OF 1887).

Yamagata was named to his first term as prime minister (December 1889–May 1891) in the same year that he was promoted to the rank of full general, and he was a field marshal when he led his second cabinet from November 1898 to October 1900. His two prime ministerships reflected his conservative view that the government should act as a responsible servant of the emperor, not of the people, and that political parties should be prevented from infiltrating the bureaucracy, forming cabinets, or holding executive power. During his first term, he was the moving force behind the 1890 IMPERIAL RESCRIPT ON EDUCATION. In 1899, during his second term, civil service laws that denied key posts in the bureaucracy to political party members were issued. The following year his cabinet passed the PUBLIC ORDER AND POLICE LAW OF 1900 to suppress labor and peasant agitation.

Yamagata's greatest satisfaction came from his contributions to Japan's achievement of a new place in the international

order. A month after the outbreak of the SINO-JAPANESE WAR OF 1894–1895, he was appointed commander of the First Army. However, his field service was cut short by serious illness. In 1896 he led a diplomatic mission to Moscow that produced the YAMAGATA-LOBANOV AGREEMENT, giving Russia and Japan equal rights and privileges in Korea. During the RUSSO-JAPANESE WAR (1904–05) he served as chief of the General Staff. For his services to the nation he was named prince (*kōshaku*) in 1907. During the last 20 years of his life Yamagata was the most influential member of the group of elder statesmen known as the GENRŌ. From behind the scenes he played an important advisory role in foreign affairs, spoke out on domestic issues through his disciples in the cabinet, and virtually dictated the selection of prime ministers until his death.

Yamagata Bantō　　　　山片蟠桃

(1748–1821). Ōsaka rice merchant and scholar. Real name Hasegawa Yūkyū. Born in the village of Kazume in Harima Province (now part of Hyōgo Prefecture), he went to Ōsaka when he was 13. He entered the service of the Yamagata family, owners of a rice and financial business, eventually becoming a virtual member of the family and changing his name to Yamagata Yoshihide. Bantō is his scholarly name (*gō*).

Bantō studied at the KAITOKUDŌ, a school founded by Ōsaka merchants for the education of commoners. He became the pupil of the brothers Nakai Chikuzan (1730–1804) and NAKAI RIKEN, as well as of the physician and astronomer ASADA GŌRYŪ.

Bantō attained a firm grounding in Western science as it was known to the Japan of his day (see WESTERN LEARNING). He developed his own theory of a market economy, based on his experience as a rice merchant. He also developed an understanding of Western-style medicine and argued for simplification of the Japanese writing system. As a thinker Bantō insisted on concrete proof of the accuracy of historical documents. He despised all superstition and denied the existence of the soul after death. He saw religious leaders as his enemies and criticized their inaccurate use of historical references. In matters of daily life, however, he approved of the feudal system and revered TOKUGAWA IEYASU, who had brought an age of peace to the nation. Bantō's magnum opus, *Yume no shiro* (Instead of Dreams), which was completed in 1820, consists of talks that he gave to his own children and to shopkeepers after hours. Only after Bantō's death did his ideas begin to spread to government and educational circles, and it was not until the Meiji period (1868–1912) that part of *Yume no shiro* finally saw publication. In the post–World War II years, there was an increased appreciation of Bantō as a thinker of universal stature.

Yamagata Basin　　　　山形盆地

(Yamagata Bonchi). In central Yamagata Prefecture, northern Honshū. Flanked by the Ōu and Asahi mountains, it consists of an alluvial fan below the fault scarp of the Ōu Mountains and the floodplain of the river Mogamigawa's upper reaches. The area produces rice, apples, cherries, grapes, and vegetables. The major city is Yamagata. Length: 40 km (25 mi); width: 12 km (7 mi).

Yamagata Daini　　　　山県大弐

(1725–67). Also known as Yamagata Ryūsō. Radical Confucian thinker who advocated rebellion against the Tokugawa shogunate (1603–1867) and who was executed for treason in the MEIWA INCIDENT. Born in Kai Province (now Yamanashi Prefecture), he practiced medicine in Edo (now Tōkyō). He gained appointment as a shogunal intendant (*daikan*) under junior councillor (*wakadoshiyori*) Ōoka Tadamitsu (1709–60) but severed ties with the shogunate around 1760 and opened a private academy at his Edo residence. While still in shogunal employ, Yamagata wrote his famous treatise *Ryūshi shinron* (1759), advocating the overthrow of the very government he served, describing it as corrupt and cruel to the peasantry and relying on military force rather than moral suasion to sustain its rule. He was arrested after plotting revolt in 1766 and was executed the following year.

Yamagata-Lobanov Agreement
山県・ロバノフ協定

(Yamagata-Robanofu Kyōtei). Pact concerning Japanese and Russian interests in Korea; signed by Army Minister YAMAGATA ARITOMO and Russian Foreign Minister Aleksei Lobanov-Rostovski (1824–96) on 9 June 1896. Because of anti-Japanese and pro-Russian sentiments in Korea, Japan made large concessions in the agreement. Japan was able to exact more favorable terms in the NISHI-ROSEN AGREEMENT of April 1898.

Yamagata Masao
山県昌夫

(1898–1981). Naval architect whose basic research in naval architecture, particularly in hull design, laid the foundation for the rapid development of Japan's modern shipbuilding industry. Born in Tōkyō, he graduated from Tōkyō University in 1921. After serving in the Ships Bureau of the Ministry of Transport, he taught at Tōkyō University from 1947 to 1958 and was dean of engineering from 1956 to 1958. He received the Order of Culture in 1967.

Yamagata Prefecture
山形県

(Yamagata Ken). Located in northeastern Honshū and bordered to the north by Akita Prefecture, to the east by Miyagi and Fukushima prefectures, to the south by Fukushima and Niigata prefectures, and to the west by the Sea of Japan. The terrain is predominantly mountainous, with the ŌU MOUNTAINS running north and south along the eastern edge of the prefecture and the Dewa and Asahi mountain ranges rising along the coast on the west. Between these mountain chains the river Mogamigawa flows northward and then westward, emptying into the Sea of Japan at Sakata. The estuary of the Mogamigawa forms Shōnai Plain, and most of the prefecture's level areas are located along this river. The climate is characterized by warm summers and snowy winters.

The Yamagata area was still occupied by EZO tribesmen during the formative years of the Japanese nation. The central government gradually extended its control, and in 712 the area became part of the newly established province of Dewa. During the late Heian period (794–1185) it came under the domination of the ŌSHŪ FUJIWARA FAMILY, who in turn yielded to a succession of warlords. For most of the feudal period it was divided into several smaller domains. The present name and borders were established in 1876 after the Meiji Restoration.

A predominantly rural prefecture, it is one of Japan's major rice-producers. There are numerous orchards, and forestry is a major component of the economy. Manufacturing,

concentrated around the cities of Sakata and Yamagata, centers on food processing, textiles, machinery, woodworking, and chemicals.

Attractions include Bandai-Asahi National Park and Zaō, Chōkai, and Kurikoma quasi-national parks. ZAŌZAN is one of Honshū's principal ski areas. The hot-spring resorts of Zaō, Kaminoyama, Higashine, Ginzan, and Akakura are well known. Area: 9,326 sq km (3,600 sq mi); pop: 1,258,390; capital: Yamagata. Other major cities include Yonezawa, Tsuruoka, Sakata, and Tendō.

Yamagishi Akira
山岸章

(1929–). Labor leader. Born in Ōsaka. In 1950 he participated in the formation of the labor union Zendentsū (Japan Telecommunications Workers Union), becoming general secretary of the organization in 1982 and president in 1989. In 1986 he became president of Jōhō Tsūshin Rōren (now Jōhō Sangyō Rōdō Kumiai Rengōkai; Japan Federation of Communications, Electronic Information, and Allied Workers) and in 1989 he became the first president of RENGŌ, Japan's largest federation of labor unions.

Yamagishikai
山岸会

Utopian movement initiated in 1953 by Yamagishi Miyozō (1901–61) and others, with headquarters in the city of Yokkaichi, Mie Prefecture. The movement's goal is peaceful achievement of the "Z Revolution" (Zetto Kakumei), whereby government policy would be determined by unanimous agreement of the people, use of money abolished, unemployment alleviated by planned production, and society based on mutual trust. Members join 1 of 30 farm communes, to which they donate all their wealth. Within the communes, decisions are reached by group consensus and there are no permanent leaders; responsibility for the chief functions of the commune changes hands every six months.

Yamagiwa Katsusaburō
山極勝三郎

(1863–1930). Pathologist. Born in Shinano Province (now Nagano Prefecture); graduate of and professor at Tōkyō University. In 1915, by continuously applying tar to the ears of rabbits, Yamagiwa and Ichikawa Kōichi (1888–1948) succeeded in inducing chemical carcinogenesis for the first time. For this achievement Yamagiwa received the Japan Academy Prize and a German award.

Yamaguchi
山口[市]

Capital of Yamaguchi Prefecture, western Honshū. Yamaguchi was a flourishing castle town and port under the rule of the ŌUCHI FAMILY from the 14th to 16th centuries. However, when the MŌRI FAMILY, which replaced the Ōuchi in 1555, transferred its base to Hagi, the town began to decline. The principal agricultural product is rice. Of interest are the St. Francis Xavier Memorial Cathedral, built in 1952 to commemorate his missionary work; the garden of the Jōeiji temple; the Yamaguchi Gion Festival held at Yasaka Shrine in July; and the Yuda Hot Spring located to the southwest. Yamaguchi is also the base for tours to the plateau AKIYOSHIDAI. Pop: 129,461.

Yamaguchi Basin
山口盆地

(Yamaguchi Bonchi). In central Yamaguchi Prefecture, western Honshū. Extending along a fault line, it consists of small alluvial fans along the river Fushinogawa's upper

reaches and of its floodplain. Rice is the principal product. Numerous Yayoi-period (ca 300 BC–AD 300) graves and relics have been discovered here. The major city is Yamaguchi. Area: approximately 40 sq km (15 sq mi).

Yamaguchi Hitomi
山口瞳

(1926–). Novelist and essayist. Born in Tōkyō; graduate of Kokugakuin University. He won the Naoki Prize in 1963 for *Eburimanshi no yūga na seikatsu* (The Refined Lifestyle of Mr. Everyman), his novel about an average white-collar worker. A similar novel is *Majime ningen* (1965, A Serious Person). Reflecting the modest circumstances of the prewar Tokyoites among whom he grew up and the bitter experiences of his generation during World War II, his writings mock the affluent Japanese urban society of the 1960s. Other works include a series of essays that he has published since 1963 up to the present under the general title *Dansei jishin* (Man Himself).

Yamaguchi Hōshun
山口蓬春

(1893–1971). Japanese-style (NIHONGA) painter. Born Yamaguchi Saburō in Hokkaidō, he graduated from Tōkyō Bijutsu Gakkō (now the Tōkyō University of Fine Arts and Music). He learned the YAMATO-E style of painting while studying under the *nihonga* painter MATSUOKA EIKYŪ. He won the Imperial Fine Arts Academy (Teikoku Bijutsuin) Prize in 1926. He infused traditional *nihonga* with a modern sense of color. In 1965 he was awarded the Order of Culture.

Yamaguchi Kaoru
山口薫

(1907–68). Western-style painter. Born in Gumma Prefecture; studied Western-style painting (YŌGA) at the Tōkyō Bijutsu Gakkō (now Tōkyō University of Fine Arts and Music). After graduating in 1930 he spent three years in Europe, where he was strongly influenced by the styles of the Paris school. On his return to Japan Yamaguchi participated in the founding of the Shinjidai (New Age) group in 1934 and the Jiyū Bijutsuka Kyōkai (Free Artists Association) in 1937. In 1950 he helped to organize the Modern Art Association. He began teaching at the Tōkyō University of Fine Arts and Music in 1953 and was appointed professor in 1964.

Yamaguchi Kayō
山口華楊

(1899–1984). Japanese-style (NIHONGA) painter. Real name Yamaguchi Yonejirō. Known for his paintings of birds and flowers and of animals. Born in Kyōto, Yamaguchi graduated from the Kyōto Municipal School of Fine Arts and Crafts (now Kyōto City University of Arts). In 1916, the year he enrolled in the school, his painting *Nichigo* (Noon)

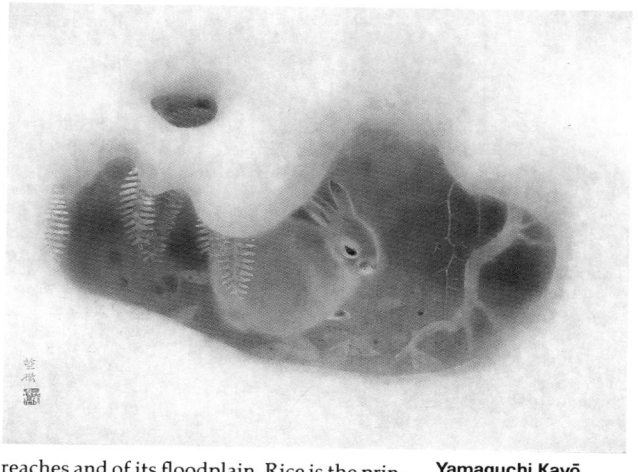

Yamaguchi Kayō
Waiting for Spring is a characteristic example of this *nihonga* painter's subject matter. 1978. Colors on paper. 49 × 68 cm. Private collection.

Yamagata Prefecture
Location and Prefectural Crest

Yamaguchi Prefecture
Location and
Prefectural Crest

Yamaguchi Seishi
This poet incorporates
motifs from contempo-
rary life into his *haiku*.

was selected for exhibition at the BUNTEN (Ministry of Education Fine Arts Exhibition). After graduating he studied with TAKEUCHI SEIHŌ. He taught at his alma mater from 1926 to 1949. He became a member of the Japan Art Academy in 1971 and received the Order of Culture in 1981. His painting *Kouma* (1955, Colts) won the Japan Art Academy Prize in 1956.

Yamaguchi no Atai Ōguchi
山口費大口

(fl 7th century). Buddhist sculptor. According to the NIHON SHOKI (720), one of Japan's first historical chronicles, he carved 1,000 images of Buddha (SENTAI BUTSU) by order of Emperor Kōtoku (r 645–654) in 650. His name also appears in the inscription on the halo (*kōhai*) of the image of Kōmokuten, one of the Four Heavenly Kings (Shitennō), in the *kondō* (main hall) of the Nara temple HŌRYŪJI.

Yamaguchi Prefecture
山口県

(Yamaguchi Ken). Located at the western tip of Honshū and bordered by the Sea of Japan to the north, Shimane and Hiroshima prefectures to the east, the Inland Sea to the south, and the Hibiki Sea to the west. The city of SHIMONOSEKI is connected to Kyūshū by both a tunnel and a bridge. The prefecture is divided into an industrial area along the Inland Sea coast to the south and a rural area along the Sea of Japan coast to the north. The terrain consists mostly of low mountains and plateaus, and the coastline is rocky and heavily indented. The climate is generally mild, especially along the seacoast. Typhoons are relatively frequent.

Its proximity to the Korean peninsula and its strategic location between western Honshū and Kyūshū led to its early development. It was formerly divided into the two provinces of Suō and Nagato. These provinces flourished under the rule of the ŌUCHI FAMILY and later the MŌRI FAMILY during the feudal period, and came to be known together as Chōshū. *Samurai* from Chōshū, such as ITŌ HIROBUMI, INOUE KAORU, and KIDO TAKAYOSHI, played a leading role in the overthrow of the Tokugawa shogunate in the closing years of the Edo period (1600–1868). The present prefectural name and boundaries were established in 1871.

Rice is the major crop in Yamaguchi; citrus and other fruits are also grown. The Inland Sea coast area has rapidly developed as a center for numerous heavy and chemical industries. Tourist attractions include its coastline, both on the Inland Sea and the Sea of Japan. YAMAGUCHI and HAGI retain traces of their past as castle towns. Akiyoshidai Quasi-National Park is noted for its karst (limestone) topography (see AKIYOSHIDAI). Hot-spring resorts include Yuda and Yumoto. Area: 6,108 sq km (2,358 sq mi); pop: 1,572,616; capital: Yamaguchi. Other major cities include Shimonoseki, UBE, TOKUYAMA, IWAKUNI, HŌFU, and Hagi.

Yamaguchi Yoshiko
This film actress began
a political career with
her election to the
House of Councillors
in 1974.

Yamaguchi Seishi
山口誓子

(1901–). HAIKU poet. Real name Yamaguchi Chikahiko. Born in Kyōto; graduate of Tōkyō University. He contributed to the haiku magazine HOTOTOGISU. However, he was opposed to the objective description of nature advocated by *Hototogisu* and left the group in 1935 to join *Ashibi*, a coterie founded by MIZUHARA SHŪŌSHI. In 1948 Yamaguchi left the *Ashibi* group and founded the magazine *Tenrō*. In his poems Yamaguchi attempted to make haiku more relevant and personal by incorporating motifs from contemporary urban life. His principal collections are *Tōkō* (1932), *Wafuku* (1955), and *Setsugaku* (1985).

Yamaguchi Sodō
山口素堂

(1642–1716). HAIKU poet of the early Edo period (1600–1868). Born Yamaguchi Nobuaki in Kai Province (now Yamanashi Prefecture), he was a close friend of the haiku poet BASHŌ, whose early stylistic development he is believed to have influenced. A student of the Confucian scholar HAYASHI GAHŌ, he retired early in life to devote himself to poetry, calligraphy, and the tea ceremony. A collection of his haiku is found in *Tokutoku no kuawase* (1735).

Yamaguchi Yoshiko
山口淑子

(1920–). Film actress and singer. Real name Ōtaka Yoshiko. Born in Fushun, Manchuria. She made her motion picture debut under the Japanized Chinese name Ri Kōran (Ch: Li Xianglan or Li Hsiang-lan). She played leading roles in such films as Watanabe Kunio's (b 1899) *Byakuran no uta* (1939, Song of the White Orchid) and *Nessa no chikai* (1940, Promise in the Hot Sand) and Fushimizu Shu's (1910–42) *Shina no yoru* (1940, China Nights). After World War II, she made a new start as Yamaguchi Yoshiko but was never able to recapture her prewar popularity. In 1974 she was elected to the House of Councillors and was a member of that house until 1992.

Yamaha Corporation
ヤマハ[株]

(Yamaha). Musical instrument manufacturer. It is the world's largest musical instrument maker in sales volume. Among its products are pianos, organs, electronic organs, guitars, audio equipment, wooden furniture, home fixtures (including bathtubs, basins, mirrors, and cabinet units), plywood, and special metal alloys. It also operates leisure and recreational facilities.

Established in 1887 by Yamaha Torakusu (1851–1916), the company began production of upright pianos in 1900. It grew rapidly after World War II as a result of the wide dissemination of music education in Japan. In 1958 the company established its first overseas subsidiary in Mexico City. By 1989 it had over 40 overseas subsidiaries in Europe, Asia, and North and South America. Recent business emphasis has been on its leisure department—the production and sale of leisure goods and the operation of hotels and recreational facilities. The firm has also carried out a wide range of demand-creating activities centered on various music popularization programs. Sales for the fiscal year ending March 1991 totaled ¥383.5 billion (US $2.8 billion). It was capitalized at ¥16.1 billion (US $117.3 million) in the same year. Headquarters are in Hamamatsu, Shizuoka Prefecture. See also YAMAHA MOTOR CO, LTD.

Yamaha Motor Co, Ltd
ヤマハ発動機[株]

(Yamaha Hatsudōki). Yamaha Motor was incorporated as a motorcycle manufacturer in 1955 after being separated from YAMAHA CORPORATION. Its engine technology has since been applied to the development and manufacture of outboard motors, diesel engines, snowmobiles, racing karts, golf carts, and multipurpose engines. The company's product diversification efforts have reached into such new fields as high-performance automobile engines, industrial robots, and air conditioners. Yamaha products are manufactured in 82 factories in 45 countries. Total sales for the fiscal year ending March 1991 were ¥452.4 billion (US $3.3 billion). The company was capitalized at ¥22.8 billion (US $166.2 million) in the same year. Headquarters are in Iwata, Shizuoka Prefecture.

Yamaichi Securities Co, Ltd
山一証券[株]

(Yamaichi Shōken). One of the "Big Four" Japanese securities houses. Established in 1897, Yamaichi is the oldest of the major Japanese securities houses. It has over 10,000 employees, 116 domestic branches, and 24 overseas networks covering all major financial centers. Yamaichi services Japanese corporations as well as international customers through its overseas outlets. In addition to its activities in the more conventional areas of brokering, dealing, distributing, and underwriting securities, Yamaichi is also involved in such aspects of modern financial technology as investment management and merger and acquisition services. Sales for the fiscal year ending March 1991 totaled ¥360.2 billion (US $2.6 billion), and capitalization stood at ¥126.4 billion (US $921.3 million). Headquarters are in Tōkyō.

Yamaji Aizan
山路愛山

(1864–1917). Journalist. Original name Yamaji Yakichi. Born in Edo (now Tōkyō) into the family of a shogunate retainer, Yamaji became a Christian soon after his graduation from Tōkyō Eiwa Gakkō (now Aoyama Gakuin University) and was briefly an editor for the Methodist magazine *Gokyo* (Defending the Faith). In 1892 he joined the Min'yūsha, the publishing house founded by TOKUTOMI SOHŌ. Yamaji later worked for the newspaper *Shinano mainichi shimbun*, and in 1903 he founded his own magazine, *Dokuritsu hyōron* (Independent Review). In 1905, with the journalist Shiba Teikichi (1869–1939), Yamaji founded the Kokka Shakaitō (National Socialist Party) to oppose Marxism. Besides contributing to such journals as CHŪŌ KŌRON and *Taiyō*, Yamaji wrote many books, including *Shakai shugi kanken* (1906, A Personal View of Socialism), *Gendai kinken shi* (1907, The Power of Money in Recent History), and *Ashikaga Takauji* (1909).

Yamakawa Hitoshi
山川均

(1880–1958). Marxist writer and theoretician whose life spanned much of Japanese socialist history. Born in Kurashiki, Okayama Prefecture. Like many other Japanese socialists, Yamakawa first became interested in social reform when he came into contact with Christianity. He studied at DŌSHISHA UNIVERSITY in Kyōto from 1895 to 1897. After leaving Dōshisha, Yamakawa went to Tōkyō. With two other young men he began a small monthly paper for young people in 1900. Because of articles criticizing the arranged marriage of the crown prince, Yamakawa was imprisoned for almost four years. In prison he turned seriously to socialism. In 1906 he joined the newly founded JAPAN SOCIALIST PARTY and came under the influence of KŌTOKU SHŪSUI, who was redirecting the movement from Christian socialism to anarcho-syndicalism. Yamakawa became an assistant editor of the HEIMIN SHIMBUN, contributing articles on anarchism and the concept of the "general strike." To a successor newspaper in 1908 he contributed a long serialized article on *Das Kapital,* the first exposition of Marxist economics to appear in Japanese. Arrested in the RED FLAG INCIDENT OF 1908, he was imprisoned for the next two years and thereby escaped being implicated in the HIGH TREASON INCIDENT OF 1910.

From 1918 to 1921 Yamakawa was the foremost writer in Japan on Lenin and the Bolsheviks. He participated in the founding of the JAPAN COMMUNIST PARTY (JCP) in 1922. In his famous article "Musan kaikyū undō no hōkō tenkan" ("A Change of Direction for the Proletarian Movement"), which exerted great influence on Japanese workers and intellectuals, Yamakawa acknowledged the failure of anarcho-syndicalism to attract workers and advocated a broadly based proletarian political movement. Yamakawa was one of the party leaders who favored the dissolution of the JCP in 1924, and he refused to participate in the reestablishment of the illegal party, believing that a mass-based, legal proletarian party was more appropriate to the conditions pertaining in Japan. In 1927 Yamakawa and his followers, who came to be known as the RŌNŌHA (Labor-Farmer faction) after their magazine, *Rōnō,* worked to unite the Left behind this program but failed because of ideological clashes with other activists. After World War II, Yamakawa called for the formation of a "democratic united front" embracing both socialist and communist positions, but he again refused to join the JCP, helping instead to revive the Japan Socialist Party.

Yamakawa Kenjirō　　山川健次郎

(1854–1931). Physicist. Born in Aizu domain (now Fukushima Prefecture). Yamakawa was sent by the Meiji-period (1868–1912) government to study at Yale University. Upon his return to Japan he taught physics at Tōkyō University and in 1879 he became Japan's first professor of physics. From the Meiji through the Taishō (1912–26) period he served at various times as president of Tōkyō, Kyōto, and Kyūshū universities. Yamakawa played a key role in introducing Western physics to Japan and in natural sciences administration.

Yamakawa Kikue　　山川菊栄

(1890–1980). Socialist and feminist. Born in Tōkyō as Morita Kikue; later took the surname Aoyama. She graduated from Joshi Eigaku Juku (now Tsuda College) and soon after began to publish essays in such magazines as the feminist *Seitō* (see SEITŌSHA) and the socialist *Shinshakai* (New Society). In 1916 she married socialist YAMAKAWA HITOSHI. In 1921 she helped found the SEKIRANKAI (Red Wave Society), Japan's first women's socialist organization. She also helped her husband edit socialist journals, including *Rōnō* (Labor-Farmer).

After World War II, she joined the newly organized Japan Socialist Party. From 1947 to 1951 she served as the first director of the new Women's and Minors' Bureau in the Ministry of Labor. Her writings include *Musansha undō to fujin no mondai* (1928, The Proletarian Movement and Problems of Women) and her autobiography, *Onna nidai no ki* (1956, A Story of Mother and Daughter).

Yamakunigawa　　山国川

River in northern Ōita Prefecture, Kyūshū, originating in the mountain Hikosan and flowing through the Nakatsu Plain into the Suō Sea. The gorge YABAKEI is located on the upper and middle reaches. Length: 56 km (35

mi); area of drainage basin: 540 sq km (208 sq mi).

yamamba　　山姥

Sometimes called *yamauba.* Female demon believed to live in the mountains. The *yamamba* is thought to have originally been a mountain deity (YAMA NO KAMI) or a mountain deity's female servant. Commonly described as a female demon who devours humans, the *yamamba* sometimes appears in legends and folklore as a humorous, stupid old hag.

Yamamoto Baiitsu　　山本梅逸

(1783–1856). Third-generation BUNJINGA painter who specialized in decorative BIRD-AND-FLOWER PAINTING (*kachōga*) as well as landscapes in the Chinese style. Real name Yamamoto Shinryō. Born in Nagoya, in his youth Baiitsu studied with practitioners of a variety of painting schools, including the NAGASAKI SCHOOL, KANŌ SCHOOL, and MARUYAMA-SHIJŌ SCHOOL. As a teenager he became the protégé of Kamiya Ten'yū (dates unknown), a rich Nagoya businessman and collector of Chinese paintings. In 1802 Baiitsu went to Kyōto with fellow painter NAKABAYASHI CHIKUTŌ to study Chinese painting. Baiitsu was subsequently active in both Kyōto and Edo (now Tōkyō) and formed a painting society with TANI BUNCHŌ. His best work is characterized by a genuine sensitivity to natural forms combined with unsurpassed technical mastery of brushwork on silk.

Yamamoto Fujiko　　山本富士子

(1931–). Film actress. Born in Ōsaka. She made her debut in Mori Kazuo's (1911–89) *Hana no Kōdōkan* (1953, The Glorious Kōdōkan). Until 1962 she was a leading star for Daiei Productions, appearing in such films as KINUGASA TEINOSUKE's *Yushima no shiraume* (1955, The Romance of Yushima), YOSHIMURA KŌZABURŌ's *Yoru no kawa* (1956, Undercurrent), and MASUMURA YASUZŌ's *Hyōheki* (1958, Ice Precipice). In 1963, after her requested release from her exclusive contract with Daiei was denied, she publicly criticized this common film industry restriction and found herself blacklisted. Even after Daiei's bankruptcy in 1971, she refused to return to acting in films, but remained active in theater and television.

Yamamoto Gombei → Yamamoto Gonnohyōe

Yamamoto Gonnohyōe　　山本権兵衛

(1852–1933). Admiral and political leader of the Meiji (1868–1912) and Taishō (1912–26) periods and twice prime minister (1913–14; 1923–24). Also known as Yamamoto Gombei. Son of a *samurai* family in the Satsuma domain (now Kagoshima Prefecture). During the MEIJI RESTORATION of 1868, Yamamoto served in the Eighth Satsuma Rifle Corps. He graduated from the Naval Training Academy in 1874. He became one of the most influential figures in planning naval strategy during the SINO-JAPANESE WAR OF 1894–1895 and in the administration of the Navy Ministry. Promoted to rear admiral in 1895, he became navy minister in the second YAMAGATA ARITOMO cabinet of 1898, a post he held in successive cabinets for six years.

In 1913, during the TAISHŌ POLITICAL CRISIS, Yamamoto was appointed prime minister. His cabinet abolished the administrative rule that allowed only officers on active duty to

serve as army and navy ministers (see GUMBU DAIJIN GEN'EKI BUKAN SEI). The SIEMENS INCIDENT of 1914, a scandal involving naval officers, forced Yamamoto's resignation. In 1923, however, he was again summoned to form a cabinet. Assuming responsibility for the TORANOMON INCIDENT, an assassination attempt on the prince regent, Yamamoto resigned on 7 January 1924 and withdrew from politics completely.

Yamamoto Hokuzan　　山本北山

(1752–1812). Confucian scholar of the Edo period (1600–1868). Born in Edo (now Tōkyō). Hokuzan established his reputation at age 21 with *Kōkyō shūsetsu* (Lectures on the *Xiao jing* [*Hsiao ching*]). Influenced by the SETCHŪGAKUHA, a syncretic school of Confucianism, he opposed the shogunate's policy (known as the Kansei Igaku no Kin) of employing only adherents of the Zhu Xi (Chu Hsi) school of Neo-Confucianism.

Yamamoto Hōsui　　山本芳翠

(1850–1906). Western-style painter. Real name Yamamoto Tamenosuke. Born in Mino (now part of Gifu Prefecture), he started out by studying Japanese literati painting (BUNJINGA) in Kyōto. He studied Western art with Goseda Hōryū (1827–92), Charles WIRGMAN, and Antonio FONTANESI. From 1878 to 1887 he studied in Paris at the Ecole des Beaux Arts under Jean Léon Gérôme (1824–1904). Upon his return to Japan he taught Western-style painting and opened his own private school, the Seikōkan. He helped to found two artist groups, Meiji Bijutsukai (1889) and the HAKUBAKAI (1896). His last years were spent as a stage designer. He is remembered for his oils in the academic Barbizon-school style of 19th-century France.

Yamamoto Isoroku　　山本五十六

(1884–1943). Naval officer and commander in chief of the Combined Fleet during World War II. Born in Nagaoka, Niigata Prefecture, the sixth son of Takano Teikichi (dates unknown), a school principal, he later was adopted by the Yamamoto family. Upon graduating from the Naval Academy he served in the RUSSO-JAPANESE WAR of 1904–05 and was wounded in the Battle of TSUSHIMA in May 1905.

After the war Yamamoto saw several assignments at sea as a gunnery officer. He graduated from the Naval War College in 1916. Three years later he was ordered to study abroad; he spent his first year at Harvard University and his second at the Japanese Embassy in Washington. He served again in Washington from 1926 to 1928 as naval attaché. As vice-minister of the navy from 1936, he strongly opposed the proposed TRIPARTITE PACT on the grounds that this would invite a war between the United States and Japan.

Yamamoto, seeing that war was inevitable, proposed a surprise attack on Pearl Harbor, the US naval base in Hawaii (see PEARL HARBOR, ATTACK ON), which devastated the US Pacific Fleet. However, the June 1942 invasion of Midway Island planned by Yamamoto ended in defeat. The Battle of MIDWAY marked the turning of the tide; American forces began their counteroffensive in the Solomon Islands in August 1942. On 18 April 1943, while on his way to inspect front-line units, Yamamoto was killed when his plane was shot down by US fighter planes.

Yamakawa Kikue This feminist helped found Japan's first women's socialist organization.

Yamamoto Gonnohyōe A figure of enormous prestige in the navy, this admiral served twice as prime minister during the early years of the 20th century.

Yamamoto Isoroku This naval officer who proposed the surprise attack on Pearl Harbor had earlier spent a number of years in the United States, first as a student and later as naval attaché.

Yamamoto Kansai
This fashion designer has gained international attention for his bold and colorful style.

Yamamoto Senji
This biologist and politician was an advocate of birth control and an opponent of the oppressive Peace Preservation Law of 1925.

Yamamoto Yasue
This stage actress created the role of Tsū in Kinoshita Junji's *Twilight Crane*, giving 1,000 performances between 1949 and 1984.

Yamamoto Jōtarō　山本条太郎

(1867–1936). Businessman and politician. Born in what is now Fukui Prefecture. After finishing elementary school he joined the MITSUI company in 1881, becoming its managing director in 1909. He was obliged to resign in 1914 after becoming implicated in the SIEMENS INCIDENT, a bribery case involving a German firm, naval officers, and Mitsui. In 1920 he was elected to the Diet as a member of the RIKKEN SEIYŪKAI party and was reelected five times. As president of the SOUTH MANCHURIA RAILWAY from 1927 to 1929, he worked to promote Japanese economic expansion in northeast China.

Yamamoto Kajirō　山本嘉次郎

(1902–74). Film director. Born in Tōkyō. In 1922 he left Keiō University and joined the film production company Nippon Katsudō Shashin (later the NIKKATSU CORPORATION). Yamamoto acted in comedies and wrote many scripts between 1926 and 1932, when he switched to directing. In 1934 he moved to PCL (a company that later merged with others to form TŌHŌ CO, LTD), where his work on a popular musical-comedy series starring ENOMOTO KEN'ICHI confirmed that he was a first-rank director. The semidocumentary realism Yamamoto introduced with *Uma* (1941, Horse), on which he worked closely with assistant director KUROSAWA AKIRA, was well received by the critics, as was *Hawai-Marē oki kaisen* (1942, The War at Sea from Hawaii to Malaya). Other directors who trained under Yamamoto include Taniguchi Senkichi (b 1912) and Honda Ishirō (b 1911). Most of the films Yamamoto directed after World War II were comedies. His most notable works include *Tōjūrō no koi* (1938, The Loves of a Kabuki Actor) and *Tsuzurikata kyōshitsu* (1938, Composition Class).

Yamamoto Kansai　やまもと寛斎

(1944–　). Fashion designer. Born in Kanagawa Prefecture; attended Nihon University. His designs are avant-garde, colorful, and marked by freedom in silhouette. He was the first Japanese designer to hold a fashion show in London (1971).

Yamamoto Kenkichi　山本健吉

(1907–88). Literary critic. Real name Ishibashi Teikichi. Born in Nagasaki Prefecture; son of Meiji-period (1868–1912) novelist ISHIBASHI NINGETSU. After graduating from Keiō Gijuku (now Keiō University), he worked as an editor before helping to found *Hihyō*, a coterie magazine of a group of critics, in 1939. His reputation was established with *Shishōsetsu sakka ron* (1943), a collection of essays on modern writers and the I-NOVEL. He developed a literary theory based upon his concept of aesthetic archetypes, which he believed transcended individual authors. In 1966 he received the Japan Art Academy Prize, and in 1969 he became a member of that academy. His principal critical works are a study on HAIKU, *Junsui haiku* (1952), and *Kakinomoto no Hitomaro* (1958–61), a critical work on the late-7th-century poet of that name. He was awarded the Order of Culture in 1983.

Yamamoto Kiyoshi　山本貴誉司

(1892–1963). Agronomist and a leader of the Japanese immigrant community in Brazil. Born in Tōkyō and graduated from Tōkyō University, Yamamoto went to Brazil in 1926 and became general manager of Casa Tozan, a subsidiary of the MITSUBISHI CORPORATION. He was the founder and first president of the Japanese Culture Society of Brazil (Sociedade Brasileira de Cultura Japonesa) and the Brazilian-Japanese Cultural Association (Aliança Cultural Brasil-Japão).

Yamamoto Kyūjin　山本丘人

(1900–1986). Japanese-style (NIHONGA) painter. Real name Yamamoto Masayoshi. Born in Tōkyō, he graduated from Tōkyō Bijutsu Gakkō (now Tōkyō University of Fine Arts and Music) and studied under the *nihonga* painter MATSUOKA EIKYŪ. Yamamoto founded the Creative Painting Society (Sōgakai). Known for his bold, vigorously composed landscapes, Yamamoto turned to a more lyrical palette reminiscent of traditional YAMATO-E in his later years. He received the Order of Culture in 1977.

Yamamoto Sanehiko　山本実彦

(1885–1952). Publisher and politician. Born in Kagoshima Prefecture, he founded the publishing company Kaizōsha in 1919 and began the magazine KAIZŌ, which played an important role in disseminating democratic and socialist ideas during the Taishō (1912–26) and early Shōwa (1926–89) periods. In the late 1920s, he published the *Gendai Nippon bungaku zenshū* series, the first inexpensive editions of modern Japanese literature (see EMPON). Kaizōsha was dissolved in 1944 because of military pressure, but Yamamoto revived the company after the war.

Yamamoto Satsuo　山本薩夫

(1910–83). Film director; known for his treatment of timely social and political themes. One hallmark of his style is length; many of his films run longer than two and a half hours. He joined SHŌCHIKU CO, LTD, in 1933 and served for a time as assistant to NARUSE MIKIO, later moving with Naruse to TŌHŌ CO, LTD. At Tōhō after World War II he became embroiled in labor disputes as a union leader, and the company eventually fired him.

Social and political "message films" were Yamamoto's forte. His *Shinkū chitai* (1952, Vacuum Zone) is regarded as one of Japan's most powerfully effective antiwar films. *Shiroi kyotō* (1966, The Ivory Tower), about corruption at the highest levels of the medical profession, won a Kinema Jumpō Award in 1966. *Kareinaru ichizoku* (1974, The Family), about abuses in the banking industry; *Kinkanshoku* (1975, Solar Eclipse), about election fraud; and *Fumō chitai* (1976, Barren Zone), an account of the LOCKHEED SCANDAL, all met with great popular success.

Yamamoto Senji　山本宣治

(1889–1929). Biologist, social activist, and politician. Born in Kyōto, Yamamoto went to Canada as a youth to work and study. After his return to Japan in 1911, he took a degree in zoology at Tōkyō University and became a lecturer at Kyōto and Dōshisha universities. Influenced by Margaret SANGER, the American advocate of family planning, he became active in the birth control movement. Late in 1925 he was ousted from his teaching positions in the wake of the so-called Kyōto University Gakuren Incident, in which several dozen leftist students were arrested under the new PEACE PRESERVATION LAW OF 1925. In 1928 he was elected to the Diet as a member of the RŌDŌ NŌMINTŌ (Labor-Farmer Party). He opposed the revision of the Peace Preservation Law to establish capital punishment for subversive activities and also spoke out against the government's China policy. Yamamoto was stabbed to death by a right-wing terrorist on the day the revision passed the Diet.

Yamamoto Shūgorō　山本周五郎

(1903–67). Novelist and short-story writer known chiefly for his stories of common people. His works enshrine the popular virtues of traditional Japan and are marked by sympathy for the underdog, dislike of authority, delicacy of description, and humor. Born Shimizu Satomu in Hatsukari in Yamanashi Prefecture, he came from a humble family. In 1926 he made his debut with the story "Sumadera fukin" and published a three-act drama, *Hōrinji iki*. His early work was written mainly for children, but in 1932 he wrote "Dadara Dambei," his first popular story for adults. He wrote mainly juvenile and detective stories until around 1945. The years from around 1940 to 1945 also yielded short stories on *samurai* themes, as well as a series of stories for women entitled *Nihon fudōki* (1942–45). Notable products of the years from 1945 to 1950 include the historical novels *Otafuku monogatari* (1949–51) and *Uso'a tsukanee* (1950). *Yamabiko otome* (1951) showed a rare nostalgia for his home district. During the 1950s his work included *Momi no ki wa nokotta* (1954–56), a long political-historical novel. *Nagai saka* (1964–66) is largely autobiographical. From *Chikushōdani* (1959) a religious tendency became more pronounced and was carried on in *Sabu* (1963) and *Ogosoka na kawaki* (1967). His works are collected in *Yamamoto Shūgorō zenshū* (1967–70).

Yamamoto Tamesaburō　山本為三郎

(1893–1966). Businessman. Born in Ōsaka Prefecture. Taking over his family's bottle-making business, Yamamoto established Nippon Bottle Manufacturing in 1918. He later served as managing director of Nippon Brewery and Mineral Water and executive director of Dai Nippon Breweries. In 1949 Yamamoto became president of ASAHI BREWERIES, LTD, when Dai Nippon Breweries split into two separate firms. He also operated hotels, played an active role in the business-industrial community, and served as a patron of the arts.

Yamamoto Tarō　山本太郎

(1925–88). Poet. Born in Tōkyō. Graduate of Tōkyō University. Yamamoto served on the staff of the monthly poetry magazine REKITEI. Grand in scale, his works express a longing to stay in touch with the origins of mankind. His principal poetry collections are *Hokōsha no inori no uta* (1954, Prayers of an Itinerant), *Gorira* (1960, Gorilla), and *Yurishīzu* (1975, Ulysses). Yamamoto was the nephew of the poet KITAHARA HAKUSHŪ.

Yamamoto Yasue　山本安英

(1906–　). Actress. Born in Kanda, Tōkyō. In 1921 she entered the Gendaigeki Joyū Yōseijo (School of Modern Theater Training for Actresses), headed by Ichikawa Sadanji II (1880–1940). She became a founding member of OSANAI KAORU's famous Tsukiji Shōgekijō (Tsukiji Little Theater) in 1924, playing leading roles in 67 productions. After Osanai's death in 1928 she joined Hijikata Yoshi (1898–1959) in founding the Shin Tsukiji Gekidan (New Tsukiji Theater Company). Until the end of World War II, she worked in radio broadcasting. In 1951 she was honored by the Ministry of Education for her role as Tsū in KINOSHITA JUNJI's internationally acclaimed play *Yūzuru* (1949, tr *Twilight Crane*, 1956). In 1966 she founded the Yamamoto Yasue no Kai (Yamamoto Yasue Society), dedicated to research in the recitation of contemporary stories and ancient tales. Yamamoto Yasue has a unique stage presence and polished diction.

Yamamoto Yōji 山本耀司

(1943–   ). Fashion designer. Born in Tōkyō. Graduate of Keiō University and Bunka Fashion College. Yamamoto established his own company, Y's, in 1972. His designs feature restrained colors and complex, often asymmetrical shapes with a loose fit modified by clever use of tucks and folds. He won the Mainichi Fashion Grand Prize in 1986.

Yamamoto Yūzō 山本有三

(1887–1974). Playwright and novelist. Born in Tochigi Prefecture. He studied at Tōkyō University, where, with AKUTAGAWA RYŪNOSUKE and KIKUCHI KAN, he published the third series of the *Shinshichō* literary magazine. Yamamoto translated several Strindberg plays. Three of his own plays are *Eijigoroshi* (1920; tr *A Case of Child Murder*, 1930), *Sakazaki Dewa no Kami* (1921; tr *Lord Dewa*, 1935), and *Dōshi no hitobito* (1923, The Comrades); all three were part of the SHINGEKI (new theater) movement. In 1928 he began publishing serial novels, such as *Nami* (1928, Waves), *Onna no isshō* (1932–33, A Woman's Life), and *Robō no ishi* (1937, Wayside Stones). Following World War II, he was involved in efforts to reform and simplify the Japanese language and was elected to the House of Councillors. He was awarded the Order of Culture in 1965.

Yamamura Bochō 山村暮鳥

(1884–1924). Poet and novelist. Real name Tsuchida Hakujū. Born in Gumma Prefecture. His *Sei sanryō hari* (1915, Sacred Prism) remains unique in modern Japanese poetry. Consisting of poems juxtaposing apparently unrelated images, this book shocked the Japanese literary world. The most frequently anthologized poem from it is "Fūkei" (Landscape), which skillfully uses the visual effect of typography. Among his other books of poems, *Kaze wa kusaki ni sasayaita* (1918, The Wind Whispered to the Grass and Trees) and *Kozue no su nite* (1921, In the Treetop Nest) differ from *Sei sanryō hari* in their religious tone and straightforward approach. One of his novels, *Jūjika* (1922, The Cross), describes a Christian proselytizer's illicit affair with his convert.

Yamamura Saisuke 山村才助

(1770–1807). Geographer. Real name Yamamura Masanaga. Born in Hitachi Province (now part of Ibaraki Prefecture), he studied world geography with ŌTSUKI GENTAKU, scholar of Dutch Learning. His *Teisei zōyaku sairan igen* (1802), a revision of *Sairan igen* (a geographical treatise by ARAI HAKUSEKI), is representative of the type of geographical work published during the years of NATIONAL SECLUSION.

Yamamuro Gumpei 山室軍平

(1872–1940). A founder and important leader of the Japanese branch of the SALVATION ARMY. Born in Okayama Prefecture, he became a Christian in 1887. When members of the English Salvation Army came to Japan in 1895, he helped organize its Japanese branch and the next year became its first Japanese officer, eventually rising to the rank of

commander. With his wife, YAMAMURO KIEKO, he strove to abolish public prostitution and to establish various social welfare programs. He worked to evangelize the poor and the laboring class. The best known of his many writings is *Heimin no fukuin* (1899, The People's Gospel).

Yamamuro Kieko 山室機恵子

(1874–1916). Pioneer in Japan's SALVATION ARMY (Kyūseigun). With her husband, YAMAMURO GUMPEI, she worked for Christian social reform. Born in Iwate Prefecture. She graduated in 1895 from the Meiji Girls' School and began campaigning with the KYŌFŪKAI (Japan Woman's Christian Temperance Union). In 1899 she married and became a "soldier" in the branch of the Salvation Army founded by her husband. From about 1900 Kieko and Gumpei were especially active in rehabilitating prostitutes.

Yamana family 山名氏

(Yamanashi). Warrior family of the Muromachi period (1333–1568). Descended from the Seiwa Genji branch of the MINAMOTO FAMILY through Nitta Yoshinori (dates unknown; grandson of NITTA YOSHISADA), from whose village in Kōzuke Province (now Gumma Prefecture) they took their name. After helping ASHIKAGA TAKAUJI rise to power, they were granted estates and by 1363 were military governors (SHUGO) of five provinces in western Honshū. The Yamana became one of four families (*shishiki*) who rotated as heads of the Board of Retainers (SAMURAI-DOKORO) of the MUROMACHI SHOGUNATE and briefly extended their power over 11 provinces. (As Japan then had 66 provinces, the Yamana were called "Lords of a Sixth.") Several family members rose against the shōgun ASHIKAGA YOSHIMITSU in the MEITOKU REBELLION (1391), and the Yamana lost all but two provinces. In 1441 YAMANA SŌZEN helped defeat AKAMATSU MITSUSUKE, who had assassinated the shōgun ASHIKAGA YOSHINORI, and the family temporarily regained its former holdings. The rivalry between Sōzen and the shogunal deputy (*kanrei*) HOSOKAWA KATSUMOTO was a principal cause of the ŌNIN WAR (1467–77); the Yamana survived as minor lords.

Yamanaka 山中[町]

Town in southern Ishikawa Prefecture, central Honshū. It is noted for its hot spring, said to have been discovered in the 8th century. A local lacquer ware, *yamanaka-nuri*, is well known. Pop: 11,518.

Yamanaka, Lake 山中湖

(Yamanakako). Lake in southeastern Yamanashi Prefecture, central Honshū. One of the FUJI FIVE LAKES located on the northeastern slope of Mt. Fuji (FUJISAN), it was created by lava flows from Fujisan. Carp, crucian carp, and pond smelt inhabit the lake. The *fujimarimo* (*Fuji aegagropilae*), a kind of water plant that grows here, is designated a natural monument. The lake is popular for its fine views of Fujisan. There are excellent camping grounds and recreational facilities. Area: 6.4 sq km (2.5 sq mi); circumference: 14 km (9 mi); depth: 13 m (43 ft); altitude: 981 m (3,218 ft).

Yamanaka Sadao 山中貞雄

(1909–38). Film director. His directorial career spanned only six years, but he gave a new direction to the period film by shifting the emphasis from a romantic to a more realistic treatment of the warrior culture. Rather

than portray heroic deeds and derring-do, Yamanaka concentrated on the lives of ordinary townspeople of the Edo period (1600–1868). When members of the *samurai* class were included, they were often RŌNIN (masterless samurai) in the throes of destitution.

Yamanaka's influence is reflected in the work of such later directors as KOBAYASHI MASAKI, whose period films reflect a concern for character and for ordinary lives. Yamanaka's masterpiece was *Ninjō kamifūsen* (1937, Humanity and Paper Balloons), which he completed just before being drafted into the Imperial Japanese Army. Yamanaka was sent as a foot soldier to China, where he died in 1938.

Yamanaka Shikanosuke 山中鹿之介

(1545–78). Also known as Yamanaka Yukimori. A warrior famed for his loyalty to the AMAKO FAMILY of Izumo Province (now part of Shimane Prefecture). In 1566 the Amako were conquered by the MŌRI FAMILY and Shikanosuke became a *rōnin* (masterless *samurai*). Shikanosuke persuaded Amako Katsuhisa (1553–78) to renounce the priesthood, assume the family headship, and recover his ancestral domains. In 1569 Katsuhisa and Shikanosuke reoccupied much of Izumo but were frustrated by the defection of Amako vassals to the Mōri. In 1573–74 Katsuhisa and Shikanosuke attacked the Mōri in Inaba (now part of Tottori Prefecture), probably with the covert support of ODA NOBUNAGA, but were again defeated. In 1577 Nobunaga sent TOYOTOMI HIDEYOSHI against the Mōri, and Katsuhisa and Shikanosuke were entrusted by him with the fortress of Kōzuki in Harima (now Kōzuki Chō, Hyōgo Prefecture). Kōzuki fell to a Mōri counterattack in the summer of 1578; Katsuhisa committed suicide, and Shikanosuke was killed.

Yamanashi 山梨[市]

City in central Yamanashi Prefecture, central Honshū. Its major industry is agriculture, mainly the growing of grapes and peaches. Numerous wineries are located in the city. Electrical-appliance and machine plants have been built. Pop: 31,100.

Yamanashi Prefectural Museum of Art 山梨県立美術館

(Yamanashi Kenritsu Bijutsukan). Institution in the city of Kōfu, Yamanashi Prefecture. Opened in 1978. The museum is noted for its collection of approximately 40 works by Jean-François Millet, including oil paintings, drawings, and prints. The museum also houses paintings by Jean-Baptiste-Camille Corot and Gustave Courbet and sculpture by Emile-Antoine Bourdelle and Henry Moore, as well as works by early modern and con-

Yamamoto Yōji
1 The distinctive interior of this fashion designer's main store in Tōkyō includes ingenious use of space and exposed steel beams.
2 A selection from Yamamoto's 1991–92 autumn/winter collection for men.

Yamamoto Yūzō
A playwright whose works were part of the *shingeki* ("new theater") movement, this author also published serial novels.

Yamamuro Gumpei
A founder of the Japanese branch of the Salvation Army, Yamamuro became its first Japanese officer in 1896.

temporary Japanese artists who have some connection with Yamanashi Prefecture.

Yamanashi Prefecture 山梨県

(Yamanashi Ken). Located in central Honshū and bordered by Tōkyō, Kanagawa, Shizuoka, Nagano, and Saitama prefectures. The terrain is mostly mountainous, and principal ranges include Kantō, Misaka, and Akaishi. Mt. Fuji (Fujisan), the highest peak in Japan, lies on the border with Shizuoka Prefecture. The principal level areas are the KŌFU BASIN in the center of the prefecture and the Gunnai region to the south near Fujisan. Summer and winter weather contrast sharply, and precipitation is less than average for Japan.

After the TAIKA REFORM of 645 the area was known as Kai Province. It was controlled by a succession of military families, including the Kai Minamoto, Takeda, and Asano, after the Heian period (794–1185). For most of the Edo period (1600–1868) it was directly controlled by the Tokugawa shogunate. It was given its present name and borders in 1871 following the Meiji Restoration.

Agriculture is the major activity; crops include rice, fruits, and vegetables. Its grapes are particularly well known, and the prefecture is the center of the country's wine production. Industry is largely limited to light manufacturing such as textiles and crystal processing. Since World War II, new industries have been developed, which produce electrical goods, machinery, and precision instruments.

Proximity to the Tōkyō area and a wealth of lakes and mountains make Yamanashi a popular tourist area, with the greatest attraction being Fujisan and the string of five lakes at its base (see FUJI FIVE LAKES). Three national parks, Fuji-Hakone-Izu, Chichibu-Tama, and the Southern Alps, span part of the prefecture. Hot springs include Masutomi, Sekisuiji, and Isawa. MINOBUSAN is the head temple of the NICHIREN SECT of Buddhism and attracts a large number of pilgrims and tourists. Area: 4,463 sq km (1,723 sq mi); pop: 852,966; capital: KŌFU. Other major cities include ŌTSUKI, TSURU, and FUJI YOSHIDA.

Yamana Sōzen 山名宗全

(1404–73). Military leader of the Muromachi period (1333–1568). In 1432 Sōzen became military governor (shugo) of several provinces in western Honshū. In 1441 he played a major role in the defeat of AKAMATSU MITSUSUKE, assassin of the shōgun ASHIKAGA YOSHINORI. In 1450 he became a monk, changing his name from Mochitoyo to Sōzen, but retaining all of his political power. In the shogunal succession dispute of 1465, Sōzen supported Ashikaga Yoshihisa (1465–89; son of the shōgun ASHIKAGA YOSHIMASA and HINO TOMIKO) as shogunal heir and opposed HOSOKAWA KATSUMOTO, who supported Yoshimasa's younger brother Ashikaga Yoshimi (1439–91). The dispute was a principal cause of the ŌNIN WAR (1467–77), in which Sōzen commanded troops. He died of illness in 1473.

yamane→dormouse, Japanese

yama no kami 山の神

(god of the mountain). There are various types of deities called yama no kami, each associated with a different occupational group. Farming folk venerate a mountain deity that is identical with the TA NO KAMI

(god of the paddies): The yama no kami descends from the mountains in early spring to become the ta no kami and after the harvest returns to his abode in the mountains. This particular type of yama no kami also embodies the spirits of the people's ancestors (see ANCESTOR WORSHIP). Mountain folk such as hunters, woodcutters, and charcoal makers venerate either a male or a female yama no kami, whereas lathe workers (KIJIYA, who live in the woods and tend to be itinerant) believe the yama no kami to be a married couple. As deities worshiped in Shintō, yama no kami are identified as the god Ōyamatsumi no Kami or the goddess Konohana no Sakuyahime. In general these yama no kami are fearsome and terrifying. Festivals honoring yama no kami are generally held on the 7th, 9th, 12th, or 17th day of February, October, or November.

Yamanote 山手

District of urban Tōkyō, roughly consisting of Bunkyō and Minato wards and wards between and to the west of them. The name, which means hill or bluff, designates the district as the hilly part of Tōkyō as opposed to the level district to the east, which is known as the SHITAMACHI. The Yamanote district contains many middle-class and upper-middle-class residential areas, with important shopping centers around railway stations. Modern standard Japanese is based on the language of educated speakers of the Yamanote district.

Yamanote line 山手線

(Yamanotesen). Rail line operated by the EAST JAPAN RAILWAY CO. The Yamanote line circuit is a loop of 34.5 kilometers (22.0 mi) around the central Tōkyō area. Stations of many JR rail lines, private rail lines, and subways are linked to Yamanote line stations, enabling passengers to transfer between different lines. At peak times on the Yamanote line, a train arrives every 2.5 minutes, and each day 677 trains, each 10 cars long, make a lap of the Yamanote circuit in 60 minutes. During rush hour, trains running between the Ueno and Okachimachi stations are filled to 270 percent of capacity. Ten of Japan's 20 largest rail stations, including Tōkyō Station and Shinjuku Station, are on the 29-station Yamanote circuit. It is the most heavily used rail line in the Tōkyō area.

Yamanouchi Kazutoyo 山内一豊

(1545–1605). General of the Azuchi-Momoyama period (1568–1600); founder of the Tosa domain (now Kōchi Prefecture). The son of a petty baron (dogō) of Owari Province (now part of Aichi Prefecture), Kazutoyo distinguished himself in the service of TOYOTOMI HIDEYOSHI in the Battle of SHIZUGATAKE in 1583 and the KOMAKI NAGAKUTE CAMPAIGN in 1584 and attained DAIMYŌ status in 1585. That year he was granted a 19,800-koku (see KOKUDAKA) domain at Takahama in what is now Fukui Prefecture and then was assigned as a counselor to Hideyoshi's adopted son TOYOTOMI HIDETSUGU and transferred to a 20,000-koku domain at Nagahama in what is now Shiga Prefecture. After participating in the ODAWARA CAMPAIGN of 1590, Kazutoyo was granted a 59,000-koku fief at Kakegawa in what is now Shizuoka Prefecture and made the intendant (DAIKAN) of Hideyoshi's immediate holdings (kurairichi) in that area. In 1600 Kazutoyo adhered to the future shōgun TOKUGAWA IEYASU and after Ieyasu's victory at SEKIGAHARA was rewarded with the 202,600-

koku domain of Tosa in Shikoku. Kazutoyo's wife, Kenshō In (1557–1617), is the subject of many anecdotes that portray her as the model samurai wife.

Yamanouchi Pharmaceutical Co, Ltd 山之内製薬[株]

(Yamanouchi Seiyaku). Pharmaceutical manufacturer. Incorporated in 1939. Its principal products are a diverse group of prescription and over-the-counter drugs. Yamanouchi licenses its own technologies to foreign pharmaceutical firms. It has an overseas office in New York. Sales for the fiscal year ending March 1991 totaled ¥213.2 billion (US $1.6 billion), and the company was capitalized at ¥54.3 billion (US $395.8 million). Headquarters are in Tōkyō.

Yamanouchi Sugao 山内清男

(1902–70). Archaeologist. Born in Tōkyō. After graduating from Tōkyō University in anthropology, he taught at Tōhoku University and Tōkyō University before becoming a professor at Seijō University in Tōkyō. Yamanouchi established the first comprehensive typology and chronology for JŌMON POTTERY, rejecting the chronology established by radiocarbon dating. He is also known for his studies on the design techniques used on Jōmon vessels. Many of his works are collected in Yamanouchi Sugao senshi kōkogaku rombunshū (5 vols, 1969–72).

Yamanouchi Toyoshige 山内豊信

(1827–72). Also known as Yamanouchi Yōdō. Daimyō of the Tosa domain (now Kōchi Prefecture) and a major figure in the events leading to the MEIJI RESTORATION of 1868. He became daimyō in 1848 and carried out modernizing reforms. He supported TOKUGAWA YOSHINOBU in the 1858 shogunal succession dispute and opposed the ANSEI COMMERCIAL TREATIES. Both issues were settled when II NAOSUKE became great elder (tairō), and Toyoshige was forced to resign as daimyō (1859) and placed in domiciliary confinement.

After Ii's assassination in 1860, Toyoshige returned to national politics, although he remained active in his domain as well, suppressing extremist antishogunate officials such as TAKECHI ZUIZAN. He advised the shōgun TOKUGAWA IEMOCHI and worked for reconciliation between the imperial court and the shogunate (see MOVEMENT FOR UNION OF COURT AND SHOGUNATE). When he realized the overthrow of the shogunate was inevitable, he followed the advice of his retainers GOTŌ SHŌJIRŌ and SAKAMOTO RYŌMA and convinced the new shōgun, Tokugawa Yoshinobu, to return his governing mandate to the emperor (see TAISEI HŌKAN) in November 1867. This concession failed to satisfy antishogunate forces, and Toyoshige allowed Tosa to join in the military coup that abolished the shogunate and restored imperial rule.

Yamanoue no Okura 山上憶良

(660–ca 733). Government official and major poet of the early 8th century. His name is usually pronounced Yamanoe. In 702 Okura was given a post in a mission to the court of Tang (T'ang) China. In 721, at the age of 61, he was appointed tutor to the crown prince, the future emperor SHŌMU. In 726 he was made governor of the province of Chikuzen in northern Kyūshū, where he wrote many poetic masterpieces inspired by his literary friendship with ŌTOMO NO TABITO, then serving as viceroy of the military headquarters at

Yamanashi Prefecture
Location and
Prefectural Crest

DAZAIFU. Okura returned to Nara, the capital, in 731 or 732.

Okura is one of the best-represented poets in the MAN'YŌSHŪ (ca 759), the first great anthology of vernacular Japanese poetry. His works preserved in the *Man'yōshū* include about 10 *chōka* ("long poems"), a *sedoka* ("head-turning poem"), and about 60 *tanka*. An additional group of 10 *tanka* attributed to some fisherfolk of Chikuzen are also probably his. In addition to his poetry in Japanese, the *Man'yōshū* contains two poems and a short prose essay in Chinese by him. Okura combined narrative, lyrical, and philosophical elements with a strain of Confucian-inspired didacticism and social consciousness in a manner that set him apart from the other great poets of the age. Unlike the poems of his contemporaries, Okura's verses on love and nature constitute only a small fraction of his surviving works. A broader warmth and compassion infuse his poems of social concern, as can be seen in his famous "Dialogue on Poverty" ("Hinkyū mondō").

Apart from his own verse, Okura also compiled an anthology of vernacular poetry entitled *Ruijū karin* (Classified Forest of Verse). Though not extant, it is believed to have served as a model for the compilers of the *Man'yōshū*.

Yamaoka Sōhachi   山岡荘八

(1907–78). Novelist. Born Fujino Shōzo in Niigata Prefecture. He was editor of a popular literary magazine in the 1930s, and his story "Yakusoku" (The Promise) won a prize from a weekly magazine in 1938. During World War II, he wrote propaganda stories and afterward was forbidden to publish under the OCCUPATION PURGE. Yamaoka made a comeback with his period novel *Tokugawa Ieyasu* (1950–67). During Japan's rapid economic growth in the 1960s, this work was widely read by businessmen looking for management guidelines from Ieyasu's administrative expertise. Other historical novels include *Oda Nobunaga* (1954–60) and *Haru no sakamichi* (1971).

Yamaoka Tesshū   山岡鉄舟

(1836–88). Also known as Yamaoka Tetsutarō. Swordsman and retainer of the Tokugawa shogunate; active during the MEIJI RESTORATION (1868). Born in Edo (now Tōkyō). Yamaoka studied with the master swordsman Chiba Shūsaku (1793–1855). In 1862 Yamaoka and Takahashi Deishū (1835–1903) organized a police force of skilled swordsmen to monitor antishogunate activities. When imperial forces marched on Edo in the spring of 1868 in anticipation of resistance to the new imperial regime, KATSU KAISHŪ, commander of the Tokugawa forces, commissioned Yamaoka to conduct preliminary negotiations with imperial army leader SAIGŌ TAKAMORI. After the restoration Yamaoka served in several prefectural gubernatorial posts and as an aide to Emperor MEIJI.

Yamasaki Naomasa   山崎直方

(1870–1929). Geographer. Born in Kōchi Prefecture. He graduated from Tōkyō University and studied geography in Germany and Austria. He founded departments of geography at Tōkyō University and Tōkyō Bunrika University (now Tsukuba University). Yamasaki proposed theories concerning the former existence of glaciers in Japan and the fault structure of the Japanese archipelago. With Satō Denzō he edited the 10-volume *Dai Nihon chishi* (1903–15).

Yamasa Shōyu Co, Ltd

ヤマサ醤油[株]

(Yamasa Shōyu). Manufacturer of soy sauce, flavor enhancers, and biochemicals related to nucleic acids. Incorporated in 1928, Yamasa was the founder of the nucleotide industry. Products are exported mainly to the United States, but also to Europe and Asia. Sales totaled ¥34.0 billion (US $254.6 million) in 1990, and the company was capitalized at ¥375.0 million (US $2.8 million). Headquarters are in Chōshi, Chiba Prefecture.

Yamashina Institute for Ornithology   山階鳥類研究所

(Yamashina Chōrui Kenkyūjo). Foundation engaged in the classification of species, the mapping of their distribution, and the study of their ecosystems, as well as working for the protection of birds. Located in the city of Abiko, Chiba Prefecture. Founded in 1932 by Yamashina Yoshimaro (1900–1989), it took its present name in 1942. In 1989, the institute's collection of mounted specimens numbered some 65,000.

Yamashiro Hot Spring   山代温泉

(Yamashiro Onsen). Located in the city of Kaga, Ishikawa Prefecture, central Honshū. A saline and sulfur spring; maximum water temperature 75°C (167°F). Said to have been discovered in the 8th century by the Buddhist priest GYŌGI.

Yamashiro no Kuni Ikki   山城国一揆

A league (IKKI) formed for mutual assistance by KOKUJIN (local *samurai* proprietors) and JIZAMURAI (yeoman warriors) of southern Yamashiro Province (now part of Kyōto Prefecture) in 1486, after the area had been ravaged by 20 years of strife within the Hatakeyama family. Meeting in council, the rural notables demanded the withdrawal of the opposing armies from their area, the restoration of manorial rights to their proprietors or *honke* (court aristocrats and religious institutions), and an end to the construction of toll barriers (SEKISHO). Within a week, the Hatakeyama forces had withdrawn, and the league adopted a set of regulations (*jōhō*) and designated a group of 36 leaders to administer the affairs of the region in a monthly rotation of three. This body claimed half-rights (HANZEI) over the land rents of many of the area's estates (SHŌEN), asserted the right to administer criminal justice (KENDAN), and refused to acknowledge the authority of the SHUGO (military governor). The *kokujin* league dissolved in 1493, having served its purpose. The *ikki* was in no sense a popular uprising, and some historians interpret it as a sign that the "popular energy" manifested in the peasant leagues (TSUCHI IKKI) had faded. See also KUNI IKKI.

Yamashiro no Ōe, Prince   山背大兄王

(?–643; Yamashiro no Ōe no Ō). Eldest son of the regent Prince SHŌTOKU; his mother was a daughter of SOGA NO UMAKO. After his father's death, Yamashiro no Ōe occupied an important position in political affairs. Following the death of reigning empress SUIKO in 628, he claimed the succession but was thwarted by Prince Tamura (593?–641), who ascended the throne as Emperor Jomei (r 629–641). In 643 forces under SOGA NO IRUKA attacked Yamashiro no Ōe's residence, and he and all his family were forced to commit suicide. The NIHON SHOKI and the JŌGŪ SHŌTOKU HŌŌTEI SETSU describe the prince as a tragic hero.

Yamashiro Province   山城国

(Yamashiro no Kuni). One of the five home or central (KINAI) provinces; established under the KOKUGUN SYSTEM in 646, it comprised what is now central and southern Kyōto Prefecture. The region was settled in the 5th century by the HATA FAMILY and other naturalized Koreans (KIKAJIN). From 741 to 744 Emperor SHŌMU maintained his official residence at KUNI NO MIYA in the southernmost part of the province, and Yamashiro again became the site of an imperial capital in 784 with the founding of NAGAOKAKYŌ. Ten years later the capital was moved to another location in Yamashiro: HEIANKYŌ (now the city of Kyōto) was to remain the seat of Japan's imperial government for 1,075 years. After the Meiji Restoration of 1868 the imperial capital was moved to Tōkyō, and Yamashiro was for a time divided into two prefectures, Kyōto and Yodo, but these were consolidated into Kyōto Prefecture on 22 November 1871.

Yamashiro Tomoe   山代巴

(1912–). Novelist; especially concerned with the sufferings of rural women. Born into a farm family in Hiroshima Prefecture; maiden name Tokumo Tomoe. In 1935 she married the communist Yamashiro Yoshimune (1900–1945). Both were imprisoned in 1940, and her husband died in jail. Her works include *Niguruma no uta* (1955, Handcart Songs) and *Toraware no onnatachi* (1980, Imprisoned Women, 10 vols).

Yamashiroya Incident   山城屋事件

(Yamashiroya Jiken). Scandal of the early 1870s involving Yamashiroya Wasuke (1836–72), a merchant who did business with the Army Ministry as an official purveyor (GOYŌ SHŌNIN). Taking advantage of his ties with Army Minister YAMAGATA ARITOMO (both were from Yamaguchi Prefecture), Yamashiroya was able to borrow large sums of money from the ministry. He lost most of it in the raw-silk market and with the remaining cash went to Paris, where his extravagance aroused the suspicions of Japanese consular officials and led to an investigation. Upon returning to Japan, Yamashiroya was asked by Yamagata to return the money. Unable to do so, he committed suicide.

Yamashita Isamu   山下勇

(1911–). Businessman; president of EAST JAPAN RAILWAY CO from 1987. Born in Tōkyō. After graduating from Tōkyō University in 1933, Yamashita joined the shipbuilding department of Mitsui & Co, Ltd. The department became independent in 1937 as Tama Zōsenjo (now MITSUI ENGINEERING & SHIPBUILDING CO, LTD). Yamashita became the company's president in 1970 and served as chairman from 1979 to 1986. In 1987, when the Japan National Railways was privatized, he became president of East Japan Railway Co. He became chairman of the Council for Transport Technology in 1988.

Yamashita Tarō   山下太郎

(1889–1967). Businessman and pioneer in Japan's overseas oil development efforts. Born in Akita Prefecture, he graduated from Sapporo Agricultural College (now Hokkaidō University) and then went to Manchuria, where he was successful in business. He served in executive capacities in many

Yamaoka Sōhachi
This author's period novel about the founder of the Tokugawa shogunate was popular with businessmen as a management "textbook."

Yamashita Yasuhiro
The jūdō champion displays his Olympic gold medal to reporters at a press conference following the award ceremony at the 1984 Los Angeles Olympics.

companies, including the presidencies of both Korean Chemical and Tōhoku Mining. With the support of ISHIZAKA TAIZŌ, KOBAYA-SHI ATARU, and other business leaders, in 1956 Yamashita established Japan Oil Export (now ARABIAN OIL CO, LTD) to develop oil resources in the Persian Gulf.

Yamashita Tomoyuki　山下奉文

(1885–1946). Army general. Also known as Yamashita Hōbun. Born in Kōchi Prefecture. A graduate of the Army Academy (1905) and the Army War College (1916), he rose rapidly, holding various assignments in the Army General Staff Office and abroad. In 1941 Yamashita was appointed commander of the 25th Army and sent to Malaya. He became famous for his capture of the British naval base at Singapore (see MALAYAN CAMPAIGN) on 15 February 1942. In 1944 he was sent to the Philippines to defend the Japanese-occupied islands against the Allied counteroffensive. After the war he was hanged in Manila for atrocities committed by soldiers under his command. See WAR CRIMES TRIALS.

Yamashita Yasuhiro　山下泰裕

(1957–). *Jūdō* expert (*jūdōka*). Born in Kumamoto Prefecture; graduate of Tōkai University. Yamashita was an open category gold medalist in *jūdō* at the 1984 Los Angeles Olympics. In 1985 he established a record by winning the All-Japan Jūdō Championship for the ninth time in succession, retiring the same year to devote himself to teaching at Tōkai University. Yamashita began learning *jūdō* while in the fourth grade of elementary school. As a freshman in high school he won the All-Japan High School Championship. In 1977, at the age of 19, he became the youngest contestant to win the All-Japan Jūdō Championship. His special techniques include *newaza*, *ōsotogari*, and *hidari uchimata.* He received the government's People's Honor Award in 1984.

Yamatai　邪馬台国

(Yamatai Koku). Country in the Japanese islands, visited by Chinese envoys from the year 240. It was described in the Chinese book *Sanguo zhi* (*Sankuo chih*; History of the Three Kingdoms), written by Chen Shou (Ch'en Shou; 233–297) toward the end of the 3rd century. There are a few earlier, fragmentary references to Japan in the Chinese histories, but this is the oldest extensive description of Japan in any language. Its rich lode of information on the 3rd-century Wa people, as the Chinese called the Japanese, and their fascinating queen, HIMIKO, is fundamental to any understanding of early Japanese history. This famous account is both illuminating and puzzling, largely because of the frustrating obscurity of its data on the location of Yamatai, Himiko's capital.

Chen Shou and the Wei Zhi——Rather than direct knowledge of Japan, Chen Shou apparently depended on archival records and earlier historical treatments of China's short-lived Wei dynasty (220–265), the northernmost of the three kingdoms into which China was divided for much of the 3rd century. Chen's history of Wei, the WEI ZHI (*Wei chih*; J: *Gishi*), was the first and largest part of the *Sanguo zhi.* The last volume of the *Wei zhi*, devoted to "accounts of the eastern barbarians" and covering the peoples of Manchuria, Korea, and Japan, has a section on the Japanese Wa people, or *woren* (*wo-jen*;

J: *wajin*). Among Japanese scholars this account is conventionally referred to as the *Gishi wajinden* (the *Wei zhi* Account of the Wa People).

Chen's account includes important information on the population and official titles in the key communities, an extensive statement of the manners and customs of the land of the Wa, and a brief section on administrative and social structure. Next there is a substantial statement on Queen Himiko, the character of her rule, and her close diplomatic relations with Wei from 239 until her death a short time after 247. The account then concludes with some details of the succession struggle that followed her burial.

The Land of the Wa People and Queen Himiko——The interesting ethnographic description of the Wa shows a sharply stratified society, with social and regional distinctions indicated by tattoo markings. Although living quarters were segregated according to age and sex, the mixing of the sexes in public activity appeared noteworthy to the Chinese observers. There was an intense concern with pollution and purification.

There appears to have been considerable commerce, both between Wa communities and with Korean and Chinese towns on the peninsula. There was a revenue office for the collection of various levies in grain and other products. Each community had markets under the supervision of a senior official based in Ito (ITOKOKU) in northwestern Kyūshū and appointed by Queen Himiko in Yamatai.

Queen Himiko was a personage of considerable mystery. According to the Chinese observers, the Wa had once been ruled by a king, but at some time during the 160s and 170s there had been a civil war that ended with the accession of Himiko. She devoted herself completely to religious affairs and was able to "delude the crowd." She was rarely seen but was assisted by her younger brother, who exercised power for her. If she was between 10 and 15 at her accession, she might have been in her nineties when she died in the late 240s.

Most readers have assumed that the capital, Yamatai, with its reported 70,000 households, must have been somewhere in the central or southern part of Kyūshū. However, the oldest Japanese historical works, the KOJIKI (712) and the NIHON SHOKI (720), contain nothing about Yamatai and Queen Himiko; rather the *Nihon shoki* refers to an Empress JINGŪ ruling in YAMATO, in the Nara Plain in Japan. The compilers of the *Nihon shoki* were apparently trying to reconcile the information in the *Wei zhi*, to which they refer several times, with their dogmatic view that Japan had always been ruled from Yamato. Thus the chronicle gives the impression that, if there was any diplomatic contact between Wei and a Japanese female ruler, it would have involved a legitimate female sovereign in Yamato. In effect, readers with access to both the Chinese and Japanese accounts were asked implicitly to take Empress Jingū as Himiko and Yamato as Yamatai.

Conflicting Views——The first scholar to depart from the view of the chronicles was MOTOORI NORINAGA. In his *Gyojū gaigen* (1778, An Outline on the Subduing of Foreigners), an anti-Chinese polemic on Japan's historical foreign relations, he took the *Wei zhi* directions literally and concluded that Yamatai was in Kyūshū and not to be identified with Yamato. He believed that the Wei observers were mistaken in thinking

that the queen herself was in Yamatai. Possibly they had heard of Japan's queen (Jingū), but any diplomatic representation from her must have been bogus, since in Motoori's view no Japanese ruler would ever have sent tribute to China. By dissociating the queen from Yamatai he was able to locate the latter in Kyūshū, as the *Wei zhi* seemed to require, without dishonoring the sacred Yamato tradition. Many scholars of the 19th century adopted Motoori's view. Because of the great distances indicated by the *Wei zhi*, most of the early Kyūshū theorists located Yamatai as far south as possible, in the Satsuma and Ōsumi areas (now Kagoshima Prefecture).

But this created geopolitical problems. It was hard to imagine that a regime so far removed from the major areas of Kyūshū life could have dominated those areas, which, as history, tradition, and (later) archaeology showed, were in the northwest. Moreover, the *Wei zhi* located the hostile country of Kunu south of Yamatai, but there was nothing south of Satsuma. In 1910 SHIRATORI KURAKICHI decided to reject entirely the long trip indicated by the *Wei zhi* and decided that Yamatai was in the Kumamoto area. South of that, in Satsuma, was Kunu. According to Shiratori, neither Yamatai nor Kunu was within the sphere of the main Yamato state in the KINAI (Kyōto-Ōsaka-Nara) area until their supposed conquest by Yamato sometime during the 4th century.

The Yamato Theory Reborn——Shiratori's treatment put the Kyūshū theory on much firmer philological and historical foundations than the earlier proponents had achieved. Yet, just at the time of his epochal article in 1910, NAITŌ KONAN revived the traditional Yamato, or Kinai, theory. The many localization problems of the Kyūshū theory, together with a residual belief in the basic Yamato tradition, encouraged Naitō to reexamine the *Wei zhi* text. Citing a number of instances of confusion between south and east in Chinese historical writing, he emended "south" to "east" and thus turned the itinerary toward the Kinai area. This theory had the advantage of not having to reject, as had Shiratori, the *Wei zhi*'s great distances. In bringing Yamatai back to Yamato, he could also draw on other material in the *Nihon shoki* to clarify the *Wei zhi* text.

The Significance of the Yamatai Debate——From the appearance of the articles by Shiratori and Naitō in 1910, no fundamentally new theory arose, only new arguments for the old theories. By the 1960s, most minds had been made up, and Kinai and Kyūshū theorists often seemed to be speaking only to their respective partisans. Moreover, the mass media became attracted to the issue.

But the localization of Yamatai is not a mere game, as it has sometimes seemed. If the growth and formation of the Japanese state is to be understood, it is of fundamental importance to know where Yamatai was. And yet, given the great differences in the two principal theories, and the determination and zeal with which they are advocated by very serious scholars, it is difficult to imagine that there will be an early solution.

Yamataka Shigeri　山高しげり

(1899–1977). Feminist and social reformer. Also known by her married name, Kaneko Shigeri, until her divorce in 1939. Born in Mie Prefecture, she attended Tōkyō Women's Higher Normal School (now

Ochanomizu Women's University). She first worked as a reporter in 1920 for the newspaper *Kokumin shimbun* and then for the women's magazine *Shufu no tomo*. She helped ICHIKAWA FUSAE found the FUSEN KAKUTOKU DŌMEI to campaign for women's suffrage during the 1920s. In 1934 she joined YAMADA WAKA and others to form the organization that in 1935 became the Bosei Hogo Remmei (Motherhood Protection League). She later helped organize war widows to improve their situation. In 1952 she founded the women's social reform league CHIFUREN and long served as its president (see also CONSUMER MOVEMENT). With its backing she was elected in 1962 and 1965 to the House of Councillors, where she served until 1971.

Yamatake-Honeywell Co, Ltd
山武ハネウエル[株]

(Yamatake Haneueru). Electronics company producing process-control devices and air-conditioning control devices, as well as other control and electronic equipment. Yamatake was established in 1906 and in 1920 concluded an exclusive sales agreement with Brown Instruments of the United States, which was acquired by Honeywell in 1934. In 1952 Yamatake-Honeywell concluded a licensing and joint-venture agreement with Honeywell. Sales totaled ¥118.6 billion (US $853.3 million) in the fiscal year ending September 1990. In 1991 the company was capitalized at ¥4.2 billion (US $30.6 million). Headquarters are in Tōkyō.

Yamatane Museum of Art
山種美術館

(Yamatane Bijutsukan). Located in Tōkyō. A collection of about 1,800 Japanese-style paintings from the Meiji period (1868–1912) to the present, most of them bought by Yamazaki Taneji (1893–1983), president of the Yamatane Securities Co, Ltd. The museum opened in 1966 and emphasizes works of the recent past. The gallery and the installation—the work of TANIGUCHI YOSHIRŌ—are fine examples of contemporary Japanese museum design.

Yamata no Orochi
八岐大蛇

Mythological, eight-headed, eight-tailed snakelike monster slain by SUSANOO NO MIKOTO. Susanoo, younger brother of the sun goddess AMATERASU ŌMIKAMI, had been banished from the High Celestial Plain (TAKAMAGAHARA) for his bad conduct (see TSUMI). Descending to earth in what is now part of the district of Izumo, Shimane Prefecture, he found an old couple weeping, saying that this monster, having eaten seven of their daughters, now demanded the last. After offering it rice wine, Susanoo killed it during its inebriated sleep and found in its tail the sword Ame no Murakumo no Tsurugi. The Ame no Murakumo sword, later called Kusanagi no Tsurugi, became one of the three IMPERIAL REGALIA.

Yamate Kiichirō
山手樹一郎

(1899–1978). Novelist. Born Iguchi Chōji in Tochigi Prefecture. After graduating from middle school, he worked as a magazine editor. In 1940 he published his first collection of stories, *Uguisu-zamurai* (Bush-Warbler Samurai), and a serialized novel, *Momotarō-zamurai* (1940–41, Samurai Momotarō). His postwar novels, such as *Yumesuke senryō miyage* (1947–51, Yumesuke's Thousand Pieces of Gold), are filled with optimism and human warmth, and held great emotional appeal for the war-weary Japanese.

Yamato
大和

A name that refers in its broadest sense to the country of Japan or to things Japanese, especially in contrast to things Chinese. Specifically, Yamato or Yamato Province (Yamato no Kuni) is the ancient name of Nara Prefecture. The name is generally thought to have come from *yama* (mountain) and *to* (place), but some scholars believe that Yamato is related to YAMATAI, the name of a legendary Japanese queendom. Between the 4th and 8th centuries Yamato was the center of early Japanese culture and politics (see YAMATO COURT). Historians generally divide the span of Yamato eminence into two periods. The protohistoric KOFUN PERIOD (ca 300–710) witnessed the rise of the first unified state in Japan, while the ensuing NARA PERIOD (710–794) saw the adoption of a centralized bureaucracy on the Chinese model and the rise of a civilization based on Buddhist ideology.

Yamato
大和[市]

City in central Kanagawa Prefecture, central Honshū. After World War II, Yamato was the site of a US Air Force base. It now has automobile parts and audio-equipment industries. Pop: 194,866.

Yamato
大和

Battleship of the Imperial Japanese Navy; the largest battleship ever built; completed in December 1941. Along with the battleship MUSASHI, the *Yamato* was constructed as part of the naval buildup following the abrogation of the London Naval Treaty in 1936 (see LONDON NAVAL CONFERENCES). The *Yamato*'s main features were a displacement of 64,000 tons; a main battery of nine 46-centimeter (18-in) guns; a secondary battery of twelve 15.5-centimeter (6-in) guns and a supplementary armament of twelve 12.7-centimeter (5-in), high-angle guns; six aircraft; a speed of 27 knots; a cruising range of 7,200 nautical miles; a length of 250 meters (820 ft); a beam of 39 meters (128 ft); and a crew of about 2,500.

The *Yamato* participated in the battles of MIDWAY, the PHILIPPINE SEA, and LEYTE GULF. On 7 April 1945 the *Yamato* and several escort vessels, almost all of the navy's remaining surface strength, sailed for Okinawa. Attacked by some 390 Allied planes, it was sunk off Bōnomisaki, southwest of Kyūshū. The disaster marked the end of the Imperial Japanese Navy.

Yamato Basin → Nara Basin

Yamato Bunkakan
大和文華館

A museum in the city of Nara. Opened in 1960. It houses a collection of approximately 2,000 items of East Asian art comprising paintings, sculpture, calligraphy, ceramics, lacquer, prints, and textiles. Outstanding items include the NEZAME MONOGATARI EMAKI, an EMAKIMONO (illustrated handscroll) from the Heian period (794–1185); a rare sutra, also from the Heian period; a pair of FŪZOKUGA (genre paintings) from the early Edo period (1600–1868); and Chinese paintings of the Song (Sung; 960–1297) dynasty.

Yamato court
大和朝廷

(Yamato *chōtei*). Center of the Japanese polity (ca 4th century–ca mid-7th century), situated in YAMATO (now Nara Prefecture). The Yamato ruler was not a sovereign but rather a *primus inter pares* acting in a loose confederation of similar chieftains. By the 5th century his authority extended as far as northern Kyūshū in the southwest and the Kantō plain in the northeast. Immigrant groups (KIKAJIN) from Korea became an important influence on the court during the 5th and 6th centuries.

By the 6th century a single kingly line seems to have emerged, the head of which devised a system of ranks and titles. Chieftains of important kin-groups (UJI) performed hereditary functions such as defense and worship for the court (see UJI-KABANE SYSTEM). The country was divided into *kuni* (provinces), which were subdivided into *agata*. These territorial units were governed by KUNI NO MIYATSUKO and AGATANUSHI, who were responsible for collecting tribute.

The introduction of BUDDHISM precipitated a conflict among the major court families. The pro-Buddhist faction, led by the SOGA FAMILY, triumphed in 587. SOGA NO UMAKO installed his niece, SUIKO, on the throne. The Soga were eventually overthrown in 645 by Prince Naka no Ōe (later Emperor TENJI) and FUJIWARA NO KAMATARI. These two, with the help of TAKAMUKO NO KUROMARO and the priest SŌMIN, established by means of the TAIKA REFORM (645) a centralized bureaucracy on the Chinese model and asserted the sovereignty of the emperor.

yamato-damashii
大和魂

(Japanese spirit). Phrase used until the end of World War II to describe spiritual qualities supposedly unique to the Japanese people. These range from physical and moral fortitude and courage, sincerity, and devotion, to what the Germans called *Volksgeist*.

Literary works reveal how the definition of *yamato-damashii* has changed over time. In the Heian period (794–1185) *yamato-damashii* was used to distinguish native ideas and patterns of behavior from those of China, a nation much admired and emulated at the time. In the late Edo period (1600–1868), when it was rediscovered by KOKUGAKU (National Learning) scholars, the term took on different meanings: MOTOORI NORINAGA equated *yamato-damashii* with the feminine spirit (*onnagokoro*) and held that it should counter the sycophantic attitude of pro-Chinese Japanese Confucianists. HIRATA ATSUTANE and others, however, reflecting the conditions of the time, made *yamato-damashii* synonymous with the militant idea

Yamato Sanzan The Three Hills of Yamato emerge faintly from the mist in the floor of the Nara Basin. *Left to right*: Amanokaguyama, Unebiyama, and Miminashiyama.

yama torikabuto Although every part of this plant is highly poisonous, its beautiful, helmet-shaped flowers are frequently used for decorative purposes.

of SONNŌ JŌI (Revere the Emperor, Expel the Barbarians). During the militaristic period from the early 1930s to the end of World War II, *yamato-damashii* was equated with unquestioning loyalty to emperor and nation.

yamato-e   大和絵

A term denoting Japanese-style painting. The word "Yamato" originally referred to the heartland of Japan, the region around Nara; the suffix *e* means pictures or paintings. It seems to have come into use in the mid-9th century when Japanese artists were beginning to produce works that differed from paintings produced under Chinese influence. Hence the term *yamato-e* came to be used in opposition to KARA-E ("Chinese-style painting"). Favorite themes included the passing of the seasons and the activities of the people in and around Heiankyō (now Kyōto), the capital from 794.

There was also a strong link between *yamato-e* and Japanese-style poetry, the 31-syllable WAKA. Often an artist would be asked to translate the content of a favorite poem into images on folding screens or sliding doors (see SCREEN AND WALL PAINTING). Poets, conversely, were frequently invited to compose a poem on the subject of a screen painting and add it as an inscription on the surface of the screen.

Today the term *yamato-e* encompasses not only Japanese themes but also formats and styles of painting that are considered to be distinctively Japanese. The narrative EMAKIMONO (handscroll) is now treated as a prime example of *yamato-e*, as are the various styles of painting associated with it. These include the *tsukuri-e* or "made-up picture" style (in which colors are laid on thickly) of the GENJI MONOGATARI EMAKI and the freer, more calligraphic manner of the SHIGISAN ENGI EMAKI. The term has even been applied to screens by HASEGAWA TŌHAKU and SŌTATSU.

Yamatogawa   大和川

River in Nara and Ōsaka prefectures, central Honshū, originating in the mountain Kaigahirayama and joined by numerous streams in the Nara Basin, flowing into the Ōsaka Plain to empty into Ōsaka Bay at the border of the cities of Sakai and Ōsaka. The water is used for irrigation, drinking, and industry. Length: 68 km (42 mi).

Yamatohime, Princess   倭姫命

(Yamatohime no Mikoto). Daughter of the legendary emperor Suinin and aunt of the legendary prince YAMATOTAKERU. According to tradition, she was commanded by the sun goddess AMATERASU ŌMIKAMI to go to the river Isuzugawa in Ise (now part of Mie Prefecture), build a shrine, and dedicate herself to the worship of the goddess (see ISE SHRINE). The chronicle KOJIKI (712) relates that Prince Yamatotakeru, before embarking on his eastern expedition to subdue the EZO people, stopped at the shrine to pay his respects and

received from his aunt a sacred sword that was later designated one of the three IMPERIAL REGALIA. It is important to note that, in both of these legends, Princess Yamatohime is described in the context of her relationship to the ruling dynasty of the YAMATO COURT and its mythical progenetrix, Amaterasu Ōmikami. Some scholars have identified Yamatohime with the 3rd-century ruler HIMIKO.

Yamato Kōriyama   大和郡山[市]

City in northern Nara Prefecture, central Honshū. Toyotomi Hidenaga, the brother of the hegemon TOYOTOMI HIDEYOSHI, built a castle here in 1585. A major center of goldfish breeding, there is also a growing electrical appliance industry. Attractions include the cherry blossoms at Kōriyama Castle, the garden at Jikōin, and the temple Kongōsenji. Pop: 92,949.

Yamato monogatari   大和物語

(Tales of Yamato). One of the *uta monogatari* (poem tales; see MONOGATARI BUNGAKU), a Heian-period (794–1185) genre. In most editions there are 173 episodes. It consists of a collection of anecdotes, each of which centers on one or more WAKA poems. The Yamato of the title probably refers to both the name of an ancient Japanese province and to Japan itself. The unknown compiler-editor was no doubt a Heian courtier with an interest in anecdotes about people at court and the poems they composed. It is fairly certain that the original text was revised shortly after 996 and that the work known today as *Yamato monogatari* is not the product of a single writer. It is believed that the original text was completed sometime in 951 or 952 and that additions were made in subsequent years.

In the first half of the work the poems are the central elements of the anecdotes, and the prose passages are often no more than introductory notes. The prose passages in the work's latter half are somewhat longer. *Yamato monogatari* suggests the development of Japanese literature from a series of poems, accompanied by headnotes, to the great prose narrative works with only occasional poems embellishing the text. This classic provides a picture of Heian society in the early 10th century and was a source for a number of later works.

Yamato period   大和時代

(Yamato *jidai*). A term formerly used widely to refer to the period of Japanese history from ca 300 to 710. Derived from the geographical name of the seat of government of the YAMATO COURT, it has been largely displaced by the term KOFUN PERIOD.

Yamato Province   大和国

(Yamato no Kuni). Present-day Nara Prefecture. The province was the center of government and culture from the establishment of the YAMATO COURT in the 4th century until 784, when a new capital, NAGAOKAKYŌ, was established in YAMASHIRO PROVINCE. During the Heian period (794–1185) Yamato was under the control of KŌFUKUJI, TŌDAIJI, and other great temples of the area. In the Kamakura (1185–1333) and Muromachi (1333–1568) periods, SHUGO (provincial constables, later military governors) were not appointed to the province by the shogunate and it continued to be administered by Kōfukuji. *Samurai* forces in the province expanded their power mainly under the temple's influence. In 1576, however, ODA NOBUNAGA, who had brought most of Japan, including Yamato,

under his control, appointed a *shugo* to the province. During the Edo period (1600–1868) it was divided into seven domains, but the city of Nara was administered by a shogunal commissioner (BUGYŌ).

yama torikabuto   山鳥兜

Aconitum japonicum. Also called *torikabuto*. A perennial herb of the family Ranunculaceae, it is found in wooded mountain areas of central-northern Honshū and Hokkaidō. The plant has underground tubers and a stem that grows to 100 centimeters (about 3 ft). The glossy, alternate leaves have five lobes. In late autumn clusters of helmet-shaped, bluish purple flowers blossom. The tuber of the *yama torikabuto* contains a potent poison used by the AINU people to poison the tips of arrows for bear-baiting festivals.

A similar species found growing wild in Japan is the *reijinsō* (*A. loczyanum*). It resembles the *yama torikabuto*, but its stems are more slender. Its light purple blossoms give the plant its name, since their shape resembles that of the headgear used by traditional dance performers called *reijin*. Originally from China, the *hana torikabuto* (*A. chinense*) is cultivated in Japan and used as a cut flower because of its attractive, bluish purple blossoms.

Yamato Sanzan   大和三山

(The Three Hills of Yamato). Three hills in the city of Kashihara, Nara Prefecture, central Honshū: Unebiyama (199 m; 653 ft), Amanokaguyama (152 m; 499 ft), and Miminashiyama (140 m; 459 ft). The hills, formed from igneous rocks, rise abruptly from the alluvial soil of the Nara Basin to form a triangle. They are mentioned in the MAN'YŌSHŪ, an 8th-century poetry anthology, and other ancient literature.

Yamato Takada   大和高田[市]

City in northwestern Nara Prefecture, central Honshū. In the Edo period (1600–1868) it flourished as a temple town around the temple Senryūji. It now produces textiles and foodstuffs. Pop: 68,237.

Yamatotakeru, Prince   日本武尊

(Yamatotakeru no Mikoto). Legendary hero, supposedly the son of the legendary 12th emperor KEIKŌ. Prince Yamatotakeru is said to have been responsible for extending the territory controlled by the YAMATO COURT (ca 4th century–ca mid-7th century) through his subjugation of the aboriginal KUMASO tribe in Kyūshū and the EZO people of northeastern Honshū. Yamatotakeru is thought to be an archetypal hero figure, probably developed between the 5th and 7th centuries, embodying the acts of numerous warriors.

The story of Yamatotakeru appears in the chronicles KOJIKI (712) and NIHON SHOKI (720). The *Kojiki* account (summarized here) gives a fuller description of Yamatotakeru as ancient noble hero, while the *Nihon shoki* emphasizes the growing power of the Yamato state.

In the *Kojiki* account of the legend of Yamatotakeru, Emperor Keikō is concerned about the violent behavior of his son and sends him off to Kyūshū on a campaign against the Kumaso. Before leaving, Yamatotakeru receives a sword and other gifts from his aunt YAMATOHIME, the custodial priestess at the ISE SHRINE. After successfully subduing the Kumaso, including the brothers Kumasotakeru, Yamatotakeru returns triumphantly to Yamato, suppressing an uprising by Izumotakeru in Izumo (now Shimane Prefecture) along the way.

After Yamatotakeru returns, Emperor Keikō again orders him on a subjugation campaign, this time against the Ezo in northeastern Honshū. He is sent off with a halberd made from a holly tree, a sacred tree reputed to drive away evil. Before his departure he meets again with Yamatohime and expresses to her the fear that his father wishes him an early death. Yamatohime encourages him to proceed and gives him another sword and a bag containing a piece of flint. He later uses these gifts when he is attacked by bandits and threatened with death in a prairie fire in Sagami (now Kanagawa Prefecture). He uses the sword to cut down the grass around him and sets his own fire with the flint to drive off his attackers.

Yamatotakeru later falls seriously ill, and as he awaits his death in Nobono (now northwestern Mie Prefecture) he composes four poems, one of which describes the beauty of Yamato, "the greatest of all nations, a truly beautiful land surrounded by mountains as though by a great green wall." Upon his death Yamatotakeru's soul takes the form of a swan and flies away. See also HERO WORSHIP.

Yamato Transport Co, Ltd
ヤマト運輸[株]

(Yamato Un'yu). Door-to-door parcel delivery company. Incorporated in 1929. It has a 40 percent share of the domestic door-to-door delivery business. The company has a worldwide delivery system that consists of 11 overseas subsidiaries. Sales for the fiscal year ending March 1991 totaled ¥426.2 billion (US $3.1 billion), and capitalization stood at ¥47.4 billion (US $345.5 million). Headquarters are in Tōkyō.

Yamawaki Tōyō
山脇東洋

(1705–62). Edo-period (1600–1868) physician of the classicist school of medicine (koihō) whose "trial and experimentation" doctrine helped advance premodern Japanese medicine. Original family name Shimizu. A native of Kyōto, he was adopted by Yamawaki Genshū (1646–1729), a court physician, to whose post he later succeeded. Following a suggestion of his former teacher GOTŌ KONZAN, on 30 March 1754 Yamawaki performed Japan's first officially approved dissection of a human body at the Rokkaku prison on the outskirts of Kyōto. Five years later a record of the dissection was published under the title Zōshi. Yamawaki also reprinted, in 1746, a Chinese medical work of the Tang (T'ang) dynasty (618–907), the Waitai mi yaofang (Wai-t'ai mi yao-fang, 24 vols).

Yamazaki
山崎

District in the town of Ōyamazaki, southern Kyōto Prefecture, central Honshū. Since ancient times the Yamazaki district has been a center of river and land transportation. In 1582 it was the site of an important battle between Toyotomi Hideyoshi and Akechi Mitsuhide. Now the district is a commuters' community for the cities of Kyōto, Ōsaka, and Kōbe.

Yamazaki Ansai
山崎闇斎

(1619–82). Prominent Neo-Confucian scholar and philosopher of the early Edo period (1600–1868) and the founder of Suiga Shintō (or SUIKA SHINTŌ), a syncretic combination of Ise Shintō (or WATARAI SHINTŌ) and YOSHIDA SHINTŌ theories with SHUSHIGAKU, the Neo-Confucian philosophy of Zhu Xi (Chu Hsi). Ansai's father was a samurai who had moved from Himeji to Kyōto, where Ansai was born. At age 23, shortly after becoming a priest of the Rinzai Zen sect, he attended a lecture on the Confucian classic The Doctrine of the Mean (Ch: Zhongyong or Chung-yung) given by TANI JICHŪ, a leader of the Nangakuha school; this led him to abandon Buddhism and turn to the Neo-Confucian philosophy of Zhu Xi. In 1646 he returned to secular life.

Ansai was not an original Neo-Confucian thinker. His understanding of the philosophy of Zhu Xi took the form of a rigorous moralism, with strong emphasis on the concept of TSUTSUSHIMI, or self-restraint, and the virtue of loyalty to one's lord. His Bunkai hitsuroku (1643, Reading Notes) is one of the best introductions to the philosophy of the Zhu Xi school as it developed in China and Korea.

Soon after he left the Buddhist priesthood, Ansai began the study of Shintō. Just as he regarded Zhu Xi's philosophy as the true way of China, Shintō to him was the way of Japan. He advocated, therefore, simultaneous study of Shintō and Confucianism (shinju kengaku). His Suiga Shintō was a combination of Neo-Confucian rationalism and Shintō nonrationalism. In Suiga Shintō Ansai expressed strong nationalistic sentiments that he claimed to have learned from Zhu Xi. Ansai's ideas later provided important ideological support for the leaders of the Meiji Restoration (1868).

Yamazaki Baking Co, Ltd
山崎製パン[株]

(Yamazaki Seipan). Company engaged in the baking and selling of bread, as well as Japanese- and Western-style confectioneries. Incorporated in 1948, Yamazaki is the country's largest bread-baking firm. Yamazaki has overseas offices in New York, Paris, and Taipei and is affiliated with the National Biscuit Co of the United States, whose products it sells domestically. It has recently expanded into the soft drink and convenience store businesses. Sales totaled ¥432.9 billion (US $3.2 billion) in 1990, of which 60 percent came from bread, 30 percent from confectioneries, and 10 percent from other sources. The company was capitalized at ¥11.0 billion (US $82.4 million) in the same year. Headquarters are in Tōkyō.

Yamazaki, Battle of
山崎の戦い

(Yamazaki no Tatakai). Also known as the Battle of Tennōzan. Battle fought on 2 July 1582 between TOYOTOMI HIDEYOSHI and AKECHI MITSUHIDE in the Yamazaki district near the town of Ōyamazaki on the border between Settsu and Yamashiro provinces (now parts of Ōsaka and Kyōto prefectures). Mitsuhide had assassinated ODA NOBUNAGA in the HONNŌJI INCIDENT 11 days earlier while Hideyoshi was on campaign against the powerful MŌRI FAMILY. Hideyoshi was able to disengage and march his troops with remarkable speed to the Ōsaka area, where he secured the support of Nobunaga's son Oda Nobutaka (1558–83) and several daimyō, including TAKAYAMA UKON. Mitsuhide's hoped-for allies HOSOKAWA YŪSAI and TSUTSUI JUNKEI failed to heed his call for assistance. Outnumbered and threatened with encirclement, Mitsuhide retreated to Shōryūji Castle (now the city of Nagaokakyō, Kyōto Prefecture) and fled the fort when it was surrounded, but he was killed by marauding peasants; on 3 July, Shōryūji fell. The victory at Yamazaki was the first step in Hideyoshi's campaign for national hegemony.

Yamazaki Chōun
山崎朝雲

(1867–1954). Sculptor. Born in Fukuoka Prefecture. Yamazaki studied under TAKAMURA KŌUN and, in 1907, founded the Nihon Chōkokukai (Japan Sculpture Association). He was made a member of the Imperial Fine Arts Academy (Teikoku Bijutsuin) in 1927 and of the Imperial Art Committee (Teishitsu Gigeiin) in 1934. His wooden sculptures are marked by Western-style realism and at the same time convey his own depth of feeling and freedom of spirit.

Yamazaki Masakazu
山崎正和

(1934–). Playwright and critic. Yamazaki was brought up in Manchuria during World War II and educated in philosophy at Kyōto University. His first important play, Zeami (1963), is a modern psychological and poetic recounting of the life of ZEAMI, the founder of the medieval Nō theater. The subject matter of his plays ranges from contemporary Japan to Western history. His 1972 Ō, Eroīzu! is about the famous 12th-century French cleric Abélard and his student and lover Héloïse. His 1973 Sanetomo shuppan (Sanetomo Sets Sail) has also been produced in English. In addition to his dramas, Yamazaki has written on aesthetics, history, and such literary figures as MORI ŌGAI. His critical works include Yawarakai kojinshugi no tanjō (1984, The Birth of Soft Individualism).

Yamazaki Sōkan
山崎宗鑑

(1465?–1553?). RENGA (linked verse) and HAIKU poet of the Muromachi period (1333–1568). He compiled the earliest haiku anthology, INU TSUKUBASHŪ (ca 1540), whose title, "Doggerel Tsukubashū," parodied those of the renga anthologies TSUKUBASHŪ and SHINSEN TSUKUBASHŪ. The title also indicated the comic and even licentious quality of its verses, signaled the contemporary reaction against the complicated rules and vocabulary of renga, and influenced the radical DANRIN SCHOOL of haiku. Of Sōkan himself, little is known. He is said to have been a samurai in the service of the shōgun Ashikaga Yoshihisa (1465–89), upon whose death in 1489 he became a monk and retired to Yamazaki in Kyōto, whence his name.

Yamazaki Toyoko
山崎豊子

(1924–). Novelist. Real name Sugimoto Toyoko. Born in Ōsaka Prefecture. Graduate of Kyōto Women's University. Yamazaki won the Naoki Prize for Hananoren (1958, Flowered Shop Curtain), a novel about Ōsaka merchants. Other works include Shiroi kyotō (1963–68, The Ivory Tower), which depicts problems in the medical world; Fumō chitai (1973–78; tr The Barren Zone, 1985), about the sorrows of a trading company employee involved in petroleum development in Iran; and Futatsu no sokoku (1983, Two Native Lands), the story of second-generation Japanese Americans during World War II.

yambaru tenaga kogane
山原手長黄金虫

(yambaru long-armed scarab beetle). Cheirotonus jambar Y. Kurosawa. Japan's largest

Yamazaki Masakazu This modern playwright is also known for his essays on aesthetics and history.

Yamazaki Toyoko This novelist's work is marked by a concern for contemporary social issues and by realistic depiction of the worlds of business and medicine.

yambaru tenaga kogane A male *yambaru* long-armed scarab beetle clings to the trunk of a chinquapin tree. Despite its designation as a protected species, the beetle is in danger of extinction.

native beetle, first recorded in 1984 in the northern part of the island of Okinawa. Designated a protected species in 1985. The male ranges from 47 to 62 millimeters (1.85 to 2.44 in) in length, the female from 46 to 57 millimeters (1.81 to 2.25 in). The head and pronotum are a gold green or bronze green, and the elytra are black with a greenish tinge, leaving a few dull brownish or yellowish patches along the suture and margin. The larvae are found among flakes of decaying wood that have accumulated in the hollows of old oak trees. It takes an estimated three to four years for the eggs to develop into mature insects. *Yambaru*, the name of the beetle, is an Okinawan dialect word for the terracelike hills in the northern part of the island.

Yame　　　　　　　　　　　　八女[市]

City in southern Fukuoka Prefecture, Kyūshū. It produces rice, tea, mandarin oranges, grapes, and pears; stock raising and dairy farming are active. Cottage industries produce handmade Japanese paper (*washi*), Buddhist altars, paper lanterns, carp streamers (*koinobori*), and stone lanterns. The Iwatoyama tomb, which dates from the Kofun period (ca 300–710), is located here. Pop: 39,816.

Yamizo Mountains　　　　　　八溝山地

(Yamizo Sanchi). Mountain range running north to south in northwestern Ibaraki Prefecture, central Honshū. The highest peak is Yamizosan (1,022 m; 3,353 ft). The northern part of the range, known for hot-spring spas and beautiful gorges, is part of Oku Kuji Prefectural Natural Park. Tsukubasan, the southernmost peak, is part of Suigō-Tsukuba Quasi-National Park.

Yanagawa　　　　　　　　　　柳川[市]

City in southwestern Fukuoka Prefecture, Kyūshū, at the mouth of the river Chikugogawa. An extensive network of creeks draws water from the river to irrigate farmland here. Rice and rushes are grown. There is an active farm-machinery industry. The poet KITAHARA HAKUSHŪ was born here. Pop: 43,791.

Yanagawa Seigan　　　　　　　梁川星巌

(1789–1858). Confucianist and poet of the late Edo period (1600–1868); known for *kanshi* (poems in Chinese; see POETRY AND PROSE IN CHINESE). Born Yanagawa Mōi in Mino Province (now part of Gifu Prefecture). He studied with YAMAMOTO HOKUZAN and became known for his verse in the elevated Tang (T'ang) style. Seigan's chief collection of poetry is his *Seiganshū* (1841–56).

Yanagawa Shunsan　　　　　　柳川春三

(1832–70). Late-Edo-period (1600–1868) journalist and scholar of WESTERN LEARNING

(Yōgaku). Born in Nagoya, he studied Dutch science and English and earned a reputation for his writings on Western Learning. In 1863 he was ordered by shogunate officials to submit summaries of articles concerned with Japan in English-language newspapers. In 1867 he began publishing the magazine *Seiyō zasshi*, which introduced Western things to Japan. The *Chūgai shimbun*, which he established in 1868, became the prototype for later newspapers.

yanagi → willows

Yanagida Izumi　　　　　　　　柳田泉

(1894–1969). Scholar of Japanese and English literature. Born in Aomori Prefecture. A graduate of Waseda University in English literature, he translated many works of Western writers. He helped found the Society for the Study of Meiji Civilization (Meiji Bunka Kenkyūkai) in 1924 and edited the 24-volume *Meiji bunka zenshū* (1927–30), the first important collection of materials for the study of Meiji (1868–1912) culture. His insistence on a systematic research methodology based on primary sources profoundly influenced the next generation of scholars. His principal works include *Seiji shōsetsu kenkyū* (3 vols, 1935–39), a study of early Meiji political novels, and *Tayama Katai no bungaku* (2 vols, 1957–58), a critical biography of novelist TAYAMA KATAI.

Yanagihara Byakuren　　　　　柳原白蓮

(1885–1967). *Waka* poet and social activist. Born in Tōkyō, the daughter of a count; real name Miyazaki Akiko. She began her study of traditional poetry with SASAKI NOBUTSUNA. After divorcing her first husband, she married Itō Den'emon (1860–1947), a Kyūshū mining magnate. In 1921 she left him to marry a young social reformer, Miyazaki Ryūsuke (1892–1971; son of MIYAZAKI TŌTEN), and joined her new husband in the labor movement. She attracted notice for the passionate style of her poetry in the anthologies *Fumie* (1915, Trodden Images) and *Kichō no kage* (1919, Screen Shadows), and for her autobiographical novel *Ibara no mi* (1928, The Fruit of Thorns).

Yanagi Muneyoshi　　　　　　柳宗悦

(1889–1961). Art historian and leader of the Japanese folk-craft movement (*mingei undō*). Also known as Yanagi Sōetsu. He studied at Gakushūin (Peers' School) and was a member of the so-called SHIRAKABA SCHOOL. He graduated from Tōkyō University in 1913.

While studying the arts and crafts of Korea and Japan he became aware of the beauty, until then largely ignored, of implements used in daily life; he subsequently developed a strong interest in the creative capacities of the common people. The term *mingei* (FOLK CRAFTS) was coined by him as a means of categorizing this quality of beauty. In 1926 Yanagi, TOMIMOTO KENKICHI, HAMADA SHŌJI, and KAWAI KANJIRŌ published *Nihon mingei bijutsukan setsuritsu shuisho* (Prospectus to Establish a Japan Folk-Craft Museum), which inspired a movement for the appreciation of the decorative arts deriving from folk tradition. In 1936, with the aid of ŌHARA MAGOSABURŌ and others, he established the JAPAN FOLK-CRAFT MUSEUM at Komaba in Tōkyō. His major writings are collected in *Yanagi Muneyoshi senshū*, (10 vols, 1954–55).

Yanagisawa Kien　　　　　　　柳沢淇園

(1704–58). Pioneer of literati (BUNJINGA) painting. Also known as Ryū Rikyō. Born in

the Kōriyama domain in the province of Yamato (now Nara Prefecture), the second son of a high-ranking *samurai* who served the Yanagisawa family. Kien studied not only painting but several other arts. In brushwork he was at first a pupil of a KANŌ SCHOOL master, but at age 12 decided to follow the great Chinese *bunjinga* masters.

Kien was doubtless influenced by OGYŪ SORAI, the great Confucian scholar who served the Yanagisawa family. Kien developed ties with ŌBAKU SECT Zen monks, who probably introduced him to Chinese paintings, books, and woodblock prints. He often followed the style of the Chinese academic bird-and-flower painter SHEN NANPIN (Shen Nan-p'in), who had come to Nagasaki in 1731 and transmitted his decorative and semirealistic methods to Japanese pupils. Kien was especially skilled in painting bamboo; his *Finger-Painted Bamboo* is noted for its freedom of composition and technique.

Yanagisawa Yoshiyasu　　　　　柳沢吉保

(1658–1714). Statesman of the Edo period (1600–1868). The son of a minor retainer to the future shōgun TOKUGAWA TSUNAYOSHI when the latter was *daimyō* of the Tatebayashi domain (now part of Gumma Prefecture), Yoshiyasu began his career as a page of his father's lord. In 1688 he was appointed chamberlain (SOBAYŌNIN) to the shōgun, a post created by Tsunayoshi to extend his personal authority as shōgun. As Tsunayoshi's favorite and trusted adviser, Yoshiyasu's power and influence steadily increased. He was made the daimyō of Kawagoe domain (now part of Saitama Prefecture) and given official status equal to members of the senior council (RŌJŪ). In 1701 he was granted the use of the surname Matsudaira, the original surname of the Tokugawa, and in 1704 was granted a fief in the domain of Kōfu (now part of Yamanashi Prefecture), previously held only by members of the main line of the Tokugawa family. Upon the death of Tsunayoshi in 1709, Yoshiyasu retired from official shogunate service and lived in seclusion. He has been portrayed as a corrupt and opportunistic shogunal favorite who encouraged Tsunayoshi in his extravagance and eccentricities. However, modern scholarship suggests that Yoshiyasu was faithful to Tsunayoshi's desire to promote Confucianism and Buddhism. He took into his service the Confucian scholars OGYŪ SORAI and HOSOI KŌTAKU, thus helping to convert the shogunate's policy of military rule to an emphasis on civil government.

Yanagita Kunio　　　　　　　　柳田国男

(1875–1962). Founder of Japanese FOLKLORE STUDIES (*minzokugaku*). A scholar and poet who also worked as a journalist and government bureaucrat, Yanagita's extensive research and writing established the framework for other folklore research in Japan. Born in Hyōgo Prefecture, he was the sixth son of Matsuoka Misao, a scholar, teacher, and Shintō priest. Following his graduation in law from Tōkyō University in 1900, he married into the influential family of Yanagita Naohei and took on the Yanagita name. He worked as a government bureaucrat from 1900 to 1919 and as a journalist for the *Asahi shimbun* from 1919 to 1930. An avid traveler and prolific writer (over 100 books and 1,000 articles), he contributed many articles to journals of the late Meiji period (1868–1912). His classic TŌNO MONOGATARI was published in 1910.

Yanagi Muneyoshi An art historian and founder of the Japanese folk-craft movement, Yanagi concentrated his attention on the decorative arts of Korea and Japan as embodiments of the creative energies of the common people.

Yanagita gave full attention to developing the discipline of folklore from around 1930. If there is a unifying theme to his work, it is the search for the elements of tradition that explain Japan's distinctive national character. Yanagita's selected works are contained in the 36-volume *Teihon Yanagita Kunio shū*.

Yanai   柳井[市]

City in southeastern Yamaguchi Prefecture, western Honshū. Known for the production of the fabric *yanaijima*, it was rapidly industrialized through the construction of factories by Hitachi, Ltd. The Chausuyama tomb, dating from the Kofun period (ca 300–710), is located here. Pop: 36,360.

Yanaihara Tadao   矢内原忠雄

(1893–1961). Economist and educator. Born in Ehime Prefecture. A disciple of UCHIMURA KANZŌ, founder of the Nonchurch (MUKYŌKAI) Christian movement, Yanaihara was well known for his courageous stand against Japanese militarism during the period 1931–45.

He studied at Tōkyō University and later occupied the chair of Colonial Policy in the Faculty of Economics there. He was very productive as a scholar and published such substantial books as *Shokumin oyobi shokumin seisaku* (1927, Colonization and Colonial Policy). He grew increasingly critical of Japan's official policies from the MANCHURIAN INCIDENT of 1931 on and gradually became a target of attack from right-wing scholars backed by militarists. He was pressured into resigning from Tōkyō University in December 1937, but from 1951 to 1957 he served as its president and was widely acknowledged as a major intellectual and spiritual leader. See also PACIFISM.

Yan'an (Yenan) government
延安政府

(En'an *seifu*). The Chinese communist government from the mid-1930s to 1949, the period of resistance against Japan and of the ensuing civil war with the Chinese Guomindang (Kuomintang; Nationalist Party). Forced out of their Jiangxi (Kiangsi) base by the Guomindang in late 1934, the Chinese communists arrived in northern Shaanxi (Shensi) in October 1935 after the epic Long March. At the end of 1936, Yan'an, a town in northern Shaanxi, was declared the capital of the Chinese Soviet Republic.

The Chinese communists claimed to have chosen the region as a base in order to confront Japanese aggression in North China. After the outbreak of the SINO-JAPANESE WAR OF 1937–1945, communist forces organized guerrilla resistance against Japan. NOSAKA SANZŌ, exiled leader of the Japan Communist Party, spent the war years in Yan'an, engaging in anti-Japanese activities. The Chinese communists defeated the Guomindang in the civil war that followed Japan's surrender, and on 1 October 1949 the People's Republic of China was proclaimed at the new capital, Beijing (Peking).

Yanase & Co, Ltd   [株]ヤナセ

(Yanase). Japan's largest distributor and dealer of imported cars, including Cadillac, Buick, Pontiac, Chevrolet, and Mercedes-Benz. The company supplies auto parts and maintenance and repair services and also distributes other products including boats and marine engines, fashion wear, jewelry, and petroleum. Incorporated in 1920. Sales for the fiscal year ending September 1990 totaled ¥466.3 billion (US $3.6 billion), and

capitalization stood at ¥320.0 million (US $2.3 million). Headquarters are in Tōkyō.

Yanmar Agricultural Equipment Co, Ltd   ヤンマー農機[株]

(Yammā Nōki). Seller of agricultural machinery and equipment. Incorporated in 1961. A subsidiary of the YANMAR DIESEL ENGINE CO, LTD, it exports products to over 130 countries. Sales for the fiscal year ending December 1990 totaled ¥153.3 billion (US $1.1 billion), and capitalization stood at ¥2.0 billion (US $15.0 million). Headquarters are in Ōsaka.

Yanmar Diesel Engine Co, Ltd
ヤンマーディーゼル[株]

(Yammā Dīzeru). Machinery maker that produces engines for agricultural machines and for ships, construction equipment, and small electric generators. Established in 1912 by Yamaoka Magokichi (1888–1962), it was the first company in the world to develop and commercialize the small diesel engine. After World War II, the company began production of small tractors, tilling and planting machines for rice fields, and maritime leisure equipment. Joint-venture subsidiary firms in Brazil, Indonesia, and Thailand manufacture and sell the company's products. Sales for the fiscal year ending March 1990 totaled ¥201.7 billion (US $1.5 billion), and capitalization stood at ¥2.4 billion (US $18.0 million) in the same year. Headquarters are in Ōsaka.

Yano Jun'ya   矢野絢也

(1932–). Politician. Born in Ōsaka Prefecture, Yano graduated from Kyōto University. In 1967 he was first elected to the House of Representatives as a KŌMEITŌ candidate from Ōsaka. Yano replaced TAKEIRI YOSHIKATSU as Kōmeitō party chairman in December 1986 but was forced to resign in May 1989 when some of his stock transactions aroused suspicion. Yano is known to be an advocate of the formation of a new party consisting of members of both the majority and minority parties.

Ya no ne   矢の根

(The Arrowhead). KABUKI play; one of the celebrated kabuki numbers known as the KABUKI JŪHACHIBAN. A *jidai-mono* (historical play), first performed in 1720, its author is unknown. The central character is the historical figure Soga Gorō (1174–93), who, with his brother Jūrō (1172–93), avenged the death of his father. As the key figures in a vendetta, the brothers became two of the most popular figures in tales (see SOGA MONOGATARI) and in every form of Japanese theater. In the kabuki it has been *de rigueur* since around 1700 for the New Year's program to include a play on the Soga theme. In *Ya no ne* Gorō falls asleep while polishing a giant arrowhead but awakes to rescue Jūrō from a dangerous situation.

Yano Ryūkei   矢野竜渓

(1850–1931). Writer and politician. Real name Yano Fumio. Born in what is now Ōita Prefecture; graduate of Keiō University. After working briefly for the newspaper YŪBIN HŌCHI SHIMBUN, in 1878 he entered government service under ŌKUMA SHIGENOBU, the liberal politician who was his patron. When Ōkuma was ousted in the POLITICAL CRISIS OF 1881, Yano left his post also. In 1882 he returned to the *Yūbin hōchi shimbun* as its president and made the paper the organ of the RIKKEN KAISHINTŌ (Constitutional Reform

Party). In 1883–84 he published the political novel *Keikoku bidan* (A Noble Tale of Statesmanship; see SEIJI SHŌSETSU). A romanticized version of the struggle of ancient Thebes to throw off Spartan domination, it inspired many young readers with notions of freedom and independence. In his later years Yano wrote for the newspaper *Ōsaka mainichi shimbun*.

Yanagita Kunio The founder of Japanese folklore studies in front of his Tōkyō home in 1957.

Yano Tsuneta   矢野恒太

(1866–1951). Businessman. Born in what is now Okayama Prefecture, Yano attended Tōkyō University. He served in the Ministry of Agriculture and Commerce (1898–1902) and drafted the Insurance Business Law (Hokengyō Hō) in 1900. In 1902 Yano established Daiichi Seimei, Japan's first mutual insurance firm (see DAI-ICHI MUTUAL LIFE INSURANCE CO), and guided the company to success. All other life insurance companies followed Daiichi Seimei's lead and became mutual insurance corporations after World War II.

Yanaihara Tadao A member of the Nonchurch Christian movement, this economist and educator strongly opposed Japanese militarism during the period 1931–45.

Yao   八尾[市]

City in central Ōsaka Prefecture, central Honshū; a satellite city of Ōsaka. Traditional products are toothbrushes and thread. Several medieval temples are located here. Pop: 277,568.

Yaohan Japan Corporation
[株]ヤオハンジャパン

(Yaohan Japan). Regional supermarket chain operator based in the Shizuoka area. Incorporated in 1962. In 1992 the company had a total of 26 overseas stores in Singapore, Costa Rica, Hong Kong, Malaysia, Taiwan, the United States, Brunei, Thailand, and China. Sales for the fiscal year ending May 1990 totaled ¥125.2 billion (US $815.5 million), and capitalization stood at ¥18.7 billion (US $121.8 million). Headquarters are in Numazu, Shizuoka Prefecture.

Yarigatake   槍ケ岳

Mountain on the border of Nagano and Gifu prefectures, central Honshū. It is the second highest peak in the Hida Mountains and the fourth highest mountain in Japan. The trails linking it with TSUBAKURODAKE and HOTAKADAKE are popular with climbers. Height: 3,180 m (10,433 ft).

Yasaka Shrine   八坂神社

(Yasaka Jinja). Formerly called Gionsha and Gion Tenjin. Shintō shrine in Higashiyama Ward, Kyōto; dedicated to the deity SUSANOO NO MIKOTO, his consort, and eight of their children. Although conflicting traditions exist regarding its origin, there is general agreement that the shrine was originally sacred to Gozu Tennō, a Buddhist deity. Ac-

cording to the prevailing notions of Buddhist-Shintō syncretism, the Buddhist deity Gozu was identified with the native Japanese deity Susanoo no Mikoto. By the 10th century, Gionsha had become one of the most popular shrines in Kyōto and was believed to be particularly efficacious in pacifying vengeful spirits (GORYŌ), protecting warriors, bringing prosperity, and averting illness. The main sanctuary of the shrine, known for its Gion-style architecture (see SHINTŌ ARCHITECTURE), dates from 1654. The official name of the shrine was changed to the present non-Buddhist designation in 1868. A major festival of Kyōto, the GION FESTIVAL, is held at the shrine for approximately a month in July. See also HONJI SUIJAKU.

Yasaka Yahama   八坂八浜

Rocky coastal area between the towns of Kainan and Mugi, southeastern Tokushima Prefecture, Shikoku. Located on the Pacific Ocean, it is included in Muroto-Anan Coast Quasi-National Park. A JR (Japan Railways) line and a state highway run along the coast. Length: 10 km (6 mi).

1740

Yasaka Yahama

Yasato   八郷[町]

Town in central Ibaraki Prefecture, central Honshū, on the eastern slopes of the mountain Tsukubasan. The principal activity is farming, mainly vegetables and fruits. The Magnetic Observatory of the Meteorological Agency is located here. Pop: 29,417.

Yashajin Pass   夜叉神峠

(Yashajin Tōge). Located in western Yamanashi Prefecture, central Honshū, at the northern end of the Akaishi Mountains. The pass is known for its spectacular scenery and panoramic views of the Southern Alps National Park. Altitude: 1,770 m (5,807 ft).

Yashima   屋島

Peninsula—formerly an island, now connected to the mainland—jutting into the Inland Sea northeast of the city of Takamatsu, Kagawa Prefecture, Shikoku. This scenic mesa-type plateau covered with pine trees is a historic spot, the site of many battles during the war between the Minamoto and the Taira families in 1185. It is part of the Inland Sea National Park. Elevation: 292 m (958 ft).

Yashima   八島

NŌ play. Attributed to ZEAMI. Classified as a *nibamme-mono* ("part-two play"), it is based on a story from the HEIKE MONOGATARI. A Buddhist priest (the *waki* or subordinate character) from Kyōto visits Yashima, a promontory on the Inland Sea coast of Sanuki Province and scene of a major battle in the TAIRA-MINAMOTO WAR in 1185. There he meets an old man (the *maejite* or main character at the beginning of a play) who tells of battles between the Taira and Minamoto armies, hints that he himself is the ill-fated warrior MINAMOTO NO YOSHITSUNE, and disappears. Later, as the priest sleeps, the armed figure of Yoshitsune (the *nochijite* or main character at the end of a play) appears before him in his dreams to recount episodes of fierce battle. The dream and Yoshitsune vanish with the light of dawn.

Yashio   八潮[市]

City in southeastern Saitama Prefecture, central Honshū. Formerly a farming area, it is now a residential suburb of Tōkyō, with textile, machine, and metal industries. Pop: 72,473.

Yashiro Hirokata   屋代弘賢

(1758–1841). KOKUGAKU (National Learning) scholar and calligrapher of the late Edo period (1600–1868). Born in Edo (now Tōkyō). He assisted his teacher, HANAWA HOKIICHI, in compiling a collection of historical and literary documents known as the GUNSHO RUIJŪ. Other works include a survey of social customs and the *Kokon yōrankō* (1842), an encyclopedic work on Japan and China.

Yashiro Seiichi   矢代静一

(1927–   ). Playwright. Born in Tōkyō; graduate of Waseda University. In 1949 he joined the Bungakuza (Literary Theater), a theater company organized by KISHIDA KUNIO. He won critical acclaim for his play *Kiiro to momoiro no yūgata* (1959, Evening in Yellow and Peach), about young people and conflict in postwar Japan. *Yoake ni kieta* (1968, They Vanished at Dawn) is an open testament of his conversion to Catholicism. His series of plays about famous UKIYO-E artists includes *Sharaku kō* (1971, Sharaku), which was awarded the 1972 Yomiuri Literary Prize,

Hokusai manga (1973; tr *Hokusai Sketchbook*, 1979), and *Edo no rokudenashi* (1982, An Edo No-Good).

Yaskawa Electric Corporation
[株]安川電機

(Yasukawa Denki). Company engaged in the manufacture and sale of electric machinery and equipment. Incorporated in 1915, it is well known for the production of electric motors and industrial electronic controls. It has subsidiaries in the United States, Brazil, and Germany and several offices abroad. The export ratio for its products was 16 percent in 1991. Sales for the fiscal year ending March 1991 totaled ¥150.7 billion (US $1.1 billion), and it was capitalized at ¥14.9 billion (US $108.6 million). Headquarters are in Kita Kyūshū, Fukuoka Prefecture.

Yasuda   安田

Business enterprise founded in 1880 when YASUDA ZENJIRŌ opened the Yasuda Bank; major financial combine (ZAIBATSU), whose holding company was dissolved in 1945 by the OCCUPATION authorities; enterprise grouping (KEIRETSU) of the postwar period (now known as the Fuyō group). The Yasuda *zaibatsu*'s activities were centered predominantly in finance, branching out only marginally into light industry, warehousing, real estate, and heavy industry.

From his beginnings in the 1860s as a street-corner money changer in Edo (now Tōkyō), Yasuda Zenjirō rapidly built a financial empire on the basis of his bank. In 1887 he set up the Yasuda Hozensha as a holding company and in 1899 Yasuda Shōji, Ltd, a trading company. In 1919 Yasuda subsidiaries numbered 17 banks and 16 companies, with Yasuda Hozensha acting as their holding company. Despite its lack of direct subsidiaries in industry, the Yasuda Hozensha had considerable investments in the industrial Asano *zaibatsu*. Yasuda Zenjirō made these loans almost unconditionally because of his friendship with ASANO SŌICHIRŌ, the founder of the combine. After Zenjirō's death in 1921 YŪKI TOYOTARŌ was brought in from the Bank of Japan to manage the holding company.

When the Occupation authorities called for ZAIBATSU DISSOLUTION in October 1945, the 30 Yasuda-affiliated banks and companies included such famous concerns as MARUBENI CORPORATION. Closely allied groups, such as Oki Electric and Oki Electric Stock, brought the total number of companies and subsidiaries to 59. Since the 1950s former Yasuda subsidiaries have been loosely affiliated as an enterprise group; its most notable members include FUJI BANK, LTD; YASUDA TRUST & BANKING CO, LTD; and YASUDA FIRE & MARINE INSURANCE CO, LTD.

Yasuda Fire & Marine Insurance Co, Ltd   安田火災海上保険[株]

(Yasuda Kasai Kaijō Hoken). Firm engaged in the sale of insurance other than life insurance, chiefly automobile insurance. The forerunner of the firm was a fire insurance company established in 1888. It took its current name in 1944. With 30 overseas offices, the company plans to expand its international operations. In the fiscal year ending March 1991 net insurance premiums totaled ¥724.8 billion (US $5.3 billion), of which optional automobile insurance accounted for 45 percent; fire insurance, 14 percent; compulsory automobile liability insurance, 13 percent; marine and transportation insurance, 4 percent; and other types of insurance,

24 percent. Total assets amounted to ¥3.5 trillion (US $25.5 billion), and the company was capitalized at ¥58.3 billion (US $424.9 million). Headquarters are in Tōkyō.

Yasuda Mutual Life Insurance Co
安田生命保険[相]

(Yasuda Seimei Hoken). Japan's oldest life insurance company. Incorporated in 1880. Yasuda Mutual Life is especially strong in group insurance. The company maintains representative offices in New York, London, Hong Kong, and Singapore. Assets for the fiscal year ending March 1991 totaled ¥6.2 trillion (US $45.2 billion), and premiums received totaled ¥1.4 trillion (US $10.2 billion). Headquarters are in Tōkyō.

Yasuda Trust & Banking Co, Ltd
安田信託銀行[株]

(Yasuda Shintaku Ginkō). Yasuda Trust & Banking was incorporated in 1925 and today ranks among the top 25 banks worldwide. It offers services in asset management, commercial banking, real estate brokerage and development, and other specialized areas. It has 5 overseas branches, 13 representative offices, and 7 subsidiaries. In the fiscal year ending March 1991 total available funds amounted to ¥22.0 trillion (US $160.3 billion), total assets reached ¥13.3 trillion (US $96.9 billion), and the company was capitalized at ¥136.6 billion (US $995.6 million). Headquarters are in Tōkyō.

Yasuda Yojūrō
保田与重郎

(1910–81). Literary critic. Born in Nara Prefecture; graduate of Tōkyō University. In 1932 he helped publish *Kogito* (Cogito), a coterie magazine of German-influenced romantic poets. In 1935 Yasuda organized a new coterie, the NIHON RŌMANHA, through which he advocated the reawakening of the Japanese national spirit and a traditional appreciation of beauty; he thus contributed to the rise of ultranationalism in the late 1930s and 1940s. His principal works include the critical essays *Nippon no hashi* (1936), *Go-Toba In* (1939), *Kindai no shūen* (1941), and *Bi no yōgo* (1941).

Yasuda Yukihiko
安田靫彦

(1884–1978). Japanese-style painter well known for his elegant but simple treatment of Japanese historical themes in the YAMATO-E style. Real name Yasuda Shinzaburō. Born in Tōkyō, he studied the traditional TOSA SCHOOL style under Kobori Tomoto (1864–1931) at the Tōkyō Bijutsu Gakkō (now Tōkyō University of Fine Arts and Music). The influential art scholar and critic OKAKURA KAKUZŌ recognized Yasuda's ability and sent him to Nara to study classical Japanese art. Yasuda participated in the reorganized JAPAN FINE ARTS ACADEMY from 1914. He taught at his alma mater from 1944 to 1951. In 1948 he received the Order of Culture and became a member of the JAPAN ART ACADEMY (Nihon Geijutsuin). In addition to his paintings on historical themes, he is noted for his portraits and bird-and-flower paintings.

Yasuda Zenjirō
安田善次郎

(1838–1921). Financier and founder of the YASUDA financial and industrial combine (ZAIBATSU). Born in what is now Toyama Prefecture, as a youth he went to Edo (now Tōkyō). He established a small but lucrative business as a money changer. Following the MEIJI RESTORATION of 1868, Yasuda reaped huge profits by buying up the shaky paper currency (DAJŌKAN SATSU) at a discount and selling it back to the government for full value. He soon acquired a virtual monopoly over money changing in Tōkyō, thanks to special privileges granted by the government (see SEISHŌ). Beginning in 1876 with the Third National Bank (Daisan Kokuritsu Ginkō), Yasuda founded a series of banks, most notably the Yasuda Bank (see FUJI BANK, LTD). He later diversified into railways, insurance, and other enterprises. He came to control dozens of companies, including the YASUDA FIRE & MARINE INSURANCE CO, LTD. He was assassinated in 1921 by an ultranationalist.

Yasugawa
野洲川

River in Shiga Prefecture, central Honshū, originating in the Suzuka Mountains and emptying into Lake Biwa. Deltas are well developed along the lower reaches; the Yasugawa Dam for irrigation is located on the upper reaches. Length: 61 km (38 mi).

Yasugi
安来[市]

City in eastern Shimane Prefecture, western Honshū. During the 16th century Yasugi flourished as a port for shipping iron made from ore mined nearby. It later became a post-station town. The construction of a steel mill in 1899 led to the establishment of numerous subcontracting plants. Farm products include pears and bamboo shoots. Attractions are Zuikōsan Kiyomizudera, a medieval temple, and Saginoyu Hot Spring. Pop: 32,439.

Yasuhara Teishitsu
安原貞室

(1610–73). *Haikai* (see HAIKU) poet. Real name Yasuhara Masaakira. A disciple and literary successor of MATSUNAGA TEITOKU, the founder of the Teimon school of *haikai*. He compiled the comprehensive Teimon anthology *Gyokukaishū* (1656) and was the author of a pioneering study of dialects, *Katakoto* (1650).

Yasui Santetsu → Shibukawa
Shunkai

Yasui Sokken
安井息軒

(1799–1876). Confucian scholar of the Edo period (1600–1868). Born in the Obi domain (now part of Miyazaki Prefecture). Sokken studied in Ōsaka with Confucian scholar Shinozaki Shōchiku (1781–1851) and at the SHŌHEIKŌ, the shogunate academy of Confucian studies in Edo (now Tōkyō). He taught at the Obi domain school and later at the Shōheikō. When Commodore Matthew PERRY's expedition threatened Japan's policy of national seclusion in 1853, Sokken urged military preparedness in *Kaibō shigi* (1852, A Discussion of Coastal Defense). After the overthrow of the Tokugawa shogunate in 1867, he devoted himself to writing. His other works include *Rongo shūsetsu* (1872), a commentary on the Confucian *Analects.*

Yasui Sōtarō
安井曽太郎

(1888–1955). Western-style painter. Born in Kyōto; studied painting at the Kansai Bijutsuin (Kansai Art School) under ASAI CHŪ. From 1907 to 1914 he studied in Paris, where he was strongly influenced by Cézanne. On his return to Japan he became a member of Nikakai, a major Western-style painting (YŌGA) organization. He painted mainly still lifes, landscapes, and portraits. He became a member of the Imperial Fine Arts Academy (Teikoku Bijutsuin) in 1935 and helped to found the artist group Issuikai in 1936. Yasui taught at the Tōkyō Bijutsu Gakkō (now Tōkyō University of Fine Arts and Music)

from 1944 to 1952 and was awarded the Order of Culture in 1952.

Yasui Sōtarō *Grand-daughter.* 1950. Oil on canvas. 92 × 73 cm. Ōhara Art Museum, Okayama Prefecture.

Yasui Takuma
安井琢磨

(1909–). Economist. Born in Ōsaka Prefecture. After graduating from Tōkyō University in 1931, Yasui taught at his alma mater. In 1944 he became a professor at Tōhoku University. He moved to Ōsaka University in 1965 and became head of the university's Social and Economic Research Institute. He later became a professor at the International Christian University. In 1971 Yasui was the first economist to receive the Order of Culture. His works on economics include *Yasui Takuma chosakushū* (3 vols, 1970–71; Collected Works of Yasui Takuma).

Yasui Tetsu
安井てつ

(1870–1945). Educator; Japan's first woman college president. Born in Tōkyō. A graduate of the Women's Higher Normal School (now Ochanomizu Women's University), she began her teaching career there. In 1897 she went to England for three years of study and was baptized a Christian soon after her return to Japan. From 1904 to 1907 she worked in Bangkok, Thailand, where she helped start the Queen's School. She took up teaching again in Japan at such government-sponsored institutions as the Peers' School (now Gakushūin University). In 1918 she became dean at the newly founded mission-sponsored TŌKYŌ WOMEN'S CHRISTIAN UNIVERSITY and subsequently served as its president from 1923 until 1940.

Yasukawa Daigorō
安川第五郎

(1886–1976). Business executive. Son of Yasukawa Keiichirō (1849–1934), a well-known coal mine developer. Born in Fukuoka Prefecture, he was a graduate of Tōkyō University. With his father and elder brother, Yasukawa established Yasukawa Denki Seisakusho (now YASKAWA ELECTRIC CORPORATION) in 1915 and started to manufacture motors. He became company presi-

Yasukuni Shrine The main gate and oratory of the shrine, which is dedicated to the spirits of Japanese military personnel who have died since 1853 in Japan's various wars.

Yasuoka Shōtarō This award-winning writer of novels, short stories, and essays is known for his self-deprecating tone and sharp sense of irony.

dent in 1936. He also served for a time as director of the Coal Agency after World War II, became the first director of the ATOMIC ENERGY RESEARCH INSTITUTE, JAPAN, in 1956, and devoted himself to the development of atomic energy in Japan. Yasukawa was chairman of the organizing committee of the Tōkyō Olympic Games in 1964.

Yasukuni Shrine 靖国神社

(Yasukuni Jinja). Shintō shrine in the Kudan district of Chiyoda Ward, Tōkyō. It is dedicated to the spirits of the approximately 2.4 million persons who have died since 1853 in Japan's various wars, both civil and foreign. In accordance with the wishes of Emperor Meiji (r 1867–1912), a shrine designated Shōkonsha (Shrine for Inviting the Spirits) was established in 1869, venerating all those who had died in the campaigns to reestablish imperial rule. In 1879 the Shōkonsha was renamed Yasukuni Jinja (Shrine for Establishing Peace in the Empire). The shrine became the symbolic head shrine for prefectural *shōkonsha* (these were redesignated *gokoku jinja* in 1939). For the spring and autumn memorial services, held on 22 April and 18 October, the emperor dispatches an emissary (*chokushi*) to visit the Yasukuni Shrine as his personal representative.

After Japan's defeat in 1945 the government was compelled to terminate all support for Yasukuni Shrine, which was converted into a private religious organization. Since then there has been considerable controversy about restoring government support for the shrine. See also STATE SHINTŌ.

Yasukuni Shrine official visit controversy 靖国神社公式参拝問題

(Yasukuni Jinja *kōshiki sampai mondai*). YASUKUNI SHRINE, which is dedicated to the spirits of Japan's military war dead, was used by the government during World War II to promote nationalism. Since article 20, paragraph 3, of the postwar CONSTITUTION OF JAPAN prohibits the state from engaging in any religious activity, and since article 89 prohibits state support of any religious institution, postwar prime ministers and cabinet ministers had refrained from making visits to the shrine in their official capacity as ministers of state. However, in 1985 a private advisory body to Prime Minister NAKASONE YASUHIRO issued a report claiming that official visits to the shrine were constitutional. As a result, on 15 August 1985, the 40th anniversary of the end of World War II, Prime Minister Nakasone paid the first postwar visit to Yasukuni Shrine by a prime minister in his official capacity. His visit renewed the domestic and international debate on the possible remilitarization of Japan and stirred protest demonstrations in China and other Asian countries.

yatsude The clustered flowers of this popular ornamental shrub bloom around November.

Yasumi Toshio 八住利雄

(1903–). Screenwriter. Born in Ōsaka. He is known for two outstanding films that depict manners and customs in Ōsaka: *Meoto zenzai* (1955, Marital Relations) and *Neko to Shōzō to futari no onna* (1956, A Cat, Shōzō, and Two Women). During World War II, Yasumi wrote screenplays to heighten war morale. After the war, however, Yasumi wrote screenplays such as *Minshū no teki* (1946, Enemy of the People), a film that exposed the illicit activities of business combines (ZAIBATSU) during World War II; *Sensō to heiwa* (1947, War and Peace), a full-scale antiwar picture; and *Senkan Yamato* (1953, Battleship Yamato), directed by Abe Yutaka (1895–1977). He also wrote *Banka* (1957, Dirge; directed by GOSHO HEINOSUKE). In the 1950s he began writing screenplays based on literary works, such as AN'YA KŌRO (1959, A Dark Night's Passing), which was directed by TOYODA SHIRŌ.

Yasuoka Shōtarō 安岡章太郎

(1920–). Author. Born in Kōchi Prefecture. Graduate of Keiō University. He won the 1953 Akutagawa Prize for his two short stories "Inki na tanoshimi" (Cheerless Pleasures) and "Warui nakama" (Bad Company). In 1960 his novelette *Umibe no kōkei* (1959; tr *A View by the Sea*, 1984) received the Noma Literary Prize. In 1960 he traveled to the United States at the invitation of the Rockefeller Foundation, later publishing a volume of essays based on this experience, *Amerika kanjō ryokō* (1962, A Sentimental Journey to America). In *Shiga Naoya shiron* (1968, Shiga Naoya: A Personal Appraisal) Yasuoka shed critical light on the novelist SHIGA NAOYA's relationship with his father and grandfather. He also broke new ground with the historical novel *Ryūritan* (1976–81, A Wanderer's Tale). This novel depicts the closing days of the Tokugawa shogunate (1603–1867) and the events of the Meiji Restoration (1868) through an examination of the history of his own family, who were *gōshi* (rural *samurai*). His collection of autobiographical essays, *Boku no Shōwa shi* (1979–88, My Shōwa History), a personal meditation on the history of the Shōwa period (1926–89), won the Noma Literary Prize in 1988. Yasuoka has been a member of the Japan Art Academy since 1976, when he received the Japan Art Academy Award.

Yatabe Ryōkichi 矢田部良吉

(1851–99). Botanist. Son of a doctor in Nirayama (now in Shizuoka Prefecture). He studied botany at Cornell University in New York state. Upon returning to Japan he helped establish modern botany there as director of the Tōkyō Education Museum (now the National Science Museum), as a professor at Tōkyō University, and as director of the KOISHIKAWA BOTANIC GARDEN. He founded the Tōkyō Biological Society in cooperation with the US zoologist E. S. MORSE and also participated in the founding of the Tōkyō Botanical Society.

Yatomi 弥富[町]

Town in southwestern Aichi Prefecture, central Honshū. It is fast becoming a residential town for commuters to NAGOYA. Goldfish and Java sparrows (*shiro bunchō*) are bred here. Pop: 33,188.

yatsude 八つ手

Fatsia japonica. An evergreen shrub of the ginseng family (Araliaceae). It is indigenous to coastal woods in Shikoku, Kyūshū, and central and western Honshū and also widely cultivated as a garden plant. The stems (2–3 m; 7–10 ft) grow in clusters and are topped by alternate, dark green, shiny leaves (20–40 cm [8–16 in] across). The name *yatsude* (literally, "eight-handed") is derived from the leaves' eight-lobed palmate shape, although some leaves may have seven or nine lobes. Appearing in large terminal clusters in late autumn, the blossoms have white petals with a slight yellow tint. The fruit is round and ripens to black or dark blue.

Because *yatsude* serves as a shade plant, it is commonly found in Japanese gardens and is exported to China, Europe, and America. Tea made from the dried leaves (which are rich in a kind of saponin) is used to help clear the throat of mucus.

Yatsugatake 八ケ岳

Group of volcanoes on the border of Nagano and Yamanashi prefectures, central Honshū. The group consists of eight peaks. The highest is Akadake (2,899 m; 9,511 ft). The foothills form vast plateaus where farms and resort areas have developed. The area, known for its large variety of alpine flora, comprises one of the sight-seeing centers of Yatsugatake-Chūshin Kōgen Quasi-National Park.

Yatsushiro 八代[市]

City in central Kumamoto Prefecture, Kyūshū. It developed in the Edo period (1600–1868) as a castle town. Cement, paper, pulp, and *sake* industries are active. *Igusa* (rushes) for the outer covering of floor mats (*tatami*) are grown. The sea near Yatsushiro is known for *shiranui*, an eerie glow created by the atmospheric refraction of fishing lamps above the water. Hinagu Hot Spring also attracts visitors. Pop: 108,135.

Yatsushiro Sea 八代海

(Yatsushiro Kai). Also known as the Shiranui Sea; formerly called Yatsushiro Bay (Yatsushiro Wan). Inlet of the East China Sea between the Amakusa Islands and the southwestern coast of Kumamoto Prefecture, Kyūshū. Land reclamation has long been extensively practiced in the northern part. Principal activities are shellfish and laver (*nori*) culture and fishing. Area: approximately 650 sq km (250 sq mi); deepest point: approximately 50 m (165 ft).

Yawata 八幡[市]

City in southern Kyōto Prefecture, central Honshū, on the river Yodogawa. It first developed as a shrine town around the IWASHIMIZU HACHIMAN SHRINE. Farming, the principal activity, has declined as a result of urbanization. Pop: 75,758.

Yawata 八幡

Also called Yahata. Industrial district in the northern part of the city of Kita Kyūshū, northern Fukuoka Prefecture, Kyūshū. The western sector, where there are a number of industrial plants of the Mitsubishi group, is called Yawata Nishi Ward; in Yawata Higashi Ward to the east are steel mills, chief among which is that of NIPPON STEEL CORPORATION (see YAWATA IRON AND STEEL WORKS). The KITA KYŪSHŪ INDUSTRIAL ZONE is centered on Yawata.

Yawatahama 八幡浜[市]

City in western Ehime Prefecture, Shikoku. Situated on the Uwa Sea, it is a base for trawler fishing. Seafood processing and textiles are its main industries. Pop: 38,550.

Major Yayoi Sites

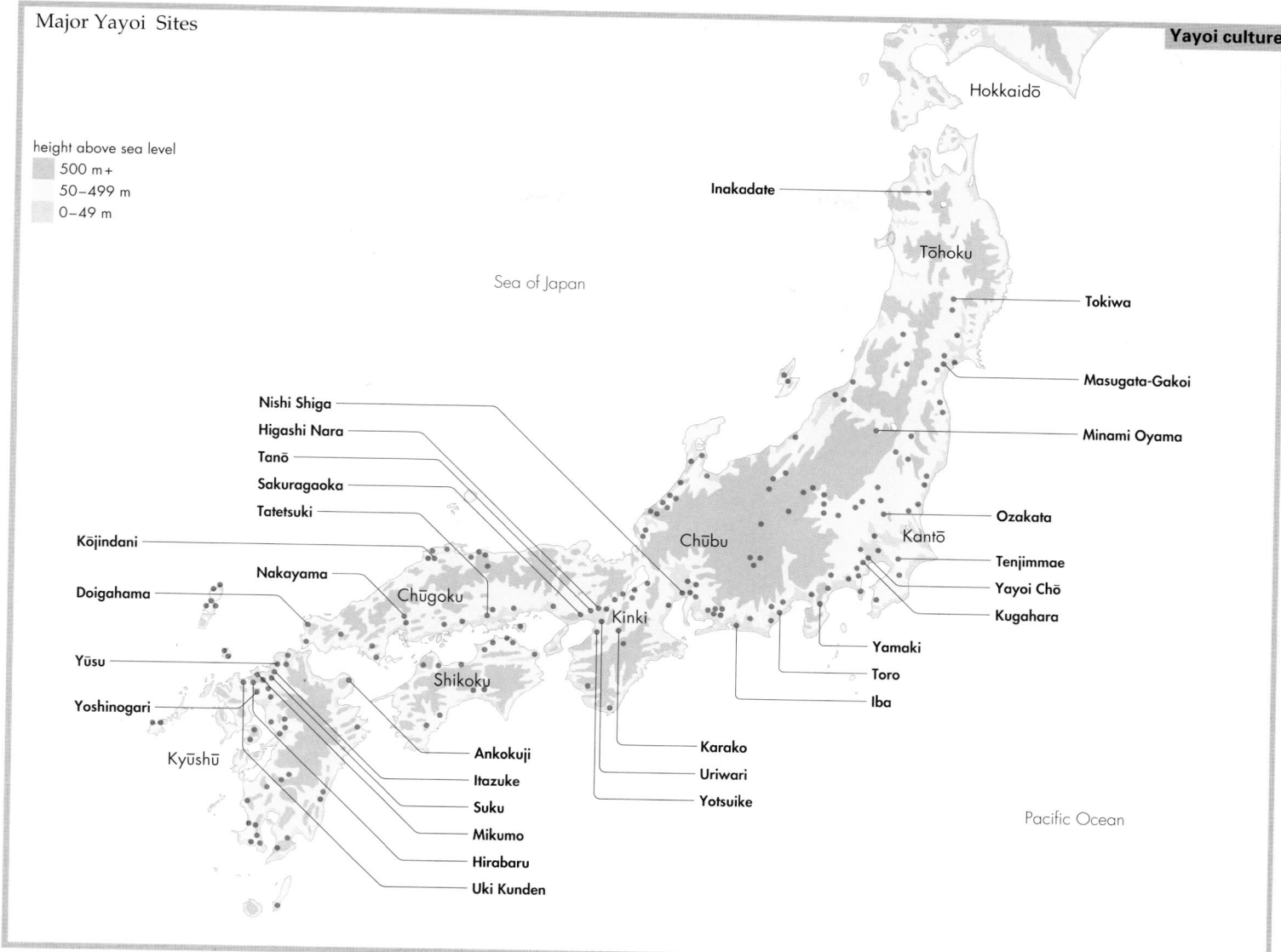

height above sea level
- 500 m+
- 50–499 m
- 0–49 m

Hokkaidō

Sea of Japan

Inakadate

Tōhoku

Tokiwa

Masugata-Gakoi

Minami Oyama

Nishi Shiga
Higashi Nara
Tanō
Sakuragaoka
Tatetsuki
Kōjindani
Nakayama
Doigahama
Chūgoku
Yūsu
Shikoku
Yoshinogari
Kyūshū

Chūbu

Kinki

Ozakata

Kantō

Tenjimmae
Yayoi Chō
Kugahara
Yamaki
Toro
Iba

Karako
Uriwari
Yotsuike

Ankokuji
Itazuke
Suku
Mikumo
Hirabaru
Uki Kunden

Pacific Ocean

Yawata Ichirō
八幡一郎

(1902–87). Archaeologist. Born in Nagano Prefecture, Yawata graduated from Tōkyō University. In 1962 he became a professor at Tōkyō University of Education, and in 1966 he became a professor at Sophia University. Yawata was a member of the team that excavated Shizuoka Prefecture's TORO SITE, a site opened in 1946 that dates to the Late Yayoi period (ca AD 100–ca AD 300). With his numerous contributions to research into Japan's Jōmon period (ca 10,000 BC–ca 300 BC), he played a leading role in Japanese archaeology. Yawata's publications include *Nihon sekki jidai bunka* (1947, The Culture of Japan's Stone Age) and *Nihon bunka no akebono* (1968, The Dawn of Japanese Culture).

Yawata Iron and Steel Works
八幡製鉄所

(Yawata Seitetsujo). Japan's largest steel mill; established in 1896 by the government in Yawata Mura (now part of the city of Kita Kyūshū), Fukuoka Prefecture, as part of the country's program to strengthen itself militarily and industrially (FUKOKU KYŌHEI). The project was placed under the Ministry of Agriculture and Commerce (Nōshōmushō), which invited German engineers to help build the mill. Construction expenses were mainly covered by public bonds and by the indemnity paid by China after the SINO-JAPANESE WAR OF 1894–1895. The mill began opera-

tions in 1901. Iron ore was imported mainly from mines in Hubei (Hupeh) Province, China, and in Korea. The mill concentrated on producing armaments and railway equipment and thus played a major role in meeting Japan's expanding military needs. In 1934 the mill merged with five private companies to form Nippon Seitetsu (Nippon Steel Co). After World War II, the company was separated into the Yawata Seitetsu and Fuji Seitetsu companies by the OCCUPATION authorities. In 1970 the two merged to form the NIPPON STEEL CORPORATION.

Yayoi culture
弥生文化

(Yayoi *bunka*). The culture of the Yayoi period (ca 300 BC–ca AD 300) is distinguished from the preceding JŌMON CULTURE by irrigated rice cultivation and the use of bronze and iron artifacts. It is supposed that the considerable contact with China and Korea during this period influenced these innovations. Social stratification developed, and by the Late Yayoi period (ca 100–ca 300) Japan was divided into a number of small political units (*kuni*) centering on regional chieftains. Some chipped STONE TOOLS of the Jōmon culture continued to be used, but the Yayoi people also knew how to smelt iron and forge simple implements. Some items were initially obtained from the continent, but by the Late Yayoi the Japanese themselves were making BRONZE MIRRORS, bronze bells (DŌTAKU), and BRONZE WEAPONS. Techniques were also developed for producing jasper and jade

magatama (see BEADS, ANCIENT). Cloth woven from flax and paper-mulberry fibers was the basic clothing material. Great dietary changes occurred in the transition from a hunting and gathering society to one primarily dependent on cultivated rice. Paddy fields were enclosed by dikes, and irrigation techniques were gradually refined. Dwellings (see PIT HOUSES) were simple structures with earthen floors and thatched roofs.

The archaeological record offers evidence of Yayoi religious festivals honoring various deities. The Yayoi people also developed the practice of secondary burial. Some time after the initial burial the bones were exhumed, washed, possibly painted with red ocher, and placed in jars; the jars were then buried, often collectively, in large pits that were sometimes surrounded by moats. The custom of burying objects with the dead also developed during this period; mirrors, beads, and bronze weapons have been discovered in DOLMEN BURIALS.

Much of our information on Late Yayoi society comes from contemporary Chinese histories such as the WEI ZHI (*Wei chih;* covering the period 220–265). They describe a highly stratified society in which wealthy landholders ruled the common people. The *Wei zhi* mentions a kingdom called YAMATAI that controlled some 30 other "countries," each ruled by a chieftain; it relates that markets flourished, taxes were collected, and a

Artist's Conception of a Yayoi-Period Settlement

This representation of a Yayoi-period settlement is based on the excavated site at Yoshinogari, Saga Prefecture. Specific features of the structures shown here are conjectural.

system of punishments was prescribed for malefactors. The society was fairly complex and well organized; political, economic, and military specialization were vigorously developing.

Yayoi (month) → calendar, dates, and time

Yayoi period   弥生時代

(ca 300 BC–ca AD 300; Yayoi *jidai*). Prehistoric period. The first period of intensive agriculture and bronze and iron use in Japanese prehistory, so called because of certain characteristic pottery discovered in the Yayoi section of Bunkyō Ward, Tōkyō, in 1884. Wet-rice technology, metallurgy, and other innovations were introduced piecemeal from the late-bronze-age cultures of the Korean peninsula into Kyūshū (see YAYOI CULTURE). From there, wet-rice cultivation spread rapidly throughout western Japan and some northern coastal regions during the Early Yayoi period (ca 300 BC–ca 100 BC) and then gradually into northeastern Japan in the Middle Yayoi (ca 100 BC–ca AD 100) and Late Yayoi (ca 100–ca 300) periods. Bronzes, however, were confined to the west, and the ceramics of northeastern Yayoi exhibit strong persistence of the traditions of the JŌMON PERIOD (ca 10,000 BC–ca 300 BC). Northeastern agriculture probably also relied much more on such nonrice crops as millet, barley, and beans. In contrast to the earlier view of Yayoi as consisting of peaceful agricultural villages (such as the well-known TORO SITE), the period is increasingly seen as one of competition and warfare, as trends toward social stratification and polity formation took hold.

Settlement—Villages in the Early Yayoi period were located near the low coastal marshlands, where rice was easily grown in diked fields with drainage canals. The grain harvest, carried out with a distinctive stone reaping knife, was supplemented with hunting, gathering, and shellfish col-

lecting in the Jōmon pattern until the agricultural intensification of the Middle Yayoi period. The development of irrigation systems and iron-edged tools at that time allowed the expansion of cultivation onto drier land, and increased harvests stimulated a massive population explosion. The numerous Middle Yayoi villages of thatched PIT HOUSES and raised granaries were often surrounded by substantial village ditches. These may have provided protection, and, from the Middle to the Late Yayoi period, settlements in upland defensive hilltop positions were common. Also, caches of bronze bells are often found on hilltops in the eastern Seto region (in what is now Aichi Prefecture) overlooking fertile agricultural land. These may have been used in fertility rites within the agricultural cycle and buried for safekeeping between ceremonies.

Material Culture—Many types of craft production of continental origin were established in Yayoi Japan: casting bronze in sandstone molds, pouring round and curved glass beads in molds, weaving paper mulberry and flax fibers, turning wooden bowls on lathes, and forging small iron tools. Native crafts included jasper and jade bead production, stone tool manufacture, and ceramic production. Many of the polished stone tools were used for working wood into architectural elements or other tools, such as pestles for pounding grain, hafts for the stone tools themselves, or hoes and spades. The Yayoi pottery tradition is a transformation of the Jōmon earthenware tradition with new techniques and shapes (long-necked jars, pedestaled bowls) from the continent. Western Yayoi pottery is decorated with combed motifs, appliqués, raised bands, and some burnished surfaces. High pedestals and stepped rims characterize the more elaborate shapes. Northeastern Yayoi pottery continued the Jōmon cord-marking tradition on Yayoi shapes, but incised-line geometrics and appliqués were also popular. All these ceramics were unglazed and fired at low temperatures in open stacks. See YAYOI POTTERY.

Burials—Each of three large regions exhibited particular burial patterns. In north-

eastern Japan secondary burials of exhumed bones were conducted, the remains being painted with ocher, placed in highly decorated jars, and buried, often collectively, in large pits. In the eastern Seto region collective primary burials in moated, mounded precincts probably represent prestigious family precincts. Adults were interred directly in pits or in wooden coffins; children were buried in small jars. These precincts are often clustered into cemeteries adjacent to the village. Western Seto had several different types of burial facilities. The practice of depositing goods with the deceased was carried out only in this region during the Yayoi period. JAR BURIALS of adults are notable in north Kyūshū in addition to cist burials, both of which might have been covered by a low dolmen structure. All these might have been accompanied by grave goods consisting of bronze weapons, beads, and many Chinese tribute goods, such as bronze mirrors. These were very much ceremonial and status goods, but the different shell bracelets worn on the arms of men and women are thought to distinguish gender.

Previously, the Yayoi period was differentiated from the KOFUN PERIOD (ca 300–710) by the presence of mounded tombs (KOFUN) in the latter. Several types of Yayoi mound burials, however, are now recognized, and the Kofun tradition is thought to have developed indigenously from these. The Yoshinogari mound burial, recently excavated in Saga Prefecture, is one of the earliest, containing a jar burial with a continental sword and blue glass beads. See DOLMEN BURIALS; FLEXED BURIALS; HŌKEI SHŪKŌBO; YOSHINOGARI SITE.

International Relations—Kyūshū was drawn into the tribute and trade network of the Chinese Lelang (Lolang) commandery on the northern Korean peninsula. Via this network, foreign goods flowed into western Japan, and information about Yayoi culture and politics was inscribed in the Chinese dynastic histories. Relatively complex political units called *kuni* are recorded, a number under the hegemony of YAMATAI, ruled by Queen HIMIKO. The Yoshinogari site is

Yayoi pottery

Jar. Itazuke site, Fukuoka Prefecture. Early Yayoi period. Height 36 cm.

Burial jar. Nagaoka site, Fukuoka Prefecture. Middle Yayoi period. Height 91 cm.

Jar with foot. Nagoya, Aichi Prefecture. Middle Yayoi period. Height 24 cm.

Jar with raised pattern. Karakami site, Nagasaki Prefecture. Middle Yayoi period. Height 41 cm.

Jar with red finish. Kugahara, Tōkyō. Late Yayoi period. Height 36 cm.

Long-necked jar. Miyaji, Kumamoto Prefecture. Late Yayoi period. Height 26 cm.

thought to embody the level of development reflected in these descriptions, having a double-moated structure complete with palisade and watchtowers.

Yayoi pottery 弥生土器

(Yayoi *doki*). The unglazed earthenware of the Yayoi period (ca 300 BC–ca AD 300). In northern Kyūshū Yayoi pottery evolved from the mixture of the local tradition of JŌMON POTTERY with the newly imported pottery of immigrant rice cultivators, probably in the 3rd century BC (see YAYOI CULTURE). In the Early Yayoi period (ca 300 BC–ca 100 BC), Yayoi pottery spread throughout Japan, replacing the earlier Jōmon period (ca 10,000 BC–ca 300 BC) pottery in western Japan but mingling with local Jōmon traditions in eastern Japan. Thus, the Yayoi styles of eastern and western Japan are very different, and Yayoi pottery was recognized as distinct from Jōmon pottery only after the excavation of the MUKŌGAOKA SHELL MOUND in 1884.

During the 1936–37 excavation of the KARAKO SITE in Nara Prefecture, five different styles of Yayoi pottery were identified for western Japan. Yayoi wares of eastern Japan are assigned type-site names rather than style names; thus the distribution of eastern Yayoi pottery types through space and time resembles that of the preceding Jōmon types. Each Yayoi style or type contains a characteristic array of shapes and decorative styles. Vessels were coil- or ring-built and not made on a potter's wheel. Few Yayoi kilns are known. The HAJI WARE of the succeeding Kofun period (ca 300–710) was a direct continuation of the Yayoi tradition. See also CERAMICS.

Yazaki Corporation 矢崎総業[株]

(Yazaki Sōgyō). Manufacturer of automotive wires, automotive measuring instruments, gas and air-conditioning equipment, solar-energy-related equipment, and gas leakage detectors. Incorporated in 1941. The company has significant market shares in tachographs, electronic taxi meters, and gas leakage detectors. Sales for the fiscal year ending June 1990 totaled ¥418.3 billion (US $2.7 billion), of which automotive components accounted for 75 percent; electric wires and cables, 14 percent; and gas equipment and other products, 11 percent. The company was capitalized at ¥2.5 billion (US $16.3 million) in the same year. Headquarters are in Tōkyō.

year-end fair 年の市

(*toshi no ichi*). Also called *sekki ichi*. Fair traditionally held in late December at shrines, temples, or in local neighborhoods, where decorations and sundry goods are sold in preparation for the NEW YEAR holidays. Originally these year-end fairs provided opportunities for farmers, fisherfolk, and mountain dwellers to exchange goods and to buy clothes and other necessities for the coming year. The *toshi no ichi* held on 17–18 December at the ASAKUSA KANNON temple in Tōkyō is one of the oldest and most famous. *Toshi no ichi* can still be seen throughout rural Japan, and modified versions have become an integral part of year-end sales at urban department stores.

"yellow peril" 黄禍論

(*kōkaron*). Phrase used to describe a presumed threat to Western civilization in the form of an Asian invasion—either military, demographic, or economic. The term appears to have originated in a direct translation of Kaiser Wilhelm II's talk of a *gelbe Gefahr* that threatened Eastern Europe and would eventually threaten all Christendom; it came into use in the United States as early as 1895. At this time the presumed threat was principally seen as coming from China. In fact, fear of a Chinese inundation of North America antedated the phrase "yellow peril" by more than a quarter century, for in the late 1860s fear and resentment of immigrants had already spawned an anti-Chinese movement on the West Coast. Only in the first half of the 20th century did the nuance of the term shift to imply a Japanese threat, a usage largely restricted to the United States, Canada, Australia, and New Zealand. With Japan's defeat in World War II, the focus of "yellow peril" fears swung back toward China, though Japan's rapid economic growth over the last few decades has at times ignited similar hysteria.

yellowtail 鰤

(*buri*). *Seriola quinqueradiata*, a migratory fish of the family Carangidae, order Perciformes, class Osteichthyes. It grows to a length of more than 1 meter (3 ft). It is distributed along the entire coast of Japan, the east and the south coasts of the Korean peninsula and the East China Sea, moving north in spring and summer and south in autumn and winter. The fry drift with

year-end fair A vendor sets up a stall of New Year's decorations to be sold at the year-end fair at the Yushima Tenjin Shrine, Tōkyō.

floating algae and are caught for culturing. Cultivation of the yellowtail is carried on more actively in western than in eastern Japan. The cultured fish is called *hamachi*, a name originally used in the Kansai (Kyōto-Ōsaka-Kōbe) area to describe the immature yellowtail. *Buri* dishes include *sashimi* (sliced raw fish) and *teriyaki* (broiled with soy sauce).

Buri was a favorite fish among the common people during the Edo period (1600–1868). Salted *buri* is a traditional New Year's dish in the Kansai area, in contrast with the salted salmon of the Kantō (Tōkyō) area. *Buri* fishing is thought to have started in the Muromachi period (1333–1568).

yen 円

(*en*). The yen was established as the unit of monetary account in Japan by the enactment of the Shinka Jōrei (New Currency Regulation) of 1871. The newly established Meiji government introduced a decimal system of currency (one-hundredth of a yen was called a *sen*, and one-tenth of a *sen* was called a *rin*) to replace the complex system of currency of the Edo period (1600–1868;

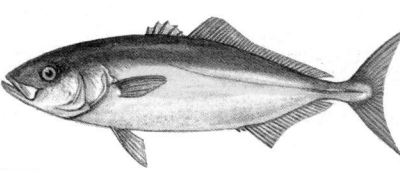

yellowtail An adult *buri*, with its conspicuous yellow marking. The yellowtail is a favorite fall and winter food, when its fat content and flavor are at their peak.

The Yen-Dollar Exchange Rate

Year	Yen per US dollar	Year	Yen per US dollar
1970	360.00	1981	220.54
1971	349.33	1982	249.08
1972	303.17*	1983	237.51
1973	271.70	1984	237.52
1974	292.08	1985	238.54
1975	296.79	1986	168.52
1976	296.55	1987	144.64
1977	268.51	1988	128.15
1978	210.44	1989	137.96
1979	219.14	1990	144.79
1980	226.74	1991	134.71

*The Smithsonian Agreement allowed for a 2.25 percent variation from the ¥308 rate it stipulated.
NOTE: From 1949 to 1970, the fixed rate of exchange was ¥360 per US dollar.
SOURCE: Bank of Japan, *Gaikoku keizai tōkei nempō* (annual): 1987 and 1992.

The Yen versus Four Major Currencies

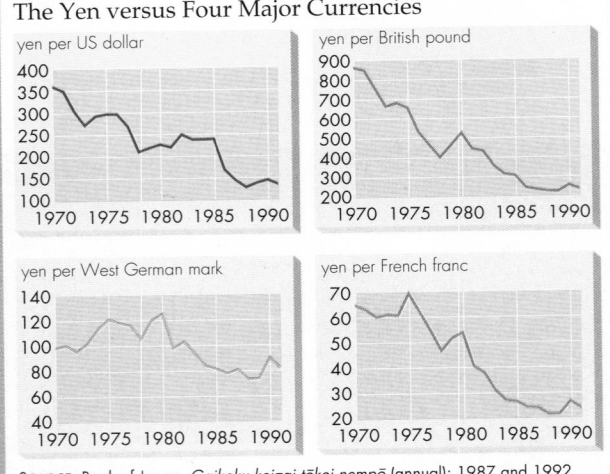

SOURCE: Bank of Japan, *Gaikoku keizai tōkei nempō* (annual): 1987 and 1992.

see MONEY, PREMODERN). The new money was named yen (*en*, meaning "round") because the coin was minted in a round shape, whereas most Edo-period coins had been oval and oblong. The new currency regulation adopted a gold standard, which pegged the yen to a parity of 1.5 grams (0.05 oz) of gold, the equivalent of one Mexican dollar (the standard unit for East Asian trade at the time). In actual practice, however, the yen was equal to 374 grams (13.2 oz) of silver, and the system functioned as a silver standard.

The outbreak of the SATSUMA REBELLION of 1877 led to a dramatic rise in inflation caused by the government's large-scale issuance of inconvertible currency in order to fund its military expenditures. Faced with the need to curb inflation and to establish a viable convertible currency system, Finance Minister MATSUKATA MASAYOSHI enacted a number of reforms of Japan's financial and currency systems. A central bank, the BANK OF JAPAN, was established in 1882 with the objective, among others, of disposing of inconvertible currency and replacing it with notes convertible to silver. The government enacted convertible currency legislation in 1884, and the following year the new Bank of Japan issued its first bank notes convertible to silver, which passed smoothly into mass circulation.

Japan returned to the gold standard through enactment of a new currency law in 1897, after the Chinese government paid the equivalent of 230 million taels of gold in British money in reparations for the SINO-JAPANESE WAR of 1894–1895. The new law also provided for the withdrawal from circulation of bank notes issued both by the government and by the national banks and reserved the issue of new bank notes as the sole right of the Bank of Japan. The value of the yen was set at 0.75 grams (0.03 oz) of gold (equivalent to US $0.50), and the Bank of Japan notes were made convertible to gold.

Japan followed the lead of other developed countries after the outbreak of World War I when in September 1917 it dropped the gold standard and prohibited the export of gold. Soon after the war the United States returned to the gold standard, but Japan was unable to do so because of a series of economic crises, including the panic of 1920 (a retrenchment following the boom period during the war) and the TŌKYŌ EARTHQUAKE OF 1923. These crises produced severe fluctuations in the exchange rate and increased pressure on the government to lift the prohibition on the export of gold. It was not until January 1930 that Japan finally reintroduced the gold standard. However, the timing of this action was unfortunate, since it coincided with the onset of the worldwide depression, and the restoration of prewar parity served only to aggravate the depression in Japan. In December 1931 Japan abandoned the gold standard and again prohibited the export of gold. This led to a rapid decline in the international value of the yen, and in order to prevent excessive flight of capital overseas the government enacted the Capital Outflow Prevention Law in 1932 and the Foreign Exchange Control Law in 1933. Japan's currency system came under increasingly tight government control, and in February 1942 a new Bank of Japan law was enacted authorizing the government to determine the maximum number of bank notes to be issued irrespective of the amount of gold held in reserve by the bank.

After World War II the Japanese economy was beset by serious inflation, which the government and Allied OCCUPATION authorities attempted to control through emergency monetary measures, including a currency reform. All old yen notes were taken out of circulation and replaced gradually with new yen notes. In April 1949 a unified exchange rate of 360 yen to one US dollar was adopted. The yen regained its status as an international currency in May 1953 when this exchange rate was officially recognized by the International Monetary Fund (IMF) and the yen's parity established at approximately 2.5 milligrams (0.0088 oz) of gold.

The gradual liberalization of foreign trade and the internationalization of the yen began around this time. Japan signed the General Agreement on Tariffs and Trade (GATT) in 1955 and joined the United Nations in 1956. In 1964, Japan agreed to article 8 of the IMF charter, obliging the country to lift all restrictions on foreign exchange transactions. During the 1960s the Japanese BALANCE OF PAYMENTS turned positive and FOREIGN CURRENCY RESERVES increased substantially.

In large part due to its deteriorating balance-of-payments situation, the US government unilaterally announced in August 1971 that the dollar would no longer be convertible to gold (see NIXON SHOCKS). Japan was then forced to modify the exchange rate that had existed since 1949; the Smithsonian Agreement of December 1971 established a new exchange rate of 308 yen to one US dollar. This agreement did not, however, succeed in redressing international trade imbalances, and in February 1973 the US dollar was again devalued against gold, and the yen and other major currencies moved to a floating exchange rate system.

From 1973 to the end of the 1970s Japan's export performance was a major influence on the value of the yen. The value of the yen against the dollar rose following growth in the trade surplus from 1976 to 1978 and fell following the contraction in export activity caused by the oil crises of 1973 and 1979. In the 1980s the pattern changed, and capital transactions in the financial markets began to have a greater effect on the yen than the trade balance. In the first half of the 1980s, the US government's efforts to control inflation through high interest rates, as well as its expansionary fiscal policy, attracted massive capital investments from overseas and kept the dollar high against the yen and other currencies. The high dollar, however, contributed to the erosion of the international competitiveness of US industry. To address this problem, the United States called a meeting of the finance ministers of the five leading industrialized countries (see G5, G7) in September 1985. This meeting produced the PLAZA ACCORD, in which members agreed to intervene collectively in the currency markets to reduce the value of the dollar. As a result the value of the yen rose from 239 yen to one US dollar in 1985 to a high of 128 yen to one US dollar in 1988.

During the 1980s the volume of international transactions and holdings denominated in yen increased dramatically. This phenomenon was considered in the report of the US-Japan Yen-Dollar Committee and in a Ministry of Finance report on financial deregulation and the internationalization of the yen, both issued in May 1984. As a result of these reports and increasing pressure for financial market liberalization from within Japan and abroad, action has been taken to deregulate interest rates, to create a yen-based banker's acceptance market, to deregulate Euroyen transactions, and to permit participation of foreign firms in Tōkyō's financial markets.

In line with Japan's growing presence in world financial markets and its role as a major creditor nation, in the 1990s increasing utilization of the yen is expected for world trade, capital transactions, and foreign currency reserves.

Yenan government → Yan'an (Yenan) government

yen credit   円借款

(*en shakkan*). Direct credit extended by the Japanese government to developing countries in the form of loans. Forty percent of Japan's official development assistance (ODA) is provided as yen credit. When yen credit is to be extended, the Japanese government reviews the request from the developing country and an agreement is concluded by an exchange of official documents specifying the basic details. Currently the loans are made through the OVERSEAS ECONOMIC COOPERATION FUND (OECF).

As a form of aid midway between outright donation and export credit, the objective of yen credit is to supply the necessary funds for large-scale projects that promote economic infrastructure building in ASEAN and other countries that already have achieved a relatively advanced stage of development. In fiscal year 1990, agreements were concluded for yen credit of ¥1.07 trillion (US $7.4 billion), which included ¥67.5 billion (US $466.2 million) in debt relief. Countries in Asia received 76.7 percent of the yen credit that year. One recent trend is the increase in "untied" loans, which do not place limitations on the use of the funds by the developing country. In fiscal year 1990, this type of credit reached 84.4 percent of the total. See also FOREIGN AID.

Yi dynasty 李朝

(J: Richō). Korea's last dynasty, founded in 1392 by YI SŎNG-GYE and ended in 1910 by the Japanese annexation of Korea. The kingdom of Korea as ruled by the Yi dynasty was called Chosŏn (J: Chōsen). Despite Japanese marauders (WAKŌ) in the 14th and 15th centuries and the Japanese INVASIONS OF KOREA IN 1592 AND 1597, the Yi dynasty remained important to Japan as a channel for trade and cultural exchange. The dynasty is divided into three major periods: Early Yi (1392–1592), from dynasty founding to maturity; Middle Yi (1592–1800), from the Japanese and Manchu invasions through the 18th-century renaissance under the kings Yŏngcho and Chŏngcho; and Late Yi (1800–1910), from dynastic decline and reforms to the Japanese occupation.

Dynasty founder General Yi Sŏng-gye (known posthumously as T'aejo) established his royal legitimacy with imperial sanction from the ruler of China's Ming dynasty (1368–1644). In 1401 the Yi dynasty was formally acknowledged as a tributary of China and remained so until the late 19th century. The state consisted of eight provinces with its capital at Seoul. As a Confucian state with a political system modeled on China's, it had a monarchical, bureaucratic, and centralized government.

In the Early Yi period, Korea was primarily concerned with security and the establishment of formal relations with Japan, then ruled by the Muromachi shogunate (1338–1573). As peaceful contacts increased, commercial and cultural exchange followed. Then, in 1592 and 1597, TOYOTOMI HIDEYOSHI, who had recently unified Japan and was determined to conquer Ming China through Korea, invaded Korea with massive forces and caused much destruction. In a treaty signed in 1609, peace was restored with Japan, then ruled by the Tokugawa shogunate (1603–1867). Between 1607 and 1811 Korea sent 12 embassies (CHŌSEN TSŪSHINSHI) to Edo (now Tōkyō), allowing Tokugawa Japan to maintain indirect contact with China despite Japan's NATIONAL SECLUSION policy. Soon after the Meiji Restoration (1868) the new Japanese government demanded that the Yi dynasty open the country to foreign trade, and in 1876 Korea was forced to conclude the unequal Treaty of KANGHWA with Japan. Japan exerted increasing control over Korean affairs, and on 5 September 1905 the Treaty of PORTSMOUTH, which concluded the RUSSO-JAPANESE WAR, confirmed Japan's "predominant" interest in Korea. In that year Japan concluded a protectorate treaty with Korea and on 22 August 1910 annexed Korea, ending the Yi dynasty.

Yi Hwang 李滉

(1501–70; J: Ri Kō). The most prominent Confucian scholar of Korea during the YI DYNASTY (1392–1910); commonly known by his pen name Yi T'oegye (Ri Taikei). During his distinguished career as a civil official he was also a prolific author of commentaries on Neo-Confucianism. Many of his writings reached Japan at the time of the INVASIONS OF KOREA IN 1592 AND 1597 and thus contributed to Neo-Confucian studies in Japan (see SHUSHIGAKU).

yen

Pictured here are the yen denominations currently in use in Japan. Bank notes are marked as samples.

Top to bottom: The nickel **¥500 coin** (1982) has a paulownia-flower design. The nickel **¥100 coin** (1967) is decorated with a cherry-blossom design. The nickel **¥50 coin** (1967) bears a design of chrysanthemum flowers. The bronze **¥10 coin** (1959) has an image of the Phoenix Hall of the temple Byōdōin. The copper **¥5 coin** (1959) is decorated with a rice-stalk design. The aluminum **¥1 coin** (1955) features a stylized sapling.

The **¥10,000 bank note** (issued from 1984) bears a portrait of the Meiji-period educator Fukuzawa Yukichi.

The **¥5,000 bank note** (1984) features Nitobe Inazō, an educator of the Meiji and Taishō periods.

The **¥1,000 bank note** (1984) portrays the literary figure Natsume Sōseki (1867–1916).

yin and yang → Ommyōdō

Yin Rugeng (Yin Ju-keng) 殷汝耕

(1889–1947; J: In Jokō). Pro-Japanese Chinese politician. Studied at Waseda University in Tōkyō. Yin participated in the Chinese Revolution of 1911 and joined the Guomindang (Kuomintang; KMT; Nationalist Party). Following the Northern Expedition mounted by CHIANG KAI-SHEK to crush the warlords in North China, he parted company with Chiang and began to develop close ties with the Japanese GUANDONG (KWANTUNG) ARMY. In November 1935 he became chairman of the Japanese-sponsored EAST HEBEI (HOPEH) ANTICOMMUNIST AUTONOMOUS GOVERNMENT, which represented part of the effort to make North China an autonomous region subject to Japanese control. In 1938 the East Hebei regime was absorbed into the PROVISIONAL GOVERNMENT OF THE REPUBLIC OF CHINA, signaling the decline of Yin Rugeng's fortunes. After the war he was captured by the Guomindang government and executed.

Yi Sam-p'yong → Ri Sampei

Yi Sŏng-gye 李成桂

(1335–1408; J: Ri Seikei). The founder of Korea's YI DYNASTY (1392–1910); reigned as King T'aejo (J: Taiso) from 1392 to 1398. As a military official of the preceding KORYŎ dynasty (935–1392), Yi led expeditions against Japanese pirates (WAKŌ). In 1388 he was ordered to expel Ming Chinese forces from Korea's northern border; he considered the effort hopeless, rebelled against the Koryŏ government, and subsequently established his own dynasty, locating his capital at Seoul.

Yi Sun-sin 李舜臣

(1545–98; J: Ri Shunshin). One of the greatest military heroes in Korean history; admiral of the YI DYNASTY's (1392–1910) navy during the Japanese INVASIONS OF KOREA IN 1592 AND 1597. His fleet of "turtle ships" (ironclad vessels resembling turtles) repeatedly cut Japanese supply lines between Tsushima and Korea in 1593, forcing the Japanese to shift to defensive tactics. He is revered as a paragon of military virtue and devotion to country. He was killed in battle against the Japanese in 1598.

Yi Wan-yong 李完用

(1858–1926; J: Ri Kan'yō). Signer of Korea's Treaty of Annexation with Japan in 1910. Pen name Iltang. The adopted son of Yi Hojun, a prominent Ubong Yi clansman and official, Yi Wan-yong passed the higher civil service examination (munkwa) in 1882. He was one of five ministers who supported the signing of the KOREAN-JAPANESE CONVENTION OF 1905. Yi was promoted to prime minister of the Korean government by ITŌ HIROBUMI, Japan's resident general of Korea from 1906 to 1909, and in August 1910 signed the treaty that incorporated Korea into the Japanese empire (see KOREA, ANNEXATION OF). Koreans view him as the man who sold their nation to Japan.

YKK → Yoshida Kōgyō KK

YMCA   キリスト教青年会

(Kirisutokyō Seinenkai). The first Young Men's Christian Association in Japan opened in Tōkyō in 1880. The Young Men's Christian Association Union of Japan (now the National Council of the YMCAs of Japan) was formed in 1903. The YMCA encourages cultural exchange among the youth of Asia through sports and other activities and sponsors Japanese language instruction in many Asian countries. In 1990 Japan had 29 city YMCAs and 33 college YMCAs, with a total membership of 138,048.

Yoake mae   夜明け前

(tr *Before the Dawn*, 1987). A lengthy historical novel by SHIMAZAKI TŌSON (1872–1943); published 1929–35. It depicts the life of Aoyama Hanzō (a character based on Tōson's own father) during the turbulent times surrounding the MEIJI RESTORATION of 1868. Hanzō lives in Magome, a post-station town along the Kiso Road (in what is now Nagano Prefecture), where he is a village headman and operates a HONJIN, or special inn for use by important officials. A fiercely patriotic KOKUGAKU (National Learning) scholar, Hanzō advocates a restoration of imperial authority over the Tokugawa shogunate. After the Restoration, however, Hanzō becomes disillusioned by the selfishness of both the new Meiji government and the peasants to whom he has given such sincere support over the years; he ultimately sees his dreams shattered and his household ruined and dies a madman. *Yoake mae*, representative of Tōson's later writing and a masterpiece of modern historical fiction, provides a unique perspective on the Meiji Restoration, depicting the intellectual activity and excitement among the wealthier farmers of the provinces (see GŌNŌ), men such as Hanzō.

yobai   夜這い

Nocturnal tryst, usually a man visiting a woman for sexual purposes before or even after their formal marriage. This was a natural consequence of an early Japanese pattern of marriage, in which the wife often continued to live with her parents (see MUKOIRIKON). The term evolved from the verb *yobu* ("to visit"), although later it came to be written with the characters for "night" and "crawl." These visits are frequently mentioned in such early literary masterpieces as the MAN'YŌSHŪ and the TALE OF GENJI. In the countryside from the 17th century onward, *yobai* became more a subject of folktales and gossip than a widespread practice. It also came to be considered immoral, and a man on a *yobai* visit was supposed to cover his face with a towel so that he could remain anonymous if he were discovered or rejected by the woman. Certain folk songs refer to *yobai* visits made by women as well. See also MARRIAGE; SEX IN JAPANESE FOLK CULTURE.

yobikō → cram schools

Yoda Yoshikata   依田義賢

(1909–91). Screenwriter. Born in Kyōto. Yoda began his career as a screenwriter at what is now the NIKKATSU CORPORATION. His first movie was MURATA MINORU's *Shiroi ane* (1931, Elder Sister). As screenwriter for MIZOGUCHI KENJI's NANIWA EREJI (1936, Ōsaka Elegy) and *Gion no shimai* (1936, Sisters of the Gion), Yoda concentrated on reproducing natural-sounding dialogues, unusual in the early period of talking pictures. Yoda wrote the majority of Mizoguchi's screenplays, including *Saikaku ichidai onna* (1952, The Life of Oharu), UGETSU MONOGATARI (1953, Ugetsu), *Sanshō-Dayū* (1954; Sanshō the Bailiff), and *Chikamatsu monogatari* (1954, A Story from Chikamatsu or Crucified Lovers). Yoda also wrote novels, poems, and essays.

Yodogawa   淀川

River in the Kinki region, central Honshū, originating in Lake Biwa, Shiga Prefecture, and emptying into Ōsaka Bay. It changes its name three times: the upper reaches are called SETAGAWA, then it is called UJIGAWA when it enters Kyōto Prefecture, and from the town of Ōyamazaki it is called Yodogawa. It was used for transportation during the medieval period (mid-12th–16th centuries) and earlier and flourished as a route between Fushimi, Kyōto's outer port, and Ōsaka in the Edo period (1600–1868). The water is used for irrigation, electric power, and drinking by many cities in Ōsaka and Hyōgo prefectures. The river also provides water to the HANSHIN INDUSTRIAL ZONE. Length: 75 km (47 mi); area of drainage basin: 8,240 sq km (3,181 sq mi).

Yodogawa Steel Works, Ltd   [株]淀川製鋼所

(Yodogawa Seikōsho). Company engaged in the manufacture, processing, and sale of steel sheets, building materials, rolls, and steel ingots. Incorporated in 1935. The company is a leading manufacturer of prepainted, galvanized steel sheets in Japan. Future plans call for the development of high-quality, surface-treated steel sheets and the expanded production and sales of household metal products. Sales totaled ¥189.4 billion (US $1.4 billion) in the fiscal year ending March 1991; the company was capitalized at ¥15.8 billion (US $115.2 million) in the same year. Headquarters are in Ōsaka.

Yodogimi   淀君

(1567–1615). More properly, Yodo no Nyōbō, "the Lady of Yodo." Concubine of TOYOTOMI HIDEYOSHI. This name refers to her residence in Yodo Castle outside Kyōto, where she lived for several years after 1589; her personal name was Chacha. She was the daughter of ODA NOBUNAGA's sister ODANI NO KATA and the *daimyō* ASAI NAGAMASA. Chacha's father was destroyed and her younger brother hunted down and executed by Nobunaga in 1573; her mother's second husband, SHIBATA KATSUIE, was destroyed by Hideyoshi in 1583, and Odani no Kata joined him in suicide; Chacha and her two sisters were thrown on Hideyoshi's mercy. It is uncertain when she was taken into Hideyoshi's household, but she became his favorite as the mother of his only two children, Tsurumatsu (1589–91) and Hideyori (see TOYOTOMI HIDEYORI). In 1599, after Hideyoshi's death, Hideyori and his entourage took up residence at Ōsaka Castle, and Yodogimi began to make her influence felt,

determined to preserve the primacy of the Toyotomi family vis-à-vis TOKUGAWA IEYASU. The Tokugawa were equally determined to eliminate the Toyotomi. The conflict was resolved in the Ōsaka Campaigns of 1614–15 (see ŌSAKA CASTLE, SIEGES OF); Hideyori and Yodogimi committed suicide on 4 June 1615 as Ōsaka Castle fell to the Tokugawa forces.

Yodoya Tatsugorō   淀屋辰五郎

The name of successive heads of an Ōsaka merchant family of the Edo period (1600–1868). Their real surname was Okamoto; their ancestor Tsuneyasu moved to Ōsaka sometime around 1619 and opened a lumber business under the trade name Yodoya. The Yodoya amassed enormous wealth as dealers in the government-controlled raw silk trade with China (ITOWAPPU) and as agents (*kuramoto*; see KURAYASHIKI) for *daimyō* in the Ōsaka rice market. In 1705 the head of the family was censured by the shogunate for extravagant living. The family fortune was confiscated and its members banished from Ōsaka. CHIKAMATSU MONZAEMON's play *Yodogoi shusse no taki nobori* (1708, The Carp of Yodo Climbs the Ladder of Success) is about this incident.

yōeki   徭役

A general term for the corvée labor levied during the 7th and 8th centuries. Initially called *edachi* or *kuwayoboro* and involving forced labor for large projects, it was formalized as an official tax after the TAIKA REFORM of 645. Under the RITSURYŌ SYSTEM of government that developed in the late 7th century, corvée labor was divided into *saieki* (annual service) and *zōyō* (miscellaneous service). Detailed regulations appeared in the TAIHŌ CODE of 701. *Saieki* was levied by the central government, while *zōyō* was levied by the provincial governors (KOKUSHI) for local projects. The labor required for *saieki* was 10 days annually but could be commuted to payment in cloth or other commodities. *Zōyō* required 60 days of labor annually and was not commutable. Within the privately held estates (SHŌEN) that grew up in the Heian period (794–1185), corvée labor came to be known as BUYAKU.

yōga   洋画

(Western-style painting). In the broadest sense, any of a variety of visual arts genres executed with techniques and materials—oils, watercolors, pastels, pen and ink, lithography, etching, etc—developed in the West. In a more limited sense, *yōga* is frequently used to refer specifically to oil painting.

The term *yōga* came into widespread use during the Meiji period (1868–1912) to distinguish Western-style art from the indigenous tradition, whose schools, styles, and technical repertoire came to be known as NIHONGA, or Japanese-style painting. Since that time, *yōga* and *nihonga* have served as the two major divisions of the visual arts in Japan, reflected in art education, the mounting of exhibitions, and the self-identification of artists. The art of contemporary Japan is the outcome of a long history of mutual influence and stimulation between these two separate traditions.

Origins—Western art and its techniques were first brought to Japan along with Christianity toward the end of the 16th century, and the first examples of Japanese *yōga* were religious paintings. However, with the persecution of Christianity and the adoption of the policy of NATIONAL SECLUSION by the

Tokugawa shogunàte (1603–1867), the influence of Western art on Japanese artists rapidly faded. With the shōgun TOKUGAWA YOSHIMUNE's relaxation of the ban on foreign books in 1720, there was a rediscovery of Western art that influenced the painters of the period in a variety of ways (among them contact with the rules of perspective), but it was not until the mid-19th century that Japanese artists were able to make direct use of Western media such as oils.

In 1855 the shogunate established the BANSHO SHIRABESHO, a translation and research bureau for Western studies, and KAWAKAMI TŌGAI was appointed head of a section for the investigation of Western art. One of his students, TAKAHASHI YUICHI, who also received instruction from the English artist Charles WIRGMAN, is regarded as Japan's first accomplished yōga painter. In 1876 the Kōbu Bijutsu Gakkō (Technological Art School) was established, becoming the first institution in Japan to specialize in research and education in Western-style painting and sculpture. The Italian painter Antonio FONTANESI served as one of the principal instructors, and his systematic instruction in the techniques of oil painting nurtured a generation of yōga painters, among them ASAI CHŪ.

During the 1880s there was a general reaction against Westernization and a revival of interest in traditional art that resulted in the temporary decline of yōga. The Kōbu Bijutsu Gakkō was forced to close in 1883 as a result of this mood and persistent financial difficulties, and when the government-sponsored Tōkyō Bijutsu Gakkō (now TŌKYŌ UNIVERSITY OF FINE ARTS AND MUSIC) was established in 1887, only courses in traditional Japanese art were offered.

Yet yōga soon reasserted itself. In 1889 the first yōga coterie, the Meiji Bijutsukai (Meiji Fine Arts Society), was formed, and in 1893 KURODA SEIKI returned from study in France to introduce a brightly toned palette and an array of new techniques that rekindled interest in Western styles. In 1896 a department of yōga was officially established at the Tōkyō Bijutsu Gakkō, and from that time forward Western-style painting may be regarded as having attained a permanent and unshakable position in the repertoire of Japanese fine art.

Yōgaku →Western Learning

Yoichi 余市[町]
Town on Ishikari Bay in western Hokkaidō. Agriculture and fishing are Yoichi's principal industries; there is also a whiskey distillery. Apples and grapes are grown in the surrounding hills. Pop: 25,266.

yojō 余情
An aesthetic ideal fostered by WAKA poets. Written with Chinese characters that literally mean "excess feeling," but usually translated as "overtones," yojō refers to the meanings a poem obliquely implies in addition to its overtly stated message. The term, pronounced yosei in premodern times, was most frequently used in waka criticism from the 11th to the 13th century. At times its connotations overlapped those of YŪGEN. With such poets as FUJIWARA NO TOSHINARI (1114–1204), his son FUJIWARA NO SADAIE (1162–1241), and KAMO NO CHŌMEI (1156?–1216), yojō became part of a complex literary aesthetic that valued poetry of rich symbolism, featuring subtle allusions, exquisite imagery, and cryptic diction.

The concept of yojō can also be observed outside waka criticism. KOMPARU ZENCHIKU (1405–70?), in discussing the art of the Nō drama, insisted that an actor's performance should "have an aura of unstated sentiment." The concept is also latent in the aesthetics of the painter Tosa Mitsuoki (1617–91), who observed that "blank space is also part of a painting," and in the poetics of the haiku master BASHŌ (1644–94). Though somewhat overshadowed by yūgen in later centuries, the term remains one of the most pervasive concepts in Japanese literature and art.

Yojōhan fusuma no shitabari trial
「四畳半襖の下張」裁判
("Yojōhan fusuma no shitabari" saiban). Obscenity trial concerning the publication of the short story "Yojōhan fusuma no shitabari" (Paper Lining of the Sliding Doors of a Four-and-a-Half-Mat Room). Allegedly written by the early-20th-century author NAGAI KAFŪ, it was published in the July 1972 issue of the magazine Omoshiro hambun by its editor, NOSAKA AKIYUKI. In 1973 Nosaka and the magazine's publisher were indicted on obscenity charges. The Tōkyō District Court in 1976 found them guilty, and both were fined. The decision was upheld on appeal by the Tōkyō High Court in 1979, and in 1980 a further appeal was rejected by the Supreme Court. See also OBSCENITY.

Yōjōkun 養生訓
(Precepts for Health). Manual on health by the Neo-Confucian scholar KAIBARA EKIKEN; written in 1713, when the author was 83. Ekiken gives specific advice on diet, sexual activity, bathing, medicinal herbs, acupuncture, and other topics. The book reflects the author's belief that cultivation of the body and spirit go hand in hand.

Yōkaichi 八日市[市]
City in central Shiga Prefecture, central Honshū. A flourishing market town from as early as the 13th century, it is still a commercial center, with numerous machinery, chemical, and textile plants. Tea and tobacco are cultivated in the surrounding areas. Pop: 40,816.

Yōkaichiba 八日市場[市]
City in northeastern Chiba Prefecture, central Honshū. An Edo-period (1600–1868) market town, it is now known for commerce and rice and vegetable farming. Pop: 32,305.

yōkan 羊羹
Jellylike confection. The most common variety, neriyōkan ("kneaded yōkan"), is made by boiling down a mixture of strained red azuki bean paste (an), sugar, agar-agar, and water. It is then poured into rectangular molds to firm. Other varieties include yōkan flavored with powdered green tea and yōkan containing chestnuts. Mizuyōkan, which melts in the mouth when eaten, is made with less agar-agar and more water. Mu-shiyōkan, in which wheat flour is used as a stiffener, is steamed.

Yokaren 予科練
(Junior Pilot Training Corps). Abbreviation for Kaigun Hikō Yoka Renshūsei (Aviation Cadets of the Imperial Japanese Navy). Established in 1930; active during the Sino-Japanese War of 1937–45 and World War II. The cadets, ranging in age from 14 to 23, took a three-to-four-year course. The main training facility was located at Kasumigaura, Ibaraki Prefecture.

Yokkaichi 四日市[市]
City in northern Mie Prefecture, central Honshū, on Ise Bay. The prefecture's largest industrial and commercial city, it developed originally as a market center and post-station town on the highway Tōkaidō during the Edo period (1600–1868). Pollution generated by its petrochemical industrial complex, built after World War II, led to an outbreak of so-called Yokkaichi asthma in the 1960s, but antipollution measures dramatically decreased the number of asthma cases of the 1980s. Pop: 274,180.

yokoana 横穴
("horizontal caverns"). A tunnel tomb or burial cavern used from the late 5th to 8th centuries. These developed simultaneously with the family, corridor-style stone chamber (see KOFUN) in the late Kofun period (ca 300–710). The stone chambers and yokoana existed in clusters and were used over long periods for multiple family interments. Two kinds of tunnel tombs are found: those dug directly into the exposed walls of cliffs or hillsides and those dug underground with an L-shaped tunnel as an entrance. The latter were prevalent in southern Kyūshū. Tunnel tombs from the Kofun period often resemble the layout of corridor-style stone chambers, with a passage leading to a main burial room. The chambers may contain platforms to receive a corpse or a variety of coffins. These included clay capsules with small trap doors and lidded clay containers supported by numerous legs. Grave articles were similar to those in the tomb mounds (kofun): SUE WARE, horse trappings (see HORSE TRAPPINGS, ANCIENT), BRONZE MIRRORS, beads (see BEADS, ANCIENT), weapons, and armor.

Yokogawa Electric Corporation
横河電機[株]
(Yokogawa Denki). Company that manufactures industrial electric equipment. Established in 1915. In 1920 it was incorporated under the name of Yokogawa Electric Works, Ltd. It became Yokogawa Hokushin Electric Corporation in 1983 through a merger with Hokushin Electric Works, Ltd, and assumed its current name in 1986. In 1963 the company established Yokogawa–Hewlett-Packard through a joint investment with Hewlett-Packard Co, USA. It estab-

1   2   3

yōkan
1 The basic variety of this jellylike sweet made with red beans is neri yōkan. Often wrapped in a bamboo-shoot husk, as pictured here, the molded loaf is sliced before serving.
2 Chilled mizu yōkan is a refreshing summertime dessert.
3 This yōkan contains chestnuts.

Yokohama
1 The 860-meter Yokohama Bay Bridge spans an arm of Tōkyō Bay. Opened in September 1989, the bridge immediately became a landmark and symbol of the city.
2 One of the five gates to Yokohama's Chinatown, a popular tourist attraction with more than 200 Chinese restaurants and grocery stores.

lished Yokogawa Medical Systems, Ltd, through a joint venture with General Electric Co, USA, in 1982. Sales for the fiscal year ending March 1991 totaled ¥199.0 billion (US $1.5 billion), and capitalization stood at ¥32.3 billion (US $235.2 million). Headquarters are in Tōkyō.

Yokogawa–Hewlett-Packard, Ltd
横河・ヒューレット・パッカード[株]

(Yokogawa–Hyūretto-Pakkādo). Manufacturer of computers, computer peripherals, medical and engineering instruments, and various electronic components. Incorporated in 1963 through a joint venture between the US firm Hewlett-Packard Co and YOKOGAWA ELECTRIC CORPORATION. The company markets its products through Hewlett-Packard's worldwide sales channels. Sales for the fiscal year ending October 1991 totaled ¥165.9 billion (US $1.3 billion), and capitalization stood at ¥7.4 billion (US $59.1 million). Headquarters are in Tōkyō.

Yokohama
横浜[市]

Capital of Kanagawa Prefecture, central Honshū, on Tōkyō Bay. It is the country's largest port. A small fishing port up to the end of the Edo period (1600–1868), with the signing of the HARRIS TREATY in 1858, Yokohama was opened to foreign trade. The first railway line in Japan was constructed between Yokohama and Tōkyō in 1872. Industrialization started in the early Taishō period (1912–1926). The city was heavily damaged during the Tōkyō Earthquake of 1923 and by Allied bombings in World War II. Today with neighboring Kawasaki, Yokohama is the center of the KEIHIN INDUSTRIAL ZONE. Huge steelmaking, automobile, chemical, oil-refining, electrical-appliance, and food-processing factories are here. The port handles the export of automobiles, cameras, and television sets and the import of oil, soybeans, and machinery. Attractions include the garden SANKEIEN, Yamashita Park, and a Chinatown district. Area: 432 sq km (167.9 sq mi); pop: 3,220,331.

Yokohama Archives of History
横浜開港資料館

(Yokohama Kaikō Shiryōkan). Collection of Japanese and foreign materials principally concerning the opening of Japan and the port of Yokohama during the late 19th century. Established by the city of Yokohama in 1981, it is housed in the former British Consulate.

Yokohama City University
横浜市立大学

(Yokohama Shiritsu Daigaku). A coeducational public university located in the city of Yokohama, Kanagawa Prefecture. Founded in 1949, the university traces its origins to the

Yokohama School of Commercial Law (founded in 1882). The university maintains faculties of economics and business administration, liberal arts and sciences, and medicine. Enrollment in 1989 was 3,151.

yokohama-e
横浜絵

(literally, "Yokohama pictures"). UKIYO-E style woodblock prints inspired by the arrival of foreigners in the early and mid-1860s at the newly opened port of Yokohama. Yokohama-e were designed in great numbers, mostly by artists of the UTAGAWA SCHOOL, and published in Edo (now Tōkyō).

In 1858 Yokohama, south of Edo, was one of the ports opened to foreign trade. The first printed views of Yokohama were published in Edo late that year. As the first foreign merchants and their families began to arrive, the Japanese became fascinated by their strange manners, costumes, attitudes, and occupations. To help satisfy public curiosity, Edo print publishers sent artists to Yokohama to sketch the foreigners and hired writers to supply descriptions, often included above the pictures when they were published as woodblock prints. The most observant and interesting of these artists was Utagawa Sadahide (1807–ca 1873), while others included Yoshiiku, Yoshikazu, and Yoshitora; most of them were pupils of UTAGAWA KUNIYOSHI.

Yokohama Incident
横浜事件

(Yokohama Jiken). A series of repressive actions against journalists taken by the SPECIAL HIGHER POLICE in Yokohama during World War II. Beginning with the arrest of HOSOKAWA KAROKU for writing an allegedly procommunist article for the magazine KAIZŌ, more than 30 journalists (most of them associated with *Kaizō*, CHŪŌ KŌRON, and the IWANAMI SHOTEN, PUBLISHERS) were arrested and jailed between 1942 and 1945 under the 1941 revision of the PEACE PRESERVATION LAW OF 1925 (Chian Iji Hō). In July 1944 *Kaizō* and *Chūō kōron* were ordered to cease publication. By the end of the war not one of the journalists had been brought to trial, although three had died from harsh treatment in prison. The rest were released shortly after the war. The affair is also known as the Tomari Incident, after Hosokawa's hometown in Toyama Prefecture. ISHIKAWA TATSUZŌ's novel, *Kaze ni soyogu ashi* (1949–51, A Reed Bowed by the Wind), is based on this incident.

Yokohama mainichi shimbun
横浜毎日新聞

Japan's first modern Japanese-language daily newspaper. It was started in 1871 by Izeki Moritome (1833–90), the governor of Kanagawa Prefecture. It evolved into a political news organ of the FREEDOM AND PEOPLE'S RIGHTS MOVEMENT (Jiyū Minken Undō). In

1879 it was bought by NUMA MORIKAZU, who moved the paper to Tōkyō, where it became the *Tōkyō-Yokohama mainichi shimbun*. It earned a reputation for calling public attention to shady government deals in Hokkaidō (see HOKKAIDŌ COLONIZATION OFFICE SCANDAL OF 1881). The banner was changed to *Mainichi shimbun* in 1886 and then to *Tōkyō mainichi shimbun* in 1906. In 1940 it was absorbed by the *Teito nichinichi shimbun*.

Yokohama National University
横浜国立大学

(Yokohama Kokuritsu Daigaku). A coeducational national university located in the city of Yokohama, Kanagawa Prefecture. Founded in 1949, the university maintains faculties of business administration, economics, education, and engineering. Its Institute of Environmental Science and Technology is nationally renowned. Enrollment in 1989 was 8,188.

Yokohama Rubber Co, Ltd
横浜ゴム[株]

(Yokohama Gomu). Manufacturer of automobile tires, industrial products, and aircraft components. Affiliated with the FURUKAWA group, the company was established in 1917 with capital furnished on an equal basis by FURUKAWA ELECTRIC CO, LTD, and B. F. Goodrich Co of the United States. The company originally manufactured automobile and bicycle tires and tubes, but after World War II it started to diversify by producing synthetic rubber, plastics, and various industrial rubber products, including belts and hoses. Sales companies are incorporated in the United States, Australia, Canada, and Germany. Sales for the fiscal year ending December 1990 totaled ¥286.0 billion (US $2.1 billion), and the export ratio was 25 percent. The company was capitalized at ¥26.9 billion (US $201.4 million) in the same year. Headquarters are in Tōkyō.

Yokohama Specie Bank
横浜正金銀行

(Yokohama Shōkin Ginkō). Established in 1880 under government auspices as a commercial bank with the twin objectives of increasing the supply of silver specie in Japan and serving the financial needs of export industries and Japanese trading companies; given semigovernmental status in 1887. It played an important role in the promotion of Japanese external trade and the acquisition of foreign exchange. After the Russo-Japanese War of 1904–05, it functioned as a colonial bank for Japanese interests in Manchuria and in the years 1909–18 represented Japan in international banking consortiums organized to provide loans to China. Early in the Shōwa period (1926–89), it served as an organ of government financial policy, helping to support the international value of the yen. In 1947, by order of the OCCUPATION authorities, it was reorganized as a commercial bank and renamed the BANK OF TŌKYŌ, LTD.

Yokoi Kinkoku
横井金谷

(1761–1832). Painter of the NANGA school. Real name Yokoi Myōdō. Born in Ōmi Province (now Shiga Prefecture) not far from the town of Ōtsu, long known for its folk paintings called *ōtsu-e*. At the age of nine he was sent to a strict Buddhist temple school. There he displayed a rebellious attitude; he eventually escaped and made his way to Edo (now Tōkyō) where he lived in a temple and then began the life of a wanderer. He settled for a few years as the only monk of a small

Yokoi Shōnan This influential reformer and political adviser to the Tokugawa shogunate called for the opening of Japan to foreign trade.

temple on Mt. Kinkoku, from which he took his art name.

Eventually Kinkoku settled in Nagoya, joined a circle of *haiku* poets, and began painting in earnest. His earliest works had been handscrolls illustrating the life of the monk HŌNEN, executed in the brightly colored style of the TOSA SCHOOL. Kinkoku soon changed to rendering landscapes in soft washes, a style more closely associated with the MARUYAMA-SHIJŌ SCHOOL. In his final 25 years Kinkoku turned to the works of the *nanga* poet-painter Yosa BUSON for inspiration.

Yokoi Shōnan　　横井小楠

(1809–69). Scholar, reformer, teacher, and political adviser; a dynamic and influential figure until the collapse of the Tokugawa shogunate in 1867–68. Real name Yokoi Tokiari. Born in the Kumamoto domain in Higo Province (now Kumamoto Prefecture).

After studying at Jishūkan, a domainal school noted for academic excellence, Shōnan was sent by the domainal government to study at Edo (now Tōkyō) in 1839. His meeting with FUJITA TŌKO of the Mito domain (now part of Ibaraki Prefecture) was decisive in spurring both on to a practical reformist course. However, after only 10 months Shōnan was recalled to Kumamoto, where he formed a group that urged the application of Neo-Confucian (see SHUSHIGAKU) scholarship to the administration of government.

In 1857 the *daimyō* MATSUDAIRA YOSHINAGA of Echizen Province (now Fukui Prefecture) invited Shōnan to teach at the domainal academy. In 1862 Yoshinaga was suddenly made acting head of the shogunal government (*seiji sōsai*) in a move to gain imperial approval of the ANSEI COMMERCIAL TREATIES (1858), which foreign powers had forced the shogunate to sign. Shōnan was called to Edo, where he advised Yoshinaga on reform within the shogunate and closer cooperation with the imperial court (see MOVEMENT FOR UNION OF COURT AND SHOGUNATE). He also called for the opening of Japan to foreign trade, a thorough reform of domainal finances to strengthen Japan's military position, and a larger voice for the more powerful domains in shogunal affairs.

Shōnan returned to Kumamoto in 1863. Because of his radical ideas, he was stripped of his *samurai* status and placed under house arrest. At the time of the MEIJI RESTORATION (1868) the new government honored him with the post of counselor (*san'yo*), but in 1869 he was assassinated by samurai who suspected him of being a Christian and of harboring republican sentiments.

Yokoi Tokiyoshi　　横井時敬

(1860–1927). Agriculturist and agricultural economist. Born in Higo Province (now Kumamoto Prefecture); graduate of Komaba Agricultural School (now part of Tōkyō University). After teaching in Fukuoka Prefecture and serving in the Ministry of Agriculture and Commerce, he taught agricultural science at Tōkyō University from 1890 to 1922. From 1911 he was also the first president of Tōkyō University of Agriculture, a private institution. Following in the tradition of Max FESCA, under whom he studied, he was a devoted teacher of agricultural science. His books include *Shōnō ni kansuru kenkyū* (1927), a study of the peasantry.

Yokoi Yayū　　横井也有

(1702–83). *Haibun* essayist and *haiku* poet. Real name Yokoi Tokitsura. Born in Na-

goya. In 1741 he was appointed chief of the *ōbangashira*, the security organization in charge of the three castles of the Tokugawa shōgun—in Edo (now Tōkyō), Ōsaka, and Kyōto. From the time of his retirement from official life at age 53, he devoted himself to study and writing. The thematic scope of Yayū's *haibun* is broad, extending from the profundities of love, death, and old age to such everyday ephemera as rice cakes and wooden sandals. The best of Yayū's *haibun* are an impressionistic mosaic of erudite allusion, the commonplace, and gentle humor presented in a rich, classical style, with a skillful display of *engo* (associative words), suggestion, and other devices of the haiku poet. His most important work was the *haibun* collection *Uzuragoromo* (Quail Cloak), which was published some years after his death.

Yokomitsu Riichi　　横光利一

(1898–1947). Novelist. One of the most important Japanese writers between 1925 and 1945. Born in Fukushima Prefecture; attended Waseda University. By 1920 or 1921 he had written the novelette *Kanashimi no daika* (The Price in Sadness), which was published posthumously in 1955. Another fine work written early in his career is the historical novelette *Nichirin* (1923, The Sun).

In 1924 Yokomitsu and other young writers formed the literary group known as the SHINKANKAKU SCHOOL (School of New Sensibilities). Yokomitsu was the group's ideological spokesman, and it was his writing style—highly polished and marked by careful attention to rhythm and symbolism and the use of startling imagery—that became known as the Shinkankaku style.

Many of Yokomitsu's early works were autobiographical. The best-known story from this period is "Haru wa basha ni notte" (1926; tr "Spring, Riding in a Carriage," 1965). Though small in scale, stories such as this one rank among the masterpieces of modern Japanese literature.

Many of the purely fictional stories of this period are satirical attacks on the Marxist idea of economic determinism. Two examples are "Shizuka naru raretsu" (1925; tr "Silent Ranks," 1965) and "Naporeon to tamushi" (1926, Napoleon's Ringworm). His one full-length novel of the period was *Shanhai* (1928–31, Shanghai).

After *Shanhai*, Yokomitsu began to experiment with a radically different style—that of the widely discussed short stories "Kikai" (1930; tr "The Machine," 1961) and "Jikan" (1931; tr "Time," 1956). This atypical style has been described as Yokomitsu's attempt at stream of consciousness; however, it more nearly resembles the psychological monologues of some of Dostoevsky's characters.

During the same time period, he had already begun *Shin'en* (1930–32, The Imperial Mausoleum); most of his fiction from this point on was written in a plainer prose style. *Monshō* (Family Crest) was published in 1934, followed by a continuation in 1940. In 1935 Yokomitsu published the essay "Junsui shōsetsu ron" (Theory of the Pure Novel), in which he asserted that if the "pure novel" were to be produced in Japan for the Japanese people it would have to be both pure and popular literature. This created a great controversy in the Japanese literary world, where a rigid distinction between pure and popular literature has been maintained.

In 1936 Yokomitsu went to Europe. The

record of his six months' travels was published as *Ōshū kikō* (1936, A European Travel Diary), but a more important result of the trip was the long, unfinished novel RYOSHŪ (1937–46, A Traveler's Sadness). Following World War II, Yokomitsu completed two fine works: *Yoru no kutsu* (1947, Shoes in the Night) and the posthumously published short story "Bishō" (1948, The Smile).

Yokomizo Seishi　　横溝正史

(1902–81). Novelist. Born in Hyōgo Prefecture; graduate of Ōsaka Pharmaceutical College. He joined the HAKUBUNKAN publishing house in 1926 but left in 1932 to devote himself full time to writing. His early novels include *Onibi* (1935) and *Ningyō Sashichi torimonochō* (1938–39). Immediately after the war, he published the mysteries *Honjin satsujin jiken* and *Chōchō satsujin jiken* (both 1946). His fiction, based on the orthodox Western detective-story format, was the model for postwar mystery writing in Japan. Other works include *Akuma ga kitarite fue o fuku* (1951–53).

Yokoo Tadanori　　横尾忠則

(1936–　). Artist; known for collage posters. Born in Hyōgo Prefecture. From childhood he showed intense interest in the colors and designs in his family's clothing store. After working briefly for a newspaper in Kōbe, he joined the Nippon Design Center, Inc, in 1961 and was recognized almost at once with awards from the Art Directors Club of Tōkyō. Influenced by the pop art and psychedelic movements, his work incorporates photos and bits from traditional Japanese, Western, and even Buddhist art, often all in the same poster. He has received numerous awards and recognitions both in Japan and abroad, including a one-man show in 1970 at the Museum of Modern Art in New York. He is also known for his essays on art and life.

Yokose Yau　　横瀬夜雨

(1878–1934). Poet. Real name Yokose Toraju; other pen name Tonemaru. Born in Ibaraki Prefecture. Crippled by rickets in childhood, he stayed home after completing grade school and submitted poems to a children's literary magazine, *Bunko*. In 1899 he published his first collection of poems, *Yūzuki*, but his second collection, *Hanamori* (1905), established his name as a poet. Melancholy and lyrical in tone, his poems are written in the simple rhythms of local folk songs. Other collections include *Nijūhasshuku* (1907).

Yokoo Tadanori Incorporating traditional elements, this work by collage poster artist Yokoo is titled *My Tour of Hell at Four Years Old: Suma Beach* (1968).

Yokomitsu Riichi This innovative novelist was a dominant figure in the Japanese literary scene of the 1930s.

Yokomizo Seishi This novelist's Western-style detective stories served as a model for postwar mystery writing in Japan.

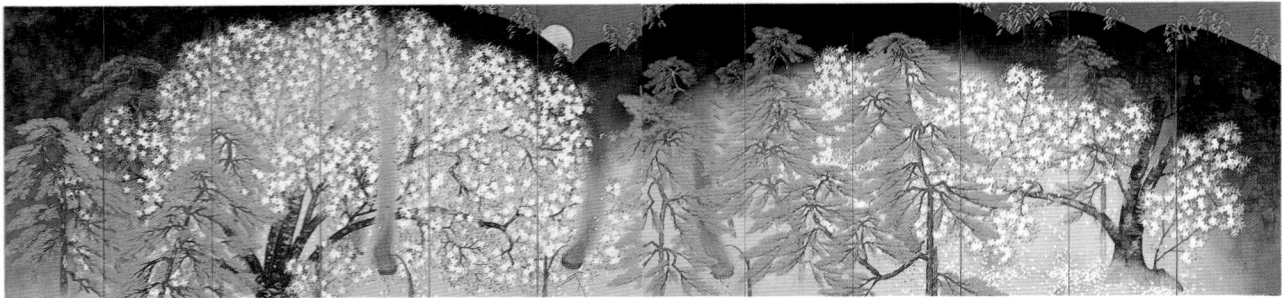

Yokosuka　　　　　横須賀[市]

City in southeastern Kanagawa Prefecture, central Honshū, situated at the mouth of Tōkyō Bay. During the Edo period (1600–1868), the Uraga commissioner's office was located here to check ships approaching the shogunal capital of Edo (now Tōkyō). It was also the site of a shipyard. From 1884 the city developed as Japan's first naval base. Since World War II, it has served as a base of the US Navy and the Japanese Maritime Self Defense Force. Its principal industries are automobile manufacturing and shipbuilding. A monument to the Englishman William ADAMS, who arrived in Japan in 1600, is in Tsukayama Park. Pop: 433,358.

Yokosuka Shipyards　　　横須賀造船所

(Yokosuka Zōsenjo). Predecessor of the Yokosuka Naval Arsenal (Kaigun Kōshō). It was originally the Yokosuka Seitetsusho, a foundry and shipyard built in 1866 at Yokosuka, in what is now Kanagawa Prefecture, by the Tokugawa shogunate under the direction of French naval engineer François VERNY (1837–1908). The shipyard was taken over by the new government immediately after the Meiji Restoration of 1868. In 1871 it was renamed the Yokosuka Zōsenjo. The shipyard was renamed the Kaigun Kōshō in 1903 and was one of the four largest arsenals in Japan until the end of World War II.

Yokota Kisaburō　　　　横田喜三郎

(1896–　). Scholar of international law and third chief justice of the Supreme Court. Born in Aichi Prefecture, he graduated from Tōkyō University in 1922. He was a professor at Tōkyō University from 1930 until 1957, when he became a member of the United Nations Committee on International Law. He served as chief justice of the Supreme Court from 1960 to 1966. After World War II, Yokota called for the removal of the emperor because of his responsibility for the war. He also took article 9 of the 1947 constitution (see RENUNCIATION OF WAR) to require complete abolition of any military capability; but later he asserted that, in accord with the right of self-defense, it was permissible for Japan to take measures to ensure its national security. His writings include *Kokusaihō* (2 vols, 1933, International Law), *Jieiken* (1951, The Right of Self-Defense), and *Kokusaihōgaku* (1955, The Study of International Law).

Yokote　　　　　　横手[市]

City in the Yokote Basin, southeastern Akita Prefecture, northern Honshū. It began as a castle town under the rule of the Onodera family during the Kamakura period (1185–1333). Local products include apples and Yokote *momen*, a traditional cotton fabric. Yokote is known for its annual winter festi-

val, in which snow huts called *kamakura* are built for children. Pop: 42,294.

Yokote Basin　　　　　横手盆地

(Yokote Bonchi). A graben basin in southeastern Akita Prefecture, northern Honshū. Bounded by the Ōu and Dewa mountain ranges, it consists of piedmont alluvial fans below the fault scarps of the Ōu Mountains and the floodplain of the river Omonogawa's upper reaches. Rice, apples, and grapes are cultivated. The major cities are Yokote, Ōmagari, and Yuzawa. Length: approximately 60 km (37 mi); maximum width: 15 km (9 mi).

Yokoyama Gennosuke　　　横山源之助

(1871–1915). Writer about social problems of the late Meiji period (1868–1912). Born in Toyama Prefecture; studied at Igirisu Hōritsu Gakkō (now Chūō University). Under the influence of the writer FUTABATEI SHIMEI, Yokoyama became interested in life at the lower levels of Japanese society. In 1894 he joined the newspaper *Mainichi shimbun* and traveled throughout the country to investigate living conditions among the poor, including urban slum dwellers, textile workers, and rural tenant farmers. He later gathered information on factory workers for the Ministry of Agriculture and Commerce. Yokoyama's *Nihon no kasō shakai* (1899, Japan's Lower Classes) is a summary of his observations.

Yokoyama Matajirō　　　横山又次郎

(1860–1942). Paleontologist. Born in the city of Nagasaki. A graduate of Tōkyō University, from 1886 to 1889 Yokoyama studied paleontology in Munich, where he wrote a study on the Mesozoic plant fossils of Niigata, Toyama, Ishikawa, and Fukui prefectures; this was the first research paper on paleontology written by a Japanese. He later did research on the mollusks of the Mesozoic and Cenozoic eras and established the foundations in Japan of biostratigraphy. The first translator into Japanese of many of the taxonomic terms of paleontology currently in use, he published *Koseibutsu kōyō* (Elements of Paleontology) in 1920.

Yokoyama Ryūichi　　　横山隆一

(1909–　). Cartoonist. Born in Kōchi Prefecture, Yokoyama studied at the Kawabata School of Drawing. In 1932 he formed an organization called the Shin Mangaha Shūdan (New Comics Group) and published many satirical comics. In the 1930s and 1940s he intermittently published *Fuku chan*, a comic with a child as its protagonist, in the *Asahi shimbun.* That work was later made into a popular motion picture. *Fuku chan* was serialized in the *Mainichi shimbun* from 1956 to 1971 as well. It was Yokoyama's most important work and the first Japanese comic in the history of the genre to be serialized for an extended period.

Yokoyama Taikan　　　横山大観

(1868–1958). Prominent painter in the movement led by OKAKURA KAKUZŌ to develop a new style of Japanese painting respectful of, but not enslaved to, past traditions. Born Sakai Hidemaro in Ibaraki Prefecture. Taikan was later adopted into his mother's family and took the name Yokoyama. He enrolled in the Tōkyō Bijutsu Gakkō (now Tōkyō University of Fine Arts and Music), which had just opened under Okakura's directorship. There he studied under the KANŌ SCHOOL painter HASHIMOTO GAHŌ.

In 1895 Taikan spent a year teaching at the Kyōto Municipal School of Fine Arts and Crafts. He returned to the Tōkyō Bijutsu Gakkō as an assistant professor of painting in 1896, but left the following year when Okakura was forced to resign. Later, Taikan, with SHIMOMURA KANZAN and HISHIDA SHUNSŌ, helped Okakura organize the JAPAN FINE ARTS ACADEMY (Nihon Bijutsuin). The academy eventually closed, but Taikan was among those to reestablish it in 1914. In the interim he traveled widely. In 1930 he was sent to Italy as an art ambassador.

After early experiments with a softly blurred style, Taikan later turned to monochrome ink painting, attracted by the unlimited tonal potential of black. An early masterpiece in this medium is his famous scroll *Seisei ruten* (1923, Wheel of Life). In 1935 he was appointed a member of the Imperial Fine Arts Academy; he received the Order of Culture in 1937.

yōkyoku —→ utai

Yōmei Bunko　　　　　陽明文庫

(Yōmei Library). A private library in the Utano district of Kyōto based on the collection of the KONOE FAMILY (also known by the name Yōmei). One of the GOSEKKE, the five branches of the Fujiwara family whose heads served for centuries as imperial regents, the Konoe built up a priceless repository, including some 100,000 manuscripts, eight National Treasures, and rare art objects. One of the gems of the collection is the original manuscript of MIDŌ KAMPAKU KI, the diary of FUJIWARA NO MICHINAGA. The modern statesman KONOE FUMIMARO established the library as a private foundation in 1938.

Yōmeigaku　　　　　陽明学

(Wang Yangming school). A system of thought expounded by the Chinese Ming dynasty (1368–1644) philosopher Wang Yangming (1472–1529; J: Ō Yōmei, hence Yōmeigaku, *gaku* meaning school). Wang Yangming emphasized the "good knowledge" (Ch: *liangzhi* or *liang-chih*; J: *ryōchi*) innate in all men and argued that awakening to this "good knowledge" was a process by which *li* (J: *ri*), the ultimate universal principle, was "realized." He also emphasized the union of thought and action, placing stress on practice (and thus putting trust in individual effort toward betterment) rather than on theory or on scholarly investigation of things in pursuit of an objective or substantive *li*. This antischolastic conception of *li* contrasted with the more intellectualist, rationalist approach of the Zhu Xi (Chu Hsi) school of Confucianism (see SHUSHIGAKU), which had the support of the Tokugawa shogunate in Japan (1603–1867).

During the Edo period (1600–1868), supporters of the Zhu Xi school were numerous in Japan, and the school played a pivotal role in the development of ideas. By contrast, adherents of the Wang Yangming school in Japan tended to be isolated from each other. Moreover, most of them drew on the doctrines of other schools in formulating and articulating their systems of thought.

The first patriarch of the Wang Yangming school in Japan was NAKAE TŌJU (1608–48). Tōju embraced the idea that the universe sprang from the "Great Emptiness" (Ch: Taixu or T'ai-hsü; J: Taikyo), over which the "Supreme Lord" rules, and maintained that "good knowledge" is the human being's sharing in the mind of the Supreme Lord. Tōju emphasized that, in our day-to-day dealings, there are appropriate times, places, and social positions for particular actions. KUMAZAWA BANZAN (1619–91), who studied in his youth with Nakae Tōju, was so attracted to Tōju's thinking about appropriate "time, place, and social position" that he made this a basic tenet in his own philosophy. Banzan put great emphasis on the practical character of Wang Yangming's teachings. Thus, he taught that wide knowledge did not guarantee successful conduct of the affairs of state; one must also understand humanity and actual social conditions. Later scholars of the Wang Yangming school included MIWA SHISSAI (1669–1744), SATŌ ISSAI (1772–1859), and ŌSHIO HEIHACHIRŌ (1793–1837).

yomeirikon　　　　　嫁入婚

Patrilocal marriage, in which the husband and wife take up residence in or near the house of the husband's parents. The practice of *yomeirikon* developed with the evolution of the warrior class in the late Heian period (794–1185). It represented a significant shift from the earlier practice of matrilocal marriage (MUKOIRIKON) and from marriages requiring relocation or even dual residences. *Yomeirikon* became more widespread during the Edo period (1600–1868). This was in part due to the dominance of government-supported Neo-Confucian philosophy in which primary emphasis was placed on the loyalty of the *samurai* to his lord and, similarly, of the wife to her husband. *Yomeirikon* was especially prevalent among samurai, who were required by social convention to marry into families of the same rank, but it became increasingly customary among commoners as well. Today a growing number of couples live apart from their parents, and the word *yomeiri* has in general come to mean marriage.

yomena　　　　　嫁菜

Kalimeris yomena. A perennial herb of the chrysanthemum family (Compositae) that grows wild in the hills, fields, and wetlands of Honshū, Shikoku, and Kyūshū. It grows 30–100 centimeters (1–3.5 ft) high. The alternate, oval to lance-shaped, serrated leaves are edible when young. Flowers (2.5 cm [1 in] wide) bloom from summer to autumn. Each flower head has yellow, disk-

shaped flowers surrounded by pale purple ray flowers. Similar species include the *nokongiku* (*Aster ageratoides* var. *ovatus*), which resembles the *yomena* but has longer hair on the fruit, and the *kongiku* (*A. ageratoides* var. *ovatus* f. *hortensis*), which bears deeper purple flowers.

yomihon　　　　　読本

(literally, "reading books"). Genre of late-18th- and early-19th-century narrative prose fiction (see GESAKU) characterized by historical settings, didactic and moralistic story lines blended with the supernatural, and heavy reliance on Chinese prose models. *Yomihon* are the immediate forerunners of the modern popular romance, but the genre included collections of short stories, full-length historical romances, and even prose discourses. The format was modeled after the UKIYO-ZŌSHI, an earlier form of prose fiction, and popular Chinese works of the Ming (1368–1644) and Qing (Ch'ing; 1644–1912) dynasties.

The origin of the *yomihon* genre can be traced to early-18th-century interest in Chinese colloquial fiction, which was stimulated by the Chinese study group organized by OGYŪ SORAI and Okajima Kanzan (1674–1728). The master *yomihon* writer Takizawa BAKIN was especially indebted to Chinese models.

Bakin's NANSŌ SATOMI HAKKENDEN (1814–42, Satomi and the Eight "Dogs") and works by UEDA AKINARI represent the culmination of the traditional art of storytelling. Other notable authors of the late 18th and early 19th centuries include TAKEBE AYATARI and SANTŌ KYŌDEN. Later authors, such as TSUBOUCHI SHŌYŌ, criticized the *yomihon* but often wrote in a style reminiscent of Akinari and Bakin.

Yomi no Kuni → afterlife

Yomitan　　　　　読谷[村]

Village on the western coast of Okinawa, Okinawa Prefecture. Much of its economy is supported by an American military base, which occupies 48 percent of the village's land. The principal farm product is sugarcane. Pop: 30,750.

Yomiuri Nippon Symphony Orchestra　　　読売日本交響楽団

(Yomiuri Nippon Kōkyō Gakudan). Orchestra established in Tōkyō in 1962 by three companies—Yomiuri Shimbun (the newspaper company), Nippon Television Network Corporation, and Yomiuri Telecasting Corporation—in order to promote international cultural exchange. Its first principal conductor was Willis Page (b 1918) of the United States. Numerous outstanding conductors from around the world have succeeded Page.

Yomiuri shimbun　　　　読売新聞

Japan's largest national daily newspaper. The *Yomiuri* was launched in 1874 by the Nisshūsha newspaper company as a small daily. During the 1880s and 1890s the paper made a name for itself as a literary arts publication by having writers such as OZAKI KŌYŌ as regular contributors. In 1924 SHŌRIKI MATSUTARŌ took over management of the company. His innovations included sensational news coverage, a full-page radio program guide, and establishment of Japan's first professional baseball team (now known as the Yomiuri Giants). Emphasis was shifted to broad news coverage aimed at readers in the local Tōkyō area. By 1941 it had the largest

circulation of any daily newspaper in the Tōkyō area. In 1942, under wartime conditions, it merged with the HŌCHI SHIMBUN and became known as the *Yomiuri-Hōchi.* In 1946 the *Yomiuri* reverted to its original name. In 1952 it began publishing in Ōsaka and then went nationwide. Circulation was 9.8 million in 1991—the largest of any newspaper in the world.

Yomiuri Telecasting Corporation　　読売テレビ放送[株]

(Yomiuri Terebi Hōsō). An Ōsaka-based commercial television-broadcasting company serving the Kyōto-Ōsaka area. It was established in 1958 with funding from the YOMIURI SHIMBUN, one of Japan's largest national daily newspapers, and other sources. The company is an affiliate of the Nippon News Network (NNN). Tōkyō's NIPPON TELEVISION NETWORK CORPORATION (NTV) is its key station. Yomiuri's programming includes dramas, documentaries, animated films, and a variety of company-produced special shows that are circulated among other network stations. The company began operation as an educational television station but is now a major general-programming station.

yomogi　　　　　蓬

(wormwood or mugwort). *Artemisia princeps.* A perennial herb of the family Compositae commonly found in fields, on mountains, and along roadsides in Honshū, Shikoku, and Kyūshū. The stem is 1.0–1.5 meters (3.3–4.9 ft) high. The leaves are alternate, oblong, and pinnate. The upper surface of the leaf is green, and the lower surface is whitish and hairy. During summer and autumn many small yellowish white flowers bloom. The entire plant has an aromatic scent that is believed to repel evil influence and bring longevity. The *yomogi* was traditionally used with leaves of the SHŌBU (sweet flag) to decorate the eaves of houses on CHILDREN'S DAY. In early spring the young *yomogi* shoots are collected, boiled, and mixed in rice cakes. The hairs on the lower surface of the leaves are used to make the combustible substance used in MOXA TREATMENT.

Yonago　　　　　米子[市]

City in western Tottori Prefecture, western Honshū. Situated on the Sea of Japan, Yonago developed as a castle town in the beginning of the 17th century and then prospered as a distribution center for iron and cotton goods. Pulp and textile mills as well as steel and food-processing plants are located in its coastal districts. The city is a base for trips to Daisen, a mountain that attracts many tourists. Kaike Hot Spring is here. Pop: 131,453.

Yonagunijima　　　　　与那国島

Island 70 km (43 mi) northwest of the island of Iriomotejima, Okinawa Prefecture. One of the YAEYAMA ISLANDS. It is the westernmost point of Japan at longitude 122°56' east. The coast is made up of raised coral reefs. The chief agricultural product is sugarcane. Area: 28.5 sq km (11 sq mi).

Yonai Mitsumasa　　　　米内光政

(1880–1948). Admiral and prime minister (1940). Born in Iwate Prefecture. A graduate of the Naval Academy, he served in numerous important navy posts, becoming commander in chief of the Combined Fleet in 1936. As navy minister in the HAYASHI SEN-

yomena The delicious young leaves of this member of the chrysanthemum family have long been used for culinary purposes. The *yomena* blooms from July through October.

yomogi This hardy and common perennial herb is distributed throughout Japan, except Hokkaidō. The small, yellowish white flowers bloom in late summer or autumn.

Yonai Mitsumasa This Imperial Japanese Navy admiral served as prime minister in 1940 and later presided over the post–World War II dissolution of Japan's naval forces.

JŪRŌ, the first KONOE FUMIMARO, and the HIRANUMA KIICHIRŌ cabinets, he took a pro-American, pro-British stance and opposed alliance with the Axis powers. He became prime minister in January 1940 but in July was forced to step down because of pressure from the pro-Axis army. He served again as navy minister in several cabinets during and immediately after World War II and presided over the dissolution of the Japanese navy.

yonaoshi rebellions　世直し一揆

(yonaoshi ikki; literally, "world renewal rebellions"). Peasant rebellions during the years 1866–69. For the most part they arose in territories directly administered by the Tokugawa shogunate (TENRYŌ) and in pro-shogunate domains of eastern Japan. Characteristically, yonaoshi revolts resembled intrapeasant civil wars, in which many poor farmers, tenants, and agricultural day laborers rose against the rich of their villages. In the largest, such as the Bushū Uprising in the Musashi Plain (now Tōkyō and Saitama prefectures) and the Shindatsu Uprising in Fukushima, both in July 1866, tens of thousands of peasants and day laborers were organized by village into units of up to 1,000 men. They marched from village to village, threatening the destruction of individuals or villages that did not accede to their demands for alms or rice. Also demanding the free return of pawned goods and mortgaged land, the rebels most often aimed their attacks at usurers, pawnbrokers, and merchants associated with the sale of silk or cotton. After considerable property damage but relatively few deaths and casualties, domainal or shogunate forces suppressed the revolts, frequently with the aid of village-recruited peasant troops. The immediate cause of the revolts was a steep rise in rice prices in 1866, exacerbated by an unstable silk market that affected wage earners and small producers. In a broader sense the yonaoshi rebellions reflected the effects of a growing commercialization of the countryside.

Yoneshirogawa　米代川

River in northern Akita Prefecture, northern Honshū, originating in the Ōu Mountains, in the northwestern part of Iwate Prefecture, and flowing west through Hanawa, Ōdate, and Takanosu basins and the Noshiro Plain, to empty into the Sea of Japan at the city of Noshiro. Large mineral deposits are located along the river. Length: 136 km (84 mi); area of drainage basin: 4,100 sq km (1,583 sq mi).

Yonezawa　米沢［市］

City in southern Yamagata Prefecture, northern Honshū. In the Edo period (1600–1868) it was a flourishing castle town belonging to the UESUGI FAMILY. It is now the most important city in the Yonezawa Basin. Long known for its yonezawa-ori silk fabrics. In recent years the manufacture of synthetic fiber cloth and wool fabrics has become predominant. Electric appliances and machinery are also manufactured. Products include rice and apples. There are numerous hot springs. It is the base camp for climbing the mountain Azumasan. Pop: 94,760.

Yonezawa Basin　米沢盆地

(Yonezawa Bonchi). A fault basin in southern Yamagata Prefecture, northern Honshū. Bounded by the Ōu and Iide mountain ranges, it consists of alluvial fans below the fault scarp and of the floodplains of the river Mogamigawa's upper reaches. Grapes, pears, and apples are cultivated. Rice is also grown. The major city is Yonezawa. Length: approximately 25 km (16 mi); width: approximately 20 km (12 mi).

yōnin　遥任

(literally, "distant appointment"). Also known as yōju. A practice whereby an appointed official, particularly a provincial governor (KOKUSHI), received the title and stipend belonging to an office but remained in the capital without taking up his assigned provincial post. In the Nara period (710–794) yōnin was permitted only in cases when appointees held concurrent positions in the capital. A deputy (mokudai) was delegated to the provincial office. From the late Heian period (794–1185) the practice became commonplace even among those who held no court appointments. The practice is considered to have been a major factor in the decline of the Chinese-style RITSURYŌ SYSTEM of government.

Yono　与野［市］

City in southeastern Saitama Prefecture, central Honshū. It is a commuter suburb of Tōkyō and manufactures automobiles. Pop: 79,060.

yoriai　寄合

1. Group meetings; especially village meetings to discuss cooperative labor, festivals, tax allotments, and local regulations. Such meetings gained importance as cultivators began to form self-governing groups (sō) in around the 14th century. They were dominated by prominent landholders (MYŌSHU and later MURA YAKUNIN), but in the Edo period (1600–1868) many villages allowed even tenant farmers to participate. Even today, village meetings are called yoriai.

2. In the Kamakura shogunate (1192–1333), an informal, secret council of important officials of the regent HŌJŌ FAMILY. Also known as the Yoriaishū, it usurped the power of the Council of State (HYŌJŌSHŪ) in the late 13th century.

3. In the Tokugawa shogunate (1603–1867), a category of direct shogunal vassal (HATAMOTO) with incomes over 3,000 koku (see KOKUDAKA) but no official posts who were responsible for miscellaneous tasks such as guard duty.

4. In linked-verse poetry (RENGA), a linking based on a close association with a word in the preceding verse.

yoriki and dōshin　与力と同心

(yoriki to dōshin). The term yoriki (literally, "strength that is offered") generally referred to a warrior who assisted another warrior superior in rank. In the Muromachi period (1333–1568) a yoriki was a samurai who served daimyō or high-ranking samurai commanders; during the 16th century the term identified a mounted samurai who commanded other samurai or ASHIGARU (foot soldiers). The Tokugawa shogunate (1603–1867) used the term yoriki to identify low-level samurai commanders analogous to modern noncommissioned officers. They headed patrol and guard units whose members were designated dōshin (literally, "like-minded" or "shared hearts"). Both yoriki and dōshin were of the GOKENIN category of vassals, but the former were of higher hereditary status, drew larger hereditary family stipends, and were entrusted with more important military duties. The hundreds of dōshin (along with the agents known as MEAKASHI) made up the basic police force of most city commissioners (MACHI BUGYŌ).

yorioya and yoriko　寄親と寄子

(yorioya to yoriko; literally, "foster parent and foster child"). Social bond between superior and inferior in premodern times modeled on the parent-child relationship. It is said to have originated in the Kamakura period (1185–1333) when the sōryō (leaders of the BUSHIDAN, or local warrior bands) enlisted warriors from outside their kin groups and expressed their ties as lord and vassal in terms of parent-child roles. In the early Muromachi period (1333–1568) this relationship was often employed by warlords to control their expanding bodies of retainers. By the Sengoku (Warring States) period (1467–1568) it had become a common basis for organizing the retainers of the great DAIMYŌ families.

Not limited to the warrior class, the yorioya-yoriko relationship appeared also in villages, both in labor-service organization and in patron-client ties between landlords and farmers. In the cities, similar bonds were widely established between artisans or merchants and their apprentices (hōkōnin) by the Edo period (1600–1868). See also OYABUN-KOBUN.

Yōrō　養老［町］

Town in southwestern Gifu Prefecture, central Honshū. On the river IBIGAWA, the town is encircled by embankments of the WAJŪ type to prevent flooding. Farming is the chief occupation. Yōrō Falls is associated with a legend about a loyal son. Pop: 33,102.

Yōrō Code　養老律令

(Yōrō Ritsuryō). Fundamental legal code of ancient Japan. A revision of the TAIHŌ CODE of 701; drafted by FUJIWARA NO FUHITO in 718 (Yōrō 2); put into effect in 757 by his grandson FUJIWARA NO NAKAMARO. The ryō, regulations for fiscal, administrative, and other aspects of government, filled 10 chapters (kan); they survive almost complete in an official commentary, RYŌ NO GIGE, and in a private commentary, RYŌ NO SHŪGE, both written in the 9th century. The ritsu, or penal regulations, in 10 chapters, survive in fragments. The Yōrō Code served as the basis of Japanese government until the early 10th century. The bureaucratic structure and names of posts in the code remained in use at the imperial court throughout the period of WARRIOR GOVERNMENT until the introduction of the modern cabinet system in 1885. See also RITSURYŌ SYSTEM.

Yōrōgawa　養老川

River in central Chiba Prefecture, central Honshū, originating in Kiyosumiyama, a small mountain near the town of Amatsu Kominato, and flowing north through the Bōsō Hills to empty into Tōkyō Bay. The upper reaches are noted for their beautiful gorges. Land reclamation projects have been implemented at the river's mouth, with the reclaimed land part of the Keiyō Industrial Region. Length: 68 km (42 mi); area of drainage basin: 258 sq km (100 sq mi).

Yoronjima　与論島

Island 25 km (16 mi) northeast of the main island of Okinawa. It is one of the AMAMI ISLANDS and is under the jurisdiction of Kagoshima Prefecture. The island is composed of raised coral reefs. Agricultural products are sugarcane and squash. Tourism is one of its main industries today. Area: 20.8 sq km (8 sq mi).

Yorozu chōhō   万朝報

Newspaper popular in the later Meiji period (1868–1912); founded in 1892 by KUROIWA RUIKŌ. It gained popularity through its probing coverage of current social problems, sensational exposés, and serialization of Kuroiwa's translations of Western novels. Its editorial staff included UCHIMURA KANZŌ, KŌTOKU SHŪSUI, and SAKAI TOSHIHIKO, all of whom campaigned against the Russo-Japanese War (1904–05) but resigned when Kuroiwa took a prowar stance. The *Yorozu* also voiced its opposition to the domain cliques (HAMBATSU). In 1940 it merged with the *Tōkyō maiyū shimbun.*

Yorozu Tetsugorō   万鉄五郎

(1885–1927). Western-style painter. Born in Iwate Prefecture. Graduate of Tōkyō Bijutsu Gakkō (now Tōkyō University of Fine Arts and Music). With the painter KISHIDA RYŪSEI and others, he participated in the Fusain Society (Hyūzankai) in 1912–13. During the late Meiji (1868–1912) and early Taishō (1912–26) periods, Yorozu developed a style influenced by fauvism and cubism. In his later years Yorozu, under the influence of the southern school of Chinese painting (*nanga*), introduced oriental techniques into his stylistic repertoire.

Yorozuya Kinnosuke   萬屋錦之介

(1932–). Movie actor. Born in Tōkyō. He is known for his roles in numerous period films (*jidaigeki*) including the very popular series *Daibosatsu Tōge* (1957–59, Daibosatsu Pass) and *Miyamoto Musashi* (1961–65, Musashi). A former KABUKI actor, he made his film debut in 1954 under the name Nakamura Kinnosuke in *Hiyodori-zōshi.* He appeared in two popular TŌEI CO, LTD, period-film series: *Fuefuki dōji* (1954) and *Benikujaku* (1954–55), and in the movie series *Isshin Tasuke* (1958–63), directed by Sawashima Tadashi (b 1926). He changed his name to Yorozuya Kinnosuke in 1972. Yorozuya has also worked on the stage and in television.

Yoru no nezame   夜の寝覚

(Nights of Fitful Waking). Also known as *Yowa no nezame* and *Nezame.* One of three tales (*monogatari*) from the mid-11th century attributed to the daughter of Sugawara no Takasue (SUGAWARA NO TAKASUE NO MUSUME), the others being SARASHINA NIKKI and HAMAMATSU CHŪNAGON MONOGATARI. Extant texts all show evidence of several missing chapters. Though written in a court style reminiscent of the TALE OF GENJI (ca 1000), this work differs remarkably in its treatment of characterization and narrative development. In contrast to the broad scope of time and place in the *Tale of Genji*, characters in *Yoru no nezame* live within their thoughts with barely a passing glance at the seasons or the world around them. Narrative development is confined largely to interior monologues. Characterization centers upon the processes of maturity in a single female character, the Lady Nezame. *Yoru no nezame* is a work devoted to examining the dual burdens of sacrifice and survival. Its theme is of survival through the process of maturation from young girl to responsible mother. The steady strengthening of resolve in a woman bred to passivity must surely have stirred the hearts of Heian-period (794–1185) readers. The fateful though steadfast attachment of Lady Nezame to her great love provides moments of balanced joy and sadness. Fragments of an illustrated handscroll of *Yoru no nezame* survive; they are among the finest achievements of Heian art.

Yoru no tsuzumi   夜の鼓

(Night Drum). A 1958 film, directed by IMAI TADASHI and starring ARIMA INEKO, MIKUNI RENTARŌ, and MORI MASAYUKI, which attacked Japan's feudal social traditions. The screenplay, by HASHIMOTO SHINOBU and SHINDŌ KANETO, based on an original play by the 18th-century dramatist CHIKAMATSU MONZAEMON, is told in a series of flashbacks. It is shot largely in close-ups, giving an emotional intensity rare in Japanese films.

In the film, the lonely wife of a provincial lord is seduced by an itinerant music teacher while the husband she loves is away. The Tokugawa social code demanded that the wife kill herself in order to spare her husband shame. Although her devoted spouse forgives her, he must carry out his obligation to the code and kill his wife when she cannot bring herself to commit suicide. To fulfill his obligation he then hunts down and kills the teacher, only to realize that he has acted not according to his own moral convictions but by society's abstract rules. In so doing he has destroyed his integrity and human worth.

yoryūdo   寄人

(literally, "dependent people"; also pronounced *yoriudo* or *yoribito*). 1. Scribes; bureaucratic staff members or clerks in the imperial ministries of the Heian period (794–1185) and the Kamakura (1192–1333) and Muromachi (1338–1573) shogunates. In the Heian government they dealt with estate (SHŌEN) management in the Records Office (KIROKU SHŌEN KENKEIJO) and poetic anthologies in the Office of Poetry (Waka-dokoro). Under the Kamakura and Muromachi shogunates they staffed the Board of Retainers (SAMURAI-DOKORO), the Administrative Board (MANDOKORO), and the Board of Inquiry (MONCHŪJO).

2. From the late 10th century through the 13th, the term was also applied to farmers and laborers who lent their services to estates other than those to which they officially belonged.

Yosa Buson → Buson

Yōsai → Eisai

Yosano Akiko   与謝野晶子

(1878–1942). Noted poet and feminist writer. Maiden name Hō Shō. Born in Sakai in Ōsaka Prefecture, she graduated from the Sakai Girls' School in 1894. When YOSANO TEKKAN began publishing a monthly, MYŌJŌ (Bright Star), Akiko was one of its first contributors. The two met in 1900, and the following year they were married. Also in 1901 Akiko produced her first volume of poems, *Midaregami* (tr *Tangled Hair,* 1971). It contained nearly 400 poems of passion and sensuality and was enthusiastically received.

Akiko published over 20 more volumes of poetry and much social commentary, including criticism of Japan's foreign aggression. She also published commentaries on classic and modern literature and translated the TALE OF GENJI into modern Japanese (1912–13, 1938–39). In 1921 she became dean and lecturer of the newly established free coeducational school Bunka Gakuin, which she had founded with Tekkan and others. She helped many new poets and writers gain their start in the literary world. Akiko's last major contribution was the *Shin man'yōshū* (New

Yorozu Tetsugorō
Nude. 1911. Oil on canvas. 162 × 97 cm. National Museum of Modern Art, Tōkyō.

Man'yōshū, 1937–39), which she compiled with 9 other leading poets. It contains 26,783 poems by 6,675 contributors dating back 60 years.

Akiko died from a stroke in 1942 at the age of 63. Her death in the midst of war went virtually unnoticed, and following the war's end her works were routinely ignored by literary historians, critics, and the general public. Although short-lived, Akiko's new poetry movement was significant in the history of Japanese poetry; she and other romantic poets infused classic poetry with new spirit and soul in fresh and novel expression, and today she is again highly regarded.

Yosano Tekkan   与謝野鉄幹

(1873–1935). Poet. Real name Yosano Hiroshi. Born in Kyōto Prefecture. Yosano was a romantic, a patriot, and a modernizer of TANKA poetry. Flamboyant masculinity is an important theme in his early poems. He established his own poetry group, Shinshisha, in 1899 with its own journal, MYŌJŌ. In the early 20th century, Yosano's coterie supported many talented poets, among them Hō Akiko, whom he married (see YOSANO AKIKO). His works include *Bōkoku no on* (1894), a collection of criticism, and *Tōzai namboku* (1896), a collection of poems.

yose   寄席

Indigenous form of vaudeville. The origins of *yose* go back to 12th-century itinerant storytellers, particularly *kōshaku* performers (see KŌDAN), and to RAKUGO performers who opened makeshift theaters in the 18th century. Most *yose* theaters operate on a traditional *iromonoseki* (mixed-bill) policy in which a variety of acts complement star storyteller performers. *Yose* embraces other oral arts, such as NANIWA-BUSHI (alternatively known as *rōkyoku;* ballads sung to musical accompaniment), two-comedian MANZAI acts, *mandan* (single stand-up comedians with routines based on topical material), and *konto* acts (a burlesque sketch or a musical parody with three to six actors). Singers, musicians, and novelty acts round out the four- to five-hour performance of 12 to 15 acts. Programs change three times a month at the typical 200-seat *yose* theater.

Yose flourished in the 19th and early 20th century as inexpensive professional enter-

Yorozuya Kinnosuke
This popular actor, best known for his roles in period films, began his acting career on the *kabuki* stage.

Yosano Akiko This poet, educator, and feminist won acclaim for her passionate and sensual reinterpretation of classical poetic forms.

tainment. *Kōdan, rakugo, manzai,* and *naniwa-bushi* became staples on radio during the 1920s, while many *yose* theaters closed due to the rapid rise in the popularity of movies. Apart from a few surviving theaters, *yose* lives on in television and radio performances and in special live concerts.

Yoshida 吉田[町]

Town in central Niigata Prefecture, central Honshū. Yoshida rose as a port on the river Nishikawa and as the chief approach to Yahiko Shrine. There are now spinning mills and electrical appliance factories; the town is also known as a producer of Western-style flatware. Pop: 23,713.

Yoshida-Acheson exchange of notes 吉田・アチソン交換公文

(Yoshida-Achison *kōkan kōbun*). Exchange of notes constituting an agreement between the United States and Japan relating to assistance to be given by Japan in support of United Nations actions. Signed on 8 September 1951 by US Secretary of State Dean Acheson and Japanese Prime Minister YOSHIDA SHIGERU, the documents expressed the desire of the United States and the willingness of Japan to permit and facilitate the support, in and about Japan, of forces engaged in United Nations actions. The exchange was a direct result of the outbreak of the KOREAN WAR in June, and it provoked a strong reaction from the Japanese public, who resented the fact that US military bases in Japan could be used to engage in international conflicts not directly involving Japan. The notes were followed by the Agreement concerning the Status of United Nations Forces in Japan, which became effective on 11 June 1954. See also UNITED STATES–JAPAN SECURITY TREATIES.

Yoshida Bungorō IV 吉田文五郎4世

(1869–1962). A principal operator of puppets in BUNRAKU (puppet theater). Born in Ōsaka Prefecture. He began training at the Bunrakuza puppet theater at the age of eight. Bungorō's genius lay in articulating through movement and gestural nuance the individuality of female characters of widely differing ages and social backgrounds such as maidens, married women, and prostitutes. His art was said to exemplify the expressive beauty of bunraku, and he was considered the leading principal bunraku operator of the first half of the 20th century. He was designated a Living National Treasure in 1955.

Yoshida Eiza I 吉田栄三1世

(1872–1945). A principal operator of puppets in BUNRAKU (puppet theater). Born in Ōsaka Prefecture. He began his bunraku training at the age of 11 and became a principal operator in 1907. By 1927 he was preeminent in the field, his only peer being YOSHIDA BUNGORŌ IV, whose specialty was *onnagata*

(female roles). Eiza devoted himself to *tachiyaku* (male leads). Eschewing theatricality and surface splendor, he carefully studied story lines and characterizations in order to reveal the humanity and inner depths of the characters. His special achievement was to bring a modern realism to the bunraku tradition.

Yoshida Hideo 吉田秀雄

(1903–63). Fourth president of the advertising agency DENTSŪ, INC. Born in Fukuoka Prefecture, he graduated from Tōkyō University and joined Nihon Dempō Tsūshinsha (now Dentsū) in 1928. In 1947 he was elected company president. He was energetic in his efforts to modernize the advertising business and established Dentsū as one of the world's major advertising agencies. He was also a driving force in early commercial radio and television broadcasting in Japan.

Yoshida Hiroshi 吉田博

(1876–1950). Western-style painter and woodblock print artist. Original family name Ueda. Born in Kurume, Fukuoka Prefecture. Yoshida first studied oil painting with Yoshida Kasaburō (dates unknown), who later adopted him, and then with Koyama Shōtarō (1857–1916). In 1902 he established the Pacific Painting Society (Taiheiyō Gakai) with other artists. He made several trips to Europe and the United States. He designed numerous woodblock prints, although he left the actual cutting and printing to craftsmen.

Yoshida Isoya 吉田五十八

(1894–1974). Architect. Born in Tōkyō. One of the creators of the modern *sukiya*-style of Japanese residential architecture (see SUKIYA-ZUKURI), Yoshida graduated in 1923 from what is now Tōkyō University of Fine Arts and Music. He introduced the *ōkabe* construction method, which hides columns within walls and frees spaces from the rigors of traditional proportion. His buildings include Kineya House (1936), the GOTŌ ART MUSEUM (1960), the YAMATO BUNKAKAN (1960), the Gyokudō Art Museum (1961), and the temple Chūgūji (1968).

Yoshida Issui 吉田一穂

(1898–1973). Poet and critic. Real name Yoshida Yoshio. Born in Hokkaidō; studied at Waseda University. He made his appearance in the poetry world after being recognized by the poet KITAHARA HAKUSHŪ. Yoshida aimed for a pure and lucid lyricism in his poetry. His collected poems include *Umi no seibo* (1926), *Koen no sho* (1930), and *Miraisha* (1948); one of his works of poetry criticism is *Kodai ryokuchi* (1958).

Yoshida Kanetomo 吉田兼倶

(1435–1511). Shintō priest. His family was the Yoshida (originally Urabe) line that served as court diviners in the Heian period (794–1185) and later as priests of the Yoshida Shrine in Kyōto. Ambitious to centralize Shintō under his family's authority, Kanetomo built an altar at the Yoshida Shrine in 1484 that he insisted would serve as a center for all the shrines in the country, later alleging that the divinity of the Ise Shrine had transferred itself to this altar. He elaborated the forms of Shintō worship, drawing on the rituals of ESOTERIC BUDDHISM. Kanetomo is considered to be the author of several works setting forth the creed that would later be known as YOSHIDA SHINTŌ and would achieve hegemony in the Shintō world during the Edo period (1600–1868).

Yoshida Kenkō 吉田兼好

(ca 1283–ca 1352). Also known as Urabe Kenkō. Author best known for his TSUREZUREGUSA (ca 1330; tr *Essays in Idleness*, 1967), a philosophical miscellany that is one of the best-loved and most-admired examples of classical Japanese prose and is ranked with SEI SHŌNAGON'S MAKURA NO SŌSHI as one of the masterpieces of the ZUIHITSU genre. His given name was Kaneyoshi; Kenkō, another reading of the same Chinese characters, was adopted when he entered religious life. He came from a family of hereditary Shintō diviners. Kenkō's father served the emperor Go-Uda (r 1274–87) in this capacity, and one of Kenkō's brothers held similar posts.

Kenkō himself, as a young man, was steward to the family of Horikawa Tomomori (dates unknown), who was the maternal grandfather of the emperor Go-Nijō (r 1301–08). In 1301 he obtained a position at court as *kurōdo*, which he held for six years; this was followed by the post of *sahyōe no suke*. At some time before 1313 he became a monk. He was not attached to any temple or master, however, and in his book he writes of monks—whether with admiration, amusement, or scorn—as an outsider. His reasons for taking the tonsure are not known. The immediate cause may well have been simply inner conviction. It is probable that he first lived in seclusion near the Shugakuin Detached Palace. In his late thirties he resided at Yokawa. At some time either in his late forties or shortly before his death he had a hermitage at a place called Narabi no Oka, near the temple Ninnaji. All of these residences were in or near Kyōto. He journeyed, however, to the Kantō region in eastern Japan on several occasions (the first probably while still a layman) and late in life visited Ise. Although a monk, he did not sever his ties with the imperial court.

Kenkō was an adherent of the conservative Nijō poetic school, which was patronized by the Daikakuji faction of the imperial house; following the accession in 1318 of the Daikakuji prince who became the emperor GO-DAIGO (r 1318–39), he became especially active in poetic circles within the capital. Kenkō was essentially an onlooker in the political arena, and after the emperor's flight into exile he accepted with equanimity the patronage of the shōgun ASHIKAGA TAKAUJI (r 1338–58) and his brother Tadayoshi (1306–52).

Writings——Kenkō was praised as one of the "four deva kings" of the poetry of the Nijō school. Over 280 WAKA appear in the anthology of his poems that he himself selected, and poems by him appear in imperial anthologies. His reputation, however, rests on his prose. *Tsurezuregusa* consists of 243 brief entries ranging in length from a single sentence to a few pages. There is no firm evidence as to when it was composed; the most generally accepted date is 1330–31, but an alternative theory that has found some acceptance is that the first 32 entries were written as early as 1319. The individual sections take varied shapes: reminiscences, anecdotes and strings of anecdotes, meditations, judgments, notes and queries on factual matters, dreamlike fragments of narrative, descriptions, and outbursts. The most profound aspect of Kenkō's thought is his sense of the transience of worldly things (MUJŌ). It is tempered, however, by his cherishing of the language, practices, and verities of the past, and in this very human irresolution lies the enduring attraction of his work.

Yoshida Kōgyō KK　吉田工業[株]

(Yoshida Kōgyō). Leader of a group of companies engaged in the manufacture of zippers, manufacturing machinery, and aluminum architectural material. Founded in 1934 by YOSHIDA TADAO. It is the world's largest manufacturer of zippers, and its sales of aluminum materials are among the highest in Japan. Its brand name, YKK, is well known in Japan and abroad. The company is not listed on the stock exchange but instead advocates a shareholding system that allocates company stock to employees and enables them to participate in management.

The company exports its products to 120 countries. It established its first overseas plant in 1959 and now has 54 plants and 114 offices in 40 countries. Sales of the YKK group were ¥552.6 billion (US $3.6 billion) in the fiscal year ending March 1990, with ¥162.0 billion (US $1.1 billion) in zippers and ¥390.6 billion (US $2.6 billion) in aluminum architectural material. Overseas sales of zippers amounted to ¥32.6 billion (US $213.0 million) in the same year. The company plans to expand its overseas operations, especially production of aluminum architectural material. Sales of the parent company for the fiscal year ending March 1992 totaled ¥235.9 billion (US $1.8 billion), and capitalization stood at ¥5.6 billion (US $42.2 million). Headquarters are in Tōkyō.

Yoshida Mitsuyoshi　吉田光由

(1598–1672). Mathematician of the Edo period (1600–1868). Born in Kyōto, he studied traditional Japanese mathematics (WASAN) under Mōri Shigeyoshi (dates unknown) and Suminokura Soan (1571–1632), a merchant-scholar to whom he was related. Mitsuyoshi adapted the Chinese *Suanfa tongzong* (*Suan-fa t'ung-tsung*; 1593, Systematic Treatise on Arithmetic) into Japanese. In 1627 he wrote *Jinkōki* (Numbers Large and Small), a textbook explaining the use of the abacus, including its practical use in computing interest and taxes. Including simple mathematical games and illustrated with color prints, this extremely popular book was important in explaining mathematics to Japanese society and was widely imitated.

Yoshida Seiichi　吉田精一

(1908–84). Scholar of Japanese literature. Born in Tōkyō; graduate of Tōkyō University. His scientific approach to literary studies emphasized close study of original texts. In 1958 he received the Japan Art Academy Award for *Shizen shugi no kenkyū*, a two-volume historical study of the Japanese naturalist literature of the early 20th century. Other works include *Akutagawa Ryūnosuke* (1942), a critical biography of the novelist Akutagawa, and *Kindai bungaku hyōron shi: Meijihen* (1974), a collection of critical essays on Meiji-period (1868–1912) literature.

Yoshida Shigeru　吉田茂

(1878–1967). Diplomat and prime minister. A diplomat until 1939, he emerged after World War II to become the most famous politician of postwar Japan, serving as prime minister for a total of 86 months between May 1946 and December 1954. Yoshida's first cabinet (May 1946–May 1947) grudgingly enacted many of the reforms demanded by Allied OCCUPATION authorities. The second through fifth Yoshida cabinets (October 1948–December 1954) oversaw Japan's transition from foreign control to restoration of sovereignty (formally attained in April 1952), and from "reform" to "reconstruction." Popularly known as the Yoshida era, this latter period was marked by the hegemony of big business, bureaucracy, and conservative party politics and witnessed the forging of Japan's tight military and economic alliance with the United States.

Born in Yokohama on 22 September 1878, Yoshida was adopted by Yoshida Kenzō, a close friend of his father, TAKENOUCHI TSUNA, a former *samurai*. He graduated from Tōkyō University in 1906. In 1909 he married Makino Yukiko, eldest daughter of MAKINO NOBUAKI.

After serving in the diplomatic service in Mukden (now Shenyang; 1907–08), London (1908–09), and Rome (1909–12), he was appointed consul in the port of Andong (Antung), on the border of Manchuria and Korea. In 1913 he became secretary to the governor-general of Korea, TERAUCHI MASATAKE. Yoshida accompanied the Japanese delegation to the Paris Peace Conference in 1919, serving as aide to Makino. From 1920 to 1922 he was first secretary in the London embassy.

As consul general in Tianjin (Tientsin) in 1922–25 and Mukden in 1925–28, he responded harshly to Chinese nationalism. In 1928 Yoshida became vice–foreign minister, remaining in that post until 1931, when he was appointed ambassador to Italy. He returned to Japan from Italy in 1935. In the wake of the FEBRUARY 26TH INCIDENT of 1936, Yoshida helped organize the first slate of proposed ministers for the HIROTA KŌKI cabinet. Hirota appointed him ambassador to Great Britain, where he remained until 1939, when he retired from the Foreign Ministry.

Yoshida opposed both the ANTI-COMINTERN PACT of 1936 and the TRIPARTITE PACT of 1940. Between 1942 and 1945 he was involved in desultory proposals to replace the TŌJŌ HIDEKI government and effect an advantageous surrender. These proposals, premised upon the belief that the war situation posed the threat of communist revolution and destruction of the national polity (*kokutai*) in Japan, culminated in the famous Konoe Memorial (Konoe Jōsōbun), a proposal submitted to the emperor by former prime minister KONOE FUMIMARO in February 1945. Largely because of his role in helping draft the Konoe Memorial, Yoshida was arrested by the military police in April 1945 and held for over two months before being released.

In September 1945 Yoshida became foreign minister. He helped arrange the meeting between Emperor SHŌWA (Hirohito) and General Douglas MACARTHUR on 27 September 1945, after which MacArthur openly supported the emperor.

In May 1946 Yoshida succeeded HATOYAMA ICHIRŌ as president of the JIYŪTŌ (Liberal Party) and thus became the next prime minister. (Hatoyama had been purged by the Occupation authorities on the eve of becoming prime minister.) Yoshida served until May 1947. In October 1948, when the cabinet of ASHIDA HITOSHI resigned following disclosure of the SHŌWA DENKŌ SCANDAL, Yoshida was returned to the premiership.

In January 1949 he called a general election and won a stunning majority victory that laid the parliamentary base for the ensuing "Yoshida era." During the tenure of this government, the shift in economic priorities from deconcentration and democratization to stabilization and reconstruction was accelerated; the labor movement was subjected to increasing restraints; the OCCUPATION PURGE of militarists and ultranationalists was gradually rescinded, while a RED PURGE involving over 20,000 individuals was carried out in 1949–50; and new domestic peace-preservation legislation was introduced. Japan also attained sovereignty under the terms of the SAN FRANCISCO PEACE TREATY signed in 1951.

Yoshida agreed to a bilateral security treaty with the United States (see UNITED STATES–JAPAN SECURITY TREATIES) under which Japan committed itself to the continued presence of US military bases in sovereign Japan and to Japan's own rearmament. Rearmament was carried out beginning with the establishment of the NATIONAL POLICE RESERVE in 1950 and accelerated with the creation of the NATIONAL SAFETY FORCES in October 1952 and the SELF DEFENSE FORCES in June 1954. In March 1954 Yoshida created a Committee to Investigate the Constitution within his party (see CONSTITUTION, DISPUTE OVER REVISION OF).

As Yoshida's political influence began to wane, his personal gestures became more flamboyant. During hearings in the Diet in February 1953, Yoshida called a socialist questioner a stupid fool (*baka yarō*); the incident led to a vote of no-confidence, which in turn led to Yoshida's dissolution of the Diet and calling of the general election that preceded the fifth Yoshida cabinet. He somewhat tarnished his reputation for personal probity by intervening in the investigation of the massive SHIPBUILDING SCANDAL OF 1954 to protect some of his political henchmen.

The UNITED STATES–JAPAN MUTUAL DEFENSE ASSISTANCE AGREEMENT (often called the Mutual Security Agreement) signed in March 1954 further defined and regulated the military, economic, and technological relationship between Japan and the United States. The Yoshida government remained pessimistic concerning the future of Japan's "shallow economy" and endeavored to encourage a broader and more purely economic "Marshall Plan for Asia" on the part of the United States. Yoshida personally carried this appeal to the United States in the autumn of 1954, but his mission was a failure in all respects. Washington was unreceptive, and Yoshida's conservative enemies at home took advantage of his absence to mobilize a final successful assault against him. Yoshida was ousted as president of the Liberal Party in November 1954 and was forced to dissolve his fifth and final cabinet in early December. Although Yoshida departed from the premiership in an atmosphere of rancor at home and uncertainty about Japan's future internationally, he lived for another 13 years—long enough to see the emergence of Japan as an economic power and to enjoy the mellow status of a venerable elder statesman. In 1964 he received the Supreme Order of the Chrysanthemum (Daikun'i Kikka Shō).

Yoshida Shigeru As prime minister of Japan during most of the immediate post–World War II period, Yoshida guided the country through the critical period of Allied Occupation.

Yoshida Shintō　吉田神道

Also called Urabe Shintō or Yuiitsu Shintō ("the only Shintō"). A school of Shintō dating from the 13th century that was transmitted within the Yoshida family, hereditary priests of the Yoshida Shrine and Hirano Shrine in Kyōto. YOSHIDA KANETOMO (1435–1511) systematized its doctrines in two important treatises, *Shintō taii* (The Gist of Shintō) and *Yuiitsu shintō myōbō yōshū* (An Anthology of the Doctrines of the Only Shintō), in which he sought to establish his family as the arbiters of Shintō orthodoxy. Kanetomo recognized three types of Shintō: (1) Honjaku Engi Shintō, or the rituals and

Yoshida Shōin This writer and imperialist ideologue, who had a strong influence on the eventual leaders of the Meiji Restoration, was executed by the shogunate in 1859.

Yoshii Isamu A *tanka* poet and playwright who was attracted to European romanticism in his early years, Yoshii later developed a more subdued poetic style.

legends associated with the various regional shrines; (2) RYŌBU SHINTŌ; and (3) "Shintō of the Original Source" (Gempon Sōgen Shintō), the formal name for Yoshida Shintō, which was so designated because of its belief that a supreme primordial deity, who preceded heaven and earth and transcended the creative forces of *in* (Ch: *yin*) and *yō* (Ch: *yang*), was the source of the myriad deities of Shintō and was also immanent in all living creatures. Yoshida Shintō is a highly eclectic school that draws upon Confucianism, Taoism, the doctrines of *yin-yang* and the five forces (or elements; see OMMYŌDŌ), and especially the elaborate rituals of SHINGON SECT Buddhism. With the emergence of STATE SHINTŌ after the Meiji Restoration in 1868, Yoshida Shintō lost its special standing with the Shintō clergy.

Yoshida Shōin   吉田松陰

(1830–59). Scholar, teacher, writer, expert in the military arts, and ideologue of the SONNŌ JŌI (Revere the Emperor, Expel the Barbarians) movement of the late Edo period (1600–1868). Real name Yoshida Norikata. Born in the village of Matsumoto on the outskirts of Hagi, the castle town of the Mōri *daimyō* of Chōshū (now Yamaguchi Prefecture), he used a variety of literary names, of which Shōin ("pine shadow") and Nijūikkai Mōshi ("21 times audacious *samurai*") were the most common.

The Yoshida family had links to YAMAGA SOKŌ (1622–85), and Shōin was deeply influenced by his teachings on both the military sciences and loyalty to the emperor. In 1854, at the instigation of SAKUMA SHŌZAN, Shōin defied the NATIONAL SECLUSION edicts and attempted to stow away on Commodore Matthew PERRY's flagship, USS *Powhatan*, at anchorage in Shimoda on the Izu Peninsula. His avowed purpose was to acquaint himself with conditions in the West in order to strengthen Japan.

This escapade, which resulted in his imprisonment and later in house arrest (1855), consolidated his thinking on *sonnō jōi* and national politics. In the Shōka Sonjuku, a private school that he established in his house, Shōin gathered a group of young samurai, including TAKASUGI SHINSAKU, KUSAKA GENZUI, ITŌ HIROBUMI, and YAMAGATA ARITOMO, who would later play key roles in the Meiji Restoration. His passionate patriotism involved him in an unsuccessful plot to assassinate the high shogunal official MANABE AKIKATSU. He was arrested once more, tried, and executed during the ANSEI PURGE (1858–60). Shōin's works include *Kaikoroku* (1855, Record of the Past), *Kōkokushi* (1858, Aspirations of a Hero), and *Ryūkonroku* (1858, Record of an Everlasting Spirit).

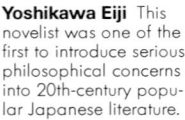

Yoshikawa Eiji This novelist was one of the first to introduce serious philosophical concerns into 20th-century popular Japanese literature.

Yoshida Tadao   吉田忠雄

(1908–   ). Businessman and founder of the company YOSHIDA KŌGYŌ KK, known for its YKK-brand products. Born in Toyama Prefecture. With only an elementary-school education, he began a fastener production venture in 1934 that developed into Yoshida Kōgyō KK. Central to the company's success was Yoshida's highly mechanized production system. He has advocated a workers' stockholding system and so does not list his company's stocks on the market.

Yoshida Tōgo   吉田東伍

(1864–1918). Historian and geographer. Born in Echigo (now Niigata Prefecture). Yoshida's *Dai Nihon chimei jisho* (1900–1907), a study of place names in Japan, earned him a position on the faculty of Waseda University. He argued in his *Zeami jūrokubushū* (1909) that ZEAMI and KAN'AMI wrote both the music and the texts of certain NŌ plays.

Yoshida Tomizō   吉田富三

(1903–73). Pathologist. Born in Fukushima Prefecture; graduate of Tōkyō University. With his teacher SASAKI TAKAOKI, Yoshida succeeded in inducing liver cancer in rats with an azo dye. He produced an ascites tumor in rats for the first time in 1943, naming it Yoshida sarcoma. Besides teaching at Nagasaki Medical College, Yoshida held posts at Tōhoku and Tōkyō universities and served as director of research at the Japanese Foundation for Cancer Research and president of the Nippon Medical Association. He received the Japan Academy Prize in 1936 and 1953 and the Order of Culture in 1959.

Yoshida Tōyō   吉田東洋

(1816–62). Also known as Yoshida Masaaki. Reformer of the Tosa domain (now Kōchi Prefecture) at the end of the Edo period (1600–1868). Given a high position by the *daimyō* YAMANOUCHI TOYOSHIGE in 1853, Yoshida planned a series of reforms in domainal administration, but conservative opposition resulted in his removal. In 1857 conditions forced domainal authorities to recall him. Yoshida planned to create a Western-style navy for the domain and to make ability, rather than birth, the basis for promotion. His proposals were opposed both by conservatives and by radical anti-Western, proimperial (SONNŌ JŌI) activists; he was assassinated by a *samurai* of the latter faction.

Yoshihara Jirō   吉原治良

(1905–72). Western-style painter. Born in Ōsaka. Yoshihara's work was first shown at the 1934 Nikaten (Exhibition of the Nika Society). His style moved toward pure abstraction and in 1934 he and other abstract artists formed an association called the Kyūshitsukai. After World War II he founded the Gutai Bijutsu Kyōkai (Concrete Art Association), a group of avant-garde artists based in the Kansai region who received international attention for their experimentation with innovative artistic media and materials.

Yoshihara Oil Mill, Ltd   吉原製油[株]

(Yoshihara Seiyu). Manufacturer of cooking oil and oil cake. Incorporated in 1934. In 1966 the company established Japan Soya Products Co jointly with Hohnen Oil Co, Ltd, to expand into the production of soybean protein. For the fiscal year ending March 1991, sales totaled ¥41.9 billion (US $305.4 million) and capitalization stood at ¥2.1 billion (US $15.3 million). Headquarters are in Ōsaka.

Yoshihara Sachiko   吉原幸子

(1932–   ). Poet. Born in Tōkyō; graduated from Tōkyō University. Yoshihara's works intelligently articulate feelings of love, betrayal, and suffering from a woman's point of view. Her poetry collections include *Yōnen rentō* (1964), *Ondīnu* (1972), and *Hirugao* (1973).

Yoshiharu Shikimoku   義治式目

Domainal law code (BUNKOKUHŌ) enacted in 1567 by the ROKKAKU FAMILY, *daimyō* of Ōmi Province (now Shiga Prefecture); known also as Rokkakushi Shikimoku. After the warlord Rokkaku Yoshiharu (1545–1612) killed one of his retainers, his chief vassals drafted this code and forced him to accept it. It carefully defines the rights and obligations of both ruler and subject and is known especially for its detailed administrative regulations.

Yoshiigawa   吉井川

River in eastern Okayama Prefecture, western Honshū, originating in the Chūgoku Mountains and flowing south through the Tsuyama Basin and Okayama Plain to empty into the Inland Sea. The water is utilized for electric power and irrigation. Tourist attractions include the Okutsukyō, a gorge on the upper reaches, and Okutsu Hot Spring. Length: 133 km (83 mi); area of drainage basin: 2,060 sq km (795 sq mi).

Yoshii Isamu   吉井勇

(1886–1960). TANKA poet and playwright. Born in Tōkyō; enrolled briefly in Waseda University in 1905. That same year he joined the New Poetry Society (Shinshisha), founded by YOSANO TEKKAN in 1899, and began contributing *tanka* to its magazine MYŌJŌ. As a member of the *Myōjō* coterie he became closely associated with such leading men of letters as MORI ŌGAI, UEDA BIN, KINOSHITA MOKUTARŌ, and KITAHARA HAKUSHŪ. He subsequently left to join the PAN NO KAI group, which shared a similar attraction for romanticism and aestheticism. In 1909 he became an editor of the poetry magazine *Subaru*, which succeeded *Myōjō*.

Yoshii early gained a reputation as a decadent poet and is perhaps best remembered for his love poetry. His early collection of *tanka*, *Sakahogai* (1910), records the joys and sorrows of a young poet overly given to wine and sexual desire. In his later years he developed a more subdued poetic style, as in the collections *Ningenkyō* (1934) and *Keieishō* (1956). *Gogo sanji* (1911) is an early collection of 11 one-act plays.

Yoshii Junji   吉井淳二

(1904–   ). Western-style painter. Born in Kagoshima Prefecture. Graduated from Tōkyō Bijutsu Gakkō (now Tōkyō University of Fine Arts and Music) and studied under WADA EISAKU. His work was first shown at the 1926 Nikaten (Exhibition of the Nika Society) and thereafter he made its sponsoring organization, the Nikakai, the center of his professional activity. Painting in a realistic style, he excelled at depicting the everyday lives of ordinary people. He was awarded the Order of Culture in 1989.

Yoshikawa Eiji   吉川英治

(1892–1962). Novelist. Real name Yoshikawa Hidetsugu. Born into an ex-*samurai* family in Kanagawa Prefecture. In his hands Japanese POPULAR FICTION, hitherto written primarily for entertainment, was elevated to something approaching a true people's literature (*kokumin bungaku*).

His father's drinking and extravagance ruined the family financially, and when he was 11 Yoshikawa left school for a succession of jobs, continuing his education in night school. His study of SENRYŪ poetry led him to write *senryū* under the pen name Kijirō. His first published work, *Enoshima monogatari* (1914), was an account of the miracle-working goddess Benzaiten (Skt: Sarasvatī). In 1921 he joined the staff of the newspaper *Maiyū shimbun*, but it failed in the chaos following the Tōkyō Earthquake of 1923. Without a job, Yoshikawa turned to writing full time.

The year 1925 saw the magazine serialization of Yoshikawa's *Kennan jonan*, a novel centering on the vendetta and love affairs of a handsome swordsman of the Edo period (1600–1868). The series proved immensely popular and was followed by several adventure novels: *Naruto hichō* (1926–27), *Edo sangokushi* (1927–29), and *Moeru Fuji* (1932–33). About this time he also wrote the autobiographical *Kankan mushi wa utau* (1930–31).

Tired of fantastic adventure stories, Yoshikawa wrote MIYAMOTO MUSASHI (1935–39; tr *Musashi*, 1981), an account of the 17th-century master swordsman Miyamoto Musashi (1584–1645). In his lifework, *Shin Heike monogatari* (1950–57, New Tales of the Heike; tr *The Heike Story*, 1956), the tumultuous power struggles of the late 12th century are seen through the eyes of a groundskeeper in the Imperial Palace.

The hallmark of Yoshikawa's writing (especially in his later works) was his basic conservatism. He believed that popular literature should aim for moral edification as well as diversion and that the realities of the present should always be seen in the light of past history, and these convictions accounted for his enormous popularity. In 1960 Yoshikawa became the first writer of popular fiction to receive the Order of Culture.

Yoshikawa Kōjirō   吉川幸次郎

(1904–80). Scholar of Chinese literature. Born in Hyōgo Prefecture, Yoshikawa was a graduate of Kyōto University. After studying in China for several years, he taught at Kyōto University from 1931 to 1967. He also translated into Japanese and annotated numerous Chinese works, including *Gen zatsugeki kenkyū* (1948), on Yuan (Yüan) dynasty (1279–1368) drama, and *Toho shiki* (1949), on the poet Du Fu (Tu Fu). He collaborated with MIYOSHI TATSUJI on *Tōshisen* (1954), a collection of translations of Tang (T'ang) dynasty (618–907) poems.

Yoshikawa Koretari   吉川惟足

(1616–94). Also known as Yoshikawa Koretaru and Kikkawa Koretari. Shintō thinker and founder of Yoshikawa Shintō. Born in Nihombashi in Edo (now Tōkyō). He went to Kyōto in 1653 and was initiated into the teachings of YOSHIDA SHINTŌ. Yoshikawa lectured on Shintō in Edo and earned the confidence of members of the Tokugawa family and various *daimyō*. In 1682 he was appointed *shintōkata* (director of Shintō affairs); this office thereafter became a hereditary office of the Yoshikawa family until the end of the Edo period (1600–1868). His theology was based mainly on Yoshida Shintō, with elements from Song (Sung) dynasty (960–1279) Confucianism. He held Shintō to be the fountainhead of all things, including

other religions. He emphasized TSUTSUSHIMI (seriousness of mind) as the way of mankind and stressed the importance of the rite of *oharai* (purification). As the teacher of YAMAZAKI ANSAI Yoshikawa greatly influenced Yamazaki's attempts to synthesize Shintō and Neo-Confucianism.

Yoshiki Masao   吉識雅夫

(1908–). Naval architect. Born in Hyōgo Prefecture. Graduate of Tōkyō University. Yoshiki taught at Tōkyō University from 1930, becoming professor emeritus in 1968. He became president of the Science University of Tōkyō in 1982. Yoshiki is internationally known for his research on the strengths and optimal positioning of oil tanker bulkheads in order to develop lighter and larger ships and to make large ships more economical. He received the Order of Culture in 1982.

yoshikiri → reed warblers

Yoshimasu Gōzō   吉増剛造

(1939–). Poet and critic. Born in Tōkyō; graduated from Keiō University. His first collection of poetry was *Shuppatsu* (1964, Departure). He received the Takami Jun Prize for *Ōgon shihen* (1971, The Golden Book of Psalms).

Yoshimasu Tōdō   吉益東洞

(1702–73). Physician of the classicist school (*koihō*) who contributed greatly to the Japanization of Chinese medicine. Real name Tamenori. Also known as Yoshimasu Shūsuke. A native of Aki (now part of Hiroshima Prefecture), Yoshimasu studied *koihō* in Kyōto and opened a practice with the help of YAMAWAKI TŌYŌ. He rejected the *yinyang* and five-elements theories (OMMYŌDŌ) of the body held by the *goseihō* ("latter-day school" of Chinese medicine in Japan; see MEDICINE), believing that medical treatment should be based on the observation of actual symptoms. He experimentally confirmed the effectiveness of treatments described in Chinese medical classics, such as the *Shang han lun* (ca 3rd century, Essay on Typhoid), publishing the methods in a book entitled *Ruijuhō* (1764). He believed that disease originated in the abdomen and that all diseases were caused by one poison (*mambyō ichidoku*), for which he proposed aggressive treatment with powerful drugs.

Yoshimi "hundred-cave" tunnel tombs   吉見百穴

(Yoshimi *hyakketsu*). A cluster of some 230 tunnel tombs (see YOKOANA) dug into the tuff cliffs along the river Ichinokawa in Yoshimichō, Saitama Prefecture; generally dated to the 6th and 7th centuries. They were first investigated in 1887 by the anthropologist TSUBOI SHŌGORŌ, who thought they were cave dwellings. Each cavern is divided into an entrance corridor and an inner chamber; the latter is equipped with a platform to receive the coffins of one generation of one family. Burial goods and skeletal remains have been recovered.

Yoshimitsu Yoshihiko   吉満義彦

(1904–45). Roman Catholic philosopher. Born in Kagoshima Prefecture, he graduated from Tōkyō University and became a professor at Sophia University. From 1928 to 1930, he studied in France under the Neothomist Jacques Maritain (1882–1973). Focusing on Thomas Aquinas, he studied medieval thought from a historical, existential point of view, thereby giving Japanese Catholicism a

firm direction. Based on the "philosophia perennis" exemplified in the Thomist "analogy of being," he criticized atheism, pantheism, and nihilism. In contrast to modern anthropocentric humanism, he propounded an "integral humanism" open to God's grace. His works include *Shi to ai no jitsuzon* (1940).

Yoshimoto Banana   吉本ばなな

(1964–). Novelist. Real name Yoshimoto Mahoko. Born in Tōkyō; daughter of the poet and critic YOSHIMOTO TAKAAKI. Graduate of Nihon University. In a detached tone Yoshimoto portrays the lives of people in desperately isolated situations. *Kitchin* (1987; partial tr "Kitchen," 1991), a novella about a girl able to sleep only in the kitchen, received the Izumi Kyōka Literary Prize. Other works include *Tsugumi* (1988–89; title appears on book in roman letters as *TUGUMI*).

Yoshimoto Takaaki   吉本隆明

(1924–). Literary critic; poet. Also known as Yoshimoto Ryūmei. Born in Tōkyō; graduate of Tōkyō Institute of Technology. With the publication of two poetry collections, *Koyūji to no taiwa* (1952) and *Ten'i no tame no juppen* (1953), he became known as a radical poet. Turning to criticism, he wrote about such issues as the validity of proletarian literary theory (see PROLETARIAN LITERATURE MOVEMENT) and the responsibility of writers for World War II. Through his independent radicalism, he exerted a significant influence on the New Left Movement of the 1960s. A prolific critic, he has written on religion, folklore, linguistics, and psychology. His principal works of literary theory include *Geijutsuteki teikō to zasetsu* (1959), *Gengo ni totte bi to wa nanika* (1965), *Kyōdō gensō ron* (1968), *Shinteki genshō ron josetsu* (1971), and *Hai imēji ron* (2 vols, 1989).

Yoshimura Akira   吉村昭

(1927–). Novelist. Born in Tōkyō; attended Gakushūin University. His *Hoshi e no tabi* (1966, Journey to the Stars), about a group of young boys who commit suicide, won the Dazai Osamu Prize. Later he turned to nonfiction and historical novels, winning the Kikuchi Kan Prize in 1973. Yoshimura's writing reflects his meticulous research and detailed knowledge of his subjects. His principal works include *Fon Shīboruto no musume* (1978, Von Siebold's Daughter); *Hagoku* (1983, Jailbreak), the story of a man who repeatedly escapes from prison; and *Tsumetai natsu, atsui natsu* (1984, Cold Summer, Hot Summer), about a relative's battle with cancer.

Yoshimura Junzō   吉村順三

(1908–). Architect. Born in Tōkyō. Yoshimura was a graduate of the Tōkyō School

Yoshimura Junzō

Yoshinogari site

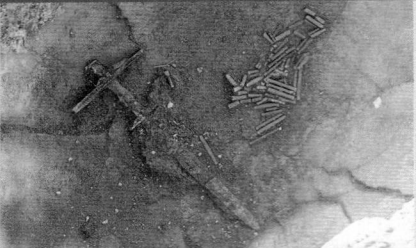

Objects found in the burial jars of the main tomb include a 45 cm decorated bronze sword and cylindrical glass beads.

Reconstructions of the remains of a watchtower (rear) and pit houses.

An aerial view of the central section of this archaeological site. Parts of the inner and outer moats are visible.

Yoshino Sakuzō
Constitutional government with "people as the base" was the cornerstone of the political ideas of this leading Taishō-period spokesman for liberal democracy.

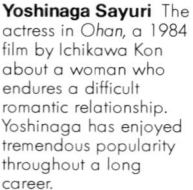

Yoshinaga Sayuri The actress in *Ohan,* a 1984 film by Ichikawa Kon about a woman who endures a difficult romantic relationship. Yoshinaga has enjoyed tremendous popularity throughout a long career.

of Fine Arts (now Tōkyō National University of Fine Arts and Music), where he taught for 25 years beginning in 1945. He is especially known as an innovative designer of houses. His works include the traditional-style Japan House (1954) at the Museum of Modern Art in New York, the Aichi Prefectural University of Arts (1971), and the Nara National Museum (1973), for which he won the Japan Art Academy Prize in 1975.

Yoshimura Kōzaburō   吉村公三郎

(1911–   ). Film director. Born in Shiga Prefecture. He began working at the film production company SHŌCHIKU CO, LTD, as an assistant to SHIMAZU YASUJIRŌ in 1929. The melodrama *Danryū* (1939, Warm Current), followed in 1940 by one of Japan's finest war films, *Nishizumi senshachō den* (1940, The Story of Tank Commander Nishizumi), helped establish Yoshimura as a director. His *Anjōke no butōkai* (1947, A Ball at the Anjō House), which depicted the aristocracy's postwar fall, won the Kinema Jumpō Award. A critic of society in his films, Yoshimura was able to elicit convincing portrayals of antagonism and discord from his actors. His *Itsuwareru seisō* (1951, Clothes of Deception), *Nishijin no shimai* (1952, Sisters of Nishijin), and *Yoru no kawa* (1956, Undercurrent) are largely about women, while *Sembazuru* (1953, A Thousand Cranes), *Yoake mae* (1953, Before the Dawn), and *Ashizuri Misaki* (1954, Cape Ashizuri) are adaptations from literature.

Yoshimura Shinkichi   吉村信吉

(1907–47). Scholar of lakes and wetlands. Born in Tōkyō. Graduate of Tōkyō University. Yoshimura was a technical official of the Central Meteorological Bureau (forerunner of the present Meteorological Agency). His nationwide field surveys of the form, water temperature, water quality, and other features of Japan's lakes and wetlands clarified their relationship to those of other countries. Yoshimura died in an ice break while investigating Lake Suwa. His works include *Koshōgaku* (1937, Study of Lakes and Wetlands).

Yoshinaga Sayuri   吉永小百合

(1945–   ). Actress. Born in Tōkyō, she graduated from Waseda University. Making her debut on a radio program in 1955, she began her film career in 1959. Specializing in playing pure-hearted, cheerful young girls, her popularity grew along with the youth films made by the Nikkatsu Corporation, and she attracted a large number of ardent fans. Among her major films are *Kyūpora no aru machi* (1962, Street of Cupolas) by Urayama Kirio (1930–85), *Ai to shi o mitsumete* (1964, Perception of Love and Death) by Saitō Buichi (b 1925), and ICHIKAWA KON's *Ohan* (1984).

Yoshinogari site   吉野ケ里遺跡

(Yoshinogari *iseki*). Yayoi-period (ca 300 BC–ca AD 300) archaeological site located in Kanzaki District, Saga Prefecture, Kyūshū. Extending across a plain at the southern foot of Mt. Sefuri (Sefuriyama), the site has an area of approximately 36 hectares (89 acres). In the spring of 1989, inner and outer oblong moats, burial jars, a mounded grave, and the remains of buildings were discovered. At a number of points along the inner moat were the remains of structures thought to have been watchtowers. The octagonal tomb mound measures about 40 by 26 meters (131 by 85 ft) and is about 4.5 meters (14.8 ft) high. Inside it were found six burial jars thought to be of members of a ruling clan. Objects found in the tomb are believed to date back to the Middle Yayoi period (ca 100 BC–ca AD 100) and include a bronze sword with an elaborately decorated hilt, a narrow-blade sword, and glass beads. Approximately 2,500 burial jars were excavated elsewhere in the site. The extent of the relics has led experts to conclude that the site was the center of a small state such as those described in the late-3rd-century Chinese chronicle WEI ZHI (*Wei chih*).

Yoshinogawa   吉野川

River in Kōchi and Tokushima prefectures, Shikoku, originating in the Shikoku Mountains and flowing east into the Kii Channel at the city of Tokushima. It is the longest river in Shikoku. The middle reaches cut through the Shikoku Mountains, forming transverse valleys and creating the Ōboke and Koboke gorges. The lower reaches form a farming area producing rice, vegetables, and flowers. Electric-power projects have resulted in the construction of dams on the upper reaches. Length: 194 km (121 mi); area of drainage basin: 3,750 sq km (1,448 sq mi).

Yoshino Hideo   吉野秀雄

(1902–67). TANKA poet. Born in Gumma Prefecture. Yoshino enrolled at Keio University but left because of illness. He studied *tanka* composition with AIZU YAICHI. His best work came after World War II in collections such as *Kansenshū* (1947, Cold Cicada). *Ryōkan Oshō no hito to uta* (1957) is his biography of the 19th-century poet-priest RYŌKAN. Like Ryōkan, he was influenced by the MAN'YŌSHŪ. Yoshino was noted for his tight, succinct style of *tanka*, and in 1958 he was awarded the Yomiuri Literary Prize for his collected poems, *Yoshino Hideo kashū* (1958).

Yoshino Hiroshi   吉野弘

(1926–   ). Poet. Born in Yamagata Prefecture; graduated from Sakata Commercial High School. Yoshino became known for his first collection of poetry, *Shōsoku* (1957, News). His poetry is a lyrical expression of the mystery and sadness of life based on a deep understanding and love of humanity. His other poetry collections include *Maboroshi; hōhō* (1959, Illusion; Method) and *Kanshō ryokō* (1971, Sentimental Journey).

Yoshino-Kumano National Park
吉野熊野国立公園

(Yoshino-Kumano Kokuritsu Kōen). Situated in central Honshū on the KII PENINSULA in Wakayama, Nara, and Mie prefectures. This park comprises the districts of Yoshino and Kumano, as well as a section of the peninsula's southeast coastline. The northern Yoshino district is characterized by mountains famed for temples of the mountain ascetic sect (SHUGENDŌ). To the south is ŌMINESAN, another center of the Shugendō sect. To the east is ŌDAIGAHARASAN, one of the wettest areas in Japan. The southern Kumano district is typified by low evergreen-covered mountains. In the east a long coastline stretches to the cape SHIONOMISAKI, the southernmost point of Honshū. The rivers KUMANOGAWA and TOTSUKAWA wind through dramatic scenery. NACHI FALLS, to the south, is one of Japan's highest waterfalls. Nearby is the Kumano Nachi Shrine, a center of the mountain ascetic sect. Area: 598 sq km (231 sq mi).

Yoshino Sakuzō   吉野作造

(1878–1933). Scholar and spokesman for liberal democratic ideas and reform during the

Taishō period (1912–26). Yoshino was the eldest son of a shopkeeper in the market town of Furukawa in Miyagi Prefecture. He was educated at the prestigious Second Higher School (1897–1900), during which time he converted to Christianity, and at Tōkyō University (1900–1904). After two years of postgraduate study, Yoshino went to China in 1906 as a tutor to Yuan Keming (Yüan K'o-ming), eldest son of YUAN SHIKAI (Yüan Shih-k'ai). From his return to Japan in 1909 until his death he was a professor in the Law Faculty at Tōkyō University.

His principal fame came with the publication in 1916 of an article entitled "Kensei no hongi o toite sono yūshū no bi o nasu no michi o ronzu" (On the Meaning of Constitutional Government and the Methods to Perfect It). He argued that, although formal sovereignty was lodged in the imperial institution, responsible representative government was still possible under the Meiji Constitution. He held that the "spirit of constitutional government" lay in *mimpon shugi* (literally, "people-as-the-base-ism"), a translation of "democracy" that he differentiated from *minshu shugi* ("popular sovereignty"), the usual translation. *Mimpon shugi* meant that the government should act on behalf of the popular welfare and that the people, through the mechanisms of elections and responsible cabinets, should be the ultimate judge of whether it did so. He was attacked from the Right by those who said that representative government was incompatible with the KOKUTAI (the state structure or polity unique to Japan as embodied in the imperial institution) and from the Left by those who said that he was an apologist for bourgeois domination.

Yoshino advocated practical political reform, urging universal manhood suffrage, greater self-rule for colonial areas such as Korea, and a peaceful and cooperative foreign policy in China. He criticized interference in politics by GENRŌ (elder statesmen) as well as such extraparliamentary powers as the HOUSE OF PEERS, the PRIVY COUNCIL, and the military high command. In the realm of social problems Yoshino favored active social welfare policies, legal recognition of labor unions, and legislation to regulate labor-employer relations, although he was critical of radical elements in the labor movement and of left-wing socialists. During his final years Yoshino turned to the study of recent Japanese history and left an enduring contribution with his compilation of the 24-volume *Meiji bunka zenshū* (1927–30), a collection of rare Meiji-period (1868–1912) historical materials.

Yoshinoyama 吉野山

Hills in the town of Yoshino, central Nara Prefecture, central Honshū, extending about 8 km (5 mi) from the river Yoshinogawa to the mountain ŌMINESAN. The area is known for its cherry blossoms and historical sites, such as the mausoleum of Emperor GO-DAIGO and the temple KIMPUSENJI. Yoshinoyama is also known as a place where MINAMOTO NO YOSHITSUNE sought refuge. It is part of Yoshino-Kumano National Park. Height: 300–850 m (985–2,790 ft).

Yoshioka Yayoi 吉岡弥生

(1871–1959). Physician, educator, public official, and founder of Japan's first medical college for women. Born in Shizuoka Prefecture. She went to Tōkyō to attend Saisei Gakusha Medical College, receiving her license in 1892. In 1895 she married Yoshioka

Arata (1868–1922). Aided by her husband, in 1900 she opened the Tōkyō Joigakkō (Tōkyō Women's Medical School). In 1912 the school became the Tōkyō Joshi Igaku Semmon Gakkō (Tōkyō Women's Medical Professional School). As its first president Yayoi fought for its full accreditation, granted in 1920. She also operated a hospital, the Tōkyō Shisei Byōin. In 1952 the school was renamed Tōkyō Joshi Ika Daigaku (TŌKYŌ WOMEN'S MEDICAL COLLEGE).

Yoshio Kōgyū 吉雄耕牛

(1724–1800). Scholar of Rangaku (Dutch Learning; see WESTERN LEARNING) and doctor of medicine. Born in Hizen Province (now Nagasaki Prefecture). Yoshio studied Western medicine, astronomy, and geography, in addition to *honzōgaku* (traditional pharmacognosy). He was named chief interpreter at Nagasaki (*ōtsūji*) in 1748 and inspector of Dutch-Japanese interpreters (Oranda *tsūji metsuki*) in 1790. He established a private academy and developed a method of Western Learning known as the Yoshio school. Among his students were MAENO RYŌTAKU, SUGITA GEMPAKU, and HIRAGA GENNAI. Yoshio was considered the leading Rangaku expert and was instrumental in its spread to all areas of Japan.

Yoshishige no Yasutane 慶滋保胤

(ca 931–1002). A man of letters and Buddhist priest who adopted the name Jakushin. His works include *Nihon ōjō gokuraku ki* (984), a collection of tales in Chinese (KAMBUN) about Japanese reborn in Amida's Western Paradise; and *Chiteiki* (982), a description, also written in Chinese, of the deterioration of the Kyōto capital that is said to have influenced KAMO NO CHŌMEI's *Hōjōki*.

Yoshitomi Pharmaceutical Industries, Ltd 吉富製薬[株]

(Yoshitomi Seiyaku). Pharmaceutical and chemical manufacturer. Incorporated in

1940. Yoshitomi has joint ventures with Japan Tobacco, Inc; Pennwalt Corporation; and M&T Chemicals, Inc. For the fiscal year ending March 1991, sales totaled ¥74.4 billion (US $542.3 million) and capitalization stood at ¥10.7 billion (US $78.0 million). Headquarters are in Ōsaka.

Yoshitsune legends 義経伝説

(Yoshitsune *densetsu*). MINAMOTO NO YOSHITSUNE, a warrior of the latter part of the Heian period (794–1185) and early part of the Kamakura period (1185–1333), has been immortalized as a tragic hero in Japanese history and legend to the point that it is often difficult to determine where history leaves off and legend begins. Yoshitsune is the subject of the GIKEIKI (ca 1400–1450; tr *Yoshitsune*, 1966) and of numerous other literary works, including Nō and *kabuki* plays. One story about Yoshitsune says that during his childhood, when he was known as Ushiwakamaru, he defeated the outlaw Benkei atop Kyōto's Gojō bridge, after which Benkei became his loyal retainer. The hero's agility is celebrated in a legend about the Battle of DANNOURA, when he is said to have jumped over eight ships. Even after Yoshitsune was said to have died, stories that he was alive and in Ezo (now Hokkaidō) or Mongolia circulated, and some legends said that Genghis Khan and Yoshitsune were the same person.

Yoshitsune sembon-zakura 義経千本桜

(The Thousand Cherry Trees of Yoshitsune). Popular title *Sembon-zakura*. KABUKI play of the *jidai-mono* category; written by Takeda Izumo II (see TAKEDA IZUMO), Miyoshi Shōraku (1696?–1772?), and Namiki Senryū (NAMIKI SŌSUKE). Originally written as a puppet play; first performed in 1747. The play's ostensible hero is MINAMOTO NO YOSHITSUNE,

Yoshioka Yayoi This pioneering physician was the founder of what is now Tōkyō Women's Medical College.

who defeats the Taira in the TAIRA-MINAMOTO WAR only to be forced to flee before the jealous wrath of his elder brother MINAMOTO NO YORITOMO, angered (according to this play) when the supposed heads of three Taira generals sent him by Yoshitsune prove to be false. The brilliant dance scenes of act 4, the *michiyuki* (journey), and the scene "At Kawazura's Residence" are perhaps the best-known parts of the play.

Yoshiya Nobuko This novelist's focus on the ideals and problems of women made her especially popular among female readers.

Yoshiyuki Junnosuke Yoshiyuki's writing is reminiscent of Edo-period popular fiction in its craftsmanship and its themes connected with the world of prostitution.

Yoshiwara 吉原

(shortened form of Shin Yoshiwara). Old name for what is now part of the Senzoku district, Taitō Ward, Tōkyō. The most famous of the government-regulated centers for PROSTITUTION in Japan for almost three-and-a-half centuries, from the early Edo period (1600–1868) until 1958. The generic term for these licensed quarters was *yūkaku* ("play quarter"), *kuruwa* ("quarter"), or *iromachi* ("love town"). Yoshiwara was founded in Edo (now Tōkyō) in 1617 when the shogunate granted a license to Shōji Jin'emon (1576–1644).

The total number of Yoshiwara prostitutes generally varied between 2,000 and 3,000 (with numerous other resident employees) in as many as 200 separate establishments. As long as it was contained within these licensed areas, prostitution was legal in Japan through 1957 when promulgation of the PROSTITUTION PREVENTION LAW abolished the licensed quarters. However, the splendors of Yoshiwara had been in decline long before the quarters were abolished. Other types of female entertainment and increasing pressure for social reform culminated in the abolition of the Yoshiwara.

Yoshiwara was a highly stratified and complex world in itself that provided the means for a very sophisticated level of entertainment. New genres of music, art, and literature developed around it, so that it played a large role in the cultural history of Edo-period Japan.

The Setting—The first location designated for the establishment of the licensed quarter in Edo was a piece of swampy land that had to be filled in before building could begin. Because of the reeds (*yoshi*) growing there, it was named Yoshiwara ("reed plain"), although the first of the two Chinese characters with which the word was written was later changed to a character meaning "auspicious." After the quarter was destroyed by the MEIREKI FIRE in 1657, it moved to another location and was named Shin (new) Yoshiwara. The original place came to be called Moto (original) Yoshiwara (now part of the Nihombashi business district of Tōkyō). The new Yoshiwara included approximately 8 hectares (20 acres) of land. The streets were laid out in a grid. As a symbol of prostitution, taken from China, willow trees were planted by the gate and on the streets within the quarter.

Like almost all of the licensed quarters, Edo's Yoshiwara was physically enclosed by a moat and walls. Access was by means of one entry called the *ōmon* (great gate) to keep customers from sneaking away without paying and to keep the prostitutes from escaping. Within these walls were the houses where the women lived and different types of teahouses where customers arranged for liaisons.

Until 1760 there were *ageya* ("houses of assignation") where guests would request that a certain prostitute be called. Then their functions were taken over by teahouses called *hikite-jaya*. Customers had to go through these teahouses in order to engage a prostitute. The guest paid the teahouse for all services, and the money for the prostitute was then passed on to the brothel owner. The customer might have already picked out a woman by looking at prostitutes sitting in rooms (*harimise*) separated from the streets by vertical wooden bars, or in more modern times he might have leafed through a selection of photographs (*shashin mitate chō*). When the customer made his choice, a teahouse servant accompanied him to the brothel where the woman resided. Entertainers called GEISHA (or *hōkan*, if they were male) could also be called by the customer. In addition to the teahouses there was a great variety of brothels (*jorōya*) of differing rank, depending on the quality of the women within them. Fees (*agedai*) varied accordingly.

The Women—There was a bewildering variety of names, both general and specific, for the different levels of prostitutes. They can be most broadly categorized as licensed (*kōshō*) or unlicensed (*shishō*). All prostitutes within quarters like Yoshiwara were *kōshō*, although the *shishō* flourished around the fringes of the licensed quarters and in other unauthorized quarters (*okabasho*), such as Shinagawa and Shinjuku.

High-ranking prostitutes walked freely about the quarters on their distinctive high clogs (GETA), whereas the other grades of women sat in the barred rooms for exhibition. Often the higher-class women were famous for both their beauty and skill in the arts. They were the subjects of many contemporary woodblock prints (UKIYO-E) and literary works. One of the grand spectacles of Yoshiwara was the *oiran dōchū*, a parade of high-class courtesans that moved in stately splendor through the main street of the quarter.

Although some prostitutes were born into the profession as daughters of prostitutes, it was very common for brothel owners to pay for girls from impoverished families. Professional procurers called *zegen* were employed for this purpose. Since the shogunate had officially banned the outright sale of persons, girls were indentured with contracts for fixed periods (commonly 10 years), but often such periods were extended and many died before the contract expired. Parents who handed over their daughters were given a sum called *minoshirokin* ("money for the body"), and the girl became almost a slave to the brothel owner. If the parents (or perhaps a patron later on) could come up with the money to buy her out of bondage, she could leave the quarter; this was known as *miuke*, or "redemption."

Yoshiya Nobuko 吉屋信子

(1896–1973). Novelist. Born in Niigata Prefecture. Yoshiya's stories began to be published while she was still in her teens, and her early work *Hana monogatari* (1916–24, The Tale of Flowers) became popular among female students. Such works as *Chi no hate made* (To the Ends of the Earth), which won the *Ōsaka asahi shimbun* prize in 1920, reflect Christian influences. Her novels focus on women's ideals, problems, and relations with other women. (She herself lived and traveled with her lifelong female companion, Momma Chiyoko.) In addition to studies of modern women writers, her principal works include *Onna no yūjō* (1933–34, Women's Friendship), *Otto no teisō* (1936–

37, A Husband's Chastity), *Onibi* (1951, Demon Fire), *Atakake no hitobito* (1951–52; tr *The Ataka Family*, 1964–65), and *Tokugawa no fujintachi* (1966, Tokugawa Ladies).

Yoshiyuki Junnosuke 吉行淳之介

(1924–). Novelist and short-story writer. Born in the city of Okayama, Yoshiyuki moved to Tōkyō with his family at the age of three. Near the end of World War II he studied English literature at Tōkyō University. Although he did not graduate, he did help publish a small literary magazine, *Ashi* (Reed). In 1954, while recovering from a bout of tuberculosis, Yoshiyuki received the Akutagawa Prize for "Shū" (tr "Sudden Shower," 1972) and decided to write full time.

Yoshiyuki employs sex as a medium to examine the nature of human existence, but his pursuit of this theme is counterbalanced by a refined prose style and sparkling wit. In his craftsmanship and partiality to themes connected with the pleasure quarters, Yoshiyuki stands in the tradition of Edo-period (1600–1868) popular fiction (GESAKU). Though he is grouped with the writers of the confessional I-NOVEL, Yoshiyuki's coolness and objectivity set him apart. His novel *Honoo no naka* (1956, In the Flames) is an autobiographical account of his life and loves in wartime Tōkyō. Other works include the best-selling *Suna no ue no shokubutsugun* (1963, Vegetable Kingdom on the Sand) and *Anshitsu* (1969; tr *The Dark Room*, 1975). In 1978 Yoshiyuki won the Noma Literary Prize for the story "Yūgure made" (Until Dusk).

Yoshizawa Ayame I 芳沢あやめ1世

(1673–1729). KABUKI actor. During the Genroku era (1688–1704), as kabuki changed from a simple show to a sophisticated form of theater, the work of Ayame I was seminal in developing the art of the *onnagata*, or specialist in female roles. Men had been playing female roles since women were banned from kabuki in 1629, but it was Ayame I who, capturing the essence of feminine emotions and movements in fine detail, perfected a new, artful mode of expression for the *onnagata*. Rather than a showy, surface imitation of women, he suggested the female with realistic art. *Ayamegusa*, a volume of his collected teachings, is an invaluable guide to the principles of *onnagata* acting.

Yoshizawa Kenkichi 芳沢謙吉

(1874–1965). Diplomat. Born in Niigata Prefecture; graduate of Tōkyō University. While minister to China from 1923 to 1929, he met with Soviet Minister Lev KARAKHAN in Beijing (Peking). These talks led to the resumption, in 1925, of formal relations between Japan and Russia for the first time since the Russian Revolution. Later ambassador to France and representative to the League of Nations, Yoshizawa became foreign minister in the cabinet of INUKAI TSUYOSHI in 1932. From 1941 to 1944 he served as ambassador to French Indochina. Purged by OCCUPATION authorities after World War II, he was appointed ambassador to the Republic of China (Taiwan) in 1952.

Yoshizumi Kosaburō IV 吉住小三郎4世

(1876–1972). Singer and composer of NAGAUTA (a major form of lyric song in KABUKI theater). The second son of Kosaburō III (1832–99), he inherited his father's name in 1890. He worked as a *nagauta* singer in kabuki until 1902 when, with the *shamisen* player Kineya Rokushirō III (later KINEYA JŌKAN II), he founded the Kenseikai Society, which worked to foster appreciation of *nagauta* on its own terms, apart from its function as accompaniment to kabuki and dance performances. He was an accomplished composer and, in collaboration with Jōkan II, wrote a number of original *nagauta.* In 1956 he was designated a Living National Treasure. He received the Order of Culture in 1957.

Yōteizan 羊蹄山

Also called Ezo Fuji. Stratovolcano in the Nasu Volcanic Zone on Oshima Peninsula, southwestern Hokkaidō. Ōgama, a crater on the summit with a diameter of 700 m (2,300 ft), changes into a crater lake when the snow melts. Yōteizan has many parasitic volcanoes and abundant alpine flora. In the foothills asparagus and potatoes are cultivated. Yōteizan is part of Shikotsu-Tōya National Park. Height: 1,898 m (6,227 ft).

Yotsukaidō 四街道[市]

City in central Chiba Prefecture, central Honshū. Before World War II it was famous as an army base; today it is a commuter town serving the city of Chiba and metropolitan Tōkyō, and many large housing developments and factories have been built here. Pop: 72,157.

youth clubs 青年団

(*seinendan*). Associations for young men and women, usually between the ages of 15 and 25. They were primarily found in rural communities. These groups developed out of the traditional youth associations (*wakamono-gumi* for men and *musume-gumi* for women) of the Edo period (1600–1868). The *seinendan* gained momentum during the Meiji period (1868–1912) and developed into vocational and study group centers as a spontaneous popular response to the trends of "modernization and enlightenment" pervasive throughout Japanese society at the time. Beginning in 1893 these centers came under government regulation and by World War II had been turned into quasi-military organizations. Toward the war's close the government replaced these organizations with student military corps (*gakutotai*). Since the Occupation period (1945–52), *seinendan* have again become voluntary youth associations for study and social activities. The movement of youth from rural communities has tended to decrease even further the role of the *seinendan,* and many young men and women now seek alternate activities in university and extracurricular-study settings. See also WAKAMONO-GUMI.

youth hostels ユースホステル

(*yūsu hosuteru*). There are approximately 450 youth hostels throughout Japan. Some 380 of these are managed and operated directly by or under private contract from Japan Youth Hostels, Inc; the balance are maintained by municipal governments. Accommodations range from large, no-frills dormitories to smaller, more personal lodgings at converted Japanese inns (*ryokan*), mountain cottages, and temples. Youth hostels observe curfews, prohibit alcoholic beverages, maintain sex-segregated sleeping quarters, and do not provide maid service. It is necessary to register with Japan Youth Hostels to stay at any of its affiliated youth hostels, but registration is not required at public hostels.

Yo wa nasake ukina no yokogushi Nakamura Baigyoku (center) as the hero and Nakamura Fukusuke (right) as his lover, in the fourth act.

Yo wa nasake ukina no yokogushi 与話情浮名横櫛

(Yosa the Carved). Popular title *Kirare Yosa.* KABUKI play of the *sewa-mono* (domestic play) category by Segawa Jokō III (see SEGAWA JOKŌ); first performed in 1853. Based on an actual incident. Acts 2, 3, and 4 (the last of these is called the "Gen'yadana" scene) remain in the kabuki repertory and recount the love story of the handsome rogue Yosaburō, adopted son of the wealthy Izuya family of Edo (now Tōkyō), and the former *geisha* Otomi. When a natural son is born to the Izuya, Yosaburō purposely enters a life of dissipation in order to allow the child to become the heir and has a torrid affair with Otomi. Tragically separated—Yosaburō disfigured (Yosa the Carved) by hoodlums and Otomi presumed dead after leaping into the sea—the two lovers cross paths momentarily years later in one of the most electric scenes in kabuki.

Yoyogi National Stadium 国立代々木競技場

(Kokuritsu Yoyogi Kyōgijō). Sports facility designed by architect TANGE KENZŌ and structural engineer Tsuboi Yoshikatsu (b 1907), comprising dynamically paired gymnasiums that were specially constructed for the 1964 Tōkyō Olympics. The larger gymnasium houses a swimming pool and the smaller a basketball court. The structure consists of a high-tensile cable and steel-suspension roof measuring 126 by 120 meters (413 by 394 ft) over a reinforced-concrete base. Originally the focus of a debate over the reconciliation of modern and traditional architecture, this facility is now considered a monument of modern international architecture.

Yoyogi Park 代々木公園

(Yoyogi Kōen). Municipal park south of Meiji Shrine in northern Shibuya Ward, Tōkyō. Until the end of World War II the area was used by the Japanese army as a parade ground (Yoyogi Rempeijō), and in the postwar era by the OCCUPATION forces for military housing (Washington Heights). The land was returned to Japan in 1964, and the Olympic Village for the TŌKYŌ OLYMPIC GAMES was built on it. In 1967 it was opened as a park, with wooded areas, sports fields, and an open-air theater. Total area: 54 hectares (133 acres).

YS-11 ワイエス-いちいち

(Waiesu-Ichiichi). Transport aircraft with two turbo-propeller engines, developed in Japan after World War II and manufactured by Nihon Aeroplane Manufacturing Co, Ltd. Its relatively short takeoff and landing ability and its seating capacity of 60 to 65 passengers make it suitable for local airport operations. The export of 76 YS-11 aircraft represented the first success for the Japanese aircraft industry in the postwar market. A total of 182 aircraft were produced before production ended in 1974. Imported equipment includes engines, propellers, and some accessories from the United Kingdom as well as some components from the United States. See also AVIATION.

Yūaikai 友愛会

(Friendship Association). A labor group organized by pioneering labor leader SUZUKI BUNJI and 14 others in August 1912. One of Japan's earliest workers' organizations, it played an important role in the growth of the Japanese labor movement. The Yūaikai ad-

YS-11 The first transport aircraft produced in postwar Japan. The YS-11 shown here was flown by All Nippon Airways Co.

vocated mutual aid through friendship and cooperation; the improvement of character, furthering of knowledge, and development of skills; and the improvement of the status of workers through unity. The organization began publishing the newspaper *Yūai shimpō* in 1912 and succeeded in attracting members from large businesses. Membership reached 2,451 in 1914, 20,000 in 1916, and 30,000 in 1918. It changed its name to Dai Nihon Rōdō Sōdōmei Yūaikai in September 1919 and included in its platform the freedom to organize labor unions and an eight-hour workday. In 1921 its name was changed to Nihon Rōdō Sōdōmei. See SŌDŌMEI.

Yuan Shikai (Yüan Shih-k'ai) 袁世凱

(1859–1916; J: En Seigai). Official of the Qing (Ch'ing) dynasty (1644–1912) and president of the Republic of China during its first years, Yuan rose to prominence while contesting Japanese initiatives in Korea in the early 1880s.

As prime minister during the Chinese Revolution of 1911, Yuan negotiated the abdication of the Qing emperor with the revolutionaries. He emerged from the revolution as president of the new republic. When Chinese civil conflict broke out in the summer of 1913, the Japanese military clandestinely assisted the anti-Yuan revolutionaries, who nonetheless failed. In May 1915 Yuan capitulated to a Japanese ultimatum in the negotiations over the TWENTY-ONE DEMANDS but managed to cast an unfavorable light on Japanese behavior. In the latter part of 1915 Yuan guided a movement to end the republic and enthrone himself. A rebellion in defense of the republic attracted official Japanese support. Although Yuan abandoned his monarchical hopes in March 1916, Japanese support for his Chinese enemies continued. Still president but preparing for exile, Yuan died in Beijing (Peking) on 6 June 1916.

Yuasa Hachirō 湯浅八郎

(1890–1981). Christian educator and entomologist; twice president of DŌSHISHA UNIVERSITY in Kyōto and the first president of INTERNATIONAL CHRISTIAN UNIVERSITY in Mitaka, Tōkyō. Born in Tōkyō. Graduating from Dōshisha Academy in 1908, young Yuasa left for the United States. He received a doctorate in entomology at the University of Illinois. Appointed to the Agriculture Faculty of Kyōto University in 1923, he was given the opportunity to travel and study in Europe. He earned a doctorate from Tōkyō University in 1931.

Dōshisha called him to be its 10th president in 1935. He resigned within two years and went to the United States. Returning to Kyōto in 1946, he again served as president of Dōshisha until 1950, when he became the first president of International Christian University, a post he held until 1962.

Yuasa Jōzan 湯浅常山

(1708–81). Confucian scholar of the Edo period (1600–1868). Born in Bizen Province (now part of Okayama Prefecture), he studied with HATTORI NANKAKU and DAZAI SHUNDAI, scholars of KOBUNJIGAKU, a school of Confucianism. Returning to Bizen, he attained high posts in the domain administration but was rebuked for expressing candid opinions. He devoted the remainder of his life to writing. His *Jōzan kidan* (1739) is a collection of anecdotes about famous warriors.

Yūbari 夕張[市]

City in central Hokkaidō. Located in the heart of the ISHIKARI COALFIELD; coal-mining operations ceased in 1990. Efforts are being made to introduce new industries. Pop: 20,969.

Yūbaridake 夕張岳

Mountain of the Yūbari Mountains, central Hokkaidō. A rugged mountain composed of Cretaceous-period sandstone, argillite, and hornfels. Alpine flora such as Yūbari gentian (Yūbari *rindō*) grow on the summit. Height: 1,668 m (5,472 ft).

Yūbari Mountains 夕張山地

(Yūbari Sanchi). Mountain range running north to south in central Hokkaidō. The principal peaks are YŪBARIDAKE (1,668 m; 5,472 ft) and ASHIBETSUDAKE (1,727 m; 5,665 ft). The mountains drop steeply to the Furano Basin in the east. The ISHIKARI COALFIELD is located along the western foothills.

Yūbin hōchi shimbun 郵便報知新聞

Newspaper founded in 1872 by MAEJIMA HISOKA and others. It was a prominent voice for the FREEDOM AND PEOPLE'S RIGHTS MOVEMENT (Jiyū Minken Undō) in the 1870s and early 1880s. Led by KURIMOTO JOUN, YANO RYŪKEI, INUKAI TSUYOSHI, and OZAKI YUKIO, it became a political tabloid for the RIKKEN KAISHINTŌ (Constitutional Reform Party). In 1886, however, the paper became more commercial. It halted publication in 1894 and was reorganized as the HŌCHI SHIMBUN.

Yu Dafu (Yü Ta-fu) 郁達夫

(1896–1945; J: Iku Tatsufu). Chinese writer. Yu studied economics at Tōkyō University, where he met other Chinese writers, including GUO MORUO (Kuo Mo-jo) and ZHANG ZIPING (Chang Tzu-p'ing). In 1921 they founded the Creation Society (Chuangzao She or Ch'uang-tsao She), a group advocating romantic literature. Yu's early writings were largely autobiographical and increasingly concerned with the problems of morality and the individual's inner life.

After the outbreak of war between China and Japan in 1937, Yu joined Guo Moruo in anti-Japanese propaganda work in Hangzhou (Hangchow), Zhejiang (Chekiang). From 1938 he worked in anti-Japanese organizations in Singapore until it fell to Japan in 1942. He then fled incognito to Sumatra, where he was forced to serve as an interpreter for the Japanese military police, who arrested and presumably killed him shortly after Japan's surrender in 1945.

Yuda Hot Spring 湯田温泉

(Yuda Onsen). Hot spring in the city of Yamaguchi, Yamaguchi Prefecture, western Honshū; widely known since the Muromachi period (1333–1568). It is a simple thermal spring with a water temperature of approximately 65°C (149°F).

Yudanaka Hot Spring 湯田中温泉

(Yudanaka Onsen). Located in the town of Yamanouchi, northeastern Nagano Prefecture, central Honshū. Simple saline and sulfur spring; water temperature 49°–97°C (120°–207°F). Part of the Yamanouchi Hot Springs.

Yudonosan 湯殿山

Also known as Yudonoyama. Mountain in central Yamagata Prefecture, northern Honshū, with Yudonosan Shrine at its summit. Yudonosan is one of the three holy mountains of Dewa, along with GASSAN and HAGUROSAN, which have long been considered sacred ground by followers of the SHUGENDŌ sect. Height: 1,504 m (4,934 ft).

Yufuin 湯布院[町]

Town in central Ōita Prefecture, Kyūshū. With many hot springs, Yufuin is known primarily as a health resort. Rice production, lumbering, and stock farming are carried out. Pop: 11,725.

Yugashima Hot Spring 湯ヶ島温泉

(Yugashima Onsen). Located in the town of Amagi Yugashima, central Izu Peninsula, eastern Shizuoka Prefecture, central Honshū. An earthy, carbonated spring; water temperature averages 50°C (122°F). Located on the upper reaches of the river Kanogawa, Yugashima is famous for such scenic spots as the Jōren Falls and the Seko Falls.

Yugawara 湯河原[町]

Town in southwestern Kanagawa Prefecture, central Honshū. It has long been known as a hot-spring resort, being mentioned in the *Man'yōshū*, the 8th-century poetry anthology. Pop: 27,717.

yūgen 幽玄

Aesthetic ideal cultivated by poets and dramatists from the 12th through the 15th century. The term *yūgen* broadly designated an ambiance of mystery, darkness, depth, elegance, ambiguity, calm, transience, and sadness. As the proportion of these components differed, the meaning of *yūgen* varied considerably within its connotations.

The word *yūgen* originated in China (Ch: *you xuan* or *yu hsüan*) to describe an object lying too deep to see or comprehend. It often appeared in a Buddhist context, referring to ultimate truth that could not be grasped through intellect. The term entered Japanese literary criticism in the early 10th century, when Ki no Yoshimochi in his Chinese preface to the KOKINSHŪ employed it in connection with the ways in which poetry had been written in ancient times.

Yūgen developed into a poetic principle in the 12th century, when it was integrated with the concept of YOJŌ, or "overtones." Underlying this was the aesthetic notion that WAKA (classical Japanese poetry) should embody emotion so delicate or subtle that it could be suggested only obliquely through overtones. FUJIWARA NO TOSHINARI (1114–1204), the foremost exponent of *yūgen* in his day, commented that "a fine poem often evokes associations not overtly expressed in word or form." An example he cited was a poem on the autumn moon that made the reader hear a deer's cry not described therein. In the 13th and 14th centuries *yūgen* came to imply a more elegant, ethereal beauty, although connotations of "overtones" persisted. This shift in emphasis was due largely to the influence of Toshinari's son FUJIWARA NO SADAIE (1162–1241). The Nō playwright ZEAMI (1363–1443) was an ardent exponent of this type of *yūgen*, so much so that he argued that all styles of Nō acting had to have it latently. In the 15th century calm resignation came into greater prominence among the components of *yūgen*. Prolonged social unrest and the influence of Zen Buddhism may have contributed to this change in emphasis.

As the central concept in medieval aesthetics, *yūgen* exerted considerable influence on artists of the succeeding centuries. WABI, a central principle of the TEA CEREMONY, and SABI, a dominant aesthetic in the form of poetry known as *haikai*, were both greatly indebted to the spirit that fostered *yūgen*.

yūgen kaisha → limited liability company

Yugyōji 遊行寺

Formal name Shōjōkōji. Head temple of the JI SECT of PURE LAND BUDDHISM, located in the city of Fujisawa, Kanagawa Prefecture. Yugyōji was established in 1325 by the fourth head of the sect, Donkai (1265–1327). Among the patrons of the temple were the shōgun ASHIKAGA TAKAUJI, Emperor Go-Komatsu (1382–1412), and the Tokugawa family. Yugyōji suffered ruin many times. It was extensively damaged by fire in 1911 and again in the Tōkyō Earthquake of 1923, losing many of its treasures. The buildings, however, have since been restored.

yūhitsu 右筆

(secretaries). Clerks whose duty was to draft and write final copies of documents for their masters; the documents were then validated by the master's signature or monogram (KAŌ). Attached to the High Court (HIKITSUKE) during the Kamakura (1192–1333) and Muromachi (1338–1573) shogunates, two ranks of *yūhitsu* evolved during the Tokugawa shogunate (1603–1867): one to handle confidential documents and one to handle ordinary government records.

yui 結

(literally, "tying"). A form of traditional cooperative labor. *Yui* is a mutual exchange of labor in which, for example, one repays a day of labor from someone by working one day for that person. In actual practice, *yui* principally occurs in farm villages during rice planting and harvesting when a large amount of labor is necessary. In many cases, a number of farm households form a *yui* association, pledging to help each other when additional labor is needed.

yuinō 結納

Engagement ceremony in which the bridegroom-to-be presents money and gifts to his fiancée. In the Kantō region it is customary for the bride-to-be to repay her fiancé with gifts of approximately half the value of those she received from him. Traditionally these exchanges were carried out by a messenger other than the go-between (NAKŌDO), but today they are usually handled by the latter.

Recently there has been a trend toward abbreviated versions of the *yuinō* ceremony, in which the go-between and the couple's families gather at a hotel or restaurant for the presentation of the engagement ring and the exchange of other keepsakes. Besides its ceremonial value, *yuinō* can have legal significance: when engagements broken off by one party are contested in court, the *yuinō* may be used as evidence that the engagement did take place. See also WEDDINGS.

Yui Shōsetsu　由井正雪

(1605–51). Teacher of military science in the early Edo period (1600–1868). Born in Suruga Province (now part of Shizuoka Prefecture). After studying military arts with Kusunoki Fuden (dates unknown), Shōsetsu opened a school in Edo (now Tōkyō). His fame gradually spread, and he counted among his students several *daimyō* and HATAMOTO. Shortly after the shōgun TOKUGAWA IEMITSU died in 1651, Shōsetsu organized RŌNIN (*samurai* who became masterless because their daimyō had been deprived of their domains) and, with MARUBASHI CHŪYA and others, plotted the overthrow of the Tokugawa shogunate (see KEIAN INCIDENT). The conspiracy was discovered, and Shōsetsu committed suicide, leaving a note explaining that he had only wanted to focus attention on the plight of the *rōnin*, not to overthrow the shogunate.

yūjo　遊女

A general term for the prostitutes serving the licensed brothel and entertainment districts that were created after TOYOTOMI HIDEYOSHI established a system of licensed prostitution in 1585. Based on their appearance, artistic accomplishments, and general cultural refinement, *yūjo* were classified as OIRAN, *tayū*, *kōshi*, or one of many other specific categories. After the Meiji period (1868–1912), *shōgi* became the general term for all types of licensed prostitutes. See also PROSTITUTION; YOSHIWARA.

yukar → Ainu language

yukata　浴衣

An unlined cotton summer *kimono. Yukata* were originally made of pure white cotton, but they were later decorated with indigo dye. Known as *yukatabira* during the Heian period (794–1185), they were worn before and after bathing. By the Edo period (1600–1868) they had come to be known as *yukata* and were worn as everyday summer clothing by the general populace. Today *yukata* are mainly worn at summer events such as the BON FESTIVAL or the temple and shrine fairs known as ENNICHI. *Yukata* are also provided to patrons at Japanese inns and hotels as after-bath or leisure wear. Children's *yukata* are usually made of a multicolored seersucker-like material.

Yukawa Hideki　湯川秀樹

(1907–81). Theoretical physicist. Renowned for his numerous pioneering works in particle physics, including the meson theory and the theory of nonlocal fields. Born in Tōkyō, he graduated from Kyōto University in 1929. He became an instructor at the newly estab-

lished physics department at Ōsaka University in 1933 and began his inquiry into the nature of elementary particles. In 1939 he joined the faculty of Kyōto University, and in 1943 he received the Order of Culture. In 1948 he was invited by J. Robert Oppenheimer (1904–67) to the United States to become visiting professor at the Institute for Advanced Study at Princeton, New Jersey. A year later he became the first Japanese to receive the Nobel Prize. Returning to Japan in 1953, he served in many high-level governmental and educational posts and was a vocal spokesman for the peaceful use of atomic energy.

Yukawa Institute for Theoretical Physics　基礎物理学研究所

(Kiso Butsurigaku Kenkyūjo). Research institute for the study of theoretical physics affiliated with Kyōto University. Founded in 1953 to commemorate YUKAWA HIDEKI's receipt in 1949 of the Nobel Prize in physics. The institute works to train theoretical physicists and to promote international exchanges of knowledge in the field of physics. Yukawa served as the institute's first director.

Yuki　湯来[町]

Town in western Hiroshima Prefecture, western Honshū. Some 90 percent of the town's area is forested. Principal activities are dairy farming, cultivation of *shiitake* (a species of mushroom), and sericulture. Two hot springs are located here. Pop: 8,002.

Yūki　結城[市]

City in western Ibaraki Prefecture, central Honshū, on the river Kinugawa. Yūki developed as a castle town and became known for its handwoven Yūki *tsumugi* silk. *Geta* (clogs) and *tansu* (chests) are also produced. Manufactures include electrical appliances and textiles. Pop: 53,288.

Yūki family　結城氏

(Yūkishi). Warrior family of the Kamakura (1185–1333) through Edo (1600–1868) periods. Descended from FUJIWARA NO HIDESATO (fl early 10th century). His 10th-generation descendant Oyama Tomomitsu (1168–1254) served MINAMOTO NO YORITOMO and was enfeoffed at Yūki in Shimōsa Province (now part of Ibaraki Prefecture), whence the family took its name. In 1289 Tomomitsu's grandson Sukehiro founded a branch of the family in Shirakawa in southern Mutsu Province (now Fukushima Prefecture). During the Muromachi period (1333–1568), the Shimōsa branch flourished while the Shirakawa branch declined (it was eventually to be destroyed by TOYOTOMI HIDEYOSHI in 1589). Yūki Shigetomo became a SENGOKU DAIMYŌ in the Yūki area. In 1556 his great-grandson Masakatsu (1504–59) drew up the domainal code YŪKIKE HATTO. In 1590 his son Harutomo (1534–1614) adopted TOKUGAWA IEYASU's son Hideyasu (1574–1607). The Yūki fought under Ieyasu at SEKIGAHARA (1600) and were enfeoffed in Echizen (now part of Fukui Prefecture). In 1626 they were granted the shogunal surname Matsudaira.

Yukiguni　雪国

(tr *Snow Country*, 1956). Novel by KAWABATA YASUNARI. Kawabata completed the first version in 1937 but added chapters and made revisions over the course of the following decade. The novel describes the handful of visits that Shimamura, a dilettantish man from Tōkyō, makes to the "snow country,"

yukata Colorful *yukata* worn by participants in a Bon dance at the town of Hachiman in Gifu Prefecture.

an area in the mountainous region near the Sea of Japan, depicted as a remote and otherworldly place. There he meets with Komako, a lively young *geisha* at a hot-spring resort, who is strongly attached to her infrequent guest. Although genuinely attracted to the passionate Komako, the strangely remote Shimamura treats her with a measure of indifference. He maintains a similar distance from Yōko, another young woman from the area, whose pure and ethereal quality appeals to his aesthetic bent. Kawabata's tendency to shift the focus from his characters to restrained descriptions of nature minimizes the importance of plot and gives *Yukiguni* the detached tone found in his other works of fiction. The first version of *Yukiguni*, acclaimed by critics and widely read by the public, established Kawabata's reputation as a major Japanese writer.

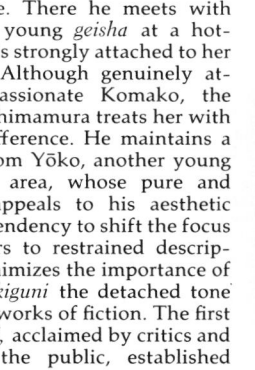

Yukawa Hideki The physicist in 1949, the year he was awarded the Nobel Prize.

Yūkike Hatto　結城家法度

(Laws of the Yūki Family). Also known as Yūkishi Shin Hatto (New Laws of the Yūki Family). A domainal law code (BUNKOKUHŌ) of the Sengoku period (1467–1568), enacted by Yūki Masakatsu (1504–59), the lord of a regional domain in Shimōsa Province (now Ibaraki Prefecture), in 1556. The code consists of a preamble, 104 articles, and a 2-article supplement; another article was added by Masakatsu's successor, Harutomo (d 1614). Not surprisingly, in view of the YŪKI FAMILY's decline in the 15th century and tenuous recovery in the 16th, the lawgiver was preoccupied with the security of his house and the loyalty of his retainers. *Samurai* are reminded that they must perform or be punished; they are also cautioned against making baseless denunciations but urged at the same time to report any suspicion of a plot against the Yūki. Extensive segments of the code deal with military preparedness. Overall, Yūki Masakatsu gives the impression that his 16th-century samurai were a drunken and disorderly lot who needed disciplining.

yuki onna　雪女

(snow woman). Also called *yuki jorō*. Apparition of a woman dressed in white, believed to appear on snowy nights and often blamed for mysterious happenings. Frequently appearing with a baby in her arms, she is associated with children and is sometimes thought to be a woman who died in childbirth. At other times the spirit is described as a woman with one eye and one leg. The *yuki onna* is thought to be a form of a deity of the New Year (TOSHIGAMI) who is said to visit people at the end or beginning of each year. See also GHOSTS.

Yūki Shōji　結城昌治

(1927–). Novelist. Real name Tamura Yukio. Born in Tōkyō; graduate of Waseda

Yumeno Kyūsaku
A wildly imaginative style characterizes this writer's detective novels of the 1920s and 1930s.

University. He gained recognition for such works as *Gomesu no na wa Gomesu* (1962), a spy novel, and *Yoru no owaru toki* (1963), a detective novel about corrupt law-enforcement officers. Known for his hard-boiled style, he received the 1970 Naoki Prize for *Gunki hatameku moto ni* (1969–70), a novel about the crimes committed by Japanese military officers during World War II; it was made into a motion picture in 1972.

Yūki Toyotarō　　　結城豊太郎

(1877–1951). Financier. Born in Yamagata Prefecture. After graduating from Tōkyō University, Yūki joined the Bank of Japan in 1903. He served as chief of various branch offices and eventually became a director. In 1921 he joined the YASUDA *zaibatsu* (financial combine). He became president of the INDUSTRIAL BANK OF JAPAN, LTD, in 1930, finance minister in 1937, and governor of the Bank of Japan from 1937 through 1944. During World War II, he worked to expand the munitions industry and to formulate and promote wartime financial and monetary policies.

yukiwarisō → misumisō

Yukuhashi　　　行橋［市］

City in northeastern Fukuoka Prefecture, Kyūshū, on the Suō Sea. Formerly a market and post-station town. Its principal products are rice, vegetables, fruit, and dairy products. Pop: 65,711.

Yumeno Kyūsaku　　　夢野久作

(1889–1936). Novelist. Real name Sugiyama Taidō. Born in Fukuoka Prefecture; attended Keiō University. Yumeno is known for his wildly imaginative and fantastic detective novels. His principal works include *Binzume jigoku* (1928, Hell in a Bottle), *Kōri no hate* (1933, The End of the Ice), and *Dogura Magura* (1935), his masterpiece.

Yumigahama　　　弓ケ浜

Also known as Yomigahama. Sandspit located in western Tottori Prefecture, western Honshū, near the cities of Sakaiminato and Yonago; separates the Miho Bay from the lagoon Nakaumi. Length: 18 km (11 mi); width: 1.5–2 km (0.9–1.2 mi).

Yumoto Hot Spring　　　湯本温泉

(Yumoto Onsen). Also known as Hakone Yumoto Hot Spring. The most popular of the HAKONE HOT SPRINGS, in the town of Hakone, Kanagawa Prefecture, central Honshū. Located at the entrance to this resort area on the site of an important Edo period (1600–1868) post-station town. It is a simple thermal spring with a water temperature of 35°–74°C (95°–165°F).

Yumoto Hot Spring　　　湯本温泉

(Yumoto Onsen). Also known as Jōban Yumoto Hot Spring. Located in the city of Iwaki, Fukushima Prefecture, central Honshū. Its present source was discovered in a mine of the JŌBAN COALFIELD in 1930, after which the area flourished as a tourist site. A common salt spring; water temperature 45°–56°C (113°–133°F).

Yumoto Hot Spring　　　湯本温泉

(Yumoto Onsen). Also known as Nagato Yumoto Hot Spring. Located in the city of Nagato, Yamaguchi Prefecture, western Honshū. A simple thermal spring; water

temperature 27°–42°C (81°–108°F). The canyon from which the spring emanates is famous for a protected species of firefly, the *genjibotaru*.

Yumoto Hot Spring　　　湯元温泉

(Yumoto Onsen). Also known as Nikkō Yumoto Hot Spring. Located on Lake Yunoko at the foot of SHIRANESAN in the city of Nikkō, Tochigi Prefecture, central Honshū. A sulfur spring; water temperature 45°–71°C (113°–160°F). A starting point for sightseeing in the NIKKŌ NATIONAL PARK.

Yumura Hot Spring　　　湯村温泉

(Yumura Onsen). Located in the city of Kōfu, Yamanashi Prefecture, central Honshū. Said to have been discovered in the 9th century by the Buddhist priest KŪKAI. Today it is a starting point for tours of the gorge SHŌSENKYŌ. A common salt spring; water temperature 40°–50°C (104°–122°F).

Yunogō Hot Spring　　　湯郷温泉

(Yunogō Onsen). Located on the west bank of the river YOSHINOGAWA in the town of Mimasaka, Okayama Prefecture, western Honshū. An alkaline spring; maximum water temperature 43°C (109°F).

Yunokawa Hot Spring　　　湯川温泉

(Yunokawa Onsen). Located at the mouth of the river Matsukuragawa, in the city of Hakodate, southwestern Hokkaidō. A common salt spring; maximum water temperature of 67°C (153°F). Discovered in the 17th century, Yunokawa Hot Spring is one of Hokkaidō's oldest.

Yunoyama Hot Spring　　　湯の山温泉

(Yunoyama Onsen). Located on the eastern slope of Gozaishoyama at an altitude of 460 m (1,509 ft), northern Mie Prefecture, central Honshū. A radium spring; water temperature 26°C (79°F). Located within Suzuka Quasi-National Park, it is said to have been discovered 1,200 years ago. This spring is a popular tourist spot with visitors from Nagoya and Ōsaka.

Yun Pong-gil　　　尹奉吉

(1908–32; J: In Hōkitsu). A member of KIM GU's Korean Patriotic League, Yun threw a bomb at Japanese dignitaries, causing deaths and injuries, during the 29 April 1932 celebration of the Japanese emperor's birthday in Shanghai. Among the injured was SHIGEMITSU MAMORU, Japan's minister to China. Yun was captured by Japanese authorities after mass arrests of Koreans in the city, tried in Ōsaka, and executed. The incident increased Chinese support for Kim Gu's anti-Japanese activities.

Yuragawa　　　由良川

River in northern Kyōto Prefecture, central Honshū, originating in the Tamba Mountains and flowing west through the Fukuchiyama Basin, where it changes to a northeastern course, to empty into Wakasa Bay. The Ōno Dam is located on the upper reaches. Length: 146 km (91 mi); area of drainage basin: 1,880 sq km (726 sq mi).

yūrei → ghosts

yuri → lilies

Yuriika　　　ユリイカ

(Eureka). Monthly magazine of poetry and criticism. Its first series consisted of 53 issues published by the bookshop Shoshi Yuriika

between October 1956 and February 1961. During this period the magazine defined the mainstream of contemporary poetry, publishing the work of young poets such as ŌOKA MAKOTO, TANIKAWA SHUNTARŌ, and Shibusawa Takasuke (b 1930). After an eight-year hiatus, *Yuriika* was revived in July 1969 by the publishing company Seidosha and continues to be an influential journal, emphasizing critical essays, a reexamination of the Japanese poetic tradition, and the introduction of Western literature and literary theory to a Japanese audience.

Yuri Kimimasa　　　由利公正

(1829–1909). Government official of the Meiji period (1868–1912). Born in the Fukui domain (now part of Fukui Prefecture). He studied under the Confucian scholar YOKOI SHŌNAN and worked for administrative reform in his domain. He joined the national government after the MEIJI RESTORATION (1868) and was the principal author of the CHARTER OATH. Yuri initiated the issuance of Japan's first national paper currency (DAJŌKAN SATSU) in 1868. He left the government the following year due to disagreements over financial policy. He accompanied the IWAKURA MISSION to Europe in 1871. He then joined ITAGAKI TAISUKE and others in petitioning for a representative assembly and in 1875 was appointed to the GENRŌIN (Chamber of Elders).

Yuriwaka legend　　　百合若伝説

(Yuriwaka *densetsu*). Folk legend, originating in the coastal regions south of Yamaguchi Prefecture. The nobleman Yuriwaka goes on an expedition to conquer demons and returns after many years of ordeals. No one recognizes him until he subdues a horse of his lord that no one else can handle. He then marries the daughter of the lord. Because of its resemblance to the story of Ulysses, some scholars believe the legend to be of foreign origin, but others contend that its themes are universal.

Yūseishō → Ministry of Posts and Telecommunications

yūsen hōsō → cable audio broadcasting

yūsoku kojitsu　　　有職故実

A term referring to the ceremonies, manners, and customs of the ancient imperial court and the medieval warrior houses, or to the study of these as precedents. In the Heian period (794–1185) the term (from *yūsoku*, "learned or cultured man," and *kojitsu*, "ancient customs") was used in reference only to the customs of the court and imperial family. However, in the Kamakura (1185–1333) and Muromachi (1333–1568) periods, the term came to include the practices of the warrior class, and later it came to mean the study of cultural and ceremonial precedents set by the court aristocracy and warrior class. Specifically, it included court ceremonies, religious rituals, the ranking system, clothing, etiquette, and arms and armor. The focus was placed on the court culture of the Engi (901–923) and Tenryaku (947–957) eras (see ENGI TENRYAKU NO CHI), and the diaries of emperors and court nobles were used as source materials. In the Edo period (1600–1868) warrior families that were well versed in traditional court customs (see KŌKE) took charge of protocol for the shogunate, establishing customs and ceremonies such as YABUSAME, KASAGAKE, INUOUMONO, and *jarai* (a

Yuya In a scene from this Nō play, the character Yuya is conveyed to a cherry-blossom viewing. The prop represents the kind of oxcart used for travel by high-ranking courtiers and *samurai*.

form of archery). The tradition of *yūsoku kojitsu* is still preserved today at the imperial court, as witnessed in the ceremony of the emperor's enthronement and in the DAIJŌSAI (a special thanksgiving ceremony held only when a new emperor is enthroned).

Yu Sŏng-nyong　柳成竜

(1542–1607; J: Ryū Seiryū). Pen name Sŏae (J: Seigai). A leading scholar-official of the Korean YI DYNASTY (1392–1910) during the Japanese INVASIONS OF KOREA IN 1592 AND 1597. Yu worked with Admiral YI SUN-SIN to rally resistance to the invasions and served as liaison between Korea's royal court and Ming Chinese armies sent to aid Korea. He is also revered in Confucian academies for his contributions to Korean Confucian scholarship.

Yü Ta-fu → Yu Dafu (Yü Ta-fu)

Yuya　熊野

NŌ play. Author unknown. It is classified as a *sambamme-mono* ("part-three play"). A female attendant (the *tsure* or "companion" character) arrives at the Taira family villa at Rokuhara near Kyōto and passes a letter to the lovely Yuya (the *shite* or main character), favorite of the warrior-courtier TAIRA NO MUNEMORI. It is from Yuya's mother, who is seriously ill and begs that her daughter return home. Munemori refuses to let her go, insisting instead that she accompany him on a cherry-blossom-viewing excursion. Yuya dances during the festivities, and, as she does so, cherry blossoms drift down around her shoulders. Inspired, she composes a poem about her mother and so impresses Munemori that he allows her to leave for home.

Yuzawa　湯沢[市]

City in southeastern Akita Prefecture, northern Honshū. Yuzawa flourished as a castle town from the early Edo period (1600–1868). The city is known for fine rice wine (*sake*) and its lumber and furniture industries. Pop: 35,539.

Yuzawa　湯沢[町]

Town in southern Niigata Prefecture, central Honshū. A post-station town during the Edo period (1600–1868). Yuzawa has rapidly developed as a resort area since the opening of several major transportation routes in the region. Attractions include hot springs and skiing at nearby Naeba. Pop: 9,986.

Yuzawa Hot Spring → Echigo
Yuzawa Hot Spring

yūzen　友禅

Abbreviation of *yūzenzome*. Textile dyeing method similar in principle to *rōkechi* (see WAX-RESIST DYEING). Originated by Miyazaki Yūzen, a late-17th-century fan painter, in Kyōto, the technique was perfected around 1720 and used throughout the Edo period (1600–1868). It allowed detailed, painterly patterns on textiles for the first time.

The hand-drawn process (*tegaki yūzen*) involves drawing a fine outline design on cloth with tracing fluid made from the *tsuyukusa* (*Commelina communis*) plant; this outline is covered with glutinous rice paste. The resulting lines, called *itome*, appear as thin white outlines after the dyeing procedure. The entire cloth is then covered with soybean milk to prevent blurring during the dyeing process. When the soybean milk dries designs are brushed on with various colored dyes. The colored portions of the design are then covered with rice paste-resist after which the cloth is brushed with dye to color the background. The dye is then fixed through steaming, and the cloth is rinsed thoroughly in running water to remove the rice paste and tracing fluid. When it is dry additional work such as embroidery can be added. The art is still carried on, primarily in Kyōto (Kyō *yūzen*) and Kanazawa (Kaga *yūzen*).

Yūzonsha　猶存社

(Survivors' Society). Political society organized in 1919 by KITA IKKI, ŌKAWA SHŪMEI, Mitsukawa Kametarō (1888–1936), and other rightists. In 1918 Mitsukawa and Ōkawa had founded the Rōsōkai (Society of the Old and the Young) to discuss social problems, and in 1919 they decided to form a small propagandist group from among its right-wing elements. The Yūzonsha called for a reorganization of Japan as outlined in Kita's secretly printed book *Nihon kaizō hōan taikō* (1923, An Outline Plan for the Reorganization of Japan). It also called for a revival of patriotic spirit and the liberation of the peoples of Asia. The membership included Kanokogi Kazunobu (1884–1949) and Yasuoka Masahiro (1898–1983), both later associated with the ultranationalist movements of the 1930s. The Yūzonsha disbanded in 1923 when Kita and Ōkawa disagreed on tactical issues. Although it accomplished little in practical terms, the Yūzonsha was the parent body of several other patriotic societies.

Yuzuki no Kimi　弓月君

(fl late 4th century?). Semilegendary ancestor of the HATA FAMILY. According to the chronicle NIHON SHOKI (720), Yuzuki came to Japan from the Korean state of PAEKCHE during the reign of Emperor ŌJIN (late 4th to early 5th century) and arranged admission of a large number of fellow immigrants (KIKAJIN). It is said that the newcomers brought gifts of gold, silver, precious stones, and silk cloth and that the emperor granted them land in Yamato Province (now Nara Prefecture). The genealogical record SHINSEN SHŌJIROKU and the chronicle *Sandai jitsuroku* claim that Yuzuki was a "prince" (J: ō; Ch: *wang*) and that his father, "Prince Gongman" (Kungman), who came to Japan during the reign of the legendary emperor Chūai, was an 11th-generation descendant of the first emperor of China's Qin (Ch'in) dynasty (221 BC–206 BC).

Yūzū Nembutsu sect　融通念仏宗

(Yūzū Nembutsu *shū*). Japanese Buddhist sect founded upon the teachings of RYŌNIN. Its doctrine holds that by practicing the NEMBUTSU (chanting of the Buddha AMIDA's name) one interfuses (*yūzū*) with other practitioners, leading to one's birth in the Pure Land of Amida. Outstanding figures in the sect include the 7th patriarch, Ryōson (1279–1349), who revived the sect from a century's dormancy, and the 46th patriarch, Yūkan (1649–1716), who wrote the first systematic exposition of *yūzū nembutsu*, *Yūzū emmonshō*.

yuzurijō　譲状

(deed of property transfer). In the history of Japanese law, a document prepared by the transferor and given to the transferee at the time of a transfer of land or other property. Used from the Heian (794–1185) through the early Muromachi (1333–1568) periods, they were also called *yuzuribumi* or *shobunjō*. In

▶ In the first step, a design is created on paper to be used as a model.

▼ After panels of cloth are basted together in the garment's final form, an outline of the pattern is drawn with fluid made from natural sap.

▲ Colors are added to the basic pattern using various sizes of brushes.

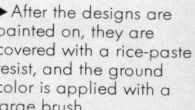

▶ After the designs are painted on, they are covered with a rice-paste resist, and the ground color is applied with a large brush.

▲ When the ground color is black, a resist is not used, and the ground color is painted on around a basic design.

◀ In the past, the resist and extra dye were removed by washing the fabric in a river as shown.

the examples that survive from the mid-Heian period, the transferee was usually a wife, child, or other relative. *Yuzurijō* were submitted for official approval in the jurisdiction to which the transferor belonged. The use of *yuzurijō* was widespread from the 13th through the 14th centuries but declined abruptly thereafter.

YWCA　キリスト教女子青年会

(Kirisutokyō Joshi Seinenkai). The Japan Young Women's Christian Association was established in 1905 and joined the World YWCA in 1906. Since World War II, the Japan YWCA has attempted to support the spirit of the Japanese constitution in a way consistent with Christianity and with the aim of protecting fundamental human rights. There were 25 city-based YWCAs in Japan and 32 school-affiliated YWCAs in participating middle and high schools in 1990. The Japan YWCA had about 15,000 members in the same year.

za 座

Trade or craft organizations of merchants, artisans, or service personnel. Originating in the 11th century, they were most active during the Muromachi period (1333–1568). *Za,* each protected by a patron in exchange for fees and services, were organized to restrict entry and competition within specific product or service markets and to ensure the economic advantage of their members. Early *za* were patronized by Buddhist temples or Shintō shrines; later, the Kyōto aristocracy and the imperial house turned to *za* patronage as a source of income. During the Muromachi period the shogunate and many of the regional DAIMYŌ also sponsored *za.* Among the best-known *za* were the Ōyamazaki oil *za* patronized by the IWASHIMIZU HACHIMAN SHRINE and the cotton *za* under the YASAKA SHRINE, both in Kyōto. Regional *za* existed in temple towns and port towns. As commercial agriculture increased, rural *za* emerged to compete with the urban and market *za.*

From the mid-16th century daimyō began to abolish *za,* toll barriers (SEKISHO), and other restrictions, which were seen to impede the expansion of trade and handicraft production. A few *za* survived into the Edo period (1600–1868) but were largely replaced by new forms of commercial organization such as the KABUNAKAMA. See also RAKUICHI AND RAKUZA.

zabuton 座布団

Small, usually rectangular cushion used for sitting on *tatami* matting or wooden floors. On the average, *zabuton* measure 59 by 63 centimeters (23 by 25 in); they are usually made in sets of five. During the Heian period (794–1185), small rectangular pieces of *tatami* with fabric borders, called *usujō,* were used as *zabuton.* The type of *zabuton* used today came into existence during the Edo period (1600–1868). Originally *zabuton* were reserved for the use of visitors during the winter months, but today they are used casually on an everyday basis, regardless of the season.

zaibatsu 財閥

Industrial and financial combines that attained a dominant position in the Japanese economy between the Meiji period (1868–1912) and World War II. Although the holding companies of those combines were officially dissolved during the OCCUPATION, the postwar corporate groupings (KEIRETSU) are often regarded as their direct successors. Westerners may refer to early-Meiji-period *zaibatsu,* but because combine-derived fortunes were accumulated only after many years, the Japanese do not speak of *zaibatsu* until the World War I period. It was in the early Meiji period, however, that the so-called Big Four *zaibatsu* (MITSUI, MITSUBISHI, SUMITOMO, and YASUDA) were set on the path to exceptional position by governmental favors. Beyond the Big Four, consensus is lacking as to which families and groupings should be called *zaibatsu.* Under the Occupation six additional combines were designated: Nissan, Asano, FURUKAWA, Ōkura, Nakajima, and Nomura.

By definition, combines are complexes of companies and subsidiaries resting on common ownership bases and operated as units. Unified direction of the member companies, the subsidiaries and subsubsidiaries, is achieved through top HOLDING COMPANIES, the command centers of the groupings. Not only

did the families retain exclusive ownership of the top holding companies in the older combines until just before World War II, but until the late 1920s and early 1930s they did not permit public shareholding of their important (or designated) subsidiaries. With Japanese expansion on the Asian mainland in the 1930s and Japan's entry into World War II in 1941, outside ownership was imperative and became substantial. When MITSUBISHI HEAVY INDUSTRIES, LTD, offered public stock in 1934, the shares were oversubscribed by a factor of 27. Whether family control was diminished was, however, another matter.

The appointment and approval of officers were further means of family control. In addition to business acumen, candidates were judged on their fealty to the controlling family. In the 1930s there were additions to the established *zaibatsu* circle, including such groupings as Nissan. These *shinkō* (new) *zaibatsu* were frequently described in popular writings as "democratic," because shareholding was fully open to the public and no family fealty was involved in officer appointments.

Credit was another control device of the combines as subsidiaries were obliged to rely primarily on the financial institutions of the combine. For instance, Mitsui Bank, Ltd (see SAKURA BANK, LTD), did not lend to a Mitsubishi subsidiary, nor did MITSUBISHI BANK, LTD, lend to a Mitsui subsidiary. However, if financial needs were in excess of what the combine could provide, it was possible—with holding-company approval—to borrow from domestic banks that were not within a rival combine network, or from abroad. Subsidiaries were also obliged to sign "sole-agency agreements" with the combine's trading companies, meaning they would do all their buying and selling through the trading company. Such centralized buying and selling brought the entire combine into each trade negotiation, protecting further the family control.

Discriminatory business practices were common under the *zaibatsu* system. Prices charged in transactions within the combine were often far lower than those charged outsiders, and, through member trading companies, combines could restrict imported technology to their own subsidiaries or undercut rivals by importing cheap foreign goods.

The power of accumulating capital, together with close political ties (cemented by cash payments from *zaibatsu* top holding companies to parties and politicians) and the absence of antidiscrimination laws, resulted in few new faces in Japan's big-business sector until the 1930s, when the industrial buildup on the Asian mainland began and the *shinkō zaibatsu* came into prominence. The major political parties of the period, the RIKKEN SEIYŪKAI and the RIKKEN MINSEITŌ, were widely regarded as little more than pawns of the Mitsui and Mitsubishi interests, respectively, provoking anti-*zaibatsu* sentiment.

After Japan's defeat in World War II, American Occupation authorities made ZAIBATSU DISSOLUTION one of the key elements in their program of preventing a recurrence of Japanese militarism and democratizing Japan's economy. Among the measures taken by the Japanese government during the Occupation were the dissolution of the holding companies of the Big Four *zaibatsu* and other large business groupings, sale to the public of the stockholdings of *zaibatsu* family members, an economic purge, and enactment of an ANTIMONOPOLY LAW and

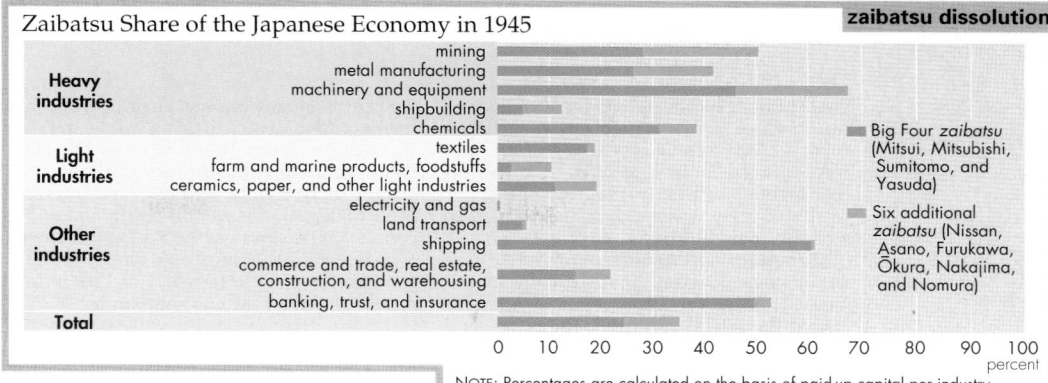

Zaibatsu Share of the Japanese Economy in 1945

Heavy industries	mining / metal manufacturing / machinery and equipment / shipbuilding / chemicals
Light industries	textiles / farm and marine products, foodstuffs / ceramics, paper, and other light industries
Other industries	electricity and gas / land transport / shipping / commerce and trade, real estate, construction, and warehousing / banking, trust, and insurance
Total	

Big Four zaibatsu (Mitsui, Mitsubishi, Sumitomo, and Yasuda)

Six additional zaibatsu (Nissan, Asano, Furukawa, Ōkura, Nakajima, and Nomura)

0 10 20 30 40 50 60 70 80 90 100 percent

NOTE: Percentages are calculated on the basis of paid-up capital per industry.
SOURCE: Noda Kazuo, *Zaibatsu* (1967).

Zaibatsu Dissolution Programs

Action taken against designated holding companies	Number of companies affected
Outright dissolution	16
Dissolution followed by reorganization	26
Reorganization without dissolution	11
None	30
Total	**83**

Stock disposal program	Value of stocks disposed
Antitrust	
Holding Company Liquidation Commission	¥8.3 billion (proceeds from sale)
Fair Trade Commission	¥1.3 billion (paid-up value)
Other	
Finance Ministry (capital tax levy)	¥1.7 billion (proceeds from sale)
Closed Institutions Liquidation Commission	¥3.1 billion (proceeds from sale)
Total	**¥14.4 billion**

Personnel program	Number of persons affected
Law for the Termination of Zaibatsu Family Control	40
Economic purge	1,535
Total	**1,575**

Reorganization under the Deconcentration Law	Number of companies affected
Companies split	11
Companies directed to make minor changes	8
Total	**19**

SOURCE: Eleanor M. Hadley, *Antitrust in Japan* (1970). Reprinted by permission of Princeton University Press. Copyright ©1970.

other legislation prohibiting excessive economic concentration.

The period following the revisions of the Antimonopoly Law in 1949 and 1953, the rescinding of the economic purge (see OCCUPATION PURGE) in 1951, and the end of the Occupation in 1952 saw a tendency for former *zaibatsu* subsidiaries to form again into groups informally centered on banks and coordinated by periodic meetings of the member companies. These corporate groupings have often been described as revived *zaibatsu*. However, this phenomenon does not necessarily constitute a *zaibatsu* revival, even though the Big Four and other business groupings having a historical *zaibatsu* base and sharing largely the same names as former *zaibatsu* are major facts of Japanese economic life. Holding companies remain outlawed under the Antimonopoly Law. There is no family domination of the complexes. Ownership is fragmented, in contrast to the prewar *zaibatsu* pattern. There is no central direction to personnel appointments; each corporation makes its own decisions. Trading and credit activities extend across group lines, and the sole-agency contract remains outlawed under the Antimonopoly Law. While it may therefore be concluded that there is not a *zaibatsu* revival, concentration is increasing in the Japanese economy as major companies and their subsidiaries hold a rising share of corporate ownership.

zaibatsu dissolution 財閥解体

(*zaibatsu kaitai*). Series of actions taken after World War II by the OCCUPATION authorities, with the Japanese government acting as intermediary, to break up the giant family-dominated financial and industrial combines known as ZAIBATSU, which had largely controlled the Japanese economy.

The Dissolution Program—By the war's end in 1945 the so-called Big Four combines—MITSUI, MITSUBISHI, SUMITOMO, and YASUDA—controlled one-fourth of the paid-up capital of the Japanese economy. American planners were convinced that *zaibatsu* dissolution was crucial to the economic democratization process in Japan.

The heart of the *zaibatsu* dissolution program was an enormous operation to dispose of the securities held by the *zaibatsu* holding companies and of those held by the *zaibatsu* family members outside the holding companies. It also included enactment of an antitrust statute, dissolution of the Mitsui and Mitsubishi trading companies, and passage of the Law for the Elimination of Excessive Concentrations of Economic Power as well as the Law for the Termination of Zaibatsu Family Control. Actions that were technically outside the program, but that had a bearing on its outcome, were the Capital Levy Law, the economic purge, the Financial Institutions Reconstruction and Reorganization Law, and the Enterprise Reconstruction and Reorganization Law.

The Yasuda Plan—The starting point of the action was an initiative taken by the Big Four *zaibatsu*. With public knowledge in Japan that General Douglas MACARTHUR, supreme commander for the Allied powers (SCAP), would call for dissolution of the *zaibatsu*, Yasuda put forward a plan in late 1945 to dissolve its holding company; it was joined by the other three combines.

Under the Yasuda plan the securities of the four top holding companies were to be turned over to a public body for sale to the public, and "directors and auditors" of the to-be-dissolved holding companies promised to "resign all offices held by them in such holding companies immediately after the transfer of securities . . . and cease forthwith to exercise any influence . . . in the management or policies." *Zaibatsu* family members offered to "resign all offices held by them in any financial, commercial, noncommercial or industrial enterprises," thus not limiting their resignations to the top holding company alone.

After review by the Japanese government, the plan was submitted to MacArthur on 4 November 1945. On 6 November MacArthur accepted it but retained freedom of action to elaborate or modify the plan. Among the measures taken at SCAP's behest to remedy the inadequacies of the original Yasuda plan was the disposal of shares held outside the holding companies by *zaibatsu* family members.

An Antitrust Statute—In accepting the Yasuda plan in November 1945, MacArthur called upon the Japanese government to submit a draft antitrust statute for the purpose of keeping the Japanese economy deconcentrated. Among the provisions of the Law concerning the Prohibition of Private Monopoly and Preservation of Fair Trade (enacted in April 1947) were the prohibition of holding companies, the prohibition of sole agency contracts, and the prohibition of cartels. In addition there were restrictions on bank shareholding in nonfinancial companies and also on interlocking directorates. The Fair Trade Commission (Kōsei Torihiki Iinkai) was established to enforce these measures. The statute was modified in 1949 and, following resumption of Japanese sovereignty, major amendments were made in 1953 and in 1977 (see ANTIMONOPOLY LAW).

Dissolution of Two Giant Trading Companies—In July 1947 MacArthur suddenly ordered the dissolution of Mitsui Trading and Mitsubishi Trading, Japan's two largest trading companies. This action was the first and only case of SCAP's ordering the dissolution of operating companies.

The Deconcentration Law—In December 1947 MacArthur succeeded in getting through the Japanese Diet the Law for the Elimination of Excessive Concentrations of Economic Power, or the Deconcentration Law, for short. Directed at large operating companies thought to pose serious barriers to market entry, the law called for the splitting of these companies into smaller successor companies. Such a hue and cry went up in the United States over the Deconcentration Law that the Deconcentration Review Board was created to review whether the proposed splits would retard Japan's economic recovery. The review board at once set about reversing the deconcentration policy.

Economic dislocation and the SCAP-directed cancellation of war indemnity payments to businesses brought virtually every Japanese corporation to the edge of bankruptcy. The Diet passed the Financial Institutions Reconstruction and Reorganization

zabuton Two of these small sitting cushions have been placed before the low table in the center of this traditional Japanese room.

Law and the Enterprise Reorganization and Reconstruction Law on 18 October 1946, putting these companies under the provisions of earlier emergency measures. Many companies were split into two or more successor companies, and most of the deconcentration of operating companies was ultimately accomplished in this manner. Furthermore, the establishment of new companies called for new boards of directors.

Economic Purge—The economic purge in January 1947, which MacArthur was ordered to carry out by the US Joint Chiefs of

Staff, came about by extension of the political purge of January 1946 (see OCCUPATION PURGE). Many senior executives of *zaibatsu* were purged or resigned as a result of MacArthur's orders. In 1951 the purge was rescinded and these individuals were free to seek any new position.

Summary and Assessment——The economic deconcentration program, implemented under the Occupation, which included the sale of securities, the purge, and reorganization of the Japanese economy under the Deconcentration Law, did not move smoothly or consistently. By 1948, with the communist victory in China imminent and with a heightening of the cold war, the United States increasingly lost interest in reforming Japan, seeking instead a strong Japan as an ally. Thus the deconcentration effort was aborted. After the Occupation ended in 1952, such former *zaibatsu* as Mitsubishi, Mitsui, and Sumitomo came together again as loose corporate groupings called KEIRETSU. *Keiretsu*, however, are substantially different from their *zaibatsu* predecessors: there are no holding companies to act as command centers for the groups, and ownership ties are far weaker than in *zaibatsu*.

The *zaibatsu* dissolution program accomplished a great deal. By making the former combine subsidiaries their own masters through the dissolution of the holding companies, the program substantially increased market competition. This increased market rivalry was a major factor in Japan's remarkable postwar economic growth.

zaigō shōnin   在郷商人

(rural merchants). Also known as *zaikata shōnin*. Merchants based in the rural hinterlands of large cities in the late EDO PERIOD (1600–1868). Active since the late 1600s, by the early 19th century *zaigō shōnin* were a nationwide phenomenon, dealing in raw and ginned cotton, cotton goods, rapeseed, cottonseed, oil, vegetables, indigo, and safflower dye as well as rice and other grains. With the support of the rural producers they were gradually able to bypass monopolistic urban merchants' associations (KABUNAKAMA) and form their own distribution networks. The banding together (see KOKUSO) in 1823 of more than 1,000 villages in the cotton-growing area of Settsu Province (now part of Ōsaka Prefecture) to protest *kabunakama* privileges greatly strengthened the *zaigō shōnin* and was one factor leading to the abolition of *kabunakama* in 1841. When the shogunate later revived *kabunakama* in 1851, it sought to combine urban and rural merchants in a single body.

zaikai   財界

(financial circles). Term used to refer to the Japanese business world, with special emphasis on the formal and informal associations linking leaders of the major corporations and financial institutions. The most important of the formal associations are KEIDANREN (Federation of Economic Organizations), a national alliance of major business firms; Keizai Dōyūkai (JAPAN ASSOCIATION OF CORPORATE EXECUTIVES), a business group whose members are individuals rather than companies, known for its policy statements; NIKKEIREN (Japan Federation of Employers' Associations), which primarily deals with labor-management relations; and Nisshō (JAPAN CHAMBER OF COMMERCE AND INDUSTRY),

the central organization of chambers of commerce and industry linking all businesses throughout Japan. Referred to as the Four Key Economic Organizations, these four groups represent the opinions and interests of virtually all of corporate Japan and wield considerable clout with the government. Keidanren is the most powerful, and its chairman is often referred to as "the prime minister of the business community."

Informal groups take a variety of forms. Some, known as *keiretsu*, are enterprise-group-based associations, such as the Mitsubishi Kin'yōkai of the Mitsubishi group and the Sumitomo Hakusuikai of the Sumitomo group. Other groups are formed around influential politicians and senior business leaders. Special-interest groups concerned with specific issues and friendship groups based on university, age group, and other ties also exist. See also PRESSURE GROUPS.

zaike   在家

(literally, "at home"). 1. Buddhist laymen who lived at home, in contrast to *shukke*, monks and nuns who lived in monasteries and temples.

2. Under the SHŌEN system of landholding in the 10th to 16th centuries, *zaike* referred to peasants attached to estate proprietors (RYŌSHU).

zaisei tōyūshi   財政投融資

(treasury investment and loans). A large governmental loan program, utilizing surplus funds from Japan's national treasury. The funds originate with government-run savings, pension, and life insurance programs and are pooled into a special account at the Ministry of Finance.

Investments and loans are made to contribute to social welfare through housing and highway construction, to improve the environment, or to add to social capital. Funds are extended to governmental financial institutions, including the GOVERNMENT HOUSING LOAN CORPORATION, PEOPLE'S FINANCE CORPORATION, SMALL BUSINESS FINANCE CORPORATION, and JAPAN DEVELOPMENT BANK; to public corporations, including the Japan Housing Corporation and the JAPAN HIGHWAY PUBLIC CORPORATION; and to local governments. The funds are extended through loans, investments, and the underwriting of bonds.

This program's total outlay of ¥32.8 trillion (US $25.1 billion) in 1989 constituted 54 percent of the general account budget of the national government. The program plays an important role in the government's efforts at economic stabilization, since its funds can be invested with great discretion and flexibility, while government expenditures require the deliberation and approval of the Diet.

zaitech   財テク

(*zaiteku*). A Japanese-coined term designating a variety of investment methods and financial instruments by which corporations attempt to maximize the productivity of their assets, thus improving their pretax profits. "Zai" is taken from the Japanese word for finance, while "tech" is from the English "technology." The term became something of a buzzword in financial and media circles after 1984, when the Ministry of Finance permitted nonfinancial institutions to raise capital by engaging in international arbitrage operations in overseas securities and foreign exchange markets.

In the 1980s Japanese companies moved into a period of steady growth and began to obtain benefits from recently liberalized fi-

nancial and investment methods (see FOREIGN EXCHANGE CONTROLS). An excess of available capital led to lower interest rates, and the stock market began an unprecedented boom. During this period Japanese companies made large profits by raising funds in the Euromarket and investing them in the Tōkyō stock market and in bond and futures markets. Another example of zaitech was the use of real estate holdings as collateral for stock market investments, a key contributory factor in the soaring land prices of the late 1980s.

The upward revaluation of the yen in 1985 (see PLAZA ACCORD) hit Japanese manufacturing industries hard, but many companies were able to weather the storm by using zaitech—creating pretax profits by financial speculation—to balance, or even completely reverse the effect of, a decline in operating profits.

One of the major results of zaitech has therefore been that it has enabled Japanese manufacturers to maintain profitability while acclimatizing themselves to the post-1986 high-yen environment. However, the dramatic fall in the value of the Tōkyō stock market in 1990, the rise in interest rate levels, and public criticism of the speculative nature of zaitech financial management policies have combined in the early 1990s to undermine the use of zaitech as a business stratagem for manufacturing industries. However, in keeping with the strict sense of the term "zaitech" ("financial technology"), financial houses continue to develop new instruments to improve the range of their services to clients.

Zama   座間[市]

City in central Kanagawa Prefecture, central Honshū. It was the site of the Army Academy from 1937 to the end of World War II and is now the site of Camp Zama, a US military base. Automobile and machinery plants are here. Recently the city has become a commuter suburb of Tōkyō and Yokohama. Pop: 112,102.

Zaō Hot Spring   蔵王温泉

(Zaō Onsen). Located in the southeastern part of the city of Yamagata, southeastern Yamagata Prefecture, northern Honshū. An alum and vitriol spring; water temperature 41°–55°C (106°–131°F). Located in the ZAŌZAN volcano group at an altitude of 880 m (2,900 ft), it is a base for excursions into the Zaō district.

Zaōzan   蔵王山

Group of volcanoes, in the Nasu Volcanic Zone, on the border of Miyagi and Yamagata prefectures, northern Honshū. The group is bisected by the Katta Pass. Kita Zaō, to the north, is a double volcano with Kumanodake and Kattadake forming its crater rims and Goshikidake (1,679 m; 5,507 ft) forming a central cone. Minami Zaō to the south includes Byōbudake (1,825 m; 5,987 ft), Mae Eboshidake, Ushiro Eboshidake, and Fubōzan. Snowfall is heavy. The area is known for its skiing, autumn foliage, ice-covered trees in winter, and hot springs. Zaōzan has been designated as Zaō Quasi-National Park. The highest peak is Kumanodake (1,841 m; 6,040 ft).

zappai   雑俳

A general term covering various forms of comic verse that evolved from *haikai* (see HAIKU) poetry during the Edo period (1600–

1868). *Zappai* became established as an independent and popular genre during the Genroku era (1688–1704), when *haikai* moved away from its original identity as a genre of humorous verse and took on a more serious character.

One type of *zappai* is *maekuzuke*, a literary amusement—in form no different from the earliest examples of linked verse—in which a *tsukeku*, or "capping stanza," of 5-7-5 syllables is linked to a given *maeku*, or "leading stanza," of 7-7 syllables; alternatively a *tsukeku* of 7-7 syllables may be linked to a *maeku* of 5-7-5 syllables. Ultimately the latter pattern predominated. Even after *maekuzuke* was superseded by the longer and more sophisticated linked-verse forms, RENGA and *haikai*, it survived both as a comic entertainment and as a device for practice by which poets could study and improve their linking techniques. As it served merely to elicit a response, the content of the *maeku* eventually became largely perfunctory.

In the *zappai* forms known as *kasazuke* and *kiriku*, a 5-syllable line is capped by a 7-5 couplet. *Kasazuke* was intended as an exercise in linking and *kiriku* as an exercise in composing an integrated verse. Similarity in form, however, led to their being considered a single type, which was referred to as *kammurizuke*, or "head capping." *Oriku* is an acrostic form in which either 2 or 3 syllables, one each for an equal number of lines, are used as head syllables. SENRYŪ is a variety of *maekuzuke* that became independent of the convention of capping.

zashiki warashi 座敷童

Household tutelary god traditionally believed to live in the homes of old and well-to-do families in northern Honshū, particularly in Iwate Prefecture. Said to appear in the form of a young boy with long hair and a red face and to bring riches to the family, it could also be mischievous.

Zasso Ketsudansho 雑訴決断所

(Court of Miscellaneous Claims). Extrastatutory board for adjudication of miscellaneous claims; established in 1333 by Emperor GO-DAIGO (r 1318–39) to impose some order on the legal chaos created by his KEMMU RESTORATION (1333–36). Like the High Court (HIKITSUKE) set up by the fallen KAMAKURA SHOGUNATE (1192–1333), it dealt chiefly with land claims. Its staff was made up largely of judiciary officials who had been attached to the now deposed shogunal deputies, the ROKUHARA TANDAI; however, warriors and courtiers also participated.

zatō 座頭

1. Heads of guilds (ZA) of entertainers or merchants in the Muromachi period (1333–1568).

2. Lowest of four ranks (*kengyō, bettō, kōtō,* and *zatō*) given to members of a guild of blind male entertainers (*tōdōza*) formed early in the Muromachi period. *Zatō* later became a general term for blind men (usually members of the *tōdōza*) who shaved their heads and wore the vestments of a Buddhist priest. They earned their living as musicians, singers, and storytellers, or as practitioners of ACUPUNCTURE or massage (see BIWA HŌSHI; AMMA). During the Edo period (1600–1868) members were permitted by the shogunate to demand payment for their services and to use their earnings (*zatōgane*) to make high-interest loans, a practice that was discontinued in 1871. *Zatō* are distinguished from GOZE, blind female entertainers.

Zatōichi 座頭市

Title of a series of films inspired by the success of *Zatōichi monogatari* (1962, The Story of Blind Ichi), directed by Misumi Kenji (1921–75) and starring KATSU SHINTARŌ. The blind hero depicted by Katsu is an itinerant masseur (ZATŌ) who also turns out to be an expert swordsman and gambler. This unusual premise and Katsu's bravura performances have earned the series enduring popularity. Twenty-five Zatōichi films for theatrical release were made before 1973, after which a Zatōichi television series was produced by the star's own Katsu Productions. After a long hiatus, the 26th Zatōichi film was released in 1989.

zatsumu sata 雑務沙汰

(literally, "miscellaneous proceedings"). A legal term of the Kamakura shogunate (1192–1333) referring to litigation over money, serfs and servants, movable property, loans (SUIKO), taxes, commercial transactions, or the forcible return of cultivators who had absconded. Cases were generally adjudicated by the Board of Inquiry (MONCHŪJO) or, within Kamakura, by the Administrative Board (MANDOKORO).

zazen → Zen

Zeami 世阿弥

(1363–1443). Also known as Seami or Kanze Motokiyo. The brilliant actor, playwright, and critic who established NŌ (*sarugaku*) as a classic theatrical art. Zeami's father, KAN'AMI, headed a SARUGAKU troupe in the province of Yamato (now Nara Prefecture). In 1374 the young shōgun ASHIKAGA YOSHIMITSU made Zeami his protégé. At Kan'ami's death Zeami took over the troupe, but it was not until 1402 that he adopted his artistic name.

In 1422 Zeami became a Sōtō Zen monk and was succeeded by KANZE MOTOMASA, his elder son. However, in 1429 ASHIKAGA YOSHINORI, a new shōgun who favored On'ami (Zeami's nephew), barred Zeami and Motomasa from his palace. In 1434 Zeami was exiled to the island of Sado, perhaps because he refused to impart his secret teach-

ings to On'ami. Zeami is credited with between 21 and 90 plays. Masterpieces definitely by Zeami include TAKASAGO, *Tadanori,* IZUTSU, and *Kinuta.* Motomasa died in 1432, and Zeami's only direct successor was his son-in-law KOMPARU ZENCHIKU.

Zeami's critical writings consist of 21 treatises (some of disputed authenticity), which were rediscovered only in the early 1900s. Aesthetic principles central to these works are *hana* (flower), a quality which distinguishes the fine actor, and *yūgen* (subtle beauty), which distinguishes the well-performed play. The best known of these treatises is FŪSHI KADEN (The Transmission of the Flower of Acting Style) in seven parts, dated from 1400 to 1418. Others are *Shikadō* (1420, The Way to the Flower), *Kakyō* (1424, The Mirror of the Flower), and *Kyūi* (undated, The Nine Grades). Like other medieval artists, Zeami understood art as a "way" toward human perfection. His ideal actor achieved flawless responsiveness to audiences and expressive freedom.

zeimusho → National Tax Administration

Zekkai Chūshin 絶海中津

(1336–1405). Poet and Zen monk of the RINZAI SECT. Born in Tosa Province (now Kōchi Prefecture). He was a disciple of MUSŌ SOSEKI. With GIDŌ SHŪSHIN, he has been called one of the "two jewels" of GOZAN LITERATURE (Chinese learning in medieval Japanese Zen monasteries). His poems are collected in the anthology *Shōkenkō.* The trend toward secularization of subject matter in Gozan literature is especially noticeable in his poetry.

zelkova 欅

(*keyaki*). *Zelkova serrata.* A deciduous tree of the elm family (Ulmaceae) that grows wild on plains and slopes in Honshū, Shikoku, and Kyūshū and is also widely cultivated. Its trunk sometimes grows to 30 meters (98 ft). The pointed, serrated leaves are lance-shaped oblongs. It develops tiny, pale yellow-green unisexual flowers.

An indigenous Japanese tree, the zelkova was formerly known as *tsuki* or *tsukinoki* in

Japanese. Favored for its shape and for both its spring and autumn foliage, it is planted along roadsides, in parks, and in the precincts of shrines and temples. Zelkova wood is strong, glossy, fine-grained, durable, warp-resistant, and easily worked. It is used for buildings, bridges, ships, furniture, and utensils. Zelkova ash is used in making ceramic wares.

Zempa 善派

(Zen school). Group of sculptors of Buddhist images active in the Nara area in the early and middle Kamakura period (1185–1333). When the prominent KEI SCHOOL sculpture workshop (BUSSHO) moved from Nara to Kyōto, sculptors remaining in the Nara area later became known as the Zen school, since many of them, such as Zen'en and Zenkei, had the character *zen* in their names. Their artistic antecedents are unclear, and their individual styles, despite a common preference for small images with finely detailed work, retain a strong personal character. The group had close ties with EIZON, the abbot of the temple Saidaiji, where a number of their sculptures may be seen.

Zen 禅

School of East Asian Buddhism that emphasizes the practice of meditation. The Zen school, known as the Chan (Ch'an) school in China, derives its name from the Sanskrit word for meditation (*dhyāna*). It arose in China out of the encounter between Buddhism and indigenous Taoist thought and was held in high regard for several centuries after having survived the persecution of Buddhism there in 845. Zen blossomed again after being brought to Japan, where it underwent further development during the Kamakura period (1185–1333). The two major sects of Japanese Zen are the SŌTŌ SECT (Ch: Caodong or Ts'ao-tung) and the RINZAI SECT (Ch: Linji or Lin-chi). Though they vary in teaching and methods, both schools assign a central role to meditation as the foundation of their spiritual practice. In 1989 Zen had an estimated following of 9.7 million and more than 21,000 temples in Japan.

History——According to legend, the meditative practices that characterize Zen Bud-

zelkova Admired for its delicate leaves and symmetrical shape, the zelkova tree (photo at top) is often planted along roadsides and in parks. The flower clusters contain both male and female flowers that bloom in April or May, with small brown berries ripening in autumn.

dhism were introduced to China by an Indian monk named Bodhidharma (d ca 532). Huineng (638–713), a patriarch of the Chan movement of the Tang (T'ang) dynasty (618–907), is considered to be the actual establisher of Zen in China. The Platform Sutra, ascribed to Huineng, clarified the essential traits of the Chan school of Buddhism. The so-called five houses of the Chan tradition were established toward the end of the Tang dynasty and during the period of the Five Dynasties (907–960). Two of these schools, the Linji and Caodong, endured and were transplanted to Japan.

The introduction of the Chan school to Japan was one of the most important events in Japanese religious history. Together with the proclamation of faith in the Buddha AMIDA and the rise of the NICHIREN SECT, it marked a renewal of Buddhism during the Kamakura period. Although Chinese Zen masters came to Japan and attempted to propagate the Chan tradition, it did not develop into a major branch of Japanese Buddhism until the time of EISAI (1141–1215) and DŌGEN (1200–1253). Eisai and Dōgen studied the way of Zen in China and then propagated its tenets in Japan. During this period, many Japanese Buddhist monks began to journey to China with the express intention of studying Zen. However, the Zen school did not become well established in Japan until it was forced to resist attacks of the powerful TENDAI SECT and SHINGON SECT of Buddhism.

The Zen movement was introduced to Japan through the two main channels of Rinzai and Sōtō. The achievements of the Rinzai school were conspicuous in the nation's imperial capital, Kyōto, and the shogunal capital, Kamakura. These cities saw the rise of the Five Great Temples (GOZAN), which were active cultural centers as well as sites of religious practice. The Gozan system originally included three monasteries in Kyōto and two in Kamakura but soon expanded to comprise five monasteries in each city. Abbots of these monasteries were often granted the title "national teacher" (*kokushi*) by the imperial court. Eisai, after founding Japan's first Rinzai temple, Shōfukuji, in the city of Hakata (now in Fukuoka Prefecture) in 1191, became the first abbot of Jufukuji in Kamakura and then of KENNINJI (founded in 1202) in Kyōto, both of which were to become part of the Gozan system. He exhorted people to practice Zen in a treatise entitled KŌZEN GOKOKU RON (1198, On Promoting Zen and Protecting the Nation).

The most outstanding Japanese figure in Rinzai Zen during this early period was ENNI Bennen (1202–80), who returned from a stay in China with the seal of enlightenment from the Yangqi (Yang-ch'i) lineage of the Linji (Rinzai) school. He served as head of the Kyōto temple TŌFUKUJI and at the same time undertook reform measures at Kenninji. The abbot NAMPO JŌMYŌ (1235–1308) received his initial training in Kamakura, studied in China, and returned to Japan, where he eventually became abbot of two of the most important Zen temples of the period, Manjuji in Kyōto and KENCHŌJI in Kamakura. A characteristic of this phase of Rinzai Zen in Japan was the activity of both Chinese and Japanese monks. In the shogunal capital of Kamakura, the Chinese masters RANKEI DŌRYŪ and Mugaku Sogen (1226–86) founded KENCHŌJI and ENGAKUJI, respectively (see also ISSAN ICHINEI). Many other Rinzai temples made significant contributions to the Zen movement of medieval Japan, and temples such as DAITOKUJI, NANZENJI, and TEN-

RYŪJI became influential centers of Japanese culture.

Dōgen is considered the founder of the Sōtō school in Japan. It was in China that he attained enlightenment and the seal of approval to succeed his master Rujing (Juching; 1163–1228) in the Sōtō lineage. After his sojourn in China, Dōgen was first active in small temples near Kyōto. He built the first completely independent Zen temple and meditation hall, Kōshō Hōrinji (also called Kōshōji), in 1233. Later, distraught by the hostility and political intrigues of the capital, he withdrew to EIHEIJI (Temple of Eternal Peace) in the district of Echizen (now Fukui Prefecture), which became the center of the Sōtō school. Another important temple of the period was SŌJIJI, founded by KEIZAN JŌKIN.

During the Muromachi period (1333–1568) Chinese cultural influence on Japan reached its highest level. Important trade relations with the Asian mainland, carried on chiefly by Buddhist monks, began to develop. At that time Zen displayed extraordinary vitality and spread broadly. The temple MYŌSHINJI, established in 1337, became a model for the strict discipline espoused by its first abbot, Kanzan Egen (1277–1360). The most famous monk of the time was MUSŌ SOSEKI (1275–1351). Soseki induced the shōgun ASHIKAGA TAKAUJI (1305–58) to issue a general decree in 1338 to build Zen temples in 66 localities—these were called "temples to pacify the country" (*ankokuji*). Although this plan was only partly realized, it was actually a continuation of the old system of provincial temples (KOKUBUNJI) that had assured the spread of Buddhism throughout Japan during the Nara period (710–794). As Zen became established under shogunal patronage, however, criticism arose from within. IKKYŪ SŌJUN (1394–1481) was perhaps the most notable monk in this regard. His iconoclastic directness in criticizing smug Buddhists, along with his eccentric behavior, made him a popular figure long remembered in Japanese Zen.

During the Muromachi period Zen exerted a formative influence on the arts of INK PAINTING (*sumi-e*), NŌ drama, the TEA CEREMONY, FLOWER ARRANGEMENT, and landscaping (see GARDENS). GOZAN LITERATURE, cultivated by monks of the Gozan temples, had a profound influence on the culture of the ruling class and included scholarship in such areas as the study of the Chinese classics of the Song (Sung) period (960–1278) and the Neo-Confucian philosophy of Zhu Xi (Chu Hsi; 1130–1200; see SHUSHIGAKU) as well as religious and secular writings in both poetry and prose.

The Edo period (1600–1868) afforded peace and an environment beneficial to the popularization of Zen. During this period, ideas based on Zen found their way into the education of the common people. As part of the religious policy of the Tokugawa shogunate, temples and members of all Buddhist sects were officially registered for the first time. The Rinzai school, divided into numerous sects, claimed fewer members than did the Sōtō school. A third branch of Zen, the ŌBAKU SECT, was introduced to Japan during the Edo period by the Chinese master Yinyuan (Yin-yüan; J: INGEN; 1592–1673). Its practice, developed during the Ming dynasty (1368–1644), is a combination of Zen and NEMBUTSU, the invocation of the name of the Buddha Amida. The Chinese architecture and ornamentation of the Ōbaku sect's central temple, MAMPUKUJI, in Uji, southeast of Kyōto, attracted much interest.

Outstanding among Rinzai monks at the beginning of the Edo period were TAKUAN SŌHŌ (1573–1645) and BANKEI YŌTAKU (1622–93). Takuan taught the affinity between Zen and swordsmanship; Bankei was responsible for making Zen accessible to the simplest of the unlettered. HAKUIN (1686–1769), one of the greatest Japanese Rinzai monks, was also renowned as an artist of exceptional achievement. His life represents a pinnacle in the history of Zen mysticism, and no other Zen master is thought to have articulated such a wealth of inner experience.

After the Meiji Restoration of 1868, the Meiji government favored the SHINTŌ religion and ordered that all syncretic associations with Buddhism be dissolved. Though adversely affected by this decree, Buddhism was already deeply rooted in Japan and soon regained a position of importance. The most prominent Rinzai figure of this period was Imakita Kōsen (1816–92), who became the abbot of ENGAKUJI in Kamakura in 1875 and went on to head the Meiji government's Bureau for Religion and Education. His successor, Shaku Sōen (1859–1919), is known as the teacher of D. T. SUZUKI (1870–1966), Zen's principal exponent in the West.

Practice and Enlightenment — Zen practice primarily consists of meditation in the lotus posture, known in Japanese as *zazen* (Ch: *zuochan* or *tso-ch'an*), and the study of KŌAN (Ch: *gongan* or *kung-an*). Practice within the Sōtō school emphasizes the sitting meditation of *zazen*. The Rinzai school also acknowledges the value of *zazen;* however, it encourages its practitioners to exhaust their thinking in the contemplation of riddlelike *kōan* to progress in meditation. The Rinzai school points out several dangers in the Sōtō emphasis on *zazen*, such as becoming attached to the practice of sitting or promoting a quietistic asceticism that goes only halfway—refining the mind but not attaining a dynamic breakthrough—and teaches that a perfect and spontaneous realization that does not rely on practice is also possible. This difference in emphasis between the Sōtō and Rinzai schools dates back to the Song dynasty in China, when there was much dispute between the two schools.

The practices of *zazen* and *kōan* study are directed toward the inner experience of enlightenment (*satori*); however, they are not necessarily linked with it in a causal relationship. The enlightenment experience can occur without a specific practice of Zen. On the other hand, practice is not to be regarded as futile, even if years of effort do not culminate in the enlightenment experience. Practice is considered worthwhile in itself.

Meditation in the lotus posture. Zazen is not entirely of Zen origin. Its basic form is taken from the Indian tradition of yoga, which covers a wide range of meditation practices. Among the numerous postures (*āsana*) of yoga, the lotus position, regarded as the most perfect posture in yoga, was adopted by the Zen school. The practitioner sits with legs crossed and drawn in, and back perfectly upright. Zen recommends breathing in a natural, rhythmical way with a prolonged exhalation. By shutting out all sense impressions and conscious thinking, the Zen practitioner seeks to attain the highest possible state of mental concentration. What is desired is an objectless meditation, devoid of conceptual thought, that can only be described in negative terms. Meditation is first of all a concentration exercise that calms the body and mind, thus supplying the requisite

conditions for higher states of consciousness.

Zazen can also be said to represent the enlightened state of mind itself. This conception is found particularly in the teachings of Dōgen and his school. The lotus posture is the external sign of enlightenment, just as the Buddha Śākyamuni and all Buddhas sitting in this posture reveal the enlightened Buddha-nature. The Zen disciple possesses Buddha-nature, or rather is the Buddha-nature, which is manifested through sitting.

Kōan study. The study of questions for meditation, *kōan*, began in China, though we can only partially determine the date of origin. The grotesque events, bizarre scenes, exchanges (*mondō*) between master and disciple, paradoxical expressions, and words of wisdom that make up the content of the *kōan* stem from the early period of Chinese Zen. But a *kōan* does not consist only of these elements. We can distinguish three phases in the formation of the *kōan*: first, the recognition that certain events or expressions could assist in awakening an experience and are appropriate for practice; next, the evolving of a method out of the formulated *kōan* questions, which were collected and handed down for practice; and, finally, the differentiation and arrangement into a system.

A *kōan* cannot be solved rationally. The practitioner is obliged to "hold" the *kōan* constantly in mind, day and night. Concentration increases until the tension causes rational thinking to give way under the pressure and a breakthrough occurs. This is the "turn back to the roots of consciousness" that opens the mind to a new way of seeing. Concentration, confrontation with an inescapable situation, and a breakthrough compose the psychological progression in this practice. Because this practice can be traumatic and requires careful monitoring to advance, *kōan* practice cannot be undertaken without the personal guidance of the master in private interviews (*dokusan*).

It was the Japanese master Hakuin who perfected the *kōan* system. His famous *kōan* "What is the sound of one hand clapping?" uniquely displays the paradoxical character of the enlightenment experience: "When you clap your hands together a sound arises. Listen to the sound of one hand."

Enlightenment. Satori is a mystical experience that does not lend itself to definition. The inner experience can only be described and interpreted. Certain characteristics are clearly evident in descriptions of *satori*, and the suddenness of the experience has been set down as one mark of Zen enlightenment. Many accounts of *satori* describe it as a merging or becoming one with the whole universe. Feelings of ecstasy accompany the experience of total unity or oneness. A surging joy—what Buddhists call "dharma rapture"—overcomes the enlightened person who, completely forgetting the self, feels at one with everything. The subjective certainty of such experiences is indubitable; however, when the master acknowledges that the experience is genuine, an immediate awareness of reality has most likely taken place. One who experiences enlightenment is thought to go beyond the trivial self of usual consciousness.

The Zen Movement Today — The numerous writings and lectures in North America and Europe of D. T. Suzuki introduced Zen Buddhism to the Western public and awakened much interest and appreciation

Zen Monks meditating at the Rinzai-sect temple Eihōji, Gifu Prefecture. Zen Buddhism, which stresses meditation and individual experience of enlightenment, has had a profound influence on many aspects of Japanese culture.

for it. Today, scholars in a variety of disciplines carry on the research he began on Zen Buddhism, but perhaps his influence is most strongly felt in the meditation movement of our day.

There are various schools and lineages within Zen Buddhism, and consequently a wide variation in practices. Hybrid forms have developed between schools, and methods are also mixed with those of other branches of Buddhism. Different forms of Zen meditation have found their way to the West, and Zen centers have been established in North America and European countries, especially in Britain, France, and Germany.

Nourished within the great Asian cultures of India and China and reaching maturity in Japan, Zen has found a deep resonance in the West. At a time when technology threatens to dominate the world, Zen awakens a demand among many for spiritual values necessary for human life. ☎ ▣▶1774–1777

Zenchiku Co, Ltd   [株]ゼンチク

(Zenchiku). Wholesaler of domestic and imported meats. Incorporated in 1948. Sales for the fiscal year ending March 1991 totaled ¥247.4 billion (US $1.8 billion), of which imported meat accounted for 52 percent; domestic beef, 19 percent; domestic pork, 19 percent; processed meat, 5 percent; ham and sausage, 3 percent; and other products, 2 percent. The company was capitalized at ¥8.4 billion (US $61.2 million) in the same year. Headquarters are in Tōkyō.

zenga   禅画

(literally, "Zen painting"). A term that is generally understood as an artistic expression of the ZEN spirit, at once simple and profound. It specifically refers to the painting and calligraphy of the great monks of the Edo period (1600–1868). Almost all these monks were Zen masters of the RINZAI SECT, SŌTŌ SECT, or ŌBAKU SECT, but the brushwork of a few monks of non-Zen sects is also considered *zenga*.

Since the Kamakura period (1185–1333), Zen monks had copied Chinese ink paintings of the Song (Sung) dynasty (960–1279), but by the end of the Muromachi period (1333–1568) the Zen artistic tradition was practiced primarily by professional painters. Some were monks attached to Zen temples, but their primary duty was painting. Their principal subject was landscapes, but they also rendered figure studies and BIRD-AND-FLOWER PAINTING, usually in ink on paper.

In the Azuchi-Momoyama period (1568–1600) ink painting of the Zen tradition was overshadowed by sumptuous golden screens, although artists such as KAIHŌ YŪSHŌ were equally adept at both. In the early Edo period Zen themes were treated by profes-

Continued on page 1778 ►

Following the Zen Path

For those who wish to embrace the way of Zen Buddhism, in few places is the training more rigorous than at the mountaintop monastery Eiheiji in Fukui Prefecture. Founded in the 13th century by Dōgen, the first patriarch of the Sōtō school of Zen in Japan, Eiheiji is renowned for the severe discipline practiced there. Each spring 110 to 120 aspiring monks dressed in the robes of pilgrims make their way up the mountain hoping to join the monastic community at Eiheiji. Many of the newcomers are young and just out of school. They must first ask permission to enter the monastery—and are loudly and repeatedly rebuffed by the senior monks. After a ritual series of requests and denials intended to fortify the newcomers' resolve, they are finally allowed to enter the monastery, where far more difficult challenges await them.

Wake-up time, 3:30 AM in summer and 4:30 AM in winter, is announced by a lone monk who runs through the monastery ringing a bell. There follows a brief sequence of signals, played on sounding boards, bells, and drums, which must be closely heeded: the rising monks must wash and arrive at the meditation hall before the sequence ends.

Morning services follow *zazen*. For over an hour those assembled intone passages from Buddhist scripture, their chants penetrating the morning calm, and dedicate their efforts to the benefit of all living beings.

Ceremonial instruments are sounded to mark the time and signal the start of various daily events. Here a monk strikes a fish-shaped drum, announcing the beginning of mealtime.

The trainees must now spend one to two weeks sequestered in the visiting monks' quarters concentrating solely on *zazen*, the meditation regimen that forms the core of Zen spiritual life. Except during short breaks for meals, toilet, chanting, and cleaning, the newcomers must remain seated in the painful cross-legged lotus position from early morning to night, under the watchful eye of a senior monk. Only those able to endure this agonizing initiation may join the community as novices.

Successful trainees scarcely have time for self-congratulation, however. Hours before dawn, the wake-up bell echoes through the monastery, rousing them to the routine discipline of Zen life.

Cleaning, like every other part of daily life, is regarded as a spiritual exercise. Called to work by the sound of a drum, the monks immerse themselves in their chores.

Washing is done in silence. Each monk is allotted one small basin of water and must take care not to waste a drop; washing one's body thus requires spiritual discipline.

Even the toilet has a role to play in the Zen lifestyle. Here, at the entrance to the latrine, a monk bows before an altar dedicated to Uzusama Myōō, a fierce deity who purifies contaminated matter.

Zazen is usually performed twice daily, in the morning and evening. By minimizing external distractions and setting aside conscious thought during meditation, practitioners seek to attain the highest possible state of mental concentration.

Meals, solemnly conducted in strict accordance with monastic rules, are punctuated with chants giving thanks for all forms of sustenance and with vows to help all beings achieve enlightenment.

Bows are exchanged whenever monks meet in the monastery's passageways. As a rule, the monks at Eiheiji greet each other silently.

Work around the monastery includes weeding, cutting branches in the mountain forest, and shoveling snow. The monks strive to maintain an attitude of active meditation in every task they perform.

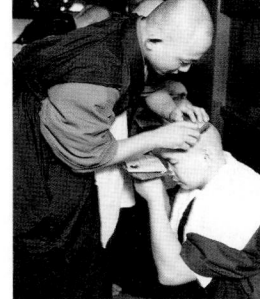

Shaving, sewing, bathing, and other personal chores are done on calendar dates containing the number 4 or 9. Shaving one's head symbolizes the severing of worldly attachments and the dedication of body and mind to the Buddhist path.

The monks beg for alms once a year. The need for charity is a reminder that they depend on the laity, and receiving donations encourages their spiritual pursuits.

Leaving the monastery after several years at Eiheiji, a monk is seen off by a comrade as he passes through the gate on his way back to the outside world. Most departing monks go on to perform religious duties at temples throughout Japan.

Practicing Zazen

A short period of focused meditation each day will make you more attuned to your environment, at home and at work.

Zazen (seated meditation) is for people who have deep questions and don't know where to turn for guidance. If this description fits you, then you have something in common with the Buddha Śākyamuni, the founder of Buddhism, who was born a prince in India more than 2,400 years ago. Tired of diversions, the young prince sought to face his doubts directly. He studied philosophy for many years, practiced austerities for a while, and finally took up the meditation we now call zazen. Seating himself under a bodhi tree, he pondered the question, "Why should there be suffering in the world?" Suddenly he was struck with the realization that all beings are enlightened and unfettered from the beginning but their delusions and preoccupations keep them from testifying to that fact.

Those delusions and preoccupations are the internal monologues of the ordinary mind. If you take up the Buddha's way of zazen, you will encounter them directly. They are like loops of audiotape, playing over and over, distracting you from your questions, and indeed from your family, work, and creative pleasures. So your first task as a Zen student is to quiet your mind.

This is a matter of concentration. It may seem like a daunting task at first. After all, as a Chinese proverb says, "The mind is like a monkey or a wild horse." But concentration does not necessarily require unusual effort. You concentrate well on many occasions in your daily life. When you take an examination, for example, or participate in an important meeting, or play at sports, you forget yourself in your devotion to your task. This natural human talent is the foundation of good zazen. As 20th-century Zen master Yamada Kōun Rōshi said, "The practice of Zen is forgetting the self in the act of uniting with something."

Sitting Positions

The model of zazen is the figure of the Buddha, sitting perfectly erect with his eyes lowered and his feet in his lap. His sitting position, known as the full lotus posture, is the most stable position for zazen. Seated on a cushion, with your knees on a mat before you, place your right foot on your left thigh, and your left foot on your right thigh. This position requires some athletic ability, and many students are never able to achieve it. Don't try to force it, or you may injure yourself. Perhaps hatha-yoga exercises can help you gradually to attain this posture.

The half lotus position is slightly less stable, but not enough to matter. Place your right foot beneath your left thigh, and left foot on your right thigh. This is not nearly as difficult as the full lotus position, but it can be demanding and should not be forced.

Besides the lotus positions, there are other acceptable postures that are less secure but can still be effective. The Burmese style is to sit as though taking a lotus position. Then instead of putting one or both feet in your lap, leave your legs and feet on the mat, one foot placed under the other thigh and the other leg folded in front.

Another position is *seiza* (quiet sitting). Turn your cushion on its edge, and kneel on it with your knees, shins, and feet resting on the mat on each side of the cushion. You can also use a *seiza* bench, a low bench that allows you to kneel but has a firm surface for your backside to rest on and space underneath for your legs and feet.

It is also possible to do zazen in a chair, or even lying down. Do the best you can with what you have and what you are. Angels can do no more.

Avoid sitting with both feet under your thighs in tailor fashion. Your legs will hurt too much after a while, and you will not be able to keep yourself erect without strain. Your lungs will be cramped, and your concentration will suffer.

Keep your eyes about one-third open. Though at first you may want to keep your eyes closed, give the model of the Buddha a good try. You will find that it offers the middle way of concentration between dreaming and visual distraction. Hold your head up and relax your eyes, so that you are looking directly forward—as though seeing through your eyelids.

Keep your hands in your lap with your palms up and your thumbs touching. Your elbows should project a little from your body. This position helps you to maintain a good balance between relaxation and tension.

Breathing

When you first sit down, take a couple of deep breaths and then breathe naturally. Swing right and left on your seat in a wide arc, and a few more times in decreasing arcs. Lean forward and back again to settle yourself.

Now count your breaths. The act of counting is the first intellectual exercise you learned as a child and is deeply embedded in your brain. Counting breaths is a perennial practice that harmonizes body, mind, will, and spirit. Breathing is an instinctive human function, which can, however, be regulated. Thus it is a link between your involuntary, physical system and your conscious will. Breath is spirit—with inspiration you take in the universe; with expiration you release it.

Count one for your inhalation, two for your exhalation, three for the next inhalation, four for the next exhalation, and so on up to ten, and up to ten again. And again.

When you have mastered this form of breath counting, count just your exhalations. Count one for your first exhalation, and keep your mind steady and clear with your inhalation; then count two for the next exhalation and so on up to ten. Most people settle on this practice of counting exhalations only, though a few find that just counting inhalations serves their purposes best. Experiment with different styles, giving each a good try.

You may think that breath-counting sounds simple, but you are likely to find it difficult. Perhaps you are able to reach ten during your first one or two sequences, but then find that you stray easily into thoughts, memories, plans, or fantasies. When you notice that you are straying, simply come back to one. Don't blame yourself for straying.

You might tend to count your breaths to ten while continuing your inner monologue. This quickly gets tiresome. Remember Yamada Rōshi's words. *Uniting* is the practice. Let there be only one in the whole universe, only two in the whole universe, only three.

Full lotus position.

Half lotus position.

Burmese position.

This circular brush stroke is a Zen symbol for the state of enlightenment. Calligraphy by Morinaga Sōkō.

Seiza position.

Using a *seiza* bench.

An alternative approach.

Become completely intimate with each number as it appears. Intimacy is a synonym for realization in Zen texts. When you are intimate, you are *one with*. When you are not intimate, you are in your head.

Practice your zazen for 25 minutes or less, before breakfast or before going to bed, or both. If you wish to sit more, get up after 25 minutes and take a break. Then return to your cushions refreshed.

When your zazen period ends, protect your meditative condition, and rise slowly. If you have been sitting in the lotus position, take hold of your ankle with one hand and your knee with the other. Lift your leg gently and place your foot on the mat before you. Exercise similar caution when getting up from other positions.

A Special Place

Zazen is not casual. It needs its own place, called the *dōjō*, a term derived from the Sanskrit *bodhimaṇḍa*, "place (or spot) of enlightenment"—originally the Buddha's seat under the bodhi tree. You can improvise your own *dōjō* as an alcove in your room, with a picture or figure that is inspiring to you. If you wish, you can add flowers, candles, and incense.

Ordinary pillows will do for your zazen, but it is probably more practical to purchase a *zabuton* and a *zafu*. The *zabuton* is a mat, usually made of black cloth, about 69 cm (27 in) by 84 cm (33 in) in size, stuffed with cotton batting. The *zafu* is a round cushion, about 36 cm (14 in) in diameter, also usually made of black cloth, stuffed with buckwheat hulls or kapok. Put the mat in front of your alcove, and place the cushion on it so that you can sit there and have space on the mat for your knees.

Wear loose-fitting clothing which you can associate with formal practice. When you sit with others, choose clothing that is unpatterned and dark in color. With each person blending in, you and your friends will have a good chance to focus entirely on the practice.

Zazen is not meant to be a form of sensory deprivation. On the contrary, when you are focused and everything else in your mind is quiet, the song of the thrush passes right through. The sound of the wind passes right through. Let your ears be open.

The Buddha himself was enlightened by the Morning Star, and all his daughters and sons are practicing with the many beings of the universe. Every person, animal, and plant is breathing together with you in your focused meditation. When you are thinking something, you are closed off and you don't hear the birds and the wind. When you are focused on each point in your count as it comes along, the birds and the wind all join you.

Yet while zazen is meditation amid sounds in the world, you must still find a way to practice in a reasonably quiet setting. You can't practice zazen, for instance, in a noisy factory. It is for this reason that monasteries are traditionally located in the mountains, where the songs of crickets, frogs, and birds frame the silence.

Sitting with Others

Most people find it difficult to practice zazen alone. This is a problem for lay students, particularly in the West where there aren't enough Zen centers to go around.

To find a zazen companion, try checking with the religion department of your local college. The instructor who teaches Buddhism or world religions might know of someone who is looking for a Zen friend. A discreet card on the bulletin board of your health food store might also bring a call.

Keep in touch with your former teachers as well. Let them encourage you. Visit libraries and bookstores and pick out translations of Zen texts that seem interesting. Treasure your Zen friends, and make up vows that can help keep you going.

If it turns out that sitting alone is your only option, think for a moment of your friends sitting at distant Zen centers. Indeed you are sitting with all beings. People on buses and in waiting rooms are doing zazen in their own ways. The cat and the dog and the birds and the trees are doing zazen in their own ways. You are not really alone at all.

Still, you can find encouragement from established Zen centers. Check one of the published guides to Buddhist organizations, and request brochures from promising Zen centers. Subscribe to their journals and newsletters, and when you can, travel to one of them on your vacation to sit with the members at a *sesshin* (retreat).

Lasting five to seven days, a *sesshin* is devoted entirely to zazen and to Zen instruction. At such a retreat, you will sit, eat, and sleep at the center, arising at 4 AM or earlier and retiring at 9 PM or later. You will have the chance for private interviews with the teacher and will attend his or her daily public talk. Occasional *sesshin*, if only once a year, can inspire your practice and your life.

The word *sesshin* means "to touch the mind." It can also mean to receive or convey the mind. The *sesshin* is a dream of the Buddha Śākyamuni and his disciples. In your mind you settle into a place of profound harmony where, as 13th-century Chinese Zen master Wumen Huikai said, your eyebrows are entangled with those of your ancestral teachers. This is not an idle notion, but a religious experience, called *makyō*, ("uncanny dimension"). Seated there on your cushions, you might find yourself in a dream of an ancient ritual. You yourself might be the central figure of the ritual and feel confirmed by it. You might even envision yourself as the Buddha, or the bodhisattva Kannon. Such experiences can be very encouraging, and you might be tempted to regard them as "the ultimate." They are not. What they represent is the promise of realization to come. Accept them as milestones on your path, and press on.

There are certain pitfalls to be mindful of. Treating *makyō* as an end-all achievement is one such pitfall. Another is the act of stepping back from the difficulties of zazen practice. You might feel that you are not up to the task. Or you might blame the task itself. Still another pitfall, known well in Christianity and other religions, is the "dark night of the soul," in which everything seems barren and tasteless, and faith in oneself and in the practice disappears completely. I wonder how many people have discontinued zazen with such feelings of discouragement. It is important to treat bleak experiences as another part of the path. They are no less a milestone than the deep dream that places you front and center in Buddhist cosmology. Nothing is static. Hang in there. Let your feelings of despair prompt you, as the birds and the wind prompt you, to stay with your practice.

You are the avatar of the Buddha, as all your ancestors assure you. Zazen is the way they followed to their deep realization, and the way you can follow as well.

Robert Aitken

zenga Titled *Circle, Triangle, Square*, this is one of the best-known works of the Zen monk Sengai Gibon, the most original of the later *zenga* artists. Early 19th century. Ink on paper. 28 × 48 cm. Idemitsu Art Gallery, Tōkyō.

— *Continued from page 1773*

sional artists of the KANŌ SCHOOL, but these works lack the vitality and spontaneity of those of the great monks of the age.

Much of the flowering of true *zenga* must be associated with calligraphy. While the monks' spontaneous ink works were largely free of excessive reliance upon painting traditions, they were at the same time disciplined by calligraphic mastery of brush and ink. The TEA CEREMONY, at which an appropriate scroll would be hung in the TOKONOMA, also helped stimulate Zen painting. The works of such notable abbots as TAKUAN SŌHŌ and Kōgetsu Sōgan (1570–1643) were considered ideal for viewing during the tea ceremony. The blossoming of Zen painting was spurred by the arrival in Japan of much of the Chinese Huangbo (Huang-po; J: Ōbaku) sect in the mid-17th century. Many Ōbaku monks were poets, seal carvers, painters, and calligraphers. The chief factor in the rise of *zenga*, however, was the interest of the great Zen monks such as HAKUIN in communicating directly through brush and ink. The most original of later *zenga* artists was SENGAI GIBON, whose delightful humor is typical of much *zenga*. See also BUDDHIST ART; INK PAINTING; CALLIGRAPHY.

Zengakuren 全学連

(Abbreviation of Zen Nihon Gakusei Jichikai Sōrengō; All-Japan Federation of Student Self-Governing Associations). National organization of Japanese university student-government groups, founded on 18 September 1948, that developed into the primary organizational vehicle of Japan's powerful left-wing STUDENT MOVEMENT.

The Zengakuren was founded by student members of the JAPAN COMMUNIST PARTY (JCP), and for a decade its activities were closely coordinated with official JCP policy. A turning point came in 1958, when anti-JCP activists coalesced into the Communist League (nicknamed the "Bund") and seized control of the Zengakuren—the origin of the so-called New Left in Japan.

The Zengakuren was dominated by the Bund through the Security Treaty Crisis of 1960 (see UNITED STATES–JAPAN SECURITY TREATIES) but then splintered into several rival factions. Pro-JCP elements formed the MINSEI Zengakuren; the anti-JCP New Left forces fragmented into a number of rival groups such as Kakumaru, Chūkaku, and Kaihō Dōmei. These factions played a key role in the UNIVERSITY UPHEAVALS OF 1968–1969 but in-

creasingly turned against each other in a series of bloody interfactional disputes that also spawned the terrorist RED ARMY FACTION. Since that time radical student politics have increasingly lost momentum and support, and the Zengakuren has reverted to its original role as an association of student government organizations.

Zenitaka Corporation [株]銭高組

(Zenitaka-Gumi). General construction company. Incorporated in 1931. With extensive participation in urban development, housing projects, and road and bridge construction, sales are well distributed between the public and private sectors. Sales for the fiscal year ending March 1991 totaled ¥298.9 billion (US $2.2 billion), and the company was capitalized at ¥3.7 billion (US $27.0 million). Headquarters are in Ōsaka.

Zeniya Gohei 銭屋五兵衛

(1773–1852). Wealthy merchant-trader of the Edo period (1600–1868); born in Kaga Province (now Ishikawa Prefecture), where his family had a money-changing business, hence the name Zeniya ("money shop"). Gohei established a lucrative business transporting goods on the new sea routes connecting Ezo (now Hokkaidō) and Aizu (now Fukushima Prefecture) with the major ports of Japan. About 1830 he received a license to act as trade agent for the Kaga domain, and, working closely with Okumura Hidezane (dates unknown) and other high Kaga officials, he reaped huge profits. At his peak Gohei is said to have owned 20 large ships, as well as numerous smaller vessels. In his later years Gohei fell from grace, having failed in a project to reclaim the Kahoku marshes; all of his assets were confiscated, and he was thrown into prison, where he died.

zeniza → kinza, ginza, and zeniza

Zenkōji 善光寺

Buddhist temple in the city of Nagano, Nagano Prefecture; affiliated with both the TENDAI SECT and JŌDO SECT of Buddhism. Its principal object of worship, the Ikkō Sanzon (the Buddha Amida flanked by two bodhisattvas), allegedly was the first Buddhist image to arrive in Japan (552). In 585, because of the MONONOBE FAMILY's suppression of Buddhism, the image was cast into the sea. According to legend, it was retrieved by one Honda Yoshimitsu (another reading of Yoshimitsu is Zenkō, hence the temple's name), who brought it to his home in Nagano, where Zenkōji was built in 642 to house the image. The Amida statue, renowned for miraculous

powers, was installed temporarily in various temples, including Shin Zenkōji (New Zenkōji) in Kai Province (now Yamanashi Prefecture), built in 1568 by TAKEDA SHINGEN. It subsequently was in the possession of ODA NOBUNAGA and, later, TOYOTOMI HIDEYOSHI, until 1598, when Hideyoshi returned it to Zenkōji. The main hall (*kondō*) of Zenkōji dates from the reconstruction of 1707 and has been designated a National Treasure. There are now 62 temples named Zenkōji and many more copies of the main images scattered throughout Japan—evidence of the enormous popularity of the Zenkōji cult.

Zenkōjidaira → Nagano Basin

Zenkunen no Eki → Earlier Nine Years' War

Zen Nihon Bukkyō Kai 全日本仏教会

(Japan Buddhist Federation). Formed in 1954 through the unification of the Nihon Bukkyō Rengōkai (Japan Buddhist League), Sekai Bukkyōto Nihon Remmei (World Fellowship of Buddhists, Japan Center), and prefectural Buddhist associations for the purpose of coordinating Japanese Buddhist activities. Ōtani Kōchō (b 1903) served as its first president. To advance the aims of supporting Buddhist activities in Japan and promoting international cultural contacts through Buddhism, the federation holds an annual national convention and participates in the biennial congress of the World Fellowship of Buddhists.

Zen no kenkyū 善の研究

(tr *A Study of Good*, 1960). The first major work of NISHIDA KITARŌ (1870–1945), the most prominent modern Japanese philosopher. Published in 1911, the book comprised four essays: "Pure Experience," "Reality," "Good," and "Religion." Nishida developed his ideas for the work while teaching at the Fourth Higher School in Kanazawa and conducting a rigorous personal discipline of Zen meditation. Although the title of the work would indicate that Nishida's main concern is with ethics, actually the first of the essays, "Pure Experience," constitutes the kernel of Nishida's thought. He sought in "pure experience" that which was prior to the separation or opposition of subject and object, mind and body, and spirit and matter. From this "pure experience" as the basis, he attempted to deduce the principles underlying epistemology, ethics, and religion.

Zenrinkoku hōki 善隣国宝記

(Precious Record of Friendly Relations with Neighboring Countries). Three-volume collection of documents concerning Japanese diplomatic and religious contacts with China and Korea during the Muromachi period (1333–1568). It was compiled in 1470 with commentaries by Zuikei Shūhō (1391–1473), an adviser to the shōgun, ASHIKAGA YOSHIMASA (r 1449–74).

Zenrōren 全労連

(abbreviation for Zenkoku Rōdō Kumiai Sōrengō; National Confederation of Trade Unions). National federation of trade unions aligned with the JAPAN COMMUNIST PARTY; formed in 1989 when its predecessor, Tōitsu Rōsokon (Conference of Trade Unions for a United Front), was joined by unions formerly affiliated with SŌHYŌ (General Council of Trade Unions of Japan), which disbanded at that time. Tōitsu Rōsokon was formed in 1974 by a number of unions opposed to moves to create a unified national labor organization. Beginning in 1983 it campaigned against the proposed creation of RENGŌ (Japanese Trade Union Confederation) as well as against the prospect of Sōhyō's joining such an organization. In 1987, when Rengō was formed, Tōitsu Rōsokon set out to build its own "working-class-based national labor center" in opposition. This led to the creation of Zenrōren, which in 1990 claimed to have 1.4 million members in 41 regional divisions and 27 industry unions.

Zensen Dōmei　　ゼンセン同盟

(Japan Federation of Textile Industry Workers' Unions). Formed in 1946 as a federation of textile workers' unions, recently it has expanded to include distribution, retail, and consumer-product manufacturing unions. Zensen Dōmei was a member of Dōmei (Japanese Confederation of Labor) until that organization disbanded in 1987. It then joined RENGŌ (Japanese Trade Union Confederation). Zensen Dōmei had 530,000 members in 1989. It has been a leader of the right-wing sector of Japanese labor since the end of World War II. A member of the International Confederation of Free Trade Unions through Rengō, it is also affiliated with the International Textile, Garment, and Leather Workers' Federation.

Zenshinza　　前進座

Theatrical company, left-wing in ideology, founded in 1931 by KABUKI actors, such as Kawarasaki Chōjūrō II (1902–81) and Nakamura Kan'emon III (1901–82), and a number of SHINGEKI actors. The kabuki actors in particular were profoundly dissatisfied with the hierarchical and highly commercialized organization of the kabuki theater. The principles of equality enunciated at the founding meeting of Zenshinza, however, soon proved impossible to sustain in the theatrical world of the early 1930s. Financial stability was assured by stage productions (and later film versions) of classical kabuki plays, many of which received high critical praise. Zenshinza's activities during the rest of the 1930s may be divided into four parts: kabuki, *shingeki* (mainly historical plays), *taishūgeki* (popular drama), and films. Despite a number of defections over ideological differences in the late 1930s, Zenshinza managed to continue performing during World War II and in the difficult postwar years promoted its very successful Youth Theater Movement (Seinen Gekijō Undō). In 1949 the Zenshinza members decided to join the Japan Communist Party. Subsequent performances on tour were often linked with appearances at political demonstrations. During the 1960s and 1970s Zenshinza concentrated on productions of classical kabuki. It initiated several new projects (including "study" productions of CHIKAMATSU MONZAEMON dramas) and appeared often on television.

Zentsūji　　善通寺［市］

City in Kagawa Prefecture, Shikoku. The birthplace of KŪKAI, the founder of the Shingon sect of Buddhism, it developed as a temple town. It was the site of an imperial army base from 1896 through World War II. Pop: 38,423.

Zentsūji　　善通寺

Head temple of the Zentsūji branch of the SHINGON SECT of Buddhism, located in the city of Zentsūji, Kagawa Prefecture. The oldest Shingon temple, it was allegedly built in 806

by KŪKAI, the sect's founder, and was destroyed in several fires. Its 17th-century *kondō* (main hall) and *mieidō* (portrait hall) house a statue of Yakushi Nyorai (Skt: Bhaiṣajyaguru; the Buddha of healing) and a portrait of Kūkai, respectively. In 1931 Zentsūji became the head temple of the Ono branch of Shingon, from that time called the Zentsūji branch. The temple is one of Shingon's three sacred places, along with KŌYASAN and TŌJI, and is 1 of 88 temples associated with Kūkai in Shikoku (see PILGRIMAGES). The Zentsūji branch claimed about 295,000 followers in 1989.

Zero Fighter　　零戦

(Zerosen). Principal fighter plane of the Imperial Japanese Navy in World War II. In 1937 Mitsubishi Heavy Industries was entrusted with the development of a fighter plane that could be used on aircraft carriers. The plane was officially adopted in July 1940 and designated the Reishiki Kanjō Sentōki (Zero-type Carrier-based Fighter), or Zerosen for short. Its maximum range of 420 nautical miles was extraordinary for that era. A modified version was used at the beginning of the Pacific War; the power of its 20-millimeter (0.8-in) machine guns and its long cruising range initially brought great strategic advantages, but from 1942 onward, it was overtaken by such American fighters as the P-38, F4U, F6F, and P-51. Toward the end of the war the Zerosen was used to carry out dive-bombing attacks and suicide missions (see KAMIKAZE SPECIAL ATTACK FORCE). Nearly 10,400 were produced during the war.

Zexel Corporation　　［株］ゼクセル

(Zekuseru). Formerly Diesel Kiki Co, Ltd. Automobile parts maker producing diesel-engine fuel pumps, automobile air conditioners and heaters, and automobile electronic systems. It dominates the market for diesel fuel pumps in Japan. It was incorporated in 1939 with capital provided by MITSUBISHI HEAVY INDUSTRIES, LTD, Tōkyō Jidōsha Kōgyō (now ISUZU MOTORS, LTD), and other major engine makers. It has technical tie-ups with Bosch of Germany and the Bendix Corporation of the United States. Annual sales for the fiscal year ending March 1991 totaled ¥258.7 billion (US $1.9 billion), and the company was capitalized at ¥20.9 billion (US $152.3 million) in the same year. Headquarters are in Tōkyō.

Zhanggufeng (Chang-ku-feng) Incident　　張鼓峰事件

(J: Chōkohō Jiken). A clash in July 1938 between Russian and Japanese armies on the boundary of the Japanese puppet state of MANCHUKUO (Manchuria) and Russian Siberia. This incident, in which Japan gave up the hill Zhanggufeng to the Russians, and the NOMONHAN INCIDENT of 1939 led Japan to shift its strategic orientation from Northeast Asia to Southeast Asia (see SOUTHERN EXPANSION DOCTRINE) after 1941.

Zhang Xueliang (Chang Hsüeh-liang)　　張学良

(1898–　; J: Chō Gakuryō). Manchurian leader; known as the Young Marshal. Eldest son of ZHANG ZUOLIN (Chang Tso-lin), the Chinese warlord based in Manchuria. Zhang succeeded to the leadership of Manchuria after his father's assassination in 1928. Despite Japanese warnings not to subordinate Manchuria to the Nationalist government at Nanjing (Nanking), Zhang pledged allegiance to it and cooperated with CHIANG KAI-

SHEK to weaken the Japanese position in Manchuria. His actions were one cause of the MANCHURIAN INCIDENT of 1931.

Zhang gradually became convinced that the anticommunist struggle was not in China's interest and that all Chinese should unite to resist Japan. In December 1936 he seized Chiang Kai-shek and forced him to meet with the Chinese Communist Party (see XI'AN [SIAN] INCIDENT). Although he agreed to end his nonresistance policy, Chiang Kai-shek imprisoned Zhang. When the Nationalists fled to Taiwan in 1949, they took Zhang with them. He was formally freed in 1961.

Zhang Ziping (Chang Tzu-p'ing)　　張資平

(1895–?; J: Chō Shihei). Chinese writer of modern, popular romantic fiction who, during the SINO-JAPANESE WAR OF 1937–1945, served in the Japanese-sponsored, collaborationist government of WANG JINGWEI (Wang Ching-wei). Zhang went to Japan in 1912 and received a degree in geology from Tōkyō University in 1922. After his return to China he wrote, taught geology and literature, and engaged in business ventures. Following Japan's defeat in World War II, in 1947 Zhang was arrested and tried by the Guomindang (Kuomintang; Nationalist Party) government for his cooperation with Wang's collaborationist reorganized government (1940–45; see REORGANIZED NATIONAL GOVERNMENT OF THE REPUBLIC OF CHINA). The outcome of his trial is unknown. His works include *Qunxing luanfei* (Ch'ün-hsing luan-fei; 1931) and *Ziping zizhuan* (Tzu-p'ing tzu-chuan; 1934).

Zenkōji The main hall of the temple Zenkōji. Dating from the reconstruction of 1707, this building is a rarity in traditional Japanese architecture, as its depth (54 m) exceeds its width (24 m). National Treasure.

Zero Fighter The range and maneuverability of the Zero made it the mainstay of Japan's naval air forces and one of the most famous fighter planes of World War II.

Zhang Ziping (Chang Tzu-p'ing)

zōni This traditional New Year's soup, which features *mochi*, appears during the holiday season in a number of regional variations.

Zhang Zuolin (Chang Tso-lin)
張作霖

(1873–1928; J: Chō Sakurin). Chinese warlord who ruled Manchuria from 1920 until his assassination in June 1928. Father of ZHANG XUELIANG (Chang Hsüeh-liang). After 1920 the Japanese government provided continuing aid to Zhang to help him preserve order and promote Japanese interests in Manchuria. Japan intervened to assure the defeat of an attempt by GUO SONGLING (Kuo Sung-ling) to overthrow Zhang in 1925. At the same time, Japanese military and political leaders warned Zhang against involvement in Beijing (Peking) political struggles, for fear of adverse effects on Manchurian stability.

In 1928, when CHIANG KAI-SHEK's armies were pushing north to drive Zhang from power, Japanese officials in Manchuria and the TANAKA GIICHI government in Tōkyō disagreed over how best to protect and strengthen Japanese interests in Manchuria. In late May 1928 Prime Minister Tanaka ruled against military intervention. That decision so incensed some extremist military officers in Manchuria that they decided to assassinate Zhang and exploit the subsequent turmoil to Japan's advantage. Colonel Kōmoto Daisaku (1882–1955), a staff officer in the GUANDONG (KWANTUNG) ARMY, organized a plot to blow up Zhang's train as it was returning to Mukden (now Shenyang) on 4 June. Zhang died a few days later.

Zheng Chenggong (Cheng Ch'eng-kung)
鄭成功

(1624–62; J: Tei Seikō). Chinese warlord loyal to the Ming dynasty (1368–1644) of China after its fall to the Qing (Ch'ing) in 1644. Known to Westerners as Coxinga or Koxinga. His father was a Chinese maritime warlord named Zheng Zhilong (Cheng Chihlung), and his mother was a Japanese woman from the island of Hirado (in what is now Nagasaki Prefecture). Zheng was born on Hirado but soon joined his father in China. Seeking to restore the Ming dynasty, Zheng made an unsuccessful attempt to capture Nanjing (Nanking) in 1659 and then established a base on Taiwan, from which he continued to mount attacks on mainland China. Zheng is better known to Japanese as Kokusen'ya (Ch: Guo Xingye or Kuo Hsingyeh). He is the hero of CHIKAMATSU MONZAEMON's play *Kokusen'ya kassen* (1715; tr *The Battles of Coxinga*, 1951).

Zheng Xiaoxu (Cheng Hsiao-hsü)
鄭孝胥

(1860–1938; J: Tei Kōsho). Chinese official with intense loyalty to the Manchu Qing (Ch'ing) dynasty (1644–1912). From 1932 to 1935 he served as premier in the restoration of the last Qing emperor, PUYI (P'u-i), in the puppet state of MANCHUKUO.

From 1891 to 1894 Zheng served in Qing-dynasty consulates at Tōkyō, Kōbe, and Ōsaka. In 1923 he joined Puyi, who had been deposed in 1912, and helped arrange his flight from warlord-dominated Beijing (Peking) to the Japanese settlement in Tianjin (Tientsin). In 1931 Japan began negotiations with Puyi for the establishment of an independent Manchu state. In November 1931 Zheng went secretly with Puyi to Port Arthur (Ch: Lüshun; now part of Lüda) in Japanese-controlled Guandong (Kwantung). Puyi became chief executive of Manchukuo on 9 March 1932. During his tenure as premier, Zheng often disagreed with the Japanese, who maintained control of the Manchukuo government, and he resigned in May 1935.

Zhong Gui (Chung Kuei)→Shō Ki

Zhou Enlai (Chou En-lai)
周恩来

(1898–1976; J: Shū Onrai). Chinese communist leader. A native of Shaoxing (Shaohsing), Zhejiang (Chekiang) Province. He studied at Japan's Waseda University and then Kyōto University. After the nationalist demonstrations against Japan in the MAY FOURTH MOVEMENT of 1919, Zhou returned to China. In the winter of 1919–20 he joined a Marxist discussion group of which MAO ZEDONG (Mao Tse-tung) was also a member. In 1920 Zhou was imprisoned for his part in an anti-Japanese demonstration. Upon his release he left for France and devoted himself to the European operations of the Chinese Communist Party.

In 1924 Zhou returned to China. The communists were then working closely with SUN YAT-SEN and the Guomindang (Kuomintang; KMT; Nationalist Party). Zhou was appointed deputy political director of the Huangpu (Whampoa) Military Academy, which CHIANG KAI-SHEK directed.

After Chiang's attack on the communists Zhou went underground, emerging among the top leadership of the Jiangxi (Kiangsi) Soviet in the early 1930s. In 1934–35 Zhou took part in the Long March to Yan'an (Yenan). In 1937 he helped to forge a new alliance with the KMT, and served as the principal communist liaison to the wartime nationalist capital of Chongqing (Chungking) during the war against Japan. Following the communist victory in 1949 Zhou served as premier of the People's Republic of China until his death.

Zhou Hongqing (Chou Hung-ch'ing) Incident
周鴻慶事件

(J: Shū Kōkei Jiken). Diplomatic crisis between Japan and the Republic of China (Taiwan) begun in October 1963 when Zhou Hongqing, an interpreter for a delegation of industrial officials from the People's Republic of China touring Japan, sought asylum in the Soviet embassy in Tōkyō. He was handed over to Japanese authorities, to whom he expressed a desire to go to Taiwan. He then changed his mind, first seeking to stay in Japan and later asking to be sent back to the People's Republic of China. The Japanese returned him to the People's Republic in January 1964 despite a protest by Taiwan that Japan had acted against Zhou's will. Taiwan temporarily recalled all staff officers from its Tōkyō embassy and canceled governmental procurement contracts in Japan.

Zhou Zuoren (Chou Tso-jen)
周作人

(1885–1966; J: Shū Sakujin). Modern Chinese essayist, scholar, and translator. Zhou Zuoren joined his brother LU XUN (Lu Hsün) in literary activities in Japan and China and, during the SINO-JAPANESE WAR OF 1937–1945, held educational posts under the Japanese puppet governments in North China.

In 1906 Zhou Zuoren went to Japan, where he studied Western and Japanese literature at Rikkyō University and, with Lu Xun and others, studied under the Chinese scholar-revolutionary Zhang Binglin (Chang Ping-lin; 1868–1936). Zhou returned to China in 1911. He taught at various universities and continued to translate and write. Zhou remained in North China after its fall to Japan in the Sino-Japanese War, becoming chancellor at Beijing (Peking) University in 1939 and minister of education in the collaborationist government of WANG JINGWEI (Wang Ching-wei) in 1940. After his trial on a charge of treason following Japan's defeat in 1945, Zhou's death sentence was commuted to imprisonment; in 1949 he was pardoned and released.

Zhu Xi (Chu Hsi) school→
Shushigaku

Zōjōji
増上寺

High-ranking temple of the JŌDO SECT of Buddhism, located in Minato Ward, Tōkyō. Originally known as Kōmyōji, it presumably was established by Shūei (809–884), a disciple of KŪKAI, founder of the Shingon sect. In 1393 Zōjōji was switched to a Jōdo affiliation by the converted abbot Shōsō (1366–1440). Throughout the Edo period (1600–1868) Zōjōji enjoyed great prestige from its status as the Tokugawa shogunate's family temple and burial ground. The temple declined after the Meiji Restoration in 1868 and suffered extensive damage during the 1945 air raids. The reconstruction of Zōjōji on a smaller scale was completed in 1974.

zōkibayashi
雑木林

Deciduous thickets that consist mainly of *konara* (*Quercus serrata*) and *kunugi* (*Quercus acutissima*). *Zōkibayashi* grow in low-altitude regions, often surrounding farm fields and houses and functioning as windbreaks. They also provide fallen leaves for compost, wood for making charcoal, and firewood. Formerly, *zōkibayashi* were periodically cut and regenerated with young offshoots from the original main stock, providing a picturesque forest landscape. The *zōkibayashi* of the MUSASHINO PLATEAU in Tōkyō Prefecture are especially well known. Recently, however, *zōkibayashi* have been neglected, and many have been destroyed by rapid urbanization. If neglected over a long period of time, the deciduous *zōkibayashi* will gradually be overrun by evergreens and other plants.

zōni
雑煮

Traditional New Year's soup, the principal ingredient of which is MOCHI (rice cake). *Mochi* has long been thought to bring good fortune, and *zōni* is the most auspicious food eaten at New Year's. The custom of eating *zōni* is thought to have originated in the 15th century and was considered a ritual partaking of food with the gods, to whom it was also offered. In the Kantō region (east-central Honshū), *zōni* is customarily made by adding a grilled square of *mochi* to clear soup (*sumashijiru*); other ingredients include chicken, KAMABOKO (steamed fish paste), shrimp, and leafy greens. In the Kansai region (Kyōto-Ōsaka-Kōbe), boiled round *mochi* as well as yam, burdock, and other ingredients are added to a soup made with white MISO.

zoological gardens 動物園

(*dōbutsuen*). In 1990 there were 95 zoological gardens in Japan. Over 50 of these zoos housed 100 or more species of animals. The oldest Japanese zoo is the UENO ZOOLOGICAL GARDENS, established in Tōkyō in 1882; it houses over 400 species of animals. The Higashiyama Zoo in Nagoya, another well-known zoo, houses over 500 species of animals. The TAMA ZOOLOGICAL PARK, in Tōkyō Prefecture, was one of the first natural-habitat zoos in Japan. The JAPAN MONKEY CENTER, in Aichi Prefecture, operates a special zoo that houses only monkeys and apes.

zōri 草履

A kind of thonged sandals. *Zōri* have been used widely in Japan for at least a millennium. Today they are still regarded as the most appropriate footwear for use with KIMONO. Women's *zōri* consist of a wedged sole covered with leather, cloth, or vinyl and thongs made of the same material. Those used by men are covered with the same woven rush material as *tatami* mats, with cloth or leather thongs, and are commonly called *setta*. See also FOOTGEAR, TRADITIONAL.

Zōsen Gigoku → Shipbuilding Scandal of 1954

zōshiki 雑色

1. General term for low-ranking hereditary occupational groups under the RITSURYŌ SYSTEM of administration instituted in the late 7th century. In a narrower sense *zōshiki* referred to the *tomobe* (servants of the imperial family) and the *zakko* (or *zōko*; skilled craftsmen). These were considered the lowest strata of the free commoners (RYŌMIN). With the breakdown of the *ritsuryō* system, most were absorbed into private estates (SHŌEN; see also SEMMIN).

2. Under the Kamakura (1192–1333) and Muromachi (1338–1573) shogunates the lowest class of *banshū* (swordsmen) were called *zōshiki*.

3. From the end of the Muromachi period through the Edo period (1600–1868) the term *zōshiki* was applied to a semiofficial organization that assisted the shōgun's Kyōto deputy (KYŌTO SHOSHIDAI) with the administration, police duties, and judicial matters of Kyōto.

zōsui 雑炊

In Japanese cooking, a kind of gruel made by simmering cooked white rice in seasoned *dashi* (stock) with one or more additional ingredients, such as chicken, shrimp, and mushrooms. *Zōsui* is sometimes flavored with MISO (bean paste). Beaten eggs may also be added to hot *zōsui* immediately before serving.

Zou Taofen (Tsou T'ao-fen) 鄒韜奮

(1895–1944; J: Sū Tōfun). Chinese journalist. Editor (1926–33) of the *Shenghuo zhoukan* (*Sheng-huo chou-k'an*; Life Weekly) in Shanghai, civil liberties advocate, and a leader of the NATIONAL SALVATION ASSOCIATION for unified Chinese resistance to Japanese aggression in China. Zou urged opposition to Japan after the 1931 MANCHURIAN INCIDENT,

criticizing the conciliatory policy of the Guomindang (Kuomintang; Nationalist Party) government under CHIANG KAI-SHEK. The Guomindang closed Zou's *Shenghuo zhoukan* in 1933.

Zou was arrested by the Guomindang in 1936 and held until the war with Japan began in July 1937, after which the official Guomindang policy also became one of resistance to Japan. Zou moved to Chongqing (Chungking) with the Guomindang government, but press censorship forced him to flee to Hong Kong in 1941. When that city fell to Japan, he went to communist-held Jiangsu (Kiangsu), where he continued to advocate united resistance to Japan and the establishment of a democratic government in China.

zuihitsu 随筆

(random jottings; literally, "following the brush"). An important Japanese literary genre. A *zuihitsu* is typically a random essay or loose collection of jottings with no clear structure other than association of ideas; written on the spur of the moment to express the author's thoughts on such subjects as people, nature, and art. Personal in nature, the *zuihitsu* discloses the unembellished, individual character of its author. The *zuihitsu*, along with NIKKI BUNGAKU, or diary literature, occupies an important position in Japanese literary history.

The first collection of *zuihitsu* to be recognized as a work of literature was the MAKURA NO SŌSHI (tr *The Pillow Book of Sei Shōnagon*, 1967) of the late-10th-century court lady SEI SHŌNAGON, considered one of the three masterworks in the genre together with the *Hōjōki* (1212; tr *The Ten-Foot Square Hut*, 1928) by KAMO NO CHŌMEI and the *Tsurezuregusa* (ca 1330; tr *Essays in Idleness*, 1967) by YOSHIDA KENKŌ. In the Edo period (1600–1868) it became customary for scholars of the Chinese or Japanese classics and for poets to write *zuihitsu*; the Confucian scholar MURO KYŪSŌ, the scholar of native literature MOTOORI NORINAGA, the poet YOKOI YAYŪ, and the political reformer MATSUDAIRA SADANOBU resorted to the genre. In the modern era not only literati but also scientists and journalists have written in the plastic and evocative style of the *zuihitsu*.

Zuisenji 瑞泉寺

Temple in the city of Kamakura, Kanagawa Prefecture, belonging to the ENGAKUJI branch of the RINZAI SECT of ZEN Buddhism. Regarded as one of the 10 major Rinzai monasteries in eastern Japan, Zuisenji was founded in 1327 by MUSŌ SOSEKI, a distinguished Zen monk, and was richly patronized by the Ashikaga family, beginning with the military leader Ashikaga Motouji (1340–67). The temple is

noted for its superb garden, which is said to have been designed by Musō Soseki. A statue of him, carved from a single block of wood, is one of the temple's many treasures.

zuryō 受領

Resident provincial administrators or deputy governors in the latter half of the HEIAN PERIOD (794–1185) who carried out administrative duties while titular governors (*yōnin kokushi*; see KOKUSHI) remained in the capital. As the RITSURYŌ SYSTEM of government broke down and members of the FUJIWARA FAMILY monopolized the higher posts, lower-ranking nobles competed for appointment as *zuryō*. They were able to enrich themselves through taxation, and the word *zuryō* (which is often translated as "tax manager," though it originally meant "receiver of administration") acquired strong connotations of avarice and greed. Some *zuryō* purchased renewal of their appointments (*chōnin*) or returned to the capital wealthy; others remained as provincial magnates, often becoming leaders of warrior bands (BUSHIDAN). With the appointment to the provinces of SHUGO ("constables," later military governors) by the KAMAKURA SHOGUNATE (1192–1333), the *zuryō* were shorn of their power.

Zushi 逗子[市]

City in southeastern Kanagawa Prefecture, central Honshū. On the western coast of scenic Miura Peninsula and convenient to Tōkyō, Zushi has long been a residential and resort town. It is the setting for several works by TOKUTOMI ROKA. Pop: 56,704.

Zushoryō 図書寮

(Bureau of Books and Charts). Also known as Toshoryō. Archival library created under the TAIHŌ CODE of 701; the earliest known official archive in Japan. The Zushoryō preserved the records of the eight ministries of the imperial government and was nominally responsible for compiling the official histories of Japan (see RIKKOKUSHI). It served also as a general secretariat—a selecting, compiling, and copying agency—for the Ministry of Central Imperial Affairs (Nakatsukasashō), to which it was attached.

The functions of the Zushoryō were greatly reduced during the period of warrior rule (1192–1868), but the bureau was revived in 1884 under the restored Imperial Household Ministry (Kunaishō). After World War II, the Zushoryō was merged with the Bureau of Imperial Mausolea (Shoryōryō) to form the ARCHIVES AND MAUSOLEA DEPARTMENT, IMPERIAL HOUSEHOLD AGENCY.

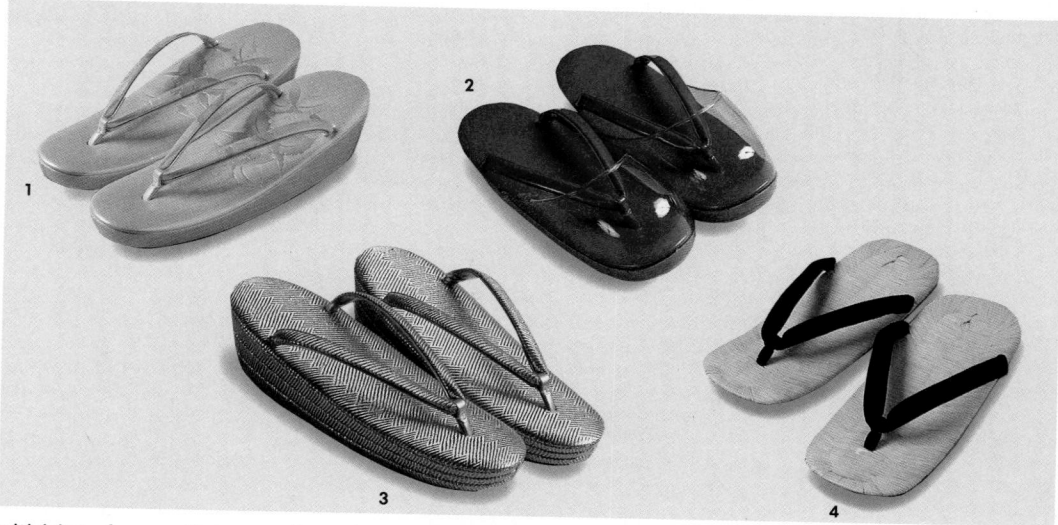

zōri

1 These women's leather *zōri* would be worn with a matching handbag for a stylish look.

2 Women's *zōri* for inclement weather. The shoes have cork and rubber soles and a plastic shield over the toes.

3 A pair of women's silk brocade *zōri* for formal wear. The fabric is known as Saga nishiki.

4 A pair of setta, or *zōri* for men. The sole is generally covered with leather, and a metal fitting at the back protects the heel.

1782

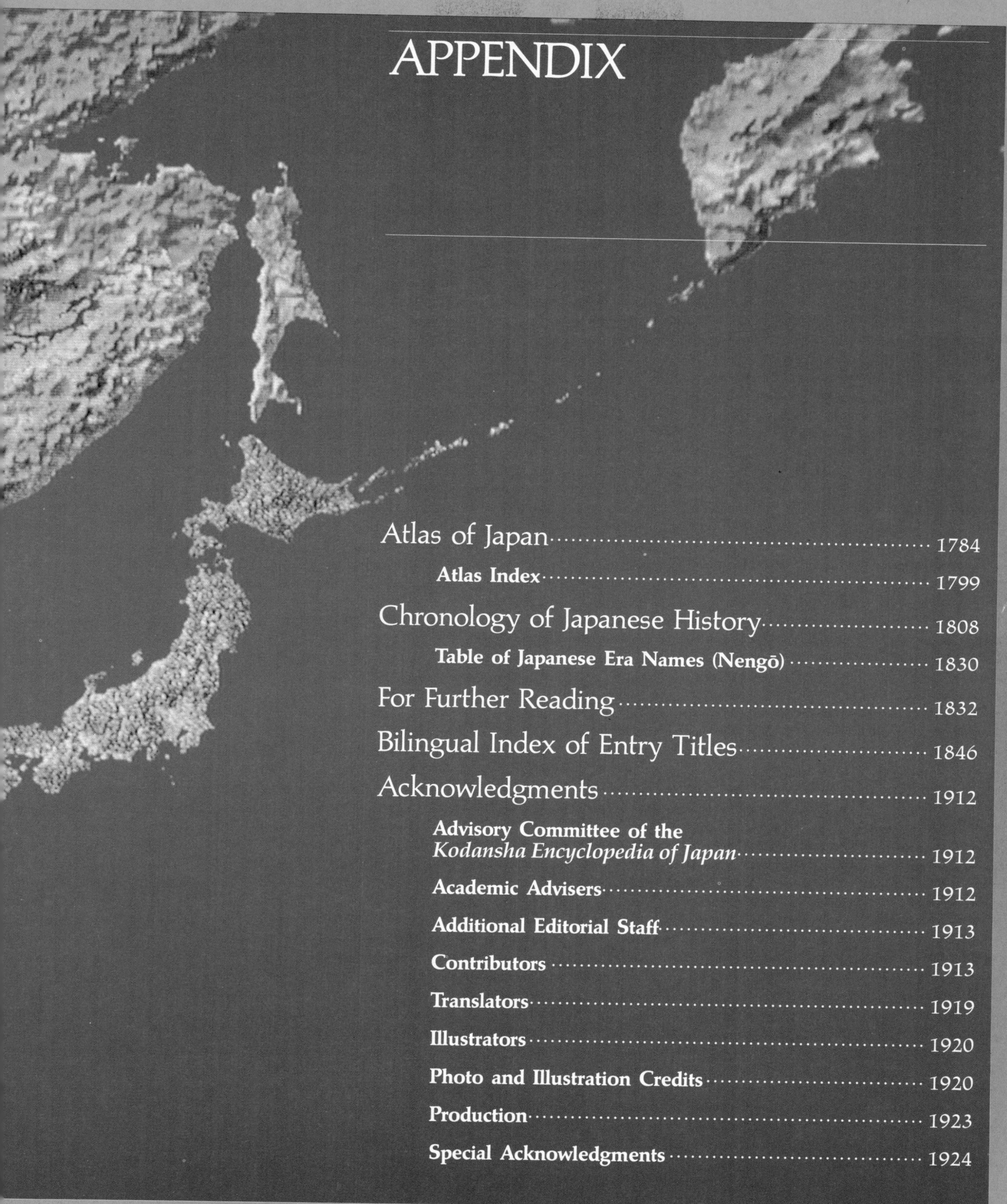

APPENDIX

ATLAS OF JAPAN

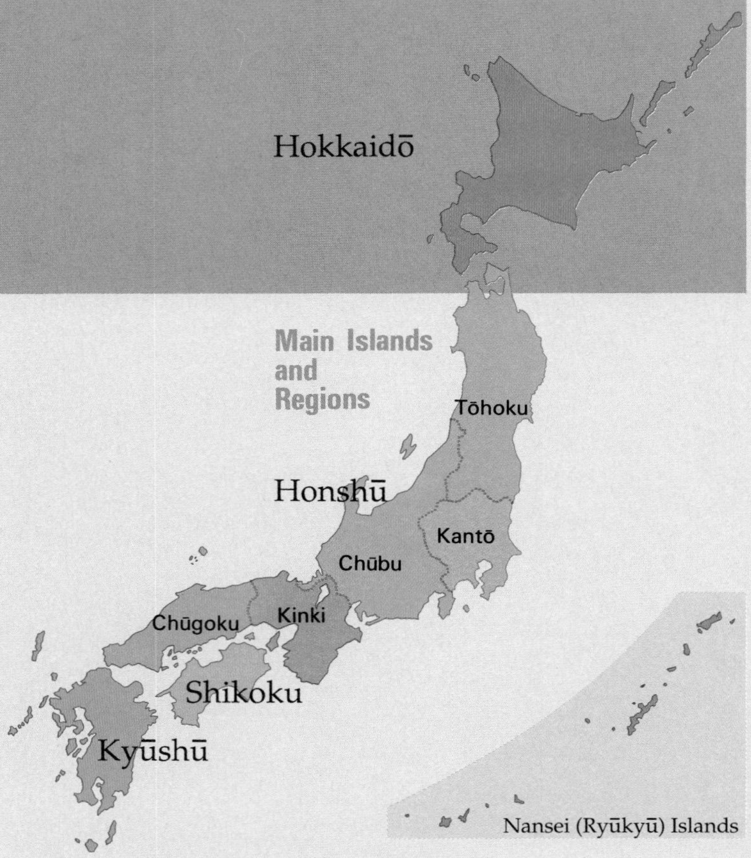

Hokkaidō

Main Islands and Regions

Tōhoku

Honshū

Kantō

Chūbu

Chūgoku

Kinki

Shikoku

Kyūshū

Nansei (Ryūkyū) Islands

Contents

Viewed from afar, as in the map on the facing page, Japan consists of the four main islands of Hokkaidō, Honshū, Shikoku, and Kyūshū (each with its smaller surrounding islands) and the Nansei, or Ryūkyū, island chain. Looked at in terms of political divisions, as in the map on page 1798, it consists of 47 prefectures. Thirty-four of these are in Honshū, 7 in Kyūshū, and 4 in Shikoku. The remaining 2 are the island of Hokkaidō, all of which is treated as one prefecture, and Okinawa Prefecture, which occupies the major portion of the Nansei (Ryūkyū) Islands. (Some of the islands are part of Kagoshima Prefecture in Kyūshū.) Most Japanese, however, think of their country in terms of the regional divisions used in the six two-page maps that make up the heart of this atlas. Honshū is divided into five regions, covering three of the maps: Tōhoku in the northeast, Kantō and Chūbu in the middle, and Kinki and Chūgoku in the southeast. Shikoku appears on the same map as the Kinki and Chūgoku regions of Honshū. The other three maps are devoted to Hokkaidō, Kyūshū, and the Nansei (Ryūkyū) Islands. Please note, however, that there is considerable overlap between some of the maps, each of which is named for its main regions. For the boundaries between regions, which are not shown on the maps, see the key map above. Please note also that the map of Hokkaidō is drawn to a different scale than the other regional maps.

Regional Map Symbols

Cities, Towns, and Villages

Cities are ranked by population in descending order.

◉ **Kita Kyūshū**	Over 1,000,000
◎ **Sagamihara**	500,000–1,000,000
◉ Iwakuni	100,000–500,000
◉ Nikkō	Under 100,000
• Hakone	Towns and Villages
	Urban Area

Other Political Units

Chiba	Prefecture
Sendai	Prefectural Capital

Boundaries

——	Prefectural
········	National Parks

Hydrographic Features

	Shoreline
Shirakawa	River
Lake Inawashiro	Lake
⌁ Nachi Falls	Waterfall
♨ Awazu	Hot Spring

Topographic Features

Kunimidake ▲1739	Mountain (elevation above sea level in meters)
⋈ Harinoki Pass	Mountain Pass
Kuroshima	Island
Shionomisaki	Cape

Miscellaneous Cultural Features

Shikotsu-Tōya National Park	National Park
◆ Sandankyō	Point of Interest

Transportation

——	Shinkansen Railway Line
——	Primary Railway
—◁—▷—	Railway Tunnel
——	Expressway
-----	Planned Expressway
——	Primary Road
✈	International Airport
✈	Domestic Airport

Depth below Sea Level in Meters

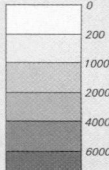

	0
	200
	1000
	2000
	4000
	6000

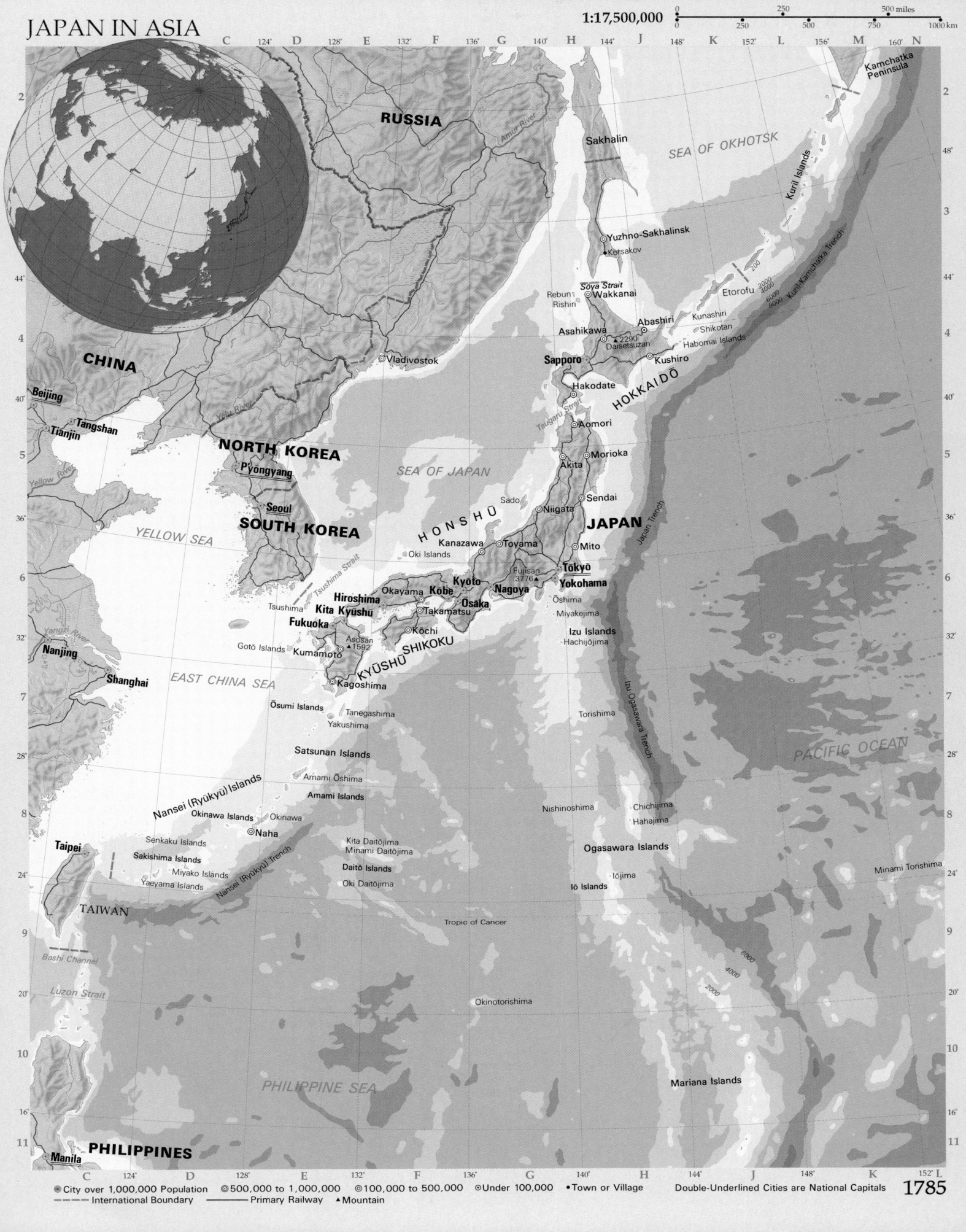

JAPAN IN ASIA

1:17,500,000

250   500 miles

250   500   750   1000 km

RUSSIA

SEA OF OKHOTSK

Kamchatka Peninsula

Sakhalin

Yuzhno-Sakhalinsk
Korsakov

Kuril Islands

CHINA

Vladivostok

Sōya Strait
Rebun   Wakkanai
Rishiri
Asahikawa   Abashiri   Kunashiri
▲2290   Shikotan
Daisetsuzan   Habomai Islands
Sapporo   Kushiro
Hakodate   **HOKKAIDŌ**
Tsugaru Strait

Etorofu

200
2000
4000
6000
Kuril-Kamchatka Trench

Beijing
Tangshan
Tianjin

Aomori

Morioka

Akita

NORTH KOREA

Pyongyang

SEA OF JAPAN

Sado
Niigata
JAPAN
Sendai

Seoul
SOUTH KOREA

YELLOW SEA

HONSHŪ

Kanazawa   Toyama
Oki Islands
Fujisan   Mito
Tōkyō
3776▲   **Yokohama**

Japan Trench

Tsushima Strait
Tsushima
Hiroshima   Okayama   **Kōbe**   **Kyōto**
Kita Kyūshū   Takamatsu   **Ōsaka**   **Nagoya**
Fukuoka   Kōchi   Ōshima
Asosan   **SHIKOKU**   Miyakejima
Gotō Islands   ▲1592   Kumamoto
KYŪSHŪ

Izu Islands
Hachijōjima

Nanjing

Shanghai

EAST CHINA SEA

Kagoshima
Ōsumi Islands
Tanegashima
Yakushima

Torishima

Izu-Ogasawara Trench

PACIFIC OCEAN

Satsunan Islands

Amami Ōshima

Nishinoshima   Chichijima
Hahajima

Amami Islands

Nansei (Ryūkyū) Islands
Okinawa Islands   Okinawa
Naha

Ogasawara Islands

Taipei

Senkaku Islands   Kita Daitōjima
Sakishima Islands   Minami Daitōjima
Miyako Islands   Daitō Islands
Yaeyama Islands   Oki Daitōjima

Iōjima
Iō Islands

Minami Torishima

Nansei (Ryūkyū) Trench

TAIWAN

Tropic of Cancer

6000

Bashi Channel

4000

Luzon Strait

Okinotorishima

2000

10
PHILIPPINE SEA

Mariana Islands

PHILIPPINES
Manila

● City over 1,000,000 Population ◉ 500,000 to 1,000,000 ◎ 100,000 to 500,000 ◌ Under 100,000 • Town or Village   Double-Underlined Cities are National Capitals
--- International Boundary   — Primary Railway   ▲ Mountain

1785

NANSEI (RYŪKYŪ) ISLANDS

CHINA

EAST CHINA SEA

Kagoshima ◎ Kyūshū

Ōsumi Islands Tanegashima

Yakushima

Kagoshima

Tokara Islands

Satsunan Islands

Naze
Amami Ōshima ◎

Nansei (Ryūkyū) Islands

Tokunoshima

Amami Islands

Okinoerabujima

Okinawa Islands

Okinawa

Naha

TAIWAN

Senkaku Islands

Okinawa

PACIFIC OCEAN

Miyakojima

Yaeyama Islands Miyako Islands

Yonagunijima Ishigakijima

Iriomotejima Sakishima Islands

EAST CHINA SEA

Torishima

Okinoerabujima

Wadomari

China

Yoronjima

Iheyajima Yoron

Iheya

Izenajima

Hedomisaki

Iejima Nakijin Kunigami

Motobu Ōgimi

Okinawa Islands

Torishima Agunijima Nago

Nago Bay

Okinawa

Onna Kin

Kin Okinawa

Yomitan Ishikawa

Kadena Kin Bay

Tonakijima Okinawa ◎ Gushikawa

Zamamijima Ginowan ◎ Yonagusuku

Urasoe ◎

Naha ◎ Nakagusuku Bay

Yonabaru

Tokashikijima Tomigusuku Chinen

Itoman ●

Kerama Islands

Kyammisaki

PACIFIC OCEAN

1786

● City over 1,000,000 Population   ◎ 500,000 to 1,000,000   ◎ 100,000 to 500,000   ◎ Under 100,000   ● Town or Village   Underlined Cities are Prefectural Capitals

— Primary Railway   Expressway   Primary Road

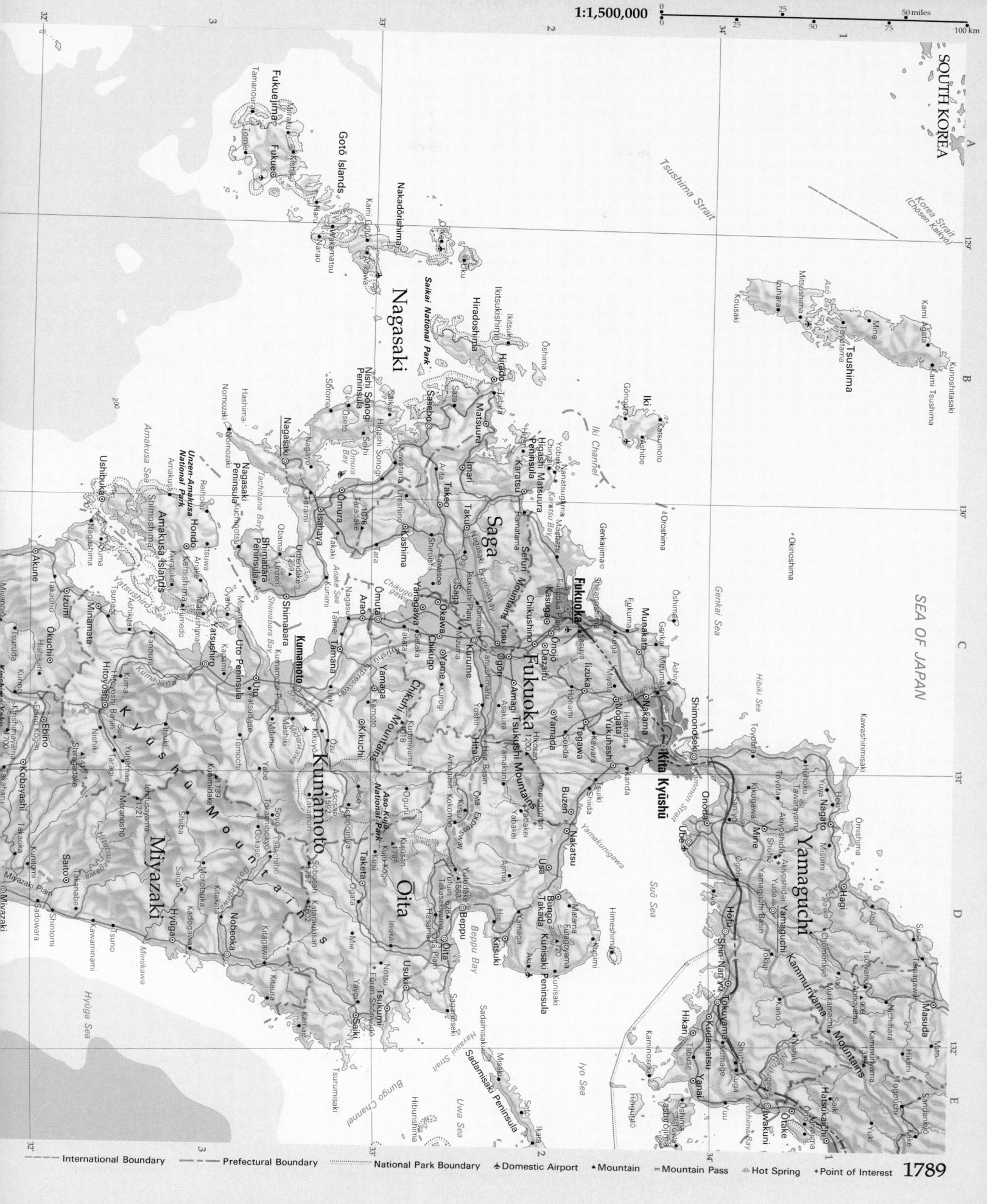

1:1,500,000

0   25   50 miles

0   25   50   75   100 km

SOUTH KOREA

A

SEA OF JAPAN

Korea Strait
(Chosen Kaikyo)

Tsushima Strait

Kunoshitasaki

Kami Agata

Kami Tsushima

Izuhara

Mitsushima

Tsushima

Mine

Kousaki

B

Korea Strait

Tamanoura
Fukuejima

Minakata

Fukue

Tomie

Gotō Islands

Nakadōrishima

Kami Goto

Narao

Wakamatsu

Arikawa

Oku

Saikai National Park

Nagasaki

Hirado

Hiradoshima

Ikitsuki

Ikitsukishima

Higashi

Sasebo

Ōshima

Iki

Katsumoto

Ashibe

Genkaijima

Oroshima

Okinoshima

Genkai Sea

SEA OF JAPAN

C

Nishi Sonogi Peninsula

Higashi Sonogi Peninsula

Seihi

Nagayo

Ōmura Bay

Chinzei

Nanatsugama

Matsuura

Karatsu

Yobuto

Machaya

Fukuoka Plain

Kasuga

Fukuoka

Onojo
Dazaifu

Munakata

Mizumaki

Ashiya

Oshima

Fukuma

Hibiki Sea

Kawashirimisaki

Toyoura

Shimonoseki

Kita Kyūshū

Onoda

Ube

Yamaguchi

Omishima

Misumi

Hagi

Masuda

Nagasaki

Saikai

Sofuku

Ōseto

Hashima

Nomozaki

Nagasaki Peninsula

Obama

Unzen-Amakusa National Park

Reihoku

Hondo

Kamishima

Amakusa

Shimoshima

Amakusa Islands

Amakusa Sea

Ushibuka

Nagashima

Izumi

Akune

Minamata

Ebino

Kobayashi

Miyakonojo

Kyūshū Mountains

Miyazaki

Kumamoto

Saga

Saga

Kurume

Chikushino
Tosu

Yame

Chikugo

Fukuoka

Hita

Yamada

Nakama

Nōgata

Tagawa

Yukuhashi

Buzen

Nakatsu

Usa

Bungo Takada

Kunisaki Peninsula

Kitakyushu

Suō Sea

Himeshima

Beppu Bay

Ōita

Ōita

Usuki

Saiki

Aso-Kujū National Park

Taketa

Beppu

Yufuin

Tsukumi

Bungo Channel

Hyūga Sea

International Boundary — — —   **Prefectural Boundary** – – –   **National Park Boundary** ········   ✈ **Domestic Airport**   ▲ **Mountain**   = **Mountain Pass**   ♨ **Hot Spring**   ♦ **Point of Interest**   **1789**

KINKI–CHŪGOKU–SHIKOKU

SEA OF JAPAN

SEA OF JAPAN

Oki Islands

Oki Islands

Daisen-Oki National Park

Dōgo
Goka • Fuse
Saigō
Tsuma

Nishinoshima
Ama • Nakanoshima
Dōzen
Chiburishima • Chibu

Daisen-Oki National Park

Mihonoseki • Jizōzaki
Shimane Peninsula **Matsue** Sakaiminato
Kashima Nawa
Hinomisaki Hirata Higashi Izumo Yonago Yumigahama Akas
Taisha Izumo Izumo Plain Shinji Tamatsukuri Kaike Daisen
Nima Taki Mitoya • Kisuki Hirose Saihaku ▲1729
Yunotsu Ōda Sambesan Yokota Nichinan Hino
Shimane ▲1126 ▲1142 Kamba F
Gōtsu Akagi Sentsuzan Dōgoyama ▲1209 Ōsa
Tatamigaura Hamada Dangyokei Hibayama Chūgoku Mountains Nijmi
Misumi Iwami Kawamoto ▲1299 Hokul
Masuda Ōsa Shōbara Tetta
Mito Geihoku Kōda Taishakukyō Takahashi
Hikimi Sandankyō Kake Yoshida Jinseki Yuki Bitchū Nariwa
Susa Tamagawa Togōchi Yachiyo Kibi Kōgen Ibara
Nichihara Kammuriyama Yuki Mitsugi Shin ichi Fuchū Kannabe San-yō Expressway
Abu ▲908 ▲1339 Hiroshima Plain Kōchi Kasaok
Tsuwano Aonoyama Mountains Fuchū Higashi Hiroshima San-yō Shinkansen Fukuyama
Hagi Atō Muikaichi **Hiroshima** Kaita Takehara Mihara Onomichi Numakuma
Heki Chōmonkyō Saiki Miyajima Kumano Kurose Akitsu Setoda Innoshima Sensuijima
Yuya Nagato Misumi Itsukushima Yasuura Ōmishima Innoshima Shin
Hōhoku Yamaguchi Ōno Ōtake Nōmijima Bingo Sea
Toyota Akiyoshidō Yamaguchi Nishiki Iwakuni Ogaki Ondo Geiyo Islands Inland Sea National Park Taku
Akiyoshidai Yuda Kano Shūtō Kurahashijima Ōshima Shisakajima Kan'o
Kikugawa Shūhō Yamaguchi Basin Tokuji Kuga Toyoham
Toyoura Mine Ogōri Hōfu Shin Nan'yō Tokuyama Kumage Nakajima Imabari
San-yō Aio Kudamatsu Kikuma Hiuchi
Shimonoseki Onoda Shin Nan'yō Tabuse Yanai Ōshima Niihama
Kammon Strait Ube Hikari Towa Hōjō Tōyo Saijō Doi Iyo Mish
Kita Kyūshū Yashirojima Dōgo Komatsu Matsuyama Expressway Kawanoe
Ōshima Ashiya Suō Sea Kaminoseki Heigunto Matsuyama Plain Ishizuchisan Kamegamori Mountains
Genkai Mizumaki Nakama Iyo Tobe ▲1982 ▲1896 Sameura Dam
Munakata Hiraodai Kanda Shigenobu Ishizuchi Mountains Shikoku
Fukuma Nōgata Yukuhashi Himeshima Kuma Shikoku Karst **Kōchi**
Koga Miyata Tsuiki Kunimi Nagahama Omogokei Tosa Yam
Kasuya Iizuka Kawara Shiida Matama Ōzu Iyo Sea Uchiko Niyodo Nank
Fukuoka Honami Tagawa Buzen Futagoyama **Ehime** Shikoku Karst **Kōchi**
Fukuoka Plain Soeda ▲720 Kunisaki Ikata Seto Haruno Katsurah
Kasuga Onojō Yamada Usa Bungo Kunisaki Peninsula Misaki Hijikawa Sakawa Tosa
Chikushino Dazaifu Hikosan Nakatsu Takada Aki Yawatahama Mima Yusuhara Susaki
Tosu Ōgōri ▲1200 Yabakei Yamaga Ajimu Hiji Kitsuki Sadamisaki Peninsula Uwa Hiyoshi
Fukuoka Amagi Tsukushi Mountains Yabakei Kitsuki Sadasaki Yawatahama Uwa Nishi Tosa
Tsukushi Plain Tanushimaru Asakura Yamakuni Hita Basin Ōita Expressway Uwajima Ōgata
Kanzaki Yoshii Hita Ōita Ōita Nametoko Keikoku
Saga Kurume Mizuma Kusu Beppu Bay Uwa Sea Ashizuri-Uwakai National Park Tosa Ba
Ōkawa Setaka Yufuin Beppu Saganoseki Hiburishima Saga
Yame Kurogi Yufudake Takasakiyama Ōita Tsushima Nakamura
Yanagawa Takata ▲1583 ▲628 Ōita Plain Hayasui Strait
Ōmuta Kōmori Kumamiyama Oguni Kujūsan Hasama Usuki Mishō Shimantogawa
Araō Yamaga ▲1018 Aso-Kujū ▲1791 Inukai Jōhen Ōgata
Nagasu Chikuhi Mountains National Park Kujū Kōgen Usuki Sukumo Sukumo Bay
Taimei Tamana Kumamoto Kikuchi Aso **Ōita** Notsu Tsukumi Ōtsuki
Kunimi Ōzu Aso Ichinomiya Taketa Yayoi Saiki Ashizurimisaki Tosa Shimizu
Kumamoto Kikuyō Asosan Ogata Mie Tsurumisaki Okinoshima
Shimabara ▲1592 Sobosan Katamukiyama Kamae
Shimabara Bay Kumamoto Plain Mashiki **Miyazaki** ▲1757 ▲1602 Kitaura Ashizurimisaki
Arie • Uto Mifune Soyō Takachihokyō Takachiho Kitagawa

Dōzo
Nakanoshima

1790

City over 1,000,000 Population   500,000 to 1,000,000   100,000 to 500,000   Under 100,000   • Town or Village   Underlined Cities are Prefectural Capitals

—— Shinkansen Railway Line   — Primary Railway   ‑‑‑‑ Railway Tunnel   ——▶ Expressway   —— Primary Road   ‑‑‑‑ Planned Expressway

KANTŌ–CHŪBU

SEA OF JAPAN

Nanatsujima

Rokkōzaki
Suzumisaki
Sosogi Coast
Suzu
Wajima
Monzen
Uchiura
Noto Peninsula
Noto
Anamizu
Nakajima
Nanao Bay
Togi
Wakura
Notoshima
Shika
Nanao

Teradomari
Izumozaki
Mitsuk
Nishiyama
Nagaoka
Koshiji
Kashiwazaki
Ojiyao
Kakizaki
993
Yoneyama
Kawaguchi
Ōgata
Niigata
Nadachi
Nō
Jōetsu
Tōkamachi
Matsuda
Itoigawa
Ōmi
Oyashirazu
Hokuriku Expressway
Araï
Matsunoyama
Tsunan
Muika
Shiozaw
Yuza
Echigo Yuzawa
Hakui
Shio
Nyūzen
Kurobe
Unazuki
Akakura
Myōkōsan 2454
Myōkō Kōgen
Nozawa Onsen
Nozawa 19
Naebasan 2145
Jōshin'etsu Kōgen National Park
Himi
Shimminato
Uozu
Unazuki
Iiyama
Takamatsu
Takaoka
Toyama Plain
Namerikawa
Kamichi
Shirumadake 2932
Otari
Togakushiyama 1911
Izunayama 1917
Shinano
Shibu
Mikuni Mountain
Shima
Ōyabe
Kosugi Fuchū
Toyama
Tateyama
Tsurugidake 2998
Yarigatake 2889
Togakushi Kōgen
Hakuba
Nakano
Obuse
Suzaka
Manza
Naganohara
Kurikara Pass Tonami
Yatsuo
Ōyama
Tateyama 3015
Kurobe Dam
Harinoki Pass
Sugadaira
Nagano Basin
Nagano
Kusatsu
Nakanojō
Kanazawa
Jōhana
Midagahara
Eboshidake 2627
Chūbu Sangaku National Park
Ōmachi
Kōshoku
Togura Sakaki
Asamayama 2354
Azumayasan 2568
Harunam 1448
Mattō
Nonoichi
Kamioka
Tsubakurodake 2763
Yarigatake 3180
Ikeda
Kamiyamada
Ueda
Tōbu
Maruko
Onioshidashi
Hanamaganuma 1655
Ishikawa
Tsurugi
Neagari
Kamitakara 2455
Hotakadake Toyoshina
Kakey
Komoro
Karuizawa
Usui Pass
Myōgisan
Annah
Kaga
Awazu
Yamashiro
Shiramine
Hakusan National Park
Furukawa
Yakedake 2455
Hotaka 3190
Asama
Nagato
Mochizuki
Saku
Atafuneyama 1423
Usuda
Tomio
Shimor
Tōjimbō
Mikuni
Katayamazu
Awara
Hakusan 2702
Shōkawa
Hirayu
Azumi Kamikōchi
Matsumoto Basin
Matsumoto
Wada Pass
Saku Basin
Sakai
Maruoka
Eiheiji
Miboro Dam
Shirakawa
Norikuradake 3026
Shirahone
Shiojiri
Shiojiri Pass
Shimo Suwa
Kirigamine
Koumi
Fukui Plain
Fukui
Miyama
Izumi
Shirotori
Kuguno
Nomugi Pass
Hirayu
Okaya
Tateshina Kōgen
Minamimaki
Nakatsu
Shimizu
Sabae
Ōno
Osaka
Takayama
Ōsaka
Suwa
Tatsuno
Chino
Yatsugatake 2899
Kōbushigadake 2475
Echizemmisaki
Echizen
Katsuyama
Nōgo Hakusan 1617
Hagiwata
Ontakesan 3067
Kaida
Kiso
Torii Pass
Minowa
Chūō Expressway
Masutomi 2599
Chichibu-Tar National Pa
Takefu
Imadate
Ryōhaku Mountains
Gifu
Gero
Kiso Fukushima
Komagatake 2956
Ina
Takatō
Kobuchizawa
Sudama
Tsuruga
Hachiman
Nakayama Shiojiri
Ōtaki
Nezamenotoko
Agematsu
Komagane 3033
Nirasaki
Hōzan 2841
Yamanashi
Enzan
Mihama
Mikata
Yogo
Kinomoto
Neo
Miyama
Mugi
Shirakawa
Sakashita
Ina Basin
Kitadake 3192
Kōfu
Katsunuma
Mikata Five Lakes
Kanayama
Tsukechi
Nagiso
Senjōgatake 2967
Yashajin Pass
Shirane
Kōfu Basin
Isawa
Sotomo
Ibigawa
Seki
Mino Kamo
Yaotsu
Kisogawa
Okuwa
Akaishi Mountains
Shiomidake 3047
Kajikazawa
Ichikawa Daimon
Tsur
Fukuy
Ōbama
Nishi Azai
Mino
Kani
Mitake
Ena
Mizunami
Iwamura
Southern Alps National Park
Ōshika
Yoshil
Takahama
Ōi
Azai
Kakamigahara
Inuyama
Tajimi
Toki
Yamanashi
Fuji Five Lakes
Kaminaka
Natashō
Nagahama
Sekigahara
Ōgaki
Komaki
Kasamatsu
Kōnan
Akechi
Mizunami
Asahi
Inaba
Chausuyama 1415
Tenryū
Minobu
Lake Yaman
Imazu
Maihara
Hashima
Bisai
Ichinomiya
Kōmaki
Seto
Owari Asahi
Mino Mikawa Kōgen
Asuke
Sumatakyō
Asagiri Kōgen
Fujisan 3776
Fuji-Hakone National Pa
Shiraito Falls
Tamba Mountains
Miyama
Hikone
Taga
Yōrō
Nobi Plain
Inazawa
Tsushima
Nagoya
Toyota
Shitara
Sakuma Dam
Hon Kawane
Fujinomiya
Kyōto
Adogawa
Hieizan 848
Azuchi
Notogawa
Taga
Hōkusei
Tōkai
Toyoake
Miyoshi
Sakuma
Fuji
Suson
Mish
Sonobe
Keihoku
Ōmi Hachiman
Yōkaichi
Gozaisho 1212
Komono
Yunoyama
Kuwana
Tokai
Kariya
Okazaki
Hōraijisan 695
Haruno
Kakegawa
Shimizu
Kambara
Abekawa
Numazu
Kameoka
Ōtsu
Kyōto
Kusatsu
Shiga
Suzuka Mountains
Suzuka Pass
Yokkaichi
Ōbu
Chiryū
Aichi
Inasa
Shizuoka
Shimizu
Shizuoka
Miho no Matsubara
Hedal
Yagi
Hiyoshi
Moriyama
Shigaraki
Higashi Meihan Expressway
Suzuka
Kameyama
Takahama
Handa
Anjō
Hekinan
Kōta
Shinshiro
Mikkabi
Mori Kanaya
Shimada
Fujieda
Nihondaira
Ma
Osaka
Muko
Uji
Jōyō
Iga
Kōka
Tokoname
Nishio
Gamagōri
Toyokawa
Iwatahara
Kakegawa
Yaizu
Dōgoshima
Yug
Takatsuki
Ibaraki
Minakuchi
Ueno
Tsu
Chita Peninsula
Taketoyo
Mihama
Nishiura
Toyohashi
Kosai
Mikatahara
Iwata
Fukuroi
Sagara
Omaezaki
Toyonaka
Suita
Neyagawa
Kizugawa
Akogiura
Kōsai
Makinohara
Ōmaezaki
Daitō
Ikoma
Nara
Tsukigase
Hisai
Minami Chita
Tahara
Hamaoka
Habikino
Yao
Yamato Kōriyama
Aoyama
Ise Bay
Nabari
Ise Expressway
Atsumi Peninsula
Arai Maisaka
Hamamatsu
Tondabayashi
Tenri
Muro
48 Falls of Akame
Ureshino
Matsusaka
Meiwa
Atsumi
Tragomisaki
Kawachi Nagano 1125
Gose
Sakurai
Kashihara
Asuka
Haibara
Takami
Miyagawa
Minami Izu
Irōzaki
Kongōsan
Kimi Pass
Gojō
Hashimoto
Higashi Yoshino
Odai
Mie
Takamisan 1249
Iinan
Tsu
Ise
Toba
Futami
Shima Peninsula
Nishi Yoshino
Yoshinoyama
Ōmiya
Ise-Shima National Park
Nantō
Daiōzaki
Nansei
Ago Bay

Toyama
Toyama Bay
Kahokugata
Kurobegawa
Kuzuryūgawa
Wakasa Bay
Lake Biwa
Ise Bay
Mikawa Bay
Suruga Bay
Enshū Sea

1792

TŌHOKU

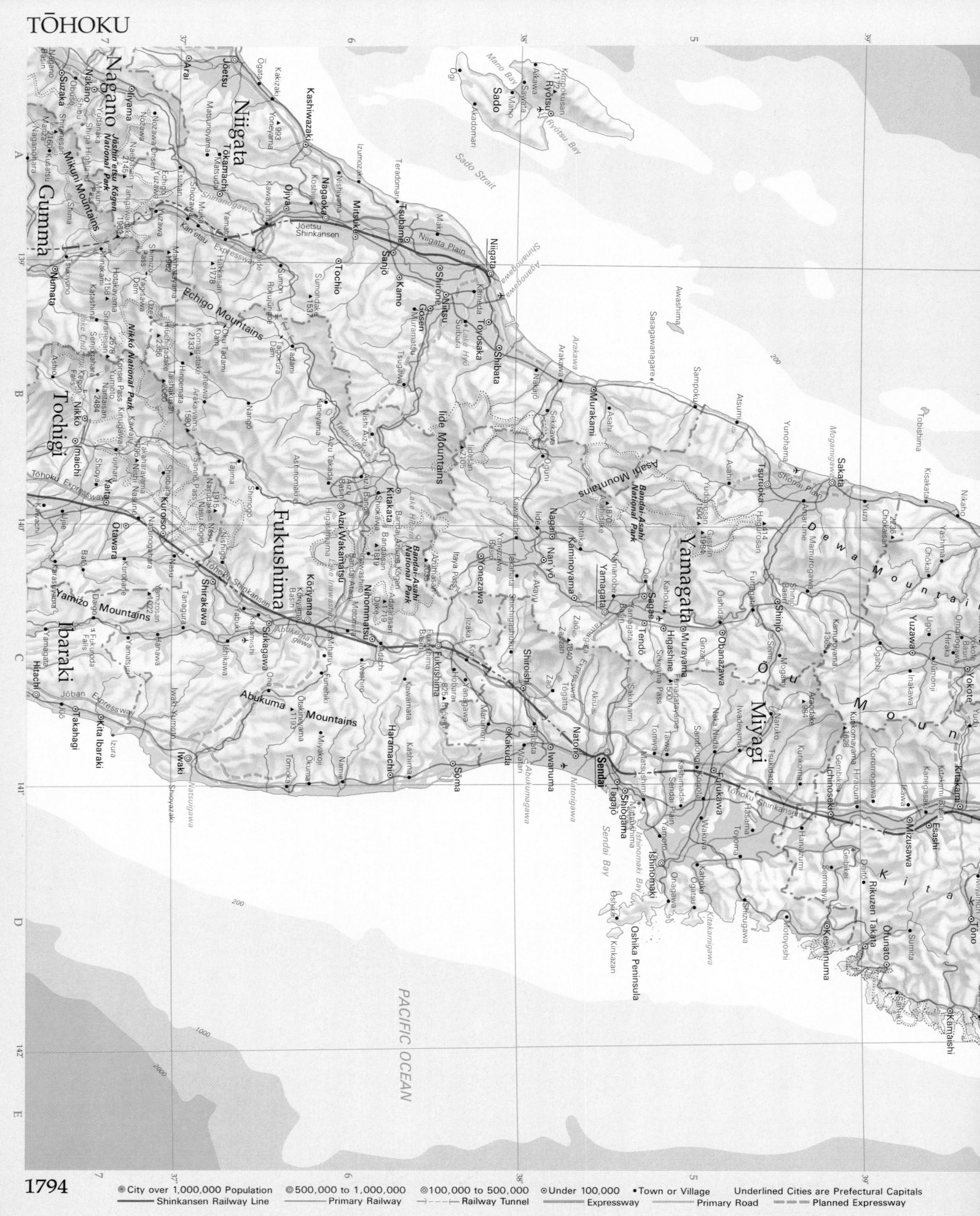

◎ City over 1,000,000 Population   ◎ 500,000 to 1,000,000   ◎ 100,000 to 500,000   ○ Under 100,000   • Town or Village   Underlined Cities are Prefectural Capitals

⎯⎯ Shinkansen Railway Line   ⎯⎯ Primary Railway   ⊢⊣ Railway Tunnel   ⎯⎯ Expressway   ⎯⎯ Primary Road   ⎯ ⎯ Planned Expressway

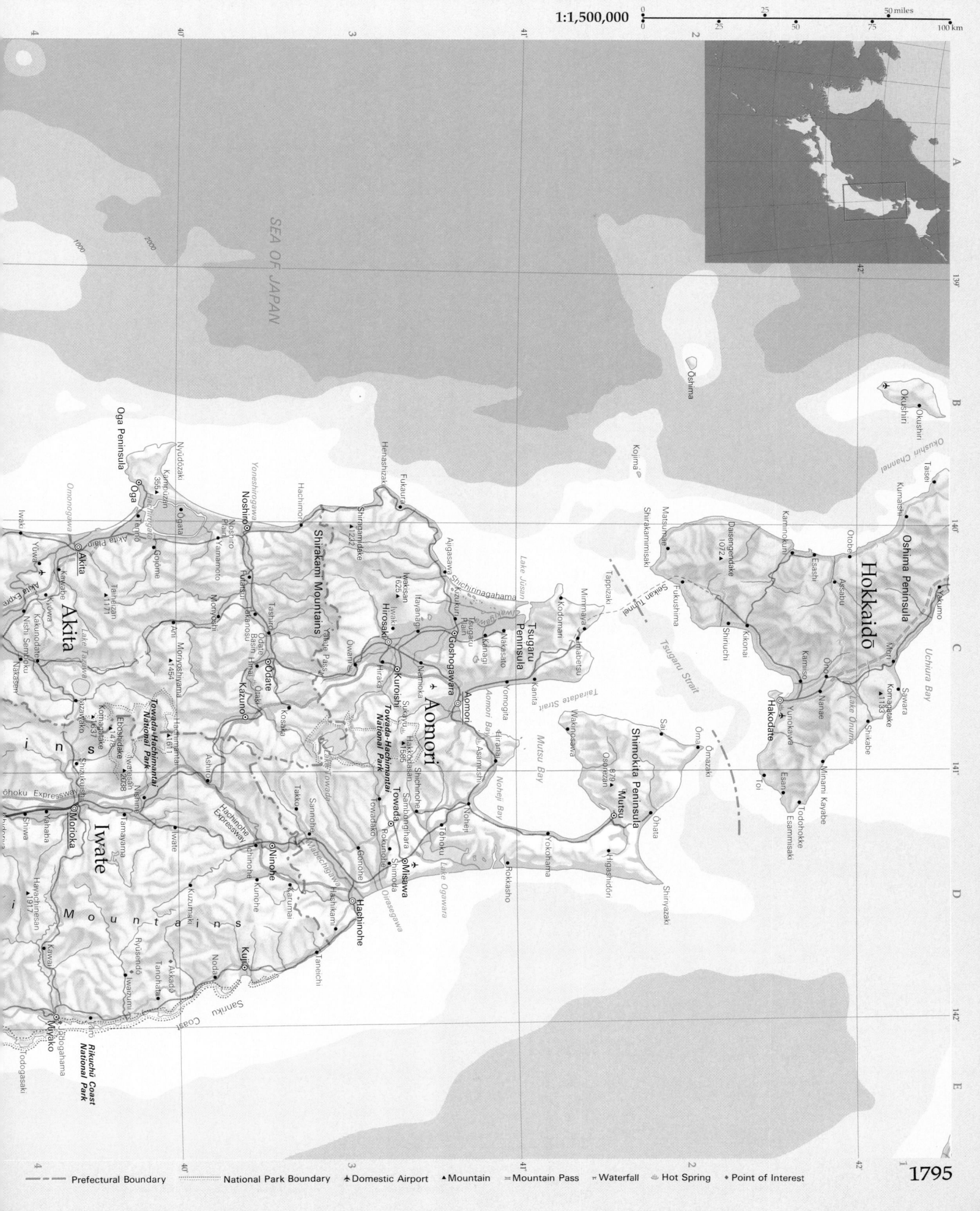

HOKKAIDŌ

SEA OF JAPAN

Sōya Strait

Sōyamisaki
Noshappumisaki
Wakkanai
Sarufutsu
Hamatombetsu

Rebun
Rishiri-Rebun-Sarobetsu National Park
Rebun
Rishiri Fuji
Rishiri Rishirizan ▲1721
Rishiri
Rishiri Channel
Sarobetsu Plain
Toyotomi
Naka Tombetsu
Esashi
Horonobe
Teshio Plain
Teshiogawa
Teshio
Nakagawa
Utanobori
Ōmu
Okoppe
Mombetsu
Embetsu
Otoineppu ▲1129 Hakodake
Bifuka
Shosambetsu
Nishi Okoppe
Teuri Yagishiri
Haboro
Nayoro
Fūren
Shimokawa
Yūbetsu
Tomamae
Kami Yūbetsu
Shibetsu
Takinoue
Maruseppu
Engaru
Sarom
Kembuchi
Asahi
Teshiodake ▲1568
Ikutahara
Shirataki
Rubeshibe
Obira
Horokanai
Wassamu
Kitami Pass
Kunneppu
Rumoi
Pippu
Kamikawa
Sōunkyō
Oketo
Mashike
Takasu
Tōma
Sekihoku Pass
Numata
Asahikawa
Daisetsuzan ▲2290
Higashikawa
Daisetsuzan National Park
Rikubetsu
Shokambetsudake ▲1491 Hokuryū
Moseushi
Kamikawa Basin
Biei
Tenninkyō
▲1967 Ishikaridake
Hamamasu
Fukagawa
Takikawa
Akabira
Ashibetsu
Ishikari Mountains
Lake Nukabira
Shin Totsukawa
Utashinai
Atsuta
Sunagawa
Kami Furano
Tokachidake ▲2077
Kami Shihoro
Ashoro
Tsukigata
Bibai
Naka Furano
Shihoro
Yūbari Mountains
Furano
Ishikari
Mikasa
Ashibetsudake ▲1727
Minami Furano
Kankachi Pass
Kamuimisaki
Shakotammisaki
Iwamizawa
Shintoku
Shakaoi
Shakotan
Furubira
Tōbetsu
Kurisawa
Yūbaridake ▲1668
Otofuke
Shakotan Peninsula
Yoichi
Ebetsu
Kuriyama Yūbari
Shimukappu
Shimizu
Ikeda
Kamoenai
Niki
Otaru
Sapporo
Hiroshima
Ishikari Plain
Teineyama ▲1024
Akaigawa
Ishikari Bay
Tomari
Jōzankei
Kyowa
Kutchan
Nishapp... Nissho Pass
Hidaka
Memurodake ▲1754
Obihiro
Makubetsu
Iwanai
Kyōko
Nakayama Pass
Eniwa
Chitose
Oiwake
Yoichidake ▲1488
Shiribetsugawa
Raiden'yama ▲1212
Yōteizan ▲1898
Kimobetsu
Eniwadake ▲1320
Hayakita
Tokachi Plain
Tōyokoro
Suttsu
Rankoshi
Rusutsu
Lake Shikotsu
Hōbetsu
Poroshiridake ▲2052
Niseko ▲1045
Tarumaezan ▲1041
Atsuma
Naka Satsunai
Shimamaki
Kombudake
Tōya
Ōtaki
Mukawa
Biratori
Karibayama ▲1520
Lake Tōya Shōwa Shinzan
Shikotsu-Tōya National Park
Tomakomai
Sarabetsu
Kuromatsunai
Abuta ▲737 Usuzan ▲402
Lake Kuttara
Shiraoi
Sarugawa Mombetsu
Chūrui
Setana
Imakane
Oshamambe
Noboribetsu
Kamuidake ▲1600
Taiki
Kita Hiyama
Date
Niikappu
Shizunai
Hidaka Mountains
Noboribetsu
Uchiura Bay
Muroran
Chikiumisaki
Mitsuishi
Urakawa
Rakkodake ▲1472
Hiroo
Yakumo
Okushiri
Okushiri Channel
Taisei
Samani
Kumaishi
Oshima Peninsula
Sawara
Komagatake ▲1133
Erimomisaki
Mori
Shikabe
Otobe
Lake Onuma
Esashi
Assabu
Ōno Nanae Minami Kayabe
Kamiiso Todohokke
Kaminokuni
Yunokawa Esan Esammisaki
Hakodate Toi
Daisengendake ▲1072
Kikonai
Shiriuchi
Matsumae
Tsugaru Strait
Fukushima
Shirakamimisaki
Ōmazaki
Ōma
Aomori
Shimokita Peninsula
Shiriyazaki

City over 1,000,000 Population   **500,000 to 1,000,000**   **100,000 to 500,000**
Expressway   Primary Road   Planned Expressway

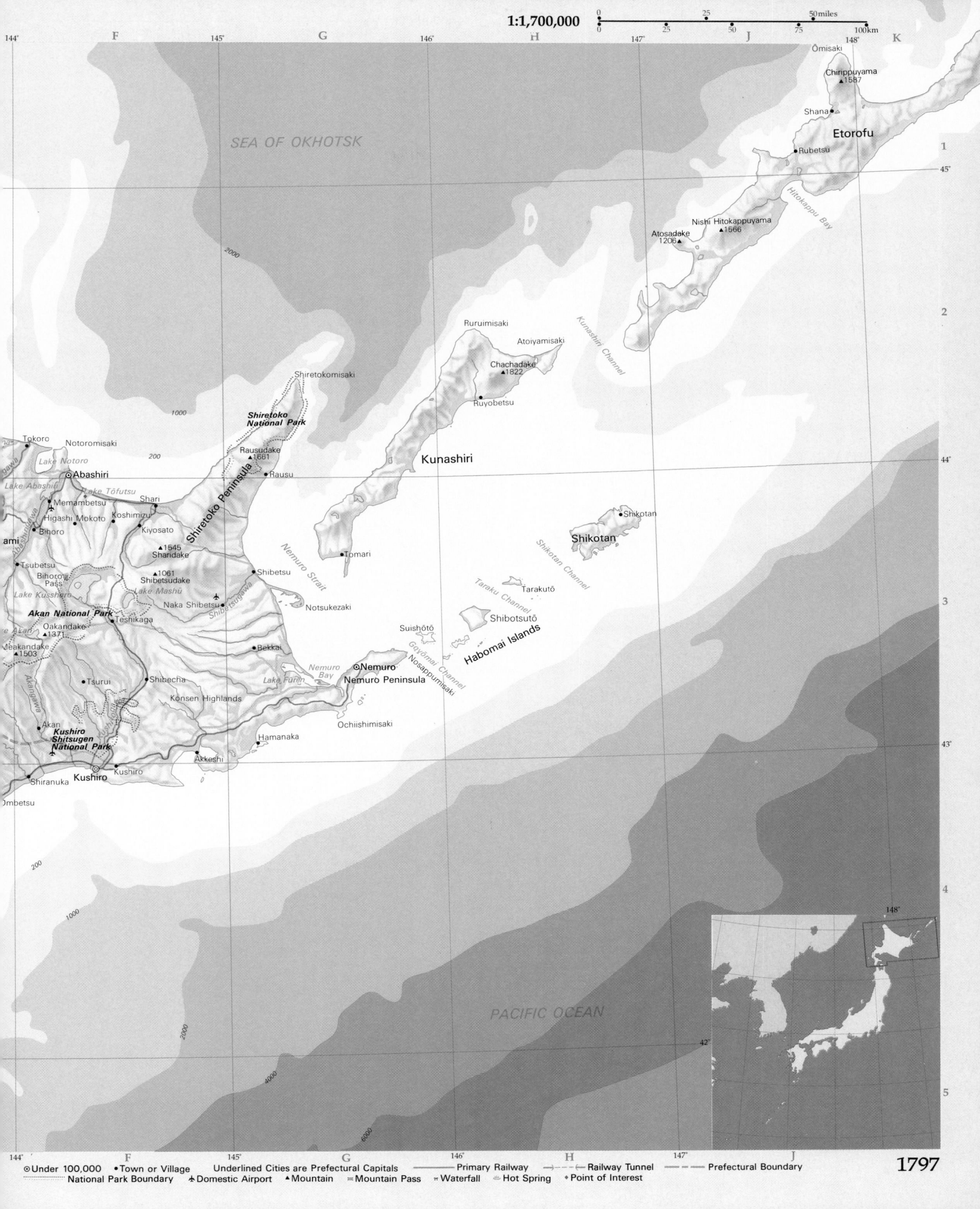

1:1,700,000

0   25   50miles

0   25   50   75   100km

SEA OF OKHOTSK

Ōmisaki

Chirippuyama
▲1587

Shana

Etorofu

Rubetsu

Hitokappu Bay

Nishi Hitokappuyama
▲1566

Atosadake
1206▲

Kunashiri Channel

Ruruimisaki

Atoiyamisaki

Chachadake
▲1822

Ruyobetsu

Shiretokomisaki

Shiretoko
National Park

Kunashiri

2000

1000

Tokoro   Notoromisaki

Lake Notoro

200

Rausudake
▲1661

Rausu

Shikotan

Shikotan
▲

⊙Abashiri

Lake Abashiri   Lake Tōfutsu   Shari

Memambetsu

Koshimizu

Higashi Mokoto

Bihoro   Kiyosato

ami

Tsubetsu

▲1545
Sharidake

▲1061
Shibetsudake

Bihoro
Pass

Lake Mashū

Naka Shibetsu

Shibetsu

Shiretoko Peninsula

Nemuro Strait

Shibetsugawa

Shikotan

Shikotan Channel

Taraku Channel

Tarakutō

Shibotsutō

Habomai Islands

Notsukezaki

Akan National Park

Oakandake
▲1371

Meakandake
▲1503

e Akan

Teshikaga

Lake Kusharo

Tsuruı

Shibecha

Kōnsen Highlands

Bekkai

Lake Fūren

Nemuro
Bay

⊙Nemuro

Nemuro Peninsula

Nosappumisaki

Suishōtō

Goyōmai Channel

Kushiro
Shitsugen
National Park

Akan

Akangawa

Hamanaka

Ochiishimisaki

Shiranuka   Kushiro

⊙Kushiro

Akkeshi

Ombetsu

200

1000

2000

PACIFIC OCEAN

4000

6000

148°

148°

42°

42°

43°

44°

45°

1

2

3

4

5

144°   F   145°   G   146°   H   147°   J   148°   K

1797

⊙ Under 100,000   • Town or Village   Underlined Cities are Prefectural Capitals   —— Primary Railway   ⊢–⊣ Railway Tunnel   ——— Prefectural Boundary

⋯⋯ National Park Boundary   ✈ Domestic Airport   ▲ Mountain   ⚌ Mountain Pass   ≈ Waterfall   ♨ Hot Spring   ◆ Point of Interest

PREFECTURES OF JAPAN

1:6,700,000

0 ⌈ 100 miles
0 ⌈ 100 200 300 400 500 km

SEA OF OKHOTSK

EAST CHINA SEA

Tanegashima

Yakushima

Kagoshima

Hokkaidō

• Sapporo

Amami Ōshima

Tokunoshima

Okinoerabujima

Yoronjima

Kumejima

Okinawa

• Naha

PACIFIC OCEAN

Aomori
• Aomori

Okinawa

Akita
• Akita

• Morioka
Iwate

Miyakojima

Yamagata
Yamagata •

Miyagi

• Sendai

Yonagunijima

Ishigakijima

Iriomotejima

Senkaku Islands

Sado

• Niigata
Niigata

Fukushima •
Fukushima

SEA OF JAPAN

Takeshima

Oki Islands

Ishikawa
Kanazawa

• Toyama
Toyama

Nagano •
Nagano

Gumma
Maebashi •

Tochigi
Utsunomiya •
• Mito

Ibaraki

Tottori
Tottori •

Matsue •

• Fukui
Fukui

Gifu

Gifu •

Saitama
Urawa •
Kōfu •

Tōkyō
• Tōkyō

Chiba
• Chiba

Shimane

Okayama
• Okayama

Kyōto
Kyōto •

Shiga
• Ōtsu

Yamanashi

Yokohama •

Kanagawa

Chiba

Hyōgo

Kōbe • Ōsaka •

Aichi
• Nagoya

Shizuoka •
Shizuoka

Hiroshima
• Hiroshima

Nara
Nara •

Ōsaka

Mie
Tsu •

Ōshima

Miyakejima

Yamaguchi
• Yamaguchi

Kagawa
• Takamatsu

Tokushima
Tokushima •

Wakayama
Wakayama •

Tōkyō

SEA OF OKHOTSK

Tsushima

Iki

Fukuoka
• Fukuoka

Matsuyama •

Ehime

Kōchi
• Kōchi

Hachijōjima

Etorofu

Nagasaki

Saga
Saga •

Ōita
Ōita •

Nagasaki •

Kumamoto
Kumamoto •

Miyazaki

Hokkaidō

Kunashiri

Shikotan

Kagoshima
Kagoshima •

• Miyazaki

PACIFIC OCEAN

PACIFIC OCEAN

1798

• Prefectural Capital   ----- Prefectural Boundary

In the index listings below, the page number is given first, then the letter and number coordinates for the location, followed by the place name. When two or more places have the same name, the first one listed is the largest political unit (e.g., the prefecture of Nagano comes before the city of Nagano) or the one with the greatest physical prominence (e.g., the river Arakawa in Saitama Prefecture is longer than the river Arakawa in Niigata Prefecture, and so the former is listed first). When two or more cities or towns or villages have identical names, the one with the largest population is listed first, followed by the others in descending order of population. To help in distinguishing between places that have the same name, the type of place (city, town, river, etc) or the name of the prefecture it is located in, or both, is given in parentheses after the name.

A

1797	F2	Abashiri
1797	F3	Abashirigawa
1797	F3	Abashiri, Lake
1792	D4	Abekawa
1793	F3	Abiko
1792	C2	Abō Pass
1790	B2	Abu
1790	B2	Abugawa
1794	C5	Abukumagawa
1794	C6	Abukuma Mountains
1796	B4	Abuta
1792	C3	Achi
1794	C6	Adachi
1794	C6	Adatarasan
1791	G1	Adogawa
1794	B6	Aganogawa
1792	D2	Agatsumagawa
1792	C3	Agematsu
1793	E3	Ageo
1791	G2	Ago
1791	G2	Ago Bay
1786	C4	Agunijima
1792	C4	Aichi
1793	E3	Aikawa (Kanagawa)
1794	A5	Aikawa (Niigata)
1790	B2	Aio
1791	E2	Aioi
1788	C4	Aira
1794	B6	Aizu Bange
1794	B6	Aizu Basin
1791	E2	Aizumi
1794	B6	Aizu Takada
1794	B6	Aizu Wakamatsu
1795	C3	Ajigasawa
1789	D2	Ajimu
1796	D3	Akabira
1794	A6	Akadomari
1790	C2	Akagi
1793	E2	Akagisan
1796	B3	Akaigawa
1792	D3	Akaishidake
1792	D3	Akaishi Mountains
1792	D2	Akakura
1791	G2	Akame, 48 Falls of
1797	F3	Akan
1797	F3	Akangawa
1797	F3	Akan, Lake
1797	F3	Akan National Park
1791	D3	Akaoka
1790	D1	Akasaki
1791	F2	Akashi
1791	F2	Akashi Strait
1794	C5	Akayu
1792	C3	Akechi
1791	D3	Aki (Kōchi)
1789	D2	Aki (Ōita)
1795	C4	Akita (Prefecture)
1795	C4	Akita (City)
1795	C4	Akita Expressway

1795	C4	Akita Plain
1790	C2	Akitsu
1794	C5	Akiu
1790	B2	Akiyoshidai
1790	B2	Akiyoshidō
1795	D4	Akkadō
1797	F3	Akkeshi
1791	E2	Akō
1791	G2	Akogiura
1789	C3	Akune
1788	B6	Akusekijima
1790	K5	Ama
1791	F2	Amagasaki
1789	D2	Amagase
1789	C2	Amagi (Fukuoka)
1787	D3	Amagi (Kagoshima)
1792	D4	Amagi Pass
1793	D4	Amagisan
1792	D4	Amagi Yugashima
1789	B3	Amakusa
1789	C3	Amakusa Islands
1789	B3	Amakusa Sea
1787	D2	Amami Islands
1787	E2	Amami Ōshima
1791	F1	Amanohashidate
1794	B5	Amarume
1793	F3	Amatsu Kominato
1793	F2	Ami
1791	F1	Amino
1792	B1	Anamizu
1791	E3	Anan
1791	E3	Anan Coast
1795	C4	Ani
1792	C4	Anjō
1792	D2	Annaka
1791	G2	Anō
1793	J7	Aogashima (Village)
1793	J7	Aogashima (Island)
1795	C3	Aomori (Prefecture)
1795	C3	Aomori (City)
1795	C3	Aomori Bay
1789	D2	Aonodōmon
1790	B2	Aonoyama
1788	D4	Aoshima
1791	D1	Aoya
1791	G2	Aoyama
1792	D2	Arafuneyama
1792	D1	Arai (Niigata)
1792	C4	Arai (Shizuoka)
1793	E1	Arakaiyama
1794	B5	Arakawa (Town, Niigata)
1793	E2	Arakawa (River, Saitama)
1794	B5	Arakawa (River, Niigata)
1789	C3	Arao
1794	C5	Araodake
1789	C3	Ariake
1789	C3	Ariake Sea
1791	F2	Arida
1791	F2	Aridagawa
1789	C3	Arie
1789	B3	Arikawa
1791	F2	Arima
1789	B2	Arita

1792	D3	Asagiri Kōgen
1791	E1	Asago
1793	F3	Asahi (Chiba)
1794	B5	Asahi (Yamagata)
1792	C3	Asahi (Aichi)
1796	D2	Asahi (Hokkaidō)
1794	B5	Asahi (Niigata)
1791	D2	Asahigawa
1796	D3	Asahikawa
1794	B5	Asahi Mountains
1794	B5	Asahidake
1793	E3	Asaka
1789	C2	Asakura
1792	C2	Asama
1792	D2	Asamayama
1795	C3	Asamushi
1789	B2	Ashibe
1796	D3	Ashibetsu
1796	D3	Ashibetsudake
1793	E2	Ashikaga
1789	C3	Ashikita
1793	E3	Ashinoko, Lake
1794	B6	Ashinomaki
1793	E2	Ashio
1793	E2	Ashio Mountains
1795	D3	Ashiro
1791	F2	Ashiya (Hyōgo)
1789	C2	Ashiya (Fukuoka)
1790	D4	Ashizurimisaki
1790	C3	Ashizuri-Uwakai National Park
1796	E3	Ashoro
1789	D3	Aso
1793	F3	Asō
1789	B1	Asō Bay
1789	D2	Aso-Kujū National Park
1789	D3	Asosan
1796	B5	Assabu
1791	F2	Asuka
1792	C3	Asuke
1793	E4	Atagawa
1793	E3	Atami
1790	B2	Atō
1797	H2	Atoiyamisaki
1797	J2	Atosadake
1793	E3	Atsugi
1796	C4	Atsuma
1792	C4	Atsumi (Aichi)
1794	B5	Atsumi (Yamagata)
1792	C4	Atsumi Peninsula
1796	C3	Atsuta
1791	E2	Awa
1791	F2	Awaji
1791	E2	Awajishima
1792	B2	Awara
1794	B5	Awashima
1792	B2	Awazu
1791	F1	Ayabe
1793	E3	Ayase
1791	G1	Azai
1791	G1	Azuchi
1789	C3	Azuma
1794	C6	Azumasan

1792	D2	Azumayasan
1792	C2	Azumi
1792	C2	Azusagawa

B

1794	C6	Bandai-Asahi National Park
1794	C6	Bandai Atami
1794	C6	Bandai Azuma Kōgen
1794	C6	Bandaisan
1793	F2	Batō
1797	G3	Bekkai
1789	D2	Beppu
1789	D2	Beppu Bay
1796	C3	Bibai
1796	D3	Biei
1796	D2	Bifuka
1797	F3	Bihoro
1797	F3	Bihoro Pass
1790	D2	Bingo Sea
1796	D4	Biratori
1788	D4	Birōjima
1792	B3	Bisai
1790	D2	Bitchū
1791	G1	Biwa, Lake
1791	E2	Bizen
1788	C4	Bōnomisaki
1788	C4	Bōnotsu
1793	F3	Bōsō Peninsula
1793	E3	Bukōzan
1790	C3	Bungo Channel
1789	D2	Bungo Takada
1789	D2	Buzen
1793	F3	Byōbugaura

C

1797	H2	Chachadake
1792	C3	Chausuyama
1793	F3	Chiba (Prefecture)
1793	F3	Chiba (City)
1790	K5	Chibu
1790	J5	Chiburishima
1793	E2	Chichibu
1792	D3	Chichibu-Tama National Park
1793	K8	Chichijima
1793	K8	Chichijima Islands
1793	E3	Chigasaki
1796	B4	Chikiumisaki
1789	C2	Chikugo
1789	C2	Chikugogawa
1789	C2	Chikuhi Mountains
1792	D2	Chikumagawa
1793	E4	Chikura
1789	C2	Chikushino
1786	D3	China
1786	C4	Chinen

I

J

K

1793	F3	Kamisu
1792	C2	Kamitakara
1791	F3	Kami Tonda
1789	B1	Kami Tsushima
1788	C5	Kami Yaku
1796	E2	Kami Yūbetsu
1790	B3	Kammon Strait
1790	C2	Kammuriyama
1790	B2	Kammuriyama Mountains
1793	E1	Kamo
1791	E3	Kamodamisaki
1796	B3	Kamoenai
1790	D2	Kamogata
1793	F3	Kamogawa
1791	E2	Kamojima
1789	C3	Kamoto
1795	B4	Kampūzan
1796	D4	Kamuidake
1796	B3	Kamuimisaki
1794	C5	Kamuroyama
1793	E3	Kanagawa
1795	C3	Kanagi (Aomori)
1790	C2	Kanagi (Shimane)
1792	D4	Kanaya
1792	C3	Kanayama
1792	B2	Kanazawa
1789	C2	Kanda
1794	D4	Kanegasaki
1792	D1	Kan'etsu Expressway
1794	B6	Kaneyama
1792	C3	Kani
1795	C2	Kanita
1791	E2	Kankakei
1790	D2	Kannabe
1793	D3	Kannami
1790	B2	Kano
1792	D3	Kanogawa
1790	D2	Kan'onji
1788	C4	Kanoya
1793	E3	Kanōzan
1792	D3	Kantō Mountains
1793	E2	Kantō Plain
1793	E2	Kanuma
1789	C2	Kanzaki (Saga)
1791	E1	Kanzaki (Hyōgo)
1793	F2	Karasuyama
1789	B2	Karatsu
1789	B2	Karatsu Bay
1796	A4	Karibayama
1796	D3	Karikachi Pass
1792	C4	Kariya
1792	D2	Karuizawa
1795	D3	Karumai
1791	E2	Kasai
1793	F2	Kasama
1792	B3	Kasamatsu
1790	D2	Kasaoka
1787	E2	Kasari
1787	E2	Kasarizaki
1788	C4	Kasasa
1788	C4	Kaseda
1791	F2	Kashihara
1789	C2	Kashima (Saga)
1793	F3	Kashima (Ibaraki)
1794	C6	Kashima (Fukushima)
1790	D1	Kashima (Shimane)
1788	B4	Kashima (Kagoshima)
1794	D5	Kashimadai
1793	F2	Kashima Sea
1793	F2	Kashimaura
1792	C2	Kashima Yarigatake
1792	C3	Kashimo
1793	E3	Kashiwa
1792	D1	Kashiwazaki
1789	C2	Kasuga (Fukuoka)
1791	F1	Kasuga (Hyōgo)
1792	B3	Kasugai
1793	E3	Kasukabe
1791	E1	Kasumi
1793	F2	Kasumigaura
1789	C2	Kasuya
1789	D3	Katamukisan
1793	E2	Katashina
1792	B2	Katayamazu
1789	B2	Katsumoto
1792	D3	Katsunuma
1790	D3	Katsurahama
1793	F2	Katsuta
1793	F3	Katsuura (Chiba)
1791	E3	Katsuura (Tokushima)
1792	B2	Katsuyama (Fukui)
1791	D1	Katsuyama (Okayama)
1795	C4	Kawabe
1793	E2	Kawachi
1791	F2	Kawachi Nagano
1791	G2	Kawage
1793	E3	Kawagoe
1793	E3	Kawaguchi (Saitama)
1792	D1	Kawaguchi (Niigata)
1792	D3	Kawaguchi, Lake
1795	D4	Kawai
1793	E2	Kawaji
1794	C6	Kawamata
1789	D3	Kawaminami
1790	C2	Kawamoto
1788	C4	Kawanabe
1792	D4	Kawane
1791	F2	Kawanishi (Hyōgo)
1794	C5	Kawanishi (Yamagata)
1790	D2	Kawanoe
1789	C2	Kawara
1793	E3	Kawasaki
1790	A2	Kawashirimisaki
1789	C2	Kawasoe
1789	B2	Kawatana
1791	F1	Kaya
1791	D2	Kayō
1793	E2	Kazo
1795	C3	Kazuno
1789	C4	Kedōin
1793	E2	Kegon Falls
1791	F1	Keihoku
1796	D2	Kembuchi
1786	C4	Kerama Islands
1794	D5	Kesennuma
1791	E1	Ketaka
1790	D2	Kibi Kōgen
1791	F3	Kihō
1791	E3	Kii Channel
1791	F2	Kii Mountains
1791	G2	Kii Nagashima
1791	F3	Kii Peninsula
1788	C4	Kiire
1787	E2	Kikai
1787	F2	Kikaishima
1796	B5	Kikonai
1789	C3	Kikuchi
1792	D4	Kikugawa (Shizuoka)
1790	B2	Kikugawa (Yamaguchi)
1790	C2	Kikuma
1789	C3	Kikuyō
1791	F2	Kimi Pass
1793	E3	Kimitsu
1796	B4	Kimobetsu
1788	C4	Kimotsuki Mountains
1794	A5	Kimpokusan
1792	D3	Kimpusan
1786	C4	Kin
1786	C4	Kin Bay
1794	D5	Kinkazan
1791	F2	Kinokawa
1791	G1	Kinomoto
1791	E1	Kinosaki
1793	E2	Kinugawa (River)
1793	G2	Kinugawa (Hot Spring)
1792	D2	Kirigamine
1788	C4	Kirishima
1789	C3	Kirishima-Yaku National Park
1789	C3	Kirishimayama
1793	E2	Kiryū
1790	D2	Kisa
1794	B4	Kisakata
1793	E3	Kisarazu
1791	F2	Kishigawa
1789	A3	Kishiku
1791	F2	Kishiwada
1792	C3	Kiso
1792	C3	Kiso Fukushima
1792	C3	Kisogawa
1792	C3	Kiso Mountains
1790	C1	Kisuki
1787	M6	Kita Daitōjima
1792	D3	Kitadake (Yamanashi)
1788	C4	Kitadake (Kagoshima)
1789	D3	Kitagawa
1796	A4	Kita Hiyama
1793	F2	Kita Ibaraki
1794	D4	Kitakami
1794	D4	Kitakami Basin
1794	D5	Kitakamigawa
1794	D4	Kitakami Mountains
1794	B6	Kitakata (Fukushima)
1789	D3	Kitakata (Miyazaki)
1789	C2	Kita Kyūshū
1797	E3	Kitami
1796	D2	Kitami Mountains
1796	D3	Kitami Pass
1793	E2	Kitamoto
1789	D3	Kitaura (Town)
1793	F2	Kitaura (Lake)
1791	E3	Kitō
1789	D2	Kitsuki
1797	F3	Kiyosato
1793	F3	Kiyosumiyama
1788	D4	Kiyotake
1791	F2	Kizu
1791	F2	Kizugawa
1795	C3	Kizukuri
1787	J5	Kobamajima
1789	C4	Kobayashi
1791	F2	Kōbe
1792	D3	Kobuchizawa
1792	D3	Kobushigadake
1790	D3	Kōchi (Prefecture)
1790	D3	Kōchi (City, Kōchi)
1790	C2	Kōchi (Town, Hiroshima)
1790	D3	Kōchi Expressway
1790	D3	Kōchi Plain
1790	C2	Kōda
1793	E2	Kodama
1795	C2	Kodomari
1792	D3	Kōfu
1792	D3	Kōfu Basin
1793	E2	Koga (Ibaraki)
1789	C2	Koga (Fukuoka)
1791	E1	Kōge
1794	D5	Kogota
1793	D1	Koide
1795	B2	Kojima
1788	D4	Kōjima
1791	E2	Kojima Bay
1791	G2	Kōka
1791	F2	Kokawa
1789	D2	Kokonoe
1788	C4	Kokubu
1793	E3	Kokubunji
1792	C3	Komagane
1792	D3	Komagatake (Yamanashi)
1792	C3	Komagatake (Nagano)
1794	B6	Komagatake (Fukushima)
1795	C4	Komagatake (Akita)
1796	B4	Komagatake (Hokkaidō)
1792	B3	Komaki
1792	B2	Komatsu (Ishikawa)
1790	D3	Komatsu (Ehime)
1791	E3	Komatsushima
1796	B4	Kombudake
1791	G2	Komono
1792	D2	Komoro
1792	B3	Kōnan
1791	F2	Kongōsan
1793	E2	Kōnosu
1793	E2	Konsei Pass
1797	F3	Konsen Highlands
1791	D2	Kōrakuen
1789	A1	Korea Strait
1794	C6	Kōri
1794	C6	Kōriyama
1794	C6	Kōriyama Basin
1794	D4	Koromogawa
1792	C4	Kosai
1795	C3	Kosaka
		Kōsaki see Kousaki
1793	E3	Koshigaya
1792	D1	Koshiji
1788	B4	Koshikijima Islands
1797	F3	Koshimizu
1792	D2	Kōshoku
1792	C2	Kosugi
1792	C4	Kōta
1791	D2	Kotohira
1792	D2	Koumi
1789	B1	Kousaki
1788	C4	Kōyama
1791	F2	Kōyasan
1791	F3	Koza
1793	J5	Kōzushima (Village)
1793	J5	Kōzushima (Island)
1790	D3	Kubokawa
1788	C5	Kuchinoerabujima
1788	B6	Kuchinoshima
1789	C3	Kuchinotsu
1790	B2	Kudamatsu
1790	C2	Kuga
1792	C2	Kuguno
1795	D3	Kuji
1793	F2	Kujigawa
1789	D2	Kujū
1789	D2	Kujū Kōgen
1793	F3	Kujūkurihama
1789	D2	Kujūsan
1793	E2	Kuki
1790	C3	Kuma (Ehime)
1789	C3	Kuma (Kumamoto)
1789	C3	Kumagawa
1793	E2	Kumagaya
1790	B2	Kumage
1796	A4	Kumaishi
1789	C3	Kumamoto (Prefecture)
1789	C3	Kumamoto (City)
1789	C3	Kumamoto Plain
1791	G3	Kumano (Mie)
1790	C2	Kumano (Hiroshima)
1791	G3	Kumanogawa
1791	G3	Kumano Sea
1791	D1	Kume
1786	B4	Kumejima
1791	E1	Kumihama
1793	D3	Kumotoriyama
1797	G2	Kunashiri
1797	H2	Kunashiri Channel
1786	D4	Kunigami
1789	C3	Kunimi (Nagasaki)
1789	D2	Kunimi (Ōita)
1789	D3	Kunimidake
1789	C2	Kunimiyama
1789	D2	Kunisaki
1789	D2	Kunisaki Peninsula
1789	D4	Kunitomi
1796	E3	Kunneppu
1795	D3	Kunohe
1789	B1	Kunoshitasaki
1790	C2	Kurahashijima
1791	D2	Kurashiki
1789	C3	Kuratake
1791	D1	Kurayoshi
1791	D1	Kurayoshi Plain
1790	C2	Kure
1792	B2	Kurikara Pass
1794	C5	Kurikoma
1794	C5	Kurikomayama
1789	C4	Kurino
1796	C3	Kurisawa
1796	C3	Kuriyama
1793	F2	Kurobane
1792	C2	Kurobe
1792	C2	Kurobe Dam
1792	C2	Kurobegawa
1792	C2	Kurobe Kyōkoku
1789	C2	Kurogi
1792	D2	Kurohimeyama
1795	C3	Kuroishi
1793	F2	Kuroiso
1796	B4	Kuromatsunai
1790	C2	Kurose
1788	B5	Kuroshima (Kagoshima)
1787	K5	Kuroshima (Okinawa)
1789	C2	Kurume
1791	F2	Kusatsu (Shiga)
1792	D2	Kusatsu (Gumma)
1788	C4	Kushikino
1788	D4	Kushima
1791	F3	Kushimoto
1788	C4	Kushira
1797	F4	Kushiro (City)
1797	F4	Kushiro (Town)
1797	F3	Kushirogawa
1797	F3	Kushiro Shitsugen National Park
1797	F3	Kussharo, Lake
1789	D2	Kusu
1796	B4	Kutchan

1796	C4	Kuttara, Lake
1791	G1	Kuwana
1795	D3	Kuzumaki
1792	B2	Kuzuryūgawa
1793	E2	Kuzuu
1786	C4	Kyammisaki
1791	F1	Kyōgamisaki
1796	B4	Kyōgoku
1793	E3	Kyonan
1791	F1	Kyōto (Prefecture)
1791	F1	Kyōto (City)
1795	C4	Kyōwa (Akita)
1796	B4	Kyōwa (Hokkaidō)
1789	C2	Kyūshū Expressway
1789	C3	Kyūshū Mountains

M

1795	D3	Mabechigawa
1793	E3	Machida
1789	C2	Maebaru
1793	E2	Maebashi
1788	C5	Magejima
1795	C4	Mahirudake
1791	G1	Maihara
1792	C4	Maisaka
1791	F1	Maizuru
1791	F1	Maizuru Expressway
1793	F2	Makabe
1794	A6	Maki
1793	D2	Makihatayama
1792	D4	Makinohara
1788	C4	Makizono
1796	E4	Makubetsu
1788	C4	Makurazaki
1792	D2	Mamba
1794	C5	Mamurogawa
1793	E3	Manatsuru
1791	D2	Mannō Pond
1794	A6	Mano
1794	A6	Mano Bay
1792	B2	Manza
1791	D2	Marugame
1792	D2	Maruko
1794	C6	Marumori
1792	B2	Maruoka
1796	E2	Maruseppu
1791	E1	Maruyamagawa
1796	C3	Mashike
1789	C3	Mashiki
1793	F2	Mashiko
1797	F3	Mashū, Lake
1790	B2	Masuda
1792	D3	Masutomi
1789	D2	Matama
1789	C3	Matsubase
1792	D1	Matsudai
1793	E3	Matsudo
1790	D1	Matsue
1790	D1	Matsue Plain
1792	D2	Matsuida
1792	C3	Matsukawa
1796	B5	Matsumae
1792	C2	Matsumoto
1792	C2	Matsumoto Basin
1792	D1	Matsunoyama
1791	G2	Matsusaka
1794	D5	Matsushima (Miyagi)
1789	C3	Matsushima (Kumamoto)
1789	B2	Matsuura
1790	C3	Matsuyama
1790	D3	Matsuyama Expressway
1790	C3	Matsuyama Plain
1792	D4	Matsuzaki
1792	B2	Mattō
1797	F3	Meakandake
1791	E2	Megijima
1791	G1	Meishin Expressway
1791	G2	Meiwa
1797	F3	Memambetsu
1796	E4	Memuro
1796	D4	Memurodake
1789	D3	Meranoshō
1792	B2	Miboro Dam
1793	E2	Mibu

1792	C2	Midagahara
1789	C3	Midorikawa
1791	G2	Mie (Prefecture)
1789	D3	Mie (Town, Ōita)
1789	C3	Mifune
1792	B4	Mihama (Aichi)
1792	A3	Mihama (Fukui)
1791	G3	Mihama (Mie)
1790	D2	Mihara (Hiroshima)
1791	E2	Mihara (Hyōgo)
1793	E4	Miharayama
1794	C6	Miharu
1792	D4	Miho no Matsubara
1790	D1	Mihonoseki
1789	A3	Miiraku
1791	D2	Mikamo
1796	C3	Mikasa
1792	A3	Mikata
1792	A3	Mikata Five Lakes
1792	C4	Mikatahara
1792	C4	Mikawa Bay
1791	E2	Miki (Hyōgo)
1791	E2	Miki (Kagawa)
1792	C4	Mikkabi
1792	B2	Mikuni
1792	D2	Mikuni Mountains
1792	D2	Mikuni Pass
1793	J6	Mikurajima (Village)
1793	J6	Mikurajima (Island)
1791	E2	Mima (Tokushima)
1790	C3	Mima (Ehime)
1791	E2	Mimasaka
1788	D4	Mimata
1789	D3	Mimikawa
1795	C2	Mimmaya
1791	F3	Minabe
1793	D2	Minakami
1791	G2	Minakuchi
1789	C3	Minamata
1793	E3	Minami Ashigara
1792	B4	Minami Chita
1787	M6	Minami Daitōjima
1796	D3	Minami Furano
1792	D4	Minami Izu
1796	B5	Minami Kayabe
1792	D2	Minamimaki
1788	C5	Minami Tane
1785	L8	Minami Torishima
1793	E2	Minano
1790	B2	Mine (Yamaguchi)
1789	B1	Mine (Nagasaki)
1791	F1	Mineyama
1787	K5	Minnashima
1792	B3	Mino
1792	D3	Minobu
1792	C3	Mino Kamo
1792	C3	Mino Mikawa Kōgen
1792	C3	Minowa
1791	F2	Misaki (Ōsaka)
1790	C3	Misaki (Ehime)
1791	D1	Misasa
1793	E3	Misato
1795	D3	Misawa
1792	D3	Mishima (City)
1790	B2	Mishima (Island)
1790	C4	Mishō
1789	C3	Misumi (Kumamoto)
1790	B2	Misumi (Shimane)
1790	B2	Misumi (Yamaguchi)
1792	C3	Mitake
1793	F2	Mito (Ibaraki)
1790	B2	Mito (Shimane)
1790	C1	Mitoya
1790	D2	Mitsugi
1796	D4	Mitsuishi
1793	E2	Mitsukaidō
1792	D1	Mitsuke
1789	B1	Mitsushima
1793	E3	Miura
1793	E3	Miura Peninsula
1791	G2	Miyagawa (Mie)
1792	C2	Miyagawa (Gifu)
1794	C5	Miyagi
1790	C2	Miyajima
1793	J5	Miyake
1793	J5	Miyakejima
1795	D4	Miyako
1787	L5	Miyako Islands

1794	C6	Miyakoji
1787	L5	Miyakojima
1788	D4	Miyakonojō
1788	D4	Miyakonojō Basin
1792	B3	Miyama (Gifu)
1792	B3	Miyama (Fukui)
1791	F1	Miyama (Kyōto)
1791	F3	Miyama (Wakayama)
1794	D4	Miyamori
1789	C4	Miyanojō
1788	C5	Miyanouradake
1789	C2	Miyata
1789	D3	Miyazaki (Prefecture)
1789	D4	Miyazaki (City)
1789	D4	Miyazaki Plain
1791	F1	Miyazu
1790	C2	Miyoshi (Hiroshima)
1792	C3	Miyoshi (Aichi)
1790	C2	Miyoshi Basin
1789	C2	Mizuma
1789	C2	Mizumaki
1792	C3	Mizunami
1794	D4	Mizusawa
1793	F3	Mobara
1792	D2	Mochizuki
1794	C5	Mogami
1794	B5	Mogamigawa
1793	F2	Mōka
1796	E2	Mombetsu (City)
1796	D4	Mombetsu (Town)
1791	D3	Monobe
1792	B1	Monzen
1792	C4	Mori (Shizuoka)
1796	B4	Mori (Hokkaidō)
1795	D4	Morioka
1791	F1	Moriyama
1795	C3	Moriyoshi
1795	C4	Moriyoshiyama
1789	D3	Morotsuka
1796	C3	Moseushi
1793	F2	Motegi
1786	C4	Motobu
1794	C6	Motomiya
1794	D5	Motoyoshi
1791	E3	Mugi (Tokushima)
1792	C3	Mugi (Gifu)
1792	D1	Muika
1790	B2	Muikaichi
1796	C4	Mukawa (Town)
1796	D4	Mukawa (River)
1791	F2	Mukō
1791	F2	Mukogawa
1793	K8	Mukojima Islands
1789	C2	Munakata
1794	B5	Murakami
1794	B6	Muramatsu
1791	E1	Muraoka
1794	C5	Murayama
1791	G2	Murō
1796	B4	Muroran
1791	E3	Muroto
1791	E3	Murotozaki
1795	D2	Mutsu
1795	C2	Mutsu Bay
1792	D2	Myōgisan
1792	D2	Myōkō Kōgen
1792	D2	Myōkōsan

N

1791	G2	Nabari
1791	F3	Nachi Falls
1791	F3	Nachi-Katsuura
1791	F3	Nachisan
1792	D1	Nadachi
1792	D2	Naebasan
1791	G1	Nagahama (Shiga)
1790	C3	Nagahama (Ehime)
1794	C5	Nagai
1792	C2	Nagano (Prefecture)
1792	D2	Nagano (City)
1792	D2	Nagano Basin
1792	D2	Naganohara
1791	E2	Nagao
1792	D1	Nagaoka

1792	B3	Nagaragawa
1789	B2	Nagasaki (Prefecture)
1789	B3	Nagasaki (City)
1788	C4	Nagasakibana
1789	C2	Nagasaki Expressway
1789	B3	Nagasaki Peninsula
1789	C3	Nagashima
1789	C3	Nagasu
1790	B2	Nagato (Yamaguchi)
1792	D2	Nagato (Nagano)
1793	E2	Nagatoro
1789	B3	Nagayo
1791	E1	Nagi
1791	E1	Nagisan
1792	C3	Nagiso
1786	C4	Nago
1786	C4	Nago Bay
1792	B3	Nagoya
1786	C4	Naha
1791	E3	Nahari
1793	F2	Naka (Ibaraki)
1791	E1	Naka (Hyōgo)
1789	B2	Nakadōrishima
1796	D3	Naka Furano
1791	E3	Nakagawa (Town, Tokushima)
1796	D2	Nakagawa (Town, Hokkaidō)
1793	F2	Nakagawa (River, Ibaraki)
1791	E3	Nakagawa (River, Tokushima)
1786	C4	Nakagusuku Bay
1792	B1	Nakajima (Town)
1790	C3	Nakajima (Island)
1794	B5	Nakajō
1789	C2	Nakama
1793	F2	Nakaminato
1790	C4	Nakamura
1794	C5	Naka Niida
1792	D2	Nakano
1792	D2	Nakanojō
1788	B6	Nakanoshima (Kagoshima)
1790	K5	Nakanoshima (Shimane)
1795	C3	Nakasato
1796	E4	Naka Satsunai
1795	C4	Nakasen
1797	F3	Naka Shibetsu
1788	C5	Naka Tane
1796	D2	Naka Tombetsu
1789	D2	Nakatsu
1792	C3	Nakatsugawa
1792	D3	Nakatsukyō
1790	D1	Nakaumi
1796	C4	Nakayama Pass
1792	C3	Nakayama Shichiri
1786	C4	Nakijin
1792	D3	Nambu
1792	C2	Namerikawa
1790	C3	Nametoko Keikoku
1794	C6	Namie
1795	C3	Namioka
1796	B5	Nanae
1792	B1	Nanao
1792	B1	Nanao Bay
1789	B2	Nanatsugama
1792	B1	Nanatsujima
1791	E2	Nandan
1788	D4	Nangō (Miyazaki)
1794	B6	Nangō (Fukushima)
1790	D3	Nankoku
1791	G2	Nansei
1785	D8	Nansei (Ryūkyū) Islands
1793	E2	Nantaisan
1791	G2	Nantō
1794	C5	Nan'yō
1791	E2	Naoshima Islands
1791	F2	Nara (Prefecture)
1791	F2	Nara (City)
1789	B3	Narao
1793	F3	Narashino
1793	F3	Narita
1790	D2	Nariwa
1789	A3	Naru
1794	C5	Naruko
1791	E2	Naruto
1793	F3	Narutō
1791	E2	Naruto Strait
1793	F1	Nasu (Town)
1793	E1	Nasu (Hot Spring)

1793	E3	Uenohara
1794	C4	Ugo
1791	F2	Uji
1791	F2	Ujigawa
1793	E2	Ujiie
1788	B4	Uji Islands
1787	E2	Uken
1789	B2	Uku
1793	F3	Unakami
1792	C2	Unazuki (Town)
1792	C2	Unazuki (Hot Spring)
1789	C3	Unzen
1789	B3	Unzen-Amakusa National Park
1789	C3	Unzendake
1792	C2	Uozu
1793	E3	Uraga Channel
1796	E4	Urahoro
1796	D4	Urakawa
1786	C4	Urasoe
1793	E3	Urawa
1793	E3	Urayasu
1789	B2	Ureshino (Saga)
1791	G2	Ureshino (Mie)
1796	C3	Uryūgawa
1789	D2	Usa
1789	C3	Ushibuka
1793	F3	Ushiku
1791	E2	Ushimado
1791	E1	Ushiroyama
1792	D2	Usuda
1792	D2	Usui Pass
1789	D2	Usuki
1796	B4	Usuzan
1796	D2	Utanobori
1796	D3	Utashinai
1789	C3	Uto
1789	C3	Uto Peninsula
1792	D2	Utsukushigahara
1793	E2	Utsunomiya
1790	C3	Uwa
1790	C3	Uwajima
1790	C3	Uwa Sea

W

1791	F1	Wachi
1793	F3	Wada
1792	D2	Wada Pass
1791	E1	Wadayama
1786	D3	Wadomari
1792	B1	Wajima
1789	B3	Wakamatsu
1791	F2	Wakanoura
1791	E1	Wakasa
1792	A3	Wakasa Bay
1791	F3	Wakayama (Prefecture)
1791	F2	Wakayama (City)
1791	F2	Wakayama Plain
1791	E2	Wake
1791	E2	Waki

1795	C2	Wakinosawa
1796	C1	Wakkanai
1792	B1	Wakura
1794	D5	Wakuya
1788	D4	Wanitsuka Mountains
1791	D2	Washūzan
1796	D2	Wassamu
1793	E2	Watarasegawa
1794	C5	Watari

Y

1789	D2	Yabakei (Town)
1789	D2	Yabakei (Gorge)
1789	C3	Yabe
1794	C6	Yabuki
1793	F3	Yachimata
1793	F3	Yachiyo (Chiba)
1790	C2	Yachiyo (Hiroshima)
1787	J5	Yaeyama Islands
1791	F1	Yagi
1793	E2	Yagisawa Dam
1796	C2	Yagishiri
1795	D4	Yahaba
1793	E2	Yaita
1792	D4	Yaizu
1790	D2	Yakage
1792	C2	Yakedake
1788	C5	Yaku
1796	B4	Yakumo
1791	F1	Yakuno
1788	C5	Yakushima
1789	C2	Yamada (Fukuoka)
1795	D4	Yamada (Iwate)
1789	C2	Yamaga (Kumamoto)
1789	D2	Yamaga (Ōita)
1794	C5	Yamagata (Prefecture)
1794	C5	Yamagata (City, Yamagata)
1793	F2	Yamagata (Town, Ibaraki)
1794	C5	Yamagata Basin
1794	C5	Yamagata Expressway
1788	C4	Yamagawa
1790	B2	Yamaguchi (Prefecture)
1790	B2	Yamaguchi (City)
1790	B2	Yamaguchi Basin
1791	E2	Yamakawa
1789	D2	Yamakuni
1789	D2	Yamakunigawa
1795	C3	Yamamoto
1792	B2	Yamanaka
1792	D3	Yamanaka, Lake
1792	D3	Yamanashi (Prefecture)
1792	D3	Yamanashi (City)
1794	C5	Yamanobe
1791	E2	Yamasaki
1791	D3	Yamashiro (Town)
1792	B2	Yamashiro (Hot Spring)
1793	E3	Yamato (Kanagawa)
1792	D1	Yamato (Niigata)
1787	E2	Yamato (Kagoshima)
1791	F2	Yamato Kōriyama

1794	C7	Yamatsuri
1789	C2	Yame
1793	F2	Yamizo Mountains
1793	F2	Yamizosan
1794	D5	Yamoto
1789	C2	Yanagawa (Saga)
1794	C6	Yanagawa (Fukushima)
1791	E2	Yanahara
1790	C3	Yanai
1791	F2	Yao
1792	C3	Yaotsu
1792	C2	Yarigatake
1793	F2	Yasato
1792	D3	Yashajin Pass
1794	C4	Yashima (Akita)
1791	E2	Yashima (Kagawa)
1791	E2	Yashiro
1790	C3	Yashirojima
1791	D3	Yasuda
1790	D1	Yasugi
1790	C2	Yasuura
1795	C3	Yatate Pass
1792	B3	Yatomi
1792	D3	Yatsugatake
1792	C2	Yatsuo
1789	C3	Yatsushiro
1789	C3	Yatsushiro Sea
1791	F2	Yawata
1790	C3	Yawatahama
1789	D3	Yayoi
1789	B2	Yobuko
1791	F2	Yodogawa
1791	G1	Yogo
1796	B3	Yoichi
1796	B3	Yoichidake
1791	E1	Yōka
1791	G1	Yōkaichi
1793	F3	Yōkaichiba
1791	G2	Yokkaichi
1787	E2	Yokoatejima
1793	E3	Yokohama (Kanagawa)
1795	D2	Yokohama (Aomori)
1793	E3	Yokosuka
1790	D1	Yokota
1794	C4	Yokote
1794	C4	Yokote Basin
1786	C4	Yomitan
1795	C3	Yomogita
1786	C4	Yonabaru
1790	D1	Yonago
1790	D1	Yonago Expressway
1787	J5	Yonaguni
1787	H5	Yonagunijima
1786	C4	Yonagusuku
1795	B3	Yoneshirogawa
1792	D1	Yoneyama
1794	C6	Yonezawa
1794	C6	Yonezawa Basin
1793	E3	Yono
1793	E2	Yorii
1792	B3	Yōrō
1793	F3	Yōrōgawa
1786	D3	Yoron
1786	D3	Yoronjima

1790	C3	Yoshida (Ehime)
1790	C2	Yoshida (Hiroshima)
1788	C4	Yoshida (Kagoshima)
1793	D2	Yoshii (Gumma)
1789	C2	Yoshii (Fukuoka)
1791	E2	Yoshii (Okayama)
1791	E2	Yoshiigawa
1791	E2	Yoshinogawa
1791	G3	Yoshino-Kumano National Park
1791	F2	Yoshinoyama
1796	B4	Yōteizan
1793	F3	Yotsukaidō
1791	F2	Yuasa
1791	D1	Yubara
1796	C3	Yūbari
1796	D3	Yūbaridake
1796	D3	Yūbari Mountains
1796	E2	Yūbetsu
1796	E2	Yūbetsugawa
1794	C4	Yuda (Town)
1790	B2	Yuda (Hot Spring)
1792	D2	Yudanaka
1794	B5	Yudonosan
1789	D2	Yufudake
1789	D2	Yufuin
1793	D4	Yugashima
1793	E3	Yugawara
1790	C2	Yuki (Town, Hiroshima)
1790	D2	Yuki (Town, Hiroshima)
1793	E2	Yūki
1789	C2	Yukuhashi
1790	D1	Yumigahama
1793	E2	Yumoto
1791	E1	Yumura
1791	E2	Yunogō
1794	B5	Yunohama
1796	B5	Yunokawa
1789	C3	Yunomae
1790	C1	Yunotsu
1791	G2	Yunoyama
1791	F3	Yura
1791	F1	Yuragawa
1790	C3	Yusuhara
1790	C2	Yuu
1795	C4	Yūwa
1790	B2	Yuya
1794	B4	Yuza
1794	C4	Yuzawa (Akita)
1792	D2	Yuzawa (Niigata)

Z

1793	E3	Zama
1786	C4	Zamamijima
1794	C5	Zaō (Town)
1794	C5	Zaō (Hot Spring)
1794	C5	Zaōzan
1791	D2	Zentsūji
1793	E3	Zushi

CHRONOLOGY OF JAPANESE HISTORY

Western Calendar	Major Periods of Japanese History
	Paleolithic (pre-10,000 BC)
10,000 BC—	Jōmon (ca 10,000 BC–ca 300 BC)
300 BC—	Yayoi (ca 300 BC–ca AD 300)
AD 300—	Kofun (ca 300–710)
400—	
500—	
600—	
700—	
800—	Nara (710–794)
900—	
1000—	Heian (794–1185)
1100—	
1200—	
1300—	Kamakura (1185–1333)
1400—	Muromachi (1333–1568)
1500—	
1600—	Azuchi-Momoyama (1568–1600)
1700—	Edo (1600–1868)
1800—	
1900—	Meiji (1868–1912)
	Taishō (1912–1926)
	Shōwa (1926–1989)
	Heisei (1989–)

The pages that follow are an illustrated outline of Japanese history.

The main column charts Japan's development as a society, recording major incidents and events, the formation and activities of political, economic, and religious institutions, and developments in literature, the arts, education, and science and technology. The central column illustrates the first with a variety of photographs and reproductions of works of art. The third column lists significant events in world history that provide the background against which events in Japan have unfolded and help place the course of Japanese history in its global context.

Together with the Bilingual Index of Entry Titles and the Reader's Guide to the Encyclopedia, the chronology also functions as a key to individual entries in the main text of this book, which are in most cases cross-referenced with SMALL CAPITALS when their titles are mentioned.

Japanese History   **World History**

Prehistory
(before ca AD 300)

Before 30,000 BC • PALEOLITHIC CULTURE; crude STONE TOOLS produced by a preceramic hunting and gathering society.

Ca 10,000 BC • Manufacture of JŌMON POTTERY and polished STONE TOOLS marks the beginning of the JŌMON PERIOD.

Ca 300 BC • YAYOI CULTURE emerges in northern Kyūshū with the introduction of wet-rice cultivation from the Korean peninsula.

Ca 100 BC • YAYOI CULTURE reaches the Kantō region in central Honshū (see also YAYOI PERIOD).

Ca 1 AD • Japan mentioned in Chinese historical records as the land of WA, composed of a number of states (see also WEI ZHI [Wei chih]).

57 • King of the state of Na (NAKOKU) in Wa offers tribute to Emperor Guangwu of the Chinese Later Han dynasty (25–220) and is awarded a seal in return (see KAN NO WA NO NA NO KOKUŌ NO IN).

Ca 180 • The various states of WA join in a league under the headship of HIMIKO, queen of YAMATAI.

239 • HIMIKO, queen of YAMATAI, sends an envoy to the kingdom of Wei in China, receiving from Emperor Ming a gold seal and the title *qin wei wowang* (J: *shingi waō*; WA ruler friendly to Wei).

Jōmon period   Example of Jōmon pottery from the Middle Jōmon period (ca 3500 BC–ca 2500 BC; also dated as ca 3500 BC–ca 2000 BC).

Ca 1300 BC • Chinese characters engraved on tortoise shells and animal bones (see KANJI).

Ca 528 BC • Historical Buddha Gautama gives his first sermon.

Ca 520 BC • Confucius begins his career as a teacher.

334 BC • Alexander the Great begins his conquest of the East.

Kofun period
(ca 300–710)

The KOFUN PERIOD was characterized by the construction of large tomb mounds (KOFUN), indicating the stratification of the agricultural society inherited from the YAYOI PERIOD. Many of these tombs were decorated with the hollow clay sculptures known as HANIWA. The Kofun period witnessed the introduction of BUDDHISM and the Chinese writing system from the Asian continent and the rise of the YAMATO COURT, a powerful dynasty which established Japan's earliest unified state. The last century of the Kofun period is called the ASUKA PERIOD, which is generally considered Japan's first historical age. During this period, a series of institutional innovations, most notably the TAIKA REFORM, created a centralized bureaucratic state based on the Chinese model.

350 • By this time the **YAMATO COURT** has been established in what is now Nara Prefecture.

372 • Chogo, king of **PAEKCHE** in Korea, sends an emissary to **WA** to present a seven-pronged sword (**SHICHISHITŌ**) now held by the **ISONOKAMI SHRINE** in Nara Prefecture.

421 • **WA** ruler San dispatches an embassy to the kingdom of the Chinese Liu-Song dynasty (420–479); this marks the beginning of the era of the **FIVE KINGS OF WA**, who send emissaries bearing tribute to Liu-Song- and Liang-dynasty (502–557) emperors.

527 • Rebellion by Iwai, governor of the province of Tsukushi, Kyūshū (527–528; see **IWAI, REBELLION OF**); this is the first recorded rebellion against the **YAMATO COURT**.

552 • Traditional date of introduction of **BUDDHISM** to Japan, when Buddhist images and sutras are sent from Korea by King Sŏng of **PAEKCHE**. An earlier date, 538, is assigned to this event by many scholars.

587 • Factions form for and against the recognition of Buddhism; **SOGA NO UMAKO**, supported by Umayado no Miko (later Prince **SHŌTOKU**), kills **MONONOBE NO MORIYA**, leader of the anti-Buddhist faction, and establishes the **SOGA FAMILY**'s dominance over the court.

592 • **SOGA NO UMAKO** engineers the assassination of Emperor Sushun, whose accession he had arranged.

593 • Prince **SHŌTOKU** appointed regent by Empress **SUIKO**.

600 • First embassy to Sui-dynasty (589–618) China dispatched (see **SUI AND TANG [T'ANG] CHINA, EMBASSIES TO**).

604 • **KAN'I JŪNIKAI** system of court ranks instituted. Prince **SHŌTOKU** promulgates **SEVENTEEN-ARTICLE CONSTITUTION**.

607 • **ONO NO IMOKO** appointed leader of the second embassy to Sui China (see **SUI AND TANG [T'ANG] CHINA, EMBASSIES TO**).
• Construction of the Buddhist temple **HŌRYŪJI** completed.

620 • Prince **SHŌTOKU** and **SOGA NO UMAKO** said to have compiled the histories **TENNŌKI AND KOKKI**, no longer extant.

630 • First embassy to Tang-dynasty (618–907) China dispatched (see **SUI AND TANG [T'ANG] CHINA, EMBASSIES TO**).

645 • Prince Naka no Ōe (later Emperor **TENJI**) and Nakatomi no Kamatari (later **FUJIWARA NO KAMATARI**) destroy the **SOGA FAMILY** and initiate the **TAIKA REFORM**.
• First year of the Taika era; use of era names (**NENGŌ**) instituted.

663 • Japanese forces sent to aid the Korean kingdom of **PAEKCHE** are defeated in the Battle of **HAKUSUKINOE** off the southwestern coast of the Korean peninsula by a Tang Chinese fleet allied with the Korean kingdom of **SILLA**.

667 • Imperial palace **ŌTSU NO MIYA** established by Prince Naka no Ōe (later Emperor **TENJI**) on the southwestern shore of Lake Biwa. Capital until 672.

668 • Unification of Korea by the kingdom of **SILLA** spurs immigration to Japan by refugees from **PAEKCHE** and **KOGURYŎ** (see **KIKAJIN**).

672 • Prince Ōama (later Emperor **TEMMU**) usurps the throne from his nephew and designated heir Prince Ōtomo (see **JINSHIN DISTURBANCE**); establishes residence at **ASUKA KIYOMI-HARA NO MIYA**.

684 • System of eight cognomens (**YAKUSA NO KABANE**) instituted, under which members of lineage groups (**UJI**) are assigned titles of rank, forming a social pyramid with the emperor at its apex.

694 • Capital city **FUJIWARAKYŌ** established. Capital until 710.

701 • Compilation of the **TAIHŌ CODE** of penal and administrative laws completed; becomes effective the following year (see also **RITSURYŌ SYSTEM**).

708 • Minting of the **WADŌ KAIHŌ** initiated; it is the first coinage minted in Japan.

Kofun period A *haniwa* sculpture from the latter part of the period.

593 • Prince Shōtoku Detail of an 8th-century portrait of the 6th-century statesman (center).

708 • Wadō kaihō A copper example of this first coinage to be minted in Japan.

476 • Romulus Augustulus, the last emperor of the Western Roman Empire, deposed by the Goths under Odoacer.

589 • Beginning of the Sui dynasty (589–618) in China.

622 • Prophet Muhammad arrives in Medina; the Islamic Era begins.

624 • China unified under the Tang dynasty (618–907).

668 • SILLA unifies Korea with the assistance of Tang China; the Chinese are driven out of the peninsula in 676.

Nara period
(710–794)

The establishment of the capital city HEIJŌKYŌ (NARA) marked the beginning of the NARA PERIOD, which was characterized by the maturation of the Chinese-inspired RITSURYŌ SYSTEM of government and the active adoption of other aspects of Chinese culture and technology. Buddhism gained official recognition as the state religion, and temples were constructed throughout Japan in an effort to buttress the authority of the central state. This period also saw the flowering of the arts known as TEMPYŌ CULTURE, the compilation of Japan's first historical chronicles, the KOJIKI and NIHON SHOKI, and the first of the great anthologies of Japanese poetry, the MAN'YŌSHŪ.

710 • Capital city **HEIJŌKYŌ (NARA)** established. Capital until 784.

712 • Compilation of the historical narrative **KOJIKI**, Japan's oldest extant chronicle, is completed by **Ō NO YASUMARO**.

720 • Historical narrative **NIHON SHOKI** (also known as the *Nihongi*) completed.

723 • **SANZE ISSHIN NO HŌ** put into effect; this marks the first government recognition of private ownership of reclaimed lands, which had been prohibited under the **HANDEN SHŪJU SYSTEM**.

724 • Taga no Ki (later known as **TAGAJŌ**) established in northern Honshū as a military outpost from which defensive operations and forays against the **EZO** tribesmen are mounted.

727 • First embassy from the north Asian kingdom of **BOHAI** (Po-hai) arrives in Japan.

733 • Regional gazetteer *Izumo fudoki* completed (see **FUDOKI**).

741 • Emperor **SHŌMU** decrees construction of two state temples in each province (see **KOKUBUNJI**).

743 • **KONDEN EISEI SHIZAI HŌ** promulgated; recognizing the permanent privatization of reclaimed lands, this law lays the legal basis for the emergence of the landed estates called **SHŌEN**.
　　• Construction of a huge Buddha image (**DAIBUTSU**) at the temple **TŌDAIJI** initiated by imperial decree; it is completed in 752.

751 • **KAIFŪSŌ** compiled; it is the oldest extant collection of Chinese poetry by Japanese poets.

754 • Buddhist priest Jianzhen (J: **GANJIN**) arrives in Japan from China.

756 • Empress **KŌMYŌ** donates to the temple **TŌDAIJI** some 600 valuable objects used by her late husband Emperor **SHŌMU** and his court; more than 100 of these objects become the core of the **SHŌSŌIN** treasure house collection.

759 • **GANJIN** founds the temple **TŌSHŌDAIJI**.
　　• The **MAN'YŌSHŪ**, the oldest extant anthology of Japanese poetry, is completed around this time. (The last of its dated poems is from this year.)

784 • Capital moved to **NAGAOKAKYŌ**. Capital until 794.

788 • **SAICHŌ**, founder of the Japanese **TENDAI SECT** of Buddhism, establishes the temple **ENRYAKUJI**.

743 • Great Buddha at Tōdaiji This enormous image has been extensively restored several times since its completion in 752.

Ca 750 • Tang poets Li Bo and Du Fu active.

Heian period
(794–1185)

The HEIAN PERIOD, which began with the establishment of the imperial capital at HEIANKYŌ (KYŌTO), saw the full assimilation of Chinese influences and the flowering of an indigenous aristocratic culture. The development of the Japanese KANA syllabary gave birth to a truly native literary tradition, including some of the finest works of Japanese poetry and prose, such as MURASAKI SHIKIBU's masterpiece, the TALE OF GENJI. Politically, the Heian period was characterized by the domination of the imperial court by regents of the FUJIWARA FAMILY. This age also witnessed the growing power of provincial warrior bands and the proliferation of private estates (SHŌEN), which together brought about the disintegration of the RITSURYŌ SYSTEM of centralized government.

794 • Capital moved to **HEIANKYŌ (KYŌTO)**. Capital until 1868.

801 • **SAKANOUE NO TAMURAMARO** sets out on a campaign in the north against the **EZO** tribesmen.

810 • **KUSUKO INCIDENT:** the Hokke branch of the **FUJIWARA FAMILY** gains political ascendancy at the imperial court.

823 • **KŪKAI**, founder of the **SHINGON SECT** of Buddhism, appointed abbot of **TŌJI**, which becomes the sect's head temple.

866 • **ŌTEMMON CONSPIRACY: FUJIWARA NO YOSHIFUSA** establishes himself as the first non-royal holder of the office of regent (see **REGENCY GOVERNMENT**) and destroys his political rivals.

903 • Poet and political figure **SUGAWARA NO MICHIZANE** dies in exile in **DAZAIFU**; he had been falsely accused two years earlier of plotting against the throne.

823 • Kūkai Detail of an idealized 14th-century portrait.

800 • Charlemagne crowned by Pope Leo III as Charles I, emperor of the Holy Roman Empire.

905 • The **KOKINSHŪ**, the first imperial anthology of **WAKA** verse, is completed.

935 • **KI NO TSURAYUKI** composes the **TOSA NIKKI**, a poetical travel diary written in the native **KANA** syllabary.

938 • The Buddhist monk **KŪYA**, known for his popularization of **PURE LAND BUDDHISM**, begins chanting the **NEMBUTSU** in the streets of **KYŌTO**.

940 • Rebellion by **TAIRA NO MASAKADO** in Hitachi Province; this is the first major rebellion of the rising warrior class against the government.

974 • Approximate date of completion of the **KAGERŌ NIKKI**, a court lady's diary.

985 • The Buddhist monk **GENSHIN** completes the religious tract **ŌJŌYŌSHŪ**; the work contributes to the spread of **PURE LAND BUDDHISM** among the aristocracy.

995 • **FUJIWARA NO MICHINAGA** becomes head of the **FUJIWARA FAMILY**; golden age of its domination of the imperial court begins.

996 • A portion of **SEI SHŌNAGON**'s **MAKURA NO SŌSHI** is now in circulation; this elegant and whimsical diary brings alive the social and aesthetic values of the court aristocracy.

1008 • Entry in **MURASAKI SHIKIBU**'s diary indicates that a substantial part of the **TALE OF GENJI**, her long novel depicting the lives of the aristocracy, has now been written.

1051 • **EARLIER NINE YEARS' WAR** (1051–62) begins in the far north of Honshū against **ABE NO YORITOKI** and his sons.

1053 • Construction of the Hōōdō (Phoenix Hall), dedicated to the Buddha **AMIDA**, completed at the temple **BYŌDŌIN**; **JŌCHŌ** sculpts its main icon.

1059 • Probable date of completion of the **SARASHINA NIKKI**, a court lady's diary.

1083 • **LATER THREE YEARS' WAR** (1083–87) begins against the Kiyohara family in northeastern Honshū.

1087 • Emperor **SHIRAKAWA** abdicates, establishes the system of "cloister government" (**INSEI**).

1156 • **HŌGEN DISTURBANCE**: rivalry between the **TAIRA FAMILY** and the **MINAMOTO FAMILY** for political power at court begins.

1160 • **HEIJI DISTURBANCE**: influence of the **TAIRA FAMILY** over the imperial court established.

1175 • **HŌNEN** begins to preach in **KYŌTO** and founds the **JŌDO SECT** of Buddhism.

1180 • **TAIRA NO KIYOMORI**'s grandson accedes as Emperor **ANTOKU**.
• **MINAMOTO NO YORIMASA**, **MINAMOTO NO YORITOMO**, and **MINAMOTO NO YOSHINAKA** rise against the forces of Kiyomori; **TAIRA-MINAMOTO WAR** begins.

1183 • **MINAMOTO NO YOSHINAKA** defeats the Taira army and enters **KYŌTO**; Taira forces retreat to southwestern Honshū.

1008 • Murasaki Shikibu This 17th-century painting portrays the celebrated Heian-period (794–1185) author at work on her masterpiece, the *Tale of Genji*.

1180 • Taira no Kiyomori Depicted here in a detail of a Kamakura-period (1185–1333) hanging scroll, this warrior solidified his control over the imperial court when his grandson acceded to the throne.

935 • Wang Kŏn establishes the hegemony of the kingdom of **KORYŎ** over the Korean peninsula.

960 • Beginning of the Northern Song dynasty (960–1126) in China.

1066 • William, duke of Normandy, defeats King Harold at the Battle of Hastings and is crowned king of England.

1127 • Beginning of the Southern Song dynasty (1127–1279) in China.

Ca 1150 • Khmer monarch Suryavarman II completes the temple complex of Angkor Wat.

Ca 1167 • Oxford University established.

Kamakura period
(1185–1333)

MINAMOTO NO YORITOMO's victory in the TAIRA-MINAMOTO WAR heralded the beginning of the KAMAKURA PERIOD and the rise to political power of the provincial warrior class. His appointment of provincial governors (SHUGO) and estate stewards (JITŌ) established the foundations of the KAMAKURA SHOGUNATE, the first in a series of military governments that would rule Japan until the mid-19th century. Other developments of this period included the eventual political ascendancy of the HŌJŌ FAMILY, the MONGOL INVASIONS OF JAPAN, the introduction of ZEN Buddhism, and the emergence of new popular sects that spread the Buddhist religion among the common people.

1185 • **MINAMOTO NO YOSHITSUNE** annihilates the Taira army in the Battle of **DANNOURA**; his brother **MINAMOTO NO YORITOMO** is now the most powerful figure in Japan.
• **MINAMOTO NO YORITOMO** receives from the imperial court the right to appoint provincial constables (**SHUGO**) and estate stewards (**JITŌ**), consolidating and extending nationwide the warrior governmental organization (later known as the **KAMAKURA SHOGUNATE**) that he had established at **KAMAKURA** in 1180.

1189 • **MINAMOTO NO YORITOMO** destroys the **ŌSHŪ FUJIWARA FAMILY**, gains control over northern Japan.

1191 • **EISAI**, the founder of the **RINZAI SECT** of **ZEN** Buddhism in Japan, returns from four years of study in China and begins to advocate Chinese Zen teachings in Japan.

1192 • **MINAMOTO NO YORITOMO** appointed **SHŌGUN** by Emperor **GO-TOBA**.

1199 • **MINAMOTO NO YORITOMO** dies; **HŌJŌ FAMILY** achieves control of the **KAMAKURA SHOGUNATE**.

1203 • **HŌJŌ TOKIMASA** assumes the office of shogunal regent (**SHIKKEN**).

1185 • Minamoto no Yoritomo The founder of the Kamakura shogunate as portrayed in a detail of a late-12th-century hanging scroll.

Ca 1200 • Printing spreads in China.

1203 • KAIKEI, UNKEI, and other members of the KEI SCHOOL sculpt the pair of guardian deities housed in the Great South Gate at the temple TŌDAIJI in Nara.

1205 • The SHIN KOKINSHŪ, the most important of the imperial anthologies of WAKA poetry after the KOKINSHŪ, is submitted to the throne.

1212 • KAMO NO CHŌMEI completes his masterwork, the contemplative essay HŌJŌKI.

1218 • Early versions of the HEIKE MONOGATARI in existence by about this time.

1219 • MINAMOTO NO SANETOMO assassinated, ending the line of Minamoto shōguns. Members of the HŌJŌ FAMILY continue to rule as regents for a series of figurehead shōguns.

1221 • JŌKYŪ DISTURBANCE: abdicated emperors GO-TOBA and JUNTOKU sent into exile by the shogunate.

1224 • SHINRAN thought to have completed the earliest version of his major work, the KYŌGYŌSHINSHŌ; this event is considered to mark his founding of the JŌDO SHIN SECT of Buddhism.

1226 • Government office HYŌJŌSHŪ established by shogunal regent HŌJŌ YASUTOKI; this institutes government by council.

1227 • DŌGEN establishes the SŌTŌ SECT of ZEN Buddhism.

1232 • GOSEIBAI SHIKIMOKU promulgated; it is the first codification of warrior house law.

1242 • Emperor Shijō dies without an heir, and the shogunate intercedes to force the accession of Emperor GO-SAGA; Go-Saga's princes, who later become the emperors GO-FUKAKUSA and KAMEYAMA, initiate the succession dispute that culminates in 1337 in the establishment of the NORTHERN AND SOUTHERN COURTS.

1252 • Construction of the Kamakura Daibutsu, a giant seated image of the Buddha Amida, begins at the temple Kōtokuin in KAMAKURA (see DAIBUTSU).

1253 • NICHIREN establishes the NICHIREN SECT of Buddhism.

1274 • First of the MONGOL INVASIONS OF JAPAN.

1281 • Second of the MONGOL INVASIONS OF JAPAN.

1297 • TOKUSEI decree issued by the KAMAKURA SHOGUNATE: debts canceled to protect shogunal retainers from the alienation of their lands to creditors.

1318 • Emperor GO-DAIGO ascends the throne.

1324 • SHŌCHŪ CONSPIRACY, led by Emperor GO-DAIGO against the KAMAKURA SHOGUNATE, fails.

1330 • YOSHIDA KENKŌ completes his masterwork, the collection of essays TSUREZUREGUSA, around this time.

1331 • GENKŌ INCIDENT: Emperor GO-DAIGO fails a second time to wrest power from the KAMAKURA SHOGUNATE; he is exiled to the island of Oki the following year.

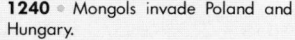

1215 • Magna Carta issued, under duress, by King John of England.

1240 • Mongols invade Poland and Hungary.

1318 • Emperor Go-Daigo Detail of an early-14th-century portrait.

1271 • Marco Polo sets out on his journey to the court of the Mongol emperor Kublai Khan.

1279 • Kublai Khan conquers the Southern Song and establishes the Yuan dynasty (1279–1368) in China.

Muromachi period
(1333–1568)

The destruction of the KAMAKURA SHOGUNATE by the forces of ASHIKAGA TAKAUJI signified the beginning of the MUROMACHI PERIOD, an era of great cultural achievement and persistent social instability. The first decades of the MUROMACHI SHOGUNATE were disrupted by conflict between two rival imperial lines (see NORTHERN AND SOUTHERN COURTS). The shogunate was unable to restrain the ambitions of powerful provincial governors (SHUGO DAIMYŌ) and collapsed entirely after the ŌNIN WAR, which ushered in a century of civil strife known as the SENGOKU PERIOD (1467–1568). At the same time, the Muromachi period saw the impressive development of new artistic forms such as NŌ and KYŌGEN, as well as ZEN-inspired arts such as the TEA CEREMONY, FLOWER ARRANGEMENT, and INK PAINTING.

1333 • KAMAKURA SHOGUNATE collapses; power restored to Emperor GO-DAIGO (see KEMMU RESTORATION).

1335 • ASHIKAGA TAKAUJI turns against Emperor GO-DAIGO.

1336 • Battle of MINATOGAWA: ASHIKAGA TAKAUJI defeats the imperial loyalist armies of NITTA YOSHISADA and KUSUNOKI MASASHIGE and enters Kyōto; Takauji forces Emperor GO-DAIGO to relinquish the IMPERIAL REGALIA to Prince Toyohito, installs the latter as Emperor KŌMYŌ, and confines Go-Daigo at the Kazan Palace.
   • The KEMMU SHIKIMOKU, a code of governmental principles, is promulgated by ASHIKAGA TAKAUJI.

1337 • Emperor GO-DAIGO escapes to Yoshino; declaring that the regalia he had surrendered to Prince Toyohito were imitations and denying his abdication, he establishes the Southern Court (see NORTHERN AND SOUTHERN COURTS).

1335 • Ashikaga Takauji Detail of a 14th-century painting thought to be of Takauji.

1337 • Hundred Years' War, waged by England against France, begins.

1338 • ASHIKAGA TAKAUJI receives the title of SHŌGUN from the Northern Court, founds the MUROMACHI SHOGUNATE.

1343 • KITABATAKE CHIKAFUSA concludes his imperial loyalist history of Japan, JINNŌ SHŌTŌ KI.

1350 • KANNŌ DISTURBANCE (1350–52): ASHIKAGA TADAYOSHI rebels against his brother, the shōgun ASHIKAGA TAKAUJI.

1356 • NIJŌ YOSHIMOTO and GUSAI begin compilation of the RENGA (linked verse) collection TSUKUBASHŪ.

1370 • From around this time fleets of Japanese pirates (WAKŌ) pillage coastal areas of China and the Korean kingdom of KORYŎ.

1391 • MEITOKU REBELLION (1391–92): the YAMANA FAMILY threatens shogunal ascendancy and is defeated by the shōgun ASHIKAGA YOSHIMITSU.

1392 • NORTHERN AND SOUTHERN COURTS reconciled with the acceptance of Emperor GO-KOMATSU as sole sovereign.

1397 • Shōgun ASHIKAGA YOSHIMITSU begins construction of the temple KINKAKUJI in Kyōto.

1399 • ŌEI REBELLION (1399–1400): the powerful ŌUCHI FAMILY defeated by the shōgun ASHIKAGA YOSHIMITSU.

1400 • ZEAMI completes the first three chapters of his FŪSHI KADEN, a treatise on NŌ drama.

1401 • Shōgun ASHIKAGA YOSHIMITSU dispatches an embassy to Ming-dynasty (1368–1644) China; diplomatic relations established the following year.

1404 • TALLY TRADE initiated with Ming-dynasty (1368–1644) China.

1415 • Ryūkyū Kingdom establishes entrepôt trade with Japan.

1419 • ŌEI INVASION: fleet dispatched by Yi-dynasty (1392–1910) Korea attacks pirate (WAKŌ) base on the Japanese island of Tsushima.

1428 • Peasant uprising (TSUCHI IKKI) in Kyōto and surrounding provinces; cancellation of debts (TOKUSEI) sought.

1441 • AKAMATSU MITSUSUKE assassinates the shōgun ASHIKAGA YOSHINORI.

1467 • ŌNIN WAR begins (1467–77); Kyōto laid waste.

1471 • Buddhist monk RENNYO establishes base for proselytizing in Yoshizaki, Echizen Province; as a result of his efforts the JŌDO SHIN SECT spreads through northwestern Honshū.

1483 • Retired shōgun ASHIKAGA YOSHIMASA settles at the villa that later becomes the temple GINKAKUJI; located in the Higashiyama section of Kyōto, this becomes known as the center of HIGASHIYAMA CULTURE.

1486 • A league of SAMURAI gains control over much of Yamashiro Province (see YAMASHIRO NO KUNI IKKI).

1488 • SŌGI, SHŌHAKU, and SŌCHŌ compose the hundred-link poem MINASE SANGIN HYAKUIN, a masterpiece of RENGA.
• Adherents of the JŌDO SHIN SECT of Buddhism vanquish the army of the governor (SHUGO) of Kaga Province and establish autonomous rule there (see IKKŌ IKKI).

1495 • Ink painter SESSHŪ TŌYŌ produces his best-known work, *Haboku sansuizu* (Haboku Landscape).

1523 • Envoys of the HOSOKAWA FAMILY and the ŌUCHI FAMILY clash in Ningbo, China, over rights to TALLY TRADE with Ming-dynasty (1368–1644) China; the Ōuchi family gains the monopoly.

1536 • TEMMON HOKKE REBELLION: an autonomous government established in Kyōto by adherents of the NICHIREN SECT is brought to a violent end by WARRIOR-MONKS of the TENDAI SECT temple ENRYAKUJI.
• From around this time Japanese pirates (WAKŌ) pillage coastal and inland areas of Ming-dynasty (1368–1644) China.

1543 • Matchlock muskets (HINAWAJŪ) are introduced to Japan by the Portuguese on the island of Tanegashima off the coast of Kyūshū.

1549 • Francis XAVIER establishes Japan's first Christian mission at Kagoshima.

1397 • Kinkakuji The Golden Pavilion, which gives this celebrated temple its popular name.

1483 • Ginkakuji The Silver Pavilion, now part of a Kyōto temple, is designated as a National Treasure.

1347 • Black Death rages in Europe (1347–51).

1368 • Zhu Yuanzhang founds the Ming dynasty (1368–1644) in China and drives the Mongols from the capital city Dadu (now Beijing).

1392 • YI SŎNG-GYE declares himself king of Korea, founds the YI DYNASTY (1392–1910).

1400 • Geoffrey Chaucer dies before completing *The Canterbury Tales*.

Ca 1455 • Johannes Gutenberg completes the Forty-Two Line Bible, the earliest book printed in Europe from movable type.

1492 • Christopher Columbus lands in the Bahamas.

1498 • Vasco da Gama, after a voyage around the Cape of Good Hope, reaches Calicut in India.

1517 • Martin Luther nails the Ninety-Five Theses to the church door at Wittenberg.

1534 • Founding of the Society of Jesus (JESUITS) by Ignatius of Loyola.

1553 • First of the Battles of **KAWANAKAJIMA** between the warlords **UESUGI KENSHIN** and **TAKEDA SHINGEN**.

1559 • **ŌTOMO SŌRIN** opens the port of Funai in Bungo Province to Western trade ships.

1560 • Battle of **OKEHAZAMA**: the future hegemon **ODA NOBUNAGA** defeats **IMAGAWA YOSHI-MOTO**.

1563 • Jesuit missionary Luis **FROIS** arrives in Japan; he later writes *Historia de Japam*, which covers the years 1549–93 and, though chiefly a history of Jesuit activities, provides much information about contemporary Japan.

1557 • Portuguese establish an entre-pôt at Macao for trade with China and Japan.

Azuchi-Momoyama period (1568–1600)

The AZUCHI-MOMOYAMA PERIOD was defined by the rise of three successive hegemons, ODA NOBUNAGA, TOYOTOMI HIDEYOSHI, and TOKUGAWA IEYASU, who brought about the political unification of Japan following a century of civil war. Warrior patronage supported the construction of CASTLES throughout the country and a spectacular flourishing of the decorative arts, epitomized by the opulent style of artists such as KANŌ EITOKU. During this brief period, Japan was also exposed to Western (NAMBAN) culture through contact with European traders and missionaries.

1568 • **ODA NOBUNAGA** enters Kyōto, installs **ASHIKAGA YOSHIAKI** as shōgun; Yoshiaki driven into exile in 1573.

1570 • Battle of **ANEGAWA**: **ODA NOBUNAGA** and **TOKUGAWA IEYASU** defeat **ASAI NAGAMASA**.

1571 • First Portuguese merchant ship arrives to trade at Nagasaki (see **NAGASAKI TRADE**).
• **ODA NOBUNAGA** attacks and burns the temple **ENRYAKUJI**.

1575 • Battle of **NAGASHINO**: the 3,000 musketeers deployed by **ODA NOBUNAGA** in his victory over **TAKEDA KATSUYORI** mark Japan's shift to modern warfare.

1576 • **ODA NOBUNAGA** begins construction of **AZUCHI CASTLE**.

1579 • Alessandro **VALIGNANO**, visitor (supervisor) of the Jesuit missions in Asia, arrives in Japan.

1580 • **ODA NOBUNAGA** captures the heavily fortified **JŌDO SHIN SECT** temple **ISHIYAMA HONGANJI**, political center of an area ranging over several provinces.

1582 • Four Christian Japanese boys are sent to Rome at the urging of Alessandro **VALIGNANO** for an audience with Pope Gregory XIII (see **MISSION TO EUROPE OF 1582**).
• **HONNŌJI INCIDENT**: hegemon **ODA NOBUNAGA** commits suicide after a surprise attack by his vassal **AKECHI MITSUHIDE**.
• **TOYOTOMI HIDEYOSHI** defeats Mitsuhide in the Battle of **YAMAZAKI**.
• Hideyoshi initiates the Taikō *kenchi*, a national survey of lands and their productive capacity (see **KENCHI**).

1583 • National unifier **TOYOTOMI HIDEYOSHI** defeats **SHIBATA KATSUIE** in the Battle of **SHIZUGATAKE**.
• **TOYOTOMI HIDEYOSHI** begins construction of **ŌSAKA CASTLE**.

1587 • **TOYOTOMI HIDEYOSHI** issues an edict expelling all Christian missionaries from Japan; it is neither obeyed nor enforced (see **ANTI-CHRISTIAN EDICTS**).
• **SEN NO RIKYŪ** and **TSUDA SŌGYŪ** officiate at a grand outdoor **TEA CEREMONY** held by **TOYOTOMI HIDEYOSHI** on the grounds of the **KITANO SHRINE**.

1588 • **TOYOTOMI HIDEYOSHI** issues an edict prohibiting possession of weapons by peasants (see **SWORD HUNT**).

1590 • **TOYOTOMI HIDEYOSHI** destroys the Later Hōjō family, pacifies all of Japan (see **ODAWARA CAMPAIGN**).

1592 • First of the **INVASIONS OF KOREA IN 1592 AND 1597**.

1596 • **SAN FELIPE INCIDENT**: **TOYOTOMI HIDEYOSHI** confiscates the Spanish galleon *San Felipe*, inaugurating his persecution of Catholic missionaries.

1597 • Twenty-six Japanese and foreign Christians crucified at Nagasaki by order of **TOYOTOMI HIDEYOSHI** (see **TWENTY-SIX MARTYRS**).
• Second of the **INVASIONS OF KOREA IN 1592 AND 1597**.

1598 • **TOYOTOMI HIDEYOSHI** dies.
• Following the second of the **INVASIONS OF KOREA IN 1592 AND 1597**, **TOYOTOMI HIDEYOSHI**'s generals return to Japan with Korean potters who establish the traditions of **SATSUMA WARE**, **ARITA WARE**, and **HAGI WARE** (see also **RI SAMPEI**).

1571 • Spain founds Manila.

1568 • Oda Nobunaga Detail of a 1583 posthumous portrait of the hegemon.

1583 • Toyotomi Hideyoshi The 16th-century unifier of Japan is seen here in a detail of an early-Edo-period (1600–1868) posthumous portrait.

Edo period
(1600–1868)

Victory in the Battle of SEKIGAHARA established TOKUGAWA IEYASU's hegemony over Japan, commencing the EDO PERIOD. Over two centuries of peace followed under the rule of the TOKUGAWA SHOGUNATE, which instituted a political structure known as the BAKUHAN SYSTEM and isolated Japan from potentially disruptive foreign influences through its policy of NATIONAL SECLUSION. The vibrant bourgeois spirit of the period's thriving merchant class (CHŌNIN) found expression in dramatic forms such as KABUKI and BUNRAKU, in the popular literature known as GESAKU, and in artistic genres such as UKIYO-E. In the turbulent period following Commodore Matthew PERRY's arrival in 1853, the shogunate lost its ability to assert national authority, and the Tokugawa regime collapsed.

1600 • English mariner William **ADAMS**, who becomes a valued adviser to **TOKUGAWA IEYASU**, arrives in Japan aboard the disabled Dutch vessel **LIEFDE**.
• Battle of **SEKIGAHARA**: **TOKUGAWA IEYASU** establishes hegemony over Japan.

1601 • Around this time **TOKUGAWA IEYASU** begins to issue licenses for the **VERMILION SEAL SHIP TRADE**, which had been initiated by **TOYOTOMI HIDEYOSHI**.

1602 • The Spanish galleon *Espiritu Santo*, blown off course in a storm, arrives in Shimizu Harbor in Tosa Province; **TOKUGAWA IEYASU**, who seeks trade with New Spain (Mexico), releases the crew.

1603 • **TOKUGAWA IEYASU** is granted the title of **SHŌGUN**, founds the **TOKUGAWA SHOGUNATE**.
• **OKUNI** stages hugely successful dance dramas in Kyōto (see **KABUKI**).
• The **JESUIT MISSION PRESS** commences publication of a Japanese-Portuguese dictionary (see **NIPPO JISHO**).

1604 • Jesuit missionary João **RODRIGUES** begins publication of *Arte da Lingoa de Iapam*, a comprehensive introduction in Portuguese to written and spoken Japanese.

1607 • Arrival in Edo of the first embassy from **YI DYNASTY** (1392–1910) Korea to the Tokugawa shogunate (see **CHŌSEN TSŪSHINSHI**).

1609 • With the approval of the shogunate, the **SHIMAZU FAMILY**, lords of the Satsuma domain, mount a military expedition against the Ryūkyū Islands; the Ryūkyūs become a vassal state of Satsuma in 1611 (see **OKINAWA**).
• **DUTCH FACTORY** established at Hirado; **DUTCH TRADE** begins.
• **MADRE DE DEUS INCIDENT**: **TOKUGAWA IEYASU** orders the arrest of the captain of the Portuguese ship *Madre de Deus*; the following year the captain destroys his ship rather than surrender.

1610 • **TANAKA SHŌSUKE** receives permission from **TOKUGAWA IEYASU** to accompany Rodrigo **VIVERO Y VELASCO** on his return to New Spain (Mexico).

1611 • Sebastian **VISCAINO**, envoy of the viceroy of New Spain (Mexico), is granted an audience with the retired shōgun **TOKUGAWA IEYASU** and the shōgun **TOKUGAWA HIDETADA**.

1612 • Shogunate issues directives aimed at restricting Christianity (see **ANTI-CHRISTIAN EDICTS**).

1613 • John **SARIS** arrives in Japan with credentials from King James I of England; he petitions **TOKUGAWA IEYASU** and receives permission for the English to trade.
• **DATE MASAMUNE**, *daimyō* of Sendai, dispatches an embassy led by **HASEKURA TSUNENAGA** to Spain to petition Philip III (unsuccessfully) for the establishment of trade relations with New Spain (Mexico).

1614 • Ban on Christianity extended nationwide.
• First of the Sieges of Ōsaka Castle begins (see **ŌSAKA CASTLE, SIEGES OF**).

1615 • Second of the Sieges of Ōsaka Castle; **TOYOTOMI HIDEYOSHI**'s son and appointed heir **TOYOTOMI HIDEYORI** commits suicide (see **ŌSAKA CASTLE, SIEGES OF**).
• Shogunate issues an order limiting castles to one per domain (**IKKOKU ICHIJŌ REI**), promulgates the **BUKE SHOHATTO** (Laws for the Military Houses) and **KINCHŪ NARABI NI KUGE SHOHATTO** (Laws Governing the Imperial Court and Nobility).

1616 • **TOKUGAWA IEYASU** dies.
• European shipping limited to the ports of Nagasaki and **HIRADO**.

1624 • English Factory in **HIRADO** closes due to poor business (see **COCKS, RICHARD**).
• Spanish ships prohibited from calling at Japanese ports; persecution of Christians intensifies.

1635 • Tokugawa shōguns adopt the title of *taikun*.
• All foreign shipping restricted to the port of Nagasaki (nonetheless, the **DUTCH FACTORY** remains active in **HIRADO**); overseas travel by Japanese prohibited; Japanese residents abroad prohibited from returning to Japan; capacity of newly constructed ships limited to 500 *koku* (49 gross tons).
• Revision of the **BUKE SHOHATTO** (Laws for the Military Houses); system of mandatory alternate residence in Edo by *daimyō* formalized (see **SANKIN KŌTAI**).

1636 • Buildings on the artificial island of **DEJIMA** at Nagasaki completed; Portuguese merchants, who since 1571 had lived freely in the city, are removed there.

1603 • Tokugawa Ieyasu Detail of an early-Edo-period (1600–1868) posthumous portrait of the founder of the Tokugawa shogunate.

1636 • Dejima Detail of a late-17th-century folding screen showing this artificial island.

1600 British East India Company incorporated by royal charter.

1602 Dutch government grants the Dutch East India Company a monopoly on trade in the East Indies.

1607 English settlement established in North America at Jamestown, Virginia.

1609 Johannes Kepler publishes the first two of his three laws of planetary motion in *Astronomia Nova*.

1616 William Shakespeare dies.

1619 Dutch Factory established at Batavia in Java; it becomes the headquarters of the Dutch East India Company.

1637 • SHIMABARA UPRISING (1637–38) mounted by overtaxed peasants.

1639 • Edicts establishing NATIONAL SECLUSION are completed: Portuguese merchants are evicted from DEJIMA; Portuguese ships are banned from Japan; all Westerners except the Dutch are prohibited from entering Japan.

1641 • DUTCH FACTORY shifted from HIRADO to DEJIMA in Nagasaki.

1643 • TAHATA EITAI BAIBAI KINSHI REI, an ordinance prohibiting the sale and purchase of farmland, issued by the TOKUGAWA SHOGUNATE.

1651 • YUI SHŌSETSU plots a coup d'état against the Tokugawa shogunate (KEIAN INCIDENT); it is unsuccessful.
 • Around this time the population of RŌNIN (masterless *samurai*) in Edo swells; bands of ruffians called HATAMOTO YAKKO and MACHI YAKKO create problems of public order.

1657 • MEIREKI FIRE ravages Edo, killing more than 100,000 people; much of EDO CASTLE and more than 350 shrines and temples burn.
 • Compilation of the national history DAI NIHON SHI begins (it is completed in 1906).

1665 • TOKUGAWA SHOGUNATE orders *daimyō* to conduct a yearly inquisition of Christians (see SHŪMON ARATAME).

1682 • Ihara SAIKAKU publishes the amorous adventure tale KŌSHOKU ICHIDAI OTOKO.

1685 • First of the SHŌRUI AWAREMI NO REI (Edicts on Compassion for Living Things) issued by the shōgun TOKUGAWA TSUNAYOSHI.

1688 • Beginning of the GENROKU ERA (1688–1704), a time of cultural flowering known in particular as the golden age of KABUKI and BUNRAKU.
 • YANAGISAWA YOSHIYASU appointed SOBAYŌNIN (grand chamberlain) to the shōgun TOKUGAWA TSUNAYOSHI.

1689 • Matsuo BASHŌ departs on the journey through northern Honshū that he later chronicles in the *haiku* travel diary OKU NO HOSOMICHI.

1690 • German physician Engelbert KAEMPFER arrives at Nagasaki to serve at the Dutch Factory; his two-volume *History of Japan*, first published in English in 1727, is the standard European work on Japan until the 19th century.

1703 • Band of former retainers of the Akō domain, under the leadership of ŌISHI YOSHIO, carry out a vendetta against KIRA YOSHINAKA (see FORTY-SEVEN RŌNIN INCIDENT).
 • First performance of SONEZAKI SHINJŪ, CHIKAMATSU MONZAEMON's BUNRAKU drama (later a KABUKI drama) about a love suicide.

1707 • Last eruption of FUJISAN (as of 1993).

1708 • Jesuit missionary Giovanni Battista SIDOTTI is arrested, transported to Edo, and interrogated by ARAI HAKUSEKI.

1709 • ARAI HAKUSEKI becomes a key shogunal adviser; commencement of the series of reforms known as the SHŌTOKU NO CHI (1709–16).

1715 • New regulations issued restricting foreign trade with the Chinese and Dutch at Nagasaki; Chinese limited to 30 and Dutch to 2 trade ships annually (see SHŌTOKU NAGASAKI SHINREI).
 • Shogunal adviser ARAI HAKUSEKI completes the first draft of his study of Western geography, *Seiyō kibun*.

1716 • TOKUGAWA YOSHIMUNE becomes shōgun; KYŌHŌ REFORMS (1716–45) commence.

1718 • Fire brigades of townsmen (*machi hikeshi*) formed in Edo (see HIKESHI).

1721 • A box (MEYASUBAKO) is posted to receive commoner appeals to the shōgun.

1723 • Rash of love suicides (SHINJŪ) leads to government attempts to discourage them.

1732 • Locust plague and unseasonable weather cause KYŌHŌ FAMINE in southwestern Japan.

1736 • Chinese trade ships limited to 25 vessels annually to reduce the flow of copper out of Japan.

1748 • First performance of the BUNRAKU drama (later a KABUKI drama) KANADEHON CHŪSHINGURA, a historical work based on the FORTY-SEVEN RŌNIN INCIDENT of 1703.

1767 • TANUMA OKITSUGU becomes SOBAYŌNIN (grand chamberlain) and attempts to increase shogunal income through the expansion of commerce; he falls from power in 1786.
 • Around this time, peasant uprisings (HYAKUSHŌ IKKI) and urban riots (UCHIKOWASHI) occur with increasing frequency.

1657 • Meireki Fire The catastrophic fire depicted in an illustration from the 1661 book *Musashi abumi*.

1689 • Bashō Detail of a 1693 hanging scroll thought to depict the poet on his journey through northern Honshū.

1641 • Dutch capture Malacca from the Portuguese.

1644 • Manchus establish the Qing dynasty (1644–1912) in China.

1689 • English Bill of Rights enacted; the levying of taxes requires the consent of Parliament.

1694 • Bank of England incorporated.

1699 • Chinese permit the English to conduct annual trade operations at Guangzhou.

1703 • Tsar Peter I of Russia founds St. Petersburg and gains a sea outlet to the West.

1712 • Thomas Newcomen erects a steam engine to pump water from a mine in Staffordshire, England.

1751 • Denis Diderot begins publication of the 35-volume *Encyclopédie*.

1774 • Anatomical text **KAITAI SHINSHO** published by **SUGITA GEMPAKU** and **MAENO RYŌTAKU**; it is the first complete Japanese translation of a Western medical work.

1776 • **UEDA AKINARI** publishes **UGETSU MONOGATARI**, a collection of supernatural tales.

1782 • **TEMMEI FAMINE** begins; estimates of the nationwide death toll during the five years of its duration range from 200,000 to 900,000.

1783 • **ASAMAYAMA** erupts, causing some 20,000 deaths; falling ash brings low summer temperatures and poor crops, exacerbating the famine that had commenced the previous year.

1787 • **MATSUDAIRA SADANOBU** becomes senior shogunal councillor (**RŌJŪ**); **KANSEI REFORMS** (1787–93) initiated.

1789 • Debt moratoriums (**KIENREI**) declared to save shogunal retainers from destitution.

1790 • **UKIYO-E** artist Kitagawa **UTAMARO** begins producing his most distinctive and memorable designs at about this time.

1791 • Shogunate prohibits communal bathing of men and women at public bathhouses in Edo.

1792 • **HAYASHI SHIHEI** placed under house arrest; the shogunate confiscates the printing blocks and all copies of his book *Kaikoku heidan* (1791), in which he discusses the possibility of foreign incursions into Edo Bay.
  • Adam Erikovich **LAXMAN** arrives at Nemuro in eastern Ezo (now Hokkaidō) with **DAIKOKUYA KŌDAYŪ**; the following year Laxman negotiates unsuccessfully with shogunal officials in **MATSUMAE** for the establishment of trade relations between Japan and Russia.

1796 • **INAMURA SAMPAKU** and others publish the Dutch-Japanese dictionary **HARUMA WAGE**.

1798 • **MOTOORI NORINAGA** completes the *Kojiki den*, a comprehensive annotation of the early historical narrative **KOJIKI** and a major work in the **KOKUGAKU** (National Learning) movement.
  • **KONDŌ JŪZŌ** explores the **KURIL ISLANDS**.

1799 • **TAKATAYA KAHEI** establishes a shipping route to **ETOROFU**. Shogunate establishes direct administrative control over the southern part of **EZO** (see **HAKODATE BUGYŌ**).

1800 • **INŌ TADATAKA** begins his cartographic survey of all Japan; it is completed in 1816.

1802 • **JIPPENSHA IKKU** publishes the first volume of his serial comic novel **TŌKAIDŌCHŪ HIZAKURIGE**, which describes the adventures of two wayfarers on the road from Edo to Ōsaka.

1804 • Russian envoy Nikolai Petrovich **REZANOV** reaches Nagasaki, unsuccessfully seeks the establishment of trade relations with Japan.

1807 • Kyokutei **BAKIN** begins publication of the adventure tale **CHINSETSU YUMIHARIZUKI**.

1808 • British warship *Phaeton* enters Nagasaki Harbor under a Dutch flag, takes two Dutch prisoners who are released in exchange for food and water; the incident exacerbates shogunal fears of encroachment from the West (see **PHAETON INCIDENT**).

1809 • **MAMIYA RINZŌ** discovers the Tatar Strait, proving that Sakhalin is an island.

1811 • Vasilii Mikhailovich **GOLOVNIN**, captain of the Russian naval vessel *Diana*, is captured and imprisoned by the Japanese while surveying the **KURIL ISLANDS** (he is released in 1813). His account of his experiences, published in 1816, is translated into English in 1818 as *Narrative of My Captivity in Japan, during the Years 1811, 1812, and 1813* and is widely read.

1812 • **TAKATAYA KAHEI** is taken captive by a Russian warship off **KUNASHIRI** in the **KURIL ISLANDS**; freed in 1813, he negotiates the release of Vasilii Mikhailovich **GOLOVNIN**.

1814 • Kurozumi Munetada founds the religious sect **KUROZUMIKYŌ**.

1820 • Kobayashi **ISSA** completes the poetical diary **ORAGA HARU**; its theme is the author's love for his infant daughter Sato and the grief aroused by her sudden death.

1823 • Philipp Franz von **SIEBOLD** arrives in Japan to serve as physician to the Dutch Factory; the following year he opens the boarding school Narutakijuku and teaches Western medicine and science to **TAKANO CHŌEI**, **ITŌ GEMBOKU**, and **ITŌ KEISUKE**.

1825 • Shogunate issues the **GAIKOKUSEN UCHIHARAI REI** (Order for the Repelling of Foreign Ships).

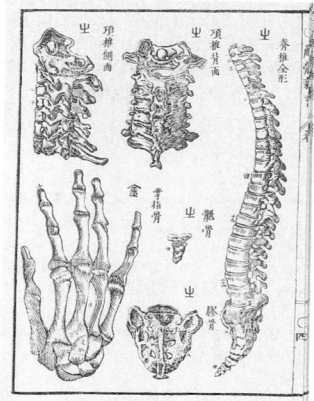

1774 • Kaitai shinsho An illustration from this anatomical text.

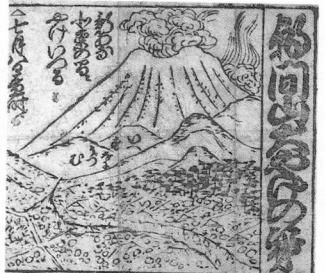

1783 • Asamayama The 1783 eruption as depicted in a contemporary newssheet.

1798 • Motoori Norinaga The scholar in a detail of a 1790 self-portrait.

1776 • Continental Congress issues the US Declaration of Independence.

1785 • Edmund Cartwright patents a power loom.

1789 • George Washington becomes the first president of the United States.
  • French Revolution begins.

1796 • Edward Jenner performs first smallpox inoculation.

1799 • Metric system instituted in France.

1804 • Napoleon crowns himself emperor of France.

1807 • Robert Fulton initiates steamboat service on the Hudson River.

1819 • British found Singapore.

1823 • US president James Monroe proclaims the Monroe Doctrine.

1829 ● Physician Philipp Franz von **SIEBOLD** placed under house arrest at **DEJIMA** for receiving maps of the Japanese archipelago from **TAKAHASHI KAGEYASU**. Siebold is subsequently banished from Japan; after returning to Europe he writes the encyclopedic study of Japan, *Nippon, Archiv zur Beschreibung von Japan*, as well as *Fauna Japonica* and *Flora Japonica*.

1831 ● Katsushika **HOKUSAI**'s series of **UKIYO-E** landscapes *Fugaku sanjūrokkei* (Thirty-Six Views of Mt. Fuji) begins to appear by about this time.

1832 ● **TAMENAGA SHUNSUI** begins publication of the romantic novel **SHUNSHOKU UMEGOYOMI**, which is to be influential in the development of the modern Japanese novel.

1833 ● **TEMPŌ FAMINE** (1833–36) begins; by 1836 rice harvests are estimated to have been only one-third of the normal crop; some 200,000 to 300,000 people are thought to have died of starvation and disease.
● Publication of Andō **HIROSHIGE**'s **UKIYO-E** landscape series *Tōkaidō gojūsantsugi* (Fifty-Three Stations of the Tōkaidō Road) begins.

1837 ● Rebellion of **ŌSHIO HEIHACHIRŌ**, a Confucian ideologue who seeks famine relief for the peasantry.
● Rebellion of **IKUTA YOROZU**, who seeks relief for starving farmers.
● US merchant ship carrying Japanese castaways is fired on as it attempts to enter Uraga Bay near Edo (now Tōkyō) and then Kagoshima Bay in Kyūshū (see **MORRISON INCIDENT**).

1838 ● **NAKAYAMA MIKI** founds the religious sect **TENRIKYŌ**.

1839 ● Shogunate crackdown on scholars of **WESTERN LEARNING** (see **BANSHA NO GOKU**).

1841 ● **TEMPŌ REFORMS** (1841–43) initiated by senior shogunal councillor **MIZUNO TADAKUNI**.
● Fisherman **NAKAHAMA MANJIRŌ**, shipwrecked on a Pacific island, is rescued by an American whaler and taken to the United States.

1842 ● **GAIKOKUSEN UCHIHARAI REI** (Order for the Repelling of Foreign Ships) revoked; shogunate orders the provision of food, water, and firewood to foreign ships (**SHINSUI KYŌYO REI**).

1843 ● Peasants in Edo ordered to return to their farmlands (see **HITOGAESHI**).
● **AGECHIREI** (Land Requisition Orders) issued as part of the **TEMPŌ REFORMS** and then rescinded; fall of **MIZUNO TADAKUNI**.

1844 ● Dutch warship arrives in Nagasaki with a letter from the king of the Netherlands advising the shogunate to open Japan to trade with the West; the following year the shogunate sends a letter of refusal.
● Garrison and battery established at Hakodate in **EZO**; garrison established on Kunashiri in the **KURIL ISLANDS**.

1846 ● Foreign warships and whaling vessels enter Japanese waters with increasing frequency; the shogunate and a number of domains give greater attention to coastal defenses.

1852 ● Jan Hendrik **DONKER CURTIUS**, the last overseer of the **DUTCH FACTORY**, arrives in Japan.

1853 ● Four warships of the US East India Squadron, commanded by Commodore Matthew **PERRY**, call at Uraga at the mouth of Edo Bay.
● Russian Vice Admiral Evfimii Vasil'evich **PUTIATIN** calls at Nagasaki with the flagship *Pallada* and four other warships.

1854 ● Fleet of nine US naval vessels, led by Commodore Matthew **PERRY**, anchors in Edo Bay.
● Treaty of Peace and Amity between the United States and the Empire of Japan (**KANAGAWA TREATY**) signed; similar treaties concluded with Great Britain (1854), Russia (1855), and the Netherlands (1856).

1855 ● Ansei Earthquake; more than 7,000 die in Edo.
● Naval-officer training school (**KAIGUN DENSHŪJO**) established at Nagasaki.

1856 ● Establishment of the **BANSHO SHIRABESHO** (Institute for the Investigation of Barbarian Books).
● US consul general Townsend **HARRIS** arrives at Shimoda to initiate negotiations with the shogunate on what will become the **HARRIS TREATY**.
● **YOSHIDA SHŌIN** begins to teach his imperial loyalist philosophy to young *samurai* of the Chōshū domain.

1857 ● Reverberatory furnace (**HANSHARO**) for the production of steel completed at Nirayama on the Izu Peninsula.

1858 ● **II NAOSUKE** becomes senior adviser to the shōgun (see **TAIRŌ**).
● **ANSEI COMMERCIAL TREATIES** are concluded between the shogunate and the United States, the Netherlands, Russia, Great Britain, and France.
● Beginning of the **ANSEI PURGE** (1858–60) of opponents to the shogunate's opening of Japan to the West.

1829 ● Philipp Franz von Siebold A portrait of the 19th-century physician by his friend and associate, the artist Kawahara Keiga.

1833 ● Hiroshige The *Keishi* print from the artist's series *Fifty-Three Stations of the Tōkaidō Road*.

1853 ● Matthew Perry A photo of the American naval officer taken after his return from his mission to Japan.

1831 ● Michael Faraday invents the dynamo.

1837 ● Victoria becomes queen of England (1837–1901).

1839 ● Opium War begins in China (1839–42).

1844 ● Telegraph line links Washington and Baltimore.

1851 ● British news agency Reuters founded.

1858 ● China signs Treaties of Tianjin with Great Britain, France, Russia, and the United States. ● Government of India Act formally transfers control over India to British crown.

1859 • British consul general Rutherford **ALCOCK** arrives in Japan; *The Capital of the Tycoon,* his account of his dealings with the shogunate, is published in 1863.
• British merchant Thomas Blake **GLOVER** arrives in Japan; Glover and Co supplies arms to the domains of Satsuma and Chōshū, centers of antishogunal activity.
• James Curtis **HEPBURN** arrives in Japan; his *Japanese and English Dictionary* (1867; J: *Waei gorin shūsei*) is the first Japanese-English dictionary.
• Kawate Bunjirō founds the religious sect **KONKŌKYŌ**.

1860 • Shogunal mission to the United States (see **UNITED STATES, MISSION OF 1860 TO**) leaves aboard the American ship *Powhatan* to ratify the **HARRIS TREATY**. It is accompanied by the **KANRIN MARU**, with a Japanese crew under the command of **KATSU KAISHŪ**.
• Assassination of **II NAOSUKE** (see **SAKURADAMONGAI**).
• From about this time large quantities of **UKIYO-E** prints are exported to Europe; the influence of Japanese art begins to be felt in the West (see **JAPONISME**).

1861 • Publication of the *Nagasaki Shipping List and Advertiser*, Japan's first modern newspaper, begins (see **NEWSPAPERS**); it is in English.

1862 • First regularly published Japanese-language newspaper, **KAMPAN BATABIYA SHIMBUN**, translated from the Dutch *Javasche Courant* at the **BANSHO SHIRABESHO**, begins publication.
• Assassination attempt on **ANDŌ NOBUMASA**, leading senior councillor (**RŌJŪ**) of the shogunate (see **SAKASHITAMONGAI INCIDENT**), in reaction to the planned marriage of the shōgun **TOKUGAWA IEMOCHI** to Princess **KAZU**, sister of Emperor **KŌMEI**. The marriage in fact takes place later this year.
• **RICHARDSON AFFAIR**: murder of a British merchant by retainers of the Satsuma domain.
• **NISHI AMANE** and **TSUDA MAMICHI**, the first students dispatched overseas by the shogunate, depart for the Netherlands.
• Publication of the first English-Japanese dictionary, *Eiwa taiyaku shūchin jisho*.

1863 • **KAGOSHIMA BOMBARDMENT**: British warships attack the Satsuma domain in retaliation for the **RICHARDSON AFFAIR**.
• **COUP D'ETAT OF 30 SEPTEMBER 1863**: radical proimperial *samurai* of the Chōshū domain driven from Kyōto.

1864 • **MITO CIVIL WAR**: proimperial uprising devastates the Mito domain.
• **IKEDAYA INCIDENT**: clash in Kyōto between proimperial *samurai*, many from the Chōshū domain, and the shogunal **SHINSENGUMI** police force.
• **HAMAGURI GOMON INCIDENT**: proimperial Chōshū domain extremists attempt to force their way into Kyōto; the imperial court orders the shogunate to mount a punitive expedition against Chōshū (see **CHŌSHŪ EXPEDITIONS**).
• **SHIMONOSEKI BOMBARDMENT**: naval expedition by the Western powers against the Chōshū domain in retaliation for attacks on its ships passing through the Shimonoseki Strait.

1865 • British minister plenipotentiary Sir Harry Smith **PARKES** arrives in Japan; Ernest Mason **SATOW** and William George **ASTON**, who later earn renown as Japanologists, serve him as interpreters.

1866 • **SATSUMA-CHŌSHŪ ALLIANCE** formed against the **TOKUGAWA SHOGUNATE**.
• **KAIZEI YAKUSHO** (Tariff Convention) signed with Great Britain, France, the Netherlands, and the United States.
• Shogunal army engages forces of the Chōshū domain in the second of the **CHŌSHŪ EXPEDITIONS**; the shogunate's failure to bring the campaign to a successful conclusion severely damages its prestige.

1867 • Formal return of political authority to the emperor by the last shōgun, **TOKUGAWA YOSHINOBU** (see **TAISEI HŌKAN**).

1859 • French forces occupy Saigon. Construction of the Suez Canal begins; completed in 1869. • Charles Darwin publishes *On the Origin of Species*.

1860 • Kanrin maru The storm-tossed vessel is depicted in this painting by a member of the shogunal mission to the United States.

1861 • Civil War begins in the United States (1861–65). • Unification of Italy.

1863 • Cambodia is made a protectorate of France.

1864 • The International Workingmen's Association (commonly known as the First International) is founded in London.

1867 • Tokugawa Yoshinobu A contemporary photograph of the last Tokugawa shōgun.

1867 • Alfred Nobel patents dynamite in Great Britain. • Karl Marx publishes the first volume of *Das Kapital* in Berlin.

Meiji period (1868–1912)

The MEIJI RESTORATION of direct imperial rule commenced the MEIJI PERIOD and began Japan's transformation into a modern industrial society. Restoration leaders welded former feudal domains into a modern nation-state, established a centralized bureaucracy, enacted a new land tax system, and created a modern conscript army. Abolition of feudal classes and the establishment of universal education helped create a unified national polity. The 1889 CONSTITUTION OF THE EMPIRE OF JAPAN established the first parliamentary government in Asia. During the latter part of the period Japan emerged as a major imperialist power through victories in the SINO-JAPANESE WAR OF 1894–1895 and the RUSSO-JAPANESE WAR and the annexation of Korea in 1910.

1868 • Restoration of imperial rule (see **MEIJI RESTORATION; ŌSEI FUKKO**).
• **BOSHIN CIVIL WAR** (1868–69): shogunate loyalist forces are defeated in a series of battles.
• **CHARTER OATH** promulgated; **GOBŌ NO KEIJI** (Five Public Notices) issued by Emperor **MEIJI**.
• Buddhist priests serving at Shintō shrines are ordered to abandon their vows and return to the laity (see **SHINTŌ AND BUDDHISM, SEPARATION OF**).
• **SEITAISHO** (Constitution of 1868) issued.
• **DAJŌKAN** (Grand Council of State) becomes the central organ of the new imperial government.
• First national paper currency issued (**DAJŌKAN SATSU**).

1868 • The city of Edo is renamed **TŌKYŌ** ("eastern capital"); it becomes the official seat of government the following year.
  • The emperor adopts the era name (**NENGŌ**) Meiji ("Enlightened Rule").
  • The emperor makes a preliminary visit to Tōkyō; he formally moves his residence from Kyōto to the new capital the following year.

1869 • Formal return of domainal registers to Emperor **MEIJI** (**HANSEKI HŌKAN**).
  • The shrine Shōkonsha (now **YASUKUNI SHRINE**) is established in Tōkyō to enshrine Japanese who died in war from 1853 on.
  • **EZO**, the region to the north of the main island of Honshū, is renamed **HOKKAIDŌ**; the **KAITAKUSHI** (Hokkaidō Colonization Office) is opened.

1870 • Telegraph line links Tōkyō and Yokohama (see **TELECOMMUNICATIONS SYSTEMS**).
  • Imperial rescript (the Daikyō Sempu) declares **SHINTŌ** beliefs to be the basis for national unity.
  • Commoners (**HEIMIN**) are permitted to assume surnames.

1871 • First Japanese-language daily newspaper, **YOKOHAMA MAINICHI SHIMBUN**, begins publication.
  • **POSTAL SERVICE** established.
  • Family Registration Law (Koseki Hō) enacted (see **JINSHIN KOSEKI**); the **SHŪMON ARATAME** system of census registration suspended.
  • Under the Shinka Jōrei (New Currency Regulation) the **YEN** is established as Japan's official monetary unit and the gold standard is adopted.
  • Domains dissolved and prefectures established (see **PREFECTURAL SYSTEM, ESTABLISHMENT OF**).
  • *Samurai* permitted to cut their topknots (see **DAMPATSUREI**) and cast off their swords; samurai and aristocrats permitted to marry commoners; the designations *eta* and **HININ**, assigned to the lowest social classes, are abolished.
  • **IWAKURA MISSION** departs Japan on an 18-month tour to study the social systems of the United States and European nations.

1872 • Implementation of the **JINSHIN KOSEKI**, the first nationwide census registration conducted by the Meiji government; the population in this year is given as 33,110,825.
  • Shogunate ordinance forbidding the sale and purchase of farmland (**TAHATA EITAI BAIBAI KINSHI REI**) is revoked.
  • Creation of the **ARMY MINISTRY** and the **NAVY MINISTRY**.
  • Railroad begins operation between Tōkyō and Yokohama (see **RAILWAYS**).
  • **MARIA LUZ INCIDENT** results in the recognition, on the basis of international law, of the equality of Japan among nations.
  • Asiatic Society of Japan is founded in Yokohama; numerous papers by Ernest Mason **SATOW**, William George **ASTON**, and Basil Hall **CHAMBERLAIN** are subsequently published in the *Transactions of the Asiatic Society of Japan*.
  • The **EDUCATION ORDER OF 1872** establishes Japan's first modern school system.

1873 • Gregorian calendar adopted on 1 January (Meiji 5.12.3 according to the lunar calendar; see **CALENDAR, DATES, AND TIME**).
  • **CONSCRIPTION ORDINACE OF 1873** enacted; antidraft riots ensue (see **KETSUZEI IKKI**).
  • Basil Hall **CHAMBERLAIN** arrives in Japan; from 1886 he teaches Japanese and philology at Tōkyō University; in 1890 he publishes *Things Japanese*.
  • Land Tax Reform Law issued (see **LAND TAX REFORM OF 1873–1881**).
  • **SAIGŌ TAKAMORI** and other dissidents resign from the government after the rejection of their plan for an expedition against Korea (see **SEIKANRON**).
  • **HOME MINISTRY** established.

1874 • **ITAGAKI TAISUKE** and others submit the Tosa Memorial, calling for the establishment of an elected national assembly (see **FREEDOM AND PEOPLE'S RIGHTS MOVEMENT**).
  • **SAGA REBELLION** by disaffected *samurai*.
  • **MEIROKUSHA** society founded to introduce Western thought.
  • **TAIWAN EXPEDITION OF 1874**.
  • During this year and the next, **FOREIGN EMPLOYEES OF THE MEIJI PERIOD**, hired by the government as teachers, technicians, and advisers, reach a peak of some 520.

1875 • **ŌSAKA CONFERENCE OF 1875**: establishment of a representative assembly discussed.
  • Treaty of **ST. PETERSBURG** gives **SAKHALIN** to Russia and the **KURIL ISLANDS** to Japan.
  • Tōkyō Meteorological Observatory established.
  • **LIBEL LAW OF 1875** and **PRESS ORDINANCE OF 1875** issued.

1876 • Treaty of **KANGHWA**, signed with Korea, gains unequal privileges for Japan.
  • Edict issued prohibiting the wearing of swords (**HAITŌREI**).
  • Erwin von **BÄLZ** arrives in Japan to teach physiology at Tōkyō University Medical School; in 1902 he becomes physician-in-waiting to the imperial household.
  • William Smith **CLARK** arrives in Japan to serve as the vice president of Sapporo Agricultural College (now part of **HOKKAIDŌ UNIVERSITY**).
  • **JIMPŪREN REBELLION, AKIZUKI REBELLION OF 1876, HAGI REBELLION** mounted by discontented *samurai*.
  • Uprisings in Ibaraki and Mie prefectures by peasants who demand a land tax reduction; lower rates implemented in 1877.

1868 • Emperor Meiji A photograph of the emperor taken when he was around 20 years old.

1871 • Iwakura mission The leaders of this mission as photographed in 1872.

1873 • Saigō Takamori An 1883 posthumous portrait of this leader of the Meiji Restoration who later became one of the first rebels against the regime he helped create.

1869 • Transcontinental railroad completed in the United States.

1870 • Franco-Prussian War (1870–71) begins.

1871 • Unification of Germany.

1876 • The first successful telephone transmission is achieved by Alexander Graham Bell.

1877 • SATSUMA REBELLION; SAIGŌ TAKAMORI commits suicide.
- Anglican missionary John BATCHELOR arrives in Japan; in 1889 he publishes *An Ainu English Japanese Dictionary*.

1878 • Home Minister ŌKUBO TOSHIMICHI assassinated by disaffected former *samurai* of Satsuma.
- Ernest Francisco FENOLLOSA arrives in Japan to teach philosophy and political economy at Tōkyō University; he will eventually bring an appreciation of traditional Japanese art to the West and contribute to the reassessment of Japanese art within Japan.
- TAKEHASHI INSURRECTION by some 260 government soldiers.

1879 • Part of the Ryūkyū Islands incorporated into Japan as Okinawa Prefecture (see OKINAWA).

1880 • Formation of the LEAGUE FOR ESTABLISHING A NATIONAL ASSEMBLY.
- SHŪKAI JŌREI (Public Assembly Ordinance) issued to control the FREEDOM AND PEOPLE'S RIGHTS MOVEMENT.

1881 • HOKKAIDŌ COLONIZATION OFFICE SCANDAL OF 1881.
- Expulsion of ŌKUMA SHIGENOBU from the government (see POLITICAL CRISIS OF 1881).
- Imperial rescript promises the promulgation of a constitution and the convening of a national assembly within a decade.
- JIYŪTŌ (Liberal Party), Japan's first national political party, is formed.
- MATSUKATA MASAYOSHI becomes minister of finance and begins to implement the MATSUKATA FISCAL POLICY.

1882 • RIKKEN KAISHINTŌ (Constitutional Reform Party) founded.
- BANK OF JAPAN established.
- IMO MUTINY: revolt of traditionalist Korean troops in reaction to the Japanese-inspired modernization of the Korean army. In the Treaty of CHEMULP'O, signed with Korea later that year, Japan receives reparations for loss of Japanese lives and property during the revolt.
- Publication of the *Shintaishi shō*, the first poetry anthology to include translations of Western verse (see SHINTAISHI).

1883 • Completion of the ROKUMEIKAN, a two-story brick building designed by Josiah CONDER; it is the site for Western-style social events attended by prominent Japanese and foreigners.

1884 • Peerage Act issued: 508 titles of nobility conferred (see PEERAGE).
- Typhoon lashes the Pacific coast of Japan; nearly 2,000 die in Kyōto.
- KABASAN INCIDENT: radical members of the JIYŪTŌ (Liberal Party) clash with police and government troops in Ibaraki Prefecture.
- CHICHIBU INCIDENT: peasants in Saitama Prefecture, led by members of the FREEDOM AND PEOPLE'S RIGHTS MOVEMENT, rise against the government.
- KAPSIN POLITICAL COUP mounted in Korea with the support of Japanese.

1885 • First group of Japanese emigrants to Hawaii departs.
- TIANJIN (TIENTSIN) CONVENTION: agreement reached between China and Japan concerning their interests in Korea.
- ŌSAKA INCIDENT: leaders of a plot to mount a coup d'état in Korea arrested and tried.
- Cabinet system adopted; the new cabinet supersedes the DAJŌKAN (Grand Council of State) as the central organ of the Japanese state (see PRIME MINISTER AND CABINET).

1886 • NORMANTON INCIDENT: all 23 Japanese passengers on the British freighter *Normanton* drown; the British crew escape in lifeboats.

1887 • FUTABATEI SHIMEI begins publication of UKIGUMO (Drifting Clouds), a work regarded as Japan's first modern novel.
- DAIDŌ DANKETSU MOVEMENT seeks reorganization of political parties in preparation for the establishment of a parliamentary system.
- SANDAI JIKEN KEMPAKU MOVEMENT proposes revision of the Unequal Treaties with the Western powers (see UNEQUAL TREATIES, REVISION OF).
- PEACE PRESERVATION LAW OF 1887 issued to suppress political agitation; outdoor gatherings and public demonstrations are subject to prior police permission.

1888 • PRIVY COUNCIL established.
- The volcano BANDAISAN erupts; 444 people die.

1889 • CONSTITUTION OF THE EMPIRE OF JAPAN promulgated.
- IMPERIAL HOUSEHOLD LAW enacted.

1890 • MORI ŌGAI publishes the short story "Maihime" (The Dancing Girl); this marks the debut of a major voice in modern Japanese literature.
- Lafcadio HEARN arrives in Tōkyō; *Glimpses of an Unfamiliar Japan* (1894) will establish his reputation as a writer on Japan.
- First general election (see ELECTIONS).
- IMPERIAL RESCRIPT ON EDUCATION distributed to all schools.

1883 • Rokumeikan In this detail of an 1889 woodblock print, Japanese musicians perform on Western instruments during an event at the Rokumeikan.

1887 • Futabatei Shimei The author of Japan's first modern novel.

1882 • Tuition-free compulsory elementary education instituted in France.

1883 • SINO-FRENCH WAR (1883–85) begins; in 1885 China recognizes Vietnam as a protectorate of France.

1886 • Britain annexes Burma.

1887 • Karl Benz sells his first internal-combustion automobile.

1889 • The Second Socialist International, meeting in Paris, declares May Day an international labor day.

1890 • First session of the **IMPERIAL DIET** convened.
- **KITASATO SHIBASABURŌ** cooperates with Emil Behring in Germany in developing serum therapies for the treatment of diphtheria and tetanus.

1891 • **ŌTSU INCIDENT**: assassination attempt on Russian Crown Prince Nicholas Alexandrovitch, who is on a pleasure tour of Japan.
- Earthquake in Gifu and Aichi prefectures; 7,273 people die.
- **TANAKA SHŌZŌ** submits query to the Diet concerning environmental pollution in Tochigi Prefecture (see **ASHIO COPPER MINE INCIDENT**).

1892 • **DEGUCHI NAO** founds the religious sect **ŌMOTO**.

1893 • **TONGHAK REBELLION**, a peasant uprising, breaks out in Korea. (China and Japan intervene in 1894, commencing the **SINO-JAPANESE WAR OF 1894–1895**.)
- Artist **KURODA SEIKI** returns from study in Paris and introduces impressionism to Japan.

1894 • **ANGLO-JAPANESE COMMERCIAL TREATY OF 1894** signed; the first treaty revision with a signatory of the **KAIZEI YAKUSHO** (Tariff Convention) of 1866, it abolishes extraterritoriality and restores partial tariff autonomy to Japan.
- **SINO-JAPANESE WAR OF 1894–1895** begins.

1895 • Treaty of **SHIMONOSEKI** ends hostilities between China and Japan.
- **TRIPARTITE INTERVENTION**: Japan forced by Russia, France, and Germany to relinquish territory ceded to it by China.
- **TAIWAN** becomes a Japanese colony as part of China's terms of surrender at the end of the **SINO-JAPANESE WAR OF 1894–1895**.
- Assassination of Queen **MIN** of Korea by Japanese troops.

1897 • **JAPAN TIMES**, the first English-language newspaper owned and edited by Japanese, commences publication.
- **SHOKKŌ GIYŪKAI** (Workers' Fraternal Society), Japan's first modern labor organization, is founded.

1898 • **KENSEITŌ** (Constitutional Party) formed.
- **SHAKAI SHUGI KENKYŪKAI** (Society for the Study of Socialism) formed.

1899 • First Japanese-made motion picture shown at the Kabukiza theater in Tōkyō.
- **NITOBE INAZŌ** publishes *Bushido: The Soul of Japan* in Philadelphia.

1900 • **PUBLIC ORDER AND POLICE LAW OF 1900** enacted.
- Poetry journal **MYŌJŌ** (Bright Star) begins publication under the editorship of **YOSANO TEKKAN**.
- System established under which only military men on active duty can serve as army or navy ministers (**GUMBU DAIJIN GEN'EKI BUKAN SEI**).
- **BOXER REBELLION** in China; Russia occupies Manchuria, threatening Japanese colonial ambitions on the Asian continent.
- **RIKKEN SEIYŪKAI** (Friends of Constitutional Government Party) formed by **ITŌ HIROBUMI**.

1901 • Ultranationalist **AMUR RIVER SOCIETY** founded to promote Japanese expansion in Asia.
- **SHAKAI MINSHUTŌ** (Socialist Democratic Party) formed.
- **YOSANO AKIKO** publishes *Midaregami* (Tangled Hair), a collection of passionate **TANKA** verse.

1902 • **ANGLO-JAPANESE ALLIANCE** signed.
- **TEXTBOOK SCANDAL OF 1902–1903**: government officials accused of accepting bribes from publishers.

1903 • **HEIMINSHA** (Society of Commoners), a socialist organization, founded.

1904 • **RUSSO-JAPANESE WAR** (1904–05) begins.
- **KŌTOKU SHŪSUI** and **SAKAI TOSHIHIKO** publish the first Japanese translation of Karl Marx and Friedrich Engels's *Communist Manifesto* in their socialist newspaper **HEIMIN SHIMBUN**.
- George Bailey **SANSOM** arrives in Japan; he later publishes *Japan: A Short Cultural History* (1931) and the three-volume *History of Japan* (1958–63).

1905 • **NATSUME SŌSEKI** begins serialization in the magazine **HOTOTOGISU** of **WAGAHAI WA NEKO DE ARU** (I Am a Cat), a satirical novel whose narrator is a cat.
- Treaty of **PORTSMOUTH** ends the **RUSSO-JAPANESE WAR**.
- **HIBIYA INCENDIARY INCIDENT**: demonstrators protest the terms of the Treaty of Portsmouth.
- **KOREAN-JAPANESE CONVENTION OF 1905**: Korea becomes a Japanese protectorate.

1906 • Office of the **RESIDENT GENERAL IN KOREA** established.
- **JAPAN SOCIALIST PARTY** formed; it is banned by the government in 1907.
- **SHIMAZAKI TŌSON** publishes the naturalist novel **HAKAI** (The Broken Commandment), which deals with the plight of a young man who is a member of the oppressed class of **BURAKUMIN**.
- **OKAKURA KAKUZŌ** publishes *The Book of Tea* in New York City.

1891 • Tsar Alexander III issues rescript initiating construction of the Trans-Siberian Railway.

1893 • France annexes Laos.

1896 • First modern Olympic Games held at Athens.

1898 • China leases Dalian and Port Arthur to Russia (see **TRIPARTITE INTERVENTION**). • Spanish-American War; Spain cedes the Philippines, Guam, and Puerto Rico to the United States. • United States annexes Hawaii.

1899 • US secretary of state John Hay sends his Open Door notes concerning China to Great Britain, Germany, France, Russia, Italy, and Japan.

1901 • Yosano Akiko Known chiefly as a *tanka* poet, Yosano was also an interpreter of classical Japanese literature.

1903 • Wilbur and Orville Wright achieve the first sustained flight in a power-driven airplane.

1905 • Albert Einstein announces his special theory of relativity.

1904 • Russo-Japanese War Japanese artillery fires on Port Arthur, a strategic Russian-held position in eastern China.

1906 • Japanese government protests the segregation of Japanese children in San Francisco schools (see **SEGREGATION OF JAPANESE SCHOOLCHILDREN IN THE UNITED STATES**).
• **SOUTH MANCHURIA RAILWAY** incorporated.

1907 • **ITŌ HIROBUMI**, the Japanese resident general in Korea, forces Korean king **KOJONG**'s abdication and the signing of the Korean-Japanese Convention of 1907, giving Japan effective control of Korea's internal affairs (see **KOREA AND JAPAN**).

1908 • First group of Japanese emigrants to Brazil departs from Kōbe.
• **TAKAHIRA-ROOT AGREEMENT**: Japan gains US recognition of its special status in Manchuria.

1909 • English potter Bernard **LEACH** arrives in Japan; his *Potter's Book* (1940) introduces East Asian glaze and kiln technology to the West.
• Government of the city of Tōkyō gives more than 2,000 flowering cherry saplings as a goodwill present to Washington, DC.
• **ITŌ HIROBUMI** assassinated on his arrival at Harbin in Manchuria by Korean nationalist **AN CHUNG-GŬN**.

1910 • Shirase Nobu The leader of Japan's first successful Antarctic research expedition.

1910 • **RIKKEN KOKUMINTŌ** (Constitutional Nationalist Party) formed.
• **HIGH TREASON INCIDENT OF 1910**: **KŌTOKU SHŪSUI** implicated in a plot to assassinate Emperor **MEIJI**; he is executed the following year.
• Folklorist **YANAGITA KUNIO** publishes **TŌNO MONOGATARI** (The Legends of Tōno), a study of northern Honshū village life and lore.
• Korea is made a colony of Japan (see **KOREA, ANNEXATION OF**); **GOVERNMENT-GENERAL OF KOREA** established.
• Expedition headed by **SHIRASE NOBU** departs Japan to explore Antarctica.
• **ISHIKAWA TAKUBOKU** publishes his first collection of **TANKA** verse, *Ichiaku no suna* (A Handful of Sand).

1911 • Government historical debate over the legitimacy of the imperial **NORTHERN AND SOUTHERN COURTS** (1337–92; see **NAMBOKUCHŌ SEIJUN RON**).
• Philosopher **NISHIDA KITARŌ** publishes **ZEN NO KENKYŪ** (A Study of Good).
• Treaties signed with the Western powers that restore tariff autonomy to Japan.
• **FACTORY LAW OF 1911** enacted to protect laborers.
• Feminist organization **SEITŌSHA** (Bluestocking Society) founded.

1911 • Nishida Kitarō Japan's most important 20th-century philosopher strove to fuse Western methods and Buddhist traditions.

Taishō period
(1912–1926)

The TAISHŌ PERIOD was marked by the advent of true party government, increased popular involvement in politics, the growth of organized labor and left-wing movements, and a domestic economic boom fueled by WORLD WAR I. The democratic tendencies of the period, often referred to as TAISHŌ DEMOCRACY, were supported by the emergence of an educated urban middle class and the rise of new forms of mass media such as radio, large-circulation newspapers, magazines, and paperback books. Eventually, however, an economic downturn and authoritarian measures such as the enactment of the PEACE PRESERVATION LAW OF 1925 and the expansion of the SPECIAL HIGHER POLICE began to erode the gains made by Japan's first experiment with democracy.

1912 • Japan sends two athletes to the 5th Summer Olympic Games at Stockholm.
• Death of Emperor **MEIJI**; accession of Emperor **TAISHŌ**.
• **YŪAIKAI** (Friendship Association) formed, begins the organization of Japanese labor.
• First **MOVEMENT TO PROTECT CONSTITUTIONAL GOVERNMENT** founded.

1913 • Third **KATSURA TARŌ** cabinet toppled by the **MOVEMENT TO PROTECT CONSTITUTIONAL GOVERNMENT** (see **TAISHŌ POLITICAL CRISIS**).

1914 • **SIEMENS INCIDENT**: politicians charged with bribery; resignation of the first **YAMAMOTO GONNOHYŌE** cabinet.
• Japan enters **WORLD WAR I** on the side of Great Britain and its allies.

1915 • Japan presents China with its **TWENTY-ONE DEMANDS** for territorial and other concessions.

1916 • Rabindranath **TAGORE**, the first Asian to receive the Nobel Prize for literature, makes his first visit to Japan.
• Serge **ELISSÉEFF** is appointed lecturer in Japanese at the University of St. Petersburg; he later becomes a professor at the Ecole des Hautes Etudes of the Sorbonne and at Harvard University.

1917 • **LANSING-ISHII AGREEMENT**: the United States and Japan agree to uphold the **OPEN DOOR POLICY** in China; Japan gains recognition of its "special interest in China" (the agreement is annulled in 1923).

1918 • Commencement of the **SIBERIAN INTERVENTION** (1918–22).
• **RICE RIOTS OF 1918**, provoked by spiraling inflation, lead to the collapse of the **TERAUCHI MASATAKE** cabinet.

1919 • **SAMIL INDEPENDENCE MOVEMENT** (1919–20) begins in Korea; it is viciously suppressed by the Japanese.
• As a victor nation in **WORLD WAR I**, Japan is a signatory to the Treaty of **VERSAILLES**.
• **ARISHIMA TAKEO** publishes the melodramatic novel **ARU ONNA** (A Certain Woman), which depicts the self-destruction of a strong-willed woman.

1912 • Republic of China established with **SUN YAT-SEN** as president; Emperor **PUYI** (P'ui) abdicates.

1913 • Niels Bohr clarifies the structure of the atom.

1914 • Archduke Francis Ferdinand assassinated at Sarajevo; **WORLD WAR I** begins. • Panama Canal completed.

1917 • October Revolution in Russia.

1919 • Mohandas K. Gandhi initiates a civil disobedience campaign in India.
• Participants in the **MAY FOURTH MOVEMENT** in China protest the decision reached at the Paris Peace Conference to award Germany's rights and leases in China to Japan (see also **VERSAILLES, TREATY OF**).

1920 • League of Nations established; Japan is granted permanent membership in the League Council (see **LEAGUE OF NATIONS AND JAPAN**).
• **MORITO INCIDENT: MORITO TATSUO**, an assistant professor at Tōkyō University, is imprisoned for three months for publishing an article on the social theory of the anarchist Peter Alekseevich Kropotkin.
• **NIKOLAEVSK INCIDENT:** Japanese residents of the town of Nikolaevsk near the mouth of the Amur River are massacred.
• Labor activists gather in Tōkyō's Ueno Park for the first celebration of May Day in Japan.
• **NIHON SHAKAI SHUGI DŌMEI** (Japan Socialist League) founded; the government orders it to dissolve in 1921.

1921 • **SHIGA NAOYA** begins serialization of his masterwork, the novel **AN'YA KŌRO** (A Dark Night's Passing).
• **YŪAIKAI** (Friendship Association) becomes the **SŌDŌMEI** (Japan Federation of Labor).
• Prime Minister **HARA TAKASHI** assassinated.
• **WASHINGTON CONFERENCE** (1921–22) begins; it will result in the signing of the **FOUR-POWER TREATY**, the **NINE-POWER TREATY**, and the **WASHINGTON NAVAL TREATY OF 1922**.
• Crown Prince Hirohito (later Emperor **SHŌWA**) becomes regent to the ailing Emperor **TAISHŌ**.

1922 • Suiheisha (Society of Levelers) founded to fight discrimination against **BURAKUMIN**.
• **JAPAN COMMUNIST PARTY** established; frequently suppressed by the government, it is not legally constituted until after World War II.
• **IMPERIAL HOTEL**, designed by Frank Lloyd **WRIGHT**, is completed.

1923 • **TŌKYŌ EARTHQUAKE OF 1923**; in its wake several thousand Koreans in Japan massacred by vigilante groups and police; Japanese radicals murdered by the military police (see **KAMEIDO INCIDENT; ŌSUGI SAKAE**).
• **TORANOMON INCIDENT:** assassination attempt on Prince Regent Hirohito.

1924 • Second **MOVEMENT TO PROTECT CONSTITUTIONAL GOVERNMENT; GOKEN SAMPA NAI-KAKU** (Cabinet of Three Groups Supporting the Constitution) formed.

1925 • **SOVIET-JAPANESE BASIC CONVENTION** signed: diplomatic relations between Japan and the Soviet Union established.
• Enactment of the **PEACE PRESERVATION LAW OF 1925**; freedoms of speech and assembly severely restricted.
• Universal Manhood Suffrage Law passed (see **UNIVERSAL MANHOOD SUFFRAGE MOVEMENT**).
• First regular radio broadcasting begun by the Tōkyō Broadcasting Station, a predecessor of Japan's public network, **NHK**, which was formed the following year.
• **INSTITUTE OF PACIFIC RELATIONS** established; its Japan Council is organized in 1926.
• Arthur David **WALEY** publishes the first volume of his six-volume translation of the **TALE OF GENJI**.

1920 • Women granted suffrage in the United States.

1921 • Hara Takashi This early-20th-century politician was among the architects of party government in modern Japan.

1922 • Benito Mussolini forms a cabinet of Fascists and Nationalists in Italy.

1923 • Tōkyō Earthquake of 1923 The ruins of this tower—once a landmark of the Asakusa district of Tōkyō—attest to the damage caused by the quake.

Shōwa period (1926–1989)

The SHŌWA PERIOD was one of the most turbulent in Japanese history. In its first decades an ultranationalist coalition of right-wing politicans and army officers seized control of the country, engaging in domestic political repression and setting Japan on a course of militarist expansionism in continental Asia that culminated in the SINO-JAPANESE WAR OF 1937–1945 and entry into WORLD WAR II. Japan's defeat ushered in a period of OCCUPATION by Allied military forces and sweeping democratic reforms that included a new CONSTITUTION OF JAPAN. The postwar decades saw recovery from the war, reentry into the international community, and phenomenal economic growth that transformed Japan into the world's second largest economy by the end of the period.

1926 • **RŌDŌ NŌMINTŌ** (Labor-Farmer Party) formed.
• **SHAKAI MINSHŪTŌ** (Socialist People's Party) formed.
• **NIHON RŌNŌTŌ** (Japan Labor-Farmer Party) formed.
• Death of Emperor **TAISHŌ**; accession of Emperor **SHŌWA**.

1927 • **FINANCIAL CRISIS OF 1927**.
• **NANJING (NANKING) INCIDENT:** Japanese, British, and US consulates in Nanjing attacked by Chinese Nationalist soldiers.
• **TANAKA GIICHI** cabinet dispatches troops to Shandong Province in China.

1928 • **MARCH 15TH INCIDENT:** 1,658 suspected communists arrested; charges brought against 483.
• Manchurian warlord **ZHANG ZUOLIN** (Chang Tso-lin) assassinated by Japanese army officers.
• **KELLOGG-BRIAND PACT** signed by Japan and 14 other countries; it provokes criticism in Japan for the use of the phrase "in the names of their respective peoples," which some Japanese take to be an assault on the sovereignty of the emperor.

1929 • **APRIL 16TH INCIDENT:** six hundred to 700 suspected communists arrested, charges brought against 339.

1930 • **SHŌWA DEPRESSION** (1930–35) begins.
• First of the **LONDON NAVAL CONFERENCES**; terms of the resulting naval arms limitation treaty provoke intense criticism of the government by the military (see **TŌSUIKEN**).
• **ŌHARA MUSEUM OF ART**, Japan's first museum of modern Western art, established.

1927 • **CHIANG KAI-SHEK**, commander of the National Revolutionary Army, purges his Communist allies and sets up a Nationalist government in Nanjing.
• Charles Lindbergh flies across the Atlantic Ocean.

1929 • US stock market crashes, prolonged depression begins.

1930 • Prime Minister **HAMAGUCHI OSACHI** mortally wounded at Tōkyō Station by a right-wing radical.

1931 • **MARCH INCIDENT:** planned coup by rightist army officers and civilians aborted.
• **GOSHO HEINOSUKE** directs Japan's first successful sound film, *Madamu to nyōbō* (The Neighbor's Wife and Mine).
• **LIUTIAOGOU (LIU-T'IAO-KOU) INCIDENT:** conquest of Manchuria by the Japanese **GUANDONG (KWANTUNG) ARMY** begins (1931–33; see **MANCHURIAN INCIDENT**).
• **OCTOBER INCIDENT:** leaders of a planned military coup arrested.

1932 • **SAKURADAMON INCIDENT:** assassination attempt made on Emperor **SHŌWA**.
• **SHANGHAI INCIDENT:** Chinese and Japanese troops clash in Shanghai.
• **GUANDONG (KWANTUNG) ARMY** establishes the state of **MANCHUKUO**; the last Qing-dynasty (1644–1912) emperor, **PUYI** (P'u-i), appointed as head of state.
• **LEAGUE OF BLOOD INCIDENT:** prominent politicians and businessmen murdered by members of an ultranationalist society.
• **MAY 15TH INCIDENT:** Prime Minister **INUKAI TSUYOSHI** assassinated during an attempted coup by young naval officers.
• **NIHON SHIHON SHUGI HATTATSU SHI KŌZA**, a series of works by Marxist scholars dealing with the development of Japanese capitalism, begins publication.
• **DAI NIPPON KOKUBŌ FUJINKAI** (National Defense Women's Association), a patriotic women's organization, founded.

1933 • Japan withdraws from the League of Nations to express its opposition to a report criticizing it as an aggressor in Manchuria (see **LYTTON COMMISSION; LEAGUE OF NATIONS AND JAPAN**).
• **TANGGU (TANGKU) TRUCE:** armistice agreement between Chinese officials and officers of the Japanese **GUANDONG (KWANTUNG) ARMY**.
• **SHIMPEITAI INCIDENT:** leaders of a planned coup arrested.

1934 • **TEIJIN INCIDENT:** government officials implicated in a stock scandal.
• **WASHINGTON NAVAL TREATY OF 1922** abrogated by Japan.

1935 • Controversy arises over the constitutional status of the emperor (see **TENNŌ KIKAN SETSU**).
• **HE-UMEZU (HO-UMEZU) AGREEMENT** concluded in North China.
• The prestigious literary awards **AKUTAGAWA PRIZE** and **NAOKI PRIZE** instituted.

1936 • Second of the **LONDON NAVAL CONFERENCES**; Japan withdraws after rejection of its proposal that the Japanese fleet be granted full parity with the fleets of Britain and the United States.
• **FEBRUARY 26TH INCIDENT:** 1,400 troops participate in an unsuccessful coup d'état.
• Observance of May Day prohibited in Japan.

1937 • Publication in book form of the novels **YUKIGUNI** (Snow Country) by **KAWABATA YASUNARI** and **BOKUTŌ KIDAN** (A Strange Tale from East of the River) by **NAGAI KAFŪ**.
• **MARCO POLO BRIDGE INCIDENT: SINO-JAPANESE WAR OF 1937–1945** commences.
• **NANJING (NANKING) MASSACRE** (1937–38): some 140,000 Chinese civilians and prisoners of war are estimated to have been murdered by Japanese forces following the taking of Nanjing.
• **POPULAR FRONT INCIDENT** (1937–38): some 400 liberals and leftists arrested.

1938 • Prime Minister **KONOE FUMIMARO** declares a policy of nonrecognition of Nationalist China and calls for "the establishment of a new order in East Asia" (see **TŌA SHINCHITSUJO**).
• *Ikite iru heitai* (Living Soldiers), a novella by **ISHIKAWA TATSUZŌ** dealing with the taking of Nanjing by Japanese forces, is banned.
• Passage of the **NATIONAL MOBILIZATION LAW**.
• Daisetz Teitarō **SUZUKI** publishes *Zen Buddhism and Its Influence on Japanese Culture* in Kyōto.

1939 • **NOMONHAN INCIDENT:** heavy fighting between Japanese and Soviet troops along the Manchurian-Mongolian border ends in a rout of Japanese forces.
• **NATIONAL SERVICE DRAFT ORDINANCE** issued to assure an adequate supply of labor in strategic industries.

1940 • **TSUDA SŌKICHI**'s revisionist study of the prehistory of Japan, *Jindaishi no kenkyū*, is banned.
• **TRIPARTITE PACT** signed by Japan, Germany, and Italy.
• **IMPERIAL RULE ASSISTANCE ASSOCIATION** formed.
• Treasures of the **SHŌSŌIN** are publicly exhibited for the first time.

1941 • Compulsory school system of **KOKUMIN GAKKŌ** established to train "loyal subjects of the emperor."
• **SOVIET-JAPANESE NEUTRALITY PACT** signed.
• Talks between Ambassador **NOMURA KICHISABURŌ** and Secretary of State Cordell **HULL** begin in an attempt to resolve the stalemate in US-Japan relations.
• **SORGE INCIDENT:** German journalist taken into custody by the Tōkyō police and charged with spying for the Soviet Union.

1932 • May 15th Incident Guards posted outside the prime minister's official residence in the wake of Prime Minister Inukai's assassination.

1936 • February 26th Incident Rebellious troops surround the Diet Building as part of this abortive coup d'état.

1933 • Adolf Hitler becomes chancellor of Germany.

1936 • **XI'AN (SIAN) INCIDENT:** troops of Manchurian warlord **ZHANG XUELIANG** detain **CHIANG KAI-SHEK**; Communist leaders effect his release, and cooperation between Nationalists and Communists against Japanese aggression is agreed upon (see **SECOND UNITED FRONT**).

1939 • Germany invades Poland; **WORLD WAR II** (1939–45) begins in Europe.

1941 • Japanese attack Pearl Harbor, the Malay Peninsula, and the Philippines; war declared against the United States, Great Britain, and the Netherlands (see **PEARL HARBOR, ATTACK ON; WORLD WAR II**).

1942 • Japanese forces occupy the Philippines, Malaya, Singapore, the Dutch East Indies, and Burma.
• Japanese naval fleet defeated in the Battle of **MIDWAY**.
• Railway tunnel completed beneath the **KAMMON STRAIT** connecting southwestern Honshū and northern Kyūshū.

1943 • Japanese forces withdraw from **GUADALCANAL**.
• Serialization of **SASAMEYUKI** (The Makioka Sisters), **TANIZAKI JUN'ICHIRŌ**'s novel about four upper-middle-class sisters, is suspended under pressure from the military.
• Death of Admiral **YAMAMOTO ISOROKU**.
• Japanese forces on the island of **ATTU** in the Aleutians annihilated.
• Late-Yayoi-period (ca AD 100–ca AD 300) **TORO SITE** discovered.

1944 • Saipan falls; large-scale US bombing raids on the Japanese main islands begin.
• Japanese naval fleet defeated in the Battle of **LEYTE GULF**.

1945 • Iōjima falls (see **IŌJIMA [IWOJIMA], BATTLE OF**).
• Okinawa falls.
• **ATOMIC BOMB** dropped on Hiroshima and Nagasaki.
• Japan accepts the terms of the **POTSDAM DECLARATION**.
• Emperor **SHŌWA** announces the end of hostilities in a national radio broadcast.
• Douglas **MACARTHUR**, supreme commander for the Allied powers (**SCAP**), arrives at Atsugi Airfield near Tōkyō to oversee the **OCCUPATION** of Japan (1945–52).
• Instrument of Surrender signed aboard the USS *Missouri* (see **SURRENDER, INSTRUMENT OF**).
• **SCAP** headquarters orders the arrest of suspected Japanese war criminals (see **WAR CRIMES TRIALS**), issues directives aimed at the democratization of Japan that include the release of political prisoners and the breakup of industrial and financial combines (see **ZAIBATSU DISSOLUTION**).
• Revival of the **JAPAN SOCIALIST PARTY** and the **JAPAN COMMUNIST PARTY**.
• New election law promulgated; women given the vote (see **WOMEN'S SUFFRAGE**).
• Labor Union Law issued (see **LABOR LAWS; LABOR REFORMS OF 1945–1947**).

1946 • Emperor **SHŌWA** renounces his divinity in New Year's address to the Japanese people (see **EMPEROR, RENUNCIATION OF DIVINITY BY**).
• **OCCUPATION PURGE** of prewar and wartime Japanese leaders.
• Implementation of the **LAND REFORMS OF 1946** begins.
• Emergency anti-inflation measures issued by **SCAP**; "new yen" currency reform.
• Emperor **SHŌWA** begins a series of goodwill tours of the country.
• First of the **UNITED STATES EDUCATION MISSIONS TO JAPAN** arrives.
• Commencement of the International Military Tribunal for the Far East (1946–48; see **WAR CRIMES TRIALS**).
• **SHOKURYŌ MĒDĒ** (Food May Day): 300,000 people demonstrate in front of the Imperial Palace.
• Formation of **KEIDANREN** (Federation of Economic Organizations).
• **CONSTITUTION OF JAPAN** promulgated; it goes into effect in 1947.
• **AIZAWA TADAHIRO** discovers the **IWAJUKU SITE**, the first recognized paleolithic site in Japan.
• Ruth Fulton **BENEDICT** publishes *The Chrysanthemum and the Sword*, a sociological study of the Japanese.

1947 • SCAP bans the **GENERAL STRIKE OF 1947**.
• Enactment of the Fundamental Law of Education (see **EDUCATION, FUNDAMENTAL LAW OF**), the Labor Standards Law (see **LABOR LAWS**), the **ANTIMONOPOLY LAW**, the Local Autonomy Law (see **LOCAL AUTONOMY**), and the **CHILD WELFARE LAW**.
• **DAZAI OSAMU** publishes the novel **SHAYŌ** (The Setting Sun).

1948 • **NIKKEIREN** (Japan Federation of Employers' Associations) founded.
• **SHŌWA DENKŌ SCANDAL**: government officials charged with the receipt of bribes.
• **EUGENIC PROTECTION LAW** enacted; it contains provisions governing abortion and sterilization.
• **NINE PRINCIPLES FOR ECONOMIC STABILIZATION** issued.

1949 • Comprehensive anti-inflation measures introduced (see **DODGE LINE**); a constant exchange rate of ¥360 to US $1 established (see **FOREIGN EXCHANGE CONTROLS**).
• **TAIRA INCIDENT; SHIMOYAMA INCIDENT; MITAKA INCIDENT; MATSUKAWA INCIDENT**; public opinion turns against the **JAPAN COMMUNIST PARTY**; emphasis of Occupation reforms shifts from democratization to economic growth.
• **SHOUP MISSION** gives recommendations on Japan's tax structure; foundation laid for the present system of direct taxation.
• **YUKAWA HIDEKI** awarded the Nobel Prize for physics; he is the first Japanese to receive a Nobel Prize.

1950 • Jiyūtō (**LIBERAL PARTY**) formed.
• Public Office Election Law enacted (see **ELECTIONS**).

1941 • attack on Pearl Harbor The *West Virginia* was one of eight US battleships sunk or crippled in Japan's surprise raid.

1945 • atomic bomb A mushroom cloud rises into the sky over Hiroshima following the detonation of the atomic bomb there.

1946 • Emperor Shōwa (Hirohito) The emperor's goodwill tours of the country included this public appearance in Saitama Prefecture.

1942 • Nazi bureaucrats plan "final solution" of the "Jewish question" at the Wannsee Conference.

1945 • United Nations Charter signed at San Francisco by delegates from 50 nations; Japan joins in 1956 (see **UNITED NATIONS AND JAPAN**). • US president Harry Truman, Soviet premier Joseph Stalin, and British prime minister Winston Churchill call for the unconditional surrender of Japan in the **POTSDAM DECLARATION**. • **SUKARNO** and Mohammad **HATTA** proclaim the independence of the Republic of Indonesia. • Ho Chi Minh proclaims the independence of Vietnam.

1946 • Republic of the Philippines inaugurated with Manuel Roxas as its first president. • UNESCO established; Japan joins in 1951.

1947 • Pakistan and India become sovereign nations.

1948 • Republic of Korea established in the southern part of the Korean peninsula and the Democratic People's Republic of Korea in the north.

1949 • North Atlantic Treaty Organization (NATO) founded. • People's Republic of China established.

1950 • **KOREAN WAR** begins (1950–53).

1950 • SŌHYŌ (General Council of Trade Unions of Japan) founded.
- RED PURGE: 1,177 government employees who are JAPAN COMMUNIST PARTY members removed from their positions.
- NATIONAL POLICE RESERVE created.

1951 • SAN FRANCISCO PEACE TREATY and the first of the UNITED STATES–JAPAN SECURITY TREATIES signed.

1952 • UNITED STATES–JAPAN ADMINISTRATIVE AGREEMENT signed.
- SAN FRANCISCO PEACE TREATY goes into effect; OCCUPATION ends and Japan regains its sovereignty.
- MAY DAY INCIDENT: 1,232 demonstrating workers arrested under the Riot Law.
- SUBVERSIVE ACTIVITIES PREVENTION LAW enacted.
- Japan sends a team of athletes, the first in the post–World War II period, to participate in the 15th Summer Olympic Games at Helsinki.
- First exchange of scholars between Japan and the United States conducted under the auspices of the Fulbright Commission (see JAPAN-UNITED STATES EDUCATIONAL COMMISSION).
- INTERNATIONAL HOUSE OF JAPAN founded by the journalist MATSUMOTO SHIGEHARU.
- UCHINADA INCIDENT (1952–53): villagers in Uchinada, Ishikawa Prefecture, protest the establishment of a US Army firing range.
- National Police Reserve reorganized as the National Safety Forces (forerunner of the SELF DEFENSE FORCES).

1952 • May Day Incident Demonstrators in the vicinity of the Imperial Palace.

1953 • TELEVISION broadcasting begins in Japan.
- First case of Minamata disease reported (see POLLUTION-RELATED DISEASES).

1953 • The Soviet Union announces its successful testing of a hydrogen bomb.

1954 • Excavation of the 8th-century imperial palace at HEIJŌKYŌ (NARA) begins.
- SHIPBUILDING SCANDAL OF 1954 contributes to the fall of the fifth YOSHIDA SHIGERU cabinet.
- LUCKY DRAGON INCIDENT: Japanese fishing boat contaminated by fallout from a US atomic test on Bikini in the Marshall Islands.
- UNITED STATES–JAPAN MUTUAL DEFENSE ASSISTANCE AGREEMENT signed.
- The MINISTRY OF EDUCATION establishes a scholarship system to support study by foreign students in Japan.
- *Jigokumon* (Gate of Hell), a film by KINUGASA TEINOSUKE, receives the Grand Prix at the Cannes Film Festival.
- DEFENSE AGENCY and the SELF DEFENSE FORCES established.

1954 • John Foster Dulles announces the US policy of massive nuclear retaliation.

1955 • First Atomic Disasters Anniversary World Conference against Atomic and Hydrogen Bombs held in Hiroshima (see ATOMIC WEAPONS, MOVEMENT TO BAN).
- First transistor radios go on sale (see ELECTRONICS).
- Japan joins GATT (General Agreement on Tariffs and Trade).
- LIBERAL DEMOCRATIC PARTY formed.

1955 • United States begins providing direct military aid to South Vietnam, Cambodia, and Laos. • Mutual defense organization of the Soviet Union and its satellites established under the Warsaw Pact.

1956 • MISHIMA YUKIO publishes the novel KINKAKUJI (The Temple of the Golden Pavilion), a psychological portrait of a priest who sets fire to the temple he serves.
- MAKI ARITSUNE leads a party of Japanese climbers who make the first ascent of Mt. Manaslu in the Himalayas.
- PROSTITUTION PREVENTION LAW passed.
- The 1956 WHITE PAPER ON THE ECONOMY declares an "end to the postwar period."
- SOVIET-JAPANESE JOINT DECLARATION reestablishes diplomatic relations between the two countries.
- Japan granted membership in the United Nations (see UNITED NATIONS AND JAPAN).

1958 • Tōkyō Tower The tower is Tōkyō's tallest structure.

1957 • Japanese expedition establishes Shōwa Station, a base camp in Antarctica (see ANTARCTIC RESEARCH).

1957 • Soviet Union launches the first space satellite, Sputnik 1.

1958 • JETRO, an organization for the promotion of Japan's foreign trade, is established under the administration of the MINISTRY OF INTERNATIONAL TRADE AND INDUSTRY.
- Construction of TŌKYŌ TOWER completed.

1959 • Metric system adopted officially by Japan (see WEIGHTS AND MEASURES).
- Beginning of protests against the revision of the United States–Japan Security Treaty (see PEACE MOVEMENT; UNITED STATES–JAPAN SECURITY TREATIES).
- Ise Bay Typhoon crosses central Honshū; some 5,000 people reported dead or missing.

1960 • Organization of Petroleum Exporting Countries (OPEC) formed.

1960 • DEMOCRATIC SOCIALIST PARTY formed.
- MIIKE STRIKE: 282-day strike at Miike Coal Mines.
- Second of the UNITED STATES–JAPAN SECURITY TREATIES signed in Washington; demonstrators against ratification of the treaty besiege the National Diet Building in Tōkyō.
- Japan Socialist Party chairman ASANUMA INEJIRŌ assassinated by a right-wing youth.

1961 • Military junta led by PAK CHŎNG-HŬI and others overthrows the civilian government of South Korea. • Construction of the Berlin Wall begins. • Organization for Economic Cooperation and Development (OECD) organized; Japan joins in 1964.

1961 • SHIMANAKA INCIDENT: right-wing zealot attempts to murder the publisher of the magazine CHŪŌ KŌRON.
- Edwin O. REISCHAUER becomes United States ambassador to Japan.

1960 • United States–Japan security treaties The ratification of the 1960 treaty on 20 May prompted a massive protest in front of the National Diet Building that day.

1962 • ABE KŌBŌ publishes the avant-garde novel SUNA NO ONNA (The Woman in the Dunes).
- Sale of thalidomide in Japan halted (see THALIDOMIDE CHILDREN).

1962 • Algeria gains independence from France. • Cuban missile crisis causes acute tension between the Soviet Union and the United States.

1964 • High-speed **SHINKANSEN** trains begin operations between Tōkyō and Ōsaka.
  • Eighteenth Summer Olympic Games, the first sponsored by an Asian city, held in Tōkyō (see **TŌKYŌ OLYMPIC GAMES**).
  • **KŌMEITŌ** (Clean Government Party) formed.

1965 • Formation of Gensuikin (Japan Congress against Atomic and Hydrogen Bombs; see **ATOMIC WEAPONS, MOVEMENT TO BAN**).
  • First demonstrations by the **PEACE FOR VIETNAM COMMITTEE**.
  • **KOREA-JAPAN TREATY OF 1965** signed; diplomatic relations between Japan and the Republic of Korea restored.
  • **TOMONAGA SHIN'ICHIRŌ** shares the Nobel Prize for physics.

1966 • **ENDŌ SHŪSAKU** publishes the novel **CHIMMOKU** (Silence), a depiction of the persecution of Christians in late-17th-century Japan.
  • The Beatles perform at the Nippon Budōkan in Tōkyō; some 2,000 policemen provide security at each of the five concerts.
  • **IBUSE MASUJI** completes serialization of the novel **KUROI AME** (Black Rain), a study of the horrific consequences of the atomic bombing at Hiroshima.

1968 • **UNIVERSITY UPHEAVALS OF 1968–1969** begin.
  • Basic Law for Consumer Protection enacted (see **CONSUMER PROTECTION LAWS**).
  • **OGASAWARA ISLANDS** returned to Japanese sovereignty by the United States.
  • **KAWABATA YASUNARI** wins the Nobel Prize for literature.

1969 • **SATŌ-NIXON COMMUNIQUÉ**: agreement reached on the reversion of **OKINAWA** to Japanese sovereignty in 1972.

1970 • **EXPO '70** opens in Ōsaka.
  • Automatic renewal of the United States–Japan Security Treaty (see **UNITED STATES–JAPAN SECURITY TREATIES**).
  • Novelist **MISHIMA YUKIO** leads his private ultranationalist group Tate no Kai in an attempt to provoke an uprising by Ground Self Defense Forces; failing, he commits suicide.

1971 • **ENVIRONMENT AGENCY** established.
  • Revaluation of the **YEN** (¥308 = US $1) depresses the Japanese economy.

1972 • **RED ARMY FACTION** incidents: 2 policemen are killed during an arrest; subsequent interrogations reveal 14 other murders committed by faction members in the course of internal disputes; 24 die in a Japanese Red Army attack on Lod Airport in Tel Aviv, Israel.
  • **OKINAWA** returned to Japanese sovereignty by the United States.
  • **CHINA-JAPAN JOINT COMMUNIQUÉ OF 1972** issued; it announces the establishment of diplomatic relations between Japan and the People's Republic of China (see **CHINA AND JAPAN**).
  • **TAKAMATSUZUKA TOMB** excavated; its polychrome wall paintings date to ca AD 700.
  • **JAPAN FOUNDATION** established.

1973 • Floating exchange rate introduced (see **YEN**).
  • Prime Minister **TANAKA KAKUEI** bestows a grant totaling $10 million on major US universities engaged in Japanese studies.
  • Sapporo District Court decision in the **NAGANUMA CASE** rules the **SELF DEFENSE FORCES** to be unconstitutional (reversed by the Sapporo High Court in 1976).
  • **OIL CRISIS OF 1973**: oil prices spiral.
  • **ESAKI REONA** shares the Nobel Prize for physics.

1974 • **NATIONAL LAND AGENCY** established to plan land use.
  • Former prime minister **SATŌ EISAKU** receives the Nobel Peace Prize.
  • Resignation of Prime Minister **TANAKA KAKUEI** amid allegations of involvement in financial scandals.

1975 • At the invitation of US president Gerald R. Ford, Emperor **SHŌWA** and Empress **NAGAKO** make a state visit to the United States.

1976 • **LOCKHEED SCANDAL**: Japanese government officials charged with taking bribes from Lockheed Aircraft Corporation.

1977 • Japan sets its territorial limit at 12 nautical miles from its coasts and its **FISHERY ZONE** at 200 nautical miles from its coasts.

1978 • **UNITED SOCIAL DEMOCRATIC PARTY** formed.
  • **NEW TŌKYŌ INTERNATIONAL AIRPORT** (Narita Airport) opens.
  • **CHINA-JAPAN PEACE AND FRIENDSHIP TREATY** signed.

1979 • It is divulged that convicted war criminals (see **WAR CRIMES TRIALS**) are enshrined at **YASUKUNI SHRINE**.

1980 • Japanese automobile production outpaces that of the United States.

1964 • Tōkyō Olympic Games A torch bearer prepares to light Tōkyō's Olympic flame.

1968 • Kawabata Yasunari The novelist receiving the Nobel Prize in literature.

1970 • Mishima Yukio Shortly before committing suicide, the novelist exhorts members of the Japanese Self Defense Forces to revolt.

1965 • US airplanes begin bombing North Vietnam.

1966 • Cultural Revolution sweeps across China.

1969 • US Apollo 11 spacecraft puts the first man on the moon.

1972 • The United States and China announce rapprochement in the Shanghai Communiqué. • The United States and the Soviet Union conclude the first round of Strategic Arms Limitation Talks (SALT I).

1973 • Fourth Arab-Israeli War triggers the **OIL CRISIS OF 1973**.

1975 • Khmer Rouge take Phnom Penh. • North Vietnam achieves the unification of Vietnam.

1979 • Ayatollah Ruhollah Khomeini establishes an Islamic republic in Iran. • Peace treaty signed by Egypt and Israel.

1980 • Iran-Iraq War commences (1980–88).

1981 • Ministry of Health and Welfare sponsors the visit to Japan of the first group of **DISPLACED JAPANESE WAR ORPHANS IN CHINA** to search for family members.
  • **FUKUI KEN'ICHI** shares the Nobel Prize for chemistry.

1982 • Chinese and South Korean governments protest the content of Japanese history textbooks; the Japanese government agrees to revise certain of the disputed passages (see **TEXTBOOK ISSUE**).
  • **SECOND PROVISIONAL COMMISSION FOR ADMINISTRATIVE REFORM** proposes **PRIVATIZATION** of Japan's three major public corporations.

1983 • **TŌKYŌ DISNEYLAND** opens.

1984 • Korean president Chŏn Du-hwan makes state visit to Japan; in reference to Korea-Japan relations, Emperor **SHŌWA** expresses "regret" over the "unfortunate past."

1985 • Amendment to the Nationality Law goes into effect; eligibility for Japanese citizenship through either the maternal or paternal line is legally recognized (see **JAPANESE NATIONALITY**).
  • First cases of **AIDS** reported in Japan.
  • Enactment of the **EQUAL EMPLOYMENT OPPORTUNITY LAW FOR MEN AND WOMEN**; it becomes effective the following year.
  • **NAKASONE YASUHIRO** becomes the first prime minister since World War II to visit Yasukuni Shrine in his official capacity (see **YASUKUNI SHRINE OFFICIAL VISIT CONTROVERSY**).

1987 • **INTERNATIONAL RESEARCH CENTER FOR JAPANESE STUDIES** founded in Kyōto.
  • **TONEGAWA SUSUMU** wins the Nobel Prize for physiology and medicine.
  • **RENGŌ** (Japanese Trade Union Confederation) formed.

1988 • **RECRUIT SCANDAL**: it comes to light that the staffs of a number of leading politicians received gifts of stock shares from Recruit Co in 1986.
  • Consumption Tax Law pushed through the Diet by a **LIBERAL DEMOCRATIC PARTY** majority; 3-percent **CONSUMPTION TAX** goes into effect the following year.

1983 • Tōkyō Disneyland Representatives from Japan, the United States, and the world of Disney attend the ribbon-cutting.

1984 • China and the United Kingdom announce the signing of an agreement stipulating the restoration of Hong Kong to China on 1 July 1997.

1985 • Mikhail Gorbachev elected general secretary of the Communist Party of the Soviet Union.

1986 • Ferdinand Marcos is deposed and Corazon Aquino assumes the presidency of the Philippines. • Nuclear accident at Chernobyl in the Soviet Union.

1988 • US Congress passes the Civil Liberties Act of 1988; it stipulates that an official apology and $20,000 be given to each Japanese American interned by the US government during World War II (see **JAPANESE AMERICANS, WARTIME RELOCATION OF**).

Heisei period
(1989–   )

1989 • Death of Emperor **SHŌWA**; accession of Emperor **AKIHITO**.
  • **STRUCTURAL IMPEDIMENTS INITIATIVE TALKS** between the United States and Japan begin.
  • **SŌHYŌ** (General Council of Trade Unions of Japan) disbands and is largely absorbed into **RENGŌ** (Japanese Trade Union Confederation).

1990 • Formal enthronement of Emperor **AKIHITO**.
  • Journalist Akiyama Toyohiro joins the crew of Soyuz TM-11; he is the first Japanese to enter outer space.

1992 • Law on Cooperation in United Nations Peacekeeping Operations passed by the Diet in June; Japanese **SELF DEFENSE FORCES** personnel are permitted to participate in peacekeeping operations in foreign lands (see **UNITED NATIONS AND JAPAN**). By October, some 600 members of the Ground Self Defense Forces had been sent to Cambodia on such a mission.
  • The American space shuttle *Endeavor II* is launched; among those aboard is Japan's first astronaut, Mōri Mamoru.
  • Emperor **AKIHITO** and Empress **MICHIKO** make their first official visit to China as emperor and empress.

1990 • Emperor Akihito The emperor proclaims his enthronement from the dais-of-state on 12 November.

1989 • Tiananmen Square Incident; thousands of demonstrators for democratization in China are killed by government troops in and around the square.
  • Vietnam withdraws the last of its forces from Cambodia. • Berlin Wall demolished.

1990 • Persian Gulf War commences with Iraq's invasion of Kuwait (1990–91). • Reunification of Germany.

1991 • Warsaw Treaty Organization dissolved. • North and South Korea admitted to the United Nations. • Soviet Union dissolved.

1992 • United Nations Transitional Authority in Cambodia (UNTAC) begins operations under the leadership of **AKASHI YASUSHI**. • United Nations Conference on Environment and Development (UNCED) held in Rio de Janeiro.

Table of Japanese Era Names (Nengō)

Listed here in alphabetical order are the era names (NENGŌ) that are still commonly used in Japan for dating purposes alongside the Western calendar. Each era name is followed by the Chinese characters used to write it and the corresponding dates in the Western calendar for its beginning and ending years.

For some eras prior to the adoption of the Western calendar on 1 January 1873, two sets of dates are given. In these cases the first set are the commonly accepted dates that appear in most standard Japa-

nese reference works. These dates have not necessarily been corrected precisely for discrepancies between the old Japanese lunar calendar and the Western solar calendar as to when a new year begins. The second set (in parentheses) are the correctly converted dates. The conventional Japanese practice is to assign the first year of an era to the Western year within which the lunar rather than solar first month began. Thus a discrepancy of only a few days between the lunar and solar months can lead to a difference of one in counting solar calendar years.

Because they are so widely accepted, it is these conventional dates that are, as a rule, given throughout this encyclopedia whenever era names are identified. One notable exception is the table of historical periods that appears in the main-text entry PERIODIZATION: the era-name dates in that table are the correctly converted ones. Throughout the encyclopedia the dates of specific events, as opposed to eras, have been precisely converted to the Western calendar whenever possible.

A

An'ei	安永	1772–1781
Angen	安元	1175–1177
Anna	安和	968–970
Ansei	安政	1854–1860
		(1855–1860)
Antei	安貞	1227–1229
		(1228–1229)

B

Bummei	文明	1469–1487
Bumpō	文保	1317–1319
Bun'an	文安	1444–1449
Bunchū (S)	文中	1372–1375
Bun'ei	文永	1264–1275
Bunji	文治	1185–1190
Bunka	文化	1804–1818
Bunki	文亀	1501–1504
Bunkyū	文久	1861–1864
Bunna (N)	文和	1352–1356
Bun'ō	文応	1260–1261
Bunroku	文禄	1592–1596
		(1593–1596)
Bunryaku	文暦	1234–1235
Bunsei	文政	1818–1830
		(1818–1831)
Bunshō	文正	1466–1467

C

Chōgen	長元	1028–1037
Chōhō	長保	999–1004
Chōji	長治	1104–1106
Chōkan	長寛	1163–1165
Chōkyō	長享	1487–1489
Chōkyū	長久	1040–1044
Chōroku	長禄	1457–1460
		(1457–1461)
Chōryaku	長暦	1037–1040
Chōshō	長承	1132–1135
Chōtoku	長徳	995–999
Chōwa	長和	1012–1017
		(1013–1017)

D

Daidō	大同	806–810
Daiji	大治	1126–1131

E

Eichō	永長	1096–1097
		(1097)
Eien	永延	987–989
Eiho	永保	1081–1084
Eiji	永治	1141–1142
Eijō	永承	1046–1053
Eikan	永観	983–985
Eikyō	永享	1429–1441
Eikyū	永久	1113–1118
Eiman	永万	1165–1166
Einin	永仁	1293–1299
Eiroku	永禄	1558–1570
Eiryaku	永暦	1160–1161
Eishō	永正	1504–1521
Eiso	永祚	989–990
Eitoku (N)	永徳	1381–1384
Eiwa (N)	永和	1375–1379
Embun (N)	延文	1356–1361
Empō	延宝	1673–1681
Enchō	延長	923–931
Engen (S)	延元	1336–1340
Engi	延喜	901–923
Enkyō	延慶	1308–1311
Enkyō	延享	1744–1748
Enkyū	延久	1069–1074
En'ō	延応	1239–1240
Enryaku	延暦	782–806
Entoku	延徳	1489–1492

G

Gangyō	元慶	877–885
Gembun	元文	1736–1741
Genchū (S)	元中	1384–1392
Gen'ei	元永	1118–1120
Genji	元治	1864–1865
Genki	元亀	1570–1573
Genkō	元享	1321–1324
Genkō (S)	元弘	1331–1334

(continued)

Genkyū	元久	1204–1206
Genna	元和	1615–1624
Gennin	元仁	1224–1225
Gen'ō	元応	1319–1321
Genroku	元禄	1688–1704
Genryaku	元暦	1184–1185
Gentoku	元徳	1329–1332

H

Hakuchi	白雉	650–654
Heiji	平治	1159–1160
Heisei	平成	1989–
Hōan	保安	1120–1124
Hōei	宝永	1704–1711
Hōen	保延	1135–1141
Hōgen	保元	1156–1159
Hōji	宝治	1247–1249
Hōki	宝亀	770–781
Hōreki	宝暦	1751–1764
Hōtoku	宝徳	1449–1452

J

Jian	治安	1021–1024
Jingo Keiun	神護景雲	767–770
Jinki	神亀	724–729
Jiryaku	治暦	1065–1069
Jishō	治承	1177–1181
Jōan	承安	1171–1175
Jōei	貞永	1232–1233
Jōgan	貞観	859–877
Jōgen	貞元	976–978
Jōgen	承元	1207–1211
Jōhei	承平	931–938
Jōhō	承保	1074–1077
Jōji (N)	貞治	1362–1368
Jōkyō	貞享	1684–1688
Jōkyū	承久	1219–1222
Jōō	貞応	1222–1224
Jōō	承応	1652–1655
Jōryaku	承暦	1077–1081
Jōtoku	承徳	1097–1099
Jōwa	承和	834–848
Jōwa (N)	貞和	1345–1350
Juei	寿永	1182–1185

K

Kaei	嘉永	1848–1854
		(1848–1855)
Kagen	嘉元	1303–1306
		(1303–1307)
Kahō	嘉保	1094–1096
		(1095–1097)
Kajō	嘉承	1106–1108
Kakitsu	嘉吉	1441–1444
Kakyō (N)	嘉慶	1387–1389
Kambun	寛文	1661–1673
Kampō	寛保	1741–1744
Kampyō	寛平	889–898
Kan'ei	寛永	1624–1644
		(1624–1645)
Kan'en	寛延	1748–1751
Kangen	寛元	1243–1247
Kangi	寛喜	1229–1232
Kanji	寛治	1087–1094
		(1087–1095)
Kankō	寛弘	1004–1012
		(1004–1013)
Kanna	寛和	985–987
Kannin	寛仁	1017–1021
Kannō (N)	観応	1350–1352
Kansei	寛政	1789–1801
Kanshō	寛正	1460–1466
		(1461–1466)
Kantoku	寛徳	1044–1046
Kaō	嘉応	1169–1171
Karoku	嘉禄	1225–1227
		(1225–1228)
Karyaku	嘉暦	1326–1329
Kashō	嘉祥	848–851
Katei	嘉禎	1235–1238
Keian	慶安	1648–1652
Keichō	慶長	1596–1615
Keiō	慶応	1865–1868
Keiun	慶雲	704–708
Kemmu	建武	1334–1338
Kempō	建保	1213–1219
		(1214–1219)
Kenchō	建長	1249–1256
Ken'ei	建永	1206–1207
Kengen	乾元	1302–1303
Kenji	建治	1275–1278
Kenkyū	建久	1190–1199
Kennin	建仁	1201–1204
Kenryaku	建暦	1211–1213
		(1211–1214)
Kentoku (S)	建徳	1370–1372
Kōan	弘安	1278–1288
Kōan (N)	康安	1361–1362
Kōchō	弘長	1261–1264
Kōei (N)	康永	1342–1345
Kōgen	康元	1256–1257
Kōhei	康平	1058–1065
Kōhō	康保	964–968
Kōji	康治	1142–1144
Kōji	弘治	1555–1558

Kōka	弘化	1844–1848
		(1845–1848)
Kōkoku (S)	興国	1340–1346
		(1340–1347)
Kōnin	弘仁	810–824
Kōō (N)	康応	1389–1390
Kōryaku (N)	康暦	1379–1381
Kōshō	康正	1455–1457
Kōwa	康和	1099–1104
Kōwa (S)	弘和	1381–1384
Kyōhō	享保	1716–1736
Kyōroku	享禄	1528–1532
Kyōtoku	享徳	1452–1455
Kyōwa	享和	1801–1804
Kyūan	久安	1145–1151
Kyūju	久寿	1154–1156

M

Man'en	万延	1860–1861
Manji	万治	1658–1661
Manju	万寿	1024–1028
Meiji	明治	1868–1912
Meiō	明応	1492–1501
Meireki	明暦	1655–1658
Meitoku (N)	明徳	1390–1394
Meiwa	明和	1764–1772

N

Nimbyō	仁平	1151–1154
Nin'an	仁安	1166–1169
Ninji	仁治	1240–1243
Ninju	仁寿	851–854
Ninna	仁和	885–889

O

Ōan (N)	応安	1368–1375
Ōchō	応長	1311–1312
Ōei	応永	1394–1428
Ōho	応保	1161–1163
Ōnin	応仁	1467–1469
Ōtoku	応徳	1084–1087
Ōwa	応和	961–964

R

Reiki	霊亀	715–717
Ryakunin	暦仁	1238–1239
Ryakuō (N)	暦応	1338–1342

S

Saikō	斉衡	854–857
Shitoku (N)	至徳	1384–1387
Shōan	正安	1299–1302
Shōchō	正長	1428–1429
Shōchū	正中	1324–1326
Shōgen	正元	1259–1260
Shōhei (S)	正平	1346–1370
		(1347–1370)

Shōhō	正保	1644–1648
		(1645–1648)
Shōji	正治	1199–1201
Shōka	正嘉	1257–1259
Shōkyō (N)	正慶	1332–1333
Shōō	正応	1288–1293
Shōryaku	正暦	990–995
Shōtai	昌泰	898–901
Shōtoku	正徳	1711–1716
Shōwa	正和	1312–1317
Shōwa	昭和	1926–1989
Shuchō	朱鳥	686
		(686–687)

T

Taiei	大永	1521–1528
Taihō	大宝	701–704
Taika	大化	645–650
Taishō	大正	1912–1926
Tembun	天文	1532–1555
Temmei	天明	1781–1789
Tempō	天保	1830–1844
		(1831–1845)
Tempuku	天福	1233–1234
Tempyō	天平	729–749
Tempyō Hōji	天平宝字	757–765
Tempyō Jingo	天平神護	765–767
Tempyō Kampō	天平感宝	749
Tempyō Shōhō	天平勝宝	749–757
Ten'an	天安	857–859
Tenchō	天長	824–834
Ten'ei	天永	1110–1113
Ten'en	天延	973–976
		(974–976)
Tengen	天元	978–983
Tengi	天喜	1053–1058
Tengyō	天慶	938–947
Tenji	天治	1124–1126
Tenju	天授	1375–1381
Tenna	天和	1681–1684
Tennin	天仁	1108–1110
Ten'ō	天応	781–782
Tenroku	天禄	970–973
		(970–974)
Tenryaku	天暦	947–957
Tenshō	天承	1131–1132
Tenshō	天正	1573–1592
		(1573–1593)
Tentoku	天徳	957–961
Ten'yō	天養	1144–1145
Tokuji	徳治	1306–1308
		(1307–1308)

W

Wadō	和同	708–715

Y

Yōrō	養老	717–724
Yōwa	養和	1181–1182

NOTE: (N) indicates era names used by the "Northern Court" and (S) those used by the "Southern Court" during the period of division into rival courts in the 14th century. The period of Northern and Southern Courts is defined in this encyclopedia as having begun in 1337, when Emperor Go-Daigo (r 1318–39) left Kyōto and established his Southern Court in Yoshino, and as having ended in 1392, when the two courts were reunified. However, even before 1337, Go-Daigo's enemies had set up rival emperors (Kōgon from 1331 to 1333 and Kōmyō in 1336), and it is common to use the word "northern" to distinguish these two courts from Go-Daigo's "southern" one. The Southern Court era names are widely regarded as more legitimate.

There had already been one earlier instance of overlapping era names of rival courts—namely the Juei era (1182–1185) of Emperor Antoku (r 1180–85) and the Genryaku era (1184–1185) of the rival emperor Go-Toba (r 1183–98). On the other hand, two early eras, Hakuchi (650–654) and Shuchō (686), were each followed by a number of years during which there was no era name.

FOR FURTHER READING

BY FRANK JOSEPH SHULMAN

The number of books available in English on contemporary Japan and on Japanese history and culture continues to grow rapidly. The following list was compiled to help the general reader make sensible choices for follow-up reading on the topics covered in this encyclopedia. A diamond (•) before a title indicates that it would be a good book to read first on that particular topic. With a few exceptions, only books that focus chiefly on Japan–as opposed to comparative studies of several nations–have been included.

The reading list is divided into 23 sections, or categories. The first of these, GENERAL WORKS, consists of books that provide an overview of Japan as a whole–its customs, culture, and place in the world at large. The last section contains a list of PERIODICALS AND NEWSPAPERS that feature articles on Japan. The intervening 21 sections are arranged in alphabetical order, from ART AND ARCHITECTURE to WOMEN. Many sections are subdivided to help the reader find specific areas of interest.

Because of space limitations, books that could have been listed in more than one section are listed only in one. Some cross-references to other sections have been provided. However, the reader should be aware that, with some exceptions, books in the social sciences with a historical orientation are listed under HISTORY. Within HISTORY itself, books containing information on a particular period may, because of overlapping subject matter, be found in the sections on the preceding or following periods. Similarly, some books on Japan's modern history are listed under INTERNATIONAL RELATIONS.

Within sections or subsections, books are listed alphabetically by title. The one exception is the subsection on the MODERN PERIOD within LITERATURE, which is subdivided alphabetically by author, with works by each author listed alphabetically under the author's name. Works about an author appear after the author's own works.

Alphabetization follows the word-by-word system rather than the letter-by-letter system that is used in alphabetizing the entry titles in this encyclopedia. (For example, in this reading list, ''Japan Today'' would come before ''Japanese Culture,'' whereas, if alphabetized letter-by-letter, ''Japanese Culture'' would come first.)

Annotations have been provided only when necessary for clarification. When appropriate, both US and British imprints are indicated. Normally the edition listed is the most recent. Reprints of older works are identified when known. Names of translators have been included whenever possible.

This list does not include books published after early 1992. Articles are omitted entirely. However, the section on PERIODICALS AND NEWSPAPERS includes publications that carry articles about Japan on a wide range of topics, from art and religion to business and foreign affairs.

Readers who want to find additional books on a particular topic should consult the subsections listing reference works and bibliographies that appear at the end of some sections, as well as the subsection REFERENCE WORKS AND BIBLIOGRAPHIES at the end of the GENERAL WORKS section.

GENERAL WORKS

See also ECONOMICS: GENERAL WORKS; HISTORY: POST–WORLD WAR II; GOVERNMENT AND POLITICS; SOCIETY.

All-Japan: The Catalogue of Everything Japanese. Liza Dalby et al. New York: William Morrow; Bromley, Kent: Columbus Books, 1984. 224 pp.
• *Cultural Atlas of Japan.* Martin Collcutt, Marius Jansen, and Isao Kumakura. Oxford: Phaidon; New York: Facts on File, 1988. 240 pp. An illustrated overview of Japan's cultural history.
Discover Japan: Words, Customs and Concepts. Japan Culture Institute (Nihon Bunka Kenkyujo). Tokyo and New York: Kodansha International, 1982–83. 2 vols.
In the Realm of a Dying Emperor. Norma Field. New York: Pantheon Books, 1991. 273 pp. Japan in the late 1980s.
Inside Japan: Wealth, Work and Power in the New Japanese Empire. Peter Tasker. London: Sidgwick and Jackson, 1987; New York: E. P. Dutton, 1988. 312 pp. Published in the United States as *The Japanese: A Major Exploration of Modern Japan* and as *The Japanese: Portrait of a Nation.*
Inside the Japanese System: Readings on Contemporary Society and Political Economy. Edited by Daniel I. Okimoto and Thomas P. Rohlen. Stanford, Calif.: Stanford University Press, 1988. 286 pp.

An Introduction to Japanese Civilization. Edited by Arthur E. Tiedemann. New York and London: Columbia University Press; Lexington, Mass.: D. C. Heath, 1974. 622 pp.
• *Japan: A Postindustrial Power.* Ardath W. Burks. Boulder, Colo., and Oxford: Westview Press, 1991. 3d ed. 234 pp.
• *Japan as Number One: Lessons for America.* Ezra F. Vogel. Cambridge, Mass., and London: Harvard University Press, 1979. 272 pp.
• *Japan: The Fragile Superpower.* Frank Gibney. New York: New American Library, 1985. 2d ed., rev. 430 pp.
• *Japan Today.* Roger Buckley. Cambridge and New York: Cambridge University Press, 1990. 2d ed. 155 pp.
The Japanese and the Jews. Isaiah Ben-Dasan (pseud.), translated by Richard L. Gage. Tokyo and New York: Weatherhill, 1972. 193 pp.
• *Japanese Culture.* H. Paul Varley. Honolulu: University of Hawaii Press, 1984. 3d ed. 331 pp.
• *The Japanese Mind: The Goliath Explained.* Robert C. Christopher. New York: Simon & Schuster, Linden Press, 1983. 352 pp.
• *The Japanese Today: Change and Continuity.* Edwin O. Reischauer. Cambridge, Mass., and London: Harvard University Press, Belknap Press, 1988. 426 pp.
The Other Japan: Postwar Realities. Edited by E. Patricia Tsurumi for the *Bulletin of Concerned Asian Scholars.* Armonk, N.Y., and London: M. E. Sharpe, 1988. 163 pp.

Shadows of the Rising Sun: A Critical View of the ''Japanese Miracle.'' Jared Taylor. New York: William Morrow, 1983. 336 pp.
• *Sources of Japanese Tradition.* Compiled by Ryusaku Tsunoda, William Theodore de Bary, and Donald Keene. New York: Columbia University Press; London: Oxford University Press, 1958. 928 pp. A collection of readings in Japanese religion, philosophy, history, and culture.

REFERENCE WORKS AND BIBLIOGRAPHIES

Bibliography of Asian Studies. Ann Arbor, Mich.: Association for Asian Studies, 1941– . Annual. Contains bibliographical listings of books and articles about Japan written in Western languages.
Catalogue of Books in English on Japan, 1945–1981. Compiled by the Japan Foundation (Kokusai Kōryū Kikin). Tokyo: Japan Foundation, 1986. 726 pp.
Doctoral Dissertations on Asia: An Annotated Bibliographical Journal of Current International Research. Ann Arbor, Mich.: Association for Asian Studies, 1975– . Annual.
Everything Japanese. Boye De Mente. Lincolnwood, Ill.: Passport Books; London: Harrap, 1989. 319 pp. Originally published as *Passport's Japan Almanac.*
Facts and Figures of Japan. Tokyo: Foreign Press Center/Japan, 1977– . Published in alternate years.

Handbook of Japanese Popular Culture. Edited by Richard Gid Powers and Hidetoshi Kato; associate editor, Bruce Stronach. New York and London: Greenwood Press, 1989. 350 pp.

♦ *Japan.* Frank Joseph Shulman. Oxford and Santa Barbara, Calif.: Clio Press, 1989. 876 pp. Annotated bibliography of some 1,900 English-language books about Japan.

Japan: A Country Study. Edited by Ronald E. Dolan and Robert L. Worden. Washington, D.C.: Headquarters, Department of the Army, 1992. 5th ed. 610 pp. For sale by the U.S. Government Printing Office.

Japan Statistical Yearbook (Nihon tōkei nenkan). Edited by Statistics Bureau, Prime Minister's Office (Sōrifu, Tōkeikyoku). Tokyo: Sōrifu, Tōkeikyoku, 1949– . Annual.

Japan through Children's Literature: An Annotated Bibliography. Compiled by Yasuko Makino, with Roberta K. Gumport. Westport, Conn., and London: Greenwood Press, 1985. Enlarged 2d ed. 144 pp.

♦ *Kodansha Encyclopedia of Japan.* Gen Itasaka, editor in chief; executive editors: Alan Campbell, Gyō Furuta, and Takeshi Kokubo. Tokyo and New York: Kodansha, Ltd., 1983. 9 vols. Supplement, 1st ed. Tokyo and New York: Kodansha, Ltd., 1986. 59 pp.

Mock Joya's Things Japanese. Mock Joya. Tokyo: Japan Times, 1985. New ed. 728 pp.

Nippon: A Charted Survey of Japan. Edited by the Tsuneta Yano Memorial Society (Yano Tsuneta Kinenkai). Tokyo: Kokuseisha, 1936– . Annual. Brief essays about contemporary Japan combined with statistical charts and tables.

Pictorial Encyclopedia of Japanese Culture: The Soul and Heritage of Japan. Tokyo: Gakken, 1987. 130 pp.

White Papers of Japan: Annual Abstract of Official Reports and Statistics of the Japanese Government. Edited by the Japan Institute of International Affairs (Nihon Kokusai Mondai Kenkyūjo). Tokyo: Japan Institute of International Affairs, 1969– . Annual.

ART AND ARCHITECTURE

GENERAL WORKS

♦ *The Art and Architecture of Japan.* Robert Treat Paine and Alexander Soper. Rev. and updated by David B. Waterhouse and Bunji Kobayashi. Harmondsworth, Middlesex, and Baltimore, Md.: Penguin Books, 1981. 3d ed. 524 pp.

♦ *The Arts of Japan. Volume 1: Ancient and Medieval. Volume 2: Late Medieval to Modern.* Seiroku Noma, translated and adapted by John Rosenfield and Glenn T. Webb, photographs by Bin Takahashi. Tokyo and New York: Kodansha International, 1978. 1st standard ed. 2 vols.

Asuka Buddhist Art: Horyu-ji. Seiichi Mizuno, translated by Richard L. Gage. New York and Tokyo: Weatherhill/Heibonsha, 1974. 172 pp.

A Century of Japanese Photography. Japan Photographers Association (Nihon Shashinka Kyōkai). New York: Pantheon, 1980. 385 pp.

A Concise History of Japanese Art. Peter C. Swann. Tokyo and New York: Kodansha International, 1979. 332 pp.

The Enduring Art of Japan. Langdon Warner. Cambridge: Harvard University Press, 1952. 113 pp.

The Genius of Japanese Design. Sherman E. Lee. Tokyo and New York: Kodansha International, 1981. 203 pp.

The Great Japan Exhibition: Art of the Edo Period 1600–1868. Edited by William Watson. London:

Royal Academy of Art; New York: Alpine Fine Arts Collection, 1981. 365 pp.

♦ *The Heritage of Japanese Art.* Masao Ishizawa et al. Tokyo and New York: Kodansha International, 1982. 208 pp.

A History of Far Eastern Art. Sherman E. Lee. Englewood Cliffs, N.J.: Prentice-Hall and Harry N. Abrams (New York), 1982. 4th ed. 548 pp.

Japan: The Shaping of Daimyo Culture, 1185–1868. Edited by Yoshiaki Shimizu. New York: George Braziller; Washington, D.C.: National Gallery of Art, 1988. 402 pp.

Japanese Art. Joan Stanley-Baker. London and New York: Thames and Hudson, 1984. 216 pp.

Japanese Art: Masterpieces in the British Museum. Lawrence Smith, Victor Harris, and Timothy Clark. London: British Museum Publications; New York: Oxford University Press, 1990. 256 pp.

A Thousand Cranes: Treasures of Japanese Art. Seattle Art Museum. Seattle: Seattle Art Museum; San Francisco: Chronicle Books, 1987. 239 pp.

APPLIED AND DECORATIVE ARTS

Art of Netsuke Carving. Masatoshi (Tokisada Nakamura), as told by Raymond Bushell. Tokyo and New York: Kodansha International, 1981. 236 pp.

Bamboo. Robert Austin and Kōichirō Ueda, photographs by Dana Levy. New York and Tokyo: Weatherhill, 1970. 215 pp.

The Book of Kimono. Norio Yamanaka. Tokyo and New York: Kodansha International, 1982. 139 pp.

Forms, Textures, Images: Traditional Japanese Craftsmanship in Everyday Life. A Photo-Essay. Takeji Iwamiya, edited by Mitsukuni Yoshida, translated by Susan Carol Barberi. New York and Tokyo: Weatherhill/Tankosha, 1979. 303 pp.

Hamada, Potter. Bernard Leach. Tokyo and New York: Kodansha International; London: Thames and Hudson, 1975. 305 pp. Biography of the renowned potter Hamada Shōji (1894–1978).

How to Wrap Five More Eggs: Traditional Japanese Packaging. Hideyuki Oka, photographs by Michikazu Sakai. New York and Tokyo: Weatherhill, 1975. 215 pp.

An Introduction to Netsuke. Raymond Bushell. Rutland, Vt., and Tokyo: Tuttle, 1971. 78 pp.

Japanese Costume and Textile Arts. Seiroku Noma, translated by Armins Nikovskis. New York and Tokyo: Weatherhill/Heibonsha, 1974. 168 pp.

Japanese Costume and the Makers of Its Elegant Tradition. Helen Benton Minnich, with Shōjirō Nomura. Rutland, Vt., and Tokyo: Tuttle, 1963. 374 pp. Reprinted, Tuttle, 1986.

Japanese Crafts. John Lowe, photographs by Mark Lowe. London: John Murray; New York: Van Nostrand Reinhold, 1983. 175 pp.

Japanese Painted Porcelain: Modern Masterpieces in Overglaze Enamel. Edited by the National Museum of Modern Art, Tokyo (Tōkyō Kokuritsu Kindai Bijutsukan), translated by Richard L. Gage. New York and Tokyo: Weatherhill/Tankosha, 1980. 245 pp.

Japanese Papermaking: Traditions, Tools, and Techniques. Timothy Barrett, with Winifred Lutz. New York and Tokyo: Weatherhill, 1983. 317 pp.

The Japanese Sword. Kanzan Satō, translated and adapted by Joe Earle. Tokyo and New York: Kodansha International and Shibundo, 1983. 210 pp.

Kanban: Shop Signs of Japan. Photographs by Dana Levy, commentaries by Lea Sneider. New York and Tokyo: Weatherhill, 1983. 167 pp.

Shigaraki, Potters' Valley. Louise Allison Cort. Tokyo and New York: Kodansha International, 1979. 428 pp. Account of the stoneware produced in the Shigaraki Valley near Kyōto.

Tansu: Traditional Japanese Cabinetry. Ty Heineken

and Kiyoko Heineken. New York and Tokyo: Weatherhill, 1981. 247 pp.

Traditional Japanese Furniture. Kazuko Koizumi, translated by Alfred Birnbaum. Tokyo and New York: Kodansha International, 1986. 223 pp.

The Unknown Craftsman: A Japanese Insight into Beauty. Sōetsu Yanagi, adapted by Bernard Leach. Tokyo and New York: Kodansha International, 1989. Rev. ed. 230 pp.

The Way of the Carpenter: Tools and Japanese Architecture. William H. Coaldrake. New York: Weatherhill, 1990. 204 pp.

The World of Japanese Ceramics. Herbert H. Sanders, with Kenkichi Tomimoto. Tokyo and Palo Alto, Calif.: Kodansha International, 1967. 267 pp. Reprinted, Tokyo and New York: Kodansha International, 1982.

ARCHITECTURE AND GARDENS

The Classic Tradition in Japanese Architecture: Modern Versions of the Sukiya Style. Teiji Itoh, translated by Richard L. Gage, photographs by Yukio Futagawa. New York and Tokyo: Weatherhill/ Tankosha, 1972. 279 pp.

Contemporary Japanese Architecture: Its Development and Challenge. Botond Bognar. New York: Van Nostrand Reinhold, 1985. 363 pp.

Feudal Architecture of Japan. Kiyoshi Hirai, translated by Hiroaki Sato and Jeannine Ciliotta. New York and Tokyo: Weatherhill/Heibonsha, 1973. 166 pp.

♦ *The Gardens of Japan.* Teiji Itoh. Tokyo and New York: Kodansha International, 1984. 228 pp.

Ise: Prototype of Japanese Architecture. Kenzō Tange and Noboru Kawazoe, photographs by Yoshio Watanabe. Cambridge: MIT Press, 1965. 212 pp. On the architectural characteristics of the Ise Shrine.

Japanese Castles. Motoo Hinago, translated and adapted by William H. Coaldrake. Tokyo and New York: Kodansha International and Shibundo, 1986. 200 pp.

The Japanese Garden: An Approach to Nature. Teiji Itoh, photographs by Takeji Iwamiya. New Haven, Conn.: Yale University Press; Tokyo: Zokeisha, 1972. 205 pp.

A Japanese Touch for Your Garden. Kiyoshi Seike and Masanobu Kudo, with David H. Engel, photographs by Haruzo Ōhashi. Tokyo and New York: Kodansha International, 1980. 80 pp.

Katsura: A Princely Retreat. Akira Naitō, translated by Charles S. Terry, photographs by Takeshi Nishikawa. Tokyo and New York: Kodansha International, 1977. 182 pp. Covers the architectural and cultural history of the Katsura Detached Palace near Kyōto.

The Making of a Modern Japanese Architecture: 1868 to the Present. David B. Stewart. Tokyo and New York: Kodansha International, 1987. 304 pp.

Minka: Traditional Houses of Rural Japan. Chūji Kawashima, translated by Lynne E. Riggs. Tokyo and New York: Kodansha International, 1986. 260 pp.

The Roots of Japanese Architecture: A Photographic Quest. Yukio Futagawa, text and commentaries by Teiji Itoh, translated by Paul Konya. New York and London: Harper & Row, 1963. 207 pp.

Space and Illusion in the Japanese Garden. Teiji Itoh, photographs by Sōsei Kuzunishi, translated and adapted by Ralph Friedrich and Masajiro Shimamura. New York and Tokyo: Weatherhill/ Tankosha, 1973. 229 pp.

♦ *What Is Japanese Architecture?* Kazuo Nishi and Kazuo Hozumi, translated by H. Mack Horton. Tokyo and New York: Kodansha International, 1985. 144 pp.

♦ *The World of the Japanese Garden: From Chinese Origins to Modern Landscape Art.* Loraine Kuck, photographs by Takeji Iwamiya. New York and

Tokyo: Walker/Weatherhill, 1968. 414 pp.
Reprinted, Weatherhill, 1980.

PAINTING, CALLIGRAPHY, AND WOODBLOCK PRINTS

The Art of Hokusai in Book Illustration. Jack Ronald Hillier. Berkeley: University of California Press; London: Sotheby Parke Bernet, 1980. 288 pp.

The Art of Sumi-e: Appreciation, Techniques, and Application. Shōzō Satō, with Thomas A. Heenan. Tokyo and New York: Kodansha International, 1984. 329 pp.

The Art of Zen: Paintings and Calligraphy by Japanese Monks, 1600–1925. Stephen Addiss. New York: Abrams, 1989. 223 pp.

The History of Japanese Printing and Book Illustration. David Chibbett. Tokyo and New York: Kodansha International, 1977. 264 pp.

• *Images from the Floating World: The Japanese Print; Including an Illustrated Dictionary of Ukiyo-e.* Richard Lane. New York: Putnam; Secaucus, N.J.: Chartwell Books, 1978. 364 pp.

Japanese Ink Painting: Shubun to Sesshu. Ichimatsu Tanaka, translated by Bruce Darling. New York and Tokyo: Weatherhill/Heibonsha, 1972. 174 pp.

Masters of Calligraphy, 8th–19th Century. Yoshiaki Shimizu and John M. Rosenfield. New York: Asia Society Galleries; Japan House Gallery, 1984. 340 pp.

Masters of the Japanese Print. Richard Lane. Garden City, N.Y.: Doubleday; London: Thames and Hudson, 1962. 319 pp.

Modern Japanese Prints: An Art Reborn. Oliver Statler. Rutland, Vt., and Tokyo: Tuttle, 1956. 209 pp.

The Namban Art of Japan. Yoshitomo Okamoto, translated by Ronald K. Jones. New York and Tokyo: Weatherhill/Heibonsha, 1972. 156 pp.

One Hundred Famous Views of Edo. Andō Hiroshige, introductory essays by Henry D. Smith, II, and Amy G. Poster. New York: George Braziller; London: Thames and Hudson, 1986. 256 pp.

The World of the Meiji Print: Impressions of a New Civilization. Julia Meech-Pekarik. New York and Tokyo: Weatherhill, 1986. 259 pp.

Zen Painting & Calligraphy: An Exhibition of Works of Art Lent by Temples, Private Collectors, and Public and Private Museums in Japan, Organized in Collaboration with the Agency for Cultural Affairs of the Japanese Government. Jan Fontein and Money L. Hickman. Boston: Museum of Fine Arts, 1970. 173 pp.

SCULPTURE

The Great Age of Japanese Buddhist Sculpture, AD 600–1300. Kyōtarō Nishikawa and Emily J. Sano. Fort Worth, Tex.: Kimbell Art Museum; New York: Japan Society, 1982. 151 pp.

Nara Buddhist Art: Todai-ji. Takeshi Kobayashi, translated and adapted by Richard L. Gage. New York and Tokyo: Weatherhill/Heibonsha, 1975. 157 pp.

Temples of Nara and Their Art. Minoru Ōoka, translated by Dennis Lishka. New York and Tokyo: Weatherhill/Heibonsha, 1973. 184 pp.

REFERENCE WORKS AND BIBLIOGRAPHIES

Biographical Dictionary of Japanese Art. Supervising editor, Yutaka Tazawa. Tokyo: International Society for Educational Information, in collaboration with Kodansha International, 1981. 825 pp.

A Dictionary of Japanese Artists: Painting, Sculpture, Ceramics, Prints, Lacquer. Laurence P. Roberts. New York and Tokyo: Weatherhill, 1976. 299 pp.

The History and Practice of Japanese Printmaking: A Selectively Annotated Bibliography of English Language Materials. Leslie E. Abrams. Westport, Conn., and London: Greenwood Press, 1984. 197 pp.

Roberts' Guide to Japanese Museums of Art and Archaeology. Laurence P. Roberts. Tokyo: Simul Press, 1987. 384 pp.

ECONOMICS

See also HISTORY: POST–WORLD WAR II; GOVERNMENT AND POLITICS; INTERNATIONAL RELATIONS; SOCIETY.

GENERAL WORKS

• *America versus Japan: A Comparative Study of Business-Government Relations Conducted at the Harvard Business School.* Edited by Thomas K. McCraw. Boston: Harvard Business School Press, 1986. 463 pp.

Asia's New Giant: How the Japanese Economy Works. Edited by Hugh Patrick and Henry Rosovsky. Washington, D.C.: Brookings Institution, 1976. 943 pp.

The Business of the Japanese State: Energy Markets in Comparative and Historical Perspective. Richard J. Samuels. Ithaca, N.Y., and London: Cornell University Press, 1987. 359 pp.

The Competition: Dealing with Japan. Thomas Pepper, Merit E. Janow, and Jimmy W. Wheeler. New York and Eastbourne, Sussex: Praeger, 1985. 374 pp.

The Economic Development of Japan: A Quantitative Study. Ryōshin Minami, translated by Ralph Thompson and Ryōshin Minami, with the assistance of David Merriman. London: Macmillan; New York: St. Martin's Press, 1986. 487 pp.

The Era of High-Speed Growth: Notes on the Postwar Japanese Economy. Yutaka Kōsai, translated by Jacqueline Kaminski. Tokyo: University of Tokyo Press, 1986. 223 pp.

Flexible Rigidities: Industrial Policy and Structural Adjustment in the Japanese Economy, 1970–80. Ronald Dore. Stanford, Calif.: Stanford University Press; London: Athlone Press, 1986. 278 pp.

Fueling Growth: The Energy Revolution and Economic Policy in Postwar Japan. Laura E. Hein. Cambridge: Council on East Asian Studies, Harvard University, 1990. 423 pp.

Japan: Facing Economic Maturity. Edward J. Lincoln. Washington, D.C.: Brookings Institution, 1988. 298 pp.

Japan in the World Economy. Bela Balassa and Marcus Noland. Washington, D.C.: Institute for International Economics, 1988. 290 pp.

Japanese Economic Development: A Short Introduction. Kunio Yoshihara. Tokyo, Oxford, and New York: Oxford University Press, 1979. 153 pp.

The Japanese Economy. George Cyril Allen. New York: St. Martin's Press; London: Weidenfeld and Nicolson, 1981. 226 pp.

Japan's Economy: Coping with Change in the International Environment. Edited by Daniel I. Okimoto. Boulder, Colo.: Westview Press, 1982. 304 pp.

Miracle by Design: The Real Reasons behind Japan's Economic Success. Frank Gibney. New York: Times Books; Toronto: Fitzhenry and Whiteside, 1982. 239 pp.

• *The Political Economy of Japan. Volume 1: The Domestic Transformation,* edited by Kozo Yamamura and Yasukichi Yasuba. *Volume 2: The Changing International Context,* edited by Takashi

Inoguchi and Daniel I. Okimoto. *Volume 3: Cultural and Social Dynamics,* edited by Shumpei Kumon and Henry Rosovsky. Stanford, Calif.: Stanford University Press, 1987–90. 3 vols.

Politics & Productivity: The Real Story of Why Japan Works. Edited by Chalmers Johnson, Laura D'Andrea Tyson, and John Zysman. Cambridge, Mass.: Ballinger, 1989. 332 pp.

The Postwar Japanese Economy: Its Development and Structure. Takafusa Nakamura, translated by Jacqueline Kaminski. Tokyo: University of Tokyo Press, 1981. 277 pp.

The Sun Also Sets: The Limits to Japan's Economic Power. Bill Emmott. New York: Times Books; London: Simon & Schuster, 1989. 292 pp.

Taking Japan Seriously: A Confucian Perspective on Leading Economic Issues. Ronald Dore. London: Athlone Press; Stanford, Calif.: Stanford University Press, 1987. 264 pp.

Why Has Japan "Succeeded"? Western Technology and the Japanese Ethos. Michio Morishima. Cambridge and New York: Cambridge University Press, 1982. 207 pp.

AGRICULTURE

The Agricultural Development of Japan: A Century's Perspective. Yūjirō Hayami and Saburō Yamada. Tokyo: University of Tokyo Press, 1991. 276 pp.

Can Japanese Agriculture Survive? A Historical and Comparative Approach. Takekazu Ogura. Tokyo: Agricultural Policy Research Center, 1982. 3d ed. 880 pp.

Japanese Agriculture: A Comparative Economic Analysis. Cornelius L. J. van der Meer and Saburō Yamada. London and New York: Routledge, 1990. 217 pp.

Japanese Agriculture under Siege: The Political Economy of Agricultural Policies. Yūjirō Hayami. New York: St. Martin's Press; London: Macmillan, 1988. 145 pp.

BUSINESS AND COMMERCE

Business and Society in Japan: Fundamentals for Businessmen. Edited by Bradley M. Richardson and Taizō Ueda. New York: Praeger, 1981. 334 pp.

The Development of Japanese Business, 1600–1980. Johannes Hirschmeier and Tsunehiko Yui. London and Boston: Allen and Unwin, 1981. 2d ed. 406 pp.

• *From Bonsai to Levi's. When West Meets East: An Insider's Surprising Account of How the Japanese Live.* George Fields. New York: Macmillan, 1983. 213 pp. On Japanese consumer buying habits.

Gaijin Kaisha: Running a Foreign Business in Japan. Jackson N. Huddleston, Jr. Armonk, N.Y., and London: M. E. Sharpe, 1990. 270 pp.

Gucci on the Ginza: Japan's New Consumer Generation. George Fields. Tokyo and New York: Kodansha International; Tokyo: Japan Times, 1989. 267 pp. Also published by Japan Times as *The Japanese Market Culture.*

• *How to Do Business with the Japanese.* Mark Zimmerman. New York: Random House, 1985. 316 pp. London: Allen and Unwin, 1985. 320 pp. Published in the United Kingdom as *Dealing with the Japanese.*

How to Do Business with the Japanese: A Complete Guide to Japanese Customs and Business Practices. Boye De Mente. Lincolnwood, Ill.: NTC Business Books, 1987. 269 pp.

The Invisible Link: Japan's Sogo Shosha and the Organization of Trade. Michael Y. Yoshino and Thomas B. Lifson. Cambridge, Mass., and London: MIT Press, 1986. 291 pp.

• *The Japanese Company.* Rodney Clark. New Haven,

Conn., and London: Yale University Press, 1979. 282 pp.

Japanese Etiquette & Ethics in Business. Boye De Mente. Lincolnwood, Ill.: Passport Books, 1987. 5th ed. 182 pp.

Japanese Takeovers: The Global Contest for Corporate Control. W. Carl Kester. Boston: Harvard Business School Press, 1991. 298 pp.

◆*Kaisha: The Japanese Corporation.* James C. Abegglen and George Stalk, Jr. New York: Basic Books, 1985; London: Taurus, 1986. 309 pp.

Second to None: American Companies in Japan. Robert C. Christopher. New York: Crown, 1986. 258 pp.

◆*Smart Bargaining: Doing Business with the Japanese.* John L. Graham and Yoshihiro Sano. New York: Harper & Row, Ballinger Division, 1989. Rev. ed. 212 pp.

◆*Sogo Shosha: The Vanguard of the Japanese Economy.* Kunio Yoshihara. Tokyo, Oxford, and New York: Oxford University Press, 1982. 358 pp.

The Spirit of Japanese Capitalism. Shichihei Yamamoto, translated by Lynne E. Riggs and Manabu Takeuchi. Lanham, Md.: Madison Books, 1992. 276 pp.

The Strategy of Japanese Business. James C. Abegglen. Cambridge, Mass.: Ballinger, 1984. 227 pp.

FINANCE AND BANKING

Banking and Finance in Japan: An Introduction to the Tokyo Market. Kazuo Tatewaki. London and New York: Routledge, 1991. 220 pp.

The Emerging Power of Japanese Money. Aron Viner. Homewood, Ill.: Dow Jones-Irwin; London: Kogan Page, 1988. 254 pp.

The Financial Behavior of Japanese Corporations. Robert J. Ballon and Iwao Tomita. Tokyo and New York: Kodansha International, 1988. 268 pp.

Financial Politics in Contemporary Japan. Frances McCall Rosenbluth. Ithaca, N.Y., and London: Cornell University Press, 1989. 237 pp.

Financial Reporting in Japan: Regulation, Practice and Environment. T. E. Cooke and M. Kikuya. Oxford: Blackwell, 1992. 356 pp.

The House of Nomura: The Inside Story of the Legendary Japanese Financial Dynasty. Albert J. Alletzhauser. New York: Arcade; London: Bloomsbury, 1990. 343 pp.

◆*Inside Japanese Financial Markets.* Aron Viner. London: Economist Publications, 1987. 274 pp. Homewood, Ill.: Dow Jones-Irwin, 1988. 364 pp.

Japanese Capital Markets: Analysis and Characteristics of Equity, Debt, and Financial Futures Markets. Edited by Edwin J. Elton and Martin J. Gruber. New York: Harper & Row, Ballinger Division, 1990. 371 pp.

◆*The Japanese Financial System.* Edited by Yoshio Suzuki. Oxford and New York: Oxford University Press, 1987. 358 pp.

The Japanese Tax System. Hiromitsu Ishi. Oxford: Clarendon Press; New York: Oxford University Press, 1989. 347 pp.

Public Finance in Japan. Edited by Tokue Shibata. Tokyo: University of Tokyo Press, 1986. 195 pp.

Tokyo: A World Financial Centre. Brian Robins. London: Euromoney Publications, 1987. 285 pp.

INDUSTRY

Between MITI and the Market: Japanese Industrial Policy for High Technology. Daniel I. Okimoto. Stanford, Calif.: Stanford University Press, 1989. 267 pp.

Industrial Organization in Japan. Richard E. Caves and Masu Uekusa. Washington, D.C.: Brookings Institution, 1976. 169 pp.

Industrial Policy of Japan. Edited by Ryūtarō Komiya, Masahiro Okuno, and Kōtarō Suzumura;

translated under the supervision of Kazuo Satō. Tokyo: Academic Press Japan; San Diego, Calif., and London: Academic Press, 1988. 590 pp.

The Japanese Automobile Industry: Technology and Management at Nissan and Toyota. Michael A. Cusumano. Cambridge: Council on East Asian Studies, Harvard University, 1985. 487 pp.

Japanese Manufacturing Techniques: Nine Hidden Lessons in Simplicity. Richard J. Schonberger. New York: Free Press; London: Collier Macmillan, 1982. 260 pp.

Japanese Participation in British Industry. John H. Dunning. London and Dover, N.H.: Croom Helm, 1986. 207 pp.

Kikkoman: Company, Clan, and Community. W. Mark Fruin. Cambridge, Mass., and London: Harvard University Press, 1983. 358 pp.

Made in Japan: Akio Morita and Sony. Akio Morita, with Edwin M. Reingold and Mitsuko Shimomura. New York: E. P. Dutton, 1986; London: Collins, 1987. 309 pp.

The Misunderstood Miracle: Industrial Development and Political Change in Japan. David Friedman. Ithaca, N.Y., and London: Cornell University Press, 1988. 265 pp.

The Reckoning. David Halberstam. New York: William Morrow, 1986; London: Bloomsbury, 1987. 752 pp. A comparison of Nissan and Ford, the number-two automobile manufacturers in Japan and the United States.

LABOR AND MANAGEMENT

◆*The Art of Japanese Management: Applications for American Executives.* Richard Tanner Pascale and Anthony G. Athos. New York: Simon & Schuster, 1981; London: Allen Lane, 1982. 221 pp.

◆*British Factory–Japanese Factory: The Origins of National Diversity in Industrial Relations.* Ronald Dore. London: Allen and Unwin; Berkeley: University of California Press, 1973. 432 pp. Reprinted, University of California Press, 1990.

Contemporary Industrial Relations in Japan. Edited by Taishirō Shirai. Madison and London: University of Wisconsin Press, 1983. 421 pp.

Honda Motor: The Men, the Management, the Machines. Tetsuo Sakiya, translated by Kiyoshi Ikemi, adapted by Timothy Porter. Tokyo and New York: Kodansha International, 1982. 242 pp.

Industrial Relations in Japan: The Peripheral Workforce. Norma J. Chalmers. London and New York: Routledge, 1989. 283 pp.

Japan in the Passing Lane: An Insider's Account of Life in a Japanese Auto Factory. Satoshi Kamata, translated and edited by Tatsuru Akimoto. New York: Pantheon; London: Allen and Unwin, 1983. 211 pp.

Japanese Blue Collar: The Changing Tradition. Robert E. Cole. Berkeley and London: University of California Press, 1971. 300 pp.

Japanese-Style Management: An Insider's Analysis. Keitarō Hasegawa. Tokyo and New York: Kodansha International, 1986. 162 pp.

Labor Relations in Japan Today. Tadashi Hanami. Tokyo and New York: Kodansha International, 1979. 253 pp.

Management and Worker: The Japanese Solution. James C. Abegglen. Tokyo: Sophia University, in cooperation with Kodansha International, 1973. 200 pp.

The Management Challenge: Japanese Views. Edited by Lester C. Thurow. Cambridge, Mass., and London: MIT Press, 1985. 237 pp.

Managing Innovation: A Study of British and Japanese Factories. D. H. Whittaker. Cambridge and New York: Cambridge University Press, 1990. 205 pp.

Strategy and Structure of Japanese Enterprises. Toyohiro Kōno. London: Macmillan; Armonk, N.Y.: M. E. Sharpe, 1984. 352 pp.

Theory Z: How American Business Can Meet the Japanese Challenge. William G. Ouchi. Reading, Mass.: Addison-Wesley, 1981. 283 pp.

Understanding Industrial Relations in Modern Japan. Kazuo Koike, translated by Mary Saso. Basingstoke, Hampshire: Macmillan; New York: St. Martin's Press, 1988. 306 pp.

Work, Mobility, and Participation: A Comparative Study of American and Japanese Industry. Robert E. Cole. Berkeley and London: University of California Press, 1979. 302 pp.

REFERENCE WORKS AND BIBLIOGRAPHIES

Japan Company Handbook. Tokyo: Toyo Keizai Inc. (The Oriental Economist), 1936– . Quarterly.

Japan 1992: An International Comparison. Editor in chief, Kokichi Morimoto. Tokyo: Keizai Koho Center (Japan Institute for Social and Economic Affairs), 1991. 100 pp. An annual statistical overview for general readers.

Japan's Economic Challenge: A Bibliographic Sourcebook. Michael Keresztesi and Gary R. Cocozzoli. New York and London: Garland, 1988. 440 pp.

Japan's Economy: A Bibliography of Its Past and Present. William D. Wray. New York: Markus Wiener, 1989. 303 pp.

Postwar Industrial Policy in Japan: An Annotated Bibliography. Karl Boger. Metuchen, N.J., and London: Scarecrow Press, 1988. 208 pp.

EDUCATION

Child Development and Education in Japan. Edited by Harold Stevenson, Hiroshi Azuma, and Kenji Hakuta. New York: W. H. Freeman, 1986. 315 pp.

Education and Equality in Japan. William K. Cummings. Princeton, N.J., and Guildford, Surrey: Princeton University Press, 1980. 305 pp.

Education Reform in Japan: A Case of Immobilist Politics. Leonard J. Schoppa. London and New York: Routledge, 1991. 319 pp.

Educational Choice and Labor Markets in Japan. Mary Jean Bowman, with Hideo Ikeda and Yasumasa Tomoda. Chicago and London: University of Chicago Press, 1981. 367 pp.

Educational Policies in Crisis: Japanese and American Perspectives. Edited by William K. Cummings et al. New York and London: Praeger, in association with the East-West Center (Honolulu), 1986. 308 pp.

How the Japanese Learn to Work. Ronald P. Dore and Mari Sako. London and New York: Routledge, 1989. 158 pp. On vocational education.

◆*Japanese Education Today: A Report from the U.S. Study of Education in Japan.* Prepared by a special task force of the OERI (Office of Educational Research and Improvement) Japan Study Team; edited by Cynthia Hearn Dorfman. Washington, D.C.: U.S. Department of Education, 1987. 95 pp.

◆*The Japanese Educational Challenge: A Commitment to Children.* Merry White. New York: Free Press; London: Collier Macmillan, 1987. 210 pp.

Japanese Educational Productivity. Edited by Robert Leestma and Herbert J. Walberg. Ann Arbor: Center for Japanese Studies, University of Michigan, 1992. 425 pp.

The Japanese School: Lessons for Industrial America. Benjamin Duke. New York and London: Praeger, 1986. 242 pp.

◆*Japan's High Schools.* Thomas P. Rohlen. Berkeley and London: University of California Press, 1983. 363 pp.

Japan's "International Youth": The Emergence of a New Class of Schoolchildren. Roger Goodman. New

York: Oxford University Press; Oxford: Clarendon Press, 1990. 283 pp.

Learning to Go to School in Japan: The Transition from Home to Preschool Life. Lois Peak. Berkeley and London: University of California Press, 1991. 310 pp.

Society and Education in Japan. Herbert Passin. New York: Teachers College Press and East Asian Institute, Columbia University, 1965. 347 pp. Reprinted, Tokyo and New York: Kodansha International, 1983.

Transcending Stereotypes: Discovering Japanese Culture and Education. Edited by Barbara Finkelstein, Anne E. Imamura, and Joseph J. Tobin. Yarmouth, Me.: Intercultural Press, 1991. 221 pp.

REFERENCE WORKS AND BIBLIOGRAPHIES

Education in Japan: A Source Book. Edward R. Beauchamp and Richard Rubinger. New York and London: Garland, 1989. 300 pp.

Japanese Colleges and Universities 1989: A Guide to Institutions of Higher Education in Japan. Compiled and edited by the Association of International Education, Japan (Nihon Kokusai Kyōiku Kyōkai), in collaboration with the Association of National Universities (Kokuritsu Daigaku Kyōkai), the Association of Public Universities (Kōritsu Daigaku Kyōkai), and the Federation of Japanese Private Colleges and Universities Associations (Shiritsu Daigaku Dantai Rengōkai). Tokyo: Maruzen, 1989. 731 pp.

FOOD AND DRINK

The Book of Sushi. Kinjirō Ōmae and Yuzuru Tachibana. Tokyo and New York: Kodansha International, 1981. 127 pp. Reprinted, Kodansha International, 1988.

• *Japanese Cooking: A Simple Art.* Shizuo Tsuji, with Mary Sutherland. Tokyo and New York: Kodansha International, 1980. 517 pp.

Saké: A Drinker's Guide. Hiroshi Kondō. Tokyo and New York: Kodansha International, 1984. 128 pp.

A Taste of Japan. Donald Richie. Tokyo and New York: Kodansha International, 1985. 112 pp. Essays on various types of Japanese cuisine.

GEOGRAPHY AND ENVIRONMENT

See also TRAVEL AND DESCRIPTION.

Environmental Protest and Citizen Politics in Japan. Margaret A. McKean. Berkeley and London: University of California Press, 1981. 291 pp.

Garbage Management in Japan: Leading the Way. Allen Hershkowitz and Eugene Salerni. New York: INFORM, 1987. 131 pp.

Geography of Japan. Edited by the Association of Japanese Geographers (Nihon Chiri Gakkai). Tokyo: Teikoku Shoin, 1980. 440 pp.

In the Shadow of Fujisan: Japan and Its Wildlife. Jo Stewart-Smith, photographs by Simon McBride. Harmondsworth, Middlesex, and New York: Viking, 1987. 208 pp.

Island of Dreams: Environmental Crisis in Japan. Norie Huddle and Michael Reich, with Nahum Stiskin. New York and Tokyo: Autumn Press, 1975. 351 pp. Reprinted, Cambridge, Mass.: Schenkman Books, 1987.

Japan: A Geography. Glenn T. Trewartha. Madison: University of Wisconsin Press; London: Methuen, 1965. Rev. ed. 652 pp.

Japan: Geographical Background to Urban-Industrial Development. David Kornhauser. Harlow, Essex: Longman Scientific and Technical; New York: John Wiley, 1982. 2d ed. 189 pp.

Minamata. W. Eugene Smith and Aileen M. Smith. New York: Holt, Rinehart, and Winston; London: Chatto and Windus, 1975. 192 pp. On the methyl-mercury poisoning of the residents of the city of Minamata, Kumamoto Prefecture, during the 1950s and 1960s.

REFERENCE WORKS

A Field Guide to the Birds of Japan. Wild Bird Society of Japan (Nihon Yachō no Kai), Joseph A. Massey et al.; edited by Kōichiro Sonobe and Jane Washburn Robinson. Tokyo and New York: Wild Bird Society of Japan and Kodansha International, 1982. 336 pp.

Japan: A Bilingual Atlas. Tokyo and New York: Kodansha International, 1991. 128 pp.

National Parks of Japan. Mary Sutherland and Dorothy Britton. Tokyo and New York: Kodansha International, 1980. 148 pp.

• *Teikoku's Complete Atlas of Japan.* Editorial Department of Teikoku-Shoin Co, Ltd. (Teikoku Shoin Henshūbu), with the editorial collaboration of Yoshio Moriya. Tokyo: Teikoku Shoin, 1989. 10th ed. 55 pp.

GOVERNMENT AND POLITICS

See also HISTORY.

Communism in Japan: A Case of Political Naturalization. Paul F. Langer. Stanford, Calif.: Hoover Institution Press, 1972. 112 pp.

Crisis and Compensation: Public Policy and Political Stability in Japan, 1949–1986. Kent E. Calder. Princeton, N.J., and Guildford, Surrey: Princeton University Press, 1988. 557 pp.

The Death of an Emperor: Japan at the Crossroads. Thomas Crump. Oxford and New York: Oxford University Press, 1991. 250 pp.

Democracy in Japan. Edited by Takeshi Ishida and Ellis S. Krauss. Pittsburgh, Penn.: University of Pittsburgh Press, 1989. 354 pp.

Election Campaigning Japanese Style. Gerald L. Curtis. New York and London: Columbia University Press, 1971. 275 pp.

The Enigma of Japanese Power: People and Politics in a Stateless Nation. Karel van Wolferen. New York: Knopf; London: Macmillan London, 1989. 496 pp.

How the Conservatives Rule Japan. Nathaniel B. Thayer. Princeton, N.J.: Princeton University Press, 1969. 349 pp.

The Human Face of Japanese Leadership: Twelve Portraits. Martin E. Weinstein. New York and London: Praeger, 1989. 410 pp.

• *The Japanese Party System.* Ronald J. Hrebenar. Boulder, Colo., and Oxford: Westview Press, 1992. 2d ed. 319 pp.

• *The Japanese Way of Politics.* Gerald L. Curtis. New York and London: Columbia University Press, 1988. 301 pp.

Japan's Administrative Elite. Byung Chol Koh. Berkeley and London: University of California Press, 1989. 297 pp.

Japan's Political System. Robert E. Ward. Englewood Cliffs, N.J.: Prentice-Hall, 1978. 2d ed. 253 pp.

Japan's Public Policy Companies. Chalmers Johnson. Washington, D.C.: American Enterprise Institute for Public Policy Research; Stanford, Calif.: Hoover Institution on War, Revolution and Peace, Stanford University, 1978. 173 pp.

Local Government in Japan. Kurt Steiner. Stanford, Calif.: Stanford University Press, 1965. 564 pp.

Losing Face: Status Politics in Japan. Susan J. Pharr. Berkeley and London: University of California Press, 1990. 266 pp.

Party in Power: The Japanese Liberal-Democrats and Policy-Making. Haruhiro Fukui. Berkeley: University of California Press; Canberra, A.C.T.: Australian National University Press, 1970. 301 pp.

Party Politics in Japan. Hans H. Baerwald. London and Boston: Allen and Unwin, 1986. 204 pp.

Policy and Politics in Japan: Creative Conservatism. T. J. Pempel. Philadelphia: Temple University Press, 1982. 330 pp.

Politics and Government in Japan. Theodore H. McNelly. Lanham, Md., and London: University Press of America, 1984. 3d ed. 274 pp.

Politics in Japan. Bradley M. Richardson and Scott C. Flanagan. Boston and Toronto: Little, Brown, 1984. 459 pp.

Public Administration in Japan. Edited by Kiyoaki Tsuji. Tokyo: University of Tokyo Press, 1984. 271 pp.

Suburban Tokyo: A Comparative Study in Politics and Social Change. Gary D. Allinson. Berkeley and London: University of California Press, 1979. 258 pp.

Thought and Behaviour in Modern Japanese Politics. Masao Maruyama, edited by Ivan Morris, translations by Ivan Morris et al. London and New York: Oxford University Press, 1969. Expanded ed. 407 pp.

HISTORY

See also the GENERAL WORKS category at the beginning of this bibliography; ECONOMICS; GOVERNMENT AND POLITICS; INTERNATIONAL RELATIONS; WOMEN.

GENERAL WORKS

• *The Cambridge History of Japan.* General editors: John W. Hall, Marius B. Jansen, Madoka Kanai, and Denis Twitchett. *Volume 1: Ancient Japan*, edited by Delmer M. Brown. *Volume 2: Heian Japan*, edited by William McCullough and Donald H. Shively. *Volume 3: Medieval Japan*, edited by Kozo Yamamura. *Volume 4: Sengoku and Edo*, edited by John W. Hall. *Volume 5: The Nineteenth Century*, edited by Marius B. Jansen. *Volume 6: The Twentieth Century*, edited by Peter Duus. Cambridge and New York: Cambridge University Press, 1989– . 6 vols. projected.

The Emergence of Modern Japan: An Introductory History since 1853. Janet Hunter. London and New York: Longman, 1989. 356 pp.

A History of Japan. George B. Sansom. Stanford, Calif.: Stanford University Press; London: Cresset Press, 1958–63. 3 vols. From prehistory through 1867.

Japan: A History in Art. Bradley Smith. New York: Simon & Schuster; London: Weidenfeld and Nicolson, 1965. 295 pp. From prehistory through 1912.

• *Japan: A Short Cultural History.* George B. Sansom. New York: Appleton-Century-Crofts, 1943. Rev. ed. 554 pp. Reprinted, Stanford, Calif.: Stanford University Press, 1978. From prehistory through 1867.

• *Japan and Its World: Two Centuries of Change.* Marius B. Jansen. Princeton, N.J., and Guildford, Surrey: Princeton University Press, 1980. 128 pp.

Japan before Perry: A Short History. Conrad Totman. Berkeley and London: University of California Press, 1981. 246 pp.

Japan: From Prehistory to Modern Times. John Whitney Hall. New York: Delacorte Press; London: Weidenfeld and Nicolson, 1970. 395 pp. Reprinted, Ann Arbor: Center for Japanese Studies, University of Michigan, 1991.

◆*Japan: The Story of a Nation.* Edwin O. Reischauer. New York: McGraw-Hill, 1989. 4th ed. 401 pp.

◆*Japan: Tradition and Transformation.* Edwin O. Reischauer and Albert M. Craig. Boston: Houghton Mifflin; London: Allen and Unwin, 1989. Rev. ed. 352 pp.

◆*Japanese Inn.* Oliver Statler. New York: Random House; London: Secker and Warburg, 1961. 360 pp. Reprinted, Honolulu: University of Hawaii Press, 1982. A literary recreation of Japanese social history from the 17th to the 20th century.

Mitsui: Three Centuries of Japanese Business. John G. Roberts. New York and Tokyo: Weatherhill, 1989. 2d ed. 578 pp.

◆*The Nobility of Failure: Tragic Heroes in the History of Japan.* Ivan Morris. New York: Holt, Rinehart, and Winston; London: Secker and Warburg, 1975. 500 pp.

Okinawa: The History of an Island People. George H. Kerr. Rutland, Vt., and Tokyo: Tuttle, 1958. 542 pp.

PREHISTORY THROUGH 1600

Buddhism and the State in Sixteenth-Century Japan. Neil McMullin. Princeton, N.J., and Guildford, Surrey: Princeton University Press, 1984. 441 pp.

The Christian Century in Japan, 1549–1650. Charles R. Boxer. Berkeley: University of California Press; London: Cambridge University Press, 1951. 535 pp. Reprinted, University of California Press, 1974.

Court and Bakufu in Japan: Essays in Kamakura History. Edited by Jeffrey P. Mass. New Haven, Conn., and London: Yale University Press, 1982. 322 pp.

◆*Feudalism in Japan.* Peter Duus. New York: Knopf, 1976. 2d ed. 124 pp.

Government and Local Power in Japan, 500 to 1700: A Study Based on Bizen Province. John Whitney Hall. Princeton, N.J.: Princeton University Press, 1966. 446 pp. Reprinted, Princeton University Press, 1980.

Hideyoshi. Mary Elizabeth Berry. Cambridge, Mass., and London: Harvard University Press, 1982. 293 pp.

Insei: Abdicated Sovereigns in the Politics of Late Heian Japan, 1086–1185. G. Cameron Hurst, III. New York and London: Columbia University Press, 1976. 337 pp.

Japan before Tokugawa: Political Consolidation and Economic Growth, 1500 to 1650. Edited by John Whitney Hall, Keiji Nagahara, and Kozo Yamamura. Princeton, N.J., and Guildford, Surrey: Princeton University Press, 1981. 392 pp.

Japan in the Muromachi Age. Edited by John W. Hall and Takeshi Toyoda. Berkeley and London: University of California Press, 1977. 376 pp.

Kojiki. Translated by Donald L. Philippi. Tokyo: University of Tokyo Press, 1968; Princeton, N.J.: Princeton University Press, 1969. 655 pp.

Medieval Japan: Essays in Institutional History. Edited by John W. Hall and Jeffrey P. Mass. New Haven, Conn., and London: Yale University Press, 1974. 269 pp. Reprinted, Stanford, Calif.: Stanford University Press, 1988.

◆*Premodern Japan: A Historical Survey.* Mikiso Hane. Boulder, Colo., and London: Westview Press, 1991. 258 pp.

Rodrigues the Interpreter: An Early Jesuit in Japan and China. Michael Cooper. New York and Tokyo: Weatherhill, 1974. 416 pp.

Science and Culture in Traditional Japan, A.D. 600–1854. Masayoshi Sugimoto and David L. Swain. Cambridge, Mass., and London: MIT Press, 1978. 498 pp.

Sugawara no Michizane and the Early Heian Court. Robert Borgen. Cambridge: Council on East Asian Studies, Harvard University, 1986. 431 pp.

They Came to Japan: An Anthology of European Reports on Japan, 1543–1640. Edited by Michael Cooper. London: Thames and Hudson; Berkeley: University of California Press, 1965. 439 pp. Reprinted, University of California Press, 1981.

Warlords, Artists, and Commoners: Japan in the Sixteenth Century. Edited by George Elison and Bardwell L. Smith. Honolulu: University Press of Hawaii, 1981. 356 pp.

Warrior Government in Early Medieval Japan: A Study of the Kamakura Bakufu, Shugo, and Jitō. Jeffrey P. Mass. New Haven, Conn., and London: Yale University Press, 1974. 257 pp.

◆*The Way of the Samurai.* Richard Storry, photographs by Werner Forman. London: Orbis; New York: Putnam, 1978. 128 pp.

Windows on the Japanese Past: Studies in Archaeology and Prehistory. Edited by Richard J. Pearson, with Gina Lee Barnes and Karl L. Hutterer. Ann Arbor: Center for Japanese Studies, University of Michigan, 1986. 629 pp.

◆*The World of the Shining Prince: Court Life in Ancient Japan.* Ivan Morris. New York: Knopf; Oxford: Oxford University Press, 1964. 336 pp.

EDO PERIOD (1600–1868)

The Agrarian Origins of Modern Japan. Thomas C. Smith. Stanford, Calif.: Stanford University Press, 1959. 250 pp. Reprinted, Stanford University Press, 1984.

The Collapse of the Tokugawa Bakufu, 1862–1868. Conrad Totman. Honolulu: University Press of Hawaii, 1980. 588 pp.

Deus Destroyed: The Image of Christianity in Early Modern Japan. George Elison. Cambridge: Harvard University Press, 1973. 542 pp. Reprinted, Council on East Asian Studies, Harvard University, 1988.

Economic and Demographic Change in Preindustrial Japan, 1600–1868. Susan B. Hanley and Kozo Yamamura. Princeton, N.J., and Guildford, Surrey: Princeton University Press, 1978. 409 pp.

Education in Tokugawa Japan. Ronald P. Dore. Berkeley: University of California Press, 1965. 346 pp. Reprinted, London: Athlone Press; Ann Arbor: Center for Japanese Studies, University of Michigan, 1984.

Everyday Life in Traditional Japan. Charles J. Dunn. London: Batsford; New York: Putnam, 1969. 198 pp.

Japan in Transition: From Tokugawa to Meiji. Edited by Marius B. Jansen and Gilbert Rozman. Princeton, N.J., and Guildford, Surrey: Princeton University Press, 1986. 485 pp.

Japan: The Dutch Experience. Grant K. Goodman. London and Dover, N.H.: Athlone Press, 1986. 304 pp.

◆*The Meiji Restoration.* William Gerald Beasley. Stanford, Calif.: Stanford University Press, 1972; London: Oxford University Press, 1973. 513 pp.

Nakahara: Family Farming and Population in a Japanese Village, 1717–1830. Thomas C. Smith, with Robert Y. Eng and Robert T. Lundy. Stanford, Calif.: Stanford University Press, 1977. 183 pp.

Peasant Protests and Uprisings in Tokugawa Japan. Stephen Vlastos. Berkeley and London: University of California Press, 1986. 184 pp.

Politics in the Tokugawa Bakufu, 1600–1843. Conrad D. Totman. Cambridge: Harvard University Press, 1967. 346 pp. Reprinted, Berkeley and London: University of California Press, 1989.

Shogunal Politics: Arai Hakuseki and the Premises of Tokugawa Rule. Kate Wildman Nakai. Cambridge: Council on East Asian Studies, Harvard University, 1988. 427 pp.

Tokugawa Japan: The Social and Economic Antecedents of Modern Japan. Edited by Chie Nakane and Shinzaburō Ōishi. Tokyo: University of Tokyo Press, 1990. 240 pp.

MEIJI, TAISHŌ, AND EARLY SHŌWA PERIODS (1868–1945)

Agricultural Development and Tenancy Disputes in Japan, 1870–1940. Richard J. Smethurst. Princeton, N.J., and Guildford, Surrey: Princeton University Press, 1986. 472 pp.

The Atomic Bombs: Voices from Hiroshima and Nagasaki. Edited by Kyoko and Mark Selden. Armonk, N.Y., and London: M. E. Sharpe, 1989. 257 pp.

◆*The Autobiography of Yukichi Fukuzawa.* Yukichi Fukuzawa, revised translation by Eiichi Kiyooka. New York and London: Columbia University Press, 1966. 407 pp. Reprinted, Lanham, Md.: Madison Books, 1992.

Christian Converts and Social Protest in Meiji Japan. Irwin Scheiner. Berkeley and London: University of California Press, 1970. 268 pp.

Clara's Diary: An American Girl in Meiji Japan. Clara A. N. Whitney, edited by M. William Steele and Tamiko Ichimata. Tokyo and New York: Kodansha International, 1979. 353 pp.

The Day Man Lost: Hiroshima, 6 August 1945. Pacific War Research Society (Bungei Shunjū Senshi Kenkyūkai). Tokyo and Palo Alto, Calif.: Kodansha International, 1972. 312 pp.

A Diplomat's Wife in Japan: Sketches at the Turn of the Century. Mary Crawford Fraser, edited by Hugh Cortazzi. New York and Tokyo: Weatherhill, 1982. 351 pp.

East to America: A History of the Japanese in the United States. Robert A. Wilson and Bill Hosokawa. New York: William Morrow, 1980. 351 pp.

The Economic Development of Japan c.1868–1941. W. J. Macpherson. Basingstoke, Hampshire: Macmillan Education, 1987. 93 pp.

The Economic Development of Japan: Growth and Structural Change. William W. Lockwood. Princeton, N.J.: Princeton University Press, 1968. Expanded ed. 686 pp.

Economic Growth in Prewar Japan. Takafusa Nakamura, translated by Robert A. Feldman. New Haven, Conn., and London: Yale University Press, 1983. 326 pp.

The Emperor's Adviser: Saionji Kinmochi and Pre-War Japanese Politics. Lesley Connors. London and Wolfeboro, N.H.: Croom Helm, 1987. 260 pp.

The Evolution of Labor Relations in Japan: Heavy Industry, 1853–1955. Andrew Gordon. Cambridge: Council on East Asian Studies, Harvard University, 1985. 524 pp.

Foundations of Constitutional Government in Modern Japan, 1868–1900. George Akita. Cambridge: Harvard University Press, 1967. 292 pp.

Hara Kei in the Politics of Compromise, 1905–1915. Tetsuo Najita. Cambridge: Harvard University Press, 1967. 314 pp.

◆*Hiroshima.* John Hersey. New York: Knopf, 1985. New ed. 196 pp.

◆*A History of Modern Japan.* Richard Storry. Harmondsworth, Middlesex, and New York: Penguin Books, 1982. Rev. ed. 304 pp.

Imitation and Innovation: The Transfer of Western Organizational Patterns to Meiji Japan. D. Eleanor Westney. Cambridge, Mass., and London: Harvard University Press, 1987. 252 pp.

Japan Examined: Perspectives on Modern Japanese History. Edited by Harry Wray and Hilary Conroy. Honolulu: University of Hawaii Press, 1983. 411 pp.

Japan Prepares for Total War: The Search for Economic Security, 1919–1941. Michael A. Barnhart. Ithaca,

N.Y., and London: Cornell University Press, 1987. 290 pp.

The Japanese Colonial Empire, 1895–1945. Edited by Ramon H. Myers and Mark R. Peattie. Princeton, N.J., and Guildford, Surrey: Princeton University Press, 1984. 540 pp.

The Japanese Communist Party, 1922–1945. George M. Beckmann and Genji Okubo. Stanford, Calif.: Stanford University Press, 1969. 453 pp.

The Japanese Enlightenment: A Study of the Writings of Fukuzawa Yukichi. Carmen Blacker. Cambridge: Cambridge University Press, 1964. 186 pp.

Japanese Industrialization and Its Social Consequences. Edited by Hugh Patrick, with Larry Meissner. Berkeley and London: University of California Press, 1976. 505 pp.

Japanese Marxist: A Portrait of Kawakami Hajime, 1879–1946. Gail Lee Bernstein. Cambridge, Mass., and London: Harvard University Press, 1976. 222 pp.

Japanese Urbanism: Industry and Politics in Kariya, 1872–1972. Gary D. Allinson. Berkeley and London: University of California Press, 1975. 276 pp.

Japan's Modern Myths: Ideology in the Late Meiji Period. Carol Gluck. Princeton, N.J., and Guildford, Surrey: Princeton University Press, 1985. 407 pp.

Konoe Fumimaro: A Political Biography. Yoshitake Oka, translated by Shumpei Okamoto and Patricia Murray. Tokyo: University of Tokyo Press, 1983. 214 pp. Reprinted, Lanham, Md.: Madison Books, 1992.

Kōtoku Shūsui: Portrait of a Japanese Radical. Frederick G. Notehelfer. Cambridge and New York: Cambridge University Press, 1971. 227 pp.

Labor and Imperial Democracy in Prewar Japan. Andrew Gordon. Berkeley and Oxford: University of California Press, 1991. 364 pp.

Liberalism in Modern Japan: Ishibashi Tanzan and His Teachers, 1905–1960. Sharon H. Nolte. Berkeley and London: University of California Press, 1987. 378 pp.

Low City, High City: Tokyo from Edo to the Earthquake. Edward Seidensticker. New York: Knopf; London: Lane, 1983. 302 pp.

◆*Modern Japan: A Historical Survey.* Mikiso Hane. Boulder, Colo., and London: Westview Press, 1992. 473 pp.

The Modernizers: Overseas Students, Foreign Employees, and Meiji Japan. Edited by Ardath W. Burks. Boulder, Colo., and London: Westview Press, 1985. 450 pp.

Mori Arinori: A Reconsideration. Ivan Parker Hall. Cambridge: Harvard University Press, 1973. 535 pp.

The New Generation in Meiji Japan: Problems of Cultural Identity, 1885–1895. Kenneth B. Pyle. Stanford, Calif.: Stanford University Press, 1969. 240 pp.

Organized Workers and Socialist Politics in Interwar Japan. Stephen S. Large. Cambridge and New York: Cambridge University Press, 1981. 326 pp.

Origins of the Modern Japanese State: Selected Writings of E. H. Norman. Egerton Herbert Norman, edited by John W. Dower. New York: Pantheon, 1975. 497 pp.

Palace and Politics in Prewar Japan. David Anson Titus. New York and London: Columbia University Press, 1974. 360 pp.

Parties out of Power in Japan, 1931–1941. Gordon Mark Berger. Princeton, N.J., and Guildford, Surrey: Princeton University Press, 1977. 413 pp.

Party Rivalry and Political Change in Taishō Japan. Peter Duus. Cambridge: Harvard University Press, 1968. 317 pp.

◆*Peasants, Rebels, and Outcasts: The Underside of Modern Japan.* Mikiso Hane. New York: Pantheon; London: Scolar Press, 1982. 297 pp.

Rebellion and Democracy in Meiji Japan: A Study of Commoners in the Popular Rights Movement. Roger W. Bowen. Berkeley and London: University of California Press, 1980. 367 pp.

The Reluctant Admiral: Yamamoto and the Imperial Navy. Hiroyuki Agawa, translated by John Bester. Tokyo and New York: Kodansha International, 1979. 397 pp.

Revolt in Japan: The Young Officers and the February 26, 1936 Incident. Ben-Ami Shillony. Princeton, N.J.: Princeton University Press, 1973. 263 pp.

Rioters and Citizens: Mass Protest in Imperial Japan. Michael Lewis. Berkeley and London: University of California Press. 1990. 314 pp.

◆*The Rise of Modern Japan.* William Gerald Beasley. New York: St. Martin's Press; London: Weidenfeld and Nicolson, 1990. 306 pp. Rev. ed. of *The Modern History of Japan.*

Samurai and Silk: A Japanese and American Heritage. Haru Matsukata Reischauer. Cambridge, Mass., and London: Harvard University Press, Belknap Press, 1986. 371 pp.

Schooldays in Imperial Japan: A Study in the Culture of a Student Elite. Donald Roden. Berkeley and London: University of California Press, 1980. 300 pp.

The Self-Made Man in Meiji Japanese Thought: From Samurai to Salary Man. Earl H. Kinmonth. Berkeley and London: University of California Press, 1981. 385 pp.

◆*A Short Economic History of Modern Japan.* George Cyril Allen. London: Macmillan; New York: St. Martin's Press, 1981. 4th ed. 305 pp.

A Social Basis for Prewar Japanese Militarism: The Army and the Rural Community. Richard J. Smethurst. Berkeley and London: University of California Press, 1974. 202 pp.

The Social Democratic Movement in Prewar Japan. George Oakley Totten, III. New Haven, Conn., and London: Yale University Press, 1966. 455 pp.

Soldiers of the Sun: The Rise and Fall of the Imperial Japanese Army. Meirion Harries and Susie Harries. New York: Random House; London: William Heinemann, 1991. 569 pp.

The State and Labor in Modern Japan. Sheldon Garon. Berkeley and London: University of California Press, 1988. 326 pp.

Technology and Agricultural Development in Pre-War Japan. Penelope Francks. New Haven, Conn., and London: Yale University Press, 1984. 322 pp.

Tokutomi Sohō, 1863–1957: A Journalist for Modern Japan. John D. Pierson. Princeton, N.J., and London: Princeton University Press, 1980. 453 pp.

Tokyo Rising: The City since the Great Earthquake. Edward Seidensticker. New York: Knopf, 1990. 362 pp.

Valley of Darkness: The Japanese People and World War Two. Thomas R. H. Havens. New York: Norton, 1978. 280 pp.

Yamagata Aritomo in the Rise of Modern Japan, 1838–1922. Roger F. Hackett. Cambridge: Harvard University Press, 1971. 377 pp.

POST–WORLD WAR II

Aftermath of War: Americans and the Remaking of Japan, 1945–1952. Howard B. Schonberger. Kent, Ohio, and London: Kent State University Press, 1989. 347 pp.

◆*Beneath the Eagle's Wings: Americans in Occupied Japan.* John Curtis Perry. New York: Dodd, Mead, 1980. 253 pp.

Democratizing Japan: The Allied Occupation. Edited by Robert E. Ward and Yoshikazu Sakamoto. Honolulu: University of Hawaii Press, 1987. 456 pp.

Empire and Aftermath: Yoshida Shigeru and the Japanese Experience, 1878–1954. John W. Dower. Cambridge: Council on East Asian Studies, Harvard University, 1979. 618 pp.

A Financial History of the New Japan. Thomas Francis Morton Adams and Iwao Hoshii. Tokyo and Palo Alto, Calif.: Kodansha International, 1972. 547 pp.

GHQ Tokyo: The Occupation Headquarters and Its Influence on Post-War Japan. Eiji Takemae, translated by Sebastian Swann. London and Atlantic Highlands, N.J.: Athlone Press, 1990. 224 pp.

Inventing Japan: The Making of a Postwar Civilization. William Chapman. New York: Prentice Hall Press, 1991. 330 pp.

◆*Japan's American Interlude.* Kazuo Kawai. Chicago: University of Chicago Press, 1960. 257 pp.

◆*MITI and the Japanese Miracle: The Growth of Industrial Policy, 1925–1975.* Chalmers Johnson. Stanford, Calif.: Stanford University Press, 1982. 393 pp.

Remaking Japan: The American Occupation as New Deal. Theodore Cohen, edited by Herbert Passin. New York: Free Press, 1987. 533 pp.

Sheathing the Sword: The Demilitarization of Post-War Japan. Meirion Harries and Susie Harries. New York: Macmillan; London: Hamish Hamilton, 1987. 384 pp.

Showa: The Japan of Hirohito. Edited by Carol Gluck and Stephen R. Graubard. New York: Norton, 1992. 315 pp.

Windows for the Crown Prince. Elizabeth Gray Vining. Philadelphia: Lippincott; London: Michael Joseph, 1952. 320 pp. Reprinted, Rutland, Vt., and Tokyo: Tuttle, 1989. Vining's four-year tutorship of Crown Prince (now Emperor) Akihito.

Winners in Peace: MacArthur, Yoshida, and Postwar Japan. Richard B. Finn. Berkeley: University of California Press, 1992. 413 pp.

REFERENCE WORKS AND BIBLIOGRAPHIES

The Allied Occupation of Japan, 1945–1952: An Annotated Bibliography of Western-Language Materials. Compiled and edited by Robert E. Ward and Frank Joseph Shulman with Masashi Nishihara and Mary Tobin Espey. Chicago: American Library Association, 1974. 867 pp. Reprinted, Tokyo: Nihon Tosho Center, 1990.

Biographical Dictionary of Japanese History. Supervising editor, Seiichi Iwao; translated by Burton Watson. Tokyo and New York: Kodansha International, in collaboration with the International Society for Educational Information (Tokyo), 1978. 655 pp.

Concise Dictionary of Modern Japanese History. Compiled by Janet E. Hunter. Berkeley and London: University of California Press, 1984. 347 pp.

Japanese History & Culture from Ancient to Modern Times: Seven Basic Bibliographies. John W. Dower. New York: Markus Wiener; Manchester, Eng.: Manchester University Press, 1986. 232 pp.

INTERNATIONAL RELATIONS

See also ECONOMICS; HISTORY.

GENERAL WORKS

Japan and China: From War to Peace, 1894–1972. Marius B. Jansen. Chicago: Rand McNally, 1975. 547 pp.

Mutual Images: Essays in American-Japanese Relations. Edited by Akira Iriye. Cambridge, Mass., and London: Harvard University Press, 1975. 304 pp.

My Life between Japan and America. Edwin O. Reischauer. New York and London: Harper & Row, 1986. 367 pp.

Neighbors across the Pacific: Canadian-Japanese Relations 1870–1982. Klaus H. Pringsheim.

Westport, Conn.: Greenwood Press; Oakville, Ont.: Mosaic Press, 1983. 241 pp.

BEFORE 1945

Alliance in Decline: A Study in Anglo-Japanese Relations, 1908–23. Ian H. Nish. London: Athlone Press, 1972. 424 pp.

The Anglo-Japanese Alliance: The Diplomacy of Two Island Empires, 1894–1907. Ian Nish. London and Dover, N.H.: Athlone Press, 1985. 2d ed. 420 pp.

As We Saw Them: The First Japanese Embassy to the United States (1860). Masao Miyoshi. Berkeley and London: University of California Press, 1979. 232 pp.

◆*At Dawn We Slept: The Untold Story of Pearl Harbor.* Gordon W. Prange, with Donald M. Goldstein and Katherine V. Dillon. New York: McGraw-Hill, 1981; London: Joseph, 1982. 873 pp.

Britain and Japan, 1858–1883. Grace Fox. Oxford: Clarendon Press, 1969. 627 pp.

The Chinese and the Japanese: Essays in Political and Cultural Interactions. Edited by Akira Iriye. Princeton, N.J., and Guildford, Surrey: Princeton University Press, 1979. 368 pp.

Defiance in Manchuria: The Making of Japanese Foreign Policy, 1931–1932. Sadako N. Ogata. Berkeley: University of California Press, 1964. 259 pp. Reprinted, Westport, Conn.: Greenwood Press, 1984.

Eagle against the Sun: The American War with Japan. Ronald H. Spector. New York: Free Press, 1985. 589 pp.

Great Britain and the Opening of Japan, 1834–1858. William G. Beasley. London: Luzac, 1951. 227 pp.

Japan and the Decline of the West in Asia 1894–1943. Richard Storry. London: Macmillan; New York: St. Martin's Press, 1979. 186 pp.

The Japan Expedition, 1852–1854: The Personal Journal of Commodore Matthew C. Perry. Matthew C. Perry, edited by Roger Pineau. Washington, D.C.: Smithsonian Institution Press, 1968. 241 pp.

◆*Japanese Foreign Policy 1869–1942: Kasumigaseki to Miyakezaka.* Ian Nish. London and Boston: Routledge and Kegan Paul, 1977. 346 pp.

◆*Japanese Imperialism, 1894–1945.* William G. Beasley. Oxford: Clarendon Press; New York: Oxford University Press, 1987. 279 pp.

Japanese International Negotiating Style. Michael Blaker. New York and Guildford, Surrey: Columbia University Press, 1977. 253 pp.

The Japanese Oligarchy and the Russo-Japanese War. Shumpei Okamoto. New York and London: Columbia University Press, 1970. 358 pp.

Japan's Quest for Autonomy: National Security and Foreign Policy, 1930–1938. James B. Crowley. Princeton, N.J.: Princeton University Press, 1966. 428 pp.

Japan's Southward Advance and Australia: From the Sixteenth Century to World War II. Henry P. Frei. Honolulu: University of Hawaii Press, 1991. 303 pp.

The Origins of the Russo-Japanese War. Ian Nish. London and New York: Longman, 1985. 274 pp.

Pacific Estrangement: Japanese and American Expansion, 1897–1911. Akira Iriye. Cambridge: Harvard University Press, 1972. 290 pp.

Pearl Harbor as History: Japanese-American Relations, 1931–1941. Edited by Dorothy Borg and Shumpei Okamoto, with Dale K. A. Finlayson. New York and London: Columbia University Press, 1973. 801 pp.

Power and Culture: The Japanese-American War, 1941–1945. Akira Iriye. Cambridge, Mass., and London: Harvard University Press, 1981. 304 pp.

◆*The Rising Sun: The Decline and Fall of the Japanese Empire, 1936–1945.* John Toland. New York: Random House, 1970; London: Cassell, 1971. 954 pp.

The Shimoda Story. Oliver Statler. New York: Random House, 1969. 627 pp. Reprinted, Honolulu: University of Hawaii Press, 1986. On Townsend Harris's efforts to negotiate the first commercial treaty between the United States and Japan, 1856–58.

Tanaka Giichi and Japan's China Policy. William Fitch Morton. New York: St. Martin's Press; Folkstone, Kent: Dawson, 1980. 329 pp.

The Troubled Encounter: The United States and Japan. Charles E. Neu. New York and London: Wiley, 1975. 257 pp.

◆*War without Mercy: Race and Power in the Pacific War.* John W. Dower. New York: Pantheon; London: Faber and Faber, 1986. 398 pp.

The Western World and Japan: A Study in the Interaction of European and Asiatic Cultures. George B. Sansom. New York: Knopf, 1950. 504 pp.

Yankees in the Land of the Gods: Commodore Perry and the Opening of Japan. Peter Booth Wiley, with Ichiro Korogi. New York: Viking, 1990. 578 pp.

SINCE 1945

Beyond Trade Friction: Japan-U.S. Economic Relations. Edited by Ryūzō Sato and Julianne Nelson. Cambridge and New York: Cambridge University Press, 1989. 201 pp.

China Eyes Japan. Allen S. Whiting. Berkeley and London: University of California Press, 1989. 228 pp.

Coming to Terms: The Politics of Australia's Trade with Japan, 1945–57. Alan Rix. Sydney, N.S.W., and London: Allen and Unwin, 1986. 267 pp.

Destinies Shared: U.S.-Japanese Relations. Edited by Paul Gordon Lauren and Raymond F. Wylie. Boulder, Colo., and London: Westview Press, 1989. 198 pp.

The Eagle and the Rising Sun: America and Japan in the Twentieth Century. John K. Emmerson and Harrison M. Holland. Reading, Mass.: Addison-Wesley, 1988. 199 pp.

The Emergence of Japan's Foreign Aid Power. Robert M. Orr, Jr. New York: Columbia University Press, 1990. 178 pp.

An Empire in Eclipse: Japan in the Postwar American Alliance System; a Study in the Interaction of Domestic Politics and Foreign Policy. John Welfield. London and Atlantic Highlands, N.J.: Athlone Press, 1988. 513 pp.

For Richer, for Poorer: The New U.S.-Japan Relationship. Ellen L. Frost. New York: Council on Foreign Relations, 1987. 199 pp.

The Foreign Policy of Modern Japan. Edited by Robert A. Scalapino. Berkeley and London: University of California Press, 1977. 426 pp.

Head to Head: The Coming Economic Battle among Japan, Europe, and America. Lester Thurow. New York: William Morrow, 1992. 336 pp.

Japan and Korea: The Political Dimensions. Chong-Sik Lee. Stanford, Calif.: Hoover Institution Press, 1985. 234 pp.

Japan and the Pacific Quadrille: The Major Powers in East Asia. Edited by Herbert J. Ellison. Boulder, Colo., and London: Westview Press, 1987. 252 pp.

The Japanese through American Eyes. Sheila K. Johnson. Stanford, Calif.: Stanford University Press, 1988. 191 pp.

Japan's Economic Performance and International Role. Yoshio Suzuki. Tokyo: University of Tokyo Press, 1989. 177 pp.

Japan's Economic Security. Edited by Nobutoshi Akao. New York: St. Martin's Press; Aldershot, Hampshire: Gower, 1983. 279 pp. Published in the United Kingdom as *Japan's Economic Security: Resources as a Factor in Foreign Policy.*

Japan's Foreign Relations: A Global Search for Economic Security. Edited by Robert S. Ozaki and Walter Arnold. Boulder, Colo., and London: Westview Press, 1985. 240 pp.

Japan's Growing Predominance over East Asia and the World Economy. William R. Nester. New York: St. Martin's Press; Basingstoke, Hampshire: Macmillan, 1990. 282 pp.

Japan's Postwar Defense Policy, 1947–1968. Martin E. Weinstein. New York and London: Columbia University Press, 1971. 160 pp.

Japan's Quest for Comprehensive Security: Defence, Diplomacy and Dependence. John W. M. Chapman, Reinhard Drifte, and Ian T. M. Gow. London: Frances Pinter; New York: St. Martin's Press, 1982. 259 pp.

Japan's Trade Policies 1945 to the Present Day. Takashi Shiraishi. London and Atlantic Highlands, N.J.: Athlone Press, 1989. 228 pp.

Japan's Unequal Trade. Edward J. Lincoln. Washington, D.C.: Brookings Institution, 1990. 223 pp. Focuses on U.S.-Japanese trade.

Managing Diplomacy: The United States and Japan. Harrison M. Holland. Stanford, Calif.: Hoover Institution Press, 1984. 251 pp.

The Politics of Canadian-Japanese Economic Relations, 1952–1983. Frank Langdon. Vancouver: University of British Columbia Press, 1983. 180 pp.

Protest in Tokyo: The Security Treaty Crisis of 1960. George R. Packard, III. Princeton, N.J.: Princeton University Press, 1966. 423 pp.

Rivals beyond Trade: America versus Japan in Global Competition. Dennis J. Encarnation. Ithaca, N.Y., and London: Cornell University Press, 1992. 222 pp.

Sharing World Leadership? A New Era for America and Japan. Edited by John H. Makin and Donald C. Hellmann. Washington, D.C.: American Enterprise Institute for Public Policy Research, 1989. 274 pp.

Soviet Policy towards Japan: An Analysis of Trends in the 1970s and 1980s. Myles L. C. Robertson. Cambridge and New York: Cambridge University Press, 1988. 234 pp.

The Soviet Union and Postwar Japan: Escalating Challenge and Response. Rodger Swearingen. Stanford, Calif.: Hoover Institution Press, 1978. 340 pp.

Trade and Investment Relations among the United States, Canada, and Japan. Edited by Robert M. Stern. Chicago: University of Chicago Press, 1989. 448 pp.

Trade War: Greed, Power, and Industrial Policy on Opposite Sides of the Pacific. Steven Schlosstein. New York: Congdon and Weed, 1984. 296 pp.

Trading Places: How We Allowed Japan to Take the Lead. Clyde V. Prestowitz, Jr. New York: Basic Books, 1988. 365 pp.

The United States and Japan in the Postwar World. Edited by Akira Iriye and Warren I. Cohen. Lexington: University Press of Kentucky, 1989. 237 pp.

The United States–Japan Economic Problem. C. Fred Bergsten and William R. Cline. Washington, D.C.: Institute for International Economics, 1987. 2d ed. 180 pp.

U.S.-Japanese Energy Relations: Cooperation and Competition. Edited by Charles K. Ebinger and Ronald A. Morse. Boulder, Colo., and London: Westview Press, 1984. 239 pp.

Zaibatsu America: How Japanese Firms Are Colonizing Vital U.S. Industries. Robert L. Kearns. New York: Free Press; Oxford: Maxwell Macmillan International, 1992. 256 pp.

BIBLIOGRAPHIES

U.S./Japan Foreign Trade: An Annotated Bibliography of Socioeconomic Perspectives. Rita E. Neri. New York and London: Garland, 1988. 306 pp.

The War against Japan, 1941–1945: An Annotated Bibliography. John J. Sbrega. New York and London: Garland, 1989. 1,050 pp.

LANGUAGE AND DICTIONARIES

Essential Kanji: 2,000 Basic Japanese Characters Systematically Arranged for Learning and Reference. Patrick Geoffrey O'Neill. New York and Tokyo: Weatherhill, 1973. 325 pp.

An Introduction to Modern Japanese. Edited by Osamu Mizutani and Nobuko Mizutani. Tokyo: Japan Times, 1977. 425 pp.

♦*Japanese for Busy People. Japanese for Busy People II: Intermediate Level.* Compiled by the Association for Japanese-Language Teaching (Kokusai Nihongo Fukyū Kyōkai). Tokyo and New York: Kodansha International, 1984–89. 2 vols.

♦*The Japanese Language.* Roy Andrew Miller. Chicago and London: University of Chicago Press, 1967. 428 pp. Reprinted, University of Chicago Press, 1980.

The Japanese Language in Contemporary Japan: Some Sociolinguistic Observations. Roy Andrew Miller. Washington, D.C.: American Enterprise Institute for Public Policy Research; Stanford, Calif.: Hoover Institution on War, Revolution, and Peace, 1977. 105 pp.

Japanese Language Patterns: A Structural Approach. Anthony Alfonso, with Yoshisuke Hirabayashi et al. Tokyo: Sophia University L. L. Center of Applied Linguistics, 1966. 2 vols.

Japanese Names: A Comprehensive Index by Characters and Readings. Patrick Geoffrey O'Neill. New York and Tokyo: Weatherhill, 1972. 359 pp.

♦*Japanese: The Spoken Language.* Eleanor Harz Jorden, with Mari Noda. New Haven, Conn., and London: Yale University Press, 1987–90. 3 vols.

Japanese: The Spoken Language in Japanese Life. Osamu Mizutani, translated by Janet Ashby. Tokyo: Japan Times, 1981. 180 pp.

Japanese Words and Their Uses. Akira Miura. Rutland, Vt., and Tokyo: Tuttle, 1983. 240 pp.

Kanji and Kana: A Handbook and Dictionary of the Japanese Writing System. Wolfgang Hadamitzky and Mark Spahn. Rutland, Vt., and Tokyo: Tuttle, 1981. 392 pp.

Kenkyusha's New English-Japanese Dictionary. Editor in chief, Yoshio Koine. Tokyo: Kenkyusha, 1980. 5th ed. 2,477 pp.

Kenkyusha's New Japanese-English Dictionary. General editor, Koh Masuda. Tokyo: Kenkyusha, 1974. 4th ed. 2,110 pp.

The Languages of Japan. Masayoshi Shibatani. Cambridge and New York: Cambridge University Press, 1990. 411 pp.

Martin's Pocket Dictionary, English-Japanese, Japanese-English: All Romanized. Samuel E. Martin. Rutland, Vt.: Tuttle, 1990. 724 pp.

The Modern Reader's Japanese-English Character Dictionary. Andrew Nathaniel Nelson. Rutland, Vt., and Tokyo: Tuttle, 1974. 2d rev. ed. 1,109 pp.

Reading Japanese. Eleanor Harz Jorden and Hamako Ito Chaplin. New Haven, Conn., and London: Yale University Press, 1976. 609 pp.

A Reference Grammar of Japanese. Samuel E. Martin. New Haven, Conn., and London: Yale University Press, 1976. 1,198 pp. Reprinted, Rutland, Vt.: Tuttle, 1988.

LAW

Authority without Power: Law and the Japanese Paradox. John Owen Haley. New York and Oxford: Oxford University Press, 1991. 258 pp.

Conciliation and Japanese Law: Tokugawa and Modern. Dan Fenno Henderson. Seattle: University of Washington Press; Tokyo: University of Tokyo Press, 1965. 2 vols.

The Constitution of Japan: Its First Twenty Years, 1947–1967. Edited by Dan Fenno Henderson. Seattle and London: University of Washington Press, 1968. 323 pp.

Freedom of Expression in Japan: A Study in Comparative Law, Politics, and Society. Lawrence Ward Beer. Tokyo and New York: Kodansha International, 1984. 415 pp.

Japanese International Trade and Investment Law. Mitsuo Matsushita and Thomas J. Schoenbaum. Tokyo: University of Tokyo Press, 1989. 238 pp.

The Japanese Supreme Court: Constitutional Policies since 1947. Hiroshi Itoh. New York: Markus Wiener, 1989. 307 pp.

Law and Social Change in Postwar Japan. Frank K. Upham. Cambridge, Mass., and London: Harvard University Press, 1987. 269 pp.

REFERENCE WORKS AND BIBLIOGRAPHIES

An Index to Japanese Law: A Bibliography of Western Language Materials, 1867–1973. Compiled by Rex Coleman and John Owen Haley. Tokyo: University of Tokyo Press, 1975. 167 pp. (*Law in Japan: An Annual*, special issue, 1975)

Japanese Labor Law. Kazuo Sugeno, translated by Leo Kanowitz. Seattle and London: University of Washington Press, 1992. 714 pp.

LITERATURE

See also PERFORMING ARTS: THEATER AND DRAMA.

GENERAL WORKS

Ancient Tales in Modern Japan: An Anthology of Japanese Folk Tales. Selected and translated by Fanny Hagin Mayer. Bloomington: Indiana University Press, 1985. 360 pp.

♦*Anthology of Japanese Literature. Volume 1: From the Earliest Era to the Mid-Nineteenth Century. Volume 2: Modern Japanese Literature.* Compiled and edited by Donald Keene. New York: Grove Press; London: Allen and Unwin, 1955–56. 2 vols.

Classical Japanese Prose: An Anthology. Compiled by Helen Craig McCullough. Stanford, Calif.: Stanford University Press, 1990. 578 pp.

♦*From the Country of Eight Islands: An Anthology of Japanese Poetry.* Edited and translated by Hiroaki Sato and Burton Watson. Seattle: University of Washington Press; Garden City, N.Y.: Anchor Books, 1981. 652 pp.

A History of Japanese Literature. Volume 1: The First Thousand Years. Volume 2: The Years of Isolation. Volume 3: The Modern Years. Shūichi Katō, translated by David Chibbett (vol. 1) and Don Sanderson (vols. 2–3). London: Macmillan; Tokyo and New York: Kodansha International, 1979–83. 3 vols.

A History of Japanese Literature. Volume 1: The Archaic and Ancient Ages. Volume 2: The Early Middle Ages. Volume 3: The High Middle Ages. Jin'ichi Konishi, translated by Aileen Gatten and Nicholas Teele, edited by Earl Miner. Princeton, N.J., and Guildford, Surrey: Princeton University Press, 1984– . 5 vols. projected.

♦*Japanese Literature: An Introduction for Western Readers.* Donald Keene. London: John Murray, 1953. 114 pp.

Japanese Poetic Diaries. Selected and translated by Earl Miner. Berkeley and London: University of California Press, 1969. 211 pp.

Landscapes and Portraits: Appreciations of Japanese Culture. Donald Keene. Tokyo and Palo Alto, Calif.: Kodansha International, 1971; London:

Secker and Warburg, 1972. 343 pp. Reprinted as *Appreciations of Japanese Culture.* Tokyo and New York: Kodansha International, 1981. On Japanese literature between the 13th and 20th centuries.

The Penguin Book of Japanese Verse. Translated by Geoffrey Bownas and Anthony Thwaite. Harmondsworth, Middlesex, and Baltimore, Md.: Penguin Books, 1964. 242 pp.

♦*The Pleasures of Japanese Literature.* Donald Keene. New York and Guildford, Surrey: Columbia University Press, 1988. 133 pp.

♦*A Reader's Guide to Japanese Literature.* J. Thomas Rimer. Tokyo and New York: Kodansha International, 1988. 208 pp.

Some Japanese Portraits. Donald Keene. Tokyo and New York: Kodansha International, 1978. 228 pp. Focuses on writers active between the early 1400s and late 1800s.

Traditional Japanese Poetry: An Anthology. Translated by Steven D. Carter. Stanford, Calif.: Stanford University Press, 1991. 514 pp.

Travelers of a Hundred Ages. Donald Keene. New York: Henry Holt, 1989. 468 pp. An overview of Japanese diaries between the Heian and Edo periods.

EARLY, HEIAN, AND MEDIEVAL PERIODS (TO 1600)

As I Crossed a Bridge of Dreams: Recollections of a Woman in Eleventh-Century Japan. Sugawara Takasue no Musume, translated by Ivan Morris. New York: Dial Press; London: Oxford University Press, 1971. 159 pp.

Brocade by Night: Kokin Wakashū and the Court Style in Japanese Classical Poetry. Helen Craig McCullough. Stanford, Calif.: Stanford University Press, 1985. 591 pp.

The Confessions of Lady Nijō. Nakanoin Masatada no Musume, translated by Karen Brazell. Garden City, N.Y.: Anchor Books, 1973. 288 pp.

Essays in Idleness: The Tsurezuregusa of Kenkō. Yoshida Kenkō, translated by Donald Keene. New York and London: Columbia University Press, 1967. 213 pp.

The Gossamer Years: The Diary of a Noblewoman of Heian Japan. Fujiwara Michitsuna no Haha, translated by Edward Seidensticker. Rutland, Vt., and Tokyo: Tuttle, 1964. 201 pp.

An Introduction to Japanese Court Poetry. Earl Miner, with translations by Earl Miner and Robert H. Brower. Stanford, Calif.: Stanford University Press, 1968. 173 pp.

Japanese Court Poetry. Robert H. Brower and Earl Miner. Stanford, Calif.: Stanford University Press, 1961; London: Cresset Press, 1962. 527 pp.

Japanese Linked Poetry: An Account with Translations of Renga and Haikai Sequences. Earl Miner. Princeton, N.J., and Guildford, Surrey: Princeton University Press, 1979. 376 pp.

Japanese Tales. Selected, edited, and translated by Royall Tyler. New York: Pantheon Books, 1987. 341 pp. Selections from medieval collections of *setsuwa bungaku* ("tale literature").

The Karma of Words: Buddhism and the Literary Arts in Medieval Japan. William R. LaFleur. Berkeley and London: University of California Press, 1983. 204 pp.

Kokin Wakashū: The First Imperial Anthology of Japanese Poetry; with Tosa Nikki and Shinsen Waka. Translated by Helen Craig McCullough. Stanford, Calif.: Stanford University Press, 1985. 388 pp.

The Manyōshū: The Nippon Gakujutsu Shinkōkai Translation of One Thousand Poems. New York and London: Columbia University Press, 1965. 502 pp.

Mirror for the Moon: A Selection of Poems. Saigyō, translated by William R. LaFleur. New York: New Directions, 1978. 100 pp.

Murasaki Shikibu: The Tale of Genji. Richard

Bowring. Cambridge and New York: Cambridge University Press, 1988. 111 pp.

Ōkagami, the Great Mirror: Fujiwara Michinaga (966–1027) and His Times. A Study and Translation. Helen Craig McCullough. Princeton, N.J., and Guildford, Surrey: Princeton University Press; Tokyo: University of Tokyo Press, 1980. 381 pp.

The Pillow Book of Sei Shōnagon. Sei Shōnagon, translated and edited by Ivan Morris. New York: Columbia University Press; London: Oxford University Press, 1967. 2 vols.

The Taiheiki: A Chronicle of Medieval Japan. Translated by Helen Craig McCullough. New York: Columbia University Press; London: Oxford University Press, 1959. 401 pp.

A Tale of Flowering Fortunes: Annals of Japanese Aristocratic Life in the Heian Period. Translated by William H. McCullough and Helen Craig McCullough. Stanford, Calif.: Stanford University Press, 1980. 910 pp.

◆*The Tale of Genji.* Murasaki Shikibu, translated by Edward G. Seidensticker. New York: Knopf; London: Secker and Warburg, 1976. 2 vols.

The Tale of Genji. Murasaki Shikibu, translated by Arthur Waley. London: Allen and Unwin; Boston: Houghton Mifflin, 1935. 1,135 pp. Reprinted many times.

The Tale of the Heike. Translated by Helen Craig McCullough. Stanford, Calif.: Stanford University Press, 1988. 489 pp.

Tales of Ise: Lyrical Episodes from Tenth-Century Japan. Translated by Helen Craig McCullough. Stanford, Calif.: Stanford University Press; Tokyo: University of Tokyo Press, 1968. 277 pp.

Tales of Times Now Past: Sixty-Two Stories from a Medieval Japanese Collection. Translated by Marian Ury. Berkeley and London: University of California Press, 1979. 199 pp. Translation of stories from the *Konjaku monogatari*.

EDO PERIOD (1600–1868)

The Floating World in Japanese Fiction. Howard Hibbett. London and New York: Oxford University Press, 1959. 232 pp. Reprinted, Rutland, Vt., and Tokyo: Tuttle, 1975.

The Great Mirror of Male Love. Ihara Saikaku, translated by Paul Gordon Schalow. Stanford, Calif.: Stanford University Press, 1990. 371 pp.

An Introduction to Haiku: An Anthology of Poems and Poets from Bashō to Shiki. Harold G. Henderson. Garden City, N.Y.: Doubleday, 1958. 190 pp.

The Life of an Amorous Woman and Other Writings. Ihara Saikaku, edited and translated by Ivan Morris. London: Chapman and Hall; New York: New Directions, 1963. 403 pp.

Matsuo Bashō. Makoto Ueda. New York: Twayne, 1970. 202 pp. Reprinted, Tokyo and New York: Kodansha International, 1983.

The Monkey's Straw Raincoat and Other Poetry of the Bashō School. Translated by Earl Miner and Hiroko Odagiri. Princeton, N.J., and Guildford, Surrey: Princeton University Press, 1981. 394 pp.

◆*The Narrow Road to the Deep North and Other Travel Sketches.* Matsuo Bashō, translated by Nobuyuki Yuasa. Harmondsworth, Middlesex, and Baltimore, Md.: Penguin Books, 1966. 167 pp.

Ugetsu Monogatari: Tales of Moonlight and Rain. A Complete English Version of the Eighteenth-Century Japanese Collection of Tales of the Supernatural. Ueda Akinari, translated and edited by Leon M. Zolbrod. London: Allen and Unwin; Vancouver: University of British Columbia Press, 1974. 280 pp.

◆*World Within Walls: Japanese Literature of the Pre-Modern Era, 1600–1867.* Donald Keene. New York: Holt, Rinehart, and Winston; London: Secker and Warburg, 1976. 606 pp.

MODERN PERIOD (1868–PRESENT)

General Works

Accomplices of Silence: The Modern Japanese Novel. Masao Miyoshi. Berkeley and London: University of California Press, 1974. 194 pp.

◆*Dawn to the West: Japanese Literature of the Modern Era. Volume 1: Fiction. Volume 2: Poetry, Drama, Criticism.* Donald Keene. New York: Holt, Rinehart, and Winston, 1984. 2 vols.

The Japanese Novel of the Meiji Period and the Ideal of Individualism. Janet A. Walker. Princeton, N.J., and Guildford, Surrey: Princeton University Press, 1979. 315 pp.

◆*Modern Japanese Fiction and Its Traditions: An Introduction.* J. Thomas Rimer. Princeton, N.J., and Guildford, Surrey: Princeton University Press, 1978. 313 pp.

Modern Japanese Writers and the Nature of Literature. Makoto Ueda. Stanford, Calif.: Stanford University Press, 1976. 292 pp.

The Rhetoric of Confession: Shishōsetsu in Early Twentieth-Century Japanese Fiction. Edward Fowler. Berkeley: University of California Press, 1988. 333 pp.

Individual Authors

Abe Kōbō

The Box Man. Translated by E. Dale Saunders. New York: Knopf, 1974. 178 pp.

The Ruined Map. Translated by E. Dale Saunders. New York: Knopf, 1969. 299 pp.

The Woman in the Dunes. Translated by E. Dale Saunders. New York: Knopf, 1964; London: Secker and Warburg, 1965. 214 pp.

Akutagawa Ryūnosuke

Kappa: A Novel. Translated by Geoffrey Bownas. London: Peter Owen, 1970. 141 pp.

Arishima Takeo

A Certain Woman. Translated by Kenneth Strong. Tokyo: University of Tokyo Press, 1978. 382 pp.

Ariyoshi Sawako

The Doctor's Wife. Translated by Wakako Hironaka and Ann Siller Kostant. Tokyo and New York: Kodansha International, 1978. 174 pp.

Dazai Osamu

No Longer Human. Translated by Donald Keene. London: Peter Owen, 1957; Norfolk, Conn.: New Directions, 1958. 154 pp.

The Setting Sun. Translated by Donald Keene. Norfolk, Conn.: New Directions, 1956; London: Peter Owen, 1958. 175 pp.

The Saga of Dazai Osamu: A Critical Study with Translations. Phyllis I. Lyons. Stanford, Calif.: Stanford University Press, 1985. 410 pp.

Enchi Fumiko

The Waiting Years. Translated by John Bester. Tokyo and Palo Alto, Calif.: Kodansha International, 1971. 203 pp.

Endō Shūsaku

Silence. Translated by William Johnston. Tokyo: Sophia University, in cooperation with Tuttle (Rutland, Vt., and Tokyo), 1969. 306 pp.

Futabatei Shimei

Japan's First Modern Novel: Ukigumo of Futabatei Shimei. Translated by Marleigh Grayer Ryan. New York and London: Columbia University Press, 1967. 381 pp.

Higuchi Ichiyō

In the Shade of Spring Leaves: The Life and Writings of Higuchi Ichiyō, a Woman of Letters in Meiji Japan. Robert Lyons Danly. New Haven, Conn., and London: Yale University Press, 1981. 355 pp.

Ibuse Masuji

◆*Black Rain.* Translated by John Bester. Tokyo and Palo Alto, Calif.: Kodansha International, 1969; London: Secker and Warburg, 1971. 300 pp.

Ishikawa Jun

The Bodhisattva; or, Samantabhadra. Translated by William Jefferson Tyler. New York: Columbia University Press, 1990. 180 pp.

Kawabata Yasunari

Beauty and Sadness. Translated by Howard Hibbett. New York: Knopf; London: Secker and Warburg, 1975. 206 pp.

The Master of Go. Translated by Edward G. Seidensticker. New York: Knopf, 1972; London: Secker and Warburg, 1973. 188 pp.

◆*Snow Country.* Translated by Edward G. Seidensticker. New York: Knopf, 1956. 175 pp. London: Secker and Warburg, 1957. 188 pp.

◆*The Sound of the Mountain.* Translated by Edward G. Seidensticker. New York: Knopf; London: Peter Owen, 1970. 276 pp.

Thousand Cranes. Translated by Edward G. Seidensticker. New York: Knopf; London: Secker and Warburg, 1959. 147 pp.

Mishima Yukio

After the Banquet. Translated by Donald Keene. New York: Knopf; London: Secker and Warburg, 1963. 270 pp.

Confessions of a Mask. Translated by Meredith Weatherby. New York: New Directions, 1958; London: Peter Owen, 1960. 254 pp.

The Sailor Who Fell from Grace with the Sea. Translated by John Nathan. New York: Knopf, 1965. 181 pp.; London: Secker and Warburg, 1966. 150 pp.

The Sea of Fertility: A Cycle of Four Novels. Volume 1: Spring Snow, translated by Michael Gallagher. *Volume 2: Runaway Horses,* translated by Michael Gallagher. *Volume 3: The Temple of Dawn,* translated by E. Dale Saunders and Cecilia Segawa Seigle. *Volume 4: The Decay of the Angel,* translated by Edward G. Seidensticker. New York: Knopf; London: Secker and Warburg, 1972–74. 4 vols.

The Sound of Waves. Translated by Meredith Weatherby. New York: Knopf, 1956; London: Secker and Warburg, 1957. 182 pp.

◆*The Temple of the Golden Pavilion.* Translated by Ivan Morris. New York: Knopf; London: Secker and Warburg, 1959. 262 pp.

Mishima: A Biography. John Nathan. Boston: Little, Brown, 1974; London: Hamilton, 1975. 300 pp.

Mori Ōgai

The Historical Literature of Mori Ōgai. Volume 1: The Incident at Sakai and Other Stories. Volume 2: Saiki kōi and Other Stories. Edited by David Dilworth and J. Thomas Rimer, translated by the editors et al. Honolulu: University Press of Hawaii, 1977. 2 vols.

The Wild Geese. Translated by Kingo Ochiai and Sanford Goldstein. Rutland, Vt., and Tokyo: Tuttle, 1959. 119 pp.

Mori Ōgai and the Modernization of Japanese Culture. Richard John Bowring. Cambridge, Eng., and New York: Cambridge University Press, 1979. 297 pp.

Nagai Kafū

◆*Kafū the Scribbler: The Life and Writings of Nagai Kafū, 1879–1959.* Edward Seidensticker. Stanford, Calif.: Stanford University Press, 1965. 360 pp.

Natsume Sōseki

Botchan. Translated by Alan Turney. Tokyo and Palo Alto, Calif.: Kodansha International, 1972. 173 pp.

I Am a Cat. Translated by Aiko Itō and Graeme Wilson. Rutland, Vt., and Tokyo: Tuttle, 1972–85. 3 vols.

◆*Kokoro: A Novel and Selected Essays.* Translated by Edwin McClellan; essays translated by Jay Rubin. Lanham, Md.: Madison Books, 1992. 322 pp.

Ōe Kenzaburō

A Personal Matter. Translated by John Nathan. New York: Grove Press, 1968; London: Weidenfeld and Nicolson, 1969. 214 pp.

The Silent Cry. Translated by John Bester. Tokyo and New York: Kodansha International, 1974. 274 pp.

Ōoka Shōhei

Fires on the Plain. Translated by Ivan Morris. New York: Knopf, 1957. 246 pp.; London: Secker and Warburg, 1957. 212 pp.

Shiga Naoya

A Dark Night's Passing. Translated by Edwin McClellan. Tokyo and New York: Kodansha International, 1976. 408 pp.

The Shiga Hero. William F. Sibley. Chicago and London: University of Chicago Press, 1979. 221 pp. An analysis of Shiga's writings.

Shimazaki Tōson

Before the Dawn. Translated by William E. Naff. Honolulu: University of Hawaii Press, 1987. 798 pp.

The Family. Translated by Cecilia Segawa Seigle. Tokyo: University of Tokyo Press, 1976. 311 pp.

Tanizaki Jun'ichirō

Diary of a Mad Old Man. Translated by Howard Hibbett. New York: Knopf, 1965. 177 pp. London: Secker and Warburg, 1966. 203 pp.

◆*The Makioka Sisters.* Translated by Edward G. Seidensticker. New York: Knopf, 1957; London: Secker and Warburg, 1958. 530 pp.

◆*In Praise of Shadows.* Translated by Thomas J. Harper and Edward G. Seidensticker. New Haven, Conn.: Leete's Island Books, 1977. 48 pp. The novelist's essay on Japanese aesthetics.

◆*Some Prefer Nettles.* Translated by Edward G. Seidensticker. New York: Knopf, 1955; London: Secker and Warburg, 1956. 202 pp.

Visions of Desire: Tanizaki's Fictional Worlds. Ken K. Ito. Stanford, Calif.: Stanford University Press, 1991. 305 pp. A critical interpretation of Tanizaki's writings.

Anthologies

◆*Contemporary Japanese Literature: An Anthology of Fiction, Film, and Other Writing since 1945.* Edited by Howard Hibbett. New York: Knopf, 1977. 468 pp.

Japanese Women Writers: Twentieth-Century Short Fiction. Translated and edited by Noriko Mizuta Lippit and Kyoko Iriye Selden. Armonk, N.Y., and London: M. E. Sharpe, 1991. 285 pp. A revised and expanded edition of *Stories by Contemporary Japanese Women Writers* (M. E. Sharpe, 1982).

Modern Japanese Haiku: An Anthology. Compiled and translated by Makoto Ueda. Toronto and Buffalo, N.Y.: University of Toronto Press, 1976. 265 pp.

Modern Japanese Poetry. Translated by James Kirkup, edited by A. R. Davis. St. Lucia, Queensland: University of Queensland Press, 1978; Milton Keynes, Eng.: Open University Press, 1979. 323 pp.

The Modern Japanese Prose Poem: An Anthology of Six Poets. Translated by Dennis Keene. Princeton,

N.J., and Guildford, Surrey: Princeton University Press, 1980. 187 pp.

Modern Japanese Stories: An Anthology. Edited by Ivan Morris; translated by Edward Seidensticker, George Saito, Geoffrey Sargent, and Ivan Morris. London: Eyre and Spottiswoode, 1961. 527 pp.; Rutland, Vt., and Tokyo: Tuttle, 1962. 512 pp.

The Shōwa Anthology: Modern Japanese Short Stories. Volume 1: 1929–1961. Volume 2: 1961–1984. Edited by Van C. Gessel and Tomone Matsumoto. Tokyo and New York: Kodansha International, 1985. 2 vols.

REFERENCE WORKS AND BIBLIOGRAPHIES

Biographical Dictionary of Japanese Literature. Sen'ichi Hisamatsu. Tokyo and New York: Kodansha International, in collaboration with the International Society for Educational Information (Tokyo), 1976. 437 pp.

Guide to Japanese Drama. Leonard C. Pronko. Boston: G. K. Hall, 1984. 2d ed. 149 pp.

Guide to Japanese Poetry. J. Thomas Rimer and Robert E. Morrell. Boston: G. K. Hall, 1984. 2d ed. 189 pp.

Guide to Japanese Prose. Alfred H. Marks and Barry D. Bort. Boston: G. K. Hall, 1984. 2d ed. 186 pp.

Guide to the Tale of Genji by Murasaki Shikibu. William J. Puette. Rutland, Vt., and Tokyo: Tuttle, 1983. 196 pp.

Japanese Folk Literature: A Core Collection and Reference Guide. Joanne P. Algarin. New York and London: Bowker, 1982. 226 pp.

Japanese Literature in Foreign Languages 1945–1990. Compiled by the Japan P.E.N. Club (Nihon Pen Kurabu). Tokyo: Japan Book Publishers Association, 1990. 383 pp.

The Princeton Companion to Classical Japanese Literature. Earl Miner, Hiroko Odagiri, and Robert E. Morrell. Princeton, N.J., and Guildford, Surrey: Princeton University Press, 1985. 570 pp.

Studies in Japanese Literature and Language: A Bibliography of English Materials. Compiled by Yasuhiro Yoshizaki. Tokyo: Nichigai Associates, 1979. 451 pp.

MASS MEDIA

50 Years of Japanese Broadcasting. Edited by NHK, Radio and TV Culture Research Institute, History Compilation Room (Nippon Hōsō Kyōkai, Sōgo Hōsō Bunka Kenkyūjo), with the Mainichi Newspapers. Tokyo: NHK Radio and TV Culture Research Institute, 1977. 429 pp.

Japanese Journalists and Their World. Young C. Kim. Charlottesville: University Press of Virgina, 1981. 226 pp.

Manga! Manga! The World of Japanese Comic Books. Frederik L. Schodt. Tokyo and New York: Kodansha International, 1983. 260 pp.

MEDICINE AND HEALTH

Death in Life: Survivors of Hiroshima. Robert Jay Lifton. New York: Random House, 1967. 594 pp. Reprinted, New York: Basic Books, 1982.

East Asian Medicine in Urban Japan: Varieties of Medical Experience. Margaret M. Lock. Berkeley and London: University of California Press, 1980. 311 pp.

Health Care in Japan. Margaret Powell and Masahira Anesaki. London and New York: Routledge, 1990. 264 pp.

Hiroshima and Nagasaki: The Physical, Medical, and Social Effects of the Atomic Bombings. Committee for the Compilation of Materials on Damage Caused by the Atomic Bombs in Hiroshima and Nagasaki (Hiroshima-shi Nagasaki-shi Genbaku Saigaishi Henshū Iinkai), translated by Eisei Ishikawa and David L. Swain. New York: Basic Books; London: Hutchinson; Tokyo: Iwanami Shoten, 1981. 706 pp.

Illness and Culture in Contemporary Japan: An Anthropological View. Emiko Ohnuki-Tierney. Cambridge and New York: Cambridge University Press, 1984. 242 pp.

The Quiet Therapies: Japanese Pathways to Personal Growth. David K. Reynolds. Honolulu: University Press of Hawaii, 1980. 135 pp.

PERFORMING ARTS

CINEMA

The Films of Akira Kurosawa. Donald Richie, with additional material by Joan Mellen. Berkeley and London: University of California Press, 1984. Rev. ed. 255 pp.

◆*Japanese Cinema: An Introduction.* Donald Richie. Hong Kong, Oxford, and New York: Oxford University Press, 1990. 102 pp.

◆*The Japanese Film: Art and Industry.* Joseph L. Anderson and Donald Richie. Princeton, N.J., and Guildford, Surrey: Princeton University Press, 1982. Expanded ed. 526 pp.

Japanese Film Directors. Audie Bock. Tokyo and New York: Kodansha International, 1985. Updated ed. 378 pp.

Japanese Films: Filmography and Commentary, 1921–1989. Beverley Bare Buehrer. Jefferson, N.C.: McFarland, 1990. 328 pp.

The Japanese Movie: An Illustrated History. Donald Richie. Tokyo and New York: Kodansha International, 1982. Rev. ed. 212 pp.

Voices from the Japanese Cinema. Joan Mellen. New York: Liveright, 1975. 295 pp.

MUSIC AND DANCE

A History of Japanese Music. Eta Harich-Schneider. London and New York: Oxford University Press, 1973. 720 pp.

The Japanese Dance. Eiryo (Hidesato) Ashihara. Tokyo: Japan Travel Bureau, 1964. Reprinted, New York: Books for Libraries, 1980. 164 pp.

◆*Japanese Music and Musical Instruments.* William P. Malm. Rutland, Vt., and Tokyo: Tuttle, 1959. 299 pp.

THEATER AND DRAMA

After Apocalypse: Four Japanese Plays of Hiroshima and Nagasaki. Kiyomi Hotta et al., translated by David G. Goodman. New York and Guildford, Surrey: Columbia University Press, 1986. 325 pp.

The Art of Kabuki: Famous Plays in Performance. Translated by Samuel L. Leiter. Berkeley and London: University of California Press, 1979. 298 pp.

Backstage at Bunraku: A Behind-the-Scenes Look at Japan's Traditional Puppet Theatre. Barbara C. Adachi, photographs by Joel Sackett. New York and Tokyo: Weatherhill, 1985. 192 pp.

◆*Bunraku: The Art of the Japanese Puppet Theatre.* Donald Keene, photographs by Hiroshi Kaneko. Tokyo and New York: Kodansha International,

1965. 287 pp. Rev. paperback ed.: Kodansha International, 1973. 88 pp.

Chūshingura (The Treasury of Loyal Retainers): A Puppet Play. Takeda Izumo II, Miyoshi Shōraku and Namiki Senryū, translated by Donald Keene. New York and London: Columbia University Press, 1971. 183 pp.

The Japanese Theatre: From Shamanistic Ritual to Contemporary Pluralism. Benito Ortolani. Leiden and New York: E. J. Brill, 1990. 352 pp.

Kabuki. Masakatsu Gunji, photographs by Chiaki Yoshida. Tokyo and New York: Kodansha International, 1985. New ed. 223 pp.

♦ *The Kabuki Theatre.* Earle Ernst. London: Secker and Warburg; New York: Oxford University Press, 1956. 296 pp. Reprinted, Honolulu: University Press of Hawaii, 1974.

♦ *Major Plays of Chikamatsu.* Chikamatsu Monzaemon, translated by Donald Keene. New York and London: Columbia University Press, 1961. 485 pp. Abbreviated edition published as *Four Major Plays of Chikamatsu.* New York and London: Columbia University Press, 1964. 220 pp.

Masterworks of the Nō Theater. Kenneth Yasuda. Bloomington: Indiana University Press, 1989. 585 pp.

Modern Japanese Drama: An Anthology. Edited and translated by Ted T. Takaya. New York and Guildford, Surrey: Columbia University Press, 1979. 277 pp.

♦ *Nō: The Classical Theatre of Japan.* Donald Keene, photographs by Hiroshi Kaneko. Tokyo and Palo Alto, Calif.: Kodansha International, 1966. 311 pp.

The Noh Theater: Principles and Perspectives. Kunio Komparu, translated by Jane Corddry and Stephen Comee. New York and Tokyo: Weatherhill/Tankosha, 1983. 376 pp.

Studies in Kabuki: Its Acting, Music, and Historical Context. James R. Brandon, William P. Malm, and Donald H. Shively. Honolulu: University Press of Hawaii, 1978. 183 pp.

Toward a Modern Japanese Theatre: Kishida Kunio. J. Thomas Rimer. Princeton, N.J.: Princeton University Press, 1974. 306 pp.

The Traditional Theater of Japan. Yoshinobu Inoura and Toshio Kawatake. New York and Tokyo: Weatherhill, in collaboration with the Japan Foundation, 1981. 259 pp.

Twenty Plays of the Nō Theatre. Edited by Donald Keene, assisted by Royall Tyler. New York and London: Columbia University Press, 1970. 336 pp.

BIBLIOGRAPHIES

Japanese Music: An Annotated Bibliography. Gen'ichi Tsuge. New York and London: Garland, 1986. 161 pp.

RELIGION AND PHILOSOPHY

Buddhism: Japan's Cultural Identity. Stuart D. B. Picken. Tokyo and New York: Kodansha International, 1982. 80 pp.

Christianity and Japan: Meeting, Conflict, Hope. Stuart D. B. Picken. Tokyo and New York: Kodansha International, 1983. 80 pp.

Confucianism and Tokugawa Culture. Edited by Peter Nosco. Princeton, N.J., and Guildford, Surrey: Princeton University Press, 1984. 290 pp.

Five Mountains: The Rinzai Zen Monastic Institution in Medieval Japan. Martin Collcutt. Cambridge: Council on East Asian Studies, Harvard University, 1981. 399 pp.

Folk Religion in Japan: Continuity and Change. Ichirō Hori, edited by Joseph M. Kitagawa and Alan L. Miller. Chicago and London: University of

Chicago Press; Tokyo: University of Tokyo Press, 1968. 278 pp.

Foundation of Japanese Buddhism. Volume 1: The Aristocratic Age. Volume 2: The Mass Movement (Kamakura and Muromachi Periods). Daigan Matsunaga and Alicia Matsunaga. Los Angeles and Tokyo: Buddhist Books International, 1974–76. 2 vols.

From the Rising of the Sun: Christians and Society in Contemporary Japan. James M. Phillips. Maryknoll, N.Y.: Orbis Books, 1981. 307 pp.

Hagakure: The Book of the Samurai. Tsunetomo Yamamoto, translated by William Scott Wilson. Tokyo and New York: Kodansha International, 1979. 180 pp.

A History of Christianity in Japan. Richard Henry Drummond. Grand Rapids, Mich.: William B. Eerdmans, 1971. 397 pp.

♦ *Japanese Religion: A Cultural Perspective.* Robert S. Ellwood and Richard Pilgrim. Englewood Cliffs, N.J.: Prentice-Hall, 1985. 162 pp.

♦ *Japanese Religion: Unity and Diversity.* H. Byron Earhart. Belmont, Calif.: Wadsworth, 1982. 3d ed. 272 pp.

Kurozumikyō and the New Religions of Japan. Helen Hardacre. Princeton, N.J., and Guildford, Surrey: Princeton University Press, 1986. 212 pp.

Motoori Norinaga, 1730–1801. Shigeru Matsumoto. Cambridge: Harvard University Press, 1970. 261 pp.

Nishida Kitarō. Keiji Nishitani, translated by Seisaku Yamamoto and James W. Heisig. Berkeley and Oxford: University of California Press, 1991. 238 pp. On a major 20th-century thinker from the Kyōto school of philosophy.

Pacifism in Japan: The Christian and Socialist Tradition. Edited by Nobuya Bamba and John F. Howes. Vancouver: University of British Columbia Press; Kyoto: Minerva Press, 1978. 300 pp.

Religion in Contemporary Japan. Ian Reader. Honolulu: University of Hawaii Press; Basingstoke, Hampshire: Macmillan, 1991. 277 pp.

♦ *Religion in Japanese History.* Joseph M. Kitagawa. New York and London: Columbia University Press, 1966. 475 pp.

♦ *Religions of Japan: Many Traditions within One Sacred Way.* H. Byron Earhart. San Francisco and London: Harper & Row, 1984. 142 pp.

Shintō and the State, 1868–1988. Helen Hardacre. Princeton, N.J., and Oxford: Princeton University Press, 1989. 203 pp.

Shinto: Japan's Spiritual Roots. Stuart D. B. Picken. Tokyo and New York: Kodansha International, 1980. 80 pp.

The Sōkagakkai and Mass Society. James W. White. Stanford, Calif.: Stanford University Press, 1970. 376 pp.

Tokugawa Religion: The Values of Pre-Industrial Japan. Robert N. Bellah. Glencoe, Ill.: Free Press, 1957. 249 pp. Reprinted as *Tokugawa Religion: The Cultural Roots of Modern Japan.* New York: Free Press; London: Collier Macmillan, 1985.

♦ *Zen and Japanese Culture.* Daisetz T. Suzuki. Princeton, N.J.: Princeton University Press, 1959; London: Routledge and Kegan Paul, 1960. 2d ed., rev. and enlarged. 478 pp.

♦ *Zen Buddhism: A History. Volume 2: Japan.* Heinrich Dumoulin, translated by James W. Heisig and Paul Knitter. New York: Macmillan; London: Collier Macmillan, 1990. 509 pp.

A Zen Forest: Sayings of the Masters. Compiled and translated by Sōiku Shigematsu. New York and Tokyo: Weatherhill, 1981. 177 pp.

BIBLIOGRAPHIES

The New Religions of Japan: A Bibliography of Western-Language Materials. H. Byron Earhart. Ann Arbor: Center for Japanese Studies,

University of Michigan, 1983. 2d ed. 213 pp.

Shintō Bibliography in Western Languages: Bibliography of Shintō and Religious Sects, Intellectual Schools and Movements Influenced by Shintoism. Arcadio Schwade. Leiden: Brill, 1986. 124 pp.

SCIENCE AND TECHNOLOGY

The Amazing Race: Winning the Technorivalry with Japan. William H. Davidson. New York and Chichester, Sussex: Wiley, 1984. 270 pp.

Arms Production in Japan: The Military Applications of Civilian Technology. Reinhard Drifte. Boulder, Colo., and London: Westview Press, 1986. 134 pp.

Biotechnology in Japan. Malcolm Vernon Brock. London and New York: Routledge, 1989. 156 pp.

Biotechnology Japan. Mark D. Dibner and R. Steven White. New York: McGraw-Hill, 1989. 313 pp.

Computers Inc.: Japan's Challenge to IBM. Marie Anchordoguy. Cambridge: Council on East Asian Studies, Harvard University, 1989. 273 pp.

The Formation of Science in Japan: Building a Research Tradition. James R. Bartholomew. New Haven, Conn., and London: Yale University Press, 1989. 369 pp.

Gaining Ground: Japan's Strides in Science and Technology. George Gamota and Wendy Frieman. Cambridge, Mass.: Ballinger, 1988. 180 pp.

Innovation and Technology Transfer in Japan and Europe: Industry-Academic Interactions. Glyn O. Phillips, assisted by Michael Hughes. London and New York: Routledge, 1989. 282 pp.

Inside the Robot Kingdom: Japan, Mechatronics, and the Coming Robotopia. Frederik L. Schodt. Tokyo and New York: Kodansha International, 1988. 256 pp.

Japanese Technology: Getting the Best for the Least. Masanori Moritani, translated by Simul International. Tokyo: Simul Press, 1982. 237 pp.

Japan's Software Factories: A Challenge to U.S. Management. Michael A. Cusumano. Oxford and New York: Oxford University Press, 1991. 513 pp.

Science and Technology in Japan. Alun M. Anderson. Harlow, Essex: Longman, 1984. 421 pp.

U.S.-Japan Science and Technology Exchange: Patterns of Interdependence. Edited by Cecil H. Uyehara. Boulder, Colo., and London: Westview Press, in cooperation with the Japan-America Society of Washington, 1988. 279 pp.

BIBLIOGRAPHIES

Japan's High Technology: An Annotated Guide to English-Language Information Sources. Dawn E. Talbot. Phoenix, Ariz.: Oryx Press, 1991. 171 pp.

SOCIETY

See also HISTORY: POST–WORLD WAR II; WOMEN.

♦ *The Anatomy of Dependence.* Takeo Doi, translated by John Bester. Tokyo and New York: Kodansha International, 1973. 170 pp.

The Anatomy of Self: The Individual versus Society. Takeo Doi, translated by Mark A. Harbison. Tokyo and New York: Kodansha International, 1986. 163 pp.

Becoming Japanese: The World of the Pre-School Child. Joy Hendry. Honolulu: University of Hawaii Press; Manchester, Eng.: Manchester University Press, 1986. 194 pp.

♦ *The Chrysanthemum and the Sword: Patterns of Japanese Culture.* Ruth Benedict. Boston:

Houghton Mifflin, 1946; London: Secker and Warburg, 1947. 324 pp. Reprinted, Houghton Mifflin, 1989.

City Life in Japan: A Study of a Tokyo Ward. Ronald P. Dore. Berkeley: University of California Press; London: Routledge and Kegan Paul, 1958. 472 pp.

Communicative Styles of Japanese and Americans: Images and Realities. Dean C. Barnlund. Belmont, Calif.: Wadsworth, 1989. 218 pp.

Conflict in Japan. Edited by Ellis S. Krauss, Thomas P. Rohlen, and Patricia G. Steinhoff. Honolulu: University of Hawaii Press, 1984. 417 pp.

Crafting Selves: Power, Gender and Discourses of Identity in a Japanese Workplace. Dorinne K. Kondo. Chicago and London: University of Chicago Press, 1990. 346 pp. Anthropological study of work in a confectionary factory.

Crested Kimono: Power and Love in the Japanese Business Family. Matthews Masayuki Hamabata. Ithaca, N.Y., and London: Cornell University Press, 1990. 191 pp.

For Harmony and Strength: Japanese White-Collar Organization in Anthropological Perspective. Thomas P. Rohlen. Berkeley and London: University of California Press, 1974. 285 pp.

The Honorable Elders Revisited: A Revised Cross-Cultural Analysis of Aging in Japan. Erdman B. Palmore and Daisaku Maeda. Durham, N.C.: Duke University Press, 1985. 135 pp.

How Policies Change: The Japanese Government and the Aging Society. John Creighton Campbell. Princeton, N.J., and Oxford: Princeton University Press, 1992. 418 pp.

◆*Japan: An Anthropological Introduction.* Harumi Befu. San Francisco: Chandler; New York: Harper & Row, 1971. 210 pp.

◆*Japanese Culture and Behavior: Selected Readings.* Edited by Takie Sugiyama Lebra and William P. Lebra. Honolulu: University of Hawaii Press, 1986. Rev. ed. 428 pp.

The Japanese Overseas: Can They Go Home Again? Merry White. New York: Free Press; London: Collier Macmillan, 1988. 179 pp.

Japanese Patterns of Behavior. Takie Sugiyama Lebra. Honolulu: University Press of Hawaii, 1976. 295 pp.

The Japanese Police System Today: An American Perspective. L. Craig Parker, Jr. Tokyo and New York: Kodansha International, 1984. 220 pp.

◆*The Japanese Social Structure: Its Evolution in the Modern Century.* Tadashi Fukutake, translated by Ronald P. Dore. Tokyo: University of Tokyo Press, 1989. 2d ed. 232 pp.

◆*Japanese Society.* Chie Nakane. Harmondsworth, Middlesex: Penguin Books, 1973. Rev. ed. 162 pp. Reprinted, Rutland, Vt., and Tokyo: Tuttle, 1984.

Japanese Society: Tradition, Self, and the Social Order. Robert J. Smith. Cambridge and New York: Cambridge University Press, 1983. 176 pp.

Japan's New Middle Class: The Salaryman and His Family in a Tokyo Suburb. Ezra F. Vogel. Berkeley and London: University of California Press, 1971. 2d ed. 313 pp.

Kurusu: The Price of Progress in a Japanese Village, 1951–1975. Robert J. Smith. Stanford, Calif.: Stanford University Press, 1978. 269 pp.

◆*Long Engagements: Maturity in Modern Japan.* David W. Plath. Stanford, Calif.: Stanford University Press, 1980. 235 pp.

Marriage in Changing Japan: Community and Society. Joy Hendry. London: Croom Helm; New York: St. Martin's Press, 1981. 274 pp.

Mirror, Sword and Jewel: A Study of Japanese Characteristics. Kurt Singer, edited by Richard Storry. London: Croom Helm; New York: George Braziller, 1973. 174 pp. Reprinted as *Mirror, Sword and Jewel: The Geometry of Japanese Life.* Tokyo and New York: Kodansha International, 1981.

Modern Japan through Its Weddings: Gender, Person, and Society in Ritual Portrayal. Walter Edwards. Stanford, Calif.: Stanford University Press, 1989. 173 pp.

The Myth of Japanese Uniqueness. Peter Dale. London: Croom Helm; New York: St. Martin's Press, 1986. 233 pp.

◆*Neighborhood Tokyo.* Theodore C. Bestor. Stanford, Calif.: Stanford University Press, 1989. 347 pp.

The Price of Affluence: Dilemmas of Contemporary Japan. Rokurō Hidaka, translated and edited by Gavan McCormack et al. Tokyo and New York: Kodansha International, 1984. 176 pp.

Rural Society in Japan. Tadashi Fukutake, translated by the staff of the *Japan Interpreter.* Tokyo: University of Tokyo Press, 1980. 218 pp.

◆*Shinohata: A Portrait of a Japanese Village.* Ronald P. Dore. London: Allen Lane; New York: Pantheon, 1978. 322 pp.

Six Lives, Six Deaths: Portraits from Modern Japan. Robert Jay Lifton, Shūichi Katō, and Michael R. Reich. New Haven, Conn., and London: Yale University Press, 1979. 305 pp.

Suye Mura: A Japanese Village. John F. Embree. Chicago: University of Chicago Press, 1939. 354 pp. Reprinted, University of Chicago Press, 1964.

Together with the Ainu: A Vanishing People. M. Inez Hilger, with Chiye Sano and Midori Yamaha. Norman: University of Oklahoma Press, 1971. 223 pp.

Understanding Japanese Society. Joy Hendry. London and New York: Croom Helm, 1987. 218 pp.

Yakuza: The Explosive Account of Japan's Criminal Underworld. David E. Kaplan and Alec Dubro. Reading, Mass.: Addison-Wesley, 1986; London: Macdonald, 1987. 336 pp.

SPORTS AND MARTIAL ARTS

A Book of Five Rings. Miyamoto Musashi, translated by Victor Harris. Woodstock, N.Y.: Overlook Press; London: Allison and Busby, 1974. 95 pp. A classic work on "the Way of the sword."

Classical Budo. Donn F. Draeger. New York and Tokyo: Weatherhill, 1973. 127 pp.

Classical Bujutsu. Donn F. Draeger. New York and Tokyo: Weatherhill, 1973. 109 pp.

Grand Sumo: The Living Sport and Tradition. Lora Sharnoff. New York and Tokyo: Weatherhill, 1989. 235 pp.

Modern Bujutsu and Budo. Donn F. Draeger. New York and Tokyo: Weatherhill, 1974. 190 pp.

You Gotta Have Wa. Robert Whiting. New York: Macmillan; London: Collier Macmillan, 1989. 339 pp. An account of Japanese-style baseball.

TRADITIONAL ARTS

Bonsai: The Complete Guide to Art and Technique. Paul Lesniewicz, translated by Susan Simpson. Poole, Dorset: Blandford Press, 1984. 194 pp.

The Book of Tea. Kakuzō Okakura. Rutland, Vt., and Tokyo: Tuttle, 1956. 133 pp. Classic essay on the aesthetic, philosophical, and religious significance of the tea ceremony.

Chado: The Japanese Way of Tea. Soshitsu Sen, translated and edited by Masuo Yamaguchi et al. New York and Tokyo: Weatherhill/Tankosha, 1979. 186 pp.

Flower Arrangement: The Ikebana Way. Minobu Ohi, Senei Ikenobō, Hōun Ohara, and Sōfū Teshigahara; translated by Seiko Aoyama et al.; edited by William C. Steere. Tokyo: Shufunotomo; New York: Grosset and Dunlap; London: Souvenir Press, 1972. 286 pp.

The Masters' Book of Bonsai. Compiled by the directors of the Japan Bonsai Association (Nippon Bonsai Kyōkai). Tokyo and Palo Alto, Calif.:

Kodansha International, 1967. 144 pp. Reprinted, Tokyo and New York: Kodansha International, 1983.

Tea Ceremony Utensils. Ryōichi Fujioka, with Masaki Nakano, Hirokazu Arakawa, and Seizō Hayashiya, translated and adapted by Louise Allison Cort. New York and Tokyo: Weatherhill/Shibundo, 1973. 142 pp.

◆*The Way of Tea.* Rand Castile. New York and Tokyo: Weatherhill, 1971. 329 pp.

TRAVEL AND DESCRIPTION

See also GEOGRAPHY AND ENVIRONMENT.

A Day in the Life of Japan: Photographed by 100 of the World's Leading Photojournalists on One Day, June 7, 1985. Project directed by Rick Smolan and David Cohen. Toronto and New York: Collins, 1985. 236 pp.

Gateway to Japan. June Kinoshita and Nicholas Palevsky. Tokyo and New York: Kodansha International, 1992. Rev. ed. 541 pp.

◆*The Inland Sea.* Donald Richie, photographs by Yōichi Midorikawa. New York and Tokyo: Weatherhill, 1971. 290 pp. Reprinted, London: Century, 1986.

The Insider's Guide to Japan. Peter Popham, photographs by Nik Wheeler. Edison, N.J.: Hunter Publishing, 1992. 2d ed., rev. 211 pp.

Introducing Japan. Donald Richie. Tokyo and New York: Kodansha International, 1990. 2d rev. ed. 72 pp.

◆*Japan.* Peter Spry-Leverton and Peter Kornicki, photographs by Joel Sackett. London: Michael O'Mara Books, 1987; New York: Facts on File, 1988. 192 pp.

Japan: Patterns of Continuity. Fosco Maraini. Tokyo and Palo Alto, Calif.: Kodansha International, 1971; London: Hamish Hamilton, 1972. 240 pp.

Japan Solo: The Independent Traveller's Passport to Singular Adventure. Eiji Kanno and Constance O'Keefe. New York: Warner Books, 1988. Rev. ed. 392 pp.

Japan: The New Official Guide. Japan Travel Bureau (Nihon Kōtsū Kōsha), edited with the cooperation of the Japan National Tourist Organization. Tokyo: Japan Travel Bureau, 1991. 968 + 120 pp.

Japan Unescorted. James K. Weatherly. Tokyo and New York: Kodansha International, in cooperation with Japan Air Lines, 1990. Rev. ed. 213 pp.

Kyoto: A Contemplative Guide. Gouverneur Mosher. Rutland, Vt., and Tokyo: Tuttle, 1978. Rev. ed. 368 pp.

Kyoto: Seven Paths to the Heart of the City. Diane Durston. Tokyo and New York: Kodansha International, 1987. 64 pp.

The Roads to Sata: A 2000-Mile Walk through Japan. Alan Booth. New York and Tokyo: Weatherhill, 1985. 281 pp.

Tokyo City Guide. Judith Connor and Mayumi Yoshida. Tokyo and New York: Ryuko Tsushin, in cooperation with Kodansha International, 1987. Rev. ed. 363 pp.

Tokyo Now and Then: An Explorer's Guide. Paul Waley. New York and Tokyo: Weatherhill, 1984. 502 pp.

WOMEN

Flowers in Salt: The Beginnings of Feminist Consciousness in Modern Japan. Sharon L. Sievers. Stanford, Calif.: Stanford University Press, 1983. 240 pp.

◆*Geisha.* Liza Crihfield Dalby. Berkeley and London: University of California Press, 1983. 347 pp. An ethnological study of the world of professional female entertainers in Kyōto.

◆*Haruko's World: A Japanese Farm Woman and Her Community.* Gail Lee Bernstein. Stanford, Calif.: Stanford University Press, 1983. 199 pp.

The Hidden Sun: Women of Modern Japan. Dorothy Robins-Mowry. Boulder, Colo.: Westview Press; Epping, Essex: Bowker, 1983. 394 pp.

Japanese Women: Constraint and Fulfillment. Takie Sugiyama Lebra. Honolulu: University of Hawaii Press, 1984. 348 pp.

Political Women in Japan: The Search for a Place in Political Life. Susan J. Pharr. Berkeley and London: University of California Press, 1981. 239 pp.

Recreating Japanese Women, 1600–1945. Edited by Gail Lee Bernstein. Berkeley and Oxford: University of California Press, 1991. 340 pp.

◆*Reflections on the Way to the Gallows: Rebel Women in Prewar Japan.* Translated and edited by Mikiso Hane. Berkeley and London: University of California Press, with Pantheon Books, 1988. 274 pp.

Urban Housewives: At Home and in the Community. Anne E. Imamura. Honolulu: University of Hawaii Press, 1987. 193 pp.

BIBLIOGRAPHIES

Japanese Women Writers in English Translation: An Annotated Bibliography. Claire Zebroski Mamola. New York and London: Garland, 1989. 469 pp.

PERIODICALS AND NEWSPAPERS

Arts of Asia. Kowloon, Hong Kong: Arts of Asia Publications, 1971– . Bimonthly.

Asian Art. New York: Oxford University Press, in association with the Arthur M. Sackler Gallery, Smithsonian Institution, 1987/88– . Quarterly.

Asian Survey: A Monthly Review of Contemporary Affairs. Berkeley: University of California Press, 1961– . Monthly.

Asian Wall Street Journal. Hong Kong: Dow Jones, 1976– . Daily.

Business Japan. Tokyo: Nihon Kōgyō Shimbun, 1971– . Monthly.

Chanoyu Quarterly: Tea and the Arts of Japan. Kyoto: Urasenke Foundation; New York: Urasenke Chanoyu Center, 1970– . Quarterly.

The East. Tokyo: East Publications, 1964– . Bimonthly.

Economic Eye: A Quarterly Digest of Views from Japan. Tokyo: Keizai Koho Center (Japan Institute for Social and Economic Affairs), 1980– . Quarterly.

◆*Far Eastern Economic Review.* Hong Kong: Far Eastern Economic Review Ltd., 1946– . Weekly.

Japan Architect: International Edition of Shinkenchiku. Tokyo: Shinkenchikusha, 1956– . Monthly.

◆*Japan Echo.* Tokyo: Japan Echo, Inc., 1974– . Quarterly.

Japan Economic Journal. Tokyo and New York: Nihon Keizai Shimbun, 1963– . Weekly.

Japan Forum. Oxford: Oxford University Press for the British Association for Japanese Studies, 1989– . Semiannual.

Japan Pictorial. Tokyo: Japan Graphic, Inc., 1978– . Quarterly.

◆*Japan Quarterly.* Tokyo: Asahi Shimbun, 1954– . Quarterly.

Japan Review of International Affairs. Tokyo: Japan Institute of International Affairs, 1987– . Semiannual.

◆*Japan Times.* Tokyo: Japan Times, 1897– . Daily.

Japan Update. Tokyo: Keizai Kōho Center (Japan Institute for Social and Economic Affairs), 1986– . Monthly.

Japanese Economic Studies. Armonk, N.Y.: M. E. Sharpe, 1972– . Quarterly.

Japanese Journal of Religious Studies. Nagoya: Nanzan Institute for Religion and Culture, 1974– . Quarterly.

Journal of American-East Asian Relations. Chicago: Imprint Publications, 1992– . Quarterly.

Journal of Asian Studies. Ann Arbor, Mich.: Association for Asian Studies, 1941– . Quarterly.

Journal of Japanese Studies. Seattle: Society for Japanese Studies, University of Washington, 1974– . Semiannual.

Journal of Japanese Trade and Industry. Tokyo: Japan Economic Foundation (Kokusai Keizai Kōryū Zaidan), 1982– . Bimonthly.

Journal of the Association of Teachers of Japanese. Madison, Wisc.: Association of Teachers of Japanese, 1964– . Semiannual.

Journal of the Japanese and International Economy. Duluth, Minn.: Academic Press, 1987– . Quarterly.

Look Japan. Tokyo: Look Japan, Ltd., 1956– . Monthly.

◆*Monumenta Nipponica: Studies in Japanese Culture.* Tokyo: Sophia University, 1938–43, 1951– . Quarterly.

Orientations: The Monthly Magazine for Collectors and Connoisseurs of Oriental Art. Hong Kong: Orientations Magazine, Ltd., 1970– . Monthly.

Pacific Affairs. Vancouver: University of British Columbia, 1928– . Quarterly.

Science and Technology in Japan. Tokyo: Three "I" Publications, Ltd., 1982– . Quarterly.

◆*Tokyo Business Today: A Monthly Magazine of Japan's Business and Finance.* Tokyo: Toyo Keizai Inc. (The Oriental Economist), 1986– . Monthly.

BILINGUAL INDEX OF ENTRY TITLES

This index is essentially a list of the titles of the main-text entries in this encyclopedia, which appear here in bold type with their equivalents in Japanese writing and the page number on which the entry begins. In addition, cross-references are provided from the Japanese equivalents of English entry titles and, when appropriate, the English equivalents of Japanese entry titles. The bilingual nature of these cross-references should make it possible in many cases for a reader to find a subject from either its Japanese or its English name. Cross-references from alternate names for entry titles (such as alternate readings of Japanese names) are also provided. These three types of cross-references consist of words in ordinary type followed by an arrow indicating the main-text entry title (in bold type) and page number. In a few cases, an additional type of cross-reference is provided consisting of Japanese words in ordinary type followed by the words *see under* and an entry title (in bold type) with page number. These are intended mainly as a guide to Japanese readers who might not know under which English headings to look for these topics.

C

H

J

K

S

U

X

Y

ACKNOWLEDGMENTS

ADVISORY COMMITTEE OF THE
KODANSHA ENCYCLOPEDIA OF JAPAN

The editors would like to express special thanks to the advisory committee and editor in chief of the nine-volume *Kodansha Encyclopedia of Japan*, on which the present book is based. They are listed here as they appeared in the original 1983 edition.

UNITED STATES

Edwin O. Reischauer (Chairman)
Harvard University

Gerald L. Curtis
Columbia University

Ronald P. Dore
Sussex University, England

John W. Hall
Yale University

Howard S. Hibbett
Harvard University

Akira Iriye
University of Chicago

Masatoshi Nagatomi
Harvard University

Hugh T. Patrick
Yale University

John M. Rosenfield
Harvard University

Donald H. Shively
Harvard University

Ezra F. Vogel
Harvard University

Michael Y. Yoshino
Harvard University

JAPAN

Tsuru Shigeto (Chairman)
Hitotsubashi University

Etō Jun
Tōkyō Institute of Technology

Inoue Mitsusada
National Museum of Japanese History

Katō Ichirō
Tōkyō University

Mitani Taichirō
Tōkyō University

Moriguchi Shigeichi
Tōkyō University

Mukaibō Takashi
Tōkyō University

Nakane Chie
Tōkyō University

Takashina Shūji
Tōkyō University

Umesao Tadao
National Museum of Ethnology

Watanabe Itaru
Keiō University

Editor in Chief
Gen Itasaka

ACADEMIC ADVISERS

The scholars listed here assisted in the selection and review of articles for *Japan: An Illustrated Encyclopedia* and are identified by their fields of specialization.

Amano Ikuo
Education

Asai Kiyoshi
Literature

Asai Motofumi
International Relations

Fujitake Akira
Mass Communications

Fukushima Yasuto
Military Science

Furuta Gyō
Philosophy and Thought, Religion

Hara Hiroko
Women

Harada Katsumasa
History

Hoshikawa Kiyochika
Agriculture

Ichibangase Yasuko
Social Problems

Imaizumi Yoshiharu
Animals

Inoue Shun
Leisure

Ishiyama Akira
Clothing

Iwasa Yoshizumi
Plants

Iwata Keiji
Anthropology, Folklore, Manners and Customs

Kanai Madoka
History

Kawatake Toshio
Performing Arts

Kurita Ken
Economics

Miyawaki Mayumi
Architecture, Housing

Mizutani Osamu
Language

Nakajima Mineo
International Relations

Nishikawa Osamu
Geography

Ogura Michio
Marine Industry

Okamura Tadao
Government and Politics

Saitō Tadashi
Archaeology

Sono Kazuaki
Law

Suzuki Masatoshi
Economics

Takada Seiji
Science and Technology

Tsuchiya Kenzaburō
Medicine

Tsuji Nobuo
Fine Arts

Tsuji Shizuo
Food

Watanabe Tōru
Sports

Yazaki Mitsukuni
Law

ADDITIONAL EDITORIAL STAFF

Carl Arnold
Stephen Barkhimer
Gwendolynne Barr
Joanne Bauer
Ann K. Bradley
Justin Doebele
Endō Akio
Enomoto Fumiyo
Patricia Farr
Fukushima Kiyoka
Fukushima Takayuki

Reiko Giffords
Hashimoto Taka
Hayashi Mariko
Ishikawa Yasumasa
Joshua Jancourtz
Simon Charles Kaner
Kariya Yōko
Kojima Chizuko
Kozawa Kuniko
Minakawa Naomi
Miyamoto Toshiyuki

Mizuochi Kimiko
Mochida Keiko
Ed Moran
Nakada Miwako
Nakajō Susumu
Nakayama Kiwako
Ono Hiroaki
Lisa Sartori
Sugai Yūko
Suzuki Takae
Suzuki Yōko

Tachikawa Masao
Takehara Yūko
Tamano Naho
Tanizaki Seiichi
Toshima Junko
Urade Rumiko
Wakui Takashi
Watanabe Naoko
Yamaguchi Satoko
Yano Mihoko
Yoshidome Yūichi

CONTRIBUTORS

This list includes both the hundreds of contributors to the *Kodansha Encyclopedia of Japan* whose work was condensed and updated for the present volume and the authors of articles and features newly commissioned for this encyclopedia.

A

Abe Gihei
Abe Hiromu
Abe Mikio
Abe Takeshi
Abe Tokiharu
Abe Yasushi
James C. Abegglen
Achiwa Gorō
Barbara C. Adachi
Adachi Tetsuo
Stephen Addiss
Aida Kō

Robert Aitken
Akashi Yōji
Akiba Tadatoshi
Akiyama Terukazu
Amagi Isao
Amano Ikuo
Amano Takashi
Amemiya Natsuo
Amenomori Isamu
Walter Ames
Anai Masahiro
J. L. Anderson
Nancy Andrew
Allan A. Andrews

Anzai Shin
Haruo Aoki
Michiko Y. Aoki
Aoki Tamotsu
Aomi Jun'ichi
Aoyagi Tamotsu
Ara Hide
Arai Eiji
Arai Naoyuki
James T. Araki
Aramaki Shigeo
Arase Yutaka
Diane Wright Arimoto
Arimoto Takafumi

Arioka Makoto
Ariyama Teruo
Barbara L. Arnn
Paul H. Aron
Aruga Yūshō
Asai Kiyoshi
Asai Motofumi
Asajima Shōichi
Asano Toshihisa
Janet Ashby
Awaji Takehisa
Awaya Kentarō
Azuma Hiroshi

B

Jane BACHNIK
Robert L. BACKUS
Frederick BAEKELAND
Hans H. BAERWALD
BAI Kōichi
Robert J. BALLON
BAMBA Nobuya
BAN Toshikazu
BANNO Junji
Gina Lee BARNES
Mary W. BASKETT
James C. BAXTER
Ellen Cary BEARN
Edward R. BEAUCHAMP
Johanna BECKER
George BEDELL
Lawrence W. BEER
Burton F. BEERS
Harumi BEFU
BEKKI Atsuhiko
Stephen BENFEY
John W. BENNETT
Gordon M. BERGER
Gail Lee BERNSTEIN
Paul BERRY
Jonathan W. BEST
John BESTER
Theodore C. BESTOR
Monica BETHE
J. D. BISIGNANI
BITŌ Masahide
Carmen BLACKER
Dorothy BLAIR
Peter BLEED
Alfred BLOOM
Tuvia BLUMENTHAL
Audie BOCK
Felicia G. BOCK
Harold BOLITHO
Andrea BOLTHO
Robert BORGEN
Adriana BOSCARO
Roger W. BOWEN
Gordon T. BOWLES
C. R. BOXER
John H. BOYLE
Karen BRAZELL
Martin BRONFENBRENNER
Robert H. BROWER
Delmer M. BROWN
Philip BROWN
Sidney DeVere BROWN
Michael Lee BROWNE
Yasuko Yabe BUSH

C

James CAHILL
Keith CAHOON
Carlo CALDAROLA

Kent E. CALDER
Alan CAMPBELL
John Creighton CAMPBELL
Jeanne CARREAU
William R. CARTER
Ann B. CARY
Otis CARY
Richard T. CHANG
Edward I-te CHEN
John J. CHEW
Madeleine CHI
CHIBA Shigeo
Soon Sung CHO
Kee Il CHOI
Robert C. CHRISTOPHER
Thomas W. CLEAVER
Diane Shaver CLEMENS
Richard S. CLEVELAND
Maida S. COALDRAKE
William H. COALDRAKE
Bruce A. COATS
Joel COHN
Robert E. COLE
Rex COLEMAN
Samuel J. COLEMAN
Martin C. COLLCUTT
Walter Ames COMPTON
Ellen P. CONANT
Hilary CONROY
Michael COOPER
Louise Allison CORT
Teruko CRAIG
Lloyd CRAIGHILL
Edwin A. CRANSTON
Sydney CRAWCOUR
Doris CROISSANT
William K. CUMMINGS
Louisa CUNNINGHAM
Michael CUNNINGHAM
Michael A. CUSUMANO
Frederick F. CZUPRYNA

D

Liza Crihfield DALBY
Kenneth J. DALE
Donald J. DALY
Eugene A. DANAHER
Roger DANIELS
James DAVIES
Mary Brett DE BARY
Barbara S. DECKER
George DEVOS
Roger DINGMAN
Donna L. DOANE
Miyoko DOCHERTY
Paula DOE
DOI Teruo
Michael W. DONNELLY
Ronald P. DORE
Grisha DOTZENKO
John W. DOWER

Peter DRYSDALE
Heinrich DUMOULIN
Charles DUNN
Diane DURSTON
Jerry DUSENBURY
Mary DUSENBURY
David DUTCHER
Masayo Umezawa DUUS
Peter DUUS
Richard E. DYCK
Yoshiko Kurata DYKSTRA

E

H. Byron EARHART
David M. EARL
Lane R. EARNS
EBARA Akinori
EDAGAWA Kōichi
EGASHIRA Kenjirō
David G. EGLER
EJIMA Yasunori
EJIRI Kōichi
Jurgis ELISONAS
ENDŌ Gen
ENDŌ Hiroshi
ENDŌ Masafumi
ENDŌ Takeshi
Gerhild ENDRESS
ENOKI Kazuo
Robert ENTENMANN
Frances ERGEN
Mark D. ERICSON
Steven J. ERICSON
Earle ERNST
ETŌ Fumio
ETŌ Kyōji
Robert EVANS, JR

F

Maggie FARLEY
Lee W. FARNSWORTH
Wayne FARRIS
Dallas FINN
Richard B. FINN
Jerry K. FISHER
Patricia FISTER
Scott C. FLANAGAN
William Miles FLETCHER III
James H. FOARD
Grace FOX
Andrew FRASER
Cal FRENCH
Peter FROST
FUCHI Kazuhiro
FUJII Toshiko
FUJIKAWA Kinji
FUJIKURA Kōichirō
FUJIMURA Michio
FUJINO Ichirō
FUJITA Hiroshi
FUJITA Tomio

FUJITAKE Akira
FUJITSU Shigeo
FUJIWARA Chika
FUKAGAWA Tsuneyoshi
FUKUDA Hideichi
FUKUDA Kizō
Haruhiro FUKUI
Glen S. FUKUSHIMA
FUKUSHIMA Kōka
FUKUSHIMA Shingo
FUKUSHIMA Yasuto
FUNAKOSHI Tōru
Jean FUNATSU
FURUTA Hikaru
Soichi FURUTA
FURUYA Kōzō
Toyomasa FUSÉ

G

GANBE Eiichi
C. Harvey GARDINER
Kenneth GARDNER
Richard GARDNER
Robert GARFIAS
B. J. GEORGE, JR
Van C. GESSEL
Kalyan Kumar GHOSH
GŌDA Yoshimasa
David I. GOLDBERG
Grant K. GOODMAN
Theodore W. GOOSSEN
Andrew GORDON
GOTŌ Kazuhiko
GOTŌ Masayuki
Patricia J. GRAHAM
Allan G. GRAPARD
Maribeth GRAYBILL
Judith Connor GREER
Edward G. GRIFFIN
Jane T. GRIFFIN
Peter M. GRILLI
Willem A. GROOTAERS
Christine GUTH

H

HABE Tadashige
Roger F. HACKETT
Eleanor M. HADLEY
HAGA Namio
HAGA Noboru
HAGA Tōru
Kanji HAITANI
Yoshito S. HAKEDA
David HALE
John O. HALEY
Ivan P. HALL
John W. HALL
Robert B. HALL, JR
Robert King HALL
HAMADA Nobuo
HAMAGUCHI Kōichi

Hamakawa Yoshihiro
Hamano Takuya
Hanami Tadashi
Hanamura Masaru
Mikiso Hane
Susan B. Hanley
Harada Katsumasa
Harada Yukihiro
Helen Hardacre
Eileen Hargadine
Phillip T. Harries
Haruhara Akihiko
Hasegawa Sakae
Hashikawa Bunzō
Hashimoto Nobuyuki
Hashimoto Sumiko
Hasumi Otohiko
Hata Ikuhiko
Hatakeyama Hirobumi
Hatori Tetsuya
Milan Hauner
William B. Hauser
T. R. H. Havens
Hayakawa Kunihiko
Hayakawa Zenjirō
Hayashi Hikaru
Hayashi Kunio
Hayashi Kyōhei
Hayashi Michio
Hayashi Ryōichi
Hayashi Shigeju
Hayashi Takeji
Hayashi Yasaka
Hayashi Yutaka
Hayashi Yūzō
Benjamin H. Hazard
Graham Healey
Waldo Heinrichs
Hemmi Takemitsu
Dan Fenno Henderson
Paul Henriques
Howard S. Hibbett
Hibi Yutaka
Brian Hickman
Money Hickman
Hidano Tadashi
Higasa Katsushi
Higashi Jutarō
Hijikata Kazuo
Hinotani Akihiko
Noburu Hiraga
Atsuko Hirai
Hirano Kunio
Hirano Ryūichi
Hirasawa Yutaka
Hirata Masami
Hiratsuka Masunori
Hiroi Nobuko
Hironaka Wakako
Hirosaki Yoshitsugu
Hirose Hideo

Hirota Teruhisa
Johannes Hirschmeier
Hitotsumatsu Shin
Frank Hoff
Hōjō Yoshio
Hokama Hiroshi
Wendy Holden
Leon Hollerman
Inger-Johanne Holmboe
Homma Yasuhei
William D. Hoover
Kyotsu Hori
Horiuchi Mamoru
H. Mack Horton
Hoshikawa Kiyochika
Hoshino Akira
Hoshino Eiki
Hoshino Takashi
Hosoda Kazuo
Hosokawa Izumi
Hosoya Chihiro
Hosoya Toshio
John F. Howes
Hoyanagi Mutsumi
Francis L. K. Hsu
Thomas M. Huber
David W. Hughes
G. Cameron Hurst III
Julia Hutt

I

Ibaragi Naoko
Ichikawa Kenjirō
Ichikawa Miyabi
Ichiki Toshio
Iida Ken'ichi
Iino Sadao
Fumiko Ikawa-Smith
Hiroko Ikeda
Ikegawa Satoshi
Ikei Nozomu
Imai Jun
Imai Shigeru
Imaizumi Yoshiharu
Imaizumi Yoshinori
Imamichi Tomonobu
Imamura Yoshio
Imazeki Rokuya
Inaba Eiko
Inagaki Shisei
Inō Tentarō
Inokuchi Shōji
Inoue Hiroshi
Inoue Kaoru
Inoue Keizō
Inoue Kōichirō
Inoue Munemichi
Inoue Shōbi
Inoue Shun
Inoue Teruko
Daniel K. Inouye

Akira Iriye
Mitsuko Iriye
Ishibashi Chie
Chiyoko Ishibashi
Ishibashi Katsuyo
Hoyu Ishida
Ishida Ichirō
Ishida Shōji
Ishige Naomichi
Ishii Ryōsuke
Ishii Susumu
Ishikawa Minoru
Ishimine Keitetsu
Ishimura Zensuke
Ishiyama Akira
Ishizaka Etsuo
Ishizaki Jūrō
Ishizaki Takashi
Isobe Kiichi
Itasaka Tsuyoshi
Itō Hajime
Itō Masami
Itō Mikiharu
Itō Nobuo
Itō Shigeo
Itō Shōken
Itō Yukiyoshi
Itō Zen'ichi
Hiroshi Itoh
Iwadare Hiroshi
Iwai Hiroaki
Iwamoto Tokuichi
Yoshio Iwamoto
Iwanaga Masaya
Iwanaga Shinkichi
Iwasa Yoshizumi
Iwashima Hisao
Masakazu Iwata
Tōru Iwatake
Iyanaga Teizō

J

Marius B. Jansen
Donald Jenkins
Jimbo Genji
Chalmers Johnson
Gine Johnson
Eleanor H. Jorden
John Junkerman

K

Kagesato Tetsurō
Kai Michitarō
Kainuma Keiji
Kakegawa Tomiko
Yoshiko Kakudō
Kamachi Noriko
Kaminogō Michiko
Kanai Madoka
Kanaseki Hiroshi
Kanazawa Yoshio

James Kanda
Kaneko Hiroshi
Kaneko Yoshimasa
Kanno Kōki
Kanō Hisashi
Kanō Kazuo
David E. Kaplan
Eugene J. Kaplan
Catherine Kaputa
Karasawa Tomitarō
Karatsu Hajime
Karita Yoshio
Kariya Takehiko
Kasaki Hideo
Kata Kōji
Katagiri Kazuo
Katō Etsuko
Katō Hiroaki
Katō Hiromi
Katō Hiroshi
Katō Ichirō
Katō Jōji
Katō Kōji
Katō Kōzaburō
Katō Masashi
Katō Shunjirō
Katō Shunpei
Katō Tadoru
Katō Tsuneo
Katō Yoshiko
Katori Tadahiko
Katsura Yoshio
Kawabe Kōji
Kawachi Hachirō
Kawada Jōji
Kawahara Sumiyuki
Kawai Takeshi
Kawakami Hiroshi
Kawamoto Akira
Kawamoto Ichirō
Kawamoto Takashi
Fujiya Kawashima
Kawashima Nobuki
Kawazoe Noboru
Donald Keene
Rick Kennedy
James T. Kenney
Roger Keyes
Kida Hiroshi
Kida Jun'ichirō
J. Edward Kidder, Jr
Kido Toshirō
Kikkawa Shūhei
Cornelius J. Kiley
Hee-Jin Kim
Yongdeok Kim
Kimura Eiichi
Kimura Hidemasa
Kimura Hiroshi
Kimura Kiyotaka
Kimura Masanori

Kimura Shigemitsu
Kimura Tsuyoshi
June Kinoshita
Masako Kinoshita
Kinouchi Kiyoko
Maurine A. Kirkpatrick
Kisaka Jun'ichirō
Kishino Hisashi
Sandy Kita
Joseph M. Kitagawa
Kitahara Yasusada
John Kitahara-Frisch
Kitamura Bunji
Kitazawa Masahiro
Gisaburō N. Kiyose
Jill Kleinberg
Lothar G. Knauth
Kobayakawa Yōichi
Kobayashi Kazuhiro
Kobayashi Manabu
Kobayashi Saburō
T. James Kodera
Kogiku Kiichirō
Byung Chul Koh
Koike Chie
Koishi Yoshio
Koizumi Iwao
Kojima Kazuto
Kojima Takeshi
Kojima Tomiko
Kokubo Takeshi
Akira Komai
Komata Yūsuke
Komatsu Sakyō
Komine Takao
Kondō Shinji
Konishi Jin'ichi
Kōno Motomichi
Kōno Tomomi
Koshiba Harumi
Kotani Kōzō
Kōuchi Saburō
Koura Kazutake
Koyanagi Shun'ichirō
Koyasu Nobukuni
Kozawa Tadahiro
Klaus Kracht
Ellis S. Krauss
Hyman Kublin
Kubo Fuminae
Kubota Kinuko
Kubota Takeshi
Kudō Masanobu
Kuma Rakuya
Fumie Kumagai
Kumagai Hiroshi
Kumakura Isao
Kumatori Toshiyuki
Kunimasa Takeshige
Kurahashi Tōru
Kuranishi Shigeru

Kurata Bunsaku
Kurauchi Shirō
Kurihara Harumi
Kurita Ken
Kuriyama Shigehisa
Kuroda Nobuyuki
Michio Kushi
Kuwata Tadachika
George Kuwayama
Patricia Hagan Kuwayama

L

William R. LaFleur
Whalen Lai
Harry J. Lamley
H. G. Lamont
Richard Lane
Betty B. Lanham
T. C. Larkin
Joyce C. Lebra
Takie Sugiyama Lebra
Gari Ledyard
Changsoo Lee
George Alexander Lensen
Gerald K. LeTendre
Robert W. Leutner
Solomon B. Levine
Young Ick Lew
Bruno H. Lewin
Olof Lidin
Thomas B. Lifson
Anthony V. Liman
Edward J. Lincoln
Howard A. Link
Noriko Mizuta Lippit
Victor D. Lippit
Jeannie P. C. Lo
David J. Lu
Jack A. Lucken
Leonard Lynn

M

Kathleen McCarthy
Paul McCarthy
James D. McCawley
Harold A. McCleery
Edwin McClellan
Aya Louisa McDonald
Terry Edward MacDougall
Miles K. McElrath
Machida Yōji
James McMullen
Theodore McNelly
Wayne C. McWilliams
Maeda Kazutoshi
Maeda Kiyoshi
Maeda Maiko
Maeda Wakaki
Makabe Tetsuo
John M. Maki
Maki Masami

Makino Noboru
William P. Malm
Robert M. March
Alfred H. Marks
Susan H. Marsh
Byron K. Marshall
Samuel E. Martin
Maruoka Hideko
Penelope E. Mason
Jeffrey Mass
Masuda Shōzō
Masuda Yoshio
Masuda Yūji
Masui Ken'ichi
Masunaga Shizuto
Francis Mathy
Susan Matisoff
Matsubara Mitsunori
Naoko Matsubara
Matsuda Michihiro
Matsuda Osamu
Matsuda Saburō
Matsui Hideji
Amy T. Matsumoto
Matsumoto Masao
Matsumoto Saburō
Tomone Matsumoto
Matsunaga Seiji
Matsunami Yoshihiro
Matsuo Shigeo
Matsuo Takayoshi
Matsushita Mitsuo
Matsuura Fumihiko
Matsuura Kaoru
Matsuzaki Akira
Marlene J. Mayo
Mayuzumi Hiromichi
Meron Medzini
Julia Meech
Joan Mellen
Richard L. Mellott
Mera Kōichi
Charles M. Mergentime
Daniel A. Metraux
Mihara Takeshi
Mikami Terumi
Miki Seiichirō
Frank O. Miller
Roy Andrew Miller
Douglas E. Mills
Minamizuka Shingo
Richard H. Minear
Minegishi Kentarō
Minegishi Sumio
Earl Miner
Sharon A. Minichiello
Misumi Haruo
Arthur M. Mitchell
C. H. Mitchell
Richard H. Mitchell
Miyachi Seiya

Hiroshi Miyaji
Miyake Hitoshi
Miyake Masahiko
Miyamoto Mataji
Miyamoto Mizuo
Miyano Nobuyuki
Miyao Shigeo
Miyata Setsuko
Dixon Y. Miyauchi
Miyawaki Ayumu
Miyawaki Mayumi
Miyawaki Osamu
Miyazawa Ken'ichi
Masao Miyoshi
Mizoguchi Toshiyuki
Mizubayashi Takeshi
Mizuochi Kiyoshi
Mizutani Osamu
Mochida Minoru
Brian Moeran
Robert Moes
Kathleen Molony
Momose Hiroto
Momose Kesao
Tazuko Monane
Betty Iverson Monroe
Wilbur F. Monroe
Mori Masumi
Mori Shigeo
Morimoto Minoru
Morinaga Hiroshi
James R. Morita
Moriyama Tsuneo
Carol Morland
Robert E. Morrell
Mark Morris
Helmut Morsbach
Anne Nishimura Morse
Ronald A. Morse
William F. Morton
William G. Morton
Karl Moskowitz
Motegi Kiyoko
Frank T. Motofuji
Motomura Kazuko
Ross Mouer
Mozai Torao
Chieko Mulhern
Jane Munro
Hugo Münsterberg
Murakami Shigeyoshi
Murakami Yumi
Murakoshi Sueo
Muramatsu Teijirō
Muranaka Kyōko
Murata Hiroshi
Susan Murata
Murata Yoshio
Patricia Murray
Mutō Shunkō

N

William E. Naff
Nagahama Yōichi
Nagahara Keiji
Nagai Hiroo
Nagano Gorō
Nagao Masakazu
Nagao Ryūichi
Susumu Nagara
Nagasawa Katsuo
Nagasawa Mitsuo
Nagase Akira
Nagashima Atsushi
Nagatoya Yōji
Nagazumi Akira
Naitō Kinju
Naitō Motoo
Tetsuo Najita
Nakagawa Kōji
Nakagawa Masayuki
Nakagawa Satoshi
Nakagawa Toshihiko
Kate Nakai
Yoshiyuki Nakai
Nakajima Kawatarō
Nakajima Kenzō
Nakajima Mineo
Nakajima Naotada
Nakamura Hajime
Nakamura Kiichi
Kyōko Motomochi Nakamura
Nakamura Masanori
Nakane Chie
Nakane Takehiko
Don T. Nakanishi
Nakao Takehiko
Nakasa Hideo
Nakasato Toshikatsu
Nakauchi Tsuneo
Shigeru Nakayama
Nakazato Michiko
Dick K. Nanto
Naoi Atsushi
Naramoto Tatsuya
Narita Katsuya
Narita Yoriaki
Nasu Hiroshi
Karin C. Nelson
Nemoto Junkichi
Margret Neuss-Kaneko
J. V. Neustupný
C. W. Nicol
Niimi Ikubumi
Niira Satoshi
Niki Isao
Ninomiya Masato
Ian Nish
Nishida Makoto
Nishida Shunji
Nishii Kazuo

Nishijima Sadao
Nishikawa Osamu
Nishimata Sōhei
Nishimizu Mieko
Nishimoto Yōichi
Nishimura Makoto
Nishino Teruhiko
Harry K. Nishio
Tamako Niwa
Niwa Toshio
Niwata Noriaki
Agnes M. Niyekawa
Noda Kazuo
Noguchi Takehiko
Noguchi Takenori
Noguchi Yukio
Nohara Hiroshi
Sharon Nolte
Nomura Tadao
Nomura Yoshihiro
Edward Norbeck
Nose Takayuki
F. G. Notehelfer
Nozaki Shigeru
Numata Satoshi

O

Obara Satoru
James A. O'Brien
Ochiai Shigenobu
Oda Takeo
Oda Yukiko
Oda Yukio
Odaka Kōnosuke
Ogasawara Nobuo
Ogata Shijūrō
Ogawa Kōichi
Ogawa Yoshio
Ōguchi Yūjirō
Ogura Michio
Oguri Junko
Ōhara Satoshi
Oka Takashi
Okada Yasushi
Okajima Tōru
Shumpei Okamoto
Frank Masao Okamura
Okamura Tadao
Okano Hisateru
Ōki Yasue
Daniel I. Okimoto
Okonogi Masao
Oku Takeo
Okuda Shinjō
Okudaira Yasuhiro
Ōmae Kinjirō
Ōmori Kazuko
Ōnami Yūji
P. G. O'Neill
Ōnishi Harutaka
Ono Kōji

Ōno Tōru
Ōno Tsutomu
Onoda Yōichi
Onodera Jun
Herman Ooms
Alfred C. Oppler
Orita Kōji
Masako M. Ōsako
Osanai Satoru
Ōshima Mitsuo
Ōshima Shigemasa
Ōsumi Seiji
Ōta Rin'ichirō
Ōta Yoshimaro
Yūzō Ōta
Ōtō Tokihiko
Ōtsuka Shigeru
Ōtsuka Shigeru
Ōtsuka Sueko
Ōtsuka Yasuo
Ōuchi Eishin
Ōuchi Minoru
Owada Hisashi
Ōwaki Hiroki
David Owens
Ozaki Hotsuki
Robert S. Ozaki
Ozawa Terutomo

P

George R. Packard
Allan Palmer
Minja Yang Paringaux
Hugh Patrick
Erich Pauer
Diana Paul
Mark R. Peattie
Joseph A. Pechman
T. J. Pempel
Susan J. Pharr
Rulan Chao Pian
Stuart D. B. Picken
John D. Pierson
Ernest D. Piryns
Joseph Pittau
David W. Plath
Herbert E. Plutschow
Christian Polak
David Pollack
Junko Sato Pollack
Edythe Polster
Barbara Porter
Brian Powell
Irena Powell
Cyril H. Powles

Q

C. Kenneth Quinones

R

Judith N. Rabinovitch
Robert B. Radin
Esperanza Ramirez-Christensen
Daniel B. Ramsdell
William V. Rapp
C. Tait Ratcliffe
Kirsten Refsing
Michael R. Reich
Haru Reischauer
David K. Reynolds
Robert Rhodes
Richard Rice
Kenneth L. Richard
Bradley Richardson
Donald Richie
J. T. Rimer
Alan Rix
Laurance P. Roberts
Gary E. Robertson
B. W. Robinson
Lawrence W. Rogers
Thomas P. Rohlen
Thomas Rohlich
Robert Rolf
John M. Rosenfield
Eugene Rotwein
Gilbert Rozman
Barbara Ruch
Marleigh Grayer Ryan
Carole A. Ryavec

S

Saeki Arikiyo
Saeki Shōichi
Sagara Iichi
Sagara Tōru
Saiki Kazuma
Saitō Chikako
Saitō Hikaru
Saitō Hiroshi
Saitō Kenjirō
Saitō Masako
Saitō Ryōsuke
Saitō Shizuo
Saitō Shōji
Saitō Tadashi
Saitō Tetsuo
Sakaguchi Nobuhiko
Akira Sakai
Robert K. Sakai
Sakai Shizu
Sakai Tadayasu
Hiroshi Sakamoto
Sakanoue Masanobu
Mitsugu Sakihara
Sakurabayashi Makoto
Sakurada Katsunori
Ralph Samuelson
Saneyoshi Tatsuo

James H. Sanford
Sanuki Matao
Sanuki Yurindo
Saotome Masahiro
Sasabuchi Tomoichi
Sasaki Kinzō
Sasaki Tadayoshi
Sasayama Haruo
Elizabeth S. Satō
Satō Hideo
Hiroaki Satō
Kazuo Satō
Satō Kōji
Satō Mitsunobu
Satō Naoyuki
Ryūzō Satō
Satō Seizaburō
Satō Tadao
Satō Tadashi
Satō Tamotsu
Toshihiko Satō
E. Dale Saunders
Sawa Shigehisa
Sawada Keisuke
Sawada Takahiro
Sawaki Takao
Sawamura Kazuhiko
Sawanobori Toshio
Sawayama Hiroshi
Gary R. Saxonhouse
C. Franklin Sayre
Paul Schalow
Wolfgang Schamoni
Irwin Scheiner
Frederik L. Schodt
Kim Schuefftan
A. C. Scott
Christopher Seeley
Edward G. Seidensticker
Seike Kiyosi
Sekiguchi Hiromasa
Kyōko Iriye Selden
Senda Akihiko
Sengen Ryūichirō
Senshū Shin'ichi
Carl Sesar
Joseph Seubert
Jack Seward
Nancy Shatzman-Steinhardt
Charles D. Sheldon
Paul Shepherd
James E. Sheridan
Shibanuma Susumu
Shibata Takao
Shibusawa Sachiko
Shigematsu Itsuzō
Shiina Kazuo
Shiki Masahide
Ben-Ami Shillony
Shimada Jirō
Shimada Masahiko

Shimazono Susumu
Shimazu Hiroshi
Shimbori Michiya
Shimizu Hideo
Shimizu Tetsuo
Shimizu Tsutomu
Yoshiaki Shimizu
Shimmi Hiroshi
Shimohira Kazuo
Shimokawa Kōichi
Shinada Yutaka
Shinagawa Fujirō
Shinji Isoya
Minoru Shinoda
Shinomiya Toshiyuki
Shinra Ichirō
Shioda Nagahide
Hiroki Shioji
Shiono Hiroshi
Shirai Kunihiko
Shirai Yoshio
Shiraishi Masaya
Shiraishi Teizō
Zenryū Shirakawa
Ichirō Shirato
Shirota Fumihiko
Shishido Toshio
Donald H. Shively
Shōjima Yumiko
William F. Sibley
Jeanne Sigée
George A. R. Silver
Bradford L. Simcock
Robert T. Singer
Patricia Sippel
Joseph W. Slade
Richard Smethurst
Henry D. Smith II
Lawrence Smith
Malcolm D. Smith
Robert J. Smith
Michael J. Smitka
Sōda Hajime
Soeda Yoshiya
Michael Solomon
Someya Shirō
Sone Ken'ya
Sonoda Hidehiro
Sonoda Minoru
Isao Soranaka
Eugene Soviak
Dennis M. Spackman
Douglas E. Sparks
Norman Sparnon
Robert M. Spaulding
Thomas A. Stanley
Richard Stanley-Baker
Oliver Statler
M. William Steele
Kurt Steiner
Patricia G. Steinhoff

John J. Stephan
William E. Steslicke
Margo Stipe
J. A. A. Stockwin
Richard Storry
Giuliana Stramigioli
Tal Streeter
Kenneth Strong
Nathan O. Strong
Suchi Tokuhei
Suda Ken
Sudō Haruo
Suenaka Tetsuo
Sugawara Kunika
Sugawara Norio
Sugeno Kazuo
Sugihara Shirō
Sugiyama Akio
Sugiyama Tadayoshi
Sugiyama Yasushi
Glenn Sullivan
Suyama Kazuyuki
Suzuki Eiichi
Suzuki Hiroaki
Suzuki Kazuyoshi
Suzuki Kōichi
Suzuki Masao
Suzuki Masatoshi
Suzuki Mitsuru
Suzuki Norihisa
Suzuki Ryōichi
Suzuki Yoshio
Suzuki Yukihisa
Suzuki Zenji
David L. Swain
Barbara Bowles Swann
Thomas E. Swann
Thomas D. Swift
R. C. F. Swinnerton
Elizabeth de Sabato Swinton

T

Kenneth M. Tagawa
Taguchi Yoshiaki
Mildred Tahara
Kōji Taira
Takabatake Michitoshi
Takada Seiji
Takagi Noritsune
Takagi Shōsaku
Takahashi Katsuhide
Takahashi Ken'ichi
Takahashi Kimiko
Takahashi Masao
Takahashi Naoki
Takahashi Tōru
Takahashi Yūzō
Takakura Shō
Takakuwa Yasuo
Takami Kenshirō
Takamura Hisao

Takano Keiichi
Takano Shinji
Takashima Shizuo
Ted T. Takaya
Takayama Shigeru
Takebe Yoshiaki
Takeda Fumio
Takeda Katsuhiko
Takeda Yukimatsu
Takehisa Yoshihiko
Takenaka Kazurō
Takeuchi Akio
Takeuchi Hitoshi
Melinda Takeuchi
Takeuchi Rizō
Takishima Isao
Takuma Shinpei
Takumi Hideo
Tamai Kensuke
Tamaru Noriyoshi
Tamiya Hiroshi
Tanabe Akira
George J. Tanabe, Jr
Atsuko Tanabe de Baba
Tanaka Akira
Tanaka Jirō
Tanaka Masaaki
Tanaka Minoru
Tanaka Nobue
Tanaka Shigeaki
Tanaka Takeo
Tanaka Tsutomu
Tanaka Yōnosuke
Tanaka Yutaka
Tanigawa Atsushi
Taniguchi Yasuhei
Tanikawa Hisashi
Tanji Kenzō
Tansō Akinobu
Tashimo Masaaki
Tashiro Hikaru
Peter Tasker
Tatsuki Mariko
Tatsuta Misao
Taura Takeo
Terai Minako
Terasaki Masao
Tezuka Yōko
John E. Thayer III
Sarah Thompson
Arthur H. Thornhill III
Donald R. Thurston
David A. Titus
Toba Reijirō
Ronald P. Toby
Toda Yoshio
Togai Yoshio
Toganoo Shōzui
Tokuzen Yoshikazu
Tomatsu Hidenori
Tomiki Kenji

Tomisawa Konomi
Tomita Torao
Tonami Kōji
Tonoki Keiichi
Tonooka Shin'ichirō
Conrad Totman
George Oakley Totten III
Glyndon Townhill
Toyoda Takeshi
Tozawa Fuyuki
Tsuchida Mitsufumi
Tsuchida Naoshige
Tsuchida Tomoaki
Tsuchiya Rokurō
Tsuchiya Shin'ichi
Tsuda Hideo
Tsuda Mamoru
Tsuji Shizuo
Matsuo Tsukada
Toshio G. Tsukahira
Reiko Tsukimura
Tsukuba Hisaharu
Tsumori Makoto
Tsumura Akinobu
Tsumura Kenshirō
E. Patricia Tsurumi
Yoshihiro Tsurumi
Kinya Tsuruta
Tsutsui Michio
Royall Tyler
William J. Tyler

U

Uchida Eiji
Uchida Michio
Uchikawa Yoshimi
Udagawa Akihito
Udagawa Masaru
Ueda Kenji
Ueda Kiichi
Makoto Ueda
Ueda Masaaki
Ueda Nobuhiro
Ueda Sumako
Ueda Yasuo
Toyoaki Uehara
Ueno Yoshiya

Ukai Nobushige
Umetani Noboru
J. Marshall Unger
Unno Fukuju
Taitetsu Unno
Unno Yoshirō
Frank K. Upham
Urano Tatsuo
Marian Ury
Sharlie Conroy Ushioda
Ushiogi Morikazu
Ushiro Masatake
Usui Katsumi
Usuki Masaharu
Uwano Zendō
Allie Marie Uyehara
Cecil H. Uyehara

V

H. Paul Varley
Susan Downing Videen
Valdo H. Viglielmo
Savitri Vishwanathan
Ezra F. Vogel
Suzanne H. Vogel
Frits Vos

W

Meredith Waddell
Hiroshi Wagatsuma
Wagatsuma Takashi
Wakasugi Akira
Wakasugi Takaaki
Wakita Osamu
Watanabe Akira
Watanabe Hiroshi
Watanabe Hiroshi
Watanabe Hirotaka
Watanabe Hitoshi
Watanabe Ichirō
Watanabe Shinji
Watanabe Tadashi
Watanabe Takeshi
Watanabe Tōru
Tsugumichi Watanabe
Watanabe Yoshirō
David B. Waterhouse

Glenn T. Webb
Herschel Webb
Peter Weber-Schäfer
C. G. Weeramantry
Gail Capitol Weigl
Lucie R. Weinstein
Stanley Weinstein
Theodore F. Welch
D. Eleanor Westney
William Wetherall
Carolyn Wheelwright
John A. White
Merry I. White
George M. Wilson
William R. Wilson
Manfred Wimmer
Clark Worswick

Y

Yagi Atsuru
Yagi Natsuhiko
Yamada Katsumi
Yamada Katsumi
Yamada Kōshō
Yamada Makiko
Yamada Terutane
Yamada Tokubei
Yamada Toshio
Yamagishi Shunsuke
Yamaguchi Kazuo
Yamaguchi Makoto
Yamaguchi Masahiro
Yamaguchi Osamu
Yamakawa Yoshio
George K. Yamamoto
Yamamoto Tadashi
Yamamoto Takeo
Yamamoto Toshiaki
Kozo Yamamura
Yamanaka Seigō
Yamano Aiko
Yamanobe Tomoyuki
Yamaryō Kenji
Yamashita Aiko
Yamashita Kaoru
Yamashita Kikuko
Yamashita Ryūji

Yamashita Yūji
Yamazaki Isao
Yamazaki Yukio
Philip Yampolsky
Minoru Yanagihashi
Yanai Kenji
Yanai Madoka
Yano Tōru
Yano Yōko
Richard Yasko
Kenneth Yasuda
Yasuda Motohisa
Yauchi Yoshiaki
Yazawa Taiji
M. Yochum
Yokote Masahiko
Karl G. Yoneda
Yonekura Mamoru
Yonemoto Kanji
Ann Yonemura
Yorida Tadashi
Yoshida Akio
Yoshida Aya
Yoshida Hiroo
Yoshida Hiroshi
Yoshida Yoshio
Takehiko Yoshihashi
Yoshikawa Yōko
Yoshikoshi Tatsuo
I. Roger Yoshino
Masatoshi M. Yoshino
Michael Y. Yoshino
Yoshino Sōhei
Yoshitake Yoshinori
Yoshitoshi Yawara
Yoshizawa Akira
Ernest P. Young
John Young
Yuasa Michio
Nobuyuki Yuasa
Yui Tsunehiko
Yukawa Osamu

Z

Zakō Jun
Leon M. Zolbrod

TRANSLATORS

Megan Backus
Barry Duell

Elizabeth Fragala
Ikeda Hiroshi

Joseph Thomas Johnson
Dan L. Kanagy

Kanai Hiroo
E. Barry Keehn

Stephen J. McKay
Joseph Mann
Meihō Gaigo Center

J. Scott Miller
Alison M. Murray
New Tec, Inc

Lucy Petermark
Lynne E. Riggs
Tsuruoka Atsuo

Frederick M. Uleman
Michael J. Verretto

ILLUSTRATORS

Amagi Shigeharu
Chō Jinsei
Endō Kōetsu
Fujishima Junzō
Fukatsu Shin'ya
Futakuchi Yoshio
Hozumi Kazuo
Ishido Tadashi
Ishikawa Mieko
Izawa Motoharu
Kabayama Sachikazu

Kamoshita Chōko
Kimura Zugei Co
Makino Yoshikichi
Matsui Kōji
Miyamoto Takashi
Murase Naoko
Narashima Tomoyuki
Nemoto Empitsu
Oda Noritsugu
Oda Otoya
Odagiri Akira

Ōkata Tadaaki
Okumura Teiichi
Ōta Yōai
Sasaki Keisuke
Satō Kōki
Satō Michihiko
Shimazoe Toshi
Shirao Mitsuo
Sugai Minoru
Takeshima Kōji
Tateishi Tetsuomi

Andrew Thomas
Tomori Ukei
Tsurukai Shinsuke
Watanabe Kaku
Yabuuchi Masayuki
Yamamoto Takumi
Yamashita Fumihito
Yamazaki Renzō
Yogi Mayuko
Yonai Suihō
Yotsumoto Fumio

PHOTO AND ILLUSTRATION CREDITS

Abe Tsuyoshi
Adachi Woodblock Printing Research
  Center
Administrative Headquarters of Sōtō
  Zen Buddhism
Advanced Robot Technology
  Research Association
Agency for Cultural Affairs
Aji Kicchō
Akama Shrine
Akira Committee
Akira Ikeda Gallery, Tōkyō
Akita Prefectural Museum
Akiyama Gallery, Tōkyō
Akiyama Minoru
Als Planning
Anzai Shigeo
Aoki Shinji
Aoyama Ōzushi Co, Ltd
Aoyama San'u
Arakawa Shūsaku
Araki Kenji
Araki Nobuyoshi
Aramaki Masayuki
Argus, Inc

Ars Photo Planning
Art Bank
Asaba Katsumi
Asahi National Broadcasting Co, Ltd
Asahi Optical Co, Ltd
Asahi shimbun
Asama Shrine
Asukaen
Awa Museum of Chiba Prefecture
Awazu Kiyoshi
Ay-O
Azumazeki Stable
Ba Photo Library
Frank Baldwin
Bank of Japan
Banshō Kurakatsu
Benridō Co, Ltd
Bon Color Photo Agency Co, Ltd
Bungakuza
Bunka Gakuen
Bunraku Kyōkai
Byōdōin
Canon, Inc
Canon Sales Co, Inc
Chiba City Education Committee

Chion'in
Chishakuin
Chiyoda Toshokan, Uchida Bunko
Chōgo Sonshiji
Chōkōji
Chūgūji
Chūō Kōron Sha, Inc
Chūsonji
Cinema Plaset
Communications Museum
Cosmo Photo Office
Currency Museum
Daigoji
Dai-Ichi Kangyō Bank, Ltd
Daisen'in
Daitokuji
Daitōkyū Memorial Library
Defense Agency
Domon Ken
Eisei Bunko Museum
Endō Toshikatsu
Engakuji
Enryakuji
Estate of Yasuo Kuniyoshi
Ezaki Haru

Fotony Associates, Inc
Freer Gallery of Art, Smithsonian
  Institution
Fuji Heavy Industries, Ltd
Fuji Photo Film Co, Ltd
Fuji Television Gallery, Tōkyō
Fujihata Masaki
Fujiko F Fujio
Fujiko Fujio A
Fujimori Takeshi
Fujita Art Museum
Fujita Masahisa
Fujitsū, Ltd
Fukase Masahisa
Fukuda Naotake
Fukuda Shigeo
Fukuda Sōhei
Fukui Prefectural Museum
Fukuinkan Shoten, Publishers, Inc
Fukuoka Art Museum
Fukuoka City Board of Education
Fukuoka City Museum
Fukuoka Prefectural Board of
  Education
Fukutake Publishing Co, Ltd

Furuichi Tomoyuki
Fushin'an Teahouse (Omote Senke)
Gallery Takagi, Nagoya
Gallery Yamaguchi, Ōsaka
General Library, Tōkyō University Library System
Geographic Photo
Gotō Art Museum
Gumma Prefectural Board of Education
Gumma Prefectural Museum of History
Gyokuzōin
Haga Library
Hakodate Municipal Museum
Hakuhōdō, Inc
Hamada Shinsaku
Hamaya Hiroshi
Hanamura
Hanazono University
Hara Museum
Hashimoto Akiko
Hatakeyama Museum
Hayashi Ryōichi
Hayashi Shigeo
Hayashi Yoshikatsu
Hayashibara Museum of Art
Heibonsha, Ltd, Publishers
Hibino Kōhō
Hidaka Seiichi
Higashiyama Kaii
Hino Agency
Hirano Jirō
Hirata Nui
Hirayama Ikuo
Hirosaki City Museum
Hiroshima Peace Culture Foundation
Historical Museum of Hokkaidō
Hokkaidō Hakodate Museum of Art
Hokkeji
Hōmasa
Honda Motor Co, Ltd
Honda Museum
Honolulu Academy of Arts
Hori Kōsai
Hōryūji
Hōsa Bunko
Hosoe Eikō
Hosokawa Takeshi
Hosoya Gan
Hot-shot
Hyōgo Prefectural Museum of Modern Art
Ichijōji
Idemitsu Art Gallery
Ie-no-Hikari
Igarashi Yumiko
Iino Hachiman Shrine
Ikeda Katsuya
Ikeda Masuo
Ikeda Yōko

Ikenobō
Ikezaki Isao
Imai Kyōji
Imperial Household Agency
Ina Eiji
Inagaki Shin'ichi
Inō Tadataka Memorial Hall
Inoue Hiromichi
Inoue Keijirō
Irie Masahiko
Ise Shrine
Isetan Co, Ltd
Isetatsu
Ishibashi Museum of Art
Ishiguro Takaaki
Ishii Kenji
Ishikawa Ken History Museum
Ishimatsu Takeo
Ishimoto Yasuhiro
Ishioka Eiko
Ishiyachō Gallery, Kyōto
Ishiyamadera
Island, Inc
Isonokami Shrine
Itami Productions
Itō Masakazu
Itō Midori
Itō Tomonori
Itsukushima Shrine
Iwagō Mitsuaki
Iwasaki Shoten
Iwata Tsuneo
Japan Art Exhibition (Nitten)
Japan Automobile Research Institute, Inc
Japan Folk-Craft Museum
Japan Foundation
Japan Motor Industrial Federation, Inc
Japan Newspapers Publishers and Editors Association
Japan Photo Research Center
Japan Stage Players' Association
Japan Sumō Association
Japan Toys Museum
Japan Weather Association
Jean Jean
Jingoji
Jingū Bunko
Jingū Chōkokan Nōgyōkan
Jisaku
Jukōin
K. Mikimoto & Co, Ltd
Kagoshima Masae
Kajima Corporation
Kakimori Bunko
Kamakura Museum of Modern Art
Kamekura Yūsaku
Kanagawa Prefectural Museum
Kanazawa Sōya

Kanegafuchi Chemical Industry Co, Ltd
Kaneko Ōtei
Kankikōji
Kansai University
Karasawa Tomitarō
Kashiwakura Shinkichi
Kasori Shell Mound Site Museum
Kasugano Stable
Kataoka Tamako
Katsui Mitsuo
Kawabata Kimiko
Kawabata Yasunari Kinen Kai
Kawada Kikuji
Kawada Masaaki
Kawaguchi Kaiji
Kawai Mitsuo
Kawai Suyako
Kawakami Shirō
Kawamata Tadashi
Kawashima Kiyoshi
Kayama Matazō
Keiō University
Kenninji
Kimura Hisako
Kinema Jumpōsha Co, Ltd
Kitahara Teruhisa
Kiyomizudera
Kobayashi Kokei Hozonkai
Kobayashi Toan
Kobayashi Tsunehiro
Kōbe City Museum
Kōdaiji
Kodaka Kazuyoshi
Kōdansha PEC, Ltd
Kōdōin
Kōfukuji
Kokugakuin University
Komai Yoshiko
Kōryūji
Koyama Hotarō
Koyano Masayoshi
Kōyasan Jimyōin
Kōyasan Jōkeiin
Kōzanji
Kudō Tomomichi
Kumakiri Keisuke
Kurakazu Sōkaku
Kusama Yayoi
Kushimoto Marine Park
Kuwayama Tadaaki
Kyōcera Corporation
Kyōdō Photo Service
Kyōto Marubeni Co, Ltd
Kyōto Museum of Contemporary Art
Kyōto National Museum
Kyōto University
Kyōto University Research Institute for Humanistic Studies
U-Fan Lee
Machida City Museum

Maeda Ikutoku-kai Foundation
Maeda Sue
Mainichi shimbun
Maki Naomi
Mamiya Masaaki
Marlborough International Fine Art Est.
Maruki Gallery for the Hiroshima Murals
Maruki Iri
Mashima Mitsuhide
Masuda Shōzō
Matsuda Film Productions
Matsudaira Kōekikai
Matsukage Hiroyuki
Matsumoto Sadako
Matsumura Sōki
Matsushige Yoshito
Matsuzawa Yutaka
Mazda Motor Corporation
Meiji Gakuin Higashi Murayama Senior High School
Meiji Memorial Picture Gallery
Meiji Mura
Migishi Setsuko
Mimatsu Masao
Minolta Camera Co, Ltd
Minowa Studio
Mint Museum
Mitsubishi Heavy Industries, Ltd, Nagasaki Shipyard and Machinery Works
Mitsubishi Motors Corporation
Mitsui Bunko
Mitsui Shinako
Mitsukoshi, Ltd
Miyai Co, Ltd
Miyajima Tatsuo
Miyajima Yasuhiko
Miyake Design Studio
Miyake Seisuke
Miyawaki Aiko
Mizuki Kyōko
Mizuno Katsuhiko
MOA Museum of Art
Mōri Museum
Morinaga Sōko
Moriyama Daidō
Munakata Chiya
Munakata Museum
Munakata Shrine
Murai Osamu
Muraoka Saburō
Musée des Arts décoratifs, Paris
Musée d'Orsay, Paris
Museum of Fine Arts, Boston
Museum of Modern Art, Ibaraki Prefecture
Museum of Motoori Norinaga
Museum of Musical Instruments, Musashino College of Music

Myōhōin
Myōhokkeji
Myōkian
Myōshinji Taizōin
NAGAI Kazumasa
Nagaoka Municipal Science Museum
Nagasaki Holland Village–Huis Ten Bosch
Nagasaki Municipal Museum
Nagasaki Photo Service
NAGAYASU Takumi
Nagoya Castle
Nagoya Railroad Co, Ltd
NAITŌ Masatoshi
Naitō Museum of Pharmaceutical Science and Industry
NAKAGAWA Einosuke
NAKAHARA Kōdai
NAKANISHI Natsuyuki
NAKATA Akira
NAKAYAMA Masako
Namban Bunkakan
Nantenshi Gallery
Nara City Hall
Nara National Museum
Nara National Research Institute of Cultural Properties
Nara Prefectural Kashihara Archaeological Institute
Nara Prefectural Museum of Art
NARITA Hiromu
National Archives
National Association of Commercial Broadcasting in Japan
National Diet Library
National Galleries of Scotland, Edinburgh
National Laboratory for High Energy Physics
National Museum of Art, Ōsaka
National Museum of Japanese History
National Museum of Modern Art, Kyōto
National Museum of Modern Art, Tōkyō
National Nō Theater
National Racing Public Relations Center
National Science Museum
National Space Development Agency of Japan
Nature Production
NEC Corporation
Newsweek Japan
Nezu Art Museum
NHK Symphony Orchestra
Nibariki-Tokumashoten
Nigensha Publishing Co, Ltd
Nihon Mengyō Kurabu

Nihon Shashinkai
Niigata Prefectural Museum of Modern Art
Nikaidō Ukiyo-e Bunko
Nikkatsu Corporation
Nikon Corporation
Nippon Color Engineers
Nippon Crown
Nippon Design Center
Nippon Phonogram Co, Ltd
Nippon Telegraph and Telephone Corporation
Nisei Week
Nishi Honganji
NISHIDA Kei
NISHIKAWA Fujino
Nissan Motor Co, Ltd
NODA Tetsuya
NOGUCHI Hiromi
NOMURA Hitoshi
North Point Press
OBARA Noboru
Ōbayashi Corporation
Ōbunsha Publishing Co, Ltd
ODA Noritsugu
ODA Yukie
Oguro Planning Co, Ltd
Ōhara Museum of Art
Ohara school
ŌHASHI Haruzō
OKAMOTO Shigeo
OKAMOTO Tarō
Okazaki Castle
OKAZAKI Chiyo
Okazaki Tamako Gallery, Tōkyō
Okinawa Prefectural Museum
OKUMURA Tadashi
Ōkura Shūkokan Museum
Old Tamba Pottery Museum
Olympus Optical Co, Ltd
ŌMICHI Jiichi
Ōmiya Municipal Cartoon Museum
Orikomi Service
Orion Press
Ōsaka Castle Museum
Ōsaka Prefectural Board of Education
Ōsaka Prefecture
Ōshima Productions Ltd
Österreichische Galerie, Vienna
ŌTA Takeshi
Ōtani Memorial Art Museum
ŌTOMO Katsuhiro
ŌTORI Ranzaburō
Ōura Church
ŌYAMA Akira
ŌYAMA Yukio
PANA Photo Library (Jiji Press)
Paper Museum
Parliamentary Museum
Peace Society for the Fifth Fukuryū-Maru

Pentax Gallery Camera Museum
Photo Atelier Sadanori
Photo Eyes
Photo Library Genryō
Photo Research Co, Ltd
Photo Stock Nagano
PPS Photo Library
Presarto
Prime Minister's Office
Q Photo International, Inc
Railway Technical Research Institute
Research Institute for Publications
Reuters Sun
Rokuharamitsuji
Rokuonji
Ryōkan Kinenkan
Ryūshi Memorial Hall
SADAYASU Kei
Saga Prefectural Board of Education
Saga Prefectural Museum
Saitama Prefectural Museum
SAITŌ Kazuki
SAITŌ Makoto
SAKAMOTO Masafumi
SAKATA Sōrei
Sakitama Archaeological and Folk-loristic Data Museum
SAKURAI Nao
SAKURAI Tadahisa
San'ei Photo Library
SASAKI Hikaru
SASAKI Keita
Satani Gallery, Tōkyō
SATŌ Chie
SATŌ Tokihiro
Sawanotsuru Co, Ltd
SEEDS
Seikyōji
Sekai Bunka Photo
Seki Photos
SEKIDO Kōga
SEKINE Nobuo
Sendai City Museum
Sezon Museum of Art
Shakaishisō-sha, Ltd
Sharp Corporation
SHIBATA Toshio
Shikōsha
Shimada Art Museum
SHIMADA Kōryō
Shimane Prefectural Education Committee
SHIMIZU Kazuyoshi
SHIMIZU Yukio
SHIMMOTO Teiko
SHIMOMURA Makoto
Shinjuan
Shinkenchiku-sha Co, Ltd
SHINODA Morio
SHINOHARA Ushio
SHINOYAMA Kishin

Shinshōgokurakuji
Shinshūsha Co, Ltd
Shinwa Bank, Ltd
SHIRAGA Kazuo
SHIROSHITA Ruiko
Shiseidō Co, Ltd
Shōchiku Co, Ltd
Shōeidō
Shōgakukan, Inc
Shōko Dō
Shōsōin
Shūkan Tsuri Nyūsu Sha
Shuri Castle Restoration Committee
Sōgetsu Shuppan, Inc
Sōgetsukai Foundation
SONOBE Kiyoshi
Sony Corporation
Sony Music Entertainment, Inc
Sōtōshū Shūmuchō
SPDA, Tōkyō
Spirit Photos
Sport Photo Life
Suda Hachiman Shrine
SUGA Hiroshi
SUGA Kishio
SUGIURA Kōhei
SUGIYAMA Yoshinosuke
Sumiya
Suntory Museum of Art
Suō Sarumawashi Association
SUZUKI Asako
SUZUKI Jūzō
SUZUKI Kiyoshi
SUZUKI Mitsuhiko
SUZUKI Tokiko
SUZUKI Yutaka
Synapse Co, Ltd
TADA Toshikatsu
Tahara Museum
Taiyō Fishery Co, Ltd
TAKAHASHI Rumiko
TAKANASHI Yutaka
TAKANO Akira
TAKATA Shizuo
Takatsuki, City of
Takayama Museum of Local History
Takehisa Yumeji Ikaho Memorial Hall
TAKEUCHI Takeji
TAKEUCHI Toshinobu
TAMURA Kitoko
TANAKA Ikkō
TANAKA Noriyuki
TANAKA Shigeru
TANAKA Toshiaki
Tawaraya Ryokan
Teito Rapid Transit Authority
Tekisui Museum
Tenkawa Shrine
Tenri Central Library
Tenri University Sankōkan Museum
TESHIMA Tairoku

Tezuka Production Co, Ltd
Tobacco and Salt Museum
Tōdaiji
Tōei Animation Co, Ltd
Tōei Co, Ltd
Tōhō Co, Ltd
Tōhoku University
Tōji
Tōkō Museum of Contemporary Art, Tōkyō
Tokugawa Art Museum (Tokugawa Reimei-kai)
Tokugawa Tsunetaka
Tokuma Shoten Publishing Co, Ltd
Tokushu Paper Mfg Co, Ltd
Tōkyō Electric Power Co, Inc
Tōkyō Gakuen
Tōkyō Gas Co, Ltd
Tōkyō Metropolitan Art Museum
Tōkyō Metropolitan Art Space
Tōkyō Metropolitan Symphony Orchestra
Tōkyō National Museum
Tōkyō National Research Institute of Cultural Properties
Tōkyō University Historiographical Institute
Tōkyō University of Fine Arts and Music

Tōkyō Zoological Park Society
Tōmatsu Shōmei
Tomiyama Haruo
Tōnai Hiroaki
Toppan Printing Co, Ltd
Toshiba Corporation
Toshimaen Co
Tōshōdaiji
Tōshōgu
Toya Shigeo
Tōyama Takayuki
Toyoda Automatic Loom Works, Ltd
Toyota Motor Corporation
Toyotaka Ryūzō
Tsubouchi Memorial Theater Museum of Waseda University
Tsuburaya Productions Co, Ltd
Tsuchida Hiromi
Tsuda College
Tsujitome
Tsukuda Original Co, Ltd
Tsunoda Kunihiro
Tsunokami Yūji
Ueda Shōji
Uematsu Keiji
Uemura Shōko
Uesugi Shrine
Umehara Shōichi
Umezawa Memorial Gallery

Umezawa Shigeaki
UNAC Tōkyō
Union des Arts Decoratifs Service Photographique
UPI Sun
Uragami Sōkyū-dō Co, Ltd
Ushioda Shōzō
VAGA, New York
Virgin Japan, Ltd
Wakabayashi Isamu
Wakuden
Walt Disney Co
Waseda University
Watanabe Yoshio
Wep Co, Ltd
Wild Bird Society of Japan
Yabumoto Kōzō
Yagi Yoshimitsu
Yagishita Hiroshi
Yakushiji
Yamada Hajime
Yamada Hiroko
Yamada Jumpei
Yamada Seizō
Yamagata Museum of Art
Yamaguchi Prefectural Archives
Yamaguchi Shizuno
Yamahata Shōgo
Yamamoto Sōroku

Yamamoto Tadasu
Yamashiro Ryūichi
Yamashita Hiroaki
Yamatane Museum of Art
Yamato Bunkakan
Yamazaki Hiroshi
Yano Masayoshi
Yano Tatehiko
Yano Yutaka
Yasuda Ken'ichi
Yasui Miharu
Yasuo Kuniyoshi Museum
Yohji Yamamoto, Inc
Yokoo Tadanori
Yokoyama Ryōichi
Yōmei Bunko
Yomiuri shimbun
Yonezawa, City of
Yoshino Yūsuke
Yoshitoku Collection
Yuki Museum of Art
Yume no Yūminsha
Yumura Teruhiko
Yūshi Hachimankō Jūhakkain, Kōyasan
Yūzenshikai
Zakuro
Zuihōin
Zuiyō Co, Ltd

PRODUCTION

Art and Design
Hirakawa Akira
Kabaya Takao
Morioka Kaori
Motoki Masako
Murata Yukiko
Ōtake Sakito
Suzuki Fumie
Terai Keiji

Graphics and Cartography
Asakura Yasue
Heibonsha Cartographic Publishing Co, Ltd
Kobayashi Tamiji
Matsushima Shūichi
Ogawa Tetsunari
Shiramasa Akiyoshi
Shiramasa Tsukasa
Sun Gabō
Yang Huichi

Color Proofing
Nikken Kōsei
Vanfu, Inc

Typesetting
ComCom, Inc
Dai Nippon Uniprocess Co, Ltd
Inoue Kiyoaki

Printing
Dai Nippon Printing Co, Ltd
DNP America, Inc

SPECIAL ACKNOWLEDGMENTS

The editors give special thanks to the following individuals and organizations for valuable advice, consultation, and editorial assistance.

Aoki Takao
Chiran Toshirō
Valerie L. Durham
Richard Emmert
Eshi Yasunari
Furukawa Takayoshi
Richard Gardner
Gotō Takeo
Hashimoto Kōichi
Hayashi Tōru
Judith Herd
Samuel T. Hicks
Hida Yoshifumi
Hidaka Kaori
Higuchi Norio
Hirosaki Yoshitsugi
Mark Hudson
Imai Tomomasa
Information & Public Affairs Co, Ltd
 (IPA)
Inoue Kō
Inoue Yōichi
Inoue Yoshie
Irisawa Makoto
Ishii Kenji
Ishii Tatsurō
Ishiwatari Seiko
Itō Sachio
Kamata Nanao

Kanai Hiroo
Kaneko Yuzuru
Kasahara Chizuko
Katakura Nobuhiro
Frederick Hiroshi Katayama
Katō Nobuaki
Katō Takao
Kawatsu Yukiko
Timothy M. Kelly
Kitahara Hisakuni
Kobayashi Machiko
Kohari Susumu
Kojima Satoshi
Kokubo Takeshi
Ronald G. Korver
Kubota Hiroko
Kudō Takashi
Suzanne Mantell
Matsubara Yasuo
Matsumoto Akira
Mimura Keiko
Miyake Michiko
Mori Kunihisa
Morita Tomoko
Regina Mylan
Nagasawa Kazutoshi
Nagiyama Kiyoshi
Nakajima Hiroo
Nakayama Kiwako

Oka Namiki
Onodera Jun
Osanai Tōru
Ōta Katsuhiko
Sasaki Yoshio
Satō Naoyuki
Sawa Shigehisa
Sawamura Kazuhiko
Shamoto Osamu
Shimbara Chisa
Shōkei Takashi
So Eitetsu
Sueki Fumihiko
Sugiyama Mitsuko
Tada Yūji
Takahashi Tomoko
Tanabe Kazuo
Tanaka Junji
Tanaka Manabu
Taniuchi Tōru
Terachi Goichi
Tobita Shigeo
Tsuchiya Haruhito
Uchida Masao
Ura Senke
Bob Tadashi Wakabayashi
Watanabe Kimiko
Yamamoto Sumie
Yellow Reports Co, Ltd

Yokomichi Mario
Yoshino Kenji
Erika Young
R. Jules Young
Yūki Jun'ichi

Sachem Publishing Associates Staff
Carol O. Behrman
Jeremy Brenner
Suzanne Stone Burke
Alan Clark
Eileen M. Gaffney
Robert Halasz
Elizabeth J. Jewell
Walter O. Jewell
Leah Raechel Killeen
Carol Lucas
Rebecca Lyon
Julie Marsh
Lisa Nielsen
Laurie Romanik
Marie-Josée A. Schorp
Carl Sesar
William Shapiro
Christine Lindberg Stevens
Adrienne Suddard
Diane Bell Surprenant
David Travers
Georg Zappler

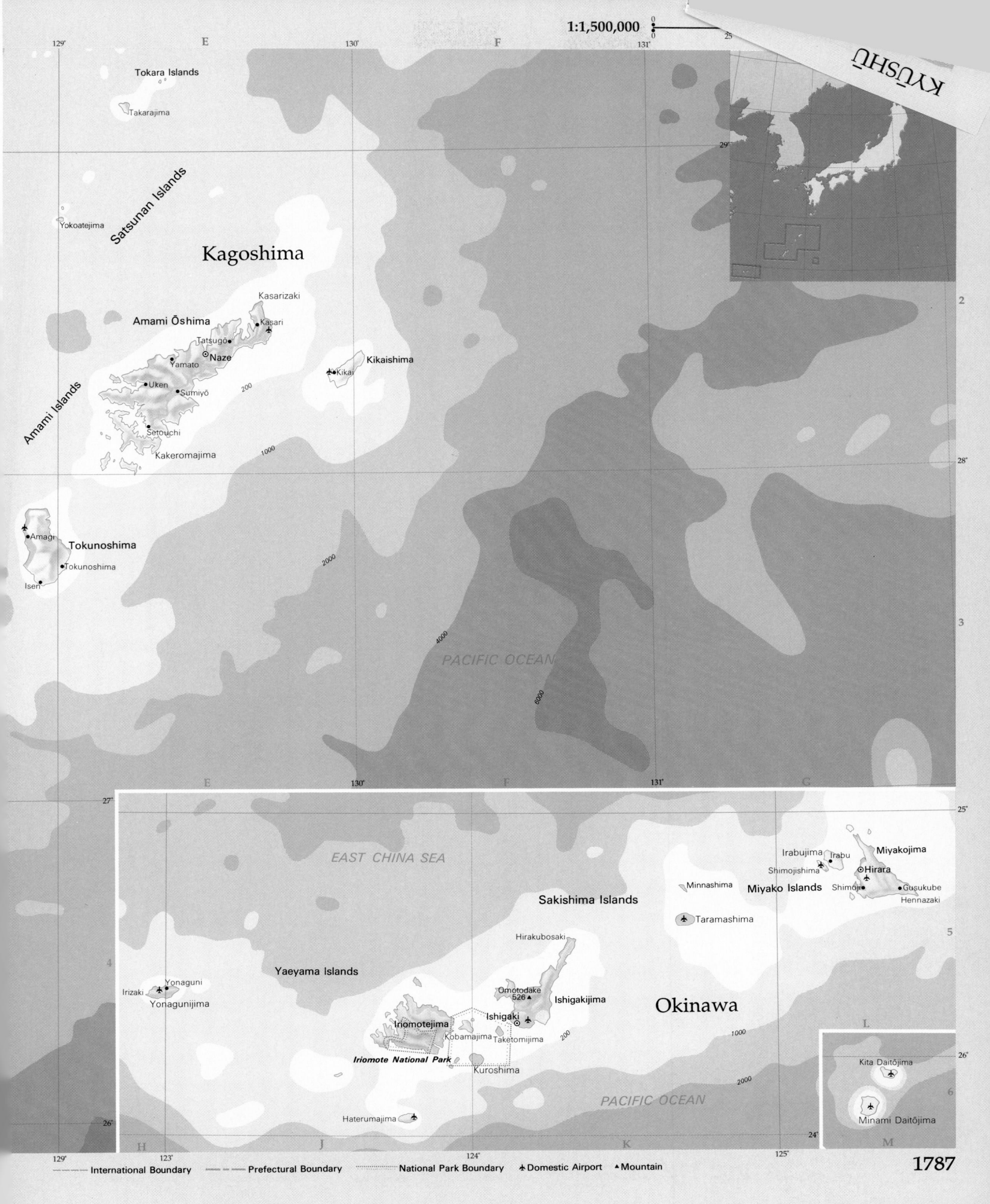

1:1,500,000

0   25

Tokara Islands

Takarajima

Satsunan Islands

Yokoatejima

Kagoshima

Amami Islands

Kasarizaki

Amami Ōshima   Kasari

Tatsugō

Yamato   ⊙Naze

Uken

Sumiyō

Setouchi

Kakeromajima

Kikai   Kikaishima

200

1000

Amagi

Tokunoshima

Tokunoshima

Isen

2000

4000

PACIFIC OCEAN

6000

EAST CHINA SEA

Irabujima   Irabu   **Miyakojima**

Shimojishima

Minnashima   ⊙Hirara

Miyako Islands   Shimoji   Gusukube

Hennazaki

Sakishima Islands

Taramashima

Hirakubosaki

Yaeyama Islands

Omotodake   **Ishigakijima**

526 ▲

Irizaki   Yonaguni   **Okinawa**

Yonagunijima

Ishigaki ⊙

Iriomotejima

Kobamajima   Taketomijima

Iriomote National Park   200

Kuroshima   1000

L

Kita Daitōjima

2000

PACIFIC OCEAN

Haterumajima

Minami Daitōjima   M

1787

— International Boundary   — — Prefectural Boundary   ⋯⋯ National Park Boundary   ✈ Domestic Airport   ▲ Mountain

EAST CHINA SEA

A

12°

B

Takarajima

Tokara Islands

Kashima
Kami Koshiki
Shimo Koshikijima

Shimo Koshiki

Koshikijima
Islands

Akusekijima

Gajashima

Suwanosejima

Nakanoshima

Kuchinoshima

Satsunan Islands

Nomamisaki
Bōnomisaki

Bōnotsu

Kaseda
Kasasa

Fukiagehama

Fukiage

Kushikino
Yoshida

Iriki

Hiwaki

Satsuma Peninsula

Sendai

Kushikino

Higashi Ichiki

C

30°

Kuroshima

Iōjima

Takeshima

Magejima

Ōsumi Strait

Kuchinoerabujima

Yakushima

Miyanouradake
1935▲

Kirishima-Yaku
National Park

Yaku

Kami Yaku

Ōsumi Islands

Kagoshima

Kimotsuki Mountains

Ōsumi Peninsula

Satamisaki

Sata

Makurazaki

Chiran

Kaimondake
921▲

Ei

Ibusuki

Kamondake
"Nagasakibana"

Yamagata

Onejima

Kire

Tarumizu

Lake Ikeda

Fukuyama

Sakurajima

Aira

Kaiki

Kirishima
1117▲

Kitabe

Kagoshima

Kokubu

Makizono

Hayato

Kushima

Kanoya

Koyama

Kushira

Shibushi

Bir̄ojima

Ōsumi

Uchinoura

Suеyoshi

Takarabe

Miyakonojō

Mimata

Takaō

Tanegashima Strait

Minami Tane

Naka Tane

Tanegashima

Nishinoomote

200

13°

1000

2000

Shibushi Bay

Toimisaki

Wanitsuka Mountains

Kushima

Kōjima

Nichinan

Kōjima

Nichinan
Coast

Aoshima

PACIFIC OCEAN

4000

D

E

132°

30°

◉ City over 1,000,000 Population   ◎ 500,000 to 1,000,000   ◉ 100,000 to 500,000   ◉ Under 100,000   • Town or Village   Underlined Cities are Prefectural Capitals
── Shinkansen Railway Line   ──── Primary Railway   ↦─← Railway Tunnel   ──── Expressway   ──── Primary Road   ───── Planned Expressway